[OFF]ICIAL®

[PRICE G]UIDE TO

BASEBALL CARDS

DR. JAMES BECKETT

TWENTY-NINTH EDITION

House of Collectibles
New York

Important Notice: All of the information, including valuations, in this book has been compiled from reliable sources, and efforts have been made to eliminate errors and questionable data. Nevertheless, the possibility of error, in a work of such immense scope, always exists. The publisher will not be held responsible for losses that may occur in the purchase, sale, or other transaction of items because of information contained herein. Readers who feel they have discovered errors are invited to *write* and inform us, so they may be corrected in subsequent editions. Those seeking further information on the topics covered in this book are advised to refer to the complete line of *Official Price Guides* published by the House of Collectibles.

House of Collectibles and colophon are trademarks of Random House, Inc.

Random House is a registered trademark of Random House, Inc.
Please address inquiries about electronic licensing of any products for use on a network, in software, or on CD-ROM to the Subsidiary Rights Department,
Random House Information Group, fax 212-572-6003.

This book is available for special discounts for bulk purchases for sales promotions or premiums. Special editions, including personalized covers, excerpts of existing books, and corporate imprints, can be created in large quantities for special needs. For more information, write to Random House, Inc., Special Markets/Premium Sales, 1745 Broadway, MD 6-2, New York, NY 10019 or e-mail specialmarkets@randomhouse.com

www.houseofcollectibles.com

Manufactured in the United States of America

ISSN: 1062-7138

ISBN: 978-0-375-72313-1

10 9 8 7 6 5 4 3 2 1

Twenty-Ninth Edition: April 2009

Table of Contents

About the Author

Jim Beckett, the leading authority on sports card values in the United States, maintains a wide range of activities in the world of sports. He possesses one of the finest collections of sports cards and autographs in the world, has made numerous appearances on radio and television, and has been frequently cited in many national publications. He was awarded the first "Special Achievement Award" for Contributions to the Hobby by the National Sports Collectors Convention in 1980, the "Jock Jaspersen Award" for Hobby Dedication in 1983, and the "Buck Barker, Spirit of the Hobby" award in 1991.

Dr. Beckett is the author of *Beckett Baseball Card Price Guide, The Official Price Guide to Baseball Cards, Price Guide to Baseball Collectibles, The Sport Americana Baseball Memorabilia and Autograph Price Guide, Beckett Almanac of Baseball Cards and Collectibles, Beckett Football Card Price Guide, The Official Price Guide to Football Cards, Beckett Hockey Card Price Guide, The Official Price Guide to Hockey Cards, Beckett Basketball Card Price Guide, The Official Price Guide to Basketball Cards, The Beckett Baseball Card Alphabetical Checklist, The Beckett Basketball Card Alphabetical Checklist,* and *The Beckett Football Card Alphabetical Checklist.* In addition, he is the founder, publisher, and editor of *Beckett Baseball Card Monthly, Beckett Basketball Monthly, Beckett Football Card Monthly, Beckett Hockey Collector, Beckett Sports Collectibles,* and *Beckett Racing and Motorsports Marketplace.*

Jim Beckett received his Ph.D. in Statistics from Southern Methodist University in 1975. Prior to starting Beckett Publications in 1984, Dr. Beckett served as an Associate Professor of Statistics at Bowling Green State University and as a vice president of a consulting firm in Dallas, Texas.

How to Use This Book

Isn't it great? Every year this book gets better with all the new sets coming out. But even more exciting is that every year there are more options in collecting the cards we love so much. This edition has been enhanced and expanded from the previous edition. The cards you collect — who appears on them, what they look like, where they are from, and (most important to most of you) what their current values are — are enumerated within. Many of the features contained in the other *Beckett Price Guides* have been incorporated into this volume since condition grading, terminology, and many other aspects of collecting are common to the card hobby in general. We hope you find the book both interesting and useful in your collecting pursuits.

The Beckett Guide has been successful where other attempts have failed because it is complete, current, and valid. This price guide contains not just one, but three prices by condition for all the baseball cards listed. The prices were added to the card lists just prior to printing and reflect not the author's opinions or desires but the going retail prices for each card, based on the marketplace (sports memorabilia conventions and shows, sports card shops, hobby papers, current mail-order catalogs, local club meetings, auction results, and other firsthand reportings of actually realized prices).

What is the best price guide available on the market today? Of course, card sellers prefer the price guide with the highest prices, while card buyers naturally prefer the one with the lowest prices. Accuracy, however, is the true test. Use the price guide trusted by more collectors and dealers than all the others combined. Look for the Beckett® name. I won't put my name on anything I won't stake my reputation on. Not the lowest and not the highest — but the most accurate, with integrity.

To facilitate your use of this book, read the complete introductory section on the following pages before going to the pricing pages. Every collectible field has its own terminology; we've tried to capture most of these terms and definitions in our glossary. Please read carefully the section on grading and the condition of your cards, as you cannot determine which price column is appropriate for a given card without first knowing its condition.

Welcome to the world of baseball cards.

How to Collect

Each collection is personal and reflects the individuality of its owner. There are no set rules on how to collect cards. Since card collecting is a hobby or leisure pastime, what you collect, how much you collect, and how much time and money you spend collecting are entirely up to you. The funds you have available for collecting and your own personal taste should determine how you collect. Information and ideas presented here are intended to help you get the most enjoyment from this hobby.

It is impossible to collect every card ever produced. Therefore, beginners as well as intermediate and advanced collectors usually specialize in some way. One of the reasons this hobby is popular is that individual collectors can define and tailor their collecting methods to match their own tastes. To give you some idea of the various approaches to collecting, we will list some of the more popular areas of specialization.

Many collectors select complete sets from particular years. For example, they may concentrate on assembling complete sets from all the years since their birth or since they became avid sports fans. They may try to collect a card for every player during that specified period of time.

Many others wish to acquire only certain players. Usually such players are the superstars of the sport, but occasionally collectors will specialize in all the cards of players who attended a particular college or came from a certain town. Some collectors are interested in only the first cards or Rookie Cards of certain players. A handy guide for collectors interested in pursuing the hobby this way is *The Sport Americana Baseball Card Alphabetical Checklist.*

Another fun way to collect cards is by team. Most fans have a favorite team, and it is natural for that loyalty to be translated into a desire for cards of the players on that favorite team. For most of the recent years, team sets (all the cards from a given team for that year) are readily available at a reasonable price. *The Sport Americana Team Baseball Card Checklist* will open up this field to the collector.

Obtaining Cards

Several avenues are open to card collectors. Cards still can be purchased in the traditional way: by the pack at the local candy, grocery, drug, or major discount store.

But there are also thousands of card shops across the country that specialize in selling cards individually or by the pack, box, or set. Another alternative is the thousands of card shows held each month around the country, which feature anywhere from 8 to 800 tables of sports cards and memorabilia for sale.

For many years, it has been possible to purchase complete sets of baseball cards through mail-order advertisers found in traditional sports media publications, such as the *Sporting News, Baseball Digest*, and *Street & Smith* yearbooks. These sets also are advertised in the card collecting periodicals. Many collectors will begin by subscribing to at least one of the hobby periodicals, all with good up-to-date information. In fact, subscription offers can be found in the advertising section of this book.

Most serious card collectors obtain old (and new) cards from one or more of several main sources: (1) trading or buying from other collectors or dealers; (2) responding to sale or auction ads in the hobby publications; (3) buying at a local hobby store; (4) attending sports collectibles shows or conventions; and (5) purchasing cards over the Internet.

We advise that you try all five methods since each has its own distinct advantages: (1) trading is a great way to make new friends; (2) hobby periodicals help you keep up with what's going on in the hobby (including when and where the conventions are happening); (3) stores provide the opportunity to enjoy personalized service and consider a great diversity of material in a relaxed sports-oriented atmosphere; (4) shows allow you to choose from multiple dealers and thousands of cards under one roof in a competitive situation; and (5) the Internet allows one to purchase cards in a convenient manner from almost anywhere in the world.

Preserving Your Cards

Cards are fragile. They must be handled properly in order to retain their value. Careless handling can easily result in creased or bent cards. It is, however, not recommended that tweezers or tongs be used to pick up your cards since such utensils might mar or indent card surfaces and thus reduce those cards´ conditions and values.

In general, your cards should be handled directly as little as possible. This is sometimes easier to say than to do.

Although there are still many who use custom boxes, storage trays, or even shoe boxes, plastic sheets are the preferred method of many collectors for storing cards.

A collection stored in plastic pages in a three-ring album allows you to view your collection at any time without the need to touch the cards themselves. Cards can also be kept in single holders (of various types and thicknesses) designed for the enjoyment of each card individually.

For a large collection, some collectors may use a combination of the above methods. When purchasing plastic sheets for your cards, be sure that you find the pocket size that fits the cards snugly. Don´t put your 1951 Bowman in a sheet designed to fit 1981 Topps.

Most hobby and collectibles shops and virtually all collectors´ conventions will have these plastic pages available in quantity for the various sizes offered, or you can purchase them directly from the advertisers in this book.

Also, remember that pocket size isn´t the only factor to consider when looking for plastic sheets. Other factors such as safety, economy, appearance, availability, or personal preference also may influence which types of sheets a collector may want to buy.

Damp, sunny, and/or hot conditions — no, this is not a weather forecast — are three elements to avoid in extremes if you are interested in preserving your collection. Too much (or too little) humidity can cause the gradual deterioration of a card. Direct, bright sun (or fluorescent light) over time will bleach out the color of a card. Extreme heat accelerates the decomposition of the card. On the other hand, many cards have lasted more than 75 years without much scientific intervention. So be cautious, even if the above factors typically present a problem only when present in the extreme. It never hurts to be prudent.

Collecting vs. Investing

Collecting individual players and collecting complete sets are both popular vehicles for investment and speculation.

Most investors and speculators stock up on complete sets or on quantities of players they think have good investment potential.

There is obviously no guarantee in this book, or anywhere else for that matter, that cards will outperform the stock market or other investment alternatives in the future. After all, baseball cards do not pay quarterly dividends and cards cannot be sold at their "current values" as easily as stocks or bonds.

Nevertheless, investors have noticed a favorable long-term trend in the past performance of baseball and other sports collectibles, and certain cards and sets have outperformed just about any other investment in some years.

Many hobbyists maintain that the best investment is and always will be the building of a collection, which traditionally has held up better than outright speculation.

Some of the obvious questions are: Which cards? When to buy? When to sell? The best investment you can make is in your own education.

The more you know about your collection and the hobby, the more informed the decisions you will be able to make. We´re not selling investment tips. We´re selling information about the current value of baseball cards. It´s up to you to use that information to your best advantage.

Terminology

Each hobby has its own language to describe its area of interest. The nomenclature traditionally used for trading cards is derived from the American Card Catalog, published in 1960 by Nostalgia Press. That catalog, written by Jefferson Burdick (who is called the "Father of Card Collecting" for his pioneering work), uses letter and number designations for each separate set of cards. The letter used in the ACC designation refers to the generic type of card. While both sport and nonsport issues are classified in the ACC, we shall confine ourselves to the sport issues. The following list defines the letters and their meanings as used by the American Card Catalog.

(none) or N - 19th Century U.S. Tobacco.
B - Blankets.
D - Bakery Inserts Including Bread.
E - Early Candy and Gum.
F - Food Inserts.
H - Advertising.
M - Periodicals.
PC - Postcards.
R - Candy and Gum since 1930.
T - Tobacco.

Following the letter prefix and an optional hyphen are one-, two-, or three-digit numbers, R(-)999. These typically represent the company or entity issuing the cards. In several cases, the ACC number is extended by an additional hyphen and another one- or two-digit numerical suffix. For example, the 1957 Topps regular-series baseball card issue carries an ACC designation of R414-11. The "R" indicates a Candy or Gum card produced since 1930. The "414" is the ACC designation for Topps Chewing Gum baseball card issues, and the "11" is the ACC designation for the 1957 regular issue (Topps´ eleventh baseball set). Like other traditional methods of identification, this system provides order to the process of cataloging cards; however, most serious collectors learn the ACC designation of the popular sets by repetition and familiarity, rather than by attempting to "figure out" what they might or should be. From 1948 forward, collectors and dealers commonly refer to all sets by their year, maker, type of issue, and any other distinguishing characteristic. For example, such a characteristic could be an unusual issue or one of several regular issues put out by a specific maker in a single year. Regional issues are usually referred to by year, maker, and sometimes by title or theme of the set.

Glossary/Legend

Our glossary defines terms used in the card collecting hobby and in this book. Many of these terms are also common to other types of sports memorabilia collecting. Some terms may have several meanings depending on use and context.

ACETATE—A transparent plastic.

AS—All-Star card. A card portraying an All-Star Player of the previous year that says "All-Star" on its face.

ATG—All-Time Great card.

ATL—All-Time Leaders card.

AU(TO)—Autographed card.

AW—Award Winner.

BB—Building Blocks.

BC—Bonus Card.

BF—Bright Futures.

BL—Blue Letters.

BNR—Banner Season.

BOX CARD—Card issued on a box (e.g., 1987 Topps Box Bottoms).

BRICK—A group of 50 or more cards having common characteristics that is intended to be bought, sold, or traded as a unit.

CABINETS—Popular and highly valuable photographs on thick card stock produced in the 19th and early 20th centuries.

CC—Curtain Call.

CG—Cornerstones of the Game.

CHECKLIST—A list of the cards contained in a particular set. The list is always in numerical order if the cards are numbered. Some unnumbered sets are artificially numbered in alphabetical order, by team and alphabetically within the team, or by uniform number for convenience.

CL—Checklist card. A card that lists in order the cards and players in the set or series. Older checklist cards in Mint condition that have not been marked are very desirable and command premiums.

CO—Coach.

COMM—Commissioner.

COMMON CARD—The typical card of any set; it has no premium value accruing from subject matter, numerical scarcity, popular demand, or anomaly.

CONVENTION—A gathering of dealers and collectors at a single location for the purpose of buying, selling, and trading sports memorabilia items. Conventions are open to the public and sometimes feature autograph guests, door prizes, contests, seminars, etc. They are frequently referred to simply as "shows."

COOP—Cooperstown.

COR—Corrected card.

CP—Changing Places.

CT—Cooperstown.

CY—Cy Young Award.

DD—Decade of Dominance.

DEALER—A person who engages in buying, selling, and trading sports collectibles or supplies. A dealer may also be a collector, but as a dealer, his main goal is to earn a profit.

DIE-CUT—A card with part of its stock partially cut, allowing one or more parts to be folded or removed. After removal or appropriate folding, the remaining part of the card can frequently be made to stand up.

DK—Diamond King.

DL—Division Leaders.

DP—Double Print (a card that was printed in double the quantity compared to the other cards in the same series) or a Draft Pick card.

DT—Dream Team.

DUFEX—A method of card manufacturing technology patented by Pinnacle Brands, Inc. It involves a refractive quality to a card with a foil coating.

ERA—Earned Run Average.

ERR—Error card. A card with erroneous information, spelling, or depiction on either side of the card. Most errors are not corrected by the producing card company.

FC—Fan Club.

FDP—First or First-Round Draft Pick.

FF—Future Foundation.

FOIL—Foil embossed stamp on card.

FOLD—Foldout.

FP—Franchise Player.

FR—Franchise.

FS—Father/son card.

FS—Future Star.

FUN—Fun cards.

FY—First Year.

GL—Green Letters.

GLOSS—A card with luster; a shiny finish as in a card with UV coating.

HG—Heroes of the Game.

HH—Hometown Heroes.

HIGH NUMBER—The cards in the last series of numbers in a year in which such higher-numbered cards were printed or distributed in significantly lesser amounts than the lower-numbered cards. The high-number designation refers to a scarcity of the high-numbered cards. Not all years have high numbers in terms of this definition.

HL—Highlight card.

HOF—Hall of Fame, or a card that portrays a Hall of Famer (HOFer).

HOLOGRAM—A three-dimensional photographic image.

HOR—Horizontal pose on card as opposed to the standard vertical orientation found on most cards.

IA—In Action card.

IF—Infielder.

INSERT—A card of a different type or any other sports collectible (typically a poster or sticker) contained and sold in the same package along with a card or cards of a major set. An insert card is either unnumbered or not numbered in the same sequence as the major set. Sometimes the inserts are randomly distributed and are not found in every pack.

INTERACTIVE—A concept that involves collector participation.

IRT—International Road Trip.

ISSUE—Synonymous with set, but usually used in conjunction with a manufacturer, e.g., a Topps issue.

JSY—Jersey.

KM—K-Men.

LHP—Left-handed Pitcher.

LL—League Leaders or large letters on card.

LUM—Lumberjack.

MAJOR SET—A set produced by a national manufacturer of cards containing a large number of cards. Usually 100 or more different cards constitute a major set.

MB—Master Blasters.

MEM—Memorial card. For example, the 1990 Donruss and Topps Bart Giamatti cards.

METALLIC—A glossy design method that enhances card features.

MG—Manager.

MI—Maximum Impact.

MINI—A small card; for example, a 1975 Topps card of identical design but smaller dimensions than the regular Topps issue of 1975.

ML—Major League.

MM—Memorable Moments.

MULTI-PLAYER CARD—A single card depicting two or more players (but not a team card).

MVP—Most Valuable Player.

NAU—No autograph on card.

NG—Next Game.

NH—No-Hitter.

NNOF—No name on front.

NOF—Name on front.

NOTCHING—The grooving of the card, usually caused by fingernails, rubber bands, or bumping card edges against other objects.

NT—Now and Then.

NV—Novato.

OF—Outfield or Outfielder.

OLY—Olympics Card.

P—Pitcher or Pitching pose.

P1—First Printing.
P2—Second Printing.
P3—Third Printing.
PACKS—A means by which cards are issued in terms of pack type (wax, cello, foil, rack, etc.) and channel of distribution (hobby, retail, etc.).
PARALLEL— A card that is similar in design to its counterpart from a basic set but that has a distinguishing quality.
PF—Profiles.
PG—Postseason Glory.
PLASTIC SHEET—A clear, plastic page that is punched for insertion into a binder (with standard three-ring spacing) containing pockets for displaying cards. Many different styles of sheets exist with pockets of varying sizes to hold the many differing card formats. Also called a display sheet or storage sheet.
PLATINUM—A metallic element used in the process of creating a glossy card.
PP—Power Passion.
PR—Printed name on back.
PREMIUM—A card, sometimes on photographic stock, that is purchased or obtained in conjunction with, or redemption for, another card or product. The premium is not packaged in the same unit as the primary item.
PRES—President.
PRISMATIC/PRISM—A glossy or bright design that refracts or disperses light.
PS—Pace Setters.
PT—Power Tools.
PUZZLE CARD—A card whose back contains a part of a picture which, when joined correctly with other puzzle cards, forms the completed picture.
PUZZLE PIECE—A die-cut piece designed to interlock with similar pieces (e.g., early 1980s Donruss).
PVC—Polyvinyl chloride, a substance used to make many of the popular card display protective sheets. Non PVC sheets are considered preferable for long-term storage of cards by many.
RARE—A card or series of cards of very limited availability. Unfortunately, "rare" is a subjective term frequently used indiscriminately to hype value. "Rare" cards are harder to obtain than "scarce" cards.
RB—Record Breaker.
RC—Rookie Card.
REDEMPTION—A program established by multiple card manufacturers that allows collectors to mail in a special card (usually a random insert) in return for special cards, sets, or other prizes not available through conventional channels.
REFRACTOR—A card that features a design element that enhances (distorts) its color/appearance through deflecting light.
REV NEG—Reversed or flopped photo side of the card. This is a major type of error card, but only some are corrected.
RHP—Right-handed Pitcher.
RHW—Rookie Home Whites.
RIF—Rifleman.
RPM—Rookie Premiere Materials.
RR—Rated Rookie.
ROO—Rookie.
ROY—Rookie of the Year.
RP—Relief Pitcher.
RTC—Rookie True Colors.
SA—Super Action card.
SASE—Self-Addressed, Stamped Envelope.

SB—Scrapbook.
SB—Stolen Bases.
SCARCE—A card or series of cards of limited availability. This subjective term is sometimes used indiscriminately to hype value. "Scarce" cards are not as difficult to obtain as "rare" cards.
SCR—Script name on back.
SD—San Diego Padres.
SEMI-HIGH—A card from the next-to-last series of a sequentially issued set. It has more value than an average card and generally less value than a high number. A card is not called a semi-high unless the next-to-last series in which it exists has an additional premium attached to it.
SERIES—The entire set of cards issued by a particular producer in a particular year; e.g., the 1971 Topps series. Also, within a particular set, series can refer to a group of (consecutively numbered) cards printed at the same time, e.g., the first series of the 1957 Topps issue (#1 through #88).
SET—One each of the entire run of cards of the same type produced by a particular manufacturer during a single year. In other words, if you have a complete set of 1976 Topps then you have every card from #1 up to and including #660; i.e., all the different cards that were produced.
SF—Starflics.
SH—Season Highlight.
SHEEN—Brightness or luster emitted by card.
SKIP-NUMBERED—A set that has many unissued card numbers between the lowest number in the set and the highest number in the set, e.g., the 1948 Leaf baseball set contains ninety-eight cards skip-numbered from #1 to #168. A major set in which a few numbers were not printed is not considered to be skip-numbered.
SP—Single or Short Print (a card that was printed in lesser quantity compared to the other cards in the same series; see also DP and TP).
SPECIAL CARD—A card that portrays something other than a single player or team, for example, a card that portrays the previous year's statistical leaders or the results from the previous year's World Series.
SS—Shortstop.
STANDARD SIZE—Most modern sports cards measure 2-1/2 by 3-1/2 inches. Exceptions are noted in card descriptions throughout this book.
STAR CARD—A card that portrays a player of some repute, usually determined by his ability; but sometimes referring to sheer popularity.
STOCK—The cardboard or paper on which the card is printed.
SUPERIMPOSED—Affixed on top of something; i.e., a player photo over a solid background.
SUPERSTAR CARD—A card that portrays a superstar, e.g., a Hall of Famer or player with strong Hall of Fame potential.
TC—Team Checklist.
TEAM CARD—A card that depicts an entire team.
THREE-DIMENSIONAL (3D)—A visual image that provides an illusion of depth and perspective.
TOPICAL—A subset or group of cards that have a common theme (e.g., MVP award winners).
TP—Triple Print (a card that was printed in triple the quantity compared to the other cards in the same series).
TR—Trade reference on card.
TRANSPARENT—Clear, see-through.
UDCA—Upper Deck Classic Alumni.
UER—Uncorrected Error.
UMP—Umpire.

USA—Team USA.
UV—Ultraviolet, a glossy coating used in producing cards.
VAR—Variation card. One of two or more cards from the same series with the same number (or player with identical pose if the series is unnumbered) differing from one another by some aspect, the different feature stemming from the printing or stock of the card. This can be caused when the manufacturer of the cards notices an error in one or more of the cards, makes the changes, and then resumes the print run. In this case there will be two versions or variations of the same card. Sometimes one of the variations is relatively scarce.
VERT—Vertical pose on card.
WAS—Washington National League (1974 Topps).
WC—What´s the Call?
WL—White letters on front.
WS—World Series card.
YL—Yellow letters on front.
YT—Yellow team name on front.
*—to denote multi-sport sets.

Understanding Card Values

Determining Value

Why are some cards more valuable than others? Obviously, the economic laws of supply and demand are applicable to card collecting just as they are to any other field where a commodity is bought, sold, or traded in a free, unregulated market.

Supply (the number of cards available on the market) is less than the total number of cards originally produced since attrition diminishes that original quantity. Each year a percentage of cards is typically thrown away, destroyed, or otherwise lost to collectors. This percentage is much, much smaller today than it was in the past because more and more people have become increasingly aware of the value of their cards.

For those who collect only Mint condition cards, the supply of older cards can be quite small indeed. Until recently, collectors were not so conscious of the need to preserve the condition of their cards. For this reason, it is difficult to know exactly how many 1953 Topps are currently available, Mint or otherwise. It is generally accepted that there are fewer 1953 Topps available than 1963, 1973, or 1983 Topps cards. If demand were equal for each of these sets, the law of supply and demand would increase the price for the least available sets. Demand, however, is never equal for all sets, so price correlations can be complicated. The demand for a card is influenced by many factors. These include: (1) the age of the card; (2) the number of cards printed; (3) the player(s) portrayed on the card; (4) the attractiveness and popularity of the set; and (5) the physical condition of the card.

In general, (1) the older the card, (2) the fewer the number of the cards printed, (3) the more famous, popular, and talented the player, (4) the more attractive and popular the set, and (5) the better the condition of the card, the higher the value of the card will be. There are exceptions to all but one of these factors: the condition of the card. Given two cards similar in all respects except condition, the one in the best condition will always be valued higher.

While those guidelines help to establish the value of a card, the countless exceptions and peculiarities make any simple, direct mathematical formula to determine card values impossible.

Regional Variation

Since the market varies from region to region, prices may be higher. This is known as a regional premium. How significant the premium is — and if there is any premium at all — depends on the local popularity of the team and the player.

The largest regional premiums usually do not apply to superstars, who often are so well known nationwide that the prices of their key cards are too high for local dealers to realize a premium.

Lesser stars often command the strongest premiums. Their popularity is concentrated in their home regions, creating local demand that greatly exceeds overall demand.

Regional premiums can apply to popular retired players and sometimes can be found in the areas where the players grew up or starred in college.

A regional discount is the converse of a regional premium. Regional discounts occur when a player has been so popular in his region for so long that local collectors and dealers have accumulated quantities of his key cards. The abundant supply may make the cards available in that area at the lowest prices anywhere.

Set Prices

A somewhat paradoxical situation exists regarding the price of a complete set versus the combined cost of the individual cards in the set. In nearly every case, the sum of the prices for the individual cards is higher than the cost for the complete set. This especially true of cards from the last few years. The reasons for this apparent anomaly stem from the habits of collectors and from the carrying costs to dealers. Today, each card in a set normally is produced in the same quantity as all other cards in its set.

Many collectors pick up only stars, superstars, and particular teams. As a result, the dealer is left with a shortage of certain player cards and an abundance of others. He therefore incurs an expense in simply "carrying" these less desirable cards in stock. On the other hand, if he sells a complete set, he gets rid of large numbers of cards at one time. For this reason, he generally is willing to receive less money for a complete set. By doing this, he recovers all of his costs and also makes a profit.

The disparity between the price of the complete set and the sum of the prices of the individual cards also has been influenced by the fact that some of the major manufacturers now are pre-collating card sets. Since "pulling" individual cards from the sets involves a specific type of labor (and cost), the singles or star card market is not affected significantly by pre-collation.

Set prices also do not include rare card varieties, unless specifically stated. Of course, the prices for sets do include one example of each type for the given set, but this is the least expensive variety.

Scarce Series

Scarce series occur because cards issued before 1974 were made available to the public each year in several series of finite numbers of cards, rather than all cards of the set being available for purchase at one time. At some point during the year, usually toward the end of the baseball season, interest in current year baseball cards waned. Consequently, the manufacturers produced smaller numbers of these later-series cards.

Nearly all nationwide issues from post–World War II manufacturers (1948 to 1973) exhibit these series variations. In the past, Topps, for example, may have issued series consisting of many different numbers of cards, including 55, 66, 80, 88, and others. Recently, Topps has settled on what is now its standard sheet size of 132 cards, six of which constitute its 792-card set.

While the number of cards within a given series is usually the same as the number of cards on one printed sheet, this is not always the case. For example, Bowman used 36 cards on its standard printed sheets, but in 1948 substituted 12 cards during later print runs of that year's baseball cards. Twelve of the cards from the initial sheet of 36 cards were removed and replaced by 12 different cards, giving, in effect, a first series of 36 cards and a second series of 12 new cards. This replacement produced a scarcity of 24 cards — the 12 cards removed from the original sheet and the 12 new cards added to the sheet. A full sheet of 1948 Bowman cards (second printing) shows that card numbers 37 through 48 have replaced 12 of the cards on the first printing sheet.

The Topps Company also has created scarcities and/or excesses of certain cards in many of its sets. Topps, however, has most frequently gone the other direction by double printing some of the cards. Double printing causes in abundance of cards of the players who are on the same sheet more than one time. During the years 1978 to 1981, Topps double printed 66 cards out of its large 726-card set. The Topps practice of double printing cards in earlier years is the most logical explanation for the known scarcities of particular cards in some of these Topps sets.

From 1988 through 1990, Donruss short printed and double printed certain cards in its major sets. Ostensibly this was because of its addition of bonus team MVP cards in its regular-issue wax packs.

We are always looking for information about or photographs of printing sheets of cards for research. Each year, we try to update the hobby's knowledge of distribution anomalies. Please let us know at the address in this book if you have firsthand knowledge that would be helpful in this pursuit.

Grading Your Cards

Each hobby — stamps, coins, comic books, record collecting, etc. — has its own grading terminology. Collectors of sports cards are no exception. The one invariable criterion for determining the value of a card is its condition: The better the condition of the card, the more valuable it is. Condition grading, however, is subjective. Individual card dealers and collectors differ in the strictness of their grading, but the stated condition of a card should be determined without regard to whether it is being bought or sold.

No allowance is made for age. A 1952 card is judged by the same standards as a 1992 card. But there are specific sets and cards that are condition-sensitive (marked with "!" in the Price Guide) because of their border color, consistently poor centering, etc. Such cards and sets sometimes command premiums above the listed percentages in Mint condition.

Centering

Current centering terminology uses numbers representing the percentage of border on either side of the main design. Obviously, centering is diminished in importance for borderless cards such as Stadium Club.

Slightly Off-Center (60/40): A slightly off-center card is one that, upon close inspection, is found to have one border bigger than the opposite border. This degree once was offensive only to purists, but now some hobbyists try to avoid cards that are anything other than perfectly centered.

Off-Center (70/30): An off-center card has one border that is noticeably more than twice as wide as the opposite border.

Badly Off-Center (80/20 or worse): A badly off-center card has virtually no border on one side of the card.

Miscut: A miscut card actually shows part of the adjacent card in its larger border and consequently a corresponding amount of its card is cut off.

Corner Wear

Corner wear is the most scrutinized grading criteria in the hobby. These are the major categories of corner wear:

Corner with a slight touch of wear: The corner still is sharp, but there is a slight touch of wear showing. On a dark-bordered card, this shows as a dot of white.

Fuzzy corner: The corner still comes to a point, but the point has just begun to fray. A slightly "dinged" corner is considered the same as a fuzzy corner.

Slightly rounded corner: The fraying of the corner has increased to where there is only a hint of a point. Mild layering may be evident. A "dinged" corner is considered the same as a slightly rounded corner.

Rounded corner: The point is completely gone. Some layering is noticeable.

Badly rounded corner: The corner is completely round and rough. Severe layering is evident.

Creases

A third common defect is the crease. The degree of creasing in a card is difficult to show in a drawing or picture. On giving the specific condition of an expensive card for sale, the seller should note any creases additionally. Creases can be categorized as to severity according to the following scale:

Light Crease: A light crease is a crease that is barely noticeable upon close inspection. In fact, when cards are in plastic sheets or holders, a light crease may not be seen (until the card is taken out of the holder). A light crease on the front is much more serious than a light crease on the card back only.

Medium Crease: A medium crease is noticeable when held and studied at arm´s length by the naked eye, but does not overly detract from the appearance of the card. It is an obvious crease, but not one that breaks the picture surface of the card.

Heavy Crease: A heavy crease is one that has torn or broken through the card´s picture surface; i.e., puts a tear in the photo surface.

Alterations

Deceptive Trimming: This occurs when someone alters the card in order (1) to shave off edge wear, (2) to improve the sharpness of the corners, or (3) to improve centering — obviously their objective is to falsely increase the perceived value of the card to an unsuspecting buyer. The shrinkage usually is evident only if the trimmed card is compared to an adjacent full-size card or if the trimmed card is itself measured.

Obvious Trimming: Obvious trimming is noticeable and unfortunate. It is usually performed by noncollectors who give no thought to the present or future value of their cards.

Deceptively Retouched Borders: This occurs when the borders (especially on those cards with dark borders) are touched up on the edges and corners with magic marker or crayons of appropriate color in order to make the card appear Mint.

Categorization of Defects—Miscellaneous Flaws

The following are common minor flaws that, depending on severity, lower a card´s condition by one to four grades and often render it no better than Excellent-Mint: bubbles (lumps in surface), gum and wax stains, diamond cutting (slanted borders), notching, off-centered backs, paper wrinkles, scratched-off cartoons or puzzles on back, rubber band marks, scratches, surface impressions, and warping.

The following are common serious flaws that, depending on severity, lower a card´s condition at least four grades and often render it no better than Good: chemical or sun fading, erasure marks, mildew, miscutting (severe off-centering), holes, bleached or retouched borders, tape marks, tears, trimming, water or coffee stains, and writing.

Condition Guide

Grades

Mint (Mt)—A card with no flaws or wear. The card has four perfect corners, 60/40 or better centering from top to bottom and from left to right, original gloss, smooth edges, and original color borders. A Mint card does not have print spots or color or focus imperfections.

Near Mint-Mint (NrMt-Mt)—A card with one minor flaw. Any one of the following would lower a Mint card to Near Mint-Mint: one corner with a slight touch of wear, barely noticeable print spots, or color or focus imperfections. The card must have

60/40 or better centering in both directions, original gloss, smooth edges, and original color borders.

Near Mint (NrMt)—A card with one minor flaw. Any one of the following would lower a Mint card to Near Mint: one fuzzy corner or two to four corners with slight touches of wear, 70/30 to 60/40 centering, slightly rough edges, minor print spots, color or focus imperfections. The card must have original gloss and original color borders.

Excellent-Mint (ExMt)—A card with two or three fuzzy, but not rounded, corners and centering no worse than 80/20. The card may have no more than two of the following: slightly rough edges, very slightly discolored borders, minor print spots, color or focus imperfections. The card must have original gloss.

Excellent (Ex)—A card with four fuzzy but definitely not rounded corners and centering no worse than 80/20. The card may have a small amount of original gloss lost, rough edges, slightly discolored borders, and minor print spots or color or focus imperfections.

Very Good (Vg)—A card that has been handled but not abused: slightly rounded corners with slight layering, slight notching on edges, a significant amount of gloss lost from the surface (but no scuffing) and moderate discoloration of borders. The card may have a few light creases.

Good (G), Fair (F), Poor (P)—A well-worn, mishandled, or abused card: badly rounded and layered corners, scuffing, most or all original gloss missing, seriously discolored borders, moderate or heavy creases, and one or more serious flaws. The grade of Good, Fair, or Poor depends on the severity of wear and flaws. Good, Fair, and Poor cards generally are used only as fillers.

The most widely used grades are defined above. Obviously, many cards will not perfectly fit one of the definitions.

Therefore, categories between the major grades known as in-between grades are used, such as Good to Very Good (G-Vg), Very Good to Excellent (VgEx), and Excellent-Mint to Near Mint (ExMt-NrMt). Such grades indicate a card with all qualities of the lower category but with at least a few qualities of the higher category.

Beckett Baseball Card Price Guide lists each card and set in two grades, with the middle grade valued at about 40%–45% of the top grade.

The value of cards that fall between the listed columns can also be calculated using a percentage of the top grade. For example, a card that falls between the top and middle grades (Ex, ExMt, or NrMt in most cases) will generally be valued at anywhere from 50% to 90% of the top grade.

Similarly, a card that falls between the middle and bottom grades (G-Vg, Vg, or VgEx in most cases) will generally be valued at anywhere from 20%–40% of the top grade.

There are also cases where cards are in better condition than the top grade or worse than the bottom grade. Cards that grade worse than the lowest grade are generally valued at 5%–10% of the top grade.

When a card exceeds the top grade by one — such as NrMt-Mt when the top grade is NrMt, or Mint when the top grade is NrMt-Mt — a premium of up to 50% is possible, with 10%–20% the usual norm.

When a card exceeds the top grade by two — such as Mint when the top grade is NrMt, or NrMt-Mt when the top grade is ExMt — a premium of 25%–50% is the usual norm. But certain condition-sensitive cards or sets, particularly those from the pre-war era, can bring premiums of up to 100% or even more.

Unopened packs, boxes, and factory-collated sets are considered Mint in their unknown (and presumed perfect) state. Once opened, however, each card can be graded (and valued) in its own right by taking into account any defects that may be present in spite of the fact that the card has never been handled.

Selling Your Cards

Just about every collector sells cards or will sell cards eventually. Someday you may be interested in selling your duplicates or maybe even your whole collection. You may sell to other collectors, friends, or dealers. You may even sell cards you purchased from a certain dealer back to that same dealer. In any event, it helps to know some of the mechanics of the typical transaction between buyer and seller.

Dealers will buy cards in order to resell them to other collectors who are interested in the cards. Dealers will always pay a higher percentage for items that (in their opinion) can be resold quickly, and a much lower percentage for those items that are perceived as having low demand and hence are slow moving. In either case, dealers must buy at a price that allows for the expense of doing business and a margin for profit.

If you have cards for sale, the best advice we can give is that you get several offers for your cards — either from card shops or at a card show — and take the best offer, all things considered. Note, the "best" offer may not be the one for the highest amount. And remember, if a dealer really wants your cards, he won't let you get away without making his best competitive offer. Another alternative is to place your cards in an auction as one or several lots.

Many people think nothing of going into a department store and paying $15 for an item of clothing for which the store paid $5. But if you were selling your $15 card to a dealer and he offered you $5 for it, you might consider his markup unreasonable. To complete the analogy: Most department stores (and card dealers) that consistently pay $10 for $15 items eventually go out of business. An exception is when the dealer has lined up a willing buyer for the item(s) you are attempting to sell, or if the cards are so hot that it's likely he'll have to hold the cards for just a short period of time.

In those cases, an offer of up to 75% of book value still will allow the dealer to make a reasonable profit considering the short time he will need to hold the merchandise. In general, however, most cards and collections will bring offers in the range of 25%–50% of retail price. Also consider that most material from the last five to ten years is plentiful. If that's what you're selling, don't be surprised if your best offer is well below that range.

Interesting Notes

The first card numerically of an issue is the single card most likely to obtain excessive wear.

Consequently, you typically will find the price on the #1 card (in NrMt or Mint condition) somewhat higher than might otherwise be the case.

Similarly, but to a lesser extent (because normally the less important, reverse side of the card is the one exposed), the last card numerically in an issue also is prone to abnormal wear. This extra wear and tear occurs because the first and last cards are exposed to the elements (human element included) more than any of the other cards. They are generally end cards in any brick formations and are subject to rubber bandings, stackings on wet surfaces, and like activities.

Sports cards have no intrinsic value. The value of a card, like the value of other collectibles, can be determined only by you and your enjoyment in viewing and possessing these cardboard treasures.

Remember, the buyer ultimately determines the price of each baseball card. You are the determining price factor because you have the ability to say "No" to the price of any card by not exchanging your hard-earned money for a given issue. When the cost of a trading card exceeds the enjoyment you will receive from it, your answer should be "No." We assess and report the prices. You set them!

We are always interested in receiving the price input of collectors and dealers. We happily credit major contributors.

We welcome your opinions, since your contributions assist us in ensuring a better guide each year.

If you would like to join our survey list for the next editions of this book and others authored by Dr. Beckett, please send your name and address to Dr. James Beckett, 15850 Dallas Parkway, Dallas, TX 75248.

History of Baseball Cards

Today's version of the baseball card, with its colorful and oftentimes high-tech front and back, is a far cry from its earliest predecessors. The issue remains cloudy as to which was the very first baseball card ever produced, but the institution of base-

Centering

Well-centered

Slightly Off-centered

Off-centered

Badly Off-centered

Miscut

ball cards dates from the latter half of the 19th century, more than 100 years ago. Early issues, generally printed on heavy cardboard, were of poor quality, with photographs, drawings, and printing far short of today´s standards.

Goodwin & Co., of New York, makers of Gypsy Queen, Old Judge, and other cigarette brands, is considered by many to be the first issuer of baseball and other sports cards. Its issues, predominantly sized 1-1/2 by 2-1/2 inches, generally consisted of photographs of baseball players, boxers, wrestlers, and other subjects mounted on stiff cardboard. More than 2,000 different photos of baseball players alone have been identified. These "Old Judges," a collective name commonly used for the Goodwin & Co. cards, were issued from 1886 to 1890 and are treasured parts of many collections today.

Among the other cigarette companies that issued baseball cards still attracting attention today are Allen & Ginter, D. Buchner & Co. (Gold Coin Chewing Tobacco), and P. H. Mayo & Brother. Cards from the first two companies bear colored line drawings, while the Mayos are sepia photographs on black cardboard. In addition to the small-size cards from this era, several tobacco companies issued cabinet-size baseball cards. These "cabinets" were considerably larger than the small cards, usually about 4-1/4 by 6-1/2 inches, and were printed on heavy stock. Goodwin & Co.´s Old Judge cabinets and the National Tobacco Works´ "Newsboy" baseball photos are two that remain popular today.

By 1895, the American Tobacco Company began to dominate its competition. They discontinued baseball card inserts in their cigarette packages (actually slide boxes in those days). The lack of competition in the cigarette market had made these inserts unnecessary. This marked the end of the first era of baseball cards. At the dawn of the 20th century, few baseball cards were being issued. But once again, it was the cigarette companies, particularly, the American Tobacco Company, followed to a lesser extent by the candy and gum makers that revived the practice of including baseball cards with their products. The bulk of these cards, identified in the American Card Catalog (designated hereafter as ACC) as T or E cards for 20th century "Tobacco" or "Early Candy and Gum" issues, respectively, were released from 1909 to 1915.

This romantic and popular era of baseball card collecting produced many desirable items. The most outstanding is the fabled T-206 Honus Wagner card. Other perennial favorites among collectors are the T-206 Eddie Plank card, and the T-206 Magee error card. The former was once the second most valuable card and only recently relinquished that position to a more distinctive and aesthetically pleasing Napoleon Lajoie card from the 1933–34 Goudey Gum series. The latter misspells the player´s name as "Magie"; the most famous and most valuable blooper card.

The ingenuity and distinctiveness of this era has yet to be surpassed. Highlights include:

- The T-202 Hassan triple-folders, one of the best looking and the most distinctive cards ever issued;
- The durable T-201 Mecca double-folders, one of the first sets with players´ records on the reverse;
- The T-3 Turkey Reds, the hobby´s most popular cabinet card;
- The E-145 Cracker Jacks, the only major set containing Federal League player cards; and
- The T-204 Ramlys, with their distinctive black-and-white oval photos and ornate gold borders.

These are but a few of the varieties issued during this period.

Increasing Popularity

While the American Tobacco Company dominated the field, several other tobacco companies, as well as clothing manufacturers, newspapers and periodicals, game makers, and companies whose identities remain anonymous, also issued cards during this period. In fact, the Collins-McCarthy Candy Company, makers of Zeenuts Pacific Coast League baseball cards, issued cards yearly from 1911 to 1938. Its record for continuous annual card production has been exceeded only by the Topps Chewing Gum Company. The era of the tobacco card issues closed with the onset of World War I, with the exception of the Red Man chewing tobacco sets produced from 1952 to 1955.

Corner Wear

The partial cards here have been photographed at 300%. This was done in order to magnify each card's corner wear to such a degree that differences could be shown on a printed page.

The 1962 Topps Mickey Mantle card definitely has a rounded corner. Some may say that this card is badly rounded, but that is a judgment call.

The 1962 Topps Hank Aaron card has a slightly rounded corner. Note that there is definite corner wear evident by the fraying and that the corner no longer sports a sharp point.

The 1962 Topps Gil Hodges card has corner wear; it is slightly better than the Aaron card above. Nevertheless, some collectors might classify this Hodges corner as slightly rounded.

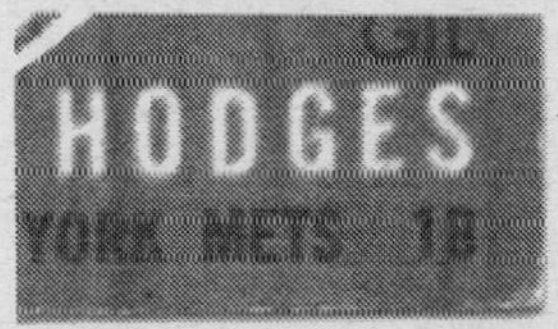

The 1962 Topps Manager's Dream card showing Mantle and Mays has slight corner wear. This is not a fuzzy corner as very slight wear is noticeable on the card's photo surface.

The 1962 Topps Don Mossi card has very slight corner wear such that it might be called a fuzzy corner. A close look at the original card shows the corner is not perfect, but almost. However, note that the issue of corner wear is somewhat academic with respect to this card. As you can plainly see, the heavy crease going across his name breaks through the photo surface.

The next flurry of card issues came in the roaring and prosperous 1920s, the era of the E card. The caramel companies (National Caramel, American Caramel, York Caramel) were the leading distributors of these E cards. In addition, the strip card, a continuous strip with several cards divided by dotted lines or other sectioning features, flourished during this time. While the E cards and the strip cards generally are considered less imaginative than the T cards or the recent candy and gum issues, they still are pursued by many advanced collectors.

Another significant event of the 1920s was the introduction of the arcade card. Taking its designation from its issuer, the Exhibit Supply Company of Chicago, it is usually known as the "Exhibit" card. Once a trademark of the penny arcades, amusement parks, and county fairs across the country, Exhibit machines dispensed nearly postcard-size photos on thick stock for one penny. These picture cards bore likenesses of a favorite cowboy, actor, actress, or baseball player. Exhibit Supply and its associated companies produced baseball cards during a longer time span, although discontinuous, than any other manufacturer. Its first cards appeared in 1921, while its last issue was in 1966. In 1979, the Exhibit Supply Company was bought and somewhat revived by a collector/dealer who has since reprinted Exhibit photos of the past.

If the T card period, from 1909 to 1915, can be designated the "Golden Age" of baseball card collecting, then perhaps the "Silver Age" commenced with the introduction of the Big League Gum series of 239 cards in 1933 (a 240th card was added in 1934). These are the forerunners of today's baseball gum cards, and the Goudey Gum Company of Boston is responsible for their success. This era spanned the period from the Depression days of 1933 to America's formal involvement in World War II in 1941.

Goudey's attractive designs, with full-color line drawings on thick card stock, greatly influenced other cards being issued at that time. As a result, the most attractive and popular vintage cards in history were produced in this "Silver Age." The 1933 Goudey Big League Gum series also owes its popularity to the more than forty Hall of Fame players in the set. These include four cards of Babe Ruth and two of Lou Gehrig. Goudey's reign continued in 1934, when it issued a 96-card set in color, together with the single remaining card from the 1933 series, #106, the Napoleon Lajoie card.

In addition to Goudey, several other bubblegum manufacturers issued baseball cards during this era. DeLong Gum Company issued an extremely attractive set in 1933. National Chicle Company's 192-card "Batter-Up" series of 1934-36 became the largest die-cut set in card history. In addition, that company offered the popular "Diamond Stars" series during the same period. Other popular sets included the "Tattoo Orbit" set of sixty color cards issued in 1933 and Gum Products' 75-card "Double Play" set, featuring sepia depictions of two players per card.

In 1939, Gum Inc., which later became Bowman Gum, replaced Goudey Gum as the leading baseball card producer. In 1939 and the following year, it issued two important sets of black-and-white cards. In 1939, its "Play Ball America" set consisted of 162 cards. The larger, 240-card "Play Ball" set of 1940 still is considered by many to be the most attractive black-and-white cards ever produced. That firm introduced its only color set in 1941, consisting of 72 cards titled "Play Ball Sports Hall of Fame." Many of these were colored repeats of poses from the black-and-white 1940 series.

In addition to regular gum cards, many manufacturers distributed premium issues during the 1930s. These premiums were printed on paper or photographic stock, rather than card stock. They were much larger than the regular cards and were sold for a penny across the counter with gum (which was packaged separately from the premium). They often were redeemed at the store or through the mail in exchange for the wrappers of previously purchased gum cards, like proof-of-purchase box-top premiums today. The gum premiums are scarcer than the card issues of the 1930s and in most cases no manufacturer's name is present.

World War II brought an end to this popular era of card collecting when paper and rubber shortages curtailed the production of bubblegum baseball cards. They were resurrected again in 1948 by the Bowman Gum Company (the direct descendent of Gum Inc.). This marked the beginning of the modern era of card collecting.

In 1948, Bowman Gum issued a 48-card set in black and white consisting of one card and one slab of gum in every 1-cent pack. That same year, the Leaf Gum Company also issued a set of cards. Although rather poor in quality, these cards were issued in color. A squabble over the rights to use players´ pictures developed between Bowman and Leaf. Eventually Leaf dropped out of the card market, but not before it had left a lasting heritage to the hobby by issuing some of the rarest cards now in existence. Leaf´s baseball card series of 1948-49 contained 98 cards, skip numbered to #168 (not all numbers were printed). Of these 98 cards, 49 are relatively plentiful; the other 49, however, are rare and quite valuable.

Bowman continued its production of cards in 1949 with a color series of 240 cards. Because there are many scarce "high numbers," this series remains the most difficult Bowman regular issue to complete. Although the set was printed in color and commands great interest due to its scarcity, it is considered aesthetically inferior to the Goudey and National Chicle issues of the 1930s. In addition to the regular issue of 1949, Bowman also produced a set of 36 Pacific Coast League players. Although this was not a regular issue, it still is prized by collectors. In fact, it has become the most valuable Bowman series.

In 1950 (representing Bowman´s one-year monopoly of the baseball card market), the company began a string of top-quality cards that continued until its demise in 1955. The 1950 series was itself something of an oddity because the low numbers, rather than the traditional high numbers, were the more difficult cards to obtain.

The year 1951 marked the beginning of the most competitive and perhaps the highest quality period of baseball card production. In that year, Topps Chewing Gum Company of Brooklyn entered the market. Topps´ 1951 series consisted of two sets of 52 cards each, one set with red backs and the other with blue backs. In addition, Topps also issued 31 insert cards, three of which remain the rarest Topps cards ("Current All-Stars" Konstanty, Roberts, and Stanky). The 1951 Topps cards were unattractive and paled in comparison to the 1951 Bowman issues. They were successful, however, and Topps has continued to produce cards ever since.

Intensified Competition

Topps issued a larger and more attractive card set in 1952. This larger size became standard for the next five years. (Bowman followed with larger-size baseball cards in 1953.) This 1952 Topps set has become, like the 1933 Goudey series and the T-206 white border series, the classic set of its era. The 407-card set is a collector´s dream of scarcities, rarities, errors, and variations. It also contains the first Topps issues of Mickey Mantle and Willie Mays.

As with Bowman and Leaf in the late 1940s, competition over player rights arose. Ensuing court battles occurred between Topps and Bowman. The market split due to stiff competition, and in January 1956, Topps bought out Bowman. (Topps, using the Bowman name, resurrected Bowman as a label in 1989.) Topps remained essentially unchallenged as the primary producer of baseball cards through 1980. So, the story of major baseball card sets from 1956 through 1980 is by and large the story of Topps´ issues. Notable exceptions include the small sets produced by Fleer Gum in 1959, 1960, 1961, and 1963, and the Kellogg´s Cereal and Hostess Cakes baseball cards issued to promote their products.

A court decision in 1980 paved the way for two other large gum companies to enter (or reenter, in Fleer´s case) the baseball card arena. Fleer, which had last made photo cards in 1963, and the Donruss Company (then a division of General Mills) secured rights to produce baseball cards of current players, thus breaking Topps´ monopoly. Each company issued major card sets in 1981 with bubblegum products.

Then a higher court decision in that year overturned the lower court ruling against Topps. It appeared that Topps had regained its sole position as a producer of baseball cards. Undaunted by the revocation ruling, Fleer and Donruss continued to issue cards in 1982 but without bubblegum or any other edible product. Fleer issued its current player baseball cards with "team logo stickers," while Donruss issued its cards with a piece of a baseball jigsaw puzzle.

Sharing the Pie

Since 1981, these three major baseball card producers all have thrived, sharing relatively equal recognition. Each has steadily increased its involvement in terms of numbers of issues per year. To the delight of collectors, their competition has generated novel, and in some cases exceptional, issues of current Major League Baseball players. Collectors also eagerly accepted the debut efforts of Score (1988) and Upper Deck (1989). These five companies were about to embark on a wild ride through the 1990s.

Upper Deck's successful entry into the market turned out to be very important. The company's card stock, photography, packaging, and marketing gave baseball cards a new standard for quality and began the "premium card" trend that continues today. The second premium baseball card set to be issued was the 1990 Leaf set, named for and issued by the parent company of Donruss. To gauge the significance of the premium card trend, one need only note that two of the most valuable post-1986 regular-issue cards in the hobby are the 1989 Upper Deck Ken Griffey Jr. and 1990 Leaf Frank Thomas Rookie Cards.

The impressive debut of Leaf in 1990 was followed by those of Studio, Ultra, and Stadium Club in 1991. Of those, Stadium Club with its dramatic borderless photos and uncoated card fronts made the biggest impact. In 1992, Bowman and Pinnacle joined the premium fray. In 1992, Donruss and Fleer abandoned the traditional 50-cent pack market and instead produced premium sets comparable to (and presumably designed to compete against) Upper Deck's set. Those moves, combined with the almost instantaneous spread of premium cards to the other major team sports cards, serve as strong indicators that premium cards were here to stay. Bowman had been a lower-level product from 1989 to 1991.

In 1993, Fleer, Topps, and Upper Deck produced the first "super premium" cards with Flair, Finest, and SP, respectively. The success of all three products was an indication the baseball card market was headed toward even higher price levels, and that turned out to be the case in 1994 with the introduction of Bowman's Best (a Topps hybrid of prospect-oriented Bowman and the superpremium Finest) and Leaf Limited. Other 1994 debuts included Upper Deck's entry-level Collector's Choice and Pinnacle's hobby-only Select.

Overall, inserts continued to dominate the hobby scene. Specifically, the parallel chase cards introduced in 1992 with Topps Gold became the latest major hobby trend. Topps Gold was followed by 1993 Finest Refractors (at the time the scarcest insert ever produced and still a landmark set) and the one-per-box Stadium Club First Day Issue.

Of course, the biggest on-field news of 1994 was the owner-provoked players' strike that halted the season prematurely. While the baseball card hobby suffered noticeably from the strike, there was no catastrophic market crash as some had feared. However, the strike drastically slowed down a market that was both strong and growing and contributed to a serious hobby contraction that continues to this day.

By 1995, parallel insert sets were commonplace and had taken on a new complexion: the most popular ones were those that had announced (or at least suspected) print runs of 500 or less, such as Finest Refractors and Select Artist's Proofs.

This trend continued in 1996, with several parallel inserts that were printed in quantities of 250 or less, such as Finest Gold Refractors, Fleer Circa Rave, Studio Silver Press Proofs, and three of the six Select Certified parallels. It could be argued that the high price tags on these extremely limited parallel cards (many exceeded the $1,000 plateau) were driving many single-player collectors to frustration, and even completely out of the hobby. At the same time, average pack prices soared while average number of cards per pack dropped, making the baseball card hobby increasingly expensive.

On the positive side, two trends from 1996 clearly brought in new collectors: Topps' Mickey Mantle retrospective inserts in both series of Topps and Stadium Club and Leaf's Signature Series, which included one certified autograph per pack. Although the Mantle craze following his passing seemed to be a short-term phenomenon, the inclusion of autographs in packs seemed to have more long-term significance.

In 1997 the print runs in selected sets got even lower. Both Fleer/SkyBox and Pinnacle brands issued cards of which only one exists.

The growth in popularity of autographs also continued. Many products had autographed cards in their packs. A very positive trend was a return to basics. Many collectors bought Rookie Cards, as they understood that concept, and worked on finishing sets.

There was also an increase in international players collecting. Hideo Nomo was incredibly popular in Japan while Chan Ho Park was in demand in Korea. This bodes well for an international growth in the hobby.

Clearly, 1998 was a year of rebirth and growth for the hobby. The big boost came from the home run chase being conducted by Mark McGwire and Sammy Sosa, as well as the continued brilliance of stalwarts like Ken Griffey Jr. and Roger Clemens. The baseball card hobby received a great deal of positive publicity from the renewed interest in the game.

Rookie Cards of the key players of 1998 made significant gains in value as the hobby once again turned to Rookie Cards as the collectible of choice. Also, cards professionally graded by companies such as PSA and SGC were becoming more heavily traded in both older and newer material.

In addition, the Internet and various services such as eBay contributed to the strong growth in collecting interest over the year.

There were downsides in 1998, though. Pinnacle Brands folded, leaving a legacy of innovation and promotions not seen by other companies. In addition, there still was the problem of collectors being frustrated by the extremely short printed cards of their favorite players, making set completion almost impossible.

During 1998, Pacific received a full baseball license and added many innovations to the card market. Their 1998 OnLine set is the most comprehensive set issued in the last five years and many veteran collectors applauded Pacific´s continuing attempts to get as many players as possible into their sets.

In the last couple of years, card companies have been printing specific subsets (usually young players or Rookie Cards) in shorter supply than the regular cards. This is not in every set, but in many sets produced since 1998.

In 1999, many of the trends of the last couple of years continued to gain strength. Buying, selling, and trading cards over the Internet became a dominant factor in the secondary market. Beckett Media LP began its own Marketplace, offering the collectors a chance to search across inventory from many of the finest dealers nationwide in one comprehensive on-line database; eBay continued to flourish, while many other parties began to reap the benefits of the burgeoning online auction market. The Barry Halper collection was auctioned off, bringing many museum quality items to the market and giving the older memorabilia market a significant boost as many treasures were made available to collectors.

Also, the boom in Internet trading created a perfect fit for professionally graded cards, as buyers and sellers traded cards sight unseen with the confidence established by a third-party grader.

From a field of almost a dozen contenders, three companies emerged in 1999 to dominate the field of professional grading, BGS (Beckett Grading Services), PSA (Professional Sports Authenticator), and SGC (Sportscard Guaranty L.L.C.). In 1999 these companies made dramatic expansions in on-site grading and submissions at card shows throughout the nation. In response to the widespread acceptance of graded cards, the line of monthly Beckett Price Guides each added a separate section within the price guide area for professionally graded cards.

Similar to 1998, four licensed manufacturers (Fleer/SkyBox, Pacific, Topps, and Upper Deck) produced slightly more than fifty different products for 1999.

Perhaps the biggest hit of the 1999 card season was created by Topps. Card #220 within the basic issue first series 1999 Topps brand featured Home Run King Mark McGwire in 70 variations, one for each homer he slugged in 1998, and many collectors went after the whole set. Continuing a legacy as strong as the Yankees, the basic Topps issue was one of the most popular sets released in 1999.

Closely trailing the Topps McGwire promotion was Upper Deck´s dynamic A Piece of History bat card promotion. The card that kicked off the frenzy was the Babe Ruth A Piece of History distributed in 1999 Upper Deck series 1 packs. Upper Deck actually purchased a cracked game-used Babe Ruth bat for $24,000 and proceeded to cut it up into approximately 350-400 chips of wood to create the now famous Ruth bat card. The card instantly created polar opposites of opinion among hobbyists. Traditional collectors howled at the sacrilegious act of destroying such a historic piece of memorabilia while more open-minded collectors jumped at the opportunity to chase such an important card. The Ruth card was followed up by the cross-brand "500 Club" bat card promotion, whereby UD produced bat cards from every major league ballplayer who hit 500 or more home runs in his career (except for Mark McGwire, who hit his 500th in the midst of the 1999 season and promptly stated that he did not support Upper Deck's promotion).

More memorabilia cards than ever were offered to collectors in 1999 as Fleer/SkyBox kicked up their efforts to match the standards set by Upper Deck in previous years. Batting gloves, hats, and shoes joined the typical bats and jerseys as pieces of game-used equipment to be featured on trading cards. Sets like E-X Century Authen-Kicks and Fleer Mystique Feel the Game typified the new offerings.

Topps only dabbled with memorabilia cards in 1999, but continued to offer some of the hottest autographed inserts, highlighted by the Topps Stars Rookie Reprint Autographs and the Topps Nolan Ryan Autographs.

Pacific made a clear decision to steer free of memorabilia and autograph inserts, instead focusing on offering collectors a wide selection of beautifully designed insert and parallel cards. Those themes worked beautifully with their established presence for making comprehensive sets, providing collectors with the necessary challenge to pursue regional stars and a favorite team in addition to the typical superstars.

An astounding total of 264 players made their first appearance on a major league licensed trading card in 1999. What may go down as the deepest class of Rookie Cards of all time features a cornucopia of talented youngsters led by Rick Ankiel, Josh Beckett, Pat Burrell, Josh Hamilton, Eric Munson, Corey Patterson, and Alfonso Soriano.

As in years past, Topps continued to provide collectors with a fistful of Rookie Cards within their Bowman, Bowman Chrome, and Bowman's Best brands. In a trend established in 1998 by Fleer when they released their Fleer Update set (fueled largely by a J. D. Drew Rookie Card), hobbyists enjoyed a bevy of late-season sets chock full of RC's. Fleer/SkyBox made an all-out effort by stuffing more than 100 Rookie Cards into their 1999 Fleer Update set. Topps produced their first boxed Traded set since 1994. Each 1999 Topps Traded set contained 1 of 75 different cards autographed by a rookie prospect. Considering how much wider the selection of Rookie Cards became in 1999, it's amazing to see that so few of these RC's were serial numbered. When one looks at the success established with serial numbered Rookie Cards in the basketball and football card markets with brands like SP Authentic and SPx Finite, one can only scratch his head when realizing that Fleer Mystique was the only brand to offer baseball collectors serial numbered RC's. Thus, it's not surprising to see that despite having twenty-five different Rookie Cards issued in 1999, Pat Burrell's Fleer Mystique RC (#'d of 2,999) had been established as his "best" RC by year's end.

Youngsters weren't the only players in the limelight in 1999 as retired stars and Hall of Famers were featured on more cards than any other year during the 1990s. Upper Deck's Century Legends brand, featuring the top fifty active and top fifty retired players of the decade as chosen by the Sporting News was a runaway hit.

Perhaps the most popular insert set of the year, outpacing all of the dazzling high-dollar memorabilia cards, was Topps Gallery Heritage. Utilizing the design and painting style of artist Gerry Dvorak from the classic 1953 Topps set, these modern masterpieces proved that insert cards can still be a hot commodity in the secondary market, albeit assuming they're well conceived and well made, an unfortunate rarity these days.

The spate of basic issue sets with short-printed subsets continued across many brands in 1999. In reaction to many frustrated dealers and collectors struggling to complete these sets, Fleer/SkyBox created dual versions of each prospect card for the 1999 SkyBox Premium set, an action shot was short-printed and a posed shot was seeded at the same rate as other basic issue cards. The idea was well received by collectors but enjoyed a surprisingly short-lived period of active trading in the secondary market.

The year 2000 was marked by several major developments that would continue shaping the future of our hobby. First off, Pacific decided to forfeit their baseball card license on January 1st, 2000, in an effort to more sharply focus their production expenditures into football and hockey.

In a separate development, Wizards of the Coast (primarily known for their non-sport gaming cards) was granted a license to produce baseball trading cards and debuted their MLB Showdown brand. The cards proved to be quite successful in that they were collected as a set by veteran collectors and played as a game by children (and some adults) both inside and outside of the typical collecting community.

By year's end, Fleer fazed out their SkyBox and Flair brand names in an effort to take full advantage of the historic significance and brand recognition of their flagship Fleer sets issued sporadically during the late 1950s-1970s and consistently from 1981 to the present.

Almost sixty brands of MLB-licensed cards, issued by five manufacturers, were produced in 2000. In addition, Just Minors and Team Best produced a variety of attractive minor league products. Most shop owners continued to generate their income primarily through the sales of packs and boxes of new product, and, as in years past, they had to make careful decisions as to what to keep in stock for customers and what to pass up in fear of a low sell through.

Vintage (or retro-themed) sets dominated the market highlighted by Fleer Greats of the Game, Upper Deck Yankees Legends, and the run of 3,000 hit club and Joe DiMaggio game-used cards issued by Fleer and Upper Deck. In 2001, Topps Heritage (mimicking the style of the classic '52 Topps cards), Upper Deck Vintage (in an homage to '63 Topps baseball), and the return of Topps Archives (after a six-year hiatus) added fuel to the fire.

Using the vintage-theme to tap into a base of wealthy consumers, Upper Deck rolled out their line of Master Collection products (which debuted in basketball a year prior with a Michael Jordan set). Both the Yankees Master Collection and Brooklyn Dodgers Master Collection sets carried initial SRP's of $4,000 or more, marking the most expensive "factory set" of alltime. Each of these sets was serial numbered (500 Yankees and 250 Dodgers), came in a stylish wood box and contained an assortment of game-used and autograph cards from legends of days gone by.

Game-used memorabilia cards became more abundant in all products to the point where a few early 2001 releases (2001 Pacific Private Stock and 2001 SP Game Bat Edition both carrying SRP's in the $15-$20 range) included them at a rate of one per pack. Both products enjoyed a dynamic sell through and proved to be very popular in the secondary market. The result, however, on the secondary market values of game-used memorabilia cards has been dramatic. An Alex Rodriguez or Ken Griffey Jr. game bat or game jersey card that sold for $200+ in 1999 could be had for as little as $25-$50 in early 2001.

Patch cards (a swatch of jersey that contains part of a multicolored patch) really caught on by year's end as the market formalized premium values on these cards. Upper Deck was the first to create separate "super-premium" jersey Patch inserts within 2000 Upper Deck 1 and 2000 Upper Deck Game Jersey Edition (aka series 2). Pacific followed suit with their Game Gear patch subset within the invincible brand.

By early 2001, Major League Baseball Properties had gotten involved with the trading card autograph and memorabilia programs. From 2001 on, all MLB-licensed trading cards produced by the manufacturers that involved an autograph or game-used memorabilia item had to have the procurement of the item witnessed by a representative of Andersen Consulting, a firm hired by MLB to oversee this historic program. Never before had the league and manufacturers made such an effort to offer autographed or game-used memorabilia trading cards of such authentic provenance.

Short-printed subset cards, a trend started in 1999, continued to be a common element in most basic sets. The trend, however, evolved to the point where these short prints were now being serial numbered, autographed by the player, or incorporating an element of game-used material onto the card. The result was higher values on the key singles, but lower odds of actually finding a good RC in a pack. By year's end, a general sentiment of frustration over not being able to pull good Rookie Cards from a box was beginning to be heard more and more often from collectors.

Rookie Cards incorporating game-used material debuted at year's end in 2000 Black Diamond Rookie Edition. Also, Rookie Cards signed by the player, introduced within the basketball and football card markets in 1999 (with Upper Deck's SPx brand), made their baseball debut in 2000 SPx. Serial-numbered Rookie Cards grew in total usage, but shrank in print run numbers as production figures reached an all-time low of 999 copies for a basic issue RC within the 2000 Pacific Omega set.

Year-end boxed sets, a trend brought back from a four-year hiatus by Fleer in 1998 with its Fleer Update set, continued to expand as Topps issued its Bowman Draft Picks and Bowman Chrome Draft Picks sets to cap the now single-series accompanying standard Bowman and Bowman Chrome products.

Fleer broke new ground by blending a 1980s "old-school" concept with some postmodern angles in their 2000 Fleer Glossy boxed set. Harkening back to the run of Glossy parallel factory sets produced from 1987 to 1989, the 2000 Fleer Glossy set included a parallel version of the complete 400-card basic 2000 Fleer set. In addition, 50 new cards (card #'s 401-450, each serial numbered to 1,000 copies) featuring a selection of prospects and rookies were created. Each Glossy factory set contained 5 of the 50 new cards, making it a real challenge to complete the Glossy set.

In a first of its kind for the baseball market, Upper Deck issued a product in December 2000 called Rookie Update that incorporated new cards for three separate popular brands (SP Authentic, SPx, and UD Pros and Prospects) into each pack of cards.

Upper Deck came to terms with Major League Baseball for a license to produce cards featuring members of past and present Team USA squads (bringing back a run of cards last seen in 1993 Topps Traded). That allowed Upper Deck the opportunity to radically expand their production of "true" Rookie Cards in year-end 2000 products, adding a spate of cards featuring heroes from the Olympics in Sydney, Australia, like Ben Sheets. Not surprisingly, the number of prospects making their Rookie Card debut in 2000 sets jumped from about 280 players in 1999 to slightly more than 350 players in 2000.

The influence of sports card dealers and collectors from the Far East (and most noticeably Japan) continued to grow in 2000 as stateside buying approached frenzied levels over scarce Hideo Nomo and Kazuhiro Sasaki cards. A much-traveled starter these days, Nomo's first-ever certified autograph card (issued within the Fleer Mystique Fresh Ink insert set) was the hottest card in the hobby for two months (initially trading for as much as $600-$800).

Not all trends were met with success this year. In particular, low-end products geared towards the youth audience (like 2000 Impact by Fleer) were roundly ignored. The hobby still faces a tough road ahead to keep new waves of collectors involved from generation to generation. Part of the Catch-22 with creating affordable brands catered to youths is that the same customers are most interested in the high-end, expensive material.

Also, Upper Deck's PowerDeck product faced an indifferent audience for a second year in a row, as collectors and even general sports enthusiasts outside the hobby failed to get excited over the CD-ROM cards. More success was met by UD's e-Card insert program, whereby collectors who pulled an e-Card from a pack of UD cards had to go to UD's Website and check the serial number printed on the card to see whether it could evolve into an autograph, game jersey, or game jersey autograph exchange.

The Internet continued to have profound ramifications on shaping the destiny of sports card collecting. By 2000, nearly every dealer (and hard-core collector) was buying or selling cards to some degree in online auctions. Auction sales had become so prolific that they were now having a strong effect on the secondary market sales levels of trading cards in arenas entirely outside of cyberspace, like shops, shows, and mail order.

The eBay site continued to dominate the online auction action, introducing what appears to be a popular "Buy It Now" option to their already established auction format. The Pit.com opened in mid-year with their concept of buying and selling a portfolio of professionally graded sports cards through their Web site. The concept is based almost exactly upon the methodology used for buying and selling stocks through a brokerage house, with daily ebbs and flows in posted buy and sell prices on your inventory.

Beckett.com made radical improvements to their Marketplace search engines and expanded their inventory of sports cards to the point where they were providing both a wider and a deeper selection of trading cards than any site on the Internet. In addition, a company-wide effort to provide daily news content on their site (coupled with a weekly newsletter sent to over 400,000 collectors) began at year's end, and the hobby has reaped the benefits ever since.

As the 2001 season approached, hobbyists waited with bated breath for seven-time Japanese batting champ Ichiro Suzuki to make his debut in the Seattle Mariner's outfield. And what a stunning debut it was. Ichiro led the league in hitting, led the Mariners to their best record ever, and walked off with the A.L. Rookie of the Year and Most Valuable Player awards. Upper Deck obtained the exclusive rights to produce his autograph cards and they hit a grand slam in midsummer by releasing his SPx Rookie Card, featuring a game jersey swatch and a cut signature autograph. In a year studded with notable cards, this one was likely the most memorable.

In the National League, 37-year-old San Francisco Giants superstar Barry Bonds captivated the nation by bashing a jaw dropping 73 home runs, shattering Mark McGwire's 1998 single-season home run record.

Cardinals' rookie Albert Pujols emerged out of the low minor leagues to become an instant hobby superstar and walk away with N.L. Rookie of the Year honors.

The year 2001 was a tumultuous one for sports cards. Topps started the year off with a bang by celebrating their 50th anniversary producing baseball cards. Pacific forfeited its license to make baseball cards after an eight-year run to focus on football and hockey cards. Playoff, a company based out of Grand Prairie, Texas, that had earned its stripes by producing football cards in the late 1990s, purchased the rights to the much-hallowed Donruss corporate name and became a formal MLB licensee in the spring of 2001. Their entrance into the baseball card market heralded the return of benchmark brands like Donruss, Donruss Signature, and Leaf.

Competition was fiercer than ever among the four primary licensees (Donruss-Playoff, Fleer, Topps, and Upper Deck) as they cranked out almost 80 different products over the course of 2001.

Of all these, likely the most historically important product, Upper Deck Prospect Premieres, was widely overlooked upon release. In a bold move, Upper Deck created a set of 102 prospects, none of which had played a day in the majors. Each player was pictured, however, in the major league uniforms of their parent ballclubs and signed to individual contracts. Because no active major leaguers were featured, Upper Deck did not have to include licensing rights from the MLB Players Association, though they did get licensing from Major League Properties. The industry had never seen a major release featuring active ballplayers marketed to the mainstream audience that lacked licensing from the MLBPA. Because of its lack of historical predecessors and a mixed reception from collectors, the cards were tagged by Beckett Baseball Card Monthly as XRC's (or Extended Rookie Cards), a term that had not been used since 1989.

UD's Prospect Premieres was the first major effort by a manufacturer to level the playing field between Topps and everyone else in that Topps has exclusive rights from the MLBPA to include minor leaguers in their basic brands.

Rookie Cards continued to fascinate collectors, especially in a year with talents like Ichiro and Albert Pujols. The number of players featured on Rookie Cards in 2001 ballooned to an almost absurd figure of 505.

Exchange cards became more prevalent than ever, as manufacturers expanded their use from autograph cards that didn't get returned in time for pack out to slots within basic sets left open in brands released early in the year to fill in with late-season rookie call-ups.

Certified autograph cards remained a huge player in how brands were structured, but the quality of the players suffered greatly as autograph fees continued to spiral out of control. Signatures from superstars like Barry Bonds and Derek Jeter were now being featured on cards with minuscule print runs of 25 or 50 copies while unknown (and often aging and talentless) prospects signed their serial-numbered

Rookies Cards by the hundred count.

More serial-numbered Rookie Cards were produced than ever before, but the quantities produced kept sinking lower and lower as companies tried to create secondary market value by simply limiting supply, a dangerous move to say the least. Donruss-Playoff produced the scarcest Rookie Cards of the year, a handful of Game Base cards (including Ichiro) each serial #'d to a scant 100 copies, within their Leaf Limited set.

After a six-month delay, Topps released their much awaited e-Topps program, a product sold entirely on their Web site whereby trading is conducted in a similar fashion to the buying and selling of stocks, in September.

Several products incorporated non-card memorabilia such as signed caps, bobbing head dolls, and signed baseballs with mixed results.

Memorabilia cards continued their slide into mediocrity as the number of cards featuring various bits and pieces of balls, bases, bats, jerseys, pants, shoes, seats, and whatever else could be dreamt up continued to be offered to consumers, who found the cards less appealing with each passing month. To battle consumer apathy, companies often started to offer combination memorabilia cards featuring notable teammates or several pieces of equipment from a notable star.

Retro-themed cards continued to grow in popularity, and some of the innovations seen in these sets were remarkable. Of particular note was Upper Deck's SP Legendary Cuts Autographs set, featuring 84 deceased players. The set required UD to purchase more than 3,300 autograph cuts, which were then incorporated into a windowpane card design. The result was the first certified autograph cards for legends like Roger Maris, Satchell Paige, and Jackie Robinson. Also, Topps Tribute released at year's end and carrying a hefty $40 per pack suggested retail was widely hailed as one of the most beautiful retro-themed cards ever designed, with their crystal-board fronts encasing full-color, razor-sharp photos.

Pack prices continued to escalate, but surprisingly, the public did not balk as long as they delivered value. The most notable high-end product to hit the market in 2001 was Upper Deck Ultimate Collection with a suggested retail of $100 per pack.

September 11th, 2001, is a day that will go down as one of the most devastating in the history of the United States of America. The game of baseball and the hobby of collecting sports cards were rightfully cast aside as the nation mourned the tragic loss of lives in New York, Pennsylvania, and Washington, D.C. America's economy tumbled as airline traveling ground to a near halt and threats of anthrax crippled the mail system. An economy threatening to slip into recession at the beginning of the year dove headlong into it. The sports card market, along with many other industries, felt the hit for several months. Slowly, Americans looked to move past the grief and the sports card industry, steeped in American nostalgia, provided an ideal retreat for many.

The Arizona Diamondbacks beat the New York Yankees in one of the finest World Series ever played, a much-needed diversion for a grief-stricken nation and a calling card for the dramatic power and glory of our National Pastime.

2002 was a relatively quiet one for baseball cards. Dodger's rookie pitcher Kazuhisa Ishii got off to a blazing first half start and his cards carried many releases through to the All-Star break. Ishii stumbled badly in the second half and no notable rookies were in place to pick up market interest. Cubs hurler Mark Prior created a stir, and his 2001 Rookie Cards were red hot at mid-season. For the second straight season, Barry Bonds was the most dominant star in our sport. His early cards continued to outpace all others in volume trading and professional grading submissions.

The number of players featured on Rookie Cards (or Extended Rookie Cards) reached an all-time high of 524 in 2002 as the manufacturers continued to push the envelope toward more immediate coverage of the current year draft. Though few collectors took notice at the time of release, Upper Deck's incorporation of collegiate Team USA athletes into several year-end brands may take hold and grow into a more prominent position in our industry for collegiate ballplayers. The results of these trends, however, are cards that feature a lot of talented youngsters whom most collectors, unfortunately, have never heard of and won't see in a major league uniform for several years.

To make up for the void in excitement generated by rookies and prospects, the manufacturers made some interesting innovations in product distribution and brand development. In general, base sets got noticeably bigger (including Upper Deck's 1,182 card 40-Man brand and Topps 990-card Topps Total brand). In addition, brands like Topps 206, Leaf Rookies and Stars, and Fleer Fall Classics started to incorporate variations of the base cards directly into the basic issue set (different images, switched out teams, etc.).

One of the bigger surprise hits of the year was the aforementioned Topps 206 brand, which borrowed design elements and set composition from the legendary T-206 tobacco set. Other brands continued to successfully mine from cards and eras long since passed.

Donruss continued to push the creative envelope by incorporating 8½" by 11" framed signature pieces directly into boxes of their Playoff Absolute brand. After a four-year hiatus, Fleer brought back their eponymous "Fleer" name brand with a 540-card set. Donruss introduced their wildly successful Diamond Kings brand, which featured a 150-card painted set. Fleer's Box Score brand was also a popular debut utilizing a unique box-inside-a-box distribution concept. Popular brands like SP Legendary Cuts, Leaf Certified, Topps Heritage, and Topps Tribute all received warm welcomes for their follow ups to their successes achieved the prior year.

The 2004 season continued to bring us again a growing number of sets with price points ranging from $1.29 to $150. There were also many new heroes during the 2003 season as players such as Josh Beckett, Miguel Cabrera, and Dontrelle Willis of the World Champion Florida Marlins were very strong sellers.

Hideki Matsui, who was the most anticipated rookie for the 2003 season, had a very fine year for the American League Champion Yankees but did not draw the same interest from collectors as Ichiro Suzuki did during the 2001 season.

The 2005 season was most notable for the departure of both Fleer and Donruss/Playoff from the ranks of major manufacturers. One of the issues in recent years has been the staggering amount of sets as well as the complexities of those sets. With some direction from the licensors, the baseball card market was reduced and a maximum of 40 products are expected to be released during the 2006 calendar year.

Despite the struggles the sport of baseball has endured; in recent years, the baseball card market has stepped back to the forefront of the card-collecting hobby, outpacing football, basketball, hockey, golf, and motor sports in volume dollars. As the hobby of collecting baseball cards evolves, we continue to face a market that is blessed with bold creativity and superlative quality; and also challenged with the need to reach new consumers both in mass retail and in cyberspace to continue its growth.

Additional Reading

Each year Beckett Media LP produces comprehensive annual price guides for several sports: *Beckett Baseball Card Price Guide, Beckett Basketball Card Price Guide, Beckett Football Card Price Guide, Beckett Hockey Card Price Guide, Beckett Racing Price Guide,* and a line of *Beckett Alphabetical Checklists* books have been released as well. The aim of these annual guides is to provide information and accurate pricing on a wide array of sports cards, ranging from main issues by the major card manufacturers to various regional, promotional, and food issues. Alphabetical checklist books are published to assist the collector in identifying all the cards of any particular player. The seasoned collector will find these tools valuable sources of information that will enable him to pursue his hobby interests.

In addition, abridged editions of the *Beckett Price Guides* have been published for each of these major sports as part of the House of Collectibles series: *The Official Price Guide to Baseball Cards, The Official Price Guide to Football Cards,* and *The Official Price Guide to Basketball Cards.* Published in a convenient mass-market paperback format, these price guides provide information and accurate pricing on all the main issues by the major card manufacturers.

Prices in This Guide

Prices found in this guide reflect current retail rates just prior to the printing of this book. They do not reflect the FOR SALE prices of the author, the publisher, the distributors, the advertisers, or any card dealers associated with this guide. No one is obligated in any way to buy, sell, or trade his or her cards based on these prices. The price listings were compiled by the author from actual buy/sell transactions at sports conventions, sports card shops, buy/sell advertisements in the hobby papers, for sale prices from dealer catalogs and price lists, and discussions with leading hobbyists in the United States and Canada. All prices are in U.S. dollars.

Acknowledgments

A great deal of diligence, hard work, and dedicated effort went into this year´s volume. However, the high standards to which we hold ourselves could not have been met without the expert input and generous amount of time contributed by many people. Our sincere thanks are extended to each and every one of you.

A complete list of these invaluable contributors appears after the **Price Guide** section.

2006 Artifacts

❑	COMPLETE SET (100)	40.00	15.00
❑	COMMON CARD (1-100)	.50	.20
❑	COMMON ROOKIE	.75	.30
❑	1 Luis Gonzalez	.60	.25
❑	2 Conor Jackson (RC)	1.25	.50
❑	3 Joey Devine RC	.75	.30
❑	4 Andruw Jones	.75	.30
❑	5 Chipper Jones	1.25	.50
❑	6 John Smoltz	.75	.30
❑	7 Jeff Francoeur	1.25	.50
❑	8 Brian Roberts	.50	.20
❑	9 Miguel Tejada	.50	.20
❑	10 Nick Markakis (RC)	1.25	.50
❑	11 Curt Schilling	.75	.30
❑	12 David Ortiz	1.25	.50
❑	13 Johnny Damon	.75	.30
❑	14 Manny Ramirez	.75	.30
❑	15 Jonathan Papelbon (RC)	4.00	1.50
❑	16 Aramis Ramirez	.50	.20
❑	17 Carlos Zambrano	.50	.20
❑	18 Derrek Lee	.50	.20
❑	19 Greg Maddux	2.00	.75
❑	20 Mark Prior	.75	.30
❑	21 Mark Buehrle	.50	.20
❑	22 Paul Konerko	.50	.20
❑	23 Adam Dunn	.50	.20
❑	24 Ken Griffey Jr.	2.00	.75
❑	25 Travis Hafner	.50	.20
❑	26 Victor Martinez	.50	.20
❑	27 Todd Helton	.75	.30
❑	28 Ivan Rodriguez	.75	.30
❑	29 Jeremy Bonderman	.50	.20
❑	30 Jeremy Hermida (RC)	.75	.30
❑	31 Carlos Delgado	.50	.20
❑	32 Dontrelle Willis	.50	.20
❑	33 Josh Beckett	.50	.20
❑	34 Miguel Cabrera	.75	.30
❑	35 Craig Biggio	.75	.30
❑	36 Lance Berkman	.50	.20
❑	37 Roger Clemens	2.50	1.00
❑	38 Roy Oswalt	.50	.20
❑	39 Josh Willingham (RC)	.75	.30
❑	40 Hanley Ramirez (RC)	2.00	.75
❑	41 Prince Fielder (RC)	3.00	1.25
❑	42 Zack Greinke	.50	.20
❑	43 Francisco Rodriguez	.50	.20
❑	44 Vladimir Guerrero	1.25	.50
❑	45 Tim Hamulack (RC)	.75	.30
❑	46 Jeff Kent	.50	.20
❑	47 Ben Sheets	.50	.20
❑	48 Rickie Weeks	.50	.20
❑	49 Francisco Liriano (RC)	4.00	1.50
❑	50 Joe Mauer	.75	.30
❑	51 Johan Santana	.75	.30
❑	52 Justin Morneau	.50	.20
❑	53 Torii Hunter	.50	.20
❑	54 Carlos Beltran	.50	.20
❑	55 David Wright	2.00	.75
❑	56 Jose Reyes	1.25	.50
❑	57 Mike Piazza	1.25	.50
❑	58 Pedro Martinez	.75	.30
❑	59 Alex Rodriguez	2.00	.75
❑	60 Derek Jeter	3.00	1.25
❑	61 Hideki Matsui	1.25	.50
❑	62 Randy Johnson	1.25	.50
❑	63 Justin Verlander (RC)	3.00	1.25
❑	64 Bobby Crosby	.50	.20
❑	65 Eric Chavez	.50	.20
❑	66 Brian Anderson (RC)	.75	.30
❑	67 Bobby Abreu	.50	.20
❑	68 Pat Burrell	.50	.20
❑	69 Jason Bay	.50	.20
❑	70 Oliver Perez	.50	.20
❑	71 Chuck James (RC)	1.25	.50
❑	72 Brian Giles	.50	.20
❑	73 Jake Peavy	.50	.20
❑	74 Khalil Greene	.75	.30
❑	75 Jason Schmidt	.50	.20
❑	76 Kenji Johjima RC	4.00	1.50
❑	77 Jeremy Accardo RC	.75	.30
❑	78 Adrian Beltre	.50	.20
❑	79 Ichiro Suzuki	2.00	.75
❑	80 Jeff Harris RC	.75	.30
❑	81 Felix Hernandez	.75	.30
❑	82 Albert Pujols	2.50	1.00
❑	83 Chris Carpenter	.50	.20
❑	84 Jim Edmonds	.75	.30
❑	85 Scott Rolen	.75	.30
❑	86 Mike Jacobs (RC)	.75	.30
❑	87 Carl Crawford	.50	.20
❑	88 Anderson Hernandez (RC)	.75	.30
❑	89 Scott Kazmir	.75	.30
❑	90 Josh Rupe (RC)	.75	.30
❑	91 Scott Feldman RC	.75	.30
❑	92 Alfonso Soriano	.50	.20
❑	93 Hank Blalock	.50	.20
❑	94 Mark Teixeira	.75	.30
❑	95 Michael Young	.50	.20
❑	96 Roy Halladay	.50	.20
❑	97 Vernon Wells	.50	.20
❑	98 Jason Bergmann RC	.75	.30
❑	99 Ryan Zimmerman (RC)	5.00	2.00
❑	100 Jose Vidro	.50	.20

2007 Artifacts

❑	COMPLETE SET (100)	40.00	15.00
❑	COMMON CARD (1-70)	.40	.15
❑	COMMON ROOKIE (71-100)	.75	.30
❑	1 Miguel Tejada	.40	.15
❑	2 David Ortiz	1.00	.40
❑	3 Manny Ramirez	.60	.25
❑	4 Curt Schilling	.60	.25
❑	5 Jim Thome	.60	.25
❑	6 Paul Konerko	.40	.15
❑	7 Jermaine Dye	.40	.15
❑	8 Travis Hafner	.40	.15
❑	9 Victor Martinez	.40	.15
❑	10 Grady Sizemore	.60	.25
❑	11 Ivan Rodriguez	.60	.25
❑	12 Magglio Ordonez	.40	.15
❑	13 Justin Verlander	1.00	.40
❑	14 Mark Teahen	.40	.15
❑	15 Vladimir Guerrero	1.00	.40
❑	16 Jered Weaver	.60	.25
❑	17 Justin Morneau	.40	.15
❑	18 Joe Mauer	.60	.25
❑	19 Torii Hunter	.40	.15
❑	20 Johan Santana	.60	.25
❑	21 Derek Jeter	2.50	1.00
❑	22 Alex Rodriguez	1.50	.60
❑	23 Johnny Damon	.60	.25
❑	24 Huston Street	.40	.15
❑	25 Nick Swisher	.40	.15
❑	26 Ichiro Suzuki	1.50	.60
❑	27 Richie Sexson	.40	.15
❑	28 Carl Crawford	.40	.15
❑	29 Scott Kazmir	.60	.25
❑	30 Michael Young	.40	.15
❑	31 Mark Teixeira	.60	.25
❑	32 Vernon Wells	.40	.15
❑	33 Roy Halladay	.40	.15
❑	34 Brandon Webb	.40	.15
❑	35 Stephen Drew	.60	.25
❑	36 Chipper Jones	1.00	.40
❑	37 Andruw Jones	.60	.25
❑	38 Derrek Lee	.40	.15
❑	39 Aramis Ramirez	.40	.15
❑	40 Ken Griffey Jr.	1.50	.60
❑	41 Adam Dunn	.40	.15
❑	42 Todd Helton	.60	.25
❑	43 Matt Holliday	.50	.20
❑	44 Miguel Cabrera	.60	.25
❑	45 Hanley Ramirez	.60	.25
❑	46 Dontrelle Willis	.40	.15
❑	47 Lance Berkman	.40	.15
❑	48 Roy Oswalt	.40	.15
❑	49 Craig Biggio	.60	.25
❑	50 Nomar Garciaparra	1.00	.40
❑	51 Derek Lowe	.40	.15
❑	52 Prince Fielder	1.00	.40
❑	53 Rickie Weeks	.40	.15
❑	54 Jose Reyes	1.00	.40
❑	55 David Wright	1.50	.60
❑	56 Carlos Beltran	.40	.15
❑	57 Ryan Howard	1.50	.60
❑	58 Chase Utley	1.00	.40
❑	59 Jimmy Rollins	.40	.15
❑	60 Jason Bay	.40	.15
❑	61 Freddy Sanchez	.40	.15
❑	62 Trevor Hoffman	.40	.15
❑	63 Adrian Gonzalez	.40	.15
❑	64 Omar Vizquel	.60	.25
❑	65 Matt Cain	.60	.25
❑	66 Albert Pujols	2.00	.75
❑	67 Jim Edmonds	.60	.25
❑	68 Chris Carpenter	.40	.15
❑	69 David Eckstein	.40	.15
❑	70 Ryan Zimmerman	1.00	.40
❑	71 Alexi Casilla RC	1.25	.50
❑	72 Andrew Miller RC	5.00	2.00
❑	73 Andy Cannizaro RC	.75	.30
❑	74 Brian Stokes (RC)	.75	.30
❑	75 Carlos Maldonado (RC)	.75	.30
❑	76 Cesar Jimenez RC	.75	.30
❑	77 Daisuke Matsuzaka RC	8.00	3.00
❑	78 Delmon Young (RC)	1.25	.50
❑	79 Delwyn Young (RC)	.75	.30
❑	80 Fred Lewis (RC)	1.25	.50
❑	81 Glen Perkins (RC)	.75	.30
❑	82 Jeff Baker (RC)	.75	.30
❑	83 Jeff Fiorentino (RC)	.75	.30
❑	84 Jeff Salazar (RC)	.75	.30
❑	85 Jerry Owens (RC)	.75	.30
❑	86 Josh Fields (RC)	.75	.30
❑	87 Juan Perez RC	.75	.30
❑	88 Juan Salas (RC)	.75	.30
❑	89 Justin Hampson (RC)	.75	.30
❑	90 Kevin Kouzmanoff (RC)	.75	.30
❑	91 Michael Bourn (RC)	.75	.30
❑	92 Miguel Montero (RC)	.75	.30
❑	93 Mike Rabelo RC	.75	.30
❑	94 Oswaldo Navarro RC	.75	.30
❑	95 Philip Humber (RC)	.75	.30
❑	96 Ryan Braun RC	.75	.30
❑	97 Ryan Sweeney (RC)	.75	.30
❑	98 Sean Henn (RC)	.75	.30
❑	99 Jose Reyes RC	.75	.30
❑	100 Troy Tulowitzki (RC)	2.00	.75

1948 Bowman

❑	COMPLETE SET (48)	5000.00	3000.00
❑	COMMON CARD (1-36)	20.00	10.00
❑	COMMON CARD (37-48)	30.00	15.00
❑	WRAPPER (5-CENT)	700.00	600.00
❑	WRAPPER (1-CENT)		
❑	1 Bob Elliott RC	125.00	75.00
❑	2 Ewell Blackwell RC	60.00	35.00
❑	3 Ralph Kiner RC	250.00	150.00
❑	4 Johnny Mize RC	125.00	75.00

❑ 5 Bob Feller RC	250.00	150.00
❑ 6 Yogi Berra RC	800.00	500.00
❑ 7 Pete Reiser SP RC	125.00	75.00
❑ 8 Phil Rizzuto SP RC	350.00	200.00
❑ 9 Walker Cooper RC	20.00	10.00
❑ 10 Buddy Rosar RC	20.00	10.00
❑ 11 Johnny Lindell RC	25.00	12.50
❑ 12 Johnny Sain RC	80.00	50.00
❑ 13 Willard Marshall SP RC	40.00	20.00
❑ 14 Allie Reynolds RC	60.00	35.00
❑ 15 Eddie Joost	20.00	10.00
❑ 16 Jack Lohrke SP RC	40.00	20.00
❑ 17 Enos Slaughter RC	100.00	60.00
❑ 18 Warren Spahn RC	300.00	175.00
❑ 19 Tommy Henrich	60.00	35.00
❑ 20 Buddy Kerr SP RC	40.00	20.00
❑ 21 Ferris Fain RC	40.00	20.00
❑ 22 Floyd Bevens SP RC	50.00	30.00
❑ 23 Larry Jansen RC	25.00	12.50
❑ 24 Dutch Leonard SP	40.00	20.00
❑ 25 Barney McCosky	20.00	10.00
❑ 26 Frank Shea SP RC	50.00	30.00
❑ 27 Sid Gordon RC	25.00	12.50
❑ 28 Emil Verban SP RC	40.00	20.00
❑ 29 Joe Page SP RC	80.00	50.00
❑ 30 Whitey Lockman SP RC	50.00	30.00
❑ 31 Bill McCahan RC	20.00	10.00
❑ 32 Bill Rigney RC	20.00	10.00
❑ 33 Bill Johnson RC	25.00	12.50
❑ 34 Sheldon Jones SP RC	40.00	20.00
❑ 35 Snuffy Stirnweiss RC	40.00	20.00
❑ 36 Stan Musial RC	800.00	500.00
❑ 37 Clint Hartung RC	30.00	15.00
❑ 38 Red Schoendienst RC	200.00	125.00
❑ 39 Augie Galan RC	30.00	15.00
❑ 40 Marty Marion RC	80.00	50.00
❑ 41 Rex Barney RC	60.00	35.00
❑ 42 Ray Poat RC	30.00	15.00
❑ 43 Bruce Edwards RC	40.00	20.00
❑ 44 Johnny Wyrostek RC	30.00	15.00
❑ 45 Hank Sauer RC	60.00	35.00
❑ 46 Herman Wehmeier RC	30.00	15.00
❑ 47 Bobby Thomson RC	100.00	60.00
❑ 48 Dave Koslo RC	80.00	50.00

1949 Bowman

❑ COMP. MASTER SET (252)	16000.00	10000.00
❑ COMPLETE SET (240)	15000.00	10000.00
❑ COMMON CARD (1-144)	15.00	7.50
❑ COMMON CARD (145-240)	50.00	30.00
❑ WRAPPER (1-CENT,Rd,Wh,Bl)		
❑ WRAPPER (5-CENT, GR.)	250.00	200.00
❑ WRAPPER (5-CENT, BL.)	200.00	150.00
❑ 1 Vern Bickford RC	125.00	75.00
❑ 2 Whitey Lockman	40.00	20.00
❑ 3 Bob Porterfield RC	15.00	7.50
❑ 4A Jerry Priddy NNOF RC	15.00	7.50
❑ 4B Jerry Priddy NOF	50.00	30.00
❑ 5 Hank Sauer	40.00	20.00
❑ 6 Phil Cavarretta RC	40.00	20.00
❑ 7 Joe Dobson RC	15.00	7.50
❑ 8 Murry Dickson RC	15.00	7.50
❑ 9 Ferris Fain	40.00	20.00
❑ 10 Ted Gray RC	15.00	7.50
❑ 11 Lou Boudreau MG RC	80.00	50.00
❑ 12 Cass Michaels RC	15.00	7.50
❑ 13 Bob Chesnes RC	15.00	7.50
❑ 14 Curt Simmons RC	40.00	20.00
❑ 15 Ned Garver RC	15.00	7.50
❑ 16 Al Kozar RC	15.00	7.50
❑ 17 Earl Torgeson RC	15.00	7.50
❑ 18 Bobby Thomson	40.00	20.00
❑ 19 Bobby Brown RC	60.00	35.00
❑ 20 Gene Hermanski RC	15.00	7.50
❑ 21 Frank Baumholtz RC	25.00	12.50
❑ 22 Peanuts Lowrey RC	15.00	7.50
❑ 23 Bobby Doerr	80.00	50.00
❑ 24 Stan Musial	600.00	350.00
❑ 25 Carl Scheib RC	15.00	7.50
❑ 26 George Kell RC	80.00	50.00
❑ 27 Bob Feller	300.00	200.00
❑ 28 Don Kolloway RC	15.00	7.50
❑ 29 Ralph Kiner	125.00	75.00
❑ 30 Andy Seminick	40.00	20.00
❑ 31 Dick Kokos RC	15.00	7.50
❑ 32 Eddie Yost RC	60.00	35.00
❑ 33 Warren Spahn	200.00	125.00
❑ 34 Dave Koslo	15.00	7.50
❑ 35 Vic Raschi RC	60.00	35.00
❑ 36 Pee Wee Reese	200.00	125.00
❑ 37 Johnny Wyrostek	15.00	7.50
❑ 38 Emil Verban	15.00	7.50
❑ 39 Billy Goodman RC	25.00	12.50
❑ 40 George Munger RC	15.00	7.50
❑ 41 Lou Brissie RC	15.00	7.50
❑ 42 Hoot Evers RC	15.00	7.50
❑ 43 Dale Mitchell RC	40.00	20.00
❑ 44 Dave Philley RC	15.00	7.50
❑ 45 Wally Westlake RC	15.00	7.50
❑ 46 Robin Roberts RC	250.00	150.00
❑ 47 Johnny Sain	60.00	35.00
❑ 48 Willard Marshall	15.00	7.50
❑ 49 Frank Shea	25.00	12.50
❑ 50 Jackie Robinson RC	1500.00	900.00
❑ 51 Herman Wehmeier	15.00	7.50
❑ 52 Johnny Schmitz RC	15.00	7.50
❑ 53 Jack Kramer RC	15.00	7.50
❑ 54 Marty Marion	60.00	35.00
❑ 55 Eddie Joost	15.00	7.50
❑ 56 Pat Mullin RC	15.00	7.50
❑ 57 Gene Bearden RC	40.00	20.00
❑ 58 Bob Elliott	40.00	20.00
❑ 59 Jack Lohrke	15.00	7.50
❑ 60 Yogi Berra	300.00	175.00
❑ 61 Rex Barney	40.00	20.00
❑ 62 Grady Hatton RC	15.00	7.50
❑ 63 Andy Pafko RC	40.00	20.00
❑ 64 Dom DiMaggio	60.00	35.00
❑ 65 Enos Slaughter	80.00	50.00
❑ 66 Elmer Valo RC	15.00	7.50
❑ 67 Alvin Dark RC	40.00	20.00
❑ 68 Sheldon Jones	15.00	7.50
❑ 69 Tommy Henrich	40.00	20.00
❑ 70 Carl Furillo RC	150.00	90.00
❑ 71 Vern Stephens RC	15.00	7.50
❑ 72 Tommy Holmes RC	40.00	20.00
❑ 73 Billy Cox RC	40.00	20.00
❑ 74 Tom McBride RC	15.00	7.50
❑ 75 Eddie Mayo RC	15.00	7.50
❑ 76 Bill Nicholson RC	25.00	12.50
❑ 77 Ernie Bonham RC	15.00	7.50
❑ 78A Sam Zoldak NNOF RC	15.00	7.50
❑ 78B Sam Zoldak NOF	50.00	30.00
❑ 79 Ron Northey RC	15.00	7.50
❑ 80 Bill McCahan	15.00	7.50
❑ 81 Virgil Stallcup RC	15.00	7.50
❑ 82 Joe Page	60.00	35.00
❑ 83A Bob Scheffing NNOF RC	15.00	7.50
❑ 83B Bob Scheffing NOF	50.00	30.00
❑ 84 Roy Campanella RC	800.00	500.00
❑ 85A Johnny Mize NNOF	100.00	60.00
❑ 85B Johnny Mize NOF	150.00	90.00
❑ 86 Johnny Pesky RC	60.00	35.00
❑ 87 Randy Gumpert RC	15.00	7.50
❑ 88A Bill Salkeld NNOF RC	15.00	7.50
❑ 88B Bill Salkeld NOF	50.00	30.00
❑ 89 Mizell Platt RC	15.00	7.50
❑ 90 Gil Coan RC	15.00	7.50
❑ 91 Dick Wakefield RC	15.00	7.50
❑ 92 Willie Jones RC	40.00	20.00
❑ 93 Ed Stevens RC	15.00	7.50
❑ 94 Mickey Vernon RC	40.00	20.00
❑ 95 Howie Pollet RC	15.00	7.50
❑ 96 Taft Wright	15.00	7.50
❑ 97 Danny Litwhiler RC	15.00	7.50
❑ 98A Phil Rizzuto NNOF	200.00	125.00
❑ 98B Phil Rizzuto NOF	250.00	150.00
❑ 99 Frank Gustine RC	15.00	7.50
❑ 100 Gil Hodges RC	250.00	150.00
❑ 101 Sid Gordon	15.00	7.50
❑ 102 Stan Spence RC	15.00	7.50
❑ 103 Joe Tipton RC	15.00	7.50
❑ 104 Eddie Stanky RC	40.00	20.00
❑ 105 Bill Kennedy RC	15.00	7.50
❑ 106 Jake Early RC	15.00	7.50
❑ 107 Eddie Lake RC	15.00	7.50
❑ 108 Ken Heintzelman RC	15.00	7.50
❑ 109A Ed Fitzgerald SCR RC	15.00	7.50
❑ 109B Ed Fitzgerald PR	60.00	35.00
❑ 110 Early Wynn RC	150.00	90.00
❑ 111 Red Schoendienst	100.00	60.00
❑ 112 Sam Chapman	40.00	20.00
❑ 113 Ray LaManno RC	15.00	7.50
❑ 114 Allie Reynolds	60.00	35.00
❑ 115 Dutch Leonard	15.00	7.50
❑ 116 Joe Hatten RC	15.00	7.50
❑ 117 Walker Cooper	15.00	7.50
❑ 118 Sam Mele RC	15.00	7.50
❑ 119 Floyd Baker RC	15.00	7.50
❑ 120 Cliff Fannin RC	15.00	7.50
❑ 121 Mark Christman RC	15.00	7.50
❑ 122 George Vico RC	15.00	7.50
❑ 123 Johnny Blatnik	15.00	7.50
❑ 124A D.Murtaugh SCR RC	40.00	20.00
❑ 124B D.Murtaugh PR	60.00	35.00
❑ 125 Ken Keltner RC	25.00	12.50
❑ 126A Al Brazle SCR RC	15.00	7.50
❑ 126B Al Brazle PR	60.00	35.00
❑ 127A Hank Majeski SCR RC	15.00	7.50
❑ 127B Hank Majeski PR	60.00	35.00
❑ 128 Johnny VanderMeer	60.00	35.00
❑ 129 Bill Johnson	40.00	20.00
❑ 130 Harry Walker RC	15.00	7.50
❑ 131 Paul Lehner RC	15.00	7.50
❑ 132A Al Evans SCR RC	15.00	7.50
❑ 132B Al Evans PR	60.00	35.00
❑ 133 Aaron Robinson RC	15.00	7.50
❑ 134 Hank Borowy RC	15.00	7.50
❑ 135 Stan Rojek RC	15.00	7.50
❑ 136 Hank Edwards RC	15.00	7.50
❑ 137 Ted Wilks RC	15.00	7.50
❑ 138 Buddy Rosar	15.00	7.50
❑ 139 Hank Arft RC	15.00	7.50
❑ 140 Ray Scarborough RC	15.00	7.50
❑ 141 Tony Lupien RC	15.00	7.50
❑ 142 Eddie Waitkus RC	40.00	20.00
❑ 143A Bob Dillinger SCR RC	25.00	12.50
❑ 143B Bob Dillinger PR	60.00	35.00
❑ 144 Mickey Haefner RC	15.00	7.50
❑ 145 Sylvester Donnelly RC	50.00	30.00
❑ 146 Mike McCormick RC	50.00	30.00
❑ 147 Bert Singleton RC	50.00	30.00
❑ 148 Bob Swift RC	50.00	30.00
❑ 149 Roy Partee RC	50.00	30.00
❑ 150 Allie Clark RC	50.00	30.00
❑ 151 Mickey Harris RC	50.00	30.00
❑ 152 Clarence Maddern RC	50.00	30.00
❑ 153 Phil Masi RC	50.00	30.00
❑ 154 Clint Hartung	60.00	35.00
❑ 155 Mickey Guerra RC	50.00	30.00
❑ 156 Al Zarilla RC	50.00	30.00
❑ 157 Walt Masterson RC	50.00	30.00
❑ 158 Harry Brecheen RC	60.00	35.00

- ❑ 159 Glen Moulder RC 50.00 30.00
- ❑ 160 Jim Blackburn RC 50.00 30.00
- ❑ 161 Jocko Thompson RC 50.00 30.00
- ❑ 162 Preacher Roe RC 125.00 75.00
- ❑ 163 Clyde McCullough RC 50.00 30.00
- ❑ 164 Vic Wertz RC 80.00 50.00
- ❑ 165 Snuffy Stirnweiss 80.00 50.00
- ❑ 166 Mike Tresh RC 50.00 30.00
- ❑ 167 Babe Martin RC 50.00 30.00
- ❑ 168 Doyle Lade RC 50.00 30.00
- ❑ 169 Jeff Heath RC 60.00 35.00
- ❑ 170 Bill Rigney 60.00 35.00
- ❑ 171 Dick Fowler RC 50.00 30.00
- ❑ 172 Eddie Pellagrini RC 50.00 30.00
- ❑ 173 Eddie Stewart RC 50.00 30.00
- ❑ 174 Terry Moore RC 80.00 50.00
- ❑ 175 Luke Appling 150.00 90.00
- ❑ 176 Ken Raffensberger RC 50.00 30.00
- ❑ 177 Stan Lopata RC 60.00 35.00
- ❑ 178 Tom Brown RC 60.00 35.00
- ❑ 179 Hugh Casey 80.00 50.00
- ❑ 180 Connie Berry 50.00 30.00
- ❑ 181 Gus Niarhos RC 50.00 30.00
- ❑ 182 Hal Peck RC 50.00 30.00
- ❑ 183 Lou Stringer RC 50.00 30.00
- ❑ 184 Bob Chipman RC 50.00 30.00
- ❑ 185 Pete Reiser 80.00 50.00
- ❑ 186 Buddy Kerr 50.00 30.00
- ❑ 187 Phil Marchildon RC 50.00 30.00
- ❑ 188 Karl Drews RC 50.00 30.00
- ❑ 189 Earl Wooten RC 50.00 30.00
- ❑ 190 Jim Hearn RC 50.00 30.00
- ❑ 191 Joe Haynes RC 50.00 30.00
- ❑ 192 Harry Gumbert 50.00 30.00
- ❑ 193 Ken Trinkle RC 50.00 30.00
- ❑ 194 Ralph Branca RC 100.00 60.00
- ❑ 195 Eddie Bockman RC 50.00 30.00
- ❑ 196 Fred Hutchinson RC 60.00 35.00
- ❑ 197 Johnny Lindell 60.00 35.00
- ❑ 198 Steve Gromek RC 50.00 30.00
- ❑ 199 Tex Hughson RC 50.00 30.00
- ❑ 200 Jess Dobernic RC 50.00 30.00
- ❑ 201 Sibby Sisti RC 50.00 30.00
- ❑ 202 Larry Jansen 60.00 35.00
- ❑ 203 Barney McCosky 50.00 30.00
- ❑ 204 Bob Savage RC 50.00 30.00
- ❑ 205 Dick Sisler RC 60.00 35.00
- ❑ 206 Bruce Edwards 50.00 30.00
- ❑ 207 Johnny Hopp RC 50.00 30.00
- ❑ 208 Dizzy Trout 60.00 35.00
- ❑ 209 Charlie Keller 80.00 50.00
- ❑ 210 Joe Gordon RC 80.00 50.00
- ❑ 211 Boo Ferriss RC 50.00 30.00
- ❑ 212 Ralph Hamner RC 50.00 30.00
- ❑ 213 Red Barrett RC 50.00 30.00
- ❑ 214 Richie Ashburn RC 600.00 350.00
- ❑ 215 Kirby Higbe 50.00 30.00
- ❑ 216 Schoolboy Rowe 60.00 35.00
- ❑ 217 Marino Pieretti RC 50.00 30.00
- ❑ 218 Dick Kryhoski RC 50.00 30.00
- ❑ 219 Virgil Trucks RC 60.00 35.00
- ❑ 220 Johnny McCarthy 50.00 30.00
- ❑ 221 Bob Muncrief RC 50.00 30.00
- ❑ 222 Alex Kellner RC 50.00 30.00
- ❑ 223 Bobby Hofman RC 50.00 30.00
- ❑ 224 Satchel Paige RC 1500.00 1000.00
- ❑ 225 Jerry Coleman RC 80.00 50.00
- ❑ 226 Duke Snider RC 1000.00 600.00
- ❑ 227 Fritz Ostermueller 50.00 30.00
- ❑ 228 Jackie Mayo RC 50.00 30.00
- ❑ 229 Ed Lopat RC 150.00 90.00
- ❑ 230 Augie Galan 60.00 35.00
- ❑ 231 Earl Johnson RC 50.00 30.00
- ❑ 232 George McQuinn 60.00 35.00
- ❑ 233 Larry Doby RC 300.00 175.00
- ❑ 234 Rip Sewell RC 50.00 30.00
- ❑ 235 Jim Russell RC 50.00 30.00
- ❑ 236 Fred Sanford RC 50.00 30.00
- ❑ 237 Monte Kennedy RC 50.00 30.00
- ❑ 238 Bob Lemon RC 200.00 125.00
- ❑ 239 Frank McCormick 50.00 30.00
- ❑ 240 Babe Young UER 100.00 60.00

1950 Bowman

- ❑ COMPLETE SET (252) 8500.00 6000.00
- ❑ COMMON CARD (1-72) 50.00 30.00
- ❑ COMMON CARD (73-252) 15.00 7.50
- ❑ WRAPPER (1-CENT) 250.00 200.00
- ❑ WRAPPER (5-CENT) 250.00 200.00
- ❑ 1 Mel Parnell RC 150.00 90.00
- ❑ 2 Vern Stephens 60.00 35.00
- ❑ 3 Dom DiMaggio 80.00 50.00
- ❑ 4 Gus Zernial RC 60.00 35.00
- ❑ 5 Bob Kuzava RC 50.00 30.00
- ❑ 6 Bob Feller 300.00 175.00
- ❑ 7 Jim Hegan 60.00 35.00
- ❑ 8 George Kell 80.00 50.00
- ❑ 9 Vic Wertz 60.00 35.00
- ❑ 10 Tommy Henrich 80.00 50.00
- ❑ 11 Phil Rizzuto 300.00 175.00
- ❑ 12 Joe Page 80.00 50.00
- ❑ 13 Ferris Fain 60.00 35.00
- ❑ 14 Alex Kellner 50.00 30.00
- ❑ 15 Al Kozar 50.00 30.00
- ❑ 16 Roy Sievers RC 80.00 50.00
- ❑ 17 Sid Hudson 50.00 30.00
- ❑ 18 Eddie Robinson RC 50.00 30.00
- ❑ 19 Warren Spahn 300.00 175.00
- ❑ 20 Bob Elliott 60.00 35.00
- ❑ 21 Pee Wee Reese 300.00 175.00
- ❑ 22 Jackie Robinson 1200.00 700.00
- ❑ 23 Don Newcombe RC 150.00 90.00
- ❑ 24 Johnny Schmitz 50.00 30.00
- ❑ 25 Hank Sauer 60.00 35.00
- ❑ 26 Grady Hatton 50.00 30.00
- ❑ 27 Herman Wehmeier 50.00 30.00
- ❑ 28 Bobby Thomson 80.00 50.00
- ❑ 29 Eddie Stanky 60.00 35.00
- ❑ 30 Eddie Waitkus 60.00 35.00
- ❑ 31 Del Ennis 80.00 50.00
- ❑ 32 Robin Roberts 150.00 90.00
- ❑ 33 Ralph Kiner 100.00 60.00
- ❑ 34 Murry Dickson 50.00 30.00
- ❑ 35 Enos Slaughter 100.00 60.00
- ❑ 36 Eddie Kazak RC 60.00 35.00
- ❑ 37 Luke Appling 80.00 50.00
- ❑ 38 Bill Wight RC 50.00 30.00
- ❑ 39 Larry Doby 100.00 60.00
- ❑ 40 Bob Lemon 80.00 50.00
- ❑ 41 Hoot Evers 50.00 30.00
- ❑ 42 Art Houtteman RC 50.00 30.00
- ❑ 43 Bobby Doerr 80.00 50.00
- ❑ 44 Joe Dobson 50.00 30.00
- ❑ 45 Al Zarilla 50.00 30.00
- ❑ 46 Yogi Berra 400.00 250.00
- ❑ 47 Jerry Coleman 80.00 50.00
- ❑ 48 Lou Brissie 50.00 30.00
- ❑ 49 Elmer Valo 50.00 30.00
- ❑ 50 Dick Kokos 50.00 30.00
- ❑ 51 Ned Garver 60.00 35.00
- ❑ 52 Sam Mele 50.00 30.00
- ❑ 53 Clyde Vollmer RC 50.00 30.00
- ❑ 54 Gil Coan 50.00 30.00
- ❑ 55 Buddy Kerr 50.00 30.00
- ❑ 56 Del Crandall RC 60.00 35.00
- ❑ 57 Vern Bickford 50.00 30.00
- ❑ 58 Carl Furillo 80.00 50.00
- ❑ 59 Ralph Branca 80.00 50.00
- ❑ 60 Andy Pafko 60.00 35.00
- ❑ 61 Bob Rush RC 50.00 30.00
- ❑ 62 Ted Kluszewski 125.00 75.00
- ❑ 63 Ewell Blackwell 60.00 35.00
- ❑ 64 Alvin Dark 60.00 35.00
- ❑ 65 Dave Koslo 50.00 30.00
- ❑ 66 Larry Jansen 60.00 35.00
- ❑ 67 Willie Jones 60.00 35.00
- ❑ 68 Curt Simmons 60.00 35.00
- ❑ 69 Wally Westlake 50.00 30.00
- ❑ 70 Bob Chesnes 50.00 30.00
- ❑ 71 Red Schoendienst 80.00 50.00
- ❑ 72 Howie Pollet 50.00 30.00
- ❑ 73 Willard Marshall 15.00 7.50
- ❑ 74 Johnny Antonelli RC 60.00 35.00
- ❑ 75 Roy Campanella 300.00 175.00
- ❑ 76 Rex Barney 40.00 20.00
- ❑ 77 Duke Snider 300.00 175.00
- ❑ 78 Mickey Owen 25.00 12.50
- ❑ 79 Johnny VanderMeer 40.00 20.00
- ❑ 80 Howard Fox RC 15.00 7.50
- ❑ 81 Ron Northey 15.00 7.50
- ❑ 82 Whitey Lockman 25.00 12.50
- ❑ 83 Sheldon Jones 15.00 7.50
- ❑ 84 Richie Ashburn 125.00 75.00
- ❑ 85 Ken Heintzelman 15.00 7.50
- ❑ 86 Stan Rojek 15.00 7.50
- ❑ 87 Bill Werle RC 15.00 7.50
- ❑ 88 Marty Marion 40.00 20.00
- ❑ 89 George Munger 15.00 7.50
- ❑ 90 Harry Brecheen 40.00 20.00
- ❑ 91 Cass Michaels 15.00 7.50
- ❑ 92 Hank Majeski 15.00 7.50
- ❑ 93 Gene Bearden 40.00 20.00
- ❑ 94 Lou Boudreau MG 60.00 35.00
- ❑ 95 Aaron Robinson 15.00 7.50
- ❑ 96 Virgil Trucks 25.00 12.50
- ❑ 97 Maurice McDermott RC 15.00 7.50
- ❑ 98 Ted Williams 1000.00 600.00
- ❑ 99 Billy Goodman 25.00 12.50
- ❑ 100 Vic Raschi 60.00 35.00
- ❑ 101 Bobby Brown 60.00 35.00
- ❑ 102 Billy Johnson 25.00 12.50
- ❑ 103 Eddie Joost 15.00 7.50
- ❑ 104 Sam Chapman 15.00 7.50
- ❑ 105 Bob Dillinger 15.00 7.50
- ❑ 106 Cliff Fannin 15.00 7.50
- ❑ 107 Sam Dente RC 15.00 7.50
- ❑ 108 Ray Scarborough 15.00 7.50
- ❑ 109 Sid Gordon 15.00 7.50
- ❑ 110 Tommy Holmes 25.00 12.50
- ❑ 111 Walker Cooper 15.00 7.50
- ❑ 112 Gil Hodges 125.00 75.00
- ❑ 113 Gene Hermanski 15.00 7.50
- ❑ 114 Wayne Terwilliger RC 15.00 7.50
- ❑ 115 Roy Smalley 15.00 7.50
- ❑ 116 Virgil Stallcup 15.00 7.50
- ❑ 117 Bill Rigney 15.00 7.50
- ❑ 118 Clint Hartung 15.00 7.50
- ❑ 119 Dick Sisler 25.00 12.50
- ❑ 120 John Thompson 15.00 7.50
- ❑ 121 Andy Seminick 25.00 12.50
- ❑ 122 Johnny Hopp 25.00 12.50
- ❑ 123 Dino Restelli RC 15.00 7.50
- ❑ 124 Clyde McCullough 15.00 7.50
- ❑ 125 Del Rice RC 15.00 7.50
- ❑ 126 Al Brazle 15.00 7.50
- ❑ 127 Dave Philley 15.00 7.50
- ❑ 128 Phil Masi 15.00 7.50
- ❑ 129 Joe Gordon 25.00 12.50
- ❑ 130 Dale Mitchell 25.00 12.50
- ❑ 131 Steve Gromek 15.00 7.50
- ❑ 132 Mickey Vernon 25.00 12.50
- ❑ 133 Don Kolloway 15.00 7.50
- ❑ 134 Paul Trout 15.00 7.50
- ❑ 135 Pat Mullin 15.00 7.50
- ❑ 136 Buddy Rosar 15.00 7.50
- ❑ 137 Johnny Pesky 25.00 12.50
- ❑ 138 Allie Reynolds 60.00 35.00
- ❑ 139 Johnny Mize 80.00 50.00
- ❑ 140 Pete Suder RC 15.00 7.50
- ❑ 141 Joe Coleman RC 25.00 12.50
- ❑ 142 Sherman Lollar RC 40.00 20.00
- ❑ 143 Eddie Stewart 15.00 7.50
- ❑ 144 Al Evans 15.00 7.50
- ❑ 145 Jack Graham RC 15.00 7.50
- ❑ 146 Floyd Baker 15.00 7.50
- ❑ 147 Mike Garcia RC 40.00 20.00
- ❑ 148 Early Wynn 80.00 50.00
- ❑ 149 Bob Swift 15.00 7.50

❑ 150 George Vico 15.00 7.50
❑ 151 Fred Hutchinson 25.00 12.50
❑ 152 Ellis Kinder RC 15.00 7.50
❑ 153 Walt Masterson 15.00 7.50
❑ 154 Gus Niarhos 15.00 7.50
❑ 155 Frank Shea 25.00 12.50
❑ 156 Fred Sanford 25.00 12.50
❑ 157 Mike Guerra 15.00 7.50
❑ 158 Paul Lehner 15.00 7.50
❑ 159 Joe Tipton 15.00 7.50
❑ 160 Mickey Harris 15.00 7.50
❑ 161 Sherry Robertson RC 15.00 7.50
❑ 162 Eddie Yost 25.00 12.50
❑ 163 Earl Torgeson 15.00 7.50
❑ 164 Sibby Sisti 15.00 7.50
❑ 165 Bruce Edwards 15.00 7.50
❑ 166 Joe Hatton 15.00 7.50
❑ 167 Preacher Roe 60.00 35.00
❑ 168 Bob Scheffing 15.00 7.50
❑ 169 Hank Edwards 15.00 7.50
❑ 170 Dutch Leonard 15.00 7.50
❑ 171 Harry Gumbert 15.00 7.50
❑ 172 Peanuts Lowrey 15.00 7.50
❑ 173 Lloyd Merriman RC 15.00 7.50
❑ 174 Hank Thompson RC 40.00 20.00
❑ 175 Monte Kennedy 15.00 7.50
❑ 176 Sylvester Donnelly 15.00 7.50
❑ 177 Hank Borowy 15.00 7.50
❑ 178 Ed Fitzgerald 15.00 7.50
❑ 179 Chuck Diering RC 15.00 7.50
❑ 180 Harry Walker 25.00 12.50
❑ 181 Marino Pieretti 15.00 7.50
❑ 182 Sam Zoldak 15.00 7.50
❑ 183 Mickey Haefner 15.00 7.50
❑ 184 Randy Gumpert 15.00 7.50
❑ 185 Howie Judson RC 15.00 7.50
❑ 186 Ken Keltner 25.00 12.50
❑ 187 Lou Stringer 15.00 7.50
❑ 188 Earl Johnson 15.00 7.50
❑ 189 Owen Friend RC 15.00 7.50
❑ 190 Ken Wood RC 15.00 7.50
❑ 191 Dick Starr RC 15.00 7.50
❑ 192 Bob Chipman 15.00 7.50
❑ 193 Pete Reiser 40.00 20.00
❑ 194 Billy Cox 60.00 35.00
❑ 195 Phil Cavarretta 40.00 20.00
❑ 196 Doyle Lade 15.00 7.50
❑ 197 Johnny Wyrostek 15.00 7.50
❑ 198 Danny Litwhiler 15.00 7.50
❑ 199 Jack Kramer 15.00 7.50
❑ 200 Kirby Higbe 25.00 12.50
❑ 201 Pete Castiglione RC 15.00 7.50
❑ 202 Cliff Chambers RC 15.00 7.50
❑ 203 Danny Murtaugh 25.00 12.50
❑ 204 Granny Hamner RC 40.00 20.00
❑ 205 Mike Goliat RC 15.00 7.50
❑ 206 Stan Lopata 25.00 12.50
❑ 207 Max Lanier RC 15.00 7.50
❑ 208 Jim Hearn 15.00 7.50
❑ 209 Johnny Lindell 15.00 7.50
❑ 210 Ted Gray 15.00 7.50
❑ 211 Charlie Keller 40.00 20.00
❑ 212 Jerry Priddy 15.00 7.50
❑ 213 Carl Scheib 15.00 7.50
❑ 214 Dick Fowler 15.00 7.50
❑ 215 Ed Lopat 60.00 35.00
❑ 216 Bob Porterfield 25.00 12.50
❑ 217 Casey Stengel MG 125.00 75.00
❑ 218 Cliff Mapes RC 25.00 12.50
❑ 219 Hank Bauer RC 100.00 60.00
❑ 220 Leo Durocher MG 60.00 35.00
❑ 221 Don Mueller RC 40.00 20.00
❑ 222 Bobby Morgan RC 15.00 7.50
❑ 223 Jim Russell 15.00 7.50
❑ 224 Jack Banta RC 15.00 7.50
❑ 225 Eddie Sawyer MG RC 25.00 12.50
❑ 226 Jim Konstanty RC 60.00 35.00
❑ 227 Bob Miller RC 25.00 12.50
❑ 228 Bill Nicholson 25.00 12.50
❑ 229 Frankie Frisch MG 60.00 35.00
❑ 230 Bill Serena RC 15.00 7.50
❑ 231 Preston Ward RC 15.00 7.50
❑ 232 Al Rosen RC 60.00 35.00
❑ 233 Allie Clark 15.00 7.50
❑ 234 Bobby Shantz RC 60.00 35.00
❑ 235 Harold Gilbert RC 15.00 7.50
❑ 236 Bob Cain RC 15.00 7.50
❑ 237 Bill Salkeld 15.00 7.50
❑ 238 Nippy Jones RC 15.00 7.50
❑ 239 Bill Howerton RC 15.00 7.50
❑ 240 Eddie Lake 15.00 7.50
❑ 241 Neil Berry RC 15.00 7.50
❑ 242 Dick Kryhoski 15.00 7.50
❑ 243 Johnny Groth RC 15.00 7.50
❑ 244 Dale Coogan RC 15.00 7.50
❑ 245 Al Papai RC 15.00 7.50
❑ 246 Walt Dropo RC 40.00 20.00
❑ 247 Irv Noren RC 25.00 12.50
❑ 248 Sam Jethroe RC 60.00 35.00
❑ 249 Snuffy Stirnweiss 25.00 12.50
❑ 250 Ray Coleman RC 15.00 7.50
❑ 251 Les Moss RC 15.00 7.50
❑ 252 Billy DeMars RC 60.00 35.00

1951 Bowman

❑ COMPLETE SET (324) 20000.00 15000.00
❑ COMMON CARD (1-252) 20.00 10.00
❑ COMMON CARD (253-324) 50.00 30.00
❑ WRAPPER (1-CENT) 200.00 150.00
❑ WRAPPER (5-CENT) 250.00 200.00
❑ 1 Whitey Ford RC 2500.00 1500.00
❑ 2 Yogi Berra 400.00 250.00
❑ 3 Robin Roberts 100.00 60.00
❑ 4 Del Ennis 25.00 12.50
❑ 5 Dale Mitchell 25.00 12.50
❑ 6 Don Newcombe 60.00 35.00
❑ 7 Gil Hodges 125.00 75.00
❑ 8 Paul Lehner 20.00 10.00
❑ 9 Sam Chapman 20.00 10.00
❑ 10 Red Schoendienst 60.00 35.00
❑ 11 George Munger 20.00 10.00
❑ 12 Hank Majeski 20.00 10.00
❑ 13 Eddie Stanky 25.00 12.50
❑ 14 Alvin Dark 40.00 20.00
❑ 15 Johnny Pesky 25.00 12.50
❑ 16 Maurice McDermott 20.00 10.00
❑ 17 Pete Castiglione 20.00 10.00
❑ 18 Gil Coan 20.00 10.00
❑ 19 Sid Gordon 20.00 10.00
❑ 20 Del Crandall UER 25.00 12.50
❑ 21 Snuffy Stirnweiss 25.00 12.50
❑ 22 Hank Sauer 25.00 12.50
❑ 23 Hoot Evers 20.00 10.00
❑ 24 Ewell Blackwell 40.00 20.00
❑ 25 Vic Raschi 60.00 35.00
❑ 26 Phil Rizzuto 150.00 90.00
❑ 27 Jim Konstanty 25.00 12.50
❑ 28 Eddie Waitkus 20.00 10.00
❑ 29 Allie Clark 20.00 10.00
❑ 30 Bob Feller 125.00 75.00
❑ 31 Roy Campanella 300.00 175.00
❑ 32 Duke Snider 250.00 150.00
❑ 33 Bob Hooper RC 20.00 10.00
❑ 34 Marty Marion MG 40.00 20.00
❑ 35 Al Zarilla 20.00 10.00
❑ 36 Joe Dobson 20.00 10.00
❑ 37 Whitey Lockman 40.00 20.00
❑ 38 Al Evans 20.00 10.00
❑ 39 Ray Scarborough 20.00 10.00
❑ 40 Gus Bell RC 60.00 35.00
❑ 41 Eddie Yost 25.00 12.50
❑ 42 Vern Bickford 20.00 10.00
❑ 43 Billy DeMars 20.00 10.00
❑ 44 Roy Smalley 20.00 10.00
❑ 45 Art Houtteman 20.00 10.00
❑ 46 George Kell UER 60.00 35.00
❑ 47 Grady Hatton 20.00 10.00
❑ 48 Ken Raffensberger 20.00 10.00
❑ 49 Jerry Coleman 25.00 12.50
❑ 50 Johnny Mize 80.00 50.00
❑ 51 Andy Seminick 20.00 10.00
❑ 52 Dick Sisler 40.00 20.00
❑ 53 Bob Lemon 60.00 35.00
❑ 54 Ray Boone RC 40.00 20.00
❑ 55 Gene Hermanski 20.00 10.00
❑ 56 Ralph Branca 60.00 35.00
❑ 57 Alex Kellner 20.00 10.00
❑ 58 Enos Slaughter 60.00 35.00
❑ 59 Randy Gumpert 20.00 10.00
❑ 60 Chico Carrasquel RC 60.00 35.00
❑ 61 Jim Hearn 25.00 12.50
❑ 62 Lou Boudreau MG 60.00 35.00
❑ 63 Bob Dillinger 20.00 10.00
❑ 64 Bill Werle 20.00 10.00
❑ 65 Mickey Vernon 40.00 20.00
❑ 66 Bob Elliott 25.00 12.50
❑ 67 Roy Sievers 25.00 12.50
❑ 68 Dick Kokos 20.00 10.00
❑ 69 Johnny Schmitz 20.00 10.00
❑ 70 Ron Northey 20.00 10.00
❑ 71 Jerry Priddy 20.00 10.00
❑ 72 Lloyd Merriman 20.00 10.00
❑ 73 Tommy Byrne RC 20.00 10.00
❑ 74 Billy Johnson 25.00 12.50
❑ 75 Russ Meyer RC 25.00 12.50
❑ 76 Stan Lopata 25.00 12.50
❑ 77 Mike Goliat 20.00 10.00
❑ 78 Early Wynn 60.00 35.00
❑ 79 Jim Hegan 25.00 12.50
❑ 80 Pee Wee Reese 200.00 125.00
❑ 81 Carl Furillo 60.00 35.00
❑ 82 Joe Tipton 20.00 10.00
❑ 83 Carl Scheib 20.00 10.00
❑ 84 Barney McCosky 20.00 10.00
❑ 85 Eddie Kazak 20.00 10.00
❑ 86 Harry Brecheen 25.00 12.50
❑ 87 Floyd Baker 20.00 10.00
❑ 88 Eddie Robinson 20.00 10.00
❑ 89 Hank Thompson 25.00 12.50
❑ 90 Dave Koslo 20.00 10.00
❑ 91 Clyde Vollmer 20.00 10.00
❑ 92 Vern Stephens 25.00 12.50
❑ 93 Danny O'Connell RC 20.00 10.00
❑ 94 Clyde McCullough 20.00 10.00
❑ 95 Sherry Robertson 20.00 10.00
❑ 96 Sandy Consuegra RC 20.00 10.00
❑ 97 Bob Kuzava 20.00 10.00
❑ 98 Willard Marshall 20.00 10.00
❑ 99 Earl Torgeson 20.00 10.00
❑ 100 Sherm Lollar 25.00 12.50
❑ 101 Owen Friend 20.00 10.00
❑ 102 Dutch Leonard 20.00 10.00
❑ 103 Andy Pafko 40.00 20.00
❑ 104 Virgil Trucks 25.00 12.50
❑ 105 Don Kolloway 20.00 10.00
❑ 106 Pat Mullin 20.00 10.00
❑ 107 Johnny Wyrostek 20.00 10.00
❑ 108 Virgil Stallcup 20.00 10.00
❑ 109 Allie Reynolds 60.00 35.00
❑ 110 Bobby Brown 40.00 20.00
❑ 111 Curt Simmons 25.00 12.50
❑ 112 Willie Jones 20.00 10.00
❑ 113 Bill Nicholson 20.00 10.00
❑ 114 Sam Zoldak 20.00 10.00
❑ 115 Steve Gromek 20.00 10.00
❑ 116 Bruce Edwards 20.00 10.00
❑ 117 Eddie Miksis RC 20.00 10.00
❑ 118 Preacher Roe 60.00 35.00
❑ 119 Eddie Joost 20.00 10.00
❑ 120 Joe Coleman 25.00 12.50
❑ 121 Gerry Staley RC 20.00 10.00
❑ 122 Joe Garagiola RC 100.00 60.00
❑ 123 Howie Judson 20.00 10.00
❑ 124 Gus Niarhos 20.00 10.00
❑ 125 Bill Rigney 25.00 12.50
❑ 126 Bobby Thomson 60.00 35.00
❑ 127 Sal Maglie RC 60.00 35.00
❑ 128 Ellis Kinder 20.00 10.00
❑ 129 Matt Batts 20.00 10.00

❑	130 Tom Saffell RC	20.00	10.00
❑	131 Cliff Chambers	20.00	10.00
❑	132 Cass Michaels	20.00	10.00
❑	133 Sam Dente	20.00	10.00
❑	134 Warren Spahn	150.00	90.00
❑	135 Walker Cooper	20.00	10.00
❑	136 Ray Coleman	20.00	10.00
❑	137 Dick Starr	20.00	10.00
❑	138 Phil Cavarretta	25.00	12.50
❑	139 Doyle Lade	20.00	10.00
❑	140 Eddie Lake	20.00	10.00
❑	141 Fred Hutchinson	25.00	12.50
❑	142 Aaron Robinson	20.00	10.00
❑	143 Ted Kluszewski	80.00	50.00
❑	144 Herman Wehmeier	20.00	10.00
❑	145 Fred Sanford	25.00	12.50
❑	146 Johnny Hopp	25.00	12.50
❑	147 Ken Heintzelman	20.00	10.00
❑	148 Granny Hamner	20.00	10.00
❑	149 Bubba Church RC	20.00	10.00
❑	150 Mike Garcia	25.00	12.50
❑	151 Larry Doby	60.00	35.00
❑	152 Cal Abrams RC	20.00	10.00
❑	153 Rex Barney	25.00	12.50
❑	154 Pete Suder	20.00	10.00
❑	155 Lou Brissie	20.00	10.00
❑	156 Del Rice	20.00	10.00
❑	157 Al Brazle	20.00	10.00
❑	158 Chuck Diering	20.00	10.00
❑	159 Eddie Stewart	20.00	10.00
❑	160 Phil Masi	20.00	10.00
❑	161 Wes Westrum RC	20.00	10.00
❑	162 Larry Jansen	25.00	12.50
❑	163 Monte Kennedy	20.00	10.00
❑	164 Bill Wight	20.00	10.00
❑	165 Ted Williams UER	800.00	500.00
❑	166 Stan Rojek	20.00	10.00
❑	167 Murry Dickson	20.00	10.00
❑	168 Sam Mele	20.00	10.00
❑	169 Sid Hudson	20.00	10.00
❑	170 Sibby Sisti	20.00	10.00
❑	171 Buddy Kerr	20.00	10.00
❑	172 Ned Garver	20.00	10.00
❑	173 Hank Arft	20.00	10.00
❑	174 Mickey Owen	25.00	12.50
❑	175 Wayne Terwilliger	20.00	10.00
❑	176 Vic Wertz	40.00	20.00
❑	177 Charlie Keller	25.00	12.50
❑	178 Ted Gray	20.00	10.00
❑	179 Danny Litwhiler	20.00	10.00
❑	180 Howie Fox	20.00	10.00
❑	181 Casey Stengel MG	80.00	50.00
❑	182 Tom Ferrick RC	20.00	10.00
❑	183 Hank Bauer	60.00	35.00
❑	184 Eddie Sawyer MG	40.00	20.00
❑	185 Jimmy Bloodworth	20.00	10.00
❑	186 Richie Ashburn	100.00	60.00
❑	187 Al Rosen	40.00	20.00
❑	188 Bobby Avila RC	25.00	12.50
❑	189 Erv Palica RC	20.00	10.00
❑	190 Joe Hatten	20.00	10.00
❑	191 Billy Hitchcock RC	20.00	10.00
❑	192 Hank Wyse RC	20.00	10.00
❑	193 Ted Wilks	20.00	10.00
❑	194 Peanuts Lowrey	20.00	10.00
❑	195 Paul Richards MG	25.00	12.50
❑	196 Billy Pierce RC	60.00	35.00
❑	197 Bob Cain	20.00	10.00
❑	198 Monte Irvin RC	125.00	75.00
❑	199 Sheldon Jones	20.00	10.00
❑	200 Jack Kramer	20.00	10.00
❑	201 Steve O'Neill MG RC	20.00	10.00
❑	202 Mike Guerra	20.00	10.00
❑	203 Vern Law RC	60.00	35.00
❑	204 Vic Lombardi RC	20.00	10.00
❑	205 Mickey Grasso RC	20.00	10.00
❑	206 Conrado Marrero RC	20.00	10.00
❑	207 Billy Southworth MG RC	20.00	10.00
❑	208 Blix Donnelly	20.00	10.00
❑	209 Ken Wood	20.00	10.00
❑	210 Les Moss	20.00	10.00
❑	211 Hal Jeffcoat RC	20.00	10.00
❑	212 Bob Rush	20.00	10.00
❑	213 Neil Berry	20.00	10.00
❑	214 Bob Swift	20.00	10.00
❑	215 Ken Peterson	20.00	10.00
❑	216 Connie Ryan RC	20.00	10.00
❑	217 Joe Page	25.00	12.50
❑	218 Ed Lopat	60.00	35.00
❑	219 Gene Woodling RC	60.00	35.00
❑	220 Bob Miller	20.00	10.00
❑	221 Dick Whitman RC	20.00	10.00
❑	222 Thurman Tucker RC	20.00	10.00
❑	223 Johnny VanderMeer	40.00	20.00
❑	224 Billy Cox	25.00	12.50
❑	225 Dan Bankhead RC	40.00	20.00
❑	226 Jimmie Dykes MG	20.00	10.00
❑	227 Bobby Shantz UER	25.00	12.50
❑	228 Cloyd Boyer RC	25.00	12.50
❑	229 Bill Howerton	20.00	10.00
❑	230 Max Lanier	20.00	10.00
❑	231 Luis Aloma RC	20.00	10.00
❑	232 Nellie Fox RC	250.00	150.00
❑	233 Leo Durocher MG	60.00	35.00
❑	234 Clint Hartung	25.00	12.50
❑	235 Jack Lohrke	20.00	10.00
❑	236 Buddy Rosar	20.00	10.00
❑	237 Billy Goodman	25.00	12.50
❑	238 Pete Reiser	40.00	20.00
❑	239 Bill MacDonald RC	20.00	10.00
❑	240 Joe Haynes	20.00	10.00
❑	241 Irv Noren	25.00	12.50
❑	242 Sam Jethroe	25.00	12.50
❑	243 Johnny Antonelli	25.00	12.50
❑	244 Cliff Fannin	20.00	10.00
❑	245 John Berardino RC	60.00	35.00
❑	246 Bill Serena	20.00	10.00
❑	247 Bob Ramazzotti RC	20.00	10.00
❑	248 Johnny Klippstein RC	20.00	10.00
❑	249 Johnny Groth	20.00	10.00
❑	250 Hank Borowy	20.00	10.00
❑	251 Willard Ramsdell RC	20.00	10.00
❑	252 Dixie Howell RC	20.00	10.00
❑	253 Mickey Mantle RC	8000.00	5000.00
❑	254 Jackie Jensen RC	100.00	60.00
❑	255 Milo Candini RC	50.00	30.00
❑	256 Ken Silvestri RC	50.00	30.00
❑	257 Birdie Tebbetts RC	60.00	35.00
❑	258 Luke Easter RC	60.00	35.00
❑	259 Chuck Dressen MG	60.00	35.00
❑	260 Carl Erskine RC	100.00	60.00
❑	261 Wally Moses	60.00	35.00
❑	262 Gus Zernial	60.00	35.00
❑	263 Howie Pollet	60.00	35.00
❑	264 Don Richmond RC	50.00	30.00
❑	265 Steve Bilko RC	50.00	30.00
❑	266 Harry Dorish RC	50.00	30.00
❑	267 Ken Holcombe RC	50.00	30.00
❑	268 Don Mueller	60.00	35.00
❑	269 Ray Noble RC	50.00	30.00
❑	270 Willard Nixon RC	50.00	30.00
❑	271 Tommy Wright RC	50.00	30.00
❑	272 Billy Meyer MG RC	50.00	30.00
❑	273 Danny Murtaugh	60.00	35.00
❑	274 George Metkovich RC	50.00	30.00
❑	275 Bucky Harris MG	80.00	50.00
❑	276 Frank Quinn RC	50.00	30.00
❑	277 Roy Hartsfield RC	50.00	30.00
❑	278 Norman Roy RC	50.00	30.00
❑	279 Jim Delsing RC	50.00	30.00
❑	280 Frank Overmire	50.00	30.00
❑	281 Al Widmar RC	50.00	30.00
❑	282 Frankie Frisch MG	100.00	60.00
❑	283 Walt Dubiel RC	50.00	30.00
❑	284 Gene Bearden	60.00	35.00
❑	285 Johnny Lipon RC	50.00	30.00
❑	286 Bob Usher RC	50.00	30.00
❑	287 Jim Blackburn	50.00	30.00
❑	288 Bobby Adams	50.00	30.00
❑	289 Cliff Mapes	60.00	35.00
❑	290 Bill Dickey CO	150.00	90.00
❑	291 Tommy Henrich CO	80.00	50.00
❑	292 Eddie Pellagrini	50.00	30.00
❑	293 Ken Johnson RC	50.00	30.00
❑	294 Jocko Thompson	50.00	30.00
❑	295 Al Lopez MG RC	125.00	75.00
❑	296 Bob Kennedy RC	60.00	35.00
❑	297 Dave Philley	50.00	30.00
❑	298 Joe Astroth RC	50.00	30.00
❑	299 Clyde King RC	50.00	30.00
❑	300 Hal Rice RC	50.00	30.00
❑	301 Tommy Glaviano RC	50.00	30.00
❑	302 Jim Busby RC	50.00	30.00
❑	303 Marv Rotblatt RC	50.00	30.00
❑	304 Al Gettell RC	50.00	30.00
❑	305 Willie Mays RC	2500.00	1800.00
❑	306 Jimmy Piersall RC	125.00	75.00
❑	307 Walt Masterson	50.00	30.00
❑	308 Ted Beard RC	50.00	30.00
❑	309 Mel Queen RC	50.00	30.00
❑	310 Erv Dusak RC	50.00	30.00
❑	311 Mickey Harris	50.00	30.00
❑	312 Gene Mauch RC	60.00	35.00
❑	313 Ray Mueller RC	50.00	30.00
❑	314 Johnny Sain	80.00	50.00
❑	315 Zack Taylor MG	50.00	30.00
❑	316 Duane Pillette RC	50.00	30.00
❑	317 Smoky Burgess RC	80.00	50.00
❑	318 Warren Hacker RC	50.00	30.00
❑	319 Red Rolfe MG	60.00	35.00
❑	320 Hal White RC	50.00	30.00
❑	321 Earl Johnson	50.00	30.00
❑	322 Luke Sewell MG	60.00	35.00
❑	323 Joe Adcock RC	80.00	50.00
❑	324 Johnny Pramesa RC	125.00	75.00

1952 Bowman

❑	COMPLETE SET (252)	8500.00	5500.00
❑	COMMON CARD (1-216)	15.00	7.50
❑	COMMON CARD (217-252)	60.00	35.00
❑	WRAPPER (1-CENT)	200.00	150.00
❑	WRAPPER (5-CENT)	100.00	75.00
❑	1 Yogi Berra	600.00	350.00
❑	2 Bobby Thomson	40.00	20.00
❑	3 Fred Hutchinson	25.00	12.50
❑	4 Robin Roberts	80.00	50.00
❑	5 Minnie Minoso RC	125.00	75.00
❑	6 Virgil Stallcup	15.00	7.50
❑	7 Mike Garcia	25.00	12.50
❑	8 Pee Wee Reese	150.00	90.00
❑	9 Vern Stephens	25.00	12.50
❑	10 Bob Hooper	15.00	7.50
❑	11 Ralph Kiner	60.00	35.00
❑	12 Max Surkont RC	15.00	7.50
❑	13 Cliff Mapes	15.00	7.50
❑	14 Cliff Chambers	15.00	7.50
❑	15 Sam Mele	15.00	7.50
❑	16 Turk Lown RC	15.00	7.50
❑	17 Ed Lopat	40.00	20.00
❑	18 Don Mueller	25.00	12.50
❑	19 Bob Cain	15.00	7.50
❑	20 Willie Jones	15.00	7.50
❑	21 Nellie Fox	100.00	60.00
❑	22 Willard Ramsdell	15.00	7.50
❑	23 Bob Lemon	60.00	35.00
❑	24 Carl Furillo	40.00	20.00
❑	25 Mickey McDermott	15.00	7.50
❑	26 Eddie Joost	15.00	7.50
❑	27 Joe Garagiola	40.00	20.00
❑	28 Roy Hartsfield	15.00	7.50
❑	29 Ned Garver	15.00	7.50
❑	30 Red Schoendienst	60.00	35.00
❑	31 Eddie Yost	25.00	12.50
❑	32 Eddie Miksis	15.00	7.50
❑	33 Gil McDougald RC	80.00	50.00
❑	34 Alvin Dark	25.00	12.50
❑	35 Granny Hamner	15.00	7.50
❑	36 Cass Michaels	15.00	7.50
❑	37 Vic Raschi	25.00	12.50
❑	38 Whitey Lockman	25.00	12.50

❑ 39 Vic Wertz 25.00 12.50
❑ 40 Bubba Church 15.00 7.50
❑ 41 Chico Carrasquel 25.00 12.50
❑ 42 Johnny Wyrostek 15.00 7.50
❑ 43 Bob Feller 150.00 90.00
❑ 44 Roy Campanella 250.00 150.00
❑ 45 Johnny Pesky 25.00 12.50
❑ 46 Carl Scheib 15.00 7.50
❑ 47 Pete Castiglione 15.00 7.50
❑ 48 Vern Bickford 15.00 7.50
❑ 49 Jim Hearn 15.00 7.50
❑ 50 Gerry Staley 15.00 7.50
❑ 51 Gil Coan 15.00 7.50
❑ 52 Phil Rizzuto 150.00 90.00
❑ 53 Richie Ashburn 125.00 75.00
❑ 54 Billy Pierce 25.00 12.50
❑ 55 Ken Raffensberger 15.00 7.50
❑ 56 Clyde King 25.00 12.50
❑ 57 Clyde Vollmer 15.00 7.50
❑ 58 Hank Majeski 15.00 7.50
❑ 59 Murry Dickson 15.00 7.50
❑ 60 Sid Gordon 15.00 7.50
❑ 61 Tommy Byrne 15.00 7.50
❑ 62 Joe Presko RC 15.00 7.50
❑ 63 Irv Noren 15.00 7.50
❑ 64 Roy Smalley 15.00 7.50
❑ 65 Hank Bauer 40.00 20.00
❑ 66 Sal Maglie 25.00 12.50
❑ 67 Johnny Groth 15.00 7.50
❑ 68 Jim Busby 15.00 7.50
❑ 69 Joe Adcock 25.00 12.50
❑ 70 Carl Erskine 40.00 20.00
❑ 71 Vern Law 25.00 12.50
❑ 72 Earl Torgeson 15.00 7.50
❑ 73 Jerry Coleman 25.00 12.50
❑ 74 Wes Westrum 25.00 12.50
❑ 75 George Kell 60.00 35.00
❑ 76 Del Ennis 25.00 12.50
❑ 77 Eddie Robinson 15.00 7.50
❑ 78 Lloyd Merriman 15.00 7.50
❑ 79 Lou Brissie 15.00 7.50
❑ 80 Gil Hodges 100.00 60.00
❑ 81 Billy Goodman 25.00 12.50
❑ 82 Gus Zernial 25.00 12.50
❑ 83 Howie Pollet 15.00 7.50
❑ 84 Sam Jethroe 25.00 12.50
❑ 85 Marty Marion CO 25.00 12.50
❑ 86 Cal Abrams 15.00 7.50
❑ 87 Mickey Vernon 25.00 12.50
❑ 88 Bruce Edwards 15.00 7.50
❑ 89 Billy Hitchcock 15.00 7.50
❑ 90 Larry Jansen 25.00 12.50
❑ 91 Don Kolloway 15.00 7.50
❑ 92 Eddie Waitkus 25.00 12.50
❑ 93 Paul Richards MG 25.00 12.50
❑ 94 Luke Sewell MG 25.00 12.50
❑ 95 Luke Easter 25.00 12.50
❑ 96 Ralph Branca 25.00 12.50
❑ 97 Willard Marshall 15.00 7.50
❑ 98 Jimmie Dykes MG 25.00 12.50
❑ 99 Clyde McCullough 15.00 7.50
❑ 100 Sibby Sisti 15.00 7.50
❑ 101 Mickey Mantle 2500.00 1500.00
❑ 102 Peanuts Lowrey 15.00 7.50
❑ 103 Joe Haynes 15.00 7.50
❑ 104 Hal Jeffcoat 15.00 7.50
❑ 105 Bobby Brown 25.00 12.50
❑ 106 Randy Gumpert 15.00 7.50
❑ 107 Del Rice 15.00 7.50
❑ 108 George Metkovich 15.00 7.50
❑ 109 Tom Morgan RC 15.00 7.50
❑ 110 Max Lanier 15.00 7.50
❑ 111 Hoot Evers 15.00 7.50
❑ 112 Smoky Burgess 25.00 12.50
❑ 113 Al Zarilla 15.00 7.50
❑ 114 Frank Hiller RC 15.00 7.50
❑ 115 Larry Doby 60.00 35.00
❑ 116 Duke Snider 200.00 125.00
❑ 117 Bill Wight 15.00 7.50
❑ 118 Ray Murray RC 15.00 7.50
❑ 119 Bill Howerton 15.00 7.50
❑ 120 Chet Nichols RC 15.00 7.50
❑ 121 Al Corwin RC 15.00 7.50
❑ 122 Billy Johnson 15.00 7.50
❑ 123 Sid Hudson 15.00 7.50
❑ 124 Birdie Tebbetts 15.00 7.50
❑ 125 Howie Fox 15.00 7.50
❑ 126 Phil Cavarretta 25.00 12.50
❑ 127 Dick Sisler 15.00 7.50
❑ 128 Don Newcombe 60.00 35.00
❑ 129 Gus Niarhos 15.00 7.50
❑ 130 Allie Clark 15.00 7.50
❑ 131 Bob Swift 15.00 7.50
❑ 132 Dave Cole RC 15.00 7.50
❑ 133 Dick Kryhoski 15.00 7.50
❑ 134 Al Brazle 15.00 7.50
❑ 135 Mickey Harris 15.00 7.50
❑ 136 Gene Hermanski 15.00 7.50
❑ 137 Stan Rojek 15.00 7.50
❑ 138 Ted Wilks 15.00 7.50
❑ 139 Jerry Priddy 15.00 7.50
❑ 140 Ray Scarborough 15.00 7.50
❑ 141 Hank Edwards 15.00 7.50
❑ 142 Early Wynn 60.00 35.00
❑ 143 Sandy Consuegra 15.00 7.50
❑ 144 Joe Hatton 15.00 7.50
❑ 145 Johnny Mize 60.00 35.00
❑ 146 Leo Durocher MG 60.00 35.00
❑ 147 Marlin Stuart RC 15.00 7.50
❑ 148 Ken Heintzelman 15.00 7.50
❑ 149 Howie Judson 15.00 7.50
❑ 150 Herman Wehmeier 15.00 7.50
❑ 151 Al Rosen 25.00 12.50
❑ 152 Billy Cox 15.00 7.50
❑ 153 Fred Hatfield RC 15.00 7.50
❑ 154 Ferris Fain 25.00 12.50
❑ 155 Billy Meyer MG 15.00 7.50
❑ 156 Warren Spahn 125.00 75.00
❑ 157 Jim Delsing 15.00 7.50
❑ 158 Bucky Harris MG 40.00 20.00
❑ 159 Dutch Leonard 15.00 7.50
❑ 160 Eddie Stanky 25.00 12.50
❑ 161 Jackie Jensen 40.00 20.00
❑ 162 Monte Irvin 60.00 35.00
❑ 163 Johnny Lipon 15.00 7.50
❑ 164 Connie Ryan 15.00 7.50
❑ 165 Saul Rogovin RC 15.00 7.50
❑ 166 Bobby Adams 15.00 7.50
❑ 167 Bobby Avila 25.00 12.50
❑ 168 Preacher Roe 25.00 12.50
❑ 169 Walt Dropo 25.00 12.50
❑ 170 Joe Astroth 15.00 7.50
❑ 171 Mel Queen 15.00 7.50
❑ 172 Ebba St.Claire RC 15.00 7.50
❑ 173 Gene Bearden 15.00 7.50
❑ 174 Mickey Grasso 15.00 7.50
❑ 175 Randy Jackson RC 15.00 7.50
❑ 176 Harry Brecheen 25.00 12.50
❑ 177 Gene Woodling 25.00 12.50
❑ 178 Dave Williams RC 25.00 12.50
❑ 179 Pete Suder 15.00 7.50
❑ 180 Ed Fitzgerald 15.00 7.50
❑ 181 Joe Collins RC 25.00 12.50
❑ 182 Dave Koslo 15.00 7.50
❑ 183 Pat Mullin 15.00 7.50
❑ 184 Curt Simmons 25.00 12.50
❑ 185 Eddie Stewart 15.00 7.50
❑ 186 Frank Smith RC 15.00 7.50
❑ 187 Jim Hegan 25.00 12.50
❑ 188 Chuck Dressen MG 25.00 12.50
❑ 189 Jimmy Piersall 25.00 12.50
❑ 190 Dick Fowler 15.00 7.50
❑ 191 Bob Friend RC 40.00 20.00
❑ 192 John Cusick RC 15.00 7.50
❑ 193 Bobby Young RC 15.00 7.50
❑ 194 Bob Porterfield 15.00 7.50
❑ 195 Frank Baumholtz 15.00 7.50
❑ 196 Stan Musial 500.00 300.00
❑ 197 Charlie Silvera RC 15.00 7.50
❑ 198 Chuck Diering 15.00 7.50
❑ 199 Ted Gray 15.00 7.50
❑ 200 Ken Silvestri 15.00 7.50
❑ 201 Ray Coleman 15.00 7.50
❑ 202 Harry Perkowski RC 15.00 7.50
❑ 203 Steve Gromek 15.00 7.50
❑ 204 Andy Pafko 25.00 12.50
❑ 205 Walt Masterson 15.00 7.50
❑ 206 Elmer Valo 15.00 7.50
❑ 207 George Strickland RC 15.00 7.50
❑ 208 Walker Cooper 15.00 7.50
❑ 209 Dick Littlefield RC 15.00 7.50
❑ 210 Archie Wilson RC 15.00 7.50
❑ 211 Paul Minner RC 15.00 7.50
❑ 212 Solly Hemus RC 15.00 7.50
❑ 213 Monte Kennedy 15.00 7.50
❑ 214 Ray Boone 15.00 7.50
❑ 215 Sheldon Jones 15.00 7.50
❑ 216 Matt Batts 15.00 7.50
❑ 217 Casey Stengel MG 150.00 90.00
❑ 218 Willie Mays 1500.00 900.00
❑ 219 Neil Berry 60.00 35.00
❑ 220 Russ Meyer 60.00 35.00
❑ 221 Lou Kretlow RC 60.00 35.00
❑ 222 Dixie Howell 60.00 35.00
❑ 223 Harry Simpson RC 60.00 35.00
❑ 224 Johnny Schmitz 60.00 35.00
❑ 225 Del Wilber RC 60.00 35.00
❑ 226 Alex Kellner 60.00 35.00
❑ 227 Clyde Sukeforth CO RC 60.00 35.00
❑ 228 Bob Chipman 60.00 35.00
❑ 229 Hank Arft 60.00 35.00
❑ 230 Frank Shea 60.00 35.00
❑ 231 Dee Fondy RC 60.00 35.00
❑ 232 Enos Slaughter 100.00 60.00
❑ 233 Bob Kuzava 60.00 35.00
❑ 234 Fred Fitzsimmons CO 60.00 35.00
❑ 235 Steve Souchock RC 60.00 35.00
❑ 236 Tommy Brown 60.00 35.00
❑ 237 Sherm Lollar 60.00 35.00
❑ 238 Roy McMillan RC 60.00 35.00
❑ 239 Dale Mitchell 60.00 35.00
❑ 240 Billy Loes RC 60.00 35.00
❑ 241 Mel Parnell 60.00 35.00
❑ 242 Everett Kell RC 60.00 35.00
❑ 243 George Munger 60.00 35.00
❑ 244 Lew Burdette RC 80.00 50.00
❑ 245 George Schmees RC 60.00 35.00
❑ 246 Jerry Snyder RC 60.00 35.00
❑ 247 Johnny Pramesa 60.00 35.00
❑ 248 Bill Werle Full Name 60.00 35.00
❑ 248A Bill Werle No W 60.00 35.00
❑ 249 Hank Thompson 60.00 35.00
❑ 250 Ike Delock RC 60.00 35.00
❑ 251 Jack Lohrke 60.00 35.00
❑ 252 Frank Crosetti CO 125.00 75.00

1953 Bowman Black and White

❑ COMPLETE SET (64) 3000.00 2000.00
❑ WRAPPER (1-CENT) 350.00 300.00
❑ 1 Gus Bell 125.00 75.00
❑ 2 Willard Nixon 40.00 25.00
❑ 3 Bill Rigney 40.00 25.00
❑ 4 Pat Mullin 40.00 25.00
❑ 5 Dee Fondy 40.00 25.00
❑ 6 Ray Murray 40.00 25.00
❑ 7 Andy Seminick 40.00 25.00
❑ 8 Pete Suder 40.00 25.00
❑ 9 Walt Masterson 40.00 25.00
❑ 10 Dick Sisler 60.00 35.00
❑ 11 Dick Gernert 40.00 25.00
❑ 12 Randy Jackson 40.00 25.00
❑ 13 Joe Tipton 40.00 25.00
❑ 14 Bill Nicholson 60.00 35.00
❑ 15 Johnny Mize 125.00 75.00
❑ 16 Stu Miller RC 60.00 35.00
❑ 17 Virgil Trucks 60.00 35.00
❑ 18 Billy Hoeft 40.00 25.00
❑ 19 Paul LaPalme 40.00 25.00
❑ 20 Eddie Robinson 40.00 25.00

21 Clarence Podbielan	40.00	25.00
22 Matt Batts	40.00	25.00
23 Wilmer Mizell	60.00	35.00
24 Del Wilber	40.00	25.00
25 Johnny Sain	80.00	50.00
26 Preacher Roe	80.00	50.00
27 Bob Lemon	175.00	100.00
28 Hoyt Wilhelm	125.00	75.00
29 Sid Hudson	40.00	25.00
30 Walker Cooper	40.00	25.00
31 Gene Woodling	80.00	50.00
32 Rocky Bridges	40.00	25.00
33 Bob Kuzava	40.00	25.00
34 Ebba St.Claire	40.00	25.00
35 Johnny Wyrostek	40.00	25.00
36 Jimmy Piersall	80.00	50.00
37 Hal Jeffcoat	40.00	25.00
38 Dave Cole	40.00	25.00
39 Casey Stengel MG	350.00	200.00
40 Larry Jansen	60.00	35.00
41 Bob Ramazzotti	40.00	25.00
42 Howie Judson	40.00	25.00
43 Hal Bevan ERR RC	40.00	25.00
43A Hal Bevan COR	40.00	25.00
44 Jim Delsing	40.00	25.00
45 Irv Noren	60.00	35.00
46 Bucky Harris MG	80.00	50.00
47 Jack Lohrke	40.00	25.00
48 Steve Ridzik RC	40.00	25.00
49 Floyd Baker	40.00	25.00
50 Dutch Leonard	40.00	25.00
51 Lew Burdette	80.00	50.00
52 Ralph Branca	80.00	50.00
53 Morrie Martin	40.00	25.00
54 Bill Miller	40.00	25.00
55 Don Johnson	40.00	25.00
56 Roy Smalley	40.00	25.00
57 Andy Pafko	60.00	35.00
58 Jim Konstanty	60.00	35.00
59 Duane Pillette	40.00	25.00
60 Billy Cox	80.00	50.00
61 Tom Gorman RC	40.00	25.00
62 Keith Thomas RC	40.00	25.00
63 Steve Gromek	40.00	25.00
64 Andy Hansen	80.00	50.00

1953 Bowman Color

COMPLETE SET (160)	15000.00	9000.00
COMMON CARD (1-112)	40.00	20.00
COMMON CARD (113-128)	80.00	50.00
COMMON CARD (129-160)	75.00	45.00
WRAPPER (1-CENT)	400.00	300.00
WRAPPER (5-CENT)	300.00	250.00
1 Davey Williams	175.00	100.00
2 Vic Wertz	50.00	30.00
3 Sam Jethroe	50.00	30.00
4 Art Houtteman	40.00	20.00
5 Sid Gordon	40.00	20.00
6 Joe Ginsberg	40.00	20.00
7 Harry Chiti RC	40.00	20.00
8 Al Rosen	50.00	30.00
9 Phil Rizzuto	225.00	150.00
10 Richie Ashburn	150.00	90.00
11 Bobby Shantz	50.00	30.00
12 Carl Erskine	60.00	35.00
13 Gus Zernial	50.00	30.00
14 Billy Loes	50.00	30.00
15 Jim Busby	40.00	20.00
16 Bob Friend	50.00	30.00
17 Gerry Staley	40.00	20.00
18 Nellie Fox	150.00	90.00
19 Alvin Dark	50.00	30.00
20 Don Lenhardt	40.00	20.00
21 Joe Garagiola	60.00	35.00
22 Bob Porterfield	40.00	20.00
23 Herman Wehmeier	40.00	20.00
24 Jackie Jensen	60.00	35.00
25 Hoot Evers	40.00	20.00
26 Roy McMillan	50.00	30.00
27 Vic Raschi	60.00	35.00
28 Smoky Burgess	50.00	30.00
29 Bobby Avila	50.00	30.00
30 Phil Cavarretta	50.00	30.00
31 Jimmy Dykes MG	50.00	30.00
32 Stan Musial	600.00	350.00
33 Pee Wee Reese	1000.00	500.00
34 Gil Coan	40.00	20.00
35 Maurice McDermott	40.00	20.00
36 Minnie Minoso	80.00	50.00
37 Jim Wilson	40.00	20.00
38 Harry Byrd RC	40.00	20.00
39 Paul Richards MG	50.00	30.00
40 Larry Doby	100.00	60.00
41 Sammy White	40.00	20.00
42 Tommy Brown	40.00	20.00
43 Mike Garcia	50.00	30.00
44 Bauer/Berra/Mantle	800.00	500.00
45 Walt Dropo	50.00	30.00
46 Roy Campanella	350.00	200.00
47 Ned Garver	40.00	20.00
48 Hank Sauer	50.00	30.00
49 Eddie Stanky MG	50.00	30.00
50 Lou Kretlow	40.00	20.00
51 Monte Irvin	80.00	50.00
52 Marty Marion MG	50.00	30.00
53 Del Rice	40.00	20.00
54 Chico Carrasquel	40.00	20.00
55 Leo Durocher MG	80.00	50.00
56 Bob Cain	40.00	20.00
57 Lou Boudreau MG	80.00	50.00
58 Willard Marshall	40.00	20.00
59 Mickey Mantle	2000.00	1200.00
60 Granny Hamner	40.00	20.00
61 George Kell	80.00	50.00
62 Ted Kluszewski	100.00	60.00
63 Gil McDougald	80.00	50.00
64 Curt Simmons	50.00	30.00
65 Robin Roberts	125.00	75.00
66 Mel Parnell	50.00	30.00
67 Mel Clark RC	40.00	20.00
68 Allie Reynolds	60.00	35.00
69 Charlie Grimm MG	50.00	30.00
70 Clint Courtney RC	40.00	20.00
71 Paul Minner	40.00	20.00
72 Ted Gray	40.00	20.00
73 Billy Pierce	50.00	30.00
74 Don Mueller	50.00	30.00
75 Saul Rogovin	40.00	20.00
76 Jim Hearn	40.00	20.00
77 Mickey Grasso	40.00	20.00
78 Carl Furillo	60.00	35.00
79 Ray Boone	50.00	30.00
80 Ralph Kiner	100.00	60.00
81 Enos Slaughter	100.00	60.00
82 Joe Astroth	40.00	20.00
83 Jack Daniels RC	40.00	20.00
84 Hank Bauer	60.00	35.00
85 Solly Hemus	40.00	20.00
86 Harry Simpson	40.00	20.00
87 Harry Perkowski	40.00	20.00
88 Joe Dobson	40.00	20.00
89 Sandy Consuegra	40.00	20.00
90 Joe Nuxhall	50.00	30.00
91 Steve Souchock	40.00	20.00
92 Gil Hodges	300.00	175.00
93 P.Rizzuto/B.Martin	300.00	175.00
94 Bob Addis	40.00	20.00
95 Wally Moses CO	50.00	30.00
96 Sal Maglie	50.00	30.00
97 Eddie Mathews	350.00	200.00
98 Hector Rodriguez RC	40.00	20.00
99 Warren Spahn	350.00	200.00
100 Bill Wight	40.00	20.00
101 Red Schoendienst	80.00	50.00
102 Jim Hegan	50.00	30.00
103 Del Ennis	50.00	30.00
104 Luke Easter	50.00	30.00
105 Eddie Joost	40.00	20.00
106 Ken Raffensberger	40.00	20.00
107 Alex Kellner	40.00	20.00
108 Bobby Adams	40.00	20.00
109 Ken Wood	40.00	20.00
110 Bob Rush	40.00	20.00
111 Jim Dyck RC	40.00	20.00
112 Toby Atwell	40.00	20.00
113 Karl Drews	80.00	50.00
114 Bob Feller	500.00	350.00
115 Cloyd Boyer	80.00	50.00
116 Eddie Yost	100.00	60.00
117 Duke Snider	600.00	350.00
118 Billy Martin	400.00	250.00
119 Dale Mitchell	100.00	60.00
120 Marlin Stuart	80.00	50.00
121 Yogi Berra	800.00	500.00
122 Bill Serena	80.00	50.00
123 Johnny Lipon	80.00	50.00
124 Chuck Dressen MG	100.00	60.00
125 Fred Hatfield	80.00	50.00
126 Al Corwin	80.00	50.00
127 Dick Kryhoski	80.00	50.00
128 Whitey Lockman	100.00	60.00
129 Russ Meyer	75.00	45.00
130 Cass Michaels	75.00	45.00
131 Connie Ryan	75.00	45.00
132 Fred Hutchinson	90.00	60.00
133 Willie Jones	75.00	45.00
134 Johnny Pesky	90.00	60.00
135 Bobby Morgan	75.00	45.00
136 Jim Brideweser RC	75.00	45.00
137 Sam Dente	75.00	45.00
138 Bubba Church	75.00	45.00
139 Pete Runnels	90.00	60.00
140 Al Brazle	75.00	45.00
141 Frank Shea	75.00	45.00
142 Larry Miggins RC	75.00	45.00
143 Al Lopez MG	110.00	70.00
144 Warren Hacker	75.00	45.00
145 George Shuba	90.00	60.00
146 Early Wynn	200.00	125.00
147 Clem Koshorek	75.00	45.00
148 Billy Goodman	90.00	60.00
149 Al Corwin	75.00	45.00
150 Carl Scheib	75.00	45.00
151 Joe Adcock	110.00	70.00
152 Clyde Vollmer	75.00	45.00
153 Whitey Ford	800.00	500.00
154 Turk Lown	75.00	45.00
155 Allie Clark	75.00	45.00
156 Max Surkont	75.00	45.00
157 Sherm Lollar	90.00	60.00
158 Howard Fox	75.00	45.00
159 Mickey Vernon UER	90.00	60.00
160 Cal Abrams	500.00	300.00

1954 Bowman

COMPLETE SET (224)	4000.00	2500.00
WRAP.(1-CENT, DATED)	150.00	100.00
WRAP.(1-CENT, UNDAT)	200.00	150.00
WRAP.(5-CENT, DATED)	150.00	100.00
WRAP.(5-CENT, UNDAT)	60.00	50.00
1 Phil Rizzuto	175.00	100.00
2 Jackie Jensen	30.00	15.00

❑ 3 Marion Fricano 12.00 6.00
❑ 4 Bob Hooper 12.00 6.00
❑ 5 Billy Hunter 12.00 6.00
❑ 6 Nellie Fox 80.00 50.00
❑ 7 Walt Dropo 20.00 10.00
❑ 8 Jim Busby 12.00 6.00
❑ 9 Dave Williams 12.00 6.00
❑ 10 Carl Erskine 20.00 10.00
❑ 11 Sid Gordon 12.00 6.00
❑ 12A Roy McMillan 551 /1290 At Bat 20.00 10.00
❑ 12B Roy McMillan 557 /1296 At Bat 20.00 10.00
❑ 13 Paul Minner 12.00 6.00
❑ 14 Gerry Staley 12.00 6.00
❑ 15 Richie Ashburn 80.00 50.00
❑ 16 Jim Wilson 12.00 6.00
❑ 17 Tom Gorman 12.00 6.00
❑ 18 Hoot Evers 12.00 6.00
❑ 19 Bobby Shantz 20.00 10.00
❑ 20 Art Houtteman 12.00 6.00
❑ 21 Vic Wertz 20.00 10.00
❑ 22A Sam Mele 213/1661 Putouts 12.006.00
❑ 22B Sam Mele 217/1665 Putouts 12.006.00
❑ 23 Harvey Kuenn RC 30.00 15.00
❑ 24 Bob Porterfield 12.00 6.00
❑ 25A Wes Westrum 1.000 /.987 Fielding Avg. 20.00 10.00
❑ 25B Wes Westrum .982 /986 Fielding Avg. 20.00 10.00
❑ 26A Billy Cox 1.000 /.960 Fielding Avg. 20.00 10.00
❑ 26B Billy Cox .972/.960 Fielding Avg. 20.00 10.00
❑ 27 Dick Cole RC 12.00 6.00
❑ 28A Jim Greengrass Birthplace Addison, NJ 12.00 6.00
❑ 28B Jim Greengrass Birthplace Addison, NY 12.00 6.00
❑ 29 Johnny Klippstein 12.00 6.00
❑ 30 Del Rice 12.00 6.00
❑ 31 Smoky Burgess 20.00 10.00
❑ 32 Del Crandall 20.00 10.00
❑ 33A Vic Raschi No Trade 20.00 10.00
❑ 33B Vic Raschi Traded to St.Louis 30.00 15.00
❑ 34 Sammy White 12.00 6.00
❑ 35A Eddie Joost Quiz Answer is 8 12.00 6.00
❑ 35B Eddie Joost Quiz Answer is 33 12.00 6.00
❑ 36 George Strickland 12.00 6.00
❑ 37 Dick Kokos 12.00 6.00
❑ 38A Minnie Minoso .895 /.961 Fielding Avg. 30.00 15.00
❑ 38B Minnie Minoso .963 /.963 Fielding Avg. 30.00 15.00
❑ 39 Ned Garver 12.00 6.00
❑ 40 Gil Coan 12.00 6.00
❑ 41A Alvin Dark .986/960 Fielding Avg. 20.00 10.00
❑ 41B Alvin Dark .968/.960 Fielding Avg. 20.00 10.00
❑ 42 Billy Loes 20.00 10.00
❑ 43A Bob Friend 20 Shutouts in Quiz 20.00 10.00
❑ 43B Bob Friend 16 Shutouts in Quiz 20.00 10.00
❑ 44 Harry Perkowski 12.00 6.00
❑ 45 Ralph Kiner 50.00 25.00
❑ 46 Rip Repulski 12.00 6.00
❑ 47A Granny Hamner .970 /.953 Fielding Avg. 12.00 6.00
❑ 47B Granny Hamner .953 /.951 Fielding Avg. 12.00 6.00
❑ 48 Jack Dittmer 12.00 6.00
❑ 49 Harry Byrd 12.00 6.00
❑ 50 George Kell 50.00 25.00
❑ 51 Alex Kellner 12.00 6.00
❑ 52 Joe Ginsberg 12.00 6.00
❑ 53A Don Lenhardt .969 /.984 Fielding Avg. 12.00 6.00
❑ 53B Don Lenhardt .966 /.983 Fielding Avg. 12.00 6.00
❑ 54 Chico Carrasquel 12.00 6.00
❑ 55 Jim Delsing 12.00 6.00
❑ 56 Maurice McDermott 12.00 6.00
❑ 57 Hoyt Wilhelm 50.00 25.00
❑ 58 Pee Wee Reese 80.00 50.00
❑ 59 Bob Schultz 12.00 6.00
❑ 60 Fred Baczewski RC 12.00 6.00
❑ 61A Eddie Miksis .954 /.962 Fielding Avg. 12.00 6.00
❑ 61B Eddie Miksis .954 /.961 Fielding Avg. 12.00 6.00
❑ 62 Enos Slaughter 50.00 25.00
❑ 63 Earl Torgeson 12.00 6.00
❑ 64 Eddie Mathews 80.00 50.00
❑ 65 Mickey Mantle 1500.00 900.00
❑ 66A Ted Williams 3000.001800.00
❑ 66B Jimmy Piersall 80.00 50.00
❑ 67A Carl Scheib .306 Pct. Two Lines under Bio 12.00 6.00
❑ 67B Carl Scheib .306 Pct. One Line under Bio 12.00 6.00
❑ 67C Carl Scheib .300 Pct. 12.00 6.00
❑ 68 Bobby Avila 20.00 10.00
❑ 69 Clint Courtney 12.00 6.00
❑ 70 Willard Marshall 12.00 6.00
❑ 71 Ted Gray 12.00 6.00
❑ 72 Eddie Yost 20.00 10.00
❑ 73 Don Mueller 20.00 10.00
❑ 74 Jim Gilliam 30.00 15.00
❑ 75 Max Surkont 12.00 6.00
❑ 76 Joe Nuxhall 20.00 10.00
❑ 77 Bob Rush 12.00 6.00
❑ 78 Sal Yvars 12.00 6.00
❑ 79 Curt Simmons 20.00 10.00
❑ 80A Johnny Logan 106 Runs 12.00 6.00
❑ 80B Johnny Logan 100 Runs 12.00 6.00
❑ 81A Jerry Coleman 1.000 /.975 Fielding Avg. 20.00 10.00
❑ 81B Jerry Coleman .952 /.975 Fielding Avg. 20.00 10.00
❑ 82A Bill Goodman .965 /.986 Fielding Avg. 20.00 10.00
❑ 82B Bill Goodman .972 /.985 Fielding Avg. 20.00 10.00
❑ 83 Ray Murray 12.00 6.00
❑ 84 Larry Doby 50.00 25.00
❑ 85A Jim Dyck .926/.956 Fielding Avg. 12.00 6.00
❑ 85B Jim Dyck .947/.960 Fielding Avg. 12.00 6.00
❑ 86 Harry Dorish 12.00 6.00
❑ 87 Don Lund 12.00 6.00
❑ 88 Tom Umphlett RC 12.00 6.00
❑ 89 Willie Mays 500.00 300.00
❑ 90 Roy Campanella 150.00 90.00
❑ 91 Cal Abrams 12.00 6.00
❑ 92 Ken Raffensberger 12.00 6.00
❑ 93A Bill Serena .983 /.966 Fielding Avg. 12.00 6.00
❑ 93B Bill Serena .977 /.966 Fielding Avg. 12.00 6.00
❑ 94A Solly Hemus 476/1343 Assists 12.00 6.00
❑ 94B Solly Hemus 477/1343 Assists 12.00 6.00
❑ 95 Robin Roberts 50.00 25.00
❑ 96 Joe Adcock 20.00 10.00
❑ 97 Gil McDougald 20.00 10.00
❑ 98 Ellis Kinder 12.00 6.00
❑ 99A Peter Suder .985 /.974 Fielding Avg. 12.00 6.00
❑ 99B Peter Suder .978 /.974 Fielding Avg. 12.00 6.00
❑ 100 Mike Garcia 20.00 10.00
❑ 101 Don Larsen RC 80.00 50.00
❑ 102 Billy Pierce 20.00 10.00
❑ 103A Stephen Souchock 144 /1192 Putouts 12.00 6.00
❑ 103B Stephen Souchock 147 /1195 Putouts 12.00 6.00
❑ 104 Frank Shea 12.00 6.00
❑ 105A Sal Maglie Quiz Answer is 8 20.00 10.00
❑ 105B Sal Maglie Quiz Answer is 1904 20.00 10.00
❑ 106 Clem Labine 20.00 10.00
❑ 107 Paul LaPalme 12.00 6.00
❑ 108 Bobby Adams 12.00 6.00
❑ 109 Roy Smalley 12.00 6.00
❑ 110 Red Schoendienst 50.00 25.00
❑ 111 Murry Dickson 12.00 6.00
❑ 112 Andy Pafko 20.00 10.00
❑ 113 Allie Reynolds 20.00 10.00
❑ 114 Willard Nixon 12.00 6.00
❑ 115 Don Bollweg 12.00 6.00
❑ 116 Luke Easter 20.00 10.00
❑ 117 Dick Kryhoski 12.00 6.00
❑ 118 Bob Boyd 12.00 6.00
❑ 119 Fred Hatfield 12.00 6.00
❑ 120 Mel Hoderlein RC 12.00 6.00
❑ 121 Ray Katt RC 12.00 6.00
❑ 122 Carl Furillo 30.00 15.00
❑ 123 Toby Atwell 12.00 6.00
❑ 124A Gus Bell 15/27 Errors 20.00 10.00
❑ 124B Gus Bell 11/26 Errors 20.00 10.00
❑ 125 Warren Hacker 12.00 6.00
❑ 126 Cliff Chambers 12.00 6.00
❑ 127 Del Ennis 20.00 10.00
❑ 128 Ebba St.Claire 12.00 6.00
❑ 129 Hank Bauer 30.00 15.00
❑ 130 Milt Bolling 12.00 6.00
❑ 131 Joe Astroth 12.00 6.00
❑ 132 Bob Feller 80.00 50.00
❑ 133 Duane Pillette 12.00 6.00
❑ 134 Luis Aloma 12.00 6.00
❑ 135 Johnny Pesky 20.00 10.00
❑ 136 Clyde Vollmer 12.00 6.00
❑ 137 Al Corwin 12.00 6.00
❑ 138A Gil Hodges .993 /.991 Fielding Avg. 80.00 50.00
❑ 138B Gil Hodges .992 /.991 Fielding Avg. 80.00 50.00
❑ 139A Preston Ward .961 /.992 Fielding Avg. 12.00 6.00
❑ 139B Preston Ward .990 /.992 Fielding Avg. 12.00 6.00
❑ 140A Saul Rogovin 7-12 W-L 2 Strikeouts 12.00 6.00
❑ 140B Saul Rogovin 7-12 W-L 62 Strikeouts 12.00 6.00
❑ 140C Saul Rogovin 8-12 W-L 12.00 6.00
❑ 141 Joe Garagiola 30.00 15.00
❑ 142 Al Brazle 12.00 6.00
❑ 143 Willie Jones 12.00 6.00
❑ 144 Ernie Johnson RC 30.00 15.00
❑ 145A Billy Martin .985 /.983 Fielding Avg. 80.00 50.00
❑ 145B Billy Martin .983 /.982 Fielding Avg. 80.00 50.00
❑ 146 Dick Gernert 12.00 6.00
❑ 147 Joe DeMaestri 12.00 6.00
❑ 148 Dale Mitchell 20.00 10.00
❑ 149 Bob Young 12.00 6.00
❑ 150 Cass Michaels 12.00 6.00
❑ 151 Pat Mullin 12.00 6.00
❑ 152 Mickey Vernon 20.00 10.00
❑ 153A Whitey Lockman 100/331 Assists 20.00 10.00
❑ 153B Whitey Lockman 102/333 Assists 20.00 10.00
❑ 154 Don Newcombe 30.00 15.00
❑ 155 Frank Thomas RC 20.00 10.00
❑ 156A Rocky Bridges 320/467 Assists 12.00 6.00
❑ 156B Rocky Bridges 328/475 Assists 12.00 6.00
❑ 157 Turk Lown 12.00 6.00
❑ 158 Stu Miller 20.00 10.00
❑ 159 Johnny Lindell 12.00 6.00
❑ 160 Danny O'Connell 12.00 6.00
❑ 161 Yogi Berra 175.00 100.00
❑ 162 Ted Lepcio 12.00 6.00
❑ 163A Dave Philley No Trade 152 Games 20.00 10.00
❑ 163B Dave Philley Traded to Cleveland 152 Games 30.0015.00
❑ 163C Dave Philley Traded to Cleveland 157 Games 30.00 15.00
❑ 164 Early Wynn 50.00 25.00
❑ 165 Johnny Groth 12.00 6.00
❑ 166 Sandy Consuegra 12.00 6.00
❑ 167 Billy Hoeft 12.00 6.00
❑ 168 Ed Fitzgerald 12.00 6.00
❑ 169 Larry Jansen 20.00 10.00
❑ 170 Duke Snider 250.00 150.00
❑ 171 Carlos Bernier 12.00 6.00
❑ 172 Andy Seminick 12.00 6.00
❑ 173 Dee Fondy 12.00 6.00
❑ 174A Pete Castiglione .966 /.959 Fielding Avg. 12.00 6.00
❑ 174B Pete Castiglione .970 /.959 Fielding Avg. 12.00 6.00
❑ 175 Mel Clark 12.00 6.00
❑ 176 Vern Bickford 12.00 6.00
❑ 177 Whitey Ford 100.00 60.00

❑ 178 Del Wilber	12.00	6.00
❑ 179A Morris Martin 44 ERA	12.00	6.00
❑ 179B Morris Martin 4.44 ERA	12.00	6.00
❑ 180 Joe Tipton	12.00	6.00
❑ 181 Les Moss	12.00	6.00
❑ 182 Sherm Lollar	20.00	10.00
❑ 183 Matt Batts	12.00	6.00
❑ 184 Mickey Grasso	12.00	6.00
❑ 185A Daryl Spencer .941 /.944 Fielding Avg. RC	12.00	6.00
❑ 185B Daryl Spencer .933 /.936 Fielding Avg.	12.00	6.00
❑ 186 Russ Meyer	12.00	6.00
❑ 187 Vern Law	20.00	10.00
❑ 188 Frank Smith	12.00	6.00
❑ 189 Randy Jackson	12.00	6.00
❑ 190 Joe Presko	12.00	6.00
❑ 191 Karl Drews	12.00	6.00
❑ 192 Lew Burdette	20.00	10.00
❑ 193 Eddie Robinson	12.00	6.00
❑ 194 Sid Hudson	12.00	6.00
❑ 195 Bob Cain	12.00	6.00
❑ 196 Bob Lemon	50.00	25.00
❑ 197 Lou Kretlow	12.00	6.00
❑ 198 Virgil Trucks	12.00	6.00
❑ 199 Steve Gromek	12.00	6.00
❑ 200 Conrado Marrero	12.00	6.00
❑ 201 Bobby Thomson	30.00	15.00
❑ 202 George Shuba	20.00	10.00
❑ 203 Vic Janowicz	20.00	10.00
❑ 204 Jack Collum RC	12.00	6.00
❑ 205 Hal Jeffcoat	12.00	6.00
❑ 206 Steve Bilko	12.00	6.00
❑ 207 Stan Lopata	12.00	6.00
❑ 208 Johnny Antonelli	20.00	10.00
❑ 209 Gene Woodling UER Reversed Photo	12.00	6.00
❑ 210 Jimmy Piersall	30.00	15.00
❑ 211 Al Robertson RC	12.00	6.00
❑ 212A Owen Friend .964 /.957 Fielding Avg.	12.00	6.00
❑ 212B Owen Friend .967 /.958 Fielding Avg.	12.00	6.00
❑ 213 Dick Littlefield	12.00	6.00
❑ 214 Ferris Fain	20.00	10.00
❑ 215 Johnny Bucha	12.00	6.00
❑ 216A Jerry Snyder .988 /.988 Fielding Avg.	12.00	6.00
❑ 216B Jerry Snyder .968 /.968 Fielding Avg.	12.00	6.00
❑ 217A Henry Thompson .956 /.951 Fielding Avg.	20.00	10.00
❑ 217B Henry Thompson .958 /.952 Fielding Avg.	20.00	10.00
❑ 218 Preacher Roe	20.00	10.00
❑ 219 Hal Rice	12.00	6.00
❑ 220 Hobie Landrith RC	12.00	6.00
❑ 221 Frank Baumholtz	12.00	6.00
❑ 222 Memo Luna RC	12.00	6.00
❑ 223 Steve Ridzik	12.00	6.00
❑ 224 Bill Bruton	50.00	25.00

1955 Bowman

❑ COMPLETE SET (320)	6000.00	3500.00
❑ COMMON CARD (1-96)	12.00	6.00
❑ COM. CARD (97-224)	10.00	5.00
❑ COM. CARD (225-320)	15.00	7.50
❑ COM. UMPIRE (225-320)	30.00	18.00
❑ WRAPPER (1-CENT)	60.00	50.00
❑ WRAPPER (5-CENT)	60.00	50.00
❑ 1 Hoyt Wilhelm	100.00	60.00
❑ 2 Alvin Dark	15.00	7.50
❑ 3 Joe Coleman	15.00	7.50
❑ 4 Eddie Waitkus	15.00	7.50
❑ 5 Jim Robertson	12.00	6.00
❑ 6 Pete Suder	12.00	6.00
❑ 7 Gene Baker RC	12.00	6.00
❑ 8 Warren Hacker	12.00	6.00
❑ 9 Gil McDougald	20.00	10.00
❑ 10 Phil Rizzuto	125.00	75.00
❑ 11 Bill Bruton	15.00	7.50
❑ 12 Andy Pafko	15.00	7.50
❑ 13 Clyde Vollmer	12.00	6.00
❑ 14 Gus Keriazakos RC	12.00	6.00
❑ 15 Frank Sullivan RC	12.00	6.00
❑ 16 Jimmy Piersall	20.00	10.00
❑ 17 Del Ennis	15.00	7.50
❑ 18 Stan Lopata	12.00	6.00
❑ 19 Bobby Avila	15.00	7.50
❑ 20 Al Smith	15.00	7.50
❑ 21 Don Hoak	12.00	6.00
❑ 22 Roy Campanella	125.00	75.00
❑ 23 Al Kaline	150.00	90.00
❑ 24 Al Aber	12.00	6.00
❑ 25 Minnie Minoso	30.00	15.00
❑ 26 Virgil Trucks	15.00	7.50
❑ 27 Preston Ward	12.00	6.00
❑ 28 Dick Cole	12.00	6.00
❑ 29 Red Schoendienst	30.00	15.00
❑ 30 Bill Sarni	12.00	6.00
❑ 31 Johnny Temple RC	15.00	7.50
❑ 32 Wally Post	15.00	7.50
❑ 33 Nellie Fox	50.00	30.00
❑ 34 Clint Courtney	12.00	6.00
❑ 35 Bill Tuttle RC	12.00	6.00
❑ 36 Wayne Belardi RC	12.00	6.00
❑ 37 Pee Wee Reese	100.00	60.00
❑ 38 Early Wynn	30.00	15.00
❑ 39 Bob Darnell RC	15.00	7.50
❑ 40 Vic Wertz	15.00	7.50
❑ 41 Mel Clark	12.00	6.00
❑ 42 Bob Greenwood RC	12.00	6.00
❑ 43 Bob Buhl	15.00	7.50
❑ 44 Danny O'Connell	12.00	6.00
❑ 45 Tom Umphlett	12.00	6.00
❑ 46 Mickey Vernon	15.00	7.50
❑ 47 Sammy White	12.00	6.00
❑ 48A Milt Bolling ERR	20.00	10.00
❑ 48B Milt Bolling COR	20.00	10.00
❑ 49 Jim Greengrass	12.00	6.00
❑ 50 Hobie Landrith	12.00	6.00
❑ 51 Elvin Tappe RC	12.00	6.00
❑ 52 Hal Rice	12.00	6.00
❑ 53 Alex Kellner	12.00	6.00
❑ 54 Don Bollweg	12.00	6.00
❑ 55 Cal Abrams	12.00	6.00
❑ 56 Billy Cox	15.00	7.50
❑ 57 Bob Friend	15.00	7.50
❑ 58 Frank Thomas	15.00	7.50
❑ 59 Whitey Ford	100.00	60.00
❑ 60 Enos Slaughter	30.00	15.00
❑ 61 Paul LaPalme	12.00	6.00
❑ 62 Royce Lint RC	12.00	6.00
❑ 63 Irv Noren	15.00	7.50
❑ 64 Curt Simmons	15.00	7.50
❑ 65 Don Zimmer RC	20.00	10.00
❑ 66 George Shuba	20.00	10.00
❑ 67 Don Larsen	20.00	10.00
❑ 68 Elston Howard RC	80.00	50.00
❑ 69 Billy Hunter	12.00	6.00
❑ 70 Lew Burdette	20.00	10.00
❑ 71 Dave Jolly	12.00	6.00
❑ 72 Chet Nichols	12.00	6.00
❑ 73 Eddie Yost	15.00	7.50
❑ 74 Jerry Snyder	12.00	6.00
❑ 75 Brooks Lawrence RC	12.00	6.00
❑ 76 Tom Poholsky	12.00	6.00
❑ 77 Jim McDonald RC	12.00	6.00
❑ 78 Gil Coan	12.00	6.00
❑ 79 Willie Miranda	12.00	6.00
❑ 80 Lou Limmer	12.00	6.00
❑ 81 Bobby Morgan	12.00	6.00
❑ 82 Lee Walls RC	12.00	6.00
❑ 83 Max Surkont	12.00	6.00
❑ 84 George Freese RC	12.00	6.00
❑ 85 Cass Michaels	12.00	6.00
❑ 86 Ted Gray	12.00	6.00
❑ 87 Randy Jackson	12.00	6.00
❑ 88 Steve Bilko	12.00	6.00
❑ 89 Lou Boudreau MG	30.00	15.00
❑ 90 Art RC	12.00	6.00
❑ 91 Dick Marlowe RC	12.00	6.00
❑ 92 George Zuverink	12.00	6.00
❑ 93 Andy Seminick	12.00	6.00
❑ 94 Hank Thompson	15.00	7.50
❑ 95 Sal Maglie	15.00	7.50
❑ 96 Ray Narleski RC	12.00	6.00
❑ 97 Johnny Podres	30.00	15.00
❑ 98 Jim Gilliam	20.00	10.00
❑ 99 Jerry Coleman	15.00	7.50
❑ 100 Tom Morgan	10.00	5.00
❑ 101A Don Johnson ERR	20.00	10.00
❑ 101B Don Johnson COR	20.00	10.00
❑ 102 Bobby Thomson	15.00	7.50
❑ 103 Eddie Mathews	80.00	50.00
❑ 104 Bob Porterfield	10.00	5.00
❑ 105 Johnny Schmitz	10.00	5.00
❑ 106 Del Rice	10.00	5.00
❑ 107 Solly Hemus	10.00	5.00
❑ 108 Lou Kretlow	10.00	5.00
❑ 109 Vern Stephens	15.00	7.50
❑ 110 Bob Miller	10.00	5.00
❑ 111 Steve Ridzik	10.00	5.00
❑ 112 Granny Hamner	10.00	5.00
❑ 113 Bob Hall RC	10.00	5.00
❑ 114 Vic Janowicz	15.00	7.50
❑ 115 Roger Bowman RC	10.00	5.00
❑ 116 Sandy Consuegra	10.00	5.00
❑ 117 Johnny Groth	10.00	5.00
❑ 118 Bobby Adams	10.00	5.00
❑ 119 Joe Astroth	10.00	5.00
❑ 120 Ed Burtschy RC	10.00	5.00
❑ 121 Rufus Crawford RC	10.00	5.00
❑ 122 Al Corwin	10.00	5.00
❑ 123 Marv Grissom RC	10.00	5.00
❑ 124 Johnny Antonelli	15.00	7.50
❑ 125 Paul Giel RC	15.00	7.50
❑ 126 Billy Goodman	15.00	7.50
❑ 127 Hank Majeski	10.00	5.00
❑ 128 Mike Garcia	15.00	7.50
❑ 129 Hal Naragon RC	10.00	5.00
❑ 130 Richie Ashburn	50.00	30.00
❑ 131 Willard Marshall	10.00	5.00
❑ 132A Harvey Kueen ERR	50.00	30.00
❑ 132B Harvey Kuenn COR	30.00	15.00
❑ 133 Charles King RC	10.00	5.00
❑ 134 Bob Feller	80.00	50.00
❑ 135 Lloyd Merriman	10.00	5.00
❑ 136 Rocky Bridges	10.00	5.00
❑ 137 Bob Talbot	10.00	5.00
❑ 138 Davey Williams	15.00	7.50
❑ 139 W.Shantz/B.Shantz	15.00	7.50
❑ 140 Bobby Shantz	15.00	7.50
❑ 141 Wes Westrum	15.00	7.50
❑ 142 Rudy Regalado RC	10.00	5.00
❑ 143 Don Newcombe	30.00	15.00
❑ 144 Art Houtteman	10.00	5.00
❑ 145 Bob Nieman RC	10.00	5.00
❑ 146 Don Liddle	10.00	5.00
❑ 147 Sam Mele	10.00	5.00
❑ 148 Bob Chakales	10.00	5.00
❑ 149 Cloyd Boyer	10.00	5.00
❑ 150 Billy Klaus RC	10.00	5.00
❑ 151 Jim Brideweser	10.00	5.00
❑ 152 Johnny Klippstein	10.00	5.00
❑ 153 Eddie Robinson	10.00	5.00
❑ 154 Frank Lary RC	15.00	7.50
❑ 155 Gerry Staley	10.00	5.00
❑ 156 Jim Hughes	15.00	7.50
❑ 157A Ernie Johnson ERR	20.00	10.00
❑ 157B Ernie Johnson COR	20.00	10.00
❑ 158 Gil Hodges	50.00	30.00
❑ 159 Harry Byrd	10.00	5.00
❑ 160 Bill Skowron	20.00	10.00
❑ 161 Matt Batts	10.00	5.00
❑ 162 Charlie Maxwell	10.00	5.00
❑ 163 Sid Gordon	15.00	7.50
❑ 164 Toby Atwell	10.00	5.00
❑ 165 Maurice McDermott	10.00	5.00
❑ 166 Jim Busby	10.00	5.00

❏ 167 Bob Grim RC 20.00 10.00
❏ 168 Yogi Berra 125.00 75.00
❏ 169 Carl Furillo 30.00 15.00
❏ 170 Carl Erskine 20.00 10.00
❏ 171 Robin Roberts 50.00 30.00
❏ 172 Willie Jones 10.00 5.00
❏ 173 Chico Carrasquel 10.00 5.00
❏ 174 Sherm Lollar 15.00 7.50
❏ 175 Wilmer Shantz RC 10.00 5.00
❏ 176 Joe DeMaestri 10.00 5.00
❏ 177 Willard Nixon 10.00 5.00
❏ 178 Tom Brewer RC 10.00 5.00
❏ 179 Hank Aaron 250.00 150.00
❏ 180 Johnny Logan 15.00 7.50
❏ 181 Eddie Miksis 10.00 5.00
❏ 182 Bob Rush 10.00 5.00
❏ 183 Ray Katt 10.00 5.00
❏ 184 Willie Mays 250.00 150.00
❏ 185 Vic Raschi 10.00 5.00
❏ 186 Alex Grammas 10.00 5.00
❏ 187 Fred Hatfield 10.00 5.00
❏ 188 Ned Garver 10.00 5.00
❏ 189 Jack Collum 10.00 5.00
❏ 190 Fred Baczewski 10.00 5.00
❏ 191 Bob Lemon 30.00 15.00
❏ 192 George Strickland 10.00 5.00
❏ 193 Howie Judson 10.00 5.00
❏ 194 Joe Nuxhall 15.00 7.50
❏ 195A Erv Palica 15.00 7.50
❏ 195B Erv Palica TR 40.00 20.00
❏ 196 Russ Meyer 15.00 7.50
❏ 197 Ralph Kiner 30.00 15.00
❏ 198 Dave Pope RC 10.00 5.00
❏ 199 Vern Law 15.00 7.50
❏ 200 Dick Littlefield 10.00 5.00
❏ 201 Allie Reynolds 20.00 10.00
❏ 202 Mickey Mantle UER 800.00 500.00
❏ 203 Steve Gromek 10.00 5.00
❏ 204A Frank Bolling ERR RC 20.00 10.00
❏ 204B Frank Bolling COR 20.00 10.00
❏ 205 Rip Repulski 10.00 5.00
❏ 206 Ralph Beard RC 10.00 5.00
❏ 207 Frank Shea 10.00 5.00
❏ 208 Ed Fitzgerald 10.00 5.00
❏ 209 Smoky Burgess 15.00 7.50
❏ 210 Earl Torgeson 10.00 5.00
❏ 211 Sonny Dixon RC 10.00 5.00
❏ 212 Jack Dittmer 10.00 5.00
❏ 213 George Kell 30.00 15.00
❏ 214 Billy Pierce 15.00 7.50
❏ 215 Bob Kuzava 10.00 5.00
❏ 216 Preacher Roe 20.00 10.00
❏ 217 Del Crandall 15.00 7.50
❏ 218 Joe Adcock 15.00 7.50
❏ 219 Whitey Lockman 15.00 7.50
❏ 220 Jim Hearn 10.00 5.00
❏ 221 Hector Brown 10.00 5.00
❏ 222 Russ Kemmerer RC 10.00 5.00
❏ 223 Hal Jeffcoat 10.00 5.00
❏ 224 Dee Fondy 10.00 5.00
❏ 225 Paul Richards MG 15.00 7.50
❏ 226 Bill McKinley UMP 30.00 18.00
❏ 227 Frank Baumholtz 15.00 7.50
❏ 228 John Phillips RC 15.00 7.50
❏ 229 Jim Brosnan RC 20.00 10.00
❏ 230 Al Brazle 15.00 7.50
❏ 231 Jim Konstanty 20.00 10.00
❏ 232 Birdie Tebbetts MG 20.00 10.00
❏ 233 Bill Serena 15.00 7.50
❏ 234 Dick Bartell CO 20.00 10.00
❏ 235 Joe Paparella UMP 30.00 18.00
❏ 236 Murry Dickson 15.00 7.50
❏ 237 Johnny Wyrostek 15.00 7.50
❏ 238 Eddie Stanky MG 20.00 10.00
❏ 239 Edwin Rommel UMP 40.00 20.00
❏ 240 Billy Loes 20.00 10.00
❏ 241 Johnny Pesky 20.00 10.00
❏ 242 Ernie Banks 350.00 200.00
❏ 243 Gus Bell 20.00 10.00
❏ 244 Duane Pillette 15.00 7.50
❏ 245 Bill Miller 15.00 7.50
❏ 246 Hank Bauer 30.00 15.00
❏ 247 Dutch Leonard CO 15.00 7.50
❏ 248 Harry Dorish 15.00 7.50
❏ 249 Billy Gardner RC 20.00 10.00
❏ 250 Larry Napp UMP 30.00 18.00
❏ 251 Stan Jok 15.00 7.50
❏ 252 Roy Smalley 15.00 7.50
❏ 253 Jim Wilson 15.00 7.50
❏ 254 Bennett Flowers RC 15.00 7.50
❏ 255 Pete Runnels 20.00 10.00
❏ 256 Owen Friend 15.00 7.50
❏ 257 Tom Alston RC 15.00 7.50
❏ 258 John Stevens UMP 30.00 18.00
❏ 259 Don Mossi RC 30.00 15.00
❏ 260 Edwin Hurley UMP 30.00 18.00
❏ 261 Walt Moryn RC 20.00 10.00
❏ 262 Jim Lemon FBC 15.00 7.50
❏ 263 Eddie Joost 15.00 7.50
❏ 264 Bill Henry RC 15.00 7.50
❏ 265 Al Barlick UMP 80.00 50.00
❏ 266 Mike Fornieles 15.00 7.50
❏ 267 J.Honochick UMP 80.00 50.00
❏ 268 Roy Lee Hawes RC 15.00 7.50
❏ 269 Joe Amalfitano RC 20.00 10.00
❏ 270 Chico Fernandez RC 20.00 10.00
❏ 271 Bob Hooper 15.00 7.50
❏ 272 John Flaherty UMP 30.00 18.00
❏ 273 Bubba Church 15.00 7.50
❏ 274 Jim Delsing 15.00 7.50
❏ 275 William Grieve UMP 30.00 18.00
❏ 276 Ike Delock 15.00 7.50
❏ 277 Ed Runge UMP 30.00 18.00
❏ 278 Charlie Neal RC 40.00 20.00
❏ 279 Hank Soar UMP 40.00 20.00
❏ 280 Clyde McCullough 15.00 7.50
❏ 281 Charles Berry UMP 40.00 20.00
❏ 282 Phil Cavarretta MG 20.00 10.00
❏ 283 Nestor Chylak UMP 80.00 50.00
❏ 284 Bill Jackowski UMP 30.00 18.00
❏ 285 Walt Dropo 20.00 10.00
❏ 286 Frank Secory UMP 30.00 18.00
❏ 287 Ron Mrozinski RC 15.00 7.50
❏ 288 Dick Smith RC 15.00 7.50
❏ 289 Arthur Gore UMP 30.00 18.00
❏ 290 Hershell Freeman RC 15.00 7.50
❏ 291 Frank Dascoli UMP 30.00 18.00
❏ 292 Marv Blaylock RC 15.00 7.50
❏ 293 Thomas Gorman UMP 40.00 20.00
❏ 294 Wally Moses CO 15.00 7.50
❏ 295 Lee Ballanfant UMP 30.00 18.00
❏ 296 Bill Virdon RC 30.00 15.00
❏ 297 Dusty Boggess UMP 30.00 18.00
❏ 298 Charlie Grimm 20.00 10.00
❏ 299 Lon Warneke UMP 40.00 20.00
❏ 300 Tommy Byrne 20.00 10.00
❏ 301 William Engeln UMP 30.00 18.00
❏ 302 Frank Malzone RC 30.00 15.00
❏ 303 Jocko Conlan UMP 80.00 50.00
❏ 304 Harry Chiti 15.00 7.50
❏ 305 Frank Umont UMP 30.00 18.00
❏ 306 Bob Cerv 20.00 10.00
❏ 307 Babe Pinelli UMP 40.00 20.00
❏ 308 Al Lopez MG 50.00 30.00
❏ 309 Hal Dixon UMP 30.00 18.00
❏ 310 Ken Lehman RC 15.00 7.50
❏ 311 Lawrence Goetz UMP 30.00 18.00
❏ 312 Bill Wight 15.00 7.50
❏ 313 Augie Donatelli UMP 50.00 30.00
❏ 314 Dale Mitchell 20.00 10.00
❏ 315 Cal Hubbard UMP 80.00 50.00
❏ 316 Marion Fricano 15.00 7.50
❏ 317 William Summers UMP 20.00 10.00
❏ 318 Sid Hudson 15.00 7.50
❏ 319 Al Schroll RC 15.00 7.50
❏ 320 George Susce RC 50.00 30.00

1989 Bowman

❏ COMPLETE SET (484) 25.00 10.00
❏ COMP.FACT.SET (484) 25.00 10.00
❏ 1 Oswald Peraza .05 .01
❏ 2 Brian Holton .05 .01
❏ 3 Jose Bautista RC .10 .02
❏ 4 Pete Harnisch RC .25 .08
❏ 5 Dave Schmidt .05 .01
❏ 6 Gregg Olson RC .25 .08
❏ 7 Jeff Ballard .05 .01
❏ 8 Bob Melvin .05 .01
❏ 9 Cal Ripken .75 .30
❏ 10 Randy Milligan .05 .01
❏ 11 Juan Bell RC .10 .02
❏ 12 Billy Ripken .05 .01
❏ 13 Jim Traber .05 .01
❏ 14 Pete Stanicek .05 .01
❏ 15 Steve Finley RC .75 .30
❏ 16 Larry Sheets .05 .01
❏ 17 Phil Bradley .05 .01
❏ 18 Brady Anderson RC .40 .15
❏ 19 Lee Smith .10 .02
❏ 20 Tom Fischer .05 .01
❏ 21 Mike Boddicker .05 .01
❏ 22 Rob Murphy .05 .01
❏ 23 Wes Gardner .05 .01
❏ 24 John Dopson .05 .01
❏ 25 Bob Stanley .05 .01
❏ 26 Roger Clemens 1.00 .40
❏ 27 Rich Gedman .05 .01
❏ 28 Marty Barrett .05 .01
❏ 29 Luis Rivera .05 .01
❏ 30 Jody Reed .05 .01
❏ 31 Nick Esasky .05 .01
❏ 32 Wade Boggs .15 .05
❏ 33 Jim Rice .10 .02
❏ 34 Mike Greenwell .05 .01
❏ 35 Dwight Evans .15 .05
❏ 36 Ellis Burks .10 .02
❏ 37 Chuck Finley .10 .02
❏ 38 Kirk McCaskill .05 .01
❏ 39 Jim Abbott RC 1.00 .40
❏ 40 Bryan Harvey RC .25 .08
❏ 41 Bert Blyleven .10 .02
❏ 42 Mike Witt .05 .01
❏ 43 Bob McClure .05 .01
❏ 44 Bill Schroeder .05 .01
❏ 45 Lance Parrish .10 .02
❏ 46 Dick Schofield .05 .01
❏ 47 Wally Joyner .10 .02
❏ 48 Jack Howell .05 .01
❏ 49 Johnny Ray .05 .01
❏ 50 Chili Davis .10 .02
❏ 51 Tony Armas .10 .02
❏ 52 Claudell Washington .05 .01
❏ 53 Brian Downing .10 .02
❏ 54 Devon White .10 .02
❏ 55 Bobby Thigpen .05 .01
❏ 56 Bill Long .05 .01
❏ 57 Jerry Reuss .05 .01
❏ 58 Shawn Hillegas .05 .01
❏ 59 Melido Perez .05 .01
❏ 60 Jeff Bittiger .05 .01
❏ 61 Jack McDowell .10 .02
❏ 62 Carlton Fisk .15 .05
❏ 63 Steve Lyons .05 .01
❏ 64 Ozzie Guillen .10 .02
❏ 65 Robin Ventura RC .75 .30
❏ 66 Fred Manrique .05 .01
❏ 67 Dan Pasqua .05 .01
❏ 68 Ivan Calderon .05 .01
❏ 69 Ron Kittle .05 .01
❏ 70 Daryl Boston .05 .01
❏ 71 Dave Gallagher .05 .01
❏ 72 Harold Baines .10 .02
❏ 73 Charles Nagy RC .25 .08
❏ 74 John Farrell .05 .01
❏ 75 Kevin Wickander .05 .01
❏ 76 Greg Swindell .05 .01
❏ 77 Mike Walker .05 .01
❏ 78 Doug Jones .05 .01
❏ 79 Rich Yett .05 .01

❑	80	Tom Candiotti	.05	.01
❑	81	Jesse Orosco	.05	.01
❑	82	Bud Black	.05	.01
❑	83	Andy Allanson	.05	.01
❑	84	Pete O'Brien	.05	.01
❑	85	Jerry Browne	.05	.01
❑	86	Brook Jacoby	.05	.01
❑	87	Mark Lewis RC	.25	.08
❑	88	Luis Aguayo	.05	.01
❑	89	Cory Snyder	.05	.01
❑	90	Oddibe McDowell	.05	.01
❑	91	Joe Carter	.10	.02
❑	92	Frank Tanana	.10	.02
❑	93	Jack Morris	.10	.02
❑	94	Doyle Alexander	.05	.01
❑	95	Steve Searcy	.05	.01
❑	96	Randy Bockus	.05	.01
❑	97	Jeff M. Robinson	.05	.01
❑	98	Mike Henneman	.05	.01
❑	99	Paul Gibson	.05	.01
❑	100	Frank Williams	.05	.01
❑	101	Matt Nokes	.05	.01
❑	102	Rico Brogna RC	.40	.15
❑	103	Lou Whitaker	.10	.02
❑	104	Al Pedrique	.05	.01
❑	105	Alan Trammell	.10	.02
❑	106	Chris Brown	.05	.01
❑	107	Pat Sheridan	.05	.01
❑	108	Chet Lemon	.10	.02
❑	109	Keith Moreland	.05	.01
❑	110	Mel Stottlemyre Jr.	.05	.01
❑	111	Bret Saberhagen	.10	.02
❑	112	Floyd Bannister	.05	.01
❑	113	Jeff Montgomery	.05	.01
❑	114	Steve Farr	.05	.01
❑	115	Tom Gordon UER RC	.40	.15
❑	116	Charlie Leibrandt	.05	.01
❑	117	Mark Gubicza	.05	.01
❑	118	Mike Macfarlane RC *	.25	.08
❑	119	Bob Boone	.10	.02
❑	120	Kurt Stillwell	.05	.01
❑	121	George Brett	.60	.25
❑	122	Frank White	.10	.02
❑	123	Kevin Seitzer	.05	.01
❑	124	Willie Wilson	.10	.02
❑	125	Pat Tabler	.05	.01
❑	126	Bo Jackson	.25	.08
❑	127	Hugh Walker RC	.10	.02
❑	128	Danny Tartabull	.05	.01
❑	129	Teddy Higuera	.05	.01
❑	130	Don August	.05	.01
❑	131	Juan Nieves	.05	.01
❑	132	Mike Birkbeck	.05	.01
❑	133	Dan Plesac	.05	.01
❑	134	Chris Bosio	.05	.01
❑	135	Bill Wegman	.05	.01
❑	136	Chuck Crim	.05	.01
❑	137	B.J. Surhoff	.10	.02
❑	138	Joey Meyer	.05	.01
❑	139	Dale Sveum	.05	.01
❑	140	Paul Molitor	.10	.02
❑	141	Jim Gantner	.05	.01
❑	142	Gary Sheffield RC	1.50	.60
❑	143	Greg Brock	.05	.01
❑	144	Robin Yount	.40	.15
❑	145	Glenn Braggs	.05	.01
❑	146	Rob Deer	.05	.01
❑	147	Fred Toliver	.05	.01
❑	148	Jeff Reardon	.10	.02
❑	149	Allan Anderson	.05	.01
❑	150	Frank Viola	.10	.02
❑	151	Shane Rawley	.05	.01
❑	152	Juan Berenguer	.05	.01
❑	153	Johnny Ard	.05	.01
❑	154	Tim Laudner	.05	.01
❑	155	Brian Harper	.05	.01
❑	156	Al Newman	.05	.01
❑	157	Kent Hrbek	.10	.02
❑	158	Gary Gaetti	.10	.02
❑	159	Wally Backman	.05	.01
❑	160	Gene Larkin	.05	.01
❑	161	Greg Gagne	.05	.01
❑	162	Kirby Puckett	.25	.08
❑	163	Dan Gladden	.05	.01
❑	164	Randy Bush	.05	.01
❑	165	Dave LaPoint	.05	.01
❑	166	Andy Hawkins	.05	.01
❑	167	Dave Righetti	.10	.02
❑	168	Lance McCullers	.05	.01
❑	169	Jimmy Jones	.05	.01
❑	170	Al Leiter	.25	.08
❑	171	John Candelaria	.05	.01
❑	172	Don Slaught	.05	.01
❑	173	Jamie Quirk	.05	.01
❑	174	Rafael Santana	.05	.01
❑	175	Mike Pagliarulo	.05	.01
❑	176	Don Mattingly	.60	.25
❑	177	Ken Phelps	.05	.01
❑	178	Steve Sax	.05	.01
❑	179	Dave Winfield	.10	.02
❑	180	Stan Jefferson	.05	.01
❑	181	Rickey Henderson	.25	.08
❑	182	Bob Brower	.05	.01
❑	183	Roberto Kelly	.05	.01
❑	184	Curt Young	.05	.01
❑	185	Gene Nelson	.05	.01
❑	186	Bob Welch	.10	.02
❑	187	Rick Honeycutt	.05	.01
❑	188	Dave Stewart	.10	.02
❑	189	Mike Moore	.05	.01
❑	190	Dennis Eckersley	.15	.05
❑	191	Eric Plunk	.05	.01
❑	192	Storm Davis	.05	.01
❑	193	Terry Steinbach	.10	.02
❑	194	Ron Hassey	.05	.01
❑	195	Stan Royer RC	.10	.02
❑	196	Walt Weiss	.05	.01
❑	197	Mark McGwire	1.00	.40
❑	198	Carney Lansford	.10	.02
❑	199	Glenn Hubbard	.05	.01
❑	200	Dave Henderson	.05	.01
❑	201	Jose Canseco	.25	.08
❑	202	Dave Parker	.10	.02
❑	203	Scott Bankhead	.05	.01
❑	204	Tom Niedenfuer	.05	.01
❑	205	Mark Langston	.05	.01
❑	206	Erik Hanson RC	.25	.08
❑	207	Mike Jackson	.05	.01
❑	208	Dave Valle	.05	.01
❑	209	Scott Bradley	.05	.01
❑	210	Harold Reynolds	.10	.02
❑	211	Tino Martinez RC	2.00	.75
❑	212	Rich Renteria	.05	.01
❑	213	Rey Quinones	.05	.01
❑	214	Jim Presley	.05	.01
❑	215	Alvin Davis	.05	.01
❑	216	Edgar Martinez	.25	.08
❑	217	Darnell Coles	.05	.01
❑	218	Jeffrey Leonard	.05	.01
❑	219	Jay Buhner	.10	.02
❑	220	Ken Griffey Jr. RC	6.00	2.50
❑	221	Drew Hall	.05	.01
❑	222	Bobby Witt	.05	.01
❑	223	Jamie Moyer	.10	.02
❑	224	Charlie Hough	.10	.02
❑	225	Nolan Ryan	1.00	.40
❑	226	Jeff Russell	.05	.01
❑	227	Jim Sundberg	.10	.02
❑	228	Julio Franco	.10	.02
❑	229	Buddy Bell	.10	.02
❑	230	Scott Fletcher	.05	.01
❑	231	Jeff Kunkel	.05	.01
❑	232	Steve Buechele	.05	.01
❑	233	Monty Fariss	.05	.01
❑	234	Rick Leach	.05	.01
❑	235	Ruben Sierra	.10	.02
❑	236	Cecil Espy	.05	.01
❑	237	Rafael Palmeiro	.25	.08
❑	238	Pete Incaviglia	.05	.01
❑	239	Dave Stieb	.10	.02
❑	240	Jeff Musselman	.05	.01
❑	241	Mike Flanagan	.05	.01
❑	242	Todd Stottlemyre	.05	.01
❑	243	Jimmy Key	.10	.02
❑	244	Tony Castillo RC	.10	.02
❑	245	Alex Sanchez RC	.05	.01
❑	246	Tom Henke	.05	.01
❑	247	John Cerutti	.05	.01
❑	248	Ernie Whitt	.05	.01
❑	249	Bob Brenly	.05	.01
❑	250	Rance Mulliniks	.05	.01
❑	251	Kelly Gruber	.05	.01
❑	252	Ed Sprague RC	.25	.08
❑	253	Fred McGriff	.15	.05
❑	254	Tony Fernandez	.05	.01
❑	255	Tom Lawless	.05	.01
❑	256	George Bell	.10	.02
❑	257	Jesse Barfield	.10	.02
❑	258	Roberto Alomar w/Dad	.15	.05
❑	259	Ken Griffey Sr./Jr.	1.00	.40
❑	260	Cal Ripken Sr./Jr.	.25	.08
❑	261	M.Stottlemyre Jr./Sr.	.05	.01
❑	262	Zane Smith	.05	.01
❑	263	Charlie Puleo	.05	.01
❑	264	Derek Lilliquist RC	.10	.02
❑	265	Paul Assenmacher	.05	.01
❑	266	John Smoltz RC	1.50	.60
❑	267	Tom Glavine	.25	.08
❑	268	Steve Avery RC	.25	.08
❑	269	Pete Smith	.05	.01
❑	270	Jody Davis	.05	.01
❑	271	Bruce Benedict	.05	.01
❑	272	Andres Thomas	.05	.01
❑	273	Gerald Perry	.05	.01
❑	274	Ron Gant	.10	.02
❑	275	Darrell Evans	.10	.02
❑	276	Dale Murphy	.15	.05
❑	277	Dion James	.05	.01
❑	278	Lonnie Smith	.05	.01
❑	279	Geronimo Berroa	.05	.01
❑	280	Steve Wilson RC	.10	.02
❑	281	Rick Sutcliffe	.10	.02
❑	282	Kevin Coffman	.05	.01
❑	283	Mitch Williams	.05	.01
❑	284	Greg Maddux	.50	.20
❑	285	Paul Kilgus	.05	.01
❑	286	Mike Harkey RC	.10	.02
❑	287	Lloyd McClendon	.05	.01
❑	288	Damon Berryhill	.05	.01
❑	289	Ty Griffin	.05	.01
❑	290	Ryne Sandberg	.40	.15
❑	291	Mark Grace	.25	.08
❑	292	Curt Wilkerson	.05	.01
❑	293	Vance Law	.05	.01
❑	294	Shawon Dunston	.05	.01
❑	295	Jerome Walton RC	.25	.08
❑	296	Mitch Webster	.05	.01
❑	297	Dwight Smith RC	.25	.08
❑	298	Andre Dawson	.10	.02
❑	299	Jeff Sellers	.05	.01
❑	300	Jose Rijo	.10	.02
❑	301	John Franco	.10	.02
❑	302	Rick Mahler	.05	.01
❑	303	Ron Robinson	.05	.01
❑	304	Danny Jackson	.05	.01
❑	305	Rob Dibble RC	.40	.15
❑	306	Tom Browning	.05	.01
❑	307	Bo Diaz	.05	.01
❑	308	Manny Trillo	.05	.01
❑	309	Chris Sabo RC *	.40	.15
❑	310	Ron Oester	.05	.01
❑	311	Barry Larkin	.15	.05
❑	312	Todd Denzinger	.05	.01
❑	313	Paul O'Neill	.15	.05
❑	314	Kal Daniels	.05	.01
❑	315	Joel Youngblood	.05	.01
❑	316	Eric Davis	.10	.02
❑	317	Dave Smith	.05	.01
❑	318	Mark Portugal	.05	.01
❑	319	Brian Meyer	.05	.01
❑	320	Jim Deshaies	.05	.01
❑	321	Juan Agosto	.05	.01
❑	322	Mike Scott	.10	.02
❑	323	Rick Rhoden	.05	.01
❑	324	Jim Clancy	.05	.01
❑	325	Larry Andersen	.05	.01
❑	326	Alex Trevino	.05	.01
❑	327	Alan Ashby	.05	.01
❑	328	Craig Reynolds	.05	.01
❑	329	Bill Doran	.05	.01
❑	330	Rafael Ramirez	.05	.01
❑	331	Glenn Davis	.05	.01
❑	332	Willie Ansley RC	.10	.02
❑	333	Gerald Young	.05	.01
❑	334	Cameron Drew	.05	.01
❑	335	Jay Howell	.05	.01
❑	336	Tim Belcher	.05	.01
❑	337	Fernando Valenzuela	.10	.02

❑ 338 Ricky Horton	.05	.01
❑ 339 Tim Leary	.05	.01
❑ 340 Bill Bene	.05	.01
❑ 341 Orel Hershiser	.10	.02
❑ 342 Mike Scioscia	.10	.02
❑ 343 Rick Dempsey	.05	.01
❑ 344 Willie Randolph	.10	.02
❑ 345 Alfredo Griffin	.05	.01
❑ 346 Eddie Murray	.25	.08
❑ 347 Mickey Hatcher	.05	.01
❑ 348 Mike Sharperson	.05	.01
❑ 349 John Shelby	.05	.01
❑ 350 Mike Marshall	.05	.01
❑ 351 Kirk Gibson	.10	.02
❑ 352 Mike Davis	.05	.01
❑ 353 Bryn Smith	.05	.01
❑ 354 Pascual Perez	.05	.01
❑ 355 Kevin Gross	.05	.01
❑ 356 Andy McGaffigan	.05	.01
❑ 357 Brian Holman RC *	.10	.02
❑ 358 Dave Wainhouse RC	.10	.02
❑ 359 Dennis Martinez	.10	.02
❑ 360 Tim Burke	.05	.01
❑ 361 Nelson Santovenia	.05	.01
❑ 362 Tim Wallach	.05	.01
❑ 363 Spike Owen	.05	.01
❑ 364 Rex Hudler	.05	.01
❑ 365 Andres Galarraga	.10	.02
❑ 366 Otis Nixon	.05	.01
❑ 367 Hubie Brooks	.05	.01
❑ 368 Mike Aldrete	.05	.01
❑ 369 Tim Raines	.10	.02
❑ 370 Dave Martinez	.05	.01
❑ 371 Bob Ojeda	.05	.01
❑ 372 Ron Darling	.10	.02
❑ 373 Wally Whitehurst RC	.10	.02
❑ 374 Randy Myers	.10	.02
❑ 375 David Cone	.10	.02
❑ 376 Dwight Gooden	.10	.02
❑ 377 Sid Fernandez	.05	.01
❑ 378 Dave Proctor	.05	.01
❑ 379 Gary Carter	.10	.02
❑ 380 Keith Miller	.05	.01
❑ 381 Gregg Jefferies	.05	.01
❑ 382 Tim Teufel	.05	.01
❑ 383 Kevin Elster	.05	.01
❑ 384 Dave Magadan	.05	.01
❑ 385 Keith Hernandez	.10	.02
❑ 386 Mookie Wilson	.10	.02
❑ 387 Darryl Strawberry	.10	.02
❑ 388 Kevin McReynolds	.05	.01
❑ 389 Mark Carreon	.05	.01
❑ 390 Jeff Parrett	.05	.01
❑ 391 Mike Maddux	.05	.01
❑ 392 Don Carman	.05	.01
❑ 393 Bruce Ruffin	.05	.01
❑ 394 Ken Howell	.05	.01
❑ 395 Steve Bedrosian	.05	.01
❑ 396 Floyd Youmans	.05	.01
❑ 397 Larry McWilliams	.05	.01
❑ 398 Pat Combs RC *	.10	.02
❑ 399 Steve Lake	.05	.01
❑ 400 Dickie Thon	.05	.01
❑ 401 Ricky Jordan RC *	.25	.08
❑ 402 Mike Schmidt	.50	.20
❑ 403 Tom Herr	.05	.01
❑ 404 Chris James	.05	.01
❑ 405 Juan Samuel	.05	.01
❑ 406 Von Hayes	.05	.01
❑ 407 Ron Jones	.10	.02
❑ 408 Curt Ford	.05	.01
❑ 409 Bob Walk	.05	.01
❑ 410 Jeff D. Robinson	.05	.01
❑ 411 Jim Gott	.05	.01
❑ 412 Scott Medvin	.05	.01
❑ 413 John Smiley	.05	.01
❑ 414 Bob Kipper	.05	.01
❑ 415 Brian Fisher	.05	.01
❑ 416 Doug Drabek	.05	.01
❑ 417 Mike LaValliere	.05	.01
❑ 418 Ken Oberkfell	.05	.01
❑ 419 Sid Bream	.05	.01
❑ 420 Austin Manahan	.05	.01
❑ 421 Jose Lind	.05	.01
❑ 422 Bobby Bonilla	.10	.02
❑ 423 Glenn Wilson	.05	.01
❑ 424 Andy Van Slyke	.15	.05
❑ 425 Gary Redus	.05	.01
❑ 426 Barry Bonds	1.50	.60
❑ 427 Don Heinkel	.05	.01
❑ 428 Ken Dayley	.05	.01
❑ 429 Todd Worrell	.05	.01
❑ 430 Brad DuVall	.05	.01
❑ 431 Jose DeLeon	.05	.01
❑ 432 Joe Magrane	.05	.01
❑ 433 John Ericks	.05	.01
❑ 434 Frank DiPino	.05	.01
❑ 435 Tony Pena	.05	.01
❑ 436 Ozzie Smith	.40	.15
❑ 437 Terry Pendleton	.10	.02
❑ 438 Jose Oquendo	.05	.01
❑ 439 Tim Jones	.05	.01
❑ 440 Pedro Guerrero	.10	.02
❑ 441 Milt Thompson	.05	.01
❑ 442 Willie McGee	.10	.02
❑ 443 Vince Coleman	.05	.01
❑ 444 Tom Brunansky	.05	.01
❑ 445 Walt Terrell	.05	.01
❑ 446 Eric Show	.05	.01
❑ 447 Mark Davis	.05	.01
❑ 448 Andy Benes RC	.40	.15
❑ 449 Ed Whitson	.05	.01
❑ 450 Dennis Rasmussen	.05	.01
❑ 451 Bruce Hurst	.05	.01
❑ 452 Pat Clements	.05	.01
❑ 453 Benito Santiago	.10	.02
❑ 454 Sandy Alomar Jr. RC	.40	.15
❑ 455 Garry Templeton	.10	.02
❑ 456 Jack Clark	.10	.02
❑ 457 Tim Flannery	.05	.01
❑ 458 Roberto Alomar	.25	.08
❑ 459 Carmelo Martinez	.05	.01
❑ 460 John Kruk	.10	.02
❑ 461 Tony Gwynn	.30	.10
❑ 462 Jerald Clark RC	.10	.02
❑ 463 Don Robinson	.05	.01
❑ 464 Craig Lefferts	.05	.01
❑ 465 Kelly Downs	.05	.01
❑ 466 Rick Reuschel	.10	.02
❑ 467 Scott Garrelts	.05	.01
❑ 468 Wil Tejada	.05	.01
❑ 469 Kirt Manwaring	.05	.01
❑ 470 Terry Kennedy	.05	.01
❑ 471 Jose Uribe	.05	.01
❑ 472 Royce Clayton RC	.40	.15
❑ 473 Robby Thompson	.05	.01
❑ 474 Kevin Mitchell	.10	.02
❑ 475 Ernie Riles	.05	.01
❑ 476 Will Clark	.15	.05
❑ 477 Donell Nixon	.05	.01
❑ 478 Candy Maldonado	.05	.01
❑ 479 Tracy Jones	.05	.01
❑ 480 Brett Butler	.10	.02
❑ 481 Checklist 1-121	.05	.01
❑ 482 Checklist 122-242	.05	.01
❑ 483 Checklist 243-363	.05	.01
❑ 484 Checklist 364-484	.05	.01

1990 Bowman

❑ COMPLETE SET (528)	25.00	10.00
❑ COMP.FACT.SET (528)	25.00	10.00
❑ 1 Tommy Greene RC	.10	.02
❑ 2 Tom Glavine	.15	.05
❑ 3 Andy Nezelek	.05	.01
❑ 4 Mike Stanton RC	.25	.08
❑ 5 Rick Luecken RC	.05	.01
❑ 6 Kent Mercker RC	.25	.08
❑ 7 Derek Lilliquist	.05	.01
❑ 8 Charlie Leibrandt	.05	.01
❑ 9 Steve Avery	.05	.01
❑ 10 John Smoltz	.25	.08
❑ 11 Mark Lemke	.05	.01
❑ 12 Lonnie Smith	.05	.01
❑ 13 Oddibe McDowell	.05	.01
❑ 14 Tyler Houston RC	.25	.08
❑ 15 Jeff Blauser	.05	.01
❑ 16 Ernie Whitt	.05	.01
❑ 17 Alexis Infante	.05	.01
❑ 18 Jim Presley	.05	.01
❑ 19 Dale Murphy	.15	.05
❑ 20 Nick Esasky	.05	.01
❑ 21 Rick Sutcliffe	.10	.02
❑ 22 Mike Bielecki	.05	.01
❑ 23 Steve Wilson	.05	.01
❑ 24 Kevin Blankenship	.05	.01
❑ 25 Mitch Williams	.05	.01
❑ 26 Dean Wilkins RC	.05	.01
❑ 27 Greg Maddux	.40	.15
❑ 28 Mike Harkey	.06	.01
❑ 29 Mark Grace	.15	.05
❑ 30 Ryne Sandberg	.40	.15
❑ 31 Greg Smith RC	.05	.01
❑ 32 Dwight Smith	.05	.01
❑ 33 Damon Berryhill	.05	.01
❑ 34 Earl Cunningham UER RC	.10	.02
❑ 35 Jerome Walton	.05	.01
❑ 36 Lloyd McClendon	.05	.01
❑ 37 Ty Griffin	.05	.01
❑ 38 Shawon Dunston	.05	.01
❑ 39 Andre Dawson	.10	.02
❑ 40 Luis Salazar	.05	.01
❑ 41 Tim Layana RC	.05	.01
❑ 42 Rob Dibble	.10	.02
❑ 43 Tom Browning	.05	.01
❑ 44 Danny Jackson	.05	.01
❑ 45 Jose Rijo	.05	.01
❑ 46 Scott Scudder	.05	.01
❑ 47 Randy Myers UER (Career ERA .274, should be 2.74	.10	.02
❑ 48 Brian Lane RC	.10	.02
❑ 49 Paul O'Neill	.15	.05
❑ 50 Barry Larkin	.15	.05
❑ 51 Reggie Jefferson RC	.25	.08
❑ 52 Jeff Branson RC	.10	.02
❑ 53 Chris Sabo	.05	.01
❑ 54 Joe Oliver	.05	.01
❑ 55 Todd Benzinger	.05	.01
❑ 56 Rolando Roomes	.05	.01
❑ 57 Hal Morris	.05	.01
❑ 58 Eric Davis	.10	.02
❑ 59 Scott Bryant RC	.05	.01
❑ 60 Ken Griffey Sr.	.10	.02
❑ 61 Darryl Kile RC	.50	.20
❑ 62 Dave Smith	.05	.01
❑ 63 Mark Portugal	.05	.01
❑ 64 Jeff Juden RC	.10	.02
❑ 65 Bill Gullickson	.05	.01
❑ 66 Danny Darwin	.05	.01
❑ 67 Larry Andersen	.05	.01
❑ 68 Jose Cano RC	.05	.01
❑ 69 Dan Schatzeder	.05	.01
❑ 70 Jim Deshaies	.05	.01
❑ 71 Mike Scott	.05	.01
❑ 72 Gerald Young	.05	.01
❑ 73 Ken Caminiti	.10	.02
❑ 74 Ken Oberkfell	.05	.01
❑ 75 Dave Rohde RC	.05	.01
❑ 76 Bill Doran	.05	.01
❑ 77 Andujar Cedeno RC	.10	.02
❑ 78 Craig Biggio	.25	.08
❑ 79 Karl Rhodes RC	.25	.08
❑ 80 Glenn Davis	.05	.01
❑ 81 Eric Anthony RC	.10	.02
❑ 82 John Wetteland	.25	.08
❑ 83 Jay Howell	.05	.01
❑ 84 Orel Hershiser	.10	.02
❑ 85 Tim Belcher	.05	.01
❑ 86 Kiki Jones RC	.05	.01
❑ 87 Mike Hartley RC	.05	.01

❑ 88	Ramon Martinez	.05	.01
❑ 89	Mike Scioscia	.05	.01
❑ 90	Willie Randolph	.10	.02
❑ 91	Juan Samuel	.05	.01
❑ 92	Jose Offerman RC	.25	.08
❑ 93	Dave Hansen RC	.25	.08
❑ 94	Jeff Hamilton	.05	.01
❑ 95	Alfredo Griffin	.05	.01
❑ 96	Tom Goodwin RC	.25	.08
❑ 97	Kirk Gibson	.10	.02
❑ 98	Jose Vizcaino RC	.25	.08
❑ 99	Kal Daniels	.05	.01
❑ 100	Hubie Brooks	.05	.01
❑ 101	Eddie Murray	.25	.08
❑ 102	Dennis Boyd	.05	.01
❑ 103	Tim Burke	.05	.01
❑ 104	Bill Sampen RC	.05	.01
❑ 105	Brett Gideon	.05	.01
❑ 106	Mark Gardner RC	.10	.02
❑ 107	Howard Farmer RC	.05	.01
❑ 108	Mel Rojas RC	.10	.02
❑ 109	Kevin Gross	.05	.01
❑ 110	Dave Schmidt	.05	.01
❑ 111	Dennis Martinez	.10	.02
❑ 112	Jerry Goff RC	.05	.01
❑ 113	Andres Galarraga	.10	.02
❑ 114	Tim Wallach	.05	.01
❑ 115	Marquis Grissom RC	.50	.20
❑ 116	Spike Owen	.05	.01
❑ 117	Larry Walker RC	1.00	.40
❑ 118	Tim Raines	.10	.02
❑ 119	Delino DeShields RC	.25	.08
❑ 120	Tom Foley	.05	.01
❑ 121	Dave Martinez	.05	.01
❑ 122	Frank Viola UER (Career ERA .384 should be 3.84	.05	.01
❑ 123	Julio Valera RC	.05	.01
❑ 124	Alejandro Pena	.05	.01
❑ 125	David Cone	.10	.02
❑ 126	Dwight Gooden	.10	.02
❑ 127	Kevin D. Brown RC	.05	.01
❑ 128	John Franco	.10	.02
❑ 129	Terry Bross RC	.05	.01
❑ 130	Blaine Beatty RC	.05	.01
❑ 131	Sid Fernandez	.05	.01
❑ 132	Mike Marshall	.05	.01
❑ 133	Howard Johnson	.05	.01
❑ 134	Jaime Roseboro RC	.05	.01
❑ 135	Alan Zinter RC	.10	.02
❑ 136	Keith Miller	.05	.01
❑ 137	Kevin Elster	.05	.01
❑ 138	Kevin McReynolds	.05	.01
❑ 139	Barry Lyons	.05	.01
❑ 140	Gregg Jefferies	.10	.02
❑ 141	Darryl Strawberry	.10	.02
❑ 142	Todd Hundley RC	.25	.08
❑ 143	Scott Service	.05	.01
❑ 144	Chuck Malone RC	.05	.01
❑ 145	Steve Ontiveros	.05	.01
❑ 146	Roger McDowell	.05	.01
❑ 147	Ken Howell	.05	.01
❑ 148	Pat Combs	.05	.01
❑ 149	Jeff Parrett	.05	.01
❑ 150	Chuck McElroy RC	.10	.02
❑ 151	Jason Grimsley RC	.10	.02
❑ 152	Len Dykstra	.10	.02
❑ 153	Mickey Morandini RC	.25	.08
❑ 154	John Kruk	.10	.02
❑ 155	Dickie Thon	.05	.01
❑ 156	Ricky Jordan	.05	.01
❑ 157	Jeff Jackson RC	.10	.02
❑ 158	Darren Daulton	.10	.02
❑ 159	Tom Herr	.05	.01
❑ 160	Von Hayes	.05	.01
❑ 161	Dave Hollins RC	.25	.08
❑ 162	Carmelo Martinez	.05	.01
❑ 163	Bob Walk	.05	.01
❑ 164	Doug Drabek	.05	.01
❑ 165	Walt Terrell	.05	.01
❑ 166	Bill Landrum	.05	.01
❑ 167	Scott Ruskin RC	.05	.01
❑ 168	Bob Patterson	.05	.01
❑ 169	Bobby Bonilla	.10	.02
❑ 170	Jose Lind	.05	.01
❑ 171	Andy Van Slyke	.15	.05
❑ 172	Mike LaValliere	.05	.01
❑ 173	Willie Greene RC	.10	.02
❑ 174	Jay Bell	.10	.02
❑ 175	Sid Bream	.05	.01
❑ 176	Tom Prince	.05	.01
❑ 177	Wally Backman	.05	.01
❑ 178	Moises Alou RC	.75	.30
❑ 179	Steve Carter	.05	.01
❑ 180	Gary Redus	.05	.01
❑ 181	Barry Bonds	1.00	.40
❑ 182	Don Slaught UER (Card back shows headings for a	.05	.01
❑ 183	Joe Magrane	.05	.01
❑ 184	Bryn Smith	.05	.01
❑ 185	Todd Worrell	.05	.01
❑ 186	Jose DeLeon	.05	.01
❑ 187	Frank DiPino	.05	.01
❑ 188	John Tudor	.05	.01
❑ 189	Howard Hilton RC	.05	.01
❑ 190	John Ericks	.05	.01
❑ 191	Ken Dayley	.05	.01
❑ 192	Ray Lankford RC	.30	.20
❑ 193	Todd Zeile	.10	.02
❑ 194	Willie McGee	.10	.02
❑ 195	Ozzie Smith	.40	.15
❑ 196	Milt Thompson	.05	.01
❑ 197	Terry Pendleton	.10	.02
❑ 198	Vince Coleman	.05	.01
❑ 199	Paul Coleman RC	.10	.02
❑ 200	Jose Oquendo	.05	.01
❑ 201	Pedro Guerrero	.05	.01
❑ 202	Tom Brunansky	.05	.01
❑ 203	Roger Smithberg RC	.05	.01
❑ 204	Eddie Whitson	.05	.01
❑ 205	Dennis Rasmussen	.05	.01
❑ 206	Craig Lefferts	.05	.01
❑ 207	Andy Benes	.10	.02
❑ 208	Bruce Hurst	.05	.01
❑ 209	Eric Show	.05	.01
❑ 210	Rafael Valdez RC	.05	.01
❑ 211	Joey Cora	.10	.02
❑ 212	Thomas Howard	.05	.01
❑ 213	Rob Nelson	.05	.01
❑ 214	Jack Clark	.10	.02
❑ 215	Garry Templeton	.05	.01
❑ 216	Fred Lynn	.05	.01
❑ 217	Tony Gwynn	.30	.10
❑ 218	Benito Santiago	.10	.02
❑ 219	Mike Pagliarulo	.05	.01
❑ 220	Joe Carter	.10	.02
❑ 221	Roberto Alomar	.15	.05
❑ 222	Bip Roberts	.05	.01
❑ 223	Rick Reuschel	.05	.01
❑ 224	Russ Swan RC	.05	.01
❑ 225	Eric Gunderson RC	.05	.01
❑ 226	Steve Bedrosian	.05	.01
❑ 227	Mike Remlinger RC	.05	.01
❑ 228	Scott Garrelts	.05	.01
❑ 229	Ernie Camacho	.05	.01
❑ 230	Andres Santana RC	.10	.02
❑ 231	Will Clark	.15	.05
❑ 232	Kevin Mitchell	.05	.01
❑ 233	Robby Thompson	.05	.01
❑ 234	Bill Bathe	.05	.01
❑ 235	Tony Perezchica	.05	.01
❑ 236	Gary Carter	.10	.02
❑ 237	Brett Butler	.10	.02
❑ 238	Matt Williams	.10	.02
❑ 239	Earnie Riles	.05	.01
❑ 240	Kevin Bass	.05	.01
❑ 241	Terry Kennedy	.05	.01
❑ 242	Steve Hosey RC	.10	.02
❑ 243	Ben McDonald RC	.25	.08
❑ 244	Jeff Ballard	.05	.01
❑ 245	Joe Price	.05	.01
❑ 246	Curt Schilling	1.00	.40
❑ 247	Pete Harnisch	.05	.01
❑ 248	Mark Williamson	.05	.01
❑ 249	Gregg Olson	.10	.02
❑ 250	Chris Myers RC	.05	.01
❑ 251A	David Segui ERR	.50	.20
❑ 251B	David Segui COR RC	.50	.20
❑ 252	Joe Orsulak	.05	.01
❑ 253	Craig Worthington	.05	.01
❑ 254	Mickey Tettleton	.05	.01
❑ 255	Cal Ripken	.75	.30
❑ 256	Bill Ripken	.05	.01
❑ 257	Randy Milligan	.05	.01
❑ 258	Brady Anderson	.10	.02
❑ 259	Chris Hoiles RC	.25	.08
❑ 260	Mike Devereaux	.05	.01
❑ 261	Phil Bradley	.05	.01
❑ 262	Leo Gomez RC	.10	.02
❑ 263	Lee Smith	.10	.02
❑ 264	Mike Rochford	.05	.01
❑ 265	Jeff Reardon	.10	.02
❑ 266	Wes Gardner	.05	.01
❑ 267	Mike Boddicker	.05	.01
❑ 268	Roger Clemens	1.00	.40
❑ 269	Rob Murphy	.05	.01
❑ 270	Mickey Pina RC	.05	.01
❑ 271	Tony Pena	.05	.01
❑ 272	Jody Reed	.05	.01
❑ 273	Kevin Romine	.05	.01
❑ 274	Mike Greenwell	.05	.01
❑ 275	Mo Vaughn RC	1.00	.40
❑ 276	Danny Heep	.05	.01
❑ 277	Scott Cooper RC	.10	.02
❑ 278	Greg Blosser RC	.10	.02
❑ 279	Dwight Evans UER (* by 1990 Team Breakdown)	.15	.05
❑ 280	Ellis Burks	.15	.05
❑ 281	Wade Boggs	.15	.05
❑ 282	Marty Barrett	.05	.01
❑ 283	Kirk McCaskill	.05	.01
❑ 284	Mark Langston	.05	.01
❑ 285	Bert Blyleven	.10	.02
❑ 286	Mike Fetters RC	.25	.08
❑ 287	Kyle Abbott RC	.05	.01
❑ 288	Jim Abbott	.15	.05
❑ 289	Chuck Finley	.10	.02
❑ 290	Gary DiSarcina RC	.25	.08
❑ 291	Dick Schofield	.05	.01
❑ 292	Devon White	.10	.02
❑ 293	Bobby Rose	.05	.01
❑ 294	Brian Downing	.05	.01
❑ 295	Lance Parrish	.05	.01
❑ 296	Jack Howell	.05	.01
❑ 297	Claudell Washington	.05	.01
❑ 298	John Orton RC	.10	.02
❑ 299	Wally Joyner	.10	.02
❑ 300	Lee Stevens	.10	.02
❑ 301	Chili Davis	.10	.02
❑ 302	Johnny Ray	.05	.01
❑ 303	Greg Hibbard RC	.10	.02
❑ 304	Eric King	.05	.01
❑ 305	Jack McDowell	.05	.01
❑ 306	Bobby Thigpen	.05	.01
❑ 307	Adam Peterson	.05	.01
❑ 308	Scott Radinsky RC	.25	.08
❑ 309	Wayne Edwards RC	.05	.01
❑ 310	Melido Perez	.05	.01
❑ 311	Robin Ventura	.25	.08
❑ 312	Sammy Sosa RC	3.00	1.25
❑ 313	Dan Pasqua	.05	.01
❑ 314	Carlton Fisk	.15	.05
❑ 315	Ozzie Guillen	.10	.02
❑ 316	Ivan Calderon	.05	.01
❑ 317	Daryl Boston	.05	.01
❑ 318	Craig Grebeck RC	.25	.08
❑ 319	Scott Fletcher	.05	.01
❑ 320	Frank Thomas RC	2.00	.75
❑ 321	Steve Lyons	.05	.01
❑ 322	Carlos Martinez	.05	.01
❑ 323	Joe Skalski	.05	.01
❑ 324	Tom Candiotti	.05	.01
❑ 325	Greg Swindell	.05	.01
❑ 326	Steve Olin RC	.25	.08
❑ 327	Kevin Wickander	.05	.01
❑ 328	Doug Jones	.05	.01
❑ 329	Jeff Shaw	.05	.01
❑ 330	Kevin Bearse RC	.05	.01
❑ 331	Dion James	.05	.01
❑ 332	Jerry Browne	.05	.01
❑ 333	Albert Belle	.25	.08
❑ 334	Felix Fermin	.05	.01
❑ 335	Candy Maldonado	.05	.01
❑ 336	Cory Snyder	.05	.01
❑ 337	Sandy Alomar Jr.	.10	.02
❑ 338	Mark Lewis	.05	.01

	Card	Price 1	Price 2
❑	339 Carlos Baerga RC	.25	.08
❑	340 Chris James	.05	.01
❑	341 Brook Jacoby	.05	.01
❑	342 Keith Hernandez	.10	.02
❑	343 Frank Tanana	.05	.01
❑	344 Scott Aldred RC	.05	.01
❑	345 Mike Henneman	.05	.01
❑	346 Steve Wapnick RC	.05	.01
❑	347 Greg Gohr RC	.10	.02
❑	348 Eric Stone RC	.05	.01
❑	349 Brian DuBois RC	.05	.01
❑	350 Kevin Ritz RC	.05	.01
❑	351 Rico Brogna	.25	.08
❑	352 Mike Heath	.05	.01
❑	353 Alan Trammell	.10	.02
❑	354 Chet Lemon	.05	.01
❑	355 Dave Bergman	.05	.01
❑	356 Lou Whitaker	.10	.02
❑	357 Cecil Fielder UER	.10	.02
❑	358 Milt Cuyler RC	.10	.02
❑	359 Tony Phillips	.05	.01
❑	360 Travis Fryman RC	.50	.20
❑	361 Ed Romero	.05	.01
❑	362 Lloyd Moseby	.05	.01
❑	363 Mark Gubicza	.05	.01
❑	364 Bret Saberhagen	.10	.02
❑	365 Tom Gordon	.10	.02
❑	366 Steve Farr	.05	.01
❑	367 Kevin Appier	.10	.02
❑	368 Storm Davis	.05	.01
❑	369 Mark Davis	.05	.01
❑	370 Jeff Montgomery	.10	.02
❑	371 Frank White	.10	.02
❑	372 Brent Mayne RC	.25	.08
❑	373 Bob Boone	.10	.02
❑	374 Jim Eisenreich	.05	.01
❑	375 Danny Tartabull	.05	.01
❑	376 Kurt Stillwell	.05	.01
❑	377 Bill Pecota	.05	.01
❑	378 Bo Jackson	.25	.08
❑	379 Bob Hamelin RC	.25	.08
❑	380 Kevin Seitzer	.05	.01
❑	381 Rey Palacios	.05	.01
❑	382 George Brett	.60	.25
❑	383 Gerald Perry	.05	.01
❑	384 Teddy Higuera	.05	.01
❑	385 Tom Filer	.05	.01
❑	386 Dan Plesac	.05	.01
❑	387 Cal Eldred RC	.25	.08
❑	388 Jaime Navarro	.05	.01
❑	389 Chris Bosio	.05	.01
❑	390 Randy Veres	.05	.01
❑	391 Gary Sheffield	.25	.08
❑	392 George Canale RC	.05	.01
❑	393 B.J. Surhoff	.10	.02
❑	394 Tim McIntosh RC	.05	.01
❑	395 Greg Brock	.05	.01
❑	396 Greg Vaughn	.05	.01
❑	397 Darryl Hamilton	.05	.01
❑	398 Dave Parker	.10	.02
❑	399 Paul Molitor	.10	.02
❑	400 Jim Gantner	.05	.01
❑	401 Rob Deer	.05	.01
❑	402 Billy Spiers	.05	.01
❑	403 Glenn Braggs	.05	.01
❑	404 Robin Yount	.40	.15
❑	405 Rick Aguilera	.10	.02
❑	406 Johnny Ard	.05	.01
❑	407 Kevin Tapani RC	.25	.08
❑	408 Park Pittman RC	.05	.01
❑	409 Allan Anderson	.05	.01
❑	410 Juan Berenguer	.05	.01
❑	411 Willie Banks RC	.10	.02
❑	412 Rich Yett	.05	.01
❑	413 Dave West	.05	.01
❑	414 Greg Gagne	.05	.01
❑	415 Chuck Knoblauch RC	.50	.20
❑	416 Randy Bush	.05	.01
❑	417 Gary Gaetti	.10	.02
❑	418 Kent Hrbek	.10	.02
❑	419 Al Newman	.05	.01
❑	420 Danny Gladden	.05	.01
❑	421 Paul Sorrento RC	.25	.08
❑	422 Derek Parks RC	.10	.02
❑	423 Scott Leius RC	.10	.02
❑	424 Kirby Puckett	.25	.08
❑	425 Willie Smith	.05	.01
❑	426 Dave Righetti	.05	.01
❑	427 Jeff D. Robinson	.05	.01
❑	428 Alan Mills RC	.10	.02
❑	429 Tim Leary	.05	.01
❑	430 Pascual Perez	.05	.01
❑	431 Alvaro Espinoza	.05	.01
❑	432 Dave Winfield	.10	.02
❑	433 Jesse Barfield	.05	.01
❑	434 Randy Velarde	.05	.01
❑	435 Rick Cerone	.05	.01
❑	436 Steve Balboni	.05	.01
❑	437 Mel Hall	.05	.01
❑	438 Bob Geren	.05	.01
❑	439 Bernie Williams RC	1.50	.60
❑	440 Kevin Maas RC	.25	.08
❑	441 Mike Blowers RC	.10	.02
❑	442 Steve Sax	.05	.01
❑	443 Don Mattingly	.60	.25
❑	444 Roberto Kelly	.05	.01
❑	445 Mike Moore	.05	.01
❑	446 Reggie Harris RC	.10	.02
❑	447 Scott Sanderson	.05	.01
❑	448 Dave Otto	.05	.01
❑	449 Dave Stewart	.10	.02
❑	450 Rick Honeycutt	.05	.01
❑	451 Dennis Eckersley	.10	.02
❑	452 Carney Lansford	.10	.02
❑	453 Scott Hemond RC	.10	.02
❑	454 Mark McGwire	1.00	.40
❑	455 Felix Jose	.05	.01
❑	456 Terry Steinbach	.05	.01
❑	457 Rickey Henderson	.25	.08
❑	458 Dave Henderson	.05	.01
❑	459 Mike Gallego	.05	.01
❑	460 Jose Canseco	.15	.05
❑	461 Walt Weiss	.05	.01
❑	462 Ken Phelps	.05	.01
❑	463 Darren Lewis RC	.10	.02
❑	464 Ron Hassey	.05	.01
❑	465 Roger Salkeld RC	.10	.02
❑	466 Scott Bankhead	.05	.01
❑	467 Keith Comstock	.05	.01
❑	468 Randy Johnson	.50	.20
❑	469 Erik Hanson	.05	.01
❑	470 Mike Schooler	.05	.01
❑	471 Gary Eave RC	.05	.01
❑	472 Jeffrey Leonard	.05	.01
❑	473 Dave Valle	.05	.01
❑	474 Omar Vizquel	.25	.08
❑	475 Pete O'Brien	.05	.01
❑	476 Henry Cotto	.05	.01
❑	477 Jay Buhner	.10	.02
❑	478 Harold Reynolds	.10	.02
❑	479 Alvin Davis	.05	.01
❑	480 Darnell Coles	.05	.01
❑	481 Ken Griffey Jr.	.75	.30
❑	482 Greg Briley	.05	.01
❑	483 Scott Bradley	.05	.01
❑	484 Tino Martinez	.50	.20
❑	485 Jeff Russell	.05	.01
❑	486 Nolan Ryan	1.00	.40
❑	487 Robb Nen RC	.50	.20
❑	488 Kevin Brown	.10	.02
❑	489 Brian Bohanon RC	.10	.02
❑	490 Ruben Sierra	.10	.02
❑	491 Pete Incaviglia	.05	.01
❑	492 Juan Gonzalez RC	1.00	.40
❑	493 Steve Buechele	.05	.01
❑	494 Scott Coolbaugh	.05	.01
❑	495 Geno Petralli	.05	.01
❑	496 Rafael Palmeiro	.15	.05
❑	497 Julio Franco	.10	.02
❑	498 Gary Pettis	.05	.01
❑	499 Donald Harris RC	.05	.01
❑	500 Monty Fariss	.05	.01
❑	501 Harold Baines	.10	.02
❑	502 Cecil Espy	.05	.01
❑	503 Jack Daugherty RC	.05	.01
❑	504 Willie Blair RC	.10	.02
❑	505 Dave Stieb	.10	.02
❑	506 Tom Henke	.05	.01
❑	507 John Cerutti	.05	.01
❑	508 Paul Kilgus	.05	.01
❑	509 Jimmy Key	.10	.02
❑	510 John Olerud RC	1.00	.40
❑	511 Ed Sprague	.10	.02
❑	512 Manuel Lee	.05	.01
❑	513 Fred McGriff	.25	.08
❑	514 Glenallen Hill	.05	.01
❑	515 George Bell	.05	.01
❑	516 Mookie Wilson	.10	.02
❑	517 Luis Sojo RC	.25	.08
❑	518 Nelson Liriano	.05	.01
❑	519 Kelly Gruber	.05	.01
❑	520 Greg Myers	.05	.01
❑	521 Pat Borders	.05	.01
❑	522 Junior Felix	.05	.01
❑	523 Eddie Zosky RC	.10	.02
❑	524 Tony Fernandez	.05	.01
❑	525 Checklist 1-132 UER (No copyright mark on the ba	.05	.01
❑	526 Checklist 133-264	.05	.01
❑	527 Checklist 265-396	.05	.01
❑	528 Checklist 397-528	.05	.01

1991 Bowman

	Card	Price 1	Price 2
❑	COMPLETE SET (704)	40.00	15.00
❑	COMP.FACT.SET (704)	40.00	15.00
❑	1 Rod Carew I	.15	.05
❑	2 Rod Carew II	.15	.05
❑	3 Rod Carew III	.15	.05
❑	4 Rod Carew IV	.15	.05
❑	5 Rod Carew V	.15	.05
❑	6 Willie Fraser	.05	.01
❑	7 John Olerud	.10	.02
❑	8 William Suero RC	.05	.01
❑	9 Roberto Alomar	.15	.05
❑	10 Todd Stottlemyre	.05	.01
❑	11 Joe Carter	.10	.02
❑	12 Steve Karsay RC	.50	.20
❑	13 Mark Whiten	.05	.01
❑	14 Pat Borders	.05	.01
❑	15 Mike Timlin RC	.50	.20
❑	16 Tom Henke	.05	.01
❑	17 Eddie Zosky	.05	.01
❑	18 Kelly Gruber	.05	.01
❑	19 Jimmy Key	.10	.02
❑	20 Jerry Schunk RC	.05	.01
❑	21 Manuel Lee	.05	.01
❑	22 Dave Stieb	.05	.01
❑	23 Pat Hentgen RC	.50	.20
❑	24 Glenallen Hill	.05	.01
❑	25 Rene Gonzales	.05	.01
❑	26 Ed Sprague	.05	.01
❑	27 Ken Dayley	.05	.01
❑	28 Pat Tabler	.05	.01
❑	29 Denis Boucher RC	.15	.05
❑	30 Devon White	.10	.02
❑	31 Dante Bichette	.10	.02
❑	32 Paul Molitor	.10	.02
❑	33 Greg Vaughn	.05	.01
❑	34 Dan Plesac	.05	.01
❑	35 Chris George RC	.15	.05
❑	36 Tim McIntosh	.05	.01
❑	37 Franklin Stubbs	.05	.01
❑	38 Bo Dodson RC	.15	.05
❑	39 Ron Robinson	.05	.01
❑	40 Ed Nunez	.05	.01
❑	41 Greg Brock	.05	.01
❑	42 Jaime Navarro	.05	.01
❑	43 Chris Bosio	.05	.01
❑	44 B.J. Surhoff	.10	.02

❑ 45 Chris Johnson RC .05 .01
❑ 46 Willie Randolph .10 .02
❑ 47 Narciso Elvira RC .05 .01
❑ 48 Jim Gantner .05 .01
❑ 49 Kevin Brown .05 .01
❑ 50 Julio Machado .05 .01
❑ 51 Chuck Crim .05 .01
❑ 52 Gary Sheffield .10 .02
❑ 53 Angel Miranda RC .15 .05
❑ 54 Ted Higuera .05 .01
❑ 55 Robin Yount .40 .15
❑ 56 Cal Eldred .05 .01
❑ 57 Sandy Alomar Jr. .05 .01
❑ 58 Greg Swindell .05 .01
❑ 59 Brook Jacoby .05 .01
❑ 60 Efrain Valdez RC .05 .01
❑ 61 Ever Magallanes RC .05 .01
❑ 62 Tom Candiotti .05 .01
❑ 63 Eric King .05 .01
❑ 64 Alex Cole .05 .01
❑ 65 Charles Nagy .05 .01
❑ 66 Mitch Webster .05 .01
❑ 67 Chris James .05 .01
❑ 68 Jim Thome RC 4.00 1.50
❑ 69 Carlos Baerga .05 .01
❑ 70 Mark Lewis .05 .01
❑ 71 Jerry Browne .05 .01
❑ 72 Jesse Orosco .05 .01
❑ 73 Mike Huff .05 .01
❑ 74 Jose Escobar RC .05 .01
❑ 75 Jeff Manto .05 .01
❑ 76 Turner Ward RC .15 .05
❑ 77 Doug Jones .05 .01
❑ 78 Bruce Egloff RC .05 .01
❑ 79 Tim Costo RC .15 .05
❑ 80 Beau Allred .05 .01
❑ 81 Albert Belle .10 .02
❑ 82 John Farrell .05 .01
❑ 83 Glenn Davis .05 .01
❑ 84 Joe Orsulak .05 .01
❑ 85 Mark Williamson .05 .01
❑ 86 Ben McDonald .05 .01
❑ 87 Billy Ripken .05 .01
❑ 88 Leo Gomez .05 .01
❑ 89 Bob Melvin .05 .01
❑ 90 Jeff M. Robinson .05 .01
❑ 91 Jose Mesa .05 .01
❑ 92 Gregg Olson .05 .01
❑ 93 Mike Devereaux .05 .01
❑ 94 Luis Mercedes RC .15 .05
❑ 95 Arthur Rhodes RC .50 .20
❑ 96 Juan Bell .05 .01
❑ 97 Mike Mussina RC 4.00 1.50
❑ 98 Jeff Ballard .05 .01
❑ 99 Chris Hoiles .05 .01
❑ 100 Brady Anderson .10 .02
❑ 101 Bob Milacki .05 .01
❑ 102 David Segui .05 .01
❑ 103 Dwight Evans .15 .05
❑ 104 Cal Ripken .75 .30
❑ 105 Mike Linskey RC .05 .01
❑ 106 Jeff Tackett RC .15 .05
❑ 107 Jeff Reardon .10 .02
❑ 108 Dana Kiecker .05 .01
❑ 109 Ellis Burks .10 .02
❑ 110 Dave Owen .05 .01
❑ 111 Danny Darwin .05 .01
❑ 112 Mo Vaughn .10 .02
❑ 113 Jeff McNeely RC .15 .05
❑ 114 Tom Bolton .05 .01
❑ 115 Greg Blosser .05 .01
❑ 116 Mike Greenwell .05 .01
❑ 117 Phil Plantier RC .15 .05
❑ 118 Roger Clemens .75 .30
❑ 119 John Marzano .05 .01
❑ 120 Jody Reed .05 .01
❑ 121 Scott Taylor RC .15 .05
❑ 122 Jack Clark .10 .02
❑ 123 Derek Livernois RC .05 .01
❑ 124 Tony Pena .05 .01
❑ 125 Tom Brunansky .05 .01
❑ 126 Carlos Quintana .05 .01
❑ 127 Tim Naehring .05 .01
❑ 128 Matt Young .05 .01
❑ 129 Wade Boggs .15 .05
❑ 130 Kevin Morton RC .05 .01
❑ 131 Pete Incaviglia .05 .01
❑ 132 Rob Deer .05 .01
❑ 133 Bill Gullickson .05 .01
❑ 134 Rico Brogna .05 .01
❑ 135 Lloyd Moseby .05 .01
❑ 136 Cecil Fielder .10 .02
❑ 137 Tony Phillips .05 .01
❑ 138 Mark Leiter RC .15 .05
❑ 139 John Cerutti .05 .01
❑ 140 Mickey Tettleton .05 .01
❑ 141 Milt Cuyler .05 .01
❑ 142 Greg Gohr .05 .01
❑ 143 Tony Bernazard .05 .01
❑ 144 Dan Gakeler RC .05 .01
❑ 145 Travis Fryman .10 .02
❑ 146 Dan Petry .05 .01
❑ 147 Scott Aldred .05 .01
❑ 148 John DeSilva RC .05 .01
❑ 149 Rusty Meacham RC .15 .05
❑ 150 Lou Whitaker .10 .02
❑ 151 Dave Haas RC .05 .01
❑ 152 Luis de los Santos .05 .01
❑ 153 Ivan Cruz RC .05 .01
❑ 154 Alan Trammell .10 .02
❑ 155 Pat Kelly RC .05 .01
❑ 156 Carl Everett RC 1.50 .60
❑ 157 Greg Cadaret .05 .01
❑ 158 Kevin Maas .05 .01
❑ 159 Jeff Johnson RC .05 .01
❑ 160 Willie Smith .05 .01
❑ 161 Gerald Williams RC .50 .20
❑ 162 Mike Humphreys RC .15 .05
❑ 163 Alvaro Espinoza .05 .01
❑ 164 Matt Nokes .05 .01
❑ 165 Wade Taylor RC .05 .01
❑ 166 Roberto Kelly .05 .01
❑ 167 John Habyan .05 .01
❑ 168 Steve Farr .05 .01
❑ 169 Jesse Barfield .05 .01
❑ 170 Steve Sax .05 .01
❑ 171 Jim Leyritz .05 .01
❑ 172 Robert Eenhoorn RC .15 .05
❑ 173 Bernie Williams .25 .08
❑ 174 Scott Lusader .05 .01
❑ 175 Torey Lovullo .05 .01
❑ 176 Chuck Cary .05 .01
❑ 177 Scott Sanderson .05 .01
❑ 178 Don Mattingly .60 .25
❑ 179 Mel Hall .05 .01
❑ 180 Juan Gonzalez .25 .08
❑ 181 Hensley Meulens .05 .01
❑ 182 Jose Offerman .05 .01
❑ 183 Jeff Bagwell RC 3.00 1.25
❑ 184 Jeff Conine RC 1.00 .40
❑ 185 Henry Rodriguez RC .50 .20
❑ 186 Jimmy Reese CO .10 .02
❑ 187 Kyle Abbott .05 .01
❑ 188 Lance Parrish .10 .02
❑ 189 Rafael Montalvo RC .05 .01
❑ 190 Floyd Bannister .05 .01
❑ 191 Dick Schofield .05 .01
❑ 192 Scott Lewis RC .05 .01
❑ 193 Jeff D. Robinson .05 .01
❑ 194 Kent Anderson .05 .01
❑ 195 Wally Joyner .10 .02
❑ 196 Chuck Finley .10 .02
❑ 197 Luis Sojo .05 .01
❑ 198 Jeff Richardson RC .05 .01
❑ 199 Dave Parker .10 .02
❑ 200 Jim Abbott .15 .05
❑ 201 Junior Felix .05 .01
❑ 202 Mark Langston .05 .01
❑ 203 Tim Salmon RC 1.50 .60
❑ 204 Cliff Young .05 .01
❑ 205 Scott Bailes .05 .01
❑ 206 Bobby Rose .05 .01
❑ 207 Gary Gaetti .10 .02
❑ 208 Ruben Amaro RC .15 .05
❑ 209 Luis Polonia .05 .01
❑ 210 Dave Winfield .10 .02
❑ 211 Bryan Harvey .05 .01
❑ 212 Mike Moore .05 .01
❑ 213 Rickey Henderson .25 .08
❑ 214 Steve Chitren RC .05 .01
❑ 215 Bob Welch .05 .01
❑ 216 Terry Steinbach .05 .01
❑ 217 Earnest Riles .05 .01
❑ 218 Todd Van Poppel RC .50 .20
❑ 219 Mike Gallego .05 .01
❑ 220 Curt Young .05 .01
❑ 221 Todd Burns .05 .01
❑ 222 Vance Law .05 .01
❑ 223 Eric Show .05 .01
❑ 224 Don Peters RC .05 .01
❑ 225 Dave Stewart .10 .02
❑ 226 Dave Henderson .05 .01
❑ 227 Jose Canseco .15 .05
❑ 228 Walt Weiss .05 .01
❑ 229 Dann Howitt .05 .01
❑ 230 Willie Wilson .05 .01
❑ 231 Harold Baines .10 .02
❑ 232 Scott Hemond .05 .01
❑ 233 Joe Slusarski RC .05 .01
❑ 234 Mark McGwire .75 .30
❑ 235 Kirk Dressendorfer RC .15 .05
❑ 236 Craig Paquette RC .50 .20
❑ 237 Dennis Eckersley .10 .02
❑ 238 Dana Allison RC .05 .01
❑ 239 Scott Bradley .05 .01
❑ 240 Brian Holman .05 .01
❑ 241 Mike Schooler .05 .01
❑ 242 Rich DeLucia RC .05 .01
❑ 243 Edgar Martinez .15 .05
❑ 244 Henry Cotto .05 .01
❑ 245 Omar Vizquel .15 .05
❑ 246 Ken Griffey Jr. .50 .20
❑ 247 Jay Buhner .10 .02
❑ 248 Bill Krueger .05 .01
❑ 249 Dave Fleming RC .15 .05
❑ 250 Patrick Lennon RC .05 .01
❑ 251 Dave Valle .05 .01
❑ 252 Harold Reynolds .10 .02
❑ 253 Randy Johnson .30 .10
❑ 254 Scott Bankhead .05 .01
❑ 255 Ken Griffey Sr. UER 246 .05 .01
❑ 256 Greg Briley .05 .01
❑ 257 Tino Martinez .25 .08
❑ 258 Alvin Davis .05 .01
❑ 259 Pete O'Brien .05 .01
❑ 260 Erik Hanson .05 .01
❑ 261 Bret Boone RC 1.50 .60
❑ 262 Roger Salkeld .05 .01
❑ 263 Dave Burba RC .50 .20
❑ 264 Kerry Woodson RC .15 .05
❑ 265 Julio Franco .10 .02
❑ 266 Dan Peltier RC .15 .05
❑ 267 Jeff Russell .05 .01
❑ 268 Steve Buechele .05 .01
❑ 269 Donald Harris .05 .01
❑ 270 Robb Nen .15 .05
❑ 271 Rich Gossage .10 .02
❑ 272 Ivan Rodriguez RC 4.00 1.50
❑ 273 Jeff Huson .05 .01
❑ 274 Kevin Brown .10 .02
❑ 275 Dan Smith RC .15 .05
❑ 276 Gary Pettis .05 .01
❑ 277 Jack Daugherty .05 .01
❑ 278 Mike Jeffcoat .05 .01
❑ 279 Brad Arnsberg .05 .01
❑ 280 Nolan Ryan 1.00 .40
❑ 281 Eric McCray RC .05 .01
❑ 282 Scott Chiamparino .05 .01
❑ 283 Ruben Sierra .10 .02
❑ 284 Geno Petralli .05 .01
❑ 285 Monty Fariss .05 .01
❑ 286 Rafael Palmeiro .15 .05
❑ 287 Bobby Witt .05 .01
❑ 288 Dean Palmer UER .10 .02
❑ 289 Tony Scruggs RC .05 .01
❑ 290 Kenny Rogers .10 .02
❑ 291 Bret Saberhagen .10 .02
❑ 292 Brian McRae RC .50 .20
❑ 293 Storm Davis .05 .01
❑ 294 Danny Tartabull .05 .01
❑ 295 David Howard RC .05 .01
❑ 296 Mike Boddicker .05 .01
❑ 297 Joel Johnston RC .15 .05
❑ 298 Tim Spehr RC .05 .01
❑ 299 Hector Wagner RC .05 .01
❑ 300 George Brett .60 .25
❑ 301 Mike Macfarlane .05 .01
❑ 302 Kirk Gibson .10 .02

❑ 303 Harvey Pulliam RC .15 .05
❑ 304 Jim Eisenreich .05 .01
❑ 305 Kevin Seitzer .05 .01
❑ 306 Mark Davis .05 .01
❑ 307 Kurt Stillwell .05 .01
❑ 308 Jeff Montgomery .05 .01
❑ 309 Kevin Appier .10 .02
❑ 310 Bob Hamelin .05 .01
❑ 311 Tom Gordon .05 .01
❑ 312 Kerwin Moore RC .15 .05
❑ 313 Hugh Walker .05 .01
❑ 314 Terry Shumpert .05 .01
❑ 315 Warren Cromartie .05 .01
❑ 316 Gary Thurman .05 .01
❑ 317 Steve Bedrosian .05 .01
❑ 318 Danny Gladden .05 .01
❑ 319 Jack Morris .10 .02
❑ 320 Kirby Puckett .25 .08
❑ 321 Kent Hrbek .10 .02
❑ 322 Kevin Tapani .05 .01
❑ 323 Denny Neagle RC .50 .20
❑ 324 Rich Garces RC .15 .05
❑ 325 Larry Casian RC .05 .01
❑ 326 Shane Mack .05 .01
❑ 327 Allan Anderson .05 .01
❑ 328 Junior Ortiz .05 .01
❑ 329 Paul Abbott RC .15 .05
❑ 330 Chuck Knoblauch .10 .02
❑ 331 Chili Davis .10 .02
❑ 332 Todd Ritchie RC .50 .20
❑ 333 Brian Harper .05 .01
❑ 334 Rick Aguilera .10 .02
❑ 335 Scott Erickson .05 .01
❑ 336 Pedro Munoz RC .15 .05
❑ 337 Scott Leius .05 .01
❑ 338 Greg Gagne .05 .01
❑ 339 Mike Pagliarulo .05 .01
❑ 340 Terry Leach .05 .01
❑ 341 Willie Banks .05 .01
❑ 342 Bobby Thigpen .05 .01
❑ 343 Roberto Hernandez RC .50 .20
❑ 344 Melido Perez .05 .01
❑ 345 Carlton Fisk .15 .05
❑ 346 Norberto Martin RC .05 .01
❑ 347 Johnny Ruffin RC .15 .05
❑ 348 Jeff Carter .05 .01
❑ 349 Lance Johnson .05 .01
❑ 350 Sammy Sosa .25 .08
❑ 351 Alex Fernandez .05 .01
❑ 352 Jack McDowell .05 .01
❑ 353 Bob Wickman RC 1.50 .60
❑ 354 Wilson Alvarez .05 .01
❑ 355 Charlie Hough .10 .02
❑ 356 Ozzie Guillen .10 .02
❑ 357 Cory Snyder .05 .01
❑ 358 Robin Ventura .10 .02
❑ 359 Scott Fletcher .05 .01
❑ 360 Cesar Bernhardt RC .05 .01
❑ 361 Dan Pasqua .05 .01
❑ 362 Tim Raines .10 .02
❑ 363 Brian Drahman RC .05 .01
❑ 364 Wayne Edwards .05 .01
❑ 365 Scott Radinsky .05 .01
❑ 366 Frank Thomas .25 .08
❑ 367 Cecil Fielder SLUG .05 .01
❑ 368 Julio Franco SLUG .05 .01
❑ 369 Kelly Gruber SLUG .05 .01
❑ 370 Alan Trammell SLUG .10 .02
❑ 371 Rickey Henderson SLUG .15 .05
❑ 372 Jose Canseco SLUG .10 .02
❑ 373 Ellis Burks SLUG .05 .01
❑ 374 Lance Parrish SLUG .05 .01
❑ 375 Dave Parker SLUG .05 .01
❑ 376 Eddie Murray SLUG .15 .05
❑ 377 Ryne Sandberg SLUG .25 .08
❑ 378 Matt Williams SLUG .05 .01
❑ 379 Barry Larkin SLUG .10 .02
❑ 380 Barry Bonds SLUG .50 .20
❑ 381 Bobby Bonilla SLUG .05 .01
❑ 382 Darryl Strawberry SLUG .05 .01
❑ 383 Benny Santiago SLUG .05 .01
❑ 384 Don Robinson SLUG .05 .01
❑ 385 Paul Coleman .05 .01
❑ 386 Milt Thompson .05 .01
❑ 387 Lee Smith .10 .02
❑ 388 Ray Lankford .10 .02
❑ 389 Tom Pagnozzi .05 .01
❑ 390 Ken Hill .05 .01
❑ 391 Jamie Moyer .10 .02
❑ 392 Greg Carmona RC .05 .01
❑ 393 John Ericks .05 .01
❑ 394 Bob Tewksbury .05 .01
❑ 395 Jose Oquendo .05 .01
❑ 396 Rheal Cormier RC .15 .05
❑ 397 Mike Milchin RC .05 .01
❑ 398 Ozzie Smith .40 .15
❑ 399 Aaron Holbert RC .15 .05
❑ 400 Jose DeLeon .05 .01
❑ 401 Felix Jose .05 .01
❑ 402 Juan Agosto .05 .01
❑ 403 Pedro Guerrero .10 .02
❑ 404 Todd Zeile .05 .01
❑ 405 Gerald Perry .05 .01
❑ 406 Donovan Osborne UER RC .15 .05
❑ 407 Bryn Smith .05 .01
❑ 408 Bernard Gilkey .05 .01
❑ 409 Rex Hudler .05 .01
❑ 410 Thomson/Branca FOIL .25 .08
❑ 411 Lance Dickson RC .15 .05
❑ 412 Danny Jackson .05 .01
❑ 413 Jerome Walton .05 .01
❑ 414 Sean Cheetham RC .05 .01
❑ 415 Joe Girardi .05 .01
❑ 416 Ryne Sandberg .40 .15
❑ 417 Mike Harkey .05 .01
❑ 418 George Bell .05 .01
❑ 419 Rick Wilkins RC .15 .05
❑ 420 Earl Cunningham .05 .01
❑ 421 Heathcliff Slocumb RC .15 .05
❑ 422 Mike Bielecki .05 .01
❑ 423 Jessie Hollins RC .15 .05
❑ 424 Shawon Dunston .05 .01
❑ 425 Dave Smith .05 .01
❑ 426 Greg Maddux .40 .15
❑ 427 Jose Vizcaino .05 .01
❑ 428 Luis Salazar .05 .01
❑ 429 Andre Dawson .10 .02
❑ 430 Rick Sutcliffe .10 .02
❑ 431 Paul Assenmacher .05 .01
❑ 432 Erik Pappas RC .05 .01
❑ 433 Mark Grace .15 .05
❑ 434 Dennis Martinez .10 .02
❑ 435 Marquis Grissom .10 .02
❑ 436 Wil Cordero RC .50 .20
❑ 437 Tim Wallach .05 .01
❑ 438 Brian Barnes RC .05 .01
❑ 439 Barry Jones .05 .01
❑ 440 Ivan Calderon .05 .01
❑ 441 Stan Spencer RC .05 .01
❑ 442 Larry Walker .25 .08
❑ 443 Chris Haney RC .15 .05
❑ 444 Hector Rivera RC .05 .01
❑ 445 Delino DeShields .10 .02
❑ 446 Andres Galarraga .10 .02
❑ 447 Gilberto Reyes .05 .01
❑ 448 Willie Greene .05 .01
❑ 449 Greg Colbrunn RC .50 .20
❑ 450 Rondell White RC 1.00 .40
❑ 451 Steve Frey .05 .01
❑ 452 Shane Andrews RC .15 .05
❑ 453 Mike Fitzgerald .05 .01
❑ 454 Spike Owen .05 .01
❑ 455 Dave Martinez .05 .01
❑ 456 Dennis Boyd .05 .01
❑ 457 Eric Bullock .05 .01
❑ 458 Reid Cornelius RC .15 .05
❑ 459 Chris Nabholz .05 .01
❑ 460 David Cone .10 .02
❑ 461 Hubie Brooks .05 .01
❑ 462 Sid Fernandez .05 .01
❑ 463 Doug Simons RC .05 .01
❑ 464 Howard Johnson .05 .01
❑ 465 Chris Donnels RC .05 .01
❑ 466 Anthony Young RC .15 .05
❑ 467 Todd Hundley .05 .01
❑ 468 Rick Cerone .05 .01
❑ 469 Kevin Elster .05 .01
❑ 470 Wally Whitehurst .05 .01
❑ 471 Vince Coleman .05 .01
❑ 472 Dwight Gooden .10 .02
❑ 473 Charlie O'Brien .05 .01
❑ 474 Jeromy Burnitz RC 1.00 .40
❑ 475 John Franco .10 .02
❑ 476 Daryl Boston .05 .01
❑ 477 Frank Viola .10 .02
❑ 478 D.J. Dozier .05 .01
❑ 479 Kevin McReynolds .05 .01
❑ 480 Tom Herr .05 .01
❑ 481 Gregg Jefferies .05 .01
❑ 482 Pete Schourek RC .15 .05
❑ 483 Ron Darling .05 .01
❑ 484 Dave Magadan .05 .01
❑ 485 Andy Ashby RC .50 .20
❑ 486 Dale Murphy .15 .05
❑ 487 Von Hayes .05 .01
❑ 488 Kim Batiste RC .15 .05
❑ 489 Tony Longmire RC .15 .05
❑ 490 Wally Backman .05 .01
❑ 491 Jeff Jackson .05 .01
❑ 492 Mickey Morandini .05 .01
❑ 493 Darrel Akerfelds .05 .01
❑ 494 Ricky Jordan .05 .01
❑ 495 Randy Ready .05 .01
❑ 496 Darrin Fletcher .05 .01
❑ 497 Chuck Malone .05 .01
❑ 498 Pat Combs .05 .01
❑ 499 Dickie Thon .05 .01
❑ 500 Roger McDowell .05 .01
❑ 501 Len Dykstra .10 .02
❑ 502 Joe Boever .05 .01
❑ 503 John Kruk .10 .02
❑ 504 Terry Mulholland .05 .01
❑ 505 Wes Chamberlain RC .15 .05
❑ 506 Mike Lieberthal RC 1.00 .40
❑ 507 Darren Daulton .10 .02
❑ 508 Charlie Hayes .05 .01
❑ 509 John Smiley .05 .01
❑ 510 Gary Varsho .05 .01
❑ 511 Curt Wilkerson .05 .01
❑ 512 Orlando Merced RC .15 .05
❑ 513 Barry Bonds 1.00 .40
❑ 514 Mike LaValliere .05 .01
❑ 515 Doug Drabek .05 .01
❑ 516 Gary Redus .05 .01
❑ 517 William Pennyfeather RC .15 .05
❑ 518 Randy Tomlin RC .05 .01
❑ 519 Mike Zimmerman RC .15 .05
❑ 520 Jeff King .05 .01
❑ 521 Kurt Miller RC .15 .05
❑ 522 Jay Bell .10 .02
❑ 523 Bill Landrum .05 .01
❑ 524 Zane Smith .05 .01
❑ 525 Bobby Bonilla .10 .02
❑ 526 Bob Walk .05 .01
❑ 527 Austin Manahan .05 .01
❑ 528 Joe Ausanio RC .05 .01
❑ 529 Andy Van Slyke .15 .05
❑ 530 Jose Lind .05 .01
❑ 531 Carlos Garcia RC .15 .05
❑ 532 Don Slaught .05 .01
❑ 533 Gen.Colin Powell .50 .20
❑ 534 Frank Bolick RC .15 .05
❑ 535 Gary Scott RC .05 .01
❑ 536 Nikco Riesgo RC .05 .01
❑ 537 Reggie Sanders RC 1.50 .60
❑ 538 Tim Howard RC .15 .05
❑ 539 Ryan Bowen RC .15 .05
❑ 540 Eric Anthony .05 .01
❑ 541 Jim Deshaies .05 .01
❑ 542 Tom Nevers RC .15 .05
❑ 543 Ken Caminiti .10 .02
❑ 544 Karl Rhodes .05 .01
❑ 545 Xavier Hernandez .05 .01
❑ 546 Mike Scott .05 .01
❑ 547 Jeff Juden .05 .01
❑ 548 Darryl Kile .10 .02
❑ 549 Willie Ansley .05 .01
❑ 550 Luis Gonzalez RC 1.50 .60
❑ 551 Mike Simms RC .05 .01
❑ 552 Mark Portugal .05 .01
❑ 553 Jimmy Jones .05 .01
❑ 554 Jim Clancy .05 .01
❑ 555 Pete Harnisch .05 .01
❑ 556 Craig Biggio .15 .05
❑ 557 Eric Yelding .05 .01
❑ 558 Dave Rohde .05 .01
❑ 559 Casey Candaele .05 .01
❑ 560 Curt Schilling .25 .08

❑	561	Steve Finley	.10	.02
❑	562	Javier Ortiz	.05	.01
❑	563	Andujar Cedeno	.05	.01
❑	564	Rafael Ramirez	.05	.01
❑	565	Kenny Lofton RC	1.50	.60
❑	566	Steve Avery	.05	.01
❑	567	Lonnie Smith	.05	.01
❑	568	Kent Mercker	.05	.01
❑	569	Chipper Jones RC	6.00	2.50
❑	570	Terry Pendleton	.10	.02
❑	571	Otis Nixon	.05	.01
❑	572	Juan Berenguer	.05	.01
❑	573	Charlie Leibrandt	.05	.01
❑	574	David Justice	.10	.02
❑	575	Keith Mitchell RC	.15	.05
❑	576	Tom Glavine	.15	.05
❑	577	Greg Olson	.05	.01
❑	578	Rafael Belliard	.05	.01
❑	579	Ben Rivera RC	.15	.05
❑	580	John Smoltz	.15	.05
❑	581	Tyler Houston	.05	.01
❑	582	Mark Wohlers RC	.50	.20
❑	583	Ron Gant	.10	.02
❑	584	Ramon Caraballo RC	.15	.05
❑	585	Sid Bream	.05	.01
❑	586	Jeff Treadway	.05	.01
❑	587	Javy Lopez RC	3.00	1.25
❑	588	Deion Sanders	.15	.05
❑	589	Mike Heath	.05	.01
❑	590	Ryan Klesko RC	1.00	.40
❑	591	Bob Ojeda	.05	.01
❑	592	Alfredo Griffin	.05	.01
❑	593	Raul Mondesi RC	1.00	.40
❑	594	Greg Smith	.05	.01
❑	595	Orel Hershiser	.10	.02
❑	596	Juan Samuel	.05	.01
❑	597	Brett Butler	.10	.02
❑	598	Gary Carter	.10	.02
❑	599	Stan Javier	.05	.01
❑	600	Kal Daniels	.05	.01
❑	601	Jamie McAndrew RC	.15	.05
❑	602	Mike Sharperson	.05	.01
❑	603	Jay Howell	.05	.01
❑	604	Eric Karros RC	1.50	.60
❑	605	Tim Belcher	.05	.01
❑	606	Dan Opperman RC	.05	.01
❑	607	Lenny Harris	.05	.01
❑	608	Tom Goodwin	.05	.01
❑	609	Darryl Strawberry	.10	.02
❑	610	Ramon Martinez	.05	.01
❑	611	Kevin Gross	.05	.01
❑	612	Zakary Shinall RC	.05	.01
❑	613	Mike Scioscia	.05	.01
❑	614	Eddie Murray	.25	.08
❑	615	Ronnie Walden RC	.15	.05
❑	616	Will Clark	.15	.05
❑	617	Adam Hyzdu RC	.50	.20
❑	618	Matt Williams	.10	.02
❑	619	Don Robinson	.05	.01
❑	620	Jeff Brantley	.05	.01
❑	621	Greg Litton	.05	.01
❑	622	Steve Decker RC	.05	.01
❑	623	Robby Thompson	.05	.01
❑	624	Mark Leonard RC	.05	.01
❑	625	Kevin Bass	.05	.01
❑	626	Scott Garrelts	.05	.01
❑	627	Jose Uribe	.05	.01
❑	628	Eric Gunderson	.05	.01
❑	629	Steve Hosey	.05	.01
❑	630	Trevor Wilson	.05	.01
❑	631	Terry Kennedy	.05	.01
❑	632	Dave Righetti	.10	.02
❑	633	Kelly Downs	.05	.01
❑	634	Johnny Ard	.05	.01
❑	635	Eric Christopherson RC	.15	.05
❑	636	Kevin Mitchell	.05	.01
❑	637	John Burkett	.05	.01
❑	638	Kevin Rogers RC	.15	.05
❑	639	Bud Black	.05	.01
❑	640	Willie McGee	.10	.02
❑	641	Royce Clayton	.05	.01
❑	642	Tony Fernandez	.05	.01
❑	643	Ricky Bones RC	.15	.05
❑	644	Thomas Howard	.05	.01
❑	645	Dave Staton RC	.15	.05
❑	646	Jim Presley	.05	.01
❑	647	Tony Gwynn	.30	.10
❑	648	Marty Barrett	.05	.01
❑	649	Scott Coolbaugh	.05	.01
❑	650	Craig Lefferts	.05	.01
❑	651	Eddie Whitson	.05	.01
❑	652	Oscar Azocar	.05	.01
❑	653	Wes Gardner	.05	.01
❑	654	Bip Roberts	.05	.01
❑	655	Robbie Beckett RC	.15	.05
❑	656	Benito Santiago	.10	.02
❑	657	Greg W.Harris	.05	.01
❑	658	Jerald Clark	.05	.01
❑	659	Fred McGriff	.15	.05
❑	660	Larry Andersen	.05	.01
❑	661	Bruce Hurst	.05	.01
❑	662	Steve Martin UER RC	.15	.05
❑	663	Rafael Valdez	.05	.01
❑	664	Paul Faries RC	.05	.01
❑	665	Andy Benes	.05	.01
❑	666	Randy Myers	.05	.01
❑	667	Rob Dibble	.10	.02
❑	668	Glenn Sutko RC	.05	.01
❑	669	Glenn Braggs	.05	.01
❑	670	Billy Hatcher	.05	.01
❑	671	Joe Oliver	.05	.01
❑	672	Freddie Benavides RC	.15	.05
❑	673	Barry Larkin	.15	.05
❑	674	Chris Sabo	.05	.01
❑	675	Mariano Duncan	.05	.01
❑	676	Chris Jones RC	.05	.01
❑	677	Gino Minutelli RC	.05	.01
❑	678	Reggie Jefferson	.05	.01
❑	679	Jack Armstrong	.05	.01
❑	680	Chris Hammond	.05	.01
❑	681	Jose Rijo	.05	.01
❑	682	Bill Doran	.05	.01
❑	683	Terry Lee RC	.05	.01
❑	684	Tom Browning	.05	.01
❑	685	Paul O'Neill	.15	.05
❑	686	Eric Davis	.10	.02
❑	687	Dan Wilson RC	.50	.20
❑	688	Ted Power	.05	.01
❑	689	Tim Layana	.05	.01
❑	690	Norm Charlton	.05	.01
❑	691	Hal Morris	.05	.01
❑	692	Rickey Henderson RB	.15	.05
❑	693	Sam Militello RC	.15	.05
❑	694	Matt Mieske RC	.15	.05
❑	695	Paul Russo RC	.15	.05
❑	696	Domingo Mota MVP	.05	.01
❑	697	Todd Guggiana RC	.15	.05
❑	698	Marc Newfield RC	.15	.05
❑	699	Checklist 1-122	.05	.01
❑	700	Checklist 123-244	.05	.01
❑	701	Checklist 245-366	.05	.01
❑	702	Checklist 367-471	.05	.01
❑	703	Checklist 472-593	.05	.01
❑	704	Checklist 594-704	.05	.01

1992 Bowman

❑		COMPLETE SET (705)	150.00	75.00
❑	1	Ivan Rodriguez	1.25	.50
❑	2	Kirk McCaskill	.50	.20
❑	3	Scott Livingstone	.50	.20
❑	4	Salomon Torres RC	.50	.20
❑	5	Carlos Hernandez	.50	.20
❑	6	Dave Hollins	.50	.20
❑	7	Scott Fletcher	.50	.20
❑	8	Jorge Fabregas RC	.50	.20
❑	9	Andujar Cedeno	.50	.20
❑	10	Howard Johnson	.50	.20
❑	11	Trevor Hoffman RC	10.00	4.00
❑	12	Roberto Kelly	.50	.20
❑	13	Gregg Jefferies	.50	.20
❑	14	Marquis Grissom	.50	.20
❑	15	Mike Ignasiak	.50	.20
❑	16	Jack Morris	.50	.20
❑	17	William Pennyfeather	.50	.20
❑	18	Todd Stottlemyre	.50	.20
❑	19	Chito Martinez	.50	.20
❑	20	Roberto Alomar	.75	.30
❑	21	Sam Militello	.50	.20
❑	22	Hector Fajardo RC	.50	.20
❑	23	Paul Quantrill RC	.50	.20
❑	24	Chuck Knoblauch	.50	.20
❑	25	Reggie Jefferson	.50	.20
❑	26	Jeremy McGarity RC	.50	.20
❑	27	Jerome Walton	.50	.20
❑	28	Chipper Jones	12.00	5.00
❑	29	Brian Barber RC	.50	.20
❑	30	Ron Darling	.50	.20
❑	31	Roberto Petagine RC	.50	.20
❑	32	Chuck Finley	.50	.20
❑	33	Edgar Martinez	.75	.30
❑	34	Napoleon Robinson	.50	.20
❑	35	Andy Van Slyke	.75	.30
❑	36	Bobby Thigpen	.50	.20
❑	37	Travis Fryman	.50	.20
❑	38	Eric Christopherson	.50	.20
❑	39	Terry Mulholland	.50	.20
❑	40	Darryl Strawberry	.50	.20
❑	41	Manny Alexander RC	.50	.20
❑	42	Tracy Sanders RC	.50	.20
❑	43	Pete Incaviglia	.50	.20
❑	44	Kim Batiste	.50	.20
❑	45	Frank Rodriguez	.50	.20
❑	46	Greg Swindell	.50	.20
❑	47	Delino DeShields	.50	.20
❑	48	John Ericks	.50	.20
❑	49	Franklin Stubbs	.50	.20
❑	50	Tony Gwynn	1.50	.60
❑	51	Clifton Garrett RC	.50	.20
❑	52	Mike Gardella	.50	.20
❑	53	Scott Erickson	.50	.20
❑	54	Gary Caraballo RC	.50	.20
❑	55	Jose Oliva RC	.50	.20
❑	56	Brook Fordyce	.50	.20
❑	57	Mark Whiten	.50	.20
❑	58	Joe Slusarski	.50	.20
❑	59	J.R. Phillips RC	.50	.20
❑	60	Barry Bonds	4.00	1.50
❑	61	Bob Milacki	.50	.20
❑	62	Keith Mitchell	.50	.20
❑	63	Angel Miranda	.50	.20
❑	64	Raul Mondesi	.50	.20
❑	65	Brian Koelling RC	.50	.20
❑	66	Brian McRae	.50	.20
❑	67	John Patterson RC	.50	.20
❑	68	John Wetteland	.50	.20
❑	69	Wilson Alvarez	.50	.20
❑	70	Wade Boggs	.75	.30
❑	71	Darryl Ratliff RC	.50	.20
❑	72	Jeff Jackson	.50	.20
❑	73	Jeremy Hernandez RC	.50	.20
❑	74	Darryl Hamilton	.50	.20
❑	75	Rafael Belliard	.50	.20
❑	76	Rick Trlicek RC	.50	.20
❑	77	Felipe Crespo RC	.50	.20
❑	78	Carney Lansford	.50	.20
❑	79	Ryan Long RC	.50	.20
❑	80	Kirby Puckett	1.25	.50
❑	81	Earl Cunningham	.50	.20
❑	82	Pedro Martinez	10.00	4.00
❑	83	Scott Hatteberg RC	1.00	.40
❑	84	Juan Gonzalez	.75	.30
❑	85	Robert Nutting RC	.50	.20
❑	86	Pokey Reese RC	1.00	.40
❑	87	Dave Silvestri	.50	.20
❑	88	Scott Ruffcorn RC	.50	.20
❑	89	Rick Aguilera	.50	.20
❑	90	Cecil Fielder	.50	.20
❑	91	Kirk Dressendorfer	.50	.20
❑	92	Jerry DiPoto RC	.50	.20
❑	93	Mike Felder	.50	.20

❑ 94	Craig Paquette	.50	.20
❑ 95	Elvin Paulino RC	.50	.20
❑ 96	Donovan Osborne	.50	.20
❑ 97	Hubie Brooks	.50	.20
❑ 98	Derek Lowe RC	4.00	1.50
❑ 99	David Zancanaro	.50	.20
❑ 100	Ken Griffey Jr.	2.00	.75
❑ 101	Todd Hundley	.50	.20
❑ 102	Mike Trombley RC	.50	.20
❑ 103	Ricky Gutierrez RC	1.00	.40
❑ 104	Braulio Castillo	.50	.20
❑ 105	Craig Lefferts	.50	.20
❑ 106	Rick Sutcliffe	.50	.20
❑ 107	Dean Palmer	.50	.20
❑ 108	Henry Rodriguez	.50	.20
❑ 109	Mark Clark RC	1.00	.40
❑ 110	Kenny Lofton	.75	.30
❑ 111	Mark Carreon	.50	.20
❑ 112	J.T. Bruett	.50	.20
❑ 113	Gerald Williams	.50	.20
❑ 114	Frank Thomas	1.25	.50
❑ 115	Kevin Reimer	.50	.20
❑ 116	Sammy Sosa	1.25	.50
❑ 117	Mickey Tettleton	.50	.20
❑ 118	Reggie Sanders	.50	.20
❑ 119	Trevor Wilson	.50	.20
❑ 120	Cliff Brantley	.50	.20
❑ 121	Spike Owen	.50	.20
❑ 122	Jeff Montgomery	.50	.20
❑ 123	Alex Sutherland	.50	.20
❑ 124	Brien Taylor RC	1.00	.40
❑ 125	Brian Williams RC	.50	.20
❑ 126	Kevin Seitzer	.50	.20
❑ 127	Carlos Delgado RC	12.00	5.00
❑ 128	Gary Scott	.50	.20
❑ 129	Scott Cooper	.50	.20
❑ 130	Domingo Jean RC	.50	.20
❑ 131	Pat Mahomes RC	1.00	.40
❑ 132	Mike Boddicker	.50	.20
❑ 133	Roberto Hernandez	.50	.20
❑ 134	Dave Valle	.50	.20
❑ 135	Kurt Stillwell	.50	.20
❑ 136	Brad Pennington RC	.50	.20
❑ 137	Jermaine Swinton RC	.50	.20
❑ 138	Ryan Hawblitzel RC	.50	.20
❑ 139	Tito Navarro RC	.50	.20
❑ 140	Sandy Alomar Jr.	.50	.20
❑ 141	Todd Benzinger	.50	.20
❑ 142	Danny Jackson	.50	.20
❑ 143	Melvin Nieves RC	.50	.20
❑ 144	Jim Campanis	.50	.20
❑ 145	Luis Gonzalez	.50	.20
❑ 146	Dave Doorneweerd RC	.50	.20
❑ 147	Charlie Hayes	.50	.20
❑ 148	Greg Maddux	2.00	.75
❑ 149	Brian Harper	.50	.20
❑ 150	Brent Miller RC	.50	.20
❑ 151	Shawn Estes RC	1.00	.40
❑ 152	Mike Williams RC	1.00	.40
❑ 153	Charlie Hough	.50	.20
❑ 154	Randy Myers	.50	.20
❑ 155	Kevin Young RC	1.00	.40
❑ 156	Rick Wilkins	.50	.20
❑ 157	Terry Shumpert	.50	.20
❑ 158	Steve Karsay	.50	.20
❑ 159	Gary DiSarcina	.50	.20
❑ 160	Deion Sanders	.75	.30
❑ 161	Tom Browning	.50	.20
❑ 162	Dickie Thon	.50	.20
❑ 163	Luis Mercedes	.50	.20
❑ 164	Riccardo Ingram	.50	.20
❑ 165	Tavo Alvarez RC	.50	.20
❑ 166	Rickey Henderson	1.25	.50
❑ 167	Jaime Navarro	.50	.20
❑ 168	Billy Ashley RC	.50	.20
❑ 169	Phil Dauphin RC	.50	.20
❑ 170	Ivan Cruz	.50	.20
❑ 171	Harold Baines	.50	.20
❑ 172	Bryan Harvey	.50	.20
❑ 173	Alex Cole	.50	.20
❑ 174	Curtis Shaw RC	.50	.20
❑ 175	Matt Williams	.50	.20
❑ 176	Felix Jose	.50	.20
❑ 177	Sam Horn	.50	.20
❑ 178	Randy Johnson	1.25	.50
❑ 179	Ivan Calderon	.50	.20
❑ 180	Steve Avery	.50	.20
❑ 181	William Suero	.50	.20
❑ 182	Bill Swift	.50	.20
❑ 183	Howard Battle RC	.50	.20
❑ 184	Ruben Amaro	.50	.20
❑ 185	Jim Abbott	.75	.30
❑ 186	Mike Fitzgerald	.50	.20
❑ 187	Bruce Hurst	.50	.20
❑ 188	Jeff Juden	.50	.20
❑ 189	Jeromy Burnitz	.50	.20
❑ 190	Dave Burba	.50	.20
❑ 191	Kevin Brown	.50	.20
❑ 192	Patrick Lennon	.50	.20
❑ 193	Jeff McNeely	.50	.20
❑ 194	Wil Cordero	.50	.20
❑ 195	Chili Davis	.50	.20
❑ 196	Milt Cuyler	.50	.20
❑ 197	Von Hayes	.50	.20
❑ 198	Todd Revenig RC	.50	.20
❑ 199	Joel Johnston	.50	.20
❑ 200	Jeff Bagwell	1.25	.50
❑ 201	Alex Fernandez	.50	.20
❑ 202	Todd Jones RC	2.50	1.00
❑ 203	Charles Nagy	.50	.20
❑ 204	Tim Raines	.50	.20
❑ 205	Kevin Maas	.50	.20
❑ 206	Julio Franco	.50	.20
❑ 207	Randy Velarde	.50	.20
❑ 208	Lance Johnson	.50	.20
❑ 209	Scott Leius	.50	.20
❑ 210	Derek Lee	.50	.20
❑ 211	Joe Sondrini RC	.50	.20
❑ 212	Royce Clayton	.50	.20
❑ 213	Chris George	.50	.20
❑ 214	Gary Sheffield	.50	.20
❑ 215	Mark Gubicza	.50	.20
❑ 216	Mike Moore	.50	.20
❑ 217	Rick Huisman RC	.50	.20
❑ 218	Jeff Russell	.50	.20
❑ 219	D.J. Dozier	.50	.20
❑ 220	Dave Martinez	.50	.20
❑ 221	Alan Newman RC	.50	.20
❑ 222	Nolan Ryan	4.00	1.50
❑ 223	Teddy Higuera	.50	.20
❑ 224	Damon Buford RC	.50	.20
❑ 225	Ruben Sierra	.50	.20
❑ 226	Tom Nevers	.50	.20
❑ 227	Tommy Greene	.50	.20
❑ 228	Nigel Wilson RC	.50	.20
❑ 229	John DeSilva	.50	.20
❑ 230	Bobby Witt	.50	.20
❑ 231	Greg Cadaret	.50	.20
❑ 232	John Vander Wal RC	1.00	.40
❑ 233	Jack Clark	.50	.20
❑ 234	Bill Doran	.50	.20
❑ 235	Bobby Bonilla	.50	.20
❑ 236	Steve Olin	.50	.20
❑ 237	Derek Bell	.50	.20
❑ 238	David Cone	.50	.20
❑ 239	Victor Cole	.50	.20
❑ 240	Rod Bolton RC	.50	.20
❑ 241	Tom Pagnozzi	.50	.20
❑ 242	Rob Dibble	.50	.20
❑ 243	Michael Carter RC	.50	.20
❑ 244	Don Peters	.50	.20
❑ 245	Mike LaValliere	.50	.20
❑ 246	Joe Perona RC	.50	.20
❑ 247	Mitch Williams	.50	.20
❑ 248	Jay Buhner	.50	.20
❑ 249	Andy Benes	.50	.20
❑ 250	Alex Ochoa RC	.50	.20
❑ 251	Greg Blosser	.50	.20
❑ 252	Jack Armstrong	.50	.20
❑ 253	Juan Samuel	.50	.20
❑ 254	Terry Pendleton	.50	.20
❑ 255	Ramon Martinez	.50	.20
❑ 256	Rico Brogna	.50	.20
❑ 257	John Smiley	.50	.20
❑ 258	Carl Everett	.75	.30
❑ 259	Tim Salmon	.75	.30
❑ 260	Will Clark	.75	.30
❑ 261	Ugueth Urbina RC	1.00	.40
❑ 262	Jason Wood RC	.50	.20
❑ 263	Dave Magadan	.50	.20
❑ 264	Dante Bichette	.50	.20
❑ 265	Jose DeLeon	.50	.20
❑ 266	Mike Neill RC	1.00	.40
❑ 267	Paul O'Neill	.75	.30
❑ 268	Anthony Young	.50	.20
❑ 269	Greg W. Harris	.50	.20
❑ 270	Todd Van Poppel	.50	.20
❑ 271	Pedro Castellano RC	.50	.20
❑ 272	Tony Phillips	.50	.20
❑ 273	Mike Gallego	.50	.20
❑ 274	Steve Cooke RC	.50	.20
❑ 275	Robin Ventura	.50	.20
❑ 276	Kevin Mitchell	.50	.20
❑ 277	Doug Linton RC	.50	.20
❑ 278	Robert Eenhoorn	.50	.20
❑ 279	Gabe White RC	.50	.20
❑ 280	Dave Stewart	.50	.20
❑ 281	Mo Sanford	.50	.20
❑ 282	Greg Perschke	.50	.20
❑ 283	Kevin Flora RC	.50	.20
❑ 284	Jeff Williams RC	1.00	.40
❑ 285	Keith Miller	.50	.20
❑ 286	Andy Ashby	.50	.20
❑ 287	Doug Dascenzo	.50	.20
❑ 288	Eric Karros	.50	.20
❑ 289	Glenn Murray RC	.50	.20
❑ 290	Troy Percival RC	3.00	1.25
❑ 291	Orlando Merced	.50	.20
❑ 292	Peter Hoy	.50	.20
❑ 293	Tony Fernandez	.50	.20
❑ 294	Juan Guzman	.50	.20
❑ 295	Jesse Barfield	.50	.20
❑ 296	Sid Fernandez	.50	.20
❑ 297	Scott Cepicky	.50	.20
❑ 298	Garret Anderson RC	5.00	2.00
❑ 299	Cal Eldred	.50	.20
❑ 300	Ryne Sandberg	2.50	1.00
❑ 301	Jim Gantner	.50	.20
❑ 302	Mariano Rivera RC	25.00	10.00
❑ 303	Ron Lockett RC	.50	.20
❑ 304	Jose Offerman	.50	.20
❑ 305	Dennis Martinez	.50	.20
❑ 306	Luis Ortiz RC	.50	.20
❑ 307	David Howard	.50	.20
❑ 308	Russ Springer RC	1.00	.40
❑ 309	Chris Howard	.50	.20
❑ 310	Kyle Abbott	.50	.20
❑ 311	Aaron Sele RC	1.00	.40
❑ 312	David Justice	.50	.20
❑ 313	Pete O'Brien	.50	.20
❑ 314	Greg Hansell RC	.50	.20
❑ 315	Dave Winfield	.50	.20
❑ 316	Lance Dickson	.50	.20
❑ 317	Eric King	.50	.20
❑ 318	Vaughn Eshelman RC	.50	.20
❑ 319	Tim Belcher	.50	.20
❑ 320	Andres Galarraga	.50	.20
❑ 321	Scott Bullett RC	.50	.20
❑ 322	Doug Strange	.50	.20
❑ 323	Jerald Clark	.50	.20
❑ 324	Dave Righetti	.50	.20
❑ 325	Greg Hibbard	.50	.20
❑ 326	Eric Hillman RC	.50	.20
❑ 327	Shane Reynolds RC	1.00	.40
❑ 328	Chris Hammond	.50	.20
❑ 329	Albert Belle	.50	.20
❑ 330	Rich Becker RC	.50	.20
❑ 331	Ed Williams	.50	.20
❑ 332	Donald Harris	.50	.20
❑ 333	Dave Smith	.50	.20
❑ 334	Steve Fireovid	.50	.20
❑ 335	Steve Buechele	.50	.20
❑ 336	Mike Schooler	.50	.20
❑ 337	Kevin McReynolds	.50	.20
❑ 338	Hensley Meulens	.50	.20
❑ 339	Benji Gil RC	1.00	.40
❑ 340	Don Mattingly	3.00	1.25
❑ 341	Alvin Davis	.50	.20
❑ 342	Alan Mills	.50	.20
❑ 343	Kelly Downs	.50	.20
❑ 344	Leo Gomez	.50	.20
❑ 345	Tarrik Brock RC	.50	.20
❑ 346	Ryan Turner RC	.50	.20
❑ 347	John Smoltz	.75	.30
❑ 348	Bill Sampen	.50	.20
❑ 349	Paul Byrd RC	3.00	1.25
❑ 350	Mike Bordick	.50	.20
❑ 351	Jose Lind	.50	.20

352	David Wells	.50	.20
353	Barry Larkin	.75	.30
354	Bruce Ruffin	.50	.20
355	Luis Rivera	.50	.20
356	Sid Bream	.50	.20
357	Julian Vasquez RC	.50	.20
358	Jason Bere RC	1.00	.40
359	Ben McDonald	.50	.20
360	Scott Stahoviak RC	.50	.20
361	Kirt Manwaring	.50	.20
362	Jeff Johnson	.50	.20
363	Rob Deer	.50	.20
364	Tony Pena	.50	.20
365	Melido Perez	.50	.20
366	Clay Parker	.50	.20
367	Dale Sveum	.50	.20
368	Mike Scioscia	.50	.20
369	Roger Salkeld	.50	.20
370	Mike Stanley	.50	.20
371	Jack McDowell	.50	.20
372	Tim Wallach	.50	.20
373	Billy Ripken	.50	.20
374	Mike Christopher	.50	.20
375	Paul Molitor	.50	.20
376	Dave Stieb	.50	.20
377	Pedro Guerrero	.50	.20
378	Russ Swan	.50	.20
379	Bob Ojeda	.50	.20
380	Donn Pall	.50	.20
381	Eddie Zosky	.50	.20
382	Darnell Coles	.50	.20
383	Tom Smith RC	.50	.20
384	Mark McGwire	3.00	1.25
385	Gary Carter	.50	.20
386	Rich Amaral RC	.50	.20
387	Alan Embree RC	1.00	.40
388	Jonathan Hurst RC	.50	.20
389	Bobby Jones RC	1.00	.40
390	Rico Rossy	.50	.20
391	Dan Smith	.50	.20
392	Terry Steinbach	.50	.20
393	Jon Farrell RC	.50	.20
394	Dave Anderson	.50	.20
395	Benny Santiago	.50	.20
396	Mark Wohlers	.50	.20
397	Mo Vaughn	.50	.20
398	Randy Kramer	.50	.20
399	John Jaha RC	1.00	.40
400	Cal Ripken	4.00	1.50
401	Ryan Bowen	.50	.20
402	Tim McIntosh	.50	.20
403	Bernard Gilkey	.50	.20
404	Junior Felix	.50	.20
405	Cris Colon RC	.50	.20
406	Marc Newfield	.50	.20
407	Bernie Williams	.75	.30
408	Jay Howell	.50	.20
409	Zane Smith	.50	.20
410	Jeff Shaw	.50	.20
411	Kerry Woodson	.50	.20
412	Wes Chamberlain	.50	.20
413	Dave Mlicki RC	1.00	.40
414	Benny Distefano	.50	.20
415	Kevin Rogers	.50	.20
416	Tim Naehring	.50	.20
417	Clemente Nunez RC	.50	.20
418	Luis Sojo	.50	.20
419	Kevin Ritz	.50	.20
420	Omar Olivares	.50	.20
421	Manuel Lee	.50	.20
422	Julio Valera	.50	.20
423	Omar Vizquel	.75	.30
424	Darren Burton RC	.50	.20
425	Mel Hall	.50	.20
426	Dennis Powell	.50	.20
427	Lee Stevens	.50	.20
428	Glenn Davis	.50	.20
429	Willie Greene	.50	.20
430	Kevin Wickander	.50	.20
431	Dennis Eckersley	.50	.20
432	Joe Orsulak	.50	.20
433	Eddie Murray	1.25	.50
434	Matt Stairs RC	1.00	.40
435	Wally Joyner	.50	.20
436	Rondell White	.50	.20
437	Rob Maurer	.50	.20
438	Joe Redfield	.50	.20
439	Mark Lewis	.50	.20
440	Darren Daulton	.50	.20
441	Mike Henneman	.50	.20
442	John Cangelosi	.50	.20
443	Vincent Moore RC	.50	.20
444	John Wehner	.50	.20
445	Kent Hrbek	.50	.20
446	Mark McLemore	.50	.20
447	Bill Wegman	.50	.20
448	Robby Thompson	.50	.20
449	Mark Anthony RC	.50	.20
450	Archi Cianfrocco RC	.50	.20
451	Johnny Ruffin	.50	.20
452	Javy Lopez	2.00	.75
453	Greg Gohr	.50	.20
454	Tim Scott	.50	.20
455	Stan Belinda	.50	.20
456	Darrin Jackson	.50	.20
457	Chris Gardner	.50	.20
458	Esteban Beltre	.50	.20
459	Phil Plantier	.50	.20
460	Jim Thome	8.00	3.00
461	Mike Piazza RC	25.00	10.00
462	Matt Sinatro	.50	.20
463	Scott Servais	.50	.20
464	Brian Jordan RC	2.00	.75
465	Doug Drabek	.50	.20
466	Carl Willis	.50	.20
467	Bret Barberie	.50	.20
468	Hal Morris	.50	.20
469	Steve Sax	.50	.20
470	Jerry Willard	.50	.20
471	Dan Wilson	.50	.20
472	Chris Hoiles	.50	.20
473	Rheal Cormier	.50	.20
474	John Morris	.50	.20
475	Jeff Reardon	.50	.20
476	Mark Leiter	.50	.20
477	Tom Gordon	.50	.20
478	Kent Bottenfield RC	1.00	.40
479	Gene Larkin	.50	.20
480	Dwight Gooden	.50	.20
481	B.J. Surhoff	.50	.20
482	Andy Stankiewicz	.50	.20
483	Tino Martinez	.75	.30
484	Craig Biggio	.75	.30
485	Denny Neagle	.50	.20
486	Rusty Meacham	.50	.20
487	Kal Daniels	.50	.20
488	Dave Henderson	.50	.20
489	Tim Costo	.50	.20
490	Doug Davis	.50	.20
491	Frank Viola	.50	.20
492	Cory Snyder	.50	.20
493	Chris Martin	.50	.20
494	Dion James	.50	.20
495	Randy Tomlin	.50	.20
496	Greg Vaughn	.50	.20
497	Dennis Cook	.50	.20
498	Rosario Rodriguez	.50	.20
499	Dave Staton	.50	.20
500	George Brett	3.00	1.25
501	Brian Barnes	.50	.20
502	Butch Henry RC	.50	.20
503	Harold Reynolds	.50	.20
504	David Nied RC	.50	.20
505	Lee Smith	.50	.20
506	Steve Chitren	.50	.20
507	Ken Hill	.50	.20
508	Robbie Beckett	.50	.20
509	Troy Afenir	.50	.20
510	Kelly Gruber	.50	.20
511	Bret Boone	.75	.30
512	Jeff Branson	.50	.20
513	Mike Jackson	.50	.20
514	Pete Harnisch	.50	.20
515	Chad Kreuter	.50	.20
516	Joe Vitko RC	.50	.20
517	Orel Hershiser	.50	.20
518	John Doherty RC	.50	.20
519	Jay Bell	.50	.20
520	Mark Langston	.50	.20
521	Dann Howitt	.50	.20
522	Bobby Reed RC	.50	.20
523	Bobby Munoz RC	.50	.20
524	Todd Ritchie	.50	.20
525	Bip Roberts	.50	.20
526	Pat Listach RC	1.00	.40
527	Scott Brosius RC	2.00	.75
528	John Roper RC	.50	.20
529	Phil Hiatt RC	.50	.20
530	Denny Walling	.50	.20
531	Carlos Baerga	.50	.20
532	Manny Ramirez RC	20.00	8.00
533	Pat Clements UER	.50	.20
534	Ron Gant	.50	.20
535	Pat Kelly	.50	.20
536	Bill Spiers	.50	.20
537	Darren Reed	.50	.20
538	Ken Caminiti	.50	.20
539	Butch Huskey RC	.50	.20
540	Matt Nokes	.50	.20
541	John Kruk	.50	.20
542	John Jaha FOIL	.50	.20
543	Justin Thompson RC	.50	.20
544	Steve Hosey	.50	.20
545	Joe Kmak	.50	.20
546	John Franco	.50	.20
547	Devon White	.50	.20
548	Elston Hansen FOIL SP RC	.50	.20
549	Ryan Klesko	.50	.20
550	Danny Tartabull	.50	.20
551	Frank Thomas FOIL	1.25	.50
552	Kevin Tapani	.50	.20
553	Willie Banks	.50	.20
554	B.J.Wallace FOIL RC	.50	.20
555	Orlando Miller RC	.50	.20
556	Mark Smith RC	.50	.20
557	Tim Wallach FOIL	.50	.20
558	Bill Gullickson	.50	.20
559	Derek Bell FOIL	.50	.20
560	Joe Randa FOIL RC	3.00	1.25
561	Frank Seminara RC	.50	.20
562	Mark Gardner	.50	.20
563	Rick Greene FOIL RC	.50	.20
564	Gary Gaetti	.50	.20
565	Ozzie Guillen	.50	.20
566	Charles Nagy FOIL	.50	.20
567	Mike Milchin	.50	.20
568	Ben Shelton RC	.50	.20
569	Chris Roberts FOIL	.50	.20
570	Ellis Burks	.50	.20
571	Scott Scudder	.50	.20
572	Jim Abbott FOIL	.75	.30
573	Joe Carter	.50	.20
574	Steve Finley	.50	.20
575	Jim Olander FOIL	.50	.20
576	Carlos Garcia	.50	.20
577	Gregg Olson	.50	.20
578	Greg Swindell FOIL	.50	.20
579	Matt Williams FOIL	.50	.20
580	Mark Grace	.75	.30
581	Howard House FOIL RC	.50	.20
582	Luis Polonia	.50	.20
583	Erik Hanson	.50	.20
584	Salomon Torres FOIL	.50	.20
585	Carlton Fisk	.75	.30
586	Bret Saberhagen	.50	.20
587	Chad McConnell FOIL RC	.50	.20
588	Jimmy Key	.50	.20
589	Mike Macfarlane	.50	.20
590	Barry Bonds FOIL	4.00	1.50
591	Jamie McAndrew	.50	.20
592	Shane Mack	.50	.20
593	Kerwin Moore	.50	.20
594	Joe Oliver	.50	.20
595	Chris Sabo	.50	.20
596	Alex Gonzalez RC	1.00	.40
597	Brett Butler	.50	.20
598	Mark Hutton RC	.50	.20
599	Andy Benes FOIL	.50	.20
600	Jose Canseco	.75	.30
601	Darryl Kile	.50	.20
602	Matt Stairs FOIL	.50	.20
603	Rob Butler FOIL RC	.50	.20
604	Willie McGee	.50	.20
605	Jack McDowell FOIL	.50	.20
606	Tom Candiotti	.50	.20
607	Ed Martel RC	.50	.20
608	Matt Mieske FOIL	.50	.20
609	Darrin Fletcher	.50	.20

610	Rafael Palmeiro	.75	.30
611	Bill Swift FOIL	.50	.20
612	Mike Mussina	1.25	.50
613	Vince Coleman	.50	.20
614	Scott Cepicky COR	.50	.20
614A	Scott Cepicky FOIL UER	.50	.20
615	Mike Greenwell	.50	.20
616	Kevin McGehee RC	.50	.20
617	Jeffrey Hammonds FOIL	.50	.20
618	Scott Taylor	.50	.20
619	Dave Otto	.50	.20
620	Mark McGwire FOIL	3.00	1.25
621	Kevin Tatar RC	.50	.20
622	Steve Farr	.50	.20
623	Ryan Klesko FOIL	.50	.20
624	Dave Fleming	.50	.20
625	Andre Dawson	.50	.20
626	Tino Martinez FOIL SP	.75	.30
627	Chad Curtis RC	1.00	.40
628	Mickey Morandini	.50	.20
629	Gregg Olson FOIL SP	.50	.20
630	Lou Whitaker	.50	.20
631	Arthur Rhodes	.50	.20
632	Brandon Wilson RC	.50	.20
633	Lance Jennings RC	.50	.20
634	Allen Watson RC	.50	.20
635	Len Dykstra	.50	.20
636	Joe Girardi	.50	.20
637	Kiki Hernandez FOIL RC	.50	.20
638	Mike Hampton RC	2.00	.75
639	Al Osuna	.50	.20
640	Kevin Appier	.50	.20
641	Rick Helling FOIL	.50	.20
642	Jody Reed	.50	.20
643	Ray Lankford	.50	.20
644	John Olerud	.50	.20
645	Paul Molitor FOIL	.50	.20
646	Pat Borders	.50	.20
647	Mike Morgan	.50	.20
648	Larry Walker	.75	.30
649	Pedro Castellano FOIL	.50	.20
650	Fred McGriff	.75	.30
651	Walt Weiss	.50	.20
652	Calvin Murray FOIL RC	1.00	.40
653	Dave Nilsson	.50	.20
654	Greg Pirkl RC	.50	.20
655	Robin Ventura FOIL	.50	.20
656	Mark Portugal	.50	.20
657	Roger McDowell	.50	.20
658	Rick Hirtensteiner FOIL RC	.50	.20
659	Glenallen Hill	.50	.20
660	Greg Gagne	.50	.20
661	Charles Johnson FOIL	.50	.20
662	Brian Hunter	.50	.20
663	Mark Lemke	.50	.20
664	Tim Belcher FOIL SP	.50	.20
665	Rich DeLucia	.50	.20
666	Bob Walk	.50	.20
667	Joe Carter FOIL	.50	.20
668	Jose Guzman	.50	.20
669	Otis Nixon	.50	.20
670	Phil Nevin FOIL	.50	.20
671	Eric Davis	.50	.20
672	Damion Easley RC	1.00	.40
673	Will Clark FOIL	.75	.30
674	Mark Kiefer RC	.50	.20
675	Ozzie Smith	2.00	.75
676	Manny Ramirez FOIL	12.00	5.00
677	Gregg Olson	.50	.20
678	Cliff Floyd RC	3.00	1.25
679	Duane Singleton RC	.50	.20
680	Jose Rijo	.50	.20
681	Willie Randolph	.50	.20
682	Michael Tucker FOIL RC	1.00	.40
683	Darren Lewis	.50	.20
684	Dale Murphy	.75	.30
685	Mike Pagliarulo	.50	.20
686	Paul Miller RC	.50	.20
687	Mike Robertson RC	.50	.20
688	Mike Devereaux	.50	.20
689	Pedro Astacio RC	1.00	.40
690	Alan Trammell	.50	.20
691	Roger Clemens	2.50	1.00
692	Bud Black	.50	.20
693	Turk Wendell RC	1.00	.40
694	Barry Larkin FOIL	.75	.30
695	Todd Zeile	.50	.20
696	Pat Hentgen	.50	.20
697	Eddie Taubensee RC	1.00	.40
698	Guillermo Velasquez RC	.50	.20
699	Tom Glavine	.75	.30
700	Robin Yount	2.00	.75
701	Checklist 1-141	.50	.20
702	Checklist 142-282	.50	.20
703	Checklist 283-423	.50	.20
704	Checklist 424-564	.50	.20
705	Checklist 565-705	.50	.20

1993 Bowman

	COMPLETE SET (708)	40.00	15.00
1	Glenn Davis	.15	.05
2	Hector Roa RC	.25	.08
3	Ken Ryan RC	.25	.08
4	Derek Wallace RC	.25	.08
5	Jorge Fabregas	.15	.05
6	Joe Oliver	.15	.05
7	Brandon Wilson	.15	.05
8	Mark Thompson RC	.25	.08
9	Tracy Sanders	.15	.05
10	Rich Renteria	.15	.05
11	Lou Whitaker	.30	.10
12	Brian L. Hunter RC	.50	.20
13	Joe Vitiello	.15	.05
14	Eric Karros	.30	.10
15	Joe Kmak	.15	.05
16	Tavo Alvarez	.15	.05
17	Steve Dunn RC	.25	.08
18	Tony Fernandez	.15	.05
19	Melido Perez	.15	.05
20	Mike Lieberthal	.30	.10
21	Terry Steinbach	.15	.05
22	Stan Belinda	.15	.05
23	Jay Buhner	.30	.10
24	Allen Watson	.15	.05
25	Daryl Henderson RC	.25	.08
26	Ray McDavid RC	.25	.08
27	Shawn Green	1.00	.40
28	Bud Black	.15	.05
29	Sherman Obando RC	.25	.08
30	Mike Hostetler RC	.25	.08
31	Nate Minchey RC	.25	.08
32	Randy Myers	.15	.05
33	Brian Grebeck	.15	.05
34	John Roper	.15	.05
35	Larry Thomas	.15	.05
36	Alex Cole	.15	.05
37	Tom Kramer RC	.25	.08
38	Matt Whisenant RC	.25	.08
39	Chris Gomez RC	.50	.20
40	Luis Gonzalez	.30	.10
41	Kevin Appier	.30	.10
42	Omar Daal RC	.25	.08
43	Duane Singleton	.15	.05
44	Bill Risley	.15	.05
45	Pat Meares RC	.50	.20
46	Butch Huskey	.15	.05
47	Bobby Munoz	.15	.05
48	Juan Bell	.15	.05
49	Scott Lydy RC	.25	.08
50	Dennis Moeller	.15	.05
51	Marc Newfield	.15	.05
52	Tripp Cromer RC	.25	.08
53	Kurt Miller	.15	.05
54	Jim Pena	.15	.05
55	Juan Guzman	.15	.05
56	Matt Williams	.30	.10
57	Harold Reynolds	.30	.10
58	Donnie Elliott RC	.25	.08
59	Jon Shave RC	.25	.08
60	Kevin Roberson RC	.25	.08
61	Hilly Hathaway RC	.25	.08
62	Jose Rijo	.15	.05
63	Kerry Taylor RC	.15	.05
64	Ryan Hawblitzel	.15	.05
65	Glenallen Hill	.15	.05
66	Ramon D. Martinez RC	.25	.08
67	Travis Fryman	.30	.10
68	Tom Nevers	.15	.05
69	Phil Hiatt	.15	.05
70	Tim Wallach	.15	.05
71	B.J. Surhoff	.30	.10
72	Rondell White	.30	.10
73	Denny Hocking RC	.50	.20
74	Mike Oquist RC	.25	.08
75	Paul O'Neill	.50	.20
76	Willie Banks	.15	.05
77	Bob Welch	.15	.05
78	Jose Sandoval RC	.25	.08
79	Bill Haselman	.15	.05
80	Rheal Cormier	.15	.05
81	Dean Palmer	.30	.10
82	Pat Gomez RC	.25	.08
83	Steve Karsay	.15	.05
84	Carl Hanselman RC	.25	.08
85	T.R. Lewis RC	.25	.08
86	Chipper Jones	.75	.30
87	Scott Hatteberg	.15	.05
88	Greg Hibbard	.15	.05
89	Lance Painter RC	.25	.08
90	Chad Mottola RC	.50	.20
91	Jason Bere	.15	.05
92	Dante Bichette	.30	.10
93	Sandy Alomar Jr.	.15	.05
94	Carl Everett	.30	.10
95	Danny Bautista RC	.50	.20
96	Steve Finley	.30	.10
97	David Cone	.30	.10
98	Todd Hollandsworth	.15	.05
99	Matt Mieske	.15	.05
100	Larry Walker	.30	.10
101	Shane Mack	.15	.05
102	Aaron Ledesma RC	.25	.08
103	Andy Pettitte RC	8.00	3.00
104	Kevin Stocker	.15	.05
105	Mike Mohler RC	.25	.08
106	Tony Menendez	.15	.05
107	Derek Lowe	.30	.10
108	Basil Shabazz	.15	.05
109	Dan Smith	.15	.05
110	Scott Sanders RC	.50	.20
111	Todd Stottlemyre	.15	.05
112	Benji Simonton RC	.25	.08
113	Rick Sutcliffe	.30	.10
114	Lee Heath RC	.25	.08
115	Jeff Russell	.15	.05
116	Dave Stevens RC	.25	.08
117	Mark Holzemer RC	.25	.08
118	Tim Belcher	.15	.05
119	Bobby Thigpen	.15	.05
120	Roger Bailey RC	.25	.08
121	Tony Mitchell RC	.25	.08
122	Junior Felix	.15	.05
123	Rich Robertson RC	.25	.08
124	Andy Cook RC	.25	.08
125	Brian Bevil RC	.25	.08
126	Darryl Strawberry	.30	.10
127	Cal Eldred	.15	.05
128	Cliff Floyd	.30	.10
129	Alan Newman	.15	.05
130	Howard Johnson	.15	.05
131	Jim Abbott	.50	.20
132	Chad McConnell	.15	.05
133	Miguel Jimenez RC	.25	.08
134	Brett Backlund RC	.25	.08
135	John Cummings RC	.25	.08
136	Brian Barber	.15	.05
137	Rafael Palmeiro	.50	.20
138	Tim Worrell RC	.25	.08
139	Jose Pett RC	.25	.08
140	Barry Bonds	2.00	.75

❑ 141 Damon Buford .15 .05
❑ 142 Jeff Blauser .15 .05
❑ 143 Frankie Rodriguez .15 .05
❑ 144 Mike Morgan .15 .05
❑ 145 Gary DiSarcina .15 .05
❑ 146 Pokey Reese .15 .05
❑ 147 Johnny Ruffin .15 .05
❑ 148 David Nied .15 .05
❑ 149 Charles Nagy .15 .05
❑ 150 Mike Myers RC .25 .08
❑ 151 Kenny Carlyle RC .25 .08
❑ 152 Eric Anthony .15 .05
❑ 153 Jose Lind .15 .05
❑ 154 Pedro Martinez 1.50 .60
❑ 155 Mark Kiefer .15 .05
❑ 156 Tim Laker RC .25 .08
❑ 157 Pat Mahomes .15 .05
❑ 158 Bobby Bonilla .30 .10
❑ 159 Domingo Jean .15 .05
❑ 160 Darren Daulton .30 .10
❑ 161 Mark McGwire 2.00 .75
❑ 162 Jason Kendall RC 2.00 .75
❑ 163 Desi Relaford .15 .05
❑ 164 Ozzie Canseco .15 .05
❑ 165 Rick Helling .15 .05
❑ 166 Steve Pegues RC .25 .08
❑ 167 Paul Molitor .30 .10
❑ 168 Larry Carter RC .15 .05
❑ 169 Arthur Rhodes .15 .05
❑ 170 Damon Hollins RC .50 .20
❑ 171 Frank Viola .30 .10
❑ 172 Steve Trachsel RC 1.00 .40
❑ 173 J.T.Snow RC 1.00 .40
❑ 174 Keith Gordon RC .25 .08
❑ 175 Carlton Fisk .50 .20
❑ 176 Jason Bates RC .25 .08
❑ 177 Mike Crosby RC .25 .08
❑ 178 Benny Santiago .30 .10
❑ 179 Mike Moore .15 .05
❑ 180 Jeff Juden .15 .05
❑ 181 Darren Burton .15 .05
❑ 182 Todd Williams RC .50 .20
❑ 183 John Jaha .15 .05
❑ 184 Mike Lansing RC .50 .20
❑ 185 Pedro Grifol RC .25 .08
❑ 186 Vince Coleman .15 .05
❑ 187 Pat Kelly .15 .05
❑ 188 Clemente Alvarez RC .25 .08
❑ 189 Ron Darling .15 .05
❑ 190 Orlando Merced .15 .05
❑ 191 Chris Bosio .15 .05
❑ 192 Steve Dixon RC .25 .08
❑ 193 Doug Dascenzo .15 .05
❑ 194 Ray Holbert RC .25 .08
❑ 195 Howard Battle .15 .05
❑ 196 Willie McGee .30 .10
❑ 197 John O'Donoghue RC .25 .08
❑ 198 Steve Avery .15 .05
❑ 199 Greg Blosser .15 .05
❑ 200 Ryne Sandberg 1.25 .50
❑ 201 Joe Grahe .15 .05
❑ 202 Dan Wilson .30 .10
❑ 203 Domingo Martinez RC .25 .08
❑ 204 Andres Galarraga .30 .10
❑ 205 Jamie Taylor RC .25 .08
❑ 206 Darrell Whitmore RC .25 .08
❑ 207 Ben Blomdahl RC .25 .08
❑ 208 Doug Drabek .15 .05
❑ 209 Keith Miller .15 .05
❑ 210 Billy Ashley .15 .05
❑ 211 Mike Farrell RC .25 .08
❑ 212 John Wetteland .30 .10
❑ 213 Randy Tomlin .15 .05
❑ 214 Sid Fernandez .15 .05
❑ 215 Quilvio Veras RC .50 .20
❑ 216 Dave Hollins .15 .05
❑ 217 Mike Neill .15 .05
❑ 218 Andy Van Slyke .50 .20
❑ 219 Bret Boone .30 .10
❑ 220 Tom Pagnozzi .15 .05
❑ 221 Mike Welch RC .25 .08
❑ 222 Frank Seminara .15 .05
❑ 223 Ron Villone .15 .05
❑ 224 D.J.Thielen RC .25 .08
❑ 225 Cal Ripken 2.50 1.00
❑ 226 Pedro Borbon Jr. RC .25 .08
❑ 227 Carlos Quintana .15 .05
❑ 228 Tommy Shields .15 .05
❑ 229 Tim Salmon .50 .20
❑ 230 John Smiley .15 .05
❑ 231 Ellis Burks .30 .10
❑ 232 Pedro Castellano .15 .05
❑ 233 Paul Byrd .30 .10
❑ 234 Bryan Harvey .15 .05
❑ 235 Scott Livingstone .15 .05
❑ 236 James Mouton RC .25 .08
❑ 237 Joe Randa .30 .10
❑ 238 Pedro Astacio .15 .05
❑ 239 Darryl Hamilton .15 .05
❑ 240 Joey Eischen RC .25 .08
❑ 241 Edgar Herrera RC .25 .08
❑ 242 Dwight Gooden .30 .10
❑ 243 Sam Militello .15 .05
❑ 244 Ron Blazier RC .25 .08
❑ 245 Ruben Sierra .30 .10
❑ 246 Al Martin .15 .05
❑ 247 Mike Felder .15 .05
❑ 248 Bob Tewksbury .15 .05
❑ 249 Craig Lefferts .15 .05
❑ 250 Luis Lopez RC .25 .08
❑ 251 Devon White .30 .10
❑ 252 Will Clark .50 .20
❑ 253 Mark Smith .15 .05
❑ 254 Terry Pendleton .30 .10
❑ 255 Aaron Sele .15 .05
❑ 256 Jose Viera RC .25 .08
❑ 257 Damion Easley .15 .05
❑ 258 Rod Lofton RC .25 .08
❑ 259 Chris Snopek RC .25 .08
❑ 260 Quinton McCracken RC .50 .20
❑ 261 Mike Matthews RC .25 .08
❑ 262 Hector Carrasco RC .25 .08
❑ 263 Rick Greene .15 .05
❑ 264 Chris Holt RC .50 .20
❑ 265 George Brett 2.00 .75
❑ 266 Rick Gorecki RC .25 .08
❑ 267 Francisco Gamez RC .25 .08
❑ 268 Marquis Grissom .30 .10
❑ 269 Kevin Tapani UER .15 .05
❑ 270 Ryan Thompson .15 .05
❑ 271 Gerald Williams .15 .05
❑ 272 Paul Fletcher RC .25 .08
❑ 273 Lance Blankenship .15 .05
❑ 274 Marty Neff RC .25 .08
❑ 275 Shawn Estes .15 .05
❑ 276 Rene Arocha RC .50 .20
❑ 277 Scott Eyre RC .25 .08
❑ 278 Phil Plantier .15 .05
❑ 279 Paul Spoljaric RC .25 .08
❑ 280 Chris Gambs .15 .05
❑ 281 Harold Baines .30 .10
❑ 282 Jose Oliva .15 .05
❑ 283 Matt Whiteside RC .25 .08
❑ 284 Brant Brown RC .50 .20
❑ 285 Russ Springer .15 .05
❑ 286 Chris Sabo .15 .05
❑ 287 Ozzie Guillen .30 .10
❑ 288 Marcus Moore RC .25 .08
❑ 289 Chad Ogea .15 .05
❑ 290 Walt Weiss .15 .05
❑ 291 Brian Edmondson .15 .05
❑ 292 Jimmy Gonzalez .15 .05
❑ 293 Danny Miceli RC .50 .20
❑ 294 Jose Offerman .15 .05
❑ 295 Greg Vaughn .15 .05
❑ 296 Frank Bolick .15 .05
❑ 297 Mike Maksudian RC .25 .08
❑ 298 John Franco .30 .10
❑ 299 Danny Tartabull .15 .05
❑ 300 Len Dykstra .30 .10
❑ 301 Bobby Witt .15 .05
❑ 302 Trey Beamon RC .25 .08
❑ 303 Tino Martinez .50 .20
❑ 304 Aaron Holbert .15 .05
❑ 305 Juan Gonzalez .30 .10
❑ 306 Billy Hall RC .25 .08
❑ 307 Duane Ward .15 .05
❑ 308 Rod Beck .15 .05
❑ 309 Jose Mercedes RC .25 .08
❑ 310 Otis Nixon .15 .05
❑ 311 Gettys Glaze RC .25 .08
❑ 312 Candy Maldonado .15 .05
❑ 313 Chad Curtis .15 .05
❑ 314 Tim Costo .15 .05
❑ 315 Mike Robertson .15 .05
❑ 316 Nigel Wilson .15 .05
❑ 317 Greg McMichael RC .50 .20
❑ 318 Scott Pose RC .25 .08
❑ 319 Ivan Cruz .15 .05
❑ 320 Greg Swindell .15 .05
❑ 321 Kevin McReynolds .15 .05
❑ 322 Tom Candiotti .15 .05
❑ 323 Rob Wishnevski RC .25 .08
❑ 324 Ken Hill .15 .05
❑ 325 Kirby Puckett .75 .30
❑ 326 Tim Bogar RC .25 .08
❑ 327 Mariano Rivera 2.50 1.00
❑ 328 Mitch Williams .15 .05
❑ 329 Craig Paquette .15 .05
❑ 330 Jay Bell .30 .10
❑ 331 Jose Martinez RC .25 .08
❑ 332 Rob Deer .15 .05
❑ 333 Brook Fordyce .15 .05
❑ 334 Matt Nokes .15 .05
❑ 335 Derek Lee .15 .05
❑ 336 Paul Ellis RC .25 .08
❑ 337 Desi Wilson RC .25 .08
❑ 338 Roberto Alomar .50 .20
❑ 339 Jim Tatum FOIL RC .25 .08
❑ 340 J.T.Snow FOIL 1.00 .40
❑ 341 Tim Salmon FOIL .50 .20
❑ 342 Russ Davis FOIL RC .50 .20
❑ 343 Javy Lopez FOIL .50 .20
❑ 344 Troy O'Leary FOIL RC .50 .20
❑ 345 Marty Cordova FOIL RC .50 .20
❑ 346 Bubba Smith RC FOIL .25 .08
❑ 347 Chipper Jones FOIL .75 .30
❑ 348 Jessie Hollins FOIL .15 .05
❑ 349 Willie Greene FOIL .15 .05
❑ 350 Mark Thompson FOIL .15 .05
❑ 351 Nigel Wilson FOIL .15 .05
❑ 352 Todd Jones FOIL .30 .10
❑ 353 Raul Mondesi FOIL .30 .10
❑ 354 Cliff Floyd FOIL .30 .10
❑ 355 Bobby Jones FOIL .30 .10
❑ 356 Kevin Stocker FOIL .15 .05
❑ 357 Midre Cummings FOIL .15 .05
❑ 358 Allen Watson FOIL .15 .05
❑ 359 Ray McDavid FOIL .15 .05
❑ 360 Steve Hosey FOIL .15 .05
❑ 361 Brad Pennington FOIL .15 .05
❑ 362 Frankie Rodriguez FOIL .15 .05
❑ 363 Troy Percival FOIL .50 .20
❑ 364 Jason Bere FOIL .15 .05
❑ 365 Manny Ramirez FOIL 1.25 .50
❑ 366 Justin Thompson FOIL .15 .05
❑ 367 Joe Vitiello FOIL .15 .05
❑ 368 Tyrone Hill FOIL .15 .05
❑ 369 David McCarty FOIL .15 .05
❑ 370 Brien Taylor FOIL .15 .05
❑ 371 Todd Van Poppel FOIL .15 .05
❑ 372 Marc Newfield FOIL .15 .05
❑ 373 Terrell Lowery FOIL RC .50 .20
❑ 374 Alex Gonzalez FOIL .15 .05
❑ 375 Ken Griffey Jr. 1.25 .50
❑ 376 Donovan Osborne .15 .05
❑ 377 Ritchie Moody RC .25 .08
❑ 378 Shane Andrews .15 .05
❑ 379 Carlos Delgado .75 .30
❑ 380 Bill Swift .15 .05
❑ 381 Leo Gomez .15 .05
❑ 382 Ron Gant .30 .10
❑ 383 Scott Fletcher .15 .05
❑ 384 Matt Walbeck RC .50 .20
❑ 385 Chuck Finley .30 .10
❑ 386 Kevin Mitchell .15 .05
❑ 387 Wilson Alvarez UER .15 .05
❑ 388 John Burke RC .25 .08
❑ 389 Alan Embree .15 .05
❑ 390 Trevor Hoffman .75 .30
❑ 391 Alan Trammell .30 .10
❑ 392 Todd Jones .30 .10
❑ 393 Felix Jose .15 .05
❑ 394 Orel Hershiser .30 .10
❑ 395 Pat Listach .15 .05
❑ 396 Gabe White .15 .05
❑ 397 Dan Serafini RC .25 .08
❑ 398 Todd Hundley .15 .05

❑ 399 Wade Boggs .50 .20
❑ 400 Tyler Green .15 .05
❑ 401 Mike Bordick .15 .05
❑ 402 Scott Bullett .15 .05
❑ 403 LaGrande Russell RC .25 .08
❑ 404 Ray Lankford .30 .10
❑ 405 Nolan Ryan 3.00 1.25
❑ 406 Robbie Beckett .15 .05
❑ 407 Brent Bowers RC .25 .08
❑ 408 Adell Davenport RC .25 .08
❑ 409 Brady Anderson .30 .10
❑ 410 Tom Glavine .50 .20
❑ 411 Doug Hecker RC .25 .08
❑ 412 Jose Guzman .15 .05
❑ 413 Luis Polonia .15 .05
❑ 414 Brian Williams .15 .05
❑ 415 Bo Jackson .75 .30
❑ 416 Eric Young .15 .05
❑ 417 Kenny Lofton .30 .10
❑ 418 Orestes Destrade .15 .05
❑ 419 Tony Phillips .15 .05
❑ 420 Jeff Bagwell .50 .20
❑ 421 Mark Gardner .15 .05
❑ 422 Brett Butler .30 .10
❑ 423 Graeme Lloyd RC .50 .20
❑ 424 Delino DeShields .15 .05
❑ 425 Scott Erickson .15 .05
❑ 426 Jeff Kent .75 .30
❑ 427 Jimmy Key .30 .10
❑ 428 Mickey Morandini .15 .05
❑ 429 Marcos Armas RC .25 .08
❑ 430 Don Slaught .15 .05
❑ 431 Randy Johnson .75 .30
❑ 432 Omar Olivares .15 .05
❑ 433 Charlie Leibrandt .15 .05
❑ 434 Kurt Stillwell .15 .05
❑ 435 Scott Brow RC .25 .08
❑ 436 Robby Thompson .15 .05
❑ 437 Ben McDonald .15 .05
❑ 438 Deion Sanders .50 .20
❑ 439 Tony Pena .15 .05
❑ 440 Mark Grace .50 .20
❑ 441 Eduardo Perez .15 .05
❑ 442 Tim Pugh RC .25 .08
❑ 443 Scott Ruffcorn .15 .05
❑ 444 Jay Gainer RC .25 .08
❑ 445 Albert Belle .30 .10
❑ 446 Bret Barberie .15 .05
❑ 447 Justin Mashore .15 .05
❑ 448 Pete Harnisch .15 .05
❑ 449 Greg Gagne .15 .05
❑ 450 Eric Davis .30 .10
❑ 451 Dave Mlicki .15 .05
❑ 452 Moises Alou .30 .10
❑ 453 Rick Aguilera .15 .05
❑ 454 Eddie Murray .75 .30
❑ 455 Bob Wickman .15 .05
❑ 456 Wes Chamberlain .15 .05
❑ 457 Brent Gates .15 .05
❑ 458 Paul Wagner .15 .05
❑ 459 Mike Hampton .30 .10
❑ 460 Ozzie Smith 1.25 .50
❑ 461 Tom Henke .15 .05
❑ 462 Ricky Gutierrez .15 .05
❑ 463 Jack Morris .30 .10
❑ 464 Joel Chimelis .15 .05
❑ 465 Gregg Olson .15 .05
❑ 466 Javy Lopez .50 .20
❑ 467 Scott Cooper .15 .05
❑ 468 Willie Wilson .15 .05
❑ 469 Mark Langston .15 .05
❑ 470 Barry Larkin .50 .20
❑ 471 Rod Bolton .15 .05
❑ 472 Freddie Benavides .15 .05
❑ 473 Ken Ramos RC .25 .08
❑ 474 Chuck Carr .15 .05
❑ 475 Cecil Fielder .30 .10
❑ 476 Eddie Taubensee .15 .05
❑ 477 Chris Eddy RC .25 .08
❑ 478 Greg Hansell .15 .05
❑ 479 Kevin Reimer .15 .05
❑ 480 Dennis Martinez .30 .10
❑ 481 Chuck Knoblauch .30 .10
❑ 482 Mike Draper .15 .05
❑ 483 Spike Owen .15 .05
❑ 484 Terry Mulholland .15 .05
❑ 485 Dennis Eckersley .30 .10
❑ 486 Blas Minor .15 .05
❑ 487 Dave Fleming .15 .05
❑ 488 Dan Cholowsky .15 .05
❑ 489 Ivan Rodriguez .50 .20
❑ 490 Gary Sheffield .30 .10
❑ 491 Ed Sprague .15 .05
❑ 492 Steve Hosey .15 .05
❑ 493 Jimmy Haynes RC .50 .20
❑ 494 John Smoltz .50 .20
❑ 495 Andre Dawson .30 .10
❑ 496 Rey Sanchez .15 .05
❑ 497 Ty Van Burkleo .15 .05
❑ 498 Bobby Ayala RC .25 .08
❑ 499 Tim Raines .30 .10
❑ 500 Charlie Hayes .15 .05
❑ 501 Paul Sorrento .15 .05
❑ 502 Richie Lewis RC .25 .08
❑ 503 Jason Pfaff RC .25 .08
❑ 504 Ken Caminiti .30 .10
❑ 505 Mike Macfarlane .15 .05
❑ 506 Jody Reed .15 .05
❑ 507 Bobby Hughes RC .25 .08
❑ 508 Wil Cordero .15 .05
❑ 509 George Tsamis RC .25 .08
❑ 510 Bret Saberhagen .30 .10
❑ 511 Derek Jeter RC 25.00 10.00
❑ 512 Gene Schall .15 .05
❑ 513 Curtis Shaw .15 .05
❑ 514 Steve Cooke .15 .05
❑ 515 Edgar Martinez .50 .20
❑ 516 Mike Milchin .15 .05
❑ 517 Billy Ripken .15 .05
❑ 518 Andy Benes .15 .05
❑ 519 Juan de la Rosa RC .25 .08
❑ 520 John Burkett .15 .05
❑ 521 Alex Ochoa .15 .05
❑ 522 Tony Tarasco RC .50 .20
❑ 523 Luis Ortiz .15 .05
❑ 524 Rick Wilkins .15 .05
❑ 525 Chris Turner RC .25 .08
❑ 526 Rob Dibble .30 .10
❑ 527 Jack McDowell .15 .05
❑ 528 Daryl Boston .15 .05
❑ 529 Bill Wertz RC .25 .08
❑ 530 Charlie Hough .30 .10
❑ 531 Sean Bergman .15 .05
❑ 532 Doug Jones .15 .05
❑ 533 Jeff Montgomery .15 .05
❑ 534 Roger Cedeno RC .50 .20
❑ 535 Robin Yount 1.25 .50
❑ 536 Mo Vaughn .30 .10
❑ 537 Brian Harper .15 .05
❑ 538 Juan Castillo RC .15 .05
❑ 539 Steve Farr .15 .05
❑ 540 John Kruk .30 .10
❑ 541 Troy Neel .15 .05
❑ 542 Danny Clyburn RC .25 .08
❑ 543 Jim Converse RC .25 .08
❑ 544 Gregg Jefferies .15 .05
❑ 545 Jose Canseco .50 .20
❑ 546 Julio Bruno RC .25 .08
❑ 547 Rob Butler .15 .05
❑ 548 Royce Clayton .15 .05
❑ 549 Chris Hoiles .15 .05
❑ 550 Greg Maddux 1.25 .50
❑ 551 Joe Ciccarella RC .25 .08
❑ 552 Ozzie Timmons .15 .05
❑ 553 Chili Davis .30 .10
❑ 554 Brian Koelling .15 .05
❑ 555 Frank Thomas .75 .30
❑ 556 Vinny Castilla .75 .30
❑ 557 Reggie Jefferson .15 .05
❑ 558 Rob Natal .15 .05
❑ 559 Mike Henneman .15 .05
❑ 560 Craig Biggio .50 .20
❑ 561 Billy Brewer .15 .05
❑ 562 Dan Melendez .15 .05
❑ 563 Kenny Felder RC .25 .08
❑ 564 Miguel Batista RC 1.00 .40
❑ 565 Dave Winfield .30 .10
❑ 566 Al Shirley .15 .05
❑ 567 Robert Eenhoorn .15 .05
❑ 568 Mike Williams .15 .05
❑ 569 Tanyon Sturtze RC .50 .20
❑ 570 Tim Wakefield .75 .30
❑ 571 Greg Pirkl .15 .05
❑ 572 Sean Lowe RC .25 .08
❑ 573 Terry Burrows RC .25 .08
❑ 574 Kevin Higgins .15 .05
❑ 575 Joe Carter .30 .10
❑ 576 Kevin Rogers .15 .05
❑ 577 Manny Alexander .15 .05
❑ 578 David Justice .30 .10
❑ 579 Brian Conroy RC .25 .08
❑ 580 Jessie Hollins .15 .05
❑ 581 Ron Watson RC .25 .08
❑ 582 Bip Roberts .15 .05
❑ 583 Tom Urbani RC .25 .08
❑ 584 Jason Hutchins RC .25 .08
❑ 585 Carlos Baerga .15 .05
❑ 586 Jeff Mutis .15 .05
❑ 587 Justin Thompson .15 .05
❑ 588 Orlando Miller .15 .05
❑ 589 Brian McRae .15 .05
❑ 590 Ramon Martinez .15 .05
❑ 591 Dave Nilsson .15 .05
❑ 592 Jose Vidro RC 2.00 .75
❑ 593 Rich Becker .15 .05
❑ 594 Preston Wilson RC 1.50 .60
❑ 595 Don Mattingly 2.00 .75
❑ 596 Tony Longmire .15 .05
❑ 597 Kevin Seitzer .15 .05
❑ 598 Midre Cummings RC .25 .08
❑ 599 Omar Vizquel .50 .20
❑ 600 Lee Smith .30 .10
❑ 601 David Hulse RC .25 .08
❑ 602 Darrell Sherman RC .25 .08
❑ 603 Alex Gonzalez .15 .05
❑ 604 Geronimo Pena .15 .05
❑ 605 Mike Devereaux .15 .05
❑ 606 Sterling Hitchcock RC .50 .20
❑ 607 Mike Greenwell .15 .05
❑ 608 Steve Buechele .15 .05
❑ 609 Troy Percival .50 .20
❑ 610 Roberto Kelly .15 .05
❑ 611 James Baldwin RC .50 .20
❑ 612 Jerald Clark .15 .05
❑ 613 Albie Lopez RC .25 .08
❑ 614 Dave Magadan .15 .05
❑ 615 Mickey Tettleton .15 .05
❑ 616 Sean Runyan RC .25 .08
❑ 617 Bob Hamelin .15 .05
❑ 618 Raul Mondesi .30 .10
❑ 619 Tyrone Hill .15 .05
❑ 620 Darrin Fletcher .15 .05
❑ 621 Mike Trombley .15 .05
❑ 622 Jeromy Burnitz .30 .10
❑ 623 Bernie Williams .50 .20
❑ 624 Mike Farmer RC .25 .08
❑ 625 Rickey Henderson .75 .30
❑ 626 Carlos Garcia .15 .05
❑ 627 Jeff Darwin RC .25 .08
❑ 628 Todd Zeile .15 .05
❑ 629 Benji Gil .15 .05
❑ 630 Tony Gwynn 1.00 .40
❑ 631 Aaron Small RC 1.00 .40
❑ 632 Joe Rosselli RC .25 .08
❑ 633 Mike Mussina .50 .20
❑ 634 Ryan Klesko .30 .10
❑ 635 Roger Clemens 1.50 .60
❑ 636 Sammy Sosa .75 .30
❑ 637 Orlando Palmeiro RC .25 .08
❑ 638 Willie Greene .15 .05
❑ 639 George Bell .15 .05
❑ 640 Garvin Alston RC .25 .08
❑ 641 Pete Janicki RC .25 .08
❑ 642 Chris Sheff RC .25 .08
❑ 643 Felipe Lira RC .25 .08
❑ 644 Roberto Petagine .15 .05
❑ 645 Wally Joyner .30 .10
❑ 646 Mike Piazza 3.00 1.25
❑ 647 Jaime Navarro .15 .05
❑ 648 Jeff Hartsock .15 .05
❑ 649 David McCarty .15 .05
❑ 650 Bobby Jones .30 .10
❑ 651 Mark Hutton .15 .05
❑ 652 Kyle Abbott .15 .05
❑ 653 Steve Cox RC .25 .08
❑ 654 Jeff King .15 .05
❑ 655 Norm Charlton .15 .05
❑ 656 Mike Gulan RC .25 .08

657	Julio Franco	.30	.10
658	Cameron Cairncross RC	.25	.08
659	John Olerud	.30	.10
660	Salomon Torres	.15	.05
661	Brad Pennington	.15	.05
662	Melvin Nieves	.15	.05
663	Ivan Calderon	.15	.05
664	Turk Wendell	.15	.05
665	Chris Pritchett	.15	.05
666	Reggie Sanders	.30	.10
667	Robin Ventura	.30	.10
668	Joe Girardi	.15	.05
669	Manny Ramirez	1.25	.50
670	Jeff Conine	.30	.10
671	Greg Gohr	.15	.05
672	Andujar Cedeno	.15	.05
673	Les Norman RC	.25	.08
674	Mike James RC	.25	.08
675	Marshall Boze RC	.25	.08
676	B.J. Wallace	.15	.05
677	Kent Hrbek	.30	.10
678	Jack Voigt RC	.25	.08
679	Brien Taylor	.15	.05
680	Curt Schilling	.30	.10
681	Todd Van Poppel	.15	.05
682	Kevin Young	.30	.10
683	Tommy Adams	.15	.05
684	Bernard Gilkey	.15	.05
685	Kevin Brown	.30	.10
686	Fred McGriff	.50	.20
687	Pat Borders	.15	.05
688	Kirt Manwaring	.15	.05
689	Sid Bream	.15	.05
690	John Valentin	.15	.05
691	Steve Olsen RC	.25	.08
692	Roberto Mejia RC	.25	.08
693	Carlos Delgado FOIL	.75	.30
694	Steve Gibralter FOIL RC	.25	.08
695	Gary Mota FOIL RC	.25	.08
696	Jose Malave FOIL RC	.25	.08
697	Larry Sutton FOIL RC	.25	.08
698	Dan Frye FOIL RC	.25	.08
699	Tim Clark FOIL RC	.25	.08
700	Brian Hupp FOIL RC	.25	.08
701	Felipe/Moises Alou FOIL	.30	.10
702	Barry/Bobby Bonds FOIL	1.00	.40
703	Ken Griffey Jr./Sr. FOIL	.75	.30
704	Brian/Hal McRae FOIL	.15	.05
705	Checklist 1	.15	.05
706	Checklist 2	.15	.05
707	Checklist 3	.15	.05
708	Checklist 4	.15	.05

1994 Bowman

	COMPLETE SET (682)	60.00	30.00
1	Joe Carter	.40	.15
2	Marcus Moore	.25	.08
3	Doug Creek RC	.40	.15
4	Pedro Martinez	1.00	.40
5	Ken Griffey Jr.	1.50	.60
6	Greg Swindell	.25	.08
7	J.J. Johnson	.25	.08
8	Homer Bush RC	.40	.15
9	Arquimedez Pozo RC	.40	.15
10	Bryan Harvey	.25	.08
11	J.T. Snow	.40	.15
12	Alan Benes RC	1.00	.40
13	Chad Kreuter	.25	.08
14	Eric Karros	.40	.15
15	Frank Thomas	1.00	.40
16	Bret Saberhagen	.40	.15
17	Terrell Lowery	.25	.08
18	Rod Bolton	.25	.08
19	Harold Baines	.40	.15
20	Matt Walbeck	.25	.08
21	Tom Glavine	.60	.25
22	Todd Jones	.25	.08
23	Alberto Castillo RC	.40	.15
24	Ruben Sierra	.40	.15
25	Don Mattingly	2.50	1.00
26	Mike Morgan	.25	.08
27	Jim Musselwhite RC	.40	.15
28	Matt Brunson RC	.40	.15
29	Adam Meinershagen RC	.40	.15
30	Joe Girardi	.25	.08
31	Shane Halter	.25	.08
32	Jose Paniagua RC	1.00	.40
33	Paul Perkins RC	.40	.15
34	John Hudek RC	.40	.15
35	Frank Viola	.40	.15
36	David Lamb RC	.40	.15
37	Marshall Boze	.25	.08
38	Jorge Posada RC	8.00	3.00
39	Brian Anderson RC	1.00	.40
40	Mark Whiten	.25	.08
41	Sean Bergman	.25	.08
42	Jose Parra RC	.40	.15
43	Mike Robertson	.25	.08
44	Pete Walker RC	.40	.15
45	Juan Gonzalez	.40	.15
46	Cleveland Ladell RC	.40	.15
47	Mark Smith	.25	.08
48	Kevin Jarvis RC UER	.40	.15
49	Amaury Telemaco RC	.40	.15
50	Andy Van Slyke	.60	.25
51	Rikkert Faneyte RC	.40	.15
52	Curtis Shaw	.25	.08
53	Matt Drews RC	.40	.15
54	Wilson Alvarez	.25	.08
55	Manny Ramirez	1.00	.40
56	Bobby Munoz	.25	.08
57	Ed Sprague	.25	.08
58	Jamey Wright RC	1.00	.40
59	Jeff Montgomery	.25	.08
60	Kirk Rueter	.25	.08
61	Edgar Martinez	.60	.25
62	Luis Gonzalez	.40	.15
63	Tim Vanegmond RC	.40	.15
64	Bip Roberts	.25	.08
65	John Jaha	.25	.08
66	Chuck Carr	.25	.08
67	Chuck Finley	.40	.15
68	Aaron Holbert	.25	.08
69	Cecil Fielder	.40	.15
70	Tom Engle RC	.40	.15
71	Ron Karkovice	.25	.08
72	Joe Orsulak	.25	.08
73	Duff Brumley RC	.40	.15
74	Craig Clayton RC	.40	.15
75	Cal Ripken	3.00	1.25
76	Brad Fullmer RC	1.00	.40
77	Tony Tarasco	.25	.08
78	Terry Farrar RC	.40	.15
79	Matt Williams	.40	.15
80	Rickey Henderson	1.00	.40
81	Terry Mulholland	.25	.08
82	Sammy Sosa	1.00	.40
83	Paul Sorrento	.25	.08
84	Pete Incaviglia	.25	.08
85	Darren Hall RC	.40	.15
86	Scott Klingenbeck	.25	.08
87	Dario Perez RC	.40	.15
88	Ugueth Urbina	.25	.08
89	Dave Vanhof RC	.40	.15
90	Domingo Jean	.25	.08
91	Otis Nixon	.25	.08
92	Andres Berumen	.25	.08
93	Jose Valentin	.25	.08
94	Edgar Renteria RC	5.00	2.00
95	Chris Turner	.25	.08
96	Ray Lankford	.40	.15
97	Danny Bautista	.25	.08
98	Chan Ho Park RC	1.50	.60
99	Glenn DiSarcina RC	.40	.15
100	Butch Huskey	.25	.08
101	Ivan Rodriguez	.60	.25
102	Johnny Ruffin	.25	.08
103	Alex Ochoa	.25	.08
104	Torii Hunter RC	5.00	2.00
105	Ryan Klesko	.40	.15
106	Jay Bell	.40	.15
107	Kurt Peltzer RC	.40	.15
108	Miguel Jimenez	.25	.08
109	Russ Davis	.25	.08
110	Derek Wallace	.25	.08
111	Keith Lockhart RC	1.00	.40
112	Mike Lieberthal	.40	.15
113	Dave Stewart	.40	.15
114	Tom Schmidt	.25	.08
115	Brian McRae	.25	.08
116	Moises Alou	.40	.15
117	Dave Fleming	.25	.08
118	Jeff Bagwell	.60	.25
119	Luis Ortiz	.25	.08
120	Tony Gwynn	1.25	.50
121	Jaime Navarro	.25	.08
122	Benito Santiago	.40	.15
123	Darrell Whitmore	.25	.08
124	John Mabry RC	1.00	.40
125	Mickey Tettleton	.25	.08
126	Tom Candiotti	.25	.08
127	Tim Raines	.40	.15
128	Bobby Bonilla	.40	.15
129	John Dettmer	.25	.08
130	Hector Carrasco	.25	.08
131	Chris Hoiles	.25	.08
132	Rick Aguilera	.25	.08
133	David Justice	.40	.15
134	Esteban Loaiza RC	1.50	.60
135	Barry Bonds	2.50	1.00
136	Bob Welch	.25	.08
137	Mike Stanley	.25	.08
138	Roberto Hernandez	.25	.08
139	Sandy Alomar Jr.	.25	.08
140	Darren Daulton	.40	.15
141	Angel Martinez RC	.40	.15
142	Howard Johnson	.25	.08
143	Bob Hamelin	.25	.08
144	J.J.Thobe RC	.40	.15
145	Roger Salkeld	.25	.08
146	Orlando Miller	.25	.08
147	Dmitri Young	.40	.15
148	Tim Hyers RC	.40	.15
149	Mark Loretta RC	5.00	2.00
150	Chris Hammond	.25	.08
151	Joel Moore RC	.40	.15
152	Todd Zeile	.25	.08
153	Wil Cordero	.25	.08
154	Chris Smith	.25	.08
155	James Baldwin	.25	.08
156	Edgardo Alfonzo RC	1.00	.40
157	Kym Ashworth RC	.40	.15
158	Paul Bako RC	.40	.15
159	Rick Krivda RC	.40	.15
160	Pat Mahomes	.25	.08
161	Damon Hollins	.25	.08
162	Felix Martinez RC	.40	.15
163	Jason Myers RC	.40	.15
164	Izzy Molina RC	.40	.15
165	Brien Taylor	.25	.08
166	Kevin Orie RC	.40	.15
167	Casey Whitten RC	.40	.15
168	Tony Longmire	.25	.08
169	John Olerud	.40	.15
170	Mark Thompson	.25	.08
171	Jorge Fabregas	.25	.08
172	John Wetteland	.40	.15
173	Dan Wilson	.25	.08
174	Doug Drabek	.25	.08
175	Jeff McNeely	.25	.08
176	Melvin Nieves	.25	.08
177	Doug Glanville RC	1.00	.40
178	Javier De La Hoya RC	.40	.15
179	Chad Curtis	.25	.08
180	Brian Barber	.25	.08
181	Mike Henneman	.25	.08
182	Jose Offerman	.25	.08
183	Robert Ellis RC	.40	.15
184	John Franco	.40	.15
185	Benji Gil	.25	.08

❑ 186	Hal Morris	.25	.08
❑ 187	Chris Sabo	.25	.08
❑ 188	Blaise Ilsley RC	.40	.15
❑ 189	Steve Avery	.25	.08
❑ 190	Rick White RC	.40	.15
❑ 191	Rod Beck	.25	.08
❑ 192	Mark McGwire UER NNO	2.50	1.00
❑ 193	Jim Abbott	.60	.25
❑ 194	Randy Myers	.25	.08
❑ 195	Kenny Lofton	.40	.15
❑ 196	Mariano Duncan	.25	.08
❑ 197	Lee Daniels RC	.40	.15
❑ 198	Armando Reynoso	.25	.08
❑ 199	Joe Randa	.40	.15
❑ 200	Cliff Floyd	.40	.15
❑ 201	Tim Harkrider RC	.40	.15
❑ 202	Kevin Gallaher RC	.40	.15
❑ 203	Scott Cooper	.25	.08
❑ 204	Phil Stidham RC	.40	.15
❑ 205	Jeff D'Amico RC	.40	.15
❑ 206	Matt Whisenant	.25	.08
❑ 207	De Shawn Warren	.25	.08
❑ 208	Rene Arocha	.25	.08
❑ 209	Tony Clark RC	1.50	.60
❑ 210	Jason Jacome RC	.40	.15
❑ 211	Scott Christman RC	.40	.15
❑ 212	Bill Pulsipher	.40	.15
❑ 213	Dean Palmer	.40	.15
❑ 214	Chad Mottola	.25	.08
❑ 215	Manny Alexander	.25	.08
❑ 216	Rich Becker	.25	.08
❑ 217	Andre King RC	.40	.15
❑ 218	Carlos Garcia	.25	.08
❑ 219	Ron Pezzoni RC	.40	.15
❑ 220	Steve Karsay	.25	.08
❑ 221	Jose Musset RC	.40	.15
❑ 222	Karl Rhodes	.25	.08
❑ 223	Frank Cimorelli RC	.40	.15
❑ 224	Kevin Jordan RC	.40	.15
❑ 225	Duane Ward	.25	.08
❑ 226	John Burke	.25	.08
❑ 227	Mike Macfarlane	.25	.08
❑ 228	Mike Lansing	.25	.08
❑ 229	Chuck Knoblauch	.40	.15
❑ 230	Ken Caminiti	.40	.15
❑ 231	Gar Finnvold RC	.40	.15
❑ 232	Derrek Lee RC	8.00	3.00
❑ 233	Brady Anderson	.40	.15
❑ 234	Vic Darensbourg RC	.40	.15
❑ 235	Mark Langston	.25	.08
❑ 236	T.J.Mathews RC	.40	.15
❑ 237	Lou Whitaker	.40	.15
❑ 238	Roger Cedeno	.25	.08
❑ 239	Alex Fernandez	.25	.08
❑ 240	Ryan Thompson	.25	.08
❑ 241	Kerry Lacy RC	.40	.15
❑ 242	Reggie Sanders	.40	.15
❑ 243	Brad Pennington	.25	.08
❑ 244	Bryan Eversgerd RC	.40	.15
❑ 245	Greg Maddux	1.50	.60
❑ 246	Jason Kendall	.40	.15
❑ 247	J.R. Phillips	.25	.08
❑ 248	Bobby Witt	.25	.08
❑ 249	Paul O'Neill	.60	.25
❑ 250	Ryne Sandberg	1.50	.60
❑ 251	Charles Nagy	.25	.08
❑ 252	Kevin Stocker	.25	.08
❑ 253	Shawn Green	1.00	.40
❑ 254	Charlie Hayes	.25	.08
❑ 255	Donnie Elliott	.25	.08
❑ 256	Rob Fitzpatrick RC	.40	.15
❑ 257	Tim Davis	.25	.08
❑ 258	James Mouton	.25	.08
❑ 259	Mike Greenwell	.25	.08
❑ 260	Ray McDavid	.25	.08
❑ 261	Mike Kelly	.25	.08
❑ 262	Andy Larkin RC	.40	.15
❑ 263	Marquis Riley UER	.25	.08
❑ 264	Bob Tewksbury	.25	.08
❑ 265	Brian Edmondson	.25	.08
❑ 266	Eduardo Lantigua RC	.40	.15
❑ 267	Brandon Wilson	.25	.08
❑ 268	Mike Welch	.25	.08
❑ 269	Tom Henke	.25	.08
❑ 270	Pokey Reese	.25	.08
❑ 271	Gregg Zaun RC	1.00	.40
❑ 272	Todd Ritchie	.25	.08
❑ 273	Javier Lopez	.40	.15
❑ 274	Kevin Young	.25	.08
❑ 275	Kirt Manwaring	.25	.08
❑ 276	Bill Taylor RC	.40	.15
❑ 277	Robert Eenhoorn	.25	.08
❑ 278	Jessie Hollins	.25	.08
❑ 279	Julian Tavarez RC	1.00	.40
❑ 280	Gene Schall	.25	.08
❑ 281	Paul Molitor	.40	.15
❑ 282	Neifi Perez RC	1.00	.40
❑ 283	Greg Gagne	.25	.08
❑ 284	Marquis Grissom	.40	.15
❑ 285	Randy Johnson	1.00	.40
❑ 286	Pete Harnisch	.25	.08
❑ 287	Joel Bennett RC	.40	.15
❑ 288	Derek Bell	.25	.08
❑ 289	Darryl Hamilton	.25	.08
❑ 290	Gary Sheffield	.40	.15
❑ 291	Eduardo Perez	.25	.08
❑ 292	Basil Shabazz	.25	.08
❑ 293	Eric Davis	.40	.15
❑ 294	Pedro Astacio	.25	.08
❑ 295	Robin Ventura	.40	.15
❑ 296	Jeff Kent	.60	.25
❑ 297	Rick Helling	.25	.08
❑ 298	Joe Oliver	.25	.08
❑ 299	Lee Smith	.40	.15
❑ 300	Dave Winfield	.40	.15
❑ 301	Deion Sanders	.60	.25
❑ 302	Ravelo Manzanillo RC	.40	.15
❑ 303	Mark Portugal	.25	.08
❑ 304	Brent Gates	.25	.08
❑ 305	Wade Boggs	.60	.25
❑ 306	Rick Wilkins	.25	.08
❑ 307	Carlos Baerga	.25	.08
❑ 308	Curt Schilling	.40	.15
❑ 309	Shannon Stewart	1.00	.40
❑ 310	Darren Holmes	.25	.08
❑ 311	Robert Toth RC	.40	.15
❑ 312	Gabe White	.25	.08
❑ 313	Mac Suzuki RC	1.00	.40
❑ 314	Alvin Morman RC	.40	.15
❑ 315	Mo Vaughn	.40	.15
❑ 316	Bryce Florie RC	.40	.15
❑ 317	Gabby Martinez RC	.40	.15
❑ 318	Carl Everett	.40	.15
❑ 319	Kerwin Moore	.25	.08
❑ 320	Tom Pagnozzi	.25	.08
❑ 321	Chris Gomez	.25	.08
❑ 322	Todd Williams	.25	.08
❑ 323	Pat Hentgen	.25	.08
❑ 324	Kirk Presley RC	.40	.15
❑ 325	Kevin Brown	.40	.15
❑ 326	Jason Isringhausen RC	3.00	1.25
❑ 327	Rick Forney RC	.40	.15
❑ 328	Carlos Pulido RC	.40	.15
❑ 329	Terrell Wade RC	.40	.15
❑ 330	Al Martin	.25	.08
❑ 331	Dan Carlson RC	.40	.15
❑ 332	Mark Acre RC	.40	.15
❑ 333	Sterling Hitchcock	.25	.08
❑ 334	Jon Ratliff RC	.40	.15
❑ 335	Alex Ramirez RC	.40	.15
❑ 336	Phil Geisler RC	.25	.08
❑ 337	Eddie Zambrano FOIL RC	.40	.15
❑ 338	Jim Thome FOIL	.60	.25
❑ 339	James Mouton FOIL	.25	.08
❑ 340	Cliff Floyd FOIL	.40	.15
❑ 341	Carlos Delgado FOIL	.60	.25
❑ 342	Roberto Petagine FOIL	.25	.08
❑ 343	Tim Clark FOIL	.25	.08
❑ 344	Bubba Smith FOIL	.25	.08
❑ 345	Randy Curtis FOIL RC	.40	.15
❑ 346	Joe Biasucci FOIL RC	.40	.15
❑ 347	D.J. Boston FOIL RC	.40	.15
❑ 348	Ruben Rivera FOIL RC	.40	.15
❑ 349	Bryan Link FOIL RC	.40	.15
❑ 350	Mike Bell FOIL RC	.40	.15
❑ 351	Marty Watson FOIL RC	.40	.15
❑ 352	Jason Myers FOIL	.25	.08
❑ 353	Chipper Jones FOIL	1.00	.40
❑ 354	Brooks Kieschnick FOIL	.40	.15
❑ 355	Pokey Reese FOIL	.25	.08
❑ 356	John Burke FOIL	.25	.08
❑ 357	Kurt Miller FOIL	.25	.08
❑ 358	Orlando Miller FOIL	.25	.08
❑ 359	Todd Hollandsworth FOIL	.25	.08
❑ 360	Rondell White FOIL	.40	.15
❑ 361	Bill Pulsipher FOIL	.40	.15
❑ 362	Tyler Green FOIL	.25	.08
❑ 363	Midre Cummings FOIL	.25	.08
❑ 364	Brian Barber FOIL	.25	.08
❑ 365	Melvin Nieves FOIL	.25	.08
❑ 366	Salomon Torres FOIL	.25	.08
❑ 367	Alex Ochoa FOIL	.25	.08
❑ 368	Frankie Rodriguez FOIL	.25	.08
❑ 369	Brian Anderson FOIL	.40	.15
❑ 370	James Baldwin FOIL	.25	.08
❑ 371	Manny Ramirez FOIL	1.00	.40
❑ 372	Justin Thompson FOIL	.25	.08
❑ 373	Johnny Damon FOIL	.60	.25
❑ 374	Jeff D'Amico FOIL	.40	.15
❑ 375	Rich Becker FOIL	.25	.08
❑ 376	Derek Jeter FOIL	3.00	1.25
❑ 377	Steve Karsay FOIL	.25	.08
❑ 378	Mac Suzuki FOIL	.40	.15
❑ 379	Benji Gil FOIL	.25	.08
❑ 380	Alex Gonzalez FOIL	.25	.08
❑ 381	Jason Bere FOIL	.25	.08
❑ 382	Brett Butler FOIL	.40	.15
❑ 383	Jeff Conine FOIL	.40	.15
❑ 384	Darren Daulton FOIL	.40	.15
❑ 385	Jeff Kent FOIL	.60	.25
❑ 386	Don Mattingly FOIL	2.50	1.00
❑ 387	Mike Piazza FOIL	2.00	.75
❑ 388	Ryne Sandberg FOIL	1.50	.60
❑ 389	Rich Amaral	.25	.08
❑ 390	Craig Biggio	.60	.25
❑ 391	Jeff Suppan RC	2.00	.75
❑ 392	Andy Benes	.25	.08
❑ 393	Cal Eldred	.25	.08
❑ 394	Jeff Conine	.40	.15
❑ 395	Tim Salmon	.60	.25
❑ 396	Ray Suplee RC	.40	.15
❑ 397	Tony Phillips	.25	.08
❑ 398	Ramon Martinez	.25	.08
❑ 399	Julio Franco	.40	.15
❑ 400	Dwight Gooden	.40	.15
❑ 401	Kevin Loman RC	.40	.15
❑ 402	Jose Rijo	.25	.08
❑ 403	Mike Devereaux	.25	.08
❑ 404	Mike Zolecki RC	.40	.15
❑ 405	Fred McGriff	.60	.25
❑ 406	Danny Clyburn	.25	.08
❑ 407	Robby Thompson	.25	.08
❑ 408	Terry Steinbach	.25	.08
❑ 409	Luis Polonia	.25	.08
❑ 410	Mark Grace	.60	.25
❑ 411	Albert Belle	.40	.15
❑ 412	John Kruk	.40	.15
❑ 413	Scott Spiezio RC	1.00	.40
❑ 414	Ellis Burks UER	.40	.15
❑ 415	Joe Vitiello	.25	.08
❑ 416	Tim Costo	.25	.08
❑ 417	Marc Newfield	.25	.08
❑ 418	Oscar Henriquez RC	.40	.15
❑ 419	Matt Perisho RC	.40	.15
❑ 420	Julio Bruno	.25	.08
❑ 421	Kenny Felder	.25	.08
❑ 422	Tyler Green	.25	.08
❑ 423	Jim Edmonds	1.00	.40
❑ 424	Ozzie Smith	1.50	.60
❑ 425	Rick Greene	.25	.08
❑ 426	Todd Hollandsworth	.25	.08
❑ 427	Eddie Pearson RC	.40	.15
❑ 428	Quilvio Veras	.25	.08
❑ 429	Kenny Rogers	.40	.15
❑ 430	Willie Greene	.25	.08
❑ 431	Vaughn Eshelman	.25	.08
❑ 432	Pat Meares	.25	.08
❑ 433	Jermaine Dye RC	6.00	2.50
❑ 434	Steve Cooke	.25	.08
❑ 435	Bill Swift	.25	.08
❑ 436	Fausto Cruz RC	.40	.15
❑ 437	Mark Hutton	.25	.08
❑ 438	Brooks Kieschnick RC	.40	.15
❑ 439	Yorkis Perez	.25	.08
❑ 440	Len Dykstra	.40	.15
❑ 441	Pat Borders	.25	.08
❑ 442	Doug Walls RC	.40	.15
❑ 443	Wally Joyner	.40	.15

❑ 444	Ken Hill	.25	.08
❑ 445	Eric Anthony	.25	.08
❑ 446	Mitch Williams	.25	.08
❑ 447	Cory Bailey RC	.40	.15
❑ 448	Dave Staton	.25	.08
❑ 449	Greg Vaughn	.25	.08
❑ 450	Dave Magadan	.25	.08
❑ 451	Chili Davis	.40	.15
❑ 452	Gerald Santos RC	.40	.15
❑ 453	Joe Perona	.25	.08
❑ 454	Delino DeShields	.25	.08
❑ 455	Jack McDowell	.25	.08
❑ 456	Todd Hundley	.25	.08
❑ 457	Ritchie Moody	.25	.08
❑ 458	Bret Boone	.40	.15
❑ 459	Ben McDonald	.25	.08
❑ 460	Kirby Puckett	1.00	.40
❑ 461	Gregg Olson	.25	.08
❑ 462	Rich Aude RC	.40	.15
❑ 463	John Burkett	.25	.08
❑ 464	Troy Neel	.25	.08
❑ 465	Jimmy Key	.40	.15
❑ 466	Ozzie Timmons	.25	.08
❑ 467	Eddie Murray	1.00	.40
❑ 468	Mark Tranberg RC	.40	.15
❑ 469	Alex Gonzalez	.25	.08
❑ 470	David Nied	.25	.08
❑ 471	Barry Larkin	.60	.25
❑ 472	Brian Looney RC	.40	.15
❑ 473	Shawn Estes	.25	.08
❑ 474	A.J.Sager RC	.40	.15
❑ 475	Roger Clemens	2.00	.75
❑ 476	Vince Moore	.25	.08
❑ 477	Scott Karl RC	.40	.15
❑ 478	Kurt Miller	.25	.08
❑ 479	Garret Anderson	1.00	.40
❑ 480	Allen Watson	.25	.08
❑ 481	Jose Lima RC	1.00	.40
❑ 482	Rick Gorecki	.25	.08
❑ 483	Jimmy Hurst RC	.40	.15
❑ 484	Preston Wilson	.40	.15
❑ 485	Will Clark	.60	.25
❑ 486	Mike Ferry RC	.40	.15
❑ 487	Curtis Goodwin RC	.40	.15
❑ 488	Mike Myers	.25	.08
❑ 489	Chipper Jones	1.00	.40
❑ 490	Jeff King	.25	.08
❑ 491	W.VanLandingham RC	.40	.15
❑ 492	Carlos Reyes RC	.40	.15
❑ 493	Andy Pettitte	1.00	.40
❑ 494	Brant Brown	.25	.08
❑ 495	Daron Kirkreit	.25	.08
❑ 496	Ricky Bottalico RC	.40	.15
❑ 497	Devon White	.40	.15
❑ 498	Jason Johnson RC	1.00	.40
❑ 499	Vince Coleman	.25	.08
❑ 500	Larry Walker	.40	.15
❑ 501	Bobby Ayala	.25	.08
❑ 502	Steve Finley	.40	.15
❑ 503	Scott Fletcher	.25	.08
❑ 504	Brad Ausmus	.60	.25
❑ 505	Scott Talanoa RC	.40	.15
❑ 506	Orestes Destrade	.25	.08
❑ 507	Gary DiSarcina	.25	.08
❑ 508	Willie Smith RC	.40	.15
❑ 509	Alan Trammell	.40	.15
❑ 510	Mike Piazza	2.00	.75
❑ 511	Ozzie Guillen	.40	.15
❑ 512	Jeromy Burnitz	.40	.15
❑ 513	Darren Oliver RC	1.00	.40
❑ 514	Kevin Mitchell	.25	.08
❑ 515	Rafael Palmeiro	.60	.25
❑ 516	David McCarty	.25	.08
❑ 517	Jeff Blauser	.25	.08
❑ 518	Trey Beamon	.25	.08
❑ 519	Royce Clayton	.25	.08
❑ 520	Dennis Eckersley	.40	.15
❑ 521	Bernie Williams	.60	.25
❑ 522	Steve Buechele	.25	.08
❑ 523	Dennis Martinez	.40	.15
❑ 524	Dave Hollins	.25	.08
❑ 525	Joey Hamilton	.25	.08
❑ 526	Andres Galarraga	.40	.15
❑ 527	Jeff Granger	.25	.08
❑ 528	Joey Eischen	.25	.08
❑ 529	Desi Relaford	.25	.08
❑ 530	Roberto Petagine	.25	.08
❑ 531	Andre Dawson	.40	.15
❑ 532	Ray Holbert	.25	.08
❑ 533	Duane Singleton	.25	.08
❑ 534	Kurt Abbott RC	.40	.15
❑ 535	Bo Jackson	1.00	.40
❑ 536	Gregg Jefferies	.25	.08
❑ 537	David Mysel	.25	.08
❑ 538	Raul Mondesi	.40	.15
❑ 539	Chris Snopek	.25	.08
❑ 540	Brook Fordyce	.25	.08
❑ 541	Ron Frazier RC	.40	.15
❑ 542	Brian Koelling	.25	.08
❑ 543	Jimmy Haynes	.25	.08
❑ 544	Marty Cordova	.25	.08
❑ 545	Jason Green RC	.40	.15
❑ 546	Orlando Merced	.25	.08
❑ 547	Lou Pote RC	.40	.15
❑ 548	Todd Van Poppel	.25	.08
❑ 549	Pat Kelly	.25	.08
❑ 550	Turk Wendell	.25	.08
❑ 551	Herbert Perry RC	.40	.15
❑ 552	Ryan Karp RC	.40	.15
❑ 553	Juan Guzman	.25	.08
❑ 554	Bryan Rekar RC	.40	.15
❑ 555	Kevin Appier	.40	.15
❑ 556	Chris Schwab RC	.40	.15
❑ 557	Jay Buhner	.40	.15
❑ 558	Andujar Cedeno	.25	.08
❑ 559	Ryan McGuire RC	.40	.15
❑ 560	Ricky Gutierrez	.25	.08
❑ 561	Keith Kimsey RC	.40	.15
❑ 562	Tim Clark	.25	.08
❑ 563	Damion Easley	.25	.08
❑ 564	Clint Davis RC	.40	.15
❑ 565	Mike Moore	.25	.08
❑ 566	Orel Hershiser	.40	.15
❑ 567	Jason Bere	.25	.08
❑ 568	Kevin McReynolds	.25	.08
❑ 569	Leland Macon RC	.40	.15
❑ 570	John Courtright RC	.40	.15
❑ 571	Sid Fernandez	.25	.08
❑ 572	Chad Roper	.25	.08
❑ 573	Terry Pendleton	.40	.15
❑ 574	Danny Miceli	.25	.08
❑ 575	Joe Rosselli	.25	.08
❑ 576	Mike Bordick	.25	.08
❑ 577	Danny Tartabull	.25	.08
❑ 578	Jose Guzman	.25	.08
❑ 579	Omar Vizquel	.60	.25
❑ 580	Tommy Greene	.25	.08
❑ 581	Paul Spoljaric	.25	.08
❑ 582	Walt Weiss	.25	.08
❑ 583	Oscar Jimenez RC	.40	.15
❑ 584	Rod Henderson	.25	.08
❑ 585	Derek Lowe	.40	.15
❑ 586	Richard Hidalgo RC	1.00	.40
❑ 587	Shayne Bennett RC	.40	.15
❑ 588	Tim Belk RC	.40	.15
❑ 589	Matt Mieske	.25	.08
❑ 590	Nigel Wilson	.25	.08
❑ 591	Jeff Knox RC	.40	.15
❑ 592	Bernard Gilkey	.25	.08
❑ 593	David Cone	.40	.15
❑ 594	Paul LoDuca RC	5.00	2.00
❑ 595	Scott Ruffcorn	.25	.08
❑ 596	Chris Roberts	.25	.08
❑ 597	Oscar Munoz RC	.40	.15
❑ 598	Scott Sullivan RC	.40	.15
❑ 599	Matt Jarvis RC	.40	.15
❑ 600	Jose Canseco	.60	.25
❑ 601	Tony Graffanino RC	1.50	.60
❑ 602	Don Slaught	.25	.08
❑ 603	Brett King RC	.40	.15
❑ 604	Jose Herrera RC	.40	.15
❑ 605	Melido Perez	.25	.08
❑ 606	Mike Hubbard RC	.40	.15
❑ 607	Chad Ogea	.25	.08
❑ 608	Wayne Gomes RC	1.00	.40
❑ 609	Roberto Alomar	.60	.25
❑ 610	Angel Echevarria RC	.40	.15
❑ 611	Jose Lind	.25	.08
❑ 612	Darrin Fletcher	.25	.08
❑ 613	Chris Bosio	.25	.08
❑ 614	Darryl Kile	.40	.15
❑ 615	Frankie Rodriguez	.25	.08
❑ 616	Phil Plantier	.25	.08
❑ 617	Pat Listach	.25	.08
❑ 618	Charlie Hough	.40	.15
❑ 619	Ryan Hancock RC	.40	.15
❑ 620	Darrel Deak RC	.40	.15
❑ 621	Travis Fryman	.40	.15
❑ 622	Brett Butler	.40	.15
❑ 623	Lance Johnson	.25	.08
❑ 624	Pete Smith	.25	.08
❑ 625	James Hurst RC	.40	.15
❑ 626	Roberto Kelly	.25	.08
❑ 627	Mike Mussina	.60	.25
❑ 628	Kevin Tapani	.25	.08
❑ 629	John Smoltz	.60	.25
❑ 630	Midre Cummings	.25	.08
❑ 631	Salomon Torres	.25	.08
❑ 632	Willie Adams	.25	.08
❑ 633	Derek Jeter	3.00	1.25
❑ 634	Steve Trachsel	.25	.08
❑ 635	Albie Lopez	.25	.08
❑ 636	Jason Moler	.25	.08
❑ 637	Carlos Delgado	.60	.25
❑ 638	Roberto Mejia	.25	.08
❑ 639	Darren Burton	.25	.08
❑ 640	B.J. Wallace	.25	.08
❑ 641	Brad Clontz RC	.40	.15
❑ 642	Billy Wagner RC	4.00	1.50
❑ 643	Aaron Sele	.25	.08
❑ 644	Cameron Cairncross	.25	.08
❑ 645	Brian Harper	.25	.08
❑ 646	Marc Valdes UER NNO	.25	.08
❑ 647	Mark Ratekin	.25	.08
❑ 648	Terry Bradshaw RC	.40	.15
❑ 649	Justin Thompson	.25	.08
❑ 650	Mike Busch RC	.40	.15
❑ 651	Joe Hall RC	.40	.15
❑ 652	Bobby Jones	.25	.08
❑ 653	Kelly Stinnett RC	1.00	.40
❑ 654	Rod Steph RC	.40	.15
❑ 655	Jay Powell RC	1.00	.40
❑ 656	Keith Garagozzo RC	.40	.15
❑ 657	Todd Dunn	.25	.08
❑ 658	Charles Peterson RC	.40	.15
❑ 659	Darren Lewis	.25	.08
❑ 660	John Wasdin RC	.40	.15
❑ 661	Tate Seefried RC	.40	.15
❑ 662	Hector Trinidad RC	.40	.15
❑ 663	John Carter RC	.25	.08
❑ 664	Larry Mitchell	.25	.08
❑ 665	David Catlett RC	.40	.15
❑ 666	Dante Bichette	.40	.15
❑ 667	Felix Jose	.25	.08
❑ 668	Rondell White	.40	.15
❑ 669	Tino Martinez	.60	.25
❑ 670	Brian L.Hunter	.25	.08
❑ 671	Jose Malave	.25	.08
❑ 672	Archi Cianfrocco	.25	.08
❑ 673	Mike Matheny RC	1.50	.60
❑ 674	Bret Barberie	.25	.08
❑ 675	Andrew Lorraine RC	.40	.15
❑ 676	Brian Jordan	.40	.15
❑ 677	Tim Belcher	.25	.08
❑ 678	Antonio Osuna RC	.40	.15
❑ 679	Checklist	.25	.08
❑ 680	Checklist	.25	.08
❑ 681	Checklist	.25	.08
❑ 682	Checklist	.25	.08

1995 Bowman

❑	COMPLETE SET (439)	150.00	90.00
❑ 1	Billy Wagner	.75	.30
❑ 2	Chris Widger	.25	.08
❑ 3	Brent Bowers	.25	.08
❑ 4	Bob Abreu RC	8.00	3.00
❑ 5	Lou Collier RC	1.00	.40
❑ 6	Juan Acevedo RC	.50	.20
❑ 7	Jason Kelley RC	.50	.20
❑ 8	Brian Sackinsky	.25	.08
❑ 9	Scott Christman	.25	.08
❑ 10	Damon Hollins	.25	.08
❑ 11	Willis Otanez RC	.50	.20
❑ 12	Jason Ryan RC	.50	.20
❑ 13	Jason Giambi	.75	.30
❑ 14	Andy Taulbee RC	.50	.20
❑ 15	Mark Thompson	.25	.08
❑ 16	Hugo Pivaral RC	.50	.20

❑	17	Brien Taylor	.25	.08
❑	18	Antonio Osuna	.25	.08
❑	19	Edgardo Alfonzo	.25	.08
❑	20	Carl Everett	.50	.20
❑	21	Matt Drews	.25	.08
❑	22	Bartolo Colon RC	4.00	1.50
❑	23	Andruw Jones RC	25.00	10.00
❑	24	Robert Person RC	1.00	.40
❑	25	Derrek Lee	1.25	.50
❑	26	John Ambrose RC	.50	.20
❑	27	Eric Knowles RC	.50	.20
❑	28	Chris Roberts	.25	.08
❑	29	Don Wengert	.25	.08
❑	30	Marcus Jensen RC	1.00	.40
❑	31	Brian Barber	.25	.08
❑	32	Kevin Brown C	.50	.20
❑	33	Benji Gil	.25	.08
❑	34	Mike Hubbard	.25	.08
❑	35	Bart Evans RC	.50	.20
❑	36	Enrique Wilson RC	.50	.20
❑	37	Brian Buchanan RC	.50	.20
❑	38	Ken Ray RC	.50	.20
❑	39	Micah Franklin RC	.50	.20
❑	40	Ricky Otero RC	.50	.20
❑	41	Jason Kendall	.50	.20
❑	42	Jimmy Hurst	.25	.08
❑	43	Jerry Wolak RC	.50	.20
❑	44	Jayson Peterson RC	.50	.20
❑	45	Allen Battle RC	.50	.20
❑	46	Scott Stahoviak	.25	.08
❑	47	Steve Schrenk RC	.50	.20
❑	48	Travis Miller RC	.50	.20
❑	49	Eddie Rios RC	.50	.20
❑	50	Mike Hampton	.50	.20
❑	51	Chad Frontera RC	.50	.20
❑	52	Tom Evans	.25	.08
❑	53	C.J. Nitkowski	.25	.08
❑	54	Clay Caruthers RC	.50	.20
❑	55	Shannon Stewart	.50	.20
❑	56	Jorge Posada	1.25	.50
❑	57	Aaron Holbert	.25	.08
❑	58	Harry Berrios RC	.50	.20
❑	59	Steve Rodriguez	.25	.08
❑	60	Shane Andrews	.25	.08
❑	61	Will Cunnane RC	.50	.20
❑	62	Richard Hidalgo	.25	.08
❑	63	Bill Selby RC	.50	.20
❑	64	Jay Cranford RC	.50	.20
❑	65	Jeff Suppan	.50	.20
❑	66	Curtis Goodwin	.25	.08
❑	67	John Thomson RC	1.00	.40
❑	68	Justin Thompson	.25	.08
❑	69	Troy Percival	.50	.20
❑	70	Matt Wagner RC	.50	.20
❑	71	Terry Bradshaw	.25	.08
❑	72	Greg Hansell	.25	.08
❑	73	John Burke	.25	.08
❑	74	Jeff D'Amico	.25	.08
❑	75	Ernie Young	.25	.08
❑	76	Jason Bates	.25	.08
❑	77	Chris Stynes	.25	.08
❑	78	Cade Gaspar RC	.50	.20
❑	79	Melvin Nieves	.25	.08
❑	80	Rick Gorecki	.25	.08
❑	81	Felix Rodriguez RC	.50	.20
❑	82	Ryan Hancock	.25	.08
❑	83	Chris Carpenter RC	8.00	3.00
❑	84	Ray McDavid	.25	.08
❑	85	Chris Wimmer	.25	.08
❑	86	Doug Glanville	.25	.08
❑	87	DeShawn Warren	.25	.08
❑	88	Damian Moss RC	.50	.20
❑	89	Rafael Orellano RC	.50	.20
❑	90	Vladimir Guerrero RC !	30.00	12.50
❑	91	Raul Casanova RC	.50	.20
❑	92	Karim Garcia RC	.50	.20
❑	93	Bryce Florie	.25	.08
❑	94	Kevin Orie	.25	.08
❑	95	Ryan Nye RC	.50	.20
❑	96	Matt Sachse RC	.50	.20
❑	97	Ivan Arteaga RC	.50	.20
❑	98	Glenn Murray	.25	.08
❑	99	Stacy Hollins RC	.50	.20
❑	100	Jim Pittsley	.25	.08
❑	101	Craig Mattson RC	.50	.20
❑	102	Neifi Perez	.25	.08
❑	103	Keith Williams	.25	.08
❑	104	Roger Cedeno	.25	.08
❑	105	Tony Terry RC	.50	.20
❑	106	Jose Malave	.25	.08
❑	107	Joe Rosselli	.25	.08
❑	108	Kevin Jordan	.25	.08
❑	109	Sid Roberson RC	.50	.20
❑	110	Alan Embree	.25	.08
❑	111	Terrell Wade	.25	.08
❑	112	Bob Wolcott	.25	.08
❑	113	Carlos Perez RC	1.00	.40
❑	114	Mike Bovee RC	.50	.20
❑	115	Tommy Davis RC	.50	.20
❑	116	Jeremey Kendall RC	.50	.20
❑	117	Rich Aude	.25	.08
❑	118	Rick Huisman	.25	.08
❑	119	Tim Belk	.25	.08
❑	120	Edgar Renteria	.50	.20
❑	121	Calvin Maduro RC	.50	.20
❑	122	Jerry Martin RC	.50	.20
❑	123	Ramon Fermin RC	.50	.20
❑	124	Kimera Bartee RC	.50	.20
❑	125	Mark Farris	.25	.08
❑	126	Frank Rodriguez	.25	.08
❑	127	Bob Higginson RC	2.00	.75
❑	128	Bret Wagner	.25	.08
❑	129	Edwin Diaz RC	.50	.20
❑	130	Jimmy Haynes	.25	.08
❑	131	Chris Weinke RC QB	1.00	.40
❑	132	Damian Jackson RC	.50	.20
❑	133	Felix Martinez	.25	.08
❑	134	Edwin Hurtado RC	.50	.20
❑	135	Matt Raleigh RC	.50	.20
❑	136	Paul Wilson	.25	.08
❑	137	Ron Villone	.25	.08
❑	138	Eric Stuckenschneider RC	.50	.20
❑	139	Tate Seefried	.25	.08
❑	140	Rey Ordonez RC	2.00	.75
❑	141	Eddie Pearson	.25	.08
❑	142	Kevin Gallaher	.25	.08
❑	143	Torii Hunter	.75	.30
❑	144	Daron Kirkreit	.25	.08
❑	145	Craig Wilson	.25	.08
❑	146	Ugueth Urbina	.25	.08
❑	147	Chris Snopek	.25	.08
❑	148	Kym Ashworth	.25	.08
❑	149	Wayne Gomes	.25	.08
❑	150	Mark Loretta	.50	.20
❑	151	Ramon Morel RC	.50	.20
❑	152	Trot Nixon	.50	.20
❑	153	Desi Relaford	.25	.08
❑	154	Scott Sullivan	.25	.08
❑	155	Marc Barcelo	.25	.08
❑	156	Willie Adams	.25	.08
❑	157	Derrick Gibson RC	.50	.20
❑	158	Brian Meadows RC	.50	.20
❑	159	Julian Tavarez	.25	.08
❑	160	Bryan Rekar	.25	.08
❑	161	Steve Gibralter	.25	.08
❑	162	Esteban Loaiza	.25	.08
❑	163	John Wasdin	.25	.08
❑	164	Kirk Presley	.25	.08
❑	165	Mariano Rivera	1.50	.60
❑	166	Andy Larkin	.25	.08
❑	167	Sean Whiteside RC	.50	.20
❑	168	Matt Apana RC	.50	.20
❑	169	Shawn Senior RC	.50	.20
❑	170	Scott Gentile	.25	.08
❑	171	Quilvio Veras	.25	.08
❑	172	Eli Marrero RC	1.50	.60
❑	173	Mendy Lopez RC	.50	.20
❑	174	Homer Bush	.25	.08
❑	175	Brian Stephenson RC	.50	.20
❑	176	Jon Nunnally	.25	.08
❑	177	Jose Herrera	.25	.08
❑	178	Corey Avrard RC	.50	.20
❑	179	David Bell	.25	.08
❑	180	Jason Isringhausen	.50	.20
❑	181	Jamey Wright	.25	.08
❑	182	Lonell Roberts RC	.25	.08
❑	183	Marty Cordova	.25	.08
❑	184	Amaury Telemaco	.25	.08
❑	185	John Mabry	.25	.08
❑	186	Andrew Vessel RC	.50	.20
❑	187	Jim Cole RC	.50	.20
❑	188	Marquis Riley	.25	.08
❑	189	Todd Dunn	.25	.08
❑	190	John Carter	.25	.08
❑	191	Donnie Sadler RC	1.00	.40
❑	192	Mike Bell	.25	.08
❑	193	Chris Cumberland RC	.50	.20
❑	194	Jason Schmidt	1.25	.50
❑	195	Matt Brunson	.25	.08
❑	196	James Baldwin	.25	.08
❑	197	Bill Simas RC	.50	.20
❑	198	Gus Gandarillas	.25	.08
❑	199	Mac Suzuki	.25	.08
❑	200	Rick Holifield RC	.50	.20
❑	201	Fernando Lunar RC	.50	.20
❑	202	Kevin Jarvis	.25	.08
❑	203	Everett Stull	.25	.08
❑	204	Steve Wojciechowski	.25	.08
❑	205	Shawn Estes	.25	.08
❑	206	Jermaine Dye	.50	.20
❑	207	Marc Kroon	.25	.08
❑	208	Peter Munro RC	1.00	.40
❑	209	Pat Watkins	.25	.08
❑	210	Matt Smith	.25	.08
❑	211	Joe Vitiello	.25	.08
❑	212	Gerald Witasick Jr.	.25	.08
❑	213	Freddy Adrian Garcia RC	.50	.20
❑	214	Glenn Dishman RC	.50	.20
❑	215	Jay Canizaro RC	.50	.20
❑	216	Angel Martinez	.25	.08
❑	217	Yamil Benitez RC	.50	.20
❑	218	Fausto Macey RC	.50	.20
❑	219	Eric Owens	.25	.08
❑	220	Checklist	.25	.08
❑	221	Dwayne Hosey FOIL RC	.50	.20
❑	222	Brad Woodall FOIL RC	.50	.20
❑	223	Billy Ashley FOIL	.25	.08
❑	224	Mark Grudzielanek FOIL RC	2.00	.75
❑	225	Mark Johnson FOIL RC	1.00	.40
❑	226	Tim Unroe FOIL RC	.50	.20
❑	227	Todd Greene FOIL	.25	.08
❑	228	Larry Sutton FOIL	.25	.08
❑	229	Derek Jeter FOIL	4.00	1.50
❑	230	Sal Fasano FOIL RC	.50	.20
❑	231	Ruben Rivera FOIL	.25	.08
❑	232	Chris Truby FOIL RC	.50	.20
❑	233	John Donati FOIL	.25	.08
❑	234	Decomba Conner FOIL RC	.50	.20
❑	235	Sergio Nunez FOIL RC	.50	.20
❑	236	Ray Brown FOIL RC	.50	.20
❑	237	Juan Melo FOIL RC	.50	.20
❑	238	Hideo Nomo FOIL RC	5.00	2.00
❑	239	Jaime Bluma RC FOIL	.50	.20
❑	240	Jay Payton FOIL RC	2.00	.75
❑	241	Paul Konerko FOIL	4.00	1.50
❑	242	Scott Elarton FOIL RC	1.00	.40
❑	243	Jeff Abbott FOIL RC	1.00	.40
❑	244	Jim Brower FOIL RC	.50	.20
❑	245	Geoff Blum FOIL RC	2.00	.75
❑	246	Aaron Boone FOIL RC	2.00	.75
❑	247	J.R. Phillips FOIL	.25	.08
❑	248	Alex Ochoa FOIL	.25	.08
❑	249	Nomar Garciaparra FOIL	4.00	1.50
❑	250	Garret Anderson FOIL	.50	.20
❑	251	Ray Durham FOIL	.50	.20
❑	252	Paul Shuey FOIL	.25	.08
❑	253	Tony Clark FOIL	.25	.08
❑	254	Johnny Damon FOIL	.75	.30
❑	255	Duane Singleton FOIL	.25	.08
❑	256	LaTroy Hawkins FOIL	.25	.08

❑ 257	Andy Pettitte FOIL	.75	.30
❑ 258	Ben Grieve FOIL	.25	.08
❑ 259	Marc Newfield FOIL	.25	.08
❑ 260	Terrell Lowery FOIL	.25	.08
❑ 261	Shawn Green FOIL	.50	.20
❑ 262	Chipper Jones FOIL	1.25	.50
❑ 263	Brooks Kieschnick FOIL	.25	.08
❑ 264	Pokey Reese FOIL	.25	.08
❑ 265	Doug Million FOIL	.25	.08
❑ 266	Marc Valdes FOIL	.25	.08
❑ 267	Brian L.Hunter FOIL	.25	.08
❑ 268	Todd Hollandsworth FOIL	.25	.08
❑ 269	Rod Henderson FOIL	.25	.08
❑ 270	Bill Pulsipher FOIL	.25	.08
❑ 271	Scott Rolen FOIL RC	12.00	5.00
❑ 272	Trey Beamon FOIL	.25	.08
❑ 273	Alan Benes FOIL	.25	.08
❑ 274	Dustin Hermanson FOIL	.25	.08
❑ 275	Ricky Bottalico	.25	.08
❑ 276	Albert Belle	.50	.20
❑ 277	Deion Sanders	.75	.30
❑ 278	Matt Williams	.50	.20
❑ 279	Jeff Bagwell	.75	.30
❑ 280	Kirby Puckett	1.25	.50
❑ 281	Dave Hollins	.25	.08
❑ 282	Don Mattingly	3.00	1.25
❑ 283	Joey Hamilton	.25	.08
❑ 284	Bobby Bonilla	.50	.20
❑ 285	Moises Alou	.50	.20
❑ 286	Tom Glavine	.75	.30
❑ 287	Brett Butler	.50	.20
❑ 288	Chris Hoiles	.25	.08
❑ 289	Kenny Rogers	.50	.20
❑ 290	Larry Walker	.50	.20
❑ 291	Tim Raines	.50	.20
❑ 292	Kevin Appier	.50	.20
❑ 293	Roger Clemens	2.50	1.00
❑ 294	Chuck Carr	.25	.08
❑ 295	Randy Myers	.25	.08
❑ 296	Dave Nilsson	.25	.08
❑ 297	Joe Carter	.50	.20
❑ 298	Chuck Finley	.50	.20
❑ 299	Ray Lankford	.50	.20
❑ 300	Roberto Kelly	.25	.08
❑ 301	Jon Lieber	.25	.08
❑ 302	Travis Fryman	.50	.20
❑ 303	Mark McGwire	3.00	1.25
❑ 304	Tony Gwynn	1.50	.60
❑ 305	Kenny Lofton	.50	.20
❑ 306	Mark Whiten	.25	.08
❑ 307	Doug Drabek	.25	.08
❑ 308	Terry Steinbach	.25	.08
❑ 309	Ryan Klesko	.50	.20
❑ 310	Mike Piazza	2.00	.75
❑ 311	Ben McDonald	.25	.08
❑ 312	Reggie Sanders	.50	.20
❑ 313	Alex Fernandez	.25	.08
❑ 314	Aaron Sele	.25	.08
❑ 315	Gregg Jefferies	.25	.08
❑ 316	Rickey Henderson	1.25	.50
❑ 317	Brian Anderson	.25	.08
❑ 318	Jose Valentin	.25	.08
❑ 319	Rod Beck	.25	.08
❑ 320	Marquis Grissom	.50	.20
❑ 321	Ken Griffey Jr.	2.00	.75
❑ 322	Bret Saberhagen	.50	.20
❑ 323	Juan Gonzalez	.50	.20
❑ 324	Paul Molitor	.50	.20
❑ 325	Gary Sheffield	.50	.20
❑ 326	Darren Daulton	.50	.20
❑ 327	Bill Swift	.25	.08
❑ 328	Brian McRae	.25	.08
❑ 329	Robin Ventura	.50	.20
❑ 330	Lee Smith	.50	.20
❑ 331	Fred McGriff	.75	.30
❑ 332	Delino DeShields	.25	.08
❑ 333	Edgar Martinez	.75	.30
❑ 334	Mike Mussina	.75	.30
❑ 335	Orlando Merced	.25	.08
❑ 336	Carlos Baerga	.25	.08
❑ 337	Wil Cordero	.25	.08
❑ 338	Tom Pagnozzi	.25	.08
❑ 339	Pat Hentgen	.25	.08
❑ 340	Chad Curtis	.25	.08
❑ 341	Darren Lewis	.25	.08
❑ 342	Jeff Kent	.50	.20

❑ 343	Bip Roberts	.25	.08
❑ 344	Ivan Rodriguez	.75	.30
❑ 345	Jeff Montgomery	.25	.08
❑ 346	Hal Morris	.25	.08
❑ 347	Danny Tartabull	.25	.08
❑ 348	Raul Mondesi	.50	.20
❑ 349	Ken Hill	.25	.08
❑ 350	Pedro Martinez	.75	.30
❑ 351	Frank Thomas	1.25	.50
❑ 352	Manny Ramirez	.75	.30
❑ 353	Tim Salmon	.75	.30
❑ 354	W. VanLandingham	.25	.08
❑ 355	Andres Galarraga	.50	.20
❑ 356	Paul O'Neill	.75	.30
❑ 357	Brady Anderson	.50	.20
❑ 358	Ramon Martinez	.25	.08
❑ 359	John Olerud	.50	.20
❑ 360	Ruben Sierra	.50	.20
❑ 361	Cal Eldred	.25	.08
❑ 362	Jay Buhner	.50	.20
❑ 363	Jay Bell	.50	.20
❑ 364	Wally Joyner	.50	.20
❑ 365	Chuck Knoblauch	.50	.20
❑ 366	Len Dykstra	.50	.20
❑ 367	John Wetteland	.50	.20
❑ 368	Roberto Alomar	.75	.30
❑ 369	Craig Biggio	.75	.30
❑ 370	Ozzie Smith	2.00	.75
❑ 371	Terry Pendleton	.50	.20
❑ 372	Sammy Sosa	1.25	.50
❑ 373	Carlos Garcia	.25	.08
❑ 374	Jose Rijo	.25	.08
❑ 375	Chris Gomez	.25	.08
❑ 376	Barry Bonds	3.00	1.25
❑ 377	Steve Avery	.25	.08
❑ 378	Rick Wilkins	.25	.08
❑ 379	Pete Harnisch	.25	.08
❑ 380	Dean Palmer	.50	.20
❑ 381	Bob Hamelin	.25	.08
❑ 382	Jason Bere	.25	.08
❑ 383	Jimmy Key	.50	.20
❑ 384	Dante Bichette	.50	.20
❑ 385	Rafael Palmeiro	.75	.30
❑ 386	David Justice	.50	.20
❑ 387	Chili Davis	.50	.20
❑ 388	Mike Greenwell	.25	.08
❑ 389	Todd Zeile	.25	.08
❑ 390	Jeff Conine	.50	.20
❑ 391	Rick Aguilera	.25	.08
❑ 392	Eddie Murray	1.25	.50
❑ 393	Mike Stanley	.25	.08
❑ 394	Cliff Floyd UER	.50	.20
❑ 395	Randy Johnson	1.25	.50
❑ 396	David Nied	.25	.08
❑ 397	Devon White	.50	.20
❑ 398	Royce Clayton	.25	.08
❑ 399	Andy Benes	.25	.08
❑ 400	John Hudek	.25	.08
❑ 401	Bobby Jones	.25	.08
❑ 402	Eric Karros	.50	.20
❑ 403	Will Clark	.75	.30
❑ 404	Mark Langston	.25	.08
❑ 405	Kevin Brown	.50	.20
❑ 406	Greg Maddux	2.00	.75
❑ 407	David Cone	.50	.20
❑ 408	Wade Boggs	.75	.30
❑ 409	Steve Trachsel	.25	.08
❑ 410	Greg Vaughn	.25	.08
❑ 411	Mo Vaughn	.50	.20
❑ 412	Wilson Alvarez	.25	.08
❑ 413	Cal Ripken	4.00	1.50
❑ 414	Rico Brogna	.25	.08
❑ 415	Barry Larkin	.75	.30
❑ 416	Cecil Fielder	.50	.20
❑ 417	Jose Canseco	.75	.30
❑ 418	Jack McDowell	.25	.08
❑ 419	Mike Lieberthal	.50	.20
❑ 420	Andrew Lorraine	.25	.08
❑ 421	Rich Becker	.25	.08
❑ 422	Tony Phillips	.25	.08
❑ 423	Scott Ruffcorn	.25	.08
❑ 424	Jeff Granger	.25	.08
❑ 425	Greg Pirkl	.25	.08
❑ 426	Dennis Eckersley	.50	.20
❑ 427	Jose Lima	.25	.08
❑ 428	Russ Davis	.25	.08

❑ 429	Armando Benitez	.25	.08
❑ 430	Alex Gonzalez	.25	.08
❑ 431	Carlos Delgado	.50	.20
❑ 432	Chan Ho Park	.50	.20
❑ 433	Mickey Tettleton	.25	.08
❑ 434	Dave Winfield	.50	.20
❑ 435	John Burkett	.25	.08
❑ 436	Orlando Miller	.25	.08
❑ 437	Rondell White	.50	.20
❑ 438	Jose Oliva	.25	.08
❑ 439	Checklist	.25	.08

1996 Bowman

❑	COMPLETE SET (385)	50.00	20.00
❑ 1	Cal Ripken	2.50	1.00
❑ 2	Ray Durham	.30	.10
❑ 3	Ivan Rodriguez	.50	.20
❑ 4	Fred McGriff	.50	.20
❑ 5	Hideo Nomo	.75	.30
❑ 6	Troy Percival	.30	.10
❑ 7	Moises Alou	.30	.10
❑ 8	Mike Stanley	.30	.10
❑ 9	Jay Buhner	.30	.10
❑ 10	Shawn Green	.30	.10
❑ 11	Ryan Klesko	.30	.10
❑ 12	Andres Galarraga	.30	.10
❑ 13	Dean Palmer	.30	.10
❑ 14	Jeff Conine	.30	.10
❑ 15	Brian L.Hunter	.30	.10
❑ 16	J.T. Snow	.30	.10
❑ 17	Larry Walker	.30	.10
❑ 18	Barry Larkin	.50	.20
❑ 19	Alex Gonzalez	.30	.10
❑ 20	Edgar Martinez	.50	.20
❑ 21	Mo Vaughn	.30	.10
❑ 22	Mark McGwire	2.00	.75
❑ 23	Jose Canseco	.50	.20
❑ 24	Jack McDowell	.30	.10
❑ 25	Dante Bichette	.30	.10
❑ 26	Wade Boggs	.50	.20
❑ 27	Mike Piazza	1.25	.50
❑ 28	Ray Lankford	.30	.10
❑ 29	Craig Biggio	.50	.20
❑ 30	Rafael Palmeiro	.50	.20
❑ 31	Ron Gant	.30	.10
❑ 32	Javy Lopez	.30	.10
❑ 33	Brian Jordan	.30	.10
❑ 34	Paul O'Neill	.50	.20
❑ 35	Mark Grace	.50	.20
❑ 36	Matt Williams	.30	.10
❑ 37	Pedro Martinez	.50	.20
❑ 38	Rickey Henderson	.75	.30
❑ 39	Bobby Bonilla	.30	.10
❑ 40	Todd Hollandsworth	.30	.10
❑ 41	Jim Thome	.50	.20
❑ 42	Gary Sheffield	.75	.30
❑ 43	Tim Salmon	.50	.20
❑ 44	Gregg Jefferies	.30	.10
❑ 45	Roberto Alomar	.50	.20
❑ 46	Carlos Baerga	.30	.10
❑ 47	Mark Grudzielanek	.30	.10
❑ 48	Randy Johnson	.75	.30
❑ 49	Tino Martinez	.50	.20
❑ 50	Robin Ventura	.30	.10
❑ 51	Ryne Sandberg	1.25	.50
❑ 52	Jay Bell	.30	.10
❑ 53	Jason Schmidt	.50	.20
❑ 54	Frank Thomas	.75	.30

- ❑ 55 Kenny Lofton .30 .10
- ❑ 56 Ariel Prieto .30 .10
- ❑ 57 David Cone .30 .10
- ❑ 58 Reggie Sanders .30 .10
- ❑ 59 Michael Tucker .30 .10
- ❑ 60 Vinny Castilla .30 .10
- ❑ 61 Len Dykstra .30 .10
- ❑ 62 Todd Hundley .30 .10
- ❑ 63 Brian McRae .30 .10
- ❑ 64 Dennis Eckersley .30 .10
- ❑ 65 Rondell White .30 .10
- ❑ 66 Eric Karros .30 .10
- ❑ 67 Greg Maddux 1.25 .50
- ❑ 68 Kevin Appier .30 .10
- ❑ 69 Eddie Murray .75 .30
- ❑ 70 John Olerud .30 .10
- ❑ 71 Tony Gwynn 1.00 .40
- ❑ 72 David Justice .30 .10
- ❑ 73 Ken Caminiti .30 .10
- ❑ 74 Terry Steinbach .30 .10
- ❑ 75 Alan Benes .30 .10
- ❑ 76 Chipper Jones .75 .30
- ❑ 77 Jeff Bagwell .50 .20
- ❑ 78 Barry Bonds 2.00 .75
- ❑ 79 Ken Griffey Jr. 1.50 .60
- ❑ 80 Roger Cedeno .30 .10
- ❑ 81 Joe Carter .30 .10
- ❑ 82 Henry Rodriguez .30 .10
- ❑ 83 Jason Isringhausen .30 .10
- ❑ 84 Chuck Knoblauch .30 .10
- ❑ 85 Manny Ramirez .50 .20
- ❑ 86 Tom Glavine .50 .20
- ❑ 87 Jeffrey Hammonds .30 .10
- ❑ 88 Paul Molitor .30 .10
- ❑ 89 Roger Clemens 1.50 .60
- ❑ 90 Greg Vaughn .30 .10
- ❑ 91 Marty Cordova .30 .10
- ❑ 92 Albert Belle .30 .10
- ❑ 93 Mike Mussina .50 .20
- ❑ 94 Garret Anderson .30 .10
- ❑ 95 Juan Gonzalez .30 .10
- ❑ 96 John Valentin .30 .10
- ❑ 97 Jason Giambi .30 .10
- ❑ 98 Kirby Puckett .75 .30
- ❑ 99 Jim Edmonds .30 .10
- ❑ 100 Cecil Fielder .30 .10
- ❑ 101 Mike Aldrete .30 .10
- ❑ 102 Marquis Grissom .30 .10
- ❑ 103 Derek Bell .30 .10
- ❑ 104 Raul Mondesi .30 .10
- ❑ 105 Sammy Sosa .75 .30
- ❑ 106 Travis Fryman .30 .10
- ❑ 107 Rico Brogna .30 .10
- ❑ 108 Will Clark .50 .20
- ❑ 109 Bernie Williams .50 .20
- ❑ 110 Brady Anderson .30 .10
- ❑ 111 Torii Hunter .30 .10
- ❑ 112 Derek Jeter 2.00 .75
- ❑ 113 Mike Kusiewicz RC .50 .20
- ❑ 114 Scott Rolen .75 .30
- ❑ 115 Ramon Castro .30 .10
- ❑ 116 Jose Guillen RC 3.00 1.25
- ❑ 117 Wade Walker RC .50 .20
- ❑ 118 Shawn Senior .30 .10
- ❑ 119 Onan Masaoka RC 1.00 .40
- ❑ 120 Marlon Anderson RC 1.00 .40
- ❑ 121 Katsuhiro Maeda RC 1.00 .40
- ❑ 122 Garrett Stephenson RC .50 .20
- ❑ 123 Butch Huskey .30 .10
- ❑ 124 D'Angelo Jimenez RC 1.00 .40
- ❑ 125 Tony Mounce RC .50 .20
- ❑ 126 Jay Canizaro .30 .10
- ❑ 127 Juan Melo .30 .10
- ❑ 128 Steve Gibralter .30 .10
- ❑ 129 Freddy Adrian Garcia .30 .10
- ❑ 130 Julio Santana .30 .10
- ❑ 131 Richard Hidalgo .30 .10
- ❑ 132 Jermaine Dye .30 .10
- ❑ 133 Willie Adams .30 .10
- ❑ 134 Everett Stull .30 .10
- ❑ 135 Ramon Morel .30 .10
- ❑ 136 Chan Ho Park .30 .10
- ❑ 137 Jamey Wright .30 .10
- ❑ 138 Luis R.Garcia RC .50 .20
- ❑ 139 Dan Serafini .30 .10
- ❑ 140 Ryan Dempster RC 2.00 .75
- ❑ 141 Tate Seefried .30 .10
- ❑ 142 Jimmy Hurst .30 .10
- ❑ 143 Travis Miller .30 .10
- ❑ 144 Curtis Goodwin .30 .10
- ❑ 145 Rocky Coppinger RC .50 .20
- ❑ 146 Enrique Wilson .30 .10
- ❑ 147 Jaime Bluma .30 .10
- ❑ 148 Andrew Vessel .30 .10
- ❑ 149 Damian Moss .30 .10
- ❑ 150 Shawn Gallagher RC .50 .20
- ❑ 151 Pat Watkins .30 .10
- ❑ 152 Jose Paniagua .30 .10
- ❑ 153 Danny Graves .30 .10
- ❑ 154 Bryon Gainey RC .50 .20
- ❑ 155 Steve Soderstrom .30 .10
- ❑ 156 Cliff Brumbaugh RC .50 .20
- ❑ 157 Eugene Kingsale RC .50 .20
- ❑ 158 Lou Collier .30 .10
- ❑ 159 Todd Walker .30 .10
- ❑ 160 Kris Detmers RC .50 .20
- ❑ 161 Josh Booty RC .50 .20
- ❑ 162 Greg Whiteman RC .50 .20
- ❑ 163 Damian Jackson .30 .10
- ❑ 164 Tony Clark .30 .10
- ❑ 165 Jeff D'Amico .30 .10
- ❑ 166 Johnny Damon .50 .20
- ❑ 167 Rafael Orellano .30 .10
- ❑ 168 Ruben Rivera .30 .10
- ❑ 169 Alex Ochoa .30 .10
- ❑ 170 Jay Powell .30 .10
- ❑ 171 Tom Evans .30 .10
- ❑ 172 Ron Villone .30 .10
- ❑ 173 Shawn Estes .30 .10
- ❑ 174 John Wasdin .30 .10
- ❑ 175 Bill Simas .30 .10
- ❑ 176 Kevin Brown .30 .10
- ❑ 177 Shannon Stewart .30 .10
- ❑ 178 Todd Greene .30 .10
- ❑ 179 Bob Wolcott .30 .10
- ❑ 180 Chris Snopek .30 .10
- ❑ 181 Nomar Garciaparra 1.50 .60
- ❑ 182 Cameron Smith RC .50 .20
- ❑ 183 Matt Drews .30 .10
- ❑ 184 Jimmy Haynes .30 .10
- ❑ 185 Chris Carpenter .50 .20
- ❑ 186 Desi Relaford .30 .10
- ❑ 187 Ben Grieve .30 .10
- ❑ 188 Mike Bell .30 .10
- ❑ 189 Luis Castillo RC 1.50 .60
- ❑ 190 Ugueth Urbina .30 .10
- ❑ 191 Paul Wilson .30 .10
- ❑ 192 Andruw Jones 1.25 .50
- ❑ 193 Wayne Gomes .30 .10
- ❑ 194 Craig Counsell RC 1.50 .60
- ❑ 195 Jim Cole .30 .10
- ❑ 196 Brooks Kieschnick .30 .10
- ❑ 197 Trey Beamon .30 .10
- ❑ 198 Marino Santana RC .50 .20
- ❑ 199 Bob Abreu .75 .30
- ❑ 200 Pokey Reese .30 .10
- ❑ 201 Dante Powell .30 .10
- ❑ 202 George Arias .30 .10
- ❑ 203 Jorge Velandia RC .50 .20
- ❑ 204 George Lombard RC .50 .20
- ❑ 205 Byron Browne RC .50 .20
- ❑ 206 John Frascatore .30 .10
- ❑ 207 Terry Adams .30 .10
- ❑ 208 Wilson Delgado RC .50 .20
- ❑ 209 Billy McMillon .30 .10
- ❑ 210 Jeff Abbott .30 .10
- ❑ 211 Trot Nixon .30 .10
- ❑ 212 Amaury Telemaco .30 .10
- ❑ 213 Scott Sullivan .30 .10
- ❑ 214 Justin Thompson .30 .10
- ❑ 215 Decomba Conner .30 .10
- ❑ 216 Ryan McGuire .30 .10
- ❑ 217 Matt Luke .30 .10
- ❑ 218 Doug Million .30 .10
- ❑ 219 Jason Dickson RC .50 .20
- ❑ 220 Ramon Hernandez RC 2.00 .75
- ❑ 221 Mark Bellhorn RC 2.00 .75
- ❑ 222 Eric Ludwick RC .50 .20
- ❑ 223 Luke Wilcox RC .50 .20
- ❑ 224 Marty Malloy RC .50 .20
- ❑ 225 Gary Coffee RC .50 .20
- ❑ 226 Wendell Magee RC .50 .20
- ❑ 227 Brett Tomko RC 1.00 .40
- ❑ 228 Derek Lowe .30 .10
- ❑ 229 Jose Rosado RC .50 .20
- ❑ 230 Steve Bourgeois RC .50 .20
- ❑ 231 Neil Weber RC .50 .20
- ❑ 232 Jeff Ware .30 .10
- ❑ 233 Edwin Diaz .30 .10
- ❑ 234 Greg Norton .30 .10
- ❑ 235 Aaron Boone .30 .10
- ❑ 236 Jeff Suppan .30 .10
- ❑ 237 Bret Wagner .30 .10
- ❑ 238 Elieser Marrero .30 .10
- ❑ 239 Will Cunnane .30 .10
- ❑ 240 Brian Barkley RC .50 .20
- ❑ 241 Jay Payton .30 .10
- ❑ 242 Marcus Jensen .30 .10
- ❑ 243 Ryan Nye .30 .10
- ❑ 244 Chad Mottola .30 .10
- ❑ 245 Scott McClain RC .50 .20
- ❑ 246 Jesse Ibarra RC .50 .20
- ❑ 247 Mike Darr RC .50 .20
- ❑ 248 Bobby Estalella RC .50 .20
- ❑ 249 Michael Barrett .30 .10
- ❑ 250 Jamie Lopiccolo RC .50 .20
- ❑ 251 Shane Spencer RC 1.00 .40
- ❑ 252 Ben Petrick RC .50 .20
- ❑ 253 Jason Bell RC .50 .20
- ❑ 254 Arnold Gooch RC .50 .20
- ❑ 255 T.J. Mathews .30 .10
- ❑ 256 Jason Ryan .30 .10
- ❑ 257 Pat Cline RC .50 .20
- ❑ 258 Rafael Carmona RC .50 .20
- ❑ 259 Carl Pavano RC 2.00 .75
- ❑ 260 Ben Davis .30 .10
- ❑ 261 Matt Lawton RC 1.00 .40
- ❑ 262 Kevin Sefcik RC .50 .20
- ❑ 263 Chris Fussell RC .50 .20
- ❑ 264 Mike Cameron RC 1.50 .60
- ❑ 265 Marty Janzen RC .50 .20
- ❑ 266 Livan Hernandez RC 2.00 .75
- ❑ 267 Raul Ibanez RC 2.00 .75
- ❑ 268 Juan Encarnacion .30 .10
- ❑ 269 David Yocum RC .50 .20
- ❑ 270 Jonathan Johnson RC .50 .20
- ❑ 271 Reggie Taylor .30 .10
- ❑ 272 Danny Buxbaum RC .50 .20
- ❑ 273 Jacob Cruz .30 .10
- ❑ 274 Bobby Morris RC .50 .20
- ❑ 275 Andy Fox RC .50 .20
- ❑ 276 Greg Keagle .30 .10
- ❑ 277 Charles Peterson .30 .10
- ❑ 278 Derrek Lee .50 .20
- ❑ 279 Bryant Nelson RC .50 .20
- ❑ 280 Antone Williamson .30 .10
- ❑ 281 Scott Elarton .30 .10
- ❑ 282 Shad Williams RC .50 .20
- ❑ 283 Rich Hunter RC .50 .20
- ❑ 284 Chris Sheff .30 .10
- ❑ 285 Derrick Gibson .30 .10
- ❑ 286 Felix Rodriguez .30 .10
- ❑ 287 Brian Banks RC .50 .20
- ❑ 288 Jason McDonald .30 .10
- ❑ 289 Glendon Rusch RC 1.00 .40
- ❑ 290 Gary Rath .30 .10
- ❑ 291 Peter Munro .30 .10
- ❑ 292 Tom Fordham .30 .10
- ❑ 293 Jason Kendall .30 .10
- ❑ 294 Russ Johnson .30 .10
- ❑ 295 Joe Long .30 .10
- ❑ 296 Robert Smith RC .50 .20
- ❑ 297 Jarrod Washburn RC 1.50 .60
- ❑ 298 Dave Coggin RC .50 .20
- ❑ 299 Jeff Yoder RC .50 .20
- ❑ 300 Jed Hansen RC .50 .20
- ❑ 301 Matt Morris RC 2.50 1.00
- ❑ 302 Josh Bishop RC .50 .20
- ❑ 303 Dustin Hermanson .30 .10
- ❑ 304 Mike Gulan .30 .10
- ❑ 305 Felipe Crespo .30 .10
- ❑ 306 Quinton McCracken .30 .10
- ❑ 307 Jim Bonnici RC .50 .20
- ❑ 308 Sal Fasano .30 .10
- ❑ 309 Gabe Alvarez RC .50 .20
- ❑ 310 Heath Murray RC .50 .20
- ❑ 311 Javier Valentin RC .50 .20
- ❑ 312 Bartolo Colon .75 .30

❑ 313 Olmedo Saenz	.30	.10
❑ 314 Norm Hutchins RC	.50	.20
❑ 315 Chris Holt	.30	.10
❑ 316 David Doster RC	.50	.20
❑ 317 Robert Person	.30	.10
❑ 318 Donne Wall RC	.50	.20
❑ 319 Adam Riggs RC	.50	.20
❑ 320 Homer Bush	.30	.10
❑ 321 Brad Rigby RC	.50	.20
❑ 322 Lou Merloni RC	.50	.20
❑ 323 Neifi Perez	.30	.10
❑ 324 Chris Cumberland	.30	.10
❑ 325 Alvie Shepherd RC	.50	.20
❑ 326 Jarrod Patterson RC	.50	.20
❑ 327 Ray Ricken RC	.50	.20
❑ 328 Danny Klassen RC	.50	.20
❑ 329 David Miller RC	.50	.20
❑ 330 Chad Alexander RC	.50	.20
❑ 331 Matt Beaumont	.30	.10
❑ 332 Damon Hollins	.30	.10
❑ 333 Todd Dunn	.30	.10
❑ 334 Mike Sweeney RC	2.00	.75
❑ 335 Richie Sexson	.50	.20
❑ 336 Billy Wagner	.30	.10
❑ 337 Ron Wright RC	.50	.20
❑ 338 Paul Konerko	.75	.30
❑ 339 Tommy Phelps RC	.50	.20
❑ 340 Karim Garcia	.30	.10
❑ 341 Mike Grace RC	.50	.20
❑ 342 Russell Branyan RC	1.00	.40
❑ 343 Randy Winn RC	1.50	.60
❑ 344 A.J. Pierzynski RC	4.00	1.50
❑ 345 Mike Busby RC	.50	.20
❑ 346 Matt Beech RC	.50	.20
❑ 347 Jose Cepeda RC	.50	.20
❑ 348 Brian Stephenson	.30	.10
❑ 349 Rey Ordonez	.30	.10
❑ 350 Rich Aurilia RC	1.00	.40
❑ 351 Edgard Velazquez RC	.50	.20
❑ 352 Raul Casanova	.30	.10
❑ 353 Carlos Guillen RC	2.00	.75
❑ 354 Bruce Aven RC	.50	.20
❑ 355 Ryan Jones RC	.50	.20
❑ 356 Derek Aucoin RC	.50	.20
❑ 357 Brian Rose RC	.50	.20
❑ 358 Richard Almanzar RC	.50	.20
❑ 359 Fletcher Bates RC	.50	.20
❑ 360 Russ Ortiz RC	1.50	.60
❑ 361 Wilton Guerrero RC	.50	.20
❑ 362 Geoff Jenkins RC	1.50	.60
❑ 363 Pete Janicki	.30	.10
❑ 364 Yamil Benitez	.30	.10
❑ 365 Aaron Holbert	.30	.10
❑ 366 Tim Belk	.30	.10
❑ 367 Terrell Wade	.30	.10
❑ 368 Terrence Long	.30	.10
❑ 369 Brad Fullmer	.30	.10
❑ 370 Matt Wagner	.30	.10
❑ 371 Craig Wilson RC	.50	.20
❑ 372 Mark Loretta	.30	.10
❑ 373 Eric Owens	.30	.10
❑ 374 Vladimir Guerrero	1.50	.60
❑ 375 Tommy Davis	.30	.10
❑ 376 Donnie Sadler	.30	.10
❑ 377 Edgar Renteria	.30	.10
❑ 378 Todd Helton	1.50	.60
❑ 379 Ralph Milliard RC	.50	.20
❑ 380 Darin Blood RC	.50	.20
❑ 381 Shayne Bennett	.30	.10
❑ 382 Mark Redman	.30	.10
❑ 383 Felix Martinez	.30	.10
❑ 384 Sean Watkins RC	.50	.20
❑ 385 Oscar Henriquez	.30	.10
❑ M20 52 Bowman Mantle	5.00	2.00
❑ NNO Unnumbered Checklists	.30	.10

1997 Bowman

❑ COMPLETE SET (441)	60.00	25.00
❑ COMPLETE SERIES 1 (221)	30.00	12.50
❑ COMPLETE SERIES 2 (220)	30.00	12.50
❑ 1 Derek Jeter	2.00	.75
❑ 2 Edgar Renteria	.30	.10
❑ 3 Chipper Jones	.75	.30
❑ 4 Hideo Nomo	.75	.30
❑ 5 Tim Salmon	.50	.20
❑ 6 Jason Giambi	.30	.10

❑ 7 Robin Ventura	.30	.10
❑ 8 Tony Clark	.30	.10
❑ 9 Barry Larkin	.50	.20
❑ 10 Paul Molitor	.30	.10
❑ 11 Bernard Gilkey	.30	.10
❑ 12 Jack McDowell	.30	.10
❑ 13 Andy Benes	.30	.10
❑ 14 Ryan Klesko	.30	.10
❑ 15 Mark McGwire	2.00	.75
❑ 16 Ken Griffey Jr.	1.25	.50
❑ 17 Robb Nen	.30	.10
❑ 18 Cal Ripken	2.50	1.00
❑ 19 John Valentin	.30	.10
❑ 20 Ricky Bottalico	.30	.10
❑ 21 Mike Lansing	.30	.10
❑ 22 Ryne Sandberg	1.25	.50
❑ 23 Carlos Delgado	.30	.10
❑ 24 Craig Biggio	.50	.20
❑ 25 Eric Karros	.30	.10
❑ 26 Kevin Appier	.30	.10
❑ 27 Mariano Rivera	.75	.30
❑ 28 Vinny Castilla	.30	.10
❑ 29 Juan Gonzalez	.30	.10
❑ 30 Al Martin	.30	.10
❑ 31 Jeff Cirillo	.30	.10
❑ 32 Eddie Murray	.75	.30
❑ 33 Ray Lankford	.30	.10
❑ 34 Manny Ramirez	.50	.20
❑ 35 Roberto Alomar	.50	.20
❑ 36 Will Clark	.50	.20
❑ 37 Chuck Knoblauch	.30	.10
❑ 38 Harold Baines	.30	.10
❑ 39 Trevor Hoffman	.30	.10
❑ 40 Edgar Martinez	.50	.20
❑ 41 Geronimo Berroa	.30	.10
❑ 42 Rey Ordonez	.30	.10
❑ 43 Mike Stanley	.30	.10
❑ 44 Mike Mussina	.50	.20
❑ 45 Kevin Brown	.30	.10
❑ 46 Dennis Eckersley	.30	.10
❑ 47 Henry Rodriguez	.30	.10
❑ 48 Tino Martinez	.50	.20
❑ 49 Eric Young	.30	.10
❑ 50 Bret Boone	.30	.10
❑ 51 Raul Mondesi	.30	.10
❑ 52 Sammy Sosa	.75	.30
❑ 53 John Smoltz	.50	.20
❑ 54 Billy Wagner	.30	.10
❑ 55 Jeff D'Amico	.30	.10
❑ 56 Ken Caminiti	.30	.10
❑ 57 Jason Kendall	.30	.10
❑ 58 Wade Boggs	.50	.20
❑ 59 Andres Galarraga	.30	.10
❑ 60 Jeff Brantley	.30	.10
❑ 61 Mel Rojas	.30	.10
❑ 62 Brian L. Hunter	.30	.10
❑ 63 Bobby Bonilla	.30	.10
❑ 64 Roger Clemens	1.50	.60
❑ 65 Jeff Kent	.30	.10
❑ 66 Matt Williams	.30	.10
❑ 67 Albert Belle	.30	.10
❑ 68 Jeff King	.30	.10
❑ 69 John Wetteland	.30	.10
❑ 70 Deion Sanders	.50	.20
❑ 71 Bubba Trammell RC	.60	.25
❑ 72 Felix Heredia RC	.40	.15
❑ 73 Billy Koch RC	1.00	.40
❑ 74 Sidney Ponson RC	1.00	.40

❑ 75 Ricky Ledee RC	.60	.25
❑ 76 Brett Tomko	.30	.10
❑ 77 Braden Looper RC	.40	.15
❑ 78 Damian Jackson	.30	.10
❑ 79 Jason Dickson	.30	.10
❑ 80 Chad Green RC	.40	.15
❑ 81 R.A. Dickey RC	.40	.15
❑ 82 Jeff Liefer	.30	.10
❑ 83 Matt Wagner	.30	.10
❑ 84 Richard Hidalgo	.30	.10
❑ 85 Adam Riggs	.30	.10
❑ 86 Robert Smith	.30	.10
❑ 87 Chad Hermansen RC	.40	.15
❑ 88 Felix Martinez	.30	.10
❑ 89 J.J. Johnson	.30	.10
❑ 90 Todd Dunwoody	.30	.10
❑ 91 Katsuhiro Maeda	.30	.10
❑ 92 Darin Erstad	.30	.10
❑ 93 Elieser Marrero	.30	.10
❑ 94 Bartolo Colon	.30	.10
❑ 95 Chris Fussell	.30	.10
❑ 96 Ugueth Urbina	.30	.10
❑ 97 Josh Paul RC	.40	.15
❑ 98 Jaime Bluma	.30	.10
❑ 99 Seth Greisinger RC	.40	.15
❑ 100 Jose Cruz Jr. RC	.60	.25
❑ 101 Todd Dunn	.30	.10
❑ 102 Joe Young RC	.40	.15
❑ 103 Jonathan Johnson	.30	.10
❑ 104 Justin Towle RC	.40	.15
❑ 105 Brian Rose	.30	.10
❑ 106 Jose Guillen	.30	.10
❑ 107 Andruw Jones	.50	.20
❑ 108 Mark Kotsay RC	1.50	.60
❑ 109 Wilton Guerrero	.30	.10
❑ 110 Jacob Cruz	.30	.10
❑ 111 Mike Sweeney	.30	.10
❑ 112 Julio Mosquera	.30	.10
❑ 113 Matt Morris	.30	.10
❑ 114 Wendell Magee	.30	.10
❑ 115 John Thomson	.30	.10
❑ 116 Javier Valentin	.30	.10
❑ 117 Tom Fordham	.30	.10
❑ 118 Ruben Rivera	.30	.10
❑ 119 Mike Drumright RC	.40	.15
❑ 120 Chris Holt	.30	.10
❑ 121 Sean Maloney	.30	.10
❑ 122 Michael Barrett	.30	.10
❑ 123 Tony Saunders RC	.40	.15
❑ 124 Kevin Brown C	.30	.10
❑ 125 Richard Almanzar	.30	.10
❑ 126 Mark Redman	.30	.10
❑ 127 Anthony Sanders RC	.40	.15
❑ 128 Jeff Abbott	.30	.10
❑ 129 Eugene Kingsale	.30	.10
❑ 130 Paul Konerko	.50	.20
❑ 131 Randall Simon RC	.60	.25
❑ 132 Andy Larkin	.30	.10
❑ 133 Rafael Medina	.30	.10
❑ 134 Mendy Lopez	.30	.10
❑ 135 Freddy Adrian Garcia	.30	.10
❑ 136 Karim Garcia	.30	.10
❑ 137 Larry Rodriguez RC	.40	.15
❑ 138 Carlos Guillen	.30	.10
❑ 139 Aaron Boone	.30	.10
❑ 140 Donnie Sadler	.30	.10
❑ 141 Brooks Kieschnick	.30	.10
❑ 142 Scott Spiezio	.30	.10
❑ 143 Everett Stull	.30	.10
❑ 144 Enrique Wilson	.30	.10
❑ 145 Milton Bradley RC	2.00	.75
❑ 146 Kevin Orie	.30	.10
❑ 147 Derek Wallace	.30	.10
❑ 148 Russ Johnson	.30	.10
❑ 149 Joe Lagarde RC	.40	.15
❑ 150 Luis Castillo	.30	.10
❑ 151 Jay Payton	.30	.10
❑ 152 Joe Long	.30	.10
❑ 153 Livan Hernandez	.30	.10
❑ 154 Vladimir Nunez RC	.60	.25
❑ 155 Pokey Reese UER	.30	.10
❑ 156 George Arias	.30	.10
❑ 157 Homer Bush	.30	.10
❑ 158 Chris Carpenter UER	.30	.10
❑ 159 Eric Milton RC	.60	.25
❑ 160 Richie Sexson	.30	.10

❑ 161 Carl Pavano .30 .10
❑ 162 Chris Gissell RC .40 .15
❑ 163 Mac Suzuki .30 .10
❑ 164 Pat Cline .30 .10
❑ 165 Ron Wright .30 .10
❑ 166 Dante Powell .30 .10
❑ 167 Mark Bellhorn .30 .10
❑ 168 George Lombard .30 .10
❑ 169 Pee Wee Lopez RC .40 .15
❑ 170 Paul Wilder RC .40 .15
❑ 171 Brad Fullmer .30 .10
❑ 172 Willie Martinez RC .40 .15
❑ 173 Dario Veras RC .40 .15
❑ 174 Dave Coggin .30 .10
❑ 175 Kris Benson RC 1.00 .40
❑ 176 Torii Hunter .30 .10
❑ 177 D.T. Cromer .30 .10
❑ 178 Nelson Figueroa RC .40 .15
❑ 179 Hiram Bocachica RC .40 .15
❑ 180 Shane Monahan .30 .10
❑ 181 Jimmy Anderson RC .40 .15
❑ 182 Juan Melo .30 .10
❑ 183 Pablo Ortega RC .40 .15
❑ 184 Calvin Pickering RC .40 .15
❑ 185 Reggie Taylor .30 .10
❑ 186 Jeff Farnsworth RC .40 .15
❑ 187 Terrence Long .30 .10
❑ 188 Geoff Jenkins .30 .10
❑ 189 Steve Rain RC .40 .15
❑ 190 Nerio Rodriguez RC .40 .15
❑ 191 Derrick Gibson .30 .10
❑ 192 Darin Blood .30 .10
❑ 193 Ben Davis .30 .10
❑ 194 Adrian Beltre RC 3.00 1.25
❑ 195 Damian Sapp RC UER .40 .15
❑ 196 Kerry Wood RC 5.00 2.00
❑ 197 Nate Rolison RC .40 .15
❑ 198 Fernando Tatis RC .40 .15
❑ 199 Brad Penny RC 3.00 1.25
❑ 200 Jake Westbrook RC 1.00 .40
❑ 201 Edwin Diaz .30 .10
❑ 202 Joe Fontenot RC .60 .25
❑ 203 Matt Halloran RC .40 .15
❑ 204 Blake Stein RC .40 .15
❑ 205 Onan Masaoka .30 .10
❑ 206 Ben Petrick .30 .10
❑ 207 Matt Clement RC 1.00 .40
❑ 208 Todd Greene .30 .10
❑ 209 Ray Ricken .30 .10
❑ 210 Eric Chavez RC 4.00 1.50
❑ 211 Edgard Velazquez .30 .10
❑ 212 Bruce Chen RC 1.00 .40
❑ 213 Danny Patterson .30 .10
❑ 214 Jeff Yoder .30 .10
❑ 215 Luis Ordaz RC .40 .15
❑ 216 Chris Widger .30 .10
❑ 217 Jason Brester .30 .10
❑ 218 Carlton Loewer .30 .10
❑ 219 Chris Reitsma RC .60 .25
❑ 220 Neifi Perez .30 .10
❑ 221 Hideki Irabu RC .60 .25
❑ 222 Ellis Burks .30 .10
❑ 223 Pedro Martinez .50 .20
❑ 224 Kenny Lofton .30 .10
❑ 225 Randy Johnson .75 .30
❑ 226 Terry Steinbach .30 .10
❑ 227 Bernie Williams .50 .20
❑ 228 Dean Palmer .30 .10
❑ 229 Alan Benes .30 .10
❑ 230 Marquis Grissom .30 .10
❑ 231 Gary Sheffield .30 .10
❑ 232 Curt Schilling .30 .10
❑ 233 Reggie Sanders .30 .10
❑ 234 Bobby Higginson .30 .10
❑ 235 Moises Alou .30 .10
❑ 236 Tom Glavine .50 .20
❑ 237 Mark Grace .50 .20
❑ 238 Ramon Martinez .30 .10
❑ 239 Rafael Palmeiro .50 .20
❑ 240 John Olerud .30 .10
❑ 241 Dante Bichette .30 .10
❑ 242 Greg Vaughn .30 .10
❑ 243 Jeff Bagwell .50 .20
❑ 244 Barry Bonds 2.00 .75
❑ 245 Pat Hentgen .30 .10
❑ 246 Jim Thome .50 .20
❑ 247 Jermaine Allensworth .30 .10
❑ 248 Andy Pettitte .50 .20
❑ 249 Jay Bell .30 .10
❑ 250 John Jaha .30 .10
❑ 251 Jim Edmonds .30 .10
❑ 252 Ron Gant .30 .10
❑ 253 David Cone .30 .10
❑ 254 Jose Canseco .50 .20
❑ 255 Jay Buhner .30 .10
❑ 256 Greg Maddux 1.25 .50
❑ 257 Brian McRae .30 .10
❑ 258 Lance Johnson .30 .10
❑ 259 Travis Fryman .30 .10
❑ 260 Paul O'Neill .50 .20
❑ 261 Ivan Rodriguez .50 .20
❑ 262 Gregg Jefferies .30 .10
❑ 263 Fred McGriff .50 .20
❑ 264 Derek Bell .30 .10
❑ 265 Jeff Conine .30 .10
❑ 266 Mike Piazza 1.25 .50
❑ 267 Mark Grudzielanek .30 .10
❑ 268 Brady Anderson .30 .10
❑ 269 Marty Cordova .30 .10
❑ 270 Ray Durham .30 .10
❑ 271 Joe Carter .30 .10
❑ 272 Brian Jordan .30 .10
❑ 273 David Justice .30 .10
❑ 274 Tony Gwynn 1.00 .40
❑ 275 Larry Walker .30 .10
❑ 276 Cecil Fielder .30 .10
❑ 277 Mo Vaughn .30 .10
❑ 278 Alex Fernandez .30 .10
❑ 279 Michael Tucker .30 .10
❑ 280 Jose Valentin .30 .10
❑ 281 Sandy Alomar Jr. .30 .10
❑ 282 Todd Hollandsworth .30 .10
❑ 283 Rico Brogna .30 .10
❑ 284 Rusty Greer .30 .10
❑ 285 Roberto Hernandez .30 .10
❑ 286 Hal Morris .30 .10
❑ 287 Johnny Damon .50 .20
❑ 288 Todd Hundley .30 .10
❑ 289 Rondell White .30 .10
❑ 290 Frank Thomas .75 .30
❑ 291 Don Denbow RC .40 .15
❑ 292 Derrek Lee .50 .20
❑ 293 Todd Walker .30 .10
❑ 294 Scott Rolen .50 .20
❑ 295 Wes Helms .30 .10
❑ 296 Bob Abreu .50 .20
❑ 297 John Patterson RC 1.50 .60
❑ 298 Alex Gonzalez RC 1.00 .40
❑ 299 Grant Roberts RC .40 .15
❑ 300 Jeff Suppan .30 .10
❑ 301 Luke Wilcox .30 .10
❑ 302 Marlon Anderson .30 .10
❑ 303 Ray Brown .30 .10
❑ 304 Mike Caruso RC .40 .15
❑ 305 Sam Marsonek RC .40 .15
❑ 306 Brady Raggio RC .40 .15
❑ 307 Kevin McGlinchy RC .60 .25
❑ 308 Roy Halladay RC 5.00 2.00
❑ 309 Jeremi Gonzalez RC .40 .15
❑ 310 Aramis Ramirez RC 4.00 1.50
❑ 311 Dee Brown RC .40 .15
❑ 312 Justin Thompson .30 .10
❑ 313 Jay Tessmer RC .40 .15
❑ 314 Mike Johnson RC .40 .15
❑ 315 Danny Clyburn .30 .10
❑ 316 Bruce Aven .30 .10
❑ 317 Keith Foulke RC 1.50 .60
❑ 318 Jimmy Osting RC .60 .25
❑ 319 Valerio De Los Santos RC .40 .15
❑ 320 Shannon Stewart .30 .10
❑ 321 Willie Adams .30 .10
❑ 322 Larry Barnes RC .40 .15
❑ 323 Mark Johnson RC .40 .15
❑ 324 Chris Stowers RC .40 .15
❑ 325 Brandon Reed .30 .10
❑ 326 Randy Winn .30 .10
❑ 327 Steve Chavez RC .40 .15
❑ 328 Nomar Garciaparra 1.25 .50
❑ 329 Jacque Jones RC 1.50 .60
❑ 330 Chris Clemons .30 .10
❑ 331 Todd Helton .75 .30
❑ 332 Ryan Brannan RC .40 .15
❑ 333 Alex Sanchez RC .60 .25
❑ 334 Arnold Gooch .30 .10
❑ 335 Russell Branyan .30 .10
❑ 336 Daryle Ward .40 .15
❑ 337 John LeRoy RC .40 .15
❑ 338 Steve Cox .30 .10
❑ 339 Kevin Witt .30 .10
❑ 340 Norm Hutchins .30 .10
❑ 341 Gabby Martinez .30 .10
❑ 342 Kris Detmers .30 .10
❑ 343 Mike Villano RC .40 .15
❑ 344 Preston Wilson .30 .10
❑ 345 James Manias RC .40 .15
❑ 346 Deivi Cruz RC .60 .25
❑ 347 Donzell McDonald RC .40 .15
❑ 348 Rod Myers RC .40 .15
❑ 349 Shawn Chacon RC 1.00 .40
❑ 350 Elvin Hernandez RC .60 .25
❑ 351 Orlando Cabrera RC 1.50 .60
❑ 352 Brian Banks .30 .10
❑ 353 Robbie Bell .40 .15
❑ 354 Brad Rigby .30 .10
❑ 355 Scott Elarton .30 .10
❑ 356 Kevin Sweeney RC .40 .15
❑ 357 Steve Soderstrom .30 .10
❑ 358 Ryan Nye .30 .10
❑ 359 Marlon Allen RC .40 .15
❑ 360 Donny Leon RC .40 .15
❑ 361 Garrett Neubart RC .60 .25
❑ 362 Abraham Nunez RC .60 .25
❑ 363 Adam Eaton RC 1.00 .40
❑ 364 Octavio Dotel RC .60 .25
❑ 365 Dean Crow RC .40 .15
❑ 366 Jason Baker RC .40 .15
❑ 367 Sean Casey 1.00 .40
❑ 368 Joe Lawrence RC .40 .15
❑ 369 Adam Johnson RC .40 .15
❑ 370 Scott Schoeneweis RC .60 .25
❑ 371 Gerald Witasick Jr. .30 .10
❑ 372 Ronnie Belliard RC 1.25 .50
❑ 373 Russ Ortiz .30 .10
❑ 374 Robert Stratton RC .60 .25
❑ 375 Bobby Estalella .30 .10
❑ 376 Corey Lee RC .40 .15
❑ 377 Carlos Beltran 2.00 .75
❑ 378 Mike Cameron .30 .10
❑ 379 Scott Randall RC .40 .15
❑ 380 Corey Erickson RC .40 .15
❑ 381 Jay Canizaro .30 .10
❑ 382 Kerry Robinson RC .40 .15
❑ 383 Todd Noel RC .40 .15
❑ 384 A.J. Zapp RC .40 .15
❑ 385 Jarrod Washburn .30 .10
❑ 386 Ben Grieve .30 .10
❑ 387 Javier Vazquez RC 1.50 .60
❑ 388 Tony Graffanino .30 .10
❑ 389 Travis Lee RC .60 .25
❑ 390 DaRond Stovall .30 .10
❑ 391 Dennis Reyes RC .60 .25
❑ 392 Danny Buxbaum .30 .10
❑ 393 Marc Lewis RC .40 .15
❑ 394 Kelvim Escobar RC 1.00 .40
❑ 395 Danny Klassen .30 .10
❑ 396 Ken Cloude RC .40 .15
❑ 397 Gabe Alvarez .30 .10
❑ 398 Jaret Wright RC .60 .25
❑ 399 Raul Casanova .30 .10
❑ 400 Clayton Bruner RC .40 .15
❑ 401 Jason Marquis RC 1.00 .40
❑ 402 Marc Kroon .30 .10
❑ 403 Jamey Wright .30 .10
❑ 404 Matt Snyder RC .40 .15
❑ 405 Josh Garrett RC .40 .15
❑ 406 Juan Encarnacion .30 .10
❑ 407 Heath Murray .30 .10
❑ 408 Brett Herbison RC .60 .25
❑ 409 Brent Butler RC .40 .15
❑ 410 Danny Peoples RC .40 .15
❑ 411 Miguel Tejada RC 5.00 2.00
❑ 412 Damian Moss .30 .10
❑ 413 Jim Pittsley .30 .10
❑ 414 Dmitri Young .30 .10
❑ 415 Glendon Rusch .30 .10
❑ 416 Vladimir Guerrero .75 .30
❑ 417 Cole Liniak RC .60 .25
❑ 418 Ramon Hernandez .30 .10

❑ 419	Cliff Politte RC	.40	.15
❑ 420	Mel Rosario RC	.40	.15
❑ 421	Jorge Carrion RC	.40	.15
❑ 422	John Barnes RC	.40	.15
❑ 423	Chris Stowe RC	.40	.15
❑ 424	Vernon Wells RC	5.00	2.00
❑ 425	Brett Caradonna RC	.40	.15
❑ 426	Scott Hodges RC	.60	.25
❑ 427	Jon Garland RC	2.50	1.00
❑ 428	Nathan Haynes RC	.40	.15
❑ 429	Geoff Goetz RC	.40	.15
❑ 430	Adam Kennedy RC	1.00	.40
❑ 431	T.J. Tucker RC	.40	.15
❑ 432	Aaron Akin RC	.40	.15
❑ 433	Jayson Werth RC	1.00	.40
❑ 434	Glenn Davis RC	.40	.15
❑ 435	Mark Mangum RC	.40	.15
❑ 436	Troy Cameron RC	.40	.15
❑ 437	J.J. Davis RC	.40	.15
❑ 438	Lance Berkman RC	10.00	4.00
❑ 439	Jason Standridge RC	.40	.15
❑ 440	Jason Dellaero RC	.60	.25
❑ 441	Hideki Irabu	.60	.25

1998 Bowman

❑	COMPLETE SET (441)	50.00	20.00
❑	COMPLETE SERIES 1 (221)	25.00	10.00
❑	COMPLETE SERIES 2 (220)	25.00	10.00
❑ 1	Nomar Garciaparra	1.25	.50
❑ 2	Scott Rolen	.50	.20
❑ 3	Andy Pettitte	.50	.20
❑ 4	Ivan Rodriguez	.50	.20
❑ 5	Mark McGwire	2.00	.75
❑ 6	Jason Dickson	.30	.10
❑ 7	Jose Cruz Jr.	.30	.10
❑ 8	Jeff Kent	.30	.10
❑ 9	Mike Mussina	.50	.20
❑ 10	Jason Kendall	.30	.10
❑ 11	Brett Tomko	.30	.10
❑ 12	Jeff King	.30	.10
❑ 13	Brad Radke	.30	.10
❑ 14	Robin Ventura	.30	.10
❑ 15	Jeff Bagwell	.50	.20
❑ 16	Greg Maddux	1.25	.50
❑ 17	John Jaha	.30	.10
❑ 18	Mike Piazza	1.25	.50
❑ 19	Edgar Martinez	.50	.20
❑ 20	David Justice	.30	.10
❑ 21	Todd Hundley	.30	.10
❑ 22	Tony Gwynn	1.00	.40
❑ 23	Larry Walker	.30	.10
❑ 24	Bernie Williams	.50	.20
❑ 25	Edgar Renteria	.30	.10
❑ 26	Rafael Palmeiro	.50	.20
❑ 27	Tim Salmon	.50	.20
❑ 28	Matt Morris	.30	.10
❑ 29	Shawn Estes	.30	.10
❑ 30	Vladimir Guerrero	.75	.30
❑ 31	Fernando Tatis	.30	.10
❑ 32	Justin Thompson	.30	.10
❑ 33	Ken Griffey Jr.	1.25	.50
❑ 34	Edgardo Alfonzo	.30	.10
❑ 35	Mo Vaughn	.30	.10
❑ 36	Marty Cordova	.30	.10
❑ 37	Craig Biggio	.50	.20
❑ 38	Roger Clemens	1.50	.60
❑ 39	Mark Grace	.50	.20
❑ 40	Ken Caminiti	.30	.10
❑ 41	Tony Womack	.30	.10
❑ 42	Albert Belle	.30	.10
❑ 43	Tino Martinez	.50	.20
❑ 44	Sandy Alomar Jr.	.30	.10
❑ 45	Jeff Cirillo	.30	.10
❑ 46	Jason Giambi	.30	.10
❑ 47	Darin Erstad	.30	.10
❑ 48	Livan Hernandez	.30	.10
❑ 49	Mark Grudzielanek	.30	.10
❑ 50	Sammy Sosa	.75	.30
❑ 51	Curt Schilling	.30	.10
❑ 52	Brian Hunter	.30	.10
❑ 53	Neifi Perez	.30	.10
❑ 54	Todd Walker	.30	.10
❑ 55	Jose Guillen	.30	.10
❑ 56	Jim Thome	.50	.20
❑ 57	Tom Glavine	.50	.20
❑ 58	Todd Greene	.30	.10
❑ 59	Rondell White	.30	.10
❑ 60	Roberto Alomar	.50	.20
❑ 61	Tony Clark	.30	.10
❑ 62	Vinny Castilla	.30	.10
❑ 63	Barry Larkin	.50	.20
❑ 64	Hideki Irabu	.30	.10
❑ 65	Johnny Damon	.50	.20
❑ 66	Juan Gonzalez	.30	.10
❑ 67	John Olerud	.30	.10
❑ 68	Gary Sheffield	.30	.10
❑ 69	Raul Mondesi	.30	.10
❑ 70	Chipper Jones	.75	.30
❑ 71	David Ortiz	2.50	1.00
❑ 72	Warren Morris RC	.40	.15
❑ 73	Alex Gonzalez	.30	.10
❑ 74	Nick Bierbrodt	.30	.10
❑ 75	Roy Halladay	.30	.10
❑ 76	Danny Buxbaum	.30	.10
❑ 77	Adam Kennedy	.30	.10
❑ 78	Jared Sandberg	.30	.10
❑ 79	Michael Barrett	.30	.10
❑ 80	Gil Meche	.60	.25
❑ 81	Jayson Werth	.30	.10
❑ 82	Abraham Nunez	.30	.10
❑ 83	Ben Petrick	.30	.10
❑ 84	Brett Caradonna	.30	.10
❑ 85	Mike Lowell RC	3.00	1.25
❑ 86	Clayton Bruner	.30	.10
❑ 87	John Curtice RC	.60	.25
❑ 88	Bobby Estalella	.30	.10
❑ 89	Juan Melo	.30	.10
❑ 90	Arnold Gooch	.30	.10
❑ 91	Kevin Millwood RC	1.50	.60
❑ 92	Richie Sexson	.30	.10
❑ 93	Orlando Cabrera	.30	.10
❑ 94	Pat Cline	.30	.10
❑ 95	Anthony Sanders	.30	.10
❑ 96	Russ Johnson	.30	.10
❑ 97	Ben Grieve	.30	.10
❑ 98	Kevin McGlinchy	.30	.10
❑ 99	Paul Wilder	.30	.10
❑ 100	Russ Ortiz	.30	.10
❑ 101	Ryan Jackson RC	.40	.15
❑ 102	Heath Murray	.30	.10
❑ 103	Brian Rose	.30	.10
❑ 104	Ryan Radmanovich RC	.40	.15
❑ 105	Ricky Ledee	.30	.10
❑ 106	Jeff Wallace RC	.40	.15
❑ 107	Ryan Minor RC	.40	.15
❑ 108	Dennis Reyes	.30	.10
❑ 109	James Manias	.30	.10
❑ 110	Chris Carpenter	.30	.10
❑ 111	Daryle Ward	.30	.10
❑ 112	Vernon Wells	.30	.10
❑ 113	Chad Green	.30	.10
❑ 114	Mike Stoner RC	.40	.15
❑ 115	Brad Fullmer	.30	.10
❑ 116	Adam Eaton	.30	.10
❑ 117	Jeff Liefer	.30	.10
❑ 118	Corey Koskie RC	1.00	.40
❑ 119	Todd Helton	.50	.20
❑ 120	Jaime Jones RC	.40	.15
❑ 121	Mel Rosario	.30	.10
❑ 122	Geoff Goetz	.30	.10
❑ 123	Adrian Beltre	.30	.10
❑ 124	Jason Dellaero	.30	.10
❑ 125	Gabe Kapler RC	1.00	.40
❑ 126	Scott Schoeneweis	.30	.10
❑ 127	Ryan Brannan	.30	.10
❑ 128	Aaron Akin	.30	.10
❑ 129	Ryan Anderson RC	.40	.15
❑ 130	Brad Penny	.30	.10
❑ 131	Bruce Chen	.30	.10
❑ 132	Eli Marrero	.30	.10
❑ 133	Eric Chavez	.30	.10
❑ 134	Troy Glaus RC	4.00	1.50
❑ 135	Troy Cameron	.30	.10
❑ 136	Brian Sikorski RC	.40	.15
❑ 137	Mike Kinkade RC	.40	.15
❑ 138	Braden Looper	.30	.10
❑ 139	Mark Mangum	.30	.10
❑ 140	Danny Peoples	.30	.10
❑ 141	J.J. Davis	.30	.10
❑ 142	Ben Davis	.30	.10
❑ 143	Jacque Jones	.30	.10
❑ 144	Derrick Gibson	.30	.10
❑ 145	Bronson Arroyo	1.50	.60
❑ 146	Luis De Los Santos RC	.40	.15
❑ 147	Jeff Abbott	.30	.10
❑ 148	Mike Cuddyer RC	1.50	.60
❑ 149	Jason Romano	.30	.10
❑ 150	Shane Monahan	.30	.10
❑ 151	Ntema Ndungidi RC	.40	.15
❑ 152	Alex Sanchez	.30	.10
❑ 153	Jack Cust RC	2.00	.75
❑ 154	Brent Butler	.30	.10
❑ 155	Ramon Hernandez	.30	.10
❑ 156	Norm Hutchins	.30	.10
❑ 157	Jason Marquis	.30	.10
❑ 158	Jacob Cruz	.30	.10
❑ 159	Rob Burger RC	.40	.15
❑ 160	Dave Coggin	.30	.10
❑ 161	Preston Wilson	.30	.10
❑ 162	Jason Fitzgerald RC	.40	.15
❑ 163	Dan Serafini	.30	.10
❑ 164	Peter Munro	.30	.10
❑ 165	Trot Nixon	.30	.10
❑ 166	Homer Bush	.30	.10
❑ 167	Dermal Brown	.30	.10
❑ 168	Chad Hermansen	.30	.10
❑ 169	Julio Moreno RC	.40	.15
❑ 170	John Roskos RC	.40	.15
❑ 171	Grant Roberts	.30	.10
❑ 172	Ken Cloude	.30	.10
❑ 173	Jason Brester	.30	.10
❑ 174	Jason Conti	.30	.10
❑ 175	Jon Garland	.30	.10
❑ 176	Robbie Bell	.30	.10
❑ 177	Nathan Haynes	.30	.10
❑ 178	Ramon Ortiz RC	.60	.25
❑ 179	Shannon Stewart	.30	.10
❑ 180	Pablo Ortega	.30	.10
❑ 181	Jimmy Rollins RC	6.00	2.50
❑ 182	Sean Casey	.30	.10
❑ 183	Ted Lilly RC	1.00	.40
❑ 184	Chris Enochs RC	.40	.15
❑ 185	Magglio Ordonez UER RC	5.00	2.00
❑ 186	Mike Drumright	.30	.10
❑ 187	Aaron Boone	.30	.10
❑ 188	Matt Clement	.30	.10
❑ 189	Todd Dunwoody	.30	.10
❑ 190	Larry Rodriguez	.30	.10
❑ 191	Todd Noel	.30	.10
❑ 192	Geoff Jenkins	.30	.10
❑ 193	George Lombard	.30	.10
❑ 194	Lance Berkman	.30	.10
❑ 195	Marcus McCain	.30	.10
❑ 196	Ryan McGuire	.30	.10
❑ 197	Jhensy Sandoval	.30	.10
❑ 198	Corey Lee	.30	.10
❑ 199	Mario Valdez	.30	.10
❑ 200	Robert Fick RC	.60	.25
❑ 201	Donnie Sadler	.30	.10
❑ 202	Marc Kroon	.30	.10
❑ 203	David Miller	.30	.10
❑ 204	Jarrod Washburn	.30	.10
❑ 205	Miguel Tejada	.75	.30
❑ 206	Raul Ibanez	.30	.10
❑ 207	John Patterson	.30	.10
❑ 208	Calvin Pickering	.30	.10
❑ 209	Felix Martinez	.30	.10
❑ 210	Mark Redman	.30	.10
❑ 211	Scott Elarton	.30	.10
❑ 212	Jose Amado RC	.40	.15

❑	213	Kerry Wood	.30	.10
❑	214	Dante Powell	.30	.10
❑	215	Aramis Ramirez	.30	.10
❑	216	A.J. Hinch	.30	.10
❑	217	Dustin Carr RC	.40	.15
❑	218	Mark Kotsay	.30	.10
❑	219	Jason Standridge	.30	.10
❑	220	Luis Ordaz	.30	.10
❑	221	Orlando Hernandez RC	2.00	.75
❑	222	Cal Ripken	2.50	1.00
❑	223	Paul Molitor	.30	.10
❑	224	Derek Jeter	2.00	.75
❑	225	Barry Bonds	2.00	.75
❑	226	Jim Edmonds	.30	.10
❑	227	John Smoltz	.50	.20
❑	228	Eric Karros	.30	.10
❑	229	Ray Lankford	.30	.10
❑	230	Rey Ordonez	.30	.10
❑	231	Kenny Lofton	.30	.10
❑	232	Alex Rodriguez	1.25	.50
❑	233	Dante Bichette	.30	.10
❑	234	Pedro Martinez	.50	.20
❑	235	Carlos Delgado	.30	.10
❑	236	Rod Beck	.30	.10
❑	237	Matt Williams	.30	.10
❑	238	Charles Johnson	.30	.10
❑	239	Rico Brogna	.30	.10
❑	240	Frank Thomas	.75	.30
❑	241	Paul O'Neill	.50	.20
❑	242	Jaret Wright	.30	.10
❑	243	Brant Brown	.30	.10
❑	244	Ryan Klesko	.30	.10
❑	245	Chuck Finley	.30	.10
❑	246	Derek Bell	.30	.10
❑	247	Delino DeShields	.30	.10
❑	248	Chan Ho Park	.30	.10
❑	249	Wade Boggs	.50	.20
❑	250	Jay Buhner	.30	.10
❑	251	Butch Huskey	.30	.10
❑	252	Steve Finley	.30	.10
❑	253	Will Clark	.50	.20
❑	254	John Valentin	.30	.10
❑	255	Bobby Higginson	.30	.10
❑	256	Darryl Strawberry	.30	.10
❑	257	Randy Johnson	.75	.30
❑	258	Al Martin	.30	.10
❑	259	Travis Fryman	.30	.10
❑	260	Fred McGriff	.50	.20
❑	261	Jose Valentin	.30	.10
❑	262	Andruw Jones	.50	.20
❑	263	Kenny Rogers	.30	.10
❑	264	Moises Alou	.30	.10
❑	265	Denny Neagle	.30	.10
❑	266	Ugueth Urbina	.30	.10
❑	267	Derrek Lee	.50	.20
❑	268	Ellis Burks	.30	.10
❑	269	Mariano Rivera	.75	.30
❑	270	Dean Palmer	.30	.10
❑	271	Eddie Taubensee	.30	.10
❑	272	Brady Anderson	.30	.10
❑	273	Brian Giles	.30	.10
❑	274	Quinton McCracken	.30	.10
❑	275	Henry Rodriguez	.30	.10
❑	276	Andres Galarraga	.30	.10
❑	277	Jose Canseco	.50	.20
❑	278	David Segui	.30	.10
❑	279	Bret Saberhagen	.30	.10
❑	280	Kevin Brown	.50	.20
❑	281	Chuck Knoblauch	.30	.10
❑	282	Jeromy Burnitz	.30	.10
❑	283	Jay Bell	.30	.10
❑	284	Manny Ramirez	.50	.20
❑	285	Rick Helling	.30	.10
❑	286	Francisco Cordova	.30	.10
❑	287	Bob Abreu	.30	.10
❑	288	J.T. Snow	.30	.10
❑	289	Hideo Nomo	.75	.30
❑	290	Brian Jordan	.30	.10
❑	291	Javy Lopez	.30	.10
❑	292	Travis Lee	.30	.10
❑	293	Russell Branyan	.30	.10
❑	294	Paul Konerko	.30	.10
❑	295	Masato Yoshii RC	.60	.25
❑	296	Kris Benson	.30	.10
❑	297	Juan Encarnacion	.30	.10
❑	298	Eric Milton	.30	.10
❑	299	Mike Caruso	.30	.10
❑	300	Ricardo Aramboles RC	.40	.15
❑	301	Bobby Smith	.30	.10
❑	302	Billy Koch	.30	.10
❑	303	Richard Hidalgo	.30	.10
❑	304	Justin Baughman RC	.40	.15
❑	305	Chris Gissell	.30	.10
❑	306	Donnie Bridges RC	.40	.15
❑	307	Nelson Lara RC	.40	.15
❑	308	Randy Wolf RC	.60	.25
❑	309	Jason LaRue RC	.60	.25
❑	310	Jason Gooding RC	.40	.15
❑	311	Edgard Clemente	.30	.10
❑	312	Andrew Vessel	.30	.10
❑	313	Chris Reitsma	.30	.10
❑	314	Jesus Sanchez RC	.40	.15
❑	315	Buddy Carlyle RC	.40	.15
❑	316	Randy Winn	.30	.10
❑	317	Luis Rivera RC	.40	.15
❑	318	Marcus Thames RC	2.50	1.00
❑	319	A.J. Pierzynski	.30	.10
❑	320	Scott Randall	.30	.10
❑	321	Damian Sapp	.30	.10
❑	322	Ed Yarnall RC	.40	.15
❑	323	Luke Allen RC	.40	.15
❑	324	J.D. Smart	.30	.10
❑	325	Willie Martinez	.30	.10
❑	326	Alex Ramirez	.30	.10
❑	327	Eric DuBose RC	.40	.15
❑	328	Kevin Witt	.30	.10
❑	329	Dan McKinley RC	.40	.15
❑	330	Cliff Politte	.30	.10
❑	331	Vladimir Nunez	.30	.10
❑	332	John Halama RC	.40	.15
❑	333	Nerio Rodriguez	.30	.10
❑	334	Desi Relaford	.30	.10
❑	335	Robinson Checo	.30	.10
❑	336	John Nicholson	.50	.20
❑	337	Tom LaRosa RC	.40	.15
❑	338	Kevin Nicholson RC	.40	.15
❑	339	Javier Vazquez	.30	.10
❑	340	A.J. Zapp	.30	.10
❑	341	Tom Evans	.30	.10
❑	342	Kerry Robinson	.30	.10
❑	343	Gabe Gonzalez RC	.40	.15
❑	344	Ralph Milliard	.30	.10
❑	345	Enrique Wilson	.30	.10
❑	346	Elvin Hernandez	.30	.10
❑	347	Mike Lincoln RC	.40	.15
❑	348	Cesar King RC	.40	.15
❑	349	Cristian Guzman RC	.60	.25
❑	350	Donzell McDonald	.30	.10
❑	351	Jim Parque RC	.40	.15
❑	352	Mike Saipe RC	.40	.15
❑	353	Carlos Febles RC	.60	.25
❑	354	Dernell Stenson RC	.40	.15
❑	355	Mark Osborne RC	.40	.15
❑	356	Odalis Perez RC	1.50	.60
❑	357	Jason Dewey RC	.40	.15
❑	358	Joe Fontenot	.30	.10
❑	359	Jason Grilli RC	.40	.15
❑	360	Kevin Haverbusch RC	.40	.15
❑	361	Jay Yennaco RC	.40	.15
❑	362	Brian Buchanan	.30	.10
❑	363	John Barnes	.30	.10
❑	364	Chris Fussell	.30	.10
❑	365	Kevin Gibbs RC	.40	.15
❑	366	Joe Lawrence	.30	.10
❑	367	DaRond Stovall	.30	.10
❑	368	Brian Fuentes RC	.40	.15
❑	369	Jimmy Anderson	.30	.10
❑	370	Lariel Gonzalez RC	.40	.15
❑	371	Scott Williamson RC	.40	.15
❑	372	Milton Bradley	.30	.10
❑	373	Jason Halper RC	.40	.15
❑	374	Brent Billingsley RC	.40	.15
❑	375	Joe DePastino RC	.40	.15
❑	376	Jake Westbrook	.30	.10
❑	377	Octavio Dotel	.30	.10
❑	378	Jason Williams RC	.40	.15
❑	379	Julio Ramirez RC	.40	.15
❑	380	Seth Greisinger	.30	.10
❑	381	Mike Judd RC	.40	.15
❑	382	Ben Ford RC	.40	.15
❑	383	Tom Bennett RC	.40	.15
❑	384	Adam Butler RC	.40	.15
❑	385	Wade Miller RC	1.00	.40
❑	386	Kyle Peterson RC	.40	.15
❑	387	Tommy Peterman RC	.40	.15
❑	388	Onan Masaoka	.30	.10
❑	389	Jason Rakers RC	.40	.15
❑	390	Rafael Medina	.30	.10
❑	391	Luis Lopez RC	.40	.15
❑	392	Jeff Yoder	.30	.10
❑	393	Vance Wilson RC	.40	.15
❑	394	Fernando Seguignol RC	.40	.15
❑	395	Ron Wright	.30	.10
❑	396	Ruben Mateo RC	.40	.15
❑	397	Steve Lomasney RC	.60	.25
❑	398	Damian Jackson	.30	.10
❑	399	Mike Jerzembeck RC	.40	.15
❑	400	Luis Rivas RC	1.00	.40
❑	401	Kevin Burford RC	.40	.15
❑	402	Glenn Davis	.30	.10
❑	403	Robert Luce RC	.40	.15
❑	404	Cole Liniak	.30	.10
❑	405	Matt LeCroy RC	.60	.25
❑	406	Jeremy Giambi RC	.60	.25
❑	407	Shawn Chacon	.30	.10
❑	408	Dewayne Wise RC	.40	.15
❑	409	Steve Woodard	.30	.10
❑	410	Francisco Cordero RC	1.00	.40
❑	411	Damon Minor RC	.40	.15
❑	412	Lou Collier	.30	.10
❑	413	Justin Towle	.30	.10
❑	414	Juan LeBron	.30	.10
❑	415	Michael Coleman	.30	.10
❑	416	Felix Rodriguez	.30	.10
❑	417	Paul Ah Yat RC	.40	.15
❑	418	Kevin Barker RC	.40	.15
❑	419	Brian Meadows	.30	.10
❑	420	Darnell McDonald RC	.40	.15
❑	421	Matt Kinney RC	.40	.15
❑	422	Mike Vavrek RC	.40	.15
❑	423	Courtney Duncan RC	.40	.15
❑	424	Kevin Millar RC	1.50	.60
❑	425	Ruben Rivera	.30	.10
❑	426	Steve Shoemaker RC	.40	.15
❑	427	Dan Reichert RC	.40	.15
❑	428	Carlos Lee RC	3.00	1.25
❑	429	Rod Barajas	1.00	.40
❑	430	Pablo Ozuna RC	.60	.25
❑	431	Todd Belitz RC	.40	.15
❑	432	Sidney Ponson	.30	.10
❑	433	Steve Carver RC	.40	.15
❑	434	Esteban Yan RC	.60	.25
❑	435	Cedrick Bowers	.30	.10
❑	436	Marlon Anderson	.30	.10
❑	437	Carl Pavano	.30	.10
❑	438	Jae Weong Seo RC	.60	.25
❑	439	Jose Taveras RC	.40	.15
❑	440	Matt Anderson RC	.40	.15
❑	441	Darron Ingram RC	.40	.15
❑	NNO	S.Hasegawa '91 BBM	10.00	4.00
❑	NNO	H.Irabu '91 BBM	10.00	4.00
❑	NNO	H.Nomo '91 BBM	25.00	10.00

1999 Bowman

❑	COMPLETE SET (440)	80.00	30.00
❑	COMPLETE SERIES 1 (220)	30.00	12.50
❑	COMPLETE SERIES 2 (220)	50.00	20.00
❑	1 Ben Grieve	.30	.10
❑	2 Kerry Wood	.30	.10
❑	3 Ruben Rivera	.30	.10

❑	4	Sandy Alomar Jr.	.30	.10
❑	5	Cal Ripken	2.50	1.00
❑	6	Mark McGwire	2.00	.75
❑	7	Vladimir Guerrero	.75	.30
❑	8	Moises Alou	.30	.10
❑	9	Jim Edmonds	.30	.10
❑	10	Greg Maddux	1.25	.50
❑	11	Gary Sheffield	.30	.10
❑	12	John Valentin	.30	.10
❑	13	Chuck Knoblauch	.30	.10
❑	14	Tony Clark	.30	.10
❑	15	Rusty Greer	.30	.10
❑	16	Al Leiter	.30	.10
❑	17	Travis Lee	.30	.10
❑	18	Jose Cruz Jr.	.30	.10
❑	19	Pedro Martinez	.50	.10
❑	20	Paul O'Neill	.50	.20
❑	21	Todd Walker	.30	.10
❑	22	Vinny Castilla	.30	.10
❑	23	Barry Larkin	.50	.20
❑	24	Curt Schilling	.30	.10
❑	25	Jason Kendall	.30	.10
❑	26	Scott Erickson	.30	.10
❑	27	Andres Galarraga	.30	.10
❑	28	Jeff Shaw	.30	.10
❑	29	John Olerud	.30	.10
❑	30	Orlando Hernandez	.30	.10
❑	31	Larry Walker	.30	.10
❑	32	Andruw Jones	.50	.20
❑	33	Jeff Cirillo	.30	.10
❑	34	Barry Bonds	2.00	.75
❑	35	Manny Ramirez	.50	.20
❑	36	Mark Kotsay	.30	.10
❑	37	Ivan Rodriguez	.50	.20
❑	38	Jeff King	.30	.10
❑	39	Brian Hunter	.30	.10
❑	40	Ray Durham	.30	.10
❑	41	Bernie Williams	.50	.20
❑	42	Darin Erstad	.30	.10
❑	43	Chipper Jones	.75	.30
❑	44	Pat Hentgen	.30	.10
❑	45	Eric Young	.30	.10
❑	46	Jaret Wright	.30	.10
❑	47	Juan Guzman	.30	.10
❑	48	Jorge Posada	.50	.20
❑	49	Bobby Higginson	.30	.10
❑	50	Jose Guillen	.30	.10
❑	51	Trevor Hoffman	.30	.10
❑	52	Ken Griffey Jr.	1.25	.50
❑	53	David Justice	.30	.10
❑	54	Matt Williams	.30	.10
❑	55	Eric Karros	.30	.10
❑	56	Derek Bell	.30	.10
❑	57	Ray Lankford	.30	.10
❑	58	Mariano Rivera	.75	.30
❑	59	Brett Tomko	.30	.10
❑	60	Mike Mussina	.50	.20
❑	61	Kenny Lofton	.30	.10
❑	62	Chuck Finley	.30	.10
❑	63	Alex Gonzalez	.30	.10
❑	64	Mark Grace	.50	.20
❑	65	Raul Mondesi	.30	.10
❑	66	David Cone	.30	.10
❑	67	Brad Fullmer	.30	.10
❑	68	Andy Benes	.30	.10
❑	69	John Smoltz	.50	.20
❑	70	Shane Reynolds	.30	.10
❑	71	Bruce Chen	.30	.10
❑	72	Adam Kennedy	.30	.10
❑	73	Jack Cust	.30	.10
❑	74	Matt Clement	.30	.10
❑	75	Derrick Gibson	.30	.10
❑	76	Darnell McDonald	.30	.10
❑	77	Adam Everett RC	1.00	.40
❑	78	Ricardo Aramboles	.30	.10
❑	79	Mark Quinn RC	.40	.15
❑	80	Jason Rakers	.30	.10
❑	81	Seth Etherton RC	.40	.15
❑	82	Jeff Urban RC	.60	.25
❑	83	Manny Aybar	.30	.10
❑	84	Mike Nannini RC	.40	.15
❑	85	Onan Masaoka	.30	.10
❑	86	Rod Barajas	.30	.10
❑	87	Mike Frank	.30	.10
❑	88	Scott Randall	.30	.10
❑	89	Justin Bowles RC	.40	.15
❑	90	Chris Haas	.30	.10
❑	91	Arturo McDowell RC	.40	.15
❑	92	Matt Belisle RC	.40	.15
❑	93	Scott Elarton	.30	.10
❑	94	Vernon Wells	.30	.10
❑	95	Pat Cline	.30	.10
❑	96	Ryan Anderson	.30	.10
❑	97	Kevin Barker	.30	.10
❑	98	Ruben Mateo	.30	.10
❑	99	Robert Fick	.30	.10
❑	100	Corey Koskie	.30	.10
❑	101	Ricky Ledee	.30	.10
❑	102	Rick Elder RC	.40	.15
❑	103	Jack Cressend RC	.40	.15
❑	104	Joe Lawrence	.30	.10
❑	105	Mike Lincoln	.30	.10
❑	106	Kit Pellow RC	.40	.15
❑	107	Matt Burch RC	.60	.25
❑	108	Cole Liniak	.30	.10
❑	109	Jason Dewey	.30	.10
❑	110	Cesar King	.30	.10
❑	111	Julio Ramirez	.30	.10
❑	112	Jake Westbrook	.30	.10
❑	113	Eric Valent RC	.60	.25
❑	114	Roosevelt Brown RC	.40	.15
❑	115	Choo Freeman RC	.60	.25
❑	116	Juan Melo	.30	.10
❑	117	Jason Grilli	.30	.10
❑	118	Jared Sandberg	.30	.10
❑	119	Glenn Davis	.30	.10
❑	120	David Riske RC	.40	.15
❑	121	Jacque Jones	.30	.10
❑	122	Corey Lee	.30	.10
❑	123	Michael Barrett	.30	.10
❑	124	Lariel Gonzalez	.30	.10
❑	125	Mitch Meluskey	.30	.10
❑	126	F.Adnan Garcia	.30	.10
❑	127	Tony Torcato RC	.40	.15
❑	128	Jeff Liefer	.30	.10
❑	129	Ntema Ndungidi	.30	.10
❑	130	Andy Brown RC	.40	.15
❑	131	Ryan Mills RC	.40	.15
❑	132	Andy Abad RC	.40	.15
❑	133	Carlos Febles	.30	.10
❑	134	Jason Tyner RC	.40	.15
❑	135	Mark Osborne	.30	.10
❑	136	Phil Norton RC	.40	.15
❑	137	Nathan Haynes	.30	.10
❑	138	Roy Halladay	.30	.10
❑	139	Juan Encarnacion	.30	.10
❑	140	Brad Penny	.30	.10
❑	141	Grant Roberts	.30	.10
❑	142	Aramis Ramirez	.30	.10
❑	143	Cristian Guzman	.30	.10
❑	144	Mamon Tucker RC	.40	.15
❑	145	Ryan Bradley	.30	.10
❑	146	Brian Simmons	.30	.10
❑	147	Dan Reichert	.30	.10
❑	148	Russ Branyan	.30	.10
❑	149	Victor Valencia RC	.50	.20
❑	150	Scott Schoeneweis	.30	.10
❑	151	Sean Spencer RC	.40	.15
❑	152	Odalis Perez	.30	.10
❑	153	Joe Fontenot	.30	.10
❑	154	Milton Bradley	.30	.10
❑	155	Josh McKinley RC	.40	.15
❑	156	Terrence Long	.30	.10
❑	157	Danny Klassen	.30	.10
❑	158	Paul Hoover RC	.60	.25
❑	159	Ron Belliard	.30	.10
❑	160	Armando Rios	.30	.10
❑	161	Ramon Hernandez	.30	.10
❑	162	Jason Conti	.30	.10
❑	163	Chad Hermansen	.30	.10
❑	164	Jason Standridge	.30	.10
❑	165	Jason Dellaero	.30	.10
❑	166	John Curtice	.30	.10
❑	167	Clayton Andrews RC	.40	.15
❑	168	Jeremy Giambi	.30	.10
❑	169	Alex Ramirez	.30	.10
❑	170	Gabe Molina RC	.40	.15
❑	171	Mario Encarnacion RC	.40	.15
❑	172	Mike Zywica RC	.40	.15
❑	173	Chip Ambres RC	.40	.15
❑	174	Trot Nixon	.30	.10
❑	175	Pat Burrell RC	3.00	1.25
❑	176	Jeff Yoder	.30	.10
❑	177	Chris Jones RC	.40	.15
❑	178	Kevin Witt	.30	.10
❑	179	Keith Luuloa RC	.40	.15
❑	180	Billy Koch	.30	.10
❑	181	Damaso Marte RC	.40	.15
❑	182	Ryan Glynn RC	.40	.15
❑	183	Calvin Pickering	.30	.10
❑	184	Michael Cuddyer	.30	.10
❑	185	Nick Johnson RC	2.00	.75
❑	186	Doug Mientkiewicz RC	1.00	.40
❑	187	Nate Cornejo RC	.40	.15
❑	188	Octavio Dotel	.30	.10
❑	189	Wes Helms	.30	.10
❑	190	Nelson Lara	.30	.10
❑	191	Chuck Abbott RC	.40	.15
❑	192	Tony Armas Jr.	.30	.10
❑	193	Gil Meche	.30	.10
❑	194	Ben Petrick	.30	.10
❑	195	Chris George RC	.40	.15
❑	196	Scott Hunter RC	.40	.15
❑	197	Ryan Brannan	.30	.10
❑	198	Amaury Garcia RC	.60	.25
❑	199	Chris Gissell	.30	.10
❑	200	Austin Kearns RC	3.00	1.25
❑	201	Alex Gonzalez	.30	.10
❑	202	Wade Miller	.30	.10
❑	203	Scott Williamson	.30	.10
❑	204	Chris Enochs	.30	.10
❑	205	Fernando Seguignol	.30	.10
❑	206	Marlon Anderson	.30	.10
❑	207	Todd Sears RC	.40	.15
❑	208	Nate Bump RC	.40	.15
❑	209	J.M. Gold RC	.40	.15
❑	210	Matt LeCroy	.30	.10
❑	211	Alex Hernandez	.30	.10
❑	212	Luis Rivera	.30	.10
❑	213	Troy Cameron	.30	.10
❑	214	Alex Escobar RC	.60	.25
❑	215	Jason LaRue	.30	.10
❑	216	Kyle Peterson	.30	.10
❑	217	Brent Butler	.30	.10
❑	218	Dernell Stenson	.30	.10
❑	219	Adrian Beltre	.30	.10
❑	220	Daryle Ward	.30	.10
❑	221	Jim Thome	.50	.20
❑	222	Cliff Floyd	.30	.10
❑	223	Rickey Henderson	.75	.30
❑	224	Garret Anderson	.30	.10
❑	225	Ken Caminiti	.30	.10
❑	226	Bret Boone	.30	.10
❑	227	Jeromy Burnitz	.30	.10
❑	228	Steve Finley	.30	.10
❑	229	Miguel Tejada	.30	.10
❑	230	Greg Vaughn	.30	.10
❑	231	Jose Offerman	.30	.10
❑	232	Andy Ashby	.30	.10
❑	233	Albert Belle	.30	.10
❑	234	Fernando Tatis	.30	.10
❑	235	Todd Helton	.50	.20
❑	236	Sean Casey	.30	.10
❑	237	Brian Giles	.30	.10
❑	238	Andy Pettitte	.50	.20
❑	239	Fred McGriff	.50	.20
❑	240	Roberto Alomar	.50	.20
❑	241	Edgar Martinez	.50	.20
❑	242	Lee Stevens	.30	.10
❑	243	Shawn Green	.30	.10
❑	244	Ryan Klesko	.30	.10
❑	245	Sammy Sosa	.75	.30
❑	246	Todd Hundley	.30	.10
❑	247	Shannon Stewart	.30	.10
❑	248	Randy Johnson	.75	.30
❑	249	Rondell White	.30	.10
❑	250	Mike Piazza	1.25	.50
❑	251	Craig Biggio	.50	.20
❑	252	David Wells	.30	.10
❑	253	Brian Jordan	.30	.10
❑	254	Edgar Renteria	.30	.10
❑	255	Bartolo Colon	.30	.10
❑	256	Frank Thomas	.75	.30
❑	257	Will Clark	.50	.20
❑	258	Dean Palmer	.30	.10
❑	259	Dmitri Young	.30	.10
❑	260	Scott Rolen	.50	.20
❑	261	Jeff Kent	.30	.10

❑	262	Dante Bichette	.30	.10
❑	263	Nomar Garciaparra	1.25	.50
❑	264	Tony Gwynn	1.00	.40
❑	265	Alex Rodriguez	1.25	.50
❑	266	Jose Canseco	.50	.20
❑	267	Jason Giambi	.30	.10
❑	268	Jeff Bagwell	.50	.20
❑	269	Carlos Delgado	.30	.10
❑	270	Tom Glavine	.50	.20
❑	271	Eric Davis	.30	.10
❑	272	Edgardo Alfonzo	.30	.10
❑	273	Tim Salmon	.50	.20
❑	274	Johnny Damon	.50	.20
❑	275	Rafael Palmeiro	.50	.20
❑	276	Denny Neagle	.30	.10
❑	277	Neifi Perez	.30	.10
❑	278	Roger Clemens	1.50	.60
❑	279	Brant Brown	.30	.10
❑	280	Kevin Brown	.50	.20
❑	281	Jay Bell	.30	.10
❑	282	Jay Buhner	.30	.10
❑	283	Matt Lawton	.30	.10
❑	284	Robin Ventura	.30	.10
❑	285	Juan Gonzalez	.30	.10
❑	286	Mo Vaughn	.30	.10
❑	287	Kevin Millwood	.30	.10
❑	288	Tino Martinez	.50	.20
❑	289	Justin Thompson	.30	.10
❑	290	Derek Jeter	2.00	.75
❑	291	Ben Davis	.30	.10
❑	292	Mike Lowell	.30	.10
❑	293	Calvin Murray	.30	.10
❑	294	Micah Bowie RC	.40	.15
❑	295	Lance Berkman	.30	.10
❑	296	Jason Marquis	.30	.10
❑	297	Chad Green	.30	.10
❑	298	Dee Brown	.30	.10
❑	299	Jerry Hairston Jr.	.30	.10
❑	300	Gabe Kapler	.30	.10
❑	301	Brent Stentz RC	.60	.25
❑	302	Scott Mullen RC	.40	.15
❑	303	Brandon Reed	.30	.10
❑	304	Shea Hillenbrand RC	1.50	.60
❑	305	J.D. Closser RC	.60	.25
❑	306	Gary Matthews Jr.	.30	.10
❑	307	Toby Hall RC	.60	.25
❑	308	Jason Phillips RC	.40	.15
❑	309	Jose Macias RC	.40	.15
❑	310	Jung Bong RC	.40	.15
❑	311	Ramon Soler RC	.40	.15
❑	312	Kelly Dransfeldt RC	.40	.15
❑	313	Carlos E. Hernandez RC	.60	.25
❑	314	Kevin Haverbusch	.30	.10
❑	315	Aaron Myette RC	.40	.15
❑	316	Chad Harville RC	.40	.15
❑	317	Kyle Farnsworth RC	.60	.25
❑	318	Gookie Dawkins RC	.60	.25
❑	319	Willie Martinez	.30	.10
❑	320	Carlos Lee	.30	.10
❑	321	Carlos Pena RC	.75	.30
❑	322	Peter Bergeron RC	.40	.15
❑	323	A.J. Burnett RC	1.50	.60
❑	324	Bucky Jacobsen RC	.60	.25
❑	325	Mo Bruce RC	.40	.15
❑	326	Reggie Taylor	.30	.10
❑	327	Jackie Rexrode	.30	.10
❑	328	Alvin Morrow RC	.40	.15
❑	329	Carlos Beltran	.50	.20
❑	330	Eric Chavez	.30	.10
❑	331	John Patterson	.30	.10
❑	332	Jayson Werth	.30	.10
❑	333	Richie Sexson	.30	.10
❑	334	Randy Wolf	.30	.10
❑	335	Eli Marrero	.30	.10
❑	336	Paul LoDuca	.30	.10
❑	337	J.D Smart	.30	.10
❑	338	Ryan Minor	.30	.10
❑	339	Kris Benson	.30	.10
❑	340	George Lombard	.30	.10
❑	341	Troy Glaus	.50	.20
❑	342	Eddie Yarnall	.30	.10
❑	343	Kip Wells RC	.60	.25
❑	344	C.C. Sabathia RC	3.00	1.25
❑	345	Sean Burroughs RC	1.00	.40
❑	346	Felipe Lopez RC	2.50	1.00
❑	347	Ryan Rupe RC	.40	.15
❑	348	Orber Moreno RC	.40	.15
❑	349	Rafael Roque RC	.40	.15
❑	350	Alfonso Soriano RC	6.00	2.50
❑	351	Pablo Ozuna	.30	.10
❑	352	Corey Patterson RC	1.50	.60
❑	353	Braden Looper	.30	.10
❑	354	Robbie Bell	.30	.10
❑	355	Mark Mulder RC	2.50	1.00
❑	356	Angel Pena	.30	.10
❑	357	Kevin McGlinchy	.30	.10
❑	358	Michael Restovich RC	.60	.25
❑	359	Eric DuBose	.30	.10
❑	360	Geoff Jenkins	.30	.10
❑	361	Mark Harriger RC	.40	.15
❑	362	Junior Herndon RC	.40	.15
❑	363	Tim Raines Jr. RC	.40	.15
❑	364	Rafael Furcal RC	2.50	1.00
❑	365	Marcus Giles RC	1.50	.60
❑	366	Ted Lilly	.30	.10
❑	367	Jorge Toca RC	.60	.25
❑	368	David Kelton RC	.40	.15
❑	369	Adam Dunn RC	5.00	2.00
❑	370	Guillermo Mota RC	.40	.15
❑	371	Brett Laxton RC	.40	.15
❑	372	Travis Harper RC	.60	.25
❑	373	Tom Davey RC	.40	.15
❑	374	Darren Blakely RC	.40	.15
❑	375	Tim Hudson RC	4.00	1.50
❑	376	Jason Romano	.30	.10
❑	377	Dan Reichert	.30	.10
❑	378	Julio Lugo RC	1.00	.40
❑	379	Jose Garcia RC	.40	.15
❑	380	Erubiel Durazo RC	.60	.25
❑	381	Jose Jimenez	.30	.10
❑	382	Chris Fussell	.30	.10
❑	383	Steve Lomasney	.30	.10
❑	384	Juan Pena RC	.60	.25
❑	385	Allen Levrault RC	.40	.15
❑	386	Juan Rivera RC	1.50	.60
❑	387	Steve Colyer RC	.40	.15
❑	388	Joe Nathan RC	2.00	.75
❑	389	Ron Walker RC	.40	.15
❑	390	Nick Bierbrodt	.30	.10
❑	391	Luke Prokopec RC	.40	.15
❑	392	Dave Roberts RC	1.00	.40
❑	393	Mike Darr	.30	.10
❑	394	Abraham Nunez RC	.60	.25
❑	395	Giuseppe Chiaramonte RC	.40	.15
❑	396	Jermaine Van Buren RC	.40	.15
❑	397	Mike Kusiewicz	.30	.10
❑	398	Matt Wise RC	.40	.15
❑	399	Joe McEwing RC	.60	.25
❑	400	Matt Holliday RC	6.00	2.50
❑	401	Willi Mo Pena RC	5.00	2.00
❑	402	Ruben Quevedo RC	.40	.15
❑	403	Rob Ryan RC	.40	.15
❑	404	Freddy Garcia RC	1.50	.60
❑	405	Kevin Eberwein RC	.40	.15
❑	406	Jesus Colome RC	.40	.15
❑	407	Chris Singleton	.30	.10
❑	408	Bubba Crosby RC	1.00	.40
❑	409	Jesus Cordero RC	.40	.15
❑	410	Donny Leon	.30	.10
❑	411	Goefrey Tomlinson RC	.60	.25
❑	412	Jeff Winchester RC	.40	.15
❑	413	Adam Piatt RC	.40	.15
❑	414	Robert Stratton	.30	.10
❑	415	T.J. Tucker	.30	.10
❑	416	Ryan Langerhans RC	1.00	.40
❑	417	Anthony Shumaker RC	.40	.15
❑	418	Matt Miller RC	.40	.15
❑	419	Doug Clark RC	.40	.15
❑	420	Kory DeHaan RC	.40	.15
❑	421	David Eckstein RC	3.00	1.25
❑	422	Brian Cooper RC	.40	.15
❑	423	Brady Clark RC	1.50	.60
❑	424	Chris Magruder RC	.60	.25
❑	425	Bobby Seay RC	.40	.15
❑	426	Aubrey Huff RC	2.00	.75
❑	427	Mike Jerzembeck	.30	.10
❑	428	Matt Blank RC	.60	.25
❑	429	Benny Agbayani RC	.60	.25
❑	430	Kevin Beirne RC	.40	.15
❑	431	Josh Hamilton RC	8.00	3.00
❑	432	Josh Girdley RC	.40	.15
❑	433	Kyle Snyder RC	.40	.15
❑	434	Mike Paradis RC	.40	.15
❑	435	Jason Jennings RC	1.00	.40
❑	436	David Walling RC	.40	.15
❑	437	Omar Ortiz RC	.60	.25
❑	438	Jay Gehrke RC	.60	.25
❑	439	Casey Burns RC	.60	.25
❑	440	Carl Crawford RC	6.00	2.50

2000 Bowman

❑		COMPLETE SET (440)	60.00	25.00
❑	1	Vladimir Guerrero	.75	.30
❑	2	Chipper Jones	.75	.30
❑	3	Todd Walker	.30	.10
❑	4	Barry Larkin	.50	.20
❑	5	Bernie Williams	.50	.20
❑	6	Todd Helton	.50	.20
❑	7	Jermaine Dye	.30	.10
❑	8	Brian Giles	.30	.10
❑	9	Freddy Garcia	.30	.10
❑	10	Greg Vaughn	.30	.10
❑	11	Alex Gonzalez	.30	.10
❑	12	Luis Gonzalez	.30	.10
❑	13	Ron Belliard	.30	.10
❑	14	Ben Grieve	.30	.10
❑	15	Carlos Delgado	.30	.10
❑	16	Brian Jordan	.30	.10
❑	17	Fernando Tatis	.30	.10
❑	18	Ryan Rupe	.30	.10
❑	19	Miguel Tejada	.30	.10
❑	20	Mark Grace	.50	.20
❑	21	Kenny Lofton	.30	.10
❑	22	Eric Karros	.30	.10
❑	23	Cliff Floyd	.30	.10
❑	24	John Halama	.30	.10
❑	25	Cristian Guzman	.30	.10
❑	26	Scott Williamson	.30	.10
❑	27	Mike Lieberthal	.30	.10
❑	28	Tim Hudson	.30	.10
❑	29	Warren Morris	.30	.10
❑	30	Pedro Martinez	.50	.20
❑	31	John Smoltz	.50	.20
❑	32	Ray Durham	.30	.10
❑	33	Chad Allen	.30	.10
❑	34	Tony Clark	.30	.10
❑	35	Tino Martinez	.50	.20
❑	36	J.T. Snow	.30	.10
❑	37	Kevin Brown	.30	.10
❑	38	Bartolo Colon	.30	.10
❑	39	Rey Ordonez	.30	.10
❑	40	Jeff Bagwell	.50	.20
❑	41	Ivan Rodriguez	.50	.20
❑	42	Eric Chavez	.30	.10
❑	43	Eric Milton	.30	.10
❑	44	Jose Canseco	.50	.20
❑	45	Shawn Green	.30	.10
❑	46	Rich Aurilia	.30	.10
❑	47	Roberto Alomar	.50	.20
❑	48	Brian Daubach	.30	.10
❑	49	Magglio Ordonez	.30	.10
❑	50	Derek Jeter	2.00	.75
❑	51	Kris Benson	.30	.10
❑	52	Albert Belle	.30	.10
❑	53	Rondell White	.30	.10
❑	54	Justin Thompson	.30	.10
❑	55	Nomar Garciaparra	1.25	.50
❑	56	Chuck Finley	.30	.10
❑	57	Omar Vizquel	.50	.20
❑	58	Luis Castillo	.30	.10

❑ 59 Richard Hidalgo .30 .10
❑ 60 Barry Bonds 2.00 .75
❑ 61 Craig Biggio .50 .20
❑ 62 Doug Glanville .30 .10
❑ 63 Gabe Kapler .30 .10
❑ 64 Johnny Damon .50 .20
❑ 65 Pokey Reese .30 .10
❑ 66 Andy Pettitte .50 .20
❑ 67 B.J. Surhoff .30 .10
❑ 68 Richie Sexson .30 .10
❑ 69 Javy Lopez .30 .10
❑ 70 Raul Mondesi .30 .10
❑ 71 Darin Erstad .30 .10
❑ 72 Kevin Millwood .30 .10
❑ 73 Ricky Ledee .30 .10
❑ 74 John Olerud .30 .10
❑ 75 Sean Casey .30 .10
❑ 76 Carlos Febles .30 .10
❑ 77 Paul O'Neill .50 .20
❑ 78 Bob Abreu .30 .10
❑ 79 Neifi Perez .30 .10
❑ 80 Tony Gwynn 1.00 .40
❑ 81 Russ Ortiz .30 .10
❑ 82 Matt Williams .30 .10
❑ 83 Chris Carpenter .30 .10
❑ 84 Roger Cedeno .30 .10
❑ 85 Tim Salmon .50 .20
❑ 86 Billy Koch .30 .10
❑ 87 Jeromy Burnitz .30 .10
❑ 88 Edgardo Alfonzo .30 .10
❑ 89 Jay Bell .30 .10
❑ 90 Manny Ramirez .50 .20
❑ 91 Frank Thomas .75 .30
❑ 92 Mike Mussina .50 .20
❑ 93 J.D. Drew .30 .10
❑ 94 Adrian Beltre .30 .10
❑ 95 Alex Rodriguez 1.25 .50
❑ 96 Larry Walker .30 .10
❑ 97 Juan Encarnacion .30 .10
❑ 98 Mike Sweeney .30 .10
❑ 99 Rusty Greer .30 .10
❑ 100 Randy Johnson .75 .30
❑ 101 Jose Vidro .30 .10
❑ 102 Preston Wilson .30 .10
❑ 103 Greg Maddux 1.25 .50
❑ 104 Jason Giambi .30 .10
❑ 105 Cal Ripken 2.50 1.00
❑ 106 Carlos Beltran .30 .10
❑ 107 Vinny Castilla .30 .10
❑ 108 Mariano Rivera .75 .30
❑ 109 Mo Vaughn .30 .10
❑ 110 Rafael Palmeiro .50 .20
❑ 111 Shannon Stewart .30 .10
❑ 112 Mike Hampton .30 .10
❑ 113 Joe Nathan .30 .10
❑ 114 Ben Davis .30 .10
❑ 115 Andruw Jones .50 .20
❑ 116 Robin Ventura .30 .10
❑ 117 Damion Easley .30 .10
❑ 118 Jeff Cirillo .30 .10
❑ 119 Kerry Wood .30 .10
❑ 120 Scott Rolen .50 .20
❑ 121 Sammy Sosa .75 .30
❑ 122 Ken Griffey Jr. 1.25 .50
❑ 123 Shane Reynolds .30 .10
❑ 124 Troy Glaus .30 .10
❑ 125 Tom Glavine .50 .20
❑ 126 Michael Barrett .30 .10
❑ 127 Al Leiter .30 .10
❑ 128 Jason Kendall .30 .10
❑ 129 Roger Clemens 1.50 .60
❑ 130 Juan Gonzalez .30 .10
❑ 131 Corey Koskie .30 .10
❑ 132 Curt Schilling .30 .10
❑ 133 Mike Piazza 1.25 .50
❑ 134 Gary Sheffield .30 .10
❑ 135 Jim Thome .50 .20
❑ 136 Orlando Hernandez .30 .10
❑ 137 Ray Lankford .30 .10
❑ 138 Geoff Jenkins .30 .10
❑ 139 Jose Lima .30 .10
❑ 140 Mark McGwire 2.00 .75
❑ 141 Adam Piatt .30 .10
❑ 142 Pat Manning RC .30 .10
❑ 143 Marcos Castillo RC .30 .10
❑ 144 Lesli Brea RC .30 .10

❑ 145 Humberto Cota RC .50 .20
❑ 146 Ben Petrick .30 .10
❑ 147 Kip Wells .30 .10
❑ 148 Wily Pena .30 .10
❑ 149 Chris Wakeland RC .30 .10
❑ 150 Brad Baker RC .30 .10
❑ 151 Robbie Morrison RC .30 .10
❑ 152 Reggie Taylor .30 .10
❑ 153 Matt Ginter RC .30 .10
❑ 154 Peter Bergeron .30 .10
❑ 155 Roosevelt Brown .30 .10
❑ 156 Matt Cepicky RC .30 .10
❑ 157 Ramon Castro .30 .10
❑ 158 Brad Baisley RC .30 .10
❑ 159 Jeff Goldbach RC .30 .10
❑ 160 Mitch Meluskey .30 .10
❑ 161 Chad Harville .30 .10
❑ 162 Brian Cooper .30 .10
❑ 163 Marcus Giles .30 .10
❑ 164 Jim Morris .75 .30
❑ 165 Geoff Goetz .30 .10
❑ 166 Bobby Bradley RC .30 .10
❑ 167 Rob Bell .30 .10
❑ 168 Joe Crede 1.50 .60
❑ 169 Michael Restovich .30 .10
❑ 170 Quincy Foster RC .30 .10
❑ 171 Enrique Cruz RC .30 .10
❑ 172 Mark Quinn .30 .10
❑ 173 Nick Johnson .30 .10
❑ 174 Jeff Liefer .30 .10
❑ 175 Kevin Mench RC 2.00 .75
❑ 176 Steve Lomasney .30 .10
❑ 177 Jayson Werth .30 .10
❑ 178 Tim Drew .30 .10
❑ 179 Chip Ambres .30 .10
❑ 180 Ryan Anderson .30 .10
❑ 181 Matt Blank .30 .10
❑ 182 Giuseppe Chiaramonte .30 .10
❑ 183 Corey Myers RC .30 .10
❑ 184 Jeff Yoder .30 .10
❑ 185 Craig Dingman RC .30 .10
❑ 186 Jon Hamilton RC .30 .10
❑ 187 Toby Hall .30 .10
❑ 188 Russell Branyan .30 .10
❑ 189 Brian Falkenborg RC .30 .10
❑ 190 Aaron Harang RC 2.50 1.00
❑ 191 Juan Pena .30 .10
❑ 192 Travis Thompson RC .30 .10
❑ 193 Alfonso Soriano .75 .30
❑ 194 Alejandro Diaz RC .30 .10
❑ 195 Carlos Pena .30 .10
❑ 196 Kevin Nicholson .30 .10
❑ 197 Mo Bruce .30 .10
❑ 198 C.C. Sabathia .30 .10
❑ 199 Carl Crawford .30 .10
❑ 200 Rafael Furcal .30 .10
❑ 201 Andrew Beinbrink RC .30 .10
❑ 202 Jimmy Osting .30 .10
❑ 203 Aaron McNeal RC .30 .10
❑ 204 Brett Laxton .30 .10
❑ 205 Chris George .30 .10
❑ 206 Felipe Lopez .30 .10
❑ 207 Ben Sheets RC 2.50 1.00
❑ 208 Mike Meyers RC .50 .20
❑ 209 Jason Conti .30 .10
❑ 210 Milton Bradley .30 .10
❑ 211 Chris Mears RC .30 .10
❑ 212 Carlos Hernandez RC .75 .30
❑ 213 Jason Romano .30 .10
❑ 214 Geofrey Tomlinson .30 .10
❑ 215 Jimmy Rollins .30 .10
❑ 216 Pablo Ozuna .30 .10
❑ 217 Steve Cox .30 .10
❑ 218 Terrence Long .30 .10
❑ 219 Jeff DaVanon RC .50 .20
❑ 220 Rick Ankiel .30 .10
❑ 221 Jason Standridge .30 .10
❑ 222 Tony Armas Jr. .30 .10
❑ 223 Jason Tyner .30 .10
❑ 224 Ramon Ortiz .30 .10
❑ 225 Daryle Ward .30 .10
❑ 226 Enger Veras RC .30 .10
❑ 227 Chris Jones .30 .10
❑ 228 Eric Cammack RC .30 .10
❑ 229 Ruben Mateo .30 .10
❑ 230 Ken Harvey RC .50 .20

❑ 231 Jake Westbrook .30 .10
❑ 232 Rob Purvis RC .30 .10
❑ 233 Choo Freeman .30 .10
❑ 234 Aramis Ramirez .30 .10
❑ 235 A.J. Burnett .30 .10
❑ 236 Kevin Barker .30 .10
❑ 237 Chance Caple RC .30 .10
❑ 238 Jarrod Washburn .30 .10
❑ 239 Lance Berkman .30 .10
❑ 240 Michael Wenner RC .30 .10
❑ 241 Alex Sanchez .30 .10
❑ 242 Pat Daneker .30 .10
❑ 243 Grant Roberts .30 .10
❑ 244 Mark Ellis RC .50 .20
❑ 245 Donny Leon .30 .10
❑ 246 David Eckstein .30 .10
❑ 247 Dicky Gonzalez RC .30 .10
❑ 248 John Patterson .30 .10
❑ 249 Chad Green .30 .10
❑ 250 Scot Shields RC .30 .10
❑ 251 Troy Cameron .30 .10
❑ 252 Jose Molina .30 .10
❑ 253 Rob Pugmire RC .30 .10
❑ 254 Rick Elder .30 .10
❑ 255 Sean Burroughs .30 .10
❑ 256 Josh Kalinowski RC .30 .10
❑ 257 Matt LeCroy .30 .10
❑ 258 Alex Graman RC .30 .10
❑ 259 Tomo Ohka RC .50 .20
❑ 260 Brady Clark .30 .10
❑ 261 Rico Washington RC .30 .10
❑ 262 Gary Matthews Jr. .30 .10
❑ 263 Matt Wise .30 .10
❑ 264 Keith Reed RC .30 .10
❑ 265 Santiago Ramirez RC .30 .10
❑ 266 Ben Broussard RC 1.25 .50
❑ 267 Ryan Langerhans .30 .10
❑ 268 Juan Rivera .30 .10
❑ 269 Shawn Gallagher .30 .10
❑ 270 Jorge Toca .30 .10
❑ 271 Brad Lidge .50 .20
❑ 272 Leoncio Estrella RC .30 .10
❑ 273 Ruben Quevedo .30 .10
❑ 274 Jack Cust .30 .10
❑ 275 T.J. Tucker .30 .10
❑ 276 Mike Colangelo .30 .10
❑ 277 Brian Schneider .30 .10
❑ 278 Calvin Murray .30 .10
❑ 279 Josh Girdley .30 .10
❑ 280 Mike Paradis .30 .10
❑ 281 Chad Hermansen .30 .10
❑ 282 Ty Howington RC .30 .10
❑ 283 Aaron Myette .30 .10
❑ 284 D'Angelo Jimenez .30 .10
❑ 285 Dernell Stenson .30 .10
❑ 286 Jerry Hairston Jr. .30 .10
❑ 287 Gary Majewski RC .50 .20
❑ 288 Derrin Ebert .30 .10
❑ 289 Steve Fish RC .30 .10
❑ 290 Carlos E. Hernandez .30 .10
❑ 291 Allen Levrault .30 .10
❑ 292 Sean McNally RC .30 .10
❑ 293 Randey Dorame RC .30 .10
❑ 294 Wes Anderson RC .30 .10
❑ 295 B.J. Ryan .30 .10
❑ 296 Alan Webb RC .30 .10
❑ 297 Brandon Inge RC 2.00 .75
❑ 298 David Walling .30 .10
❑ 299 Sun Woo Kim RC .30 .10
❑ 300 Pat Burrell .30 .10
❑ 301 Rick Guttormson RC .30 .10
❑ 302 Gil Meche .30 .10
❑ 303 Carlos Zambrano RC 5.00 2.00
❑ 304 Eric Byrnes UER RC .50 .20
❑ 305 Robb Quinlan RC .50 .20
❑ 306 Jackie Rexrode .30 .10
❑ 307 Nate Bump .30 .10
❑ 308 Sean DePaula RC .30 .10
❑ 309 Matt Riley .30 .10
❑ 310 Ryan Minor .30 .10
❑ 311 J.J. Davis .30 .10
❑ 312 Randy Wolf .30 .10
❑ 313 Jason Jennings .30 .10
❑ 314 Scott Seabol RC .30 .10
❑ 315 Doug Davis .30 .10
❑ 316 Todd Moser RC .30 .10

❑ 317	Rob Ryan	.30	.10
❑ 318	Bubba Crosby	.30	.10
❑ 319	Lyle Overbay RC	1.25	.50
❑ 320	Mario Encarnacion	.30	.10
❑ 321	Francisco Rodriguez RC	2.50	1.00
❑ 322	Michael Cuddyer	.30	.10
❑ 323	Ed Yarnall	.30	.10
❑ 324	Cesar Saba RC	.30	.10
❑ 325	Gookie Dawkins	.30	.10
❑ 326	Alex Escobar	.30	.10
❑ 327	Julio Zuleta RC	.30	.10
❑ 328	Josh Hamilton	1.00	.40
❑ 329	Nick Neugebauer RC	.30	.10
❑ 330	Matt Belisle	.30	.10
❑ 331	Kurt Ainsworth RC	.30	.10
❑ 332	Tim Raines Jr.	.30	.10
❑ 333	Eric Munson	.30	.10
❑ 334	Donzell McDonald	.30	.10
❑ 335	Larry Bigbie RC	.75	.30
❑ 336	Matt Watson RC	.30	.10
❑ 337	Aubrey Huff	.30	.10
❑ 338	Julio Ramirez	.30	.10
❑ 339	Jason Grabowski RC	.30	.10
❑ 340	Jon Garland	.30	.10
❑ 341	Austin Kearns	.30	.10
❑ 342	Josh Pressley RC	.30	.10
❑ 343	Miguel Olivo RC	.75	.30
❑ 344	Julio Lugo	.30	.10
❑ 345	Roberto Vaz	.30	.10
❑ 346	Ramon Soler	.30	.10
❑ 347	Brandon Phillips RC	1.50	.60
❑ 348	Vince Faison RC	.30	.10
❑ 349	Mike Venafro	.30	.10
❑ 350	Rick Asadoorian RC	.50	.20
❑ 351	B.J. Garbe RC	.30	.10
❑ 352	Dan Reichert	.30	.10
❑ 353	Jason Stumm RC	.30	.10
❑ 354	Ruben Salazar RC	.30	.10
❑ 355	Francisco Cordero	.30	.10
❑ 356	Juan Guzman RC	.30	.10
❑ 357	Mike Bacsik RC	.30	.10
❑ 358	Jared Sandberg	.30	.10
❑ 359	Rod Barajas	.30	.10
❑ 360	Junior Brignac RC	.30	.10
❑ 361	J.M. Gold	.30	.10
❑ 362	Octavio Dotel	.30	.10
❑ 363	David Kelton	.30	.10
❑ 364	Scott Morgan	.30	.10
❑ 365	Wascar Serrano RC	.30	.10
❑ 366	Wilton Veras	.30	.10
❑ 367	Eugene Kingsale	.30	.10
❑ 368	Ted Lilly	.30	.10
❑ 369	George Lombard	.30	.10
❑ 370	Chris Haas	.30	.10
❑ 371	Wilton Pena RC	.30	.10
❑ 372	Vernon Wells	.30	.10
❑ 373	Jason Royer RC	.30	.10
❑ 374	Jeff Heaverlo RC	.30	.10
❑ 375	Calvin Pickering	.30	.10
❑ 376	Mike Lamb RC	.75	.30
❑ 377	Kyle Snyder	.30	.10
❑ 378	Javier Cardona RC	.30	.10
❑ 379	Aaron Rowand RC	2.00	.75
❑ 380	Dee Brown	.30	.10
❑ 381	Brett Myers RC	1.50	.60
❑ 382	Abraham Nunez	.30	.10
❑ 383	Eric Valent	.30	.10
❑ 384	Jody Gerut RC	.50	.20
❑ 385	Adam Dunn	.75	.30
❑ 386	Jay Gehrke	.30	.10
❑ 387	Omar Ortiz	.30	.10
❑ 388	Darnell McDonald	.30	.10
❑ 389	Tony Schrager RC	.30	.10
❑ 390	J.D. Closser	.30	.10
❑ 391	Ben Christensen RC	.30	.10
❑ 392	Adam Kennedy	.30	.10
❑ 393	Nick Green RC	.30	.10
❑ 394	Ramon Hernandez	.30	.10
❑ 395	Roy Oswalt RC	12.00	5.00
❑ 396	Andy Tracy RC	.30	.10
❑ 397	Eric Gagne	.75	.30
❑ 398	Michael Tejera RC	.30	.10
❑ 399	Adam Everett	.30	.10
❑ 400	Corey Patterson	.30	.10
❑ 401	Gary Knotts RC	.30	.10
❑ 402	Ryan Christianson RC	.30	.10
❑ 403	Eric Ireland RC	.30	.10
❑ 404	Andrew Good RC	.30	.10
❑ 405	Brad Penny	.30	.10
❑ 406	Jason LaRue	.30	.10
❑ 407	Kit Pellow	.30	.10
❑ 408	Kevin Beirne	.30	.10
❑ 409	Kelly Dransfeldt	.30	.10
❑ 410	Jason Grilli	.30	.10
❑ 411	Scott Downs RC	.30	.10
❑ 412	Jesus Colome	.30	.10
❑ 413	John Sneed RC	.30	.10
❑ 414	Tony McKnight	.30	.10
❑ 415	Luis Rivera	.30	.10
❑ 416	Adam Eaton	.30	.10
❑ 417	Mike MacDougal RC	.50	.20
❑ 418	Mike Nannini	.30	.10
❑ 419	Barry Zito RC	4.00	1.50
❑ 420	DeWayne Wise	.30	.10
❑ 421	Jason Dellaero	.30	.10
❑ 422	Chad Moeller	.30	.10
❑ 423	Jason Marquis	.30	.10
❑ 424	Tim Redding RC	.50	.20
❑ 425	Mark Mulder	.30	.10
❑ 426	Josh Paul	.30	.10
❑ 427	Chris Enochs	.30	.10
❑ 428	Wilfredo Rodriguez RC	.30	.10
❑ 429	Kevin Witt	.30	.10
❑ 430	Scott Sobkowiak RC	.30	.10
❑ 431	McKay Christensen	.30	.10
❑ 432	Jung Bong	.30	.10
❑ 433	Keith Evans RC	.30	.10
❑ 434	Garry Maddox Jr. RC	.30	.10
❑ 435	Ramon Santiago RC	.30	.10
❑ 436	Alex Cora	.30	.10
❑ 437	Carlos Lee	.30	.10
❑ 438	Jason Repko RC	.75	.30
❑ 439	Matt Burch	.30	.10
❑ 440	Shawn Sonnier RC	.30	.10

2000 Bowman Draft Picks

❑	COMP.FACT.SET (111)	40.00	20.00
❑	COMPLETE SET (110)	25.00	10.00
❑ 1	Pat Burrell	.30	.10
❑ 2	Rafael Furcal	.30	.10
❑ 3	Grant Roberts	.30	.10
❑ 4	Barry Zito	1.50	.60
❑ 5	Julio Zuleta	.30	.10
❑ 6	Mark Mulder	.30	.10
❑ 7	Rob Bell	.30	.10
❑ 8	Adam Piatt	.30	.10
❑ 9	Mike Lamb	.60	.25
❑ 10	Pablo Ozuna	.30	.10
❑ 11	Jason Tyner	.30	.10
❑ 12	Jason Marquis	.30	.10
❑ 13	Eric Munson	.30	.10
❑ 14	Seth Etherton	.30	.10
❑ 15	Milton Bradley	.30	.10
❑ 16	Nick Green	.30	.10
❑ 17	Chin-Feng Chen RC	.60	.25
❑ 18	Matt Boone RC	.30	.10
❑ 19	Kevin Gregg RC	.30	.10
❑ 20	Eddy Garabito RC	.30	.10
❑ 21	Aaron Capista RC	.30	.10
❑ 22	Esteban German RC	.30	.10
❑ 23	Derek Thompson RC	.30	.10
❑ 24	Phil Merrell RC	.30	.10
❑ 25	Brian O'Connor RC	.30	.10
❑ 26	Yamid Haad	.30	.10
❑ 27	Hector Mercado RC	.30	.10
❑ 28	Jason Woolf RC	.30	.10
❑ 29	Eddy Furniss RC	.30	.10
❑ 30	Cha Sueng Baek RC	.30	.10
❑ 31	Colby Lewis RC	.30	.10
❑ 32	Pasqual Coco RC	.30	.10
❑ 33	Jorge Cantu RC	2.50	1.00
❑ 34	Erasmo Ramirez RC	.30	.10
❑ 35	Bobby Kielty RC	.40	.15
❑ 36	Joaquin Benoit RC	.30	.10
❑ 37	Brian Esposito RC	.30	.10
❑ 38	Michael Wenner	.30	.10
❑ 39	Juan Rincon RC	.30	.10
❑ 40	Yorvit Torrealba RC	6.00	.25
❑ 41	Chad Durham RC	.30	.10
❑ 42	Jim Mann RC	.30	.10
❑ 43	Shane Loux RC	.30	.10
❑ 44	Luis Rivas	.30	.10
❑ 45	Ken Chenard RC	.30	.10
❑ 46	Mike Lockwood RC	.30	.10
❑ 47	Yovanny Lara RC	.30	.10
❑ 48	Bubba Carpenter RC	.30	.10
❑ 49	Ryan Dittfurth RC	.30	.10
❑ 50	John Stephens RC	.30	.10
❑ 51	Pedro Feliz RC	1.00	.40
❑ 52	Kenny Kelly RC	.30	.10
❑ 53	Neil Jenkins RC	.30	.10
❑ 54	Mike Glendenning RC	.30	.10
❑ 55	Bo Porter	.30	.10
❑ 56	Eric Byrnes	.30	.10
❑ 57	Tony Alvarez RC	.30	.10
❑ 58	Kazuhiro Sasaki RC	.60	.25
❑ 59	Chad Durbin RC	.30	.10
❑ 60	Mike Bynum RC	.30	.10
❑ 61	Travis Wilson RC	.30	.10
❑ 62	Jose Leon RC	.30	.10
❑ 63	Ryan Vogelsong RC	.30	.10
❑ 64	Geraldo Guzman RC	.30	.10
❑ 65	Craig Anderson RC	.30	.10
❑ 66	Carlos Silva RC	.40	.15
❑ 67	Brad Thomas RC	.30	.10
❑ 68	Chin-Hui Tsao RC	2.00	.75
❑ 69	Mark Buehrle RC	4.00	1.50
❑ 70	Juan Salas RC	.30	.10
❑ 71	Denny Abreu RC	.30	.10
❑ 72	Keith McDonald RC	.30	.10
❑ 73	Chris Richard RC	.30	.10
❑ 74	Tomas De la Rosa RC	.30	.10
❑ 75	Vicente Padilla RC	.40	.15
❑ 76	Justin Brunette RC	.30	.10
❑ 77	Scott Linebrink RC	.30	.10
❑ 78	Jeff Sparks RC	.30	.10
❑ 79	Tike Redman RC	.60	.25
❑ 80	John Lackey RC	2.50	1.00
❑ 81	Joe Strong RC	.30	.10
❑ 82	Brian Tollberg RC	.30	.10
❑ 83	Steve Sisco RC	.30	.10
❑ 84	Chris Clapinski RC	.30	.10
❑ 85	Augie Ojeda RC	.30	.10
❑ 86	Adrian Gonzalez RC	3.00	1.25
❑ 87	Mike Stodolka RC	.30	.10
❑ 88	Adam Johnson RC	.30	.10
❑ 89	Matt Wheatland RC	.30	.10
❑ 90	Corey Smith RC	.30	.10
❑ 91	Rocco Baldelli RC	2.00	.75
❑ 92	Keith Bucktrot RC	.30	.10
❑ 93	Adam Wainwright RC	1.25	.50
❑ 94	Blaine Boyer RC	.30	.10
❑ 95	Aaron Herr RC	.40	.15
❑ 96	Scott Thorman RC	1.00	.40
❑ 97	Bryan Digby RC	.30	.10
❑ 98	Josh Shortslef RC	.50	.20
❑ 99	Sean Smith RC	.30	.10
❑ 100	Alex Cruz RC	.30	.10
❑ 101	Marc Love RC	.30	.10
❑ 102	Kevin Lee RC	.30	.10
❑ 103	Victor Ramos RC	.30	.10
❑ 104	Jason Kaanoi RC	.30	.10
❑ 105	Luis Escobar RC	.30	.10
❑ 106	Tripper Johnson RC	.30	.10
❑ 107	Phil Dumatrait RC	.30	.10
❑ 108	Bryan Edwards RC	.30	.10
❑ 109	Grady Sizemore RC	15.00	6.00
❑ 110	Thomas Mitchell RC	.30	.10

2001 Bowman

Card	High	Low
❑ COMPLETE SET (440)	150.00	90.00
❑ COMMON CARD (1-440)	.30	.10
❑ COMMON RC	.40	.15
❑ 1 Jason Giambi	.30	.10
❑ 2 Rafael Furcal	.30	.10
❑ 3 Rick Ankiel	.30	.10
❑ 4 Freddy Garcia	.30	.10
❑ 5 Magglio Ordonez	.30	.10
❑ 6 Bernie Williams	.50	.20
❑ 7 Kenny Lofton	.30	.10
❑ 8 Al Leiter	.30	.10
❑ 9 Albert Belle	.30	.10
❑ 10 Craig Biggio	.50	.20
❑ 11 Mark Mulder	.30	.10
❑ 12 Carlos Delgado	.30	.10
❑ 13 Darin Erstad	.30	.10
❑ 14 Richie Sexson	.30	.10
❑ 15 Randy Johnson	.75	.30
❑ 16 Greg Maddux	1.25	.50
❑ 17 Cliff Floyd	.30	.10
❑ 18 Mark Buehrle	.50	.20
❑ 19 Chris Singleton	.30	.10
❑ 20 Orlando Hernandez	.30	.10
❑ 21 Javier Vazquez	.30	.10
❑ 22 Jeff Kent	.30	.10
❑ 23 Jim Thome	.50	.20
❑ 24 John Olerud	.30	.10
❑ 25 Jason Kendall	.30	.10
❑ 26 Scott Rolen	.50	.20
❑ 27 Tony Gwynn	1.00	.40
❑ 28 Edgardo Alfonzo	.30	.10
❑ 29 Pokey Reese	.30	.10
❑ 30 Todd Helton	.50	.20
❑ 31 Mark Quinn	.30	.10
❑ 32 Dan Tosca RC	.40	.15
❑ 33 Dean Palmer	.30	.10
❑ 34 Jacque Jones	.30	.10
❑ 35 Ray Durham	.30	.10
❑ 36 Rafael Palmeiro	.50	.20
❑ 37 Carl Everett	.30	.10
❑ 38 Ryan Dempster	.30	.10
❑ 39 Randy Wolf	.30	.10
❑ 40 Vladimir Guerrero	.75	.30
❑ 41 Livan Hernandez	.30	.10
❑ 42 Mo Vaughn	.30	.10
❑ 43 Shannon Stewart	.30	.10
❑ 44 Preston Wilson	.30	.10
❑ 45 Jose Vidro	.30	.10
❑ 46 Fred McGriff	.50	.20
❑ 47 Kevin Brown	.30	.10
❑ 48 Peter Bergeron	.30	.10
❑ 49 Miguel Tejada	.30	.10
❑ 50 Chipper Jones	.75	.30
❑ 51 Edgar Martinez	.50	.20
❑ 52 Tony Batista	.30	.10
❑ 53 Jorge Posada	.50	.20
❑ 54 Ricky Ledee	.30	.10
❑ 55 Sammy Sosa	.75	.30
❑ 56 Steve Cox	.30	.10
❑ 57 Tony Armas Jr.	.30	.10
❑ 58 Gary Sheffield	.30	.10
❑ 59 Bartolo Colon	.30	.10
❑ 60 Pat Burrell	.30	.10
❑ 61 Jay Payton	.30	.10
❑ 62 Sean Casey	.30	.10
❑ 63 Larry Walker	.30	.10
❑ 64 Mike Mussina	.50	.20
❑ 65 Nomar Garciaparra	1.25	.50
❑ 66 Darren Dreifort	.30	.10
❑ 67 Richard Hidalgo	.30	.10
❑ 68 Troy Glaus	.30	.10
❑ 69 Ben Grieve	.30	.10
❑ 70 Jim Edmonds	.30	.10
❑ 71 Raul Mondesi	.30	.10
❑ 72 Andruw Jones	.50	.20
❑ 73 Luis Castillo	.30	.10
❑ 74 Mike Sweeney	.30	.10
❑ 75 Derek Jeter	2.00	.75
❑ 76 Ruben Mateo	.30	.10
❑ 77 Carlos Lee	.30	.10
❑ 78 Cristian Guzman	.30	.10
❑ 79 Mike Hampton	.30	.10
❑ 80 J.D. Drew	.30	.10
❑ 81 Matt Lawton	.30	.10
❑ 82 Moises Alou	.30	.10
❑ 83 Terrence Long	.30	.10
❑ 84 Geoff Jenkins	.30	.10
❑ 85 Manny Ramirez Sox	.50	.20
❑ 86 Johnny Damon	.50	.20
❑ 87 Barry Larkin	.50	.20
❑ 88 Pedro Martinez	.50	.20
❑ 89 Juan Gonzalez	.30	.10
❑ 90 Roger Clemens	1.50	.60
❑ 91 Carlos Beltran	.30	.10
❑ 92 Brad Radke	.30	.10
❑ 93 Orlando Cabrera	.30	.10
❑ 94 Roberto Alomar	.50	.20
❑ 95 Barry Bonds	2.00	.75
❑ 96 Tim Hudson	.30	.10
❑ 97 Tom Glavine	.50	.20
❑ 98 Jeromy Burnitz	.30	.10
❑ 99 Adrian Beltre	.30	.10
❑ 100 Mike Piazza	1.25	.50
❑ 101 Kerry Wood	.30	.10
❑ 102 Steve Finley	.30	.10
❑ 103 Alex Cora	.30	.10
❑ 104 Bob Abreu	.30	.10
❑ 105 Neifi Perez	.30	.10
❑ 106 Mark Redman	.30	.10
❑ 107 Paul Konerko	.30	.10
❑ 108 Jermaine Dye	.30	.10
❑ 109 Brian Giles	.30	.10
❑ 110 Ivan Rodriguez	.50	.20
❑ 111 Vinny Castilla	.30	.10
❑ 112 Adam Kennedy	.30	.10
❑ 113 Eric Chavez	.30	.10
❑ 114 Billy Koch	.30	.10
❑ 115 Shawn Green	.30	.10
❑ 116 Matt Williams	.30	.10
❑ 117 Greg Vaughn	.30	.10
❑ 118 Gabe Kapler	.30	.10
❑ 119 Jeff Cirillo	.30	.10
❑ 120 Frank Thomas	.75	.30
❑ 121 David Justice	.30	.10
❑ 122 Cal Ripken	2.50	1.00
❑ 123 Rich Aurilia	.30	.10
❑ 124 Curt Schilling	.30	.10
❑ 125 Barry Zito	.50	.20
❑ 126 Brian Jordan	.30	.10
❑ 127 Chan Ho Park	.30	.10
❑ 128 J.T. Snow	.30	.10
❑ 129 Kazuhiro Sasaki	.30	.10
❑ 130 Alex Rodriguez	1.25	.50
❑ 131 Mariano Rivera	.75	.30
❑ 132 Eric Milton	.30	.10
❑ 133 Andy Pettitte	.50	.20
❑ 134 Scott Elarton	.30	.10
❑ 135 Ken Griffey Jr.	1.25	.50
❑ 136 Bengie Molina	.30	.10
❑ 137 Jeff Bagwell	.50	.20
❑ 138 Kevin Millwood	.30	.10
❑ 139 Tino Martinez	.50	.20
❑ 140 Mark McGwire	2.00	.75
❑ 141 Larry Barnes	.30	.10
❑ 142 John Buck RC	1.00	.40
❑ 143 Freddie Bynum RC	.40	.15
❑ 144 Abraham Nunez	.30	.10
❑ 145 Felix Diaz RC	.40	.15
❑ 146 Horacio Estrada	.30	.10
❑ 147 Ben Diggins	.30	.10
❑ 148 Tsuyoshi Shinjo RC	1.00	.40
❑ 149 Rocco Baldelli	.30	.10
❑ 150 Rod Barajas	.30	.10
❑ 151 Luis Terrero	.30	.10
❑ 152 Milton Bradley	.30	.10
❑ 153 Kurt Ainsworth	.30	.10
❑ 154 Russell Branyan	.30	.10
❑ 155 Ryan Anderson	.30	.10
❑ 156 Mitch Jones RC	.60	.25
❑ 157 Chip Ambres	.30	.10
❑ 158 Steve Bennett RC	.40	.15
❑ 159 Ivanon Coffie	.30	.10
❑ 160 Sean Burroughs	.30	.10
❑ 161 Keith Bucktrot	.30	.10
❑ 162 Tony Alvarez	.30	.10
❑ 163 Joaquin Benoit	.30	.10
❑ 164 Rick Asadoorian	.30	.10
❑ 165 Ben Broussard	.30	.10
❑ 166 Ryan Madson RC	1.25	.50
❑ 167 Dee Brown	.30	.10
❑ 168 Sergio Contreras RC	.60	.25
❑ 169 John Barnes	.30	.10
❑ 170 Ben Washburn RC	.40	.15
❑ 171 Erick Almonte RC	.40	.15
❑ 172 Shawn Fagan RC	.40	.15
❑ 173 Gary Johnson RC	.40	.15
❑ 174 Brady Clark	.30	.10
❑ 175 Grant Roberts	.30	.10
❑ 176 Tony Torcato	.30	.10
❑ 177 Ramon Castro	.30	.10
❑ 178 Esteban German	.30	.10
❑ 179 Joe Hamer RC	.60	.25
❑ 180 Nick Neugebauer	.30	.10
❑ 181 Dernell Stenson	.30	.10
❑ 182 Yhency Brazoban RC	1.00	.40
❑ 183 Aaron Myette	.30	.10
❑ 184 Juan Sosa	.30	.10
❑ 185 Brandon Inge	.30	.10
❑ 186 Domingo Guante RC	.40	.15
❑ 187 Adrian Brown	.30	.10
❑ 188 Deivi Mendez RC	.40	.15
❑ 189 Luis Matos	.30	.10
❑ 190 Pedro Liriano RC	.60	.25
❑ 191 Donnie Bridges	.30	.10
❑ 192 Alex Cintron	.30	.10
❑ 193 Jace Brewer	.30	.10
❑ 194 Ron Davenport RC	.60	.25
❑ 195 Jason Belcher RC	.40	.15
❑ 196 Adrian Hernandez RC	.40	.15
❑ 197 Bobby Kielty	.30	.10
❑ 198 Reggie Griggs RC	.60	.25
❑ 199 Reggie Abercrombie RC	1.00	.40
❑ 200 Troy Farnsworth RC	.60	.25
❑ 201 Matt Belisle	.30	.10
❑ 202 Miguel Villilo RC	.60	.25
❑ 203 Adam Everett	.30	.10
❑ 204 John Lackey	.30	.10
❑ 205 Pasqual Coco	.30	.10
❑ 206 Adam Wainwright	.30	.10
❑ 207 Matt White RC	.60	.25
❑ 208 Chin-Feng Chen	.30	.10
❑ 209 Jeff Andra RC	.40	.15
❑ 210 Willie Bloomquist	.30	.10
❑ 211 Wes Anderson	.30	.10
❑ 212 Enrique Cruz	.30	.10
❑ 213 Jerry Hairston Jr.	.30	.10
❑ 214 Mike Bynum	.30	.10
❑ 215 Brian Hitchcox RC	.40	.15
❑ 216 Ryan Christianson	.30	.10
❑ 217 J.J. Davis	.30	.10
❑ 218 Jovanny Cedeno	.30	.10
❑ 219 Elvin Nina	.30	.10
❑ 220 Alex Graman	.30	.10
❑ 221 Arturo McDowell	.30	.10
❑ 222 Deivis Santos RC	.40	.15
❑ 223 Jody Gerut	.30	.10
❑ 224 Sun Woo Kim	.30	.10
❑ 225 Jimmy Rollins	.30	.10
❑ 226 Ntema Ndungidi	.30	.10
❑ 227 Ruben Salazar	.30	.10
❑ 228 Josh Girdley	.30	.10
❑ 229 Carl Crawford	.30	.10
❑ 230 Luis Montanez RC	.75	.30
❑ 231 Ramon Carvajal RC	.60	.25
❑ 232 Matt Riley	.30	.10
❑ 233 Ben Davis	.30	.10
❑ 234 Jason Grabowski	.30	.10
❑ 235 Chris George	.30	.10

❑ 236 Hank Blalock RC	5.00	2.00
❑ 237 Roy Oswalt	.75	.30
❑ 238 Eric Reynolds RC	.40	.15
❑ 239 Brian Cole	.30	.10
❑ 240 Denny Bautista RC	1.00	.40
❑ 241 Hector Garcia RC	.40	.15
❑ 242 Joe Thurston RC	.60	.25
❑ 243 Brad Cresse	.30	.10
❑ 244 Corey Patterson	.30	.10
❑ 245 Brett Evert RC	.40	.15
❑ 246 Elpidio Guzman RC	.40	.15
❑ 247 Vernon Wells	.30	.10
❑ 248 Roberto Miniel RC	.60	.25
❑ 249 Brian Bass RC	.40	.15
❑ 250 Mark Burnett RC	.60	.25
❑ 251 Juan Silvestre	.30	.10
❑ 252 Pablo Ozuna	.30	.10
❑ 253 Jayson Werth	.30	.10
❑ 254 Russ Jacobson	.30	.10
❑ 255 Chad Hermansen	.30	.10
❑ 256 Travis Hafner RC	10.00	4.00
❑ 257 Brad Baker	.30	.10
❑ 258 Gookie Dawkins	.30	.10
❑ 259 Michael Cuddyer	.30	.10
❑ 260 Mark Buehrle	.50	.20
❑ 261 Ricardo Aramboles	.30	.10
❑ 262 Esix Snead RC	.40	.15
❑ 263 Wilson Betemit RC	3.00	1.25
❑ 264 Albert Pujols RC	60.00	30.00
❑ 265 Joe Lawrence	.30	.10
❑ 266 Ramon Ortiz	.30	.10
❑ 267 Ben Sheets	.50	.20
❑ 268 Luke Lockwood RC	.60	.25
❑ 269 Toby Hall	.30	.10
❑ 270 Jack Cust	.30	.10
❑ 271 Pedro Feliz	.30	.10
❑ 272 Noel Devarez RC	.60	.25
❑ 273 Josh Beckett	.50	.20
❑ 274 Alex Escobar	.30	.10
❑ 275 Doug Gredvig RC	.40	.15
❑ 276 Marcus Giles	.30	.10
❑ 277 Jon Rauch	.30	.10
❑ 278 Brian Schmitt RC	.40	.15
❑ 279 Seung Song RC	.60	.25
❑ 280 Kevin Mench	.30	.10
❑ 281 Adam Eaton	.30	.10
❑ 282 Shawn Sonnier	.30	.10
❑ 283 Andy Van Hekken RC	.40	.15
❑ 284 Aaron Rowand	.30	.10
❑ 285 Tony Blanco RC	.60	.25
❑ 286 Ryan Kohlmeier	.30	.10
❑ 287 C.C. Sabathia	.30	.10
❑ 288 Bubba Crosby	.30	.10
❑ 289 Josh Hamilton	.60	.25
❑ 290 Dee Haynes RC	.40	.15
❑ 291 Jason Marquis	.30	.10
❑ 292 Julio Zuleta	.30	.10
❑ 293 Carlos Hernandez	.30	.10
❑ 294 Matt Lecroy	.30	.10
❑ 295 Andy Beal RC	.40	.15
❑ 296 Carlos Pena	.30	.10
❑ 297 Reggie Taylor	.30	.10
❑ 298 Bob Keppel RC	.40	.15
❑ 299 Miguel Cabrera	1.50	.60
❑ 300 Ryan Franklin	.30	.10
❑ 301 Brandon Phillips	.30	.10
❑ 302 Victor Hall RC	.60	.25
❑ 303 Tony Pena Jr.	.30	.10
❑ 304 Jim Journell RC	.60	.25
❑ 305 Cristian Guerrero	.30	.10
❑ 306 Miguel Olivo	.30	.10
❑ 307 Jin Ho Cho	.30	.10
❑ 308 Choo Freeman	.30	.10
❑ 309 Danny Borrell RC	.40	.15
❑ 310 Doug Mientkiewicz	.30	.10
❑ 311 Aaron Herr	.30	.10
❑ 312 Keith Ginter	.30	.10
❑ 313 Felipe Lopez	.30	.10
❑ 314 Jeff Goldbach	.30	.10
❑ 315 Travis Harper	.30	.10
❑ 316 Paul LoDuca	.30	.10
❑ 317 Joe Torres	.30	.10
❑ 318 Eric Byrnes	.30	.10
❑ 319 George Lombard	.30	.10
❑ 320 Dave Krynzel	.30	.10
❑ 321 Ben Christensen	.30	.10
❑ 322 Aubrey Huff	.30	.10
❑ 323 Lyle Overbay	.30	.10
❑ 324 Sean McGowan	.30	.10
❑ 325 Jeff Heaverlo	.30	.10
❑ 326 Timo Perez	.30	.10
❑ 327 Octavio Martinez RC	.60	.25
❑ 328 Vince Faison	.30	.10
❑ 329 David Parrish RC	.40	.15
❑ 330 Bobby Bradley	.30	.10
❑ 331 Jason Miller RC	.40	.15
❑ 332 Corey Spencer RC	.40	.15
❑ 333 Craig House	.30	.10
❑ 334 Maxim St. Pierre RC	.60	.25
❑ 335 Adam Johnson	.30	.10
❑ 336 Joe Crede	.75	.30
❑ 337 Greg Nash RC	.40	.15
❑ 338 Chad Durbin	.30	.10
❑ 339 Pat Magness RC	.60	.25
❑ 340 Matt Wheatland	.30	.10
❑ 341 Julio Lugo	.30	.10
❑ 342 Grady Sizemore	1.50	.60
❑ 343 Adrian Gonzalez	.30	.10
❑ 344 Tim Raines Jr.	.30	.10
❑ 345 Ranier Olmedo RC	.60	.25
❑ 346 Phil Dumatrait	.30	.10
❑ 347 Brandon Mims RC	.40	.15
❑ 348 Jason Jennings	.30	.10
❑ 349 Phil Wilson RC	.60	.25
❑ 350 Jason Hart	.30	.10
❑ 351 Cesar Izturis	.30	.10
❑ 352 Matt Butler RC	.60	.25
❑ 353 David Kelton	.30	.10
❑ 354 Luke Prokopec	.30	.10
❑ 355 Corey Smith	.30	.10
❑ 356 Joel Pineiro	.60	.25
❑ 357 Ken Chenard	.30	.10
❑ 358 Keith Reed	.30	.10
❑ 359 David Walling	.30	.10
❑ 360 Alexis Gomez RC	.40	.15
❑ 361 Justin Morneau RC	12.00	5.00
❑ 362 Josh Fogg RC	.60	.25
❑ 363 J.R. House	.30	.10
❑ 364 Andy Tracy	.30	.10
❑ 365 Kenny Kelly	.30	.10
❑ 366 Aaron McNeal	.30	.10
❑ 367 Nick Johnson	.30	.10
❑ 368 Brian Esposito	.30	.10
❑ 369 Charles Frazier RC	.40	.15
❑ 370 Scott Heard	.30	.10
❑ 371 Pat Strange	.30	.10
❑ 372 Mike Meyers	.30	.10
❑ 373 Ryan Ludwick RC	6.00	2.50
❑ 374 Brad Wilkerson	.30	.10
❑ 375 Allen Levrault	.30	.10
❑ 376 Seth McClung RC	.60	.25
❑ 377 Joe Nathan	.30	.10
❑ 378 Rafael Soriano RC	.60	.25
❑ 379 Chris Richard	.30	.10
❑ 380 Jared Sandberg	.30	.10
❑ 381 Tike Redman	.30	.10
❑ 382 Adam Dunn	.50	.20
❑ 383 Jared Abruzzo RC	.40	.15
❑ 384 Jason Richardson RC	.40	.15
❑ 385 Matt Holliday	.40	.15
❑ 386 Darwin Cubillan RC	.40	.15
❑ 387 Mike Nannini	.30	.10
❑ 388 Blake Williams RC	.40	.15
❑ 389 Valentino Pascucci RC	.60	.25
❑ 390 Jon Garland	.30	.10
❑ 391 Josh Pressley	.30	.10
❑ 392 Jose Ortiz	.30	.10
❑ 393 Ryan Hannaman RC	.60	.25
❑ 394 Steve Smyth RC	.60	.25
❑ 395 John Patterson	.30	.10
❑ 396 Chad Petty RC	.40	.15
❑ 397 Jake Peavy UER RC	6.00	2.50
❑ 398 Onix Mercado RC	.60	.25
❑ 399 Jason Romano	.30	.10
❑ 400 Luis Torres RC	.60	.25
❑ 401 Casey Fossum RC	.40	.15
❑ 402 Eduardo Figueroa RC	.40	.15
❑ 403 Bryan Barnowski RC	.40	.15
❑ 404 Tim Redding	.30	.10
❑ 405 Jason Standridge	.30	.10
❑ 406 Marvin Seale RC	.60	.25
❑ 407 Todd Moser	.30	.10
❑ 408 Alex Gordon	.30	.10
❑ 409 Steve Smitherman RC	.60	.25
❑ 410 Ben Petrick	.30	.10
❑ 411 Eric Munson	.30	.10
❑ 412 Luis Rivas	.30	.10
❑ 413 Matt Ginter	.30	.10
❑ 414 Alfonso Soriano	.50	.20
❑ 415 Rafael Boitel RC	.40	.15
❑ 416 Dany Morban RC	.40	.15
❑ 417 Justin Woodrow RC	.60	.25
❑ 418 Wilfredo Rodriguez	.30	.10
❑ 419 Derrick Van Dusen RC	.40	.15
❑ 420 Josh Spoerl RC	.60	.25
❑ 421 Juan Pierre	.30	.10
❑ 422 J.C. Romero	.30	.10
❑ 423 Ed Rogers RC	.40	.15
❑ 424 Tomo Ohka	.30	.10
❑ 425 Ben Hendrickson RC	.40	.15
❑ 426 Carlos Zambrano	.50	.20
❑ 427 Brett Myers	.30	.10
❑ 428 Scott Seabol	.30	.10
❑ 429 Thomas Mitchell	.30	.10
❑ 430 Jose Reyes RC	15.00	6.00
❑ 431 Kip Wells	.30	.10
❑ 432 Donzell McDonald	.30	.10
❑ 433 Adam Pettyjohn RC	.40	.15
❑ 434 Austin Kearns	.30	.10
❑ 435 Rico Washington	.30	.10
❑ 436 Doug Nickle RC	.40	.15
❑ 437 Steve Lomasney	.30	.10
❑ 438 Jason Jones RC	.40	.15
❑ 439 Bobby Seay	.30	.10
❑ 440 Justin Wayne RC	.60	.25
❑ ROYR Sasaki/Furcal ROY Jsy	15.00	6.00
❑ NNO Sean Burroughs Ball/80	15.00	6.00

2001 Bowman Draft Picks

❑ COMP.FACT.SET (112)	60.00	30.00
❑ COMPLETE SET (110)	50.00	20.00
❑ BDP1 Alfredo Amezaga RC	.30	.10
❑ BDP2 Andrew Good	.30	.10
❑ BDP3 Kelly Johnson RC	3.00	1.25
❑ BDP4 Larry Bigbie	.30	.10
❑ BDP5 Matt Thompson RC	.40	.15
❑ BDP6 Wilton Chavez RC	.40	.15
❑ BDP7 Joe Borchard RC	.40	.15
❑ BDP8 David Espinosa	.30	.10
❑ BDP9 Zach Day RC	.40	.15
❑ BDP10 Brad Hawpe RC	2.50	1.00
❑ BDP11 Nate Cornejo	.30	.10
❑ BDP12 Matt Cooper RC	.40	.15
❑ BDP13 Brad Lidge	.30	.10
❑ BDP14 Angel Berroa RC	.60	.25
❑ BDP15 Lamont Matthews RC	.40	.15
❑ BDP16 Jose Garcia	.30	.10
❑ BDP17 Grant Balfour RC	.30	.10
❑ BDP18 Ron Chiavacci RC	.30	.10
❑ BDP19 Jae Seo	.30	.10
❑ BDP20 Juan Rivera	.30	.10
❑ BDP21 D'Angelo Jimenez	.30	.10
❑ BDP22 Juan A.Pena RC	.40	.15
❑ BDP23 Marlon Byrd RC	.40	.15
❑ BDP24 Sean Burnett	.30	.10
❑ BDP25 Josh Pearce RC	.40	.15
❑ BDP26 Brandon Duckworth RC	.30	.10
❑ BDP27 Jack Taschner RC	.30	.10
❑ BDP28 Marcus Thames	.30	.10
❑ BDP29 Brent Abernathy	.30	.10

❑ BDP30	David Elder RC	.30	.10
❑ BDP31	Scott Cassidy RC	.40	.15
❑ BDP32	Dennis Tankersley RC	.30	.10
❑ BDP33	Denny Stark	.30	.10
❑ BDP34	Dave Williams RC	.30	.10
❑ BDP35	Boof Bonser RC	.30	.10
❑ BDP36	Kris Foster RC	.30	.10
❑ BDP37	Luis Garcia RC	.40	.15
❑ BDP38	Shawn Chacon	.30	.10
❑ BDP39	Mike Rivera RC	.40	.15
❑ BDP40	Will Smith RC	.40	.15
❑ BDP41	Morgan Ensberg RC	2.00	.75
❑ BDP42	Ken Harvey	.30	.10
❑ BDP43	Ricardo Rodriguez RC	.40	.15
❑ BDP44	Jose Mieses RC	.40	.15
❑ BDP45	Luis Maza RC	.30	.10
❑ BDP46	Julio Perez RC	.40	.15
❑ BDP47	Dustan Mohr RC	.40	.15
❑ BDP48	Randy Flores RC	.30	.10
❑ BDP49	Covelli Crisp RC	5.00	2.00
❑ BDP50	Kevin Reese RC	.40	.15
❑ BDP51	Brad Thomas UER	.30	.10
❑ BDP52	Xavier Nady	.30	.10
❑ BDP53	Ryan Vogelsong	.30	.10
❑ BDP54	Carlos Silva	.30	.10
❑ BDP55	Dan Wright	.30	.10
❑ BDP56	Brent Butler	.30	.10
❑ BDP57	Brandon Knight RC	.30	.10
❑ BDP58	Brian Reith RC	.30	.10
❑ BDP59	Mario Valenzuela RC	.40	.15
❑ BDP60	Bobby Hill RC	.40	.15
❑ BDP61	Rich Rundles RC	.40	.15
❑ BDP62	Rick Elder	.30	.10
❑ BDP63	J.D. Closser	.30	.10
❑ BDP64	Scot Shields	.30	.10
❑ BDP65	Miguel Olivo	.30	.10
❑ BDP66	Stubby Clapp RC	.30	.10
❑ BDP67	Jerome Williams RC	.60	.25
❑ BDP68	Jason Lane RC	.60	.25
❑ BDP69	Chase Utley RC	15.00	6.00
❑ BDP70	Erik Bedard RC	5.00	2.00
❑ BDP71	Alex Herrera UER RC	.30	.10
❑ BDP72	Juan Cruz RC	.40	.15
❑ BDP73	Billy Martin RC	.30	.10
❑ BDP74	Ronnie Merrill RC	.40	.15
❑ BDP75	Jason Kinchen RC	.30	.10
❑ BDP76	Wilkin Ruan RC	.40	.15
❑ BDP77	Cody Ransom RC	.30	.10
❑ BDP78	Bud Smith RC	.30	.10
❑ BDP79	Wily Mo Pena	.30	.10
❑ BDP80	Jeff Nettles RC	.40	.15
❑ BDP81	Jamal Strong RC	.30	.10
❑ BDP82	Bill Ortega RC	.30	.10
❑ BDP83	Mike Bell	.30	.10
❑ BDP84	Ichiro Suzuki RC	8.00	3.00
❑ BDP85	Fernando Rodney RC	.30	.10
❑ BDP86	Chris Smith RC	.30	.10
❑ BDP87	John VanBenschoten RC	.40	.15
❑ BDP88	Bobby Crosby RC	4.00	1.50
❑ BDP89	Kenny Baugh RC	.30	.10
❑ BDP90	Jake Gautreau RC	.30	.10
❑ BDP91	Gabe Gross RC	.60	.25
❑ BDP92	Kris Honel RC	.40	.15
❑ BDP93	Dan Denham RC	.30	.10
❑ BDP94	Aaron Heilman RC	.40	.15
❑ BDP95	Irvin Guzman RC	4.00	1.50
❑ BDP96	Mike Jones RC	.60	.25
❑ BDP97	John-Ford Griffin RC	.40	.15
❑ BDP98	Macay McBride RC	1.00	.40
❑ BDP99	John Rheinecker RC	1.00	.40
❑ BDP100	Bronson Sardinha RC	.30	.10
❑ BDP101	Jason Weintraub RC	.30	.10
❑ BDP102	J.D. Martin RC	.30	.10
❑ BDP103	Jayson Nix RC	.40	.15
❑ BDP104	Noah Lowry RC	2.50	1.00
❑ BDP105	Richard Lewis RC	.40	.15
❑ BDP106	Brad Hennessey RC	.60	.25
❑ BDP107	Jeff Mathis RC	.60	.25
❑ BDP108	Jon Skaggs RC	.40	.15
❑ BDP109	Justin Pope RC	.40	.15
❑ BDP110	Josh Burrus RC	.40	.15

2002 Bowman

❑ COMPLETE SET (440)	80.00	40.00
❑ COMMON CARD (1-110)	.30	.10
❑ COMMON CARD (111-440)	.30	.10

❑ 1	Adam Dunn	.30	.10
❑ 2	Derek Jeter	2.00	.75
❑ 3	Alex Rodriguez	1.25	.50
❑ 4	Miguel Tejada	.30	.10
❑ 5	Nomar Garciaparra	1.25	.50
❑ 6	Toby Hall	.30	.10
❑ 7	Brandon Duckworth	.30	.10
❑ 8	Paul LoDuca	.30	.10
❑ 9	Brian Giles	.30	.10
❑ 10	C.C. Sabathia	.30	.10
❑ 11	Curt Schilling	.30	.10
❑ 12	Tsuyoshi Shinjo	.30	.10
❑ 13	Ramon Hernandez	.30	.10
❑ 14	Jose Cruz Jr.	.30	.10
❑ 15	Albert Pujols	1.50	.60
❑ 16	Joe Mays	.30	.10
❑ 17	Javy Lopez	.30	.10
❑ 18	J.T. Snow	.30	.10
❑ 19	David Segui	.30	.10
❑ 20	Jorge Posada	.50	.20
❑ 21	Doug Mientkiewicz	.30	.10
❑ 22	Jerry Hairston Jr.	.30	.10
❑ 23	Bernie Williams	.50	.20
❑ 24	Mike Sweeney	.30	.10
❑ 25	Jason Giambi	.30	.10
❑ 26	Ryan Dempster	.30	.10
❑ 27	Ryan Klesko	.30	.10
❑ 28	Mark Quinn	.30	.10
❑ 29	Jeff Kent	.30	.10
❑ 30	Eric Chavez	.30	.10
❑ 31	Adrian Beltre	.30	.10
❑ 32	Andruw Jones	.50	.20
❑ 33	Alfonso Soriano	.30	.10
❑ 34	Aramis Ramirez	.30	.10
❑ 35	Greg Maddux	1.25	.50
❑ 36	Andy Pettitte	.50	.20
❑ 37	Bartolo Colon	.30	.10
❑ 38	Ben Sheets	.30	.10
❑ 39	Bobby Higginson	.30	.10
❑ 40	Ivan Rodriguez	.50	.20
❑ 41	Brad Penny	.30	.10
❑ 42	Carlos Lee	.30	.10
❑ 43	Damion Easley	.30	.10
❑ 44	Preston Wilson	.30	.10
❑ 45	Jeff Bagwell	.50	.20
❑ 46	Eric Milton	.30	.10
❑ 47	Rafael Palmeiro	.50	.20
❑ 48	Gary Sheffield	.30	.10
❑ 49	J.D. Drew	.30	.10
❑ 50	Jim Thome	.50	.20
❑ 51	Ichiro Suzuki	1.50	.60
❑ 52	Bud Smith	.30	.10
❑ 53	Chan Ho Park	.30	.10
❑ 54	D'Angelo Jimenez	.30	.10
❑ 55	Ken Griffey Jr.	1.25	.50
❑ 56	Wade Miller	.30	.10
❑ 57	Vladimir Guerrero	.75	.30
❑ 58	Troy Glaus	.30	.10
❑ 59	Shawn Green	.30	.10
❑ 60	Kerry Wood	.30	.10
❑ 61	Jack Wilson	.30	.10
❑ 62	Kevin Brown	.30	.10
❑ 63	Marcus Giles	.30	.10
❑ 64	Pat Burrell	.30	.10
❑ 65	Larry Walker	.30	.10
❑ 66	Sammy Sosa	.75	.30
❑ 67	Raul Mondesi	.30	.10
❑ 68	Tim Hudson	.30	.10
❑ 69	Lance Berkman	.30	.10
❑ 70	Mike Mussina	.50	.20
❑ 71	Barry Zito	.30	.10
❑ 72	Jimmy Rollins	.30	.10
❑ 73	Barry Bonds	2.00	.75
❑ 74	Craig Biggio	.50	.20
❑ 75	Todd Helton	.50	.20
❑ 76	Roger Clemens	1.50	.60
❑ 77	Frank Catalanotto	.30	.10
❑ 78	Josh Towers	.30	.10
❑ 79	Roy Oswalt	.30	.10
❑ 80	Chipper Jones	.75	.30
❑ 81	Cristian Guzman	.30	.10
❑ 82	Darin Erstad	.30	.10
❑ 83	Freddy Garcia	.30	.10
❑ 84	Jason Tyner	.30	.10
❑ 85	Carlos Delgado	.30	.10
❑ 86	Jon Lieber	.30	.10
❑ 87	Juan Pierre	.30	.10
❑ 88	Matt Morris	.30	.10
❑ 89	Phil Nevin	.30	.10
❑ 90	Jim Edmonds	.30	.10
❑ 91	Magglio Ordonez	.30	.10
❑ 92	Mike Hampton	.30	.10
❑ 93	Rafael Furcal	.30	.10
❑ 94	Richie Sexson	.30	.10
❑ 95	Luis Gonzalez	.30	.10
❑ 96	Scott Rolen	.50	.20
❑ 97	Tim Redding	.30	.10
❑ 98	Moises Alou	.30	.10
❑ 99	Jose Vidro	.30	.10
❑ 100	Mike Piazza	1.25	.50
❑ 101	Pedro Martinez	.50	.20
❑ 102	Geoff Jenkins	.30	.10
❑ 103	Johnny Damon Sox	.50	.20
❑ 104	Mike Cameron	.30	.10
❑ 105	Randy Johnson	.75	.30
❑ 106	David Eckstein	.30	.10
❑ 107	Javier Vazquez	.30	.10
❑ 108	Mark Mulder	.30	.10
❑ 109	Robert Fick	.30	.10
❑ 110	Roberto Alomar	.50	.20
❑ 111	Wilson Betemit	.30	.10
❑ 112	Chris Tritle RC	.30	.10
❑ 113	Ed Rogers	.30	.10
❑ 114	Juan Pena	.30	.10
❑ 115	Josh Beckett	.40	.15
❑ 116	Juan Cruz	.30	.10
❑ 117	Noochie Varner RC	.40	.15
❑ 118	Taylor Buchholz RC	.60	.25
❑ 119	Mike Rivera	.30	.10
❑ 120	Hank Blalock	.60	.25
❑ 121	Hansel Izquierdo RC	.40	.15
❑ 122	Orlando Hudson	.30	.10
❑ 123	Bill Hall	.40	.15
❑ 124	Jose Reyes	.60	.25
❑ 125	Juan Rivera	.30	.10
❑ 126	Eric Valent	.30	.10
❑ 127	Scotty Layfield RC	.40	.15
❑ 128	Austin Kearns	.30	.10
❑ 129	Nic Jackson RC	.40	.15
❑ 130	Chris Baker RC	.40	.15
❑ 131	Chad Qualls RC	.50	.20
❑ 132	Marcus Thames	.30	.10
❑ 133	Nathan Haynes	.30	.10
❑ 134	Brett Evert	.30	.10
❑ 135	Joe Borchard	.30	.10
❑ 136	Ryan Christianson	.30	.10
❑ 137	Josh Hamilton	.60	.25
❑ 138	Corey Patterson	.30	.10
❑ 139	Travis Wilson	.30	.10
❑ 140	Alex Escobar	.30	.10
❑ 141	Alexis Gomez	.30	.10
❑ 142	Nick Johnson	.40	.15
❑ 143	Kenny Kelly	.30	.10
❑ 144	Marlon Byrd	.30	.10
❑ 145	Kory DeHaan	.30	.10
❑ 146	Matt Belisle	.30	.10
❑ 147	Carlos Hernandez	.30	.10
❑ 148	Sean Burroughs	.30	.10
❑ 149	Angel Berroa	.30	.10
❑ 150	Aubrey Huff	.40	.15
❑ 151	Travis Hafner	.40	.15
❑ 152	Brandon Berger	.30	.10
❑ 153	David Krynzel	.30	.10
❑ 154	Ruben Salazar	.30	.10

❑ 155 J.R. House .30 .10
❑ 156 Juan Silvestre .30 .10
❑ 157 Dewon Brazelton .30 .10
❑ 158 Jayson Werth .30 .10
❑ 159 Larry Barnes .30 .10
❑ 160 Elvis Pena .30 .10
❑ 161 Ruben Gotay RC .50 .20
❑ 162 Tommy Marx RC .40 .15
❑ 163 John Suomi RC .40 .15
❑ 164 Javier Colina .30 .10
❑ 165 Greg Sain RC .40 .15
❑ 166 Robert Cosby RC .40 .15
❑ 167 Angel Pagan RC .50 .20
❑ 168 Ralph Santana RC .40 .15
❑ 169 Joe Orloski RC .40 .15
❑ 170 Shayne Wright RC .40 .15
❑ 171 Jay Caligiuri RC .40 .15
❑ 172 Greg Montalbano RC .40 .15
❑ 173 Rich Harden RC 3.00 1.25
❑ 174 Rich Thompson RC .40 .15
❑ 175 Fred Bastardo RC .40 .15
❑ 176 Alejandro Giron RC .40 .15
❑ 177 Jesus Medrano RC .40 .15
❑ 178 Kevin Deaton RC .40 .15
❑ 179 Mike Rosamond RC .40 .15
❑ 180 Jon Guzman RC .40 .15
❑ 181 Gerard Oakes RC .40 .15
❑ 182 Francisco Liriano RC 8.00 3.00
❑ 183 Matt Allegra RC .40 .15
❑ 184 Mike Snyder RC .40 .15
❑ 185 James Shanks RC .40 .15
❑ 186 Anderson Hernandez RC .40 .15
❑ 187 Dan Trumble RC .40 .15
❑ 188 Luis DePaula RC .40 .15
❑ 189 Randall Shelley RC .40 .15
❑ 190 Richard Lane RC .40 .15
❑ 191 Antwon Rollins RC .40 .15
❑ 192 Ryan Bukvich RC .40 .15
❑ 193 Derrick Lewis .30 .10
❑ 194 Eric Miller RC .40 .15
❑ 195 Justin Schuda RC .40 .15
❑ 196 Brian West RC .40 .15
❑ 197 Adam Roller RC .40 .15
❑ 198 Neal Frendling RC .40 .15
❑ 199 Jeremy Hill RC .40 .15
❑ 200 James Barrett RC .40 .15
❑ 201 Brett Kay RC .40 .15
❑ 202 Ryan Mottl RC .40 .15
❑ 203 Brad Nelson RC .40 .15
❑ 204 Juan M. Gonzalez RC .40 .15
❑ 205 Curtis Legendre RC .40 .15
❑ 206 Ronald Acuna RC .40 .15
❑ 207 Chris Flinn RC .40 .15
❑ 208 Nick Alvarez RC .40 .15
❑ 209 Jason Ellison RC .75 .30
❑ 210 Blake McGinley RC .40 .15
❑ 211 Dan Phillips RC .40 .15
❑ 212 Demetrius Heath RC .40 .15
❑ 213 Eric Bruntlett RC .40 .15
❑ 214 Joe Jiannetti RC .40 .15
❑ 215 Mike Hill RC .40 .15
❑ 216 Ricardo Cordova RC .40 .15
❑ 217 Mark Hamilton RC .40 .15
❑ 218 David Mattox RC .40 .15
❑ 219 Jose Morban RC .40 .15
❑ 220 Scott Wiggins RC .30 .10
❑ 221 Steve Green .30 .10
❑ 222 Brian Rogers .30 .10
❑ 223 Chin-Hui Tsao .40 .15
❑ 224 Kenny Baugh .30 .10
❑ 225 Nate Teut .30 .10
❑ 226 Josh Wilson RC .40 .15
❑ 227 Christian Parker .30 .10
❑ 228 Tim Raines Jr. .30 .10
❑ 229 Anastacio Martinez RC .40 .15
❑ 230 Richard Lewis .30 .10
❑ 231 Tim Kalita RC .40 .15
❑ 232 Edwin Almonte RC .40 .15
❑ 233 Hee-Seop Choi .30 .10
❑ 234 Ty Howington .30 .10
❑ 235 Victor Alvarez RC .40 .15
❑ 236 Morgan Ensberg .40 .15
❑ 237 Jeff Austin RC .40 .15
❑ 238 Luis Terrero .30 .10
❑ 239 Adam Wainwright .30 .10
❑ 240 Clint Weibl RC .30 .10
❑ 241 Eric Cyr .30 .10
❑ 242 Marlyn Tisdale RC .40 .15
❑ 243 John VanBenschoten .30 .10
❑ 244 Ryan Raburn RC .40 .15
❑ 245 Miguel Cabrera 1.50 .60
❑ 246 Jung Bong .30 .10
❑ 247 Raul Chavez RC .30 .10
❑ 248 Erik Bedard .40 .15
❑ 249 Chris Snelling RC .60 .25
❑ 250 Joe Rogers RC .40 .15
❑ 251 Nate Field RC .40 .15
❑ 252 Matt Herges RC .30 .10
❑ 253 Matt Childers RC .40 .15
❑ 254 Erick Almonte .30 .10
❑ 255 Nick Neugebauer .30 .10
❑ 256 Ron Calloway RC .40 .15
❑ 257 Seung Song .30 .10
❑ 258 Brandon Phillips .30 .10
❑ 259 Cole Barthel RC .30 .10
❑ 260 Jason Lane .40 .15
❑ 261 Jae Seo .30 .10
❑ 262 Randy Flores .30 .10
❑ 263 Scott Chiasson .30 .10
❑ 264 Chase Utley 2.50 1.00
❑ 265 Tony Alvarez .30 .10
❑ 266 Ben Howard RC .40 .15
❑ 267 Nelson Castro RC .40 .15
❑ 268 Mark Lukasiewicz .30 .10
❑ 269 Eric Glaser RC .40 .15
❑ 270 Rob Henkel RC .40 .15
❑ 271 Jose Valverde RC .40 .15
❑ 272 Ricardo Rodriguez .30 .10
❑ 273 Chris Smith .30 .10
❑ 274 Mark Prior .60 .25
❑ 275 Miguel Olivo .30 .10
❑ 276 Ben Broussard .30 .10
❑ 277 Zach Sorensen .30 .10
❑ 278 Brian Mallette RC .30 .10
❑ 279 Brad Wilkerson .30 .10
❑ 280 Carl Crawford .40 .15
❑ 281 Chone Figgins RC 1.50 .60
❑ 282 Jimmy Alvarez RC .40 .15
❑ 283 Gavin Floyd RC 1.00 .40
❑ 284 Josh Bonifay RC .40 .15
❑ 285 Garrett Guzman RC .40 .15
❑ 286 Blake Williams .30 .10
❑ 287 Matt Holliday .30 .10
❑ 288 Ryan Madson .30 .10
❑ 289 Luis Torres .30 .10
❑ 290 Jeff Verplancke RC .40 .15
❑ 291 Nate Espy RC .40 .15
❑ 292 Jeff Lincoln RC .40 .15
❑ 293 Ryan Snare RC .40 .15
❑ 294 Jose Ortiz .30 .10
❑ 295 Eric Munson .30 .10
❑ 296 Denny Bautista .30 .10
❑ 297 Willy Aybar .40 .15
❑ 298 Kelly Johnson .60 .25
❑ 299 Justin Morneau .40 .15
❑ 300 Derrick Van Dusen .30 .10
❑ 301 Chad Petty .30 .10
❑ 302 Mike Restovich .30 .10
❑ 303 Shawn Fagan .30 .10
❑ 304 Yurendell DeCaster RC .40 .15
❑ 305 Justin Wayne .30 .10
❑ 306 Mike Peeples RC .30 .10
❑ 307 Joel Guzman 1.00 .40
❑ 308 Ryan Vogelsong .30 .10
❑ 309 Jorge Padilla RC .40 .15
❑ 310 Grady Sizemore 1.00 .40
❑ 311 Joe Jester RC .40 .15
❑ 312 Jim Journell .30 .10
❑ 313 Bobby Seay .30 .10
❑ 314 Ryan Church RC 1.00 .40
❑ 315 Grant Balfour .30 .10
❑ 316 Mitch Jones .30 .10
❑ 317 Travis Foley RC .40 .15
❑ 318 Bobby Crosby 1.00 .40
❑ 319 Adrian Gonzalez .30 .10
❑ 320 Ronnie Merrill .30 .10
❑ 321 Joel Pineiro .30 .10
❑ 322 John-Ford Griffin .30 .10
❑ 323 Brian Forystek RC .40 .15
❑ 324 Sean Douglass .30 .10
❑ 325 Manny Delcarmen RC .50 .20
❑ 326 Donnie Bridges .30 .10
❑ 327 Jim Kavourias RC .40 .15
❑ 328 Gabe Gross .30 .10
❑ 329 Jon Rauch .30 .10
❑ 330 Bill Ortega .30 .10
❑ 331 Joey Hammond RC .40 .15
❑ 332 Ramon Moreta RC .40 .15
❑ 333 Ron Davenport .30 .10
❑ 334 Brett Myers .40 .15
❑ 335 Carlos Pena .30 .10
❑ 336 Ezequiel Astacio RC .40 .15
❑ 337 Edwin Yan RC .40 .15
❑ 338 Josh Girdley .30 .10
❑ 339 Shaun Boyd .30 .10
❑ 340 Juan Rincon .30 .10
❑ 341 Chris Duffy RC .50 .20
❑ 342 Jason Kinchen .30 .10
❑ 343 Brad Thomas .30 .10
❑ 344 David Kelton .30 .10
❑ 345 Rafael Soriano .30 .10
❑ 346 Colin Young RC .40 .15
❑ 347 Eric Byrnes .30 .10
❑ 348 Chris Narveson RC .50 .20
❑ 349 John Rheinecker .30 .10
❑ 350 Mike Wilson RC .40 .15
❑ 351 Justin Sherrod RC .40 .15
❑ 352 Deivi Mendez .30 .10
❑ 353 Wily Mo Pena .40 .15
❑ 354 Brett Roneberg RC .40 .15
❑ 355 Trey Lunsford RC .40 .15
❑ 356 Jimmy Gobble RC .40 .15
❑ 357 Brent Butler .30 .10
❑ 358 Aaron Heilman .30 .10
❑ 359 Wilkin Ruan .30 .10
❑ 360 Brian Wolfe RC .40 .15
❑ 361 Cody Ransom .30 .10
❑ 362 Koyie Hill .30 .10
❑ 363 Scott Cassidy .30 .10
❑ 364 Tony Fontana RC .40 .15
❑ 365 Mark Teixeira 1.50 .60
❑ 366 Doug Sessions RC .40 .15
❑ 367 Victor Hall .30 .10
❑ 368 Josh Cisneros RC .40 .15
❑ 369 Kevin Mench .30 .10
❑ 370 Tike Redman .30 .10
❑ 371 Jeff Heaverlo .30 .10
❑ 372 Carlos Brackley RC .40 .15
❑ 373 Brad Hawpe .30 .10
❑ 374 Jesus Colome .30 .10
❑ 375 David Espinosa .30 .10
❑ 376 Jesse Foppert RC .50 .20
❑ 377 Ross Peeples RC .40 .15
❑ 378 Alex Requena RC .40 .15
❑ 379 Joe Mauer RC 12.00 5.00
❑ 380 Carlos Silva .30 .10
❑ 381 David Wright RC 30.00 12.50
❑ 382 Craig Kuzmic RC .40 .15
❑ 383 Pete Zamora RC .40 .15
❑ 384 Matt Parker RC .40 .15
❑ 385 Keith Ginter .30 .10
❑ 386 Gary Cates Jr. RC .40 .15
❑ 387 Justin Reid RC .40 .15
❑ 388 Jake Mauer RC .40 .15
❑ 389 Dennis Tankersley .30 .10
❑ 390 Josh Barfield RC 2.50 1.00
❑ 391 Luis Maza .30 .10
❑ 392 Henry Pichardo RC .40 .15
❑ 393 Michael Floyd RC .40 .15
❑ 394 Clint Nageotte RC .50 .20
❑ 395 Raymond Cabrera RC .40 .15
❑ 396 Mauricio Lara RC .40 .15
❑ 397 Alejandro Cadena RC .40 .15
❑ 398 Jonny Gomes RC 2.50 1.00
❑ 399 Jason Bulger RC .40 .15
❑ 400 Bobby Jenks RC 1.50 .60
❑ 401 David Gil RC .40 .15
❑ 402 Joel Crump RC .40 .15
❑ 403 Kazuhisa Ishii RC .75 .30
❑ 404 So Taguchi RC .75 .30
❑ 405 Ryan Doumit RC .60 .25
❑ 406 Macay McBride .40 .15
❑ 407 Brandon Claussen .30 .10
❑ 408 Chin-Feng Chen .40 .15
❑ 409 Josh Phelps .30 .10
❑ 410 Freddie Money RC .50 .20
❑ 411 Cliff Bartosh RC .40 .15
❑ 412 Josh Pearce .30 .10

- ❑ 413 Lyle Overbay .30 .10
- ❑ 414 Ryan Anderson .30 .10
- ❑ 415 Terrance Hill RC .40 .15
- ❑ 416 John Rodriguez RC .50 .20
- ❑ 417 Richard Stahl .30 .10
- ❑ 418 Brian Specht .30 .10
- ❑ 419 Chris Latham RC .30 .10
- ❑ 420 Carlos Cabrera RC .40 .15
- ❑ 421 Jose Bautista RC 1.00 .40
- ❑ 422 Kevin Frederick RC .40 .15
- ❑ 423 Jerome Williams .30 .10
- ❑ 424 Napoleon Calzado RC .40 .15
- ❑ 425 Benito Baez .30 .10
- ❑ 426 Xavier Nady .30 .10
- ❑ 427 Jason Botts RC .60 .25
- ❑ 428 Steve Bechler RC .40 .15
- ❑ 429 Reed Johnson RC 1.00 .40
- ❑ 430 Mark Outlaw RC .40 .15
- ❑ 431 Billy Sylvester .30 .10
- ❑ 432 Luke Lockwood .30 .10
- ❑ 433 Jake Peavy .60 .25
- ❑ 434 Alfredo Amezaga .30 .10
- ❑ 435 Aaron Cook RC .40 .15
- ❑ 436 Josh Shaffer RC .40 .15
- ❑ 437 Dan Wright .30 .10
- ❑ 438 Ryan Gripp RC .40 .15
- ❑ 439 Alex Herrera .30 .10
- ❑ 440 Jason Bay RC 5.00 2.00

2002 Bowman Draft

- ❑ COMPLETE SET (165) 50.00 25.00
- ❑ BDP1 Clint Everts RC .50 .20
- ❑ BDP2 Fred Lewis RC .40 .15
- ❑ BDP3 Jon Broxton RC 1.00 .40
- ❑ BDP4 Jason Anderson RC .40 .15
- ❑ BDP5 Mike Eusebio RC .40 .15
- ❑ BDP6 Zack Greinke RC 4.00 1.50
- ❑ BDP7 Joe Blanton RC 2.00 .75
- ❑ BDP8 Sergio Santos RC .50 .20
- ❑ BDP9 Jason Cooper RC .40 .15
- ❑ BDP10 Delwyn Young RC 1.00 .40
- ❑ BDP11 Jeremy Hermida RC 5.00 2.00
- ❑ BDP12 Dan Ortmeier RC .50 .20
- ❑ BDP13 Kevin Jepsen RC .50 .20
- ❑ BDP14 Russ Adams RC .50 .20
- ❑ BDP15 Mike Nixon RC .40 .15
- ❑ BDP16 Nick Swisher RC 5.00 2.00
- ❑ BDP17 Cole Hamels RC 15.00 6.00
- ❑ BDP18 Brian Dopirak RC 1.00 .40
- ❑ BDP19 James Loney RC 6.00 2.50
- ❑ BDP20 Denard Span RC .50 .20
- ❑ BDP21 Billy Petrick RC .40 .15
- ❑ BDP22 Jared Doyle RC .40 .15
- ❑ BDP23 Jeff Francoeur RC 15.00 6.00
- ❑ BDP24 Nick Bourgeois RC .40 .15
- ❑ BDP25 Matt Cain RC 6.00 2.50
- ❑ BDP26 John McCurdy RC .40 .15
- ❑ BDP27 Mark Kiger RC .40 .15
- ❑ BDP28 Bill Murphy RC .40 .15
- ❑ BDP29 Matt Craig RC .50 .20
- ❑ BDP30 Mike Megrew RC .40 .15
- ❑ BDP31 Ben Crockett RC .40 .15
- ❑ BDP32 Luke Hagerty RC .40 .15
- ❑ BDP33 Matt Whitney RC .40 .15
- ❑ BDP34 Dan Meyer RC .50 .20
- ❑ BDP35 Jeremy Brown RC .40 .15
- ❑ BDP36 Doug Johnson RC .40 .15
- ❑ BDP37 Steve Obenchain RC .40 .15
- ❑ BDP38 Matt Clanton RC .40 .15
- ❑ BDP39 Mark Teahen RC 1.00 .40
- ❑ BDP40 Tom Carrow RC .40 .15
- ❑ BDP41 Micah Schilling RC .40 .15
- ❑ BDP42 Blair Johnson RC .40 .15
- ❑ BDP43 Jason Pridie RC .40 .15
- ❑ BDP44 Joey Votto RC 3.00 1.25
- ❑ BDP45 Taber Lee RC .40 .15
- ❑ BDP46 Adam Peterson RC .40 .15
- ❑ BDP47 Adam Donachie RC .40 .15
- ❑ BDP48 Josh Murray RC .40 .15
- ❑ BDP49 Brent Clevlen RC 2.00 .75
- ❑ BDP50 Chad Pleiness RC .40 .15
- ❑ BDP51 Zach Hammes RC .40 .15
- ❑ BDP52 Chris Snyder RC .50 .20
- ❑ BDP53 Chris Smith RC .40 .15
- ❑ BDP54 Justin Maureau RC .40 .15
- ❑ BDP55 David Bush RC 1.00 .40
- ❑ BDP56 Tim Gilhooly RC .40 .15
- ❑ BDP57 Blair Barbier RC .40 .15
- ❑ BDP58 Zach Segovia RC .40 .15
- ❑ BDP59 Jeremy Reed RC 1.00 .40
- ❑ BDP60 Matt Pender RC .40 .15
- ❑ BDP61 Eric Thames RC .40 .15
- ❑ BDP62 Justin Jones RC .50 .20
- ❑ BDP63 Brian Slocum RC .40 .15
- ❑ BDP64 Larry Broadway RC .40 .15
- ❑ BDP65 Bo Flowers RC .40 .15
- ❑ BDP66 Scott White RC .40 .15
- ❑ BDP67 Steve Stanley RC .40 .15
- ❑ BDP68 Alex Merricks RC .40 .15
- ❑ BDP69 Josh Womack RC .40 .15
- ❑ BDP70 Dave Jensen RC .40 .15
- ❑ BDP71 Curtis Granderson RC 5.00 2.00
- ❑ BDP72 Pat Osborn RC .40 .15
- ❑ BDP73 Nic Carter RC .40 .15
- ❑ BDP74 Mitch Talbot RC .40 .15
- ❑ BDP75 Don Murphy RC .40 .15
- ❑ BDP76 Val Majewski RC .40 .15
- ❑ BDP77 Javy Rodriguez RC .40 .15
- ❑ BDP78 Fernando Pacheco RC .40 .15
- ❑ BDP79 Steve Russell RC .40 .15
- ❑ BDP80 Jon Slack RC .40 .15
- ❑ BDP81 John Baker RC .40 .15
- ❑ BDP82 Aaron Coonrod RC .40 .15
- ❑ BDP83 Josh Johnson RC 5.00 2.00
- ❑ BDP84 Jake Blalock RC 5.00 2.00
- ❑ BDP85 Alex Hart RC .40 .15
- ❑ BDP86 Wes Bankston RC 2.00 .75
- ❑ BDP87 Josh Rupe RC .40 .15
- ❑ BDP88 Dan Cevette RC .40 .15
- ❑ BDP89 Kiel Fisher RC .50 .20
- ❑ BDP90 Alan Rick RC .40 .15
- ❑ BDP91 Charlie Morton RC .40 .15
- ❑ BDP92 Chad Spann RC .40 .15
- ❑ BDP93 Kyle Boyer RC .40 .15
- ❑ BDP94 Bob Malek RC .40 .15
- ❑ BDP95 Ryan Rodriguez RC .40 .15
- ❑ BDP96 Jordan Renz RC .40 .15
- ❑ BDP97 Randy Frye RC .40 .15
- ❑ BDP98 Rich Hill RC 5.00 2.00
- ❑ BDP99 B.J. Upton RC 5.00 2.00
- ❑ BDP100 Dan Christensen RC .40 .15
- ❑ BDP101 Casey Kotchman RC 1.00 .40
- ❑ BDP102 Eric Good RC .30 .10
- ❑ BDP103 Mike Fontenot RC .40 .15
- ❑ BDP104 John Webb RC .40 .15
- ❑ BDP105 Jason Dubois RC .50 .20
- ❑ BDP106 Ryan Kibler RC .40 .15
- ❑ BDP107 Jhonny Peralta RC 2.50 1.00
- ❑ BDP108 Kirk Saarloos RC .40 .15
- ❑ BDP109 Rhett Parrott RC .40 .15
- ❑ BDP110 Jason Grove RC .40 .15
- ❑ BDP111 Colt Griffin RC .40 .15
- ❑ BDP112 Dallas McPherson RC 1.00 .40
- ❑ BDP113 Oliver Perez RC 1.00 .40
- ❑ BDP114 Marshall McDougall RC .40 .15
- ❑ BDP115 Mike Wood RC .40 .15
- ❑ BDP116 Scott Hairston RC .50 .20
- ❑ BDP117 Jason Simontacchi RC .40 .15
- ❑ BDP118 Taggert Bozied RC .50 .20
- ❑ BDP119 Shelley Duncan RC 3.00 1.25
- ❑ BDP120 Dontrelle Willis RC 5.00 2.00
- ❑ BDP121 Sean Burnett .30 .10
- ❑ BDP122 Aaron Cook .30 .10
- ❑ BDP123 Brett Evert .30 .10
- ❑ BDP124 Jimmy Journell .30 .10
- ❑ BDP125 Brett Myers .30 .10
- ❑ BDP126 Brad Baker .30 .10
- ❑ BDP127 Billy Traber RC .40 .15
- ❑ BDP128 Adam Wainwright .30 .10
- ❑ BDP129 Jason Young RC .30 .10
- ❑ BDP130 John Buck .30 .10
- ❑ BDP131 Kevin Cash RC .40 .15
- ❑ BDP132 Jason Stokes RC .50 .20
- ❑ BDP133 Drew Henson .30 .10
- ❑ BDP134 Chad Tracy RC 1.00 .40
- ❑ BDP135 Orlando Hudson .30 .10
- ❑ BDP136 Brandon Phillips .30 .10
- ❑ BDP137 Joe Borchard .30 .10
- ❑ BDP138 Marlon Byrd .30 .10
- ❑ BDP139 Carl Crawford .30 .10
- ❑ BDP140 Michael Restovich .30 .10
- ❑ BDP141 Corey Hart RC 1.50 .60
- ❑ BDP142 Edwin Almonte .30 .10
- ❑ BDP143 Francis Beltran RC .40 .15
- ❑ BDP144 Jorge De La Rosa RC .40 .15
- ❑ BDP145 Gerardo Garcia RC .40 .15
- ❑ BDP146 Franklyn German RC .40 .15
- ❑ BDP147 Francisco Liriano 3.00 1.25
- ❑ BDP148 Francisco Rodriguez .30 .10
- ❑ BDP149 Ricardo Rodriguez .30 .10
- ❑ BDP150 Seung Song .30 .10
- ❑ BDP151 John Stephens .30 .10
- ❑ BDP152 Justin Huber RC .75 .30
- ❑ BDP153 Victor Martinez .75 .30
- ❑ BDP154 Hee Seop Choi .30 .10
- ❑ BDP155 Justin Morneau .30 .10
- ❑ BDP156 Miguel Cabrera 1.25 .50
- ❑ BDP157 Victor Diaz RC .75 .30
- ❑ BDP158 Jose Reyes .50 .20
- ❑ BDP159 Omar Infante .30 .10
- ❑ BDP160 Angel Berroa .30 .10
- ❑ BDP161 Tony Alvarez .30 .10
- ❑ BDP162 Shin Soo Choo RC .75 .30
- ❑ BDP163 Wily Mo Pena .30 .10
- ❑ BDP164 Andres Torres .30 .10
- ❑ BDP165 Jose Lopez RC 2.00 .75

2003 Bowman

- ❑ COMPLETE SET (330) 60.00 25.00
- ❑ COMMON CARD (1-155) .30 .10
- ❑ COMMON CARD (156-330) .30 .10
- ❑ 1 Garret Anderson .30 .10
- ❑ 2 Derek Jeter 2.00 .75
- ❑ 3 Gary Sheffield .30 .10
- ❑ 4 Matt Morris .30 .10
- ❑ 5 Derek Lowe .30 .10
- ❑ 6 Andy Van Hekken .30 .10
- ❑ 7 Sammy Sosa .75 .30
- ❑ 8 Ken Griffey Jr. 1.25 .50
- ❑ 9 Omar Vizquel .50 .20
- ❑ 10 Jorge Posada .50 .20
- ❑ 11 Lance Berkman .30 .10
- ❑ 12 Mike Sweeney .30 .10
- ❑ 13 Adrian Beltre .30 .10
- ❑ 14 Richie Sexson .30 .10
- ❑ 15 A.J. Pierzynski .30 .10
- ❑ 16 Bartolo Colon .30 .10
- ❑ 17 Mike Mussina .50 .20
- ❑ 18 Paul Byrd .30 .10
- ❑ 19 Bobby Abreu .30 .10
- ❑ 20 Miguel Tejada .30 .10
- ❑ 21 Aramis Ramirez .30 .10

❑ 22 Edgardo Alfonzo	.30	.10
❑ 23 Edgar Martinez	.50	.20
❑ 24 Albert Pujols	1.50	.60
❑ 25 Carl Crawford	.30	.10
❑ 26 Eric Hinske	.30	.10
❑ 27 Tim Salmon	.50	.20
❑ 28 Luis Gonzalez	.30	.10
❑ 29 Jay Gibbons	.30	.10
❑ 30 John Smoltz	.50	.20
❑ 31 Tim Wakefield	.30	.10
❑ 32 Mark Prior	.50	.20
❑ 33 Magglio Ordonez	.30	.10
❑ 34 Adam Dunn	.30	.10
❑ 35 Larry Walker	.30	.10
❑ 36 Luis Castillo	.30	.10
❑ 37 Wade Miller	.30	.10
❑ 38 Carlos Beltran	.30	.10
❑ 39 Odalis Perez	.30	.10
❑ 40 Alex Sanchez	.30	.10
❑ 41 Torii Hunter	.30	.10
❑ 42 Cliff Floyd	.30	.10
❑ 43 Andy Pettitte	.50	.20
❑ 44 Francisco Rodriguez	.30	.10
❑ 45 Eric Chavez	.30	.10
❑ 46 Kevin Millwood	.30	.10
❑ 47 Dennis Tankersley	.30	.10
❑ 48 Hideo Nomo	.75	.30
❑ 49 Freddy Garcia	.30	.10
❑ 50 Randy Johnson	.75	.30
❑ 51 Aubrey Huff	.30	.10
❑ 52 Carlos Delgado	.30	.10
❑ 53 Troy Glaus	.30	.10
❑ 54 Junior Spivey	.30	.10
❑ 55 Mike Hampton	.30	.10
❑ 56 Sidney Ponson	.30	.10
❑ 57 Aaron Boone	.30	.10
❑ 58 Kerry Wood	.30	.10
❑ 59 Runelvys Hernandez	.30	.10
❑ 60 Nomar Garciaparra	1.25	.50
❑ 61 Todd Helton	.50	.20
❑ 62 Mike Lowell	.30	.10
❑ 63 Roy Oswalt	.30	.10
❑ 64 Raul Ibanez	.30	.10
❑ 65 Brian Jordan	.30	.10
❑ 66 Geoff Jenkins	.30	.10
❑ 67 Jermaine Dye	.30	.10
❑ 68 Tom Glavine	.50	.20
❑ 69 Bernie Williams	.50	.20
❑ 70 Vladimir Guerrero	.75	.30
❑ 71 Mark Mulder	.30	.10
❑ 72 Jimmy Rollins	.30	.10
❑ 73 Oliver Perez	.30	.10
❑ 74 Rich Aurilia	.30	.10
❑ 75 Joel Pineiro	.30	.10
❑ 76 J.D. Drew	.30	.10
❑ 77 Ivan Rodriguez	.50	.20
❑ 78 Josh Phelps	.30	.10
❑ 79 Darin Erstad	.30	.10
❑ 80 Curt Schilling	.30	.10
❑ 81 Paul Lo Duca	.30	.10
❑ 82 Marty Cordova	.30	.10
❑ 83 Manny Ramirez	.50	.20
❑ 84 Bobby Hill	.30	.10
❑ 85 Paul Konerko	.30	.10
❑ 86 Austin Kearns	.30	.10
❑ 87 Jason Jennings	.30	.10
❑ 88 Brad Penny	.30	.10
❑ 89 Jeff Bagwell	.50	.20
❑ 90 Shawn Green	.30	.10
❑ 91 Jason Schmidt	.30	.10
❑ 92 Doug Mientkiewicz	.30	.10
❑ 93 Jose Vidro	.30	.10
❑ 94 Bret Boone	.30	.10
❑ 95 Jason Giambi	.30	.10
❑ 96 Barry Zito	.30	.10
❑ 97 Roy Halladay	.30	.10
❑ 98 Pat Burrell	.30	.10
❑ 99 Sean Burroughs	.30	.10
❑ 100 Barry Bonds	2.00	.75
❑ 101 Kazuhiro Sasaki	.30	.10
❑ 102 Fernando Vina	.30	.10
❑ 103 Chan Ho Park	.30	.10
❑ 104 Andruw Jones	.50	.20
❑ 105 Adam Kennedy	.30	.10
❑ 106 Shea Hillenbrand	.30	.10
❑ 107 Greg Maddux	1.25	.50
❑ 108 Jim Edmonds	.30	.10
❑ 109 Pedro Martinez	.50	.20
❑ 110 Moises Alou	.30	.10
❑ 111 Jeff Weaver	.30	.10
❑ 112 C.C. Sabathia	.30	.10
❑ 113 Robert Fick	.30	.10
❑ 114 A.J. Burnett	.30	.10
❑ 115 Jeff Kent	.30	.10
❑ 116 Kevin Brown	.30	.10
❑ 117 Rafael Furcal	.30	.10
❑ 118 Cristian Guzman	.30	.10
❑ 119 Brad Wilkerson	.30	.10
❑ 120 Mike Piazza	1.25	.50
❑ 121 Alfonso Soriano	.30	.10
❑ 122 Mark Ellis	.30	.10
❑ 123 Vicente Padilla	.30	.10
❑ 124 Eric Gagne	.30	.10
❑ 125 Ryan Klesko	.30	.10
❑ 126 Ichiro Suzuki	1.50	.60
❑ 127 Tony Batista	.30	.10
❑ 128 Roberto Alomar	.50	.20
❑ 129 Alex Rodriguez	1.25	.50
❑ 130 Jim Thome	.50	.20
❑ 131 Jarrod Washburn	.30	.10
❑ 132 Orlando Hudson	.30	.10
❑ 133 Chipper Jones	.75	.30
❑ 134 Rodrigo Lopez	.30	.10
❑ 135 Johnny Damon	.50	.20
❑ 136 Matt Clement	.30	.10
❑ 137 Frank Thomas	.75	.30
❑ 138 Ellis Burks	.30	.10
❑ 139 Carlos Pena	.30	.10
❑ 140 Josh Beckett	.30	.10
❑ 141 Joe Randa	.30	.10
❑ 142 Brian Giles	.30	.10
❑ 143 Kazuhisa Ishii	.30	.10
❑ 144 Corey Koskie	.30	.10
❑ 145 Orlando Cabrera	.30	.10
❑ 146 Mark Buehrle	.30	.10
❑ 147 Roger Clemens	1.50	.60
❑ 148 Tim Hudson	.30	.10
❑ 149 Randy Wolf	.30	.10
❑ 150 Josh Fogg	.30	.10
❑ 151 Phil Nevin	.30	.10
❑ 152 John Olerud	.30	.10
❑ 153 Scott Rolen	.50	.20
❑ 154 Joe Kennedy	.30	.10
❑ 155 Rafael Palmeiro	.50	.20
❑ 156 Chad Hutchinson	.30	.10
❑ 157 Quincy Carter XRC	.40	.15
❑ 158 Hee Seop Choi	.30	.10
❑ 159 Joe Borchard	.30	.10
❑ 160 Brandon Phillips	.30	.10
❑ 161 Wily Mo Pena	.30	.10
❑ 162 Victor Martinez	.50	.20
❑ 163 Jason Stokes	.30	.10
❑ 164 Ken Harvey	.30	.10
❑ 165 Juan Rivera	.30	.10
❑ 166 Jose Contreras RC	1.50	.60
❑ 167 Dan Haren RC	1.00	.40
❑ 168 Michel Hernandez RC	.40	.15
❑ 169 Eider Torres RC	.40	.15
❑ 170 Chris De La Cruz RC	.40	.15
❑ 171 Ramon Nivar-Martinez RC	.40	.15
❑ 172 Mike Adams RC	.40	.15
❑ 173 Justin Arneson RC	.40	.15
❑ 174 Jamie Athas RC	.40	.15
❑ 175 Dwaine Bacon RC	.40	.15
❑ 176 Clint Barmes RC	1.00	.40
❑ 177 B.J. Barns RC	.40	.15
❑ 178 Tyler Johnson RC	.40	.15
❑ 179 Bobby Basham RC	.40	.15
❑ 180 T.J. Bohn RC	.40	.15
❑ 181 J.D. Durbin RC	.40	.15
❑ 182 Brandon Bowe RC	.40	.15
❑ 183 Craig Brazell RC	.40	.15
❑ 184 Dusty Brown RC	.40	.15
❑ 185 Brian Bruney RC	.50	.20
❑ 186 Greg Bruso RC	.40	.15
❑ 187 Jaime Bubela RC	.40	.15
❑ 188 Bryan Bullington RC	.40	.15
❑ 189 Brian Burgamy RC	.40	.15
❑ 190 Eny Cabreja RC	1.25	.50
❑ 191 Daniel Cabrera RC	.75	.30
❑ 192 Ryan Cameron RC	.40	.15
❑ 193 Lance Caraccioli RC	.40	.15
❑ 194 David Cash RC	.40	.15
❑ 195 Bernie Castro RC	.40	.15
❑ 196 Ismael Castro RC	.50	.20
❑ 197 Daryl Clark RC	.40	.15
❑ 198 Jeff Clark RC	.40	.15
❑ 199 Chris Colton RC	.40	.15
❑ 200 Dexter Cooper RC	.40	.15
❑ 201 Callix Crabbe RC	.50	.20
❑ 202 Chien-Ming Wang RC	6.00	2.50
❑ 203 Eric Crozier RC	.50	.20
❑ 204 Nook Logan RC	.50	.20
❑ 205 David DeJesus RC	.75	.30
❑ 206 Matt DeMarco RC	.40	.15
❑ 207 Chris Duncan RC	4.00	1.50
❑ 208 Eric Eckenstahler	.30	.10
❑ 209 Willie Eyre RC	.40	.15
❑ 210 Evel Bastida-Martinez RC	.40	.15
❑ 211 Chris Fallon RC	.40	.15
❑ 212 Mike Flannery RC	.40	.15
❑ 213 Mike Oâ ™Keefe RC	.40	.15
❑ 214 Ben Francisco RC	.40	.15
❑ 215 Kason Gabbard RC	.40	.15
❑ 216 Mike Gallo RC	.40	.15
❑ 217 Jairo Garcia RC	.50	.20
❑ 218 Angel Garcia RC	.50	.20
❑ 219 Michael Garciaparra RC	.30	.10
❑ 220 Joey Gomes RC	.40	.15
❑ 221 Dusty Gomon RC	.50	.20
❑ 222 Bryan Grace RC	.40	.15
❑ 223 Tyson Graham RC	.40	.15
❑ 224 Henry Guerrero RC	.40	.15
❑ 225 Franklin Gutierrez RC	1.00	.40
❑ 226 Carlos Guzman RC	.50	.20
❑ 227 Matthew Hagen RC	.40	.15
❑ 228 Josh Hall RC	.40	.15
❑ 229 Rob Hammock RC	.40	.15
❑ 230 Brendan Harris RC	.50	.20
❑ 231 Gary Harris RC	.40	.15
❑ 232 Clay Hensley RC	.40	.15
❑ 233 Michael Hinckley RC	.50	.20
❑ 234 Luis Hodge RC	.40	.15
❑ 235 Donnie Hood RC	.50	.20
❑ 236 Travis Ishikawa RC	1.00	.40
❑ 237 Edwin Jackson RC	.50	.20
❑ 238 Ardley Jansen RC	.50	.20
❑ 239 Ferenc Jongejan RC	.40	.15
❑ 240 Matt Kata RC	.40	.15
❑ 241 Kazuhiro Takeoka RC	.40	.15
❑ 242 Beau Kemp RC	.40	.15
❑ 243 Il Kim RC	.40	.15
❑ 244 Brennan King RC	.40	.15
❑ 245 Chris Kroski RC	.40	.15
❑ 246 Jason Kubel RC	2.00	.75
❑ 247 Pete LaForest RC	.40	.15
❑ 248 Wil Ledezma RC	.40	.15
❑ 249 Jeremy Bonderman RC	3.00	1.25
❑ 250 Gonzalo Lopez RC	.40	.15
❑ 251 Brian Luderer RC	.40	.15
❑ 252 Ruddy Lugo RC	.40	.15
❑ 253 Wayne Lydon RC	.40	.15
❑ 254 Mark Malaska RC	.40	.15
❑ 255 Andy Marte RC	3.00	1.25
❑ 256 Tyler Martin RC	.40	.15
❑ 257 Branden Florence RC	.40	.15
❑ 258 Aneudis Mateo RC	.40	.15
❑ 259 Derell McCall RC	.40	.15
❑ 260 Brian McCann RC	8.00	3.00
❑ 261 Mike McNutt RC	.40	.15
❑ 262 Jacabo Meque RC	.40	.15
❑ 263 Derek Michaelis RC	.40	.15
❑ 264 Aaron Miles RC	.50	.20
❑ 265 Jose Morales RC	.40	.15
❑ 266 Dustin Moseley RC	.40	.15
❑ 267 Adrian Myers RC	.40	.15
❑ 268 Dan Neil RC	.40	.15
❑ 269 Jon Nelson RC	.50	.20
❑ 270 Mike Neu RC	.40	.15
❑ 271 Leigh Neuage RC	.40	.15
❑ 272 Wes O'Brien RC	.40	.15
❑ 273 Trent Oeltjen RC	.50	.20
❑ 274 Tim Olson RC	.40	.15
❑ 275 David Pahucki RC	.40	.15
❑ 276 Nathan Panther RC	.40	.15
❑ 277 Arnie Munoz RC	.40	.15
❑ 278 Dave Pember RC	.40	.15
❑ 279 Jason Perry RC	.50	.20

❑ 280 Matthew Peterson RC .40 .15
❑ 281 Ryan Shealy RC 2.50 1.00
❑ 282 Jorge Piedra RC .50 .20
❑ 283 Simon Pond RC .40 .15
❑ 284 Aaron Rakers RC .40 .15
❑ 285 Hanley Ramirez RC 5.00 2.00
❑ 286 Manuel Ramirez RC .50 .20
❑ 287 Kevin Randel RC .40 .15
❑ 288 Darrell Rasner RC .40 .15
❑ 289 Prentice Redman RC .40 .15
❑ 290 Eric Reed RC .40 .15
❑ 291 Wilton Reynolds RC .50 .20
❑ 292 Eric Riggs RC .50 .20
❑ 293 Carlos Rijo RC .40 .15
❑ 294 Rajai Davis RC .40 .15
❑ 295 Aron Weston RC .40 .15
❑ 296 Arturo Rivas RC .40 .15
❑ 297 Kyle Roat RC .40 .15
❑ 298 Bubba Nelson RC .50 .20
❑ 299 Levi Robinson RC .40 .15
❑ 300 Ray Sadler RC .40 .15
❑ 301 Gary Schneidmiller RC .40 .15
❑ 302 Jon Schuerholz RC .40 .15
❑ 303 Corey Shafer RC .40 .15
❑ 304 Brian Shackelford RC .40 .15
❑ 305 Bill Simon RC .40 .15
❑ 306 Haj Turay RC .30 .10
❑ 307 Sean Smith RC .50 .20
❑ 308 Ryan Spataro RC .40 .15
❑ 309 Jemel Spearman RC .40 .15
❑ 310 Keith Stamler RC .40 .15
❑ 311 Luke Steidlmayer RC .40 .15
❑ 312 Adam Stern RC .30 .10
❑ 313 Jay Sitzman RC .40 .15
❑ 314 Thomari Story-Harden RC .50 .20
❑ 315 Terry Tiffee RC .40 .15
❑ 316 Nick Trzesniak RC .40 .15
❑ 317 Denny Tussen RC .40 .15
❑ 318 Scott Tyler RC .50 .20
❑ 319 Shane Victorino RC .75 .30
❑ 320 Doug Waechter RC .50 .20
❑ 321 Brandon Watson RC .40 .15
❑ 322 Todd Wellemeyer RC .40 .15
❑ 323 Eli Whiteside RC .40 .15
❑ 324 Josh Willingham RC 1.00 .40
❑ 325 Travis Wong RC .50 .20
❑ 326 Brian Wright RC .40 .15
❑ 327 Kevin Youkilis RC 3.00 1.25
❑ 328 Andy Sisco RC .30 .10
❑ 329 Dustin Yount RC .50 .20
❑ 330 Andrew Dominique RC .40 .15
❑ NNO Hinske/Jennings ROY Relic 15.00 6.00

2003 Bowman Draft

❑ COMPLETE SET (165) 50.00 20.00
❑ 1 Dontrelle Willis .75 .30
❑ 2 Freddy Sanchez .30 .10
❑ 3 Miguel Cabrera .75 .30
❑ 4 Ryan Ludwick .30 .10
❑ 5 Ty Wigginton .30 .10
❑ 6 Mark Teixeira .50 .20
❑ 7 Trey Hodges .30 .10
❑ 8 Laynce Nix .30 .10
❑ 9 Antonio Perez .30 .10
❑ 10 Jody Gerut .30 .10
❑ 11 Jae Weong Seo .30 .10
❑ 12 Erick Almonte .30 .10
❑ 13 Lyle Overbay .30 .10
❑ 14 Billy Traber .30 .10
❑ 15 Andres Torres .30 .10
❑ 16 Jose Valverde .30 .10
❑ 17 Aaron Heilman .30 .10
❑ 18 Brandon Larson .30 .10
❑ 19 Jung Bong .30 .10
❑ 20 Jesse Foppert .30 .10
❑ 21 Angel Berroa .30 .10
❑ 22 Jeff DaVanon .30 .10
❑ 23 Kurt Ainsworth .30 .10
❑ 24 Brandon Claussen .30 .10
❑ 25 Xavier Nady .30 .10
❑ 26 Travis Hafner .30 .10
❑ 27 Jerome Williams .30 .10
❑ 28 Jose Reyes .30 .10
❑ 29 Sergio Mitre RC .50 .20
❑ 30 Bo Hart RC .40 .15
❑ 31 Adam Miller RC 2.50 1.00
❑ 32 Brian Finch RC .40 .15
❑ 33 Taylor Mattingly RC .50 .20
❑ 34 Daric Barton RC 2.50 1.00
❑ 35 Chris Ray RC 1.00 .40
❑ 36 Jarrod Saltalamacchia RC 8.00 3.00
❑ 37 Dennis Dove RC .50 .20
❑ 38 James Houser RC .50 .20
❑ 39 Clint King RC .50 .20
❑ 40 Lou Palmisano RC .50 .20
❑ 41 Dan Moore RC .40 .15
❑ 42 Craig Stansberry RC .50 .20
❑ 43 Jo Jo Reyes RC 1.25 .50
❑ 44 Jake Stevens RC .50 .20
❑ 45 Tom Gorzelanny RC 1.25 .50
❑ 46 Brian Marshall RC .40 .15
❑ 47 Scott Beerer RC .40 .15
❑ 48 Javi Herrera RC .50 .20
❑ 49 Steve LeRud RC .50 .20
❑ 50 Josh Banks RC .75 .30
❑ 51 Jon Papelbon RC 12.00 5.00
❑ 52 Juan Valdes RC .50 .20
❑ 53 Beau Vaughan RC .50 .20
❑ 54 Matt Chico RC .50 .20
❑ 55 Todd Jennings RC .50 .20
❑ 56 Anthony Gwynn RC 1.25 .50
❑ 57 Matt Harrison RC .75 .30
❑ 58 Aaron Marsden RC .50 .20
❑ 59 Casey Abrams RC .40 .15
❑ 60 Cory Stuart RC .40 .15
❑ 61 Mike Wagner RC .40 .15
❑ 62 Jordan Pratt RC .50 .20
❑ 63 Andre Randolph RC .50 .20
❑ 64 Blake Balkcom RC .50 .20
❑ 65 Josh Muecke RC .40 .15
❑ 66 Jamie D'Antona RC .75 .30
❑ 67 Cole Seifrig RC .40 .15
❑ 68 Josh Anderson RC .50 .20
❑ 69 Matt Lorenzo RC .50 .20
❑ 70 Nate Spears RC .50 .20
❑ 71 Chris Goodman RC .40 .15
❑ 72 Brian McFall RC .40 .15
❑ 73 Billy Hogan RC .50 .20
❑ 74 Jamie Romak RC .50 .20
❑ 75 Jeff Cook RC .50 .20
❑ 76 Brooks McNiven RC .40 .15
❑ 77 Xavier Paul RC .50 .20
❑ 78 Bob Zimmerman RC .40 .15
❑ 79 Mickey Hall RC .50 .20
❑ 80 Shaun Marcum RC .50 .20
❑ 81 Matt Nachreiner RC .50 .20
❑ 82 Chris Kinsey RC .40 .15
❑ 83 Jonathan Fulton RC .50 .20
❑ 84 Edgardo Baez RC .50 .20
❑ 85 Robert Valido RC .50 .20
❑ 86 Kenny Lewis RC .50 .20
❑ 87 Trent Peterson RC .40 .15
❑ 88 Johnny Woodard RC .50 .20
❑ 89 Wes Littleton RC .50 .20
❑ 90 Sean Rodriguez RC 1.50 .60
❑ 91 Kyle Pearson RC .40 .15
❑ 92 Josh Rainwater RC .50 .20
❑ 93 Travis Schlichting RC .50 .20
❑ 94 Tim Battle RC .75 .30
❑ 95 Aaron Hill RC 1.50 .60
❑ 96 Bob McCrory RC .40 .15
❑ 97 Rick Guarno RC .50 .20
❑ 98 Brandon Yarbrough RC .40 .15
❑ 99 Peter Stonard RC .40 .15
❑ 100 Darin Downs RC .50 .20
❑ 101 Matt Bruback RC .30 .10
❑ 102 Danny Garcia RC .40 .15
❑ 103 Cory Stewart RC .40 .15
❑ 104 Ferdin Tejeda RC .40 .15
❑ 105 Kade Johnson RC .40 .15
❑ 106 Andrew Brown RC .50 .20
❑ 107 Aquilino Lopez RC .40 .15
❑ 108 Stephen Randolph RC .40 .15
❑ 109 Dave Matranga RC .40 .15
❑ 110 Dustin McGowan RC .50 .20
❑ 111 Juan Camacho RC .40 .15
❑ 112 Cliff Lee .30 .10
❑ 113 Jeff Duncan RC .40 .15
❑ 114 C.J. Wilson .30 .10
❑ 115 Brandon Roberson RC .40 .15
❑ 116 David Corrente RC .40 .15
❑ 117 Kevin Beavers RC .40 .15
❑ 118 Anthony Webster RC .50 .20
❑ 119 Oscar Villarreal RC .40 .15
❑ 120 Hong-Chih Kuo RC 2.50 1.00
❑ 121 Josh Barfield .30 .10
❑ 122 Denny Bautista .30 .10
❑ 123 Chris Burke RC 1.25 .50
❑ 124 Robinson Cano RC 8.00 3.00
❑ 125 Jose Castillo .30 .10
❑ 126 Neal Cotts .30 .10
❑ 127 Jorge De La Rosa .30 .10
❑ 128 J.D. Durbin .40 .15
❑ 129 Edwin Encarnacion 1.00 .40
❑ 130 Gavin Floyd .30 .10
❑ 131 Alexis Gomez .30 .10
❑ 132 Edgar Gonzalez RC .40 .15
❑ 133 Khalil Greene .75 .30
❑ 134 Zack Greinke .30 .10
❑ 135 Franklin Gutierrez .50 .20
❑ 136 Rich Harden .50 .20
❑ 137 J.J. Hardy RC 5.00 2.00
❑ 138 Ryan Howard RC 15.00 6.00
❑ 139 Justin Huber .30 .10
❑ 140 David Kelton .30 .10
❑ 141 Dave Krynzel .30 .10
❑ 142 Pete LaForest .40 .15
❑ 143 Adam LaRoche .30 .10
❑ 144 Preston Larrison RC .50 .20
❑ 145 John Maine RC 5.00 2.00
❑ 146 Andy Marte 1.25 .50
❑ 147 Jeff Mathis .30 .10
❑ 148 Joe Mauer .75 .30
❑ 149 Clint Nageotte .30 .10
❑ 150 Chris Narveson .30 .10
❑ 151 Ramon Nivar .40 .15
❑ 152 Felix Pie RC 5.00 2.00
❑ 153 Guillermo Quiroz RC .40 .15
❑ 154 Rene Reyes .30 .10
❑ 155 Royce Ring .30 .10
❑ 156 Alexis Rios 1.00 .40
❑ 157 Grady Sizemore .75 .30
❑ 158 Stephen Smitherman .30 .10
❑ 159 Seung Song .30 .10
❑ 160 Scott Thorman .30 .10
❑ 161 Chad Tracy .30 .10
❑ 162 Chin Hui Tsao .30 .10
❑ 163 John VanBenschoten .30 .10
❑ 164 Kevin Youkilis 4.00 1.50
❑ 165 Chien-Ming Wang 5.00 2.00

2004 Bowman

❑ COMPLETE SET (330)	80.00	40.00
❑ ROY ODDS 1:829 H, 1:284 HTA, 1:1632 R		
❑ 1 Garret Anderson	.30	.10
❑ 2 Larry Walker	.30	.10
❑ 3 Derek Jeter	1.50	.60
❑ 4 Curt Schilling	.50	.20
❑ 5 Carlos Zambrano	.30	.10
❑ 6 Shawn Green	.30	.10
❑ 7 Manny Ramirez	.50	.20
❑ 8 Randy Johnson	.75	.30
❑ 9 Jeremy Bonderman	.30	.10
❑ 10 Alfonso Soriano	.30	.10
❑ 11 Scott Rolen	.50	.20
❑ 12 Kerry Wood	.30	.10
❑ 13 Eric Gagne	.30	.10
❑ 14 Ryan Klesko	.30	.10
❑ 15 Kevin Millar	.30	.10
❑ 16 Ty Wigginton	.30	.10
❑ 17 David Ortiz	.75	.30
❑ 18 Luis Castillo	.30	.10
❑ 19 Bernie Williams	.50	.20
❑ 20 Edgar Renteria	.30	.10
❑ 21 Matt Kata	.30	.10
❑ 22 Bartolo Colon	.30	.10
❑ 23 Derrek Lee	.50	.20
❑ 24 Gary Sheffield	.30	.10
❑ 25 Nomar Garciaparra	1.25	.50
❑ 26 Kevin Millwood	.30	.10
❑ 27 Corey Patterson	.30	.10
❑ 28 Carlos Beltran	.30	.10
❑ 29 Mike Lieberthal	.30	.10
❑ 30 Troy Glaus	.30	.10
❑ 31 Preston Wilson	.30	.10
❑ 32 Jorge Posada	.50	.20
❑ 33 Bo Hart	.30	.10
❑ 34 Mark Prior	.50	.20
❑ 35 Hideo Nomo	.75	.30
❑ 36 Jason Kendall	.30	.10
❑ 37 Roger Clemens	1.50	.60
❑ 38 Dmitri Young	.30	.10
❑ 39 Jason Giambi	.30	.10
❑ 40 Jim Edmonds	.30	.10
❑ 41 Ryan Ludwick	.30	.10
❑ 42 Brandon Webb	.30	.10
❑ 43 Todd Helton	.50	.20
❑ 44 Jacque Jones	.30	.10
❑ 45 Jamie Moyer	.30	.10
❑ 46 Tim Salmon	.50	.20
❑ 47 Kelvim Escobar	.30	.10
❑ 48 Tony Batista	.30	.10
❑ 49 Nick Johnson	.30	.10
❑ 50 Jim Thome	.50	.20
❑ 51 Casey Blake	.30	.10
❑ 52 Trot Nixon	.30	.10
❑ 53 Luis Gonzalez	.30	.10
❑ 54 Dontrelle Willis	.50	.20
❑ 55 Mike Mussina	.50	.20
❑ 56 Carl Crawford	.30	.10
❑ 57 Mark Buehrle	.30	.10
❑ 58 Scott Podsednik	.30	.10
❑ 59 Brian Giles	.30	.10
❑ 60 Rafael Furcal	.30	.10
❑ 61 Miguel Cabrera	.50	.20
❑ 62 Rich Harden	.30	.10
❑ 63 Mark Teixeira	.50	.20
❑ 64 Frank Thomas	.75	.30
❑ 65 Johan Santana	.75	.30
❑ 66 Jason Schmidt	.30	.10
❑ 67 Aramis Ramirez	.30	.10
❑ 68 Jose Reyes	.30	.10
❑ 69 Maggio Ordonez	.30	.10
❑ 70 Mike Sweeney	.30	.10
❑ 71 Eric Chavez	.30	.10
❑ 72 Rocco Baldelli	.30	.10
❑ 73 Sammy Sosa	.75	.30
❑ 74 Javy Lopez	.30	.10
❑ 75 Roy Oswalt	.30	.10
❑ 76 Raul Ibanez	.30	.10
❑ 77 Ivan Rodriguez	.50	.20
❑ 78 Jerome Williams	.30	.10
❑ 79 Carlos Lee	.30	.10
❑ 80 Geoff Jenkins	.30	.10
❑ 81 Sean Burroughs	.30	.10
❑ 82 Marcus Giles	.30	.10
❑ 83 Mike Lowell	.30	.10
❑ 84 Barry Zito	.30	.10
❑ 85 Aubrey Huff	.30	.10
❑ 86 Esteban Loaiza	.30	.10
❑ 87 Torii Hunter	.30	.10
❑ 88 Phil Nevin	.30	.10
❑ 89 Andruw Jones	.50	.20
❑ 90 Josh Beckett	.30	.10
❑ 91 Mark Mulder	.30	.10
❑ 92 Hank Blalock	.30	.10
❑ 93 Jason Phillips	.30	.10
❑ 94 Russ Ortiz	.30	.10
❑ 95 Juan Pierre	.30	.10
❑ 96 Tom Glavine	.50	.20
❑ 97 Gil Meche	.30	.10
❑ 98 Ramon Ortiz	.30	.10
❑ 99 Richie Sexson	.30	.10
❑ 100 Albert Pujols	1.50	.60
❑ 101 Javier Vazquez	.30	.10
❑ 102 Johnny Damon	.50	.20
❑ 103 Alex Rodriguez Yanks	1.25	.50
❑ 104 Omar Vizquel	.50	.20
❑ 105 Chipper Jones	.75	.30
❑ 106 Lance Berkman	.30	.10
❑ 107 Tim Hudson	.30	.10
❑ 108 Carlos Delgado	.30	.10
❑ 109 Austin Kearns	.30	.10
❑ 110 Orlando Cabrera	.30	.10
❑ 111 Edgar Martinez	.50	.20
❑ 112 Melvin Mora	.30	.10
❑ 113 Jeff Bagwell	.50	.20
❑ 114 Marlon Byrd	.30	.10
❑ 115 Vernon Wells	.30	.10
❑ 116 C.C. Sabathia	.30	.10
❑ 117 Cliff Floyd	.30	.10
❑ 118 Ichiro Suzuki	1.50	.60
❑ 119 Miguel Olivo	.30	.10
❑ 120 Mike Piazza	1.25	.50
❑ 121 Adam Dunn	.30	.10
❑ 122 Paul Lo Duca	.30	.10
❑ 123 Brett Myers	.30	.10
❑ 124 Michael Young	.30	.10
❑ 125 Sidney Ponson	.30	.10
❑ 126 Greg Maddux	1.25	.50
❑ 127 Vladimir Guerrero	.75	.30
❑ 128 Miguel Tejada	.30	.10
❑ 129 Andy Pettitte	.50	.20
❑ 130 Rafael Palmeiro	.50	.20
❑ 131 Ken Griffey Jr.	1.25	.50
❑ 132 Shannon Stewart	.30	.10
❑ 133 Joel Pineiro	.30	.10
❑ 134 Luis Matos	.30	.10
❑ 135 Jeff Kent	.30	.10
❑ 136 Randy Wolf	.30	.10
❑ 137 Chris Woodward	.30	.10
❑ 138 Jody Gerut	.30	.10
❑ 139 Jose Vidro	.30	.10
❑ 140 Bret Boone	.30	.10
❑ 141 Bill Mueller	.30	.10
❑ 142 Angel Berroa	.30	.10
❑ 143 Bobby Abreu	.30	.10
❑ 144 Roy Halladay	.30	.10
❑ 145 Delmon Young	.50	.20
❑ 146 Jonny Gomes	.30	.10
❑ 147 Rickie Weeks	.30	.10
❑ 148 Edwin Jackson	.30	.10
❑ 149 Neal Cotts	.30	.10
❑ 150 Jason Bay	.30	.10
❑ 151 Khalil Greene	.50	.20
❑ 152 Joe Mauer	.75	.30
❑ 153 Bobby Jenks	.30	.10
❑ 154 Chin-Feng Chen	.30	.10
❑ 155 Chien-Ming Wang	1.00	.40
❑ 156 Mickey Hall	.30	.10
❑ 157 James Houser	.30	.10
❑ 158 Jay Sborz	.30	.10
❑ 159 Jonathan Fulton	.30	.10
❑ 160 Steven Lerud	.30	.10
❑ 161 Grady Sizemore	.75	.30
❑ 162 Felix Pie	.50	.20
❑ 163 Dustin McGowan	.30	.10
❑ 164 Chris Lubanski	.30	.10
❑ 165 Tom Gorzelanny	.30	.10
❑ 166 Rudy Guillen FY RC	.75	.30
❑ 167 Bobby Brownlie FY RC	1.00	.40
❑ 168 Conor Jackson FY RC	3.00	1.25
❑ 169 Matt Moses FY RC	1.00	.40
❑ 170 Ervin Santana FY RC	1.50	.60
❑ 171 Merkin Valdez FY RC	.50	.20
❑ 172 Erick Aybar FY RC	1.00	.40
❑ 173 Brad Sullivan FY RC	.50	.20
❑ 174 David Aardsma FY RC	.50	.20
❑ 175 Brad Snyder FY RC	1.00	.40
❑ 176 Alberto Callaspo FY RC	.75	.30
❑ 177 Brandon Medders FY RC	.40	.15
❑ 178 Zach Miner FY RC	1.25	.50
❑ 179 Charlie Zink FY RC	.30	.10
❑ 180 Adam Greenberg FY RC	.75	.30
❑ 181 Kevin Howard FY RC	.50	.20
❑ 182 Wanell Severino FY RC	.30	.10
❑ 183 Kevin Kouzmanoff FY RC	2.00	.75
❑ 184 Joel Zumaya FY RC	5.00	2.00
❑ 185 Skip Schumaker FY RC	.40	.15
❑ 186 Nic Ungs FY RC	.40	.15
❑ 187 Todd Self FY RC	.50	.20
❑ 188 Brian Steffek FY RC	.30	.10
❑ 189 Brock Peterson FY RC	.40	.15
❑ 190 Greg Thissen FY RC	.40	.15
❑ 191 Frank Brooks FY RC	.30	.10
❑ 192 Estee Harris FY RC	.50	.20
❑ 193 Chris Mabeus FY RC	.40	.15
❑ 194 Dan Giese FY RC	.40	.15
❑ 195 Jared Wells FY RC	.30	.10
❑ 196 Carlos Sosa FY RC	.40	.15
❑ 197 Bobby Madritsch FY	.30	.10
❑ 198 Calvin Hayes FY RC	.50	.20
❑ 199 Omar Quintanilla FY RC	.50	.20
❑ 200 Chris O'Riordan FY RC	.40	.15
❑ 201 Tim Hutting FY RC	.30	.10
❑ 202 Carlos Quentin FY RC	2.50	1.00
❑ 203 Brayan Pena FY RC	.40	.15
❑ 204 Jeff Salazar FY RC	1.00	.40
❑ 205 David Murphy FY RC	.75	.30
❑ 206 Alberto Garcia FY RC	.50	.20
❑ 207 Ramon Ramirez FY RC	.40	.15
❑ 208 Luis Bolivar FY RC	.50	.20
❑ 209 Rodney Choy Foo FY RC	.30	.10
❑ 210 Kyle Sleeth FY RC	.50	.20
❑ 211 Anthony Acevedo FY RC	.40	.15
❑ 212 Chad Santos FY RC	.40	.15
❑ 213 Jason Frasor FY RC	.40	.15
❑ 214 Jesse Roman FY RC	.30	.10
❑ 215 James Tomlin FY RC	.40	.15
❑ 216 Josh Labandeira FY RC	.40	.15
❑ 217 Joaquin Arias FY RC	.75	.30
❑ 218 Don Sutton FY UER RC	1.00	.40
❑ 219 Danny Gonzalez FY RC	.30	.10
❑ 220 Javier Guzman FY RC	.50	.20
❑ 221 Anthony Lerew FY RC	.75	.30
❑ 222 Jon Knott FY RC	.40	.15
❑ 223 Jesse English FY RC	.40	.15
❑ 224 Felix Hernandez FY RC	8.00	3.00
❑ 225 Travis Hanson FY RC	.50	.20
❑ 226 Jesse Floyd FY RC	.40	.15
❑ 227 Nick Gorneault FY RC	.50	.20
❑ 228 Craig Ansman FY RC	.40	.15
❑ 229 Wardell Starling FY RC	.40	.15
❑ 230 Carl Loadenthal FY RC	.50	.20
❑ 231 Dave Crouthers FY RC	.30	.10
❑ 232 Harvey Garcia FY RC	.30	.10
❑ 233 Casey Kopitzke FY RC	.30	.10
❑ 234 Ricky Nolasco FY RC	1.25	.50
❑ 235 Miguel Perez FY RC	.40	.15
❑ 236 Ryan Mulhern FY RC	.40	.15
❑ 237 Chris Aguila FY RC	.40	.15
❑ 238 Brooks Conrad FY RC	.50	.20
❑ 239 Damaso Espino FY RC	.30	.10
❑ 240 Jereme Milons FY RC	.50	.20
❑ 241 Luke Hughes FY RC	.30	.10
❑ 242 Kory Casto FY RC	.50	.20
❑ 243 Jose Valdez FY RC	.40	.15
❑ 244 J.T. Stotts FY RC	.30	.10
❑ 245 Lee Gwaltney FY RC	.30	.10
❑ 246 Yoann Torrealba FY RC	.30	.10
❑ 247 Omar Falcon FY RC	.40	.15
❑ 248 Jon Coutlangus FY RC	.30	.10
❑ 249 George Sherrill FY RC	.40	.15
❑ 250 John Santor FY RC	.30	.10
❑ 251 Tony Richie FY RC	.40	.15
❑ 252 Kevin Richardson FY RC	.30	.10
❑ 253 Tim Bittner FY RC	.40	.15
❑ 254 Dustin Nippert FY RC	1.25	.50
❑ 255 Jose Capellan FY RC	.50	.20
❑ 256 Donald Levinski FY RC	.30	.10

❑ 257 Jerome Gamble FY RC .30 .10
❑ 258 Jeff Keppinger FY RC 2.00 .75
❑ 259 Jason Szuminski FY RC .30 .10
❑ 260 Akinori Otsuka FY RC .40 .15
❑ 261 Ryan Budde FY RC .40 .15
❑ 262 Shingo Takatsu FY RC .75 .30
❑ 263 Jeff Allison FY RC .40 .15
❑ 264 Hector Gimenez FY RC .30 .10
❑ 265 Tim Frend FY RC .40 .15
❑ 266 Tom Farmer FY RC .40 .15
❑ 267 Shawn Hill FY RC .40 .15
❑ 268 Lastings Milledge FY RC 5.00 2.00
❑ 269 Scott Proctor FY RC .50 .20
❑ 270 Jorge Mejia FY RC .40 .15
❑ 271 Terry Jones FY RC .50 .20
❑ 272 Zach Duke FY RC 2.00 .75
❑ 273 Tim Stauffer FY RC .75 .30
❑ 274 Luke Anderson FY RC .30 .10
❑ 275 Hunter Brown FY RC .30 .10
❑ 276 Matt Lemanczyk FY RC .40 .15
❑ 277 Fernando Cortez FY RC .30 .10
❑ 278 Vince Perkins FY RC .50 .20
❑ 279 Tommy Murphy FY RC .40 .15
❑ 280 Mike Gosling FY RC .30 .10
❑ 281 Paul Bacot FY RC .50 .20
❑ 282 Matt Capps FY RC .40 .15
❑ 283 Juan Gutierrez FY RC .40 .15
❑ 284 Teodoro Encarnacion FY RC .50 .20
❑ 285 Juan Cedeno FY RC .40 .15
❑ 286 Matt Creighton FY RC .40 .15
❑ 287 Ryan Hankins FY RC .30 .10
❑ 288 Leo Nunez FY RC .40 .15
❑ 289 Dave Wallace FY RC .40 .15
❑ 290 Rob Tejeda FY RC .75 .30
❑ 291 Lincoln Holdzkom FY RC .40 .15
❑ 292 Jason Hirsh FY RC 1.50 .60
❑ 293 Tydus Meadows FY RC .40 .15
❑ 294 Khalid Ballouli FY RC .30 .10
❑ 295 Benji DeQuin FY RC .30 .10
❑ 296 Tyler Davidson FY RC 1.50 .60
❑ 297 Brant Colamarino FY RC .75 .30
❑ 298 Marcus McBeth FY RC .30 .10
❑ 299 Brad Eldred FY RC .60 .25
❑ 300 David Pauley FY RC 1.25 .50
❑ 301 Yadier Molina FY RC 1.50 .60
❑ 302 Chris Shelton FY RC 1.25 .50
❑ 303 Travis Blackley FY RC .40 .15
❑ 304 Jon DeVries FY RC .40 .15
❑ 305 Sheldon Fulse FY RC .30 .10
❑ 306 Vito Chiaravalloti FY RC .40 .15
❑ 307 Warner Madrigal FY RC .75 .30
❑ 308 Reid Gorecki FY RC .40 .15
❑ 309 Sung Jung FY RC .30 .10
❑ 310 Pete Shier FY RC .30 .10
❑ 311 Michael Mooney FY RC .40 .15
❑ 312 Kenny Perez FY RC .40 .15
❑ 313 Michael Mallory FY RC .40 .15
❑ 314 Ben Himes FY RC .30 .10
❑ 315 Ivan Ochoa FY RC .40 .15
❑ 316 Donald Kelly FY RC .40 .15
❑ 317 Logan Kensing FY RC .40 .15
❑ 318 Kevin Davidson FY RC .30 .10
❑ 319 Brian Pilkington FY RC .30 .10
❑ 320 Alex Romero FY RC .40 .15
❑ 321 Chad Chop FY RC .40 .15
❑ 322 Dioner Navarro FY RC .75 .30
❑ 323 Casey Myers FY RC .30 .10
❑ 324 Mike Rouse FY RC .40 .15
❑ 325 Sergio Silva FY RC .30 .10
❑ 326 J.J. Furmaniak FY RC .75 .30
❑ 327 Brad Vericker FY RC .40 .15
❑ 328 Blake Hawksworth FY RC .50 .20
❑ 329 Brock Jacobsen FY RC .30 .10
❑ 330 Alec Zumwalt FY RC .30 .10
❑ BW Berroa Bat/Willis Jsy ROY 15.00 6.00

2004 Bowman Draft

❑ COMPLETE SET (165) 40.00 15.00
❑ COMMON CARD (1-165) .30 .10
❑ COMMON RC (1-165) .30 .10
❑ COMMON RC YR .30 .10
❑ PLATES ODDS 1:559 HOBBY
❑ PLATES PRINT RUN 1 SERIAL #'d SET
❑ BLACK-CYAN-MAGENTA-YELLOW EXIST
❑ NO PLATES PRICING DUE TO SCARCITY
❑ 1 Lyle Overbay .30 .10

❑ 2 David Newhan .30 .10
❑ 3 J.R. House .30 .10
❑ 4 Chad Tracy .30 .10
❑ 5 Humberto Quintero .30 .10
❑ 6 Dave Bush .30 .10
❑ 7 Scott Hairston .30 .10
❑ 8 Mike Wood .30 .10
❑ 9 Alexis Rios .30 .10
❑ 10 Sean Burnett .30 .10
❑ 11 Wilson Valdez .30 .10
❑ 12 Lew Ford .30 .10
❑ 13 Freddy Thon RC .40 .15
❑ 14 Zack Greinke .30 .10
❑ 15 Bucky Jacobsen .30 .10
❑ 16 Kevin Youkilis .30 .10
❑ 17 Grady Sizemore .75 .30
❑ 18 Denny Bautista .30 .10
❑ 19 David DeJesus .30 .10
❑ 20 Casey Kotchman .30 .10
❑ 21 David Kelton .30 .10
❑ 22 Charles Thomas RC .40 .15
❑ 23 Kazuhito Tadano RC .50 .20
❑ 24 Justin Leone RC .50 .20
❑ 25 Eduardo Villacis RC .40 .15
❑ 26 Brian Dallimore RC .30 .10
❑ 27 Nick Green .30 .10
❑ 28 Sam McConnell RC .40 .15
❑ 29 Brad Halsey RC .50 .20
❑ 30 Roman Colon RC .30 .10
❑ 31 Josh Fields RC 2.00 .75
❑ 32 Cody Bunkelman RC .50 .20
❑ 33 Jay Rainville RC 1.25 .50
❑ 34 Richie Robnett RC 1.00 .40
❑ 35 Jon Peterson RC .75 .30
❑ 36 Huston Street RC 2.00 .75
❑ 37 Erick San Pedro RC .40 .15
❑ 38 Cory Dunlap RC 1.25 .50
❑ 39 Kurt Suzuki RC 1.00 .40
❑ 40 Anthony Swarzak RC .75 .30
❑ 41 Ian Desmond RC 1.25 .50
❑ 42 Chris Covington RC .50 .20
❑ 43 Christian Garcia RC .75 .30
❑ 44 Gaby Hernandez RC 1.25 .50
❑ 45 Steven Register RC .40 .15
❑ 46 Eduardo Morlan RC .75 .30
❑ 47 Collin Balester RC .50 .20
❑ 48 Nathan Phillips RC .50 .20
❑ 49 Dan Schwartzbauer RC .50 .20
❑ 50 Rafael Gonzalez RC .40 .15
❑ 51 K.C. Herren RC .75 .30
❑ 52 William Susdorf RC .40 .15
❑ 53 Rob Johnson RC .50 .20
❑ 54 Louis Marson RC .75 .30
❑ 55 Joe Koshansky RC 2.00 .75
❑ 56 Jamar Walton RC .75 .30
❑ 57 Mark Lowe RC 1.50 .60
❑ 58 Matt Macri RC 1.00 .40
❑ 59 Donny Lucy RC .40 .15
❑ 60 Mike Ferris RC .50 .20
❑ 61 Mike Nickeas RC .50 .20
❑ 62 Eric Hurley RC 1.00 .40
❑ 63 Scott Elbert RC 1.00 .40
❑ 64 Blake DeWitt RC 1.50 .60
❑ 65 Danny Putnam RC .75 .30
❑ 66 J.P. Howell RC 1.00 .40
❑ 67 John Wiggins RC .40 .15
❑ 68 Justin Orenduff RC .75 .30
❑ 69 Ray Liotta RC 1.25 .50
❑ 70 Billy Buckner RC .50 .20
❑ 71 Eric Campbell RC 2.00 .75
❑ 72 Olin Wick RC .75 .30
❑ 73 Sean Gamble RC .50 .20
❑ 74 Seth Smith RC 1.00 .40
❑ 75 Wade Davis RC 1.50 .60
❑ 76 Joe Jacobitz RC .40 .15
❑ 77 J.A. Happ RC .75 .30
❑ 78 Eric Ridener RC .40 .15
❑ 79 Matt Tuiasosopo RC 2.00 .75
❑ 80 Brad Bergesen RC .40 .15
❑ 81 Javy Guerra RC .50 .20
❑ 82 Buck Shaw RC .50 .20
❑ 83 Paul Janish RC .75 .30
❑ 84 Sean Kazmar RC .40 .15
❑ 85 Josh Johnson RC .50 .20
❑ 86 Angel Salome RC 1.25 .50
❑ 87 Jordan Parraz RC .75 .30
❑ 88 Kelvin Vazquez RC .40 .15
❑ 89 Grant Hansen RC .40 .15
❑ 90 Matt Fox RC .40 .15
❑ 91 Trevor Plouffe RC 1.25 .50
❑ 92 Wes Whisler RC .40 .15
❑ 93 Curtis Thigpen RC .75 .30
❑ 94 Donnie Smith RC .50 .20
❑ 95 Luis Rivera RC .60 .20
❑ 96 Jesse Hoover RC .50 .20
❑ 97 Jason Vargas RC 1.50 .60
❑ 98 Clary Carlsen RC .40 .15
❑ 99 Mark Robinson RC .40 .15
❑ 100 J.C. Holt RC .50 .20
❑ 101 Chad Blackwell RC .40 .15
❑ 102 Daryl Jones RC 1.00 .40
❑ 103 Jonathan Tierce RC .40 .15
❑ 104 Patrick Bryant RC .40 .15
❑ 105 Eddie Prasch RC .50 .20
❑ 106 Mitch Einertson RC .50 .20
❑ 107 Kyle Waldrop RC 1.00 .40
❑ 108 Jeff Marquez RC .50 .20
❑ 109 Zach Jackson RC .75 .30
❑ 110 Josh Wahpepah RC .40 .15
❑ 111 Adam Lind RC 2.00 .75
❑ 112 Kyle Bloom RC .50 .20
❑ 113 Ben Harrison RC .40 .15
❑ 114 Taylor Tankersley RC .50 .20
❑ 115 Steven Jackson RC .40 .15
❑ 116 David Purcey RC .75 .30
❑ 117 Jacob McGee RC 1.00 .40
❑ 118 Lucas Harrell RC .40 .15
❑ 119 Brandon Allen RC 1.00 .40
❑ 120 Van Pope RC .50 .20
❑ 121 Jeff Francis .30 .10
❑ 122 Joe Blanton .30 .10
❑ 123 Wil Ledezma .30 .10
❑ 124 Bryan Bullington .30 .10
❑ 125 Jairo Garcia .30 .10
❑ 126 Matt Cain 1.00 .40
❑ 127 Arnie Munoz .30 .10
❑ 128 Clint Everts .30 .10
❑ 129 Jesus Cota .30 .10
❑ 130 Gavin Floyd .30 .10
❑ 131 Edwin Encarnacion .30 .10
❑ 132 Koyie Hill .30 .10
❑ 133 Ruben Gotay .30 .10
❑ 134 Jeff Mathis .30 .10
❑ 135 Andy Marte .50 .20
❑ 136 Dallas McPherson .30 .10
❑ 137 Justin Morneau .30 .10
❑ 138 Rickie Weeks .30 .10
❑ 139 Joel Guzman .50 .20
❑ 140 Shin Soo Choo .30 .10
❑ 141 Yusmeiro Petit RC 2.00 .75
❑ 142 Jorge Cortes RC .40 .15
❑ 143 Val Majewski .30 .10
❑ 144 Felix Pie .50 .20
❑ 145 Aaron Hill .30 .10
❑ 146 Jose Capellan .30 .10
❑ 147 Dioner Navarro .50 .20
❑ 148 Fausto Carmona RC 1.50 .60
❑ 149 Robinzon Diaz RC .40 .15
❑ 150 Felix Hernandez 4.00 1.50
❑ 151 Andres Blanco RC .40 .15
❑ 152 Jason Kubel .30 .10
❑ 153 Willy Taveras RC 1.00 .40
❑ 154 Merkin Valdez .50 .20
❑ 155 Robinson Cano .75 .30

❑ 156 Bill Murphy .30 .10
❑ 157 Chris Burke .30 .10
❑ 158 Kyle Sleeth .30 .10
❑ 159 B.J. Upton .50 .20
❑ 160 Tim Stauffer .50 .20
❑ 161 David Wright 2.00 .75
❑ 162 Conor Jackson 1.25 .50
❑ 163 Brad Thompson RC .75 .30
❑ 164 Delmon Young .50 .20
❑ 165 Jeremy Reed .30 .10

2005 Bowman

❑ COMPLETE SET (330) 80.00 40.00
❑ COMMON CARD (1-140) .30 .10
❑ COMMON CARD (141-165) .40 .15
❑ COMMON CARD (166-330) .40 .15
❑ PLATE ODDS 1:695 HOBBY, 1:177 HTA
❑ PLATE PRINT RUN 1 SET PER COLOR
❑ BLACK-CYAN-MAGENTA-YELLOW ISSUED
❑ NO PLATE PRICING DUE TO SCARCITY
❑ ROY ODDS 1:668 H, 1:248 HTA, 1:1535 R
❑ 1 Gavin Floyd .30 .10
❑ 2 Eric Chavez .30 .10
❑ 3 Miguel Tejada .30 .10
❑ 4 Dmitri Young .30 .10
❑ 5 Hank Blalock .30 .10
❑ 6 Kerry Wood .30 .10
❑ 7 Andy Pettitte .50 .20
❑ 8 Pat Burrell .30 .10
❑ 9 Johnny Estrada .30 .10
❑ 10 Frank Thomas .75 .30
❑ 11 Juan Pierre .30 .10
❑ 12 Tom Glavine .50 .20
❑ 13 Lyle Overbay .30 .10
❑ 14 Jim Edmonds .30 .10
❑ 15 Steve Finley .30 .10
❑ 16 Jermaine Dye .30 .10
❑ 17 Omar Vizquel .50 .20
❑ 18 Nick Johnson .30 .10
❑ 19 Brian Giles .30 .10
❑ 20 Justin Morneau .30 .10
❑ 21 Preston Wilson .30 .10
❑ 22 Wily Mo Pena .30 .10
❑ 23 Rafael Palmeiro .50 .20
❑ 24 Scott Kazmir .30 .10
❑ 25 Derek Jeter 1.50 .60
❑ 26 Barry Zito .30 .10
❑ 27 Mike Lowell .30 .10
❑ 28 Jason Bay .30 .10
❑ 29 Ken Harvey .30 .10
❑ 30 Nomar Garciaparra .75 .30
❑ 31 Roy Halladay .30 .10
❑ 32 Todd Helton .50 .20
❑ 33 Mark Kotsay .30 .10
❑ 34 Jake Peavy .30 .10
❑ 35 David Wright 1.25 .50
❑ 36 Dontrelle Willis .30 .10
❑ 37 Marcus Giles .30 .10
❑ 38 Chone Figgins .30 .10
❑ 39 Sidney Ponson .30 .10
❑ 40 Randy Johnson .75 .30
❑ 41 John Smoltz .50 .20
❑ 42 Kevin Millar .30 .10
❑ 43 Mark Teixeira .50 .20
❑ 44 Alex Rios .30 .10
❑ 45 Mike Piazza .75 .30
❑ 46 Victor Martinez .30 .10
❑ 47 Jeff Bagwell .50 .20
❑ 48 Shawn Green .30 .10
❑ 49 Ivan Rodriguez .50 .20
❑ 50 Alex Rodriguez 1.25 .50
❑ 51 Kazuo Matsui .30 .10
❑ 52 Mark Mulder .30 .10
❑ 53 Michael Young .30 .10
❑ 54 Javy Lopez .30 .10
❑ 55 Johnny Damon .50 .20
❑ 56 Jeff Francis .30 .10
❑ 57 Rich Harden .30 .10
❑ 58 Bobby Abreu .30 .10
❑ 59 Mark Loretta .30 .10
❑ 60 Gary Sheffield .30 .10
❑ 61 Jamie Moyer .30 .10
❑ 62 Garret Anderson .30 .10
❑ 63 Vernon Wells .30 .10
❑ 64 Orlando Cabrera .30 .10
❑ 65 Magglio Ordonez .30 .10
❑ 66 Ronnie Belliard .30 .10
❑ 67 Carlos Lee .30 .10
❑ 68 Carl Pavano .30 .10
❑ 69 Jon Lieber .30 .10
❑ 70 Aubrey Huff .30 .10
❑ 71 Rocco Baldelli .30 .10
❑ 72 Jason Schmidt .30 .10
❑ 73 Bernie Williams .50 .20
❑ 74 Hideki Matsui 1.25 .50
❑ 75 Ken Griffey Jr. 1.25 .50
❑ 76 Josh Beckett .30 .10
❑ 77 Mark Buehrle .30 .10
❑ 78 David Ortiz .75 .30
❑ 79 Luis Gonzalez .30 .10
❑ 80 Scott Rolen .50 .20
❑ 81 Joe Mauer .75 .30
❑ 82 Jose Reyes .30 .10
❑ 83 Adam Dunn .30 .10
❑ 84 Greg Maddux 1.25 .50
❑ 85 Bartolo Colon .30 .10
❑ 86 Bret Boone .30 .10
❑ 87 Mike Mussina .50 .20
❑ 88 Ben Sheets .30 .10
❑ 89 Lance Berkman .30 .10
❑ 90 Miguel Cabrera .50 .20
❑ 91 C.C. Sabathia .30 .10
❑ 92 Mike Maroth .30 .10
❑ 93 Andruw Jones .50 .20
❑ 94 Jack Wilson .30 .10
❑ 95 Ichiro Suzuki 1.50 .60
❑ 96 Geoff Jenkins .30 .10
❑ 97 Zack Greinke .30 .10
❑ 98 Jorge Posada .50 .20
❑ 99 Travis Hafner .30 .10
❑ 100 Barry Bonds 2.00 .75
❑ 101 Aaron Rowand .30 .10
❑ 102 Aramis Ramirez .30 .10
❑ 103 Curt Schilling .50 .20
❑ 104 Melvin Mora .30 .10
❑ 105 Albert Pujols 1.50 .60
❑ 106 Austin Kearns .30 .10
❑ 107 Shannon Stewart .30 .10
❑ 108 Carl Crawford .30 .10
❑ 109 Carlos Zambrano .30 .10
❑ 110 Roger Clemens 1.25 .50
❑ 111 Javier Vazquez .30 .10
❑ 112 Randy Wolf .30 .10
❑ 113 Chipper Jones .75 .30
❑ 114 Larry Walker .50 .20
❑ 115 Alfonso Soriano .30 .10
❑ 116 Brad Wilkerson .30 .10
❑ 117 Bobby Crosby .30 .10
❑ 118 Jim Thome .50 .20
❑ 119 Oliver Perez .30 .10
❑ 120 Vladimir Guerrero .75 .30
❑ 121 Roy Oswalt .30 .10
❑ 122 Torii Hunter .30 .10
❑ 123 Rafael Furcal .30 .10
❑ 124 Luis Castillo .30 .10
❑ 125 Carlos Beltran .30 .10
❑ 126 Mike Sweeney .30 .10
❑ 127 Johan Santana .75 .30
❑ 128 Tim Hudson .30 .10
❑ 129 Troy Glaus .30 .10
❑ 130 Manny Ramirez .50 .20
❑ 131 Jeff Kent .30 .10
❑ 132 Jose Vidro .30 .10
❑ 133 Edgar Renteria .30 .10
❑ 134 Russ Ortiz .30 .10
❑ 135 Sammy Sosa .75 .30
❑ 136 Carlos Delgado .30 .10
❑ 137 Richie Sexson .30 .10
❑ 138 Pedro Martinez .50 .20
❑ 139 Adrian Beltre .30 .10
❑ 140 Mark Prior .50 .20
❑ 141 Omar Quintanilla .40 .15
❑ 142 Carlos Quentin .50 .20
❑ 143 Dan Johnson .50 .20
❑ 144 Jake Stevens .40 .15
❑ 145 Nate Schierholtz .50 .20
❑ 146 Neil Walker .40 .15
❑ 147 Bill Bray .40 .15
❑ 148 Taylor Tankersley .40 .15
❑ 149 Trevor Plouffe .50 .20
❑ 150 Felix Hernandez 2.00 .75
❑ 151 Philip Hughes .50 .20
❑ 152 James Houser .40 .15
❑ 153 David Murphy .40 .15
❑ 154 Ervin Santana .40 .15
❑ 155 Anthony Whittington .40 .15
❑ 156 Chris Lambert .40 .15
❑ 157 Jeremy Sowers .50 .20
❑ 158 Giovanny Gonzalez .40 .15
❑ 159 Blake DeWitt .50 .20
❑ 160 Thomas Diamond .50 .20
❑ 161 Greg Golson .40 .15
❑ 162 David Aardsma .40 .15
❑ 163 Paul Maholm .40 .15
❑ 164 Mark Rogers .50 .20
❑ 165 Homer Bailey .50 .20
❑ 166 Chip Cannon FY RC 1.00 .40
❑ 167 Tony Giarratano FY RC .50 .20
❑ 168 Darren Fenster FY RC .50 .20
❑ 169 Elvys Quezada FY RC .50 .20
❑ 170 Glen Perkins FY RC 1.00 .40
❑ 171 Ian Kinsler FY RC 3.00 1.25
❑ 172 Mike Bourn FY RC 1.00 .40
❑ 173 Jeremy West FY RC .75 .30
❑ 174 Justin Verlander FY RC 5.00 2.00
❑ 175 Kevin West FY RC .50 .20
❑ 176 Luis Hernandez FY RC .50 .20
❑ 177 Matt Campbell FY RC .50 .20
❑ 178 Nate McLouth FY RC 1.00 .40
❑ 179 Ryan Goleski FY RC .75 .30
❑ 180 Matthew Lindstrom FY RC .50 .20
❑ 181 Matt DeSalvo FY RC .75 .30
❑ 182 Kole Strayhorn FY RC .50 .20
❑ 183 Jose Vaquedano FY RC .50 .20
❑ 184 James Jurries FY RC .75 .30
❑ 185 Ian Bladergroen FY RC .75 .30
❑ 186 Eric Nielsen FY RC .50 .20
❑ 187 Chris Vines FY RC .50 .20
❑ 188 Chris Denorfia FY RC 1.00 .40
❑ 189 Kevin Melillo FY RC 1.00 .40
❑ 190 Melky Cabrera FY RC 2.50 1.00
❑ 191 Ryan Sweeney FY RC 1.25 .50
❑ 192 Sean Marshall FY RC 2.00 .75
❑ 193 Andy LaRoche FY RC 4.00 1.50
❑ 194 Tyler Pelland FY RC .75 .30
❑ 195 Mike Morse FY RC .60 .25
❑ 196 Wes Swackhamer FY RC .50 .20
❑ 197 Wade Robinson FY RC .50 .20
❑ 198 Dan Santin FY RC .50 .20
❑ 199 Steve Doetsch FY RC .75 .30
❑ 200 Shane Costa FY RC .50 .20
❑ 201 Scott Mathieson FY RC 1.00 .40
❑ 202 Ben Jones FY RC 1.00 .40
❑ 203 Michael Rogers FY RC .50 .20
❑ 204 Matt Rogelstad FY RC .50 .20
❑ 205 Luis Ramirez FY RC .50 .20
❑ 206 Landon Powell FY RC .75 .30
❑ 207 Erik Cordier FY RC .50 .20
❑ 208 Chris Seddon FY RC .50 .20
❑ 209 Chris Roberson FY RC .50 .20
❑ 210 Thomas Oldham FY RC .50 .20
❑ 211 Dana Eveland FY RC .50 .20
❑ 212 Cody Haerther FY RC .50 .20
❑ 213 Danny Core FY RC .50 .20
❑ 214 Craig Tatum FY RC .50 .20
❑ 215 Elliot Johnson FY RC .50 .20
❑ 216 Ender Chavez FY RC .50 .20
❑ 217 Errol Simonitsch FY RC .75 .30
❑ 218 Matt Van Der Bosch FY RC .50 .20
❑ 219 Eulogio de la Cruz FY RC .50 .20

220	C.J. Smith FY RC	.50	.20
221	Adam Boeve FY RC	.50	.20
222	Adam Harben FY RC	.75	.30
223	Baltazar Lopez FY RC	.50	.20
224	Russ Martin FY RC	2.00	.75
225	Brian Bannister FY RC	1.00	.40
226	Brian Miller FY RC	.50	.20
227	Casey McGehee FY RC	.50	.20
228	Humberto Sanchez FY RC	2.00	.75
229	Javon Moran FY RC	.50	.20
230	Brandon McCarthy FY RC	1.50	.60
231	Danny Zell FY RC	.50	.20
232	Jake Postlewait FY RC	.50	.20
233	Juan Tejeda FY RC	.50	.20
234	Keith Ramsey FY RC	.50	.20
235	Lorenzo Scott FY RC	.50	.20
236	Wladimir Balentien FY RC	1.00	.40
237	Martin Prado FY RC	.50	.20
238	Matt Albers FY RC	1.25	.50
239	Brian Schweiger FY RC	.50	.20
240	Brian Stavisky FY RC	.50	.20
241	Pat Misch FY RC	.50	.20
242	Pat Osborn FY	.40	.15
243	Ryan Feierabend FY RC	.50	.20
244	Chaun Maroum FY	.40	.15
245	Kevin Collins FY RC	.50	.20
246	Stuart Pomeranz FY RC	.50	.20
247	Tetsu Yofu FY RC	.50	.20
248	Hernan Iribarren FY RC	.75	.30
249	Mike Spidale FY RC	.50	.20
250	Tony Arnerich FY RC	.50	.20
251	Manny Parra FY RC	1.25	.50
252	Drew Anderson FY RC	.50	.20
253	T.J. Beam FY RC	1.00	.40
254	Pedro Lopez FY RC	.50	.20
255	Andy Sides FY RC	.50	.20
256	Bear Bay FY RC	.75	.30
257	Bill McCarthy FY RC	.50	.20
258	Daniel Haigwood FY RC	1.00	.40
259	Brian Sprout FY RC	1.00	.40
260	Bryan Triplett FY RC	.50	.20
261	Steven Bondurant FY RC	.50	.20
262	Darwinson Salazar FY RC	.50	.20
263	David Shepard FY RC	.50	.20
264	Johan Silva FY RC	.50	.20
265	J.B. Thurmond FY RC	.50	.20
266	Brandon Moorhead FY RC	.50	.20
267	Kyle Nichols FY RC	.75	.30
268	Jonathan Sanchez FY RC	1.25	.50
269	Mike Esposito FY RC	.50	.20
270	Erik Schindewolf FY RC	.50	.20
271	Peeter Ramos FY RC	.50	.20
272	Juan Senreiso FY RC	.50	.20
273	Matthew Kemp FY RC	4.00	1.50
274	Vinny Rottino FY RC	.50	.20
275	Micah Furtado FY RC	.50	.20
276	George Kottaras FY RC	1.00	.40
277	Billy Butler FY RC	4.00	1.50
278	Buck Coats FY RC	.50	.20
279	Kenny Durost FY RC	.50	.20
280	Nick Touchstone FY RC	.50	.20
281	Jerry Owens FY RC	.75	.30
282	Stefan Bailie FY RC	.50	.20
283	Jesse Gutierrez FY RC	.50	.20
284	Chuck Tiffany FY RC	1.25	.50
285	Brendan Ryan FY RC	.50	.20
286	Hayden Penn FY RC	1.00	.40
287	Shawn Bowman FY RC	.75	.30
288	Alexander Smit FY RC	.50	.20
289	Micah Schnurstein FY RC	.50	.20
290	Jared Gothreaux FY RC	.50	.20
291	Jair Jurrjens FY RC	1.50	.60
292	Bobby Livingston FY RC	.50	.20
293	Ryan Speier FY RC	.50	.20
294	Zach Parker FY RC	.50	.20
295	Christian Colonel FY RC	.50	.20
296	Scott Mitchinson FY RC	.50	.20
297	Neil Wilson FY RC	.50	.20
298	Chuck James FY RC	2.00	.75
299	Heath Totten FY RC	.50	.20
300	Sean Tracey FY RC	.50	.20
301	Ismael Ramirez FY RC	.50	.20
302	Matt Brown FY RC	.50	.20
303	Franklin Morales FY RC	.75	.30
304	Brandon Sing FY RC	.75	.30
305	D.J. Houlton FY RC	.50	.20
306	Jayce Tingler FY RC	.50	.20
307	Mitchell Arnold FY RC	.50	.20
308	Jim Burt FY RC	.50	.20
309	Jason Motte FY RC	.50	.20
310	David Gassner FY RC	.50	.20
311	Andy Santana FY RC	.50	.20
312	Kelvin Pichardo FY RC	.50	.20
313	Carlos Carrasco FY RC	1.25	.50
314	Willy Mota FY RC	.50	.20
315	Frank Mata FY RC	.50	.20
316	Carlos Gonzalez FY RC	3.00	1.25
317	Jeff Niemann FY RC	1.00	.40
318	Chris B.Young FY RC	2.50	1.00
319	Billy Sadler FY RC	.50	.20
320	Ricky Barrett FY RC	.50	.20
321	Ben Harrison FY	.40	.15
322	Steve Nelson FY RC	.50	.20
323	Daryl Thompson FY RC	.50	.20
324	Philip Humber FY RC	1.00	.40
325	Jeremy Harts FY RC	.50	.20
326	Nick Masset FY RC	.50	.20
327	Mike Rodriguez FY RC	.50	.20
328	Mike Garber FY RC	.50	.20
329	Kennard Bibbs FY RC	.50	.20
330	Ryan Garko FY RC	1.50	.60
BC	Bay Bat/Crosby Bat ROY	15.00	6.00

2005 Bowman Draft

COMPLETE SET (165)	40.00	15.00
COMMON CARD (1-165)	.30	.10
COMMON RC	.30	.10
COMMON RC YR	.30	.10
OVERALL PLATE ODDS 1:826 HOBBY		
PLATE PRINT RUN 1 SET PER COLOR		
BLACK-CYAN-MAGENTA-YELLOW ISSUED		
NO PLATE PRICING DUE TO SCARCITY		

1	Rickie Weeks	.30	.10
2	Kyle Davies	.30	.10
3	Garrett Atkins	.30	.10
4	Chien-Ming Wang	1.00	.40
5	Dallas McPherson	.30	.10
6	Dan Johnson	.30	.10
7	Andy Sisco	.30	.10
8	Ryan Doumit	.30	.10
9	J.P. Howell	.30	.10
10	Tim Stauffer	.30	.10
11	Willy Taveras	.30	.10
12	Aaron Hill	.30	.10
13	Victor Diaz	.30	.10
14	Wilson Betemit	.30	.10
15	Ervin Santana	.30	.10
16	Mike Morse	.30	.10
17	Yadier Molina	.30	.10
18	Kelly Johnson	.30	.10
19	Clint Barmes	.30	.10
20	Robinson Cano	.50	.20
21	Brad Thompson	.30	.10
22	Jorge Cantu	.30	.10
23	Brad Halsey	.30	.10
24	Lance Niekro	.30	.10
25	D.J. Houlton	.30	.10
26	Ryan Church	.30	.10
27	Hayden Penn	.75	.30
28	Chris Young	.30	.10
29	Chad Orvella RC	.30	.10
30	Mark Teahen	.30	.10
31	Mark McCormick FY RC	.50	.20
32	Jay Bruce FY RC	8.00	3.00
33	Beau Jones FY RC	.50	.20
34	Tyler Greene FY RC	.75	.30
35	Zach Ward FY RC	.30	.10
36	Josh Bell FY RC	.75	.30
37	Josh Wall FY RC	.50	.20
38	Nick Webber FY RC	.30	.10
39	Travis Buck FY RC	1.00	.40
40	Kyle Winters FY RC	.50	.20
41	Mitch Boggs FY RC	.30	.10
42	Tommy Mendoza FY RC	.75	.30
43	Brad Corley FY RC	.50	.20
44	Drew Butera FY RC	.30	.10
45	Ryan Mount FY RC	.75	.30
46	Tyler Herron FY RC	.50	.20
47	Nick Weglarz FY RC	.50	.20
48	Brandon Erbe FY RC	1.00	.40
49	Cody Allen FY RC	.30	.10
50	Eric Fowler FY RC	.30	.10
51	James Boone FY RC	.50	.20
52	Josh Flores FY RC	1.25	.50
53	Brandon Monk FY RC	.50	.20
54	Kieron Pope FY RC	.75	.30
55	Kyle Cofield FY RC	.30	.10
56	Brent Lillibridge FY RC	.50	.20
57	Daryl Jones FY	.30	.10
58	Eli Iorg FY RC	.50	.20
59	Brett Hayes FY RC	.30	.10
60	Mike Durant FY RC	.75	.30
61	Michael Bowden FY RC	2.00	.75
62	Paul Kelly FY RC	.50	.20
63	Andrew McCutchen FY RC	2.00	.75
64	Travis Wood FY RC	1.00	.40
65	Cesar Ramos FY RC	.50	.20
66	Chaz Roe FY RC	.50	.20
67	Matt Torra FY RC	.50	.20
68	Kevin Slowey FY RC	1.50	.60
69	Trayvon Robinson FY RC	.50	.20
70	Reid Engel FY RC	.30	.10
71	Kris Harvey FY RC	.50	.20
72	Craig Italiano FY RC	.75	.30
73	Matt Maloney FY RC	1.00	.40
74	Sean West FY RC	.75	.30
75	Henry Sanchez FY RC	.50	.20
76	Scott Blue FY RC	.30	.10
77	Jordan Schafer FY RC	1.50	.60
78	Chris Robinson FY RC	.50	.20
79	Chris Hobdy FY RC	.30	.10
80	Brandon Durden FY RC	.30	.10
81	Clay Buchholz FY RC	6.00	2.50
82	Josh Geer FY RC	.30	.10
83	Sam LeCure FY RC	.30	.10
84	Justin Thomas FY RC	.30	.10
85	Brett Gardner FY RC	.50	.20
86	Tommy Manzella FY RC	.30	.10
87	Matt Green FY RC	.30	.10
88	Yunel Escobar FY RC	2.00	.75
89	Mike Costanzo FY RC	.75	.30
90	Nick Hundley FY RC	.30	.10
91	Zach Simons FY RC	.30	.10
92	Jacob Marceaux FY RC	.30	.10
93	Jed Lowrie FY RC	.50	.20
94	Brandon Snyder FY RC	1.00	.40
95	Matt Goyen FY RC	.30	.10
96	Jon Egan FY RC	.50	.20
97	Drew Thompson FY RC	.50	.20
98	Bryan Anderson FY RC	1.00	.40
99	Clayton Richard FY RC	.30	.10
100	Jimmy Shull FY RC	.50	.20
101	Mark Pawelek FY RC	1.50	.60
102	P.J. Phillips FY RC	.75	.30
103	John Drennen FY RC	1.25	.50
104	Nolan Reimold FY RC	1.00	.40
105	Troy Tulowitzki FY RC	4.00	1.50
106	Kevin Whelan FY RC	.40	.15
107	Wade Townsend FY RC	.50	.20
108	Micah Owings FY RC	1.25	.50
109	Ryan Tucker FY RC	.50	.20
110	Jeff Clement FY RC	1.50	.60
111	Josh Sullivan FY RC	.30	.10
112	Jeff Lyman FY RC	.50	.20
113	Brian Bogusevic FY RC	.30	.10
114	Trevor Bell FY RC	.50	.20
115	Brent Cox FY RC	.50	.20
116	Michael Billek FY RC	.30	.10
117	Garrett Olson FY RC	.50	.20
118	Steven Johnson FY RC	.30	.10

❑ 119	Chase Headley FY RC	.75	.30
❑ 120	Daniel Carte FY RC	.50	.20
❑ 121	Francisco Liriano PROS	1.50	.60
❑ 122	Fausto Carmona PROS	.30	.10
❑ 123	Zach Jackson PROS	.30	.10
❑ 124	Adam Loewen PROS	.30	.10
❑ 125	Chris Lambert PROS	.30	.10
❑ 126	Scott Mathieson FY	.30	.10
❑ 127	Paul Maholm PROS	.30	.10
❑ 128	Fernando Nieve PROS	.30	.10
❑ 129	Justin Verlander FY	1.50	.60
❑ 130	Yusmeiro Petit PROS	.50	.20
❑ 131	Joel Zumaya PROS	.30	.10
❑ 132	Merkin Valdez PROS	.30	.10
❑ 133	Ryan Garko FY	.50	.20
❑ 134	Edison Volquez FY RC	4.00	1.50
❑ 135	Russ Martin FY	.75	.30
❑ 136	Conor Jackson PROS	.30	.10
❑ 137	Miguel Montero FY RC	1.00	.40
❑ 138	Josh Barfield PROS	.30	.10
❑ 139	Delmon Young PROS	.50	.20
❑ 140	Andy LaRoche FY	.75	.30
❑ 141	William Bergolla PROS	.30	.10
❑ 142	B.J. Upton PROS	.30	.10
❑ 143	Hernan Iribarren FY	.30	.10
❑ 144	Brandon Wood PROS	.75	.30
❑ 145	Jose Bautista PROS	.30	.10
❑ 146	Edwin Encarnacion PROS	.30	.10
❑ 147	Javier Herrera FY RC	.75	.30
❑ 148	Jeremy Hermida PROS	.75	.30
❑ 149	Frank Diaz PROS RC	.30	.10
❑ 150	Chris B.Young FY	1.00	.40
❑ 151	Shin-Soo Choo PROS	.30	.10
❑ 152	Kevin Thompson PROS RC	.30	.10
❑ 153	Hanley Ramirez PROS	.50	.20
❑ 154	Lastings Milledge PROS	.30	.10
❑ 155	Luis Montanez PROS	.30	.10
❑ 156	Justin Huber PROS	.30	.10
❑ 157	Zach Duke PROS	.50	.20
❑ 158	Jeff Francoeur PROS	.75	.30
❑ 159	Melky Cabrera FY	1.00	.40
❑ 160	Bobby Jenks PROS	.30	.10
❑ 161	Ian Snell PROS	.30	.10
❑ 162	Fernando Cabrera PROS	.30	.10
❑ 163	Troy Patton PROS	.50	.20
❑ 164	Anthony Lerew PROS	.30	.10
❑ 165	Nelson Cruz FY RC	.75	.30

2006 Bowman

❑ COMP.SET w/o AU's (220)	40.00	15.00
❑ COMP.SET w/PROS (330)	80.00	40.00
❑ COMMON CARD (1-200)	.30	.10
❑ SEMISTARS 1-220	.50	.20
❑ UNLISTED STARS 1-220	.75	.30
❑ COMMON ROOKIE (201-220)	.40	.15
❑ ROOKIE SEMIS 201-220	.60	.25

❑ 219-220 AU ODDS 1:1150 HOBBY, 1:699 HTA

❑ COMMON AUTO (221-231)	10.00	4.00

❑ 221-231 AU ODDS 1:82 HOBBY, 1:40 HTA
❑ 1-220 PLATE ODDS 1:588 HOBBY, 1:575 HTA
❑ 221-231 AU PLATES 1:15,700 H, 1:4100 HTA
❑ PLATE PRINT RUN 1 SET PER COLOR
❑ BLACK-CYAN-MAGENTA-YELLOW ISSUED
❑ NO PLATE PRICING DUE TO SCARCITY

❑ 1	Nick Swisher	.30	.12
❑ 2	Ted Lilly	.30	.12
❑ 3	John Smoltz	.50	.20
❑ 4	Lyle Overbay	.30	.12
❑ 5	Alfonso Soriano	.30	.12
❑ 6	Javier Vazquez	.30	.12
❑ 7	Ronnie Belliard	.30	.12
❑ 8	Jose Reyes	.75	.30
❑ 9	Brian Roberts	.30	.12
❑ 10	Curt Schilling	.50	.20
❑ 11	Adam Dunn	.30	.12
❑ 12	Zack Greinke	.30	.12
❑ 13	Carlos Guillen	.30	.12
❑ 14	Jon Garland	.30	.12
❑ 15	Robinson Cano	.50	.20
❑ 16	Chris Burke	.30	.10
❑ 17	Barry Zito	.30	.10
❑ 18	Russ Adams	.30	.10
❑ 19	Chris Capuano	.30	.10
❑ 20	Scott Rolen	.50	.20
❑ 21	Kerry Wood	.30	.10
❑ 22	Scott Kazmir	.50	.20
❑ 23	Brandon Webb	.30	.10
❑ 24	Jeff Kent	.30	.10
❑ 25	Albert Pujols	1.50	.60
❑ 26	C.C. Sabathia	.30	.10
❑ 27	Adrian Beltre	.30	.10
❑ 28	Brad Wilkerson	.30	.10
❑ 29	Randy Wolf	.30	.10
❑ 30	Jason Bay	.30	.10
❑ 31	Austin Kearns	.30	.10
❑ 32	Clint Barmes	.30	.10
❑ 33	Mike Sweeney	.30	.10
❑ 34	Justin Verlander	1.25	.50
❑ 35	Justin Morneau	.30	.10
❑ 36	Scott Podsednik	.30	.10
❑ 37	Jason Giambi	.30	.10
❑ 38	Steve Finley	.30	.10
❑ 39	Morgan Ensberg	.30	.10
❑ 40	Eric Chavez	.30	.10
❑ 41	Roy Halladay	.30	.10
❑ 42	Horacio Ramirez	.30	.10
❑ 43	Ben Sheets	.30	.10
❑ 44	Chris Carpenter	.30	.10
❑ 45	Andruw Jones	.50	.20
❑ 46	Carlos Zambrano	.30	.10
❑ 47	Jonny Gomes	.30	.10
❑ 48	Shawn Green	.30	.10
❑ 49	Moises Alou	.30	.10
❑ 50	Ichiro Suzuki	1.25	.50
❑ 51	Juan Pierre	.30	.10
❑ 52	Grady Sizemore	.50	.20
❑ 53	Kazuo Matsui	.30	.10
❑ 54	Jose Vidro	.30	.10
❑ 55	Jake Peavy	.30	.10
❑ 56	Dallas Mcpherson	.30	.10
❑ 57	Ryan Howard	1.25	.50
❑ 58	Zach Duke	.30	.10
❑ 59	Michael Young	.30	.10
❑ 60	Todd Helton	.50	.20
❑ 61	David Dejesus	.30	.10
❑ 62	Ivan Rodriguez	.50	.20
❑ 63	Johan Santana	.50	.20
❑ 64	Danny Haren	.30	.10
❑ 65	Derek Jeter	2.00	.75
❑ 66	Greg Maddux	1.25	.50
❑ 67	Jorge Cantu	.30	.10
❑ 68	Conor Jackson	.30	.10
❑ 69	Victor Martinez	.30	.10
❑ 70	David Wright	1.25	.50
❑ 71	Ryan Church	.30	.10
❑ 72	Khalil Greene	.50	.20
❑ 73	Jimmy Rollins	.30	.10
❑ 74	Hank Blalock	.30	.10
❑ 75	Pedro Martinez	.50	.20
❑ 76	Jon Papelbon	2.00	.75
❑ 77	Felipe Lopez	.30	.10
❑ 78	Jeff Francis	.30	.10
❑ 79	Andy Sisco	.30	.10
❑ 80	Hideki Matsui	1.25	.50
❑ 81	Ken Griffey Jr.	1.25	.50
❑ 82	Nomar Garciaparra	.75	.30
❑ 83	Kevin Millwood	.30	.10
❑ 84	Paul Konerko	.30	.10
❑ 85	A.J. Burnett	.30	.10
❑ 86	Mike Piazza	.75	.30
❑ 87	Brian Giles	.30	.10
❑ 88	Johnny Damon	.50	.20
❑ 89	Jim Thome	.50	.20
❑ 90	Roger Clemens	1.50	.60
❑ 91	Aaron Rowand	.30	.10
❑ 92	Rafael Furcal	.30	.10
❑ 93	Gary Sheffield	.30	.10
❑ 94	Mike Cameron	.30	.10
❑ 95	Carlos Delgado	.30	.10
❑ 96	Jorge Posada	.50	.20
❑ 97	Denny Bautista	.30	.10
❑ 98	Mike Maroth	.30	.10
❑ 99	Brad Radke	.30	.10
❑ 100	Alex Rodriguez	1.25	.50
❑ 101	Freddy Garcia	.30	.10
❑ 102	Oliver Perez	.30	.10
❑ 103	Jon Lieber	.30	.10
❑ 104	Melvin Mora	.30	.10
❑ 105	Travis Hafner	.30	.10
❑ 106	Matt Cain	.50	.20
❑ 107	Derek Lowe	.30	.10
❑ 108	Luis Castillo	.30	.10
❑ 109	Livan Hernandez	.30	.10
❑ 110	Tadahito Iguchi	.30	.10
❑ 111	Shawn Chacon	.30	.10
❑ 112	Frank Thomas	.75	.30
❑ 113	Josh Beckett	.30	.12
❑ 114	Aubrey Huff	.30	.10
❑ 115	Derrek Lee	.30	.10
❑ 116	Chien-Ming Wang	1.25	.50
❑ 117	Joe Crede	.30	.10
❑ 118	Torii Hunter	.30	.10
❑ 119	J.D. Drew	.30	.10
❑ 120	Troy Glaus	.30	.10
❑ 121	Sean Casey	.30	.10
❑ 122	Edgar Renteria	.30	.10
❑ 123	Craig Wilson	.30	.10
❑ 124	Adam Eaton	.30	.10
❑ 125	Jeff Francoeur	.75	.30
❑ 126	Bruce Chen	.30	.10
❑ 127	Cliff Floyd	.30	.10
❑ 128	Jeremy Reed	.30	.10
❑ 129	Jake Westbrook	.30	.10
❑ 130	Wily Mo Pena	.30	.10
❑ 131	Toby Hall	.30	.10
❑ 132	David Ortiz	.75	.30
❑ 133	David Eckstein	.30	.10
❑ 134	Brady Clark	.30	.10
❑ 135	Marcus Giles	.30	.10
❑ 136	Aaron Hill	.30	.10
❑ 137	Mark Kotsay	.30	.10
❑ 138	Carlos Lee	.30	.10
❑ 139	Roy Oswalt	.30	.10
❑ 140	Chone Figgins	.30	.10
❑ 141	Mike Mussina	.50	.20
❑ 142	Orlando Hernandez	.30	.10
❑ 143	Magglio Ordonez	.30	.10
❑ 144	Jim Edmonds	.50	.20
❑ 145	Bobby Abreu	.30	.10
❑ 146	Nick Johnson	.30	.10
❑ 147	Carlos Beltran	.30	.10
❑ 148	Jhonny Peralta	.30	.10
❑ 149	Pedro Feliz	.30	.10
❑ 150	Miguel Tejada	.30	.10
❑ 151	Luis Gonzalez	.30	.10
❑ 152	Carl Crawford	.30	.10
❑ 153	Yadier Molina	.30	.10
❑ 154	Rich Harden	.30	.10
❑ 155	Tim Wakefield	.30	.10
❑ 156	Rickie Weeks	.30	.10
❑ 157	Johnny Estrada	.30	.10
❑ 158	Gustavo Chacin	.30	.10
❑ 159	Dan Johnson	.30	.10
❑ 160	Willy Taveras	.30	.10
❑ 161	Garret Anderson	.30	.10
❑ 162	Randy Johnson	.75	.30
❑ 163	Jermaine Dye	.30	.10
❑ 164	Joe Mauer	.50	.20
❑ 165	Ervin Santana	.30	.10
❑ 166	Jeremy Bonderman	.30	.10
❑ 167	Garrett Atkins	.30	.10
❑ 168	Manny Ramirez	.50	.20
❑ 169	Brad Eldred	.30	.10
❑ 170	Chase Utley	.75	.30
❑ 171	Mark Loretta	.30	.10
❑ 172	John Patterson	.30	.10
❑ 173	Tom Glavine	.50	.20
❑ 174	Dontrelle Willis	.30	.10
❑ 175	Mark Teixeira	.50	.20
❑ 176	Felix Hernandez	.50	.20

❑ 177 Cliff Lee .30 .10
❑ 178 Jason Schmidt .30 .10
❑ 179 Chad Tracy .30 .10
❑ 180 Rocco Baldelli .30 .10
❑ 181 Aramis Ramirez .30 .10
❑ 182 Andy Pettitte .50 .20
❑ 183 Mark Mulder .30 .10
❑ 184 Geoff Jenkins .30 .10
❑ 185 Chipper Jones .75 .30
❑ 186 Vernon Wells .30 .10
❑ 187 Bobby Crosby .30 .10
❑ 188 Lance Berkman .30 .10
❑ 189 Vladimir Guerrero .75 .30
❑ 190 Jose Capellan .30 .10
❑ 191 Brad Penny .30 .10
❑ 192 Jose Guillen .30 .10
❑ 193 Brett Myers .30 .10
❑ 194 Miguel Cabrera .50 .20
❑ 195 Bartolo Colon .30 .10
❑ 196 Craig Biggio .50 .20
❑ 197 Tim Hudson .30 .10
❑ 198 Mark Prior .50 .20
❑ 199 Mark Buehrle .30 .10
❑ 200 Barry Bonds 2.00 .75
❑ 201 Anderson Hernandez (RC) .40 .15
❑ 202 Charlton Jimerson (RC) .40 .15
❑ 203 Jeremy Accardo RC .40 .15
❑ 204 Hanley Ramirez (RC) 1.00 .40
❑ 205 Matt Capps (RC) .40 .15
❑ 206 John-Ford Griffin (RC) .40 .15
❑ 207 Chuck James (RC) .60 .25
❑ 208 Jaime Bubela (RC) .40 .15
❑ 209 Mark Woodyard (RC) .40 .15
❑ 210 Jason Botts (RC) .40 .15
❑ 211 Chris Demaria RC .40 .15
❑ 212 Miguel Perez (RC) .40 .15
❑ 213 Tom Gorzelanny (RC) .40 .15
❑ 214 Adam Wainwright (RC) .40 .15
❑ 215 Ryan Garko (RC) .40 .15
❑ 216 Jason Bergmann RC .40 .15
❑ 217 J.J. Furmaniak (RC) .40 .15
❑ 218 Francisco Liriano (RC) 2.00 .75
❑ 219 Kenji Johjima RC 2.00 .75
❑ 219a Kenji Johjima AU 80.00 30.00
❑ 220 Craig Hansen RC 1.50 .60
❑ 220a Craig Hansen AU 50.00 20.00
❑ 221 Ryan Zimmerman AU (RC) 50.00 20.00
❑ 222 Joey Devine AU RC 10.00 4.00
❑ 223 Scott Olsen AU (RC) 10.00 4.00
❑ 224 Darrel Rasner AU (RC) 10.00 4.00
❑ 225 Craig Breslow AU RC 10.00 4.00
❑ 226 Reggie Abercrombie AU (RC) 10.00 4.00
❑ 227 Dan Uggla AU (RC) 15.00 6.00
❑ 228 Willie Eyre AU (RC) 10.00 4.00
❑ 229 Joel Zumaya AU (RC) 30.00 12.50
❑ 230 Ricky Nolasco AU (RC) 10.00 4.00
❑ 231 Ian Kinsler AU (RC) 25.00 10.00

2006 Bowman Draft

❑ COMPLETE SET (55) 15.00 6.00
❑ COMMON RC (1-55) .40 .15
❑ RC SEMIS 1-55 .60 .25
❑ RC UNLISTED 1-55 1.00 .40
❑ APPX. TWO PER HOBBY/RETAL PACK
❑ ODDS INFO PROVIDED BY BECKETT
❑ OVERALL PLATE ODDS 1:990 HOBBY
❑ PLATE PRINT RUN 1 SET PER COLOR
❑ BLACK-CYAN-MAGENTA-YELLOW ISSUED
❑ NO PLATE PRICING DUE TO SCARCITY
❑ 1 Matt Kemp (RC) .60 .25
❑ 2 Taylor Tankersley (RC) .40 .15
❑ 3 Mike Napoli RC 1.00 .40
❑ 4 Brian Bannister (RC) .40 .15
❑ 5 Melky Cabrera (RC) .60 .25
❑ 6 Bill Bray (RC) .40 .15
❑ 7 Brian Anderson (RC) .40 .15
❑ 8 Jered Weaver (RC) 1.25 .50
❑ 9 Chris Duncan (RC) .60 .25
❑ 10 Boof Bonser (RC) .60 .25
❑ 11 Mike Rouse (RC) .40 .15
❑ 12 David Pauley (RC) .40 .15
❑ 13 Russ Martin (RC) .60 .25
❑ 14 Jeremy Sowers (RC) .40 .15
❑ 15 Kevin Reese (RC) .40 .15
❑ 16 John Rheinecker (RC) .40 .15
❑ 17 Tommy Murphy (RC) .40 .15
❑ 18 Sean Marshall (RC) .40 .15
❑ 19 Jason Kubel (RC) .40 .15
❑ 20 Chad Billingsley (RC) .60 .25
❑ 21 Kendry Morales (RC) .60 .25
❑ 22 Jon Lester RC 1.25 .50
❑ 23 Brandon Fahey RC .40 .15
❑ 24 Josh Johnson (RC) .60 .25
❑ 25 Kevin Frandsen (RC) .40 .15
❑ 26 Casey Janssen RC .60 .25
❑ 27 Scott Thorman (RC) .40 .15
❑ 28 Scott Mathieson (RC) .40 .15
❑ 29 Jeremy Hermida (RC) .40 .15
❑ 30 Dustin Nippert (RC) .40 .15
❑ 31 Kevin Thompson (RC) .40 .15
❑ 32 Bobby Livingston (RC) .40 .15
❑ 33 Travis Ishikawa (RC) .40 .15
❑ 34 Jeff Mathis (RC) .40 .15
❑ 35 Charlie Haeger RC .60 .25
❑ 36 Josh Willingham (RC) .40 .15
❑ 37 Taylor Buchholz (RC) .40 .15
❑ 38 Joel Guzman (RC) .40 .15
❑ 39 Zach Jackson (RC) .40 .15
❑ 40 Howie Kendrick (RC) 1.00 .40
❑ 41 T.J. Beam (RC) .40 .15
❑ 42 Ty Taubenheim RC .60 .25
❑ 43 Erick Aybar (RC) .40 .15
❑ 44 Anibal Sanchez (RC) .60 .25
❑ 45 Michael Pelfrey RC 1.50 .60
❑ 46 Shawn Hill (RC) .40 .15
❑ 47 Chris Roberson (RC) .40 .15
❑ 48 Carlos Villanueva RC .40 .15
❑ 49 Andre Ethier (RC) 1.00 .40
❑ 50 Anthony Reyes (RC) .60 .25
❑ 51 Franklin Gutierrez (RC) .40 .15
❑ 52 Angel Guzman (RC) .40 .15
❑ 53 Michael O'Connor RC .40 .15
❑ 54 James Shields RC .40 .15
❑ 55 Nate McLouth (RC) .40 .15

2007 Bowman

❑ COMP.SET w/o AU's (221) 50.00 20.00
❑ COMMON CARD (1-200) .30 .12
❑ COMMON ROOKIE (201-220) .40 .15
❑ COMMON AUTO (221-236) 10.00 4.00
❑ 219/221-236 AU ODDS 1:98 HOBBY, 1:25 HTA
❑ BONDS ODDS 1:51 HTA, 1:610 RETAIL
❑ 1-220 PLATE ODDS 1:1468 H, 1:212 HTA
❑ 221-231 AU PLATES 1:8200 H, 1:1150 HTA
❑ BONDS PLATE ODDS 1:106,000 HTA
❑ PLATE PRINT RUN 1 SET PER COLOR
❑ BLACK-CYAN-MAGENTA-YELLOW ISSUED
❑ NO PLATE PRICING DUE TO SCARCITY
❑ 1 Hanley Ramirez .50 .20
❑ 2 Justin Verlander .75 .30
❑ 3 Ryan Zimmerman .75 .30
❑ 4 Jered Weaver .50 .20
❑ 5 Stephen Drew .50 .20
❑ 6 Jonathan Papelbon .75 .30
❑ 7 Melky Cabrera .30 .12
❑ 8 Francisco Liriano .75 .30
❑ 9 Prince Fielder .75 .30
❑ 10 Dan Uggla .50 .20
❑ 11 Jeremy Sowers .30 .12
❑ 12 Carlos Quentin .30 .12
❑ 13 Chuck James .30 .12
❑ 14 Andre Ethier .50 .20
❑ 15 Cole Hamels UER .75 .30
❑ 16 Kenji Johjima .75 .30
❑ 17 Chad Billingsley .30 .12
❑ 18 Ian Kinsler .30 .12
❑ 19 Jason Hirsh .30 .12
❑ 20 Nick Markakis .50 .20
❑ 21 Jeremy Hermida .30 .12
❑ 22 Ryan Shealy .30 .12
❑ 23 Scott Olsen .30 .12
❑ 24 Russell Martin .30 .12
❑ 25 Conor Jackson .30 .12
❑ 26 Erik Bedard .30 .12
❑ 27 Brian McCann .30 .12
❑ 28 Michael Barrett .30 .12
❑ 29 Brandon Phillips .30 .12
❑ 30 Garrett Atkins .30 .12
❑ 31 Freddy Garcia .30 .12
❑ 32 Mark Loretta .30 .12
❑ 33 Craig Biggio .50 .20
❑ 34 Jeremy Bonderman .30 .12
❑ 35 Johan Santana .50 .20
❑ 36 Jorge Posada .50 .20
❑ 37 Brian Bannister .30 .12
❑ 38 Carlos Delgado .30 .12
❑ 39 Gary Matthews Jr. .30 .12
❑ 40 Mike Cameron .30 .12
❑ 41 Adrian Beltre .30 .12
❑ 42 Freddy Sanchez .30 .12
❑ 43 Austin Kearns .30 .12
❑ 44 Mark Buehrle .30 .12
❑ 45 Miguel Cabrera .50 .20
❑ 46 Josh Beckett .50 .20
❑ 47 Chone Figgins .30 .12
❑ 48 Edgar Renteria .30 .12
❑ 49 Derek Lowe .30 .12
❑ 50 Ryan Howard 1.25 .50
❑ 51 Shawn Green .30 .12
❑ 52 Jason Giambi .30 .12
❑ 53 Ervin Santana .30 .12
❑ 54 Jack Wilson .30 .12
❑ 55 Roy Oswalt .30 .12
❑ 56 Dan Haren .30 .12
❑ 57 Jose Vidro .30 .12
❑ 58 Kevin Millwood .30 .12
❑ 59 Jim Edmonds .50 .20
❑ 60 Carl Crawford .30 .12
❑ 61 Randy Wolf .30 .12
❑ 62 Paul LoDuca .30 .12
❑ 63 Johnny Estrada .30 .12
❑ 64 Brian Roberts .30 .12
❑ 65 Manny Ramirez .50 .20
❑ 66 Jose Contreras .30 .12
❑ 67 Josh Barfield .30 .12
❑ 68 Juan Pierre .30 .12
❑ 69 David DeJesus .30 .12
❑ 70 Gary Sheffield .30 .12
❑ 71 Jon Lieber .30 .12
❑ 72 Randy Johnson .75 .30
❑ 73 Rickie Weeks .30 .12
❑ 74 Brian Giles .30 .12
❑ 75 Ichiro Suzuki 1.25 .50
❑ 76 Nick Swisher .30 .12
❑ 77 Justin Morneau .30 .12
❑ 78 Scott Kazmir .50 .20
❑ 79 Lyle Overbay .30 .12
❑ 80 Alfonso Soriano .30 .12
❑ 81 Brandon Webb .30 .12
❑ 82 Joe Crede .30 .12
❑ 83 Corey Patterson .30 .12
❑ 84 Kenny Rogers .30 .12

❑ 85 Ken Griffey Jr 1.25 .50
❑ 86 Cliff Lee .30 .12
❑ 87 Mike Lowell .30 .12
❑ 88 Marcus Giles .30 .12
❑ 89 Orlando Cabrera .30 .12
❑ 90 Derek Jeter 2.00 .75
❑ 91 Josh Johnson .30 .12
❑ 92 Carlos Guillen .30 .12
❑ 93 Bill Hall .30 .12
❑ 94 Michael Cuddyer .30 .12
❑ 95 Miguel Tejada .30 .12
❑ 96 Todd Helton .50 .20
❑ 97 C.C. Sabathia .30 .12
❑ 98 Tadahito Iguchi .30 .12
❑ 99 Jose Reyes .75 .30
❑ 100 David Wright 1.25 .50
❑ 101 Barry Zito .30 .12
❑ 102 Jake Peavy .30 .12
❑ 103 Richie Sexson .30 .12
❑ 104 A.J. Burnett .30 .12
❑ 105 Eric Chavez .30 .12
❑ 106 Jorge Cantu .30 .12
❑ 107 Grady Sizemore .50 .20
❑ 108 Bronson Arroyo .30 .12
❑ 109 Mike Mussina .50 .20
❑ 110 Magglio Ordonez .30 .12
❑ 111 Anibal Sanchez .30 .12
❑ 112 Jeff Francoeur .75 .30
❑ 113 Kevin Youkilis .30 .12
❑ 114 Aubrey Huff .30 .12
❑ 115 Carlos Zambrano .30 .12
❑ 116 Mark Teahen .30 .12
❑ 117 Carlos Silva .30 .12
❑ 118 Pedro Martinez .50 .20
❑ 119 Hideki Matsui .75 .30
❑ 120 Mike Piazza .75 .30
❑ 121 Jason Schmidt .30 .12
❑ 122 Greg Maddux 1.25 .50
❑ 123 Joe Blanton .30 .12
❑ 124 Chris Carpenter .30 .12
❑ 125 David Ortiz .75 .30
❑ 126 Alex Rios .30 .12
❑ 127 Nick Johnson .30 .12
❑ 128 Carlos Lee .30 .12
❑ 129 Pat Burrell .30 .12
❑ 130 Ben Sheets .30 .12
❑ 131 Kazuo Matsui .30 .12
❑ 132 Adam Dunn .30 .12
❑ 133 Jermaine Dye .30 .12
❑ 134 Curt Schilling .50 .20
❑ 135 Chad Tracy .30 .12
❑ 136 Vladimir Guerrero .75 .30
❑ 137 Melvin Mora .30 .12
❑ 138 John Smoltz .50 .20
❑ 139 Craig Monroe .30 .12
❑ 140 Dontrelle Willis .30 .12
❑ 141 Jeff Francis .30 .12
❑ 142 Chipper Jones .75 .30
❑ 143 Frank Thomas .75 .30
❑ 144 Brett Myers .30 .12
❑ 145 Xavier Nady .30 .12
❑ 146 Robinson Cano .50 .20
❑ 147 Jeff Kent .30 .12
❑ 148 Scott Rolen .50 .20
❑ 149 Roy Halladay .30 .12
❑ 150 Joe Mauer .50 .20
❑ 151 Bobby Abreu .30 .12
❑ 152 Matt Cain .50 .20
❑ 153 Hank Blalock .30 .12
❑ 154 Chris Capuano .30 .12
❑ 155 Jake Westbrook .30 .12
❑ 156 Javier Vazquez .30 .12
❑ 157 Garret Anderson .30 .12
❑ 158 Aramis Ramirez .30 .12
❑ 159 Mark Kotsay .30 .12
❑ 160 Matt Kemp .30 .12
❑ 161 Adrian Gonzalez .30 .12
❑ 162 Felix Hernandez .50 .20
❑ 163 David Eckstein .30 .12
❑ 164 Curtis Granderson .30 .12
❑ 165 Paul Konerko .30 .12
❑ 166 Orlando Hudson .30 .12
❑ 167 Tim Hudson .30 .12
❑ 168 J.D. Drew .30 .12
❑ 169 Chien-Ming Wang 1.25 .50
❑ 170 Jimmy Rollins .30 .12
❑ 171 Matt Morris .30 .12
❑ 172 Raul Ibanez .30 .12
❑ 173 Mark Teixeira .50 .20
❑ 174 Ted Lilly .30 .12
❑ 175 Albert Pujols 1.50 .60
❑ 176 Carlos Beltran .30 .12
❑ 177 Lance Berkman .30 .12
❑ 178 Ivan Rodriguez .50 .20
❑ 179 Torii Hunter .30 .12
❑ 180 Johnny Damon .50 .20
❑ 181 Chase Utley .75 .30
❑ 182 Jason Bay .30 .12
❑ 183 Jeff Weaver .30 .12
❑ 184 Troy Glaus .30 .12
❑ 185 Rocco Baldelli .30 .12
❑ 186 Rafael Furcal .30 .12
❑ 187 Jim Thome .50 .20
❑ 188 Travis Hafner .30 .12
❑ 189 Matt Holliday .75 .30
❑ 190 Andruw Jones .50 .20
❑ 191 Ramon Hernandez .30 .12
❑ 192 Victor Martinez .30 .12
❑ 193 Aaron Hill .30 .12
❑ 194 Michael Young .30 .12
❑ 195 Vernon Wells .30 .12
❑ 196 Mark Mulder .30 .12
❑ 197 Derrek Lee .30 .12
❑ 198 Tom Glavine .50 .20
❑ 199 Chris Young .30 .12
❑ 200 Alex Rodriguez 1.25 .50
❑ 201 Delmon Young (RC) .60 .25
❑ 202 Alexi Casilla RC .60 .25
❑ 203 Shawn Riggans (RC) .40 .15
❑ 204 Jeff Baker (RC) .40 .15
❑ 205 Hector Gimenez (RC) .40 .15
❑ 206 Ubaldo Jimenez (RC) .40 .15
❑ 207 Adam Lind (RC) .40 .15
❑ 208 Joaquin Arias (RC) .40 .15
❑ 209 David Murphy (RC) .40 .15
❑ 210 Daisuke Matsuzaka RC 5.00 2.00
❑ 211 Jerry Owens (RC) .40 .15
❑ 212 Ryan Sweeney (RC) .40 .15
❑ 213 Kei Igawa RC 1.50 .60
❑ 214 Fred Lewis (RC) .60 .25
❑ 215 Philip Humber (RC) .40 .15
❑ 216 Kevin Hooper (RC) .40 .15
❑ 217 Jeff Fiorentino (RC) .40 .15
❑ 218 Michael Bourn (RC) .40 .15
❑ 219 Hideki Okajima RC 2.00 .75
❑ 219b H.Okajima English AU 40.00 15.00
❑ 219c H.Okajima Japan AU 60.00 30.00
❑ 220 Josh Fields (RC) .40 .15
❑ 221 Andrew Miller AU RC 25.00 10.00
❑ 222 Troy Tulowitzki AU (RC) 30.00 12.50
❑ 223 Ryan Braun AU RC 25.00 10.00
❑ 224 Oswaldo Navarro AU RC 10.00 4.00
❑ 225 Philip Humber AU (RC) 10.00 4.00
❑ 226 Mitch Maier AU RC 10.00 4.00
❑ 227 Jerry Owens AU (RC) 10.00 4.00
❑ 228 Mike Rabelo AU RC 10.00 4.00
❑ 229 Delwyn Young AU (RC) 10.00 4.00
❑ 230 Miguel Montero AU (RC) 10.00 4.00
❑ 231 Akinori Iwamura AU RC 25.00 10.00
❑ 232 Matt Lindstrom AU (RC) 10.00 4.00
❑ 233 Josh Hamilton AU (RC) 40.00 15.00
❑ 235 Elijah Dukes AU RC 15.00 6.00
❑ 236 Sean Henn AU (RC) 10.00 4.00
❑ 237 Barry Bonds 1.50 .60

2007 Bowman Draft

❑ COMMON RC (1-54) .40 .15
❑ SEE 07 BOWMAN FOR BONDS PRICING
❑ OVERALL PLATE ODDS 1:1294 HOBBY
❑ PLATE PRINT RUN 1 SET PER COLOR
❑ BLACK-CYAN-MAGENTA-YELLOW ISSUED
❑ NO PLATE PRICING DUE TO SCARCITY
❑ BDP1 Travis Buck (RC) .40 .15
❑ BDP2 Matt Chico (RC) .40 .15
❑ BDP3 Justin Upton RC 2.50 1.00
❑ BDP4 Chase Wright RC 1.00 .40
❑ BDP5 Kevin Kouzmanoff (RC) .40 .15
❑ BDP6 John Danks RC .40 .15
❑ BDP7 Alejandro De Aza RC .60 .25
❑ BDP8 Jamie Vermilyea RC .40 .15
❑ BDP9 Jesus Flores RC .40 .15
❑ BDP10 Glen Perkins (RC) .40 .15

❑ BDP11 Tim Lincecum RC 3.00 1.25
❑ BDP12 Cameron Maybin RC 2.00 .75
❑ BDP13 Brandon Morrow RC 1.00 .40
❑ BDP14 Mike Rabelo RC .40 .15
❑ BDP15 Alex Gordon RC 2.00 .75
❑ BDP16 Zack Segovia (RC) .40 .15
❑ BDP17 Jon Knott (RC) .40 .15
❑ BDP18 Joba Chamberlain RC 4.00 1.50
❑ BDP19 Danny Putnam (RC) .40 .15
❑ BDP20 Matt DeSalvo (RC) .40 .15
❑ BDP21 Fred Lewis (RC) .60 .25
❑ BDP22 Sean Gallagher (RC) .40 .15
❑ BDP23 Brandon Wood (RC) .40 .15
❑ BDP24 Dennis Dove (RC) .40 .15
❑ BDP25 Hunter Pence (RC) 2.00 .75
❑ BDP26 Jarrod Saltalamacchia (RC) .60 .25
❑ BDP27 Ben Francisco (RC) .40 .15
❑ BDP28 Doug Slaten RC .40 .15
❑ BDP29 Tony Abreu RC 1.00 .40
❑ BDP30 Billy Butler (RC) .60 .25
❑ BDP31 Jesse Litsch RC .60 .25
❑ BDP32 Nate Schierholtz (RC) .40 .15
❑ BDP33 Jared Burton RC .40 .15
❑ BDP34 Matt Brown RC .40 .15
❑ BDP35 Dallas Braden RC .60 .25
❑ BDP36 Carlos Gomez RC .60 .25
❑ BDP37 Brian Stokes (RC) .40 .15
❑ BDP38 Kory Casto (RC) .40 .15
❑ BDP39 Mark McLemore (RC) .40 .15
❑ BDP40 Andy LaRoche (RC) .40 .15
❑ BDP41 Tyler Clippard (RC) .60 .25
❑ BDP42 Curtis Thigpen (RC) .40 .15
❑ BDP43 Yunel Escobar (RC) .40 .15
❑ BDP44 Andy Sonnanstine RC .40 .15
❑ BDP45 Felix Pie (RC) .40 .15
❑ BDP46 Homer Bailey (RC) .60 .25
❑ BDP47 Kyle Kendrick RC 1.00 .40
❑ BDP48 Angel Sanchez RC .40 .15
❑ BDP49 Phil Hughes (RC) 2.00 .75
❑ BDP50 Ryan Braun (RC) 2.50 1.00
❑ BDP51 Kevin Slowey (RC) 1.00 .40
❑ BDP52 Brendan Ryan (RC) .40 .15
❑ BDP53 Yovani Gallardo (RC) 1.25 .50
❑ BDP54 Mark Reynolds RC 1.50 .60

2008 Bowman

❑ COMP.SET w/o AU's (220) 25.00 10.00
❑ COMMON CARD (1-200) .30 .12
❑ COMMON ROOKIE (201-220) .40 .15
❑ COMMON AUTO (221-230) 10.00 4.00
❑ AU RC ODDS 1:233 HOBBY

❑			
❑	1-220 PLATE ODDS 1:732 HOBBY		
❑	221-231 AU PLATES 1:4700 HOBBY		
❑	PLATE PRINT RUN 1 SET PER COLOR		
❑	BLACK-CYAN-MAGENTA-YELLOW ISSUED		
❑	NO PLATE PRICING DUE TO SCARCITY		
❑	1 Ryan Braun	1.00	.40
❑	2 David DeJesus	.30	.12
❑	3 Brandon Phillips	.30	.12
❑	4 Mark Teixeira	.50	.20
❑	5 Daisuke Matsuzaka	1.25	.50
❑	6 Justin Upton	.75	.30
❑	7 Jered Weaver	.30	.12
❑	8 Todd Helton	.50	.20
❑	9 Cameron Maybin	.75	.30
❑	10 Erik Bedard	.30	.12
❑	11 Jason Bay	.30	.12
❑	12 Cole Hamels	.50	.20
❑	13 Bobby Abreu	.30	.12
❑	14 Carlos Zambrano	.30	.12
❑	15 Vladimir Guerrero	.75	.30
❑	16 Joe Blanton	.30	.12
❑	17 Bengie Molina	.30	.12
❑	18 Paul Maholm	.30	.12
❑	19 Adrian Gonzalez	.50	.20
❑	20 Brandon Webb	.30	.12
❑	21 Carl Crawford	.30	.12
❑	22 A.J. Burnett	.30	.12
❑	23 Dmitri Young	.30	.12
❑	24 Jeremy Hermida	.30	.12
❑	25 C.C. Sabathia	.30	.12
❑	26 Adam Dunn	.30	.12
❑	27 Matt Garza	.30	.12
❑	28 Adrian Beltre	.30	.12
❑	29 Kevin Milwood	.30	.12
❑	30 Manny Ramirez	.75	.30
❑	31 Javier Vazquez	.30	.12
❑	32 Carlos Delgado	.30	.12
❑	33 Jason Schmidt	.30	.12
❑	34 Torii Hunter	.30	.12
❑	35 Ivan Rodriguez	.50	.20
❑	36 Nick Markakis	.50	.20
❑	37 Gil Meche	.30	.12
❑	38 Garrett Atkins	.30	.12
❑	39 Fausto Carmona	.30	.12
❑	40 Joe Mauer	.50	.20
❑	41 Tom Glavine	.50	.20
❑	42 Hideki Matsui	.75	.30
❑	43 Scott Rolen	.50	.20
❑	44 Tim Lincecum	.75	.30
❑	45 Prince Fielder	.75	.30
❑	46 Ted Lilly	.30	.12
❑	47 Frank Thomas	.75	.30
❑	48 Tom Gorzelanny	.30	.12
❑	49 Lance Berkman	.50	.20
❑	50 David Ortiz	.75	.30
❑	51 Dontrelle Willis	.30	.12
❑	52 Travis Hafner	.30	.12
❑	53 Aaron Harang	.30	.12
❑	54 Chris Young	.30	.12
❑	55 Vernon Wells	.30	.12
❑	56 Francisco Liriano	.50	.20
❑	57 Eric Chavez	.30	.12
❑	58 Phil Hughes	1.00	.40
❑	59 Melvin Mora	.30	.12
❑	60 Johan Santana	.75	.30
❑	61 Brian McCann	.50	.20
❑	62 Pat Burrell	.30	.12
❑	63 Chris Carpenter	.30	.12
❑	64 Brian Giles	.30	.12
❑	65 Jose Reyes	.50	.20
❑	66 Hanley Ramirez	.75	.30
❑	67 Ubaldo Jimenez	.30	.12
❑	68 Felix Pie	.30	.12
❑	69 Jeremy Bonderman	.30	.12
❑	70 Jimmy Rollins	.50	.20
❑	71 Miguel Tejada	.30	.12
❑	72 Derek Lowe	.30	.12
❑	73 Alex Gordon	.75	.30
❑	74 John Maine	.30	.12
❑	75 Alfonso Soriano	.50	.20
❑	76 Richie Sexson	.30	.12
❑	77 Ben Sheets	.50	.20
❑	78 Hunter Pence	.75	.30
❑	79 Magglio Ordonez	.50	.20
❑	80 Josh Beckett	.50	.20
❑	81 Victor Martinez	.30	.12
❑	82 Mark Buehrle	.30	.12
❑	83 Jason Varitek	.75	.30
❑	84 Chien-Ming Wang	1.25	.50
❑	85 Ken Griffey Jr.	1.25	.50
❑	86 Billy Butler	.30	.12
❑	87 Brad Penny	.30	.12
❑	88 Carlos Beltran	.30	.12
❑	89 Curt Schilling	.50	.20
❑	90 Jorge Posada	.50	.20
❑	91 Andruw Jones	.30	.12
❑	92 Bobby Crosby	.30	.12
❑	93 Freddy Sanchez	.30	.12
❑	94 Barry Zito	.30	.12
❑	95 Miguel Cabrera	.50	.20
❑	96 B.J. Upton	.50	.20
❑	97 Matt Cain	.30	.12
❑	98 Lyle Overbay	.30	.12
❑	99 Austin Kearns	.30	.12
❑	100 Alex Rodriguez	1.25	.50
❑	101 Rich Harden	.30	.12
❑	102 Justin Morneau	.30	.12
❑	103 Oliver Perez	.30	.12
❑	104 Gary Matthews	.30	.12
❑	105 Matt Holliday	.50	.20
❑	106 Justin Verlander	.50	.20
❑	107 Orlando Cabrera	.30	.12
❑	108 Rich Hill	.30	.12
❑	109 Tim Hudson	.30	.12
❑	110 Ryan Zimmerman	.50	.20
❑	111 Roy Oswalt	.30	.12
❑	112 Nick Swisher	.30	.12
❑	113 Raul Ibanez	.30	.12
❑	114 Kelly Johnson	.30	.12
❑	115 Alex Rios	.30	.12
❑	116 John Lackey	.30	.12
❑	117 Robinson Cano	.50	.20
❑	118 Michael Young	.30	.12
❑	119 Jeff Francis	.30	.12
❑	120 Grady Sizemore	.50	.20
❑	121 Mike Lowell	.30	.12
❑	122 Aramis Ramirez	.30	.12
❑	123 Stephen Drew	.30	.12
❑	124 Yovani Gallardo	.30	.12
❑	125 Chase Utley	.75	.30
❑	126 Dan Haren	.30	.12
❑	127 Jose Vidro	.30	.12
❑	128 Ronnie Belliard	.30	.12
❑	129 Yunel Escobar	.30	.12
❑	130 Greg Maddux	1.00	.40
❑	131 Garret Anderson	.30	.12
❑	132 Aubrey Huff	.30	.12
❑	133 Paul Konerko	.30	.12
❑	134 Dan Uggla	.50	.20
❑	135 Roy Halladay	.30	.12
❑	136 Andre Ethier	.50	.20
❑	137 Orlando Hernandez	.30	.12
❑	138 Troy Tulowitzki	.50	.20
❑	139 Carlos Guillen	.30	.12
❑	140 Scott Kazmir	.50	.20
❑	141 Aaron Rowand	.30	.12
❑	142 Jim Edmonds	.50	.20
❑	143 Jermaine Dye	.30	.12
❑	144 Orlando Hudson	.30	.12
❑	145 Derrek Lee	.50	.20
❑	146 Travis Buck	.30	.12
❑	147 Zack Greinke	.30	.12
❑	148 Jeff Kent	.30	.12
❑	149 John Smoltz	.75	.30
❑	150 David Wright	1.00	.40
❑	151 Joba Chamberlain	2.00	.75
❑	152 Adam LaRoche	.30	.12
❑	153 Kevin Youkilis	.50	.20
❑	154 Troy Glaus	.50	.20
❑	155 Nick Johnson	.30	.12
❑	156 J.J. Hardy	.30	.12
❑	157 Felix Hernandez	.50	.20
❑	158 Khalil Greene	.50	.20
❑	159 Gary Sheffield	.30	.12
❑	160 Albert Pujols	1.50	.60
❑	161 Chuck James	.30	.12
❑	162 Rocco Baldelli	.30	.12
❑	163 Eric Byrnes	.30	.12
❑	164 Brad Hawpe	.30	.12
❑	165 Delmon Young	.50	.20
❑	166 Chris Young	.30	.12
❑	167 Brian Roberts	.50	.20
❑	168 Russell Martin	.30	.12
❑	169 Hank Blalock	.30	.12
❑	170 Yadier Molina	.50	.20
❑	171 Jeremy Guthrie	.30	.12
❑	172 Chipper Jones	1.00	.40
❑	173 Johnny Damon	.50	.20
❑	174 Ryan Garko	.30	.12
❑	175 Jake Peavy	.30	.12
❑	176 Chone Figgins	.30	.12
❑	177 Edgar Renteria	.30	.12
❑	178 Jim Thome	.50	.20
❑	179 Carlos Pena	.30	.12
❑	180 Corey Patterson	.30	.12
❑	181 Dustin Pedroia	.50	.20
❑	182 Brett Myers	.30	.12
❑	183 Josh Hamilton	1.00	.40
❑	184 Randy Johnson	.75	.30
❑	185 Ichiro Suzuki	1.25	.50
❑	186 Aaron Hill	.30	.12
❑	187 Jarrod Saltalamacchia	.30	.12
❑	188 Michael Cuddyer	.30	.12
❑	189 Jeff Francoeur	.50	.20
❑	190 Derek Jeter	2.00	.75
❑	191 Curtis Granderson	.50	.20
❑	192 James Loney	.50	.20
❑	193 Brian Bannister	.30	.12
❑	194 Carlos Lee	.30	.12
❑	195 Pedro Martinez	.50	.20
❑	196 Asdrubal Cabrera	.30	.12
❑	197 Kenji Johjima	.30	.12
❑	198 Bartolo Colon	.30	.12
❑	199 Jacoby Ellsbury	1.25	.50
❑	200 Ryan Howard	1.00	.40
❑	201 Radhames Liz RC	.60	.25
❑	202 Justin Ruggiano RC	.60	.25
❑	203 Lance Broadway (RC)	.40	.15
❑	204 Joey Votto (RC)	.60	.25
❑	205 Billy Buckner (RC)	.40	.15
❑	206 Joe Koshansky (RC)	.40	.15
❑	207 Ross Detwiler RC	1.00	.40
❑	208 Chin-Lung Hu (RC)	.60	.25
❑	209 Luke Hochevar RC	1.25	.50
❑	210 Jeff Clement (RC)	.40	.15
❑	211 Troy Patton (RC)	.40	.15
❑	212 Hiroki Kuroda RC	.60	.25
❑	213 Emilio Bonifacio RC	.60	.25
❑	214 Armando Galarraga RC	.60	.25
❑	215 Josh Anderson (RC)	.40	.15
❑	216 Nick Blackburn RC	.60	.25
❑	217 Seth Smith (RC)	.40	.15
❑	218 Jonathan Meloan RC	.60	.25
❑	219 Alberto Gonzalez RC	.60	.25
❑	220 Josh Banks (RC)	.40	.15
❑	221 Clay Buchholz AU (RC)	15.00	6.00
❑	222 Nyjer Morgan AU (RC)	10.00	4.00
❑	223 Brandon Jones AU RC	10.00	4.00
❑	224 Sam Fuld AU (RC)	10.00	4.00
❑	225 Dane Barton AU (RC)	10.00	4.00
❑	226 Chris Seddon AU (RC)	10.00	4.00
❑	227 J.R. Towles AU RC	10.00	4.00
❑	228 Steve Pearce AU RC	10.00	4.00
❑	229 Ross Ohlendorf AU RC	10.00	4.00
❑	230 Clint Sammons AU (RC)	10.00	4.00

1997 Bowman Chrome

❑			
❑	COMPLETE SET (300)	150.00	75.00
❑	1 Derek Jeter	3.00	1.25
❑	2 Chipper Jones	1.25	.50

3	Hideo Nomo	1.25	.50
4	Tim Salmon	.75	.30
5	Robin Ventura	.50	.20
6	Tony Clark	.50	.20
7	Barry Larkin	.75	.30
8	Paul Molitor	.50	.20
9	Andy Benes	.50	.20
10	Ryan Klesko	.50	.20
11	Mark McGwire	3.00	1.25
12	Ken Griffey Jr.	2.00	.75
13	Robb Nen	.50	.20
14	Cal Ripken	4.00	1.50
15	John Valentin	.50	.20
16	Ricky Bottalico	.50	.20
17	Mike Lansing	.50	.20
18	Ryne Sandberg	2.00	.75
19	Carlos Delgado	.50	.20
20	Craig Biggio	.75	.30
21	Eric Karros	.50	.20
22	Kevin Appier	.50	.20
23	Mariano Rivera	1.25	.50
24	Vinny Castilla	.50	.20
25	Juan Gonzalez	.50	.20
26	Al Martin	.50	.20
27	Jeff Cirillo	.50	.20
28	Ray Lankford	.50	.20
29	Manny Ramirez	.75	.30
30	Roberto Alomar	.75	.30
31	Will Clark	.75	.30
32	Chuck Knoblauch	.50	.20
33	Harold Baines	.50	.20
34	Edgar Martinez	.75	.30
35	Mike Mussina	.75	.30
36	Kevin Brown	.50	.20
37	Dennis Eckersley	.50	.20
38	Tino Martinez	.75	.30
39	Raul Mondesi	.50	.20
40	Sammy Sosa	1.25	.50
41	John Smoltz	.75	.30
42	Billy Wagner	.50	.20
43	Ken Caminiti	.50	.20
44	Wade Boggs	.75	.30
45	Andres Galarraga	.50	.20
46	Roger Clemens	2.50	1.00
47	Matt Williams	.50	.20
48	Albert Belle	.50	.20
49	Jeff King	.50	.20
50	John Wetteland	.50	.20
51	Deion Sanders	.75	.30
52	Ellis Burks	.50	.20
53	Pedro Martinez	.75	.30
54	Kenny Lofton	.50	.20
55	Randy Johnson	1.25	.50
56	Bernie Williams	.75	.30
57	Marquis Grissom	.50	.20
58	Gary Sheffield	.50	.20
59	Curt Schilling	.50	.20
60	Reggie Sanders	.50	.20
61	Bobby Higginson	.50	.20
62	Moises Alou	.50	.20
63	Tom Glavine	.75	.30
64	Mark Grace	.75	.30
65	Rafael Palmeiro	.75	.30
66	John Olerud	.50	.20
67	Dante Bichette	.50	.20
68	Jeff Bagwell	.75	.30
69	Barry Bonds	3.00	1.25
70	Pat Hentgen	.50	.20
71	Jim Thome	.75	.30
72	Andy Pettitte	.75	.30
73	Jay Bell	.50	.20
74	Jim Edmonds	.50	.20
75	Ron Gant	.50	.20
76	David Cone	.50	.20
77	Jose Canseco	.75	.30
78	Jay Buhner	.50	.20
79	Greg Maddux	2.00	.75
80	Lance Johnson	.50	.20
81	Travis Fryman	.50	.20
82	Paul O'Neill	.75	.30
83	Ivan Rodriguez	.75	.30
84	Fred McGriff	.75	.30
85	Mike Piazza	2.00	.75
86	Brady Anderson	.50	.20
87	Marty Cordova	.50	.20
88	Joe Carter	.50	.20
89	Brian Jordan	.50	.20
90	David Justice	.50	.20
91	Tony Gwynn	1.50	.60
92	Larry Walker	.50	.20
93	Mo Vaughn	.50	.20
94	Sandy Alomar Jr.	.50	.20
95	Rusty Greer	.50	.20
96	Roberto Hernandez	.50	.20
97	Hal Morris	.50	.20
98	Todd Hundley	.50	.20
99	Rondell White	.50	.20
100	Frank Thomas	1.25	.50
101	Bubba Trammell RC	1.50	.60
102	Sidney Ponson RC	2.50	1.00
103	Ricky Ledee RC	1.50	.60
104	Brett Tomko	.50	.20
105	Braden Looper RC	1.00	.40
106	Jason Dickson	.50	.20
107	Chad Green RC	1.00	.40
108	R.A. Dickey RC	1.00	.40
109	Jeff Liefer	.50	.20
110	Richard Hidalgo	.50	.20
111	Chad Hermansen RC	1.00	.40
112	Felix Martinez	.50	.20
113	J.J. Johnson	.50	.20
114	Todd Dunwoody	.50	.20
115	Katsuhiro Maeda	.50	.20
116	Darin Erstad	.50	.20
117	Elieser Marrero	.50	.20
118	Bartolo Colon	.50	.20
119	Ugueth Urbina	.50	.20
120	Jaime Bluma	.50	.20
121	Seth Greisinger RC	1.00	.40
122	Jose Cruz Jr. RC	1.50	.60
123	Todd Dunn	.50	.20
124	Justin Towle RC	1.00	.40
125	Brian Rose	.50	.20
126	Jose Guillen	.50	.20
127	Andruw Jones	.75	.30
128	Mark Kotsay RC	4.00	1.50
129	Wilton Guerrero	.50	.20
130	Jacob Cruz	.50	.20
131	Mike Sweeney	.50	.20
132	Matt Morris	.50	.20
133	John Thomson	.50	.20
134	Javier Valentin	.50	.20
135	Mike Drumright RC	1.00	.40
136	Michael Barrett	.50	.20
137	Tony Saunders RC	1.00	.40
138	Kevin Brown	.50	.20
139	Anthony Sanders RC	1.00	.40
140	Jeff Abbott	.50	.20
141	Eugene Kingsale	.50	.20
142	Paul Konerko	.75	.30
143	Randall Simon RC	1.50	.60
144	Freddy Adrian Garcia	.50	.20
145	Karim Garcia	.50	.20
146	Carlos Guillen	.50	.20
147	Aaron Boone	.50	.20
148	Donnie Sadler	.50	.20
149	Brooks Kieschnick	.50	.20
150	Scott Spiezio	.50	.20
151	Kevin Orie	.50	.20
152	Russ Johnson	.50	.20
153	Livan Hernandez	.50	.20
154	Vladimir Nunez RC	1.00	.40
155	Pokey Reese	.50	.20
156	Chris Carpenter	.50	.20
157	Eric Milton RC	1.50	.60
158	Richie Sexson	.50	.20
159	Carl Pavano	.50	.20
160	Pat Cline	.50	.20
161	Ron Wright	.50	.20
162	Dante Powell	.50	.20
163	Mark Bellhorn	.50	.20
164	George Lombard	.50	.20
165	Paul Wilder RC	1.00	.40
166	Brad Fullmer	.50	.20
167	Kris Benson RC	2.50	1.00
168	Torii Hunter	.50	.20
169	D.T. Cromer RC	1.00	.40
170	Nelson Figueroa RC	1.00	.40
171	Hiram Bocachica RC	1.00	.40
172	Shane Monahan	.50	.20
173	Juan Melo	.50	.20
174	Calvin Pickering RC	1.00	.40
175	Reggie Taylor	.50	.20
176	Geoff Jenkins	.50	.20
177	Steve Rain RC	1.00	.40
178	Nerio Rodriguez RC	1.00	.40
179	Derrick Gibson	.50	.20
180	Darin Blood	.50	.20
181	Ben Davis	.50	.20
182	Adrian Beltre RC	8.00	3.00
183	Kerry Wood RC	12.00	5.00
184	Nate Rolison RC	1.00	.40
185	Fernando Tatis RC	1.00	.40
186	Jake Westbrook RC	2.50	1.00
187	Edwin Diaz	.50	.20
188	Joe Fontenot RC	1.00	.40
189	Matt Halloran RC	1.00	.40
190	Matt Clement RC	2.50	1.00
191	Todd Greene	.50	.20
192	Eric Chavez RC	10.00	4.00
193	Edgard Velazquez	.50	.20
194	Bruce Chen RC	2.50	1.00
195	Jason Brester	.50	.20
196	Chris Reitsma RC	1.50	.60
197	Neifi Perez	.50	.20
198	Hideki Irabu RC	1.50	.60
199	Don Denbow RC	1.00	.40
200	Derrek Lee	.75	.30
201	Todd Walker	.50	.20
202	Scott Rolen	.75	.30
203	Wes Helms	.50	.20
204	Bob Abreu	.75	.30
205	John Patterson RC	4.00	1.50
206	Alex Gonzalez RC	2.50	1.00
207	Grant Roberts RC	1.00	.40
208	Jeff Suppan	.50	.20
209	Luke Wilcox	.50	.20
210	Marlon Anderson	.50	.20
211	Mike Caruso RC	1.00	.40
212	Roy Halladay RC	10.00	4.00
213	Jeremi Gonzalez RC	1.00	.40
214	Aramis Ramirez RC	10.00	4.00
215	Dee Brown RC	1.00	.40
216	Justin Thompson	.50	.20
217	Danny Clyburn	.50	.20
218	Bruce Aven	.50	.20
219	Keith Foulke RC	4.00	1.50
220	Shannon Stewart	.50	.20
221	Larry Barnes RC	1.00	.40
222	Mark Johnson RC	1.00	.40
223	Randy Winn	.50	.20
224	Nomar Garciaparra	2.00	.75
225	Jacque Jones RC	4.00	1.50
226	Chris Clemons	.50	.20
227	Todd Helton	1.25	.50
228	Ryan Brannan RC	1.00	.40
229	Alex Sanchez RC	1.50	.60
230	Russell Branyan	.50	.20
231	Daryle Ward	1.00	.40
232	Kevin Witt	.50	.20
233	Gabby Martinez	.50	.20
234	Preston Wilson	.50	.20
235	Donzell McDonald RC	1.00	.40
236	Orlando Cabrera RC	4.00	1.50
237	Brian Banks	.50	.20
238	Robbie Bell	1.00	.40
239	Brad Rigby	.50	.20
240	Scott Elarton	.50	.20
241	Donny Leon RC	1.00	.40
242	Abraham Nunez RC	1.00	.40
243	Adam Eaton RC	2.50	1.00
244	Octavio Dotel RC	1.50	.60
245	Sean Casey	2.50	1.00
246	Joe Lawrence RC	1.00	.40
247	Adam Johnson RC	1.00	.40
248	Ronnie Belliard RC	3.00	1.25
249	Bobby Estalella	.50	.20
250	Corey Lee RC	1.00	.40
251	Mike Cameron	.50	.20
252	Kerry Robinson RC	1.00	.40
253	A.J. Zapp RC	1.00	.40
254	Jarrod Washburn	.50	.20
255	Ben Grieve	.50	.20
256	Javier Vazquez RC	4.00	1.50
257	Travis Lee RC	1.50	.60
258	Dennis Reyes RC	1.00	.40
259	Danny Buxbaum	.50	.20
260	Kelvim Escobar RC	2.50	1.00

❑ 261	Danny Klassen	.50	.20
❑ 262	Ken Cloude RC	1.00	.40
❑ 263	Gabe Alvarez	.50	.20
❑ 264	Clayton Bruner RC	1.00	.40
❑ 265	Jason Marquis RC	2.50	1.00
❑ 266	Jamey Wright	.50	.20
❑ 267	Matt Snyder RC	1.00	.40
❑ 268	Josh Garrett RC	1.00	.40
❑ 269	Juan Encarnacion	.50	.20
❑ 270	Heath Murray	.50	.20
❑ 271	Brent Butler RC	1.00	.40
❑ 272	Danny Peoples RC	1.00	.40
❑ 273	Miguel Tejada RC	12.00	5.00
❑ 274	Jim Pittsley	.50	.20
❑ 275	Dmitri Young	.50	.20
❑ 276	Vladimir Guerrero	1.25	.50
❑ 277	Cole Liniak RC	1.00	.40
❑ 278	Ramon Hernandez	.50	.20
❑ 279	Cliff Politte RC	1.00	.40
❑ 280	Mel Rosario RC	1.00	.40
❑ 281	Jorge Carrion RC	1.00	.40
❑ 282	John Barnes RC	1.00	.40
❑ 283	Chris Stowe RC	1.00	.40
❑ 284	Vernon Wells RC	12.00	5.00
❑ 285	Brett Caradonna RC	1.00	.40
❑ 286	Scott Hodges RC	1.00	.40
❑ 287	Jon Garland RC	6.00	2.50
❑ 288	Nathan Haynes RC	1.00	.40
❑ 289	Geoff Goetz RC	1.00	.40
❑ 290	Adam Kennedy RC	2.50	1.00
❑ 291	T.J. Tucker RC	1.00	.40
❑ 292	Aaron Akin RC	1.00	.40
❑ 293	Jayson Werth RC	2.50	1.00
❑ 294	Glenn Davis RC	1.00	.40
❑ 295	Mark Mangum RC	1.00	.40
❑ 296	Troy Cameron RC	1.00	.40
❑ 297	J.J. Davis RC	1.00	.40
❑ 298	Lance Berkman RC	15.00	6.00
❑ 299	Jason Standridge RC	1.00	.40
❑ 300	Jason Dellaero RC	1.00	.40

1998 Bowman Chrome

❑	COMPLETE SET (441)	160.00	60.00
❑	COMPLETE SERIES 1 (221)	80.00	30.00
❑	COMPLETE SERIES 2 (220)	80.00	30.00
❑ 1	Nomar Garciaparra	2.00	.75
❑ 2	Scott Rolen	.75	.30
❑ 3	Andy Pettitte	.75	.30
❑ 4	Ivan Rodriguez	.75	.30
❑ 5	Mark McGwire	3.00	1.25
❑ 6	Jason Dickson	.50	.20
❑ 7	Jose Cruz Jr.	.50	.20
❑ 8	Jeff Kent	.50	.20
❑ 9	Mike Mussina	.75	.30
❑ 10	Jason Kendall	.50	.20
❑ 11	Brett Tomko	.50	.20
❑ 12	Jeff King	.50	.20
❑ 13	Brad Radke	.50	.20
❑ 14	Robin Ventura	.50	.20
❑ 15	Jeff Bagwell	.75	.30
❑ 16	Greg Maddux	2.00	.75
❑ 17	John Jaha	.50	.20
❑ 18	Mike Piazza	2.00	.75
❑ 19	Edgar Martinez	.75	.30
❑ 20	David Justice	.50	.20
❑ 21	Todd Hundley	.50	.20
❑ 22	Tony Gwynn	1.50	.60
❑ 23	Larry Walker	.50	.20
❑ 24	Bernie Williams	.75	.30
❑ 25	Edgar Renteria	.50	.20
❑ 26	Rafael Palmeiro	.75	.30
❑ 27	Tim Salmon	.75	.30
❑ 28	Matt Morris	.50	.20
❑ 29	Shawn Estes	.50	.20
❑ 30	Vladimir Guerrero	1.25	.50
❑ 31	Fernando Tatis	.50	.20
❑ 32	Justin Thompson	.50	.20
❑ 33	Ken Griffey Jr.	2.00	.75
❑ 34	Edgardo Alfonzo	.50	.20
❑ 35	Mo Vaughn	.50	.20
❑ 36	Marty Cordova	.50	.20
❑ 37	Craig Biggio	.75	.30
❑ 38	Roger Clemens	2.50	1.00
❑ 39	Mark Grace	.75	.30
❑ 40	Ken Caminiti	.50	.20
❑ 41	Tony Womack	.50	.20
❑ 42	Albert Belle	.50	.20
❑ 43	Tino Martinez	.75	.30
❑ 44	Sandy Alomar Jr.	.50	.20
❑ 45	Jeff Cirillo	.50	.20
❑ 46	Jason Giambi	.50	.20
❑ 47	Darin Erstad	.50	.20
❑ 48	Livan Hernandez	.50	.20
❑ 49	Mark Grudzielanek	.50	.20
❑ 50	Sammy Sosa	1.25	.50
❑ 51	Curt Schilling	.50	.20
❑ 52	Brian Hunter	.50	.20
❑ 53	Neifi Perez	.50	.20
❑ 54	Todd Walker	.50	.20
❑ 55	Jose Guillen	.50	.20
❑ 56	Jim Thome	.75	.30
❑ 57	Tom Glavine	.75	.30
❑ 58	Todd Greene	.50	.20
❑ 59	Rondell White	.50	.20
❑ 60	Roberto Alomar	.75	.30
❑ 61	Tony Clark	.50	.20
❑ 62	Vinny Castilla	.50	.20
❑ 63	Barry Larkin	.75	.30
❑ 64	Hideki Irabu	.50	.20
❑ 65	Johnny Damon	.75	.30
❑ 66	Juan Gonzalez	.50	.20
❑ 67	John Olerud	.50	.20
❑ 68	Gary Sheffield	.50	.20
❑ 69	Raul Mondesi	.50	.20
❑ 70	Chipper Jones	1.25	.50
❑ 71	David Ortiz	6.00	2.50
❑ 72	Warren Morris RC	1.00	.40
❑ 73	Alex Gonzalez	.50	.20
❑ 74	Nick Bierbrodt	.50	.20
❑ 75	Roy Halladay	.50	.20
❑ 76	Danny Buxbaum	.50	.20
❑ 77	Adam Kennedy	.50	.20
❑ 78	Jared Sandberg	.50	.20
❑ 79	Michael Barrett	.50	.20
❑ 80	Gil Meche	1.50	.60
❑ 81	Jayson Werth	.50	.20
❑ 82	Abraham Nunez	.50	.20
❑ 83	Ben Petrick	.50	.20
❑ 84	Brett Caradonna	.50	.20
❑ 85	Mike Lowell RC	6.00	2.50
❑ 86	Clay Bruner	.50	.20
❑ 87	John Curtice RC	1.50	.60
❑ 88	Bobby Estalella	.50	.20
❑ 89	Juan Melo	.50	.20
❑ 90	Arnold Gooch	.50	.20
❑ 91	Kevin Millwood RC	4.00	1.50
❑ 92	Richie Sexson	.50	.20
❑ 93	Orlando Cabrera	.50	.20
❑ 94	Pat Cline	.50	.20
❑ 95	Anthony Sanders	.50	.20
❑ 96	Russ Johnson	.50	.20
❑ 97	Ben Grieve	.50	.20
❑ 98	Kevin McGlinchy	.50	.20
❑ 99	Paul Wilder	.50	.20
❑ 100	Russ Ortiz	.50	.20
❑ 101	Ryan Jackson RC	1.00	.40
❑ 102	Heath Murray	.50	.20
❑ 103	Brian Rose	.50	.20
❑ 104	Ryan Radmanovich RC	1.00	.40
❑ 105	Ricky Ledee	.50	.20
❑ 106	Jeff Wallace RC	1.00	.40
❑ 107	Ryan Minor RC	1.00	.40
❑ 108	Dennis Reyes	.50	.20
❑ 109	James Manias	.50	.20
❑ 110	Chris Carpenter	.50	.20
❑ 111	Daryle Ward	.50	.20
❑ 112	Vernon Wells	.50	.20
❑ 113	Chad Green	.50	.20
❑ 114	Mike Stoner RC	1.00	.40
❑ 115	Brad Fullmer	.50	.20
❑ 116	Adam Eaton	.50	.20
❑ 117	Jeff Liefer	.50	.20
❑ 118	Corey Koskie RC	2.50	1.00
❑ 119	Todd Helton	.75	.30
❑ 120	Jaime Jones RC	1.00	.40
❑ 121	Mel Rosario	.50	.20
❑ 122	Geoff Goetz	.50	.20
❑ 123	Adrian Beltre	.50	.20
❑ 124	Jason Dellaero	.50	.20
❑ 125	Gabe Kapler RC	2.50	1.00
❑ 126	Scott Schoeneweis	.50	.20
❑ 127	Ryan Brannan	.50	.20
❑ 128	Aaron Akin	.50	.20
❑ 129	Ryan Anderson RC	1.00	.40
❑ 130	Brad Penny	.50	.20
❑ 131	Bruce Chen	.50	.20
❑ 132	Eli Marrero	.50	.20
❑ 133	Eric Chavez	.50	.20
❑ 134	Troy Glaus RC	8.00	3.00
❑ 135	Troy Cameron	.50	.20
❑ 136	Brian Sikorski RC	1.00	.40
❑ 137	Mike Kinkade RC	1.00	.40
❑ 138	Braden Looper	.50	.20
❑ 139	Mark Mangum	.50	.20
❑ 140	Danny Peoples	.50	.20
❑ 141	J.J. Davis	.50	.20
❑ 142	Ben Davis	.50	.20
❑ 143	Jacque Jones	.50	.20
❑ 144	Derrick Gibson	.50	.20
❑ 145	Bronson Arroyo	4.00	1.50
❑ 146	Luis De Los Santos RC	1.00	.40
❑ 147	Jeff Abbott	.50	.20
❑ 148	Mike Cuddyer RC	4.00	1.50
❑ 149	Jason Romano	.50	.20
❑ 150	Shane Monahan	.50	.20
❑ 151	Ntema Ndungidi RC	1.00	.40
❑ 152	Alex Sanchez	.50	.20
❑ 153	Jack Cust RC	8.00	3.00
❑ 154	Brent Butler	.50	.20
❑ 155	Ramon Hernandez	.50	.20
❑ 156	Norm Hutchins	.50	.20
❑ 157	Jason Marquis	.50	.20
❑ 158	Jacob Cruz	.50	.20
❑ 159	Rob Burger RC	1.00	.40
❑ 160	Dave Coggin	.50	.20
❑ 161	Preston Wilson	.50	.20
❑ 162	Jason Fitzgerald RC	1.00	.40
❑ 163	Dan Serafini	.50	.20
❑ 164	Pete Munro	.50	.20
❑ 165	Trot Nixon	.50	.20
❑ 166	Homer Bush	.50	.20
❑ 167	Dermal Brown	.50	.20
❑ 168	Chad Hermansen	.50	.20
❑ 169	Julio Moreno RC	1.00	.40
❑ 170	John Roskos RC	1.00	.40
❑ 171	Grant Roberts	.50	.20
❑ 172	Ken Cloude	.50	.20
❑ 173	Jason Brester	.50	.20
❑ 174	Jason Conti	.50	.20
❑ 175	Jon Garland	.50	.20
❑ 176	Robbie Bell	.50	.20
❑ 177	Nathan Haynes	.50	.20
❑ 178	Ramon Ortiz RC	1.50	.60
❑ 179	Shannon Stewart	.50	.20
❑ 180	Pablo Ortega	.50	.20
❑ 181	Jimmy Rollins RC	10.00	4.00
❑ 182	Sean Casey	.50	.20
❑ 183	Ted Lilly RC	2.50	1.00
❑ 184	Chris Enochs RC	1.00	.40
❑ 185	Magglio Ordonez UER RC	10.00	4.00
❑ 186	Mike Drumright	.50	.20
❑ 187	Aaron Boone	.50	.20
❑ 188	Matt Clement	.50	.20
❑ 189	Todd Dunwoody	.50	.20
❑ 190	Larry Rodriguez	.50	.20
❑ 191	Todd Noel	.50	.20
❑ 192	Geoff Jenkins	.50	.20
❑ 193	George Lombard	.50	.20
❑ 194	Lance Berkman	.50	.20
❑ 195	Marcus McCain	.50	.20

❑ 196 Ryan McGuire .50 .20
❑ 197 Jhensy Sandoval .50 .20
❑ 198 Corey Lee .50 .20
❑ 199 Mario Valdez .50 .20
❑ 200 Robert Fick RC 1.50 .60
❑ 201 Donnie Sadler .50 .20
❑ 202 Marc Kroon .50 .20
❑ 203 David Miller .50 .20
❑ 204 Jarrod Washburn .50 .20
❑ 205 Miguel Tejada 1.25 .50
❑ 206 Raul Ibanez .50 .20
❑ 207 John Patterson .50 .20
❑ 208 Calvin Pickering .50 .20
❑ 209 Felix Martinez .50 .20
❑ 210 Mark Redman .50 .20
❑ 211 Scott Elarton .50 .20
❑ 212 Jose Amado RC 1.00 .40
❑ 213 Kerry Wood .50 .20
❑ 214 Dante Powell .50 .20
❑ 215 Aramis Ramirez .50 .20
❑ 216 A.J. Hinch .50 .20
❑ 217 Dustin Carr RC 1.00 .40
❑ 218 Mark Kotsay .50 .20
❑ 219 Jason Standridge .50 .20
❑ 220 Luis Ordaz .50 .20
❑ 221 Orlando Hernandez RC 5.00 2.00
❑ 222 Cal Ripken 4.00 1.50
❑ 223 Paul Molitor .50 .20
❑ 224 Derek Jeter 3.00 1.25
❑ 225 Barry Bonds 3.00 1.25
❑ 226 Jim Edmonds .50 .20
❑ 227 John Smoltz .75 .30
❑ 228 Eric Karros .50 .20
❑ 229 Ray Lankford .50 .20
❑ 230 Rey Ordonez .50 .20
❑ 231 Kenny Lofton .50 .20
❑ 232 Alex Rodriguez 2.00 .75
❑ 233 Dante Bichette .50 .20
❑ 234 Pedro Martinez .75 .30
❑ 235 Carlos Delgado .50 .20
❑ 236 Rod Beck .50 .20
❑ 237 Matt Williams .50 .20
❑ 238 Charles Johnson .50 .20
❑ 239 Rico Brogna .50 .20
❑ 240 Frank Thomas 1.25 .50
❑ 241 Paul O'Neill .75 .30
❑ 242 Jaret Wright .50 .20
❑ 243 Brant Brown .50 .20
❑ 244 Ryan Klesko .50 .20
❑ 245 Chuck Finley .50 .20
❑ 246 Derek Bell .50 .20
❑ 247 Delino DeShields .50 .20
❑ 248 Chan Ho Park .50 .20
❑ 249 Wade Boggs .75 .30
❑ 250 Jay Buhner .50 .20
❑ 251 Butch Huskey .50 .20
❑ 252 Steve Finley .50 .20
❑ 253 Will Clark .75 .30
❑ 254 John Valentin .50 .20
❑ 255 Bobby Higginson .50 .20
❑ 256 Darryl Strawberry .50 .20
❑ 257 Randy Johnson 1.25 .50
❑ 258 Al Martin .50 .20
❑ 259 Travis Fryman .50 .20
❑ 260 Fred McGriff .75 .30
❑ 261 Jose Valentin .50 .20
❑ 262 Andruw Jones .75 .30
❑ 263 Kenny Rogers .50 .20
❑ 264 Moises Alou .50 .20
❑ 265 Denny Neagle .50 .20
❑ 266 Ugueth Urbina .50 .20
❑ 267 Derrek Lee .75 .30
❑ 268 Ellis Burks .50 .20
❑ 269 Mariano Rivera 1.25 .50
❑ 270 Dean Palmer .50 .20
❑ 271 Eddie Taubensee .50 .20
❑ 272 Brady Anderson .50 .20
❑ 273 Brian Giles .50 .20
❑ 274 Quinton McCracken .50 .20
❑ 275 Henry Rodriguez .50 .20
❑ 276 Andres Galarraga .50 .20
❑ 277 Jose Canseco .75 .30
❑ 278 David Segui .50 .20
❑ 279 Bret Saberhagen .50 .20
❑ 280 Kevin Brown .75 .30
❑ 281 Chuck Knoblauch .50 .20
❑ 282 Jeromy Burnitz .50 .20
❑ 283 Jay Bell .50 .20
❑ 284 Manny Ramirez .75 .30
❑ 285 Rick Helling .50 .20
❑ 286 Francisco Cordova .50 .20
❑ 287 Bob Abreu .50 .20
❑ 288 J.T. Snow .50 .20
❑ 289 Hideo Nomo 1.25 .50
❑ 290 Brian Jordan .50 .20
❑ 291 Javy Lopez .50 .20
❑ 292 Travis Lee .50 .20
❑ 293 Russell Branyan .50 .20
❑ 294 Paul Konerko .50 .20
❑ 295 Masato Yoshii RC 1.50 .60
❑ 296 Kris Benson .50 .20
❑ 297 Juan Encarnacion .50 .20
❑ 298 Eric Milton .50 .20
❑ 299 Mike Caruso .50 .20
❑ 300 Ricardo Aramboles RC 1.00 .40
❑ 301 Bobby Smith .50 .20
❑ 302 Billy Koch .50 .20
❑ 303 Richard Hidalgo .50 .20
❑ 304 Justin Baughman RC 1.00 .40
❑ 305 Chris Gissell .50 .20
❑ 306 Donnie Bridges RC 1.00 .40
❑ 307 Nelson Lara RC 1.00 .40
❑ 308 Randy Wolf RC 1.50 .60
❑ 309 Jason LaRue RC 1.50 .60
❑ 310 Jason Gooding RC 1.00 .40
❑ 311 Edgard Clemente .50 .20
❑ 312 Andrew Vessel .50 .20
❑ 313 Chris Reitsma .50 .20
❑ 314 Jesus Sanchez RC 1.00 .40
❑ 315 Buddy Carlyle RC 1.00 .40
❑ 316 Randy Winn .50 .20
❑ 317 Luis Rivera RC 1.00 .40
❑ 318 Marcus Thames RC 6.00 2.50
❑ 319 A.J. Pierzynski .50 .20
❑ 320 Scott Randall .50 .20
❑ 321 Damian Sapp .50 .20
❑ 322 Ed Yarnall RC 1.00 .40
❑ 323 Luke Allen RC 1.00 .40
❑ 324 J.D. Smart .50 .20
❑ 325 Willie Martinez .50 .20
❑ 326 Alex Ramirez .50 .20
❑ 327 Eric DuBose RC 1.00 .40
❑ 328 Kevin Witt .50 .20
❑ 329 Dan McKinley RC 1.00 .40
❑ 330 Cliff Politte .50 .20
❑ 331 Vladimir Nunez .50 .20
❑ 332 John Halama RC 1.00 .40
❑ 333 Nerio Rodriguez .50 .20
❑ 334 Desi Relaford .50 .20
❑ 335 Robinson Checo .50 .20
❑ 336 John Nicholson .75 .30
❑ 337 Tom LaRosa RC 1.00 .40
❑ 338 Kevin Nicholson RC 1.00 .40
❑ 339 Javier Vazquez .50 .20
❑ 340 A.J. Zapp .50 .20
❑ 341 Tom Evans .50 .20
❑ 342 Kerry Robinson .50 .20
❑ 343 Gabe Gonzalez RC 1.00 .40
❑ 344 Ralph Milliard .50 .20
❑ 345 Enrique Wilson .50 .20
❑ 346 Elvin Hernandez .50 .20
❑ 347 Mike Lincoln RC 1.00 .40
❑ 348 Cesar King RC 1.00 .40
❑ 349 Cristian Guzman RC 1.50 .60
❑ 350 Donzell McDonald .50 .20
❑ 351 Jim Parque RC 1.00 .40
❑ 352 Mike Saipe RC 1.00 .40
❑ 353 Carlos Febles RC 1.50 .60
❑ 354 Dernell Stenson RC 1.00 .40
❑ 355 Mark Osborne RC 1.00 .40
❑ 356 Odalis Perez RC 4.00 1.50
❑ 357 Jason Dewey RC 1.00 .40
❑ 358 Joe Fontenot .50 .20
❑ 359 Jason Grilli RC 1.00 .40
❑ 360 Kevin Haverbusch RC 1.00 .40
❑ 361 Jay Yennaco RC 1.00 .40
❑ 362 Brian Buchanan .50 .20
❑ 363 John Barnes .50 .20
❑ 364 Chris Fussell .50 .20
❑ 365 Kevin Gibbs RC 1.00 .40
❑ 366 Joe Lawrence .50 .20
❑ 367 DaRond Stovall .50 .20
❑ 368 Brian Fuentes RC 1.00 .40
❑ 369 Jimmy Anderson .50 .20
❑ 370 Lariel Gonzalez RC 1.00 .40
❑ 371 Scott Williamson RC 1.00 .40
❑ 372 Milton Bradley .50 .20
❑ 373 Jason Halper RC 1.00 .40
❑ 374 Brent Billingsley RC 1.00 .40
❑ 375 Joe DePastino RC 1.00 .40
❑ 376 Jake Westbrook .50 .20
❑ 377 Octavio Dotel .50 .20
❑ 378 Jason Williams RC 1.00 .40
❑ 379 Julio Ramirez RC 1.00 .40
❑ 380 Seth Greisinger .50 .20
❑ 381 Mike Judd RC 1.00 .40
❑ 382 Ben Ford RC 1.00 .40
❑ 383 Tom Bennett RC 1.00 .40
❑ 384 Adam Butler RC 1.00 .40
❑ 385 Wade Miller RC 2.50 1.00
❑ 386 Kyle Peterson RC 1.00 .40
❑ 387 Tommy Peterman RC 1.00 .40
❑ 388 Onan Masaoka .50 .20
❑ 389 Jason Rakers RC 1.00 .40
❑ 390 Rafael Medina .50 .20
❑ 391 Luis Lopez RC 1.00 .40
❑ 392 Jeff Yoder .50 .20
❑ 393 Vance Wilson RC 1.00 .40
❑ 394 Fernando Seguignol RC 1.00 .40
❑ 395 Ron Wright .50 .20
❑ 396 Ruben Mateo RC 1.00 .40
❑ 397 Steve Lomasney RC 1.50 .60
❑ 398 Damian Jackson .50 .20
❑ 399 Mike Jerzembeck RC 1.00 .40
❑ 400 Luis Rivas RC 2.50 1.00
❑ 401 Kevin Burford RC 1.00 .40
❑ 402 Glenn Davis .50 .20
❑ 403 Robert Luce RC 1.00 .40
❑ 404 Cole Liniak .50 .20
❑ 405 Matt LeCroy RC 1.50 .60
❑ 406 Jeremy Giambi RC 1.50 .60
❑ 407 Shawn Chacon .50 .20
❑ 408 Dewayne Wise RC 1.00 .40
❑ 409 Steve Woodard .50 .20
❑ 410 Francisco Cordero RC 2.50 1.00
❑ 411 Damon Minor RC 1.00 .40
❑ 412 Lou Collier .50 .20
❑ 413 Justin Towle .50 .20
❑ 414 Juan LeBron .50 .20
❑ 415 Michael Coleman .50 .20
❑ 416 Felix Rodriguez .50 .20
❑ 417 Paul Ah Yat RC 1.00 .40
❑ 418 Kevin Barker RC 1.00 .40
❑ 419 Brian Meadows .50 .20
❑ 420 Darnell McDonald RC 1.00 .40
❑ 421 Matt Kinney RC 1.00 .40
❑ 422 Mike Vavrek RC 1.00 .40
❑ 423 Courtney Duncan RC 1.00 .40
❑ 424 Kevin Millar RC 4.00 1.50
❑ 425 Ruben Rivera .50 .20
❑ 426 Steve Shoemaker RC 1.00 .40
❑ 427 Dan Reichert RC 1.00 .40
❑ 428 Carlos Lee RC 6.00 2.50
❑ 429 Rod Barajas 2.50 1.00
❑ 430 Pablo Ozuna RC 1.50 .60
❑ 431 Todd Belitz RC 1.00 .40
❑ 432 Sidney Ponson .50 .20
❑ 433 Steve Carver RC 1.00 .40
❑ 434 Esteban Yan RC 1.50 .60
❑ 435 Cedrick Bowers .50 .20
❑ 436 Marlon Anderson .50 .20
❑ 437 Carl Pavano .50 .20
❑ 438 Jae Weong Seo RC 1.50 .60
❑ 439 Jose Taveras RC 1.00 .40
❑ 440 Matt Anderson RC 1.00 .40
❑ 441 Darron Ingram RC 1.00 .40

1999 Bowman Chrome

❑ COMPLETE SET (440) 200.00 100.00
❑ COMPLETE SERIES 1 (220) 80.00 40.00
❑ COMPLETE SERIES 2 (220) 120.00 60.00
❑ 1 Ben Grieve .50 .20
❑ 2 Kerry Wood .50 .20
❑ 3 Ruben Rivera .50 .20
❑ 4 Sandy Alomar Jr. .50 .20
❑ 5 Cal Ripken 4.00 1.50
❑ 6 Mark McGwire 3.00 1.25
❑ 7 Vladimir Guerrero 1.25 .50

❑	8	Moises Alou	.50	.20
❑	9	Jim Edmonds	.50	.20
❑	10	Greg Maddux	2.00	.75
❑	11	Gary Sheffield	.50	.20
❑	12	John Valentin	.50	.20
❑	13	Chuck Knoblauch	.50	.20
❑	14	Tony Clark	.50	.20
❑	15	Rusty Greer	.50	.20
❑	16	Al Leiter	.50	.20
❑	17	Travis Lee	.50	.20
❑	18	Jose Cruz Jr.	.50	.20
❑	19	Pedro Martinez	.75	.30
❑	20	Paul O'Neill	.75	.30
❑	21	Todd Walker	.50	.20
❑	22	Vinny Castilla	.50	.20
❑	23	Barry Larkin	.75	.30
❑	24	Curt Schilling	.50	.20
❑	25	Jason Kendall	.50	.20
❑	26	Scott Erickson	.50	.20
❑	27	Andres Galarraga	.50	.20
❑	28	Jeff Shaw	.50	.20
❑	29	John Olerud	.50	.20
❑	30	Orlando Hernandez	.50	.20
❑	31	Larry Walker	.50	.20
❑	32	Andruw Jones	.75	.30
❑	33	Jeff Cirillo	.50	.20
❑	34	Barry Bonds	3.00	1.25
❑	35	Manny Ramirez	.75	.30
❑	36	Mark Kotsay	.50	.20
❑	37	Ivan Rodriguez	.75	.30
❑	38	Jeff King	.50	.20
❑	39	Brian Hunter	.50	.20
❑	40	Ray Durham	.50	.20
❑	41	Bernie Williams	.75	.30
❑	42	Darin Erstad	.50	.20
❑	43	Chipper Jones	1.25	.50
❑	44	Pat Hentgen	.50	.20
❑	45	Eric Young	.50	.20
❑	46	Jaret Wright	.50	.20
❑	47	Juan Guzman	.50	.20
❑	48	Jorge Posada	.75	.30
❑	49	Bobby Higginson	.50	.20
❑	50	Jose Guillen	.50	.20
❑	51	Trevor Hoffman	.50	.20
❑	52	Ken Griffey Jr.	2.00	.75
❑	53	David Justice	.50	.20
❑	54	Matt Williams	.50	.20
❑	55	Eric Karros	.50	.20
❑	56	Derek Bell	.50	.20
❑	57	Ray Lankford	.50	.20
❑	58	Mariano Rivera	1.25	.50
❑	59	Brett Tomko	.50	.20
❑	60	Mike Mussina	.75	.30
❑	61	Kenny Lofton	.50	.20
❑	62	Chuck Finley	.50	.20
❑	63	Alex Gonzalez	.50	.20
❑	64	Mark Grace	.75	.30
❑	65	Raul Mondesi	.50	.20
❑	66	David Cone	.50	.20
❑	67	Brad Fullmer	.50	.20
❑	68	Andy Benes	.50	.20
❑	69	John Smoltz	.75	.30
❑	70	Shane Reynolds	.50	.20
❑	71	Bruce Chen	.50	.20
❑	72	Adam Kennedy	.50	.20
❑	73	Jack Cust	.50	.20
❑	74	Matt Clement	.50	.20
❑	75	Derrick Gibson	.50	.20
❑	76	Darnell McDonald	.50	.20
❑	77	Adam Everett RC	2.50	1.00
❑	78	Ricardo Aramboles	.50	.20
❑	79	Mark Quinn RC	1.00	.40
❑	80	Jason Rakers	.50	.20
❑	81	Seth Etherton RC	1.00	.40
❑	82	Jeff Urban RC	1.00	.40
❑	83	Manny Aybar	.50	.20
❑	84	Mike Nannini RC	1.00	.40
❑	85	Onan Masaoka	.50	.20
❑	86	Rod Barajas	.50	.20
❑	87	Mike Frank	.50	.20
❑	88	Scott Randall	.50	.20
❑	89	Justin Bowles RC	1.00	.40
❑	90	Chris Haas	.50	.20
❑	91	Arturo McDowell RC	1.00	.40
❑	92	Matt Belisle RC	1.00	.40
❑	93	Scott Elarton	.50	.20
❑	94	Vernon Wells	.50	.20
❑	95	Pat Cline	.50	.20
❑	96	Ryan Anderson	.50	.20
❑	97	Kevin Barker	.50	.20
❑	98	Ruben Mateo	.50	.20
❑	99	Robert Fick	.50	.20
❑	100	Corey Koskie	.50	.20
❑	101	Ricky Ledee	.50	.20
❑	102	Rick Elder RC	1.00	.40
❑	103	Jack Cressend RC	1.00	.40
❑	104	Joe Lawrence	.50	.20
❑	105	Mike Lincoln	.50	.20
❑	106	Kit Pellow RC	1.00	.40
❑	107	Matt Burch RC	1.00	.40
❑	108	Cole Liniak	.50	.20
❑	109	Jason Dewey	.50	.20
❑	110	Cesar King	.50	.20
❑	111	Julio Ramirez	.50	.20
❑	112	Jake Westbrook	.50	.20
❑	113	Eric Valent RC	1.50	.60
❑	114	Roosevelt Brown RC	1.00	.40
❑	115	Choo Freeman RC	1.50	.60
❑	116	Juan Melo	.50	.20
❑	117	Jason Grilli	.50	.20
❑	118	Jared Sandberg	.50	.20
❑	119	Glenn Davis	.50	.20
❑	120	David Riske RC	1.00	.40
❑	121	Jacque Jones	.50	.20
❑	122	Corey Lee	.50	.20
❑	123	Michael Barrett	.50	.20
❑	124	Lariel Gonzalez	.50	.20
❑	125	Mitch Meluskey	.50	.20
❑	126	F.Adrian Garcia	.50	.20
❑	127	Tony Torcato RC	1.00	.40
❑	128	Jeff Liefer	.50	.20
❑	129	Ntema Ndungidi	.50	.20
❑	130	Andy Brown RC	1.00	.40
❑	131	Ryan Mills RC	1.00	.40
❑	132	Andy Abad RC	1.00	.40
❑	133	Carlos Febles	.50	.20
❑	134	Jason Tyner RC	1.00	.40
❑	135	Mark Osborne	.50	.20
❑	136	Phil Norton RC	1.00	.40
❑	137	Nathan Haynes	.50	.20
❑	138	Roy Halladay	.50	.20
❑	139	Juan Encarnacion	.50	.20
❑	140	Brad Penny	.50	.20
❑	141	Grant Roberts	.50	.20
❑	142	Aramis Ramirez	.50	.20
❑	143	Cristian Guzman	.50	.20
❑	144	Mamon Tucker RC	1.00	.40
❑	145	Ryan Bradley	.50	.20
❑	146	Brian Simmons	.50	.20
❑	147	Dan Reichert	.50	.20
❑	148	Russell Branyan	.50	.20
❑	149	Victor Valencia RC	1.00	.40
❑	150	Scott Schoeneweis	.50	.20
❑	151	Sean Spencer RC	1.00	.40
❑	152	Odalis Perez	.50	.20
❑	153	Joe Fontenot	.50	.20
❑	154	Milton Bradley	.50	.20
❑	155	Josh McKinley RC	1.00	.40
❑	156	Terrence Long	.50	.20
❑	157	Danny Klassen	.50	.20
❑	158	Paul Hoover RC	1.00	.40
❑	159	Ron Belliard	.50	.20
❑	160	Armando Rios	.50	.20
❑	161	Ramon Hernandez	.50	.20
❑	162	Jason Conti	.50	.20
❑	163	Chad Hermansen	.50	.20
❑	164	Jason Standridge	.50	.20
❑	165	Jason Dellaero	.50	.20
❑	166	John Curtice	.50	.20
❑	167	Clayton Andrews RC	1.00	.40
❑	168	Jeremy Giambi	.50	.20
❑	169	Alex Ramirez	.50	.20
❑	170	Gabe Molina RC	1.00	.40
❑	171	Mario Encarnacion RC	1.00	.40
❑	172	Mike Zywica RC	1.00	.40
❑	173	Chip Ambres RC	1.00	.40
❑	174	Trot Nixon	.50	.20
❑	175	Pat Burrell RC	8.00	3.00
❑	176	Jeff Yoder	.50	.20
❑	177	Chris Jones RC	1.00	.40
❑	178	Kevin Witt	.50	.20
❑	179	Keith Luuloa RC	1.00	.40
❑	180	Billy Koch	.50	.20
❑	181	Damaso Marte RC	1.00	.40
❑	182	Ryan Glynn RC	1.00	.40
❑	183	Calvin Pickering	.50	.20
❑	184	Michael Cuddyer	.50	.20
❑	185	Nick Johnson RC	5.00	2.00
❑	186	Doug Mientkiewicz RC	2.50	1.00
❑	187	Nate Cornejo RC	1.00	.40
❑	188	Octavio Dotel	.50	.20
❑	189	Wes Helms	.50	.20
❑	190	Nelson Lara	.50	.20
❑	191	Chuck Abbott RC	1.00	.40
❑	192	Tony Armas Jr.	.50	.20
❑	193	Gil Meche	.50	.20
❑	194	Ben Petrick	.50	.20
❑	195	Chris George RC	1.00	.40
❑	196	Scott Hunter RC	1.00	.40
❑	197	Ryan Brannan	.50	.20
❑	198	Amaury Garcia RC	1.00	.40
❑	199	Chris Gissell	.50	.20
❑	200	Austin Kearns RC	8.00	3.00
❑	201	Alex Gonzalez	.50	.20
❑	202	Wade Miller	.50	.20
❑	203	Scott Williamson	.50	.20
❑	204	Chris Enochs	.50	.20
❑	205	Fernando Seguignol	.50	.20
❑	206	Marlon Anderson	.50	.20
❑	207	Todd Sears RC	1.00	.40
❑	208	Nate Bump RC	1.00	.40
❑	209	J.M. Gold RC	1.00	.40
❑	210	Matt LeCroy	.50	.20
❑	211	Alex Hernandez	.50	.20
❑	212	Luis Rivera	.50	.20
❑	213	Troy Cameron	.50	.20
❑	214	Alex Escobar RC	1.50	.60
❑	215	Jason LaRue	.50	.20
❑	216	Kyle Peterson	.50	.20
❑	217	Brent Butler	.50	.20
❑	218	Dernell Stenson	.50	.20
❑	219	Adrian Beltre	.50	.20
❑	220	Daryle Ward	.50	.20
❑	221	Jim Thome	.75	.30
❑	222	Cliff Floyd	.50	.20
❑	223	Rickey Henderson	1.25	.50
❑	224	Garret Anderson	.50	.20
❑	225	Ken Caminiti	.50	.20
❑	226	Bret Boone	.50	.20
❑	227	Jeromy Burnitz	.50	.20
❑	228	Steve Finley	.50	.20
❑	229	Miguel Tejada	.50	.20
❑	230	Greg Vaughn	.50	.20
❑	231	Jose Offerman	.50	.20
❑	232	Andy Ashby	.50	.20
❑	233	Albert Belle	.50	.20
❑	234	Fernando Tatis	.50	.20
❑	235	Todd Helton	.75	.30
❑	236	Sean Casey	.50	.20
❑	237	Brian Giles	.50	.20
❑	238	Andy Pettitte	.75	.30
❑	239	Fred McGriff	.75	.30
❑	240	Roberto Alomar	.75	.30
❑	241	Edgar Martinez	.75	.30
❑	242	Lee Stevens	.50	.20
❑	243	Shawn Green	.50	.20
❑	244	Ryan Klesko	.50	.20
❑	245	Sammy Sosa	1.25	.50
❑	246	Todd Hundley	.50	.20
❑	247	Shannon Stewart	.50	.20

248	Randy Johnson	1.25	.50
249	Rondell White	.50	.20
250	Mike Piazza	2.00	.75
251	Craig Biggio	.75	.30
252	David Wells	.50	.20
253	Brian Jordan	.50	.20
254	Edgar Renteria	.50	.20
255	Bartolo Colon	.50	.20
256	Frank Thomas	1.25	.50
257	Will Clark	.75	.30
258	Dean Palmer	.50	.20
259	Dmitri Young	.50	.20
260	Scott Rolen	.75	.30
261	Jeff Kent	.50	.20
262	Dante Bichette	.50	.20
263	Nomar Garciaparra	2.00	.75
264	Tony Gwynn	1.50	.60
265	Alex Rodriguez	2.00	.75
266	Jose Canseco	.75	.30
267	Jason Giambi	.50	.20
268	Jeff Bagwell	.75	.30
269	Carlos Delgado	.50	.20
270	Tom Glavine	.75	.30
271	Eric Davis	.50	.20
272	Edgardo Alfonzo	.50	.20
273	Tim Salmon	.75	.30
274	Johnny Damon	.75	.30
275	Rafael Palmeiro	.75	.30
276	Denny Neagle	.50	.20
277	Neifi Perez	.50	.20
278	Roger Clemens	2.50	1.00
279	Brant Brown	.50	.20
280	Kevin Brown	.75	.30
281	Jay Bell	.50	.20
282	Jay Buhner	.50	.20
283	Matt Lawton	.50	.20
284	Robin Ventura	.50	.20
285	Juan Gonzalez	.50	.20
286	Mo Vaughn	.50	.20
287	Kevin Millwood	.50	.20
288	Tino Martinez	.75	.30
289	Justin Thompson	.50	.20
290	Derek Jeter	3.00	1.25
291	Ben Davis	.50	.20
292	Mike Lowell	.50	.20
293	Calvin Murray	.50	.20
294	Micah Bowie RC	1.00	.40
295	Lance Berkman	.50	.20
296	Jason Marquis	.50	.20
297	Chad Green	.50	.20
298	Dee Brown	.50	.20
299	Jerry Hairston Jr.	.50	.20
300	Gabe Kapler	.50	.20
301	Brent Stentz RC	1.00	.40
302	Scott Mullen RC	1.00	.40
303	Brandon Reed	.50	.20
304	Shea Hillenbrand RC	4.00	1.50
305	J.D. Closser RC	1.50	.60
306	Gary Matthews Jr.	.50	.20
307	Toby Hall RC	1.50	.60
308	Jason Phillips RC	1.00	.40
309	Jose Macias RC	1.00	.40
310	Jung Bong RC	1.00	.40
311	Ramon Soler RC	1.00	.40
312	Kelly Dransfeldt RC	1.00	.40
313	Carlos E. Hernandez RC	1.50	.60
314	Kevin Haverbusch	.50	.20
315	Aaron Myette RC	1.00	.40
316	Chad Harville RC	1.00	.40
317	Kyle Farnsworth RC	1.50	.60
318	Gookie Dawkins RC	1.50	.60
319	Willie Martinez	.50	.20
320	Carlos Lee	.50	.20
321	Carlos Pena RC	3.00	1.25
322	Peter Bergeron RC	1.00	.40
323	A.J. Burnett RC	4.00	1.50
324	Bucky Jacobsen RC	1.50	.60
325	Mo Bruce RC	1.00	.40
326	Reggie Taylor	.50	.20
327	Jackie Rexrode	.50	.20
328	Alvin Morrow RC	1.00	.40
329	Carlos Beltran	.75	.30
330	Eric Chavez	.50	.20
331	John Patterson	.50	.20
332	Jayson Werth	.50	.20
333	Richie Sexson	.50	.20
334	Randy Wolf	.50	.20
335	Eli Marrero	.50	.20
336	Paul LoDuca	.50	.20
337	J.D Smart	.50	.20
338	Ryan Minor	.50	.20
339	Kris Benson	.50	.20
340	George Lombard	.50	.20
341	Troy Glaus	.75	.30
342	Eddie Yarnall	.50	.20
343	Kip Wells RC	1.50	.60
344	C.C. Sabathia RC	10.00	4.00
345	Sean Burroughs RC	2.50	1.00
346	Felipe Lopez RC	6.00	2.50
347	Ryan Rupe RC	1.00	.40
348	Orber Moreno RC	1.00	.40
349	Rafael Roque RC	1.00	.40
350	Alfonso Soriano RC	12.00	5.00
351	Pablo Ozuna	.50	.20
352	Corey Patterson RC	4.00	1.50
353	Braden Looper	.50	.20
354	Robbie Bell	.50	.20
355	Mark Mulder RC	6.00	2.50
356	Angel Pena	.50	.20
357	Kevin McGlinchy	.50	.20
358	Michael Restovich RC	1.50	.60
359	Eric DuBose	.50	.20
360	Geoff Jenkins	.50	.20
361	Mark Harriger RC	1.00	.40
362	Junior Herndon RC	1.00	.40
363	Tim Raines Jr. RC	1.00	.40
364	Rafael Furcal RC	6.00	2.50
365	Marcus Giles RC	4.00	1.50
366	Ted Lilly	.50	.20
367	Jorge Toca RC	1.50	.60
368	David Kelton RC	1.00	.40
369	Adam Dunn RC	12.00	5.00
370	Guillermo Mota RC	1.00	.40
371	Brett Laxton RC	1.00	.40
372	Travis Harper RC	1.00	.40
373	Tom Davey RC	1.00	.40
374	Darren Blakely RC	1.00	.40
375	Tim Hudson RC	8.00	3.00
376	Jason Romano	.50	.20
377	Dan Reichert	.50	.20
378	Julio Lugo RC	2.50	1.00
379	Jose Garcia RC	1.00	.40
380	Erubiel Durazo RC	1.50	.60
381	Jose Jimenez	.50	.20
382	Chris Fussell	.50	.20
383	Steve Lomasney	.50	.20
384	Juan Pena RC	1.00	.40
385	Allen Levrault RC	1.00	.40
386	Juan Rivera RC	4.00	1.50
387	Steve Colyer RC	1.00	.40
388	Joe Nathan RC	5.00	2.00
389	Ron Walker RC	1.00	.40
390	Nick Bierbrodt	.50	.20
391	Luke Prokopec RC	1.00	.40
392	Dave Roberts RC	2.50	1.00
393	Mike Darr	.50	.20
394	Abraham Nunez RC	1.50	.60
395	Giuseppe Chiaramonte RC	1.00	.40
396	Jermaine Van Buren RC	1.00	.40
397	Mike Kusiewicz	.50	.20
398	Matt Wise RC	1.00	.40
399	Joe McEwing RC	1.50	.60
400	Matt Holliday RC	12.00	5.00
401	Willi Mo Pena RC	12.00	5.00
402	Ruben Quevedo RC	1.00	.40
403	Rob Ryan RC	1.00	.40
404	Freddy Garcia RC	4.00	1.50
405	Kevin Eberwein RC	1.00	.40
406	Jesus Colome RC	1.00	.40
407	Chris Singleton	.50	.20
408	Bubba Crosby RC	2.50	1.00
409	Jesus Cordero RC	1.00	.40
410	Donny Leon	.50	.20
411	Goefrey Tomlinson RC	1.00	.40
412	Jeff Winchester RC	1.00	.40
413	Adam Piatt RC	1.00	.40
414	Robert Stratton	.50	.20
415	T.J. Tucker	.50	.20
416	Ryan Langerhans RC	2.50	1.00
417	Anthony Shumaker RC	1.00	.40
418	Matt Miller RC	1.00	.40
419	Doug Clark RC	1.00	.40
420	Kory DeHaan RC	1.00	.40
421	David Eckstein RC	8.00	3.00
422	Brian Cooper RC	1.00	.40
423	Brady Clark RC	4.00	1.50
424	Chris Magruder RC	1.00	.40
425	Bobby Seay RC	1.00	.40
426	Aubrey Huff RC	5.00	2.00
427	Mike Jerzembeck	.50	.20
428	Matt Blank RC	1.00	.40
429	Benny Agbayani RC	1.50	.60
430	Kevin Beirne RC	1.00	.40
431	Josh Hamilton RC	30.00	12.50
432	Josh Girdley RC	1.00	.40
433	Kyle Snyder RC	1.00	.40
434	Mike Paradis RC	1.00	.40
435	Jason Jennings RC	2.50	1.00
436	David Walling RC	1.00	.40
437	Omar Ortiz RC	1.00	.40
438	Jay Gehrke RC	1.50	.60
439	Casey Burns RC	1.00	.40
440	Carl Crawford RC	15.00	6.00

2000 Bowman Chrome

	COMPLETE SET (440)	120.00	60.00
1	Vladimir Guerrero	1.25	.50
2	Chipper Jones	1.25	.50
3	Todd Walker	.50	.20
4	Barry Larkin	.75	.30
5	Bernie Williams	.75	.30
6	Todd Helton	.75	.30
7	Jermaine Dye	.50	.20
8	Brian Giles	.50	.20
9	Freddy Garcia	.50	.20
10	Greg Vaughn	.50	.20
11	Alex Gonzalez	.50	.20
12	Luis Gonzalez	.50	.20
13	Ron Belliard	.50	.20
14	Ben Grieve	.50	.20
15	Carlos Delgado	.50	.20
16	Brian Jordan	.50	.20
17	Fernando Tatis	.50	.20
18	Ryan Rupe	.50	.20
19	Miguel Tejada	.50	.20
20	Mark Grace	.75	.30
21	Kenny Lofton	.50	.20
22	Eric Karros	.50	.20
23	Cliff Floyd	.50	.20
24	John Halama	.50	.20
25	Cristian Guzman	.50	.20
26	Scott Williamson	.50	.20
27	Mike Lieberthal	.50	.20
28	Tim Hudson	.50	.20
29	Warren Morris	.50	.20
30	Pedro Martinez	.75	.30
31	John Smoltz	.75	.30
32	Ray Durham	.50	.20
33	Chad Allen	.50	.20
34	Tony Clark	.50	.20
35	Tino Martinez	.75	.30
36	J.T. Snow	.50	.20
37	Kevin Brown	.75	.30
38	Bartolo Colon	.50	.20
39	Rey Ordonez	.50	.20
40	Jeff Bagwell	.75	.30
41	Ivan Rodriguez	.75	.30
42	Eric Chavez	.50	.20
43	Eric Milton	.50	.20
44	Jose Canseco	.75	.30

❑ 45	Shawn Green	.50	.20
❑ 46	Rich Aurilia	.50	.20
❑ 47	Roberto Alomar	.75	.30
❑ 48	Brian Daubach	.50	.20
❑ 49	Magglio Ordonez	.50	.20
❑ 50	Derek Jeter	3.00	1.25
❑ 51	Kris Benson	.50	.20
❑ 52	Albert Belle	.50	.20
❑ 53	Rondell White	.50	.20
❑ 54	Justin Thompson	.50	.20
❑ 55	Nomar Garciaparra	2.00	.75
❑ 56	Chuck Finley	.50	.20
❑ 57	Omar Vizquel	.75	.30
❑ 58	Luis Castillo	.50	.20
❑ 59	Richard Hidalgo	.50	.20
❑ 60	Barry Bonds	3.00	1.25
❑ 61	Craig Biggio	.75	.30
❑ 62	Doug Glanville	.50	.20
❑ 63	Gabe Kapler	.50	.20
❑ 64	Johnny Damon	.75	.30
❑ 65	Pokey Reese	.50	.20
❑ 66	Andy Pettitte	.75	.30
❑ 67	B.J. Surhoff	.50	.20
❑ 68	Richie Sexson	.50	.20
❑ 69	Javy Lopez	.50	.20
❑ 70	Raul Mondesi	.50	.20
❑ 71	Darin Erstad	.50	.20
❑ 72	Kevin Millwood	.50	.20
❑ 73	Ricky Ledee	.50	.20
❑ 74	John Olerud	.50	.20
❑ 75	Sean Casey	.50	.20
❑ 76	Carlos Febles	.50	.20
❑ 77	Paul O'Neill	.75	.30
❑ 78	Bob Abreu	.50	.20
❑ 79	Neifi Perez	.50	.20
❑ 80	Tony Gwynn	1.50	.60
❑ 81	Russ Ortiz	.50	.20
❑ 82	Matt Williams	.50	.20
❑ 83	Chris Carpenter	.50	.20
❑ 84	Roger Cedeno	.50	.20
❑ 85	Tim Salmon	.75	.30
❑ 86	Billy Koch	.50	.20
❑ 87	Jeromy Burnitz	.50	.20
❑ 88	Edgardo Alfonzo	.50	.20
❑ 89	Jay Bell	.50	.20
❑ 90	Manny Ramirez	.75	.30
❑ 91	Frank Thomas	1.25	.50
❑ 92	Mike Mussina	.75	.30
❑ 93	J.D. Drew	.50	.20
❑ 94	Adrian Beltre	.50	.20
❑ 95	Alex Rodriguez	2.00	.75
❑ 96	Larry Walker	.50	.20
❑ 97	Juan Encarnacion	.50	.20
❑ 98	Mike Sweeney	.50	.20
❑ 99	Rusty Greer	.50	.20
❑ 100	Randy Johnson	1.25	.50
❑ 101	Jose Vidro	.50	.20
❑ 102	Preston Wilson	.50	.20
❑ 103	Greg Maddux	2.00	.75
❑ 104	Jason Giambi	.50	.20
❑ 105	Cal Ripken	4.00	1.50
❑ 106	Carlos Beltran	.50	.20
❑ 107	Vinny Castilla	.50	.20
❑ 108	Mariano Rivera	1.25	.50
❑ 109	Mo Vaughn	.50	.20
❑ 110	Rafael Palmeiro	.75	.30
❑ 111	Shannon Stewart	.50	.20
❑ 112	Mike Hampton	.50	.20
❑ 113	Joe Nathan	.50	.20
❑ 114	Ben Davis	.50	.20
❑ 115	Andruw Jones	.75	.30
❑ 116	Robin Ventura	.50	.20
❑ 117	Damion Easley	.50	.20
❑ 118	Jeff Cirillo	.50	.20
❑ 119	Kerry Wood	.50	.20
❑ 120	Scott Rolen	.75	.30
❑ 121	Sammy Sosa	1.25	.50
❑ 122	Ken Griffey Jr.	2.00	.75
❑ 123	Shane Reynolds	.50	.20
❑ 124	Troy Glaus	.50	.20
❑ 125	Tom Glavine	.75	.30
❑ 126	Michael Barrett	.50	.20
❑ 127	Al Leiter	.50	.20
❑ 128	Jason Kendall	.50	.20
❑ 129	Roger Clemens	2.50	1.00
❑ 130	Juan Gonzalez	.50	.20
❑ 131	Corey Koskie	.50	.20
❑ 132	Curt Schilling	.50	.20
❑ 133	Mike Piazza	2.00	.75
❑ 134	Gary Sheffield	.50	.20
❑ 135	Jim Thome	.75	.30
❑ 136	Orlando Hernandez	.50	.20
❑ 137	Ray Lankford	.50	.20
❑ 138	Geoff Jenkins	.50	.20
❑ 139	Jose Lima	.50	.20
❑ 140	Mark McGwire	3.00	1.25
❑ 141	Adam Piatt	.50	.20
❑ 142	Pat Manning RC	.75	.30
❑ 143	Marcos Castillo RC	.75	.30
❑ 144	Lesli Brea RC	.75	.30
❑ 145	Humberto Cota RC	1.25	.50
❑ 146	Ben Petrick	.50	.20
❑ 147	Kip Wells	.50	.20
❑ 148	Wily Pena	.50	.20
❑ 149	Chris Wakeland RC	.75	.30
❑ 150	Brad Baker RC	.75	.30
❑ 151	Robbie Morrison RC	.75	.30
❑ 152	Reggie Taylor	.50	.20
❑ 153	Matt Ginter RC	.75	.30
❑ 154	Peter Bergeron	.50	.20
❑ 155	Roosevelt Brown	.50	.20
❑ 156	Matt Cepicky RC	.75	.30
❑ 157	Ramon Castro	.50	.20
❑ 158	Brad Baisley RC	.75	.30
❑ 159	Jason Hart RC	.75	.30
❑ 160	Mitch Meluskey	.50	.20
❑ 161	Chad Harville	.50	.20
❑ 162	Brian Cooper	.50	.20
❑ 163	Marcus Giles	.50	.20
❑ 164	Jim Morris	1.25	.50
❑ 165	Geoff Goetz	.50	.20
❑ 166	Bobby Bradley RC	.75	.30
❑ 167	Rob Bell	.50	.20
❑ 168	Joe Crede	2.50	1.00
❑ 169	Michael Restovich	.50	.20
❑ 170	Quincy Foster RC	.75	.30
❑ 171	Enrique Cruz RC	.75	.30
❑ 172	Mark Quinn	.50	.20
❑ 173	Nick Johnson	.50	.20
❑ 174	Jeff Liefer	.50	.20
❑ 175	Kevin Mench RC	5.00	2.00
❑ 176	Steve Lomasney	.50	.20
❑ 177	Jayson Werth	.50	.20
❑ 178	Tim Drew	.50	.20
❑ 179	Chip Ambres	.50	.20
❑ 180	Ryan Anderson	.50	.20
❑ 181	Matt Blank	.50	.20
❑ 182	Giuseppe Chiaramonte	.50	.20
❑ 183	Corey Myers RC	.75	.30
❑ 184	Jeff Yoder	.50	.20
❑ 185	Craig Dingman RC	.75	.30
❑ 186	Jon Hamilton RC	.75	.30
❑ 187	Toby Hall	.50	.20
❑ 188	Russell Branyan	.50	.20
❑ 189	Brian Falkenborg RC	.75	.30
❑ 190	Aaron Harang RC	5.00	2.00
❑ 191	Juan Pena	.50	.20
❑ 192	Chin-Hui Tsao RC	5.00	2.00
❑ 193	Alfonso Soriano	1.25	.50
❑ 194	Alejandro Diaz RC	.75	.30
❑ 195	Carlos Pena	.50	.20
❑ 196	Kevin Nicholson	.50	.20
❑ 197	Mo Bruce	.50	.20
❑ 198	C.C. Sabathia	.50	.20
❑ 199	Carl Crawford	.50	.20
❑ 200	Rafael Furcal	.50	.20
❑ 201	Andrew Beinbrink RC	.75	.30
❑ 202	Jimmy Osting	.50	.20
❑ 203	Aaron McNeal RC	.75	.30
❑ 204	Brett Laxton	.50	.20
❑ 205	Chris George	.50	.20
❑ 206	Felipe Lopez	.50	.20
❑ 207	Ben Sheets RC	6.00	2.50
❑ 208	Mike Meyers RC	1.25	.50
❑ 209	Jason Conti	.50	.20
❑ 210	Milton Bradley	.50	.20
❑ 211	Chris Mears RC	.75	.30
❑ 212	Carlos Hernandez RC	1.25	.50
❑ 213	Jason Romano	.50	.20
❑ 214	Geofrey Tomlinson	.50	.20
❑ 215	Jimmy Rollins	.50	.20
❑ 216	Pablo Ozuna	.50	.20
❑ 217	Steve Cox	.50	.20
❑ 218	Terrence Long	.50	.20
❑ 219	Jeff DaVanon RC	1.25	.50
❑ 220	Rick Ankiel	.50	.20
❑ 221	Jason Standridge	.50	.20
❑ 222	Tony Armas Jr.	.50	.20
❑ 223	Jason Tyner	.50	.20
❑ 224	Ramon Ortiz	.50	.20
❑ 225	Daryle Ward	.50	.20
❑ 226	Enger Veras RC	.75	.30
❑ 227	Chris Jones	.50	.20
❑ 228	Eric Cammack RC	.75	.30
❑ 229	Ruben Mateo	.50	.20
❑ 230	Ken Harvey RC	1.25	.50
❑ 231	Jake Westbrook	.50	.20
❑ 232	Rob Purvis RC	.75	.30
❑ 233	Choo Freeman	.50	.20
❑ 234	Aramis Ramirez	.50	.20
❑ 235	A.J. Burnett	.50	.20
❑ 236	Kevin Barker	.50	.20
❑ 237	Chance Caple RC	.75	.30
❑ 238	Jarrod Washburn	.50	.20
❑ 239	Lance Berkman	.50	.20
❑ 240	Michael Wenner RC	.75	.30
❑ 241	Alex Sanchez	.50	.20
❑ 242	Pat Daneker	.50	.20
❑ 243	Grant Roberts	.50	.20
❑ 244	Mark Ellis RC	1.25	.50
❑ 245	Donny Leon	.50	.20
❑ 246	David Eckstein	.50	.20
❑ 247	Dicky Gonzalez RC	.75	.30
❑ 248	John Patterson	.50	.20
❑ 249	Chad Green	.50	.20
❑ 250	Scot Shields RC	.75	.30
❑ 251	Troy Cameron	.50	.20
❑ 252	Jose Molina	.50	.20
❑ 253	Rob Pugmire RC	.75	.30
❑ 254	Rick Elder	.50	.20
❑ 255	Sean Burroughs	.50	.20
❑ 256	Josh Kalinowski RC	.75	.30
❑ 257	Matt LeCroy	.50	.20
❑ 258	Alex Graman RC	.75	.30
❑ 259	Juan Silvestre RC	.75	.30
❑ 260	Brady Clark	.50	.20
❑ 261	Rico Washington RC	.75	.30
❑ 262	Gary Matthews Jr.	.50	.20
❑ 263	Matt Wise	.50	.20
❑ 264	Keith Reed RC	.75	.30
❑ 265	Santiago Ramirez RC	.75	.30
❑ 266	Ben Broussard RC	3.00	1.25
❑ 267	Ryan Langerhans	.50	.20
❑ 268	Juan Rivera	.50	.20
❑ 269	Shawn Gallagher	.50	.20
❑ 270	Jorge Toca	.50	.20
❑ 271	Brad Lidge	.75	.30
❑ 272	Leoncio Estrella RC	.75	.30
❑ 273	Ruben Quevedo	.50	.20
❑ 274	Jack Cust	.50	.20
❑ 275	T.J. Tucker	.50	.20
❑ 276	Mike Colangelo	.50	.20
❑ 277	Brian Schneider	.50	.20
❑ 278	Calvin Murray	.50	.20
❑ 279	Josh Girdley	.50	.20
❑ 280	Mike Paradis	.50	.20
❑ 281	Chad Hermansen	.50	.20
❑ 282	Ty Howington RC	.75	.30
❑ 283	Aaron Myette	.50	.20
❑ 284	D'Angelo Jimenez	.50	.20
❑ 285	Dernell Stenson	.50	.20
❑ 286	Jerry Hairston Jr.	.50	.20
❑ 287	Gary Majewski RC	1.25	.50
❑ 288	Derrin Ebert	.50	.20
❑ 289	Steve Fish RC	.75	.30
❑ 290	Carlos E. Hernandez	.50	.20
❑ 291	Allen Levrault	.50	.20
❑ 292	Sean McNally RC	.75	.30
❑ 293	Randey Dorame RC	.75	.30
❑ 294	Wes Anderson RC	.75	.30
❑ 295	B.J. Ryan	.50	.20
❑ 296	Alan Webb RC	.75	.30
❑ 297	Brandon Inge RC	5.00	2.00
❑ 298	David Walling	.50	.20
❑ 299	Sun Woo Kim RC	.75	.30
❑ 300	Pat Burrell	.50	.20
❑ 301	Rick Guttormson RC	.75	.30
❑ 302	Gil Meche	.50	.20

❑ 303 Carlos Zambrano RC 12.00 5.00
❑ 304 Eric Byrnes UER RC 1.00 .40
❑ 305 Robb Quinlan RC 1.25 .50
❑ 306 Jackie Rexrode .50 .20
❑ 307 Nate Bump .50 .20
❑ 308 Sean DePaula RC .75 .30
❑ 309 Matt Riley .50 .20
❑ 310 Ryan Minor .50 .20
❑ 311 J.J. Davis .50 .20
❑ 312 Randy Wolf .50 .20
❑ 313 Jason Jennings .50 .20
❑ 314 Scott Seabol RC .75 .30
❑ 315 Doug Davis .50 .20
❑ 316 Todd Moser RC .75 .30
❑ 317 Rob Ryan .50 .20
❑ 318 Bubba Crosby .50 .20
❑ 319 Lyle Overbay RC 3.00 1.25
❑ 320 Mario Encarnacion .50 .20
❑ 321 Francisco Rodriguez RC 6.00 2.50
❑ 322 Michael Cuddyer .50 .20
❑ 323 Ed Yarnall .50 .20
❑ 324 Cesar Saba RC .75 .30
❑ 325 Gookie Dawkins .50 .20
❑ 326 Alex Escobar .50 .20
❑ 327 Julio Zuleta RC .75 .30
❑ 328 Josh Hamilton 1.50 .60
❑ 329 Carlos Urquiola RC .75 .30
❑ 330 Matt Belisle .50 .20
❑ 331 Kurt Ainsworth RC .75 .30
❑ 332 Tim Raines Jr. .50 .20
❑ 333 Eric Munson .50 .20
❑ 334 Donzell McDonald .50 .20
❑ 335 Larry Bigbie RC 2.00 .75
❑ 336 Matt Watson RC .75 .30
❑ 337 Aubrey Huff .50 .20
❑ 338 Julio Ramirez .50 .20
❑ 339 Jason Grabowski RC .75 .30
❑ 340 Jon Garland .50 .20
❑ 341 Austin Kearns .50 .20
❑ 342 Josh Pressley RC .75 .30
❑ 343 Miguel Olivo RC 2.00 .75
❑ 344 Julio Lugo .50 .20
❑ 345 Roberto Vaz .50 .20
❑ 346 Ramon Soler .50 .20
❑ 347 Brandon Phillips RC 4.00 1.50
❑ 348 Vince Faison RC .75 .30
❑ 349 Mike Venafro .50 .20
❑ 350 Rick Asadoorian RC 1.25 .50
❑ 351 B.J. Garbe RC .75 .30
❑ 352 Dan Reichert .50 .20
❑ 353 Jason Stumm RC .75 .30
❑ 354 Ruben Salazar RC .75 .30
❑ 355 Francisco Cordero .50 .20
❑ 356 Juan Guzman RC .75 .30
❑ 357 Mike Bacsik RC .75 .30
❑ 358 Jared Sandberg .50 .20
❑ 359 Rod Barajas .50 .20
❑ 360 Junior Brignac RC .75 .30
❑ 361 J.M. Gold .50 .20
❑ 362 Octavio Dotel .50 .20
❑ 363 David Kelton .50 .20
❑ 364 Scott Morgan .50 .20
❑ 365 Wascar Serrano RC .75 .30
❑ 366 Wilton Veras .50 .20
❑ 367 Eugene Kingsale .50 .20
❑ 368 Ted Lilly .50 .20
❑ 369 George Lombard .50 .20
❑ 370 Chris Haas .50 .20
❑ 371 Wilton Pena RC .75 .30
❑ 372 Vernon Wells .50 .20
❑ 373 Keith Ginter RC .75 .30
❑ 374 Jeff Heaverlo RC .75 .30
❑ 375 Calvin Pickering .50 .20
❑ 376 Mike Lamb RC 2.00 .75
❑ 377 Kyle Snyder .50 .20
❑ 378 Javier Cardona RC .75 .30
❑ 379 Aaron Rowand RC 5.00 2.00
❑ 380 Dee Brown .50 .20
❑ 381 Brett Myers RC 4.00 1.50
❑ 382 Abraham Nunez .50 .20
❑ 383 Eric Valent .50 .20
❑ 384 Jody Gerut RC 1.25 .50
❑ 385 Adam Dunn 1.25 .50
❑ 386 Jay Gehrke .50 .20
❑ 387 Omar Ortiz .50 .20
❑ 388 Darnell McDonald .50 .20
❑ 389 Tony Schrager RC .75 .30
❑ 390 J.D. Closser .50 .20
❑ 391 Ben Christensen RC .75 .30
❑ 392 Adam Kennedy .50 .20
❑ 393 Nick Green RC .75 .30
❑ 394 Ramon Hernandez .50 .20
❑ 395 Roy Oswalt RC 25.00 10.00
❑ 396 Andy Tracy RC .75 .30
❑ 397 Eric Gagne 1.25 .50
❑ 398 Michael Tejera RC .75 .30
❑ 399 Adam Everett .50 .20
❑ 400 Corey Patterson .50 .20
❑ 401 Gary Knotts RC .75 .30
❑ 402 Ryan Christianson RC .75 .30
❑ 403 Eric Ireland RC .75 .30
❑ 404 Andrew Good RC .75 .30
❑ 405 Brad Penny .50 .20
❑ 406 Jason LaRue .50 .20
❑ 407 Kit Pellow .50 .20
❑ 408 Kevin Beirne .50 .20
❑ 409 Kelly Dransfeldt .50 .20
❑ 410 Jason Grilli .50 .20
❑ 411 Scott Downs RC .75 .30
❑ 412 Jesus Colome .50 .20
❑ 413 John Sneed RC .75 .30
❑ 414 Tony McKnight .50 .20
❑ 415 Luis Rivera .50 .20
❑ 416 Adam Eaton .50 .20
❑ 417 Mike MacDougal RC 1.25 .50
❑ 418 Mike Nannini .50 .20
❑ 419 Barry Zito RC 10.00 4.00
❑ 420 DeWayne Wise .50 .20
❑ 421 Jason Dellaero .50 .20
❑ 422 Chad Moeller .50 .20
❑ 423 Jason Marquis .50 .20
❑ 424 Tim Redding RC 1.25 .50
❑ 425 Mark Mulder .50 .20
❑ 426 Josh Paul .50 .20
❑ 427 Chris Enochs .50 .20
❑ 428 Wilfredo Rodriguez RC .75 .30
❑ 429 Kevin Witt .50 .20
❑ 430 Scott Sobkowiak RC .75 .30
❑ 431 McKay Christensen .50 .20
❑ 432 Jung Bong .50 .20
❑ 433 Keith Evans RC .75 .30
❑ 434 Garry Maddox Jr. RC .75 .30
❑ 435 Ramon Santiago RC .75 .30
❑ 436 Alex Cora .50 .20
❑ 437 Carlos Lee .50 .20
❑ 438 Jason Repko RC 2.00 .75
❑ 439 Matt Burch .50 .20
❑ 440 Shawn Sonnier RC .75 .30

2000 Bowman Chrome Draft Picks

❑ COMP.FACT.SET (110) 50.00 20.00
❑ 1 Pat Burrell .50 .20
❑ 2 Rafael Furcal .50 .20
❑ 3 Grant Roberts .50 .20
❑ 4 Barry Zito 4.00 1.50
❑ 5 Julio Zuleta .50 .20
❑ 6 Mark Mulder .50 .20
❑ 7 Rob Bell .50 .20
❑ 8 Adam Piatt .50 .20
❑ 9 Mike Lamb .75 .30
❑ 10 Pablo Ozuna .50 .20
❑ 11 Jason Tyner .50 .20
❑ 12 Jason Marquis .50 .20
❑ 13 Eric Munson .50 .20
❑ 14 Seth Etherton .50 .20
❑ 15 Milton Bradley .50 .20
❑ 16 Nick Green .50 .20
❑ 17 Chin-Feng Chen RC 1.50 .60
❑ 18 Matt Boone RC .50 .20
❑ 19 Kevin Gregg RC .50 .20
❑ 20 Eddy Garabito RC .50 .20
❑ 21 Aaron Capista RC .50 .20
❑ 22 Esteban German RC .50 .20
❑ 23 Derek Thompson RC .50 .20
❑ 24 Phil Merrell RC .50 .20
❑ 25 Brian O'Connor RC .50 .20
❑ 26 Yamid Haad .50 .20
❑ 27 Hector Mercado RC .50 .20
❑ 28 Jason Woolf RC .50 .20
❑ 29 Eddy Furniss RC .50 .20
❑ 30 Cha Sueng Baek RC .50 .20
❑ 31 Colby Lewis RC .50 .20
❑ 32 Pasqual Coco RC .50 .20
❑ 33 Jorge Cantu RC 5.00 2.00
❑ 34 Erasmo Ramirez RC .50 .20
❑ 35 Bobby Kielty RC 1.00 .40
❑ 36 Joaquin Benoit RC .50 .20
❑ 37 Brian Esposito RC .50 .20
❑ 38 Michael Wenner .50 .20
❑ 39 Juan Rincon RC .50 .20
❑ 40 Yorvit Torrealba RC 1.00 .40
❑ 41 Chad Durham RC .50 .20
❑ 42 Jim Mann RC .50 .20
❑ 43 Shane Loux RC .50 .20
❑ 44 Luis Rivas .50 .20
❑ 45 Ken Chenard RC .50 .20
❑ 46 Mike Lockwood RC .50 .20
❑ 47 Yovanny Lara RC .50 .20
❑ 48 Bubba Carpenter RC .50 .20
❑ 49 Ryan Dittfurth RC .50 .20
❑ 50 John Stephens RC .50 .20
❑ 51 Pedro Feliz RC 2.50 1.00
❑ 52 Kenny Kelly RC .50 .20
❑ 53 Neil Jenkins RC .50 .20
❑ 54 Mike Glendenning RC .50 .20
❑ 55 Bo Porter .50 .20
❑ 56 Eric Byrnes .50 .20
❑ 57 Tony Alvarez RC .50 .20
❑ 58 Kazuhiro Sasaki RC 1.50 .60
❑ 59 Chad Durbin RC .50 .20
❑ 60 Mike Bynum RC .50 .20
❑ 61 Travis Wilson RC .50 .20
❑ 62 Jose Leon RC .50 .20
❑ 63 Ryan Vogelsong RC .50 .20
❑ 64 Geraldo Guzman RC .50 .20
❑ 65 Craig Anderson RC .50 .20
❑ 66 Carlos Silva RC 1.00 .40
❑ 67 Brad Thomas RC .50 .20
❑ 68 Chin-Hui Tsao 1.50 .60
❑ 69 Mark Buehrle RC 8.00 3.00
❑ 70 Juan Salas RC .50 .20
❑ 71 Denny Abreu RC .50 .20
❑ 72 Keith McDonald RC .50 .20
❑ 73 Chris Richard RC .50 .20
❑ 74 Tomas De la Rosa RC .50 .20
❑ 75 Vicente Padilla RC 1.00 .40
❑ 76 Justin Brunette RC .50 .20
❑ 77 Scott Linebrink RC .50 .20
❑ 78 Jeff Sparks RC .50 .20
❑ 79 Tike Redman RC 1.50 .60
❑ 80 John Lackey RC 5.00 2.00
❑ 81 Joe Strong RC .50 .20
❑ 82 Brian Tollberg RC .50 .20
❑ 83 Steve Sisco RC .50 .20
❑ 84 Chris Clapinski RC .50 .20
❑ 85 Augie Ojeda RC .50 .20
❑ 86 Adrian Gonzalez RC 6.00 2.50
❑ 87 Mike Stodolka RC .50 .20
❑ 88 Adam Johnson RC .50 .20
❑ 89 Matt Wheatland RC .50 .20
❑ 90 Corey Smith RC .50 .20
❑ 91 Rocco Baldelli RC 5.00 2.00
❑ 92 Keith Bucktrot RC .50 .20
❑ 93 Adam Wainwright RC 2.50 1.00
❑ 94 Blaine Boyer RC .50 .20
❑ 95 Aaron Herr RC 1.00 .40
❑ 96 Scott Thorman RC 2.50 1.00
❑ 97 Bryan Digby RC .50 .20
❑ 98 Josh Shortslef RC .50 .20

❑ 99 Sean Smith RC .50 .20
❑ 100 Alex Cruz RC .50 .20
❑ 101 Marc Love RC .50 .20
❑ 102 Kevin Lee RC .50 .20
❑ 103 Timo Perez RC 1.00 .40
❑ 104 Alex Cabrera RC 1.00 .40
❑ 105 Shane Heams RC .50 .20
❑ 106 Tripper Johnson RC .50 .20
❑ 107 Brent Abernathy RC .50 .20
❑ 108 John Cotton RC .50 .20
❑ 109 Brad Wilkerson RC 2.50 1.00
❑ 110 Jon Rauch RC .50 .20

2001 Bowman Chrome

❑ COMP.SET w/o SP's (220) 50.00 20.00
❑ COMMON (1-110/201-310) .50 .20
❑ COM.REF (111-200/311-330) 5.00 2.00
❑ COMMON AU REF (331-350) 50.00 20.00
❑ 1 Jason Giambi .50 .20
❑ 2 Rafael Furcal .50 .20
❑ 3 Bernie Williams .75 .30
❑ 4 Kenny Lofton .50 .20
❑ 5 Al Leiter .50 .20
❑ 6 Albert Belle .50 .20
❑ 7 Craig Biggio .75 .30
❑ 8 Mark Mulder .50 .20
❑ 9 Carlos Delgado .50 .20
❑ 10 Darin Erstad .50 .20
❑ 11 Richie Sexson .50 .20
❑ 12 Randy Johnson 1.25 .50
❑ 13 Greg Maddux 2.00 .75
❑ 14 Orlando Hernandez .50 .20
❑ 15 Javier Vazquez .50 .20
❑ 16 Jeff Kent .50 .20
❑ 17 Jim Thome .75 .30
❑ 18 John Olerud .50 .20
❑ 19 Jason Kendall .50 .20
❑ 20 Scott Rolen .75 .30
❑ 21 Tony Gwynn 1.50 .60
❑ 22 Edgardo Alfonzo .50 .20
❑ 23 Pokey Reese .50 .20
❑ 24 Todd Helton .75 .30
❑ 25 Mark Quinn .50 .20
❑ 26 Dean Palmer .50 .20
❑ 27 Ray Durham .50 .20
❑ 28 Rafael Palmeiro .75 .30
❑ 29 Carl Everett .50 .20
❑ 30 Vladimir Guerrero 1.25 .50
❑ 31 Livan Hernandez .50 .20
❑ 32 Preston Wilson .50 .20
❑ 33 Jose Vidro .50 .20
❑ 34 Fred McGriff .75 .30
❑ 35 Kevin Brown .50 .20
❑ 36 Miguel Tejada .50 .20
❑ 37 Chipper Jones 1.25 .50
❑ 38 Edgar Martinez .75 .30
❑ 39 Tony Batista .50 .20
❑ 40 Jorge Posada .75 .30
❑ 41 Sammy Sosa 1.25 .50
❑ 42 Gary Sheffield .50 .20
❑ 43 Bartolo Colon .50 .20
❑ 44 Pat Burrell .50 .20
❑ 45 Jay Payton .50 .20
❑ 46 Mike Mussina .75 .30
❑ 47 Nomar Garciaparra 2.00 .75
❑ 48 Darren Dreifort .50 .20
❑ 49 Richard Hidalgo .50 .20
❑ 50 Troy Glaus .50 .20
❑ 51 Ben Grieve .50 .20
❑ 52 Jim Edmonds .50 .20
❑ 53 Raul Mondesi .50 .20
❑ 54 Andruw Jones .75 .30
❑ 55 Mike Sweeney .50 .20
❑ 56 Derek Jeter 3.00 1.25
❑ 57 Ruben Mateo .50 .20
❑ 58 Cristian Guzman .50 .20
❑ 59 Mike Hampton .50 .20
❑ 60 J.D. Drew .50 .20
❑ 61 Matt Lawton .50 .20
❑ 62 Moises Alou .50 .20
❑ 63 Terrence Long .50 .20
❑ 64 Geoff Jenkins .50 .20
❑ 65 Manny Ramirez Sox .75 .30
❑ 66 Johnny Damon .75 .30
❑ 67 Pedro Martinez .75 .30
❑ 68 Juan Gonzalez .50 .20
❑ 69 Roger Clemens 2.50 1.00
❑ 70 Carlos Beltran .50 .20
❑ 71 Roberto Alomar .75 .30
❑ 72 Barry Bonds 3.00 1.25
❑ 73 Tim Hudson .50 .20
❑ 74 Tom Glavine .75 .30
❑ 75 Jeromy Burnitz .50 .20
❑ 76 Adrian Beltre .50 .20
❑ 77 Mike Piazza 2.00 .75
❑ 78 Kerry Wood .50 .20
❑ 79 Steve Finley .50 .20
❑ 80 Bob Abreu .50 .20
❑ 81 Neifi Perez .50 .20
❑ 82 Mark Redman .50 .20
❑ 83 Paul Konerko .50 .20
❑ 84 Jermaine Dye .50 .20
❑ 85 Brian Giles .50 .20
❑ 86 Ivan Rodriguez .75 .30
❑ 87 Adam Kennedy .50 .20
❑ 88 Eric Chavez .50 .20
❑ 89 Billy Koch .50 .20
❑ 90 Shawn Green .50 .20
❑ 91 Matt Williams .50 .20
❑ 92 Greg Vaughn .50 .20
❑ 93 Jeff Cirillo .50 .20
❑ 94 Frank Thomas 1.25 .50
❑ 95 David Justice .50 .20
❑ 96 Cal Ripken 4.00 1.50
❑ 97 Curt Schilling .50 .20
❑ 98 Barry Zito .75 .30
❑ 99 Brian Jordan .50 .20
❑ 100 Chan Ho Park .50 .20
❑ 101 J.T. Snow .50 .20
❑ 102 Kazuhiro Sasaki .50 .20
❑ 103 Alex Rodriguez 2.00 .75
❑ 104 Mariano Rivera 1.25 .50
❑ 105 Eric Milton .50 .20
❑ 106 Andy Pettitte .75 .30
❑ 107 Ken Griffey Jr. 2.00 .75
❑ 108 Bengie Molina .50 .20
❑ 109 Jeff Bagwell .75 .30
❑ 110 Mark McGwire 3.00 1.25
❑ 111 Dan Tosca RC 5.00 2.00
❑ 112 Sergio Contreras RC 8.00 3.00
❑ 113 Mitch Jones RC 8.00 3.00
❑ 114 Ramon Carvajal RC 8.00 3.00
❑ 115 Ryan Madson RC 10.00 4.00
❑ 116 Hank Blalock RC 30.00 12.50
❑ 117 Ben Washburn RC 5.00 2.00
❑ 118 Erick Almonte RC 5.00 2.00
❑ 119 Shawn Fagan RC 8.00 3.00
❑ 120 Gary Johnson RC 5.00 2.00
❑ 121 Brett Evert RC 5.00 2.00
❑ 122 Joe Hamer RC 8.00 3.00
❑ 123 Yhency Brazoban RC 10.00 4.00
❑ 124 Domingo Guante RC 5.00 2.00
❑ 125 Deivi Mendez RC 5.00 2.00
❑ 126 Adrian Hernandez RC 5.00 2.00
❑ 127 Reggie Abercrombie RC 10.00 4.00
❑ 128 Steve Bennett RC 5.00 2.00
❑ 129 Matt White RC 8.00 3.00
❑ 130 Brian Hitchcox RC 5.00 2.00
❑ 131 Deivis Santos RC 5.00 2.00
❑ 133 Eric Reynolds RC 5.00 2.00
❑ 134 Denny Bautista RC 10.00 4.00
❑ 135 Hector Garcia RC 5.00 2.00
❑ 136 Joe Thurston RC 8.00 3.00
❑ 137 Tsuyoshi Shinjo RC 10.00 4.00
❑ 138 Elpidio Guzman RC 5.00 2.00
❑ 139 Brian Bass RC 5.00 2.00
❑ 140 Mark Burnett RC 8.00 3.00
❑ 141 Russ Jacobson UER 5.00 2.00
❑ 142 Travis Hafner RC 30.00 12.50
❑ 143 Wilson Betemit RC 15.00 6.00
❑ 144 Luke Lockwood RC 8.00 3.00
❑ 145 Noel Devarez RC 8.00 3.00
❑ 146 Doug Gredvig RC 5.00 2.00
❑ 147 Seung Song RC 8.00 3.00
❑ 148 Andy Van Hekken RC 5.00 2.00
❑ 149 Ryan Kohlmeier 5.00 2.00
❑ 150 Dee Haynes RC 5.00 2.00
❑ 151 Jim Journell RC 8.00 3.00
❑ 152 Chad Petty RC 5.00 2.00
❑ 153 Danny Borrell RC 5.00 2.00
❑ 154 Dave Krynzel 5.00 2.00
❑ 155 Octavio Martinez RC 8.00 3.00
❑ 156 David Parrish RC 5.00 2.00
❑ 157 Jason Miller RC 5.00 2.00
❑ 158 Corey Spencer RC 5.00 2.00
❑ 159 Maxim St. Pierre RC 8.00 3.00
❑ 160 Pat Magness RC 8.00 3.00
❑ 161 Ranier Olmedo RC 8.00 3.00
❑ 162 Brandon Mims RC 5.00 2.00
❑ 163 Phil Wilson RC 8.00 3.00
❑ 164 Jose Reyes RC 150.00 75.00
❑ 165 Matt Butler RC 8.00 3.00
❑ 166 Joel Pineiro 8.00 3.00
❑ 167 Ken Chenard 5.00 2.00
❑ 168 Alexis Gomez RC 5.00 2.00
❑ 169 Justin Morneau RC 80.00 40.00
❑ 170 Josh Fogg RC 8.00 3.00
❑ 171 Charles Frazier RC 5.00 2.00
❑ 172 Ryan Ludwick RC 25.00 10.00
❑ 173 Seth McClung RC 8.00 3.00
❑ 174 Justin Wayne RC 8.00 3.00
❑ 175 Rafael Soriano RC 8.00 3.00
❑ 176 Jared Abruzzo RC 5.00 2.00
❑ 177 Jason Richardson RC 5.00 2.00
❑ 178 Darwin Cubillan RC 5.00 2.00
❑ 179 Blake Williams RC 5.00 2.00
❑ 180 Valentino Pascucci RC 8.00 3.00
❑ 181 Ryan Hannaman RC 8.00 3.00
❑ 182 Steve Smyth RC 8.00 3.00
❑ 183 Jake Peavy RC 60.00 30.00
❑ 184 Onix Mercado RC 8.00 3.00
❑ 185 Luis Torres RC 8.00 3.00
❑ 186 Casey Fossum RC 5.00 2.00
❑ 187 Eduardo Figueroa RC 5.00 2.00
❑ 188 Bryan Barnowski RC 5.00 2.00
❑ 189 Jason Standridge 5.00 2.00
❑ 190 Marvin Seale RC 8.00 3.00
❑ 191 Steve Smitherman RC 8.00 3.00
❑ 192 Rafael Boitel RC 5.00 2.00
❑ 193 Dany Morban RC 5.00 2.00
❑ 194 Justin Woodrow RC 8.00 3.00
❑ 195 Ed Rogers RC 5.00 2.00
❑ 196 Ben Hendrickson RC 5.00 2.00
❑ 197 Thomas Mitchell 5.00 2.00
❑ 198 Adam Pettyjohn RC 5.00 2.00
❑ 199 Doug Nickle RC 5.00 2.00
❑ 200 Jason Jones RC 5.00 2.00
❑ 201 Larry Barnes .50 .20
❑ 202 Ben Diggins .50 .20
❑ 203 Dee Brown .50 .20
❑ 204 Rocco Baldelli .50 .20
❑ 205 Luis Terrero .50 .20
❑ 206 Milton Bradley .50 .20
❑ 207 Kurt Ainsworth .50 .20
❑ 208 Sean Burroughs .50 .20
❑ 209 Rick Asadoorian .50 .20
❑ 210 Ramon Castro .50 .20
❑ 211 Nick Neugebauer .50 .20
❑ 212 Aaron Myette .50 .20
❑ 213 Luis Matos .50 .20
❑ 214 Donnie Bridges .50 .20
❑ 215 Alex Cintron .50 .20
❑ 216 Bobby Kielty .50 .20
❑ 217 Matt Belisle .50 .20
❑ 218 Adam Everett .50 .20
❑ 219 John Lackey .50 .20
❑ 220 Adam Wainwright .50 .20
❑ 221 Jerry Hairston Jr. .50 .20
❑ 222 Mike Bynum .50 .20
❑ 223 Ryan Christianson .50 .20

❑	224	J.J. Davis	.50	.20
❑	225	Alex Graman	.50	.20
❑	226	Abraham Nunez	.50	.20
❑	227	Sun Woo Kim	.50	.20
❑	228	Jimmy Rollins	.50	.20
❑	229	Ruben Salazar	.50	.20
❑	230	Josh Girdley	.50	.20
❑	231	Carl Crawford	.50	.20
❑	232	Ben Davis	.50	.20
❑	233	Jason Grabowski	.50	.20
❑	234	Chris George	.50	.20
❑	235	Roy Oswalt	1.25	.50
❑	236	Brian Cole	.50	.20
❑	237	Corey Patterson	.50	.20
❑	238	Vernon Wells	.50	.20
❑	239	Brad Baker	.50	.20
❑	240	Gookie Dawkins	.50	.20
❑	241	Michael Cuddyer	.50	.20
❑	242	Ricardo Aramboles	.50	.20
❑	243	Ben Sheets	.75	.30
❑	244	Toby Hall	.50	.20
❑	245	Jack Cust	.50	.20
❑	246	Pedro Feliz	.50	.20
❑	247	Josh Beckett	.75	.30
❑	248	Alex Escobar	.50	.20
❑	249	Marcus Giles	.50	.20
❑	250	Jon Rauch	.50	.20
❑	251	Kevin Mench	.50	.20
❑	252	Shawn Sonnier	.50	.20
❑	253	Aaron Rowand	.50	.20
❑	254	C.C. Sabathia	.50	.20
❑	255	Bubba Crosby	.50	.20
❑	256	Josh Hamilton	1.00	.40
❑	257	Carlos Hernandez	.50	.20
❑	258	Carlos Pena	.50	.20
❑	259	Miguel Cabrera	4.00	1.50
❑	260	Brandon Phillips	.50	.20
❑	261	Tony Pena Jr.	.50	.20
❑	262	Cristian Guerrero	.50	.20
❑	263	Jin Ho Cho	.50	.20
❑	264	Aaron Herr	.50	.20
❑	265	Keith Ginter	.50	.20
❑	266	Felipe Lopez	.50	.20
❑	267	Travis Harper	.50	.20
❑	268	Joe Torres	.50	.20
❑	269	Eric Byrnes	.50	.20
❑	270	Ben Christensen	.50	.20
❑	271	Aubrey Huff	.50	.20
❑	272	Lyle Overbay	.50	.20
❑	273	Vince Faison	.50	.20
❑	274	Bobby Bradley	.50	.20
❑	275	Joe Crede	1.25	.50
❑	276	Matt Wheatland	.50	.20
❑	277	Grady Sizemore	2.00	.75
❑	278	Adrian Gonzalez	.50	.20
❑	279	Tim Raines Jr.	.50	.20
❑	280	Phil Dumatrait	.50	.20
❑	281	Jason Hart	.50	.20
❑	282	David Kelton	.50	.20
❑	283	David Walling	.50	.20
❑	284	J.R. House	.50	.20
❑	285	Kenny Kelly	.50	.20
❑	286	Aaron McNeal	.50	.20
❑	287	Nick Johnson	.50	.20
❑	288	Scott Heard	.50	.20
❑	289	Brad Wilkerson	.50	.20
❑	290	Allen Levrault	.50	.20
❑	291	Chris Richard	.50	.20
❑	292	Jared Sandberg	.50	.20
❑	293	Tike Redman	.50	.20
❑	294	Adam Dunn	.75	.30
❑	295	Josh Pressley	.50	.20
❑	296	Jose Ortiz	.50	.20
❑	297	Jason Romano	.50	.20
❑	298	Tim Redding	.50	.20
❑	299	Alex Gordon	.50	.20
❑	300	Ben Petrick	.50	.20
❑	301	Eric Munson	.50	.20
❑	302	Luis Rivas	.50	.20
❑	303	Matt Ginter	.50	.20
❑	304	Alfonso Soriano	.75	.30
❑	305	Wilfredo Rodriguez	.50	.20
❑	306	Brett Myers	.50	.20
❑	307	Scott Seabol	.50	.20
❑	308	Tony Alvarez	.50	.20
❑	309	Donzell McDonald	.50	.20
❑	310	Austin Kearns	.50	.20
❑	311	Will Ohman RC	8.00	3.00
❑	312	Ryan Soules RC	5.00	2.00
❑	313	Cody Ross RC	5.00	2.00
❑	314	Bill Whitecotton RC	5.00	2.00
❑	315	Mike Burns RC	8.00	3.00
❑	316	Manuel Acosta RC	5.00	2.00
❑	317	Lance Niekro RC	10.00	4.00
❑	318	Travis Thompson RC	8.00	3.00
❑	319	Zach Sorensen RC	8.00	3.00
❑	320	Austin Evans RC	5.00	2.00
❑	321	Brad Stiles RC	5.00	2.00
❑	322	Joe Kennedy RC	10.00	4.00
❑	323	Luke Martin RC	8.00	3.00
❑	324	Juan Diaz RC	8.00	3.00
❑	325	Pat Hallmark RC	5.00	2.00
❑	326	Christian Parker RC	5.00	2.00
❑	327	Ronny Corona RC	8.00	3.00
❑	328	Jermaine Clark RC	5.00	2.00
❑	329	Scott Dunn RC	8.00	3.00
❑	330	Scott Chiasson RC	8.00	3.00
❑	331	Greg Nash AU RC	50.00	20.00
❑	332	Brad Cresse AU	50.00	20.00
❑	333	John Buck AU RC	80.00	40.00
❑	334	Freddie Bynum AU RC	50.00	20.00
❑	335	Felix Diaz AU RC	50.00	20.00
❑	336	Jason Belcher AU RC	50.00	20.00
❑	337	Troy Farnsworth AU RC	50.00	20.00
❑	338	Roberto Miniel AU RC	50.00	20.00
❑	339	Esix Snead AU RC	50.00	20.00
❑	340	Albert Pujols AU RC	2500.00	2000.00
❑	341	Jeff Andra AU RC	50.00	20.00
❑	342	Victor Hall AU RC	50.00	20.00
❑	343	Pedro Liriano AU RC	50.00	20.00
❑	344	Andy Beal AU RC	50.00	20.00
❑	345	Bob Keppel AU RC	50.00	20.00
❑	346	Brian Schmitt AU RC	50.00	20.00
❑	347	Ron Davenport AU RC	150.00	90.00
❑	348	Tony Blanco AU RC	50.00	20.00
❑	349	Reggie Griggs AU RC	50.00	20.00
❑	350	Derrick Van Dusen AU RC	50.00	20.00
❑	351A	Ichiro Suzuki English RC	100.00	60.00
❑	351B	Ichiro Suzuki Japan RC	100.00	60.00

2002 Bowman Chrome

❑		COMP.RED SET (110)	40.00	15.00
❑		COMP.BLUE w/o SP's (110)	40.00	15.00
❑		COMMON RED (1-110)	.50	.20
❑		COMMON BLUE (111-383)	.75	.30
❑		COMMON AU (324B/384-405)	10.00	4.00
❑		324B/384-405 GROUP A AUTO ODDS 1:28		
❑		403-404 GROUP B AUTO ODDS 1:1290		
❑		324B/384-405 OVERALL AUTO ODDS 1:27		
❑	1	Adam Dunn	.50	.20
❑	2	Derek Jeter	3.00	1.25
❑	3	Alex Rodriguez	2.00	.75
❑	4	Miguel Tejada	.50	.20
❑	5	Nomar Garciaparra	2.00	.75
❑	6	Toby Hall	.50	.20
❑	7	Brandon Duckworth	.50	.20
❑	8	Paul LoDuca	.50	.20
❑	9	Brian Giles	.50	.20
❑	10	C.C. Sabathia	.50	.20
❑	11	Curt Schilling	.50	.20
❑	12	Tsuyoshi Shinjo	.50	.20
❑	13	Ramon Hernandez	.50	.20
❑	14	Jose Cruz Jr.	.50	.20
❑	15	Albert Pujols	2.50	1.00
❑	16	Joe Mays	.50	.20
❑	17	Javy Lopez	.50	.20
❑	18	J.T. Snow	.50	.20
❑	19	David Segui	.50	.20
❑	20	Jorge Posada	.75	.30
❑	21	Doug Mientkiewicz	.50	.20
❑	22	Jerry Hairston Jr.	.50	.20
❑	23	Bernie Williams	.75	.30
❑	24	Mike Sweeney	.50	.20
❑	25	Jason Giambi	.50	.20
❑	26	Ryan Dempster	.50	.20
❑	27	Ryan Klesko	.50	.20
❑	28	Mark Quinn	.50	.20
❑	29	Jeff Kent	.50	.20
❑	30	Eric Chavez	.50	.20
❑	31	Adrian Beltre	.50	.20
❑	32	Andruw Jones	.75	.30
❑	33	Alfonso Soriano	.50	.20
❑	34	Aramis Ramirez	.50	.20
❑	35	Greg Maddux	2.00	.75
❑	36	Andy Pettitte	.75	.30
❑	37	Bartolo Colon	.50	.20
❑	38	Ben Sheets	.50	.20
❑	39	Bobby Higginson	.50	.20
❑	40	Ivan Rodriguez	.75	.30
❑	41	Brad Penny	.50	.20
❑	42	Carlos Lee	.50	.20
❑	43	Damion Easley	.50	.20
❑	44	Preston Wilson	.50	.20
❑	45	Jeff Bagwell	.75	.30
❑	46	Eric Milton	.50	.20
❑	47	Rafael Palmeiro	.75	.30
❑	48	Gary Sheffield	.50	.20
❑	49	J.D. Drew	.50	.20
❑	50	Jim Thome	.75	.30
❑	51	Ichiro Suzuki	2.50	1.00
❑	52	Bud Smith	.50	.20
❑	53	Chan Ho Park	.50	.20
❑	54	D'Angelo Jimenez	.50	.20
❑	55	Ken Griffey Jr.	2.00	.75
❑	56	Wade Miller	.50	.20
❑	57	Vladimir Guerrero	1.25	.50
❑	58	Troy Glaus	.50	.20
❑	59	Shawn Green	.50	.20
❑	60	Kerry Wood	.50	.20
❑	61	Jack Wilson	.50	.20
❑	62	Kevin Brown	.50	.20
❑	63	Marcus Giles	.50	.20
❑	64	Pat Burrell	.50	.20
❑	65	Larry Walker	.50	.20
❑	66	Sammy Sosa	1.25	.50
❑	67	Raul Mondesi	.50	.20
❑	68	Tim Hudson	.50	.20
❑	69	Lance Berkman	.50	.20
❑	70	Mike Mussina	.75	.30
❑	71	Barry Zito	.50	.20
❑	72	Jimmy Rollins	.50	.20
❑	73	Barry Bonds	3.00	1.25
❑	74	Craig Biggio	.75	.30
❑	75	Todd Helton	.75	.30
❑	76	Roger Clemens	2.50	1.00
❑	77	Frank Catalanotto	.50	.20
❑	78	Josh Towers	.50	.20
❑	79	Roy Oswalt	.50	.20
❑	80	Chipper Jones	1.25	.50
❑	81	Cristian Guzman	.50	.20
❑	82	Darin Erstad	.50	.20
❑	83	Freddy Garcia	.50	.20
❑	84	Jason Tyner	.50	.20
❑	85	Carlos Delgado	.50	.20
❑	86	Jon Lieber	.50	.20
❑	87	Juan Pierre	.50	.20
❑	88	Matt Morris	.50	.20
❑	89	Phil Nevin	.50	.20
❑	90	Jim Edmonds	.50	.20
❑	91	Magglio Ordonez	.50	.20
❑	92	Mike Hampton	.50	.20
❑	93	Rafael Furcal	.50	.20
❑	94	Richie Sexson	.50	.20
❑	95	Luis Gonzalez	.50	.20
❑	96	Scott Rolen	.75	.30
❑	97	Tim Redding	.50	.20
❑	98	Moises Alou	.50	.20
❑	99	Jose Vidro	.50	.20
❑	100	Mike Piazza	2.00	.75
❑	101	Pedro Martinez	.75	.30

- ❑ 102 Geoff Jenkins .50 .20
- ❑ 103 Johnny Damon Sox .75 .30
- ❑ 104 Mike Cameron .50 .20
- ❑ 105 Randy Johnson 1.25 .50
- ❑ 106 David Eckstein .50 .20
- ❑ 107 Javier Vazquez .50 .20
- ❑ 108 Mark Mulder .50 .20
- ❑ 109 Robert Fick .50 .20
- ❑ 110 Roberto Alomar .75 .30
- ❑ 111 Wilson Betemit .75 .30
- ❑ 112 Chris Tritle SP RC 5.00 2.00
- ❑ 113 Ed Rogers .75 .30
- ❑ 114 Juan Pena .75 .30
- ❑ 115 Josh Beckett 1.25 .50
- ❑ 116 Juan Cruz .75 .30
- ❑ 117 Noochie Varner SP RC 5.00 2.00
- ❑ 118 Blake Williams .75 .30
- ❑ 119 Mike Rivera .75 .30
- ❑ 120 Hank Blalock 2.00 .75
- ❑ 121 Hansel Izquierdo SP RC 5.00 2.00
- ❑ 122 Orlando Hudson .75 .30
- ❑ 123 Bill Hall SP 5.00 2.00
- ❑ 124 Jose Reyes 2.00 .75
- ❑ 125 Juan Rivera .75 .30
- ❑ 126 Eric Valent .75 .30
- ❑ 127 Scotty Layfield SP RC 5.00 2.00
- ❑ 128 Austin Kearns .75 .30
- ❑ 129 Nic Jackson SP RC 5.00 2.00
- ❑ 130 Scott Chiasson .75 .30
- ❑ 131 Chad Qualls SP RC 8.00 3.00
- ❑ 132 Marcus Thames .75 .30
- ❑ 133 Nathan Haynes .75 .30
- ❑ 134 Joe Borchard .75 .30
- ❑ 135 Josh Hamilton 1.50 .60
- ❑ 136 Corey Patterson .75 .30
- ❑ 137 Travis Wilson .75 .30
- ❑ 138 Alex Escobar .75 .30
- ❑ 139 Alexis Gomez .75 .30
- ❑ 140 Nick Johnson 1.25 .50
- ❑ 141 Marlon Byrd .75 .30
- ❑ 142 Kory DeHaan .75 .30
- ❑ 143 Carlos Hernandez .75 .30
- ❑ 144 Sean Burroughs .75 .30
- ❑ 145 Angel Berroa .75 .30
- ❑ 146 Aubrey Huff 1.25 .50
- ❑ 147 Travis Hafner 1.25 .50
- ❑ 148 Brandon Berger .75 .30
- ❑ 149 J.R. House .75 .30
- ❑ 150 Dewon Brazelton .75 .30
- ❑ 151 Jayson Werth .75 .30
- ❑ 152 Larry Barnes .75 .30
- ❑ 153 Ruben Gotay SP RC 8.00 3.00
- ❑ 154 Tommy Marx SP RC 5.00 2.00
- ❑ 155 John Suomi SP RC 5.00 2.00
- ❑ 156 Javier Colina SP 5.00 2.00
- ❑ 157 Greg Sain SP RC 5.00 2.00
- ❑ 158 Robert Cosby SP RC 5.00 2.00
- ❑ 159 Angel Payan SP RC 8.00 3.00
- ❑ 160 Ralph Santana RC 1.25 .50
- ❑ 161 Joe Orloski RC 1.25 .50
- ❑ 162 Shayne Wright SP RC 5.00 2.00
- ❑ 163 Jay Caligiuri SP RC 5.00 2.00
- ❑ 164 Greg Montalbano SP RC 5.00 2.00
- ❑ 165 Rich Harden SP RC 25.00 10.00
- ❑ 166 Rich Thompson SP RC 5.00 2.00
- ❑ 167 Fred Bastardo SP RC 5.00 2.00
- ❑ 168 Alejandro Giron SP RC 5.00 2.00
- ❑ 169 Jesus Medrano SP RC 5.00 2.00
- ❑ 170 Kevin Deaton SP RC 5.00 2.00
- ❑ 171 Mike Rosamond RC 1.25 .50
- ❑ 172 Jon Guzman SP RC 5.00 2.00
- ❑ 173 Gerard Oakes SP RC 5.00 2.00
- ❑ 174 Francisco Liriano SP RC 40.00 15.00
- ❑ 175 Matt Allegra SP RC 5.00 2.00
- ❑ 176 Mike Snyder SP RC 5.00 2.00
- ❑ 177 James Shanks SP RC 5.00 2.00
- ❑ 178 Anderson Hernandez SP RC 5.00 2.00
- ❑ 179 Dan Trumble SP RC 5.00 2.00
- ❑ 180 Luis DePaula SP RC 5.00 2.00
- ❑ 181 Randall Shelley SP RC 5.00 2.00
- ❑ 182 Richard Lane SP RC 5.00 2.00
- ❑ 183 Antwon Rollins SP RC 5.00 2.00
- ❑ 184 Ryan Bukvich SP RC 5.00 2.00
- ❑ 185 Derrick Lewis SP 5.00 2.00
- ❑ 186 Eric Miller SP RC 5.00 2.00
- ❑ 187 Justin Schuda SP RC 5.00 2.00
- ❑ 188 Brian West SP RC 5.00 2.00
- ❑ 189 Brad Wilkerson .75 .30
- ❑ 190 Neal Frendling SP RC 5.00 2.00
- ❑ 191 Jeremy Hill SP RC 5.00 2.00
- ❑ 192 James Barrett SP RC 5.00 2.00
- ❑ 193 Brett Kay SP RC 5.00 2.00
- ❑ 194 Ryan Mottl SP RC 5.00 2.00
- ❑ 195 Brad Nelson SP RC 5.00 2.00
- ❑ 196 Juan M. Gonzalez SP RC 5.00 2.00
- ❑ 197 Curtis Legendre SP RC 5.00 2.00
- ❑ 198 Ronald Acuna SP RC 5.00 2.00
- ❑ 199 Chris Flinn SP RC 5.00 2.00
- ❑ 200 Nick Alvarez SP RC 5.00 2.00
- ❑ 201 Jason Ellison SP RC 10.00 4.00
- ❑ 202 Blake McGinley SP RC 5.00 2.00
- ❑ 203 Dan Phillips SP RC 5.00 2.00
- ❑ 204 Demetrius Heath SP RC 5.00 2.00
- ❑ 205 Eric Bruntlett SP RC 5.00 2.00
- ❑ 206 Joe Jiannetti SP RC 5.00 2.00
- ❑ 207 Mike Hill SP RC 5.00 2.00
- ❑ 208 Ricardo Cordova SP RC 5.00 2.00
- ❑ 209 Mark Hamilton SP RC 5.00 2.00
- ❑ 210 David Mattox SP RC 5.00 2.00
- ❑ 211 Jose Morban SP RC 5.00 2.00
- ❑ 212 Scott Wiggins SP RC 5.00 2.00
- ❑ 213 Steve Green .75 .30
- ❑ 214 Brian Rogers SP 5.00 2.00
- ❑ 215 Kenny Baugh .75 .30
- ❑ 216 Anastacio Martinez SP RC 5.00 2.00
- ❑ 217 Richard Lewis .75 .30
- ❑ 218 Tim Kalita SP RC 5.00 2.00
- ❑ 219 Edwin Almonte SP RC 5.00 2.00
- ❑ 220 Hee Seop Choi .75 .30
- ❑ 221 Ty Howington .75 .30
- ❑ 222 Victor Alvarez SP RC 5.00 2.00
- ❑ 223 Morgan Ensberg 1.25 .50
- ❑ 224 Jeff Austin SP RC 5.00 2.00
- ❑ 225 Clint Weibl SP RC 5.00 2.00
- ❑ 226 Eric Cyr .75 .30
- ❑ 227 Marlyn Tisdale SP RC 5.00 2.00
- ❑ 228 John VanBenschoten .75 .30
- ❑ 229 David Krynzel .75 .30
- ❑ 230 Raul Chavez SP RC 5.00 2.00
- ❑ 231 Brett Evert .75 .30
- ❑ 232 Joe Rogers SP RC 5.00 2.00
- ❑ 233 Adam Wainwright .75 .30
- ❑ 234 Matt Herges RC .75 .30
- ❑ 235 Matt Childers SP RC 5.00 2.00
- ❑ 236 Nick Neugebauer .75 .30
- ❑ 237 Carl Crawford 1.25 .50
- ❑ 238 Seung Song .75 .30
- ❑ 239 Randy Flores .75 .30
- ❑ 240 Jason Lane 1.25 .50
- ❑ 241 Chase Utley 10.00 4.00
- ❑ 242 Ben Howard SP RC 5.00 2.00
- ❑ 243 Eric Glaser SP RC 5.00 2.00
- ❑ 244 Josh Wilson RC 1.25 .50
- ❑ 245 Jose Valverde SP RC 5.00 2.00
- ❑ 246 Chris Smith .75 .30
- ❑ 247 Mark Prior 2.00 .75
- ❑ 248 Brian Mallette SP RC 5.00 2.00
- ❑ 249 Chone Figgins SP RC 8.00 3.00
- ❑ 250 Jimmy Alvarez SP RC 5.00 2.00
- ❑ 251 Luis Terrero .75 .30
- ❑ 252 Josh Bonifay SP RC 5.00 2.00
- ❑ 253 Garrett Guzman SP RC 5.00 2.00
- ❑ 254 Jeff Verplancke SP RC 5.00 2.00
- ❑ 255 Nate Espy SP RC 5.00 2.00
- ❑ 256 Jeff Lincoln SP RC 5.00 2.00
- ❑ 257 Ryan Snare SP RC 5.00 2.00
- ❑ 258 Jose Ortiz .75 .30
- ❑ 259 Denny Bautista .75 .30
- ❑ 260 Willy Aybar .75 .30
- ❑ 261 Kelly Johnson 3.00 1.25
- ❑ 262 Shawn Fagan .75 .30
- ❑ 263 Yurendell DeCaster SP RC 5.00 2.00
- ❑ 264 Mike Peeples SP RC 5.00 2.00
- ❑ 265 Joel Guzman 3.00 1.25
- ❑ 266 Ryan Vogelsong .75 .30
- ❑ 267 Jorge Padilla SP RC 5.00 2.00
- ❑ 268 Joe Jester SP RC 5.00 2.00
- ❑ 269 Ryan Church SP RC 10.00 4.00
- ❑ 270 Mitch Jones .75 .30
- ❑ 271 Travis Foley SP RC 5.00 2.00
- ❑ 272 Bobby Crosby 3.00 1.25
- ❑ 273 Adrian Gonzalez .75 .30
- ❑ 274 Ronnie Merrill .75 .30
- ❑ 275 Joel Pineiro .75 .30
- ❑ 276 John-Ford Griffin .75 .30
- ❑ 277 Brian Forystek SP RC 5.00 2.00
- ❑ 278 Sean Douglass .75 .30
- ❑ 279 Manny Delcarmen SP RC 8.00 3.00
- ❑ 280 Jim Kavourias SP RC 5.00 2.00
- ❑ 281 Gabe Gross .75 .30
- ❑ 282 Bill Ortega .75 .30
- ❑ 283 Joey Hammond SP RC 5.00 2.00
- ❑ 284 Brett Myers 1.25 .50
- ❑ 285 Carlos Pena .75 .30
- ❑ 286 Ezequiel Astacio SP RC 5.00 2.00
- ❑ 287 Edwin Yan SP RC 5.00 2.00
- ❑ 288 Chris Duffy SP RC 8.00 3.00
- ❑ 289 Jason Kinchen .75 .30
- ❑ 290 Rafael Soriano .75 .30
- ❑ 291 Colin Young RC 5.00 2.00
- ❑ 292 Eric Byrnes .75 .30
- ❑ 293 Chris Narveson SP RC 8.00 3.00
- ❑ 294 John Rheinecker .75 .30
- ❑ 295 Mike Wilson SP RC 5.00 2.00
- ❑ 296 Justin Sherrod SP RC 5.00 2.00
- ❑ 297 Deivi Mendez .75 .30
- ❑ 298 Wily Mo Pena 1.25 .50
- ❑ 299 Brett Roneberg SP RC 5.00 2.00
- ❑ 300 Trey Lunsford SP RC 5.00 2.00
- ❑ 301 Christian Parker .75 .30
- ❑ 302 Brent Butler .75 .30
- ❑ 303 Aaron Heilman .75 .30
- ❑ 304 Wilkin Ruan .75 .30
- ❑ 305 Kenny Kelly .75 .30
- ❑ 306 Cody Ransom .75 .30
- ❑ 307 Koyie Hill SP 5.00 2.00
- ❑ 308 Tony Fontana SP RC 5.00 2.00
- ❑ 309 Mark Teixeira 5.00 2.00
- ❑ 310 Doug Sessions SP RC 5.00 2.00
- ❑ 311 Josh Cisneros SP RC 5.00 2.00
- ❑ 312 Carlos Brackley SP RC 5.00 2.00
- ❑ 313 Tim Raines Jr. .75 .30
- ❑ 314 Ross Peeples SP RC 5.00 2.00
- ❑ 315 Alex Requena SP RC 5.00 2.00
- ❑ 316 Chin-Hui Tsao 1.25 .50
- ❑ 317 Tony Alvarez .75 .30
- ❑ 318 Craig Kuzmic SP RC 5.00 2.00
- ❑ 319 Pete Zamora SP RC 5.00 2.00
- ❑ 320 Matt Parker SP RC 5.00 2.00
- ❑ 321 Keith Ginter .75 .30
- ❑ 322 Gary Cates Jr. SP RC 5.00 2.00
- ❑ 323 Matt Belisle .75 .30
- ❑ 324A Ben Broussard .75 .30
- ❑ 324B Jake Mauer AU A RC 10.00 4.00
- ❑ 325 Dennis Tankersley .75 .30
- ❑ 326 Juan Silvestre .75 .30
- ❑ 327 Henry Pichardo SP RC 5.00 2.00
- ❑ 328 Michael Floyd SP RC 5.00 2.00
- ❑ 329 Clint Nageotte SP RC 8.00 3.00
- ❑ 330 Raymond Cabrera SP RC 5.00 2.00
- ❑ 331 Mauricio Lara SP RC 5.00 2.00
- ❑ 332 Alejandro Cadena SP RC 5.00 2.00
- ❑ 333 Jonny Gomes SP RC 15.00 6.00
- ❑ 334 Jason Bulger SP RC 5.00 2.00
- ❑ 335 Nate Teut .75 .30
- ❑ 336 David Gil SP RC 5.00 2.00
- ❑ 337 Joel Crump SP RC 5.00 2.00
- ❑ 338 Brandon Phillips .75 .30
- ❑ 339 Macay McBride 1.25 .50
- ❑ 340 Brandon Claussen .75 .30
- ❑ 341 Josh Phelps .75 .30
- ❑ 342 Freddie Money SP RC 5.00 2.00
- ❑ 343 Cliff Bartosh SP RC 5.00 2.00
- ❑ 344 Terrance Hill SP RC 5.00 2.00
- ❑ 345 John Rodriguez SP RC 8.00 3.00
- ❑ 346 Chris Latham SP RC 5.00 2.00
- ❑ 347 Carlos Cabrera SP RC 5.00 2.00
- ❑ 348 Jose Bautista SP RC 10.00 4.00
- ❑ 349 Kevin Frederick SP RC 5.00 2.00
- ❑ 350 Jerome Williams .75 .30
- ❑ 351 Napoleon Calzado SP RC 5.00 2.00
- ❑ 352 Benito Baez SP 5.00 2.00
- ❑ 353 Xavier Nady .75 .30
- ❑ 354 Jason Botts SP RC 8.00 3.00
- ❑ 355 Steve Bechler SP RC 5.00 2.00
- ❑ 356 Reed Johnson SP RC 10.00 4.00
- ❑ 357 Mark Outlaw SP RC 5.00 2.00
- ❑ 358 Jake Peavy 2.00 .75

❑ 359 Josh Shaffer SP RC	5.00	2.00
❑ 360 Dan Wright SP	5.00	2.00
❑ 361 Ryan Gripp SP RC	5.00	2.00
❑ 362 Nelson Castro SP RC	5.00	2.00
❑ 363 Jason Bay SP RC	15.00	6.00
❑ 364 Franklyn German SP RC	5.00	2.00
❑ 365 Corwin Malone SP RC	5.00	2.00
❑ 366 Kelly Ramos SP RC	5.00	2.00
❑ 367 John Ennis SP RC	5.00	2.00
❑ 368 George Perez SP	5.00	2.00
❑ 369 Rene Reyes SP RC	5.00	2.00
❑ 370 Rolando Viera SP RC	5.00	2.00
❑ 371 Earl Snyder SP RC	5.00	2.00
❑ 372 Kyle Kane SP RC	5.00	2.00
❑ 373 Mario Ramos SP RC	5.00	2.00
❑ 374 Tyler Yates SP RC	5.00	2.00
❑ 375 Jason Young SP RC	5.00	2.00
❑ 376 Chris Bootcheck SP RC	5.00	2.00
❑ 377 Jesus Cota SP RC	5.00	2.00
❑ 378 Corky Miller SP	5.00	2.00
❑ 379 Matt Erickson SP RC	5.00	2.00
❑ 380 Justin Huber SP RC	10.00	4.00
❑ 381 Felix Escalona SP RC	5.00	2.00
❑ 382 Kevin Cash SP RC	5.00	2.00
❑ 383 J.J. Putz SP RC	8.00	3.00
❑ 384 Chris Snelling AU A RC	20.00	8.00
❑ 385 David Wright AU A RC	300.00	200.00
❑ 386 Brian Wolfe AU A RC	10.00	4.00
❑ 387 Justin Reid AU A RC	10.00	4.00
❑ 389 Ryan Raburn AU A RC	10.00	4.00
❑ 390 Josh Barfield AU A RC	50.00	25.00
❑ 391 Joe Mauer AU A RC	150.00	75.00
❑ 392 Bobby Jenks AU A RC	25.00	10.00
❑ 393 Rob Henkel AU A RC	10.00	4.00
❑ 394 Jimmy Gobble AU A RC	10.00	4.00
❑ 395 Jesse Foppert AU A RC	15.00	6.00
❑ 396 Gavin Floyd AU A RC	15.00	6.00
❑ 397 Nate Field AU A RC	10.00	4.00
❑ 398 Ryan Doumit AU A RC	15.00	6.00
❑ 399 Ron Calloway AU A RC	10.00	4.00
❑ 400 Taylor Buchholz AU A RC	15.00	6.00
❑ 401 Adam Roller AU A RC	10.00	4.00
❑ 402 Cole Barthel AU A RC	10.00	4.00
❑ 403 Kazuhisa Ishii SP RC	8.00	3.00
❑ 403A Kazuhisa Ishii AU B	50.00	30.00
❑ 404 So Taguchi SP RC	8.00	3.00
❑ 404A So Taguchi AU B	50.00	30.00
❑ 405 Chris Baker AU A RC	10.00	4.00

2002 Bowman Chrome Draft

❑ COMPLETE SET (175)	350.00	200.00
❑ COMP.SET w/o AU's (165)	200.00	135.00
❑ COMMON CARD (1-165)	.40	.15
❑ COMMON CARD (166-175)	10.00	4.00
❑ 1 Clint Everts RC	1.50	.60
❑ 2 Fred Lewis RC	1.00	.40
❑ 3 Jon Broxton RC	3.00	1.25
❑ 4 Jason Anderson RC	1.00	.40
❑ 5 Mike Eusebio RC	1.00	.40
❑ 6 Zack Greinke RC	6.00	2.50
❑ 7 Joe Blanton RC	5.00	2.00
❑ 8 Sergio Santos RC	1.50	.60
❑ 9 Jason Cooper RC	1.00	.40
❑ 10 Delwyn Young RC	3.00	1.25
❑ 11 Jeremy Hermida RC	12.00	5.00
❑ 12 Dan Ortmeier RC	1.50	.60
❑ 13 Kevin Jepsen RC	1.50	.60
❑ 14 Russ Adams RC	1.50	.60
❑ 15 Mike Nixon RC	1.00	.40
❑ 16 Nick Swisher RC	15.00	6.00
❑ 17 Cole Hamels RC	40.00	15.00
❑ 18 Brian Dopirak RC	3.00	1.25
❑ 19 James Loney RC	12.00	5.00
❑ 20 Denard Span RC	1.50	.60
❑ 21 Billy Petrick RC	1.00	.40
❑ 22 Jared Doyle RC	1.00	.40
❑ 23 Jeff Francoeur RC	40.00	20.00
❑ 24 Nick Bourgeois RC	1.00	.40
❑ 25 Matt Cain RC	15.00	6.00
❑ 26 John McCurdy RC	1.00	.40
❑ 27 Mark Kiger RC	1.00	.40
❑ 28 Bill Murphy RC	1.00	.40
❑ 29 Matt Craig RC	1.50	.60
❑ 30 Mike Megrew RC	1.00	.40
❑ 31 Ben Crockett RC	1.00	.40
❑ 32 Luke Hagerty RC	1.00	.40
❑ 33 Matt Whitney RC	1.00	.40
❑ 34 Dan Meyer RC	1.50	.60
❑ 35 Jeremy Brown RC	1.00	.40
❑ 36 Doug Johnson RC	1.00	.40
❑ 37 Steve Obenchain RC	1.00	.40
❑ 38 Matt Clanton RC	1.00	.40
❑ 39 Mark Teahen RC	3.00	1.25
❑ 40 Tom Carrow RC	1.00	.40
❑ 41 Micah Schilling RC	1.00	.40
❑ 42 Blair Johnson RC	1.00	.40
❑ 43 Jason Pridie RC	1.00	.40
❑ 44 Joey Votto RC	12.00	5.00
❑ 45 Taber Lee RC	1.00	.40
❑ 46 Adam Peterson RC	1.00	.40
❑ 47 Adam Donachie RC	1.00	.40
❑ 48 Josh Murray RC	1.00	.40
❑ 49 Brent Clevlen RC	6.00	2.50
❑ 50 Chad Pleiness RC	1.00	.40
❑ 51 Zach Hammes RC	1.00	.40
❑ 52 Chris Snyder RC	1.50	.60
❑ 53 Chris Smith RC	1.00	.40
❑ 54 Justin Maureau RC	1.00	.40
❑ 55 David Bush RC	3.00	1.25
❑ 56 Tim Gilhooly RC	1.00	.40
❑ 57 Blair Barbier RC	1.00	.40
❑ 58 Zach Segovia RC	1.00	.40
❑ 59 Jeremy Reed RC	3.00	1.25
❑ 60 Matt Pender RC	1.00	.40
❑ 61 Eric Thomas RC	1.00	.40
❑ 62 Justin Jones RC	1.50	.60
❑ 63 Brian Slocum RC	1.00	.40
❑ 64 Larry Broadway RC	1.00	.40
❑ 65 Bo Flowers RC	1.00	.40
❑ 66 Scott White RC	1.00	.40
❑ 67 Steve Stanley RC	1.00	.40
❑ 68 Alex Merricks RC	1.00	.40
❑ 69 Josh Womack RC	1.00	.40
❑ 70 Dave Jensen RC	1.00	.40
❑ 71 Curtis Granderson RC	12.00	5.00
❑ 72 Pat Osborn RC	1.00	.40
❑ 73 Nic Carter RC	1.00	.40
❑ 74 Mitch Talbot RC	1.00	.40
❑ 75 Don Murphy RC	1.00	.40
❑ 76 Val Majewski RC	1.00	.40
❑ 77 Javy Rodriguez RC	1.00	.40
❑ 78 Fernando Pacheco RC	1.00	.40
❑ 79 Steve Russell RC	1.00	.40
❑ 80 Jon Slack RC	1.00	.40
❑ 81 John Baker RC	1.00	.40
❑ 82 Aaron Coonrod RC	1.00	.40
❑ 83 Josh Johnson RC	10.00	4.00
❑ 84 Jake Blalock RC	1.50	.60
❑ 85 Alex Hart RC	1.00	.40
❑ 86 Wes Bankston RC	6.00	2.50
❑ 87 Josh Rupe RC	1.00	.40
❑ 88 Dan Cevette RC	1.00	.40
❑ 89 Kiel Fisher RC	1.50	.60
❑ 90 Alan Rick RC	1.00	.40
❑ 91 Charlie Morton RC	1.00	.40
❑ 92 Chad Spann RC	1.00	.40
❑ 93 Kyle Boyer RC	1.00	.40
❑ 94 Bob Malek RC	1.00	.40
❑ 95 Ryan Rodriguez RC	1.00	.40
❑ 96 Jordan Renz RC	1.00	.40
❑ 97 Randy Frye RC	1.00	.40
❑ 98 Rich Hill RC	12.00	5.00
❑ 99 B.J. Upton RC	15.00	6.00
❑ 100 Dan Christensen RC	1.00	.40
❑ 101 Casey Kotchman RC	6.00	2.50
❑ 102 Eric Good RC	1.00	.40
❑ 103 Mike Fontenot RC	1.00	.40
❑ 104 John Webb RC	1.00	.40
❑ 105 Jason Dubois RC	1.50	.60
❑ 106 Ryan Kibler RC	1.00	.40
❑ 107 Jhonny Peralta RC	8.00	3.00
❑ 108 Kirk Saarloos RC	1.00	.40
❑ 109 Rhett Parrott RC	1.00	.40
❑ 110 Jason Grove RC	1.00	.40
❑ 111 Colt Griffin RC	1.00	.40
❑ 112 Dallas McPherson RC	3.00	1.25
❑ 113 Oliver Perez RC	3.00	1.25
❑ 114 Marshall McDougall RC	1.00	.40
❑ 115 Mike Wood RC	1.00	.40
❑ 116 Scott Hairston RC	1.50	.60
❑ 117 Jason Simontacchi RC	1.00	.40
❑ 118 Taggert Bozied RC	1.50	.60
❑ 119 Shelley Duncan RC	10.00	4.00
❑ 120 Dontrelle Willis RC	15.00	6.00
❑ 121 Sean Burnett	.40	.15
❑ 122 Aaron Cook	.60	.25
❑ 123 Brett Evert	.40	.15
❑ 124 Jimmy Journell	.40	.15
❑ 125 Brett Myers	.60	.25
❑ 126 Brad Baker	.40	.15
❑ 127 Billy Traber RC	1.00	.40
❑ 128 Adam Wainwright	.40	.15
❑ 129 Jason Young	1.00	.40
❑ 130 John Buck	.40	.15
❑ 131 Kevin Cash	1.00	.40
❑ 132 Jason Stokes RC	1.50	.60
❑ 133 Drew Henson	.40	.15
❑ 134 Chad Tracy RC	5.00	2.00
❑ 135 Orlando Hudson	.40	.15
❑ 136 Brandon Phillips	.40	.15
❑ 137 Joe Borchard	.40	.15
❑ 138 Marlon Byrd	.40	.15
❑ 139 Carl Crawford	.60	.25
❑ 140 Michael Restovich	.40	.15
❑ 141 Corey Hart RC	5.00	2.00
❑ 142 Edwin Almonte	.60	.25
❑ 143 Francis Beltran RC	1.00	.40
❑ 144 Jorge De La Rosa RC	1.00	.40
❑ 145 Gerardo Garcia RC	1.00	.40
❑ 146 Franklyn German RC	1.00	.40
❑ 147 Francisco Liriano	10.00	4.00
❑ 148 Francisco Rodriguez	.60	.25
❑ 149 Ricardo Rodriguez	.40	.15
❑ 150 Seung Song	.40	.15
❑ 151 John Stephens	.40	.15
❑ 152 Justin Huber RC	2.50	1.00
❑ 153 Victor Martinez	1.50	.60
❑ 154 Hee Seop Choi	.40	.15
❑ 155 Justin Morneau	.60	.25
❑ 156 Miguel Cabrera	2.50	1.00
❑ 157 Victor Diaz RC	2.50	1.00
❑ 158 Jose Reyes	1.00	.40
❑ 159 Omar Infante	.40	.15
❑ 160 Angel Berroa	.40	.15
❑ 161 Tony Alvarez	.40	.15
❑ 162 Shin Soo Choo RC	2.50	1.00
❑ 163 Wily Mo Pena	.60	.25
❑ 164 Andres Torres	.40	.15
❑ 165 Jose Lopez RC	6.00	2.50
❑ 166 Scott Moore AU RC	15.00	6.00
❑ 167 Chris Gruler AU RC	10.00	4.00
❑ 168 Joe Saunders AU RC	20.00	8.00
❑ 169 Jeff Francis AU RC	50.00	20.00
❑ 170 Royce Ring AU RC	10.00	4.00
❑ 171 Greg Miller AU RC	15.00	6.00
❑ 172 Brandon Weeden AU RC	10.00	4.00
❑ 173 Drew Meyer AU RC	10.00	4.00
❑ 174 Khalil Greene AU RC	60.00	30.00
❑ 175 Mark Schramek AU RC	10.00	4.00

2003 Bowman Chrome

❑ COMPLETE SET (351)	500.00	300.00
❑ COMP.SET w/o AU's (331)	150.00	75.00
❑ COMMON CARD (1-165)	.50	.20
❑ COMMON CARD (166-330)	.50	.20
❑ COMMON RC (156-330)	1.00	.40
❑ COMP.SET w/o AU'S INCLUDES 351 MAYS		
❑ MAYS AU IS NOT PART OF 351-CARD SET		
❑ 1 Garret Anderson	.50	.20

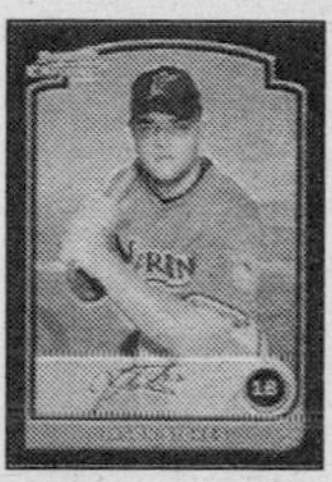

❑ 2	Derek Jeter	3.00	1.25
❑ 3	Gary Sheffield	.50	.20
❑ 4	Matt Morris	.50	.20
❑ 5	Derek Lowe	.50	.20
❑ 6	Andy Van Hekken	.50	.20
❑ 7	Sammy Sosa	1.25	.50
❑ 8	Ken Griffey Jr.	2.00	.75
❑ 9	Omar Vizquel	.75	.30
❑ 10	Jorge Posada	.75	.30
❑ 11	Lance Berkman	.50	.20
❑ 12	Mike Sweeney	.50	.20
❑ 13	Adrian Beltre	.50	.20
❑ 14	Richie Sexson	.50	.20
❑ 15	A.J. Pierzynski	.50	.20
❑ 16	Bartolo Colon	.50	.20
❑ 17	Mike Mussina	.75	.30
❑ 18	Paul Byrd	.50	.20
❑ 19	Bobby Abreu	.50	.20
❑ 20	Miguel Tejada	.50	.20
❑ 21	Aramis Ramirez	.50	.20
❑ 22	Edgardo Alfonzo	.50	.20
❑ 23	Edgar Martinez	.75	.30
❑ 24	Albert Pujols	2.50	1.00
❑ 25	Carl Crawford	.50	.20
❑ 26	Eric Hinske	.50	.20
❑ 27	Tim Salmon	.75	.30
❑ 28	Luis Gonzalez	.50	.20
❑ 29	Jay Gibbons	.50	.20
❑ 30	John Smoltz	.50	.20
❑ 31	Tim Wakefield	.50	.20
❑ 32	Mark Prior	.75	.30
❑ 33	Maggio Ordonez	.50	.20
❑ 34	Adam Dunn	.50	.20
❑ 35	Larry Walker	.50	.20
❑ 36	Luis Castillo	.50	.20
❑ 37	Wade Miller	.50	.20
❑ 38	Carlos Beltran	.50	.20
❑ 39	Odalis Perez	.50	.20
❑ 40	Alex Sanchez	.50	.20
❑ 41	Torii Hunter	.50	.20
❑ 42	Cliff Floyd	.50	.20
❑ 43	Andy Pettitte	.75	.30
❑ 44	Francisco Rodriguez	.50	.20
❑ 45	Eric Chavez	.50	.20
❑ 46	Kevin Millwood	.50	.20
❑ 47	Dennis Tankersley	.50	.20
❑ 48	Hideo Nomo	1.25	.50
❑ 49	Freddy Garcia	.50	.20
❑ 50	Randy Johnson	1.25	.50
❑ 51	Aubrey Huff	.50	.20
❑ 52	Carlos Delgado	.50	.20
❑ 53	Troy Glaus	.50	.20
❑ 54	Junior Spivey	.50	.20
❑ 55	Mike Hampton	.50	.20
❑ 56	Sidney Ponson	.50	.20
❑ 57	Aaron Boone	.50	.20
❑ 58	Kerry Wood	.50	.20
❑ 59	Willie Harris	.50	.20
❑ 60	Nomar Garciaparra	2.00	.75
❑ 61	Todd Helton	.75	.30
❑ 62	Mike Lowell	.50	.20
❑ 63	Roy Oswalt	.50	.20
❑ 64	Raul Ibanez	.50	.20
❑ 65	Brian Jordan	.50	.20
❑ 66	Geoff Jenkins	.50	.20
❑ 67	Jermaine Dye	.50	.20
❑ 68	Tom Glavine	.75	.30
❑ 69	Bernie Williams	.75	.30
❑ 70	Vladimir Guerrero	1.25	.50
❑ 71	Mark Mulder	.50	.20
❑ 72	Jimmy Rollins	.50	.20
❑ 73	Oliver Perez	.50	.20
❑ 74	Rich Aurilia	.50	.20
❑ 75	Joel Pineiro	.50	.20
❑ 76	J.D. Drew	.50	.20
❑ 77	Ivan Rodriguez	.75	.30
❑ 78	Josh Phelps	.50	.20
❑ 79	Darin Erstad	.50	.20
❑ 80	Curt Schilling	.50	.20
❑ 81	Paul Lo Duca	.50	.20
❑ 82	Marty Cordova	.50	.20
❑ 83	Manny Ramirez	.75	.30
❑ 84	Bobby Hill	.50	.20
❑ 85	Paul Konerko	.50	.20
❑ 86	Austin Kearns	.50	.20
❑ 87	Jason Jennings	.50	.20
❑ 88	Brad Penny	.50	.20
❑ 89	Jeff Bagwell	.75	.30
❑ 90	Shawn Green	.50	.20
❑ 91	Jason Schmidt	.50	.20
❑ 92	Doug Mientkiewicz	.50	.20
❑ 93	Jose Vidro	.50	.20
❑ 94	Bret Boone	.50	.20
❑ 95	Jason Giambi	.50	.20
❑ 96	Barry Zito	.50	.20
❑ 97	Roy Halladay	.50	.20
❑ 98	Pat Burrell	.50	.20
❑ 99	Sean Burroughs	.50	.20
❑ 100	Barry Bonds	3.00	1.25
❑ 101	Kazuhiro Sasaki	.50	.20
❑ 102	Fernando Vina	.50	.20
❑ 103	Chan Ho Park	.50	.20
❑ 104	Andruw Jones	.75	.30
❑ 105	Adam Kennedy	.50	.20
❑ 106	Shea Hillenbrand	.50	.20
❑ 107	Greg Maddux	2.00	.75
❑ 108	Jim Edmonds	.50	.20
❑ 109	Pedro Martinez	.75	.30
❑ 110	Moises Alou	.50	.20
❑ 111	Jeff Weaver	.50	.20
❑ 112	C.C. Sabathia	.50	.20
❑ 113	Robert Fick	.50	.20
❑ 114	A.J. Burnett	.50	.20
❑ 115	Jeff Kent	.50	.20
❑ 116	Kevin Brown	.50	.20
❑ 117	Rafael Furcal	.50	.20
❑ 118	Cristian Guzman	.50	.20
❑ 119	Brad Wilkerson	.50	.20
❑ 120	Mike Piazza	2.00	.75
❑ 121	Alfonso Soriano	.50	.20
❑ 122	Mark Ellis	.50	.20
❑ 123	Vicente Padilla	.50	.20
❑ 124	Eric Gagne	.50	.20
❑ 125	Ryan Klesko	.50	.20
❑ 126	Ichiro Suzuki	2.50	1.00
❑ 127	Tony Batista	.50	.20
❑ 128	Roberto Alomar	.75	.30
❑ 129	Alex Rodriguez	2.00	.75
❑ 130	Jim Thome	.75	.30
❑ 131	Jarrod Washburn	.50	.20
❑ 132	Orlando Hudson	.50	.20
❑ 133	Chipper Jones	1.25	.50
❑ 134	Rodrigo Lopez	.50	.20
❑ 135	Johnny Damon	.75	.30
❑ 136	Matt Clement	.50	.20
❑ 137	Frank Thomas	1.25	.50
❑ 138	Ellis Burks	.50	.20
❑ 139	Carlos Pena	.50	.20
❑ 140	Josh Beckett	.50	.20
❑ 141	Joe Randa	.50	.20
❑ 142	Brian Giles	.50	.20
❑ 143	Kazuhisa Ishii	.50	.20
❑ 144	Corey Koskie	.50	.20
❑ 145	Orlando Cabrera	.50	.20
❑ 146	Mark Buehrle	.50	.20
❑ 147	Roger Clemens	2.50	1.00
❑ 148	Tim Hudson	.50	.20
❑ 149	Randy Wolf	.50	.20
❑ 150	Josh Fogg	.50	.20
❑ 151	Phil Nevin	.50	.20
❑ 152	John Olerud	.50	.20
❑ 153	Scott Rolen	.75	.30
❑ 154	Joe Kennedy	.50	.20
❑ 155	Rafael Palmeiro	.75	.30
❑ 156	Chad Hutchinson	.50	.20
❑ 157	Quincy Carter XRC	1.50	.60
❑ 158	Hee Seop Choi	.50	.20
❑ 159	Joe Borchard	.50	.20
❑ 160	Brandon Phillips	.50	.20
❑ 161	Wily Mo Pena	.50	.20
❑ 162	Victor Martinez	.75	.30
❑ 163	Jason Stokes	.50	.20
❑ 164	Ken Harvey	.50	.20
❑ 165	Juan Rivera	.50	.20
❑ 166	Joe Valentine RC	1.50	.60
❑ 168	Michel Hernandez RC	1.50	.60
❑ 169	Eider Torres RC	1.50	.60
❑ 170	Chris De La Cruz RC	1.50	.60
❑ 171	Ramon Nivar-Martinez RC	1.50	.60
❑ 172	Mike Adams RC	1.50	.60
❑ 173	Justin Arneson RC	1.50	.60
❑ 174	Jamie Athas RC	1.50	.60
❑ 175	Dwaine Bacon RC	1.50	.60
❑ 176	Clint Barmes RC	4.00	1.50
❑ 177	B.J. Barns RC	1.50	.60
❑ 178	Tyler Johnson RC	1.50	.60
❑ 179	Brandon Webb RC	15.00	6.00
❑ 180	T.J. Bohn RC	1.50	.60
❑ 181	Ozzie Chavez RC	1.50	.60
❑ 182	Brandon Bowe RC	1.50	.60
❑ 183	Craig Brazell RC	1.50	.60
❑ 184	Dusty Brown RC	1.50	.60
❑ 185	Brian Bruney RC	2.00	.75
❑ 186	Greg Bruso RC	1.50	.60
❑ 187	Jaime Bubela RC	1.50	.60
❑ 188	Matt Diaz RC	3.00	1.25
❑ 189	Brian Burgamy RC	1.50	.60
❑ 190	Eny Cabreja RC	5.00	2.00
❑ 191	Daniel Cabrera RC	3.00	1.25
❑ 192	Ryan Cameron RC	1.50	.60
❑ 193	Lance Caraccioli RC	1.50	.60
❑ 194	David Cash RC	1.50	.60
❑ 195	Bernie Castro RC	1.50	.60
❑ 196	Ismael Castro RC	2.00	.75
❑ 197	Cory Doyne RC	1.50	.60
❑ 198	Jeff Clark RC	1.50	.60
❑ 199	Chris Colton RC	1.50	.60
❑ 200	Dexter Cooper RC	1.50	.60
❑ 201	Callix Crabbe RC	2.00	.75
❑ 202	Chien-Ming Wang RC	15.00	6.00
❑ 203	Eric Crozier RC	2.00	.75
❑ 204	Nook Logan RC	2.00	.75
❑ 205	David DeJesus RC	3.00	1.25
❑ 206	Matt DeMarco RC	1.50	.60
❑ 207	Chris Duncan RC	12.00	5.00
❑ 208	Eric Eckenstahler	.50	.20
❑ 209	Willie Eyre RC	1.50	.60
❑ 210	Evel Bastida-Martinez RC	1.50	.60
❑ 211	Chris Fallon RC	1.50	.60
❑ 212	Mike Flannery RC	1.50	.60
❑ 213	Mike Oâ ™Keefe RC	1.50	.60
❑ 214	Lew Ford RC	2.00	.75
❑ 215	Kason Gabbard RC	1.50	.60
❑ 216	Mike Gallo RC	1.50	.60
❑ 217	Jairo Garcia RC	2.00	.75
❑ 218	Angel Garcia RC	2.00	.75
❑ 219	Michael Garciaparra RC	1.50	.60
❑ 220	Jeremy Griffiths RC	1.50	.60
❑ 221	Dusty Gomon RC	2.00	.75
❑ 222	Bryan Grace RC	1.50	.60
❑ 223	Tyson Graham RC	1.50	.60
❑ 224	Henry Guerrero RC	1.50	.60
❑ 225	Franklin Gutierrez RC	4.00	1.50
❑ 226	Carlos Guzman RC	2.00	.75
❑ 227	Matthew Hagen RC	1.50	.60
❑ 228	Josh Hall RC	1.50	.60
❑ 229	Rob Hammock RC	1.50	.60
❑ 230	Brendan Harris RC	2.00	.75
❑ 231	Gary Harris RC	1.50	.60
❑ 232	Clay Hensley RC	1.50	.60
❑ 233	Michael Hinckley RC	2.00	.75
❑ 234	Luis Hodge RC	1.50	.60
❑ 235	Donnie Hood RC	2.00	.75
❑ 236	Matt Hensley RC	1.50	.60
❑ 237	Edwin Jackson RC	2.00	.75
❑ 238	Ardley Jansen RC	2.00	.75
❑ 239	Ferenc Jongejan RC	1.50	.60
❑ 240	Matt Kata RC	1.50	.60
❑ 241	Kazuhiro Takeoka RC	1.50	.60
❑ 242	Charlie Manning RC	1.50	.60

❑ 243 Il Kim RC 1.50 .60
❑ 244 Brennan King RC 1.50 .60
❑ 245 Chris Kroski RC 1.50 .60
❑ 246 David Martinez RC 1.50 .60
❑ 247 Pete LaForest RC 1.50 .60
❑ 248 Wil Ledezma RC 1.50 .60
❑ 249 Jeremy Bonderman RC 10.00 4.00
❑ 250 Gonzalo Lopez RC 1.50 .60
❑ 251 Brian Luderer RC 1.50 .60
❑ 252 Ruddy Lugo RC 1.50 .60
❑ 253 Wayne Lydon RC 1.50 .60
❑ 254 Mark Malaska RC 1.50 .60
❑ 255 Andy Marte RC 10.00 4.00
❑ 256 Tyler Martin RC 1.50 .60
❑ 257 Branden Florence RC 1.50 .60
❑ 258 Aneudis Mateo RC 1.50 .60
❑ 259 Derell McCall RC 1.50 .60
❑ 260 Elizardo Ramirez RC 2.00 .75
❑ 261 Mike McNutt RC 1.50 .60
❑ 262 Jacobo Meque RC 1.50 .60
❑ 263 Derek Michaelis RC 1.50 .60
❑ 264 Aaron Miles RC 2.00 .75
❑ 265 Jose Morales RC 1.50 .60
❑ 266 Dustin Moseley RC 1.50 .60
❑ 267 Adrian Myers RC 1.50 .60
❑ 268 Dan Neil RC 1.50 .60
❑ 269 Jon Nelson RC 2.00 .75
❑ 270 Mike Neu RC 1.50 .60
❑ 271 Leigh Neuage RC 1.50 .60
❑ 272 Wes O'Brien RC 1.50 .60
❑ 273 Trent Oeltjen RC 2.00 .75
❑ 274 Tim Olson RC 1.50 .60
❑ 275 David Pahucki RC 1.50 .60
❑ 276 Nathan Panther RC 1.50 .60
❑ 277 Arnie Munoz RC 1.50 .60
❑ 278 Dave Pember RC 1.50 .60
❑ 279 Jason Perry RC 2.00 .75
❑ 280 Matthew Peterson RC 1.50 .60
❑ 281 Greg Aquino RC 1.50 .60
❑ 282 Jorge Piedra RC 2.00 .75
❑ 283 Simon Pond RC 1.50 .60
❑ 284 Aaron Rakers RC 1.50 .60
❑ 285 Felix Sanchez RC 1.50 .60
❑ 286 Manuel Ramirez RC 2.00 .75
❑ 287 Kevin Randel RC 1.50 .60
❑ 288 Kelly Shoppach RC 3.00 1.25
❑ 289 Prentice Redman RC 1.50 .60
❑ 290 Eric Reed RC 1.50 .60
❑ 291 Wilton Reynolds RC 2.00 .75
❑ 292 Eric Riggs RC 2.00 .75
❑ 293 Carlos Rijo RC 1.50 .60
❑ 294 Tyler Adamczyk RC 1.50 .60
❑ 295 Jon-Mark Sprowl RC 1.50 .60
❑ 296 Arturo Rivas RC 1.50 .60
❑ 297 Kyle Roat RC 1.50 .60
❑ 298 Bubba Nelson RC .75 .30
❑ 299 Levi Robinson RC 1.50 .60
❑ 300 Ray Sadler RC 1.50 .60
❑ 301 Rylan Reed RC 1.50 .60
❑ 302 Jon Schuerholz RC 1.50 .60
❑ 303 Nobuaki Yoshida RC 1.50 .60
❑ 304 Brian Shackelford RC 1.50 .60
❑ 305 Bill Simon RC 1.50 .60
❑ 306 Haj Turay RC 1.00 .40
❑ 307 Sean Smith RC 2.00 .75
❑ 308 Ryan Spataro RC 1.50 .60
❑ 309 Jemel Spearman RC 1.50 .60
❑ 310 Keith Stamler RC 1.50 .60
❑ 311 Luke Steidlmayer RC 1.50 .60
❑ 312 Adam Stern RC 1.00 .40
❑ 313 Jay Sitzman RC 1.50 .60
❑ 314 Mike Wodnicki RC 1.50 .60
❑ 315 Terry Tiffee RC 1.50 .60
❑ 316 Nick Trzesniak RC 1.50 .60
❑ 317 Denny Tussen RC 1.50 .60
❑ 318 Scott Tyler RC 2.00 .75
❑ 319 Shane Victorino RC 3.00 1.25
❑ 320 Doug Waechter RC 2.00 .75
❑ 321 Brandon Watson RC 1.50 .60
❑ 322 Todd Wellemeyer RC 1.50 .60
❑ 323 Eli Whiteside RC 1.50 .60
❑ 324 Josh Willingham RC 4.00 1.50
❑ 325 Travis Wong RC 2.00 .75
❑ 326 Brian Wright RC 1.50 .60
❑ 327 Felix Pie RC 12.00 5.00
❑ 328 Andy Sisco RC .50 .20
❑ 329 Dustin Yount RC 2.00 .75
❑ 330 Andrew Dominique RC 1.50 .60
❑ 331 Brian McCann AU A RC 120.00 60.00
❑ 332 Jose Contreras AU B RC 150.00 90.00
❑ 333 Corey Shafer AU A RC 10.00 4.00
❑ 334 Hanley Ramirez AU A RC 250.00 150.00
❑ 335 Ryan Shealy AU A RC 30.00 12.50
❑ 336 Kevin Youkilis AU A RC 50.00 20.00
❑ 337 Jason Kubel AU A RC 30.00 12.50
❑ 338 Aron Weston AU A RC 10.00 4.00
❑ 338B Rajai Davis AU A ERR
❑ 339 J.D. Durbin AU A RC 10.00 4.00
❑ 340 Gary Schneidmiller AU A RC 10.004.00
❑ 341 Travis Ishikawa AU A RC 15.00 6.00
❑ 342 Ben Francisco AU A RC 10.00 4.00
❑ 343 Bobby Basham AU A RC 10.00 4.00
❑ 344 Joey Gomes AU A RC 10.00 4.00
❑ 345 Beau Kemp AU A RC 10.00 4.00
❑ 346 T.Story-Harden AU A RC 10.00 4.00
❑ 347 Daryl Clark AU A RC 10.00 4.00
❑ 348 Bryan Bullington AU A RC 10.00 4.00
❑ 349 Rajai Davis AU A RC 10.00 4.00
❑ 350 Darrell Rasner AU A RC 10.00 4.00
❑ 351 Willie Mays 2.00 .75
❑ 351AU Willie Mays AU 250.00 150.00

2003 Bowman Chrome Draft

❑ COMPLETE SET (176) 550.00 400.00
❑ COMP.SET w/o AU's (165) 100.00 50.00
❑ COMMON CARD (1-165) .40 .15
❑ 1-165 TWO PER BOWMAN DRAFT PACK
❑ COMMON CARD (166-176) 10.00 4.00
❑ 166-176 STATED ODDS 1:41 H/R
❑ LUBANSKI IS AN SP BY 1000 COPIES
❑ 1 Dontrelle Willis 1.50 .60
❑ 2 Freddy Sanchez .40 .15
❑ 3 Miguel Cabrera 1.50 .60
❑ 4 Ryan Ludwick .40 .15
❑ 5 Ty Wigginton .40 .15
❑ 6 Mark Teixeira 1.00 .40
❑ 7 Trey Hodges .40 .15
❑ 8 Laynce Nix .60 .25
❑ 9 Antonio Perez .40 .15
❑ 10 Jody Gerut .40 .15
❑ 11 Jae Weong Seo .40 .15
❑ 12 Erick Almonte .40 .15
❑ 13 Lyle Overbay .40 .15
❑ 14 Billy Traber .40 .15
❑ 15 Andres Torres .40 .15
❑ 16 Jose Valverde .40 .15
❑ 17 Aaron Heilman .40 .15
❑ 18 Brandon Larson .40 .15
❑ 19 Jung Bong .40 .15
❑ 20 Jesse Foppert .40 .15
❑ 21 Angel Berroa .40 .15
❑ 22 Jeff DaVanon .40 .15
❑ 23 Kurt Ainsworth .40 .15
❑ 24 Brandon Claussen .40 .15
❑ 25 Xavier Nady .40 .15
❑ 26 Travis Hafner .60 .25
❑ 27 Jerome Williams .40 .15
❑ 28 Jose Reyes .60 .25
❑ 29 Sergio Mitre RC 1.50 .60
❑ 30 Bo Hart RC 1.00 .40
❑ 31 Adam Miller RC 10.00 4.00
❑ 32 Brian Finch RC 1.00 .40
❑ 33 Taylor Mattingly RC 1.50 .60
❑ 34 Daric Barton RC 6.00 2.50
❑ 35 Chris Ray RC 3.00 1.25
❑ 36 Jarrod Saltalamacchia RC 15.00 6.00
❑ 37 Dennis Dove RC 1.50 .60
❑ 38 James Houser RC 1.50 .60
❑ 39 Clint King RC 1.50 .60
❑ 40 Lou Palmisano RC 1.50 .60
❑ 41 Dan Moore RC 1.00 .40
❑ 42 Craig Stansberry RC 1.50 .60
❑ 43 Jo Jo Reyes RC 3.00 1.25
❑ 44 Jake Stevens RC 1.50 .60
❑ 45 Tom Gorzelanny RC 5.00 2.00
❑ 46 Brian Marshall RC 1.00 .40
❑ 47 Scott Beerer RC 1.00 .40
❑ 48 Javi Herrera RC 1.50 .60
❑ 49 Steve LeRud RC 1.50 .60
❑ 50 Josh Banks RC 2.50 1.00
❑ 51 Jon Papelbon RC 30.00 12.50
❑ 52 Juan Valdes RC 1.50 .60
❑ 53 Beau Vaughan RC 1.50 .60
❑ 54 Matt Chico RC 1.50 .60
❑ 55 Todd Jennings RC 1.50 .60
❑ 56 Anthony Gwynn RC 4.00 1.50
❑ 57 Matt Harrison RC 2.50 1.00
❑ 58 Aaron Marsden RC 1.50 .60
❑ 59 Casey Abrams RC 1.00 .40
❑ 60 Cory Stuart RC 1.00 .40
❑ 61 Mike Wagner RC 1.00 .40
❑ 62 Jordan Pratt RC 1.50 .60
❑ 63 Andre Randolph RC 1.50 .60
❑ 64 Blake Balkcom RC 1.50 .60
❑ 65 Josh Muecke RC 1.00 .40
❑ 66 Jamie D'Antona RC 2.50 1.00
❑ 67 Cole Seifrig RC 1.00 .40
❑ 68 Josh Anderson RC 1.50 .60
❑ 69 Matt Lorenzo RC 1.50 .60
❑ 70 Nate Spears RC 1.50 .60
❑ 71 Chris Goodman RC 1.00 .40
❑ 72 Brian McFall RC 1.00 .40
❑ 73 Billy Hogan RC 1.50 .60
❑ 74 Jamie Romak RC 1.50 .60
❑ 75 Jeff Cook RC 1.50 .60
❑ 76 Brooks McNiven RC 1.00 .40
❑ 77 Xavier Paul RC 1.50 .60
❑ 78 Bob Zimmerman RC 1.00 .40
❑ 79 Mickey Hall RC 1.50 .60
❑ 80 Shaun Marcum RC 1.50 .60
❑ 81 Matt Nachreiner RC 1.50 .60
❑ 82 Chris Kinsey RC 1.00 .40
❑ 83 Jonathan Fulton RC 1.50 .60
❑ 84 Edgardo Baez RC 1.50 .60
❑ 85 Robert Valido RC 1.50 .60
❑ 86 Kenny Lewis RC 1.50 .60
❑ 87 Trent Peterson RC 1.00 .40
❑ 88 Johnny Woodard RC 1.50 .60
❑ 89 Wes Littleton RC 1.50 .60
❑ 90 Sean Rodriguez RC 5.00 2.00
❑ 91 Kyle Pearson RC 1.00 .40
❑ 92 Josh Rainwater RC 1.50 .60
❑ 93 Travis Schlichting RC 1.50 .60
❑ 94 Tim Battle RC 2.50 1.00
❑ 95 Aaron Hill RC 5.00 2.00
❑ 96 Bob McCrory RC 1.00 .40
❑ 97 Rick Guarno RC 1.50 .60
❑ 98 Brandon Yarbrough RC 1.00 .40
❑ 99 Peter Stonard RC 1.00 .40
❑ 100 Darin Downs RC 1.50 .60
❑ 101 Matt Bruback RC 1.00 .40
❑ 102 Danny Garcia RC 1.00 .40
❑ 103 Cory Stewart RC 1.00 .40
❑ 104 Ferdin Tejeda RC 1.00 .40
❑ 105 Kade Johnson RC 1.00 .40
❑ 106 Andrew Brown RC 1.50 .60
❑ 107 Aquilino Lopez RC 1.00 .40
❑ 108 Stephen Randolph RC 1.00 .40
❑ 109 Dave Matranga RC 1.00 .40
❑ 110 Dustin McGowan RC 1.50 .60
❑ 111 Juan Camacho RC 1.00 .40
❑ 112 Cliff Lee .40 .15
❑ 113 Jeff Duncan RC 1.00 .40
❑ 114 C.J. Wilson .40 .15
❑ 115 Brandon Roberson RC 1.00 .40
❑ 116 David Corrente RC 1.00 .40
❑ 117 Kevin Beavers RC 1.00 .40
❑ 118 Anthony Webster RC 1.50 .60
❑ 119 Oscar Villarreal RC 1.00 .40

- ❑ 120 Hong-Chih Kuo RC 8.00 3.00
- ❑ 121 Josh Barfield .60 .25
- ❑ 122 Denny Bautista .40 .15
- ❑ 123 Chris Burke RC 4.00 1.50
- ❑ 124 Robinson Cano RC 25.00 10.00
- ❑ 125 Jose Castillo .40 .15
- ❑ 126 Neal Cotts .40 .15
- ❑ 127 Jorge De La Rosa .40 .15
- ❑ 128 J.D. Durbin .50 .20
- ❑ 129 Edwin Encarnacion 2.00 .75
- ❑ 130 Gavin Floyd .40 .15
- ❑ 131 Alexis Gomez .40 .15
- ❑ 132 Edgar Gonzalez RC 1.00 .40
- ❑ 133 Khalil Greene 1.50 .60
- ❑ 134 Zack Greinke .60 .25
- ❑ 135 Franklin Gutierrez 1.50 .60
- ❑ 136 Rich Harden 1.00 .40
- ❑ 137 J.J. Hardy RC 10.00 4.00
- ❑ 138 Ryan Howard RC 25.00 10.00
- ❑ 139 Justin Huber .40 .15
- ❑ 140 David Kelton .40 .15
- ❑ 141 Dave Krynzel .40 .15
- ❑ 142 Pete LaForest .50 .20
- ❑ 143 Adam LaRoche .40 .15
- ❑ 144 Preston Larrison RC 1.00 .40
- ❑ 145 John Maine RC 12.00 5.00
- ❑ 146 Andy Marte 4.00 1.50
- ❑ 147 Jeff Mathis .40 .15
- ❑ 148 Joe Mauer 1.50 .60
- ❑ 149 Clint Nageotte .40 .15
- ❑ 150 Chris Narveson .40 .15
- ❑ 151 Ramon Nivar .50 .20
- ❑ 152 Felix Pie 5.00 2.00
- ❑ 153 Guillermo Quiroz RC 1.00 .40
- ❑ 154 Rene Reyes .40 .15
- ❑ 155 Royce Ring .40 .15
- ❑ 156 Alexis Rios 3.00 1.25
- ❑ 157 Grady Sizemore 1.50 .60
- ❑ 158 Stephen Smitherman .40 .15
- ❑ 159 Seung Song .40 .15
- ❑ 160 Scott Thorman .40 .15
- ❑ 161 Chad Tracy .40 .15
- ❑ 162 Chin-Hui Tsao .60 .25
- ❑ 163 John VanBenschoten .40 .15
- ❑ 164 Kevin Youkilis 5.00 2.00
- ❑ 165 Chien-Ming Wang 6.00 2.50
- ❑ 166 Chris Lubanski AU SP RC 40.00 20.00
- ❑ 167 Ryan Harvey AU RC 30.00 12.50
- ❑ 168 Matt Murton AU RC 30.00 12.50
- ❑ 169 Jay Sborz AU RC 10.00 4.00
- ❑ 170 Brandon Wood AU RC 80.00 40.00
- ❑ 171 Nick Markakis AU RC 80.00 40.00
- ❑ 172 Rickie Weeks AU RC 50.00 20.00
- ❑ 173 Eric Duncan AU RC 30.00 12.50
- ❑ 174 Chad Billingsley AU RC 50.00 30.00
- ❑ 175 Ryan Wagner AU RC 10.00 4.00
- ❑ 176 Delmon Young AU RC 120.00 60.00

2004 Bowman Chrome

- ❑ COMPLETE SET (350) 400.00 250.00
- ❑ COMP.SET w/o AU'S (330) 120.00 60.00
- ❑ COMMON CARD (1-150) .50 .20
- ❑ COMMON CARD (151-165) .50 .20
- ❑ COMMON AUTO (331-350) 10.00 4.00
- ❑ 331-350 AU'S ARE NOT SERIAL-NUMBERED
- ❑ 331-350 PRINT RUN PROVIDED BY TOPPS
- ❑ 1 Garret Anderson .50 .20
- ❑ 2 Larry Walker .50 .20
- ❑ 3 Derek Jeter 2.50 1.00
- ❑ 4 Curt Schilling .75 .30
- ❑ 5 Carlos Zambrano .50 .20
- ❑ 6 Shawn Green .50 .20
- ❑ 7 Manny Ramirez .75 .30
- ❑ 8 Randy Johnson 1.25 .50
- ❑ 9 Jeremy Bonderman .50 .20
- ❑ 10 Alfonso Soriano .50 .20
- ❑ 11 Scott Rolen .75 .30
- ❑ 12 Kerry Wood .50 .20
- ❑ 13 Eric Gagne .50 .20
- ❑ 14 Ryan Klesko .50 .20
- ❑ 15 Kevin Millar .50 .20
- ❑ 16 Ty Wigginton .50 .20
- ❑ 17 David Ortiz 1.25 .50
- ❑ 18 Luis Castillo .50 .20
- ❑ 19 Bernie Williams .75 .30
- ❑ 20 Edgar Renteria .50 .20
- ❑ 21 Matt Kata .50 .20
- ❑ 22 Bartolo Colon .50 .20
- ❑ 23 Derrek Lee .75 .30
- ❑ 24 Gary Sheffield .50 .20
- ❑ 25 Nomar Garciaparra 2.00 .75
- ❑ 26 Kevin Millwood .50 .20
- ❑ 27 Corey Patterson .50 .20
- ❑ 28 Carlos Beltran .50 .20
- ❑ 29 Mike Lieberthal .50 .20
- ❑ 30 Troy Glaus .50 .20
- ❑ 31 Preston Wilson .50 .20
- ❑ 32 Jorge Posada .75 .30
- ❑ 33 Bo Hart .50 .20
- ❑ 34 Mark Prior .75 .30
- ❑ 35 Hideo Nomo 1.25 .50
- ❑ 36 Jason Kendall .50 .20
- ❑ 37 Roger Clemens 2.50 1.00
- ❑ 38 Dmitri Young .50 .20
- ❑ 39 Jason Giambi .50 .20
- ❑ 40 Jim Edmonds .50 .20
- ❑ 41 Ryan Ludwick .50 .20
- ❑ 42 Brandon Webb .50 .20
- ❑ 43 Todd Helton .75 .30
- ❑ 44 Jacque Jones .50 .20
- ❑ 45 Jamie Moyer .50 .20
- ❑ 46 Tim Salmon .75 .30
- ❑ 47 Kelvim Escobar .50 .20
- ❑ 48 Tony Batista .50 .20
- ❑ 49 Nick Johnson .50 .20
- ❑ 50 Jim Thome .75 .30
- ❑ 51 Casey Blake .50 .20
- ❑ 52 Trot Nixon .50 .20
- ❑ 53 Luis Gonzalez .50 .20
- ❑ 54 Dontrelle Willis .75 .30
- ❑ 55 Mike Mussina .75 .30
- ❑ 56 Carl Crawford .50 .20
- ❑ 57 Mark Buehrle .50 .20
- ❑ 58 Scott Podsednik .50 .20
- ❑ 59 Brian Giles .50 .20
- ❑ 60 Rafael Furcal .50 .20
- ❑ 61 Miguel Cabrera .75 .30
- ❑ 62 Rich Harden .50 .20
- ❑ 63 Mark Teixeira .75 .30
- ❑ 64 Frank Thomas 1.25 .50
- ❑ 65 Johan Santana 1.25 .50
- ❑ 66 Jason Schmidt .50 .20
- ❑ 67 Aramis Ramirez .50 .20
- ❑ 68 Jose Reyes .50 .20
- ❑ 69 Magglio Ordonez .50 .20
- ❑ 70 Mike Sweeney .50 .20
- ❑ 71 Eric Chavez .50 .20
- ❑ 72 Rocco Baldelli .50 .20
- ❑ 73 Sammy Sosa 1.25 .50
- ❑ 74 Javy Lopez .50 .20
- ❑ 75 Roy Oswalt .50 .20
- ❑ 76 Raul Ibanez .50 .20
- ❑ 77 Ivan Rodriguez .75 .30
- ❑ 78 Jerome Williams .50 .20
- ❑ 79 Carlos Lee .50 .20
- ❑ 80 Geoff Jenkins .50 .20
- ❑ 81 Sean Burroughs .50 .20
- ❑ 82 Marcus Giles .50 .20
- ❑ 83 Mike Lowell .50 .20
- ❑ 84 Barry Zito .50 .20
- ❑ 85 Aubrey Huff .50 .20
- ❑ 86 Esteban Loaiza .50 .20
- ❑ 87 Torii Hunter .50 .20
- ❑ 88 Phil Nevin .50 .20
- ❑ 89 Andruw Jones .75 .30
- ❑ 90 Josh Beckett .50 .20
- ❑ 91 Mark Mulder .50 .20
- ❑ 92 Hank Blalock .50 .20
- ❑ 93 Jason Phillips .50 .20
- ❑ 94 Russ Ortiz .50 .20
- ❑ 95 Juan Pierre .50 .20
- ❑ 96 Tom Glavine .75 .30
- ❑ 97 Gil Meche .50 .20
- ❑ 98 Ramon Ortiz .50 .20
- ❑ 99 Richie Sexson .50 .20
- ❑ 100 Albert Pujols 2.50 1.00
- ❑ 101 Javier Vazquez .50 .20
- ❑ 102 Johnny Damon .75 .30
- ❑ 103 Alex Rodriguez 2.00 .75
- ❑ 104 Omar Vizquel .75 .30
- ❑ 105 Chipper Jones 1.25 .50
- ❑ 106 Lance Berkman .50 .20
- ❑ 107 Tim Hudson .50 .20
- ❑ 108 Carlos Delgado .50 .20
- ❑ 109 Austin Kearns .50 .20
- ❑ 110 Orlando Cabrera .50 .20
- ❑ 111 Edgar Martinez .75 .30
- ❑ 112 Melvin Mora .50 .20
- ❑ 113 Jeff Bagwell .75 .30
- ❑ 114 Marlon Byrd .50 .20
- ❑ 115 Vernon Wells .50 .20
- ❑ 116 C.C. Sabathia .50 .20
- ❑ 117 Cliff Floyd .50 .20
- ❑ 118 Ichiro Suzuki 2.50 1.00
- ❑ 119 Miguel Olivo .50 .20
- ❑ 120 Mike Piazza 2.00 .75
- ❑ 121 Adam Dunn .50 .20
- ❑ 122 Paul Lo Duca .50 .20
- ❑ 123 Brett Myers .50 .20
- ❑ 124 Michael Young .50 .20
- ❑ 125 Sidney Ponson .50 .20
- ❑ 126 Greg Maddux 2.00 .75
- ❑ 127 Vladimir Guerrero 1.25 .50
- ❑ 128 Miguel Tejada .50 .20
- ❑ 129 Andy Pettitte .75 .30
- ❑ 130 Rafael Palmeiro .75 .30
- ❑ 131 Ken Griffey Jr. 2.00 .75
- ❑ 132 Shannon Stewart .50 .20
- ❑ 133 Joel Pineiro .50 .20
- ❑ 134 Luis Matos .50 .20
- ❑ 135 Jeff Kent .50 .20
- ❑ 136 Randy Wolf .50 .20
- ❑ 137 Chris Woodward .50 .20
- ❑ 138 Jody Gerut .50 .20
- ❑ 139 Jose Vidro .50 .20
- ❑ 140 Bret Boone .50 .20
- ❑ 141 Bill Mueller .50 .20
- ❑ 142 Angel Berroa .50 .20
- ❑ 143 Bobby Abreu .50 .20
- ❑ 144 Roy Halladay .50 .20
- ❑ 145 Delmon Young .75 .30
- ❑ 146 Jonny Gomes .50 .20
- ❑ 147 Rickie Weeks .50 .20
- ❑ 148 Edwin Jackson .50 .20
- ❑ 149 Neal Cotts .50 .20
- ❑ 150 Jason Bay .50 .20
- ❑ 151 Khalil Greene 1.00 .40
- ❑ 152 Joe Mauer 1.25 .50
- ❑ 153 Bobby Jenks .75 .30
- ❑ 154 Chin-Feng Chen .50 .20
- ❑ 155 Chien-Ming Wang 2.00 .75
- ❑ 156 Mickey Hall .50 .20
- ❑ 157 James Houser .50 .20
- ❑ 158 Jay Sborz .50 .20
- ❑ 159 Jonathan Fulton .50 .20
- ❑ 160 Steven Lerud .50 .20
- ❑ 161 Grady Sizemore 1.50 .60
- ❑ 162 Felix Pie 2.00 .75
- ❑ 163 Dustin McGowan .50 .20
- ❑ 164 Chris Lubanski .75 .30
- ❑ 165 Tom Gorzelanny .50 .20
- ❑ 166 Rudy Guillen RC 3.00 1.25
- ❑ 167 Aarom Baldiris RC 2.00 .75
- ❑ 168 Conor Jackson RC 10.00 4.00
- ❑ 169 Matt Moses RC 4.00 1.50
- ❑ 170 Ervin Santana RC 6.00 2.50
- ❑ 171 Merkin Valdez RC 2.00 .75
- ❑ 172 Erick Aybar RC 3.00 1.25
- ❑ 173 Brad Sullivan RC 2.00 .75
- ❑ 174 Joey Gathright RC 4.00 1.50

❑ 175 Brad Snyder RC 4.00 1.50
❑ 176 Alberto Callaspo RC 3.00 1.25
❑ 177 Brandon Medders RC 1.50 .60
❑ 178 Zach Miner RC 5.00 2.00
❑ 179 Charlie Zink RC 1.00 .40
❑ 180 Adam Greenberg RC 3.00 1.25
❑ 181 Kevin Howard RC 2.00 .75
❑ 182 Wanell Severino RC 1.00 .40
❑ 183 Chin-Lung Hu RC 5.00 2.00
❑ 184 Joel Zumaya RC 12.00 5.00
❑ 185 Skip Schumaker RC 1.50 .60
❑ 186 Nic Ungs RC 1.50 .60
❑ 187 Todd Self RC 2.00 .75
❑ 188 Brian Steffek RC 1.00 .40
❑ 189 Brock Peterson RC 1.50 .60
❑ 190 Greg Thissen RC 1.50 .60
❑ 191 Frank Brooks RC 1.00 .40
❑ 192 Scott Olsen RC 6.00 2.50
❑ 193 Chris Mabeus RC 1.50 .60
❑ 194 Dan Giese RC 1.50 .60
❑ 195 Jared Wells RC 1.00 .40
❑ 196 Carlos Sosa RC 1.50 .60
❑ 197 Bobby Madritsch 1.00 .40
❑ 198 Calvin Hayes RC 2.00 .75
❑ 199 Omar Quintanilla RC 2.00 .75
❑ 200 Chris O'Riordan RC 1.50 .60
❑ 201 Tim Hutting RC 1.00 .40
❑ 202 Carlos Quentin RC 10.00 4.00
❑ 203 Brayan Pena RC 1.50 .60
❑ 204 Jeff Salazar RC 4.00 1.50
❑ 205 David Murphy RC 3.00 1.25
❑ 206 Alberto Garcia RC 2.00 .75
❑ 207 Ramon Ramirez RC 1.50 .60
❑ 208 Luis Bolivar RC 1.50 .60
❑ 209 Rodney Choy Foo RC 1.00 .40
❑ 210 Fausto Carmona RC 8.00 3.00
❑ 211 Anthony Acevedo RC 1.50 .60
❑ 212 Chad Santos RC 1.50 .60
❑ 213 Jason Frasor RC 1.50 .60
❑ 214 Jesse Roman RC 1.00 .40
❑ 215 James Tomlin RC 1.50 .60
❑ 216 Josh Labandeira RC 1.50 .60
❑ 217 Ryan Meaux RC 1.50 .60
❑ 218 Don Sutton RC 4.00 1.50
❑ 219 Danny Gonzalez RC 1.00 .40
❑ 220 Javier Guzman RC 2.00 .75
❑ 221 Anthony Lerew RC 3.00 1.25
❑ 222 Jon Connolly RC 4.00 1.50
❑ 223 Jesse English RC 1.50 .60
❑ 224 Hector Madé RC 3.00 1.25
❑ 225 Travis Hanson RC 2.00 .75
❑ 226 Jesse Floyd RC 1.50 .60
❑ 227 Nick Gorneault RC 2.00 .75
❑ 228 Craig Ansman RC 1.50 .60
❑ 229 Paul McAnulty RC 3.00 1.25
❑ 230 Carl Loadenthal RC 2.00 .75
❑ 231 Dave Crouthers RC 1.00 .40
❑ 232 Harvey Garcia RC 1.00 .40
❑ 233 Casey Kopitzke RC 1.00 .40
❑ 234 Ricky Nolasco RC 5.00 2.00
❑ 235 Miguel Perez RC 1.50 .60
❑ 236 Ryan Mulhern RC 1.50 .60
❑ 237 Chris Aguila RC 1.50 .60
❑ 238 Brooks Conrad RC 2.00 .75
❑ 239 Damaso Espino RC 1.00 .40
❑ 240 Jereme Milons RC 2.00 .75
❑ 241 Luke Hughes RC 1.00 .40
❑ 242 Kory Casto RC 2.00 .75
❑ 243 Jose Valdez RC 1.50 .60
❑ 244 J.T. Stotts RC 1.00 .40
❑ 245 Lee Gwaltney RC 1.00 .40
❑ 246 Yoann Torrealba RC 1.00 .40
❑ 247 Omar Falcon RC 1.50 .60
❑ 248 Jon Coutlangus RC 1.00 .40
❑ 249 George Sherrill RC 1.50 .60
❑ 250 John Santor RC 1.00 .40
❑ 251 Tony Richie RC 1.50 .60
❑ 252 Kevin Richardson RC 1.00 .40
❑ 253 Tim Bittner RC 1.50 .60
❑ 254 Chris Saenz RC 1.50 .60
❑ 255 Jose Capellan RC 2.00 .75
❑ 256 Donald Levinski RC 1.00 .40
❑ 257 Jerome Gamble RC 1.00 .40
❑ 258 Jeff Keppinger RC 6.00 2.50
❑ 259 Jason Szuminski RC 1.00 .40
❑ 260 Akinori Otsuka RC 1.50 .60
❑ 261 Ryan Budde RC 1.50 .60
❑ 262 Marland Williams RC 2.00 .75
❑ 263 Jeff Allison RC 1.50 .60
❑ 264 Hector Gimenez RC 1.00 .40
❑ 265 Tim Frend RC 1.50 .60
❑ 266 Tom Farmer RC 1.50 .60
❑ 267 Shawn Hill RC 1.50 .60
❑ 268 Mike Huggins RC 1.50 .60
❑ 269 Scott Proctor RC 2.00 .75
❑ 270 Jorge Mejia RC 1.50 .60
❑ 271 Terry Jones RC 2.00 .75
❑ 272 Zach Duke RC 8.00 3.00
❑ 273 Jesse Crain RC 3.00 1.25
❑ 274 Luke Anderson RC 1.00 .40
❑ 275 Hunter Brown RC 1.00 .40
❑ 276 Matt Lemanczyk RC 1.50 .60
❑ 277 Fernando Cortez RC 1.00 .40
❑ 278 Vince Perkins RC 2.00 .75
❑ 279 Tommy Murphy RC 1.50 .60
❑ 280 Mike Gosling RC 1.00 .40
❑ 281 Paul Bacot RC 2.00 .75
❑ 282 Matt Capps RC 1.50 .60
❑ 283 Juan Gutierrez RC 1.50 .60
❑ 284 Teodoro Encarnacion RC 2.00 .75
❑ 285 Chad Bentz RC 1.50 .60
❑ 286 Kazuo Matsui RC 2.00 .75
❑ 287 Ryan Hankins RC 1.00 .40
❑ 288 Leo Nunez RC 1.50 .60
❑ 289 Dave Wallace RC 1.50 .60
❑ 290 Rob Tejeda RC 3.00 1.25
❑ 291 Paul Maholm RC 4.00 1.50
❑ 292 Casey Daigle RC 1.50 .60
❑ 293 Tydus Meadows RC 1.00 .40
❑ 294 Khalid Ballouli RC 1.00 .40
❑ 295 Benji DeQuin RC 1.00 .40
❑ 296 Tyler Davidson RC 2.00 .75
❑ 297 Brant Colamarino RC 3.00 1.25
❑ 298 Marcus McBeth RC 1.00 .40
❑ 299 Brad Eldred RC 2.00 .75
❑ 300 David Pauley RC 5.00 2.00
❑ 301 Yadier Molina RC 6.00 2.50
❑ 302 Chris Shelton RC 5.00 2.00
❑ 303 Nyjer Morgan RC 1.00 .40
❑ 304 Jon DeVries RC 1.50 .60
❑ 305 Sheldon Fulse RC 1.00 .40
❑ 306 Vito Chiaravalloti RC 1.50 .60
❑ 307 Warner Madrigal RC 3.00 1.25
❑ 308 Reid Gorecki RC 1.50 .60
❑ 309 Sung Jung RC 1.00 .40
❑ 310 Pete Shier RC 1.00 .40
❑ 311 Michael Mooney RC 1.50 .60
❑ 312 Kenny Perez RC 1.50 .60
❑ 313 Michael Mallory RC 1.50 .60
❑ 314 Ben Himes RC 1.00 .40
❑ 315 Ivan Ochoa RC 1.50 .60
❑ 316 Donald Kelly RC 1.50 .60
❑ 317 Tom Mastny RC 1.50 .60
❑ 318 Kevin Davidson RC 1.00 .40
❑ 319 Brian Pilkington RC 1.00 .40
❑ 320 Alex Romero RC 1.50 .60
❑ 321 Chad Chop RC 1.50 .60
❑ 322 Kody Kirkland RC 2.00 .75
❑ 323 Casey Myers RC 1.00 .40
❑ 324 Mike Rouse RC 1.50 .60
❑ 325 Sergio Silva RC 1.00 .40
❑ 326 J.J. Furmaniak RC 3.00 1.25
❑ 327 Brad Vericker RC 1.50 .60
❑ 328 Blake Hawksworth RC 2.00 .75
❑ 329 Brock Jacobsen RC 1.00 .40
❑ 330 Alec Zumwalt RC 1.00 .40
❑ 331 Wardell Starling AU RC 10.00 4.00
❑ 332 Estee Harris AU RC 10.00 4.00
❑ 333 Kyle Sleeth AU RC 10.00 4.00
❑ 334 Dioner Navarro AU RC 15.00 6.00
❑ 335 Logan Kensing AU RC 10.00 4.00
❑ 336 Travis Blackley AU RC 10.00 4.00
❑ 337 Lincoln Holdzkom AU RC 10.00 4.00
❑ 338 Jason Hirsh AU RC 25.00 10.00
❑ 339 Juan Cedeno AU RC 10.00 4.00
❑ 340 Matt Creighton AU RC 10.00 4.00
❑ 341 Tim Stauffer AU RC 15.00 6.00
❑ 342 Shingo Takatsu AU RC 15.00 6.00
❑ 343 Lastings Milledge AU RC 50.00 20.00
❑ 344 Dustin Nippert AU RC 10.00 4.00
❑ 345 Felix Hernandez AU RC 120.00 60.00
❑ 346 Joaquin Arias AU RC 15.00 6.00
❑ 347 Kevin Kouzmanoff AU RC 25.00 10.00
❑ 348 B.Brownlie AU RC 10.00 4.00
❑ 349 David Aardsma AU RC 10.00 4.00
❑ 350 Jon Knott AU RC 15.00 6.00

2004 Bowman Chrome Draft

❑ COMPLETE SET (175) 300.00 175.00
❑ COMP.SET w/o SP's (165) 100.00 50.00
❑ COMMON CARD (1-165) .40 .15
❑ COMMON RC YR .40 .15
❑ 1-165 TWO PER BOWMAN DRAFT PACK
❑ 166-175 ODDS 1:60 BOWMAN DRAFT HOBBY
❑ 166-175 ODDS 1:60 BOWMAN DRAFT RETAIL
❑ 166-175 STATED PRINT RUN 1695 SETS
❑ 166-175 ARE NOT SERIAL-NUMBERED
❑ 166-175 PRINT RUN PROVIDED BY TOPPS
❑ PLATES 1-165 ODDS 1:559 HOBBY
❑ PLATES 166-175 ODDS 1:18,354 HOBBY
❑ PLATES PRINT RUN 1 SERIAL #'d SET
❑ BLACK-CYAN-MAGENTA-YELLOW EXIST
❑ NO PLATES PRICING DUE TO SCARCITY
❑ 1 Lyle Overbay .40 .15
❑ 2 David Newhan .40 .15
❑ 3 J.R. House .40 .15
❑ 4 Chad Tracy .40 .15
❑ 5 Humberto Quintero .40 .15
❑ 6 Dave Bush .40 .15
❑ 7 Scott Hairston .40 .15
❑ 8 Mike Wood .40 .15
❑ 9 Alexis Rios .60 .25
❑ 10 Sean Burnett .40 .15
❑ 11 Wilson Valdez .40 .15
❑ 12 Lew Ford .40 .15
❑ 13 Freddy Thon RC 1.00 .40
❑ 14 Zack Greinke .60 .25
❑ 15 Bucky Jacobsen .40 .15
❑ 16 Kevin Youkilis .40 .15
❑ 17 Grady Sizemore 1.50 .60
❑ 18 Denny Bautista .40 .15
❑ 19 David DeJesus .40 .15
❑ 20 Casey Kotchman .60 .25
❑ 21 David Kelton .40 .15
❑ 22 Charles Thomas RC 1.00 .40
❑ 23 Kazuhito Tadano RC 1.50 .60
❑ 24 Justin Leone RC 1.50 .60
❑ 25 Eduardo Villacis RC 1.00 .40
❑ 26 Brian Dallimore RC 1.00 .40
❑ 27 Nick Green .40 .15
❑ 28 Sam McConnell RC 1.00 .40
❑ 29 Brad Halsey RC 1.50 .60
❑ 30 Roman Colon RC 1.00 .40
❑ 31 Josh Fields RC 6.00 2.50
❑ 32 Cody Bunkelman RC 1.50 .60
❑ 33 Jay Rainville RC 4.00 1.50
❑ 34 Richie Robnett RC 3.00 1.25
❑ 35 Jon Poterson RC 2.50 1.00
❑ 36 Huston Street RC 5.00 2.00
❑ 37 Erick San Pedro RC 1.00 .40
❑ 38 Cory Dunlap RC 3.00 1.25
❑ 39 Kurt Suzuki RC 3.00 1.25
❑ 40 Anthony Swarzak RC 2.50 1.00
❑ 41 Ian Desmond RC 4.00 1.50
❑ 42 Chris Covington RC 1.50 .60
❑ 43 Christian Garcia RC 2.50 1.00
❑ 44 Gaby Hernandez RC 4.00 1.50
❑ 45 Steven Register RC 1.00 .40
❑ 46 Eduardo Morlan RC 3.00 1.25

❑ 47 Collin Balester RC	1.50	.60
❑ 48 Nathan Phillips RC	1.50	.60
❑ 49 Dan Schwartzbauer RC	1.50	.60
❑ 50 Rafael Gonzalez RC	1.00	.40
❑ 51 K.C. Herren RC	2.50	1.00
❑ 52 William Susdorf RC	1.00	.40
❑ 53 Rob Johnson RC	1.50	.60
❑ 54 Louis Marson RC	2.50	1.00
❑ 55 Joe Koshansky RC	6.00	2.50
❑ 56 Jamar Walton RC	2.50	1.00
❑ 57 Mark Lowe RC	5.00	2.00
❑ 58 Matt Macri RC	3.00	1.25
❑ 59 Donny Lucy RC	1.00	.40
❑ 60 Mike Ferris RC	1.50	.60
❑ 61 Mike Nickeas RC	1.50	.60
❑ 62 Eric Hurley RC	3.00	1.25
❑ 63 Scott Elbert RC	3.00	1.25
❑ 64 Blake DeWitt RC	5.00	2.00
❑ 65 Danny Putnam RC	2.50	1.00
❑ 66 J.P. Howell RC	3.00	1.25
❑ 67 John Wiggins RC	1.00	.40
❑ 68 Justin Orenduff RC	2.50	1.00
❑ 69 Ray Liotta RC	3.00	1.25
❑ 70 Billy Buckner RC	1.50	.60
❑ 71 Eric Campbell RC	6.00	2.50
❑ 72 Olin Wick RC	2.50	1.00
❑ 73 Sean Gamble RC	1.50	.60
❑ 74 Seth Smith RC	3.00	1.25
❑ 75 Wade Davis RC	5.00	2.00
❑ 76 Joe Jacobitz RC	1.00	.40
❑ 77 J.A. Happ RC	2.50	1.00
❑ 78 Eric Ridener RC	1.00	.40
❑ 79 Matt Tuiasosopo RC	4.00	1.50
❑ 80 Brad Bergesen RC	1.00	.40
❑ 81 Javy Guerra RC	1.50	.60
❑ 82 Buck Shaw RC	1.50	.60
❑ 83 Paul Janish RC	2.00	.75
❑ 84 Sean Kazmar RC	1.00	.40
❑ 85 Josh Johnson RC	1.50	.60
❑ 86 Angel Salome RC	4.00	1.50
❑ 87 Jordan Parraz RC	2.50	1.00
❑ 88 Kelvin Vazquez RC	1.00	.40
❑ 89 Grant Hansen RC	1.00	.40
❑ 90 Matt Fox RC	1.00	.40
❑ 91 Trevor Plouffe RC	4.00	1.50
❑ 92 Wes Whisler RC	1.00	.40
❑ 93 Curtis Thigpen RC	2.50	1.00
❑ 94 Donnie Smith RC	1.50	.60
❑ 95 Luis Rivera RC	1.50	.60
❑ 96 Jesse Hoover RC	1.50	.60
❑ 97 Jason Vargas RC	4.00	1.50
❑ 98 Clary Carlsen RC	1.00	.40
❑ 99 Mark Robinson RC	1.00	.40
❑ 100 J.C. Holt RC	1.50	.60
❑ 101 Chad Blackwell RC	1.00	.40
❑ 102 Daryl Jones RC	3.00	1.25
❑ 103 Jonathan Tierce RC	1.00	.40
❑ 104 Patrick Bryant RC	1.00	.40
❑ 105 Eddie Prasch RC	1.50	.60
❑ 106 Mitch Einertson RC	2.00	.75
❑ 107 Kyle Waldrop RC	3.00	1.25
❑ 108 Jeff Marquez RC	1.50	.60
❑ 109 Zach Jackson RC	2.50	1.00
❑ 110 Josh Wahpepah RC	1.00	.40
❑ 111 Adam Lind RC	8.00	3.00
❑ 112 Kyle Bloom RC	1.50	.60
❑ 113 Ben Harrison RC	1.00	.40
❑ 114 Taylor Tankersley RC	1.50	.60
❑ 115 Steven Jackson RC	1.00	.40
❑ 116 David Purcey RC	2.50	1.00
❑ 117 Jacob McGee RC	5.00	2.00
❑ 118 Lucas Harrell RC	1.00	.40
❑ 119 Brandon Allen RC	3.00	1.25
❑ 120 Van Pope RC	1.50	.60
❑ 121 Jeff Francis	.60	.25
❑ 122 Joe Blanton	.60	.25
❑ 123 Wil Ledezma	.40	.15
❑ 124 Bryan Bullington	.40	.15
❑ 125 Jairo Garcia	.40	.15
❑ 126 Matt Cain	2.00	.75
❑ 127 Arnie Munoz	.40	.15
❑ 128 Clint Everts	.40	.15
❑ 129 Jesus Cota	.40	.15
❑ 130 Gavin Floyd	.40	.15
❑ 131 Edwin Encarnacion	.60	.25
❑ 132 Koyie Hill	.40	.15
❑ 133 Ruben Gotay	.40	.15
❑ 134 Jeff Mathis	.40	.15
❑ 135 Andy Marte	1.00	.40
❑ 136 Dallas McPherson	.60	.25
❑ 137 Justin Morneau	.60	.25
❑ 138 Rickie Weeks	.60	.25
❑ 139 Joel Guzman	1.00	.40
❑ 140 Shin Soo Choo	.40	.15
❑ 141 Yusmeiro Petit RC	5.00	2.00
❑ 142 Jorge Cortes RC	1.00	.40
❑ 143 Val Majewski	.40	.15
❑ 144 Felix Pie	1.00	.40
❑ 145 Aaron Hill	.40	.15
❑ 146 Jose Capellan	.60	.25
❑ 147 Dioner Navarro	1.00	.40
❑ 148 Fausto Carmona	2.50	1.00
❑ 149 Robinzon Diaz RC	1.00	.40
❑ 150 Felix Hernandez	15.00	6.00
❑ 151 Andres Blanco RC	1.00	.40
❑ 152 Jason Kubel	.40	.15
❑ 153 Willy Taveras RC	2.50	1.00
❑ 154 Merkin Valdez	1.00	.40
❑ 155 Robinson Cano	1.50	.60
❑ 156 Bill Murphy	.40	.15
❑ 157 Chris Burke	.60	.25
❑ 158 Kyle Sleeth	.40	.15
❑ 159 B.J. Upton	1.00	.40
❑ 160 Tim Stauffer	1.00	.40
❑ 161 David Wright	4.00	1.50
❑ 162 Conor Jackson	4.00	1.50
❑ 163 Brad Thompson RC	2.50	1.00
❑ 164 Delmon Young	1.00	.40
❑ 165 Jeremy Reed	.60	.25
❑ 166 Matt Bush AU RC	25.00	10.00
❑ 167 Mark Rogers AU RC	20.00	8.00
❑ 168 Thomas Diamond AU RC	15.00	6.00
❑ 169 Greg Golson AU RC	20.00	8.00
❑ 170 Homer Bailey AU RC	60.00	30.00
❑ 171 Chris Lambert AU RC	10.00	4.00
❑ 172 Neil Walker AU RC	30.00	12.50
❑ 173 Bill Bray AU RC	10.00	4.00
❑ 174 Philip Hughes AU RC	100.00	50.00
❑ 175 Gio Gonzalez AU RC	30.00	12.50

2005 Bowman Chrome

❑ COMP.SET w/o AU's (330)	120.00	60.00
❑ COMMON CARD (1-140)	.50	.20
❑ COMMON CARD (141-165)	.50	.20
❑ COMMON CARD (166-330)	1.00	.40
❑ COMMON AUTO (331-353)	10.00	4.00
❑ 1-330 PLATE ODDS 1:779 HOBBY		
❑ 331-353 AU PLATE ODDS 1:10,996 HOBBY		
❑ PLATE PRINT RUN 1 SET PER COLOR		
❑ BLACK-CYAN-MAGENTA-YELLOW ISSUED		
❑ NO PLATE PRICING DUE TO SCARCITY		
❑ 1 Gavin Floyd	.50	.20
❑ 2 Eric Chavez	.50	.20
❑ 3 Miguel Tejada	.50	.20
❑ 4 Dmitri Young	.50	.20
❑ 5 Hank Blalock	.50	.20
❑ 6 Kerry Wood	.50	.20
❑ 7 Andy Pettitte	.75	.30
❑ 8 Pat Burrell	.50	.20
❑ 9 Johnny Estrada	.50	.20
❑ 10 Frank Thomas	1.25	.50
❑ 11 Juan Pierre	.50	.20
❑ 12 Tom Glavine	.75	.30
❑ 13 Lyle Overbay	.50	.20
❑ 14 Jim Edmonds	.50	.20
❑ 15 Steve Finley	.50	.20
❑ 16 Jermaine Dye	.50	.20
❑ 17 Omar Vizquel	.75	.30
❑ 18 Nick Johnson	.50	.20
❑ 19 Brian Giles	.50	.20
❑ 20 Justin Morneau	.50	.20
❑ 21 Preston Wilson	.50	.20
❑ 22 Wily Mo Pena	.50	.20
❑ 23 Rafael Palmeiro	.75	.30
❑ 24 Scott Kazmir	.50	.20
❑ 25 Derek Jeter	2.50	1.00
❑ 26 Barry Zito	.50	.20
❑ 27 Mike Lowell	.50	.20
❑ 28 Jason Bay	.50	.20
❑ 29 Ken Harvey	.50	.20
❑ 30 Nomar Garciaparra	1.25	.50
❑ 31 Roy Halladay	.50	.20
❑ 32 Todd Helton	.75	.30
❑ 33 Mark Kotsay	.50	.20
❑ 34 Jake Peavy	.50	.20
❑ 35 David Wright	2.00	.75
❑ 36 Dontrelle Willis	.50	.20
❑ 37 Marcus Giles	.50	.20
❑ 38 Chone Figgins	.50	.20
❑ 39 Sidney Ponson	.50	.20
❑ 40 Randy Johnson	1.25	.50
❑ 41 John Smoltz	.75	.30
❑ 42 Kevin Millar	.50	.20
❑ 43 Mark Teixeira	.75	.30
❑ 44 Alex Rios	.50	.20
❑ 45 Mike Piazza	1.25	.50
❑ 46 Victor Martinez	.50	.20
❑ 47 Jeff Bagwell	.75	.30
❑ 48 Shawn Green	.50	.20
❑ 49 Ivan Rodriguez	.75	.30
❑ 50 Alex Rodriguez	2.00	.75
❑ 51 Kazuo Matsui	.50	.20
❑ 52 Mark Mulder	.50	.20
❑ 53 Michael Young	.50	.20
❑ 54 Javy Lopez	.50	.20
❑ 55 Johnny Damon	.75	.30
❑ 56 Jeff Francis	.50	.20
❑ 57 Rich Harden	.50	.20
❑ 58 Bobby Abreu	.50	.20
❑ 59 Mark Loretta	.50	.20
❑ 60 Gary Sheffield	.50	.20
❑ 61 Jamie Moyer	.50	.20
❑ 62 Garret Anderson	.50	.20
❑ 63 Vernon Wells	.50	.20
❑ 64 Orlando Cabrera	.50	.20
❑ 65 Magglio Ordonez	.50	.20
❑ 66 Ronnie Belliard	.50	.20
❑ 67 Carlos Lee	.50	.20
❑ 68 Carl Pavano	.50	.20
❑ 69 Jon Lieber	.50	.20
❑ 70 Aubrey Huff	.50	.20
❑ 71 Rocco Baldelli	.50	.20
❑ 72 Jason Schmidt	.50	.20
❑ 73 Bernie Williams	.75	.30
❑ 74 Hideki Matsui	2.00	.75
❑ 75 Ken Griffey Jr.	2.00	.75
❑ 76 Josh Beckett	.50	.20
❑ 77 Mark Buehrle	.50	.20
❑ 78 David Ortiz	1.25	.50
❑ 79 Luis Gonzalez	.50	.20
❑ 80 Scott Rolen	.75	.30
❑ 81 Joe Mauer	1.25	.50
❑ 82 Jose Reyes	.50	.20
❑ 83 Adam Dunn	.50	.20
❑ 84 Greg Maddux	2.00	.75
❑ 85 Bartolo Colon	.50	.20
❑ 86 Bret Boone	.50	.20
❑ 87 Mike Mussina	.75	.30
❑ 88 Ben Sheets	.50	.20
❑ 89 Lance Berkman	.50	.20
❑ 90 Miguel Cabrera	.75	.30
❑ 91 C.C. Sabathia	.50	.20
❑ 92 Mike Maroth	.50	.20
❑ 93 Andruw Jones	.75	.30
❑ 94 Jack Wilson	.50	.20
❑ 95 Ichiro Suzuki	2.50	1.00
❑ 96 Geoff Jenkins	.50	.20
❑ 97 Zack Greinke	.50	.20
❑ 98 Jorge Posada	.75	.30
❑ 99 Travis Hafner	.50	.20

❑ 100	Barry Bonds	3.00	1.25
❑ 101	Aaron Rowand	.50	.20
❑ 102	Aramis Ramirez	.50	.20
❑ 103	Curt Schilling	.75	.30
❑ 104	Melvin Mora	.50	.20
❑ 105	Albert Pujols	2.50	1.00
❑ 106	Austin Kearns	.50	.20
❑ 107	Shannon Stewart	.50	.20
❑ 108	Carl Crawford	.50	.20
❑ 109	Carlos Zambrano	.50	.20
❑ 110	Roger Clemens	2.00	.75
❑ 111	Javier Vazquez	.50	.20
❑ 112	Randy Wolf	.50	.20
❑ 113	Chipper Jones	1.25	.50
❑ 114	Larry Walker	.75	.30
❑ 115	Alfonso Soriano	.50	.20
❑ 116	Brad Wilkerson	.50	.20
❑ 117	Bobby Crosby	.50	.20
❑ 118	Jim Thome	.75	.30
❑ 119	Oliver Perez	.50	.20
❑ 120	Vladimir Guerrero	1.25	.50
❑ 121	Roy Oswalt	.50	.20
❑ 122	Torii Hunter	.50	.20
❑ 123	Rafael Furcal	.50	.20
❑ 124	Luis Castillo	.50	.20
❑ 125	Carlos Beltran	.50	.20
❑ 126	Mike Sweeney	.50	.20
❑ 127	Johan Santana	1.25	.50
❑ 128	Tim Hudson	.50	.20
❑ 129	Troy Glaus	.50	.20
❑ 130	Manny Ramirez	.75	.30
❑ 131	Jeff Kent	.50	.20
❑ 132	Jose Vidro	.50	.20
❑ 133	Edgar Renteria	.50	.20
❑ 134	Russ Ortiz	.50	.20
❑ 135	Sammy Sosa	1.25	.50
❑ 136	Carlos Delgado	.50	.20
❑ 137	Richie Sexson	.50	.20
❑ 138	Pedro Martinez	.75	.30
❑ 139	Adrian Beltre	.50	.20
❑ 140	Mark Prior	.75	.30
❑ 141	Omar Quintanilla	.50	.20
❑ 142	Carlos Quentin	.75	.30
❑ 143	Dan Johnson	.50	.20
❑ 144	Jake Stevens	.50	.20
❑ 145	Nate Schierholtz	.75	.30
❑ 146	Neil Walker	.50	.20
❑ 147	Bill Bray	.50	.20
❑ 148	Taylor Tankersley	.50	.20
❑ 149	Trevor Plouffe	.75	.30
❑ 150	Felix Hernandez	6.00	2.50
❑ 151	Philip Hughes	2.00	.75
❑ 152	James Houser	.50	.20
❑ 153	David Murphy	.50	.20
❑ 154	Ervin Santana	.75	.30
❑ 155	Anthony Whittington	.50	.20
❑ 156	Chris Lambert	.50	.20
❑ 157	Jeremy Sowers	.75	.30
❑ 158	Giovanny Gonzalez	.75	.30
❑ 159	Blake DeWitt	.75	.30
❑ 160	Thomas Diamond	.75	.30
❑ 161	Greg Golson	.75	.30
❑ 162	David Aardsma	.50	.20
❑ 163	Paul Maholm	.50	.20
❑ 164	Mark Rogers	.75	.30
❑ 165	Homer Bailey	.75	.30
❑ 166	Elvin Puello RC	1.50	.60
❑ 167	Tony Giarratano RC	1.50	.60
❑ 168	Darren Fenster RC	1.50	.60
❑ 169	Elvys Quezada RC	1.50	.60
❑ 170	Glen Perkins RC	3.00	1.25
❑ 171	Ian Kinsler RC	6.00	2.50
❑ 172	Adam Bostick RC	1.50	.60
❑ 173	Jeremy West RC	2.00	.75
❑ 174	Brett Harper RC	2.00	.75
❑ 175	Kevin West RC	1.50	.60
❑ 176	Luis Hernandez RC	1.50	.60
❑ 177	Matt Campbell RC	1.50	.60
❑ 178	Nate McLouth RC	4.00	1.50
❑ 179	Ryan Goleski RC	2.00	.75
❑ 180	Matthew Lindstrom RC	1.50	.60
❑ 181	Matt DeSalvo RC	2.00	.75
❑ 182	Kole Strayhorn RC	1.50	.60
❑ 183	Jose Vaquedano RC	1.50	.60
❑ 184	James Jurries RC	2.00	.75
❑ 185	Ian Bladergroen RC	2.00	.75
❑ 186	Kila Kaaihue RC	4.00	1.50
❑ 187	Luke Scott RC	6.00	2.50
❑ 188	Chris Denorfia RC	4.00	1.50
❑ 189	Jai Miller RC	2.00	.75
❑ 190	Melky Cabrera RC	8.00	3.00
❑ 191	Ryan Sweeney RC	4.00	1.50
❑ 192	Sean Marshall RC	6.00	2.50
❑ 193	Erick Abreu RC	3.00	1.25
❑ 194	Tyler Pelland RC	2.00	.75
❑ 195	Cole Armstrong RC	1.50	.60
❑ 196	John Hudgins RC	1.50	.60
❑ 197	Wade Robinson RC	1.50	.60
❑ 198	Dan Santin RC	1.50	.60
❑ 199	Steve Doetsch RC	1.50	.60
❑ 200	Shane Costa RC	1.50	.60
❑ 201	Scott Mathieson RC	3.00	1.25
❑ 202	Ben Jones RC	2.00	.75
❑ 203	Michael Rogers RC	1.50	.60
❑ 204	Matt Rogelstad RC	1.50	.60
❑ 205	Luis Ramirez RC	1.50	.60
❑ 206	Landon Powell RC	2.00	.75
❑ 207	Erik Cordier RC	1.50	.60
❑ 208	Chris Seddon RC	1.50	.60
❑ 209	Chris Roberson RC	1.50	.60
❑ 210	Thomas Oldham RC	1.50	.60
❑ 211	Dana Eveland RC	1.50	.60
❑ 212	Cody Haerther RC	1.50	.60
❑ 213	Danny Core RC	1.50	.60
❑ 214	Craig Tatum RC	1.50	.60
❑ 215	Elliot Johnson RC	1.50	.60
❑ 216	Ender Chavez RC	1.50	.60
❑ 217	Errol Simonitsch RC	2.00	.75
❑ 218	Matt Van Der Bosch RC	1.50	.60
❑ 219	Eulogio de la Cruz RC	1.50	.60
❑ 220	Drew Toussaint RC	1.50	.60
❑ 221	Adam Boeve RC	1.50	.60
❑ 222	Adam Harben RC	2.00	.75
❑ 223	Baltazar Lopez RC	1.50	.60
❑ 224	Russ Martin RC	5.00	2.00
❑ 225	Brian Bannister RC	4.00	1.50
❑ 226	Chris Walker RC	1.50	.60
❑ 227	Casey McGehee RC	1.50	.60
❑ 228	Humberto Sanchez RC	6.00	2.50
❑ 229	Javon Moran RC	1.50	.60
❑ 230	Brandon McCarthy RC	5.00	2.00
❑ 231	Danny Zell RC	1.50	.60
❑ 232	Kevin Barry RC	1.50	.60
❑ 233	Juan Tejeda RC	1.50	.60
❑ 234	Keith Ramsey RC	1.50	.60
❑ 235	Lorenzo Scott RC	1.50	.60
❑ 236	Jon Barratt RC	1.50	.60
❑ 237	Martin Prado RC	1.50	.60
❑ 238	Matt Albers RC	4.00	1.50
❑ 239	Brian Schweiger RC	1.50	.60
❑ 240	Raul Tablado RC	1.50	.60
❑ 241	Pat Misch RC	1.50	.60
❑ 242	Pat Osborn	1.50	.60
❑ 243	Ryan Feierabend RC	1.50	.60
❑ 244	Shaun Marcum	1.00	.40
❑ 245	Kevin Collins RC	1.50	.60
❑ 246	Stuart Pomeranz RC	1.50	.60
❑ 247	Tetsu Yofu RC	1.50	.60
❑ 248	Hernan Iribarren RC	2.00	.75
❑ 249	Mike Spidale RC	1.50	.60
❑ 250	Tony Americh RC	1.50	.60
❑ 251	Manny Parra RC	5.00	2.00
❑ 252	Drew Anderson RC	1.50	.60
❑ 253	T.J. Beam RC	3.00	1.25
❑ 254	Claudio Arias RC	2.00	.75
❑ 255	Andy Sides RC	1.50	.60
❑ 256	Bear Bay RC	2.00	.75
❑ 257	Bill McCarthy RC	1.50	.60
❑ 258	Daniel Haigwood RC	3.00	1.25
❑ 259	Brian Sprout RC	2.00	.75
❑ 260	Bryan Triplett RC	1.50	.60
❑ 261	Steven Bondurant RC	1.50	.60
❑ 262	Darwinson Salazar RC	1.50	.60
❑ 263	David Shepard RC	1.50	.60
❑ 264	Johan Silva RC	1.50	.60
❑ 265	J.B. Thurmond RC	1.50	.60
❑ 266	Brandon Moorhead RC	1.50	.60
❑ 267	Kyle Nichols RC	2.00	.75
❑ 268	Jonathan Sanchez RC	5.00	2.00
❑ 269	Mike Esposito RC	1.50	.60
❑ 270	Erik Schindewolf RC	1.50	.60
❑ 271	Peeter Ramos RC	1.50	.60
❑ 272	Juan Senreiso RC	1.50	.60
❑ 273	Travis Chick RC	2.00	.75
❑ 274	Vinny Rottino RC	1.50	.60
❑ 275	Micah Furtado RC	1.50	.60
❑ 276	George Kottaras RC	3.00	1.25
❑ 277	Abel Gomez RC	2.00	.75
❑ 278	Buck Coats RC	1.50	.60
❑ 279	Kenny Durost RC	1.50	.60
❑ 280	Nick Touchstone RC	1.50	.60
❑ 281	Jerry Owens RC	2.00	.75
❑ 282	Stefan Bailie RC	1.50	.60
❑ 283	Jesse Gutierrez RC	1.50	.60
❑ 284	Chuck Tiffany RC	4.00	1.50
❑ 285	Brendan Ryan RC	1.50	.60
❑ 286	Julio Pimentel RC	2.00	.75
❑ 287	Shawn Bowman RC	2.00	.75
❑ 288	Alexander Smit RC	1.50	.60
❑ 289	Micah Schnurstein RC	1.50	.60
❑ 290	Jared Gothreaux RC	1.50	.60
❑ 291	Jair Jurrjens RC	4.00	1.50
❑ 292	Bobby Livingston RC	1.50	.60
❑ 293	Ryan Speier RC	1.50	.60
❑ 294	Zach Parker RC	1.50	.60
❑ 295	Christian Colonel RC	1.50	.60
❑ 296	Scott Mitchinson RC	1.50	.60
❑ 297	Neil Wilson RC	1.50	.60
❑ 298	Chuck James RC	6.00	2.50
❑ 299	Heath Totten RC	1.50	.60
❑ 300	Sean Tracey RC	1.50	.60
❑ 301	Tadahito Iguchi RC	5.00	2.00
❑ 302	Matt Brown RC	1.50	.60
❑ 303	Franklin Morales RC	3.00	1.25
❑ 304	Brandon Sing RC	2.00	.75
❑ 305	D.J. Houlton RC	1.50	.60
❑ 306	Jayce Tingler RC	1.50	.60
❑ 307	Mitchell Arnold RC	1.50	.60
❑ 308	Jim Burt RC	1.50	.60
❑ 309	Jason Motte RC	1.50	.60
❑ 310	David Gassner RC	1.50	.60
❑ 311	Andy Santana RC	1.50	.60
❑ 312	Kelvin Pichardo RC	1.50	.60
❑ 313	Carlos Carrasco RC	5.00	2.00
❑ 314	Willy Mota RC	1.50	.60
❑ 315	Frank Mata RC	1.50	.60
❑ 316	Carlos Gonzalez RC	8.00	3.00
❑ 317	Jesse Floyd	1.00	.40
❑ 318	Chris B.Young RC	8.00	3.00
❑ 319	Billy Sadler RC	1.50	.60
❑ 320	Ricky Barrett RC	1.50	.60
❑ 321	Ben Harrison	1.50	.60
❑ 322	Steve Nelson RC	1.50	.60
❑ 323	Daryl Thompson RC	1.50	.60
❑ 324	Davis Romero RC	1.50	.60
❑ 325	Jeremy Harts RC	1.50	.60
❑ 326	Nick Masset RC	1.50	.60
❑ 327	Thomas Pauly RC	1.50	.60
❑ 328	Mike Garber RC	1.50	.60
❑ 329	Kennard Bibbs RC	1.50	.60
❑ 330	Colter Bean RC	1.50	.60
❑ 331	Justin Verlander AU RC	100.00	50.00
❑ 332	Chip Cannon AU RC	25.00	10.00
❑ 333	Kevin Melillo AU RC	15.00	6.00
❑ 334	Jake Postlewait AU RC	10.00	4.00
❑ 335	Wes Swackhamer AU RC	10.00	4.00
❑ 336	Mike Rodriguez AU RC	10.00	4.00
❑ 337	Philip Humber AU RC	25.00	10.00
❑ 338	Jeff Niemann AU RC	30.00	12.50
❑ 339	Brian Miller AU RC	10.00	4.00
❑ 340	Chris Vines AU RC	10.00	4.00
❑ 341	Andy LaRoche AU RC	50.00	20.00
❑ 342	Mike Bourn AU RC	25.00	10.00
❑ 343	Eric Nielsen AU RC	10.00	4.00
❑ 344	Wladimir Balentien AU RC	50.00	20.00
❑ 345	Ismael Ramirez AU RC	10.00	4.00
❑ 346	Pedro Lopez AU RC	10.00	4.00
❑ 347	Shawn Bowman AU	15.00	6.00
❑ 348	Hayden Penn AU RC	25.00	10.00
❑ 349	Matthew Kemp AU RC	100.00	50.00
❑ 350	Brian Stavisky AU RC	10.00	4.00
❑ 351	C.J. Smith AU RC	10.00	4.00
❑ 352	Mike Morse AU RC	12.00	5.00
❑ 353	Billy Butler AU RC	100.00	50.00

2005 Bowman Chrome Draft

- ❑ COMP.SET w/o SP's (165) 100.00 50.00
- ❑ COMMON CARD (1-165) .40 .15
- ❑ COMMON RC 1.00 .40
- ❑ COMMON RC YR .40 .15
- ❑ 1-165 TWO PER BOWMAN DRAFT PACK
- ❑ 166-180 GROUP A ODDS 1:671 H, 1:643 R
- ❑ 166-180 GROUP B ODDS 1:69 H, 1:69 R
- ❑ 1-165 PLATE ODDS 1:826 HOBBY
- ❑ 166-180 AU PLATE ODDS 1:18,411 HOBBY
- ❑ PLATE PRINT RUN 1 SET PER COLOR
- ❑ BLACK-CYAN-MAGENTA-YELLOW ISSUED
- ❑ NO PLATE PRICING DUE TO SCARCITY
- ❑ 1 Rickie Weeks .60 .25
- ❑ 2 Kyle Davies .40 .15
- ❑ 3 Garrett Atkins .40 .15
- ❑ 4 Chien-Ming Wang 2.00 .75
- ❑ 5 Dallas McPherson .40 .15
- ❑ 6 Dan Johnson .60 .25
- ❑ 7 Andy Sisco .40 .15
- ❑ 8 Ryan Doumit .40 .15
- ❑ 9 J.P. Howell .40 .15
- ❑ 10 Tim Stauffer .40 .15
- ❑ 11 Willy Taveras .60 .25
- ❑ 12 Aaron Hill .40 .15
- ❑ 13 Victor Diaz .40 .15
- ❑ 14 Wilson Betemit .40 .15
- ❑ 15 Ervin Santana .60 .25
- ❑ 16 Mike Morse .60 .25
- ❑ 17 Yadier Molina .60 .25
- ❑ 18 Kelly Johnson .40 .15
- ❑ 19 Clint Barmes .60 .25
- ❑ 20 Robinson Cano 1.00 .40
- ❑ 21 Brad Thompson .40 .15
- ❑ 22 Jorge Cantu .60 .25
- ❑ 23 Brad Halsey .40 .15
- ❑ 24 Lance Niekro .60 .25
- ❑ 25 D.J. Houlton .40 .15
- ❑ 26 Ryan Church .40 .15
- ❑ 27 Hayden Penn 1.50 .60
- ❑ 28 Chris Young .40 .15
- ❑ 29 Chad Orvella RC 1.00 .40
- ❑ 30 Mark Teahen .40 .15
- ❑ 31 Mark McCormick FY RC 1.50 .60
- ❑ 32 Jay Bruce FY RC 20.00 8.00
- ❑ 33 Beau Jones FY RC 2.50 1.00
- ❑ 34 Tyler Greene FY RC 2.50 1.00
- ❑ 35 Zach Ward FY RC 1.00 .40
- ❑ 36 Josh Bell FY RC 4.00 1.50
- ❑ 37 Josh Wall FY RC 1.50 .60
- ❑ 38 Nick Webber FY RC 1.00 .40
- ❑ 39 Travis Buck FY RC 4.00 1.25
- ❑ 40 Kyle Winters FY RC 1.50 .60
- ❑ 41 Mitch Boggs FY RC 1.00 .40
- ❑ 42 Tommy Mendoza FY RC 2.50 1.00
- ❑ 43 Brad Corley FY RC 1.50 .60
- ❑ 44 Drew Butera FY RC 1.00 .40
- ❑ 45 Ryan Mount FY RC 2.50 1.00
- ❑ 46 Tyler Herron FY RC 1.50 .60
- ❑ 47 Nick Weglarz FY RC 2.50 1.00
- ❑ 48 Brandon Erbe FY RC 4.00 1.50
- ❑ 49 Cody Allen FY RC 1.00 .40
- ❑ 50 Eric Fowler FY RC 1.00 .40
- ❑ 51 James Boone FY RC 1.50 .60
- ❑ 52 Josh Flores FY RC 4.00 1.50
- ❑ 53 Brandon Monk FY RC 1.50 .60
- ❑ 54 Kieron Pope FY RC 2.50 1.00
- ❑ 55 Kyle Cofield FY RC 1.00 .40
- ❑ 56 Brent Lillibridge FY RC 1.50 .60
- ❑ 57 Daryl Jones FY 1.00 .40
- ❑ 58 Eli Iorg FY RC 1.50 .60
- ❑ 59 Brett Hayes FY RC 1.00 .40
- ❑ 60 Mike Durant FY RC 3.00 1.25
- ❑ 61 Michael Bowden FY RC 5.00 2.00
- ❑ 62 Paul Kelly FY RC 1.50 .60
- ❑ 63 Andrew McCutchen FY RC 8.00 3.00
- ❑ 64 Travis Wood FY RC 3.00 1.25
- ❑ 65 Cesar Ramos FY RC 1.50 .60
- ❑ 66 Chaz Roe FY RC 1.50 .60
- ❑ 67 Matt Torra FY RC 1.50 .60
- ❑ 68 Kevin Slowey FY RC 6.00 2.50
- ❑ 69 Trayvon Robinson FY RC 1.50 .60
- ❑ 70 Reid Engel FY RC 1.00 .40
- ❑ 71 Kris Harvey FY RC 1.50 .60
- ❑ 72 Craig Italiano FY RC 2.50 1.00
- ❑ 73 Matt Maloney FY RC 3.00 1.25
- ❑ 74 Sean West FY RC 3.00 1.25
- ❑ 75 Henry Sanchez FY RC 2.50 1.00
- ❑ 76 Scott Blue FY RC 1.00 .40
- ❑ 77 Jordan Schafer FY RC 8.00 0.00
- ❑ 78 Chris Robinson FY RC 1.50 .60
- ❑ 79 Chris Hobdy FY RC 1.00 .40
- ❑ 80 Brandon Durden FY RC 1.00 .40
- ❑ 81 Clay Buchholz FY RC 15.00 6.00
- ❑ 82 Josh Geer FY RC 1.00 .40
- ❑ 83 Sam LoCuro FY RC 1.00 .40
- ❑ 84 Justin Thomas FY RC 1.00 .40
- ❑ 85 Brett Gardner FY RC 2.50 1.00
- ❑ 86 Tommy Manzella FY RC 1.00 .40
- ❑ 87 Matt Green FY RC 1.00 .40
- ❑ 88 Yunel Escobar FY RC 5.00 2.00
- ❑ 89 Mike Costanzo FY RC 3.00 1.25
- ❑ 90 Nick Hundley FY RC 1.00 .40
- ❑ 91 Zach Simons FY RC 1.00 .40
- ❑ 92 Jacob Marceaux FY RC 1.00 .40
- ❑ 94 Brandon Snyder FY RC 3.00 1.25
- ❑ 95 Matt Goyen FY RC 1.00 .40
- ❑ 96 Jon Egan FY RC 1.50 .60
- ❑ 97 Drew Thompson FY RC 1.50 .60
- ❑ 98 Bryan Anderson FY RC 4.00 1.50
- ❑ 99 Clayton Richard FY RC 1.00 .40
- ❑ 100 Jimmy Shull FY RC 1.50 .60
- ❑ 101 Mark Pawelek FY RC 5.00 2.00
- ❑ 102 P.J. Phillips FY RC 2.50 1.00
- ❑ 103 John Drennen FY RC 4.00 1.50
- ❑ 104 Nolan Reimold FY RC 5.00 2.00
- ❑ 105 Troy Tulowitzki FY RC 12.00 5.00
- ❑ 106 Kevin Whelan FY RC 1.25 .50
- ❑ 107 Wade Townsend FY RC 1.50 .60
- ❑ 108 Micah Owings FY RC 2.50 1.00
- ❑ 109 Ryan Tucker FY RC 1.50 .60
- ❑ 110 Jeff Clement FY RC 8.00 3.00
- ❑ 111 Josh Sullivan FY RC 1.00 .40
- ❑ 112 Jeff Lyman FY RC 1.50 .60
- ❑ 113 Brian Bogusevic FY RC 1.00 .40
- ❑ 114 Trevor Bell FY RC 1.50 .60
- ❑ 115 Brent Cox FY RC 1.50 .60
- ❑ 116 Michael Billek FY RC 1.00 .40
- ❑ 117 Garrett Olson FY RC 1.50 .60
- ❑ 118 Steven Johnson FY RC 1.50 .60
- ❑ 119 Chase Headley FY RC 5.00 2.00
- ❑ 120 Daniel Carte FY RC 1.50 .60
- ❑ 121 Francisco Liriano PROS 2.50 1.00
- ❑ 122 Fausto Carmona PROS .40 .15
- ❑ 123 Zach Jackson PROS .40 .15
- ❑ 124 Adam Loewen PROS .40 .15
- ❑ 125 Chris Lambert PROS .40 .15
- ❑ 126 Scott Mathieson FY .60 .25
- ❑ 127 Paul Maholm PROS .60 .25
- ❑ 128 Fernando Nieve PROS .40 .15
- ❑ 129 Justin Verlander FY 4.00 1.50
- ❑ 130 Yusmeiro Petit PROS 1.00 .40
- ❑ 131 Joel Zumaya PROS 1.50 .60
- ❑ 132 Merkin Valdez PROS .40 .15
- ❑ 133 Ryan Garko FY RC 4.00 1.50
- ❑ 134 Edison Volquez FY RC 12.00 5.00
- ❑ 135 Russ Martin FY 1.50 .60
- ❑ 136 Conor Jackson PROS .60 .25
- ❑ 137 Miguel Montero FY RC 4.00 1.50
- ❑ 138 Josh Barfield PROS .60 .25
- ❑ 139 Delmon Young PROS 1.00 .40
- ❑ 140 Andy LaRoche FY 1.50 .60
- ❑ 141 William Bergolla PROS .40 .15
- ❑ 142 B.J. Upton PROS .60 .25
- ❑ 143 Hernan Iribarren FY .60 .25
- ❑ 144 Brandon Wood PROS 1.25 .50
- ❑ 145 Jose Bautista PROS .40 .15
- ❑ 146 Edwin Encarnacion PROS .60 .25
- ❑ 147 Javier Herrera FY RC 2.50 1.00
- ❑ 148 Jeremy Hermida PROS 1.50 .60
- ❑ 149 Frank Diaz PROS RC 1.00 .40
- ❑ 150 Chris B.Young FY 3.00 1.25
- ❑ 151 Shin-Soo Choo PROS .40 .15
- ❑ 152 Kevin Thompson PROS RC 1.00 .40
- ❑ 153 Hanley Ramirez PROS 1.00 .40
- ❑ 154 Lastings Milledge PROS .60 .25
- ❑ 155 Luis Montanez PROS .40 .15
- ❑ 156 Justin Huber PROS .40 .15
- ❑ 157 Zach Duke PROS .75 .30
- ❑ 158 Jeff Francoeur PROS 1.25 .50
- ❑ 159 Melky Cabrera FY 3.00 1.25
- ❑ 160 Bobby Jenks PROS .60 .25
- ❑ 161 Ian Snell PROS .40 .15
- ❑ 162 Fernando Cabrera PROS .40 .15
- ❑ 163 Troy Patton PROS 1.00 .40
- ❑ 164 Anthony Lerew PROS .60 .25
- ❑ 165 Nelson Cruz FY RC 3.00 1.25
- ❑ 166 Stephen Drew AU A RC 80.00 40.00
- ❑ 167 Jered Weaver AU A RC 60.00 30.00
- ❑ 168 Ryan Braun AU B RC 200.00 125.00
- ❑ 169 John Mayberry Jr. AU B RC 30.00 12.50
- ❑ 170 Aaron Thompson AU B RC 15.00 6.00
- ❑ 171 Cesar Carrillo AU B RC 25.00 10.00
- ❑ 172 Jacoby Ellsbury AU B RC 150.00 75.00
- ❑ 173 Matt Garza AU B RC 50.00 30.00
- ❑ 174 Cliff Pennington AU B RC 10.00 4.00
- ❑ 175 Colby Rasmus AU B RC 100.00 50.00
- ❑ 176 Chris Volstad AU B RC 30.00 12.50
- ❑ 177 Ricky Romero AU B RC 15.00 6.00
- ❑ 178 Ryan Zimmerman AU B RC 100.00 50.00
- ❑ 179 C.J. Henry AU B RC 25.00 10.00
- ❑ 180 Eddy Martinez AU B RC 15.00 6.00

2006 Bowman Chrome

- ❑ COMP.SET w/o AU's (220) 60.00 30.00
- ❑ COMMON CARD (1-200) .50 .20
- ❑ COMMON ROOKIE (201-220) .60 .25
- ❑ 219 AU ODDS 1:2734 HOBBY, 1:6617 RETAIL
- ❑ 221-224 AU ODDS 1:27 HOBBY, 1:65 RETAIL
- ❑ 1-220 PLATE ODDS 1:836 HOBBY
- ❑ 219 AU PLATE ODDS 1:292,536 HOBBY
- ❑ 221-224 AU PLATES ODDS 1:9,000 HOBBY
- ❑ PLATE PRINT RUN 1 SET PER COLOR
- ❑ BLACK-CYAN-MAGENTA-YELLOW ISSUED
- ❑ NO PLATE PRICING DUE TO SCARCITY
- ❑ 1 Nick Swisher .50 .20
- ❑ 2 Ted Lilly .50 .20
- ❑ 3 John Smoltz .75 .30
- ❑ 4 Lyle Overbay .50 .20
- ❑ 5 Alfonso Soriano .50 .20
- ❑ 6 Javier Vazquez .50 .20
- ❑ 7 Ronnie Belliard .50 .20
- ❑ 8 Jose Reyes 1.25 .50
- ❑ 9 Brian Roberts .50 .20
- ❑ 10 Curt Schilling .75 .30
- ❑ 11 Adam Dunn .50 .20
- ❑ 12 Zack Greinke .50 .20
- ❑ 13 Carlos Guillen .50 .20
- ❑ 14 Jon Garland .50 .20
- ❑ 15 Robinson Cano .75 .30

❑ 16 Chris Burke .50 .20
❑ 17 Barry Zito .50 .20
❑ 18 Russ Adams .50 .20
❑ 19 Chris Capuano .50 .20
❑ 20 Scott Rolen .75 .30
❑ 21 Kerry Wood .50 .20
❑ 22 Scott Kazmir .75 .30
❑ 23 Brandon Webb .50 .20
❑ 24 Jeff Kent .50 .20
❑ 25 Albert Pujols 2.50 1.00
❑ 26 C.C. Sabathia .50 .20
❑ 27 Adrian Beltre .50 .20
❑ 28 Brad Wilkerson .50 .20
❑ 29 Randy Wolf .50 .20
❑ 30 Jason Bay .50 .20
❑ 31 Austin Kearns .50 .20
❑ 32 Clint Barmes .50 .20
❑ 33 Mike Sweeney .50 .20
❑ 34 Kevin Youkilis .50 .20
❑ 35 Justin Morneau .50 .20
❑ 36 Scott Podsednik .50 .20
❑ 37 Jason Giambi .50 .20
❑ 38 Steve Finley .50 .20
❑ 39 Morgan Ensberg .50 .20
❑ 40 Eric Chavez .50 .20
❑ 41 Roy Halladay .50 .20
❑ 42 Horacio Ramirez .50 .20
❑ 43 Ben Sheets .50 .20
❑ 44 Chris Carpenter .50 .20
❑ 45 Andruw Jones .75 .30
❑ 46 Carlos Zambrano .50 .20
❑ 47 Jonny Gomes .50 .20
❑ 48 Shawn Green .50 .20
❑ 49 Moises Alou .50 .20
❑ 50 Ichiro Suzuki 2.00 .75
❑ 51 Juan Pierre .50 .20
❑ 52 Grady Sizemore .75 .30
❑ 53 Kazuo Matsui .50 .20
❑ 54 Jose Vidro .50 .20
❑ 55 Jake Peavy .50 .20
❑ 56 Dallas McPherson .50 .20
❑ 57 Ryan Howard 2.00 .75
❑ 58 Zach Duke .50 .20
❑ 59 Michael Young .50 .20
❑ 60 Todd Helton .75 .30
❑ 61 David DeJesus .50 .20
❑ 62 Ivan Rodriguez .75 .30
❑ 63 Johan Santana .75 .30
❑ 64 Danny Haren .50 .20
❑ 65 Derek Jeter 3.00 1.25
❑ 66 Greg Maddux 2.00 .75
❑ 67 Jorge Cantu .50 .20
❑ 68 J.J. Hardy .50 .20
❑ 69 Victor Martinez .50 .20
❑ 70 David Wright 2.00 .75
❑ 71 Ryan Church .50 .20
❑ 72 Khalil Greene .75 .30
❑ 73 Jimmy Rollins .50 .20
❑ 74 Hank Blalock .50 .20
❑ 75 Pedro Martinez .75 .30
❑ 76 Chris Shelton .50 .20
❑ 77 Felipe Lopez .50 .20
❑ 78 Jeff Francis .50 .20
❑ 79 Andy Sisco .50 .20
❑ 80 Hideki Matsui 1.25 .50
❑ 81 Ken Griffey Jr. 2.00 .75
❑ 82 Nomar Garciaparra 1.25 .50
❑ 83 Kevin Millwood .50 .20
❑ 84 Paul Konerko .50 .20
❑ 85 A.J. Burnett .50 .20
❑ 86 Mike Piazza 1.25 .50
❑ 87 Brian Giles .50 .20
❑ 88 Johnny Damon .75 .30
❑ 89 Jim Thome .75 .30
❑ 90 Roger Clemens 2.50 1.00
❑ 91 Aaron Rowand .50 .20
❑ 92 Rafael Furcal .50 .20
❑ 93 Gary Sheffield .50 .20
❑ 94 Mike Cameron .50 .20
❑ 95 Carlos Delgado .50 .20
❑ 96 Jorge Posada .75 .30
❑ 97 Denny Bautista .50 .20
❑ 98 Mike Maroth .50 .20
❑ 99 Brad Radke .50 .20
❑ 100 Alex Rodriguez 2.00 .75
❑ 101 Freddy Garcia .50 .20
❑ 102 Oliver Perez .50 .20
❑ 103 Jon Lieber .50 .20
❑ 104 Melvin Mora .50 .20
❑ 105 Travis Hafner .50 .20
❑ 106 Alex Rios .50 .20
❑ 107 Derek Lowe .50 .20
❑ 108 Luis Castillo .50 .20
❑ 109 Livan Hernandez .50 .20
❑ 110 Tadahito Iguchi .50 .20
❑ 111 Shawn Chacon .50 .20
❑ 112 Frank Thomas 1.25 .50
❑ 113 Josh Beckett .50 .20
❑ 114 Aubrey Huff .50 .20
❑ 115 Derrek Lee .50 .20
❑ 116 Chien-Ming Wang 2.00 .75
❑ 117 Joe Crede .50 .20
❑ 118 Torii Hunter .50 .20
❑ 119 J.D. Drew .50 .20
❑ 120 Troy Glaus .50 .20
❑ 121 Sean Casey .50 .20
❑ 122 Edgar Renteria .50 .20
❑ 123 Craig Wilson .50 .20
❑ 124 Adam Eaton .50 .20
❑ 125 Jeff Francoeur 1.25 .50
❑ 126 Bruce Chen .50 .20
❑ 127 Cliff Floyd .50 .20
❑ 128 Jeremy Reed .50 .20
❑ 129 Jake Westbrook .50 .20
❑ 130 Wily Mo Pena .50 .20
❑ 131 Toby Hall .50 .20
❑ 132 David Ortiz 1.25 .50
❑ 133 David Eckstein .50 .20
❑ 134 Brady Clark .50 .20
❑ 135 Marcus Giles .50 .20
❑ 136 Aaron Hill .50 .20
❑ 137 Mark Kotsay .50 .20
❑ 138 Carlos Lee .50 .20
❑ 139 Roy Oswalt .50 .20
❑ 140 Chone Figgins .50 .20
❑ 141 Mike Mussina .75 .30
❑ 142 Orlando Hernandez .50 .20
❑ 143 Magglio Ordonez .50 .20
❑ 144 Jim Edmonds .75 .30
❑ 145 Bobby Abreu .50 .20
❑ 146 Nick Johnson .50 .20
❑ 147 Carlos Beltran .50 .20
❑ 148 Jhonny Peralta .50 .20
❑ 149 Pedro Feliz .50 .20
❑ 150 Miguel Tejada .50 .20
❑ 151 Luis Gonzalez .50 .20
❑ 152 Carl Crawford .50 .20
❑ 153 Yadier Molina .50 .20
❑ 154 Rich Harden .50 .20
❑ 155 Tim Wakefield .50 .20
❑ 156 Rickie Weeks .50 .20
❑ 157 Johnny Estrada .50 .20
❑ 158 Gustavo Chacin .50 .20
❑ 159 Dan Johnson .50 .20
❑ 160 Willy Taveras .50 .20
❑ 161 Garret Anderson .50 .20
❑ 162 Randy Johnson 1.25 .50
❑ 163 Jermaine Dye .50 .20
❑ 164 Joe Mauer .75 .30
❑ 165 Ervin Santana .50 .20
❑ 166 Jeremy Bonderman .50 .20
❑ 167 Garrett Atkins .50 .20
❑ 168 Manny Ramirez .75 .30
❑ 169 Brad Eldred .50 .20
❑ 170 Chase Utley 1.25 .50
❑ 171 Mark Loretta .50 .20
❑ 172 John Patterson .50 .20
❑ 173 Tom Glavine .75 .30
❑ 174 Dontrelle Willis .50 .20
❑ 175 Mark Teixeira .75 .30
❑ 176 Felix Hernandez .75 .30
❑ 177 Cliff Lee .50 .20
❑ 178 Jason Schmidt .50 .20
❑ 179 Chad Tracy .50 .20
❑ 180 Rocco Baldelli .50 .20
❑ 181 Aramis Ramirez .50 .20
❑ 182 Andy Pettitte .75 .30
❑ 183 Mark Mulder .50 .20
❑ 184 Geoff Jenkins .50 .20
❑ 185 Chipper Jones 1.25 .50
❑ 186 Vernon Wells .50 .20
❑ 187 Bobby Crosby .50 .20
❑ 188 Lance Berkman .50 .20
❑ 189 Vladimir Guerrero 1.25 .50
❑ 190 Coco Crisp .50 .20
❑ 191 Brad Penny .50 .20
❑ 192 Jose Guillen .50 .20
❑ 193 Brett Myers .50 .20
❑ 194 Miguel Cabrera .75 .30
❑ 195 Bartolo Colon .50 .20
❑ 196 Craig Biggio .75 .30
❑ 197 Tim Hudson .50 .20
❑ 198 Mark Prior .75 .30
❑ 199 Mark Buehrle .50 .20
❑ 200 Barry Bonds 2.50 1.00
❑ 201 Anderson Hernandez (RC) .60 .25
❑ 202 Jose Capellan (RC) .60 .25
❑ 203 Jeremy Accardo RC .60 .25
❑ 204 Hanley Ramirez (RC) 1.50 .60
❑ 205 Matt Capps (RC) .60 .25
❑ 206 Jonathan Papelbon (RC) 3.00 1.25
❑ 207 Chuck James (RC) 1.00 .40
❑ 208 Matt Cain (RC) 1.00 .40
❑ 209 Cole Hamels (RC) 1.50 .60
❑ 210 Jason Botts (RC) .60 .25
❑ 211 Lastings Milledge (RC) 1.00 .40
❑ 212 Conor Jackson (RC) 1.00 .40
❑ 213 Yusmeiro Petit (RC) .60 .25
❑ 214 Alay Soler RC .60 .25
❑ 215 Willy Aybar (RC) .60 .25
❑ 216 Adam Loewen (RC) .60 .25
❑ 217 Justin Verlander (RC) 2.50 1.00
❑ 218 Francisco Liriano (RC) 1.50 .60
❑ 219 Kenji Johjima RC 3.00 1.25
❑ 219a Kenji Johjima AU 120.00 60.00
❑ 220 Craig Hansen RC 2.50 1.00
❑ 221 Prince Fielder AU (RC) 80.00 40.00
❑ 222 Josh Barfield AU (RC) 15.00 6.00
❑ 223 Fausto Carmona AU (RC) 30.00 12.50
❑ 224 James Loney AU (RC) 40.00 15.00

2006 Bowman Chrome Draft

❑ COMPLETE SET (55) 40.00 15.00
❑ COMMON RC (1-55) 1.00 .40
❑ RC SEMIS 1-55 1.50 .60
❑ RC UNLISTED 1-55 2.50 1.00
❑ APPX. ODDS 1:2 HOBBY, 1:2 RETAIL
❑ ODDS INFO PROVIDED BY BECKETT
❑ OVERALL PLATE ODDS 1:990 HOBBY
❑ PLATE PRINT RUN 1 SET PER COLOR
❑ BLACK-CYAN-MAGENTA-YELLOW ISSUED
❑ NO PLATE PRICING DUE TO SCARCITY
❑ 1 Matt Kemp (RC) 1.50 .60
❑ 2 Taylor Tankersley (RC) 1.00 .40
❑ 3 Mike Napoli RC 2.50 1.00
❑ 4 Brian Bannister (RC) 1.00 .40
❑ 5 Melky Cabrera (RC) 1.50 .60
❑ 6 Bill Bray (RC) 1.00 .40
❑ 7 Brian Anderson (RC) 1.00 .40
❑ 8 Jered Weaver (RC) 3.00 1.25
❑ 9 Chris Duncan (RC) 1.50 .60
❑ 10 Boof Bonser (RC) 1.50 .60
❑ 11 Mike Rouse (RC) 1.00 .40
❑ 12 David Pauley (RC) 1.00 .40
❑ 13 Russ Martin (RC) 1.50 .60
❑ 14 Jeremy Sowers (RC) 1.00 .40
❑ 15 Kevin Reese (RC) 1.00 .40
❑ 16 John Rheinecker (RC) 1.00 .40
❑ 17 Tommy Murphy (RC) 1.00 .40

❑ 18 Sean Marshall (RC) 1.00 .40
❑ 19 Jason Kubel (RC) 1.00 .40
❑ 20 Chad Billingsley (RC) 1.50 .60
❑ 21 Kendry Morales (RC) 1.50 .60
❑ 22 Jon Lester RC 5.00 2.00
❑ 23 Brandon Fahey RC 1.00 .40
❑ 24 Josh Johnson (RC) 1.50 .60
❑ 25 Kevin Frandsen (RC) 1.00 .40
❑ 26 Casey Janssen RC 1.50 .60
❑ 27 Scott Thorman (RC) 1.00 .40
❑ 28 Scott Mathieson (RC) 1.00 .40
❑ 29 Jeremy Hermida (RC) 1.00 .40
❑ 30 Dustin Nippert (RC) 1.00 .40
❑ 31 Kevin Thompson (RC) 1.00 .40
❑ 32 Bobby Livingston (RC) 1.00 .40
❑ 33 Travis Ishikawa (RC) 1.00 .40
❑ 34 Jeff Mathis (RC) 1.00 .40
❑ 35 Charlie Haeger RC 1.50 .60
❑ 36 Josh Willingham (RC) 1.00 .40
❑ 37 Taylor Buchholz (RC) 1.00 .40
❑ 38 Joel Guzman (RC) 1.00 .40
❑ 39 Zach Jackson (RC) 1.00 .40
❑ 40 Howie Kendrick (RC) 2.50 1.00
❑ 41 T.J. Beam (RC) 1.00 .40
❑ 42 Ty Taubenheim RC 1.50 .60
❑ 43 Erick Aybar (RC) 1.00 .40
❑ 44 Anibal Sanchez (RC) 1.50 .60
❑ 45 Michael Pelfrey RC 8.00 3.00
❑ 46 Shawn Hill (RC) 1.00 .40
❑ 47 Chris Roberson (RC) 1.00 .40
❑ 48 Carlos Villanueva RC 1.00 .40
❑ 49 Andre Ethier (RC) 2.50 1.00
❑ 50 Anthony Reyes (RC) 1.50 .60
❑ 51 Franklin Gutierrez (RC) 1.00 .40
❑ 52 Angel Guzman (RC) 1.00 .40
❑ 53 Michael O'Connor RC 1.00 .40
❑ 54 James Shields RC 1.00 .40
❑ 55 Nate McLouth (RC) 1.00 .40

2007 Bowman Chrome

❑ COMPLETE SET (220) 60.00 30.00
❑ COMMON CARD (1-190) .50 .20
❑ COMMON ROOKIE (191-220) .75 .30
❑ 1-220 PLATE ODDS 1:1054 HOBBY
❑ PLATE PRINT RUN 1 SET PER COLOR
❑ BLACK-CYAN-MAGENTA-YELLOW ISSUED
❑ NO PLATE PRICING DUE TO SCARCITY
❑ 1 Hanley Ramirez .75 .30
❑ 2 Justin Verlander 1.25 .50
❑ 3 Ryan Zimmerman 1.25 .50
❑ 4 Jered Weaver .75 .30
❑ 5 Stephen Drew .75 .30
❑ 6 Jonathan Papelbon 1.25 .50
❑ 7 Melky Cabrera .50 .20
❑ 8 Francisco Liriano 1.25 .50
❑ 9 Prince Fielder 1.25 .50
❑ 10 Dan Uggla .75 .30
❑ 11 Jeremy Sowers .50 .20
❑ 12 Carlos Quentin .50 .20
❑ 13 Chuck James .50 .20
❑ 14 Andre Ethier .75 .30
❑ 15 Cole Hamels .75 .30
❑ 16 Kenji Johjima 1.25 .50
❑ 17 Chad Billingsley .50 .20
❑ 18 Ian Kinsler .50 .20
❑ 19 Jason Hirsh .50 .20
❑ 20 Nick Markakis .75 .30
❑ 21 Jeremy Hermida .50 .20
❑ 22 Ryan Shealy .50 .20
❑ 23 Scott Olsen .50 .20
❑ 24 Russell Martin .50 .20
❑ 25 Conor Jackson .50 .20
❑ 26 Erik Bedard .50 .20
❑ 27 Brian McCann .50 .20
❑ 28 Michael Barrett .50 .20
❑ 29 Brandon Phillips .50 .20
❑ 30 Garrett Atkins .50 .20
❑ 31 Freddy Garcia .50 .20
❑ 32 Mark Loretta .50 .20
❑ 33 Craig Biggio .75 .30
❑ 34 Jeremy Bonderman .50 .20
❑ 35 Johan Santana .75 .30
❑ 36 Jorge Posada .75 .30
❑ 37 Victor Martinez .50 .20
❑ 38 Carlos Delgado .50 .20
❑ 39 Gary Matthews Jr. .50 .20
❑ 40 Mike Cameron .50 .20
❑ 41 Adrian Beltre .50 .20
❑ 42 Freddy Sanchez .50 .20
❑ 43 Austin Kearns .50 .20
❑ 44 Mark Buehrle .50 .20
❑ 45 Miguel Cabrera .75 .30
❑ 46 Josh Beckett .75 .30
❑ 47 Chone Figgins .50 .20
❑ 48 Edgar Renteria .50 .20
❑ 49 Derek Lowe .50 .20
❑ 50 Ryan Howard 2.00 .75
❑ 51 Shawn Green .50 .20
❑ 52 Jason Giambi .50 .20
❑ 53 Ervin Santana .50 .20
❑ 54 Aaron Hill .50 .20
❑ 55 Roy Oswalt .50 .20
❑ 56 Dan Haren .50 .20
❑ 57 Jose Vidro .50 .20
❑ 58 Kevin Millwood .50 .20
❑ 59 Jim Edmonds .75 .30
❑ 60 Carl Crawford .50 .20
❑ 61 Randy Wolf .50 .20
❑ 62 Paul LoDuca .50 .20
❑ 63 Johnny Estrada .50 .20
❑ 64 Brian Roberts .50 .20
❑ 65 Manny Ramirez .75 .30
❑ 66 Jose Contreras .50 .20
❑ 67 Josh Barfield .50 .20
❑ 68 Juan Pierre .50 .20
❑ 69 David DeJesus .50 .20
❑ 70 Gary Sheffield .50 .20
❑ 71 Michael Young .50 .20
❑ 72 Randy Johnson 1.25 .50
❑ 73 Rickie Weeks .50 .20
❑ 74 Brian Giles .50 .20
❑ 75 Ichiro Suzuki 2.00 .75
❑ 76 Nick Swisher .50 .20
❑ 77 Justin Morneau .50 .20
❑ 78 Scott Kazmir .75 .30
❑ 79 Lyle Overbay .50 .20
❑ 80 Alfonso Soriano .50 .20
❑ 81 Brandon Webb .50 .20
❑ 82 Joe Crede .50 .20
❑ 83 Corey Patterson .50 .20
❑ 84 Kenny Rogers .50 .20
❑ 85 Ken Griffey Jr. 2.00 .75
❑ 86 Cliff Lee .50 .20
❑ 87 Mike Lowell .50 .20
❑ 88 Marcus Giles .50 .20
❑ 89 Orlando Cabrera .50 .20
❑ 90 Derek Jeter 3.00 1.25
❑ 91 Ramon Hernandez .50 .20
❑ 92 Carlos Guillen .50 .20
❑ 93 Bill Hall .50 .20
❑ 94 Michael Cuddyer .50 .20
❑ 95 Miguel Tejada .50 .20
❑ 96 Todd Helton .75 .30
❑ 97 C.C. Sabathia .50 .20
❑ 98 Tadahito Iguchi .50 .20
❑ 99 Jose Reyes 1.25 .50
❑ 100 David Wright 2.00 .75
❑ 101 Barry Zito .50 .20
❑ 102 Jake Peavy .50 .20
❑ 103 Richie Sexson .50 .20
❑ 104 A.J. Burnett .50 .20
❑ 105 Eric Chavez .50 .20
❑ 106 Vernon Wells .50 .20
❑ 107 Grady Sizemore .75 .30
❑ 108 Bronson Arroyo .50 .20
❑ 109 Mike Mussina .75 .30
❑ 110 Magglio Ordonez .50 .20
❑ 111 Anibal Sanchez .50 .20
❑ 112 Jeff Francoeur 1.25 .50
❑ 113 Kevin Youkilis .50 .20
❑ 114 Aubrey Huff .50 .20
❑ 115 Carlos Zambrano .50 .20
❑ 116 Mark Teahen .50 .20
❑ 117 Mark Mulder .50 .20
❑ 118 Pedro Martinez .75 .30
❑ 119 Hideki Matsui 1.25 .50
❑ 120 Mike Piazza 1.25 .50
❑ 121 Jason Schmidt .50 .20
❑ 122 Greg Maddux 2.00 .75
❑ 123 Joe Blanton .50 .20
❑ 124 Chris Carpenter .50 .20
❑ 125 David Ortiz 1.25 .50
❑ 126 Alex Rios .50 .20
❑ 127 Nick Johnson .50 .20
❑ 128 Carlos Lee .50 .20
❑ 129 Pat Burrell .50 .20
❑ 130 Ben Sheets .50 .20
❑ 131 Derrek Lee .50 .20
❑ 132 Adam Dunn .50 .20
❑ 133 Jermaine Dye .50 .20
❑ 134 Curt Schilling .75 .30
❑ 135 Chad Tracy .50 .20
❑ 136 Vladimir Guerrero 1.25 .50
❑ 137 Melvin Mora .50 .20
❑ 138 John Smoltz .75 .30
❑ 139 Craig Monroe .50 .20
❑ 140 Dontrelle Willis .50 .20
❑ 141 Jeff Francis .50 .20
❑ 142 Chipper Jones 1.25 .50
❑ 143 Frank Thomas 1.25 .50
❑ 144 Brett Myers .50 .20
❑ 145 Tom Glavine .75 .30
❑ 146 Robinson Cano .75 .30
❑ 147 Jeff Kent .50 .20
❑ 148 Scott Rolen .75 .30
❑ 149 Roy Halladay .50 .20
❑ 150 Joe Mauer .75 .30
❑ 151 Bobby Abreu .50 .20
❑ 152 Matt Cain .75 .30
❑ 153 Hank Blalock .50 .20
❑ 154 Chris Young .50 .20
❑ 155 Jake Westbrook .50 .20
❑ 156 Javier Vazquez .50 .20
❑ 157 Garret Anderson .50 .20
❑ 158 Aramis Ramirez .50 .20
❑ 159 Mark Kotsay .50 .20
❑ 160 Matt Kemp .50 .20
❑ 161 Adrian Gonzalez .50 .20
❑ 162 Felix Hernandez .75 .30
❑ 163 David Eckstein .50 .20
❑ 164 Curtis Granderson .50 .20
❑ 165 Paul Konerko .50 .20
❑ 166 Alex Rodriguez 2.00 .75
❑ 167 Tim Hudson .50 .20
❑ 168 J.D. Drew .50 .20
❑ 169 Chien-Ming Wang 2.00 .75
❑ 170 Jimmy Rollins .50 .20
❑ 171 Matt Morris .50 .20
❑ 172 Raul Ibanez .50 .20
❑ 173 Mark Teixeira .75 .30
❑ 174 Ted Lilly .50 .20
❑ 175 Albert Pujols 2.50 1.00
❑ 176 Carlos Beltran .50 .20
❑ 177 Lance Berkman .50 .20
❑ 178 Ivan Rodriguez .75 .30
❑ 179 Torii Hunter .50 .20
❑ 180 Johnny Damon .75 .30
❑ 181 Chase Utley 1.25 .50
❑ 182 Jason Bay .50 .20
❑ 183 Jeff Weaver .50 .20
❑ 184 Troy Glaus .50 .20
❑ 185 Rocco Baldelli .50 .20
❑ 186 Rafael Furcal .50 .20
❑ 187 Jim Thome .75 .30
❑ 188 Travis Hafner .50 .20
❑ 189 Matt Holliday 1.25 .50
❑ 190 Andruw Jones .75 .30
❑ 191 Andrew Miller RC 5.00 2.00
❑ 192 Ryan Braun RC .75 .30
❑ 193 Oswaldo Navarro RC .75 .30

❑ 194 Mike Rabelo RC .75 .30
❑ 195 Delwyn Young (RC) .75 .30
❑ 196 Miguel Montero (RC) .75 .30
❑ 197 Matt Lindstrom (RC) .75 .30
❑ 198 Josh Hamilton (RC) 2.00 .75
❑ 199 Elijah Dukes RC 1.25 .50
❑ 200 Sean Henn (RC) .75 .30
❑ 201 Delmon Young (RC) 1.25 .50
❑ 202 Alexi Casilla RC 1.25 .50
❑ 203 Hunter Pence (RC) 4.00 1.50
❑ 204 Jeff Baker (RC) .75 .30
❑ 205 Hector Gimenez (RC) .75 .30
❑ 206 Ubaldo Jimenez (RC) .75 .30
❑ 207 Adam Lind (RC) .75 .30
❑ 208 Joaquin Arias (RC) .75 .30
❑ 209 David Murphy (RC) .75 .30
❑ 210 Daisuke Matsuzaka RC 8.00 3.00
❑ 211 Jerry Owens (RC) .75 .30
❑ 212 Ryan Sweeney (RC) .75 .30
❑ 213 Kei Igawa RC 2.00 .75
❑ 214 Mitch Maier RC .75 .30
❑ 215 Philip Humber (RC) .75 .30
❑ 216 Troy Tulowitzki (RC) 2.00 .75
❑ 217 Tim Lincecum RC 10.00 4.00
❑ 218 Michael Bourn (RC) .75 .30
❑ 219 Hideki Okajima RC 4.00 1.50
❑ 220 Josh Fields (RC) .75 .30

2007 Bowman Chrome Draft

❑ COMPLETE SET (55) 40.00 15.00
❑ COMMON RC (1-55) .60 .25
❑ OVERALL PLATE ODDS 1:1294 HOBBY
❑ PLATE PRINT RUN 1 SET PER COLOR
❑ BLACK-CYAN-MAGENTA-YELLOW ISSUED
❑ NO PLATE PRICING DUE TO SCARCITY
❑ BDP1 Travis Buck (RC) .60 .25
❑ BDP2 Matt Chico (RC) .60 .25
❑ BDP3 Justin Upton RC 4.00 1.50
❑ BDP4 Chase Wright RC 1.50 .60
❑ BDP5 Kevin Kouzmanoff (RC) .60 .25
❑ BDP6 John Danks RC .60 .25
❑ BDP7 Alejandro De Aza RC 1.00 .40
❑ BDP8 Jamie Vermilyea RC .60 .25
❑ BDP9 Jesus Flores RC .60 .25
❑ BDP10 Glen Perkins (RC) .60 .25
❑ BDP11 Tim Lincecum RC 5.00 2.00
❑ BDP12 Cameron Maybin RC 3.00 1.25
❑ BDP13 Brandon Morrow RC 1.50 .60
❑ BDP14 Mike Rabelo RC .60 .25
❑ BDP15 Alex Gordon RC 3.00 1.25
❑ BDP16 Zack Segovia (RC) .60 .25
❑ BDP17 Jon Knott (RC) .60 .25
❑ BDP18 Joba Chamberlain RC 6.00 2.50
❑ BDP19 Danny Putnam (RC) .60 .25
❑ BDP20 Matt DeSalvo (RC) .60 .25
❑ BDP21 Fred Lewis (RC) 1.00 .40
❑ BDP22 Sean Gallagher (RC) .60 .25
❑ BDP23 Brandon Wood (RC) .60 .25
❑ BDP24 Dennis Dove (RC) .60 .25
❑ BDP25 Hunter Pence (RC) 3.00 1.25
❑ BDP26 Jarrod Saltalamacchia (RC) 1.00 .40
❑ BDP27 Ben Francisco (RC) .60 .25
❑ BDP28 Doug Slaten RC .60 .25
❑ BDP29 Tony Abreu RC 1.50 .60
❑ BDP30 Billy Butler (RC) 1.00 .40
❑ BDP31 Jesse Litsch RC 1.00 .40
❑ BDP32 Nate Schierholtz (RC) .60 .25
❑ BDP33 Jared Burton RC .60 .25
❑ BDP34 Matt Brown RC .60 .25
❑ BDP35 Dallas Braden RC 1.00 .40
❑ BDP36 Carlos Gomez RC 1.00 .40
❑ BDP37 Brian Stokes (RC) .60 .25
❑ BDP38 Kory Casto (RC) .60 .25
❑ BDP39 Mark McLemore (RC) .60 .25
❑ BDP40 Andy LaRoche (RC) .60 .25
❑ BDP41 Tyler Clippard (RC) 1.00 .40
❑ BDP42 Curtis Thigpen (RC) .60 .25
❑ BDP43 Yunel Escobar (RC) .60 .25
❑ BDP44 Andy Sonnanstine RC .60 .25
❑ BDP45 Felix Pie (RC) .60 .25
❑ BDP46 Homer Bailey (RC) 1.00 .40
❑ BDP47 Kyle Kendrick RC 1.50 .60
❑ BDP48 Angel Sanchez RC .60 .25
❑ BDP49 Phil Hughes (RC) 3.00 1.25
❑ BDP50 Ryan Braun (RC) 4.00 1.50
❑ BDP51 Kevin Slowey (RC) 1.50 .60
❑ BDP52 Brendan Ryan (RC) .60 .25
❑ BDP53 Yovani Gallardo (RC) 2.00 .75
❑ BDP54 Mark Reynolds RC 2.50 1.00
❑ 237 Barry Bonds 3.00 1.25

2008 Bowman Chrome

❑ COMMON CARD (1-190) .50 .20
❑ COMMON ROOKIE (1-220) 1.50 .60
❑ 1 Ryan Braun 1.50 .60
❑ 2 David DeJesus .50 .20
❑ 3 Brandon Phillips .50 .20
❑ 4 Mark Teixeira .75 .30
❑ 5 Daisuke Matsuzaka 2.00 .75
❑ 6 Justin Upton 1.25 .50
❑ 7 Jered Weaver .50 .20
❑ 8 Todd Helton .75 .30
❑ 9 Adam Jones .50 .20
❑ 10 Erik Bedard .50 .20
❑ 11 Jason Bay .50 .20
❑ 12 Cole Hamels .75 .30
❑ 13 Bobby Abreu .50 .20
❑ 14 Carlos Zambrano .50 .20
❑ 15 Vladimir Guerrero 1.25 .50
❑ 16 Joe Blanton .50 .20
❑ 17 Paul Maholm .50 .20
❑ 18 Adrian Gonzalez .75 .30
❑ 19 Brandon Webb .50 .20
❑ 20 Carl Crawford .50 .20
❑ 21 A.J. Burnett .50 .20
❑ 22 Dmitri Young .50 .20
❑ 23 Jeremy Hermida .50 .20
❑ 24 C.C. Sabathia .50 .20
❑ 25 Adam Dunn .50 .20
❑ 26 Matt Garza .50 .20
❑ 27 Adrian Beltre .50 .20
❑ 28 Kevin Milwood .50 .20
❑ 29 Manny Ramirez 1.25 .50
❑ 30 Javier Vazquez .50 .20
❑ 31 Carlos Delgado .50 .20
❑ 32 Torii Hunter .50 .20
❑ 33 Ivan Rodriguez .75 .30
❑ 34 Nick Markakis .75 .30
❑ 35 Gil Meche .50 .20
❑ 36 Garrett Atkins .50 .20
❑ 37 Fausto Carmona .50 .20
❑ 38 Joe Mauer .75 .30
❑ 39 Tom Glavine .75 .30
❑ 40 Hideki Matsui 1.25 .50
❑ 41 Scott Rolen .75 .30
❑ 42 Tim Lincecum 1.25 .50
❑ 43 Prince Fielder 1.25 .50
❑ 44 Kazuo Matsui .50 .20
❑ 45 Tom Gorzelanny .50 .20
❑ 46 Lance Berkman .75 .30
❑ 47 David Ortiz 1.25 .50
❑ 48 Dontrelle Willis .50 .20
❑ 49 Travis Hafner .50 .20
❑ 50 Aaron Harang .50 .20
❑ 51 Chris Young .50 .20
❑ 52 Vernon Wells .50 .20
❑ 53 Francisco Liriano .75 .30
❑ 54 Eric Chavez .50 .20
❑ 55 Phil Hughes 1.25 .50
❑ 56 Melvin Mora .50 .20
❑ 57 Johan Santana 1.25 .50
❑ 58 Brian McCann .75 .30
❑ 59 Pat Burrell .50 .20
❑ 60 Chris Carpenter .50 .20
❑ 61 Brian Giles .50 .20
❑ 62 Jose Reyes .75 .30
❑ 63 Hanley Ramirez 1.25 .50
❑ 64 Ubaldo Jimenez .50 .20
❑ 65 Felix Pie .50 .20
❑ 66 Jeremy Bonderman .50 .20
❑ 67 Jimmy Rollins .75 .30
❑ 68 Miguel Tejada .50 .20
❑ 69 Derek Lowe .50 .20
❑ 70 Alex Gordon 1.25 .50
❑ 71 John Maine .50 .20
❑ 72 Alfonso Soriano .75 .30
❑ 73 Ben Sheets .75 .30
❑ 74 Hunter Pence 1.25 .50
❑ 75 Magglio Ordonez .75 .30
❑ 76 Josh Beckett .75 .30
❑ 77 Victor Martinez .50 .20
❑ 78 Mark Buehrle .50 .20
❑ 79 Jason Varitek 1.25 .50
❑ 80 Chien-Ming Wang 1.50 .60
❑ 81 Ken Griffey Jr. 2.00 .75
❑ 82 Billy Butler .50 .20
❑ 83 Brad Penny .50 .20
❑ 84 Carlos Beltran .50 .20
❑ 85 Curt Schilling .75 .30
❑ 86 Jorge Posada .75 .30
❑ 87 Andruw Jones .50 .20
❑ 88 Bobby Crosby .50 .20
❑ 89 Freddy Sanchez .50 .20
❑ 90 Barry Zito .50 .20
❑ 91 Miguel Cabrera .75 .30
❑ 92 B.J. Upton .75 .30
❑ 93 Matt Cain .50 .20
❑ 94 Lyle Overbay .50 .20
❑ 95 Austin Kearns .50 .20
❑ 96 Alex Rodriguez 2.00 .75
❑ 97 Rich Harden .50 .20
❑ 98 Justin Morneau .75 .30
❑ 99 Oliver Perez .50 .20
❑ 100 Gary Matthews .50 .20
❑ 101 Matt Holliday .75 .30
❑ 102 Justin Verlander .75 .30
❑ 103 Orlando Cabrera .50 .20
❑ 104 Rich Hill .50 .20
❑ 105 Tim Hudson .50 .20
❑ 106 Ryan Zimmerman .75 .30
❑ 107 Roy Oswalt .50 .20
❑ 108 Nick Swisher .50 .20
❑ 109 Raul Ibanez .50 .20
❑ 110 Kelly Johnson .50 .20
❑ 111 Alex Rios .50 .20
❑ 112 John Lackey .50 .20
❑ 113 Robinson Cano .75 .30
❑ 114 Michael Young .50 .20
❑ 115 Jeff Francis .50 .20
❑ 116 Grady Sizemore .75 .30
❑ 117 Mike Lowell .50 .20
❑ 118 Aramis Ramirez .50 .20
❑ 119 Stephen Drew .50 .20
❑ 120 Yovani Gallardo .50 .20
❑ 121 Chase Utley 1.25 .50
❑ 122 Dan Haren .50 .20
❑ 123 Yunel Escobar .50 .20
❑ 124 Greg Maddux 1.50 .60
❑ 125 Garret Anderson .50 .20
❑ 126 Aubrey Huff .50 .20
❑ 127 Paul Konerko .50 .20

❑ 128 Dan Uggla .75 .30
❑ 129 Roy Halladay .50 .20
❑ 130 Andre Ethier .75 .30
❑ 131 Orlando Hernandez .50 .20
❑ 132 Troy Tulowitzki .75 .30
❑ 133 Carlos Guillen .50 .20
❑ 134 Scott Kazmir .75 .30
❑ 135 Aaron Rowand .50 .20
❑ 136 Jim Edmonds .75 .30
❑ 137 Jermaine Dye .50 .20
❑ 138 Orlando Hudson .50 .20
❑ 139 Derrek Lee .75 .30
❑ 140 Travis Buck .50 .20
❑ 141 Zack Greinke .50 .20
❑ 142 Jeff Kent .50 .20
❑ 143 John Smoltz 1.25 .50
❑ 144 David Wright 1.50 .60
❑ 145 Joba Chamberlain 2.00 .75
❑ 146 Adam LaRoche .50 .20
❑ 147 Kevin Youkilis .75 .30
❑ 148 Troy Glaus .75 .30
❑ 149 Nick Johnson .50 .20
❑ 150 J.J. Hardy .50 .20
❑ 151 Felix Hernandez .75 .30
❑ 152 Gary Sheffield .50 .20
❑ 153 Albert Pujols 2.50 1.00
❑ 154 Chuck James .50 .20
❑ 155 Kosuke Fukudome RC 10.00 4.00
❑ 155b Kosuke Fukudome Japan 10.00 4.00
❑ 155c Fukudome No Sig/1600 *
❑ 156 Eric Byrnes .50 .20
❑ 157 Brad Hawpe .50 .20
❑ 158 Delmon Young .75 .30
❑ 159 Brian Roberts .75 .30
❑ 160 Russ Martin .75 .30
❑ 161 Hank Blalock .50 .20
❑ 162 Yadier Molina .75 .30
❑ 163 Jeremy Guthrie .50 .20
❑ 164 Chipper Jones 1.50 .60
❑ 165 Johnny Damon .75 .30
❑ 166 Ryan Garko .50 .20
❑ 167 Jake Peavy .50 .20
❑ 168 Chone Figgins .50 .20
❑ 169 Edgar Renteria .50 .20
❑ 170 Jim Thome .75 .30
❑ 171 Carlos Pena .50 .20
❑ 172 Dustin Pedroia .75 .30
❑ 173 Brett Myers .50 .20
❑ 174 Josh Hamilton 1.50 .60
❑ 175 Randy Johnson 1.25 .50
❑ 176 Ichiro Suzuki 2.00 .75
❑ 177 Aaron Hill .50 .20
❑ 178 Corey Hart .50 .20
❑ 179 Jarrod Saltalamacchia .50 .20
❑ 180 Jeff Francoeur .75 .30
❑ 181 Derek Jeter 3.00 1.25
❑ 182 Curtis Granderson .75 .30
❑ 183 James Loney .75 .30
❑ 184 Brian Bannister .50 .20
❑ 185 Carlos Lee .50 .20
❑ 186 Pedro Martinez .75 .30
❑ 187 Asdrubal Cabrera .50 .20
❑ 188 Kenji Johjima .50 .20
❑ 189 Jacoby Ellsbury 2.00 .75
❑ 190 Ryan Howard 1.50 .60
❑ 191 Sean Rodriguez (RC) 1.50 .60
❑ 192 Justin Ruggiano RC 2.50 1.00
❑ 193 Jed Lowrie (RC) 2.50 1.00
❑ 194 Joey Votto (RC) 2.50 1.00
❑ 195 Denard Span (RC) 1.50 .60
❑ 196 Brad Harman RC 2.50 1.00
❑ 197 Jeff Niemann (RC) 1.50 .60
❑ 198 Chin-Lung Hu (RC) 2.50 1.00
❑ 199 Luke Hochevar RC 5.00 2.00
❑ 200 German Duran RC 1.50 .60
❑ 201 Troy Patton (RC) 1.50 .60
❑ 202 Hiroki Kuroda RC 2.50 1.00
❑ 203 David Purcey (RC) 1.50 .60
❑ 204 Armando Galarraga RC 2.50 1.00
❑ 205 John Bowker (RC) 1.50 .60
❑ 206 Nick Blackburn RC 2.50 1.00
❑ 207 Hernan Iribarren (RC) 1.50 .60
❑ 208 Greg Smith RC 2.50 1.00
❑ 209 Alberto Gonzalez RC 2.50 1.00
❑ 210 Justin Masterson RC 4.00 1.50
❑ 211 Brian Barton RC 2.50 1.00
❑ 212 Robinzon Diaz (RC) 1.50 .60
❑ 213 Clete Thomas RC 2.50 1.00
❑ 214 Kazuo Fukumori RC 2.50 1.00
❑ 215 Jayson Nix (RC) 1.50 .60
❑ 216 Evan Longoria RC 10.00 4.00
❑ 217 Johnny Cueto RC 4.00 1.50
❑ 218 Matt Tolbert RC 2.50 1.00
❑ 219 Masahide Kobayashi RC 2.50 1.00
❑ 220 Callix Crabbe (RC) 1.50 .60

2001 Bowman Heritage

❑ COMPLETE SET (440) 200.00 125.00
❑ COMP.SET w/o SP's (330) 50.00 20.00
❑ COMMON CARD (1-330) .40 .15
❑ COMMON RC (1-330) .40 .15
❑ COMMON CARD (331-440) 2.00 .75
❑ 1 Chipper Jones 1.00 .40
❑ 2 Pete Harnisch .40 .15
❑ 3 Brian Giles .40 .15
❑ 4 J.T. Snow .40 .15
❑ 5 Bartolo Colon .40 .15
❑ 6 Jorge Posada .60 .25
❑ 7 Shawn Green .40 .15
❑ 8 Derek Jeter 2.50 1.00
❑ 9 Benito Santiago .40 .15
❑ 10 Ramon Hernandez .40 .15
❑ 11 Bernie Williams .60 .25
❑ 12 Greg Maddux 1.50 .60
❑ 13 Barry Bonds 2.50 1.00
❑ 14 Roger Clemens 2.00 .75
❑ 15 Miguel Tejada .40 .15
❑ 16 Pedro Feliz .40 .15
❑ 17 Jim Edmonds .40 .15
❑ 18 Tom Glavine .60 .25
❑ 19 David Justice .40 .15
❑ 20 Rich Aurilia .40 .15
❑ 21 Jason Giambi .40 .15
❑ 22 Orlando Hernandez .40 .15
❑ 23 Shawn Estes .40 .15
❑ 24 Nelson Figueroa .40 .15
❑ 25 Terrence Long .40 .15
❑ 26 Mike Mussina .60 .25
❑ 27 Eric Davis .40 .15
❑ 28 Jimmy Rollins .40 .15
❑ 29 Andy Pettitte .60 .25
❑ 30 Shawon Dunston .40 .15
❑ 31 Tim Hudson .40 .15
❑ 32 Jeff Kent .40 .15
❑ 33 Scott Brosius .40 .15
❑ 34 Livan Hernandez .40 .15
❑ 35 Alfonso Soriano .60 .25
❑ 36 Mark McGwire 2.50 1.00
❑ 37 Russ Ortiz .40 .15
❑ 38 Fernando Vina .40 .15
❑ 39 Ken Griffey Jr. 1.50 .60
❑ 40 Edgar Renteria .40 .15
❑ 41 Kevin Brown .40 .15
❑ 42 Robb Nen .40 .15
❑ 43 Paul LoDuca .40 .15
❑ 44 Bobby Abreu .40 .15
❑ 45 Adam Dunn .60 .25
❑ 46 Osvaldo Fernandez .40 .15
❑ 47 Marvin Benard .40 .15
❑ 48 Mark Gardner .40 .15
❑ 49 Alex Rodriguez 1.50 .60
❑ 50 Preston Wilson .40 .15
❑ 51 Roberto Alomar .60 .25
❑ 52 Ben Davis .40 .15
❑ 53 Derek Bell .40 .15
❑ 54 Ken Caminiti .40 .15
❑ 55 Barry Zito .60 .25
❑ 56 Scott Rolen .60 .25
❑ 57 Geoff Jenkins .40 .15
❑ 58 Mike Cameron .40 .15
❑ 59 Ben Grieve .40 .15
❑ 60 Chuck Knoblauch .40 .15
❑ 61 Matt Lawton .40 .15
❑ 62 Chan Ho Park .40 .15
❑ 63 Lance Berkman .40 .15
❑ 64 Carlos Beltran .40 .15
❑ 65 Dean Palmer .40 .15
❑ 66 Alex Gonzalez .40 .15
❑ 67 Larry Walker .40 .15
❑ 68 Magglio Ordonez .40 .15
❑ 69 Ellis Burks .40 .15
❑ 70 Mark Mulder .40 .15
❑ 71 Randy Johnson 1.00 .40
❑ 72 John Smoltz .60 .25
❑ 73 Jerry Hairston Jr. .40 .15
❑ 74 Pedro Martinez .60 .25
❑ 75 Fred McGriff .60 .25
❑ 76 Sean Casey .40 .15
❑ 77 C.C. Sabathia .40 .15
❑ 78 Todd Helton .60 .25
❑ 79 Brad Penny .40 .15
❑ 80 Mike Sweeney .40 .15
❑ 81 Billy Wagner .40 .15
❑ 82 Mark Buehrle .60 .25
❑ 83 Cristian Guzman .40 .15
❑ 84 Jose Vidro .40 .15
❑ 85 Pat Burrell .40 .15
❑ 86 Jermaine Dye .40 .15
❑ 87 Brandon Inge .40 .15
❑ 88 David Wells .40 .15
❑ 89 Mike Piazza 1.50 .60
❑ 90 Jose Cabrera .40 .15
❑ 91 Cliff Floyd .40 .15
❑ 92 Matt Morris .40 .15
❑ 93 Raul Mondesi .40 .15
❑ 94 Joe Kennedy RC .60 .25
❑ 95 Jack Wilson RC .60 .25
❑ 96 Andruw Jones .60 .25
❑ 97 Mariano Rivera 1.00 .40
❑ 98 Mike Hampton .40 .15
❑ 99 Roger Cedeno .40 .15
❑ 100 Jose Cruz .40 .15
❑ 101 Mike Lowell .40 .15
❑ 102 Pedro Astacio .40 .15
❑ 103 Joe Mays .40 .15
❑ 104 John Franco .40 .15
❑ 105 Tim Redding .40 .15
❑ 106 Sandy Alomar Jr. .40 .15
❑ 107 Bret Boone .40 .15
❑ 108 Josh Towers RC .60 .25
❑ 109 Matt Stairs .40 .15
❑ 110 Chris Truby .40 .15
❑ 111 Jeff Suppan .40 .15
❑ 112 J.C. Romero .40 .15
❑ 113 Felipe Lopez .40 .15
❑ 114 Ben Sheets .60 .25
❑ 115 Frank Thomas 1.00 .40
❑ 116 A.J. Burnett .40 .15
❑ 117 Tony Clark .40 .15
❑ 118 Mac Suzuki .40 .15
❑ 119 Brad Radke .40 .15
❑ 120 Jeff Shaw .40 .15
❑ 121 Nick Neugebauer .40 .15
❑ 122 Kenny Lofton .40 .15
❑ 123 Jacque Jones .40 .15
❑ 124 Brent Mayne .40 .15
❑ 125 Carlos Hernandez .40 .15
❑ 126 Shane Spencer .40 .15
❑ 127 John Lackey .40 .15
❑ 128 Sterling Hitchcock .40 .15
❑ 129 Darren Dreifort .40 .15
❑ 130 Rusty Greer .40 .15
❑ 131 Michael Cuddyer .40 .15
❑ 132 Tyler Houston .40 .15
❑ 133 Chin-Feng Chen .40 .15
❑ 134 Ken Harvey .40 .15
❑ 135 Marquis Grissom .40 .15
❑ 136 Russell Branyan .40 .15
❑ 137 Eric Karros .40 .15
❑ 138 Josh Beckett .60 .25
❑ 139 Todd Zeile .40 .15

❑ 140 Corey Koskie	.40	.15
❑ 141 Steve Sparks	.40	.15
❑ 142 Bobby Seay	.40	.15
❑ 143 Tim Raines Jr.	.40	.15
❑ 144 Julio Zuleta	.40	.15
❑ 145 Jose Lima	.40	.15
❑ 146 Dante Bichette	.40	.15
❑ 147 Randy Keisler	.40	.15
❑ 148 Brent Butler	.40	.15
❑ 149 Antonio Alfonseca	.40	.15
❑ 150 Bryan Rekar	.40	.15
❑ 151 Jeffrey Hammonds	.40	.15
❑ 152 Larry Bigbie	.40	.15
❑ 153 Blake Stein	.40	.15
❑ 154 Robin Ventura	.40	.15
❑ 155 Rondell White	.40	.15
❑ 156 Juan Silvestre	.40	.15
❑ 157 Marcus Thames	.40	.15
❑ 158 Sidney Ponson	.40	.15
❑ 159 Juan A. Pena RC	.40	.15
❑ 160 C.J. Nitkowski	.40	.15
❑ 161 Adam Everett	.40	.15
❑ 162 Eric Munson	.40	.15
❑ 163 Jason Isringhausen	.40	.15
❑ 164 Brad Fullmer	.40	.15
❑ 165 Miguel Olivo	.40	.15
❑ 166 Fernando Tatis	.40	.15
❑ 167 Freddy Garcia	.40	.15
❑ 168 Tom Goodwin	.40	.15
❑ 169 Armando Benitez	.40	.15
❑ 170 Paul Konerko	.40	.15
❑ 171 Jeff Cirillo	.40	.15
❑ 172 Shane Reynolds	.40	.15
❑ 173 Kevin Tapani	.40	.15
❑ 174 Joe Crede	1.00	.40
❑ 175 Omar Infante RC	.40	.15
❑ 176 Jake Peavy RC	5.00	2.00
❑ 177 Corey Patterson	.40	.15
❑ 178 Mike Penney RC	.40	.15
❑ 179 Jeromy Burnitz	.40	.15
❑ 180 David Segui	.40	.15
❑ 181 Marcus Giles	.40	.15
❑ 182 Paul O'Neill	.60	.25
❑ 183 John Olerud	.40	.15
❑ 184 Andy Benes	.40	.15
❑ 185 Brad Cresse	.40	.15
❑ 186 Ricky Ledee	.40	.15
❑ 187 Allen Levrault UER	.40	.15
❑ 188 Royce Clayton	.40	.15
❑ 189 Kelly Johnson RC	3.00	1.25
❑ 190 Quilvio Veras	.40	.15
❑ 191 Mike Williams	.40	.15
❑ 192 Jason Lane RC	.60	.25
❑ 193 Rick Helling	.40	.15
❑ 194 Tim Wakefield	.40	.15
❑ 195 James Baldwin	.40	.15
❑ 196 Cody Ransom RC	.40	.15
❑ 197 Bobby Kielty	.40	.15
❑ 198 Bobby Jones	.40	.15
❑ 199 Steve Cox	.40	.15
❑ 200 Jamal Strong RC	.40	.15
❑ 201 Steve Lomasney	.40	.15
❑ 202 Brian Cardwell RC	.40	.15
❑ 203 Mike Matheny	.40	.15
❑ 204 Jeff Randazzo RC	.40	.15
❑ 205 Aubrey Huff	.40	.15
❑ 206 Chuck Finley	.40	.15
❑ 207 Denny Bautista RC	.60	.25
❑ 208 Terry Mulholland	.40	.15
❑ 209 Rey Ordonez	.40	.15
❑ 210 Keith Surkont RC	.40	.15
❑ 211 Orlando Cabrera	.40	.15
❑ 212 Juan Encarnacion	.40	.15
❑ 213 Dustin Hermanson	.40	.15
❑ 214 Luis Rivas	.40	.15
❑ 215 Mark Quinn	.40	.15
❑ 216 Randy Velarde	.40	.15
❑ 217 Billy Koch	.40	.15
❑ 218 Ryan Rupe	.40	.15
❑ 219 Keith Ginter	.40	.15
❑ 220 Woody Williams	.40	.15
❑ 221 Ryan Franklin	.40	.15
❑ 222 Aaron Myette	.40	.15
❑ 223 Joe Borchard RC	.40	.15
❑ 224 Nate Cornejo	.40	.15
❑ 225 Julian Tavarez	.40	.15
❑ 226 Kevin Millwood	.40	.15
❑ 227 Travis Hafner RC	5.00	2.00
❑ 228 Charles Nagy	.40	.15
❑ 229 Mike Lieberthal	.40	.15
❑ 230 Jeff Nelson	.40	.15
❑ 231 Ryan Dempster	.40.	.15
❑ 232 Andres Galarraga	.40	.15
❑ 233 Chad Durbin	.40	.15
❑ 234 Timo Perez	.40	.15
❑ 235 Troy O'Leary	.40	.15
❑ 236 Kevin Young	.40	.15
❑ 237 Gabe Kapler	.40	.15
❑ 238 Juan Cruz RC	.40	.15
❑ 239 Masato Yoshii	.40	.15
❑ 240 Aramis Ramirez	.40	.15
❑ 241 Matt Cooper RC	.40	.15
❑ 242 Randy Flores RC	.40	.15
❑ 243 Rafael Furcal	.40	.15
❑ 244 David Eckstein	.40	.15
❑ 245 Matt Clement	.40	.15
❑ 246 Craig Biggio	.60	.25
❑ 247 Rick Reed	.40	.15
❑ 248 Jose Macias	.40	.15
❑ 249 Alex Escobar	.40	.15
❑ 250 Roberto Hernandez	.40	.15
❑ 251 Andy Ashby	.40	.15
❑ 252 Tony Armas Jr.	.40	.15
❑ 253 Jamie Moyer	.40	.15
❑ 254 Jason Tyner	.40	.15
❑ 255 Charles Kegley RC	.40	.15
❑ 256 Jeff Conine	.40	.15
❑ 257 Francisco Cordova	.40	.15
❑ 258 Ted Lilly	.40	.15
❑ 259 Joe Randa	.40	.15
❑ 260 Jeff D'Amico	.40	.15
❑ 261 Albie Lopez	.40	.15
❑ 262 Kevin Appier	.40	.15
❑ 263 Richard Hidalgo	.40	.15
❑ 264 Omar Daal	.40	.15
❑ 265 Ricky Gutierrez	.40	.15
❑ 266 John Rocker	.40	.15
❑ 267 Ray Lankford	.40	.15
❑ 268 Beau Hale RC	.40	.15
❑ 269 Tony Blanco RC	.40	.15
❑ 270 Derrek Lee UER	.60	.25
❑ 271 Jamey Wright	.40	.15
❑ 272 Alex Gordon	.40	.15
❑ 273 Jeff Weaver	.40	.15
❑ 274 Jaret Wright	.40	.15
❑ 275 Jose Hernandez	.40	.15
❑ 276 Bruce Chen	.40	.15
❑ 277 Todd Hollandsworth	.40	.15
❑ 278 Wade Miller	.40	.15
❑ 279 Luke Prokopec	.40	.15
❑ 280 Rafael Soriano RC	.40	.15
❑ 281 Damion Easley	.40	.15
❑ 282 Darren Oliver	.40	.15
❑ 283 Brandon Duckworth RC	.40	.15
❑ 284 Aaron Herr	.40	.15
❑ 285 Ray Durham	.40	.15
❑ 286 Wilmy Caceras RC	.40	.15
❑ 287 Ugueth Urbina	.40	.15
❑ 288 Scott Seabol	.40	.15
❑ 289 Lance Niekro RC	.60	.25
❑ 290 Trot Nixon	.40	.15
❑ 291 Adam Kennedy	.40	.15
❑ 292 Brian Schmitt RC	.40	.15
❑ 293 Grant Roberts	.40	.15
❑ 294 Benny Agbayani	.40	.15
❑ 295 Travis Lee	.40	.15
❑ 296 Erick Almonte RC	.40	.15
❑ 297 Jim Thome	.60	.25
❑ 298 Eric Young	.40	.15
❑ 299 Dan Denham RC	.40	.15
❑ 300 Boof Bonser RC	.40	.15
❑ 301 Denny Neagle	.40	.15
❑ 302 Kenny Rogers	.40	.15
❑ 303 J.D. Closser	.40	.15
❑ 304 Chase Utley RC	10.00	4.00
❑ 305 Rey Sanchez	.40	.15
❑ 306 Sean McGowan	.40	.15
❑ 307 Justin Pope RC	.40	.15
❑ 308 Torii Hunter	.40	.15
❑ 309 B.J. Surhoff	.40	.15
❑ 310 Aaron Heilman RC	.50	.20
❑ 311 Gabe Gross RC	.60	.25
❑ 312 Lee Stevens	.40	.15
❑ 313 Todd Hundley	.40	.15
❑ 314 Macay McBride RC	1.00	.40
❑ 315 Edgar Martinez	.60	.25
❑ 316 Omar Vizquel	.60	.25
❑ 317 Reggie Sanders	.40	.15
❑ 318 John-Ford Griffin RC	.40	.15
❑ 319 T.Salmon UER Glaus Photo	.40	.15
❑ 320 Pokey Reese	.40	.15
❑ 321 Jay Payton	.40	.15
❑ 322 Doug Glanville	.40	.15
❑ 323 Greg Vaughn	.40	.15
❑ 324 Ruben Sierra	.40	.15
❑ 325 Kip Wells	.40	.15
❑ 326 Carl Everett	.40	.15
❑ 327 Garret Anderson	.40	.15
❑ 328 Jay Bell	.40	.15
❑ 329 Barry Larkin	.60	.25
❑ 330 Jeff Mathis RC	.60	.25
❑ 331 Adrian Gonzalez SP	2.00	.75
❑ 332 Juan Rivera SP	2.00	.75
❑ 333 Tony Alvarez SP	2.00	.75
❑ 334 Xavier Nady SP	2.00	.75
❑ 335 Josh Hamilton SP	4.00	1.50
❑ 336 Will Smith SP RC	2.00	.75
❑ 337 Israel Alcantara SP	2.00	.75
❑ 338 Chris George SP	2.00	.75
❑ 339 Sean Burroughs SP	2.00	.75
❑ 340 Jack Cust SP	2.00	.75
❑ 341 Henry Mateo SP RC	2.00	.75
❑ 342 Carlos Pena SP	2.00	.75
❑ 343 J.R. House SP	2.00	.75
❑ 344 Carlos Silva SP	2.00	.75
❑ 345 Mike Rivera SP RC	2.00	.75
❑ 346 Adam Johnson SP	2.00	.75
❑ 347 Scott Heard SP	2.00	.75
❑ 348 Alex Cintron SP	2.00	.75
❑ 349 Miguel Cabrera SP	8.00	3.00
❑ 350 Nick Johnson SP	2.00	.75
❑ 351 Albert Pujols SP RC	50.00	20.00
❑ 352 Ichiro Suzuki SP RC	30.00	12.50
❑ 353 Carlos Delgado SP	2.00	.75
❑ 354 Troy Glaus SP	2.00	.75
❑ 355 Sammy Sosa SP	3.00	1.25
❑ 356 Ivan Rodriguez SP	3.00	1.25
❑ 357 Vladimir Guerrero SP	3.00	1.25
❑ 358 Manny Ramirez Sox SP	3.00	1.25
❑ 359 Luis Gonzalez SP	2.00	.75
❑ 360 Roy Oswalt SP	3.00	1.25
❑ 361 Moises Alou SP	2.00	.75
❑ 362 Juan Gonzalez SP	2.00	.75
❑ 363 Tony Gwynn SP	4.00	1.50
❑ 364 Hideo Nomo SP	3.00	1.25
❑ 365 Tsuyoshi Shinjo SP RC	3.00	1.25
❑ 366 Kazuhiro Sasaki SP	2.00	.75
❑ 367 Cal Ripken SP	10.00	4.00
❑ 368 Rafael Palmeiro SP	3.00	1.25
❑ 369 J.D. Drew SP	2.00	.75
❑ 370 Doug Mientkiewicz SP	2.00	.75
❑ 371 Jeff Bagwell SP	3.00	1.25
❑ 372 Darin Erstad SP	2.00	.75
❑ 373 Tom Gordon SP	2.00	.75
❑ 374 Ben Petrick SP	2.00	.75
❑ 375 Eric Milton SP	2.00	.75
❑ 376 Nomar Garciaparra SP	5.00	2.00
❑ 377 Julio Lugo SP	2.00	.75
❑ 378 Tino Martinez SP	3.00	1.25
❑ 379 Javier Vazquez SP	2.00	.75
❑ 380 Jeremy Giambi SP	2.00	.75
❑ 381 Marty Cordova SP	2.00	.75
❑ 382 Adrian Beltre SP	2.00	.75
❑ 383 John Burkett SP	2.00	.75
❑ 384 Aaron Boone SP	2.00	.75
❑ 385 Eric Chavez SP	2.00	.75
❑ 386 Curt Schilling SP	2.00	.75
❑ 387 Cory Lidle UER SP	2.00	.75
❑ 388 Jason Schmidt SP	2.00	.75
❑ 389 Johnny Damon SP	3.00	1.25
❑ 390 Steve Finley SP	2.00	.75
❑ 391 Edgardo Alfonzo SP	2.00	.75
❑ 392 Jose Valentin SP	2.00	.75
❑ 393 Jose Canseco SP	3.00	1.25
❑ 394 Ryan Klesko SP	2.00	.75
❑ 395 David Cone SP	2.00	.75
❑ 396 Jason Kendall UER SP	2.00	.75
❑ 397 Placido Polanco SP	2.00	.75

❑	398 Glendon Rusch SP	2.00	.75
❑	399 Aaron Sele SP	2.00	.75
❑	400 D'Angelo Jimenez SP	2.00	.75
❑	401 Mark Grace SP	3.00	1.25
❑	402 Al Leiter SP	2.00	.75
❑	403 Brian Jordan SP	2.00	.75
❑	404 Phil Nevin SP	2.00	.75
❑	405 Brent Abernathy SP	2.00	.75
❑	406 Kerry Wood SP	2.00	.75
❑	407 Alex Gonzalez SP	2.00	.75
❑	408 Robert Fick SP	2.00	.75
❑	409 Dmitri Young UER SP	2.00	.75
❑	410 Wes Helms SP	2.00	.75
❑	411 Trevor Hoffman SP	2.00	.75
❑	412 Rickey Henderson SP	3.00	1.25
❑	413 Bobby Higginson SP	2.00	.75
❑	414 Gary Sheffield SP	2.00	.75
❑	415 Darryl Kile SP	2.00	.75
❑	416 Richie Sexson SP	2.00	.75
❑	417 Frank Menechino SP RC	2.00	.75
❑	418 Javy Lopez SP	2.00	.75
❑	419 Carlos Lee SP	2.00	.75
❑	420 Jon Lieber SP	2.00	.75
❑	421 Hank Blalock SP RC	6.00	2.50
❑	422 Marlon Byrd SP RC	.40	.15
❑	423 Jason Kinchen SP RC	2.00	.75
❑	424 Morgan Ensberg SP RC	5.00	2.00
❑	425 Greg Nash SP RC	2.00	.75
❑	426 Dennis Tankersley SP RC	2.00	.75
❑	427 Nate Murphy SP RC	2.00	.75
❑	428 Chris Smith SP RC	2.00	.75
❑	429 Jake Gautreau SP RC	2.00	.75
❑	430 John VanBenschoten SP RC	2.00	.75
❑	431 Travis Thompson SP RC	2.00	.75
❑	432 Orlando Hudson SP RC	3.00	1.25
❑	433 Jerome Williams SP RC	3.00	1.25
❑	434 Kevin Reese SP RC	2.00	.75
❑	435 Ed Rogers SP RC	2.00	.75
❑	436 Ryan Jamison SP RC	2.00	.75
❑	437 Adam Pettyjohn SP RC	2.00	.75
❑	438 Hee Seop Choi SP RC	3.00	1.25
❑	439 Justin Morneau SP RC	12.00	5.00
❑	440 Mitch Jones SP RC	2.00	.75

2002 Bowman Heritage

❑	COMP SET w/o SP's (324)	50.00	25.00
❑	COMMON CARD (1-439)	.40	.15
❑	COMMON SP	2.00	.75
❑	1 Brent Abernathy	.40	.15
❑	2 Jermaine Dye	.40	.15
❑	3 James Shanks RC	.40	.15
❑	4 Chris Flinn RC	.40	.15
❑	5 Mike Peeples SP RC	2.00	.75
❑	6 Gary Sheffield	.40	.15
❑	7 Livan Hernandez SP	2.00	.75
❑	8 Jeff Austin RC	.40	.15
❑	9 Jeremy Giambi	.40	.15
❑	10 Adam Roller RC	.40	.15
❑	11 Sandy Alomar Jr. SP	2.00	.75
❑	12 Matt Williams SP	2.00	.75
❑	13 Hee Seop Choi	.40	.15
❑	14 Jose Offerman	.40	.15
❑	15 Robin Ventura	.40	.15
❑	16 Craig Biggio	.60	.25
❑	17 David Wells	.40	.15
❑	18 Rob Henkel RC	.40	.15
❑	19 Edgar Martinez	.60	.25
❑	20 Matt Morris SP	2.00	.75
❑	21 Jose Valentin	.40	.15
❑	22 Barry Bonds	2.50	1.00
❑	23 Justin Schuda RC	.40	.15
❑	24 Josh Phelps	.40	.15
❑	25 John Rodriguez RC	.50	.20
❑	27 Aramis Ramirez	.40	.15
❑	28 Jack Wilson	.40	.15
❑	29 Roger Clemens	2.00	.75
❑	30 Kazuhisa Ishii RC	.50	.20
❑	31 Carlos Beltran	.40	.15
❑	32 Drew Henson SP	2.00	.75
❑	33 Kevin Young SP	2.00	.75
❑	34 Juan Cruz SP	2.00	.75
❑	35 Curtis Legendre RC	.40	.15
❑	36 Jose Morban RC	.40	.15
❑	37 Ricardo Cordova SP RC	2.00	.75
❑	38 Adam Everett	.40	.15
❑	39 Mark Prior	.60	.25
❑	40 Jose Bautista RC	1.00	.40
❑	41 Travis Foley RC	.40	.15
❑	42 Kerry Wood	.40	.15
❑	43 B.J. Surhoff	.40	.15
❑	44 Moises Alou	.40	.15
❑	45 Joey Hammond	.40	.15
❑	46 Eric Bruntlett RC	.40	.15
❑	47 Carlos Guillen	.40	.15
❑	48 Joe Crede	.40	.15
❑	49 Dan Phillips RC	.40	.15
❑	50 Jason LaRue	.40	.15
❑	51 Javy Lopez	.40	.15
❑	52 Larry Bigbie SP	2.00	.75
❑	53 Chris Baker RC	.40	.15
❑	54 Marty Cordova	.40	.15
❑	55 C.C. Sabathia	.40	.15
❑	56 Mike Piazza	1.50	.60
❑	57 Brian Giles	.40	.15
❑	58 Mike Bordick SP	2.00	.75
❑	59 Tyler Houston SP	2.00	.75
❑	60 Gabe Kapler	.40	.15
❑	61 Ben Broussard	.40	.15
❑	62 Steve Finley SP	2.00	.75
❑	63 Koyie Hill	.40	.15
❑	64 Jeff D'Amico	.40	.15
❑	65 Edwin Almonte RC	.40	.15
❑	66 Pedro Martinez	.60	.25
❑	66B Nomar Garciaparra 66	1.50	.60
❑	67 Travis Fryman SP	2.00	.75
❑	68 Brady Clark SP	2.00	.75
❑	69 Reed Johnson SP RC	4.00	1.50
❑	70 Mark Grace SP	3.00	1.25
❑	71 Tony Batista SP	2.00	.75
❑	72 Roy Oswalt	.40	.15
❑	73 Pat Burrell SP	2.00	.75
❑	74 Dennis Tankersley	.40	.15
❑	75 Ramon Ortiz	.40	.15
❑	76 Neal Frendling SP RC	2.00	.75
❑	77 Omar Vizquel SP	3.00	1.25
❑	78 Hideo Nomo	1.00	.40
❑	79 Orlando Hernandez SP	2.00	.75
❑	80 Andy Pettitte	.60	.25
❑	81 Cole Barthel RC	.40	.15
❑	82 Bret Boone	.40	.15
❑	83 Alfonso Soriano	.40	.15
❑	84 Brandon Duckworth	.40	.15
❑	85 Ben Grieve	.40	.15
❑	86 Mike Rosamond SP RC	2.00	.75
❑	87 Luke Prokopec	.40	.15
❑	88 Chone Figgins RC	1.50	.60
❑	89 Rick Ankiel SP	2.00	.75
❑	90 David Eckstein	.40	.15
❑	91 Corey Koskie	.40	.15
❑	92 David Justice	.40	.15
❑	93 Jimmy Alvarez RC	.40	.15
❑	94 Jason Schmidt	.40	.15
❑	95 Reggie Sanders	.40	.15
❑	96 Victor Alvarez RC	.40	.15
❑	97 Brett Roneberg RC	.40	.15
❑	98 D'Angelo Jimenez	.40	.15
❑	99 Hank Blalock	.60	.25
❑	100 Juan Rivera	.40	.15
❑	101 Mark Buehrle SP	2.00	.75
❑	102 Juan Uribe	.40	.15
❑	103 Royce Clayton SP	2.00	.75
❑	104 Brett Kay RC	.40	.15
❑	105 John Olerud	.40	.15
❑	106 Richie Sexson	.40	.15
❑	107 Chipper Jones	1.00	.40
❑	108 Adam Dunn	.40	.15
❑	109 Tim Salmon SP	3.00	1.25
❑	110 Eric Karros	.40	.15
❑	111 Jose Vidro	.40	.15
❑	112 Jerry Hairston Jr.	.40	.15
❑	113 Anastacio Martinez RC	.40	.15
❑	114 Robert Fick SP	2.00	.75
❑	115 Randy Johnson	1.00	.40
❑	116 Trot Nixon SP	2.00	.75
❑	117 Nick Bierbrodt SP	2.00	.75
❑	118 Jim Edmonds	.40	.15
❑	119 Rafael Palmeiro	.60	.25
❑	120 Jose Macias	.40	.15
❑	121 Josh Beckett	.40	.15
❑	122 Sean Douglass	.40	.15
❑	123 Jeff Kent	.40	.15
❑	124 Tim Redding	.40	.15
❑	125 Xavier Nady	.40	.15
❑	126 Carl Everett	.40	.15
❑	127 Joe Randa	.40	.15
❑	128 Luke Hudson SP	2.00	.75
❑	129 Eric Miller RC	.40	.15
❑	130 Melvin Mora	.40	.15
❑	131 Adrian Gonzalez	.40	.15
❑	132 Larry Walker SP	2.00	.75
❑	133 Nic Jackson SP RC	2.00	.75
❑	134 Mike Lowell SP	2.00	.75
❑	135 Jim Thome	.60	.25
❑	136 Eric Milton	.40	.15
❑	137 Rich Thompson SP RC	2.00	.75
❑	138 Placido Polanco SP	2.00	.75
❑	139 Juan Pierre	.40	.15
❑	140 David Segui	.40	.15
❑	141 Chuck Finley	.40	.15
❑	142 Felipe Lopez	.40	.15
❑	143 Toby Hall	.40	.15
❑	144 Fred Bastardo RC	.40	.15
❑	145 Troy Glaus	.40	.15
❑	146 Todd Helton	.60	.25
❑	147 Ruben Gotay SP RC	3.00	1.25
❑	148 Darin Erstad	.40	.15
❑	149 Ryan Gripp SP RC	2.00	.75
❑	150 Orlando Cabrera	.40	.15
❑	151 Jason Young RC	.40	.15
❑	152 Sterling Hitchcock SP	2.00	.75
❑	153 Miguel Tejada	.40	.15
❑	154 Al Leiter	.40	.15
❑	155 Taylor Buchholz RC	.50	.20
❑	156 Juan M. Gonzalez RC	.40	.15
❑	157 Damion Easley	.40	.15
❑	158 Jimmy Gobble RC	.40	.15
❑	159 Dennis Ulacia SP RC	2.00	.75
❑	160 Shane Reynolds SP	2.00	.75
❑	161 Javier Colina	.40	.15
❑	162 Frank Thomas	1.00	.40
❑	163 Chuck Knoblauch	.40	.15
❑	164 Sean Burroughs	.40	.15
❑	165 Greg Maddux	1.50	.60
❑	166 Jason Ellison RC	.75	.30
❑	167 Tony Womack	.40	.15
❑	168 Randall Shelley SP RC	2.00	.75
❑	169 Jason Marquis	.40	.15
❑	170 Brian Jordan	.40	.15
❑	171 Vicente Padilla	.40	.15
❑	172 Barry Zito	.40	.15
❑	173 Matt Allegra SP RC	2.00	.75
❑	174 Ralph Santana SP RC	2.00	.75
❑	175 Carlos Lee	.40	.15
❑	176 Richard Hidalgo SP	2.00	.75
❑	177 Kevin Deaton RC	.40	.15
❑	178 Juan Encarnacion	.40	.15
❑	179 Mark Quinn	.40	.15
❑	180 Rafael Furcal	.40	.15
❑	181 G.Anderson UER Figgins	.40	.15
❑	182 David Wright RC	20.00	8.00
❑	183 Jose Reyes	.60	.25
❑	184 Mario Ramos SP RC	2.00	.75
❑	185 J.D. Drew	.40	.15
❑	186 Juan Gonzalez	.40	.15
❑	187 Nick Neugebauer	.40	.15
❑	188 Alejandro Giron RC	.40	.15
❑	189 John Burkett	.40	.15
❑	190 Ben Sheets	.40	.15
❑	191 Vinny Castilla SP	2.00	.75
❑	192 Cory Lidle	.40	.15

❑ 193 Fernando Vina	.40	.15
❑ 194 Russell Branyan SP	2.00	.75
❑ 195 Ben Davis	.40	.15
❑ 196 Angel Berroa	.40	.15
❑ 197 Alex Gonzalez	.40	.15
❑ 198 Jared Sandberg	.40	.15
❑ 199 Travis Lee SP	2.00	.75
❑ 200 Luis DePaula SP RC	2.00	.75
❑ 201 Ramon Hernandez SP	2.00	.75
❑ 202 Brandon Inge	.40	.15
❑ 203 Aubrey Huff	.40	.15
❑ 204 Mike Rivera	.40	.15
❑ 205 Brad Nelson RC	.40	.15
❑ 206 Colt Griffin SP RC	2.00	.75
❑ 207 Joel Pineiro	.40	.15
❑ 208 Adam Pettyjohn	.40	.15
❑ 209 Mark Redman	.40	.15
❑ 210 Roberto Alomar SP	3.00	1.25
❑ 211 Denny Neagle	.40	.15
❑ 212 Adam Kennedy	.40	.15
❑ 213 Jason Arnold SP RC	2.00	.75
❑ 214 Jamie Moyer	.40	.15
❑ 215 Aaron Boone	.40	.15
❑ 216 Doug Glanville	.40	.15
❑ 217 Nick Johnson SP	2.00	.75
❑ 218 Mike Cameron SP	2.00	.75
❑ 219 Tim Wakefield SP	2.00	.75
❑ 220 Todd Stottlemyre SP	2.00	.75
❑ 221 Mo Vaughn SP	2.00	.75
❑ 222 Vladimir Guerrero	1.00	.40
❑ 223 Bill Ortega	.40	.15
❑ 224 Kevin Brown	.40	.15
❑ 225 Peter Bergeron SP	2.00	.75
❑ 226 Shannon Stewart SP	2.00	.75
❑ 227 Eric Chavez	.40	.15
❑ 228 Clint Weibl RC	.40	.15
❑ 229 Todd Hollandsworth SP	2.00	.75
❑ 230 Jeff Bagwell	.60	.25
❑ 231 Chad Qualls RC	.50	.20
❑ 232 Ben Howard RC	.40	.15
❑ 233 Rondell White SP	2.00	.75
❑ 234 Fred McGriff	.60	.25
❑ 235 Steve Cox SP	2.00	.75
❑ 236 Chris Tritle RC	.40	.15
❑ 237 Eric Valent	.40	.15
❑ 238 Joe Mauer RC	8.00	3.00
❑ 239 Shawn Green	.40	.15
❑ 240 Jimmy Rollins	.40	.15
❑ 241 Edgar Renteria	.40	.15
❑ 242 Edwin Yan RC	.40	.15
❑ 243 Noochie Varner RC	.40	.15
❑ 244 Kris Benson SP	2.00	.75
❑ 245 Mike Hampton	.40	.15
❑ 246 So Taguchi RC	.50	.20
❑ 247 Sammy Sosa	1.00	.40
❑ 248 Terrence Long	.40	.15
❑ 249 Jason Bay RC	5.00	2.00
❑ 250 Kevin Millar SP	2.00	.75
❑ 251 Albert Pujols	2.00	.75
❑ 252 Chris Latham RC	.40	.15
❑ 253 Eric Byrnes	.40	.15
❑ 254 Napoleon Calzado SP RC	2.00	.75
❑ 255 Bobby Higginson	.40	.15
❑ 256 Ben Molina	.40	.15
❑ 257 Torii Hunter SP	2.00	.75
❑ 258 Jason Giambi	.40	.15
❑ 259 Bartolo Colon	.40	.15
❑ 260 Benito Baez	.40	.15
❑ 261 Ichiro Suzuki	2.00	.75
❑ 262 Mike Sweeney	.40	.15
❑ 263 Brian West RC	.40	.15
❑ 264 Brad Penny	.40	.15
❑ 265 Kevin Millwood SP	2.00	.75
❑ 266 Orlando Hudson	.40	.15
❑ 267 Doug Mientkiewicz	.40	.15
❑ 268 Luis Gonzalez SP	2.00	.75
❑ 269 Jay Caligiuri RC	.40	.15
❑ 270 Nate Cornejo SP	2.00	.75
❑ 271 Lee Stevens	.40	.15
❑ 272 Eric Hinske	.40	.15
❑ 273 Antwon Rollins RC	.40	.15
❑ 274 Bobby Jenks RC	1.50	.60
❑ 275 Joe Mays	.40	.15
❑ 276 Josh Shaffer RC	.40	.15
❑ 277 Jonny Gomes RC	2.50	1.00
❑ 278 Bernie Williams	.60	.25
❑ 279 Ed Rogers	.40	.15
❑ 280 Carlos Delgado	.40	.15
❑ 281 Raul Mondesi SP	2.00	.75
❑ 282 Jose Ortiz	.40	.15
❑ 283 Cesar Izturis	.40	.15
❑ 284 Ryan Dempster SP	2.00	.75
❑ 285 Brian Daubach	.40	.15
❑ 286 Hansel Izquierdo RC	.40	.15
❑ 287 Mike Lieberthal SP	2.00	.75
❑ 288 Marcus Thames	.40	.15
❑ 289 Nomar Garciaparra	1.50	.60
❑ 290 Brad Fullmer	.40	.15
❑ 291 Tino Martinez	.60	.25
❑ 292 James Barrett RC	.40	.15
❑ 293 Jacque Jones	.40	.15
❑ 294 Nick Alvarez SP RC	2.00	.75
❑ 295 Jason Grove SP RC	2.00	.75
❑ 296 Mike Wilson SP RC	2.00	.75
❑ 297 J.T. Snow	.40	.15
❑ 298 Cliff Floyd	.40	.15
❑ 299 Todd Hundley SP	2.00	.75
❑ 300 Tony Clark SP	2.00	.75
❑ 301 Demetrius Heath RC	.40	.15
❑ 302 Morgan Ensberg	.40	.15
❑ 303 Cristian Guzman	.40	.15
❑ 304 Frank Catalanotto	.40	.15
❑ 305 Jeff Weaver	.40	.15
❑ 306 Tim Hudson	.40	.15
❑ 307 Scott Wiggins SP RC	2.00	.75
❑ 308 Shea Hillenbrand SP	2.00	.75
❑ 309 Todd Walker SP	2.00	.75
❑ 310 Tsuyoshi Shinjo	.40	.15
❑ 311 Adrian Beltre	.40	.15
❑ 312 Craig Kuzmic RC	.40	.15
❑ 313 Paul Konerko	.40	.15
❑ 314 Scott Hairston RC	.50	.20
❑ 315 Chan Ho Park	.40	.15
❑ 316 Jorge Posada	.60	.25
❑ 317 Chris Snelling RC	.75	.30
❑ 318 Keith Foulke	.40	.15
❑ 319 John Smoltz	.60	.25
❑ 320 Ryan Church SP RC	4.00	1.50
❑ 321 Mike Mussina	.60	.25
❑ 322 Tony Armas Jr. SP	2.00	.75
❑ 323 Craig Counsell	.40	.15
❑ 324 Marcus Giles	.40	.15
❑ 325 Greg Vaughn	.40	.15
❑ 326 Curt Schilling	.40	.15
❑ 327 Jeromy Burnitz	.40	.15
❑ 328 Eric Byrnes	.40	.15
❑ 329 Johnny Damon Sox	.60	.25
❑ 330 Michael Floyd SP RC	2.00	.75
❑ 331 Edgardo Alfonzo	.40	.15
❑ 332 Jeremy Hill RC	.40	.15
❑ 333 Josh Bonifay RC	.40	.15
❑ 334 Byung-Hyun Kim	.40	.15
❑ 335 Keith Ginter	.40	.15
❑ 336 Ronald Acuna SP RC	2.00	.75
❑ 337 Mike Hill SP RC	2.00	.75
❑ 338 Sean Casey	.40	.15
❑ 339 Matt Anderson SP	2.00	.75
❑ 340 Dan Wright	.40	.15
❑ 341 Ben Petrick	.40	.15
❑ 342 Mike Sirotka SP	2.00	.75
❑ 343 Alex Rodriguez	1.50	.60
❑ 344 Einar Diaz	.40	.15
❑ 345 Derek Jeter	2.50	1.00
❑ 346 Jeff Conine	.40	.15
❑ 347 Ray Durham SP	2.00	.75
❑ 348 Wilson Betemit SP	2.00	.75
❑ 349 Jeffrey Hammonds	.40	.15
❑ 350 Dan Trumble RC	.40	.15
❑ 351 Phil Nevin SP	2.00	.75
❑ 352 A.J. Burnett	.40	.15
❑ 353 Bill Mueller	.40	.15
❑ 354 Charles Nagy	.40	.15
❑ 355 Rusty Greer SP	2.00	.75
❑ 356 Jason Botts RC	.50	.20
❑ 357 Magglio Ordonez	.40	.15
❑ 358 Kevin Appier	.40	.15
❑ 359 Brad Radke	.40	.15
❑ 360 Chris George	.40	.15
❑ 361 Chris Piersoll RC	.40	.15
❑ 362 Ivan Rodriguez	.60	.25
❑ 363 Jim Kavourias RC	.40	.15
❑ 364 Rick Helling SP	2.00	.75
❑ 365 Dean Palmer	.40	.15
❑ 366 Rich Aurilia SP	2.00	.75
❑ 367 Ryan Vogelsong	.40	.15
❑ 368 Matt Lawton	.40	.15
❑ 369 Wade Miller	.40	.15
❑ 370 Dustin Hermanson	.40	.15
❑ 371 Craig Wilson	.40	.15
❑ 372 Todd Zeile SP	2.00	.75
❑ 373 Jon Guzman RC	.40	.15
❑ 374 Ellis Burks	.40	.15
❑ 375 Robert Cosby SP RC	2.00	.75
❑ 376 Jason Kendall	.40	.15
❑ 377 Scott Rolen SP	3.00	1.25
❑ 378 Andruw Jones	.60	.25
❑ 379 Greg Sain RC	.40	.15
❑ 380 Paul LoDuca	.40	.15
❑ 381 Scotty Layfield RC	.40	.15
❑ 382 Tomo Ohka	.40	.15
❑ 383 Garrett Guzman RC	.40	.15
❑ 384 Jack Cust SP	2.00	.75
❑ 385 Shayne Wright RC	.40	.15
❑ 386 Derrek Lee	.60	.25
❑ 387 Jesus Medrano RC	.40	.15
❑ 388 Javier Vazquez	.40	.15
❑ 389 Preston Wilson SP	2.00	.75
❑ 390 Gavin Floyd RC	1.00	.40
❑ 391 Sidney Ponson SP	2.00	.75
❑ 392 Jose Hernandez	.40	.15
❑ 393 Scott Erickson SP	2.00	.75
❑ 394 Jose Valverde RC	.40	.15
❑ 395 Mark Hamilton SP RC	2.00	.75
❑ 396 Brad Cresse	.40	.15
❑ 397 Danny Bautista	.40	.15
❑ 398 Ray Lankford SP	2.00	.75
❑ 399 Miguel Batista SP	2.00	.75
❑ 400 Brent Butler	.40	.15
❑ 401 Manny Delcarmen SP RC	3.00	1.25
❑ 402 Kyle Farnsworth SP	2.00	.75
❑ 403 Freddy Garcia	.40	.15
❑ 404 Joe Jiannetti RC	.40	.15
❑ 405 Josh Barfield RC	2.50	1.00
❑ 406 Corey Patterson	.40	.15
❑ 407 Josh Towers	.40	.15
❑ 408 Carlos Pena	.40	.15
❑ 409 Jeff Cirillo	.40	.15
❑ 410 Jon Lieber	.40	.15
❑ 411 Woody Williams SP	2.00	.75
❑ 412 Richard Lane SP RC	2.00	.75
❑ 413 Alex Gonzalez	.40	.15
❑ 414 Wilkin Ruan	.40	.15
❑ 415 Geoff Jenkins	.40	.15
❑ 416 Carlos Hernandez	.40	.15
❑ 417 Matt Clement SP	2.00	.75
❑ 418 Jose Cruz Jr.	.40	.15
❑ 419 Jake Mauer RC	.40	.15
❑ 420 Matt Childers RC	.40	.15
❑ 421 Tom Glavine SP	3.00	1.25
❑ 422 Ken Griffey Jr.	1.50	.60
❑ 423 Anderson Hernandez RC	.40	.15
❑ 424 John Suomi RC	.40	.15
❑ 425 Doug Sessions RC	.40	.15
❑ 426 Jaret Wright	.40	.15
❑ 427 Rolando Viera SP RC	2.00	.75
❑ 428 Aaron Sele	.40	.15
❑ 429 Dmitri Young	.40	.15
❑ 430 Ryan Klesko	.40	.15
❑ 431 Kevin Tapani SP	2.00	.75
❑ 432 Joe Kennedy	.40	.15
❑ 433 Austin Kearns	.40	.15
❑ 434 Roger Cedeno SP	2.00	.75
❑ 435 Lance Berkman	.40	.15
❑ 436 Frank Menechino	.40	.15
❑ 437 Brett Myers	.40	.15
❑ 438 Bob Abreu	.40	.15
❑ 439 Shawn Estes SP	2.00	.75

2003 Bowman Heritage

❑ COMPLETE SET (300)	120.00	60.00
❑ 1 Jorge Posada	.60	.25
❑ 2 Todd Helton	.60	.25
❑ 3 Marcus Giles	.40	.15
❑ 4 Eric Chavez	.40	.15
❑ 5 Edgar Martinez	.60	.25
❑ 6 Luis Gonzalez	.40	.15
❑ 7 Corey Patterson	.40	.15
❑ 8 Preston Wilson	.40	.15

9	Ryan Klesko	.40	.15
10	Randy Johnson	1.00	.40
11	Jose Guillen	.40	.15
12	Carlos Lee	.40	.15
13	Steve Finley	.40	.15
14	A.J. Pierzynski	.40	.15
15	Troy Glaus	.40	.15
16	Darin Erstad	.40	.15
17	Moises Alou	.40	.15
18	Torii Hunter	.40	.15
19	Marlon Byrd	.40	.15
20	Mark Prior	.60	.25
21	Shannon Stewart	.40	.15
22	Craig Biggio	.60	.25
23	Johnny Damon	.60	.25
24	Robert Fick	.40	.15
25	Jason Giambi	.40	.15
26	Fernando Vina	.40	.15
27	Aubrey Huff	.40	.15
28	Benito Santiago	.40	.15
29	Jay Gibbons	.40	.15
30	Ken Griffey Jr.	1.50	.60
31	Rocco Baldelli	.40	.15
32	Pat Burrell	.40	.15
33	A.J. Burnett	.40	.15
34	Omar Vizquel	.60	.25
35	Greg Maddux	1.50	.60
36	Cliff Floyd	.40	.15
37	C.C. Sabathia	.40	.15
38	Geoff Jenkins	.40	.15
39	Ty Wigginton	.40	.15
40	Jeff Kent	.40	.15
41	Orlando Hudson	.40	.15
42	Edgardo Alfonzo	.40	.15
43	Greg Myers	.40	.15
44	Melvin Mora	.40	.15
45	Sammy Sosa	1.00	.40
46	Russ Ortiz	.40	.15
47	Josh Beckett	.40	.15
48	David Wells	.40	.15
49	Woody Williams	.40	.15
50	Alex Rodriguez	1.50	.60
51	Randy Wolf	.40	.15
52	Carlos Beltran	.40	.15
53	Austin Kearns	.40	.15
54	Trot Nixon	.40	.15
55	Ivan Rodriguez	.60	.25
56	Shea Hillenbrand	.40	.15
57	Roberto Alomar	.60	.25
58	John Olerud	.40	.15
59	Michael Young	.60	.25
60	Garret Anderson	.40	.15
61	Mike Lieberthal	.40	.15
62	Adam Dunn	.40	.15
63	Raul Ibanez	.40	.15
64	Kenny Lofton	.40	.15
65	Ichiro Suzuki	2.00	.75
66	Jarrod Washburn	.40	.15
67	Shawn Chacon	.40	.15
68	Alex Gonzalez	.40	.15
69	Roy Halladay	.40	.15
70	Vladimir Guerrero	1.00	.40
71	Hee Seop Choi	.40	.15
72	Jody Gerut	.40	.15
73	Ray Durham	.40	.15
74	Mark Teixeira	.60	.25
75	Hank Blalock	.40	.15
76	Jerry Hairston Jr.	.40	.15
77	Erubiel Durazo	.40	.15
78	Frank Catalanotto	.40	.15
79	Jacque Jones	.40	.15
80	Bobby Abreu	.40	.15
81	Mike Hampton	.40	.15
82	Zach Day	.40	.15
83	Jimmy Rollins	.40	.15
84	Joel Pineiro	.40	.15
85	Brett Myers	.40	.15
86	Frank Thomas	1.00	.40
87	Aramis Ramirez	.40	.15
88	Paul Lo Duca	.40	.15
89	Dmitri Young	.40	.15
90	Brian Giles	.40	.15
91	Jose Cruz Jr.	.40	.15
92	Derek Lowe	.40	.15
93	Mark Buehrle	.40	.15
94	Wade Miller	.40	.15
95	Derek Jeter	2.50	1.00
96	Bret Boone	.40	.15
97	Tony Batista	.40	.15
98	Sean Casey	.40	.15
99	Eric Hinske	.40	.15
100	Albert Pujols	2.00	.75
101	Runelvys Hernandez	.40	.15
102	Vernon Wells	.40	.15
103	Kerry Wood	.40	.15
104	Lance Berkman	.40	.15
105	Alfonso Soriano	.40	.15
106	Bill Mueller	.40	.15
107	Bartolo Colon	.40	.15
108	Andy Pettitte	.60	.25
109	Rafael Furcal	.40	.15
110	Dontrelle Willis	1.00	.40
111	Carl Crawford	.40	.15
112	Scott Rolen	.60	.25
113	Chipper Jones	1.00	.40
114	Magglio Ordonez	.40	.15
115	Bernie Williams	.60	.25
116	Roy Oswalt	.40	.15
117	Kevin Brown	.40	.15
118	Cristian Guzman	.40	.15
119	Kazuhisa Ishii	.40	.15
120	Larry Walker	.40	.15
121	Miguel Tejada	.40	.15
122	Manny Ramirez	.60	.25
123	Mike Mussina	.60	.25
124	Mike Lowell	.40	.15
125	Scott Podsednik	.40	.15
126	Aaron Boone	.40	.15
127	Carlos Delgado	.40	.15
128	Jose Vidro	.40	.15
129	Brad Radke	.40	.15
130	Rafael Palmeiro	.60	.25
131	Mark Mulder	.40	.15
132	Jason Schmidt	.40	.15
133	Gary Sheffield	.40	.15
134	Richie Sexson	.40	.15
135	Barry Zito	.40	.15
136	Tom Glavine	.60	.25
137	Jim Edmonds	.40	.15
138	Andruw Jones	.60	.25
139	Pedro Martinez	.60	.25
140	Curt Schilling	.40	.15
141	Phil Nevin	.40	.15
142	Nomar Garciaparra	1.50	.60
143	Vicente Padilla	.40	.15
144	Kevin Millwood	.40	.15
145	Shawn Green	.40	.15
146	Jeff Bagwell	.60	.25
147	Hideo Nomo	1.00	.40
148	Fred McGriff	.60	.25
149	Matt Morris	.40	.15
150	Roger Clemens	2.00	.75
151	Jerome Williams	.40	.15
152	Orlando Cabrera	.40	.15
153	Tim Hudson	.40	.15
154	Mike Sweeney	.40	.15
155	Jim Thome	.60	.25
156	Rich Aurilia	.40	.15
157	Mike Piazza	1.50	.60
158	Edgar Renteria	.40	.15
159	Javy Lopez	.40	.15
160	Jamie Moyer	.40	.15
161	Miguel Cabrera DI	1.00	.40
162	Adam Loewen DI RC	1.00	.40
163	Jose Reyes DI	.40	.15
164	Zack Greinke DI	.40	.15
165	Gavin Floyd DI	.40	.15
166	Jeremy Guthrie DI	.40	.15
167	Victor Martinez DI	.60	.25
168	Rich Harden DI	.60	.25
169	Joe Mauer DI	1.00	.40
170	Khalil Greene DI	1.00	.40
171A	Willie Mays	2.00	.75
171B	Willie Mays DI	2.00	.75
171C	Willie Mays KN	2.00	.75
172A	Phil Rizzuto	.60	.25
172B	Phil Rizzuto DI	.60	.25
172C	Phil Rizzuto KN	.60	.25
173A	Al Kaline	1.00	.40
173B	Al Kaline DI	1.00	.40
173C	Al Kaline KN	1.00	.40
174A	Warren Spahn	.60	.25
174B	Warren Spahn DI	.60	.25
174C	Warren Spahn KN	.60	.25
175A	Jimmy Piersall	.40	.15
175B	Jimmy Piersall DI	.40	.15
175C	Jimmy Piersall KN	.40	.15
176A	Luis Aparicio	.40	.15
176B	Luis Aparicio DI	.40	.15
176C	Luis Aparicio KN	.40	.15
177A	Whitey Ford	.60	.25
177B	Whitey Ford DI	.60	.25
177C	Whitey Ford KN	.60	.25
178A	Harmon Killebrew	1.00	.40
178B	Harmon Killebrew DI	1.00	.40
178C	Harmon Killebrew KN	1.00	.40
179A	Duke Snider	.60	.25
179B	Duke Snider DI	.60	.25
179C	Duke Snider KN	.60	.25
180A	Roberto Clemente	2.50	1.00
180B	Roberto Clemente DI	2.50	1.00
180C	Roberto Clemente KN	2.50	1.00
181	David Martinez KN RC	.40	.15
182	Felix Pie KN RC	4.00	1.50
183	Kevin Correia KN RC	.40	.15
184	Brandon Webb KN RC	2.50	1.00
185	Matt Diaz KN RC	.75	.30
186	Lew Ford KN RC	.50	.20
187	Jeremy Griffiths KN RC	.40	.15
188	Matt Hensley KN RC	.40	.15
189	Danny Garcia KN RC	.40	.15
190	Elizardo Ramirez KN RC	.50	.20
191	Greg Aquino KN RC	.40	.15
192	Felix Sanchez KN RC	.40	.15
193	Kelly Shoppach KN RC	.75	.30
194	Bubba Nelson KN RC	.50	.20
195	Mike Oâ ™Keefe KN RC	.40	.15
196	Hanley Ramirez KN RC	4.00	1.50
197	Todd Wellemeyer KN RC	.40	.15
198	Dustin Moseley KN RC	.40	.15
199	Eric Crozier KN RC	.50	.20
200	Ryan Shealy KN RC	2.50	1.00
201	Jeremy Bonderman KN RC	2.50	1.00
202	Bo Hart KN RC	.40	.15
203	Dusty Brown KN RC	.40	.15
204	Rob Hammock KN RC	.40	.15
205	Jorge Piedra KN RC	.50	.20
206	Jason Kubel KN RC	1.50	.60
207	Stephen Randolph KN RC	.40	.15
208	Andy Sisco KN RC	.40	.15
209	Matt Kata KN RC	.40	.15
210	Robinson Cano KN RC	8.00	3.00
211	Ben Francisco KN RC	.40	.15
212	Arnie Munoz KN RC	.40	.15
213	Ozzie Chavez KN RC	.40	.15
214	Beau Kemp KN RC	.40	.15
215	Travis Wong KN RC	.50	.20
216	Brian McCann KN RC	6.00	2.50
217	Aquilino Lopez KN RC	.40	.15
218	Bobby Basham KN RC	.40	.15
219	Tim Olson KN RC	.40	.15
220	Nathan Panther KN RC	.40	.15
221	Wil Ledezma KN RC	.40	.15
222	Josh Willingham KN RC	1.00	.40
223	David Cash KN RC	.40	.15
224	Oscar Villarreal KN RC	.40	.15
225	Jeff Duncan KN RC	.40	.15
226	Dan Haren KN RC	1.00	.40
227	Michel Hernandez KN RC	.40	.15
228	Matt Murton KN RC	2.00	.75

❑ 229 Clay Hensley KN RC	.40	.15
❑ 230 Tyler Johnson KN RC	.40	.15
❑ 231 Tyler Martin KN RC	.40	.15
❑ 232 J.D. Durbin KN RC	.40	.15
❑ 233 Shane Victorino KN RC	.75	.30
❑ 234 Rajai Davis KN RC	.40	.15
❑ 235 Chien-Ming Wang KN RC	5.00	2.00
❑ 236 Travis Ishikawa KN RC	.75	.30
❑ 237 Eric Eckenstahler KN	.40	.15
❑ 238 Dustin McGowan KN RC	.50	.20
❑ 239 Prentice Redman KN RC	.40	.15
❑ 240 Haj Turay KN RC	.40	.15
❑ 241 Matt DeMarco KN RC	.40	.15
❑ 242 Lou Palmisano KN RC	.50	.20
❑ 243 Eric Reed KN RC	.40	.15
❑ 244 Willie Eyre KN RC	.40	.15
❑ 245 Ferdin Tejeda KN RC	.40	.15
❑ 246 Michael Garciaparra KN RC	.40	.15
❑ 247 Michael Hinckley KN RC	.50	.20
❑ 248 Branden Florence KN RC	.40	.15
❑ 249 Trent Oeltjen KN RC	.50	.20
❑ 250 Mike Neu KN RC	.40	.15
❑ 251 Chris Lubanski KN RC	1.00	.40
❑ 252 Brandon Wood KN RC	10.00	4.00
❑ 253 Delmon Young KN RC	5.00	2.00
❑ 254 Matt Harrison KN RC	.75	.30
❑ 255 Chad Billingsley KN RC	3.00	1.25
❑ 256 Josh Anderson KN RC	.50	.20
❑ 257 Brian McFall KN RC	.40	.15
❑ 258 Ryan Wagner KN RC	.40	.15
❑ 259 Billy Hogan KN RC	.50	.20
❑ 260 Nate Spears KN RC	.50	.20
❑ 261 Ryan Harvey KN RC	2.00	.75
❑ 262 Wes Littleton KN RC	.50	.20
❑ 263 Xavier Paul KN RC	.50	.20
❑ 264 Sean Rodriguez KN RC	2.00	.75
❑ 265 Brian Finch KN RC	.40	.15
❑ 266 Josh Rainwater KN RC	.50	.20
❑ 267 Brian Snyder KN RC	.50	.20
❑ 268 Eric Duncan KN RC	2.00	.75
❑ 269 Rickie Weeks KN RC	3.00	1.25
❑ 270 Tim Battle KN RC	.75	.30
❑ 271 Scott Beerer KN RC	.40	.15
❑ 272 Aaron Hill KN RC	.75	.30
❑ 273 Casey Abrams KN RC	.40	.15
❑ 274 Jonathan Fulton KN RC	.50	.20
❑ 275 Todd Jennings KN RC	.50	.20
❑ 276 Jordan Pratt KN RC	.50	.20
❑ 277 Tom Gorzelanny KN RC	1.25	.50
❑ 278 Matt Lorenzo KN RC	.50	.20
❑ 279 Jarrod Saltalamacchia KN RC	5.00	2.00
❑ 280 Mike Wagner KN RC	.40	.15

2004 Bowman Heritage

❑ COMPLETE SET (351)	300.00	175.00
❑ COMP.SET w/o SP's (300)	50.00	25.00

❑ SP STATED ODDS 1:3 HOBBY, 1:3 RETAIL
❑ SP's: 2/9/13/21/25/40B/46/48B/50/55/61
❑ SP's: 77/80/87/89/95/100/104/109/127/130
❑ SP's: 132/141/183A/189/204/206/208/210
❑ SP's: 213/216/220/224/228/234/240/243
❑ SP's: 246/249/259/268/270-271/282/291
❑ SP's: 304/318/327/334/342/348
❑ PLATES STATED ODDS 1:240 HOBBY
❑ PLATES PRINT RUN 1 #'d SET PER COLOR
❑ PLATES: BLACK, CYAN, MAGENTA & YELLOW
❑ NO PLATES PRICING DUE TO SCARCITY
❑ ROOP BINDER ODDS 1:240 HOBBY
❑ ROOP BINDER EXCH.DEADLINE 12/31/05

❑ 1 Tom Glavine	.60	.25
❑ 2 Mike Piazza SP	8.00	3.00
❑ 3 Sidney Ponson	.40	.15
❑ 4 Jerry Hairston Jr.	.40	.15
❑ 5 Jermaine Dye	.40	.15
❑ 6 Bobby Crosby	.40	.15
❑ 7 Carlos Zambrano	.40	.15
❑ 8 Moises Alou	.40	.15
❑ 9 Alex Rodriguez SP	8.00	3.00
❑ 10 Derek Jeter	2.00	.75
❑ 11 Rafael Furcal	.40	.15
❑ 12 J.D. Drew	.40	.15
❑ 13 Joe Mauer SP	6.00	2.50
❑ 14 Brad Radke	.40	.15
❑ 15 Johnny Damon	.60	.25
❑ 16 Derek Lowe	.40	.15
❑ 17 Pat Burrell	.40	.15
❑ 18 Mike Lieberthal	.40	.15
❑ 19 Cliff Lee	.40	.15
❑ 20 Ronnie Belliard	.40	.15
❑ 21 Eric Gagne SP	5.00	2.00
❑ 22 Brad Penny	.40	.15
❑ 23 Al Kaline RET	1.50	.60
❑ 24 Mike Maroth	.40	.15
❑ 25 Magglio Ordonez SP	5.00	2.00
❑ 26 Mark Buehrle	.40	.15
❑ 27 Jack Wilson	.40	.15
❑ 28 Oliver Perez	.40	.15
❑ 29 Red Schoendienst RET	.60	.25
❑ 30 Yadier Molina FY RC	2.00	.75
❑ 31 Ryan Freel	.40	.15
❑ 32 Adam Dunn	.40	.15
❑ 33 Paul Konerko	.40	.15
❑ 34 Esteban Loaiza	.40	.15
❑ 35 Ivan Rodriguez	.60	.25
❑ 36 Carlos Guillen	.40	.15
❑ 37 Adrian Beltre	.40	.15
❑ 38 C.C. Sabathia	.40	.15
❑ 39 Hideo Nomo	1.00	.40
❑ 40A Victor Martinez	.40	.15
❑ 40B V.Martinez Pedro Stats SP	5.00	2.00
❑ 41 Bobby Abreu	.40	.15
❑ 42 Randy Wolf	.40	.15
❑ 43 Johnny Estrada	.40	.15
❑ 44 Russ Ortiz	.40	.15
❑ 45 Kenny Rogers	.40	.15
❑ 46 Hank Blalock SP	5.00	2.00
❑ 47 David Ortiz	1.00	.40
❑ 48A Pedro Martinez	.60	.25
❑ 48B P.Martinez Victor Stats SP	8.00	3.00
❑ 49 Austin Kearns	.40	.15
❑ 50 Ken Griffey Jr. SP	8.00	3.00
❑ 51 Mark Prior	.60	.25
❑ 52 Kerry Wood	.40	.15
❑ 53 Eric Chavez	.40	.15
❑ 54 Tim Hudson	.40	.15
❑ 55 Rafael Palmeiro SP	8.00	3.00
❑ 56 Javy Lopez	.40	.15
❑ 57 Jason Bay	.40	.15
❑ 58 Craig Wilson	.40	.15
❑ 59 Whitey Ford RET	1.00	.40
❑ 60 Jason Giambi	.40	.15
❑ 61 Scott Rolen SP	8.00	3.00
❑ 62 Matt Morris	.40	.15
❑ 63 Javier Vazquez	.40	.15
❑ 64 Jim Thome	.60	.25
❑ 65 Don Zimmer RET	.60	.25
❑ 66 Shawn Green	.40	.15
❑ 67 Don Larsen RET	1.00	.40
❑ 68 Gary Sheffield	.40	.15
❑ 69 Jorge Posada	.60	.25
❑ 70 Bernie Williams	.60	.25
❑ 71 Chipper Jones	1.00	.40
❑ 72 Andruw Jones	.60	.25
❑ 73 John Thomson	.40	.15
❑ 74 Jim Edmonds	.40	.15
❑ 75 Albert Pujols	2.00	.75
❑ 76 Chris Carpenter	.40	.15
❑ 77 Aubrey Huff SP	5.00	2.00
❑ 78 Carl Crawford	.40	.15
❑ 79 Victor Zambrano	.40	.15
❑ 80 Alfonso Soriano SP	5.00	2.00
❑ 81 Lance Berkman	.40	.15
❑ 82 Mike Sweeney	.40	.15
❑ 83 Ken Harvey	.40	.15
❑ 84 Angel Berroa	.40	.15
❑ 85 A.J. Burnett	.40	.15
❑ 86 Mike Lowell	.40	.15
❑ 87 Miguel Cabrera SP	8.00	3.00
❑ 88 Preston Wilson	.40	.15
❑ 89 Todd Helton SP	8.00	3.00
❑ 90 Larry Walker Cards	.60	.25
❑ 91 Vladimir Guerrero	1.00	.40
❑ 92 Garret Anderson	.40	.15
❑ 93 Bartolo Colon	.40	.15
❑ 94 Scott Hairston	.40	.15
❑ 95 Richie Sexson SP	5.00	2.00
❑ 96 Sean Casey	.40	.15
❑ 97 John Podres RET	.60	.25
❑ 98 Andy Pettitte	.60	.25
❑ 99 Roy Oswalt	.40	.15
❑ 100 Roger Clemens SP	8.00	3.00
❑ 101 Scott Podsednik	.40	.15
❑ 102 Ben Sheets	.40	.15
❑ 103 Lyle Overbay	.40	.15
❑ 104 Nick Johnson SP	5.00	2.00
❑ 105 Zach Day	.40	.15
❑ 106 Jose Reyes	.40	.15
❑ 107 Khalil Greene	.60	.25
❑ 108 Sean Burroughs	.40	.15
❑ 109 David Wells SP	5.00	2.00
❑ 110 Jason Schmidt	.40	.15
❑ 111 Neifi Perez	.40	.15
❑ 112 Edgar Renteria	.40	.15
❑ 113 Rich Aurilia	.40	.15
❑ 114 Edgar Martinez	.60	.25
❑ 115 Joel Pineiro	.40	.15
❑ 116 Mark Teixeira	.60	.25
❑ 117 Michael Young	.40	.15
❑ 118 Ricardo Rodriguez	.40	.15
❑ 119 Carlos Delgado	.40	.15
❑ 120 Roy Halladay	.40	.15
❑ 121 Jose Guillen	.40	.15
❑ 122 Troy Glaus	.40	.15
❑ 123 Shea Hillenbrand	.40	.15
❑ 124 Luis Gonzalez	.40	.15
❑ 125 Horacio Ramirez	.40	.15
❑ 126 Melvin Mora	.40	.15
❑ 127 Miguel Tejada SP	5.00	2.00
❑ 128 Manny Ramirez	.60	.25
❑ 129 Tim Wakefield	.40	.15
❑ 130 Curt Schilling SP	8.00	3.00
❑ 131 Aramis Ramirez	.40	.15
❑ 132 Sammy Sosa SP	8.00	3.00
❑ 133 Matt Clement	.40	.15
❑ 134 Juan Uribe	.40	.15
❑ 135 Dontrelle Willis	.60	.25
❑ 136 Paul Lo Duca	.40	.15
❑ 137 Juan Pierre	.40	.15
❑ 138 Kevin Brown	.40	.15
❑ 139 B.Giles/M.Giles	.40	.15
❑ 140 Brian Giles	.40	.15
❑ 141 Nomar Garciaparra SP	8.00	3.00
❑ 142 Cesar Izturis	.40	.15
❑ 143 Don Newcombe RET	.60	.25
❑ 144 Craig Biggio	.60	.25
❑ 145 Carlos Beltran	.40	.15
❑ 146 Torii Hunter	.40	.15
❑ 147 Livan Hernandez	.40	.15
❑ 148 Cliff Floyd	.40	.15
❑ 149 Barry Zito	.40	.15
❑ 150 Mark Mulder	.40	.15
❑ 151 Rocco Baldelli	.40	.15
❑ 152 Bret Boone	.40	.15
❑ 153 Jamie Moyer	.40	.15
❑ 154 Ichiro Suzuki	2.00	.75
❑ 155 Brett Myers	.40	.15
❑ 156 Carl Pavano	.40	.15
❑ 157 Josh Beckett	.40	.15
❑ 158 Randy Johnson	1.00	.40
❑ 159 Trot Nixon	.40	.15
❑ 160 Dmitri Young	.40	.15
❑ 161 Jacque Jones	.40	.15
❑ 162 Lew Ford	.40	.15
❑ 163 Jose Vidro	.40	.15
❑ 164 Mark Kotsay	.40	.15
❑ 165 A.J. Pierzynski	.40	.15
❑ 166 Dewon Brazelton	.40	.15
❑ 167 Jeromy Burnitz	.40	.15
❑ 168 Johan Santana	1.00	.40
❑ 169 Greg Maddux	1.50	.60

❑ 170 Carl Erskine RET	.60	.25
❑ 171 Robin Roberts RET	.60	.25
❑ 172 Freddy Garcia	.40	.15
❑ 173 Carlos Lee	.40	.15
❑ 174 Jeff Bagwell	.60	.25
❑ 175 Jeff Kent	.40	.15
❑ 176 Kazuhisa Ishii	.40	.15
❑ 177 Orlando Cabrera	.40	.15
❑ 178 Shannon Stewart	.40	.15
❑ 179 Mike Cameron	.40	.15
❑ 180 Mike Mussina	.60	.25
❑ 181 Frank Thomas	1.00	.40
❑ 182 Jaret Wright	.40	.15
❑ 183A Alex Gonzalez Marlins SP	5.00	2.00
❑ 183B Alex Gonzalez Padres	.40	.15
❑ 184 Matt Lawton	.40	.15
❑ 185 Derrek Lee	.60	.25
❑ 186 Omar Vizquel	.60	.25
❑ 187 Jeremy Bonderman	.40	.15
❑ 188 Jake Westbrook	.40	.15
❑ 189 Zack Greinke SP	5.00	2.00
❑ 190 Chad Tracy	.40	.15
❑ 191 Rondell White	.40	.15
❑ 192 Alex Gonzalez	.40	.15
❑ 193 Geoff Jenkins	.40	.15
❑ 194 Ralph Kiner RET	1.00	.40
❑ 195 Al Leiter	.40	.15
❑ 196 Kevin Millwood	.40	.15
❑ 197 Jason Kendall	.40	.15
❑ 198 Kris Benson	.40	.15
❑ 199 Ryan Klesko	.40	.15
❑ 200 Mark Loretta	.40	.15
❑ 201 Richard Hidalgo	.40	.15
❑ 202 Reed Johnson	.40	.15
❑ 203 Luis Castillo	.40	.15
❑ 204 Jon Zeringue DP SP RC	5.00	2.00
❑ 205 Matt Bush DP RC	2.50	1.00
❑ 206 Kurt Suzuki DP SP RC	6.00	2.50
❑ 207 Mark Rogers DP RC	2.00	.75
❑ 208 Jason Vargas DP SP RC	5.00	2.00
❑ 209 Homer Bailey DP RC	4.00	1.50
❑ 210 Ray Liotta DP SP RC	5.00	2.00
❑ 211 Eric Campbell DP RC	3.00	1.25
❑ 212 Thomas Diamond DP RC	2.50	1.00
❑ 213 Gaby Hernandez DP SP RC	8.00	3.00
❑ 214 Neil Walker DP RC	2.00	.75
❑ 215 Bill Bray DP RC	.75	.30
❑ 216 Wade Davis DP SP RC	8.00	3.00
❑ 217 David Purcey DP RC	1.50	.60
❑ 218 Scott Elbert DP RC	2.00	.75
❑ 219 Josh Fields DP RC	4.00	1.50
❑ 220 Josh Johnson DP SP RC	5.00	2.00
❑ 221 Chris Lambert DP RC	1.00	.40
❑ 222 Trevor Plouffe DP RC	2.50	1.00
❑ 223 Bruce Froemming UMP	.50	.20
❑ 224 Matt Macri DP SP RC	4.00	1.50
❑ 225 Greg Golson DP RC	2.50	1.00
❑ 226 Philip Hughes DP RC	10.00	4.00
❑ 227 Kyle Waldrop DP RC	2.00	.75
❑ 228 Matt Tuiasosopo DP SP RC	8.00	3.00
❑ 229 Richie Robnett DP RC	2.00	.75
❑ 230 Taylor Tankersley DP RC	1.00	.40
❑ 231 Blake DeWitt DP RC	3.00	1.25
❑ 232 Charlie Reliford UMP	.50	.20
❑ 233 Eric Hurley DP RC	2.00	.75
❑ 234 Jordan Parraz DP SP RC	5.00	2.00
❑ 235 J.P. Howell DP RC	2.00	.75
❑ 236 Dana DeMuth UMP	.50	.20
❑ 237 Zach Jackson DP RC	1.50	.60
❑ 238 Justin Orenduff DP RC	1.50	.60
❑ 239 Brad Thompson FY RC	.75	.30
❑ 240 J.C. Holt DP SP RC	5.00	2.00
❑ 241 Matt Fox DP RC	.75	.30
❑ 242 Danny Putnam DP RC	1.50	.60
❑ 243 Daryl Jones DP SP RC	5.00	2.00
❑ 244 Jon Poterson DP RC	.75	.30
❑ 245 Gio Gonzalez DP RC	2.50	1.00
❑ 246 Lucas Harrell DP SP RC	5.00	2.00
❑ 247 Jerry Crawford UMP	.50	.20
❑ 248 Jay Rainville DP RC	2.50	1.00
❑ 249 Donnie Smith DP SP RC	5.00	2.00
❑ 250 Huston Street DP RC	3.00	1.25
❑ 251 Jeff Marquez DP RC	1.00	.40
❑ 252 Reid Brignac DP RC	3.00	1.25
❑ 253 Yusmeiro Petit FY RC	2.00	.75
❑ 254 K.C. Herren DP RC	1.50	.60
❑ 255 Dale Scott UMP	.50	.20
❑ 256 Erick San Pedro DP RC	.75	.30
❑ 257 Ed Montague UMP	.50	.20
❑ 258 Billy Buckner DP RC	1.00	.40
❑ 259 Mitch Einertson DP SP RC	5.00	2.00
❑ 260 Aarom Baldiris FY RC	.50	.20
❑ 261 Conor Jackson FY RC	3.00	1.25
❑ 262 Rick Reed UMP	.50	.20
❑ 263 Ervin Santana FY RC	2.00	.75
❑ 264 Gerry Davis UMP	.50	.20
❑ 265 Merkin Valdez FY RC	.50	.20
❑ 266 Joey Gathright FY RC	1.00	.40
❑ 267 Alberto Callaspo FY RC	.75	.30
❑ 268 Carlos Quentin FY SP RC	10.00	4.00
❑ 269 Gary Darling UMP	.50	.20
❑ 270 Jeff Salazar FY SP RC	5.00	2.00
❑ 271 Akinori Otsuka FY SP RC	5.00	2.00
❑ 272 Joe Brinkman UMP	.50	.20
❑ 273 Omar Quintanilla FY RC	.50	.20
❑ 274 Brian Runge UMP	.50	.20
❑ 275 Tom Mastny FY RC	.40	.15
❑ 276 John Hirschbeck UMP	.50	.20
❑ 277 Warner Madrigal FY RC	.75	.30
❑ 278 Joe West UMP	.50	.20
❑ 279 Paul Maholm FY RC	1.00	.40
❑ 280 Larry Young UMP	.50	.20
❑ 281 Mike Reilly UMP	.50	.20
❑ 282 Kazuo Matsui FY SP RC	5.00	2.00
❑ 283 Randy Marsh UMP	.50	.20
❑ 284 Frank Francisco FY RC	.40	.15
❑ 285 Zach Duke FY RC	2.00	.75
❑ 286 Tim McClelland UMP	.50	.20
❑ 287 Jesse Crain FY RC	.75	.30
❑ 288 Hector Gimenez FY RC	.40	.15
❑ 289 Marland Williams FY RC	.50	.20
❑ 290 Brian Gorman UMP	.50	.20
❑ 291 Jose Capellan FY SP RC	5.00	2.00
❑ 292 Tim Welke UMP	.50	.20
❑ 293 Javier Guzman FY RC	.50	.20
❑ 294 Paul McAnulty FY RC	.75	.30
❑ 295 Hector Made FY RC	.75	.30
❑ 296 Jon Connolly FY RC	1.00	.40
❑ 297 Don Sutton FY RC	1.00	.40
❑ 298 Fausto Carmona FY RC	2.00	.75
❑ 299 Ramon Ramirez FY RC	.40	.15
❑ 300 Brad Snyder FY RC	1.00	.40
❑ 301 Chin-Lung Hu FY RC	1.25	.50
❑ 302 Rudy Guillen FY RC	.75	.30
❑ 303 Matt Moses FY RC	1.00	.40
❑ 304 Brad Halsey FY SP RC	5.00	2.00
❑ 305 Erick Aybar FY RC	1.00	.40
❑ 306 Brad Sullivan FY RC	.50	.20
❑ 307 Nick Gorneault FY RC	.50	.20
❑ 308 Craig Ansman FY RC	.40	.15
❑ 309 Ricky Nolasco FY RC	1.25	.50
❑ 310 Luke Hughes FY RC	.40	.15
❑ 311 Danny Gonzalez FY RC	.40	.15
❑ 312 Josh Labandeira FY RC	.40	.15
❑ 313 Donald Levinski FY RC	.40	.15
❑ 314 Vince Perkins FY RC	.50	.20
❑ 315 Tommy Murphy FY RC	.40	.15
❑ 316 Chad Bentz FY RC	.40	.15
❑ 317 Chris Shelton FY RC	2.00	.75
❑ 318 Nyjer Morgan FY SP RC	5.00	2.00
❑ 319 Kody Kirkland FY RC	.50	.20
❑ 320 Blake Hawksworth FY RC	.50	.20
❑ 321 Alex Romero FY RC	.40	.15
❑ 322 Mike Gosling FY RC	.40	.15
❑ 323 Ryan Budde FY RC	.40	.15
❑ 324 Kevin Howard FY RC	.50	.20
❑ 325 Wanell Macia FY RC	.40	.15
❑ 326 Travis Blackley FY RC	.40	.15
❑ 327 Kazuhito Tadano FY SP RC	5.00	2.00
❑ 328 Shingo Takatsu FY RC	.75	.30
❑ 329 Joaquin Arias FY RC	.75	.30
❑ 330 Juan Cedeno FY RC	.40	.15
❑ 331 Bobby Brownlie FY RC	1.00	.40
❑ 332 Lastings Milledge FY RC	5.00	2.00
❑ 333 Estee Harris FY RC	.50	.20
❑ 334 Tim Stauffer FY SP RC	5.00	2.00
❑ 335 Jon Knott FY RC	.40	.15
❑ 336 David Aardsma FY RC	.50	.20
❑ 337 Wardell Starling FY RC	.40	.15
❑ 338 Dioner Navarro FY RC	.75	.30
❑ 339 Logan Kensing FY RC	.40	.15
❑ 340 Jason Hirsh FY RC	2.00	.75
❑ 341 Matt Creighton FY RC	.40	.15
❑ 342 Felix Hernandez FY SP RC	20.00	8.00
❑ 343 Kyle Sleeth FY RC	.50	.20
❑ 344 Dustin Nippert FY RC	.50	.20
❑ 345 Anthony Lerew FY RC	.75	.30
❑ 346 Chris Saenz FY RC	.40	.15
❑ 347 Steve Palermo SUP	1.00	.40
❑ 348 Barry Bonds SP	15.00	6.00
❑ MJ Roop Binder EXCH		

2005 Bowman Heritage

❑ COMPLETE SET (350)	300.00	175.00
❑ COMP.SET w/o SP's (300)	50.00	25.00
❑ COMMON CARD (1-300)	.40	.15
❑ COMMON RC (1-300)	.40	.15
❑ COMMON SP (301-350)	5.00	2.00
❑ COM.SP RC (301-350)	5.00	2.00

❑ 301-350 SP ODDS 1:3 H, 1:3 R
❑ PLATES STATED ODDS 1:343 HOBBY
❑ PLATES PRINT RUN 1 #'d SET PER COLOR
❑ PLATES: BLACK, CYAN, MAGENTA & YELLOW
❑ NO PLATES PRICING DUE TO SCARCITY
❑ ROOP BINDER EXCH ODDS 1:240 H
❑ ROOP BINDER EXCH.DEADLINE 12/31/07

❑ 1 Steven White FY RC	.40	.15
❑ 2 Jorge Posada	.60	.25
❑ 3 Brett Myers	.40	.15
❑ 4 Pat Burrell	.40	.15
❑ 5 Grady Sizemore	.60	.25
❑ 6 Jeff Weaver	.40	.15
❑ 7 Jeff Kent	.40	.15
❑ 8 Mark Kotsay	.40	.15
❑ 9 Nick Swisher	.60	.25
❑ 10 Scott Rolen	.60	.25
❑ 11 Matt Morris	.40	.15
❑ 12 Luis Castillo	.40	.15
❑ 13 Pedro Feliz	.40	.15
❑ 14 Omar Vizquel	.60	.25
❑ 15 Edgar Renteria	.40	.15
❑ 16 David Wells	.40	.15
❑ 17 Chad Cordero	.40	.15
❑ 18 Brad Wilkerson	.40	.15
❑ 19 Kelly Johnson	.40	.15
❑ 20 Johnny Estrada	.40	.15
❑ 21 Brian Roberts	.40	.15
❑ 22 Jeromy Burnitz	.40	.15
❑ 23 Magglio Ordonez	.40	.15
❑ 24 Adam Dunn	.40	.15
❑ 25 Randy Johnson	1.00	.40
❑ 26 Derek Jeter	2.00	.75
❑ 27 Jon Lieber	.40	.15
❑ 28 Jim Thome	.60	.25
❑ 29 Ronnie Belliard	.40	.15
❑ 30 Jake Westbrook	.40	.15
❑ 31 Bengie Molina	.40	.15
❑ 32 J.D. Drew	.40	.15
❑ 33 Rich Harden	.40	.15
❑ 34 David Eckstein	.40	.15
❑ 35 Scott Podsednik	.40	.15
❑ 36 Mark Buehrle	.40	.15
❑ 37 Barry Bonds	2.50	1.00
❑ 38 Brian Schneider	.40	.15
❑ 39 Tim Wakefield	.40	.15
❑ 40 Craig Wilson	.40	.15
❑ 41 Jose Vidro	.40	.15
❑ 42 Jacque Jones	.40	.15
❑ 43 Felix Hernandez	1.00	.40
❑ 44 Nomar Garciaparra	1.00	.40

❑ 45 Neifi Perez .40 .15
❑ 46 Brandon Inge .40 .15
❑ 47 Felipe Lopez .40 .15
❑ 48 Ken Griffey Jr. 1.50 .60
❑ 49 Robinson Cano .60 .25
❑ 50 Jason Giambi .40 .15
❑ 51 Mike Lieberthal .40 .15
❑ 52 Bobby Abreu .40 .15
❑ 53 C.C. Sabathia .40 .15
❑ 54 Aaron Boone .40 .15
❑ 55 Milton Bradley .40 .15
❑ 56 Derek Lowe .40 .15
❑ 57 Barry Zito .40 .15
❑ 58 Jim Edmonds .40 .15
❑ 59 Jon Garland .40 .15
❑ 60 Tadahito Iguchi RC 1.50 .60
❑ 61 Jason Schmidt .40 .15
❑ 62 David Ortiz 1.00 .40
❑ 63 Matt Lawton .40 .15
❑ 64 Zach Duke .60 .25
❑ 65 Gary Sheffield .40 .15
❑ 66 Chipper Jones 1.00 .40
❑ 67 Sammy Sosa 1.00 .40
❑ 68 Rafael Palmeiro .60 .25
❑ 69 Carlos Zambrano .40 .15
❑ 70 Aramis Ramirez .40 .15
❑ 71 Chris Shelton .60 .25
❑ 72 Wily Mo Pena .40 .15
❑ 73 Mike Mussina .60 .25
❑ 74 Chien-Ming Wang 1.50 .60
❑ 75 Randy Wolf .40 .15
❑ 76 Jimmy Rollins .40 .15
❑ 77 Chase Utley .60 .25
❑ 78 Kevin Millwood .40 .15
❑ 79 Victor Martinez .40 .15
❑ 80 Morgan Ensberg .40 .15
❑ 81 Bartolo Colon .40 .15
❑ 82 Bobby Crosby .40 .15
❑ 83 Dan Johnson .40 .15
❑ 84 Dan Haren .40 .15
❑ 85 Yadier Molina .40 .15
❑ 86 Mark Mulder .40 .15
❑ 87 Russell Branyan .40 .15
❑ 88 Lyle Overbay .40 .15
❑ 89 Edgardo Alfonzo .40 .15
❑ 90 Mike Matheny .40 .15
❑ 91 J.T. Snow .40 .15
❑ 92 Curt Schilling .60 .25
❑ 93 Oliver Perez .40 .15
❑ 94 Mark Redman .40 .15
❑ 95 Esteban Loaiza .40 .15
❑ 96 Livan Hernandez .40 .15
❑ 97 Ryan Church .40 .15
❑ 98 Kyle Davies .40 .15
❑ 99 Mike Hampton .40 .15
❑ 100 Jeff Francoeur 1.00 .40
❑ 101 Javy Lopez .40 .15
❑ 102 Mark Prior .60 .25
❑ 103 Kerry Wood .40 .15
❑ 104 Carlos Guillen .40 .15
❑ 105 Dmitri Young .40 .15
❑ 106 David Wright 1.50 .60
❑ 107 Cliff Floyd .40 .15
❑ 108 Carlos Beltran .40 .15
❑ 109 Melky Cabrera RC 2.00 .75
❑ 110 Carl Pavano .40 .15
❑ 111 Jamie Moyer .40 .15
❑ 112 Joel Pineiro .40 .15
❑ 113 Adrian Beltre .40 .15
❑ 114 Jhonny Peralta .40 .15
❑ 115 Travis Hafner .40 .15
❑ 116 Cesar Izturis .40 .15
❑ 117 Brad Penny .40 .15
❑ 118 Garret Anderson .40 .15
❑ 119 Scott Kazmir .40 .15
❑ 120 Aubrey Huff .40 .15
❑ 121 Larry Walker .60 .25
❑ 122 Albert Pujols 2.00 .75
❑ 123 Paul Konerko .40 .15
❑ 124 Frank Thomas 1.00 .40
❑ 125 Phil Nevin .40 .15
❑ 126 Brian Giles .40 .15
❑ 127 Ramon Hernandez .40 .15
❑ 128 Johnny Damon .60 .25
❑ 129 Trot Nixon .40 .15
❑ 130 Rocco Baldelli .40 .15
❑ 131 Carl Crawford .40 .15
❑ 132 Alfonso Soriano .40 .15
❑ 133 Mark Teixeira .60 .25
❑ 134 Gustavo Chacin .40 .15
❑ 135 Vernon Wells .40 .15
❑ 136 Erik Bedard .40 .15
❑ 137 Daniel Cabrera .40 .15
❑ 138 Michael Barrett .40 .15
❑ 139 Greg Maddux 1.50 .60
❑ 140 Javier Vazquez .40 .15
❑ 141 Chad Tracy .40 .15
❑ 142 Michael Young .40 .15
❑ 143 Kenny Rogers .40 .15
❑ 144 Mike Piazza 1.00 .40
❑ 145 Jose Reyes .40 .15
❑ 146 Geoff Jenkins .40 .15
❑ 147 Carlos Lee .40 .15
❑ 148 Brady Clark .40 .15
❑ 149 Torii Hunter .40 .15
❑ 150 Johan Santana 1.00 .40
❑ 151 Steve Finley .40 .15
❑ 152 Darin Erstad .40 .15
❑ 153 Jake Peavy .40 .15
❑ 154 Xavier Nady .40 .15
❑ 155 Ryan Klesko .40 .15
❑ 156 Ichiro Suzuki 2.00 .75
❑ 157 Richie Sexson .40 .15
❑ 158 Raul Ibanez .40 .15
❑ 159 Freddy Garcia .40 .15
❑ 160 Brad Hawpe .40 .15
❑ 161 Jeff Francis .40 .15
❑ 162 Todd Helton .60 .25
❑ 163 Clint Barmes .40 .15
❑ 164 Rodrigo Lopez .40 .15
❑ 165 Melvin Mora .40 .15
❑ 166 Brandon Webb .40 .15
❑ 167 Shawn Green .40 .15
❑ 168 Moises Alou .40 .15
❑ 169 Matt Clement .40 .15
❑ 170 John Smoltz .60 .25
❑ 171 Rafael Furcal .40 .15
❑ 172 Jeff Bagwell .60 .25
❑ 173 Roger Clemens 1.50 .60
❑ 174 Dontrelle Willis .40 .15
❑ 175 Paul Lo Duca .40 .15
❑ 176 Zack Greinke .40 .15
❑ 177 David DeJesus .40 .15
❑ 178 Mike Sweeney .40 .15
❑ 179 Ben Sheets .40 .15
❑ 180 Doug Davis .40 .15
❑ 181 Mike Cameron .40 .15
❑ 182 Lance Berkman .40 .15
❑ 183 Craig Biggio .60 .25
❑ 184 Shannon Stewart .40 .15
❑ 185 Joe Mauer 1.00 .40
❑ 186 Justin Morneau .40 .15
❑ 187 Mike Maroth .40 .15
❑ 188 Ivan Rodriguez .60 .25
❑ 189 Luis Gonzalez .40 .15
❑ 190 Troy Glaus .40 .15
❑ 191 Adam Eaton .40 .15
❑ 192 Khalil Greene .60 .25
❑ 193 Mike Lowell .40 .15
❑ 194 Miguel Cabrera .60 .25
❑ 195 Roy Halladay .40 .15
❑ 196 Ted Lilly .40 .15
❑ 197 Alex Rios .40 .15
❑ 198 Josh Beckett .40 .15
❑ 199 A.J. Burnett .40 .15
❑ 200 Juan Pierre .40 .15
❑ 201 Marcus Giles .40 .15
❑ 202 Craig Tatum FY RC .40 .15
❑ 203 Hayden Penn FY RC .75 .30
❑ 204 C.J. Smith FY RC .40 .15
❑ 205 Matt Albers FY RC 1.00 .40
❑ 206 Jared Gothreaux FY RC .40 .15
❑ 207 Mike Rodriguez FY RC .40 .15
❑ 208 Hernan Iribarren FY RC .50 .20
❑ 209 Manny Parra FY RC .30 .12
❑ 210 Kevin Collins FY RC .40 .15
❑ 211 Buck Coats FY RC .40 .15
❑ 212 Jeremy West FY RC .75 .30
❑ 213 Ian Bladergroen FY RC .50 .20
❑ 214 Chuck Tiffany FY RC 1.00 .40
❑ 215 Andy LaRoche FY RC 3.00 1.25
❑ 216 Frank Diaz FY RC .40 .15
❑ 217 Jai Miller FY RC .50 .20
❑ 218 Tony Giarratano FY RC .40 .15
❑ 219 Danny Zell FY RC .40 .15
❑ 220 Justin Verlander FY RC 4.00 1.50
❑ 221 Ryan Sweeney FY RC 1.00 .40
❑ 222 Brandon McCarthy FY RC 1.25 .50
❑ 223 Jerry Owens FY RC .50 .20
❑ 224 Glen Perkins FY RC .75 .30
❑ 225 Kevin West FY RC .40 .15
❑ 226 Billy Butler FY RC 4.00 1.50
❑ 227 Shane Costa FY RC .40 .15
❑ 228 Erik Schindewolf FY RC .40 .15
❑ 229 Miguel Montero FY RC 1.25 .50
❑ 230 Stephen Drew FY RC 5.00 2.00
❑ 231 Matt DeSalvo FY RC .50 .20
❑ 232 Ben Jones FY RC .50 .20
❑ 233 Bill McCarthy FY RC .40 .15
❑ 234 Chuck James FY RC 1.50 .60
❑ 235 Brandon Sing FY RC .50 .20
❑ 236 Andy Santana FY RC .40 .15
❑ 237 Brendan Ryan FY RC .40 .15
❑ 238 Wes Swackhamer FY RC .40 .15
❑ 239 Jeff Niemann FY RC .75 .30
❑ 240 Ian Kinsler FY RC 2.50 1.00
❑ 241 Micah Furtado FY RC .40 .15
❑ 242 Ryan Mount FY RC .75 .30
❑ 243 P.J. Phillips FY RC .75 .30
❑ 244 Trevor Bell FY RC .75 .30
❑ 245 Jered Weaver FY RC 5.00 2.00
❑ 246 Eddy Martinez FY RC 1.00 .40
❑ 247 Brian Bannister FY RC .75 .30
❑ 248 Philip Humber FY RC .75 .30
❑ 249 Michael Rogers FY RC .40 .15
❑ 250 Landon Powell FY RC .50 .20
❑ 251 Kennard Bibbs FY RC .40 .15
❑ 252 Nelson Cruz FY RC 1.25 .50
❑ 253 Paul Kelly FY RC .50 .20
❑ 254 Kevin Slowey FY RC 1.25 .50
❑ 255 Brandon Snyder FY RC 1.50 .60
❑ 256 Nolan Reimold FY RC 1.25 .50
❑ 257 Brian Stavisky FY RC .40 .15
❑ 258 Javier Herrera FY RC 2.00 .75
❑ 259 Russ Martin FY RC 1.25 .50
❑ 260 Matthew Kemp FY RC 5.00 2.00
❑ 261 Wade Townsend FY RC .50 .20
❑ 262 Nick Touchstone FY RC .40 .15
❑ 263 Ryan Feierabend FY RC .40 .15
❑ 264 Bobby Livingston FY RC .40 .15
❑ 265 Wladimir Balentien FY RC .75 .30
❑ 266 Keiichi Yabu FY RC .40 .15
❑ 267 Craig Italiano FY RC .75 .30
❑ 268 Ryan Goleski FY RC .40 .15
❑ 269 Ryan Garko FY RC 1.25 .50
❑ 270 Mike Bourn FY RC .75 .30
❑ 271 Scott Mathieson FY RC .75 .30
❑ 272 Scott Mitchinson FY RC .40 .15
❑ 273 Tyler Greene FY RC .75 .30
❑ 274 Mark McCormick FY RC .50 .20
❑ 275 Daryl Jones FY .40 .15
❑ 276 Travis Chick FY RC .50 .20
❑ 277 Luis Hernandez FY RC .40 .15
❑ 278 Steve Doetsch FY RC .40 .15
❑ 279 Chris Vines FY RC .40 .15
❑ 280 Mike Costanzo FY RC 1.25 .50
❑ 281 Matt Maloney FY RC 1.00 .40
❑ 282 Matt Goyen FY RC .40 .15
❑ 283 Jacob Marceaux FY RC .40 .15
❑ 284 David Gassner FY RC .40 .15
❑ 285 Ricky Barrett FY RC .40 .15
❑ 286 Jon Egan FY RC .50 .20
❑ 287 Scott Blue FY RC .40 .15
❑ 288 Steven Bondurant FY RC .40 .15
❑ 289 Kevin Melillo FY RC .75 .30
❑ 290 Brad Corley FY RC .50 .20
❑ 291 Brent Lillibridge FY RC .40 .15
❑ 292 Mike Morse FY RC .75 .30
❑ 293 Justin Thomas FY RC .40 .15
❑ 294 Nick Webber FY RC .40 .15
❑ 295 Mitch Boggs FY RC .40 .15
❑ 296 Jeff Lyman FY RC .50 .20
❑ 297 Jordan Schafer FY RC 1.00 .40
❑ 298 Ismael Ramirez FY RC .40 .15
❑ 299 Chris B.Young FY RC 2.00 .75
❑ 300 Brian Miller FY RC .40 .15
❑ 301 Jason Bay SP 5.00 2.00
❑ 302 Tim Hudson SP 5.00 2.00

❑ 303 Miguel Tejada SP 5.00 2.00
❑ 304 Jeremy Bonderman SP 5.00 2.00
❑ 305 Alex Rodriguez SP 8.00 3.00
❑ 306 Rickie Weeks SP 5.00 2.00
❑ 307 Manny Ramirez SP 8.00 3.00
❑ 308 Nick Johnson SP 5.00 2.00
❑ 309 Andruw Jones SP 8.00 3.00
❑ 310 Hideki Matsui SP 6.00 2.50
❑ 311 Jeremy Reed SP 5.00 2.00
❑ 312 Dallas McPherson SP 5.00 2.00
❑ 313 Vladimir Guerrero SP 8.00 3.00
❑ 314 Eric Chavez SP 5.00 2.00
❑ 315 Chris Carpenter SP 5.00 2.00
❑ 316 Aaron Hill SP 5.00 2.00
❑ 317 Derrek Lee SP 8.00 3.00
❑ 318 Mark Loretta SP 5.00 2.00
❑ 319 Garrett Atkins SP 5.00 2.00
❑ 320 Hank Blalock SP 5.00 2.00
❑ 321 Chris Young SP 5.00 2.00
❑ 322 Roy Oswalt SP 5.00 2.00
❑ 323 Carlos Delgado SP 5.00 2.00
❑ 324 Pedro Martinez SP 8.00 3.00
❑ 325 Jeff Clement FY SP RC 10.00 4.00
❑ 326 Jimmy Shull FY SP RC 5.00 2.00
❑ 327 Daniel Carte FY SP RC 5.00 2.00
❑ 328 Travis Buck FY SP RC 6.00 2.50
❑ 329 Chris Volstad FY SP RC 5.00 2.00
❑ 330 A.McCutchen FY SP RC 10.00 4.00
❑ 331 Cliff Pennington FY SP RC 5.00 2.00
❑ 332 John Mayberry Jr. FY SP RC 5.00 2.00
❑ 333 C.J. Henry FY SP RC 8.00 3.00
❑ 334 Ricky Romero FY SP RC 5.00 2.00
❑ 335 Aaron Thompson FY SP RC 5.00 2.00
❑ 336 Cesar Carrillo FY SP RC 5.00 2.00
❑ 337 Jacoby Ellsbury FY SP RC 20.00 8.00
❑ 338 Matt Garza FY SP RC 8.00 3.00
❑ 339 Colby Rasmus FY SP RC 12.00 5.00
❑ 340 Ryan Zimmerman FY SP RC 15.006.00
❑ 341 Ryan Braun FY SP RC 15.00 6.00
❑ 342 Brent Lillibridge FY SP 5.00 2.00
❑ 343 Jay Bruce FY SP RC 15.00 6.00
❑ 344 Matt Green FY SP RC 5.00 2.00
❑ 345 Brent Cox FY SP RC 5.00 2.00
❑ 346 Jed Lowrie FY SP RC 5.00 2.00
❑ 347 Beau Jones FY SP RC 5.00 2.00
❑ 348 Eli Iorg FY SP RC 5.00 2.00
❑ 349 Chaz Roe FY SP RC 5.00 2.00
❑ 350 Mystery Redemption SP 25.00 10.00
❑ NNO Roop Binder Redemption 15.00 6.00

2006 Bowman Heritage

❑ COMPLETE SET (300) 150.00 75.00
❑ COMP.SET w/o SP's (250) 40.00 15.00
❑ COMMON CARD (1-300) .40 .15
❑ SEMISTARS 1-300 .60 .25
❑ UNLISTED 1-300 1.00 .40
❑ COMMON RC (1-300) .40 .15
❑ RC UNLISTED 1-300 1.00 .40
❑ COMMON SP (202-300) 5.00 2.00
❑ SP SEMIS 202-300 8.00 3.00
❑ SP UNL 202-300 8.00 3.00
❑ COM.SP RC (202-300) 5.00 2.00
❑ SP RC SEMI 202-300 5.00 2.00
❑ SP RC UNL 202-300 5.00 2.00
❑ 202-300 SP ODDS 1:3 H, 1:3 R
❑ SP CL: EVEN #s B/WN 202-300
❑ OVERALL PLATE ODDS 1:497 HOBBY
❑ PLATE PRINT RUN 1 SET PER COLOR
❑ BLACK-CYAN-MAGENTA-YELLOW ISSUED
❑ NO PLATE PRICING DUE TO SCARCITY
❑ 1 David Wright 1.50 .60
❑ 2 Andruw Jones .60 .25
❑ 3 Ryan Howard 1.50 .60
❑ 4 Jason Bay .40 .15
❑ 5 Paul Konerko .40 .15
❑ 6 Jake Peavy .40 .15
❑ 7 Todd Jones .40 .15
❑ 8 Troy Glaus .40 .15
❑ 9 Rocco Baldelli .40 .15
❑ 10 Rafael Furcal .40 .15
❑ 11 Freddy Sanchez .40 .15
❑ 12 Jermaine Dye .40 .15
❑ 13 A.J. Burnett .40 .15
❑ 14 Michael Cuddyer .40 .15
❑ 15 Barry Zito .40 .15
❑ 16 Chipper Jones 1.00 .40
❑ 17 Paul LoDuca .40 .15
❑ 18 Mark Mulder .40 .15
❑ 19 Raul Ibanez .40 .15
❑ 20 Carlos Delgado .40 .15
❑ 21 Marcus Giles .40 .15
❑ 22 Dan Haren .40 .15
❑ 23 Justin Morneau .40 .15
❑ 24 Livan Hernandez .40 .15
❑ 25 Ken Griffey Jr. 1.50 .60
❑ 26 Aaron Hill .40 .15
❑ 27 Tadahito Iguchi .40 .15
❑ 28 Nate Robertson .40 .15
❑ 29 Kevin Millwood .40 .15
❑ 30 Jim Thome .60 .25
❑ 31 Aubrey Huff .40 .15
❑ 32 Dontrelle Willis .40 .15
❑ 33 Khalil Greene .60 .25
❑ 34 Doug Davis .40 .15
❑ 35 Ivan Rodriguez .60 .25
❑ 36 Rickie Weeks .40 .15
❑ 37 Jhonny Peralta .40 .15
❑ 38 Yadier Molina .40 .15
❑ 39 Eric Chavez .40 .15
❑ 40 Alfonso Soriano .40 .15
❑ 41 Pat Burrell .40 .15
❑ 42 B.J. Ryan .40 .15
❑ 43 Carl Crawford .40 .15
❑ 44 Preston Wilson .40 .15
❑ 45 Jorge Posada .60 .25
❑ 46 Carlos Zambrano .40 .15
❑ 47 Mark Teahen .40 .15
❑ 48 Nick Johnson .40 .15
❑ 49 Mark Kotsay .40 .15
❑ 50 Derek Jeter 2.50 1.00
❑ 51 Moises Alou .40 .15
❑ 52 Ryan Freel .40 .15
❑ 53 Shannon Stewart .40 .15
❑ 54 Casey Blake .40 .15
❑ 55 Edgar Renteria .40 .15
❑ 56 Frank Thomas 1.00 .40
❑ 57 Ty Wigginton .40 .15
❑ 58 Jeff Kent .40 .15
❑ 59 Chien-Ming Wang 1.50 .60
❑ 60 Josh Beckett .40 .15
❑ 61 Chase Utley 1.00 .40
❑ 62 Gary Matthews .40 .15
❑ 63 Torii Hunter .40 .15
❑ 64 Bobby Jenks .40 .15
❑ 65 Wilson Betemit .40 .15
❑ 66 Jeremy Bonderman .40 .15
❑ 67 Scott Rolen .60 .25
❑ 68 Brad Penny .40 .15
❑ 69 Jacque Jones .40 .15
❑ 70 Jose Reyes .40 .15
❑ 71 Brian Roberts .40 .15
❑ 72 John Smoltz .60 .25
❑ 73 Johnny Estrada .40 .15
❑ 74 Ronnie Belliard .40 .15
❑ 75 Vladimir Guerrero 1.00 .40
❑ 76 A.J. Pierzynski .40 .15
❑ 77 Garrett Atkins .40 .15
❑ 78 Adam LaRoche .40 .15
❑ 79 Mark Loretta .40 .15
❑ 80 Todd Helton .60 .25
❑ 81 Jose Vidro .40 .15
❑ 82 Carlos Guillen .40 .15
❑ 83 Michael Barrett .40 .15
❑ 84 Lyle Overbay .40 .15
❑ 85 Travis Hafner .40 .15
❑ 86 Shea Hillenbrand .40 .15
❑ 87 Julio Lugo .40 .15
❑ 88 Tim Hudson .40 .15
❑ 89 Scott Podsednik .40 .15
❑ 90 Roy Halladay .40 .15
❑ 91 Bartolo Colon .40 .15
❑ 92 Ryan Langerhans .40 .15
❑ 93 Tom Glavine .60 .25
❑ 94 Kenny Rogers .40 .15
❑ 95 Robinson Cano .60 .25
❑ 96 Mark Prior .60 .25
❑ 97 Jason Schmidt .40 .15
❑ 98 Bengie Molina .40 .15
❑ 99 Jon Lieber .40 .15
❑ 100 Alex Rodriguez 1.50 .60
❑ 101 Scott Kazmir .60 .25
❑ 102 Jeff Francoeur 1.00 .40
❑ 103 Chris Carpenter .40 .15
❑ 104 Juan Uribe .40 .15
❑ 105 Mariano Rivera 1.00 .40
❑ 106 Rich Harden .40 .15
❑ 107 Jack Wilson .40 .15
❑ 108 Austin Kearns .40 .15
❑ 109 Marcus Thames .40 .15
❑ 110 Miguel Tejada .40 .15
❑ 111 Chone Figgins .40 .15
❑ 112 Bronson Arroyo .40 .15
❑ 113 Chad Cordero .40 .15
❑ 114 Bill Hall .40 .15
❑ 115 Curt Schilling .60 .25
❑ 116 David Eckstein .40 .15
❑ 117 Ramon Hernandez .40 .15
❑ 118 Eric Byrnes .40 .15
❑ 119 Clint Barmes .40 .15
❑ 120 Bobby Abreu .40 .15
❑ 121 Joe Crede .40 .15
❑ 122 Derek Lowe .40 .15
❑ 123 Jason Marquis .40 .15
❑ 124 Erik Bedard .40 .15
❑ 125 Derrek Lee .40 .15
❑ 126 Brian McCann .40 .15
❑ 127 Magglio Ordonez .40 .15
❑ 128 Ben Sheets .40 .15
❑ 129 Brandon Inge .40 .15
❑ 130 Miguel Cabrera .60 .25
❑ 131 Jim Edmonds .60 .25
❑ 132 John Lackey .40 .15
❑ 133 Kevin Mench .40 .15
❑ 134 Adrian Beltre .40 .15
❑ 135 Curtis Granderson .40 .15
❑ 136 Shawn Green .40 .15
❑ 137 Jose Contreras .40 .15
❑ 138 Joe Nathan .40 .15
❑ 139 Bobby Crosby .40 .15
❑ 140 Johnny Damon .60 .25
❑ 141 Brad Hawpe .40 .15
❑ 142 Brandon Phillips .40 .15
❑ 143 Victor Martinez .40 .15
❑ 144 Jimmy Rollins .40 .15
❑ 145 Corey Patterson .40 .15
❑ 146 Grady Sizemore .60 .25
❑ 147 Placido Polanco .40 .15
❑ 148 Mike Lowell .40 .15
❑ 149 Francisco Rodriguez .40 .15
❑ 150 Ichiro Suzuki 1.50 .60
❑ 151 Kris Benson .40 .15
❑ 152 Scott Hatteberg .40 .15
❑ 153 Akinori Otsuka .40 .15
❑ 154 Cesar Izturis .40 .15
❑ 155 Roger Clemens 2.00 .75
❑ 156 Kerry Wood .40 .15
❑ 157 Tom Gordon .40 .15
❑ 158 Sean Casey .40 .15
❑ 159 Jose Lopez .40 .15
❑ 160 Orlando Hernandez .40 .15
❑ 161 Aramis Ramirez .40 .15
❑ 162 J.D. Drew .40 .15
❑ 163 David DeJesus .40 .15
❑ 164 Craig Biggio .60 .25
❑ 165 Brett Myers .40 .15
❑ 166 C.C. Sabathia .40 .15
❑ 167 Zach Duke .40 .15
❑ 168 Luis Castillo .40 .15
❑ 169 Hideki Matsui 1.00 .40
❑ 170 Brian Giles .40 .15

❑ 171 Coco Crisp	.40	.15
❑ 172 Richie Sexson	.40	.15
❑ 173 Nomar Garciaparra	1.00	.40
❑ 174 Roy Oswalt	.40	.15
❑ 175 David Ortiz	1.00	.40
❑ 176 Matt Morris	.40	.15
❑ 177 Felipe Lopez	.40	.15
❑ 178 Garret Anderson	.40	.15
❑ 179 Kevin Youkilis	.40	.15
❑ 180 Alex Rios	.40	.15
❑ 181 Jon Garland	.40	.15
❑ 182 Luis Gonzalez	.40	.15
❑ 183 Cliff Floyd	.40	.15
❑ 184 Juan Encarnacion	.40	.15
❑ 185 Nick Swisher	.40	.15
❑ 186 Mike Cameron	.40	.15
❑ 187 Jose Castillo	.40	.15
❑ 188 Ray Durham	.40	.15
❑ 189 Jorge Cantu	.40	.15
❑ 190 Andy Pettitte	.40	.15
❑ 191 Chad Tracy	.40	.15
❑ 192 Adrian Gonzalez	.40	.15
❑ 193 Jose Valentin	.40	.15
❑ 194 Mark Buehrle	.40	.15
❑ 195 Huston Street	.40	.15
❑ 196 Chris Capuano	.40	.15
❑ 197 Aaron Rowand	.40	.15
❑ 198 Billy Wagner	.40	.15
❑ 199 Orlando Cabrera	.40	.15
❑ 200 Albert Pujols	2.00	.75
❑ 201 Dan Uggla (RC)	1.00	.40
❑ 202 Alay Soler SP RC	5.00	2.00
❑ 203 Matt Kemp (RC)	.60	.25
❑ 204 Mike Napoli SP RC	5.00	2.00
❑ 205 Joel Zumaya (RC)	1.00	.40
❑ 206 Mike Pelfrey SP RC	8.00	3.00
❑ 207 Ian Kinsler (RC)	.60	.25
❑ 208 Josh Willingham SP (RC)	5.00	2.00
❑ 209 Erick Aybar (RC)	.40	.15
❑ 210 Willie Eyre SP (RC)	5.00	2.00
❑ 211 Kendry Morales (RC)	.60	.25
❑ 212 Scott Thorman SP (RC)	5.00	2.00
❑ 213 Hanley Ramirez (RC)	1.00	.40
❑ 214 Boof Bonser SP (RC)	5.00	2.00
❑ 215 Anthony Reyes (RC)	.60	.25
❑ 216 Justin Huber SP (RC)	5.00	2.00
❑ 217 Yusmeiro Petit (RC)	.40	.15
❑ 218 Jason Bartlett SP (RC)	5.00	2.00
❑ 219 Shin-Soo Choo (RC)	.60	.25
❑ 220 Francisco Liriano SP (RC)	5.00	2.00
❑ 221 Craig Hansen RC	1.50	.60
❑ 222 Ricky Nolasco SP (RC)	5.00	2.00
❑ 223 Adam Loewen (RC)	.40	.15
❑ 224 Scott Olsen SP (RC)	5.00	2.00
❑ 225 Cole Hamels (RC)	1.00	.40
❑ 226 Martin Prado SP (RC)	5.00	2.00
❑ 227 James Loney (RC)	.60	.25
❑ 228 Kevin Thompson SP (RC)	5.00	2.00
❑ 229 Adam Jones RC	1.25	.50
❑ 230 Josh Johnson SP (RC)	5.00	2.00
❑ 231 Anderson Hernandez (RC)	.40	.15
❑ 232 Tony Gwynn Jr. SP (RC)	5.00	2.00
❑ 233 Casey Janssen RC	.60	.25
❑ 234 Taylor Tankersley SP (RC)	5.00	2.00
❑ 235 Mike Thompson RC	.40	.15
❑ 236 Jeremy Sowers SP (RC)	5.00	2.00
❑ 237 Anibal Sanchez (RC)	.60	.25
❑ 238 Adam Wainwright SP (RC)	5.00	2.00
❑ 239 Rich Hill (RC)	.40	.15
❑ 240 Russ Martin SP (RC)	5.00	2.00
❑ 241 Joe Inglett RC	.40	.15
❑ 242 Tony Pena SP (RC)	5.00	2.00
❑ 243 Josh Sharpless RC	.40	.15
❑ 244 Darrell Rasner SP (RC)	5.00	2.00
❑ 245 Joe Saunders (RC)	.40	.15
❑ 246 Jon Lester SP RC	5.00	2.00
❑ 247 Jeremy Hermida (RC)	.40	.15
❑ 248 Chad Billingsley SP (RC)	5.00	2.00
❑ 249 Bobby Livingston (RC)	.40	.15
❑ 250 Justin Verlander SP (RC)	5.00	2.00
❑ 251 Mickey Mantle	8.00	3.00
❑ 252 Hank Blalock SP	5.00	2.00
❑ 253 Manny Ramirez	.60	.25
❑ 254 Mike Mussina SP	8.00	3.00
❑ 255 Greg Maddux	1.50	.60
❑ 256 Jason Giambi SP	5.00	2.00
❑ 257 Mark Teixeira	.60	.25
❑ 258 Carlos Beltran SP	5.00	2.00
❑ 259 Matt Holliday	.50	.20
❑ 260 Pedro Martinez SP	8.00	3.00
❑ 261 Joe Mauer	.60	.25
❑ 262 Melvin Mora SP	5.00	2.00
❑ 263 Mike Piazza	1.00	.40
❑ 264 B.J. Upton SP	5.00	2.00
❑ 265 Vernon Wells	.40	.15
❑ 266 Gary Sheffield SP	5.00	2.00
❑ 267 Randy Johnson	1.00	.40
❑ 268 Ryan Zimmerman SP	5.00	2.00
❑ 269 Lance Berkman	.40	.15
❑ 270 Johan Santana SP	8.00	3.00
❑ 271 Carlos Lee	.40	.15
❑ 272 Brandon Webb SP	5.00	2.00
❑ 273 Adam Dunn	.40	.15
❑ 274 Michael Young SP	5.00	2.00
❑ 275 Barry Bonds	2.00	.75
❑ 276 Jonathan Papelbon SP (RC)	5.00	2.00
❑ 277 Howie Kendrick (RC)	1.00	.40
❑ 278 Melky Cabrera SP (RC)	5.00	2.00
❑ 279 Jered Weaver (RC)	1.25	.50
❑ 280 Josh Barfield SP (RC)	5.00	2.00
❑ 281 Chuck James (RC)	.60	.25
❑ 282 Lastings Milledge SP (RC)	5.00	2.00
❑ 283 Nick Markakis (RC)	.60	.25
❑ 284 Jose Capellan SP (RC)	5.00	2.00
❑ 285 Prince Fielder (RC)	1.50	.60
❑ 286 Jason Botts SP (RC)	5.00	2.00
❑ 287 Eliezer Alfonzo RC	.40	.15
❑ 288 Sean Marshall SP (RC)	5.00	2.00
❑ 289 Ryan Garko (RC)	.40	.15
❑ 290 Stephen Drew SP (RC)	5.00	2.00
❑ 291 Joel Guzman (RC)	.40	.15
❑ 292 Hong-Chih Kuo SP (RC)	5.00	2.00
❑ 293 Zach Miner (RC)	.40	.15
❑ 294 Angel Guzman SP (RC)	5.00	2.00
❑ 295 Andre Ethier (RC)	1.00	.40
❑ 296 Fausto Carmona SP (RC)	5.00	2.00
❑ 297 Ronny Paulino (RC)	.40	.15
❑ 298 Matt Cain SP (RC)	5.00	2.00
❑ 299 Carlos Quentin (RC)	.60	.25
❑ 300 Kenji Johjima SP RC	5.00	2.00

2007 Bowman Heritage

❑ COMP.SET w/o SPs (251)	40.00	15.00
❑ COMMON CARD (1-200)	.40	.15
❑ COMMON ROOKIE (201-251)	.50	.20
❑ COMMON SP (181-200)	3.00	1.25
❑ COMMON SP RC (226-250)	4.00	1.50
❑ SP ODDS 1:3 HOBBY		
❑ NO SIG CARDS ARE SHORT PRINTS		
❑ COMP.SET INCLUDES ALL MANTLE VAR.		
❑ OVERALL PLATE ODDS 1:463 HOBBY		
❑ PLATE PRINT RUN 1 SET PER COLOR		
❑ BLACK-CYAN-MAGENTA-YELLOW ISSUED		
❑ NO PLATE PRICING DUE TO SCARCITY		
❑ 1 Jeff Francoeur	1.00	.40
❑ 2 Jered Weaver	.60	.25
❑ 3 Derrek Lee	.40	.15
❑ 4 Todd Helton	.60	.25
❑ 5 Shawn Hill	.40	.15
❑ 6 Ivan Rodriguez	.60	.25
❑ 7 Mickey Mantle	5.00	2.00
❑ 8 Ramon Hernandez	.40	.15
❑ 9 Randy Johnson	1.00	.40
❑ 10 Jermaine Dye	.40	.15
❑ 11 Brian Roberts	.40	.15
❑ 12 Hank Blalock	.40	.15
❑ 13 Chien-Ming Wang	1.50	.60
❑ 14 Mike Lowell	.40	.15
❑ 15 Brandon Webb	.40	.15
❑ 16 Kelly Johnson	.40	.15
❑ 17 Nick Johnson	.40	.15
❑ 18 Zach Duke	.40	.15
❑ 19 Aaron Hill	.40	.15
❑ 20 Miguel Tejada	.40	.15
❑ 21 Mark Buehrle	.40	.15
❑ 22 Michael Young	.40	.15
❑ 23 Carlos Delgado	.40	.15
❑ 24 Anibal Sanchez	.40	.15
❑ 25 Vladimir Guerrero	1.00	.40
❑ 26 Russell Martin	.40	.15
❑ 27 Lance Berkman	.40	.15
❑ 28 Bobby Crosby	.40	.15
❑ 29 Javier Vazquez	.40	.15
❑ 30 Manny Ramirez	.60	.25
❑ 31 Rich Hill	.40	.15
❑ 32 Mike Sweeney	.40	.15
❑ 33 Jeff Kent	.40	.15
❑ 34 Noah Lowry	.40	.15
❑ 35 Alfonso Soriano	.40	.15
❑ 36 Paul Lo Duca	.40	.15
❑ 37 J.D. Drew	.40	.15
❑ 38 C.C Sabathia	.40	.15
❑ 39 Craig Biggio	.60	.25
❑ 40 Adam Dunn	.40	.15
❑ 41 Josh Beckett	.60	.25
❑ 42 Carlos Guillen	.40	.15
❑ 43 Jeff Francis	.40	.15
❑ 44 Orlando Hudson	.40	.15
❑ 45 Grady Sizmore	.60	.25
❑ 46 Jason Jennings	.40	.15
❑ 47 Mark Teixeira	.60	.25
❑ 48 Freddy Garcia	.40	.15
❑ 49 Adrian Gonzalez	.40	.15
❑ 50 Albert Pujols	2.00	.75
❑ 51 Tom Glavine	.60	.25
❑ 52 J.J. Hardy	.40	.15
❑ 53 Bobby Abreu	.40	.15
❑ 54 Bartolo Colon	.40	.15
❑ 55 Garrett Atkins	.40	.15
❑ 56 Moises Alou	.40	.15
❑ 57 Cliff Lee	.40	.15
❑ 58 Michael Cuddyer	.40	.15
❑ 59 Brandon Phillips	.40	.15
❑ 60 Jeremy Bonderman	.40	.15
❑ 61 Rickie Weeks	.40	.15
❑ 62 Chris Carpenter	.40	.15
❑ 63 Frank Thomas	1.00	.40
❑ 64 Victor Martinez	.40	.15
❑ 65 Dontrelle Willis	.40	.15
❑ 66 Jim Thome	.60	.25
❑ 67 Aaron Rowand	.40	.15
❑ 68 Andy Pettitte	.60	.25
❑ 69 Brian McCann	.40	.15
❑ 70 Roger Clemens	1.50	.60
❑ 71 Gary Matthews	.40	.15
❑ 72 Bronson Arroyo	.40	.15
❑ 73 Jeremy Hermida	.40	.15
❑ 74 Eric Chavez	.40	.15
❑ 75 David Ortiz	1.00	.40
❑ 76 Stephen Drew	.60	.25
❑ 77 Ronnie Belliard	.40	.15
❑ 78 James Shields	.40	.15
❑ 79 Richie Sexson	.40	.15
❑ 80 Johan Santana	.60	.25
❑ 81 Orlando Cabrera	.40	.15
❑ 82 Aramis Ramirez	.40	.15
❑ 83 Greg Maddux	1.50	.60
❑ 84 Reggie Sanders	.40	.15
❑ 85 Carlos Zambrano	.40	.15
❑ 86 Bengie Molina	.40	.15
❑ 87 David DeJesus	.40	.15
❑ 88 Adam Wainwright	.40	.15
❑ 89 Conor Jackson	.40	.15
❑ 90 David Wright	1.50	.60
❑ 91 Ryan Garko	.40	.15
❑ 92 Bill Hall	.40	.15
❑ 93 Marcus Giles	.40	.15
❑ 94 Kenny Rogers	.40	.15
❑ 95 Joe Mauer	.60	.25
❑ 96 Hanley Ramirez	.60	.25

❑ 97 Brian Giles .40 .15
❑ 98 Dan Haren .40 .15
❑ 99 Robinson Cano .60 .25
❑ 100 Ryan Howard 1.50 .60
❑ 101 Andruw Jones .60 .25
❑ 102 Aaron Harang .40 .15
❑ 103 Hideki Matsui 1.00 .40
❑ 104 Nick Swisher .40 .15
❑ 105 Pedro Martinez .60 .25
❑ 106 Felipe Lopez .40 .15
❑ 107 Erik Bedard .40 .15
❑ 108 Rafael Furcal .40 .15
❑ 109 Curt Schilling .60 .25
❑ 110 Jose Reyes 1.00 .40
❑ 111 Adam LaRoche .40 .15
❑ 112 Mike Mussina .60 .25
❑ 113 Melvin Mora .40 .15
❑ 114 Zack Greinke .40 .15
❑ 115 Justin Morneau .40 .15
❑ 116 Ervin Santana .40 .15
❑ 117 Ken Griffey Jr. 1.50 .60
❑ 118 David Eckstein .40 .15
❑ 119 Jamie Moyer .40 .15
❑ 120 Jorge Posada .60 .25
❑ 121 Justin Verlander 1.00 .40
❑ 122 Sammy Sosa 1.00 .40
❑ 123 Jason Schmidt .40 .15
❑ 124 Josh Willingham .40 .15
❑ 125 Roy Oswalt .40 .15
❑ 126 Travis Hafner .40 .15
❑ 127 John Maine .40 .15
❑ 128 Willy Taveras .40 .15
❑ 129 Magglio Ordonez .40 .15
❑ 130 Barry Zito .40 .15
❑ 131 Prince Fielder 1.00 .40
❑ 132 Michael Barrett .40 .15
❑ 133 Livan Hernandez .40 .15
❑ 134 Troy Glaus .40 .15
❑ 135 Rocco Baldelli .40 .15
❑ 136 Jason Giambi .40 .15
❑ 137 Austin Kearns .40 .15
❑ 138 Dan Uggla .60 .25
❑ 139 Pat Burrell .40 .15
❑ 140 Carlos Beltran .40 .15
❑ 141 Carlos Quentin .40 .15
❑ 142 Johnny Estrada .40 .15
❑ 143 Torii Hunter .40 .15
❑ 144 Carlos Lee .40 .15
❑ 145 Mike Piazza 1.00 .40
❑ 146 Mark Teahen .40 .15
❑ 147 Juan Pierre .40 .15
❑ 148 Paul Konerko .40 .15
❑ 149 Freddy Sanchez .40 .15
❑ 150 Derek Jeter 2.50 1.00
❑ 151 Orlando Hernandez .40 .15
❑ 152 Raul Ibanez .40 .15
❑ 153 John Smoltz .60 .25
❑ 154 Scott Rolen .60 .25
❑ 155 Jimmy Rollins .40 .15
❑ 156 A.J. Burnett .40 .15
❑ 157 Jason Varitek 1.00 .40
❑ 158 Ben Sheets .40 .15
❑ 159 Matt Cain .60 .25
❑ 160 Carl Crawford .40 .15
❑ 161 Jeff Suppan .40 .15
❑ 162 Tadahito Iguchi .40 .15
❑ 163 Kevin Millwood .40 .15
❑ 164 Chris Duncan .40 .15
❑ 165 Rich Harden .40 .15
❑ 166 Joe Crede .40 .15
❑ 167 Chipper Jones 1.00 .40
❑ 168 Gary Sheffield .40 .15
❑ 169 Cole Hamels .60 .25
❑ 170 Jason Bay .40 .15
❑ 171 Jhonny Peralta .40 .15
❑ 172 Aubrey Huff .40 .15
❑ 173 Xavier Nady .40 .15
❑ 174 Kazuo Matsui .40 .15
❑ 175 Vernon Wells .40 .15
❑ 176 Johnny Damon .60 .25
❑ 177 Jim Edmonds .60 .25
❑ 178 Jose Vidro .40 .15
❑ 179 Garret Anderson .40 .15
❑ 180 Alex Rios .40 .15
❑ 181a Ichiro Suzuki 1.50 .60
❑ 181b Ichiro Suzuki SP 8.00 3.00
❑ 182a Jake Peavy .40 .15
❑ 182b Jake Peavy SP 4.00 1.25
❑ 183a Ian Kinsler .40 .15
❑ 183b Ian Kinsler SP 4.00 1.25
❑ 184a Tom Gorzelanny .40 .15
❑ 184b Tom Gorzelanny SP 4.00 1.25
❑ 185a Miguel Cabrera .60 .25
❑ 185b Miguel Cabrera SP 5.00 2.00
❑ 186a Scott Kazmir .60 .25
❑ 186b Scott Kazmir SP 5.00 2.00
❑ 187a Matt Holliday 1.00 .40
❑ 187b Matt Holliday SP 5.00 2.00
❑ 188a Roy Halladay .40 .15
❑ 188b Roy Halladay SP 4.00 1.25
❑ 189a Ryan Zimmerman 1.00 .40
❑ 189b Ryan Zimmerman SP 5.00 2.00
❑ 190a Alex Rodriguez 1.50 .60
❑ 190b Alex Rodriguez SP 8.00 3.00
❑ 191a Kenji Johjima 1.00 .40
❑ 191b Kenji Johjima SP 5.00 2.00
❑ 192a Gil Meche .40 .15
❑ 192b Gil Meche SP 4.00 1.25
❑ 193a Chase Utley 1.00 .40
❑ 193b Chase Utley SP 5.00 2.00
❑ 194a Jeremy Sowers .40 .15
❑ 194b Jeremy Sowers SP 3.00 1.25
❑ 195a John Lackey .40 .15
❑ 195b John Lackey SP 3.00 1.25
❑ 196a Nick Markakis .60 .25
❑ 196b Nick Markakis SP 5.00 2.00
❑ 197a Tim Hudson .40 .15
❑ 197b Tim Hudson SP 3.00 1.25
❑ 198a B.J. Upton .40 .15
❑ 198b B.J. Upton SP 3.00 1.25
❑ 199a Felix Hernandez .60 .25
❑ 199b Felix Hernandez SP 5.00 2.00
❑ 200a Barry Bonds 2.00 .75
❑ 200b Barry Bonds SP 10.00 4.00
❑ 201 Jarrod Saltalamacchia (RC) .75 .30
❑ 202 Tim Lincecum RC 4.00 1.50
❑ 203 Kory Casto (RC) .50 .20
❑ 204 Sean Henn (RC) .50 .20
❑ 205 Hector Gimenez (RC) .50 .20
❑ 206 Homer Bailey (RC) .75 .30
❑ 207 Yunel Escobar (RC) .50 .20
❑ 208 Matt Lindstrom (RC) .50 .20
❑ 209 Tyler Clippard (RC) .75 .30
❑ 210 Joe Smith RC .50 .20
❑ 211 Tony Abreu RC 1.25 .50
❑ 212 Billy Butler (RC) .75 .30
❑ 213 Gustavo Molina RC .50 .20
❑ 214 Brian Stokes (RC) .50 .20
❑ 215 Kevin Slowey (RC) 1.25 .50
❑ 216 Curtis Thigpen (RC) .50 .20
❑ 217 Carlos Gomez RC .75 .30
❑ 218 Rick Vanden Hurk RC .75 .30
❑ 219 Michael Bourn (RC) .50 .20
❑ 220 Jeff Baker (RC) .50 .20
❑ 221 Andy LaRoche (RC) .50 .20
❑ 222 Andy Sonnanstine RC .50 .20
❑ 223 Chase Wright RC 1.25 .50
❑ 224 Mark Reynolds RC 2.00 .75
❑ 225 Matt Chico (RC) .50 .20
❑ 226a Hunter Pence (RC) 2.50 1.00
❑ 226b Hunter Pence SP 8.00 3.00
❑ 227a John Danks RC .50 .20
❑ 227b John Danks SP 4.00 1.50
❑ 228a Elijah Dukes RC .75 .30
❑ 228b Elijah Dukes SP 6.00 2.50
❑ 229a Kei Igawa RC 1.25 .50
❑ 229b Kei Igawa SP 6.00 2.50
❑ 230a Felix Pie (RC) .50 .20
❑ 230b Felix Pie SP 4.00 1.50
❑ 231a Jesus Flores RC .50 .20
❑ 231b Jesus Flores SP 4.00 1.50
❑ 232a Dallas Braden RC .75 .30
❑ 232b Dallas Braden SP 6.00 2.50
❑ 233a Akinori Iwamura RC 1.25 .50
❑ 233b Akinori Iwamura SP 6.00 2.50
❑ 234a Ryan Braun (RC) 3.00 1.25
❑ 234b Ryan Braun SP 8.00 3.00
❑ 235a Alex Gordon RC 2.50 1.00
❑ 235b Alex Gordon SP 8.00 3.00
❑ 236a Micah Owings (RC) .50 .20
❑ 236b Micah Owings SP 4.00 1.50
❑ 237a Kevin Kouzmanoff (RC) .50 .20
❑ 237b Kevin Kouzmanoff SP 4.00 1.50
❑ 238a Glen Perkins (RC) .50 .20
❑ 238b Glen Perkins SP 4.00 1.50
❑ 239a Danny Putnam (RC) .50 .20
❑ 239b Danny Putnam SP 4.00 1.50
❑ 240a Philip Hughes (RC) 2.50 1.00
❑ 240b Philip Hughes SP 8.00 3.00
❑ 241a Ryan Sweeney (RC) .50 .20
❑ 241b Ryan Sweeney SP 4.00 1.50
❑ 242a Josh Hamilton (RC) 1.25 .50
❑ 242b Josh Hamilton SP 12.00 5.00
❑ 243a Hideki Okajima RC 2.50 1.00
❑ 243b Hideki Okajima SP 8.00 3.00
❑ 244a Adam Lind (RC) .50 .20
❑ 244b Adam Lind SP 4.00 1.50
❑ 245a Travis Buck (RC) .50 .20
❑ 245b Travis Buck SP 4.00 1.50
❑ 246a Miguel Montero (RC) .50 .20
❑ 246b Miguel Montero SP 4.00 1.50
❑ 247a Brandon Morrow RC 1.00 .40
❑ 247b Brandon Morrow SP 6.00 2.50
❑ 248a Troy Tulowitzki (RC) 1.25 .50
❑ 248b Troy Tulowitzki SP 6.00 2.50
❑ 249a Delmon Young (RC) .75 .30
❑ 249b Delmon Young SP 6.00 2.50
❑ 250a Daisuke Matsuzaka RC 5.00 2.00
❑ 250b Daisuke Matsuzaka SP 10.00 4.00
❑ 251 Joba Chamberlain RC 8.00 3.00

2004 Bowman Sterling

❑ FY ODDS APPX.TWO PER HOBBY PACK
❑ FY AU ODDS APPX.ONE PER HOBBY PACK
❑ AU-GU ODDS APPX.ONE PER HOBBY PACK
❑ AU-GU 1:2 WRAPPER ODDS IS AN ERROR
❑ GU ODDS APPX. 1.5 PER HOBBY PACK
❑ GU 1:2 WRAPPER ODDS IS AN ERROR
❑ AB Angel Berroa Bat 5.00 2.00
❑ ABA Aarom Baldiris FY RC 5.00 2.00
❑ AC Alberto Callaspo FY AU RC 20.00 8.00
❑ AD Adam Dunn Bat 5.00 2.00
❑ AER Alex Rodriguez Bat 15.00 6.00
❑ AJ Andruw Jones Jsy 8.00 3.00
❑ AK Austin Kearns Jsy 5.00 2.00
❑ ANR Aramis Ramirez Bat 5.00 2.00
❑ AP Albert Pujols Jsy 20.00 8.00
❑ AR Alex Romero FY AU RC 8.00 3.00
❑ AW Adam Wainwright AU Jsy 25.00 10.00
❑ AWH A.Whittington FY RC 5.00 2.00
❑ AZ Alec Zumwalt FY AU RC 8.00 3.00
❑ BB Brian Bixler AU Jsy RC 10.00 4.00
❑ BBR Bill Bray FY RC 4.00 1.50
❑ BBU Billy Buckner FY RC 5.00 2.00
❑ BC2 Bobby Crosby Jsy 5.00 2.00
❑ BD Blake DeWitt AU Jsy RC 30.00 12.50
❑ BE Brad Eldred FY RC 5.00 2.00
❑ BH B.Hawksworth FY AU RC 10.00 4.00
❑ BT Brad Thompson FY RC 5.00 2.00
❑ BU B.J. Upton AU Bat 25.00 10.00
❑ BW Bernie Williams Jsy 8.00 3.00
❑ CA Chris Aguila FY AU RC 8.00 3.00
❑ CB Craig Biggio Jsy 8.00 3.00
❑ CC Chad Cordero AU Jsy 15.00 6.00
❑ CG Christian Garcia AU Jsy RC 15.00 6.00
❑ CH Chin-Lung Hu FY RC 15.00 6.00
❑ CIB Carlos Beltran Bat 5.00 2.00
❑ CJ Conor Jackson FY RC 20.00 8.00
❑ CL Chris Lubanski AU Bat 10.00 4.00
❑ CLA Chris Lambert FY RC 5.00 2.00

- ❑ CN Chris Nelson FY RC 8.00 3.00
- ❑ CQ Carlos Quentin FY AU RC 30.00 12.50
- ❑ CT Curtis Thigpen FY RC 5.00 2.00
- ❑ DD David DeJesus AU Jsy 15.00 6.00
- ❑ DP Danny Putnam AU Jsy RC 10.00 4.00
- ❑ DPU David Purcey FY RC 5.00 2.00
- ❑ DW David Wright AU Jsy 50.00 30.00
- ❑ DWW Dontrelle Willis Jsy 8.00 3.00
- ❑ DY Delmon Young AU Bat 30.00 12.50
- ❑ EG Eric Gagne Jsy 5.00 2.00
- ❑ EH Eric Hurley FY RC 5.00 2.00
- ❑ ESP Erick San Pedro FY RC 4.00 1.50
- ❑ FC Fausto Carmona FY RC 10.00 4.00
- ❑ FG Freddy Guzman FY RC 4.00 1.50
- ❑ FH Felix Hernandez FY RC 30.00 12.50
- ❑ FP Felix Pie AU Jsy 25.00 10.00
- ❑ FT Frank Thomas Bat 8.00 3.00
- ❑ GG Greg Golson FY RC 8.00 3.00
- ❑ GH Gaby Hernandez FY RC 8.00 3.00
- ❑ GIG Gio Gonzalez FY RC 8.00 3.00
- ❑ GS Gary Sheffield Bat 5.00 2.00
- ❑ HB Homer Bailey AU Jsy RC 40.00 15.00
- ❑ HC Hee Seop Choi Bat 5.00 2.00
- ❑ HG Hector Gimenez FY AU RC 8.00 3.00
- ❑ HJB Hank Blalock Bat 5.00 2.00
- ❑ HM Hector Made FY RC 5.00 2.00
- ❑ HS Huston Street AU Jsy RC 25.00 10.00
- ❑ IR Ivan Rodriguez Bat 8.00 3.00
- ❑ JB Jeff Bagwell Jsy 8.00 3.00
- ❑ JC Jose Capellan FY RC 5.00 2.00
- ❑ JCR Jesse Crain FY RC 5.00 2.00
- ❑ JD Johnny Damon Bat 8.00 3.00
- ❑ JE Johnny Estrada Bat 5.00 2.00
- ❑ JFI Josh Fields FY RC 12.00 5.00
- ❑ JG Joey Gathright FY RC 5.00 2.00
- ❑ JH Jesse Hoover FY RC 5.00 2.00
- ❑ JK Jason Kendall Bat 5.00 2.00
- ❑ JM Jeff Marquez AU Jsy RC 15.00 6.00
- ❑ JO Justin Orenduff FY RC 5.00 2.00
- ❑ JP Juan Pierre Bat 5.00 2.00
- ❑ JPH J.P. Howell FY RC 5.00 2.00
- ❑ JR Jay Rainville FY AU RC 12.00 5.00
- ❑ JS Jeremy Sowers FY AU RC 30.00 15.00
- ❑ JZ Jon Zeringue FY RC 5.00 2.00
- ❑ KCH K.C. Herren FY RC 5.00 2.00
- ❑ KS Kurt Suzuki FY RC 6.00 2.50
- ❑ KT Kazuhito Tadano FY RC 5.00 2.00
- ❑ KW Kerry Wood Jsy 5.00 2.00
- ❑ KWA Kyle Waldrop AU Jsy RC 15.00 6.00
- ❑ LB Lance Berkman Jsy 5.00 2.00
- ❑ LC Luis Castillo Jsy 5.00 2.00
- ❑ LH Linc Holdzkom FY AU RC 8.00 3.00
- ❑ LN Laynce Nix Bat 5.00 2.00
- ❑ MA Moises Alou Bat 5.00 2.00
- ❑ MAM Mark Mulder Jsy 5.00 2.00
- ❑ MAR Manny Ramirez Bat 8.00 3.00
- ❑ MB Matt Bush AU Jsy RC 25.00 10.00
- ❑ MC Miguel Cabrera Bat 8.00 3.00
- ❑ MCT Mark Teixeira Bat 8.00 3.00
- ❑ ME Mitch Einertson FY RC 5.00 2.00
- ❑ MF Mike Ferris FY RC 5.00 2.00
- ❑ MFO Matt Fox FY RC 4.00 1.50
- ❑ MJP Mike Piazza Bat 8.00 3.00
- ❑ MM Matt Moses FY AU RC 15.00 6.00
- ❑ MMC Matt Macri FY RC 6.00 2.50
- ❑ MP Mark Prior Jsy 8.00 3.00
- ❑ MR Mike Rouse FY AU RC 8.00 3.00
- ❑ MRO Mark Rogers FY RC 8.00 3.00
- ❑ MT M.Tuiasosopo AU Bat RC 30.00 12.50
- ❑ MT1 Miguel Tejada Bat 5.00 2.00
- ❑ MT2 Miguel Tejada Jsy 5.00 2.00
- ❑ MW Marland Williams FY RC 5.00 2.00
- ❑ MY Michael Young Bat 5.00 2.00
- ❑ NJ Nick Johnson Bat 5.00 2.00
- ❑ NM Nyjer Morgan FY RC 4.00 1.50
- ❑ NS Nate Schierholtz FY RC 8.00 3.00
- ❑ NW Neil Walker FY RC 8.00 3.00
- ❑ OQ Omar Quintanilla FY RC 5.00 2.00
- ❑ PGM Paul Maholm FY RC 8.00 3.00
- ❑ PH Philip Hughes FY RC 25.00 10.00
- ❑ PL Paul LoDuca Bat 5.00 2.00
- ❑ PR Pokey Reese Bat 5.00 2.00
- ❑ RB Rocco Baldelli Bat 5.00 2.00
- ❑ RBR Reid Brignac FY RC 10.00 4.00
- ❑ RC Robinson Cano AU Jsy 50.00 20.00
- ❑ RH Ryan Harvey AU Bat 15.00 6.00
- ❑ RJH Richard Hidalgo Bat 5.00 2.00
- ❑ RM Ryan Meaux FY AU RC 8.00 3.00
- ❑ RO Russ Ortiz Jsy 5.00 2.00
- ❑ RP Rafael Palmeiro Bat 8.00 3.00
- ❑ SK Scott Kazmir AU Jsy RC 50.00 20.00
- ❑ SO Scott Olsen AU Jsy RC 30.00 15.00
- ❑ SS Sammy Sosa Jsy 8.00 3.00
- ❑ SSM Seth Smith FY RC 8.00 3.00
- ❑ TD Thomas Diamond FY RC 8.00 3.00
- ❑ TG Troy Glaus Bat 5.00 2.00
- ❑ TLH Todd Helton Bat 8.00 3.00
- ❑ TM Tino Martinez Bat 8.00 3.00
- ❑ TMG Tom Glavine Jsy 8.00 3.00
- ❑ TP Trevor Plouffe AU Jsy RC 15.00 6.00
- ❑ TT T.Tankersley AU Jsy RC 10.00 4.00
- ❑ VG Vladimir Guerrero Bat 8.00 3.00
- ❑ VP Vince Perkins FY AU RC 10.00 4.00
- ❑ YP Yusmeiro Petit FY RC 10.00 4.00
- ❑ ZD Zach Duke FY RC 10.00 4.00
- ❑ ZJ Zach Jackson FY RC 5.00 2.00

2005 Bowman Sterling

- ❑ COMMON CARD 4.00 1.50
- ❑ BASIC CARDS APPX.TWO PER HOBBY PACK
- ❑ BASIC CARDS APPX.TWO PER RETAIL PACK
- ❑ AU GROUP A ODDS 1:2 HOBBY
- ❑ AU GROUP B ODDS 1:3 HOBBY
- ❑ AU-GU GROUP A ODDS 1:2 H, 1:2 R
- ❑ AU-GU GROUP B ODDS 1:37 H, 1:37 R
- ❑ AU-GU GROUP C ODDS 1:11 H, 1:11 R
- ❑ AU-GU GROUP D ODDS 1:10 H, 1:10 R
- ❑ AU-GU GROUP E ODDS 1:27 H, 1:27 R
- ❑ AU-GU GROUP F ODDS 1:13 H, 1:13 R
- ❑ GU GROUP A ODDS 1:3 H, 1:3 R
- ❑ GU GROUP B ODDS 1:5 H, 1:5 R
- ❑ GU GROUP C ODDS 1:6 H, 1:6 R
- ❑ ACL Andy LaRoche RC 8.00 3.00
- ❑ AL Adam Lind AU Bat B 25.00 10.00
- ❑ AM A.McCutchen AU Jsy D RC 50.00 20.00
- ❑ AP Albert Pujols Jsy B 15.00 6.00
- ❑ AR Alex Rodriguez Jsy B UER 15.00 6.00
- ❑ ARA Aramis Ramirez Bat A 5.00 2.00
- ❑ AS Alfonso Soriano Bat A 5.00 2.00
- ❑ AT Aaron Thompson AU A RC 10.00 4.00
- ❑ BA Brian Anderson RC 6.00 2.50
- ❑ BB Billy Buckner AU Jsy A 10.00 4.00
- ❑ BBU Billy Butler RC 12.00 5.00
- ❑ BC Brent Cox AU Jsy D RC 15.00 6.00
- ❑ BCR Brad Corley RC 5.00 2.00
- ❑ BE Brad Eldred AU Jsy C 10.00 4.00
- ❑ BH Brett Hayes RC 4.00 1.50
- ❑ BJ Beau Jones AU Jsy A RC 20.00 8.00
- ❑ BL B.Livingston AU Jsy A RC 10.00 4.00
- ❑ BLB Barry Bonds Jsy C 15.00 6.00
- ❑ BM B.McCarthy AU Jsy A RC 25.00 10.00
- ❑ BMU Bill Mueller Jsy C 5.00 2.00
- ❑ BRB Brian Bogusevic RC 4.00 1.50
- ❑ BS Brandon Sing AU A RC 10.00 4.00
- ❑ BSN Brandon Snyder RC 8.00 3.00
- ❑ BZ Barry Zito Uni A 5.00 2.00
- ❑ CB Carlos Beltran Bat A 5.00 2.00
- ❑ CBU Clay Buchholz RC 30.00 12.50
- ❑ CC Cesar Carrillo RC 6.00 2.50
- ❑ CD Carlos Delgado Jsy A 5.00 2.00
- ❑ CH C.J. Henry AU B RC 12.00 5.00
- ❑ CHE Chase Headley RC 8.00 3.00
- ❑ CI Craig Italiano RC 5.00 2.00
- ❑ CJ Chuck James RC 10.00 4.00
- ❑ CLT Chuck Tiffany RC 5.00 2.00
- ❑ CN Chris Nelson AU Jsy A 10.00 4.00
- ❑ CP Cliff Pennington AU B RC 10.00 4.00
- ❑ CPP C.Pignatiello AU Jsy A RC 10.00 4.00
- ❑ CR Colby Rasmus AU Jsy A RC 80.00 40.00
- ❑ CRA Cesar Ramos RC 5.00 2.00
- ❑ CRO Chaz Roe AU Jsy A RC 15.00 6.00
- ❑ CS C.J. Smith AU Jsy A RC 10.00 4.00
- ❑ CSU Curt Schilling Jsy C 8.00 3.00
- ❑ CT Curtis Thigpen AU Jsy A 10.00 4.00
- ❑ CV Chris Volstad AU B RC 10.00 4.00
- ❑ DC Dan Carte RC 5.00 2.00
- ❑ DL Derrek Lee Bat A 8.00 3.00
- ❑ DO David Ortiz Bat A 8.00 3.00
- ❑ DP Dustin Pedroia AU Jsy A 100.00 50.00
- ❑ DT Drew Thompson RC 5.00 2.00
- ❑ DW Dontrelle Willis Jsy C 5.00 2.00
- ❑ EC Eric Chavez Uni B 5.00 2.00
- ❑ EI Eli Iorg AU Jsy C RC 15.00 6.00
- ❑ EM Eddy Martinez AU A RC 10.00 4.00
- ❑ GK George Kottaras AU A RC 10.00 4.00
- ❑ GM Greg Maddux Jsy C 10.00 4.00
- ❑ GO Garrett Olson AU A RC 15.00 6.00
- ❑ GS Gary Sheffield Bat A 5.00 2.00
- ❑ HAS Henry Sanchez RC 6.00 2.50
- ❑ HB Hank Blalock Bat A 5.00 2.00
- ❑ HI Hernan Iribarren RC 5.00 2.00
- ❑ HM Hideki Matsui AS Jsy C 15.00 6.00
- ❑ HS Hum Sanchez AU A RC 20.00 8.00
- ❑ IR Ivan Rodriguez Bat A 8.00 3.00
- ❑ JB Jay Bruce AU Jsy D RC 100.00 50.00
- ❑ JBE Josh Beckett Uni A 5.00 2.00
- ❑ JC Jeff Clement RC 15.00 6.00
- ❑ JCN John Nelson AU Uni A RC 10.00 4.00
- ❑ JD Johnny Damon Bat A 8.00 3.00
- ❑ JDR John Drennen RC 8.00 3.00
- ❑ JE J.Ellsbury AU Jsy E RC 120.00 60.00
- ❑ JEG Jon Egan RC 5.00 2.00
- ❑ JF Josh Fields AU Jsy A 12.00 5.00
- ❑ JG Josh Geer AU Jsy A RC 10.00 4.00
- ❑ JGI Josh Gibson Seat C 15.00 6.00
- ❑ JL Jed Lowrie AU Jsy F RC 50.00 20.00
- ❑ JLY Jeff Lyman RC 5.00 2.00
- ❑ JM John Mayberry Jr. AU A RC 15.00 6.00
- ❑ JMA Jacob Marceaux RC 4.00 1.50
- ❑ JN Jeff Niemann AU Jsy A RC 15.00 6.00
- ❑ JO Justin Olson AU Jsy A RC 10.00 4.00
- ❑ JP Jorge Posada Bat A 8.00 3.00
- ❑ JPE Jim Edmonds Jsy B 5.00 2.00
- ❑ JS John Smoltz Jsy A 8.00 3.00
- ❑ JV J.Verlander AU Jsy A RC 60.00 30.00
- ❑ JW Josh Wall RC 5.00 2.00
- ❑ JWE Jered Weaver RC 15.00 6.00
- ❑ KG Khalil Greene Jsy B 8.00 3.00
- ❑ KM Kevin Millar Bat A 5.00 2.00
- ❑ KS Kevin Slowey RC 15.00 6.00
- ❑ KW Kevin Whelan RC 5.00 2.00
- ❑ LWJ Chipper Jones Bat A 8.00 3.00
- ❑ MA Matt Albers AU A RC 10.00 4.00
- ❑ MAM Matt Maloney RC 6.00 2.50
- ❑ MB M.Bowden AU Jsy A RC 50.00 20.00
- ❑ MC Mike Conroy AU Jsy A RC 10.00 4.00
- ❑ MCA Miguel Cabrera Jsy A 8.00 3.00
- ❑ MCO Mike Costanzo RC 8.00 3.00
- ❑ MG Matt Green AU A RC 8.00 3.00
- ❑ MGA Matt Garza RC 10.00 4.00
- ❑ MGI Marcus Giles AS Jsy B 5.00 2.00
- ❑ MM Mark Mulder Uni B 5.00 2.00
- ❑ MMC Mark McCormick RC 5.00 2.00
- ❑ MP Mike Piazza Bat A 8.00 3.00
- ❑ MPR Mark Prior Jsy B 8.00 3.00
- ❑ MR Manny Ramirez Bat A 8.00 3.00
- ❑ MT Miguel Tejada Uni A 5.00 2.00
- ❑ MTE Mark Teixeira Bat A 8.00 3.00
- ❑ MTO Matt Torra RC 5.00 2.00
- ❑ MY Michael Young Bat A 5.00 2.00
- ❑ NH Nick Hundley RC 4.00 1.50
- ❑ NR Nolan Reimold RC 8.00 3.00
- ❑ NW Nick Webber RC 4.00 1.50
- ❑ PH Philip Humber AU Jsy A RC 25.00 10.00
- ❑ PK Paul Kelly RC 5.00 2.00
- ❑ PL Paul Lo Duca Bat A 5.00 2.00
- ❑ PM Pedro Martinez Jsy A 8.00 3.00
- ❑ PP P.J. Phillips RC 5.00 2.00
- ❑ RB Ryan Braun AU A RC 120.00 60.00
- ❑ RBE Ronnie Belliard Bat A 5.00 2.00

❑ RF Rafael Furcal Jsy A 5.00 2.00
❑ RM Russ Martin AU Jsy F RC 40.00 15.00
❑ RMO Ryan Mount RC 5.00 2.00
❑ RR Ricky Romero RC 5.00 2.00
❑ RT Raul Tablado AU Jsy A RC 10.00 4.00
❑ RZ Ryan Zimmerman RC 25.00 10.00
❑ SD Stephen Drew RC 20.00 8.00
❑ SE Scott Elbert AU Jsy A 10.00 4.00
❑ SM Steve Marek AU Jsy A RC 10.00 4.00
❑ SR Scott Rolen Jsy B 8.00 3.00
❑ SS Sammy Sosa Bat A 8.00 3.00
❑ SW Steven White AU B RC 8.00 3.00
❑ TB Trevor Bell AU Jsy C RC 15.00 6.00
❑ TBU Travis Buck RC 8.00 3.00
❑ TC Travis Chick AU A RC 8.00 3.00
❑ TG Tyler Greene RC 5.00 2.00
❑ TH Torii Hunter Bat A 5.00 2.00
❑ THE Tyler Herron RC 5.00 2.00
❑ THU Tim Hudson Uni A 5.00 2.00
❑ TI Tadahito Iguchi RC 5.00 2.00
❑ TLH Todd Helton Jsy B 8.00 3.00
❑ TM Tyler Minges AU Jsy A RC 10.00 4.00
❑ TM Tino Martinez Bat A 8.00 3.00
❑ TN Trot Nixon Bat A 5.00 2.00
❑ TT Troy Tulowitzki RC 15.00 6.00
❑ TW Travis Wood RC 6.00 2.50
❑ VG Vladimir Guerrero Bat A 8.00 3.00
❑ VM Victor Martinez Bat A 5.00 2.00
❑ WT Wade Townsend RC 5.00 2.00
❑ YE Yunel Escobar RC 15.00 6.00
❑ ZS Zach Simons RC 4.00 1.50

2006 Bowman Sterling

❑ COMMON ROOKIE 3.00 1.25
❑ COMMON AUTO RC 8.00 3.00
❑ AU RC AUTO ODDS 1:4 HOBBY
❑ COMMON AU-GU RC 10.00 4.00
❑ AU-GU RC ODDS 1:4 HOBBY
❑ COMMON GU VET 6.00 2.50
❑ GU VET ODDS 1:4 HOBBY
❑ OVERALL PLATE ODDS 1:23 BOXES
❑ PLATE PRINT RUN 1 SET PER COLOR
❑ BLACK-CYAN-MAGENTA-YELLOW ISSUED
❑ NO PLATE PRICING DUE TO SCARCITY
❑ EXCHANGE DEADLINE 12/31/08
❑ AD Adam Dunn Jsy 6.00 2.50
❑ AE Andre Ethier AU (RC) 25.00 10.00
❑ AER Alex Rodriguez Bat 25.00 10.00
❑ AJ Andruw Jones Jsy 8.00 3.00
❑ ALR A.Reyes Jsy AU (RC) EXCH 15.00 6.00
❑ ALS Alay Soler RC 3.00 1.25
❑ AP Albert Pujols Jsy 20.00 8.00
❑ AP2 Albert Pujols Bat 20.00 8.00
❑ APS Alfonso Soriano Bat 10.00 4.00
❑ AR Aramis Ramirez Bat UER 8.00 3.00
❑ AS Anibal Sanchez (RC) 4.00 1.50
❑ BA Brian Anderson (RC) 3.00 1.25
❑ BB Brian Bannister (RC) 3.00 1.25
❑ BL B.Livingston Jsy AU (RC) 10.00 4.00
❑ BLB Barry Bonds Bat 15.00 6.00
❑ BON Boof Bonser (RC) 4.00 1.50
❑ BR Brian Roberts Jsy 6.00 2.50
❑ BZ Ben Zobrist (RC) 4.00 1.50
❑ CB Carlos Beltran Jsy 6.00 2.50
❑ CB2 Carlos Beltran Bat 6.00 2.50
❑ CC Chris Carpenter Jsy 10.00 4.00
❑ CH Cole Hamels Jsy AU (RC) 40.00 15.00
❑ CHJ Chuck James (RC) 4.00 1.50
❑ CI Chris Iannetta Jsy AU RC 20.00 8.00
❑ CJ Conor Jackson (RC) 4.00 1.50
❑ CJJ Casey Janssen RC 4.00 1.50
❑ CQ Carlos Quentin (RC) 4.00 1.50
❑ CRB Chad Billingsley (RC) 4.00 1.50
❑ CRH Craig Hansen RC 5.00 2.00
❑ CS Curt Schilling Jsy 8.00 3.00
❑ DG David Gassner (RC) 3.00 1.25
❑ DO David Ortiz Bat 10.00 4.00
❑ DP David Pauley (RC) 3.00 1.25
❑ DU Dan Uggla (RC) 5.00 2.00
❑ DW David Wright Jsy 15.00 6.00
❑ DWW Dontrelle Willis Jsy 6.00 2.50
❑ EC Eric Chavez Pants 6.00 2.50
❑ EG Enrique Gonzalez (RC) 3.00 1.25
❑ FG Franklin Gutierrez (RC) 3.00 1.25
❑ FL Francisco Liriano (RC) 6.00 2.50
❑ GS Grady Sizemore Jsy 10.00 4.00
❑ HB Hank Blalock Jsy 6.00 2.50
❑ HK1 Howie Kendrick (RC) 5.00 2.00
❑ HK2 H.Kendrick Jsy AU (RC) EXCH 20.00 8.00
❑ HM Hideki Matsui Bat 15.00 6.00
❑ HP Hayden Penn (RC) 3.00 1.25
❑ HR Hanley Ramirez (RC) 5.00 2.00
❑ IK Ian Kinsler AU (RC) 25.00 10.00
❑ IR Ivan Rodriguez Jsy 8.00 3.00
❑ IS Ichiro Suzuki Jsy 25.00 10.00
❑ JAS Johan Santana Jsy 10.00 4.00
❑ JB J.Bulger Jsy AU (RC) EXCH 10.00 4.00
❑ JBS Jeremy Sowers (RC) 3.00 1.25
❑ JCB Jason Botts AU (RC) 8.00 3.00
❑ JD Joey Devine RC 3.00 1.25
❑ JDD Johnny Damon Bat 10.00 4.00
❑ JHT Jim Thome Bat 10.00 4.00
❑ JI Joe Inglett AU RC 12.00 5.00
❑ JJ Josh Johnson (RC) 4.00 1.50
❑ JK Jeff Karstens RC 5.00 2.00
❑ JL James Loney (RC) 4.00 1.50
❑ JLB Josh Barfield AU (RC) 8.00 3.00
❑ JM Jeff Mathis (RC) 3.00 1.25
❑ JP Jonathan Papelbon (RC) 8.00 3.00
❑ JRH Rich Harden Jsy 6.00 2.50
❑ JS James Shields RC 3.00 1.25
❑ JT Jack Taschner Jsy AU (RC) 10.00 4.00
❑ JTA Jordan Tata RC 3.00 1.25
❑ JTL Jon Lester Jsy AU RC 50.00 20.00
❑ JV Justin Verlander (RC) 8.00 3.00
❑ JW Jered Weaver (RC) 6.00 2.50
❑ JZ Joel Zumaya (RC) 5.00 2.00
❑ KF Kevin Frandsen (RC) 3.00 1.25
❑ KJ Kenji Johjima RC 8.00 3.00
❑ KM Kendry Morales (RC) 4.00 1.50
❑ LB Lance Berkman Jsy 8.00 3.00
❑ LM Lastings Milledge AU (RC) 20.00 8.00
❑ LWJ Chipper Jones Jsy 10.00 4.00
❑ MC Miguel Cabrera Jsy 8.00 3.00
❑ MC2 Miguel Cabrera Bat 8.00 3.00
❑ MCC Melky Cabrera (RC) 4.00 1.50
❑ MCM Mickey Mantle Bat 100.00 50.00
❑ MCT Mark Teixeira Bat 8.00 3.00
❑ ME Morgan Ensberg Jsy 6.00 2.50
❑ MJP Mike Piazza Bat 10.00 4.00
❑ MK Matt Kemp (RC) 4.00 1.50
❑ MM Mark Mulder Pants 6.00 2.50
❑ MN Mike Napoli Jsy AU RC EXCH 15.00 6.00
❑ MP Martin Prado Jsy AU (RC) 20.00 8.00
❑ MPP Mike Pelfrey RC 15.00 6.00
❑ MR Manny Ramirez Jsy 10.00 4.00
❑ MR2 Manny Ramirez Bat 10.00 4.00
❑ MS Matt Smith (RC) 4.00 1.50
❑ MT Miguel Tejada Pants 6.00 2.50
❑ NM Nick Markakis (RC) 4.00 1.50
❑ PF Prince Fielder Jsy AU (RC) 80.00 40.00
❑ PK Paul Konerko Bat 8.00 3.00
❑ PM Pedro Martinez Pants 8.00 3.00
❑ RC Robinson Cano Bat 12.00 5.00
❑ RH Ryan Howard Jsy 20.00 8.00
❑ RK Ryan Garko (RC) 3.00 1.25
❑ RM Russ Martin (RC) 4.00 1.50
❑ RN Ricky Nolasco AU (RC) 8.00 3.00
❑ RP Ronny Paulino Jsy AU (RC) 15.00 6.00
❑ RZ Ryan Zimmerman (RC) 8.00 3.00
❑ SD Stephen Drew (RC) 5.00 2.00
❑ SM Scott Mathieson (RC) 3.00 1.25
❑ SO Scott Olsen (RC) 3.00 1.25
❑ SR Scott Rolen Pants 8.00 3.00
❑ ST S.Thoman Jsy AU (RC) EXCH 12.00 5.00
❑ TGJ Tony Gwynn Jr (RC) 6.00 2.50
❑ TH Todd Helton Jsy 8.00 3.00
❑ TT Taylor Tankersley (RC) 3.00 1.25
❑ VG Vladimir Guerrero Jsy 8.00 3.00
❑ WA Willy Aybar (RC) 3.00 1.25
❑ YP Yusmeiro Petit Jsy AU (RC) 10.00 4.00
❑ ZM Zach Miner AU (RC) 8.00 3.00

2007 Bowman Sterling

❑ COMMON ROOKIE 2.50 1.00
❑ COMMON AUTO RC 8.00 3.00
❑ AU RC AUTO ODDS 1:2 PACKS
❑ COMMON GU VET 6.00 2.50
❑ GU VET GROUP A ODDS 1:5 PACKS
❑ GU VET GROUP B ODDS 1:3 PACKS
❑ GU VET GROUP C ODDS 1:253 PACKS
❑ PRINTING PLATE ODDS 1:29 BOXES
❑ PRINTING PLATE AU ODDS 1:41 BOXES
❑ PLATE PRINT RUN 1 SET PER COLOR
❑ BLACK-CYAN-MAGENTA-YELLOW ISSUED
❑ NO PLATE PRICING DUE TO SCARCITY
❑ AAL Adam Lind (RC) 2.50 1.00
❑ AER Alex Rodriguez Bat A 15.00 6.00
❑ AG Alex Gordon RC 6.00 2.50
❑ AI Akinori Iwamura RC 4.00 1.50
❑ AJ Andruw Jones Bat B 6.00 2.50
❑ AL Andy LaRoche (RC) 2.50 1.00
❑ AM Andrew Miller RC 6.00 2.50
❑ AP Albert Pujols Jsy A 12.00 5.00
❑ AR Alex Rios Jsy B 6.00 2.50
❑ AS Alfonso Soriano Bat B 6.00 2.50
❑ AS Andy Sonnanstine RC 2.50 1.00
❑ BB Billy Butler (RC) 3.00 1.25
❑ BF Ben Francisco (RC) 2.50 1.00
❑ BLB Barry Bonds Pants A 10.00 4.00
❑ BP Brad Penny Jsy B 6.00 2.50
❑ BR Brian Roberts Jsy A 6.00 2.50
❑ BS Brian Stokes (RC) 2.50 1.00
❑ BU B.J. Upton Bat B 6.00 2.50
❑ BW Brandon Webb Jsy B 6.00 2.50
❑ BW Brandon Wood (RC) 2.50 1.00
❑ CAB Craig Biggio Jsy B 8.00 3.00
❑ CAG Carlos Guillen Jsy B 6.00 2.50
❑ CG Carlos Gomez RC 3.00 1.25
❑ CH Cole Hamels Jsy A 8.00 3.00
❑ CH Chase Headley AU (RC) 8.00 3.00
❑ CL Carlos Lee Jsy B 6.00 2.50
❑ CM Cameron Maybin AU RC 20.00 8.00
❑ CMS Curt Schilling Jsy B 6.00 2.50
❑ CT Curtis Thigpen (RC) 2.50 1.00
❑ DDY Dmitri Young Jsy B 6.00 2.50
❑ DM Daisuke Matsuzaka RC 8.00 3.00
❑ DMM David Murphy (RC) 2.50 1.00
❑ DO David Ortiz Bat B 8.00 3.00
❑ DP Danny Putnam (RC) 2.50 1.00
❑ DW David Wright Bat B 10.00 4.00
❑ DWW Dontrelle Willis Jsy B 6.00 2.50
❑ DY Delmon Young (RC) 3.00 1.25
❑ EC Eric Chavez Pants B 6.00 2.50
❑ FL Fred Lewis (RC) 3.00 1.25
❑ FP Felix Pie AU (RC) 10.00 4.00
❑ GO Garrett Olson (RC) 2.50 1.00
❑ GP Glen Perkins AU (RC) 8.00 3.00
❑ HB Homer Bailey AU (RC) 12.00 5.00
❑ HG Hector Gimenez (RC) 2.50 1.00
❑ HO Hideki Okajima RC 6.00 2.50
❑ HP Hunter Pence (RC) 6.00 2.50

❑ IS Ichiro Suzuki Bat B 12.00 5.00
❑ JAV Jason Varitek Jsy B 8.00 3.00
❑ JB Jeff Baker (RC) 2.50 1.00
❑ JBR Jose Reyes Jsy A 8.00 3.00
❑ JC1 Joba Chamberlain RC 12.00 5.00
❑ JC2 Joba Chamberlain AU 100.00 50.00
❑ JD John Danks AU RC 8.00 3.00
❑ JDF Josh Fields (RC) 2.50 1.00
❑ JE Jim Edmonds Jsy B 8.00 3.00
❑ JE Jacoby Ellsbury (RC) 12.00 5.00
❑ JF Jesus Flores RC 2.50 1.00
❑ JH Josh Hamilton AU (RC) 50.00 20.00
❑ JL Jesse Litsch AU RC 8.00 3.00
❑ JQF Jake Fox RC 2.50 1.00
❑ JR Jo-Jo Reyes (RC) 2.50 1.00
❑ JS Johan Santana Jsy A 8.00 3.00
❑ JS Jarrod Saltalamacchia AU (RC) 10.00 4.00
❑ JU Justin Upton RC 6.00 2.50
❑ JV Justin Verlander Jsy B 8.00 3.00
❑ KI Kei Igawa RC 4.00 1.50
❑ KK Kevin Kouzmanoff (RC) 2.50 1.00
❑ KKS Kurt Suzuki AU (RC) 8.00 3.00
❑ KRK Kyle Kendrick AU RC 10.00 4.00
❑ KS Kevin Slowey AU (RC) 10.00 4.00
❑ LB Lance Berkman Jsy B 6.00 2.50
❑ MAR Manny Ramirez Bat B 6.00 2.50
❑ MB Michael Bourn (RC) 2.50 1.00
❑ MC Melky Cabrera Bat B 6.00 2.50
❑ MC Matt Chico AU (RC) 8.00 3.00
❑ MCT Mark Teixeira Bat A 6.00 2.50
❑ MF Mike Fontenot (RC) 2.50 1.00
❑ MH Matt Holliday Jsy B 8.00 3.00
❑ MJO Magglio Ordonez Bat B 6.00 2.50
❑ MK Masumi Kuwata RC 3.00 1.25
❑ MM Mickey Mantle Jsy C 80.00 40.00
❑ MM Miguel Montero (RC) 2.50 1.00
❑ MO Micah Owings (RC) 2.50 1.00
❑ MP Manny Parra (RC) 2.50 1.00
❑ MR Mark Reynolds RC 6.00 2.50
❑ MSM Mark McLemore (RC) 2.50 1.00
❑ MT Miguel Tejada Pants B 6.00 2.50
❑ MY Michael Young Jsy B 6.00 2.50
❑ NG Nick Gorneault AU (RC) 8.00 3.00
❑ NS Nate Schierholtz AU (RC) 8.00 3.00
❑ OC Orlando Cabrera Jsy 6.00 2.50
❑ PF Prince Fielder Jsy A 8.00 3.00
❑ PH Phil Hughes (RC) 6.00 2.50
❑ PH Phil Hughes AU (RC) 30.00 12.50
❑ RB Rocco Baldelli Jsy B 6.00 2.50
❑ RB Ryan Braun AU (RC) 50.00 20.00
❑ RC Roger Clemens Jsy B 10.00 4.00
❑ RJC Robinson Cano Bat B 8.00 3.00
❑ RJH Ryan Howard Bat A 10.00 4.00
❑ RS Ryan Sweeney (RC) 2.50 1.00
❑ RV Rick Vanden Hurk RC 3.00 1.25
❑ RZ Ryan Zimmerman Bat B 8.00 3.00
❑ SD Shelley Duncan (RC) 2.50 1.00
❑ SG Sean Gallagher (RC) 2.50 1.00
❑ SK Scott Kazmir Jsy B 6.00 2.50
❑ TA Tony Abreu RC 4.00 1.50
❑ TB Travis Buck (RC) 2.50 1.00
❑ TC Tyler Clippard (RC) 3.00 1.25
❑ TH Tim Hudson Jsy B 6.00 2.50
❑ TL Tim Lincecum AU RC 80.00 40.00
❑ TLH Todd Helton Bat A 6.00 2.50
❑ TM Travis Metcalf RC 3.00 1.25
❑ TW Tim Wakefield Jsy B 6.00 2.50
❑ UJ Ubaldo Jimenez (RC) 2.50 1.00
❑ VG Vladimir Guerrero Jsy A 6.00 2.50
❑ YE Yunel Escobar (RC) 2.50 1.00
❑ YG Yovani Gallardo AU (RC) 15.00 6.00

1994 Bowman's Best

❑ COMPLETE SET (200) 40.00 15.00
❑ B1 Chipper Jones 1.25 .50
❑ B2 Derek Jeter 4.00 1.50
❑ B3 Bill Pulsipher .50 .20
❑ B4 James Baldwin .25 .08
❑ B5 Brooks Kieschnick RC .50 .20
❑ B6 Justin Thompson .25 .08
❑ B7 Midre Cummings .25 .08
❑ B8 Joey Hamilton .25 .08
❑ B9 Pokey Reese .25 .08
❑ B10 Brian Barber .25 .08
❑ B11 John Burke .25 .08
❑ B12 DeShawn Warren .25 .08

❑ B13 Edgardo Alfonzo RC 1.00 .40
❑ B14 Eddie Pearson RC .50 .20
❑ B15 Jimmy Haynes .25 .08
❑ B16 Danny Bautista .25 .08
❑ B17 Roger Cedeno .25 .08
❑ B18 Jon Lieber .50 .20
❑ B19 Billy Wagner RC 5.00 2.00
❑ B20 Tate Seefried RC .50 .20
❑ B21 Chad Mottola .25 .08
❑ B22 Jose Malave .25 .08
❑ B23 Terrell Wade RC .50 .20
❑ B24 Shane Andrews .25 .08
❑ B25 Chan Ho Park RC 1.50 .60
❑ B26 Kirk Presley RC .50 .20
❑ B27 Robbie Beckett .25 .08
❑ B28 Orlando Miller .25 .08
❑ B29 Jorge Posada RC 10.00 4.00
❑ B30 Frankie Rodriguez .25 .08
❑ B31 Brian L. Hunter .25 .08
❑ B32 Billy Ashley .25 .08
❑ B33 Rondell White .50 .20
❑ B34 John Roper .25 .08
❑ B35 Marc Valdes .25 .08
❑ B36 Scott Ruffcorn .25 .08
❑ B37 Rod Henderson .25 .08
❑ B38 Curtis Goodwin RC .50 .20
❑ B39 Russ Davis .25 .08
❑ B40 Rick Gorecki .25 .08
❑ B41 Johnny Damon 1.25 .50
❑ B42 Roberto Petagine .25 .08
❑ B43 Chris Snopek .25 .08
❑ B44 Mark Acre RC .50 .20
❑ B45 Todd Hollandsworth .25 .08
❑ B46 Shawn Green 1.25 .50
❑ B47 John Carter RC .50 .20
❑ B48 Jim Pittsley RC .50 .20
❑ B49 John Wasdin RC .50 .20
❑ B50 D.J. Boston RC .50 .20
❑ B51 Tim Clark .25 .08
❑ B52 Alex Ochoa .25 .08
❑ B53 Chad Roper .25 .08
❑ B54 Mike Kelly .25 .08
❑ B55 Brad Fullmer RC 1.00 .40
❑ B56 Carl Everett .50 .20
❑ B57 Tim Belk RC .50 .20
❑ B58 Jimmy Hurst RC .50 .20
❑ B59 Mac Suzuki RC 1.00 .40
❑ B60 Mike Moore .25 .08
❑ B61 Alan Benes RC .50 .20
❑ B62 Tony Clark RC 1.50 .60
❑ B63 Edgar Renteria RC 5.00 2.00
❑ B64 Trey Beamon .25 .08
❑ B65 LaTroy Hawkins RC 1.00 .40
❑ B66 Wayne Gomes RC 1.00 .40
❑ B67 Ray McDavid .25 .08
❑ B68 John Dettmer .25 .08
❑ B69 Willie Greene .25 .08
❑ B70 Dave Stevens .25 .08
❑ B71 Kevin Orie RC .25 .08
❑ B72 Chad Ogea .25 .08
❑ B73 Ben Van Ryn RC .50 .20
❑ B74 Kym Ashworth RC .50 .20
❑ B75 Dmitri Young .50 .20
❑ B76 Herbert Perry RC .50 .20
❑ B77 Joey Eischen .25 .08
❑ B78 Arquimedez Pozo RC .50 .20
❑ B79 Ugueth Urbina .25 .08
❑ B80 Keith Williams RC .50 .20
❑ B81 John Frascatore RC .50 .20
❑ B82 Garey Ingram RC .50 .20
❑ B83 Aaron Small .50 .20
❑ B84 Olmedo Saenz RC .50 .20
❑ B85 Jesus Tavarez RC .50 .20
❑ B86 Jose Silva RC 1.00 .40
❑ B87 Jay Witasick RC .50 .20
❑ B88 Jay Maldonado RC .50 .20
❑ B89 Keith Heberling RC .50 .20
❑ B90 Rusty Greer RC 1.50 .60
❑ R1 Paul Molitor .50 .20
❑ R2 Eddie Murray 1.25 .50
❑ R3 Ozzie Smith 2.00 .75
❑ R4 Rickey Henderson 1.25 .50
❑ R5 Lee Smith .50 .20
❑ R6 Dave Winfield .50 .20
❑ R7 Roberto Alomar .75 .30
❑ R8 Matt Williams .50 .20
❑ R9 Mark Grace .75 .30
❑ R10 Lance Johnson .25 .08
❑ R11 Darren Daulton .50 .20
❑ R12 Tom Glavine .75 .30
❑ R13 Gary Sheffield .50 .20
❑ R14 Rod Beck .25 .08
❑ R15 Fred McGriff .75 .30
❑ R16 Joe Carter .50 .20
❑ R17 Dante Bichette .50 .20
❑ R18 Danny Tartabull .25 .08
❑ R19 Juan Gonzalez .50 .20
❑ R20 Steve Avery .25 .08
❑ R21 John Wetteland .50 .20
❑ R22 Ben McDonald .25 .08
❑ R23 Jack McDowell .25 .08
❑ R24 Jose Canseco .75 .30
❑ R25 Tim Salmon .75 .30
❑ R26 Wilson Alvarez .25 .08
❑ R27 Gregg Jefferies .25 .08
❑ R28 John Burkett .25 .08
❑ R29 Greg Vaughn .25 .08
❑ R30 Robin Ventura .50 .20
❑ R31 Paul O'Neill .75 .30
❑ R32 Cecil Fielder .50 .20
❑ R33 Kevin Mitchell .25 .08
❑ R34 Jeff Conine .50 .20
❑ R35 Carlos Baerga .25 .08
❑ R36 Greg Maddux 2.00 .75
❑ R37 Roger Clemens 2.50 1.00
❑ R38 Deion Sanders .75 .30
❑ R39 Delino DeShields .25 .08
❑ R40 Ken Griffey Jr. 2.00 .75
❑ R41 Albert Belle .50 .20
❑ R42 Wade Boggs .75 .30
❑ R43 Andres Galarraga .50 .20
❑ R44 Aaron Sele .25 .08
❑ R45 Don Mattingly 3.00 1.25
❑ R46 David Cone .50 .20
❑ R47 Len Dykstra .50 .20
❑ R48 Brett Butler .50 .20
❑ R49 Bill Swift .25 .08
❑ R50 Bobby Bonilla .50 .20
❑ R51 Rafael Palmeiro .75 .30
❑ R52 Moises Alou .50 .20
❑ R53 Jeff Bagwell .75 .30
❑ R54 Mike Mussina .75 .30
❑ R55 Frank Thomas 1.25 .50
❑ R56 Jose Rijo .25 .08
❑ R57 Ruben Sierra .50 .20
❑ R58 Randy Myers .25 .08
❑ R59 Barry Bonds 3.00 1.25
❑ R60 Jimmy Key .50 .20
❑ R61 Travis Fryman .50 .20
❑ R62 John Olerud .50 .20
❑ R63 David Justice .50 .20
❑ R64 Ray Lankford .50 .20
❑ R65 Bob Tewksbury .25 .08
❑ R66 Chuck Carr .25 .08
❑ R67 Jay Buhner .50 .20
❑ R68 Kenny Lofton .50 .20
❑ R69 Marquis Grissom .50 .20
❑ R70 Sammy Sosa 1.25 .50
❑ R71 Cal Ripken 4.00 1.50
❑ R72 Ellis Burks .50 .20
❑ R73 Jeff Montgomery .25 .08
❑ R74 Julio Franco .50 .20
❑ R75 Kirby Puckett 1.25 .50
❑ R76 Larry Walker .50 .20

❑ R77	Andy Van Slyke	.75	.30
❑ R78	Tony Gwynn	1.50	.60
❑ R79	Will Clark	.75	.30
❑ R80	Mo Vaughn	.50	.20
❑ R81	Mike Piazza	2.50	1.00
❑ R82	James Mouton	.25	.08
❑ R83	Carlos Delgado	.75	.30
❑ R84	Ryan Klesko	.50	.20
❑ R85	Javier Lopez	.50	.20
❑ R86	Raul Mondesi	.50	.20
❑ R87	Cliff Floyd	.50	.20
❑ R88	Manny Ramirez	1.25	.50
❑ R89	Hector Carrasco	.25	.08
❑ R90	Jeff Granger	.25	.08
❑ X91	F.Thomas/D.Young	.75	.30
❑ X92	F.McGriff/B.Kieschnick	.50	.20
❑ X93	M.Williams/S.Andrews	.25	.08
❑ X94	C.Ripken/K.Orie	2.00	.75
❑ X95	D.Jeter/B.Larkin	2.00	.75
❑ X96	K.Griffey Jr./J.Damon	1.00	.40
❑ X97	B.Bonds/R.White	1.50	.60
❑ X98	A.Belle/J.Hurst	.50	.20
❑ X99	R.Rivera RC/R.Mondesi	.50	.20
❑ X100	R.Clemens/S.Ruffcorn	1.25	.50
❑ X101	G.Maddux/J.Wasdin	1.25	.50
❑ X102	T.Salmon/C.Mottola	.75	.30
❑ X103	C.Baerga/A.Pozo	.25	.08
❑ X104	M.Piazza/B.Hughes	1.25	.50
❑ X105	C.Delgado/M.Nieves	.75	.30
❑ X106	J.Posada/J.Lopez	2.50	1.00
❑ X107	M.Ramirez/J.Malave	1.25	.50
❑ X108	C.Jones/T.Fryman	.75	.30
❑ X109	S.Avery/B.Pulsipher	.25	.08
❑ X110	J.Olerud/S.Green	1.25	.50

1995 Bowman's Best

❑	COMPLETE SET (195)	250.00	125.00
❑	COMMON CARD (B1-R90)	.50	.20
❑	COMMON CARD (X1-X15)	.50	.20
❑ B1	Derek Jeter	3.00	1.25
❑ B2	Vladimir Guerrero RC	50.00	20.00
❑ B3	Bob Abreu RC	12.00	5.00
❑ B4	Chan Ho Park	.50	.20
❑ B5	Paul Wilson	.50	.20
❑ B6	Chad Ogea	.50	.20
❑ B7	Andruw Jones RC	25.00	10.00
❑ B8	Brian Barber	.50	.20
❑ B9	Andy Larkin	.50	.20
❑ B10	Richie Sexson RC	10.00	4.00
❑ B11	Everett Stull	.50	.20
❑ B12	Brooks Kieschnick	.50	.20
❑ B13	Matt Murray	.50	.20
❑ B14	John Wasdin	.50	.20
❑ B15	Shannon Stewart	.50	.20
❑ B16	Luis Ortiz	.50	.20
❑ B17	Marc Kroon	.50	.20
❑ B18	Todd Greene	.50	.20
❑ B19	Juan Acevedo RC	1.00	.40
❑ B20	Tony Clark	.50	.20
❑ B21	Jermaine Dye	.50	.20
❑ B22	Derrek Lee	1.25	.50
❑ B23	Pat Watkins	.50	.20
❑ B24	Pokey Reese	.50	.20
❑ B25	Ben Grieve	.50	.20
❑ B26	Julio Santana RC	.50	.20
❑ B27	Felix Rodriguez RC	1.00	.40
❑ B28	Paul Konerko	8.00	3.00
❑ B29	Nomar Garciaparra	5.00	2.00
❑ B30	Pat Ahearne RC	.50	.20
❑ B31	Jason Schmidt	1.25	.50
❑ B32	Billy Wagner	.75	.30
❑ B33	Rey Ordonez RC	3.00	1.25
❑ B34	Curtis Goodwin	.50	.20
❑ B35	Sergio Nunez RC	1.00	.40
❑ B36	Tim Belk	.50	.20
❑ B37	Scott Elarton RC	2.00	.75
❑ B38	Jason Isringhausen	.50	.20
❑ B39	Trot Nixon	.50	.20
❑ B40	Sid Roberson RC	1.00	.40
❑ B41	Ron Villone	.50	.20
❑ B42	Ruben Rivera	.50	.20
❑ B43	Rick Huisman	.50	.20
❑ B44	Todd Hollandsworth	.50	.20
❑ B45	Johnny Damon	.75	.30
❑ B46	Garret Anderson	.50	.20
❑ B47	Jeff D'Amico	.50	.20
❑ B48	Dustin Hermanson	.50	.20
❑ B49	Juan Encarnacion RC	3.00	1.25
❑ B50	Andy Pettitte	.75	.30
❑ B51	Chris Stynes	.50	.20
❑ B52	Troy Percival	.50	.20
❑ B53	LaTroy Hawkins	.50	.20
❑ B54	Roger Cedeno	.50	.20
❑ B55	Alan Benes	.50	.20
❑ B56	Karim Garcia RC	1.00	.40
❑ B57	Andrew Lorraine	.50	.20
❑ B58	Gary Rath RC	1.00	.40
❑ B59	Bret Wagner	.50	.20
❑ B60	Jeff Suppan	.50	.20
❑ B61	Bill Pulsipher	.50	.20
❑ B62	Jay Payton RC	3.00	1.25
❑ B63	Alex Ochoa	.50	.20
❑ B64	Ugueth Urbina	.50	.20
❑ B65	Armando Benitez	.50	.20
❑ B66	George Arias	.50	.20
❑ B67	Raul Casanova RC	1.00	.40
❑ B68	Matt Drews	.50	.20
❑ B69	Jimmy Haynes	.50	.20
❑ B70	Jimmy Hurst	.50	.20
❑ B71	C.J. Nitkowski	.50	.20
❑ B72	Tommy Davis RC	1.00	.40
❑ B73	Bartolo Colon RC	8.00	3.00
❑ B74	Chris Carpenter RC	12.00	5.00
❑ B75	Trey Beamon	.50	.20
❑ B76	Bryan Rekar	.50	.20
❑ B77	James Baldwin	.50	.20
❑ B78	Marc Valdes	.50	.20
❑ B79	Tom Fordham RC	1.00	.40
❑ B80	Marc Newfield	.50	.20
❑ B81	Angel Martinez	.50	.20
❑ B82	Brian L. Hunter	.50	.20
❑ B83	Jose Herrera	.50	.20
❑ B84	Glenn Dishman RC	1.00	.40
❑ B85	Jacob Cruz RC	2.00	.75
❑ B86	Paul Shuey	.50	.20
❑ B87	Scott Rolen RC	20.00	8.00
❑ B88	Doug Million	.50	.20
❑ B89	Desi Relaford	.50	.20
❑ B90	Michael Tucker	.50	.20
❑ R1	Randy Johnson	1.25	.50
❑ R2	Joe Carter	.50	.20
❑ R3	Chili Davis	.50	.20
❑ R4	Moises Alou	.50	.20
❑ R5	Gary Sheffield	.50	.20
❑ R6	Kevin Appier	.50	.20
❑ R7	Denny Neagle	.50	.20
❑ R8	Ruben Sierra	.50	.20
❑ R9	Darren Daulton	.50	.20
❑ R10	Cal Ripken	4.00	1.50
❑ R11	Bobby Bonilla	.50	.20
❑ R12	Manny Ramirez	.75	.30
❑ R13	Barry Bonds	3.00	1.25
❑ R14	Eric Karros	.50	.20
❑ R15	Greg Maddux	2.00	.75
❑ R16	Jeff Bagwell	.75	.30
❑ R17	Paul Molitor	.50	.20
❑ R18	Ray Lankford	.50	.20
❑ R19	Mark Grace	.75	.30
❑ R20	Kenny Lofton	.50	.20
❑ R21	Tony Gwynn	1.50	.60
❑ R22	Will Clark	.75	.30
❑ R23	Roger Clemens	2.50	1.00
❑ R24	Dante Bichette	.50	.20
❑ R25	Barry Larkin	.75	.30
❑ R26	Wade Boggs	.75	.30
❑ R27	Kirby Puckett	1.25	.50
❑ R28	Cecil Fielder	.50	.20
❑ R29	Jose Canseco	.75	.30
❑ R30	Juan Gonzalez	.50	.20
❑ R31	David Cone	.50	.20
❑ R32	Craig Biggio	.75	.30
❑ R33	Tim Salmon	.75	.30
❑ R34	David Justice	.50	.20
❑ R35	Sammy Sosa	1.25	.50
❑ R36	Mike Piazza	2.00	.75
❑ R37	Carlos Baerga	.50	.20
❑ R38	Jeff Conine	.50	.20
❑ R39	Rafael Palmeiro	.75	.30
❑ R40	Bret Saberhagen	.50	.20
❑ R41	Len Dykstra	.50	.20
❑ R42	Mo Vaughn	.50	.20
❑ R43	Wally Joyner	.50	.20
❑ R44	Chuck Knoblauch	.50	.20
❑ R45	Robin Ventura	.50	.20
❑ R46	Don Mattingly	3.00	1.25
❑ R47	Dave Hollins	.50	.20
❑ R48	Andy Benes	.50	.20
❑ R49	Ken Griffey Jr.	2.00	.75
❑ R50	Albert Belle	.50	.20
❑ R51	Matt Williams	.50	.20
❑ R52	Rondell White	.50	.20
❑ R53	Raul Mondesi	.50	.20
❑ R54	Brian Jordan	.50	.20
❑ R55	Greg Vaughn	.50	.20
❑ R56	Fred McGriff	.75	.30
❑ R57	Roberto Alomar	.75	.30
❑ R58	Dennis Eckersley	.50	.20
❑ R59	Lee Smith	.50	.20
❑ R60	Eddie Murray	1.25	.50
❑ R61	Kenny Rogers	.50	.20
❑ R62	Ron Gant	.50	.20
❑ R63	Larry Walker	.50	.20
❑ R64	Chad Curtis	.50	.20
❑ R65	Frank Thomas	1.25	.50
❑ R66	Paul O'Neill	.75	.30
❑ R67	Kevin Seitzer	.50	.20
❑ R68	Marquis Grissom	.50	.20
❑ R69	Mark McGwire	4.00	1.50
❑ R70	Travis Fryman	.50	.20
❑ R71	Andres Galarraga	.50	.20
❑ R72	Carlos Perez RC	2.00	.75
❑ R73	Tyler Green	.50	.20
❑ R74	Marty Cordova	.50	.20
❑ R75	Shawn Green	.50	.20
❑ R76	Vaughn Eshelman	.50	.20
❑ R77	John Mabry	.50	.20
❑ R78	Jason Bates	.50	.20
❑ R79	Jon Nunnally	.50	.20
❑ R80	Ray Durham	.50	.20
❑ R81	Edgardo Alfonzo	.50	.20
❑ R82	Esteban Loaiza	.50	.20
❑ R83	Hideo Nomo RC	8.00	3.00
❑ R84	Orlando Miller	.50	.20
❑ R85	Alex Gonzalez	.50	.20
❑ R86	Mark Grudzielanek RC	3.00	1.25
❑ R87	Julian Tavarez	.50	.20
❑ R88	Benji Gil	.50	.20
❑ R89	Quilvio Veras	.50	.20
❑ R90	Ricky Bottalico	.50	.20
❑ X1	B.Davis RC/I.Rodriguez	1.50	.60
❑ X2	M.Redman RC/M.Ramirez	1.50	.60
❑ X3	R.Taylor RC/D.Sanders	1.50	.60
❑ X4	R.Jaroncyk RC/S.Green	.50	.20
❑ X5	C.Beltran UER/J.Gonz	8.00	3.00
❑ X6	T.McKnight RC/C.Biggio	.50	.20
❑ X7	M.Barrett RC/T.Fryman	1.50	.60
❑ X8	C.Jenkins RC/M.Vaughn	.50	.20
❑ X9	R.Rivera/F.Thomas	1.25	.50
❑ X10	C.Goodwin/K.Lofton	.50	.20
❑ X11	B.Hunter/T.Gwynn	.75	.30
❑ X12	T.Greene/K.Griffey Jr.	1.25	.50
❑ X13	K.Garcia/M.Williams	.50	.20
❑ X14	B.Wagner/R.Johnson	.75	.30
❑ X15	P.Watkins/J.Bagwell	.75	.30

1996 Bowman's Best

❑	COMPLETE SET (180)	40.00	15.00
❑ 1	Hideo Nomo	1.00	.40
❑ 2	Edgar Martinez	.60	.25
❑ 3	Cal Ripken	3.00	1.25

❑ 4 Wade Boggs	.60	.25
❑ 5 Cecil Fielder	.40	.15
❑ 6 Albert Belle	.40	.15
❑ 7 Chipper Jones	1.00	.40
❑ 8 Ryne Sandberg	1.50	.60
❑ 9 Tim Salmon	.60	.25
❑ 10 Barry Bonds	2.50	1.00
❑ 11 Ken Caminiti	.40	.15
❑ 12 Ron Gant	.40	.15
❑ 13 Frank Thomas	1.00	.40
❑ 14 Dante Bichette	.40	.15
❑ 15 Jason Kendall	.40	.15
❑ 16 Mo Vaughn	.40	.15
❑ 17 Rey Ordonez	.40	.15
❑ 18 Henry Rodriguez	.40	.15
❑ 19 Ryan Klesko	.40	.15
❑ 20 Jeff Bagwell	.60	.25
❑ 21 Randy Johnson	1.00	.40
❑ 22 Jim Edmonds	.40	.15
❑ 23 Kenny Lofton	.40	.15
❑ 24 Andy Pettitte	.60	.25
❑ 25 Brady Anderson	.40	.15
❑ 26 Mike Piazza	1.50	.60
❑ 27 Greg Vaughn	.40	.15
❑ 28 Joe Carter	.40	.15
❑ 29 Jason Giambi	.40	.15
❑ 30 Ivan Rodriguez	.60	.25
❑ 31 Jeff Conine	.40	.15
❑ 32 Rafael Palmeiro	.60	.25
❑ 33 Roger Clemens UER	2.00	.75
❑ 34 Chuck Knoblauch	.40	.15
❑ 35 Reggie Sanders	.40	.15
❑ 36 Andres Galarraga	.40	.15
❑ 37 Paul O'Neill	.60	.25
❑ 38 Tony Gwynn	1.25	.50
❑ 39 Paul Wilson	.40	.15
❑ 40 Garret Anderson	.40	.15
❑ 41 David Justice	.40	.15
❑ 42 Eddie Murray	1.00	.40
❑ 43 Mike Grace RC	.50	.20
❑ 44 Marty Cordova	.40	.15
❑ 45 Kevin Appier	.40	.15
❑ 46 Raul Mondesi	.40	.15
❑ 47 Jim Thome	.60	.25
❑ 48 Sammy Sosa	1.00	.40
❑ 49 Craig Biggio	.60	.25
❑ 50 Marquis Grissom	.40	.15
❑ 51 Alan Benes	.40	.15
❑ 52 Manny Ramirez	.60	.25
❑ 53 Gary Sheffield	.40	.15
❑ 54 Mike Mussina	.60	.25
❑ 55 Robin Ventura	.40	.15
❑ 56 Johnny Damon	.60	.25
❑ 57 Jose Canseco	.60	.25
❑ 58 Juan Gonzalez	.40	.15
❑ 59 Tino Martinez	.60	.25
❑ 60 Brian Hunter	.40	.15
❑ 61 Fred McGriff	.60	.25
❑ 62 Jay Buhner	.40	.15
❑ 63 Carlos Delgado	.40	.15
❑ 64 Moises Alou	.40	.15
❑ 65 Roberto Alomar	.60	.25
❑ 66 Barry Larkin	.60	.25
❑ 67 Vinny Castilla	.40	.15
❑ 68 Ray Durham	.40	.15
❑ 69 Travis Fryman	.40	.15
❑ 70 Jason Isringhausen	.40	.15
❑ 71 Ken Griffey Jr.	1.50	.60
❑ 72 John Smoltz	.60	.25
❑ 73 Matt Williams	.40	.15
❑ 74 Chan Ho Park	.40	.15
❑ 75 Mark McGwire	3.00	1.25
❑ 76 Jeffrey Hammonds	.40	.15
❑ 77 Will Clark	.60	.25
❑ 78 Kirby Puckett	1.00	.40
❑ 79 Derek Jeter	2.50	1.00
❑ 80 Derek Bell	.40	.15
❑ 81 Eric Karros	.40	.15
❑ 82 Len Dykstra	.40	.15
❑ 83 Larry Walker	.40	.15
❑ 84 Mark Grudzielanek	.40	.15
❑ 85 Greg Maddux	1.50	.60
❑ 86 Carlos Baerga	.40	.15
❑ 87 Paul Molitor	.40	.15
❑ 88 John Valentin	.40	.15
❑ 89 Mark Grace	.60	.25
❑ 90 Ray Lankford	.40	.15
❑ 91 Andruw Jones	1.50	.60
❑ 92 Nomar Garciaparra	2.00	.75
❑ 93 Alex Ochoa	.40	.15
❑ 94 Derrick Gibson	.40	.15
❑ 95 Jeff D'Amico	.40	.15
❑ 96 Ruben Rivera	.40	.15
❑ 97 Vladimir Guerrero	2.00	.75
❑ 98 Pokey Reese	.40	.15
❑ 99 Richard Hidalgo	.40	.15
❑ 100 Bartolo Colon	1.00	.40
❑ 101 Karim Garcia	.40	.15
❑ 102 Ben Davis	.40	.15
❑ 103 Jay Powell	.40	.15
❑ 104 Chris Snopek	.40	.15
❑ 105 Glendon Rusch RC	1.00	.40
❑ 106 Enrique Wilson	.40	.15
❑ 107 Antonio Alfonseca RC	1.00	.40
❑ 108 Wilton Guerrero RC	.50	.20
❑ 109 Jose Guillen RC	4.00	1.50
❑ 110 Miguel Mejia RC	.50	.20
❑ 111 Jay Payton	.40	.15
❑ 112 Scott Elarton	.40	.15
❑ 113 Brooks Kieschnick	.40	.15
❑ 114 Dustin Hermanson	.40	.15
❑ 115 Roger Cedeno	.40	.15
❑ 116 Matt Wagner	.40	.15
❑ 117 Lee Daniels	.40	.15
❑ 118 Ben Grieve	.40	.15
❑ 119 Ugueth Urbina	.40	.15
❑ 120 Danny Graves	.40	.15
❑ 121 Dan Donato RC	.50	.20
❑ 122 Matt Ruebel RC	.50	.20
❑ 123 Mark Sievert RC	.50	.20
❑ 124 Chris Stynes	.40	.15
❑ 125 Jeff Abbott	.40	.15
❑ 126 Rocky Coppinger RC	.50	.20
❑ 127 Jermaine Dye	.40	.15
❑ 128 Todd Greene	.40	.15
❑ 129 Chris Carpenter	.60	.25
❑ 130 Edgar Renteria	.40	.15
❑ 131 Matt Drews	.40	.15
❑ 132 Edgard Velazquez RC	.50	.20
❑ 133 Casey Whitten	.40	.15
❑ 134 Ryan Jones RC	.50	.20
❑ 135 Todd Walker	.40	.15
❑ 136 Geoff Jenkins RC	2.00	.75
❑ 137 Matt Morris RC	4.00	1.50
❑ 138 Richie Sexson	.60	.25
❑ 139 Todd Dunwoody RC	.50	.20
❑ 140 Gabe Alvarez RC	.50	.20
❑ 141 J.J. Johnson	.40	.15
❑ 142 Shannon Stewart	.40	.15
❑ 143 Brad Fullmer	.40	.15
❑ 144 Julio Santana	.40	.15
❑ 145 Scott Rolen	1.00	.40
❑ 146 Amaury Telemaco	.40	.15
❑ 147 Trey Beamon	.40	.15
❑ 148 Billy Wagner	.40	.15
❑ 149 Todd Hollandsworth	.40	.15
❑ 150 Doug Million	.40	.15
❑ 151 Javier Valentin RC	.50	.20
❑ 152 Wes Helms RC	1.00	.40
❑ 153 Jeff Suppan	.40	.15
❑ 154 Luis Castillo RC	1.50	.60
❑ 155 Bob Abreu	1.00	.40
❑ 156 Paul Konerko	1.00	.40
❑ 157 Jamey Wright	.40	.15
❑ 158 Eddie Pearson	.40	.15
❑ 159 Jimmy Haynes	.40	.15
❑ 160 Derrek Lee	.60	.25
❑ 161 Damian Moss	.40	.15
❑ 162 Carlos Guillen RC	2.50	1.00
❑ 163 Chris Fussell RC	.50	.20
❑ 164 Mike Sweeney RC	2.50	1.00
❑ 165 Donnie Sadler	.40	.15
❑ 166 Desi Relaford	.40	.15
❑ 167 Steve Gibralter	.40	.15
❑ 168 Neifi Perez	.40	.15
❑ 169 Antone Williamson	.40	.15
❑ 170 Marty Janzen RC	.50	.20
❑ 171 Todd Helton	2.00	.75
❑ 172 Raul Ibanez RC	2.00	.75
❑ 173 Bill Selby	.40	.15
❑ 174 Shane Monahan RC	.50	.20
❑ 175 Robin Jennings	.40	.15
❑ 176 Bobby Chouinard	.40	.15
❑ 177 Einar Diaz	.40	.15
❑ 178 Jason Thompson RC	.40	.15
❑ 179 Rafael Medina RC	.50	.20
❑ 180 Kevin Orie	.40	.15
❑ NNO 1952 Mantle Atomic Ref.	10.00	4.00
❑ NNO 1952 Mantle Refractor	5.00	2.00
❑ NNO 1952 Mantle Chrome	2.50	1.00

1997 Bowman's Best

❑ COMPLETE SET (200)	40.00	15.00
❑ 1 Ken Griffey Jr.	1.50	.60
❑ 2 Cecil Fielder	.40	.15
❑ 3 Albert Belle	.40	.15
❑ 4 Todd Hundley	.40	.15
❑ 5 Mike Piazza	1.50	.60
❑ 6 Matt Williams	.40	.15
❑ 7 Mo Vaughn	.40	.15
❑ 8 Ryne Sandberg	1.50	.60
❑ 9 Chipper Jones	1.00	.40
❑ 10 Edgar Martinez	.60	.25
❑ 11 Kenny Lofton	.40	.15
❑ 12 Ron Gant	.40	.15
❑ 13 Moises Alou	.40	.15
❑ 14 Pat Hentgen	.40	.15
❑ 15 Steve Finley	.40	.15
❑ 16 Mark Grace	.60	.25
❑ 17 Jay Buhner	.40	.15
❑ 18 Jeff Conine	.40	.15
❑ 19 Jim Edmonds	.40	.15
❑ 20 Todd Hollandsworth	.40	.15
❑ 21 Andy Pettitte	.60	.25
❑ 22 Jim Thome	.60	.25
❑ 23 Eric Young	.40	.15
❑ 24 Ray Lankford	.40	.15
❑ 25 Marquis Grissom	.40	.15
❑ 26 Tony Clark	.40	.15
❑ 27 Jermaine Allensworth	.40	.15
❑ 28 Ellis Burks	.40	.15
❑ 29 Tony Gwynn	1.25	.50
❑ 30 Barry Larkin	.60	.25
❑ 31 John Olerud	.40	.15
❑ 32 Mariano Rivera	1.00	.40
❑ 33 Paul Molitor	.40	.15
❑ 34 Ken Caminiti	.40	.15
❑ 35 Gary Sheffield	.40	.15
❑ 36 Al Martin	.40	.15
❑ 37 John Valentin	.40	.15
❑ 38 Frank Thomas	1.00	.40
❑ 39 John Jaha	.40	.15

❑ 40 Greg Maddux 1.50 .60
❑ 41 Alex Fernandez .40 .15
❑ 42 Dean Palmer .40 .15
❑ 43 Bernie Williams .60 .25
❑ 44 Deion Sanders .60 .25
❑ 45 Mark McGwire 3.00 1.25
❑ 46 Brian Jordan .40 .15
❑ 47 Bernard Gilkey .40 .15
❑ 48 Will Clark .60 .25
❑ 49 Kevin Appier .40 .15
❑ 50 Tom Glavine .60 .25
❑ 51 Chuck Knoblauch .40 .15
❑ 52 Rondell White .40 .15
❑ 53 Greg Vaughn .40 .15
❑ 54 Mike Mussina .60 .25
❑ 55 Brian McRae .40 .15
❑ 56 Chili Davis .40 .15
❑ 57 Wade Boggs .60 .25
❑ 58 Jeff Bagwell .60 .25
❑ 59 Roberto Alomar .60 .25
❑ 60 Dennis Eckersley .40 .15
❑ 61 Ryan Klesko .40 .15
❑ 62 Manny Ramirez .60 .25
❑ 63 John Wetteland .40 .15
❑ 64 Cal Ripken 3.00 1.25
❑ 65 Edgar Renteria .40 .15
❑ 66 Tino Martinez .60 .25
❑ 67 Larry Walker .40 .15
❑ 68 Gregg Jefferies .40 .15
❑ 69 Lance Johnson .40 .15
❑ 70 Carlos Delgado .40 .15
❑ 71 Craig Biggio .60 .25
❑ 72 Jose Canseco .60 .25
❑ 73 Barry Bonds 2.50 1.00
❑ 74 Juan Gonzalez .40 .15
❑ 75 Eric Karros .40 .15
❑ 76 Reggie Sanders .40 .15
❑ 77 Robin Ventura .40 .15
❑ 78 Hideo Nomo 1.00 .40
❑ 79 David Justice .40 .15
❑ 80 Vinny Castilla .40 .15
❑ 81 Travis Fryman .40 .15
❑ 82 Derek Jeter 2.50 1.00
❑ 83 Sammy Sosa 1.00 .40
❑ 84 Ivan Rodriguez .60 .25
❑ 85 Rafael Palmeiro .60 .25
❑ 86 Roger Clemens 2.00 .75
❑ 87 Jason Giambi .40 .15
❑ 88 Andres Galarraga .40 .15
❑ 89 Jermaine Dye .40 .15
❑ 90 Joe Carter .40 .15
❑ 91 Brady Anderson .40 .15
❑ 92 Derek Bell .40 .15
❑ 93 Randy Johnson 1.00 .40
❑ 94 Fred McGriff .60 .25
❑ 95 John Smoltz .60 .25
❑ 96 Harold Baines .40 .15
❑ 97 Raul Mondesi .40 .15
❑ 98 Tim Salmon .60 .25
❑ 99 Carlos Baerga .40 .15
❑ 100 Dante Bichette .40 .15
❑ 101 Vladimir Guerrero 1.00 .40
❑ 102 Richard Hidalgo .40 .15
❑ 103 Paul Konerko .60 .25
❑ 104 Alex Gonzalez RC 1.00 .40
❑ 105 Jason Dickson .40 .15
❑ 106 Jose Rosado .40 .15
❑ 107 Todd Walker .40 .15
❑ 108 Seth Greisinger RC .40 .15
❑ 109 Todd Helton 1.00 .40
❑ 110 Ben Davis .40 .15
❑ 111 Bartolo Colon .40 .15
❑ 112 Elieser Marrero .40 .15
❑ 113 Jeff D'Amico .40 .15
❑ 114 Miguel Tejada RC 4.00 1.50
❑ 115 Darin Erstad .40 .15
❑ 116 Kris Benson RC 1.00 .40
❑ 117 Adrian Beltre RC 3.00 1.25
❑ 118 Neifi Perez .40 .15
❑ 119 Pokey Reese .40 .15
❑ 120 Carl Pavano .40 .15
❑ 121 Juan Melo .40 .15
❑ 122 Kevin McGlinchy RC .40 .15
❑ 123 Pat Cline .40 .15
❑ 124 Felix Heredia RC .40 .15
❑ 125 Aaron Boone .40 .15
❑ 126 Glendon Rusch .40 .15
❑ 127 Mike Cameron .40 .15
❑ 128 Justin Thompson .40 .15
❑ 129 Chad Hermansen RC .40 .15
❑ 130 Sidney Ponson RC 1.00 .40
❑ 131 Willie Martinez RC .40 .15
❑ 132 Paul Wilder RC .40 .15
❑ 133 Geoff Jenkins .40 .15
❑ 134 Roy Halladay RC 4.00 1.50
❑ 135 Carlos Guillen .40 .15
❑ 136 Tony Batista .40 .15
❑ 137 Todd Greene .40 .15
❑ 138 Luis Castillo .40 .15
❑ 139 Jimmy Anderson RC .40 .15
❑ 140 Edgard Velazquez .40 .15
❑ 141 Chris Snopek .40 .15
❑ 142 Ruben Rivera .40 .15
❑ 143 Javier Valentin .40 .15
❑ 144 Brian Rose .40 .15
❑ 145 Fernando Tatis RC .40 .15
❑ 146 Dean Crow RC .40 .15
❑ 147 Karim Garcia .40 .15
❑ 148 Dante Powell .40 .15
❑ 149 Hideki Irabu RC .60 .25
❑ 150 Matt Morris .40 .15
❑ 151 Wes Helms .40 .15
❑ 152 Russ Johnson .40 .15
❑ 153 Jarrod Washburn .40 .15
❑ 154 Kerry Wood RC 4.00 1.50
❑ 155 Joe Fontenot RC .40 .15
❑ 156 Eugene Kingsale .40 .15
❑ 157 Terrence Long .40 .15
❑ 158 Calvin Maduro .40 .15
❑ 159 Jeff Suppan .40 .15
❑ 160 DaRond Stovall .40 .15
❑ 161 Mark Redman .40 .15
❑ 162 Ken Cloude RC .40 .15
❑ 163 Bobby Estalella .40 .15
❑ 164 Abraham Nunez RC .40 .15
❑ 165 Derrick Gibson .40 .15
❑ 166 Mike Drumright RC .40 .15
❑ 167 Katsuhiro Maeda .40 .15
❑ 168 Jeff Liefer .40 .15
❑ 169 Ben Grieve .40 .15
❑ 170 Bob Abreu .60 .25
❑ 171 Shannon Stewart .40 .15
❑ 172 Braden Looper RC .75 .30
❑ 173 Brant Brown .40 .15
❑ 174 Marlon Anderson .40 .15
❑ 175 Brad Fullmer .40 .15
❑ 176 Carlos Beltran 2.00 .75
❑ 177 Nomar Garciaparra 1.50 .60
❑ 178 Derrek Lee .60 .25
❑ 179 Valerio De Los Santos RC .40 .15
❑ 180 Dmitri Young .40 .15
❑ 181 Jamey Wright .40 .15
❑ 182 Hiram Bocachica RC .40 .15
❑ 183 Wilton Guerrero .40 .15
❑ 184 Chris Carpenter .40 .15
❑ 185 Scott Spiezio .40 .15
❑ 186 Andruw Jones .60 .25
❑ 187 Travis Lee RC .60 .25
❑ 188 Jose Cruz Jr. RC .60 .25
❑ 189 Jose Guillen .40 .15
❑ 190 Jeff Abbott .40 .15
❑ 191 Ricky Ledee RC .60 .25
❑ 192 Mike Sweeney .40 .15
❑ 193 Donnie Sadler .40 .15
❑ 194 Scott Rolen .60 .25
❑ 195 Kevin Orie .40 .15
❑ 196 Jason Conti RC .40 .15
❑ 197 Mark Kotsay RC 1.50 .60
❑ 198 Eric Milton RC .60 .25
❑ 199 Russell Branyan .40 .15
❑ 200 Alex Sanchez RC .60 .25

1998 Bowman's Best

❑ COMPLETE SET (200) 40.00 15.00
❑ 1 Mark McGwire 2.50 1.00
❑ 2 Jeromy Burnitz .40 .15
❑ 3 Barry Bonds 2.50 1.00
❑ 4 Dante Bichette .40 .15
❑ 5 Chipper Jones 1.00 .40
❑ 6 Frank Thomas 1.00 .40
❑ 7 Kevin Brown .60 .25
❑ 8 Juan Gonzalez .40 .15
❑ 9 Jay Buhner .40 .15
❑ 10 Chuck Knoblauch .40 .15
❑ 11 Cal Ripken 3.00 1.25
❑ 12 Matt Williams .40 .15
❑ 13 Jim Edmonds .40 .15
❑ 14 Manny Ramirez .60 .25
❑ 15 Tony Clark .40 .15
❑ 16 Mo Vaughn .40 .15
❑ 17 Bernie Williams .60 .25
❑ 18 Scott Rolen .60 .25
❑ 19 Gary Sheffield .40 .15
❑ 20 Albert Belle .40 .15
❑ 21 Mike Piazza 1.50 .60
❑ 22 John Olerud .40 .15
❑ 23 Tony Gwynn 1.25 .50
❑ 24 Jay Bell .40 .15
❑ 25 Jose Cruz Jr. .40 .15
❑ 26 Justin Thompson .40 .15
❑ 27 Ken Griffey Jr. 1.50 .60
❑ 28 Sandy Alomar Jr. .40 .15
❑ 29 Mark Grudzielanek .40 .15
❑ 30 Mark Grace .60 .25
❑ 31 Ron Gant .40 .15
❑ 32 Javy Lopez .40 .15
❑ 33 Jeff Bagwell .60 .25
❑ 34 Fred McGriff .60 .25
❑ 35 Rafael Palmeiro .60 .25
❑ 36 Vinny Castilla .40 .15
❑ 37 Andy Benes .40 .15
❑ 38 Pedro Martinez .60 .25
❑ 39 Andy Pettitte .60 .25
❑ 40 Marty Cordova .40 .15
❑ 41 Rusty Greer .40 .15
❑ 42 Kevin Orie .40 .15
❑ 43 Chan Ho Park .40 .15
❑ 44 Ryan Klesko .40 .15
❑ 45 Alex Rodriguez 1.50 .60
❑ 46 Travis Fryman .40 .15
❑ 47 Jeff King .40 .15
❑ 48 Roger Clemens 2.00 .75
❑ 49 Darin Erstad .40 .15
❑ 50 Brady Anderson .40 .15
❑ 51 Jason Kendall .40 .15
❑ 52 John Valentin .40 .15
❑ 53 Ellis Burks .40 .15
❑ 54 Brian Hunter .40 .15
❑ 55 Paul O'Neill .60 .25
❑ 56 Ken Caminiti .40 .15
❑ 57 David Justice .40 .15
❑ 58 Eric Karros .40 .15
❑ 59 Pat Hentgen .40 .15
❑ 60 Greg Maddux 1.50 .60
❑ 61 Craig Biggio .60 .25
❑ 62 Edgar Martinez .60 .25
❑ 63 Mike Mussina .60 .25
❑ 64 Larry Walker .40 .15
❑ 65 Tino Martinez .60 .25
❑ 66 Jim Thome .60 .25
❑ 67 Tom Glavine .60 .25
❑ 68 Raul Mondesi .40 .15
❑ 69 Marquis Grissom .40 .15
❑ 70 Randy Johnson 1.00 .40
❑ 71 Steve Finley .40 .15
❑ 72 Jose Guillen .40 .15
❑ 73 Nomar Garciaparra 1.50 .60
❑ 74 Wade Boggs .60 .25
❑ 75 Bobby Higginson .40 .15
❑ 76 Robin Ventura .40 .15

❑ 77 Derek Jeter 2.50 1.00
❑ 78 Andruw Jones .60 .25
❑ 79 Ray Lankford .40 .15
❑ 80 Vladimir Guerrero 1.00 .40
❑ 81 Kenny Lofton .40 .15
❑ 82 Ivan Rodriguez .60 .25
❑ 83 Neifi Perez .40 .15
❑ 84 John Smoltz .60 .25
❑ 85 Tim Salmon .60 .25
❑ 86 Carlos Delgado .40 .15
❑ 87 Sammy Sosa 1.00 .40
❑ 88 Jaret Wright .40 .15
❑ 89 Roberto Alomar .60 .25
❑ 90 Paul Molitor .40 .15
❑ 91 Dean Palmer .40 .15
❑ 92 Barry Larkin .60 .25
❑ 93 Jason Giambi .40 .15
❑ 94 Curt Schilling .40 .15
❑ 95 Eric Young .40 .15
❑ 96 Denny Neagle .40 .15
❑ 97 Moises Alou .40 .15
❑ 98 Livan Hernandez .40 .15
❑ 99 Todd Hundley .40 .15
❑ 100 Andres Galarraga .40 .15
❑ 101 Travis Lee .40 .15
❑ 102 Lance Berkman .40 .15
❑ 103 Orlando Cabrera .40 .15
❑ 104 Mike Lowell RC 3.00 1.25
❑ 105 Ben Grieve .40 .15
❑ 106 Jae Weong Seo RC .60 .25
❑ 107 Richie Sexson .40 .15
❑ 108 Eli Marrero .40 .15
❑ 109 Aramis Ramirez .40 .15
❑ 110 Paul Konerko .40 .15
❑ 111 Carl Pavano .40 .15
❑ 112 Brad Fullmer .40 .15
❑ 113 Matt Clement .40 .15
❑ 114 Donzell McDonald .40 .15
❑ 115 Todd Helton .60 .25
❑ 116 Mike Caruso .40 .15
❑ 117 Donnie Sadler .40 .15
❑ 118 Bruce Chen .40 .15
❑ 119 Jarrod Washburn .40 .15
❑ 120 Adrian Beltre .40 .15
❑ 121 Ryan Jackson RC .40 .15
❑ 122 Kevin Millar RC 1.50 .60
❑ 123 Corey Koskie RC 1.00 .40
❑ 124 Dermal Brown .40 .15
❑ 125 Kerry Wood .40 .15
❑ 126 Juan Melo .40 .15
❑ 127 Ramon Hernandez .40 .15
❑ 128 Roy Halladay .40 .15
❑ 129 Ron Wright .40 .15
❑ 130 Darnell McDonald RC .60 .25
❑ 131 Odalis Perez RC 1.50 .60
❑ 132 Alex Cora RC .60 .25
❑ 133 Justin Towle .40 .15
❑ 134 Juan Encarnacion .40 .15
❑ 135 Brian Rose .40 .15
❑ 136 Russell Branyan .40 .15
❑ 137 Cesar King RC .40 .15
❑ 138 Ruben Rivera .40 .15
❑ 139 Ricky Ledee .40 .15
❑ 140 Vernon Wells .40 .15
❑ 141 Luis Rivas RC 1.00 .40
❑ 142 Brent Butler .40 .15
❑ 143 Karim Garcia .40 .15
❑ 144 George Lombard .40 .15
❑ 145 Masato Yoshii RC .60 .25
❑ 146 Braden Looper .40 .15
❑ 147 Alex Sanchez .40 .15
❑ 148 Kris Benson .40 .15
❑ 149 Mark Kotsay .40 .15
❑ 150 Richard Hidalgo .40 .15
❑ 151 Scott Elarton .40 .15
❑ 152 Ryan Minor RC .40 .15
❑ 153 Troy Glaus RC 4.00 1.50
❑ 154 Carlos Lee RC 3.00 1.25
❑ 155 Michael Coleman .40 .15
❑ 156 Jason Grilli RC .40 .15
❑ 157 Julio Ramirez RC .40 .15
❑ 158 Randy Wolf RC .60 .25
❑ 159 Ryan Brannan .40 .15
❑ 160 Edgard Clemente .40 .15
❑ 161 Miguel Tejada 1.00 .40
❑ 162 Chad Hermansen .40 .15
❑ 163 Ryan Anderson RC .40 .15
❑ 164 Ben Petrick .40 .15
❑ 165 Alex Gonzalez .40 .15
❑ 166 Ben Davis .40 .15
❑ 167 John Patterson .40 .15
❑ 168 Cliff Politte .40 .15
❑ 169 Randall Simon .40 .15
❑ 170 Javier Vazquez .40 .15
❑ 171 Kevin Witt .40 .15
❑ 172 Geoff Jenkins .40 .15
❑ 173 David Ortiz 4.00 1.50
❑ 174 Derrick Gibson .40 .15
❑ 175 Abraham Nunez .40 .15
❑ 176 A.J. Hinch .40 .15
❑ 177 Ruben Mateo RC .40 .15
❑ 178 Magglio Ordonez RC 5.00 2.00
❑ 179 Todd Dunwoody .40 .15
❑ 180 Daryle Ward .40 .15
❑ 181 Mike Kinkade RC .40 .15
❑ 182 Willie Martinez .40 .15
❑ 183 Orlando Hernandez RC 2.00 .75
❑ 184 Eric Milton .40 .15
❑ 185 Eric Chavez .40 .15
❑ 186 Damian Jackson .40 .15
❑ 187 Jim Parque RC .60 .25
❑ 188 Dan Reichert RC .60 .25
❑ 189 Mike Drumright .40 .15
❑ 190 Todd Walker .40 .15
❑ 191 Shane Monahan .40 .15
❑ 192 Derrek Lee .60 .25
❑ 193 Jeremy Giambi RC .60 .25
❑ 194 Dan McKinley RC .40 .15
❑ 195 Tony Armas Jr. RC .60 .25
❑ 196 Matt Anderson RC .40 .15
❑ 197 Jim Chamblee RC .40 .15
❑ 198 Francisco Cordero RC 1.00 .40
❑ 199 Calvin Pickering .40 .15
❑ 200 Reggie Taylor .40 .15

1999 Bowman's Best

❑ COMPLETE SET (200) 40.00 15.00
❑ COMP.SET w/o SP's (150) 25.00 10.00
❑ COMMON CARD (1-150) .40 .15
❑ COMMON ROOKIE (151-200) .50 .20
❑ 1 Chipper Jones 1.00 .40
❑ 2 Brian Jordan .40 .15
❑ 3 David Justice .40 .15
❑ 4 Jason Kendall .40 .15
❑ 5 Mo Vaughn .40 .15
❑ 6 Jim Edmonds .40 .15
❑ 7 Wade Boggs .60 .25
❑ 8 Jeromy Burnitz .40 .15
❑ 9 Todd Hundley .40 .15
❑ 10 Rondell White .40 .15
❑ 11 Cliff Floyd .40 .15
❑ 12 Sean Casey .40 .15
❑ 13 Bernie Williams .60 .25
❑ 14 Dante Bichette .40 .15
❑ 15 Greg Vaughn .40 .15
❑ 16 Andres Galarraga .40 .15
❑ 17 Ray Durham .40 .15
❑ 18 Jim Thome .60 .25
❑ 19 Gary Sheffield .40 .15
❑ 20 Frank Thomas 1.00 .40
❑ 21 Orlando Hernandez .40 .15
❑ 22 Ivan Rodriguez .60 .25
❑ 23 Jose Cruz Jr. .40 .15
❑ 24 Jason Giambi .40 .15
❑ 25 Craig Biggio .60 .25
❑ 26 Kerry Wood .40 .15
❑ 27 Manny Ramirez .60 .25
❑ 28 Curt Schilling .40 .15
❑ 29 Mike Mussina .60 .25
❑ 30 Tim Salmon .60 .25
❑ 31 Mike Piazza 1.50 .60
❑ 32 Roberto Alomar .60 .25
❑ 33 Larry Walker .40 .15
❑ 34 Barry Larkin .60 .25
❑ 35 Nomar Garciaparra 1.50 .60
❑ 36 Paul O'Neill .60 .25
❑ 37 Todd Walker .40 .15
❑ 38 Eric Karros .40 .15
❑ 39 Brad Fullmer .40 .15
❑ 40 John Olerud .40 .15
❑ 41 Todd Helton .60 .25
❑ 42 Raul Mondesi .40 .15
❑ 43 Jose Canseco .60 .25
❑ 44 Matt Williams .40 .15
❑ 45 Ray Lankford .40 .15
❑ 46 Carlos Delgado .40 .15
❑ 47 Darin Erstad .40 .15
❑ 48 Vladimir Guerrero 1.00 .40
❑ 49 Robin Ventura .40 .15
❑ 50 Alex Rodriguez 1.50 .60
❑ 51 Vinny Castilla .40 .15
❑ 52 Tony Clark .40 .15
❑ 53 Pedro Martinez .60 .25
❑ 54 Rafael Palmeiro .60 .25
❑ 55 Scott Rolen .60 .25
❑ 56 Tino Martinez .60 .25
❑ 57 Tony Gwynn 1.25 .50
❑ 58 Barry Bonds 2.50 1.00
❑ 59 Kenny Lofton .40 .15
❑ 60 Javy Lopez .40 .15
❑ 61 Mark Grace .60 .25
❑ 62 Travis Lee .40 .15
❑ 63 Kevin Brown .60 .25
❑ 64 Al Leiter .40 .15
❑ 65 Albert Belle .40 .15
❑ 66 Sammy Sosa 1.00 .40
❑ 67 Greg Maddux 1.50 .60
❑ 68 Mark Kotsay .40 .15
❑ 69 Dmitri Young .40 .15
❑ 70 Mark McGwire 2.50 1.00
❑ 71 Juan Gonzalez .40 .15
❑ 72 Andruw Jones .60 .25
❑ 73 Derek Jeter 2.50 1.00
❑ 74 Randy Johnson 1.00 .40
❑ 75 Cal Ripken 3.00 1.25
❑ 76 Shawn Green .40 .15
❑ 77 Moises Alou .40 .15
❑ 78 Tom Glavine .60 .25
❑ 79 Sandy Alomar Jr. .40 .15
❑ 80 Ken Griffey Jr. 1.50 .60
❑ 81 Ryan Klesko .40 .15
❑ 82 Jeff Bagwell .60 .25
❑ 83 Ben Grieve .40 .15
❑ 84 John Smoltz .60 .25
❑ 85 Roger Clemens 2.00 .75
❑ 86 Ken Griffey Jr. BP 1.00 .40
❑ 87 Roger Clemens BP 1.00 .40
❑ 88 Derek Jeter BP 1.25 .50
❑ 89 Nomar Garciaparra BP .75 .30
❑ 90 Mark McGwire BP 1.25 .50
❑ 91 Sammy Sosa BP .60 .25
❑ 92 Alex Rodriguez BP .75 .30
❑ 93 Greg Maddux BP .75 .30
❑ 94 Vladimir Guerrero BP .60 .25
❑ 95 Chipper Jones BP .60 .25
❑ 96 Kerry Wood BP .40 .15
❑ 97 Ben Grieve BP .40 .15
❑ 98 Tony Gwynn BP .60 .25
❑ 99 Juan Gonzalez BP .40 .15
❑ 100 Mike Piazza BP .75 .30
❑ 101 Eric Chavez .40 .15
❑ 102 Billy Koch .40 .15
❑ 103 Dernell Stenson .40 .15
❑ 104 Marlon Anderson .40 .15
❑ 105 Ron Belliard .40 .15
❑ 106 Bruce Chen .40 .15
❑ 107 Carlos Beltran .60 .25
❑ 108 Chad Hermansen .40 .15
❑ 109 Ryan Anderson .40 .15
❑ 110 Michael Barrett .40 .15

❑ 111 Matt Clement .40 .15
❑ 112 Ben Davis .40 .15
❑ 113 Calvin Pickering .40 .15
❑ 114 Brad Penny .40 .15
❑ 115 Paul Konerko .40 .15
❑ 116 Alex Gonzalez .40 .15
❑ 117 George Lombard .40 .15
❑ 118 John Patterson .40 .15
❑ 119 Rob Bell .40 .15
❑ 120 Ruben Mateo .40 .15
❑ 121 Troy Glaus .60 .25
❑ 122 Ryan Bradley .40 .15
❑ 123 Carlos Lee .40 .15
❑ 124 Gabe Kapler .40 .15
❑ 125 Ramon Hernandez .40 .15
❑ 126 Carlos Febles .40 .15
❑ 127 Mitch Meluskey .40 .15
❑ 128 Michael Cuddyer .40 .15
❑ 129 Pablo Ozuna .40 .15
❑ 130 Jayson Werth .40 .15
❑ 131 Ricky Ledee .40 .15
❑ 132 Jeremy Giambi .40 .15
❑ 133 Danny Klassen .40 .15
❑ 134 Mark DeRosa .40 .15
❑ 135 Randy Wolf .40 .15
❑ 136 Roy Halladay .40 .15
❑ 137 Derrick Gibson .40 .15
❑ 138 Ben Petrick .40 .15
❑ 139 Warren Morris .40 .15
❑ 140 Lance Berkman .40 .15
❑ 141 Russell Branyan .40 .15
❑ 142 Adrian Beltre .40 .15
❑ 143 Juan Encarnacion .40 .15
❑ 144 Fernando Seguignol .40 .15
❑ 145 Corey Koskie .40 .15
❑ 146 Preston Wilson .40 .15
❑ 147 Homer Bush .40 .15
❑ 148 Daryle Ward .40 .15
❑ 149 Joe McEwing RC .60 .25
❑ 150 Peter Bergeron RC .50 .20
❑ 151 Pat Burrell RC 3.00 1.25
❑ 152 Choo Freeman RC .60 .25
❑ 153 Matt Belisle RC .50 .20
❑ 154 Carlos Pena RC .75 .30
❑ 155 A.J. Burnett RC 1.50 .60
❑ 156 Doug Mientkiewicz RC 1.00 .40
❑ 157 Sean Burroughs RC 1.00 .40
❑ 158 Mike Zywica RC .50 .20
❑ 159 Corey Patterson RC 1.50 .60
❑ 160 Austin Kearns RC 3.00 1.25
❑ 161 Chip Ambres RC .50 .20
❑ 162 Kelly Dransfeldt RC .50 .20
❑ 163 Mike Nannini RC .50 .20
❑ 164 Mark Mulder RC 2.50 1.00
❑ 165 Jason Tyner RC .50 .20
❑ 166 Bobby Seay RC .50 .20
❑ 167 Alex Escobar RC .60 .25
❑ 168 Nick Johnson RC 1.50 .60
❑ 169 Alfonso Soriano RC 8.00 3.00
❑ 170 Clayton Andrews RC .50 .20
❑ 171 C.C. Sabathia RC 4.00 1.50
❑ 172 Matt Holliday RC 8.00 3.00
❑ 173 Brad Lidge RC 4.00 1.50
❑ 174 Kit Pellow RC .50 .20
❑ 175 J.M. Gold RC .50 .20
❑ 176 Roosevelt Brown RC .50 .20
❑ 177 Eric Valent RC .60 .25
❑ 178 Adam Everett RC 1.00 .40
❑ 179 Jorge Toca RC .60 .25
❑ 180 Matt Roney RC .50 .20
❑ 181 Andy Brown RC .50 .20
❑ 182 Phil Norton RC .50 .20
❑ 183 Mickey Lopez RC .50 .20
❑ 184 Chris George RC .50 .20
❑ 185 Arturo McDowell RC .50 .20
❑ 186 Jose Fernandez RC .50 .20
❑ 187 Seth Etherton RC .50 .20
❑ 188 Josh McKinley RC .50 .20
❑ 189 Nate Cornejo RC .50 .20
❑ 190 Giuseppe Chiaramonte RC .50 .20
❑ 191 Mamon Tucker RC .50 .20
❑ 192 Ryan Mills RC .50 .20
❑ 193 Chad Moeller RC .50 .20
❑ 194 Tony Torcato RC .50 .20
❑ 195 Jeff Winchester RC .50 .20
❑ 196 Rick Elder RC .50 .20
❑ 197 Matt Burch RC .60 .25
❑ 198 Jeff Urban RC .60 .25
❑ 199 Chris Jones RC .50 .20
❑ 200 Masao Kida RC .60 .25

2000 Bowman's Best

❑ COMP.SET w/o RC's (150) 40.00 15.00
❑ COMMON CARD (1-150) .40 .15
❑ COMMON ROOKIE (151-200) 5.00 2.00
❑ 1 Nomar Garciaparra 1.50 .60
❑ 2 Chipper Jones 1.00 .40
❑ 3 Tony Clark .40 .15
❑ 4 Bernie Williams .60 .25
❑ 5 Barry Bonds 2.50 1.00
❑ 6 Jermaine Dye .40 .15
❑ 7 John Olerud .40 .15
❑ 8 Mike Hampton .40 .15
❑ 9 Cal Ripken 3.00 1.25
❑ 10 Jeff Bagwell .60 .25
❑ 11 Troy Glaus .40 .15
❑ 12 J.D. Drew .40 .15
❑ 13 Jeromy Burnitz .40 .15
❑ 14 Carlos Delgado .40 .15
❑ 15 Shawn Green .40 .15
❑ 16 Kevin Millwood .40 .15
❑ 17 Rondell White .40 .15
❑ 18 Scott Rolen .60 .25
❑ 19 Jeff Cirillo .40 .15
❑ 20 Barry Larkin .60 .25
❑ 21 Brian Giles .40 .15
❑ 22 Roger Clemens 2.00 .75
❑ 23 Manny Ramirez .60 .25
❑ 24 Alex Gonzalez .40 .15
❑ 25 Mark Grace .60 .25
❑ 26 Fernando Tatis .40 .15
❑ 27 Randy Johnson 1.00 .40
❑ 28 Roger Cedeno .40 .15
❑ 29 Brian Jordan .40 .15
❑ 30 Kevin Brown .40 .15
❑ 31 Greg Vaughn .40 .15
❑ 32 Roberto Alomar .60 .25
❑ 33 Larry Walker .40 .15
❑ 34 Rafael Palmeiro .60 .25
❑ 35 Curt Schilling .40 .15
❑ 36 Orlando Hernandez .40 .15
❑ 37 Todd Walker .40 .15
❑ 38 Juan Gonzalez .40 .15
❑ 39 Sean Casey .40 .15
❑ 40 Tony Gwynn 1.25 .50
❑ 41 Albert Belle .40 .15
❑ 42 Gary Sheffield .40 .15
❑ 43 Michael Barrett .40 .15
❑ 44 Preston Wilson .40 .15
❑ 45 Jim Thome .60 .25
❑ 46 Shannon Stewart .40 .15
❑ 47 Mo Vaughn .40 .15
❑ 48 Ben Grieve .40 .15
❑ 49 Adrian Beltre .40 .15
❑ 50 Sammy Sosa 1.00 .40
❑ 51 Bob Abreu .40 .15
❑ 52 Edgardo Alfonzo .40 .15
❑ 53 Carlos Febles .40 .15
❑ 54 Frank Thomas 1.00 .40
❑ 55 Alex Rodriguez 1.50 .60
❑ 56 Cliff Floyd .40 .15
❑ 57 Jose Canseco .60 .25
❑ 58 Erubiel Durazo .40 .15
❑ 59 Tim Hudson .40 .15
❑ 60 Craig Biggio .60 .25
❑ 61 Eric Karros .40 .15
❑ 62 Mike Mussina .60 .25
❑ 63 Robin Ventura .40 .15
❑ 64 Carlos Beltran .40 .15
❑ 65 Pedro Martinez .60 .25
❑ 66 Gabe Kapler .40 .15
❑ 67 Jason Kendall .40 .15
❑ 68 Derek Jeter 2.50 1.00
❑ 69 Magglio Ordonez .40 .15
❑ 70 Mike Piazza 1.50 .60
❑ 71 Mike Lieberthal .40 .15
❑ 72 Andres Galarraga .40 .15
❑ 73 Raul Mondesi .40 .15
❑ 74 Eric Chavez .40 .15
❑ 75 Greg Maddux 1.50 .60
❑ 76 Matt Williams .40 .15
❑ 77 Kris Benson .40 .15
❑ 78 Ivan Rodriguez .60 .25
❑ 79 Pokey Reese .40 .15
❑ 80 Vladimir Guerrero 1.00 .40
❑ 81 Mark McGwire 2.50 1.00
❑ 82 Vinny Castilla .40 .15
❑ 83 Todd Helton .60 .25
❑ 84 Andruw Jones .60 .25
❑ 85 Ken Griffey Jr. 1.50 .60
❑ 86 Mark McGwire BP 1.25 .50
❑ 87 Derek Jeter BP 1.25 .50
❑ 88 Chipper Jones BP .60 .25
❑ 89 Nomar Garciaparra BP 1.00 .40
❑ 90 Sammy Sosa BP .60 .25
❑ 91 Cal Ripken BP 1.50 .60
❑ 92 Juan Gonzalez BP .40 .15
❑ 93 Alex Rodriguez BP 1.00 .40
❑ 94 Barry Bonds BP 1.25 .50
❑ 95 Sean Casey BP .40 .15
❑ 96 Vladimir Guerrero BP .60 .25
❑ 97 Mike Piazza BP 1.00 .40
❑ 98 Shawn Green BP .40 .15
❑ 99 Jeff Bagwell BP .40 .15
❑ 100 Ken Griffey Jr. BP 1.00 .40
❑ 101 Rick Ankiel .40 .15
❑ 102 John Patterson .40 .15
❑ 103 David Walling .40 .15
❑ 104 Michael Restovich .40 .15
❑ 105 A.J. Burnett .40 .15
❑ 106 Pablo Ozuna .40 .15
❑ 107 Chad Hermansen .40 .15
❑ 108 Choo Freeman .40 .15
❑ 109 Mark Quinn .40 .15
❑ 110 Corey Patterson .40 .15
❑ 111 Ramon Ortiz .40 .15
❑ 112 Vernon Wells .40 .15
❑ 113 Milton Bradley .40 .15
❑ 114 Gookie Dawkins .40 .15
❑ 115 Sean Burroughs .40 .15
❑ 116 Wily Mo Pena .40 .15
❑ 117 Dee Brown .40 .15
❑ 118 C.C. Sabathia .40 .15
❑ 119 Adam Kennedy .40 .15
❑ 120 Octavio Dotel .40 .15
❑ 121 Kip Wells .40 .15
❑ 122 Ben Petrick .40 .15
❑ 123 Mark Mulder .40 .15
❑ 124 Jason Standridge .40 .15
❑ 125 Adam Platt .40 .15
❑ 126 Steve Lomasney .40 .15
❑ 127 Jayson Werth .40 .15
❑ 128 Alex Escobar .40 .15
❑ 129 Ryan Anderson .40 .15
❑ 130 Adam Dunn 1.00 .40
❑ 131 Ted Lilly .40 .15
❑ 132 Brad Penny .40 .15
❑ 133 Daryle Ward .40 .15
❑ 134 Eric Munson .40 .15
❑ 135 Nick Johnson .40 .15
❑ 136 Jason Jennings .40 .15
❑ 137 Tim Raines Jr. .40 .15
❑ 138 Ruben Mateo .40 .15
❑ 139 Jack Cust .40 .15
❑ 140 Rafael Furcal .40 .15
❑ 141 Eric Gagne 1.00 .40
❑ 142 Tony Armas Jr. .40 .15
❑ 143 Mike Paradis .40 .15
❑ 144 Peter Bergeron .40 .15
❑ 145 Alfonso Soriano 1.00 .40

❑ 146 Josh Hamilton 1.50 .60
❑ 147 Michael Cuddyer .40 .15
❑ 148 Jay Gehrke .40 .15
❑ 149 Josh Girdley .40 .15
❑ 150 Pat Burrell .40 .15
❑ 151 Brett Myers RC 12.00 5.00
❑ 152 Scott Seabol RC 5.00 2.00
❑ 153 Keith Reed RC 5.00 2.00
❑ 154 Francisco Rodriguez RC 20.00 8.00
❑ 155 Barry Zito RC 30.00 12.50
❑ 156 Pat Manning RC 5.00 2.00
❑ 157 Ben Christensen RC 5.00 2.00
❑ 158 Corey Myers RC 5.00 2.00
❑ 159 Wascar Serrano RC 5.00 2.00
❑ 160 Wes Anderson RC 5.00 2.00
❑ 161 Andy Tracy RC 5.00 2.00
❑ 162 Cesar Saba RC 5.00 2.00
❑ 163 Mike Lamb RC 8.00 3.00
❑ 164 Bobby Bradley RC 5.00 2.00
❑ 165 Vince Faison RC 5.00 2.00
❑ 166 Ty Howington RC 5.00 2.00
❑ 167 Ken Harvey RC 5.00 2.00
❑ 168 Josh Kalinowski RC 5.00 2.00
❑ 169 Ruben Salazar RC 5.00 2.00
❑ 170 Aaron Rowand RC 10.00 4.00
❑ 171 Ramon Santiago RC 5.00 2.00
❑ 172 Scott Sobkowiak RC 5.00 2.00
❑ 173 Lyle Overbay RC 8.00 3.00
❑ 174 Rico Washington RC 5.00 2.00
❑ 175 Rick Asadoorian RC 5.00 2.00
❑ 176 Matt Ginter RC 5.00 2.00
❑ 177 Jason Stumm RC 5.00 2.00
❑ 178 B.J. Garbe RC 5.00 2.00
❑ 179 Mike MacDougal RC 5.00 2.00
❑ 180 Ryan Christianson RC 5.00 2.00
❑ 181 Kurt Ainsworth RC 5.00 2.00
❑ 182 Brad Baisley RC 5.00 2.00
❑ 183 Ben Broussard RC 12.00 5.00
❑ 184 Aaron McNeal RC 5.00 2.00
❑ 185 John Sneed RC 5.00 2.00
❑ 186 Junior Brignac RC 5.00 2.00
❑ 187 Chance Caple RC 5.00 2.00
❑ 188 Scott Downs RC 5.00 2.00
❑ 189 Matt Cepicky RC 5.00 2.00
❑ 190 Chin-Feng Chen RC 30.00 15.00
❑ 191 Johan Santana RC 80.00 40.00
❑ 192 Brad Baker RC 5.00 2.00
❑ 193 Jason Repko RC 8.00 3.00
❑ 194 Craig Dingman RC 5.00 2.00
❑ 195 Chris Wakeland RC 5.00 2.00
❑ 196 Rogelio Arias RC 5.00 2.00
❑ 197 Luis Matos RC 5.00 2.00
❑ 198 Rob Ramsay 5.00 2.00
❑ 199 Willie Bloomquist RC 30.00 15.00
❑ 200 Tony Pena Jr. RC 5.00 2.00

2001 Bowman's Best

❑ COMP.SET w/o SP's (150) 50.00 20.00
❑ COMMON CARD (1-150) .40 .15
❑ COMMON CARD (151-200) 5.00 2.00
❑ 1 Vladimir Guerrero 1.00 .40
❑ 2 Miguel Tejada .40 .15
❑ 3 Geoff Jenkins .40 .15
❑ 4 Jeff Bagwell .60 .25
❑ 5 Todd Helton .60 .25
❑ 6 Ken Griffey Jr. 1.50 .60
❑ 7 Nomar Garciaparra 1.50 .60
❑ 8 Chipper Jones 1.00 .40
❑ 9 Darin Erstad .40 .15
❑ 10 Frank Thomas 1.00 .40
❑ 11 Jim Thome .60 .25
❑ 12 Preston Wilson .40 .15
❑ 13 Kevin Brown .40 .15
❑ 14 Derek Jeter 2.50 1.00
❑ 15 Scott Rolen .60 .25
❑ 16 Ryan Klesko .40 .15
❑ 17 Jeff Kent .40 .15
❑ 18 Raul Mondesi .40 .15
❑ 19 Greg Vaughn .40 .15
❑ 20 Bernie Williams .60 .25
❑ 21 Mike Piazza 1.50 .60
❑ 22 Richard Hidalgo .40 .15
❑ 23 Dean Palmer .40 .15
❑ 24 Roberto Alomar .60 .25
❑ 25 Sammy Sosa 1.00 .40
❑ 26 Randy Johnson 1.00 .40
❑ 27 Manny Ramirez Sox .60 .25
❑ 28 Roger Clemens 2.00 .75
❑ 29 Terrence Long .40 .15
❑ 30 Jason Kendall .40 .15
❑ 31 Richie Sexson .40 .15
❑ 32 David Wells .40 .15
❑ 33 Andruw Jones .60 .25
❑ 34 Pokey Reese .40 .15
❑ 35 Juan Gonzalez .40 .15
❑ 36 Carlos Beltran .40 .15
❑ 37 Shawn Green .40 .15
❑ 38 Mariano Rivera 1.00 .40
❑ 39 John Olerud .40 .15
❑ 40 Jim Edmonds .40 .15
❑ 41 Andres Galarraga .40 .15
❑ 42 Carlos Delgado .40 .15
❑ 43 Kris Benson .40 .15
❑ 44 Andy Pettitte .60 .25
❑ 45 Jeff Cirillo .40 .15
❑ 46 Magglio Ordonez .40 .15
❑ 47 Tom Glavine .60 .25
❑ 48 Garret Anderson .40 .15
❑ 49 Cal Ripken 3.00 1.25
❑ 50 Pedro Martinez .60 .25
❑ 51 Barry Bonds 2.50 1.00
❑ 52 Alex Rodriguez 1.50 .60
❑ 53 Ben Grieve .40 .15
❑ 54 Edgar Martinez .60 .25
❑ 55 Jason Giambi .40 .15
❑ 56 Jeromy Burnitz .40 .15
❑ 57 Mike Mussina .60 .25
❑ 58 Moises Alou .40 .15
❑ 59 Sean Casey .40 .15
❑ 60 Greg Maddux 1.50 .60
❑ 61 Tim Hudson .40 .15
❑ 62 Mark McGwire 2.50 1.00
❑ 63 Rafael Palmeiro .60 .25
❑ 64 Tony Batista .40 .15
❑ 65 Kazuhiro Sasaki .40 .15
❑ 66 Jorge Posada .60 .25
❑ 67 Johnny Damon .60 .25
❑ 68 Brian Giles .40 .15
❑ 69 Jose Vidro .40 .15
❑ 70 Jermaine Dye .40 .15
❑ 71 Craig Biggio .60 .25
❑ 72 Larry Walker .40 .15
❑ 73 Eric Chavez .40 .15
❑ 74 David Segui .40 .15
❑ 75 Tim Salmon .60 .25
❑ 76 Javy Lopez .40 .15
❑ 77 Paul Konerko .40 .15
❑ 78 Barry Larkin .60 .25
❑ 79 Mike Hampton .40 .15
❑ 80 Bobby Higginson .40 .15
❑ 81 Mark Mulder .40 .15
❑ 82 Pat Burrell .40 .15
❑ 83 Kerry Wood .40 .15
❑ 84 J.T. Snow .40 .15
❑ 85 Ivan Rodriguez .60 .25
❑ 86 Edgardo Alfonzo .40 .15
❑ 87 Orlando Hernandez .40 .15
❑ 88 Gary Sheffield .40 .15
❑ 89 Mike Sweeney .40 .15
❑ 90 Carlos Lee .40 .15
❑ 91 Rafael Furcal .40 .15
❑ 92 Troy Glaus .40 .15
❑ 93 Bartolo Colon .40 .15
❑ 94 Cliff Floyd .40 .15
❑ 95 Barry Zito .60 .25
❑ 96 J.D. Drew .40 .15
❑ 97 Eric Karros .40 .15
❑ 98 Jose Valentin .40 .15
❑ 99 Ellis Burks .40 .15
❑ 100 David Justice .40 .15
❑ 101 Larry Barnes .40 .15
❑ 102 Rod Barajas .40 .15
❑ 103 Tony Pena Jr. .40 .15
❑ 104 Jerry Hairston Jr. .40 .15
❑ 105 Keith Ginter .40 .15
❑ 106 Corey Patterson .40 .15
❑ 107 Aaron Rowand .40 .15
❑ 108 Miguel Olivo .40 .15
❑ 109 Gookie Dawkins .40 .15
❑ 110 C.C. Sabathia .40 .15
❑ 111 Ben Petrick .40 .15
❑ 112 Eric Munson .40 .15
❑ 113 Ramon Castro .40 .15
❑ 114 Alex Escobar .40 .15
❑ 115 Josh Hamilton .75 .30
❑ 116 Jason Marquis .40 .15
❑ 117 Ben Davis .40 .15
❑ 118 Alex Cintron .40 .15
❑ 119 Julio Zuleta .40 .15
❑ 120 Ben Broussard .40 .15
❑ 121 Adam Everett .40 .15
❑ 122 Ramon Carvajal RC .40 .15
❑ 123 Felipe Lopez .40 .15
❑ 124 Alfonso Soriano .60 .25
❑ 125 Jayson Werth .40 .15
❑ 126 Donzell McDonald .40 .15
❑ 127 Jason Hart .40 .15
❑ 128 Joe Crede 1.00 .40
❑ 129 Sean Burroughs .40 .15
❑ 130 Jack Cust .40 .15
❑ 131 Corey Smith .40 .15
❑ 132 Adrian Gonzalez .40 .15
❑ 133 J.R. House .40 .15
❑ 134 Steve Lomasney .40 .15
❑ 135 Tim Raines Jr. .40 .15
❑ 136 Tony Alvarez .40 .15
❑ 137 Doug Mientkiewicz .40 .15
❑ 138 Rocco Baldelli .40 .15
❑ 139 Jason Romano .40 .15
❑ 140 Vernon Wells .40 .15
❑ 141 Mike Bynum .40 .15
❑ 142 Xavier Nady .40 .15
❑ 143 Brad Wilkerson .40 .15
❑ 144 Ben Diggins .40 .15
❑ 145 Aubrey Huff .40 .15
❑ 146 Eric Byrnes .40 .15
❑ 147 Alex Gordon .40 .15
❑ 148 Roy Oswalt 1.00 .40
❑ 149 Brian Esposito .40 .15
❑ 150 Scott Seabol .40 .15
❑ 151 Erick Almonte RC 5.00 2.00
❑ 152 Gary Johnson RC 5.00 2.00
❑ 153 Pedro Liriano RC 5.00 2.00
❑ 154 Matt White RC 5.00 2.00
❑ 156 Brad Cresse 5.00 2.00
❑ 157 Wilson Betemit RC 8.00 3.00
❑ 158 Octavio Martinez RC 5.00 2.00
❑ 159 Adam Pettyjohn RC 5.00 2.00
❑ 160 Corey Spencer RC 5.00 2.00
❑ 161 Mark Burnett RC 5.00 2.00
❑ 162 Ichiro Suzuki RC 50.00 25.00
❑ 163 Alexis Gomez RC 5.00 2.00
❑ 164 Greg Nash RC 5.00 2.00
❑ 165 Roberto Miniel RC 5.00 2.00
❑ 166 Justin Morneau RC 40.00 20.00
❑ 167 Ben Washburn RC 5.00 2.00
❑ 168 Bob Keppel RC 5.00 2.00
❑ 169 Deivi Mendez RC 5.00 2.00
❑ 170 Tsuyoshi Shinjo RC 8.00 3.00
❑ 171 Jared Abruzzo RC 5.00 2.00
❑ 172 Derrick Van Dusen RC 5.00 2.00
❑ 173 Hee Seop Choi RC 8.00 3.00
❑ 174 Albert Pujols RC 250.00 125.00
❑ 175 Travis Hafner RC 30.00 15.00
❑ 176 Ron Davenport RC 5.00 2.00
❑ 177 Luis Torres RC 5.00 2.00
❑ 178 Jake Peavy RC 25.00 10.00
❑ 179 Elvis Corporan RC 5.00 2.00
❑ 180 Dave Krynzel 5.00 2.00
❑ 181 Tony Blanco RC 5.00 2.00

❑ 182 Elpidio Guzman RC 5.00 2.00
❑ 183 Matt Butler RC 5.00 2.00
❑ 184 Joe Thurston RC 5.00 2.00
❑ 185 Andy Beal RC 5.00 2.00
❑ 186 Kevin Nulton RC 5.00 2.00
❑ 187 Sneideer Santos RC 5.00 2.00
❑ 188 Joe Dillon RC 5.00 2.00
❑ 189 Jeremy Blevins RC 5.00 2.00
❑ 190 Chris Amador RC 5.00 2.00
❑ 191 Mark Hendrickson RC 5.00 2.00
❑ 192 Willy Aybar RC 15.00 6.00
❑ 193 Antoine Cameron RC 5.00 2.00
❑ 194 J.J. Johnson RC 5.00 2.00
❑ 195 Ryan Kotchner RC 5.00 2.00
❑ 196 Bjorn Ivy RC 5.00 2.00
❑ 197 Josh Kroeger RC 5.00 2.00
❑ 198 Ty Wigginton RC 8.00 3.00
❑ 199 Stubby Clapp RC 5.00 2.00
❑ 200 Jerrod Riggan RC 5.00 2.00

2002 Bowman's Best

❑ COMP.SET w/o SP's (90) 100.00 40.00
❑ COMMON CARD (1-90) .75 .30
❑ COMMON AUTO A (91-180) 8.00 3.00
❑ AUTO GROUP A ODDS 1:3
❑ COMMON AUTO B (91-180) 10.00 4.00
❑ AUTO GROUP B ODDS 1:19
❑ COMMON BAT (91-180) 5.00 2.00
❑ 91-180 BAT STATED ODDS 1:5
❑ 181 ISHII BAT EXCHANGE ODDS 1:131
❑ 1 Josh Beckett .75 .30
❑ 2 Derek Jeter 5.00 2.00
❑ 3 Alex Rodriguez 3.00 1.25
❑ 4 Miguel Tejada .75 .30
❑ 5 Nomar Garciaparra 3.00 1.25
❑ 6 Aramis Ramirez .75 .30
❑ 7 Jeremy Giambi .75 .30
❑ 8 Bernie Williams 1.25 .50
❑ 9 Juan Pierre .75 .30
❑ 10 Chipper Jones 2.00 .75
❑ 11 Jimmy Rollins .75 .30
❑ 12 Alfonso Soriano .75 .30
❑ 13 Mark Prior 1.25 .50
❑ 14 Paul Konerko .75 .30
❑ 15 Tim Hudson .75 .30
❑ 16 Doug Mientkiewicz .75 .30
❑ 17 Todd Helton 1.25 .50
❑ 18 Moises Alou .75 .30
❑ 19 Juan Gonzalez .75 .30
❑ 20 Jorge Posada 1.25 .50
❑ 21 Jeff Kent .75 .30
❑ 22 Roger Clemens 4.00 1.50
❑ 23 Phil Nevin .75 .30
❑ 24 Brian Giles .75 .30
❑ 25 Carlos Delgado .75 .30
❑ 26 Jason Giambi .75 .30
❑ 27 Vladimir Guerrero 2.00 .75
❑ 28 Cliff Floyd .75 .30
❑ 29 Shea Hillenbrand .75 .30
❑ 30 Ken Griffey Jr. 3.00 1.25
❑ 31 Mike Piazza 3.00 1.25
❑ 32 Carlos Pena .75 .30
❑ 33 Larry Walker .75 .30
❑ 34 Magglio Ordonez .75 .30
❑ 35 Mike Mussina 1.25 .50
❑ 36 Andruw Jones 1.25 .50
❑ 37 Nick Johnson .75 .30
❑ 38 Curt Schilling .75 .30
❑ 39 Eric Chavez .75 .30
❑ 40 Bartolo Colon .75 .30
❑ 41 Eric Hinske .75 .30
❑ 42 Sean Burroughs .75 .30
❑ 43 Randy Johnson 2.00 .75
❑ 44 Adam Dunn .75 .30
❑ 45 Pedro Martinez 1.25 .50
❑ 46 Garret Anderson .75 .30
❑ 47 Jim Thome 1.25 .50
❑ 48 Gary Sheffield .75 .30
❑ 49 Tsuyoshi Shinjo .75 .30
❑ 50 Albert Pujols 4.00 1.50
❑ 51 Ichiro Suzuki 4.00 1.50
❑ 52 C.C. Sabathia .75 .30
❑ 53 Bobby Abreu .75 .30
❑ 54 Ivan Rodriguez 1.25 .50
❑ 55 J.D. Drew .75 .30
❑ 56 Jacque Jones .75 .30
❑ 57 Jason Kendall .75 .30
❑ 58 Javier Vazquez .75 .30
❑ 59 Jeff Bagwell 1.25 .50
❑ 60 Greg Maddux 3.00 1.25
❑ 61 Jim Edmonds .75 .30
❑ 62 Hank Blalock 1.25 .50
❑ 63 Jose Vidro .75 .30
❑ 64 Kevin Brown .75 .30
❑ 65 Mark Teixeira 2.00 .75
❑ 66 Sammy Sosa 2.00 .75
❑ 67 Lance Berkman .75 .30
❑ 68 Mark Mulder .75 .30
❑ 69 Marty Cordova .75 .30
❑ 70 Frank Thomas 2.00 .75
❑ 71 Mike Cameron .75 .30
❑ 72 Mike Sweeney .75 .30
❑ 73 Barry Bonds 5.00 2.00
❑ 74 Troy Glaus .75 .30
❑ 75 Barry Zito .75 .30
❑ 76 Pat Burrell .75 .30
❑ 77 Paul LoDuca .75 .30
❑ 78 Rafael Palmeiro 1.25 .50
❑ 79 Austin Kearns .75 .30
❑ 80 Darin Erstad .75 .30
❑ 81 Richie Sexson .75 .30
❑ 82 Roberto Alomar 1.25 .50
❑ 83 Roy Oswalt .75 .30
❑ 84 Ryan Klesko .75 .30
❑ 85 Luis Gonzalez .75 .30
❑ 86 Scott Rolen 1.25 .50
❑ 87 Shannon Stewart .75 .30
❑ 88 Shawn Green .75 .30
❑ 89 Toby Hall .75 .30
❑ 90 Bret Boone .75 .30
❑ 91 Casey Kotchman Bat RC 8.00 3.00
❑ 92 Jose Valverde AU A RC 8.00 3.00
❑ 93 Cole Barthel Bat RC 5.00 2.00
❑ 94 Brad Nelson AU A RC 8.00 3.00
❑ 95 Mauricio Lara AU A RC 8.00 3.00
❑ 96 Ryan Gripp Bat RC 5.00 2.00
❑ 97 Brian West AU A RC 8.00 3.00
❑ 98 Chris Piersoll AU B RC 10.00 4.00
❑ 99 Ryan Church AU B RC 15.00 6.00
❑ 100 Javier Colina AU A 8.00 3.00
❑ 101 Juan M. Gonzalez AU A RC 8.00 3.00
❑ 102 Benito Baez AU A 8.00 3.00
❑ 103 Mike Hill Bat RC 5.00 2.00
❑ 104 Jason Grove AU B RC 10.00 4.00
❑ 105 Koyie Hill AU B 10.00 4.00
❑ 106 Mark Outlaw AU A RC 8.00 3.00
❑ 107 Jason Bay Bat RC 25.00 10.00
❑ 108 Jorge Padilla AU A RC 8.00 3.00
❑ 109 Pete Zamora AU A RC 8.00 3.00
❑ 110 Joe Mauer AU A RC 80.00 40.00
❑ 111 Franklyn German AU A RC 8.00 3.00
❑ 112 Chris Flinn AU A RC 8.00 3.00
❑ 113 David Wright Bat RC 80.00 50.00
❑ 114 Anastacio Martinez AU A RC 8.00 3.00
❑ 115 Nic Jackson Bat RC 5.00 2.00
❑ 116 Rene Reyes AU A RC 8.00 3.00
❑ 117 Colin Young AU A RC 8.00 3.00
❑ 118 Joe Orloski AU A RC 8.00 3.00
❑ 119 Mike Wilson AU A RC 8.00 3.00
❑ 120 Rich Thompson AU A RC 8.00 3.00
❑ 121 Jake Mauer AU B RC 10.00 4.00
❑ 122 Mario Ramos AU A RC 8.00 3.00
❑ 123 Doug Sessions AU B RC 10.00 4.00
❑ 124 Doug Devore Bat RC 5.00 2.00
❑ 125 Travis Foley AU A RC 8.00 3.00
❑ 126 Chris Baker AU A RC 8.00 3.00
❑ 127 Michael Floyd AU A RC 8.00 3.00
❑ 128 Josh Barfield Bat RC 10.00 4.00
❑ 129 Jose Bautista Bat RC 8.00 3.00
❑ 130 Gavin Floyd AU A RC 15.00 6.00
❑ 131 Jason Botts Bat RC 5.00 2.00
❑ 132 Clint Nageotte AU A RC 10.00 4.00
❑ 133 Jesus Cota AU B RC 10.00 4.00
❑ 134 Ron Calloway Bat RC 5.00 2.00
❑ 135 Kevin Cash Bat RC 5.00 2.00
❑ 136 Jonny Gomes AU B RC 25.00 10.00
❑ 137 Dennis Ulacia AU A RC 8.00 3.00
❑ 138 Ryan Snare AU A RC 8.00 3.00
❑ 139 Kevin Deaton AU A RC 8.00 3.00
❑ 140 Bobby Jenks AU B RC 15.00 6.00
❑ 141 Casey Kotchman AU A RC 15.00 6.00
❑ 142 Adam Walker AU A RC 8.00 3.00
❑ 143 Mike Gonzalez AU A RC 8.00 3.00
❑ 144 Ruben Gotay Bat RC 8.00 3.00
❑ 145 Jason Grove Bat RC 5.00 2.00
❑ 146 Freddy Sanchez AU B RC 30.00 12.50
❑ 147 Jason Arnold AU B RC 10.00 4.00
❑ 148 Scott Hairston AU A RC 10.00 4.00
❑ 149 Jason St. Clair AU B RC 10.00 4.00
❑ 150 Chris Tritle Bat RC 5.00 2.00
❑ 151 Edwin Yan Bat RC 5.00 2.00
❑ 152 Freddy Sanchez Bat RC 12.00 5.00
❑ 153 Greg Sain Bat RC 5.00 2.00
❑ 154 Yurendell De Caster Bat RC 5.00 2.00
❑ 155 Noochie Varner Bat RC 5.00 2.00
❑ 156 Nelson Castro AU B RC 10.00 4.00
❑ 157 Randall Shelley Bat RC 5.00 2.00
❑ 158 Reed Johnson Bat RC 8.00 3.00
❑ 159 Ryan Raburn AU A RC 8.00 3.00
❑ 160 Jose Morban Bat RC 5.00 2.00
❑ 161 Justin Schuda AU A RC 8.00 3.00
❑ 162 Henry Pichardo AU A RC 8.00 3.00
❑ 163 Josh Bard AU A RC 8.00 3.00
❑ 164 Josh Bonifay AU A RC 8.00 3.00
❑ 165 Brandon League AU B RC 10.00 4.00
❑ 166 Jor-Jul DePaula AU A RC 8.00 3.00
❑ 167 Todd Linden AU B RC 15.00 6.00
❑ 168 Francisco Liriano AU A RC 120.00 60.00
❑ 169 Chris Snelling AU A RC 12.00 5.00
❑ 170 Blake McGinley AU A RC 8.00 3.00
❑ 171 Cody McKay AU A RC 8.00 3.00
❑ 172 Jason Stanford AU A RC 8.00 3.00
❑ 173 Lenny Dinardo AU A RC 8.00 3.00
❑ 174 Greg Montalbano AU A RC 8.00 3.00
❑ 175 Earl Snyder AU A RC 8.00 3.00
❑ 176 Justin Huber AU A RC 15.00 6.00
❑ 177 Chris Narveson AU A RC 8.00 3.00
❑ 178 Jon Switzer AU A RC 8.00 3.00
❑ 179 Ronald Acuna AU A RC 8.00 3.00
❑ 180 Chris Duffy Bat RC 8.00 3.00
❑ 181 Kazuhisa Ishii Bat RC 8.00 3.00

2003 Bowman's Best

❑ COMP.SET w/o SP's (50) 40.00 15.00
❑ COMMON CARD 1.00 .40
❑ COMMON AUTO 8.00 3.00
❑ COMMON BAT 4.00 1.50
❑ AB Andrew Brown FY AU RC 10.00 4.00
❑ AK Austin Kearns 1.00 .40
❑ AM Aneudis Mateo FY AU RC 8.00 3.00
❑ AP Albert Pujols 3.00 1.25
❑ AR Alex Rodriguez 2.50 1.00

- ❑ AS Alfonso Soriano 1.00 .40
- ❑ AW Aron Weston FY AU RC 8.00 3.00
- ❑ BB Bryan Bullington FY AU RC 8.00 3.00
- ❑ BC Bernie Castro FY RC 1.00 .40
- ❑ BFL Branden Florence FY AU RC 8.00 3.00
- ❑ BFR Ben Francisco FY AU RC 8.00 3.00
- ❑ BH Brendan Harris FY AU RC 10.00 4.00
- ❑ BJH Bo Hart FY RC 1.00 .40
- ❑ BK Beau Kemp FY AU RC 8.00 3.00
- ❑ BLB Barry Bonds 4.00 1.50
- ❑ BM Brian McCann FY AU RC 50.00 20.00
- ❑ BSG Brian Giles 1.00 .40
- ❑ BWB Bobby Basham FY AU RC 8.00 3.00
- ❑ BZ Barry Zito 1.00 .40
- ❑ CAD Carlos Duran FY AU RC 8.00 3.00
- ❑ CDC Chris De La Cruz FY AU RC 8.00 3.00
- ❑ CJ Chipper Jones 1.50 .60
- ❑ CJW C.J. Wilson FY AU 8.00 3.00
- ❑ CM Charlie Manning FY AU RC 8.00 3.00
- ❑ CMS Curt Schilling 1.00 .40
- ❑ CS Cory Stewart FY AU RC 8.00 3.00
- ❑ CSS Corey Shafer FY AU RC 8.00 3.00
- ❑ CW Chien-Ming Wang FY RC 12.00 5.00
- ❑ CWA Chien-Ming Wang FY AU 250.00 150.00
- ❑ DAM Dustin Moseley FY AU RC 8.00 3.00
- ❑ DC David Cash FY AU RC 8.00 3.00
- ❑ DH Dan Haren FY AU RC 25.00 10.00
- ❑ DJ Derek Jeter 4.00 1.50
- ❑ DM David Martinez FY AU RC 8.00 3.00
- ❑ DMM Dust. McGowan FY AU RC 10.00 4.00
- ❑ DR Darrell Rasner FY AU RC 8.00 3.00
- ❑ DW Doug Waechter FY AU RC 10.00 4.00
- ❑ DY Dustin Yount FY RC 1.50 .60
- ❑ ERA Elizardo Ramirez FY AU RC 10.00 4.00
- ❑ ERI Eric Riggs FY AU RC 10.00 4.00
- ❑ ET Eider Torres FY AU RC 8.00 3.00
- ❑ FP Felix Pie FY AU RC 100.00 50.00
- ❑ FS Felix Sanchez FY AU RC 8.00 3.00
- ❑ FT Ferdin Tejeda FY AU RC 8.00 3.00
- ❑ GA Greg Aquino FY AU RC 8.00 3.00
- ❑ GB Gregor Blanco FY AU RC 8.00 3.00
- ❑ GJA Garret Anderson 1.00 .40
- ❑ GM Greg Maddux 2.50 1.00
- ❑ GS Gary Schneidmiller FY AU RC 8.00 3.00
- ❑ HR Hanley Ramirez FY AU RC 120.00 60.00
- ❑ HRB Hanley Ramirez FY Bat 25.00 10.00
- ❑ HT Haj Turay FY RC 1.00 .40
- ❑ IS Ichiro Suzuki 3.00 1.25
- ❑ JB Jeremy Bonderman FY RC 4.00 1.50
- ❑ JC Jose Contreras FY RC 1.50 .60
- ❑ JDD J.D. Durbin FY AU RC 8.00 3.00
- ❑ JFK Jeff Kent 1.00 .40
- ❑ JG Joey Gomes FY AU RC 8.00 3.00
- ❑ JGB Joey Gomes FY Bat 4.00 1.50
- ❑ JGG Jason Giambi 1.00 .40
- ❑ JK Jason Kubel FY AU RC 25.00 10.00
- ❑ JKB Jason Kubel FY Bat 6.00 2.50
- ❑ JLB Jaime Bubela FY AU RC 8.00 3.00
- ❑ JM Jose Morales FY AU RC 8.00 3.00
- ❑ JMS Jon-Mark Sprowl FY RC 1.00 .40
- ❑ JRG Jeremy Griffiths FY AU RC 8.00 3.00
- ❑ JT Jim Thome 1.00 .40
- ❑ JV Joe Valentine FY AU RC 8.00 3.00
- ❑ JW Josh Willingham FY AU RC 25.00 10.00
- ❑ KBS Kelly Shoppach FY Bat 5.00 2.00
- ❑ KG Ken Griffey Jr. 2.50 1.00
- ❑ KJ Kade Johnson FY AU RC 8.00 3.00
- ❑ KS Kelly Shoppach FY AU RC 10.00 4.00
- ❑ KY Kevin Youkilis FY AU RC 40.00 15.00
- ❑ KYE Kevin Youkilis FY Bat 15.00 6.00
- ❑ LB Lance Berkman 1.00 .40
- ❑ LF Lew Ford FY AU RC 10.00 4.00
- ❑ LFJ Lew Ford FY Bat 5.00 2.00
- ❑ LW Larry Walker 1.00 .40
- ❑ MB Matt Bruback FY RC 1.00 .40
- ❑ MD Matt Diaz FY RC 2.00 .75
- ❑ MDA Matt Diaz FY AU 10.00 4.00
- ❑ MDH Matt Hensley FY AU RC 8.00 3.00
- ❑ MDM Mark Malaska FY AU RC 8.00 3.00
- ❑ MH Michel Hernandez FY AU RC 8.00 3.00
- ❑ MHI Michael Hinckley FY AU RC 10.00 4.00
- ❑ MJP Mike Piazza 2.50 1.00
- ❑ MK Matt Kata FY AU RC 8.00 3.00
- ❑ MNH Matt Hagen FY AU RC 8.00 3.00
- ❑ MO Mike O'Keefe FY RC 1.00 .40
- ❑ MOR Maggio Ordonez 1.00 .40
- ❑ MP Mark Prior 1.00 .40
- ❑ MR Manny Ramirez 1.00 .40
- ❑ MS Mike Sweeney 1.00 .40
- ❑ MT Miguel Tejada 1.00 .40
- ❑ NG Nomar Garciaparra 2.50 1.00
- ❑ NL Nook Logan FY AU RC 10.00 4.00
- ❑ OC Ozzie Chavez FY AU RC 8.00 3.00
- ❑ PB Pat Burrell 1.00 .40
- ❑ PL Pete LaForest FY AU RC 8.00 3.00
- ❑ PM Pedro Martinez 1.00 .40
- ❑ PR Prentice Redman FY AU RC 8.00 3.00
- ❑ RC Ryan Cameron FY AU RC 8.00 3.00
- ❑ RD Rajai Davis FY AU RC 8.00 3.00
- ❑ RH Ryan Howard FY AU RC 250.00 150.00
- ❑ RHJ Ryan Howard FY Bat 60.00 30.00
- ❑ RJ Randy Johnson 1.50 .60
- ❑ RLD Rajai Davis FY Bat 4.00 1.50
- ❑ RM Ramon Nivar-Martinez FY RC 1.00 .40
- ❑ RS Ryan Shealy FY AU RC 30.00 12.50
- ❑ RSB Ryan Shealy FY Bat 12.00 5.00
- ❑ RWH Robbie Hammock FY AU RC 8.00 3.00
- ❑ SG Shawn Green 1.00 .40
- ❑ SS Sammy Sosa 1.50 .60
- ❑ ST Scott Tyler FY AU RC 10.00 4.00
- ❑ SV Shane Victorino FY RC 2.00 .75
- ❑ TA Tyler Adamczyk FY AU RC 8.00 3.00
- ❑ TH Todd Helton 1.00 .40
- ❑ TI Travis Ishikawa FY AU RC 10.00 4.00
- ❑ TJ Tyler Johnson FY AU RC 8.00 3.00
- ❑ TJB T.J. Bohn FY RC 1.00 .40
- ❑ TKH Torii Hunter 1.00 .40
- ❑ TO Tim Olson FY AU RC 8.00 3.00
- ❑ TS T.Story-Harden FY AU RC 8.00 3.00
- ❑ TSB T.Story-Harden FY Bat 4.00 1.50
- ❑ TT Terry Tiffee FY RC 1.00 .40
- ❑ VG Vladimir Guerrero 1.50 .60
- ❑ WE Willie Eyre FY AU RC 8.00 3.00
- ❑ WL Wil Ledezma FY AU RC 8.00 3.00
- ❑ WRC Roger Clemens 3.00 1.25
- ❑ NNO B.Bullington Opened Box AU 25.00 10.00
- ❑ NNO B.Bullington Sealed Box AU

2004 Bowman's Best

- ❑ COMP.SET w/o SP'S (50) 25.00 10.00
- ❑ COMMON CARD 1.00 .40
- ❑ COMMON RC 1.00 .40
- ❑ ONE AUTO PER HOBBY PACK
- ❑ ONE RELIC PER BOX-LOADER PACK
- ❑ ONE BOX-LOADER PACK PER HOBBY BOX
- ❑ STAUFFER BOX RANDOM IN HOBBY CASES
- ❑ OVERALL AU PLATE ODDS 1:391 HOBBY
- ❑ AU PLATE PRINT RUN 1 SET PER COLOR
- ❑ BLACK-CYAN-MAGENTA-YELLOW ISSUED
- ❑ NO AU PLATE PRICING DUE TO SCARCITY
- ❑ AER Alex Rodriguez 2.50 1.00
- ❑ AG Adam Greenberg FY AU RC 10.00 4.00
- ❑ AL Anthony Lerew FY RC 1.50 .60
- ❑ AO Akinori Otsuka FY RC 1.00 .40
- ❑ AP Albert Pujols 3.00 1.25
- ❑ AS Alfonso Soriano 1.00 .40
- ❑ BB Bobby Brownlie FY AU RC 10.00 4.00
- ❑ BEM Brandon Medders FY AU RC 8.00 3.00
- ❑ BG Brian Giles 1.00 .40
- ❑ BMS Brad Snyder FY AU RC 10.00 4.00
- ❑ BP Brayan Pena FY AU RC 8.00 3.00
- ❑ BS Brad Sullivan FY AU RC 10.00 4.00
- ❑ CB Carlos Beltran 1.00 .40
- ❑ CD Carlos Delgado 1.00 .40
- ❑ CJ Conor Jackson FY AU RC 25.00 10.00
- ❑ CLH Chin-Lung Hu FY RC 2.50 1.00
- ❑ CMA Craig Ansman FY AU RC 8.00 3.00
- ❑ CMS Curt Schilling 1.00 .40
- ❑ CZ Charlie Zink FY AU RC 8.00 3.00
- ❑ DA David Aardsma FY AU RC 10.00 4.00
- ❑ DC Dave Crouthers FY AU RC 8.00 3.00
- ❑ DDN Dustin Nippert FY AU RC 10.00 4.00
- ❑ DG Danny Gonzalez FY RC 1.00 .40
- ❑ DK Donald Kelly FY AU RC 8.00 3.00
- ❑ DL Donald Levinski FY AU RC 8.00 3.00
- ❑ DM David Murphy FY AU RC 15.00 6.00
- ❑ DN Dioner Navarro FY AU RC 10.00 4.00
- ❑ DS Don Sutton FY RC 2.50 1.00
- ❑ EA Erick Aybar FY AU RC 15.00 6.00
- ❑ EC Eric Chavez 1.00 .40
- ❑ EH Estee Harris FY AU RC 10.00 4.00
- ❑ ES Ervin Santana FY AU RC 25.00 10.00
- ❑ FH Felix Hernandez FY AU RC 60.00 30.00
- ❑ GA Garret Anderson 1.00 .40
- ❑ HB Hank Blalock 1.00 .40
- ❑ HM Hector Made FY RC 1.50 .60
- ❑ IR Ivan Rodriguez 1.00 .40
- ❑ IS Ichiro Suzuki 3.00 1.25
- ❑ JA Joaquin Arias FY AU RC 10.00 6.00
- ❑ JAV Jose Vidro 1.00 .40
- ❑ JC Juan Cedeno FY AU RC 8.00 3.00
- ❑ JDS Jason Schmidt 1.00 .40
- ❑ JE Jesse English FY AU RC 8.00 3.00
- ❑ JGG Jason Giambi 1.00 .40
- ❑ JH Jason Hirsh FY AU RC 25.00 10.00
- ❑ JJC Jon Connolly FY RC 2.00 .75
- ❑ JK Jon Knott FY AU RC 8.00 3.00
- ❑ JL Josh Labandeira FY AU RC 8.00 3.00
- ❑ JLO Javy Lopez 1.00 .40
- ❑ JP Jorge Posada 1.00 .40
- ❑ JRG Joey Gathright FY RC 2.00 .75
- ❑ JS Jeff Salazar FY AU RC 10.00 4.00
- ❑ JSZ Jason Szuminski FY AU RC 8.00 3.00
- ❑ JT Jim Thome 1.00 .40
- ❑ KC Kory Casto FY AU RC 15.00 6.00
- ❑ KK Kevin Kouzmanoff FY AU RC 40.00 15.00
- ❑ KM Kazuo Matsui FY Uni RC 5.00 2.00
- ❑ KRK Kody Kirkland FY Bat RC 5.00 2.00
- ❑ KS Kyle Sleeth FY RC 1.50 .60
- ❑ KT Kazuhito Tadano FY Jsy RC 8.00 3.00
- ❑ LK Logan Kensing FY AU RC 8.00 3.00
- ❑ LM Lastings Milledge FY AU RC 40.00 15.00
- ❑ LO Lyle Overbay 1.00 .40
- ❑ LTH Luke Hughes FY AU RC 8.00 3.00
- ❑ LWJ Chipper Jones 1.50 .60
- ❑ MAR Manny Ramirez 1.00 .40
- ❑ MDC Matt Creighton FY AU RC 8.00 3.00
- ❑ MG Mike Gosling FY RC 1.00 .40
- ❑ MJP Mike Piazza 2.50 1.00
- ❑ MO Magglio Ordonez 1.00 .40
- ❑ MT Miguel Tejada 1.00 .40
- ❑ MTC Miguel Cabrera 1.00 .40
- ❑ MV Merkin Valdez FY AU RC 8.00 3.00
- ❑ MWP Mark Prior 1.00 .40
- ❑ MY Michael Young 1.00 .40
- ❑ NAG Nomar Garciaparra 2.50 1.00
- ❑ NG Nick Gorneault FY RC 1.50 .60
- ❑ NU Nic Ungs FY AU RC 8.00 3.00
- ❑ OQ Omar Quintanilla FY AU RC 10.00 4.00
- ❑ PM Paul Maholm FY AU RC 25.00 10.00
- ❑ PMM Paul McAnulty FY RC 1.50 .60
- ❑ RB Ryan Budde FY AU RC 8.00 3.00
- ❑ RC Roger Clemens 3.00 1.25
- ❑ RG Rudy Guillen FY AU RC 10.00 4.00
- ❑ RJ Randy Johnson 1.50 .60
- ❑ RN Ricky Nolasco FY AU RC 20.00 8.00
- ❑ RR Ramon Ramirez FY AU RC 8.00 3.00
- ❑ RS Richie Sexson 1.00 .40
- ❑ RT Rob Tejeda FY AU RC 15.00 6.00
- ❑ SH Shawn Hill FY AU RC 8.00 3.00
- ❑ SR Scott Rolen 1.00 .40
- ❑ SS Sammy Sosa 1.50 .60
- ❑ ST Shingo Takatsu FY Jsy RC 8.00 3.00
- ❑ TB Travis Blackley FY Jsy RC 5.00 2.00
- ❑ TD Tyler Davidson FY AU RC 10.00 4.00
- ❑ TJ Terry Jones FY RC 1.50 .60
- ❑ TJS Tim Stauffer FY AU RC 10.00 4.00
- ❑ TLH Todd Helton 1.00 .40
- ❑ TOH Travis Hanson FY AU RC 10.00 4.00
- ❑ TRM Tom Mastny FY AU RC 8.00 3.00

❑ TS Todd Self FY RC 1.50 .60
❑ VC Vito Chiaravalloti FY AU RC 8.00 3.00
❑ VG Vladimir Guerrero 1.50 .60
❑ WM Warner Madrigal FY RC 1.50 .60
❑ WS Wardell Starling FY AU RC 8.00 3.00
❑ YM Yadier Molina FY AU RC 20.00 8.00
❑ ZD Zach Duke FY AU RC 40.00 20.00
❑ NNO Tim Stauffer AU Box/100 25.00 10.00

2005 Bowman's Best

❑ COMP.SET w/o SP's (100) 50.00 25.00
❑ COMMON CARD (1-30) .50 .20
❑ COMMON CARD (31-100) 1.00 .40
❑ COMMON AU (101-143) 8.00 3.00
❑ OVERALL 1-100 PLATE ODDS 1:345 H
❑ OVERALL 101-143 AU PLATE ODDS 1:805 H
❑ PLATE PRINT RUN 1 SET PER COLOR
❑ BLACK-CYAN-MAGENTA-YELLOW ISSUED
❑ NO PLATE PRICING DUE TO SCARCITY
❑ 1 Jose Vidro .50 .20
❑ 2 Adam Dunn .50 .20
❑ 3 Manny Ramirez .75 .30
❑ 4 Miguel Tejada .50 .20
❑ 5 Ken Griffey Jr. 2.00 .75
❑ 6 Pedro Martinez .75 .30
❑ 7 Alex Rodriguez 2.00 .75
❑ 8 Ichiro Suzuki 2.50 1.00
❑ 9 Alfonso Soriano .50 .20
❑ 10 Brian Giles .50 .20
❑ 11 Roger Clemens 2.00 .75
❑ 12 Todd Helton .75 .30
❑ 13 Ivan Rodriguez .75 .30
❑ 14 David Ortiz .75 .30
❑ 15 Sammy Sosa 1.25 .50
❑ 16 Chipper Jones 1.25 .50
❑ 17 Mark Buehrle .50 .20
❑ 18 Miguel Cabrera .75 .30
❑ 19 Johan Santana 1.25 .50
❑ 20 Randy Johnson 1.25 .50
❑ 21 Jim Thome .75 .30
❑ 22 Vladimir Guerrero 1.25 .50
❑ 23 Dontrelle Willis .50 .20
❑ 24 Nomar Garciaparra 1.25 .50
❑ 25 Barry Bonds 3.00 1.25
❑ 26 Curt Schilling .75 .30
❑ 27 Carlos Beltran .50 .20
❑ 28 Albert Pujols 2.50 1.00
❑ 29 Mark Prior .75 .30
❑ 30 Derek Jeter 2.50 1.00
❑ 31 Ryan Garko FY RC 3.00 1.25
❑ 32 Eulogio De La Cruz FY RC 1.00 .40
❑ 33 Luke Scott FY RC 3.00 1.25
❑ 34 Shane Costa FY RC 1.00 .40
❑ 35 Casey McGehee FY RC 1.00 .40
❑ 36 Jered Weaver FY RC 12.00 5.00
❑ 37 Kevin Melillo FY RC 2.00 .75
❑ 38 D.J. Houlton FY RC 1.00 .40
❑ 39 Brandon Moorhead FY RC 1.00 .40
❑ 40 Jerry Owens FY RC 1.50 .60
❑ 41 Elliot Johnson FY RC 1.00 .40
❑ 42 Kevin West FY RC 1.00 .40
❑ 43 Hernan Iribarren FY RC 1.50 .60
❑ 44 Miguel Montero FY RC 5.00 2.00
❑ 45 Craig Tatum FY RC 1.00 .40
❑ 46 Ryan Sweeney FY RC 2.50 1.00
❑ 47 Micah Furtado FY RC 1.00 .40
❑ 48 Cody Haerther FY RC 1.00 .40
❑ 49 Erick Abreu FY RC 2.00 .75
❑ 50 Chuck Tiffany FY RC 2.50 1.00
❑ 51 Tadahito Iguchi FY RC 4.00 1.50
❑ 52 Frank Diaz FY RC 1.00 .40
❑ 53 Errol Simonitsch FY RC 1.50 .60
❑ 54 Wade Robinson FY RC 1.00 .40
❑ 55 Adam Boeve FY RC 1.00 .40
❑ 56 Steven Bondurant FY RC 1.00 .40
❑ 57 Jason Motte FY RC 1.00 .40
❑ 58 Juan Senreiso FY RC 1.00 .40
❑ 59 Vinny Rottino FY RC 1.00 .40
❑ 60 Jai Miller FY RC 1.50 .60
❑ 61 Thomas Pauly FY RC 1.00 .40
❑ 62 Tony Giarratano FY RC 1.00 .40
❑ 63 Alexander Smit FY RC 1.00 .40
❑ 64 Keiichi Yabu FY RC 1.00 .40
❑ 65 Brian Bannister FY RC 2.50 1.00
❑ 66 Kennard Bibbs FY RC 1.00 .40
❑ 67 Anthony Reyes FY RC 5.00 2.00
❑ 68 Thomas Oldham FY RC 1.00 .40
❑ 69 Ben Harrison FY 1.00 .40
❑ 70 Daryl Thompson FY RC 1.00 .40
❑ 71 Kevin Collins FY RC 1.00 .40
❑ 72 Wes Swackhamer FY RC 1.00 .40
❑ 73 Landon Powell FY RC 1.50 .60
❑ 74 Matt Brown FY RC 1.00 .40
❑ 75 Russ Martin FY RC 3.00 1.25
❑ 76 Nick Touchstone FY RC 1.00 .40
❑ 77 Steven White FY RC 1.00 .40
❑ 78 Ian Bladergroen FY RC 1.50 .60
❑ 79 Sean Marshall FY RC 4.00 1.50
❑ 80 Nick Masset FY RC 1.00 .40
❑ 81 Ryan Goleski FY RC 1.00 .40
❑ 82 Matt Campbell FY RC 1.00 .40
❑ 83 Manny Parra FY RC 2.50 1.00
❑ 84 Melky Cabrera FY RC 5.00 2.00
❑ 85 Ryan Feierabend FY RC 1.00 .40
❑ 86 Nate McLouth FY RC 1.50 .60
❑ 87 Glen Perkins FY RC 2.00 .75
❑ 88 Kila Kaaihue FY RC 2.50 1.00
❑ 89 Dana Eveland FY RC 1.00 .40
❑ 90 Tyler Pelland FY RC 1.50 .60
❑ 91 Matt Van Der Bosch FY RC 1.00 .40
❑ 92 Andy Santana FY RC 1.00 .40
❑ 93 Eric Nielsen FY RC 1.00 .40
❑ 94 Brendan Ryan FY RC 1.00 .40
❑ 95 Ian Kinsler FY RC 8.00 3.00
❑ 96 Matthew Kemp FY RC 8.00 3.00
❑ 97 Stephen Drew FY RC 10.00 4.00
❑ 98 Peeter Ramos FY RC 1.00 .40
❑ 99 Chris Seddon FY RC 1.00 .40
❑ 100 Chuck James FY RC 4.00 1.50
❑ 101 Travis Chick FY AU RC 10.00 4.00
❑ 102 Justin Verlander FY AU RC 50.00 20.00
❑ 103 Billy Butler FY AU RC 50.00 20.00
❑ 104 Chris B.Young FY AU RC 60.00 35.00
❑ 105 Jake Postlewait FY AU RC 8.00 3.00
❑ 106 C.J. Smith FY AU RC 8.00 3.00
❑ 107 Mike Rodriguez FY AU RC 8.00 3.00
❑ 108 Philip Humber FY AU RC 25.00 10.00
❑ 109 Jeff Niemann FY AU RC 10.00 4.00
❑ 110 Brian Miller FY AU RC 8.00 3.00
❑ 111 Chris Vines FY AU RC 8.00 3.00
❑ 112 Andy LaRoche FY AU RC 30.00 12.50
❑ 113 Mike Bourn FY AU RC 10.00 4.00
❑ 114 Wlad Balentein FY AU RC 30.00 12.50
❑ 115 Ismael Ramirez FY AU RC 8.00 3.00
❑ 116 Hayden Penn FY AU RC 10.00 4.00
❑ 117 Pedro Lopez FY AU RC 8.00 3.00
❑ 118 Shawn Bowman FY AU RC 10.00 4.00
❑ 119 Chad Orvella FY AU RC 8.00 3.00
❑ 120 Sean Tracey FY AU RC 8.00 3.00
❑ 121 Bobby Livingston FY AU RC 8.00 3.00
❑ 122 Michael Rogers FY AU RC 8.00 3.00
❑ 123 Willy Mota FY AU RC 8.00 3.00
❑ 124 Bran McCarthy FY AU RC 25.00 10.00
❑ 125 Mike Morse FY AU RC 8.00 3.00
❑ 126 Matt Lindstrom FY AU RC 8.00 3.00
❑ 127 Brian Stavisky FY AU RC 8.00 3.00
❑ 128 Richie Gardner FY AU RC 8.00 3.00
❑ 129 Scott Mitchinson FY AU RC 8.00 3.00
❑ 130 Billy McCarthy FY AU RC 8.00 3.00
❑ 131 Brandon Sing FY AU RC 10.00 4.00
❑ 132 Matt Albers FY AU RC 10.00 4.00
❑ 133 George Kottaras FY AU RC 10.00 4.00
❑ 134 Luis Hernandez FY AU RC 8.00 3.00
❑ 135 Hum Sanchez FY AU RC 30.00 12.50
❑ 136 Buck Coats FY AU RC 8.00 3.00
❑ 137 Jon Barratt FY AU RC 8.00 3.00
❑ 138 Raul Tablado FY AU RC 8.00 3.00
❑ 139 Jake Mullinax FY AU RC 8.00 3.00
❑ 140 Edgar Varela FY AU RC 8.00 3.00
❑ 141 Ryan Garko FY AU 15.00 6.00
❑ 142 Nate McLouth FY AU 25.00 10.00
❑ 143 Shane Costa FY AU 8.00 3.00

2007 Bowman's Best

❑ COMP.SET w/o AU (33) 15.00 6.00
❑ COMMON CARD (1-33) .50 .20
❑ COMMON AU VET VAR (23-33) 15.00 6.00
❑ AU VET VAR GROUP A 1:15 PACKS
❑ AU VET VAR GROUP B 1:122 PACKS
❑ AU VET VAR GROUP C 1:381 PACKS
❑ AU VET VAR GROUP D 1:113 PACKS
❑ COMMON AU VET (34-51) 8.00 3.00
❑ AU VET ODDS 1:2 PACKS
❑ COMMON RC (52-81) 1.00 .40
❑ RC ODDS 1:2 PACKS
❑ RC PRINT RUN 799 SER.#'D SETS
❑ GU-RC ODDS 1:35 PACKS
❑ COMMON AU VAR RC (71-81) 8.00 3.00
❑ AU VAR RC ODDS 1:11 PACKS
❑ COMMON AU RC (82-99) 8.00 3.00
❑ AU RC ODDS 1:2 PACKS
❑ PRINTING PLATE ODDS 1:88 PACKS
❑ PRINTING PLATE AU ODDS 1:173 PACKS
❑ PRINTING PLATE GU ODDS 1:8945 PACKS
❑ PLATE PRINT RUN 1 SET PER COLOR
❑ BLACK-CYAN-MAGENTA-YELLOW ISSUED
❑ NO PLATE PRICING DUE TO SCARCITY
❑ 1 Jose Reyes 1.25 .50
❑ 2 Derek Jeter 3.00 1.25
❑ 3 Vladimir Guerrero 1.25 .50
❑ 4 Ichiro Suzuki 2.00 .75
❑ 5 Jason Bay .50 .20
❑ 6 Joe Mauer .75 .30
❑ 7 Alfonso Soriano .50 .20
❑ 8 David Ortiz 1.25 .50
❑ 9 Andruw Jones .75 .30
❑ 10 Roger Clemens 2.00 .75
❑ 11 Grady Sizemore .75 .30
❑ 12 Magglio Ordonez .50 .20
❑ 13 Carl Crawford .50 .20
❑ 14 Chase Utley 1.25 .50
❑ 15 Mark Teixeira .75 .30
❑ 16 Ryan Zimmerman 1.25 .50
❑ 17 Ken Griffey Jr. 2.00 .75
❑ 18 Derrek Lee .50 .20
❑ 19 Barry Bonds 2.50 1.00
❑ 20 Chipper Jones 1.25 .50
❑ 21 Vernon Wells .50 .20
❑ 22 Manny Ramirez .75 .30
❑ 23a Alex Rodriguez 2.00 .75
❑ 23b Alex Rodriguez AU A 150.00 90.00
❑ 24a Ryan Howard 2.00 .75
❑ 24b Ryan Howard AU B 50.00 20.00
❑ 25a Tom Glavine .75 .30
❑ 25b Tom Glavine AU D 40.00 15.00
❑ 26a Gary Sheffield .50 .20
❑ 26b Gary Sheffield AU A 20.00 8.00
❑ 27a Miguel Cabrera .75 .30
❑ 27b Miguel Cabrera AU A 20.00 8.00
❑ 28a Robinson Cano .75 .30
❑ 28b Robinson Cano AU A 25.00 10.00
❑ 29a David Wright 2.00 .75

❑ 29b	David Wright AU A	50.00	20.00
❑ 30a	Jim Thome	.75	.30
❑ 30b	Jim Thome AU A	25.00	10.00
❑ 31a	Albert Pujols	2.50	1.00
❑ 31b	Albert Pujols AU C	200.00	150.00
❑ 32	Jorge Posada	.75	.30
❑ 33a	Brian McCann	.50	.20
❑ 33b	Brian McCann AU A	15.00	6.00
❑ 34	Josh Barfield AU	8.00	3.00
❑ 35	Melky Cabrera AU	20.00	8.00
❑ 36	Bill Hall AU	8.00	3.00
❑ 37	Cole Hamels AU	20.00	8.00
❑ 38	Adam LaRoche AU	8.00	3.00
❑ 39	Matt Holliday AU	20.00	8.00
❑ 40	Jeremy Hermida AU	8.00	3.00
❑ 41	Jonathan Papelbon AU	20.00	8.00
❑ 42	Hanley Ramirez AU	25.00	10.00
❑ 43	Justin Verlander AU	20.00	8.00
❑ 44	Andre Ethier AU	12.00	5.00
❑ 46	Erik Bedard AU	12.00	5.00
❑ 47	Freddy Sanchez AU	8.00	3.00
❑ 48	Adrian Gonzalez AU	12.00	5.00
❑ 49	Russell Martin AU	12.00	5.00
❑ 50	B.J. Upton AU	12.00	5.00
❑ 51	Prince Fielder AU	40.00	15.00
❑ 52	Tony Abreu RC	2.50	1.00
❑ 53	Ben Francisco (RC)	1.00	.40
❑ 54	Billy Butler (RC)	1.50	.60
❑ 55	Philip Hughes (RC)	5.00	2.00
❑ 56	Josh Fields (RC)	1.00	.40
❑ 57	Carlos Gomez RC	1.50	.60
❑ 58	Akinori Iwamura RC	2.50	1.00
❑ 59	Matt Brown RC	1.00	.40
❑ 60	Jesus Flores RC	1.00	.40
❑ 61	Mike Fontenot (RC)	1.00	.40
❑ 62	Ryan Feierabend (RC)	1.00	.40
❑ 63	Miguel Montero (RC)	1.00	.40
❑ 64a	Daisuke Matsuzaka RC	10.00	4.00
❑ 64b	Daisuke Matsuzaka Jsy	25.00	10.00
❑ 65	Kei Igawa RC	2.50	1.00
❑ 66	Shawn Riggans (RC)	1.00	.40
❑ 67	Masumi Kuwata RC	8.00	3.00
❑ 68	Kevin Slowey (RC)	2.50	1.00
❑ 69	Josh Hamilton (RC)	2.50	1.00
❑ 70	Curtis Thigpen (RC)	1.00	.40
❑ 71a	Justin Upton RC	6.00	2.50
❑ 71b	Justin Upton AU	80.00	40.00
❑ 72a	Delmon Young (RC)	1.50	.60
❑ 72b	Delmon Young AU	20.00	8.00
❑ 73a	Brandon Wood (RC)	1.00	.40
❑ 73b	Brandon Wood AU	15.00	6.00
❑ 74a	Felix Pie (RC)	1.00	.40
❑ 74b	Felix Pie AU	10.00	4.00
❑ 75a	Alex Gordon RC	5.00	2.00
❑ 75b	Alex Gordon AU	40.00	15.00
❑ 76a	Mark Reynolds RC	4.00	1.50
❑ 76b	Mark Reynolds AU	50.00	20.00
❑ 77a	Tyler Clippard (RC)	1.50	.60
❑ 77b	Tyler Clippard AU	10.00	4.00
❑ 78a	Adam Lind (RC)	1.00	.40
❑ 78b	Adam Lind AU	8.00	3.00
❑ 79a	Hunter Pence (RC)	5.00	2.00
❑ 79b	Hunter Pence AU	50.00	20.00
❑ 80	Micah Owings (RC)	1.00	.40
❑ 81a	Jarrod Saltalamacchia (RC)	1.50	.60
❑ 81b	Jarrod Saltalamacchia AU	15.00	6.00
❑ 82	Kevin Kouzmanoff AU (RC)	8.00	3.00
❑ 83	Glen Perkins AU (RC)	8.00	3.00
❑ 84	Michael Bourn AU (RC)	8.00	3.00
❑ 85	Andrew Miller AU RC	15.00	6.00
❑ 86	Fred Lewis AU (RC)	8.00	3.00
❑ 88	Joba Chamberlain AU RC	100.00	50.00
❑ 89	Hideki Okajima AU RC	40.00	15.00
❑ 90	Troy Tulowitzki AU (RC)	25.00	10.00
❑ 91	Ryan Sweeney AU (RC)	8.00	3.00
❑ 92	Matt Lindstrom AU (RC)	8.00	3.00
❑ 93	Tim Lincecum AU RC	80.00	40.00
❑ 94	Homer Bailey AU (RC)	10.00	4.00
❑ 95	Matt DeSalvo AU (RC)	8.00	3.00
❑ 96	Alejandro De Aza AU RC	8.00	3.00
❑ 97	Ryan Braun AU (RC)	60.00	30.00
❑ 99	Andy LaRoche AU (RC)	15.00	6.00

1914 Cracker Jack

❑ 1	Otto Knabe	600.00	300.00
❑ 2	Frank Baker	1500.00	750.00

❑ 3	Joe Tinker	2000.00	1000.00
❑ 4	Larry Doyle	400.00	200.00
❑ 5	Ward Miller	400.00	200.00
❑ 6	Eddie Plank	1500.00	750.00
❑ 7	Eddie Collins	1500.00	750.00
❑ 8	Rube Oldring	400.00	200.00
❑ 9	Artie Hoffman	400.00	200.00
❑ 10	John McInnis	400.00	200.00
❑ 11	George Stovall	400.00	200.00
❑ 12	Connie Mack MG	1500.00	750.00
❑ 13	Art Wilson	400.00	200.00
❑ 14	Sam Crawford	1500.00	750.00
❑ 15	Reb Russell	400.00	200.00
❑ 16	Howie Camnitz	400.00	200.00
❑ 17	Roger Bresnahan	1500.00	750.00
❑ 18	Johnny Evers	1500.00	750.00
❑ 19	Chief Bender	1500.00	750.00
❑ 20	Cy Falkenberg	400.00	200.00
❑ 21	Heinie Zimmerman	400.00	200.00
❑ 22	Joe Wood	2500.00	1250.00
❑ 23	Charles Comiskey	1500.00	750.00
❑ 24	George Mullen	400.00	200.00
❑ 25	Michael Simon	400.00	200.00
❑ 26	James Scott	400.00	200.00
❑ 27	Bill Carrigan	400.00	200.00
❑ 28	Jack Barry	400.00	200.00
❑ 29	Vean Gregg	400.00	200.00
❑ 30	Ty Cobb	10000.00	5000.00
❑ 31	Heinie Wagner	400.00	200.00
❑ 32	Mordecai Brown	1500.00	750.00
❑ 33	Amos Strunk	400.00	200.00
❑ 34	Ira Thomas	600.00	300.00
❑ 35	Harry Hooper	1500.00	750.00
❑ 36	Ed Walsh	1500.00	750.00
❑ 37	Grover C. Alexander	4000.00	2000.00
❑ 38	Red Dooin	400.00	200.00
❑ 39	Chick Gandil	1500.00	750.00
❑ 40	Jimmy Austin	400.00	200.00
❑ 41	Tommy Leach	400.00	200.00
❑ 42	Al Bridwell	400.00	200.00
❑ 43	Rube Marquard	1500.00	750.00
❑ 44	Jeff (Charles) Tesreau	400.00	200.00
❑ 45	Fred Luderus	400.00	200.00
❑ 46	Bob Groom	400.00	200.00
❑ 47	Josh Devore	400.00	200.00
❑ 48	Harry Lord	600.00	300.00
❑ 49	John Miller	400.00	200.00
❑ 50	John Hummell	400.00	200.00
❑ 51	Nap Rucker	400.00	200.00
❑ 52	Zach Wheat	1500.00	750.00
❑ 53	Otto Miller	400.00	200.00
❑ 54	Marty O'Toole	400.00	200.00
❑ 55	Dick Hoblitzel	400.00	200.00
❑ 56	Clyde Milan	400.00	200.00
❑ 57	Walter Johnson	4000.00	2000.00
❑ 58	Wally Schang	400.00	200.00
❑ 59	Harry Gessler	400.00	200.00
❑ 60	Rollie Zeider	600.00	300.00
❑ 61	Ray Schalk	2000.00	1000.00
❑ 62	Jay Cashion	600.00	300.00
❑ 63	Babe Adams	400.00	200.00
❑ 64	Jimmy Archer	400.00	200.00
❑ 65	Tris Speaker	1500.00	750.00
❑ 66	Napoleon Lajoie	2500.00	1250.00
❑ 67	Otis Crandall	400.00	200.00
❑ 68	Honus Wagner	8000.00	4000.00
❑ 69	John McGraw	1500.00	750.00
❑ 70	Fred Clarke	1200.00	600.00
❑ 71	Chief Meyers	400.00	200.00
❑ 72	John Boehling	400.00	200.00
❑ 73	Max Carey	1500.00	750.00
❑ 74	Frank Owens	400.00	200.00
❑ 75	Miller Huggins	1200.00	600.00
❑ 76	Claude Hendrix	400.00	200.00
❑ 77	Hughie Jennings MG	1500.00	750.00
❑ 78	Fred Merkle	400.00	200.00
❑ 79	Ping Bodie	400.00	200.00
❑ 80	Ed Ruelbach	400.00	200.00
❑ 81	Jim Delahanty	400.00	200.00
❑ 82	Gavvy Cravath	400.00	200.00
❑ 83	Russ Ford	400.00	200.00
❑ 84	Elmer E. Knetzer	400.00	200.00
❑ 85	Buck Herzog	400.00	200.00
❑ 86	Burt Shotton	400.00	200.00
❑ 87	Forrest Cady	400.00	200.00
❑ 88	Christy Mathewson	50000.00	20000.00
❑ 89	Lawrence Cheney	400.00	200.00
❑ 90	Frank Smith	400.00	200.00
❑ 91	Roger Peckinpaugh	400.00	200.00
❑ 92	Al Demaree	400.00	200.00
❑ 93	Del Pratt	400.00	200.00
❑ 94	Eddie Cicotte	1500.00	750.00
❑ 95	Ray Keating	400.00	200.00
❑ 96	Beals Becker	400.00	200.00
❑ 97	John (Rube) Benton	400.00	200.00
❑ 98	Frank LaPorte	400.00	200.00
❑ 99	Frank Chance	4000.00	2000.00
❑ 100	Thomas Seaton	400.00	200.00
❑ 101	Frank Schulte	400.00	200.00
❑ 102	Ray Fisher	400.00	200.00
❑ 103	Joe Jackson	20000.00	10000.00
❑ 104	Vic Saier	400.00	200.00
❑ 105	James Lavender	400.00	200.00
❑ 106	Joe Birmingham	400.00	200.00
❑ 107	Tom Downey	400.00	200.00
❑ 108	Sherry Magee	400.00	200.00
❑ 109	Fred Blanding	400.00	200.00
❑ 110	Bob Bescher	400.00	200.00
❑ 111	Jim Callahan	400.00	200.00
❑ 112	Ed Sweeney	400.00	200.00
❑ 113	George Suggs	400.00	200.00
❑ 114	George Moriarity	400.00	200.00
❑ 115	Addison Brennan	400.00	200.00
❑ 116	Rollie Zeider	400.00	200.00
❑ 117	Ted Easterly	400.00	200.00
❑ 118	Ed Konetchy	400.00	200.00
❑ 119	George Perring	400.00	200.00
❑ 120	Mike Doolan	400.00	200.00
❑ 121	Hub Perdue	400.00	200.00
❑ 122	Owen Bush	400.00	200.00
❑ 123	Slim Sallee	400.00	200.00
❑ 124	Earl Moore	400.00	200.00
❑ 125	Bert Niehoff	400.00	200.00
❑ 126	Walter Blair	400.00	200.00
❑ 127	Butch Schmidt	400.00	200.00
❑ 128	Steve Evans	400.00	200.00
❑ 129	Ray Caldwell	400.00	200.00
❑ 130	Ivy Wingo	400.00	200.00
❑ 131	George Baumgardner	400.00	200.00
❑ 132	Les Nunamaker	400.00	200.00
❑ 133	Branch Rickey MG	2000.00	1000.00
❑ 134	Armando Marsans	400.00	200.00
❑ 135	Bill Killefer	400.00	200.00
❑ 136	Rabbit Maranville	1500.00	750.00
❑ 137	William Rariden	400.00	200.00
❑ 138	Hank Gowdy	400.00	200.00
❑ 139	Rebel Oakes	400.00	200.00
❑ 140	Danny Murphy	400.00	200.00
❑ 141	Cy Barger	400.00	200.00
❑ 142	Eugene Packard	400.00	200.00
❑ 143	Jake Daubert	400.00	200.00
❑ 144	James C. Walsh	800.00	400.00

1915 Cracker Jack

❑	COMPLETE SET (176)	70000.00	35000.00
❑	COMMON CARD (1-144)	200.00	100.00
❑	COMMON CARD(145-176)	250.00	125.00
❑ 1	Otto Knabe	600.00	300.00
❑ 2	Frank Baker	1000.00	500.00
❑ 3	Joe Tinker	800.00	400.00
❑ 4	Larry Doyle	250.00	125.00
❑ 5	Ward Miller	200.00	100.00
❑ 6	Eddie Plank	1500.00	750.00
❑ 7	Eddie Collins	800.00	400.00

❑ 8 Rube Oldring 200.00 100.00
❑ 9 Artie Hoffman 200.00 100.00
❑ 10 John McInnis 200.00 100.00
❑ 11 George Stovall 200.00 100.00
❑ 12 Connie Mack MG 800.00 400.00
❑ 13 Art Wilson 200.00 100.00
❑ 14 Sam Crawford 800.00 400.00
❑ 15 Reb Russell 200.00 100.00
❑ 16 Howie Camnitz 200.00 100.00
❑ 17 Roger Bresnahan 600.00 300.00
❑ 18 Johnny Evers 800.00 400.00
❑ 19 Chief Bender 800.00 400.00
❑ 20 Cy Falkenberg 200.00 100.00
❑ 21 Heinie Zimmerman 200.00 100.00
❑ 22 Joe Wood 1000.00 500.00
❑ 23 Charles Comiskey 1000.00 500.00
❑ 24 George Mullen 200.00 100.00
❑ 25 Michael Simon 200.00 100.00
❑ 26 James Scott 200.00 100.00
❑ 27 Bill Carrigan 200.00 100.00
❑ 28 Jack Barry 250.00 125.00
❑ 29 Vean Gregg 200.00 100.00
❑ 30 Ty Cobb 6000.00 3000.00
❑ 31 Heinie Wagner 200.00 100.00
❑ 32 Mordecai Brown 1000.00 500.00
❑ 33 Amos Strunk 200.00 100.00
❑ 34 Ira Thomas 200.00 100.00
❑ 35 Harry Hooper 600.00 300.00
❑ 36 Ed Walsh 800.00 400.00
❑ 37 Grover C. Alexander 2000.00 1000.00
❑ 38 Red Dooin 200.00 100.00
❑ 39 Chick Gandil 800.00 400.00
❑ 40 Jimmy Austin 250.00 125.00
❑ 41 Tommy Leach 200.00 100.00
❑ 42 Al Bridwell 200.00 100.00
❑ 43 Rube Marquard 600.00 300.00
❑ 44 Jeff (Charles) Tesreau 200.00 100.00
❑ 45 Fred Luderus 200.00 100.00
❑ 46 Bob Groom 200.00 100.00
❑ 47 Josh Devore 200.00 100.00
❑ 48 Steve O'Neill 200.00 100.00
❑ 49 John Miller 200.00 100.00
❑ 50 John Hummell 200.00 100.00
❑ 51 Nap Rucker 200.00 100.00
❑ 52 Zach Wheat 600.00 300.00
❑ 53 Otto Miller 200.00 100.00
❑ 54 Marty O'Toole 200.00 100.00
❑ 55 Dick Hoblitzel 200.00 100.00
❑ 56 Clyde Milan 200.00 100.00
❑ 57 Walter Johnson 3000.00 1500.00
❑ 58 Wally Schang 200.00 100.00
❑ 59 Harry Gessler 200.00 100.00
❑ 60 Oscar Dugey 200.00 100.00
❑ 61 Ray Schalk 800.00 400.00
❑ 62 Willie Mitchell 200.00 100.00
❑ 63 Babe Adams 200.00 100.00
❑ 64 Jimmy Archer 200.00 100.00
❑ 65 Tris Speaker 1500.00 750.00
❑ 66 Napoleon Lajoie 1200.00 600.00
❑ 67 Otis Crandall 200.00 100.00
❑ 68 Honus Wagner 6000.00 3000.00
❑ 69 John McGraw MG 800.00 400.00
❑ 70 Fred Clarke 600.00 300.00
❑ 71 Chief Meyers 250.00 125.00
❑ 72 John Boehling 200.00 100.00
❑ 73 Max Carey 800.00 400.00
❑ 74 Frank Owens 200.00 100.00
❑ 75 Miller Huggins 600.00 300.00
❑ 76 Claude Hendrix 200.00 100.00
❑ 77 Hughie Jennings MG 600.00 300.00
❑ 78 Fred Merkle 200.00 100.00
❑ 79 Ping Bodie 200.00 100.00
❑ 80 Ed Ruelbach 200.00 100.00
❑ 81 Jim Delahanty 200.00 100.00
❑ 82 Gavvy Cravath 200.00 100.00
❑ 83 Russ Ford 200.00 100.00
❑ 84 Elmer E. Knetzer 200.00 100.00
❑ 85 Buck Herzog 200.00 100.00
❑ 86 Burt Shotton 200.00 100.00
❑ 87 Forrest Cady 200.00 100.00
❑ 88 Christy Mathewson 3500.00 1750.00
❑ 89 Lawrence Cheney 200.00 100.00
❑ 90 Frank Smith 200.00 100.00
❑ 91 Roger Peckinpaugh 200.00 100.00
❑ 92 Al Demaree 200.00 100.00
❑ 93 Del Pratt 250.00 125.00
❑ 94 Eddie Cicotte 900.00 450.00
❑ 95 Ray Keating 200.00 100.00
❑ 96 Beals Becker 250.00 125.00
❑ 97 John (Rube) Benton 200.00 100.00
❑ 98 Frank LaPorte 200.00 100.00
❑ 99 Hal Chase 500.00 250.00
❑ 100 Thomas Seaton 200.00 100.00
❑ 101 Frank Schulte 200.00 100.00
❑ 102 Ray Fisher 200.00 100.00
❑ 103 Joe Jackson 15000.00 7500.00
❑ 104 Vic Saier 200.00 100.00
❑ 105 James Lavender 200.00 100.00
❑ 106 Joe Birmingham 200.00 100.00
❑ 107 Thomas Downey 200.00 100.00
❑ 108 Sherry Magee 200.00 100.00
❑ 109 Fred Blanding 200.00 100.00
❑ 110 Bob Bescher 200.00 100.00
❑ 111 Herbie Moran 200.00 100.00
❑ 112 Ed Sweeney 200.00 100.00
❑ 113 George Suggs 200.00 100.00
❑ 114 George Moriarity 200.00 100.00
❑ 115 Addison Brennan 200.00 100.00
❑ 116 Rollie Zeider 200.00 100.00
❑ 117 Ted Easterly 200.00 100.00
❑ 118 Ed Konetchy 200.00 100.00
❑ 119 George Perring 200.00 100.00
❑ 120 Mike Doolan 200.00 100.00
❑ 121 Hub Perdue 200.00 100.00
❑ 122 Owen Bush 200.00 100.00
❑ 123 Slim Sallee 200.00 100.00
❑ 124 Earl Moore 200.00 100.00
❑ 125 Bert Niehoff 200.00 100.00
❑ 126 Walter Blair 200.00 100.00
❑ 127 Butch Schmidt 200.00 100.00
❑ 128 Steve Evans 200.00 100.00
❑ 129 Ray Caldwell 200.00 100.00
❑ 130 Ivy Wingo 200.00 100.00
❑ 131 Geo. Baumgardner 200.00 100.00
❑ 132 Les Nunamaker 200.00 100.00
❑ 133 Branch Rickey MG 1200.00 600.00
❑ 134 Armando Marsans 250.00 125.00
❑ 135 William Killefer 200.00 100.00
❑ 136 Rabbit Maranville 600.00 300.00
❑ 137 William Rariden 200.00 100.00
❑ 138 Hank Gowdy 200.00 100.00
❑ 139 Rebel Oakes 200.00 100.00
❑ 140 Danny Murphy 200.00 100.00
❑ 141 Cy Barger 200.00 100.00
❑ 142 Eugene Packard 200.00 100.00
❑ 143 Jake Daubert 200.00 100.00
❑ 144 James C. Walsh 200.00 100.00
❑ 145 Ted Cather 250.00 125.00
❑ 146 George Tyler 250.00 125.00
❑ 147 Lee Magee 250.00 125.00
❑ 148 Owen Wilson 250.00 125.00
❑ 149 Hal Janvrin 250.00 125.00
❑ 150 Doc Johnston 250.00 125.00
❑ 151 George Whitted 250.00 125.00
❑ 152 George McQuillen 250.00 125.00
❑ 153 Bill James 250.00 125.00
❑ 154 Dick Rudolph 250.00 125.00
❑ 155 Joe Connolly 250.00 125.00
❑ 156 Jean Dubuc 250.00 125.00
❑ 157 George Kaiserling 250.00 125.00
❑ 158 Fritz Maisel 250.00 125.00
❑ 159 Heinie Groh 250.00 125.00
❑ 160 Benny Kauff 250.00 125.00
❑ 161 Edd Roush 1000.00 500.00
❑ 162 George Stallings MG 250.00 125.00
❑ 163 Bert Whaling 250.00 125.00
❑ 164 Bob Shawkey 250.00 125.00
❑ 165 Eddie Murphy 250.00 125.00
❑ 166 Joe Bush 250.00 125.00
❑ 167 Clark Griffith 600.00 300.00
❑ 168 Vin Campbell 250.00 125.00
❑ 169 Raymond Collins 250.00 125.00
❑ 170 Hans Lobert 250.00 125.00
❑ 171 Earl Hamilton 250.00 125.00
❑ 172 Erskine Mayer 250.00 125.00
❑ 173 Tilly Walker 250.00 125.00
❑ 174 Robert Veach 250.00 125.00
❑ 175 Joseph Benz 250.00 125.00
❑ 176 Hippo Vaughn 600.00 300.00

1981 Donruss

❑ COMPLETE SET (605) 50.00 20.00
❑ 1 Ozzie Smith 3.00 1.25
❑ 2 Rollie Fingers .25 .08
❑ 3 Rick Wise .10 .02
❑ 4 Gene Richards .10 .02
❑ 5 Alan Trammell .50 .20
❑ 6 Tom Brookens .10 .02
❑ 7A Duffy Dyer P1 .25 .08
❑ 7B Duffy Dyer P2 .10 .02
❑ 8 Mark Fidrych .25 .08
❑ 9 Dave Rozema .10 .02
❑ 10 Ricky Peters RC .10 .02
❑ 11 Mike Schmidt 2.50 1.00
❑ 12 Willie Stargell .50 .20
❑ 13 Tim Foli .10 .02
❑ 14 Manny Sanguillen .25 .08
❑ 15 Grant Jackson .10 .02
❑ 16 Eddie Solomon .10 .02
❑ 17 Omar Moreno .10 .02
❑ 18 Joe Morgan .50 .20
❑ 19 Rafael Landestoy .10 .02
❑ 20 Bruce Bochy .10 .02
❑ 21 Joe Sambito .10 .02
❑ 22 Manny Trillo .10 .02
❑ 23A Dave Smith P1 .50 .20
❑ 23B Dave Smith P2 RC .50 .20
❑ 24 Terry Puhl .10 .02
❑ 25 Bump Wills .10 .02
❑ 26A John Ellis P1 ERR .50 .20
❑ 26B John Ellis P2 COR .25 .08
❑ 27 Jim Kern .10 .02
❑ 28 Richie Zisk .10 .02
❑ 29 John Mayberry .10 .02
❑ 30 Bob Davis .10 .02
❑ 31 Jackson Todd .10 .02
❑ 32 Alvis Woods .10 .02
❑ 33 Steve Carlton .50 .20
❑ 34 Lee Mazzilli .25 .08
❑ 35 John Stearns .10 .02
❑ 36 Roy Lee Jackson RC .10 .02
❑ 37 Mike Scott .25 .08
❑ 38 Lamar Johnson .10 .02
❑ 39 Kevin Bell .10 .02
❑ 40 Ed Farmer .10 .02
❑ 41 Ross Baumgarten .10 .02
❑ 42 Leo Sutherland RC .10 .02
❑ 43 Dan Meyer .10 .02
❑ 44 Ron Reed .10 .02
❑ 45 Mario Mendoza .10 .02
❑ 46 Rick Honeycutt .10 .02
❑ 47 Glenn Abbott .10 .02

❑ 48 Leon Roberts .10 .02
❑ 49 Rod Carew .50 .20
❑ 50 Bert Campaneris .25 .08
❑ 51A Tom Donahue P1 ERR .25 .08
❑ 51B Tom Donohue P2 RC .10 .02
❑ 52 Dave Frost .10 .02
❑ 53 Ed Halicki .10 .02
❑ 54 Dan Ford .10 .02
❑ 55 Garry Maddox .10 .02
❑ 56A Steve Garvey P1 25HR .25 .08
❑ 56B Steve Garvey P2 21HR .25 .08
❑ 57 Bill Russell .25 .08
❑ 58 Don Sutton .25 .08
❑ 59 Reggie Smith .25 .08
❑ 60 Rick Monday .25 .08
❑ 61 Ray Knight .25 .08
❑ 62 Johnny Bench 1.00 .40
❑ 63 Mario Soto .25 .08
❑ 64 Doug Bair .10 .02
❑ 65 George Foster .25 .08
❑ 66 Jeff Burroughs .25 .08
❑ 67 Keith Hernandez .25 .08
❑ 68 Tom Herr .10 .02
❑ 69 Bob Forsch .10 .02
❑ 70 John Fulgham .10 .02
❑ 71A Bobby Bonds P1 ERR 1.00 .40
❑ 71B Bobby Bonds P2 COR .50 .20
❑ 72A Rennie Stennett P1 .25 .08
❑ 72B Rennie Stennett P2 .10 .02
❑ 73 Joe Strain .10 .02
❑ 74 Ed Whitson .10 .02
❑ 75 Tom Griffin .10 .02
❑ 76 Billy North .10 .02
❑ 77 Gene Garber .10 .02
❑ 78 Mike Hargrove .10 .02
❑ 79 Dave Rosello .10 .02
❑ 80 Ron Hassey .10 .02
❑ 81 Sid Monge .10 .02
❑ 82A Joe Charboneau P1 1.00 .40
❑ 82B Joe Charboneau P2 RC 1.00 .40
❑ 83 Cecil Cooper .25 .08
❑ 84 Sal Bando .25 .08
❑ 85 Moose Haas .10 .02
❑ 86 Mike Caldwell .10 .02
❑ 87A Larry Hisle P1 .25 .08
❑ 87B Larry Hisle P2 .10 .02
❑ 88 Luis Gomez .10 .02
❑ 89 Larry Parrish .10 .02
❑ 90 Gary Carter .50 .20
❑ 91 Bill Gullickson RC .50 .20
❑ 92 Fred Norman .10 .02
❑ 93 Tommy Hutton .10 .02
❑ 94 Carl Yastrzemski 1.50 .60
❑ 95 Glenn Hoffman RC .10 .02
❑ 96 Dennis Eckersley .50 .20
❑ 97A Tom Burgmeier P1 .25 .08
❑ 97B Tom Burgmeier P2 .10 .02
❑ 98 Win Remmerswaal RC .10 .02
❑ 99 Bob Horner .25 .08
❑ 100 George Brett 2.50 1.00
❑ 101 Dave Chalk .10 .02
❑ 102 Dennis Leonard .10 .02
❑ 103 Renie Martin .10 .02
❑ 104 Amos Otis .25 .08
❑ 105 Graig Nettles .25 .08
❑ 106 Eric Soderholm .10 .02
❑ 107 Tommy John .25 .08
❑ 108 Tom Underwood .10 .02
❑ 109 Lou Piniella .25 .08
❑ 110 Mickey Klutts .10 .02
❑ 111 Bobby Murcer .25 .08
❑ 112 Eddie Murray 1.50 .60
❑ 113 Rick Dempsey .10 .02
❑ 114 Scott McGregor .10 .02
❑ 115 Ken Singleton .25 .08
❑ 116 Gary Roenicke .10 .02
❑ 117 Dave Revering .10 .02
❑ 118 Mike Norris .10 .02
❑ 119 Rickey Henderson 6.00 2.50
❑ 120 Mike Heath .10 .02
❑ 121 Dave Cash .10 .02
❑ 122 Randy Jones .25 .08
❑ 123 Eric Rasmussen .10 .02
❑ 124 Jerry Mumphrey .10 .02
❑ 125 Richie Hebner .10 .02
❑ 126 Mark Wagner .10 .02
❑ 127 Jack Morris .50 .20
❑ 128 Dan Petry .10 .02
❑ 129 Bruce Robbins .10 .02
❑ 130 Champ Summers .10 .02
❑ 131 Pete Rose 3.00 1.25
❑ 131B Pete Rose P2 2.00 .75
❑ 132 Willie Stargell .50 .20
❑ 133 Ed Ott .10 .02
❑ 134 Jim Bibby .10 .02
❑ 135 Bert Blyleven .25 .08
❑ 136 Dave Parker .25 .08
❑ 137 Bill Robinson .10 .02
❑ 138 Enos Cabell .10 .02
❑ 139 Dave Bergman .10 .02
❑ 140 J.R. Richard .25 .08
❑ 141 Ken Forsch .10 .02
❑ 142 Larry Bowa UER .25 .08
❑ 143 Frank LaCorte UER .10 .02
❑ 144 Denny Walling .10 .02
❑ 145 Buddy Bell .25 .08
❑ 146 Fergie Jenkins .25 .08
❑ 147 Dannny Darwin .25 .08
❑ 148 John Grubb .10 .02
❑ 149 Alfredo Griffin .10 .02
❑ 150 Jerry Garvin .10 .02
❑ 151 Paul Mirabella RC .10 .02
❑ 152 Rick Bosetti .10 .02
❑ 153 Dick Ruthven .10 .02
❑ 154 Frank Taveras .10 .02
❑ 155 Craig Swan .10 .02
❑ 156 Jeff Reardon RC 1.00 .40
❑ 157 Steve Henderson .10 .02
❑ 158 Jim Morrison .10 .02
❑ 159 Glenn Borgmann .10 .02
❑ 160 LaMarr Hoyt RC .50 .20
❑ 161 Rich Wortham .10 .02
❑ 162 Thad Bosley .10 .02
❑ 163 Julio Cruz .10 .02
❑ 164A Del Unser P1 .25 .08
❑ 164B Del Unser P2 .10 .02
❑ 165 Jim Anderson .10 .02
❑ 166 Jim Beattie .10 .02
❑ 167 Shane Rawley .10 .02
❑ 168 Joe Simpson .10 .02
❑ 169 Rod Carew .50 .20
❑ 170 Fred Patek .10 .02
❑ 171 Frank Tanana .25 .08
❑ 172 Alfredo Martinez RC .10 .02
❑ 173 Chris Knapp .10 .02
❑ 174 Joe Rudi .25 .08
❑ 175 Greg Luzinski .25 .08
❑ 176 Steve Garvey .50 .20
❑ 177 Joe Ferguson .10 .02
❑ 178 Bob Welch .25 .08
❑ 179 Dusty Baker .25 .08
❑ 180 Rudy Law .10 .02
❑ 181 Dave Concepcion .25 .08
❑ 182 Johnny Bench 1.00 .40
❑ 183 Mike LaCoss .10 .02
❑ 184 Ken Griffey .25 .08
❑ 185 Dave Collins .10 .02
❑ 186 Brian Asselstine .10 .02
❑ 187 Garry Templeton .25 .08
❑ 188 Mike Phillips .10 .02
❑ 189 Pete Vuckovich .10 .02
❑ 190 John Urrea .10 .02
❑ 191 Tony Scott .10 .02
❑ 192 Darrell Evans .25 .08
❑ 193 Milt May .10 .02
❑ 194 Bob Knepper .10 .02
❑ 195 Randy Moffitt .10 .02
❑ 196 Larry Herndon .10 .02
❑ 197 Rick Camp .10 .02
❑ 198 Andre Thornton .25 .08
❑ 199 Tom Veryzer .10 .02
❑ 200 Gary Alexander .10 .02
❑ 201 Rick Waits .10 .02
❑ 202 Rick Manning .10 .02
❑ 203 Paul Molitor 1.00 .40
❑ 204 Jim Gantner .10 .02
❑ 205 Paul Mitchell .10 .02
❑ 206 Reggie Cleveland .10 .02
❑ 207 Sixto Lezcano .10 .02
❑ 208 Bruce Benedict .10 .02
❑ 209 Rodney Scott .10 .02
❑ 210 John Tamargo .10 .02
❑ 211 Bill Lee .25 .08
❑ 212 Andre Dawson .50 .20
❑ 213 Rowland Office .10 .02
❑ 214 Carl Yastrzemski 1.50 .60
❑ 215 Jerry Remy .10 .02
❑ 216 Mike Torrez .10 .02
❑ 217 Skip Lockwood .10 .02
❑ 218 Fred Lynn .25 .08
❑ 219 Chris Chambliss .25 .08
❑ 220 Willie Aikens .10 .02
❑ 221 John Wathan .10 .02
❑ 222 Dan Quisenberry .10 .02
❑ 223 Willie Wilson .25 .08
❑ 224 Clint Hurdle .10 .02
❑ 225 Bob Watson .10 .02
❑ 226 Jim Spencer .10 .02
❑ 227 Ron Guidry .25 .08
❑ 228 Reggie Jackson 1.00 .40
❑ 229 Oscar Gamble .10 .02
❑ 230 Jeff Cox RC .10 .02
❑ 231 Luis Tiant .25 .08
❑ 232 Rich Dauer .10 .02
❑ 233 Dan Graham .10 .02
❑ 234 Mike Flanagan .10 .02
❑ 235 John Lowenstein .10 .02
❑ 236 Benny Ayala .10 .02
❑ 237 Wayne Gross .10 .02
❑ 238 Rick Langford .10 .02
❑ 239 Tony Armas .25 .08
❑ 240A Bob Lacy P1 ERR .50 .20
❑ 240B Bob Lacey P2 COR .10 .02
❑ 241 Gene Tenace .25 .08
❑ 242 Bob Shirley .10 .02
❑ 243 Gary Lucas RC .10 .02
❑ 244 Jerry Turner .10 .02
❑ 245 John Wockenfuss .10 .02
❑ 246 Stan Papi .10 .02
❑ 247 Milt Wilcox .10 .02
❑ 248 Dan Schatzeder .10 .02
❑ 249 Steve Kemp .10 .02
❑ 250 Jim Lentine RC .10 .02
❑ 251 Pete Rose 3.00 1.25
❑ 252 Bill Madlock .25 .08
❑ 253 Dale Berra .10 .02
❑ 254 Kent Tekulve .10 .02
❑ 255 Enrique Romo .10 .02
❑ 256 Mike Easler .10 .02
❑ 257 Chuck Tanner MG .10 .02
❑ 258 Art Howe .10 .02
❑ 259 Alan Ashby .10 .02
❑ 260 Nolan Ryan 5.00 2.00
❑ 261A Vern Ruhle P1 ERR .50 .20
❑ 261B Vern Ruhle P2 COR .25 .08
❑ 262 Bob Boone .25 .08
❑ 263 Cesar Cedeno .25 .08
❑ 264 Jeff Leonard .25 .08
❑ 265 Pat Putnam .10 .02
❑ 266 Jon Matlack .10 .02
❑ 267 Dave Rajsich .10 .02
❑ 268 Billy Sample .10 .02
❑ 269 Damaso Garcia RC .10 .02
❑ 270 Tom Buskey .10 .02
❑ 271 Joey McLaughlin .10 .02
❑ 272 Barry Bonnell .10 .02
❑ 273 Tug McGraw .25 .08
❑ 274 Mike Jorgensen .10 .02
❑ 275 Pat Zachry .10 .02
❑ 276 Neil Allen .10 .02
❑ 277 Joel Youngblood .10 .02
❑ 278 Greg Pryor .10 .02
❑ 279 Britt Burns RC .10 .02
❑ 280 Rich Dotson RC .10 .02
❑ 281 Chet Lemon .25 .08
❑ 282 Rusty Kuntz RC .10 .02
❑ 283 Ted Cox .10 .02
❑ 284 Sparky Lyle .25 .08
❑ 285 Larry Cox .10 .02
❑ 286 Floyd Bannister .10 .02
❑ 287 Byron McLaughlin .10 .02
❑ 288 Rodney Craig .10 .02
❑ 289 Bobby Grich .25 .08
❑ 290 Dickie Thon .10 .02
❑ 291 Mark Clear .10 .02
❑ 292 Dave Lemanczyk .10 .02
❑ 293 Jason Thompson .10 .02
❑ 294 Rick Miller .10 .02

❑	295	Lonnie Smith	.25	.08
❑	296	Ron Cey	.25	.08
❑	297	Steve Yeager	.25	.08
❑	298	Bobby Castillo	.10	.02
❑	299	Manny Mota	.25	.08
❑	300	Jay Johnstone	.10	.02
❑	301	Dan Driessen	.10	.02
❑	302	Joe Nolan RC	.10	.02
❑	303	Paul Householder RC	.10	.02
❑	304	Harry Spilman	.10	.02
❑	305	Cesar Geronimo	.10	.02
❑	306A	Gary Mathews P1 ERR	.50	.20
❑	306B	Gary Matthews P2 COR	.25	.08
❑	307	Ken Reitz	.10	.02
❑	308	Ted Simmons	.25	.08
❑	309	John Littlefield RC	.10	.02
❑	310	George Frazier	.10	.02
❑	311	Dane Iorg	.10	.02
❑	312	Mike Ivie	.10	.02
❑	313	Dennis Littlejohn	.10	.02
❑	314	Gary Lavelle	.10	.02
❑	315	Jack Clark	.25	.08
❑	316	Jim Wohlford	.10	.02
❑	317	Rick Matula	.10	.02
❑	318	Toby Harrah	.25	.08
❑	319A	Dwane Kuiper P1 ERR	.25	.08
❑	319B	Duane Kuiper P2 COR	.10	.02
❑	320	Len Barker	.25	.08
❑	321	Victor Cruz	.10	.02
❑	322	Dell Alston	.10	.02
❑	323	Robin Yount	1.50	.60
❑	324	Charlie Moore	.10	.02
❑	325	Lary Sorensen	.10	.02
❑	326A	Gorman Thomas P1	.50	.20
❑	326B	Gorman Thomas P2	.25	.08
❑	327	Bob Rodgers MG	.10	.02
❑	328	Phil Niekro	.25	.08
❑	329	Chris Speier	.10	.02
❑	330A	Steve Rodgers P1	.25	.08
❑	330B	Steve Rogers P2 COR	.25	.08
❑	331	Woodie Fryman	.10	.02
❑	332	Warren Cromartie	.10	.02
❑	333	Jerry White	.10	.02
❑	334	Tony Perez	.50	.20
❑	335	Carlton Fisk	.50	.20
❑	336	Dick Drago	.10	.02
❑	337	Steve Renko	.10	.02
❑	338	Jim Rice	.25	.08
❑	339	Jerry Royster	.10	.02
❑	340	Frank White	.25	.08
❑	341	Jamie Quirk	.10	.02
❑	342A	Paul Spittorff P1 ERR	.25	.08
❑	342B	Paul Splittorff P2 COR	.10	.02
❑	343	Marty Pattin	.10	.02
❑	344	Pete LaCock	.10	.02
❑	345	Willie Randolph	.25	.08
❑	346	Rick Cerone	.10	.02
❑	347	Rich Gossage	.25	.08
❑	348	Reggie Jackson	1.00	.40
❑	349	Ruppert Jones	.10	.02
❑	350	Dave McKay RC	.10	.02
❑	351	Yogi Berra CO	1.00	.40
❑	352	Doug DeCinces	.10	.02
❑	353	Jim Palmer	.50	.20
❑	354	Tippy Martinez	.10	.02
❑	355	Al Bumbry	.10	.02
❑	356	Earl Weaver MG	.25	.08
❑	357A	Bob Picciolo P1 ERR	.25	.08
❑	357B	Rob Picciolo P2 COR	.10	.02
❑	358	Matt Keough	.10	.02
❑	359	Dwayne Murphy	.10	.02
❑	360	Brian Kingman	.10	.02
❑	361	Bill Fahey	.10	.02
❑	362	Steve Mura	.10	.02
❑	363	Dennis Kinney RC	.10	.02
❑	364	Dave Winfield	.50	.20
❑	365	Lou Whitaker	.50	.20
❑	366	Lance Parrish	.25	.08
❑	367	Tim Corcoran	.10	.02
❑	368	Pat Underwood	.10	.02
❑	369	Al Cowens	.10	.02
❑	370	Sparky Anderson MG	.25	.08
❑	371	Pete Rose	3.00	1.25
❑	372	Phil Garner	.25	.08
❑	373	Steve Nicosia	.10	.02
❑	374	John Candelaria	.25	.08
❑	375	Don Robinson	.10	.02
❑	376	Lee Lacy	.10	.02
❑	377	John Milner	.10	.02
❑	378	Craig Reynolds	.10	.02
❑	379A	Luis Pujois P1 ERR	.25	.08
❑	379B	Luis Pujols P2 COR	.10	.02
❑	380	Joe Niekro	.10	.02
❑	381	Joaquin Andujar	.25	.08
❑	382	Keith Moreland RC	.10	.02
❑	383	Jose Cruz	.25	.08
❑	384	Bill Virdon MG	.10	.02
❑	385	Jim Sundberg	.25	.08
❑	386	Doc Medich	.10	.02
❑	387	Al Oliver	.25	.08
❑	388	Jim Norris	.10	.02
❑	389	Bob Bailor	.10	.02
❑	390	Ernie Whitt	.10	.02
❑	391	Otto Velez	.10	.02
❑	392	Roy Howell	.10	.02
❑	393	Bob Walk RC	.50	.20
❑	394	Doug Flynn	.10	.02
❑	395	Pete Falcone	.10	.02
❑	396	Tom Hausman	.10	.02
❑	397	Elliott Maddox	.10	.02
❑	398	Mike Squires	.10	.02
❑	399	Marvis Foley RC	.10	.02
❑	400	Steve Trout	.10	.02
❑	401	Wayne Nordhagen	.10	.02
❑	402	Tony LaRussa MG	.25	.08
❑	403	Bruce Bochte	.10	.02
❑	404	Bake McBride	.25	.08
❑	405	Jerry Narron	.10	.02
❑	406	Rob Dressler	.10	.02
❑	407	Dave Heaverlo	.10	.02
❑	408	Tom Paciorek	.10	.02
❑	409	Carney Lansford	.25	.08
❑	410	Brian Downing	.25	.08
❑	411	Don Aase	.10	.02
❑	412	Jim Barr	.10	.02
❑	413	Don Baylor	.25	.08
❑	414	Jim Fregosi MG	.10	.02
❑	415	Dallas Green MG	.10	.02
❑	416	Dave Lopes	.25	.08
❑	417	Jerry Reuss	.10	.02
❑	418	Rick Sutcliffe	.25	.08
❑	419	Derrel Thomas	.10	.02
❑	420	Tom Lasorda MG	.50	.20
❑	421	Charlie Leibrandt RC	.50	.20
❑	422	Tom Seaver	1.00	.40
❑	423	Ron Oester	.10	.02
❑	424	Junior Kennedy	.10	.02
❑	425	Tom Seaver	1.00	.40
❑	426	Bobby Cox MG	.25	.08
❑	427	Leon Durham RC	.50	.20
❑	428	Terry Kennedy	.10	.02
❑	429	Silvio Martinez	.10	.02
❑	430	George Hendrick	.25	.08
❑	431	Red Schoendienst MG	.50	.20
❑	432	Johnnie LeMaster	.10	.02
❑	433	Vida Blue	.25	.08
❑	434	John Montefusco	.10	.02
❑	435	Terry Whitfield	.10	.02
❑	436	Dave Bristol MG	.10	.02
❑	437	Dale Murphy	.50	.20
❑	438	Jerry Dybzinski RC	.10	.02
❑	439	Jorge Orta	.10	.02
❑	440	Wayne Garland	.10	.02
❑	441	Miguel Dilone	.10	.02
❑	442	Dave Garcia MG	.10	.02
❑	443	Don Money	.10	.02
❑	444A	Buck Martinez P1 ERR	.25	.08
❑	444B	Buck Martinez P2 COR	.10	.02
❑	445	Jerry Augustine	.10	.02
❑	446	Ben Oglivie	.25	.08
❑	447	Jim Slaton	.10	.02
❑	448	Doyle Alexander	.10	.02
❑	449	Tony Bernazard	.10	.02
❑	450	Scott Sanderson	.10	.02
❑	451	David Palmer	.10	.02
❑	452	Stan Bahnsen	.10	.02
❑	453	Dick Williams MG	.10	.02
❑	454	Rick Burleson	.10	.02
❑	455	Gary Allenson	.10	.02
❑	456	Bob Stanley	.10	.02
❑	457A	John Tudor ERR	1.00	.40
❑	457B	John Tudor RC	1.00	.40
❑	458	Dwight Evans	.50	.20
❑	459	Glenn Hubbard	.10	.02
❑	460	U.L. Washington	.10	.02
❑	461	Larry Gura	.10	.02
❑	462	Rich Gale	.10	.02
❑	463	Hal McRae	.25	.08
❑	464	Jim Frey MG RC	.10	.02
❑	465	Bucky Dent	.25	.08
❑	466	Dennis Werth RC	.10	.02
❑	467	Ron Davis	.10	.02
❑	468	Reggie Jackson	1.00	.40
❑	469	Bobby Brown	.10	.02
❑	470	Mike Davis RC	.50	.20
❑	471	Gaylord Perry	.25	.08
❑	472	Mark Belanger	.10	.02
❑	473	Jim Palmer	.50	.20
❑	474	Sammy Stewart	.10	.02
❑	475	Tim Stoddard	.10	.02
❑	476	Steve Stone	.10	.02
❑	477	Jeff Newman	.10	.02
❑	478	Steve McCatty	.10	.02
❑	479	Billy Martin MG	.50	.20
❑	480	Mitchell Page	.10	.02
❑	481	Steve Carlton CY	.25	.08
❑	482	Bill Buckner	.25	.08
❑	483A	Ivan DeJesus P1 ERR	.25	.08
❑	483B	Ivan DeJesus P2 COR	.10	.02
❑	484	Cliff Johnson	.10	.02
❑	485	Lenny Randle	.10	.02
❑	486	Larry Milbourne	.10	.02
❑	487	Roy Smalley	.10	.02
❑	488	John Castino	.10	.02
❑	489	Ron Jackson	.10	.02
❑	490A	Dave Roberts P1	.25	.08
❑	490B	Dave Roberts P2	.10	.02
❑	491	George Brett MVP	1.50	.60
❑	492	Mike Cubbage	.10	.02
❑	493	Rob Wilfong	.10	.02
❑	494	Danny Goodwin	.10	.02
❑	495	Jose Morales	.10	.02
❑	496	Mickey Rivers	.10	.02
❑	497	Mike Edwards	.10	.02
❑	498	Mike Sadek	.10	.02
❑	499	Lenn Sakata	.10	.02
❑	500	Gene Michael MG	.10	.02
❑	501	Dave Roberts	.10	.02
❑	502	Steve Dillard	.10	.02
❑	503	Jim Essian	.10	.02
❑	504	Rance Mulliniks	.10	.02
❑	505	Darrell Porter	.10	.02
❑	506	Joe Torre MG	.25	.08
❑	507	Terry Crowley	.10	.02
❑	508	Bill Travers	.10	.02
❑	509	Nelson Norman	.10	.02
❑	510	Bob McClure	.10	.02
❑	511	Steve Howe RC	.50	.20
❑	512	Dave Rader	.10	.02
❑	513	Mick Kelleher	.10	.02
❑	514	Kiko Garcia	.10	.02
❑	515	Larry Biittner	.10	.02
❑	516A	Willie Norwood P1	.25	.08
❑	516B	Willie Norwood P2	.10	.02
❑	517	Bo Diaz	.10	.02
❑	518	Juan Beniquez	.10	.02
❑	519	Scot Thompson	.10	.02
❑	520	Jim Tracy RC	1.00	.40
❑	521	Carlos Lezcano RC	.10	.02
❑	522	Joe Amalfitano MG	.10	.02
❑	523	Preston Hanna	.10	.02
❑	524A	Ray Burris P1	.25	.08
❑	524B	Ray Burris P2	.10	.02
❑	525	Broderick Perkins	.10	.02
❑	526	Mickey Hatcher	.10	.02
❑	527	John Goryl MG	.10	.02
❑	528	Dick Davis	.10	.02
❑	529	Butch Wynegar	.10	.02
❑	530	Sal Butera RC	.10	.02
❑	531	Jerry Koosman	.25	.08
❑	532A	Geoff Zahn P1	.25	.08
❑	532B	Geoff Zahn P2	.10	.02
❑	533	Dennis Martinez	.25	.08
❑	534	Gary Thomasson	.10	.02
❑	535	Steve Macko	.10	.02
❑	536	Jim Kaat	.25	.08
❑	537	G.Brett/R.Carew	1.50	.60
❑	538	Tim Raines RC	2.50	1.00

❑ 539 Keith Smith .10 .02
❑ 540 Ken Macha .10 .02
❑ 541 Burt Hooton .10 .02
❑ 542 Butch Hobson .10 .02
❑ 543 Bill Stein .10 .02
❑ 544 Dave Stapleton RC .10 .02
❑ 545 Bob Pate RC .10 .02
❑ 546 Doug Corbett RC .10 .02
❑ 547 Darrell Jackson .10 .02
❑ 548 Pete Redfern .10 .02
❑ 549 Roger Erickson .10 .02
❑ 550 Al Hrabosky .25 .08
❑ 551 Dick Tidrow .10 .02
❑ 552 Dave Ford RC .10 .02
❑ 553 Dave Kingman .25 .08
❑ 554A Mike Vail P1 .25 .08
❑ 554B Mike Vail P2 .10 .02
❑ 555A Jerry Martin P1 .25 .08
❑ 555B Jerry Martin P2 .10 .02
❑ 556A Jesus Figueroa P1 .25 .08
❑ 556B Jesus Figueroa P2 RC .10 .02
❑ 557 Don Stanhouse .10 .02
❑ 558 Barry Foote .10 .02
❑ 559 Tim Blackwell .10 .02
❑ 560 Bruce Sutter .50 .20
❑ 561 Rick Reuschel .25 .08
❑ 562 Lynn McGlothen .10 .02
❑ 563A Bob Owchinko P1 .25 .08
❑ 563B Bob Owchinko P2 .10 .02
❑ 564 John Verhoeven .10 .02
❑ 565 Ken Landreaux .10 .02
❑ 566A Glen Adams P1 ERR .25 .08
❑ 566B Glenn Adams P2 COR .10 .02
❑ 567 Hosken Powell .10 .02
❑ 568 Dick Noles .10 .02
❑ 569 Danny Ainge RC 3.00 1.25
❑ 570 Bobby Mattick MG RC .10 .02
❑ 571 Joe Lefebvre RC .10 .02
❑ 572 Bobby Clark .10 .02
❑ 573 Dennis Lamp .10 .02
❑ 574 Randy Lerch .10 .02
❑ 575 Mookie Wilson RC 3.00 1.25
❑ 576 Ron LeFlore .25 .08
❑ 577 Jim Dwyer .10 .02
❑ 578 Bill Castro .10 .02
❑ 579 Greg Minton .10 .02
❑ 580 Mark Littell .10 .02
❑ 581 Andy Hassler .10 .02
❑ 582 Dave Stieb .25 .08
❑ 583 Ken Oberkfell .10 .02
❑ 584 Larry Bradford .10 .02
❑ 585 Fred Stanley .10 .02
❑ 586 Bill Caudill .10 .02
❑ 587 Doug Capilla .10 .02
❑ 588 George Riley RC .10 .02
❑ 589 Willie Hernandez .10 .02
❑ 590 Mike Schmidt MVP 2.50 1.00
❑ 591 Steve Stone CY .10 .02
❑ 592 Rick Sofield .10 .02
❑ 593 Bombo Rivera .10 .02
❑ 594 Gary Ward .10 .02
❑ 595A Dave Edwards P1 .25 .08
❑ 595B Dave Edwards P2 .10 .02
❑ 596 Mike Proly .10 .02
❑ 597 Tommy Boggs .10 .02
❑ 598 Greg Gross .10 .02
❑ 599 Elias Sosa .10 .02
❑ 600 Pat Kelly .10 .02
❑ 601A Checklist 1-120 P1 .25 .08
❑ 601B Checklist 1-120 P2 .50 .20
❑ 602 Checklist 121-240 NNO .25 .08
❑ 603A Checklist 241-360 P1 .25 .08
❑ 603B Checklist 241-360 P2 .25 .08
❑ 604A Checklist 361-480 P1 .25 .08
❑ 604B Checklist 361-480 P2 .25 .08
❑ 605A Checklist 481-600 P1 .25 .08
❑ 605B Checklist 481-600 P2 .25 .08

1982 Donruss

❑ COMPLETE SET (660) 60.00 30.00
❑ COMP.FACT.SET (660) 60.00 30.00
❑ COMP.RUTH PUZZLE 10.00 5.00
❑ 1 Pete Rose DK 2.50 1.00
❑ 2 Gary Carter DK .20 .07
❑ 3 Steve Garvey DK .20 .07
❑ 4 Vida Blue DK .20 .07

❑ 5 Alan Trammell DK .20 .07
❑ 5A Alan Trammel DK ERR .20 .07
❑ 6 Len Barker DK .10 .02
❑ 7 Dwight Evans DK .40 .15
❑ 8 Rod Carew DK .40 .15
❑ 9 George Hendrick DK .20 .07
❑ 10 Phil Niekro DK .20 .07
❑ 11 Richie Zisk DK .10 .02
❑ 12 Dave Parker DK .20 .07
❑ 13 Nolan Ryan DK 4.00 1.50
❑ 14 Ivan DeJesus DK .10 .02
❑ 15 George Brett DK 2.00 .75
❑ 16 Tom Seaver DK .40 .15
❑ 17 Dave Kingman DK .20 .07
❑ 18 Dave Winfield DK .20 .07
❑ 19 Mike Norris DK .10 .02
❑ 20 Carlton Fisk DK .40 .15
❑ 21 Ozzie Smith DK 1.50 .60
❑ 22 Roy Smalley DK .10 .02
❑ 23 Buddy Bell DK .20 .07
❑ 24 Ken Singleton DK .20 .07
❑ 25 John Mayberry DK .10 .02
❑ 26 Gorman Thomas DK .20 .07
❑ 27 Earl Weaver MG .20 .07
❑ 28 Rollie Fingers .20 .07
❑ 29 Sparky Anderson MG .20 .07
❑ 30 Dennis Eckersley .40 .15
❑ 31 Dave Winfield .20 .07
❑ 32 Burt Hooton .10 .02
❑ 33 Rick Waits .10 .02
❑ 34 George Brett 2.00 .75
❑ 35 Steve McCatty .10 .02
❑ 36 Steve Rogers .20 .07
❑ 37 Bill Stein .10 .02
❑ 38 Steve Renko .10 .02
❑ 39 Mike Squires .10 .02
❑ 40 George Hendrick .20 .07
❑ 41 Bob Knepper .10 .02
❑ 42 Steve Carlton .40 .15
❑ 43 Larry Biittner .10 .02
❑ 44 Chris Welsh .10 .02
❑ 45 Steve Nicosia .10 .02
❑ 46 Jack Clark .20 .07
❑ 47 Chris Chambliss .20 .07
❑ 48 Ivan DeJesus .10 .02
❑ 49 Lee Mazzilli .20 .07
❑ 50 Julio Cruz .10 .02
❑ 51 Pete Redfern .10 .02
❑ 52 Dave Stieb .20 .07
❑ 53 Doug Corbett .10 .02
❑ 54 George Bell RC 1.00 .40
❑ 55 Joe Simpson .10 .02
❑ 56 Rusty Staub .20 .07
❑ 57 Hector Cruz .10 .02
❑ 58 Claudell Washington .10 .02
❑ 59 Enrique Romo .10 .02
❑ 60 Gary Lavelle .10 .02
❑ 61 Tim Flannery .10 .02
❑ 62 Joe Nolan .10 .02
❑ 63 Larry Bowa .20 .07
❑ 64 Sixto Lezcano .10 .02
❑ 65 Joe Sambito .10 .02
❑ 66 Bruce Kison .10 .02
❑ 67 Wayne Nordhagen .10 .02
❑ 68 Woodie Fryman .10 .02
❑ 69 Billy Sample .10 .02
❑ 70 Amos Otis .20 .07
❑ 71 Matt Keough .10 .02
❑ 72 Toby Harrah .20 .07
❑ 73 Dave Righetti RC 1.50 .60
❑ 74 Carl Yastrzemski 1.25 .50
❑ 75 Bob Welch .20 .07
❑ 76 Alan Trammell .20 .07
❑ 76A Alan Trammel ERR .20 .07
❑ 77 Rick Dempsey .10 .02
❑ 78 Paul Molitor .20 .07
❑ 79 Dennis Martinez .20 .07
❑ 80 Jim Slaton .10 .02
❑ 81 Champ Summers .10 .02
❑ 82 Carney Lansford .20 .07
❑ 83 Barry Foote .10 .02
❑ 84 Steve Garvey .20 .07
❑ 85 Rick Manning .10 .02
❑ 86 John Wathan .10 .02
❑ 87 Brian Kingman .10 .02
❑ 88 Andre Dawson .20 .07
❑ 89 Jim Kern .10 .02
❑ 90 Bobby Grich .20 .07
❑ 91 Bob Forsch .10 .02
❑ 92 Art Howe .10 .02
❑ 93 Marty Bystrom .10 .02
❑ 94 Ozzie Smith 1.50 .60
❑ 95 Dave Parker .20 .07
❑ 96 Doyle Alexander .10 .02
❑ 97 Al Hrabosky .10 .02
❑ 98 Frank Taveras .10 .02
❑ 99 Tim Blackwell .10 .02
❑ 100 Floyd Bannister .10 .02
❑ 101 Alfredo Griffin .10 .02
❑ 102 Dave Engle .10 .02
❑ 103 Mario Soto .20 .07
❑ 104 Ross Baumgarten .10 .02
❑ 105 Ken Singleton .20 .07
❑ 106 Ted Simmons .20 .07
❑ 107 Jack Morris .20 .07
❑ 108 Bob Watson .10 .02
❑ 109 Dwight Evans .40 .15
❑ 110 Tom Lasorda MG .40 .15
❑ 111 Bert Blyleven .20 .07
❑ 112 Dan Quisenberry .10 .02
❑ 113 Rickey Henderson 2.50 1.00
❑ 114 Gary Carter .20 .07
❑ 115 Brian Downing .20 .07
❑ 116 Al Oliver .20 .07
❑ 117 LaMarr Hoyt .10 .02
❑ 118 Cesar Cedeno .20 .07
❑ 119 Keith Moreland .10 .02
❑ 120 Bob Shirley .10 .02
❑ 121 Terry Kennedy .10 .02
❑ 122 Frank Pastore .10 .02
❑ 123 Gene Garber .10 .02
❑ 124 Tony Pena .20 .07
❑ 125 Allen Ripley .10 .02
❑ 126 Randy Martz .10 .02
❑ 127 Richie Zisk .10 .02
❑ 128 Mike Scott .20 .07
❑ 129 Lloyd Moseby .10 .02
❑ 130 Rob Wilfong .10 .02
❑ 131 Tim Stoddard .10 .02
❑ 132 Gorman Thomas .20 .07
❑ 133 Dan Petry .10 .02
❑ 134 Bob Stanley .10 .02
❑ 135 Lou Piniella .20 .07
❑ 136 Pedro Guerrero .20 .07
❑ 137 Len Barker .10 .02
❑ 138 Rich Gale .10 .02
❑ 139 Wayne Gross .10 .02
❑ 140 Tim Wallach RC 1.00 .40
❑ 141 Gene Mauch MG .10 .02
❑ 142 Doc Medich .10 .02
❑ 143 Tony Bernazard .10 .02
❑ 144 Bill Virdon MG .10 .02
❑ 145 John Littlefield .10 .02
❑ 146 Dave Bergman .10 .02
❑ 147 Dick Davis .10 .02
❑ 148 Tom Seaver .75 .30
❑ 149 Matt Sinatro .10 .02
❑ 150 Chuck Tanner MG .10 .02
❑ 151 Leon Durham .10 .02
❑ 152 Gene Tenace .20 .07
❑ 153 Al Bumbry .10 .02
❑ 154 Mark Brouhard .10 .02
❑ 155 Rick Peters .10 .02
❑ 156 Jerry Remy .10 .02

❑ 157	Rick Reuschel	.20	.07
❑ 158	Steve Howe	.10	.02
❑ 159	Alan Bannister	.10	.02
❑ 160	U.L. Washington	.10	.02
❑ 161	Rick Langford	.10	.02
❑ 162	Bill Gullickson	.10	.02
❑ 163	Mark Wagner	.10	.02
❑ 164	Geoff Zahn	.10	.02
❑ 165	Ron LeFlore	.20	.07
❑ 166	Dane Iorg	.10	.02
❑ 167	Joe Niekro	.10	.02
❑ 168	Pete Rose	2.50	1.00
❑ 169	Dave Collins	.10	.02
❑ 170	Rick Wise	.10	.02
❑ 171	Jim Bibby	.10	.02
❑ 172	Larry Herndon	.10	.02
❑ 173	Bob Horner	.20	.07
❑ 174	Steve Dillard	.10	.02
❑ 175	Mookie Wilson	.20	.07
❑ 176	Dan Meyer	.10	.02
❑ 177	Fernando Arroyo	.10	.02
❑ 178	Jackson Todd	.10	.02
❑ 179	Darrell Jackson	.10	.02
❑ 180	Alvis Woods	.10	.02
❑ 181	Jim Anderson	.10	.02
❑ 182	Dave Kingman	.20	.07
❑ 183	Steve Henderson	.10	.02
❑ 184	Brian Asselstine	.10	.02
❑ 185	Rod Scurry	.10	.02
❑ 186	Fred Breining	.10	.02
❑ 187	Danny Boone	.10	.02
❑ 188	Junior Kennedy	.10	.02
❑ 189	Sparky Lyle	.20	.07
❑ 190	Whitey Herzog MG	.20	.07
❑ 191	Dave Smith	.10	.02
❑ 192	Ed Ott	.10	.02
❑ 193	Greg Luzinski	.20	.07
❑ 194	Bill Lee	.20	.07
❑ 195	Don Zimmer MG	.20	.07
❑ 196	Hal McRae	.20	.07
❑ 197	Mike Norris	.10	.02
❑ 198	Duane Kuiper	.10	.02
❑ 199	Rick Cerone	.10	.02
❑ 200	Jim Rice	.20	.07
❑ 201	Steve Yeager	.20	.07
❑ 202	Tom Brookens	.10	.02
❑ 203	Jose Morales	.10	.02
❑ 204	Roy Howell	.10	.02
❑ 205	Tippy Martinez	.10	.02
❑ 206	Moose Haas	.10	.02
❑ 207	Al Cowens	.10	.02
❑ 208	Dave Stapleton	.10	.02
❑ 209	Bucky Dent	.20	.07
❑ 210	Ron Cey	.20	.07
❑ 211	Jorge Orta	.10	.02
❑ 212	Jamie Quirk	.10	.02
❑ 213	Jeff Jones	.10	.02
❑ 214	Tim Raines	.40	.15
❑ 215	Jon Matlack	.10	.02
❑ 216	Rod Carew	.40	.15
❑ 217	Jim Kaat	.20	.07
❑ 218	Joe Pittman	.10	.02
❑ 219	Larry Christenson	.10	.02
❑ 220	Juan Bonilla RC	.15	.05
❑ 221	Mike Easler	.10	.02
❑ 222	Vida Blue	.20	.07
❑ 223	Rick Camp	.10	.02
❑ 224	Mike Jorgensen	.10	.02
❑ 225	Jody Davis	.10	.02
❑ 226	Mike Parrott	.10	.02
❑ 227	Jim Clancy	.10	.02
❑ 228	Hosken Powell	.10	.02
❑ 229	Tom Hume	.10	.02
❑ 230	Britt Burns	.10	.02
❑ 231	Jim Palmer	.20	.07
❑ 232	Bob Rodgers MG	.10	.02
❑ 233	Milt Wilcox	.10	.02
❑ 234	Dave Revering	.10	.02
❑ 235	Mike Torrez	.10	.02
❑ 236	Robert Castillo	.10	.02
❑ 237	Von Hayes RC	.50	.20
❑ 238	Renie Martin	.10	.02
❑ 239	Dwayne Murphy	.10	.02
❑ 240	Rodney Scott	.10	.02
❑ 241	Fred Patek	.10	.02
❑ 242	Mickey Rivers	.10	.02
❑ 243	Steve Trout	.10	.02
❑ 244	Jose Cruz	.20	.07
❑ 245	Manny Trillo	.10	.02
❑ 246	Lary Sorensen	.10	.02
❑ 247	Dave Edwards	.10	.02
❑ 248	Dan Driessen	.10	.02
❑ 249	Tommy Boggs	.10	.02
❑ 250	Dale Berra	.10	.02
❑ 251	Ed Whitson	.10	.02
❑ 252	Lee Smith RC	2.00	.75
❑ 253	Tom Paciorek	.10	.02
❑ 254	Pat Zachry	.10	.02
❑ 255	Luis Leal	.10	.02
❑ 256	John Castino	.10	.02
❑ 257	Rich Dauer	.10	.02
❑ 258	Cecil Cooper	.20	.07
❑ 259	Dave Rozema	.10	.02
❑ 260	John Tudor	.20	.07
❑ 261	Jerry Mumphrey	.10	.02
❑ 262	Jay Johnstone	.10	.02
❑ 263	Bo Diaz	.10	.02
❑ 264	Dennis Leonard	.10	.02
❑ 265	Jim Spencer	.10	.02
❑ 266	John Milner	.10	.02
❑ 267	Don Aase	.10	.02
❑ 268	Jim Sundberg	.20	.07
❑ 269	Lamar Johnson	.10	.02
❑ 270	Frank LaCorte	.10	.02
❑ 271	Barry Evans	.10	.02
❑ 272	Enos Cabell	.10	.02
❑ 273	Del Unser	.10	.02
❑ 274	George Foster	.20	.07
❑ 275	Brett Butler RC	1.00	.40
❑ 276	Lee Lacy	.10	.02
❑ 277	Ken Reitz	.10	.02
❑ 278	Keith Hernandez	.20	.07
❑ 279	Doug DeCinces	.10	.02
❑ 280	Charlie Moore	.10	.02
❑ 281	Lance Parrish	.20	.07
❑ 282	Ralph Houk MG	.10	.02
❑ 283	Rich Gossage	.20	.07
❑ 284	Jerry Reuss	.10	.02
❑ 285	Mike Stanton	.10	.02
❑ 286	Frank White	.20	.07
❑ 287	Bob Owchinko	.10	.02
❑ 288	Scott Sanderson	.10	.02
❑ 289	Bump Wills	.10	.02
❑ 290	Dave Frost	.10	.02
❑ 291	Chet Lemon	.20	.07
❑ 292	Tito Landrum	.10	.02
❑ 293	Vern Ruhle	.10	.02
❑ 294	Mike Schmidt	2.00	.75
❑ 295	Sam Mejias	.10	.02
❑ 296	Gary Lucas	.10	.02
❑ 297	John Candelaria	.10	.02
❑ 298	Jerry Martin	.10	.02
❑ 299	Dale Murphy	.40	.15
❑ 300	Mike Lum	.10	.02
❑ 301	Tom Hausman	.10	.02
❑ 302	Glenn Abbott	.10	.02
❑ 303	Roger Erickson	.10	.02
❑ 304	Otto Velez	.10	.02
❑ 305	Danny Goodwin	.10	.02
❑ 306	John Mayberry	.10	.02
❑ 307	Lenny Randle	.10	.02
❑ 308	Bob Bailor	.10	.02
❑ 309	Jerry Morales	.10	.02
❑ 310	Rufino Linares	.10	.02
❑ 311	Kent Tekulve	.10	.02
❑ 312	Joe Morgan	.20	.07
❑ 313	John Urrea	.10	.02
❑ 314	Paul Householder	.10	.02
❑ 315	Garry Maddox	.10	.02
❑ 316	Mike Ramsey	.10	.02
❑ 317	Alan Ashby	.10	.02
❑ 318	Bob Clark	.10	.02
❑ 319	Tony LaRussa MG	.20	.07
❑ 320	Charlie Lea	.10	.02
❑ 321	Danny Darwin	.10	.02
❑ 322	Cesar Geronimo	.10	.02
❑ 323	Tom Underwood	.10	.02
❑ 324	Andre Thornton	.10	.02
❑ 325	Rudy May	.10	.02
❑ 326	Frank Tanana	.20	.07
❑ 327	Dave Lopes	.20	.07
❑ 328	Richie Hebner	.10	.02
❑ 329	Mike Flanagan	.10	.02
❑ 330	Mike Caldwell	.10	.02
❑ 331	Scott McGregor	.10	.02
❑ 332	Jerry Augustine	.10	.02
❑ 333	Stan Papi	.10	.02
❑ 334	Rick Miller	.10	.02
❑ 335	Graig Nettles	.20	.07
❑ 336	Dusty Baker	.20	.07
❑ 337	Dave Garcia MG	.10	.02
❑ 338	Larry Gura	.10	.02
❑ 339	Cliff Johnson	.10	.02
❑ 340	Warren Cromartie	.10	.02
❑ 341	Steve Comer	.10	.02
❑ 342	Rick Burleson	.10	.02
❑ 343	John Martin RC	.15	.05
❑ 344	Craig Reynolds	.10	.02
❑ 345	Mike Proly	.10	.02
❑ 346	Ruppert Jones	.10	.02
❑ 347	Omar Moreno	.10	.02
❑ 348	Greg Minton	.10	.02
❑ 349	Rick Mahler	.10	.02
❑ 350	Alex Trevino	.10	.02
❑ 351	Mike Krukow	.10	.02
❑ 352A	Shane Rawley ERR (Photo actually Jim Anderson)	.40	.15
❑ 352B	Shane Rawley COR	.10	.02
❑ 353	Garth Iorg	.10	.02
❑ 354	Pete Mackanin	.10	.02
❑ 355	Paul Moskau	.10	.02
❑ 356	Richard Dotson	.10	.02
❑ 357	Steve Stone	.10	.02
❑ 358	Larry Hisle	.10	.02
❑ 359	Aurelio Lopez	.10	.02
❑ 360	Oscar Gamble	.10	.02
❑ 361	Tom Burgmeier	.10	.02
❑ 362	Terry Forster	.20	.07
❑ 363	Joe Charboneau	.20	.07
❑ 364	Ken Brett	.10	.02
❑ 365	Tony Armas	.20	.07
❑ 366	Chris Speier	.10	.02
❑ 367	Fred Lynn	.20	.07
❑ 368	Buddy Bell	.20	.07
❑ 369	Jim Essian	.10	.02
❑ 370	Terry Puhl	.10	.02
❑ 371	Greg Gross	.10	.02
❑ 372	Bruce Sutter	.40	.15
❑ 373	Joe Lefebvre	.10	.02
❑ 374	Ray Knight	.20	.07
❑ 375	Bruce Benedict	.10	.02
❑ 376	Tim Foli	.10	.02
❑ 377	Al Holland	.10	.02
❑ 378	Ken Kravec	.10	.02
❑ 379	Jeff Burroughs	.10	.02
❑ 380	Pete Falcone	.10	.02
❑ 381	Ernie Whitt	.10	.02
❑ 382	Brad Havens	.10	.02
❑ 383	Terry Crowley	.10	.02
❑ 384	Don Money	.10	.02
❑ 385	Dan Schatzeder	.10	.02
❑ 386	Gary Allenson	.10	.02
❑ 387	Yogi Berra CO	.75	.30
❑ 388	Ken Landreaux	.10	.02
❑ 389	Mike Hargrove	.10	.02
❑ 390	Darryl Motley	.10	.02
❑ 391	Dave McKay	.10	.02
❑ 392	Stan Bahnsen	.10	.02
❑ 393	Ken Forsch	.10	.02
❑ 394	Mario Mendoza	.10	.02
❑ 395	Jim Morrison	.10	.02
❑ 396	Mike Ivie	.10	.02
❑ 397	Broderick Perkins	.10	.02
❑ 398	Darrell Evans	.20	.07
❑ 399	Ron Reed	.10	.02
❑ 400	Johnny Bench	.75	.30
❑ 401	Steve Bedrosian RC	.50	.20
❑ 402	Bill Robinson	.10	.02
❑ 403	Bill Buckner	.20	.07
❑ 404	Ken Oberkfell	.10	.02
❑ 405	Cal Ripken RC	30.00	12.50
❑ 406	Jim Gantner	.10	.02
❑ 407	Kirk Gibson	.75	.30
❑ 408	Tony Perez	.40	.15
❑ 409	Tommy John	.20	.07
❑ 410	Dave Stewart RC	1.50	.60
❑ 411	Dan Spillner	.10	.02

❑	412	Willie Aikens	.10	.02
❑	413	Mike Heath	.10	.02
❑	414	Ray Burris	.10	.02
❑	415	Leon Roberts	.10	.02
❑	416	Mike Witt	.50	.20
❑	417	Bob Molinaro	.10	.02
❑	418	Steve Braun	.10	.02
❑	419	Nolan Ryan	4.00	1.50
❑	420	Tug McGraw	.20	.07
❑	421	Dave Concepcion	.20	.07
❑	422A	Juan Eichelberger ERR (Photo actually Gary Lucas	.40	.15
❑	422B	Juan Eichelberger COR	.10	.02
❑	423	Rick Rhoden	.10	.02
❑	424	Frank Robinson MG	.40	.15
❑	425	Eddie Miller	.10	.02
❑	426	Bill Caudill	.10	.02
❑	427	Doug Flynn	.10	.02
❑	428	Larry Andersen UER (Misspelled Anderson on card	.10	.02
❑	429	Al Williams	.10	.02
❑	430	Jerry Garvin	.10	.02
❑	431	Glenn Adams	.10	.02
❑	432	Barry Bonnell	.10	.02
❑	433	Jerry Narron	.10	.02
❑	434	John Stearns	.10	.02
❑	435	Mike Tyson	.10	.02
❑	436	Glenn Hubbard	.10	.02
❑	437	Eddie Solomon	.10	.02
❑	438	Jeff Leonard	.10	.02
❑	439	Randy Bass	.50	.20
❑	440	Mike LaCoss	.10	.02
❑	441	Gary Matthews	.20	.07
❑	442	Mark Littell	.10	.02
❑	443	Don Sutton	.20	.07
❑	444	John Harris	.10	.02
❑	445	Vada Pinson CO	.20	.07
❑	446	Elias Sosa	.10	.02
❑	447	Charlie Hough	.20	.07
❑	448	Willie Wilson	.20	.07
❑	449	Fred Stanley	.10	.02
❑	450	Tom Veryzer	.10	.02
❑	451	Ron Davis	.10	.02
❑	452	Mark Clear	.10	.02
❑	453	Bill Russell	.20	.07
❑	454	Lou Whitaker	.20	.07
❑	455	Dan Graham	.10	.02
❑	456	Reggie Cleveland	.10	.02
❑	457	Sammy Stewart	.10	.02
❑	458	Pete Vuckovich	.10	.02
❑	459	John Wockenfuss	.10	.02
❑	460	Glenn Hoffman	.10	.02
❑	461	Willie Randolph	.20	.07
❑	462	Fernando Valenzuela	.75	.30
❑	463	Ron Hassey	.10	.02
❑	464	Paul Splittorff	.10	.02
❑	465	Rob Picciolo	.10	.02
❑	466	Larry Parrish	.10	.02
❑	467	Johnny Grubb	.10	.02
❑	468	Dan Ford	.10	.02
❑	469	Silvio Martinez	.10	.02
❑	470	Kiko Garcia	.10	.02
❑	471	Bob Boone	.20	.07
❑	472	Luis Salazar	.10	.02
❑	473	Randy Niemann	.10	.02
❑	474	Tom Griffin	.10	.02
❑	475	Phil Niekro	.20	.07
❑	476	Hubie Brooks	.10	.02
❑	477	Dick Tidrow	.10	.02
❑	478	Jim Beattie	.10	.02
❑	479	Damaso Garcia	.10	.02
❑	480	Mickey Hatcher	.10	.02
❑	481	Joe Price	.10	.02
❑	482	Ed Farmer	.10	.02
❑	483	Eddie Murray	.75	.30
❑	484	Ben Oglivie	.20	.07
❑	485	Kevin Saucier	.10	.02
❑	486	Bobby Murcer	.20	.07
❑	487	Bill Campbell	.10	.02
❑	488	Reggie Smith	.20	.07
❑	489	Wayne Garland	.10	.02
❑	490	Jim Wright	.10	.02
❑	491	Billy Martin MG	.40	.15
❑	492	Jim Fanning MG	.10	.02
❑	493	Don Baylor	.20	.07
❑	494	Rick Honeycutt	.10	.02
❑	495	Carlton Fisk	.40	.15
❑	496	Denny Walling	.10	.02
❑	497	Bake McBride	.20	.07
❑	498	Darrell Porter	.10	.02
❑	499	Gene Richards	.10	.02
❑	500	Ron Oester	.10	.02
❑	501	Ken Dayley	.10	.02
❑	502	Jason Thompson	.10	.02
❑	503	Milt May	.10	.02
❑	504	Doug Bird	.10	.02
❑	505	Bruce Bochte	.10	.02
❑	506	Neil Allen	.10	.02
❑	507	Joey McLaughlin	.10	.02
❑	508	Butch Wynegar	.10	.02
❑	509	Gary Roenicke	.10	.02
❑	510	Robin Yount	1.25	.50
❑	511	Dave Tobik	.10	.02
❑	512	Rich Gedman	.50	.20
❑	513	Gene Nelson	.10	.02
❑	514	Rick Monday	.20	.07
❑	515	Miguel Dilone	.10	.02
❑	516	Clint Hurdle	.10	.02
❑	517	Jeff Newman	.10	.02
❑	518	Grant Jackson	.10	.02
❑	519	Andy Hassler	.10	.02
❑	520	Pat Putnam	.10	.02
❑	521	Greg Pryor	.10	.02
❑	522	Tony Scott	.10	.02
❑	523	Steve Mura	.10	.02
❑	524	Johnnie LeMaster	.10	.02
❑	525	Dick Ruthven	.10	.02
❑	526	John McNamara MG	.10	.02
❑	527	Larry McWilliams	.10	.02
❑	528	Johnny Ray RC	.50	.20
❑	529	Pat Tabler	.10	.02
❑	530	Tom Herr	.10	.02
❑	531A	SD Chicken ERR	1.00	.40
❑	531B	SD Chicken COR	1.00	.40
❑	532	Sal Butera	.10	.02
❑	533	Mike Griffin	.10	.02
❑	534	Kelvin Moore	.10	.02
❑	535	Reggie Jackson	.40	.15
❑	536	Ed Romero	.10	.02
❑	537	Derrel Thomas	.10	.02
❑	538	Mike O'Berry	.10	.02
❑	539	Jack O'Connor	.10	.02
❑	540	Bob Ojeda RC	.50	.20
❑	541	Roy Lee Jackson	.10	.02
❑	542	Lynn Jones	.10	.02
❑	543	Gaylord Perry	.20	.07
❑	544A	Phil Garner ERR (Reverse negative)	.20	.07
❑	544B	Phil Garner COR	.20	.07
❑	545	Garry Templeton	.20	.07
❑	546	Rafael Ramirez	.10	.02
❑	547	Jeff Reardon	.20	.07
❑	548	Ron Guidry	.20	.07
❑	549	Tim Laudner	.10	.02
❑	550	John Henry Johnson	.10	.02
❑	551	Chris Bando	.10	.02
❑	552	Bobby Brown	.10	.02
❑	553	Larry Bradford	.10	.02
❑	554	Scott Fletcher RC	.50	.20
❑	555	Jerry Royster	.10	.02
❑	556	Shooty Babitt UER (Spelled Babbitt on front)	.10	.02
❑	557	Kent Hrbek RC	1.00	.40
❑	558	R.Guidry/T.John	.20	.07
❑	559	Mark Bomback	.10	.02
❑	560	Julio Valdez	.10	.02
❑	561	Buck Martinez	.10	.02
❑	562	Mike A. Marshall RC	.50	.20
❑	563	Rennie Stennett	.10	.02
❑	564	Steve Crawford	.10	.02
❑	565	Bob Babcock	.10	.02
❑	566	Johnny Podres CO	.20	.07
❑	567	Paul Serna	.10	.02
❑	568	Harold Baines	.20	.07
❑	569	Dave LaRoche	.10	.02
❑	570	Lee May	.10	.02
❑	571	Gary Ward	.10	.02
❑	572	John Denny	.10	.02
❑	573	Roy Smalley	.10	.02
❑	574	Bob Brenly RC	1.00	.40
❑	575	R.Jackson/D.Winfield	.20	.07
❑	576	Luis Pujols	.10	.02
❑	577	Butch Hobson	.10	.02
❑	578	Harvey Kuenn MG	.10	.02
❑	579	Cal Ripken Sr. CO	.20	.07
❑	580	Juan Berenguer	.10	.02
❑	581	Benny Ayala	.10	.02
❑	582	Vance Law	.10	.02
❑	583	Rick Leach	.10	.02
❑	584	George Frazier	.10	.02
❑	585	P.Rose/M.Schmidt	1.50	.60
❑	586	Joe Rudi	.20	.07
❑	587	Juan Beniquez	.10	.02
❑	588	Luis DeLeon	.10	.02
❑	589	Craig Swan	.10	.02
❑	590	Dave Chalk	.10	.02
❑	591	Billy Gardner MG	.10	.02
❑	592	Sal Bando	.20	.07
❑	593	Bert Campaneris	.20	.07
❑	594	Steve Kemp	.10	.02
❑	595A	Randy Lerch ERR (Braves)	.40	.15
❑	595B	Randy Lerch COR (Brewers)	.10	.02
❑	596	Bryan Clark RC	.15	.05
❑	597	Dave Ford	.10	.02
❑	598	Mike Scioscia	.20	.07
❑	599	John Lowenstein	.10	.02
❑	600	Rene Lachemann MG	.10	.02
❑	601	Mick Kelleher	.10	.02
❑	602	Ron Jackson	.10	.02
❑	603	Jerry Koosman	.20	.07
❑	604	Dave Goltz	.10	.02
❑	605	Ellis Valentine	.10	.02
❑	606	Lonnie Smith	.10	.02
❑	607	Joaquin Andujar	.20	.07
❑	608	Garry Hancock	.10	.02
❑	609	Jerry Turner	.10	.02
❑	610	Bob Bonner	.10	.02
❑	611	Jim Dwyer	.10	.02
❑	612	Terry Bulling	.10	.02
❑	613	Joel Youngblood	.10	.02
❑	614	Larry Milbourne	.10	.02
❑	615	Gene Roof UER (Name on front is Phil Roof)	.10	.02
❑	616	Keith Drumwright	.10	.02
❑	617	Dave Rosello	.10	.02
❑	618	Rickey Keeton	.10	.02
❑	619	Dennis Lamp	.10	.02
❑	620	Sid Monge	.10	.02
❑	621	Jerry White	.10	.02
❑	622	Luis Aguayo	.10	.02
❑	623	Jamie Easterly	.10	.02
❑	624	Steve Sax RC	1.00	.40
❑	625	Dave Roberts	.10	.02
❑	626	Rick Bosetti	.10	.02
❑	627	Terry Francona RC	3.00	1.25
❑	628	T.Seaver/J.Bench	.75	.30
❑	629	Paul Mirabella	.10	.02
❑	630	Rance Mulliniks	.10	.02
❑	631	Kevin Hickey RC	.15	.05
❑	632	Reid Nichols	.10	.02
❑	633	Dave Geisel	.10	.02
❑	634	Ken Griffey	.20	.07
❑	635	Bob Lemon MG	.40	.15
❑	636	Orlando Sanchez	.10	.02
❑	637	Bill Almon	.10	.02
❑	638	Danny Ainge	.20	.07
❑	639	Willie Stargell	.40	.15
❑	640	Bob Sykes	.10	.02
❑	641	Ed Lynch	.10	.02
❑	642	John Ellis	.10	.02
❑	643	Fergie Jenkins	.20	.07
❑	644	Lenn Sakata	.10	.02
❑	645	Julio Gonzalez	.10	.02
❑	646	Jesse Orosco	.10	.02
❑	647	Jerry Dybzinski	.10	.02
❑	648	Tommy Davis CO	.20	.07
❑	649	Ron Gardenhire RC	.50	.20
❑	650	Felipe Alou CO	.20	.07
❑	651	Harvey Haddix CO	.20	.07
❑	652	Willie Upshaw	.50	.20
❑	653	Bill Madlock	.20	.07

❑ 654A DK Checklist 1-26 ERR (Unnumbered) (With Trammel	.40	.15
❑ 654B DK Checklist 1-26 COR (Unnumbered) (With Trammel	.20	.07
❑ 655 Checklist 27-130 (Unnumbered)	.20	.07
❑ 656 Checklist 131-234 (Unnumbered)	.20	.07
❑ 657 Checklist 235-338 (Unnumbered)	.20	.07
❑ 658 Checklist 339-442 (Unnumbered)	.20	.07
❑ 659 Checklist 443-544 (Unnumbered)	.20	.07
❑ 660 Checklist 545-650 (Unnumbered)	.20	.07

1983 Donruss

❑ COMPLETE SET (660)	60.00	30.00
❑ COMP.FACT.SET (660)	80.00	40.00
❑ COMP.COBB PUZZLE	5.00	2.00
❑ 1 Fernando Valenzuela DK	.20	.07
❑ 2 Rollie Fingers DK	.20	.07
❑ 3 Reggie Jackson DK	.40	.15
❑ 4 Jim Palmer DK	.20	.07
❑ 5 Jack Morris DK	.20	.07
❑ 6 George Foster DK	.20	.07
❑ 7 Jim Sundberg DK	.20	.07
❑ 8 Willie Stargell DK	.40	.15
❑ 9 Dave Stieb DK	.20	.07
❑ 10 Joe Niekro DK	.10	.02
❑ 11 Rickey Henderson DK	1.50	.60
❑ 12 Dale Murphy DK	.40	.15
❑ 13 Toby Harrah DK	.20	.07
❑ 14 Bill Buckner DK	.20	.07
❑ 15 Willie Wilson DK	.20	.07
❑ 16 Steve Carlton DK	.40	.15
❑ 17 Ron Guidry DK	.20	.07
❑ 18 Steve Rogers DK	.20	.07
❑ 19 Kent Hrbek DK	.20	.07
❑ 20 Keith Hernandez DK	.20	.07
❑ 21 Floyd Bannister DK	.10	.02
❑ 22 Johnny Bench DK	.75	.30
❑ 23 Britt Burns DK	.10	.02
❑ 24 Joe Morgan DK	.20	.07
❑ 25 Carl Yastrzemski DK	.75	.30
❑ 26 Terry Kennedy DK	.10	.02
❑ 27 Gary Roenicke	.10	.02
❑ 28 Dwight Bernard	.10	.02
❑ 29 Pat Underwood	.10	.02
❑ 30 Gary Allenson	.10	.02
❑ 31 Ron Guidry	.20	.07
❑ 32 Burt Hooton	.10	.02
❑ 33 Chris Bando	.10	.02
❑ 34 Vida Blue	.20	.07
❑ 35 Rickey Henderson	1.50	.60
❑ 36 Ray Burris	.10	.02
❑ 37 John Butcher	.10	.02
❑ 38 Don Aase	.10	.02
❑ 39 Jerry Koosman	.20	.07
❑ 40 Bruce Sutter	.40	.15
❑ 41 Jose Cruz	.20	.07
❑ 42 Pete Rose	2.50	1.00
❑ 43 Cesar Cedeno	.20	.07
❑ 44 Floyd Chiffer	.10	.02
❑ 45 Larry McWilliams	.10	.02
❑ 46 Alan Fowlkes	.10	.02
❑ 47 Dale Murphy	.40	.15
❑ 48 Doug Bird	.10	.02
❑ 49 Hubie Brooks	.10	.02
❑ 50 Floyd Bannister	.10	.02
❑ 51 Jack O'Connor	.10	.02
❑ 52 Steve Senteney	.10	.02
❑ 53 Gary Gaetti RC	1.00	.40
❑ 54 Damaso Garcia	.10	.02
❑ 55 Gene Nelson	.10	.02
❑ 56 Mookie Wilson	.20	.07
❑ 57 Allen Ripley	.10	.02
❑ 58 Bob Horner	.20	.07
❑ 59 Tony Pena	.10	.02
❑ 60 Gary Lavelle	.10	.02
❑ 61 Tim Lollar	.10	.02
❑ 62 Frank Pastore	.10	.02
❑ 63 Garry Maddox	.10	.02
❑ 64 Bob Forsch	.10	.02
❑ 65 Harry Spilman	.10	.02
❑ 66 Geoff Zahn	.10	.02
❑ 67 Salome Barojas	.10	.02
❑ 68 David Palmer	.10	.02
❑ 69 Charlie Hough	.20	.07
❑ 70 Dan Quisenberry	.10	.02
❑ 71 Tony Armas	.20	.07
❑ 72 Rick Sutcliffe	.20	.07
❑ 73 Steve Balboni	.10	.02
❑ 74 Jerry Remy	.10	.02
❑ 75 Mike Scioscia	.20	.07
❑ 76 John Wockenfuss	.10	.02
❑ 77 Jim Palmer	.20	.07
❑ 78 Rollie Fingers	.20	.07
❑ 79 Joe Nolan	.10	.02
❑ 80 Pete Vuckovich	.10	.02
❑ 81 Rick Leach	.10	.02
❑ 82 Rick Miller	.10	.02
❑ 83 Graig Nettles	.20	.07
❑ 84 Ron Cey	.20	.07
❑ 85 Miguel Dilone	.10	.02
❑ 86 John Wathan	.10	.02
❑ 87 Kelvin Moore	.10	.02
❑ 88A Bryn Smith FDC Byrn	.20	.07
❑ 88B Bryn Smith FDC COR	.40	.15
❑ 89 Dave Hostetler	.10	.02
❑ 90 Rod Carew	.40	.15
❑ 91 Lonnie Smith	.10	.02
❑ 92 Bob Knepper	.10	.02
❑ 93 Marty Bystrom	.10	.02
❑ 94 Chris Welsh	.10	.02
❑ 95 Jason Thompson	.10	.02
❑ 96 Tom O'Malley	.10	.02
❑ 97 Phil Niekro	.20	.07
❑ 98 Neil Allen	.10	.02
❑ 99 Bill Buckner	.20	.07
❑ 100 Ed VandeBerg	.10	.02
❑ 101 Jim Clancy	.10	.02
❑ 102 Robert Castillo	.10	.02
❑ 103 Bruce Berenyi	.10	.02
❑ 104 Carlton Fisk	.40	.15
❑ 105 Mike Flanagan	.10	.02
❑ 106 Cecil Cooper	.20	.07
❑ 107 Jack Morris	.20	.07
❑ 108 Mike Morgan	.10	.02
❑ 109 Luis Aponte	.10	.02
❑ 110 Pedro Guerrero	.20	.07
❑ 111 Len Barker	.10	.02
❑ 112 Willie Wilson	.20	.07
❑ 113 Dave Beard	.10	.02
❑ 114 Mike Gates	.10	.02
❑ 115 Reggie Jackson	.40	.15
❑ 116 George Wright RC	.50	.20
❑ 117 Vance Law	.10	.02
❑ 118 Nolan Ryan	4.00	1.50
❑ 119 Mike Krukow	.10	.02
❑ 120 Ozzie Smith	1.25	.50
❑ 121 Broderick Perkins	.10	.02
❑ 122 Tom Seaver	.75	.30
❑ 123 Chris Chambliss	.20	.07
❑ 124 Chuck Tanner MG	.10	.02
❑ 125 Johnnie LeMaster	.10	.02
❑ 126 Mel Hall RC	.50	.20
❑ 127 Bruce Bochte	.10	.02
❑ 128 Charlie Puleo	.10	.02
❑ 129 Luis Leal	.10	.02
❑ 130 John Pacella	.10	.02
❑ 131 Glenn Gulliver	.10	.02
❑ 132 Don Money	.10	.02
❑ 133 Dave Rozema	.10	.02
❑ 134 Bruce Hurst	.10	.02
❑ 135 Rudy May	.10	.02
❑ 136 Tom Lasorda MG	.40	.15
❑ 137 Dan Spillner UER (Photo actually Ed Whitson)	.10	.02
❑ 138 Jerry Martin	.10	.02
❑ 139 Mike Norris	.10	.02
❑ 140 Al Oliver	.20	.07
❑ 141 Daryl Sconiers	.10	.02
❑ 142 Lamar Johnson	.10	.02
❑ 143 Harold Baines	.20	.07
❑ 144 Alan Ashby	.10	.02
❑ 145 Garry Templeton	.20	.07
❑ 146 Al Holland	.10	.02
❑ 147 Bo Diaz	.10	.02
❑ 148 Dave Concepcion	.20	.07
❑ 149 Rick Camp	.10	.02
❑ 150 Jim Morrison	.10	.02
❑ 151 Randy Martz	.10	.02
❑ 152 Keith Hernandez	.20	.07
❑ 153 John Lowenstein	.10	.02
❑ 154 Mike Caldwell	.10	.02
❑ 155 Milt Wilcox	.10	.02
❑ 156 Rich Gedman	.10	.02
❑ 157 Rich Gossage	.20	.07
❑ 158 Jerry Reuss	.10	.02
❑ 159 Ron Hassey	.10	.02
❑ 160 Larry Gura	.10	.02
❑ 161 Dwayne Murphy	.10	.02
❑ 162 Woodie Fryman	.10	.02
❑ 163 Steve Comer	.10	.02
❑ 164 Ken Forsch	.10	.02
❑ 165 Dennis Lamp	.10	.02
❑ 166 David Green RC	.50	.20
❑ 167 Terry Puhl	.10	.02
❑ 168 Mike Schmidt	2.00	.75
❑ 169 Eddie Milner	.10	.02
❑ 170 John Curtis	.10	.02
❑ 171 Don Robinson	.10	.02
❑ 172 Rich Gale	.10	.02
❑ 173 Steve Bedrosian	.10	.02
❑ 174 Willie Hernandez	.10	.02
❑ 175 Ron Gardenhire	.10	.02
❑ 176 Jim Beattie	.10	.02
❑ 177 Tim Laudner	.10	.02
❑ 178 Buck Martinez	.10	.02
❑ 179 Kent Hrbek	.20	.07
❑ 180 Alfredo Griffin	.10	.02
❑ 181 Larry Andersen	.10	.02
❑ 182 Pete Falcone	.10	.02
❑ 183 Jody Davis	.10	.02
❑ 184 Glenn Hubbard	.10	.02
❑ 185 Dale Berra	.10	.02
❑ 186 Greg Minton	.10	.02
❑ 187 Gary Lucas	.10	.02
❑ 188 Dave Van Gorder	.10	.02
❑ 189 Bob Dernier	.10	.02
❑ 190 Willie McGee RC	1.50	.60
❑ 191 Dickie Thon	.10	.02
❑ 192 Bob Boone	.20	.07
❑ 193 Britt Burns	.10	.02
❑ 194 Jeff Reardon	.20	.07
❑ 195 Jon Matlack	.10	.02
❑ 196 Don Slaught RC	.50	.20
❑ 197 Fred Stanley	.10	.02
❑ 198 Rick Manning	.10	.02
❑ 199 Dave Righetti	.20	.07
❑ 200 Dave Stapleton	.10	.02
❑ 201 Steve Yeager	.20	.07
❑ 202 Enos Cabell	.10	.02
❑ 203 Sammy Stewart	.10	.02
❑ 204 Moose Haas	.10	.02
❑ 205 Lenn Sakata	.10	.02
❑ 206 Charlie Moore	.10	.02
❑ 207 Alan Trammell	.20	.07
❑ 208 Jim Rice	.20	.07
❑ 209 Roy Smalley	.10	.02
❑ 210 Bill Russell	.20	.07
❑ 211 Andre Thornton	.10	.02
❑ 212 Willie Aikens	.10	.02
❑ 213 Dave McKay	.10	.02
❑ 214 Tim Blackwell	.10	.02

❑	215	Buddy Bell	.20	.07
❑	216	Doug DeCinces	.10	.02
❑	217	Tom Herr	.10	.02
❑	218	Frank LaCorte	.10	.02
❑	219	Steve Carlton	.40	.15
❑	220	Terry Kennedy	.10	.02
❑	221	Mike Easler	.10	.02
❑	222	Jack Clark	.20	.07
❑	223	Gene Garber	.10	.02
❑	224	Scott Holman	.10	.02
❑	225	Mike Proly	.10	.02
❑	226	Terry Bulling	.10	.02
❑	227	Jerry Garvin	.10	.02
❑	228	Ron Davis	.10	.02
❑	229	Tom Hume	.10	.02
❑	230	Marc Hill	.10	.02
❑	231	Dennis Martinez	.20	.07
❑	232	Jim Gantner	.10	.02
❑	233	Larry Pashnick	.10	.02
❑	234	Dave Collins	.10	.02
❑	235	Tom Burgmeier	.10	.02
❑	236	Ken Landreaux	.10	.02
❑	237	John Denny	.10	.02
❑	238	Hal McRae	.20	.07
❑	239	Matt Keough	.10	.02
❑	240	Doug Flynn	.10	.02
❑	241	Fred Lynn	.20	.07
❑	242	Billy Sample	.10	.02
❑	243	Tom Paciorek	.10	.02
❑	244	Joe Sambito	.10	.02
❑	245	Sid Monge	.10	.02
❑	246	Ken Oberkfell	.10	.02
❑	247	Joe Pittman UER (Photo actually Juan Eichelberge	.10	.02
❑	248	Mario Soto	.20	.07
❑	249	Claudell Washington	.10	.02
❑	250	Rick Rhoden	.10	.02
❑	251	Darrell Evans	.20	.07
❑	252	Steve Henderson	.10	.02
❑	253	Manny Castillo	.10	.02
❑	254	Craig Swan	.10	.02
❑	255	Joey McLaughlin	.10	.02
❑	256	Pete Redfern	.10	.02
❑	257	Ken Singleton	.20	.07
❑	258	Robin Yount	1.25	.50
❑	259	Elias Sosa	.10	.02
❑	260	Bob Ojeda	.10	.02
❑	261	Bobby Murcer	.20	.07
❑	262	Candy Maldonado RC	.50	.20
❑	263	Rick Waits	.10	.02
❑	264	Greg Pryor	.10	.02
❑	265	Bob Owchinko	.10	.02
❑	266	Chris Speier	.10	.02
❑	267	Bruce Kison	.10	.02
❑	268	Mark Wagner	.10	.02
❑	269	Steve Kemp	.10	.02
❑	270	Phil Garner	.20	.07
❑	271	Gene Richards	.10	.02
❑	272	Renie Martin	.10	.02
❑	273	Dave Roberts	.10	.02
❑	274	Dan Driessen	.10	.02
❑	275	Rufino Linares	.10	.02
❑	276	Lee Lacy	.10	.02
❑	277	Ryne Sandberg RC	10.00	4.00
❑	278	Darrell Porter	.10	.02
❑	279	Cal Ripken	6.00	2.50
❑	280	Jamie Easterly	.10	.02
❑	281	Bill Fahey	.10	.02
❑	282	Glenn Hoffman	.10	.02
❑	283	Willie Randolph	.20	.07
❑	284	Fernando Valenzuela	.20	.07
❑	285	Alan Bannister	.10	.02
❑	286	Paul Splittorff	.10	.02
❑	287	Joe Rudi	.20	.07
❑	288	Bill Gullickson	.10	.02
❑	289	Danny Darwin	.10	.02
❑	290	Andy Hassler	.10	.02
❑	291	Ernesto Escarrega	.10	.02
❑	292	Steve Mura	.10	.02
❑	293	Tony Scott	.10	.02
❑	294	Manny Trillo	.10	.02
❑	295	Greg Harris	.10	.02
❑	296	Luis DeLeon	.10	.02
❑	297	Kent Tekulve	.10	.02
❑	298	Atlee Hammaker	.10	.02
❑	299	Bruce Benedict	.10	.02
❑	300	Fergie Jenkins	.20	.07
❑	301	Dave Kingman	.20	.07
❑	302	Bill Caudill	.10	.02
❑	303	John Castino	.10	.02
❑	304	Ernie Whitt	.10	.02
❑	305	Randy Johnson	.10	.02
❑	306	Garth Iorg	.10	.02
❑	307	Gaylord Perry	.20	.07
❑	308	Ed Lynch	.10	.02
❑	309	Keith Moreland	.10	.02
❑	310	Rafael Ramirez	.10	.02
❑	311	Bill Madlock	.20	.07
❑	312	Milt May	.10	.02
❑	313	John Montefusco	.10	.02
❑	314	Wayne Krenchicki	.10	.02
❑	315	George Vukovich	.10	.02
❑	316	Joaquin Andujar	.20	.07
❑	317	Craig Reynolds	.10	.02
❑	318	Rick Burleson	.10	.02
❑	319	Richard Dotson	.10	.02
❑	320	Steve Rogers	.20	.07
❑	321	Dave Schmidt	.10	.02
❑	322	Bud Black RC	.50	.20
❑	323	Jeff Burroughs	.10	.02
❑	324	Von Hayes	.10	.02
❑	325	Butch Wynegar	.10	.02
❑	326	Carl Yastrzemski	1.25	.50
❑	327	Ron Roenicke	.10	.02
❑	328	Howard Johnson RC	1.00	.40
❑	329	Rick Dempsey UER (Posing as a left-handed batte	.10	.02
❑	330A	Jim Slaton (Bio printed black on white)	.10	.02
❑	330B	Jim Slaton (Bio printed black on yellow)	.20	.07
❑	331	Benny Ayala	.10	.02
❑	332	Ted Simmons	.20	.07
❑	333	Lou Whitaker	.20	.07
❑	334	Chuck Rainey	.10	.02
❑	335	Lou Piniella	.20	.07
❑	336	Steve Sax	.20	.07
❑	337	Toby Harrah	.20	.07
❑	338	George Brett	2.00	.75
❑	339	Dave Lopes	.20	.07
❑	340	Gary Carter	.20	.07
❑	341	John Grubb	.10	.02
❑	342	Tim Foli	.10	.02
❑	343	Jim Kaat	.20	.07
❑	344	Mike LaCoss	.10	.02
❑	345	Larry Christenson	.10	.02
❑	346	Juan Bonilla	.10	.02
❑	347	Omar Moreno	.10	.02
❑	348	Chili Davis	.20	.07
❑	349	Tommy Boggs	.10	.02
❑	350	Rusty Staub	.20	.07
❑	351	Bump Wills	.10	.02
❑	352	Rick Sweet	.10	.02
❑	353	Jim Gott RC	.50	.20
❑	354	Terry Felton	.10	.02
❑	355	Jim Kern	.10	.02
❑	356	Bill Almon UER (Expos/Mets in 1983, not Padres/M	.10	.02
❑	357	Tippy Martinez	.10	.02
❑	358	Roy Howell	.10	.02
❑	359	Dan Petry	.10	.02
❑	360	Jerry Mumphrey	.10	.02
❑	361	Mark Clear	.10	.02
❑	362	Mike Marshall	.10	.02
❑	363	Lary Sorensen	.10	.02
❑	364	Amos Otis	.20	.07
❑	365	Rick Langford	.10	.02
❑	366	Brad Mills	.10	.02
❑	367	Brian Downing	.20	.07
❑	368	Mike Richardt	.10	.02
❑	369	Aurelio Rodriguez	.10	.02
❑	370	Dave Smith	.10	.02
❑	371	Tug McGraw	.20	.07
❑	372	Doug Bair	.10	.02
❑	373	Ruppert Jones	.10	.02
❑	374	Alex Trevino	.10	.02
❑	375	Ken Dayley	.10	.02
❑	376	Rod Scurry	.10	.02
❑	377	Bob Brenly	.10	.02
❑	378	Scot Thompson	.10	.02
❑	379	Julio Cruz	.10	.02
❑	380	John Stearns	.10	.02
❑	381	Dale Murray	.10	.02
❑	382	Frank Viola RC	1.50	.60
❑	383	Al Bumbry	.10	.02
❑	384	Ben Oglivie	.20	.07
❑	385	Dave Tobik	.10	.02
❑	386	Bob Stanley	.10	.02
❑	387	Andre Robertson	.10	.02
❑	388	Jorge Orta	.10	.02
❑	389	Ed Whitson	.10	.02
❑	390	Don Hood	.10	.02
❑	391	Tom Underwood	.10	.02
❑	392	Tim Wallach	.20	.07
❑	393	Steve Renko	.10	.02
❑	394	Mickey Rivers	.10	.02
❑	395	Greg Luzinski	.20	.07
❑	396	Art Howe	.10	.02
❑	397	Alan Wiggins	.10	.02
❑	398	Jim Barr	.10	.02
❑	399	Ivan DeJesus	.10	.02
❑	400	Tom Lawless	.10	.02
❑	401	Bob Walk	.10	.02
❑	402	Jimmy Smith	.10	.02
❑	403	Lee Smith	.40	.15
❑	404	George Hendrick	.20	.07
❑	405	Eddie Murray	.75	.30
❑	406	Marshall Edwards	.10	.02
❑	407	Lance Parrish	.20	.07
❑	408	Carney Lansford	.20	.07
❑	409	Dave Winfield	.20	.07
❑	410	Bob Welch	.20	.07
❑	411	Larry Milbourne	.10	.02
❑	412	Dennis Leonard	.10	.02
❑	413	Dan Meyer	.10	.02
❑	414	Charlie Lea	.10	.02
❑	415	Rick Honeycutt	.10	.02
❑	416	Mike Witt	.10	.02
❑	417	Steve Trout	.10	.02
❑	418	Glenn Brummer	.10	.02
❑	419	Denny Walling	.10	.02
❑	420	Gary Matthews	.20	.07
❑	421	Charlie Leibrandt UER (Liebrandt on front of car	.10	.02
❑	422	Juan Eichelberger UER (Photo actually Joe Pittma	.10	.02
❑	423	Cecilio Guante UER (Listed as Matt on card)	.10	.02
❑	424	Bill Laskey	.10	.02
❑	425	Jerry Royster	.10	.02
❑	426	Dickie Noles	.10	.02
❑	427	George Foster	.20	.07
❑	428	Mike Moore RC	.50	.20
❑	429	Gary Ward	.10	.02
❑	430	Barry Bonnell	.10	.02
❑	431	Ron Washington	.10	.02
❑	432	Rance Mulliniks	.10	.02
❑	433	Mike Stanton	.10	.02
❑	434	Jesse Orosco	.10	.02
❑	435	Larry Bowa	.20	.07
❑	436	Biff Pocoroba	.10	.02
❑	437	Johnny Ray	.10	.02
❑	438	Joe Morgan	.20	.07
❑	439	Eric Show RC	.50	.20
❑	440	Larry Biittner	.10	.02
❑	441	Greg Gross	.10	.02
❑	442	Gene Tenace	.20	.07
❑	443	Danny Heep	.10	.02
❑	444	Bobby Clark	.10	.02
❑	445	Kevin Hickey	.10	.02
❑	446	Scott Sanderson	.10	.02
❑	447	Frank Tanana	.20	.07
❑	448	Cesar Geronimo	.10	.02
❑	449	Jimmy Sexton	.10	.02
❑	450	Mike Hargrove	.10	.02
❑	451	Doyle Alexander	.10	.02
❑	452	Dwight Evans	.40	.15
❑	453	Terry Forster	.20	.07
❑	454	Tom Brookens	.10	.02
❑	455	Rich Dauer	.10	.02

Card	Price	Price
❑ 456 Rob Picciolo	.10	.02
❑ 457 Terry Crowley	.10	.02
❑ 458 Ned Yost	.10	.02
❑ 459 Kirk Gibson	.20	.07
❑ 460 Reid Nichols	.10	.02
❑ 461 Oscar Gamble	.10	.02
❑ 462 Dusty Baker	.20	.07
❑ 463 Jack Perconte	.10	.02
❑ 464 Frank White	.20	.07
❑ 465 Mickey Klutts	.10	.02
❑ 466 Warren Cromartie	.10	.02
❑ 467 Larry Parrish	.10	.02
❑ 468 Bobby Grich	.20	.07
❑ 469 Dane Iorg	.10	.02
❑ 470 Joe Niekro	.10	.02
❑ 471 Ed Farmer	.10	.02
❑ 472 Tim Flannery	.10	.02
❑ 473 Dave Parker	.20	.07
❑ 474 Jeff Leonard	.10	.02
❑ 475 Al Hrabosky	.10	.02
❑ 476 Ron Hodges	.10	.02
❑ 477 Leon Durham	.10	.02
❑ 478 Jim Essian	.10	.02
❑ 479 Roy Lee Jackson	.10	.02
❑ 480 Brad Havens	.10	.02
❑ 481 Joe Price	.10	.02
❑ 482 Tony Bernazard	.10	.02
❑ 483 Scott McGregor	.10	.02
❑ 484 Paul Molitor	.20	.07
❑ 485 Mike Ivie	.10	.02
❑ 486 Ken Griffey	.20	.07
❑ 487 Dennis Eckersley	.40	.15
❑ 488 Steve Garvey	.20	.07
❑ 489 Mike Fischlin	.10	.02
❑ 490 U.L. Washington	.10	.02
❑ 491 Steve McCatty	.10	.02
❑ 492 Roy Johnson	.10	.02
❑ 493 Don Baylor	.20	.07
❑ 494 Bobby Johnson	.10	.02
❑ 495 Mike Squires	.10	.02
❑ 496 Bert Roberge	.10	.02
❑ 497 Dick Ruthven	.10	.02
❑ 498 Tito Landrum	.10	.02
❑ 499 Sixto Lezcano	.10	.02
❑ 500 Johnny Bench	.75	.30
❑ 501 Larry Whisenton	.10	.02
❑ 502 Manny Sarmiento	.10	.02
❑ 503 Fred Breining	.10	.02
❑ 504 Bill Campbell	.10	.02
❑ 505 Todd Cruz	.10	.02
❑ 506 Bob Bailor	.10	.02
❑ 507 Dave Stieb	.20	.07
❑ 508 Al Williams	.10	.02
❑ 509 Dan Ford	.10	.02
❑ 510 Gorman Thomas	.20	.07
❑ 511 Chet Lemon	.20	.07
❑ 512 Mike Torrez	.10	.02
❑ 513 Shane Rawley	.10	.02
❑ 514 Mark Belanger	.10	.02
❑ 515 Rodney Craig	.10	.02
❑ 516 Onix Concepcion	.10	.02
❑ 517 Mike Heath	.10	.02
❑ 518 Andre Dawson	.20	.07
❑ 519 Luis Sanchez	.10	.02
❑ 520 Terry Bogener	.10	.02
❑ 521 Rudy Law	.10	.02
❑ 522 Ray Knight	.20	.07
❑ 523 Joe Lefebvre	.10	.02
❑ 524 Jim Wohlford	.10	.02
❑ 525 Julio Franco RC	6.00	2.50
❑ 526 Ron Oester	.10	.02
❑ 527 Rick Mahler	.10	.02
❑ 528 Steve Nicosia	.10	.02
❑ 529 Junior Kennedy	.10	.02
❑ 530A Whitey Herzog MG (Bio printed black on white)	.20	.07
❑ 530B Whitey Herzog MG (Bio printed black on yellow)	.20	.07
❑ 531A Don Sutton	.20	.07
❑ 531B Don Sutton	.20	.07
❑ 532 Mark Brouhard	.10	.02
❑ 533A Sparky Anderson MG (Bio printed black on white)	.20	.07

Card	Price	Price
❑ 533B Sparky Anderson MG (Bio printed black on yellow)	.20	.07
❑ 534 Roger LaFrancois	.10	.02
❑ 535 George Frazier	.10	.02
❑ 536 Tom Niedenfuer	.10	.02
❑ 537 Ed Glynn	.10	.02
❑ 538 Lee May	.10	.02
❑ 539 Bob Kearney	.10	.02
❑ 540 Tim Raines	.20	.07
❑ 541 Paul Mirabella	.10	.02
❑ 542 Luis Tiant	.20	.07
❑ 543 Ron LeFlore	.20	.07
❑ 544 Dave LaPoint	.10	.02
❑ 545 Randy Moffitt	.10	.02
❑ 546 Luis Aguayo	.10	.02
❑ 547 Brad Lesley	.15	.05
❑ 548 Luis Salazar	.10	.02
❑ 549 John Candelaria	.10	.02
❑ 550 Dave Bergman	.10	.02
❑ 551 Bob Watson	.10	.02
❑ 552 Pat Tabler	.10	.02
❑ 553 Brent Gaff	.10	.02
❑ 554 Al Cowens	.10	.02
❑ 555 Tom Brunansky	.20	.07
❑ 556 Lloyd Moseby	.10	.02
❑ 557A Pascual Perez ERR Twins	2.00	.75
❑ 557B Pascual Perez COR (Braves in glove)	.20	.07
❑ 558 Willie Upshaw	.10	.02
❑ 559 Richie Zisk	.10	.02
❑ 560 Pat Zachry	.10	.02
❑ 561 Jay Johnstone	.10	.02
❑ 562 Carlos Diaz RC	.15	.05
❑ 563 John Tudor	.20	.07
❑ 564 Frank Robinson MG	.40	.15
❑ 565 Dave Edwards	.10	.02
❑ 566 Paul Householder	.10	.02
❑ 567 Ron Reed	.10	.02
❑ 568 Mike Ramsey	.10	.02
❑ 569 Kiko Garcia	.10	.02
❑ 570 Tommy John	.20	.07
❑ 571 Tony LaRussa MG	.20	.07
❑ 572 Joel Youngblood	.10	.02
❑ 573 Wayne Tolleson	.10	.02
❑ 574 Keith Creel	.10	.02
❑ 575 Billy Martin MG	.40	.15
❑ 576 Jerry Dybzinski	.10	.02
❑ 577 Rick Cerone	.10	.02
❑ 578 Tony Perez	.40	.15
❑ 579 Greg Brock	.10	.02
❑ 580 Glenn Wilson	.50	.20
❑ 581 Tim Stoddard	.10	.02
❑ 582 Bob McClure	.10	.02
❑ 583 Jim Dwyer	.10	.02
❑ 584 Ed Romero	.10	.02
❑ 585 Larry Herndon	.10	.02
❑ 586 Wade Boggs RC	10.00	4.00
❑ 587 Jay Howell	.10	.02
❑ 588 Dave Stewart	.20	.07
❑ 589 Bert Blyleven	.20	.07
❑ 590 Dick Howser MG	.10	.02
❑ 591 Wayne Gross	.10	.02
❑ 592 Terry Francona	.20	.07
❑ 593 Don Werner	.10	.02
❑ 594 Bill Stein	.10	.02
❑ 595 Jesse Barfield	.20	.07
❑ 596 Bob Molinaro	.10	.02
❑ 597 Mike Vail	.10	.02
❑ 598 Tony Gwynn RC	15.00	6.00
❑ 599 Gary Rajsich	.10	.02
❑ 600 Jerry Ujdur	.10	.02
❑ 601 Cliff Johnson	.10	.02
❑ 602 Jerry White	.10	.02
❑ 603 Bryan Clark	.10	.02
❑ 604 Joe Ferguson	.10	.02
❑ 605 Guy Sularz	.10	.02
❑ 606A Ozzie Virgil (Green border on photo)	.20	.07
❑ 606B Ozzie Virgil (Orange border on photo)	.20	.07
❑ 607 Terry Harper	.10	.02
❑ 608 Harvey Kuenn MG	.10	.02
❑ 609 Jim Sundberg	.20	.07

Card	Price	Price
❑ 610 Willie Stargell	.40	.15
❑ 611 Reggie Smith	.20	.07
❑ 612 Rob Wilfong	.10	.02
❑ 613 Niekro Brothers	.20	.07
❑ 614 Lee Elia MG	.10	.02
❑ 615 Mickey Hatcher	.10	.02
❑ 616 Jerry Hairston	.10	.02
❑ 617 John Martin	.10	.02
❑ 618 Wally Backman	.10	.02
❑ 619 Storm Davis RC	.50	.20
❑ 620 Alan Knicely	.10	.02
❑ 621 John Stuper	.10	.02
❑ 622 Matt Sinatro	.10	.02
❑ 623 Geno Petralli	.50	.20
❑ 624 Duane Walker	.10	.02
❑ 625 Dick Williams MG	.10	.02
❑ 626 Pat Corrales MG	.10	.02
❑ 627 Vern Ruhle	.10	.02
❑ 628 Joe Torre MG	.20	.07
❑ 629 Anthony Johnson	.10	.02
❑ 630 Steve Howe	.10	.02
❑ 631 Gary Woods	.10	.02
❑ 632 LaMarr Hoyt	.10	.02
❑ 633 Steve Swisher	.10	.02
❑ 634 Terry Leach	.10	.02
❑ 635 Jeff Newman	.10	.02
❑ 636 Brett Butler	.20	.07
❑ 637 Gary Gray	.10	.02
❑ 638 Lee Mazzilli	.20	.07
❑ 639A Ron Jackson ERR A's	20.00	8.00
❑ 639B Ron Jackson COR (Angels in glove& red border on	.10	.02
❑ 639C Ron Jackson COR (Angels in glove& green border	.40	.15
❑ 640 Juan Beniquez	.10	.02
❑ 641 Dave Rucker	.10	.02
❑ 642 Luis Pujols	.10	.02
❑ 643 Rick Monday	.20	.07
❑ 644 Hosken Powell	.10	.02
❑ 645 The Chicken	.40	.15
❑ 646 Dave Engle	.10	.02
❑ 647 Dick Davis	.10	.02
❑ 648 F.Robby/V.Blue/J.Morgan	.40	.15
❑ 649 Al Chambers	.10	.02
❑ 650 Jesus Vega	.10	.02
❑ 651 Jeff Jones	.10	.02
❑ 652 Marvis Foley	.10	.02
❑ 653 Ty Cobb Puzzle	.75	.30
❑ 654A Dick Perez/DK CL	.40	.15
❑ 654B Dick Perez/DK CL	.40	.15
❑ 655 Checklist 27-130 (Unnumbered)	.10	.02
❑ 656 Checklist 131-234 (Unnumbered)	.10	.02
❑ 657 Checklist 235-338 (Unnumbered)	.10	.02
❑ 658 Checklist 339-442 (Unnumbered)	.10	.02
❑ 659 Checklist 443-544 (Unnumbered)	.10	.02
❑ 660 Checklist 545-653 (Unnumbered)	.10	.02

1984 Donruss

KEITH HERNANDEZ 1B

Set	Price	Price
❑ COMPLETE SET (660)	120.00	70.00
❑ COMP.FACT.SET (658)	120.00	70.00

❑ COMP.SNIDER PUZZLE	5.00	2.00
❑ 1 Robin Yount DK	2.50	1.00
❑ 1A Robin Yount DK ERR	5.00	2.00
❑ 2 Dave Concepcion DK	.75	.30
❑ 2A Dave Concepcion DK ERR	.75	.30
❑ 3 Dwayne Murphy DK	.25	.08
❑ 3A Dwayne Murphy DK ERR	.25	.08
❑ 4 John Castino DK	.25	.08
❑ 4A John Castino DK ERR	.25	.08
❑ 5 Leon Durham DK	.75	.30
❑ 5A Leon Durham DK ERR	.25	.08
❑ 6 Rusty Staub DK	.75	.30
❑ 6A Rusty Staub DK ERR	.75	.30
❑ 7 Jack Clark DK	.75	.30
❑ 7A Jack Clark DK ERR	.75	.30
❑ 8 Dave Dravecky DK	.25	.08
❑ 8A Dave Dravecky DK ERR	.25	.08
❑ 9 Al Oliver DK	.75	.30
❑ 9A Al Oliver DK ERR	.75	.30
❑ 10 Dave Righetti DK	.75	.30
❑ 10A Dave Righetti DK ERR	.75	.30
❑ 11 Hal McRae DK	.75	.30
❑ 11A Hal McRae DK ERR	.75	.30
❑ 12 Ray Knight DK	.75	.30
❑ 12A Ray Knight DK ERR	.75	.30
❑ 13 Bruce Sutter DK	1.50	.60
❑ 13A Bruce Sutter DK ERR	1.50	.60
❑ 14 Bob Horner DK	.75	.30
❑ 14A Bob Horner DK ERR	.75	.30
❑ 15 Lance Parrish DK	.75	.30
❑ 15A Lance Parrish DK ERR	.75	.30
❑ 16 Matt Young DK	.75	.30
❑ 16A Matt Young DK ERR	.75	.30
❑ 17 Fred Lynn DK	.75	.30
❑ 17A Fred Lynn DK ERR	.75	.30
❑ 18 Ron Kittle DK	.25	.08
❑ 18A Ron Kittle DK ERR	.25	.08
❑ 19 Jim Clancy DK	.25	.08
❑ 19A Jim Clancy DK ERR	.25	.08
❑ 20 Bill Madlock DK	.75	.30
❑ 20A Bill Madlock DK ERR	.75	.30
❑ 21 Larry Parrish DK	.25	.08
❑ 21A Larry Parrish DK ERR	.25	.08
❑ 22 Eddie Murray DK	3.00	1.25
❑ 22A Eddie Murray DK ERR	3.00	1.25
❑ 23 Mike Schmidt DK	5.00	2.00
❑ 23A Mike Schmidt DK ERR	5.00	2.00
❑ 24 Pedro Guerrero DK	.75	.30
❑ 24A Pedro Guerrero DK ERR	.75	.30
❑ 25 Andre Thornton DK	.25	.08
❑ 25A Andre Thornton DK ERR	.25	.08
❑ 26 Wade Boggs DK	3.00	1.25
❑ 26A Wade Boggs DK ERR	3.00	1.25
❑ 27 Joel Skinner RC	.25	.08
❑ 28 Tommy Dunbar RC	.25	.08
❑ 29A Mike Stenhouse ERR RC	.25	.08
❑ 29B Mike Stenhouse COR	3.00	1.25
❑ 30A Ron Darling ERR RC	2.00	.75
❑ 30B Ron Darling COR	3.00	1.25
❑ 31 Dion James RC	.25	.08
❑ 32 Tony Fernandez RC	2.00	.75
❑ 33 Angel Salazar RC	.25	.08
❑ 34 Kevin McReynolds RC	2.00	.75
❑ 35 Dick Schofield RC	1.00	.40
❑ 36 Brad Komminsk RC	.25	.08
❑ 37 Tim Teufel RC	1.00	.40
❑ 38 Doug Frobel RC	.25	.08
❑ 39 Greg Gagne RC	1.00	.40
❑ 40 Mike Fuentes RC	.25	.08
❑ 41 Joe Carter RC	8.00	3.00
❑ 42 Mike C. Brown RC	.25	.08
❑ 43 Mike Jeffcoat RC	.25	.08
❑ 44 Sid Fernandez RC !	2.00	.75
❑ 45 Brian Dayett RC	.25	.08
❑ 46 Chris Smith RC	.25	.08
❑ 47 Eddie Murray	3.00	1.25
❑ 48 Robin Yount	5.00	2.00
❑ 49 Lance Parrish	1.50	.60
❑ 50 Jim Rice	.75	.30
❑ 51 Dave Winfield	.75	.30
❑ 52 Fernando Valenzuela	.75	.30
❑ 53 George Brett	8.00	3.00
❑ 54 Rickey Henderson	5.00	2.00
❑ 55 Gary Carter	.75	.30
❑ 56 Buddy Bell	.75	.30
❑ 57 Reggie Jackson	1.50	.60
❑ 58 Harold Baines	.75	.30
❑ 59 Ozzie Smith	5.00	2.00
❑ 60 Nolan Ryan	15.00	6.00
❑ 61 Pete Rose	10.00	4.00
❑ 62 Ron Oester	.25	.08
❑ 63 Steve Garvey	.75	.30
❑ 64 Jason Thompson	.25	.08
❑ 65 Jack Clark	.75	.30
❑ 66 Dale Murphy	1.50	.60
❑ 67 Leon Durham	.25	.08
❑ 68 Darryl Strawberry RC	8.00	3.00
❑ 69 Richie Zisk	.25	.08
❑ 70 Kent Hrbek	.75	.30
❑ 71 Dave Stieb	.75	.30
❑ 72 Ken Schrom	.25	.08
❑ 73 George Bell	.75	.30
❑ 74 John Moses	.25	.08
❑ 75 Ed Lynch	.25	.08
❑ 76 Chuck Rainey	.25	.08
❑ 77 Biff Pocoroba	.25	.08
❑ 78 Cecilio Guante	.25	.08
❑ 79 Jim Barr	.25	.08
❑ 80 Kurt Bevacqua	.25	.08
❑ 81 Tom Foley	.25	.08
❑ 82 Joe Lefebvre	.25	.08
❑ 83 Andy Van Slyke RC	4.00	1.50
❑ 84 Bob Lillis MG	.25	.08
❑ 85 Ricky Adams	.25	.08
❑ 86 Jerry Hairston	.25	.08
❑ 87 Bob James	.25	.08
❑ 88 Joe Altobelli MG	.25	.08
❑ 89 Ed Romero	.25	.08
❑ 90 John Grubb	.25	.08
❑ 91 John Henry Johnson	.25	.08
❑ 92 Juan Espino	.25	.08
❑ 93 Candy Maldonado	.25	.08
❑ 94 Andre Thornton	.25	.08
❑ 95 Onix Concepcion	.25	.08
❑ 96 Donnie Hill UER (Listed as P, should be 2B)	.25	.08
❑ 97 Andre Dawson	.75	.30
❑ 98 Frank Tanana	.75	.30
❑ 99 Curt Wilkerson	.25	.08
❑ 100 Larry Gura	.25	.08
❑ 101 Dwayne Murphy	.25	.08
❑ 102 Tom Brennan	.25	.08
❑ 103 Dave Righetti	.75	.30
❑ 104 Steve Sax	.25	.08
❑ 105 Dan Petry	.75	.30
❑ 106 Cal Ripken	12.00	5.00
❑ 107 Paul Molitor	.75	.30
❑ 108 Fred Lynn	.75	.30
❑ 109 Neil Allen	.25	.08
❑ 110 Joe Niekro	.25	.08
❑ 111 Steve Carlton	1.50	.60
❑ 112 Terry Kennedy	.25	.08
❑ 113 Bill Madlock	.75	.30
❑ 114 Chili Davis	.75	.30
❑ 115 Jim Gantner	.25	.08
❑ 116 Tom Seaver	3.00	1.25
❑ 117 Bill Buckner	.75	.30
❑ 118 Bill Caudill	.25	.08
❑ 119 Jim Clancy	.25	.08
❑ 120 John Castino	.25	.08
❑ 121 Dave Concepcion	.75	.30
❑ 122 Greg Luzinski	.75	.30
❑ 123 Mike Boddicker	.25	.08
❑ 124 Pete Ladd	.25	.08
❑ 125 Juan Berenguer	.25	.08
❑ 126 John Montefusco	.25	.08
❑ 127 Ed Jurak	.25	.08
❑ 128 Tom Niedenfuer	.25	.08
❑ 129 Bert Blyleven	.75	.30
❑ 130 Bud Black	.25	.08
❑ 131 Gorman Heimueller	.25	.08
❑ 132 Dan Schatzeder	.25	.08
❑ 133 Ron Jackson	.25	.08
❑ 134 Tom Henke RC	2.00	.75
❑ 135 Kevin Hickey	.25	.08
❑ 136 Mike Scott	.75	.30
❑ 137 Bo Diaz	.25	.08
❑ 138 Glenn Brummer	.25	.08
❑ 139 Sid Monge	.25	.08
❑ 140 Rich Gale	.25	.08
❑ 141 Brett Butler	.75	.30
❑ 142 Brian Harper RC	1.00	.40
❑ 143 John Rabb	.25	.08
❑ 144 Gary Woods	.25	.08
❑ 145 Pat Putnam	.25	.08
❑ 146 Jim Acker	.25	.08
❑ 147 Mickey Hatcher	.25	.08
❑ 148 Todd Cruz	.25	.08
❑ 149 Tom Tellmann	.25	.08
❑ 150 John Wockenfuss	.25	.08
❑ 151 Wade Boggs	8.00	3.00
❑ 152 Don Baylor	.75	.30
❑ 153 Bob Welch	.75	.30
❑ 154 Alan Bannister	.25	.08
❑ 155 Willie Aikens	.25	.08
❑ 156 Jeff Burroughs	.25	.08
❑ 157 Bryan Little	.25	.08
❑ 158 Bob Boone	.75	.30
❑ 159 Dave Hostetler	.25	.08
❑ 160 Jerry Dybzinski	.25	.08
❑ 161 Mike Madden	.25	.08
❑ 162 Luis DeLeon	.25	.08
❑ 163 Willie Hernandez	.25	.08
❑ 164 Frank Pastore	.25	.08
❑ 165 Rick Camp	.25	.08
❑ 166 Lee Mazzilli	.75	.30
❑ 167 Scot Thompson	.25	.08
❑ 168 Bob Forsch	.25	.08
❑ 169 Mike Flanagan	.25	.08
❑ 170 Rick Manning	.25	.08
❑ 171 Chet Lemon	.75	.30
❑ 172 Jerry Remy	.25	.08
❑ 173 Ron Guidry	.75	.30
❑ 174 Pedro Guerrero	.75	.30
❑ 175 Willie Wilson	.75	.30
❑ 176 Carney Lansford	.75	.30
❑ 177 Al Oliver	.75	.30
❑ 178 Jim Sundberg	.75	.30
❑ 179 Bobby Grich	.75	.30
❑ 180 Rich Dotson	.25	.08
❑ 181 Joaquin Andujar	.75	.30
❑ 182 Jose Cruz	.75	.30
❑ 183 Mike Schmidt	8.00	3.00
❑ 184 Gary Redus RC	1.00	.40
❑ 185 Garry Templeton	.75	.30
❑ 186 Tony Pena	.25	.08
❑ 187 Greg Minton	.25	.08
❑ 188 Phil Niekro	.75	.30
❑ 189 Fergie Jenkins	.75	.30
❑ 190 Mookie Wilson	.75	.30
❑ 191 Jim Beattie	.25	.08
❑ 192 Gary Ward	.25	.08
❑ 193 Jesse Barfield	.75	.30
❑ 194 Pete Filson	.25	.08
❑ 195 Roy Lee Jackson	.25	.08
❑ 196 Rick Sweet	.25	.08
❑ 197 Jesse Orosco	.25	.08
❑ 198 Steve Lake	.25	.08
❑ 199 Ken Dayley	.25	.08
❑ 200 Manny Sarmiento	.25	.08
❑ 201 Mark Davis	.25	.08
❑ 202 Tim Flannery	.25	.08
❑ 203 Bill Scherrer	.25	.08
❑ 204 Al Holland	.25	.08
❑ 205 Dave Von Ohlen	.25	.08
❑ 206 Mike LaCoss	.25	.08
❑ 207 Juan Beniquez	.25	.08
❑ 208 Juan Agosto	.25	.08
❑ 209 Bobby Ramos	.25	.08
❑ 210 Al Bumbry	.25	.08
❑ 211 Mark Brouhard	.25	.08
❑ 212 Howard Bailey	.25	.08
❑ 213 Bruce Hurst	.25	.08
❑ 214 Bob Shirley	.25	.08
❑ 215 Pat Zachry	.25	.08
❑ 216 Julio Franco	3.00	1.25
❑ 217 Mike Armstrong	.25	.08
❑ 218 Dave Beard	.25	.08
❑ 219 Steve Rogers	.75	.30
❑ 220 John Butcher	.25	.08
❑ 221 Mike Smithson	.25	.08
❑ 222 Frank White	.75	.30
❑ 223 Mike Heath	.25	.08
❑ 224 Chris Bando	.25	.08
❑ 225 Roy Smalley	.25	.08
❑ 226 Dusty Baker	.75	.30
❑ 227 Lou Whitaker	.75	.30

❑ 228 John Lowenstein .25 .08
❑ 229 Ben Oglivie .75 .30
❑ 230 Doug DeCinces .25 .08
❑ 231 Lonnie Smith .25 .08
❑ 232 Ray Knight .75 .30
❑ 233 Gary Matthews .75 .30
❑ 234 Juan Bonilla .25 .08
❑ 235 Rod Scurry .25 .08
❑ 236 Atlee Hammaker .25 .08
❑ 237 Mike Caldwell .25 .08
❑ 238 Keith Hernandez .75 .30
❑ 239 Larry Bowa .75 .30
❑ 240 Tony Bernazard .25 .08
❑ 241 Damaso Garcia .25 .08
❑ 242 Tom Brunansky .25 .08
❑ 243 Dan Driessen .25 .08
❑ 244 Ron Kittle .25 .08
❑ 245 Tim Stoddard .25 .08
❑ 246 Bob L. Gibson RC (Brewers Pitcher) .25 .08
❑ 247 Marty Castillo .25 .08
❑ 248 Don Mattingly RC 30.00 12.50
❑ 249 Jeff Newman .25 .08
❑ 250 Alejandro Pena RC 2.00 .75
❑ 251 Toby Harrah .75 .30
❑ 252 Cesar Geronimo .25 .08
❑ 253 Tom Underwood .25 .08
❑ 254 Doug Flynn .25 .08
❑ 255 Andy Hassler .25 .08
❑ 256 Odell Jones .25 .08
❑ 257 Rudy Law .25 .08
❑ 258 Harry Spilman .25 .08
❑ 259 Marty Bystrom .25 .08
❑ 260 Dave Rucker .25 .08
❑ 261 Ruppert Jones .25 .08
❑ 262 Jeff R. Jones (Reds OF) .25 .08
❑ 263 Gerald Perry 1.00 .40
❑ 264 Gene Tenace .75 .30
❑ 265 Brad Wellman .25 .08
❑ 266 Dickie Noles .25 .08
❑ 267 Jamie Allen .25 .08
❑ 268 Jim Gott .25 .08
❑ 269 Ron Davis .25 .08
❑ 270 Benny Ayala .25 .08
❑ 271 Ned Yost .25 .08
❑ 272 Dave Rozema .25 .08
❑ 273 Dave Stapleton .25 .08
❑ 274 Lou Piniella .75 .30
❑ 275 Jose Morales .25 .08
❑ 276 Broderick Perkins .25 .08
❑ 277 Butch Davis RC .25 .08
❑ 278 Tony Phillips RC 2.00 .75
❑ 279 Jeff Reardon .75 .30
❑ 280 Ken Forsch .25 .08
❑ 281 Pete O'Brien RC 1.00 .40
❑ 282 Tom Paciorek .25 .08
❑ 283 Frank LaCorte .25 .08
❑ 284 Tim Lollar .25 .08
❑ 285 Greg Gross .25 .08
❑ 286 Alex Trevino .25 .08
❑ 287 Gene Garber .25 .08
❑ 288 Dave Parker .75 .30
❑ 289 Lee Smith .75 .30
❑ 290 Dave LaPoint .25 .08
❑ 291 John Shelby .25 .08
❑ 292 Charlie Moore .25 .08
❑ 293 Alan Trammell .75 .30
❑ 294 Tony Armas .75 .30
❑ 295 Shane Rawley .25 .08
❑ 296 Greg Brock .25 .08
❑ 297 Hal McRae .75 .30
❑ 298 Mike Davis .25 .08
❑ 299 Tim Raines .75 .30
❑ 300 Bucky Dent .75 .30
❑ 301 Tommy John .75 .30
❑ 302 Carlton Fisk 1.50 .60
❑ 303 Darrell Porter .25 .08
❑ 304 Dickie Thon .25 .08
❑ 305 Garry Maddox .25 .08
❑ 306 Cesar Cedeno .75 .30
❑ 307 Gary Lucas .25 .08
❑ 308 Johnny Ray .25 .08
❑ 309 Andy McGaffigan .25 .08
❑ 310 Claudell Washington .25 .08
❑ 311 Ryne Sandberg 12.00 5.00
❑ 312 George Foster .75 .30
❑ 313 Spike Owen RC 1.00 .40
❑ 314 Gary Gaetti 1.50 .60
❑ 315 Willie Upshaw .25 .08
❑ 316 Al Williams .25 .08
❑ 317 Jorge Orta .25 .08
❑ 318 Orlando Mercado .25 .08
❑ 319 Junior Ortiz .25 .08
❑ 320 Mike Proly .25 .08
❑ 321 Randy Johnson UER ('72-'82 stats are from Twins' .25 .08
❑ 322 Jim Morrison .25 .08
❑ 323 Max Venable .25 .08
❑ 324 Tony Gwynn 12.00 5.00
❑ 325 Duane Walker .25 .08
❑ 326 Ozzie Virgil .25 .08
❑ 327 Jeff Lahti .25 .08
❑ 328 Bill Dawley .25 .08
❑ 329 Rob Wilfong .25 .08
❑ 330 Marc Hill .25 .08
❑ 331 Ray Burris .25 .08
❑ 332 Allan Ramirez .25 .08
❑ 333 Chuck Porter .25 .08
❑ 334 Wayne Krenchicki .25 .08
❑ 335 Gary Allenson .25 .08
❑ 336 Bobby Meacham .25 .08
❑ 337 Joe Beckwith .25 .08
❑ 338 Rick Sutcliffe .75 .30
❑ 339 Mark Huismann .25 .08
❑ 340 Tim Conroy .25 .08
❑ 341 Scott Sanderson .25 .08
❑ 342 Larry Biittner .25 .08
❑ 343 Dave Stewart .75 .30
❑ 344 Darryl Motley .25 .08
❑ 345 Chris Codiroli .25 .08
❑ 346 Rich Behenna .25 .08
❑ 347 Andre Robertson .25 .08
❑ 348 Mike Marshall .25 .08
❑ 349 Larry Herndon .75 .30
❑ 350 Rich Dauer .25 .08
❑ 351 Cecil Cooper .75 .30
❑ 352 Rod Carew 1.50 .60
❑ 353 Willie McGee .75 .30
❑ 354 Phil Garner .75 .30
❑ 355 Joe Morgan .75 .30
❑ 356 Luis Salazar .25 .08
❑ 357 John Candelaria .25 .08
❑ 358 Bill Laskey .25 .08
❑ 359 Bob McClure .25 .08
❑ 360 Dave Kingman .75 .30
❑ 361 Ron Cey .75 .30
❑ 362 Matt Young RC 1.00 .40
❑ 363 Lloyd Moseby .25 .08
❑ 364 Frank Viola 1.50 .60
❑ 365 Eddie Milner .25 .08
❑ 366 Floyd Bannister .25 .08
❑ 367 Dan Ford .25 .08
❑ 368 Moose Haas .25 .08
❑ 369 Doug Bair .25 .08
❑ 370 Ray Fontenot .25 .08
❑ 371 Luis Aponte .25 .08
❑ 372 Jack Fimple .25 .08
❑ 373 Neal Heaton .25 .08
❑ 374 Greg Pryor .25 .08
❑ 375 Wayne Gross .25 .08
❑ 376 Charlie Lea .25 .08
❑ 377 Steve Lubratich .25 .08
❑ 378 Jon Matlack .25 .08
❑ 379 Julio Cruz .25 .08
❑ 380 John Mizerock .25 .08
❑ 381 Kevin Gross RC 1.00 .40
❑ 382 Mike Ramsey .25 .08
❑ 383 Doug Gwosdz .25 .08
❑ 384 Kelly Paris .25 .08
❑ 385 Pete Falcone .25 .08
❑ 386 Milt May .25 .08
❑ 387 Fred Breining .25 .08
❑ 388 Craig Lefferts RC .25 .08
❑ 389 Steve Henderson .25 .08
❑ 390 Randy Moffitt .25 .08
❑ 391 Ron Washington .25 .08
❑ 392 Gary Roenicke .25 .08
❑ 393 Tom Candiotti RC 2.00 .75
❑ 394 Larry Pashnick .25 .08
❑ 395 Dwight Evans 1.50 .60
❑ 396 Rich Gossage .75 .30
❑ 397 Derrel Thomas .25 .08
❑ 398 Juan Eichelberger .25 .08
❑ 399 Leon Roberts .25 .08
❑ 400 Dave Lopes .75 .30
❑ 401 Bill Gullickson .25 .08
❑ 402 Geoff Zahn .25 .08
❑ 403 Billy Sample .25 .08
❑ 404 Mike Squires .25 .08
❑ 405 Craig Reynolds .25 .08
❑ 406 Eric Show .25 .08
❑ 407 John Denny .25 .08
❑ 408 Dann Bilardello .25 .08
❑ 409 Bruce Benedict .25 .08
❑ 410 Kent Tekulve .25 .08
❑ 411 Mel Hall .75 .30
❑ 412 John Stuper .25 .08
❑ 413 Rick Dempsey .25 .08
❑ 414 Don Sutton .75 .30
❑ 415 Jack Morris .75 .30
❑ 416 John Tudor .75 .30
❑ 417 Willie Randolph .75 .30
❑ 418 Jerry Reuss .25 .08
❑ 419 Don Slaught .75 .30
❑ 420 Steve McCatty .25 .08
❑ 421 Tim Wallach .25 .08
❑ 422 Larry Parrish .25 .08
❑ 423 Brian Downing .75 .30
❑ 424 Britt Burns .25 .08
❑ 425 David Green .25 .08
❑ 426 Jerry Mumphrey .25 .08
❑ 427 Ivan DeJesus .25 .08
❑ 428 Mario Soto .75 .30
❑ 429 Gene Richards .25 .08
❑ 430 Dale Berra .25 .08
❑ 431 Darrell Evans .75 .30
❑ 432 Glenn Hubbard .25 .08
❑ 433 Jody Davis .25 .08
❑ 434 Danny Heep .25 .08
❑ 435 Edwin Nunez RC .25 .08
❑ 436 Bobby Castillo .25 .08
❑ 437 Ernie Whitt .25 .08
❑ 438 Scott Ullger .25 .08
❑ 439 Doyle Alexander .25 .08
❑ 440 Domingo Ramos .25 .08
❑ 441 Craig Swan .25 .08
❑ 442 Warren Brusstar .25 .08
❑ 443 Len Barker .25 .08
❑ 444 Mike Easler .25 .08
❑ 445 Renie Martin .25 .08
❑ 446 Dennis Rasmussen RC 1.00 .40
❑ 447 Ted Power .25 .08
❑ 448 Charles Hudson .25 .08
❑ 449 Danny Cox RC .25 .08
❑ 450 Kevin Bass .25 .08
❑ 451 Daryl Sconiers .25 .08
❑ 452 Scott Fletcher .25 .08
❑ 453 Bryn Smith .25 .08
❑ 454 Jim Dwyer .25 .08
❑ 455 Rob Picciolo .25 .08
❑ 456 Enos Cabell .25 .08
❑ 457 Dennis Boyd .75 .30
❑ 458 Butch Wynegar .25 .08
❑ 459 Burt Hooton .25 .08
❑ 460 Ron Hassey .25 .08
❑ 461 Danny Jackson RC 1.00 .40
❑ 462 Bob Kearney .25 .08
❑ 463 Terry Francona .75 .30
❑ 464 Wayne Tolleson .25 .08
❑ 465 Mickey Rivers .25 .08
❑ 466 John Wathan .25 .08
❑ 467 Bill Almon .25 .08
❑ 468 George Vukovich .25 .08
❑ 469 Steve Kemp .25 .08
❑ 470 Ken Landreaux .25 .08
❑ 471 Milt Wilcox .25 .08
❑ 472 Tippy Martinez .25 .08
❑ 473 Ted Simmons .75 .30
❑ 474 Tim Foli .25 .08
❑ 475 George Hendrick .75 .30
❑ 476 Terry Puhl .25 .08
❑ 477 Von Hayes .25 .08
❑ 478 Bobby Brown .25 .08
❑ 479 Lee Lacy .25 .08
❑ 480 Joel Youngblood .25 .08
❑ 481 Jim Slaton .25 .08

❑ 482 Mike Fitzgerald .25 .08
❑ 483 Keith Moreland .25 .08
❑ 484 Ron Roenicke .25 .08
❑ 485 Luis Leal .25 .08
❑ 486 Bryan Oelkers .25 .08
❑ 487 Bruce Berenyi .25 .08
❑ 488 LaMarr Hoyt .25 .08
❑ 489 Joe Nolan .25 .08
❑ 490 Marshall Edwards .25 .08
❑ 491 Mike Laga .75 .30
❑ 492 Rick Cerone .25 .08
❑ 493 Rick Miller UER (Listed as Mike on card front) .25 .08
❑ 494 Rick Honeycutt .25 .08
❑ 495 Mike Hargrove .25 .08
❑ 496 Joe Simpson .25 .08
❑ 497 Keith Atherton .25 .08
❑ 498 Chris Welsh .25 .08
❑ 499 Bruce Kison .25 .08
❑ 500 Bobby Johnson .25 .08
❑ 501 Jerry Koosman .75 .30
❑ 502 Frank DiPino .25 .08
❑ 503 Tony Perez 1.50 .60
❑ 504 Ken Oberkfell .25 .08
❑ 505 Mark Thurmond .25 .08
❑ 506 Joe Price .25 .08
❑ 507 Pascual Perez .25 .08
❑ 508 Marvell Wynne 1.00 .40
❑ 509 Mike Krukow .25 .08
❑ 510 Dick Ruthven .25 .08
❑ 511 Al Cowens .25 .08
❑ 512 Cliff Johnson .25 .08
❑ 513 Randy Bush .25 .08
❑ 514 Sammy Stewart .25 .08
❑ 515 Bill Schroeder .25 .08
❑ 516 Aurelio Lopez .75 .30
❑ 517 Mike C. Brown .25 .08
❑ 518 Graig Nettles .75 .30
❑ 519 Dave Sax .25 .08
❑ 520 Jerry Willard .25 .08
❑ 521 Paul Splittorff .25 .08
❑ 522 Tom Burgmeier .25 .08
❑ 523 Chris Speier .25 .08
❑ 524 Bobby Clark .25 .08
❑ 525 George Wright .25 .08
❑ 526 Dennis Lamp .25 .08
❑ 527 Tony Scott .25 .08
❑ 528 Ed Whitson .25 .08
❑ 529 Ron Reed .25 .08
❑ 530 Charlie Puleo .25 .08
❑ 531 Jerry Royster .25 .08
❑ 532 Don Robinson .25 .08
❑ 533 Steve Trout .25 .08
❑ 534 Bruce Sutter 1.50 .60
❑ 535 Bob Horner ! .75 .30
❑ 536 Pat Tabler .25 .08
❑ 537 Chris Chambliss .75 .30
❑ 538 Bob Ojeda .25 .08
❑ 539 Alan Ashby .25 .08
❑ 540 Jay Johnstone .25 .08
❑ 541 Bob Dernier .25 .08
❑ 542 Brook Jacoby 1.00 .40
❑ 543 U.L. Washington .25 .08
❑ 544 Danny Darwin .25 .08
❑ 545 Kiko Garcia .25 .08
❑ 546 Vance Law UER (Listed as P on card front) .25 .08
❑ 547 Tug McGraw .75 .30
❑ 548 Dave Smith .25 .08
❑ 549 Len Matuszek .25 .08
❑ 550 Tom Hume .25 .08
❑ 551 Dave Dravecky .25 .08
❑ 552 Rick Rhoden .25 .08
❑ 553 Duane Kuiper .25 .08
❑ 554 Rusty Staub .75 .30
❑ 555 Bill Campbell .25 .08
❑ 556 Mike Torrez .25 .08
❑ 557 Dave Henderson .75 .30
❑ 558 Len Whitehouse .25 .08
❑ 559 Barry Bonnell .25 .08
❑ 560 Rick Lysander .25 .08
❑ 561 Garth Iorg .25 .08
❑ 562 Bryan Clark .25 .08
❑ 563 Brian Giles .25 .08
❑ 564 Vern Ruhle .25 .08
❑ 565 Steve Bedrosian .25 .08
❑ 566 Larry McWilliams .25 .08
❑ 567 Jeff Leonard UER (Listed as P on card front) .25 .08
❑ 568 Alan Wiggins .25 .08
❑ 569 Jeff Russell RC 1.00 .40
❑ 570 Salome Barojas .25 .08
❑ 571 Dane Iorg .25 .08
❑ 572 Bob Knepper .25 .08
❑ 573 Gary Lavelle .25 .08
❑ 574 Gorman Thomas .75 .30
❑ 575 Manny Trillo .25 .08
❑ 576 Jim Palmer .75 .30
❑ 577 Dale Murray .25 .08
❑ 578 Tom Brookens .75 .30
❑ 579 Rich Gedman .25 .08
❑ 580 Bill Doran RC 1.00 .40
❑ 581 Steve Yeager .75 .30
❑ 582 Dan Spillner .25 .08
❑ 583 Dan Quisenberry .25 .08
❑ 584 Rance Mulliniks .25 .08
❑ 585 Storm Davis .25 .08
❑ 586 Dave Schmidt .25 .08
❑ 587 Bill Russell .75 .30
❑ 588 Pat Sheridan .25 .08
❑ 589 Rafael Ramirez UER (A's on front) .25 .08
❑ 590 Bud Anderson .25 .08
❑ 591 George Frazier .25 .08
❑ 592 Lee Tunnell .25 .08
❑ 593 Kirk Gibson 3.00 1.25
❑ 594 Scott McGregor .25 .08
❑ 595 Bob Bailor .25 .08
❑ 596 Tommy Herr .25 .08
❑ 597 Luis Sanchez .25 .08
❑ 598 Dave Engle .25 .08
❑ 599 Craig McMurtry .25 .08
❑ 600 Carlos Diaz .25 .08
❑ 601 Tom O'Malley .25 .08
❑ 602 Nick Esasky .25 .08
❑ 603 Ron Hodges .25 .08
❑ 604 Ed VandeBerg .25 .08
❑ 605 Alfredo Griffin .25 .08
❑ 606 Glenn Hoffman .25 .08
❑ 607 Hubie Brooks .25 .08
❑ 608 Richard Barnes UER (Photo actually Neal Heaton) .25 .08
❑ 609 Greg Walker 1.00 .40
❑ 610 Ken Singleton .75 .30
❑ 611 Mark Clear .25 .08
❑ 612 Buck Martinez .25 .08
❑ 613 Ken Griffey .75 .30
❑ 614 Reid Nichols .25 .08
❑ 615 Doug Sisk .25 .08
❑ 616 Bob Brenly .25 .08
❑ 617 Joey McLaughlin .25 .08
❑ 618 Glenn Wilson .75 .30
❑ 619 Bob Stoddard .25 .08
❑ 620 Lenn Sakata UER (Listed as Len on card front) .25 .08
❑ 621 Mike Young RC .25 .08
❑ 622 John Stefero .25 .08
❑ 623 Carmelo Martinez .25 .08
❑ 624 Dave Bergman .25 .08
❑ 625 Ozzie Smith/W.McGee 3.00 1.25
❑ 626 Rudy May .25 .08
❑ 627 Matt Keough .25 .08
❑ 628 Jose DeLeon RC 1.00 .40
❑ 629 Jim Essian .25 .08
❑ 630 Darnell Coles RC 1.00 .40
❑ 631 Mike Warren .25 .08
❑ 632 Del Crandall MG .25 .08
❑ 633 Dennis Martinez .75 .30
❑ 634 Mike Moore .25 .08
❑ 635 Lary Sorensen .25 .08
❑ 636 Ricky Nelson .25 .08
❑ 637 Omar Moreno .25 .08
❑ 638 Charlie Hough .75 .30
❑ 639 Dennis Eckersley ! 1.50 .60
❑ 640 Walt Terrell .25 .08
❑ 641 Denny Walling .25 .08
❑ 642 Dave Anderson RC .25 .08
❑ 643 Jose Oquendo RC 1.00 .40
❑ 644 Bob Stanley .25 .08
❑ 645 Dave Geisel .25 .08
❑ 646 Scott Garrelts .25 .08
❑ 647 Gary Pettis .25 .08
❑ 648 Duke Snider Puzzle 1.50 .60
❑ 649 Johnnie LeMaster .25 .08
❑ 650 Dave Collins .25 .08
❑ 651 The Chicken 1.50 .60
❑ 652 DK Checklist 1-26 (Unnumbered) .75 .30
❑ 653 Checklist 27-130 (Unnumbered) .25 .08
❑ 654 Checklist 131-234 (Unnumbered) .25 .08
❑ 655 Checklist 235-338 (Unnumbered) .25 .08
❑ 656 Checklist 339-442 (Unnumbered) .25 .08
❑ 657 Checklist 443-546 (Unnumbered) .25 .08
❑ 658 Checklist 547-651 (Unnumbered) .25 .08
❑ A G.Perry/R.Fingers SP 2.50 1.00
❑ B J.Bench/C.Yastrzemski SP 5.00 2.00

1985 Donruss

❑ COMPLETE SET (660) 60.00 30.00
❑ COMP.FACT.SET (660) 100.00 50.00
❑ COMP.GEHRIG PUZZLE 4.00 1.50
❑ 1 Ryne Sandberg DK 1.25 .50
❑ 2 Doug DeCinces DK .15 .05
❑ 3 Richard Dotson DK .15 .05
❑ 4 Bert Blyleven DK .40 .15
❑ 5 Lou Whitaker DK .40 .15
❑ 6 Dan Quisenberry DK .15 .05
❑ 7 Don Mattingly DK 2.50 1.00
❑ 8 Carney Lansford DK .40 .15
❑ 9 Frank Tanana DK .40 .15
❑ 10 Willie Upshaw DK .15 .05
❑ 11 Claudell Washington DK .15 .05
❑ 12 Mike Marshall DK .15 .05
❑ 13 Joaquin Andujar DK .40 .15
❑ 14 Cal Ripken DK 2.50 1.00
❑ 15 Jim Rice DK .40 .15
❑ 16 Don Sutton DK .40 .15
❑ 17 Frank Viola DK .40 .15
❑ 18 Alvin Davis DK .40 .15
❑ 19 Mario Soto DK .40 .15
❑ 20 Jose Cruz DK .40 .15
❑ 21 Charlie Lea DK .15 .05
❑ 22 Jesse Orosco DK .15 .05
❑ 23 Juan Samuel DK .15 .05
❑ 24 Tony Pena DK .15 .05
❑ 25 Tony Gwynn DK 1.25 .50
❑ 26 Bob Brenly DK .15 .05
❑ 27 Danny Tartabull RC 1.00 .40
❑ 28 Mike Bielecki RC .25 .08
❑ 29 Steve Lyons RC .50 .20
❑ 30 Jeff Reed RC .25 .08
❑ 31 Tony Brewer RC .25 .08
❑ 32 John Morris RC .25 .08
❑ 33 Daryl Boston RC .25 .08
❑ 34 Al Pulido RC .25 .08
❑ 35 Steve Kiefer RC .25 .08
❑ 36 Larry Sheets RC .25 .08
❑ 37 Scott Bradley RC .25 .08
❑ 38 Calvin Schiraldi RC .50 .20

❑ 39 Shawon Dunston RC 1.00 .40
❑ 40 Charlie Mitchell RC .25 .08
❑ 41 Billy Hatcher RC .50 .20
❑ 42 Russ Stephans RC .25 .08
❑ 43 Alejandro Sanchez RC .25 .08
❑ 44 Steve Jeltz RC .25 .08
❑ 45 Jim Traber RC .25 .08
❑ 46 Doug Loman RC .25 .08
❑ 47 Eddie Murray 1.25 .50
❑ 48 Robin Yount 2.00 .75
❑ 49 Lance Parrish .40 .15
❑ 50 Jim Rice .40 .15
❑ 51 Dave Winfield .40 .15
❑ 52 Fernando Valenzuela .40 .15
❑ 53 George Brett 3.00 1.25
❑ 54 Dave Kingman .40 .15
❑ 55 Gary Carter .40 .15
❑ 56 Buddy Bell .40 .15
❑ 57 Reggie Jackson .75 .30
❑ 58 Harold Baines .40 .15
❑ 59 Ozzie Smith 2.00 .75
❑ 60 Nolan Ryan 6.00 2.50
❑ 61 Mike Schmidt 3.00 1.25
❑ 62 Dave Parker .40 .15
❑ 63 Tony Gwynn 2.50 1.00
❑ 64 Tony Pena .15 .05
❑ 65 Jack Clark .40 .15
❑ 66 Dale Murphy .75 .30
❑ 67 Ryne Sandberg 2.50 1.00
❑ 68 Keith Hernandez .40 .15
❑ 69 Alvin Davis RC* .50 .20
❑ 70 Kent Hrbek .40 .15
❑ 71 Willie Upshaw .15 .05
❑ 72 Dave Engle .15 .05
❑ 73 Alfredo Griffin .15 .05
❑ 74A Jack Perconte (Career Highlights takes four line .15 .05
❑ 74B Jack Perconte (Career Highlights takes three lin .15 .05
❑ 75 Jesse Orosco .15 .05
❑ 76 Jody Davis .15 .05
❑ 77 Bob Horner .40 .15
❑ 78 Larry McWilliams .15 .05
❑ 79 Joel Youngblood .15 .05
❑ 80 Alan Wiggins .15 .05
❑ 81 Ron Oester .15 .05
❑ 82 Ozzie Virgil .15 .05
❑ 83 Ricky Horton .15 .05
❑ 84 Bill Doran .15 .05
❑ 85 Rod Carew .75 .30
❑ 86 LaMarr Hoyt .15 .05
❑ 87 Tim Wallach .15 .05
❑ 88 Mike Flanagan .15 .05
❑ 89 Jim Sundberg .40 .15
❑ 90 Chet Lemon .40 .15
❑ 91 Bob Stanley .15 .05
❑ 92 Willie Randolph .40 .15
❑ 93 Bill Russell .40 .15
❑ 94 Julio Franco .40 .15
❑ 95 Dan Quisenberry .15 .05
❑ 96 Bill Caudill .15 .05
❑ 97 Bill Gullickson .15 .05
❑ 98 Danny Darwin .15 .05
❑ 99 Curtis Wilkerson .15 .05
❑ 100 Bud Black .15 .05
❑ 101 Tony Phillips .15 .05
❑ 102 Tony Bernazard .15 .05
❑ 103 Jay Howell .15 .05
❑ 104 Burt Hooton .15 .05
❑ 105 Milt Wilcox .15 .05
❑ 106 Rich Dauer .15 .05
❑ 107 Don Sutton .40 .15
❑ 108 Mike Witt .15 .05
❑ 109 Bruce Sutter .40 .15
❑ 110 Enos Cabell .15 .05
❑ 111 John Denny .15 .05
❑ 112 Dave Dravecky .15 .05
❑ 113 Marvell Wynne .15 .05
❑ 114 Johnnie LeMaster .15 .05
❑ 115 Chuck Porter .15 .05
❑ 116 John Gibbons RC .15 .05
❑ 117 Keith Moreland .15 .05
❑ 118 Darnell Coles .15 .05
❑ 119 Dennis Lamp .15 .05
❑ 120 Ron Davis .15 .05
❑ 121 Nick Esasky .15 .05
❑ 122 Vance Law .15 .05
❑ 123 Gary Roenicke .15 .05
❑ 124 Bill Schroeder .15 .05
❑ 125 Dave Rozema .15 .05
❑ 126 Bobby Meacham .15 .05
❑ 127 Marty Barrett .15 .05
❑ 128 R.J. Reynolds .15 .05
❑ 129 Ernie Camacho UER (Photo actually Rich Thompson) .15 .05
❑ 130 Jorge Orta .15 .05
❑ 131 Lary Sorensen .15 .05
❑ 132 Terry Francona .40 .15
❑ 133 Fred Lynn .40 .15
❑ 134 Bob Jones .15 .05
❑ 135 Jerry Hairston .15 .05
❑ 136 Kevin Bass .15 .05
❑ 137 Garry Maddox .15 .05
❑ 138 Dave LaPoint .15 .05
❑ 139 Kevin McReynolds .40 .15
❑ 140 Wayne Krenchicki .15 .05
❑ 141 Rafael Ramirez .15 .05
❑ 142 Rod Scurry .15 .05
❑ 143 Greg Minton .15 .05
❑ 144 Tim Stoddard .15 .05
❑ 145 Steve Henderson .15 .05
❑ 146 George Bell .40 .15
❑ 147 Dave Meier .15 .05
❑ 148 Sammy Stewart .15 .05
❑ 149 Mark Brouhard .15 .05
❑ 150 Larry Herndon .15 .05
❑ 151 Oil Can Boyd .15 .05
❑ 152 Brian Dayett .15 .05
❑ 153 Tom Niedenfuer .15 .05
❑ 154 Brook Jacoby .15 .05
❑ 155 Onix Concepcion .15 .05
❑ 156 Tim Conroy .15 .05
❑ 157 Joe Hesketh .15 .05
❑ 158 Brian Downing .40 .15
❑ 159 Tommy Dunbar .15 .05
❑ 160 Marc Hill .15 .05
❑ 161 Phil Garner .40 .15
❑ 162 Jerry Davis .15 .05
❑ 163 Bill Campbell .15 .05
❑ 164 John Franco RC 1.00 .40
❑ 165 Len Barker .15 .05
❑ 166 Benny Distefano .15 .05
❑ 167 George Frazier .15 .05
❑ 168 Tito Landrum .15 .05
❑ 169 Cal Ripken 5.00 2.00
❑ 170 Cecil Cooper .40 .15
❑ 171 Alan Trammell .40 .15
❑ 172 Wade Boggs 1.25 .50
❑ 173 Don Baylor .40 .15
❑ 174 Pedro Guerrero .40 .15
❑ 175 Frank White .40 .15
❑ 176 Rickey Henderson 1.50 .60
❑ 177 Charlie Lea .15 .05
❑ 178 Pete O'Brien .15 .05
❑ 179 Doug DeCinces .15 .05
❑ 180 Ron Kittle .15 .05
❑ 181 George Hendrick .40 .15
❑ 182 Joe Niekro .15 .05
❑ 183 Juan Samuel .15 .05
❑ 184 Mario Soto .40 .15
❑ 185 Goose Gossage .40 .15
❑ 186 Johnny Ray .15 .05
❑ 187 Bob Brenly .15 .05
❑ 188 Craig McMurtry .15 .05
❑ 189 Leon Durham .15 .05
❑ 190 Dwight Gooden RC 3.00 1.25
❑ 191 Barry Bonnell .15 .05
❑ 192 Tim Teufel .15 .05
❑ 193 Dave Stieb .40 .15
❑ 194 Mickey Hatcher .15 .05
❑ 195 Jesse Barfield .40 .15
❑ 196 Al Cowens .15 .05
❑ 197 Hubie Brooks .15 .05
❑ 198 Steve Trout .15 .05
❑ 199 Glenn Hubbard .15 .05
❑ 200 Bill Madlock .40 .15
❑ 201 Jeff D. Robinson .15 .05
❑ 202 Eric Show .15 .05
❑ 203 Dave Concepcion .40 .15
❑ 204 Ivan DeJesus .15 .05
❑ 205 Neil Allen .15 .05
❑ 206 Jerry Mumphrey .15 .05
❑ 207 Mike C. Brown .15 .05
❑ 208 Carlton Fisk .75 .30
❑ 209 Bryn Smith .15 .05
❑ 210 Tippy Martinez .15 .05
❑ 211 Dion James .15 .05
❑ 212 Willie Hernandez .15 .05
❑ 213 Mike Easler .15 .05
❑ 214 Ron Guidry .40 .15
❑ 215 Rick Honeycutt .15 .05
❑ 216 Brett Butler .40 .15
❑ 217 Larry Gura .15 .05
❑ 218 Ray Burris .15 .05
❑ 219 Steve Rogers .40 .15
❑ 220 Frank Tanana UER (Bats Left listed twice on card .40 .15
❑ 221 Ned Yost .15 .05
❑ 222 Bret Saberhagen RC 1.50 .60
❑ 223 Mike Davis .15 .05
❑ 224 Bert Blyleven .40 .15
❑ 225 Steve Kemp .15 .05
❑ 226 Jerry Reuss .15 .05
❑ 227 Darrell Evans UER (80 homers in 1980) .40 .15
❑ 228 Wayne Gross .15 .05
❑ 229 Jim Gantner .15 .05
❑ 230 Bob Boone .40 .15
❑ 231 Lonnie Smith .15 .05
❑ 232 Frank DiPino .15 .05
❑ 233 Jerry Koosman .40 .15
❑ 234 Graig Nettles .40 .15
❑ 235 John Tudor .40 .15
❑ 236 John Rabb .15 .05
❑ 237 Rick Manning .15 .05
❑ 238 Mike Fitzgerald .15 .05
❑ 239 Gary Matthews .40 .15
❑ 240 Jim Presley .50 .20
❑ 241 Dave Collins .15 .05
❑ 242 Gary Gaetti .40 .15
❑ 243 Dann Bilardello .15 .05
❑ 244 Rudy Law .15 .05
❑ 245 John Lowenstein .15 .05
❑ 246 Tom Tellmann .15 .05
❑ 247 Howard Johnson .40 .15
❑ 248 Ray Fontenot .15 .05
❑ 249 Tony Armas .40 .15
❑ 250 Candy Maldonado .15 .05
❑ 251 Mike Jeffcoat .15 .05
❑ 252 Dane Iorg .15 .05
❑ 253 Bruce Bochte .15 .05
❑ 254 Pete Rose Expos 4.00 1.50
❑ 255 Don Aase .15 .05
❑ 256 George Wright .15 .05
❑ 257 Britt Burns .15 .05
❑ 258 Mike Scott .40 .15
❑ 259 Len Matuszek .15 .05
❑ 260 Dave Rucker .15 .05
❑ 261 Craig Lefferts .15 .05
❑ 262 Jay Tibbs .15 .05
❑ 263 Bruce Benedict .15 .05
❑ 264 Don Robinson .15 .05
❑ 265 Gary Lavelle .15 .05
❑ 266 Scott Sanderson .15 .05
❑ 267 Matt Young .15 .05
❑ 268 Ernie Whitt .15 .05
❑ 269 Houston Jimenez .15 .05
❑ 270 Ken Dixon .15 .05
❑ 271 Pete Ladd .15 .05
❑ 272 Juan Berenguer .15 .05
❑ 273 Roger Clemens RC 20.00 8.00
❑ 274 Rick Cerone .15 .05
❑ 275 Dave Anderson .15 .05
❑ 276 George Vukovich .15 .05
❑ 277 Greg Pryor .15 .05
❑ 278 Mike Warren .15 .05
❑ 279 Bob James .15 .05
❑ 280 Bobby Grich .40 .15
❑ 281 Mike Mason RC .25 .08
❑ 282 Ron Reed .15 .05
❑ 283 Alan Ashby .15 .05
❑ 284 Mark Thurmond .15 .05
❑ 285 Joe Lefebvre .15 .05
❑ 286 Ted Power .15 .05

❑ 287 Chris Chambliss .40 .15
❑ 288 Lee Tunnell .15 .05
❑ 289 Rich Bordi .15 .05
❑ 290 Glenn Brummer .15 .05
❑ 291 Mike Boddicker .15 .05
❑ 292 Rollie Fingers .40 .15
❑ 293 Lou Whitaker .40 .15
❑ 294 Dwight Evans .75 .30
❑ 295 Don Mattingly 5.00 2.00
❑ 296 Mike Marshall .15 .05
❑ 297 Willie Wilson .40 .15
❑ 298 Mike Heath .15 .05
❑ 299 Tim Raines .40 .15
❑ 300 Larry Parrish .15 .05
❑ 301 Geoff Zahn .15 .05
❑ 302 Rich Dotson .15 .05
❑ 303 David Green .15 .05
❑ 304 Jose Cruz .40 .15
❑ 305 Steve Carlton .40 .15
❑ 306 Gary Redus .15 .05
❑ 307 Steve Garvey .40 .15
❑ 308 Jose DeLeon .15 .05
❑ 309 Randy Lerch .15 .05
❑ 310 Claudell Washington .15 .05
❑ 311 Lee Smith .40 .15
❑ 312 Darryl Strawberry 1.25 .50
❑ 313 Jim Beattie .15 .05
❑ 314 John Butcher .15 .05
❑ 315 Damaso Garcia .15 .05
❑ 316 Mike Smithson .15 .05
❑ 317 Luis Leal .15 .05
❑ 318 Ken Phelps .15 .05
❑ 319 Wally Backman .15 .05
❑ 320 Ron Cey .40 .15
❑ 321 Brad Komminsk .15 .05
❑ 322 Jason Thompson .15 .05
❑ 323 Frank Williams .15 .05
❑ 324 Tim Lollar .15 .05
❑ 325 Eric Davis RC 3.00 1.25
❑ 326 Von Hayes .15 .05
❑ 327 Andy Van Slyke .75 .30
❑ 328 Craig Reynolds .15 .05
❑ 329 Dick Schofield .15 .05
❑ 330 Scott Fletcher .15 .05
❑ 331 Jeff Reardon .40 .15
❑ 332 Rick Dempsey .15 .05
❑ 333 Ben Oglivie .40 .15
❑ 334 Dan Petry .15 .05
❑ 335 Jackie Gutierrez .15 .05
❑ 336 Dave Righetti .40 .15
❑ 337 Alejandro Pena .15 .05
❑ 338 Mel Hall .15 .05
❑ 339 Pat Sheridan .15 .05
❑ 340 Keith Atherton .15 .05
❑ 341 David Palmer .15 .05
❑ 342 Gary Ward .15 .05
❑ 343 Dave Stewart .40 .15
❑ 344 Mark Gubicza RC* .50 .20
❑ 345 Carney Lansford .40 .15
❑ 346 Jerry Willard .15 .05
❑ 347 Ken Griffey .40 .15
❑ 348 Franklin Stubbs .15 .05
❑ 349 Aurelio Lopez .15 .05
❑ 350 Al Bumbry .15 .05
❑ 351 Charlie Moore .15 .05
❑ 352 Luis Sanchez .15 .05
❑ 353 Darrell Porter .15 .05
❑ 354 Bill Dawley .15 .05
❑ 355 Charles Hudson .15 .05
❑ 356 Garry Templeton .40 .15
❑ 357 Cecilio Guante .15 .05
❑ 358 Jeff Leonard .15 .05
❑ 359 Paul Molitor .40 .15
❑ 360 Ron Gardenhire .15 .05
❑ 361 Larry Bowa .40 .15
❑ 362 Bob Kearney .15 .05
❑ 363 Garth Iorg .15 .05
❑ 364 Tom Brunansky .15 .05
❑ 365 Brad Gulden .15 .05
❑ 366 Greg Walker .15 .05
❑ 367 Mike Young .15 .05
❑ 368 Rick Waits .15 .05
❑ 369 Doug Bair .15 .05
❑ 370 Bob Shirley .15 .05
❑ 371 Bob Ojeda .15 .05
❑ 372 Bob Welch .40 .15
❑ 373 Neal Heaton .15 .05
❑ 374 Danny Jackson UER
(Photo actually
Frank Wills) .15 .05
❑ 375 Donnie Hill .15 .05
❑ 376 Mike Stenhouse .15 .05
❑ 377 Bruce Kison .15 .05
❑ 378 Wayne Tolleson .15 .05
❑ 379 Floyd Bannister .15 .05
❑ 380 Vern Ruhle .15 .05
❑ 381 Tim Corcoran .15 .05
❑ 382 Kurt Kepshire .15 .05
❑ 383 Bobby Brown .15 .05
❑ 384 Dave Van Gorder .15 .05
❑ 385 Rick Mahler .15 .05
❑ 386 Lee Mazzilli .40 .15
❑ 387 Bill Laskey .15 .05
❑ 388 Thad Bosley .15 .05
❑ 389 Al Chambers .15 .05
❑ 390 Tony Fernandez .40 .15
❑ 391 Ron Washington .15 .05
❑ 392 Bill Swaggerty .15 .05
❑ 393 Bob L. Gibson .15 .05
❑ 394 Marty Castillo .15 .05
❑ 395 Steve Crawford .15 .05
❑ 396 Clay Christiansen .15 .05
❑ 397 Bob Bailor .15 .05
❑ 398 Mike Hargrove .15 .05
❑ 399 Charlie Leibrandt .15 .05
❑ 400 Tom Burgmeier .15 .05
❑ 401 Razor Shines .15 .05
❑ 402 Rob Wilfong .15 .05
❑ 403 Tom Henke .40 .15
❑ 404 Al Jones .15 .05
❑ 405 Mike LaCoss .15 .05
❑ 406 Luis DeLeon .15 .05
❑ 407 Greg Gross .15 .05
❑ 408 Tom Hume .15 .05
❑ 409 Rick Camp .15 .05
❑ 410 Milt May .15 .05
❑ 411 Henry Cotto RC .25 .08
❑ 412 David Von Ohlen .15 .05
❑ 413 Scott McGregor .15 .05
❑ 414 Ted Simmons .40 .15
❑ 415 Jack Morris .40 .15
❑ 416 Bill Buckner .40 .15
❑ 417 Butch Wynegar .15 .05
❑ 418 Steve Sax .15 .05
❑ 419 Steve Balboni .15 .05
❑ 420 Dwayne Murphy .15 .05
❑ 421 Andre Dawson .40 .15
❑ 422 Charlie Hough .40 .15
❑ 423 Tommy John .40 .15
❑ 424A Tom Seaver ERR .75 .30
❑ 424B Tom Seaver COR 10.00 4.00
❑ 425 Tommy Herr .15 .05
❑ 426 Terry Puhl .15 .05
❑ 427 Al Holland .15 .05
❑ 428 Eddie Milner .15 .05
❑ 429 Terry Kennedy .15 .05
❑ 430 John Candelaria .15 .05
❑ 431 Manny Trillo .15 .05
❑ 432 Ken Oberkfell .15 .05
❑ 433 Rick Sutcliffe .40 .15
❑ 434 Ron Darling .40 .15
❑ 435 Spike Owen .15 .05
❑ 436 Frank Viola .40 .15
❑ 437 Lloyd Moseby .15 .05
❑ 438 Kirby Puckett RC 10.00 4.00
❑ 439 Jim Clancy .15 .05
❑ 440 Mike Moore .15 .05
❑ 441 Doug Sisk .15 .05
❑ 442 Dennis Eckersley .75 .30
❑ 443 Gerald Perry .15 .05
❑ 444 Dale Berra .15 .05
❑ 445 Dusty Baker .40 .15
❑ 446 Ed Whitson .15 .05
❑ 447 Cesar Cedeno .40 .15
❑ 448 Rick Schu .15 .05
❑ 449 Joaquin Andujar .40 .15
❑ 450 Mark Bailey .15 .05
❑ 451 Ron Romanick .15 .05
❑ 452 Julio Cruz .15 .05
❑ 453 Miguel Dilone .15 .05
❑ 454 Storm Davis .15 .05
❑ 455 Jaime Cocanower .15 .05
❑ 456 Barbaro Garbey .15 .05
❑ 457 Rich Gedman .15 .05
❑ 458 Phil Niekro .40 .15
❑ 459 Mike Scioscia .40 .15
❑ 460 Pat Tabler .15 .05
❑ 461 Darryl Motley .15 .05
❑ 462 Chris Codiroli .15 .05
❑ 463 Doug Flynn .15 .05
❑ 464 Billy Sample .15 .05
❑ 465 Mickey Rivers .15 .05
❑ 466 John Wathan .15 .05
❑ 467 Bill Krueger .15 .05
❑ 468 Andre Thornton .15 .05
❑ 469 Rex Hudler .15 .05
❑ 470 Sid Bream RC .50 .20
❑ 471 Kirk Gibson .40 .15
❑ 472 John Shelby .15 .05
❑ 473 Moose Haas .15 .05
❑ 474 Doug Corbett .15 .05
❑ 475 Willie McGee .40 .15
❑ 476 Bob Knepper .15 .05
❑ 477 Kevin Gross .15 .05
❑ 478 Carmelo Martinez .15 .05
❑ 479 Kent Tekulve .15 .05
❑ 480 Chili Davis .40 .15
❑ 481 Bobby Clark .15 .05
❑ 482 Mookie Wilson .40 .15
❑ 483 Dave Owen .15 .05
❑ 484 Ed Nunez .15 .05
❑ 485 Rance Mulliniks .15 .05
❑ 486 Ken Schrom .15 .05
❑ 487 Jeff Russell .15 .05
❑ 488 Tom Paciorek .15 .05
❑ 489 Dan Ford .15 .05
❑ 490 Mike Caldwell .15 .05
❑ 491 Scottie Earl .15 .05
❑ 492 Jose Rijo RC 1.00 .40
❑ 493 Bruce Hurst .15 .05
❑ 494 Ken Landreaux .15 .05
❑ 495 Mike Fischlin .15 .05
❑ 496 Don Slaught .15 .05
❑ 497 Steve McCatty .15 .05
❑ 498 Gary Lucas .15 .05
❑ 499 Gary Pettis .15 .05
❑ 500 Marvis Foley .15 .05
❑ 501 Mike Squires .15 .05
❑ 502 Jim Pankovits .15 .05
❑ 503 Luis Aguayo .15 .05
❑ 504 Ralph Citarella .15 .05
❑ 505 Bruce Bochy .15 .05
❑ 506 Bob Owchinko .15 .05
❑ 507 Pascual Perez .15 .05
❑ 508 Lee Lacy .15 .05
❑ 509 Atlee Hammaker .15 .05
❑ 510 Bob Dernier .15 .05
❑ 511 Ed VandeBerg .15 .05
❑ 512 Cliff Johnson .15 .05
❑ 513 Len Whitehouse .15 .05
❑ 514 Dennis Martinez .40 .15
❑ 515 Ed Romero .15 .05
❑ 516 Rusty Kuntz .15 .05
❑ 517 Rick Miller .15 .05
❑ 518 Dennis Rasmussen .15 .05
❑ 519 Steve Yeager .40 .15
❑ 520 Chris Bando .15 .05
❑ 521 U.L. Washington .15 .05
❑ 522 Curt Young .15 .05
❑ 523 Angel Salazar .15 .05
❑ 524 Curt Kaufman .15 .05
❑ 525 Odell Jones .15 .05
❑ 526 Juan Agosto .15 .05
❑ 527 Denny Walling .15 .05
❑ 528 Andy Hawkins .15 .05
❑ 529 Sixto Lezcano .15 .05
❑ 530 Skeeter Barnes RC .25 .08
❑ 531 Randy Johnson .15 .05
❑ 532 Jim Morrison .15 .05
❑ 533 Warren Brusstar .15 .05
❑ 534A Jeff Pendleton ERR RC 1.00 .40
❑ 534B Terry Pendleton COR 1.00 .40
❑ 535 Vic Rodriguez .15 .05
❑ 536 Bob McClure .15 .05
❑ 537 Dave Bergman .15 .05
❑ 538 Mark Clear .15 .05
❑ 539 Mike Pagliarulo .15 .05
❑ 540 Terry Whitfield .15 .05

❑	541 Joe Beckwith	.15	.05
❑	542 Jeff Burroughs	.15	.05
❑	543 Dan Schatzeder	.15	.05
❑	544 Donnie Scott	.15	.05
❑	545 Jim Slaton	.15	.05
❑	546 Greg Luzinski	.40	.15
❑	547 Mark Salas	.15	.05
❑	548 Dave Smith	.15	.05
❑	549 John Wockenfuss	.15	.05
❑	550 Frank Pastore	.15	.05
❑	551 Tim Flannery	.15	.05
❑	552 Rick Rhoden	.15	.05
❑	553 Mark Davis	.15	.05
❑	554 Jeff Dedmon	.15	.05
❑	555 Gary Woods	.15	.05
❑	556 Danny Heep	.15	.05
❑	557 Mark Langston RC	1.00	.40
❑	558 Darrell Brown	.15	.05
❑	559 Jimmy Key RC	1.00	.40
❑	560 Rick Lysander	.15	.05
❑	561 Doyle Alexander	.15	.05
❑	562 Mike Stanton	.15	.05
❑	563 Sid Fernandez	.40	.15
❑	564 Richie Hebner	.15	.05
❑	565 Alex Trevino	.15	.05
❑	566 Brian Harper	.15	.05
❑	567 Dan Gladden RC	.50	.20
❑	568 Luis Salazar	.15	.05
❑	569 Tom Foley	.15	.05
❑	570 Larry Andersen	.15	.05
❑	571 Danny Cox	.15	.05
❑	572 Joe Sambito	.15	.05
❑	573 Juan Beniquez	.15	.05
❑	574 Joel Skinner	.15	.05
❑	575 Randy St.Claire	.15	.05
❑	576 Floyd Rayford	.15	.05
❑	577 Roy Howell	.15	.05
❑	578 John Grubb	.15	.05
❑	579 Ed Jurak	.15	.05
❑	580 John Montefusco	.15	.05
❑	581 Orel Hershiser RC	3.00	1.25
❑	582 Tom Waddell	.15	.05
❑	583 Mark Huismann	.15	.05
❑	584 Joe Morgan	.40	.15
❑	585 Jim Wohlford	.15	.05
❑	586 Dave Schmidt	.15	.05
❑	587 Jeff Kunkel	.15	.05
❑	588 Hal McRae	.40	.15
❑	589 Bill Almon	.15	.05
❑	590 Carmelo Castillo	.15	.05
❑	591 Omar Moreno	.15	.05
❑	592 Ken Howell	.15	.05
❑	593 Tom Brookens	.15	.05
❑	594 Joe Nolan	.15	.05
❑	595 Willie Lozado	.15	.05
❑	596 Tom Nieto	.15	.05
❑	597 Walt Terrell	.15	.05
❑	598 Al Oliver	.40	.15
❑	599 Shane Rawley	.15	.05
❑	600 Denny Gonzalez	.15	.05
❑	601 Mark Grant	.15	.05
❑	602 Mike Armstrong	.15	.05
❑	603 George Foster	.40	.15
❑	604 Dave Lopes	.40	.15
❑	605 Salome Barojas	.15	.05
❑	606 Roy Lee Jackson	.15	.05
❑	607 Pete Filson	.15	.05
❑	608 Duane Walker	.15	.05
❑	609 Glenn Wilson	.15	.05
❑	610 Rafael Santana	.15	.05
❑	611 Roy Smith	.15	.05
❑	612 Ruppert Jones	.15	.05
❑	613 Joe Cowley	.15	.05
❑	614 Al Nipper UER (Photo actually Mike Brown)	.15	.05
❑	615 Gene Nelson	.15	.05
❑	616 Joe Carter	1.25	.50
❑	617 Ray Knight	.40	.15
❑	618 Chuck Rainey	.15	.05
❑	619 Dan Driessen	.15	.05
❑	620 Daryl Sconiers	.15	.05
❑	621 Bill Stein	.15	.05
❑	622 Roy Smalley	.15	.05
❑	623 Ed Lynch	.15	.05
❑	624 Jeff Stone RC	.15	.05
❑	625 Bruce Berenyi	.15	.05
❑	626 Kelvin Chapman	.15	.05
❑	627 Joe Price	.15	.05
❑	628 Steve Bedrosian	.15	.05
❑	629 Vic Mata	.15	.05
❑	630 Mike Krukow	.15	.05
❑	631 Phil Bradley	.50	.20
❑	632 Jim Gott	.15	.05
❑	633 Randy Bush	.15	.05
❑	634 Tom Browning RC	.50	.20
❑	635 Lou Gehrig Puzzle	1.25	.50
❑	636 Reid Nichols	.15	.05
❑	637 Dan Pasqua RC	.50	.20
❑	638 German Rivera	.15	.05
❑	639 Don Schulze	.15	.05
❑	640A Mike Jones (Career Highlights& takes five lines)	.15	.05
❑	640B Mike Jones (Career Highlights& takes four lines)	.15	.05
❑	641 Pete Rose	4.00	1.50
❑	642 Wade Rowdon	.15	.05
❑	643 Jerry Narron	.15	.05
❑	644 Darrell Miller	.15	.05
❑	645 Tim Hulett RC	.25	.08
❑	646 Andy McGaffigan	.15	.05
❑	647 Kurt Bevacqua	.15	.05
❑	648 John Russell	.15	.05
❑	649 Ron Robinson	.15	.05
❑	650 Donnie Moore	.15	.05
❑	651A D.Mattingly/D.Winfield YL	2.00	.75
❑	651B D.Mattingly/D.Winfield WL	5.00	2.00
❑	652 Tim Laudner	.15	.05
❑	653 Steve Farr RC	.50	.20
❑	654 DK Checklist 1-26 (Unnumbered)	.15	.05
❑	655 Checklist 27-130 (Unnumbered)	.15	.05
❑	656 Checklist 131-234 (Unnumbered)	.15	.05
❑	657 Checklist 235-338 (Unnumbered)	.15	.05
❑	658 Checklist 339-442 (Unnumbered)	.15	.05
❑	659 Checklist 443-546 (Unnumbered)	.15	.05
❑	660 Checklist 547-653 (Unnumbered)	.15	.05

1986 Donruss

❑	COMPLETE SET (660)	40.00	15.00
❑	COMP.FACT.SET (660)	40.00	15.00
❑	COMP.AARON PUZZLE	2.00	.75
❑	1 Kirk Gibson DK	.25	.08
❑	2 Goose Gossage DK	.25	.08
❑	3 Willie McGee DK	.25	.08
❑	4 George Bell DK	.25	.08
❑	5 Tony Armas DK	.25	.08
❑	6 Chili Davis DK	.25	.08
❑	7 Cecil Cooper DK	.25	.08
❑	8 Mike Boddicker DK	.15	.05
❑	9 Dave Lopes DK	.25	.08
❑	10 Bill Doran DK	.15	.05
❑	11 Bret Saberhagen DK	.25	.08
❑	12 Brett Butler DK	.25	.08
❑	13 Harold Baines DK	.25	.08
❑	14 Mike Davis DK	.15	.05
❑	15 Tony Perez DK	.50	.20
❑	16 Willie Randolph DK	.25	.08
❑	17 Bob Boone DK	.25	.08
❑	18 Orel Hershiser DK	.50	.20
❑	19 Johnny Ray DK	.15	.05
❑	20 Gary Ward DK	.15	.05
❑	21 Rick Mahler DK	.15	.05
❑	22 Phil Bradley DK	.15	.05
❑	23 Jerry Koosman DK	.25	.08
❑	24 Tom Brunansky DK	.15	.05
❑	25 Andre Dawson DK	.15	.05
❑	26 Dwight Gooden DK	.75	.30
❑	27 Kal Daniels RC	.50	.20
❑	28 Fred McGriff RC	8.00	3.00
❑	29 Cory Snyder	.15	.05
❑	30 Jose Guzman RC	.15	.05
❑	31 Ty Gainey RC	.15	.05
❑	32 Johnny Abrego RC	.15	.05
❑	33A Andres Galarraga RC	1.50	.60
❑	33B Andres Galarraga RC	1.50	.60
❑	34 Dave Shipanoff RC	.15	.05
❑	35 Mark McLemore RC	1.00	.40
❑	36 Marty Clary RC	.15	.05
❑	37 Paul O'Neill RC	4.00	1.50
❑	38 Danny Tartabull	.25	.08
❑	39 Jose Canseco RC	10.00	4.00
❑	40 Juan Nieves RC	.15	.05
❑	41 Lance McCullers RC	.15	.05
❑	42 Rick Surhoff RC	.15	.05
❑	43 Todd Worrell RC	.50	.20
❑	44 Bob Kipper RC	.15	.05
❑	45 John Habyan RC	.15	.05
❑	46 Mike Woodard RC	.15	.05
❑	47 Mike Boddicker	.15	.05
❑	48 Robin Yount	1.25	.50
❑	49 Lou Whitaker	.25	.08
❑	50 Oil Can Boyd	.15	.05
❑	51 Rickey Henderson	.75	.30
❑	52 Mike Marshall	.15	.05
❑	53 George Brett	2.00	.75
❑	54 Dave Kingman	.25	.08
❑	55 Hubie Brooks	.15	.05
❑	56 Oddibe McDowell	.15	.05
❑	57 Doug DeCinces	.15	.05
❑	58 Britt Burns	.15	.05
❑	59 Ozzie Smith	1.25	.50
❑	60 Jose Cruz	.25	.08
❑	61 Mike Schmidt	2.00	.75
❑	62 Pete Rose	2.50	1.00
❑	63 Steve Garvey	.25	.08
❑	64 Tony Pena	.15	.05
❑	65 Chili Davis	.25	.08
❑	66 Dale Murphy	.50	.20
❑	67 Ryne Sandberg	1.50	.60
❑	68 Gary Carter	.25	.08
❑	69 Alvin Davis	.15	.05
❑	70 Kent Hrbek	.25	.08
❑	71 George Bell	.25	.08
❑	72 Kirby Puckett	2.00	.75
❑	73 Lloyd Moseby	.15	.05
❑	74 Bob Kearney	.15	.05
❑	75 Dwight Gooden	.75	.30
❑	76 Gary Matthews	.25	.08
❑	77 Rick Mahler	.15	.05
❑	78 Benny Distefano	.15	.05
❑	79 Jeff Leonard	.15	.05
❑	80 Kevin McReynolds	.25	.08
❑	81 Ron Oester	.15	.05
❑	82 John Russell	.15	.05
❑	83 Tommy Herr	.15	.05
❑	84 Jerry Mumphrey	.15	.05
❑	85 Ron Romanick	.15	.05
❑	86 Daryl Boston	.15	.05
❑	87 Andre Dawson	.25	.08
❑	88 Eddie Murray	.75	.30
❑	89 Dion James	.15	.05
❑	90 Chet Lemon	.25	.08
❑	91 Bob Stanley	.15	.05
❑	92 Willie Randolph	.25	.08
❑	93 Mike Scioscia	.25	.08
❑	94 Tom Waddell	.15	.05
❑	95 Danny Jackson	.15	.05
❑	96 Mike Davis	.15	.05
❑	97 Mike Fitzgerald	.15	.05
❑	98 Gary Ward	.15	.05
❑	99 Pete O'Brien	.15	.05

❑	100	Bret Saberhagen	.25	.08
❑	101	Alfredo Griffin	.15	.05
❑	102	Brett Butler	.25	.08
❑	103	Ron Guidry	.25	.08
❑	104	Jerry Reuss	.15	.05
❑	105	Jack Morris	.25	.08
❑	106	Rick Dempsey	.15	.05
❑	107	Ray Burris	.15	.05
❑	108	Brian Downing	.25	.08
❑	109	Willie McGee	.25	.08
❑	110	Bill Doran	.15	.05
❑	111	Kent Tekulve	.15	.05
❑	112	Tony Gwynn	1.25	.50
❑	113	Marvell Wynne	.15	.05
❑	114	David Green	.15	.05
❑	115	Jim Gantner	.15	.05
❑	116	George Foster	.25	.08
❑	117	Steve Trout	.15	.05
❑	118	Mark Langston	.25	.08
❑	119	Tony Fernandez	.15	.05
❑	120	John Butcher	.15	.05
❑	121	Ron Robinson	.15	.05
❑	122	Dan Spillner	.15	.05
❑	123	Mike Young	.15	.05
❑	124	Paul Molitor	.25	.08
❑	125	Kirk Gibson	.25	.08
❑	126	Ken Griffey	.25	.08
❑	127	Tony Armas	.25	.08
❑	128	Mariano Duncan RC	.50	.20
❑	129	Pat Tabler	.15	.05
❑	130	Frank White	.25	.08
❑	131	Carney Lansford	.25	.08
❑	132	Vance Law	.15	.05
❑	133	Dick Schofield	.15	.05
❑	134	Wayne Tolleson	.15	.05
❑	135	Greg Walker	.15	.05
❑	136	Denny Walling	.15	.05
❑	137	Ozzie Virgil	.15	.05
❑	138	Ricky Horton	.15	.05
❑	139	LaMarr Hoyt	.15	.05
❑	140	Wayne Krenchicki	.15	.05
❑	141	Glenn Hubbard	.15	.05
❑	142	Cecilio Guante	.15	.05
❑	143	Mike Krukow	.15	.05
❑	144	Lee Smith	.25	.08
❑	145	Edwin Nunez	.15	.05
❑	146	Dave Stieb	.25	.08
❑	147	Mike Smithson	.15	.05
❑	148	Ken Dixon	.15	.05
❑	149	Danny Darwin	.15	.05
❑	150	Chris Pittaro	.15	.05
❑	151	Bill Buckner	.25	.08
❑	152	Mike Pagliarulo	.15	.05
❑	153	Bill Russell	.25	.08
❑	154	Brook Jacoby	.15	.05
❑	155	Pat Sheridan	.15	.05
❑	156	Mike Gallego RC	.15	.05
❑	157	Jim Wohlford	.15	.05
❑	158	Gary Pettis	.15	.05
❑	159	Toby Harrah	.25	.08
❑	160	Richard Dotson	.15	.05
❑	161	Bob Knepper	.15	.05
❑	162	Dave Dravecky	.15	.05
❑	163	Greg Gross	.15	.05
❑	164	Eric Davis	.75	.30
❑	165	Gerald Perry	.15	.05
❑	166	Rick Rhoden	.15	.05
❑	167	Keith Moreland	.15	.05
❑	168	Jack Clark	.25	.08
❑	169	Storm Davis	.15	.05
❑	170	Cecil Cooper	.25	.08
❑	171	Alan Trammell	.25	.08
❑	172	Roger Clemens	5.00	2.00
❑	173	Don Mattingly	2.50	1.00
❑	174	Pedro Guerrero	.25	.08
❑	175	Willie Wilson	.25	.08
❑	176	Dwayne Murphy	.15	.05
❑	177	Tim Raines	.25	.08
❑	178	Larry Parrish	.15	.05
❑	179	Mike Witt	.15	.05
❑	180	Harold Baines	.25	.08
❑	181	Vince Coleman UER RC	1.00	.40
❑	182	Jeff Heathcock	.15	.05
❑	183	Steve Carlton	.25	.08
❑	184	Mario Soto	.25	.08
❑	185	Goose Gossage	.25	.08
❑	186	Johnny Ray	.15	.05
❑	187	Dan Gladden	.15	.05
❑	188	Bob Horner	.25	.08
❑	189	Rick Sutcliffe	.25	.08
❑	190	Keith Hernandez	.25	.08
❑	191	Phil Bradley	.15	.05
❑	192	Tom Brunansky	.15	.05
❑	193	Jesse Barfield	.25	.08
❑	194	Frank Viola	.25	.08
❑	195	Willie Upshaw	.15	.05
❑	196	Jim Beattie	.15	.05
❑	197	Darryl Strawberry	.50	.20
❑	198	Ron Cey	.25	.08
❑	199	Steve Bedrosian	.15	.05
❑	200	Steve Kemp	.15	.05
❑	201	Manny Trillo	.15	.05
❑	202	Garry Templeton	.25	.08
❑	203	Dave Parker	.25	.08
❑	204	John Denny	.15	.05
❑	205	Terry Pendleton	.25	.08
❑	206	Terry Puhl	.15	.05
❑	207	Bobby Grich	.25	.08
❑	208	Ozzie Guillen RC	2.00	.75
❑	209	Jeff Reardon	.25	.08
❑	210	Cal Ripken	3.00	1.25
❑	211	Bill Schroeder	.15	.05
❑	212	Dan Petry	.15	.05
❑	213	Jim Rice	.25	.08
❑	214	Dave Righetti	.25	.08
❑	215	Fernando Valenzuela	.25	.08
❑	216	Julio Franco	.25	.08
❑	217	Darryl Motley	.15	.05
❑	218	Dave Collins	.15	.05
❑	219	Tim Wallach	.15	.05
❑	220	George Wright	.15	.05
❑	221	Tommy Dunbar	.15	.05
❑	222	Steve Balboni	.15	.05
❑	223	Jay Howell	.15	.05
❑	224	Joe Carter	.25	.08
❑	225	Ed Whitson	.15	.05
❑	226	Orel Hershiser	.75	.30
❑	227	Willie Hernandez	.15	.05
❑	228	Lee Lacy	.15	.05
❑	229	Rollie Fingers	.25	.08
❑	230	Bob Boone	.25	.08
❑	231	Joaquin Andujar	.25	.08
❑	232	Craig Reynolds	.15	.05
❑	233	Shane Rawley	.15	.05
❑	234	Eric Show	.15	.05
❑	235	Jose DeLeon	.15	.05
❑	236	Jose Uribe	.15	.05
❑	237	Moose Haas	.15	.05
❑	238	Wally Backman	.15	.05
❑	239	Dennis Eckersley	.50	.20
❑	240	Mike Moore	.15	.05
❑	241	Damaso Garcia	.15	.05
❑	242	Tim Teufel	.15	.05
❑	243	Dave Concepcion	.25	.08
❑	244	Floyd Bannister	.15	.05
❑	245	Fred Lynn	.25	.08
❑	246	Charlie Moore	.15	.05
❑	247	Walt Terrell	.15	.05
❑	248	Dave Winfield	.25	.08
❑	249	Dwight Evans	.50	.20
❑	250	Dennis Powell	.15	.05
❑	251	Andre Thornton	.15	.05
❑	252	Onix Concepcion	.15	.05
❑	253	Mike Heath	.15	.05
❑	254A	David Palmer ERR (Position 2B)	.15	.05
❑	254B	David Palmer COR (Position P)	.50	.20
❑	255	Donnie Moore	.15	.05
❑	256	Curtis Wilkerson	.15	.05
❑	257	Julio Cruz	.15	.05
❑	258	Nolan Ryan	4.00	1.50
❑	259	Jeff Stone	.15	.05
❑	260	John Tudor	.25	.08
❑	261	Mark Thurmond	.15	.05
❑	262	Jay Tibbs	.15	.05
❑	263	Rafael Ramirez	.15	.05
❑	264	Larry McWilliams	.15	.05
❑	265	Mark Davis	.15	.05
❑	266	Bob Dernier	.15	.05
❑	267	Matt Young	.15	.05
❑	268	Jim Clancy	.15	.05
❑	269	Mickey Hatcher	.15	.05
❑	270	Sammy Stewart	.15	.05
❑	271	Bob L. Gibson	.15	.05
❑	272	Nelson Simmons	.15	.05
❑	273	Rich Gedman	.15	.05
❑	274	Butch Wynegar	.15	.05
❑	275	Ken Howell	.15	.05
❑	276	Mel Hall	.15	.05
❑	277	Jim Sundberg	.25	.08
❑	278	Chris Codiroli	.15	.05
❑	279	Herm Winningham	.15	.05
❑	280	Rod Carew	.50	.20
❑	281	Don Slaught	.15	.05
❑	282	Scott Fletcher	.15	.05
❑	283	Bill Dawley	.15	.05
❑	284	Andy Hawkins	.15	.05
❑	285	Glenn Wilson	.15	.05
❑	286	Nick Esasky	.15	.05
❑	287	Claudell Washington	.15	.05
❑	288	Lee Mazzilli	.25	.08
❑	289	Jody Davis	.15	.05
❑	290	Darrell Porter	.15	.05
❑	291	Scott McGregor	.15	.05
❑	292	Ted Simmons	.25	.08
❑	293	Aurelio Lopez	.15	.05
❑	294	Marty Barrett	.15	.05
❑	295	Dale Berra	.15	.05
❑	296	Greg Brock	.15	.05
❑	297	Charlie Leibrandt	.15	.05
❑	298	Bill Krueger	.15	.05
❑	299	Bryn Smith	.15	.05
❑	300	Burt Hooton	.15	.05
❑	301	Stu Cliburn	.15	.05
❑	302	Luis Salazar	.15	.05
❑	303	Ken Dayley	.15	.05
❑	304	Frank DiPino	.15	.05
❑	305	Von Hayes	.15	.05
❑	306	Gary Redus	.15	.05
❑	307	Craig Lefferts	.15	.05
❑	308	Sammy Khalifa	.15	.05
❑	309	Scott Garrelts	.15	.05
❑	310	Rick Cerone	.15	.05
❑	311	Shawon Dunston	.25	.08
❑	312	Howard Johnson	.25	.08
❑	313	Jim Presley	.15	.05
❑	314	Gary Gaetti	.25	.08
❑	315	Luis Leal	.15	.05
❑	316	Mark Salas	.15	.05
❑	317	Bill Caudill	.15	.05
❑	318	Dave Henderson	.15	.05
❑	319	Rafael Santana	.15	.05
❑	320	Leon Durham	.15	.05
❑	321	Bruce Sutter	.25	.08
❑	322	Jason Thompson	.15	.05
❑	323	Bob Brenly	.15	.05
❑	324	Carmelo Martinez	.15	.05
❑	325	Eddie Milner	.15	.05
❑	326	Juan Samuel	.15	.05
❑	327	Tom Nieto	.15	.05
❑	328	Dave Smith	.15	.05
❑	329	Urbano Lugo	.15	.05
❑	330	Joel Skinner	.15	.05
❑	331	Bill Gullickson	.15	.05
❑	332	Floyd Rayford	.15	.05
❑	333	Ben Oglivie	.25	.08
❑	334	Lance Parrish	.25	.08
❑	335	Jackie Gutierrez	.15	.05
❑	336	Dennis Rasmussen	.15	.05
❑	337	Terry Whitfield	.15	.05
❑	338	Neal Heaton	.15	.05
❑	339	Jorge Orta	.15	.05
❑	340	Donnie Hill	.15	.05
❑	341	Joe Hesketh	.15	.05
❑	342	Charlie Hough	.25	.08
❑	343	Dave Rozema	.15	.05
❑	344	Greg Pryor	.15	.05
❑	345	Mickey Tettleton RC	.50	.20
❑	346	George Vukovich	.15	.05
❑	347	Don Baylor	.25	.08
❑	348	Carlos Diaz	.15	.05
❑	349	Barbaro Garbey	.15	.05
❑	350	Larry Sheets	.15	.05
❑	351	Teddy Higuera RC*	.50	.20
❑	352	Juan Beniquez	.15	.05
❑	353	Bob Forsch	.15	.05
❑	354	Mark Bailey	.15	.05

❑ 355 Larry Andersen .15 .05
❑ 356 Terry Kennedy .15 .05
❑ 357 Don Robinson .15 .05
❑ 358 Jim Gott .15 .05
❑ 359 Earnie Riles .15 .05
❑ 360 John Christensen .15 .05
❑ 361 Ray Fontenot .15 .05
❑ 362 Spike Owen .15 .05
❑ 363 Jim Acker .15 .05
❑ 364 Ron Davis .15 .05
❑ 365 Tom Hume .15 .05
❑ 366 Carlton Fisk .50 .20
❑ 367 Nate Snell .15 .05
❑ 368 Rick Manning .15 .05
❑ 369 Darrell Evans .25 .08
❑ 370 Ron Hassey .15 .05
❑ 371 Wade Boggs .50 .20
❑ 372 Rick Honeycutt .15 .05
❑ 373 Chris Bando .15 .05
❑ 374 Bud Black .15 .05
❑ 375 Steve Henderson .15 .05
❑ 376 Charlie Lea .15 .05
❑ 377 Reggie Jackson .50 .20
❑ 378 Dave Schmidt .15 .05
❑ 379 Bob James .15 .05
❑ 380 Glenn Davis .15 .05
❑ 381 Tim Corcoran .15 .05
❑ 382 Danny Cox .15 .05
❑ 383 Tim Flannery .15 .05
❑ 384 Tom Browning .15 .05
❑ 385 Rick Camp .15 .05
❑ 386 Jim Morrison .15 .05
❑ 387 Dave LaPoint .15 .05
❑ 388 Dave Lopes .25 .08
❑ 389 Al Cowens .15 .05
❑ 390 Doyle Alexander .15 .05
❑ 391 Tim Laudner .15 .05
❑ 392 Don Aase .15 .05
❑ 393 Jaime Cocanower .15 .05
❑ 394 Randy O'Neal .15 .05
❑ 395 Mike Easler .15 .05
❑ 396 Scott Bradley .15 .05
❑ 397 Tom Niedenfuer .15 .05
❑ 398 Jerry Willard .15 .05
❑ 399 Lonnie Smith .15 .05
❑ 400 Bruce Bochte .15 .05
❑ 401 Terry Francona .25 .08
❑ 402 Jim Slaton .15 .05
❑ 403 Bill Stein .15 .05
❑ 404 Tim Hulett .15 .05
❑ 405 Alan Ashby .15 .05
❑ 406 Tim Stoddard .15 .05
❑ 407 Garry Maddox .15 .05
❑ 408 Ted Power .15 .05
❑ 409 Len Barker .15 .05
❑ 410 Denny Gonzalez .15 .05
❑ 411 George Frazier .15 .05
❑ 412 Andy Van Slyke .50 .20
❑ 413 Jim Dwyer .15 .05
❑ 414 Paul Householder .15 .05
❑ 415 Alejandro Sanchez .15 .05
❑ 416 Steve Crawford .15 .05
❑ 417 Dan Pasqua .15 .05
❑ 418 Enos Cabell .15 .05
❑ 419 Mike Jones .15 .05
❑ 420 Steve Kiefer .15 .05
❑ 421 Tim Burke .15 .05
❑ 422 Mike Mason .15 .05
❑ 423 Ruppert Jones .15 .05
❑ 424 Jerry Hairston .15 .05
❑ 425 Tito Landrum .15 .05
❑ 426 Jeff Calhoun .15 .05
❑ 427 Don Carman .15 .05
❑ 428 Tony Perez .50 .20
❑ 429 Jerry Davis .15 .05
❑ 430 Bob Walk .15 .05
❑ 431 Brad Wellman .15 .05
❑ 432 Terry Forster .25 .08
❑ 433 Billy Hatcher .15 .05
❑ 434 Clint Hurdle .15 .05
❑ 435 Ivan Calderon RC* .50 .20
❑ 436 Pete Filson .15 .05
❑ 437 Tom Henke .25 .08
❑ 438 Dave Engle .15 .05
❑ 439 Tom Filer .15 .05
❑ 440 Gorman Thomas .25 .08
❑ 441 Rick Aguilera RC .50 .20
❑ 442 Scott Sanderson .15 .05
❑ 443 Jeff Dedmon .15 .05
❑ 444 Joe Orsulak RC* .50 .20
❑ 445 Atlee Hammaker .15 .05
❑ 446 Jerry Royster .15 .05
❑ 447 Buddy Bell .25 .08
❑ 448 Dave Rucker .15 .05
❑ 449 Ivan DeJesus .15 .05
❑ 450 Jim Pankovits .15 .05
❑ 451 Jerry Narron .15 .05
❑ 452 Bryan Little .15 .05
❑ 453 Gary Lucas .15 .05
❑ 454 Dennis Martinez .25 .08
❑ 455 Ed Romero .15 .05
❑ 456 Bob Melvin .15 .05
❑ 457 Glenn Hoffman .15 .05
❑ 458 Bob Shirley .15 .05
❑ 459 Bob Welch .25 .08
❑ 460 Carmen Castillo .15 .05
❑ 461 Dave Leeper OF .15 .05
❑ 462 Tim Birtsas .15 .05
❑ 463 Randy St.Claire .15 .05
❑ 464 Chris Welsh .15 .05
❑ 465 Greg Harris .15 .05
❑ 466 Lynn Jones .15 .05
❑ 467 Dusty Baker .25 .08
❑ 468 Roy Smith .15 .05
❑ 469 Andre Robertson .15 .05
❑ 470 Ken Landreaux .15 .05
❑ 471 Dave Bergman .15 .05
❑ 472 Gary Roenicke .15 .05
❑ 473 Pete Vuckovich .15 .05
❑ 474 Kirk McCaskill RC .50 .20
❑ 475 Jeff Lahti .15 .05
❑ 476 Mike Scott .25 .08
❑ 477 Darren Daulton RC 1.00 .40
❑ 478 Graig Nettles .25 .08
❑ 479 Bill Almon .15 .05
❑ 480 Greg Minton .15 .05
❑ 481 Randy Ready .15 .05
❑ 482 Len Dykstra RC 1.50 .60
❑ 483 Thad Bosley .15 .05
❑ 484 Harold Reynolds RC 1.50 .60
❑ 485 Al Oliver .25 .08
❑ 486 Roy Smalley .15 .05
❑ 487 John Franco .25 .08
❑ 488 Juan Agosto .15 .05
❑ 489 Al Pardo .15 .05
❑ 490 Bill Wegman RC .15 .05
❑ 491 Frank Tanana .25 .08
❑ 492 Brian Fisher RC .15 .05
❑ 493 Mark Clear .15 .05
❑ 494 Len Matuszek .15 .05
❑ 495 Ramon Romero .15 .05
❑ 496 John Wathan .15 .05
❑ 497 Rob Picciolo .15 .05
❑ 498 U.L. Washington .15 .05
❑ 499 John Candelaria .15 .05
❑ 500 Duane Walker .15 .05
❑ 501 Gene Nelson .15 .05
❑ 502 John Mizerock .15 .05
❑ 503 Luis Aguayo .15 .05
❑ 504 Kurt Kepshire .15 .05
❑ 505 Ed Wojna .15 .05
❑ 506 Joe Price .15 .05
❑ 507 Milt Thompson RC .50 .20
❑ 508 Junior Ortiz .15 .05
❑ 509 Vida Blue .25 .08
❑ 510 Steve Engel .15 .05
❑ 511 Karl Best .15 .05
❑ 512 Cecil Fielder RC 2.00 .75
❑ 513 Frank Eufemia .15 .05
❑ 514 Tippy Martinez .15 .05
❑ 515 Billy Joe Robidoux .15 .05
❑ 516 Bill Scherrer .15 .05
❑ 517 Bruce Hurst .15 .05
❑ 518 Rich Bordi .15 .05
❑ 519 Steve Yeager .25 .08
❑ 520 Tony Bernazard .15 .05
❑ 521 Hal McRae .25 .08
❑ 522 Jose Rijo .25 .08
❑ 523 Mitch Webster .15 .05
❑ 524 Jack Howell .15 .05
❑ 525 Alan Bannister .15 .05
❑ 526 Ron Kittle .15 .05
❑ 527 Phil Garner .25 .08
❑ 528 Kurt Bevacqua .15 .05
❑ 529 Kevin Gross .15 .05
❑ 530 Bo Diaz .15 .05
❑ 531 Ken Oberkfell .15 .05
❑ 532 Rick Reuschel .25 .08
❑ 533 Ron Meridith .15 .05
❑ 534 Steve Braun .15 .05
❑ 535 Wayne Gross .15 .05
❑ 536 Ray Searage .15 .05
❑ 537 Tom Brookens .15 .05
❑ 538 Al Nipper .15 .05
❑ 539 Billy Sample .15 .05
❑ 540 Steve Sax .15 .05
❑ 541 Dan Quisenberry .15 .05
❑ 542 Tony Phillips .15 .05
❑ 543 Floyd Youmans .15 .05
❑ 544 Steve Buechele RC .50 .20
❑ 545 Craig Gerber .15 .05
❑ 546 Joe DeSa .15 .05
❑ 547 Brian Harper .15 .05
❑ 548 Kevin Bass .15 .05
❑ 549 Tom Foley .15 .05
❑ 550 Dave Van Gorder .15 .05
❑ 551 Bruce Bochy .15 .05
❑ 552 R.J. Reynolds .15 .05
❑ 553 Chris Brown RC .15 .05
❑ 554 Bruce Benedict .15 .05
❑ 555 Warren Brusstar .15 .05
❑ 556 Danny Heep .15 .05
❑ 557 Darnell Coles .15 .05
❑ 558 Greg Gagne .15 .05
❑ 559 Ernie Whitt .15 .05
❑ 560 Ron Washington .15 .05
❑ 561 Jimmy Key .25 .08
❑ 562 Bill Swift .15 .05
❑ 563 Ron Darling .25 .08
❑ 564 Dick Ruthven .15 .05
❑ 565 Zane Smith .15 .05
❑ 566 Sid Bream .15 .05
❑ 567A Joel Youngblood ERR (Position P) .15 .05
❑ 567B Joel Youngblood COR (Position IF) .50 .20
❑ 568 Mario Ramirez .15 .05
❑ 569 Tom Runnells .15 .05
❑ 570 Rick Schu .15 .05
❑ 571 Bill Campbell .15 .05
❑ 572 Dickie Thon .15 .05
❑ 573 Al Holland .15 .05
❑ 574 Reid Nichols .15 .05
❑ 575 Bert Roberge .15 .05
❑ 576 Mike Flanagan .15 .05
❑ 577 Tim Leary .15 .05
❑ 578 Mike Laga .15 .05
❑ 579 Steve Lyons .15 .05
❑ 580 Phil Niekro .25 .08
❑ 581 Gilberto Reyes .15 .05
❑ 582 Jamie Easterly .15 .05
❑ 583 Mark Gubicza .15 .05
❑ 584 Stan Javier RC .50 .20
❑ 585 Bill Laskey .15 .05
❑ 586 Jeff Russell .15 .05
❑ 587 Dickie Noles .15 .05
❑ 588 Steve Farr .15 .05
❑ 589 Steve Ontiveros RC .15 .05
❑ 590 Mike Hargrove .15 .05
❑ 591 Marty Bystrom .15 .05
❑ 592 Franklin Stubbs .15 .05
❑ 593 Larry Herndon .15 .05
❑ 594 Bill Swaggerty .15 .05
❑ 595 Carlos Ponce .15 .05
❑ 596 Pat Perry .15 .05
❑ 597 Ray Knight .25 .08
❑ 598 Steve Lombardozzi .15 .05
❑ 599 Brad Havens .15 .05
❑ 600 Pat Clements .15 .05
❑ 601 Joe Niekro .15 .05
❑ 602 Hank Aaron Puzzle .75 .30
❑ 603 Dwayne Henry .15 .05
❑ 604 Mookie Wilson .25 .08
❑ 605 Buddy Biancalana .15 .05
❑ 606 Rance Mulliniks .15 .05
❑ 607 Alan Wiggins .15 .05
❑ 608 Joe Cowley .15 .05
❑ 609 Tom Seaver .50 .20

❑ 609B Tom Seaver YL 2.00 .75
❑ 610 Neil Allen .15 .05
❑ 611 Don Sutton .25 .08
❑ 612 Fred Toliver .15 .05
❑ 613 Jay Baller .15 .05
❑ 614 Marc Sullivan .15 .05
❑ 615 John Grubb .15 .05
❑ 616 Bruce Kison .15 .05
❑ 617 Bill Madlock .25 .08
❑ 618 Chris Chambliss .25 .08
❑ 619 Dave Stewart .25 .08
❑ 620 Tim Lollar .15 .05
❑ 621 Gary Lavelle .15 .05
❑ 622 Charles Hudson .15 .05
❑ 623 Joel Davis .15 .05
❑ 624 Joe Johnson .15 .05
❑ 625 Sid Fernandez .15 .05
❑ 626 Dennis Lamp .15 .05
❑ 627 Terry Harper .15 .05
❑ 628 Jack Lazorko .15 .05
❑ 629 Roger McDowell RC* .50 .20
❑ 630 Mark Funderburk .15 .05
❑ 631 Ed Lynch .15 .05
❑ 632 Rudy Law .15 .05
❑ 633 Roger Mason RC .15 .05
❑ 634 Mike Felder RC .15 .05
❑ 635 Ken Schrom .15 .05
❑ 636 Bob Ojeda .15 .05
❑ 637 Ed VandeBerg .15 .05
❑ 638 Bobby Meacham .15 .05
❑ 639 Cliff Johnson .15 .05
❑ 640 Garth Iorg .15 .05
❑ 641 Dan Driessen .15 .05
❑ 642 Mike Brown OF .15 .05
❑ 643 John Shelby .15 .05
❑ 644 Pete Rose RB .75 .30
❑ 645 The Knuckle Brothers .25 .08
❑ 646 Jesse Orosco .15 .05
❑ 647 Billy Beane RC 1.00 .40
❑ 648 Cesar Cedeno .25 .08
❑ 649 Bert Blyleven .25 .08
❑ 650 Max Venable .15 .05
❑ 651 Fleet Feet
Vince Coleman
Willie McGee .15 .05
❑ 652 Calvin Schiraldi .15 .05
❑ 653 Pete Rose KING .75 .30
❑ 654 Diamond Kings CL 1-26
(Unnumbered) .15 .05
❑ 655A CL 1: 27-130
(Unnumbered)
(45 Beane ERR) .15 .05
❑ 655B CL 1: 27-130
(Unnumbered)
(45 Habyan COR) .15 .05
❑ 656 CL 2: 131-234
(Unnumbered) .15 .05
❑ 657 CL 3: 235-338
(Unnumbered) .15 .05
❑ 658 CL 4: 339-442
(Unnumbered) .15 .05
❑ 659 CL 5: 443-546
(Unnumbered) .15 .05
❑ 660 CL 6: 547-653
(Unnumbered) .15 .05

1987 Donruss

❑ COMPLETE SET (660) 40.00 15.00
❑ COMP.FACT.SET (660) 50.00 20.00
❑ COMP.CLEMENTE PUZZLE 1.50 .60
❑ 1 Wally Joyner DK .40 .15
❑ 2 Roger Clemens DK 2.00 .75
❑ 3 Dale Murphy DK .25 .08
❑ 4 Darryl Strawberry DK .15 .05
❑ 5 Ozzie Smith DK .60 .25
❑ 6 Jose Canseco DK 1.00 .40
❑ 7 Charlie Hough DK .15 .05
❑ 8 Brook Jacoby DK .10 .02
❑ 9 Fred Lynn DK .15 .05
❑ 10 Rick Rhoden DK .10 .02
❑ 11 Chris Brown DK .10 .02
❑ 12 Von Hayes DK .10 .02
❑ 13 Jack Morris DK .15 .05
❑ 14A Kevin McReynolds DK ERR .40 .15
❑ 14B Kevin McReynolds DK COR .10 .02
❑ 15 George Brett DK 1.00 .40
❑ 16 Ted Higuera DK .10 .02
❑ 17 Hubie Brooks DK .10 .02
❑ 18 Mike Scott DK .15 .05
❑ 19 Kirby Puckett DK .75 .30
❑ 20 Dave Winfield DK .15 .05
❑ 21 Lloyd Moseby DK .10 .02
❑ 22A Eric Davis DK ERR .40 .15
❑ 22B Eric Davis DK COR .25 .08
❑ 23 Jim Presley DK .10 .02
❑ 24 Keith Moreland DK .10 .02
❑ 25A Greg Walker DK ERR .40 .15
❑ 25B Greg Walker DK COR .10 .02
❑ 26 Steve Sax DK .10 .02
❑ 27 DK Checklist 1-26 .10 .02
❑ 28 B.J. Surhoff RC .60 .25
❑ 29 Randy Myers RC .60 .25
❑ 30 Ken Gerhart RC .15 .05
❑ 31 Benito Santiago .15 .05
❑ 32 Greg Swindell RC .40 .15
❑ 33 Mike Birkbeck RC .15 .05
❑ 34 Terry Steinbach RC .60 .25
❑ 35 Bo Jackson RC 5.00 2.00
❑ 36 Greg Maddux RC 10.00 4.00
❑ 37 Jim Lindeman RC .15 .05
❑ 38 Devon White RC .60 .25
❑ 39 Eric Bell RC .15 .05
❑ 40 Willie Fraser RC .15 .05
❑ 41 Jerry Browne RC .15 .05
❑ 42 Chris James RC * .15 .05
❑ 43 Rafael Palmeiro RC 5.00 2.00
❑ 44 Pat Dodson RC .15 .05
❑ 45 Duane Ward RC * .40 .15
❑ 46 Mark McGwire 8.00 3.00
❑ 47 Bruce Fields UER RC .15 .05
❑ 48 Eddie Murray .40 .15
❑ 49 Ted Higuera .10 .02
❑ 50 Kirk Gibson .15 .05
❑ 51 Oil Can Boyd .10 .02
❑ 52 Don Mattingly 1.25 .50
❑ 53 Pedro Guerrero .15 .05
❑ 54 George Brett 1.00 .40
❑ 55 Jose Rijo .15 .05
❑ 56 Tim Raines .15 .05
❑ 57 Ed Correa .10 .02
❑ 58 Mike Witt .10 .02
❑ 59 Greg Walker .10 .02
❑ 60 Ozzie Smith .60 .25
❑ 61 Glenn Davis .10 .02
❑ 62 Glenn Wilson .10 .02
❑ 63 Tom Browning .10 .02
❑ 64 Tony Gwynn .60 .25
❑ 65 R.J. Reynolds .10 .02
❑ 66 Will Clark RC 1.50 .60
❑ 67 Ozzie Virgil .10 .02
❑ 68 Rick Sutcliffe .15 .05
❑ 69 Gary Carter .15 .05
❑ 70 Mike Moore .10 .02
❑ 71 Bert Blyleven .15 .05
❑ 72 Tony Fernandez .10 .02
❑ 73 Kent Hrbek .15 .05
❑ 74 Lloyd Moseby .10 .02
❑ 75 Alvin Davis .10 .02
❑ 76 Keith Hernandez .15 .05
❑ 77 Ryne Sandberg .75 .30
❑ 78 Dale Murphy .25 .08
❑ 79 Sid Bream .10 .02
❑ 80 Chris Brown .10 .02
❑ 81 Steve Garvey .15 .05
❑ 82 Mario Soto .15 .05
❑ 83 Shane Rawley .10 .02
❑ 84 Willie McGee .15 .05
❑ 85 Jose Cruz .15 .05
❑ 86 Brian Downing .15 .05
❑ 87 Ozzie Guillen .25 .08
❑ 88 Hubie Brooks .10 .02
❑ 89 Cal Ripken 1.50 .60
❑ 90 Juan Nieves .10 .02
❑ 91 Lance Parrish .15 .05
❑ 92 Jim Rice .15 .05
❑ 93 Ron Guidry .15 .05
❑ 94 Fernando Valenzuela .15 .05
❑ 95 Andy Allanson RC .10 .02
❑ 96 Willie Wilson .15 .05
❑ 97 Jose Canseco 1.00 .40
❑ 98 Jeff Reardon .15 .05
❑ 99 Bobby Witt RC .40 .15
❑ 100 Checklist 28-133 .10 .02
❑ 101 Jose Guzman .10 .02
❑ 102 Steve Balboni .10 .02
❑ 103 Tony Phillips .10 .02
❑ 104 Brook Jacoby .10 .02
❑ 105 Dave Winfield .15 .05
❑ 106 Orel Hershiser .25 .08
❑ 107 Lou Whitaker .15 .05
❑ 108 Fred Lynn .15 .05
❑ 109 Bill Wegman .10 .02
❑ 110 Donnie Moore .10 .02
❑ 111 Jack Clark .15 .05
❑ 112 Bob Knepper .10 .02
❑ 113 Von Hayes .10 .02
❑ 114 Bip Roberts RC .40 .15
❑ 115 Tony Pena .10 .02
❑ 116 Scott Garrelts .10 .02
❑ 117 Paul Molitor .15 .05
❑ 118 Darryl Strawberry .15 .05
❑ 119 Shawon Dunston .10 .02
❑ 120 Jim Presley .10 .02
❑ 121 Jesse Barfield .15 .05
❑ 122 Gary Gaetti .15 .05
❑ 123 Kurt Stillwell .10 .02
❑ 124 Joel Davis .10 .02
❑ 125 Mike Boddicker .10 .02
❑ 126 Robin Yount .60 .25
❑ 127 Alan Trammell .15 .05
❑ 128 Dave Righetti .15 .05
❑ 129 Dwight Evans .25 .08
❑ 130 Mike Scioscia .15 .05
❑ 131 Julio Franco .15 .05
❑ 132 Bret Saberhagen .15 .05
❑ 133 Mike Davis .10 .02
❑ 134 Joe Hesketh .10 .02
❑ 135 Wally Joyner RC .60 .25
❑ 136 Don Slaught .10 .02
❑ 137 Daryl Boston .10 .02
❑ 138 Nolan Ryan 2.00 .75
❑ 139 Mike Schmidt 1.00 .40
❑ 140 Tommy Herr .10 .02
❑ 141 Garry Templeton .15 .05
❑ 142 Kal Daniels .10 .02
❑ 143 Billy Sample .10 .02
❑ 144 Johnny Ray .10 .02
❑ 145 Robby Thompson RC * .40 .15
❑ 146 Bob Dernier .10 .02
❑ 147 Danny Tartabull .10 .02
❑ 148 Ernie Whitt .10 .02
❑ 149 Kirby Puckett .75 .30
❑ 150 Mike Young .10 .02
❑ 151 Ernest Riles .10 .02
❑ 152 Frank Tanana .15 .05
❑ 153 Rich Gedman .10 .02
❑ 154 Willie Randolph .15 .05
❑ 155 Bill Madlock .15 .05
❑ 156 Joe Carter .15 .05
❑ 157 Danny Jackson .10 .02
❑ 158 Carney Lansford .15 .05
❑ 159 Bryn Smith .10 .02
❑ 160 Gary Pettis .10 .02
❑ 161 Oddibe McDowell .10 .02
❑ 162 John Cangelosi .10 .02
❑ 163 Mike Scott .15 .05
❑ 164 Eric Show .10 .02
❑ 165 Juan Samuel .10 .02
❑ 166 Nick Esasky .10 .02

❑ 167 Zane Smith	.10	.02
❑ 168 Mike C. Brown OF	.10	.02
❑ 169 Keith Moreland	.10	.02
❑ 170 John Tudor	.15	.05
❑ 171 Ken Dixon	.10	.02
❑ 172 Jim Gantner	.10	.02
❑ 173 Jack Morris	.15	.05
❑ 174 Bruce Hurst	.10	.02
❑ 175 Dennis Rasmussen	.10	.02
❑ 176 Mike Marshall	.10	.02
❑ 177 Dan Quisenberry	.10	.02
❑ 178 Eric Plunk	.10	.02
❑ 179 Tim Wallach	.10	.02
❑ 180 Steve Buechele	.10	.02
❑ 181 Don Sutton	.15	.05
❑ 182 Dave Schmidt	.10	.02
❑ 183 Terry Pendleton	.15	.05
❑ 184 Jim Deshaies RC *	.15	.05
❑ 185 Steve Bedrosian	.10	.02
❑ 186 Pete Rose	1.25	.50
❑ 187 Dave Dravecky	.10	.02
❑ 188 Rick Reuschel	.15	.05
❑ 189 Dan Gladden	.10	.02
❑ 190 Rick Mahler	.10	.02
❑ 191 Thad Bosley	.10	.02
❑ 192 Ron Darling	.15	.05
❑ 193 Matt Young	.10	.02
❑ 194 Tom Brunansky	.10	.02
❑ 195 Dave Stieb	.15	.05
❑ 196 Frank Viola	.15	.05
❑ 197 Tom Henke	.10	.02
❑ 198 Karl Best	.10	.02
❑ 199 Dwight Gooden	.25	.08
❑ 200 Checklist 134-239	.10	.02
❑ 201 Steve Trout	.10	.02
❑ 202 Rafael Ramirez	.10	.02
❑ 203 Bob Walk	.10	.02
❑ 204 Roger Mason	.10	.02
❑ 205 Terry Kennedy	.10	.02
❑ 206 Ron Oester	.10	.02
❑ 207 John Russell	.10	.02
❑ 208 Greg Mathews	.10	.02
❑ 209 Charlie Kerfeld	.10	.02
❑ 210 Reggie Jackson	.25	.08
❑ 211 Floyd Bannister	.10	.02
❑ 212 Vance Law	.10	.02
❑ 213 Rich Bordi	.10	.02
❑ 214 Dan Plesac	.10	.02
❑ 215 Dave Collins	.10	.02
❑ 216 Bob Stanley	.10	.02
❑ 217 Joe Niekro	.10	.02
❑ 218 Tom Niedenfuer	.10	.02
❑ 219 Brett Butler	.15	.05
❑ 220 Charlie Leibrandt	.10	.02
❑ 221 Steve Ontiveros	.10	.02
❑ 222 Tim Burke	.10	.02
❑ 223 Curtis Wilkerson	.10	.02
❑ 224 Pete Incaviglia RC *	.40	.15
❑ 225 Lonnie Smith	.10	.02
❑ 226 Chris Codiroli	.10	.02
❑ 227 Scott Bailes	.10	.02
❑ 228 Rickey Henderson	.40	.15
❑ 229 Ken Howell	.10	.02
❑ 230 Darnell Coles	.10	.02
❑ 231 Don Aase	.10	.02
❑ 232 Tim Leary	.10	.02
❑ 233 Bob Boone	.15	.05
❑ 234 Ricky Horton	.10	.02
❑ 235 Mark Bailey	.10	.02
❑ 236 Kevin Gross	.10	.02
❑ 237 Lance McCullers	.10	.02
❑ 238 Cecilio Guante	.10	.02
❑ 239 Bob Melvin	.10	.02
❑ 240 Billy Joe Robidoux	.10	.02
❑ 241 Roger McDowell	.10	.02
❑ 242 Leon Durham	.10	.02
❑ 243 Ed Nunez	.10	.02
❑ 244 Jimmy Key	.15	.05
❑ 245 Mike Smithson	.10	.02
❑ 246 Bo Diaz	.10	.02
❑ 247 Carlton Fisk	.25	.08
❑ 248 Larry Sheets	.10	.02
❑ 249 Juan Castillo RC	.15	.05
❑ 250 Eric King	.10	.02
❑ 251 Doug Drabek RC	.60	.25
❑ 252 Wade Boggs	.25	.08
❑ 253 Mariano Duncan	.10	.02
❑ 254 Pat Tabler	.10	.02
❑ 255 Frank White	.15	.05
❑ 256 Alfredo Griffin	.10	.02
❑ 257 Floyd Youmans	.10	.02
❑ 258 Rob Wilfong	.10	.02
❑ 259 Pete O'Brien	.10	.02
❑ 260 Tim Hulett	.10	.02
❑ 261 Dickie Thon	.10	.02
❑ 262 Darren Daulton	.15	.05
❑ 263 Vince Coleman	.10	.02
❑ 264 Andy Hawkins	.10	.02
❑ 265 Eric Davis	.25	.08
❑ 266 Andres Thomas	.10	.02
❑ 267 Mike Diaz	.10	.02
❑ 268 Chili Davis	.15	.05
❑ 269 Jody Davis	.10	.02
❑ 270 Phil Bradley	.10	.02
❑ 271 George Bell	.15	.05
❑ 272 Keith Atherton	.10	.02
❑ 273 Storm Davis	.10	.02
❑ 274 Rob Deer	.10	.02
❑ 275 Walt Terrell	.10	.02
❑ 276 Roger Clemens	2.00	.75
❑ 277 Mike Easler	.10	.02
❑ 278 Steve Sax	.10	.02
❑ 279 Andre Thornton	.10	.02
❑ 280 Jim Sundberg	.15	.05
❑ 281 Bill Bathe	.10	.02
❑ 282 Jay Tibbs	.10	.02
❑ 283 Dick Schofield	.10	.02
❑ 284 Mike Mason	.10	.02
❑ 285 Jerry Hairston	.10	.02
❑ 286 Bill Doran	.10	.02
❑ 287 Tim Flannery	.10	.02
❑ 288 Gary Redus	.10	.02
❑ 289 John Franco	.15	.05
❑ 290 Paul Assenmacher	.40	.15
❑ 291 Joe Orsulak	.10	.02
❑ 292 Lee Smith	.15	.05
❑ 293 Mike Laga	.10	.02
❑ 294 Rick Dempsey	.10	.02
❑ 295 Mike Felder	.10	.02
❑ 296 Tom Brookens	.10	.02
❑ 297 Al Nipper	.10	.02
❑ 298 Mike Pagliarulo	.10	.02
❑ 299 Franklin Stubbs	.10	.02
❑ 300 Checklist 240-345	.10	.02
❑ 301 Steve Farr	.10	.02
❑ 302 Bill Mooneyham	.10	.02
❑ 303 Andres Galarraga	.15	.05
❑ 304 Scott Fletcher	.10	.02
❑ 305 Jack Howell	.10	.02
❑ 306 Russ Morman	.10	.02
❑ 307 Todd Worrell	.10	.02
❑ 308 Dave Smith	.10	.02
❑ 309 Jeff Stone	.10	.02
❑ 310 Ron Robinson	.10	.02
❑ 311 Bruce Bochy	.10	.02
❑ 312 Jim Winn	.10	.02
❑ 313 Mark Davis	.10	.02
❑ 314 Jeff Dedmon	.10	.02
❑ 315 Jamie Moyer RC	1.00	.40
❑ 316 Wally Backman	.10	.02
❑ 317 Ken Phelps	.10	.02
❑ 318 Steve Lombardozzi	.10	.02
❑ 319 Rance Mulliniks	.10	.02
❑ 320 Tim Laudner	.10	.02
❑ 321 Mark Eichhorn	.10	.02
❑ 322 Lee Guetterman	.10	.02
❑ 323 Sid Fernandez	.10	.02
❑ 324 Jerry Mumphrey	.10	.02
❑ 325 David Palmer	.10	.02
❑ 326 Bill Almon	.10	.02
❑ 327 Candy Maldonado	.10	.02
❑ 328 John Kruk RC	1.00	.40
❑ 329 John Denny	.10	.02
❑ 330 Milt Thompson	.10	.02
❑ 331 Mike LaValliere RC *	.40	.15
❑ 332 Alan Ashby	.10	.02
❑ 333 Doug Corbett	.10	.02
❑ 334 Ron Karkovice RC	.40	.15
❑ 335 Mitch Webster	.10	.02
❑ 336 Lee Lacy	.10	.02
❑ 337 Glenn Braggs RC	.15	.05
❑ 338 Dwight Lowry	.10	.02
❑ 339 Don Baylor	.15	.05
❑ 340 Brian Fisher	.10	.02
❑ 341 Reggie Williams	.10	.02
❑ 342 Tom Candiotti	.10	.02
❑ 343 Rudy Law	.10	.02
❑ 344 Curt Young	.10	.02
❑ 345 Mike Fitzgerald	.10	.02
❑ 346 Ruben Sierra RC	1.00	.40
❑ 347 Mitch Williams RC *	.40	.15
❑ 348 Jorge Orta	.10	.02
❑ 349 Mickey Tettleton	.10	.02
❑ 350 Ernie Camacho	.10	.02
❑ 351 Ron Kittle	.10	.02
❑ 352 Ken Landreaux	.10	.02
❑ 353 Chet Lemon	.15	.05
❑ 354 John Shelby	.10	.02
❑ 355 Mark Clear	.10	.02
❑ 356 Doug DeCinces	.10	.02
❑ 357 Ken Dayley	.10	.02
❑ 358 Phil Garner	.15	.05
❑ 359 Steve Jeltz	.10	.02
❑ 360 Ed Whitson	.10	.02
❑ 361 Barry Bonds RC	12.00	5.00
❑ 362 Vida Blue	.15	.05
❑ 363 Cecil Cooper	.15	.05
❑ 364 Bob Ojeda	.10	.02
❑ 365 Dennis Eckersley	.25	.08
❑ 366 Mike Morgan	.10	.02
❑ 367 Willie Upshaw	.10	.02
❑ 368 Allan Anderson RC	.10	.02
❑ 369 Bill Gullickson	.10	.02
❑ 370 Bobby Thigpen RC	.40	.15
❑ 371 Juan Beniquez	.10	.02
❑ 372 Charlie Moore	.10	.02
❑ 373 Dan Petry	.10	.02
❑ 374 Rod Scurry	.10	.02
❑ 375 Tom Seaver	.25	.08
❑ 376 Ed VandeBerg	.10	.02
❑ 377 Tony Bernazard	.10	.02
❑ 378 Greg Pryor	.10	.02
❑ 379 Dwayne Murphy	.10	.02
❑ 380 Andy McGaffigan	.10	.02
❑ 381 Kirk McCaskill	.10	.02
❑ 382 Greg Harris	.10	.02
❑ 383 Rich Dotson	.10	.02
❑ 384 Craig Reynolds	.10	.02
❑ 385 Greg Gross	.10	.02
❑ 386 Tito Landrum	.10	.02
❑ 387 Craig Lefferts	.10	.02
❑ 388 Dave Parker	.15	.05
❑ 389 Bob Horner	.15	.05
❑ 390 Pat Clements	.10	.02
❑ 391 Jeff Leonard	.10	.02
❑ 392 Chris Speier	.10	.02
❑ 393 John Moses	.10	.02
❑ 394 Garth Iorg	.10	.02
❑ 395 Greg Gagne	.10	.02
❑ 396 Nate Snell	.10	.02
❑ 397 Bryan Clutterbuck	.10	.02
❑ 398 Darrell Evans	.15	.05
❑ 399 Steve Crawford	.10	.02
❑ 400 Checklist 346-451	.10	.02
❑ 401 Phil Lombardi	.10	.02
❑ 402 Rick Honeycutt	.10	.02
❑ 403 Ken Schrom	.10	.02
❑ 404 Bud Black	.10	.02
❑ 405 Donnie Hill	.10	.02
❑ 406 Wayne Krenchicki	.10	.02
❑ 407 Chuck Finley RC	.60	.25
❑ 408 Toby Harrah	.15	.05
❑ 409 Steve Lyons	.10	.02
❑ 410 Kevin Bass	.10	.02
❑ 411 Marvell Wynne	.10	.02
❑ 412 Ron Roenicke	.10	.02
❑ 413 Tracy Jones	.10	.02
❑ 414 Gene Garber	.10	.02
❑ 415 Mike Bielecki	.10	.02
❑ 416 Frank DiPino	.10	.02
❑ 417 Andy Van Slyke	.25	.08
❑ 418 Jim Dwyer	.10	.02
❑ 419 Ben Oglivie	.15	.05
❑ 420 Dave Bergman	.10	.02
❑ 421 Joe Sambito	.10	.02
❑ 422 Bob Tewksbury RC *	.40	.15
❑ 423 Len Matuszek	.10	.02
❑ 424 Mike Kingery RC	.15	.05

❑ 425 Dave Kingman .15 .05
❑ 426 Al Newman RC .10 .02
❑ 427 Gary Ward .10 .02
❑ 428 Ruppert Jones .10 .02
❑ 429 Harold Baines .15 .05
❑ 430 Pat Perry .10 .02
❑ 431 Terry Puhl .10 .02
❑ 432 Don Carman .10 .02
❑ 433 Eddie Milner .10 .02
❑ 434 LaMarr Hoyt .10 .02
❑ 435 Rick Rhoden .10 .02
❑ 436 Jose Uribe .10 .02
❑ 437 Ken Oberkfell .10 .02
❑ 438 Ron Davis .10 .02
❑ 439 Jesse Orosco .10 .02
❑ 440 Scott Bradley .10 .02
❑ 441 Randy Bush .10 .02
❑ 442 John Cerutti .10 .02
❑ 443 Roy Smalley .10 .02
❑ 444 Kelly Gruber .10 .02
❑ 445 Bob Kearney .10 .02
❑ 446 Ed Hearn RC .10 .02
❑ 447 Scott Sanderson .10 .02
❑ 448 Bruce Benedict .10 .02
❑ 449 Junior Ortiz .10 .02
❑ 450 Mike Aldrete .10 .02
❑ 451 Kevin McReynolds .10 .02
❑ 452 Rob Murphy .10 .02
❑ 453 Kent Tekulve .10 .02
❑ 454 Curt Ford .10 .02
❑ 455 Dave Lopes .15 .05
❑ 456 Bob Grich .15 .05
❑ 457 Jose DeLeon .10 .02
❑ 458 Andre Dawson .15 .05
❑ 459 Mike Flanagan .10 .02
❑ 460 Joey Meyer .15 .05
❑ 461 Chuck Cary .10 .02
❑ 462 Bill Buckner .15 .05
❑ 463 Bob Shirley .10 .02
❑ 464 Jeff Hamilton .10 .02
❑ 465 Phil Niekro .15 .05
❑ 466 Mark Gubicza .10 .02
❑ 467 Jerry Willard .10 .02
❑ 468 Bob Sebra .10 .02
❑ 469 Larry Parrish .10 .02
❑ 470 Charlie Hough .15 .05
❑ 471 Hal McRae .15 .05
❑ 472 Dave Leiper .10 .02
❑ 473 Mel Hall .10 .02
❑ 474 Dan Pasqua .10 .02
❑ 475 Bob Welch .15 .05
❑ 476 Johnny Grubb .10 .02
❑ 477 Jim Traber .10 .02
❑ 478 Chris Bosio RC .40 .15
❑ 479 Mark McLemore .15 .05
❑ 480 John Morris .10 .02
❑ 481 Billy Hatcher .10 .02
❑ 482 Dan Schatzeder .10 .02
❑ 483 Rich Gossage .15 .05
❑ 484 Jim Morrison .10 .02
❑ 485 Bob Brenly .10 .02
❑ 486 Bill Schroeder .10 .02
❑ 487 Mookie Wilson .15 .05
❑ 488 Dave Martinez RC .40 .15
❑ 489 Harold Reynolds .15 .05
❑ 490 Jeff Hearron .10 .02
❑ 491 Mickey Hatcher .10 .02
❑ 492 Barry Larkin RC 1.50 .60
❑ 493 Bob James .10 .02
❑ 494 John Habyan .10 .02
❑ 495 Jim Adduci .10 .02
❑ 496 Mike Heath .10 .02
❑ 497 Tim Stoddard .10 .02
❑ 498 Tony Armas .15 .05
❑ 499 Dennis Powell .10 .02
❑ 500 Checklist 452-557 .10 .02
❑ 501 Chris Bando .10 .02
❑ 502 David Cone RC 1.00 .40
❑ 503 Jay Howell .10 .02
❑ 504 Tom Foley .10 .02
❑ 505 Ray Chadwick .10 .02
❑ 506 Mike Loynd RC .15 .05
❑ 507 Neil Allen .10 .02
❑ 508 Danny Darwin .10 .02
❑ 509 Rick Schu .10 .02
❑ 510 Jose Oquendo .10 .02
❑ 511 Gene Walter .10 .02
❑ 512 Terry McGriff .10 .02
❑ 513 Ken Griffey .15 .05
❑ 514 Benny Distefano .10 .02
❑ 515 Terry Mulholland RC .40 .15
❑ 516 Ed Lynch .10 .02
❑ 517 Bill Swift .10 .02
❑ 518 Manny Lee .10 .02
❑ 519 Andre David .10 .02
❑ 520 Scott McGregor .10 .02
❑ 521 Rick Manning .10 .02
❑ 522 Willie Hernandez .10 .02
❑ 523 Marty Barrett .10 .02
❑ 524 Wayne Tolleson .10 .02
❑ 525 Jose Gonzalez RC .15 .05
❑ 526 Cory Snyder .10 .02
❑ 527 Buddy Biancalana .10 .02
❑ 528 Moose Haas .10 .02
❑ 529 Wilfredo Tejada .10 .02
❑ 530 Stu Cliburn .10 .02
❑ 531 Dale Mohorcic .10 .02
❑ 532 Ron Hassey .10 .02
❑ 533 Ty Gainey .10 .02
❑ 534 Jerry Royster .10 .02
❑ 535 Mike Maddux RC .10 .02
❑ 536 Ted Power .10 .02
❑ 537 Ted Simmons .15 .05
❑ 538 Rafael Belliard RC .40 .15
❑ 539 Chico Walker .10 .02
❑ 540 Bob Forsch .10 .02
❑ 541 John Stefero .10 .02
❑ 542 Dale Sveum .10 .02
❑ 543 Mark Thurmond .10 .02
❑ 544 Jeff Sellers .10 .02
❑ 545 Joel Skinner .10 .02
❑ 546 Alex Trevino .10 .02
❑ 547 Randy Kutcher .10 .02
❑ 548 Joaquin Andujar .15 .05
❑ 549 Casey Candaele .10 .02
❑ 550 Jeff Russell .10 .02
❑ 551 John Candelaria .10 .02
❑ 552 Joe Cowley .10 .02
❑ 553 Danny Cox .10 .02
❑ 554 Denny Walling .10 .02
❑ 555 Bruce Ruffin RC .15 .05
❑ 556 Buddy Bell .15 .05
❑ 557 Jimmy Jones RC .15 .05
❑ 558 Bobby Bonilla RC .60 .25
❑ 559 Jeff D. Robinson .10 .02
❑ 560 Ed Olwine .10 .02
❑ 561 Glenallen Hill RC .40 .15
❑ 562 Lee Mazzilli .15 .05
❑ 563 Mike G. Brown P .10 .02
❑ 564 George Frazier .10 .02
❑ 565 Mike Sharperson RC .15 .05
❑ 566 Mark Portugal RC * .40 .15
❑ 567 Rick Leach .10 .02
❑ 568 Mark Langston .10 .02
❑ 569 Rafael Santana .10 .02
❑ 570 Manny Trillo .10 .02
❑ 571 Cliff Speck .10 .02
❑ 572 Bob Kipper .10 .02
❑ 573 Kelly Downs RC .15 .05
❑ 574 Randy Asadoor .10 .02
❑ 575 Dave Magadan RC .40 .15
❑ 576 Marvin Freeman RC .15 .05
❑ 577 Jeff Lahti .10 .02
❑ 578 Jeff Calhoun .10 .02
❑ 579 Gus Polidor .10 .02
❑ 580 Gene Nelson .10 .02
❑ 581 Tim Teufel .10 .02
❑ 582 Odell Jones .10 .02
❑ 583 Mark Ryal .10 .02
❑ 584 Randy O'Neal .10 .02
❑ 585 Mike Greenwell RC .40 .15
❑ 586 Ray Knight .15 .05
❑ 587 Ralph Bryant .10 .02
❑ 588 Carmen Castillo .10 .02
❑ 589 Ed Wojna .10 .02
❑ 590 Stan Javier .10 .02
❑ 591 Jeff Musselman .10 .02
❑ 592 Mike Stanley RC .40 .15
❑ 593 Darrell Porter .10 .02
❑ 594 Drew Hall .10 .02
❑ 595 Rob Nelson .10 .02
❑ 596 Bryan Oelkers .10 .02
❑ 597 Scott Nielsen .10 .02
❑ 598 Brian Holton .10 .02
❑ 599 Kevin Mitchell RC * .60 .25
❑ 600 Checklist 558-660 .10 .02
❑ 601 Jackie Gutierrez .10 .02
❑ 602 Barry Jones .10 .02
❑ 603 Jerry Narron .10 .02
❑ 604 Steve Lake .10 .02
❑ 605 Jim Pankovits .10 .02
❑ 606 Ed Romero .10 .02
❑ 607 Dave LaPoint .10 .02
❑ 608 Don Robinson .10 .02
❑ 609 Mike Krukow .10 .02
❑ 610 Dave Valle RC ** .15 .05
❑ 611 Len Dykstra .15 .05
❑ 612 Roberto Clemente PUZ .50 .20
❑ 613 Mike Trujillo .10 .02
❑ 614 Damaso Garcia .10 .02
❑ 615 Neal Heaton .10 .02
❑ 616 Juan Berenguer .10 .02
❑ 617 Steve Carlton .15 .05
❑ 618 Gary Lucas .10 .02
❑ 619 Geno Petralli .10 .02
❑ 620 Rick Aguilera .10 .02
❑ 621 Fred McGriff .75 .30
❑ 622 Dave Henderson .10 .02
❑ 623 Dave Clark RC .15 .05
❑ 624 Angel Salazar .10 .02
❑ 625 Randy Hunt .10 .02
❑ 626 John Gibbons .10 .02
❑ 627 Kevin Brown RC 1.50 .60
❑ 628 Bill Dawley .10 .02
❑ 629 Aurelio Lopez .10 .02
❑ 630 Charles Hudson .10 .02
❑ 631 Ray Soff .10 .02
❑ 632 Ray Hayward .10 .02
❑ 633 Spike Owen .10 .02
❑ 634 Glenn Hubbard .10 .02
❑ 635 Kevin Elster RC .40 .15
❑ 636 Mike LaCoss .10 .02
❑ 637 Dwayne Henry .10 .02
❑ 638 Rey Quinones .10 .02
❑ 639 Jim Clancy .10 .02
❑ 640 Larry Andersen .10 .02
❑ 641 Calvin Schiraldi .10 .02
❑ 642 Stan Jefferson .10 .02
❑ 643 Marc Sullivan .10 .02
❑ 644 Mark Grant .10 .02
❑ 645 Cliff Johnson .10 .02
❑ 646 Howard Johnson .15 .05
❑ 647 Dave Sax .10 .02
❑ 648 Dave Stewart .15 .05
❑ 649 Danny Heep .10 .02
❑ 650 Joe Johnson .10 .02
❑ 651 Bob Brower .10 .02
❑ 652 Rob Woodward .10 .02
❑ 653 John Mizerock .10 .02
❑ 654 Tim Pyznarski .10 .02
❑ 655 Luis Aquino .10 .02
❑ 656 Mickey Brantley .10 .02
❑ 657 Doyle Alexander .10 .02
❑ 658 Sammy Stewart .10 .02
❑ 659 Jim Acker .10 .02
❑ 660 Pete Ladd .10 .02

1988 Donruss

❑ COMPLETE SET (660) 10.00 4.00
❑ COMP.FACT.SET (660) 15.00 6.00

❑ COMMON CARD (1-660) .05 .01
❑ COMMON SP (648-660) .10 .02
❑ 1 Mark McGwire DK .75 .30
❑ 2 Tim Raines DK .10 .02
❑ 3 Benito Santiago DK .10 .02
❑ 4 Alan Trammell DK .10 .02
❑ 5 Danny Tartabull DK .05 .01
❑ 6 Ron Darling DK .10 .02
❑ 7 Paul Molitor DK .10 .02
❑ 8 Devon White DK .10 .02
❑ 9 Andre Dawson DK .05 .01
❑ 10 Julio Franco DK .10 .02
❑ 11 Scott Fletcher DK .05 .01
❑ 12 Tony Fernandez DK .05 .01
❑ 13 Shane Rawley DK .05 .01
❑ 14 Kal Daniels DK .05 .01
❑ 15 Jack Clark DK .10 .02
❑ 16 Dwight Evans DK .15 .05
❑ 17 Tommy John DK .10 .02
❑ 18 Andy Van Slyke DK .15 .05
❑ 19 Gary Gaetti DK .10 .02
❑ 20 Mark Langston DK .05 .01
❑ 21 Will Clark DK .20 .07
❑ 22 Glenn Hubbard DK .05 .01
❑ 23 Billy Hatcher DK .05 .01
❑ 24 Bob Welch DK .10 .02
❑ 25 Ivan Calderon DK .05 .01
❑ 26 Cal Ripken DK .40 .15
❑ 27 DK Checklist 1-26 .05 .01
❑ 28 Mackey Sasser RC .25 .08
❑ 29 Jeff Treadway RC .25 .08
❑ 30 Mike Campbell RR .05 .01
❑ 31 Lance Johnson RC .25 .08
❑ 32 Nelson Liriano RR .05 .01
❑ 33 Shawn Abner RR .05 .01
❑ 34 Roberto Alomar RC 2.00 .75
❑ 35 Shawn Hillegas RR .05 .01
❑ 36 Joey Meyer RR .05 .01
❑ 37 Kevin Elster RR .05 .01
❑ 38 Jose Lind RC .25 .08
❑ 39 Kirt Manwaring RC .25 .08
❑ 40 Mark Grace RC 2.00 .75
❑ 41 Jody Reed RC .25 .08
❑ 42 John Farrell RR RC .10 .02
❑ 43 Al Leiter RC .75 .30
❑ 44 Gary Thurman RR .05 .01
❑ 45 Vicente Palacios RR .05 .01
❑ 46 Eddie Williams RC .10 .02
❑ 47 Jack McDowell RC .40 .15
❑ 48 Ken Dixon .05 .01
❑ 49 Mike Birkbeck .05 .01
❑ 50 Eric King .05 .01
❑ 51 Roger Clemens 1.00 .40
❑ 52 Pat Clements .05 .01
❑ 53 Fernando Valenzuela .10 .02
❑ 54 Mark Gubicza .05 .01
❑ 55 Jay Howell .05 .01
❑ 56 Floyd Youmans .05 .01
❑ 57 Ed Correa .05 .01
❑ 58 DeWayne Buice .05 .01
❑ 59 Jose DeLeon .05 .01
❑ 60 Danny Cox .05 .01
❑ 61 Nolan Ryan 1.00 .40
❑ 62 Steve Bedrosian .05 .01
❑ 63 Tom Browning .05 .01
❑ 64 Mark Davis .05 .01
❑ 65 R.J. Reynolds .05 .01
❑ 66 Kevin Mitchell .10 .02
❑ 67 Ken Oberkfell .05 .01
❑ 68 Rick Sutcliffe .10 .02
❑ 69 Dwight Gooden .10 .02
❑ 70 Scott Bankhead .05 .01
❑ 71 Bert Blyleven .10 .02
❑ 72 Jimmy Key .10 .02
❑ 73 Les Straker .05 .01
❑ 74 Jim Clancy .05 .01
❑ 75 Mike Moore .05 .01
❑ 76 Ron Darling .10 .02
❑ 77 Ed Lynch .05 .01
❑ 78 Dale Murphy .15 .05
❑ 79 Doug Drabek .05 .01
❑ 80 Scott Garrelts .05 .01
❑ 81 Ed Whitson .05 .01
❑ 82 Rob Murphy .05 .01
❑ 83 Shane Rawley .05 .01
❑ 84 Greg Mathews .05 .01
❑ 85 Jim Deshaies .05 .01
❑ 86 Mike Witt .05 .01
❑ 87 Donnie Hill .05 .01
❑ 88 Jeff Reed .05 .01
❑ 89 Mike Boddicker .05 .01
❑ 90 Ted Higuera .05 .01
❑ 91 Walt Terrell .05 .01
❑ 92 Bob Stanley .05 .01
❑ 93 Dave Righetti .10 .02
❑ 94 Orel Hershiser .10 .02
❑ 95 Chris Bando .05 .01
❑ 96 Bret Saberhagen .10 .02
❑ 97 Curt Young .05 .01
❑ 98 Tim Burke .05 .01
❑ 99 Charlie Hough .10 .02
❑ 100A Checklist 28-137 .05 .01
❑ 100B Checklist 28-133 .05 .01
❑ 101 Bobby Witt .05 .01
❑ 102 George Brett .50 .20
❑ 103 Mickey Tettleton .05 .01
❑ 104 Scott Bailes .05 .01
❑ 105 Mike Pagliarulo .05 .01
❑ 106 Mike Scioscia .10 .02
❑ 107 Tom Brookens .05 .01
❑ 108 Ray Knight .10 .02
❑ 109 Dan Plesac .05 .01
❑ 110 Wally Joyner .10 .02
❑ 111 Bob Forsch .05 .01
❑ 112 Mike Scott .10 .02
❑ 113 Kevin Gross .05 .01
❑ 114 Benito Santiago .10 .02
❑ 115 Bob Kipper .05 .01
❑ 116 Mike Krukow .05 .01
❑ 117 Chris Bosio .05 .01
❑ 118 Sid Fernandez .05 .01
❑ 119 Jody Davis .05 .01
❑ 120 Mike Morgan .05 .01
❑ 121 Mark Eichhorn .05 .01
❑ 122 Jeff Reardon .10 .02
❑ 123 John Franco .10 .02
❑ 124 Richard Dotson .05 .01
❑ 125 Eric Bell .05 .01
❑ 126 Juan Nieves .05 .01
❑ 127 Jack Morris .10 .02
❑ 128 Rick Rhoden .05 .01
❑ 129 Rich Gedman .05 .01
❑ 130 Ken Howell .05 .01
❑ 131 Brook Jacoby .05 .01
❑ 132 Danny Jackson .05 .01
❑ 133 Gene Nelson .05 .01
❑ 134 Neal Heaton .05 .01
❑ 135 Willie Fraser .05 .01
❑ 136 Jose Guzman .05 .01
❑ 137 Ozzie Guillen .10 .02
❑ 138 Bob Knepper .05 .01
❑ 139 Mike Jackson RC* .25 .08
❑ 140 Joe Magrane RC* .25 .08
❑ 141 Jimmy Jones .05 .01
❑ 142 Ted Power .05 .01
❑ 143 Ozzie Virgil .05 .01
❑ 144 Felix Fermin .05 .01
❑ 145 Kelly Downs .05 .01
❑ 146 Shawon Dunston .05 .01
❑ 147 Scott Bradley .05 .01
❑ 148 Dave Stieb .10 .02
❑ 149 Frank Viola .10 .02
❑ 150 Terry Kennedy .05 .01
❑ 151 Bill Wegman .05 .01
❑ 152 Matt Nokes RC* .25 .08
❑ 153 Wade Boggs .15 .05
❑ 154 Wayne Tolleson .05 .01
❑ 155 Mariano Duncan .05 .01
❑ 156 Julio Franco .10 .02
❑ 157 Charlie Leibrandt .05 .01
❑ 158 Terry Steinbach .10 .02
❑ 159 Mike Fitzgerald .05 .01
❑ 160 Jack Lazorko .05 .01
❑ 161 Mitch Williams .05 .01
❑ 162 Greg Walker .05 .01
❑ 163 Alan Ashby .05 .01
❑ 164 Tony Gwynn .30 .10
❑ 165 Bruce Ruffin .05 .01
❑ 166 Ron Robinson .05 .01
❑ 167 Zane Smith .05 .01
❑ 168 Junior Ortiz .05 .01
❑ 169 Jamie Moyer .10 .02
❑ 170 Tony Pena .05 .01
❑ 171 Cal Ripken .75 .30
❑ 172 B.J. Surhoff .10 .02
❑ 173 Lou Whitaker .10 .02
❑ 174 Ellis Burks RC .40 .15
❑ 175 Ron Guidry .10 .02
❑ 176 Steve Sax .05 .01
❑ 177 Danny Tartabull .05 .01
❑ 178 Carney Lansford .10 .02
❑ 179 Casey Candaele .05 .01
❑ 180 Scott Fletcher .05 .01
❑ 181 Mark McLemore .05 .01
❑ 182 Ivan Calderon .05 .01
❑ 183 Jack Clark .10 .02
❑ 184 Glenn Davis .05 .01
❑ 185 Luis Aguayo .05 .01
❑ 186 Bo Diaz .05 .01
❑ 187 Stan Jefferson .05 .01
❑ 188 Sid Bream .05 .01
❑ 189 Bob Brenly .05 .01
❑ 190 Dion James .05 .01
❑ 191 Leon Durham .05 .01
❑ 192 Jesse Orosco .05 .01
❑ 193 Alvin Davis .05 .01
❑ 194 Gary Gaetti .10 .02
❑ 195 Fred McGriff .20 .07
❑ 196 Steve Lombardozzi .05 .01
❑ 197 Rance Mulliniks .05 .01
❑ 198 Rey Quinones .05 .01
❑ 199 Gary Carter .10 .02
❑ 200A Checklist 138-247 .05 .01
❑ 200B Checklist 134-239 .05 .01
❑ 201 Keith Moreland .05 .01
❑ 202 Ken Griffey .10 .02
❑ 203 Tommy Gregg .05 .01
❑ 204 Will Clark .20 .07
❑ 205 John Kruk .10 .02
❑ 206 Buddy Bell .10 .02
❑ 207 Von Hayes .05 .01
❑ 208 Tommy Herr .05 .01
❑ 209 Craig Reynolds .05 .01
❑ 210 Gary Pettis .05 .01
❑ 211 Harold Baines .10 .02
❑ 212 Vance Law .05 .01
❑ 213 Ken Gerhart .05 .01
❑ 214 Jim Gantner .05 .01
❑ 215 Chet Lemon .10 .02
❑ 216 Dwight Evans .15 .05
❑ 217 Don Mattingly .60 .25
❑ 218 Franklin Stubbs .05 .01
❑ 219 Pat Tabler .05 .01
❑ 220 Bo Jackson .20 .07
❑ 221 Tony Phillips .05 .01
❑ 222 Tim Wallach .05 .01
❑ 223 Ruben Sierra .10 .02
❑ 224 Steve Buechele .05 .01
❑ 225 Frank White .10 .02
❑ 226 Alfredo Griffin .05 .01
❑ 227 Greg Swindell .05 .01
❑ 228 Willie Randolph .10 .02
❑ 229 Mike Marshall .05 .01
❑ 230 Alan Trammell .10 .02
❑ 231 Eddie Murray .20 .07
❑ 232 Dale Sveum .05 .01
❑ 233 Dick Schofield .05 .01
❑ 234 Jose Oquendo .05 .01
❑ 235 Bill Doran .05 .01
❑ 236 Milt Thompson .05 .01
❑ 237 Marvell Wynne .05 .01
❑ 238 Bobby Bonilla .10 .02
❑ 239 Chris Speier .05 .01
❑ 240 Glenn Braggs .05 .01
❑ 241 Wally Backman .05 .01
❑ 242 Ryne Sandberg .40 .15
❑ 243 Phil Bradley .05 .01
❑ 244 Kelly Gruber .05 .01
❑ 245 Tom Brunansky .05 .01
❑ 246 Ron Oester .05 .01
❑ 247 Bobby Thigpen .05 .01
❑ 248 Fred Lynn .10 .02
❑ 249 Paul Molitor .10 .02
❑ 250 Darrell Evans .10 .02
❑ 251 Gary Ward .05 .01
❑ 252 Bruce Hurst .05 .01
❑ 253 Bob Welch .10 .02
❑ 254 Joe Carter .10 .02

	No.	Player		
❑	255	Willie Wilson	.10	.02
❑	256	Mark McGwire	1.50	.60
❑	257	Mitch Webster	.05	.01
❑	258	Brian Downing	.10	.02
❑	259	Mike Stanley	.05	.01
❑	260	Carlton Fisk	.15	.05
❑	261	Billy Hatcher	.05	.01
❑	262	Glenn Wilson	.05	.01
❑	263	Ozzie Smith	.30	.10
❑	264	Randy Ready	.05	.01
❑	265	Kurt Stillwell	.05	.01
❑	266	David Palmer	.05	.01
❑	267	Mike Diaz	.05	.01
❑	268	Robby Thompson	.05	.01
❑	269	Andre Dawson	.10	.02
❑	270	Lee Guetterman	.05	.01
❑	271	Willie Upshaw	.05	.01
❑	272	Randy Bush	.05	.01
❑	273	Larry Sheets	.05	.01
❑	274	Rob Deer	.05	.01
❑	275	Kirk Gibson	.20	.07
❑	276	Marty Barrett	.05	.01
❑	277	Rickey Henderson	.20	.07
❑	278	Pedro Guerrero	.10	.02
❑	279	Brett Butler	.10	.02
❑	280	Kevin Seitzer	.05	.01
❑	281	Mike Davis	.05	.01
❑	282	Andres Galarraga	.10	.02
❑	283	Devon White	.10	.02
❑	284	Pete O'Brien	.05	.01
❑	285	Jerry Hairston	.05	.01
❑	286	Kevin Bass	.05	.01
❑	287	Carmelo Martinez	.05	.01
❑	288	Juan Samuel	.05	.01
❑	289	Kal Daniels	.05	.01
❑	290	Albert Hall	.05	.01
❑	291	Andy Van Slyke	.15	.05
❑	292	Lee Smith	.10	.02
❑	293	Vince Coleman	.05	.01
❑	294	Tom Niedenfuer	.05	.01
❑	295	Robin Yount	.30	.10
❑	296	Jeff M. Robinson	.05	.01
❑	297	Todd Benzinger RC*	.25	.08
❑	298	Dave Winfield	.10	.02
❑	299	Mickey Hatcher	.05	.01
❑	300A	Checklist 248-357	.05	.01
❑	300B	Checklist 240-345	.05	.01
❑	301	Bud Black	.05	.01
❑	302	Jose Canseco	.50	.20
❑	303	Tom Foley	.05	.01
❑	304	Pete Incaviglia	.05	.01
❑	305	Bob Boone	.10	.02
❑	306	Bill Long	.05	.01
❑	307	Willie McGee	.10	.02
❑	308	Ken Caminiti RC	2.00	.75
❑	309	Darren Daulton	.10	.02
❑	310	Tracy Jones	.05	.01
❑	311	Greg Booker	.05	.01
❑	312	Mike LaValliere	.05	.01
❑	313	Chili Davis	.10	.02
❑	314	Glenn Hubbard	.05	.01
❑	315	Paul Noce	.05	.01
❑	316	Keith Hernandez	.10	.02
❑	317	Mark Langston	.05	.01
❑	318	Keith Atherton	.05	.01
❑	319	Tony Fernandez	.05	.01
❑	320	Kent Hrbek	.10	.02
❑	321	John Cerutti	.05	.01
❑	322	Mike Kingery	.05	.01
❑	323	Dave Magadan	.05	.01
❑	324	Rafael Palmeiro	.40	.15
❑	325	Jeff Dedmon	.05	.01
❑	326	Barry Bonds	2.00	.75
❑	327	Jeffrey Leonard	.05	.01
❑	328	Tim Flannery	.05	.01
❑	329	Dave Concepcion	.10	.02
❑	330	Mike Schmidt	.50	.20
❑	331	Bill Dawley	.05	.01
❑	332	Larry Andersen	.05	.01
❑	333	Jack Howell	.05	.01
❑	334	Ken Williams	.05	.01
❑	335	Bryn Smith	.05	.01
❑	336	Bill Ripken RC*	.25	.08
❑	337	Greg Brock	.05	.01
❑	338	Mike Heath	.05	.01
❑	339	Mike Greenwell	.05	.01
❑	340	Claudell Washington	.05	.01
❑	341	Jose Gonzalez	.05	.01
❑	342	Mel Hall	.05	.01
❑	343	Jim Eisenreich	.05	.01
❑	344	Tony Bernazard	.05	.01
❑	345	Tim Raines	.10	.02
❑	346	Bob Brower	.05	.01
❑	347	Larry Parrish	.05	.01
❑	348	Thad Bosley	.05	.01
❑	349	Dennis Eckersley	.15	.05
❑	350	Cory Snyder	.05	.01
❑	351	Rick Cerone	.05	.01
❑	352	John Shelby	.05	.01
❑	353	Larry Herndon	.05	.01
❑	354	John Habyan	.05	.01
❑	355	Chuck Crim	.05	.01
❑	356	Gus Polidor	.05	.01
❑	357	Ken Dayley	.05	.01
❑	358	Danny Darwin	.05	.01
❑	359	Lance Parrish	.10	.02
❑	360	James Steels	.05	.01
❑	361	Al Pedrique	.05	.01
❑	362	Mike Aldrete	.05	.01
❑	363	Juan Castillo	.05	.01
❑	364	Len Dykstra	.10	.02
❑	365	Luis Quinones	.05	.01
❑	366	Jim Presley	.05	.01
❑	367	Lloyd Moseby	.05	.01
❑	368	Kirby Puckett	.20	.07
❑	369	Eric Davis	.10	.02
❑	370	Gary Redus	.05	.01
❑	371	Dave Schmidt	.05	.01
❑	372	Mark Clear	.05	.01
❑	373	Dave Bergman	.05	.01
❑	374	Charles Hudson	.05	.01
❑	375	Calvin Schiraldi	.05	.01
❑	376	Alex Trevino	.05	.01
❑	377	Tom Candiotti	.05	.01
❑	378	Steve Farr	.05	.01
❑	379	Mike Gallego	.05	.01
❑	380	Andy McGaffigan	.05	.01
❑	381	Kirk McCaskill	.05	.01
❑	382	Oddibe McDowell	.05	.01
❑	383	Floyd Bannister	.05	.01
❑	384	Denny Walling	.05	.01
❑	385	Don Carman	.05	.01
❑	386	Todd Worrell	.05	.01
❑	387	Eric Show	.05	.01
❑	388	Dave Parker	.10	.02
❑	389	Rick Mahler	.05	.01
❑	390	Mike Dunne	.05	.01
❑	391	Candy Maldonado	.05	.01
❑	392	Bob Dernier	.05	.01
❑	393	Dave Valle	.05	.01
❑	394	Ernie Whitt	.05	.01
❑	395	Juan Berenguer	.05	.01
❑	396	Mike Young	.05	.01
❑	397	Mike Felder	.05	.01
❑	398	Willie Hernandez	.05	.01
❑	399	Jim Rice	.10	.02
❑	400A	Checklist 358-467	.05	.01
❑	400B	Checklist 346-451	.05	.01
❑	401	Tommy John	.10	.02
❑	402	Brian Holton	.05	.01
❑	403	Carmen Castillo	.05	.01
❑	404	Jamie Quirk	.05	.01
❑	405	Dwayne Murphy	.05	.01
❑	406	Jeff Parrett	.05	.01
❑	407	Don Sutton	.10	.02
❑	408	Jerry Browne	.05	.01
❑	409	Jim Winn	.05	.01
❑	410	Dave Smith	.05	.01
❑	411	Shane Mack	.05	.01
❑	412	Greg Gross	.05	.01
❑	413	Nick Esasky	.05	.01
❑	414	Damaso Garcia	.05	.01
❑	415	Brian Fisher	.05	.01
❑	416	Brian Dayett	.05	.01
❑	417	Curt Ford	.05	.01
❑	418	Mark Williamson	.05	.01
❑	419	Bill Schroeder	.05	.01
❑	420	Mike Henneman RC*	.25	.08
❑	421	John Marzano	.05	.01
❑	422	Ron Kittle	.05	.01
❑	423	Matt Young	.05	.01
❑	424	Steve Balboni	.05	.01
❑	425	Luis Polonia RC*	.25	.08
❑	426	Randy St.Claire	.05	.01
❑	427	Greg Harris	.05	.01
❑	428	Johnny Ray	.05	.01
❑	429	Ray Searage	.05	.01
❑	430	Ricky Horton	.05	.01
❑	431	Gerald Young	.05	.01
❑	432	Rick Schu	.05	.01
❑	433	Paul O'Neill	.15	.05
❑	434	Rich Gossage	.10	.02
❑	435	John Cangelosi	.05	.01
❑	436	Mike LaCoss	.05	.01
❑	437	Gerald Perry	.05	.01
❑	438	Dave Martinez	.05	.01
❑	439	Darryl Strawberry	.10	.02
❑	440	John Moses	.05	.01
❑	441	Greg Gagne	.05	.01
❑	442	Jesse Barfield	.10	.02
❑	443	George Frazier	.05	.01
❑	444	Garth Iorg	.05	.01
❑	445	Ed Nunez	.05	.01
❑	446	Rick Aguilera	.05	.01
❑	447	Jerry Mumphrey	.05	.01
❑	448	Rafael Ramirez	.05	.01
❑	449	John Smiley RC*	.25	.08
❑	450	Atlee Hammaker	.05	.01
❑	451	Lance McCullers	.05	.01
❑	452	Guy Hoffman	.05	.01
❑	453	Chris James	.05	.01
❑	454	Terry Pendleton	.10	.02
❑	455	Dave Meads	.05	.01
❑	456	Bill Buckner	.10	.02
❑	457	John Pawlowski	.05	.01
❑	458	Bob Sebra	.05	.01
❑	459	Jim Dwyer	.05	.01
❑	460	Jay Aldrich	.05	.01
❑	461	Frank Tanana	.10	.02
❑	462	Oil Can Boyd	.05	.01
❑	463	Dan Pasqua	.05	.01
❑	464	Tim Crews RC	.25	.08
❑	465	Andy Allanson	.05	.01
❑	466	Bill Pecota RC*	.10	.02
❑	467	Steve Ontiveros	.05	.01
❑	468	Hubie Brooks	.05	.01
❑	469	Paul Kilgus	.05	.01
❑	470	Dale Mohorcic	.05	.01
❑	471	Dan Quisenberry	.05	.01
❑	472	Dave Stewart	.10	.02
❑	473	Dave Clark	.05	.01
❑	474	Joel Skinner	.05	.01
❑	475	Dave Anderson	.05	.01
❑	476	Dan Petry	.05	.01
❑	477	Carl Nichols	.05	.01
❑	478	Ernest Riles	.05	.01
❑	479	George Hendrick	.10	.02
❑	480	John Morris	.05	.01
❑	481	Manny Hernandez	.05	.01
❑	482	Jeff Stone	.05	.01
❑	483	Chris Brown	.05	.01
❑	484	Mike Bielecki	.05	.01
❑	485	Dave Dravecky	.05	.01
❑	486	Rick Manning	.05	.01
❑	487	Bill Almon	.05	.01
❑	488	Jim Sundberg	.10	.02
❑	489	Ken Phelps	.05	.01
❑	490	Tom Henke	.05	.01
❑	491	Dan Gladden	.05	.01
❑	492	Barry Larkin	.15	.05
❑	493	Fred Manrique	.05	.01
❑	494	Mike Griffin	.05	.01
❑	495	Mark Knudson	.05	.01
❑	496	Bill Madlock	.10	.02
❑	497	Tim Stoddard	.05	.01
❑	498	Sam Horn RC	.10	.02
❑	499	Tracy Woodson RC	.10	.02
❑	500A	Checklist 468-577	.05	.01
❑	500B	Checklist 452-557	.05	.01
❑	501	Ken Schrom	.05	.01
❑	502	Angel Salazar	.05	.01
❑	503	Eric Plunk	.05	.01
❑	504	Joe Hesketh	.05	.01
❑	505	Greg Minton	.05	.01
❑	506	Geno Petralli	.05	.01
❑	507	Bob James	.05	.01
❑	508	Robbie Wine	.05	.01
❑	509	Jeff Calhoun	.05	.01

- ❑ 510 Steve Lake .05 .01
- ❑ 511 Mark Grant .05 .01
- ❑ 512 Frank Williams .05 .01
- ❑ 513 Jeff Blauser RC .25 .08
- ❑ 514 Bob Walk .05 .01
- ❑ 515 Craig Lefferts .05 .01
- ❑ 516 Manny Trillo .05 .01
- ❑ 517 Jerry Reed .05 .01
- ❑ 518 Rick Leach .05 .01
- ❑ 519 Mark Davidson .05 .01
- ❑ 520 Jeff Ballard .05 .01
- ❑ 521 Dave Stapleton .05 .01
- ❑ 522 Pat Sheridan .05 .01
- ❑ 523 Al Nipper .05 .01
- ❑ 524 Steve Trout .05 .01
- ❑ 525 Jeff Hamilton .05 .01
- ❑ 526 Tommy Hinzo .05 .01
- ❑ 527 Lonnie Smith .05 .01
- ❑ 528 Greg Cadaret .05 .01
- ❑ 529 Bob McClure UER (%%Rob~ on front) .05 .01
- ❑ 530 Chuck Finley .10 .02
- ❑ 531 Jeff Russell .05 .01
- ❑ 532 Steve Lyons .05 .01
- ❑ 533 Terry Puhl .05 .01
- ❑ 534 Eric Nolte .05 .01
- ❑ 535 Kent Tekulve .05 .01
- ❑ 536 Pat Pacillo .05 .01
- ❑ 537 Charlie Puleo .05 .01
- ❑ 538 Tom Prince .05 .01
- ❑ 539 Greg Maddux 1.00 .40
- ❑ 540 Jim Lindeman .05 .01
- ❑ 541 Pete Stanicek .05 .01
- ❑ 542 Steve Kiefer .05 .01
- ❑ 543A Jim Morrison ERR (No decimal before lifetime ave .15 .05
- ❑ 543B Jim Morrison COR .05 .01
- ❑ 544 Spike Owen .05 .01
- ❑ 545 Jay Buhner RC .50 .20
- ❑ 546 Mike Devereaux RC .25 .08
- ❑ 547 Jerry Don Gleaton .05 .01
- ❑ 548 Jose Rijo .10 .02
- ❑ 549 Dennis Martinez .10 .02
- ❑ 550 Mike Loynd .05 .01
- ❑ 551 Darrell Miller .05 .01
- ❑ 552 Dave LaPoint .05 .01
- ❑ 553 John Tudor .10 .02
- ❑ 554 Rocky Childress .05 .01
- ❑ 555 Wally Ritchie .05 .01
- ❑ 556 Terry McGriff .05 .01
- ❑ 557 Dave Leiper .05 .01
- ❑ 558 Jeff D. Robinson .05 .01
- ❑ 559 Jose Uribe .05 .01
- ❑ 560 Ted Simmons .10 .02
- ❑ 561 Les Lancaster .05 .01
- ❑ 562 Keith Miller RC .25 .08
- ❑ 563 Harold Reynolds .10 .02
- ❑ 564 Gene Larkin RC* .25 .08
- ❑ 565 Cecil Fielder .10 .02
- ❑ 566 Roy Smalley .05 .01
- ❑ 567 Duane Ward .05 .01
- ❑ 568 Bill Wilkinson .05 .01
- ❑ 569 Howard Johnson .10 .02
- ❑ 570 Frank DiPino .05 .01
- ❑ 571 Pete Smith RC .10 .02
- ❑ 572 Darnell Coles .05 .01
- ❑ 573 Don Robinson .05 .01
- ❑ 574 Rob Nelson UER (Career 0 RBI& but 1 RBI in '87) .05 .01
- ❑ 575 Dennis Rasmussen .05 .01
- ❑ 576 Steve Jeltz UER (Photo actually Juan Samuel; Sam .05 .01
- ❑ 577 Tom Pagnozzi RC .10 .02
- ❑ 578 Ty Gainey .05 .01
- ❑ 579 Gary Lucas .05 .01
- ❑ 580 Ron Hassey .05 .01
- ❑ 581 Herm Winningham .05 .01
- ❑ 582 Rene Gonzales RC .10 .02
- ❑ 583 Brad Komminsk .05 .01
- ❑ 584 Doyle Alexander .05 .01
- ❑ 585 Jeff Sellers .05 .01
- ❑ 586 Bill Gullickson .05 .01
- ❑ 587 Tim Belcher .05 .01
- ❑ 588 Doug Jones RC .25 .08
- ❑ 589 Melido Perez RC .25 .08
- ❑ 590 Rick Honeycutt .05 .01
- ❑ 591 Pascual Perez .05 .01
- ❑ 592 Curt Wilkerson .05 .01
- ❑ 593 Steve Howe .05 .01
- ❑ 594 John Davis .05 .01
- ❑ 595 Storm Davis .05 .01
- ❑ 596 Sammy Stewart .05 .01
- ❑ 597 Neil Allen .05 .01
- ❑ 598 Alejandro Pena .05 .01
- ❑ 599 Mark Thurmond .05 .01
- ❑ 600A Checklist 578-660/BC1-BC26 .05 .01
- ❑ 600B Checklist 558-660 .05 .01
- ❑ 601 Jose Mesa RC .25 .08
- ❑ 602 Don August .05 .01
- ❑ 603 Terry Leach SP .10 .02
- ❑ 604 Tom Newell .05 .01
- ❑ 605 Randall Byers SP .10 .02
- ❑ 606 Jim Gott .05 .01
- ❑ 607 Harry Spilman .05 .01
- ❑ 608 John Candelaria .05 .01
- ❑ 609 Mike Brumley .05 .01
- ❑ 610 Mickey Brantley .05 .01
- ❑ 611 Jose Nunez SP .10 .02
- ❑ 612 Tom Nieto .05 .01
- ❑ 613 Rick Reuschel .10 .02
- ❑ 614 Lee Mazzilli SP .10 .02
- ❑ 615 Scott Lusader .05 .01
- ❑ 616 Bobby Meacham .05 .01
- ❑ 617 Kevin McReynolds SP .10 .02
- ❑ 618 Gene Garber .05 .01
- ❑ 619 Barry Lyons SP .10 .02
- ❑ 620 Randy Myers .10 .02
- ❑ 621 Donnie Moore .05 .01
- ❑ 622 Domingo Ramos .05 .01
- ❑ 623 Ed Romero .05 .01
- ❑ 624 Greg Myers RC .25 .08
- ❑ 625 The Ripken Family .40 .15
- ❑ 626 Pat Perry .05 .01
- ❑ 627 Andres Thomas SP .10 .02
- ❑ 628 Matt Williams RC .75 .30
- ❑ 629 Dave Hengel .05 .01
- ❑ 630 Jeff Musselman SP .10 .02
- ❑ 631 Tim Laudner .05 .01
- ❑ 632 Bob Ojeda SP .10 .02
- ❑ 633 Rafael Santana .05 .01
- ❑ 634 Wes Gardner .05 .01
- ❑ 635 Roberto Kelly SP RC .25 .08
- ❑ 636 Mike Flanagan SP .10 .02
- ❑ 637 Jay Bell RC .40 .15
- ❑ 638 Bob Melvin .05 .01
- ❑ 639 Damon Berryhill RC .25 .08
- ❑ 640 David Wells RC 1.00 .40
- ❑ 641 Stan Musial Puzzle .20 .07
- ❑ 642 Doug Sisk .05 .01
- ❑ 643 Keith Hughes .05 .01
- ❑ 644 Tom Glavine RC 2.50 1.00
- ❑ 645 Al Newman .05 .01
- ❑ 646 Scott Sanderson .05 .01
- ❑ 647 Scott Terry .05 .01
- ❑ 648 Tim Teufel SP .10 .02
- ❑ 649 Garry Templeton SP .10 .02
- ❑ 650 Manny Lee SP .10 .02
- ❑ 651 Roger McDowell SP .10 .02
- ❑ 652 Mookie Wilson SP .10 .02
- ❑ 653 David Cone .10 .02
- ❑ 654 Ron Gant RC .40 .15
- ❑ 655 Joe Price SP .10 .02
- ❑ 656 George Bell SP .10 .02
- ❑ 657 Gregg Jefferies RC .25 .08
- ❑ 658 Todd Stottlemyre RC .25 .08
- ❑ 659 Geronimo Berroa RC .25 .08
- ❑ 660 Jerry Royster SP .10 .02
- ❑ XX Kirby Puckett Blister Pack 1.25 .50

1989 Donruss

- ❑ COMPLETE SET (660) 25.00 10.00
- ❑ COMP.FACT.SET (672) 25.00 10.00
- ❑ 1 Mike Greenwell DK .05 .01
- ❑ 2 Bobby Bonilla DK DP .10 .02
- ❑ 3 Pete Incaviglia DK .05 .01
- ❑ 4 Chris Sabo DK DP .10 .02
- ❑ 5 Robin Yount DK .40 .15
- ❑ 6 Tony Gwynn DK DP .15 .05
- ❑ 7 Carlton Fisk DK UER .15 .05
- ❑ 8 Cory Snyder DK .05 .01
- ❑ 9 David Cone DK UER .10 .02
- ❑ 10 Kevin Seitzer DK .05 .01
- ❑ 11 Rick Reuschel DK .10 .02
- ❑ 12 Johnny Ray DK .05 .01
- ❑ 13 Dave Schmidt DK .05 .01
- ❑ 14 Andres Galarraga DK .10 .02
- ❑ 15 Kirk Gibson DK .10 .02
- ❑ 16 Fred McGriff DK .15 .05
- ❑ 17 Mark Grace DK .25 .08
- ❑ 18 Jeff M. Robinson DK .05 .01
- ❑ 19 Vince Coleman DK DP .05 .01
- ❑ 20 Dave Henderson DK .05 .01
- ❑ 21 Harold Reynolds DK .10 .02
- ❑ 22 Gerald Perry DK .05 .01
- ❑ 23 Frank Viola DK .10 .02
- ❑ 24 Steve Bedrosian DK .05 .01
- ❑ 25 Glenn Davis DK .05 .01
- ❑ 26 Don Mattingly DK .30 .10
- ❑ 27 DK Checklist 1-26 DP .05 .01
- ❑ 28 Sandy Alomar Jr. RC .40 .15
- ❑ 29 Steve Searcy RR .05 .01
- ❑ 30 Cameron Drew RR .05 .01
- ❑ 31 Gary Sheffield RC 1.50 .60
- ❑ 32 Erik Hanson RC .25 .08
- ❑ 33 Ken Griffey Jr. RC 8.00 3.00
- ❑ 34 Greg W.Harris RC .10 .02
- ❑ 35 Gregg Jefferies .05 .01
- ❑ 36 Luis Medina RR .05 .01
- ❑ 37 Carlos Quintana RC .10 .02
- ❑ 38 Felix Jose RC .10 .02
- ❑ 39 Eric Carpenter RC * .10 .02
- ❑ 40 Ron Jones RR .10 .02
- ❑ 41 Dave West RC .10 .02
- ❑ 42 Randy Johnson RC 2.00 .75
- ❑ 43 Mike Harkey RC .10 .02
- ❑ 44 Pete Harnisch RC .25 .08
- ❑ 45 Tom Gordon RC .50 .20
- ❑ 46 Gregg Olson DP RC .25 .08
- ❑ 47 Alex Sanchez RC .05 .01
- ❑ 48 Ruben Sierra .10 .02
- ❑ 49 Rafael Palmeiro .25 .08
- ❑ 50 Ron Gant .10 .02
- ❑ 51 Cal Ripken .75 .30
- ❑ 52 Wally Joyner .10 .02
- ❑ 53 Gary Carter .10 .02
- ❑ 54 Andy Van Slyke .15 .05
- ❑ 55 Robin Yount .40 .15
- ❑ 56 Pete Incaviglia .05 .01
- ❑ 57 Greg Brock .05 .01
- ❑ 58 Melido Perez .05 .01
- ❑ 59 Craig Lefferts .05 .01
- ❑ 60 Gary Pettis .05 .01
- ❑ 61 Danny Tartabull .05 .01
- ❑ 62 Guillermo Hernandez .05 .01
- ❑ 63 Ozzie Smith .40 .15
- ❑ 64 Gary Gaetti .10 .02
- ❑ 65 Mark Davis .05 .01
- ❑ 66 Lee Smith .10 .02
- ❑ 67 Dennis Eckersley .15 .05
- ❑ 68 Wade Boggs .15 .05
- ❑ 69 Mike Scott .10 .02
- ❑ 70 Fred McGriff .15 .05
- ❑ 71 Tom Browning .05 .01
- ❑ 72 Claudell Washington .05 .01
- ❑ 73 Mel Hall .05 .01
- ❑ 74 Don Mattingly .60 .25

❑ 75 Steve Bedrosian	.05	.01
❑ 76 Juan Samuel	.05	.01
❑ 77 Mike Scioscia	.10	.02
❑ 78 Dave Righetti	.10	.02
❑ 79 Alfredo Griffin	.05	.01
❑ 80 Eric Davis UER (165 games in 1988, should be 135	.10	.02
❑ 81 Juan Berenguer	.05	.01
❑ 82 Todd Worrell	.05	.01
❑ 83 Joe Carter	.10	.02
❑ 84 Steve Sax	.05	.01
❑ 85 Frank White	.10	.02
❑ 86 John Kruk	.10	.02
❑ 87 Rance Mulliniks	.05	.01
❑ 88 Alan Ashby	.05	.01
❑ 89 Charlie Leibrandt	.05	.01
❑ 90 Frank Tanana	.10	.02
❑ 91 Jose Canseco	.25	.08
❑ 92 Barry Bonds	1.50	.60
❑ 93 Harold Reynolds	.10	.02
❑ 94 Mark McLemore	.05	.01
❑ 95 Mark McGwire	1.00	.40
❑ 96 Eddie Murray	.25	.08
❑ 97 Tim Raines	.10	.02
❑ 98 Robby Thompson	.05	.01
❑ 99 Kevin McReynolds	.05	.01
❑ 100 Checklist 28-137	.05	.01
❑ 101 Carlton Fisk	.15	.05
❑ 102 Dave Martinez	.05	.01
❑ 103 Glenn Braggs	.05	.01
❑ 104 Dale Murphy	.15	.05
❑ 105 Ryne Sandberg	.40	.15
❑ 106 Dennis Martinez	.10	.02
❑ 107 Pete O'Brien	.05	.01
❑ 108 Dick Schofield	.05	.01
❑ 109 Henry Cotto	.05	.01
❑ 110 Mike Marshall	.05	.01
❑ 111 Keith Moreland	.05	.01
❑ 112 Tom Brunansky	.05	.01
❑ 113 Kelly Gruber UER (Wrong birthdate)	.05	.01
❑ 114 Brook Jacoby	.05	.01
❑ 115 Keith Brown	.05	.01
❑ 116 Matt Nokes	.05	.01
❑ 117 Keith Hernandez	.10	.02
❑ 118 Bob Forsch	.05	.01
❑ 119 Bert Blyleven UER (... 3000 strikeouts in 1987&	.10	.02
❑ 120 Willie Wilson	.10	.02
❑ 121 Tommy Gregg	.05	.01
❑ 122 Jim Rice	.10	.02
❑ 123 Bob Knepper	.05	.01
❑ 124 Danny Jackson	.05	.01
❑ 125 Eric Plunk	.05	.01
❑ 126 Brian Fisher	.05	.01
❑ 127 Mike Pagliarulo	.05	.01
❑ 128 Tony Gwynn	.30	.10
❑ 129 Lance McCullers	.05	.01
❑ 130 Andres Galarraga	.10	.02
❑ 131 Jose Uribe	.05	.01
❑ 132 Kirk Gibson UER	.10	.02
❑ 133 David Palmer	.05	.01
❑ 134 R.J. Reynolds	.05	.01
❑ 135 Greg Walker	.05	.01
❑ 136 Kirk McCaskill UER (Wrong birthdate)	.05	.01
❑ 137 Shawon Dunston	.05	.01
❑ 138 Andy Allanson	.05	.01
❑ 139 Rob Murphy	.05	.01
❑ 140 Mike Aldrete	.05	.01
❑ 141 Terry Kennedy	.05	.01
❑ 142 Scott Fletcher	.05	.01
❑ 143 Steve Balboni	.05	.01
❑ 144 Bret Saberhagen	.10	.02
❑ 145 Ozzie Virgil	.05	.01
❑ 146 Dale Sveum	.05	.01
❑ 147 Darryl Strawberry	.10	.02
❑ 148 Harold Baines	.10	.02
❑ 149 George Bell	.10	.02
❑ 150 Dave Parker	.10	.02
❑ 151 Bobby Bonilla	.10	.02
❑ 152 Mookie Wilson	.10	.02
❑ 153 Ted Power	.05	.01
❑ 154 Nolan Ryan	1.00	.40
❑ 155 Jeff Reardon	.10	.02
❑ 156 Tim Wallach	.05	.01
❑ 157 Jamie Moyer	.10	.02
❑ 158 Rich Gossage	.10	.02
❑ 159 Dave Winfield	.10	.02
❑ 160 Von Hayes	.05	.01
❑ 161 Willie McGee	.10	.02
❑ 162 Rich Gedman	.05	.01
❑ 163 Tony Pena	.05	.01
❑ 164 Mike Morgan	.05	.01
❑ 165 Charlie Hough	.10	.02
❑ 166 Mike Stanley	.05	.01
❑ 167 Andre Dawson	.10	.02
❑ 168 Joe Boever	.05	.01
❑ 169 Pete Stanicek	.05	.01
❑ 170 Bob Boone	.10	.02
❑ 171 Ron Darling	.10	.02
❑ 172 Bob Walk	.05	.01
❑ 173 Rob Deer	.05	.01
❑ 174 Steve Buechele	.05	.01
❑ 175 Ted Higuera	.05	.01
❑ 176 Ozzie Guillen	.10	.02
❑ 177 Candy Maldonado	.05	.01
❑ 178 Doyle Alexander	.05	.01
❑ 179 Mark Gubicza	.05	.01
❑ 180 Alan Trammell	.10	.02
❑ 181 Vince Coleman	.05	.01
❑ 182 Kirby Puckett	.25	.08
❑ 183 Chris Brown	.05	.01
❑ 184 Marty Barrett	.05	.01
❑ 185 Stan Javier	.05	.01
❑ 186 Mike Greenwell	.05	.01
❑ 187 Billy Hatcher	.05	.01
❑ 188 Jimmy Key	.10	.02
❑ 189 Nick Esasky	.05	.01
❑ 190 Don Slaught	.05	.01
❑ 191 Cory Snyder	.05	.01
❑ 192 John Candelaria	.05	.01
❑ 193 Mike Schmidt	.50	.20
❑ 194 Kevin Gross	.05	.01
❑ 195 John Tudor	.10	.02
❑ 196 Neil Allen	.05	.01
❑ 197 Orel Hershiser	.10	.02
❑ 198 Kal Daniels	.05	.01
❑ 199 Kent Hrbek	.10	.02
❑ 200 Checklist 138-247	.05	.01
❑ 201 Joe Magrane	.05	.01
❑ 202 Scott Bailes	.05	.01
❑ 203 Tim Belcher	.05	.01
❑ 204 George Brett	.60	.25
❑ 205 Benito Santiago	.10	.02
❑ 206 Tony Fernandez	.05	.01
❑ 207 Gerald Young	.05	.01
❑ 208 Bo Jackson	.25	.08
❑ 209 Chet Lemon	.10	.02
❑ 210 Storm Davis	.05	.01
❑ 211 Doug Drabek	.05	.01
❑ 212 Mickey Brantley UER (Photo actually Nelson Simmo	.05	.01
❑ 213 Devon White	.10	.02
❑ 214 Dave Stewart	.10	.02
❑ 215 Dave Schmidt	.05	.01
❑ 216 Bryn Smith	.05	.01
❑ 217 Brett Butler	.10	.02
❑ 218 Bob Ojeda	.05	.01
❑ 219 Steve Rosenberg	.05	.01
❑ 220 Hubie Brooks	.05	.01
❑ 221 B.J. Surhoff	.10	.02
❑ 222 Rick Mahler	.05	.01
❑ 223 Rick Sutcliffe	.10	.02
❑ 224 Neal Heaton	.05	.01
❑ 225 Mitch Williams	.05	.01
❑ 226 Chuck Finley	.10	.02
❑ 227 Mark Langston	.05	.01
❑ 228 Jesse Orosco	.05	.01
❑ 229 Ed Whitson	.05	.01
❑ 230 Terry Pendleton	.10	.02
❑ 231 Lloyd Moseby	.05	.01
❑ 232 Greg Swindell	.05	.01
❑ 233 John Franco	.10	.02
❑ 234 Jack Morris	.10	.02
❑ 235 Howard Johnson	.10	.02
❑ 236 Glenn Davis	.05	.01
❑ 237 Frank Viola	.10	.02
❑ 238 Kevin Seitzer	.05	.01
❑ 239 Gerald Perry	.05	.01
❑ 240 Dwight Evans	.15	.05
❑ 241 Jim Deshaies	.05	.01
❑ 242 Bo Diaz	.05	.01
❑ 243 Carney Lansford	.10	.02
❑ 244 Mike LaValliere	.05	.01
❑ 245 Rickey Henderson	.25	.08
❑ 246 Roberto Alomar	.25	.08
❑ 247 Jimmy Jones	.05	.01
❑ 248 Pascual Perez	.05	.01
❑ 249 Will Clark	.15	.05
❑ 250 Fernando Valenzuela	.10	.02
❑ 251 Shane Rawley	.05	.01
❑ 252 Sid Bream	.05	.01
❑ 253 Steve Lyons	.05	.01
❑ 254 Brian Downing	.10	.02
❑ 255 Mark Grace	.25	.08
❑ 256 Tom Candiotti	.05	.01
❑ 257 Barry Larkin	.15	.05
❑ 258 Mike Krukow	.05	.01
❑ 259 Billy Ripken	.05	.01
❑ 260 Cecilio Guante	.05	.01
❑ 261 Scott Bradley	.05	.01
❑ 262 Floyd Bannister	.05	.01
❑ 263 Pete Smith	.05	.01
❑ 264 Jim Gantner UER (Wrong birthdate)	.05	.01
❑ 265 Roger McDowell	.05	.01
❑ 266 Bobby Thigpen	.05	.01
❑ 267 Jim Clancy	.05	.01
❑ 268 Terry Steinbach	.10	.02
❑ 269 Mike Dunne	.05	.01
❑ 270 Dwight Gooden	.10	.02
❑ 271 Mike Heath	.05	.01
❑ 272 Dave Smith	.05	.01
❑ 273 Keith Atherton	.05	.01
❑ 274 Tim Burke	.05	.01
❑ 275 Damon Berryhill	.05	.01
❑ 276 Vance Law	.05	.01
❑ 277 Rich Dotson	.05	.01
❑ 278 Lance Parrish	.10	.02
❑ 279 Denny Walling	.05	.01
❑ 280 Roger Clemens	1.00	.40
❑ 281 Greg Mathews	.05	.01
❑ 282 Tom Niedenfuer	.05	.01
❑ 283 Paul Kilgus	.05	.01
❑ 284 Jose Guzman	.05	.01
❑ 285 Calvin Schiraldi	.05	.01
❑ 286 Charlie Puleo UER (Career ERA 4.24& should be 4.	.05	.01
❑ 287 Joe Orsulak	.05	.01
❑ 288 Jack Howell	.05	.01
❑ 289 Kevin Elster	.05	.01
❑ 290 Jose Lind	.05	.01
❑ 291 Paul Molitor	.10	.02
❑ 292 Cecil Espy	.05	.01
❑ 293 Bill Wegman	.05	.01
❑ 294 Dan Pasqua	.05	.01
❑ 295 Scott Garrelts UER (Wrong birthdate)	.05	.01
❑ 296 Walt Terrell	.05	.01
❑ 297 Ed Hearn	.05	.01
❑ 298 Lou Whitaker	.10	.02
❑ 299 Ken Dayley	.05	.01
❑ 300 Checklist 248-357	.05	.01
❑ 301 Tommy Herr	.05	.01
❑ 302 Mike Brumley	.05	.01
❑ 303 Ellis Burks	.10	.02
❑ 304 Curt Young UER (Wrong birthdate)	.05	.01
❑ 305 Jody Reed	.05	.01
❑ 306 Bill Doran	.05	.01
❑ 307 David Wells	.10	.02
❑ 308 Ron Robinson	.05	.01
❑ 309 Rafael Santana	.05	.01
❑ 310 Julio Franco	.10	.02
❑ 311 Jack Clark	.10	.02
❑ 312 Chris James	.05	.01
❑ 313 Milt Thompson	.05	.01
❑ 314 John Shelby	.05	.01
❑ 315 Al Leiter	.25	.08
❑ 316 Mike Davis	.05	.01
❑ 317 Chris Sabo RC *	.40	.15
❑ 318 Greg Gagne	.05	.01
❑ 319 Jose Oquendo	.05	.01

❑ 320 John Farrell .05 .01
❑ 321 Franklin Stubbs .05 .01
❑ 322 Kurt Stillwell .05 .01
❑ 323 Shawn Abner .05 .01
❑ 324 Mike Flanagan .05 .01
❑ 325 Kevin Bass .05 .01
❑ 326 Pat Tabler .05 .01
❑ 327 Mike Henneman .05 .01
❑ 328 Rick Honeycutt .05 .01
❑ 329 John Smiley .05 .01
❑ 330 Rey Quinones .05 .01
❑ 331 Johnny Ray .05 .01
❑ 332 Bob Welch .10 .02
❑ 333 Larry Sheets .05 .01
❑ 334 Jeff Parrett .05 .01
❑ 335 Rick Reuschel UER (For Don Robinson& should be J .10 .02
❑ 336 Randy Myers .10 .02
❑ 337 Ken Williams .05 .01
❑ 338 Andy McGaffigan .05 .01
❑ 339 Joey Meyer .05 .01
❑ 340 Dion James .05 .01
❑ 341 Les Lancaster .05 .01
❑ 342 Tom Foley .05 .01
❑ 343 Geno Petralli .05 .01
❑ 344 Dan Petry .05 .01
❑ 345 Alvin Davis .05 .01
❑ 346 Mickey Hatcher .05 .01
❑ 347 Marvell Wynne .05 .01
❑ 348 Danny Cox .05 .01
❑ 349 Dave Stieb .10 .02
❑ 350 Jay Bell .10 .02
❑ 351 Jeff Treadway .05 .01
❑ 352 Luis Salazar .05 .01
❑ 353 Len Dykstra .10 .02
❑ 354 Juan Agosto .05 .01
❑ 355 Gene Larkin .05 .01
❑ 356 Steve Farr .05 .01
❑ 357 Paul Assenmacher .05 .01
❑ 358 Todd Benzinger .05 .01
❑ 359 Larry Andersen .05 .01
❑ 360 Paul O'Neill .15 .05
❑ 361 Ron Hassey .05 .01
❑ 362 Jim Gott .05 .01
❑ 363 Ken Phelps .05 .01
❑ 364 Tim Flannery .05 .01
❑ 365 Randy Ready .05 .01
❑ 366 Nelson Santovenia .05 .01
❑ 367 Kelly Downs .05 .01
❑ 368 Danny Heep .05 .01
❑ 369 Phil Bradley .05 .01
❑ 370 Jeff D. Robinson .05 .01
❑ 371 Ivan Calderon .05 .01
❑ 372 Mike Witt .05 .01
❑ 373 Greg Maddux .50 .20
❑ 374 Carmen Castillo .05 .01
❑ 375 Jose Rijo .10 .02
❑ 376 Joe Price .05 .01
❑ 377 Rene Gonzales .05 .01
❑ 378 Oddibe McDowell .05 .01
❑ 379 Jim Presley .05 .01
❑ 380 Brad Wellman .05 .01
❑ 381 Tom Glavine .25 .08
❑ 382 Dan Plesac .05 .01
❑ 383 Wally Backman .05 .01
❑ 384 Dave Gallagher .05 .01
❑ 385 Tom Henke .05 .01
❑ 386 Luis Polonia .05 .01
❑ 387 Junior Ortiz .05 .01
❑ 388 David Cone .10 .02
❑ 389 Dave Bergman .05 .01
❑ 390 Danny Darwin .05 .01
❑ 391 Dan Gladden .05 .01
❑ 392 John Dopson .05 .01
❑ 393 Frank DiPino .05 .01
❑ 394 Al Nipper .05 .01
❑ 395 Willie Randolph .10 .02
❑ 396 Don Carman .05 .01
❑ 397 Scott Terry .05 .01
❑ 398 Rick Cerone .05 .01
❑ 399 Tom Pagnozzi .05 .01
❑ 400 Checklist 358-467 .05 .01
❑ 401 Mickey Tettleton .05 .01
❑ 402 Curtis Wilkerson .05 .01
❑ 403 Jeff Russell .05 .01
❑ 404 Pat Perry .05 .01
❑ 405 Jose Alvarez RC .10 .02
❑ 406 Rick Schu .05 .01
❑ 407 Sherman Corbett .05 .01
❑ 408 Dave Magadan .05 .01
❑ 409 Bob Kipper .05 .01
❑ 410 Don August .05 .01
❑ 411 Bob Brower .05 .01
❑ 412 Chris Bosio .05 .01
❑ 413 Jerry Reuss .05 .01
❑ 414 Atlee Hammaker .05 .01
❑ 415 Jim Walewander .05 .01
❑ 416 Mike Macfarlane RC * .25 .08
❑ 417 Pat Sheridan .05 .01
❑ 418 Pedro Guerrero .10 .02
❑ 419 Allan Anderson .05 .01
❑ 420 Mark Parent .05 .01
❑ 421 Bob Stanley .05 .01
❑ 422 Mike Gallego .05 .01
❑ 423 Bruce Hurst .05 .01
❑ 424 Dave Meads .05 .01
❑ 425 Jesse Barfield .10 .02
❑ 426 Rob Dibble RC .40 .15
❑ 427 Joel Skinner .05 .01
❑ 428 Ron Kittle .05 .01
❑ 429 Rick Rhoden .05 .01
❑ 430 Bob Dernier .05 .01
❑ 431 Steve Jeltz .05 .01
❑ 432 Rick Dempsey .05 .01
❑ 433 Roberto Kelly .05 .01
❑ 434 Dave Anderson .05 .01
❑ 435 Herm Winningham .05 .01
❑ 436 Al Newman .05 .01
❑ 437 Jose DeLeon .05 .01
❑ 438 Doug Jones .05 .01
❑ 439 Brian Holton .05 .01
❑ 440 Jeff Montgomery .05 .01
❑ 441 Dickie Thon .05 .01
❑ 442 Cecil Fielder .10 .02
❑ 443 John Fishel .05 .01
❑ 444 Jerry Don Gleaton .05 .01
❑ 445 Paul Gibson .05 .01
❑ 446 Walt Weiss .05 .01
❑ 447 Glenn Wilson .05 .01
❑ 448 Mike Moore .05 .01
❑ 449 Chili Davis .10 .02
❑ 450 Dave Henderson .05 .01
❑ 451 Jose Bautista RC .10 .02
❑ 452 Rex Hudler .05 .01
❑ 453 Bob Brenly .05 .01
❑ 454 Mackey Sasser .05 .01
❑ 455 Daryl Boston .05 .01
❑ 456 Mike R. Fitzgerald .05 .01
❑ 457 Jeffrey Leonard .05 .01
❑ 458 Bruce Sutter .10 .02
❑ 459 Mitch Webster .05 .01
❑ 460 Joe Hesketh .05 .01
❑ 461 Bobby Witt .05 .01
❑ 462 Stu Cliburn .05 .01
❑ 463 Scott Bankhead .05 .01
❑ 464 Ramon Martinez RC .25 .08
❑ 465 Dave Leiper .05 .01
❑ 466 Luis Alicea RC * .25 .08
❑ 467 John Cerutti .05 .01
❑ 468 Ron Washington .05 .01
❑ 469 Jeff Reed .05 .01
❑ 470 Jeff M. Robinson .05 .01
❑ 471 Sid Fernandez .05 .01
❑ 472 Terry Puhl .05 .01
❑ 473 Charlie Lea .05 .01
❑ 474 Israel Sanchez .05 .01
❑ 475 Bruce Benedict .05 .01
❑ 476 Oil Can Boyd .05 .01
❑ 477 Craig Reynolds .05 .01
❑ 478 Frank Williams .05 .01
❑ 479 Greg Cadaret .05 .01
❑ 480 Randy Kramer .05 .01
❑ 481 Dave Eiland .05 .01
❑ 482 Eric Show .05 .01
❑ 483 Garry Templeton .10 .02
❑ 484 Wallace Johnson .05 .01
❑ 485 Kevin Mitchell .10 .02
❑ 486 Tim Crews .05 .01
❑ 487 Mike Maddux .05 .01
❑ 488 Dave LaPoint .05 .01
❑ 489 Fred Manrique .05 .01
❑ 490 Greg Minton .05 .01
❑ 491 Doug Dascenzo UER (Photo actually Damon Berryhil .05 .01
❑ 492 Willie Upshaw .05 .01
❑ 493 Jack Armstrong RC * .25 .08
❑ 494 Kirt Manwaring .05 .01
❑ 495 Jeff Ballard .05 .01
❑ 496 Jeff Kunkel .05 .01
❑ 497 Mike Campbell .05 .01
❑ 498 Gary Thurman .05 .01
❑ 499 Zane Smith .05 .01
❑ 500 Checklist 468-577 DP .05 .01
❑ 501 Mike Birkbeck .05 .01
❑ 502 Terry Leach .05 .01
❑ 503 Shawn Hillegas .05 .01
❑ 504 Manny Lee .05 .01
❑ 505 Doug Jennings .05 .01
❑ 506 Ken Oberkfell .05 .01
❑ 507 Tim Teufel .05 .01
❑ 508 Tom Brookens .05 .01
❑ 509 Rafael Ramirez .05 .01
❑ 510 Fred Toliver .05 .01
❑ 511 Brian Holman RC * .10 .02
❑ 512 Mike Bielecki .05 .01
❑ 513 Jeff Pico .05 .01
❑ 514 Charles Hudson .05 .01
❑ 515 Bruce Ruffin .05 .01
❑ 516 Larry McWilliams UER (New Richland& should be No .05 .01
❑ 517 Jeff Sellers .05 .01
❑ 518 John Costello .05 .01
❑ 519 Brady Anderson RC .40 .15
❑ 520 Craig McMurtry .05 .01
❑ 521 Ray Hayward DP .05 .01
❑ 522 Drew Hall DP .05 .01
❑ 523 Mark Lemke DP RC .40 .15
❑ 524 Oswald Peraza DP .05 .01
❑ 525 Bryan Harvey DP RC * .25 .08
❑ 526 Rick Aguilera DP .05 .01
❑ 527 Tom Prince DP .05 .01
❑ 528 Mark Clear DP .05 .01
❑ 529 Jerry Browne DP .05 .01
❑ 530 Juan Castillo DP .05 .01
❑ 531 Jack McDowell DP .10 .02
❑ 532 Chris Speier DP .05 .01
❑ 533 Darrell Evans DP .10 .02
❑ 534 Luis Aquino DP .05 .01
❑ 535 Eric King DP .05 .01
❑ 536 Ken Hill DP RC .25 .08
❑ 537 Randy Bush DP .05 .01
❑ 538 Shane Mack DP .05 .01
❑ 539 Tom Bolton DP .05 .01
❑ 540 Gene Nelson DP .05 .01
❑ 541 Wes Gardner DP .05 .01
❑ 542 Ken Caminiti DP .15 .05
❑ 543 Duane Ward DP .05 .01
❑ 544 Norm Charlton DP RC .25 .08
❑ 545 Hal Morris DP RC .25 .08
❑ 546 Rich Yett DP .05 .01
❑ 547 Hensley Meulens DP RC .10 .02
❑ 548 Greg A. Harris DP .05 .01
❑ 549 Darren Daulton .10 .02
❑ 550 Jeff Hamilton DP .05 .01
❑ 551 Luis Aguayo DP .05 .01
❑ 552 Tim Leary DP (Resembles M.Marshall) .05 .01
❑ 553 Ron Oester DP .05 .01
❑ 554 Steve Lombardozzi DP .05 .01
❑ 555 Tim Jones DP .05 .01
❑ 556 Bud Black DP .05 .01
❑ 557 Alejandro Pena DP .05 .01
❑ 558 Jose DeJesus DP .05 .01
❑ 559 Dennis Rasmussen DP .05 .01
❑ 560 Pat Borders DP RC * .25 .08
❑ 561 Craig Biggio RC 3.00 1.25
❑ 562 Luis DeLosSantos DP .05 .01
❑ 563 Fred Lynn DP .10 .02
❑ 564 Todd Burns DP .05 .01
❑ 565 Felix Fermin DP .05 .01
❑ 566 Darnell Coles DP .05 .01
❑ 567 Willie Fraser DP .05 .01
❑ 568 Glenn Hubbard DP .05 .01
❑ 569 Craig Worthington DP .05 .01
❑ 570 Johnny Paredes DP .05 .01

❑ 571 Don Robinson DP .05 .01
❑ 572 Barry Lyons DP .05 .01
❑ 573 Bill Long DP .05 .01
❑ 574 Tracy Jones DP .05 .01
❑ 575 Juan Nieves DP .05 .01
❑ 576 Andres Thomas DP .05 .01
❑ 577 Rolando Roomes DP .05 .01
❑ 578 Luis Rivera UER DP
(Wrong birthdate) .05 .01
❑ 579 Chad Kreuter RC .25 .08
❑ 580 Tony Armas DP .10 .02
❑ 581 Jay Buhner .10 .02
❑ 582 Ricky Horton DP .05 .01
❑ 583 Andy Hawkins DP .05 .01
❑ 584 Sil Campusano .05 .01
❑ 585 Dave Clark .05 .01
❑ 586 Van Snider DP .05 .01
❑ 587 Todd Frohwirth DP .05 .01
❑ 588 Warren Spahn Puzzle DP .15 .05
❑ 589 William Brennan .05 .01
❑ 590 German Gonzalez .05 .01
❑ 591 Ernie Whitt DP .05 .01
❑ 592 Jeff Blauser .05 .01
❑ 593 Spike Owen DP .05 .01
❑ 594 Matt Williams .25 .08
❑ 595 Lloyd McClendon DP .05 .01
❑ 596 Steve Ontiveros .05 .01
❑ 597 Scott Medvin .05 .01
❑ 598 Hipolito Pena DP .05 .01
❑ 599 Jerald Clark DP RC .10 .02
❑ 600A Checklist 578-660 DP .05 .01
❑ 600B Checklist 578-660 DP .05 .01
❑ 600C Checklist 578-660 DP .05 .01
❑ 601 Carmelo Martinez DP .05 .01
❑ 602 Mike LaCoss .05 .01
❑ 603 Mike Devereaux .05 .01
❑ 604 Alex Madrid DP .05 .01
❑ 605 Gary Redus DP .05 .01
❑ 606 Lance Johnson .05 .01
❑ 607 Terry Clark DP .05 .01
❑ 608 Manny Trillo DP .05 .01
❑ 609 Scott Jordan RC .25 .08
❑ 610 Jay Howell DP .05 .01
❑ 611 Francisco Melendez .05 .01
❑ 612 Mike Boddicker .05 .01
❑ 613 Kevin Brown .25 .08
❑ 614 Dave Valle .05 .01
❑ 615 Tim Laudner DP .05 .01
❑ 616 Andy Nezelek UER
(Wrong birthdate) .05 .01
❑ 617 Chuck Crim .05 .01
❑ 618 Jack Savage DP .05 .01
❑ 619 Adam Peterson .05 .01
❑ 620 Todd Stottlemyre .05 .01
❑ 621 Lance Blankenship RC .10 .02
❑ 622 Miguel Garcia DP .05 .01
❑ 623 Keith A. Miller DP .05 .01
❑ 624 Ricky Jordan DP RC * .25 .08
❑ 625 Ernest Riles DP .05 .01
❑ 626 John Moses DP .05 .01
❑ 627 Nelson Liriano DP .05 .01
❑ 628 Mike Smithson DP .05 .01
❑ 629 Scott Sanderson .05 .01
❑ 630 Dale Mohorcic .05 .01
❑ 631 Marvin Freeman DP .05 .01
❑ 632 Mike Young DP .05 .01
❑ 633 Dennis Lamp .05 .01
❑ 634 Dante Bichette RC .40 .15
❑ 635 Curt Schilling RC 4.00 1.50
❑ 636 Scott May DP .05 .01
❑ 637 Mike Schooler .05 .01
❑ 638 Rick Leach .05 .01
❑ 639 Tom Lampkin UER
(Throws Left& should
be Throws R .05 .01
❑ 640 Brian Meyer .05 .01
❑ 641 Brian Harper .05 .01
❑ 642 John Smoltz RC 1.50 .60
❑ 643 Jose Canseco 40/40 .25 .08
❑ 644 Bill Schroeder .05 .01
❑ 645 Edgar Martinez .25 .08
❑ 646 Dennis Cook RC .25 .08
❑ 647 Barry Jones .05 .01
❑ 648 Orel Hershiser
(59 and Counting) .10 .02
❑ 649 Rod Nichols .05 .01
❑ 650 Jody Davis .05 .01
❑ 651 Bob Milacki .05 .01
❑ 652 Mike Jackson .05 .01
❑ 653 Derek Lilliquist RC .10 .02
❑ 654 Paul Mirabella .05 .01
❑ 655 Mike Diaz .05 .01
❑ 656 Jeff Musselman .05 .01
❑ 657 Jerry Reed .05 .01
❑ 658 Kevin Blankenship .05 .01
❑ 659 Wayne Tolleson .05 .01
❑ 660 Eric Hetzel .05 .01
❑ BC Jose Canseco
Blister Pack 2.00 .75

1990 Donruss

❑ COMPLETE SET (716) 15.00 6.00
❑ COMP.FACT.SET (728) 15.00 6.00
❑ COMP.YAZ PUZZLE 1.00 .40
❑ 1 Bo Jackson DK .15 .05
❑ 2 Steve Sax DK .05 .01
❑ 3A Ruben Sierra DK ERR .10 .02
❑ 3B Ruben Sierra DK COR .10 .02
❑ 4 Ken Griffey Jr. DK .40 .15
❑ 5 Mickey Tettleton DK .05 .01
❑ 6 Dave Stewart DK .05 .01
❑ 7 Jim Deshaies DK DP .05 .01
❑ 8 John Smoltz DK .25 .08
❑ 9 Mike Bielecki DK .05 .01
❑ 10A Brian Downing DK ERR .15 .05
❑ 10B Brian Downing DK COR .05 .01
❑ 11 Kevin Mitchell DK .05 .01
❑ 12 Kelly Gruber DK .05 .01
❑ 13 Joe Magrane DK .05 .01
❑ 14 John Franco DK .10 .02
❑ 15 Ozzie Guillen DK .10 .02
❑ 16 Lou Whitaker DK .05 .01
❑ 17 John Smiley DK .05 .01
❑ 18 Howard Johnson DK .05 .01
❑ 19 Willie Randolph DK .10 .02
❑ 20 Chris Bosio DK .05 .01
❑ 21 Tommy Herr DK DP .05 .01
❑ 22 Dan Gladden DK .05 .01
❑ 23 Ellis Burks DK .10 .02
❑ 24 Pete O'Brien DK .05 .01
❑ 25 Bryn Smith DK .05 .01
❑ 26 Ed Whitson DK DP .05 .01
❑ 27 DK Checklist 1-27 DP
(Comments on Perez-
Steele .05 .01
❑ 28 Robin Ventura .25 .08
❑ 29 Todd Zeile .10 .02
❑ 30 Sandy Alomar Jr. .10 .02
❑ 31 Kent Mercker RC .25 .08
❑ 32 Ben McDonald RC .25 .08
❑ 33A Juan Gonzalez RevNg RC 2.00 .75
❑ 33B Juan Gonzalez COR RC 1.00 .40
❑ 34 Eric Anthony RC .10 .02
❑ 35 Mike Fetters RC .25 .08
❑ 36 Marquis Grissom RC .40 .15
❑ 37 Greg Vaughn .05 .01
❑ 38 Brian DuBois RC .10 .02
❑ 39 Steve Avery .05 .01
❑ 40 Mark Gardner RC .10 .02
❑ 41 Andy Benes .10 .02
❑ 42 Delino DeShields RC .25 .08
❑ 43 Scott Coolbaugh RC .10 .02
❑ 44 Pat Combs DP .05 .01
❑ 45 Alex Sanchez DP .05 .01
❑ 46 Kelly Mann DP RC .10 .02
❑ 47 Julio Machado RC .10 .02
❑ 48 Pete Incaviglia .05 .01
❑ 49 Shawon Dunston .05 .01
❑ 50 Jeff Treadway .05 .01
❑ 51 Jeff Ballard .05 .01
❑ 52 Claudell Washington .05 .01
❑ 53 Juan Samuel .05 .01
❑ 54 John Smiley .05 .01
❑ 55 Rob Deer .05 .01
❑ 56 Geno Petralli .05 .01
❑ 57 Chris Bosio .05 .01
❑ 58 Carlton Fisk .15 .05
❑ 59 Kirt Manwaring .05 .01
❑ 60 Chet Lemon .05 .01
❑ 61 Bo Jackson .25 .08
❑ 62 Doyle Alexander .05 .01
❑ 63 Pedro Guerrero .05 .01
❑ 64 Allan Anderson .05 .01
❑ 65 Greg W. Harris .05 .01
❑ 66 Mike Greenwell .05 .01
❑ 67 Walt Weiss .05 .01
❑ 68 Wade Boggs .15 .05
❑ 69 Jim Clancy .05 .01
❑ 70 Junior Felix .05 .01
❑ 71 Barry Larkin .15 .05
❑ 72 Dave LaPoint .05 .01
❑ 73 Joel Skinner .05 .01
❑ 74 Jesse Barfield .05 .01
❑ 75 Tommy Herr .05 .01
❑ 76 Ricky Jordan .05 .01
❑ 77 Eddie Murray .25 .08
❑ 78 Steve Sax .05 .01
❑ 79 Tim Belcher .05 .01
❑ 80 Danny Jackson .05 .01
❑ 81 Kent Hrbek .10 .02
❑ 82 Milt Thompson .05 .01
❑ 83 Brook Jacoby .05 .01
❑ 84 Mike Marshall .05 .01
❑ 85 Kevin Seitzer .05 .01
❑ 86 Tony Gwynn .30 .10
❑ 87 Dave Stieb .10 .02
❑ 88 Dave Smith .05 .01
❑ 89 Bret Saberhagen .10 .02
❑ 90 Alan Trammell .10 .02
❑ 91 Tony Phillips .05 .01
❑ 92 Doug Drabek .05 .01
❑ 93 Jeffrey Leonard .05 .01
❑ 94 Wally Joyner .10 .02
❑ 95 Carney Lansford .10 .02
❑ 96 Cal Ripken .75 .30
❑ 97 Andres Galarraga .10 .02
❑ 98 Kevin Mitchell .05 .01
❑ 99 Howard Johnson .05 .01
❑ 100A Checklist 28-129 .05 .01
❑ 100B Checklist 28-125 .05 .01
❑ 101 Melido Perez .05 .01
❑ 102 Spike Owen .05 .01
❑ 103 Paul Molitor .10 .02
❑ 104 Geronimo Berroa .05 .01
❑ 105 Ryne Sandberg .40 .15
❑ 106 Bryn Smith .05 .01
❑ 107 Steve Buechele .05 .01
❑ 108 Jim Abbott .15 .05
❑ 109 Alvin Davis .05 .01
❑ 110 Lee Smith .10 .02
❑ 111 Roberto Alomar .15 .05
❑ 112 Rick Reuschel .05 .01
❑ 113A Kelly Gruber ERR
(Born 2/22) .05 .01
❑ 113B Kelly Gruber COR
(Born 2/26; corrected
in factor .05 .01
❑ 114 Joe Carter .10 .02
❑ 115 Jose Rijo .05 .01
❑ 116 Greg Minton .05 .01
❑ 117 Bob Ojeda .05 .01
❑ 118 Glenn Davis .05 .01
❑ 119 Jeff Reardon .10 .02
❑ 120 Kurt Stillwell .05 .01
❑ 121 John Smoltz .25 .08
❑ 122 Dwight Evans .15 .05
❑ 123 Eric Yelding RC .05 .01
❑ 124 John Franco .10 .02
❑ 125 Jose Canseco .15 .05
❑ 126 Barry Bonds 1.00 .40

❑ 127 Lee Guetterman	.05	.01
❑ 128 Jack Clark	.10	.02
❑ 129 Dave Valle	.05	.01
❑ 130 Hubie Brooks	.05	.01
❑ 131 Ernest Riles	.05	.01
❑ 132 Mike Morgan	.05	.01
❑ 133 Steve Jeltz	.05	.01
❑ 134 Jeff D. Robinson	.05	.01
❑ 135 Ozzie Guillen	.10	.02
❑ 136 Chili Davis	.10	.02
❑ 137 Mitch Webster	.05	.01
❑ 138 Jerry Browne	.05	.01
❑ 139 Bo Diaz	.05	.01
❑ 140 Robby Thompson	.05	.01
❑ 141 Craig Worthington	.05	.01
❑ 142 Julio Franco	.10	.02
❑ 143 Brian Holman	.05	.01
❑ 144 George Brett	.60	.25
❑ 145 Tom Glavine	.15	.05
❑ 146 Robin Yount	.40	.15
❑ 147 Gary Carter	.10	.02
❑ 148 Ron Kittle	.05	.01
❑ 149 Tony Fernandez	.05	.01
❑ 150 Dave Stewart	.10	.02
❑ 151 Gary Gaetti	.10	.02
❑ 152 Kevin Elster	.05	.01
❑ 153 Gerald Perry	.05	.01
❑ 154 Jesse Orosco	.05	.01
❑ 155 Wally Backman	.05	.01
❑ 156 Dennis Martinez	.10	.02
❑ 157 Rick Sutcliffe	.10	.02
❑ 158 Greg Maddux	.40	.15
❑ 159 Andy Hawkins	.05	.01
❑ 160 John Kruk	.10	.02
❑ 161 Jose Oquendo	.05	.01
❑ 162 John Dopson	.05	.01
❑ 163 Joe Magrane	.05	.01
❑ 164 Bill Ripken	.05	.01
❑ 165 Fred Manrique	.05	.01
❑ 166 Nolan Ryan	1.00	.40
❑ 167 Damon Berryhill	.05	.01
❑ 168 Dale Murphy	.15	.05
❑ 169 Mickey Tettleton	.05	.01
❑ 170A Kirk McCaskill ERR (Born 4/19)	.05	.01
❑ 170B Kirk McCaskill COR (Born 4/9; corrected in facto	.05	.01
❑ 171 Dwight Gooden	.10	.02
❑ 172 Jose Lind	.05	.01
❑ 173 B.J. Surhoff	.10	.02
❑ 174 Ruben Sierra	.10	.02
❑ 175 Dan Plesac	.05	.01
❑ 176 Dan Pasqua	.05	.01
❑ 177 Kelly Downs	.05	.01
❑ 178 Matt Nokes	.05	.01
❑ 179 Luis Aquino	.05	.01
❑ 180 Frank Tanana	.05	.01
❑ 181 Tony Pena	.05	.01
❑ 182 Dan Gladden	.05	.01
❑ 183 Bruce Hurst	.05	.01
❑ 184 Roger Clemens	1.00	.40
❑ 185 Mark McGwire	1.00	.40
❑ 186 Rob Murphy	.05	.01
❑ 187 Jim Deshaies	.05	.01
❑ 188 Fred McGriff	.25	.08
❑ 189 Rob Dibble	.10	.02
❑ 190 Don Mattingly	.60	.25
❑ 191 Felix Fermin	.05	.01
❑ 192 Roberto Kelly	.05	.01
❑ 193 Dennis Cook	.05	.01
❑ 194 Darren Daulton	.10	.02
❑ 195 Alfredo Griffin	.05	.01
❑ 196 Eric Plunk	.05	.01
❑ 197 Orel Hershiser	.10	.02
❑ 198 Paul O'Neill	.15	.05
❑ 199 Randy Bush	.05	.01
❑ 200A Checklist 130-231	.05	.01
❑ 200B Checklist 126-223	.05	.01
❑ 201 Ozzie Smith	.40	.15
❑ 202 Pete O'Brien	.05	.01
❑ 203 Jay Howell	.05	.01
❑ 204 Mark Gubicza	.05	.01
❑ 205 Ed Whitson	.05	.01
❑ 206 George Bell	.05	.01
❑ 207 Mike Scott	.05	.01
❑ 208 Charlie Leibrandt	.05	.01
❑ 209 Mike Heath	.05	.01
❑ 210 Dennis Eckersley	.10	.02
❑ 211 Mike LaValliere	.05	.01
❑ 212 Darnell Coles	.05	.01
❑ 213 Lance Parrish	.05	.01
❑ 214 Mike Moore	.05	.01
❑ 215 Steve Finley	.10	.02
❑ 216 Tim Raines	.10	.02
❑ 217A Scott Garrelts ERR (Born 10/20)	.05	.01
❑ 217B Scott Garrelts COR (Born 10/30; corrected in fac	.05	.01
❑ 218 Kevin McReynolds	.05	.01
❑ 219 Dave Gallagher	.05	.01
❑ 220 Tim Wallach	.05	.01
❑ 221 Chuck Crim	.05	.01
❑ 222 Lonnie Smith	.05	.01
❑ 223 Andre Dawson	.10	.02
❑ 224 Nelson Santovenia	.05	.01
❑ 225 Rafael Palmeiro	.15	.05
❑ 226 Devon White	.10	.02
❑ 227 Harold Reynolds	.10	.02
❑ 228 Ellis Burks	.15	.05
❑ 229 Mark Parent	.05	.01
❑ 230 Will Clark	.15	.05
❑ 231 Jimmy Key	.10	.02
❑ 232 John Farrell	.05	.01
❑ 233 Eric Davis	.10	.02
❑ 234 Johnny Ray	.05	.01
❑ 235 Darryl Strawberry	.10	.02
❑ 236 Bill Doran	.05	.01
❑ 237 Greg Gagne	.05	.01
❑ 238 Jim Eisenreich	.05	.01
❑ 239 Tommy Gregg	.05	.01
❑ 240 Marty Barrett	.05	.01
❑ 241 Rafael Ramirez	.05	.01
❑ 242 Chris Sabo	.05	.01
❑ 243 Dave Henderson	.05	.01
❑ 244 Andy Van Slyke	.15	.05
❑ 245 Alvaro Espinoza	.05	.01
❑ 246 Garry Templeton	.05	.01
❑ 247 Gene Harris	.05	.01
❑ 248 Kevin Gross	.05	.01
❑ 249 Brett Butler	.10	.02
❑ 250 Willie Randolph	.10	.02
❑ 251 Roger McDowell	.05	.01
❑ 252 Rafael Belliard	.05	.01
❑ 253 Steve Rosenberg	.05	.01
❑ 254 Jack Howell	.05	.01
❑ 255 Marvell Wynne	.05	.01
❑ 256 Tom Candiotti	.05	.01
❑ 257 Todd Benzinger	.05	.01
❑ 258 Don Robinson	.05	.01
❑ 259 Phil Bradley	.05	.01
❑ 260 Cecil Espy	.05	.01
❑ 261 Scott Bankhead	.05	.01
❑ 262 Frank White	.10	.02
❑ 263 Andres Thomas	.05	.01
❑ 264 Glenn Braggs	.05	.01
❑ 265 David Cone	.10	.02
❑ 266 Bobby Thigpen	.05	.01
❑ 267 Nelson Liriano	.05	.01
❑ 268 Terry Steinbach	.05	.01
❑ 269 Kirby Puckett	.25	.08
❑ 270 Gregg Jefferies	.10	.02
❑ 271 Jeff Blauser	.05	.01
❑ 272 Cory Snyder	.05	.01
❑ 273 Roy Smith	.05	.01
❑ 274 Tom Foley	.05	.01
❑ 275 Mitch Williams	.05	.01
❑ 276 Paul Kilgus	.05	.01
❑ 277 Don Slaught	.05	.01
❑ 278 Von Hayes	.05	.01
❑ 279 Vince Coleman	.05	.01
❑ 280 Mike Boddicker	.05	.01
❑ 281 Ken Dayley	.05	.01
❑ 282 Mike Devereaux	.05	.01
❑ 283 Kenny Rogers	.10	.02
❑ 284 Jeff Russell	.05	.01
❑ 285 Jerome Walton	.05	.01
❑ 286 Derek Lilliquist	.05	.01
❑ 287 Joe Orsulak	.05	.01
❑ 288 Dick Schofield	.05	.01
❑ 289 Ron Darling	.05	.01
❑ 290 Bobby Bonilla	.10	.02
❑ 291 Jim Gantner	.05	.01
❑ 292 Bobby Witt	.05	.01
❑ 293 Greg Brock	.05	.01
❑ 294 Ivan Calderon	.05	.01
❑ 295 Steve Bedrosian	.05	.01
❑ 296 Mike Henneman	.05	.01
❑ 297 Tom Gordon	.10	.02
❑ 298 Lou Whitaker	.10	.02
❑ 299 Terry Pendleton	.10	.02
❑ 300A Checklist 232-333	.05	.01
❑ 300B Checklist 224-321	.05	.01
❑ 301 Juan Berenguer	.05	.01
❑ 302 Mark Davis	.05	.01
❑ 303 Nick Esasky	.05	.01
❑ 304 Rickey Henderson	.25	.08
❑ 305 Rick Cerone	.05	.01
❑ 306 Craig Biggio	.25	.08
❑ 307 Duane Ward	.05	.01
❑ 308 Tom Browning	.05	.01
❑ 309 Walt Terrell	.05	.01
❑ 310 Greg Swindell	.05	.01
❑ 311 Dave Righetti	.05	.01
❑ 312 Mike Maddux	.05	.01
❑ 313 Len Dykstra	.10	.02
❑ 314 Jose Gonzalez	.05	.01
❑ 315 Steve Balboni	.05	.01
❑ 316 Mike Scioscia	.05	.01
❑ 317 Ron Oester	.05	.01
❑ 318 Gary Wayne	.05	.01
❑ 319 Todd Worrell	.05	.01
❑ 320 Doug Jones	.05	.01
❑ 321 Jeff Hamilton	.05	.01
❑ 322 Danny Tartabull	.05	.01
❑ 323 Chris James	.05	.01
❑ 324 Mike Flanagan	.05	.01
❑ 325 Gerald Young	.05	.01
❑ 326 Bob Boone	.10	.02
❑ 327 Frank Williams	.05	.01
❑ 328 Dave Parker	.10	.02
❑ 329 Sid Bream	.05	.01
❑ 330 Mike Schooler	.05	.01
❑ 331 Bert Blyleven	.10	.02
❑ 332 Bob Welch	.05	.01
❑ 333 Bob Milacki	.05	.01
❑ 334 Tim Burke	.05	.01
❑ 335 Jose Uribe	.05	.01
❑ 336 Randy Myers	.10	.02
❑ 337 Eric King	.05	.01
❑ 338 Mark Langston	.05	.01
❑ 339 Teddy Higuera	.05	.01
❑ 340 Oddibe McDowell	.05	.01
❑ 341 Lloyd McClendon	.05	.01
❑ 342 Pascual Perez	.05	.01
❑ 343 Kevin Brown UER (Signed is misspelled as signeed	.10	.02
❑ 344 Chuck Finley	.10	.02
❑ 345 Erik Hanson	.05	.01
❑ 346 Rich Gedman	.05	.01
❑ 347 Bip Roberts	.05	.01
❑ 348 Matt Williams	.10	.02
❑ 349 Tom Henke	.05	.01
❑ 350 Brad Komminsk	.05	.01
❑ 351 Jeff Reed	.05	.01
❑ 352 Brian Downing	.05	.01
❑ 353 Frank Viola	.05	.01
❑ 354 Terry Puhl	.05	.01
❑ 355 Brian Harper	.05	.01
❑ 356 Steve Farr	.05	.01
❑ 357 Joe Boever	.05	.01
❑ 358 Danny Heep	.05	.01
❑ 359 Larry Andersen	.05	.01
❑ 360 Rolando Roomes	.05	.01
❑ 361 Mike Gallego	.05	.01
❑ 362 Bob Kipper	.05	.01
❑ 363 Clay Parker	.05	.01
❑ 364 Mike Pagliarulo	.05	.01
❑ 365 Ken Griffey Jr.	.75	.30
❑ 366 Rex Hudler	.05	.01
❑ 367 Pat Sheridan	.05	.01
❑ 368 Kirk Gibson	.10	.02
❑ 369 Jeff Parrett	.05	.01
❑ 370 Bob Walk	.05	.01
❑ 371 Ken Patterson	.05	.01
❑ 372 Bryan Harvey	.05	.01

❑ 373 Mike Bielecki .05 .01
❑ 374 Tom Magrann RC .05 .01
❑ 375 Rick Mahler .05 .01
❑ 376 Craig Lefferts .05 .01
❑ 377 Gregg Olson .10 .02
❑ 378 Jamie Moyer .10 .02
❑ 379 Randy Johnson .50 .20
❑ 380 Jeff Montgomery .10 .02
❑ 381 Marty Clary .05 .01
❑ 382 Bill Spiers .05 .01
❑ 383 Dave Magadan .05 .01
❑ 384 Greg Hibbard RC .10 .02
❑ 385 Ernie Whitt .05 .01
❑ 386 Rick Honeycutt .05 .01
❑ 387 Dave West .05 .01
❑ 388 Keith Hernandez .10 .02
❑ 389 Jose Alvarez .05 .01
❑ 390 Albert Belle .25 .08
❑ 391 Rick Aguilera .10 .02
❑ 392 Mike Fitzgerald .05 .01
❑ 393 Dwight Smith .05 .01
❑ 394 Steve Wilson .05 .01
❑ 395 Bob Geren .05 .01
❑ 396 Randy Ready .05 .01
❑ 397 Ken Hill .10 .02
❑ 398 Jody Reed .05 .01
❑ 399 Tom Brunansky .05 .01
❑ 400A Checklist 334-435 .05 .01
❑ 400B Checklist 322-419 .05 .01
❑ 401 Rene Gonzales .05 .01
❑ 402 Harold Baines .10 .02
❑ 403 Cecilio Guante .05 .01
❑ 404 Joe Girardi .15 .05
❑ 405A Sergio Valdez ERR RC .05 .01
❑ 405B Sergio Valdez COR RC .05 .01
❑ 406 Mark Williamson .05 .01
❑ 407 Glenn Hoffman .05 .01
❑ 408 Jeff Innis RC .05 .01
❑ 409 Randy Kramer .05 .01
❑ 410 Charlie O'Brien .05 .01
❑ 411 Charlie Hough .10 .02
❑ 412 Gus Polidor .05 .01
❑ 413 Ron Karkovice .05 .01
❑ 414 Trevor Wilson .05 .01
❑ 415 Kevin Ritz RC .05 .01
❑ 416 Gary Thurman .05 .01
❑ 417 Jeff M. Robinson .05 .01
❑ 418 Scott Terry .05 .01
❑ 419 Tim Laudner .05 .01
❑ 420 Dennis Rasmussen .05 .01
❑ 421 Luis Rivera .05 .01
❑ 422 Jim Corsi .05 .01
❑ 423 Dennis Lamp .05 .01
❑ 424 Ken Caminiti .10 .02
❑ 425 David Wells .10 .02
❑ 426 Norm Charlton .05 .01
❑ 427 Deion Sanders .25 .08
❑ 428 Dion James .05 .01
❑ 429 Chuck Cary .05 .01
❑ 430 Ken Howell .05 .01
❑ 431 Steve Lake .05 .01
❑ 432 Kal Daniels .05 .01
❑ 433 Lance McCullers .05 .01
❑ 434 Lenny Harris .05 .01
❑ 435 Scott Scudder .05 .01
❑ 436 Gene Larkin .05 .01
❑ 437 Dan Quisenberry .05 .01
❑ 438 Steve Olin RC .25 .08
❑ 439 Mickey Hatcher .05 .01
❑ 440 Willie Wilson .05 .01
❑ 441 Mark Grant .05 .01
❑ 442 Mookie Wilson .10 .02
❑ 443 Alex Trevino .05 .01
❑ 444 Pat Tabler .05 .01
❑ 445 Dave Bergman .05 .01
❑ 446 Todd Burns .05 .01
❑ 447 R.J. Reynolds .05 .01
❑ 448 Jay Buhner .10 .02
❑ 449 Lee Stevens .10 .02
❑ 450 Ron Hassey .05 .01
❑ 451 Bob Melvin .05 .01
❑ 452 Dave Martinez .05 .01
❑ 453 Greg Litton .05 .01
❑ 454 Mark Carreon .05 .01
❑ 455 Scott Fletcher .05 .01
❑ 456 Otis Nixon .05 .01
❑ 457 Tony Fossas RC .05 .01
❑ 458 John Russell .05 .01
❑ 459 Paul Assenmacher .05 .01
❑ 460 Zane Smith .05 .01
❑ 461 Jack Daugherty RC .05 .01
❑ 462 Rich Monteleone .05 .01
❑ 463 Greg Briley .05 .01
❑ 464 Mike Smithson .05 .01
❑ 465 Benito Santiago .10 .02
❑ 466 Jeff Brantley .05 .01
❑ 467 Jose Nunez .05 .01
❑ 468 Scott Bailes .05 .01
❑ 469 Ken Griffey Sr. .10 .02
❑ 470 Bob McClure .05 .01
❑ 471 Mackey Sasser .05 .01
❑ 472 Glenn Wilson .05 .01
❑ 473 Kevin Tapani RC .25 .08
❑ 474 Bill Buckner .05 .01
❑ 475 Ron Gant .10 .02
❑ 476 Kevin Romine .05 .01
❑ 477 Juan Agosto .05 .01
❑ 478 Herm Winningham .05 .01
❑ 479 Storm Davis .05 .01
❑ 480 Jeff King .05 .01
❑ 481 Kevin Mmahat RC .05 .01
❑ 482 Carmelo Martinez .05 .01
❑ 483 Omar Vizquel .25 .08
❑ 484 Jim Dwyer .05 .01
❑ 485 Bob Knepper .05 .01
❑ 486 Dave Anderson .05 .01
❑ 487 Ron Jones .05 .01
❑ 488 Jay Bell .10 .02
❑ 489 Sammy Sosa RC 2.50 1.00
❑ 490 Kent Anderson .05 .01
❑ 491 Domingo Ramos .05 .01
❑ 492 Dave Clark .05 .01
❑ 493 Tim Birtsas .05 .01
❑ 494 Ken Oberkfell .05 .01
❑ 495 Larry Sheets .05 .01
❑ 496 Jeff Kunkel .05 .01
❑ 497 Jim Presley .05 .01
❑ 498 Mike Macfarlane .05 .01
❑ 499 Pete Smith .05 .01
❑ 500A Checklist 436-537 DP .05 .01
❑ 500B Checklist 420-517 .05 .01
❑ 501 Gary Sheffield .25 .08
❑ 502 Terry Bross RC .05 .01
❑ 503 Jerry Kutzler RC .05 .01
❑ 504 Lloyd Moseby .05 .01
❑ 505 Curt Young .05 .01
❑ 506 Al Newman .05 .01
❑ 507 Keith Miller .05 .01
❑ 508 Mike Stanton RC .25 .08
❑ 509 Rich Yett .05 .01
❑ 510 Tim Drummond RC .05 .01
❑ 511 Joe Hesketh .05 .01
❑ 512 Rick Wrona .05 .01
❑ 513 Luis Salazar .05 .01
❑ 514 Hal Morris .05 .01
❑ 515 Terry Mulholland .05 .01
❑ 516 John Morris .05 .01
❑ 517 Carlos Quintana .05 .01
❑ 518 Frank DiPino .05 .01
❑ 519 Randy Milligan .05 .01
❑ 520 Chad Kreuter .05 .01
❑ 521 Mike Jeffcoat .05 .01
❑ 522 Mike Harkey .05 .01
❑ 523A Andy Nezelek ERR
(Wrong birth year) .05 .01
❑ 523B Andy Nezelek COR
(Finally corrected
in factory s .15 .05
❑ 524 Dave Schmidt .05 .01
❑ 525 Tony Armas .05 .01
❑ 526 Barry Lyons .05 .01
❑ 527 Rick Reed RC .25 .08
❑ 528 Jerry Reuss .05 .01
❑ 529 Dean Palmer RC .25 .08
❑ 530 Jeff Peterek RC .05 .01
❑ 531 Carlos Martinez .05 .01
❑ 532 Atlee Hammaker .05 .01
❑ 533 Mike Brumley .05 .01
❑ 534 Terry Leach .05 .01
❑ 535 Doug Strange RC .05 .01
❑ 536 Jose DeLeon .05 .01
❑ 537 Shane Rawley .05 .01
❑ 538 Joey Cora .10 .02
❑ 539 Eric Hetzel .05 .01
❑ 540 Gene Nelson .05 .01
❑ 541 Wes Gardner .05 .01
❑ 542 Mark Portugal .05 .01
❑ 543 Al Leiter .25 .08
❑ 544 Jack Armstrong .05 .01
❑ 545 Greg Cadaret .05 .01
❑ 546 Rod Nichols .05 .01
❑ 547 Luis Polonia .05 .01
❑ 548 Charlie Hayes .05 .01
❑ 549 Dickie Thon .05 .01
❑ 550 Tim Crews .05 .01
❑ 551 Dave Winfield .10 .02
❑ 552 Mike Davis .05 .01
❑ 553 Ron Robinson .05 .01
❑ 554 Carmen Castillo .05 .01
❑ 555 John Costello .05 .01
❑ 556 Bud Black .05 .01
❑ 557 Rick Dempsey .05 .01
❑ 558 Jim Acker .05 .01
❑ 559 Eric Show .05 .01
❑ 560 Pat Borders .05 .01
❑ 561 Danny Darwin .05 .01
❑ 562 Rick Luecken RC .05 .01
❑ 563 Edwin Nunez .05 .01
❑ 564 Felix Jose .05 .01
❑ 565 John Cangelosi .05 .01
❑ 566 Bill Swift .05 .01
❑ 567 Bill Schroeder .05 .01
❑ 568 Stan Javier .05 .01
❑ 569 Jim Traber .05 .01
❑ 570 Wallace Johnson .05 .01
❑ 571 Donell Nixon .05 .01
❑ 572 Sid Fernandez .05 .01
❑ 573 Lance Johnson .05 .01
❑ 574 Andy McGaffigan .05 .01
❑ 575 Mark Knudson .05 .01
❑ 576 Tommy Greene RC .10 .02
❑ 577 Mark Grace .15 .05
❑ 578 Larry Walker RC 1.00 .40
❑ 579 Mike Stanley .05 .01
❑ 580 Mike Witt DP .05 .01
❑ 581 Scott Bradley .05 .01
❑ 582 Greg A. Harris .05 .01
❑ 583A Kevin Hickey ERR .25 .08
❑ 583B Kevin Hickey COR .05 .01
❑ 584 Lee Mazzilli .05 .01
❑ 585 Jeff Pico .05 .01
❑ 586 Joe Oliver .05 .01
❑ 587 Willie Fraser DP .05 .01
❑ 588 Carl Yastrzemski Puzzle .25 .08
❑ 589 Kevin Bass DP .05 .01
❑ 590 John Moses DP .05 .01
❑ 591 Tom Pagnozzi DP .05 .01
❑ 592 Tony Castillo DP .05 .01
❑ 593 Jerald Clark DP .05 .01
❑ 594 Dan Schatzeder .05 .01
❑ 595 Luis Quinones DP .05 .01
❑ 596 Pete Harnisch DP .05 .01
❑ 597 Gary Redus .05 .01
❑ 598 Mel Hall .05 .01
❑ 599 Rick Schu .05 .01
❑ 600A Checklist 538-639 .05 .01
❑ 600B Checklist 518-617 .05 .01
❑ 601 Mike Kingery DP .05 .01
❑ 602 Terry Kennedy DP .05 .01
❑ 603 Mike Sharperson DP .05 .01
❑ 604 Don Carman DP .05 .01
❑ 605 Jim Gott .05 .01
❑ 606 Donn Pall DP .05 .01
❑ 607 Rance Mulliniks .05 .01
❑ 608 Curt Wilkerson DP .05 .01
❑ 609 Mike Felder DP .05 .01
❑ 610 Guillermo Hernandez DP .05 .01
❑ 611 Candy Maldonado DP .05 .01
❑ 612 Mark Thurmond DP .05 .01
❑ 613 Rick Leach DP RC .05 .01
❑ 614 Jerry Reed DP .05 .01
❑ 615 Franklin Stubbs .05 .01
❑ 616 Billy Hatcher DP .05 .01
❑ 617 Don August DP .05 .01
❑ 618 Tim Teufel .05 .01
❑ 619 Shawn Hillegas DP .05 .01
❑ 620 Manny Lee .05 .01
❑ 621 Gary Ward DP .05 .01

❑ 622 Mark Guthrie DP RC .05 .01
❑ 623 Jeff Musselman DP .05 .01
❑ 624 Mark Lemke DP .05 .01
❑ 625 Fernando Valenzuela .10 .02
❑ 626 Paul Sorrento DP RC .25 .08
❑ 627 Glenallen Hill DP .05 .01
❑ 628 Les Lancaster DP .05 .01
❑ 629 Vance Law DP .05 .01
❑ 630 Randy Velarde DP .05 .01
❑ 631 Todd Frohwirth DP .05 .01
❑ 632 Willie McGee .10 .02
❑ 633 Dennis Boyd DP .05 .01
❑ 634 Cris Carpenter DP .05 .01
❑ 635 Brian Holton .05 .01
❑ 636 Tracy Jones DP .05 .01
❑ 637A Terry Steinbach AS (Recent Major League Performa .05 .01
❑ 637B Terry Steinbach AS (All-Star Game Performance) .05 .01
❑ 638 Brady Anderson .10 .02
❑ 639A Jack Morris ERR (Card front shows black line cro .10 .02
❑ 639B Jack Morris COR .10 .02
❑ 640 Jaime Navarro .05 .01
❑ 641 Darrin Jackson .05 .01
❑ 642 Mike Dyer RC .05 .01
❑ 643 Mike Schmidt .50 .20
❑ 644 Henry Cotto .05 .01
❑ 645 John Cerutti .05 .01
❑ 646 Francisco Cabrera .05 .01
❑ 647 Scott Sanderson .05 .01
❑ 648 Brian Meyer .05 .01
❑ 649 Ray Searage .05 .01
❑ 650A Bo Jackson AS ERR .25 .08
❑ 650B Bo Jackson AS COR .25 .08
❑ 651 Steve Lyons .05 .01
❑ 652 Mike LaCoss .05 .01
❑ 653 Ted Power .05 .01
❑ 654A Howard Johnson AS (Recent Major League Performan .05 .01
❑ 654B Howard Johnson AS (All-Star Game Performance) .05 .01
❑ 655 Mauro Gozzo RC .05 .01
❑ 656 Mike Blowers RC .10 .02
❑ 657 Paul Gibson .05 .01
❑ 658 Neal Heaton .05 .01
❑ 659 Nolan Ryan 5000K .50 .20
❑ 659A Nolan Ryan 5000K ERR 1.50 .60
❑ 660A H.Baines AS ERR/ERR .75 .30
❑ 660B H.Baines AS ERR/COR 1.00 .40
❑ 660C H.Baines AS COR/ERR .25 .08
❑ 660D Harold Baines AS (Black line behind star on fron .05 .01
❑ 661 Gary Pettis .05 .01
❑ 662 Clint Zavaras RC .05 .01
❑ 663A Rick Reuschel AS (Recent Major League Performanc .05 .01
❑ 663B Rick Reuschel AS (All-Star Game Performance) .05 .01
❑ 664 Alejandro Pena .05 .01
❑ 665 Nolan Ryan KING .50 .20
❑ 665A Nolan Ryan KING ERR 1.50 .60
❑ 665C Nolan Ryan KING NNO .75 .30
❑ 666 Ricky Horton .05 .01
❑ 667 Curt Schilling 1.00 .40
❑ 668 Bill Landrum .05 .01
❑ 669 Todd Stottlemyre .10 .02
❑ 670 Tim Leary .05 .01
❑ 671 John Wetteland .25 .08
❑ 672 Calvin Schiraldi .05 .01
❑ 673A Ruben Sierra AS ERR .05 .01
❑ 673B Ruben Sierra AS COR .05 .01
❑ 674A Pedro Guerrero AS (Recent Major League Performan .05 .01
❑ 674B Pedro Guerrero AS (All-Star Game Performance) .05 .01
❑ 675 Ken Phelps .05 .01
❑ 676A Cal Ripken AS .40 .15
❑ 676B Cal Ripken AS ERR .75 .30
❑ 677 Denny Walling .05 .01
❑ 678 Goose Gossage .10 .02
❑ 679 Gary Mielke RC .05 .01
❑ 680 Bill Bathe .05 .01
❑ 681 Tom Lawless .05 .01
❑ 682 Xavier Hernandez RC .05 .01
❑ 683A Kirby Puckett AS ERR .15 .05
❑ 683B Kirby Puckett AS COR .15 .05
❑ 684 Mariano Duncan .05 .01
❑ 685 Ramon Martinez .05 .01
❑ 686 Tim Jones .05 .01
❑ 687 Tom Filer .05 .01
❑ 688 Steve Lombardozzi .05 .01
❑ 689 Bernie Williams RC 1.50 .60
❑ 690 Chip Hale RC .05 .01
❑ 691 Beau Allred RC .05 .01
❑ 692A Ryne Sandberg AS ERR .25 .08
❑ 692B Ryne Sandberg AS COR .25 .08
❑ 693 Jeff Huson RC .10 .02
❑ 694 Curt Ford .05 .01
❑ 695A Eric Davis AS (Recent Major League Performance) .05 .01
❑ 695B Eric Davis AS (All-Star Game Performance) .05 .01
❑ 696 Scott Lusader .05 .01
❑ 697A Mark McGwire AS ERR .50 .20
❑ 697B Mark McGwire AS COR .50 .20
❑ 698 Steve Cummings RC .05 .01
❑ 699 George Canale RC .05 .01
❑ 700A Checklist w/out 716 .25 .08
❑ 700B Checklist with 716 .10 .02
❑ 700C Checklist 618-716 .05 .01
❑ 701A Julio Franco AS (Recent Major League Performance .05 .01
❑ 701B Julio Franco AS (All-Star Game Performance) .05 .01
❑ 702 Dave Wayne Johnson RC .05 .01
❑ 703A Dave Stewart AS ERR .05 .01
❑ 703B Dave Stewart AS COR .05 .01
❑ 704 David Justice RC .50 .20
❑ 705 Tony Gwynn AS .15 .05
❑ 705A Tony Gwynn AS ERR .15 .05
❑ 706 Greg Myers .05 .01
❑ 707A Will Clark AS ERR .15 .05
❑ 707B Will Clark AS COR .15 .05
❑ 708A Benito Santiago AS .05 .01
❑ 708B Benito Santiago AS .05 .01
❑ 709 Larry McWilliams .05 .01
❑ 710A Ozzie Smith AS ML Perf .25 .08
❑ 710B Ozzie Smith AS Perf .25 .08
❑ 711 John Olerud RC .50 .20
❑ 712A Wade Boggs AS ERR .10 .02
❑ 712B Wade Boggs AS COR .10 .02
❑ 713 Gary Eave RC .05 .01
❑ 714 Bob Tewksbury .05 .01
❑ 715A Kevin Mitchell AS (Recent Major League Performan .05 .01
❑ 715B Kevin Mitchell AS (All-Star Game Performance) .05 .01
❑ 716 Bart Giamatti MEM .25 .08

1991 Donruss

❑ COMPLETE SET (770) 8.00 3.00
❑ COMP.FACT.w/LEAF PREV 10.00 4.00
❑ COMP.FACT.w/STUDIO PREV 10.00 4.00
❑ COMP.STARGELL PUZZLE 1.00 .40
❑ 1 Dave Stieb DK .05 .01
❑ 2 Craig Biggio DK .10 .02
❑ 3 Cecil Fielder DK .05 .01
❑ 4 Barry Bonds DK .50 .20
❑ 5 Barry Larkin DK .10 .02
❑ 6 Dave Parker DK .05 .01
❑ 7 Len Dykstra DK .05 .01
❑ 8 Bobby Thigpen DK .05 .01
❑ 9 Roger Clemens DK .40 .15
❑ 10 Ron Gant DK UER .10 .02
❑ 11 Delino DeShields DK .05 .01

❑ 12 Roberto Alomar DK UER .10 .02
❑ 13 Sandy Alomar Jr. DK .05 .01
❑ 14 Ryne Sandberg DK UER .25 .08
❑ 15 Ramon Martinez DK .05 .01
❑ 16 Edgar Martinez DK .15 .05
❑ 17 Dave Magadan DK .05 .01
❑ 18 Matt Williams DK .05 .01
❑ 19 Rafael Palmeiro DK UER .10 .02
❑ 20 Bob Welch DK .05 .01
❑ 21 Dave Righetti DK .05 .01
❑ 22 Brian Harper DK .05 .01
❑ 23 Gregg Olson DK .05 .01
❑ 24 Kurt Stillwell DK .05 .01
❑ 25 Pedro Guerrero DK UER .05 .01
❑ 26 Chuck Finley DK UER .10 .02
❑ 27 DK Checklist 1-27 .05 .01
❑ 28 Tino Martinez RR .25 .08
❑ 29 Mark Lewis RR .05 .01
❑ 30 Bernard Gilkey RR .05 .01
❑ 31 Hensley Meulens RR .05 .01
❑ 32 Derek Bell RR .10 .02
❑ 33 Jose Offerman RR .05 .01
❑ 34 Terry Bross RR .05 .01
❑ 35 Leo Gomez RR .05 .01
❑ 36 Derrick May RR .05 .01
❑ 37 Kevin Morton RR RC .05 .01
❑ 38 Moises Alou RR .10 .02
❑ 39 Julio Valera RR .05 .01
❑ 40 Milt Cuyler RR .05 .01
❑ 41 Phil Plantier RR RC .25 .08
❑ 42 Scott Chiamparino RR .05 .01
❑ 43 Ray Lankford RR .10 .02
❑ 44 Mickey Morandini RR .05 .01
❑ 45 Dave Hansen RR .05 .01
❑ 46 Kevin Belcher RR RC .05 .01
❑ 47 Darrin Fletcher RR .05 .01
❑ 48 Steve Sax AS .05 .01
❑ 49 Ken Griffey Jr. AS .25 .08
❑ 50A Jose Canseco AS ERR .10 .02
❑ 50B Jose Canseco AS COR .15 .05
❑ 51 Sandy Alomar Jr. AS .05 .01
❑ 52 Cal Ripken AS .40 .15
❑ 53 Rickey Henderson AS .15 .05
❑ 54 Bob Welch AS .05 .01
❑ 55 Wade Boggs AS .10 .02
❑ 56 Mark McGwire AS .40 .15
❑ 57A Jack McDowell ERR .25 .08
❑ 57B Jack McDowell COR .50 .20
❑ 58 Jose Lind .05 .01
❑ 59 Alex Fernandez .05 .01
❑ 60 Pat Combs .05 .01
❑ 61 Mike Walker .05 .01
❑ 62 Juan Samuel .05 .01
❑ 63 Mike Blowers UER .05 .01
❑ 64 Mark Guthrie .05 .01
❑ 65 Mark Salas .05 .01
❑ 66 Tim Jones .05 .01
❑ 67 Tim Leary .05 .01
❑ 68 Andres Galarraga .10 .02
❑ 69 Bob Milacki .05 .01
❑ 70 Tim Belcher .05 .01
❑ 71 Todd Zeile .05 .01
❑ 72 Jerome Walton .05 .01
❑ 73 Kevin Seitzer .05 .01
❑ 74 Jerald Clark .05 .01
❑ 75 John Smoltz UER .15 .05
❑ 76 Mike Henneman .05 .01
❑ 77 Ken Griffey Jr. .50 .20

❑ 78 Jim Abbott .15 .05
❑ 79 Gregg Jefferies .05 .01
❑ 80 Kevin Reimer .05 .01
❑ 81 Roger Clemens .75 .30
❑ 82 Mike Fitzgerald .05 .01
❑ 83 Bruce Hurst UER .05 .01
❑ 84 Eric Davis .10 .02
❑ 85 Paul Molitor .10 .02
❑ 86 Will Clark .15 .05
❑ 87 Mike Bielecki .05 .01
❑ 88 Bret Saberhagen .10 .02
❑ 89 Nolan Ryan 1.00 .40
❑ 90 Bobby Thigpen .05 .01
❑ 91 Dickie Thon .05 .01
❑ 92 Duane Ward .05 .01
❑ 93 Luis Polonia .05 .01
❑ 94 Terry Kennedy .05 .01
❑ 95 Kent Hrbek .10 .02
❑ 96 Danny Jackson .05 .01
❑ 97 Sid Fernandez .05 .01
❑ 98 Jimmy Key .10 .02
❑ 99 Franklin Stubbs .05 .01
❑ 100 Checklist 28-103 .05 .01
❑ 101 R.J. Reynolds .05 .01
❑ 102 Dave Stewart .10 .02
❑ 103 Dan Pasqua .05 .01
❑ 104 Dan Plesac .05 .01
❑ 105 Mark McGwire .75 .30
❑ 106 John Farrell .05 .01
❑ 107 Don Mattingly .60 .25
❑ 108 Carlton Fisk .15 .05
❑ 109 Ken Oberkfell .05 .01
❑ 110 Darrel Akerfelds .05 .01
❑ 111 Gregg Olson .05 .01
❑ 112 Mike Scioscia .05 .01
❑ 113 Bryn Smith .05 .01
❑ 114 Bob Geren .05 .01
❑ 115 Tom Candiotti .05 .01
❑ 116 Kevin Tapani .05 .01
❑ 117 Jeff Treadway .05 .01
❑ 118 Alan Trammell .10 .02
❑ 119 Pete O'Brien UER .05 .01
❑ 120 Joel Skinner .05 .01
❑ 121 Mike LaValliere .05 .01
❑ 122 Dwight Evans .15 .05
❑ 123 Jody Reed .05 .01
❑ 124 Lee Guetterman .05 .01
❑ 125 Tim Burke .05 .01
❑ 126 Dave Johnson .05 .01
❑ 127 Fernando Valenzuela UER .10 .02
❑ 128 Jose DeLeon .05 .01
❑ 129 Andre Dawson .10 .02
❑ 130 Gerald Perry .05 .01
❑ 131 Greg W. Harris .05 .01
❑ 132 Tom Glavine .15 .05
❑ 133 Lance McCullers .05 .01
❑ 134 Randy Johnson .30 .10
❑ 135 Lance Parrish UER .10 .02
❑ 136 Mackey Sasser .05 .01
❑ 137 Geno Petralli .05 .01
❑ 138 Dennis Lamp .05 .01
❑ 139 Dennis Martinez .10 .02
❑ 140 Mike Pagliarulo .05 .01
❑ 141 Hal Morris .05 .01
❑ 142 Dave Parker .10 .02
❑ 143 Brett Butler .10 .02
❑ 144 Paul Assenmacher .05 .01
❑ 145 Mark Gubicza .05 .01
❑ 146 Charlie Hough .10 .02
❑ 147 Sammy Sosa .25 .08
❑ 148 Randy Ready .05 .01
❑ 149 Kelly Gruber .05 .01
❑ 150 Devon White .10 .02
❑ 151 Gary Carter .10 .02
❑ 152 Gene Larkin .05 .01
❑ 153 Chris Sabo .05 .01
❑ 154 David Cone .10 .02
❑ 155 Todd Stottlemyre .05 .01
❑ 156 Glenn Wilson .05 .01
❑ 157 Bob Walk .05 .01
❑ 158 Mike Gallego .05 .01
❑ 159 Greg Hibbard .05 .01
❑ 160 Chris Bosio .05 .01
❑ 161 Mike Moore .05 .01
❑ 162 Jerry Browne UER .05 .01
❑ 163 Steve Sax UER .05 .01
❑ 164 Melido Perez .05 .01
❑ 165 Danny Darwin .05 .01
❑ 166 Roger McDowell .05 .01
❑ 167 Bill Ripken .05 .01
❑ 168 Mike Sharperson .05 .01
❑ 169 Lee Smith .10 .02
❑ 170 Matt Nokes .05 .01
❑ 171 Jesse Orosco .05 .01
❑ 172 Rick Aguilera .10 .02
❑ 173 Jim Presley .05 .01
❑ 174 Lou Whitaker .10 .02
❑ 175 Harold Reynolds .10 .02
❑ 176 Brook Jacoby .05 .01
❑ 177 Wally Backman .05 .01
❑ 178 Wade Boggs .15 .05
❑ 179 Chuck Cary UER .05 .01
❑ 180 Tom Foley .05 .01
❑ 181 Pete Harnisch .05 .01
❑ 182 Mike Morgan .05 .01
❑ 183 Bob Tewksbury .05 .01
❑ 184 Joe Girardi .05 .01
❑ 185 Storm Davis .05 .01
❑ 186 Ed Whitson .05 .01
❑ 187 Steve Avery UER .05 .01
❑ 188 Lloyd Moseby .05 .01
❑ 189 Scott Bankhead .05 .01
❑ 190 Mark Langston .05 .01
❑ 191 Kevin McReynolds .05 .01
❑ 192 Julio Franco .10 .02
❑ 193 John Dopson .05 .01
❑ 194 Dennis Boyd .05 .01
❑ 195 Bip Roberts .05 .01
❑ 196 Billy Hatcher .05 .01
❑ 197 Edgar Diaz .05 .01
❑ 198 Greg Litton .05 .01
❑ 199 Mark Grace .15 .05
❑ 200 Checklist 104-179 .05 .01
❑ 201 George Brett .60 .25
❑ 202 Jeff Russell .05 .01
❑ 203 Ivan Calderon .05 .01
❑ 204 Ken Howell .05 .01
❑ 205 Tom Henke .05 .01
❑ 206 Bryan Harvey .05 .01
❑ 207 Steve Bedrosian .05 .01
❑ 208 Al Newman .05 .01
❑ 209 Randy Myers .05 .01
❑ 210 Daryl Boston .05 .01
❑ 211 Manny Lee .05 .01
❑ 212 Dave Smith .05 .01
❑ 213 Don Slaught .05 .01
❑ 214 Walt Weiss .05 .01
❑ 215 Donn Pall .05 .01
❑ 216 Jaime Navarro .05 .01
❑ 217 Willie Randolph .10 .02
❑ 218 Rudy Seanez .05 .01
❑ 219 Jim Leyritz .05 .01
❑ 220 Ron Karkovice .05 .01
❑ 221 Ken Caminiti .10 .02
❑ 222 Von Hayes .05 .01
❑ 223 Cal Ripken .75 .30
❑ 224 Lenny Harris .05 .01
❑ 225 Milt Thompson .05 .01
❑ 226 Alvaro Espinoza .05 .01
❑ 227 Chris James .05 .01
❑ 228 Dan Gladden .05 .01
❑ 229 Jeff Blauser .05 .01
❑ 230 Mike Heath .05 .01
❑ 231 Omar Vizquel .15 .05
❑ 232 Doug Jones .05 .01
❑ 233 Jeff King .05 .01
❑ 234 Luis Rivera .05 .01
❑ 235 Ellis Burks .10 .02
❑ 236 Greg Cadaret .05 .01
❑ 237 Dave Martinez .05 .01
❑ 238 Mark Williamson .05 .01
❑ 239 Stan Javier .05 .01
❑ 240 Ozzie Smith .40 .15
❑ 241 Shawn Boskie .05 .01
❑ 242 Tom Gordon .05 .01
❑ 243 Tony Gwynn .30 .10
❑ 244 Tommy Gregg .05 .01
❑ 245 Jeff M. Robinson .05 .01
❑ 246 Keith Comstock .05 .01
❑ 247 Jack Howell .05 .01
❑ 248 Keith Miller .05 .01
❑ 249 Bobby Witt .05 .01
❑ 250 Rob Murphy UER .05 .01
❑ 251 Spike Owen .05 .01
❑ 252 Garry Templeton .05 .01
❑ 253 Glenn Braggs .05 .01
❑ 254 Ron Robinson .05 .01
❑ 255 Kevin Mitchell .05 .01
❑ 256 Les Lancaster .05 .01
❑ 257 Mel Stottlemyre Jr. .05 .01
❑ 258 Kenny Rogers UER .10 .02
❑ 259 Lance Johnson .05 .01
❑ 260 John Kruk .10 .02
❑ 261 Fred McGriff .15 .05
❑ 262 Dick Schofield .05 .01
❑ 263 Trevor Wilson .05 .01
❑ 264 David West .05 .01
❑ 265 Scott Scudder .05 .01
❑ 266 Dwight Gooden .10 .02
❑ 267 Willie Blair .05 .01
❑ 268 Mark Portugal .05 .01
❑ 269 Doug Drabek .05 .01
❑ 270 Dennis Eckersley .10 .02
❑ 271 Eric King .05 .01
❑ 272 Robin Yount .40 .15
❑ 273 Carney Lansford .10 .02
❑ 274 Carlos Baerga .05 .01
❑ 275 Dave Righetti .10 .02
❑ 276 Scott Fletcher .05 .01
❑ 277 Eric Yelding .05 .01
❑ 278 Charlie Hayes .05 .01
❑ 279 Jeff Ballard .05 .01
❑ 280 Orel Hershiser .10 .02
❑ 281 Jose Oquendo .05 .01
❑ 282 Mike Witt .05 .01
❑ 283 Mitch Webster .05 .01
❑ 284 Greg Gagne .05 .01
❑ 285 Greg Olson .05 .01
❑ 286 Tony Phillips UER .05 .01
❑ 287 Scott Bradley .05 .01
❑ 288 Cory Snyder UER .05 .01
❑ 289 Jay Bell UER .10 .02
❑ 290 Kevin Romine .05 .01
❑ 291 Jeff D. Robinson .05 .01
❑ 292 Steve Frey UER .05 .01
❑ 293 Craig Worthington .05 .01
❑ 294 Tim Crews .05 .01
❑ 295 Joe Magrane .05 .01
❑ 296 Hector Villanueva .05 .01
❑ 297 Terry Shumpert .05 .01
❑ 298 Joe Carter .10 .02
❑ 299 Kent Mercker UER .05 .01
❑ 300 Checklist 180-255 .05 .01
❑ 301 Chet Lemon .05 .01
❑ 302 Mike Schooler .05 .01
❑ 303 Dante Bichette .10 .02
❑ 304 Kevin Elster .05 .01
❑ 305 Jeff Huson .05 .01
❑ 306 Greg A. Harris .05 .01
❑ 307 Marquis Grissom UER .10 .02
❑ 308 Calvin Schiraldi .05 .01
❑ 309 Mariano Duncan .05 .01
❑ 310 Bill Spiers .05 .01
❑ 311 Scott Garrelts .05 .01
❑ 312 Mitch Williams .05 .01
❑ 313 Mike Macfarlane .05 .01
❑ 314 Kevin Brown .10 .02
❑ 315 Robin Ventura .10 .02
❑ 316 Darren Daulton .10 .02
❑ 317 Pat Borders .05 .01
❑ 318 Mark Eichhorn .05 .01
❑ 319 Jeff Brantley .05 .01
❑ 320 Shane Mack .05 .01
❑ 321 Rob Dibble .10 .02
❑ 322 John Franco .10 .02
❑ 323 Junior Felix .05 .01
❑ 324 Casey Candaele .05 .01
❑ 325 Bobby Bonilla .10 .02
❑ 326 Dave Henderson .05 .01
❑ 327 Wayne Edwards .05 .01
❑ 328 Mark Knudson .05 .01
❑ 329 Terry Steinbach .05 .01
❑ 330 Colby Ward UER RC .05 .01
❑ 331 Oscar Azocar .05 .01
❑ 332 Scott Radinsky .05 .01
❑ 333 Eric Anthony .05 .01
❑ 334 Steve Lake .05 .01
❑ 335 Bob Melvin .05 .01

❑ 336 Kal Daniels .05 .01
❑ 337 Tom Pagnozzi .05 .01
❑ 338 Alan Mills .05 .01
❑ 339 Steve Olin .05 .01
❑ 340 Juan Berenguer .05 .01
❑ 341 Francisco Cabrera .05 .01
❑ 342 Dave Bergman .05 .01
❑ 343 Henry Cotto .05 .01
❑ 344 Sergio Valdez .05 .01
❑ 345 Bob Patterson .05 .01
❑ 346 John Marzano .05 .01
❑ 347 Dana Kiecker .05 .01
❑ 348 Dion James .05 .01
❑ 349 Hubie Brooks .05 .01
❑ 350 Bill Landrum .05 .01
❑ 351 Bill Sampen .05 .01
❑ 352 Greg Briley .05 .01
❑ 353 Paul Gibson .05 .01
❑ 354 Dave Eiland .05 .01
❑ 355 Steve Finley .10 .02
❑ 356 Bob Boone .10 .02
❑ 357 Steve Buechele .05 .01
❑ 358 Chris Hoiles RC .05 .01
❑ 359 Larry Walker .25 .08
❑ 360 Frank DiPino .05 .01
❑ 361 Mark Grant .05 .01
❑ 362 Dave Magadan .05 .01
❑ 363 Robby Thompson .05 .01
❑ 364 Lonnie Smith .05 .01
❑ 365 Steve Farr .05 .01
❑ 366 Dave Valle .05 .01
❑ 367 Tim Naehring .05 .01
❑ 368 Jim Acker .05 .01
❑ 369 Jeff Reardon UER .10 .02
❑ 370 Tim Teufel .05 .01
❑ 371 Juan Gonzalez .25 .08
❑ 372 Luis Salazar .05 .01
❑ 373 Rick Honeycutt .05 .01
❑ 374 Greg Maddux .40 .15
❑ 375 Jose Uribe UER .05 .01
❑ 376 Donnie Hill .05 .01
❑ 377 Don Carman .05 .01
❑ 378 Craig Grebeck .05 .01
❑ 379 Willie Fraser .05 .01
❑ 380 Glenallen Hill .05 .01
❑ 381 Joe Oliver .05 .01
❑ 382 Randy Bush .05 .01
❑ 383 Alex Cole .05 .01
❑ 384 Norm Charlton .05 .01
❑ 385 Gene Nelson .05 .01
❑ 386 Checklist 256-331 .05 .01
❑ 387 Rickey Henderson MVP .15 .05
❑ 388 Lance Parrish MVP .05 .01
❑ 389 Fred McGriff MVP .10 .02
❑ 390 Dave Parker MVP .05 .01
❑ 391 Candy Maldonado MVP .05 .01
❑ 392 Ken Griffey Jr. MVP .25 .08
❑ 393 Gregg Olson MVP .05 .01
❑ 394 Rafael Palmeiro MVP .10 .02
❑ 395 Roger Clemens MVP .40 .15
❑ 396 George Brett MVP .25 .08
❑ 397 Cecil Fielder MVP .05 .01
❑ 398 Brian Harper MVP UER .05 .01
❑ 399 Bobby Thigpen MVP .05 .01
❑ 400 Roberto Kelly MVP UER .05 .01
❑ 401 Danny Darwin MVP .05 .01
❑ 402 David Justice MVP .05 .01
❑ 403 Lee Smith MVP .05 .01
❑ 404 Ryne Sandberg MVP .25 .08
❑ 405 Eddie Murray MVP .15 .05
❑ 406 Tim Wallach MVP .05 .01
❑ 407 Kevin Mitchell MVP .05 .01
❑ 408 Darryl Strawberry MVP .05 .01
❑ 409 Joe Carter MVP .05 .01
❑ 410 Len Dykstra MVP .05 .01
❑ 411 Doug Drabek MVP .05 .01
❑ 412 Chris Sabo MVP .05 .01
❑ 413 Paul Marak RR RC .05 .01
❑ 414 Tim McIntosh RR .05 .01
❑ 415 Brian Barnes RR RC .10 .02
❑ 416 Eric Gunderson RR .05 .01
❑ 417 Mike Gardiner RR RC .05 .01
❑ 418 Steve Carter RR .05 .01
❑ 419 Gerald Alexander RR RC .05 .01
❑ 420 Rich Garces RR RC .10 .02
❑ 421 Chuck Knoblauch .10 .02
❑ 422 Scott Aldred RR .05 .01
❑ 423 Wes Chamberlain RR RC .25 .08
❑ 424 Lance Dickson RR RC .10 .02
❑ 425 Greg Colbrunn RR RC .25 .08
❑ 426 Rich DeLucia RR UER RC .05 .01
❑ 427 Jeff Conine RR RC .40 .15
❑ 428 Steve Decker RR RC .05 .01
❑ 429 Turner Ward RR RC .25 .08
❑ 430 Mo Vaughn .10 .02
❑ 431 Steve Chitren RR RC .05 .01
❑ 432 Mike Benjamin RR .05 .01
❑ 433 Ryne Sandberg AS .25 .08
❑ 434 Len Dykstra AS .05 .01
❑ 435 Andre Dawson AS .05 .01
❑ 436A Mike Scioscia AS White .05 .01
❑ 436B Mike Scioscia AS Yellow .05 .01
❑ 437 Ozzie Smith AS .25 .08
❑ 438 Kevin Mitchell AS .05 .01
❑ 439 Jack Armstrong AS .05 .01
❑ 440 Chris Sabo AS .05 .01
❑ 441 Will Clark AS .10 .02
❑ 442 Mel Hall .05 .01
❑ 443 Mark Gardner .05 .01
❑ 444 Mike Devereaux .05 .01
❑ 445 Kirk Gibson .10 .02
❑ 446 Terry Pendleton .10 .02
❑ 447 Mike Harkey .05 .01
❑ 448 Jim Eisenreich .05 .01
❑ 449 Benito Santiago .10 .02
❑ 450 Oddibe McDowell .05 .01
❑ 451 Cecil Fielder .10 .02
❑ 452 Ken Griffey Sr. .10 .02
❑ 453 Bert Blyleven .10 .02
❑ 454 Howard Johnson .05 .01
❑ 455 Monty Fariss UER .05 .01
❑ 456 Tony Pena .05 .01
❑ 457 Tim Raines .10 .02
❑ 458 Dennis Rasmussen .05 .01
❑ 459 Luis Quinones .05 .01
❑ 460 B.J. Surhoff .10 .02
❑ 461 Ernest Riles .05 .01
❑ 462 Rick Sutcliffe .10 .02
❑ 463 Danny Tartabull .05 .01
❑ 464 Pete Incaviglia .05 .01
❑ 465 Carlos Martinez .05 .01
❑ 466 Ricky Jordan .05 .01
❑ 467 John Cerutti .05 .01
❑ 468 Dave Winfield .10 .02
❑ 469 Francisco Oliveras .05 .01
❑ 470 Roy Smith .05 .01
❑ 471 Barry Larkin .15 .05
❑ 472 Ron Darling .05 .01
❑ 473 David Wells .10 .02
❑ 474 Glenn Davis .05 .01
❑ 475 Neal Heaton .05 .01
❑ 476 Ron Hassey .05 .01
❑ 477 Frank Thomas .25 .08
❑ 478 Greg Vaughn .05 .01
❑ 479 Todd Burns .05 .01
❑ 480 Candy Maldonado .05 .01
❑ 481 Dave LaPoint .05 .01
❑ 482 Alvin Davis .05 .01
❑ 483 Mike Scott .05 .01
❑ 484 Dale Murphy .15 .05
❑ 485 Ben McDonald .05 .01
❑ 486 Jay Howell .05 .01
❑ 487 Vince Coleman .05 .01
❑ 488 Alfredo Griffin .05 .01
❑ 489 Sandy Alomar Jr. .05 .01
❑ 490 Kirby Puckett .25 .08
❑ 491 Andres Thomas .05 .01
❑ 492 Jack Morris .10 .02
❑ 493 Matt Young .05 .01
❑ 494 Greg Myers .05 .01
❑ 495 Barry Bonds 1.00 .40
❑ 496 Scott Cooper UER .05 .01
❑ 497 Dan Schatzeder .05 .01
❑ 498 Jesse Barfield .05 .01
❑ 499 Jerry Goff .05 .01
❑ 500 Checklist 332-408 .05 .01
❑ 501 Anthony Telford RC .05 .01
❑ 502 Eddie Murray .25 .08
❑ 503 Omar Olivares RC .25 .08
❑ 504 Ryne Sandberg .40 .15
❑ 505 Jeff Montgomery .05 .01
❑ 506 Mark Parent .05 .01
❑ 507 Ron Gant .10 .02
❑ 508 Frank Tanana .05 .01
❑ 509 Jay Buhner .10 .02
❑ 510 Max Venable .05 .01
❑ 511 Wally Whitehurst .05 .01
❑ 512 Gary Pettis .05 .01
❑ 513 Tom Brunansky .05 .01
❑ 514 Tim Wallach .05 .01
❑ 515 Craig Lefferts .05 .01
❑ 516 Tim Layana .05 .01
❑ 517 Darryl Hamilton .05 .01
❑ 518 Rick Reuschel .05 .01
❑ 519 Steve Wilson .05 .01
❑ 520 Kurt Stillwell .05 .01
❑ 521 Rafael Palmeiro .15 .05
❑ 522 Ken Patterson .05 .01
❑ 523 Len Dykstra .10 .02
❑ 524 Tony Fernandez .05 .01
❑ 525 Kent Anderson .05 .01
❑ 526 Mark Leonard RC .05 .01
❑ 527 Allan Anderson .05 .01
❑ 528 Tom Browning .05 .01
❑ 529 Frank Viola .10 .02
❑ 530 John Olerud .10 .02
❑ 531 Juan Agosto .05 .01
❑ 532 Zane Smith .05 .01
❑ 533 Scott Sanderson .05 .01
❑ 534 Barry Jones .05 .01
❑ 535 Mike Felder .05 .01
❑ 536 Jose Canseco .15 .05
❑ 537 Felix Fermin .05 .01
❑ 538 Roberto Kelly .05 .01
❑ 539 Brian Holman .05 .01
❑ 540 Mark Davidson .05 .01
❑ 541 Terry Mulholland .05 .01
❑ 542 Randy Milligan .05 .01
❑ 543 Jose Gonzalez .05 .01
❑ 544 Craig Wilson RC .05 .01
❑ 545 Mike Hartley .05 .01
❑ 546 Greg Swindell .05 .01
❑ 547 Gary Gaetti .10 .02
❑ 548 David Justice .10 .02
❑ 549 Steve Searcy .05 .01
❑ 550 Erik Hanson .05 .01
❑ 551 Dave Stieb .05 .01
❑ 552 Andy Van Slyke .15 .05
❑ 553 Mike Greenwell .05 .01
❑ 554 Kevin Maas .05 .01
❑ 555 Delino DeShields .10 .02
❑ 556 Curt Schilling .25 .08
❑ 557 Ramon Martinez .05 .01
❑ 558 Pedro Guerrero .10 .02
❑ 559 Dwight Smith .05 .01
❑ 560 Mark Davis .05 .01
❑ 561 Shawn Abner .05 .01
❑ 562 Charlie Leibrandt .05 .01
❑ 563 John Shelby .05 .01
❑ 564 Bill Swift .05 .01
❑ 565 Mike Fetters .05 .01
❑ 566 Alejandro Pena .05 .01
❑ 567 Ruben Sierra .10 .02
❑ 568 Carlos Quintana .05 .01
❑ 569 Kevin Gross .05 .01
❑ 570 Derek Lilliquist .05 .01
❑ 571 Jack Armstrong .05 .01
❑ 572 Greg Brock .05 .01
❑ 573 Mike Kingery .05 .01
❑ 574 Greg Smith .05 .01
❑ 575 Brian McRae RC .25 .08
❑ 576 Jack Daugherty .05 .01
❑ 577 Ozzie Guillen .10 .02
❑ 578 Joe Boever .05 .01
❑ 579 Luis Sojo .05 .01
❑ 580 Chili Davis .10 .02
❑ 581 Don Robinson .05 .01
❑ 582 Brian Harper .05 .01
❑ 583 Paul O'Neill .15 .05
❑ 584 Bob Ojeda .05 .01
❑ 585 Mookie Wilson .10 .02
❑ 586 Rafael Ramirez .05 .01
❑ 587 Gary Redus .05 .01
❑ 588 Jamie Quirk .05 .01
❑ 589 Shawn Hillegas .05 .01
❑ 590 Tom Edens RC .05 .01
❑ 591 Joe Klink .05 .01
❑ 592 Charles Nagy .05 .01

❑ 593 Eric Plunk	.05	.01
❑ 594 Tracy Jones	.05	.01
❑ 595 Craig Biggio	.15	.05
❑ 596 Jose DeJesus	.05	.01
❑ 597 Mickey Tettleton	.05	.01
❑ 598 Chris Gwynn	.05	.01
❑ 599 Rex Hudler	.05	.01
❑ 600 Checklist 409-506	.05	.01
❑ 601 Jim Gott	.05	.01
❑ 602 Jeff Manto	.05	.01
❑ 603 Nelson Liriano	.05	.01
❑ 604 Mark Lemke	.05	.01
❑ 605 Clay Parker	.05	.01
❑ 606 Edgar Martinez	.15	.05
❑ 607 Mark Whiten	.05	.01
❑ 608 Ted Power	.05	.01
❑ 609 Tom Bolton	.05	.01
❑ 610 Tom Herr	.05	.01
❑ 611 Andy Hawkins UER	.05	.01
❑ 612 Scott Ruskin	.05	.01
❑ 613 Ron Kittle	.05	.01
❑ 614 John Wetteland	.10	.02
❑ 615 Mike Perez RC	.10	.02
❑ 616 Dave Clark	.05	.01
❑ 617 Brent Mayne	.05	.01
❑ 618 Jack Clark	.10	.02
❑ 619 Marvin Freeman	.05	.01
❑ 620 Edwin Nunez	.05	.01
❑ 621 Russ Swan	.05	.01
❑ 622 Johnny Ray	.05	.01
❑ 623 Charlie O'Brien	.05	.01
❑ 624 Joe Bitker RC	.05	.01
❑ 625 Mike Marshall	.05	.01
❑ 626 Otis Nixon	.05	.01
❑ 627 Andy Benes	.05	.01
❑ 628 Ron Oester	.05	.01
❑ 629 Ted Higuera	.05	.01
❑ 630 Kevin Bass	.05	.01
❑ 631 Damon Berryhill	.05	.01
❑ 632 Bo Jackson	.25	.08
❑ 633 Brad Arnsberg	.05	.01
❑ 634 Jerry Willard	.05	.01
❑ 635 Tommy Greene	.05	.01
❑ 636 Bob MacDonald RC	.05	.01
❑ 637 Kirk McCaskill	.05	.01
❑ 638 John Burkett	.05	.01
❑ 639 Paul Abbott RC	.05	.01
❑ 640 Todd Benzinger	.05	.01
❑ 641 Todd Hundley	.05	.01
❑ 642 George Bell	.05	.01
❑ 643 Javier Ortiz	.05	.01
❑ 644 Sid Bream	.05	.01
❑ 645 Bob Welch	.05	.01
❑ 646 Phil Bradley	.05	.01
❑ 647 Bill Krueger	.05	.01
❑ 648 Rickey Henderson	.25	.08
❑ 649 Kevin Wickander	.05	.01
❑ 650 Steve Balboni	.05	.01
❑ 651 Gene Harris	.05	.01
❑ 652 Jim Deshales	.05	.01
❑ 653 Jason Grimsley	.05	.01
❑ 654 Joe Orsulak	.05	.01
❑ 655 Jim Poole	.05	.01
❑ 656 Felix Jose	.05	.01
❑ 657 Denis Cook	.05	.01
❑ 658 Tom Brookens	.05	.01
❑ 659 Junior Ortiz	.05	.01
❑ 660 Jeff Parrett	.05	.01
❑ 661 Jerry Don Gleaton	.05	.01
❑ 662 Brent Knackert	.05	.01
❑ 663 Rance Mulliniks	.05	.01
❑ 664 John Smiley	.05	.01
❑ 665 Larry Andersen	.05	.01
❑ 666 Willie McGee	.10	.02
❑ 667 Chris Nabholz	.05	.01
❑ 668 Brady Anderson	.10	.02
❑ 669 Darren Holmes UER RC	.25	.08
❑ 670 Ken Hill	.05	.01
❑ 671 Gary Varsho	.05	.01
❑ 672 Bill Pecota	.05	.01
❑ 673 Fred Lynn	.05	.01
❑ 674 Kevin D. Brown	.05	.01
❑ 675 Dan Petry	.05	.01
❑ 676 Mike Jackson	.05	.01
❑ 677 Wally Joyner	.10	.02
❑ 678 Danny Jackson	.05	.01
❑ 679 Bill Haselman RC	.05	.01
❑ 680 Mike Boddicker	.05	.01
❑ 681 Mel Rojas	.05	.01
❑ 682 Roberto Alomar	.15	.05
❑ 683 David Justice ROY	.05	.01
❑ 684 Chuck Crim	.05	.01
❑ 685 Matt Williams	.10	.02
❑ 686 Shawon Dunston	.05	.01
❑ 687 Jeff Schulz RC	.05	.01
❑ 688 John Barfield	.05	.01
❑ 689 Gerald Young	.05	.01
❑ 690 Luis Gonzalez RC	.50	.20
❑ 691 Frank Wills	.05	.01
❑ 692 Chuck Finley	.10	.02
❑ 693 Sandy Alomar Jr. ROY	.05	.01
❑ 694 Tim Drummond	.05	.01
❑ 695 Herm Winningham	.05	.01
❑ 696 Darryl Strawberry	.10	.02
❑ 697 Al Leiter	.10	.02
❑ 698 Karl Rhodes	.05	.01
❑ 699 Stan Belinda	.05	.01
❑ 700 Checklist 507-604	.05	.01
❑ 701 Lance Blankenship	.05	.01
❑ 702 Willie Stargell PUZ	.15	.05
❑ 703 Jim Gantner	.05	.01
❑ 704 Reggie Harris	.05	.01
❑ 705 Rob Ducey	.05	.01
❑ 706 Tim Hulett	.05	.01
❑ 707 Atlee Hammaker	.05	.01
❑ 708 Xavier Hernandez	.05	.01
❑ 709 Chuck McElroy	.05	.01
❑ 710 John Mitchell	.05	.01
❑ 711 Carlos Hernandez	.05	.01
❑ 712 Geronimo Pena	.05	.01
❑ 713 Jim Neidlinger RC	.05	.01
❑ 714 John Orton	.05	.01
❑ 715 Terry Leach	.05	.01
❑ 716 Mike Stanton	.05	.01
❑ 717 Walt Terrell	.05	.01
❑ 718 Luis Aquino	.05	.01
❑ 719 Bud Black UER	.05	.01
❑ 720 Bob Kipper	.05	.01
❑ 721 Jeff Gray RC	.05	.01
❑ 722 Jose Rijo	.05	.01
❑ 723 Curt Young	.05	.01
❑ 724 Jose Vizcaino	.05	.01
❑ 725 Randy Tomlin RC	.10	.02
❑ 726 Junior Noboa	.05	.01
❑ 727 Bob Welch CY	.05	.01
❑ 728 Gary Ward	.05	.01
❑ 729 Rob Deer UER	.05	.01
❑ 730 David Segui	.05	.01
❑ 731 Mark Carreon	.05	.01
❑ 732 Vicente Palacios	.05	.01
❑ 733 Sam Horn	.05	.01
❑ 734 Howard Farmer	.05	.01
❑ 735 Ken Dayley UER	.05	.01
❑ 736 Kelly Mann	.05	.01
❑ 737 Joe Grahe RC	.10	.02
❑ 738 Kelly Downs	.05	.01
❑ 739 Jimmy Kremers	.05	.01
❑ 740 Kevin Appier	.10	.02
❑ 741 Jeff Reed	.05	.01
❑ 742 Jose Rijo WS	.05	.01
❑ 743 Dave Rohde	.05	.01
❑ 744 L.Dykstra/D.Murphy UER	.15	.05
❑ 745 Paul Sorrento	.05	.01
❑ 746 Thomas Howard	.05	.01
❑ 747 Matt Stark RC	.05	.01
❑ 748 Harold Baines	.10	.02
❑ 749 Doug Dascenzo	.05	.01
❑ 750 Doug Drabek CY	.05	.01
❑ 751 Gary Sheffield	.10	.02
❑ 752 Terry Lee RC	.05	.01
❑ 753 Jim Vatcher RC	.05	.01
❑ 754 Lee Stevens	.05	.01
❑ 755 Randy Veres	.05	.01
❑ 756 Bill Doran	.05	.01
❑ 757 Gary Wayne	.05	.01
❑ 758 Pedro Munoz RC	.10	.02
❑ 759 Chris Hammond FDC	.05	.01
❑ 760 Checklist 605-702	.05	.01
❑ 761 Rickey Henderson MVP	.15	.05
❑ 762 Barry Bonds MVP	.50	.20
❑ 763 Billy Hatcher WS UER	.05	.01
❑ 764 Julio Machado	.05	.01
❑ 765 Jose Mesa	.05	.01
❑ 766 Willie Randolph WS	.05	.01
❑ 767 Scott Erickson	.05	.01
❑ 768 Travis Fryman	.10	.02
❑ 769 Rich Rodriguez RC	.05	.01
❑ 770 Checklist 703-770/BC1-BC22	.05	.01

1992 Donruss

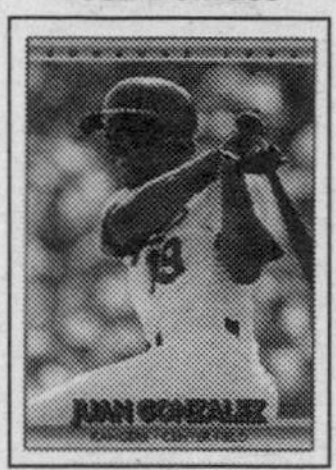

❑ COMPLETE SET (784)	10.00	4.00
❑ COMP.HOBBY SET (788)	10.00	4.00
❑ COMP.RETAIL SET (788)	10.00	4.00
❑ COMPLETE SERIES 1 (396)	5.00	2.00
❑ COMPLETE SERIES 2 (388)	5.00	2.00
❑ COMP.CAREW PUZZLE	1.00	.40
❑ 1 Mark Wohlers RR	.05	.01
❑ 2 Wil Cordero	.05	.01
❑ 3 Kyle Abbott RR	.05	.01
❑ 4 Dave Nilsson	.05	.01
❑ 5 Kenny Lofton	.15	.05
❑ 6 Luis Mercedes RR	.05	.01
❑ 7 Roger Salkeld RR	.05	.01
❑ 8 Eddie Zosky RR	.05	.01
❑ 9 Todd Van Poppel	.05	.01
❑ 10 Frank Seminara RR RC	.10	.02
❑ 11 Andy Ashby	.05	.01
❑ 12 Reggie Jefferson RR	.05	.01
❑ 13 Ryan Klesko	.10	.02
❑ 14 Carlos Garcia	.05	.01
❑ 15 John Ramos RR	.05	.01
❑ 16 Eric Karros	.10	.02
❑ 17 Patrick Lennon RR	.05	.01
❑ 18 Eddie Taubensee RR RC	.25	.08
❑ 19 Roberto Hernandez RR	.05	.01
❑ 20 D.J. Dozier RR	.05	.01
❑ 21 Dave Henderson AS	.05	.01
❑ 22 Cal Ripken AS	.40	.15
❑ 23 Wade Boggs AS	.10	.02
❑ 24 Ken Griffey Jr. AS	.25	.08
❑ 25 Jack Morris AS	.05	.01
❑ 26 Danny Tartabull AS	.05	.01
❑ 27 Cecil Fielder AS	.05	.01
❑ 28 Roberto Alomar AS	.10	.02
❑ 29 Sandy Alomar Jr. AS	.05	.01
❑ 30 Rickey Henderson AS	.15	.05
❑ 31 Ken Hill	.05	.01
❑ 32 John Habyan	.05	.01
❑ 33 Otis Nixon HL	.05	.01
❑ 34 Tim Wallach	.05	.01
❑ 35 Cal Ripken	.75	.30
❑ 36 Gary Carter	.10	.02
❑ 37 Juan Agosto	.05	.01
❑ 38 Doug Dascenzo	.05	.01
❑ 39 Kirk Gibson	.10	.02
❑ 40 Benito Santiago	.10	.02
❑ 41 Otis Nixon	.05	.01
❑ 42 Andy Allanson	.05	.01
❑ 43 Brian Holman	.05	.01
❑ 44 Dick Schofield	.05	.01
❑ 45 Dave Magadan	.05	.01
❑ 46 Rafael Palmeiro	.15	.05
❑ 47 Jody Reed	.05	.01
❑ 48 Ivan Calderon	.05	.01
❑ 49 Greg W. Harris	.05	.01
❑ 50 Chris Sabo	.05	.01
❑ 51 Paul Molitor	.10	.02
❑ 52 Robby Thompson	.05	.01
❑ 53 Dave Smith	.05	.01
❑ 54 Mark Davis	.05	.01

❑	55	Kevin Brown	.10	.02
❑	56	Donn Pall	.05	.01
❑	57	Len Dykstra	.10	.02
❑	58	Roberto Alomar	.15	.05
❑	59	Jeff D. Robinson	.05	.01
❑	60	Willie McGee	.10	.02
❑	61	Jay Buhner	.10	.02
❑	62	Mike Pagliarulo	.05	.01
❑	63	Paul O'Neill	.15	.05
❑	64	Hubie Brooks	.05	.01
❑	65	Kelly Gruber	.05	.01
❑	66	Ken Caminiti	.10	.02
❑	67	Gary Redus	.05	.01
❑	68	Harold Baines	.10	.02
❑	69	Charlie Hough	.10	.02
❑	70	B.J. Surhoff	.10	.02
❑	71	Walt Weiss	.05	.01
❑	72	Shawn Hillegas	.05	.01
❑	73	Roberto Kelly	.05	.01
❑	74	Jeff Ballard	.05	.01
❑	75	Craig Biggio	.15	.05
❑	76	Pat Combs	.05	.01
❑	77	Jeff M. Robinson	.05	.01
❑	78	Tim Belcher	.05	.01
❑	79	Cris Carpenter	.05	.01
❑	80	Checklist 1-79	.05	.01
❑	81	Steve Avery	.05	.01
❑	82	Chris James	.05	.01
❑	83	Brian Harper	.05	.01
❑	84	Charlie Leibrandt	.05	.01
❑	85	Mickey Tettleton	.05	.01
❑	86	Pete O'Brien	.05	.01
❑	87	Danny Darwin	.05	.01
❑	88	Bob Walk	.05	.01
❑	89	Jeff Reardon	.10	.02
❑	90	Bobby Rose	.05	.01
❑	91	Danny Jackson	.05	.01
❑	92	John Morris	.05	.01
❑	93	Bud Black	.05	.01
❑	94	Tommy Greene HL	.05	.01
❑	95	Rick Aguilera	.10	.02
❑	96	Gary Gaetti	.10	.02
❑	97	David Cone	.10	.02
❑	98	John Olerud	.10	.02
❑	99	Joel Skinner	.05	.01
❑	100	Jay Bell	.10	.02
❑	101	Bob Milacki	.05	.01
❑	102	Norm Charlton	.05	.01
❑	103	Chuck Crim	.05	.01
❑	104	Terry Steinbach	.05	.01
❑	105	Juan Samuel	.05	.01
❑	106	Steve Howe	.05	.01
❑	107	Rafael Belliard	.05	.01
❑	108	Joey Cora	.05	.01
❑	109	Tommy Greene	.05	.01
❑	110	Gregg Olson	.05	.01
❑	111	Frank Tanana	.05	.01
❑	112	Lee Smith	.10	.02
❑	113	Greg A. Harris	.05	.01
❑	114	Dwayne Henry	.05	.01
❑	115	Chili Davis	.10	.02
❑	116	Kent Mercker	.05	.01
❑	117	Brian Barnes	.05	.01
❑	118	Rich DeLucia	.05	.01
❑	119	Andre Dawson	.10	.02
❑	120	Carlos Baerga	.05	.01
❑	121	Mike LaValliere	.05	.01
❑	122	Jeff Gray	.05	.01
❑	123	Bruce Hurst	.05	.01
❑	124	Alvin Davis	.05	.01
❑	125	John Candelaria	.05	.01
❑	126	Matt Nokes	.05	.01
❑	127	George Bell	.05	.01
❑	128	Bret Saberhagen	.10	.02
❑	129	Jeff Russell	.05	.01
❑	130	Jim Abbott	.15	.05
❑	131	Bill Gullickson	.05	.01
❑	132	Todd Zeile	.05	.01
❑	133	Dave Winfield	.10	.02
❑	134	Wally Whitehurst	.05	.01
❑	135	Matt Williams	.10	.02
❑	136	Tom Browning	.05	.01
❑	137	Marquis Grissom	.10	.02
❑	138	Erik Hanson	.05	.01
❑	139	Rob Dibble	.10	.02
❑	140	Don August	.05	.01
❑	141	Tom Henke	.05	.01
❑	142	Dan Pasqua	.05	.01
❑	143	George Brett	.60	.25
❑	144	Jerald Clark	.05	.01
❑	145	Robin Ventura	.10	.02
❑	146	Dale Murphy	.15	.05
❑	147	Dennis Eckersley	.10	.02
❑	148	Eric Yelding	.05	.01
❑	149	Mario Diaz	.05	.01
❑	150	Casey Candaele	.05	.01
❑	151	Steve Olin	.05	.01
❑	152	Luis Salazar	.05	.01
❑	153	Kevin Maas	.05	.01
❑	154	Nolan Ryan HL	.50	.20
❑	155	Barry Jones	.05	.01
❑	156	Chris Hoiles	.05	.01
❑	157	Bob Ojeda	.05	.01
❑	158	Pedro Guerrero	.10	.02
❑	159	Paul Assenmacher	.05	.01
❑	160	Checklist 80-157	.05	.01
❑	161	Mike Macfarlane	.05	.01
❑	162	Craig Lefferts	.05	.01
❑	163	Brian Hunter	.05	.01
❑	164	Alan Trammell	.10	.02
❑	165	Ken Griffey Jr.	.40	.15
❑	166	Lance Parrish	.10	.02
❑	167	Brian Downing	.05	.01
❑	168	John Barfield	.05	.01
❑	169	Jack Clark	.10	.02
❑	170	Chris Nabholz	.05	.01
❑	171	Tim Teufel	.05	.01
❑	172	Chris Hammond	.05	.01
❑	173	Robin Yount	.40	.15
❑	174	Dave Righetti	.10	.02
❑	175	Joe Girardi	.05	.01
❑	176	Mike Boddicker	.05	.01
❑	177	Dean Palmer	.10	.02
❑	178	Greg Hibbard	.05	.01
❑	179	Randy Ready	.05	.01
❑	180	Devon White	.10	.02
❑	181	Mark Eichhorn	.05	.01
❑	182	Mike Felder	.05	.01
❑	183	Joe Klink	.05	.01
❑	184	Steve Bedrosian	.05	.01
❑	185	Barry Larkin	.15	.05
❑	186	John Franco	.10	.02
❑	187	Ed Sprague	.05	.01
❑	188	Mark Portugal	.05	.01
❑	189	Jose Lind	.05	.01
❑	190	Bob Welch	.05	.01
❑	191	Alex Fernandez	.05	.01
❑	192	Gary Sheffield	.10	.02
❑	193	Rickey Henderson	.25	.08
❑	194	Rod Nichols	.05	.01
❑	195	Scott Kamieniecki	.05	.01
❑	196	Mike Flanagan	.05	.01
❑	197	Steve Finley	.10	.02
❑	198	Darren Daulton	.10	.02
❑	199	Leo Gomez	.05	.01
❑	200	Mike Morgan	.05	.01
❑	201	Bob Tewksbury	.05	.01
❑	202	Sid Bream	.05	.01
❑	203	Sandy Alomar Jr.	.05	.01
❑	204	Greg Gagne	.05	.01
❑	205	Juan Berenguer	.05	.01
❑	206	Cecil Fielder	.10	.02
❑	207	Randy Johnson	.25	.08
❑	208	Tony Pena	.05	.01
❑	209	Doug Drabek	.05	.01
❑	210	Wade Boggs	.15	.05
❑	211	Bryan Harvey	.05	.01
❑	212	Jose Vizcaino	.05	.01
❑	213	Alonzo Powell	.05	.01
❑	214	Will Clark	.15	.05
❑	215	Rickey Henderson HL	.15	.05
❑	216	Jack Morris	.10	.02
❑	217	Junior Felix	.05	.01
❑	218	Vince Coleman	.05	.01
❑	219	Jimmy Key	.10	.02
❑	220	Alex Cole	.05	.01
❑	221	Bill Landrum	.05	.01
❑	222	Randy Milligan	.05	.01
❑	223	Jose Rijo	.05	.01
❑	224	Greg Vaughn	.05	.01
❑	225	Dave Stewart	.10	.02
❑	226	Lenny Harris	.05	.01
❑	227	Scott Sanderson	.05	.01
❑	228	Jeff Blauser	.05	.01
❑	229	Ozzie Guillen	.10	.02
❑	230	John Kruk	.10	.02
❑	231	Bob Melvin	.05	.01
❑	232	Milt Cuyler	.05	.01
❑	233	Felix Jose	.05	.01
❑	234	Ellis Burks	.10	.02
❑	235	Pete Harnisch	.05	.01
❑	236	Kevin Tapani	.05	.01
❑	237	Terry Pendleton	.10	.02
❑	238	Mark Gardner	.05	.01
❑	239	Harold Reynolds	.10	.02
❑	240	Checklist 158-237	.05	.01
❑	241	Mike Harkey	.05	.01
❑	242	Felix Fermin	.05	.01
❑	243	Barry Bonds	1.00	.40
❑	244	Roger Clemens	.50	.20
❑	245	Dennis Rasmussen	.05	.01
❑	246	Jose DeLeon	.05	.01
❑	247	Orel Hershiser	.10	.02
❑	248	Mel Hall	.05	.01
❑	249	Rick Wilkins	.05	.01
❑	250	Tom Gordon	.05	.01
❑	251	Kevin Reimer	.05	.01
❑	252	Luis Polonia	.05	.01
❑	253	Mike Henneman	.05	.01
❑	254	Tom Pagnozzi	.05	.01
❑	255	Chuck Finley	.10	.02
❑	256	Mackey Sasser	.05	.01
❑	257	John Burkett	.05	.01
❑	258	Hal Morris	.05	.01
❑	259	Larry Walker	.15	.05
❑	260	Bill Swift	.05	.01
❑	261	Joe Oliver	.05	.01
❑	262	Julio Machado	.05	.01
❑	263	Todd Stottlemyre	.05	.01
❑	264	Matt Merullo	.05	.01
❑	265	Brent Mayne	.05	.01
❑	266	Thomas Howard	.05	.01
❑	267	Lance Johnson	.05	.01
❑	268	Terry Mulholland	.05	.01
❑	269	Rick Honeycutt	.05	.01
❑	270	Luis Gonzalez	.10	.02
❑	271	Jose Guzman	.05	.01
❑	272	Jimmy Jones	.05	.01
❑	273	Mark Lewis	.05	.01
❑	274	Rene Gonzales	.05	.01
❑	275	Jeff Johnson	.05	.01
❑	276	Dennis Martinez HL	.05	.01
❑	277	Delino DeShields	.05	.01
❑	278	Sam Horn	.05	.01
❑	279	Kevin Gross	.05	.01
❑	280	Jose Oquendo	.05	.01
❑	281	Mark Grace	.15	.05
❑	282	Mark Gubicza	.05	.01
❑	283	Fred McGriff	.15	.05
❑	284	Ron Gant	.10	.02
❑	285	Lou Whitaker	.10	.02
❑	286	Edgar Martinez	.15	.05
❑	287	Ron Tingley	.05	.01
❑	288	Kevin McReynolds	.05	.01
❑	289	Ivan Rodriguez	.25	.08
❑	290	Mike Gardiner	.05	.01
❑	291	Chris Haney	.05	.01
❑	292	Darrin Jackson	.05	.01
❑	293	Bill Doran	.05	.01
❑	294	Ted Higuera	.05	.01
❑	295	Jeff Brantley	.05	.01
❑	296	Les Lancaster	.05	.01
❑	297	Jim Eisenreich	.05	.01
❑	298	Ruben Sierra	.10	.02
❑	299	Scott Radinsky	.05	.01
❑	300	Jose DeJesus	.05	.01
❑	301	Mike Timlin	.05	.01
❑	302	Luis Sojo	.05	.01
❑	303	Kelly Downs	.05	.01
❑	304	Scott Bankhead	.05	.01
❑	305	Pedro Munoz	.05	.01
❑	306	Scott Scudder	.05	.01
❑	307	Kevin Elster	.05	.01
❑	308	Duane Ward	.05	.01
❑	309	Darryl Kile	.10	.02
❑	310	Orlando Merced	.05	.01
❑	311	Dave Henderson	.05	.01
❑	312	Tim Raines	.10	.02

❑ 313 Mark Lee .05 .01
❑ 314 Mike Gallego .05 .01
❑ 315 Charles Nagy .05 .01
❑ 316 Jesse Barfield .05 .01
❑ 317 Todd Frohwirth .05 .01
❑ 318 Al Osuna .05 .01
❑ 319 Darrin Fletcher .05 .01
❑ 320 Checklist 238-316 .05 .01
❑ 321 David Segui .05 .01
❑ 322 Stan Javier .05 .01
❑ 323 Bryn Smith .05 .01
❑ 324 Jeff Treadway .05 .01
❑ 325 Mark Whiten .05 .01
❑ 326 Kent Hrbek .10 .02
❑ 327 David Justice .10 .02
❑ 328 Tony Phillips .05 .01
❑ 329 Rob Murphy .05 .01
❑ 330 Kevin Morton .05 .01
❑ 331 John Smiley .05 .01
❑ 332 Luis Rivera .05 .01
❑ 333 Wally Joyner .10 .02
❑ 334 Heathcliff Slocumb .05 .01
❑ 335 Rick Cerone .05 .01
❑ 336 Mike Remlinger .05 .01
❑ 337 Mike Moore .05 .01
❑ 338 Lloyd McClendon .05 .01
❑ 339 Al Newman .05 .01
❑ 340 Kirk McCaskill .05 .01
❑ 341 Howard Johnson .05 .01
❑ 342 Greg Myers .05 .01
❑ 343 Kal Daniels .05 .01
❑ 344 Bernie Williams .15 .05
❑ 345 Shane Mack .05 .01
❑ 346 Gary Thurman .05 .01
❑ 347 Dante Bichette .10 .02
❑ 348 Mark McGwire .60 .25
❑ 349 Travis Fryman .10 .02
❑ 350 Ray Lankford .10 .02
❑ 351 Mike Jeffcoat .05 .01
❑ 352 Jack McDowell .05 .01
❑ 353 Mitch Williams .05 .01
❑ 354 Mike Devereaux .05 .01
❑ 355 Andres Galarraga .10 .02
❑ 356 Henry Cotto .05 .01
❑ 357 Scott Bailes .05 .01
❑ 358 Jeff Bagwell .25 .08
❑ 359 Scott Leius .05 .01
❑ 360 Zane Smith .05 .01
❑ 361 Bill Pecota .05 .01
❑ 362 Tony Fernandez .05 .01
❑ 363 Glenn Braggs .05 .01
❑ 364 Bill Spiers .05 .01
❑ 365 Vicente Palacios .05 .01
❑ 366 Tim Burke .05 .01
❑ 367 Randy Tomlin .05 .01
❑ 368 Kenny Rogers .10 .02
❑ 369 Brett Butler .10 .02
❑ 370 Pat Kelly .05 .01
❑ 371 Bip Roberts .05 .01
❑ 372 Gregg Jefferies .05 .01
❑ 373 Kevin Bass .05 .01
❑ 374 Ron Karkovice .05 .01
❑ 375 Paul Gibson .05 .01
❑ 376 Bernard Gilkey .05 .01
❑ 377 Dave Gallagher .05 .01
❑ 378 Bill Wegman .05 .01
❑ 379 Pat Borders .05 .01
❑ 380 Ed Whitson .05 .01
❑ 381 Gilberto Reyes .05 .01
❑ 382 Russ Swan .05 .01
❑ 383 Andy Van Slyke .15 .05
❑ 384 Wes Chamberlain .05 .01
❑ 385 Steve Chitren .05 .01
❑ 386 Greg Olson .05 .01
❑ 387 Brian McRae .05 .01
❑ 388 Rich Rodriguez .05 .01
❑ 389 Steve Decker .05 .01
❑ 390 Chuck Knoblauch .10 .02
❑ 391 Bobby Witt .05 .01
❑ 392 Eddie Murray .25 .08
❑ 393 Juan Gonzalez .15 .05
❑ 394 Scott Ruskin .05 .01
❑ 395 Jay Howell .05 .01
❑ 396 Checklist 317-396 .05 .01
❑ 397 Royce Clayton RR .05 .01
❑ 398 John Jaha RR RC .25 .08
❑ 399 Dan Wilson RR .05 .01
❑ 400 Archie Corbin .05 .01
❑ 401 Barry Manuel RR .05 .01
❑ 402 Kim Batiste RR .05 .01
❑ 403 Pat Mahomes RR RC .25 .08
❑ 404 Dave Fleming .05 .01
❑ 405 Jeff Juden RR .05 .01
❑ 406 Jim Thome .25 .08
❑ 407 Sam Militello RR .05 .01
❑ 408 Jeff Nelson RR RC .40 .15
❑ 409 Anthony Young .05 .01
❑ 410 Tino Martinez RR .15 .05
❑ 411 Jeff Mutis RR .05 .01
❑ 412 Rey Sanchez RR RC .25 .08
❑ 413 Chris Gardner RR .05 .01
❑ 414 John Vander Wal RR .05 .01
❑ 415 Reggie Sanders .10 .02
❑ 416 Brian Williams RR RC .10 .02
❑ 417 Mo Sanford RR .05 .01
❑ 418 David Weathers RR RC .40 .15
❑ 419 Hector Fajardo RR RC .10 .02
❑ 420 Steve Foster RR .05 .01
❑ 421 Lance Dickson RR .05 .01
❑ 422 Andre Dawson AS .05 .01
❑ 423 Ozzie Smith AS .25 .08
❑ 424 Chris Sabo AS .05 .01
❑ 425 Tony Gwynn AS .15 .05
❑ 426 Tom Glavine AS .10 .02
❑ 427 Bobby Bonilla AS .05 .01
❑ 428 Will Clark AS .10 .02
❑ 429 Ryne Sandberg AS .25 .08
❑ 430 Benito Santiago AS .05 .01
❑ 431 Ivan Calderon AS .05 .01
❑ 432 Ozzie Smith .40 .15
❑ 433 Tim Leary .05 .01
❑ 434 Bret Saberhagen HL .05 .01
❑ 435 Mel Rojas .05 .01
❑ 436 Ben McDonald .05 .01
❑ 437 Tim Crews .05 .01
❑ 438 Rex Hudler .05 .01
❑ 439 Chico Walker .05 .01
❑ 440 Kurt Stillwell .05 .01
❑ 441 Tony Gwynn .30 .10
❑ 442 John Smoltz .15 .05
❑ 443 Lloyd Moseby .05 .01
❑ 444 Mike Schooler .05 .01
❑ 445 Joe Grahe .05 .01
❑ 446 Dwight Gooden .10 .02
❑ 447 Oil Can Boyd .05 .01
❑ 448 John Marzano .05 .01
❑ 449 Bret Barberie .05 .01
❑ 450 Mike Maddux .05 .01
❑ 451 Jeff Reed .05 .01
❑ 452 Dale Sveum .05 .01
❑ 453 Jose Uribe .05 .01
❑ 454 Bob Scanlan .05 .01
❑ 455 Kevin Appier .10 .02
❑ 456 Jeff Huson .05 .01
❑ 457 Ken Patterson .05 .01
❑ 458 Ricky Jordan .05 .01
❑ 459 Tom Candiotti .05 .01
❑ 460 Lee Stevens .05 .01
❑ 461 Rod Beck RC .25 .08
❑ 462 Dave Valle .05 .01
❑ 463 Scott Erickson .05 .01
❑ 464 Chris Jones .05 .01
❑ 465 Mark Carreon .05 .01
❑ 466 Rob Ducey .05 .01
❑ 467 Jim Corsi .05 .01
❑ 468 Jeff King .05 .01
❑ 469 Curt Young .05 .01
❑ 470 Bo Jackson .25 .08
❑ 471 Chris Bosio .05 .01
❑ 472 Jamie Quirk .05 .01
❑ 473 Jesse Orosco .05 .01
❑ 474 Alvaro Espinoza .05 .01
❑ 475 Joe Orsulak .05 .01
❑ 476 Checklist 397-477 .05 .01
❑ 477 Gerald Young .05 .01
❑ 478 Wally Backman .05 .01
❑ 479 Juan Bell .05 .01
❑ 480 Mike Scioscia .05 .01
❑ 481 Omar Olivares .05 .01
❑ 482 Francisco Cabrera .05 .01
❑ 483 Greg Swindell UER
(Shown on Indians&
but listed .05 .01
❑ 484 Terry Leach .05 .01
❑ 485 Tommy Gregg .05 .01
❑ 486 Scott Aldred .05 .01
❑ 487 Greg Briley .05 .01
❑ 488 Phil Plantier .05 .01
❑ 489 Curtis Wilkerson .05 .01
❑ 490 Tom Brunansky .05 .01
❑ 491 Mike Fetters .05 .01
❑ 492 Frank Castillo .05 .01
❑ 493 Joe Boever .05 .01
❑ 494 Kirt Manwaring .05 .01
❑ 495 Wilson Alvarez HL .05 .01
❑ 496 Gene Larkin .05 .01
❑ 497 Gary DiSarcina .05 .01
❑ 498 Frank Viola .10 .02
❑ 499 Manuel Lee .05 .01
❑ 500 Albert Belle .10 .02
❑ 501 Stan Belinda .05 .01
❑ 502 Dwight Evans .15 .05
❑ 503 Eric Davis .10 .02
❑ 504 Darren Holmes .05 .01
❑ 505 Mike Bordick .05 .01
❑ 506 Dave Hansen .05 .01
❑ 507 Lee Guetterman .05 .01
❑ 508 Keith Mitchell .05 .01
❑ 509 Melido Perez .05 .01
❑ 510 Dickie Thon .05 .01
❑ 511 Mark Williamson .05 .01
❑ 512 Mark Salas .05 .01
❑ 513 Milt Thompson .05 .01
❑ 514 Mo Vaughn .10 .02
❑ 515 Jim Deshaies .05 .01
❑ 516 Rich Garces .05 .01
❑ 517 Lonnie Smith .05 .01
❑ 518 Spike Owen .05 .01
❑ 519 Tracy Jones .05 .01
❑ 520 Greg Maddux .40 .15
❑ 521 Carlos Martinez .05 .01
❑ 522 Neal Heaton .05 .01
❑ 523 Mike Greenwell .05 .01
❑ 524 Andy Benes .05 .01
❑ 525 Jeff Schaefer UER .05 .01
❑ 526 Mike Sharperson .05 .01
❑ 527 Wade Taylor .05 .01
❑ 528 Jerome Walton .05 .01
❑ 529 Storm Davis .05 .01
❑ 530 Jose Hernandez RC .25 .08
❑ 531 Mark Langston .05 .01
❑ 532 Rob Deer .05 .01
❑ 533 Geronimo Pena .05 .01
❑ 534 Juan Guzman .05 .01
❑ 535 Pete Schourek .05 .01
❑ 536 Todd Benzinger .05 .01
❑ 537 Billy Hatcher .05 .01
❑ 538 Tom Foley .05 .01
❑ 539 Dave Cochrane .05 .01
❑ 540 Mariano Duncan .05 .01
❑ 541 Edwin Nunez .05 .01
❑ 542 Rance Mulliniks .05 .01
❑ 543 Carlton Fisk .15 .05
❑ 544 Luis Aquino .05 .01
❑ 545 Ricky Bones .05 .01
❑ 546 Craig Grebeck .05 .01
❑ 547 Charlie Hayes .05 .01
❑ 548 Jose Canseco .15 .05
❑ 549 Andujar Cedeno .05 .01
❑ 550 Geno Petralli .05 .01
❑ 551 Javier Ortiz .05 .01
❑ 552 Rudy Seanez .05 .01
❑ 553 Rich Gedman .05 .01
❑ 554 Eric Plunk .05 .01
❑ 555 N.Ryan/G.Gossage HL .40 .15
❑ 556 Checklist 478-555 .05 .01
❑ 557 Greg Colbrunn .05 .01
❑ 558 Chito Martinez .05 .01
❑ 559 Darryl Strawberry .10 .02
❑ 560 Luis Alicea .05 .01
❑ 561 Dwight Smith .05 .01
❑ 562 Torry Shumport .05 .01
❑ 563 Jim Vatcher .05 .01
❑ 564 Deion Sanders .15 .05
❑ 565 Walt Terrell .05 .01
❑ 566 Dave Burba .05 .01
❑ 567 Dave Howard .05 .01
❑ 568 Todd Hundley .05 .01

❑ 569 Jack Daugherty .05 .01
❑ 570 Scott Cooper .05 .01
❑ 571 Bill Sampen .05 .01
❑ 572 Jose Melendez .05 .01
❑ 573 Freddie Benavides .05 .01
❑ 574 Jim Gantner .05 .01
❑ 575 Trevor Wilson .05 .01
❑ 576 Ryne Sandberg .40 .15
❑ 577 Kevin Seitzer .05 .01
❑ 578 Gerald Alexander .05 .01
❑ 579 Mike Huff .05 .01
❑ 580 Von Hayes .05 .01
❑ 581 Derek Bell .10 .02
❑ 582 Mike Stanley .05 .01
❑ 583 Kevin Mitchell .05 .01
❑ 584 Mike Jackson .05 .01
❑ 585 Dan Gladden .05 .01
❑ 586 Ted Power UER
(Wrong year given for
signing with .05 .01
❑ 587 Jeff Innis .05 .01
❑ 588 Bob MacDonald .05 .01
❑ 589 Jose Tolentino .05 .01
❑ 590 Bob Patterson .05 .01
❑ 591 Scott Brosius RC .40 .15
❑ 592 Frank Thomas .25 .08
❑ 593 Darryl Hamilton .05 .01
❑ 594 Kirk Dressendorfer .05 .01
❑ 595 Jeff Shaw .05 .01
❑ 596 Don Mattingly .60 .25
❑ 597 Glenn Davis .05 .01
❑ 598 Andy Mota .05 .01
❑ 599 Jason Grimsley .05 .01
❑ 600 Jim Poole .05 .01
❑ 601 Jim Gott .05 .01
❑ 602 Stan Royer .05 .01
❑ 603 Marvin Freeman .05 .01
❑ 604 Denis Boucher .05 .01
❑ 605 Denny Neagle .10 .02
❑ 606 Mark Lemke .05 .01
❑ 607 Jerry Don Gleaton .05 .01
❑ 608 Brent Knackert .05 .01
❑ 609 Carlos Quintana .05 .01
❑ 610 Bobby Bonilla .10 .02
❑ 611 Joe Hesketh .05 .01
❑ 612 Daryl Boston .05 .01
❑ 613 Shawon Dunston .05 .01
❑ 614 Danny Cox .05 .01
❑ 615 Darren Lewis .05 .01
❑ 616 Mercker/Pena/Wohlers UER .05 .01
❑ 617 Kirby Puckett .25 .08
❑ 618 Franklin Stubbs .05 .01
❑ 619 Chris Donnels .05 .01
❑ 620 David Wells UER .10 .02
❑ 621 Mike Aldrete .05 .01
❑ 622 Bob Kipper .05 .01
❑ 623 Anthony Telford .05 .01
❑ 624 Randy Myers .05 .01
❑ 625 Willie Randolph .10 .02
❑ 626 Joe Slusarski .05 .01
❑ 627 John Wetteland .10 .02
❑ 628 Greg Cadaret .05 .01
❑ 629 Tom Glavine .15 .05
❑ 630 Wilson Alvarez .05 .01
❑ 631 Wally Ritchie .05 .01
❑ 632 Mike Mussina .25 .08
❑ 633 Mark Leiter .05 .01
❑ 634 Gerald Perry .05 .01
❑ 635 Matt Young .05 .01
❑ 636 Checklist 556-635 .05 .01
❑ 637 Scott Hemond .05 .01
❑ 638 David West .05 .01
❑ 639 Jim Clancy .05 .01
❑ 640 Doug Piatt UER
(Not born in 1955 as
on card; inc .05 .01
❑ 641 Omar Vizquel .15 .05
❑ 642 Rick Sutcliffe .10 .02
❑ 643 Glenallen Hill .05 .01
❑ 644 Gary Varsho .05 .01
❑ 645 Tony Fossas .05 .01
❑ 646 Jack Howell .05 .01
❑ 647 Jim Campanis .05 .01
❑ 648 Chris Gwynn .05 .01
❑ 649 Jim Leyritz .05 .01
❑ 650 Chuck McElroy .05 .01
❑ 651 Sean Berry .05 .01
❑ 652 Donald Harris .05 .01
❑ 653 Don Slaught .05 .01
❑ 654 Rusty Meacham .05 .01
❑ 655 Scott Terry .05 .01
❑ 656 Ramon Martinez .05 .01
❑ 657 Keith Miller .05 .01
❑ 658 Ramon Garcia .05 .01
❑ 659 Milt Hill .05 .01
❑ 660 Steve Frey .05 .01
❑ 661 Bob McClure .05 .01
❑ 662 Ced Landrum .05 .01
❑ 663 Doug Henry RC .10 .02
❑ 664 Candy Maldonado .05 .01
❑ 665 Carl Willis .05 .01
❑ 666 Jeff Montgomery .05 .01
❑ 667 Craig Shipley .05 .01
❑ 668 Warren Newson .05 .01
❑ 669 Mickey Morandini .05 .01
❑ 670 Brook Jacoby .05 .01
❑ 671 Ryan Bowen .05 .01
❑ 672 Bill Krueger .05 .01
❑ 673 Rob Mallicoat .05 .01
❑ 674 Doug Jones .05 .01
❑ 675 Scott Livingstone .05 .01
❑ 676 Danny Tartabull .05 .01
❑ 677 Joe Carter HL .05 .01
❑ 678 Cecil Espy .05 .01
❑ 679 Randy Velarde .05 .01
❑ 680 Bruce Ruffin .05 .01
❑ 681 Ted Wood .05 .01
❑ 682 Dan Plesac .05 .01
❑ 683 Eric Bullock .05 .01
❑ 684 Junior Ortiz .05 .01
❑ 685 Dave Hollins .05 .01
❑ 686 Dennis Martinez .10 .02
❑ 687 Larry Andersen .05 .01
❑ 688 Doug Simons .05 .01
❑ 689 Tim Spehr .05 .01
❑ 690 Calvin Jones .05 .01
❑ 691 Mark Guthrie .05 .01
❑ 692 Alfredo Griffin .05 .01
❑ 693 Joe Carter .10 .02
❑ 694 Terry Mathews .05 .01
❑ 695 Pascual Perez .05 .01
❑ 696 Gene Nelson .05 .01
❑ 697 Gerald Williams .05 .01
❑ 698 Chris Cron .05 .01
❑ 699 Steve Buechele .05 .01
❑ 700 Paul McClellan .05 .01
❑ 701 Jim Lindeman .05 .01
❑ 702 Francisco Oliveras .05 .01
❑ 703 Rob Maurer .05 .01
❑ 704 Pat Hentgen .05 .01
❑ 705 Jaime Navarro .05 .01
❑ 706 Mike Magnante RC .10 .02
❑ 707 Nolan Ryan 1.00 .40
❑ 708 Bobby Thigpen .05 .01
❑ 709 John Cerutti .05 .01
❑ 710 Steve Wilson .05 .01
❑ 711 Hensley Meulens .05 .01
❑ 712 Rheal Cormier .05 .01
❑ 713 Scott Bradley .05 .01
❑ 714 Mitch Webster .05 .01
❑ 715 Roger Mason .05 .01
❑ 716 Checklist 636-716 .05 .01
❑ 717 Jeff Fassero .05 .01
❑ 718 Cal Eldred .05 .01
❑ 719 Sid Fernandez .05 .01
❑ 720 Bob Zupcic RC .10 .02
❑ 721 Jose Offerman .05 .01
❑ 722 Cliff Brantley .05 .01
❑ 723 Ron Darling .05 .01
❑ 724 Dave Stieb .05 .01
❑ 725 Hector Villanueva .05 .01
❑ 726 Mike Hartley .05 .01
❑ 727 Arthur Rhodes .05 .01
❑ 728 Randy Bush .05 .01
❑ 729 Steve Sax .05 .01
❑ 730 Dave Otto .05 .01
❑ 731 John Wehner .05 .01
❑ 732 Dave Martinez .05 .01
❑ 733 Ruben Amaro .05 .01
❑ 734 Billy Ripken .05 .01
❑ 735 Steve Farr .05 .01
❑ 736 Shawn Abner .05 .01
❑ 737 Gil Heredia RC .25 .08
❑ 738 Ron Jones .05 .01
❑ 739 Tony Castillo .05 .01
❑ 740 Sammy Sosa .25 .08
❑ 741 Julio Franco .10 .02
❑ 742 Tim Naehring .05 .01
❑ 743 Steve Wapnick .05 .01
❑ 744 Craig Wilson .05 .01
❑ 745 Darrin Chapin .05 .01
❑ 746 Chris George .05 .01
❑ 747 Mike Simms .05 .01
❑ 748 Rosario Rodriguez .05 .01
❑ 749 Skeeter Barnes .05 .01
❑ 750 Roger McDowell .05 .01
❑ 751 Dann Howitt .05 .01
❑ 752 Paul Sorrento .05 .01
❑ 753 Braulio Castillo .05 .01
❑ 754 Yorkis Perez .05 .01
❑ 755 Willie Fraser .05 .01
❑ 756 Jeremy Hernandez RC .10 .02
❑ 757 Curt Schilling .15 .05
❑ 758 Steve Lyons .05 .01
❑ 759 Dave Anderson .05 .01
❑ 760 Willie Banks .05 .01
❑ 761 Mark Leonard .05 .01
❑ 762 Jack Armstrong
(Listed on Indians&
but shown on .05 .01
❑ 763 Scott Servais .05 .01
❑ 764 Ray Stephens .05 .01
❑ 765 Junior Noboa .05 .01
❑ 766 Jim Olander .05 .01
❑ 767 Joe Magrane .05 .01
❑ 768 Lance Blankenship .05 .01
❑ 769 Mike Humphreys .05 .01
❑ 770 Jarvis Brown .05 .01
❑ 771 Damon Berryhill .05 .01
❑ 772 Alejandro Pena .05 .01
❑ 773 Jose Mesa .05 .01
❑ 774 Gary Cooper .05 .01
❑ 775 Carney Lansford .10 .02
❑ 776 Mike Bielecki
(Shown on Cubs&
but listed on Brav .05 .01
❑ 777 Charlie O'Brien .05 .01
❑ 778 Carlos Hernandez .05 .01
❑ 779 Howard Farmer .05 .01
❑ 780 Mike Stanton .05 .01
❑ 781 Reggie Harris .05 .01
❑ 782 Xavier Hernandez .05 .01
❑ 783 Bryan Hickerson RC .10 .02
❑ 784 Checklist 717-784
and BC1-BC8 .05 .01

1993 Donruss

❑ COMPLETE SET (792) 30.00 12.00
❑ COMPLETE SERIES 1 (396) 15.00 6.00
❑ COMPLETE SERIES 2 (396) 15.00 6.00
❑ 1 Craig Lefferts .10 .02
❑ 2 Kent Mercker .10 .02
❑ 3 Phil Plantier .10 .02
❑ 4 Alex Arias .10 .02
❑ 5 Julio Valera .10 .02
❑ 6 Dan Wilson .20 .07
❑ 7 Frank Thomas .50 .20
❑ 8 Eric Anthony .10 .02
❑ 9 Derek Lilliquist .10 .02
❑ 10 Rafael Bournigal .10 .02

❑ 11	Manny Alexander	.10	.02
❑ 12	Bret Barberie	.10	.02
❑ 13	Mickey Tettleton	.10	.02
❑ 14	Anthony Young	.10	.02
❑ 15	Tim Spehr	.10	.02
❑ 16	Bob Ayrault	.10	.02
❑ 17	Bill Wegman	.10	.02
❑ 18	Jay Bell	.20	.07
❑ 19	Rick Aguilera	.10	.02
❑ 20	Todd Zeile	.10	.02
❑ 21	Steve Farr	.10	.02
❑ 22	Andy Benes	.10	.02
❑ 23	Lance Blankenship	.10	.02
❑ 24	Ted Wood	.10	.02
❑ 25	Omar Vizquel	.30	.10
❑ 26	Steve Avery	.10	.02
❑ 27	Brian Bohanon	.10	.02
❑ 28	Rick Wilkins	.10	.02
❑ 29	Devon White	.20	.07
❑ 30	Bobby Ayala RC	.10	.02
❑ 31	Leo Gomez	.10	.02
❑ 32	Mike Simms	.10	.02
❑ 33	Ellis Burks	.20	.07
❑ 34	Steve Wilson	.10	.02
❑ 35	Jim Abbott	.30	.10
❑ 36	Tim Wallach	.10	.02
❑ 37	Wilson Alvarez	.10	.02
❑ 38	Daryl Boston	.10	.02
❑ 39	Sandy Alomar Jr.	.10	.02
❑ 40	Mitch Williams	.10	.02
❑ 41	Rico Brogna	.10	.02
❑ 42	Gary Varsho	.10	.02
❑ 43	Kevin Appier	.20	.07
❑ 44	Eric Wedge RC	.10	.02
❑ 45	Dante Bichette	.20	.07
❑ 46	Jose Oquendo	.10	.02
❑ 47	Mike Trombley	.10	.02
❑ 48	Dan Walters	.10	.02
❑ 49	Gerald Williams	.10	.02
❑ 50	Bud Black	.10	.02
❑ 51	Bobby Witt	.10	.02
❑ 52	Mark Davis	.10	.02
❑ 53	Shawn Barton RC	.10	.02
❑ 54	Paul Assenmacher	.10	.02
❑ 55	Kevin Reimer	.10	.02
❑ 56	Billy Ashley	.10	.02
❑ 57	Eddie Zosky	.10	.02
❑ 58	Chris Sabo	.10	.02
❑ 59	Billy Ripken	.10	.02
❑ 60	Scooter Tucker	.10	.02
❑ 61	Tim Wakefield	.50	.20
❑ 62	Mitch Webster	.10	.02
❑ 63	Jack Clark	.20	.07
❑ 64	Mark Gardner	.10	.02
❑ 65	Lee Stevens	.10	.02
❑ 66	Todd Hundley	.10	.02
❑ 67	Bobby Thigpen	.10	.02
❑ 68	Dave Hollins	.10	.02
❑ 69	Jack Armstrong	.10	.02
❑ 70	Alex Cole	.10	.02
❑ 71	Mark Carreon	.10	.02
❑ 72	Todd Worrell	.10	.02
❑ 73	Steve Shifflett	.10	.02
❑ 74	Jerald Clark	.10	.02
❑ 75	Paul Molitor	.20	.07
❑ 76	Larry Carter RC	.10	.02
❑ 77	Rich Rowland	.10	.02
❑ 78	Damon Berryhill	.10	.02
❑ 79	Willie Banks	.10	.02
❑ 80	Hector Villanueva	.10	.02
❑ 81	Mike Gallego	.10	.02
❑ 82	Tim Belcher	.10	.02
❑ 83	Mike Bordick	.10	.02
❑ 84	Craig Biggio	.30	.10
❑ 85	Lance Parrish	.20	.07
❑ 86	Brett Butler	.20	.07
❑ 87	Mike Timlin	.10	.02
❑ 88	Brian Barnes	.10	.02
❑ 89	Brady Anderson	.20	.07
❑ 90	D.J. Dozier	.10	.02
❑ 91	Frank Viola	.20	.07
❑ 92	Darren Daulton	.20	.07
❑ 93	Chad Curtis	.10	.02
❑ 94	Zane Smith	.10	.02
❑ 95	George Bell	.10	.02
❑ 96	Rex Hudler	.10	.02
❑ 97	Mark Whiten	.10	.02
❑ 98	Tim Teufel	.10	.02
❑ 99	Kevin Ritz	.10	.02
❑ 100	Jeff Brantley	.10	.02
❑ 101	Jeff Conine	.20	.07
❑ 102	Vinny Castilla	.50	.20
❑ 103	Greg Vaughn	.10	.02
❑ 104	Steve Buechele	.10	.02
❑ 105	Darren Reed	.10	.02
❑ 106	Bip Roberts	.10	.02
❑ 107	John Habyan	.10	.02
❑ 108	Scott Servais	.10	.02
❑ 109	Walt Weiss	.10	.02
❑ 110	J.T.Snow RC	.30	.10
❑ 111	Jay Buhner	.20	.07
❑ 112	Darryl Strawberry	.20	.07
❑ 113	Roger Pavlik	.10	.02
❑ 114	Chris Nabholz	.10	.02
❑ 115	Pat Borders	.10	.02
❑ 116	Pat Howell	.10	.02
❑ 117	Gregg Olson	.10	.02
❑ 118	Curt Schilling	.20	.07
❑ 119	Roger Clemens	1.00	.40
❑ 120	Victor Cole	.10	.02
❑ 121	Gary DiSarcina	.10	.02
❑ 122	Checklist 1-80 Gary Carter and Kirt Manwaring	.10	.02
❑ 123	Steve Sax	.10	.02
❑ 124	Chuck Carr	.10	.02
❑ 125	Mark Lewis	.10	.02
❑ 126	Tony Gwynn	.60	.25
❑ 127	Travis Fryman	.20	.07
❑ 128	Dave Burba	.10	.02
❑ 129	Wally Joyner	.20	.07
❑ 130	John Smoltz	.30	.10
❑ 131	Cal Eldred	.10	.02
❑ 132	Checklist 81-159 (Roberto Alomar and Devon White	.20	.07
❑ 133	Arthur Rhodes	.10	.02
❑ 134	Jeff Blauser	.10	.02
❑ 135	Scott Cooper	.10	.02
❑ 136	Doug Strange	.10	.02
❑ 137	Luis Sojo	.10	.02
❑ 138	Jeff Branson	.10	.02
❑ 139	Alex Fernandez	.10	.02
❑ 140	Ken Caminiti	.20	.07
❑ 141	Charles Nagy	.10	.02
❑ 142	Tom Candiotti	.10	.02
❑ 143	Willie Greene	.10	.02
❑ 144	John Vander Wal	.10	.02
❑ 145	Kurt Knudsen	.10	.02
❑ 146	John Franco	.20	.07
❑ 147	Eddie Pierce RC	.10	.02
❑ 148	Kim Batiste	.10	.02
❑ 149	Darren Holmes	.10	.02
❑ 150	Steve Cooke	.10	.02
❑ 151	Terry Jorgensen	.10	.02
❑ 152	Mark Clark	.10	.02
❑ 153	Randy Velarde	.10	.02
❑ 154	Greg W. Harris	.10	.02
❑ 155	Kevin Campbell	.10	.02
❑ 156	John Burkett	.10	.02
❑ 157	Kevin Mitchell	.10	.02
❑ 158	Deion Sanders	.30	.10
❑ 159	Jose Canseco	.30	.10
❑ 160	Jeff Hartsock	.10	.02
❑ 161	Tom Quinlan RC	.10	.02
❑ 162	Tim Pugh RC	.10	.02
❑ 163	Glenn Davis	.10	.02
❑ 164	Shane Reynolds	.10	.02
❑ 165	Jody Reed	.10	.02
❑ 166	Mike Sharperson	.10	.02
❑ 167	Scott Lewis	.10	.02
❑ 168	Dennis Martinez	.20	.07
❑ 169	Scott Radinsky	.10	.02
❑ 170	Dave Gallagher	.10	.02
❑ 171	Jim Thome	.30	.10
❑ 172	Terry Mulholland	.10	.02
❑ 173	Milt Cuyler	.10	.02
❑ 174	Bob Patterson	.10	.02
❑ 175	Jeff Montgomery	.10	.02
❑ 176	Tim Salmon	.30	.10
❑ 177	Franklin Stubbs	.10	.02
❑ 178	Donovan Osborne	.10	.02
❑ 179	Jeff Reboulet	.10	.02
❑ 180	Jeremy Hernandez	.10	.02
❑ 181	Charlie Hayes	.10	.02
❑ 182	Matt Williams	.20	.07
❑ 183	Mike Raczka	.10	.02
❑ 184	Francisco Cabrera	.10	.02
❑ 185	Rich DeLucia	.10	.02
❑ 186	Sammy Sosa	.50	.20
❑ 187	Ivan Rodriguez	.30	.10
❑ 188	Bret Boone	.20	.07
❑ 189	Juan Guzman	.10	.02
❑ 190	Tom Browning	.10	.02
❑ 191	Randy Milligan	.10	.02
❑ 192	Steve Finley	.20	.07
❑ 193	John Patterson RR	.10	.02
❑ 194	Kip Gross	.10	.02
❑ 195	Tony Fossas	.10	.02
❑ 196	Ivan Calderon	.10	.02
❑ 197	Junior Felix	.10	.02
❑ 198	Pete Schourek	.10	.02
❑ 199	Craig Grebeck	.10	.02
❑ 200	Juan Bell	.10	.02
❑ 201	Glenallen Hill	.10	.02
❑ 202	Danny Jackson	.10	.02
❑ 203	John Kiely	.10	.02
❑ 204	Bob Tewksbury	.10	.02
❑ 205	Kevin Koslofski	.10	.02
❑ 206	Craig Shipley	.10	.02
❑ 207	John Jaha	.10	.02
❑ 208	Royce Clayton	.10	.02
❑ 209	Mike Piazza	3.00	1.25
❑ 210	Ron Gant	.20	.07
❑ 211	Scott Erickson	.10	.02
❑ 212	Doug Dascenzo	.10	.02
❑ 213	Andy Stankiewicz	.10	.02
❑ 214	Geronimo Berroa	.10	.02
❑ 215	Dennis Eckersley	.20	.07
❑ 216	Al Osuna	.10	.02
❑ 217	Tino Martinez	.30	.10
❑ 218	Henry Rodriguez	.10	.02
❑ 219	Ed Sprague	.10	.02
❑ 220	Ken Hill	.10	.02
❑ 221	Chito Martinez	.10	.02
❑ 222	Bret Saberhagen	.20	.07
❑ 223	Mike Greenwell	.10	.02
❑ 224	Mickey Morandini	.10	.02
❑ 225	Chuck Finley	.20	.07
❑ 226	Denny Neagle	.20	.07
❑ 227	Kirk McCaskill	.10	.02
❑ 228	Rheal Cormier	.10	.02
❑ 229	Paul Sorrento	.10	.02
❑ 230	Darrin Jackson	.10	.02
❑ 231	Rob Deer	.10	.02
❑ 232	Bill Swift	.10	.02
❑ 233	Kevin McReynolds	.10	.02
❑ 234	Terry Pendleton	.20	.07
❑ 235	Dave Nilsson	.10	.02
❑ 236	Chuck McElroy	.10	.02
❑ 237	Derek Parks	.10	.02
❑ 238	Norm Charlton	.10	.02
❑ 239	Matt Nokes	.10	.02
❑ 240	Juan Guerrero	.10	.02
❑ 241	Jeff Parrett	.10	.02
❑ 242	Ryan Thompson	.10	.02
❑ 243	Dave Fleming	.10	.02
❑ 244	Dave Hansen	.10	.02
❑ 245	Monty Fariss	.10	.02
❑ 246	Archi Cianfrocco	.10	.02
❑ 247	Pat Hentgen	.10	.02
❑ 248	Bill Pecota	.10	.02
❑ 249	Ben McDonald	.10	.02
❑ 250	Cliff Brantley	.10	.02
❑ 251	John Valentin	.10	.02
❑ 252	Jeff King	.10	.02
❑ 253	Reggie Williams	.10	.02
❑ 254	Checklist 160-238	.10	.02
❑ 255	Ozzie Guillen	.20	.07
❑ 256	Mike Perez	.10	.02
❑ 257	Thomas Howard	.10	.02
❑ 258	Kurt Stillwell	.10	.02
❑ 259	Mike Henneman	.10	.02
❑ 260	Steve Decker	.10	.02
❑ 261	Brent Mayne	.10	.02
❑ 262	Otis Nixon	.10	.02
❑ 263	Mark Kiefer	.10	.02
❑ 264	Checklist 239-317		

(Don Mattingly
and Mike Bordic .30 .10
❑ 265 Richie Lewis RC .10 .02
❑ 266 Pat Gomez RC .10 .02
❑ 267 Scott Taylor .10 .02
❑ 268 Shawon Dunston .10 .02
❑ 269 Greg Myers .10 .02
❑ 270 Tim Costo .10 .02
❑ 271 Greg Hibbard .10 .02
❑ 272 Pete Harnisch .10 .02
❑ 273 Dave Mlicki .10 .02
❑ 274 Orel Hershiser .20 .07
❑ 275 Sean Berry RR .10 .02
❑ 276 Doug Simons .10 .02
❑ 277 John Doherty .10 .02
❑ 278 Eddie Murray .50 .20
❑ 279 Chris Haney .10 .02
❑ 280 Stan Javier .10 .02
❑ 281 Jaime Navarro .10 .02
❑ 282 Orlando Merced .10 .02
❑ 283 Kent Hrbek .20 .07
❑ 284 Bernard Gilkey .10 .02
❑ 285 Russ Springer .10 .02
❑ 286 Mike Maddux .10 .02
❑ 287 Eric Fox .10 .02
❑ 288 Mark Leonard .10 .02
❑ 289 Tim Leary .10 .02
❑ 290 Brian Hunter .10 .02
❑ 291 Donald Harris .10 .02
❑ 292 Bob Scanlan .10 .02
❑ 293 Turner Ward .10 .02
❑ 294 Hal Morris .10 .02
❑ 295 Jimmy Poole .10 .02
❑ 296 Doug Jones .10 .02
❑ 297 Tony Pena .10 .02
❑ 298 Ramon Martinez .10 .02
❑ 299 Tim Fortugno .10 .02
❑ 300 Marquis Grissom .20 .07
❑ 301 Lance Johnson .10 .02
❑ 302 Jeff Kent .50 .20
❑ 303 Reggie Jefferson .10 .02
❑ 304 Wes Chamberlain .10 .02
❑ 305 Shawn Hare .10 .02
❑ 306 Mike LaValliere .10 .02
❑ 307 Gregg Jefferies .10 .02
❑ 308 Troy Neel .10 .02
❑ 309 Pat Listach .10 .02
❑ 310 Geronimo Pena .10 .02
❑ 311 Pedro Munoz .10 .02
❑ 312 Guillermo Velasquez .10 .02
❑ 313 Roberto Kelly .10 .02
❑ 314 Mike Jackson .10 .02
❑ 315 Rickey Henderson .50 .20
❑ 316 Mark Lemke .10 .02
❑ 317 Erik Hanson .10 .02
❑ 318 Derrick May .10 .02
❑ 319 Geno Petralli .10 .02
❑ 320 Melvin Nieves .10 .02
❑ 321 Doug Linton .10 .02
❑ 322 Rob Dibble .20 .07
❑ 323 Chris Hoiles .10 .02
❑ 324 Jimmy Jones .10 .02
❑ 325 Dave Staton .10 .02
❑ 326 Pedro Martinez 1.00 .40
❑ 327 Paul Quantrill .10 .02
❑ 328 Greg Colbrunn .10 .02
❑ 329 Hilly Hathaway RC .10 .02
❑ 330 Jeff Innis .10 .02
❑ 331 Ron Karkovice .10 .02
❑ 332 Keith Shepherd RC .10 .02
❑ 333 Alan Embree .10 .02
❑ 334 Paul Wagner .10 .02
❑ 335 Dave Haas .10 .02
❑ 336 Ozzie Canseco .10 .02
❑ 337 Bill Sampen .10 .02
❑ 338 Rich Rodriguez .10 .02
❑ 339 Dean Palmer .20 .07
❑ 340 Greg Litton .10 .02
❑ 341 Jim Tatum RC .10 .02
❑ 342 Todd Haney RC .10 .02
❑ 343 Larry Casian .10 .02
❑ 344 Ryne Sandberg .75 .30
❑ 345 Sterling Hitchcock RC .20 .07
❑ 346 Chris Hammond .10 .02
❑ 347 Vince Horsman .10 .02
❑ 348 Butch Henry .10 .02
❑ 349 Dann Howitt .10 .02
❑ 350 Roger McDowell .10 .02
❑ 351 Jack Morris .20 .07
❑ 352 Bill Krueger .10 .02
❑ 353 Cris Colon .10 .02
❑ 354 Joe Vitko .10 .02
❑ 355 Willie McGee .20 .07
❑ 356 Jay Baller .10 .02
❑ 357 Pat Mahomes .10 .02
❑ 358 Roger Mason .10 .02
❑ 359 Jerry Nielsen .10 .02
❑ 360 Tom Pagnozzi .10 .02
❑ 361 Kevin Baez .10 .02
❑ 362 Tim Scott .10 .02
❑ 363 Domingo Martinez RC .10 .02
❑ 364 Kirt Manwaring .10 .02
❑ 365 Rafael Palmeiro .30 .10
❑ 366 Ray Lankford .20 .07
❑ 367 Tim McIntosh .10 .02
❑ 368 Jessie Hollins .10 .02
❑ 369 Scott Leius .10 .02
❑ 370 Bill Doran .10 .02
❑ 371 Sam Militello .10 .02
❑ 372 Ryan Bowen .10 .02
❑ 373 Dave Henderson .10 .02
❑ 374 Dan Smith .10 .02
❑ 375 Steve Reed RC .10 .02
❑ 376 Jose Offerman .10 .02
❑ 377 Kevin Brown .20 .07
❑ 378 Darrin Fletcher .10 .02
❑ 379 Duane Ward .10 .02
❑ 380 Wayne Kirby .10 .02
❑ 381 Steve Scarsone .10 .02
❑ 382 Mariano Duncan .10 .02
❑ 383 Ken Ryan RC .10 .02
❑ 384 Lloyd McClendon .10 .02
❑ 385 Brian Holman .10 .02
❑ 386 Braulio Castillo .10 .02
❑ 387 Danny Leon .10 .02
❑ 388 Omar Olivares .10 .02
❑ 389 Kevin Wickander .10 .02
❑ 390 Fred McGriff .30 .10
❑ 391 Phil Clark .10 .02
❑ 392 Darren Lewis .10 .02
❑ 393 Phil Hiatt .10 .02
❑ 394 Mike Morgan .10 .02
❑ 395 Shane Mack .10 .02
❑ 396 Checklist 318-396
(Dennis Eckersley
and Art Kusn .20 .07
❑ 397 David Segui .10 .02
❑ 398 Rafael Belliard .10 .02
❑ 399 Tim Naehring .10 .02
❑ 400 Frank Castillo .10 .02
❑ 401 Joe Grahe .10 .02
❑ 402 Reggie Sanders .20 .07
❑ 403 Roberto Hernandez .10 .02
❑ 404 Luis Gonzalez .20 .07
❑ 405 Carlos Baerga .10 .02
❑ 406 Carlos Hernandez .10 .02
❑ 407 Pedro Astacio .10 .02
❑ 408 Mel Rojas .10 .02
❑ 409 Scott Livingstone .10 .02
❑ 410 Chico Walker .10 .02
❑ 411 Brian McRae .10 .02
❑ 412 Ben Rivera .10 .02
❑ 413 Ricky Bones .10 .02
❑ 414 Andy Van Slyke .30 .10
❑ 415 Chuck Knoblauch .20 .07
❑ 416 Luis Alicea .10 .02
❑ 417 Bob Wickman .10 .02
❑ 418 Doug Brocail .10 .02
❑ 419 Scott Brosius .20 .07
❑ 420 Rod Beck .10 .02
❑ 421 Edgar Martinez .30 .10
❑ 422 Ryan Klesko .20 .07
❑ 423 Nolan Ryan 2.00 .75
❑ 424 Rey Sanchez .10 .02
❑ 425 Roberto Alomar .30 .10
❑ 426 Barry Larkin .30 .10
❑ 427 Mike Mussina .30 .10
❑ 428 Jeff Bagwell .30 .10
❑ 429 Mo Vaughn .20 .07
❑ 430 Eric Karros .20 .07
❑ 431 John Orton .10 .02
❑ 432 Wil Cordero .10 .02
❑ 433 Jack McDowell .10 .02
❑ 434 Howard Johnson .10 .02
❑ 435 Albert Belle .20 .07
❑ 436 John Kruk .20 .07
❑ 437 Skeeter Barnes .10 .02
❑ 438 Don Slaught .10 .02
❑ 439 Rusty Meacham .10 .02
❑ 440 Tim Laker RC .10 .02
❑ 441 Robin Yount .75 .30
❑ 442 Brian Jordan .20 .07
❑ 443 Kevin Tapani .10 .02
❑ 444 Gary Sheffield .20 .07
❑ 445 Rich Monteleone .10 .02
❑ 446 Will Clark .30 .10
❑ 447 Jerry Browne .10 .02
❑ 448 Jeff Treadway .10 .02
❑ 449 Mike Schooler .10 .02
❑ 450 Mike Harkey .10 .02
❑ 451 Julio Franco .20 .07
❑ 452 Kevin Young .20 .07
❑ 453 Kelly Gruber .10 .02
❑ 454 Jose Rijo .10 .02
❑ 455 Mike Devereaux .10 .02
❑ 456 Andujar Cedeno .10 .02
❑ 457 Damion Easley RR .10 .02
❑ 458 Kevin Gross .10 .02
❑ 459 Matt Young .10 .02
❑ 460 Matt Stairs .10 .02
❑ 461 Luis Polonia .10 .02
❑ 462 Dwight Gooden .20 .07
❑ 463 Warren Newson .10 .02
❑ 464 Jose DeLeon .10 .02
❑ 465 Jose Mesa .10 .02
❑ 466 Danny Cox .10 .02
❑ 467 Dan Gladden .10 .02
❑ 468 Gerald Perry .10 .02
❑ 469 Mike Boddicker .10 .02
❑ 470 Jeff Gardner .10 .02
❑ 471 Doug Henry .10 .02
❑ 472 Mike Benjamin .10 .02
❑ 473 Dan Peltier .10 .02
❑ 474 Mike Stanton .10 .02
❑ 475 John Smiley .10 .02
❑ 476 Dwight Smith .10 .02
❑ 477 Jim Leyritz .10 .02
❑ 478 Dwayne Henry .10 .02
❑ 479 Mark McGwire 1.25 .50
❑ 480 Pete Incaviglia .10 .02
❑ 481 Dave Cochrane .10 .02
❑ 482 Eric Davis .20 .07
❑ 483 John Olerud .20 .07
❑ 484 Kent Bottenfield .10 .02
❑ 485 Mark McLemore .10 .02
❑ 486 Dave Magadan .10 .02
❑ 487 John Marzano .10 .02
❑ 488 Ruben Amaro .10 .02
❑ 489 Rob Ducey .10 .02
❑ 490 Stan Belinda .10 .02
❑ 491 Dan Pasqua .10 .02
❑ 492 Joe Magrane .10 .02
❑ 493 Brook Jacoby .10 .02
❑ 494 Gene Harris .10 .02
❑ 495 Mark Leiter .10 .02
❑ 496 Bryan Hickerson .10 .02
❑ 497 Tom Gordon .10 .02
❑ 498 Pete Smith .10 .02
❑ 499 Chris Bosio .10 .02
❑ 500 Shawn Boskie .10 .02
❑ 501 Dave West .10 .02
❑ 502 Milt Hill .10 .02
❑ 503 Pat Kelly .10 .02
❑ 504 Joe Boever .10 .02
❑ 505 Terry Steinbach .10 .02
❑ 506 Butch Huskey .10 .02
❑ 507 David Valle .10 .02
❑ 508 Mike Scioscia .10 .02
❑ 509 Kenny Rogers .20 .07
❑ 510 Moises Alou .20 .07
❑ 511 David Wells .20 .07
❑ 512 Mackey Sasser .10 .02
❑ 513 Todd Frohwirth .10 .02
❑ 514 Ricky Jordan .10 .02
❑ 515 Mike Gardiner .10 .02
❑ 516 Gary Redus .10 .02
❑ 517 Gary Gaetti .20 .07
❑ 518 Checklist .10 .02

❑	519	Carlton Fisk	.30	.10
❑	520	Ozzie Smith	.75	.30
❑	521	Rod Nichols	.10	.02
❑	522	Benito Santiago	.20	.07
❑	523	Bill Gullickson	.10	.02
❑	524	Robby Thompson	.10	.02
❑	525	Mike Macfarlane	.10	.02
❑	526	Sid Bream	.10	.02
❑	527	Darryl Hamilton	.10	.02
❑	528	Checklist	.10	.02
❑	529	Jeff Tackett	.10	.02
❑	530	Greg Olson	.10	.02
❑	531	Bob Zupcic	.10	.02
❑	532	Mark Grace	.30	.10
❑	533	Steve Frey	.10	.02
❑	534	Dave Martinez	.10	.02
❑	535	Robin Ventura	.20	.07
❑	536	Casey Candaele	.10	.02
❑	537	Kenny Lofton	.20	.07
❑	538	Jay Howell	.10	.02
❑	539	Fernando Ramsey RC	.10	.02
❑	540	Larry Walker	.20	.07
❑	541	Cecil Fielder	.20	.07
❑	542	Lee Guetterman	.10	.02
❑	543	Keith Miller	.10	.02
❑	544	Len Dykstra	.20	.07
❑	545	B.J. Surhoff	.20	.07
❑	546	Bob Walk	.10	.02
❑	547	Brian Harper	.10	.02
❑	548	Lee Smith	.20	.07
❑	549	Danny Tartabull	.10	.02
❑	550	Frank Seminara	.10	.02
❑	551	Henry Mercedes	.10	.02
❑	552	Dave Righetti	.20	.07
❑	553	Ken Griffey Jr.	.75	.30
❑	554	Tom Glavine	.30	.10
❑	555	Juan Gonzalez	.20	.07
❑	556	Jim Bullinger	.10	.02
❑	557	Derek Bell	.10	.02
❑	558	Cesar Hernandez	.10	.02
❑	559	Cal Ripken	1.50	.60
❑	560	Eddie Taubensee	.10	.02
❑	561	John Flaherty	.10	.02
❑	562	Todd Benzinger	.10	.02
❑	563	Hubie Brooks	.10	.02
❑	564	Delino DeShields	.10	.02
❑	565	Tim Raines	.20	.07
❑	566	Sid Fernandez	.10	.02
❑	567	Steve Olin	.10	.02
❑	568	Tommy Greene	.10	.02
❑	569	Buddy Groom	.10	.02
❑	570	Randy Tomlin	.10	.02
❑	571	Hipolito Pichardo	.10	.02
❑	572	Rene Arocha RC	.20	.07
❑	573	Mike Fetters	.10	.02
❑	574	Felix Jose	.10	.02
❑	575	Gene Larkin	.10	.02
❑	576	Bruce Hurst	.10	.02
❑	577	Bernie Williams	.30	.10
❑	578	Trevor Wilson	.10	.02
❑	579	Bob Welch	.10	.02
❑	580	David Justice	.20	.07
❑	581	Randy Johnson	.50	.20
❑	582	Jose Vizcaino	.10	.02
❑	583	Jeff Huson	.10	.02
❑	584	Rob Maurer	.10	.02
❑	585	Todd Stottlemyre	.10	.02
❑	586	Joe Oliver	.10	.02
❑	587	Bob Milacki	.10	.02
❑	588	Rob Murphy	.10	.02
❑	589	Greg Pirkl	.10	.02
❑	590	Lenny Harris	.10	.02
❑	591	Luis Rivera	.10	.02
❑	592	John Wetteland	.20	.07
❑	593	Mark Langston	.10	.02
❑	594	Bobby Bonilla	.20	.07
❑	595	Esteban Beltre	.10	.02
❑	596	Mike Hartley	.10	.02
❑	597	Felix Fermin	.10	.02
❑	598	Carlos Garcia	.10	.02
❑	599	Frank Tanana	.10	.02
❑	600	Pedro Guerrero	.20	.07
❑	601	Terry Shumpert	.10	.02
❑	602	Wally Whitehurst	.10	.02
❑	603	Kevin Seitzer	.10	.02
❑	604	Chris James	.10	.02
❑	605	Greg Gohr	.10	.02
❑	606	Mark Wohlers	.10	.02
❑	607	Kirby Puckett	.50	.20
❑	608	Greg Maddux	.75	.30
❑	609	Don Mattingly	1.25	.50
❑	610	Greg Cadaret	.10	.02
❑	611	Dave Stewart	.20	.07
❑	612	Mark Portugal	.10	.02
❑	613	Pete O'Brien	.10	.02
❑	614	Bob Ojeda	.10	.02
❑	615	Joe Carter	.20	.07
❑	616	Pete Young	.10	.02
❑	617	Sam Horn	.10	.02
❑	618	Vince Coleman	.10	.02
❑	619	Wade Boggs	.30	.10
❑	620	Todd Pratt RC	.20	.07
❑	621	Ron Tingley	.10	.02
❑	622	Doug Drabek	.10	.02
❑	623	Scott Hemond	.10	.02
❑	624	Tim Jones	.10	.02
❑	625	Dennis Cook	.10	.02
❑	626	Jose Melendez	.10	.02
❑	627	Mike Munoz	.10	.02
❑	628	Jim Pena	.10	.02
❑	629	Gary Thurman	.10	.02
❑	630	Charlie Leibrandt	.10	.02
❑	631	Scott Fletcher	.10	.02
❑	632	Andre Dawson	.20	.07
❑	633	Greg Gagne	.10	.02
❑	634	Greg Swindell	.10	.02
❑	635	Kevin Maas	.10	.02
❑	636	Xavier Hernandez	.10	.02
❑	637	Ruben Sierra	.20	.07
❑	638	Dmitri Young	.20	.07
❑	639	Harold Reynolds	.20	.07
❑	640	Tom Goodwin	.10	.02
❑	641	Todd Burns	.10	.02
❑	642	Jeff Fassero	.10	.02
❑	643	Dave Winfield	.20	.07
❑	644	Willie Randolph	.20	.07
❑	645	Luis Mercedes	.10	.02
❑	646	Dale Murphy	.30	.10
❑	647	Danny Darwin	.10	.02
❑	648	Dennis Moeller	.10	.02
❑	649	Chuck Crim	.10	.02
❑	650	Checklist	.10	.02
❑	651	Shawn Abner	.10	.02
❑	652	Tracy Woodson	.10	.02
❑	653	Scott Scudder	.10	.02
❑	654	Tom Lampkin	.10	.02
❑	655	Alan Trammell	.20	.07
❑	656	Cory Snyder	.10	.02
❑	657	Chris Gwynn	.10	.02
❑	658	Lonnie Smith	.10	.02
❑	659	Jim Austin	.10	.02
❑	660	Rob Picciolo CL	.10	.02
❑	661	Tim Hulett	.10	.02
❑	662	Marvin Freeman	.10	.02
❑	663	Greg A. Harris	.10	.02
❑	664	Heathcliff Slocumb	.10	.02
❑	665	Mike Butcher	.10	.02
❑	666	Steve Foster	.10	.02
❑	667	Donn Pall	.10	.02
❑	668	Darryl Kile	.20	.07
❑	669	Jesse Levis	.10	.02
❑	670	Jim Gott	.10	.02
❑	671	Mark Hutton	.10	.02
❑	672	Brian Drahman	.10	.02
❑	673	Chad Kreuter	.10	.02
❑	674	Tony Fernandez	.10	.02
❑	675	Jose Lind	.10	.02
❑	676	Kyle Abbott	.10	.02
❑	677	Dan Plesac	.10	.02
❑	678	Barry Bonds	1.50	.60
❑	679	Chili Davis	.20	.07
❑	680	Stan Royer	.10	.02
❑	681	Scott Kamieniecki	.10	.02
❑	682	Carlos Martinez	.10	.02
❑	683	Mike Moore	.10	.02
❑	684	Candy Maldonado	.10	.02
❑	685	Jeff Nelson	.10	.02
❑	686	Lou Whitaker	.20	.07
❑	687	Jose Guzman	.10	.02
❑	688	Manuel Lee	.10	.02
❑	689	Bob MacDonald	.10	.02
❑	690	Scott Bankhead	.10	.02
❑	691	Alan Mills	.10	.02
❑	692	Brian Williams	.10	.02
❑	693	Tom Brunansky	.10	.02
❑	694	Lenny Webster	.10	.02
❑	695	Greg Briley	.10	.02
❑	696	Paul O'Neill	.30	.10
❑	697	Joey Cora	.10	.02
❑	698	Charlie O'Brien	.10	.02
❑	699	Junior Ortiz	.10	.02
❑	700	Ron Darling	.10	.02
❑	701	Tony Phillips	.10	.02
❑	702	William Pennyfeather	.10	.02
❑	703	Mark Gubicza	.10	.02
❑	704	Steve Hosey	.10	.02
❑	705	Henry Cotto	.10	.02
❑	706	David Hulse RC	.10	.02
❑	707	Mike Pagliarulo	.10	.02
❑	708	Dave Stieb	.10	.02
❑	709	Melido Perez	.10	.02
❑	710	Jimmy Key	.20	.07
❑	711	Jeff Russell	.10	.02
❑	712	David Cone	.20	.07
❑	713	Russ Swan	.10	.02
❑	714	Mark Guthrie	.10	.02
❑	715	Checklist	.10	.02
❑	716	Al Martin	.10	.02
❑	717	Randy Knorr	.10	.02
❑	718	Mike Stanley	.10	.02
❑	719	Rick Sutcliffe	.20	.07
❑	720	Terry Leach	.10	.02
❑	721	Chipper Jones	.50	.20
❑	722	Jim Eisenreich	.10	.02
❑	723	Tom Henke	.10	.02
❑	724	Jeff Frye	.10	.02
❑	725	Harold Baines	.20	.07
❑	726	Scott Sanderson	.10	.02
❑	727	Tom Foley	.10	.02
❑	728	Bryan Harvey	.10	.02
❑	729	Tom Edens	.10	.02
❑	730	Eric Young	.10	.02
❑	731	Dave Weathers	.10	.02
❑	732	Spike Owen	.10	.02
❑	733	Scott Aldred	.10	.02
❑	734	Cris Carpenter	.10	.02
❑	735	Dion James	.10	.02
❑	736	Joe Girardi	.10	.02
❑	737	Nigel Wilson	.10	.02
❑	738	Scott Chiamparino	.10	.02
❑	739	Jeff Reardon	.20	.07
❑	740	Willie Blair	.10	.02
❑	741	Jim Corsi	.10	.02
❑	742	Ken Patterson	.10	.02
❑	743	Andy Ashby	.10	.02
❑	744	Rob Natal	.10	.02
❑	745	Kevin Bass	.10	.02
❑	746	Freddie Benavides	.10	.02
❑	747	Chris Donnels	.10	.02
❑	748	Kerry Woodson	.10	.02
❑	749	Calvin Jones	.10	.02
❑	750	Gary Scott	.10	.02
❑	751	Joe Orsulak	.10	.02
❑	752	Armando Reynoso	.10	.02
❑	753	Monty Fariss	.10	.02
❑	754	Billy Hatcher	.10	.02
❑	755	Denis Boucher	.10	.02
❑	756	Walt Weiss	.10	.02
❑	757	Mike Fitzgerald	.10	.02
❑	758	Rudy Seanez	.10	.02
❑	759	Bret Barberie	.10	.02
❑	760	Mo Sanford	.10	.02
❑	761	Pedro Castellano	.10	.02
❑	762	Chuck Carr	.10	.02
❑	763	Steve Howe	.10	.02
❑	764	Andres Galarraga	.20	.07
❑	765	Jeff Conine	.20	.07
❑	766	Ted Power	.10	.02
❑	767	Butch Henry	.10	.02
❑	768	Steve Decker	.10	.02
❑	769	Storm Davis	.10	.02
❑	770	Vinny Castilla	.50	.20
❑	771	Junior Felix	.10	.02
❑	772	Walt Terrell	.10	.02
❑	773	Brad Ausmus	.50	.20
❑	774	Jamie McAndrew	.10	.02
❑	775	Milt Thompson	.10	.02
❑	776	Charlie Hayes	.10	.02

❑ 777 Jack Armstrong .10 .02
❑ 778 Dennis Rasmussen .10 .02
❑ 779 Darren Holmes .10 .02
❑ 780 Alex Arias .10 .02
❑ 781 Randy Bush .10 .02
❑ 782 Javy Lopez .30 .10
❑ 783 Dante Bichette .20 .07
❑ 784 John Johnstone RC .10 .02
❑ 785 Rene Gonzales .10 .02
❑ 786 Alex Cole .10 .02
❑ 787 Jeromy Burnitz .20 .07
❑ 788 Michael Huff .10 .02
❑ 789 Anthony Telford .10 .02
❑ 790 Jerald Clark .10 .02
❑ 791 Joel Johnston .10 .02
❑ 792 David Nied .10 .02

1994 Donruss

❑ COMPLETE SET (660) 30.00 12.00
❑ COMPLETE SERIES 1 (330) 15.00 6.00
❑ COMPLETE SERIES 2 (330) 15.00 6.00
❑ 1 Nolan Ryan Salute 4.00 1.50
❑ 2 Mike Piazza 1.50 .60
❑ 3 Moises Alou .30 .10
❑ 4 Ken Griffey Jr. 1.25 .50
❑ 5 Gary Sheffield .30 .10
❑ 6 Roberto Alomar .50 .20
❑ 7 John Kruk .30 .10
❑ 8 Gregg Olson .15 .05
❑ 9 Gregg Jefferies .15 .05
❑ 10 Tony Gwynn 1.00 .40
❑ 11 Chad Curtis .15 .05
❑ 12 Craig Biggio .50 .20
❑ 13 John Burkett .15 .05
❑ 14 Carlos Baerga .15 .05
❑ 15 Robin Yount 1.25 .50
❑ 16 Dennis Eckersley .30 .10
❑ 17 Dwight Gooden .30 .10
❑ 18 Ryne Sandberg 1.25 .50
❑ 19 Rickey Henderson .75 .30
❑ 20 Jack McDowell .15 .05
❑ 21 Jay Bell .30 .10
❑ 22 Kevin Brown .30 .10
❑ 23 Robin Ventura .30 .10
❑ 24 Paul Molitor .30 .10
❑ 25 David Justice .30 .10
❑ 26 Rafael Palmeiro .50 .20
❑ 27 Cecil Fielder .30 .10
❑ 28 Chuck Knoblauch .30 .10
❑ 29 Dave Hollins .15 .05
❑ 30 Jimmy Key .30 .10
❑ 31 Mark Langston .15 .05
❑ 32 Darryl Kile .30 .10
❑ 33 Ruben Sierra .30 .10
❑ 34 Ron Gant .30 .10
❑ 35 Ozzie Smith 1.25 .50
❑ 36 Wade Boggs .50 .20
❑ 37 Marquis Grissom .30 .10
❑ 38 Will Clark .50 .20
❑ 39 Kenny Lofton .30 .10
❑ 40 Cal Ripken 2.50 1.00
❑ 41 Steve Avery .15 .05
❑ 42 Mo Vaughn .30 .10
❑ 43 Brian McRae .15 .05
❑ 44 Mickey Tettleton .15 .05
❑ 45 Barry Larkin .50 .20
❑ 46 Charlie Hayes .15 .05
❑ 47 Kevin Appier .30 .10
❑ 48 Robby Thompson .15 .05
❑ 49 Juan Gonzalez .30 .10
❑ 50 Paul O'Neill .50 .20
❑ 51 Marcos Armas .15 .05
❑ 52 Mike Butcher .15 .05
❑ 53 Ken Caminiti .30 .10
❑ 54 Pat Borders .15 .05
❑ 55 Pedro Munoz .15 .05
❑ 56 Tim Belcher .15 .05
❑ 57 Paul Assenmacher .15 .05
❑ 58 Damon Berryhill .15 .05
❑ 59 Ricky Bones .15 .05
❑ 60 Rene Arocha .15 .05
❑ 61 Shawn Boskie .15 .05
❑ 62 Pedro Astacio .15 .05
❑ 63 Frank Bolick .15 .05
❑ 64 Bud Black .15 .05
❑ 65 Sandy Alomar Jr. .15 .05
❑ 66 Rich Amaral .15 .05
❑ 67 Luis Aquino .15 .05
❑ 68 Kevin Baez .15 .05
❑ 69 Mike Devereaux .15 .05
❑ 70 Andy Ashby .15 .05
❑ 71 Larry Andersen .15 .05
❑ 72 Steve Cooke .15 .05
❑ 73 Mario Diaz .15 .05
❑ 74 Rob Deer .15 .05
❑ 75 Bobby Ayala .15 .05
❑ 76 Freddie Benavides .15 .05
❑ 77 Stan Belinda .15 .05
❑ 78 John Doherty .15 .05
❑ 79 Willie Banks .15 .05
❑ 80 Spike Owen .15 .05
❑ 81 Mike Bordick .15 .05
❑ 82 Chili Davis .30 .10
❑ 83 Luis Gonzalez .30 .10
❑ 84 Ed Sprague .15 .05
❑ 85 Jeff Reboulet .15 .05
❑ 86 Jason Bere .15 .05
❑ 87 Mark Hutton .15 .05
❑ 88 Jeff Blauser .15 .05
❑ 89 Cal Eldred .15 .05
❑ 90 Bernard Gilkey .15 .05
❑ 91 Frank Castillo .15 .05
❑ 92 Jim Gott .15 .05
❑ 93 Greg Colbrunn .15 .05
❑ 94 Jeff Brantley .15 .05
❑ 95 Jeremy Hernandez .15 .05
❑ 96 Norm Charlton .15 .05
❑ 97 Alex Arias .15 .05
❑ 98 John Franco .30 .10
❑ 99 Chris Hoiles .15 .05
❑ 100 Brad Ausmus .50 .20
❑ 101 Wes Chamberlain .15 .05
❑ 102 Mark Dewey .15 .05
❑ 103 Benji Gil .15 .05
❑ 104 John Dopson .15 .05
❑ 105 John Smiley .15 .05
❑ 106 David Nied .15 .05
❑ 107 George Brett Salute 2.00 .75
❑ 108 Kirk Gibson .30 .10
❑ 109 Larry Casian .15 .05
❑ 110 Ryne Sandberg CL .75 .30
❑ 111 Brent Gates .15 .05
❑ 112 Damion Easley .15 .05
❑ 113 Pete Harnisch .15 .05
❑ 114 Danny Cox .15 .05
❑ 115 Kevin Tapani .15 .05
❑ 116 Roberto Hernandez .15 .05
❑ 117 Domingo Jean .15 .05
❑ 118 Sid Bream .15 .05
❑ 119 Doug Henry .15 .05
❑ 120 Omar Olivares .15 .05
❑ 121 Mike Harkey .15 .05
❑ 122 Carlos Hernandez .15 .05
❑ 123 Jeff Fassero .15 .05
❑ 124 Dave Burba .15 .05
❑ 125 Wayne Kirby .15 .05
❑ 126 John Cummings .15 .05
❑ 127 Bret Barberie .15 .05
❑ 128 Todd Hundley .15 .05
❑ 129 Tim Hulett .15 .05
❑ 130 Phil Clark .15 .05
❑ 131 Danny Jackson .15 .05
❑ 132 Tom Foley .15 .05
❑ 133 Donald Harris .15 .05
❑ 134 Scott Fletcher .15 .05
❑ 135 Johnny Ruffin .15 .05
❑ 136 Jerald Clark .15 .05
❑ 137 Billy Brewer .15 .05
❑ 138 Dan Gladden .15 .05
❑ 139 Eddie Guardado .30 .10
❑ 140 Cal Ripken CL .75 .30
❑ 141 Scott Hemond .15 .05
❑ 142 Steve Frey .15 .05
❑ 143 Xavier Hernandez .15 .05
❑ 144 Mark Eichhorn .15 .05
❑ 145 Ellis Burks .30 .10
❑ 146 Jim Leyritz .15 .05
❑ 147 Mark Lemke .15 .05
❑ 148 Pat Listach .15 .05
❑ 149 Donovan Osborne .15 .05
❑ 150 Glenallen Hill .15 .05
❑ 151 Orel Hershiser .30 .10
❑ 152 Darrin Fletcher .15 .05
❑ 153 Royce Clayton .15 .05
❑ 154 Derek Lilliquist .15 .05
❑ 155 Mike Felder .15 .05
❑ 156 Jeff Conine .30 .10
❑ 157 Ryan Thompson .15 .05
❑ 158 Ben McDonald .15 .05
❑ 159 Ricky Gutierrez .15 .05
❑ 160 Terry Mulholland .15 .05
❑ 161 Carlos Garcia .15 .05
❑ 162 Tom Henke .15 .05
❑ 163 Mike Greenwell .15 .05
❑ 164 Thomas Howard .15 .05
❑ 165 Joe Girardi .15 .05
❑ 166 Hubie Brooks .15 .05
❑ 167 Greg Gohr .15 .05
❑ 168 Chip Hale .15 .05
❑ 169 Rick Honeycutt .15 .05
❑ 170 Hilly Hathaway .15 .05
❑ 171 Todd Jones .15 .05
❑ 172 Tony Fernandez .15 .05
❑ 173 Bo Jackson .75 .30
❑ 174 Bobby Munoz .15 .05
❑ 175 Greg McMichael .15 .05
❑ 176 Graeme Lloyd .15 .05
❑ 177 Tom Pagnozzi .15 .05
❑ 178 Derrick May .15 .05
❑ 179 Pedro Martinez .75 .30
❑ 180 Ken Hill .15 .05
❑ 181 Bryan Hickerson .15 .05
❑ 182 Jose Mesa .15 .05
❑ 183 Dave Fleming .15 .05
❑ 184 Henry Cotto .15 .05
❑ 185 Jeff Kent .50 .20
❑ 186 Mark McLemore .15 .05
❑ 187 Trevor Hoffman .50 .20
❑ 188 Todd Pratt .15 .05
❑ 189 Blas Minor .15 .05
❑ 190 Charlie Leibrandt .15 .05
❑ 191 Tony Pena .15 .05
❑ 192 Larry Luebbers RC .15 .05
❑ 193 Greg W. Harris .15 .05
❑ 194 David Cone .30 .10
❑ 195 Bill Gullickson .15 .05
❑ 196 Brian Harper .15 .05
❑ 197 Steve Karsay .15 .05
❑ 198 Greg Myers .15 .05
❑ 199 Mark Portugal .15 .05
❑ 200 Pat Hentgen .15 .05
❑ 201 Mike LaValliere .15 .05
❑ 202 Mike Stanley .15 .05
❑ 203 Kent Mercker .15 .05
❑ 204 Dave Nilsson .15 .05
❑ 205 Erik Pappas .15 .05
❑ 206 Mike Morgan .15 .05
❑ 207 Roger McDowell .15 .05
❑ 208 Mike Lansing .15 .05
❑ 209 Kirt Manwaring .15 .05
❑ 210 Randy Milligan .15 .05
❑ 211 Erik Hanson .15 .05
❑ 212 Orestes Destrade .15 .05
❑ 213 Mike Maddux .15 .05
❑ 214 Alan Mills .15 .05
❑ 215 Tim Mauser .15 .05
❑ 216 Ben Rivera .15 .05
❑ 217 Don Slaught .15 .05
❑ 218 Bob Patterson .15 .05
❑ 219 Carlos Quintana .15 .05

❑ 220	Tim Raines CL	.15	.05
❑ 221	Hal Morris	.15	.05
❑ 222	Darren Holmes	.15	.05
❑ 223	Chris Gwynn	.15	.05
❑ 224	Chad Kreuter	.15	.05
❑ 225	Mike Hartley	.15	.05
❑ 226	Scott Lydy	.15	.05
❑ 227	Eduardo Perez	.15	.05
❑ 228	Greg Swindell	.15	.05
❑ 229	Al Leiter	.30	.10
❑ 230	Scott Radinsky	.15	.05
❑ 231	Bob Wickman	.15	.05
❑ 232	Otis Nixon	.15	.05
❑ 233	Kevin Reimer	.15	.05
❑ 234	Geronimo Pena	.15	.05
❑ 235	Kevin Roberson	.15	.05
❑ 236	Jody Reed	.15	.05
❑ 237	Kirk Rueter	.15	.05
❑ 238	Willie McGee	.30	.10
❑ 239	Charles Nagy	.15	.05
❑ 240	Tim Leary	.15	.05
❑ 241	Carl Everett	.30	.10
❑ 242	Charlie O'Brien	.15	.05
❑ 243	Mike Pagliarulo	.15	.05
❑ 244	Kerry Taylor	.15	.05
❑ 245	Kevin Stocker	.15	.05
❑ 246	Joel Johnston	.15	.05
❑ 247	Geno Petralli	.15	.05
❑ 248	Jeff Russell	.15	.05
❑ 249	Joe Oliver	.15	.05
❑ 250	Roberto Mejia	.15	.05
❑ 251	Chris Haney	.15	.05
❑ 252	Bill Krueger	.15	.05
❑ 253	Shane Mack	.15	.05
❑ 254	Terry Steinbach	.15	.05
❑ 255	Luis Polonia	.15	.05
❑ 256	Eddie Taubensee	.15	.05
❑ 257	Dave Stewart	.30	.10
❑ 258	Tim Raines	.30	.10
❑ 259	Bernie Williams	.50	.20
❑ 260	John Smoltz	.50	.20
❑ 261	Kevin Seitzer	.15	.05
❑ 262	Bob Tewksbury	.15	.05
❑ 263	Bob Scanlan	.15	.05
❑ 264	Henry Rodriguez	.15	.05
❑ 265	Tim Scott	.15	.05
❑ 266	Scott Sanderson	.15	.05
❑ 267	Eric Plunk	.15	.05
❑ 268	Edgar Martinez	.50	.20
❑ 269	Charlie Hough	.30	.10
❑ 270	Joe Orsulak	.15	.05
❑ 271	Harold Reynolds	.30	.10
❑ 272	Tim Teufel	.15	.05
❑ 273	Bobby Thigpen	.15	.05
❑ 274	Randy Tomlin	.15	.05
❑ 275	Gary Redus	.15	.05
❑ 276	Ken Ryan	.15	.05
❑ 277	Tim Pugh	.15	.05
❑ 278	Jayhawk Owens	.15	.05
❑ 279	Phil Hiatt	.15	.05
❑ 280	Alan Trammell	.30	.10
❑ 281	David McCarty	.15	.05
❑ 282	Bob Welch	.15	.05
❑ 283	J.T.Snow	.30	.10
❑ 284	Brian Williams	.15	.05
❑ 285	Devon White	.30	.10
❑ 286	Steve Sax	.15	.05
❑ 287	Tony Tarasco	.15	.05
❑ 288	Bill Spiers	.15	.05
❑ 289	Allen Watson	.15	.05
❑ 290	Rickey Henderson CL	.50	.20
❑ 291	Jose Vizcaino	.15	.05
❑ 292	Darryl Strawberry	.30	.10
❑ 293	John Wetteland	.30	.10
❑ 294	Bill Swift	.15	.05
❑ 295	Jeff Treadway	.15	.05
❑ 296	Tino Martinez	.50	.20
❑ 297	Richie Lewis	.15	.05
❑ 298	Bret Saberhagen	.30	.10
❑ 299	Arthur Rhodes	.15	.05
❑ 300	Guillermo Velasquez	.15	.05
❑ 301	Milt Thompson	.15	.05
❑ 302	Doug Strange	.15	.05
❑ 303	Aaron Sele	.15	.05
❑ 304	Bip Roberts	.15	.05
❑ 305	Bruce Ruffin	.15	.05
❑ 306	Jose Lind	.15	.05
❑ 307	David Wells	.30	.10
❑ 308	Bobby Witt	.15	.05
❑ 309	Mark Wohlers	.15	.05
❑ 310	B.J. Surhoff	.30	.10
❑ 311	Mark Whiten	.15	.05
❑ 312	Turk Wendell	.15	.05
❑ 313	Raul Mondesi	.30	.10
❑ 314	Brian Turang RC	.15	.05
❑ 315	Chris Hammond	.15	.05
❑ 316	Tim Bogar	.15	.05
❑ 317	Brad Pennington	.15	.05
❑ 318	Tim Worrell	.15	.05
❑ 319	Mitch Williams	.15	.05
❑ 320	Rondell White	.30	.10
❑ 321	Frank Viola	.30	.10
❑ 322	Manny Ramirez	.75	.30
❑ 323	Gary Wayne	.15	.05
❑ 324	Mike Macfarlane	.15	.05
❑ 325	Russ Springer	.15	.05
❑ 326	Tim Wallach	.15	.05
❑ 327	Salomon Torres	.15	.05
❑ 328	Omar Vizquel	.50	.20
❑ 329	Andy Tomberlin RC	.15	.05
❑ 330	Chris Sabo	.15	.05
❑ 331	Mike Mussina	.50	.20
❑ 332	Andy Benes	.15	.05
❑ 333	Darren Daulton	.30	.10
❑ 334	Orlando Merced	.15	.05
❑ 335	Mark McGwire	2.00	.75
❑ 336	Dave Winfield	.30	.10
❑ 337	Sammy Sosa	.75	.30
❑ 338	Eric Karros	.30	.10
❑ 339	Greg Vaughn	.15	.05
❑ 340	Don Mattingly	2.00	.75
❑ 341	Frank Thomas	.75	.30
❑ 342	Fred McGriff	.50	.20
❑ 343	Kirby Puckett	.75	.30
❑ 344	Roberto Kelly	.15	.05
❑ 345	Wally Joyner	.30	.10
❑ 346	Andres Galarraga	.30	.10
❑ 347	Bobby Bonilla	.30	.10
❑ 348	Benito Santiago	.30	.10
❑ 349	Barry Bonds	2.00	.75
❑ 350	Delino DeShields	.15	.05
❑ 351	Albert Belle	.30	.10
❑ 352	Randy Johnson	.75	.30
❑ 353	Tim Salmon	.50	.20
❑ 354	John Olerud	.30	.10
❑ 355	Dean Palmer	.30	.10
❑ 356	Roger Clemens	1.50	.60
❑ 357	Jim Abbott	.50	.20
❑ 358	Mark Grace	.50	.20
❑ 359	Ozzie Guillen	.30	.10
❑ 360	Lou Whitaker	.30	.10
❑ 361	Jose Rijo	.15	.05
❑ 362	Jeff Montgomery	.15	.05
❑ 363	Chuck Finley	.30	.10
❑ 364	Tom Glavine	.50	.20
❑ 365	Jeff Bagwell	.50	.20
❑ 366	Joe Carter	.30	.10
❑ 367	Ray Lankford	.30	.10
❑ 368	Ramon Martinez	.15	.05
❑ 369	Jay Buhner	.30	.10
❑ 370	Matt Williams	.30	.10
❑ 371	Larry Walker	.30	.10
❑ 372	Jose Canseco	.50	.20
❑ 373	Lenny Dykstra	.30	.10
❑ 374	Bryan Harvey	.15	.05
❑ 375	Andy Van Slyke	.50	.20
❑ 376	Ivan Rodriguez	.50	.20
❑ 377	Kevin Mitchell	.15	.05
❑ 378	Travis Fryman	.30	.10
❑ 379	Duane Ward	.15	.05
❑ 380	Greg Maddux	1.25	.50
❑ 381	Scott Servais	.15	.05
❑ 382	Greg Olson	.15	.05
❑ 383	Rey Sanchez	.15	.05
❑ 384	Tom Kramer	.15	.05
❑ 385	David Valle	.15	.05
❑ 386	Eddie Murray	.75	.30
❑ 387	Kevin Higgins	.15	.05
❑ 388	Dan Wilson	.15	.05
❑ 389	Todd Frohwirth	.15	.05
❑ 390	Gerald Williams	.15	.05
❑ 391	Hipolito Pichardo	.15	.05
❑ 392	Pat Meares	.15	.05
❑ 393	Luis Lopez	.15	.05
❑ 394	Ricky Jordan	.15	.05
❑ 395	Bob Walk	.15	.05
❑ 396	Sid Fernandez	.15	.05
❑ 397	Todd Worrell	.15	.05
❑ 398	Darryl Hamilton	.15	.05
❑ 399	Randy Myers	.15	.05
❑ 400	Rod Brewer	.15	.05
❑ 401	Lance Blankenship	.15	.05
❑ 402	Steve Finley	.30	.10
❑ 403	Phil Leftwich RC	.15	.05
❑ 404	Juan Guzman	.15	.05
❑ 405	Anthony Young	.15	.05
❑ 406	Jeff Gardner	.15	.05
❑ 407	Ryan Bowen	.15	.05
❑ 408	Fernando Valenzuela	.30	.10
❑ 409	David West	.15	.05
❑ 410	Kenny Rogers	.30	.10
❑ 411	Bob Zupcic	.15	.05
❑ 412	Eric Young	.15	.05
❑ 413	Bret Boone	.30	.10
❑ 414	Danny Tartabull	.15	.05
❑ 415	Bob MacDonald	.15	.05
❑ 416	Ron Karkovice	.15	.05
❑ 417	Scott Cooper	.15	.05
❑ 418	Dante Bichette	.30	.10
❑ 419	Tripp Cromer	.15	.05
❑ 420	Billy Ashley	.15	.05
❑ 421	Roger Smithberg	.15	.05
❑ 422	Dennis Martinez	.30	.10
❑ 423	Mike Blowers	.15	.05
❑ 424	Darren Lewis	.15	.05
❑ 425	Junior Ortiz	.15	.05
❑ 426	Butch Huskey	.15	.05
❑ 427	Jimmy Poole	.15	.05
❑ 428	Walt Weiss	.15	.05
❑ 429	Scott Bankhead	.15	.05
❑ 430	Deion Sanders	.50	.20
❑ 431	Scott Bullett	.15	.05
❑ 432	Jeff Huson	.15	.05
❑ 433	Tyler Green	.15	.05
❑ 434	Billy Hatcher	.15	.05
❑ 435	Bob Hamelin	.15	.05
❑ 436	Reggie Sanders	.30	.10
❑ 437	Scott Erickson	.15	.05
❑ 438	Steve Reed	.15	.05
❑ 439	Randy Velarde	.15	.05
❑ 440	Tony Gwynn CL	.50	.20
❑ 441	Terry Leach	.15	.05
❑ 442	Danny Bautista	.15	.05
❑ 443	Kent Hrbek	.30	.10
❑ 444	Rick Wilkins	.15	.05
❑ 445	Tony Phillips	.15	.05
❑ 446	Dion James	.15	.05
❑ 447	Joey Cora	.15	.05
❑ 448	Andre Dawson	.30	.10
❑ 449	Pedro Castellano	.15	.05
❑ 450	Tom Gordon	.15	.05
❑ 451	Rob Dibble	.30	.10
❑ 452	Ron Darling	.15	.05
❑ 453	Chipper Jones	.75	.30
❑ 454	Joe Grahe	.15	.05
❑ 455	Domingo Cedeno	.15	.05
❑ 456	Tom Edens	.15	.05
❑ 457	Mitch Webster	.15	.05
❑ 458	Jose Bautista	.15	.05
❑ 459	Troy O'Leary	.15	.05
❑ 460	Todd Zeile	.15	.05
❑ 461	Sean Berry	.15	.05
❑ 462	Brad Holman RC	.15	.05
❑ 463	Dave Martinez	.15	.05
❑ 464	Mark Lewis	.15	.05
❑ 465	Paul Carey	.15	.05
❑ 466	Jack Armstrong	.15	.05
❑ 467	David Telgheder	.15	.05
❑ 468	Gene Harris	.15	.05
❑ 469	Danny Darwin	.15	.05
❑ 470	Kim Batiste	.15	.05
❑ 471	Tim Wakefield	.50	.20
❑ 472	Craig Lefferts	.15	.05
❑ 473	Jacob Brumfield	.15	.05
❑ 474	Lance Painter	.15	.05
❑ 475	Milt Cuyler	.15	.05
❑ 476	Melido Perez	.15	.05
❑ 477	Derek Parks	.15	.05

❑ 478 Gary DiSarcina .15 .05
❑ 479 Steve Bedrosian .15 .05
❑ 480 Eric Anthony .15 .05
❑ 481 Julio Franco .30 .10
❑ 482 Tommy Greene .15 .05
❑ 483 Pat Kelly .15 .05
❑ 484 Nate Minchey .15 .05
❑ 485 William Pennyfeather .15 .05
❑ 486 Harold Baines .30 .10
❑ 487 Howard Johnson .15 .05
❑ 488 Angel Miranda .15 .05
❑ 489 Scott Sanders .15 .05
❑ 490 Shawon Dunston .15 .05
❑ 491 Mel Rojas .15 .05
❑ 492 Jeff Nelson .15 .05
❑ 493 Archi Cianfrocco .15 .05
❑ 494 Al Martin .15 .05
❑ 495 Mike Gallego .15 .05
❑ 496 Mike Henneman .15 .05
❑ 497 Armando Reynoso .15 .05
❑ 498 Mickey Morandini .15 .05
❑ 499 Rick Renteria .15 .05
❑ 500 Rick Sutcliffe .30 .10
❑ 501 Bobby Jones .15 .05
❑ 502 Gary Gaetti .30 .10
❑ 503 Rick Aguilera .15 .05
❑ 504 Todd Stottlemyre .15 .05
❑ 505 Mike Mohler .15 .05
❑ 506 Mike Stanton .15 .05
❑ 507 Jose Guzman .15 .05
❑ 508 Kevin Rogers .15 .05
❑ 509 Chuck Carr .15 .05
❑ 510 Chris Jones .15 .05
❑ 511 Brent Mayne .15 .05
❑ 512 Greg Harris .15 .05
❑ 513 Dave Henderson .15 .05
❑ 514 Eric Hillman .15 .05
❑ 515 Dan Peltier .15 .05
❑ 516 Craig Shipley .15 .05
❑ 517 John Valentin .15 .05
❑ 518 Wilson Alvarez .15 .05
❑ 519 Andujar Cedeno .15 .05
❑ 520 Troy Neel .15 .05
❑ 521 Tom Candiotti .15 .05
❑ 522 Matt Mieske .15 .05
❑ 523 Jim Thome .50 .20
❑ 524 Lou Frazier .15 .05
❑ 525 Mike Jackson .15 .05
❑ 526 Pedro A.Martinez RC .15 .05
❑ 527 Roger Pavlik .15 .05
❑ 528 Kent Bottenfield .15 .05
❑ 529 Felix Jose .15 .05
❑ 530 Mark Guthrie .15 .05
❑ 531 Steve Farr .15 .05
❑ 532 Craig Paquette .15 .05
❑ 533 Doug Jones .15 .05
❑ 534 Luis Alicea .15 .05
❑ 535 Cory Snyder .15 .05
❑ 536 Paul Sorrento .15 .05
❑ 537 Nigel Wilson .15 .05
❑ 538 Jeff King .15 .05
❑ 539 Willie Greene .15 .05
❑ 540 Kirk McCaskill .15 .05
❑ 541 Al Osuna .15 .05
❑ 542 Greg Hibbard .15 .05
❑ 543 Brett Butler .30 .10
❑ 544 Jose Valentin .15 .05
❑ 545 Wil Cordero .15 .05
❑ 546 Chris Bosio .15 .05
❑ 547 Jamie Moyer .30 .10
❑ 548 Jim Eisenreich .15 .05
❑ 549 Vinny Castilla .30 .10
❑ 550 Dave Winfield CL .15 .05
❑ 551 John Roper .15 .05
❑ 552 Lance Johnson .15 .05
❑ 553 Scott Kamieniecki .15 .05
❑ 554 Mike Moore .15 .05
❑ 555 Steve Buechele .15 .05
❑ 556 Terry Pendleton .30 .10
❑ 557 Todd Van Poppel .15 .05
❑ 558 Rob Butler .15 .05
❑ 559 Zane Smith .15 .05
❑ 560 David Hulse .15 .05
❑ 561 Tim Costo .15 .05
❑ 562 John Habyan .15 .05
❑ 563 Terry Jorgensen .15 .05
❑ 564 Matt Nokes .15 .05
❑ 565 Kevin McReynolds .15 .05
❑ 566 Phil Plantier .15 .05
❑ 567 Chris Turner .15 .05
❑ 568 Carlos Delgado .50 .20
❑ 569 John Jaha .15 .05
❑ 570 Dwight Smith .15 .05
❑ 571 John Vander Wal .15 .05
❑ 572 Trevor Wilson .15 .05
❑ 573 Felix Fermin .15 .05
❑ 574 Marc Newfield .15 .05
❑ 575 Jeromy Burnitz .30 .10
❑ 576 Leo Gomez .15 .05
❑ 577 Curt Schilling .30 .10
❑ 578 Kevin Young .15 .05
❑ 579 Jerry Spradlin RC .15 .05
❑ 580 Curt Leskanic .15 .05
❑ 581 Carl Willis .15 .05
❑ 582 Alex Fernandez .15 .05
❑ 583 Mark Holzemer .15 .05
❑ 584 Domingo Martinez .15 .05
❑ 585 Pete Smith .15 .05
❑ 586 Brian Jordan .30 .10
❑ 587 Kevin Gross .15 .05
❑ 588 J.R. Phillips .15 .05
❑ 589 Chris Nabholz .15 .05
❑ 590 Bill Wertz .15 .05
❑ 591 Derek Bell .15 .05
❑ 592 Brady Anderson .30 .10
❑ 593 Matt Turner .15 .05
❑ 594 Pete Incaviglia .15 .05
❑ 595 Greg Gagne .15 .05
❑ 596 John Flaherty .15 .05
❑ 597 Scott Livingstone .15 .05
❑ 598 Rod Bolton .15 .05
❑ 599 Mike Perez .15 .05
❑ 600 Roger Clemens CL .75 .30
❑ 601 Tony Castillo .15 .05
❑ 602 Henry Mercedes .15 .05
❑ 603 Mike Fetters .15 .05
❑ 604 Rod Beck .15 .05
❑ 605 Damon Buford .15 .05
❑ 606 Matt Whiteside .15 .05
❑ 607 Shawn Green .75 .30
❑ 608 Midre Cummings .15 .05
❑ 609 Jeff McNeely .15 .05
❑ 610 Danny Sheaffer .15 .05
❑ 611 Paul Wagner .15 .05
❑ 612 Torey Lovullo .15 .05
❑ 613 Javier Lopez .30 .10
❑ 614 Mariano Duncan .15 .05
❑ 615 Doug Brocail .15 .05
❑ 616 Dave Hansen .15 .05
❑ 617 Ryan Klesko .30 .10
❑ 618 Eric Davis .30 .10
❑ 619 Scott Ruffcorn .15 .05
❑ 620 Mike Trombley .15 .05
❑ 621 Jaime Navarro .15 .05
❑ 622 Rheal Cormier .15 .05
❑ 623 Jose Offerman .15 .05
❑ 624 David Segui .15 .05
❑ 625 Robb Nen .30 .10
❑ 626 Dave Gallagher .15 .05
❑ 627 Julian Tavarez RC .30 .10
❑ 628 Chris Gomez .15 .05
❑ 629 Jeffrey Hammonds .15 .05
❑ 630 Scott Brosius .30 .10
❑ 631 Willie Blair .15 .05
❑ 632 Doug Drabek .15 .05
❑ 633 Bill Wegman .15 .05
❑ 634 Jeff McKnight .15 .05
❑ 635 Rich Rodriguez .15 .05
❑ 636 Steve Trachsel .15 .05
❑ 637 Buddy Groom .15 .05
❑ 638 Sterling Hitchcock .15 .05
❑ 639 Chuck McElroy .15 .05
❑ 640 Rene Gonzales .15 .05
❑ 641 Dan Plesac .15 .05
❑ 642 Jeff Branson .15 .05
❑ 643 Darrell Whitmore .15 .05
❑ 644 Paul Quantrill .15 .05
❑ 645 Rich Rowland .15 .05
❑ 646 Curtis Pride RC .30 .10
❑ 647 Erik Plantenberg RC .15 .05
❑ 648 Albie Lopez .15 .05
❑ 649 Rich Batchelor RC .15 .05
❑ 650 Lee Smith .30 .10
❑ 651 Cliff Floyd .30 .10
❑ 652 Pete Schourek .15 .05
❑ 653 Reggie Jefferson .15 .05
❑ 654 Bill Haselman .15 .05
❑ 655 Steve Hosey .15 .05
❑ 656 Mark Clark .15 .05
❑ 657 Mark Davis .15 .05
❑ 658 Dave Magadan .15 .05
❑ 659 Candy Maldonado .15 .05
❑ 660 Mark Langston CL .15 .05

1995 Donruss

❑ COMPLETE SET (550) 30.00 12.00
❑ COMPLETE SERIES 1 (330) 20.00 8.00
❑ COMPLETE SERIES 2 (220) 10.00 4.00
❑ 1 David Justice .30 .10
❑ 2 Rene Arocha .15 .05
❑ 3 Sandy Alomar Jr. .15 .05
❑ 4 Luis Lopez .15 .05
❑ 5 Mike Piazza 1.25 .50
❑ 6 Bobby Jones .15 .05
❑ 7 Damion Easley .15 .05
❑ 8 Barry Bonds 2.00 .75
❑ 9 Mike Mussina .50 .20
❑ 10 Kevin Seitzer .15 .05
❑ 11 John Smiley .15 .05
❑ 12 Wm.VanLandingham .15 .05
❑ 13 Ron Darling .15 .05
❑ 14 Walt Weiss .15 .05
❑ 15 Mike Lansing .15 .05
❑ 16 Allen Watson .15 .05
❑ 17 Aaron Sele .15 .05
❑ 18 Randy Johnson .75 .30
❑ 19 Dean Palmer .30 .10
❑ 20 Jeff Bagwell .50 .20
❑ 21 Curt Schilling .30 .10
❑ 22 Darrell Whitmore .15 .05
❑ 23 Steve Trachsel .15 .05
❑ 24 Dan Wilson .15 .05
❑ 25 Steve Finley .30 .10
❑ 26 Bret Boone .30 .10
❑ 27 Charles Johnson .30 .10
❑ 28 Mike Stanton .15 .05
❑ 29 Ismael Valdes .15 .05
❑ 30 Salomon Torres .15 .05
❑ 31 Eric Anthony .15 .05
❑ 32 Spike Owen .15 .05
❑ 33 Joey Cora .15 .05
❑ 34 Robert Eenhoorn .15 .05
❑ 35 Rick White .15 .05
❑ 36 Omar Vizquel .50 .20
❑ 37 Carlos Delgado .30 .10
❑ 38 Eddie Williams .15 .05
❑ 39 Shawon Dunston .15 .05
❑ 40 Darrin Fletcher .15 .05
❑ 41 Leo Gomez .15 .05
❑ 42 Juan Gonzalez .30 .10
❑ 43 Luis Alicea .15 .05
❑ 44 Ken Ryan .15 .05
❑ 45 Lou Whitaker .30 .10
❑ 46 Mike Blowers .15 .05
❑ 47 Willie Blair .15 .05
❑ 48 Todd Van Poppel .15 .05
❑ 49 Roberto Alomar .50 .20
❑ 50 Ozzie Smith 1.25 .50
❑ 51 Sterling Hitchcock .15 .05
❑ 52 Mo Vaughn .30 .10

❑ 53 Rick Aguilera	.15	.05
❑ 54 Kent Mercker	.15	.05
❑ 55 Don Mattingly	2.00	.75
❑ 56 Bob Scanlan	.15	.05
❑ 57 Wilson Alvarez	.15	.05
❑ 58 Jose Mesa	.15	.05
❑ 59 Scott Kamieniecki	.15	.05
❑ 60 Todd Jones	.15	.05
❑ 61 John Kruk	.30	.10
❑ 62 Mike Stanley	.15	.05
❑ 63 Tino Martinez	.50	.20
❑ 64 Eddie Zambrano	.15	.05
❑ 65 Todd Hundley	.15	.05
❑ 66 Jamie Moyer	.30	.10
❑ 67 Rich Amaral	.15	.05
❑ 68 Jose Valentin	.15	.05
❑ 69 Alex Gonzalez	.15	.05
❑ 70 Kurt Abbott	.15	.05
❑ 71 Delino DeShields	.15	.05
❑ 72 Brian Anderson	.15	.05
❑ 73 John Vander Wal	.15	.05
❑ 74 Turner Ward	.15	.05
❑ 75 Tim Raines	.30	.10
❑ 76 Mark Acre	.15	.05
❑ 77 Jose Offerman	.15	.05
❑ 78 Jimmy Key	.30	.10
❑ 79 Mark Whiten	.15	.05
❑ 80 Mark Gubicza	.15	.05
❑ 81 Darren Hall	.15	.05
❑ 82 Travis Fryman	.30	.10
❑ 83 Cal Ripken	2.50	1.00
❑ 84 Geronimo Berroa	.15	.05
❑ 85 Bret Barberie	.15	.05
❑ 86 Andy Ashby	.15	.05
❑ 87 Steve Avery	.15	.05
❑ 88 Rich Becker	.15	.05
❑ 89 John Valentin	.15	.05
❑ 90 Glenallen Hill	.15	.05
❑ 91 Carlos Garcia	.15	.05
❑ 92 Dennis Martinez	.30	.10
❑ 93 Pat Kelly	.15	.05
❑ 94 Orlando Miller	.15	.05
❑ 95 Felix Jose	.15	.05
❑ 96 Mike Kingery	.15	.05
❑ 97 Jeff Kent	.30	.10
❑ 98 Pete Incaviglia	.15	.05
❑ 99 Chad Curtis	.15	.05
❑ 100 Thomas Howard	.15	.05
❑ 101 Hector Carrasco	.15	.05
❑ 102 Tom Pagnozzi	.15	.05
❑ 103 Danny Tartabull	.15	.05
❑ 104 Donnie Elliott	.15	.05
❑ 105 Danny Jackson	.15	.05
❑ 106 Steve Dunn	.15	.05
❑ 107 Roger Salkeld	.15	.05
❑ 108 Jeff King	.15	.05
❑ 109 Cecil Fielder	.30	.10
❑ 110 Paul Molitor CL	.15	.05
❑ 111 Denny Neagle	.30	.10
❑ 112 Troy Neel	.15	.05
❑ 113 Rod Beck	.15	.05
❑ 114 Alex Rodriguez	2.00	.75
❑ 115 Joey Eischen	.15	.05
❑ 116 Tom Candiotti	.15	.05
❑ 117 Ray McDavid	.15	.05
❑ 118 Vince Coleman	.15	.05
❑ 119 Pete Harnisch	.15	.05
❑ 120 David Nied	.15	.05
❑ 121 Pat Rapp	.15	.05
❑ 122 Sammy Sosa	.75	.30
❑ 123 Steve Reed	.15	.05
❑ 124 Jose Oliva	.15	.05
❑ 125 Ricky Bottalico	.15	.05
❑ 126 Jose DeLeon	.15	.05
❑ 127 Pat Hentgen	.15	.05
❑ 128 Will Clark	.50	.20
❑ 129 Mark Dewey	.15	.05
❑ 130 Greg Vaughn	.15	.05
❑ 131 Darren Dreifort	.15	.05
❑ 132 Ed Sprague	.15	.05
❑ 133 Lee Smith	.30	.10
❑ 134 Charles Nagy	.15	.05
❑ 135 Phil Plantier	.15	.05
❑ 136 Jason Jacome	.15	.05
❑ 137 Jose Lima	.15	.05
❑ 138 J.R. Phillips	.15	.05
❑ 139 J.T. Snow	.30	.10
❑ 140 Michael Huff	.15	.05
❑ 141 Billy Brewer	.15	.05
❑ 142 Jeromy Burnitz	.30	.10
❑ 143 Ricky Bones	.15	.05
❑ 144 Carlos Rodriguez	.15	.05
❑ 145 Luis Gonzalez	.30	.10
❑ 146 Mark Lemke	.15	.05
❑ 147 Al Martin	.15	.05
❑ 148 Mike Bordick	.15	.05
❑ 149 Robb Nen	.30	.10
❑ 150 Wil Cordero	.15	.05
❑ 151 Edgar Martinez	.50	.20
❑ 152 Gerald Williams	.15	.05
❑ 153 Esteban Beltre	.15	.05
❑ 154 Mike Moore	.15	.05
❑ 155 Mark Langston	.15	.05
❑ 156 Mark Clark	.15	.05
❑ 157 Bobby Ayala	.15	.05
❑ 158 Rick Wilkins	.15	.05
❑ 159 Bobby Munoz	.15	.05
❑ 160 Brett Butler CL	.15	.05
❑ 161 Scott Erickson	.15	.05
❑ 162 Paul Molitor	.30	.10
❑ 163 Jon Lieber	.15	.05
❑ 164 Jason Grimsley	.15	.05
❑ 165 Norberto Martin	.15	.05
❑ 166 Javier Lopez	.30	.10
❑ 167 Brian McRae	.15	.05
❑ 168 Gary Sheffield	.30	.10
❑ 169 Marcus Moore	.15	.05
❑ 170 John Hudek	.15	.05
❑ 171 Kelly Stinnett	.15	.05
❑ 172 Chris Gomez	.15	.05
❑ 173 Rey Sanchez	.15	.05
❑ 174 Juan Guzman	.15	.05
❑ 175 Chan Ho Park	.30	.10
❑ 176 Terry Shumpert	.15	.05
❑ 177 Steve Ontiveros	.15	.05
❑ 178 Brad Ausmus	.30	.10
❑ 179 Tim Davis	.15	.05
❑ 180 Billy Ashley	.15	.05
❑ 181 Vinny Castilla	.30	.10
❑ 182 Bill Spiers	.15	.05
❑ 183 Randy Knorr	.15	.05
❑ 184 Brian L.Hunter	.15	.05
❑ 185 Pat Meares	.15	.05
❑ 186 Steve Buechele	.15	.05
❑ 187 Kirt Manwaring	.15	.05
❑ 188 Tim Naehring	.15	.05
❑ 189 Matt Mieske	.15	.05
❑ 190 Josias Manzanillo	.15	.05
❑ 191 Greg McMichael	.15	.05
❑ 192 Chuck Carr	.15	.05
❑ 193 Midre Cummings	.15	.05
❑ 194 Darryl Strawberry	.30	.10
❑ 195 Greg Gagne	.15	.05
❑ 196 Steve Cooke	.15	.05
❑ 197 Woody Williams	.15	.05
❑ 198 Ron Karkovice	.15	.05
❑ 199 Phil Leftwich	.15	.05
❑ 200 Jim Thome	.50	.20
❑ 201 Brady Anderson	.30	.10
❑ 202 Pedro A.Martinez	.15	.05
❑ 203 Steve Karsay	.15	.05
❑ 204 Reggie Sanders	.30	.10
❑ 205 Bill Risley	.15	.05
❑ 206 Jay Bell	.30	.10
❑ 207 Kevin Brown	.30	.10
❑ 208 Tim Scott	.15	.05
❑ 209 Lenny Dykstra	.30	.10
❑ 210 Willie Greene	.15	.05
❑ 211 Jim Eisenreich	.15	.05
❑ 212 Cliff Floyd	.30	.10
❑ 213 Otis Nixon	.15	.05
❑ 214 Eduardo Perez	.15	.05
❑ 215 Manuel Lee	.15	.05
❑ 216 Armando Benitez	.15	.05
❑ 217 Dave McCarty	.15	.05
❑ 218 Scott Livingstone	.15	.05
❑ 219 Chad Kreuter	.15	.05
❑ 220 Don Mattingly CL	1.00	.40
❑ 221 Brian Jordan	.30	.10
❑ 222 Matt Whiteside	.15	.05
❑ 223 Jim Edmonds	.50	.20
❑ 224 Tony Gwynn	1.00	.40
❑ 225 Jose Lind	.15	.05
❑ 226 Marvin Freeman	.15	.05
❑ 227 Ken Hill	.15	.05
❑ 228 David Hulse	.15	.05
❑ 229 Joe Hesketh	.15	.05
❑ 230 Roberto Petagine	.15	.05
❑ 231 Jeffrey Hammonds	.15	.05
❑ 232 John Jaha	.15	.05
❑ 233 John Burkett	.15	.05
❑ 234 Hal Morris	.15	.05
❑ 235 Tony Castillo	.15	.05
❑ 236 Ryan Bowen	.15	.05
❑ 237 Wayne Kirby	.15	.05
❑ 238 Brent Mayne	.15	.05
❑ 239 Jim Bullinger	.15	.05
❑ 240 Mike Lieberthal	.30	.10
❑ 241 Barry Larkin	.50	.20
❑ 242 David Segui	.15	.05
❑ 243 Jose Bautista	.15	.05
❑ 244 Hector Fajardo	.15	.05
❑ 245 Orel Hershiser	.30	.10
❑ 246 James Mouton	.15	.05
❑ 247 Scott Leius	.15	.05
❑ 248 Tom Glavine	.50	.20
❑ 249 Danny Bautista	.15	.05
❑ 250 Jose Mercedes	.15	.05
❑ 251 Marquis Grissom	.30	.10
❑ 252 Charlie Hayes	.15	.05
❑ 253 Ryan Klesko	.30	.10
❑ 254 Vicente Palacios	.15	.05
❑ 255 Matias Carrillo	.15	.05
❑ 256 Gary DiSarcina	.15	.05
❑ 257 Kirk Gibson	.30	.10
❑ 258 Garey Ingram	.15	.05
❑ 259 Alex Fernandez	.15	.05
❑ 260 John Mabry	.15	.05
❑ 261 Chris Howard	.15	.05
❑ 262 Miguel Jimenez	.15	.05
❑ 263 Heathcliff Slocumb	.15	.05
❑ 264 Albert Belle	.30	.10
❑ 265 Dave Clark	.15	.05
❑ 266 Joe Orsulak	.15	.05
❑ 267 Joey Hamilton	.15	.05
❑ 268 Mark Portugal	.15	.05
❑ 269 Kevin Tapani	.15	.05
❑ 270 Sid Fernandez	.15	.05
❑ 271 Steve Dreyer	.15	.05
❑ 272 Denny Hocking	.15	.05
❑ 273 Troy O'Leary	.15	.05
❑ 274 Milt Cuyler	.15	.05
❑ 275 Frank Thomas	.75	.30
❑ 276 Jorge Fabregas	.15	.05
❑ 277 Mike Gallego	.15	.05
❑ 278 Mickey Morandini	.15	.05
❑ 279 Roberto Hernandez	.15	.05
❑ 280 Henry Rodriguez	.15	.05
❑ 281 Garret Anderson	.30	.10
❑ 282 Bob Wickman	.15	.05
❑ 283 Gar Finnvold	.15	.05
❑ 284 Paul O'Neill	.50	.20
❑ 285 Royce Clayton	.15	.05
❑ 286 Chuck Knoblauch	.30	.10
❑ 287 Johnny Ruffin	.15	.05
❑ 288 Dave Nilsson	.15	.05
❑ 289 David Cone	.30	.10
❑ 290 Chuck McElroy	.15	.05
❑ 291 Kevin Stocker	.15	.05
❑ 292 Jose Rijo	.15	.05
❑ 293 Sean Berry	.15	.05
❑ 294 Ozzie Guillen	.30	.10
❑ 295 Chris Hoiles	.15	.05
❑ 296 Kevin Foster	.15	.05
❑ 297 Jeff Frye	.15	.05
❑ 298 Lance Johnson	.15	.05
❑ 299 Mike Kelly	.15	.05
❑ 300 Ellis Burks	.30	.10
❑ 301 Roberto Kelly	.15	.05
❑ 302 Dante Bichette	.30	.10
❑ 303 Alvaro Espinoza	.15	.05
❑ 304 Alex Cole	.15	.05
❑ 305 Rickey Henderson	.75	.30
❑ 306 Dave Weathers	.15	.05
❑ 307 Shane Reynolds	.15	.05
❑ 308 Bobby Bonilla	.30	.10
❑ 309 Junior Felix	.15	.05
❑ 310 Jeff Fassero	.15	.05

❑ 311 Darren Lewis	.15	.05
❑ 312 John Doherty	.15	.05
❑ 313 Scott Servais	.15	.05
❑ 314 Rick Helling	.15	.05
❑ 315 Pedro Martinez	.50	.20
❑ 316 Wes Chamberlain	.15	.05
❑ 317 Bryan Eversgerd	.15	.05
❑ 318 Trevor Hoffman	.30	.10
❑ 319 John Patterson	.15	.05
❑ 320 Matt Walbeck	.15	.05
❑ 321 Jeff Montgomery	.15	.05
❑ 322 Mel Rojas	.15	.05
❑ 323 Eddie Taubensee	.15	.05
❑ 324 Ray Lankford	.30	.10
❑ 325 Jose Vizcaino	.15	.05
❑ 326 Carlos Baerga	.15	.05
❑ 327 Jack Voigt	.15	.05
❑ 328 Julio Franco	.30	.10
❑ 329 Brent Gates	.15	.05
❑ 330 Kirby Puckett CL	.50	.20
❑ 331 Greg Maddux	1.25	.50
❑ 332 Jason Bere	.15	.05
❑ 333 Bill Wegman	.15	.05
❑ 334 Tuffy Rhodes	.15	.05
❑ 335 Kevin Young	.15	.05
❑ 336 Andy Benes	.15	.05
❑ 337 Pedro Astacio	.15	.05
❑ 338 Reggie Jefferson	.15	.05
❑ 339 Tim Belcher	.15	.05
❑ 340 Ken Griffey Jr.	1.25	.50
❑ 341 Mariano Duncan	.15	.05
❑ 342 Andres Galarraga	.30	.10
❑ 343 Rondell White	.30	.10
❑ 344 Cory Bailey	.15	.05
❑ 345 Bryan Harvey	.15	.05
❑ 346 John Franco	.30	.10
❑ 347 Greg Swindell	.15	.05
❑ 348 David West	.15	.05
❑ 349 Fred McGriff	.50	.20
❑ 350 Jose Canseco	.50	.20
❑ 351 Orlando Merced	.15	.05
❑ 352 Rheal Cormier	.15	.05
❑ 353 Carlos Pulido	.15	.05
❑ 354 Terry Steinbach	.15	.05
❑ 355 Wade Boggs	.50	.20
❑ 356 B.J. Surhoff	.30	.10
❑ 357 Rafael Palmeiro	.50	.20
❑ 358 Anthony Young	.15	.05
❑ 359 Tom Brunansky	.15	.05
❑ 360 Todd Stottlemyre	.15	.05
❑ 361 Chris Turner	.15	.05
❑ 362 Joe Boever	.15	.05
❑ 363 Jeff Blauser	.15	.05
❑ 364 Derek Bell	.15	.05
❑ 365 Matt Williams	.30	.10
❑ 366 Jeromy Hernandez	.15	.05
❑ 367 Joe Girardi	.15	.05
❑ 368 Mike Devereaux	.15	.05
❑ 369 Jim Abbott	.50	.20
❑ 370 Manny Ramirez	.50	.20
❑ 371 Kenny Lofton	.30	.10
❑ 372 Mark Smith	.15	.05
❑ 373 Dave Fleming	.15	.05
❑ 374 Dave Stewart	.30	.10
❑ 375 Roger Pavlik	.15	.05
❑ 376 Hipolito Pichardo	.15	.05
❑ 377 Bill Taylor	.15	.05
❑ 378 Robin Ventura	.30	.10
❑ 379 Bernard Gilkey	.15	.05
❑ 380 Kirby Puckett	.75	.30
❑ 381 Steve Howe	.15	.05
❑ 382 Devon White	.30	.10
❑ 383 Roberto Mejia	.15	.05
❑ 384 Darrin Jackson	.15	.05
❑ 385 Mike Morgan	.15	.05
❑ 386 Rusty Meacham	.15	.05
❑ 387 Bill Swift	.15	.05
❑ 388 Lou Frazier	.15	.05
❑ 389 Andy Van Slyke	.50	.20
❑ 390 Brett Butler	.30	.10
❑ 391 Bobby Witt	.15	.05
❑ 392 Jeff Conine	.30	.10
❑ 393 Tim Hyers	.15	.05
❑ 394 Terry Pendleton	.30	.10
❑ 395 Ricky Jordan	.15	.05
❑ 396 Eric Plunk	.15	.05
❑ 397 Melido Perez	.15	.05
❑ 398 Darryl Kile	.30	.10
❑ 399 Mark McLemore	.15	.05
❑ 400 Greg W.Harris	.15	.05
❑ 401 Jim Leyritz	.15	.05
❑ 402 Doug Strange	.15	.05
❑ 403 Tim Salmon	.50	.20
❑ 404 Terry Mulholland	.15	.05
❑ 405 Robby Thompson	.15	.05
❑ 406 Ruben Sierra	.30	.10
❑ 407 Tony Phillips	.15	.05
❑ 408 Moises Alou	.30	.10
❑ 409 Felix Fermin	.15	.05
❑ 410 Pat Listach	.15	.05
❑ 411 Kevin Bass	.15	.05
❑ 412 Ben McDonald	.15	.05
❑ 413 Scott Cooper	.15	.05
❑ 414 Jody Reed	.15	.05
❑ 415 Deion Sanders	.50	.20
❑ 416 Ricky Gutierrez	.15	.05
❑ 417 Gregg Jefferies	.15	.05
❑ 418 Jack McDowell	.15	.05
❑ 419 Al Leiter	.30	.10
❑ 420 Tony Longmire	.15	.05
❑ 421 Paul Wagner	.15	.05
❑ 422 Geronimo Pena	.15	.05
❑ 423 Ivan Rodriguez	.50	.20
❑ 424 Kevin Gross	.15	.05
❑ 425 Kirk McCaskill	.15	.05
❑ 426 Greg Myers	.15	.05
❑ 427 Roger Clemens	1.50	.60
❑ 428 Chris Hammond	.15	.05
❑ 429 Randy Myers	.15	.05
❑ 430 Roger Mason	.15	.05
❑ 431 Bret Saberhagen	.30	.10
❑ 432 Jeff Reboulet	.15	.05
❑ 433 John Olerud	.30	.10
❑ 434 Bill Gullickson	.15	.05
❑ 435 Eddie Murray	.75	.30
❑ 436 Pedro Munoz	.15	.05
❑ 437 Charlie O'Brien	.15	.05
❑ 438 Jeff Nelson	.15	.05
❑ 439 Mike Macfarlane	.15	.05
❑ 440 Don Mattingly CL	1.00	.40
❑ 441 Derrick May	.15	.05
❑ 442 John Roper	.15	.05
❑ 443 Darryl Hamilton	.15	.05
❑ 444 Dan Miceli	.15	.05
❑ 445 Tony Eusebio	.15	.05
❑ 446 Jerry Browne	.15	.05
❑ 447 Wally Joyner	.30	.10
❑ 448 Brian Harper	.15	.05
❑ 449 Scott Fletcher	.15	.05
❑ 450 Bip Roberts	.15	.05
❑ 451 Pete Smith	.15	.05
❑ 452 Chili Davis	.30	.10
❑ 453 Dave Hollins	.15	.05
❑ 454 Tony Pena	.15	.05
❑ 455 Butch Henry	.15	.05
❑ 456 Craig Biggio	.50	.20
❑ 457 Zane Smith	.15	.05
❑ 458 Ryan Thompson	.15	.05
❑ 459 Mike Jackson	.15	.05
❑ 460 Mark McGwire	2.00	.75
❑ 461 John Smoltz	.50	.20
❑ 462 Steve Scarsone	.15	.05
❑ 463 Greg Colbrunn	.15	.05
❑ 464 Shawn Green	.30	.10
❑ 465 David Wells	.30	.10
❑ 466 Jose Hernandez	.15	.05
❑ 467 Chip Hale	.15	.05
❑ 468 Tony Tarasco	.15	.05
❑ 469 Kevin Mitchell	.15	.05
❑ 470 Billy Hatcher	.15	.05
❑ 471 Jay Buhner	.30	.10
❑ 472 Ken Caminiti	.30	.10
❑ 473 Tom Henke	.15	.05
❑ 474 Todd Worrell	.15	.05
❑ 475 Mark Eichhorn	.15	.05
❑ 476 Bruce Ruffin	.15	.05
❑ 477 Chuck Finley	.30	.10
❑ 478 Marc Newfield	.15	.05
❑ 479 Paul Shuey	.15	.05
❑ 480 Bob Tewksbury	.15	.05
❑ 481 Ramon J.Martinez	.15	.05
❑ 482 Melvin Nieves	.15	.05
❑ 483 Todd Zeile	.15	.05
❑ 484 Benito Santiago	.30	.10
❑ 485 Stan Javier	.15	.05
❑ 486 Kirk Rueter	.15	.05
❑ 487 Andre Dawson	.30	.10
❑ 488 Eric Karros	.30	.10
❑ 489 Dave Magadan	.15	.05
❑ 490 Joe Carter CL	.15	.05
❑ 491 Randy Velarde	.15	.05
❑ 492 Larry Walker	.30	.10
❑ 493 Cris Carpenter	.15	.05
❑ 494 Tom Gordon	.15	.05
❑ 495 Dave Burba	.15	.05
❑ 496 Darren Bragg	.15	.05
❑ 497 Darren Daulton	.30	.10
❑ 498 Don Slaught	.15	.05
❑ 499 Pat Borders	.15	.05
❑ 500 Lenny Harris	.15	.05
❑ 501 Joe Ausanio	.15	.05
❑ 502 Alan Trammell	.30	.10
❑ 503 Mike Fetters	.15	.05
❑ 504 Scott Ruffcorn	.15	.05
❑ 505 Rich Rowland	.15	.05
❑ 506 Juan Samuel	.15	.05
❑ 507 Bo Jackson	.75	.30
❑ 508 Jeff Branson	.15	.05
❑ 509 Bernie Williams	.50	.20
❑ 510 Paul Sorrento	.15	.05
❑ 511 Dennis Eckersley	.30	.10
❑ 512 Pat Mahomes	.15	.05
❑ 513 Rusty Greer	.30	.10
❑ 514 Luis Polonia	.15	.05
❑ 515 Willie Banks	.15	.05
❑ 516 John Wetteland	.30	.10
❑ 517 Mike LaValliere	.15	.05
❑ 518 Tommy Greene	.15	.05
❑ 519 Mark Grace	.50	.20
❑ 520 Bob Hamelin	.15	.05
❑ 521 Scott Sanderson	.15	.05
❑ 522 Joe Carter	.30	.10
❑ 523 Jeff Brantley	.15	.05
❑ 524 Andrew Lorraine	.15	.05
❑ 525 Rico Brogna	.15	.05
❑ 526 Shane Mack	.15	.05
❑ 527 Mark Wohlers	.15	.05
❑ 528 Scott Sanders	.15	.05
❑ 529 Chris Bosio	.15	.05
❑ 530 Andujar Cedeno	.15	.05
❑ 531 Kenny Rogers	.30	.10
❑ 532 Doug Drabek	.15	.05
❑ 533 Curt Leskanic	.15	.05
❑ 534 Craig Shipley	.15	.05
❑ 535 Craig Grebeck	.15	.05
❑ 536 Cal Eldred	.15	.05
❑ 537 Mickey Tettleton	.15	.05
❑ 538 Harold Baines	.30	.10
❑ 539 Tim Wallach	.15	.05
❑ 540 Damon Buford	.15	.05
❑ 541 Lenny Webster	.15	.05
❑ 542 Kevin Appier	.30	.10
❑ 543 Raul Mondesi	.30	.10
❑ 544 Eric Young	.15	.05
❑ 545 Russ Davis	.15	.05
❑ 546 Mike Benjamin	.15	.05
❑ 547 Mike Greenwell	.15	.05
❑ 548 Scott Brosius	.30	.10
❑ 549 Brian Dorsett	.15	.05
❑ 550 Chili Davis CL	.15	.05

1996 Donruss

❑ COMPLETE SET (550)	40.00	16.00
❑ COMPLETE SERIES 1 (330)	25.00	10.00
❑ COMPLETE SERIES 2 (220)	15.00	6.00
❑ 1 Frank Thomas	.75	.30
❑ 2 Jason Bates	.30	.10
❑ 3 Steve Sparks	.30	.10
❑ 4 Scott Servais	.30	.10
❑ 5 Angelo Encarnacion RC	.30	.10
❑ 6 Scott Sanders	.30	.10
❑ 7 Billy Ashley	.30	.10
❑ 8 Alex Rodriguez	1.50	.60
❑ 9 Sean Bergman	.30	.10
❑ 10 Brad Radke	.30	.10
❑ 11 Andy Van Slyke	.50	.20
❑ 12 Joe Girardi	.30	.10
❑ 13 Mark Grudzielanek	.30	.10

❑	14	Rick Aguilera	.30	.10
❑	15	Randy Veres	.30	.10
❑	16	Tim Bogar	.30	.10
❑	17	Dave Veres	.30	.10
❑	18	Kevin Stocker	.30	.10
❑	19	Marquis Grissom	.30	.10
❑	20	Will Clark	.50	.20
❑	21	Jay Bell	.30	.10
❑	22	Allen Battle	.30	.10
❑	23	Frank Rodriguez	.30	.10
❑	24	Terry Steinbach	.30	.10
❑	25	Gerald Williams	.30	.10
❑	26	Sid Roberson	.30	.10
❑	27	Greg Zaun	.30	.10
❑	28	Ozzie Timmons	.30	.10
❑	29	Vaughn Eshelman	.30	.10
❑	30	Ed Sprague	.30	.10
❑	31	Gary DiSarcina	.30	.10
❑	32	Joe Boever	.30	.10
❑	33	Steve Avery	.30	.10
❑	34	Brad Ausmus	.30	.10
❑	35	Kirt Manwaring	.30	.10
❑	36	Gary Sheffield	.30	.10
❑	37	Jason Bere	.30	.10
❑	38	Jeff Manto	.30	.10
❑	39	David Cone	.30	.10
❑	40	Manny Ramirez	.50	.20
❑	41	Sandy Alomar Jr.	.30	.10
❑	42	Curtis Goodwin	.30	.10
❑	43	Tino Martinez	.50	.20
❑	44	Woody Williams	.30	.10
❑	45	Dean Palmer	.30	.10
❑	46	Hipolito Pichardo	.30	.10
❑	47	Jason Giambi	.30	.10
❑	48	Lance Johnson	.30	.10
❑	49	Bernard Gilkey	.30	.10
❑	50	Kirby Puckett	.75	.30
❑	51	Tony Fernandez	.30	.10
❑	52	Alex Gonzalez	.30	.10
❑	53	Bret Saberhagen	.30	.10
❑	54	Lyle Mouton	.30	.10
❑	55	Brian McRae	.30	.10
❑	56	Mark Gubicza	.30	.10
❑	57	Sergio Valdez	.30	.10
❑	58	Darrin Fletcher	.30	.10
❑	59	Steve Parris	.30	.10
❑	60	Johnny Damon	.50	.20
❑	61	Rickey Henderson	.75	.30
❑	62	Darrell Whitmore	.30	.10
❑	63	Roberto Petagine	.30	.10
❑	64	Trenidad Hubbard	.30	.10
❑	65	Heathcliff Slocumb	.30	.10
❑	66	Steve Finley	.30	.10
❑	67	Mariano Rivera	.75	.30
❑	68	Brian L.Hunter	.30	.10
❑	69	Jamie Moyer	.30	.10
❑	70	Ellis Burks	.30	.10
❑	71	Pat Kelly	.30	.10
❑	72	Mickey Tettleton	.30	.10
❑	73	Garret Anderson	.30	.10
❑	74	Andy Pettitte	.50	.20
❑	75	Glenallen Hill	.30	.10
❑	76	Brent Gates	.30	.10
❑	77	Lou Whitaker	.30	.10
❑	78	David Segui	.30	.10
❑	79	Dan Wilson	.30	.10
❑	80	Pat Listach	.30	.10
❑	81	Jeff Bagwell	.50	.20
❑	82	Ben McDonald	.30	.10
❑	83	John Valentin	.30	.10
❑	84	John Jaha	.30	.10
❑	85	Pete Schourek	.30	.10
❑	86	Bryce Florie	.30	.10
❑	87	Brian Jordan	.30	.10
❑	88	Ron Karkovice	.30	.10
❑	89	Al Leiter	.30	.10
❑	90	Tony Longmire	.30	.10
❑	91	Nelson Liriano	.30	.10
❑	92	David Bell	.30	.10
❑	93	Kevin Gross	.30	.10
❑	94	Tom Candiotti	.30	.10
❑	95	Dave Martinez	.30	.10
❑	96	Greg Myers	.30	.10
❑	97	Rheal Cormier	.30	.10
❑	98	Chris Hammond	.30	.10
❑	99	Randy Myers	.30	.10
❑	100	Bill Pulsipher	.30	.10
❑	101	Jason Isringhausen	.30	.10
❑	102	Dave Stevens	.30	.10
❑	103	Roberto Alomar	.50	.20
❑	104	Bob Higginson	.30	.10
❑	105	Eddie Murray	.75	.30
❑	106	Matt Walbeck	.30	.10
❑	107	Mark Wohlers	.30	.10
❑	108	Jeff Nelson	.30	.10
❑	109	Tom Goodwin	.30	.10
❑	110	Cal Ripken CL	1.25	.50
❑	111	Rey Sanchez	.30	.10
❑	112	Hector Carrasco	.30	.10
❑	113	B.J. Surhoff	.30	.10
❑	114	Dan Miceli	.30	.10
❑	115	Dean Hartgraves	.30	.10
❑	116	John Burkett	.30	.10
❑	117	Gary Gaetti	.30	.10
❑	118	Ricky Bones	.30	.10
❑	119	Mike Macfarlane	.30	.10
❑	120	Bip Roberts	.30	.10
❑	121	Dave Mlicki	.30	.10
❑	122	Chili Davis	.30	.10
❑	123	Mark Whiten	.30	.10
❑	124	Herbert Perry	.30	.10
❑	125	Butch Henry	.30	.10
❑	126	Derek Bell	.30	.10
❑	127	Al Martin	.30	.10
❑	128	John Franco	.30	.10
❑	129	W. VanLandingham	.30	.10
❑	130	Mike Bordick	.30	.10
❑	131	Mike Mordecai	.30	.10
❑	132	Robby Thompson	.30	.10
❑	133	Greg Colbrunn	.30	.10
❑	134	Domingo Cedeno	.30	.10
❑	135	Chad Curtis	.30	.10
❑	136	Jose Hernandez	.30	.10
❑	137	Scott Klingenbeck	.30	.10
❑	138	Ryan Klesko	.30	.10
❑	139	John Smiley	.30	.10
❑	140	Charlie Hayes	.30	.10
❑	141	Jay Buhner	.30	.10
❑	142	Doug Drabek	.30	.10
❑	143	Roger Pavlik	.30	.10
❑	144	Todd Worrell	.30	.10
❑	145	Cal Ripken	2.50	1.00
❑	146	Steve Reed	.30	.10
❑	147	Chuck Finley	.30	.10
❑	148	Mike Blowers	.30	.10
❑	149	Orel Hershiser	.30	.10
❑	150	Allen Watson	.30	.10
❑	151	Ramon Martinez	.30	.10
❑	152	Melvin Nieves	.30	.10
❑	153	Tripp Cromer	.30	.10
❑	154	Yorkis Perez	.30	.10
❑	155	Stan Javier	.30	.10
❑	156	Mel Rojas	.30	.10
❑	157	Aaron Sele	.30	.10
❑	158	Eric Karros	.30	.10
❑	159	Robb Nen	.30	.10
❑	160	Raul Mondesi	.30	.10
❑	161	John Wetteland	.30	.10
❑	162	Tim Scott	.30	.10
❑	163	Kenny Rogers	.30	.10
❑	164	Melvin Bunch	.30	.10
❑	165	Rod Beck	.30	.10
❑	166	Andy Benes	.30	.10
❑	167	Lenny Dykstra	.30	.10
❑	168	Orlando Merced	.30	.10
❑	169	Tomas Perez	.30	.10
❑	170	Xavier Hernandez	.30	.10
❑	171	Ruben Sierra	.30	.10
❑	172	Alan Trammell	.30	.10
❑	173	Mike Fetters	.30	.10
❑	174	Wilson Alvarez	.30	.10
❑	175	Erik Hanson	.30	.10
❑	176	Travis Fryman	.30	.10
❑	177	Jim Abbott	.50	.20
❑	178	Bret Boone	.30	.10
❑	179	Sterling Hitchcock	.30	.10
❑	180	Pat Mahomes	.30	.10
❑	181	Mark Acre	.30	.10
❑	182	Charles Nagy	.30	.10
❑	183	Rusty Greer	.30	.10
❑	184	Mike Stanley	.30	.10
❑	185	Jim Bullinger	.30	.10
❑	186	Shane Andrews	.30	.10
❑	187	Brian Keyser	.30	.10
❑	188	Tyler Green	.30	.10
❑	189	Mark Grace	.50	.20
❑	190	Bob Hamelin	.30	.10
❑	191	Luis Ortiz	.30	.10
❑	192	Joe Carter	.30	.10
❑	193	Eddie Taubensee	.30	.10
❑	194	Brian Anderson	.30	.10
❑	195	Edgardo Alfonzo	.30	.10
❑	196	Pedro Munoz	.30	.10
❑	197	David Justice	.30	.10
❑	198	Trevor Hoffman	.30	.10
❑	199	Bobby Ayala	.30	.10
❑	200	Tony Eusebio	.30	.10
❑	201	Jeff Russell	.30	.10
❑	202	Mike Hampton	.30	.10
❑	203	Walt Weiss	.30	.10
❑	204	Joey Hamilton	.30	.10
❑	205	Roberto Hernandez	.30	.10
❑	206	Greg Vaughn	.30	.10
❑	207	Felipe Lira	.30	.10
❑	208	Harold Baines	.30	.10
❑	209	Tim Wallach	.30	.10
❑	210	Manny Alexander	.30	.10
❑	211	Tim Laker	.30	.10
❑	212	Chris Haney	.30	.10
❑	213	Brian Maxcy	.30	.10
❑	214	Eric Young	.30	.10
❑	215	Darryl Strawberry	.30	.10
❑	216	Barry Bonds	2.00	.75
❑	217	Tim Naehring	.30	.10
❑	218	Scott Brosius	.30	.10
❑	219	Reggie Sanders	.30	.10
❑	220	Eddie Murray CL	.50	.20
❑	221	Luis Alicea	.30	.10
❑	222	Albert Belle	.30	.10
❑	223	Benji Gil	.30	.10
❑	224	Dante Bichette	.30	.10
❑	225	Bobby Bonilla	.30	.10
❑	226	Todd Stottlemyre	.30	.10
❑	227	Jim Edmonds	.30	.10
❑	228	Todd Jones	.30	.10
❑	229	Shawn Green	.30	.10
❑	230	Javier Lopez	.30	.10
❑	231	Ariel Prieto	.30	.10
❑	232	Tony Phillips	.30	.10
❑	233	James Mouton	.30	.10
❑	234	Jose Oquendo	.30	.10
❑	235	Royce Clayton	.30	.10
❑	236	Chuck Carr	.30	.10
❑	237	Doug Jones	.30	.10
❑	238	Mark McLemore	.30	.10
❑	239	Bill Swift	.30	.10
❑	240	Scott Leius	.30	.10
❑	241	Russ Davis	.30	.10
❑	242	Ray Durham	.30	.10
❑	243	Matt Mieske	.30	.10
❑	244	Brent Mayne	.30	.10
❑	245	Thomas Howard	.30	.10
❑	246	Troy O'Leary	.30	.10
❑	247	Jacob Brumfield	.30	.10
❑	248	Mickey Morandini	.30	.10
❑	249	Todd Hundley	.30	.10
❑	250	Chris Bosio	.30	.10
❑	251	Omar Vizquel	.50	.20
❑	252	Mike Lansing	.30	.10
❑	253	John Mabry	.30	.10

❑ 254 Mike Perez .30 .10
❑ 255 Delino DeShields .30 .10
❑ 256 Wil Cordero .30 .10
❑ 257 Mike James .30 .10
❑ 258 Todd Van Poppel .30 .10
❑ 259 Joey Cora .30 .10
❑ 260 Andre Dawson .30 .10
❑ 261 Jerry DiPoto .30 .10
❑ 262 Rick Krivda .30 .10
❑ 263 Glenn Dishman .30 .10
❑ 264 Mike Mimbs .30 .10
❑ 265 John Ericks .30 .10
❑ 266 Jose Canseco .50 .20
❑ 267 Jeff Branson .30 .10
❑ 268 Curt Leskanic .30 .10
❑ 269 Jon Nunnally .30 .10
❑ 270 Scott Stahoviak .30 .10
❑ 271 Jeff Montgomery .30 .10
❑ 272 Hal Morris .30 .10
❑ 273 Esteban Loaiza .30 .10
❑ 274 Rico Brogna .30 .10
❑ 275 Dave Winfield .30 .10
❑ 276 J.R. Phillips .30 .10
❑ 277 Todd Zeile .30 .10
❑ 278 Tom Pagnozzi .30 .10
❑ 279 Mark Lemke .30 .10
❑ 280 Dave Magadan .30 .10
❑ 281 Greg McMichael .30 .10
❑ 282 Mike Morgan .30 .10
❑ 283 Moises Alou .30 .10
❑ 284 Dennis Martinez .30 .10
❑ 285 Jeff Kent .30 .10
❑ 286 Mark Johnson .30 .10
❑ 287 Darren Lewis .30 .10
❑ 288 Brad Clontz .30 .10
❑ 289 Chad Fonville .30 .10
❑ 290 Paul Sorrento .30 .10
❑ 291 Lee Smith .30 .10
❑ 292 Tom Glavine .50 .20
❑ 293 Antonio Osuna .30 .10
❑ 294 Kevin Foster .30 .10
❑ 295 Sandy Martinez .30 .10
❑ 296 Mark Leiter .30 .10
❑ 297 Julian Tavarez .30 .10
❑ 298 Mike Kelly .30 .10
❑ 299 Joe Oliver .30 .10
❑ 300 John Flaherty .30 .10
❑ 301 Don Mattingly 2.00 .75
❑ 302 Pat Meares .30 .10
❑ 303 John Doherty .30 .10
❑ 304 Joe Vitiello .30 .10
❑ 305 Vinny Castilla .30 .10
❑ 306 Jeff Brantley .30 .10
❑ 307 Mike Greenwell .30 .10
❑ 308 Midre Cummings .30 .10
❑ 309 Curt Schilling .30 .10
❑ 310 Ken Caminiti .30 .10
❑ 311 Scott Erickson .30 .10
❑ 312 Carl Everett .30 .10
❑ 313 Charles Johnson .30 .10
❑ 314 Alex Diaz .30 .10
❑ 315 Jose Mesa .30 .10
❑ 316 Mark Carreon .30 .10
❑ 317 Carlos Perez .30 .10
❑ 318 Ismael Valdes .30 .10
❑ 319 Frank Castillo .30 .10
❑ 320 Tom Henke .30 .10
❑ 321 Spike Owen .30 .10
❑ 322 Joe Orsulak .30 .10
❑ 323 Paul Menhart .30 .10
❑ 324 Pedro Borbon .30 .10
❑ 325 Paul Molitor CL .30 .10
❑ 326 Jeff Cirillo .30 .10
❑ 327 Edwin Hurtado .30 .10
❑ 328 Orlando Miller .30 .10
❑ 329 Steve Ontiveros .30 .10
❑ 330 Kirby Puckett CL .50 .20
❑ 331 Scott Bullett .30 .10
❑ 332 Andres Galarraga .30 .10
❑ 333 Cal Eldred .30 .10
❑ 334 Sammy Sosa .75 .30
❑ 335 Don Slaught .30 .10
❑ 336 Jody Reed .30 .10
❑ 337 Roger Cedeno .30 .10
❑ 338 Ken Griffey Jr. 1.25 .50
❑ 339 Todd Hollandsworth .30 .10
❑ 340 Mike Trombley .30 .10
❑ 341 Gregg Jefferies .30 .10
❑ 342 Larry Walker .30 .10
❑ 343 Pedro Martinez .50 .20
❑ 344 Dwayne Hosey .30 .10
❑ 345 Terry Pendleton .30 .10
❑ 346 Pete Harnisch .30 .10
❑ 347 Tony Castillo .30 .10
❑ 348 Paul Quantrill .30 .10
❑ 349 Fred McGriff .50 .20
❑ 350 Ivan Rodriguez .50 .20
❑ 351 Butch Huskey .30 .10
❑ 352 Ozzie Smith 1.25 .50
❑ 353 Marty Cordova .30 .10
❑ 354 John Wasdin .30 .10
❑ 355 Wade Boggs .50 .20
❑ 356 Dave Nilsson .30 .10
❑ 357 Rafael Palmeiro .50 .20
❑ 358 Luis Gonzalez .30 .10
❑ 359 Reggie Jefferson .30 .10
❑ 360 Carlos Delgado .30 .10
❑ 361 Orlando Palmeiro .30 .10
❑ 362 Chris Gomez .30 .10
❑ 363 John Smoltz .50 .20
❑ 364 Marc Newfield .30 .10
❑ 365 Matt Williams .30 .10
❑ 366 Jesus Tavarez .30 .10
❑ 367 Bruce Ruffin .30 .10
❑ 368 Sean Berry .30 .10
❑ 369 Randy Velarde .30 .10
❑ 370 Tony Pena .30 .10
❑ 371 Jim Thome .50 .20
❑ 372 Jeffrey Hammonds .30 .10
❑ 373 Bob Wolcott .30 .10
❑ 374 Juan Guzman .30 .10
❑ 375 Juan Gonzalez .30 .10
❑ 376 Michael Tucker .30 .10
❑ 377 Doug Johns .30 .10
❑ 378 Mike Cameron RC .60 .25
❑ 379 Ray Lankford .30 .10
❑ 380 Jose Parra .30 .10
❑ 381 Jimmy Key .30 .10
❑ 382 John Olerud .30 .10
❑ 383 Kevin Ritz .30 .10
❑ 384 Tim Raines .30 .10
❑ 385 Rich Amaral .30 .10
❑ 386 Keith Lockhart .30 .10
❑ 387 Steve Scarsone .30 .10
❑ 388 Cliff Floyd .30 .10
❑ 389 Rich Aude .30 .10
❑ 390 Hideo Nomo .75 .30
❑ 391 Geronimo Berroa .30 .10
❑ 392 Pat Rapp .30 .10
❑ 393 Dustin Hermanson .30 .10
❑ 394 Greg Maddux 1.25 .50
❑ 395 Darren Daulton .30 .10
❑ 396 Kenny Lofton .30 .10
❑ 397 Ruben Rivera .30 .10
❑ 398 Billy Wagner .30 .10
❑ 399 Kevin Brown .30 .10
❑ 400 Mike Kingery .30 .10
❑ 401 Bernie Williams .50 .20
❑ 402 Otis Nixon .30 .10
❑ 403 Damion Easley .30 .10
❑ 404 Paul O'Neill .50 .20
❑ 405 Deion Sanders .50 .20
❑ 406 Dennis Eckersley .30 .10
❑ 407 Tony Clark .30 .10
❑ 408 Rondell White .30 .10
❑ 409 Luis Sojo .30 .10
❑ 410 David Hulse .30 .10
❑ 411 Shane Reynolds .30 .10
❑ 412 Chris Hoiles .30 .10
❑ 413 Lee Tinsley .30 .10
❑ 414 Scott Karl .30 .10
❑ 415 Ron Gant .30 .10
❑ 416 Brian Johnson .30 .10
❑ 417 Jose Oliva .30 .10
❑ 418 Jack McDowell .30 .10
❑ 419 Paul Molitor .30 .10
❑ 420 Ricky Bottalico .30 .10
❑ 421 Paul Wagner .30 .10
❑ 422 Terry Bradshaw .30 .10
❑ 423 Bob Tewksbury .30 .10
❑ 424 Mike Piazza 1.25 .50
❑ 425 Luis Andujar .30 .10
❑ 426 Mark Langston .30 .10
❑ 427 Stan Belinda .30 .10
❑ 428 Kurt Abbott .30 .10
❑ 429 Shawon Dunston .30 .10
❑ 430 Bobby Jones .30 .10
❑ 431 Jose Vizcaino .30 .10
❑ 432 Matt Lawton RC .40 .15
❑ 433 Pat Hentgen .30 .10
❑ 434 Cecil Fielder .30 .10
❑ 435 Carlos Baerga .30 .10
❑ 436 Rich Becker .30 .10
❑ 437 Chipper Jones .75 .30
❑ 438 Bill Risley .30 .10
❑ 439 Kevin Appier .30 .10
❑ 440 Wade Boggs CL .30 .10
❑ 441 Jaime Navarro .30 .10
❑ 442 Barry Larkin .50 .20
❑ 443 Jose Valentin .30 .10
❑ 444 Bryan Rekar .30 .10
❑ 445 Rick Wilkins .30 .10
❑ 446 Quilvio Veras .30 .10
❑ 447 Greg Gagne .30 .10
❑ 448 Mark Kiefer .30 .10
❑ 449 Bobby Witt .30 .10
❑ 450 Andy Ashby .30 .10
❑ 451 Alex Ochoa .30 .10
❑ 452 Jorge Fabregas .30 .10
❑ 453 Gene Schall .30 .10
❑ 454 Ken Hill .30 .10
❑ 455 Tony Tarasco .30 .10
❑ 456 Donnie Wall .30 .10
❑ 457 Carlos Garcia .30 .10
❑ 458 Ryan Thompson .30 .10
❑ 459 Marvin Benard RC .40 .15
❑ 460 Jose Herrera .30 .10
❑ 461 Jeff Blauser .30 .10
❑ 462 Chris Hook .30 .10
❑ 463 Jeff Conine .30 .10
❑ 464 Devon White .30 .10
❑ 465 Danny Bautista .30 .10
❑ 466 Steve Trachsel .30 .10
❑ 467 C.J. Nitkowski .30 .10
❑ 468 Mike Devereaux .30 .10
❑ 469 David Wells .30 .10
❑ 470 Jim Eisenreich .30 .10
❑ 471 Edgar Martinez .50 .20
❑ 472 Craig Biggio .50 .20
❑ 473 Jeff Frye .30 .10
❑ 474 Karim Garcia .30 .10
❑ 475 Jimmy Haynes .30 .10
❑ 476 Darren Holmes .30 .10
❑ 477 Tim Salmon .50 .20
❑ 478 Randy Johnson .75 .30
❑ 479 Eric Plunk .30 .10
❑ 480 Scott Cooper .30 .10
❑ 481 Chan Ho Park .30 .10
❑ 482 Ray McDavid .30 .10
❑ 483 Mark Petkovsek .30 .10
❑ 484 Greg Swindell .30 .10
❑ 485 George Williams .30 .10
❑ 486 Yamil Benitez .30 .10
❑ 487 Tim Wakefield .30 .10
❑ 488 Kevin Tapani .30 .10
❑ 489 Derrick May .30 .10
❑ 490 Ken Griffey Jr. CL .75 .30
❑ 491 Derek Jeter 2.00 .75
❑ 492 Jeff Fassero .30 .10
❑ 493 Benito Santiago .30 .10
❑ 494 Tom Gordon .30 .10
❑ 495 Jamie Brewington RC .30 .10
❑ 496 Vince Coleman .30 .10
❑ 497 Kevin Jordan .30 .10
❑ 498 Jeff King .30 .10
❑ 499 Mike Simms .30 .10
❑ 500 Jose Rijo .30 .10
❑ 501 Denny Neagle .30 .10
❑ 502 Jose Lima .30 .10
❑ 503 Kevin Seitzer .30 .10
❑ 504 Alex Fernandez .30 .10
❑ 505 Mo Vaughn .30 .10
❑ 506 Phil Nevin .30 .10
❑ 507 J.T. Snow .30 .10
❑ 508 Andujar Cedeno .30 .10
❑ 509 Ozzie Guillen .30 .10
❑ 510 Mark Clark .30 .10
❑ 511 Mark McGwire 2.00 .75

❑ 512	Jeff Reboulet	.30	.10
❑ 513	Armando Benitez	.30	.10
❑ 514	LaTroy Hawkins	.30	.10
❑ 515	Brett Butler	.30	.10
❑ 516	Tavo Alvarez	.30	.10
❑ 517	Chris Snopek	.30	.10
❑ 518	Mike Mussina	.50	.20
❑ 519	Darryl Kile	.30	.10
❑ 520	Wally Joyner	.30	.10
❑ 521	Willie McGee	.30	.10
❑ 522	Kent Mercker	.30	.10
❑ 523	Mike Jackson	.30	.10
❑ 524	Troy Percival	.30	.10
❑ 525	Tony Gwynn	1.00	.40
❑ 526	Ron Coomer	.30	.10
❑ 527	Darryl Hamilton	.30	.10
❑ 528	Phil Plantier	.30	.10
❑ 529	Norm Charlton	.30	.10
❑ 530	Craig Paquette	.30	.10
❑ 531	Dave Burba	.30	.10
❑ 532	Mike Henneman	.30	.10
❑ 533	Terrell Wade	.30	.10
❑ 534	Eddie Williams	.30	.10
❑ 535	Robin Ventura	.30	.10
❑ 536	Chuck Knoblauch	.30	.10
❑ 537	Les Norman	.30	.10
❑ 538	Brady Anderson	.30	.10
❑ 539	Roger Clemens	1.50	.60
❑ 540	Mark Portugal	.30	.10
❑ 541	Mike Matheny	.30	.10
❑ 542	Jeff Parrett	.30	.10
❑ 543	Roberto Kelly	.30	.10
❑ 544	Damon Buford	.30	.10
❑ 545	Chad Ogea	.30	.10
❑ 546	Jose Offerman	.30	.10
❑ 547	Brian Barber	.30	.10
❑ 548	Danny Tartabull	.30	.10
❑ 549	Duane Singleton	.30	.10
❑ 550	Tony Gwynn CL	.50	.20

1997 Donruss

❑	COMPLETE SET (450)	50.00	20.00
❑	COMPLETE SERIES 1 (270)	25.00	10.00
❑	COMPLETE UPDATE (180)	25.00	10.00
❑ 1	Juan Gonzalez	.30	.10
❑ 2	Jim Edmonds	.30	.10
❑ 3	Tony Gwynn	1.00	.40
❑ 4	Andres Galarraga	.30	.10
❑ 5	Joe Carter	.30	.10
❑ 6	Raul Mondesi	.30	.10
❑ 7	Greg Maddux	1.25	.50
❑ 8	Travis Fryman	.30	.10
❑ 9	Brian Jordan	.30	.10
❑ 10	Henry Rodriguez	.30	.10
❑ 11	Manny Ramirez	.50	.20
❑ 12	Mark McGwire	2.00	.75
❑ 13	Marc Newfield	.30	.10
❑ 14	Craig Biggio	.50	.20
❑ 15	Sammy Sosa	.75	.30
❑ 16	Brady Anderson	.30	.10
❑ 17	Wade Boggs	.50	.20
❑ 18	Charles Johnson	.30	.10
❑ 19	Matt Williams	.30	.10
❑ 20	Denny Neagle	.30	.10
❑ 21	Ken Griffey Jr.	1.25	.50
❑ 22	Robin Ventura	.30	.10
❑ 23	Barry Larkin	.50	.20
❑ 24	Todd Zeile	.30	.10

❑ 25	Chuck Knoblauch	.30	.10
❑ 26	Todd Hundley	.30	.10
❑ 27	Roger Clemens	1.50	.60
❑ 28	Michael Tucker	.30	.10
❑ 29	Rondell White	.30	.10
❑ 30	Osvaldo Fernandez	.30	.10
❑ 31	Ivan Rodriguez	.50	.20
❑ 32	Alex Fernandez	.30	.10
❑ 33	Jason Isringhausen	.30	.10
❑ 34	Chipper Jones	.75	.30
❑ 35	Paul O'Neill	.50	.20
❑ 36	Hideo Nomo	.75	.30
❑ 37	Roberto Alomar	.50	.20
❑ 38	Derek Bell	.30	.10
❑ 39	Paul Molitor	.30	.10
❑ 40	Andy Benes	.30	.10
❑ 41	Steve Trachsel	.30	.10
❑ 42	J.T. Snow	.30	.10
❑ 43	Jason Kendall	.30	.10
❑ 44	Alex Rodriguez	1.25	.50
❑ 45	Joey Hamilton	.30	.10
❑ 46	Carlos Delgado	.30	.10
❑ 47	Jason Giambi	.30	.10
❑ 48	Larry Walker	.30	.10
❑ 49	Derek Jeter	2.00	.75
❑ 50	Kenny Lofton	.30	.10
❑ 51	Devon White	.30	.10
❑ 52	Matt Mieske	.30	.10
❑ 53	Melvin Nieves	.30	.10
❑ 54	Jose Canseco	.50	.20
❑ 55	Tino Martinez	.50	.20
❑ 56	Rafael Palmeiro	.50	.20
❑ 57	Edgardo Alfonzo	.30	.10
❑ 58	Jay Buhner	.30	.10
❑ 59	Shane Reynolds	.30	.10
❑ 60	Steve Finley	.30	.10
❑ 61	Bobby Higginson	.30	.10
❑ 62	Dean Palmer	.30	.10
❑ 63	Terry Pendleton	.30	.10
❑ 64	Marquis Grissom	.30	.10
❑ 65	Mike Stanley	.30	.10
❑ 66	Moises Alou	.30	.10
❑ 67	Ray Lankford	.30	.10
❑ 68	Marty Cordova	.30	.10
❑ 69	John Olerud	.30	.10
❑ 70	David Cone	.30	.10
❑ 71	Benito Santiago	.30	.10
❑ 72	Ryne Sandberg	1.25	.50
❑ 73	Rickey Henderson	.75	.30
❑ 74	Roger Cedeno	.30	.10
❑ 75	Wilson Alvarez	.30	.10
❑ 76	Tim Salmon	.50	.20
❑ 77	Orlando Merced	.30	.10
❑ 78	Vinny Castilla	.30	.10
❑ 79	Ismael Valdes	.30	.10
❑ 80	Dante Bichette	.30	.10
❑ 81	Kevin Brown	.30	.10
❑ 82	Andy Pettitte	.50	.20
❑ 83	Scott Stahoviak	.30	.10
❑ 84	Mickey Tettleton	.30	.10
❑ 85	Jack McDowell	.30	.10
❑ 86	Tom Glavine	.50	.20
❑ 87	Gregg Jefferies	.30	.10
❑ 88	Chili Davis	.30	.10
❑ 89	Randy Johnson	.75	.30
❑ 90	John Mabry	.30	.10
❑ 91	Billy Wagner	.30	.10
❑ 92	Jeff Cirillo	.30	.10
❑ 93	Trevor Hoffman	.30	.10
❑ 94	Juan Guzman	.30	.10
❑ 95	Geronimo Berroa	.30	.10
❑ 96	Bernard Gilkey	.30	.10
❑ 97	Danny Tartabull	.30	.10
❑ 98	Johnny Damon	.50	.20
❑ 99	Charlie Hayes	.30	.10
❑ 100	Reggie Sanders	.30	.10
❑ 101	Robby Thompson	.30	.10
❑ 102	Bobby Bonilla	.30	.10
❑ 103	Reggie Jefferson	.30	.10
❑ 104	John Smoltz	.50	.20
❑ 105	Jim Thome	.50	.20
❑ 106	Ruben Rivera	.30	.10
❑ 107	Darren Oliver	.30	.10
❑ 108	Mo Vaughn	.30	.10
❑ 109	Roger Pavlik	.30	.10
❑ 110	Terry Steinbach	.30	.10

❑ 111	Jermaine Dye	.30	.10
❑ 112	Mark Grudzielanek	.30	.10
❑ 113	Rick Aguilera	.30	.10
❑ 114	Jamey Wright	.30	.10
❑ 115	Eddie Murray	.75	.30
❑ 116	Brian L. Hunter	.30	.10
❑ 117	Hal Morris	.30	.10
❑ 118	Tom Pagnozzi	.30	.10
❑ 119	Mike Mussina	.50	.20
❑ 120	Mark Grace	.50	.20
❑ 121	Cal Ripken	2.50	1.00
❑ 122	Tom Goodwin	.30	.10
❑ 123	Paul Sorrento	.30	.10
❑ 124	Jay Bell	.30	.10
❑ 125	Todd Hollandsworth	.30	.10
❑ 126	Edgar Martinez	.50	.20
❑ 127	George Arias	.30	.10
❑ 128	Greg Vaughn	.30	.10
❑ 129	Roberto Hernandez	.30	.10
❑ 130	Delino DeShields	.30	.10
❑ 131	Bill Pulsipher	.30	.10
❑ 132	Joey Cora	.30	.10
❑ 133	Mariano Rivera	.75	.30
❑ 134	Mike Piazza	1.25	.50
❑ 135	Carlos Baerga	.30	.10
❑ 136	Jose Mesa	.30	.10
❑ 137	Will Clark	.50	.20
❑ 138	Frank Thomas	.75	.30
❑ 139	John Wetteland	.30	.10
❑ 140	Shawn Estes	.30	.10
❑ 141	Garret Anderson	.30	.10
❑ 142	Andre Dawson	.30	.10
❑ 143	Eddie Taubensee	.30	.10
❑ 144	Ryan Klesko	.30	.10
❑ 145	Rocky Coppinger	.30	.10
❑ 146	Jeff Bagwell	.50	.20
❑ 147	Donovan Osborne	.30	.10
❑ 148	Greg Myers	.30	.10
❑ 149	Brant Brown	.30	.10
❑ 150	Kevin Elster	.30	.10
❑ 151	Bob Wells	.30	.10
❑ 152	Wally Joyner	.30	.10
❑ 153	Rico Brogna	.30	.10
❑ 154	Dwight Gooden	.30	.10
❑ 155	Jermaine Allensworth	.30	.10
❑ 156	Ray Durham	.30	.10
❑ 157	Cecil Fielder	.30	.10
❑ 158	John Burkett	.30	.10
❑ 159	Gary Sheffield	.30	.10
❑ 160	Albert Belle	.30	.10
❑ 161	Tomas Perez	.30	.10
❑ 162	David Doster	.30	.10
❑ 163	John Valentin	.30	.10
❑ 164	Danny Graves	.30	.10
❑ 165	Jose Paniagua	.30	.10
❑ 166	Brian Giles RC	1.50	.60
❑ 167	Barry Bonds	2.00	.75
❑ 168	Sterling Hitchcock	.30	.10
❑ 169	Bernie Williams	.50	.20
❑ 170	Fred McGriff	.50	.20
❑ 171	George Williams	.30	.10
❑ 172	Amaury Telemaco	.30	.10
❑ 173	Ken Caminiti	.30	.10
❑ 174	Ron Gant	.30	.10
❑ 175	Dave Justice	.30	.10
❑ 176	James Baldwin	.30	.10
❑ 177	Pat Hentgen	.30	.10
❑ 178	Ben McDonald	.30	.10
❑ 179	Tim Naehring	.30	.10
❑ 180	Jim Eisenreich	.30	.10
❑ 181	Ken Hill	.30	.10
❑ 182	Paul Wilson	.30	.10
❑ 183	Marvin Benard	.30	.10
❑ 184	Alan Benes	.30	.10
❑ 185	Ellis Burks	.30	.10
❑ 186	Scott Servais	.30	.10
❑ 187	David Segui	.30	.10
❑ 188	Scott Brosius	.30	.10
❑ 189	Jose Offerman	.30	.10
❑ 190	Eric Davis	.30	.10
❑ 191	Brett Butler	.30	.10
❑ 192	Curtis Pride	.30	.10
❑ 193	Yamil Benitez	.30	.10
❑ 194	Chan Ho Park	.30	.10
❑ 195	Bret Boone	.30	.10
❑ 196	Omar Vizquel	.50	.20

❑ 197 Orlando Miller .30 .10
❑ 198 Ramon Martinez .30 .10
❑ 199 Harold Baines .30 .10
❑ 200 Eric Young .30 .10
❑ 201 Fernando Vina .30 .10
❑ 202 Alex Gonzalez .30 .10
❑ 203 Fernando Valenzuela .30 .10
❑ 204 Steve Avery .30 .10
❑ 205 Ernie Young .30 .10
❑ 206 Kevin Appier .30 .10
❑ 207 Randy Myers .30 .10
❑ 208 Jeff Suppan .30 .10
❑ 209 James Mouton .30 .10
❑ 210 Russ Davis .30 .10
❑ 211 Al Martin .30 .10
❑ 212 Troy Percival .30 .10
❑ 213 Al Leiter .30 .10
❑ 214 Dennis Eckersley .30 .10
❑ 215 Mark Johnson .30 .10
❑ 216 Eric Karros .30 .10
❑ 217 Royce Clayton .30 .10
❑ 218 Tony Phillips .30 .10
❑ 219 Tim Wakefield .30 .10
❑ 220 Alan Trammell .30 .10
❑ 221 Eduardo Perez .30 .10
❑ 222 Butch Huskey .30 .10
❑ 223 Tim Belcher .30 .10
❑ 224 Jamie Moyer .30 .10
❑ 225 F.P. Santangelo .30 .10
❑ 226 Rusty Greer .30 .10
❑ 227 Jeff Brantley .30 .10
❑ 228 Mark Langston .30 .10
❑ 229 Ray Montgomery .30 .10
❑ 230 Rich Becker .30 .10
❑ 231 Ozzie Smith 1.25 .50
❑ 232 Rey Ordonez .30 .10
❑ 233 Ricky Otero .30 .10
❑ 234 Mike Cameron .30 .10
❑ 235 Mike Sweeney .30 .10
❑ 236 Mark Lewis .30 .10
❑ 237 Luis Gonzalez .30 .10
❑ 238 Marcus Jensen .30 .10
❑ 239 Ed Sprague .30 .10
❑ 240 Jose Valentin .30 .10
❑ 241 Jeff Frye .30 .10
❑ 242 Charles Nagy .30 .10
❑ 243 Carlos Garcia .30 .10
❑ 244 Mike Hampton .30 .10
❑ 245 B.J. Surhoff .30 .10
❑ 246 Wilton Guerrero .30 .10
❑ 247 Frank Rodriguez .30 .10
❑ 248 Gary Gaetti .30 .10
❑ 249 Lance Johnson .30 .10
❑ 250 Darren Bragg .30 .10
❑ 251 Darryl Hamilton .30 .10
❑ 252 John Jaha .30 .10
❑ 253 Craig Paquette .30 .10
❑ 254 Jaime Navarro .30 .10
❑ 255 Shawon Dunston .30 .10
❑ 256 Mark Loretta .30 .10
❑ 257 Tim Belk .30 .10
❑ 258 Jeff Darwin .30 .10
❑ 259 Ruben Sierra .30 .10
❑ 260 Chuck Finley .30 .10
❑ 261 Darryl Strawberry .30 .10
❑ 262 Shannon Stewart .30 .10
❑ 263 Pedro Martinez .50 .20
❑ 264 Neifi Perez .30 .10
❑ 265 Jeff Conine .30 .10
❑ 266 Orel Hershiser .30 .10
❑ 267 Eddie Murray CL .50 .20
❑ 268 Paul Molitor CL .30 .10
❑ 269 Barry Bonds CL 1.00 .40
❑ 270 Mark McGwire CL 1.00 .40
❑ 271 Matt Williams .30 .10
❑ 272 Todd Zeile .30 .10
❑ 273 Roger Clemens 1.50 .60
❑ 274 Michael Tucker .30 .10
❑ 275 J.T. Snow .30 .10
❑ 276 Kenny Lofton .30 .10
❑ 277 Jose Canseco .50 .20
❑ 278 Marquis Grissom .30 .10
❑ 279 Moises Alou .30 .10
❑ 280 Benito Santiago .30 .10
❑ 281 Willie McGee .30 .10
❑ 282 Chili Davis .30 .10
❑ 283 Ron Coomer .30 .10
❑ 284 Orlando Merced .30 .10
❑ 285 Delino DeShields .30 .10
❑ 286 John Wetteland .30 .10
❑ 287 Darren Daulton .30 .10
❑ 288 Lee Stevens .30 .10
❑ 289 Albert Belle .30 .10
❑ 290 Sterling Hitchcock .30 .10
❑ 291 David Justice .30 .10
❑ 292 Eric Davis .30 .10
❑ 293 Brian Hunter .30 .10
❑ 294 Darryl Hamilton .30 .10
❑ 295 Steve Avery .30 .10
❑ 296 Joe Vitiello .30 .10
❑ 297 Jaime Navarro .30 .10
❑ 298 Eddie Murray .75 .30
❑ 299 Randy Myers .30 .10
❑ 300 Francisco Cordova .30 .10
❑ 301 Javier Lopez .30 .10
❑ 302 Geronimo Berroa .30 .10
❑ 303 Jeffrey Hammonds .30 .10
❑ 304 Deion Sanders .50 .20
❑ 305 Jeff Fassero .30 .10
❑ 306 Curt Schilling .30 .10
❑ 307 Robb Nen .30 .10
❑ 308 Mark McLemore .30 .10
❑ 309 Jimmy Key .30 .10
❑ 310 Quilvio Veras .30 .10
❑ 311 Bip Roberts .30 .10
❑ 312 Esteban Loaiza .30 .10
❑ 313 Andy Ashby .30 .10
❑ 314 Sandy Alomar Jr. .30 .10
❑ 315 Shawn Green .30 .10
❑ 316 Luis Castillo .30 .10
❑ 317 Benji Gil .30 .10
❑ 318 Otis Nixon .30 .10
❑ 319 Aaron Sele .30 .10
❑ 320 Brad Ausmus .30 .10
❑ 321 Troy O'Leary .30 .10
❑ 322 Terrell Wade .30 .10
❑ 323 Jeff King .30 .10
❑ 324 Kevin Seitzer .30 .10
❑ 325 Mark Wohlers .30 .10
❑ 326 Edgar Renteria .30 .10
❑ 327 Dan Wilson .30 .10
❑ 328 Brian McRae .30 .10
❑ 329 Rod Beck .30 .10
❑ 330 Julio Franco .30 .10
❑ 331 Dave Nilsson .30 .10
❑ 332 Glenallen Hill .30 .10
❑ 333 Kevin Elster .30 .10
❑ 334 Joe Girardi .30 .10
❑ 335 David Wells .30 .10
❑ 336 Jeff Blauser .30 .10
❑ 337 Darryl Kile .30 .10
❑ 338 Jeff Kent .30 .10
❑ 339 Jim Leyritz .30 .10
❑ 340 Todd Stottlemyre .30 .10
❑ 341 Tony Clark .30 .10
❑ 342 Chris Hoiles .30 .10
❑ 343 Mike Lieberthal .30 .10
❑ 344 Matt Lawton .30 .10
❑ 345 Alex Ochoa .30 .10
❑ 346 Chris Snopek .30 .10
❑ 347 Rudy Pemberton .30 .10
❑ 348 Eric Owens .30 .10
❑ 349 Joe Randa .30 .10
❑ 350 John Olerud .30 .10
❑ 351 Steve Karsay .30 .10
❑ 352 Mark Whiten .30 .10
❑ 353 Bob Abreu .50 .20
❑ 354 Bartolo Colon .30 .10
❑ 355 Vladimir Guerrero .75 .30
❑ 356 Darin Erstad .30 .10
❑ 357 Scott Rolen .50 .20
❑ 358 Andruw Jones .50 .20
❑ 359 Scott Spiezio .30 .10
❑ 360 Karim Garcia .30 .10
❑ 361 Hideki Irabu RC .40 .15
❑ 362 Nomar Garciaparra 1.25 .50
❑ 363 Dmitri Young .30 .10
❑ 364 Bubba Trammell RC .40 .15
❑ 365 Kevin Orie .30 .10
❑ 366 Jose Rosado .30 .10
❑ 367 Jose Guillen .30 .10
❑ 368 Brooks Kieschnick .30 .10
❑ 369 Pokey Reese .30 .10
❑ 370 Glendon Rusch .30 .10
❑ 371 Jason Dickson .30 .10
❑ 372 Todd Walker .30 .10
❑ 373 Justin Thompson .30 .10
❑ 374 Todd Greene .30 .10
❑ 375 Jeff Suppan .30 .10
❑ 376 Trey Beamon .30 .10
❑ 377 Damon Mashore .30 .10
❑ 378 Wendell Magee .30 .10
❑ 379 Shigetoshi Hasegawa RC .50 .20
❑ 380 Bill Mueller RC 1.25 .50
❑ 381 Chris Widger .30 .10
❑ 382 Tony Graffanino .30 .10
❑ 383 Derrek Lee .50 .20
❑ 384 Brian Moehler RC .40 .15
❑ 385 Quinton McCracken .30 .10
❑ 386 Matt Morris .30 .10
❑ 387 Marvin Benard .30 .10
❑ 388 Deivi Cruz RC .40 .15
❑ 389 Javier Valentin .30 .10
❑ 390 Todd Dunwoody .30 .10
❑ 391 Derrick Gibson .30 .10
❑ 392 Raul Casanova .30 .10
❑ 393 George Arias .30 .10
❑ 394 Tony Womack RC .40 .15
❑ 395 Antone Williamson .30 .10
❑ 396 Jose Cruz Jr. RC .40 .15
❑ 397 Desi Relaford .30 .10
❑ 398 Frank Thomas HIT .50 .20
❑ 399 Ken Griffey Jr. HIT .75 .30
❑ 400 Cal Ripken HIT 1.25 .50
❑ 401 Chipper Jones HIT .50 .20
❑ 402 Mike Piazza HIT .75 .30
❑ 403 Gary Sheffield HIT .30 .10
❑ 404 Alex Rodriguez HIT .75 .30
❑ 405 Wade Boggs HIT .30 .10
❑ 406 Juan Gonzalez HIT .30 .10
❑ 407 Tony Gwynn HIT .50 .20
❑ 408 Edgar Martinez HIT .30 .10
❑ 409 Jeff Bagwell HIT .30 .10
❑ 410 Larry Walker HIT .30 .10
❑ 411 Kenny Lofton HIT .30 .10
❑ 412 Manny Ramirez HIT .30 .10
❑ 413 Mark McGwire HIT 1.00 .40
❑ 414 Roberto Alomar HIT .30 .10
❑ 415 Derek Jeter HIT 1.00 .40
❑ 416 Brady Anderson HIT .30 .10
❑ 417 Paul Molitor HIT .30 .10
❑ 418 Dante Bichette HIT .30 .10
❑ 419 Jim Edmonds HIT .30 .10
❑ 420 Mo Vaughn HIT .30 .10
❑ 421 Barry Bonds HIT 1.00 .40
❑ 422 Rusty Greer HIT .30 .10
❑ 423 Greg Maddux KING .75 .30
❑ 424 Andy Pettitte KING .30 .10
❑ 425 John Smoltz KING .30 .10
❑ 426 Randy Johnson KING .50 .20
❑ 427 Hideo Nomo KING .30 .10
❑ 428 Roger Clemens KING .75 .30
❑ 429 Tom Glavine KING .30 .10
❑ 430 Pat Hentgen KING .30 .10
❑ 431 Kevin Brown KING .30 .10
❑ 432 Mike Mussina KING .30 .10
❑ 433 Alex Fernandez KING .30 .10
❑ 434 Kevin Appier KING .30 .10
❑ 435 David Cone KING .30 .10
❑ 436 Jeff Fassero KING .30 .10
❑ 437 John Wetteland KING .30 .10
❑ 438 B.Bonds/I.Rodriguez IS 1.00 .40
❑ 439 K.Griffey Jr./A.Galarraga IS .75 .30
❑ 440 F.McGriff/R.Palmeiro IS .30 .10
❑ 441 B.Larkin/J.Thome IS .50 .20
❑ 442 S.Sosa/A.Belle IS .50 .20
❑ 443 B.Williams/T.Hundley IS .30 .10
❑ 444 C.Knoblauch/B.Jordan IS .30 .10
❑ 445 M.Vaughn/J.Conine IS .30 .10
❑ 446 K.Caminiti/J.Giambi IS .30 .10
❑ 447 R.Mondesi/T.Salmon IS .30 .10
❑ 448 Cal Ripken CL 1.25 .50
❑ 449 Greg Maddux CL .75 .30
❑ 450 Ken Griffey Jr. CL .75 .30

1998 Donruss

❑ COMPLETE SET (420)	50.00	20.00
❑ COMPLETE SERIES 1 (170)	20.00	8.00
❑ COMPLETE UPDATE (250)	30.00	12.50
❑ 1 Paul Molitor	.25	.08
❑ 2 Juan Gonzalez	.25	.08
❑ 3 Darryl Kile	.25	.08
❑ 4 Randy Johnson	.60	.25
❑ 5 Tom Glavine	.40	.15
❑ 6 Pat Hentgen	.25	.08
❑ 7 David Justice	.25	.08
❑ 8 Kevin Brown	.40	.15
❑ 9 Mike Mussina	.40	.15
❑ 10 Ken Caminiti	.25	.08
❑ 11 Todd Hundley	.25	.08
❑ 12 Frank Thomas	.60	.25
❑ 13 Ray Lankford	.25	.08
❑ 14 Justin Thompson	.25	.08
❑ 15 Jason Dickson	.25	.08
❑ 16 Kenny Lofton	.25	.08
❑ 17 Ivan Rodriguez	.40	.15
❑ 18 Pedro Martinez	.40	.15
❑ 19 Brady Anderson	.25	.08
❑ 20 Barry Larkin	.40	.15
❑ 21 Chipper Jones	.60	.25
❑ 22 Tony Gwynn	.75	.30
❑ 23 Roger Clemens	1.25	.50
❑ 24 Sandy Alomar Jr.	.25	.08
❑ 25 Tino Martinez	.40	.15
❑ 26 Jeff Bagwell	.40	.15
❑ 27 Shawn Estes	.25	.08
❑ 28 Ken Griffey Jr.	1.00	.40
❑ 29 Javier Lopez	.25	.08
❑ 30 Denny Neagle	.25	.08
❑ 31 Mike Piazza	1.00	.40
❑ 32 Andres Galarraga	.25	.08
❑ 33 Larry Walker	.25	.08
❑ 34 Alex Rodriguez	1.00	.40
❑ 35 Greg Maddux	1.00	.40
❑ 36 Albert Belle	.25	.08
❑ 37 Barry Bonds	1.50	.60
❑ 38 Mo Vaughn	.25	.08
❑ 39 Kevin Appier	.25	.08
❑ 40 Wade Boggs	.40	.15
❑ 41 Garret Anderson	.25	.08
❑ 42 Jeffrey Hammonds	.25	.08
❑ 43 Marquis Grissom	.25	.08
❑ 44 Jim Edmonds	.25	.08
❑ 45 Brian Jordan	.25	.08
❑ 46 Raul Mondesi	.25	.08
❑ 47 John Valentin	.25	.08
❑ 48 Brad Radke	.25	.08
❑ 49 Ismael Valdes	.25	.08
❑ 50 Matt Stairs	.25	.08
❑ 51 Matt Williams	.25	.08
❑ 52 Reggie Jefferson	.25	.08
❑ 53 Alan Benes	.25	.08
❑ 54 Charles Johnson	.25	.08
❑ 55 Chuck Knoblauch	.25	.08
❑ 56 Edgar Martinez	.40	.15
❑ 57 Nomar Garciaparra	1.00	.40
❑ 58 Craig Biggio	.40	.15
❑ 59 Bernie Williams	.40	.15
❑ 60 David Cone	.25	.08
❑ 61 Cal Ripken	2.00	.75
❑ 62 Mark McGwire	1.50	.60
❑ 63 Roberto Alomar	.40	.15
❑ 64 Fred McGriff	.40	.15
❑ 65 Eric Karros	.25	.08
❑ 66 Robin Ventura	.25	.08
❑ 67 Darin Erstad	.25	.08
❑ 68 Michael Tucker	.25	.08
❑ 69 Jim Thome	.40	.15
❑ 70 Mark Grace	.40	.15
❑ 71 Lou Collier	.25	.08
❑ 72 Karim Garcia	.25	.08
❑ 73 Alex Fernandez	.25	.08
❑ 74 J.T. Snow	.25	.08
❑ 75 Reggie Sanders	.25	.08
❑ 76 John Smoltz	.40	.15
❑ 77 Tim Salmon	.40	.15
❑ 78 Paul O'Neill	.40	.15
❑ 79 Vinny Castilla	.25	.08
❑ 80 Rafael Palmeiro	.40	.15
❑ 81 Jaret Wright	.25	.08
❑ 82 Jay Buhner	.25	.08
❑ 83 Brett Butler	.25	.08
❑ 84 Todd Greene	.25	.08
❑ 85 Scott Rolen	.40	.15
❑ 86 Sammy Sosa	.60	.25
❑ 87 Jason Giambi	.25	.08
❑ 88 Carlos Delgado	.25	.08
❑ 89 Deion Sanders	.40	.15
❑ 90 Wilton Guerrero	.25	.08
❑ 91 Andy Pettitte	.40	.15
❑ 92 Brian Giles	.25	.08
❑ 93 Dmitri Young	.25	.08
❑ 94 Ron Coomer	.25	.08
❑ 95 Mike Cameron	.25	.08
❑ 96 Edgardo Alfonzo	.25	.08
❑ 97 Jimmy Key	.25	.08
❑ 98 Ryan Klesko	.25	.08
❑ 99 Andy Benes	.25	.08
❑ 100 Derek Jeter	1.50	.60
❑ 101 Jeff Fassero	.25	.08
❑ 102 Neifi Perez	.25	.08
❑ 103 Hideo Nomo	.60	.25
❑ 104 Andruw Jones	.40	.15
❑ 105 Todd Helton	.40	.15
❑ 106 Livan Hernandez	.25	.08
❑ 107 Brett Tomko	.25	.08
❑ 108 Shannon Stewart	.25	.08
❑ 109 Bartolo Colon	.25	.08
❑ 110 Matt Morris	.25	.08
❑ 111 Miguel Tejada	.60	.25
❑ 112 Pokey Reese	.25	.08
❑ 113 Fernando Tatis	.25	.08
❑ 114 Todd Dunwoody	.25	.08
❑ 115 Jose Cruz Jr.	.25	.08
❑ 116 Chan Ho Park	.25	.08
❑ 117 Kevin Young	.25	.08
❑ 118 Rickey Henderson	.60	.25
❑ 119 Hideki Irabu	.25	.08
❑ 120 Francisco Cordova	.25	.08
❑ 121 Al Martin	.25	.08
❑ 122 Tony Clark	.25	.08
❑ 123 Curt Schilling	.25	.08
❑ 124 Rusty Greer	.25	.08
❑ 125 Jose Canseco	.40	.15
❑ 126 Edgar Renteria	.25	.08
❑ 127 Todd Walker	.25	.08
❑ 128 Wally Joyner	.25	.08
❑ 129 Bill Mueller	.25	.08
❑ 130 Jose Guillen	.25	.08
❑ 131 Manny Ramirez	.40	.15
❑ 132 Bobby Higginson	.25	.08
❑ 133 Kevin Orie	.25	.08
❑ 134 Will Clark	.40	.15
❑ 135 Dave Nilsson	.25	.08
❑ 136 Jason Kendall	.25	.08
❑ 137 Ivan Cruz	.25	.08
❑ 138 Gary Sheffield	.25	.08
❑ 139 Bubba Trammell	.25	.08
❑ 140 Vladimir Guerrero	.60	.25
❑ 141 Dennis Reyes	.25	.08
❑ 142 Bobby Bonilla	.25	.08
❑ 143 Ruben Rivera	.25	.08
❑ 144 Ben Grieve	.25	.08
❑ 145 Moises Alou	.25	.08
❑ 146 Tony Womack	.25	.08
❑ 147 Eric Young	.25	.08
❑ 148 Paul Konerko	.25	.08
❑ 149 Dante Bichette	.25	.08
❑ 150 Joe Carter	.25	.08
❑ 151 Rondell White	.25	.08
❑ 152 Chris Holt	.25	.08
❑ 153 Shawn Green	.25	.08
❑ 154 Mark Grudzielanek	.25	.08
❑ 155 Jermaine Dye	.25	.08
❑ 156 Ken Griffey Jr. FC	.60	.25
❑ 157 Frank Thomas FC	.40	.15
❑ 158 Chipper Jones FC	.40	.15
❑ 159 Mike Piazza FC	.60	.25
❑ 160 Cal Ripken FC	1.00	.40
❑ 161 Greg Maddux FC	.60	.25
❑ 162 Juan Gonzalez FC	.25	.08
❑ 163 Alex Rodriguez FC	.60	.25
❑ 164 Mark McGwire FC	.75	.30
❑ 165 Derek Jeter FC	.75	.30
❑ 166 Larry Walker CL	.25	.08
❑ 167 Tony Gwynn CL	.40	.15
❑ 168 Tino Martinez CL	.25	.08
❑ 169 Scott Rolen CL	.25	.08
❑ 170 Nomar Garciaparra CL	.60	.25
❑ 171 Mike Sweeney	.25	.08
❑ 172 Dustin Hermanson	.25	.08
❑ 173 Darren Dreifort	.25	.08
❑ 174 Ron Gant	.25	.08
❑ 175 Todd Hollandsworth	.25	.08
❑ 176 John Jaha	.25	.08
❑ 177 Kerry Wood	.30	.10
❑ 178 Chris Stynes	.25	.08
❑ 179 Kevin Elster	.25	.08
❑ 180 Derek Bell	.25	.08
❑ 181 Darryl Strawberry	.25	.08
❑ 182 Damion Easley	.25	.08
❑ 183 Jeff Cirillo	.25	.08
❑ 184 John Thomson	.25	.08
❑ 185 Dan Wilson	.25	.08
❑ 186 Jay Bell	.25	.08
❑ 187 Bernard Gilkey	.25	.08
❑ 188 Marc Valdes	.25	.08
❑ 189 Ramon Martinez	.25	.08
❑ 190 Charles Nagy	.25	.08
❑ 191 Derek Lowe	.25	.08
❑ 192 Andy Benes	.25	.08
❑ 193 Delino DeShields	.25	.08
❑ 194 Ryan Jackson RC	.25	.08
❑ 195 Kenny Lofton	.25	.08
❑ 196 Chuck Knoblauch	.25	.08
❑ 197 Andres Galarraga	.25	.08
❑ 198 Jose Canseco	.40	.15
❑ 199 John Olerud	.25	.08
❑ 200 Lance Johnson	.25	.08
❑ 201 Darryl Kile	.25	.08
❑ 202 Luis Castillo	.25	.08
❑ 203 Joe Carter	.25	.08
❑ 204 Dennis Eckersley	.25	.08
❑ 205 Steve Finley	.25	.08
❑ 206 Esteban Loaiza	.25	.08
❑ 207 Ryan Christenson RC	.25	.08
❑ 208 Deivi Cruz	.25	.08
❑ 209 Mariano Rivera	.60	.25
❑ 210 Mike Judd RC	.30	.10
❑ 211 Billy Wagner	.25	.08
❑ 212 Scott Spiezio	.25	.08
❑ 213 Russ Davis	.25	.08
❑ 214 Jeff Suppan	.25	.08
❑ 215 Doug Glanville	.25	.08
❑ 216 Dmitri Young	.25	.08
❑ 217 Rey Ordonez	.25	.08
❑ 218 Cecil Fielder	.25	.08
❑ 219 Masato Yoshii RC	.30	.10
❑ 220 Raul Casanova	.25	.08
❑ 221 Rolando Arrojo RC	.30	.10
❑ 222 Ellis Burks	.25	.08
❑ 223 Butch Huskey	.25	.08
❑ 224 Brian Hunter	.25	.08
❑ 225 Marquis Grissom	.25	.08
❑ 226 Kevin Brown	.40	.15
❑ 227 Joe Randa	.25	.08
❑ 228 Henry Rodriguez	.25	.08
❑ 229 Omar Vizquel	.40	.15
❑ 230 Fred McGriff	.40	.15
❑ 231 Matt Williams	.25	.08
❑ 232 Moises Alou	.25	.08
❑ 233 Travis Fryman	.25	.08
❑ 234 Wade Boggs	.40	.15
❑ 235 Pedro Martinez	.40	.15

❑	236 Rickey Henderson	.60	.25
❑	237 Bubba Trammell	.25	.08
❑	238 Mike Caruso	.25	.08
❑	239 Wilson Alvarez	.25	.08
❑	240 Geronimo Berroa	.25	.08
❑	241 Eric Milton	.25	.08
❑	242 Scott Erickson	.25	.08
❑	243 Todd Erdos RC	.25	.08
❑	244 Bobby Hughes	.25	.08
❑	245 Dave Hollins	.25	.08
❑	246 Dean Palmer	.25	.08
❑	247 Carlos Baerga	.25	.08
❑	248 Jose Silva	.25	.08
❑	249 Jose Cabrera RC	.25	.08
❑	250 Tom Evans	.25	.08
❑	251 Marty Cordova	.25	.08
❑	252 Hanley Frias RC	.25	.08
❑	253 Javier Valentin	.25	.08
❑	254 Mario Valdez	.25	.08
❑	255 Joey Cora	.25	.08
❑	256 Mike Lansing	.25	.08
❑	257 Jeff Kent	.25	.08
❑	258 Dave Dellucci RC	.50	.20
❑	259 Curtis King RC	.25	.08
❑	260 David Segui	.25	.08
❑	261 Royce Clayton	.25	.08
❑	262 Jeff Blauser	.25	.08
❑	263 Manny Aybar RC	.25	.08
❑	264 Mike Cather RC	.25	.08
❑	265 Todd Zeile	.25	.08
❑	266 Richard Hidalgo	.25	.08
❑	267 Dante Powell	.25	.08
❑	268 Mike DeJean RC	.25	.08
❑	269 Ken Cloude	.25	.08
❑	270 Danny Klassen	.25	.08
❑	271 Sean Casey	.25	.08
❑	272 A.J. Hinch	.25	.08
❑	273 Rich Butler RC	.25	.08
❑	274 Ben Ford RC	.25	.08
❑	275 Billy McMillon	.25	.08
❑	276 Wilson Delgado	.25	.08
❑	277 Orlando Cabrera	.25	.08
❑	278 Geoff Jenkins	.25	.08
❑	279 Enrique Wilson	.25	.08
❑	280 Derrek Lee	.40	.15
❑	281 Marc Pisciotta RC	.25	.08
❑	282 Abraham Nunez	.25	.08
❑	283 Aaron Boone	.25	.08
❑	284 Brad Fullmer	.25	.08
❑	285 Rob Stanifer RC	.25	.08
❑	286 Preston Wilson	.25	.08
❑	287 Greg Norton	.25	.08
❑	288 Bobby Smith	.25	.08
❑	289 Josh Booty	.25	.08
❑	290 Russell Branyan	.25	.08
❑	291 Jeremi Gonzalez	.25	.08
❑	292 Michael Coleman	.25	.08
❑	293 Cliff Politte	.25	.08
❑	294 Eric Ludwick	.25	.08
❑	295 Rafael Medina	.25	.08
❑	296 Jason Varitek	.60	.25
❑	297 Ron Wright	.25	.08
❑	298 Mark Kotsay	.25	.08
❑	299 David Ortiz	.75	.30
❑	300 Frank Catalanotto RC	.50	.20
❑	301 Robinson Checo	.25	.08
❑	302 Kevin Millwood RC	.75	.30
❑	303 Jacob Cruz	.25	.08
❑	304 Javier Vazquez	.25	.08
❑	305 Magglio Ordonez RC	2.50	1.00
❑	306 Kevin Witt	.25	.08
❑	307 Derrick Gibson	.25	.08
❑	308 Shane Monahan	.25	.08
❑	309 Brian Rose	.25	.08
❑	310 Bobby Estalella	.25	.08
❑	311 Felix Heredia	.25	.08
❑	312 Desi Relaford	.25	.08
❑	313 Esteban Yan RC	.30	.10
❑	314 Ricky Ledee	.25	.08
❑	315 Steve Woodard	.25	.08
❑	316 Pat Watkins	.25	.08
❑	317 Damian Moss	.25	.08
❑	318 Bob Abreu	.25	.08
❑	319 Jeff Abbott	.25	.08
❑	320 Miguel Cairo	.25	.08
❑	321 Rigo Beltran RC	.25	.08
❑	322 Tony Saunders	.25	.08
❑	323 Randall Simon	.25	.08
❑	324 Hiram Bocachica	.25	.08
❑	325 Richie Sexson	.25	.08
❑	326 Karim Garcia	.25	.08
❑	327 Mike Lowell RC	1.25	.50
❑	328 Pat Cline	.25	.08
❑	329 Matt Clement	.25	.08
❑	330 Scott Elarton	.25	.08
❑	331 Manuel Barrios RC	.25	.08
❑	332 Bruce Chen	.25	.08
❑	333 Juan Encarnacion	.25	.08
❑	334 Travis Lee	.25	.08
❑	335 Wes Helms	.25	.08
❑	336 Chad Fox RC	.25	.08
❑	337 Donnie Sadler	.25	.08
❑	338 Carlos Mendoza RC	.25	.08
❑	339 Damian Jackson	.25	.08
❑	340 Julio Ramirez RC	.25	.08
❑	341 John Halama RC	.30	.10
❑	342 Edwin Diaz	.25	.08
❑	343 Felix Martinez	.25	.08
❑	344 Eli Marrero	.25	.08
❑	345 Carl Pavano	.25	.08
❑	346 Vladimir Guerrero HL	.40	.15
❑	347 Barry Bonds HL	.75	.30
❑	348 Darin Erstad HL	.25	.08
❑	349 Albert Belle HL	.25	.08
❑	350 Kenny Lofton HL	.25	.08
❑	351 Mo Vaughn HL	.25	.08
❑	352 Jose Cruz Jr. HL	.25	.08
❑	353 Tony Clark HL	.25	.08
❑	354 Roberto Alomar HL	.25	.08
❑	355 Manny Ramirez HL	.25	.08
❑	356 Paul Molitor HL	.25	.08
❑	357 Jim Thome HL	.25	.08
❑	358 Tino Martinez HL	.25	.08
❑	359 Tim Salmon HL	.25	.08
❑	360 David Justice HL	.25	.08
❑	361 Raul Mondesi HL	.25	.08
❑	362 Mark Grace HL	.25	.08
❑	363 Craig Biggio HL	.25	.08
❑	364 Larry Walker HL	.25	.08
❑	365 Mark McGwire HL	.75	.30
❑	366 Juan Gonzalez HL	.25	.08
❑	367 Derek Jeter HL	.75	.30
❑	368 Chipper Jones HL	.40	.15
❑	369 Frank Thomas HL	.40	.15
❑	370 Alex Rodriguez HL	.60	.25
❑	371 Mike Piazza HL	.60	.25
❑	372 Tony Gwynn HL	.40	.15
❑	373 Jeff Bagwell HL	.25	.08
❑	374 Nomar Garciaparra HL	.60	.25
❑	375 Ken Griffey Jr. HL	.60	.25
❑	376 Livan Hernandez UN	.25	.08
❑	377 Chan Ho Park UN	.25	.08
❑	378 Mike Mussina UN	.25	.08
❑	379 Andy Pettitte UN	.25	.08
❑	380 Greg Maddux UN	.60	.25
❑	381 Hideo Nomo UN	.40	.15
❑	382 Roger Clemens UN	.60	.25
❑	383 Randy Johnson UN	.40	.15
❑	384 Pedro Martinez UN	.40	.15
❑	385 Jaret Wright UN	.25	.08
❑	386 Ken Griffey Jr. SG	.60	.25
❑	387 Todd Helton SG	.25	.08
❑	388 Paul Konerko SG	.25	.08
❑	389 Cal Ripken SG	1.00	.40
❑	390 Larry Walker SG	.25	.08
❑	391 Ken Caminiti SG	.25	.08
❑	392 Jose Guillen SG	.25	.08
❑	393 Jim Edmonds SG	.25	.08
❑	394 Barry Larkin SG	.25	.08
❑	395 Bernie Williams SG	.25	.08
❑	396 Tony Clark SG	.25	.08
❑	397 Jose Cruz Jr. SG	.25	.08
❑	398 Ivan Rodriguez SG	.25	.08
❑	399 Darin Erstad SG	.25	.08
❑	400 Scott Rolen SG	.25	.08
❑	401 Mark McGwire SG	.75	.30
❑	402 Andruw Jones SG	.25	.08
❑	403 Juan Gonzalez SG	.25	.08
❑	404 Derek Jeter SG	.75	.30
❑	405 Chipper Jones SG	.40	.15
❑	406 Greg Maddux SG	.60	.25
❑	407 Frank Thomas SG	.40	.15
❑	408 Alex Rodriguez SG	.60	.25
❑	409 Mike Piazza SG	.60	.25
❑	410 Tony Gwynn SG	.40	.15
❑	411 Jeff Bagwell SG	.25	.08
❑	412 Nomar Garciaparra SG	.60	.25
❑	413 Hideo Nomo SG	.40	.15
❑	414 Barry Bonds SG	.75	.30
❑	415 Ben Grieve SG	.25	.08
❑	416 Barry Bonds CL	.75	.30
❑	417 Mark McGwire CL	.75	.30
❑	418 Roger Clemens CL	.60	.25
❑	419 Livan Hernandez CL	.25	.08
❑	420 Ken Griffey Jr. CL	.60	.25

2001 Donruss

❑	COMP.SET w/o SP's (150)	25.00	10.00
❑	COMMON CARD (1-150)	.30	.10
❑	COMMON CARD (151-200)	8.00	3.00
❑	COMMON CARD (201-220)	2.50	1.00
❑	1 Alex Rodriguez	1.25	.50
❑	2 Barry Bonds	2.00	.75
❑	3 Cal Ripken	2.50	1.00
❑	4 Chipper Jones	.75	.30
❑	5 Derek Jeter	2.00	.75
❑	6 Troy Glaus	.30	.10
❑	7 Frank Thomas	.75	.30
❑	8 Greg Maddux	1.25	.50
❑	9 Ivan Rodriguez	.50	.20
❑	10 Jeff Bagwell	.50	.20
❑	11 Jose Canseco	.50	.20
❑	12 Todd Helton	.50	.20
❑	13 Ken Griffey Jr.	1.25	.50
❑	14 Manny Ramirez Sox	.50	.20
❑	15 Mark McGwire	2.00	.75
❑	16 Mike Piazza	1.25	.50
❑	17 Nomar Garciaparra	1.25	.50
❑	18 Pedro Martinez	.50	.20
❑	19 Randy Johnson	.75	.30
❑	20 Rick Ankiel	.30	.10
❑	21 Rickey Henderson	.75	.30
❑	22 Roger Clemens	1.50	.60
❑	23 Sammy Sosa	.75	.30
❑	24 Tony Gwynn	1.00	.40
❑	25 Vladimir Guerrero	.75	.30
❑	26 Eric Davis	.30	.10
❑	27 Roberto Alomar	.30	.10
❑	28 Mark Mulder	.30	.10
❑	29 Pat Burrell	.30	.10
❑	30 Harold Baines	.30	.10
❑	31 Carlos Delgado	.30	.10
❑	32 J.D. Drew	.30	.10
❑	33 Jim Edmonds	.30	.10
❑	34 Darin Erstad	.30	.10
❑	35 Jason Giambi	.30	.10
❑	36 Tom Glavine	.50	.20
❑	37 Juan Gonzalez	.30	.10
❑	38 Mark Grace	.50	.20
❑	39 Shawn Green	.30	.10
❑	40 Tim Hudson	.30	.10
❑	41 Andruw Jones	.50	.20
❑	42 David Justice	.30	.10
❑	43 Jeff Kent	.30	.10
❑	44 Barry Larkin	.50	.20
❑	45 Pokey Reese	.30	.10
❑	46 Mike Mussina	.50	.20
❑	47 Hideo Nomo	.75	.30
❑	48 Rafael Palmeiro	.50	.20
❑	49 Adam Piatt	.30	.10

❑	50 Scott Rolen	.50	.20
❑	51 Gary Sheffield	.30	.10
❑	52 Bernie Williams	.50	.20
❑	53 Bob Abreu	.30	.10
❑	54 Edgardo Alfonzo	.30	.10
❑	55 Jermaine Clark RC	.50	.20
❑	56 Albert Belle	.30	.10
❑	57 Craig Biggio	.50	.20
❑	58 Andres Galarraga	.30	.10
❑	59 Edgar Martinez	.50	.20
❑	60 Fred McGriff	.50	.20
❑	61 Magglio Ordonez	.30	.10
❑	62 Jim Thome	.50	.20
❑	63 Matt Williams	.30	.10
❑	64 Kerry Wood	.30	.10
❑	65 Moises Alou	.30	.10
❑	66 Brady Anderson	.30	.10
❑	67 Garret Anderson	.30	.10
❑	68 Tony Armas Jr.	.30	.10
❑	69 Tony Batista	.30	.10
❑	70 Jose Cruz Jr.	.30	.10
❑	71 Carlos Beltran	.30	.10
❑	72 Adrian Beltre	.30	.10
❑	73 Kris Benson	.30	.10
❑	74 Lance Berkman	.30	.10
❑	75 Kevin Brown	.30	.10
❑	76 Jay Buhner	.30	.10
❑	77 Jeromy Burnitz	.30	.10
❑	78 Ken Caminiti	.30	.10
❑	79 Sean Casey	.30	.10
❑	80 Luis Castillo	.30	.10
❑	81 Eric Chavez	.30	.10
❑	82 Jeff Cirillo	.30	.10
❑	83 Bartolo Colon	.30	.10
❑	84 David Cone	.30	.10
❑	85 Freddy Garcia	.30	.10
❑	86 Johnny Damon	.50	.20
❑	87 Ray Durham	.30	.10
❑	88 Jermaine Dye	.30	.10
❑	89 Juan Encarnacion	.30	.10
❑	90 Terrence Long	.30	.10
❑	91 Carl Everett	.30	.10
❑	92 Steve Finley	.30	.10
❑	93 Cliff Floyd	.30	.10
❑	94 Brad Fullmer	.30	.10
❑	95 Brian Giles	.30	.10
❑	96 Luis Gonzalez	.30	.10
❑	97 Rusty Greer	.30	.10
❑	98 Jeffrey Hammonds	.30	.10
❑	99 Mike Hampton	.30	.10
❑	100 Orlando Hernandez	.30	.10
❑	101 Richard Hidalgo	.30	.10
❑	102 Geoff Jenkins	.30	.10
❑	103 Jacque Jones	.30	.10
❑	104 Brian Jordan	.30	.10
❑	105 Gabe Kapler	.30	.10
❑	106 Eric Karros	.30	.10
❑	107 Jason Kendall	.30	.10
❑	108 Adam Kennedy	.30	.10
❑	109 Byung-Hyun Kim	.30	.10
❑	110 Ryan Klesko	.30	.10
❑	111 Chuck Knoblauch	.30	.10
❑	112 Paul Konerko	.30	.10
❑	113 Carlos Lee	.30	.10
❑	114 Kenny Lofton	.30	.10
❑	115 Javy Lopez	.30	.10
❑	116 Tino Martinez	.50	.20
❑	117 Ruben Mateo	.30	.10
❑	118 Kevin Millwood	.30	.10
❑	119 Ben Molina	.30	.10
❑	120 Raul Mondesi	.30	.10
❑	121 Trot Nixon	.30	.10
❑	122 John Olerud	.30	.10
❑	123 Paul O'Neill	.50	.20
❑	124 Chan Ho Park	.30	.10
❑	125 Andy Pettitte	.50	.20
❑	126 Jorge Posada	.50	.20
❑	127 Mark Quinn	.30	.10
❑	128 Aramis Ramirez	.30	.10
❑	129 Mariano Rivera	.75	.30
❑	130 Tim Salmon	.50	.20
❑	131 Curt Schilling	.30	.10
❑	132 Richie Sexson	.30	.10
❑	133 John Smoltz	.50	.20
❑	134 J.T. Snow	.30	.10
❑	135 Jay Payton	.30	.10
❑	136 Shannon Stewart	.30	.10
❑	137 B.J. Surhoff	.30	.10
❑	138 Mike Sweeney	.30	.10
❑	139 Fernando Tatis	.30	.10
❑	140 Miguel Tejada	.30	.10
❑	141 Jason Varitek	.75	.30
❑	142 Greg Vaughn	.30	.10
❑	143 Mo Vaughn	.30	.10
❑	144 Robin Ventura	.30	.10
❑	145 Jose Vidro	.30	.10
❑	146 Omar Vizquel	.50	.20
❑	147 Larry Walker	.30	.10
❑	148 David Wells	.30	.10
❑	149 Rondell White	.30	.10
❑	150 Preston Wilson	.30	.10
❑	151 Brent Abernathy RR	8.00	3.00
❑	152 Cory Aldridge RR RC	8.00	3.00
❑	153 Gene Altman RR RC	8.00	3.00
❑	154 Josh Beckett RR	10.00	4.00
❑	155 Wilson Betemit RR RC	10.00	4.00
❑	156 Albert Pujols RR/500 RC	250.00	125.00
❑	157 Joe Crede RR	10.00	4.00
❑	158 Jack Cust RR	8.00	3.00
❑	159 Ben Sheets RR/500	40.00	15.00
❑	160 Alex Escobar RR	8.00	3.00
❑	161 Adrian Hernandez RR RC	8.00	3.00
❑	162 Pedro Feliz RR	8.00	3.00
❑	163 Nate Frese RR RC	8.00	3.00
❑	164 Carlos Garcia RR RC	8.00	3.00
❑	165 Marcus Giles RR	8.00	3.00
❑	166 Alexis Gomez RR RC	8.00	3.00
❑	167 Jason Hart RR	8.00	3.00
❑	168 Eric Hinske RR RC	10.00	4.00
❑	169 Cesar Izturis RR	8.00	3.00
❑	170 Nick Johnson RR	8.00	3.00
❑	171 Mike Young RR	10.00	4.00
❑	172 Brian Lawrence RR RC	8.00	3.00
❑	173 Steve Lomasney RR	8.00	3.00
❑	174 Nick Maness RR	8.00	3.00
❑	175 Jose Mieses RR RC	8.00	3.00
❑	176 Greg Miller RR RC	8.00	3.00
❑	177 Eric Munson RR	8.00	3.00
❑	178 Xavier Nady RR	8.00	3.00
❑	179 Blaine Neal RR RC	8.00	3.00
❑	180 Abraham Nunez RR	8.00	3.00
❑	181 Jose Ortiz RR	8.00	3.00
❑	182 Jeremy Owens RR RC	8.00	3.00
❑	183 Pablo Ozuna RR	8.00	3.00
❑	184 Corey Patterson RR	8.00	3.00
❑	185 Carlos Pena RR	8.00	3.00
❑	186 Wily Mo Pena RR	8.00	3.00
❑	187 Timo Perez RR	8.00	3.00
❑	188 Adam Pettyjohn RR RC	8.00	3.00
❑	189 Luis Rivas RR	8.00	3.00
❑	190 Jackson Melian RR RC	8.00	3.00
❑	191 Wilken Ruan RR RC	8.00	3.00
❑	192 Duaner Sanchez RR RC	8.00	3.00
❑	193 Alfonso Soriano RR	10.00	4.00
❑	194 Rafael Soriano RR RC	8.00	3.00
❑	195 Ichiro Suzuki RR RC	60.00	30.00
❑	196 Billy Sylvester RR RC	8.00	3.00
❑	197 Juan Uribe RR RC	10.00	4.00
❑	198 Eric Valent RR	8.00	3.00
❑	199 Carlos Valderrama RR RC	8.00	3.00
❑	200 Matt White RR RC	8.00	3.00
❑	201 Alex Rodriguez FC	6.00	2.50
❑	202 Barry Bonds FC	10.00	4.00
❑	203 Cal Ripken FC	12.00	5.00
❑	204 Chipper Jones FC	4.00	1.50
❑	205 Derek Jeter FC	10.00	4.00
❑	206 Troy Glaus FC	2.50	1.00
❑	207 Frank Thomas FC	4.00	1.50
❑	208 Greg Maddux FC	6.00	2.50
❑	209 Ivan Rodriguez FC	2.50	1.00
❑	210 Jeff Bagwell FC	2.50	1.00
❑	211 Todd Helton FC	2.50	1.00
❑	212 Ken Griffey Jr. FC	6.00	2.50
❑	213 Manny Ramirez Sox FC	2.50	1.00
❑	214 Mark McGwire FC	10.00	4.00
❑	215 Mike Piazza FC	6.00	2.50
❑	216 Pedro Martinez FC	2.50	1.00
❑	217 Sammy Sosa FC	4.00	1.50
❑	218 Tony Gwynn FC	5.00	2.00
❑	219 Vladimir Guerrero FC	4.00	1.50
❑	220 Nomar Garciaparra FC	6.00	2.50
❑	NNO BB Best Coupon	2.00	.75
❑	NNO The Rookies Coupon	.50	.20

2002 Donruss

❑	COMPLETE SET (220)	150.00	60.00
❑	COMP.SET w/o SP'S (150)	25.00	10.00
❑	COMMON CARD (1-150)	.30	.10
❑	COMMON CARD (151-200)	3.00	1.25
❑	COMMON CARD (201-220)	1.50	.60
❑	1 Alex Rodriguez	1.25	.50
❑	2 Barry Bonds	2.00	.75
❑	3 Derek Jeter	2.00	.75
❑	4 Robert Fick	.30	.10
❑	5 Juan Pierre	.30	.10
❑	6 Torii Hunter	.30	.10
❑	7 Todd Helton	.50	.20
❑	8 Cal Ripken	2.50	1.00
❑	9 Manny Ramirez	.50	.20
❑	10 Johnny Damon	.50	.20
❑	11 Mike Piazza	1.25	.50
❑	12 Nomar Garciaparra	1.25	.50
❑	13 Pedro Martinez	.50	.20
❑	14 Brian Giles	.30	.10
❑	15 Albert Pujols	1.50	.60
❑	16 Roger Clemens	1.50	.60
❑	17 Sammy Sosa	.75	.30
❑	18 Vladimir Guerrero	.75	.30
❑	19 Tony Gwynn	1.00	.40
❑	20 Pat Burrell	.30	.10
❑	21 Carlos Delgado	.30	.10
❑	22 Tino Martinez	.50	.20
❑	23 Jim Edmonds	.30	.10
❑	24 Jason Giambi	.30	.10
❑	25 Tom Glavine	.50	.20
❑	26 Mark Grace	.50	.20
❑	27 Tony Armas Jr.	.30	.10
❑	28 Andruw Jones	.50	.20
❑	29 Ben Sheets	.30	.10
❑	30 Jeff Kent	.30	.10
❑	31 Barry Larkin	.50	.20
❑	32 Joe Mays	.30	.10
❑	33 Mike Mussina	.50	.20
❑	34 Hideo Nomo	.75	.30
❑	35 Rafael Palmeiro	.50	.20
❑	36 Scott Brosius	.30	.10
❑	37 Scott Rolen	.50	.20
❑	38 Gary Sheffield	.30	.10
❑	39 Bernie Williams	.50	.20
❑	40 Bob Abreu	.30	.10
❑	41 Edgardo Alfonzo	.30	.10
❑	42 C.C. Sabathia	.30	.10
❑	43 Jeremy Giambi	.30	.10
❑	44 Craig Biggio	.50	.20
❑	45 Andres Galarraga	.30	.10
❑	46 Edgar Martinez	.50	.20
❑	47 Fred McGriff	.50	.20
❑	48 Magglio Ordonez	.30	.10
❑	49 Jim Thome	.50	.20
❑	50 Matt Williams	.30	.10
❑	51 Kerry Wood	.30	.10
❑	52 Moises Alou	.30	.10
❑	53 Brady Anderson	.30	.10
❑	54 Garret Anderson	.30	.10
❑	55 Juan Gonzalez	.30	.10
❑	56 Bret Boone	.30	.10
❑	57 Jose Cruz Jr.	.30	.10
❑	58 Carlos Beltran	.30	.10
❑	59 Adrian Beltre	.30	.10

❑ 60 Joe Kennedy	.30	.10
❑ 61 Lance Berkman	.30	.10
❑ 62 Kevin Brown	.30	.10
❑ 63 Tim Hudson	.30	.10
❑ 64 Jeromy Burnitz	.30	.10
❑ 65 Jarrod Washburn	.30	.10
❑ 66 Sean Casey	.30	.10
❑ 67 Eric Chavez	.30	.10
❑ 68 Bartolo Colon	.30	.10
❑ 69 Freddy Garcia	.30	.10
❑ 70 Jermaine Dye	.30	.10
❑ 71 Terrence Long	.30	.10
❑ 72 Cliff Floyd	.30	.10
❑ 73 Luis Gonzalez	.30	.10
❑ 74 Ichiro Suzuki	1.50	.60
❑ 75 Mike Hampton	.30	.10
❑ 76 Richard Hidalgo	.30	.10
❑ 77 Geoff Jenkins	.30	.10
❑ 78 Gabe Kapler	.30	.10
❑ 79 Ken Griffey Jr.	1.25	.50
❑ 80 Jason Kendall	.30	.10
❑ 81 Josh Towers	.30	.10
❑ 82 Ryan Klesko	.30	.10
❑ 83 Paul Konerko	.30	.10
❑ 84 Carlos Lee	.30	.10
❑ 85 Kenny Lofton	.30	.10
❑ 86 Josh Beckett	.30	.10
❑ 87 Raul Mondesi	.30	.10
❑ 88 Trot Nixon	.30	.10
❑ 89 John Olerud	.30	.10
❑ 90 Paul O'Neill	.50	.20
❑ 91 Chan Ho Park	.30	.10
❑ 92 Andy Pettitte	.50	.20
❑ 93 Jorge Posada	.50	.20
❑ 94 Mark Quinn	.30	.10
❑ 95 Aramis Ramirez	.30	.10
❑ 96 Curt Schilling	.30	.10
❑ 97 Richie Sexson	.30	.10
❑ 98 John Smoltz	.50	.20
❑ 99 Wilson Betemit	.30	.10
❑ 100 Shannon Stewart	.30	.10
❑ 101 Alfonso Soriano	.30	.10
❑ 102 Mike Sweeney	.30	.10
❑ 103 Miguel Tejada	.30	.10
❑ 104 Greg Vaughn	.30	.10
❑ 105 Robin Ventura	.30	.10
❑ 106 Jose Vidro	.30	.10
❑ 107 Larry Walker	.30	.10
❑ 108 Preston Wilson	.30	.10
❑ 109 Corey Patterson	.30	.10
❑ 110 Mark Mulder	.30	.10
❑ 111 Tony Clark	.30	.10
❑ 112 Roy Oswalt	.30	.10
❑ 113 Jimmy Rollins	.30	.10
❑ 114 Kazuhiro Sasaki	.30	.10
❑ 115 Barry Zito	.30	.10
❑ 116 Javier Vazquez	.30	.10
❑ 117 Mike Cameron	.30	.10
❑ 118 Phil Nevin	.30	.10
❑ 119 Bud Smith	.30	.10
❑ 120 Cristian Guzman	.30	.10
❑ 121 Al Leiter	.30	.10
❑ 122 Brad Radke	.30	.10
❑ 123 Bobby Higginson	.30	.10
❑ 124 Robert Person	.30	.10
❑ 125 Adam Dunn	.30	.10
❑ 126 Ben Grieve	.30	.10
❑ 127 Rafael Furcal	.30	.10
❑ 128 Jay Gibbons	.30	.10
❑ 129 Paul LoDuca	.30	.10
❑ 130 Wade Miller	.30	.10
❑ 131 Tsuyoshi Shinjo	.30	.10
❑ 132 Eric Milton	.30	.10
❑ 133 Rickey Henderson	.75	.30
❑ 134 Roberto Alomar	.50	.20
❑ 135 Darin Erstad	.30	.10
❑ 136 J.D. Drew	.30	.10
❑ 137 Shawn Green	.30	.10
❑ 138 Randy Johnson	.75	.30
❑ 139 Austin Kearns	.30	.10
❑ 140 Jose Canseco	.50	.20
❑ 141 Jeff Bagwell	.50	.20
❑ 142 Greg Maddux	1.25	.50
❑ 143 Mark Buehrle	.30	.10
❑ 144 Ivan Rodriguez	.50	.20
❑ 145 Frank Thomas	.75	.30
❑ 146 Rich Aurilia	.30	.10
❑ 147 Troy Glaus	.30	.10
❑ 148 Ryan Dempster	.30	.10
❑ 149 Chipper Jones	.75	.30
❑ 150 Matt Morris	.30	.10
❑ 151 Marlon Byrd RR	3.00	1.25
❑ 152 Ben Howard RR RC	3.00	1.25
❑ 153 Brandon Backe RR RC	3.00	1.25
❑ 154 Jorge De La Rosa RR RC	3.00	1.25
❑ 155 Corky Miller RR	3.00	1.25
❑ 156 Dennis Tankersley RR	3.00	1.25
❑ 157 Kyle Kane RR RC	3.00	1.25
❑ 158 Justin Duchscherer RR	3.00	1.25
❑ 159 Brian Mallette RR RC	3.00	1.25
❑ 160 Chris Baker RR RC	3.00	1.25
❑ 161 Jason Lane RR	3.00	1.25
❑ 162 Hee Seop Choi RR	3.00	1.25
❑ 163 Juan Cruz RR	3.00	1.25
❑ 164 Rodrigo Rosario RR RC	3.00	1.25
❑ 165 Matt Guerrier RR	3.00	1.25
❑ 166 Anderson Machado RR RC	3.00	1.25
❑ 167 Geronimo Gil RR	3.00	1.25
❑ 168 Dewon Brazelton RR	3.00	1.25
❑ 169 Mark Prior RR	4.00	1.50
❑ 170 Bill Hall RR	3.00	1.25
❑ 171 Jorge Padilla RR RC	3.00	1.25
❑ 172 Jose Cueto RR	3.00	1.25
❑ 173 Allan Simpson RR RC	3.00	1.25
❑ 174 Doug Devore RR RC	3.00	1.25
❑ 175 Josh Pearce RR	3.00	1.25
❑ 176 Angel Berroa RR	3.00	1.25
❑ 177 Steve Bechler RR RC	3.00	1.25
❑ 178 Antonio Perez RR	3.00	1.25
❑ 179 Mark Teixeira RR	4.00	1.50
❑ 180 Erick Almonte RR	3.00	1.25
❑ 181 Orlando Hudson RR	3.00	1.25
❑ 182 Michael Rivera RR	3.00	1.25
❑ 183 Raul Chavez RR RC	3.00	1.25
❑ 184 Juan Pena RR	3.00	1.25
❑ 185 Travis Hughes RR RC	3.00	1.25
❑ 186 Ryan Ludwick RR	3.00	1.25
❑ 187 Ed Rogers RR	3.00	1.25
❑ 188 Andy Pratt RR RC	3.00	1.25
❑ 189 Nick Neugebauer RR	3.00	1.25
❑ 190 Tom Shearn RR RC	3.00	1.25
❑ 191 Eric Cyr RR	3.00	1.25
❑ 192 Victor Martinez RR	4.00	1.50
❑ 193 Brandon Berger RR	3.00	1.25
❑ 194 Erik Bedard RR	3.00	1.25
❑ 195 Fernando Rodney RR	3.00	1.25
❑ 196 Joe Thurston RR	3.00	1.25
❑ 197 John Buck RR	3.00	1.25
❑ 198 Jeff Deardorff RR	3.00	1.25
❑ 199 Ryan Jamison RR	3.00	1.25
❑ 200 Alfredo Amezaga RR	3.00	1.25
❑ 201 Luis Gonzalez FC	1.50	.60
❑ 202 Roger Clemens FC	5.00	2.00
❑ 203 Barry Zito FC	1.50	.60
❑ 204 Bud Smith FC	1.50	.60
❑ 205 Magglio Ordonez FC	1.50	.60
❑ 206 Kerry Wood FC	1.50	.60
❑ 207 Freddy Garcia FC	1.50	.60
❑ 208 Adam Dunn FC	1.50	.60
❑ 209 Curt Schilling FC	1.50	.60
❑ 210 Lance Berkman FC	1.50	.60
❑ 211 Rafael Palmeiro FC	1.50	.60
❑ 212 Ichiro Suzuki FC	5.00	2.00
❑ 213 Bob Abreu FC	1.50	.60
❑ 214 Mark Mulder FC	1.50	.60
❑ 215 Roy Oswalt FC	1.50	.60
❑ 216 Mike Sweeney FC	1.50	.60
❑ 217 Paul LoDuca FC	1.50	.60
❑ 218 Aramis Ramirez FC	1.50	.60
❑ 219 Randy Johnson FC	2.50	1.00
❑ 220 Albert Pujols FC	5.00	2.00

2003 Donruss

❑ COMPLETE SET (400)	50.00	25.00
❑ COMMON CARD (71-400)	.30	.10
❑ COMMON CARD (1-20)	.50	.20
❑ COMMON CARD (21-70)	.50	.20
❑ 1 Vladimir Guerrero DK	.75	.30
❑ 2 Derek Jeter DK	2.00	.75
❑ 3 Adam Dunn DK	.50	.20
❑ 4 Greg Maddux DK	1.25	.50
❑ 5 Lance Berkman DK	.50	.20
❑ 6 Ichiro Suzuki DK	1.50	.60
❑ 7 Mike Piazza DK	1.25	.50
❑ 8 Alex Rodriguez DK	1.25	.50
❑ 9 Tom Glavine DK	.50	.20
❑ 10 Randy Johnson DK	.75	.30
❑ 11 Nomar Garciaparra DK	1.25	.50
❑ 12 Jason Giambi DK	.50	.20
❑ 13 Sammy Sosa DK	.75	.30
❑ 14 Barry Zito DK	.50	.20
❑ 15 Chipper Jones DK	.75	.30
❑ 16 Magglio Ordonez DK	.50	.20
❑ 17 Larry Walker DK	.50	.20
❑ 18 Alfonso Soriano DK	.50	.20
❑ 19 Curt Schilling DK	.50	.20
❑ 20 Barry Bonds DK	2.00	.75
❑ 21 Joe Borchard RR	.50	.20
❑ 22 Chris Snelling RR	.50	.20
❑ 23 Brian Tallet RR	.50	.20
❑ 24 Cliff Lee RR	.50	.20
❑ 25 Freddy Sanchez RR	.50	.20
❑ 26 Chone Figgins RR	.50	.20
❑ 27 Kevin Cash RR	.50	.20
❑ 28 Josh Bard RR	.50	.20
❑ 29 Jeriome Robertson RR	.50	.20
❑ 30 Jeremy Hill RR	.50	.20
❑ 31 Shane Nance RR	.50	.20
❑ 32 Jake Peavy RR	.50	.20
❑ 33 Trey Hodges RR	.50	.20
❑ 34 Eric Eckenstahler RR	.50	.20
❑ 35 Jim Rushford RR	.50	.20
❑ 36 Oliver Perez RR	.50	.20
❑ 37 Kirk Saarloos RR	.50	.20
❑ 38 Hank Blalock RR	.50	.20
❑ 39 Francisco Rodriguez RR	.50	.20
❑ 40 Runelvys Hernandez RR	.50	.20
❑ 41 Aaron Cook RR	.50	.20
❑ 42 Josh Hancock RR	.50	.20
❑ 43 P.J. Bevis RR	.50	.20
❑ 44 Jon Adkins RR	.50	.20
❑ 45 Tim Kalita RR	.50	.20
❑ 46 Nelson Castro RR	.50	.20
❑ 47 Colin Young RR	.50	.20
❑ 48 Adrian Burnside RR	.50	.20
❑ 49 Luis Martinez RR	.50	.20
❑ 50 Pete Zamora RR	.50	.20
❑ 51 Todd Donovan RR	.50	.20
❑ 52 Jeremy Ward RR	.50	.20
❑ 53 Wilson Valdez RR	.50	.20
❑ 54 Eric Good RR	.50	.20
❑ 55 Jeff Baker RR	.50	.20
❑ 56 Mitch Wylie RR	.50	.20
❑ 57 Ron Calloway RR	.50	.20
❑ 58 Jose Valverde RR	.50	.20
❑ 59 Jason Davis RR	.50	.20
❑ 60 Scotty Layfield RR	.50	.20
❑ 61 Matt Thornton RR	.50	.20
❑ 62 Adam Walker RR	.50	.20
❑ 63 Gustavo Chacin RR	.50	.20
❑ 64 Ron Chiavacci RR	.50	.20
❑ 65 Wiki Nieves RR	.50	.20
❑ 66 Cliff Bartosh RR	.50	.20
❑ 67 Mike Gonzalez RR	.50	.20
❑ 68 Justin Wayne RR	.50	.20
❑ 69 Eric Junge RR	.50	.20
❑ 70 Ben Kozlowski RR	.50	.20
❑ 71 Darin Erstad	.30	.10
❑ 72 Garret Anderson	.30	.10
❑ 73 Troy Glaus	.30	.10

❑ 74 David Eckstein .30 .10
❑ 75 Adam Kennedy .30 .10
❑ 76 Kevin Appier .30 .10
❑ 77 Jarrod Washburn .30 .10
❑ 78 Scott Spiezio .30 .10
❑ 79 Tim Salmon .50 .20
❑ 80 Ramon Ortiz .30 .10
❑ 81 Bengie Molina .30 .10
❑ 82 Brad Fullmer .30 .10
❑ 83 Troy Percival .30 .10
❑ 84 David Segui .30 .10
❑ 85 Jay Gibbons .30 .10
❑ 86 Tony Batista .30 .10
❑ 87 Scott Erickson .30 .10
❑ 88 Jeff Conine .30 .10
❑ 89 Melvin Mora .30 .10
❑ 90 Buddy Groom .30 .10
❑ 91 Rodrigo Lopez .30 .10
❑ 92 Marty Cordova .30 .10
❑ 93 Geronimo Gil .30 .10
❑ 94 Kenny Lofton .30 .10
❑ 95 Shea Hillenbrand .30 .10
❑ 96 Manny Ramirez .50 .20
❑ 97 Pedro Martinez .50 .20
❑ 98 Nomar Garciaparra 1.25 .50
❑ 99 Rickey Henderson .75 .30
❑ 100 Johnny Damon .50 .20
❑ 101 Trot Nixon .30 .10
❑ 102 Derek Lowe .30 .10
❑ 103 Hee Seop Choi .30 .10
❑ 104 Mark Teixeira .50 .20
❑ 105 Tim Wakefield .30 .10
❑ 106 Jason Varitek .75 .30
❑ 107 Frank Thomas .75 .30
❑ 108 Joe Crede .30 .10
❑ 109 Magglio Ordonez .30 .10
❑ 110 Ray Durham .30 .10
❑ 111 Mark Buehrle .30 .10
❑ 112 Paul Konerko .30 .10
❑ 113 Jose Valentin .30 .10
❑ 114 Carlos Lee .30 .10
❑ 115 Royce Clayton .30 .10
❑ 116 C.C. Sabathia .30 .10
❑ 117 Ellis Burks .30 .10
❑ 118 Omar Vizquel .50 .20
❑ 119 Jim Thome .50 .20
❑ 120 Matt Lawton .30 .10
❑ 121 Travis Fryman .30 .10
❑ 122 Earl Snyder .30 .10
❑ 123 Ricky Gutierrez .30 .10
❑ 124 Einar Diaz .30 .10
❑ 125 Danys Baez .30 .10
❑ 126 Robert Fick .30 .10
❑ 127 Bobby Higginson .30 .10
❑ 128 Steve Sparks .30 .10
❑ 129 Mike Rivera .30 .10
❑ 130 Wendell Magee .30 .10
❑ 131 Randall Simon .30 .10
❑ 132 Carlos Pena .30 .10
❑ 133 Mark Redman .30 .10
❑ 134 Juan Acevedo .30 .10
❑ 135 Mike Sweeney .30 .10
❑ 136 Aaron Guiel .30 .10
❑ 137 Carlos Beltran .30 .10
❑ 138 Joe Randa .30 .10
❑ 139 Paul Byrd .30 .10
❑ 140 Shawn Sedlacek .30 .10
❑ 141 Raul Ibanez .30 .10
❑ 142 Michael Tucker .30 .10
❑ 143 Torii Hunter .30 .10
❑ 144 Jacque Jones .30 .10
❑ 145 David Ortiz .75 .30
❑ 146 Corey Koskie .30 .10
❑ 147 Brad Radke .30 .10
❑ 148 Doug Mientkiewicz .30 .10
❑ 149 A.J. Pierzynski .30 .10
❑ 150 Dustan Mohr .30 .10
❑ 151 Michael Cuddyer .30 .10
❑ 152 Eddie Guardado .30 .10
❑ 153 Cristian Guzman .30 .10
❑ 154 Derek Jeter 2.00 .75
❑ 155 Bernie Williams .50 .20
❑ 156 Roger Clemens 1.50 .60
❑ 157 Mike Mussina .50 .20
❑ 158 Jorge Posada .50 .20
❑ 159 Alfonso Soriano .30 .10
❑ 160 Jason Giambi .30 .10
❑ 161 Robin Ventura .30 .10
❑ 162 Andy Pettitte .50 .20
❑ 163 David Wells .30 .10
❑ 164 Nick Johnson .30 .10
❑ 165 Jeff Weaver .30 .10
❑ 166 Raul Mondesi .30 .10
❑ 167 Rondell White .30 .10
❑ 168 Tim Hudson .30 .10
❑ 169 Barry Zito .30 .10
❑ 170 Mark Mulder .30 .10
❑ 171 Miguel Tejada .30 .10
❑ 172 Eric Chavez .30 .10
❑ 173 Billy Koch .30 .10
❑ 174 Jermaine Dye .30 .10
❑ 175 Scott Hatteberg .30 .10
❑ 176 Terrence Long .30 .10
❑ 177 David Justice .30 .10
❑ 178 Ramon Hernandez .30 .10
❑ 179 Ted Lilly .30 .10
❑ 180 Ichiro Suzuki 1.50 .60
❑ 181 Edgar Martinez .50 .20
❑ 182 Mike Cameron .30 .10
❑ 183 John Olerud .30 .10
❑ 184 Bret Boone .30 .10
❑ 185 Dan Wilson .30 .10
❑ 186 Freddy Garcia .30 .10
❑ 187 Jamie Moyer .30 .10
❑ 188 Carlos Guillen .30 .10
❑ 189 Ruben Sierra .30 .10
❑ 190 Kazuhiro Sasaki .30 .10
❑ 191 Mark McLemore .30 .10
❑ 192 John Halama .30 .10
❑ 193 Joel Pineiro .30 .10
❑ 194 Jeff Cirillo .30 .10
❑ 195 Rafael Soriano .30 .10
❑ 196 Ben Grieve .30 .10
❑ 197 Aubrey Huff .30 .10
❑ 198 Steve Cox .30 .10
❑ 199 Toby Hall .30 .10
❑ 200 Randy Winn .30 .10
❑ 201 Brent Abernathy .30 .10
❑ 202 Chris Gomez .30 .10
❑ 203 John Flaherty .30 .10
❑ 204 Paul Wilson .30 .10
❑ 205 Chan Ho Park .30 .10
❑ 206 Alex Rodriguez 1.25 .50
❑ 207 Juan Gonzalez .30 .10
❑ 208 Rafael Palmeiro .50 .20
❑ 209 Ivan Rodriguez .50 .20
❑ 210 Rusty Greer .30 .10
❑ 211 Kenny Rogers .30 .10
❑ 212 Ismael Valdes .30 .10
❑ 213 Frank Catalanotto .30 .10
❑ 214 Hank Blalock .30 .10
❑ 215 Michael Young .50 .20
❑ 216 Kevin Mench .30 .10
❑ 217 Herbert Perry .30 .10
❑ 218 Gabe Kapler .30 .10
❑ 219 Carlos Delgado .30 .10
❑ 220 Shannon Stewart .30 .10
❑ 221 Eric Hinske .30 .10
❑ 222 Roy Halladay .30 .10
❑ 223 Felipe Lopez .30 .10
❑ 224 Vernon Wells .30 .10
❑ 225 Josh Phelps .30 .10
❑ 226 Jose Cruz .30 .10
❑ 227 Curt Schilling .30 .10
❑ 228 Randy Johnson .75 .30
❑ 229 Luis Gonzalez .30 .10
❑ 230 Mark Grace .50 .20
❑ 231 Junior Spivey .30 .10
❑ 232 Tony Womack .30 .10
❑ 233 Matt Williams .30 .10
❑ 234 Steve Finley .30 .10
❑ 235 Byung-Hyun Kim .30 .10
❑ 236 Craig Counsell .30 .10
❑ 237 Greg Maddux 1.25 .50
❑ 238 Tom Glavine .50 .20
❑ 239 John Smoltz .50 .20
❑ 240 Chipper Jones .75 .30
❑ 241 Gary Sheffield .30 .10
❑ 242 Andruw Jones .50 .20
❑ 243 Vinny Castilla .30 .10
❑ 244 Damian Moss .30 .10
❑ 245 Rafael Furcal .30 .10
❑ 246 Javy Lopez .30 .10
❑ 247 Kevin Millwood .30 .10
❑ 248 Kerry Wood .30 .10
❑ 249 Fred McGriff .50 .20
❑ 250 Sammy Sosa .75 .30
❑ 251 Alex Gonzalez .30 .10
❑ 252 Corey Patterson .30 .10
❑ 253 Moises Alou .30 .10
❑ 254 Juan Cruz .30 .10
❑ 255 Jon Lieber .30 .10
❑ 256 Matt Clement .30 .10
❑ 257 Mark Prior .50 .20
❑ 258 Ken Griffey Jr. 1.25 .50
❑ 259 Barry Larkin .50 .20
❑ 260 Adam Dunn .30 .10
❑ 261 Sean Casey .30 .10
❑ 262 Jose Rijo .30 .10
❑ 263 Elmer Dessens .30 .10
❑ 264 Austin Kearns .30 .10
❑ 265 Corky Miller .30 .10
❑ 266 Todd Walker .30 .10
❑ 267 Chris Reitsma .30 .10
❑ 268 Ryan Dempster .30 .10
❑ 269 Aaron Boone .30 .10
❑ 270 Danny Graves .30 .10
❑ 271 Brandon Larson .30 .10
❑ 272 Larry Walker .30 .10
❑ 273 Todd Helton .50 .20
❑ 274 Juan Uribe .30 .10
❑ 275 Juan Pierre .30 .10
❑ 276 Mike Hampton .30 .10
❑ 277 Todd Zeile .30 .10
❑ 278 Todd Hollandsworth .30 .10
❑ 279 Jason Jennings .30 .10
❑ 280 Josh Beckett .30 .10
❑ 281 Mike Lowell .30 .10
❑ 282 Derrek Lee .50 .20
❑ 283 A.J. Burnett .30 .10
❑ 284 Luis Castillo .30 .10
❑ 285 Tim Raines .30 .10
❑ 286 Preston Wilson .30 .10
❑ 287 Juan Encarnacion .30 .10
❑ 288 Charles Johnson .30 .10
❑ 289 Jeff Bagwell .50 .20
❑ 290 Craig Biggio .50 .20
❑ 291 Lance Berkman .30 .10
❑ 292 Daryle Ward .30 .10
❑ 293 Roy Oswalt .30 .10
❑ 294 Richard Hidalgo .30 .10
❑ 295 Octavio Dotel .30 .10
❑ 296 Wade Miller .30 .10
❑ 297 Julio Lugo .30 .10
❑ 298 Billy Wagner .30 .10
❑ 299 Shawn Green .30 .10
❑ 300 Adrian Beltre .30 .10
❑ 301 Paul Lo Duca .30 .10
❑ 302 Eric Karros .30 .10
❑ 303 Kevin Brown .30 .10
❑ 304 Hideo Nomo .75 .30
❑ 305 Odalis Perez .30 .10
❑ 306 Eric Gagne .30 .10
❑ 307 Brian Jordan .30 .10
❑ 308 Cesar Izturis .30 .10
❑ 309 Mark Grudzielanek .30 .10
❑ 310 Kazuhisa Ishii .30 .10
❑ 311 Geoff Jenkins .30 .10
❑ 312 Richie Sexson .30 .10
❑ 313 Jose Hernandez .30 .10
❑ 314 Ben Sheets .30 .10
❑ 315 Ruben Quevedo .30 .10
❑ 316 Jeffrey Hammonds .30 .10
❑ 317 Alex Sanchez .30 .10
❑ 318 Eric Young .30 .10
❑ 319 Takahito Nomura .30 .10
❑ 320 Vladimir Guerrero .75 .30
❑ 321 Jose Vidro .30 .10
❑ 322 Orlando Cabrera .30 .10
❑ 323 Michael Barrett .30 .10
❑ 324 Javier Vazquez .30 .10
❑ 325 Tony Armas Jr. .30 .10
❑ 326 Andres Galarraga .30 .10
❑ 327 Tomo Ohka .30 .10
❑ 328 Bartolo Colon .30 .10
❑ 329 Fernando Tatis .30 .10
❑ 330 Brad Wilkerson .30 .10
❑ 331 Masato Yoshii .30 .10

❑ 332 Mike Piazza	1.25	.50
❑ 333 Jeromy Burnitz	.30	.10
❑ 334 Roberto Alomar	.50	.20
❑ 335 Mo Vaughn	.30	.10
❑ 336 Al Leiter	.30	.10
❑ 337 Pedro Astacio	.30	.10
❑ 338 Edgardo Alfonzo	.30	.10
❑ 339 Armando Benitez	.30	.10
❑ 340 Timo Perez	.30	.10
❑ 341 Jay Payton	.30	.10
❑ 342 Roger Cedeno	.30	.10
❑ 343 Rey Ordonez	.30	.10
❑ 344 Steve Trachsel	.30	.10
❑ 345 Satoru Komiyama	.30	.10
❑ 346 Scott Rolen	.50	.20
❑ 347 Pat Burrell	.30	.10
❑ 348 Bobby Abreu	.30	.10
❑ 349 Mike Lieberthal	.30	.10
❑ 350 Brandon Duckworth	.30	.10
❑ 351 Jimmy Rollins	.30	.10
❑ 352 Marlon Anderson	.30	.10
❑ 353 Travis Lee	.30	.10
❑ 354 Vicente Padilla	.30	.10
❑ 355 Randy Wolf	.30	.10
❑ 356 Jason Kendall	.30	.10
❑ 357 Brian Giles	.30	.10
❑ 358 Aramis Ramirez	.30	.10
❑ 359 Pokey Reese	.30	.10
❑ 360 Kip Wells	.30	.10
❑ 361 Josh Fogg	.30	.10
❑ 362 Mike Williams	.30	.10
❑ 363 Jack Wilson	.30	.10
❑ 364 Craig Wilson	.30	.10
❑ 365 Kevin Young	.30	.10
❑ 366 Ryan Klesko	.30	.10
❑ 367 Phil Nevin	.30	.10
❑ 368 Brian Lawrence	.30	.10
❑ 369 Mark Kotsay	.30	.10
❑ 370 Brett Tomko	.30	.10
❑ 371 Trevor Hoffman	.30	.10
❑ 372 Deivi Cruz	.30	.10
❑ 373 Bubba Trammell	.30	.10
❑ 374 Sean Burroughs	.30	.10
❑ 375 Barry Bonds	2.00	.75
❑ 376 Jeff Kent	.30	.10
❑ 377 Rich Aurilia	.30	.10
❑ 378 Tsuyoshi Shinjo	.30	.10
❑ 379 Benito Santiago	.30	.10
❑ 380 Kirk Rueter	.30	.10
❑ 381 Livan Hernandez	.30	.10
❑ 382 Russ Ortiz	.30	.10
❑ 383 David Bell	.30	.10
❑ 384 Jason Schmidt	.30	.10
❑ 385 Reggie Sanders	.30	.10
❑ 386 J.T. Snow	.30	.10
❑ 387 Robb Nen	.30	.10
❑ 388 Ryan Jensen	.30	.10
❑ 389 Jim Edmonds	.30	.10
❑ 390 J.D. Drew	.30	.10
❑ 391 Albert Pujols	1.50	.60
❑ 392 Fernando Vina	.30	.10
❑ 393 Tino Martinez	.50	.20
❑ 394 Edgar Renteria	.30	.10
❑ 395 Matt Morris	.30	.10
❑ 396 Woody Williams	.30	.10
❑ 397 Jason Isringhausen	.30	.10
❑ 398 Placido Polanco	.30	.10
❑ 399 Eli Marrero	.30	.10
❑ 400 Jason Simontacchi	.30	.10

2004 Donruss

❑ COMPLETE SET (400)	150.00	75.00
❑ COMP.SET w/o SP's (300)	25.00	10.00
❑ COMMON CARD (71-370)	.30	.10
❑ COMMON CARD (1-25/371-400)	2.00	.75
❑ COMMON CARD (26-70)	2.00	.75
❑ 1-70/370-400 RANDOM INSERTS IN PACKS		
❑ 1 Derek Jeter DK	4.00	1.50
❑ 2 Greg Maddux DK	3.00	1.25
❑ 3 Albert Pujols DK	4.00	1.50
❑ 4 Ichiro Suzuki DK	4.00	1.50
❑ 5 Alex Rodriguez DK	3.00	1.25
❑ 6 Roger Clemens DK	4.00	1.50
❑ 7 Andruw Jones DK	2.00	.75
❑ 8 Barry Bonds DK	5.00	2.00

❑ 9 Jeff Bagwell DK	2.00	.75
❑ 10 Randy Johnson DK	2.00	.75
❑ 11 Scott Rolen DK	2.00	.75
❑ 12 Lance Berkman DK	2.00	.75
❑ 13 Barry Zito DK	2.00	.75
❑ 14 Manny Ramirez DK	2.00	.75
❑ 15 Carlos Delgado DK	2.00	.75
❑ 16 Alfonso Soriano DK	2.00	.75
❑ 17 Todd Helton DK	2.00	.75
❑ 18 Mike Mussina DK	2.00	.75
❑ 19 Austin Kearns DK	2.00	.75
❑ 20 Nomar Garciaparra DK	3.00	1.25
❑ 21 Chipper Jones DK	2.00	.75
❑ 22 Mark Prior DK	2.00	.75
❑ 23 Jim Thome DK	2.00	.75
❑ 24 Vladimir Guerrero DK	2.00	.75
❑ 25 Pedro Martinez DK	2.00	.75
❑ 26 Sergio Mitre RR	2.00	.75
❑ 27 Adam Loewen RR	2.00	.75
❑ 28 Alfredo Gonzalez RR	2.00	.75
❑ 29 Miguel Ojeda RR	2.00	.75
❑ 30 Rosman Garcia RR	2.00	.75
❑ 31 Arnie Munoz RR	2.00	.75
❑ 32 Andrew Brown RR	2.00	.75
❑ 33 Josh Hall RR	2.00	.75
❑ 34 Josh Stewart RR	2.00	.75
❑ 35 Clint Barmes RR	3.00	1.25
❑ 36 Brandon Webb RR	2.00	.75
❑ 37 Chien-Ming Wang RR	8.00	3.00
❑ 38 Edgar Gonzalez RR	2.00	.75
❑ 39 Alejandro Machado RR	2.00	.75
❑ 40 Jeremy Griffiths RR	2.00	.75
❑ 41 Craig Brazell RR	2.00	.75
❑ 42 Daniel Cabrera RR	2.00	.75
❑ 43 Fernando Cabrera RR	2.00	.75
❑ 44 Terrmel Sledge RR	2.00	.75
❑ 45 Rob Hammock RR	2.00	.75
❑ 46 Francisco Rosario RR	2.00	.75
❑ 47 Francisco Cruceta RR	2.00	.75
❑ 48 Rett Johnson RR	2.00	.75
❑ 49 Guillermo Quiroz RR	2.00	.75
❑ 50 Hong-Chih Kuo RR	3.00	1.25
❑ 51 Ian Ferguson RR	2.00	.75
❑ 52 Tim Olson RR	2.00	.75
❑ 53 Todd Wellemeyer RR	2.00	.75
❑ 54 Rich Fischer RR	2.00	.75
❑ 55 Phil Seibel RR	2.00	.75
❑ 56 Joe Valentine RR	2.00	.75
❑ 57 Matt Kata RR	2.00	.75
❑ 58 Michael Hessman RR	2.00	.75
❑ 59 Michel Hernandez RR	2.00	.75
❑ 60 Doug Waechter RR	2.00	.75
❑ 61 Prentice Redman RR	2.00	.75
❑ 62 Nook Logan RR	2.00	.75
❑ 63 Oscar Villarreal RR	2.00	.75
❑ 64 Pete LaForest RR	2.00	.75
❑ 65 Matt Bruback RR	2.00	.75
❑ 66 Dan Haren RR	2.00	.75
❑ 67 Greg Aquino RR	2.00	.75
❑ 68 Lew Ford RR	2.00	.75
❑ 69 Jeff Duncan RR	2.00	.75
❑ 70 Ryan Wagner RR	2.00	.75
❑ 71 Bengie Molina	.30	.10
❑ 72 Brad Fullmer	.30	.10
❑ 73 Darin Erstad	.30	.10
❑ 74 David Eckstein	.30	.10
❑ 75 Garret Anderson	.30	.10
❑ 76 Jarrod Washburn	.30	.10
❑ 77 Kevin Appier	.30	.10
❑ 78 Scott Spiezio	.30	.10
❑ 79 Tim Salmon	.50	.20
❑ 80 Troy Glaus	.30	.10
❑ 81 Troy Percival	.30	.10
❑ 82 Jason Johnson	.30	.10
❑ 83 Jay Gibbons	.30	.10
❑ 84 Melvin Mora	.30	.10
❑ 85 Sidney Ponson	.30	.10
❑ 86 Tony Batista	.30	.10
❑ 87 Bill Mueller	.30	.10
❑ 88 Byung-Hyun Kim	.30	.10
❑ 89 David Ortiz	.75	.30
❑ 90 Derek Lowe	.30	.10
❑ 91 Johnny Damon	.50	.20
❑ 92 Casey Fossum	.30	.10
❑ 93 Manny Ramirez	.50	.20
❑ 94 Nomar Garciaparra	1.25	.50
❑ 95 Pedro Martinez	.50	.20
❑ 96 Todd Walker	.30	.10
❑ 97 Trot Nixon	.30	.10
❑ 98 Bartolo Colon	.30	.10
❑ 99 Carlos Lee	.30	.10
❑ 100 D'Angelo Jimenez	.30	.10
❑ 101 Esteban Loaiza	.30	.10
❑ 102 Frank Thomas	.75	.30
❑ 103 Joe Crede	.30	.10
❑ 104 Jose Valentin	.30	.10
❑ 105 Magglio Ordonez	.30	.10
❑ 106 Mark Buehrle	.30	.10
❑ 107 Paul Konerko	.30	.10
❑ 108 Brandon Phillips	.30	.10
❑ 109 C.C Sabathia	.30	.10
❑ 110 Ellis Burks	.30	.10
❑ 111 Jeremy Guthrie	.30	.10
❑ 112 Josh Bard	.30	.10
❑ 113 Matt Lawton	.30	.10
❑ 114 Milton Bradley	.30	.10
❑ 115 Omar Vizquel	.50	.20
❑ 116 Travis Hafner	.30	.10
❑ 117 Bobby Higginson	.30	.10
❑ 118 Carlos Pena	.30	.10
❑ 119 Dmitri Young	.30	.10
❑ 120 Eric Munson	.30	.10
❑ 121 Jeremy Bonderman	.30	.10
❑ 122 Nate Cornejo	.30	.10
❑ 123 Omar Infante	.30	.10
❑ 124 Ramon Santiago	.30	.10
❑ 125 Angel Berroa	.30	.10
❑ 126 Carlos Beltran	.30	.10
❑ 127 Desi Relaford	.30	.10
❑ 128 Jeremy Affeldt	.30	.10
❑ 129 Joe Randa	.30	.10
❑ 130 Ken Harvey	.30	.10
❑ 131 Mike MacDougal	.30	.10
❑ 132 Michael Tucker	.30	.10
❑ 133 Mike Sweeney	.30	.10
❑ 134 Raul Ibanez	.30	.10
❑ 135 Runelvys Hernandez	.30	.10
❑ 136 A.J. Pierzynski	.30	.10
❑ 137 Brad Radke	.30	.10
❑ 138 Corey Koskie	.30	.10
❑ 139 Cristian Guzman	.30	.10
❑ 140 Doug Mientkiewicz	.30	.10
❑ 141 Dustan Mohr	.30	.10
❑ 142 Jacque Jones	.30	.10
❑ 143 Kenny Rogers	.30	.10
❑ 144 Bobby Kielty	.30	.10
❑ 145 Kyle Lohse	.30	.10
❑ 146 Luis Rivas	.30	.10
❑ 147 Torii Hunter	.30	.10
❑ 148 Alfonso Soriano	.30	.10
❑ 149 Andy Pettitte	.50	.20
❑ 150 Bernie Williams	.50	.20
❑ 151 David Wells	.30	.10
❑ 152 Derek Jeter	1.50	.60
❑ 153 Hideki Matsui	1.25	.50
❑ 154 Jason Giambi	.30	.10
❑ 155 Jorge Posada	.50	.20
❑ 156 Jose Contreras	.30	.10
❑ 157 Mike Mussina	.50	.20
❑ 158 Nick Johnson	.30	.10
❑ 159 Robin Ventura	.30	.10
❑ 160 Roger Clemens	1.50	.60
❑ 161 Barry Zito	.30	.10
❑ 162 Chris Singleton	.30	.10

❑	163	Eric Byrnes	.30	.10
❑	164	Eric Chavez	.30	.10
❑	165	Erubiel Durazo	.30	.10
❑	166	Keith Foulke	.30	.10
❑	167	Mark Ellis	.30	.10
❑	168	Miguel Tejada	.30	.10
❑	169	Mark Mulder	.30	.10
❑	170	Ramon Hernandez	.30	.10
❑	171	Ted Lilly	.30	.10
❑	172	Terrence Long	.30	.10
❑	173	Tim Hudson	.30	.10
❑	174	Bret Boone	.30	.10
❑	175	Carlos Guillen	.30	.10
❑	176	Dan Wilson	.30	.10
❑	177	Edgar Martinez	.50	.20
❑	178	Freddy Garcia	.30	.10
❑	179	Gil Meche	.30	.10
❑	180	Ichiro Suzuki	1.50	.60
❑	181	Jamie Moyer	.30	.10
❑	182	Joel Pineiro	.30	.10
❑	183	John Olerud	.30	.10
❑	184	Mike Cameron	.30	.10
❑	185	Randy Winn	.30	.10
❑	186	Ryan Franklin	.30	.10
❑	187	Kazuhiro Sasaki	.30	.10
❑	188	Aubrey Huff	.30	.10
❑	189	Carl Crawford	.30	.10
❑	190	Joe Kennedy	.30	.10
❑	191	Marlon Anderson	.30	.10
❑	192	Rey Ordonez	.30	.10
❑	193	Rocco Baldelli	.30	.10
❑	194	Toby Hall	.30	.10
❑	195	Travis Lee	.30	.10
❑	196	Alex Rodriguez	1.25	.50
❑	197	Carl Everett	.30	.10
❑	198	Chan Ho Park	.30	.10
❑	199	Einar Diaz	.30	.10
❑	200	Hank Blalock	.30	.10
❑	201	Ismael Valdes	.30	.10
❑	202	Juan Gonzalez	.30	.10
❑	203	Mark Teixeira	.50	.20
❑	204	Mike Young	.30	.10
❑	205	Rafael Palmeiro	.50	.20
❑	206	Carlos Delgado	.30	.10
❑	207	Kelvim Escobar	.30	.10
❑	208	Eric Hinske	.30	.10
❑	209	Frank Catalanotto	.30	.10
❑	210	Josh Phelps	.30	.10
❑	211	Orlando Hudson	.30	.10
❑	212	Roy Halladay	.30	.10
❑	213	Shannon Stewart	.30	.10
❑	214	Vernon Wells	.30	.10
❑	215	Carlos Baerga	.30	.10
❑	216	Curt Schilling	.30	.10
❑	217	Junior Spivey	.30	.10
❑	218	Luis Gonzalez	.30	.10
❑	219	Lyle Overbay	.30	.10
❑	220	Mark Grace	.50	.20
❑	221	Matt Williams	.30	.10
❑	222	Randy Johnson	.75	.30
❑	223	Shea Hillenbrand	.30	.10
❑	224	Steve Finley	.30	.10
❑	225	Andruw Jones	.50	.20
❑	226	Chipper Jones	.75	.30
❑	227	Gary Sheffield	.30	.10
❑	228	Greg Maddux	1.25	.50
❑	229	Javy Lopez	.30	.10
❑	230	John Smoltz	.50	.20
❑	231	Marcus Giles	.30	.10
❑	232	Mike Hampton	.30	.10
❑	233	Rafael Furcal	.30	.10
❑	234	Robert Fick	.30	.10
❑	235	Russ Ortiz	.30	.10
❑	236	Alex Gonzalez	.30	.10
❑	237	Carlos Zambrano	.30	.10
❑	238	Corey Patterson	.30	.10
❑	239	Hee Seop Choi	.30	.10
❑	240	Kerry Wood	.30	.10
❑	241	Mark Bellhorn	.30	.10
❑	242	Mark Prior	.50	.20
❑	243	Moises Alou	.30	.10
❑	244	Sammy Sosa	.75	.30
❑	245	Aaron Boone	.30	.10
❑	246	Adam Dunn	.30	.10
❑	247	Austin Kearns	.30	.10
❑	248	Barry Larkin	.50	.20
❑	249	Felipe Lopez	.30	.10
❑	250	Jose Guillen	.30	.10
❑	251	Ken Griffey Jr.	1.25	.50
❑	252	Jason LaRue	.30	.10
❑	253	Scott Williamson	.30	.10
❑	254	Sean Casey	.30	.10
❑	255	Shawn Chacon	.30	.10
❑	256	Chris Stynes	.30	.10
❑	257	Jason Jennings	.30	.10
❑	258	Jay Payton	.30	.10
❑	259	Jose Hernandez	.30	.10
❑	260	Larry Walker	.30	.10
❑	261	Preston Wilson	.30	.10
❑	262	Ronnie Belliard	.30	.10
❑	263	Todd Helton	.50	.20
❑	264	A.J. Burnett	.30	.10
❑	265	Alex Gonzalez	.30	.10
❑	266	Brad Penny	.30	.10
❑	267	Derrek Lee	.50	.20
❑	268	Ivan Rodriguez	.50	.20
❑	269	Josh Beckett	.30	.10
❑	270	Juan Encarnacion	.30	.10
❑	271	Juan Pierre	.30	.10
❑	272	Luis Castillo	.30	.10
❑	273	Mike Lowell	.30	.10
❑	274	Todd Hollandsworth	.30	.10
❑	275	Billy Wagner	.30	.10
❑	276	Brad Ausmus	.30	.10
❑	277	Craig Biggio	.50	.20
❑	278	Jeff Bagwell	.50	.20
❑	279	Jeff Kent	.30	.10
❑	280	Lance Berkman	.30	.10
❑	281	Richard Hidalgo	.30	.10
❑	282	Roy Oswalt	.30	.10
❑	283	Wade Miller	.30	.10
❑	284	Adrian Beltre	.30	.10
❑	285	Brian Jordan	.30	.10
❑	286	Cesar Izturis	.30	.10
❑	287	Dave Roberts	.30	.10
❑	288	Eric Gagne	.30	.10
❑	289	Fred McGriff	.50	.20
❑	290	Hideo Nomo	.75	.30
❑	291	Kazuhisa Ishii	.30	.10
❑	292	Kevin Brown	.30	.10
❑	293	Paul Lo Duca	.30	.10
❑	294	Shawn Green	.30	.10
❑	295	Ben Sheets	.30	.10
❑	296	Geoff Jenkins	.30	.10
❑	297	Rey Sanchez	.30	.10
❑	298	Richie Sexson	.30	.10
❑	299	Wes Helms	.30	.10
❑	300	Brad Wilkerson	.30	.10
❑	301	Claudio Vargas	.30	.10
❑	302	Endy Chavez	.30	.10
❑	303	Fernando Tatis	.30	.10
❑	304	Javier Vazquez	.30	.10
❑	305	Jose Vidro	.30	.10
❑	306	Michael Barrett	.30	.10
❑	307	Orlando Cabrera	.30	.10
❑	308	Tony Armas Jr.	.30	.10
❑	309	Vladimir Guerrero	.75	.30
❑	310	Zach Day	.30	.10
❑	311	Al Leiter	.30	.10
❑	312	Cliff Floyd	.30	.10
❑	313	Jae Weong Seo	.30	.10
❑	314	Jeromy Burnitz	.30	.10
❑	315	Mike Piazza	1.25	.50
❑	316	Mo Vaughn	.30	.10
❑	317	Roberto Alomar	.50	.20
❑	318	Roger Cedeno	.30	.10
❑	319	Tom Glavine	.50	.20
❑	320	Jose Reyes	.30	.10
❑	321	Bobby Abreu	.30	.10
❑	322	Brett Myers	.30	.10
❑	323	David Bell	.30	.10
❑	324	Jim Thome	.50	.20
❑	325	Jimmy Rollins	.30	.10
❑	326	Kevin Millwood	.30	.10
❑	327	Marlon Byrd	.30	.10
❑	328	Mike Lieberthal	.30	.10
❑	329	Pat Burrell	.30	.10
❑	330	Randy Wolf	.30	.10
❑	331	Aramis Ramirez	.30	.10
❑	332	Brian Giles	.30	.10
❑	333	Jason Kendall	.30	.10
❑	334	Kenny Lofton	.30	.10
❑	335	Kip Wells	.30	.10
❑	336	Kris Benson	.30	.10
❑	337	Randall Simon	.30	.10
❑	338	Reggie Sanders	.30	.10
❑	339	Albert Pujols	1.50	.60
❑	340	Edgar Renteria	.30	.10
❑	341	Fernando Vina	.30	.10
❑	342	J.D. Drew	.30	.10
❑	343	Jim Edmonds	.30	.10
❑	344	Matt Morris	.30	.10
❑	345	Mike Matheny	.30	.10
❑	346	Scott Rolen	.50	.20
❑	347	Tino Martinez	.50	.20
❑	348	Woody Williams	.30	.10
❑	349	Brian Lawrence	.30	.10
❑	350	Mark Kotsay	.30	.10
❑	351	Mark Loretta	.30	.10
❑	352	Ramon Vazquez	.30	.10
❑	353	Rondell White	.30	.10
❑	354	Ryan Klesko	.30	.10
❑	355	Sean Burroughs	.30	.10
❑	356	Trevor Hoffman	.30	.10
❑	357	Xavier Nady	.30	.10
❑	358	Andres Galarraga	.30	.10
❑	359	Barry Bonds	2.00	.75
❑	360	Benito Santiago	.30	.10
❑	361	Deivi Cruz	.30	.10
❑	362	Edgardo Alfonzo	.30	.10
❑	363	J.T. Snow	.30	.10
❑	364	Jason Schmidt	.30	.10
❑	365	Kirk Rueter	.30	.10
❑	366	Kurt Ainsworth	.30	.10
❑	367	Marquis Grissom	.30	.10
❑	368	Ray Durham	.30	.10
❑	369	Rich Aurilia	.30	.10
❑	370	Tim Worrell	.30	.10
❑	371	Troy Glaus TC	2.00	.75
❑	372	Melvin Mora TC	2.00	.75
❑	373	Nomar Garciaparra TC	3.00	1.25
❑	374	Magglio Ordonez TC	2.00	.75
❑	375	Omar Vizquel TC	2.00	.75
❑	376	Dmitri Young TC	2.00	.75
❑	377	Mike Sweeney TC	2.00	.75
❑	378	Torii Hunter TC	2.00	.75
❑	379	Derek Jeter TC	4.00	1.50
❑	380	Barry Zito TC	2.00	.75
❑	381	Ichiro Suzuki TC	4.00	1.50
❑	382	Rocco Baldelli TC	2.00	.75
❑	383	Alex Rodriguez TC	3.00	1.25
❑	384	Carlos Delgado TC	2.00	.75
❑	385	Randy Johnson TC	2.00	.75
❑	386	Greg Maddux TC	3.00	1.25
❑	387	Sammy Sosa TC	2.00	.75
❑	388	Ken Griffey Jr. TC	3.00	1.25
❑	389	Todd Helton TC	2.00	.75
❑	390	Ivan Rodriguez TC	2.00	.75
❑	391	Jeff Bagwell TC	2.00	.75
❑	392	Hideo Nomo TC	2.00	.75
❑	393	Richie Sexson TC	2.00	.75
❑	394	Vladimir Guerrero TC	2.00	.75
❑	395	Mike Piazza TC	3.00	1.25
❑	396	Jim Thome TC	2.00	.75
❑	397	Jason Kendall TC	2.00	.75
❑	398	Albert Pujols TC	4.00	1.50
❑	399	Ryan Klesko TC	2.00	.75
❑	400	Barry Bonds TC	5.00	2.00

2005 Donruss

Card		
❑ COMPLETE SET (400)	150.00	75.00
❑ COMP.SET w/o SP's (300)	25.00	10.00
❑ COMMON CARD (71-370)	.30	.10
❑ COMMON (1-25/371-400)	2.00	.75
❑ COMMON CARD (26-70)	2.00	.75
❑ 1-25 STATED ODDS 1:6		
❑ 26-70 STATED ODDS 1:6		
❑ 371-400 STATED ODDS 1:6		
❑ 1 Garret Anderson DK	2.00	.75
❑ 2 Vladimir Guerrero DK	2.00	.75
❑ 3 Manny Ramirez DK	2.00	.75
❑ 4 Kerry Wood DK	2.00	.75
❑ 5 Sammy Sosa DK	2.00	.75
❑ 6 Magglio Ordonez DK	2.00	.75
❑ 7 Adam Dunn DK	2.00	.75
❑ 8 Todd Helton DK	2.00	.75
❑ 9 Josh Beckett DK	2.00	.75
❑ 10 Miguel Cabrera DK	2.00	.75
❑ 11 Lance Berkman DK	2.00	.75
❑ 12 Carlos Beltran DK	2.00	.75
❑ 13 Shawn Green DK	2.00	.75
❑ 14 Roger Clemens DK	3.00	1.25
❑ 15 Mike Piazza DK	2.00	.75
❑ 16 Alex Rodriguez DK	3.00	1.25
❑ 17 Derek Jeter DK	4.00	1.50
❑ 18 Mark Mulder DK	2.00	.75
❑ 19 Jim Thome DK	2.00	.75
❑ 20 Albert Pujols DK	4.00	1.50
❑ 21 Scott Rolen DK	2.00	.75
❑ 22 Aubrey Huff DK	2.00	.75
❑ 23 Alfonso Soriano DK	2.00	.75
❑ 24 Hank Blalock DK	2.00	.75
❑ 25 Vernon Wells DK	2.00	.75
❑ 26 Kazuo Matsui RR	3.00	1.25
❑ 27 B.J. Upton RR	5.00	2.00
❑ 28 Charles Thomas RR	2.00	.75
❑ 29 Akinori Otsuka RR	3.00	1.25
❑ 30 David Aardsma RR	2.00	.75
❑ 31 Travis Blackley RR	2.00	.75
❑ 32 Brad Halsey RR	2.00	.75
❑ 33 David Wright RR	8.00	3.00
❑ 34 Kazuhito Tadano RR	3.00	1.25
❑ 35 Casey Kotchman RR	3.00	1.25
❑ 36 Khalil Greene RR	5.00	2.00
❑ 37 Adrian Gonzalez RR	2.00	.75
❑ 38 Zack Greinke RR	2.00	.75
❑ 39 Chad Cordero RR	2.00	.75
❑ 40 Scott Kazmir RR	5.00	2.00
❑ 41 Jeremy Guthrie RR	2.00	.75
❑ 42 Noah Lowry RR	3.00	1.25
❑ 43 Chase Utley RR	5.00	2.00
❑ 44 Billy Traber RR	2.00	.75
❑ 45 Aarom Baldiris RR	2.00	.75
❑ 46 Abe Alvarez RR	2.00	.75
❑ 47 Angel Chavez RR	2.00	.75
❑ 48 Joe Mauer RR	5.00	2.00
❑ 49 Joey Gathright RR	3.00	1.25
❑ 50 John Gall RR	2.00	.75
❑ 51 Ronald Bolisario RR	2.00	.75
❑ 52 Ryan Wing RR	2.00	.75
❑ 53 Scott Proctor RR	2.00	.75
❑ 54 Yadier Molina RR	3.00	1.25
❑ 55 Carlos Hines RR	2.00	.75
❑ 56 Frankie Francisco RR	2.00	.75
❑ 57 Graham Koonce RR	2.00	.75
❑ 58 Jake Woods RR	2.00	.75
❑ 59 Jason Bartlett RR	2.00	.75
❑ 60 Mike Rouse RR	2.00	.75
❑ 61 Phil Stockman RR	2.00	.75
❑ 62 Renyel Pinto RR	2.00	.75
❑ 63 Roberto Novoa RR	2.00	.75
❑ 64 Ryan Meaux RR	2.00	.75
❑ 65 Dave Crouthers RR	2.00	.75
❑ 66 Justin Knoedler RR	2.00	.75
❑ 67 Justin Leone RR	2.00	.75
❑ 68 Nick Regilio RR	2.00	.75
❑ 69 Mike Gosling RR	2.00	.75
❑ 70 Onil Joseph RR	2.00	.75
❑ 71 Bartolo Colon	.30	.10
❑ 72 Brad Fullmer	.30	.10
❑ 73 Chone Figgins	.30	.10
❑ 74 Darin Erstad	.30	.10
❑ 75 Francisco Rodriguez	.30	.10
❑ 76 Garret Anderson	.30	.10
❑ 77 Jarrod Washburn	.30	.10
❑ 78 John Lackey	.30	.10
❑ 79 Jose Guillen	.30	.10
❑ 80 Robb Quinlan	.30	.10
❑ 81 Tim Salmon	.50	.20
❑ 82 Troy Glaus	.30	.10
❑ 83 Troy Percival	.30	.10
❑ 84 Vladimir Guerrero	.75	.30
❑ 85 Brandon Webb	.30	.10
❑ 86 Casey Fossum	.30	.10
❑ 87 Luis Gonzalez	.30	.10
❑ 88 Randy Johnson	.75	.30
❑ 89 Richie Sexson	.30	.10
❑ 90 Robby Hammock	.30	.10
❑ 91 Roberto Alomar	.50	.20
❑ 92 Adam LaRoche	.30	.10
❑ 93 Andruw Jones	.50	.20
❑ 94 Bubba Nelson	.30	.10
❑ 95 Chipper Jones	.75	.30
❑ 96 J.D. Drew	.30	.10
❑ 97 John Smoltz	.50	.20
❑ 98 Johnny Estrada	.30	.10
❑ 99 Marcus Giles	.30	.10
❑ 100 Mike Hampton	.30	.10
❑ 101 Nick Green	.30	.10
❑ 102 Rafael Furcal	.30	.10
❑ 103 Russ Ortiz	.30	.10
❑ 104 Adam Loewen	.30	.10
❑ 105 Brian Roberts	.30	.10
❑ 106 Javy Lopez	.30	.10
❑ 107 Jay Gibbons	.30	.10
❑ 108 L.Bigbie UER Roberts	.30	.10
❑ 109 Luis Matos	.30	.10
❑ 110 Melvin Mora	.30	.10
❑ 111 Miguel Tejada	.30	.10
❑ 112 Rafael Palmeiro	.50	.20
❑ 113 Rodrigo Lopez	.30	.10
❑ 114 Sidney Ponson	.30	.10
❑ 115 Bill Mueller	.30	.10
❑ 116 Byung-Hyun Kim	.30	.10
❑ 117 Curt Schilling	.50	.20
❑ 118 David Ortiz	.75	.30
❑ 119 Derek Lowe	.30	.10
❑ 120 Doug Mientkiewicz	.30	.10
❑ 121 Jason Varitek	.75	.30
❑ 122 Johnny Damon	.50	.20
❑ 123 Keith Foulke	.30	.10
❑ 124 Kevin Youkilis	.30	.10
❑ 125 Manny Ramirez	.50	.20
❑ 126 Orlando Cabrera	.30	.10
❑ 127 Pedro Martinez	.50	.20
❑ 128 Trot Nixon	.30	.10
❑ 129 Aramis Ramirez	.30	.10
❑ 130 Carlos Zambrano	.30	.10
❑ 131 Corey Patterson	.30	.10
❑ 132 Derrek Lee	.50	.20
❑ 133 Greg Maddux	1.25	.50
❑ 134 Kerry Wood	.30	.10
❑ 135 Mark Prior	.50	.20
❑ 136 Matt Clement	.30	.10
❑ 137 Moises Alou	.30	.10
❑ 138 Nomar Garciaparra	.75	.30
❑ 139 Sammy Sosa	.75	.30
❑ 140 Todd Walker	.30	.10
❑ 141 Angel Guzman	.30	.10
❑ 142 Billy Koch	.30	.10
❑ 143 Carlos Lee	.30	.10
❑ 144 Frank Thomas	.75	.30
❑ 145 Magglio Ordonez	.30	.10
❑ 146 Mark Buehrle	.30	.10
❑ 147 Paul Konerko	.30	.10
❑ 148 Wilson Valdez	.30	.10
❑ 149 Adam Dunn	.30	.10
❑ 150 Austin Kearns	.30	.10
❑ 151 Barry Larkin	.50	.20
❑ 152 Benito Santiago	.30	.10
❑ 153 Jason LaRue	.30	.10
❑ 154 Ken Griffey Jr.	1.25	.50
❑ 155 Ryan Wagner	.30	.10
❑ 156 Sean Casey	.30	.10
❑ 157 Brandon Phillips	.30	.10
❑ 158 Brian Tallet	.30	.10
❑ 159 C.C. Sabathia	.30	.10
❑ 160 Cliff Lee	.30	.10
❑ 161 Jeremy Guthrie	.30	.10
❑ 162 Jody Gerut	.30	.10
❑ 163 Matt Lawton	.30	.10
❑ 164 Omar Vizquel	.50	.20
❑ 165 Travis Hafner	.30	.10
❑ 166 Victor Martinez	.30	.10
❑ 167 Charles Johnson	.30	.10
❑ 168 Garrett Atkins	.30	.10
❑ 169 Jason Jennings	.30	.10
❑ 170 Jay Payton	.30	.10
❑ 171 Jeromy Burnitz	.30	.10
❑ 172 Joe Kennedy	.30	.10
❑ 173 Larry Walker	.50	.20
❑ 174 Preston Wilson	.30	.10
❑ 175 Todd Helton	.50	.20
❑ 176 Vinny Castilla	.30	.10
❑ 177 Bobby Higginson	.30	.10
❑ 178 Brandon Inge	.30	.10
❑ 179 Carlos Guillen	.30	.10
❑ 180 Carlos Pena	.30	.10
❑ 181 Craig Monroe	.30	.10
❑ 182 Dmitri Young	.30	.10
❑ 183 Eric Munson	.30	.10
❑ 184 Fernando Vina	.30	.10
❑ 185 Ivan Rodriguez	.50	.20
❑ 186 Jeremy Bonderman	.30	.10
❑ 187 Rondell White	.30	.10
❑ 188 A.J. Burnett	.30	.10
❑ 189 Dontrelle Willis	.30	.10
❑ 190 Guillermo Mota	.30	.10
❑ 191 Hee Seop Choi	.30	.10
❑ 192 Jeff Conine	.30	.10
❑ 193 Josh Beckett	.30	.10
❑ 194 Juan Encarnacion	.30	.10
❑ 195 Juan Pierre	.30	.10
❑ 196 Luis Castillo	.30	.10
❑ 197 Miguel Cabrera	.50	.20
❑ 198 Mike Lowell	.30	.10
❑ 199 Paul Lo Duca	.30	.10
❑ 200 Andy Pettitte	.50	.20
❑ 201 Brad Ausmus	.30	.10
❑ 202 Carlos Beltran	.30	.10
❑ 203 Chris Burke	.30	.10
❑ 204 Craig Biggio	.50	.20
❑ 205 Jeff Bagwell	.50	.20
❑ 206 Jeff Kent	.30	.10
❑ 207 Lance Berkman	.30	.10
❑ 208 Morgan Ensberg	.30	.10
❑ 209 Octavio Dotel	.30	.10
❑ 210 Roger Clemens	1.25	.50
❑ 211 Roy Oswalt	.30	.10
❑ 212 Tim Redding	.30	.10
❑ 213 Angel Berroa	.30	.10
❑ 214 Juan Gonzalez	.30	.10
❑ 215 Ken Harvey	.30	.10
❑ 216 Mike Sweeney	.30	.10
❑ 217 Adrian Beltre	.30	.10
❑ 218 Brad Penny	.30	.10
❑ 219 Eric Gagne	.30	.10
❑ 220 Hideo Nomo	.75	.30
❑ 221 Hong-Chih Kuo	.30	.10
❑ 222 Jeff Weaver	.30	.10
❑ 223 Kazuhisa Ishii	.30	.10
❑ 224 Milton Bradley	.30	.10
❑ 225 Shawn Green	.30	.10
❑ 226 Steve Finley	.30	.10
❑ 227 Danny Kolb	.30	.10
❑ 228 Geoff Jenkins	.30	.10
❑ 229 Junior Spivey	.30	.10
❑ 230 Lyle Overbay	.30	.10
❑ 231 Rickie Weeks	.30	.10
❑ 232 Scott Podsednik	.30	.10
❑ 233 Brad Radke	.30	.10
❑ 234 Corey Koskie	.30	.10
❑ 235 Cristian Guzman	.30	.10
❑ 236 Dustan Mohr	.30	.10
❑ 237 Eddie Guardado	.30	.10
❑ 238 J.D. Durbin	.30	.10
❑ 239 Jacque Jones	.30	.10
❑ 240 Joe Nathan	.30	.10
❑ 241 Johan Santana	.75	.30
❑ 242 Lew Ford	.30	.10
❑ 243 Michael Cuddyer	.30	.10
❑ 244 Shannon Stewart	.30	.10
❑ 245 Torii Hunter	.30	.10
❑ 246 Brad Wilkerson	.30	.10
❑ 247 Carl Everett	.30	.10
❑ 248 Jeff Fassero	.30	.10
❑ 249 Jose Vidro	.30	.10
❑ 250 Livan Hernandez	.30	.10

❑ 251 Michael Barrett .30 .10
❑ 252 Tony Batista .30 .10
❑ 253 Zach Day .30 .10
❑ 254 Al Leiter .30 .10
❑ 255 Cliff Floyd .30 .10
❑ 256 Jae Weong Seo .30 .10
❑ 257 John Olerud .30 .10
❑ 258 Jose Reyes .30 .10
❑ 259 Mike Cameron .30 .10
❑ 260 Mike Piazza .75 .30
❑ 261 Richard Hidalgo .30 .10
❑ 262 Tom Glavine .50 .20
❑ 263 Vance Wilson .30 .10
❑ 264 Alex Rodriguez 1.25 .50
❑ 265 Armando Benitez .30 .10
❑ 266 Bernie Williams .50 .20
❑ 267 Bubba Crosby .30 .10
❑ 268 Chien-Ming Wang 1.25 .50
❑ 269 Derek Jeter 1.50 .60
❑ 270 Esteban Loaiza .30 .10
❑ 271 Gary Sheffield .30 .10
❑ 272 Hideki Matsui 1.25 .50
❑ 273 Jason Giambi .30 .10
❑ 274 Javier Vazquez .30 .10
❑ 275 Jorge Posada .50 .20
❑ 276 Jose Contreras .30 .10
❑ 277 Kenny Lofton .30 .10
❑ 278 Kevin Brown .30 .10
❑ 279 Mariano Rivera .75 .30
❑ 280 Mike Mussina .50 .20
❑ 281 Barry Zito .30 .10
❑ 282 Bobby Crosby .30 .10
❑ 283 Eric Byrnes .30 .10
❑ 284 Eric Chavez .30 .10
❑ 285 Erubiel Durazo .30 .10
❑ 286 Jermaine Dye .30 .10
❑ 287 Mark Kotsay .30 .10
❑ 288 Mark Mulder .30 .10
❑ 289 Rich Harden .30 .10
❑ 290 Tim Hudson .30 .10
❑ 291 Billy Wagner .30 .10
❑ 292 Bobby Abreu .30 .10
❑ 293 Brett Myers .30 .10
❑ 294 Eric Milton .30 .10
❑ 295 Jim Thome .50 .20
❑ 296 Jimmy Rollins .30 .10
❑ 297 Kevin Millwood .30 .10
❑ 298 Marlon Byrd .30 .10
❑ 299 Mike Lieberthal .30 .10
❑ 300 Pat Burrell .30 .10
❑ 301 Randy Wolf .30 .10
❑ 302 Craig Wilson .30 .10
❑ 303 Jack Wilson .30 .10
❑ 304 Jacob Cruz .30 .10
❑ 305 Jason Bay .30 .10
❑ 306 Jason Kendall .30 .10
❑ 307 Jose Castillo .30 .10
❑ 308 Kip Wells .30 .10
❑ 309 Brian Giles .30 .10
❑ 310 Brian Lawrence .30 .10
❑ 311 Chris Oxspring .30 .10
❑ 312 David Wells .30 .10
❑ 313 Freddy Guzman .30 .10
❑ 314 Jake Peavy .30 .10
❑ 315 Mark Loretta .30 .10
❑ 316 Ryan Klesko .30 .10
❑ 317 Sean Burroughs .30 .10
❑ 318 Trevor Hoffman .30 .10
❑ 319 Xavier Nady .30 .10
❑ 320 A.J. Pierzynski .30 .10
❑ 321 Edgardo Alfonzo .30 .10
❑ 322 J.T. Snow .30 .10
❑ 323 Jason Schmidt .30 .10
❑ 324 Jerome Williams .30 .10
❑ 325 Kirk Rueter .30 .10
❑ 326 Bret Boone .30 .10
❑ 327 Bucky Jacobsen .30 .10
❑ 328 Edgar Martinez .50 .20
❑ 329 Freddy Garcia .30 .10
❑ 330 Ichiro Suzuki 1.50 .60
❑ 331 Jamie Moyer .30 .10
❑ 332 Joel Pineiro .30 .10
❑ 333 Scott Spiezio .30 .10
❑ 334 Shigetoshi Hasegawa .30 .10
❑ 335 Albert Pujols 1.50 .60
❑ 336 Edgar Renteria .30 .10
❑ 337 Jason Isringhausen .30 .10
❑ 338 Jim Edmonds .30 .10
❑ 339 Matt Morris .30 .10
❑ 340 Mike Matheny .30 .10
❑ 341 Reggie Sanders .30 .10
❑ 342 Scott Rolen .50 .20
❑ 343 Woody Williams .30 .10
❑ 344 Jeff Suppan .30 .10
❑ 345 Aubrey Huff .30 .10
❑ 346 Carl Crawford .30 .10
❑ 347 Chad Gaudin .30 .10
❑ 348 Delmon Young .50 .20
❑ 349 Dewon Brazelton .30 .10
❑ 350 Jose Cruz Jr. .30 .10
❑ 351 Rocco Baldelli .30 .10
❑ 352 Tino Martinez .50 .20
❑ 353 Toby Hall .30 .10
❑ 354 Alfonso Soriano .30 .10
❑ 355 Brian Jordan .30 .10
❑ 356 Francisco Cordero .30 .10
❑ 357 Hank Blalock .30 .10
❑ 358 Kenny Rogers .30 .10
❑ 359 Kevin Mench .30 .10
❑ 360 Laynce Nix .30 .10
❑ 361 Mark Teixeira .50 .20
❑ 362 Michael Young .30 .10
❑ 363 Alex S. Gonzalez .30 .10
❑ 364 Alexis Rios .30 .10
❑ 365 Carlos Delgado .30 .10
❑ 366 Eric Hinske .30 .10
❑ 367 Frank Catalanotto .30 .10
❑ 368 Josh Phelps .30 .10
❑ 369 Roy Halladay .30 .10
❑ 370 Vernon Wells .30 .10
❑ 371 Vladimir Guerrero TC 2.00 .75
❑ 372 Randy Johnson TC 2.00 .75
❑ 373 Chipper Jones TC 2.00 .75
❑ 374 Miguel Tejada TC 2.00 .75
❑ 375 Pedro Martinez TC 2.00 .75
❑ 376 Sammy Sosa TC 2.00 .75
❑ 377 Frank Thomas TC 2.00 .75
❑ 378 Ken Griffey Jr. TC 3.00 1.25
❑ 379 Victor Martinez TC 2.00 .75
❑ 380 Todd Helton TC 2.00 .75
❑ 381 Ivan Rodriguez TC 2.00 .75
❑ 382 Miguel Cabrera TC 2.00 .75
❑ 383 Roger Clemens TC 3.00 1.25
❑ 384 Ken Harvey TC 2.00 .75
❑ 385 Eric Gagne TC 2.00 .75
❑ 386 Lyle Overbay TC 2.00 .75
❑ 387 Shannon Stewart TC 2.00 .75
❑ 388 Brad Wilkerson TC 2.00 .75
❑ 389 Mike Piazza TC 2.00 .75
❑ 390 Alex Rodriguez TC 3.00 1.25
❑ 391 Mark Mulder TC 2.00 .75
❑ 392 Jim Thome TC 2.00 .75
❑ 393 Jack Wilson TC 2.00 .75
❑ 394 Khalil Greene TC 2.00 .75
❑ 395 Jason Schmidt TC 2.00 .75
❑ 396 Ichiro Suzuki TC 4.00 1.50
❑ 397 Albert Pujols TC 4.00 1.50
❑ 398 Rocco Baldelli TC 2.00 .75
❑ 399 Alfonso Soriano TC 2.00 .75
❑ 400 Vernon Wells TC 2.00 .75

2003 Donruss Elite Extra Edition

❑ 1 Adam Loewen RC 5.00 2.00
❑ 2 Brandon Webb RC 10.00 4.00
❑ 3 Chien-Ming Wang RC 40.00 15.00
❑ 4 Hong-Chih Kuo RC 20.00 8.00
❑ 5 Clint Barmes RC 5.00 2.00
❑ 6 Guillermo Quiroz RC 4.00 1.50
❑ 7 Edgar Gonzalez RC 4.00 1.50
❑ 8 Todd Wellemeyer RC 5.00 2.00
❑ 9 Alfredo Gonzalez RC 4.00 1.50
❑ 10 Craig Brazell RC 4.00 1.50
❑ 11 Tim Olson RC 4.00 1.50
❑ 12 Rich Fischer RC 4.00 1.50
❑ 13 Daniel Cabrera RC 5.00 2.00
❑ 14 Francisco Rosario RC 4.00 1.50
❑ 15 Francisco Cruceta RC 4.00 1.50
❑ 16 Alejandro Machado RC 4.00 1.50
❑ 17 Andrew Brown RC 5.00 2.00
❑ 18 Rob Hammock RC 4.00 1.50
❑ 19 Arnie Munoz RC 4.00 1.50
❑ 20 Felix Sanchez RC 4.00 1.50
❑ 21 Nook Logan RC 5.00 2.00
❑ 22 Cory Stewart RC 4.00 1.50
❑ 23 Michel Hernandez RC 4.00 1.50
❑ 24 Rett Johnson RC 4.00 1.50
❑ 25 Josh Hall RC 4.00 1.50
❑ 26 Doug Waechter RC 5.00 2.00
❑ 27 Matt Kata RC 4.00 1.50
❑ 28 Dan Haren RC 5.00 2.00
❑ 29 Dontrelle Willis 5.00 2.00
❑ 30 Ramon Nivar RC 4.00 1.50
❑ 31 Chad Gaudin RC 4.00 1.50
❑ 32 Rickie Weeks RC 10.00 4.00
❑ 33 Ryan Wagner RC 4.00 1.50
❑ 34 Kevin Correia RC 4.00 1.50
❑ 35 Bo Hart RC 4.00 1.50
❑ 36 Oscar Villarreal RC 4.00 1.50
❑ 37 Josh Willingham RC 8.00 3.00
❑ 38 Jeff Duncan RC 4.00 1.50
❑ 39 David DeJesus RC 5.00 2.00
❑ 40 Dustin McGowan RC 5.00 2.00
❑ 41 Preston Larrison RC 5.00 2.00
❑ 43 Kevin Youkilis RC 8.00 3.00
❑ 44 Bubba Nelson RC 5.00 2.00
❑ 45 Chris Burke RC 5.00 2.00
❑ 46 J.D. Durbin RC 4.00 1.50
❑ 47 Ryan Howard RC 60.00 30.00
❑ 48 Jason Kubel RC 5.00 2.00
❑ 49 Brendan Harris RC 5.00 2.00
❑ 50 Brian Bruney RC 5.00 2.00
❑ 52 Byron Gettis RC 4.00 1.50
❑ 53 Edwin Jackson RC 5.00 2.00
❑ 55 Daniel Garcia RC 4.00 1.50
❑ 57 Chad Cordero RC 8.00 3.00
❑ 58 Delmon Young RC 25.00 10.00

2004 Donruss Elite Extra Edition

❑ COMP.SET w/o SP's (150) 25.00 10.00
❑ COMMON CARD (1-150) .30 .10
❑ COMMON CARD (206-215) 3.00 1.25
❑ 206-215 RANDOM INSERTS IN PACKS
❑ 206-215 PRINT RUN 1000 SERIAL #'d SETS
❑ COMMON NO AU (234-254) 4.00 1.50
❑ NO AU 234-254 RANDOM IN PACKS
❑ NO AU 234-254 PRINT RUN 1000 #'d SETS
❑ 216-355 OVERALL AU-GU ODDS 1:4
❑ 216-355 PRINT RUNS B/WN 260-1617 PER

❑ DO NOT EXIST: 151-205/232/236-238/240
❑ DO NOT EXIST: 241/245/248-249/251/255
❑ DO NOT EXIST: 274/339

	Card	Nm-Mt	Ex-Mt
❑	1 Troy Glaus	.30	.10
❑	2 John Lackey	.30	.10
❑	3 Garret Anderson	.30	.10
❑	4 Francisco Rodriguez	.30	.10
❑	5 Casey Kotchman	.30	.10
❑	6 Jose Guillen	.30	.10
❑	7 Miguel Tejada	.30	.10
❑	8 Rafael Palmeiro	.50	.20
❑	9 Jay Gibbons	.30	.10
❑	10 Melvin Mora	.30	.10
❑	11 Javy Lopez	.30	.10
❑	12 Pedro Martinez	.50	.20
❑	13 Curt Schilling	.50	.20
❑	14 David Ortiz	.75	.30
❑	15 Manny Ramirez	.50	.20
❑	16 Nomar Garciaparra	1.25	.50
❑	17 Magglio Ordonez	.30	.10
❑	18 Frank Thomas	.75	.30
❑	19 Esteban Loaiza	.30	.10
❑	20 Paul Konerko	.30	.10
❑	21 Mark Buehrle	.30	.10
❑	22 Jody Gerut	.30	.10
❑	23 Victor Martinez	.30	.10
❑	24 C.C. Sabathia	.30	.10
❑	25 Travis Hafner	.30	.10
❑	26 Cliff Lee	.30	.10
❑	27 Jeremy Bonderman	.30	.10
❑	28 Dallas McPherson	.30	.10
❑	29 Jermaine Dye	.30	.10
❑	30 Carlos Guillen	.30	.10
❑	31 Carlos Beltran	.30	.10
❑	32 Ken Harvey	.30	.10
❑	33 Mike Sweeney	.30	.10
❑	34 Angel Berroa	.30	.10
❑	35 Joe Nathan	.30	.10
❑	36 Johan Santana	.75	.30
❑	37 Jacque Jones	.30	.10
❑	38 Shannon Stewart	.30	.10
❑	39 Torii Hunter	.30	.10
❑	40 Derek Jeter	1.50	.60
❑	41 Jason Giambi	.30	.10
❑	42 Danny Graves	.30	.10
❑	43 Alfonso Soriano	.30	.10
❑	44 Gary Sheffield	.30	.10
❑	45 Mike Mussina	.50	.20
❑	46 Jorge Posada	.50	.20
❑	47 Hideki Matsui	1.25	.50
❑	48 Francisco Cordero	.30	.10
❑	49 Javier Vazquez	.30	.10
❑	50 Mariano Rivera	.75	.30
❑	51 Eric Chavez	.30	.10
❑	52 Tim Hudson	.30	.10
❑	53 Mark Mulder	.30	.10
❑	54 Barry Zito	.30	.10
❑	55 Ichiro Suzuki	1.50	.60
❑	56 Edgar Martinez	.50	.20
❑	57 Bret Boone	.30	.10
❑	58 Lew Ford	.30	.10
❑	59 B.J. Upton	.50	.20
❑	60 Aubrey Huff	.30	.10
❑	61 Rocco Baldelli	.30	.10
❑	62 Carl Crawford	.30	.10
❑	63 Delmon Young	.50	.20
❑	64 Mark Teixeira	.50	.20
❑	65 Hank Blalock	.30	.10
❑	66 Michael Young	.30	.10
❑	67 Alex Rodriguez	1.25	.50
❑	68 Carlos Delgado	.30	.10
❑	69 Milton Bradley	.30	.10
❑	70 Roy Halladay	.30	.10
❑	71 Vernon Wells	.30	.10
❑	72 Randy Johnson	.75	.30
❑	73 Bobby Crosby	.30	.10
❑	74 Lyle Overbay	.30	.10
❑	75 Luis Gonzalez	.30	.10
❑	76 Steve Finley	.30	.10
❑	77 Chipper Jones	.75	.30
❑	78 Andruw Jones	.50	.20
❑	79 Marcus Giles	.30	.10
❑	80 Rafael Furcal	.30	.10
❑	81 J.D. Drew	.30	.10
❑	82 Sammy Sosa	.75	.30
❑	83 Kerry Wood	.30	.10
❑	84 Mark Prior	.50	.20
❑	85 Derrek Lee	.50	.20
❑	86 Moises Alou	.30	.10
❑	87 Carlos Zambrano	.30	.10
❑	88 Ken Griffey Jr.	1.25	.50
❑	89 Austin Kearns	.30	.10
❑	90 Adam Dunn	.30	.10
❑	91 Barry Larkin	.50	.20
❑	92 Todd Helton	.50	.20
❑	93 Larry Walker Cards	.50	.20
❑	94 Preston Wilson	.30	.10
❑	95 Sean Casey	.30	.10
❑	96 Luis Castillo	.30	.10
❑	97 Josh Beckett	.30	.10
❑	98 Mike Lowell	.30	.10
❑	99 Miguel Cabrera	.50	.20
❑	100 Brad Penny	.30	.10
❑	101 Dontrelle Willis	.50	.20
❑	102 Andy Pettitte	.50	.20
❑	103 Wade Miller	.30	.10
❑	104 Jeff Bagwell	.50	.20
❑	105 Craig Biggio	.50	.20
❑	106 Lance Berkman	.30	.10
❑	107 Jeff Kent	.30	.10
❑	108 Roy Oswalt	.30	.10
❑	109 Hideo Nomo	.75	.30
❑	110 Adrian Beltre	.30	.10
❑	111 Paul Lo Duca	.30	.10
❑	112 Shawn Green	.30	.10
❑	113 Roger Clemens	2.00	.75
❑	114 Eric Gagne	.30	.10
❑	115 Danny Kolb	.30	.10
❑	116 Rickie Weeks	.30	.10
❑	117 Scott Podsednik	.30	.10
❑	118 Livan Hernandez	.30	.10
❑	119 Orlando Cabrera	.30	.10
❑	120 Jose Vidro	.30	.10
❑	121 David Wright	2.00	.75
❑	122 Tom Glavine	.50	.20
❑	123 Al Leiter	.30	.10
❑	124 Mike Piazza	1.25	.50
❑	125 Jose Reyes	.30	.10
❑	126 Richard Hidalgo	.30	.10
❑	127 Eric Milton	.30	.10
❑	128 Jim Thome	.50	.20
❑	129 Mike Lieberthal	.30	.10
❑	130 Bobby Abreu	.30	.10
❑	131 Kip Wells	.30	.10
❑	132 Jack Wilson	.30	.10
❑	133 Jason Bay	.30	.10
❑	134 Brian Giles	.30	.10
❑	135 Sean Burroughs	.30	.10
❑	136 Khalil Greene	.50	.20
❑	137 Jake Peavy	.30	.10
❑	138 Jason Schmidt	.30	.10
❑	139 J.T. Snow	.30	.10
❑	140 Craig Wilson	.30	.10
❑	141 Chase Utley	.50	.20
❑	142 Jim Edmonds	.30	.10
❑	143 Albert Pujols	1.50	.60
❑	144 Edgar Renteria	.30	.10
❑	145 Scott Rolen	.50	.20
❑	146 Matt Morris	.30	.10
❑	147 Ivan Rodriguez	.50	.20
❑	148 Vladimir Guerrero	.75	.30
❑	149 Greg Maddux	1.25	.50
❑	150 Ben Sheets	.30	.10
❑	206 Will Clark RET	4.00	1.50
❑	207 Nolan Ryan RET	8.00	3.00
❑	208 Bob Feller RET	3.00	1.25
❑	209 Red Schoendienst RET	3.00	1.25
❑	210 Brooks Robinson RET	4.00	1.50
❑	211 Al Kaline RET	4.00	1.50
❑	212 Ozzie Smith RET	5.00	2.00
❑	213 Maury Wills RET	3.00	1.25
❑	214 Steve Carlton RET	3.00	1.25
❑	215 Duke Snider RET	4.00	1.50
❑	216 Scott Lewis AU/603 RC	20.00	8.00
❑	217 Josh Johnson AU/597 RC	10.00	4.00
❑	218 Jeff Fiorentino AU/597 RC	12.00	5.00
❑	219 Grant Hansen AU/599 RC	8.00	3.00
❑	220 Yov Gallardo AU/803 RC	50.00	30.00
❑	221 Eddie Prasch AU/603 RC	10.00	4.00
❑	222 Danny Hill AU/603 RC	8.00	3.00
❑	223 Chuck Lofgren AU/803 RC	15.00	6.00
❑	224 Blake Johnson AU/811 RC	10.00	4.00
❑	225 Cory Dunlap AU/599 RC	15.00	6.00
❑	226 Carlos Vasquez AU/869 RC	8.00	3.00
❑	227 Jesse Crain AU/1000 RC	8.00	3.00
❑	228 Yhency Brazoban AU/1000	8.00	3.00
❑	229 Abe Alvarez AU/1000 RC	10.00	4.00
❑	230 Scott Kazmir AU/350 RC	60.00	30.00
❑	231 J.A. Happ AU/1195 RC	20.00	8.00
❑	233 Mark Jecmen AU/1047 RC	8.00	3.00
❑	234 Kameron Loe/1000 RC	5.00	2.00
❑	235 Ervin Santana/1000 RC	8.00	3.00
❑	239 Josh Karp/1000 RC	4.00	1.50
❑	242 Alberto Callaspo/1000 RC	5.00	2.00
❑	243 Jesse Hoover AU/1191 RC	10.00	4.00
❑	246 Just Hoyman AU/1124 RC	10.00	4.00
❑	247 Juan Cedeno/1000 RC	4.00	1.50
❑	250 Jake Dittler/1000 RC	4.00	1.50
❑	252 Ben Zobrist AU/1178 RC	20.00	8.00
❑	253 Jeff Salazar/1000 RC	5.00	2.00
❑	256 Jor Vasquez AU/1000 RC	8.00	3.00
❑	257 Raf Gonzalez AU/603 RC	8.00	3.00
❑	258 Andrew Dobies AU/601 RC	25.00	10.00
❑	259 Colby Miller AU/997 RC	8.00	3.00
❑	260 K.C. Herren AU/735 RC	8.00	3.00
❑	261 Ryan Meaux AU/540 RC	8.00	3.00
❑	262 Dust Pedroia AU/1114 RC	80.00	40.00
❑	263 Fern Nieve AU/1000 RC	8.00	3.00
❑	264 Mar Gomez AU/1000 RC	8.00	3.00
❑	265 Eric Campbell AU/260 RC	120.00	70.00
❑	266 Billy Killian AU/703 RC	10.00	4.00
❑	267 Mike Rouse AU/999 RC	8.00	3.00
❑	268 Kyle Bono AU/1203 RC	8.00	3.00
❑	269 M.Einertson AU/1047 RC	15.00	6.00
❑	270 Scott Proctor AU/1000 RC	8.00	3.00
❑	271 Tim Bittner AU/1000 RC	8.00	3.00
❑	272 Christian Garcia AU/799 RC	10.00	4.00
❑	273 Yadier Molina AU/1000 RC	20.00	8.00
❑	275 C.Thomas AU/907 RC	8.00	3.00
❑	276 Trav Blackley AU/1000 RC	8.00	3.00
❑	277 F.Francisco AU/1000 RC	8.00	3.00
❑	278 Dion Navarro AU/1000 RC	8.00	3.00
❑	279 Joey Gathright AU/1000 RC	8.00	3.00
❑	280 Kaz Tadano AU/1000 RC	10.00	4.00
❑	281 Matt Bush AU/1100 RC	15.00	6.00
❑	282 David Haehnel AU/865 RC	10.00	4.00
❑	283 Tommy Hottovy AU/825 RC	10.00	4.00
❑	284 Chris Carter AU/973 RC	25.00	10.00
❑	285 Mark Rogers AU/578 RC	20.00	8.00
❑	286 Jeremy Sowers AU/537 RC	30.00	15.00
❑	287 Homer Bailey AU/1571 RC	40.00	15.00
❑	288 Mike Butia AU/825 RC	8.00	3.00
❑	289 Chris Nelson AU/465 RC	30.00	15.00
❑	290 T.Diamond AU/1055 RC	15.00	6.00
❑	291 Neil Walker AU/1343 RC	20.00	8.00
❑	292 Sean Gamble AU/1229 RC	8.00	3.00
❑	293 Bill Bray AU/1073 RC	8.00	3.00
❑	294 Reid Brignac AU/522 RC	60.00	30.00
❑	295 R.Klosterman AU/865 RC	8.00	3.00
❑	296 David Purcey AU/1485 RC	8.00	3.00
❑	297 Scott Elbert AU/1617 RC	20.00	8.00
❑	298 Josh Fields AU/961 RC	30.00	15.00
❑	299 Chris Lambert AU/954 RC	10.00	4.00
❑	300 Trevor Plouffe AU/1329 RC	10.00	4.00
❑	301 Greg Golson AU/1334 RC	10.00	4.00
❑	302 Josh Baker AU/525 RC	8.00	3.00
❑	303 Philip Hughes AU/1485 RC	80.00	40.00
❑	304 Matt Macri AU/979 RC	10.00	4.00
❑	305 Kyle Waldrop AU/823 RC	15.00	6.00
❑	306 Rich Robnett AU/1575 RC	10.00	4.00
❑	307 T.Tankersley AU/1073 RC	10.00	4.00
❑	308 Blake DeWitt AU/1562 RC	25.00	10.00
❑	309 Daryl Jones AU/575 RC	30.00	12.50
❑	310 Eric Hurley AU/1021 RC	25.00	10.00
❑	311 J.P. Howell AU/1453 RC	10.00	4.00
❑	312 Zach Jackson AU/1069 RC	8.00	3.00
❑	313 Justin Orenduff AU/473 RC	30.00	12.50
❑	314 Tyler Lumsden AU/473 RC	10.00	4.00
❑	315 Matt Fox AU/473 RC	10.00	4.00
❑	316 Danny Putnam AU/473 RC	10.00	4.00
❑	317 Jon Poterson AU/464 RC	10.00	6.00
❑	318 Gio Gonzalez AU/473 RC	25.00	10.00
❑	319 Jay Rainville AU/823 RC	25.00	10.00
❑	320 Huston Street AU/709 RC	25.00	10.00
❑	321 Jeff Marquez AU/493 RC	10.00	4.00
❑	322 Eric Beattie AU/930 RC	10.00	4.00
❑	323 B.Szymanski AU/1327 RC	10.00	4.00
❑	324 Seth Smith AU/1065 RC	10.00	4.00

❑ 325 Rob Johnson AU/790 RC 10.00 4.00
❑ 326 Wes Whisler AU/473 RC 10.00 4.00
❑ 327 Billy Buckner AU/673 RC 10.00 4.00
❑ 328 Jon Zeringue AU/473 RC 8.00 3.00
❑ 329 Curtis Thigpen AU/673 RC 30.00 12.50
❑ 330 Donny Lucy AU/573 RC 8.00 3.00
❑ 331 Mike Ferris AU/558 RC 10.00 4.00
❑ 332 A.Swarzak AU/370 RC 25.00 10.00
❑ 333 Jason Jaramillo AU/573 RC 10.00 4.00
❑ 334 Hunter Pence AU/672 RC 120.00 60.00
❑ 335 Mike Rozier AU/628 RC 10.00 4.00
❑ 336 Kurt Suzuki AU/473 RC 15.00 6.00
❑ 337 Jason Vargas AU/621 RC 20.00 8.00
❑ 338 Brian Bixler AU/665 RC 25.00 10.00
❑ 340 Dexter Fowler AU/623 RC 60.00 30.00
❑ 341 Mark Trumbo AU/1321 RC 15.00 6.00
❑ 342 Jeff Frazier AU/423 RC 10.00 4.00
❑ 343 Steve Register AU/673 RC 8.00 3.00
❑ 344 M.Schlact AU/477 RC 10.00 4.00
❑ 345 Garrett Mock AU/471 RC 10.00 4.00
❑ 346 Eric Haberer AU/473 RC 10.00 4.00
❑ 347 M.Tuiasosopo AU/473 RC 25.00 10.00
❑ 348 Jason Windsor AU/473 RC 25.00 10.00
❑ 349 Grant Johnson AU/815 RC 10.00 4.00
❑ 350 J.C. Holt AU/673 RC 10.00 4.00
❑ 351 Joe Bauserman AU/472 RC 10.00 4.00
❑ 352 Jamar Walton AU/481 RC 10.00 4.00
❑ 353 Eric Patterson AU/1571 RC 15.00 6.00
❑ 354 Tyler Johnson AU/775 RC 15.00 6.00
❑ 355 Nick Adenhart AU/653 RC 100.00 50.00

2007 Donruss Elite Extra Edition *

❑ COMP.SET w/o AU's (92) 20.00 8.00
❑ COMMON CARD (1-92) .50 .20
❑ COMMON AU (92-142) 10.00 4.00
❑ OVERALL AUTO/MEM ODDS 1:5
❑ AU PRINT RUNS B/WN 374-999 COPIES PER
❑ EXCHANGE DEADLINE 07/01/2009
❑ 1 Andrew Brackman 1.50 .60
❑ 2 Austin Gallagher .50 .20
❑ 3 Brett Cecil .50 .20
❑ 4 Darwin Barney 1.25 .50
❑ 5 David Price 2.00 .75
❑ 6 J. P. Arencibia .50 .20
❑ 7 Josh Donaldson .50 .20
❑ 8 Brandon Hicks .50 .20
❑ 9 Brian Rike .50 .20
❑ 10 Bryan Morris .50 .20
❑ 11 Cale Iorg .50 .20
❑ 12 Casey Weathers .50 .20
❑ 13 Corey Kluber .50 .20
❑ 14 Daniel Moskos .50 .20
❑ 15 Danny Payne .50 .20
❑ 16 David Kopp .50 .20
❑ 17 Dellin Betances 1.50 .60
❑ 18 Derrick Robinson .50 .20
❑ 19 Drew Stubbs .50 .20
❑ 20 Eric Eiland .50 .20
❑ 21 Francisco Pena .50 .20
❑ 22 Greg Reynolds .50 .20
❑ 24 Jess Todd .50 .20
❑ 25 John Tolisano .50 .20
❑ 26 Jordan Zimmerman .75 .30
❑ 27 Julian Sampson .50 .20
❑ 28 Luke Hochevar 1.25 .50
❑ 29 Mat Latos .50 .20
❑ 30 Matt Mangini .50 .20
❑ 31 Matt Spencer .75 .30
❑ 32 Matthew Sweeney 1.25 .50
❑ 33 Max Scherzer 2.00 .75
❑ 34 Mitch Canham .50 .20
❑ 35 Nick Schmidt .50 .20
❑ 36 Paul Kelly .50 .20
❑ 37 Ryan Pope .75 .30
❑ 38 Sam Runion .50 .20
❑ 39 Steven Souza .50 .20
❑ 40 Travis Mattair .50 .20
❑ 41 Trystan Magnuson .50 .20
❑ 42 Will Middlebrooks .75 .30
❑ 43 Zack Cozart .50 .20
❑ 44 James Adkins .50 .20
❑ 45 Cory Luebke .50 .20
❑ 46 Aaron Poreda .50 .20
❑ 47 Clayton Mortensen .50 .20
❑ 48 Bradley Suttle .75 .30
❑ 49 Tony Butler .75 .30
❑ 50 Zach Britton .50 .20
❑ 51 Scott Cousins .50 .20
❑ 52 Wendell Fairley 1.25 .50
❑ 53 Eric Sogard .50 .20
❑ 54 Jonathan Lucroy .75 .30
❑ 55 Lars Davis .50 .20
❑ 56 Demetris Nichols .50 .20
❑ 57 Aaron Gray .50 .20
❑ 58 Daequan Cook .50 .20
❑ 59 Derrick Byars .50 .20
❑ 60 Reyshawn Terry .50 .20
❑ 61 Taurean Green .50 .20
❑ 62 Don Haskins .50 .20
❑ 63 Jerry Tarkanian .50 .20
❑ 64 Rick Majerus .50 .20
❑ 65 Rollie Massimino .50 .20
❑ 66 Ara Parseghian .50 .20
❑ 67 Dale Brown .50 .20
❑ 68 Dean Smith .50 .20
❑ 69 Eddie Sutton .50 .20
❑ 70 Frank Broyles .50 .20
❑ 71 Gene Keady .50 .20
❑ 72 Jim Boeheim .50 .20
❑ 73 Norm Stewart .50 .20
❑ 74 Steve Spurrier .50 .20
❑ 75 Tom Osborne .50 .20
❑ 76 Vince Dooley .50 .20
❑ 77 Jennie Finch 1.25 .50
❑ 78 Amanda Beard .50 .20
❑ 79 Mike Powell .50 .20
❑ 80 Rebecca Lobo .50 .20
❑ 81 Brandi Chastain .50 .20
❑ 82 Clint Dolezel .50 .20
❑ 83 Elvin Hayes .50 .20
❑ 84 Cobi Jones .50 .20
❑ 85 Bill Walton .50 .20
❑ 86 Sidney Moncrief .50 .20
❑ 87 Dominique Wilkins .50 .20
❑ 88 Summer Sanders .50 .20
❑ 89 Michelle Akers .50 .20
❑ 90 Muggsy Bogues .50 .20
❑ 91 Charlie Culberson 1.50 .60
❑ 92 Jacob Smolinski .50 .20
❑ 93 Blake Beaven AU/719 15.00 6.00
❑ 94 Brad Chalk AU/613 10.00 4.00
❑ 95 Brett Anderson AU/549 40.00 15.00
❑ 96 Chris Withrow AU/700 10.00 4.00
❑ 97 Clay Fuller AU/674 10.00 4.00
❑ 98 Damon Sublett AU/674 20.00 8.00
❑ 99 Devin Mesoraco AU/674 12.00 5.00
❑ 100 Drew Cumberland AU/744 10.00 4.00
❑ 101 Jack McGeary AU/674 15.00 6.00
❑ 102 Jake Arrieta AU/949 25.00 10.00
❑ 103 James Simmons AU/624 EXCH 10.00 4.00
❑ 104 Jarrod Parker AU/499 50.00 20.00
❑ 105 Jason Dominguez AU/744 10.00 4.00
❑ 106 Jason Heyward AU/750 60.00 30.00
❑ 107 Joe Savery AU/750 12.00 5.00
❑ 108 Jon Gilmore AU/819 12.00 5.00
❑ 109 Jordan Walden AU/794 30.00 12.50
❑ 110 Josh Smoker AU/719 25.00 10.00
❑ 111 Josh Vitters AU/769 30.00 12.50
❑ 112 Julio Borbon AU/594 12.00 5.00
❑ 113 Justin Jackson AU/850 10.00 4.00
❑ 114 Kellen Kulbacki AU/549 12.00 5.00
❑ 115 Kevin Ahrens AU/794 20.00 8.00
❑ 116 Kyle Lotzkar AU/611 10.00 4.00
❑ 117 Madison Bumgarner AU/794 40.00 15.00
❑ 118 Matt Dominguez AU/769 25.00 10.00
❑ 119 Matt LaPorta AU/594 60.00 30.00
❑ 120 Matt Wieters AU/799 120.00 60.00
❑ 121 Michael Burgess AU/672 25.00 10.00
❑ 122 Michael Main AU/794 12.00 5.00
❑ 123 Mike Moustakas AU/999 60.00 30.00
❑ 124 Nathan Vineyard AU/700 12.00 5.00
❑ 125 Neil Ramirez AU/774 15.00 6.00
❑ 126 Nick Hagadone AU/544 15.00 6.00
❑ 127 Pete Kozma AU/719 10.00 4.00
❑ 128 Phillippe Aumont AU/674 40.00 15.00
❑ 129 Preston Mattingly AU/519 25.00 10.00
❑ 130 Mystery EXCH 150.00 75.00
❑ 131 Ross Detwiler AU/650 12.00 5.00
❑ 132 Tim Alderson AU/719 12.00 5.00
❑ 133 Todd Frazier AU/774 20.00 8.00
❑ 134 Wes Roemer AU/694 12.00 5.00
❑ 135 Ben Revere AU/700 15.00 6.00
❑ 136 Chris Davis AU/374 EXCH 150.00 100.00
❑ 137 Alando Tucker AU/494 10.00 4.00
❑ 138 Bryan Anderson AU/474 EXCH 10.00 4.00
❑ 139 Marc Gasol AU/474 EXCH 10.00 4.00
❑ 140 Stephane Lasme AU/674 10.00 4.00
❑ 141 Austin Jackson AU/794 80.00 40.00
❑ 142 Beau Mills AU/624 EXCH 25.00 10.00

2006 Exquisite Collection

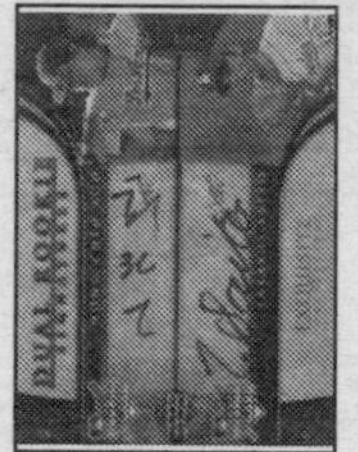

❑ COMMON AU RC (1-90) 20.00 8.00
❑ ISSUED AS EXCH CARDS IN VARIOUS
❑ 2006 UPPER DECK PRODUCTS
❑ 1-90 PRINT RUN 55 SER.#'d SETS
❑ 91-100 PRINT RUN 10 SER.#'d SETS
❑ 1-90 FEATURE ROOKIE LOGOS
❑ NO PRICING ON 91-100 DUE TO SCARCITY
❑ 1 Cabrera/Hermida
❑ 2 Hansen/Carmona 25.00 10.00
❑ 3 Ethier/Kubel 20.00 8.00
❑ 4 Billingsley/Bonser 25.00 10.00
❑ 5 Sowers/Carmona 50.00 20.00
❑ 6 Willingham/Paulino 25.00 10.00
❑ 7 Saito/Ethier 50.00 20.00
❑ 8 Hamels/Shields 60.00 30.00
❑ 9 Denorfia/Quentin 25.00 10.00
❑ 10 Hammel/Shields 25.00 10.00
❑ 11 Uggla/Kinsler 40.00 15.00
❑ 12 Accardo/Cain 40.00 15.00
❑ 13 Sowers/Maholm 25.00 10.00
❑ 14 Hamels/Sowers 50.00 20.00
❑ 15 Liriano/Bonser 40.00 15.00
❑ 16 Verlander/Zumaya 80.00 40.00
❑ 17 Ramirez/Drew 60.00 30.00
❑ 18 Soler/Bannister 25.00 10.00
❑ 19 Gassner/Bonser 25.00 10.00
❑ 20 Pagan/Theroit 60.00 30.00
❑ 21 Uggla/Hermida 30.00 12.50
❑ 22 Pelfrey/Billingsley
❑ 23 Carmona/Hamels 80.00 40.00
❑ 24 Saito/Kuo 120.00 60.00
❑ 25 Maholm/Marshall 20.00 8.00
❑ 26 Kendrick/Uggla 30.00 12.50
❑ 27 Johnson/Petit 25.00 10.00
❑ 28 Cain/Pelfrey
❑ 29 Martin/Ethier 80.00 40.00
❑ 30 Liriano/Weaver 50.00 20.00
❑ 31 Hamels/Jackson 30.00 12.50
❑ 32 Papelbon/Hansen 50.00 20.00
❑ 33 Pelfrey/Soler

❑ 34 Denorfia/Hermida 30.00 12.50
❑ 35 Willingham/Ross 25.00 10.00
❑ 36 Drew/Weaver 50.00 20.00
❑ 37 Cabrera/Nieves
❑ 38 Dunn/Shields 25.00 10.00
❑ 39 Kendrick/Morales 50.00 20.00
❑ 40 Maholm/Capps 25.00 10.00
❑ 41 Kinsler/Kendrick 25.00 10.00
❑ 42 Cain/Soler 50.00 20.00
❑ 43 Ethier/Cabrera
❑ 44 Verlander/Sowers 50.00 20.00
❑ 45 Kendrick/Weaver
❑ 46 Ramirez/Willingham 50.00 20.00
❑ 47 Ramirez/Hermida 40.00 15.00
❑ 48 Uggla/Willingham 30.00 12.50
❑ 49 Soler/Hamels 50.00 20.00
❑ 50 Kubel/Bonser 25.00 10.00
❑ 51 Jacobs/Morales 25.00 10.00
❑ 52 Saito/Papelbon 50.00 20.00
❑ 53 Papelbon/Verlander 80.00 40.00
❑ 54 Ethier/Billingsley 50.00 20.00
❑ 55 Hermida/Gwynn Jr. 30.00 12.50
❑ 56 Zimmerman/Drew 80.00 40.00
❑ 57 Gwynn Jr./Barfield 30.00 12.50
❑ 58 Hensley/Thompson 25.00 10.00
❑ 59 Verlander/Johnson 50.00 20.00
❑ 60 Verlander/Weaver
❑ 61 Gwynn Jr./Cabrera
❑ 62 Gwynn Jr./Ethier 30.00 12.50
❑ 63 Drew/Quentin 50.00 20.00
❑ 64 Jackson/Quentin 50.00 20.00
❑ 65 Zimmerman/Harris 60.00 30.00
❑ 66 Saito/Martin 50.00 20.00
❑ 67 Jacobs/Willingham 30.00 12.50
❑ 68 Jacobs/Ramiez 40.00 15.00
❑ 69 Pelfrey/Verlander
❑ 70 Pelfrey/Papelbon
❑ 71 Hansen/Hamels 50.00 20.00
❑ 72 Ramirez/Bynum 30.00 12.50
❑ 73 Gwynn Jr./Freeman
❑ 74 Nieve/Buchholz 20.00 8.00
❑ 75 Wainwright/Johnson 40.00 15.00
❑ 76 Willingham/Martin 50.00 20.00
❑ 77 Martin/Nieves 40.00 15.00
❑ 78 Johnson/Thompson 20.00 8.00
❑ 79 Jackson/Hendrickson 20.00 8.00
❑ 80 Papelbon/Zumaya 60.00 30.00
❑ 81 Hendrickson/Capellan 25.00 10.00
❑ 82 Devine/Ray 25.00 10.00
❑ 83 Pelfrey/Hernandez
❑ 84 Shoppach/Martin 50.00 20.00
❑ 85 Soler/Johnson 20.00 8.00
❑ 86 Soler/Hansen 25.00 10.00
❑ 87 Hansen/Billingsley 50.00 20.00
❑ 88 Billingsley/Cain 50.00 20.00
❑ 89 Liriano/Hansen 40.00 15.00
❑ 90 Jackson/Jacobs 30.00 12.50
❑ 91 Ken Griffey Jr. AU
❑ 92 Derek Jeter AU
❑ 93 Albert Pujols AU
❑ 94 Roger Clemens AU
❑ 95 Jim Thome AU
❑ 96 Howie Kendrick AU (RC)
❑ 97 Francisco Liriano AU (RC)
❑ 98 Jered Weaver AU (RC)
❑ 99 Justin Verlander AU (RC)
❑ 100 Stephen Drew AU (RC)

2007 Exquisite Collection Rookie Signatures

❑ COMMON CARD (1-100) 4.00 1.50
❑ ONE BASE CARD PER PACK
❑ 1-100 PRINT RUN 99 SER.#'d SETS
❑ COMMON AU RC (101-191) 10.00 4.00
❑ OVERALL FIVE AUTOS PER PACK
❑ AU RC SER.#'d B/WN 150-235 PER
❑ COMMON JSY AU RC (101-191) 15.00 6.00
❑ OVERALL FIVE AUTOS PER PACK
❑ JSY AU RC SER.#'d B/WN 125-199 PER
❑ EXCHANGE DEADLINE 12/28/2009
❑ 1 Ichiro Suzuki 15.00 6.00
❑ 2 Alex Rodriguez 15.00 6.00
❑ 3 David Wright 15.00 6.00
❑ 4 Ryan Howard 15.00 6.00
❑ 5 Ken Griffey Jr. 15.00 6.00

❑ 6 Derek Jeter 20.00 8.00
❑ 7 Vladimir Guerrero 10.00 4.00
❑ 8 Roger Clemens 12.00 5.00
❑ 9 Greg Maddux 15.00 6.00
❑ 10 Johan Santana 6.00 2.50
❑ 11 Nomar Garciaparra 10.00 4.00
❑ 12 Carlos Beltran 4.00 1.50
❑ 13 Carlos Delgado 4.00 1.50
❑ 14 Manny Ramirez 6.00 2.50
❑ 15 John Lackey 4.00 1.50
❑ 16 David Ortiz 10.00 4.00
❑ 17 Curt Schilling 6.00 2.50
❑ 18 Cal Ripken Jr. 30.00 12.00
❑ 19 Albert Pujols 15.00 6.00
❑ 20 Frank Thomas 10.00 4.00
❑ 21 Chris Carpenter 4.00 1.50
❑ 22 Prince Fielder 10.00 4.00
❑ 23 Justin Morneau 4.00 1.50
❑ 24 Joe Mauer 6.00 2.50
❑ 25 Torii Hunter 4.00 1.50
❑ 26 Jake Peavy 4.00 1.50
❑ 27 Roy Oswalt 4.00 1.50
❑ 28 Craig Biggio 6.00 2.50
❑ 29 Lance Berkman 4.00 1.50
❑ 30 Carlos Zambrano 4.00 1.50
❑ 31 Derrek Lee 4.00 1.50
❑ 32 Aramis Ramirez 4.00 1.50
❑ 33 Noah Lowry 4.00 1.50
❑ 34 Magglio Ordonez 4.00 1.50
❑ 35 Ivan Rodriguez 6.00 2.50
❑ 36 Johnny Damon 6.00 2.50
❑ 37 Justin Verlander 10.00 4.00
❑ 38 John Smoltz 6.00 2.50
❑ 39 Chipper Jones 10.00 4.00
❑ 40 Jeff Francoeur 10.00 4.00
❑ 41 Hanley Ramirez 6.00 2.50
❑ 42 Miguel Cabrera 6.00 2.50
❑ 43 Josh Beckett 6.00 2.50
❑ 44 Cole Hamels 6.00 2.50
❑ 45 Chase Utley 10.00 4.00
❑ 46 Grady Sizemore 6.00 2.50
❑ 47 Travis Hafner 4.00 1.50
❑ 48 Victor Martinez 4.00 1.50
❑ 49 Russell Martin 4.00 1.50
❑ 50 Jason Varitek 10.00 4.00
❑ 51 Hideki Matsui 10.00 4.00
❑ 52 Carl Crawford 4.00 1.50
❑ 53 Scott Kazmir 6.00 2.50
❑ 54 Miguel Tejada 4.00 1.50
❑ 55 Erik Bedard 4.00 1.50
❑ 56 Carlos Lee 4.00 1.50
❑ 57 Sammy Sosa 10.00 4.00
❑ 58 Mark Teixeira 6.00 2.50
❑ 59 Michael Young 4.00 1.50
❑ 60 Jim Thome 6.00 2.50
❑ 61 Paul Konerko 4.00 1.50
❑ 62 Jermaine Dye 4.00 1.50
❑ 63 Mark Teahen 4.00 1.50
❑ 64 Felix Hernandez 6.00 2.50
❑ 65 Andruw Jones 6.00 2.50
❑ 66 Pedro Martinez 6.00 2.50
❑ 67 Randy Johnson 10.00 4.00
❑ 68 Ryan Zimmerman 10.00 4.00
❑ 69 Matt Holliday 10.00 4.00
❑ 70 Todd Helton 6.00 2.50
❑ 71 Brian Bannister 4.00 1.50
❑ 72 Jeremy Bonderman 4.00 1.50
❑ 73 Adam Dunn 4.00 1.50
❑ 74 Aaron Harang 4.00 1.50
❑ 75 Jason Bay 4.00 1.50
❑ 76 Adam LaRoche 4.00 1.50
❑ 77 Freddy Sanchez 4.00 1.50
❑ 78 Dan Uggla 6.00 2.50
❑ 79 Joe Nathan 4.00 1.50
❑ 80 Brad Penny 4.00 1.50
❑ 81 Takashi Saito 4.00 1.50
❑ 82 Jimmy Rollins 4.00 1.50
❑ 83 Jose Reyes 10.00 4.00
❑ 84 Jered Weaver 6.00 2.50
❑ 85 Chien-Ming Wang 15.00 6.00
❑ 86 Jonathan Papelbon 10.00 4.00
❑ 87 Mariano Rivera 10.00 4.00
❑ 88 Eric Byrnes 4.00 1.50
❑ 89 Nick Markakis 6.00 2.50
❑ 90 Brian Roberts 4.00 1.50
❑ 91 Omar Vizquel 6.00 2.50
❑ 92 Vernon Wells 4.00 1.50
❑ 93 Dan Haren 4.00 1.50
❑ 94 Ben Sheets 4.00 1.50
❑ 95 B.J. Upton 4.00 1.50
❑ 96 Adrian Gonzalez 4.00 1.50
❑ 97 J.J. Hardy 4.00 1.50
❑ 98 Mike Piazza 10.00 4.00
❑ 99 Roy Halladay 4.00 1.50
❑ 100 Alfonso Soriano 4.00 1.50
❑ 101 Sean Henn AU/235 (RC) 10.00 4.00
❑ 102 Sean White AU/235 RC 10.00 4.00
❑ 103 Mike Schultz AU/234 RC 10.00 4.00
❑ 104 Michael Bourn AU/234 (RC) 10.00 4.00
❑ 105 Matt Chico AU/235 (RC) 10.00 4.00
❑ 106 Matt Lindstrom AU/235 (RC) 10.00 4.00
❑ 107 Connor Robertson AU/235 RC 10.00 4.00
❑ 108 Jay Marshall AU/235 RC 10.00 4.00
❑ 109 Jared Burton AU/235 RC 10.00 4.00
❑ 110 Juan Perez AU/235 RC 10.00 4.00
❑ 111 Scott Moore AU/235 (RC) 10.00 4.00
❑ 112 Brad Salmon AU/235 RC 10.00 4.00
❑ 113 Danny Putnam AU/235 (RC) 10.00 4.00
❑ 114 Kelvin Jimenez AU/235 RC 10.00 4.00
❑ 115 Dennis Dove AU/235 (RC) 10.00 4.00
❑ 116 Yoel Hernandez AU/234 RC 10.00 4.00
❑ 117 Devern Hansack AU/235 RC 10.00 4.00
❑ 118 Mike Rabelo AU/235 RC 10.00 4.00
❑ 119 Miguel Montero AU/235 (RC) 10.00 4.00
❑ 120 Kevin Cameron AU/235 RC 10.00 4.00
❑ 121 Joseph Bisenius AU/235 RC 10.00 4.00
❑ 122 Ryan Z. Braun AU/234 RC 10.00 4.00
❑ 123 Levale Speigner AU/235 RC 10.00 4.00
❑ 124 Lee Gardner AU/235 (RC) 10.00 4.00
❑ 125 Ryan Rowland-Smith AU/234 RC 10.00 4.00
❑ 126 Zack Segovia AU/235 (RC) 10.00 4.00
❑ 127 Rick Vanden Hurk AU/235 RC 10.00 4.00
❑ 128 Dallas Braden AU/235 RC 10.00 4.00
❑ 129 Rocky Cherry AU/234 RC 10.00 4.00
❑ 130 Andy Gonzalez AU/235 (RC) 10.00 4.00
❑ 131 Neal Musser AU/235 RC 10.00 4.00
❑ 132 Garrett Jones AU/235 (RC) 10.00 4.00
❑ 133 Ben Francisco AU/235 (RC) 10.00 4.00
❑ 134 Jon Coutlangus AU/235 (RC) 10.00 4.00
❑ 135 A.J. Murray AU/235 RC 10.00 4.00
❑ 136 Brett Carroll AU/235 RC 10.00 4.00
❑ 137 John Danks AU/235 RC 10.00 4.00
❑ 138 Kyle Kendrick AU/235 RC 15.00 6.00
❑ 139 Joaquin Arias AU/235 (RC) 10.00 4.00
❑ 140 Matt Brown AU/235 RC 10.00 4.00
❑ 141 Kurt Suzuki AU/150 (RC) 25.00 10.00
❑ 142 Curtis Thigpen AU/150 (RC) 10.00 4.00
❑ 143 Jerry Owens AU/150 (RC) 10.00 4.00
❑ 144 Billy Butler AU/150 (RC) 40.00 15.00
❑ 145 Kei Igawa AU/150 RC 40.00 15.00
❑ 146 Mike Fontenot AU/150 (RC) 15.00 6.00
❑ 147 Brandon Wood AU/150 (RC) 25.00 10.00
❑ 148 Alexi Casilla AU/150 RC 10.00 4.00
❑ 149 Jeff Baker AU/150 (RC) 10.00 4.00
❑ 150 Brian Barden AU/150 RC 10.00 4.00
❑ 151 Chris Stewart AU/150 RC 10.00 4.00
❑ 152 Jon Knott AU/150 (RC) 10.00 4.00
❑ 153 Chase Wright AU/150 RC 15.00 6.00
❑ 154 Chase Headley AU/150 (RC) 25.00 10.00
❑ 155 Jesse Litsch Jsy AU/199 RC 15.00 6.00
❑ 156 Tyler Clippard AU/150 (RC) 15.00 6.00
❑ 157 Matt DeSalvo AU/150 (RC) 10.00 4.00
❑ 158 Kory Casto AU/150 (RC) 10.00 4.00
❑ 159 J.Saltalamac.Jsy AU/199 (RC) 20.00 8.00

❑ 160 Glen Perkins AU/150 (RC) 10.00 4.00
❑ 161 Ryan Braun Jsy AU/199 (RC) 100.00 50.00
❑ 162 Justin Upton Jsy AU/199 RC 150.00 75.00
❑ 163 Tim Lincecum Jsy AU/199 RC 200.00 100.00
❑ 164 Fred Lewis AU/150 (RC) 15.00 6.00
❑ 165 Alex Gordon Jsy AU/199 RC 60.00 30.00
❑ 166 Akinori Iwamura Jsy AU/199 RC 40.00 15.00
❑ 167 Delmon Young Jsy AU/199 (RC) 30.00 12.50
❑ 168 Tulowitzki Jsy AU/199 (RC) 100.00 50.00
❑ 169 Matsuzaka Jsy AU/199 RC 300.00 175.00
❑ 170 J.Hamilton Jsy AU/199 (RC) 100.00 50.00
❑ 171 Kevin Kouzmanoff Jsy AU/199 (RC) 15.00 6.00
❑ 172 Hunter Pence Jsy AU/199 (RC) 80.00 40.00
❑ 173 Felix Pie Jsy AU/199 (RC) 15.00 6.00
❑ 174 Andrew Miller Jsy AU/199 RC 40.00 15.00
❑ 175 Gallardo Jsy AU/199 (RC) 40.00 15.00
❑ 176 Ryan Sweeney Jsy AU/199 (RC) 15.00 6.00
❑ 177 Josh Fields Jsy AU/199 (RC) 20.00 8.00
❑ 178 Mark Reynolds Jsy AU/199 RC 60.00 30.00
❑ 180 Homer Bailey AU/150 (RC) 25.00 10.00
❑ 182 Joba Chamberlain AU/150 RC 300.00 200.00
❑ 184 Travis Metcalf Jsy AU/125 RC 20.00 8.00
❑ 185 Kevin Slowey Jsy AU/199 (RC) 30.00 12.50
❑ 186 Phil Hughes AU/150 (RC) 60.00 30.00
❑ 187 Micah Owings AU/150 (RC) 25.00 10.00
❑ 188 Joe Smith AU/150 RC 10.00 4.00
❑ 189 Joakim Soria Jsy AU/199 RC 25.00 10.00
❑ 190 Adam Lind Jsy AU/199 (RC) 15.00 6.00
❑ 191 Andy LaRoche Jsy AU/199 (RC) 20.00 8.00
❑ 192 B.Morrow Jsy AU/175 RC 25.00 10.00
❑ 193 Carlos Gomez Jsy AU/125 RC 40.00 15.00
❑ 194 Yunel Escobar AU/150 (RC) 30.00 12.50

1993 Finest

❑ COMPLETE SET (199) 150.00 75.00
❑ 1 David Justice 2.50 1.00
❑ 2 Lou Whitaker 2.50 1.00
❑ 3 Bryan Harvey 1.50 .60
❑ 4 Carlos Garcia 1.50 .60
❑ 5 Sid Fernandez 1.50 .60
❑ 6 Brett Butler 2.50 1.00
❑ 7 Scott Cooper 1.50 .60
❑ 8 B.J. Surhoff 2.50 1.00
❑ 9 Steve Finley 2.50 1.00
❑ 10 Curt Schilling 2.50 1.00
❑ 11 Jeff Bagwell 4.00 1.50
❑ 12 Alex Cole 1.50 .60
❑ 13 John Olerud 2.50 1.00
❑ 14 John Smiley 1.50 .60
❑ 15 Bip Roberts 1.50 .60
❑ 16 Albert Belle 2.50 1.00
❑ 17 Duane Ward 1.50 .60
❑ 18 Alan Trammell 2.50 1.00
❑ 19 Andy Benes 1.50 .60
❑ 20 Reggie Sanders 2.50 1.00
❑ 21 Todd Zeile 1.50 .60
❑ 22 Rick Aguilera 1.50 .60
❑ 23 Dave Hollins 1.50 .60
❑ 24 Jose Rijo 1.50 .60
❑ 25 Matt Williams 2.50 1.00
❑ 26 Sandy Alomar Jr. 1.50 .60
❑ 27 Alex Fernandez 1.50 .60
❑ 28 Ozzie Smith 10.00 4.00
❑ 29 Ramon Martinez 1.50 .60
❑ 30 Bernie Williams 4.00 1.50
❑ 31 Gary Sheffield 2.50 1.00
❑ 32 Eric Karros 2.50 1.00
❑ 33 Frank Viola 2.50 1.00
❑ 34 Kevin Young 2.50 1.00
❑ 35 Ken Hill 1.50 .60
❑ 36 Tony Fernandez 1.50 .60
❑ 37 Tim Wakefield 6.00 2.50
❑ 38 John Kruk 2.50 1.00
❑ 39 Chris Sabo 1.50 .60
❑ 40 Marquis Grissom 2.50 1.00
❑ 41 Glenn Davis 1.50 .60
❑ 42 Jeff Montgomery 1.50 .60
❑ 43 Kenny Lofton 2.50 1.00
❑ 44 John Burkett 1.50 .60
❑ 45 Darryl Hamilton 1.50 .60
❑ 46 Jim Abbott 4.00 1.50
❑ 47 Ivan Rodriguez 4.00 1.50
❑ 48 Eric Young 1.50 .60
❑ 49 Mitch Williams 1.50 .60
❑ 50 Harold Reynolds 2.50 1.00
❑ 51 Brian Harper 1.50 .60
❑ 52 Rafael Palmeiro 4.00 1.50
❑ 53 Bret Saberhagen 2.50 1.00
❑ 54 Jeff Conine 2.50 1.00
❑ 55 Ivan Calderon 1.50 .60
❑ 56 Juan Guzman 1.50 .60
❑ 57 Carlos Baerga 1.50 .60
❑ 58 Charles Nagy 1.50 .60
❑ 59 Wally Joyner 2.50 1.00
❑ 60 Charlie Hayes 1.50 .60
❑ 61 Shane Mack 1.50 .60
❑ 62 Pete Harnisch 1.50 .60
❑ 63 George Brett 15.00 6.00
❑ 64 Lance Johnson 1.50 .60
❑ 65 Ben McDonald 1.50 .60
❑ 66 Bobby Bonilla 2.50 1.00
❑ 67 Terry Steinbach 1.50 .60
❑ 68 Ron Gant 2.50 1.00
❑ 69 Doug Jones 1.50 .60
❑ 70 Paul Molitor 2.50 1.00
❑ 71 Brady Anderson 2.50 1.00
❑ 72 Chuck Finley 2.50 1.00
❑ 73 Mark Grace 4.00 1.50
❑ 74 Mike Devereaux 1.50 .60
❑ 75 Tony Phillips 1.50 .60
❑ 76 Chuck Knoblauch 2.50 1.00
❑ 77 Tony Gwynn 8.00 3.00
❑ 78 Kevin Appier 2.50 1.00
❑ 79 Sammy Sosa 6.00 2.50
❑ 80 Mickey Tettleton 1.50 .60
❑ 81 Felix Jose 1.50 .60
❑ 82 Mark Langston 1.50 .60
❑ 83 Gregg Jefferies 1.50 .60
❑ 84 Andre Dawson AS 2.50 1.00
❑ 85 Greg Maddux AS 10.00 4.00
❑ 86 Rickey Henderson AS 6.00 2.50
❑ 87 Tom Glavine AS 4.00 1.50
❑ 88 Roberto Alomar AS 4.00 1.50
❑ 89 Darryl Strawberry AS 2.50 1.00
❑ 90 Wade Boggs AS 4.00 1.50
❑ 91 Bo Jackson AS 6.00 2.50
❑ 92 Mark McGwire AS 15.00 6.00
❑ 93 Robin Ventura AS 2.50 1.00
❑ 94 Joe Carter AS 2.50 1.00
❑ 95 Lee Smith AS 2.50 1.00
❑ 96 Cal Ripken AS 20.00 8.00
❑ 97 Larry Walker AS 2.50 1.00
❑ 98 Don Mattingly AS 15.00 6.00
❑ 99 Jose Canseco AS 4.00 1.50
❑ 100 Dennis Eckersley AS 2.50 1.00
❑ 101 Terry Pendleton AS 2.50 1.00
❑ 102 Frank Thomas AS 6.00 2.50
❑ 103 Barry Bonds AS 15.00 6.00
❑ 104 Roger Clemens AS 12.00 5.00
❑ 105 Ryne Sandberg AS 10.00 4.00
❑ 106 Fred McGriff AS 4.00 1.50
❑ 107 Nolan Ryan AS 25.00 10.00
❑ 108 Will Clark AS 4.00 1.50
❑ 109 Pat Listach AS 1.50 .60
❑ 110 Ken Griffey Jr. AS 10.00 4.00
❑ 111 Cecil Fielder AS 2.50 1.00
❑ 112 Kirby Puckett AS 6.00 2.50
❑ 113 Dwight Gooden AS 2.50 1.00
❑ 114 Barry Larkin AS 4.00 1.50
❑ 115 David Cone AS 2.50 1.00
❑ 116 Juan Gonzalez AS 2.50 1.00
❑ 117 Kent Hrbek 2.50 1.00
❑ 118 Tim Wallach 1.50 .60
❑ 119 Craig Biggio 4.00 1.50
❑ 120 Roberto Kelly 1.50 .60
❑ 121 Gregg Olson 1.50 .60
❑ 122 Eddie Murray 6.00 2.50
❑ 123 Wil Cordero 1.50 .60
❑ 124 Jay Buhner 2.50 1.00
❑ 125 Carlton Fisk 4.00 1.50
❑ 126 Eric Davis 2.50 1.00
❑ 127 Doug Drabek 1.50 .60
❑ 128 Ozzie Guillen 2.50 1.00
❑ 129 John Wetteland 2.50 1.00
❑ 130 Andres Galarraga 2.50 1.00
❑ 131 Ken Caminiti 2.50 1.00
❑ 132 Tom Candiotti 1.50 .60
❑ 133 Pat Borders 1.50 .60
❑ 134 Kevin Brown 2.50 1.00
❑ 135 Travis Fryman 2.50 1.00
❑ 136 Kevin Mitchell 1.50 .60
❑ 137 Greg Swindell 1.50 .60
❑ 138 Benito Santiago 2.50 1.00
❑ 139 Reggie Jefferson 1.50 .60
❑ 140 Chris Bosio 1.50 .60
❑ 141 Deion Sanders 4.00 1.50
❑ 142 Scott Erickson 1.50 .60
❑ 143 Howard Johnson 1.50 .60
❑ 144 Orestes Destrade 1.50 .60
❑ 145 Jose Guzman 1.50 .60
❑ 146 Chad Curtis 1.50 .60
❑ 147 Cal Eldred 1.50 .60
❑ 148 Willie Greene 1.50 .60
❑ 149 Tommy Greene 1.50 .60
❑ 150 Erik Hanson 1.50 .60
❑ 151 Bob Welch 1.50 .60
❑ 152 John Jaha 1.50 .60
❑ 153 Harold Baines 2.50 1.00
❑ 154 Randy Johnson 6.00 2.50
❑ 155 Al Martin 1.50 .60
❑ 156 J.T.Snow RC 4.00 1.50
❑ 157 Mike Mussina 4.00 1.50
❑ 158 Ruben Sierra 2.50 1.00
❑ 159 Dean Palmer 2.50 1.00
❑ 160 Steve Avery 1.50 .60
❑ 161 Julio Franco 2.50 1.00
❑ 162 Dave Winfield 2.50 1.00
❑ 163 Tim Salmon 4.00 1.50
❑ 164 Tom Henke 1.50 .60
❑ 165 Mo Vaughn 2.50 1.00
❑ 166 John Smoltz 4.00 1.50
❑ 167 Danny Tartabull 1.50 .60
❑ 168 Delino DeShields 1.50 .60
❑ 169 Charlie Hough 2.50 1.00
❑ 170 Paul O'Neill 4.00 1.50
❑ 171 Darren Daulton 2.50 1.00
❑ 172 Jack McDowell 1.50 .60
❑ 173 Junior Felix 1.50 .60
❑ 174 Jimmy Key 2.50 1.00
❑ 175 George Bell 1.50 .60
❑ 176 Mike Stanton 1.50 .60
❑ 177 Len Dykstra 2.50 1.00
❑ 178 Norm Charlton 1.50 .60
❑ 179 Eric Anthony 1.50 .60
❑ 180 Rob Dibble 2.50 1.00
❑ 181 Otis Nixon 1.50 .60
❑ 182 Randy Myers 1.50 .60
❑ 183 Tim Raines 2.50 1.00
❑ 184 Orel Hershiser 2.50 1.00
❑ 185 Andy Van Slyke 4.00 1.50
❑ 186 Mike Lansing RC 2.50 1.00
❑ 187 Ray Lankford 2.50 1.00
❑ 188 Mike Morgan 1.50 .60
❑ 189 Moises Alou 2.50 1.00
❑ 190 Edgar Martinez 4.00 1.50
❑ 191 John Franco 2.50 1.00
❑ 192 Robin Yount 10.00 4.00
❑ 193 Bob Tewksbury 1.50 .60
❑ 194 Jay Bell 2.50 1.00
❑ 195 Luis Gonzalez 2.50 1.00
❑ 196 Dave Fleming 1.50 .60
❑ 197 Mike Greenwell 1.50 .60
❑ 198 David Nied 1.50 .60
❑ 199 Mike Piazza 15.00 6.00

1994 Finest

❑ COMPLETE SET (440) 120.00 50.00
❑ COMPLETE SERIES 1 (220) 60.00 25.00
❑ COMPLETE SERIES 2 (220) 60.00 25.00

❑ 1	Mike Piazza FIN	6.00	2.50
❑ 2	Kevin Stocker FIN	.75	.30
❑ 3	Greg McMichael FIN	.75	.30
❑ 4	Jeff Conine FIN	1.25	.50
❑ 5	Rene Arocha FIN	.75	.30
❑ 6	Aaron Sele FIN	.75	.30
❑ 7	Brent Gates FIN	.75	.30
❑ 8	Chuck Carr FIN	.75	.30
❑ 9	Kirk Rueter FIN	.75	.30
❑ 10	Mike Lansing FIN	.75	.30
❑ 11	Al Martin FIN	.75	.30
❑ 12	Jason Bere FIN	.75	.30
❑ 13	Troy Neel FIN	.75	.30
❑ 14	Armando Reynoso FIN	.75	.30
❑ 15	Jeromy Burnitz FIN	1.25	.50
❑ 16	Rich Amaral FIN	.75	.30
❑ 17	David McCarty FIN	.75	.30
❑ 18	Tim Salmon FIN	2.00	.75
❑ 19	Steve Cooke FIN	.75	.30
❑ 20	Wil Cordero FIN	.75	.30
❑ 21	Kevin Tapani	.75	.30
❑ 22	Deion Sanders	2.00	.75
❑ 23	Jose Offerman	.75	.30
❑ 24	Mark Langston	.75	.30
❑ 25	Ken Hill	.75	.30
❑ 26	Alex Fernandez	.75	.30
❑ 27	Jeff Blauser	.75	.30
❑ 28	Royce Clayton	.75	.30
❑ 29	Brad Ausmus	2.00	.75
❑ 30	Ryan Bowen	.75	.30
❑ 31	Steve Finley	1.25	.50
❑ 32	Charlie Hayes	.75	.30
❑ 33	Jeff Kent	2.00	.75
❑ 34	Mike Henneman	.75	.30
❑ 35	Andres Galarraga	1.25	.50
❑ 36	Wayne Kirby	.75	.30
❑ 37	Joe Oliver	.75	.30
❑ 38	Terry Steinbach	.75	.30
❑ 39	Ryan Thompson	.75	.30
❑ 40	Luis Alicea	.75	.30
❑ 41	Randy Velarde	.75	.30
❑ 42	Bob Tewksbury	.75	.30
❑ 43	Reggie Sanders	1.25	.50
❑ 44	Brian Williams	.75	.30
❑ 45	Joe Orsulak	.75	.30
❑ 46	Jose Lind	.75	.30
❑ 47	Dave Hollins	.75	.30
❑ 48	Graeme Lloyd	.75	.30
❑ 49	Jim Gott	.75	.30
❑ 50	Andre Dawson	1.25	.50
❑ 51	Steve Buechele	.75	.30
❑ 52	David Cone	1.25	.50
❑ 53	Ricky Gutierrez	.75	.30
❑ 54	Lance Johnson	.75	.30
❑ 55	Tino Martinez	2.00	.75
❑ 56	Phil Hiatt	.75	.30
❑ 57	Carlos Garcia	.75	.30
❑ 58	Danny Darwin	.75	.30
❑ 59	Dante Bichette	1.25	.50
❑ 60	Scott Kamieniecki	.75	.30
❑ 61	Orlando Merced	.75	.30
❑ 62	Brian McRae	.75	.30
❑ 63	Pat Kelly	.75	.30
❑ 64	Tom Henke	.75	.30
❑ 65	Jeff King	.75	.30
❑ 66	Mike Mussina	2.00	.75
❑ 67	Tim Pugh	.75	.30
❑ 68	Robby Thompson	.75	.30
❑ 69	Paul O'Neill	2.00	.75
❑ 70	Hal Morris	.75	.30
❑ 71	Ron Karkovice	.75	.30
❑ 72	Joe Girardi	.75	.30
❑ 73	Eduardo Perez	.75	.30
❑ 74	Raul Mondesi	1.25	.50
❑ 75	Mike Gallego	.75	.30
❑ 76	Mike Stanley	.75	.30
❑ 77	Kevin Roberson	.75	.30
❑ 78	Mark McGwire	8.00	3.00
❑ 79	Pat Listach	.75	.30
❑ 80	Eric Davis	1.25	.50
❑ 81	Mike Bordick	.75	.30
❑ 82	Dwight Gooden	1.25	.50
❑ 83	Mike Moore	.75	.30
❑ 84	Phil Plantier	.75	.30
❑ 85	Darren Lewis	.75	.30
❑ 86	Rick Wilkins	.75	.30
❑ 87	Darryl Strawberry	1.25	.50
❑ 88	Rob Dibble	1.25	.50
❑ 89	Greg Vaughn	.75	.30
❑ 90	Jeff Russell	.75	.30
❑ 91	Mark Lewis	.75	.30
❑ 92	Gregg Jefferies	.75	.30
❑ 93	Jose Guzman	.75	.30
❑ 94	Kenny Rogers	1.25	.50
❑ 95	Mark Lemke	.75	.30
❑ 96	Mike Morgan	.75	.30
❑ 97	Andujar Cedeno	.75	.30
❑ 98	Orel Hershiser	1.25	.50
❑ 99	Greg Swindell	.75	.30
❑ 100	John Smoltz	2.00	.75
❑ 101	Pedro A.Martinez RC	.75	.30
❑ 102	Jim Thome	2.00	.75
❑ 103	David Segui	.75	.30
❑ 104	Charles Nagy	.75	.30
❑ 105	Shane Mack	.75	.30
❑ 106	John Jaha	.75	.30
❑ 107	Tom Candiotti	.75	.30
❑ 108	David Wells	1.25	.50
❑ 109	Bobby Jones	.75	.30
❑ 110	Bob Hamelin	.75	.30
❑ 111	Bernard Gilkey	.75	.30
❑ 112	Chili Davis	1.25	.50
❑ 113	Todd Stottlemyre	.75	.30
❑ 114	Derek Bell	.75	.30
❑ 115	Mark McLemore	.75	.30
❑ 116	Mark Whiten	.75	.30
❑ 117	Mike Devereaux	.75	.30
❑ 118	Terry Pendleton	1.25	.50
❑ 119	Pat Meares	.75	.30
❑ 120	Pete Harnisch	.75	.30
❑ 121	Moises Alou	1.25	.50
❑ 122	Jay Buhner	1.25	.50
❑ 123	Wes Chamberlain	.75	.30
❑ 124	Mike Perez	.75	.30
❑ 125	Devon White	1.25	.50
❑ 126	Ivan Rodriguez	2.00	.75
❑ 127	Don Slaught	.75	.30
❑ 128	John Valentin	.75	.30
❑ 129	Jaime Navarro	.75	.30
❑ 130	Dave Magadan	.75	.30
❑ 131	Brady Anderson	1.25	.50
❑ 132	Juan Guzman	.75	.30
❑ 133	John Wetteland	1.25	.50
❑ 134	Dave Stewart	1.25	.50
❑ 135	Scott Servais	.75	.30
❑ 136	Ozzie Smith	5.00	2.00
❑ 137	Darrin Fletcher	.75	.30
❑ 138	Jose Mesa	.75	.30
❑ 139	Wilson Alvarez	.75	.30
❑ 140	Pete Incaviglia	.75	.30
❑ 141	Chris Hoiles	.75	.30
❑ 142	Darryl Hamilton	.75	.30
❑ 143	Chuck Finley	1.25	.50
❑ 144	Archi Cianfrocco	.75	.30
❑ 145	Bill Wegman	.75	.30
❑ 146	Joey Cora	.75	.30
❑ 147	Darrell Whitmore	.75	.30
❑ 148	David Hulse	.75	.30
❑ 149	Jim Abbott	2.00	.75
❑ 150	Curt Schilling	1.25	.50
❑ 151	Bill Swift	.75	.30
❑ 152	Tommy Greene	.75	.30
❑ 153	Roberto Mejia	.75	.30
❑ 154	Edgar Martinez	2.00	.75
❑ 155	Roger Pavlik	.75	.30
❑ 156	Randy Tomlin	.75	.30
❑ 157	J.T. Snow	1.25	.50
❑ 158	Bob Welch	.75	.30
❑ 159	Alan Trammell	1.25	.50
❑ 160	Ed Sprague	.75	.30
❑ 161	Ben McDonald	.75	.30
❑ 162	Derrick May	.75	.30
❑ 163	Roberto Kelly	.75	.30
❑ 164	Bryan Harvey	.75	.30
❑ 165	Ron Gant	1.25	.50
❑ 166	Scott Erickson	.75	.30
❑ 167	Anthony Young	.75	.30
❑ 168	Scott Cooper	.75	.30
❑ 169	Rod Beck	.75	.30
❑ 170	John Franco	1.25	.50
❑ 171	Gary DiSarcina	.75	.30
❑ 172	Dave Fleming	.75	.30
❑ 173	Wade Boggs	2.00	.75
❑ 174	Kevin Appier	1.25	.50
❑ 175	Jose Bautista	.75	.30
❑ 176	Wally Joyner	1.25	.50
❑ 177	Dean Palmer	1.25	.50
❑ 178	Tony Phillips	.75	.30
❑ 179	John Smiley	.75	.30
❑ 180	Charlie Hough	1.25	.50
❑ 181	Scott Fletcher	.75	.30
❑ 182	Todd Van Poppel	.75	.30
❑ 183	Mike Blowers	.75	.30
❑ 184	Willie McGee	1.25	.50
❑ 185	Paul Sorrento	.75	.30
❑ 186	Eric Young	.75	.30
❑ 187	Bret Barberie	.75	.30
❑ 188	Manuel Lee	.75	.30
❑ 189	Jeff Branson	.75	.30
❑ 190	Jim Deshaies	.75	.30
❑ 191	Ken Caminiti	1.25	.50
❑ 192	Tim Raines	1.25	.50
❑ 193	Joe Grahe	.75	.30
❑ 194	Hipolito Pichardo	.75	.30
❑ 195	Denny Neagle	1.25	.50
❑ 196	Jeff Gardner	.75	.30
❑ 197	Mike Benjamin	.75	.30
❑ 198	Milt Thompson	.75	.30
❑ 199	Bruce Ruffin	.75	.30
❑ 200	Chris Hammond UER (Back of card has Mariners; sh	.75	.30
❑ 201	Tony Gwynn FIN	4.00	1.50
❑ 202	Robin Ventura FIN	1.25	.50
❑ 203	Frank Thomas FIN	3.00	1.25
❑ 204	Kirby Puckett FIN	3.00	1.25
❑ 205	Roberto Alomar FIN	2.00	.75
❑ 206	Dennis Eckersley FIN	1.25	.50
❑ 207	Joe Carter FIN	1.25	.50
❑ 208	Albert Belle FIN	1.25	.50
❑ 209	Greg Maddux FIN	5.00	2.00
❑ 210	Ryne Sandberg FIN	5.00	2.00
❑ 211	Juan Gonzalez FIN	1.25	.50
❑ 212	Jeff Bagwell FIN	2.00	.75
❑ 213	Randy Johnson FIN	3.00	1.25
❑ 214	Matt Williams FIN	1.25	.50
❑ 215	Dave Winfield FIN	1.25	.50
❑ 216	Larry Walker FIN	1.25	.50
❑ 217	Roger Clemens FIN	6.00	2.50
❑ 218	Kenny Lofton FIN	1.25	.50
❑ 219	Cecil Fielder FIN	1.25	.50
❑ 220	Darren Daulton FIN	1.25	.50
❑ 221	John Olerud FIN	1.25	.50
❑ 222	Jose Canseco FIN	2.00	.75
❑ 223	Rickey Henderson FIN	3.00	1.25
❑ 224	Fred McGriff FIN	2.00	.75
❑ 225	Gary Sheffield FIN	1.25	.50
❑ 226	Jack McDowell FIN	.75	.30
❑ 227	Rafael Palmeiro FIN	2.00	.75
❑ 228	Travis Fryman FIN	1.25	.50
❑ 229	Marquis Grissom FIN	1.25	.50
❑ 230	Barry Bonds FIN	8.00	3.00
❑ 231	Carlos Baerga FIN	.75	.30
❑ 232	Ken Griffey Jr. FIN	5.00	2.00
❑ 233	David Justice FIN	1.25	.50
❑ 234	Bobby Bonilla FIN	1.25	.50
❑ 235	Cal Ripken FIN	10.00	4.00
❑ 236	Sammy Sosa FIN	3.00	1.25
❑ 237	Len Dykstra FIN	1.25	.50
❑ 238	Will Clark FIN	2.00	.75
❑ 239	Paul Molitor FIN	1.25	.50

240	Barry Larkin FIN	2.00	.75
241	Bo Jackson	3.00	1.25
242	Mitch Williams	.75	.30
243	Ron Darling	.75	.30
244	Darryl Kile	1.25	.50
245	Geronimo Berroa	.75	.30
246	Gregg Olson	.75	.30
247	Brian Harper	.75	.30
248	Rheal Cormier	.75	.30
249	Rey Sanchez	.75	.30
250	Jeff Fassero	.75	.30
251	Sandy Alomar Jr.	.75	.30
252	Chris Bosio	.75	.30
253	Andy Stankiewicz	.75	.30
254	Harold Baines	1.25	.50
255	Andy Ashby	.75	.30
256	Tyler Green	.75	.30
257	Kevin Brown	1.25	.50
258	Mo Vaughn	1.25	.50
259	Mike Harkey	.75	.30
260	Dave Henderson	.75	.30
261	Kent Hrbek	1.25	.50
262	Darrin Jackson	.75	.30
263	Bob Wickman	.75	.30
264	Spike Owen	.75	.30
265	Todd Jones	.75	.30
266	Pat Borders	.75	.30
267	Tom Glavine	2.00	.75
268	Dave Nilsson	.75	.30
269	Rich Batchelor	.75	.30
270	Delino DeShields	.75	.30
271	Felix Fermin	.75	.30
272	Orestes Destrade	.75	.30
273	Mickey Morandini	.75	.30
274	Otis Nixon	.75	.30
275	Ellis Burks	1.25	.50
276	Greg Gagne	.75	.30
277	John Doherty	.75	.30
278	Julio Franco	1.25	.50
279	Bernie Williams	2.00	.75
280	Rick Aguilera	.75	.30
281	Mickey Tettleton	.75	.30
282	David Nied	.75	.30
283	Johnny Ruffin	.75	.30
284	Dan Wilson	.75	.30
285	Omar Vizquel	2.00	.75
286	Willie Banks	.75	.30
287	Erik Pappas	.75	.30
288	Cal Eldred	.75	.30
289	Bobby Witt	.75	.30
290	Luis Gonzalez	1.25	.50
291	Greg Pirkl	.75	.30
292	Alex Cole	.75	.30
293	Ricky Bones	.75	.30
294	Denis Boucher	.75	.30
295	John Burkett	.75	.30
296	Steve Trachsel	.75	.30
297	Ricky Jordan	.75	.30
298	Mark Dewey	.75	.30
299	Jimmy Key	1.25	.50
300	Mike Macfarlane	.75	.30
301	Tim Belcher	.75	.30
302	Carlos Reyes	.75	.30
303	Greg A. Harris	.75	.30
304	Brian Anderson RC	1.25	.50
305	Terry Mulholland	.75	.30
306	Felix Jose	.75	.30
307	Darren Holmes	.75	.30
308	Jose Rijo	.75	.30
309	Paul Wagner	.75	.30
310	Bob Scanlan	.75	.30
311	Mike Jackson	.75	.30
312	Jose Vizcaino	.75	.30
313	Rob Butler	.75	.30
314	Kevin Seitzer	.75	.30
315	Geronimo Pena	.75	.30
316	Hector Carrasco	.75	.30
317	Eddie Murray	3.00	1.25
318	Roger Salkeld	.75	.30
319	Todd Hundley	.75	.30
320	Danny Jackson	.75	.30
321	Kevin Young	.75	.30
322	Mike Greenwell	.75	.30
323	Kevin Mitchell	.75	.30
324	Chuck Knoblauch	1.25	.50
325	Danny Tartabull	.75	.30
326	Vince Coleman	.75	.30
327	Marvin Freeman	.75	.30
328	Andy Benes	.75	.30
329	Mike Kelly	.75	.30
330	Karl Rhodes	.75	.30
331	Allen Watson	.75	.30
332	Damion Easley	.75	.30
333	Reggie Jefferson	.75	.30
334	Kevin McReynolds	.75	.30
335	Arthur Rhodes	.75	.30
336	Brian Hunter	.75	.30
337	Tom Browning	.75	.30
338	Pedro Munoz	.75	.30
339	Billy Ripken	.75	.30
340	Gene Harris	.75	.30
341	Fernando Vina	.75	.30
342	Sean Berry	.75	.30
343	Pedro Astacio	.75	.30
344	B.J. Surhoff	1.25	.50
345	Doug Drabek	.75	.30
346	Jody Reed	.75	.30
347	Ray Lankford	1.25	.50
348	Steve Farr	.75	.30
349	Eric Anthony	.75	.30
350	Pete Smith	.75	.30
351	Lee Smith	1.25	.50
352	Mariano Duncan	.75	.30
353	Doug Strange	.75	.30
354	Tim Bogar	.75	.30
355	Dave Weathers	.75	.30
356	Eric Karros	1.25	.50
357	Randy Myers	.75	.30
358	Chad Curtis	.75	.30
359	Steve Avery	.75	.30
360	Brian Jordan	1.25	.50
361	Tim Wallach	.75	.30
362	Pedro Martinez	3.00	1.25
363	Bip Roberts	.75	.30
364	Lou Whitaker	1.25	.50
365	Luis Polonia	.75	.30
366	Benito Santiago	1.25	.50
367	Brett Butler	1.25	.50
368	Shawon Dunston	.75	.30
369	Kelly Stinnett RC	1.25	.50
370	Chris Turner	.75	.30
371	Ruben Sierra	1.25	.50
372	Greg A. Harris	.75	.30
373	Xavier Hernandez	.75	.30
374	Howard Johnson	.75	.30
375	Duane Ward	.75	.30
376	Roberto Hernandez	.75	.30
377	Scott Leius	.75	.30
378	Dave Valle	.75	.30
379	Sid Fernandez	.75	.30
380	Doug Jones	.75	.30
381	Zane Smith	.75	.30
382	Craig Biggio	2.00	.75
383	Rick White RC	.75	.30
384	Tom Pagnozzi	.75	.30
385	Chris James	.75	.30
386	Bret Boone	1.25	.50
387	Jeff Montgomery	.75	.30
388	Chad Kreuter	.75	.30
389	Greg Hibbard	.75	.30
390	Mark Grace	2.00	.75
391	Phil Leftwich RC	.75	.30
392	Don Mattingly	8.00	3.00
393	Ozzie Guillen	1.25	.50
394	Gary Gaetti	1.25	.50
395	Erik Hanson	.75	.30
396	Scott Brosius	1.25	.50
397	Tom Gordon	.75	.30
398	Bill Gullickson	.75	.30
399	Matt Mieske	.75	.30
400	Pat Hentgen	.75	.30
401	Walt Weiss	.75	.30
402	Greg Blosser	.75	.30
403	Stan Javier	.75	.30
404	Doug Henry	.75	.30
405	Ramon Martinez	.75	.30
406	Frank Viola	1.25	.50
407	Mike Hampton	1.25	.50
408	Andy Van Slyke	2.00	.75
409	Bobby Ayala	.75	.30
410	Todd Zeile	.75	.30
411	Jay Bell	1.25	.50
412	Dennis Martinez	1.25	.50
413	Mark Portugal	.75	.30
414	Bobby Munoz	.75	.30
415	Kirt Manwaring	.75	.30
416	John Kruk	1.25	.50
417	Trevor Hoffman	2.00	.75
418	Chris Sabo	.75	.30
419	Bret Saberhagen	1.25	.50
420	Chris Nabholz	.75	.30
421	James Mouton FIN	.75	.30
422	Tony Tarasco FIN	.75	.30
423	Carlos Delgado FIN	2.00	.75
424	Rondell White FIN	1.25	.50
425	Javier Lopez FIN	1.25	.50
426	Chan Ho Park FIN RC	2.00	.75
427	Cliff Floyd FIN	1.25	.50
428	Dave Staton FIN	.75	.30
429	J.R. Phillips FIN	.75	.30
430	Manny Ramirez FIN	3.00	1.25
431	Kurt Abbott FIN RC	.75	.30
432	Melvin Nieves FIN	.75	.30
433	Alex Gonzalez FIN	.75	.30
434	Rick Helling FIN	.75	.30
435	Danny Bautista FIN	.75	.30
436	Matt Walbeck FIN	.75	.30
437	Ryan Klesko FIN	1.25	.50
438	Steve Karsay FIN	.75	.30
439	Salomon Torres FIN	.75	.30
440	Scott Ruffcorn FIN	.75	.30

1995 Finest

	COMPLETE SET (330)	60.00	25.00
	COMPLETE SERIES 1 (220)	50.00	20.00
	COMPLETE SERIES 2 (110)	15.00	6.00
1	Raul Mondesi	1.00	.40
2	Kurt Abbott	.50	.20
3	Chris Gomez	.50	.20
4	Manny Ramirez	1.50	.60
5	Rondell White	1.00	.40
6	William VanLandingham	.50	.20
7	Jon Lieber	.50	.20
8	Ryan Klesko	1.00	.40
9	John Hudek	.50	.20
10	Joey Hamilton	.50	.20
11	Bob Hamelin	.50	.20
12	Brian Anderson	.50	.20
13	Mike Lieberthal	1.00	.40
14	Rico Brogna	.50	.20
15	Rusty Greer	1.00	.40
16	Carlos Delgado	1.00	.40
17	Jim Edmonds	1.50	.60
18	Steve Trachsel	.50	.20
19	Matt Walbeck	.50	.20
20	Armando Benitez	.50	.20
21	Steve Karsay	.50	.20
22	Jose Oliva	.50	.20
23	Cliff Floyd	1.00	.40
24	Kevin Foster	.50	.20
25	Javier Lopez	1.00	.40
26	Jose Valentin	.50	.20
27	James Mouton	.50	.20
28	Hector Carrasco	.50	.20
29	Orlando Miller	.50	.20
30	Garret Anderson	1.00	.40
31	Marvin Freeman	.50	.20
32	Brett Butler	1.00	.40
33	Roberto Kelly	.50	.20
34	Rod Beck	.50	.20

❑ 35 Jose Rijo	.50	.20
❑ 36 Edgar Martinez	1.50	.60
❑ 37 Jim Thome	1.50	.60
❑ 38 Rick Wilkins	.50	.20
❑ 39 Wally Joyner	1.00	.40
❑ 40 Wil Cordero	.50	.20
❑ 41 Tommy Greene	.50	.20
❑ 42 Travis Fryman	1.00	.40
❑ 43 Don Slaught	.50	.20
❑ 44 Brady Anderson	1.00	.40
❑ 45 Matt Williams	1.00	.40
❑ 46 Rene Arocha	.50	.20
❑ 47 Rickey Henderson	2.50	1.00
❑ 48 Mike Mussina	1.50	.60
❑ 49 Greg McMichael	.50	.20
❑ 50 Jody Reed	.50	.20
❑ 51 Tino Martinez	1.50	.60
❑ 52 Dave Clark	.50	.20
❑ 53 John Valentin	.50	.20
❑ 54 Bret Boone	1.00	.40
❑ 55 Walt Weiss	.50	.20
❑ 56 Kenny Lofton	1.00	.40
❑ 57 Scott Leius	.50	.20
❑ 58 Eric Karros	1.00	.40
❑ 59 John Olerud	1.00	.40
❑ 60 Chris Hoiles	.50	.20
❑ 61 Sandy Alomar Jr.	.50	.20
❑ 62 Tim Wallach	.50	.20
❑ 63 Cal Eldred	.50	.20
❑ 64 Tom Glavine	1.50	.60
❑ 65 Mark Grace	1.50	.60
❑ 66 Rey Sanchez	.50	.20
❑ 67 Bobby Ayala	.50	.20
❑ 68 Dante Bichette	1.00	.40
❑ 69 Andres Galarraga	1.00	.40
❑ 70 Chuck Carr	.50	.20
❑ 71 Bobby Witt	.50	.20
❑ 72 Steve Avery	.50	.20
❑ 73 Bobby Jones	.50	.20
❑ 74 Delino DeShields	.50	.20
❑ 75 Kevin Tapani	.50	.20
❑ 76 Randy Johnson	2.50	1.00
❑ 77 David Nied	.50	.20
❑ 78 Pat Hentgen	.50	.20
❑ 79 Tim Salmon	1.50	.60
❑ 80 Todd Zeile	.50	.20
❑ 81 John Wetteland	1.00	.40
❑ 82 Albert Belle	1.00	.40
❑ 83 Ben McDonald	.50	.20
❑ 84 Bobby Munoz	.50	.20
❑ 85 Bip Roberts	.50	.20
❑ 86 Mo Vaughn	1.00	.40
❑ 87 Chuck Finley	1.00	.40
❑ 88 Chuck Knoblauch	1.00	.40
❑ 89 Frank Thomas	2.50	1.00
❑ 90 Danny Tartabull	.50	.20
❑ 91 Dean Palmer	1.00	.40
❑ 92 Len Dykstra	1.00	.40
❑ 93 J.R. Phillips	.50	.20
❑ 94 Tom Candiotti	.50	.20
❑ 95 Marquis Grissom	1.00	.40
❑ 96 Barry Larkin	1.50	.60
❑ 97 Bryan Harvey	.50	.20
❑ 98 David Justice	1.00	.40
❑ 99 David Cone	1.00	.40
❑ 100 Wade Boggs	1.50	.60
❑ 101 Jason Bere	.50	.20
❑ 102 Hal Morris	.50	.20
❑ 103 Fred McGriff	1.50	.60
❑ 104 Bobby Bonilla	1.00	.40
❑ 105 Jay Buhner	1.00	.40
❑ 106 Allen Watson	.50	.20
❑ 107 Mickey Tettleton	.50	.20
❑ 108 Kevin Appier	1.00	.40
❑ 109 Ivan Rodriguez	1.50	.60
❑ 110 Carlos Garcia	.50	.20
❑ 111 Andy Benes	.50	.20
❑ 112 Eddie Murray	2.50	1.00
❑ 113 Mike Piazza	4.00	1.50
❑ 114 Greg Vaughn	.50	.20
❑ 115 Paul Molitor	1.00	.40
❑ 116 Terry Steinbach	.50	.20
❑ 117 Jeff Bagwell	1.50	.60
❑ 118 Ken Griffey Jr.	4.00	1.50
❑ 119 Gary Sheffield	1.00	.40
❑ 120 Cal Ripken	8.00	3.00
❑ 121 Jeff Kent	1.00	.40
❑ 122 Jay Bell	1.00	.40
❑ 123 Will Clark	1.50	.60
❑ 124 Cecil Fielder	1.00	.40
❑ 125 Alex Fernandez	.50	.20
❑ 126 Don Mattingly	6.00	2.50
❑ 127 Reggie Sanders	1.00	.40
❑ 128 Moises Alou	1.00	.40
❑ 129 Craig Biggio	1.50	.60
❑ 130 Eddie Williams	.50	.20
❑ 131 John Franco	1.00	.40
❑ 132 John Kruk	1.00	.40
❑ 133 Jeff King	.50	.20
❑ 134 Royce Clayton	.50	.20
❑ 135 Doug Drabek	.50	.20
❑ 136 Ray Lankford	1.00	.40
❑ 137 Roberto Alomar	1.50	.60
❑ 138 Todd Hundley	.50	.20
❑ 139 Alex Cole	.50	.20
❑ 140 Shawon Dunston	.50	.20
❑ 141 John Roper	.50	.20
❑ 142 Mark Langston	.50	.20
❑ 143 Tom Pagnozzi	.50	.20
❑ 144 Wilson Alvarez	.50	.20
❑ 145 Scott Cooper	.50	.20
❑ 146 Kevin Mitchell	.50	.20
❑ 147 Mark Whiten	.50	.20
❑ 148 Jeff Conine	1.00	.40
❑ 149 Chili Davis	1.00	.40
❑ 150 Luis Gonzalez	1.00	.40
❑ 151 Juan Guzman	.50	.20
❑ 152 Mike Greenwell	.50	.20
❑ 153 Mike Henneman	.50	.20
❑ 154 Rick Aguilera	.50	.20
❑ 155 Dennis Eckersley	1.00	.40
❑ 156 Darrin Fletcher	.50	.20
❑ 157 Darren Lewis	.50	.20
❑ 158 Juan Gonzalez	1.00	.40
❑ 159 Dave Hollins	.50	.20
❑ 160 Jimmy Key	1.00	.40
❑ 161 Roberto Hernandez	.50	.20
❑ 162 Randy Myers	.50	.20
❑ 163 Joe Carter	1.00	.40
❑ 164 Darren Daulton	1.00	.40
❑ 165 Mike Macfarlane	.50	.20
❑ 166 Bret Saberhagen	1.00	.40
❑ 167 Kirby Puckett	2.50	1.00
❑ 168 Lance Johnson	.50	.20
❑ 169 Mark McGwire	6.00	2.50
❑ 170 Jose Canseco	1.50	.60
❑ 171 Mike Stanley	.50	.20
❑ 172 Lee Smith	1.00	.40
❑ 173 Robin Ventura	1.00	.40
❑ 174 Greg Gagne	.50	.20
❑ 175 Brian McRae	.50	.20
❑ 176 Mike Bordick	.50	.20
❑ 177 Rafael Palmeiro	1.50	.60
❑ 178 Kenny Rogers	1.00	.40
❑ 179 Chad Curtis	.50	.20
❑ 180 Devon White	1.00	.40
❑ 181 Paul O'Neill	1.50	.60
❑ 182 Ken Caminiti	1.00	.40
❑ 183 Dave Nilsson	.50	.20
❑ 184 Tim Naehring	.50	.20
❑ 185 Roger Clemens	5.00	2.00
❑ 186 Otis Nixon	.50	.20
❑ 187 Tim Raines	1.00	.40
❑ 188 Denny Martinez	1.00	.40
❑ 189 Pedro Martinez	1.50	.60
❑ 190 Jim Abbott	1.50	.60
❑ 191 Ryan Thompson	.50	.20
❑ 192 Barry Bonds	6.00	2.50
❑ 193 Joe Girardi	.50	.20
❑ 194 Steve Finley	1.00	.40
❑ 195 John Jaha	.50	.20
❑ 196 Tony Gwynn	3.00	1.25
❑ 197 Sammy Sosa	2.50	1.00
❑ 198 John Burkett	.50	.20
❑ 199 Carlos Baerga	.50	.20
❑ 200 Ramon Martinez	.50	.20
❑ 201 Aaron Sele	.50	.20
❑ 202 Eduardo Perez	.50	.20
❑ 203 Alan Trammell	1.00	.40
❑ 204 Orlando Merced	.50	.20
❑ 205 Deion Sanders	1.50	.60
❑ 206 Robb Nen	1.00	.40
❑ 207 Jack McDowell	.50	.20
❑ 208 Ruben Sierra	1.00	.40
❑ 209 Bernie Williams	1.50	.60
❑ 210 Kevin Seitzer	.50	.20
❑ 211 Charles Nagy	.50	.20
❑ 212 Tony Phillips	.50	.20
❑ 213 Greg Maddux	4.00	1.50
❑ 214 Jeff Montgomery	.50	.20
❑ 215 Larry Walker	1.00	.40
❑ 216 Andy Van Slyke	1.50	.60
❑ 217 Ozzie Smith	4.00	1.50
❑ 218 Geronimo Pena	.50	.20
❑ 219 Gregg Jefferies	.50	.20
❑ 220 Lou Whitaker	1.00	.40
❑ 221 Chipper Jones	2.50	1.00
❑ 222 Benji Gil	.50	.20
❑ 223 Tony Phillips	.50	.20
❑ 224 Trevor Wilson	.50	.20
❑ 225 Tony Tarasco	.50	.20
❑ 226 Roberto Petagine	.50	.20
❑ 227 Mike Macfarlane	.50	.20
❑ 228 Hideo Nomo RC	10.00	4.00
❑ 229 Mark McLemore	.50	.20
❑ 230 Ron Gant	1.00	.40
❑ 231 Andujar Cedeno	.50	.20
❑ 232 Michael Mimbs RC	.50	.20
❑ 233 Jim Abbott	1.50	.60
❑ 234 Ricky Bones	.50	.20
❑ 235 Marty Cordova	.50	.20
❑ 236 Mark Johnson RC	1.25	.50
❑ 237 Marquis Grissom	1.00	.40
❑ 238 Tom Henke	.50	.20
❑ 239 Terry Pendleton	1.00	.40
❑ 240 John Wetteland	1.00	.40
❑ 241 Lee Smith	1.00	.40
❑ 242 Jaime Navarro	.50	.20
❑ 243 Luis Alicea	.50	.20
❑ 244 Scott Cooper	.50	.20
❑ 245 Gary Gaetti	1.00	.40
❑ 246 Edgardo Alfonzo	.50	.20
❑ 247 Brad Clontz	.50	.20
❑ 248 Dave Mlicki	.50	.20
❑ 249 Dave Winfield	1.00	.40
❑ 250 Mark Grudzielanek RC	2.00	.75
❑ 251 Alex Gonzalez	.50	.20
❑ 252 Kevin Brown	1.00	.40
❑ 253 Esteban Loaiza	.50	.20
❑ 254 Vaughn Eshelman	.50	.20
❑ 255 Bill Swift	.50	.20
❑ 256 Brian McRae	.50	.20
❑ 257 Bob Higginson RC	2.00	.75
❑ 258 Jack McDowell	.50	.20
❑ 259 Scott Stahoviak	.50	.20
❑ 260 Jon Nunnally	.50	.20
❑ 261 Charlie Hayes	.50	.20
❑ 262 Jacob Brumfield	.50	.20
❑ 263 Chad Curtis	.50	.20
❑ 264 Heathcliff Slocumb	.50	.20
❑ 265 Mark Whiten	.50	.20
❑ 266 Mickey Tettleton	.50	.20
❑ 267 Jose Mesa	.50	.20
❑ 268 Doug Jones	.50	.20
❑ 269 Trevor Hoffman	1.00	.40
❑ 270 Paul Sorrento	.50	.20
❑ 271 Shane Andrews	.50	.20
❑ 272 Brett Butler	1.00	.40
❑ 273 Curtis Goodwin	.50	.20
❑ 274 Larry Walker	1.00	.40
❑ 275 Phil Plantier	.50	.20
❑ 276 Ken Hill	.50	.20
❑ 277 Vinny Castilla	1.00	.40
❑ 278 Billy Ashley	.50	.20
❑ 279 Derek Jeter	6.00	2.50
❑ 280 Bob Tewksbury	.50	.20
❑ 281 Jose Offerman	.50	.20
❑ 282 Glenallen Hill	.50	.20
❑ 283 Tony Fernandez	.50	.20
❑ 284 Mike Devereaux	.50	.20
❑ 285 John Burkett	.50	.20
❑ 286 Geronimo Berroa	.50	.20
❑ 287 Quilvio Veras	.50	.20
❑ 288 Jason Bates	.50	.20
❑ 289 Lee Tinsley	.50	.20
❑ 290 Derek Bell	.50	.20
❑ 291 Jeff Fassero	.50	.20
❑ 292 Ray Durham	1.00	.40

❑ 293	Chad Ogea	.50	.20
❑ 294	Bill Pulsipher	.50	.20
❑ 295	Phil Nevin	1.00	.40
❑ 296	Carlos Perez RC	1.25	.50
❑ 297	Roberto Kelly	.50	.20
❑ 298	Tim Wakefield	1.00	.40
❑ 299	Jeff Manto	.50	.20
❑ 300	Brian L.Hunter	.50	.20
❑ 301	C.J. Nitkowski	.50	.20
❑ 302	Dustin Hermanson	.50	.20
❑ 303	John Mabry	.50	.20
❑ 304	Orel Hershiser	1.00	.40
❑ 305	Ron Villone	.50	.20
❑ 306	Sean Bergman	.50	.20
❑ 307	Tom Goodwin	.50	.20
❑ 308	Al Reyes	.50	.20
❑ 309	Todd Stottlemyre	.50	.20
❑ 310	Rich Becker	.50	.20
❑ 311	Joey Cora	.50	.20
❑ 312	Ed Sprague	.50	.20
❑ 313	John Smoltz	1.50	.60
❑ 314	Frank Castillo	.50	.20
❑ 315	Chris Hammond	.50	.20
❑ 316	Ismael Valdes	.50	.20
❑ 317	Pete Harnisch	.50	.20
❑ 318	Bernard Gilkey	.50	.20
❑ 319	John Kruk	1.00	.40
❑ 320	Marc Newfield	.50	.20
❑ 321	Brian Johnson	.50	.20
❑ 322	Mark Portugal	.50	.20
❑ 323	David Hulse	.50	.20
❑ 324	Luis Ortiz	.50	.20
❑ 325	Mike Benjamin	.50	.20
❑ 326	Brian Jordan	1.00	.40
❑ 327	Shawn Green	1.00	.40
❑ 328	Joe Oliver	.50	.20
❑ 329	Felipe Lira	.50	.20
❑ 330	Andre Dawson	1.00	.40

1996 Finest

❑ COMP.BRONZE SER.1 (110)		25.00	10.00
❑ COMP.BRONZE SER.2 (110)		25.00	10.00
❑ COMMON BRONZE		.50	.20
❑ COMMON GOLD		5.00	2.00
❑ COMMON G RC		5.00	2.00
❑ COMMON SILVER		2.50	1.00
❑ B5	Roberto Hernandez B	.50	.20
❑ B8	Terry Pendleton B	.50	.20
❑ B12	Ken Caminiti B	.50	.20
❑ B15	Dan Miceli B	.50	.20
❑ B16	Chipper Jones B	1.25	.50
❑ B17	John Wetteland B	.50	.20
❑ B19	Tim Naehring B	.50	.20
❑ B21	Eddie Murray B	1.25	.50
❑ B23	Kevin Appier B	.50	.20
❑ B24	Ken Griffey Jr. B	2.00	.75
❑ B26	Brian McRae B	.50	.20
❑ B27	Pedro Martinez B	.75	.30
❑ B28	Brian Jordan B	.50	.20
❑ B29	Mike Fetters B	.50	.20
❑ B30	Carlos Delgado B	.50	.20
❑ B31	Shane Reynolds B	.50	.20
❑ B32	Terry Steinbach B	.50	.20
❑ B34	Mark Leiter B	.50	.20
❑ B36	David Segui B	.50	.20
❑ B40	Fred McGriff B	.75	.30
❑ B44	Glenallen Hill B	.50	.20
❑ B45	Brady Anderson B	.50	.20
❑ B47	Jim Thome B	.75	.30
❑ B48	Frank Thomas B	1.25	.50
❑ B49	Chuck Knoblauch B	.50	.20
❑ B50	Len Dykstra B	.50	.20
❑ B53	Tom Pagnozzi B	.50	.20
❑ B55	Ricky Bones B	.50	.20
❑ B56	David Justice B	.50	.20
❑ B57	Steve Avery B	.50	.20
❑ B58	Robby Thompson B	.50	.20
❑ B61	Tony Gwynn B	1.50	.60
❑ B63	Denny Neagle B	.50	.20
❑ B67	Robin Ventura B	.50	.20
❑ B70	Kevin Seitzer B	.50	.20
❑ B71	Ramon Martinez B	.50	.20
❑ B75	Brian L.Hunter B	.50	.20
❑ B76	Alan Benes B	.50	.20
❑ B80	Ozzie Guillen B	.50	.20
❑ B82	Benji Gil B	.50	.20
❑ B85	Todd Hundley B	.50	.20
❑ B87	Pat Hentgen B	.50	.20
❑ B89	Chuck Finley B	.50	.20
❑ B92	Derek Jeter B	3.00	1.25
❑ B93	Paul O'Neill B	.75	.30
❑ B94	Darrin Fletcher B	.50	.20
❑ B96	Delino DeShields B	.50	.20
❑ B97	Tim Salmon B	.75	.30
❑ B98	John Olerud B	.50	.20
❑ B101	Tim Wakefield B	.50	.20
❑ B103	Dave Stevens B	.50	.20
❑ B104	Orlando Merced B	.50	.20
❑ B106	Jay Bell B	.50	.20
❑ B107	John Burkett B	.50	.20
❑ B108	Chris Hoiles B	.50	.20
❑ B110	Dave Nilsson B	.50	.20
❑ B111	Rod Beck B	.50	.20
❑ B113	Mike Piazza B	2.00	.75
❑ B114	Mark Langston B	.50	.20
❑ B116	Rico Brogna B	.50	.20
❑ B118	Tom Goodwin B	.50	.20
❑ B119	Bryan Rekar B	.50	.20
❑ B120	David Cone B	.50	.20
❑ B122	Andy Pettitte B	.75	.30
❑ B123	Chili Davis B	.50	.20
❑ B124	John Smoltz B	.75	.30
❑ B125	Heathcliff Slocumb B	.50	.20
❑ B126	Dante Bichette B	.50	.20
❑ B128	Alex Gonzalez B	.50	.20
❑ B129	Jeff Montgomery B	.50	.20
❑ B131	Denny Martinez B	.50	.20
❑ B132	Mel Rojas B	.50	.20
❑ B133	Derek Bell B	.50	.20
❑ B134	Trevor Hoffman B	.50	.20
❑ B136	Darren Daulton B	.50	.20
❑ B137	Pete Schourek B	.50	.20
❑ B138	Phil Nevin B	.50	.20
❑ B139	Andres Galarraga B	.50	.20
❑ B140	Chad Fonville B	.50	.20
❑ B144	J.T. Snow B	.50	.20
❑ B146	Barry Bonds B	3.00	1.25
❑ B147	Orel Hershiser B	.50	.20
❑ B148	Quilvio Veras B	.50	.20
❑ B149	Will Clark B	.75	.30
❑ B150	Jose Rijo B	.50	.20
❑ B152	Travis Fryman B	.50	.20
❑ B154	Alex Fernandez B	.50	.20
❑ B155	Wade Boggs B	.75	.30
❑ B156	Troy Percival B	.50	.20
❑ B157	Moises Alou B	.50	.20
❑ B158	Javy Lopez B	.50	.20
❑ B159	Jason Giambi B	.50	.20
❑ B162	Mark McGwire B	3.00	1.25
❑ B163	Eric Karros B	.50	.20
❑ B166	Mickey Tettleton B	.50	.20
❑ B167	Barry Larkin B	.75	.30
❑ B169	Ruben Sierra B	.50	.20
❑ B170	Bill Swift B	.50	.20
❑ B172	Chad Curtis B	.50	.20
❑ B173	Dean Palmer B	.50	.20
❑ B175	Bobby Bonilla B	.50	.20
❑ B176	Greg Colbrunn B	.50	.20
❑ B177	Jose Mesa B	.50	.20
❑ B178	Mike Greenwell B	.50	.20
❑ B181	Doug Drabek B	.50	.20
❑ B183	Wilson Alvarez B	.50	.20
❑ B184	Marty Cordova B	.50	.20
❑ B185	Hal Morris B	.50	.20
❑ B187	Carlos Garcia B	.50	.20
❑ B190	Marquis Grissom B	.50	.20
❑ B193	Will Clark B	.75	.30
❑ B194	Paul Molitor B	.50	.20
❑ B195	Kenny Rogers B	.50	.20
❑ B196	Reggie Sanders B	.50	.20
❑ B199	Raul Mondesi B	.50	.20
❑ B200	Lance Johnson B	.50	.20
❑ B201	Alvin Morman B	.50	.20
❑ B203	Jack McDowell B	.50	.20
❑ B204	Randy Myers B	.50	.20
❑ B205	Harold Baines B	.50	.20
❑ B206	Marty Cordova B	.50	.20
❑ B207	Rich Hunter B RC	.50	.20
❑ B208	Al Leiter B	.50	.20
❑ B209	Greg Gagne B	.50	.20
❑ B210	Ben McDonald B	.50	.20
❑ B212	Terry Adams B	.50	.20
❑ B213	Paul Sorrento B	.50	.20
❑ B214	Albert Belle B	.50	.20
❑ B215	Mike Blowers B	.50	.20
❑ B216	Jim Edmonds B	.50	.20
❑ B217	Felipe Crespo B	.50	.20
❑ B219	Shawon Dunston B	.50	.20
❑ B220	Jimmy Haynes B	.50	.20
❑ B221	Jose Canseco B	.75	.30
❑ B222	Eric Davis B	.50	.20
❑ B224	Tim Raines B	.50	.20
❑ B225	Tony Phillips B	.50	.20
❑ B226	Charlie Hayes B	.50	.20
❑ B227	Eric Owens B	.50	.20
❑ B228	Roberto Alomar B	.75	.30
❑ B233	Kenny Lofton B	.50	.20
❑ B236	Mark McGwire B	3.00	1.25
❑ B237	Jay Buhner B	.50	.20
❑ B238	Craig Biggio B	.75	.30
❑ B240	Barry Bonds B	3.00	1.25
❑ B244	Ron Gant B	.50	.20
❑ B245	Paul Wilson B	.50	.20
❑ B246	Todd Hollandsworth B	.50	.20
❑ B247	Todd Zeile B	.50	.20
❑ B248	David Justice B	.50	.20
❑ B250	Moises Alou B	.50	.20
❑ B251	Bob Wolcott B	.50	.20
❑ B252	David Wells B	.50	.20
❑ B253	Juan Gonzalez B	.50	.20
❑ B254	Andres Galarraga B	.50	.20
❑ B255	Dave Hollins B	.50	.20
❑ B257	Sammy Sosa B	1.25	.50
❑ B258	Ivan Rodriguez B	.75	.30
❑ B259	Bip Roberts B	.50	.20
❑ B260	Tino Martinez B	.75	.30
❑ B262	Mike Stanley B	.50	.20
❑ B264	Butch Huskey B	.50	.20
❑ B265	Jeff Conine B	.50	.20
❑ B267	Mark Grace B	.75	.30
❑ B268	Jason Schmidt B	.75	.30
❑ B269	Otis Nixon B	.50	.20
❑ B271	Kirby Puckett B	1.25	.50
❑ B273	Andy Benes B	.50	.20
❑ B275	Mike Piazza B	2.00	.75
❑ B276	Rey Ordonez B	.50	.20
❑ B278	Gary Gaetti B	.50	.20
❑ B280	Robin Ventura B	.50	.20
❑ B281	Cal Ripken B	4.00	1.50
❑ B282	Carlos Baerga B	.50	.20
❑ B283	Roger Cedeno B	.50	.20
❑ B285	Terrell Wade B	.50	.20
❑ B286	Kevin Brown B	.50	.20
❑ B287	Rafael Palmeiro B	.75	.30
❑ B288	Mo Vaughn B	.50	.20
❑ B292	Bob Tewksbury B	.50	.20
❑ B297	T.J. Mathews B	.50	.20
❑ B298	Manny Ramirez B	.75	.30
❑ B299	Jeff Bagwell B	.75	.30
❑ B301	Wade Boggs B	.75	.30
❑ B303	Steve Gibralter B	.50	.20
❑ B304	B.J. Surhoff B	.50	.20
❑ B306	Royce Clayton B	.50	.20
❑ B307	Sal Fasano B	.50	.20
❑ B309	Gary Sheffield B	.50	.20
❑ B310	Ken Hill B	.50	.20
❑ B311	Joe Girardi B	.50	.20
❑ B312	Matt Lawton B RC	.50	.20
❑ B314	Julio Franco B	.50	.20
❑ B315	Joe Carter B	.50	.20

❑ B316 Brooks Kieschnick B .50 .20
❑ B318 Heathcliff Slocumb B .50 .20
❑ B319 Barry Larkin B .75 .30
❑ B320 Tony Gwynn B 1.50 .60
❑ B322 Frank Thomas B 1.25 .50
❑ B323 Edgar Martinez B .75 .30
❑ B325 Henry Rodriguez B .50 .20
❑ B326 Marvin Benard B RC .50 .20
❑ B329 Ugueth Urbina B .50 .20
❑ B331 Roger Salkeld B .50 .20
❑ B332 Edgar Renteria B .50 .20
❑ B333 Ryan Klesko B .50 .20
❑ B334 Ray Lankford B .50 .20
❑ B336 Justin Thompson B .50 .20
❑ B339 Mark Clark B .50 .20
❑ B340 Ruben Rivera B .50 .20
❑ B342 Matt Williams B .50 .20
❑ B343 Francisco Cordova B RC .50 .20
❑ B344 Cecil Fielder B .50 .20
❑ B348 Mark Grudzielanek B .50 .20
❑ B349 Ron Coomer B .50 .20
❑ B351 Rich Aurilia B RC .50 .20
❑ B352 Jose Herrera B .50 .20
❑ B356 Tony Clark B .50 .20
❑ B358 Dan Naulty B .50 .20
❑ B359 Checklist B .50 .20
❑ G4 Marty Cordova G 5.00 2.00
❑ G0 Tony Gwynn G 15.00 6.00
❑ G9 Albert Belle G 5.00 2.00
❑ G18 Kirby Puckett G 12.00 5.00
❑ G20 Karim Garcia G 5.00 2.00
❑ G25 Cal Ripken G 40.00 15.00
❑ G33 Hideo Nomo G 12.00 5.00
❑ G39 Ryne Sandberg G 20.00 8.00
❑ G42 Jeff Bagwell G 4.00 1.50
❑ G51 Jason Isringhausen G 5.00 2.00
❑ G64 Mo Vaughn G 5.00 2.00
❑ G66 Dante Bichette G 5.00 2.00
❑ G74 Mark McGwire G 30.00 12.50
❑ G81 Kenny Lofton G 5.00 2.00
❑ G83 Jim Edmonds G 5.00 2.00
❑ G90 Mike Mussina G 8.00 3.00
❑ G100 Jeff Conine G 5.00 2.00
❑ G102 Johnny Damon G 8.00 3.00
❑ G105 Barry Bonds G 30.00 12.50
❑ G117 Jose Canseco G 8.00 3.00
❑ G135 Ken Griffey Jr. G 20.00 8.00
❑ G141 Chipper Jones G 12.00 5.00
❑ G145 Greg Maddux G 20.00 8.00
❑ G164 Jay Buhner G 5.00 2.00
❑ G186 Frank Thomas G 12.00 5.00
❑ G191 Checklist G 5.00 2.00
❑ G192 Chipper Jones G 12.00 5.00
❑ G197 Roberto Alomar G 8.00 3.00
❑ G198 Dennis Eckersley G 5.00 2.00
❑ G202 George Arias G 5.00 2.00
❑ G232 Hideo Nomo G 12.00 5.00
❑ G243 Chris Snopek G 5.00 2.00
❑ G249 Tim Salmon G 8.00 3.00
❑ G266 Matt Williams G 5.00 2.00
❑ G270 Randy Johnson G 12.00 5.00
❑ G279 Paul Molitor G 5.00 2.00
❑ G290 Cecil Fielder G 5.00 2.00
❑ G294 Livan Hernandez G RC 10.00 4.00
❑ G300 Marty Janzen G RC 5.00 2.00
❑ G308 Ron Gant G 5.00 2.00
❑ G321 Ryan Klesko G 5.00 2.00
❑ G324 Jermaine Dye G 5.00 2.00
❑ G330 Jason Giambi G 5.00 2.00
❑ G335 Edgar Martinez G 8.00 3.00
❑ G338 Rey Ordonez G 5.00 2.00
❑ G347 Sammy Sosa G 12.00 5.00
❑ G354 Juan Gonzalez G 5.00 2.00
❑ G355 Craig Biggio G 8.00 3.00
❑ S1 Greg Maddux S 10.00 4.00
❑ S2 Bernie Williams S 4.00 1.50
❑ S3 Ivan Rodriguez S 4.00 1.50
❑ S7 Barry Larkin S 4.00 1.50
❑ S10 Ray Lankford S 2.50 1.00
❑ S11 Mike Piazza S 10.00 4.00
❑ S13 Larry Walker S 2.50 1.00
❑ S14 Matt Williams S 2.50 1.00
❑ S22 Tim Salmon S 4.00 1.50
❑ S35 Edgar Martinez S 4.00 1.50
❑ S37 Gregg Jefferies S 2.50 1.00
❑ S38 Bill Pulsipher S 2.50 1.00
❑ S41 Shawn Green S 2.50 1.00
❑ S43 Jim Abbott S 4.00 1.50
❑ S46 Roger Clemens S 12.00 5.00
❑ S52 Rondell White S 2.50 1.00
❑ S54 Dennis Eckersley S 2.50 1.00
❑ S59 Hideo Nomo S 6.00 2.50
❑ S60 Gary Sheffield S 2.50 1.00
❑ S62 Will Clark S 4.00 1.50
❑ S65 Bret Boone S 2.50 1.00
❑ S68 Rafael Palmeiro S 4.00 1.50
❑ S69 Carlos Baerga S 2.50 1.00
❑ S72 Tom Glavine S 4.00 1.50
❑ S73 Garret Anderson S 2.50 1.00
❑ S77 Randy Johnson S 6.00 2.50
❑ S78 Jeff King S 2.50 1.00
❑ S79 Kirby Puckett S 6.00 2.50
❑ S84 Cecil Fielder S 2.50 1.00
❑ S86 Reggie Sanders S 2.50 1.00
❑ S88 Ryan Klesko S 2.50 1.00
❑ S91 John Valentin S 2.50 1.00
❑ S95 Manny Ramirez S 4.00 1.50
❑ S99 Vinny Castilla S 2.50 1.00
❑ S109 Carlos Perez S 2.50 1.00
❑ S112 Craig Biggio S 4.00 1.50
❑ S115 Juan Gonzalez S 2.50 1.00
❑ S121 Ray Durham S 2.50 1.00
❑ S127 C.J. Nitkowski S 2.50 1.00
❑ S130 Raul Mondesi S 2.50 1.00
❑ S142 Lee Smith S 2.50 1.00
❑ S143 Joe Carter S 2.50 1.00
❑ S151 Mo Vaughn S 2.50 1.00
❑ S153 Frank Rodriguez S 2.50 1.00
❑ S160 Steve Finley S 2.50 1.00
❑ S161 Jeff Bagwell S 4.00 1.50
❑ S165 Cal Ripken S 20.00 8.00
❑ S168 Lyle Mouton S 2.50 1.00
❑ S171 Sammy Sosa S 6.00 2.50
❑ S174 John Franco S 2.50 1.00
❑ S179 Greg Vaughn S 2.50 1.00
❑ S180 Mark Wohlers S 2.50 1.00
❑ S182 Paul O'Neill S 4.00 1.50
❑ S188 Albert Belle S 2.50 1.00
❑ S189 Mark Grace S 4.00 1.50
❑ S211 Ernie Young S 2.50 1.00
❑ S210 Fred McGriff S 4.00 1.50
❑ S223 Kimera Bartee S 2.50 1.00
❑ S229 Rickey Henderson S 6.00 2.50
❑ S230 Sterling Hitchcock S 2.50 1.00
❑ S231 Bernard Gilkey S 2.50 1.00
❑ S234 Ryne Sandberg S 10.00 4.00
❑ S235 Greg Maddux S 10.00 4.00
❑ S239 Todd Stottlemyre S 2.50 1.00
❑ S241 Jason Kendall S 2.50 1.00
❑ S242 Paul O'Neill S 4.00 1.50
❑ S256 Devon White S 2.50 1.00
❑ S261 Chuck Knoblauch S 2.50 1.00
❑ S263 Wally Joyner S 2.50 1.00
❑ S272 Andy Fox S 2.50 1.00
❑ S274 Sean Berry S 2.50 1.00
❑ S277 Benito Santiago S 2.50 1.00
❑ S284 Chad Mottola S 2.50 1.00
❑ S289 Dante Bichette S 2.50 1.00
❑ S291 Dwight Gooden S 2.50 1.00
❑ S293 Kevin Mitchell S 2.50 1.00
❑ S295 Russ Davis S 2.50 1.00
❑ S296 Chan Ho Park S 2.50 1.00
❑ S302 Larry Walker S 2.50 1.00
❑ S305 Ken Griffey Jr. S 10.00 4.00
❑ S313 Billy Wagner S 2.50 1.00
❑ S317 Mike Grace S RC 2.50 1.00
❑ S327 Kenny Lofton S 2.50 1.00
❑ S328 Derek Bell S 2.50 1.00
❑ S337 Gary Sheffield S 2.50 1.00
❑ S341 Mark Grace S 4.00 1.50
❑ S345 Andres Galarraga S 2.50 1.00
❑ S346 Brady Anderson S 2.50 1.00
❑ S350 Derek Jeter S 12.00 5.00
❑ S353 Jay Buhner S 2.50 1.00
❑ S357 Tino Martinez S 4.00 1.50

1997 Finest

❑ COMP.BRONZE SER.1 (100) 30.00 12.50
❑ COMP.BRONZE SER.2 (100) 30.00 12.50
❑ COM.BRON.(1-100/176-275) .50 .20
❑ COMP.SILVER SER.1 (50)
❑ COMP.SILVER SER.2 (50)

❑ COM.SILV.(101-150/276-325) 2.00 .75
❑ COMP.GOLD SER.1 (25)
❑ COMP.GOLD SER.2 (25)
❑ COM.GOLD (151-175/326-350) 5.00 2.00
❑ BICHETTE/JETER BOTH NUMBERED 155
❑ BICHETTE UER SHOULD BE NUMBER 5
❑ 1 Barry Bonds B 3.00 1.25
❑ 2 Ryne Sandberg B 2.00 .75
❑ 3 Brian Jordan B .50 .20
❑ 4 Rocky Coppinger B .50 .20
❑ 5 Dante Bichette B UER 15 .50 .20
❑ 6 Al Martin B .50 .20
❑ 7 Charles Nagy B .50 .20
❑ 8 Otis Nixon B .50 .20
❑ 9 Mark Johnson B .50 .20
❑ 10 Jeff Bagwell B .75 .30
❑ 11 Ken Hill B .50 .20
❑ 12 Willie Adams B .50 .20
❑ 13 Raul Mondesi B .50 .20
❑ 14 Reggie Sanders B .50 .20
❑ 15 Derek Jeter B 3.00 1.25
❑ 16 Jermaine Dye B .50 .20
❑ 17 Edgar Renteria B .50 .20
❑ 18 Travis Fryman B .50 .20
❑ 19 Roberto Hernandez B .50 .20
❑ 20 Sammy Sosa B 1.25 .50
❑ 21 Garret Anderson B .50 .20
❑ 22 Rey Ordonez B .50 .20
❑ 23 Glenallen Hill B .50 .20
❑ 24 Dave Nilsson B .50 .20
❑ 25 Kevin Brown B .50 .20
❑ 26 Brian McRae B .50 .20
❑ 27 Joey Hamilton B .50 .20
❑ 28 Jamey Wright B .50 .20
❑ 29 Frank Thomas B 1.25 .50
❑ 30 Mark McGwire B 3.00 1.25
❑ 31 Ramon Martinez B .50 .20
❑ 32 Jaime Bluma B .50 .20
❑ 33 Frank Rodriguez B .50 .20
❑ 34 Andy Benes B .50 .20
❑ 35 Jay Buhner B .50 .20
❑ 36 Justin Thompson B .50 .20
❑ 37 Darin Erstad B .50 .20
❑ 38 Gregg Jefferies B .50 .20
❑ 39 Jeff D'Amico B .50 .20
❑ 40 Pedro Martinez B .75 .30
❑ 41 Nomar Garciaparra B 2.00 .75
❑ 42 Jose Valentin B .50 .20
❑ 43 Pat Hentgen B .50 .20
❑ 44 Will Clark B .75 .30
❑ 45 Bernie Williams B .75 .30
❑ 46 Luis Castillo B .50 .20
❑ 47 B.J. Surhoff B .50 .20
❑ 48 Greg Gagne B .50 .20
❑ 49 Pete Schourek B .50 .20
❑ 50 Mike Piazza B 2.00 .75
❑ 51 Dwight Gooden B .50 .20
❑ 52 Javy Lopez B .50 .20
❑ 53 Chuck Finley B .50 .20
❑ 54 James Baldwin B .50 .20
❑ 55 Jack McDowell B .50 .20
❑ 56 Royce Clayton B .50 .20
❑ 57 Carlos Delgado B .50 .20
❑ 58 Neifi Perez B .50 .20
❑ 59 Eddie Taubensee B .50 .20
❑ 60 Rafael Palmeiro B .75 .30
❑ 61 Marty Cordova B .50 .20
❑ 62 Wade Boggs B .75 .30

❑ 63 Rickey Henderson B 1.25 .50
❑ 64 Mike Hampton B .50 .20
❑ 65 Troy Percival B .50 .20
❑ 66 Barry Larkin B .75 .30
❑ 67 Jermaine Allensworth B .50 .20
❑ 68 Mark Clark B .50 .20
❑ 69 Mike Lansing B .50 .20
❑ 70 Mark Grudzielanek B .50 .20
❑ 71 Todd Stottlemyre B .50 .20
❑ 72 Juan Guzman B .50 .20
❑ 73 John Burkett B .50 .20
❑ 74 Wilson Alvarez B .50 .20
❑ 75 Ellis Burks B .50 .20
❑ 76 Bobby Higginson B .50 .20
❑ 77 Ricky Bottalico B .50 .20
❑ 78 Omar Vizquel B .75 .30
❑ 79 Paul Sorrento B .50 .20
❑ 80 Denny Neagle B .50 .20
❑ 81 Roger Pavlik B .50 .20
❑ 82 Mike Lieberthal B .50 .20
❑ 83 Devon White B .50 .20
❑ 84 John Olerud B .50 .20
❑ 85 Kevin Appier B .50 .20
❑ 86 Joe Girardi B .50 .20
❑ 87 Paul O'Neill B .75 .30
❑ 88 Mike Sweeney B .50 .20
❑ 89 John Smiley B .50 .20
❑ 90 Ivan Rodriguez B .75 .30
❑ 91 Randy Myers B .50 .20
❑ 92 Bip Roberts B .50 .20
❑ 93 Jose Mesa B .50 .20
❑ 94 Paul Wilson B .50 .20
❑ 95 Mike Mussina B .75 .30
❑ 96 Ben McDonald B .50 .20
❑ 97 John Mabry B .50 .20
❑ 98 Tom Goodwin B .50 .20
❑ 99 Edgar Martinez B .75 .30
❑ 100 Andruw Jones B .75 .30
❑ 101 Jose Canseco S 3.00 1.25
❑ 102 Billy Wagner S 2.00 .75
❑ 103 Dante Bichette S 2.00 .75
❑ 104 Curt Schilling S 2.00 .75
❑ 105 Dean Palmer S 2.00 .75
❑ 106 Larry Walker S 2.00 .75
❑ 107 Bernie Williams S 3.00 1.25
❑ 108 Chipper Jones S 5.00 2.00
❑ 109 Gary Sheffield S 2.00 .75
❑ 110 Randy Johnson S 5.00 2.00
❑ 111 Roberto Alomar S 3.00 1.25
❑ 112 Todd Walker S 2.00 .75
❑ 113 Sandy Alomar Jr. S 2.00 .75
❑ 114 John Jaha S 2.00 .75
❑ 115 Ken Caminiti S 2.00 .75
❑ 116 Ryan Klesko S 2.00 .75
❑ 117 Mariano Rivera S 5.00 2.00
❑ 118 Jason Giambi S 2.00 .75
❑ 119 Lance Johnson S 2.00 .75
❑ 120 Robin Ventura S 2.00 .75
❑ 121 Todd Hollandsworth S 2.00 .75
❑ 122 Johnny Damon S 3.00 1.25
❑ 123 William VanLandingham S 2.00 .75
❑ 124 Jason Kendall S 2.00 .75
❑ 125 Vinny Castilla S 2.00 .75
❑ 126 Harold Baines S 2.00 .75
❑ 127 Joe Carter S 2.00 .75
❑ 128 Craig Biggio S 3.00 1.25
❑ 129 Tony Clark S 2.00 .75
❑ 130 Ron Gant S 2.00 .75
❑ 131 David Segui S 2.00 .75
❑ 132 Steve Trachsel S 2.00 .75
❑ 133 Scott Rolen S 3.00 1.25
❑ 134 Mike Stanley S 2.00 .75
❑ 135 Cal Ripken S 15.00 6.00
❑ 136 John Smoltz S 3.00 1.25
❑ 137 Bobby Jones S 2.00 .75
❑ 138 Manny Ramirez S 3.00 1.25
❑ 139 Ken Griffey Jr. S 8.00 3.00
❑ 140 Chuck Knoblauch S 2.00 .75
❑ 141 Mark Grace S 3.00 1.25
❑ 142 Chris Snopek S 2.00 .75
❑ 143 Hideo Nomo S 5.00 2.00
❑ 144 Tim Salmon S 3.00 1.25
❑ 145 David Cone S 2.00 .75
❑ 146 Eric Young S 2.00 .75
❑ 147 Jeff Brantley S 2.00 .75
❑ 148 Jim Thome S 3.00 1.25
❑ 149 Trevor Hoffman S 2.00 .75
❑ 150 Juan Gonzalez S 2.00 .75
❑ 151 Mike Piazza G 20.00 8.00
❑ 152 Ivan Rodriguez G 8.00 3.00
❑ 153 Mo Vaughn G 5.00 2.00
❑ 154 Brady Anderson G 5.00 2.00
❑ 155 Mark McGwire G 30.00 12.50
❑ 156 Rafael Palmeiro G 8.00 3.00
❑ 157 Barry Larkin G 8.00 3.00
❑ 158 Greg Maddux G 20.00 8.00
❑ 159 Jeff Bagwell G 8.00 3.00
❑ 160 Frank Thomas G 12.00 5.00
❑ 161 Ken Caminiti G 5.00 2.00
❑ 162 Andruw Jones G 8.00 3.00
❑ 163 Dennis Eckersley G 5.00 2.00
❑ 164 Jeff Conine G 5.00 2.00
❑ 165 Jim Edmonds G 5.00 2.00
❑ 166 Derek Jeter G 30.00 12.50
❑ 167 Vladimir Guerrero G 12.00 5.00
❑ 168 Sammy Sosa G 12.00 5.00
❑ 169 Tony Gwynn G 15.00 6.00
❑ 170 Andres Galarraga G 5.00 2.00
❑ 171 Todd Hundley G 5.00 2.00
❑ 172 Jay Buhner G 5.00 2.00
❑ 173 Paul Molitor G 5.00 2.00
❑ 174 Kenny Lofton G 5.00 2.00
❑ 175 Barry Bonds G 30.00 12.50
❑ 176 Gary Sheffield B .50 .20
❑ 177 Dmitri Young B .50 .20
❑ 178 Jay Bell B .50 .20
❑ 179 David Wells B .50 .20
❑ 180 Walt Weiss B .50 .20
❑ 181 Paul Molitor B .50 .20
❑ 182 Jose Guillen B .50 .20
❑ 183 Al Leiter B .50 .20
❑ 184 Mike Fetters B .50 .20
❑ 185 Mark Langston B .50 .20
❑ 186 Fred McGriff B .75 .30
❑ 187 Darrin Fletcher B .50 .20
❑ 188 Brant Brown B .50 .20
❑ 189 Geronimo Berroa B .50 .20
❑ 190 Jim Thome B .75 .30
❑ 191 Jose Vizcaino B .50 .20
❑ 192 Andy Ashby B .50 .20
❑ 193 Rusty Greer B .50 .20
❑ 194 Brian Hunter B .50 .20
❑ 195 Chris Hoiles B .50 .20
❑ 196 Orlando Merced B .50 .20
❑ 197 Brett Butler B .50 .20
❑ 198 Derek Bell B .50 .20
❑ 199 Bobby Bonilla B .50 .20
❑ 200 Alex Ochoa B .50 .20
❑ 201 Wally Joyner B .50 .20
❑ 202 Mo Vaughn B .50 .20
❑ 203 Doug Drabek B .50 .20
❑ 204 Tino Martinez B .75 .30
❑ 205 Roberto Alomar B .75 .30
❑ 206 Brian Giles B RC 3.00 1.25
❑ 207 Todd Worrell B .50 .20
❑ 208 Alan Benes B .50 .20
❑ 209 Jim Leyritz B .50 .20
❑ 210 Darryl Hamilton B .50 .20
❑ 211 Jimmy Key B .50 .20
❑ 212 Juan Gonzalez B .50 .20
❑ 213 Vinny Castilla B .50 .20
❑ 214 Chuck Knoblauch B .50 .20
❑ 215 Tony Phillips B .50 .20
❑ 216 Jeff Cirillo B .50 .20
❑ 217 Carlos Garcia B .50 .20
❑ 218 Brooks Kieschnick B .50 .20
❑ 219 Marquis Grissom B .50 .20
❑ 220 Dan Wilson B .50 .20
❑ 221 Greg Vaughn B .50 .20
❑ 222 John Wetteland B .50 .20
❑ 223 Andres Galarraga B .50 .20
❑ 224 Ozzie Guillen B .50 .20
❑ 225 Kevin Elster B .50 .20
❑ 226 Bernard Gilkey B .50 .20
❑ 227 Mike Macfarlane B .50 .20
❑ 228 Heathcliff Slocumb B .50 .20
❑ 229 Wendell Magee Jr. B .50 .20
❑ 230 Carlos Baerga B .50 .20
❑ 231 Kevin Seitzer B .50 .20
❑ 232 Henry Rodriguez B .50 .20
❑ 233 Roger Clemens B 2.50 1.00
❑ 234 Mark Wohlers B .50 .20
❑ 235 Eddie Murray B 1.25 .50
❑ 236 Todd Zeile B .50 .20
❑ 237 J.T. Snow B .50 .20
❑ 238 Ken Griffey Jr. B 2.00 .75
❑ 239 Sterling Hitchcock B .50 .20
❑ 240 Albert Belle B .50 .20
❑ 241 Terry Steinbach B .50 .20
❑ 242 Robb Nen B .50 .20
❑ 243 Mark McLemore B .50 .20
❑ 244 Jeff King B .50 .20
❑ 245 Tony Clark B .50 .20
❑ 246 Tim Salmon B .75 .30
❑ 247 Benito Santiago B .50 .20
❑ 248 Robin Ventura B .50 .20
❑ 249 Bubba Trammell B RC .50 .20
❑ 250 Chili Davis B .50 .20
❑ 251 John Valentin B .50 .20
❑ 252 Cal Ripken B 4.00 1.50
❑ 253 Matt Williams B .50 .20
❑ 254 Jeff Kent B .50 .20
❑ 255 Eric Karros B .50 .20
❑ 256 Ray Lankford B .50 .20
❑ 257 Ed Sprague B .50 .20
❑ 258 Shane Reynolds B .50 .20
❑ 259 Jaime Navarro B .50 .20
❑ 260 Eric Davis B .50 .20
❑ 261 Orel Hershiser B .50 .20
❑ 262 Mark Grace B .75 .30
❑ 263 Rod Beck B .50 .20
❑ 264 Ismael Valdes B .50 .20
❑ 265 Manny Ramirez B .75 .30
❑ 266 Ken Caminiti B .50 .20
❑ 267 Tim Naehring B .50 .20
❑ 268 Jose Rosado B .50 .20
❑ 269 Greg Colbrunn B .50 .20
❑ 270 Dean Palmer B .50 .20
❑ 271 David Justice B .50 .20
❑ 272 Scott Spiezio B .50 .20
❑ 273 Chipper Jones B 1.25 .50
❑ 274 Mel Rojas B .50 .20
❑ 275 Bartolo Colon B .50 .20
❑ 276 Darin Erstad S 2.00 .75
❑ 277 Sammy Sosa S 5.00 2.00
❑ 278 Rafael Palmeiro S 3.00 1.25
❑ 279 Frank Thomas S 5.00 2.00
❑ 280 Ruben Rivera S 2.00 .75
❑ 281 Hal Morris S 2.00 .75
❑ 282 Jay Buhner S 2.00 .75
❑ 283 Kenny Lofton S 2.00 .75
❑ 284 Jose Canseco S 3.00 1.25
❑ 285 Alex Fernandez S 2.00 .75
❑ 286 Todd Helton S 5.00 2.00
❑ 287 Andy Pettitte S 3.00 1.25
❑ 288 John Franco S 2.00 .75
❑ 289 Ivan Rodriguez S 3.00 1.25
❑ 290 Ellis Burks S 2.00 .75
❑ 291 Julio Franco S 2.00 .75
❑ 292 Mike Piazza S 8.00 3.00
❑ 293 Brian Jordan S 2.00 .75
❑ 294 Greg Maddux S 8.00 3.00
❑ 295 Bob Abreu S 3.00 1.25
❑ 296 Rondell White S 2.00 .75
❑ 297 Moises Alou S 2.00 .75
❑ 298 Tony Gwynn S 6.00 2.50
❑ 299 Deion Sanders S 3.00 1.25
❑ 300 Jeff Montgomery S 2.00 .75
❑ 301 Ray Durham S 2.00 .75
❑ 302 John Wasdin S 2.00 .75
❑ 303 Ryne Sandberg S 8.00 3.00
❑ 304 Delino DeShields S 2.00 .75
❑ 305 Mark McGwire S 12.00 5.00
❑ 306 Andruw Jones S 3.00 1.25
❑ 307 Kevin Orie S 2.00 .75
❑ 308 Matt Williams S 2.00 .75
❑ 309 Karim Garcia S 2.00 .75
❑ 310 Derek Jeter S 12.00 5.00
❑ 311 Mo Vaughn S 2.00 .75
❑ 312 Brady Anderson S 2.00 .75
❑ 313 Barry Bonds S 12.00 5.00
❑ 314 Steve Finley S 2.00 .75
❑ 315 Vladimir Guerrero S 5.00 2.00
❑ 316 Matt Morris S 2.00 .75
❑ 317 Tom Glavine S 3.00 1.25
❑ 318 Jeff Bagwell S 3.00 1.25
❑ 319 Albert Belle S 2.00 .75
❑ 320 Hideki Irabu S RC 2.00 .75

Card		
❑ 321 Andres Galarraga S	2.00	.75
❑ 322 Cecil Fielder S	2.00	.75
❑ 323 Barry Larkin S	3.00	1.25
❑ 324 Todd Hundley S	2.00	.75
❑ 325 Fred McGriff S	3.00	1.25
❑ 326 Gary Sheffield G	5.00	2.00
❑ 327 Craig Biggio G	8.00	3.00
❑ 328 Raul Mondesi G	5.00	2.00
❑ 329 Edgar Martinez G	8.00	3.00
❑ 330 Chipper Jones G	12.00	5.00
❑ 331 Bernie Williams G	8.00	3.00
❑ 332 Juan Gonzalez G	5.00	2.00
❑ 333 Ron Gant G	5.00	2.00
❑ 334 Cal Ripken G	40.00	15.00
❑ 335 Larry Walker G	5.00	2.00
❑ 336 Matt Williams G	5.00	2.00
❑ 337 Jose Cruz Jr. G RC	5.00	2.00
❑ 338 Joe Carter G	5.00	2.00
❑ 339 Wilton Guerrero G	5.00	2.00
❑ 340 Cecil Fielder G	5.00	2.00
❑ 341 Todd Walker G	5.00	2.00
❑ 342 Ken Griffey Jr. G	20.00	8.00
❑ 343 Ryan Klesko G	5.00	2.00
❑ 344 Roger Clemens G	25.00	10.00
❑ 345 Hideo Nomo G	12.00	5.00
❑ 346 Dante Bichette G	5.00	2.00
❑ 347 Albert Belle G	5.00	2.00
❑ 348 Randy Johnson G	12.00	5.00
❑ 349 Manny Ramirez G	8.00	3.00
❑ 350 John Smoltz G	8.00	3.00

1998 Finest

Card		
❑ COMPLETE SET (275)	50.00	20.00
❑ COMPLETE SERIES 1 (150)	25.00	10.00
❑ COMPLETE SERIES 2 (125)	25.00	10.00
❑ 1 Larry Walker	.40	.15
❑ 2 Andruw Jones	.60	.25
❑ 3 Ramon Martinez	.25	.08
❑ 4 Geronimo Berroa	.25	.08
❑ 5 David Justice	.40	.15
❑ 6 Rusty Greer	.40	.15
❑ 7 Chad Ogea	.25	.08
❑ 8 Tom Goodwin	.25	.08
❑ 9 Tino Martinez	.60	.25
❑ 10 Jose Guillen	.40	.15
❑ 11 Jeffrey Hammonds	.25	.08
❑ 12 Brian McRae	.25	.08
❑ 13 Jeremi Gonzalez	.25	.08
❑ 14 Craig Counsell	.25	.08
❑ 15 Mike Piazza	1.50	.60
❑ 16 Greg Maddux	1.50	.60
❑ 17 Todd Greene	.25	.08
❑ 18 Rondell White	.40	.15
❑ 19 Kirk Rueter	.25	.08
❑ 20 Tony Clark	.25	.08
❑ 21 Brad Radke	.40	.15
❑ 22 Jaret Wright	.25	.08
❑ 23 Carlos Delgado	.40	.15
❑ 24 Dustin Hermanson	.25	.08
❑ 25 Gary Sheffield	.40	.15
❑ 26 Jose Canseco	.60	.25
❑ 27 Kevin Young	.40	.15
❑ 28 David Wells	.40	.15
❑ 29 Mariano Rivera	1.00	.40
❑ 30 Reggie Sanders	.40	.15
❑ 31 Mike Cameron	.25	.08
❑ 32 Bobby Witt	.25	.08
❑ 33 Kevin Orie	.25	.08
❑ 34 Royce Clayton	.25	.08
❑ 35 Edgar Martinez	.60	.25
❑ 36 Neifi Perez	.25	.08
❑ 37 Kevin Appier	.40	.15
❑ 38 Darryl Hamilton	.25	.08
❑ 39 Michael Tucker	.25	.08
❑ 40 Roger Clemens	2.00	.75
❑ 41 Carl Everett	.40	.15
❑ 42 Mike Sweeney	.40	.15
❑ 43 Pat Meares	.25	.08
❑ 44 Brian Giles	.40	.15
❑ 45 Matt Morris	.40	.15
❑ 46 Jason Dickson	.25	.08
❑ 47 Rich Loiselle RC	.40	.15
❑ 48 Joe Girardi	.25	.08
❑ 49 Steve Trachsel	.25	.08
❑ 50 Ben Grieve	.25	.08
❑ 51 Brian Johnson	.25	.08
❑ 52 Hideki Irabu	.25	.08
❑ 53 J.T. Snow	.40	.15
❑ 54 Mike Hampton	.40	.15
❑ 55 Dave Nilsson	.25	.08
❑ 56 Alex Fernandez	.25	.08
❑ 57 Brett Tomko	.25	.08
❑ 58 Wally Joyner	.40	.15
❑ 59 Kelvim Escobar	.25	.08
❑ 60 Roberto Alomar	.60	.25
❑ 61 Todd Jones	.25	.08
❑ 62 Paul O'Neill	.60	.25
❑ 63 Jamie Moyer	.40	.15
❑ 64 Mark Wohlers	.25	.08
❑ 65 Jose Cruz Jr.	.25	.08
❑ 66 Troy Percival	.40	.15
❑ 67 Rick Reed	.25	.08
❑ 68 Will Clark	.60	.25
❑ 69 Jamey Wright	.25	.08
❑ 70 Mike Mussina	.60	.25
❑ 71 David Cone	.40	.15
❑ 72 Ryan Klesko	.40	.15
❑ 73 Scott Hatteberg	.25	.08
❑ 74 James Baldwin	.25	.08
❑ 75 Tony Womack	.25	.08
❑ 76 Carlos Perez	.25	.08
❑ 77 Charles Nagy	.25	.08
❑ 78 Jeromy Burnitz	.40	.15
❑ 79 Shane Reynolds	.25	.08
❑ 80 Cliff Floyd	.40	.15
❑ 81 Jason Kendall	.40	.15
❑ 82 Chad Curtis	.25	.08
❑ 83 Matt Karchner	.25	.08
❑ 84 Ricky Bottalico	.25	.08
❑ 85 Sammy Sosa	1.00	.40
❑ 86 Javy Lopez	.40	.15
❑ 87 Jeff Kent	.40	.15
❑ 88 Shawn Green	.40	.15
❑ 89 Joey Cora	.25	.08
❑ 90 Tony Gwynn	1.25	.50
❑ 91 Bob Tewksbury	.25	.08
❑ 92 Derek Jeter	2.50	1.00
❑ 93 Eric Davis	.40	.15
❑ 94 Jeff Fassero	.25	.08
❑ 95 Denny Neagle	.25	.08
❑ 96 Ismael Valdes	.25	.08
❑ 97 Tim Salmon	.60	.25
❑ 98 Mark Grudzielanek	.25	.08
❑ 99 Curt Schilling	.40	.15
❑ 100 Ken Griffey Jr.	1.50	.60
❑ 101 Edgardo Alfonzo	.25	.08
❑ 102 Vinny Castilla	.40	.15
❑ 103 Jose Rosado	.25	.08
❑ 104 Scott Erickson	.25	.08
❑ 105 Alan Benes	.25	.08
❑ 106 Shannon Stewart	.40	.15
❑ 107 Delino DeShields	.25	.08
❑ 108 Mark Loretta	.25	.08
❑ 109 Todd Hundley	.25	.08
❑ 110 Chuck Knoblauch	.40	.15
❑ 111 Todd Helton	.60	.25
❑ 112 F.P. Santangelo	.25	.08
❑ 113 Jeff Cirillo	.25	.08
❑ 114 Omar Vizquel	.60	.25
❑ 115 John Valentin	.25	.08
❑ 116 Damion Easley	.25	.08
❑ 117 Matt Lawton	.25	.08
❑ 118 Jim Thome	.60	.25
❑ 119 Sandy Alomar Jr.	.25	.08
❑ 120 Albert Belle	.40	.15
❑ 121 Chris Stynes	.25	.08
❑ 122 Butch Huskey	.25	.08
❑ 123 Shawn Estes	.25	.08
❑ 124 Terry Adams	.25	.08
❑ 125 Ivan Rodriguez	.60	.25
❑ 126 Ron Gant	.40	.15
❑ 127 John Mabry	.25	.08
❑ 128 Jeff Shaw	.25	.08
❑ 129 Jeff Montgomery	.25	.08
❑ 130 Justin Thompson	.25	.08
❑ 131 Livan Hernandez	.40	.15
❑ 132 Ugueth Urbina	.25	.08
❑ 133 Scott Servais	.25	.08
❑ 134 Troy O'Leary	.25	.08
❑ 135 Cal Ripken	3.00	1.25
❑ 136 Quilvio Veras	.25	.08
❑ 137 Pedro Astacio	.25	.08
❑ 138 Willie Greene	.25	.08
❑ 139 Lance Johnson	.25	.08
❑ 140 Nomar Garciaparra	1.50	.60
❑ 141 Jose Offerman	.25	.08
❑ 142 Scott Rolen	.60	.25
❑ 143 Derek Bell	.25	.08
❑ 144 Johnny Damon	.60	.25
❑ 145 Mark McGwire	2.50	1.00
❑ 146 Chan Ho Park	.40	.15
❑ 147 Edgar Renteria	.40	.15
❑ 148 Eric Young	.25	.08
❑ 149 Craig Biggio	.60	.25
❑ 150 Checklist (1-150)	.25	.08
❑ 151 Frank Thomas	1.00	.40
❑ 152 John Wetteland	.40	.15
❑ 153 Mike Lansing	.25	.08
❑ 154 Pedro Martinez	.60	.25
❑ 155 Rico Brogna	.25	.08
❑ 156 Kevin Brown	.60	.25
❑ 157 Alex Rodriguez	1.50	.60
❑ 158 Wade Boggs	.60	.25
❑ 159 Richard Hidalgo	.25	.08
❑ 160 Mark Grace	.60	.25
❑ 161 Jose Mesa	.25	.08
❑ 162 John Olerud	.40	.15
❑ 163 Tim Belcher	.25	.08
❑ 164 Chuck Finley	.40	.15
❑ 165 Brian Hunter	.25	.08
❑ 166 Joe Carter	.40	.15
❑ 167 Stan Javier	.25	.08
❑ 168 Jay Bell	.40	.15
❑ 169 Ray Lankford	.40	.15
❑ 170 John Smoltz	.60	.25
❑ 171 Ed Sprague	.25	.08
❑ 172 Jason Giambi	.40	.15
❑ 173 Todd Walker	.25	.08
❑ 174 Paul Konerko	.40	.15
❑ 175 Rey Ordonez	.25	.08
❑ 176 Dante Bichette	.40	.15
❑ 177 Bernie Williams	.60	.25
❑ 178 Jon Nunnally	.25	.08
❑ 179 Rafael Palmeiro	.60	.25
❑ 180 Jay Buhner	.40	.15
❑ 181 Devon White	.40	.15
❑ 182 Jeff D'Amico	.25	.08
❑ 183 Walt Weiss	.40	.15
❑ 184 Scott Spiezio	.25	.08
❑ 185 Moises Alou	.40	.15
❑ 186 Carlos Baerga	.25	.08
❑ 187 Todd Zeile	.40	.15
❑ 188 Gregg Jefferies	.25	.08
❑ 189 Mo Vaughn	.40	.15
❑ 190 Terry Steinbach	.25	.08
❑ 191 Ray Durham	.40	.15
❑ 192 Robin Ventura	.40	.15
❑ 193 Jeff Reed	.25	.08
❑ 194 Ken Caminiti	.40	.15
❑ 195 Eric Karros	.40	.15
❑ 196 Wilson Alvarez	.25	.08
❑ 197 Gary Gaetti	.40	.15
❑ 198 Andres Galarraga	.40	.15
❑ 199 Alex Gonzalez	.25	.08
❑ 200 Garret Anderson	.40	.15
❑ 201 Andy Benes	.25	.08
❑ 202 Harold Baines	.40	.15
❑ 203 Ron Coomer	.25	.08
❑ 204 Dean Palmer	.40	.15
❑ 205 Reggie Jefferson	.25	.08

❑ 206	John Burkett	.25	.08
❑ 207	Jermaine Allensworth	.25	.08
❑ 208	Bernard Gilkey	.25	.08
❑ 209	Jeff Bagwell	.60	.25
❑ 210	Kenny Lofton	.40	.15
❑ 211	Bobby Jones	.25	.08
❑ 212	Bartolo Colon	.40	.15
❑ 213	Jim Edmonds	.40	.15
❑ 214	Pat Hentgen	.25	.08
❑ 215	Matt Williams	.40	.15
❑ 216	Bob Abreu	.40	.15
❑ 217	Jorge Posada	.60	.25
❑ 218	Marty Cordova	.25	.08
❑ 219	Ken Hill	.25	.08
❑ 220	Steve Finley	.40	.15
❑ 221	Jeff King	.25	.08
❑ 222	Quinton McCracken	.25	.08
❑ 223	Matt Stairs	.25	.08
❑ 224	Darin Erstad	.40	.15
❑ 225	Fred McGriff	.60	.25
❑ 226	Marquis Grissom	.40	.15
❑ 227	Doug Glanville	.25	.08
❑ 228	Tom Glavine	.60	.25
❑ 229	John Franco	.40	.15
❑ 230	Darren Bragg	.25	.08
❑ 231	Barry Larkin	.60	.25
❑ 232	Trevor Hoffman	.40	.15
❑ 233	Brady Anderson	.40	.15
❑ 234	Al Martin	.25	.08
❑ 235	B.J. Surhoff	.40	.15
❑ 236	Ellis Burks	.40	.15
❑ 237	Randy Johnson	1.00	.40
❑ 238	Mark Clark	.25	.08
❑ 239	Tony Saunders	.25	.08
❑ 240	Hideo Nomo	1.00	.40
❑ 241	Brad Fullmer	.25	.08
❑ 242	Chipper Jones	1.00	.40
❑ 243	Jose Valentin	.25	.08
❑ 244	Manny Ramirez	.60	.25
❑ 245	Derrek Lee	.60	.25
❑ 246	Jimmy Key	.40	.15
❑ 247	Tim Naehring	.25	.08
❑ 248	Bobby Higginson	.40	.15
❑ 249	Charles Johnson	.40	.15
❑ 250	Chili Davis	.40	.15
❑ 251	Tom Gordon	.25	.08
❑ 252	Mike Lieberthal	.40	.15
❑ 253	Billy Wagner	.40	.15
❑ 254	Juan Guzman	.25	.08
❑ 255	Todd Stottlemyre	.25	.08
❑ 256	Brian Jordan	.40	.15
❑ 257	Barry Bonds	2.50	1.00
❑ 258	Dan Wilson	.25	.08
❑ 259	Paul Molitor	.40	.15
❑ 260	Juan Gonzalez	.40	.15
❑ 261	Francisco Cordova	.25	.08
❑ 262	Cecil Fielder	.40	.15
❑ 263	Travis Lee	.25	.08
❑ 264	Kevin Tapani	.25	.08
❑ 265	Raul Mondesi	.40	.15
❑ 266	Travis Fryman	.40	.15
❑ 267	Armando Benitez	.25	.08
❑ 268	Pokey Reese	.25	.08
❑ 269	Rick Aguilera	.25	.08
❑ 270	Andy Pettitte	.60	.25
❑ 271	Jose Vizcaino	.25	.08
❑ 272	Kerry Wood	.50	.20
❑ 273	Vladimir Guerrero	1.00	.40
❑ 274	John Smiley	.25	.08
❑ 275	Checklist (151-275)	.25	.08

1999 Finest

❑	COMPLETE SET (300)	80.00	30.00
❑	COMPLETE SERIES 1 (150)	40.00	15.00
❑	COMPLETE SERIES 2 (150)	40.00	15.00
❑	COMP.SER.1 w/o SP's (100)	15.00	6.00
❑	COMP.SER.2 w/o SP's (100)	15.00	6.00
❑	COMMON (1-100/151-250)	.40	.15
❑	COMMON (101-150/251-300)	.50	.20
❑ 1	Darin Erstad	.40	.15
❑ 2	Javy Lopez	.40	.15
❑ 3	Vinny Castilla	.40	.15
❑ 4	Jim Thome	.60	.25
❑ 5	Tino Martinez	.60	.25
❑ 6	Mark Grace	.60	.25
❑ 7	Shawn Green	.40	.15
❑ 8	Dustin Hermanson	.40	.15
❑ 9	Kevin Young	.40	.15
❑ 10	Tony Clark	.40	.15
❑ 11	Scott Brosius	.40	.15
❑ 12	Craig Biggio	.60	.25
❑ 13	Brian McRae	.40	.15
❑ 14	Chan Ho Park	.40	.15
❑ 15	Manny Ramirez	.60	.25
❑ 16	Chipper Jones	1.00	.40
❑ 17	Rico Brogna	.40	.15
❑ 18	Quinton McCracken	.40	.15
❑ 19	J.T. Snow	.40	.15
❑ 20	Tony Gwynn	1.25	.50
❑ 21	Juan Guzman	.40	.15
❑ 22	John Valentin	.40	.15
❑ 23	Rick Helling	.40	.15
❑ 24	Sandy Alomar Jr.	.40	.15
❑ 25	Frank Thomas	1.00	.40
❑ 26	Jorge Posada	.60	.25
❑ 27	Dmitri Young	.40	.15
❑ 28	Rick Reed	.40	.15
❑ 29	Kevin Tapani	.40	.15
❑ 30	Troy Glaus	.60	.25
❑ 31	Kenny Rogers	.40	.15
❑ 32	Jeromy Burnitz	.40	.15
❑ 33	Mark Grudzielanek	.40	.15
❑ 34	Mike Mussina	.60	.25
❑ 35	Scott Rolen	.60	.25
❑ 36	Neifi Perez	.40	.15
❑ 37	Brad Radke	.40	.15
❑ 38	Darryl Strawberry	.40	.15
❑ 39	Robb Nen	.40	.15
❑ 40	Moises Alou	.40	.15
❑ 41	Eric Young	.40	.15
❑ 42	Livan Hernandez	.40	.15
❑ 43	John Wetteland	.40	.15
❑ 44	Matt Lawton	.40	.15
❑ 45	Ben Grieve	.40	.15
❑ 46	Fernando Tatis	.40	.15
❑ 47	Travis Fryman	.40	.15
❑ 48	David Segui	.40	.15
❑ 49	Bob Abreu	.40	.15
❑ 50	Nomar Garciaparra	1.50	.60
❑ 51	Paul O'Neill	.60	.25
❑ 52	Jeff King	.40	.15
❑ 53	Francisco Cordova	.40	.15
❑ 54	John Olerud	.40	.15
❑ 55	Vladimir Guerrero	1.00	.40
❑ 56	Fernando Vina	.40	.15
❑ 57	Shane Reynolds	.40	.15
❑ 58	Chuck Finley	.40	.15
❑ 59	Rondell White	.40	.15
❑ 60	Greg Vaughn	.40	.15
❑ 61	Ryan Minor	.40	.15
❑ 62	Tom Gordon	.40	.15
❑ 63	Damion Easley	.40	.15
❑ 64	Ray Durham	.40	.15
❑ 65	Orlando Hernandez	.40	.15
❑ 66	Bartolo Colon	.40	.15
❑ 67	Jaret Wright	.40	.15
❑ 68	Royce Clayton	.40	.15
❑ 69	Tim Salmon	.60	.25
❑ 70	Mark McGwire	2.50	1.00
❑ 71	Alex Gonzalez	.40	.15
❑ 72	Tom Glavine	.60	.25
❑ 73	David Justice	.40	.15
❑ 74	Omar Vizquel	.60	.25
❑ 75	Juan Gonzalez	.40	.15
❑ 76	Bobby Higginson	.40	.15
❑ 77	Todd Walker	.40	.15
❑ 78	Dante Bichette	.40	.15
❑ 79	Kevin Millwood	.40	.15
❑ 80	Roger Clemens	2.00	.75
❑ 81	Kerry Wood	.40	.15
❑ 82	Cal Ripken	3.00	1.25
❑ 83	Jay Bell	.40	.15
❑ 84	Barry Bonds	2.50	1.00
❑ 85	Alex Rodriguez	1.50	.60
❑ 86	Doug Glanville	.40	.15
❑ 87	Jason Kendall	.40	.15
❑ 88	Sean Casey	.40	.15
❑ 89	Aaron Sele	.40	.15
❑ 90	Derek Jeter	2.50	1.00
❑ 91	Andy Ashby	.40	.15
❑ 92	Rusty Greer	.40	.15
❑ 93	Rod Beck	.40	.15
❑ 94	Matt Williams	.40	.15
❑ 95	Mike Piazza	1.50	.60
❑ 96	Wally Joyner	.40	.15
❑ 97	Barry Larkin	.60	.25
❑ 98	Eric Milton	.40	.15
❑ 99	Gary Sheffield	.40	.15
❑ 100	Greg Maddux	1.50	.60
❑ 101	Ken Griffey Jr. GEM	2.50	1.00
❑ 102	Frank Thomas GEM	1.50	.60
❑ 103	Nomar Garciaparra GEM	2.50	1.00
❑ 104	Mark McGwire GEM	4.00	1.50
❑ 105	Alex Rodriguez GEM	2.50	1.00
❑ 106	Tony Gwynn GEM	2.00	.75
❑ 107	Juan Gonzalez GEM	.60	.25
❑ 108	Jeff Bagwell GEM	1.00	.40
❑ 109	Sammy Sosa GEM	1.50	.60
❑ 110	Vladimir Guerrero GEM	1.50	.60
❑ 111	Roger Clemens GEM	3.00	1.25
❑ 112	Barry Bonds GEM	4.00	1.50
❑ 113	Darin Erstad GEM	.60	.25
❑ 114	Mike Piazza GEM	2.50	1.00
❑ 115	Derek Jeter GEM	4.00	1.50
❑ 116	Chipper Jones GEM	1.50	.60
❑ 117	Larry Walker GEM	.60	.25
❑ 118	Scott Rolen GEM	1.00	.40
❑ 119	Cal Ripken GEM	5.00	2.00
❑ 120	Greg Maddux GEM	2.50	1.00
❑ 121	Troy Glaus SENS	1.00	.40
❑ 122	Ben Grieve SENS	.50	.20
❑ 123	Ryan Minor SENS	.50	.20
❑ 124	Kerry Wood SENS	.60	.25
❑ 125	Travis Lee SENS	.50	.20
❑ 126	Adrian Beltre SENS	.60	.25
❑ 127	Brad Fullmer SENS	.50	.20
❑ 128	Aramis Ramirez SENS	.60	.25
❑ 129	Eric Chavez SENS	.60	.25
❑ 130	Todd Helton SENS	1.00	.40
❑ 131	Pat Burrell RC	3.00	1.25
❑ 132	Ryan Mills RC	.50	.20
❑ 133	Austin Kearns RC	3.00	1.25
❑ 134	Josh McKinley RC	.50	.20
❑ 135	Adam Everett RC	1.00	.40
❑ 136	Marlon Anderson	.50	.20
❑ 137	Bruce Chen	.50	.20
❑ 138	Matt Clement	.60	.25
❑ 139	Alex Gonzalez	.50	.20
❑ 140	Roy Halladay	.60	.25
❑ 141	Calvin Pickering	.50	.20
❑ 142	Randy Wolf	.50	.20
❑ 143	Ryan Anderson	.50	.20
❑ 144	Ruben Mateo	.50	.20
❑ 145	Alex Escobar RC	.60	.25
❑ 146	Jeremy Giambi	.50	.20
❑ 147	Lance Berkman	.60	.25
❑ 148	Michael Barrett	.50	.20
❑ 149	Preston Wilson	.60	.25
❑ 150	Gabe Kapler	.60	.25
❑ 151	Roger Clemens	2.00	.75
❑ 152	Jay Buhner	.40	.15
❑ 153	Brad Fullmer	.40	.15
❑ 154	Ray Lankford	.40	.15
❑ 155	Jim Edmonds	.40	.15
❑ 156	Jason Giambi	.40	.15
❑ 157	Bret Boone	.40	.15
❑ 158	Jeff Cirillo	.40	.15
❑ 159	Rickey Henderson	1.00	.40
❑ 160	Edgar Martinez	.60	.25
❑ 161	Ron Gant	.40	.15

❑ 162 Mark Kotsay .40 .15
❑ 163 Trevor Hoffman .40 .15
❑ 164 Jason Schmidt .40 .15
❑ 165 Brett Tomko .40 .15
❑ 166 David Ortiz 1.00 .40
❑ 167 Dean Palmer .40 .15
❑ 168 Hideki Irabu .40 .15
❑ 169 Mike Cameron .40 .15
❑ 170 Pedro Martinez .60 .25
❑ 171 Tom Goodwin .40 .15
❑ 172 Brian Hunter .40 .15
❑ 173 Al Leiter .40 .15
❑ 174 Charles Johnson .40 .15
❑ 175 Curt Schilling .40 .15
❑ 176 Robin Ventura .40 .15
❑ 177 Travis Lee .40 .15
❑ 178 Jeff Shaw .40 .15
❑ 179 Ugueth Urbina .40 .15
❑ 180 Roberto Alomar .60 .25
❑ 181 Cliff Floyd .40 .15
❑ 182 Adrian Beltre .40 .15
❑ 183 Tony Womack .40 .15
❑ 184 Brian Jordan .40 .15
❑ 185 Randy Johnson 1.00 .40
❑ 186 Mickey Morandini .40 .15
❑ 187 Todd Hundley .40 .15
❑ 188 Jose Valentin .40 .15
❑ 189 Eric Davis .40 .15
❑ 190 Ken Caminiti .40 .15
❑ 191 David Wells .40 .15
❑ 192 Ryan Klesko .40 .15
❑ 193 Garret Anderson .40 .15
❑ 194 Eric Karros .40 .15
❑ 195 Ivan Rodriguez .60 .25
❑ 196 Aramis Ramirez .40 .15
❑ 197 Mike Lieberthal .40 .15
❑ 198 Will Clark .60 .25
❑ 199 Rey Ordonez .40 .15
❑ 200 Ken Griffey Jr. 1.50 .60
❑ 201 Jose Guillen .40 .15
❑ 202 Scott Erickson .40 .15
❑ 203 Paul Konerko .40 .15
❑ 204 Johnny Damon .60 .25
❑ 205 Larry Walker .40 .15
❑ 206 Denny Neagle .40 .15
❑ 207 Jose Offerman .40 .15
❑ 208 Andy Pettitte .60 .25
❑ 209 Bobby Jones .40 .15
❑ 210 Kevin Brown .60 .25
❑ 211 John Smoltz .60 .25
❑ 212 Henry Rodriguez .40 .15
❑ 213 Tim Belcher .40 .15
❑ 214 Carlos Delgado .40 .15
❑ 215 Andruw Jones .60 .25
❑ 216 Andy Benes .40 .15
❑ 217 Fred McGriff .60 .25
❑ 218 Edgar Renteria .40 .15
❑ 219 Miguel Tejada .40 .15
❑ 220 Bernie Williams .60 .25
❑ 221 Justin Thompson .40 .15
❑ 222 Marty Cordova .40 .15
❑ 223 Delino DeShields .40 .15
❑ 224 Ellis Burks .40 .15
❑ 225 Kenny Lofton .40 .15
❑ 226 Steve Finley .40 .15
❑ 227 Eric Chavez .40 .15
❑ 228 Jose Cruz Jr. .40 .15
❑ 229 Marquis Grissom .40 .15
❑ 230 Jeff Bagwell .60 .25
❑ 231 Jose Canseco .60 .25
❑ 232 Edgardo Alfonzo .40 .15
❑ 233 Richie Sexson .40 .15
❑ 234 Jeff Kent .40 .15
❑ 235 Rafael Palmeiro .60 .25
❑ 236 David Cone .40 .15
❑ 237 Gregg Jefferies .40 .15
❑ 238 Mike Lansing .40 .15
❑ 239 Mariano Rivera 1.00 .40
❑ 240 Albert Belle .40 .15
❑ 241 Chuck Knoblauch .40 .15
❑ 242 Derek Bell .40 .15
❑ 243 Pat Hentgen .40 .15
❑ 244 Andres Galarraga .40 .15
❑ 245 Mo Vaughn .40 .15
❑ 246 Wade Boggs .60 .25
❑ 247 Devon White .40 .15
❑ 248 Todd Helton .60 .25
❑ 249 Raul Mondesi .40 .15
❑ 250 Sammy Sosa 1.00 .40
❑ 251 Nomar Garciaparra ST 2.50 1.00
❑ 252 Mark McGwire ST 4.00 1.50
❑ 253 Alex Rodriguez ST 2.50 1.00
❑ 254 Juan Gonzalez ST .60 .25
❑ 255 Vladimir Guerrero ST 1.50 .60
❑ 256 Ken Griffey Jr. ST 2.50 1.00
❑ 257 Mike Piazza ST 2.50 1.00
❑ 258 Derek Jeter ST 4.00 1.50
❑ 259 Albert Belle ST .60 .25
❑ 260 Greg Vaughn ST .50 .20
❑ 261 Sammy Sosa ST 1.50 .60
❑ 262 Greg Maddux ST 2.50 1.00
❑ 263 Frank Thomas ST 1.50 .60
❑ 264 Mark Grace ST 1.00 .40
❑ 265 Ivan Rodriguez ST 1.00 .40
❑ 266 Roger Clemens GM 3.00 1.25
❑ 267 Mo Vaughn GM .60 .25
❑ 268 Jim Thome GM 1.00 .40
❑ 269 Darin Erstad GM .60 .25
❑ 270 Chipper Jones GM 1.50 .60
❑ 271 Larry Walker GM .60 .25
❑ 272 Cal Ripken GM 5.00 2.00
❑ 273 Scott Rolen GM 1.00 .40
❑ 274 Randy Johnson GM 1.50 .60
❑ 275 Tony Gwynn GM 2.00 .75
❑ 276 Barry Bonds GM 4.00 1.50
❑ 277 Sean Burroughs RC 1.00 .40
❑ 278 J.M. Gold RC .50 .20
❑ 279 Carlos Lee .60 .25
❑ 280 George Lombard .50 .20
❑ 281 Carlos Beltran 1.00 .40
❑ 282 Fernando Seguignol .50 .20
❑ 283 Eric Chavez .60 .25
❑ 284 Carlos Pena RC .75 .30
❑ 285 Corey Patterson RC 1.50 .60
❑ 286 Alfonso Soriano RC 8.00 3.00
❑ 287 Nick Johnson RC 1.50 .60
❑ 288 Jorge Toca RC .60 .25
❑ 289 A.J. Burnett RC 1.50 .60
❑ 290 Andy Brown RC .50 .20
❑ 291 Doug Mientkiewicz RC 1.00 .40
❑ 292 Bobby Seay RC .50 .20
❑ 293 Chip Ambres RC .50 .20
❑ 294 C.C. Sabathia RC 4.00 1.50
❑ 295 Choo Freeman RC .60 .25
❑ 296 Eric Valent RC .60 .25
❑ 297 Matt Belisle RC .50 .20
❑ 298 Jason Tyner RC .50 .20
❑ 299 Masao Kida RC .60 .25
❑ 300 H.Aaron/M.McGwire 3.00 1.25

2000 Finest

❑ COMP.SERIES 1 w/o SP's (100) 25.00 10.00
❑ COMP.SERIES 2 w/o SP's (100) 25.00 10.00
❑ COMMON (1-100/147-246) .40 .15
❑ COMMON ROOKIE (101-120) 5.00 2.00
❑ COMMON FEATURES (121-135) 1.50 .60
❑ COMM.GEM (136-145/277-286) 2.00 .75
❑ COMMON ROOKIE (247-266) 5.00 2.00
❑ COMMON COUNTER (267-276) 1.00 .40
❑ 1 Nomar Garciaparra 1.50 .60
❑ 2 Chipper Jones 1.00 .40
❑ 3 Erubiel Durazo .40 .15
❑ 4 Robin Ventura .60 .25
❑ 5 Garret Anderson .40 .15
❑ 6 Dean Palmer .40 .15
❑ 7 Mariano Rivera 1.00 .40
❑ 8 Rusty Greer .40 .15
❑ 9 Jim Thome .60 .25
❑ 10 Jeff Bagwell .60 .25
❑ 11 Jason Giambi .40 .15
❑ 12 Jeromy Burnitz .40 .15
❑ 13 Mark Grace .60 .25
❑ 14 Russ Ortiz .40 .15
❑ 15 Kevin Brown .60 .25
❑ 16 Kevin Millwood .40 .15
❑ 17 Scott Williamson .40 .15
❑ 18 Orlando Hernandez .40 .15
❑ 19 Todd Walker .40 .15
❑ 20 Carlos Beltran .40 .15
❑ 21 Ruben Rivera .40 .15
❑ 22 Curt Schilling .40 .15
❑ 23 Brian Giles .40 .15
❑ 24 Eric Karros .40 .15
❑ 25 Preston Wilson .40 .15
❑ 26 Al Leiter .40 .15
❑ 27 Juan Encarnacion .40 .15
❑ 28 Tim Salmon .60 .25
❑ 29 B.J. Surhoff .40 .15
❑ 30 Bernie Williams .60 .25
❑ 31 Lee Stevens .40 .15
❑ 32 Pokey Reese .40 .15
❑ 33 Mike Sweeney .40 .15
❑ 34 Corey Koskie .40 .15
❑ 35 Roberto Alomar .60 .25
❑ 36 Tim Hudson .40 .15
❑ 37 Tom Glavine .60 .25
❑ 38 Jeff Kent .40 .15
❑ 39 Mike Lieberthal .40 .15
❑ 40 Barry Larkin .60 .25
❑ 41 Paul O'Neill .60 .25
❑ 42 Rico Brogna .40 .15
❑ 43 Brian Daubach .40 .15
❑ 44 Rich Aurilia .40 .15
❑ 45 Vladimir Guerrero 1.00 .40
❑ 46 Luis Castillo .40 .15
❑ 47 Bartolo Colon .40 .15
❑ 48 Kevin Appier .40 .15
❑ 49 Mo Vaughn .40 .15
❑ 50 Alex Rodriguez 1.50 .60
❑ 51 Randy Johnson 1.00 .40
❑ 52 Kris Benson .40 .15
❑ 53 Tony Clark .40 .15
❑ 54 Chad Allen .40 .15
❑ 55 Larry Walker .40 .15
❑ 56 Freddy Garcia .40 .15
❑ 57 Paul Konerko .40 .15
❑ 58 Edgardo Alfonzo .40 .15
❑ 59 Brady Anderson .40 .15
❑ 60 Derek Jeter 2.50 1.00
❑ 61 John Smoltz .60 .25
❑ 62 Doug Glanville .40 .15
❑ 63 Shannon Stewart .40 .15
❑ 64 Greg Maddux 1.50 .60
❑ 65 Mark McGwire 2.50 1.00
❑ 66 Gary Sheffield .40 .15
❑ 67 Kevin Young .40 .15
❑ 68 Tony Gwynn 1.25 .50
❑ 69 Rey Ordonez .40 .15
❑ 70 Cal Ripken 3.00 1.25
❑ 71 Todd Helton .60 .25
❑ 72 Brian Jordan .40 .15
❑ 73 Jose Canseco .60 .25
❑ 74 Luis Gonzalez .40 .15
❑ 75 Barry Bonds 2.50 1.00
❑ 76 Jermaine Dye .40 .15
❑ 77 Jose Offerman .40 .15
❑ 78 Magglio Ordonez .40 .15
❑ 79 Fred Mcgriff .60 .25
❑ 80 Ivan Rodriguez .60 .25
❑ 81 Josh Hamilton 2.00 .75
❑ 82 Vernon Wells .40 .15
❑ 83 Mark Mulder .40 .15
❑ 84 John Patterson .40 .15
❑ 85 Nick Johnson .40 .15
❑ 86 Pablo Ozuna .40 .15
❑ 87 A.J. Burnett .40 .15
❑ 88 Jack Cust .40 .15
❑ 89 Adam Piatt .40 .15
❑ 90 Rob Ryan .40 .15
❑ 91 Sean Burroughs .40 .15

- ❑ 92 D'Angelo Jimenez .40 .15
- ❑ 93 Chad Hermansen .40 .15
- ❑ 94 Robert Fick .40 .15
- ❑ 95 Ruben Mateo .40 .15
- ❑ 96 Alex Escobar .40 .15
- ❑ 97 Wily Pena .40 .15
- ❑ 98 Corey Patterson .40 .15
- ❑ 99 Eric Munson .40 .15
- ❑ 100 Pat Burrell .40 .15
- ❑ 101 Michael Tejera RC 5.00 2.00
- ❑ 102 Bobby Bradley RC 5.00 2.00
- ❑ 103 Larry Bigbie RC 8.00 3.00
- ❑ 104 B.J. Garbe RC 5.00 2.00
- ❑ 105 Josh Kalinowski RC 5.00 2.00
- ❑ 106 Brett Myers RC 8.00 3.00
- ❑ 107 Chris Mears RC 5.00 2.00
- ❑ 108 Aaron Rowand RC 10.00 4.00
- ❑ 109 Corey Myers RC 5.00 2.00
- ❑ 110 John Sneed RC 5.00 2.00
- ❑ 111 Ryan Christianson RC 5.00 2.00
- ❑ 112 Kyle Snyder 5.00 2.00
- ❑ 113 Mike Paradis 5.00 2.00
- ❑ 114 Chance Caple RC 5.00 2.00
- ❑ 115 Ben Christensen RC 5.00 2.00
- ❑ 116 Brad Baker RC 5.00 2.00
- ❑ 117 Rob Purvis RC 5.00 2.00
- ❑ 118 Rick Asadoorian RC 5.00 2.00
- ❑ 119 Ruben Salazar RC 5.00 2.00
- ❑ 120 Julio Zuleta RC 5.00 2.00
- ❑ 121 A.Rodriguez/K.Griffey Jr. 2.50 1.00
- ❑ 122 N.Garciaparra/D.Jeter 3.00 1.25
- ❑ 123 M.McGwire/S.Sosa 4.00 1.50
- ❑ 124 R.Johnson/P.Martinez 2.50 1.00
- ❑ 125 I.Rodriguez/M.Piazza 2.50 1.00
- ❑ 126 M.Ramirez/R.Alomar 1.50 .60
- ❑ 127 C.Jones/A.Jones 2.50 1.00
- ❑ 128 C.Ripken/T.Gwynn 5.00 2.00
- ❑ 129 J.Bagwell/C.Biggio 1.50 .60
- ❑ 130 B.Bonds/V.Guerrero 4.00 1.50
- ❑ 131 N.Johnson/A.Soriano 2.50 1.00
- ❑ 132 J.Hamilton/P.Burrell 10.00 4.00
- ❑ 133 C.Patterson/R.Mateo 1.50 .60
- ❑ 134 L.Walker/T.Helton 1.50 .60
- ❑ 135 R.Ordonez/E.Alfonzo 1.50 .60
- ❑ 136 Derek Jeter GEM 8.00 3.00
- ❑ 137 Alex Rodriguez GEM 5.00 2.00
- ❑ 138 Chipper Jones GEM 5.00 2.00
- ❑ 139 Mike Piazza GEM 5.00 2.00
- ❑ 140 Mark McGwire GEM 8.00 3.00
- ❑ 141 Ivan Rodriguez GEM 3.00 1.25
- ❑ 142 Cal Ripken GEM 10.00 4.00
- ❑ 143 Vladimir Guerrero GEM 5.00 2.00
- ❑ 144 Randy Johnson GEM 5.00 2.00
- ❑ 145 Jeff Bagwell GEM 3.00 1.25
- ❑ 146 Ken Griffey Jr. ACTION 1.50 .60
- ❑ 146A Ken Griffey Jr. PORT 1.50 .60
- ❑ 147 Andruw Jones .60 .25
- ❑ 148 Kerry Wood .40 .15
- ❑ 149 Jim Edmonds .40 .15
- ❑ 150 Pedro Martinez .60 .25
- ❑ 151 Warren Morris .40 .15
- ❑ 152 Trevor Hoffman .40 .15
- ❑ 153 Ryan Klesko .40 .15
- ❑ 154 Andy Pettitte .60 .25
- ❑ 155 Frank Thomas 1.00 .40
- ❑ 156 Damion Easley .40 .15
- ❑ 157 Cliff Floyd .40 .15
- ❑ 158 Ben Davis .40 .15
- ❑ 159 John Valentin .40 .15
- ❑ 160 Rafael Palmeiro .60 .25
- ❑ 161 Andy Ashby .40 .15
- ❑ 162 J.D. Drew .40 .15
- ❑ 163 Jay Bell .40 .15
- ❑ 164 Adam Kennedy .40 .15
- ❑ 165 Manny Ramirez .60 .25
- ❑ 166 John Halama .40 .15
- ❑ 167 Octavio Dotel .40 .15
- ❑ 168 Darin Erstad .40 .15
- ❑ 169 Jose Lima .40 .15
- ❑ 170 Andres Galarraga .40 .15
- ❑ 171 Scott Rolen .60 .25
- ❑ 172 Delino DeShields .40 .15
- ❑ 173 J.T. Snow .40 .15
- ❑ 174 Tony Womack .40 .15
- ❑ 175 John Olerud .40 .15
- ❑ 176 Jason Kendall .40 .15
- ❑ 177 Carlos Lee .40 .15
- ❑ 178 Eric Milton .40 .15
- ❑ 179 Jeff Cirillo .40 .15
- ❑ 180 Gabe Kapler .40 .15
- ❑ 181 Greg Vaughn .40 .15
- ❑ 182 Denny Neagle .40 .15
- ❑ 183 Tino Martinez .60 .25
- ❑ 184 Doug Mientkiewicz .40 .15
- ❑ 185 Juan Gonzalez .40 .15
- ❑ 186 Ellis Burks .40 .15
- ❑ 187 Mike Hampton .40 .15
- ❑ 188 Royce Clayton .40 .15
- ❑ 189 Mike Mussina .60 .25
- ❑ 190 Carlos Delgado .40 .15
- ❑ 191 Ben Grieve .40 .15
- ❑ 192 Fernando Tatis .40 .15
- ❑ 193 Matt Williams .40 .15
- ❑ 194 Rondell White .40 .15
- ❑ 195 Shawn Green .40 .15
- ❑ 196 Hideki Irabu .40 .15
- ❑ 197 Troy Glaus .40 .15
- ❑ 198 Roger Cedeno .40 .15
- ❑ 199 Ray Lankford .40 .15
- ❑ 200 Sammy Sosa 1.00 .40
- ❑ 201 Kenny Lofton .40 .15
- ❑ 202 Edgar Martinez .60 .25
- ❑ 203 Mark Kotsay .40 .15
- ❑ 204 David Wells .40 .15
- ❑ 205 Craig Biggio .60 .25
- ❑ 206 Ray Durham .40 .15
- ❑ 207 Troy O'Leary .40 .15
- ❑ 208 Rickey Henderson 1.00 .40
- ❑ 209 Bob Abreu .40 .15
- ❑ 210 Neifi Perez .40 .15
- ❑ 211 Carlos Febles .40 .15
- ❑ 212 Chuck Knoblauch .40 .15
- ❑ 213 Moises Alou .40 .15
- ❑ 214 Omar Vizquel .60 .25
- ❑ 215 Vinny Castilla .40 .15
- ❑ 216 Javy Lopez .40 .15
- ❑ 217 Johnny Damon .60 .25
- ❑ 218 Roger Clemens 2.00 .75
- ❑ 219 Miguel Tejada .40 .15
- ❑ 220 Carl Everett .40 .15
- ❑ 221 Matt Lawton .40 .15
- ❑ 222 Albert Belle .40 .15
- ❑ 223 Adrian Beltre .40 .15
- ❑ 224 Dante Bichette .40 .15
- ❑ 225 Raul Mondesi .40 .15
- ❑ 226 Mike Piazza 1.50 .60
- ❑ 227 Brad Penny .40 .15
- ❑ 228 Kip Wells .40 .15
- ❑ 229 Adam Everett .40 .15
- ❑ 230 Eddie Yarnall .40 .15
- ❑ 231 Matt LeCroy .40 .15
- ❑ 232 Jason Tyner .40 .15
- ❑ 233 Rick Ankiel .40 .15
- ❑ 234 Lance Berkman .40 .15
- ❑ 235 Rafael Furcal .40 .15
- ❑ 236 Dee Brown .40 .15
- ❑ 237 Gookie Dawkins .40 .15
- ❑ 238 Eric Valent .40 .15
- ❑ 239 Peter Bergeron .40 .15
- ❑ 240 Alfonso Soriano 1.00 .40
- ❑ 241 Adam Dunn 1.00 .40
- ❑ 242 Jorge Toca .40 .15
- ❑ 243 Ryan Anderson .40 .15
- ❑ 244 Jason Dellaero .40 .15
- ❑ 245 Jason Grilli .40 .15
- ❑ 246 Milton Bradley .40 .15
- ❑ 247 Scott Downs RC 5.00 2.00
- ❑ 248 Keith Reed RC 5.00 2.00
- ❑ 249 Edgar Cruz RC 5.00 2.00
- ❑ 250 Wes Anderson RC 5.00 2.00
- ❑ 251 Lyle Overbay RC 8.00 3.00
- ❑ 252 Mike Lamb RC 8.00 3.00
- ❑ 253 Vince Faison RC 5.00 2.00
- ❑ 254 Chad Alexander 5.00 2.00
- ❑ 255 Chris Wakeland RC 5.00 2.00
- ❑ 256 Aaron McNeal RC 5.00 2.00
- ❑ 257 Tomo Ohka RC 5.00 2.00
- ❑ 258 Ty Howington RC 5.00 2.00
- ❑ 259 Javier Colina RC 5.00 2.00
- ❑ 260 Jason Jennings 5.00 2.00
- ❑ 261 Ramon Santiago RC 5.00 2.00
- ❑ 262 Johan Santana RC 100.00 50.00
- ❑ 263 Quincy Foster RC 5.00 2.00
- ❑ 264 Junior Brignac RC 5.00 2.00
- ❑ 265 Rico Washington RC 5.00 2.00
- ❑ 266 Scott Sobkowiak RC 5.00 2.00
- ❑ 267 P.Martinez/R.Ankiel 1.50 .60
- ❑ 268 M.Ramirez/V.Guerrero 2.50 1.00
- ❑ 269 A.Burnett/M.Mulder 1.00 .40
- ❑ 270 M.Piazza/E.Munson 2.50 1.00
- ❑ 271 J.Hamilton/C.Patterson 3.00 1.25
- ❑ 272 K.Griffey Jr./S.Sosa 2.00 .75
- ❑ 273 D.Jeter/A.Soriano 4.00 1.50
- ❑ 274 M.McGwire/P.Burrell 4.00 1.50
- ❑ 275 C.Jones/C.Ripken 4.00 1.50
- ❑ 276 N.Garciaparra/A.Rodriguez 2.50 1.00
- ❑ 277 Pedro Martinez GEM 3.00 1.25
- ❑ 278 Tony Gwynn GEM 4.00 1.50
- ❑ 279 Barry Bonds GEM 8.00 3.00
- ❑ 280 Juan Gonzalez GEM 2.00 .75
- ❑ 281 Larry Walker GEM 2.00 .75
- ❑ 282 Nomar Garciaparra GEM 5.00 2.00
- ❑ 283 Ken Griffey Jr. GEM 5.00 2.00
- ❑ 284 Manny Ramirez GEM 3.00 1.25
- ❑ 285 Shawn Green GEM 2.00 .75
- ❑ 286 Sammy Sosa GEM 5.00 2.00

2001 Finest

- ❑ COMP.SET w/o SP's (100) 25.00 10.00
- ❑ COMMON CARD (1-110) .40 .15
- ❑ COMMON SP 10.00 4.00
- ❑ COMMON PROSPECT (111-140) 10.00 4.00
- ❑ 1 Mike Piazza SP 20.00 8.00
- ❑ 2 Andruw Jones .60 .25
- ❑ 3 Jason Giambi .40 .15
- ❑ 4 Fred McGriff .60 .25
- ❑ 5 Vladimir Guerrero SP 10.00 4.00
- ❑ 6 Adrian Gonzalez .40 .15
- ❑ 7 Pedro Martinez .60 .25
- ❑ 8 Mike Lieberthal .40 .15
- ❑ 9 Warren Morris .40 .15
- ❑ 10 Juan Gonzalez .40 .15
- ❑ 11 Jose Canseco .60 .25
- ❑ 12 Jose Valentin .40 .15
- ❑ 13 Jeff Cirillo .40 .15
- ❑ 14 Pokey Reese .40 .15
- ❑ 15 Scott Rolen .60 .25
- ❑ 16 Greg Maddux 1.50 .60
- ❑ 17 Carlos Delgado .40 .15
- ❑ 18 Rick Ankiel .40 .15
- ❑ 19 Steve Finley .40 .15
- ❑ 20 Shawn Green .40 .15
- ❑ 21 Orlando Cabrera .40 .15
- ❑ 22 Roberto Alomar .60 .25
- ❑ 23 John Olerud .40 .15
- ❑ 24 Albert Belle .40 .15
- ❑ 25 Edgardo Alfonzo .40 .15
- ❑ 26 Rafael Palmeiro .60 .25
- ❑ 27 Mike Sweeney .40 .15
- ❑ 28 Bernie Williams .60 .25
- ❑ 29 Larry Walker .40 .15
- ❑ 30 Barry Bonds SP 25.00 10.00
- ❑ 31 Orlando Hernandez .40 .15
- ❑ 32 Randy Johnson 1.00 .40
- ❑ 33 Shannon Stewart .40 .15
- ❑ 34 Mark Grace .60 .25
- ❑ 35 Alex Rodriguez SP 25.00 10.00
- ❑ 36 Tino Martinez .60 .25
- ❑ 37 Carlos Febles .40 .15
- ❑ 38 Al Leiter .40 .15

- ❑ 39 Omar Vizquel .60 .25
- ❑ 40 Chuck Knoblauch .40 .15
- ❑ 41 Tim Salmon .60 .25
- ❑ 42 Brian Jordan .40 .15
- ❑ 43 Edgar Renteria .40 .15
- ❑ 44 Preston Wilson .40 .15
- ❑ 45 Mariano Rivera 1.00 .40
- ❑ 46 Gabe Kapler .40 .15
- ❑ 47 Jason Kendall .40 .15
- ❑ 48 Rickey Henderson 1.00 .40
- ❑ 49 Luis Gonzalez .40 .15
- ❑ 50 Tom Glavine .60 .25
- ❑ 51 Jeromy Burnitz .40 .15
- ❑ 52 Garret Anderson .40 .15
- ❑ 53 Craig Biggio .60 .25
- ❑ 54 Vinny Castilla .40 .15
- ❑ 55 Jeff Kent .40 .15
- ❑ 56 Gary Sheffield .40 .15
- ❑ 57 Jorge Posada .60 .25
- ❑ 58 Sean Casey .40 .15
- ❑ 59 Johnny Damon .60 .25
- ❑ 60 Dean Palmer .40 .15
- ❑ 61 Todd Helton .60 .25
- ❑ 62 Barry Larkin .60 .25
- ❑ 63 Robin Ventura .40 .15
- ❑ 64 Kenny Lofton .40 .15
- ❑ 65 Sammy Sosa SP 10.00 4.00
- ❑ 66 Rafael Furcal .40 .15
- ❑ 67 Jay Bell .40 .15
- ❑ 68 J.T. Snow .40 .15
- ❑ 69 Jose Vidro .40 .15
- ❑ 70 Ivan Rodriguez .60 .25
- ❑ 71 Jermaine Dye .40 .15
- ❑ 72 Chipper Jones SP 10.00 4.00
- ❑ 73 Fernando Vina .40 .15
- ❑ 74 Ben Grieve .40 .15
- ❑ 75 Mark McGwire SP 25.00 10.00
- ❑ 76 Matt Williams .40 .15
- ❑ 77 Mark Grudzielanek .40 .15
- ❑ 78 Mike Hampton .40 .15
- ❑ 79 Brian Giles .40 .15
- ❑ 80 Tony Gwynn 1.25 .50
- ❑ 81 Carlos Beltran .40 .15
- ❑ 82 Ray Durham .40 .15
- ❑ 83 Brad Radke .40 .15
- ❑ 84 David Justice .40 .15
- ❑ 85 Frank Thomas 1.00 .40
- ❑ 86 Todd Zeile .40 .15
- ❑ 87 Pat Burrell .40 .15
- ❑ 88 Jim Thome .60 .25
- ❑ 89 Greg Vaughn .40 .15
- ❑ 90 Ken Griffey Jr. SP 15.00 6.00
- ❑ 91 Mike Mussina .60 .25
- ❑ 92 Magglio Ordonez .40 .15
- ❑ 93 Bob Abreu .40 .15
- ❑ 94 Alex Gonzalez .40 .15
- ❑ 95 Kevin Brown .40 .15
- ❑ 96 Jay Buhner .40 .15
- ❑ 97 Roger Clemens 2.00 .75
- ❑ 98 Nomar Garciaparra SP 15.00 6.00
- ❑ 99 Derrek Lee .60 .25
- ❑ 100 Derek Jeter SP 25.00 10.00
- ❑ 101 Adrian Beltre .40 .15
- ❑ 102 Geoff Jenkins .40 .15
- ❑ 103 Javy Lopez .40 .15
- ❑ 104 Raul Mondesi .40 .15
- ❑ 105 Troy Glaus .40 .15
- ❑ 106 Jeff Bagwell .60 .25
- ❑ 107 Eric Karros .40 .15
- ❑ 108 Mo Vaughn .40 .15
- ❑ 109 Cal Ripken 3.00 1.25
- ❑ 110 Manny Ramirez Sox .60 .25
- ❑ 111 Scott Heard PROS 10.00 4.00
- ❑ 112 Luis Montanez PROS RC 10.00 4.00
- ❑ 113 Ben Diggins PROS 10.00 4.00
- ❑ 114 Shaun Boyd PROS RC 10.00 4.00
- ❑ 115 Sean Burnett PROS 10.00 4.00
- ❑ 116 Carmen Cali PROS RC 10.00 4.00
- ❑ 117 Derek Thompson PROS 10.00 4.00
- ❑ 118 David Parrish PROS RC 10.00 4.00
- ❑ 119 Dominic Rich PROS RC 10.00 4.00
- ❑ 120 Chad Petty PROS RC 10.00 4.00
- ❑ 121 Steve Smyth PROS RC 10.00 4.00
- ❑ 122 John Lackey PROS 10.00 4.00
- ❑ 123 Matt Galante PROS RC 10.00 4.00
- ❑ 124 Danny Borrell PROS RC 10.00 4.00
- ❑ 125 Bob Keppel PROS RC 10.00 4.00
- ❑ 126 Justin Wayne PROS RC 10.00 4.00
- ❑ 127 J.R. House PROS 10.00 4.00
- ❑ 128 Brian Sellier PROS RC 10.00 4.00
- ❑ 129 Dan Moylan PROS RC 10.00 4.00
- ❑ 130 Scott Pratt PROS RC 10.00 4.00
- ❑ 131 Victor Hall PROS RC 10.00 4.00
- ❑ 132 Joel Pineiro PROS 10.00 4.00
- ❑ 133 Josh Axelson PROS RC 10.00 4.00
- ❑ 134 Jose Reyes PROS RC 150.00 90.00
- ❑ 135 Greg Runser PROS RC 10.00 4.00
- ❑ 136 Bryan Hebson PROS RC 10.00 4.00
- ❑ 137 Sammy Serrano PROS RC 10.00 4.00
- ❑ 138 Kevin Joseph PROS RC 10.00 4.00
- ❑ 139 Juan Richardson PROS RC 10.00 4.00
- ❑ 140 Mark Fischer PROS RC 10.00 4.00

2002 Finest

- ❑ COMP.SET w/o SP's (100) 25.00 10.00
- ❑ COMMON CARD (1-100) .50 .20
- ❑ COMMON CARD (101-110) 10.00 4.00
- ❑ 1 Mike Mussina .75 .30
- ❑ 2 Steve Sparks .50 .20
- ❑ 3 Randy Johnson 1.25 .50
- ❑ 4 Orlando Cabrera .50 .20
- ❑ 5 Jeff Kent .50 .20
- ❑ 6 Carlos Delgado .50 .20
- ❑ 7 Ivan Rodriguez .75 .30
- ❑ 8 Jose Cruz .50 .20
- ❑ 9 Jason Giambi .50 .20
- ❑ 10 Brad Penny .50 .20
- ❑ 11 Moises Alou .50 .20
- ❑ 12 Mike Piazza 2.00 .75
- ❑ 13 Ben Grieve .50 .20
- ❑ 14 Derek Jeter 3.00 1.25
- ❑ 15 Roy Oswalt .50 .20
- ❑ 16 Pat Burrell .50 .20
- ❑ 17 Preston Wilson .50 .20
- ❑ 18 Kevin Brown .50 .20
- ❑ 19 Barry Bonds 3.00 1.25
- ❑ 20 Phil Nevin .50 .20
- ❑ 21 Aramis Ramirez .50 .20
- ❑ 22 Carlos Beltran .50 .20
- ❑ 23 Chipper Jones 1.25 .50
- ❑ 24 Curt Schilling .50 .20
- ❑ 25 Jorge Posada .75 .30
- ❑ 26 Alfonso Soriano .50 .20
- ❑ 27 Cliff Floyd .50 .20
- ❑ 28 Rafael Palmeiro .75 .30
- ❑ 29 Terrence Long .50 .20
- ❑ 30 Ken Griffey Jr. 2.00 .75
- ❑ 31 Jason Kendall .50 .20
- ❑ 32 Jose Vidro .50 .20
- ❑ 33 Jermaine Dye .50 .20
- ❑ 34 Bobby Higginson .50 .20
- ❑ 35 Albert Pujols 2.50 1.00
- ❑ 36 Miguel Tejada .50 .20
- ❑ 37 Jim Edmonds .50 .20
- ❑ 38 Barry Zito .50 .20
- ❑ 39 Jimmy Rollins .50 .20
- ❑ 40 Rafael Furcal .50 .20
- ❑ 41 Omar Vizquel .75 .30
- ❑ 42 Kazuhiro Sasaki .50 .20
- ❑ 43 Brian Giles .50 .20
- ❑ 44 Darin Erstad .50 .20
- ❑ 45 Mariano Rivera 1.25 .50
- ❑ 46 Troy Percival .50 .20
- ❑ 47 Mike Sweeney .50 .20
- ❑ 48 Vladimir Guerrero 1.25 .50
- ❑ 49 Troy Glaus .50 .20
- ❑ 50 So Taguchi RC 2.50 1.00
- ❑ 51 Edgardo Alfonzo .50 .20
- ❑ 52 Roger Clemens 2.50 1.00
- ❑ 53 Eric Chavez .50 .20
- ❑ 54 Alex Rodriguez 2.00 .75
- ❑ 55 Cristian Guzman .50 .20
- ❑ 56 Jeff Bagwell .75 .30
- ❑ 57 Bernie Williams .75 .30
- ❑ 58 Kerry Wood .50 .20
- ❑ 59 Ryan Klesko .50 .20
- ❑ 60 Ichiro Suzuki 2.50 1.00
- ❑ 61 Larry Walker .50 .20
- ❑ 62 Nomar Garciaparra 2.00 .75
- ❑ 63 Craig Biggio .75 .30
- ❑ 64 J.D. Drew .50 .20
- ❑ 65 Juan Pierre .50 .20
- ❑ 66 Roberto Alomar .75 .30
- ❑ 67 Luis Gonzalez .50 .20
- ❑ 68 Bud Smith .50 .20
- ❑ 69 Magglio Ordonez .50 .20
- ❑ 70 Scott Rolen .75 .30
- ❑ 71 Tsuyoshi Shinjo .50 .20
- ❑ 72 Paul Konerko .50 .20
- ❑ 73 Garret Anderson .50 .20
- ❑ 74 Tim Hudson .50 .20
- ❑ 75 Adam Dunn .50 .20
- ❑ 76 Gary Sheffield .50 .20
- ❑ 77 Johnny Damon Sox .75 .30
- ❑ 78 Todd Helton .75 .30
- ❑ 79 Geoff Jenkins .50 .20
- ❑ 80 Shawn Green .50 .20
- ❑ 81 C.C. Sabathia .50 .20
- ❑ 82 Kazuhisa Ishii RC 2.50 1.00
- ❑ 83 Rich Aurilia .50 .20
- ❑ 84 Mike Hampton .50 .20
- ❑ 85 Ben Sheets .50 .20
- ❑ 86 Andruw Jones .75 .30
- ❑ 87 Richie Sexson .50 .20
- ❑ 88 Jim Thome .75 .30
- ❑ 89 Sammy Sosa 1.25 .50
- ❑ 90 Greg Maddux 2.00 .75
- ❑ 91 Pedro Martinez .75 .30
- ❑ 92 Jeromy Burnitz .50 .20
- ❑ 93 Raul Mondesi .50 .20
- ❑ 94 Bret Boone .50 .20
- ❑ 95 Jerry Hairston .50 .20
- ❑ 96 Mike Rivera .50 .20
- ❑ 97 Juan Cruz .50 .20
- ❑ 98 Morgan Ensberg .50 .20
- ❑ 99 Nathan Haynes .50 .20
- ❑ 100 Xavier Nady .50 .20
- ❑ 101 Nic Jackson FY AU RC 10.00 4.00
- ❑ 102 Mauricio Lara FY AU RC 10.00 4.00
- ❑ 103 Freddy Sanchez FY AU RC 30.00 12.50
- ❑ 104 Clint Nageotte FY AU RC 10.00 4.00
- ❑ 105 Beltran Perez FY AU RC 10.00 4.00
- ❑ 106 Garrett Gentry FY AU RC 10.00 4.00
- ❑ 107 Chad Qualls FY AU RC 10.00 4.00
- ❑ 108 Jason Bay FY AU RC 50.00 20.00
- ❑ 109 Michael Hill FY AU RC 10.00 4.00
- ❑ 110 Brian Tallet FY AU RC 10.00 4.00

2003 Finest

- ❑ COMP.SET w/o SP's (100) 25.00 10.00
- ❑ COMMON CARD (1-100) .50 .20
- ❑ COMMON CARD (101-110) 15.00 6.00

❑ 1 Sammy Sosa	1.25	.50
❑ 2 Paul Konerko	.50	.20
❑ 3 Todd Helton	.75	.30
❑ 4 Mike Lowell	.50	.20
❑ 5 Lance Berkman	.50	.20
❑ 6 Kazuhisa Ishii	.50	.20
❑ 7 A.J. Pierzynski	.50	.20
❑ 8 Jose Vidro	.50	.20
❑ 9 Roberto Alomar	.75	.30
❑ 10 Derek Jeter	3.00	1.25
❑ 11 Barry Zito	.50	.20
❑ 12 Jimmy Rollins	.50	.20
❑ 13 Brian Giles	.50	.20
❑ 14 Ryan Klesko	.50	.20
❑ 15 Rich Aurilia	.50	.20
❑ 16 Jim Edmonds	.50	.20
❑ 17 Aubrey Huff	.50	.20
❑ 18 Ivan Rodriguez	.75	.30
❑ 19 Eric Hinske	.50	.20
❑ 20 Barry Bonds	3.00	1.25
❑ 21 Darin Erstad	.50	.20
❑ 22 Curt Schilling	.50	.20
❑ 23 Andruw Jones	.75	.30
❑ 24 Jay Gibbons	.50	.20
❑ 25 Nomar Garciaparra	2.00	.75
❑ 26 Kerry Wood	.50	.20
❑ 27 Magglio Ordonez	.50	.20
❑ 28 Austin Kearns	.50	.20
❑ 29 Jason Jennings	.50	.20
❑ 30 Jason Giambi	.50	.20
❑ 31 Tim Hudson	.50	.20
❑ 32 Edgar Martinez	.75	.30
❑ 33 Carl Crawford	.50	.20
❑ 34 Hee Seop Choi	.50	.20
❑ 35 Vladimir Guerrero	1.25	.50
❑ 36 Jeff Kent	.50	.20
❑ 37 John Smoltz	.75	.30
❑ 38 Frank Thomas	1.25	.50
❑ 39 Cliff Floyd	.50	.20
❑ 40 Mike Piazza	2.00	.75
❑ 41 Mark Prior	.75	.30
❑ 42 Tim Salmon	.75	.30
❑ 43 Shawn Green	.50	.20
❑ 44 Bernie Williams	.75	.30
❑ 45 Jim Thome	.75	.30
❑ 46 John Olerud	.50	.20
❑ 47 Orlando Hudson	.50	.20
❑ 48 Mark Teixeira	.75	.30
❑ 49 Gary Sheffield	.50	.20
❑ 50 Ichiro Suzuki	2.50	1.00
❑ 51 Tom Glavine	.75	.30
❑ 52 Torii Hunter	.50	.20
❑ 53 Craig Biggio	.75	.30
❑ 54 Carlos Beltran	.50	.20
❑ 55 Bartolo Colon	.50	.20
❑ 56 Jorge Posada	.75	.30
❑ 57 Pat Burrell	.50	.20
❑ 58 Edgar Renteria	.50	.20
❑ 59 Rafael Palmeiro	.75	.30
❑ 60 Alfonso Soriano	.50	.20
❑ 61 Brandon Phillips	.50	.20
❑ 62 Luis Gonzalez	.50	.20
❑ 63 Manny Ramirez	.75	.30
❑ 64 Garret Anderson	.50	.20
❑ 65 Ken Griffey Jr.	2.00	.75
❑ 66 A.J. Burnett	.50	.20
❑ 67 Mike Sweeney	.50	.20
❑ 68 Doug Mientkiewicz	.50	.20
❑ 69 Eric Chavez	.50	.20
❑ 70 Adam Dunn	.50	.20
❑ 71 Shea Hillenbrand	.50	.20
❑ 72 Troy Glaus	.50	.20
❑ 73 Rodrigo Lopez	.50	.20
❑ 74 Moises Alou	.50	.20
❑ 75 Chipper Jones	1.25	.50
❑ 76 Bobby Abreu	.50	.20
❑ 77 Mark Mulder	.50	.20
❑ 78 Kevin Brown	.50	.20
❑ 79 Josh Beckett	.50	.20
❑ 80 Larry Walker	.50	.20
❑ 81 Randy Johnson	1.25	.50
❑ 82 Greg Maddux	2.00	.75
❑ 83 Johnny Damon	.75	.30
❑ 84 Omar Vizquel	.75	.30
❑ 85 Jeff Bagwell	.75	.30
❑ 86 Carlos Pena	.50	.20
❑ 87 Roy Oswalt	.50	.20
❑ 88 Richie Sexson	.50	.20
❑ 89 Roger Clemens	2.50	1.00
❑ 90 Miguel Tejada	.50	.20
❑ 91 Vicente Padilla	.50	.20
❑ 92 Phil Nevin	.50	.20
❑ 93 Edgardo Alfonzo	.50	.20
❑ 94 Bret Boone	.50	.20
❑ 95 Albert Pujols	2.50	1.00
❑ 96 Carlos Delgado	.50	.20
❑ 97 Jose Contreras RC	2.00	.75
❑ 98 Scott Rolen	.75	.30
❑ 99 Pedro Martinez	.75	.30
❑ 100 Alex Rodriguez	2.00	.75
❑ 101 Adam LaRoche AU	15.00	6.00
❑ 102 Andy Marte AU RC	50.00	25.00
❑ 103 Daryl Clark AU RC	10.00	4.00
❑ 104 J.D. Durbin AU RC	10.00	4.00
❑ 105 Craig Brazell AU RC	10.00	4.00
❑ 106 Brian Burgamy AU RC	10.00	4.00
❑ 107 Tyler Johnson AU RC	10.00	4.00
❑ 108 Joey Gomes AU RC	10.00	4.00
❑ 109 Bryan Bullington AU RC	15.00	6.00
❑ 110 Byron Gettis AU RC	10.00	4.00

2004 Finest

❑ COMP.SET w/o SP's (100)	25.00	10.00
❑ COMMON CARD (1-100)	.50	.20
❑ COMMON CARD (101-110)	8.00	3.00
❑ 101-110 STATED ODDS 1:7 MINI-BOXES		
❑ COMMON CARD (111-122)	10.00	4.00
❑ 111-122 STATED ODDS 1:3 MINI-BOXES		
❑ EXCHANGE DEADLINE 04/30/06		
❑ CARD 112 EXCH UNABLE TO BE FULFILLED		
❑ 04 WS HL B.THOMSON AU SENT INSTEAD		
❑ 1 Juan Pierre	.50	.20
❑ 2 Derek Jeter	2.50	1.00
❑ 3 Garret Anderson	.50	.20
❑ 4 Javy Lopez	.50	.20
❑ 5 Corey Patterson	.50	.20
❑ 6 Todd Helton	.75	.30
❑ 7 Roy Oswalt	.50	.20
❑ 8 Shawn Green	.50	.20
❑ 9 Vladimir Guerrero	1.25	.50
❑ 10 Jorge Posada	.75	.30
❑ 11 Jason Kendall	.50	.20
❑ 12 Scott Rolen	.75	.30
❑ 13 Randy Johnson	1.25	.50
❑ 14 Bill Mueller	.50	.20
❑ 15 Magglio Ordonez	.50	.20
❑ 16 Larry Walker	.50	.20
❑ 17 Lance Berkman	.50	.20
❑ 18 Richie Sexson	.50	.20
❑ 19 Orlando Cabrera	.50	.20
❑ 20 Alfonso Soriano	.50	.20
❑ 21 Kevin Millwood	.50	.20
❑ 22 Edgar Martinez	.75	.30
❑ 23 Aubrey Huff	.50	.20
❑ 24 Carlos Delgado	.50	.20
❑ 25 Vernon Wells	.50	.20
❑ 26 Mark Teixeira	.75	.30
❑ 27 Troy Glaus	.50	.20
❑ 28 Jeff Kent	.50	.20
❑ 29 Hideo Nomo	1.25	.50
❑ 30 Torii Hunter	.50	.20
❑ 31 Hank Blalock	.50	.20
❑ 32 Brandon Webb	.50	.20
❑ 33 Tony Batista	.50	.20
❑ 34 Bret Boone	.50	.20
❑ 35 Ryan Klesko	.50	.20
❑ 36 Barry Zito	.50	.20
❑ 37 Edgar Renteria	.50	.20
❑ 38 Geoff Jenkins	.50	.20
❑ 39 Jeff Bagwell	.75	.30
❑ 40 Dontrelle Willis	.75	.30
❑ 41 Adam Dunn	.50	.20
❑ 42 Mark Buehrle	.50	.20
❑ 43 Esteban Loaiza	.50	.20
❑ 44 Angel Berroa	.50	.20
❑ 45 Ivan Rodriguez	.75	.30
❑ 46 Jose Vidro	.50	.20
❑ 47 Mark Mulder	.50	.20
❑ 48 Roger Clemens	2.50	1.00
❑ 49 Jim Edmonds	.50	.20
❑ 50 Eric Gagne	.50	.20
❑ 51 Marcus Giles	.50	.20
❑ 52 Curt Schilling	.75	.30
❑ 53 Ken Griffey Jr.	2.00	.75
❑ 54 Jason Schmidt	.50	.20
❑ 55 Miguel Tejada	.50	.20
❑ 56 Dmitri Young	.50	.20
❑ 57 Mike Lowell	.50	.20
❑ 58 Mike Sweeney	.50	.20
❑ 59 Scott Podsednik	.50	.20
❑ 60 Miguel Cabrera	.75	.30
❑ 61 Johan Santana	1.25	.50
❑ 62 Bernie Williams	.75	.30
❑ 63 Eric Chavez	.50	.20
❑ 64 Bobby Abreu	.50	.20
❑ 65 Brian Giles	.50	.20
❑ 66 Michael Young	.50	.20
❑ 67 Paul Lo Duca	.50	.20
❑ 68 Austin Kearns	.50	.20
❑ 69 Jody Gerut	.50	.20
❑ 70 Kerry Wood	.50	.20
❑ 71 Luis Matos	.50	.20
❑ 72 Greg Maddux	2.00	.75
❑ 73 Alex Rodriguez Yanks	2.00	.75
❑ 74 Mike Lieberthal	.50	.20
❑ 75 Jim Thome	.75	.30
❑ 76 Javier Vazquez	.50	.20
❑ 77 Bartolo Colon	.50	.20
❑ 78 Manny Ramirez	.75	.30
❑ 79 Jacque Jones	.50	.20
❑ 80 Johnny Damon	.75	.30
❑ 81 Carlos Beltran	.50	.20
❑ 82 C.C. Sabathia	.50	.20
❑ 83 Preston Wilson	.50	.20
❑ 84 Luis Castillo	.50	.20
❑ 85 Kevin Brown	.50	.20
❑ 86 Shannon Stewart	.50	.20
❑ 87 Cliff Floyd	.50	.20
❑ 88 Mike Mussina	.75	.30
❑ 89 Rafael Furcal	.50	.20
❑ 90 Roy Halladay	.50	.20
❑ 91 Frank Thomas	1.25	.50
❑ 92 Melvin Mora	.50	.20
❑ 93 Andruw Jones	.75	.30
❑ 94 Luis Gonzalez	.50	.20
❑ 95 David Ortiz	1.25	.50
❑ 96 Gary Sheffield	.50	.20
❑ 97 Tim Hudson	.50	.20
❑ 98 Phil Nevin	.50	.20
❑ 99 Ichiro Suzuki	2.50	1.00
❑ 100 Albert Pujols	2.50	1.00
❑ 101 Nomar Garciaparra SR Jsy	15.00	6.00
❑ 102 Sammy Sosa SR Jsy	10.00	4.00
❑ 103 Josh Beckett SR Jsy	8.00	3.00
❑ 104 Jason Giambi SR Jsy	8.00	3.00
❑ 105 Rocco Baldelli SR Jsy	8.00	3.00
❑ 106 Jose Reyes SR Jsy	8.00	3.00
❑ 107 Chipper Jones SR Jsy	10.00	4.00
❑ 108 Pedro Martinez SR Jsy	10.00	4.00
❑ 109 Mike Piazza SR Jsy	15.00	6.00
❑ 110 Mark Prior SR Jsy	10.00	4.00
❑ 111 Craig Ansman AU RC	10.00	4.00
❑ 113 David Murphy AU RC	10.00	4.00
❑ 114 Jason Hirsh AU RC	25.00	10.00
❑ 115 Matt Moses AU RC	15.00	6.00
❑ 116 Estee Harris AU RC	15.00	6.00
❑ 117 Logan Kensing AU RC	10.00	4.00
❑ 118 L.Milledge AU RC	50.00	20.00
❑ 119 Merkin Valdez AU RC	10.00	4.00
❑ 120 Travis Blackley AU RC	10.00	4.00

❑ 121 Vito Chiaravalloti AU RC 10.00 4.00
❑ 122 Dioner Navarro AU RC 10.00 4.00

2005 Finest

❑ COMP.SET w/o SP's (150) 80.00 40.00
❑ COMMON CARD (1-140) .50 .20
❑ COMMON CARD (157-166) 1.00 .40
❑ AU p/r 970 ODDS 1:3 MINI BOXES
❑ AU p/r 970 PRINT RUN 970 #'d SETS
❑ AU p/r 375 ODDS 1:41 MINI BOXES
❑ AU p/r 375 PRINT RUN 375 #'d SETS
❑ OVERALL PLATE ODDS 1:51 MINI BOX
❑ OVERALL AU PLATE ODDS 1:478 MINI BOX
❑ PLATE PRINT RUN 1 SET PER COLOR
❑ BLACK-CYAN-MAGENTA-YELLOW ISSUED
❑ NO PLATE PRICING DUE TO SCARCITY
❑ 1 Alexis Rios .50 .20
❑ 2 Hank Blalock .50 .20
❑ 3 Bobby Abreu .50 .20
❑ 4 Curt Schilling .75 .30
❑ 5 Albert Pujols 2.50 1.00
❑ 6 Aaron Rowand .50 .20
❑ 7 B.J. Upton .50 .20
❑ 8 Andruw Jones .75 .30
❑ 9 Jeff Francis .50 .20
❑ 10 Sammy Sosa 1.25 .50
❑ 11 Aramis Ramirez .50 .20
❑ 12 Carl Pavano .50 .20
❑ 13 Bartolo Colon .50 .20
❑ 14 Greg Maddux 2.00 .75
❑ 15 Scott Kazmir .50 .20
❑ 16 Melvin Mora .50 .20
❑ 17 Brandon Backe .50 .20
❑ 18 Bobby Crosby .50 .20
❑ 19 Carlos Lee .50 .20
❑ 20 Carl Crawford .50 .20
❑ 21 Brian Giles .50 .20
❑ 22 Jeff Bagwell .75 .30
❑ 23 J.D. Drew .50 .20
❑ 24 C.C. Sabathia .50 .20
❑ 25 Alfonso Soriano .50 .20
❑ 26 Chipper Jones 1.25 .50
❑ 27 Austin Kearns .50 .20
❑ 28 Carlos Delgado .50 .20
❑ 29 Jack Wilson .50 .20
❑ 30 Dmitri Young .50 .20
❑ 31 Carlos Guillen .50 .20
❑ 32 Jim Thome .75 .30
❑ 33 Eric Chavez .50 .20
❑ 34 Jason Schmidt .50 .20
❑ 35 Brad Radke .50 .20
❑ 36 Frank Thomas 1.25 .50
❑ 37 Darin Erstad .50 .20
❑ 38 Javier Vazquez .50 .20
❑ 39 Garret Anderson .50 .20
❑ 40 David Ortiz 1.25 .50
❑ 41 Javy Lopez .50 .20
❑ 42 Geoff Jenkins .50 .20
❑ 43 Jose Vidro .50 .20
❑ 44 Aubrey Huff .50 .20
❑ 45 Bernie Williams .75 .30
❑ 46 Dontrelle Willis .50 .20
❑ 47 Jim Edmonds .50 .20
❑ 48 Ivan Rodriguez .75 .30
❑ 49 Gary Sheffield .50 .20
❑ 50 Alex Rodriguez 2.00 .75
❑ 51 John Buck .50 .20
❑ 52 Andy Pettitte .75 .30
❑ 53 Ichiro Suzuki 2.50 1.00
❑ 54 Johnny Estrada .50 .20
❑ 55 Jake Peavy .50 .20
❑ 56 Carlos Zambrano .50 .20
❑ 57 Jose Reyes .50 .20
❑ 58 Bret Boone .50 .20
❑ 59 Jason Bay .50 .20
❑ 60 David Wright 2.00 .75
❑ 61 Jeromy Burnitz .50 .20
❑ 62 Corey Patterson .50 .20
❑ 63 Juan Pierre .50 .20
❑ 64 Zack Greinke .50 .20
❑ 65 Mike Lowell .50 .20
❑ 66 Ken Griffey Jr. 2.00 .75
❑ 67 Marcus Giles .50 .20
❑ 68 Edgar Renteria .50 .20
❑ 69 Ken Harvey .50 .20
❑ 70 Pedro Martinez .75 .30
❑ 71 Johnny Damon .75 .30
❑ 72 Lyle Overbay .50 .20
❑ 73 Mike Maroth .50 .20
❑ 74 Jorge Posada .75 .30
❑ 75 Carlos Beltran .50 .20
❑ 76 Mark Buehrle .50 .20
❑ 77 Khalil Greene .75 .30
❑ 78 Josh Beckett .50 .20
❑ 79 Mark Loretta .50 .20
❑ 80 Rafael Palmeiro .75 .30
❑ 81 Justin Morneau .50 .20
❑ 82 Rocco Baldelli .50 .20
❑ 83 Ben Sheets .50 .20
❑ 84 Kerry Wood .50 .20
❑ 85 Miguel Tejada .50 .20
❑ 86 Magglio Ordonez .50 .20
❑ 87 Livan Hernandez .50 .20
❑ 88 Kazuo Matsui .50 .20
❑ 89 Manny Ramirez .75 .30
❑ 90 Hideki Matsui 2.00 .75
❑ 91 Jeff Kent .50 .20
❑ 92 Matt Lawton .50 .20
❑ 93 Richie Sexson .50 .20
❑ 94 Mike Mussina .75 .30
❑ 95 Adam Dunn .50 .20
❑ 96 Johan Santana 1.25 .50
❑ 97 Nomar Garciaparra 1.25 .50
❑ 98 Michael Young .50 .20
❑ 99 Victor Martinez .50 .20
❑ 100 Barry Bonds 3.00 1.25
❑ 101 Oliver Perez .50 .20
❑ 102 Randy Johnson 1.25 .50
❑ 103 Mark Mulder .50 .20
❑ 104 Pat Burrell .50 .20
❑ 105 Mike Sweeney .50 .20
❑ 106 Mark Teixeira .75 .30
❑ 107 Paul Lo Duca .50 .20
❑ 108 Jon Lieber .50 .20
❑ 109 Mike Piazza 1.25 .50
❑ 110 Roger Clemens 2.00 .75
❑ 111 Rafael Furcal .50 .20
❑ 112 Troy Glaus .50 .20
❑ 113 Miguel Cabrera .75 .30
❑ 114 Randy Wolf .50 .20
❑ 115 Lance Berkman .50 .20
❑ 116 Mark Prior .75 .30
❑ 117 Rich Harden .50 .20
❑ 118 Preston Wilson .50 .20
❑ 119 Roy Oswalt .50 .20
❑ 120 Luis Gonzalez .50 .20
❑ 121 Ronnie Belliard .50 .20
❑ 122 Sean Casey .50 .20
❑ 123 Barry Zito .50 .20
❑ 124 Larry Walker .75 .30
❑ 125 Derek Jeter 2.50 1.00
❑ 126 Tim Hudson .50 .20
❑ 127 Tom Glavine .75 .30
❑ 128 Scott Rolen .75 .30
❑ 129 Torii Hunter .50 .20
❑ 130 Paul Konerko .50 .20
❑ 131 Shawn Green .50 .20
❑ 132 Travis Hafner .50 .20
❑ 133 Vernon Wells .50 .20
❑ 134 Sidney Ponson .50 .20
❑ 135 Vladimir Guerrero 1.25 .50
❑ 136 Mark Kotsay .50 .20
❑ 137 Todd Helton .75 .30
❑ 138 Adrian Beltre .50 .20
❑ 139 Wily Mo Pena .50 .20
❑ 140 Joe Mauer 1.25 .50
❑ 141 Brian Stavisky AU/970 RC 10.00 4.00
❑ 142 Nate McLouth AU/970 RC 15.00 6.00
❑ 143 Glen Perkins AU/375 RC 20.00 8.00
❑ 144 Chip Cannon AU/970 RC 20.00 8.00
❑ 145 Shane Costa AU/970 RC 10.00 4.00
❑ 146 W.Swackhamer AU/970 RC 10.00 4.00
❑ 147 Kevin Melillo AU/970 RC 15.00 6.00
❑ 148 Billy Butler AU/970 RC 50.00 25.00
❑ 149 Landon Powell AU/970 RC 15.00 6.00
❑ 150 Scott Mathieson AU/970 RC 10.00 4.00
❑ 151 Chris Roberson AU/970 10.00 4.00
❑ 152 Chad Orvella AU/375 RC 15.00 6.00
❑ 153 Eric Nielsen AU/970 RC 10.00 4.00
❑ 154 Matt Campbell AU/970 RC 10.00 4.00
❑ 155 Mike Rogers AU/970 RC 10.00 4.00
❑ 156 Melky Cabrera AU/970 RC 40.00 20.00
❑ 157 Nolan Ryan RET 5.00 2.00
❑ 158 Bo Jackson RET 2.00 .75
❑ 159 Wade Boggs RET 1.50 .60
❑ 160 Andre Dawson RET 1.00 .40
❑ 161 Dave Winfield RET 1.00 .40
❑ 162 Reggie Jackson RET 1.50 .60
❑ 163 David Justice RET 2.00 .75
❑ 164 Dale Murphy RET 1.50 .60
❑ 165 Paul O'Neill RET 1.50 .60
❑ 166 Tom Seaver RET 1.50 .60

2006 Finest

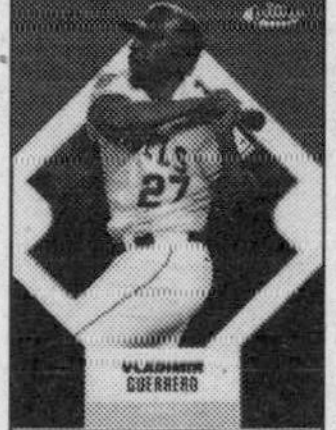

❑ COMPLETE SET (155)
❑ COMP.SET w/o AU's (140) 60.00 30.00
❑ COMMON CARD (1-131) .50 .20
❑ UNLISTED STARS 1-131 1.25 .50
❑ COMMON ROOKIE (132-140) .75 .30
❑ COMMON AUTO (141-155) 10.00 4.00
❑ 141-155 AU ODDS 1:4 MINI BOX
❑ 141-155 AU PRINT RUN 963 SETS
❑ 141-155 AU's NOT SERIAL NUMBERED
❑ PRINT RUN INFO PROVIDED BY TOPPS
❑ 1-140 PLATES RANDOM INSERTS IN PACKS
❑ AU 141-155 PLATE ODDS 1:792 MINI BOX
❑ PLATE PRINT RUN 1 SET PER COLOR
❑ BLACK-CYAN-MAGENTA-YELLOW ISSUED
❑ NO PLATE PRICING DUE TO SCARCITY
❑ 1 Vladimir Guerrero 1.25 .50
❑ 2 Troy Glaus .50 .20
❑ 3 Andruw Jones .75 .30
❑ 4 Miguel Tejada .50 .20
❑ 5 Manny Ramirez .75 .30
❑ 6 Curt Schilling .75 .30
❑ 7 Mark Prior .75 .30
❑ 8 Kerry Wood .50 .20
❑ 9 Tadahito Iguchi .50 .20
❑ 10 Freddy Garcia .50 .20
❑ 11 Ryan Howard 2.00 .75
❑ 12 Mark Buehrle .50 .20
❑ 13 Wily Mo Pena .50 .20
❑ 14 C.C. Sabathia .50 .20
❑ 15 Garret Anderson .50 .20
❑ 16 Shawn Green .50 .20
❑ 17 Rafael Furcal .50 .20
❑ 18 Jeff Francoeur 1.25 .50
❑ 19 Ken Griffey Jr. 2.00 .75
❑ 20 Derrek Lee .50 .20
❑ 21 Paul Konerko .50 .20
❑ 22 Rickie Weeks .50 .20
❑ 23 Magglio Ordonez .50 .20

Card		
❑ 24 Juan Pierre	.50	.20
❑ 25 Felix Hernandez	.75	.30
❑ 26 Roger Clemens	2.50	1.00
❑ 27 Zack Greinke	.50	.20
❑ 28 Johan Santana	.75	.30
❑ 29 Jose Reyes	1.25	.50
❑ 30 Bobby Crosby	.50	.20
❑ 31 Jason Schmidt	.50	.20
❑ 32 Khalil Greene	.75	.30
❑ 33 Richie Sexson	.50	.20
❑ 34 Mark Mulder	.50	.20
❑ 35 Mark Teixeira	.75	.30
❑ 36 Nick Johnson	.50	.20
❑ 37 Vernon Wells	.50	.20
❑ 38 Scott Kazmir	.75	.30
❑ 39 Jim Edmonds	.75	.30
❑ 40 Adrian Beltre	.50	.20
❑ 41 Dan Johnson	.50	.20
❑ 42 Carlos Lee	.50	.20
❑ 43 Lance Berkman	.50	.20
❑ 44 Josh Beckett	.50	.20
❑ 45 Morgan Ensberg	.50	.20
❑ 46 Garrett Atkins	.50	.20
❑ 47 Chase Utley	1.25	.50
❑ 48 Joe Mauer	.75	.30
❑ 49 Travis Hafner	.50	.20
❑ 50 Alex Rodriguez	2.00	.75
❑ 51 Austin Kearns	.50	.20
❑ 52 Scott Podsednik	.50	.20
❑ 53 Jose Contreras	.50	.20
❑ 54 Greg Maddux	2.00	.75
❑ 55 Hideki Matsui	2.00	.75
❑ 56 Matt Clement	.50	.20
❑ 57 Javy Lopez	.50	.20
❑ 58 Tim Hudson	.50	.20
❑ 59 Luis Gonzalez	.50	.20
❑ 60 Bartolo Colon	.50	.20
❑ 61 Marcus Giles	.50	.20
❑ 62 Justin Morneau	.50	.20
❑ 63 Nomar Garciaparra	1.25	.50
❑ 64 Robinson Cano	.75	.30
❑ 65 Ervin Santana	.50	.20
❑ 66 Brady Clark	.50	.20
❑ 67 Edgar Renteria	.50	.20
❑ 68 Jon Garland	.50	.20
❑ 69 Felipe Lopez	.50	.20
❑ 70 Ivan Rodriguez	.75	.30
❑ 71 Dontrelle Willis	.50	.20
❑ 72 Carlos Guillen	.50	.20
❑ 73 J.D. Drew	.50	.20
❑ 74 Rich Harden	.50	.20
❑ 75 Albert Pujols	2.50	1.00
❑ 76 Livan Hernandez	.50	.20
❑ 77 Roy Halladay	.50	.20
❑ 78 Hank Blalock	.50	.20
❑ 79 David Wright	2.00	.75
❑ 80 Jimmy Rollins	.50	.20
❑ 81 John Smoltz	.75	.30
❑ 82 Miguel Cabrera	.75	.30
❑ 83 David DeJesus	.50	.20
❑ 83 Zach Duke	.50	.20
❑ 84 Torii Hunter	.50	.20
❑ 85 Adam Dunn	.50	.20
❑ 86 Randy Johnson	1.25	.50
❑ 87 Roy Oswalt	.50	.20
❑ 88 Bobby Abreu	.50	.20
❑ 89 Rocco Baldelli	.50	.20
❑ 90 Ichiro Suzuki	2.00	.75
❑ 91 Jorge Cantu	.50	.20
❑ 92 Jack Wilson	.50	.20
❑ 93 Jose Vidro	.50	.20
❑ 94 Kevin Millwood	.50	.20
❑ 95 David Ortiz	1.25	.50
❑ 96 Victor Martinez	.50	.20
❑ 97 Jeremy Bonderman	.50	.20
❑ 98 Todd Helton	.75	.30
❑ 99 Carlos Beltran	.50	.20
❑ 100 Barry Bonds	3.00	1.25
❑ 101 Jeff Kent	.50	.20
❑ 102 Mike Sweeney	.50	.20
❑ 103 Ben Sheets	.50	.20
❑ 104 Melvin Mora	.50	.20
❑ 105 Gary Sheffield	.50	.20
❑ 106 Craig Wilson	.50	.20
❑ 107 Chris Carpenter	.50	.20
❑ 108 Michael Young	.50	.20
❑ 109 Gustavo Chacin	.50	.20
❑ 110 Chipper Jones	1.25	.50
❑ 111 Mark Loretta	.50	.20
❑ 112 Andy Pettitte	.75	.30
❑ 113 Carlos Delgado	.50	.20
❑ 114 Pat Burrell	.50	.20
❑ 115 Jason Bay	.50	.20
❑ 116 Brian Roberts	.50	.20
❑ 117 Joe Crede	.50	.20
❑ 118 Jake Peavy	.50	.20
❑ 119 Aubrey Huff	.50	.20
❑ 120 Pedro Martinez	.75	.30
❑ 121 Jorge Posada	.75	.30
❑ 122 Barry Zito	.50	.20
❑ 123 Scott Rolen	.75	.30
❑ 124 Brett Myers	.50	.20
❑ 125 Derek Jeter	3.00	1.25
❑ 126 Eric Chavez	.50	.20
❑ 127 Carl Crawford	.50	.20
❑ 128 Jim Thome	.75	.30
❑ 129 Johnny Damon	.75	.30
❑ 130 Alfonso Soriano	.50	.20
❑ 131 Clint Barmes	.50	.20
❑ 132 Dustin Nippert (RC)	.75	.30
❑ 133 Hanley Ramirez (RC)	2.00	.75
❑ 134 Matt Capps (RC)	.75	.30
❑ 135 Miguel Perez (RC)	.75	.30
❑ 136 Tom Gorzelanny (RC)	.75	.30
❑ 137 Charlton Jimerson (RC)	.75	.30
❑ 138 Bryan Bullington (RC)	.75	.30
❑ 139 Kenji Johjima RC	4.00	1.50
❑ 140 Craig Hansen RC	3.00	1.25
❑ 141 Craig Breslow AU/963 RC *	10.00	4.00
❑ 142 A.Wainwright AU/963 (RC) *	15.00	6.00
❑ 143 Joey Devine AU/963 RC *	10.00	4.00
❑ 144 H.Kuo AU/963 (RC) *	50.00	20.00
❑ 145 Jason Botts AU/963 (RC) *	10.00	4.00
❑ 146 J.Johnson AU/963 (RC) *	20.00	8.00
❑ 147 J.Bergmann AU/963 RC *	10.00	4.00
❑ 148 Scott Olsen AU/963 (RC) *	15.00	6.00
❑ 149 D.Rasner AU/963 (RC) *	10.00	4.00
❑ 150 Dan Ortmeier AU/963 (RC) *	10.00	4.00
❑ 151 Chuck James AU/963 (RC) *	15.00	6.00
❑ 152 Ryan Garko AU/963 (RC) *	10.00	4.00
❑ 153 Nelson Cruz AU/963 (RC) *	10.00	4.00
❑ 154 A.Lerew AU/963 (RC) *	10.00	4.00
❑ 155 F.Liriano AU/963 (RC) *	50.00	20.00

2007 Finest

Card		
❑ COMP.SET w/o AU's (150)	60.00	30.00
❑ COMMON CARD (1-135)	.40	.15
❑ COMMON ROOKIE (136-150)	1.00	.40
❑ 151-166 AU ODDS 1:3 MINI BOX		
❑ 1-150 PLATE ODDS 1:96 MINI BOX		
❑ AU 151-166 PLATE ODDS 1:909 MINI BOX		
❑ PLATE PRINT RUN 1 SET PER COLOR		
❑ BLACK-CYAN-MAGENTA-YELLOW ISSUED		
❑ NO PLATE PRICING DUE TO SCARCITY		
❑ EXCHANGE DEADLINE 02/28/09		
❑ 1 David Wright	1.50	.60
❑ 2 Jered Weaver	.60	.25
❑ 3 Chipper Jones	1.00	.40
❑ 4 Magglio Ordonez	.40	.15
❑ 5 Ben Sheets	.40	.15
❑ 6 Nick Johnson	.40	.15
❑ 7 Melvin Mora	.40	.15
❑ 8 Chien-Ming Wang	1.50	.60
❑ 9 Andre Ethier	.60	.25
❑ 10 Carlos Beltran	.40	.15
❑ 11 Ryan Zimmerman	1.00	.40
❑ 12 Troy Glaus	.40	.15
❑ 13 Hanley Ramirez	.60	.25
❑ 14 Mark Buehrle	.40	.15
❑ 15 Dan Uggla	.60	.25
❑ 16 Richie Sexson	.40	.15
❑ 17 Scott Kazmir	.60	.25
❑ 18 Garrett Atkins	.40	.15
❑ 19 Matt Cain	.60	.25
❑ 20 Jorge Posada	.60	.25
❑ 21 Brett Myers	.40	.15
❑ 22 Jeff Francoeur	1.00	.40
❑ 23 Scott Rolen	.60	.25
❑ 24 Derrek Lee	.40	.15
❑ 25 Manny Ramirez	.60	.25
❑ 26 Johnny Damon	.60	.25
❑ 27 Mark Teixeira	.60	.25
❑ 28 Mark Prior	.60	.25
❑ 29 Victor Martinez	.40	.15
❑ 30 Greg Maddux	1.50	.60
❑ 31 Prince Fielder	1.00	.40
❑ 32 Jeremy Bonderman	.40	.15
❑ 33 Paul LoDuca	.40	.15
❑ 34 Brandon Webb	.40	.15
❑ 35 Robinson Cano	.60	.25
❑ 36 Josh Beckett	.60	.25
❑ 37 David DeJesus	.40	.15
❑ 38 Kenny Rogers	.40	.15
❑ 39 Jim Thome	.60	.25
❑ 40 Brian McCann	.40	.15
❑ 41 Lance Berkman	.40	.15
❑ 42 Adam Dunn	.40	.15
❑ 43 Rocco Baldelli	.40	.15
❑ 44 Brian Roberts	.40	.15
❑ 45 Vladimir Guerrero	1.00	.40
❑ 46 Dontrelle Willis	.40	.15
❑ 47 Eric Chavez	.40	.15
❑ 48 Carlos Zambrano	.40	.15
❑ 49 Ivan Rodriguez	.60	.25
❑ 50 Alex Rodriguez	1.50	.60
❑ 51 Curt Schilling	.60	.25
❑ 52 Carlos Delgado	.40	.15
❑ 53 Matt Holliday	1.00	.40
❑ 54 Mark Teahen	.40	.15
❑ 55 Frank Thomas	1.00	.40
❑ 56 Grady Sizemore	.60	.25
❑ 57 Aramis Ramirez	.40	.15
❑ 58 Rafael Furcal	.40	.15
❑ 59 David Ortiz	1.00	.40
❑ 60 Paul Konerko	.40	.15
❑ 61 Barry Zito	.40	.15
❑ 62 Travis Hafner	.40	.15
❑ 63 Nick Swisher	.40	.15
❑ 64 Johan Santana	.60	.25
❑ 65 Miguel Tejada	.40	.15
❑ 66 Carl Crawford	.40	.15
❑ 67 Kenji Johjima	1.00	.40
❑ 68 Derek Jeter	2.50	1.00
❑ 69 Francisco Liriano	2.00	.75
❑ 70 Ken Griffey Jr.	1.50	.60
❑ 71 Pat Burrell	.40	.15
❑ 72 Adrian Gonzalez	.40	.15
❑ 73 Miguel Cabrera	.60	.25
❑ 74 Albert Pujols	2.00	.75
❑ 75 Justin Verlander	1.00	.40
❑ 76 Carlos Lee	.40	.15
❑ 77 John Smoltz	.60	.25
❑ 78 Orlando Hudson	.40	.15
❑ 79 Joe Mauer	.60	.25
❑ 80 Freddy Sanchez	.40	.15
❑ 81 Bobby Abreu	.40	.15
❑ 82 Pedro Martinez	.60	.25
❑ 83 Vernon Wells	.40	.15
❑ 84 Justin Morneau	.40	.15
❑ 85 Bill Hall	.40	.15
❑ 86 Jason Schmidt	.40	.15
❑ 87 Michael Young	.40	.15
❑ 88 Tadahito Iguchi	.40	.15
❑ 89 Kevin Millwood	.40	.15
❑ 90 Randy Johnson	1.00	.40
❑ 91 Roy Halladay	.40	.15
❑ 92 Mike Lowell	.40	.15
❑ 93 Jake Peavy	.40	.15
❑ 94 Jason Varitek	1.00	.40
❑ 95 Todd Helton	.60	.25

❑ 96 Mark Loretta .40 .15
❑ 97 Gary Matthews Jr. .40 .15
❑ 98 Ryan Howard 1.50 .60
❑ 99 Jose Reyes .40 .15
❑ 100 Chris Carpenter .40 .15
❑ 101 Hideki Matsui 1.00 .40
❑ 102 Brian Giles .40 .15
❑ 103 Torii Hunter .40 .15
❑ 104 Rich Harden .40 .15
❑ 105 Ichiro Suzuki 1.50 .60
❑ 106 Chase Utley 1.00 .40
❑ 107 Nick Markakis .60 .25
❑ 108 Marcus Giles .40 .15
❑ 109 Gary Sheffield .40 .15
❑ 110 Jim Edmonds .60 .25
❑ 111 Brandon Phillips .40 .15
❑ 112 Roy Oswalt .40 .15
❑ 113 Jeff Kent .40 .15
❑ 114 Jason Bay .40 .15
❑ 115 Raul Ibanez .40 .15
❑ 116 Stephen Drew .60 .25
❑ 117 Hank Blalock .40 .15
❑ 118 Tom Glavine .60 .25
❑ 119 Andruw Jones .60 .25
❑ 120 Alfonso Soriano .40 .15
❑ 121 Mariano Rivera 1.00 .40
❑ 122 Garret Anderson .40 .15
❑ 123 Erik Bedard UER .40 .15
❑ 124 Huston Street .40 .15
❑ 125 Austin Kearns .40 .15
❑ 126 Jermaine Dye .40 .15
❑ 127 C.C. Sabathia .40 .15
❑ 128 Joe Nathan .40 .15
❑ 129 Craig Monroe .40 .15
❑ 130 Aubrey Huff .40 .15
❑ 131 Billy Wagner .40 .15
❑ 132 Jorge Cantu .40 .15
❑ 133 Trevor Hoffman .40 .15
❑ 134 Ronnie Belliard .40 .15
❑ 135 B.J. Ryan .40 .15
❑ 136 Adam Lind (RC) 1.00 .40
❑ 137 Hector Gimenez (RC) 1.00 .40
❑ 138 Shawn Riggans UER (RC) 1.00 .40
❑ 139 Joaquin Arias (RC) 1.00 .40
❑ 140 Drew Anderson RC 1.00 .40
❑ 141 Mike Rabelo RC 1.00 .40
❑ 142 Chris Narveson (RC) 1.00 .40
❑ 143 Ryan Feierabend (RC) 1.00 .40
❑ 144 Vinny Rottino (RC) 1.00 .40
❑ 145 Jon Knott (RC) 1.00 .40
❑ 146 Oswaldo Navarro RC 1.00 .40
❑ 147 Brian Stokes (RC) 1.00 .40
❑ 148 Glen Perkins (RC) 1.00 .40
❑ 149 Mitch Maier RC 1.00 .40
❑ 150 Delmon Young (RC) 2.50 1.00
❑ 151 Andrew Miller AU RC 40.00 15.00
❑ 152 T.Tulowitzki AU (RC) 30.00 12.50
❑ 153 Philip Humber AU (RC) 15.00 6.00
❑ 154 K.Kouzmanoff AU (RC) 15.00 6.00
❑ 155 Michael Bourn AU (RC) 10.00 4.00
❑ 156 M.Montero AU (RC) EXCH 10.00 4.00
❑ 157 David Murphy AU (RC) 10.00 4.00
❑ 158 R.Sweeney AU (RC) 10.00 4.00
❑ 159 Jeff Baker AU (RC) 10.00 4.00
❑ 160 Jeff Salazar AU (RC) 10.00 4.00
❑ 161 J.Garcia AU RC EXCH 10.00 4.00
❑ 162 Josh Fields AU (RC) 10.00 4.00
❑ 163 Delwyn Young AU (RC) 10.00 4.00
❑ 164 Fred Lewis AU (RC) 10.00 4.00
❑ 165 Scott Moore AU (RC) 10.00 4.00
❑ 166 Chris Stewart AU RC 10.00 4.00

2008 Finest

❑ COMP.SET w/o AUs (150) 80.00 40.00
❑ COMMON CARD (1-125) .40 .15
❑ COMMON RC (126-150) 2.00 .75
❑ COMMON AU RC (151-166) 10.00 4.00
❑ 151-166 AU ODDS 1:3 MINI BOX
❑ 1-150 PLATE ODDS 1:82 MINI BOX
❑ AU 151-166 PLATE ODDS 1:775 MINI BOX
❑ PLATE PRINT RUN 1 SET PER COLOR
❑ BLACK-CYAN-MAGENTA-YELLOW ISSUED
❑ NO PLATE PRICING DUE TO SCARCITY
❑ 1 Daisuke Matsuzaka 2.00 .75
❑ 2 Justin Upton 1.00 .40
❑ 3 Andruw Jones .40 .15

❑ 4 John Lackey .40 .15
❑ 5 Brandon Phillips .40 .15
❑ 6 Ryan Zimmerman .60 .25
❑ 7 Tim Lincecum 1.00 .40
❑ 8 Johnny Damon .60 .25
❑ 9 Garrett Atkins .40 .15
❑ 10 Magglio Ordonez .60 .25
❑ 11 Tom Gorzelanny .40 .15
❑ 12 Eric Chavez .40 .15
❑ 13 Troy Tulowitzki .60 .25
❑ 14 Mike Lowell .40 .15
❑ 15 Brandon Webb .40 .15
❑ 16 Chipper Jones 1.25 .50
❑ 17 Alex Gordon 1.00 .40
❑ 18 Ken Griffey Jr. 1.50 .60
❑ 19 Roy Oswalt .40 .15
❑ 20 Miguel Cabrera .60 .25
❑ 21 Chase Utley 1.00 .40
❑ 22 Scott Kazmir .60 .25
❑ 23 Kenji Johjima .40 .15
❑ 24 Frank Thomas 1.00 .40
❑ 25 Ryan Braun 1.25 .50
❑ 26 Carlos Pena .40 .15
❑ 27 Robinson Cano .60 .25
❑ 28 Ben Sheets .60 .25
❑ 29 Russell Martin .40 .15
❑ 30 Joe Mauer .60 .25
❑ 31 Gary Sheffield .40 .15
❑ 32 Carlos Zambrano .40 .15
❑ 33 Jermaine Dye .40 .15
❑ 34 Dan Uggla .60 .25
❑ 35 Erik Bedard .40 .15
❑ 36 Tim Hudson .40 .15
❑ 37 David Ortiz 1.00 .40
❑ 38 Tom Glavine .60 .25
❑ 39 Adrian Gonzalez .60 .25
❑ 40 Jorge Posada .60 .25
❑ 41 Noah Lowry .40 .15
❑ 42 Vernon Wells .40 .15
❑ 43 Johan Santana 1.00 .40
❑ 44 Dmitri Young .40 .15
❑ 45 Manny Ramirez 1.00 .40
❑ 46 Jim Edmonds .60 .25
❑ 47 Roy Halladay .40 .15
❑ 48 Delmon Young .60 .25
❑ 49 Nick Swisher .40 .15
❑ 50 David Wright 1.25 .50
❑ 51 Paul Konerko .40 .15
❑ 52 Curt Schilling .60 .25
❑ 53 Torii Hunter .40 .15
❑ 54 Gary Matthews .40 .15
❑ 55 Derrek Lee .60 .25
❑ 56 John Smoltz 1.00 .40
❑ 57 Adam Dunn .40 .15
❑ 58 C.C Sabathia .40 .15
❑ 59 Chris Young .40 .15
❑ 60 Jake Peavy .40 .15
❑ 61 Joba Chamberlain 4.00 1.50
❑ 62 Jason Bay .40 .15
❑ 63 Chris Carpenter .40 .15
❑ 64 Jimmy Rollins .60 .25
❑ 65 Grady Sizemore .60 .25
❑ 66 Joe Blanton .40 .15
❑ 67 Justin Morneau .40 .15
❑ 68 Lance Berkman .60 .25
❑ 69 Jeff Francis .40 .15
❑ 70 Nick Markakis .60 .25
❑ 71 Orlando Cabrera .40 .15
❑ 72 Barry Zito .40 .15
❑ 73 Eric Byrnes .40 .15
❑ 74 Brian McCann .60 .25
❑ 75 Albert Pujols 1.50 .60
❑ 76 Josh Beckett .60 .25
❑ 77 Jim Thome .60 .25
❑ 78 Fausto Carmona .40 .15
❑ 79 Brad Hawpe .40 .15
❑ 80 Prince Fielder 1.00 .40
❑ 81 Justin Verlander .60 .25
❑ 82 Billy Butler .40 .15
❑ 83 J.J. Hardy .40 .15
❑ 84 Hideki Matsui 1.00 .40
❑ 85 Matt Holliday .60 .25
❑ 86 Bobby Crosby .40 .15
❑ 87 Orlando Hudson .40 .15
❑ 88 Ichiro Suzuki 1.50 .60
❑ 89 Troy Glaus .60 .25
❑ 90 Hanley Ramirez 1.00 .40
❑ 91 Carlos Beltran .40 .15
❑ 92 Mark Buehrle .40 .15
❑ 93 Andy Pettitte .60 .25
❑ 94 Mark Teixeira .60 .25
❑ 95 Curtis Granderson .60 .25
❑ 96 Cole Hamels .60 .25
❑ 97 Jarrod Saltalamacchia .40 .15
❑ 98 Carl Crawford .40 .15
❑ 99 Dontrelle Willis .40 .15
❑ 100 Alex Rodriguez 1.50 .60
❑ 101 Brad Penny .40 .15
❑ 102 Michael Young .40 .15
❑ 103 Greg Maddux 1.25 .50
❑ 104 Brian Roberts .60 .25
❑ 105 Hunter Pence 1.00 .40
❑ 106 Aaron Harang .40 .15
❑ 107 Ivan Rodriguez .60 .25
❑ 108 Dan Haren .40 .15
❑ 109 Freddy Sanchez .40 .15
❑ 110 Alfonso Soriano .60 .25
❑ 111 Hank Blalock .40 .15
❑ 112 Chien- Ming Wang 1.50 .60
❑ 113 Carlos Delgado .40 .15
❑ 114 Aramis Ramirez .40 .15
❑ 115 Jose Reyes .60 .25
❑ 116 Victor Martinez .40 .15
❑ 117 Carlos Lee .40 .15
❑ 118 Jeff Kent .40 .15
❑ 119 Miguel Tejada .40 .15
❑ 120 Vladimir Guerrero 1.00 .40
❑ 121 Travis Hafner .40 .15
❑ 122 Todd Helton .60 .25
❑ 123 Chris Young .40 .15
❑ 124 Derek Jeter 2.50 1.00
❑ 125 Ryan Howard 1.25 .50
❑ 126 Alberto Gonzalez RC 3.00 1.25
❑ 127 Felipe Paulino RC 3.00 1.25
❑ 128 Donny Lucy (RC) 2.00 .75
❑ 129 Nick Blackburn RC 3.00 1.25
❑ 130 Luke Hochevar RC 6.00 2.50
❑ 131 Bronson Sardinha (RC) 2.00 .75
❑ 132 Heath Phillips RC 3.00 1.25
❑ 133 Bryan Bullington (RC) 2.00 .75
❑ 134 Jeff Clement (RC) 2.00 .75
❑ 135 Josh Banks (RC) 2.00 .75
❑ 136 Emilio Bonifacio RC 3.00 1.25
❑ 137 Ryan Hanigan RC 3.00 1.25
❑ 138 Erick Threets (RC) 2.00 .75
❑ 139 Seth Smith (RC) 2.00 .75
❑ 140 Billy Buckner (RC) 2.00 .75
❑ 141 Bill Murphy (RC) 2.00 .75
❑ 142 Radhames Liz RC 3.00 1.25
❑ 143 Joey Votto (RC) 3.00 1.25
❑ 144 Mel Stocker RC 2.00 .75
❑ 145 Dan Meyer (RC) 2.00 .75
❑ 146 Rob Johnson (RC) 2.00 .75
❑ 147 Josh Newman RC 3.00 1.25
❑ 148 Dan Giese (RC) 2.00 .75
❑ 149 Luis Mendoza (RC) 2.00 .75
❑ 150 Wladimir Balentien (RC) 2.00 .75
❑ 151 B.Jones AU RC 10.00 4.00
❑ 152 Rich Thompson AU RC 10.00 4.00
❑ 153 C.Hu AU (RC) 40.00 15.00
❑ 154 Chris Seddon AU (RC) 10.00 4.00
❑ 155 S.Pearce AU RC 15.00 6.00
❑ 156 Lance Broadway AU (RC) 10.00 4.00
❑ 157 Nyjer Morgan AU (RC) 10.00 4.00

Card		
❑ 158 Jonathan Meloan AU RC	10.00	4.00
❑ 159 Josh Anderson AU (RC)	10.00	4.00
❑ 160 C.Buchholz AU (RC)	40.00	15.00
❑ 161 Joe Koshansky AU (RC)	10.00	4.00
❑ 162 Clint Sammons AU (RC)	10.00	4.00
❑ 163 Daric Barton AU (RC)	12.00	5.00
❑ 164 Ross Detwiler AU RC	12.00	5.00
❑ 165 Sam Fuld AU (RC)	10.00	4.00
❑ 166 Justin Ruggiano AU RC	10.00	4.00

1960 Fleer

Card		
❑ COMPLETE SET (79)	600.00	300.00
❑ WRAPPER (5-CENT)	100.00	50.00
❑ 1 Napoleon Lajoie DP	30.00	12.50
❑ 2 Christy Mathewson	15.00	6.00
❑ 3 Babe Ruth	100.00	50.00
❑ 4 Carl Hubbell	8.00	3.00
❑ 5 Grover C. Alexander	8.00	3.00
❑ 6 Walter Johnson DP	10.00	4.00
❑ 7 Chief Bender	4.00	1.50
❑ 8 Roger Bresnahan	4.00	1.50
❑ 9 Mordecai Brown	4.00	1.50
❑ 10 Tris Speaker	8.00	3.00
❑ 11 Arky Vaughan DP	4.00	1.50
❑ 12 Zach Wheat	4.00	1.50
❑ 13 George Sisler	4.00	1.50
❑ 14 Connie Mack	8.00	3.00
❑ 15 Clark Griffith	4.00	1.50
❑ 16 Lou Boudreau DP	8.00	3.00
❑ 17 Ernie Lombardi	4.00	1.50
❑ 18 Heinie Manush	4.00	1.50
❑ 19 Marty Marion	6.00	2.50
❑ 20 Eddie Collins DP	4.00	1.50
❑ 21 Rabbit Maranville DP	4.00	1.50
❑ 22 Joe Medwick	4.00	1.50
❑ 23 Ed Barrow	4.00	1.50
❑ 24 Mickey Cochrane	6.00	2.50
❑ 25 Jimmy Collins	4.00	1.50
❑ 26 Bob Feller DP	15.00	6.00
❑ 27 Luke Appling	6.00	2.50
❑ 28 Lou Gehrig	80.00	40.00
❑ 29 Gabby Hartnett	4.00	1.50
❑ 30 Chuck Klein	4.00	1.50
❑ 31 Tony Lazzeri DP	6.00	2.50
❑ 32 Al Simmons	4.00	1.50
❑ 33 Wilbert Robinson	4.00	1.50
❑ 34 Sam Rice	4.00	1.50
❑ 35 Herb Pennock	4.00	1.50
❑ 36 Mel Ott DP	8.00	3.00
❑ 37 Lefty O'Doul	4.00	1.50
❑ 38 Johnny Mize	8.00	3.00
❑ 39 Edmund (Bing) Miller	4.00	1.50
❑ 40 Joe Tinker	4.00	1.50
❑ 41 Frank Baker DP	4.00	1.50
❑ 42 Ty Cobb	60.00	30.00
❑ 43 Paul Derringer	4.00	1.50
❑ 44 Cap Anson	4.00	1.50
❑ 45 Jim Bottomley	4.00	1.50
❑ 46 Eddie Plank DP	4.00	1.50
❑ 47 Denton (Cy) Young	10.00	4.00
❑ 48 Hack Wilson	6.00	2.50
❑ 49 Ed Walsh UER	4.00	1.50
❑ 50 Frank Chance	4.00	1.50
❑ 51 Dazzy Vance DP	4.00	1.50
❑ 52 Bill Terry	6.00	2.50
❑ 53 Jimmie Foxx	10.00	4.00
❑ 54 Lefty Gomez	8.00	3.00
❑ 55 Branch Rickey	4.00	1.50
❑ 56 Ray Schalk DP	4.00	1.50
❑ 57 Johnny Evers	4.00	1.50
❑ 58 Charley Gehringer	6.00	2.50
❑ 59 Burleigh Grimes	4.00	1.50
❑ 60 Lefty Grove	8.00	3.00
❑ 61 Rube Waddell DP	4.00	1.50
❑ 62 Honus Wagner	15.00	6.00
❑ 63 Red Ruffing	4.00	1.50
❑ 64 Kenesaw M. Landis	4.00	1.50
❑ 65 Harry Heilmann	4.00	1.50
❑ 66 John McGraw DP	4.00	1.50
❑ 67 Hughie Jennings	4.00	1.50
❑ 68 Hal Newhouser	6.00	2.50
❑ 69 Waite Hoyt	4.00	1.50
❑ 70 Bobo Newsom	4.00	1.50
❑ 71 Earl Averill DP	4.00	1.50
❑ 72 Ted Williams	80.00	40.00
❑ 73 Warren Giles	6.00	2.50
❑ 74 Ford Frick	6.00	2.50
❑ 75 Kiki Cuyler	4.00	1.50
❑ 76 Paul Waner DP	6.00	2.50
❑ 77 Pie Traynor	4.00	1.50
❑ 78 Lloyd Waner	4.00	1.50
❑ 79 Ralph Kiner	10.00	4.00
❑ 80A P.Martin SP/Eddie Collins	2500.00	1250.00
❑ 80B P.Martin SP/Lefty Grove	2000.00	1000.00
❑ 80C P.Martin SP/Joe Tinker	2000.00	1000.00

1961 Fleer

Card		
❑ COMPLETE SET (154)	1200.00	600.00
❑ COMMON CARD (1-88)	3.00	1.25
❑ COMMON CARD (89-154)	8.00	3.00
❑ WRAPPER (5-CENT)	100.00	50.00
❑ 1 Baker/Cobb/Wheat	50.00	20.00
❑ 2 Grover C. Alexander	6.00	2.50
❑ 3 Nick Altrock	3.00	1.25
❑ 4 Cap Anson	4.00	1.50
❑ 5 Earl Averill	4.00	1.50
❑ 6 Frank Baker	4.00	1.50
❑ 7 Dave Bancroft	4.00	1.50
❑ 8 Chief Bender	4.00	1.50
❑ 9 Jim Bottomley	4.00	1.50
❑ 10 Roger Bresnahan	4.00	1.50
❑ 11 Mordecai Brown	4.00	1.50
❑ 12 Max Carey	4.00	1.50
❑ 13 Jack Chesbro	4.00	1.50
❑ 14 Ty Cobb	50.00	20.00
❑ 15 Mickey Cochrane	4.00	1.50
❑ 16 Eddie Collins	6.00	2.50
❑ 17 Earle Combs	4.00	1.50
❑ 18 Charles Comiskey	4.00	1.50
❑ 19 Kiki Cuyler	4.00	1.50
❑ 20 Paul Derringer	3.00	1.25
❑ 21 Howard Ehmke	3.00	1.25
❑ 22 Billy Evans UMP	4.00	1.50
❑ 23 Johnny Evers	4.00	1.50
❑ 24 Urban Faber	4.00	1.50
❑ 25 Bob Feller	12.00	5.00
❑ 26 Wes Ferrell	3.00	1.25
❑ 27 Lew Fonseca	3.00	1.25
❑ 28 Jimmie Foxx	6.00	2.50
❑ 29 Ford Frick	3.00	1.25
❑ 30 Frankie Frisch	4.00	1.50
❑ 31 Lou Gehrig	80.00	40.00
❑ 32 Charley Gehringer	4.00	1.50
❑ 33 Warren Giles	3.00	1.25
❑ 34 Lefty Gomez	4.00	1.50
❑ 35 Goose Goslin	4.00	1.50
❑ 36 Clark Griffith	4.00	1.50
❑ 37 Burleigh Grimes	4.00	1.50
❑ 38 Lefty Grove	6.00	2.50
❑ 39 Chick Hafey	4.00	1.50
❑ 40 Jesse Haines	4.00	1.50
❑ 41 Gabby Hartnett	4.00	1.50
❑ 42 Harry Heilmann	4.00	1.50
❑ 43 Rogers Hornsby	6.00	2.50
❑ 44 Waite Hoyt	4.00	1.50
❑ 45 Carl Hubbell	6.00	2.50
❑ 46 Miller Huggins	4.00	1.50
❑ 47 Hughie Jennings	4.00	1.50
❑ 48 Ban Johnson	4.00	1.50
❑ 49 Walter Johnson	12.00	5.00
❑ 50 Ralph Kiner	6.00	2.50
❑ 51 Chuck Klein	4.00	1.50
❑ 52 Johnny Kling	3.00	1.25
❑ 53 Kenesaw M. Landis	4.00	1.50
❑ 54 Tony Lazzeri	4.00	1.50
❑ 55 Ernie Lombardi	4.00	1.50
❑ 56 Dolf Luque	3.00	1.25
❑ 57 Heinie Manush	4.00	1.50
❑ 58 Marty Marion	3.00	1.25
❑ 59 Christy Mathewson	12.00	5.00
❑ 60 John McGraw	4.00	1.50
❑ 61 Joe Medwick	4.00	1.50
❑ 62 Edmund (Bing) Miller	3.00	1.25
❑ 63 Johnny Mize	4.00	1.50
❑ 64 John Mostil	3.00	1.25
❑ 65 Art Nehf	3.00	1.25
❑ 66 Hal Newhouser	4.00	1.50
❑ 67 Bobo Newsom	3.00	1.25
❑ 68 Mel Ott	6.00	2.50
❑ 69 Allie Reynolds	3.00	1.25
❑ 70 Sam Rice	4.00	1.50
❑ 71 Eppa Rixey	4.00	1.50
❑ 72 Edd Roush	4.00	1.50
❑ 73 Schoolboy Rowe	3.00	1.25
❑ 74 Red Ruffing	4.00	1.50
❑ 75 Babe Ruth	120.00	60.00
❑ 76 Joe Sewell	4.00	1.50
❑ 77 Al Simmons	4.00	1.50
❑ 78 George Sisler	4.00	1.50
❑ 79 Tris Speaker	4.00	1.50
❑ 80 Fred Toney	3.00	1.25
❑ 81 Dazzy Vance	4.00	1.50
❑ 82 Hippo Vaughn	3.00	1.25
❑ 83 Ed Walsh	4.00	1.50
❑ 84 Lloyd Waner	4.00	1.50
❑ 85 Paul Waner	4.00	1.50
❑ 86 Zack Wheat	4.00	1.50
❑ 87 Hack Wilson	4.00	1.50
❑ 88 Jimmy Wilson	3.00	1.25
❑ 89 G.Sisler/P.Traynor	60.00	30.00
❑ 90 Babe Adams	8.00	3.00
❑ 91 Dale Alexander	8.00	3.00
❑ 92 Jim Bagby	8.00	3.00
❑ 93 Ossie Bluege	8.00	3.00
❑ 94 Lou Boudreau	10.00	4.00
❑ 95 Tommy Bridges	8.00	3.00
❑ 96 Donie Bush	8.00	3.00
❑ 97 Dolph Camilli	8.00	3.00
❑ 98 Frank Chance	10.00	4.00
❑ 99 Jimmy Collins	10.00	4.00
❑ 100 Stan Coveleskie	10.00	4.00
❑ 101 Hugh Critz	8.00	3.00
❑ 102 Alvin Crowder	8.00	3.00
❑ 103 Joe Dugan	8.00	3.00
❑ 104 Bibb Falk	8.00	3.00
❑ 105 Rick Ferrell	10.00	4.00
❑ 106 Art Fletcher	8.00	3.00
❑ 107 Dennis Galehouse	8.00	3.00
❑ 108 Chick Galloway	8.00	3.00
❑ 109 Mule Haas	8.00	3.00
❑ 110 Stan Hack	8.00	3.00
❑ 111 Bump Hadley	8.00	3.00
❑ 112 Billy Hamilton	10.00	4.00
❑ 113 Joe Hauser	8.00	3.00
❑ 114 Babe Herman	8.00	3.00
❑ 115 Travis Jackson	10.00	4.00
❑ 116 Eddie Joost	8.00	3.00
❑ 117 Addie Joss	10.00	4.00
❑ 118 Joe Judge	8.00	3.00
❑ 119 Joe Kuhel	8.00	3.00
❑ 120 Napoleon Lajoie	12.00	5.00
❑ 121 Dutch Leonard	8.00	3.00

❑ 122 Ted Lyons	10.00	4.00
❑ 123 Connie Mack	12.00	5.00
❑ 124 Rabbit Maranville	10.00	4.00
❑ 125 Fred Marberry	8.00	3.00
❑ 126 Joe McGinnity	10.00	4.00
❑ 127 Oscar Melillo	8.00	3.00
❑ 128 Ray Mueller	8.00	3.00
❑ 129 Kid Nichols	10.00	4.00
❑ 130 Lefty O'Doul	10.00	4.00
❑ 131 Bob O'Farrell	8.00	3.00
❑ 132 Roger Peckinpaugh	8.00	3.00
❑ 133 Herb Pennock	10.00	4.00
❑ 134 George Pipgras	8.00	3.00
❑ 135 Eddie Plank	10.00	4.00
❑ 136 Ray Schalk	10.00	4.00
❑ 137 Hal Schumacher	8.00	3.00
❑ 138 Luke Sewell	8.00	3.00
❑ 139 Bob Shawkey	8.00	3.00
❑ 140 Riggs Stephenson	8.00	3.00
❑ 141 Billy Sullivan	8.00	3.00
❑ 142 Bill Terry	12.00	5.00
❑ 143 Joe Tinker	10.00	4.00
❑ 144 Pie Traynor	10.00	4.00
❑ 145 Hal Trosky	8.00	3.00
❑ 146 George Uhle	8.00	3.00
❑ 147 Johnny VanderMeer	10.00	4.00
❑ 148 Arky Vaughan	10.00	4.00
❑ 149 Rube Waddell	10.00	4.00
❑ 150 Honus Wagner	50.00	20.00
❑ 151 Dixie Walker	8.00	3.00
❑ 152 Ted Williams	120.00	60.00
❑ 153 Cy Young	40.00	15.00
❑ 154 Ross Youngs	40.00	15.00

1963 Fleer

❑ COMPLETE SET (67)	2000.00	1000.00
❑ WRAPPER (5-CENT)	100.00	50.00
❑ 1 Steve Barber	25.00	10.00
❑ 2 Ron Hansen	15.00	6.00
❑ 3 Milt Pappas	20.00	8.00
❑ 4 Brooks Robinson	100.00	50.00
❑ 5 Willie Mays	200.00	100.00
❑ 6 Lou Clinton	15.00	6.00
❑ 7 Bill Monbouquette	15.00	6.00
❑ 8 Carl Yastrzemski	100.00	50.00
❑ 9 Ray Herbert	15.00	6.00
❑ 10 Jim Landis	15.00	6.00
❑ 11 Dick Donovan	15.00	6.00
❑ 12 Tito Francona	15.00	6.00
❑ 13 Jerry Kindall	15.00	6.00
❑ 14 Frank Lary	20.00	8.00
❑ 15 Dick Howser	20.00	8.00
❑ 16 Jerry Lumpe	15.00	6.00
❑ 17 Norm Siebern	15.00	6.00
❑ 18 Don Lee	15.00	6.00
❑ 19 Albie Pearson	20.00	8.00
❑ 20 Bob Rodgers	20.00	8.00
❑ 21 Leon Wagner	15.00	6.00
❑ 22 Jim Kaat	25.00	10.00
❑ 23 Vic Power	20.00	8.00
❑ 24 Rich Rollins	20.00	8.00
❑ 25 Bobby Richardson	25.00	10.00
❑ 26 Ralph Terry	20.00	8.00
❑ 27 Tom Cheney	15.00	6.00
❑ 28 Chuck Cottier	15.00	6.00
❑ 29 Jimmy Piersall	20.00	8.00
❑ 30 Dave Stenhouse	15.00	6.00
❑ 31 Glen Hobbie	15.00	6.00
❑ 32 Ron Santo	25.00	10.00
❑ 33 Gene Freese	15.00	6.00
❑ 34 Vada Pinson	25.00	10.00
❑ 35 Bob Purkey	15.00	6.00
❑ 36 Joe Amalfitano	15.00	6.00
❑ 37 Bob Aspromonte	15.00	6.00
❑ 38 Dick Farrell	15.00	6.00
❑ 39 Al Spangler	15.00	6.00
❑ 40 Tommy Davis	20.00	8.00
❑ 41 Don Drysdale	80.00	40.00
❑ 42 Sandy Koufax	200.00	100.00
❑ 43 Maury Wills RC	100.00	50.00
❑ 44 Frank Bolling	15.00	6.00
❑ 45 Warren Spahn	80.00	40.00
❑ 46 Joe Adcock SP	150.00	75.00
❑ 47 Roger Craig	20.00	8.00
❑ 48 Al Jackson	20.00	8.00
❑ 49 Rod Kanehl	20.00	8.00
❑ 50 Ruben Amaro	15.00	6.00
❑ 51 Johnny Callison	20.00	8.00
❑ 52 Clay Dalrymple	15.00	6.00
❑ 53 Don Demeter	15.00	6.00
❑ 54 Art Mahaffey	15.00	6.00
❑ 55 Smoky Burgess	20.00	8.00
❑ 56 Roberto Clemente	200.00	100.00
❑ 57 Roy Face	20.00	8.00
❑ 58 Vern Law	20.00	8.00
❑ 59 Bill Mazeroski	30.00	12.50
❑ 60 Ken Boyer	25.00	10.00
❑ 61 Bob Gibson	80.00	40.00
❑ 62 Gene Oliver	15.00	6.00
❑ 63 Bill White	20.00	8.00
❑ 64 Orlando Cepeda	30.00	12.50
❑ 65 Jim Davenport	15.00	6.00
❑ 66 Billy O'Dell	25.00	10.00
❑ NNO Checklist SP	500.00	250.00

1981 Fleer

❑ COMPLETE SET (660)	40.00	15.00
❑ 1 Pete Rose	3.00	1.25
❑ 2 Larry Bowa	.25	.08
❑ 3 Manny Trillo	.10	.02
❑ 4 Bob Boone	.25	.08
❑ 5 Mike Schmidt	2.50	1.00
❑ 6 Steve Carlton P1	.50	.20
❑ 6B Steve Carlton P2	1.50	.60
❑ 6C Steve Carlton P3	2.00	.75
❑ 7 Tug McGraw	.25	.08
❑ 8 Larry Christenson	.10	.02
❑ 9 Bake McBride	.25	.08
❑ 10 Greg Luzinski	.25	.08
❑ 11 Ron Reed	.10	.02
❑ 12 Dickie Noles	.10	.02
❑ 13 Keith Moreland RC	.10	.02
❑ 14 Bob Walk RC	.50	.20
❑ 15 Lonnie Smith	.25	.08
❑ 16 Dick Ruthven	.10	.02
❑ 17 Sparky Lyle	.25	.08
❑ 18 Greg Gross	.10	.02
❑ 19 Garry Maddox	.10	.02
❑ 20 Nino Espinosa	.10	.02
❑ 21 George Vukovich RC	.10	.02
❑ 22 John Vukovich	.10	.02
❑ 23 Ramon Aviles	.10	.02
❑ 24A Kevin Saucier P1	.10	.02
❑ 24B Kevin Saucier P2	.10	.02
❑ 24C Kevin Saucier P3	.50	.20
❑ 25 Randy Lerch	.10	.02
❑ 26 Del Unser	.10	.02
❑ 27 Tim McCarver	.25	.08
❑ 28 George Brett	2.50	1.00
❑ 29 Willie Wilson	.25	.08
❑ 30 Paul Splittorff	.10	.02
❑ 31 Dan Quisenberry	.10	.02
❑ 32A Amos Otis P1 Batting	.25	.08
❑ 32B Amos Otis P2	.25	.08
❑ 33 Steve Busby	.10	.02
❑ 34 U.L. Washington	.10	.02
❑ 35 Dave Chalk	.10	.02
❑ 36 Darrell Porter	.10	.02
❑ 37 Marty Pattin	.10	.02
❑ 38 Larry Gura	.10	.02
❑ 39 Renie Martin	.10	.02
❑ 40 Rich Gale	.10	.02
❑ 41A Hal McRae P1	.50	.20
❑ 41B Hal McRae P2	.25	.08
❑ 42 Dennis Leonard	.10	.02
❑ 43 Willie Aikens	.10	.02
❑ 44 Frank White	.25	.08
❑ 45 Clint Hurdle	.10	.02
❑ 46 John Wathan	.10	.02
❑ 47 Pete LaCock	.10	.02
❑ 48 Rance Mulliniks	.10	.02
❑ 49 Jeff Twitty RC	.10	.02
❑ 50 Jamie Quirk	.10	.02
❑ 51 Art Howe	.10	.02
❑ 52 Ken Forsch	.10	.02
❑ 53 Vern Ruhle	.10	.02
❑ 54 Joe Niekro	.10	.02
❑ 55 Frank LaCorte	.10	.02
❑ 56 J.R. Richard	.25	.08
❑ 57 Nolan Ryan	5.00	2.00
❑ 58 Enos Cabell	.10	.02
❑ 59 Cesar Cedeno	.25	.08
❑ 60 Jose Cruz	.25	.08
❑ 61 Bill Virdon MG	.10	.02
❑ 62 Terry Puhl	.10	.02
❑ 63 Joaquin Andujar	.25	.08
❑ 64 Alan Ashby	.10	.02
❑ 65 Joe Sambito	.10	.02
❑ 66 Denny Walling	.10	.02
❑ 67 Jeff Leonard	.25	.08
❑ 68 Luis Pujols	.10	.02
❑ 69 Bruce Bochy	.10	.02
❑ 70 Rafael Landestoy	.10	.02
❑ 71 Dave Smith RC	.50	.20
❑ 72 Danny Heep RC	.10	.02
❑ 73 Julio Gonzalez	.10	.02
❑ 74 Craig Reynolds	.10	.02
❑ 75 Gary Woods	.10	.02
❑ 76 Dave Bergman	.10	.02
❑ 77 Randy Niemann	.10	.02
❑ 78 Joe Morgan	.50	.20
❑ 79 Reggie Jackson	1.00	.40
❑ 80 Bucky Dent	.25	.08
❑ 81 Tommy John	.25	.08
❑ 82 Luis Tiant	.25	.08
❑ 83 Rick Cerone	.10	.02
❑ 84 Dick Howser MG	.10	.02
❑ 85 Lou Piniella	.25	.08
❑ 86 Ron Davis	.10	.02
❑ 87A Craig Nettles P1	5.00	2.00
❑ 87B Graig Nettles COR	.25	.08
❑ 88 Ron Guidry	.25	.08
❑ 89 Rich Gossage	.25	.08
❑ 90 Rudy May	.10	.02
❑ 91 Gaylord Perry	.25	.08
❑ 92 Eric Soderholm	.10	.02
❑ 93 Bob Watson	.10	.02
❑ 94 Bobby Murcer	.25	.08
❑ 95 Bobby Brown	.10	.02
❑ 96 Jim Spencer	.10	.02
❑ 97 Tom Underwood	.10	.02
❑ 98 Oscar Gamble	.10	.02
❑ 99 Johnny Oates	.25	.08
❑ 100 Fred Stanley	.10	.02
❑ 101 Ruppert Jones	.10	.02
❑ 102 Dennis Werth RC	.10	.02
❑ 103 Joe Lefebvre RC	.10	.02
❑ 104 Brian Doyle	.10	.02
❑ 105 Aurelio Rodriguez	.10	.02
❑ 106 Doug Bird	.10	.02
❑ 107 Mike Griffin RC	.15	.05
❑ 108 Tim Lollar RC	.10	.02

❑	109	Willie Randolph	.25	.08
❑	110	Steve Garvey	.50	.20
❑	111	Reggie Smith	.25	.08
❑	112	Don Sutton	.25	.08
❑	113	Burt Hooton	.10	.02
❑	114A	Dave Lopes P1	.50	.20
❑	114B	Dave Lopes P2	.25	.08
❑	115	Dusty Baker	.25	.08
❑	116	Tom Lasorda MG	.50	.20
❑	117	Bill Russell	.25	.08
❑	118	Jerry Reuss UER	.10	.02
❑	119	Terry Forster	.25	.08
❑	120A	Bob Welch	.25	.08
❑	120B	Bob Welch (Robert)	.25	.08
❑	121	Don Stanhouse	.10	.02
❑	122	Rick Monday	.25	.08
❑	123	Derrel Thomas	.10	.02
❑	124	Joe Ferguson	.10	.02
❑	125	Rick Sutcliffe	.25	.08
❑	126A	Ron Cey P1	.25	.08
❑	126B	Ron Cey P2	.25	.08
❑	127	Dave Goltz	.10	.02
❑	128	Jay Johnstone	.10	.02
❑	129	Steve Yeager	.25	.08
❑	130	Gary Weiss RC	.10	.02
❑	131	Mike Scioscia RC	1.50	.60
❑	132	Vic Davalillo	.10	.02
❑	133	Doug Rau	.10	.02
❑	134	Pepe Frias	.10	.02
❑	135	Mickey Hatcher	.10	.02
❑	136	Steve Howe RC	.50	.20
❑	137	Robert Castillo RC	.10	.02
❑	138	Gary Thomasson	.10	.02
❑	139	Rudy Law	.10	.02
❑	140	Fernando Valenzuela RC	5.00	2.00
❑	141	Manny Mota	.25	.08
❑	142	Gary Carter	.50	.20
❑	143	Steve Rogers	.25	.08
❑	144	Warren Cromartie	.10	.02
❑	145	Andre Dawson	.50	.20
❑	146	Larry Parrish	.10	.02
❑	147	Rowland Office	.10	.02
❑	148	Ellis Valentine	.10	.02
❑	149	Dick Williams MG	.10	.02
❑	150	Bill Gullickson RC	.50	.20
❑	151	Elias Sosa	.10	.02
❑	152	John Tamargo	.10	.02
❑	153	Chris Speier	.10	.02
❑	154	Ron LeFlore	.25	.08
❑	155	Rodney Scott	.10	.02
❑	156	Stan Bahnsen	.10	.02
❑	157	Bill Lee	.25	.08
❑	158	Fred Norman	.10	.02
❑	159	Woodie Fryman	.10	.02
❑	160	David Palmer	.10	.02
❑	161	Jerry White	.10	.02
❑	162	Roberto Ramos RC	.10	.02
❑	163	John D'Acquisto	.10	.02
❑	164	Tommy Hutton	.10	.02
❑	165	Charlie Lea RC	.10	.02
❑	166	Scott Sanderson	.10	.02
❑	167	Ken Macha	.10	.02
❑	168	Tony Bernazard	.10	.02
❑	169	Jim Palmer	.50	.20
❑	170	Steve Stone	.10	.02
❑	171	Mike Flanagan	.10	.02
❑	172	Al Bumbry	.10	.02
❑	173	Doug DeCinces	.10	.02
❑	174	Scott McGregor	.10	.02
❑	175	Mark Belanger	.10	.02
❑	176	Tim Stoddard	.10	.02
❑	177A	Rick Dempsey P1	.25	.08
❑	177B	Rick Dempsey P2	.10	.02
❑	178	Earl Weaver MG	.25	.08
❑	179	Tippy Martinez	.10	.02
❑	180	Dennis Martinez	.25	.08
❑	181	Sammy Stewart	.10	.02
❑	182	Rich Dauer	.10	.02
❑	183	Lee May	.10	.02
❑	184	Eddie Murray	1.50	.60
❑	185	Benny Ayala	.10	.02
❑	186	John Lowenstein	.10	.02
❑	187	Gary Roenicke	.10	.02
❑	188	Ken Singleton	.25	.08
❑	189	Dan Graham	.10	.02
❑	190	Terry Crowley	.10	.02
❑	191	Kiko Garcia	.10	.02
❑	192	Dave Ford RC	.10	.02
❑	193	Mark Corey	.10	.02
❑	194	Lenn Sakata	.10	.02
❑	195	Doug DeCinces	.10	.02
❑	196	Johnny Bench	1.00	.40
❑	197	Dave Concepcion	.25	.08
❑	198	Ray Knight	.25	.08
❑	199	Ken Griffey	.25	.08
❑	200	Tom Seaver	1.00	.40
❑	201	Dave Collins	.10	.02
❑	202A	George Foster P1	.50	.20
❑	202B	George Foster P2	.50	.20
❑	203	Junior Kennedy	.10	.02
❑	204	Frank Pastore	.10	.02
❑	205	Dan Driessen	.10	.02
❑	206	Hector Cruz	.10	.02
❑	207	Paul Moskau	.10	.02
❑	208	Charlie Leibrandt RC	.50	.20
❑	209	Harry Spilman	.10	.02
❑	210	Joe Price RC	.10	.02
❑	211	Tom Hume	.10	.02
❑	212	Joe Nolan RC	.10	.02
❑	213	Doug Bair	.10	.02
❑	214	Mario Soto	.25	.08
❑	215A	Bill Bonham P1	.50	.20
❑	215B	Bill Bonham P2	.10	.02
❑	216	George Foster SLG	.25	.08
❑	217	Paul Householder RC	.10	.02
❑	218	Ron Oester	.10	.02
❑	219	Sam Mejias	.10	.02
❑	220	Sheldon Burnside RC	.10	.02
❑	221	Carl Yastrzemski	1.50	.60
❑	222	Jim Rice	.25	.08
❑	223	Fred Lynn	.25	.08
❑	224	Carlton Fisk	.50	.20
❑	225	Rick Burleson	.10	.02
❑	226	Dennis Eckersley	.50	.20
❑	227	Butch Hobson	.10	.02
❑	228	Tom Burgmeier	.10	.02
❑	229	Garry Hancock	.10	.02
❑	230	Don Zimmer MG	.25	.08
❑	231	Steve Renko	.10	.02
❑	232	Dwight Evans	.50	.20
❑	233	Mike Torrez	.10	.02
❑	234	Bob Stanley	.10	.02
❑	235	Jim Dwyer	.10	.02
❑	236	Dave Stapleton RC	.10	.02
❑	237	Glenn Hoffman RC	.10	.02
❑	238	Jerry Remy	.10	.02
❑	239	Dick Drago	.10	.02
❑	240	Bill Campbell	.10	.02
❑	241	Tony Perez	.50	.20
❑	242	Phil Niekro	.25	.08
❑	243	Dale Murphy	.50	.20
❑	244	Bob Horner	.25	.08
❑	245	Jeff Burroughs	.25	.08
❑	246	Rick Camp	.10	.02
❑	247	Bobby Cox MG	.25	.08
❑	248	Bruce Benedict	.10	.02
❑	249	Gene Garber	.10	.02
❑	250	Jerry Royster	.10	.02
❑	251A	Gary Matthews P1	.50	.20
❑	251B	Gary Matthews P2	.25	.08
❑	252	Chris Chambliss	.25	.08
❑	253	Luis Gomez	.10	.02
❑	254	Bill Nahorodny	.10	.02
❑	255	Doyle Alexander	.10	.02
❑	256	Brian Asselstine	.10	.02
❑	257	Biff Pocoroba	.10	.02
❑	258	Mike Lum	.10	.02
❑	259	Charlie Spikes	.10	.02
❑	260	Glenn Hubbard	.10	.02
❑	261	Tommy Boggs	.10	.02
❑	262	Al Hrabosky	.25	.08
❑	263	Rick Matula	.10	.02
❑	264	Preston Hanna	.10	.02
❑	265	Larry Bradford	.10	.02
❑	266	Rafael Ramirez RC	.10	.02
❑	267	Larry McWilliams	.10	.02
❑	268	Rod Carew	.50	.20
❑	269	Bobby Grich	.25	.08
❑	270	Carney Lansford	.25	.08
❑	271	Don Baylor	.25	.08
❑	272	Joe Rudi	.25	.08
❑	273	Dan Ford	.10	.02
❑	274	Jim Fregosi MG	.10	.02
❑	275	Dave Frost	.10	.02
❑	276	Frank Tanana	.25	.08
❑	277	Dickie Thon	.10	.02
❑	278	Jason Thompson	.10	.02
❑	279	Rick Miller	.10	.02
❑	280	Bert Campaneris	.25	.08
❑	281	Tom Donohue	.10	.02
❑	282	Brian Downing	.25	.08
❑	283	Fred Patek	.10	.02
❑	284	Bruce Kison	.10	.02
❑	285	Dave LaRoche	.10	.02
❑	286	Don Aase	.10	.02
❑	287	Jim Barr	.10	.02
❑	288	Alfredo Martinez RC	.10	.02
❑	289	Larry Harlow	.10	.02
❑	290	Andy Hassler	.10	.02
❑	291	Dave Kingman	.25	.08
❑	292	Bill Buckner	.25	.08
❑	293	Rick Reuschel	.25	.08
❑	294	Bruce Sutter	.50	.20
❑	295	Jerry Martin	.10	.02
❑	296	Scot Thompson	.10	.02
❑	297	Ivan DeJesus	.10	.02
❑	298	Steve Dillard	.10	.02
❑	299	Dick Tidrow	.10	.02
❑	300	Randy Martz RC	.10	.02
❑	301	Lenny Randle	.10	.02
❑	302	Lynn McGlothen	.10	.02
❑	303	Cliff Johnson	.10	.02
❑	304	Tim Blackwell	.10	.02
❑	305	Dennis Lamp	.10	.02
❑	306	Bill Caudill	.10	.02
❑	307	Carlos Lezcano RC	.10	.02
❑	308	Jim Tracy RC	1.00	.40
❑	309	Doug Capilla UER	.10	.02
❑	310	Willie Hernandez	.10	.02
❑	311	Mike Vail	.10	.02
❑	312	Mike Krukow RC	.10	.02
❑	313	Barry Foote	.10	.02
❑	314	Larry Biittner	.10	.02
❑	315	Mike Tyson	.10	.02
❑	316	Lee Mazzilli	.25	.08
❑	317	John Stearns	.10	.02
❑	318	Alex Trevino	.10	.02
❑	319	Craig Swan	.10	.02
❑	320	Frank Taveras	.10	.02
❑	321	Steve Henderson	.10	.02
❑	322	Neil Allen	.10	.02
❑	323	Mark Bomback RC	.10	.02
❑	324	Mike Jorgensen	.10	.02
❑	325	Joe Torre MG	.25	.08
❑	326	Elliott Maddox	.10	.02
❑	327	Pete Falcone	.10	.02
❑	328	Ray Burris	.10	.02
❑	329	Claudell Washington	.10	.02
❑	330	Doug Flynn	.10	.02
❑	331	Joel Youngblood	.10	.02
❑	332	Bill Almon RC	.10	.02
❑	333	Tom Hausman	.10	.02
❑	334	Pat Zachry	.10	.02
❑	335	Jeff Reardon RC	1.00	.40
❑	336	Wally Backman RC	.50	.20
❑	337	Dan Norman	.10	.02
❑	338	Jerry Morales	.10	.02
❑	339	Ed Farmer	.10	.02
❑	340	Bob Molinaro	.10	.02
❑	341	Todd Cruz	.10	.02
❑	342A	Britt Burns P1	.50	.20
❑	342B	Britt Burns P2 RC	.25	.08
❑	343	Kevin Bell	.10	.02
❑	344	Tony LaRussa MG	.25	.08
❑	345	Steve Trout	.10	.02
❑	346	Harold Baines RC	2.00	.75
❑	347	Richard Wortham	.10	.02
❑	348	Wayne Nordhagen	.10	.02
❑	349	Mike Squires	.10	.02
❑	350	Lamar Johnson	.10	.02
❑	351	Rickey Henderson SB	3.00	1.25
❑	352	Francisco Barrios	.10	.02
❑	353	Thad Bosley	.10	.02
❑	354	Chet Lemon	.25	.08
❑	355	Bruce Kimm	.10	.02
❑	356	Richard Dotson RC	.10	.02
❑	357	Jim Morrison	.10	.02
❑	358	Mike Proly	.10	.02

❑ 359	Greg Pryor	.10	.02
❑ 360	Dave Parker	.25	.08
❑ 361	Omar Moreno	.10	.02
❑ 362A	Kent Tekulve P1	.10	.02
❑ 362B	Kent Tekulve P2	.10	.02
❑ 363	Willie Stargell	.50	.20
❑ 364	Phil Garner	.25	.08
❑ 365	Ed Ott	.10	.02
❑ 366	Don Robinson	.10	.02
❑ 367	Chuck Tanner MG	.10	.02
❑ 368	Jim Rooker	.10	.02
❑ 369	Dale Berra	.10	.02
❑ 370	Jim Bibby	.10	.02
❑ 371	Steve Nicosia	.10	.02
❑ 372	Mike Easler	.10	.02
❑ 373	Bill Robinson	.10	.02
❑ 374	Lee Lacy	.10	.02
❑ 375	John Candelaria	.25	.08
❑ 376	Manny Sanguillen	.25	.08
❑ 377	Rick Rhoden	.10	.02
❑ 378	Grant Jackson	.10	.02
❑ 379	Tim Foli	.10	.02
❑ 380	Rod Scurry RC	.10	.02
❑ 381	Bill Madlock	.25	.08
❑ 382A	Kurt Bevacqua P1	.25	.08
❑ 382B	Kurt Bevacqua P2	.10	.02
❑ 383	Bert Blyleven	.25	.08
❑ 384	Eddie Solomon	.10	.02
❑ 385	Enrique Romo	.10	.02
❑ 386	John Milner	.10	.02
❑ 387	Mike Hargrove	.10	.02
❑ 388	Jorge Orta	.10	.02
❑ 389	Toby Harrah	.25	.08
❑ 390	Tom Veryzer	.10	.02
❑ 391	Miguel Dilone	.10	.02
❑ 392	Dan Spillner	.10	.02
❑ 393	Jack Brohamer	.10	.02
❑ 394	Wayne Garland	.10	.02
❑ 395	Sid Monge	.10	.02
❑ 396	Rick Waits	.10	.02
❑ 397	Joe Charboneau RC	1.00	.40
❑ 398	Gary Alexander	.10	.02
❑ 399	Jerry Dybzinski RC	.10	.02
❑ 400	Mike Stanton RC	.10	.02
❑ 401	Mike Paxton	.10	.02
❑ 402	Gary Gray RC	.10	.02
❑ 403	Rick Manning	.10	.02
❑ 404	Bo Diaz	.10	.02
❑ 405	Ron Hassey	.10	.02
❑ 406	Ross Grimsley	.10	.02
❑ 407	Victor Cruz	.10	.02
❑ 408	Len Barker	.25	.08
❑ 409	Bob Bailor	.10	.02
❑ 410	Otto Velez	.10	.02
❑ 411	Ernie Whitt	.10	.02
❑ 412	Jim Clancy	.10	.02
❑ 413	Barry Bonnell	.10	.02
❑ 414	Dave Stieb	.25	.08
❑ 415	Damaso Garcia RC	.10	.02
❑ 416	John Mayberry	.10	.02
❑ 417	Roy Howell	.10	.02
❑ 418	Danny Ainge RC	3.00	1.25
❑ 419A	Jesse Jefferson P1	.10	.02
❑ 419B	Jesse Jefferson P2	.10	.02
❑ 419C	Jesse Jefferson P3	.50	.20
❑ 420	Joey McLaughlin	.10	.02
❑ 421	Lloyd Moseby RC	.50	.20
❑ 422	Alvis Woods	.10	.02
❑ 423	Garth Iorg	.10	.02
❑ 424	Doug Ault	.10	.02
❑ 425	Ken Schrom RC	.10	.02
❑ 426	Mike Willis	.10	.02
❑ 427	Steve Braun	.10	.02
❑ 428	Bob Davis	.10	.02
❑ 429	Jerry Garvin	.10	.02
❑ 430	Alfredo Griffin	.10	.02
❑ 431	Bob Mattick MG RC	.10	.02
❑ 432	Vida Blue	.25	.08
❑ 433	Jack Clark	.25	.08
❑ 434	Willie McCovey	.50	.20
❑ 435	Mike Ivie	.10	.02
❑ 436A	Darrel Evans P1 ERR	.50	.20
❑ 436B	Darrell Evans P2 COR	.50	.20
❑ 437	Terry Whitfield	.10	.02
❑ 438	Rennie Stennett	.10	.02
❑ 439	John Montefusco	.10	.02
❑ 440	Jim Wohlford	.10	.02
❑ 441	Bill North	.10	.02
❑ 442	Milt May	.10	.02
❑ 443	Max Venable RC	.10	.02
❑ 444	Ed Whitson	.10	.02
❑ 445	Al Holland RC	.10	.02
❑ 446	Randy Moffitt	.10	.02
❑ 447	Bob Knepper	.10	.02
❑ 448	Gary Lavelle	.10	.02
❑ 449	Greg Minton	.10	.02
❑ 450	Johnnie LeMaster	.10	.02
❑ 451	Larry Herndon	.10	.02
❑ 452	Rich Murray RC	.10	.02
❑ 453	Joe Pettini RC	.10	.02
❑ 454	Allen Ripley	.10	.02
❑ 455	Dennis Littlejohn	.10	.02
❑ 456	Tom Griffin	.10	.02
❑ 457	Alan Hargesheimer RC	.10	.02
❑ 458	Joe Strain	.10	.02
❑ 459	Steve Kemp	.10	.02
❑ 460	Sparky Anderson MG	.25	.08
❑ 461	Alan Trammell	.50	.20
❑ 462	Mark Fidrych	.25	.08
❑ 463	Lou Whitaker	.50	.20
❑ 464	Dave Rozema	.10	.02
❑ 465	Milt Wilcox	.10	.02
❑ 466	Champ Summers	.10	.02
❑ 467	Lance Parrish	.25	.08
❑ 468	Dan Petry	.10	.02
❑ 469	Pat Underwood	.10	.02
❑ 470	Rick Peters RC	.10	.02
❑ 471	Al Cowens	.10	.02
❑ 472	John Wockenfuss	.10	.02
❑ 473	Tom Brookens	.10	.02
❑ 474	Richie Hebner	.10	.02
❑ 475	Jack Morris	.50	.20
❑ 476	Jim Lentine RC	.10	.02
❑ 477	Bruce Robbins	.10	.02
❑ 478	Mark Wagner	.10	.02
❑ 479	Tim Corcoran	.10	.02
❑ 480A	Stan Papi P1	.25	.08
❑ 480B	Stan Papi P2	.10	.02
❑ 481	Kirk Gibson RC	5.00	2.00
❑ 482	Dan Schatzeder	.10	.02
❑ 483A	Amos Otis P1	.25	.08
❑ 483B	Amos Otis P2	.25	.08
❑ 484	Dave Winfield	.50	.20
❑ 485	Rollie Fingers	.25	.08
❑ 486	Gene Richards	.10	.02
❑ 487	Randy Jones	.10	.02
❑ 488	Ozzie Smith	3.00	1.25
❑ 489	Gene Tenace	.25	.08
❑ 490	Bill Fahey	.10	.02
❑ 491	John Curtis	.10	.02
❑ 492	Dave Cash	.10	.02
❑ 493A	Tim Flannery P1	.25	.08
❑ 493B	Tim Flannery P2	.10	.02
❑ 494	Jerry Mumphrey	.10	.02
❑ 495	Bob Shirley	.10	.02
❑ 496	Steve Mura	.10	.02
❑ 497	Eric Rasmussen	.10	.02
❑ 498	Broderick Perkins	.10	.02
❑ 499	Barry Evans RC	.10	.02
❑ 500	Chuck Baker	.10	.02
❑ 501	Luis Salazar RC	.50	.20
❑ 502	Gary Lucas RC	.10	.02
❑ 503	Mike Armstrong RC	.10	.02
❑ 504	Jerry Turner	.10	.02
❑ 505	Dennis Kinney RC	.10	.02
❑ 506	Willie Montanez UER	.10	.02
❑ 507	Gorman Thomas	.25	.08
❑ 508	Ben Oglivie	.25	.08
❑ 509	Larry Hisle	.10	.02
❑ 510	Sal Bando	.25	.08
❑ 511	Robin Yount	1.50	.60
❑ 512	Mike Caldwell	.10	.02
❑ 513	Sixto Lezcano	.10	.02
❑ 514A	Bill Travers P1 ERR	.25	.08
❑ 514B	Bill Travers P2 COR	.10	.02
❑ 515	Paul Molitor	1.00	.40
❑ 516	Moose Haas	.10	.02
❑ 517	Bill Castro	.10	.02
❑ 518	Jim Slaton	.10	.02
❑ 519	Lary Sorensen	.10	.02
❑ 520	Bob McClure	.10	.02
❑ 521	Charlie Moore	.10	.02
❑ 522	Jim Gantner	.10	.02
❑ 523	Reggie Cleveland	.10	.02
❑ 524	Don Money	.10	.02
❑ 525	Bill Travers	.10	.02
❑ 526	Buck Martinez	.10	.02
❑ 527	Dick Davis	.10	.02
❑ 528	Ted Simmons	.25	.08
❑ 529	Garry Templeton	.25	.08
❑ 530	Ken Reitz	.10	.02
❑ 531	Tony Scott	.10	.02
❑ 532	Ken Oberkfell	.10	.02
❑ 533	Bob Sykes	.10	.02
❑ 534	Keith Smith	.10	.02
❑ 535	John Littlefield RC	.10	.02
❑ 536	Jim Kaat	.25	.08
❑ 537	Bob Forsch	.10	.02
❑ 538	Mike Phillips	.10	.02
❑ 539	Terry Landrum RC	.10	.02
❑ 540	Leon Durham RC	.50	.20
❑ 541	Terry Kennedy	.10	.02
❑ 542	George Hendrick	.25	.08
❑ 543	Dane Iorg	.10	.02
❑ 544	Mark Littell	.10	.02
❑ 545	Keith Hernandez	.25	.08
❑ 546	Silvio Martinez	.10	.02
❑ 547A	Don Hood P1 ERR	.25	.08
❑ 547B	Don Hood P2 COR	.10	.02
❑ 548	Bobby Bonds	.25	.08
❑ 549	Mike Ramsey RC	.15	.05
❑ 550	Tom Herr	.10	.02
❑ 551	Roy Smalley	.10	.02
❑ 552	Jerry Koosman	.25	.08
❑ 553	Ken Landreaux	.10	.02
❑ 554	John Castino	.10	.02
❑ 555	Doug Corbett RC	.10	.02
❑ 556	Bombo Rivera	.10	.02
❑ 557	Ron Jackson	.10	.02
❑ 558	Butch Wynegar	.10	.02
❑ 559	Hosken Powell	.10	.02
❑ 560	Pete Redfern	.10	.02
❑ 561	Roger Erickson	.10	.02
❑ 562	Glenn Adams	.10	.02
❑ 563	Rick Sofield	.10	.02
❑ 564	Geoff Zahn	.10	.02
❑ 565	Pete Mackanin	.10	.02
❑ 566	Mike Cubbage	.10	.02
❑ 567	Darrell Jackson	.10	.02
❑ 568	Dave Edwards	.10	.02
❑ 569	Rob Wilfong	.10	.02
❑ 570	Sal Butera RC	.10	.02
❑ 571	Jose Morales	.10	.02
❑ 572	Rick Langford	.10	.02
❑ 573	Mike Norris	.10	.02
❑ 574	Rickey Henderson	6.00	2.50
❑ 575	Tony Armas	.25	.08
❑ 576	Dave Revering	.10	.02
❑ 577	Jeff Newman	.10	.02
❑ 578	Bob Lacey	.10	.02
❑ 579	Brian Kingman	.10	.02
❑ 580	Mitchell Page	.10	.02
❑ 581	Billy Martin MG	.50	.20
❑ 582	Rob Picciolo	.10	.02
❑ 583	Mike Heath	.10	.02
❑ 584	Mickey Klutts	.10	.02
❑ 585	Orlando Gonzalez	.10	.02
❑ 586	Mike Davis RC	.50	.20
❑ 587	Wayne Gross	.10	.02
❑ 588	Matt Keough	.10	.02
❑ 589	Steve McCatty	.10	.02
❑ 590	Dwayne Murphy	.10	.02
❑ 591	Mario Guerrero	.10	.02
❑ 592	Dave McKay RC	.10	.02
❑ 593	Jim Essian	.10	.02
❑ 594	Dave Heaverlo	.10	.02
❑ 595	Maury Wills MG	.25	.08
❑ 596	Juan Beniquez	.10	.02
❑ 597	Rodney Craig	.10	.02
❑ 598	Jim Anderson	.10	.02
❑ 599	Floyd Bannister	.10	.02
❑ 600	Bruce Bochte	.10	.02
❑ 601	Julio Cruz	.10	.02
❑ 602	Ted Cox	.10	.02
❑ 603	Dan Meyer	.10	.02
❑ 604	Larry Cox	.10	.02
❑ 605	Bill Stein	.10	.02
❑ 606	Steve Garvey	.50	.20

607	Dave Roberts	.10	.02
608	Leon Roberts	.10	.02
609	Reggie Walton RC	.10	.02
610	Dave Edler RC	.10	.02
611	Larry Milbourne	.10	.02
612	Kim Allen RC	.10	.02
613	Mario Mendoza	.10	.02
614	Tom Paciorek	.10	.02
615	Glenn Abbott	.10	.02
616	Joe Simpson	.10	.02
617	Mickey Rivers	.10	.02
618	Jim Kern	.10	.02
619	Jim Sundberg	.25	.08
620	Richie Zisk	.10	.02
621	Jon Matlack	.10	.02
622	Fergie Jenkins	.25	.08
623	Pat Corrales MG	.10	.02
624	Ed Figueroa	.10	.02
625	Buddy Bell	.25	.08
626	Al Oliver	.25	.08
627	Doc Medich	.10	.02
628	Bump Wills	.10	.02
629	Rusty Staub	.25	.08
630	Pat Putnam	.10	.02
631	John Grubb	.10	.02
632	Danny Darwin	.10	.02
633	Ken Clay	.10	.02
634	Jim Norris	.10	.02
635	John Butcher RC	.10	.02
636	Dave Roberts	.10	.02
637	Billy Sample	.10	.02
638	Carl Yastrzemski	1.50	.60
639	Cecil Cooper	.25	.08
640	M.Schmidt Portrait P1	2.50	1.00
640B	M.Schmidt Portrait P2	2.50	1.00
641A	CL: Phils/Royals P1	.25	.08
641B	CL: Phils/Royals P2	.25	.08
642	CL: Astros/Yankees	.10	.02
643	CL: Expos/Dodgers	.10	.02
644A	CL: Reds/Orioles P1	.25	.08
644B	CL: Reds/Orioles P2	.25	.08
645	Rose/Bowa/Schmidt	1.50	.60
645B	Rose/Bowa/Schmidt	2.50	1.00
646	CL: Braves/Red Sox	.10	.02
647	CL: Cubs/Angels	.10	.02
648	CL: Mets/White Sox	.10	.02
649	CL: Indians/Pirates	.10	.02
650	Reggie Jackson Mr. BB	1.00	.40
650B	R.Jackson Mr. BB P2	.50	.20
651	CL: Giants/Blue Jays	.10	.02
652A	CL: Tigers/Padres P1	.25	.08
652B	CL: Tigers/Padres P2	.25	.08
653A	Willie Wilson Most Hits	.25	.08
653B	W.Wilson Hits P2	.25	.08
654A	CL:Brewers/Cards P1	.25	.08
654B	CL:Brewers/Cards P2	.25	.08
655	George Brett .390 Avg.	2.50	1.00
655B	G.Brett .390 Avg. P2	2.50	1.00
656	CL: Twins/Oakland A's	.25	.08
657A	Tug McGraw Saver	.25	.08
657B	T.McGraw Saver P2	.25	.08
658	CL: Rangers/Mariners	.10	.02
659A	Checklist P1	.10	.02
659B	Checklist P2	.10	.02
660	S.Carlton Gold Arm P1	.50	.20
660B	S.Carlton Golden Arm	2.00	.75

1982 Fleer

	COMPLETE SET (660)	50.00	20.00
1	Dusty Baker	.20	.07
2	Robert Castillo	.10	.02
3	Ron Cey	.20	.07
4	Terry Forster	.20	.07
5	Steve Garvey	.20	.07
6	Dave Goltz	.10	.02
7	Pedro Guerrero	.20	.07
8	Burt Hooton	.10	.02
9	Steve Howe	.10	.02
10	Jay Johnstone	.10	.02
11	Ken Landreaux	.10	.02
12	Dave Lopes	.20	.07
13	Mike A. Marshall RC	.50	.20
14	Bobby Mitchell	.10	.02
15	Rick Monday	.20	.07
16	Tom Niedenfuer RC	.50	.20
17	Ted Power RC	.15	.05
18	Jerry Reuss UER	.10	.02
19	Ron Roenicke	.10	.02
20	Bill Russell	.20	.07
21	Steve Sax RC	1.00	.40
22	Mike Scioscia	.20	.07
23	Reggie Smith	.20	.07
24	Dave Stewart RC	1.50	.60
25	Rick Sutcliffe	.20	.07
26	Derrel Thomas	.10	.02
27	Fernando Valenzuela	.75	.30
28	Bob Welch	.20	.07
29	Steve Yeager	.20	.07
30	Bobby Brown	.10	.02
31	Rick Cerone	.10	.02
32	Ron Davis	.10	.02
33	Bucky Dent	.20	.07
34	Barry Foote	.10	.02
35	George Frazier	.10	.02
36	Oscar Gamble	.10	.02
37	Rich Gossage	.20	.07
38	Ron Guidry	.20	.07
39	Reggie Jackson	.40	.15
40	Tommy John	.20	.07
41	Rudy May	.10	.02
42	Larry Milbourne	.10	.02
43	Jerry Mumphrey	.10	.02
44	Bobby Murcer	.20	.07
45	Gene Nelson	.10	.02
46	Graig Nettles	.20	.07
47	Johnny Oates	.20	.07
48	Lou Piniella	.20	.07
49	Willie Randolph	.20	.07
50	Rick Reuschel	.20	.07
51	Dave Revering	.10	.02
52	Dave Righetti RC	1.50	.60
53	Aurelio Rodriguez	.10	.02
54	Bob Watson	.10	.02
55	Dennis Werth	.10	.02
56	Dave Winfield	.20	.07
57	Johnny Bench	.75	.30
58	Bruce Berenyi	.10	.02
59	Larry Biittner	.10	.02
60	Scott Brown	.10	.02
61	Dave Collins	.10	.02
62	Geoff Combe	.10	.02
63	Dave Concepcion	.20	.07
64	Dan Driessen	.10	.02
65	Joe Edelen	.10	.02
66	George Foster	.20	.07
67	Ken Griffey	.20	.07
68	Paul Householder	.10	.02
69	Tom Hume	.10	.02
70	Junior Kennedy	.10	.02
71	Ray Knight	.20	.07
72	Mike LaCoss	.10	.02
73	Rafael Landestoy	.10	.02
74	Charlie Leibrandt	.10	.02
75	Sam Mejias	.10	.02
76	Paul Moskau	.10	.02
77	Joe Nolan	.10	.02
78	Mike O'Berry	.10	.02
79	Ron Oester	.10	.02
80	Frank Pastore	.10	.02
81	Joe Price	.10	.02
82	Tom Seaver	.75	.30
83	Mario Soto	.20	.07
84	Mike Vail	.10	.02
85	Tony Armas	.20	.07

86	Shooty Babitt	.10	.02
87	Dave Beard	.10	.02
88	Rick Bosetti	.10	.02
89	Keith Drumwright	.10	.02
90	Wayne Gross	.10	.02
91	Mike Heath	.10	.02
92	Rickey Henderson	2.50	1.00
93	Cliff Johnson	.10	.02
94	Jeff Jones	.10	.02
95	Matt Keough	.10	.02
96	Brian Kingman	.10	.02
97	Mickey Klutts	.10	.02
98	Rick Langford	.10	.02
99	Steve McCatty	.10	.02
100	Dave McKay	.10	.02
101	Dwayne Murphy	.10	.02
102	Jeff Newman	.10	.02
103	Mike Norris	.10	.02
104	Bob Owchinko	.10	.02
105	Mitchell Page	.10	.02
106	Rob Picciolo	.10	.02
107	Jim Spencer	.10	.02
108	Fred Stanley	.10	.02
109	Tom Underwood	.10	.02
110	Joaquin Andujar	.20	.07
111	Steve Braun	.10	.02
112	Bob Forsch	.10	.02
113	George Hendrick	.20	.07
114	Keith Hernandez	.20	.07
115	Tom Herr	.10	.02
116	Dane Iorg	.10	.02
117	Jim Kaat	.20	.07
118	Tito Landrum	.10	.02
119	Sixto Lezcano	.10	.02
120	Mark Littell	.10	.02
121	John Martin RC	.15	.05
122	Silvio Martinez	.10	.02
123	Ken Oberkfell	.10	.02
124	Darrell Porter	.10	.02
125	Mike Ramsey	.10	.02
126	Orlando Sanchez	.10	.02
127	Bob Shirley	.10	.02
128	Lary Sorensen	.10	.02
129	Bruce Sutter	.40	.15
130	Bob Sykes	.10	.02
131	Garry Templeton	.20	.07
132	Gene Tenace	.20	.07
133	Jerry Augustine	.10	.02
134	Sal Bando	.20	.07
135	Mark Brouhard	.10	.02
136	Mike Caldwell	.10	.02
137	Reggie Cleveland	.10	.02
138	Cecil Cooper	.20	.07
139	Jamie Easterly	.10	.02
140	Marshall Edwards	.10	.02
141	Rollie Fingers	.20	.07
142	Jim Gantner	.10	.02
143	Moose Haas	.10	.02
144	Larry Hisle	.10	.02
145	Roy Howell	.10	.02
146	Rickey Keeton	.10	.02
147	Randy Lerch	.10	.02
148	Paul Molitor	.20	.07
149	Don Money	.10	.02
150	Charlie Moore	.10	.02
151	Ben Oglivie	.20	.07
152	Ted Simmons	.20	.07
153	Jim Slaton	.10	.02
154	Gorman Thomas	.20	.07
155	Robin Yount	1.25	.50
156	Pete Vuckovich (Should precede Yount in the team	.10	.02
157	Benny Ayala	.10	.02
158	Mark Belanger	.10	.02
159	Al Bumbry	.10	.02
160	Terry Crowley	.10	.02
161	Rich Dauer	.10	.02
162	Doug DeCinces	.10	.02
163	Rick Dempsey	.10	.02
164	Jim Dwyer	.10	.02
165	Mike Flanagan	.10	.02
166	Dave Ford	.10	.02
167	Dan Graham	.10	.02
168	Wayne Krenchicki	.10	.02
169	John Lowenstein	.10	.02

❑ 170 Dennis Martinez	.20	.07
❑ 171 Tippy Martinez	.10	.02
❑ 172 Scott McGregor	.10	.02
❑ 173 Jose Morales	.10	.02
❑ 174 Eddie Murray	.75	.30
❑ 175 Jim Palmer	.20	.07
❑ 176 Cal Ripken RC	30.00	12.50
❑ 177 Gary Roenicke	.10	.02
❑ 178 Lenn Sakata	.10	.02
❑ 179 Ken Singleton	.20	.07
❑ 180 Sammy Stewart	.10	.02
❑ 181 Tim Stoddard	.10	.02
❑ 182 Steve Stone	.10	.02
❑ 183 Stan Bahnsen	.10	.02
❑ 184 Ray Burris	.10	.02
❑ 185 Gary Carter	.20	.07
❑ 186 Warren Cromartie	.10	.02
❑ 187 Andre Dawson	.20	.07
❑ 188 Terry Francona RC	3.00	1.25
❑ 189 Woodie Fryman	.10	.02
❑ 190 Bill Gullickson	.10	.02
❑ 191 Grant Jackson	.10	.02
❑ 192 Wallace Johnson	.10	.02
❑ 193 Charlie Lea	.10	.02
❑ 194 Bill Lee	.20	.07
❑ 195 Jerry Manuel	.10	.02
❑ 196 Brad Mills	.10	.02
❑ 197 John Milner	.10	.02
❑ 198 Rowland Office	.10	.02
❑ 199 David Palmer	.10	.02
❑ 200 Larry Parrish	.10	.02
❑ 201 Mike Phillips	.10	.02
❑ 202 Tim Raines	.40	.15
❑ 203 Bobby Ramos	.10	.02
❑ 204 Jeff Reardon	.20	.07
❑ 205 Steve Rogers	.20	.07
❑ 206 Scott Sanderson	.10	.02
❑ 207 Rodney Scott UER Raines	.40	.15
❑ 208 Elias Sosa	.10	.02
❑ 209 Chris Speier	.10	.02
❑ 210 Tim Wallach RC	1.00	.40
❑ 211 Jerry White	.10	.02
❑ 212 Alan Ashby	.10	.02
❑ 213 Cesar Cedeno	.20	.07
❑ 214 Jose Cruz	.20	.07
❑ 215 Kiko Garcia	.10	.02
❑ 216 Phil Garner	.20	.07
❑ 217 Danny Heep	.10	.02
❑ 218 Art Howe	.10	.02
❑ 219 Bob Knepper	.10	.02
❑ 220 Frank LaCorte	.10	.02
❑ 221 Joe Niekro	.10	.02
❑ 222 Joe Pittman	.10	.02
❑ 223 Terry Puhl	.10	.02
❑ 224 Luis Pujols	.10	.02
❑ 225 Craig Reynolds	.10	.02
❑ 226 J.R. Richard	.20	.07
❑ 227 Dave Roberts	.10	.02
❑ 228 Vern Ruhle	.10	.02
❑ 229 Nolan Ryan	4.00	1.50
❑ 230 Joe Sambito	.10	.02
❑ 231 Tony Scott	.10	.02
❑ 232 Dave Smith	.10	.02
❑ 233 Harry Spilman	.10	.02
❑ 234 Don Sutton	.20	.07
❑ 235 Dickie Thon	.10	.02
❑ 236 Denny Walling	.10	.02
❑ 237 Gary Woods	.10	.02
❑ 238 Luis Aguayo	.10	.02
❑ 239 Ramon Aviles	.10	.02
❑ 240 Bob Boone	.20	.07
❑ 241 Larry Bowa	.20	.07
❑ 242 Warren Brusstar	.10	.02
❑ 243 Steve Carlton	.40	.15
❑ 244 Larry Christenson	.10	.02
❑ 245 Dick Davis	.10	.02
❑ 246 Greg Gross	.10	.02
❑ 247 Sparky Lyle	.20	.07
❑ 248 Garry Maddox	.10	.02
❑ 249 Gary Matthews	.20	.07
❑ 250 Bake McBride	.20	.07
❑ 251 Tug McGraw	.20	.07
❑ 252 Keith Moreland	.10	.02
❑ 253 Dickie Noles	.10	.02
❑ 254 Mike Proly	.10	.02
❑ 255 Ron Reed	.10	.02
❑ 256 Pete Rose	2.50	1.00
❑ 257 Dick Ruthven	.10	.02
❑ 258 Mike Schmidt	2.00	.75
❑ 259 Lonnie Smith	.10	.02
❑ 260 Manny Trillo	.10	.02
❑ 261 Del Unser	.10	.02
❑ 262 George Vukovich	.10	.02
❑ 263 Tom Brookens	.10	.02
❑ 264 George Cappuzzello	.10	.02
❑ 265 Marty Castillo	.10	.02
❑ 266 Al Cowens	.10	.02
❑ 267 Kirk Gibson	.75	.30
❑ 268 Richie Hebner	.10	.02
❑ 269 Ron Jackson	.10	.02
❑ 270 Lynn Jones	.10	.02
❑ 271 Steve Kemp	.10	.02
❑ 272 Rick Leach	.10	.02
❑ 273 Aurelio Lopez	.10	.02
❑ 274 Jack Morris	.20	.07
❑ 275 Kevin Saucier	.10	.02
❑ 276 Lance Parrish	.20	.07
❑ 277 Rick Peters	.10	.02
❑ 278 Dan Petry	.10	.02
❑ 279 Dave Rozema	.10	.02
❑ 280 Stan Papi	.10	.02
❑ 281 Dan Schatzeder	.10	.02
❑ 282 Champ Summers	.10	.02
❑ 283 Alan Trammell	.20	.07
❑ 284 Lou Whitaker	.20	.07
❑ 285 Milt Wilcox	.10	.02
❑ 286 John Wockenfuss	.10	.02
❑ 287 Gary Allenson	.10	.02
❑ 288 Tom Burgmeier	.10	.02
❑ 289 Bill Campbell	.10	.02
❑ 290 Mark Clear	.10	.02
❑ 291 Steve Crawford	.10	.02
❑ 292 Dennis Eckersley	.40	.15
❑ 293 Dwight Evans	.40	.15
❑ 294 Rich Gedman	.50	.20
❑ 295 Garry Hancock	.10	.02
❑ 296 Glenn Hoffman	.10	.02
❑ 297 Bruce Hurst	.10	.02
❑ 298 Carney Lansford	.20	.07
❑ 299 Rick Miller	.10	.02
❑ 300 Reid Nichols	.10	.02
❑ 301 Bob Ojeda RC	.50	.20
❑ 302 Tony Perez	.40	.15
❑ 303 Chuck Rainey	.10	.02
❑ 304 Jerry Remy	.10	.02
❑ 305 Jim Rice	.20	.07
❑ 306 Joe Rudi	.20	.07
❑ 307 Bob Stanley	.10	.02
❑ 308 Dave Stapleton	.10	.02
❑ 309 Frank Tanana	.20	.07
❑ 310 Mike Torrez	.10	.02
❑ 311 John Tudor	.20	.07
❑ 312 Carl Yastrzemski	1.25	.50
❑ 313 Buddy Bell	.20	.07
❑ 314 Steve Comer	.10	.02
❑ 315 Danny Darwin	.10	.02
❑ 316 John Ellis	.10	.02
❑ 317 John Grubb	.10	.02
❑ 318 Rick Honeycutt	.10	.02
❑ 319 Charlie Hough	.20	.07
❑ 320 Fergie Jenkins	.20	.07
❑ 321 John Henry Johnson	.10	.02
❑ 322 Jim Kern	.10	.02
❑ 323 Jon Matlack	.10	.02
❑ 324 Doc Medich	.10	.02
❑ 325 Mario Mendoza	.10	.02
❑ 326 Al Oliver	.20	.07
❑ 327 Pat Putnam	.10	.02
❑ 328 Mickey Rivers	.10	.02
❑ 329 Leon Roberts	.10	.02
❑ 330 Billy Sample	.10	.02
❑ 331 Bill Stein	.10	.02
❑ 332 Jim Sundberg	.20	.07
❑ 333 Mark Wagner	.10	.02
❑ 334 Bump Wills	.10	.02
❑ 335 Bill Almon	.10	.02
❑ 336 Harold Baines	.20	.07
❑ 337 Ross Baumgarten	.10	.02
❑ 338 Tony Bernazard	.10	.02
❑ 339 Britt Burns	.10	.02
❑ 340 Richard Dotson	.10	.02
❑ 341 Jim Essian	.10	.02
❑ 342 Ed Farmer	.10	.02
❑ 343 Carlton Fisk	.40	.15
❑ 344 Kevin Hickey RC	.15	.05
❑ 345 LaMarr Hoyt	.10	.02
❑ 346 Lamar Johnson	.10	.02
❑ 347 Jerry Koosman	.20	.07
❑ 348 Rusty Kuntz	.10	.02
❑ 349 Dennis Lamp	.10	.02
❑ 350 Ron LeFlore	.20	.07
❑ 351 Chet Lemon	.20	.07
❑ 352 Greg Luzinski	.20	.07
❑ 353 Bob Molinaro	.10	.02
❑ 354 Jim Morrison	.10	.02
❑ 355 Wayne Nordhagen	.10	.02
❑ 356 Greg Pryor	.10	.02
❑ 357 Mike Squires	.10	.02
❑ 358 Steve Trout	.10	.02
❑ 359 Alan Bannister	.10	.02
❑ 360 Len Barker	.10	.02
❑ 361 Bert Blyleven	.20	.07
❑ 362 Joe Charboneau	.20	.07
❑ 363 John Denny	.10	.02
❑ 364 Bo Diaz	.10	.02
❑ 365 Miguel Dilone	.10	.02
❑ 366 Jerry Dybzinski	.10	.02
❑ 367 Wayne Garland	.10	.02
❑ 368 Mike Hargrove	.10	.02
❑ 369 Toby Harrah	.20	.07
❑ 370 Ron Hassey	.10	.02
❑ 371 Von Hayes RC	.50	.20
❑ 372 Pat Kelly	.10	.02
❑ 373 Duane Kuiper	.10	.02
❑ 374 Rick Manning	.10	.02
❑ 375 Sid Monge	.10	.02
❑ 376 Jorge Orta	.10	.02
❑ 377 Dave Rosello	.10	.02
❑ 378 Dan Spillner	.10	.02
❑ 379 Mike Stanton	.10	.02
❑ 380 Andre Thornton	.10	.02
❑ 381 Tom Veryzer	.10	.02
❑ 382 Rick Waits	.10	.02
❑ 383 Doyle Alexander	.10	.02
❑ 384 Vida Blue	.20	.07
❑ 385 Fred Breining	.10	.02
❑ 386 Enos Cabell	.10	.02
❑ 387 Jack Clark	.20	.07
❑ 388 Darrell Evans	.20	.07
❑ 389 Tom Griffin	.10	.02
❑ 390 Larry Herndon	.10	.02
❑ 391 Al Holland	.10	.02
❑ 392 Gary Lavelle	.10	.02
❑ 393 Johnnie LeMaster	.10	.02
❑ 394 Jerry Martin	.10	.02
❑ 395 Milt May	.10	.02
❑ 396 Greg Minton	.10	.02
❑ 397 Joe Morgan	.20	.07
❑ 398 Joe Pettini	.10	.02
❑ 399 Allen Ripley	.10	.02
❑ 400 Billy Smith	.10	.02
❑ 401 Rennie Stennett	.10	.02
❑ 402 Ed Whitson	.10	.02
❑ 403 Jim Wohlford	.10	.02
❑ 404 Willie Aikens	.10	.02
❑ 405 George Brett	2.00	.75
❑ 406 Ken Brett	.10	.02
❑ 407 Dave Chalk	.10	.02
❑ 408 Rich Gale	.10	.02
❑ 409 Cesar Geronimo	.10	.02
❑ 410 Larry Gura	.10	.02
❑ 411 Clint Hurdle	.10	.02
❑ 412 Mike Jones	.10	.02
❑ 413 Dennis Leonard	.10	.02
❑ 414 Renie Martin	.10	.02
❑ 415 Lee May	.10	.02
❑ 416 Hal McRae	.20	.07
❑ 417 Darryl Motley	.10	.02
❑ 418 Rance Mulliniks	.10	.02
❑ 419 Amos Otis	.20	.07
❑ 420 Ken Phelps	.10	.02
❑ 421 Jamie Quirk	.10	.02
❑ 422 Dan Quisenberry	.10	.02
❑ 423 Paul Splittorff	.10	.02
❑ 424 U.L. Washington	.10	.02
❑ 425 John Wathan	.10	.02
❑ 426 Frank White	.20	.07
❑ 427 Willie Wilson	.20	.07

❑	428 Brian Asselstine	.10	.02
❑	429 Bruce Benedict	.10	.02
❑	430 Tommy Boggs	.10	.02
❑	431 Larry Bradford	.10	.02
❑	432 Rick Camp	.10	.02
❑	433 Chris Chambliss	.20	.07
❑	434 Gene Garber	.10	.02
❑	435 Preston Hanna	.10	.02
❑	436 Bob Horner	.20	.07
❑	437 Glenn Hubbard	.10	.02
❑	438A All Hrabosky ERR	8.00	3.00
❑	438B Al Hrabosky ERR (Height 5'1)	.40	.15
❑	438C Al Hrabosky (Height 5'10)	.20	.07
❑	439 Rufino Linares	.10	.02
❑	440 Rick Mahler	.10	.02
❑	441 Ed Miller	.10	.02
❑	442 John Montefusco	.10	.02
❑	443 Dale Murphy	.40	.15
❑	444 Phil Niekro	.20	.07
❑	445 Gaylord Perry	.20	.07
❑	446 Biff Pocoroba	.10	.02
❑	447 Rafael Ramirez	.10	.02
❑	448 Jerry Royster	.10	.02
❑	449 Claudell Washington	.10	.02
❑	450 Don Aase	.10	.02
❑	451 Don Baylor	.20	.07
❑	452 Juan Beniquez	.10	.02
❑	453 Rick Burleson	.10	.02
❑	454 Bert Campaneris	.20	.07
❑	455 Rod Carew	.40	.15
❑	456 Bob Clark	.10	.02
❑	457 Brian Downing	.20	.07
❑	458 Dan Ford	.10	.02
❑	459 Ken Forsch	.10	.02
❑	460A Dave Frost (5 mm space before ERA)	.10	.02
❑	460B Dave Frost (1 mm space)	.10	.02
❑	461 Bobby Grich	.20	.07
❑	462 Larry Harlow	.10	.02
❑	463 John Harris	.10	.02
❑	464 Andy Hassler	.10	.02
❑	465 Butch Hobson	.10	.02
❑	466 Jesse Jefferson	.10	.02
❑	467 Bruce Kison	.10	.02
❑	468 Fred Lynn	.20	.07
❑	469 Angel Moreno	.10	.02
❑	470 Ed Ott	.10	.02
❑	471 Fred Patek	.10	.02
❑	472 Steve Renko	.10	.02
❑	473 Mike Witt	.50	.20
❑	474 Geoff Zahn	.10	.02
❑	475 Gary Alexander	.10	.02
❑	476 Dale Berra	.10	.02
❑	477 Kurt Bevacqua	.10	.02
❑	478 Jim Bibby	.10	.02
❑	479 John Candelaria	.10	.02
❑	480 Victor Cruz	.10	.02
❑	481 Mike Easler	.10	.02
❑	482 Tim Foli	.10	.02
❑	483 Lee Lacy	.10	.02
❑	484 Vance Law	.10	.02
❑	485 Bill Madlock	.20	.07
❑	486 Willie Montanez	.10	.02
❑	487 Omar Moreno	.10	.02
❑	488 Steve Nicosia	.10	.02
❑	489 Dave Parker	.20	.07
❑	490 Tony Pena	.20	.07
❑	491 Pascual Perez	.10	.02
❑	492 Johnny Ray RC	.50	.20
❑	493 Rick Rhoden	.10	.02
❑	494 Bill Robinson	.10	.02
❑	495 Don Robinson	.10	.02
❑	496 Enrique Romo	.10	.02
❑	497 Rod Scurry	.10	.02
❑	498 Eddie Solomon	.10	.02
❑	499 Willie Stargell	.40	.15
❑	500 Kent Tekulve	.10	.02
❑	501 Jason Thompson	.10	.02
❑	502 Glenn Abbott	.10	.02
❑	503 Jim Anderson	.10	.02
❑	504 Floyd Bannister	.10	.02
❑	505 Bruce Bochte	.10	.02
❑	506 Jeff Burroughs	.10	.02
❑	507 Bryan Clark RC	.15	.05
❑	508 Ken Clay	.10	.02
❑	509 Julio Cruz	.10	.02
❑	510 Dick Drago	.10	.02
❑	511 Gary Gray	.10	.02
❑	512 Dan Meyer	.10	.02
❑	513 Jerry Narron	.10	.02
❑	514 Tom Paciorek	.10	.02
❑	515 Casey Parsons	.10	.02
❑	516 Lenny Randle	.10	.02
❑	517 Shane Rawley	.10	.02
❑	518 Joe Simpson	.10	.02
❑	519 Richie Zisk	.10	.02
❑	520 Neil Allen	.10	.02
❑	521 Bob Bailor	.10	.02
❑	522 Hubie Brooks	.10	.02
❑	523 Mike Cubbage	.10	.02
❑	524 Pete Falcone	.10	.02
❑	525 Doug Flynn	.10	.02
❑	526 Tom Hausman	.10	.02
❑	527 Ron Hodges	.10	.02
❑	528 Randy Jones	.10	.02
❑	529 Mike Jorgensen	.10	.02
❑	530 Dave Kingman	.20	.07
❑	531 Ed Lynch	.10	.02
❑	532 Mike G. Marshall	.10	.02
❑	533 Lee Mazzilli	.20	.07
❑	534 Dyar Miller	.10	.02
❑	535 Mike Scott	.20	.07
❑	536 Rusty Staub	.20	.07
❑	537 John Stearns	.10	.02
❑	538 Craig Swan	.10	.02
❑	539 Frank Taveras	.10	.02
❑	540 Alex Trevino	.10	.02
❑	541 Ellis Valentine	.10	.02
❑	542 Mookie Wilson	.20	.07
❑	543 Joel Youngblood	.10	.02
❑	544 Pat Zachry	.10	.02
❑	545 Glenn Adams	.10	.02
❑	546 Fernando Arroyo	.10	.02
❑	547 John Verhoeven	.10	.02
❑	548 Sal Butera	.10	.02
❑	549 John Castino	.10	.02
❑	550 Don Cooper	.10	.02
❑	551 Doug Corbett	.10	.02
❑	552 Dave Engle	.10	.02
❑	553 Roger Erickson	.10	.02
❑	554 Danny Goodwin	.10	.02
❑	555A Darrell Jackson (Black cap)	.40	.15
❑	555B Darrell Jackson (Red cap with T)	.20	.07
❑	555C Darrell Jackson VAR3	3.00	1.25
❑	556 Pete Mackanin	.10	.02
❑	557 Jack O'Connor	.10	.02
❑	558 Hosken Powell	.10	.02
❑	559 Pete Redfern	.10	.02
❑	560 Roy Smalley	.10	.02
❑	561 Chuck Baker UER (Shortshop on front)	.10	.02
❑	562 Gary Ward	.10	.02
❑	563 Rob Wilfong	.10	.02
❑	564 Al Williams	.10	.02
❑	565 Butch Wynegar	.10	.02
❑	566 Randy Bass	.50	.20
❑	567 Juan Bonilla RC	.15	.05
❑	568 Danny Boone	.10	.02
❑	569 John Curtis	.10	.02
❑	570 Juan Eichelberger	.10	.02
❑	571 Barry Evans	.10	.02
❑	572 Tim Flannery	.10	.02
❑	573 Ruppert Jones	.10	.02
❑	574 Terry Kennedy	.10	.02
❑	575 Joe Lefebvre	.10	.02
❑	576A John Littlefield RevNg	100.00	50.00
❑	576B John Littlefield COR (Right handed)	.20	.07
❑	577 Gary Lucas	.10	.02
❑	578 Steve Mura	.10	.02
❑	579 Broderick Perkins	.10	.02
❑	580 Gene Richards	.10	.02
❑	581 Luis Salazar	.10	.02
❑	582 Ozzie Smith	1.50	.60
❑	583 John Urrea	.10	.02
❑	584 Chris Welsh	.10	.02
❑	585 Rick Wise	.10	.02
❑	586 Doug Bird	.10	.02
❑	587 Tim Blackwell	.10	.02
❑	588 Bobby Bonds	.20	.07
❑	589 Bill Buckner	.20	.07
❑	590 Bill Caudill	.10	.02
❑	591 Hector Cruz	.10	.02
❑	592 Jody Davis	.10	.02
❑	593 Ivan DeJesus	.10	.02
❑	594 Steve Dillard	.10	.02
❑	595 Leon Durham	.10	.02
❑	596 Rawly Eastwick	.20	.07
❑	597 Steve Henderson	.10	.02
❑	598 Mike Krukow	.10	.02
❑	599 Mike Lum	.10	.02
❑	600 Randy Martz	.10	.02
❑	601 Jerry Morales	.10	.02
❑	602 Ken Reitz	.10	.02
❑	603 Lee Smith RC	2.00	.75
❑	603B Lee Smith RC COR	6.00	2.50
❑	604 Dick Tidrow	.10	.02
❑	605 Jim Tracy	.20	.07
❑	606 Mike Tyson	.10	.02
❑	607 Ty Waller	.10	.02
❑	608 Danny Ainge	.20	.07
❑	609 George Bell RC	1.00	.40
❑	610 Mark Bomback	.10	.02
❑	611 Barry Bonnell	.10	.02
❑	612 Jim Clancy	.10	.02
❑	613 Damaso Garcia	.10	.02
❑	614 Jerry Garvin	.10	.02
❑	615 Alfredo Griffin	.10	.02
❑	616 Garth Iorg	.10	.02
❑	617 Luis Leal	.10	.02
❑	618 Ken Macha	.10	.02
❑	619 John Mayberry	.10	.02
❑	620 Joey McLaughlin	.10	.02
❑	621 Lloyd Moseby	.10	.02
❑	622 Dave Stieb	.20	.07
❑	623 Jackson Todd	.10	.02
❑	624 Willie Upshaw	.50	.20
❑	625 Otto Velez	.10	.02
❑	626 Ernie Whitt	.10	.02
❑	627 Alvis Woods	.10	.02
❑	628 All Star Game Cleveland, Ohio	.20	.07
❑	629 All Star Infielders Frank White Bucky Dent	.20	.07
❑	630 Big Red Machine Dan Driessen Dave Concepcion Ge	.20	.07
❑	631 Bruce Sutter Top NL Relief Pitcher	.20	.07
❑	632 Steve Carlton/C.Fisk	.20	.07
❑	633 Yaz 3000th Game	.75	.30
❑	634 J.Bench/T.Seaver	.75	.30
❑	635 West Meets East Fernando Valenzuela and Gary Car	.10	.02
❑	636A Fernando Valenzuela IA	.40	.15
❑	636B Fernando Valenzuela: NL SO King (%%the~ NL)	.40	.15
❑	637 Mike Schmidt IA	.75	.30
❑	638 Gary Carter/D.Parker	.10	.02
❑	639 Perfect Game UER Len Barker and Bo Diaz (Catche	.20	.07
❑	640 Pete and Re-Pete	.75	.30
❑	641 L.Smith/Schmidt/Carlton	.75	.30
❑	642 Red Sox Reunion Fred Lynn Dwight Evans	.40	.15
❑	643 Rickey Henderson IA	1.25	.50
❑	644 R.Fingers Most Saves	.20	.07
❑	645 Tom Seaver Most Wins	.20	.07
❑	646 R.Jackson/D.Winfield	.20	.07
❑	646B Reggie/D.Winfield	.20	.07
❑	647 CL: Yankees/Dodgers	.10	.02
❑	648 CL: A's/Reds	.10	.02
❑	649 CL: Cards/Brewers	.10	.02
❑	650 CL: Expos/Orioles	.10	.02
❑	651 CL: Astros/Phillies	.10	.02
❑	652 CL: Tigers/Red Sox	.10	.02
❑	653 CL: Rangers/White Sox	.10	.02

❑ 654 CL: Giants/Indians .10 .02
❑ 655 CL: Royals/Braves .10 .02
❑ 656 CL: Angels/Pirates .10 .02
❑ 657 CL: Mariners/Mets .10 .02
❑ 658 CL: Padres/Twins .10 .02
❑ 659 CL: Blue Jays/Cubs .10 .02
❑ 660 Specials Checklist .10 .02

1983 Fleer

❑ COMPLETE SET (660) 60.00 30.00
❑ 1 Joaquin Andujar .20 .07
❑ 2 Doug Bair .10 .02
❑ 3 Steve Braun .10 .02
❑ 4 Glenn Brummer .10 .02
❑ 5 Bob Forsch .10 .02
❑ 6 David Green RC .50 .20
❑ 7 George Hendrick .20 .07
❑ 8 Keith Hernandez .20 .07
❑ 9 Tom Herr .10 .02
❑ 10 Dane Iorg .10 .02
❑ 11 Jim Kaat .20 .07
❑ 12 Jeff Lahti .10 .02
❑ 13 Tito Landrum .10 .02
❑ 14 Dave LaPoint .10 .02
❑ 15 Willie McGee RC 1.50 .60
❑ 16 Steve Mura .10 .02
❑ 17 Ken Oberkfell .10 .02
❑ 18 Darrell Porter .10 .02
❑ 19 Mike Ramsey .10 .02
❑ 20 Gene Roof .10 .02
❑ 21 Lonnie Smith .10 .02
❑ 22 Ozzie Smith 1.25 .50
❑ 23 John Stuper .10 .02
❑ 24 Bruce Sutter .40 .15
❑ 25 Gene Tenace .20 .07
❑ 26 Jerry Augustine .10 .02
❑ 27 Dwight Bernard .10 .02
❑ 28 Mark Brouhard .10 .02
❑ 29 Mike Caldwell .10 .02
❑ 30 Cecil Cooper .20 .07
❑ 31 Jamie Easterly .10 .02
❑ 32 Marshall Edwards .10 .02
❑ 33 Rollie Fingers .20 .07
❑ 34 Jim Gantner .10 .02
❑ 35 Moose Haas .10 .02
❑ 36 Roy Howell .10 .02
❑ 37 Pete Ladd .10 .02
❑ 38 Bob McClure .10 .02
❑ 39 Doc Medich .10 .02
❑ 40 Paul Molitor .20 .07
❑ 41 Don Money .10 .02
❑ 42 Charlie Moore .10 .02
❑ 43 Ben Oglivie .20 .07
❑ 44 Ed Romero .10 .02
❑ 45 Ted Simmons .20 .07
❑ 46 Jim Slaton .10 .02
❑ 47 Don Sutton .20 .07
❑ 48 Gorman Thomas .20 .07
❑ 49 Pete Vuckovich .10 .02
❑ 50 Ned Yost .10 .02
❑ 51 Robin Yount 1.25 .50
❑ 52 Benny Ayala .10 .02
❑ 53 Bob Bonner .10 .02
❑ 54 Al Bumbry .10 .02
❑ 55 Terry Crowley .10 .02
❑ 56 Storm Davis RC .50 .20
❑ 57 Rich Dauer .10 .02
❑ 58 Rick Dempsey UER .10 .02
❑ 59 Jim Dwyer .10 .02
❑ 60 Mike Flanagan .10 .02
❑ 61 Dan Ford .10 .02
❑ 62 Glenn Gulliver .10 .02
❑ 63 John Lowenstein .10 .02
❑ 64 Dennis Martinez .20 .07
❑ 65 Tippy Martinez .10 .02
❑ 66 Scott McGregor .10 .02
❑ 67 Eddie Murray .75 .30
❑ 68 Joe Nolan .10 .02
❑ 69 Jim Palmer .20 .07
❑ 70 Cal Ripken 6.00 2.50
❑ 71 Gary Roenicke .10 .02
❑ 72 Lenn Sakata .10 .02
❑ 73 Ken Singleton .20 .07
❑ 74 Sammy Stewart .10 .02
❑ 75 Tim Stoddard .10 .02
❑ 76 Don Aase .10 .02
❑ 77 Don Baylor .20 .07
❑ 78 Juan Beniquez .10 .02
❑ 79 Bob Boone .20 .07
❑ 80 Rick Burleson .10 .02
❑ 81 Rod Carew .40 .15
❑ 82 Bobby Clark .10 .02
❑ 83 Doug Corbett .10 .02
❑ 84 John Curtis .10 .02
❑ 85 Doug DeCinces .10 .02
❑ 86 Brian Downing .20 .07
❑ 87 Joe Ferguson .10 .02
❑ 88 Tim Foli .10 .02
❑ 89 Ken Forsch .10 .02
❑ 90 Dave Goltz .10 .02
❑ 91 Bobby Grich .20 .07
❑ 92 Andy Hassler .10 .02
❑ 93 Reggie Jackson .40 .15
❑ 94 Ron Jackson .10 .02
❑ 95 Tommy John .20 .07
❑ 96 Bruce Kison .10 .02
❑ 97 Fred Lynn .20 .07
❑ 98 Ed Ott .10 .02
❑ 99 Steve Renko .10 .02
❑ 100 Luis Sanchez .10 .02
❑ 101 Rob Wilfong .10 .02
❑ 102 Mike Witt .10 .02
❑ 103 Geoff Zahn .10 .02
❑ 104 Willie Aikens .10 .02
❑ 105 Mike Armstrong .10 .02
❑ 106 Vida Blue .20 .07
❑ 107 Bud Black RC .50 .20
❑ 108 George Brett 2.00 .75
❑ 109 Bill Castro .10 .02
❑ 110 Onix Concepcion .10 .02
❑ 111 Dave Frost .10 .02
❑ 112 Cesar Geronimo .10 .02
❑ 113 Larry Gura .10 .02
❑ 114 Steve Hammond .10 .02
❑ 115 Don Hood .10 .02
❑ 116 Dennis Leonard .10 .02
❑ 117 Jerry Martin .10 .02
❑ 118 Lee May .10 .02
❑ 119 Hal McRae .20 .07
❑ 120 Amos Otis .20 .07
❑ 121 Greg Pryor .10 .02
❑ 122 Dan Quisenberry .10 .02
❑ 123 Don Slaught RC .50 .20
❑ 124 Paul Splittorff .10 .02
❑ 125 U.L. Washington .10 .02
❑ 126 John Wathan .10 .02
❑ 127 Frank White .20 .07
❑ 128 Willie Wilson .20 .07
❑ 129 Steve Bedrosian UER (Height 6'33) .10 .02
❑ 130 Bruce Benedict .10 .02
❑ 131 Tommy Boggs .10 .02
❑ 132 Brett Butler .20 .07
❑ 133 Rick Camp .10 .02
❑ 134 Chris Chambliss .20 .07
❑ 135 Ken Dayley .10 .02
❑ 136 Gene Garber .10 .02
❑ 137 Terry Harper .10 .02
❑ 138 Bob Horner .20 .07
❑ 139 Glenn Hubbard .10 .02
❑ 140 Rufino Linares .10 .02
❑ 141 Rick Mahler .10 .02
❑ 142 Dale Murphy .40 .15
❑ 143 Phil Niekro .20 .07
❑ 144 Pascual Perez .10 .02
❑ 145 Biff Pocoroba .10 .02
❑ 146 Rafael Ramirez .10 .02
❑ 147 Jerry Royster .10 .02
❑ 148 Ken Smith .10 .02
❑ 149 Bob Walk .10 .02
❑ 150 Claudell Washington .10 .02
❑ 151 Bob Watson .10 .02
❑ 152 Larry Whisenton .10 .02
❑ 153 Porfirio Altamirano .10 .02
❑ 154 Marty Bystrom .10 .02
❑ 155 Steve Carlton .40 .15
❑ 156 Larry Christenson .10 .02
❑ 157 Ivan DeJesus .10 .02
❑ 158 John Denny .10 .02
❑ 159 Bob Dernier .10 .02
❑ 160 Bo Diaz .10 .02
❑ 161 Ed Farmer .10 .02
❑ 162 Greg Gross .10 .02
❑ 163 Mike Krukow .10 .02
❑ 164 Garry Maddox .10 .02
❑ 165 Gary Matthews .20 .07
❑ 166 Tug McGraw .20 .07
❑ 167 Bob Molinaro .10 .02
❑ 168 Sid Monge .10 .02
❑ 169 Ron Reed .10 .02
❑ 170 Bill Robinson .10 .02
❑ 171 Pete Rose 2.50 1.00
❑ 172 Dick Ruthven .10 .02
❑ 173 Mike Schmidt 2.00 .75
❑ 174 Manny Trillo .10 .02
❑ 175 Ozzie Virgil .10 .02
❑ 176 George Vukovich .10 .02
❑ 177 Gary Allenson .10 .02
❑ 178 Luis Aponte .10 .02
❑ 179 Wade Boggs RC 10.00 4.00
❑ 180 Tom Burgmeier .10 .02
❑ 181 Mark Clear .10 .02
❑ 182 Dennis Eckersley .40 .15
❑ 183 Dwight Evans .40 .15
❑ 184 Rich Gedman .10 .02
❑ 185 Glenn Hoffman .10 .02
❑ 186 Bruce Hurst .10 .02
❑ 187 Carney Lansford .20 .07
❑ 188 Rick Miller .10 .02
❑ 189 Reid Nichols .10 .02
❑ 190 Bob Ojeda .10 .02
❑ 191 Tony Perez .40 .15
❑ 192 Chuck Rainey .10 .02
❑ 193 Jerry Remy .10 .02
❑ 194 Jim Rice .20 .07
❑ 195 Bob Stanley .10 .02
❑ 196 Dave Stapleton .10 .02
❑ 197 Mike Torrez .10 .02
❑ 198 John Tudor .20 .07
❑ 199 Julio Valdez .10 .02
❑ 200 Carl Yastrzemski 1.25 .50
❑ 201 Dusty Baker .20 .07
❑ 202 Joe Beckwith .10 .02
❑ 203 Greg Brock .10 .02
❑ 204 Ron Cey .20 .07
❑ 205 Terry Forster .20 .07
❑ 206 Steve Garvey .20 .07
❑ 207 Pedro Guerrero .20 .07
❑ 208 Burt Hooton .10 .02
❑ 209 Steve Howe .10 .02
❑ 210 Ken Landreaux .10 .02
❑ 211 Mike Marshall .10 .02
❑ 212 Candy Maldonado RC .50 .20
❑ 213 Rick Monday .20 .07
❑ 214 Tom Niedenfuer .10 .02
❑ 215 Jorge Orta .10 .02
❑ 216 Jerry Reuss UER (%%Home:- omitted) .10 .02
❑ 217 Ron Roenicke .10 .02
❑ 218 Vicente Romo .10 .02
❑ 219 Bill Russell .20 .07
❑ 220 Steve Sax .20 .07
❑ 221 Mike Scioscia .20 .07
❑ 222 Dave Stewart .20 .07
❑ 223 Derrel Thomas .10 .02
❑ 224 Fernando Valenzuela .20 .07
❑ 225 Bob Welch .20 .07
❑ 226 Ricky Wright .10 .02
❑ 227 Steve Yeager .20 .07
❑ 228 Bill Almon .10 .02

❑ 229 Harold Baines .20 .07
❑ 230 Salome Barojas .10 .02
❑ 231 Tony Bernazard .10 .02
❑ 232 Britt Burns .10 .02
❑ 233 Richard Dotson .10 .02
❑ 234 Ernesto Escarrega .10 .02
❑ 235 Carlton Fisk .40 .15
❑ 236 Jerry Hairston .10 .02
❑ 237 Kevin Hickey .10 .02
❑ 238 LaMarr Hoyt .10 .02
❑ 239 Steve Kemp .10 .02
❑ 240 Jim Kern .10 .02
❑ 241 Ron Kittle RC 1.00 .40
❑ 242 Jerry Koosman .20 .07
❑ 243 Dennis Lamp .10 .02
❑ 244 Rudy Law .10 .02
❑ 245 Vance Law .10 .02
❑ 246 Ron LeFlore .20 .07
❑ 247 Greg Luzinski .20 .07
❑ 248 Tom Paciorek .10 .02
❑ 249 Aurelio Rodriguez .10 .02
❑ 250 Mike Squires .10 .02
❑ 251 Steve Trout .10 .02
❑ 252 Jim Barr .10 .02
❑ 253 Dave Bergman .10 .02
❑ 254 Fred Breining .10 .02
❑ 255 Bob Brenly .10 .02
❑ 256 Jack Clark .20 .07
❑ 257 Chili Davis .20 .07
❑ 258 Darrell Evans .20 .07
❑ 259 Alan Fowlkes .10 .02
❑ 260 Rich Gale .10 .02
❑ 261 Atlee Hammaker .10 .02
❑ 262 Al Holland .10 .02
❑ 263 Duane Kuiper .10 .02
❑ 264 Bill Laskey .10 .02
❑ 265 Gary Lavelle .10 .02
❑ 266 Johnnie LeMaster .10 .02
❑ 267 Renie Martin .10 .02
❑ 268 Milt May .10 .02
❑ 269 Greg Minton .10 .02
❑ 270 Joe Morgan .20 .07
❑ 271 Tom O'Malley .10 .02
❑ 272 Reggie Smith .20 .07
❑ 273 Guy Sularz .10 .02
❑ 274 Champ Summers .10 .02
❑ 275 Max Venable .10 .02
❑ 276 Jim Wohlford .10 .02
❑ 277 Ray Burris .10 .02
❑ 278 Gary Carter .20 .07
❑ 279 Warren Cromartie .10 .02
❑ 280 Andre Dawson .20 .07
❑ 281 Terry Francona .20 .07
❑ 282 Doug Flynn .10 .02
❑ 283 Woodie Fryman .10 .02
❑ 284 Bill Gullickson .10 .02
❑ 285 Wallace Johnson .10 .02
❑ 286 Charlie Lea .10 .02
❑ 287 Randy Lerch .10 .02
❑ 288 Brad Mills .10 .02
❑ 289 Dan Norman .10 .02
❑ 290 Al Oliver .20 .07
❑ 291 David Palmer .10 .02
❑ 292 Tim Raines .20 .07
❑ 293 Jeff Reardon .20 .07
❑ 294 Steve Rogers .20 .07
❑ 295 Scott Sanderson .10 .02
❑ 296 Dan Schatzeder .10 .02
❑ 297 Bryn Smith .10 .02
❑ 298 Chris Speier .10 .02
❑ 299 Tim Wallach .20 .07
❑ 300 Jerry White .10 .02
❑ 301 Joel Youngblood .10 .02
❑ 302 Ross Baumgarten .10 .02
❑ 303 Dale Berra .10 .02
❑ 304 John Candelaria .10 .02
❑ 305 Dick Davis .10 .02
❑ 306 Mike Easler .10 .02
❑ 307 Richie Hebner .10 .02
❑ 308 Lee Lacy .10 .02
❑ 309 Bill Madlock .20 .07
❑ 310 Larry McWilliams .10 .02
❑ 311 John Milner .10 .02
❑ 312 Omar Moreno .10 .02
❑ 313 Jim Morrison .10 .02
❑ 314 Steve Nicosia .10 .02
❑ 315 Dave Parker .20 .07
❑ 316 Tony Pena .10 .02
❑ 317 Johnny Ray .10 .02
❑ 318 Rick Rhoden .10 .02
❑ 319 Don Robinson .10 .02
❑ 320 Enrique Romo .10 .02
❑ 321 Manny Sarmiento .10 .02
❑ 322 Rod Scurry .10 .02
❑ 323 Jimmy Smith .10 .02
❑ 324 Willie Stargell .40 .15
❑ 325 Jason Thompson .10 .02
❑ 326 Kent Tekulve .10 .02
❑ 327A Tom Brookens
(Short .375~ brown box
shaded in on .10 .02
❑ 327B Tom Brookens
(Longer 1.25~ brown box
shaded in o .10 .02
❑ 328 Enos Cabell .10 .02
❑ 329 Kirk Gibson .20 .07
❑ 330 Larry Herndon .10 .02
❑ 331 Mike Ivie .10 .02
❑ 332 Howard Johnson RC 1.00 .40
❑ 333 Lynn Jones .10 .02
❑ 334 Rick Leach .10 .02
❑ 335 Chet Lemon .20 .07
❑ 336 Jack Morris .20 .07
❑ 337 Lance Parrish .20 .07
❑ 338 Larry Pashnick .10 .02
❑ 339 Dan Petry .10 .02
❑ 340 Dave Rozema .10 .02
❑ 341 Dave Rucker .10 .02
❑ 342 Elias Sosa .10 .02
❑ 343 Dave Tobik .10 .02
❑ 344 Alan Trammell .20 .07
❑ 345 Jerry Turner .10 .02
❑ 346 Jerry Ujdur .10 .02
❑ 347 Pat Underwood .10 .02
❑ 348 Lou Whitaker .20 .07
❑ 349 Milt Wilcox .10 .02
❑ 350 Glenn Wilson .50 .20
❑ 351 John Wockenfuss .10 .02
❑ 352 Kurt Bevacqua .10 .02
❑ 353 Juan Bonilla .10 .02
❑ 354 Floyd Chiffer .10 .02
❑ 355 Luis DeLeon .10 .02
❑ 356 Dave Dravecky RC 1.00 .40
❑ 357 Dave Edwards .10 .02
❑ 358 Juan Eichelberger .10 .02
❑ 359 Tim Flannery .10 .02
❑ 360 Tony Gwynn RC 15.00 6.00
❑ 361 Ruppert Jones .10 .02
❑ 362 Terry Kennedy .10 .02
❑ 363 Joe Lefebvre .10 .02
❑ 364 Sixto Lezcano .10 .02
❑ 365 Tim Lollar .10 .02
❑ 366 Gary Lucas .10 .02
❑ 367 John Montefusco .10 .02
❑ 368 Broderick Perkins .10 .02
❑ 369 Joe Pittman .10 .02
❑ 370 Gene Richards .10 .02
❑ 371 Luis Salazar .10 .02
❑ 372 Eric Show RC .50 .20
❑ 373 Garry Templeton .20 .07
❑ 374 Chris Welsh .10 .02
❑ 375 Alan Wiggins .10 .02
❑ 376 Rick Cerone .10 .02
❑ 377 Dave Collins .10 .02
❑ 378 Roger Erickson .10 .02
❑ 379 George Frazier .10 .02
❑ 380 Oscar Gamble .10 .02
❑ 381 Rich Gossage .20 .07
❑ 382 Ken Griffey .20 .07
❑ 383 Ron Guidry .20 .07
❑ 384 Dave LaRoche .10 .02
❑ 385 Rudy May .10 .02
❑ 386 John Mayberry .10 .02
❑ 387 Lee Mazzilli .20 .07
❑ 388 Mike Morgan .10 .02
❑ 389 Jerry Mumphrey .10 .02
❑ 390 Bobby Murcer .20 .07
❑ 391 Graig Nettles .20 .07
❑ 392 Lou Piniella .20 .07
❑ 393 Willie Randolph .20 .07
❑ 394 Shane Rawley .10 .02
❑ 395 Dave Righetti .20 .07
❑ 396 Andre Robertson .10 .02
❑ 397 Roy Smalley .10 .02
❑ 398 Dave Winfield .20 .07
❑ 399 Butch Wynegar .10 .02
❑ 400 Chris Bando .10 .02
❑ 401 Alan Bannister .10 .02
❑ 402 Len Barker .10 .02
❑ 403 Tom Brennan .10 .02
❑ 404 Carmelo Castillo .10 .02
❑ 405 Miguel Dilone .10 .02
❑ 406 Jerry Dybzinski .10 .02
❑ 407 Mike Fischlin .10 .02
❑ 408 Ed Glynn UER .10 .02
❑ 409 Mike Hargrove .10 .02
❑ 410 Toby Harrah .20 .07
❑ 411 Ron Hassey .10 .02
❑ 412 Von Hayes .10 .02
❑ 413 Rick Manning .10 .02
❑ 414 Bake McBride .20 .07
❑ 415 Larry Milbourne .10 .02
❑ 416 Bill Nahorodny .10 .02
❑ 417 Jack Perconte .10 .02
❑ 418 Lary Sorensen .10 .02
❑ 419 Dan Spillner .10 .02
❑ 420 Rick Sutcliffe .20 .07
❑ 421 Andre Thornton .10 .02
❑ 422 Rick Waits .10 .02
❑ 423 Eddie Whitson .10 .02
❑ 424 Jesse Barfield .20 .07
❑ 425 Barry Bonnell .10 .02
❑ 426 Jim Clancy .10 .02
❑ 427 Damaso Garcia .10 .02
❑ 428 Jerry Garvin .10 .02
❑ 429 Alfredo Griffin .10 .02
❑ 430 Garth Iorg .10 .02
❑ 431 Roy Lee Jackson .10 .02
❑ 432 Luis Leal .10 .02
❑ 433 Buck Martinez .10 .02
❑ 434 Joey McLaughlin .10 .02
❑ 435 Lloyd Moseby .10 .02
❑ 436 Rance Mulliniks .10 .02
❑ 437 Dale Murray .10 .02
❑ 438 Wayne Nordhagen .10 .02
❑ 439 Geno Petralli .50 .20
❑ 440 Hosken Powell .10 .02
❑ 441 Dave Stieb .20 .07
❑ 442 Willie Upshaw .10 .02
❑ 443 Ernie Whitt .10 .02
❑ 444 Alvis Woods .10 .02
❑ 445 Alan Ashby .10 .02
❑ 446 Jose Cruz .20 .07
❑ 447 Kiko Garcia .10 .02
❑ 448 Phil Garner .20 .07
❑ 449 Danny Heep .10 .02
❑ 450 Art Howe .10 .02
❑ 451 Bob Knepper .10 .02
❑ 452 Alan Knicely .10 .02
❑ 453 Ray Knight .20 .07
❑ 454 Frank LaCorte .10 .02
❑ 455 Mike LaCoss .10 .02
❑ 456 Randy Moffitt .10 .02
❑ 457 Joe Niekro .10 .02
❑ 458 Terry Puhl .10 .02
❑ 459 Luis Pujols .10 .02
❑ 460 Craig Reynolds .10 .02
❑ 461 Bert Roberge .10 .02
❑ 462 Vern Ruhle .10 .02
❑ 463 Nolan Ryan 4.00 1.50
❑ 464 Joe Sambito .10 .02
❑ 465 Tony Scott .10 .02
❑ 466 Dave Smith .10 .02
❑ 467 Harry Spilman .10 .02
❑ 468 Dickie Thon .10 .02
❑ 469 Denny Walling .10 .02
❑ 470 Larry Andersen .10 .02
❑ 471 Floyd Bannister .10 .02
❑ 472 Jim Beattie .10 .02
❑ 473 Bruce Bochte .10 .02
❑ 474 Manny Castillo .10 .02
❑ 475 Bill Caudill .10 .02
❑ 476 Bryan Clark .10 .02
❑ 477 Al Cowens .10 .02
❑ 478 Julio Cruz .10 .02
❑ 479 Todd Cruz .10 .02
❑ 480 Gary Gray .10 .02
❑ 481 Dave Henderson .10 .02

❑ 482 Mike Moore RC .50 .20
❑ 483 Gaylord Perry .20 .07
❑ 484 Dave Revering .10 .02
❑ 485 Joe Simpson .10 .02
❑ 486 Mike Stanton .10 .02
❑ 487 Rick Sweet .10 .02
❑ 488 Ed VandeBerg .10 .02
❑ 489 Richie Zisk .10 .02
❑ 490 Doug Bird .10 .02
❑ 491 Larry Bowa .20 .07
❑ 492 Bill Buckner .20 .07
❑ 493 Bill Campbell .10 .02
❑ 494 Jody Davis .10 .02
❑ 495 Leon Durham .10 .02
❑ 496 Steve Henderson .10 .02
❑ 497 Willie Hernandez .10 .02
❑ 498 Fergie Jenkins .20 .07
❑ 499 Jay Johnstone .10 .02
❑ 500 Junior Kennedy .10 .02
❑ 501 Randy Martz .10 .02
❑ 502 Jerry Morales .10 .02
❑ 503 Keith Moreland .10 .02
❑ 504 Dickie Noles .10 .02
❑ 505 Mike Proly .10 .02
❑ 506 Allen Ripley .10 .02
❑ 507 Ryne Sandberg RC 10.00 4.00
❑ 508 Lee Smith .40 .15
❑ 509 Pat Tabler .10 .02
❑ 510 Dick Tidrow .10 .02
❑ 511 Bump Wills .10 .02
❑ 512 Gary Woods .10 .02
❑ 513 Tony Armas .20 .07
❑ 514 Dave Beard .10 .02
❑ 515 Jeff Burroughs .10 .02
❑ 516 John D'Acquisto .10 .02
❑ 517 Wayne Gross .10 .02
❑ 518 Mike Heath .10 .02
❑ 519 Rickey Henderson 1.50 .60
❑ 520 Cliff Johnson .10 .02
❑ 521 Matt Keough .10 .02
❑ 522 Brian Kingman .10 .02
❑ 523 Rick Langford .10 .02
❑ 524 Dave Lopes .20 .07
❑ 525 Steve McCatty .10 .02
❑ 526 Dave McKay .10 .02
❑ 527 Dan Meyer .10 .02
❑ 528 Dwayne Murphy .10 .02
❑ 529 Jeff Newman .10 .02
❑ 530 Mike Norris .10 .02
❑ 531 Bob Owchinko .10 .02
❑ 532 Joe Rudi .20 .07
❑ 533 Jimmy Sexton .10 .02
❑ 534 Fred Stanley .10 .02
❑ 535 Tom Underwood .10 .02
❑ 536 Neil Allen .10 .02
❑ 537 Wally Backman .10 .02
❑ 538 Bob Bailor .10 .02
❑ 539 Hubie Brooks .10 .02
❑ 540 Carlos Diaz RC .25 .08
❑ 541 Pete Falcone .10 .02
❑ 542 George Foster .20 .07
❑ 543 Ron Gardenhire .10 .02
❑ 544 Brian Giles .10 .02
❑ 545 Ron Hodges .10 .02
❑ 546 Randy Jones .10 .02
❑ 547 Mike Jorgensen .10 .02
❑ 548 Dave Kingman .20 .07
❑ 549 Ed Lynch .10 .02
❑ 550 Jesse Orosco .10 .02
❑ 551 Rick Ownbey .10 .02
❑ 552 Charlie Puleo .10 .02
❑ 553 Gary Rajsich .10 .02
❑ 554 Mike Scott .20 .07
❑ 555 Rusty Staub .20 .07
❑ 556 John Stearns .10 .02
❑ 557 Craig Swan .10 .02
❑ 558 Ellis Valentine .10 .02
❑ 559 Tom Veryzer .10 .02
❑ 560 Mookie Wilson .20 .07
❑ 561 Pat Zachry .10 .02
❑ 562 Buddy Bell .20 .07
❑ 563 John Butcher .10 .02
❑ 564 Steve Comer .10 .02
❑ 565 Danny Darwin .10 .02
❑ 566 Bucky Dent .20 .07
❑ 567 John Grubb .10 .02
❑ 568 Rick Honeycutt .10 .02
❑ 569 Dave Hostetler .10 .02
❑ 570 Charlie Hough .20 .07
❑ 571 Lamar Johnson .10 .02
❑ 572 Jon Matlack .10 .02
❑ 573 Paul Mirabella .10 .02
❑ 574 Larry Parrish .10 .02
❑ 575 Mike Richardt .10 .02
❑ 576 Mickey Rivers .10 .02
❑ 577 Billy Sample .10 .02
❑ 578 Dave Schmidt .10 .02
❑ 579 Bill Stein .10 .02
❑ 580 Jim Sundberg .20 .07
❑ 581 Frank Tanana .20 .07
❑ 582 Mark Wagner .10 .02
❑ 583 George Wright RC .50 .20
❑ 584 Johnny Bench .75 .30
❑ 585 Bruce Berenyi .10 .02
❑ 586 Larry Biittner .10 .02
❑ 587 Cesar Cedeno .20 .07
❑ 588 Dave Concepcion .20 .07
❑ 589 Dan Driessen .10 .02
❑ 590 Greg Harris .10 .02
❑ 591 Ben Hayes .10 .02
❑ 592 Paul Householder .10 .02
❑ 593 Tom Hume .10 .02
❑ 594 Wayne Krenchicki .10 .02
❑ 595 Rafael Landestoy .10 .02
❑ 596 Charlie Leibrandt .10 .02
❑ 597 Eddie Milner .10 .02
❑ 598 Ron Oester .10 .02
❑ 599 Frank Pastore .10 .02
❑ 600 Joe Price .10 .02
❑ 601 Tom Seaver .75 .30
❑ 602 Bob Shirley .10 .02
❑ 603 Mario Soto .20 .07
❑ 604 Alex Trevino .10 .02
❑ 605 Mike Vail .10 .02
❑ 606 Duane Walker .10 .02
❑ 607 Tom Brunansky .20 .07
❑ 608 Bobby Castillo .10 .02
❑ 609 John Castino .10 .02
❑ 610 Ron Davis .10 .02
❑ 611 Lenny Faedo .10 .02
❑ 612 Terry Felton .10 .02
❑ 613 Gary Gaetti RC 1.00 .40
❑ 614 Mickey Hatcher .10 .02
❑ 615 Brad Havens .10 .02
❑ 616 Kent Hrbek .20 .07
❑ 617 Randy Johnson .10 .02
❑ 618 Tim Laudner .10 .02
❑ 619 Jeff Little .10 .02
❑ 620 Bobby Mitchell .10 .02
❑ 621 Jack O'Connor .10 .02
❑ 622 John Pacella .10 .02
❑ 623 Pete Redfern .10 .02
❑ 624 Jesus Vega .10 .02
❑ 625 Frank Viola RC 1.50 .60
❑ 626 Ron Washington .10 .02
❑ 627 Gary Ward .10 .02
❑ 628 Al Williams .10 .02
❑ 629 C.Yaz/Eck/M.Clear .75 .30
❑ 630 G.Perry/T.Bulling .10 .02
❑ 631 D.Concepcion/M.Trillo .20 .07
❑ 632 R.Yount/B.Bell .75 .30
❑ 633 D.Winfield/K.Hrbek .10 .02
❑ 634 P.Rose/W.Stargell .75 .30
❑ 635 T.Harrah/A.Thornton .20 .07
❑ 636 O.Smith/Lo.Smith .75 .30
❑ 637 B.Diaz/G.Carter .10 .02
❑ 638 C.Fisk/G.Carter .20 .07
❑ 639 Rickey Henderson IA .75 .30
❑ 640 B.Oglivie/R.Jackson .40 .15
❑ 641 Joel Youngblood .10 .02
❑ 642 R.Hassey/L.Barker .20 .07
❑ 643 V.Blue/Black-Blue .20 .07
❑ 644 B.Black/Black-Blue .10 .02
❑ 645 Reggie Jackson Power .20 .07
❑ 646 Rickey Henderson Speed .75 .30
❑ 647 CL: Cards/Brewers .10 .02
❑ 648 CL: Orioles/Angels .10 .02
❑ 649 CL: Royals/Braves .10 .02
❑ 650 CL: Phillies/Red Sox .10 .02
❑ 651 CL: Dodgers/White Sox .10 .02
❑ 652 CL: Giants/Expos .10 .02
❑ 653 CL: Pirates/Tigers .10 .02
❑ 654 CL: Padres/Yankees .10 .02
❑ 655 CL: Indians/Blue Jays .10 .02
❑ 656 CL: Astros/Mariners .10 .02
❑ 657 CL: Cubs/A's .10 .02
❑ 658 CL: Mets/Rangers .10 .02
❑ 659 CL: Reds/Twins .10 .02
❑ 660 CL: Specials/Teams .10 .02

1984 Fleer

❑ COMPLETE SET (660) 50.00 25.00
❑ 1 Mike Boddicker .15 .05
❑ 2 Al Bumbry .15 .05
❑ 3 Todd Cruz .15 .05
❑ 4 Rich Dauer .15 .05
❑ 5 Storm Davis .15 .05
❑ 6 Rick Dempsey .15 .05
❑ 7 Jim Dwyer .15 .05
❑ 8 Mike Flanagan .15 .05
❑ 9 Dan Ford .15 .05
❑ 10 John Lowenstein .15 .05
❑ 11 Dennis Martinez .40 .15
❑ 12 Tippy Martinez .15 .05
❑ 13 Scott McGregor .15 .05
❑ 14 Eddie Murray 1.50 .60
❑ 15 Joe Nolan .15 .05
❑ 16 Jim Palmer .40 .15
❑ 17 Cal Ripken 10.00 4.00
❑ 18 Gary Roenicke .15 .05
❑ 19 Lenn Sakata .15 .05
❑ 20 John Shelby .15 .05
❑ 21 Ken Singleton .40 .15
❑ 22 Sammy Stewart .15 .05
❑ 23 Tim Stoddard .15 .05
❑ 24 Marty Bystrom .15 .05
❑ 25 Steve Carlton .75 .30
❑ 26 Ivan DeJesus .15 .05
❑ 27 John Denny .15 .05
❑ 28 Bob Dernier .15 .05
❑ 29 Bo Diaz .15 .05
❑ 30 Kiko Garcia .15 .05
❑ 31 Greg Gross .15 .05
❑ 32 Kevin Gross RC .50 .20
❑ 33 Von Hayes .15 .05
❑ 34 Willie Hernandez .15 .05
❑ 35 Al Holland .15 .05
❑ 36 Charles Hudson .15 .05
❑ 37 Joe Lefebvre .15 .05
❑ 38 Sixto Lezcano .15 .05
❑ 39 Garry Maddox .15 .05
❑ 40 Gary Matthews .40 .15
❑ 41 Len Matuszek .15 .05
❑ 42 Tug McGraw .40 .15
❑ 43 Joe Morgan .40 .15
❑ 44 Tony Perez .75 .30
❑ 45 Ron Reed .15 .05
❑ 46 Pete Rose 5.00 2.00
❑ 47 Juan Samuel RC 1.00 .40
❑ 48 Mike Schmidt 4.00 1.50
❑ 49 Ozzie Virgil .15 .05
❑ 50 Juan Agosto .15 .05
❑ 51 Harold Baines .40 .15
❑ 52 Floyd Bannister .15 .05
❑ 53 Salome Barojas .15 .05
❑ 54 Britt Burns .15 .05
❑ 55 Julio Cruz .15 .05
❑ 56 Richard Dotson .15 .05
❑ 57 Jerry Dybzinski .15 .05
❑ 58 Carlton Fisk .75 .30

❑ 59 Scott Fletcher .15 .05
❑ 60 Jerry Hairston .15 .05
❑ 61 Kevin Hickey .15 .05
❑ 62 Marc Hill .15 .05
❑ 63 LaMarr Hoyt .15 .05
❑ 64 Ron Kittle .15 .05
❑ 65 Jerry Koosman .40 .15
❑ 66 Dennis Lamp .15 .05
❑ 67 Rudy Law .15 .05
❑ 68 Vance Law .15 .05
❑ 69 Greg Luzinski .40 .15
❑ 70 Tom Paciorek .15 .05
❑ 71 Mike Squires .15 .05
❑ 72 Dick Tidrow .15 .05
❑ 73 Greg Walker .50 .20
❑ 74 Glenn Abbott .15 .05
❑ 75 Howard Bailey .15 .05
❑ 76 Doug Bair .15 .05
❑ 77 Juan Berenguer .15 .05
❑ 78 Tom Brookens .40 .15
❑ 79 Enos Cabell .15 .05
❑ 80 Kirk Gibson 1.50 .60
❑ 81 John Grubb .15 .05
❑ 82 Larry Herndon .40 .15
❑ 83 Wayne Krenchicki .15 .05
❑ 84 Rick Leach .15 .05
❑ 85 Chet Lemon .40 .15
❑ 86 Aurelio Lopez .40 .15
❑ 87 Jack Morris .40 .15
❑ 88 Lance Parrish .75 .30
❑ 89 Dan Petry .40 .15
❑ 90 Dave Rozema .15 .05
❑ 91 Alan Trammell .40 .15
❑ 92 Lou Whitaker .40 .15
❑ 93 Milt Wilcox .15 .05
❑ 94 Glenn Wilson .40 .15
❑ 95 John Wockenfuss .15 .05
❑ 96 Dusty Baker .40 .15
❑ 97 Joe Beckwith .15 .05
❑ 98 Greg Brock .15 .05
❑ 99 Jack Fimple .15 .05
❑ 100 Pedro Guerrero .40 .15
❑ 101 Rick Honeycutt .15 .05
❑ 102 Burt Hooton .15 .05
❑ 103 Steve Howe .15 .05
❑ 104 Ken Landreaux .15 .05
❑ 105 Mike Marshall .15 .05
❑ 106 Rick Monday .40 .15
❑ 107 Jose Morales .15 .05
❑ 108 Tom Niedenfuer .15 .05
❑ 109 Alejandro Pena RC* 1.00 .40
❑ 110 Jerry Reuss UER
(%%Home:~ omitted) .15 .05
❑ 111 Bill Russell .40 .15
❑ 112 Steve Sax .15 .05
❑ 113 Mike Scioscia .40 .15
❑ 114 Derrel Thomas .15 .05
❑ 115 Fernando Valenzuela .40 .15
❑ 116 Bob Welch .40 .15
❑ 117 Steve Yeager .40 .15
❑ 118 Pat Zachry .15 .05
❑ 119 Don Baylor .40 .15
❑ 120 Bert Campaneris .40 .15
❑ 121 Rick Cerone .15 .05
❑ 122 Ray Fontenot .15 .05
❑ 123 George Frazier .15 .05
❑ 124 Oscar Gamble .15 .05
❑ 125 Rich Gossage .40 .15
❑ 126 Ken Griffey .40 .15
❑ 127 Ron Guidry .40 .15
❑ 128 Jay Howell .15 .05
❑ 129 Steve Kemp .15 .05
❑ 130 Matt Keough .15 .05
❑ 131 Don Mattingly RC 25.00 10.00
❑ 132 John Montefusco .15 .05
❑ 133 Omar Moreno .15 .05
❑ 134 Dale Murray .15 .05
❑ 135 Graig Nettles .40 .15
❑ 136 Lou Piniella .40 .15
❑ 137 Willie Randolph .40 .15
❑ 138 Shane Rawley .15 .05
❑ 139 Dave Righetti .40 .15
❑ 140 Andre Robertson .15 .05
❑ 141 Bob Shirley .15 .05
❑ 142 Roy Smalley .15 .05
❑ 143 Dave Winfield .40 .15
❑ 144 Butch Wynegar .15 .05
❑ 145 Jim Acker .15 .05
❑ 146 Doyle Alexander .15 .05
❑ 147 Jesse Barfield .40 .15
❑ 148 George Bell .40 .15
❑ 149 Barry Bonnell .15 .05
❑ 150 Jim Clancy .15 .05
❑ 151 Dave Collins .15 .05
❑ 152 Tony Fernandez RC 1.00 .40
❑ 153 Damaso Garcia .15 .05
❑ 154 Dave Geisel .15 .05
❑ 155 Jim Gott .15 .05
❑ 156 Alfredo Griffin .15 .05
❑ 157 Garth Iorg .15 .05
❑ 158 Roy Lee Jackson .15 .05
❑ 159 Cliff Johnson .15 .05
❑ 160 Luis Leal .15 .05
❑ 161 Buck Martinez .15 .05
❑ 162 Joey McLaughlin .15 .05
❑ 163 Randy Moffitt .15 .05
❑ 164 Lloyd Moseby .15 .05
❑ 165 Rance Mulliniks .15 .05
❑ 166 Jorge Orta .15 .05
❑ 167 Dave Stieb .40 .15
❑ 168 Willie Upshaw .15 .05
❑ 169 Ernie Whitt .15 .05
❑ 170 Len Barker .15 .05
❑ 171 Steve Bedrosian .15 .05
❑ 172 Bruce Benedict .15 .05
❑ 173 Brett Butler .40 .15
❑ 174 Rick Camp .15 .05
❑ 175 Chris Chambliss .40 .15
❑ 176 Ken Dayley .15 .05
❑ 177 Pete Falcone .15 .05
❑ 178 Terry Forster .40 .15
❑ 179 Gene Garber .15 .05
❑ 180 Terry Harper .15 .05
❑ 181 Bob Horner .40 .15
❑ 182 Glenn Hubbard .15 .05
❑ 183 Randy Johnson .15 .05
❑ 184 Craig McMurtry .15 .05
❑ 185 Donnie Moore .15 .05
❑ 186 Dale Murphy .75 .30
❑ 187 Phil Niekro .40 .15
❑ 188 Pascual Perez .15 .05
❑ 189 Biff Pocoroba .15 .05
❑ 190 Rafael Ramirez .15 .05
❑ 191 Jerry Royster .15 .05
❑ 192 Claudell Washington .15 .05
❑ 193 Bob Watson .15 .05
❑ 194 Jerry Augustine .15 .05
❑ 195 Mark Brouhard .15 .05
❑ 196 Mike Caldwell .15 .05
❑ 197 Tom Candiotti RC 1.00 .40
❑ 198 Cecil Cooper .40 .15
❑ 199 Rollie Fingers .40 .15
❑ 200 Jim Gantner .15 .05
❑ 201 Bob L. Gibson RC .25 .08
❑ 202 Moose Haas .15 .05
❑ 203 Roy Howell .15 .05
❑ 204 Pete Ladd .15 .05
❑ 205 Rick Manning .15 .05
❑ 206 Bob McClure .15 .05
❑ 207 Paul Molitor .40 .15
❑ 208 Don Money .15 .05
❑ 209 Charlie Moore .15 .05
❑ 210 Ben Oglivie .40 .15
❑ 211 Chuck Porter .15 .05
❑ 212 Ed Romero .15 .05
❑ 213 Ted Simmons .40 .15
❑ 214 Jim Slaton .15 .05
❑ 215 Don Sutton .40 .15
❑ 216 Tom Tellmann .15 .05
❑ 217 Pete Vuckovich .15 .05
❑ 218 Ned Yost .15 .05
❑ 219 Robin Yount 2.50 1.00
❑ 220 Alan Ashby .15 .05
❑ 221 Kevin Bass .15 .05
❑ 222 Jose Cruz .40 .15
❑ 223 Bill Dawley .15 .05
❑ 224 Frank DiPino .15 .05
❑ 225 Bill Doran RC* .50 .20
❑ 226 Phil Garner .40 .15
❑ 227 Art Howe .15 .05
❑ 228 Bob Knepper .15 .05
❑ 229 Ray Knight .40 .15
❑ 230 Frank LaCorte .15 .05
❑ 231 Mike LaCoss .15 .05
❑ 232 Mike Madden .15 .05
❑ 233 Jerry Mumphrey .15 .05
❑ 234 Joe Niekro .15 .05
❑ 235 Terry Puhl .15 .05
❑ 236 Luis Pujols .15 .05
❑ 237 Craig Reynolds .15 .05
❑ 238 Vern Ruhle .15 .05
❑ 239 Nolan Ryan 8.00 3.00
❑ 240 Mike Scott .40 .15
❑ 241 Tony Scott .15 .05
❑ 242 Dave Smith .15 .05
❑ 243 Dickie Thon .15 .05
❑ 244 Denny Walling .15 .05
❑ 245 Dale Berra .15 .05
❑ 246 Jim Bibby .15 .05
❑ 247 John Candelaria .15 .05
❑ 248 Jose DeLeon RC .50 .20
❑ 249 Mike Easler .15 .05
❑ 250 Cecilio Guante .15 .05
❑ 251 Richie Hebner .15 .05
❑ 252 Lee Lacy .15 .05
❑ 253 Bill Madlock .40 .15
❑ 254 Milt May .15 .05
❑ 255 Lee Mazzilli .40 .15
❑ 256 Larry McWilliams .15 .05
❑ 257 Jim Morrison .15 .05
❑ 258 Dave Parker .40 .15
❑ 259 Tony Pena .15 .05
❑ 260 Johnny Ray .15 .05
❑ 261 Rick Rhoden .15 .05
❑ 262 Don Robinson .15 .05
❑ 263 Manny Sarmiento .15 .05
❑ 264 Rod Scurry .15 .05
❑ 265 Kent Tekulve .15 .05
❑ 266 Gene Tenace .40 .15
❑ 267 Jason Thompson .15 .05
❑ 268 Lee Tunnell .15 .05
❑ 269 Marvell Wynne .50 .20
❑ 270 Ray Burris .15 .05
❑ 271 Gary Carter .40 .15
❑ 272 Warren Cromartie .15 .05
❑ 273 Andre Dawson .40 .15
❑ 274 Doug Flynn .15 .05
❑ 275 Terry Francona .40 .15
❑ 276 Bill Gullickson .15 .05
❑ 277 Bob James .15 .05
❑ 278 Charlie Lea .15 .05
❑ 279 Bryan Little .15 .05
❑ 280 Al Oliver .40 .15
❑ 281 Tim Raines .40 .15
❑ 282 Bobby Ramos .15 .05
❑ 283 Jeff Reardon .40 .15
❑ 284 Steve Rogers .40 .15
❑ 285 Scott Sanderson .15 .05
❑ 286 Dan Schatzeder .15 .05
❑ 287 Bryn Smith .15 .05
❑ 288 Chris Speier .15 .05
❑ 289 Manny Trillo .15 .05
❑ 290 Mike Vail .15 .05
❑ 291 Tim Wallach .15 .05
❑ 292 Chris Welsh .15 .05
❑ 293 Jim Wohlford .15 .05
❑ 294 Kurt Bevacqua .15 .05
❑ 295 Juan Bonilla .15 .05
❑ 296 Bobby Brown .15 .05
❑ 297 Luis DeLeon .15 .05
❑ 298 Dave Dravecky .15 .05
❑ 299 Tim Flannery .15 .05
❑ 300 Steve Garvey .40 .15
❑ 301 Tony Gwynn 6.00 2.50
❑ 302 Andy Hawkins .15 .05
❑ 303 Ruppert Jones .15 .05
❑ 304 Terry Kennedy .15 .05
❑ 305 Tim Lollar .15 .05
❑ 306 Gary Lucas .15 .05
❑ 307 Kevin McReynolds RC 1.00 .40
❑ 308 Sid Monge .15 .05
❑ 309 Mario Ramirez .15 .05
❑ 310 Gene Richards .15 .05
❑ 311 Luis Salazar .15 .05
❑ 312 Eric Show .15 .05
❑ 313 Elias Sosa .15 .05
❑ 314 Garry Templeton .40 .15
❑ 315 Mark Thurmond .15 .05

❑ 316	Ed Whitson	.15	.05
❑ 317	Alan Wiggins	.15	.05
❑ 318	Neil Allen	.15	.05
❑ 319	Joaquin Andujar	.40	.15
❑ 320	Steve Braun	.15	.05
❑ 321	Glenn Brummer	.15	.05
❑ 322	Bob Forsch	.15	.05
❑ 323	David Green	.15	.05
❑ 324	George Hendrick	.40	.15
❑ 325	Tom Herr	.15	.05
❑ 326	Dane Iorg	.15	.05
❑ 327	Jeff Lahti	.15	.05
❑ 328	Dave LaPoint	.15	.05
❑ 329	Willie McGee	.40	.15
❑ 330	Ken Oberkfell	.15	.05
❑ 331	Darrell Porter	.15	.05
❑ 332	Jamie Quirk	.15	.05
❑ 333	Mike Ramsey	.15	.05
❑ 334	Floyd Rayford	.15	.05
❑ 335	Lonnie Smith	.15	.05
❑ 336	Ozzie Smith	2.50	1.00
❑ 337	John Stuper	.15	.05
❑ 338	Bruce Sutter	.75	.30
❑ 339	Andy Van Slyke RC	2.50	1.00
❑ 340	Dave Von Ohlen	.15	.05
❑ 341	Willie Aikens	.15	.05
❑ 342	Mike Armstrong	.15	.05
❑ 343	Bud Black	.15	.05
❑ 344	George Brett	4.00	1.50
❑ 345	Onix Concepcion	.15	.05
❑ 346	Keith Creel	.15	.05
❑ 347	Larry Gura	.15	.05
❑ 348	Don Hood	.15	.05
❑ 349	Dennis Leonard	.15	.05
❑ 350	Hal McRae	.40	.15
❑ 351	Amos Otis	.40	.15
❑ 352	Gaylord Perry	.40	.15
❑ 353	Greg Pryor	.15	.05
❑ 354	Dan Quisenberry	.15	.05
❑ 355	Steve Renko	.15	.05
❑ 356	Leon Roberts	.15	.05
❑ 357	Pat Sheridan	.15	.05
❑ 358	Joe Simpson	.15	.05
❑ 359	Don Slaught	.40	.15
❑ 360	Paul Splittorff	.15	.05
❑ 361	U.L. Washington	.15	.05
❑ 362	John Wathan	.15	.05
❑ 363	Frank White	.40	.15
❑ 364	Willie Wilson	.40	.15
❑ 365	Jim Barr	.15	.05
❑ 366	Dave Bergman	.15	.05
❑ 367	Fred Breining	.15	.05
❑ 368	Bob Brenly	.15	.05
❑ 369	Jack Clark	.40	.15
❑ 370	Chili Davis	.40	.15
❑ 371	Mark Davis	.15	.05
❑ 372	Darrell Evans	.40	.15
❑ 373	Atlee Hammaker	.15	.05
❑ 374	Mike Krukow	.15	.05
❑ 375	Duane Kuiper	.15	.05
❑ 376	Bill Laskey	.15	.05
❑ 377	Gary Lavelle	.15	.05
❑ 378	Johnnie LeMaster	.15	.05
❑ 379	Jeff Leonard	.15	.05
❑ 380	Randy Lerch	.15	.05
❑ 381	Renie Martin	.15	.05
❑ 382	Andy McGaffigan	.15	.05
❑ 383	Greg Minton	.15	.05
❑ 384	Tom O'Malley	.15	.05
❑ 385	Max Venable	.15	.05
❑ 386	Brad Wellman	.15	.05
❑ 387	Joel Youngblood	.15	.05
❑ 388	Gary Allenson	.15	.05
❑ 389	Luis Aponte	.15	.05
❑ 390	Tony Armas	.40	.15
❑ 391	Doug Bird	.15	.05
❑ 392	Wade Boggs	4.00	1.50
❑ 393	Dennis Boyd	.40	.15
❑ 394	Mike G. Brown UER	.25	.08
❑ 395	Mark Clear	.15	.05
❑ 396	Dennis Eckersley	.75	.30
❑ 397	Dwight Evans	.75	.30
❑ 398	Rich Gedman	.15	.05
❑ 399	Glenn Hoffman	.15	.05
❑ 400	Bruce Hurst	.15	.05
❑ 401	John Henry Johnson	.15	.05
❑ 402	Ed Jurak	.15	.05
❑ 403	Rick Miller	.15	.05
❑ 404	Jeff Newman	.15	.05
❑ 405	Reid Nichols	.15	.05
❑ 406	Bob Ojeda	.15	.05
❑ 407	Jerry Remy	.15	.05
❑ 408	Jim Rice	.40	.15
❑ 409	Bob Stanley	.15	.05
❑ 410	Dave Stapleton	.15	.05
❑ 411	John Tudor	.40	.15
❑ 412	Carl Yastrzemski	1.50	.60
❑ 413	Buddy Bell	.40	.15
❑ 414	Larry Biittner	.15	.05
❑ 415	John Butcher	.15	.05
❑ 416	Danny Darwin	.15	.05
❑ 417	Bucky Dent	.40	.15
❑ 418	Dave Hostetler	.15	.05
❑ 419	Charlie Hough	.40	.15
❑ 420	Bobby Johnson	.15	.05
❑ 421	Odell Jones	.15	.05
❑ 422	Jon Matlack	.15	.05
❑ 423	Pete O'Brien RC*	.50	.20
❑ 424	Larry Parrish	.15	.05
❑ 425	Mickey Rivers	.15	.05
❑ 426	Billy Sample	.15	.05
❑ 427	Dave Schmidt	.15	.05
❑ 428	Mike Smithson	.15	.05
❑ 429	Bill Stein	.15	.05
❑ 430	Dave Stewart	.40	.15
❑ 431	Jim Sundberg	.40	.15
❑ 432	Frank Tanana	.40	.15
❑ 433	Dave Tobik	.15	.05
❑ 434	Wayne Tolleson	.15	.05
❑ 435	George Wright	.15	.05
❑ 436	Bill Almon	.15	.05
❑ 437	Keith Atherton	.15	.05
❑ 438	Dave Beard	.15	.05
❑ 439	Tom Burgmeier	.15	.05
❑ 440	Jeff Burroughs	.15	.05
❑ 441	Chris Codiroli	.15	.05
❑ 442	Tim Conroy	.15	.05
❑ 443	Mike Davis	.15	.05
❑ 444	Wayne Gross	.15	.05
❑ 445	Garry Hancock	.15	.05
❑ 446	Mike Heath	.15	.05
❑ 447	Rickey Henderson	2.50	1.00
❑ 448	Donnie Hill	.15	.05
❑ 449	Bob Kearney	.15	.05
❑ 450	Bill Krueger RC	.25	.08
❑ 451	Rick Langford	.15	.05
❑ 452	Carney Lansford	.40	.15
❑ 453	Dave Lopes	.40	.15
❑ 454	Steve McCatty	.15	.05
❑ 455	Dan Meyer	.15	.05
❑ 456	Dwayne Murphy	.15	.05
❑ 457	Mike Norris	.15	.05
❑ 458	Ricky Peters	.15	.05
❑ 459	Tony Phillips RC	1.00	.40
❑ 460	Tom Underwood	.15	.05
❑ 461	Mike Warren	.15	.05
❑ 462	Johnny Bench	1.50	.60
❑ 463	Bruce Berenyi	.15	.05
❑ 464	Dann Bilardello	.15	.05
❑ 465	Cesar Cedeno	.40	.15
❑ 466	Dave Concepcion	.40	.15
❑ 467	Dan Driessen	.15	.05
❑ 468	Nick Esasky	.15	.05
❑ 469	Rich Gale	.15	.05
❑ 470	Ben Hayes	.15	.05
❑ 471	Paul Householder	.15	.05
❑ 472	Tom Hume	.15	.05
❑ 473	Alan Knicely	.15	.05
❑ 474	Eddie Milner	.15	.05
❑ 475	Ron Oester	.15	.05
❑ 476	Kelly Paris	.15	.05
❑ 477	Frank Pastore	.15	.05
❑ 478	Ted Power	.15	.05
❑ 479	Joe Price	.15	.05
❑ 480	Charlie Puleo	.15	.05
❑ 481	Gary Redus RC*	.50	.20
❑ 482	Bill Scherrer	.15	.05
❑ 483	Mario Soto	.40	.15
❑ 484	Alex Trevino	.15	.05
❑ 485	Duane Walker	.15	.05
❑ 486	Larry Bowa	.40	.15
❑ 487	Warren Brusstar	.15	.05
❑ 488	Bill Buckner	.40	.15
❑ 489	Bill Campbell	.15	.05
❑ 490	Ron Cey	.40	.15
❑ 491	Jody Davis	.15	.05
❑ 492	Leon Durham	.15	.05
❑ 493	Mel Hall	.40	.15
❑ 494	Fergie Jenkins	.40	.15
❑ 495	Jay Johnstone	.15	.05
❑ 496	Craig Lefferts RC	.25	.08
❑ 497	Carmelo Martinez	.15	.05
❑ 498	Jerry Morales	.15	.05
❑ 499	Keith Moreland	.15	.05
❑ 500	Dickie Noles	.15	.05
❑ 501	Mike Proly	.15	.05
❑ 502	Chuck Rainey	.15	.05
❑ 503	Dick Ruthven	.15	.05
❑ 504	Ryne Sandberg	6.00	2.50
❑ 505	Lee Smith	.40	.15
❑ 506	Steve Trout	.15	.05
❑ 507	Gary Woods	.15	.05
❑ 508	Juan Beniquez	.15	.05
❑ 509	Bob Boone	.40	.15
❑ 510	Rick Burleson	.15	.05
❑ 511	Rod Carew	.75	.30
❑ 512	Bobby Clark	.15	.05
❑ 513	John Curtis	.15	.05
❑ 514	Doug DeCinces	.15	.05
❑ 515	Brian Downing	.40	.15
❑ 516	Tim Foli	.15	.05
❑ 517	Ken Forsch	.15	.05
❑ 518	Bobby Grich	.40	.15
❑ 519	Andy Hassler	.15	.05
❑ 520	Reggie Jackson	.75	.30
❑ 521	Ron Jackson	.15	.05
❑ 522	Tommy John	.40	.15
❑ 523	Bruce Kison	.15	.05
❑ 524	Steve Lubratich	.15	.05
❑ 525	Fred Lynn	.40	.15
❑ 526	Gary Pettis	.15	.05
❑ 527	Luis Sanchez	.15	.05
❑ 528	Daryl Sconiers	.15	.05
❑ 529	Ellis Valentine	.15	.05
❑ 530	Rob Wilfong	.15	.05
❑ 531	Mike Witt	.15	.05
❑ 532	Geoff Zahn	.15	.05
❑ 533	Bud Anderson	.15	.05
❑ 534	Chris Bando	.15	.05
❑ 535	Alan Bannister	.15	.05
❑ 536	Bert Blyleven	.40	.15
❑ 537	Tom Brennan	.15	.05
❑ 538	Jamie Easterly	.15	.05
❑ 539	Juan Eichelberger	.15	.05
❑ 540	Jim Essian	.15	.05
❑ 541	Mike Fischlin	.15	.05
❑ 542	Julio Franco	.40	.15
❑ 543	Mike Hargrove	.15	.05
❑ 544	Toby Harrah	.40	.15
❑ 545	Ron Hassey	.15	.05
❑ 546	Neal Heaton	.15	.05
❑ 547	Bake McBride	.40	.15
❑ 548	Broderick Perkins	.15	.05
❑ 549	Lary Sorensen	.15	.05
❑ 550	Dan Spillner	.15	.05
❑ 551	Rick Sutcliffe	.40	.15
❑ 552	Pat Tabler	.15	.05
❑ 553	Gorman Thomas	.40	.15
❑ 554	Andre Thornton	.15	.05
❑ 555	George Vukovich	.15	.05
❑ 556	Darrell Brown	.15	.05
❑ 557	Tom Brunansky	.15	.05
❑ 558	Randy Bush	.15	.05
❑ 559	Bobby Castillo	.15	.05
❑ 560	John Castino	.15	.05
❑ 561	Ron Davis	.15	.05
❑ 562	Dave Engle	.15	.05
❑ 563	Lenny Faedo	.15	.05
❑ 564	Pete Filson	.15	.05
❑ 565	Gary Gaetti	.75	.30
❑ 566	Mickey Hatcher	.15	.05
❑ 567	Kent Hrbek	.40	.15
❑ 568	Rusty Kuntz	.15	.05
❑ 569	Tim Laudner	.15	.05
❑ 570	Rick Lysander	.15	.05
❑ 571	Bobby Mitchell	.15	.05
❑ 572	Ken Schrom	.15	.05
❑ 573	Ray Smith	.15	.05

❑ 574 Tim Teufel RC .50 .20
❑ 575 Frank Viola .75 .30
❑ 576 Gary Ward .15 .05
❑ 577 Ron Washington .15 .05
❑ 578 Len Whitehouse .15 .05
❑ 579 Al Williams .15 .05
❑ 580 Bob Bailor .15 .05
❑ 581 Mark Bradley .15 .05
❑ 582 Hubie Brooks .15 .05
❑ 583 Carlos Diaz .15 .05
❑ 584 George Foster .40 .15
❑ 585 Brian Giles .15 .05
❑ 586 Danny Heep .15 .05
❑ 587 Keith Hernandez .40 .15
❑ 588 Ron Hodges .15 .05
❑ 589 Scott Holman .15 .05
❑ 590 Dave Kingman .40 .15
❑ 591 Ed Lynch .15 .05
❑ 592 Jose Oquendo RC .50 .20
❑ 593 Jesse Orosco .15 .05
❑ 594 Junior Ortiz .15 .05
❑ 595 Tom Seaver 1.50 .60
❑ 596 Doug Sisk .15 .05
❑ 597 Rusty Staub .40 .15
❑ 598 John Stearns .15 .05
❑ 599 Darryl Strawberry RC 5.00 2.00
❑ 600 Craig Swan .15 .05
❑ 601 Walt Terrell .15 .05
❑ 602 Mike Torrez .15 .05
❑ 603 Mookie Wilson .40 .15
❑ 604 Jamie Allen .15 .05
❑ 605 Jim Beattie .15 .05
❑ 606 Tony Bernazard .15 .05
❑ 607 Manny Castillo .15 .05
❑ 608 Bill Caudill .15 .05
❑ 609 Bryan Clark .15 .05
❑ 610 Al Cowens .15 .05
❑ 611 Dave Henderson .40 .15
❑ 612 Steve Henderson .15 .05
❑ 613 Orlando Mercado .15 .05
❑ 614 Mike Moore .15 .05
❑ 615 Ricky Nelson UER (Jamie Nelson's stats on back) .15 .05
❑ 616 Spike Owen RC .50 .20
❑ 617 Pat Putnam .15 .05
❑ 618 Ron Roenicke .15 .05
❑ 619 Mike Stanton .15 .05
❑ 620 Bob Stoddard .15 .05
❑ 621 Rick Sweet .15 .05
❑ 622 Roy Thomas .15 .05
❑ 623 Ed VandeBerg .15 .05
❑ 624 Matt Young RC .50 .20
❑ 625 Richie Zisk .15 .05
❑ 626 Fred Lynn 1982 AS Game RB .40 .15
❑ 627 Manny Trillo 1983 AS Game RB .15 .05
❑ 628 Steve Garvey Iron Man .15 .05
❑ 629 Rod Carew AL RunnerUp .40 .15
❑ 630 Wade Boggs AL Champ 1.50 .60
❑ 631 Tim Raines IA .15 .05
❑ 632 Al Oliver Double Trouble .40 .15
❑ 633 Steve Sax AS Second Base .15 .05
❑ 634 Dickie Thon AS Shortstop .15 .05
❑ 635 Ace Firemen Dan Quisenberry and Tippy Martinez .15 .05
❑ 636 J.Morgan/P.Rose/T.Perez 1.50 .60
❑ 637 Backstop Stars Lance Parrish Bob Boone .75 .30
❑ 638 G.Brett/G.Perry 2.00 .75
❑ 639 1983 No Hitters Dave Righetti Mike Warren Bob F .75 .30
❑ 640 J.Bench/C.Yastrzemski 1.50 .60
❑ 641 Gaylord Perry Style .15 .05
❑ 642 Steve Carlton IA .40 .15
❑ 643 Joe Altobelli and Paul Owens World Series Manage .15 .05
❑ 644 Rick Dempsey World Series MVP .15 .05
❑ 645 Mike Boddicker WS Rookie Winner .15 .05
❑ 646 Scott McGregor WS Clincher .15 .05
❑ 647 CL: Orioles/Royals Joe Altobelli MG .15 .05
❑ 648 CL: Phillies/Giants Paul Owens MG .15 .05
❑ 649 CL: White Sox/Red Sox Tony LaRussa MG .75 .30
❑ 650 CL: Tigers/Rangers Sparky Anderson MG .75 .30
❑ 651 CL: Dodgers/A's Tommy Lasorda MG .75 .30
❑ 652 CL: Yankees/Reds Billy Martin MG .75 .30
❑ 653 CL: Blue Jays/Cubs Bobby Cox MG .40 .15
❑ 654 CL: Braves/Angels Joe Torre MG .75 .30
❑ 655 CL: Brewers/Indians Rene Lachemann MG .15 .05
❑ 656 CL: Astros/Twins Bob Lillis MG .15 .05
❑ 657 CL: Pirates/Mets Chuck Tanner MG .15 .05
❑ 658 CL: Expos/Mariners Bill Virdon MG .15 .05
❑ 659 CL: Padres/Specials Dick Williams MG .40 .15
❑ 660 CL: Cardinals/Teams Whitey Herzog MG .75 .30

1984 Fleer Update

❑ COMP.FACT.SET (132) 300.00 175.00
❑ 1 Willie Aikens 1.00 .40
❑ 2 Luis Aponte 1.00 .40
❑ 3 Mark Bailey 1.00 .40
❑ 4 Bob Bailor 1.00 .40
❑ 5 Dusty Baker 1.50 .60
❑ 6 Steve Balboni 1.00 .40
❑ 7 Alan Bannister 1.00 .40
❑ 8 Marty Barrett XRC 2.00 .75
❑ 9 Dave Beard 1.00 .40
❑ 10 Joe Beckwith 1.00 .40
❑ 11 Dave Bergman 1.00 .40
❑ 12 Tony Bernazard 1.00 .40
❑ 13 Bruce Bochte 1.00 .40
❑ 14 Barry Bonnell 1.00 .40
❑ 15 Phil Bradley 2.00 .75
❑ 16 Fred Breining 1.00 .40
❑ 17 Mike C. Brown 1.00 .40
❑ 18 Bill Buckner 1.50 .60
❑ 19 Ray Burris 1.00 .40
❑ 20 John Butcher 1.00 .40
❑ 21 Brett Butler 1.50 .60
❑ 22 Enos Cabell 1.00 .40
❑ 23 Bill Campbell 1.00 .40
❑ 24 Bill Caudill 1.00 .40
❑ 25 Bobby Clark 1.00 .40
❑ 26 Bryan Clark 1.00 .40
❑ 27 Roger Clemens XRC 150.00 90.00
❑ 28 Jaime Cocanower 1.00 .40
❑ 29 Ron Darling XRC 5.00 2.00
❑ 30 Alvin Davis XRC 2.00 .75
❑ 31 Bob Dernier 1.00 .40
❑ 32 Carlos Diaz 1.00 .40
❑ 33 Mike Easler 1.00 .40
❑ 34 Dennis Eckersley 2.50 1.00
❑ 35 Jim Essian 1.00 .40
❑ 36 Darrell Evans 1.50 .60
❑ 37 Mike Fitzgerald 1.00 .40
❑ 38 Tim Foli 1.00 .40
❑ 39 John Franco XRC 5.00 2.00
❑ 40 George Frazier 1.00 .40
❑ 41 Rich Gale 1.00 .40
❑ 42 Barbaro Garbey 1.00 .40
❑ 43 Dwight Gooden XRC 25.00 10.00
❑ 44 Rich Gossage 1.50 .60
❑ 45 Wayne Gross 1.00 .40
❑ 46 Mark Gubicza XRC 2.00 .75
❑ 47 Jackie Gutierrez 1.00 .40
❑ 48 Toby Harrah 1.50 .60
❑ 49 Ron Hassey 1.00 .40
❑ 50 Richie Hebner 1.00 .40
❑ 51 Willie Hernandez 1.00 .40
❑ 52 Ed Hodge 1.00 .40
❑ 53 Ricky Horton 1.00 .40
❑ 54 Art Howe 1.00 .40
❑ 55 Dane Iorg 1.00 .40
❑ 56 Brook Jacoby 2.00 .75
❑ 57 Dion James XRC 1.00 .40
❑ 58 Mike Jeffcoat XRC 1.00 .40
❑ 59 Ruppert Jones 1.00 .40
❑ 60 Bob Kearney 1.00 .40
❑ 61 Jimmy Key XRC 5.00 2.00
❑ 62 Dave Kingman 1.50 .60
❑ 63 Brad Komminsk XRC 1.00 .40
❑ 64 Jerry Koosman 1.50 .60
❑ 65 Wayne Krenchicki 1.00 .40
❑ 66 Rusty Kuntz 1.00 .40
❑ 67 Frank LaCorte 1.00 .40
❑ 68 Dennis Lamp 1.00 .40
❑ 69 Tito Landrum 1.00 .40
❑ 70 Mark Langston XRC 5.00 2.00
❑ 71 Rick Leach 1.00 .40
❑ 72 Craig Lefferts 1.00 .40
❑ 73 Gary Lucas 1.00 .40
❑ 74 Jerry Martin 1.00 .40
❑ 75 Carmelo Martinez 1.00 .40
❑ 76 Mike Mason XRC 1.00 .40
❑ 77 Gary Matthews 1.50 .60
❑ 78 Andy McGaffigan 1.00 .40
❑ 79 Joey McLaughlin 1.00 .40
❑ 80 Joe Morgan 1.50 .60
❑ 81 Darryl Motley 1.00 .40
❑ 82 Graig Nettles 1.50 .60
❑ 83 Phil Niekro 1.50 .60
❑ 84 Ken Oberkfell 1.00 .40
❑ 85 Al Oliver 1.50 .60
❑ 86 Jorge Orta 1.00 .40
❑ 87 Amos Otis 1.50 .60
❑ 88 Bob Owchinko 1.00 .40
❑ 89 Dave Parker 1.50 .60
❑ 90 Jack Perconte 1.00 .40
❑ 91 Tony Perez 2.50 1.00
❑ 92 Gerald Perry 2.00 .75
❑ 93 Kirby Puckett XRC 80.00 40.00
❑ 94 Shane Rawley 1.00 .40
❑ 95 Floyd Rayford 1.00 .40
❑ 96 Ron Reed 1.00 .40
❑ 97 R.J. Reynolds 1.00 .40
❑ 98 Gene Richards 1.00 .40
❑ 99 Jose Rijo XRC 5.00 2.00
❑ 100 Jeff D. Robinson 1.00 .40
❑ 101 Ron Romanick 1.00 .40
❑ 102 Pete Rose 12.00 5.00
❑ 103 Bret Saberhagen XRC 10.00 4.00
❑ 104 Scott Sanderson 1.00 .40
❑ 105 Dick Schofield XRC 2.00 .75
❑ 106 Tom Seaver 4.00 1.50
❑ 107 Jim Slaton 1.00 .40
❑ 108 Mike Smithson 1.00 .40
❑ 109 Lary Sorensen 1.00 .40
❑ 110 Tim Stoddard 1.00 .40
❑ 111 Jeff Stone XRC 1.00 .40
❑ 112 Champ Summers 1.00 .40
❑ 113 Jim Sundberg 1.50 .60
❑ 114 Rick Sutcliffe 1.50 .60
❑ 115 Craig Swan 1.00 .40
❑ 116 Derrel Thomas 1.00 .40
❑ 117 Gorman Thomas 1.50 .60

❑ 118 Alex Trevino	1.00	.40
❑ 119 Manny Trillo	1.00	.40
❑ 120 John Tudor	1.50	.60
❑ 121 Tom Underwood	1.00	.40
❑ 122 Mike Vail	1.00	.40
❑ 123 Tom Waddell	1.00	.40
❑ 124 Gary Ward	1.00	.40
❑ 125 Terry Whitfield	1.00	.40
❑ 126 Curtis Wilkerson	1.00	.40
❑ 127 Frank Williams	1.00	.40
❑ 128 Glenn Wilson	1.50	.60
❑ 129 John Wockenfuss	1.00	.40
❑ 130 Ned Yost	1.00	.40
❑ 131 Mike Young XRC	1.00	.40
❑ 132 Checklist 1-132	1.00	.40

1985 Fleer

❑ COMPLETE SET (660)	60.00	30.00
❑ COMP.FACT.SET (660)	100.00	50.00
❑ 1 Doug Bair	.15	.05
❑ 2 Juan Berenguer	.15	.05
❑ 3 Dave Bergman	.15	.05
❑ 4 Tom Brookens	.15	.05
❑ 5 Marty Castillo	.15	.05
❑ 6 Darrell Evans	.40	.15
❑ 7 Barbaro Garbey	.15	.05
❑ 8 Kirk Gibson	.40	.15
❑ 9 John Grubb	.15	.05
❑ 10 Willie Hernandez	.15	.05
❑ 11 Larry Herndon	.15	.05
❑ 12 Howard Johnson	.40	.15
❑ 13 Ruppert Jones	.15	.05
❑ 14 Rusty Kuntz	.15	.05
❑ 15 Chet Lemon	.40	.15
❑ 16 Aurelio Lopez	.15	.05
❑ 17 Sid Monge	.15	.05
❑ 18 Jack Morris	.40	.15
❑ 19 Lance Parrish	.40	.15
❑ 20 Dan Petry	.15	.05
❑ 21 Dave Rozema	.15	.05
❑ 22 Bill Scherrer	.15	.05
❑ 23 Alan Trammell	.40	.15
❑ 24 Lou Whitaker	.40	.15
❑ 25 Milt Wilcox	.15	.05
❑ 26 Kurt Bevacqua	.15	.05
❑ 27 Greg Booker	.15	.05
❑ 28 Bobby Brown	.15	.05
❑ 29 Luis DeLeon	.15	.05
❑ 30 Dave Dravecky	.15	.05
❑ 31 Tim Flannery	.15	.05
❑ 32 Steve Garvey	.40	.15
❑ 33 Rich Gossage	.40	.15
❑ 34 Tony Gwynn	2.50	1.00
❑ 35 Greg Harris	.15	.05
❑ 36 Andy Hawkins	.15	.05
❑ 37 Terry Kennedy	.15	.05
❑ 38 Craig Lefferts	.15	.05
❑ 39 Tim Lollar	.15	.05
❑ 40 Carmelo Martinez	.15	.05
❑ 41 Kevin McReynolds	.40	.15
❑ 42 Graig Nettles	.40	.15
❑ 43 Luis Salazar	.15	.05
❑ 44 Eric Show	.15	.05
❑ 45 Garry Templeton	.40	.15
❑ 46 Mark Thurmond	.15	.05
❑ 47 Ed Whitson	.15	.05
❑ 48 Alan Wiggins	.15	.05
❑ 49 Rich Bordi	.15	.05

❑ 50 Larry Bowa	.40	.15
❑ 51 Warren Brusstar	.15	.05
❑ 52 Ron Cey	.40	.15
❑ 53 Henry Cotto RC	.25	.08
❑ 54 Jody Davis	.15	.05
❑ 55 Bob Dernier	.15	.05
❑ 56 Leon Durham	.15	.05
❑ 57 Dennis Eckersley	.75	.30
❑ 58 George Frazier	.15	.05
❑ 59 Richie Hebner	.15	.05
❑ 60 Dave Lopes	.40	.15
❑ 61 Gary Matthews	.40	.15
❑ 62 Keith Moreland	.15	.05
❑ 63 Rick Reuschel	.40	.15
❑ 64 Dick Ruthven	.15	.05
❑ 65 Ryne Sandberg	2.50	1.00
❑ 66 Scott Sanderson	.15	.05
❑ 67 Lee Smith	.40	.15
❑ 68 Tim Stoddard	.15	.05
❑ 69 Rick Sutcliffe	.40	.15
❑ 70 Steve Trout	.15	.05
❑ 71 Gary Woods	.15	.05
❑ 72 Wally Backman	.15	.05
❑ 73 Bruce Berenyi	.15	.05
❑ 74 Hubie Brooks UER (Kelvin Chapman's stats on card	.15	.05
❑ 75 Kelvin Chapman	.15	.05
❑ 76 Ron Darling	.40	.15
❑ 77 Sid Fernandez	.40	.15
❑ 78 Mike Fitzgerald	.15	.05
❑ 79 George Foster	.40	.15
❑ 80 Brent Gaff	.15	.05
❑ 81 Ron Gardenhire	.15	.05
❑ 82 Dwight Gooden RC	3.00	1.25
❑ 83 Tom Gorman	.15	.05
❑ 84 Danny Heep	.15	.05
❑ 85 Keith Hernandez	.40	.15
❑ 86 Ray Knight	.40	.15
❑ 87 Ed Lynch	.15	.05
❑ 88 Jose Oquendo	.15	.05
❑ 89 Jesse Orosco	.15	.05
❑ 90 Rafael Santana	.15	.05
❑ 91 Doug Sisk	.15	.05
❑ 92 Rusty Staub	.40	.15
❑ 93 Darryl Strawberry	1.25	.50
❑ 94 Walt Terrell	.15	.05
❑ 95 Mookie Wilson	.40	.15
❑ 96 Jim Acker	.15	.05
❑ 97 Willie Aikens	.15	.05
❑ 98 Doyle Alexander	.15	.05
❑ 99 Jesse Barfield	.40	.15
❑ 100 George Bell	.40	.15
❑ 101 Jim Clancy	.15	.05
❑ 102 Dave Collins	.15	.05
❑ 103 Tony Fernandez	.40	.15
❑ 104 Damaso Garcia	.15	.05
❑ 105 Jim Gott	.15	.05
❑ 106 Alfredo Griffin	.15	.05
❑ 107 Garth Iorg	.15	.05
❑ 108 Roy Lee Jackson	.15	.05
❑ 109 Cliff Johnson	.15	.05
❑ 110 Jimmy Key RC	1.00	.40
❑ 111 Dennis Lamp	.15	.05
❑ 112 Rick Leach	.15	.05
❑ 113 Luis Leal	.15	.05
❑ 114 Buck Martinez	.15	.05
❑ 115 Lloyd Moseby	.15	.05
❑ 116 Rance Mulliniks	.15	.05
❑ 117 Dave Stieb	.40	.15
❑ 118 Willie Upshaw	.15	.05
❑ 119 Ernie Whitt	.15	.05
❑ 120 Mike Armstrong	.15	.05
❑ 121 Don Baylor	.40	.15
❑ 122 Marty Bystrom	.15	.05
❑ 123 Rick Cerone	.15	.05
❑ 124 Joe Cowley	.15	.05
❑ 125 Brian Dayett	.15	.05
❑ 126 Tim Foli	.15	.05
❑ 127 Ray Fontenot	.15	.05
❑ 128 Ken Griffey	.40	.15
❑ 129 Ron Guidry	.40	.15
❑ 130 Toby Harrah	.40	.15
❑ 131 Jay Howell	.15	.05
❑ 132 Steve Kemp	.15	.05
❑ 133 Don Mattingly	5.00	2.00

❑ 134 Bobby Meacham	.15	.05
❑ 135 John Montefusco	.15	.05
❑ 136 Omar Moreno	.15	.05
❑ 137 Dale Murray	.15	.05
❑ 138 Phil Niekro	.40	.15
❑ 139 Mike Pagliarulo	.15	.05
❑ 140 Willie Randolph	.40	.15
❑ 141 Dennis Rasmussen	.15	.05
❑ 142 Dave Righetti	.40	.15
❑ 143 Jose Rijo RC	1.00	.40
❑ 144 Andre Robertson	.15	.05
❑ 145 Bob Shirley	.15	.05
❑ 146 Dave Winfield	.40	.15
❑ 147 Butch Wynegar	.15	.05
❑ 148 Gary Allenson	.15	.05
❑ 149 Tony Armas	.40	.15
❑ 150 Marty Barrett	.15	.05
❑ 151 Wade Boggs	1.25	.50
❑ 152 Dennis Boyd	.15	.05
❑ 153 Bill Buckner	.40	.15
❑ 154 Mark Clear	.15	.05
❑ 155 Roger Clemens RC	25.00	10.00
❑ 156 Steve Crawford	.15	.05
❑ 157 Mike Easler	.15	.05
❑ 158 Dwight Evans	.75	.30
❑ 159 Rich Gedman	.15	.05
❑ 160 Jackie Gutierrez w/Boggs	.40	.15
❑ 161 Bruce Hurst	.15	.05
❑ 162 John Henry Johnson	.15	.05
❑ 163 Rick Miller	.15	.05
❑ 164 Reid Nichols	.15	.05
❑ 165 Al Nipper	.15	.05
❑ 166 Bob Ojeda	.15	.05
❑ 167 Jerry Remy	.15	.05
❑ 168 Jim Rice	.40	.15
❑ 169 Bob Stanley	.15	.05
❑ 170 Mike Boddicker	.15	.05
❑ 171 Al Bumbry	.15	.05
❑ 172 Todd Cruz	.15	.05
❑ 173 Rich Dauer	.15	.05
❑ 174 Storm Davis	.15	.05
❑ 175 Rick Dempsey	.15	.05
❑ 176 Jim Dwyer	.15	.05
❑ 177 Mike Flanagan	.15	.05
❑ 178 Dan Ford	.15	.05
❑ 179 Wayne Gross	.15	.05
❑ 180 John Lowenstein	.15	.05
❑ 181 Dennis Martinez	.40	.15
❑ 182 Tippy Martinez	.15	.05
❑ 183 Scott McGregor	.15	.05
❑ 184 Eddie Murray	1.25	.50
❑ 185 Joe Nolan	.15	.05
❑ 186 Floyd Rayford	.15	.05
❑ 187 Cal Ripken	5.00	2.00
❑ 188 Gary Roenicke	.15	.05
❑ 189 Lenn Sakata	.15	.05
❑ 190 John Shelby	.15	.05
❑ 191 Ken Singleton	.40	.15
❑ 192 Sammy Stewart	.15	.05
❑ 193 Bill Swaggerty	.15	.05
❑ 194 Tom Underwood	.15	.05
❑ 195 Mike Young	.15	.05
❑ 196 Steve Balboni	.15	.05
❑ 197 Joe Beckwith	.15	.05
❑ 198 Bud Black	.15	.05
❑ 199 George Brett	3.00	1.25
❑ 200 Onix Concepcion	.15	.05
❑ 201 Mark Gubicza RC*	.50	.20
❑ 202 Larry Gura	.15	.05
❑ 203 Mark Huismann	.15	.05
❑ 204 Dane Iorg	.15	.05
❑ 205 Danny Jackson	.15	.05
❑ 206 Charlie Leibrandt	.15	.05
❑ 207 Hal McRae	.40	.15
❑ 208 Darryl Motley	.15	.05
❑ 209 Jorge Orta	.15	.05
❑ 210 Greg Pryor	.15	.05
❑ 211 Dan Quisenberry	.15	.05
❑ 212 Bret Saberhagen RC	1.50	.60
❑ 213 Pat Sheridan	.15	.05
❑ 214 Don Slaught	.15	.05
❑ 215 U.L. Washington	.15	.05
❑ 216 John Wathan	.15	.05
❑ 217 Frank White	.40	.15
❑ 218 Willie Wilson	.40	.15
❑ 219 Neil Allen	.15	.05

❑ 220 Joaquin Andujar .40 .15
❑ 221 Steve Braun .15 .05
❑ 222 Danny Cox .15 .05
❑ 223 Bob Forsch .15 .05
❑ 224 David Green .15 .05
❑ 225 George Hendrick .40 .15
❑ 226 Tom Herr .15 .05
❑ 227 Ricky Horton .15 .05
❑ 228 Art Howe .15 .05
❑ 229 Mike Jorgensen .15 .05
❑ 230 Kurt Kepshire .15 .05
❑ 231 Jeff Lahti .15 .05
❑ 232 Tito Landrum .15 .05
❑ 233 Dave LaPoint .15 .05
❑ 234 Willie McGee .40 .15
❑ 235 Tom Nieto .15 .05
❑ 236 Terry Pendleton RC 1.00 .40
❑ 237 Darrell Porter .15 .05
❑ 238 Dave Rucker .15 .05
❑ 239 Lonnie Smith .15 .05
❑ 240 Ozzie Smith 2.00 .75
❑ 241 Bruce Sutter .40 .15
❑ 242 Andy Van Slyke UER .75 .30
❑ 243 Dave Von Ohlen .15 .05
❑ 244 Larry Andersen .15 .05
❑ 245 Bill Campbell .15 .05
❑ 246 Steve Carlton .40 .15
❑ 247 Tim Corcoran .15 .05
❑ 248 Ivan DeJesus .15 .05
❑ 249 John Denny .15 .05
❑ 250 Bo Diaz .15 .05
❑ 251 Greg Gross .15 .05
❑ 252 Kevin Gross .15 .05
❑ 253 Von Hayes .15 .05
❑ 254 Al Holland .15 .05
❑ 255 Charles Hudson .15 .05
❑ 256 Jerry Koosman .40 .15
❑ 257 Joe Lefebvre .15 .05
❑ 258 Sixto Lezcano .15 .05
❑ 259 Garry Maddox .15 .05
❑ 260 Len Matuszek .15 .05
❑ 261 Tug McGraw .40 .15
❑ 262 Al Oliver .40 .15
❑ 263 Shane Rawley .15 .05
❑ 264 Juan Samuel .15 .05
❑ 265 Mike Schmidt 3.00 1.25
❑ 266 Jeff Stone RC .15 .05
❑ 267 Ozzie Virgil .15 .05
❑ 268 Glenn Wilson .15 .05
❑ 269 John Wockenfuss .15 .05
❑ 270 Darrell Brown .15 .05
❑ 271 Tom Brunansky .15 .05
❑ 272 Randy Bush .15 .05
❑ 273 John Butcher .15 .05
❑ 274 Bobby Castillo .15 .05
❑ 275 Ron Davis .15 .05
❑ 276 Dave Engle .15 .05
❑ 277 Pete Filson .15 .05
❑ 278 Gary Gaetti .40 .15
❑ 279 Mickey Hatcher .15 .05
❑ 280 Ed Hodge .15 .05
❑ 281 Kent Hrbek .40 .15
❑ 282 Houston Jimenez .15 .05
❑ 283 Tim Laudner .15 .05
❑ 284 Rick Lysander .15 .05
❑ 285 Dave Meier .15 .05
❑ 286 Kirby Puckett RC 10.00 4.00
❑ 287 Pat Putnam .15 .05
❑ 288 Ken Schrom .15 .05
❑ 289 Mike Smithson .15 .05
❑ 290 Tim Teufel .15 .05
❑ 291 Frank Viola .40 .15
❑ 292 Ron Washington .15 .05
❑ 293 Don Aase .15 .05
❑ 294 Juan Beniquez .15 .05
❑ 295 Bob Boone .40 .15
❑ 296 Mike C. Brown .15 .05
❑ 297 Rod Carew .75 .30
❑ 298 Doug Corbett .15 .05
❑ 299 Doug DeCinces .15 .05
❑ 300 Brian Downing .40 .15
❑ 301 Ken Forsch .15 .05
❑ 302 Bobby Grich .40 .15
❑ 303 Reggie Jackson .75 .30
❑ 304 Tommy John .40 .15
❑ 305 Curt Kaufman .15 .05
❑ 306 Bruce Kison .15 .05
❑ 307 Fred Lynn .40 .15
❑ 308 Gary Pettis .15 .05
❑ 309 Ron Romanick .15 .05
❑ 310 Luis Sanchez .15 .05
❑ 311 Dick Schofield .15 .05
❑ 312 Daryl Sconiers .15 .05
❑ 313 Jim Slaton .15 .05
❑ 314 Derrel Thomas .15 .05
❑ 315 Rob Wilfong .15 .05
❑ 316 Mike Witt .15 .05
❑ 317 Geoff Zahn .15 .05
❑ 318 Len Barker .15 .05
❑ 319 Steve Bedrosian .15 .05
❑ 320 Bruce Benedict .15 .05
❑ 321 Rick Camp .15 .05
❑ 322 Chris Chambliss .40 .15
❑ 323 Jeff Dedmon .15 .05
❑ 324 Terry Forster .40 .15
❑ 325 Gene Garber .15 .05
❑ 326 Albert Hall .15 .05
❑ 327 Terry Harper .15 .05
❑ 328 Bob Horner .40 .15
❑ 329 Glenn Hubbard .15 .05
❑ 330 Randy Johnson .15 .05
❑ 331 Brad Komminsk .15 .05
❑ 332 Rick Mahler .15 .05
❑ 333 Craig McMurtry .15 .05
❑ 334 Donnie Moore .15 .05
❑ 335 Dale Murphy .75 .30
❑ 336 Ken Oberkfell .15 .05
❑ 337 Pascual Perez .15 .05
❑ 338 Gerald Perry .15 .05
❑ 339 Rafael Ramirez .15 .05
❑ 340 Jerry Royster .15 .05
❑ 341 Alex Trevino .15 .05
❑ 342 Claudell Washington .15 .05
❑ 343 Alan Ashby .15 .05
❑ 344 Mark Bailey .15 .05
❑ 345 Kevin Bass .15 .05
❑ 346 Enos Cabell .15 .05
❑ 347 Jose Cruz .40 .15
❑ 348 Bill Dawley .15 .05
❑ 349 Frank DiPino .15 .05
❑ 350 Bill Doran .15 .05
❑ 351 Phil Garner .40 .15
❑ 352 Bob Knepper .15 .05
❑ 353 Mike LaCoss .15 .05
❑ 354 Jerry Mumphrey .15 .05
❑ 355 Joe Niekro .15 .05
❑ 356 Terry Puhl .15 .05
❑ 357 Craig Reynolds .15 .05
❑ 358 Vern Ruhle .15 .05
❑ 359 Nolan Ryan 6.00 2.50
❑ 360 Joe Sambito .15 .05
❑ 361 Mike Scott .40 .15
❑ 362 Dave Smith .15 .05
❑ 363 Julio Solano .15 .05
❑ 364 Dickie Thon .15 .05
❑ 365 Denny Walling .15 .05
❑ 366 Dave Anderson .15 .05
❑ 367 Bob Bailor .15 .05
❑ 368 Greg Brock .15 .05
❑ 369 Carlos Diaz .15 .05
❑ 370 Pedro Guerrero .40 .15
❑ 371 Orel Hershiser RC 3.00 1.25
❑ 372 Rick Honeycutt .15 .05
❑ 373 Burt Hooton .15 .05
❑ 374 Ken Howell .15 .05
❑ 375 Ken Landreaux .15 .05
❑ 376 Candy Maldonado .15 .05
❑ 377 Mike Marshall .15 .05
❑ 378 Tom Niedenfuer .15 .05
❑ 379 Alejandro Pena .15 .05
❑ 380 Jerry Reuss UER
(%%Home:~ omitted) .15 .05
❑ 381 R.J. Reynolds .15 .05
❑ 382 German Rivera .15 .05
❑ 383 Bill Russell .40 .15
❑ 384 Steve Sax .15 .05
❑ 385 Mike Scioscia .40 .15
❑ 386 Franklin Stubbs .15 .05
❑ 387 Fernando Valenzuela .40 .15
❑ 388 Bob Welch .40 .15
❑ 389 Terry Whitfield .15 .05
❑ 390 Steve Yeager .40 .15
❑ 391 Pat Zachry .15 .05
❑ 392 Fred Breining .15 .05
❑ 393 Gary Carter .40 .15
❑ 394 Andre Dawson .40 .15
❑ 395 Miguel Dilone .15 .05
❑ 396 Dan Driessen .15 .05
❑ 397 Doug Flynn .15 .05
❑ 398 Terry Francona .40 .15
❑ 399 Bill Gullickson .15 .05
❑ 400 Bob James .15 .05
❑ 401 Charlie Lea .15 .05
❑ 402 Bryan Little .15 .05
❑ 403 Gary Lucas .15 .05
❑ 404 David Palmer .15 .05
❑ 405 Tim Raines .40 .15
❑ 406 Mike Ramsey .15 .05
❑ 407 Jeff Reardon .40 .15
❑ 408 Steve Rogers .40 .15
❑ 409 Dan Schatzeder .15 .05
❑ 410 Bryn Smith .15 .05
❑ 411 Mike Stenhouse .15 .05
❑ 412 Tim Wallach .15 .05
❑ 413 Jim Wohlford .15 .05
❑ 414 Bill Almon .15 .05
❑ 415 Keith Atherton .15 .05
❑ 416 Bruce Bochte .15 .05
❑ 417 Tom Burgmeier .15 .05
❑ 418 Ray Burris .15 .05
❑ 419 Bill Caudill .15 .05
❑ 420 Chris Codiroli .15 .05
❑ 421 Tim Conroy .15 .05
❑ 422 Mike Davis .15 .05
❑ 423 Jim Essian .15 .05
❑ 424 Mike Heath .15 .05
❑ 425 Rickey Henderson 1.50 .60
❑ 426 Donnie Hill .15 .05
❑ 427 Dave Kingman .40 .15
❑ 428 Bill Krueger .15 .05
❑ 429 Carney Lansford .40 .15
❑ 430 Steve McCatty .15 .05
❑ 431 Joe Morgan .40 .15
❑ 432 Dwayne Murphy .15 .05
❑ 433 Tony Phillips .15 .05
❑ 434 Lary Sorensen .15 .05
❑ 435 Mike Warren .15 .05
❑ 436 Curt Young .15 .05
❑ 437 Luis Aponte .15 .05
❑ 438 Chris Bando .15 .05
❑ 439 Tony Bernazard .15 .05
❑ 440 Bert Blyleven .40 .15
❑ 441 Brett Butler .40 .15
❑ 442 Ernie Camacho .15 .05
❑ 443 Joe Carter 1.25 .50
❑ 444 Carmelo Castillo .15 .05
❑ 445 Jamie Easterly .15 .05
❑ 446 Steve Farr RC .50 .20
❑ 447 Mike Fischlin .15 .05
❑ 448 Julio Franco .40 .15
❑ 449 Mel Hall .15 .05
❑ 450 Mike Hargrove .15 .05
❑ 451 Neal Heaton .15 .05
❑ 452 Brook Jacoby .15 .05
❑ 453 Mike Jeffcoat .15 .05
❑ 454 Don Schulze .15 .05
❑ 455 Roy Smith .15 .05
❑ 456 Pat Tabler .15 .05
❑ 457 Andre Thornton .15 .05
❑ 458 George Vukovich .15 .05
❑ 459 Tom Waddell .15 .05
❑ 460 Jerry Willard .15 .05
❑ 461 Dale Berra .15 .05
❑ 462 John Candelaria .15 .05
❑ 463 Jose DeLeon .15 .05
❑ 464 Doug Frobel .15 .05
❑ 465 Cecilio Guante .15 .05
❑ 466 Brian Harper .15 .05
❑ 467 Lee Lacy .15 .05
❑ 468 Bill Madlock .40 .15
❑ 469 Lee Mazzilli .40 .15
❑ 470 Larry McWilliams .15 .05
❑ 471 Jim Morrison .15 .05
❑ 472 Tony Pena .15 .05
❑ 473 Johnny Ray .15 .05
❑ 474 Rick Rhoden .15 .05
❑ 475 Don Robinson .15 .05
❑ 476 Rod Scurry .15 .05

❑ 477 Kent Tekulve .15 .05
❑ 478 Jason Thompson .15 .05
❑ 479 John Tudor .40 .15
❑ 480 Lee Tunnell .15 .05
❑ 481 Marvell Wynne .15 .05
❑ 482 Salome Barojas .15 .05
❑ 483 Dave Beard .15 .05
❑ 484 Jim Beattie .15 .05
❑ 485 Barry Bonnell .15 .05
❑ 486 Phil Bradley .50 .20
❑ 487 Al Cowens .15 .05
❑ 488 Alvin Davis RC* .50 .20
❑ 489 Dave Henderson .15 .05
❑ 490 Steve Henderson .15 .05
❑ 491 Bob Kearney .15 .05
❑ 492 Mark Langston RC 1.00 .40
❑ 493 Larry Milbourne .15 .05
❑ 494 Paul Mirabella .15 .05
❑ 495 Mike Moore .15 .05
❑ 496 Edwin Nunez .15 .05
❑ 497 Spike Owen .15 .05
❑ 498 Jack Perconte .15 .05
❑ 499 Ken Phelps .15 .05
❑ 500 Jim Presley .50 .20
❑ 501 Mike Stanton .15 .05
❑ 502 Bob Stoddard .15 .05
❑ 503 Gorman Thomas .40 .15
❑ 504 Ed VandeBerg .15 .05
❑ 505 Matt Young .15 .05
❑ 506 Juan Agosto .15 .05
❑ 507 Harold Baines .40 .15
❑ 508 Floyd Bannister .15 .05
❑ 509 Britt Burns .15 .05
❑ 510 Julio Cruz .15 .05
❑ 511 Richard Dotson .15 .05
❑ 512 Jerry Dybzinski .15 .05
❑ 513 Carlton Fisk .75 .30
❑ 514 Scott Fletcher .15 .05
❑ 515 Jerry Hairston .15 .05
❑ 516 Marc Hill .15 .05
❑ 517 LaMarr Hoyt .15 .05
❑ 518 Ron Kittle .15 .05
❑ 519 Rudy Law .15 .05
❑ 520 Vance Law .15 .05
❑ 521 Greg Luzinski .40 .15
❑ 522 Gene Nelson .15 .05
❑ 523 Tom Paciorek .15 .05
❑ 524 Ron Reed .15 .05
❑ 525 Bert Roberge .15 .05
❑ 526 Tom Seaver .75 .30
❑ 527 Roy Smalley .15 .05
❑ 528 Dan Spillner .15 .05
❑ 529 Mike Squires .15 .05
❑ 530 Greg Walker .15 .05
❑ 531 Cesar Cedeno .40 .15
❑ 532 Dave Concepcion .40 .15
❑ 533 Eric Davis RC 3.00 1.25
❑ 534 Nick Esasky .15 .05
❑ 535 Tom Foley .15 .05
❑ 536 John Franco UER RC 1.00 .40
❑ 537 Brad Gulden .15 .05
❑ 538 Tom Hume .15 .05
❑ 539 Wayne Krenchicki .15 .05
❑ 540 Andy McGaffigan .15 .05
❑ 541 Eddie Milner .15 .05
❑ 542 Ron Oester .15 .05
❑ 543 Bob Owchinko .15 .05
❑ 544 Dave Parker .40 .15
❑ 545 Frank Pastore .15 .05
❑ 546 Tony Perez .75 .30
❑ 547 Ted Power .15 .05
❑ 548 Joe Price .15 .05
❑ 549 Gary Redus .15 .05
❑ 550 Pete Rose 4.00 1.50
❑ 551 Jeff Russell .15 .05
❑ 552 Mario Soto .40 .15
❑ 553 Jay Tibbs .15 .05
❑ 554 Duane Walker .15 .05
❑ 555 Alan Bannister .15 .05
❑ 556 Buddy Bell .40 .15
❑ 557 Danny Darwin .15 .05
❑ 558 Charlie Hough .40 .15
❑ 559 Bobby Jones .15 .05
❑ 560 Odell Jones .15 .05
❑ 561 Jeff Kunkel .15 .05
❑ 562 Mike Mason RC .25 .08
❑ 563 Pete O'Brien .15 .05
❑ 564 Larry Parrish .15 .05
❑ 565 Mickey Rivers .15 .05
❑ 566 Billy Sample .15 .05
❑ 567 Dave Schmidt .15 .05
❑ 568 Donnie Scott .15 .05
❑ 569 Dave Stewart .40 .15
❑ 570 Frank Tanana .40 .15
❑ 571 Wayne Tolleson .15 .05
❑ 572 Gary Ward .15 .05
❑ 573 Curtis Wilkerson .15 .05
❑ 574 George Wright .15 .05
❑ 575 Ned Yost .15 .05
❑ 576 Mark Brouhard .15 .05
❑ 577 Mike Caldwell .15 .05
❑ 578 Bobby Clark .15 .05
❑ 579 Jaime Cocanower .15 .05
❑ 580 Cecil Cooper .40 .15
❑ 581 Rollie Fingers .40 .15
❑ 582 Jim Gantner .15 .05
❑ 583 Moose Haas .15 .05
❑ 584 Dion James .15 .05
❑ 585 Pete Ladd .15 .05
❑ 586 Rick Manning .15 .05
❑ 587 Bob McClure .15 .05
❑ 588 Paul Molitor .40 .15
❑ 589 Charlie Moore .15 .05
❑ 590 Ben Oglivie .40 .15
❑ 591 Chuck Porter .15 .05
❑ 592 Randy Ready RC* .25 .08
❑ 593 Ed Romero .15 .05
❑ 594 Bill Schroeder .15 .05
❑ 595 Ray Searage .15 .05
❑ 596 Ted Simmons .40 .15
❑ 597 Jim Sundberg .40 .15
❑ 598 Don Sutton .40 .15
❑ 599 Tom Tellmann .15 .05
❑ 600 Rick Waits .15 .05
❑ 601 Robin Yount 2.00 .75
❑ 602 Dusty Baker .40 .15
❑ 603 Bob Brenly .15 .05
❑ 604 Jack Clark .40 .15
❑ 605 Chili Davis .40 .15
❑ 606 Mark Davis .15 .05
❑ 607 Dan Gladden RC .50 .20
❑ 608 Atlee Hammaker .15 .05
❑ 609 Mike Krukow .15 .05
❑ 610 Duane Kuiper .15 .05
❑ 611 Bob Lacey .15 .05
❑ 612 Bill Laskey .15 .05
❑ 613 Gary Lavelle .15 .05
❑ 614 Johnnie LeMaster .15 .05
❑ 615 Jeff Leonard .15 .05
❑ 616 Randy Lerch .15 .05
❑ 617 Greg Minton .15 .05
❑ 618 Steve Nicosia .15 .05
❑ 619 Gene Richards .15 .05
❑ 620 Jeff D. Robinson .15 .05
❑ 621 Scot Thompson .15 .05
❑ 622 Manny Trillo .15 .05
❑ 623 Brad Wellman .15 .05
❑ 624 Frank Williams .15 .05
❑ 625 Joel Youngblood .15 .05
❑ 626 Cal Ripken IA 3.00 1.25
❑ 627 Mike Schmidt IA 1.25 .50
❑ 628 Giving The Signs
Sparky Anderson .40 .15
❑ 629 D.Winfield/R.Henderson .40 .15
❑ 630 M.Schmidt/R.Sandberg 2.00 .75
❑ 631 Straw/Carter/Garvey/Oz 1.25 .50
❑ 632 A-S Winning Battery
Gary Carter
Charlie Lea .15 .05
❑ 633 NL Pennant Clinchers
Steve Garvey
Rich Gossage .40 .15
❑ 634 Dwight Gooden/J.Samuel 1.25 .50
❑ 635 Toronto's Big Guns
Willie Upshaw .15 .05
❑ 636 Toronto's Big Guns
Lloyd Moseby .15 .05
❑ 637 HOLLAND: Al Holland .15 .05
❑ 638 TUNNELL: Lee Tunnell .15 .05
❑ 639 Reggie Jackson IA .40 .15
❑ 640 Pete Rose IA 1.25 .50
❑ 641 Cal Ripken Jr./Sr. 3.00 1.25
❑ 642 Cubs: Division Champs .40 .15
❑ 643 Two Perfect Games
and One No-Hitter:
Mike Witt .40 .15
❑ 644 W.Lozado RC/V.Mata RC .15 .05
❑ 645 K.Gruber RC/R.O'Neal RC .50 .20
❑ 646 J.Roman RC/J.Skinner .15 .05
❑ 647 S.Kiefer RC/D.Tartabull RC 1.00 .40
❑ 648 R.Deer RC/A.Sanchez RC .50 .20
❑ 649 B.Hatcher RC/S.Dunston RC 1.00 .40
❑ 650 R.Robinson RC/M.Bielecki RC .15 .05
❑ 651 Z.Smith RC/P.Zuvella RC .50 .20
❑ 652 J.Hesketh RC/G.Davis RC .50 .20
❑ 653 J.Russell RC/S.Jeltz RC .15 .05
❑ 654 CL: Tigers/Padres
and Cubs/Mets .15 .05
❑ 655 CL: Blue Jays/Yankees
and Red Sox/Orioles .15 .05
❑ 656 CL: Royals/Cardinals
and Phillies/Twins .15 .05
❑ 657 CL: Angels/Braves
and Astros/Dodgers .15 .05
❑ 658 CL: Expos/A's
and Indians/Pirates .15 .05
❑ 659 CL: Mariners/White Sox
and Reds/Rangers .15 .05
❑ 660 CL: Brewers/Giants
and Special Cards .15 .05

1986 Fleer

❑ COMPLETE SET (660) 40.00 15.00
❑ COMP.FACT.SET (660) 40.00 15.00
❑ 1 Steve Balboni .15 .05
❑ 2 Joe Beckwith .15 .05
❑ 3 Buddy Biancalana .15 .05
❑ 4 Bud Black .15 .05
❑ 5 George Brett 2.00 .75
❑ 6 Onix Concepcion .15 .05
❑ 7 Steve Farr .15 .05
❑ 8 Mark Gubicza .15 .05
❑ 9 Dane Iorg .15 .05
❑ 10 Danny Jackson .15 .05
❑ 11 Lynn Jones .15 .05
❑ 12 Mike Jones .15 .05
❑ 13 Charlie Leibrandt .15 .05
❑ 14 Hal McRae .25 .08
❑ 15 Omar Moreno .15 .05
❑ 16 Darryl Motley .15 .05
❑ 17 Jorge Orta .15 .05
❑ 18 Dan Quisenberry .15 .05
❑ 19 Bret Saberhagen .25 .08
❑ 20 Pat Sheridan .15 .05
❑ 21 Lonnie Smith .15 .05
❑ 22 Jim Sundberg .25 .08
❑ 23 John Wathan .15 .05
❑ 24 Frank White .25 .08
❑ 25 Willie Wilson .25 .08
❑ 26 Joaquin Andujar .25 .08
❑ 27 Steve Braun .15 .05
❑ 28 Bill Campbell .15 .05
❑ 29 Cesar Cedeno .25 .08
❑ 30 Jack Clark .25 .08
❑ 31 Vince Coleman RC 1.00 .40
❑ 32 Danny Cox .15 .05
❑ 33 Ken Dayley .15 .05
❑ 34 Ivan DeJesus .15 .05
❑ 35 Bob Forsch .15 .05
❑ 36 Brian Harper .15 .05

❑ 37 Tom Herr .15 .05
❑ 38 Ricky Horton .15 .05
❑ 39 Kurt Kepshire .15 .05
❑ 40 Jeff Lahti .15 .05
❑ 41 Tito Landrum .15 .05
❑ 42 Willie McGee .25 .08
❑ 43 Tom Nieto .15 .05
❑ 44 Terry Pendleton .25 .08
❑ 45 Darrell Porter .15 .05
❑ 46 Ozzie Smith 1.25 .50
❑ 47 John Tudor .25 .08
❑ 48 Andy Van Slyke .50 .20
❑ 49 Todd Worrell RC .50 .20
❑ 50 Jim Acker .15 .05
❑ 51 Doyle Alexander .15 .05
❑ 52 Jesse Barfield .25 .08
❑ 53 George Bell .25 .08
❑ 54 Jeff Burroughs .15 .05
❑ 55 Bill Caudill .15 .05
❑ 56 Jim Clancy .15 .05
❑ 57 Tony Fernandez .15 .05
❑ 58 Tom Filer .15 .05
❑ 59 Damaso Garcia .15 .05
❑ 60 Tom Henke .25 .08
❑ 61 Garth Iorg .15 .05
❑ 62 Cliff Johnson .15 .05
❑ 63 Jimmy Key .25 .08
❑ 64 Dennis Lamp .15 .05
❑ 65 Gary Lavelle .15 .05
❑ 66 Buck Martinez .15 .05
❑ 67 Lloyd Moseby .15 .05
❑ 68 Rance Mulliniks .15 .05
❑ 69 Al Oliver .25 .08
❑ 70 Dave Stieb .25 .08
❑ 71 Louis Thornton .15 .05
❑ 72 Willie Upshaw .15 .05
❑ 73 Ernie Whitt .15 .05
❑ 74 Rick Aguilera RC .50 .20
❑ 75 Wally Backman .15 .05
❑ 76 Gary Carter .25 .08
❑ 77 Ron Darling .25 .08
❑ 78 Len Dykstra RC 1.50 .60
❑ 79 Sid Fernandez .15 .05
❑ 80 George Foster .25 .08
❑ 81 Dwight Gooden .75 .30
❑ 82 Tom Gorman .15 .05
❑ 83 Danny Heep .15 .05
❑ 84 Keith Hernandez .25 .08
❑ 85 Howard Johnson .25 .08
❑ 86 Ray Knight .25 .08
❑ 87 Terry Leach .15 .05
❑ 88 Ed Lynch .15 .05
❑ 89 Roger McDowell RC* .50 .20
❑ 90 Jesse Orosco .15 .05
❑ 91 Tom Paciorek .15 .05
❑ 92 Ronn Reynolds .15 .05
❑ 93 Rafael Santana .15 .05
❑ 94 Doug Sisk .15 .05
❑ 95 Rusty Staub .25 .08
❑ 96 Darryl Strawberry .50 .20
❑ 97 Mookie Wilson .25 .08
❑ 98 Neil Allen .15 .05
❑ 99 Don Baylor .25 .08
❑ 100 Dale Berra .15 .05
❑ 101 Rich Bordi .15 .05
❑ 102 Marty Bystrom .15 .05
❑ 103 Joe Cowley .15 .05
❑ 104 Brian Fisher RC .15 .05
❑ 105 Ken Griffey .25 .08
❑ 106 Ron Guidry .25 .08
❑ 107 Ron Hassey .15 .05
❑ 108 Rickey Henderson .75 .30
❑ 109 Don Mattingly 2.50 1.00
❑ 110 Bobby Meacham .15 .05
❑ 111 John Montefusco .15 .05
❑ 112 Phil Niekro .25 .08
❑ 113 Mike Pagliarulo .15 .05
❑ 114 Dan Pasqua .15 .05
❑ 115 Willie Randolph .25 .08
❑ 116 Dave Righetti .25 .08
❑ 117 Andre Robertson .15 .05
❑ 118 Billy Sample .15 .05
❑ 119 Bob Shirley .15 .05
❑ 120 Ed Whitson .15 .05
❑ 121 Dave Winfield .25 .08
❑ 122 Butch Wynegar .15 .05
❑ 123 Dave Anderson .15 .05
❑ 124 Bob Bailor .15 .05
❑ 125 Greg Brock .15 .05
❑ 126 Enos Cabell .15 .05
❑ 127 Bobby Castillo .15 .05
❑ 128 Carlos Diaz .15 .05
❑ 129 Mariano Duncan RC .50 .20
❑ 130 Pedro Guerrero .25 .08
❑ 131 Orel Hershiser .75 .30
❑ 132 Rick Honeycutt .15 .05
❑ 133 Ken Howell .15 .05
❑ 134 Ken Landreaux .15 .05
❑ 135 Bill Madlock .25 .08
❑ 136 Candy Maldonado .15 .05
❑ 137 Mike Marshall .15 .05
❑ 138 Len Matuszek .15 .05
❑ 139 Tom Niedenfuer .15 .05
❑ 140 Alejandro Pena .15 .05
❑ 141 Jerry Reuss .15 .05
❑ 142 Bill Russell .25 .08
❑ 143 Steve Sax .15 .05
❑ 144 Mike Scioscia .25 .08
❑ 145 Fernando Valenzuela .25 .08
❑ 146 Bob Welch .25 .08
❑ 147 Terry Whitfield .15 .05
❑ 148 Juan Beniquez .15 .05
❑ 149 Bob Boone .25 .08
❑ 150 John Candelaria .15 .05
❑ 151 Rod Carew .50 .20
❑ 152 Stu Cliburn .15 .05
❑ 153 Doug DeCinces .15 .05
❑ 154 Brian Downing .25 .08
❑ 155 Ken Forsch .15 .05
❑ 156 Craig Gerber .15 .05
❑ 157 Bobby Grich .25 .08
❑ 158 George Hendrick .25 .08
❑ 159 Al Holland .15 .05
❑ 160 Reggie Jackson .50 .20
❑ 161 Ruppert Jones .15 .05
❑ 162 Urbano Lugo .15 .05
❑ 163 Kirk McCaskill RC .50 .20
❑ 164 Donnie Moore .15 .05
❑ 165 Gary Pettis .15 .05
❑ 166 Ron Romanick .15 .05
❑ 167 Dick Schofield .15 .05
❑ 168 Daryl Sconiers .15 .05
❑ 169 Jim Slaton .15 .05
❑ 170 Don Sutton .25 .08
❑ 171 Mike Witt .15 .05
❑ 172 Buddy Bell .25 .08
❑ 173 Tom Browning .15 .05
❑ 174 Dave Concepcion .25 .08
❑ 175 Eric Davis .75 .30
❑ 176 Bo Diaz .15 .05
❑ 177 Nick Esasky .15 .05
❑ 178 John Franco .25 .08
❑ 179 Tom Hume .15 .05
❑ 180 Wayne Krenchicki .15 .05
❑ 181 Andy McGaffigan .15 .05
❑ 182 Eddie Milner .15 .05
❑ 183 Ron Oester .15 .05
❑ 184 Dave Parker .25 .08
❑ 185 Frank Pastore .15 .05
❑ 186 Tony Perez .50 .20
❑ 187 Ted Power .15 .05
❑ 188 Joe Price .15 .05
❑ 189 Gary Redus .15 .05
❑ 190 Ron Robinson .15 .05
❑ 191 Pete Rose 2.50 1.00
❑ 192 Mario Soto .25 .08
❑ 193 John Stuper .15 .05
❑ 194 Jay Tibbs .15 .05
❑ 195 Dave Van Gorder .15 .05
❑ 196 Max Venable .15 .05
❑ 197 Juan Agosto .15 .05
❑ 198 Harold Baines .25 .08
❑ 199 Floyd Bannister .15 .05
❑ 200 Britt Burns .15 .05
❑ 201 Julio Cruz .15 .05
❑ 202 Joel Davis .15 .05
❑ 203 Richard Dotson .15 .05
❑ 204 Carlton Fisk .50 .20
❑ 205 Scott Fletcher .15 .05
❑ 206 Ozzie Guillen RC 2.00 .75
❑ 207 Jerry Hairston .15 .05
❑ 208 Tim Hulett .15 .05
❑ 209 Bob James .15 .05
❑ 210 Ron Kittle .15 .05
❑ 211 Rudy Law .15 .05
❑ 212 Bryan Little .15 .05
❑ 213 Gene Nelson .15 .05
❑ 214 Reid Nichols .15 .05
❑ 215 Luis Salazar .15 .05
❑ 216 Tom Seaver .50 .20
❑ 217 Dan Spillner .15 .05
❑ 218 Bruce Tanner .15 .05
❑ 219 Greg Walker .15 .05
❑ 220 Dave Wehrmeister .15 .05
❑ 221 Juan Berenguer .15 .05
❑ 222 Dave Bergman .15 .05
❑ 223 Tom Brookens .15 .05
❑ 224 Darrell Evans .25 .08
❑ 225 Barbaro Garbey .15 .05
❑ 226 Kirk Gibson .25 .08
❑ 227 John Grubb .15 .05
❑ 228 Willie Hernandez .15 .05
❑ 229 Larry Herndon .15 .05
❑ 230 Chet Lemon .25 .08
❑ 231 Aurelio Lopez .15 .05
❑ 232 Jack Morris .25 .08
❑ 233 Randy O'Neal .15 .05
❑ 234 Lance Parrish .25 .08
❑ 235 Dan Petry .15 .05
❑ 236 Alejandro Sanchez .15 .05
❑ 237 Bill Scherrer .15 .05
❑ 238 Nelson Simmons .15 .05
❑ 239 Frank Tanana .25 .08
❑ 240 Walt Terrell .15 .05
❑ 241 Alan Trammell .25 .08
❑ 242 Lou Whitaker .25 .08
❑ 243 Milt Wilcox .15 .05
❑ 244 Hubie Brooks .15 .05
❑ 245 Tim Burke .15 .05
❑ 246 Andre Dawson .25 .08
❑ 247 Mike Fitzgerald .15 .05
❑ 248 Terry Francona .25 .08
❑ 249 Bill Gullickson .15 .05
❑ 250 Joe Hesketh .15 .05
❑ 251 Bill Laskey .15 .05
❑ 252 Vance Law .15 .05
❑ 253 Charlie Lea .15 .05
❑ 254 Gary Lucas .15 .05
❑ 255 David Palmer .15 .05
❑ 256 Tim Raines .25 .08
❑ 257 Jeff Reardon .25 .08
❑ 258 Bert Roberge .15 .05
❑ 259 Dan Schatzeder .15 .05
❑ 260 Bryn Smith .15 .05
❑ 261 Randy St.Claire .15 .05
❑ 262 Scot Thompson .15 .05
❑ 263 Tim Wallach .15 .05
❑ 264 U.L. Washington .15 .05
❑ 265 Mitch Webster .15 .05
❑ 266 Herm Winningham .15 .05
❑ 267 Floyd Youmans .15 .05
❑ 268 Don Aase .15 .05
❑ 269 Mike Boddicker .15 .05
❑ 270 Rich Dauer .15 .05
❑ 271 Storm Davis .15 .05
❑ 272 Rick Dempsey .15 .05
❑ 273 Ken Dixon .15 .05
❑ 274 Jim Dwyer .15 .05
❑ 275 Mike Flanagan .15 .05
❑ 276 Wayne Gross .15 .05
❑ 277 Lee Lacy .15 .05
❑ 278 Fred Lynn .25 .08
❑ 279 Tippy Martinez .15 .05
❑ 280 Dennis Martinez .25 .08
❑ 281 Scott McGregor .15 .05
❑ 282 Eddie Murray .75 .30
❑ 283 Floyd Rayford .15 .05
❑ 284 Cal Ripken 3.00 1.25
❑ 285 Gary Roenicke .15 .05
❑ 286 Larry Sheets .15 .05
❑ 287 John Shelby .15 .05
❑ 288 Nate Snell .15 .05
❑ 289 Sammy Stewart .15 .05
❑ 290 Alan Wiggins .15 .05
❑ 291 Mike Young .15 .05
❑ 292 Alan Ashby .15 .05
❑ 293 Mark Bailey .15 .05
❑ 294 Kevin Bass .15 .05

❑	295	Jeff Calhoun	.15	.05
❑	296	Jose Cruz	.25	.08
❑	297	Glenn Davis	.15	.05
❑	298	Bill Dawley	.15	.05
❑	299	Frank DiPino	.15	.05
❑	300	Bill Doran	.15	.05
❑	301	Phil Garner	.25	.08
❑	302	Jeff Heathcock	.15	.05
❑	303	Charlie Kerfeld	.15	.05
❑	304	Bob Knepper	.15	.05
❑	305	Ron Mathis	.15	.05
❑	306	Jerry Mumphrey	.15	.05
❑	307	Jim Pankovits	.15	.05
❑	308	Terry Puhl	.15	.05
❑	309	Craig Reynolds	.15	.05
❑	310	Nolan Ryan	4.00	1.50
❑	311	Mike Scott	.25	.08
❑	312	Dave Smith	.15	.05
❑	313	Dickie Thon	.15	.05
❑	314	Denny Walling	.15	.05
❑	315	Kurt Bevacqua	.15	.05
❑	316	Al Bumbry	.15	.05
❑	317	Jerry Davis	.15	.05
❑	318	Luis DeLeon	.15	.05
❑	319	Dave Dravecky	.15	.05
❑	320	Tim Flannery	.15	.05
❑	321	Steve Garvey	.25	.08
❑	322	Rich Gossage	.25	.08
❑	323	Tony Gwynn	1.25	.50
❑	324	Andy Hawkins	.15	.05
❑	325	LaMarr Hoyt	.15	.05
❑	326	Roy Lee Jackson	.15	.05
❑	327	Terry Kennedy	.15	.05
❑	328	Craig Lefferts	.15	.05
❑	329	Carmelo Martinez	.15	.05
❑	330	Lance McCullers	.15	.05
❑	331	Kevin McReynolds	.15	.05
❑	332	Graig Nettles	.25	.08
❑	333	Jerry Royster	.15	.05
❑	334	Eric Show	.15	.05
❑	335	Tim Stoddard	.15	.05
❑	336	Garry Templeton	.25	.08
❑	337	Mark Thurmond	.15	.05
❑	338	Ed Wojna	.15	.05
❑	339	Tony Armas	.25	.08
❑	340	Marty Barrett	.15	.05
❑	341	Wade Boggs	.50	.20
❑	342	Dennis Boyd	.15	.05
❑	343	Bill Buckner	.25	.08
❑	344	Mark Clear	.15	.05
❑	345	Roger Clemens	5.00	2.00
❑	346	Steve Crawford	.15	.05
❑	347	Mike Easler	.15	.05
❑	348	Dwight Evans	.50	.20
❑	349	Rich Gedman	.15	.05
❑	350	Jackie Gutierrez	.15	.05
❑	351	Glenn Hoffman	.15	.05
❑	352	Bruce Hurst	.15	.05
❑	353	Bruce Kison	.15	.05
❑	354	Tim Lollar	.15	.05
❑	355	Steve Lyons	.15	.05
❑	356	Al Nipper	.15	.05
❑	357	Bob Ojeda	.15	.05
❑	358	Jim Rice	.25	.08
❑	359	Bob Stanley	.15	.05
❑	360	Mike Trujillo	.15	.05
❑	361	Thad Bosley	.15	.05
❑	362	Warren Brusstar	.15	.05
❑	363	Ron Cey	.25	.08
❑	364	Jody Davis	.15	.05
❑	365	Bob Dernier	.15	.05
❑	366	Shawon Dunston	.25	.08
❑	367	Leon Durham	.15	.05
❑	368	Dennis Eckersley	.50	.20
❑	369	Ray Fontenot	.15	.05
❑	370	George Frazier	.15	.05
❑	371	Billy Hatcher	.15	.05
❑	372	Dave Lopes	.25	.08
❑	373	Gary Matthews	.25	.08
❑	374	Ron Meridith	.15	.05
❑	375	Keith Moreland	.15	.05
❑	376	Reggie Patterson	.15	.05
❑	377	Dick Ruthven	.15	.05
❑	378	Ryne Sandberg	1.50	.60
❑	379	Scott Sanderson	.15	.05
❑	380	Lee Smith	.25	.08
❑	381	Lary Sorensen	.15	.05
❑	382	Chris Speier	.15	.05
❑	383	Rick Sutcliffe	.25	.08
❑	384	Steve Trout	.15	.05
❑	385	Gary Woods	.15	.05
❑	386	Bert Blyleven	.25	.08
❑	387	Tom Brunansky	.15	.05
❑	388	Randy Bush	.15	.05
❑	389	John Butcher	.15	.05
❑	390	Ron Davis	.15	.05
❑	391	Dave Engle	.15	.05
❑	392	Frank Eufemia	.15	.05
❑	393	Pete Filson	.15	.05
❑	394	Gary Gaetti	.25	.08
❑	395	Greg Gagne	.15	.05
❑	396	Mickey Hatcher	.15	.05
❑	397	Kent Hrbek	.25	.08
❑	398	Tim Laudner	.15	.05
❑	399	Rick Lysander	.15	.05
❑	400	Dave Meier	.15	.05
❑	401	Kirby Puckett	2.00	.75
❑	402	Mark Salas	.15	.05
❑	403	Ken Schrom	.15	.05
❑	404	Roy Smalley	.15	.05
❑	405	Mike Smithson	.15	.05
❑	406	Mike Stenhouse	.15	.05
❑	407	Tim Teufel	.15	.05
❑	408	Frank Viola	.25	.08
❑	409	Ron Washington	.15	.05
❑	410	Keith Atherton	.15	.05
❑	411	Dusty Baker	.25	.08
❑	412	Tim Birtsas	.15	.05
❑	413	Bruce Bochte	.15	.05
❑	414	Chris Codiroli	.15	.05
❑	415	Dave Collins	.15	.05
❑	416	Mike Davis	.15	.05
❑	417	Alfredo Griffin	.15	.05
❑	418	Mike Heath	.15	.05
❑	419	Steve Henderson	.15	.05
❑	420	Donnie Hill	.15	.05
❑	421	Jay Howell	.15	.05
❑	422	Tommy John	.25	.08
❑	423	Dave Kingman	.25	.08
❑	424	Bill Krueger	.15	.05
❑	425	Rick Langford	.15	.05
❑	426	Carney Lansford	.25	.08
❑	427	Steve McCatty	.15	.05
❑	428	Dwayne Murphy	.15	.05
❑	429	Steve Ontiveros RC	.15	.05
❑	430	Tony Phillips	.15	.05
❑	431	Jose Rijo	.25	.08
❑	432	Mickey Tettleton RC	.50	.20
❑	433	Luis Aguayo	.15	.05
❑	434	Larry Andersen	.15	.05
❑	435	Steve Carlton	.25	.08
❑	436	Don Carman	.15	.05
❑	437	Tim Corcoran	.15	.05
❑	438	Darren Daulton RC	1.00	.40
❑	439	John Denny	.15	.05
❑	440	Tom Foley	.15	.05
❑	441	Greg Gross	.15	.05
❑	442	Kevin Gross	.15	.05
❑	443	Von Hayes	.15	.05
❑	444	Charles Hudson	.15	.05
❑	445	Garry Maddox	.15	.05
❑	446	Shane Rawley	.15	.05
❑	447	Dave Rucker	.15	.05
❑	448	John Russell	.15	.05
❑	449	Juan Samuel	.15	.05
❑	450	Mike Schmidt	2.00	.75
❑	451	Rick Schu	.15	.05
❑	452	Dave Shipanoff	.15	.05
❑	453	Dave Stewart	.25	.08
❑	454	Jeff Stone	.15	.05
❑	455	Kent Tekulve	.15	.05
❑	456	Ozzie Virgil	.15	.05
❑	457	Glenn Wilson	.15	.05
❑	458	Jim Beattie	.15	.05
❑	459	Karl Best	.15	.05
❑	460	Barry Bonnell	.15	.05
❑	461	Phil Bradley	.15	.05
❑	462	Ivan Calderon RC*	.50	.20
❑	463	Al Cowens	.15	.05
❑	464	Alvin Davis	.15	.05
❑	465	Dave Henderson	.15	.05
❑	466	Bob Kearney	.15	.05
❑	467	Mark Langston	.25	.08
❑	468	Bob Long	.15	.05
❑	469	Mike Moore	.15	.05
❑	470	Edwin Nunez	.15	.05
❑	471	Spike Owen	.15	.05
❑	472	Jack Perconte	.15	.05
❑	473	Jim Presley	.15	.05
❑	474	Donnie Scott	.15	.05
❑	475	Bill Swift	.15	.05
❑	476	Danny Tartabull	.25	.08
❑	477	Gorman Thomas	.25	.08
❑	478	Roy Thomas	.15	.05
❑	479	Ed VandeBerg	.15	.05
❑	480	Frank Wills	.15	.05
❑	481	Matt Young	.15	.05
❑	482	Ray Burris	.15	.05
❑	483	Jaime Cocanower	.15	.05
❑	484	Cecil Cooper	.25	.08
❑	485	Danny Darwin	.15	.05
❑	486	Rollie Fingers	.25	.08
❑	487	Jim Gantner	.15	.05
❑	488	Bob L. Gibson	.15	.05
❑	489	Moose Haas	.15	.05
❑	490	Teddy Higuera RC*	.50	.20
❑	491	Paul Householder	.15	.05
❑	492	Pete Ladd	.15	.05
❑	493	Rick Manning	.15	.05
❑	494	Bob McClure	.15	.05
❑	495	Paul Molitor	.25	.08
❑	496	Charlie Moore	.15	.05
❑	497	Ben Oglivie	.25	.08
❑	498	Randy Ready	.15	.05
❑	499	Earnie Riles	.15	.05
❑	500	Ed Romero	.15	.05
❑	501	Bill Schroeder	.15	.05
❑	502	Ray Searage	.15	.05
❑	503	Ted Simmons	.25	.08
❑	504	Pete Vuckovich	.15	.05
❑	505	Rick Waits	.15	.05
❑	506	Robin Yount	1.25	.50
❑	507	Len Barker	.15	.05
❑	508	Steve Bedrosian	.15	.05
❑	509	Bruce Benedict	.15	.05
❑	510	Rick Camp	.15	.05
❑	511	Rick Cerone	.15	.05
❑	512	Chris Chambliss	.25	.08
❑	513	Jeff Dedmon	.15	.05
❑	514	Terry Forster	.25	.08
❑	515	Gene Garber	.15	.05
❑	516	Terry Harper	.15	.05
❑	517	Bob Horner	.25	.08
❑	518	Glenn Hubbard	.15	.05
❑	519	Joe Johnson	.15	.05
❑	520	Brad Komminsk	.15	.05
❑	521	Rick Mahler	.15	.05
❑	522	Dale Murphy	.50	.20
❑	523	Ken Oberkfell	.15	.05
❑	524	Pascual Perez	.15	.05
❑	525	Gerald Perry	.15	.05
❑	526	Rafael Ramirez	.15	.05
❑	527	Steve Shields	.15	.05
❑	528	Zane Smith	.15	.05
❑	529	Bruce Sutter	.25	.08
❑	530	Milt Thompson RC	.50	.20
❑	531	Claudell Washington	.15	.05
❑	532	Paul Zuvella	.15	.05
❑	533	Vida Blue	.25	.08
❑	534	Bob Brenly	.15	.05
❑	535	Chris Brown RC	.15	.05
❑	536	Chili Davis	.25	.08
❑	537	Mark Davis	.15	.05
❑	538	Rob Deer	.15	.05
❑	539	Dan Driessen	.15	.05
❑	540	Scott Garrelts	.15	.05
❑	541	Dan Gladden	.15	.05
❑	542	Jim Gott	.15	.05
❑	543	David Green	.15	.05
❑	544	Atlee Hammaker	.15	.05
❑	545	Mike Jeffcoat	.15	.05
❑	546	Mike Krukow	.15	.05
❑	547	Dave LaPoint	.15	.05
❑	548	Jeff Leonard	.15	.05
❑	549	Greg Minton	.15	.05
❑	550	Alex Trevino	.15	.05
❑	551	Manny Trillo	.15	.05
❑	552	Jose Uribe	.15	.05

❑	553	Brad Wellman	.15	.05
❑	554	Frank Williams	.15	.05
❑	555	Joel Youngblood	.15	.05
❑	556	Alan Bannister	.15	.05
❑	557	Glenn Brummer	.15	.05
❑	558	Steve Buechele RC	.50	.20
❑	559	Jose Guzman RC	.15	.05
❑	560	Toby Harrah	.25	.08
❑	561	Greg Harris	.15	.05
❑	562	Dwayne Henry	.15	.05
❑	563	Burt Hooton	.15	.05
❑	564	Charlie Hough	.25	.08
❑	565	Mike Mason	.15	.05
❑	566	Oddibe McDowell	.15	.05
❑	567	Dickie Noles	.15	.05
❑	568	Pete O'Brien	.15	.05
❑	569	Larry Parrish	.15	.05
❑	570	Dave Rozema	.15	.05
❑	571	Dave Schmidt	.15	.05
❑	572	Don Slaught	.15	.05
❑	573	Wayne Tolleson	.15	.05
❑	574	Duane Walker	.15	.05
❑	575	Gary Ward	.15	.05
❑	576	Chris Welsh	.15	.05
❑	577	Curtis Wilkerson	.15	.05
❑	578	George Wright	.15	.05
❑	579	Chris Bando	.15	.05
❑	580	Tony Bernazard	.15	.05
❑	581	Brett Butler	.25	.08
❑	582	Ernie Camacho	.15	.05
❑	583	Joe Carter	.25	.08
❑	584	Carmen Castillo	.15	.05
❑	585	Jamie Easterly	.15	.05
❑	586	Julio Franco	.25	.08
❑	587	Mel Hall	.15	.05
❑	588	Mike Hargrove	.15	.05
❑	589	Neal Heaton	.15	.05
❑	590	Brook Jacoby	.15	.05
❑	591	Otis Nixon RC	1.00	.40
❑	592	Jerry Reed	.15	.05
❑	593	Vern Ruhle	.15	.05
❑	594	Pat Tabler	.15	.05
❑	595	Rich Thompson	.15	.05
❑	596	Andre Thornton	.15	.05
❑	597	Dave Von Ohlen	.15	.05
❑	598	George Vukovich	.15	.05
❑	599	Tom Waddell	.15	.05
❑	600	Curt Wardle	.15	.05
❑	601	Jerry Willard	.15	.05
❑	602	Bill Almon	.15	.05
❑	603	Mike Bielecki	.15	.05
❑	604	Sid Bream	.15	.05
❑	605	Mike C. Brown	.15	.05
❑	606	Pat Clements	.15	.05
❑	607	Jose DeLeon	.15	.05
❑	608	Denny Gonzalez	.15	.05
❑	609	Cecilio Guante	.15	.05
❑	610	Steve Kemp	.15	.05
❑	611	Sammy Khalifa	.15	.05
❑	612	Lee Mazzilli	.25	.08
❑	613	Larry McWilliams	.15	.05
❑	614	Jim Morrison	.15	.05
❑	615	Joe Orsulak RC*	.50	.20
❑	616	Tony Pena	.15	.05
❑	617	Johnny Ray	.15	.05
❑	618	Rick Reuschel	.25	.08
❑	619	R.J. Reynolds	.15	.05
❑	620	Rick Rhoden	.15	.05
❑	621	Don Robinson	.15	.05
❑	622	Jason Thompson	.15	.05
❑	623	Lee Tunnell	.15	.05
❑	624	Jim Winn	.15	.05
❑	625	Marvell Wynne	.15	.05
❑	626	Dwight Gooden IA	.50	.20
❑	627	Don Mattingly IA	1.25	.50
❑	628	Pete Rose 4192	.50	.20
❑	629	Rod Carew 3000 Hits	.25	.08
❑	630	T.Seaver/P.Niekro	.25	.08
❑	631	Don Baylor Ouch	.25	.08
❑	632	Tim Raines/Strawberry	.25	.08
❑	633	C.Ripken/A.Trammell	1.50	.60
❑	634	Wade Boggs/G.Brett	1.00	.40
❑	635	B.Horner/D.Murphy	.50	.20
❑	636	W.McGee/V.Coleman	.25	.08
❑	637	Vince Coleman IA	.25	.08
❑	638	Pete Rose/D.Gooden	.75	.30
❑	639	Wade Boggs/D.Mattingly	1.25	.50
❑	640	Murphy/Garvey/Parker	.50	.20
❑	641	D.Gooden/F.Valenzuela	.50	.20
❑	642	Jimmy Key/D.Stieb	.25	.08
❑	643	C.Fisk/R.Gedman	.25	.08
❑	644	Benito Santiago RC	2.00	.75
❑	645	M.Woodard/C.Ward RC	.15	.05
❑	646	Paul O'Neill RC	4.00	1.50
❑	647	Andres Galarraga RC	1.50	.60
❑	648	B.Kipper/C.Ford RC	.15	.05
❑	649	Jose Canseco RC	8.00	3.00
❑	650	Mark McLemore RC	1.00	.40
❑	651	R.Woodward/M.Brantley RC	.15	.05
❑	652	B.Robidoux/M.Funderburk RC	.15	.05
❑	653	Cecil Fielder RC	2.00	.75
❑	654	CL: Royals/Cardinals Blue Jays/Mets	.15	.05
❑	655	CL: Yankees/Dodgers Angels/Reds UER (168 Darly S	.15	.05
❑	656	CL: White Sox/Tigers Expos/Orioles (279 Dennis&#	.15	.05
❑	657	CL: Astros/Padres Red Sox/Cubs	.15	.05
❑	658	CL: Twins/A's Phillies/Mariners	.15	.05
❑	659	CL: Brewers/Braves Giants/Rangers	.15	.05
❑	660	CL: Indians/Pirates Special Cards	.15	.05

1986 Fleer Update

❑		COMP.FACT.SET (132)	30.00	12.00
❑	1	Mike Aldrete XRC	.15	.05
❑	2	Andy Allanson XRC	.15	.05
❑	3	Neil Allen	.15	.05
❑	4	Joaquin Andujar	.25	.08
❑	5	Paul Assenmacher XRC	.50	.20
❑	6	Scott Bailes XRC	.15	.05
❑	7	Jay Baller XRC	.15	.05
❑	8	Scott Bankhead	.15	.05
❑	9	Bill Bathe XRC	.15	.05
❑	10	Don Baylor	.25	.08
❑	11	Billy Beane XRC	1.00	.40
❑	12	Steve Bedrosian	.15	.05
❑	13	Juan Beniquez	.15	.05
❑	14	Barry Bonds XRC	15.00	6.00
❑	15	Bobby Bonilla XRC	1.00	.40
❑	16	Rich Bordi	.15	.05
❑	17	Bill Campbell	.15	.05
❑	18	Tom Candiotti	.15	.05
❑	19	John Cangelosi XRC	.50	.20
❑	20	Jose Canseco	4.00	1.50
❑	21	Chuck Cary XRC	.15	.05
❑	22	Juan Castillo XRC	.15	.05
❑	23	Rick Cerone	.15	.05
❑	24	John Cerutti XRC	.15	.05
❑	25	Will Clark XRC	2.00	.75
❑	26	Mark Clear	.15	.05
❑	27	Darnell Coles	.15	.05
❑	28	Dave Collins	.15	.05
❑	29	Tim Conroy	.15	.05
❑	30	Ed Correa	.15	.05
❑	31	Joe Cowley	.15	.05
❑	32	Bill Dawley	.15	.05
❑	33	Rob Deer	.15	.05
❑	34	John Denny	.15	.05
❑	35	Jim Deshaies XRC	.15	.05
❑	36	Doug Drabek XRC	1.00	.40
❑	37	Mike Easler	.15	.05
❑	38	Mark Eichhorn	.15	.05
❑	39	Dave Engle	.15	.05
❑	40	Mike Fischlin	.15	.05
❑	41	Scott Fletcher	.15	.05
❑	42	Terry Forster	.25	.08
❑	43	Terry Francona	.25	.08
❑	44	Andres Galarraga	1.50	.60
❑	45	Lee Guetterman	.15	.05
❑	46	Bill Gullickson	.15	.05
❑	47	Jackie Gutierrez	.15	.05
❑	48	Moose Haas	.15	.05
❑	49	Billy Hatcher	.15	.05
❑	50	Mike Heath	.15	.05
❑	51	Guy Hoffman	.15	.05
❑	52	Tom Hume	.15	.05
❑	53	Pete Incaviglia XRC	.50	.20
❑	54	Dane Iorg	.15	.05
❑	55	Chris James XRC	.15	.05
❑	56	Stan Javier XRC*	.50	.20
❑	57	Tommy John	.25	.08
❑	58	Tracy Jones	.15	.05
❑	59	Wally Joyner XRC	1.00	.40
❑	60	Wayne Krenchicki	.15	.05
❑	61	John Kruk XRC	1.50	.60
❑	62	Mike LaCoss	.15	.05
❑	63	Pete Ladd	.15	.05
❑	64	Dave LaPoint	.15	.05
❑	65	Mike LaValliere XRC	.50	.20
❑	66	Rudy Law	.15	.05
❑	67	Dennis Leonard	.15	.05
❑	68	Steve Lombardozzi	.15	.05
❑	69	Aurelio Lopez	.15	.05
❑	70	Mickey Mahler	.15	.05
❑	71	Candy Maldonado	.15	.05
❑	72	Roger Mason XRC*	.15	.05
❑	73	Greg Mathews	.15	.05
❑	74	Andy McGaffigan	.15	.05
❑	75	Joel McKeon	.15	.05
❑	76	Kevin Mitchell XRC	1.00	.40
❑	77	Bill Mooneyham	.15	.05
❑	78	Omar Moreno	.15	.05
❑	79	Jerry Mumphrey	.15	.05
❑	80	Al Newman XRC	.25	.08
❑	81	Phil Niekro	.25	.08
❑	82	Randy Niemann	.15	.05
❑	83	Juan Nieves	.15	.05
❑	84	Bob Ojeda	.15	.05
❑	85	Rick Ownbey	.15	.05
❑	86	Tom Paciorek	.15	.05
❑	87	David Palmer	.15	.05
❑	88	Jeff Parrett XRC	.15	.05
❑	89	Pat Perry	.15	.05
❑	90	Dan Plesac	.15	.05
❑	91	Darrell Porter	.15	.05
❑	92	Luis Quinones	.15	.05
❑	93	Rey Quinones UER (Misspelled Quinonez)	.15	.05
❑	94	Gary Redus	.15	.05
❑	95	Jeff Reed	.15	.05
❑	96	Bip Roberts XRC	.50	.20
❑	97	Billy Joe Robidoux	.15	.05
❑	98	Gary Roenicke	.15	.05
❑	99	Ron Roenicke	.15	.05
❑	100	Angel Salazar	.15	.05
❑	101	Joe Sambito	.15	.05
❑	102	Billy Sample	.15	.05
❑	103	Dave Schmidt	.15	.05
❑	104	Ken Schrom	.15	.05
❑	105	Ruben Sierra XRC	1.50	.60
❑	106	Ted Simmons	.25	.08
❑	107	Sammy Stewart	.15	.05
❑	108	Kurt Stillwell	.15	.05
❑	109	Dale Sveum	.15	.05
❑	110	Tim Teufel	.15	.05
❑	111	Bob Tewksbury XRC	.50	.20
❑	112	Andres Thomas	.15	.05
❑	113	Jason Thompson	.15	.05
❑	114	Milt Thompson	.50	.20
❑	115	Robby Thompson XRC	.50	.20
❑	116	Jay Tibbs	.15	.05
❑	117	Fred Toliver	.15	.05
❑	118	Wayne Tolleson	.15	.05
❑	119	Alex Trevino	.15	.05

❑ 120 Manny Trillo	.15	.05
❑ 121 Ed VandeBerg	.15	.05
❑ 122 Ozzie Virgil	.15	.05
❑ 123 Tony Walker	.15	.05
❑ 124 Gene Walter	.15	.05
❑ 125 Duane Ward XRC	.50	.20
❑ 126 Jerry Willard	.15	.05
❑ 127 Mitch Williams XRC	.50	.20
❑ 128 Reggie Williams	.15	.05
❑ 129 Bobby Witt XRC	.50	.20
❑ 130 Marvell Wynne	.15	.05
❑ 131 Steve Yeager	.25	.08
❑ 132 Checklist 1-132	.15	.05

1987 Fleer

❑ COMPLETE SET (660)	40.00	20.00
❑ COMP.FACT.SET (672)	50.00	25.00
❑ 1 Rick Aguilera	.15	.05
❑ 2 Richard Anderson	.15	.05
❑ 3 Wally Backman	.15	.05
❑ 4 Gary Carter	.25	.08
❑ 5 Ron Darling	.25	.08
❑ 6 Len Dykstra	.25	.08
❑ 7 Kevin Elster RC	.50	.20
❑ 8 Sid Fernandez	.15	.05
❑ 9 Dwight Gooden	.40	.15
❑ 10 Ed Hearn RC	.15	.05
❑ 11 Danny Heep	.15	.05
❑ 12 Keith Hernandez	.25	.08
❑ 13 Howard Johnson	.25	.08
❑ 14 Ray Knight	.25	.08
❑ 15 Lee Mazzilli	.25	.08
❑ 16 Roger McDowell	.15	.05
❑ 17 Kevin Mitchell RC *	1.25	.50
❑ 18 Randy Niemann	.15	.05
❑ 19 Bob Ojeda	.15	.05
❑ 20 Jesse Orosco	.15	.05
❑ 21 Rafael Santana	.15	.05
❑ 22 Doug Sisk	.15	.05
❑ 23 Darryl Strawberry	.25	.08
❑ 24 Tim Teufel	.15	.05
❑ 25 Mookie Wilson	.25	.08
❑ 26 Tony Armas	.25	.08
❑ 27 Marty Barrett	.15	.05
❑ 28 Don Baylor	.25	.08
❑ 29 Wade Boggs	.40	.15
❑ 30 Oil Can Boyd	.15	.05
❑ 31 Bill Buckner	.25	.08
❑ 32 Roger Clemens	3.00	1.25
❑ 33 Steve Crawford	.15	.05
❑ 34 Dwight Evans	.40	.15
❑ 35 Rich Gedman	.15	.05
❑ 36 Dave Henderson	.15	.05
❑ 37 Bruce Hurst	.15	.05
❑ 38 Tim Lollar	.15	.05
❑ 39 Al Nipper	.15	.05
❑ 40 Spike Owen	.15	.05
❑ 41 Jim Rice	.25	.08
❑ 42 Ed Romero	.15	.05
❑ 43 Joe Sambito	.15	.05
❑ 44 Calvin Schiraldi	.15	.05
❑ 45 Tom Seaver	.40	.15
❑ 46 Jeff Sellers	.15	.05
❑ 47 Bob Stanley	.15	.05
❑ 48 Sammy Stewart	.15	.05
❑ 49 Larry Andersen	.15	.05
❑ 50 Alan Ashby	.15	.05
❑ 51 Kevin Bass	.15	.05
❑ 52 Jeff Calhoun	.15	.05
❑ 53 Jose Cruz	.25	.08
❑ 54 Danny Darwin	.15	.05
❑ 55 Glenn Davis	.15	.05
❑ 56 Jim Deshaies RC *	.25	.08
❑ 57 Bill Doran	.15	.05
❑ 58 Phil Garner	.25	.08
❑ 59 Billy Hatcher	.15	.05
❑ 60 Charlie Kerfeld	.15	.05
❑ 61 Bob Knepper	.15	.05
❑ 62 Dave Lopes	.25	.08
❑ 63 Aurelio Lopez	.15	.05
❑ 64 Jim Pankovits	.15	.05
❑ 65 Terry Puhl	.15	.05
❑ 66 Craig Reynolds	.15	.05
❑ 67 Nolan Ryan	3.00	1.25
❑ 68 Mike Scott	.25	.08
❑ 69 Dave Smith	.15	.05
❑ 70 Dickie Thon	.15	.05
❑ 71 Tony Walker	.15	.05
❑ 72 Denny Walling	.15	.05
❑ 73 Bob Boone	.25	.08
❑ 74 Rick Burleson	.15	.05
❑ 75 John Candelaria	.15	.05
❑ 76 Doug Corbett	.15	.05
❑ 77 Doug DeCinces	.15	.05
❑ 78 Brian Downing	.25	.08
❑ 79 Chuck Finley RC	1.25	.50
❑ 80 Terry Forster	.25	.08
❑ 81 Bob Grich	.25	.08
❑ 82 George Hendrick	.25	.08
❑ 83 Jack Howell	.15	.05
❑ 84 Reggie Jackson	.40	.15
❑ 85 Ruppert Jones	.15	.05
❑ 86 Wally Joyner RC	1.25	.50
❑ 87 Gary Lucas	.15	.05
❑ 88 Kirk McCaskill	.15	.05
❑ 89 Donnie Moore	.15	.05
❑ 90 Gary Pettis	.15	.05
❑ 91 Vern Ruhle	.15	.05
❑ 92 Dick Schofield	.15	.05
❑ 93 Don Sutton	.25	.08
❑ 94 Rob Wilfong	.15	.05
❑ 95 Mike Witt	.15	.05
❑ 96 Doug Drabek RC	1.25	.50
❑ 97 Mike Easler	.15	.05
❑ 98 Mike Fischlin	.15	.05
❑ 99 Brian Fisher	.15	.05
❑ 100 Ron Guidry	.25	.08
❑ 101 Rickey Henderson	.60	.25
❑ 102 Tommy John	.25	.08
❑ 103 Ron Kittle	.15	.05
❑ 104 Don Mattingly	2.00	.75
❑ 105 Bobby Meacham	.15	.05
❑ 106 Joe Niekro	.15	.05
❑ 107 Mike Pagliarulo	.15	.05
❑ 108 Dan Pasqua	.15	.05
❑ 109 Willie Randolph	.25	.08
❑ 110 Dennis Rasmussen	.15	.05
❑ 111 Dave Righetti	.25	.08
❑ 112 Gary Roenicke	.15	.05
❑ 113 Rod Scurry	.15	.05
❑ 114 Bob Shirley	.15	.05
❑ 115 Joel Skinner	.15	.05
❑ 116 Tim Stoddard	.15	.05
❑ 117 Bob Tewksbury RC *	.50	.20
❑ 118 Wayne Tolleson	.15	.05
❑ 119 Claudell Washington	.15	.05
❑ 120 Dave Winfield	.25	.08
❑ 121 Steve Buechele	.15	.05
❑ 122 Ed Correa	.15	.05
❑ 123 Scott Fletcher	.15	.05
❑ 124 Jose Guzman	.15	.05
❑ 125 Toby Harrah	.25	.08
❑ 126 Greg Harris	.15	.05
❑ 127 Charlie Hough	.25	.08
❑ 128 Pete Incaviglia RC *	.50	.20
❑ 129 Mike Mason	.15	.05
❑ 130 Oddibe McDowell	.15	.05
❑ 131 Dale Mohorcic	.15	.05
❑ 132 Pete O'Brien	.15	.05
❑ 133 Tom Paciorek	.15	.05
❑ 134 Larry Parrish	.15	.05
❑ 135 Geno Petralli	.15	.05
❑ 136 Darrell Porter	.15	.05
❑ 137 Jeff Russell	.15	.05
❑ 138 Ruben Sierra RC	2.00	.75
❑ 139 Don Slaught	.15	.05
❑ 140 Gary Ward	.15	.05
❑ 141 Curtis Wilkerson	.15	.05
❑ 142 Mitch Williams RC *	.50	.20
❑ 143 Bobby Witt RC	.50	.20
❑ 144 Dave Bergman	.15	.05
❑ 145 Tom Brookens	.15	.05
❑ 146 Bill Campbell	.15	.05
❑ 147 Chuck Cary	.15	.05
❑ 148 Darnell Coles	.15	.05
❑ 149 Dave Collins	.15	.05
❑ 150 Darrell Evans	.25	.08
❑ 151 Kirk Gibson	.25	.08
❑ 152 John Grubb	.15	.05
❑ 153 Willie Hernandez	.15	.05
❑ 154 Larry Herndon	.15	.05
❑ 155 Eric King	.15	.05
❑ 156 Chet Lemon	.25	.08
❑ 157 Dwight Lowry	.15	.05
❑ 158 Jack Morris	.25	.08
❑ 159 Randy O'Neal	.15	.05
❑ 160 Lance Parrish	.25	.08
❑ 161 Dan Petry	.15	.05
❑ 162 Pat Sheridan	.15	.05
❑ 163 Jim Slaton	.15	.05
❑ 164 Frank Tanana	.25	.08
❑ 165 Walt Terrell	.15	.05
❑ 166 Mark Thurmond	.15	.05
❑ 167 Alan Trammell	.25	.08
❑ 168 Lou Whitaker	.25	.08
❑ 169 Luis Aguayo	.15	.05
❑ 170 Steve Bedrosian	.15	.05
❑ 171 Don Carman	.15	.05
❑ 172 Darren Daulton	.25	.08
❑ 173 Greg Gross	.15	.05
❑ 174 Kevin Gross	.15	.05
❑ 175 Von Hayes	.15	.05
❑ 176 Charles Hudson	.15	.05
❑ 177 Tom Hume	.15	.05
❑ 178 Steve Jeltz	.15	.05
❑ 179 Mike Maddux RC	.15	.05
❑ 180 Shane Rawley	.15	.05
❑ 181 Gary Redus	.15	.05
❑ 182 Ron Roenicke	.15	.05
❑ 183 Bruce Ruffin RC	.25	.08
❑ 184 John Russell	.15	.05
❑ 185 Juan Samuel	.15	.05
❑ 186 Dan Schatzeder	.15	.05
❑ 187 Mike Schmidt	1.50	.60
❑ 188 Rick Schu	.15	.05
❑ 189 Jeff Stone	.15	.05
❑ 190 Kent Tekulve	.15	.05
❑ 191 Milt Thompson	.15	.05
❑ 192 Glenn Wilson	.15	.05
❑ 193 Buddy Bell	.25	.08
❑ 194 Tom Browning	.15	.05
❑ 195 Sal Butera	.15	.05
❑ 196 Dave Concepcion	.25	.08
❑ 197 Kal Daniels	.15	.05
❑ 198 Eric Davis	.40	.15
❑ 199 John Denny	.15	.05
❑ 200 Bo Diaz	.15	.05
❑ 201 Nick Esasky	.15	.05
❑ 202 John Franco	.25	.08
❑ 203 Bill Gullickson	.15	.05
❑ 204 Barry Larkin RC	3.00	1.25
❑ 205 Eddie Milner	.15	.05
❑ 206 Rob Murphy	.15	.05
❑ 207 Ron Oester	.15	.05
❑ 208 Dave Parker	.25	.08
❑ 209 Tony Perez	.40	.15
❑ 210 Ted Power	.15	.05
❑ 211 Joe Price	.15	.05
❑ 212 Ron Robinson	.15	.05
❑ 213 Pete Rose	2.00	.75
❑ 214 Mario Soto	.25	.08
❑ 215 Kurt Stillwell	.15	.05
❑ 216 Max Venable	.15	.05
❑ 217 Chris Welsh	.15	.05
❑ 218 Carl Willis RC	.25	.08
❑ 219 Jesse Barfield	.25	.08
❑ 220 George Bell	.25	.08
❑ 221 Bill Caudill	.15	.05
❑ 222 John Cerutti	.15	.05
❑ 223 Jim Clancy	.15	.05

❑ 224 Mark Eichhorn .15 .05
❑ 225 Tony Fernandez .15 .05
❑ 226 Damaso Garcia .15 .05
❑ 227 Kelly Gruber ERR
(Wrong birth year) .15 .05
❑ 228 Tom Henke .15 .05
❑ 229 Garth Iorg .15 .05
❑ 230 Joe Johnson .15 .05
❑ 231 Cliff Johnson .15 .05
❑ 232 Jimmy Key .25 .08
❑ 233 Dennis Lamp .15 .05
❑ 234 Rick Leach .15 .05
❑ 235 Buck Martinez .15 .05
❑ 236 Lloyd Moseby .15 .05
❑ 237 Rance Mulliniks .15 .05
❑ 238 Dave Stieb .25 .08
❑ 239 Willie Upshaw .15 .05
❑ 240 Ernie Whitt .15 .05
❑ 241 Andy Allanson RC .15 .05
❑ 242 Scott Bailes .15 .05
❑ 243 Chris Bando .15 .05
❑ 244 Tony Bernazard .15 .05
❑ 245 John Butcher .15 .05
❑ 246 Brett Butler .25 .08
❑ 247 Ernie Camacho .15 .05
❑ 248 Tom Candiotti .15 .05
❑ 249 Joe Carter .25 .08
❑ 250 Carmen Castillo .15 .05
❑ 251 Julio Franco .25 .08
❑ 252 Mel Hall .15 .05
❑ 253 Brook Jacoby .15 .05
❑ 254 Phil Niekro .25 .08
❑ 255 Otis Nixon .15 .05
❑ 256 Dickie Noles .15 .05
❑ 257 Bryan Oelkers .15 .05
❑ 258 Ken Schrom .15 .05
❑ 259 Don Schulze .15 .05
❑ 260 Cory Snyder .15 .05
❑ 261 Pat Tabler .15 .05
❑ 262 Andre Thornton .15 .05
❑ 263 Rich Yett .15 .05
❑ 264 Mike Aldrete .15 .05
❑ 265 Juan Berenguer .15 .05
❑ 266 Vida Blue .25 .08
❑ 267 Bob Brenly .15 .05
❑ 268 Chris Brown .15 .05
❑ 269 Will Clark RC 3.00 1.25
❑ 270 Chili Davis .25 .08
❑ 271 Mark Davis .15 .05
❑ 272 Kelly Downs RC .25 .08
❑ 273 Scott Garrelts .15 .05
❑ 274 Dan Gladden .15 .05
❑ 275 Mike Krukow .15 .05
❑ 276 Randy Kutcher .15 .05
❑ 277 Mike LaCoss .15 .05
❑ 278 Jeff Leonard .15 .05
❑ 279 Candy Maldonado .15 .05
❑ 280 Roger Mason .15 .05
❑ 281 Bob Melvin .15 .05
❑ 282 Greg Minton .15 .05
❑ 283 Jeff D. Robinson .15 .05
❑ 284 Harry Spilman .15 .05
❑ 285 Robby Thompson RC * .50 .20
❑ 286 Jose Uribe .15 .05
❑ 287 Frank Williams .15 .05
❑ 288 Joel Youngblood .15 .05
❑ 289 Jack Clark .25 .08
❑ 290 Vince Coleman .15 .05
❑ 291 Tim Conroy .15 .05
❑ 292 Danny Cox .15 .05
❑ 293 Ken Dayley .15 .05
❑ 294 Curt Ford .15 .05
❑ 295 Bob Forsch .15 .05
❑ 296 Tom Herr .15 .05
❑ 297 Ricky Horton .15 .05
❑ 298 Clint Hurdle .15 .05
❑ 299 Jeff Lahti .15 .05
❑ 300 Steve Lake .15 .05
❑ 301 Tito Landrum .15 .05
❑ 302 Mike LaValliere RC * .50 .20
❑ 303 Greg Mathews .15 .05
❑ 304 Willie McGee .25 .08
❑ 305 Jose Oquendo .15 .05
❑ 306 Terry Pendleton .25 .08
❑ 307 Pat Perry .15 .05
❑ 308 Ozzie Smith 1.00 .40
❑ 309 Ray Soff .15 .05
❑ 310 John Tudor .25 .08
❑ 311 Andy Van Slyke UER .40 .15
❑ 312 Todd Worrell .15 .05
❑ 313 Dann Bilardello .15 .05
❑ 314 Hubie Brooks .15 .05
❑ 315 Tim Burke .15 .05
❑ 316 Andre Dawson .25 .08
❑ 317 Mike Fitzgerald .15 .05
❑ 318 Tom Foley .15 .05
❑ 319 Andres Galarraga .25 .08
❑ 320 Joe Hesketh .15 .05
❑ 321 Wallace Johnson .15 .05
❑ 322 Wayne Krenchicki .15 .05
❑ 323 Vance Law .15 .05
❑ 324 Dennis Martinez .25 .08
❑ 325 Bob McClure .15 .05
❑ 326 Andy McGaffigan .15 .05
❑ 327 Al Newman RC .15 .05
❑ 328 Tim Raines .25 .08
❑ 329 Jeff Reardon .25 .08
❑ 330 Luis Rivera RC .25 .08
❑ 331 Bob Sebra .15 .05
❑ 332 Bryn Smith .15 .05
❑ 333 Jay Tibbs .15 .05
❑ 334 Tim Wallach .15 .05
❑ 335 Mitch Webster .15 .05
❑ 336 Jim Wohlford .15 .05
❑ 337 Floyd Youmans .15 .05
❑ 338 Chris Bosio RC .50 .20
❑ 339 Glenn Braggs RC .25 .08
❑ 340 Rick Cerone .15 .05
❑ 341 Mark Clear .15 .05
❑ 342 Bryan Clutterbuck .15 .05
❑ 343 Cecil Cooper .25 .08
❑ 344 Rob Deer .15 .05
❑ 345 Jim Gantner .15 .05
❑ 346 Ted Higuera .15 .05
❑ 347 John Henry Johnson .15 .05
❑ 348 Tim Leary .15 .05
❑ 349 Rick Manning .15 .05
❑ 350 Paul Molitor .25 .08
❑ 351 Charlie Moore .15 .05
❑ 352 Juan Nieves .15 .05
❑ 353 Ben Oglivie .25 .08
❑ 354 Dan Plesac .15 .05
❑ 355 Ernest Riles .15 .05
❑ 356 Billy Joe Robidoux .15 .05
❑ 357 Bill Schroeder .15 .05
❑ 358 Dale Sveum .15 .05
❑ 359 Gorman Thomas .25 .08
❑ 360 Bill Wegman .15 .05
❑ 361 Robin Yount 1.00 .40
❑ 362 Steve Balboni .15 .05
❑ 363 Scott Bankhead .15 .05
❑ 364 Buddy Biancalana .15 .05
❑ 365 Bud Black .15 .05
❑ 366 George Brett 1.50 .60
❑ 367 Steve Farr .15 .05
❑ 368 Mark Gubicza .15 .05
❑ 369 Bo Jackson RC 8.00 3.00
❑ 370 Danny Jackson .15 .05
❑ 371 Mike Kingery RC .25 .08
❑ 372 Rudy Law .15 .05
❑ 373 Charlie Leibrandt .15 .05
❑ 374 Dennis Leonard .15 .05
❑ 375 Hal McRae .25 .08
❑ 376 Jorge Orta .15 .05
❑ 377 Jamie Quirk .15 .05
❑ 378 Dan Quisenberry .15 .05
❑ 379 Bret Saberhagen .25 .08
❑ 380 Angel Salazar .15 .05
❑ 381 Lonnie Smith .15 .05
❑ 382 Jim Sundberg .25 .08
❑ 383 Frank White .25 .08
❑ 384 Willie Wilson .25 .08
❑ 385 Joaquin Andujar .25 .08
❑ 386 Doug Bair .15 .05
❑ 387 Dusty Baker .25 .08
❑ 388 Bruce Bochte .15 .05
❑ 389 Jose Canseco 1.50 .60
❑ 390 Chris Codiroli .15 .05
❑ 391 Mike Davis .15 .05
❑ 392 Alfredo Griffin .15 .05
❑ 393 Moose Haas .15 .05
❑ 394 Donnie Hill .15 .05
❑ 395 Jay Howell .15 .05
❑ 396 Dave Kingman .25 .08
❑ 397 Carney Lansford .25 .08
❑ 398 Dave Leiper .15 .05
❑ 399 Bill Mooneyham .15 .05
❑ 400 Dwayne Murphy .15 .05
❑ 401 Steve Ontiveros .15 .05
❑ 402 Tony Phillips .15 .05
❑ 403 Eric Plunk .15 .05
❑ 404 Jose Rijo .25 .08
❑ 405 Terry Steinbach RC 1.25 .50
❑ 406 Dave Stewart .25 .08
❑ 407 Mickey Tettleton .15 .05
❑ 408 Dave Von Ohlen .15 .05
❑ 409 Jerry Willard .15 .05
❑ 410 Curt Young .15 .05
❑ 411 Bruce Bochy .15 .05
❑ 412 Dave Dravecky .15 .05
❑ 413 Tim Flannery .15 .05
❑ 414 Steve Garvey .25 .08
❑ 415 Rich Gossage .25 .08
❑ 416 Tony Gwynn 1.00 .40
❑ 417 Andy Hawkins .15 .05
❑ 418 LaMarr Hoyt .15 .05
❑ 419 Terry Kennedy .15 .05
❑ 420 John Kruk RC 2.00 .75
❑ 421 Dave LaPoint .15 .05
❑ 422 Craig Lefferts .15 .05
❑ 423 Carmelo Martinez .15 .05
❑ 424 Lance McCullers .15 .05
❑ 425 Kevin McReynolds .15 .05
❑ 426 Graig Nettles .25 .08
❑ 427 Bip Roberts RC .50 .20
❑ 428 Jerry Royster .15 .05
❑ 429 Benito Santiago .25 .08
❑ 430 Eric Show .15 .05
❑ 431 Bob Stoddard .15 .05
❑ 432 Garry Templeton .25 .08
❑ 433 Gene Walter .15 .05
❑ 434 Ed Whitson .15 .05
❑ 435 Marvell Wynne .15 .05
❑ 436 Dave Anderson .15 .05
❑ 437 Greg Brock .15 .05
❑ 438 Enos Cabell .15 .05
❑ 439 Mariano Duncan .15 .05
❑ 440 Pedro Guerrero .25 .08
❑ 441 Orel Hershiser .40 .15
❑ 442 Rick Honeycutt .15 .05
❑ 443 Ken Howell .15 .05
❑ 444 Ken Landreaux .15 .05
❑ 445 Bill Madlock .25 .08
❑ 446 Mike Marshall .15 .05
❑ 447 Len Matuszek .15 .05
❑ 448 Tom Niedenfuer .15 .05
❑ 449 Alejandro Pena .15 .05
❑ 450 Dennis Powell .15 .05
❑ 451 Jerry Reuss .15 .05
❑ 452 Bill Russell .25 .08
❑ 453 Steve Sax .15 .05
❑ 454 Mike Scioscia .25 .08
❑ 455 Franklin Stubbs .15 .05
❑ 456 Alex Trevino .15 .05
❑ 457 Fernando Valenzuela .25 .08
❑ 458 Ed VandeBerg .15 .05
❑ 459 Bob Welch .25 .08
❑ 460 Reggie Williams .15 .05
❑ 461 Don Aase .15 .05
❑ 462 Juan Beniquez .15 .05
❑ 463 Mike Boddicker .15 .05
❑ 464 Juan Bonilla .15 .05
❑ 465 Rich Bordi .15 .05
❑ 466 Storm Davis .15 .05
❑ 467 Rick Dempsey .15 .05
❑ 468 Ken Dixon .15 .05
❑ 469 Jim Dwyer .15 .05
❑ 470 Mike Flanagan .15 .05
❑ 471 Jackie Gutierrez .15 .05
❑ 472 Brad Havens .15 .05
❑ 473 Lee Lacy .15 .05
❑ 474 Fred Lynn .25 .08
❑ 475 Scott McGregor .15 .05
❑ 476 Eddie Murray .60 .25
❑ 477 Tom O'Malley .15 .05
❑ 478 Cal Ripken 2.50 1.00
❑ 479 Larry Sheets .15 .05
❑ 480 John Shelby .15 .05

❑ 481 Nate Snell .15 .05
❑ 482 Jim Traber .15 .05
❑ 483 Mike Young .15 .05
❑ 484 Neil Allen .15 .05
❑ 485 Harold Baines .25 .08
❑ 486 Floyd Bannister .15 .05
❑ 487 Daryl Boston .15 .05
❑ 488 Ivan Calderon .15 .05
❑ 489 John Cangelosi .15 .05
❑ 490 Steve Carlton .25 .08
❑ 491 Joe Cowley .15 .05
❑ 492 Julio Cruz .15 .05
❑ 493 Bill Dawley .15 .05
❑ 494 Jose DeLeon .15 .05
❑ 495 Richard Dotson .15 .05
❑ 496 Carlton Fisk .40 .15
❑ 497 Ozzie Guillen .40 .15
❑ 498 Jerry Hairston .15 .05
❑ 499 Ron Hassey .15 .05
❑ 500 Tim Hulett .15 .05
❑ 501 Bob James .15 .05
❑ 502 Steve Lyons .15 .05
❑ 503 Joel McKeon .15 .05
❑ 504 Gene Nelson .15 .05
❑ 505 Dave Schmidt .15 .05
❑ 506 Ray Searage .15 .05
❑ 507 Bobby Thigpen RC .50 .20
❑ 508 Greg Walker .15 .05
❑ 509 Jim Acker .15 .05
❑ 510 Doyle Alexander .15 .05
❑ 511 Paul Assenmacher .50 .20
❑ 512 Bruce Benedict .15 .05
❑ 513 Chris Chambliss .25 .08
❑ 514 Jeff Dedmon .15 .05
❑ 515 Gene Garber .15 .05
❑ 516 Ken Griffey .25 .08
❑ 517 Terry Harper .15 .05
❑ 518 Bob Horner .25 .08
❑ 519 Glenn Hubbard .15 .05
❑ 520 Rick Mahler .15 .05
❑ 521 Omar Moreno .15 .05
❑ 522 Dale Murphy .40 .15
❑ 523 Ken Oberkfell .15 .05
❑ 524 Ed Olwine .15 .05
❑ 525 David Palmer .15 .05
❑ 526 Rafael Ramirez .15 .05
❑ 527 Billy Sample .15 .05
❑ 528 Ted Simmons .25 .08
❑ 529 Zane Smith .15 .05
❑ 530 Bruce Sutter .25 .08
❑ 531 Andres Thomas .15 .05
❑ 532 Ozzie Virgil .15 .05
❑ 533 Allan Anderson RC .15 .05
❑ 534 Keith Atherton .15 .05
❑ 535 Billy Beane .25 .08
❑ 536 Bert Blyleven .25 .08
❑ 537 Tom Brunansky .15 .05
❑ 538 Randy Bush .15 .05
❑ 539 George Frazier .15 .05
❑ 540 Gary Gaetti .25 .08
❑ 541 Greg Gagne .15 .05
❑ 542 Mickey Hatcher .15 .05
❑ 543 Neal Heaton .15 .05
❑ 544 Kent Hrbek .25 .08
❑ 545 Roy Lee Jackson .15 .05
❑ 546 Tim Laudner .15 .05
❑ 547 Steve Lombardozzi .15 .05
❑ 548 Mark Portugal RC * .50 .20
❑ 549 Kirby Puckett 1.00 .40
❑ 550 Jeff Reed .15 .05
❑ 551 Mark Salas .15 .05
❑ 552 Roy Smalley .15 .05
❑ 553 Mike Smithson .15 .05
❑ 554 Frank Viola .25 .08
❑ 555 Thad Bosley .15 .05
❑ 556 Ron Cey .25 .08
❑ 557 Jody Davis .15 .05
❑ 558 Ron Davis .15 .05
❑ 559 Bob Dernier .15 .05
❑ 560 Frank DiPino .15 .05
❑ 561 Shawon Dunston UER
(Wrong birth year
listed on c .15 .05
❑ 562 Leon Durham .15 .05
❑ 563 Dennis Eckersley .40 .15
❑ 564 Terry Francona .25 .08
❑ 565 Dave Gumpert .15 .05
❑ 566 Guy Hoffman .15 .05
❑ 567 Ed Lynch .15 .05
❑ 568 Gary Matthews .25 .08
❑ 569 Keith Moreland .15 .05
❑ 570 Jamie Moyer RC 2.00 .75
❑ 571 Jerry Mumphrey .15 .05
❑ 572 Ryne Sandberg 1.25 .50
❑ 573 Scott Sanderson .15 .05
❑ 574 Lee Smith .25 .08
❑ 575 Chris Speier .15 .05
❑ 576 Rick Sutcliffe .25 .08
❑ 577 Manny Trillo .15 .05
❑ 578 Steve Trout .15 .05
❑ 579 Karl Best .15 .05
❑ 580 Scott Bradley .15 .05
❑ 581 Phil Bradley .15 .05
❑ 582 Mickey Brantley .15 .05
❑ 583 Mike G. Brown P .15 .05
❑ 584 Alvin Davis .15 .05
❑ 585 Lee Guetterman .15 .05
❑ 586 Mark Huismann .15 .05
❑ 587 Bob Kearney .15 .05
❑ 588 Pete Ladd .15 .05
❑ 589 Mark Langston .15 .05
❑ 590 Mike Moore .15 .05
❑ 591 Mike Morgan .15 .05
❑ 592 John Moses .15 .05
❑ 593 Ken Phelps .15 .05
❑ 594 Jim Presley .15 .05
❑ 595 Rey Quinones UER
(Quinonez on front) .15 .05
❑ 596 Harold Reynolds .25 .08
❑ 597 Bill Swift .15 .05
❑ 598 Danny Tartabull .15 .05
❑ 599 Steve Yeager .25 .08
❑ 600 Matt Young .15 .05
❑ 601 Bill Almon .15 .05
❑ 602 Rafael Belliard RC .50 .20
❑ 603 Mike Bielecki .15 .05
❑ 604 Barry Bonds RC 15.00 6.00
❑ 605 Bobby Bonilla RC 1.25 .50
❑ 606 Sid Bream .15 .05
❑ 607 Mike C. Brown .15 .05
❑ 608 Pat Clements .15 .05
❑ 609 Mike Diaz .15 .05
❑ 610 Cecilio Guante .15 .05
❑ 611 Barry Jones .15 .05
❑ 612 Bob Kipper .15 .05
❑ 613 Larry McWilliams .15 .05
❑ 614 Jim Morrison .15 .05
❑ 615 Joe Orsulak .15 .05
❑ 616 Junior Ortiz .15 .05
❑ 617 Tony Pena .15 .05
❑ 618 Johnny Ray .15 .05
❑ 619 Rick Reuschel .25 .08
❑ 620 R.J. Reynolds .15 .05
❑ 621 Rick Rhoden .15 .05
❑ 622 Don Robinson .15 .05
❑ 623 Bob Walk .15 .05
❑ 624 Jim Winn .15 .05
❑ 625 J.Canseco/P.Incaviglia .75 .30
❑ 626 300 Game Winners
Don Sutton
Phil Niekro .25 .08
❑ 627 AL Firemen
Dave Righetti
Don Aase .15 .05
❑ 628 J.Canseco/W.Joyner .75 .30
❑ 629 Magic Mets .40 .15
❑ 630 NL Best Righties
Mike Scott
Mike Krukow .15 .05
❑ 631 Sensational Southpaws
Fernando Valenzuela
John F .15 .05
❑ 632 Count'Em
Bob Horner .15 .05
❑ 633 J.Canseco/Rice/Puckett .75 .30
❑ 634 R.Clemens/G.Carter .60 .25
❑ 635 Steve Carlton 4000 .25 .08
❑ 636 Eddie Murray/G.Davis .60 .25
❑ 637 W.Boggs/K.Hernandez .25 .08
❑ 638 D.Mattingly/Strawberry 1.00 .40
❑ 639 R.Sandberg/D.Parker .60 .25
❑ 640 R.Clemens/D.Gooden .60 .25
❑ 641 AL West Stoppers
Mike Witt
Charlie Hough .15 .05
❑ 642 Doubles and Triples
Juan Samuel
Tim Raines .25 .08
❑ 643 Outfielders with Punch
Harold Baines
Jesse Barfi .25 .08
❑ 644 G.Swindell/D.Clark RC .50 .20
❑ 645 R.Karkovice/R.Morman RC .50 .20
❑ 646 D.White/W.Fraser RC 1.25 .50
❑ 647 M.Stanley/J.Browne RC .50 .20
❑ 648 D.Magadan/P.Lombardi RC .50 .20
❑ 649 J.Gonzalez/R.Bryant RC .25 .08
❑ 650 J.Jones/R.Asadoor RC .25 .08
❑ 651 T.Jones/M.Freeman RC .25 .08
❑ 652 K.Seitzer/J.Stefero RC .50 .20
❑ 653 R.Nelson/S.Fireovid RC .25 .08
❑ 654 CL: Mets/Red Sox
Astros/Angels .15 .05
❑ 655 CL: Yankees/Rangers
Tigers/Phillies .15 .05
❑ 656 CL: Reds/Blue Jays
Indians/Giants
ERR (230/231 w .15 .05
❑ 657 CL: Cardinals/Expos
Brewers/Royals .15 .05
❑ 658 CL: A's/Padres
Dodgers/Orioles .15 .05
❑ 659 CL: White Sox/Braves
Twins/Cubs .15 .05
❑ 660 CL: Mariners/Pirates
Special Cards
ER (580/581 w .15 .05

1988 Fleer

❑ COMPLETE SET (660) 15.00 6.00
❑ COMP.RETAIL SET (660) 15.00 6.00
❑ COMP.HOBBY SET (672) 15.00 6.00
❑ 1 Keith Atherton .10 .02
❑ 2 Don Baylor .15 .05
❑ 3 Juan Berenguer .10 .02
❑ 4 Bert Blyleven .15 .05
❑ 5 Tom Brunansky .10 .02
❑ 6 Randy Bush .10 .02
❑ 7 Steve Carlton .15 .05
❑ 8 Mark Davidson .10 .02
❑ 9 George Frazier .10 .02
❑ 10 Gary Gaetti .15 .05
❑ 11 Greg Gagne .10 .02
❑ 12 Dan Gladden .10 .02
❑ 13 Kent Hrbek .15 .05
❑ 14 Gene Larkin RC* .40 .15
❑ 15 Tim Laudner .10 .02
❑ 16 Steve Lombardozzi .10 .02
❑ 17 Al Newman .10 .02
❑ 18 Joe Niekro .10 .02
❑ 19 Kirby Puckett .30 .10
❑ 20 Jeff Reardon .15 .05
❑ 21A Dan Schatzeder ERR
(Misspelled Schatzader
on car .15 .05
❑ 21B Dan Schatzeder COR .10 .02
❑ 22 Roy Smalley .10 .02
❑ 23 Mike Smithson .10 .02
❑ 24 Les Straker .10 .02
❑ 25 Frank Viola .15 .05

❑ 26 Jack Clark	.15	.05
❑ 27 Vince Coleman	.10	.02
❑ 28 Danny Cox	.10	.02
❑ 29 Bill Dawley	.10	.02
❑ 30 Ken Dayley	.10	.02
❑ 31 Doug DeCinces	.10	.02
❑ 32 Curt Ford	.10	.02
❑ 33 Bob Forsch	.10	.02
❑ 34 David Green	.10	.02
❑ 35 Tom Herr	.10	.02
❑ 36 Ricky Horton	.10	.02
❑ 37 Lance Johnson RC	.40	.15
❑ 38 Steve Lake	.10	.02
❑ 39 Jim Lindeman	.10	.02
❑ 40 Joe Magrane RC*	.40	.15
❑ 41 Greg Mathews	.10	.02
❑ 42 Willie McGee	.15	.05
❑ 43 John Morris	.10	.02
❑ 44 Jose Oquendo	.10	.02
❑ 45 Tony Pena	.10	.02
❑ 46 Terry Pendleton	.15	.05
❑ 47 Ozzie Smith	.50	.20
❑ 48 John Tudor	.15	.05
❑ 49 Lee Tunnell	.10	.02
❑ 50 Todd Worrell	.10	.02
❑ 51 Doyle Alexander	.10	.02
❑ 52 Dave Bergman	.10	.02
❑ 53 Tom Brookens	.10	.02
❑ 54 Darrell Evans	.15	.05
❑ 55 Kirk Gibson	.30	.10
❑ 56 Mike Heath	.10	.02
❑ 57 Mike Henneman RC*	.40	.15
❑ 58 Willie Hernandez	.10	.02
❑ 59 Larry Herndon	.10	.02
❑ 60 Eric King	.10	.02
❑ 61 Chet Lemon	.15	.05
❑ 62 Scott Lusader	.10	.02
❑ 63 Bill Madlock	.15	.05
❑ 64 Jack Morris	.15	.05
❑ 65 Jim Morrison	.10	.02
❑ 66 Matt Nokes RC*	.40	.15
❑ 67 Dan Petry	.10	.02
❑ 68A Jeff M. Robinson ERR		
(Stats for Jeff D.		
Robinson	.20	.07
❑ 68B Jeff M. Robinson COR		
(Born 12-14-61)	.10	.02
❑ 69 Pat Sheridan	.10	.02
❑ 70 Nate Snell	.10	.02
❑ 71 Frank Tanana	.15	.05
❑ 72 Walt Terrell	.10	.02
❑ 73 Mark Thurmond	.10	.02
❑ 74 Alan Trammell	.15	.05
❑ 75 Lou Whitaker	.15	.05
❑ 76 Mike Aldrete	.10	.02
❑ 77 Bob Brenly	.10	.02
❑ 78 Will Clark	.30	.10
❑ 79 Chili Davis	.15	.05
❑ 80 Kelly Downs	.10	.02
❑ 81 Dave Dravecky	.10	.02
❑ 82 Scott Garrelts	.10	.02
❑ 83 Atlee Hammaker	.10	.02
❑ 84 Dave Henderson	.10	.02
❑ 85 Mike Krukow	.10	.02
❑ 86 Mike LaCoss	.10	.02
❑ 87 Craig Lefferts	.10	.02
❑ 88 Jeff Leonard	.10	.02
❑ 89 Candy Maldonado	.10	.02
❑ 90 Eddie Milner	.10	.02
❑ 91 Bob Melvin	.10	.02
❑ 92 Kevin Mitchell	.15	.05
❑ 93 Jon Perlman	.10	.02
❑ 94 Rick Reuschel	.15	.05
❑ 95 Don Robinson	.10	.02
❑ 96 Chris Speier	.10	.02
❑ 97 Harry Spilman	.10	.02
❑ 98 Robby Thompson	.10	.02
❑ 99 Jose Uribe	.10	.02
❑ 100 Mark Wasinger	.10	.02
❑ 101 Matt Williams RC	1.50	.60
❑ 102 Jesse Barfield	.15	.05
❑ 103 George Bell	.15	.05
❑ 104 Juan Beniquez	.10	.02
❑ 105 John Cerutti	.10	.02
❑ 106 Jim Clancy	.10	.02
❑ 107 Rob Ducey	.10	.02
❑ 108 Mark Eichhorn	.10	.02
❑ 109 Tony Fernandez	.10	.02
❑ 110 Cecil Fielder	.15	.05
❑ 111 Kelly Gruber	.10	.02
❑ 112 Tom Henke	.10	.02
❑ 113A Garth Iorg ERR		
(Misspelled lorq		
on card front)	.20	.07
❑ 113B Garth Iorg COR	.10	.02
❑ 114 Jimmy Key	.15	.05
❑ 115 Rick Leach	.10	.02
❑ 116 Manny Lee	.10	.02
❑ 117 Nelson Liriano	.10	.02
❑ 118 Fred McGriff	.30	.10
❑ 119 Lloyd Moseby	.10	.02
❑ 120 Rance Mulliniks	.10	.02
❑ 121 Jeff Musselman	.10	.02
❑ 122 Jose Nunez	.10	.02
❑ 123 Dave Stieb	.15	.05
❑ 124 Willie Upshaw	.10	.02
❑ 125 Duane Ward	.10	.02
❑ 126 Ernie Whitt	.10	.02
❑ 127 Rick Aguilera	.10	.02
❑ 128 Wally Backman	.10	.02
❑ 129 Mark Carreon RC	.15	.05
❑ 130 Gary Carter	.15	.05
❑ 131 David Cone	.15	.05
❑ 132 Ron Darling	.15	.05
❑ 133 Len Dykstra	.15	.05
❑ 134 Sid Fernandez	.10	.02
❑ 135 Dwight Gooden	.15	.05
❑ 136 Keith Hernandez	.15	.05
❑ 137 Gregg Jefferies RC	.40	.15
❑ 138 Howard Johnson	.15	.05
❑ 139 Terry Leach	.10	.02
❑ 140 Barry Lyons	.10	.02
❑ 141 Dave Magadan	.10	.02
❑ 142 Roger McDowell	.10	.02
❑ 143 Kevin McReynolds	.10	.02
❑ 144 Keith Miller RC	.40	.15
❑ 145 John Mitchell RC	.15	.05
❑ 146 Randy Myers	.15	.05
❑ 147 Bob Ojeda	.10	.02
❑ 148 Jesse Orosco	.10	.02
❑ 149 Rafael Santana	.10	.02
❑ 150 Doug Sisk	.10	.02
❑ 151 Darryl Strawberry	.15	.05
❑ 152 Tim Teufel	.10	.02
❑ 153 Gene Walter	.10	.02
❑ 154 Mookie Wilson	.15	.05
❑ 155 Jay Aldrich	.10	.02
❑ 156 Chris Bosio	.10	.02
❑ 157 Glenn Braggs	.10	.02
❑ 158 Greg Brock	.10	.02
❑ 159 Juan Castillo	.10	.02
❑ 160 Mark Clear	.10	.02
❑ 161 Cecil Cooper	.15	.05
❑ 162 Chuck Crim	.10	.02
❑ 163 Rob Deer	.10	.02
❑ 164 Mike Felder	.10	.02
❑ 165 Jim Gantner	.10	.02
❑ 166 Ted Higuera	.10	.02
❑ 167 Steve Kiefer	.10	.02
❑ 168 Rick Manning	.10	.02
❑ 169 Paul Molitor	.15	.05
❑ 170 Juan Nieves	.10	.02
❑ 171 Dan Plesac	.10	.02
❑ 172 Earnest Riles	.10	.02
❑ 173 Bill Schroeder	.10	.02
❑ 174 Steve Stanicek	.10	.02
❑ 175 B.J. Surhoff	.15	.05
❑ 176 Dale Sveum	.10	.02
❑ 177 Bill Wegman	.10	.02
❑ 178 Robin Yount	.50	.20
❑ 179 Hubie Brooks	.10	.02
❑ 180 Tim Burke	.10	.02
❑ 181 Casey Candaele	.10	.02
❑ 182 Mike Fitzgerald	.10	.02
❑ 183 Tom Foley	.10	.02
❑ 184 Andres Galarraga	.15	.05
❑ 185 Neal Heaton	.10	.02
❑ 186 Wallace Johnson	.10	.02
❑ 187 Vance Law	.10	.02
❑ 188 Dennis Martinez	.15	.05
❑ 189 Bob McClure	.10	.02
❑ 190 Andy McGaffigan	.10	.02
❑ 191 Reid Nichols	.10	.02
❑ 192 Pascual Perez	.10	.02
❑ 193 Tim Raines	.15	.05
❑ 194 Jeff Reed	.10	.02
❑ 195 Bob Sebra	.10	.02
❑ 196 Bryn Smith	.10	.02
❑ 197 Randy St.Claire	.10	.02
❑ 198 Tim Wallach	.10	.02
❑ 199 Mitch Webster	.10	.02
❑ 200 Herm Winningham	.10	.02
❑ 201 Floyd Youmans	.10	.02
❑ 202 Brad Arnsberg	.10	.02
❑ 203 Rick Cerone	.10	.02
❑ 204 Pat Clements	.10	.02
❑ 205 Henry Cotto	.10	.02
❑ 206 Mike Easler	.10	.02
❑ 207 Ron Guidry	.15	.05
❑ 208 Bill Gullickson	.10	.02
❑ 209 Rickey Henderson	.30	.10
❑ 210 Charles Hudson	.10	.02
❑ 211 Tommy John	.15	.05
❑ 212 Roberto Kelly RC	.40	.15
❑ 213 Ron Kittle	.10	.02
❑ 214 Don Mattingly	1.00	.40
❑ 215 Bobby Meacham	.10	.02
❑ 216 Mike Pagliarulo	.10	.02
❑ 217 Dan Pasqua	.10	.02
❑ 218 Willie Randolph	.15	.05
❑ 219 Rick Rhoden	.10	.02
❑ 220 Dave Righetti	.15	.05
❑ 221 Jerry Royster	.10	.02
❑ 222 Tim Stoddard	.10	.02
❑ 223 Wayne Tolleson	.10	.02
❑ 224 Gary Ward	.10	.02
❑ 225 Claudell Washington	.10	.02
❑ 226 Dave Winfield	.15	.05
❑ 227 Buddy Bell	.15	.05
❑ 228 Tom Browning	.10	.02
❑ 229 Dave Concepcion	.15	.05
❑ 230 Kal Daniels	.10	.02
❑ 231 Eric Davis	.15	.05
❑ 232 Bo Diaz	.10	.02
❑ 233 Nick Esasky		
(Has a dollar sign		
before '87 SB tot	.10	.02
❑ 234 John Franco	.15	.05
❑ 235 Guy Hoffman	.10	.02
❑ 236 Tom Hume	.10	.02
❑ 237 Tracy Jones	.10	.02
❑ 238 Bill Landrum	.10	.02
❑ 239 Barry Larkin	.20	.07
❑ 240 Terry McGriff	.10	.02
❑ 241 Rob Murphy	.10	.02
❑ 242 Ron Oester	.10	.02
❑ 243 Dave Parker	.15	.05
❑ 244 Pat Perry	.10	.02
❑ 245 Ted Power	.10	.02
❑ 246 Dennis Rasmussen	.10	.02
❑ 247 Ron Robinson	.10	.02
❑ 248 Kurt Stillwell	.10	.02
❑ 249 Jeff Treadway RC	.40	.15
❑ 250 Frank Williams	.10	.02
❑ 251 Steve Balboni	.10	.02
❑ 252 Bud Black	.10	.02
❑ 253 Thad Bosley	.10	.02
❑ 254 George Brett	.75	.30
❑ 255 John Davis	.10	.02
❑ 256 Steve Farr	.10	.02
❑ 257 Gene Garber	.10	.02
❑ 258 Jerry Don Gleaton	.10	.02
❑ 259 Mark Gubicza	.10	.02
❑ 260 Bo Jackson	.30	.10
❑ 261 Danny Jackson	.10	.02
❑ 262 Ross Jones	.10	.02
❑ 263 Charlie Leibrandt	.10	.02
❑ 264 Bill Pecota RC*	.15	.05
❑ 265 Melido Perez RC	.40	.15
❑ 266 Jamie Quirk	.10	.02
❑ 267 Dan Quisenberry	.10	.02
❑ 268 Bret Saberhagen	.15	.05
❑ 269 Angel Salazar	.10	.02
❑ 270 Kevin Seitzer UER		
(Wrong birth year)	.15	.05
❑ 271 Danny Tartabull	.10	.02
❑ 272 Gary Thurman	.10	.02
❑ 273 Frank White	.15	.05

274	Willie Wilson	.15	.05
275	Tony Bernazard	.10	.02
276	Jose Canseco	.75	.30
277	Mike Davis	.10	.02
278	Storm Davis	.10	.02
279	Dennis Eckersley	.20	.07
280	Alfredo Griffin	.10	.02
281	Rick Honeycutt	.10	.02
282	Jay Howell	.10	.02
283	Reggie Jackson	.20	.07
284	Dennis Lamp	.10	.02
285	Carney Lansford	.15	.05
286	Mark McGwire	2.50	1.00
287	Dwayne Murphy	.10	.02
288	Gene Nelson	.10	.02
289	Steve Ontiveros	.10	.02
290	Tony Phillips	.10	.02
291	Eric Plunk	.10	.02
292	Luis Polonia RC*	.40	.15
293	Rick Rodriguez	.10	.02
294	Terry Steinbach	.15	.05
295	Dave Stewart	.15	.05
296	Curt Young	.10	.02
297	Luis Aguayo	.10	.02
298	Steve Bedrosian	.10	.02
299	Jeff Calhoun	.10	.02
300	Don Carman	.10	.02
301	Todd Frohwirth	.10	.02
302	Greg Gross	.10	.02
303	Kevin Gross	.10	.02
304	Von Hayes	.10	.02
305	Keith Hughes	.10	.02
306	Mike Jackson RC*	.40	.15
307	Chris James	.10	.02
308	Steve Jeltz	.10	.02
309	Mike Maddux	.10	.02
310	Lance Parrish	.15	.05
311	Shane Rawley	.10	.02
312	Wally Ritchie	.10	.02
313	Bruce Ruffin	.10	.02
314	Juan Samuel	.10	.02
315	Mike Schmidt	.75	.30
316	Rick Schu	.10	.02
317	Jeff Stone	.10	.02
318	Kent Tekulve	.10	.02
319	Milt Thompson	.10	.02
320	Glenn Wilson	.10	.02
321	Rafael Belliard	.10	.02
322	Barry Bonds	2.50	1.00
323	Bobby Bonilla	.15	.05
324	Sid Bream	.10	.02
325	John Cangelosi	.10	.02
326	Mike Diaz	.10	.02
327	Doug Drabek	.10	.02
328	Mike Dunne	.10	.02
329	Brian Fisher	.10	.02
330	Brett Gideon	.10	.02
331	Terry Harper	.10	.02
332	Bob Kipper	.10	.02
333	Mike LaValliere	.10	.02
334	Jose Lind RC	.40	.15
335	Junior Ortiz	.10	.02
336	Vicente Palacios	.10	.02
337	Bob Patterson	.10	.02
338	Al Pedrique	.10	.02
339	R.J. Reynolds	.10	.02
340	John Smiley RC*	.40	.15
341	Andy Van Slyke UER (Wrong batting and throwing l	.20	.07
342	Bob Walk	.10	.02
343	Marty Barrett	.10	.02
344	Todd Benzinger RC*	.40	.15
345	Wade Boggs	.20	.07
346	Tom Bolton	.10	.02
347	Oil Can Boyd	.10	.02
348	Ellis Burks RC	.50	.20
349	Roger Clemens	1.50	.60
350	Steve Crawford	.10	.02
351	Dwight Evans	.20	.07
352	Wes Gardner	.10	.02
353	Rich Gedman	.10	.02
354	Mike Greenwell	.10	.02
355	Sam Horn RC	.15	.05
356	Bruce Hurst	.10	.02
357	John Marzano	.10	.02
358	Al Nipper	.10	.02
359	Spike Owen	.10	.02
360	Jody Reed RC	.40	.15
361	Jim Rice	.15	.05
362	Ed Romero	.10	.02
363	Kevin Romine	.10	.02
364	Joe Sambito	.10	.02
365	Calvin Schiraldi	.10	.02
366	Jeff Sellers	.10	.02
367	Bob Stanley	.10	.02
368	Scott Bankhead	.10	.02
369	Phil Bradley	.10	.02
370	Scott Bradley	.10	.02
371	Mickey Brantley	.10	.02
372	Mike Campbell	.10	.02
373	Alvin Davis	.10	.02
374	Lee Guetterman	.10	.02
375	Dave Hengel	.10	.02
376	Mike Kingery	.10	.02
377	Mark Langston	.10	.02
378	Edgar Martinez RC	5.00	2.00
379	Mike Moore	.10	.02
380	Mike Morgan	.10	.02
381	John Moses	.10	.02
382	Donell Nixon	.10	.02
383	Edwin Nunez	.10	.02
384	Ken Phelps	.10	.02
385	Jim Presley	.10	.02
386	Rey Quinones	.10	.02
387	Jerry Reed	.10	.02
388	Harold Reynolds	.15	.05
389	Dave Valle	.10	.02
390	Bill Wilkinson	.10	.02
391	Harold Baines	.15	.05
392	Floyd Bannister	.10	.02
393	Daryl Boston	.10	.02
394	Ivan Calderon	.10	.02
395	Jose DeLeon	.10	.02
396	Richard Dotson	.10	.02
397	Carlton Fisk	.20	.07
398	Ozzie Guillen	.15	.05
399	Ron Hassey	.10	.02
400	Donnie Hill	.10	.02
401	Bob James	.10	.02
402	Dave LaPoint	.10	.02
403	Bill Lindsey	.10	.02
404	Bill Long	.10	.02
405	Steve Lyons	.10	.02
406	Fred Manrique	.10	.02
407	Jack McDowell RC	.50	.20
408	Gary Redus	.10	.02
409	Ray Searage	.10	.02
410	Bobby Thigpen	.10	.02
411	Greg Walker	.10	.02
412	Ken Williams	.10	.02
413	Jim Winn	.10	.02
414	Jody Davis	.10	.02
415	Andre Dawson	.15	.05
416	Brian Dayett	.10	.02
417	Bob Dernier	.10	.02
418	Frank DiPino	.10	.02
419	Shawon Dunston	.10	.02
420	Leon Durham	.10	.02
421	Les Lancaster	.10	.02
422	Ed Lynch	.10	.02
423	Greg Maddux	1.50	.60
424	Dave Martinez	.10	.02
425A	Keith Moreland ERR	1.50	.60
425B	Keith Moreland COR (Bat on shoulder)	.15	.05
426	Jamie Moyer	.15	.05
427	Jerry Mumphrey	.10	.02
428	Paul Noce	.10	.02
429	Rafael Palmeiro	.60	.25
430	Wade Rowdon	.10	.02
431	Ryne Sandberg	.60	.25
432	Scott Sanderson	.10	.02
433	Lee Smith	.15	.05
434	Jim Sundberg	.15	.05
435	Rick Sutcliffe	.15	.05
436	Manny Trillo	.10	.02
437	Juan Agosto	.10	.02
438	Larry Andersen	.10	.02
439	Alan Ashby	.10	.02
440	Kevin Bass	.10	.02
441	Ken Caminiti RC	3.00	1.25
442	Rocky Childress	.10	.02
443	Jose Cruz	.15	.05
444	Danny Darwin	.10	.02
445	Glenn Davis	.10	.02
446	Jim Deshaies	.10	.02
447	Bill Doran	.10	.02
448	Ty Gainey	.10	.02
449	Billy Hatcher	.10	.02
450	Jeff Heathcock	.10	.02
451	Bob Knepper	.10	.02
452	Rob Mallicoat	.10	.02
453	Dave Meads	.10	.02
454	Craig Reynolds	.10	.02
455	Nolan Ryan	1.50	.60
456	Mike Scott	.15	.05
457	Dave Smith	.10	.02
458	Denny Walling	.10	.02
459	Robbie Wine	.10	.02
460	Gerald Young	.10	.02
461	Bob Brower	.10	.02
462A	Jerry Browne ERR	1.50	.60
462B	Jerry Browne COR (Black player)	.15	.05
463	Steve Buechele	.10	.02
464	Edwin Correa	.10	.02
465	Cecil Espy RC	.10	.02
466	Scott Fletcher	.10	.02
467	Jose Guzman	.10	.02
468	Greg Harris	.10	.02
469	Charlie Hough	.15	.05
470	Pete Incaviglia	.10	.02
471	Paul Kilgus	.10	.02
472	Mike Loynd	.10	.02
473	Oddibe McDowell	.10	.02
474	Dale Mohorcic	.10	.02
475	Pete O'Brien	.10	.02
476	Larry Parrish	.10	.02
477	Geno Petralli	.10	.02
478	Jeff Russell	.10	.02
479	Ruben Sierra	.15	.05
480	Mike Stanley	.10	.02
481	Curtis Wilkerson	.10	.02
482	Mitch Williams	.10	.02
483	Bobby Witt	.10	.02
484	Tony Armas	.15	.05
485	Bob Boone	.15	.05
486	Bill Buckner	.15	.05
487	DeWayne Buice	.10	.02
488	Brian Downing	.15	.05
489	Chuck Finley	.15	.05
490	Willie Fraser UER (Wrong bio stats& for George H	.10	.02
491	Jack Howell	.10	.02
492	Ruppert Jones	.10	.02
493	Wally Joyner	.15	.05
494	Jack Lazorko	.10	.02
495	Gary Lucas	.10	.02
496	Kirk McCaskill	.10	.02
497	Mark McLemore	.10	.02
498	Darrell Miller	.10	.02
499	Greg Minton	.10	.02
500	Donnie Moore	.10	.02
501	Gus Polidor	.10	.02
502	Johnny Ray	.10	.02
503	Mark Ryal	.10	.02
504	Dick Schofield	.10	.02
505	Don Sutton	.15	.05
506	Devon White	.15	.05
507	Mike Witt	.10	.02
508	Dave Anderson	.10	.02
509	Tim Belcher	.10	.02
510	Ralph Bryant	.10	.02
511	Tim Crews RC	.40	.15
512	Mike Devereaux RC	.40	.15
513	Mariano Duncan	.10	.02
514	Pedro Guerrero	.15	.05
515	Jeff Hamilton	.10	.02
516	Mickey Hatcher	.10	.02
517	Brad Havens	.10	.02
518	Orel Hershiser	.15	.05
519	Shawn Hillegas	.10	.02
520	Ken Howell	.10	.02
521	Tim Leary	.10	.02
522	Mike Marshall	.10	.02
523	Steve Sax	.10	.02

❑ 524 Mike Scioscia .15 .05
❑ 525 Mike Sharperson .10 .02
❑ 526 John Shelby .10 .02
❑ 527 Franklin Stubbs .10 .02
❑ 528 Fernando Valenzuela .15 .05
❑ 529 Bob Welch .15 .05
❑ 530 Matt Young .10 .02
❑ 531 Jim Acker .10 .02
❑ 532 Paul Assenmacher .10 .02
❑ 533 Jeff Blauser RC .40 .15
❑ 534 Joe Boever .10 .02
❑ 535 Martin Clary .10 .02
❑ 536 Kevin Coffman .10 .02
❑ 537 Jeff Dedmon .10 .02
❑ 538 Ron Gant RC .50 .20
❑ 539 Tom Glavine RC 4.00 1.50
❑ 540 Ken Griffey .15 .05
❑ 541 Albert Hall .10 .02
❑ 542 Glenn Hubbard .10 .02
❑ 543 Dion James .10 .02
❑ 544 Dale Murphy .20 .07
❑ 545 Ken Oberkfell .10 .02
❑ 546 David Palmer .10 .02
❑ 547 Gerald Perry .10 .02
❑ 548 Charlie Puleo .10 .02
❑ 549 Ted Simmons .15 .05
❑ 550 Zane Smith .10 .02
❑ 551 Andres Thomas .10 .02
❑ 552 Ozzie Virgil .10 .02
❑ 553 Don Aase .10 .02
❑ 554 Jeff Ballard .10 .02
❑ 555 Eric Bell .10 .02
❑ 556 Mike Boddicker .10 .02
❑ 557 Ken Dixon .10 .02
❑ 558 Jim Dwyer .10 .02
❑ 559 Ken Gerhart .10 .02
❑ 560 Rene Gonzales RC .15 .05
❑ 561 Mike Griffin .10 .02
❑ 562 John Habyan UER
(Misspelled Hayban on
both sides .10 .02
❑ 563 Terry Kennedy .10 .02
❑ 564 Ray Knight .15 .05
❑ 565 Lee Lacy .10 .02
❑ 566 Fred Lynn .15 .05
❑ 567 Eddie Murray .30 .10
❑ 568 Tom Niedenfuer .10 .02
❑ 569 Bill Ripken RC* .40 .15
❑ 570 Cal Ripken 1.25 .50
❑ 571 Dave Schmidt .10 .02
❑ 572 Larry Sheets .10 .02
❑ 573 Pete Stanicek .10 .02
❑ 574 Mark Williamson .10 .02
❑ 575 Mike Young .10 .02
❑ 576 Shawn Abner .10 .02
❑ 577 Greg Booker .10 .02
❑ 578 Chris Brown .10 .02
❑ 579 Keith Comstock .10 .02
❑ 580 Joey Cora RC .40 .15
❑ 581 Mark Davis .10 .02
❑ 582 Tim Flannery
(With surfboard) .20 .07
❑ 583 Goose Gossage .15 .05
❑ 584 Mark Grant .10 .02
❑ 585 Tony Gwynn .50 .20
❑ 586 Andy Hawkins .10 .02
❑ 587 Stan Jefferson .10 .02
❑ 588 Jimmy Jones .10 .02
❑ 589 John Kruk .15 .05
❑ 590 Shane Mack .10 .02
❑ 591 Carmelo Martinez .10 .02
❑ 592 Lance McCullers UER
(6'11 tall) .10 .02
❑ 593 Eric Nolte .10 .02
❑ 594 Randy Ready .10 .02
❑ 595 Luis Salazar .10 .02
❑ 596 Benito Santiago .15 .05
❑ 597 Eric Show .10 .02
❑ 598 Garry Templeton .15 .05
❑ 599 Ed Whitson .10 .02
❑ 600 Scott Bailes .10 .02
❑ 601 Chris Bando .10 .02
❑ 602 Jay Bell RC .50 .20
❑ 603 Brett Butler .15 .05
❑ 604 Tom Candiotti .10 .02
❑ 605 Joe Carter .15 .05
❑ 606 Carmen Castillo .10 .02
❑ 607 Brian Dorsett .10 .02
❑ 608 John Farrell RC .15 .05
❑ 609 Julio Franco .15 .05
❑ 610 Mel Hall .10 .02
❑ 611 Tommy Hinzo .10 .02
❑ 612 Brook Jacoby .10 .02
❑ 613 Doug Jones RC .40 .15
❑ 614 Ken Schrom .10 .02
❑ 615 Cory Snyder .10 .02
❑ 616 Sammy Stewart .10 .02
❑ 617 Greg Swindell .10 .02
❑ 618 Pat Tabler .10 .02
❑ 619 Ed VandeBerg .10 .02
❑ 620 Eddie Williams RC .15 .05
❑ 621 Rich Yett .10 .02
❑ 622 Slugging Sophomores
Wally Joyner
Cory Snyder .15 .05
❑ 623 Dominican Dynamite
George Bell
Pedro Guerrero .10 .02
❑ 624 M.McGwire/J.Canseco 1.50 .60
❑ 625 Classic Relief
Dave Righetti
Dan Plesac .10 .02
❑ 626 All Star Righties
Bret Saberhagen
Mike Witt
Jac .15 .05
❑ 627 Game Closers
John Franco
Steve Bedrosian .10 .02
❑ 628 O.Smith/R.Sandberg .30 .10
❑ 629 Mark McGwire HL 1.25 .50
❑ 630 Greenwell/Burks/Benz .30 .10
❑ 631 Tony Gwynn/T.Raines .20 .07
❑ 632 Pitching Magic
Mike Scott
Orel Hershiser .15 .05
❑ 633 M.McGwire/P.Tabler 1.25 .50
❑ 634 Tony Gwynn/V.Coleman .20 .07
❑ 635 C.Ripken/Trammell/Fern .50 .20
❑ 636 Mike Schmidt/G.Carter .30 .10
❑ 637 D.Strawberry/E.Davis .15 .05
❑ 638 M.Nokes/K.Puckett .20 .07
❑ 639 NL All-Stars
Keith Hernandez
Dale Murphy .15 .05
❑ 640 Ripken Brothers .75 .30
❑ 641 Mark Grace RC 3.00 1.25
❑ 642 D.Berryhill/J.Montgomery RC .40 .15
❑ 643 F.Fermin/J.Reid RC .15 .05
❑ 644 G.Myers/G.Tabor RC .40 .15
❑ 645 J.Meyer/J.Eppard RC .15 .05
❑ 646 A.Peterson RC/R.Velarde RC .40 .15
❑ 647 P.Smith/C.Gwynn RC .40 .15
❑ 648 T.Newell/G.Jelks RC .15 .05
❑ 649 M.Diaz/C.Parker RC .15 .05
❑ 650 J.Savage/T.Simmons RC .15 .05
❑ 651 John Burkett RC .40 .15
❑ 652 Walt Weiss RC .50 .20
❑ 653 Jeff King RC .40 .15
❑ 654 CL: Twins/Cards
Tigers/Giants UER
(90 Bob Melvin .10 .02
❑ 655 CL: Blue Jays/Mets
Brewers/Expos UER
(Mets liste .10 .02
❑ 656 CL: Yankees/Reds
Royals/A's .10 .02
❑ 657 CL: Phillies/Pirates
Red Sox/Mariners .10 .02
❑ 658 CL: White Sox/Cubs
Astros/Rangers .10 .02
❑ 659 CL: Angels/Dodgers
Braves/Orioles .10 .02
❑ 660 CL: Padres/Indians
Rookies/Specials .10 .02

1989 Fleer

❑ COMPLETE SET (660) 15.00 6.00
❑ COMP.FACT.SET (672) 15.00 6.00
❑ 1 Don Baylor .10 .02
❑ 2 Lance Blankenship RC .10 .02
❑ 3 Todd Burns UER .05 .01
❑ 4 Greg Cadaret UER .05 .01
❑ 5 Jose Canseco .25 .08
❑ 6 Storm Davis .05 .01
❑ 7 Dennis Eckersley .15 .05
❑ 8 Mike Gallego .05 .01
❑ 9 Ron Hassey .05 .01
❑ 10 Dave Henderson .05 .01
❑ 11 Rick Honeycutt .05 .01
❑ 12 Glenn Hubbard .05 .01
❑ 13 Stan Javier .05 .01
❑ 14 Doug Jennings .05 .01
❑ 15 Felix Jose RC .10 .02
❑ 16 Carney Lansford .10 .02
❑ 17 Mark McGwire 1.00 .40
❑ 18 Gene Nelson .05 .01
❑ 19 Dave Parker .10 .02
❑ 20 Eric Plunk .05 .01
❑ 21 Luis Polonia .05 .01
❑ 22 Terry Steinbach .10 .02
❑ 23 Dave Stewart .10 .02
❑ 24 Walt Weiss .05 .01
❑ 25 Bob Welch .10 .02
❑ 26 Curt Young .05 .01
❑ 27 Rick Aguilera .05 .01
❑ 28 Wally Backman .05 .01
❑ 29 Mark Carreon UER .05 .01
❑ 30 Gary Carter .10 .02
❑ 31 David Cone .10 .02
❑ 32 Ron Darling .10 .02
❑ 33 Len Dykstra .10 .02
❑ 34 Kevin Elster .05 .01
❑ 35 Sid Fernandez .05 .01
❑ 36 Dwight Gooden .10 .02
❑ 37 Keith Hernandez .10 .02
❑ 38 Gregg Jefferies .05 .01
❑ 39 Howard Johnson .10 .02
❑ 40 Terry Leach .05 .01
❑ 41 Dave Magadan UER .05 .01
❑ 42 Bob McClure .05 .01
❑ 43 Roger McDowell UER .05 .01
❑ 44 Kevin McReynolds .05 .01
❑ 45 Keith A. Miller .05 .01
❑ 46 Randy Myers .10 .02
❑ 47 Bob Ojeda .05 .01
❑ 48 Mackey Sasser .05 .01
❑ 49 Darryl Strawberry .10 .02
❑ 50 Tim Teufel .05 .01
❑ 51 Dave West RC .10 .02
❑ 52 Mookie Wilson .10 .02
❑ 53 Dave Anderson .05 .01
❑ 54 Tim Belcher .05 .01
❑ 55 Mike Davis .05 .01
❑ 56 Mike Devereaux .05 .01
❑ 57 Kirk Gibson .10 .02
❑ 58 Alfredo Griffin .05 .01
❑ 59 Chris Gwynn .05 .01
❑ 60 Jeff Hamilton .05 .01
❑ 61A Danny Heep ERR .25 .08
❑ 61B Danny Heep COR .05 .01
❑ 62 Orel Hershiser .10 .02
❑ 63 Brian Holton .05 .01
❑ 64 Jay Howell .05 .01
❑ 65 Tim Leary .05 .01
❑ 66 Mike Marshall .05 .01
❑ 67 Ramon Martinez RC .25 .08
❑ 68 Jesse Orosco .05 .01
❑ 69 Alejandro Pena .05 .01
❑ 70 Steve Sax .05 .01

❑ 71	Mike Scioscia	.10	.02
❑ 72	Mike Sharperson	.05	.01
❑ 73	John Shelby	.05	.01
❑ 74	Franklin Stubbs	.05	.01
❑ 75	John Tudor	.10	.02
❑ 76	Fernando Valenzuela	.10	.02
❑ 77	Tracy Woodson	.05	.01
❑ 78	Marty Barrett	.05	.01
❑ 79	Todd Benzinger	.05	.01
❑ 80	Mike Boddicker UER	.05	.01
❑ 81	Wade Boggs	.15	.05
❑ 82	Oil Can Boyd	.05	.01
❑ 83	Ellis Burks	.10	.02
❑ 84	Rick Cerone	.05	.01
❑ 85	Roger Clemens	1.00	.40
❑ 86	Steve Curry	.05	.01
❑ 87	Dwight Evans	.15	.05
❑ 88	Wes Gardner	.05	.01
❑ 89	Rich Gedman	.05	.01
❑ 90	Mike Greenwell	.05	.01
❑ 91	Bruce Hurst	.05	.01
❑ 92	Dennis Lamp	.05	.01
❑ 93	Spike Owen	.05	.01
❑ 94	Larry Parrish UER	.05	.01
❑ 95	Carlos Quintana RC	.10	.02
❑ 96	Jody Reed	.05	.01
❑ 97	Jim Rice	.10	.02
❑ 98A	Kevin Romine ERR	.25	.08
❑ 98B	Kevin Romine COR	.05	.01
❑ 99	Lee Smith	.10	.02
❑ 100	Mike Smithson	.05	.01
❑ 101	Bob Stanley	.05	.01
❑ 102	Allan Anderson	.05	.01
❑ 103	Keith Atherton	.05	.01
❑ 104	Juan Berenguer	.05	.01
❑ 105	Bert Blyleven	.10	.02
❑ 106	Eric Bullock UER	.05	.01
❑ 107	Randy Bush	.05	.01
❑ 108	John Christensen	.05	.01
❑ 109	Mark Davidson	.05	.01
❑ 110	Gary Gaetti	.10	.02
❑ 111	Greg Gagne	.05	.01
❑ 112	Dan Gladden	.05	.01
❑ 113	German Gonzalez	.05	.01
❑ 114	Brian Harper	.05	.01
❑ 115	Tom Herr	.05	.01
❑ 116	Kent Hrbek	.10	.02
❑ 117	Gene Larkin	.05	.01
❑ 118	Tim Laudner	.05	.01
❑ 119	Charlie Lea	.05	.01
❑ 120	Steve Lombardozzi	.05	.01
❑ 121A	John Moses ERR	.25	.08
❑ 121B	John Moses COR	.05	.01
❑ 122	Al Newman	.05	.01
❑ 123	Mark Portugal	.05	.01
❑ 124	Kirby Puckett	.25	.08
❑ 125	Jeff Reardon	.10	.02
❑ 126	Fred Toliver	.05	.01
❑ 127	Frank Viola	.10	.02
❑ 128	Doyle Alexander	.05	.01
❑ 129	Dave Bergman	.05	.01
❑ 130A	Tom Brookens ERR	.75	.30
❑ 130B	Tom Brookens COR	.05	.01
❑ 131	Paul Gibson	.05	.01
❑ 132A	Mike Heath ERR	.75	.30
❑ 132B	Mike Heath COR	.05	.01
❑ 133	Don Heinkel	.05	.01
❑ 134	Mike Henneman	.05	.01
❑ 135	Guillermo Hernandez	.05	.01
❑ 136	Eric King	.05	.01
❑ 137	Chet Lemon	.10	.02
❑ 138	Fred Lynn UER	.10	.02
❑ 139	Jack Morris	.10	.02
❑ 140	Matt Nokes	.05	.01
❑ 141	Gary Pettis	.05	.01
❑ 142	Ted Power	.05	.01
❑ 143	Jeff M. Robinson	.05	.01
❑ 144	Luis Salazar	.05	.01
❑ 145	Steve Searcy	.05	.01
❑ 146	Pat Sheridan	.05	.01
❑ 147	Frank Tanana	.10	.02
❑ 148	Alan Trammell	.10	.02
❑ 149	Walt Terrell	.05	.01
❑ 150	Jim Walewander	.05	.01
❑ 151	Lou Whitaker	.10	.02
❑ 152	Tim Birtsas	.05	.01
❑ 153	Tom Browning	.05	.01
❑ 154	Keith Brown	.05	.01
❑ 155	Norm Charlton RC	.25	.08
❑ 156	Dave Concepcion	.10	.02
❑ 157	Kal Daniels	.05	.01
❑ 158	Eric Davis	.10	.02
❑ 159	Bo Diaz	.05	.01
❑ 160	Rob Dibble RC	.40	.15
❑ 161	Nick Esasky	.05	.01
❑ 162	John Franco	.10	.02
❑ 163	Danny Jackson	.05	.01
❑ 164	Barry Larkin	.15	.05
❑ 165	Rob Murphy	.05	.01
❑ 166	Paul O'Neill	.15	.05
❑ 167	Jeff Reed	.05	.01
❑ 168	Jose Rijo	.10	.02
❑ 169	Ron Robinson	.05	.01
❑ 170	Chris Sabo RC	.40	.15
❑ 171	Candy Sierra	.05	.01
❑ 172	Van Snider	.05	.01
❑ 173A	J.Treadway ERR Target	25.00	10.00
❑ 173B	Jeff Treadway No Target	.05	.01
❑ 174	Frank Williams UER	.05	.01
❑ 175	Herm Winningham	.05	.01
❑ 176	Jim Adduci	.05	.01
❑ 177	Don August	.05	.01
❑ 178	Mike Birkbeck	.05	.01
❑ 179	Chris Bosio	.05	.01
❑ 180	Glenn Braggs	.05	.01
❑ 181	Greg Brock	.05	.01
❑ 182	Mark Clear	.05	.01
❑ 183	Chuck Crim	.05	.01
❑ 184	Rob Deer	.05	.01
❑ 185	Tom Filer	.05	.01
❑ 186	Jim Gantner	.05	.01
❑ 187	Darryl Hamilton RC	.25	.08
❑ 188	Ted Higuera	.05	.01
❑ 189	Odell Jones	.05	.01
❑ 190	Jeffrey Leonard	.05	.01
❑ 191	Joey Meyer	.05	.01
❑ 192	Paul Mirabella	.05	.01
❑ 193	Paul Molitor	.10	.02
❑ 194	Charlie O'Brien	.05	.01
❑ 195	Dan Plesac	.05	.01
❑ 196	Gary Sheffield RC	1.50	.60
❑ 197	B.J. Surhoff	.10	.02
❑ 198	Dale Sveum	.05	.01
❑ 199	Bill Wegman	.05	.01
❑ 200	Robin Yount	.40	.15
❑ 201	Rafael Belliard	.05	.01
❑ 202	Barry Bonds	1.50	.60
❑ 203	Bobby Bonilla	.10	.02
❑ 204	Sid Bream	.05	.01
❑ 205	Benny Distefano	.05	.01
❑ 206	Doug Drabek	.05	.01
❑ 207	Mike Dunne	.05	.01
❑ 208	Felix Fermin	.05	.01
❑ 209	Brian Fisher	.05	.01
❑ 210	Jim Gott	.05	.01
❑ 211	Bob Kipper	.05	.01
❑ 212	Dave LaPoint	.05	.01
❑ 213	Mike LaValliere	.05	.01
❑ 214	Jose Lind	.05	.01
❑ 215	Junior Ortiz	.05	.01
❑ 216	Vicente Palacios	.05	.01
❑ 217	Tom Prince	.05	.01
❑ 218	Gary Redus	.05	.01
❑ 219	R.J. Reynolds	.05	.01
❑ 220	Jeff D. Robinson	.05	.01
❑ 221	John Smiley	.05	.01
❑ 222	Andy Van Slyke	.15	.05
❑ 223	Bob Walk	.05	.01
❑ 224	Glenn Wilson	.05	.01
❑ 225	Jesse Barfield	.10	.02
❑ 226	George Bell	.10	.02
❑ 227	Pat Borders RC	.25	.08
❑ 228	John Cerutti	.05	.01
❑ 229	Jim Clancy	.05	.01
❑ 230	Mark Eichhorn	.05	.01
❑ 231	Tony Fernandez	.05	.01
❑ 232	Cecil Fielder	.10	.02
❑ 233	Mike Flanagan	.05	.01
❑ 234	Kelly Gruber	.05	.01
❑ 235	Tom Henke	.05	.01
❑ 236	Jimmy Key	.10	.02
❑ 237	Rick Leach	.05	.01
❑ 238	Manny Lee UER	.05	.01
❑ 239	Nelson Liriano	.05	.01
❑ 240	Fred McGriff	.15	.05
❑ 241	Lloyd Moseby	.05	.01
❑ 242	Rance Mulliniks	.05	.01
❑ 243	Jeff Musselman	.05	.01
❑ 244	Dave Stieb	.10	.02
❑ 245	Todd Stottlemyre	.05	.01
❑ 246	Duane Ward	.05	.01
❑ 247	David Wells	.10	.02
❑ 248	Ernie Whitt UER	.05	.01
❑ 249	Luis Aguayo	.05	.01
❑ 250A	Neil Allen ERR	.75	.30
❑ 250B	Neil Allen COR	.05	.01
❑ 251	John Candelaria	.05	.01
❑ 252	Jack Clark	.10	.02
❑ 253	Richard Dotson	.05	.01
❑ 254	Rickey Henderson	.25	.08
❑ 255	Tommy John	.10	.02
❑ 256	Roberto Kelly	.05	.01
❑ 257	Al Leiter	.25	.08
❑ 258	Don Mattingly	.60	.25
❑ 259	Dale Mohorcic	.05	.01
❑ 260	Hal Morris RC	.25	.08
❑ 261	Scott Nielsen	.05	.01
❑ 262	Mike Pagliarulo UER	.05	.01
❑ 263	Hipolito Pena	.05	.01
❑ 264	Ken Phelps	.05	.01
❑ 265	Willie Randolph	.10	.02
❑ 266	Rick Rhoden	.05	.01
❑ 267	Dave Righetti	.10	.02
❑ 268	Rafael Santana	.05	.01
❑ 269	Steve Shields	.05	.01
❑ 270	Joel Skinner	.05	.01
❑ 271	Don Slaught	.05	.01
❑ 272	Claudell Washington	.05	.01
❑ 273	Gary Ward	.05	.01
❑ 274	Dave Winfield	.10	.02
❑ 275	Luis Aquino	.05	.01
❑ 276	Floyd Bannister	.05	.01
❑ 277	George Brett	.60	.25
❑ 278	Bill Buckner	.10	.02
❑ 279	Nick Capra	.05	.01
❑ 280	Jose DeJesus	.05	.01
❑ 281	Steve Farr	.05	.01
❑ 282	Jerry Don Gleaton	.05	.01
❑ 283	Mark Gubicza	.05	.01
❑ 284	Tom Gordon RC	.50	.20
❑ 285	Bo Jackson	.25	.08
❑ 286	Charlie Leibrandt	.05	.01
❑ 287	Mike Macfarlane RC	.25	.08
❑ 288	Jeff Montgomery	.05	.01
❑ 289	Bill Pecota UER	.05	.01
❑ 290	Jamie Quirk	.05	.01
❑ 291	Bret Saberhagen	.10	.02
❑ 292	Kevin Seitzer	.05	.01
❑ 293	Kurt Stillwell	.05	.01
❑ 294	Pat Tabler	.05	.01
❑ 295	Danny Tartabull	.05	.01
❑ 296	Gary Thurman	.05	.01
❑ 297	Frank White	.10	.02
❑ 298	Willie Wilson	.10	.02
❑ 299	Roberto Alomar	.25	.08
❑ 300	Sandy Alomar Jr. RC	.40	.15
❑ 301	Chris Brown	.05	.01
❑ 302	Mike Brumley UER	.05	.01
❑ 303	Mark Davis	.05	.01
❑ 304	Mark Grant	.05	.01
❑ 305	Tony Gwynn	.30	.10
❑ 306	Greg W.Harris RC	.10	.02
❑ 307	Andy Hawkins	.05	.01
❑ 308	Jimmy Jones	.05	.01
❑ 309	John Kruk	.10	.02
❑ 310	Dave Leiper	.05	.01
❑ 311	Carmelo Martinez	.05	.01
❑ 312	Lance McCullers	.05	.01
❑ 313	Keith Moreland	.05	.01
❑ 314	Dennis Rasmussen	.05	.01
❑ 315	Randy Ready UER	.05	.01
❑ 316	Benito Santiago	.10	.02
❑ 317	Eric Show	.05	.01
❑ 318	Todd Simmons	.05	.01
❑ 319	Garry Templeton	.10	.02
❑ 320	Dickie Thon	.05	.01
❑ 321	Ed Whitson	.05	.01
❑ 322	Marvell Wynne	.05	.01

❑ 323 Mike Aldrete .05 .01
❑ 324 Brett Butler .10 .02
❑ 325 Will Clark .15 .05
❑ 326 Kelly Downs UER .05 .01
❑ 327 Dave Dravecky .05 .01
❑ 328 Scott Garrelts .05 .01
❑ 329 Atlee Hammaker .05 .01
❑ 330 Charlie Hayes RC .25 .08
❑ 331 Mike Krukow .05 .01
❑ 332 Craig Lefferts .05 .01
❑ 333 Candy Maldonado .05 .01
❑ 334 Kirt Manwaring UER .05 .01
❑ 335 Bob Melvin .05 .01
❑ 336 Kevin Mitchell .10 .02
❑ 337 Donell Nixon .05 .01
❑ 338 Tony Perezchica .05 .01
❑ 339 Joe Price .05 .01
❑ 340 Rick Reuschel .10 .02
❑ 341 Earnest Riles .05 .01
❑ 342 Don Robinson .05 .01
❑ 343 Chris Speier .05 .01
❑ 344 Robby Thompson UER .05 .01
❑ 345 Jose Uribe .05 .01
❑ 346 Matt Williams .25 .08
❑ 347 Trevor Wilson RC .10 .02
❑ 348 Juan Agosto .05 .01
❑ 349 Larry Andersen .05 .01
❑ 350A Alan Ashby ERR 2.00 .75
❑ 350B Alan Ashby COR .05 .01
❑ 351 Kevin Bass .05 .01
❑ 352 Buddy Bell .10 .02
❑ 353 Craig Biggio RC 2.50 1.00
❑ 354 Danny Darwin .05 .01
❑ 355 Glenn Davis .05 .01
❑ 356 Jim Deshaies .05 .01
❑ 357 Bill Doran .05 .01
❑ 358 John Fishel .05 .01
❑ 359 Billy Hatcher .05 .01
❑ 360 Bob Knepper .05 .01
❑ 361 Louie Meadows UER .05 .01
❑ 362 Dave Meads .05 .01
❑ 363 Jim Pankovits .05 .01
❑ 364 Terry Puhl .05 .01
❑ 365 Rafael Ramirez .05 .01
❑ 366 Craig Reynolds .05 .01
❑ 367 Mike Scott .10 .02
❑ 368 Nolan Ryan 1.00 .40
❑ 369 Dave Smith .05 .01
❑ 370 Gerald Young .05 .01
❑ 371 Hubie Brooks .05 .01
❑ 372 Tim Burke .05 .01
❑ 373 John Dopson .05 .01
❑ 374 Mike R. Fitzgerald .05 .01
❑ 375 Tom Foley .05 .01
❑ 376 Andres Galarraga UER .10 .02
❑ 377 Neal Heaton .05 .01
❑ 378 Joe Hesketh .05 .01
❑ 379 Brian Holman RC .10 .02
❑ 380 Rex Hudler .05 .01
❑ 381 Randy Johnson RC 2.00 .75
❑ 381B R.Johnson Marlboro ERR 25.00 10.00
❑ 382 Wallace Johnson .05 .01
❑ 383 Tracy Jones .05 .01
❑ 384 Dave Martinez .05 .01
❑ 385 Dennis Martinez .10 .02
❑ 386 Andy McGaffigan .05 .01
❑ 387 Otis Nixon .05 .01
❑ 388 Johnny Paredes .05 .01
❑ 389 Jeff Parrett .05 .01
❑ 390 Pascual Perez .05 .01
❑ 391 Tim Raines .10 .02
❑ 392 Luis Rivera .05 .01
❑ 393 Nelson Santovenia .05 .01
❑ 394 Bryn Smith .05 .01
❑ 395 Tim Wallach .05 .01
❑ 396 Andy Allanson UER .05 .01
❑ 397 Rod Allen .05 .01
❑ 398 Scott Bailes .05 .01
❑ 399 Tom Candiotti .05 .01
❑ 400 Joe Carter .10 .02
❑ 401 Carmen Castillo UER .05 .01
❑ 402 Dave Clark UER# .05 .01
❑ 403 John Farrell UER .05 .01
❑ 404 Julio Franco .10 .02
❑ 405 Don Gordon .05 .01
❑ 406 Mel Hall .05 .01
❑ 407 Brad Havens .05 .01
❑ 408 Brook Jacoby .05 .01
❑ 409 Doug Jones .05 .01
❑ 410 Jeff Kaiser .05 .01
❑ 411 Luis Medina .05 .01
❑ 412 Cory Snyder .05 .01
❑ 413 Greg Swindell .05 .01
❑ 414 Ron Tingley UER .05 .01
❑ 415 Willie Upshaw .05 .01
❑ 416 Ron Washington .05 .01
❑ 417 Rich Yett .05 .01
❑ 418 Damon Berryhill .05 .01
❑ 419 Mike Bielecki .05 .01
❑ 420 Doug Dascenzo .05 .01
❑ 421 Jody Davis UER .05 .01
❑ 422 Andre Dawson .10 .02
❑ 423 Frank DiPino .05 .01
❑ 424 Shawon Dunston .05 .01
❑ 425 Rich Gossage .10 .02
❑ 426 Mark Grace .25 .08
❑ 427 Mike Harkey RC .10 .02
❑ 428 Darrin Jackson .10 .02
❑ 429 Les Lancaster .05 .01
❑ 430 Vance Law .05 .01
❑ 431 Greg Maddux .50 .20
❑ 432 Jamie Moyer .10 .02
❑ 433 Al Nipper .05 .01
❑ 434 Rafael Palmeiro .25 .08
❑ 435 Pat Perry .05 .01
❑ 436 Jeff Pico .05 .01
❑ 437 Ryne Sandberg .40 .15
❑ 438 Calvin Schiraldi .05 .01
❑ 439 Rick Sutcliffe .10 .02
❑ 440A Manny Trillo ERR 2.00 .75
❑ 440B Manny Trillo COR .05 .01
❑ 441 Gary Varsho UER .05 .01
❑ 442 Mitch Webster .05 .01
❑ 443 Luis Alicea RC .25 .08
❑ 444 Tom Brunansky .05 .01
❑ 445 Vince Coleman UER .05 .01
❑ 446 John Costello UER .05 .01
❑ 447 Danny Cox .05 .01
❑ 448 Ken Dayley .05 .01
❑ 449 Jose DeLeon .05 .01
❑ 450 Curt Ford .05 .01
❑ 451 Pedro Guerrero .10 .02
❑ 452 Bob Horner .10 .02
❑ 453 Tim Jones .05 .01
❑ 454 Steve Lake .05 .01
❑ 455 Joe Magrane UER .05 .01
❑ 456 Greg Mathews .05 .01
❑ 457 Willie McGee .10 .02
❑ 458 Larry McWilliams .05 .01
❑ 459 Jose Oquendo .05 .01
❑ 460 Tony Pena .05 .01
❑ 461 Terry Pendleton .10 .02
❑ 462 Steve Peters UER .05 .01
❑ 463 Ozzie Smith .40 .15
❑ 464 Scott Terry .05 .01
❑ 465 Denny Walling .05 .01
❑ 466 Todd Worrell .05 .01
❑ 467 Tony Armas UER .10 .02
❑ 468 Dante Bichette RC .40 .15
❑ 469 Bob Boone .10 .02
❑ 470 Terry Clark .05 .01
❑ 471 Stu Cliburn .05 .01
❑ 472 Mike Cook UER .05 .01
❑ 473 Sherman Corbett .05 .01
❑ 474 Chili Davis .10 .02
❑ 475 Brian Downing .10 .02
❑ 476 Jim Eppard .05 .01
❑ 477 Chuck Finley .10 .02
❑ 478 Willie Fraser .05 .01
❑ 479 Bryan Harvey UER RC .25 .08
❑ 480 Jack Howell .05 .01
❑ 481 Wally Joyner UER .10 .02
❑ 482 Jack Lazorko .05 .01
❑ 483 Kirk McCaskill .05 .01
❑ 484 Mark McLemore .05 .01
❑ 485 Greg Minton .05 .01
❑ 486 Dan Petry .05 .01
❑ 487 Johnny Ray .05 .01
❑ 488 Dick Schofield .05 .01
❑ 489 Devon White .10 .02
❑ 490 Mike Witt .05 .01
❑ 491 Harold Baines .10 .02
❑ 492 Daryl Boston .05 .01
❑ 493 Ivan Calderon UER .05 .01
❑ 494 Mike Diaz .05 .01
❑ 495 Carlton Fisk .15 .05
❑ 496 Dave Gallagher .05 .01
❑ 497 Ozzie Guillen .10 .02
❑ 498 Shawn Hillegas .05 .01
❑ 499 Lance Johnson .05 .01
❑ 500 Barry Jones .05 .01
❑ 501 Bill Long .05 .01
❑ 502 Steve Lyons .05 .01
❑ 503 Fred Manrique .05 .01
❑ 504 Jack McDowell .10 .02
❑ 505 Donn Pall .05 .01
❑ 506 Kelly Paris .05 .01
❑ 507 Dan Pasqua .05 .01
❑ 508 Ken Patterson .05 .01
❑ 509 Melido Perez .05 .01
❑ 510 Jerry Reuss .05 .01
❑ 511 Mark Salas .05 .01
❑ 512 Bobby Thigpen UER .05 .01
❑ 513 Mike Woodard .05 .01
❑ 514 Bob Brower .05 .01
❑ 515 Steve Buechele .05 .01
❑ 516 Jose Cecena .05 .01
❑ 517 Cecil Espy .05 .01
❑ 518 Scott Fletcher .05 .01
❑ 519 Cecilio Guante .05 .01
❑ 520 Jose Guzman .05 .01
❑ 521 Ray Hayward .05 .01
❑ 522 Charlie Hough .10 .02
❑ 523 Pete Incaviglia .05 .01
❑ 524 Mike Jeffcoat .05 .01
❑ 525 Paul Kilgus .05 .01
❑ 526 Chad Kreuter RC .25 .08
❑ 527 Jeff Kunkel .05 .01
❑ 528 Oddibe McDowell .05 .01
❑ 529 Pete O'Brien .05 .01
❑ 530 Geno Petralli .05 .01
❑ 531 Jeff Russell .05 .01
❑ 532 Ruben Sierra .10 .02
❑ 533 Mike Stanley .05 .01
❑ 534A Ed VandeBerg ERR 2.00 .75
❑ 534B Ed VandeBerg COR .05 .01
❑ 535 Curtis Wilkerson ERR .05 .01
❑ 536 Mitch Williams .05 .01
❑ 537 Bobby Witt UER .05 .01
❑ 538 Steve Balboni .05 .01
❑ 539 Scott Bankhead .05 .01
❑ 540 Scott Bradley .05 .01
❑ 541 Mickey Brantley .05 .01
❑ 542 Jay Buhner .10 .02
❑ 543 Mike Campbell .05 .01
❑ 544 Darnell Coles .05 .01
❑ 545 Henry Cotto .05 .01
❑ 546 Alvin Davis .05 .01
❑ 547 Mario Diaz .05 .01
❑ 548 Ken Griffey Jr. RC 10.00 4.00
❑ 549 Erik Hanson RC .25 .08
❑ 550 Mike Jackson UER .05 .01
❑ 551 Mark Langston .05 .01
❑ 552 Edgar Martinez .25 .08
❑ 553 Bill McGuire .05 .01
❑ 554 Mike Moore .05 .01
❑ 555 Jim Presley .05 .01
❑ 556 Rey Quinones .05 .01
❑ 557 Jerry Reed .05 .01
❑ 558 Harold Reynolds .10 .02
❑ 559 Mike Schooler .05 .01
❑ 560 Bill Swift .05 .01
❑ 561 Dave Valle .05 .01
❑ 562 Steve Bedrosian .05 .01
❑ 563 Phil Bradley .05 .01
❑ 564 Don Carman .05 .01
❑ 565 Bob Dernier .05 .01
❑ 566 Marvin Freeman .05 .01
❑ 567 Todd Frohwirth .05 .01
❑ 568 Greg Gross .05 .01
❑ 569 Kevin Gross .05 .01
❑ 570 Greg A. Harris .05 .01
❑ 571 Von Hayes .05 .01
❑ 572 Chris James .05 .01
❑ 573 Steve Jeltz .05 .01
❑ 574 Ron Jones UER .10 .02
❑ 575 Ricky Jordan RC .25 .08
❑ 576 Mike Maddux .05 .01

❑ 577 David Palmer .05 .01
❑ 578 Lance Parrish .10 .02
❑ 579 Shane Rawley .05 .01
❑ 580 Bruce Ruffin .05 .01
❑ 581 Juan Samuel .05 .01
❑ 582 Mike Schmidt .50 .20
❑ 583 Kent Tekulve .05 .01
❑ 584 Milt Thompson UER .05 .01
❑ 585 Jose Alvarez RC .10 .02
❑ 586 Paul Assenmacher .05 .01
❑ 587 Bruce Benedict .05 .01
❑ 588 Jeff Blauser .05 .01
❑ 589 Terry Blocker .05 .01
❑ 590 Ron Gant .10 .02
❑ 591 Tom Glavine .25 .08
❑ 592 Tommy Gregg .05 .01
❑ 593 Albert Hall .05 .01
❑ 594 Dion James .05 .01
❑ 595 Rick Mahler .05 .01
❑ 596 Dale Murphy .15 .05
❑ 597 Gerald Perry .05 .01
❑ 598 Charlie Puleo .05 .01
❑ 599 Ted Simmons .10 .02
❑ 600 Pete Smith .05 .01
❑ 601 Zane Smith .05 .01
❑ 602 John Smoltz RC 1.50 .60
❑ 603 Bruce Sutter .10 .02
❑ 604 Andres Thomas .05 .01
❑ 605 Ozzie Virgil .05 .01
❑ 606 Brady Anderson RC .40 .15
❑ 607 Jeff Ballard .05 .01
❑ 608 Jose Bautista RC .10 .02
❑ 609 Ken Gerhart .05 .01
❑ 610 Terry Kennedy .05 .01
❑ 611 Eddie Murray .25 .08
❑ 612 Carl Nichols UER .05 .01
❑ 613 Tom Niedenfuer .05 .01
❑ 614 Joe Orsulak .05 .01
❑ 615 Oswald Peraza UER .05 .01
❑ 616A Bill Ripken Rick Face 15.00 6.00
❑ 616B Bill Ripken Whiteout 120.00 60.00
❑ 616C Bill Ripken White Scribble 25.00 10.00
❑ 616D Bill Ripken Black Scribble 15.00 6.00
❑ 616E Bill Ripken Black Box 6.00 2.00
❑ 617 Cal Ripken .75 .30
❑ 618 Dave Schmidt .05 .01
❑ 619 Rick Schu .05 .01
❑ 620 Larry Sheets .05 .01
❑ 621 Doug Sisk .05 .01
❑ 622 Pete Stanicek .05 .01
❑ 623 Mickey Tettleton .05 .01
❑ 624 Jay Tibbs .05 .01
❑ 625 Jim Traber .05 .01
❑ 626 Mark Williamson .05 .01
❑ 627 Craig Worthington .05 .01
❑ 628 Jose Canseco 40/40 .25 .08
❑ 629 Tom Browning Perfect .05 .01
❑ 630 R.Alomar/S.Alomar .25 .08
❑ 631 W.Clark/R.Palmeiro .15 .05
❑ 632 D.Strawberry/W.Clark .10 .02
❑ 633 W.Boggs/C.Lansford .10 .02
❑ 634 McGwire/Cans/Stein .75 .30
❑ 635 M.Davis/D.Gooden .05 .01
❑ 636 D.Jackson/D.Cone UER .05 .01
❑ 637 C.Sabo/B.Bonilla UER .10 .02
❑ 638 A.Galarraga/G.Perry UER .05 .01
❑ 639 K.Puckett/E.Davis .15 .05
❑ 640 S.Wilson/C.Drew .05 .01
❑ 641 K.Brown/K.Reimer .25 .08
❑ 642 B.Pounders RC/J.Clark .10 .02
❑ 643 M.Capel/D.Hall .05 .01
❑ 644 J.Girardi RC/R.Roomes .40 .15
❑ 645 L.Harris RC/M.Brown .25 .08
❑ 646 L.De Los Santos/J.Campbell .05 .01
❑ 647 R.Kramer/M.Garcia .05 .01
❑ 648 T.Lovullo RC/R.Palacios .10 .02
❑ 649 J.Corsi/B.Milacki .05 .01
❑ 650 G.Hall/M.Rochford .05 .01
❑ 651 T.Taylor/V.Lovelace RC .10 .02
❑ 652 K.Hill RC/D.Cook .25 .08
❑ 653 S.Service/S.Turner .05 .01
❑ 654 CL: Oakland/Mets
Dodgers/Red Sox
(10 Henderson;# .05 .01
❑ 655A CL: Twins/Tigers ERR
Reds/Brewers
(179 Boslo and .05 .01
❑ 655B CL: Twins/Tigers COR
Reds/Brewers
(179 Boslo but .05 .01
❑ 656 CL: Pirates/Blue Jays
Yankees/Royals
(225 Jess B .05 .01
❑ 657 CL: Padres/Giants
Astros/Expos
(367/368 wrong) .05 .01
❑ 658 CL: Indians/Cubs
Cardinals/Angels
(449 Deleon) .05 .01
❑ 659 CL: White Sox/Rangers
Mariners/Phillies .05 .01
❑ 660 CL: Braves/Orioles
Specials/Checklists
(632 hyph .05 .01

1990 Fleer

❑ COMPLETE SET (660) 15.00 6.00
❑ COMP.RETAIL SET (660) 15.00 6.00
❑ COMP.HOBBY SET (672) 15.00 6.00
❑ 1 Lance Blankenship .05 .01
❑ 2 Todd Burns .05 .01
❑ 3 Jose Canseco .15 .05
❑ 4 Jim Corsi .05 .01
❑ 5 Storm Davis .05 .01
❑ 6 Dennis Eckersley .10 .02
❑ 7 Mike Gallego .05 .01
❑ 8 Ron Hassey .05 .01
❑ 9 Dave Henderson .05 .01
❑ 10 Rickey Henderson .25 .08
❑ 11 Rick Honeycutt .05 .01
❑ 12 Stan Javier .05 .01
❑ 13 Felix Jose .05 .01
❑ 14 Carney Lansford .10 .02
❑ 15 Mark McGwire 1.00 .40
❑ 16 Mike Moore .05 .01
❑ 17 Gene Nelson .05 .01
❑ 18 Dave Parker .10 .02
❑ 19 Tony Phillips .05 .01
❑ 20 Terry Steinbach .05 .01
❑ 21 Dave Stewart .10 .02
❑ 22 Walt Weiss .05 .01
❑ 23 Bob Welch .05 .01
❑ 24 Curt Young .05 .01
❑ 25 Paul Assenmacher .05 .01
❑ 26 Damon Berryhill .05 .01
❑ 27 Mike Bielecki .05 .01
❑ 28 Kevin Blankenship .05 .01
❑ 29 Andre Dawson .10 .02
❑ 30 Shawon Dunston .05 .01
❑ 31 Joe Girardi .15 .05
❑ 32 Mark Grace .15 .05
❑ 33 Mike Harkey .05 .01
❑ 34 Paul Kilgus .05 .01
❑ 35 Les Lancaster .05 .01
❑ 36 Vance Law .05 .01
❑ 37 Greg Maddux .40 .15
❑ 38 Lloyd McClendon .05 .01
❑ 39 Jeff Pico .05 .01
❑ 40 Ryne Sandberg .40 .15
❑ 41 Scott Sanderson .05 .01
❑ 42 Dwight Smith .05 .01
❑ 43 Rick Sutcliffe .10 .02
❑ 44 Jerome Walton .05 .01
❑ 45 Mitch Webster .05 .01
❑ 46 Curt Wilkerson .05 .01
❑ 47 Dean Wilkins RC .05 .01
❑ 48 Mitch Williams .05 .01
❑ 49 Steve Wilson .05 .01
❑ 50 Steve Bedrosian .05 .01
❑ 51 Mike Benjamin RC .10 .02
❑ 52 Jeff Brantley .05 .01
❑ 53 Brett Butler .10 .02
❑ 54 Will Clark UER .10 .02
❑ 55 Kelly Downs .05 .01
❑ 56 Scott Garrelts .05 .01
❑ 57 Atlee Hammaker .05 .01
❑ 58 Terry Kennedy .05 .01
❑ 59 Mike LaCoss .05 .01
❑ 60 Craig Lefferts .05 .01
❑ 61 Greg Litton .05 .01
❑ 62 Candy Maldonado .05 .01
❑ 63 Kirt Manwaring UER
(No '88 Phoenix stats
as note .05 .01
❑ 64 Randy McCament RC .05 .01
❑ 65 Kevin Mitchell .05 .01
❑ 66 Donell Nixon .05 .01
❑ 67 Ken Oberkfell .05 .01
❑ 68 Rick Reuschel .05 .01
❑ 69 Ernest Riles .05 .01
❑ 70 Don Robinson .05 .01
❑ 71 Pat Sheridan .05 .01
❑ 72 Chris Speier .05 .01
❑ 73 Robby Thompson .05 .01
❑ 74 Jose Uribe .05 .01
❑ 75 Matt Williams .10 .02
❑ 76 George Bell .05 .01
❑ 77 Pat Borders .05 .01
❑ 78 John Cerutti .05 .01
❑ 79 Junior Felix .05 .01
❑ 80 Tony Fernandez .05 .01
❑ 81 Mike Flanagan .05 .01
❑ 82 Mauro Gozzo RC .05 .01
❑ 83 Kelly Gruber .05 .01
❑ 84 Tom Henke .05 .01
❑ 85 Jimmy Key .10 .02
❑ 86 Manny Lee .05 .01
❑ 87 Nelson Liriano UER .05 .01
❑ 88 Lee Mazzilli .05 .01
❑ 89 Fred McGriff .25 .08
❑ 90 Lloyd Moseby .05 .01
❑ 91 Rance Mulliniks .05 .01
❑ 92 Alex Sanchez .05 .01
❑ 93 Dave Stieb .10 .02
❑ 94 Todd Stottlemyre .10 .02
❑ 95 Duane Ward UER .05 .01
❑ 96 David Wells .10 .02
❑ 97 Ernie Whitt .05 .01
❑ 98 Frank Wills .05 .01
❑ 99 Mookie Wilson .10 .02
❑ 100 Kevin Appier .10 .02
❑ 101 Luis Aquino .05 .01
❑ 102 Bob Boone .10 .02
❑ 103 George Brett .60 .25
❑ 104 Jose DeJesus .05 .01
❑ 105 Luis De Los Santos .05 .01
❑ 106 Jim Eisenreich .05 .01
❑ 107 Steve Farr .05 .01
❑ 108 Tom Gordon .10 .02
❑ 109 Mark Gubicza .05 .01
❑ 110 Bo Jackson .25 .08
❑ 111 Terry Leach .05 .01
❑ 112 Charlie Leibrandt .05 .01
❑ 113 Rick Luecken RC .05 .01
❑ 114 Mike Macfarlane .05 .01
❑ 115 Jeff Montgomery .10 .02
❑ 116 Bret Saberhagen .10 .02
❑ 117 Kevin Seitzer .05 .01
❑ 118 Kurt Stillwell .05 .01
❑ 119 Pat Tabler .05 .01
❑ 120 Danny Tartabull .05 .01
❑ 121 Gary Thurman .05 .01
❑ 122 Frank White .10 .02
❑ 123 Willie Wilson .05 .01
❑ 124 Matt Winters RC .05 .01
❑ 125 Jim Abbott .15 .05
❑ 126 Tony Armas .05 .01
❑ 127 Dante Bichette .10 .02
❑ 128 Bert Blyleven .10 .02
❑ 129 Chili Davis .10 .02

❑ 130 Brian Downing .05 .01
❑ 131 Mike Fetters RC .25 .08
❑ 132 Chuck Finley .10 .02
❑ 133 Willie Fraser .05 .01
❑ 134 Bryan Harvey .05 .01
❑ 135 Jack Howell .05 .01
❑ 136 Wally Joyner .10 .02
❑ 137 Jeff Manto .05 .01
❑ 138 Kirk McCaskill .05 .01
❑ 139 Bob McClure .05 .01
❑ 140 Greg Minton .05 .01
❑ 141 Lance Parrish .05 .01
❑ 142 Dan Petry .05 .01
❑ 143 Johnny Ray .05 .01
❑ 144 Dick Schofield .05 .01
❑ 145 Lee Stevens .10 .02
❑ 146 Claudell Washington .05 .01
❑ 147 Devon White .10 .02
❑ 148 Mike Witt .05 .01
❑ 149 Roberto Alomar .15 .05
❑ 150 Sandy Alomar Jr. .10 .02
❑ 151 Andy Benes .10 .02
❑ 152 Jack Clark .10 .02
❑ 153 Pat Clements .05 .01
❑ 154 Joey Cora .10 .02
❑ 155 Mark Davis .05 .01
❑ 156 Mark Grant .05 .01
❑ 157 Tony Gwynn .30 .10
❑ 158 Greg W. Harris .05 .01
❑ 159 Bruce Hurst .05 .01
❑ 160 Darrin Jackson .05 .01
❑ 161 Chris James .05 .01
❑ 162 Carmelo Martinez .05 .01
❑ 163 Mike Pagliarulo .05 .01
❑ 164 Mark Parent .05 .01
❑ 165 Dennis Rasmussen .05 .01
❑ 166 Bip Roberts .05 .01
❑ 167 Benito Santiago .10 .02
❑ 168 Calvin Schiraldi .05 .01
❑ 169 Eric Show .05 .01
❑ 170 Garry Templeton .05 .01
❑ 171 Ed Whitson .05 .01
❑ 172 Brady Anderson .10 .02
❑ 173 Jeff Ballard .05 .01
❑ 174 Phil Bradley .05 .01
❑ 175 Mike Devereaux .05 .01
❑ 176 Steve Finley .10 .02
❑ 177 Pete Harnisch .05 .01
❑ 178 Kevin Hickey .05 .01
❑ 179 Brian Holton .05 .01
❑ 180 Ben McDonald RC .25 .08
❑ 181 Bob Melvin .05 .01
❑ 182 Bob Milacki .05 .01
❑ 183 Randy Milligan UER .05 .01
❑ 184 Gregg Olson .10 .02
❑ 185 Joe Orsulak .05 .01
❑ 186 Bill Ripken .05 .01
❑ 187 Cal Ripken .75 .30
❑ 188 Dave Schmidt .05 .01
❑ 189 Larry Sheets .05 .01
❑ 190 Mickey Tettleton .05 .01
❑ 191 Mark Thurmond .05 .01
❑ 192 Jay Tibbs .05 .01
❑ 193 Jim Traber .05 .01
❑ 194 Mark Williamson .05 .01
❑ 195 Craig Worthington .05 .01
❑ 196 Don Aase .05 .01
❑ 197 Blaine Beatty RC .05 .01
❑ 198 Mark Carreon .05 .01
❑ 199 Gary Carter .10 .02
❑ 200 David Cone .10 .02
❑ 201 Ron Darling .05 .01
❑ 202 Kevin Elster .05 .01
❑ 203 Sid Fernandez .05 .01
❑ 204 Dwight Gooden .10 .02
❑ 205 Keith Hernandez .10 .02
❑ 206 Jeff Innis RC .05 .01
❑ 207 Gregg Jefferies .10 .02
❑ 208 Howard Johnson .05 .01
❑ 209 Barry Lyons UER .05 .01
❑ 210 Dave Magadan .05 .01
❑ 211 Kevin McReynolds .05 .01
❑ 212 Jeff Musselman .05 .01
❑ 213 Randy Myers .10 .02
❑ 214 Bob Ojeda .05 .01
❑ 215 Juan Samuel .05 .01
❑ 216 Mackey Sasser .05 .01
❑ 217 Darryl Strawberry .10 .02
❑ 218 Tim Teufel .05 .01
❑ 219 Frank Viola .05 .01
❑ 220 Juan Agosto .05 .01
❑ 221 Larry Andersen .05 .01
❑ 222 Eric Anthony RC .10 .02
❑ 223 Kevin Bass .05 .01
❑ 224 Craig Biggio .25 .08
❑ 225 Ken Caminiti .10 .02
❑ 226 Jim Clancy .05 .01
❑ 227 Danny Darwin .05 .01
❑ 228 Glenn Davis .05 .01
❑ 229 Jim Deshaies .05 .01
❑ 230 Bill Doran .05 .01
❑ 231 Bob Forsch .05 .01
❑ 232 Brian Meyer .05 .01
❑ 233 Terry Puhl .05 .01
❑ 234 Rafael Ramirez .05 .01
❑ 235 Rick Rhoden .05 .01
❑ 236 Dan Schatzeder .05 .01
❑ 237 Mike Scott .05 .01
❑ 238 Dave Smith .05 .01
❑ 239 Alex Trevino .05 .01
❑ 240 Glenn Wilson .05 .01
❑ 241 Gerald Young .05 .01
❑ 242 Tom Brunansky .05 .01
❑ 243 Cris Carpenter .05 .01
❑ 244 Alex Cole RC .10 .02
❑ 245 Vince Coleman .05 .01
❑ 246 John Costello .05 .01
❑ 247 Ken Dayley .05 .01
❑ 248 Jose DeLeon .05 .01
❑ 249 Frank DiPino .05 .01
❑ 250 Pedro Guerrero .05 .01
❑ 251 Ken Hill .10 .02
❑ 252 Joe Magrane .05 .01
❑ 253 Willie McGee UER .10 .02
❑ 254 John Morris .05 .01
❑ 255 Jose Oquendo .05 .01
❑ 256 Tony Pena .05 .01
❑ 257 Terry Pendleton .10 .02
❑ 258 Ted Power .05 .01
❑ 259 Dan Quisenberry .05 .01
❑ 260 Ozzie Smith .40 .15
❑ 261 Scott Terry .05 .01
❑ 262 Milt Thompson .05 .01
❑ 263 Denny Walling .05 .01
❑ 264 Todd Worrell .05 .01
❑ 265 Todd Zeile .10 .02
❑ 266 Marty Barrett .05 .01
❑ 267 Mike Boddicker .05 .01
❑ 268 Wade Boggs .15 .05
❑ 269 Ellis Burks .15 .05
❑ 270 Rick Cerone .05 .01
❑ 271 Roger Clemens 1.00 .40
❑ 272 John Dopson .05 .01
❑ 273 Nick Esasky .05 .01
❑ 274 Dwight Evans .15 .05
❑ 275 Wes Gardner .05 .01
❑ 276 Rich Gedman .05 .01
❑ 277 Mike Greenwell .05 .01
❑ 278 Danny Heep .05 .01
❑ 279 Eric Hetzel .05 .01
❑ 280 Dennis Lamp .05 .01
❑ 281 Rob Murphy UER .05 .01
❑ 282 Joe Price .05 .01
❑ 283 Carlos Quintana .05 .01
❑ 284 Jody Reed .05 .01
❑ 285 Luis Rivera .05 .01
❑ 286 Kevin Romine .05 .01
❑ 287 Lee Smith .10 .02
❑ 288 Mike Smithson .05 .01
❑ 289 Bob Stanley .05 .01
❑ 290 Harold Baines .10 .02
❑ 291 Kevin Brown .10 .02
❑ 292 Steve Buechele .05 .01
❑ 293 Scott Coolbaugh RC .05 .01
❑ 294 Jack Daugherty RC .05 .01
❑ 295 Cecil Espy .05 .01
❑ 296 Julio Franco .10 .02
❑ 297 Juan Gonzalez RC 1.00 .40
❑ 298 Cecilio Guante .05 .01
❑ 299 Drew Hall .05 .01
❑ 300 Charlie Hough .10 .02
❑ 301 Pete Incaviglia .05 .01
❑ 302 Mike Jeffcoat .05 .01
❑ 303 Chad Kreuter .05 .01
❑ 304 Jeff Kunkel .05 .01
❑ 305 Rick Leach .05 .01
❑ 306 Fred Manrique .05 .01
❑ 307 Jamie Moyer .10 .02
❑ 308 Rafael Palmeiro .15 .05
❑ 309 Geno Petralli .05 .01
❑ 310 Kevin Reimer .05 .01
❑ 311 Kenny Rogers .10 .02
❑ 312 Jeff Russell .05 .01
❑ 313 Nolan Ryan 1.00 .40
❑ 314 Ruben Sierra .10 .02
❑ 315 Bobby Witt .05 .01
❑ 316 Chris Bosio .05 .01
❑ 317 Glenn Braggs UER .05 .01
❑ 318 Greg Brock .05 .01
❑ 319 Chuck Crim .05 .01
❑ 320 Rob Deer .05 .01
❑ 321 Mike Felder .05 .01
❑ 322 Tom Filer .05 .01
❑ 323 Tony Fossas RC .05 .01
❑ 324 Jim Gantner .05 .01
❑ 325 Darryl Hamilton .05 .01
❑ 326 Teddy Higuera .05 .01
❑ 327 Mark Knudson .05 .01
❑ 328 Bill Krueger UER .05 .01
❑ 329 Tim McIntosh RC .10 .02
❑ 330 Paul Molitor .10 .02
❑ 331 Jaime Navarro .05 .01
❑ 332 Charlie O'Brien .05 .01
❑ 333 Jeff Peterek RC .05 .01
❑ 334 Dan Plesac .05 .01
❑ 335 Jerry Reuss .05 .01
❑ 336 Gary Sheffield .25 .08
❑ 337 Bill Spiers .05 .01
❑ 338 B.J. Surhoff .10 .02
❑ 339 Greg Vaughn .05 .01
❑ 340 Robin Yount .40 .15
❑ 341 Hubie Brooks .05 .01
❑ 342 Tim Burke .05 .01
❑ 343 Mike Fitzgerald .05 .01
❑ 344 Tom Foley .05 .01
❑ 345 Andres Galarraga .10 .02
❑ 346 Damaso Garcia .05 .01
❑ 347 Marquis Grissom RC .40 .15
❑ 348 Kevin Gross .05 .01
❑ 349 Joe Hesketh .05 .01
❑ 350 Jeff Huson RC .05 .01
❑ 351 Wallace Johnson .05 .01
❑ 352 Mark Langston .05 .01
❑ 353A Dave Martinez Yellow 2.00 .75
❑ 353B Dave Martinez Red .05 .01
❑ 354 Dennis Martinez UER .10 .02
❑ 355 Andy McGaffigan .05 .01
❑ 356 Otis Nixon .05 .01
❑ 357 Spike Owen .05 .01
❑ 358 Pascual Perez .05 .01
❑ 359 Tim Raines .10 .02
❑ 360 Nelson Santovenia .05 .01
❑ 361 Bryn Smith .05 .01
❑ 362 Zane Smith .05 .01
❑ 363 Larry Walker RC 1.00 .40
❑ 364 Tim Wallach .05 .01
❑ 365 Rick Aguilera .10 .02
❑ 366 Allan Anderson .05 .01
❑ 367 Wally Backman .05 .01
❑ 368 Doug Baker .05 .01
❑ 369 Juan Berenguer .05 .01
❑ 370 Randy Bush .05 .01
❑ 371 Carmelo Castillo .05 .01
❑ 372 Mike Dyer RC .05 .01
❑ 373 Gary Gaetti .10 .02
❑ 374 Greg Gagne .05 .01
❑ 375 Dan Gladden .05 .01
❑ 376 German Gonzalez UER .05 .01
❑ 377 Brian Harper .05 .01
❑ 378 Kent Hrbek .10 .02
❑ 379 Gene Larkin .05 .01
❑ 380 Tim Laudner UER .05 .01
❑ 381 John Moses .05 .01
❑ 382 Al Newman .05 .01
❑ 383 Kirby Puckett .25 .08
❑ 384 Shane Rawley .05 .01
❑ 385 Jeff Reardon .10 .02
❑ 386 Roy Smith .05 .01

❑ 387 Gary Wayne .05 .01
❑ 388 Dave West .05 .01
❑ 389 Tim Belcher .05 .01
❑ 390 Tim Crews UER .05 .01
❑ 391 Mike Davis .05 .01
❑ 392 Rick Dempsey .05 .01
❑ 393 Kirk Gibson .10 .02
❑ 394 Jose Gonzalez .05 .01
❑ 395 Alfredo Griffin .05 .01
❑ 396 Jeff Hamilton .05 .01
❑ 397 Lenny Harris .05 .01
❑ 398 Mickey Hatcher .05 .01
❑ 399 Orel Hershiser .10 .02
❑ 400 Jay Howell .05 .01
❑ 401 Mike Marshall .05 .01
❑ 402 Ramon Martinez .05 .01
❑ 403 Mike Morgan .05 .01
❑ 404 Eddie Murray .25 .08
❑ 405 Alejandro Pena .05 .01
❑ 406 Willie Randolph .10 .02
❑ 407 Mike Scioscia .05 .01
❑ 408 Ray Searage .05 .01
❑ 409 Fernando Valenzuela .10 .02
❑ 410 Jose Vizcaino RC .25 .08
❑ 411 John Wetteland .25 .08
❑ 412 Jack Armstrong .05 .01
❑ 413 Todd Benzinger UER .05 .01
❑ 414 Tim Birtsas .05 .01
❑ 415 Tom Browning .05 .01
❑ 416 Norm Charlton .05 .01
❑ 417 Eric Davis .10 .02
❑ 418 Rob Dibble .10 .02
❑ 419 John Franco .10 .02
❑ 420 Ken Griffey Sr. .10 .02
❑ 421 Chris Hammond RC .10 .02
❑ 422 Danny Jackson .05 .01
❑ 423 Barry Larkin .15 .05
❑ 424 Tim Leary .05 .01
❑ 425 Rick Mahler .05 .01
❑ 426 Joe Oliver .05 .01
❑ 427 Paul O'Neill .15 .05
❑ 428 Luis Quinones UER .05 .01
❑ 429 Jeff Reed .05 .01
❑ 430 Jose Rijo .05 .01
❑ 431 Ron Robinson .05 .01
❑ 432 Rolando Roomes .05 .01
❑ 433 Chris Sabo .05 .01
❑ 434 Scott Scudder .05 .01
❑ 435 Herm Winningham .05 .01
❑ 436 Steve Balboni .05 .01
❑ 437 Jesse Barfield .05 .01
❑ 438 Mike Blowers RC .10 .02
❑ 439 Tom Brookens .05 .01
❑ 440 Greg Cadaret .05 .01
❑ 441 Alvaro Espinoza UER .05 .01
❑ 442 Bob Geren .05 .01
❑ 443 Lee Guetterman .05 .01
❑ 444 Mel Hall .05 .01
❑ 445 Andy Hawkins .05 .01
❑ 446 Roberto Kelly .05 .01
❑ 447 Don Mattingly .60 .25
❑ 448 Lance McCullers .05 .01
❑ 449 Hensley Meulens .05 .01
❑ 450 Dale Mohorcic .05 .01
❑ 451 Clay Parker .05 .01
❑ 452 Eric Plunk .05 .01
❑ 453 Dave Righetti .05 .01
❑ 454 Deion Sanders .25 .08
❑ 455 Steve Sax .05 .01
❑ 456 Don Slaught .05 .01
❑ 457 Walt Terrell .05 .01
❑ 458 Dave Winfield .10 .02
❑ 459 Jay Bell .10 .02
❑ 460 Rafael Belliard .05 .01
❑ 461 Barry Bonds 1.00 .40
❑ 462 Bobby Bonilla .10 .02
❑ 463 Sid Bream .05 .01
❑ 464 Benny Distefano .05 .01
❑ 465 Doug Drabek .05 .01
❑ 466 Jim Gott .05 .01
❑ 467 Billy Hatcher UER .05 .01
❑ 468 Neal Heaton .05 .01
❑ 469 Jeff King .05 .01
❑ 470 Bob Kipper .05 .01
❑ 471 Randy Kramer .05 .01
❑ 472 Bill Landrum .05 .01
❑ 473 Mike LaValliere .05 .01
❑ 474 Jose Lind .05 .01
❑ 475 Junior Ortiz .05 .01
❑ 476 Gary Redus .05 .01
❑ 477 Rick Reed RC .25 .08
❑ 478 R.J. Reynolds .05 .01
❑ 479 Jeff D. Robinson .05 .01
❑ 480 John Smiley .05 .01
❑ 481 Andy Van Slyke .15 .05
❑ 482 Bob Walk .05 .01
❑ 483 Andy Allanson .05 .01
❑ 484 Scott Bailes .05 .01
❑ 485 Albert Belle .25 .08
❑ 486 Bud Black .05 .01
❑ 487 Jerry Browne .05 .01
❑ 488 Tom Candiotti .05 .01
❑ 489 Joe Carter .10 .02
❑ 490 Dave Clark
(No '84 stats) .05 .01
❑ 491 John Farrell .05 .01
❑ 492 Felix Fermin .05 .01
❑ 493 Brook Jacoby .05 .01
❑ 494 Dion James .05 .01
❑ 495 Doug Jones .05 .01
❑ 496 Brad Komminsk .05 .01
❑ 497 Rod Nichols .05 .01
❑ 498 Pete O'Brien .05 .01
❑ 499 Steve Olin RC .10 .02
❑ 500 Jesse Orosco .05 .01
❑ 501 Joel Skinner .05 .01
❑ 502 Cory Snyder .05 .01
❑ 503 Greg Swindell .05 .01
❑ 504 Rich Yett .05 .01
❑ 505 Scott Bankhead .05 .01
❑ 506 Scott Bradley .05 .01
❑ 507 Greg Briley UER .05 .01
❑ 508 Jay Buhner .10 .02
❑ 509 Darnell Coles .05 .01
❑ 510 Keith Comstock .05 .01
❑ 511 Henry Cotto .05 .01
❑ 512 Alvin Davis .05 .01
❑ 513 Ken Griffey Jr. .75 .30
❑ 514 Erik Hanson .05 .01
❑ 515 Gene Harris .05 .01
❑ 516 Brian Holman .05 .01
❑ 517 Mike Jackson .05 .01
❑ 518 Randy Johnson .50 .20
❑ 519 Jeffrey Leonard .05 .01
❑ 520 Edgar Martinez .15 .05
❑ 521 Dennis Powell .05 .01
❑ 522 Jim Presley .05 .01
❑ 523 Jerry Reed .05 .01
❑ 524 Harold Reynolds .10 .02
❑ 525 Mike Schooler .05 .01
❑ 526 Bill Swift .05 .01
❑ 527 Dave Valle .05 .01
❑ 528 Omar Vizquel .25 .08
❑ 529 Ivan Calderon .05 .01
❑ 530 Carlton Fisk UER .15 .05
❑ 531 Scott Fletcher .05 .01
❑ 532 Dave Gallagher .05 .01
❑ 533 Ozzie Guillen .10 .02
❑ 534 Greg Hibbard RC .10 .02
❑ 535 Shawn Hillegas .05 .01
❑ 536 Lance Johnson .05 .01
❑ 537 Eric King .05 .01
❑ 538 Ron Kittle .05 .01
❑ 539 Steve Lyons .05 .01
❑ 540 Carlos Martinez .05 .01
❑ 541 Tom McCarthy .05 .01
❑ 542 Matt Merullo .05 .01
❑ 543 Donn Pall UER .05 .01
❑ 544 Dan Pasqua .05 .01
❑ 545 Ken Patterson .05 .01
❑ 546 Melido Perez .05 .01
❑ 547 Steve Rosenberg .05 .01
❑ 548 Sammy Sosa RC 2.50 1.00
❑ 549 Bobby Thigpen .05 .01
❑ 550 Robin Ventura .25 .08
❑ 551 Greg Walker .05 .01
❑ 552 Don Carman .05 .01
❑ 553 Pat Combs .05 .01
❑ 554 Dennis Cook .05 .01
❑ 555 Darren Daulton .10 .02
❑ 556 Len Dykstra .10 .02
❑ 557 Curt Ford .05 .01
❑ 558 Charlie Hayes .05 .01
❑ 559 Von Hayes .05 .01
❑ 560 Tommy Herr .05 .01
❑ 561 Ken Howell .05 .01
❑ 562 Steve Jeltz .05 .01
❑ 563 Ron Jones .05 .01
❑ 564 Ricky Jordan UER .05 .01
❑ 565 John Kruk .10 .02
❑ 566 Steve Lake .05 .01
❑ 567 Roger McDowell .05 .01
❑ 568 Terry Mulholland UER .05 .01
❑ 569 Dwayne Murphy .05 .01
❑ 570 Jeff Parrett .05 .01
❑ 571 Randy Ready .05 .01
❑ 572 Bruce Ruffin .05 .01
❑ 573 Dickie Thon .05 .01
❑ 574 Jose Alvarez UER .05 .01
❑ 575 Geronimo Berroa .05 .01
❑ 576 Jeff Blauser .05 .01
❑ 577 Joe Boever .05 .01
❑ 578 Marty Clary UER .05 .01
❑ 579 Jody Davis .05 .01
❑ 580 Mark Eichhorn .05 .01
❑ 581 Darrell Evans .10 .02
❑ 582 Ron Gant .10 .02
❑ 583 Tom Glavine .15 .05
❑ 584 Tommy Greene RC .10 .02
❑ 585 Tommy Gregg .05 .01
❑ 586 David Justice RC .50 .20
❑ 587 Mark Lemke .05 .01
❑ 588 Derek Lilliquist .05 .01
❑ 589 Oddibe McDowell .05 .01
❑ 590 Kent Mercker RC .05 .01
❑ 591 Dale Murphy .15 .05
❑ 592 Gerald Perry .05 .01
❑ 593 Lonnie Smith .05 .01
❑ 594 Pete Smith .05 .01
❑ 595 John Smoltz .25 .08
❑ 596 Mike Stanton UER RC .25 .08
❑ 597 Andres Thomas .05 .01
❑ 598 Jeff Treadway .05 .01
❑ 599 Doyle Alexander .05 .01
❑ 600 Dave Bergman .05 .01
❑ 601 Brian DuBois RC .05 .01
❑ 602 Paul Gibson .05 .01
❑ 603 Mike Heath .05 .01
❑ 604 Mike Henneman .05 .01
❑ 605 Guillermo Hernandez .05 .01
❑ 606 Shawn Holman RC .05 .01
❑ 607 Tracy Jones .05 .01
❑ 608 Chet Lemon .05 .01
❑ 609 Fred Lynn .05 .01
❑ 610 Jack Morris .10 .02
❑ 611 Matt Nokes .05 .01
❑ 612 Gary Pettis .05 .01
❑ 613 Kevin Ritz RC .05 .01
❑ 614 Jeff M. Robinson .05 .01
❑ 615 Steve Searcy .05 .01
❑ 616 Frank Tanana .05 .01
❑ 617 Alan Trammell .10 .02
❑ 618 Gary Ward .05 .01
❑ 619 Lou Whitaker .10 .02
❑ 620 Frank Williams .05 .01
❑ 621A George Brett '80 ERR 2.00 .75
❑ 621B George Brett '80 .30 .10
❑ 622 Fern.Valenzuela '81 .05 .01
❑ 623 Dale Murphy '82 .15 .05
❑ 624A Cal Ripkin '83 ERR 5.00 2.00
❑ 624B Cal Ripken '83 COR .40 .15
❑ 625 Ryne Sandberg '84 .25 .08
❑ 626 Don Mattingly '85 .20 .07
❑ 627 Roger Clemens '86 .50 .20
❑ 628 George Bell '87 .05 .01
❑ 629 Jose Canseco '88 UER .10 .02
❑ 630A Will Clark '89 ERR 32 1.00 .40
❑ 630B Will Clark '89 COR 321 .15 .05
❑ 631 M.Davis/M.Williams .05 .01
❑ 632 W.Boggs/M.Greenwell .10 .02
❑ 633 M.Gubicza/J.Russell .05 .01
❑ 634 C.Ripken/T.Fernandez .25 .08
❑ 635 K.Puckett/Bo Jackson .15 .05
❑ 636 N.Ryan/M.Scott .40 .15
❑ 637 W.Clark/K.Mitchell .10 .02
❑ 638 M.McGwire/D.Mattingly .30 .10
❑ 639 R.Sandberg/H.Johnson .25 .08
❑ 640 R.Seanez RC/C.Charland RC .10 .02

❑ 641 G.Canale RC/K.Maas RC .25 .08
❑ 642 Kelly Mann RC/D.Hansen RC .25 .08
❑ 643 G.Smith RC/S.Tate RC .10 .02
❑ 644 T.Drees RC/D.Howitt RC .10 .02
❑ 645 M.Roesler RC/D.May RC .10 .02
❑ 646 S.Hemond RC/M.Gardner RC .10 .02
❑ 647 John Orton RC/S.Leius RC .10 .02
❑ 648 R.Monteleone RC/D.Williams RC .10 .02
❑ 649 M.Huff RC/S.Frey RC .10 .02
❑ 650 C.McElroy RC/M.Alou RC .75 .30
❑ 651 B.Rose RC/M.Hartley RC .25 .08
❑ 652 M.Kinzer RC/W.Edwards RC .10 .02
❑ 653 D.DeShields RC/J.Grimsley RC .25 .08
❑ 654 CL: A's/Cubs
Giants/Blue Jays .05 .01
❑ 655 CL: Royals/Angels
Padres/Orioles .05 .01
❑ 656 CL: Mets/Astros
Cards/Red Sox .05 .01
❑ 657 CL: Rangers/Brewers
Expos/Twins .05 .01
❑ 658 CL: Dodgers/Reds
Yankees/Pirates .05 .01
❑ 659 CL: Indians/Mariners
White Sox/Phillies .05 .01
❑ 660A CL: Braves/Tigers
Specials/Checklists
(Checklist .05 .01
❑ 660B CL: Braves/Tigers
Specials/Checklists
(Checklist .05 .01

1991 Fleer

❑ COMPLETE SET (720) 8.00 3.00
❑ COMP.RETAIL SET (732) 10.00 4.00
❑ COMP.HOBBY SET (732) 10.00 4.00
❑ 1 Troy Afenir RC .05 .01
❑ 2 Harold Baines .10 .02
❑ 3 Lance Blankenship .05 .01
❑ 4 Todd Burns .05 .01
❑ 5 Jose Canseco .15 .05
❑ 6 Dennis Eckersley .10 .02
❑ 7 Mike Gallego .05 .01
❑ 8 Ron Hassey .05 .01
❑ 9 Dave Henderson .05 .01
❑ 10 Rickey Henderson .25 .08
❑ 11 Rick Honeycutt .05 .01
❑ 12 Doug Jennings .05 .01
❑ 13 Joe Klink .05 .01
❑ 14 Carney Lansford .10 .02
❑ 15 Darren Lewis .05 .01
❑ 16 Willie McGee UER .10 .02
❑ 17 Mark McGwire UER .75 .30
❑ 18 Mike Moore .05 .01
❑ 19 Gene Nelson .05 .01
❑ 20 Dave Otto .05 .01
❑ 21 Jamie Quirk .05 .01
❑ 22 Willie Randolph .10 .02
❑ 23 Scott Sanderson .05 .01
❑ 24 Terry Steinbach .05 .01
❑ 25 Dave Stewart .10 .02
❑ 26 Walt Weiss .05 .01
❑ 27 Bob Welch .05 .01
❑ 28 Curt Young .05 .01
❑ 29 Wally Backman .05 .01
❑ 30 Stan Belinda UER .05 .01
❑ 31 Jay Bell .10 .02
❑ 32 Rafael Belliard .05 .01
❑ 33 Barry Bonds 1.00 .40
❑ 34 Bobby Bonilla .10 .02
❑ 35 Sid Bream .05 .01
❑ 36 Doug Drabek .05 .01
❑ 37 Carlos Garcia RC .10 .02
❑ 38 Neal Heaton .05 .01
❑ 39 Jeff King .05 .01
❑ 40 Bob Kipper .05 .01
❑ 41 Bill Landrum .05 .01
❑ 42 Mike LaValliere .05 .01
❑ 43 Jose Lind .05 .01
❑ 44 Carmelo Martinez .05 .01
❑ 45 Bob Patterson .05 .01
❑ 46 Ted Power .05 .01
❑ 47 Gary Redus .05 .01
❑ 48 R.J. Reynolds .05 .01
❑ 49 Don Slaught .05 .01
❑ 50 John Smiley .05 .01
❑ 51 Zane Smith .05 .01
❑ 52 Randy Tomlin RC .10 .02
❑ 53 Andy Van Slyke .15 .05
❑ 54 Bob Walk .05 .01
❑ 55 Jack Armstrong .05 .01
❑ 56 Todd Benzinger .05 .01
❑ 57 Glenn Braggs .05 .01
❑ 58 Keith Brown .05 .01
❑ 59 Tom Browning .05 .01
❑ 60 Norm Charlton .05 .01
❑ 61 Eric Davis .10 .02
❑ 62 Rob Dibble .10 .02
❑ 63 Bill Doran .05 .01
❑ 64 Mariano Duncan .05 .01
❑ 65 Chris Hammond .05 .01
❑ 66 Billy Hatcher .05 .01
❑ 67 Danny Jackson .05 .01
❑ 68 Barry Larkin .15 .05
❑ 69 Tim Layana UER .05 .01
❑ 70 Terry Lee RC .05 .01
❑ 71 Rick Mahler .05 .01
❑ 72 Hal Morris .05 .01
❑ 73 Randy Myers .05 .01
❑ 74 Ron Oester .05 .01
❑ 75 Joe Oliver .05 .01
❑ 76 Paul O'Neill .15 .05
❑ 77 Luis Quinones .05 .01
❑ 78 Jeff Reed .05 .01
❑ 79 Jose Rijo .05 .01
❑ 80 Chris Sabo .05 .01
❑ 81 Scott Scudder .05 .01
❑ 82 Herm Winningham .05 .01
❑ 83 Larry Andersen .05 .01
❑ 84 Marty Barrett .05 .01
❑ 85 Mike Boddicker .05 .01
❑ 86 Wade Boggs .15 .05
❑ 87 Tom Bolton .05 .01
❑ 88 Tom Brunansky .05 .01
❑ 89 Ellis Burks .10 .02
❑ 90 Roger Clemens .75 .30
❑ 91 Scott Cooper .05 .01
❑ 92 John Dopson .05 .01
❑ 93 Dwight Evans .15 .05
❑ 94 Wes Gardner .05 .01
❑ 95 Jeff Gray .05 .01
❑ 96 Mike Greenwell .05 .01
❑ 97 Greg A. Harris .05 .01
❑ 98 Daryl Irvine RC .05 .01
❑ 99 Dana Kiecker .05 .01
❑ 100 Randy Kutcher .05 .01
❑ 101 Dennis Lamp .05 .01
❑ 102 Mike Marshall .05 .01
❑ 103 John Marzano .05 .01
❑ 104 Rob Murphy .05 .01
❑ 105 Tim Naehring .05 .01
❑ 106 Tony Pena .05 .01
❑ 107 Phil Plantier RC .25 .08
❑ 108 Carlos Quintana .05 .01
❑ 109 Jeff Reardon .10 .02
❑ 110 Jerry Reed .05 .01
❑ 111 Jody Reed .05 .01
❑ 112 Luis Rivera UER .05 .01
❑ 113 Kevin Romine .05 .01
❑ 114 Phil Bradley .05 .01
❑ 115 Ivan Calderon .05 .01
❑ 116 Wayne Edwards .05 .01
❑ 117 Alex Fernandez .05 .01
❑ 118 Carlton Fisk .15 .05
❑ 119 Scott Fletcher .05 .01
❑ 120 Craig Grebeck .05 .01
❑ 121 Ozzie Guillen .10 .02
❑ 122 Greg Hibbard .05 .01
❑ 123 Lance Johnson UER .05 .01
❑ 124 Barry Jones .05 .01
❑ 125 Ron Karkovice .05 .01
❑ 126 Eric King .05 .01
❑ 127 Steve Lyons .05 .01
❑ 128 Carlos Martinez .05 .01
❑ 129 Jack McDowell UER .05 .01
❑ 130 Donn Pall .05 .01
❑ 131 Dan Pasqua .05 .01
❑ 132 Ken Patterson .05 .01
❑ 133 Melido Perez .05 .01
❑ 134 Adam Peterson .05 .01
❑ 135 Scott Radinsky .05 .01
❑ 136 Sammy Sosa .25 .08
❑ 137 Bobby Thigpen .05 .01
❑ 138 Frank Thomas .25 .08
❑ 139 Robin Ventura .10 .02
❑ 140 Daryl Boston .05 .01
❑ 141 Chuck Carr .05 .01
❑ 142 Mark Carreon .05 .01
❑ 143 David Cone .10 .02
❑ 144 Ron Darling .05 .01
❑ 145 Kevin Elster .05 .01
❑ 146 Sid Fernandez .05 .01
❑ 147 John Franco .10 .02
❑ 148 Dwight Gooden .10 .02
❑ 149 Tom Herr .05 .01
❑ 150 Todd Hundley .05 .01
❑ 151 Gregg Jefferies .05 .01
❑ 152 Howard Johnson .05 .01
❑ 153 Dave Magadan .05 .01
❑ 154 Kevin McReynolds .05 .01
❑ 155 Keith Miller UER
(Text says Rochester in
'87& st .05 .01
❑ 156 Bob Ojeda .05 .01
❑ 157 Tom O'Malley .05 .01
❑ 158 Alejandro Pena .05 .01
❑ 159 Darren Reed .05 .01
❑ 160 Mackey Sasser .05 .01
❑ 161 Darryl Strawberry .10 .02
❑ 162 Tim Teufel .05 .01
❑ 163 Kelvin Torve .05 .01
❑ 164 Julio Valera .05 .01
❑ 165 Frank Viola .10 .02
❑ 166 Wally Whitehurst .05 .01
❑ 167 Jim Acker .05 .01
❑ 168 Derek Bell .10 .02
❑ 169 George Bell .05 .01
❑ 170 Willie Blair .05 .01
❑ 171 Pat Borders .05 .01
❑ 172 John Cerutti .05 .01
❑ 173 Junior Felix .05 .01
❑ 174 Tony Fernandez .05 .01
❑ 175 Kelly Gruber UER
(Born in Houston&
should be Bel .05 .01
❑ 176 Tom Henke .05 .01
❑ 177 Glenallen Hill .05 .01
❑ 178 Jimmy Key .10 .02
❑ 179 Manny Lee .05 .01
❑ 180 Fred McGriff .15 .05
❑ 181 Rance Mulliniks .05 .01
❑ 182 Greg Myers .05 .01
❑ 183 John Olerud .10 .02
❑ 184 Luis Sojo .05 .01
❑ 185 Dave Stieb .05 .01
❑ 186 Todd Stottlemyre .05 .01
❑ 187 Duane Ward .05 .01
❑ 188 David Wells .10 .02
❑ 189 Mark Whiten .05 .01
❑ 190 Ken Williams .05 .01
❑ 191 Frank Wills .05 .01
❑ 192 Mookie Wilson .10 .02
❑ 193 Don Aase .05 .01
❑ 194 Tim Belcher UER
(Born Sparta& Ohio&
should say M .05 .01
❑ 195 Hubie Brooks .05 .01
❑ 196 Dennis Cook .05 .01
❑ 197 Tim Crews .05 .01
❑ 198 Kal Daniels .05 .01

❑	199	Kirk Gibson	.10	.02
❑	200	Jim Gott	.05	.01
❑	201	Alfredo Griffin	.05	.01
❑	202	Chris Gwynn	.05	.01
❑	203	Dave Hansen	.05	.01
❑	204	Lenny Harris	.05	.01
❑	205	Mike Hartley	.05	.01
❑	206	Mickey Hatcher	.05	.01
❑	207	Carlos Hernandez	.05	.01
❑	208	Orel Hershiser	.10	.02
❑	209	Jay Howell UER (No 1982 Yankee stats)	.05	.01
❑	210	Mike Huff	.05	.01
❑	211	Stan Javier	.05	.01
❑	212	Ramon Martinez	.05	.01
❑	213	Mike Morgan	.05	.01
❑	214	Eddie Murray	.25	.08
❑	215	Jim Neidlinger RC	.05	.01
❑	216	Jose Offerman	.05	.01
❑	217	Jim Poole	.05	.01
❑	218	Juan Samuel	.05	.01
❑	219	Mike Scioscia	.05	.01
❑	220	Ray Searage	.05	.01
❑	221	Mike Sharperson	.05	.01
❑	222	Fernando Valenzuela	.10	.02
❑	223	Jose Vizcaino	.05	.01
❑	224	Mike Aldrete	.05	.01
❑	225	Scott Anderson RC	.05	.01
❑	226	Dennis Boyd	.05	.01
❑	227	Tim Burke	.05	.01
❑	228	Delino DeShields	.10	.02
❑	229	Mike Fitzgerald	.05	.01
❑	230	Tom Foley	.05	.01
❑	231	Steve Frey	.05	.01
❑	232	Andres Galarraga	.10	.02
❑	233	Mark Gardner	.05	.01
❑	234	Marquis Grissom	.10	.02
❑	235	Kevin Gross (No date given for first Expos win)	.05	.01
❑	236	Drew Hall	.05	.01
❑	237	Dave Martinez	.05	.01
❑	238	Dennis Martinez	.10	.02
❑	239	Dale Mohorcic	.05	.01
❑	240	Chris Nabholz	.05	.01
❑	241	Otis Nixon	.05	.01
❑	242	Junior Noboa	.05	.01
❑	243	Spike Owen	.05	.01
❑	244	Tim Raines	.10	.02
❑	245	Mel Rojas UER (Stats show 3.60 ERA. bio says 3.1	.05	.01
❑	246	Scott Ruskin	.05	.01
❑	247	Bill Sampen	.05	.01
❑	248	Nelson Santovenia	.05	.01
❑	249	Dave Schmidt	.05	.01
❑	250	Larry Walker	.25	.08
❑	251	Tim Wallach	.05	.01
❑	252	Dave Anderson	.05	.01
❑	253	Kevin Bass	.05	.01
❑	254	Steve Bedrosian	.05	.01
❑	255	Jeff Brantley	.05	.01
❑	256	John Burkett	.05	.01
❑	257	Brett Butler	.10	.02
❑	258	Gary Carter	.10	.02
❑	259	Will Clark	.15	.05
❑	260	Steve Decker RC	.10	.02
❑	261	Kelly Downs	.05	.01
❑	262	Scott Garrelts	.05	.01
❑	263	Terry Kennedy	.05	.01
❑	264	Mike LaCoss	.05	.01
❑	265	Mark Leonard RC	.05	.01
❑	266	Greg Litton	.05	.01
❑	267	Kevin Mitchell	.05	.01
❑	268	Randy O'Neal	.05	.01
❑	269	Rick Parker	.05	.01
❑	270	Rick Reuschel	.05	.01
❑	271	Ernest Riles	.05	.01
❑	272	Don Robinson	.05	.01
❑	273	Robby Thompson	.05	.01
❑	274	Mark Thurmond	.05	.01
❑	275	Jose Uribe	.05	.01
❑	276	Matt Williams	.10	.02
❑	277	Trevor Wilson	.05	.01
❑	278	Gerald Alexander RC	.05	.01
❑	279	Brad Arnsberg	.05	.01
❑	280	Kevin Belcher RC	.05	.01
❑	281	Joe Bitker RC	.05	.01
❑	282	Kevin Brown	.10	.02
❑	283	Steve Buechele	.05	.01
❑	284	Jack Daugherty	.05	.01
❑	285	Julio Franco	.10	.02
❑	286	Juan Gonzalez	.25	.08
❑	287	Bill Haselman RC	.05	.01
❑	288	Charlie Hough	.10	.02
❑	289	Jeff Huson	.05	.01
❑	290	Pete Incaviglia	.05	.01
❑	291	Mike Jeffcoat	.05	.01
❑	292	Jeff Kunkel	.05	.01
❑	293	Gary Mielke	.05	.01
❑	294	Jamie Moyer	.10	.02
❑	295	Rafael Palmeiro	.15	.05
❑	296	Geno Petralli	.05	.01
❑	297	Gary Pettis	.05	.01
❑	298	Kevin Reimer	.05	.01
❑	299	Kenny Rogers	.10	.02
❑	300	Jeff Russell	.05	.01
❑	301	John Russell	.05	.01
❑	302	Nolan Ryan	1.00	.40
❑	303	Ruben Sierra	.10	.02
❑	304	Bobby Witt	.05	.01
❑	305	Jim Abbott	.15	.05
❑	306	Kent Anderson	.05	.01
❑	307	Dante Bichette	.10	.02
❑	308	Bert Blyleven	.10	.02
❑	309	Chili Davis	.10	.02
❑	310	Brian Downing	.05	.01
❑	311	Mark Eichhorn	.05	.01
❑	312	Mike Fetters	.05	.01
❑	313	Chuck Finley	.10	.02
❑	314	Willie Fraser	.05	.01
❑	315	Bryan Harvey	.05	.01
❑	316	Donnie Hill	.05	.01
❑	317	Wally Joyner	.10	.02
❑	318	Mark Langston	.05	.01
❑	319	Kirk McCaskill	.05	.01
❑	320	John Orton	.05	.01
❑	321	Lance Parrish	.10	.02
❑	322	Luis Polonia UER (1984 Madfison& should be Madis	.05	.01
❑	323	Johnny Ray	.05	.01
❑	324	Bobby Rose	.05	.01
❑	325	Dick Schofield	.05	.01
❑	326	Rick Schu	.05	.01
❑	327	Lee Stevens	.05	.01
❑	328	Devon White	.10	.02
❑	329	Dave Winfield	.10	.02
❑	330	Cliff Young	.05	.01
❑	331	Dave Bergman	.05	.01
❑	332	Phil Clark RC	.10	.02
❑	333	Darnell Coles	.05	.01
❑	334	Milt Cuyler	.05	.01
❑	335	Cecil Fielder	.10	.02
❑	336	Travis Fryman	.10	.02
❑	337	Paul Gibson	.05	.01
❑	338	Jerry Don Gleaton	.05	.01
❑	339	Mike Heath	.05	.01
❑	340	Mike Henneman	.05	.01
❑	341	Chet Lemon	.05	.01
❑	342	Lance McCullers	.05	.01
❑	343	Jack Morris	.10	.02
❑	344	Lloyd Moseby	.05	.01
❑	345	Edwin Nunez	.05	.01
❑	346	Clay Parker	.05	.01
❑	347	Dan Petry	.05	.01
❑	348	Tony Phillips	.05	.01
❑	349	Jeff M. Robinson	.05	.01
❑	350	Mark Salas	.05	.01
❑	351	Mike Schwabe	.05	.01
❑	352	Larry Sheets	.05	.01
❑	353	John Shelby	.05	.01
❑	354	Frank Tanana	.05	.01
❑	355	Alan Trammell	.10	.02
❑	356	Gary Ward	.05	.01
❑	357	Lou Whitaker	.10	.02
❑	358	Beau Allred	.05	.01
❑	359	Sandy Alomar Jr.	.05	.01
❑	360	Carlos Baerga	.05	.01
❑	361	Kevin Bearse	.05	.01
❑	362	Tom Brookens	.05	.01
❑	363	Jerry Browne UER (No dot over i in first text li	.05	.01
❑	364	Tom Candiotti	.05	.01
❑	365	Alex Cole	.05	.01
❑	366	John Farrell UER (Born in Neptune& should be Mon	.05	.01
❑	367	Felix Fermin	.05	.01
❑	368	Keith Hernandez	.10	.02
❑	369	Brook Jacoby	.05	.01
❑	370	Chris James	.05	.01
❑	371	Dion James	.05	.01
❑	372	Doug Jones	.05	.01
❑	373	Candy Maldonado	.05	.01
❑	374	Steve Olin	.05	.01
❑	375	Jesse Orosco	.05	.01
❑	376	Rudy Seanez	.05	.01
❑	377	Joel Skinner	.05	.01
❑	378	Cory Snyder	.05	.01
❑	379	Greg Swindell	.05	.01
❑	380	Sergio Valdez	.05	.01
❑	381	Mike Walker	.05	.01
❑	382	Colby Ward RC	.05	.01
❑	383	Turner Ward RC	.25	.08
❑	384	Mitch Webster	.05	.01
❑	385	Kevin Wickander	.05	.01
❑	386	Darrel Akerfelds	.05	.01
❑	387	Joe Boever	.05	.01
❑	388	Rod Booker	.05	.01
❑	389	Sil Campusano	.05	.01
❑	390	Don Carman	.05	.01
❑	391	Wes Chamberlain RC	.25	.08
❑	392	Pat Combs	.05	.01
❑	393	Darren Daulton	.10	.02
❑	394	Jose DeJesus	.05	.01
❑	395A	Len Dykstra	.10	.02
❑	395B	Len Dykstra	.10	.02
❑	396	Jason Grimsley	.05	.01
❑	397	Charlie Hayes	.05	.01
❑	398	Von Hayes	.05	.01
❑	399	Dave Hollins UER	.05	.01
❑	400	Ken Howell	.05	.01
❑	401	Ricky Jordan	.05	.01
❑	402	John Kruk	.10	.02
❑	403	Steve Lake	.05	.01
❑	404	Chuck Malone	.05	.01
❑	405	Roger McDowell UER (Says Phillies is saves& shou	.05	.01
❑	406	Chuck McElroy	.05	.01
❑	407	Mickey Morandini	.05	.01
❑	408	Terry Mulholland	.05	.01
❑	409	Dale Murphy	.15	.05
❑	410A	Randy Ready ERR (No Brewers stats listed for 198	.05	.01
❑	410B	Randy Ready COR	.05	.01
❑	411	Bruce Ruffin	.05	.01
❑	412	Dickie Thon	.05	.01
❑	413	Paul Assenmacher	.05	.01
❑	414	Damon Berryhill	.05	.01
❑	415	Mike Bielecki	.05	.01
❑	416	Shawn Boskie	.05	.01
❑	417	Dave Clark	.05	.01
❑	418	Doug Dascenzo	.05	.01
❑	419A	Andre Dawson ERR	.10	.02
❑	419B	Andre Dawson COR	.10	.02
❑	420	Shawon Dunston	.05	.01
❑	421	Joe Girardi	.05	.01
❑	422	Mark Grace	.15	.05
❑	423	Mike Harkey	.05	.01
❑	424	Les Lancaster	.05	.01
❑	425	Bill Long	.05	.01
❑	426	Greg Maddux	.40	.15
❑	427	Derrick May	.05	.01
❑	428	Jeff Pico	.05	.01
❑	429	Domingo Ramos	.05	.01
❑	430	Luis Salazar	.05	.01
❑	431	Ryne Sandberg	.40	.15
❑	432	Dwight Smith	.05	.01
❑	433	Greg Smith	.05	.01
❑	434	Rick Sutcliffe	.10	.02
❑	435	Gary Varsho	.05	.01
❑	436	Hector Villanueva	.05	.01
❑	437	Jerome Walton	.05	.01
❑	438	Curtis Wilkerson	.05	.01

❑ 439 Mitch Williams .05 .01
❑ 440 Steve Wilson .05 .01
❑ 441 Marvell Wynne .05 .01
❑ 442 Scott Bankhead .05 .01
❑ 443 Scott Bradley .05 .01
❑ 444 Greg Briley .05 .01
❑ 445 Mike Brumley UER .05 .01
❑ 446 Jay Buhner .10 .02
❑ 447 Dave Burba RC .25 .08
❑ 448 Henry Cotto .05 .01
❑ 449 Alvin Davis .05 .01
❑ 450 Ken Griffey Jr. .50 .20
❑ 450A Ken Griffey Jr. ERR 1.00 .40
❑ 451 Erik Hanson .05 .01
❑ 452 Gene Harris UER
(63 career runs&
should be 73) .05 .01
❑ 453 Brian Holman .05 .01
❑ 454 Mike Jackson .05 .01
❑ 455 Randy Johnson .30 .10
❑ 456 Jeffrey Leonard .05 .01
❑ 457 Edgar Martinez .15 .05
❑ 458 Tino Martinez .25 .08
❑ 459 Pete O'Brien UER
(1987 BA .266&
should be .286) .05 .01
❑ 460 Harold Reynolds .10 .02
❑ 461 Mike Schooler .05 .01
❑ 462 Bill Swift .05 .01
❑ 463 David Valle .05 .01
❑ 464 Omar Vizquel .15 .05
❑ 465 Matt Young .05 .01
❑ 466 Brady Anderson .10 .02
❑ 467 Jeff Ballard UER
(Missing top of right
parenthes .05 .01
❑ 468 Juan Bell .05 .01
❑ 469A Mike Devereaux
(First line of text
ends with six .10 .02
❑ 469B Mike Devereaux
(First line of text
ends with run .10 .02
❑ 470 Steve Finley .10 .02
❑ 471 Dave Gallagher .05 .01
❑ 472 Leo Gomez .05 .01
❑ 473 Rene Gonzales .05 .01
❑ 474 Pete Harnisch .05 .01
❑ 475 Kevin Hickey .05 .01
❑ 476 Chris Hoiles .05 .01
❑ 477 Sam Horn .05 .01
❑ 478 Tim Hulett
(Photo shows National
League sliding .05 .01
❑ 479 Dave Johnson .05 .01
❑ 480 Ron Kittle UER
(Edmonton misspelled
as Edmundton .05 .01
❑ 481 Ben McDonald .05 .01
❑ 482 Bob Melvin .05 .01
❑ 483 Bob Milacki .05 .01
❑ 484 Randy Milligan .05 .01
❑ 485 John Mitchell .05 .01
❑ 486 Gregg Olson .05 .01
❑ 487 Joe Orsulak .05 .01
❑ 488 Joe Price .05 .01
❑ 489 Bill Ripken .05 .01
❑ 490 Cal Ripken .75 .30
❑ 491 Curt Schilling .25 .08
❑ 492 David Segui .05 .01
❑ 493 Anthony Telford RC .05 .01
❑ 494 Mickey Tettleton .05 .01
❑ 495 Mark Williamson .05 .01
❑ 496 Craig Worthington .05 .01
❑ 497 Juan Agosto .05 .01
❑ 498 Eric Anthony .05 .01
❑ 499 Craig Biggio .15 .05
❑ 500 Ken Caminiti UER .10 .02
❑ 501 Casey Candaele .05 .01
❑ 502 Andujar Cedeno .05 .01
❑ 503 Danny Darwin .05 .01
❑ 504 Mark Davidson .05 .01
❑ 505 Glenn Davis .05 .01
❑ 506 Jim Deshaies .05 .01
❑ 507 Luis Gonzalez RC .50 .20
❑ 508 Bill Gullickson .05 .01
❑ 509 Xavier Hernandez .05 .01
❑ 510 Brian Meyer .05 .01
❑ 511 Ken Oberkfell .05 .01
❑ 512 Mark Portugal .05 .01
❑ 513 Rafael Ramirez .05 .01
❑ 514 Karl Rhodes .05 .01
❑ 515 Mike Scott .05 .01
❑ 516 Mike Simms RC .05 .01
❑ 517 Dave Smith .05 .01
❑ 518 Franklin Stubbs .05 .01
❑ 519 Glenn Wilson .05 .01
❑ 520 Eric Yelding UER
(Text has 63 steals&
stats have .05 .01
❑ 521 Gerald Young .05 .01
❑ 522 Shawn Abner .05 .01
❑ 523 Roberto Alomar .15 .05
❑ 524 Andy Benes .05 .01
❑ 525 Joe Carter .10 .02
❑ 526 Jack Clark .10 .02
❑ 527 Joey Cora .05 .01
❑ 528 Paul Faries RC .05 .01
❑ 529 Tony Gwynn .30 .10
❑ 530 Atlee Hammaker .05 .01
❑ 531 Greg W. Harris .05 .01
❑ 532 Thomas Howard .05 .01
❑ 533 Bruce Hurst .05 .01
❑ 534 Craig Lefferts .05 .01
❑ 535 Derek Lilliquist .05 .01
❑ 536 Fred Lynn .05 .01
❑ 537 Mike Pagliarulo .05 .01
❑ 538 Mark Parent .05 .01
❑ 539 Dennis Rasmussen .05 .01
❑ 540 Bip Roberts .05 .01
❑ 541 Richard Rodriguez RC .05 .01
❑ 542 Benito Santiago .10 .02
❑ 543 Calvin Schiraldi .05 .01
❑ 544 Eric Show .05 .01
❑ 545 Phil Stephenson .05 .01
❑ 546 Garry Templeton UER
(Born 3/24/57&
should be 3/2 .05 .01
❑ 547 Ed Whitson .05 .01
❑ 548 Eddie Williams .05 .01
❑ 549 Kevin Appier .10 .02
❑ 550 Luis Aquino .05 .01
❑ 551 Bob Boone .10 .02
❑ 552 George Brett .60 .25
❑ 553 Jeff Conine RC .40 .15
❑ 554 Steve Crawford .05 .01
❑ 555 Mark Davis .05 .01
❑ 556 Storm Davis .05 .01
❑ 557 Jim Eisenreich .05 .01
❑ 558 Steve Farr .05 .01
❑ 559 Tom Gordon .05 .01
❑ 560 Mark Gubicza .05 .01
❑ 561 Bo Jackson .25 .08
❑ 562 Mike Macfarlane .05 .01
❑ 563 Brian McRae RC .25 .08
❑ 564 Jeff Montgomery .05 .01
❑ 565 Bill Pecota .05 .01
❑ 566 Gerald Perry .05 .01
❑ 567 Bret Saberhagen .10 .02
❑ 568 Jeff Schulz RC .05 .01
❑ 569 Kevin Seitzer .05 .01
❑ 570 Terry Shumpert .05 .01
❑ 571 Kurt Stillwell .05 .01
❑ 572 Danny Tartabull .05 .01
❑ 573 Gary Thurman .05 .01
❑ 574 Frank White .10 .02
❑ 575 Willie Wilson .05 .01
❑ 576 Chris Bosio .05 .01
❑ 577 Greg Brock .05 .01
❑ 578 George Canale .05 .01
❑ 579 Chuck Crim .05 .01
❑ 580 Rob Deer .05 .01
❑ 581 Edgar Diaz .05 .01
❑ 582 Tom Edens RC .05 .01
❑ 583 Mike Felder .05 .01
❑ 584 Jim Gantner .05 .01
❑ 585 Darryl Hamilton .05 .01
❑ 586 Ted Higuera .05 .01
❑ 587 Mark Knudson .05 .01
❑ 588 Bill Krueger .05 .01
❑ 589 Tim McIntosh .05 .01
❑ 590 Paul Mirabella .05 .01
❑ 591 Paul Molitor .10 .02
❑ 592 Jaime Navarro .05 .01
❑ 593 Dave Parker .10 .02
❑ 594 Dan Plesac .05 .01
❑ 595 Ron Robinson .05 .01
❑ 596 Gary Sheffield .10 .02
❑ 597 Bill Spiers .05 .01
❑ 598 B.J. Surhoff .10 .02
❑ 599 Greg Vaughn .05 .01
❑ 600 Randy Veres .05 .01
❑ 601 Robin Yount .40 .15
❑ 602 Rick Aguilera .10 .02
❑ 603 Allan Anderson .05 .01
❑ 604 Juan Berenguer .05 .01
❑ 605 Randy Bush .05 .01
❑ 606 Carmelo Castillo .05 .01
❑ 607 Tim Drummond .05 .01
❑ 608 Scott Erickson .05 .01
❑ 609 Gary Gaetti .10 .02
❑ 610 Greg Gagne .05 .01
❑ 611 Dan Gladden .05 .01
❑ 612 Mark Guthrie .05 .01
❑ 613 Brian Harper .05 .01
❑ 614 Kent Hrbek .10 .02
❑ 615 Gene Larkin .05 .01
❑ 616 Terry Leach .05 .01
❑ 617 Nelson Liriano .05 .01
❑ 618 Shane Mack .05 .01
❑ 619 John Moses .05 .01
❑ 620 Pedro Munoz RC .10 .02
❑ 621 Al Newman .05 .01
❑ 622 Junior Ortiz .05 .01
❑ 623 Kirby Puckett .25 .08
❑ 624 Roy Smith .05 .01
❑ 625 Kevin Tapani .05 .01
❑ 626 Gary Wayne .05 .01
❑ 627 David West .05 .01
❑ 628 Cris Carpenter .05 .01
❑ 629 Vince Coleman .05 .01
❑ 630 Ken Dayley .05 .01
❑ 631A Jose DeLeon ERR .05 .01
❑ 631B Jose DeLeon COR .05 .01
❑ 632 Frank DiPino .05 .01
❑ 633 Bernard Gilkey .05 .01
❑ 634A Pedro Guerrero ERR .10 .02
❑ 634B Pedro Guerrero COR .10 .02
❑ 635 Ken Hill .05 .01
❑ 636 Felix Jose .05 .01
❑ 637 Ray Lankford .10 .02
❑ 638 Joe Magrane .05 .01
❑ 639 Tom Niedenfuer .05 .01
❑ 640 Jose Oquendo .05 .01
❑ 641 Tom Pagnozzi .05 .01
❑ 642 Terry Pendleton .10 .02
❑ 643 Mike Perez RC .10 .02
❑ 644 Bryn Smith .05 .01
❑ 645 Lee Smith .10 .02
❑ 646 Ozzie Smith .40 .15
❑ 647 Scott Terry .05 .01
❑ 648 Bob Tewksbury .05 .01
❑ 649 Milt Thompson .05 .01
❑ 650 John Tudor .05 .01
❑ 651 Denny Walling .05 .01
❑ 652 Craig Wilson RC .05 .01
❑ 653 Todd Worrell .05 .01
❑ 654 Todd Zeile .05 .01
❑ 655 Oscar Azocar .05 .01
❑ 656 Steve Balboni UER
(Born 1/5/57,
should be 1/16) .05 .01
❑ 657 Jesse Barfield .05 .01
❑ 658 Greg Cadaret .05 .01
❑ 659 Chuck Cary .05 .01
❑ 660 Rick Cerone .05 .01
❑ 661 Dave Eiland .05 .01
❑ 662 Alvaro Espinoza .05 .01
❑ 663 Bob Geren .05 .01
❑ 664 Lee Guetterman .05 .01
❑ 665 Mel Hall .05 .01
❑ 666 Andy Hawkins .05 .01
❑ 667 Jimmy Jones .05 .01
❑ 668 Roberto Kelly .05 .01
❑ 669 Dave LaPoint UER
(No '81 Brewers stats&
totals a .05 .01
❑ 670 Tim Leary .05 .01

❑	671 Jim Leyritz	.05	.01
❑	672 Kevin Maas	.05	.01
❑	673 Don Mattingly	.60	.25
❑	674 Matt Nokes	.05	.01
❑	675 Pascual Perez	.05	.01
❑	676 Eric Plunk	.05	.01
❑	677 Dave Righetti	.10	.02
❑	678 Jeff D. Robinson	.05	.01
❑	679 Steve Sax	.05	.01
❑	680 Mike Witt	.05	.01
❑	681 Steve Avery UER	.05	.01
❑	682 Mike Bell RC	.05	.01
❑	683 Jeff Blauser	.05	.01
❑	684 Francisco Cabrera UER (Born 10/16& should say 10	.05	.01
❑	685 Tony Castillo	.05	.01
❑	686 Marty Clary UER (Shown pitching righty& but bio	.05	.01
❑	687 Nick Esasky	.05	.01
❑	688 Ron Gant	.10	.02
❑	689 Tom Glavine	.15	.05
❑	690 Mark Grant	.05	.01
❑	691 Tommy Gregg	.05	.01
❑	692 Dwayne Henry	.05	.01
❑	693 David Justice	.10	.02
❑	694 Jimmy Kremers	.05	.01
❑	695 Charlie Leibrandt	.05	.01
❑	696 Mark Lemke	.05	.01
❑	697 Oddibe McDowell	.05	.01
❑	698 Greg Olson	.05	.01
❑	699 Jeff Parrett	.05	.01
❑	700 Jim Presley	.05	.01
❑	701 Victor Rosario RC	.05	.01
❑	702 Lonnie Smith	.05	.01
❑	703 Pete Smith	.05	.01
❑	704 John Smoltz	.15	.05
❑	705 Mike Stanton	.05	.01
❑	706 Andres Thomas	.05	.01
❑	707 Jeff Treadway	.05	.01
❑	708 Jim Vatcher RC	.05	.01
❑	709 R.Sandberg/C.Fielder	.25	.08
❑	710 K.Griffey Jr./B.Bonds	1.00	.40
❑	711 B.Bonilla/B.Larkin	.10	.02
❑	712 Top Game Savers Bobby Thigpen John Franco	.05	.01
❑	713 A.Dawson/R.Sandberg UER	.25	.08
❑	714 CL:A's/Pirates Reds/Red Sox	.05	.01
❑	715 CL:White Sox/Mets Blue Jays/Dodgers	.05	.01
❑	716 CL:Expos/Giants Rangers/Angels	.05	.01
❑	717 CL:Tigers/Indians Phillies/Cubs	.05	.01
❑	718 CL:Mariners/Orioles Astros/Padres	.05	.01
❑	719 CL:Royals/Brewers Twins/Cardinals	.05	.01
❑	720 CL:Yankees/Braves Superstars/Specials	.05	.01

1992 Fleer

❑	COMPLETE SET (720)	10.00	4.00
❑	COMP.HOBBY SET (732)	20.00	8.00
❑	COMP.RETAIL SET (732)	20.00	8.00

❑	1 Brady Anderson	.10	.02
❑	2 Jose Bautista	.10	.02
❑	3 Juan Bell	.10	.02
❑	4 Glenn Davis	.10	.02
❑	5 Mike Devereaux	.10	.02
❑	6 Dwight Evans	.15	.05
❑	7 Mike Flanagan	.10	.02
❑	8 Leo Gomez	.10	.02
❑	9 Chris Hoiles	.10	.02
❑	10 Sam Horn	.10	.02
❑	11 Tim Hulett	.10	.02
❑	12 Dave Johnson	.10	.02
❑	13 Chito Martinez	.10	.02
❑	14 Ben McDonald	.10	.02
❑	15 Bob Melvin	.10	.02
❑	16 Luis Mercedes	.10	.02
❑	17 Jose Mesa	.10	.02
❑	18 Bob Milacki	.10	.02
❑	19 Randy Milligan	.10	.02
❑	20 Mike Mussina	.25	.08
❑	21 Gregg Olson	.10	.02
❑	22 Joe Orsulak	.10	.02
❑	23 Jim Poole	.10	.02
❑	24 Arthur Rhodes	.10	.02
❑	25 Billy Ripken	.10	.02
❑	26 Cal Ripken	.75	.30
❑	27 David Segui	.10	.02
❑	28 Roy Smith	.10	.02
❑	29 Anthony Telford	.10	.02
❑	30 Mark Williamson	.10	.02
❑	31 Craig Worthington	.10	.02
❑	32 Wade Boggs	.15	.05
❑	33 Tom Bolton	.10	.02
❑	34 Tom Brunansky	.10	.02
❑	35 Ellis Burks	.10	.02
❑	36 Jack Clark	.10	.02
❑	37 Roger Clemens	.50	.20
❑	38 Danny Darwin	.10	.02
❑	39 Mike Greenwell	.10	.02
❑	40 Joe Hesketh	.10	.02
❑	41 Daryl Irvine	.10	.02
❑	42 Dennis Lamp	.10	.02
❑	43 Tony Pena	.10	.02
❑	44 Phil Plantier	.10	.02
❑	45 Carlos Quintana	.10	.02
❑	46 Jeff Reardon	.10	.02
❑	47 Jody Reed	.10	.02
❑	48 Luis Rivera	.10	.02
❑	49 Mo Vaughn	.10	.02
❑	50 Jim Abbott	.15	.05
❑	51 Kyle Abbott	.10	.02
❑	52 Ruben Amaro	.10	.02
❑	53 Scott Bailes	.10	.02
❑	54 Chris Beasley	.10	.02
❑	55 Mark Eichhorn	.10	.02
❑	56 Mike Fetters	.10	.02
❑	57 Chuck Finley	.10	.02
❑	58 Gary Gaetti	.10	.02
❑	59 Dave Gallagher	.10	.02
❑	60 Donnie Hill	.10	.02
❑	61 Bryan Harvey UER (Lee Smith led the Majors with	.10	.02
❑	62 Wally Joyner	.10	.02
❑	63 Mark Langston	.10	.02
❑	64 Kirk McCaskill	.10	.02
❑	65 John Orton	.10	.02
❑	66 Lance Parrish	.10	.02
❑	67 Luis Polonia	.10	.02
❑	68 Bobby Rose	.10	.02
❑	69 Dick Schofield	.10	.02
❑	70 Luis Sojo	.10	.02
❑	71 Lee Stevens	.10	.02
❑	72 Dave Winfield	.10	.02
❑	73 Cliff Young	.10	.02
❑	74 Wilson Alvarez	.10	.02
❑	75 Esteban Beltre	.10	.02
❑	76 Joey Cora	.10	.02
❑	77 Brian Drahman	.10	.02
❑	78 Alex Fernandez	.10	.02
❑	79 Carlton Fisk	.15	.05
❑	80 Scott Fletcher	.10	.02
❑	81 Craig Grebeck	.10	.02
❑	82 Ozzie Guillen	.10	.02
❑	83 Greg Hibbard	.10	.02
❑	84 Charlie Hough	.10	.02
❑	85 Mike Huff	.10	.02
❑	86 Bo Jackson	.25	.08
❑	87 Lance Johnson	.10	.02
❑	88 Ron Karkovice	.10	.02
❑	89 Jack McDowell	.10	.02
❑	90 Matt Merullo	.10	.02
❑	91 Warren Newson	.10	.02
❑	92 Donn Pall UER (Called Dunn on card back)	.10	.02
❑	93 Dan Pasqua	.10	.02
❑	94 Ken Patterson	.10	.02
❑	95 Melido Perez	.10	.02
❑	96 Scott Radinsky	.10	.02
❑	97 Tim Raines	.10	.02
❑	98 Sammy Sosa	.25	.08
❑	99 Bobby Thigpen	.10	.02
❑	100 Frank Thomas	.25	.08
❑	101 Robin Ventura	.10	.02
❑	102 Mike Aldrete	.10	.02
❑	103 Sandy Alomar Jr.	.10	.02
❑	104 Carlos Baerga	.10	.02
❑	105 Albert Belle	.10	.02
❑	106 Willie Blair	.10	.02
❑	107 Jerry Browne	.10	.02
❑	108 Alex Cole	.10	.02
❑	109 Felix Fermin	.10	.02
❑	110 Glenallen Hill	.10	.02
❑	111 Shawn Hillegas	.10	.02
❑	112 Chris James	.10	.02
❑	113 Reggie Jefferson	.10	.02
❑	114 Doug Jones	.10	.02
❑	115 Eric King	.10	.02
❑	116 Mark Lewis	.10	.02
❑	117 Carlos Martinez	.10	.02
❑	118 Charles Nagy UER (Throws right& but card says le	.10	.02
❑	119 Rod Nichols	.10	.02
❑	120 Steve Olin	.10	.02
❑	121 Jesse Orosco	.10	.02
❑	122 Rudy Seanez	.10	.02
❑	123 Joel Skinner	.10	.02
❑	124 Greg Swindell	.10	.02
❑	125 Jim Thome	.25	.08
❑	126 Mark Whiten	.10	.02
❑	127 Scott Aldred	.10	.02
❑	128 Andy Allanson	.10	.02
❑	129 John Cerutti	.10	.02
❑	130 Milt Cuyler	.10	.02
❑	131 Mike Dalton	.10	.02
❑	132 Rob Deer	.10	.02
❑	133 Cecil Fielder	.10	.02
❑	134 Travis Fryman	.10	.02
❑	135 Dan Gakeler	.10	.02
❑	136 Paul Gibson	.10	.02
❑	137 Bill Gullickson	.10	.02
❑	138 Mike Henneman	.10	.02
❑	139 Pete Incaviglia	.10	.02
❑	140 Mark Leiter	.10	.02
❑	141 Scott Livingstone	.10	.02
❑	142 Lloyd Moseby	.10	.02
❑	143 Tony Phillips	.10	.02
❑	144 Mark Salas	.10	.02
❑	145 Frank Tanana	.10	.02
❑	146 Walt Terrell	.10	.02
❑	147 Mickey Tettleton	.10	.02
❑	148 Alan Trammell	.10	.02
❑	149 Lou Whitaker	.10	.02
❑	150 Kevin Appier	.10	.02
❑	151 Luis Aquino	.10	.02
❑	152 Todd Benzinger	.10	.02
❑	153 Mike Boddicker	.10	.02
❑	154 George Brett	.60	.25
❑	155 Storm Davis	.10	.02
❑	156 Jim Eisenreich	.10	.02
❑	157 Kirk Gibson	.10	.02
❑	158 Tom Gordon	.10	.02
❑	159 Mark Gubicza	.10	.02
❑	160 David Howard	.10	.02
❑	161 Mike Macfarlane	.10	.02
❑	162 Brent Mayne	.10	.02
❑	163 Brian McRae	.10	.02
❑	164 Jeff Montgomery	.10	.02
❑	165 Bill Pecota	.10	.02
❑	166 Harvey Pulliam	.10	.02

❑	167	Bret Saberhagen	.10	.02
❑	168	Kevin Seitzer	.10	.02
❑	169	Terry Shumpert	.10	.02
❑	170	Kurt Stillwell	.10	.02
❑	171	Danny Tartabull	.10	.02
❑	172	Gary Thurman	.10	.02
❑	173	Dante Bichette	.10	.02
❑	174	Kevin D. Brown	.10	.02
❑	175	Chuck Crim	.10	.02
❑	176	Jim Gantner	.10	.02
❑	177	Darryl Hamilton	.10	.02
❑	178	Ted Higuera	.10	.02
❑	179	Darren Holmes	.10	.02
❑	180	Mark Lee	.10	.02
❑	181	Julio Machado	.10	.02
❑	182	Paul Molitor	.10	.02
❑	183	Jaime Navarro	.10	.02
❑	184	Edwin Nunez	.10	.02
❑	185	Dan Plesac	.10	.02
❑	186	Willie Randolph	.10	.02
❑	187	Ron Robinson	.10	.02
❑	188	Gary Sheffield	.10	.02
❑	189	Bill Spiers	.10	.02
❑	190	B.J. Surhoff	.10	.02
❑	191	Dale Sveum	.10	.02
❑	192	Greg Vaughn	.10	.02
❑	193	Bill Wegman	.10	.02
❑	194	Robin Yount	.40	.15
❑	195	Rick Aguilera	.10	.02
❑	196	Allan Anderson	.10	.02
❑	197	Steve Bedrosian	.10	.02
❑	198	Randy Bush	.10	.02
❑	199	Larry Casian	.10	.02
❑	200	Chili Davis	.10	.02
❑	201	Scott Erickson	.10	.02
❑	202	Greg Gagne	.10	.02
❑	203	Dan Gladden	.10	.02
❑	204	Brian Harper	.10	.02
❑	205	Kent Hrbek	.10	.02
❑	206	Chuck Knoblauch UER	.10	.02
❑	207	Gene Larkin	.10	.02
❑	208	Terry Leach	.10	.02
❑	209	Scott Leius	.10	.02
❑	210	Shane Mack	.10	.02
❑	211	Jack Morris	.10	.02
❑	212	Pedro Munoz	.10	.02
❑	213	Denny Neagle	.10	.02
❑	214	Al Newman	.10	.02
❑	215	Junior Ortiz	.10	.02
❑	216	Mike Pagliarulo	.10	.02
❑	217	Kirby Puckett	.25	.08
❑	218	Paul Sorrento	.10	.02
❑	219	Kevin Tapani	.10	.02
❑	220	Lenny Webster	.10	.02
❑	221	Jesse Barfield	.10	.02
❑	222	Greg Cadaret	.10	.02
❑	223	Dave Eiland	.10	.02
❑	224	Alvaro Espinoza	.10	.02
❑	225	Steve Farr	.10	.02
❑	226	Bob Geren	.10	.02
❑	227	Lee Guetterman	.10	.02
❑	228	John Habyan	.10	.02
❑	229	Mel Hall	.10	.02
❑	230	Steve Howe	.10	.02
❑	231	Mike Humphreys	.10	.02
❑	232	Scott Kamieniecki	.10	.02
❑	233	Pat Kelly	.10	.02
❑	234	Roberto Kelly	.10	.02
❑	235	Tim Leary	.10	.02
❑	236	Kevin Maas	.10	.02
❑	237	Don Mattingly	.60	.25
❑	238	Hensley Meulens	.10	.02
❑	239	Matt Nokes	.10	.02
❑	240	Pascual Perez	.10	.02
❑	241	Eric Plunk	.10	.02
❑	242	John Ramos	.10	.02
❑	243	Scott Sanderson	.10	.02
❑	244	Steve Sax	.10	.02
❑	245	Wade Taylor	.10	.02
❑	246	Randy Velarde	.10	.02
❑	247	Bernie Williams	.15	.05
❑	248	Troy Afenir	.10	.02
❑	249	Harold Baines	.10	.02
❑	250	Lance Blankenship	.10	.02
❑	251	Mike Bordick	.10	.02
❑	252	Jose Canseco	.15	.05
❑	253	Steve Chitren	.10	.02
❑	254	Ron Darling	.10	.02
❑	255	Dennis Eckersley	.10	.02
❑	256	Mike Gallego	.10	.02
❑	257	Dave Henderson	.10	.02
❑	258	Rickey Henderson	.25	.08
❑	259	Rick Honeycutt	.10	.02
❑	260	Brook Jacoby	.10	.02
❑	261	Carney Lansford	.10	.02
❑	262	Mark McGwire	.60	.25
❑	263	Mike Moore	.10	.02
❑	264	Gene Nelson	.10	.02
❑	265	Jamie Quirk	.10	.02
❑	266	Joe Slusarski	.10	.02
❑	267	Terry Steinbach	.10	.02
❑	268	Dave Stewart	.10	.02
❑	269	Todd Van Poppel	.10	.02
❑	270	Walt Weiss	.10	.02
❑	271	Bob Welch	.10	.02
❑	272	Curt Young	.10	.02
❑	273	Scott Bradley	.10	.02
❑	274	Greg Briley	.10	.02
❑	275	Jay Buhner	.10	.02
❑	276	Henry Cotto	.10	.02
❑	277	Alvin Davis	.10	.02
❑	278	Rich DeLucia	.10	.02
❑	279	Ken Griffey Jr.	.40	.15
❑	280	Erik Hanson	.10	.02
❑	281	Brian Holman	.10	.02
❑	282	Mike Jackson	.10	.02
❑	283	Randy Johnson	.25	.08
❑	284	Tracy Jones	.10	.02
❑	285	Bill Krueger	.10	.02
❑	286	Edgar Martinez	.15	.05
❑	287	Tino Martinez	.15	.05
❑	288	Rob Murphy	.10	.02
❑	289	Pete O'Brien	.10	.02
❑	290	Alonzo Powell	.10	.02
❑	291	Harold Reynolds	.10	.02
❑	292	Mike Schooler	.10	.02
❑	293	Russ Swan	.10	.02
❑	294	Bill Swift	.10	.02
❑	295	Dave Valle	.10	.02
❑	296	Omar Vizquel	.15	.05
❑	297	Gerald Alexander	.10	.02
❑	298	Brad Arnsberg	.10	.02
❑	299	Kevin Brown	.10	.02
❑	300	Jack Daugherty	.10	.02
❑	301	Mario Diaz	.10	.02
❑	302	Brian Downing	.10	.02
❑	303	Julio Franco	.10	.02
❑	304	Juan Gonzalez	.15	.05
❑	305	Rich Gossage	.10	.02
❑	306	Jose Guzman	.10	.02
❑	307	Jose Hernandez RC	.25	.08
❑	308	Jeff Huson	.10	.02
❑	309	Mike Jeffcoat	.10	.02
❑	310	Terry Mathews	.10	.02
❑	311	Rafael Palmeiro	.15	.05
❑	312	Dean Palmer	.10	.02
❑	313	Geno Petralli	.10	.02
❑	314	Gary Pettis	.10	.02
❑	315	Kevin Reimer	.10	.02
❑	316	Ivan Rodriguez	.25	.08
❑	317	Kenny Rogers	.10	.02
❑	318	Wayne Rosenthal	.10	.02
❑	319	Jeff Russell	.10	.02
❑	320	Nolan Ryan	1.00	.40
❑	321	Ruben Sierra	.10	.02
❑	322	Jim Acker	.10	.02
❑	323	Roberto Alomar	.15	.05
❑	324	Derek Bell	.10	.02
❑	325	Pat Borders	.10	.02
❑	326	Tom Candiotti	.10	.02
❑	327	Joe Carter	.10	.02
❑	328	Rob Ducey	.10	.02
❑	329	Kelly Gruber	.10	.02
❑	330	Juan Guzman	.10	.02
❑	331	Tom Henke	.10	.02
❑	332	Jimmy Key	.10	.02
❑	333	Manny Lee	.10	.02
❑	334	Al Leiter	.10	.02
❑	335	Bob MacDonald	.10	.02
❑	336	Candy Maldonado	.10	.02
❑	337	Rance Mulliniks	.10	.02
❑	338	Greg Myers	.10	.02
❑	339	John Olerud UER	.10	.02
❑	340	Ed Sprague	.10	.02
❑	341	Dave Stieb	.10	.02
❑	342	Todd Stottlemyre	.10	.02
❑	343	Mike Timlin	.10	.02
❑	344	Duane Ward	.10	.02
❑	345	David Wells	.10	.02
❑	346	Devon White	.10	.02
❑	347	Mookie Wilson	.10	.02
❑	348	Eddie Zosky	.10	.02
❑	349	Steve Avery	.10	.02
❑	350	Mike Bell	.10	.02
❑	351	Rafael Belliard	.10	.02
❑	352	Juan Berenguer	.10	.02
❑	353	Jeff Blauser	.10	.02
❑	354	Sid Bream	.10	.02
❑	355	Francisco Cabrera	.10	.02
❑	356	Marvin Freeman	.10	.02
❑	357	Ron Gant	.10	.02
❑	358	Tom Glavine	.15	.05
❑	359	Brian Hunter	.10	.02
❑	360	David Justice	.10	.02
❑	361	Charlie Leibrandt	.10	.02
❑	362	Mark Lemke	.10	.02
❑	363	Kent Mercker	.10	.02
❑	364	Keith Mitchell	.10	.02
❑	365	Greg Olson	.10	.02
❑	366	Terry Pendleton	.10	.02
❑	367	Armando Reynoso RC	.25	.08
❑	368	Deion Sanders	.15	.05
❑	369	Lonnie Smith	.10	.02
❑	370	Pete Smith	.10	.02
❑	371	John Smoltz	.15	.05
❑	372	Mike Stanton	.10	.02
❑	373	Jeff Treadway	.10	.02
❑	374	Mark Wohlers	.10	.02
❑	375	Paul Assenmacher	.10	.02
❑	376	George Bell	.10	.02
❑	377	Shawn Boskie	.10	.02
❑	378	Frank Castillo	.10	.02
❑	379	Andre Dawson	.10	.02
❑	380	Shawon Dunston	.10	.02
❑	381	Mark Grace	.15	.05
❑	382	Mike Harkey	.10	.02
❑	383	Danny Jackson	.10	.02
❑	384	Les Lancaster	.10	.02
❑	385	Ced Landrum	.10	.02
❑	386	Greg Maddux	.40	.15
❑	387	Derrick May	.10	.02
❑	388	Chuck McElroy	.10	.02
❑	389	Ryne Sandberg	.40	.15
❑	390	Heathcliff Slocumb	.10	.02
❑	391	Dave Smith	.10	.02
❑	392	Dwight Smith	.10	.02
❑	393	Rick Sutcliffe	.10	.02
❑	394	Hector Villanueva	.10	.02
❑	395	Chico Walker	.10	.02
❑	396	Jerome Walton	.10	.02
❑	397	Rick Wilkins	.10	.02
❑	398	Jack Armstrong	.10	.02
❑	399	Freddie Benavides	.10	.02
❑	400	Glenn Braggs	.10	.02
❑	401	Tom Browning	.10	.02
❑	402	Norm Charlton	.10	.02
❑	403	Eric Davis	.10	.02
❑	404	Rob Dibble	.10	.02
❑	405	Bill Doran	.10	.02
❑	406	Mariano Duncan	.10	.02
❑	407	Kip Gross	.10	.02
❑	408	Chris Hammond	.10	.02
❑	409	Billy Hatcher	.10	.02
❑	410	Chris Jones	.10	.02
❑	411	Barry Larkin	.15	.05
❑	412	Hal Morris	.10	.02
❑	413	Randy Myers	.10	.02
❑	414	Joe Oliver	.10	.02
❑	415	Paul O'Neill	.15	.05
❑	416	Ted Power	.10	.02
❑	417	Luis Quinones	.10	.02
❑	418	Jeff Reed	.10	.02
❑	419	Jose Rijo	.10	.02
❑	420	Chris Sabo	.10	.02
❑	421	Reggie Sanders	.10	.02
❑	422	Scott Scudder	.10	.02
❑	423	Glenn Sutko	.10	.02
❑	424	Eric Anthony	.10	.02

❑ 425 Jeff Bagwell .25 .08
❑ 426 Craig Biggio .15 .05
❑ 427 Ken Caminiti .10 .02
❑ 428 Casey Candaele .10 .02
❑ 429 Mike Capel .10 .02
❑ 430 Andujar Cedeno .10 .02
❑ 431 Jim Corsi .10 .02
❑ 432 Mark Davidson .10 .02
❑ 433 Steve Finley .10 .02
❑ 434 Luis Gonzalez .10 .02
❑ 435 Pete Harnisch .10 .02
❑ 436 Dwayne Henry .10 .02
❑ 437 Xavier Hernandez .10 .02
❑ 438 Jimmy Jones .10 .02
❑ 439 Darryl Kile .10 .02
❑ 440 Rob Mallicoat .10 .02
❑ 441 Andy Mota .10 .02
❑ 442 Al Osuna .10 .02
❑ 443 Mark Portugal .10 .02
❑ 444 Scott Servais .10 .02
❑ 445 Mike Simms .10 .02
❑ 446 Gerald Young .10 .02
❑ 447 Tim Belcher .10 .02
❑ 448 Brett Butler .10 .02
❑ 449 John Candelaria .10 .02
❑ 450 Gary Carter .10 .02
❑ 451 Dennis Cook .10 .02
❑ 452 Tim Crews .10 .02
❑ 453 Kal Daniels .10 .02
❑ 454 Jim Gott .10 .02
❑ 455 Alfredo Griffin .10 .02
❑ 456 Kevin Gross .10 .02
❑ 457 Chris Gwynn .10 .02
❑ 458 Lenny Harris .10 .02
❑ 459 Orel Hershiser .10 .02
❑ 460 Jay Howell .10 .02
❑ 461 Stan Javier .10 .02
❑ 462 Eric Karros .10 .02
❑ 463 Ramon Martinez UER
(Card says bats right&
should .10 .02
❑ 464 Roger McDowell UER
(Wins add up to 54&
totals ha .10 .02
❑ 465 Mike Morgan .10 .02
❑ 466 Eddie Murray .25 .08
❑ 467 Jose Offerman .10 .02
❑ 468 Bob Ojeda .10 .02
❑ 469 Juan Samuel .10 .02
❑ 470 Mike Scioscia .10 .02
❑ 471 Darryl Strawberry .10 .02
❑ 472 Bret Barberie .10 .02
❑ 473 Brian Barnes .10 .02
❑ 474 Eric Bullock .10 .02
❑ 475 Ivan Calderon .10 .02
❑ 476 Delino DeShields .10 .02
❑ 477 Jeff Fassero .10 .02
❑ 478 Mike Fitzgerald .10 .02
❑ 479 Steve Frey .10 .02
❑ 480 Andres Galarraga .10 .02
❑ 481 Mark Gardner .10 .02
❑ 482 Marquis Grissom .10 .02
❑ 483 Chris Haney .10 .02
❑ 484 Barry Jones .10 .02
❑ 485 Dave Martinez .10 .02
❑ 486 Dennis Martinez .10 .02
❑ 487 Chris Nabholz .10 .02
❑ 488 Spike Owen .10 .02
❑ 489 Gilberto Reyes .10 .02
❑ 490 Mel Rojas .10 .02
❑ 491 Scott Ruskin .10 .02
❑ 492 Bill Sampen .10 .02
❑ 493 Larry Walker .15 .05
❑ 494 Tim Wallach .10 .02
❑ 495 Daryl Boston .10 .02
❑ 496 Hubie Brooks .10 .02
❑ 497 Tim Burke .10 .02
❑ 498 Mark Carreon .10 .02
❑ 499 Tony Castillo .10 .02
❑ 500 Vince Coleman .10 .02
❑ 501 David Cone .10 .02
❑ 502 Kevin Elster .10 .02
❑ 503 Sid Fernandez .10 .02
❑ 504 John Franco .10 .02
❑ 505 Dwight Gooden .10 .02
❑ 506 Todd Hundley .10 .02
❑ 507 Jeff Innis .10 .02
❑ 508 Gregg Jefferies .10 .02
❑ 509 Howard Johnson .10 .02
❑ 510 Dave Magadan .10 .02
❑ 511 Terry McDaniel .10 .02
❑ 512 Kevin McReynolds .10 .02
❑ 513 Keith Miller .10 .02
❑ 514 Charlie O'Brien .10 .02
❑ 515 Mackey Sasser .10 .02
❑ 516 Pete Schourek .10 .02
❑ 517 Julio Valera .10 .02
❑ 518 Frank Viola .10 .02
❑ 519 Wally Whitehurst .10 .02
❑ 520 Anthony Young .10 .02
❑ 521 Andy Ashby .10 .02
❑ 522 Kim Batiste .10 .02
❑ 523 Joe Boever .10 .02
❑ 524 Wes Chamberlain .10 .02
❑ 525 Pat Combs .10 .02
❑ 526 Danny Cox .10 .02
❑ 527 Darren Daulton .10 .02
❑ 528 Jose DeJesus .10 .02
❑ 529 Len Dykstra .10 .02
❑ 530 Darrin Fletcher .10 .02
❑ 531 Tommy Greene .10 .02
❑ 532 Jason Grimsley .10 .02
❑ 533 Charlie Hayes .10 .02
❑ 534 Von Hayes .10 .02
❑ 535 Dave Hollins .10 .02
❑ 536 Ricky Jordan .10 .02
❑ 537 John Kruk .10 .02
❑ 538 Jim Lindeman .10 .02
❑ 539 Mickey Morandini .10 .02
❑ 540 Terry Mulholland .10 .02
❑ 541 Dale Murphy .15 .05
❑ 542 Randy Ready .10 .02
❑ 543 Wally Ritchie UER
(Letters in data are
cut off o .10 .02
❑ 544 Bruce Ruffin .10 .02
❑ 545 Steve Searcy .10 .02
❑ 546 Dickie Thon .10 .02
❑ 547 Mitch Williams .10 .02
❑ 548 Stan Belinda .10 .02
❑ 549 Jay Bell .10 .02
❑ 550 Barry Bonds 1.00 .40
❑ 551 Bobby Bonilla .10 .02
❑ 552 Steve Buechele .10 .02
❑ 553 Doug Drabek .10 .02
❑ 554 Neal Heaton .10 .02
❑ 555 Jeff King .10 .02
❑ 556 Bob Kipper .10 .02
❑ 557 Bill Landrum .10 .02
❑ 558 Mike LaValliere .10 .02
❑ 559 Jose Lind .10 .02
❑ 560 Lloyd McClendon .10 .02
❑ 561 Orlando Merced .10 .02
❑ 562 Bob Patterson .10 .02
❑ 563 Joe Redfield .10 .02
❑ 564 Gary Redus .10 .02
❑ 565 Rosario Rodriguez .10 .02
❑ 566 Don Slaught .10 .02
❑ 567 John Smiley .10 .02
❑ 568 Zane Smith .10 .02
❑ 569 Randy Tomlin .10 .02
❑ 570 Andy Van Slyke .15 .05
❑ 571 Gary Varsho .10 .02
❑ 572 Bob Walk .10 .02
❑ 573 John Wehner UER
(Actually played for
Carolina in .10 .02
❑ 574 Juan Agosto .10 .02
❑ 575 Cris Carpenter .10 .02
❑ 576 Jose DeLeon .10 .02
❑ 577 Rich Gedman .10 .02
❑ 578 Bernard Gilkey .10 .02
❑ 579 Pedro Guerrero .10 .02
❑ 580 Ken Hill .10 .02
❑ 581 Rex Hudler .10 .02
❑ 582 Felix Jose .10 .02
❑ 583 Ray Lankford .10 .02
❑ 584 Omar Olivares .10 .02
❑ 585 Jose Oquendo .10 .02
❑ 586 Tom Pagnozzi .10 .02
❑ 587 Geronimo Pena .10 .02
❑ 588 Mike Perez .10 .02
❑ 589 Gerald Perry .10 .02
❑ 590 Bryn Smith .10 .02
❑ 591 Lee Smith .10 .02
❑ 592 Ozzie Smith .40 .15
❑ 593 Scott Terry .10 .02
❑ 594 Bob Tewksbury .10 .02
❑ 595 Milt Thompson .10 .02
❑ 596 Todd Zeile .10 .02
❑ 597 Larry Andersen .10 .02
❑ 598 Oscar Azocar .10 .02
❑ 599 Andy Benes .10 .02
❑ 600 Ricky Bones .10 .02
❑ 601 Jerald Clark .10 .02
❑ 602 Pat Clements .10 .02
❑ 603 Paul Faries .10 .02
❑ 604 Tony Fernandez .10 .02
❑ 605 Tony Gwynn .30 .10
❑ 606 Greg W. Harris .10 .02
❑ 607 Thomas Howard .10 .02
❑ 608 Bruce Hurst .10 .02
❑ 609 Darrin Jackson .10 .02
❑ 610 Tom Lampkin .10 .02
❑ 611 Craig Lefferts .10 .02
❑ 612 Jim Lewis RC .10 .02
❑ 613 Mike Maddux .10 .02
❑ 614 Fred McGriff .15 .05
❑ 615 Jose Melendez .10 .02
❑ 616 Jose Mota .10 .02
❑ 617 Dennis Rasmussen .10 .02
❑ 618 Bip Roberts .10 .02
❑ 619 Rich Rodriguez .10 .02
❑ 620 Benito Santiago .10 .02
❑ 621 Craig Shipley .10 .02
❑ 622 Tim Teufel .10 .02
❑ 623 Kevin Ward .10 .02
❑ 624 Ed Whitson .10 .02
❑ 625 Dave Anderson .10 .02
❑ 626 Kevin Bass .10 .02
❑ 627 Rod Beck RC .40 .15
❑ 628 Bud Black .10 .02
❑ 629 Jeff Brantley .10 .02
❑ 630 John Burkett .10 .02
❑ 631 Will Clark .15 .05
❑ 632 Royce Clayton .10 .02
❑ 633 Steve Decker .10 .02
❑ 634 Kelly Downs .10 .02
❑ 635 Mike Felder .10 .02
❑ 636 Scott Garrelts .10 .02
❑ 637 Eric Gunderson .10 .02
❑ 638 Bryan Hickerson RC .10 .02
❑ 639 Darren Lewis .10 .02
❑ 640 Greg Litton .10 .02
❑ 641 Kirt Manwaring .10 .02
❑ 642 Paul McClellan .10 .02
❑ 643 Willie McGee .10 .02
❑ 644 Kevin Mitchell .10 .02
❑ 645 Francisco Oliveras .10 .02
❑ 646 Mike Remlinger .10 .02
❑ 647 Dave Righetti .10 .02
❑ 648 Robby Thompson .10 .02
❑ 649 Jose Uribe .10 .02
❑ 650 Matt Williams .10 .02
❑ 651 Trevor Wilson .10 .02
❑ 652 Tom Goodwin MLP UER .10 .02
❑ 653 Terry Bross MLP .10 .02
❑ 654 Mike Christopher MLP .10 .02
❑ 655 Kenny Lofton .15 .05
❑ 656 Chris Cron MLP .10 .02
❑ 657 Willie Banks MLP .10 .02
❑ 658 Pat Rice MLP .10 .02
❑ 659A Rob Mauer ERR .75 .30
❑ 659B Rob Maurer MLP COR .10 .02
❑ 660 Don Harris MLP .10 .02
❑ 661 Henry Rodriguez MLP .10 .02
❑ 662 Cliff Brantley MLP .10 .02
❑ 663 Mike Linskey MLP UER .10 .02
❑ 664 Gary DiSarcina MLP .10 .02
❑ 665 Gil Heredia RC .25 .08
❑ 666 Vinny Castilla RC 1.00 .40
❑ 667 Paul Abbott MLP .10 .02
❑ 668 Monty Fariss MLP UER
(Called Paul on back) .10 .02
❑ 669 Jarvis Brown MLP .10 .02
❑ 670 Wayne Kirby RC .10 .02
❑ 671 Scott Brosius RC .40 .15
❑ 672 Bob Hamelin .10 .02

❑ 673 Joel Johnston MLP .10 .02
❑ 674 Tim Spehr MLP .10 .02
❑ 675A Jeff Gardner ERR P .75 .30
❑ 675B Jeff Gardner MLP COR .10 .02
❑ 676 Rico Rossy MLP .10 .02
❑ 677 Roberto Hernandez MLP .10 .02
❑ 678 Ted Wood MLP .10 .02
❑ 679 Cal Eldred .10 .02
❑ 680 Sean Berry MLP .10 .02
❑ 681 Rickey Henderson RS .15 .05
❑ 682 Nolan Ryan RS .50 .20
❑ 683 Dennis Martinez RS .10 .02
❑ 684 Wilson Alvarez RS .10 .02
❑ 685 Joe Carter RS .10 .02
❑ 686 Dave Winfield RS .10 .02
❑ 687 David Cone RS .10 .02
❑ 688 Jose Canseco LL UER .10 .02
❑ 689 Howard Johnson LL .10 .02
❑ 690 Julio Franco LL .10 .02
❑ 691 Terry Pendleton LL .10 .02
❑ 692 Cecil Fielder LL .10 .02
❑ 693 Scott Erickson LL .10 .02
❑ 694 Tom Glavine LL .10 .02
❑ 695 Dennis Martinez LL .10 .02
❑ 696 Bryan Harvey LL .10 .02
❑ 697 Lee Smith LL .10 .02
❑ 698 Roberto/Sandy Alomar .10 .02
❑ 699 B.Bonilla/W.Clark .10 .02
❑ 700 Wohlers/Mercker/Pena .10 .02
❑ 701 B.Jackson/F.Thomas .15 .05
❑ 702 P.Molitor/Butler .10 .02
❑ 703 C.Ripken/J.Carter .40 .15
❑ 704 B.Larkin/K.Puckett .15 .05
❑ 705 M.Vaughn/C.Fielder .10 .02
❑ 706 R.Martinez/O.Guillen .10 .02
❑ 707 H.Baines/W.Boggs .10 .02
❑ 708 Robin Yount PV .25 .08
❑ 709 Ken Griffey Jr. PV .25 .08
❑ 710 Nolan Ryan PV .50 .20
❑ 711 Cal Ripken PV .40 .15
❑ 712 Frank Thomas PV .15 .05
❑ 713 David Justice PV .10 .02
❑ 714 Checklist 1-101 .10 .02
❑ 715 Checklist 102-194 .10 .02
❑ 716 Checklist 195-296 .10 .02
❑ 717 Checklist 297-397 .10 .02
❑ 718 Checklist 398-494 .10 .02
❑ 719 Checklist 495-596 .10 .02
❑ 720A Checklist 597-720 ERR (659 Rob Mauer) .10 .02
❑ 720B Checklist 597-720 COR (659 Rob Maurer) .10 .02

1993 Fleer

❑ COMPLETE SET (720) 40.00 20.00
❑ COMPLETE SERIES 1 (360) 20.00 10.00
❑ COMPLETE SERIES 2 (360) 20.00 10.00
❑ 1 Steve Avery .10 .02
❑ 2 Sid Bream .10 .02
❑ 3 Ron Gant .20 .07
❑ 4 Tom Glavine .30 .10
❑ 5 Brian Hunter .10 .02
❑ 6 Ryan Klesko .20 .07
❑ 7 Charlie Leibrandt .10 .02
❑ 8 Kent Mercker .10 .02
❑ 9 David Nied .10 .02
❑ 10 Otis Nixon .10 .02
❑ 11 Greg Olson .10 .02
❑ 12 Terry Pendleton .20 .07
❑ 13 Deion Sanders .30 .10
❑ 14 John Smoltz .30 .10
❑ 15 Mike Stanton .10 .02
❑ 16 Mark Wohlers .10 .02
❑ 17 Paul Assenmacher .10 .02
❑ 18 Steve Buechele .10 .02
❑ 19 Shawon Dunston .10 .02
❑ 20 Mark Grace .30 .10
❑ 21 Derrick May .10 .02
❑ 22 Chuck McElroy .10 .02
❑ 23 Mike Morgan .10 .02
❑ 24 Rey Sanchez .10 .02
❑ 25 Ryne Sandberg .75 .30
❑ 26 Bob Scanlan .10 .02
❑ 27 Sammy Sosa .50 .20
❑ 28 Rick Wilkins .10 .02
❑ 29 Bobby Ayala RC .10 .02
❑ 30 Tim Belcher .10 .02
❑ 31 Jeff Branson .10 .02
❑ 32 Norm Charlton .10 .02
❑ 33 Steve Foster .10 .02
❑ 34 Willie Greene .10 .02
❑ 35 Chris Hammond .10 .02
❑ 36 Milt Hill .10 .02
❑ 37 Hal Morris .10 .02
❑ 38 Joe Oliver .10 .02
❑ 39 Paul O'Neill .30 .10
❑ 40 Tim Pugh RC .10 .02
❑ 41 Jose Rijo .10 .02
❑ 42 Bip Roberts .10 .02
❑ 43 Chris Sabo .10 .02
❑ 44 Reggie Sanders .20 .07
❑ 45 Eric Anthony .10 .02
❑ 46 Jeff Bagwell .30 .10
❑ 47 Craig Biggio .30 .10
❑ 48 Joe Boever .10 .02
❑ 49 Casey Candaele .10 .02
❑ 50 Steve Finley .20 .07
❑ 51 Luis Gonzalez .20 .07
❑ 52 Pete Harnisch .10 .02
❑ 53 Xavier Hernandez .10 .02
❑ 54 Doug Jones .10 .02
❑ 55 Eddie Taubensee .10 .02
❑ 56 Brian Williams .10 .02
❑ 57 Pedro Astacio .10 .02
❑ 58 Todd Benzinger .10 .02
❑ 59 Brett Butler .20 .07
❑ 60 Tom Candiotti .10 .02
❑ 61 Lenny Harris .10 .02
❑ 62 Carlos Hernandez .10 .02
❑ 63 Orel Hershiser .20 .07
❑ 64 Eric Karros .20 .07
❑ 65 Ramon Martinez .10 .02
❑ 66 Jose Offerman .10 .02
❑ 67 Mike Scioscia .10 .02
❑ 68 Mike Sharperson .10 .02
❑ 69 Eric Young .10 .02
❑ 70 Moises Alou .20 .07
❑ 71 Ivan Calderon .10 .02
❑ 72 Archi Cianfrocco .10 .02
❑ 73 Wil Cordero .10 .02
❑ 74 Delino DeShields .10 .02
❑ 75 Mark Gardner .10 .02
❑ 76 Ken Hill .10 .02
❑ 77 Tim Laker RC .10 .02
❑ 78 Chris Nabholz .10 .02
❑ 79 Mel Rojas .10 .02
❑ 80 John Vander Wal UER (Misspelled Vander Wall in l .10 .02
❑ 81 Larry Walker .20 .07
❑ 82 Tim Wallach .10 .02
❑ 83 John Wetteland .20 .07
❑ 84 Bobby Bonilla .20 .07
❑ 85 Daryl Boston .10 .02
❑ 86 Sid Fernandez .10 .02
❑ 87 Eric Hillman .10 .02
❑ 88 Todd Hundley .10 .02
❑ 89 Howard Johnson .10 .02
❑ 90 Jeff Kent .50 .20
❑ 91 Eddie Murray .50 .20
❑ 92 Bill Pecota .10 .02
❑ 93 Bret Saberhagen .20 .07
❑ 94 Dick Schofield .10 .02
❑ 95 Pete Schourek .10 .02
❑ 96 Anthony Young .10 .02
❑ 97 Ruben Amaro .10 .02
❑ 98 Juan Bell .10 .02
❑ 99 Wes Chamberlain .10 .02
❑ 100 Darren Daulton .20 .07
❑ 101 Mariano Duncan .10 .02
❑ 102 Mike Hartley .10 .02
❑ 103 Ricky Jordan .10 .02
❑ 104 John Kruk .20 .07
❑ 105 Mickey Morandini .10 .02
❑ 106 Terry Mulholland .10 .02
❑ 107 Ben Rivera .10 .02
❑ 108 Curt Schilling .20 .07
❑ 109 Keith Shepherd RC .10 .02
❑ 110 Stan Belinda .10 .02
❑ 111 Jay Bell .20 .07
❑ 112 Barry Bonds 1.50 .60
❑ 113 Jeff King .10 .02
❑ 114 Mike LaValliere .10 .02
❑ 115 Jose Lind .10 .02
❑ 116 Roger Mason .10 .02
❑ 117 Orlando Merced .10 .02
❑ 118 Bob Patterson .10 .02
❑ 119 Don Slaught .10 .02
❑ 120 Zane Smith .10 .02
❑ 121 Randy Tomlin .10 .02
❑ 122 Andy Van Slyke .30 .10
❑ 123 Tim Wakefield .50 .20
❑ 124 Rheal Cormier .10 .02
❑ 125 Bernard Gilkey .10 .02
❑ 126 Felix Jose .10 .02
❑ 127 Ray Lankford .20 .07
❑ 128 Bob McClure .10 .02
❑ 129 Donovan Osborne .10 .02
❑ 130 Tom Pagnozzi .10 .02
❑ 131 Geronimo Pena .10 .02
❑ 132 Mike Perez .10 .02
❑ 133 Lee Smith .20 .07
❑ 134 Bob Tewksbury .10 .02
❑ 135 Todd Worrell .10 .02
❑ 136 Todd Zeile .10 .02
❑ 137 Jerald Clark .10 .02
❑ 138 Tony Gwynn .60 .25
❑ 139 Greg W. Harris .10 .02
❑ 140 Jeremy Hernandez .10 .02
❑ 141 Darrin Jackson .10 .02
❑ 142 Mike Maddux .10 .02
❑ 143 Fred McGriff .30 .10
❑ 144 Jose Melendez .10 .02
❑ 145 Rich Rodriguez .10 .02
❑ 146 Frank Seminara .10 .02
❑ 147 Gary Sheffield .20 .07
❑ 148 Kurt Stillwell .10 .02
❑ 149 Dan Walters .10 .02
❑ 150 Rod Beck .10 .02
❑ 151 Bud Black .10 .02
❑ 152 Jeff Brantley .10 .02
❑ 153 John Burkett .10 .02
❑ 154 Will Clark .30 .10
❑ 155 Royce Clayton .10 .02
❑ 156 Mike Jackson .10 .02
❑ 157 Darren Lewis .10 .02
❑ 158 Kirt Manwaring .10 .02
❑ 159 Willie McGee .20 .07
❑ 160 Cory Snyder .10 .02
❑ 161 Bill Swift .10 .02
❑ 162 Trevor Wilson .10 .02
❑ 163 Brady Anderson .20 .07
❑ 164 Glenn Davis .10 .02
❑ 165 Mike Devereaux .10 .02
❑ 166 Todd Frohwirth .10 .02
❑ 167 Leo Gomez .10 .02
❑ 168 Chris Hoiles .10 .02
❑ 169 Ben McDonald .10 .02
❑ 170 Randy Milligan .10 .02
❑ 171 Alan Mills .10 .02
❑ 172 Mike Mussina .30 .10
❑ 173 Gregg Olson .10 .02
❑ 174 Arthur Rhodes .10 .02
❑ 175 David Segui .10 .02
❑ 176 Ellis Burks .20 .07
❑ 177 Roger Clemens 1.00 .40
❑ 178 Scott Cooper .10 .02
❑ 179 Danny Darwin .10 .02
❑ 180 Tony Fossas .10 .02
❑ 181 Paul Quantrill .10 .02

❑ 182	Jody Reed	.10	.02
❑ 183	John Valentin	.10	.02
❑ 184	Mo Vaughn	.20	.07
❑ 185	Frank Viola	.20	.07
❑ 186	Bob Zupcic	.10	.02
❑ 187	Jim Abbott	.30	.10
❑ 188	Gary DiSarcina	.10	.02
❑ 189	Damion Easley	.10	.02
❑ 190	Junior Felix	.10	.02
❑ 191	Chuck Finley	.20	.07
❑ 192	Joe Grahe	.10	.02
❑ 193	Bryan Harvey	.10	.02
❑ 194	Mark Langston	.10	.02
❑ 195	John Orton	.10	.02
❑ 196	Luis Polonia	.10	.02
❑ 197	Tim Salmon	.30	.10
❑ 198	Luis Sojo	.10	.02
❑ 199	Wilson Alvarez	.10	.02
❑ 200	George Bell	.10	.02
❑ 201	Alex Fernandez	.10	.02
❑ 202	Craig Grebeck	.10	.02
❑ 203	Ozzie Guillen	.20	.07
❑ 204	Lance Johnson	.10	.02
❑ 205	Ron Karkovice	.10	.02
❑ 206	Kirk McCaskill	.10	.02
❑ 207	Jack McDowell	.10	.02
❑ 208	Scott Radinsky	.10	.02
❑ 209	Tim Raines	.20	.07
❑ 210	Frank Thomas	.50	.20
❑ 211	Robin Ventura	.20	.07
❑ 212	Sandy Alomar Jr.	.10	.02
❑ 213	Carlos Baerga	.10	.02
❑ 214	Dennis Cook	.10	.02
❑ 215	Thomas Howard	.10	.02
❑ 216	Mark Lewis	.10	.02
❑ 217	Derek Lilliquist	.10	.02
❑ 218	Kenny Lofton	.20	.07
❑ 219	Charles Nagy	.10	.02
❑ 220	Steve Olin	.10	.02
❑ 221	Paul Sorrento	.10	.02
❑ 222	Jim Thome	.30	.10
❑ 223	Mark Whiten	.10	.02
❑ 224	Milt Cuyler	.10	.02
❑ 225	Rob Deer	.10	.02
❑ 226	John Doherty	.10	.02
❑ 227	Cecil Fielder	.20	.07
❑ 228	Travis Fryman	.20	.07
❑ 229	Mike Henneman	.10	.02
❑ 230	John Kiely UER (Card has batting stats of Pat Ke	.10	.02
❑ 231	Kurt Knudsen	.10	.02
❑ 232	Scott Livingstone	.10	.02
❑ 233	Tony Phillips	.10	.02
❑ 234	Mickey Tettleton	.10	.02
❑ 235	Kevin Appier	.20	.07
❑ 236	George Brett	1.25	.50
❑ 237	Tom Gordon	.10	.02
❑ 238	Gregg Jefferies	.10	.02
❑ 239	Wally Joyner	.20	.07
❑ 240	Kevin Koslofski	.10	.02
❑ 241	Mike Macfarlane	.10	.02
❑ 242	Brian McRae	.10	.02
❑ 243	Rusty Meacham	.10	.02
❑ 244	Keith Miller	.10	.02
❑ 245	Jeff Montgomery	.10	.02
❑ 246	Hipolito Pichardo	.10	.02
❑ 247	Ricky Bones	.10	.02
❑ 248	Cal Eldred	.10	.02
❑ 249	Mike Fetters	.10	.02
❑ 250	Darryl Hamilton	.10	.02
❑ 251	Doug Henry	.10	.02
❑ 252	John Jaha	.10	.02
❑ 253	Pat Listach	.10	.02
❑ 254	Paul Molitor	.20	.07
❑ 255	Jaime Navarro	.10	.02
❑ 256	Kevin Seitzer	.10	.02
❑ 257	B.J. Surhoff	.20	.07
❑ 258	Greg Vaughn	.10	.02
❑ 259	Bill Wegman	.10	.02
❑ 260	Robin Yount	.75	.30
❑ 261	Rick Aguilera	.10	.02
❑ 262	Chili Davis	.20	.07
❑ 263	Scott Erickson	.10	.02
❑ 264	Greg Gagne	.10	.02
❑ 265	Mark Guthrie	.10	.02
❑ 266	Brian Harper	.10	.02
❑ 267	Kent Hrbek	.20	.07
❑ 268	Terry Jorgensen	.10	.02
❑ 269	Gene Larkin	.10	.02
❑ 270	Scott Leius	.10	.02
❑ 271	Pat Mahomes	.10	.02
❑ 272	Pedro Munoz	.10	.02
❑ 273	Kirby Puckett	.50	.20
❑ 274	Kevin Tapani	.10	.02
❑ 275	Carl Willis	.10	.02
❑ 276	Steve Farr	.10	.02
❑ 277	John Habyan	.10	.02
❑ 278	Mel Hall	.10	.02
❑ 279	Charlie Hayes	.10	.02
❑ 280	Pat Kelly	.10	.02
❑ 281	Don Mattingly	1.25	.50
❑ 282	Sam Militello	.10	.02
❑ 283	Matt Nokes	.10	.02
❑ 284	Melido Perez	.10	.02
❑ 285	Andy Stankiewicz	.10	.02
❑ 286	Danny Tartabull	.10	.02
❑ 287	Randy Velarde	.10	.02
❑ 288	Bob Wickman	.10	.02
❑ 289	Bernie Williams	.30	.10
❑ 290	Lance Blankenship	.10	.02
❑ 291	Mike Bordick	.10	.02
❑ 292	Jerry Browne	.10	.02
❑ 293	Dennis Eckersley	.20	.07
❑ 294	Rickey Henderson	.50	.20
❑ 295	Vince Horsman	.10	.02
❑ 296	Mark McGwire	1.25	.50
❑ 297	Jeff Parrett	.10	.02
❑ 298	Ruben Sierra	.20	.07
❑ 299	Terry Steinbach	.10	.02
❑ 300	Walt Weiss	.10	.02
❑ 301	Bob Welch	.10	.02
❑ 302	Willie Wilson	.10	.02
❑ 303	Bobby Witt	.10	.02
❑ 304	Bret Boone	.20	.07
❑ 305	Jay Buhner	.20	.07
❑ 306	Dave Fleming	.10	.02
❑ 307	Ken Griffey Jr.	.75	.30
❑ 308	Erik Hanson	.10	.02
❑ 309	Edgar Martinez	.30	.10
❑ 310	Tino Martinez	.30	.10
❑ 311	Jeff Nelson	.10	.02
❑ 312	Dennis Powell	.10	.02
❑ 313	Mike Schooler	.10	.02
❑ 314	Russ Swan	.10	.02
❑ 315	Dave Valle	.10	.02
❑ 316	Omar Vizquel	.30	.10
❑ 317	Kevin Brown	.20	.07
❑ 318	Todd Burns	.10	.02
❑ 319	Jose Canseco	.30	.10
❑ 320	Julio Franco	.20	.07
❑ 321	Jeff Frye	.10	.02
❑ 322	Juan Gonzalez	.20	.07
❑ 323	Jose Guzman	.10	.02
❑ 324	Jeff Huson	.10	.02
❑ 325	Dean Palmer	.20	.07
❑ 326	Kevin Reimer	.10	.02
❑ 327	Ivan Rodriguez	.30	.10
❑ 328	Kenny Rogers	.20	.07
❑ 329	Dan Smith	.10	.02
❑ 330	Roberto Alomar	.30	.10
❑ 331	Derek Bell	.10	.02
❑ 332	Pat Borders	.10	.02
❑ 333	Joe Carter	.20	.07
❑ 334	Kelly Gruber	.10	.02
❑ 335	Tom Henke	.10	.02
❑ 336	Jimmy Key	.20	.07
❑ 337	Manuel Lee	.10	.02
❑ 338	Candy Maldonado	.10	.02
❑ 339	John Olerud	.20	.07
❑ 340	Todd Stottlemyre	.10	.02
❑ 341	Duane Ward	.10	.02
❑ 342	Devon White	.20	.07
❑ 343	Dave Winfield	.20	.07
❑ 344	Edgar Martinez LL	.20	.07
❑ 345	Cecil Fielder LL	.10	.02
❑ 346	Kenny Lofton LL	.10	.02
❑ 347	Jack Morris LL	.10	.02
❑ 348	Roger Clemens LL	.50	.20
❑ 349	Fred McGriff RT	.20	.07
❑ 350	Barry Bonds RT	.75	.30
❑ 351	Gary Sheffield RT	.10	.02
❑ 352	Darren Daulton RT	.10	.02
❑ 353	Dave Hollins RT	.10	.02
❑ 354	P.Martinez/R.Martinez	.50	.20
❑ 355	K.Puckett/I.Rodriguez	.30	.10
❑ 356	Sandberg/Sheffield	.50	.20
❑ 357	R.Alomar/Knoblauch/Baerg	.20	.07
❑ 358	Checklist 1-120	.10	.02
❑ 359	Checklist 121-240	.10	.02
❑ 360	Checklist 241-360	.10	.02
❑ 361	Rafael Belliard	.10	.02
❑ 362	Damon Berryhill	.10	.02
❑ 363	Mike Bielecki	.10	.02
❑ 364	Jeff Blauser	.10	.02
❑ 365	Francisco Cabrera	.10	.02
❑ 366	Marvin Freeman	.10	.02
❑ 367	David Justice	.20	.07
❑ 368	Mark Lemke	.10	.02
❑ 369	Alejandro Pena	.10	.02
❑ 370	Jeff Reardon	.20	.07
❑ 371	Lonnie Smith	.10	.02
❑ 372	Pete Smith	.10	.02
❑ 373	Shawn Boskie	.10	.02
❑ 374	Jim Bullinger	.10	.02
❑ 375	Frank Castillo	.10	.02
❑ 376	Doug Dascenzo	.10	.02
❑ 377	Andre Dawson	.20	.07
❑ 378	Mike Harkey	.10	.02
❑ 379	Greg Hibbard	.10	.02
❑ 380	Greg Maddux	.75	.30
❑ 381	Ken Patterson	.10	.02
❑ 382	Jeff D. Robinson	.10	.02
❑ 383	Luis Salazar	.10	.02
❑ 384	Dwight Smith	.10	.02
❑ 385	Jose Vizcaino	.10	.02
❑ 386	Scott Bankhead	.10	.02
❑ 387	Tom Browning	.10	.02
❑ 388	Darnell Coles	.10	.02
❑ 389	Rob Dibble	.20	.07
❑ 390	Bill Doran	.10	.02
❑ 391	Dwayne Henry	.10	.02
❑ 392	Cesar Hernandez	.10	.02
❑ 393	Roberto Kelly	.10	.02
❑ 394	Barry Larkin	.30	.10
❑ 395	Dave Martinez	.10	.02
❑ 396	Kevin Mitchell	.10	.02
❑ 397	Jeff Reed	.10	.02
❑ 398	Scott Ruskin	.10	.02
❑ 399	Greg Swindell	.10	.02
❑ 400	Dan Wilson	.20	.07
❑ 401	Andy Ashby	.10	.02
❑ 402	Freddie Benavides	.10	.02
❑ 403	Dante Bichette	.20	.07
❑ 404	Willie Blair	.10	.02
❑ 405	Denis Boucher	.10	.02
❑ 406	Vinny Castilla	.50	.20
❑ 407	Braulio Castillo	.10	.02
❑ 408	Alex Cole	.10	.02
❑ 409	Andres Galarraga	.20	.07
❑ 410	Joe Girardi	.10	.02
❑ 411	Butch Henry	.10	.02
❑ 412	Darren Holmes	.10	.02
❑ 413	Calvin Jones	.10	.02
❑ 414	Steve Reed RC	.10	.02
❑ 415	Kevin Ritz	.10	.02
❑ 416	Jim Tatum RC	.10	.02
❑ 417	Jack Armstrong	.10	.02
❑ 418	Bret Barberie	.10	.02
❑ 419	Ryan Bowen	.10	.02
❑ 420	Cris Carpenter	.10	.02
❑ 421	Chuck Carr	.10	.02
❑ 422	Scott Chiamparino	.10	.02
❑ 423	Jeff Conine	.20	.07
❑ 424	Jim Corsi	.10	.02
❑ 425	Steve Decker	.10	.02
❑ 426	Chris Donnels	.10	.02
❑ 427	Monty Fariss	.10	.02
❑ 428	Bob Natal	.10	.02
❑ 429	Pat Rapp	.10	.02
❑ 430	Dave Weathers	.10	.02
❑ 431	Nigel Wilson	.10	.02
❑ 432	Ken Caminiti	.20	.07
❑ 433	Andujar Cedeno	.10	.02
❑ 434	Tom Edens	.10	.02
❑ 435	Juan Guerrero	.10	.02
❑ 436	Pete Incaviglia	.10	.02
❑ 437	Jimmy Jones	.10	.02

❑ 438 Darryl Kile .20 .07
❑ 439 Rob Murphy .10 .02
❑ 440 Al Osuna .10 .02
❑ 441 Mark Portugal .10 .02
❑ 442 Scott Servais .10 .02
❑ 443 John Candelaria .10 .02
❑ 444 Tim Crews .10 .02
❑ 445 Eric Davis .20 .07
❑ 446 Tom Goodwin .10 .02
❑ 447 Jim Gott .10 .02
❑ 448 Kevin Gross .10 .02
❑ 449 Dave Hansen .10 .02
❑ 450 Jay Howell .10 .02
❑ 451 Roger McDowell .10 .02
❑ 452 Bob Ojeda .10 .02
❑ 453 Henry Rodriguez .10 .02
❑ 454 Darryl Strawberry .20 .07
❑ 455 Mitch Webster .10 .02
❑ 456 Steve Wilson .10 .02
❑ 457 Brian Barnes .10 .02
❑ 458 Sean Berry .10 .02
❑ 459 Jeff Fassero .10 .02
❑ 460 Darrin Fletcher .10 .02
❑ 461 Marquis Grissom .20 .07
❑ 462 Dennis Martinez .20 .07
❑ 463 Spike Owen .10 .02
❑ 464 Matt Stairs .10 .02
❑ 465 Sergio Valdez .10 .02
❑ 466 Kevin Bass .10 .02
❑ 467 Vince Coleman .10 .02
❑ 468 Mark Dewey .10 .02
❑ 469 Kevin Elster .10 .02
❑ 470 Tony Fernandez .10 .02
❑ 471 John Franco .20 .07
❑ 472 Dave Gallagher .10 .02
❑ 473 Paul Gibson .10 .02
❑ 474 Dwight Gooden .20 .07
❑ 475 Lee Guetterman .10 .02
❑ 476 Jeff Innis .10 .02
❑ 477 Dave Magadan .10 .02
❑ 478 Charlie O'Brien .10 .02
❑ 479 Willie Randolph .20 .07
❑ 480 Mackey Sasser .10 .02
❑ 481 Ryan Thompson .10 .02
❑ 482 Chico Walker .10 .02
❑ 483 Kyle Abbott .10 .02
❑ 484 Bob Ayrault .10 .02
❑ 485 Kim Batiste .10 .02
❑ 486 Cliff Brantley .10 .02
❑ 487 Jose DeLeon .10 .02
❑ 488 Len Dykstra .20 .07
❑ 489 Tommy Greene .10 .02
❑ 490 Jeff Grotewold .10 .02
❑ 491 Dave Hollins .10 .02
❑ 492 Danny Jackson .10 .02
❑ 493 Stan Javier .10 .02
❑ 494 Tom Marsh .10 .02
❑ 495 Greg Mathews .10 .02
❑ 496 Dale Murphy .30 .10
❑ 497 Todd Pratt RC .20 .07
❑ 498 Mitch Williams .10 .02
❑ 499 Danny Cox .10 .02
❑ 500 Doug Drabek .10 .02
❑ 501 Carlos Garcia .10 .02
❑ 502 Lloyd McClendon .10 .02
❑ 503 Denny Neagle .20 .07
❑ 504 Gary Redus .10 .02
❑ 505 Bob Walk .10 .02
❑ 506 John Wehner .10 .02
❑ 507 Luis Alicea .10 .02
❑ 508 Mark Clark .10 .02
❑ 509 Pedro Guerrero .20 .07
❑ 510 Rex Hudler .10 .02
❑ 511 Brian Jordan .20 .07
❑ 512 Omar Olivares .10 .02
❑ 513 Jose Oquendo .10 .02
❑ 514 Gerald Perry .10 .02
❑ 515 Bryn Smith .10 .02
❑ 516 Craig Wilson .10 .02
❑ 517 Tracy Woodson .10 .02
❑ 518 Larry Andersen .10 .02
❑ 519 Andy Benes .10 .02
❑ 520 Jim Deshaies .10 .02
❑ 521 Bruce Hurst .10 .02
❑ 522 Randy Myers .10 .02
❑ 523 Benito Santiago .20 .07
❑ 524 Tim Scott .10 .02
❑ 525 Tim Teufel .10 .02
❑ 526 Mike Benjamin .10 .02
❑ 527 Dave Burba .10 .02
❑ 528 Craig Colbert .10 .02
❑ 529 Mike Felder .10 .02
❑ 530 Bryan Hickerson .10 .02
❑ 531 Chris James .10 .02
❑ 532 Mark Leonard .10 .02
❑ 533 Greg Litton .10 .02
❑ 534 Francisco Oliveras .10 .02
❑ 535 John Patterson .10 .02
❑ 536 Jim Pena .10 .02
❑ 537 Dave Righetti .20 .07
❑ 538 Robby Thompson .10 .02
❑ 539 Jose Uribe .10 .02
❑ 540 Matt Williams .20 .07
❑ 541 Storm Davis .10 .02
❑ 542 Sam Horn .10 .02
❑ 543 Tim Hulett .10 .02
❑ 544 Craig Lefferts .10 .02
❑ 545 Chito Martinez .10 .02
❑ 546 Mark McLemore .10 .02
❑ 547 Luis Mercedes .10 .02
❑ 548 Bob Milacki .10 .02
❑ 549 Joe Orsulak .10 .02
❑ 550 Billy Ripken .10 .02
❑ 551 Cal Ripken 1.50 .60
❑ 552 Rick Sutcliffe .20 .07
❑ 553 Jeff Tackett .10 .02
❑ 554 Wade Boggs .30 .10
❑ 555 Tom Brunansky .10 .02
❑ 556 Jack Clark .20 .07
❑ 557 John Dopson .10 .02
❑ 558 Mike Gardiner .10 .02
❑ 559 Mike Greenwell .10 .02
❑ 560 Greg A. Harris .10 .02
❑ 561 Billy Hatcher .10 .02
❑ 562 Joe Hesketh .10 .02
❑ 563 Tony Pena .10 .02
❑ 564 Phil Plantier .10 .02
❑ 565 Luis Rivera .10 .02
❑ 566 Herm Winningham .10 .02
❑ 567 Matt Young .10 .02
❑ 568 Bert Blyleven .20 .07
❑ 569 Mike Butcher .10 .02
❑ 570 Chuck Crim .10 .02
❑ 571 Chad Curtis .10 .02
❑ 572 Tim Fortugno .10 .02
❑ 573 Steve Frey .10 .02
❑ 574 Gary Gaetti .20 .07
❑ 575 Scott Lewis .10 .02
❑ 576 Lee Stevens .10 .02
❑ 577 Ron Tingley .10 .02
❑ 578 Julio Valera .10 .02
❑ 579 Shawn Abner .10 .02
❑ 580 Joey Cora .10 .02
❑ 581 Chris Cron .10 .02
❑ 582 Carlton Fisk .30 .10
❑ 583 Roberto Hernandez .10 .02
❑ 584 Charlie Hough .20 .07
❑ 585 Terry Leach .10 .02
❑ 586 Donn Pall .10 .02
❑ 587 Dan Pasqua .10 .02
❑ 588 Steve Sax .10 .02
❑ 589 Bobby Thigpen .10 .02
❑ 590 Albert Belle .20 .07
❑ 591 Felix Fermin .10 .02
❑ 592 Glenallen Hill .10 .02
❑ 593 Brook Jacoby .10 .02
❑ 594 Reggie Jefferson .10 .02
❑ 595 Carlos Martinez .10 .02
❑ 596 Jose Mesa .10 .02
❑ 597 Rod Nichols .10 .02
❑ 598 Junior Ortiz .10 .02
❑ 599 Eric Plunk .10 .02
❑ 600 Ted Power .10 .02
❑ 601 Scott Scudder .10 .02
❑ 602 Kevin Wickander .10 .02
❑ 603 Skeeter Barnes .10 .02
❑ 604 Mark Carreon .10 .02
❑ 605 Dan Gladden .10 .02
❑ 606 Bill Gullickson .10 .02
❑ 607 Chad Kreuter .10 .02
❑ 608 Mark Leiter .10 .02
❑ 609 Mike Munoz .10 .02
❑ 610 Rich Rowland .10 .02
❑ 611 Frank Tanana .10 .02
❑ 612 Walt Terrell .10 .02
❑ 613 Alan Trammell .20 .07
❑ 614 Lou Whitaker .20 .07
❑ 615 Luis Aquino .10 .02
❑ 616 Mike Boddicker .10 .02
❑ 617 Jim Eisenreich .10 .02
❑ 618 Mark Gubicza .10 .02
❑ 619 David Howard .10 .02
❑ 620 Mike Magnante .10 .02
❑ 621 Brent Mayne .10 .02
❑ 622 Kevin McReynolds .10 .02
❑ 623 Eddie Pierce RC .10 .02
❑ 624 Bill Sampen .10 .02
❑ 625 Steve Shifflett .10 .02
❑ 626 Gary Thurman .10 .02
❑ 627 Curt Wilkerson .10 .02
❑ 628 Chris Bosio .10 .02
❑ 629 Scott Fletcher .10 .02
❑ 630 Jim Gantner .10 .02
❑ 631 Dave Nilsson .10 .02
❑ 632 Jesse Orosco .10 .02
❑ 633 Dan Plesac .10 .02
❑ 634 Ron Robinson .10 .02
❑ 635 Bill Spiers .10 .02
❑ 636 Franklin Stubbs .10 .02
❑ 637 Willie Banks .10 .02
❑ 638 Randy Bush .10 .02
❑ 639 Chuck Knoblauch .20 .07
❑ 640 Shane Mack .10 .02
❑ 641 Mike Pagliarulo .10 .02
❑ 642 Jeff Reboulet .10 .02
❑ 643 John Smiley .10 .02
❑ 644 Mike Trombley .10 .02
❑ 645 Gary Wayne .10 .02
❑ 646 Lenny Webster .10 .02
❑ 647 Tim Burke .10 .02
❑ 648 Mike Gallego .10 .02
❑ 649 Dion James .10 .02
❑ 650 Jeff Johnson .10 .02
❑ 651 Scott Kamieniecki .10 .02
❑ 652 Kevin Maas .10 .02
❑ 653 Rich Monteleone .10 .02
❑ 654 Jerry Nielsen .10 .02
❑ 655 Scott Sanderson .10 .02
❑ 656 Mike Stanley .10 .02
❑ 657 Gerald Williams .10 .02
❑ 658 Curt Young .10 .02
❑ 659 Harold Baines .20 .07
❑ 660 Kevin Campbell .10 .02
❑ 661 Ron Darling .10 .02
❑ 662 Kelly Downs .10 .02
❑ 663 Eric Fox .10 .02
❑ 664 Dave Henderson .10 .02
❑ 665 Rick Honeycutt .10 .02
❑ 666 Mike Moore .10 .02
❑ 667 Jamie Quirk .10 .02
❑ 668 Jeff Russell .10 .02
❑ 669 Dave Stewart .20 .07
❑ 670 Greg Briley .10 .02
❑ 671 Dave Cochrane .10 .02
❑ 672 Henry Cotto .10 .02
❑ 673 Rich DeLucia .10 .02
❑ 674 Brian Fisher .10 .02
❑ 675 Mark Grant .10 .02
❑ 676 Randy Johnson .50 .20
❑ 677 Tim Leary .10 .02
❑ 678 Pete O'Brien .10 .02
❑ 679 Lance Parrish .20 .07
❑ 680 Harold Reynolds .20 .07
❑ 681 Shane Turner .10 .02
❑ 682 Jack Daugherty .10 .02
❑ 683 David Hulse RC .10 .02
❑ 684 Terry Mathews .10 .02
❑ 685 Al Newman .10 .02
❑ 686 Edwin Nunez .10 .02
❑ 687 Rafael Palmeiro .30 .10
❑ 688 Roger Pavlik .10 .02
❑ 689 Geno Petralli .10 .02
❑ 690 Nolan Ryan 2.00 .75
❑ 691 David Cone .20 .07
❑ 692 Alfredo Griffin .10 .02
❑ 693 Juan Guzman .10 .02
❑ 694 Pat Hentgen .10 .02
❑ 695 Randy Knorr .10 .02

❑	696	Bob MacDonald	.10	.02
❑	697	Jack Morris	.20	.07
❑	698	Ed Sprague	.10	.02
❑	699	Dave Stieb	.10	.02
❑	700	Pat Tabler	.10	.02
❑	701	Mike Timlin	.10	.02
❑	702	David Wells	.20	.07
❑	703	Eddie Zosky	.10	.02
❑	704	Gary Sheffield LL	.10	.02
❑	705	Darren Daulton LL	.10	.02
❑	706	Marquis Grissom LL	.10	.02
❑	707	Greg Maddux LL	.50	.20
❑	708	Bill Swift LL	.10	.02
❑	709	Juan Gonzalez RT	.10	.02
❑	710	Mark McGwire RT	.60	.25
❑	711	Cecil Fielder RT	.10	.02
❑	712	Albert Belle RT	.20	.07
❑	713	Joe Carter RT	.10	.02
❑	714	F.Thomas/C.Fielder	.30	.10
❑	715	L.Walker/D.Daulton SS	.20	.07
❑	716	E.Martinez/R.Ventura SS	.20	.07
❑	717	R.Clemens/D.Eckersley	.50	.20
❑	718	Checklist 361-480	.10	.02
❑	719	Checklist 481-600	.10	.02
❑	720	Checklist 601-720	.10	.02

1994 Fleer

❑		COMPLETE SET (720)	50.00	25.00
❑	1	Brady Anderson	.30	.10
❑	2	Harold Baines	.30	.10
❑	3	Mike Devereaux	.15	.05
❑	4	Todd Frohwirth	.15	.05
❑	5	Jeffrey Hammonds	.15	.05
❑	6	Chris Hoiles	.15	.05
❑	7	Tim Hulett	.15	.05
❑	8	Ben McDonald	.15	.05
❑	9	Mark McLemore	.15	.05
❑	10	Alan Mills	.15	.05
❑	11	Jamie Moyer	.30	.10
❑	12	Mike Mussina	.50	.20
❑	13	Gregg Olson	.15	.05
❑	14	Mike Pagliarulo	.15	.05
❑	15	Brad Pennington	.15	.05
❑	16	Jim Poole	.15	.05
❑	17	Harold Reynolds	.30	.10
❑	18	Arthur Rhodes	.15	.05
❑	19	Cal Ripken	2.50	1.00
❑	20	David Segui	.15	.05
❑	21	Rick Sutcliffe	.30	.10
❑	22	Fernando Valenzuela	.30	.10
❑	23	Jack Voigt	.15	.05
❑	24	Mark Williamson	.15	.05
❑	25	Scott Bankhead	.15	.05
❑	26	Roger Clemens	1.50	.60
❑	27	Scott Cooper	.15	.05
❑	28	Danny Darwin	.15	.05
❑	29	Andre Dawson	.30	.10
❑	30	Rob Deer	.15	.05
❑	31	John Dopson	.15	.05
❑	32	Scott Fletcher	.15	.05
❑	33	Mike Greenwell	.15	.05
❑	34	Greg A. Harris	.15	.05
❑	35	Billy Hatcher	.15	.05
❑	36	Bob Melvin	.15	.05
❑	37	Tony Pena	.15	.05
❑	38	Paul Quantrill	.15	.05
❑	39	Carlos Quintana	.15	.05
❑	40	Ernest Riles	.15	.05
❑	41	Jeff Russell	.15	.05
❑	42	Ken Ryan	.15	.05
❑	43	Aaron Sele	.15	.05
❑	44	John Valentin	.15	.05
❑	45	Mo Vaughn	.30	.10
❑	46	Frank Viola	.30	.10
❑	47	Bob Zupcic	.15	.05
❑	48	Mike Butcher	.15	.05
❑	49	Rod Correia	.15	.05
❑	50	Chad Curtis	.15	.05
❑	51	Chili Davis	.30	.10
❑	52	Gary DiSarcina	.15	.05
❑	53	Damion Easley	.15	.05
❑	54	Jim Edmonds	.75	.30
❑	55	Chuck Finley	.30	.10
❑	56	Steve Frey	.15	.05
❑	57	Rene Gonzales	.15	.05
❑	58	Joe Grahe	.15	.05
❑	59	Hilly Hathaway	.15	.05
❑	60	Stan Javier	.15	.05
❑	61	Mark Langston	.15	.05
❑	62	Phil Leftwich RC	.15	.05
❑	63	Torey Lovullo	.15	.05
❑	64	Joe Magrane	.15	.05
❑	65	Greg Myers	.15	.05
❑	66	Ken Patterson	.15	.05
❑	67	Eduardo Perez	.15	.05
❑	68	Luis Polonia	.15	.05
❑	69	Tim Salmon	.50	.20
❑	70	J.T.Snow	.30	.10
❑	71	Ron Tingley	.15	.05
❑	72	Julio Valera	.15	.05
❑	73	Wilson Alvarez	.15	.05
❑	74	Tim Belcher	.15	.05
❑	75	George Bell	.15	.05
❑	76	Jason Bere	.15	.05
❑	77	Rod Bolton	.15	.05
❑	78	Ellis Burks	.30	.10
❑	79	Joey Cora	.15	.05
❑	80	Alex Fernandez	.15	.05
❑	81	Craig Grebeck	.15	.05
❑	82	Ozzie Guillen	.30	.10
❑	83	Roberto Hernandez	.15	.05
❑	84	Bo Jackson	.75	.30
❑	85	Lance Johnson	.15	.05
❑	86	Ron Karkovice	.15	.05
❑	87	Mike LaValliere	.15	.05
❑	88	Kirk McCaskill	.15	.05
❑	89	Jack McDowell	.15	.05
❑	90	Warren Newson	.15	.05
❑	91	Dan Pasqua	.15	.05
❑	92	Scott Radinsky	.15	.05
❑	93	Tim Raines	.30	.10
❑	94	Steve Sax	.15	.05
❑	95	Jeff Schwarz	.15	.05
❑	96	Frank Thomas	.75	.30
❑	97	Robin Ventura	.30	.10
❑	98	Sandy Alomar Jr.	.15	.05
❑	99	Carlos Baerga	.15	.05
❑	100	Albert Belle	.30	.10
❑	101	Mark Clark	.15	.05
❑	102	Jerry DiPoto	.15	.05
❑	103	Alvaro Espinoza	.15	.05
❑	104	Felix Fermin	.15	.05
❑	105	Jeremy Hernandez	.15	.05
❑	106	Reggie Jefferson	.15	.05
❑	107	Wayne Kirby	.15	.05
❑	108	Tom Kramer	.15	.05
❑	109	Mark Lewis	.15	.05
❑	110	Derek Lilliquist	.15	.05
❑	111	Kenny Lofton	.30	.10
❑	112	Candy Maldonado	.15	.05
❑	113	Jose Mesa	.15	.05
❑	114	Jeff Mutis	.15	.05
❑	115	Charles Nagy	.15	.05
❑	116	Bob Ojeda	.15	.05
❑	117	Junior Ortiz	.15	.05
❑	118	Eric Plunk	.15	.05
❑	119	Manny Ramirez	.75	.30
❑	120	Paul Sorrento	.15	.05
❑	121	Jim Thome	.50	.20
❑	122	Jeff Treadway	.15	.05
❑	123	Bill Wertz	.15	.05
❑	124	Skeeter Barnes	.15	.05
❑	125	Milt Cuyler	.15	.05
❑	126	Eric Davis	.30	.10
❑	127	John Doherty	.15	.05
❑	128	Cecil Fielder	.30	.10
❑	129	Travis Fryman	.30	.10
❑	130	Kirk Gibson	.30	.10
❑	131	Dan Gladden	.15	.05
❑	132	Greg Gohr	.15	.05
❑	133	Chris Gomez	.15	.05
❑	134	Bill Gullickson	.15	.05
❑	135	Mike Henneman	.15	.05
❑	136	Kurt Knudsen	.15	.05
❑	137	Chad Kreuter	.15	.05
❑	138	Bill Krueger	.15	.05
❑	139	Scott Livingstone	.15	.05
❑	140	Bob MacDonald	.15	.05
❑	141	Mike Moore	.15	.05
❑	142	Tony Phillips	.15	.05
❑	143	Mickey Tettleton	.15	.05
❑	144	Alan Trammell	.30	.10
❑	145	David Wells	.30	.10
❑	146	Lou Whitaker	.30	.10
❑	147	Kevin Appier	.30	.10
❑	148	Stan Belinda	.15	.05
❑	149	George Brett	2.00	.75
❑	150	Billy Brewer	.15	.05
❑	151	Hubie Brooks	.15	.05
❑	152	David Cone	.30	.10
❑	153	Gary Gaetti	.30	.10
❑	154	Greg Gagne	.15	.05
❑	155	Tom Gordon	.15	.05
❑	156	Mark Gubicza	.15	.05
❑	157	Chris Gwynn	.15	.05
❑	158	John Habyan	.15	.05
❑	159	Chris Haney	.15	.05
❑	160	Phil Hiatt	.15	.05
❑	161	Felix Jose	.15	.05
❑	162	Wally Joyner	.30	.10
❑	163	Jose Lind	.15	.05
❑	164	Mike Macfarlane	.15	.05
❑	165	Mike Magnante	.15	.05
❑	166	Brent Mayne	.15	.05
❑	167	Brian McRae	.15	.05
❑	168	Kevin McReynolds	.15	.05
❑	169	Keith Miller	.15	.05
❑	170	Jeff Montgomery	.15	.05
❑	171	Hipolito Pichardo	.15	.05
❑	172	Rico Rossy	.15	.05
❑	173	Juan Bell	.15	.05
❑	174	Ricky Bones	.15	.05
❑	175	Cal Eldred	.15	.05
❑	176	Mike Fetters	.15	.05
❑	177	Darryl Hamilton	.15	.05
❑	178	Doug Henry	.15	.05
❑	179	Mike Ignasiak	.15	.05
❑	180	John Jaha	.15	.05
❑	181	Pat Listach	.15	.05
❑	182	Graeme Lloyd	.15	.05
❑	183	Matt Mieske	.15	.05
❑	184	Angel Miranda	.15	.05
❑	185	Jaime Navarro	.15	.05
❑	186	Dave Nilsson	.15	.05
❑	187	Troy O'Leary	.15	.05
❑	188	Jesse Orosco	.15	.05
❑	189	Kevin Reimer	.15	.05
❑	190	Kevin Seitzer	.15	.05
❑	191	Bill Spiers	.15	.05
❑	192	B.J. Surhoff	.30	.10
❑	193	Dickie Thon	.15	.05
❑	194	Jose Valentin	.15	.05
❑	195	Greg Vaughn	.15	.05
❑	196	Bill Wegman	.15	.05
❑	197	Robin Yount	1.25	.50
❑	198	Rick Aguilera	.15	.05
❑	199	Willie Banks	.15	.05
❑	200	Bernardo Brito	.15	.05
❑	201	Larry Casian	.15	.05
❑	202	Scott Erickson	.15	.05
❑	203	Eddie Guardado	.30	.10
❑	204	Mark Guthrie	.15	.05
❑	205	Chip Hale	.15	.05
❑	206	Brian Harper	.15	.05
❑	207	Mike Hartley	.15	.05
❑	208	Kent Hrbek	.30	.10
❑	209	Terry Jorgensen	.15	.05
❑	210	Chuck Knoblauch	.30	.10
❑	211	Gene Larkin	.15	.05
❑	212	Shane Mack	.15	.05

❑ 213 David McCarty .15 .05
❑ 214 Pat Meares .15 .05
❑ 215 Pedro Munoz .15 .05
❑ 216 Derek Parks .15 .05
❑ 217 Kirby Puckett .75 .30
❑ 218 Jeff Reboulet .15 .05
❑ 219 Kevin Tapani .15 .05
❑ 220 Mike Trombley .15 .05
❑ 221 George Tsamis .15 .05
❑ 222 Carl Willis .15 .05
❑ 223 Dave Winfield .30 .10
❑ 224 Jim Abbott .50 .20
❑ 225 Paul Assenmacher .15 .05
❑ 226 Wade Boggs .50 .20
❑ 227 Russ Davis .15 .05
❑ 228 Steve Farr .15 .05
❑ 229 Mike Gallego .15 .05
❑ 230 Paul Gibson .15 .05
❑ 231 Steve Howe .15 .05
❑ 232 Dion James .15 .05
❑ 233 Domingo Jean .15 .05
❑ 234 Scott Kamieniecki .15 .05
❑ 235 Pat Kelly .15 .05
❑ 236 Jimmy Key .30 .10
❑ 237 Jim Leyritz .15 .05
❑ 238 Kevin Maas .15 .05
❑ 239 Don Mattingly 2.00 .75
❑ 240 Rich Monteleone .15 .05
❑ 241 Bobby Munoz .15 .05
❑ 242 Matt Nokes .15 .05
❑ 243 Paul O'Neill .50 .20
❑ 244 Spike Owen .15 .05
❑ 245 Melido Perez .15 .05
❑ 246 Lee Smith .30 .10
❑ 247 Mike Stanley .15 .05
❑ 248 Danny Tartabull .15 .05
❑ 249 Randy Velarde .15 .05
❑ 250 Bob Wickman .15 .05
❑ 251 Bernie Williams .50 .20
❑ 252 Mike Aldrete .15 .05
❑ 253 Marcos Armas .15 .05
❑ 254 Lance Blankenship .15 .05
❑ 255 Mike Bordick .15 .05
❑ 256 Scott Brosius .30 .10
❑ 257 Jerry Browne .15 .05
❑ 258 Ron Darling .15 .05
❑ 259 Kelly Downs .15 .05
❑ 260 Dennis Eckersley .30 .10
❑ 261 Brent Gates .15 .05
❑ 262 Rich Gossage .30 .10
❑ 263 Scott Hemond .15 .05
❑ 264 Dave Henderson .15 .05
❑ 265 Rick Honeycutt .15 .05
❑ 266 Vince Horsman .15 .05
❑ 267 Scott Lydy .15 .05
❑ 268 Mark McGwire 2.00 .75
❑ 269 Mike Mohler .15 .05
❑ 270 Troy Neel .15 .05
❑ 271 Edwin Nunez .15 .05
❑ 272 Craig Paquette .15 .05
❑ 273 Ruben Sierra .30 .10
❑ 274 Terry Steinbach .15 .05
❑ 275 Todd Van Poppel .15 .05
❑ 276 Bob Welch .15 .05
❑ 277 Bobby Witt .15 .05
❑ 278 Rich Amaral .15 .05
❑ 279 Mike Blowers .15 .05
❑ 280 Bret Boone UER .30 .10
❑ 281 Chris Bosio .15 .05
❑ 282 Jay Buhner .30 .10
❑ 283 Norm Charlton .15 .05
❑ 284 Mike Felder .15 .05
❑ 285 Dave Fleming .15 .05
❑ 286 Ken Griffey Jr. 1.25 .50
❑ 287 Erik Hanson .15 .05
❑ 288 Bill Haselman .15 .05
❑ 289 Brad Holman RC .15 .05
❑ 290 Randy Johnson .75 .30
❑ 291 Tim Leary .15 .05
❑ 292 Greg Litton .15 .05
❑ 293 Dave Magadan .15 .05
❑ 294 Edgar Martinez .50 .20
❑ 295 Tino Martinez .50 .20
❑ 296 Jeff Nelson .15 .05
❑ 297 Erik Plantenberg RC .15 .05
❑ 298 Mackey Sasser .15 .05
❑ 299 Brian Turang RC .15 .05
❑ 300 Dave Valle .15 .05
❑ 301 Omar Vizquel .50 .20
❑ 302 Brian Bohanon .15 .05
❑ 303 Kevin Brown .30 .10
❑ 304 Jose Canseco .50 .20
❑ 305 Mario Diaz .15 .05
❑ 306 Julio Franco .30 .10
❑ 307 Juan Gonzalez .30 .10
❑ 308 Tom Henke .15 .05
❑ 309 David Hulse .15 .05
❑ 310 Manuel Lee .15 .05
❑ 311 Craig Lefferts .15 .05
❑ 312 Charlie Leibrandt .15 .05
❑ 313 Rafael Palmeiro .50 .20
❑ 314 Dean Palmer .30 .10
❑ 315 Roger Pavlik .15 .05
❑ 316 Dan Peltier .15 .05
❑ 317 Gene Petralli .15 .05
❑ 318 Gary Redus .15 .05
❑ 319 Ivan Rodriguez .50 .20
❑ 320 Kenny Rogers .30 .10
❑ 321 Nolan Ryan 3.00 1.25
❑ 322 Doug Strange .15 .05
❑ 323 Matt Whiteside .15 .05
❑ 324 Roberto Alomar .50 .20
❑ 325 Pat Borders .15 .05
❑ 326 Joe Carter .30 .10
❑ 327 Tony Castillo .15 .05
❑ 328 Darnell Coles .15 .05
❑ 329 Danny Cox .15 .05
❑ 330 Mark Eichhorn .15 .05
❑ 331 Tony Fernandez .15 .05
❑ 332 Alfredo Griffin .15 .05
❑ 333 Juan Guzman .15 .05
❑ 334 Rickey Henderson .75 .30
❑ 335 Pat Hentgen .15 .05
❑ 336 Randy Knorr .15 .05
❑ 337 Al Leiter .30 .10
❑ 338 Paul Molitor .30 .10
❑ 339 Jack Morris .30 .10
❑ 340 John Olerud .30 .10
❑ 341 Dick Schofield .15 .05
❑ 342 Ed Sprague .15 .05
❑ 343 Dave Stewart .30 .10
❑ 344 Todd Stottlemyre .15 .05
❑ 345 Mike Timlin .15 .05
❑ 346 Duane Ward .15 .05
❑ 347 Turner Ward .15 .05
❑ 348 Devon White .30 .10
❑ 349 Woody Williams .30 .10
❑ 350 Steve Avery .15 .05
❑ 351 Steve Bedrosian .15 .05
❑ 352 Rafael Belliard .15 .05
❑ 353 Damon Berryhill .15 .05
❑ 354 Jeff Blauser .15 .05
❑ 355 Sid Bream .15 .05
❑ 356 Francisco Cabrera .15 .05
❑ 357 Marvin Freeman .15 .05
❑ 358 Ron Gant .30 .10
❑ 359 Tom Glavine .50 .20
❑ 360 Jay Howell .15 .05
❑ 361 David Justice .30 .10
❑ 362 Ryan Klesko .30 .10
❑ 363 Mark Lemke .15 .05
❑ 364 Javier Lopez .30 .10
❑ 365 Greg Maddux 1.25 .50
❑ 366 Fred McGriff .50 .20
❑ 367 Greg McMichael .15 .05
❑ 368 Kent Mercker .15 .05
❑ 369 Otis Nixon .15 .05
❑ 370 Greg Olson .15 .05
❑ 371 Bill Pecota .15 .05
❑ 372 Terry Pendleton .30 .10
❑ 373 Deion Sanders .50 .20
❑ 374 Pete Smith .15 .05
❑ 375 John Smoltz .50 .20
❑ 376 Mike Stanton .15 .05
❑ 377 Tony Tarasco .15 .05
❑ 378 Mark Wohlers .15 .05
❑ 379 Jose Bautista .15 .05
❑ 380 Shawn Boskie .15 .05
❑ 381 Steve Buechele .15 .05
❑ 382 Frank Castillo .15 .05
❑ 383 Mark Grace .50 .20
❑ 384 Jose Guzman .15 .05
❑ 385 Mike Harkey .15 .05
❑ 386 Greg Hibbard .15 .05
❑ 387 Glenallen Hill .15 .05
❑ 388 Steve Lake .15 .05
❑ 389 Derrick May .15 .05
❑ 390 Chuck McElroy .15 .05
❑ 391 Mike Morgan .15 .05
❑ 392 Randy Myers .15 .05
❑ 393 Dan Plesac .15 .05
❑ 394 Kevin Roberson .15 .05
❑ 395 Rey Sanchez .15 .05
❑ 396 Ryne Sandberg 1.25 .50
❑ 397 Bob Scanlan .15 .05
❑ 398 Dwight Smith .15 .05
❑ 399 Sammy Sosa .75 .30
❑ 400 Jose Vizcaino .15 .05
❑ 401 Rick Wilkins .15 .05
❑ 402 Willie Wilson .15 .05
❑ 403 Eric Yelding .15 .05
❑ 404 Bobby Ayala .15 .05
❑ 405 Jeff Branson .15 .05
❑ 406 Tom Browning .15 .05
❑ 407 Jacob Brumfield .15 .05
❑ 408 Tim Costo .15 .05
❑ 409 Rob Dibble .30 .10
❑ 410 Willie Greene .15 .05
❑ 411 Thomas Howard .15 .05
❑ 412 Roberto Kelly .15 .05
❑ 413 Bill Landrum .15 .05
❑ 414 Barry Larkin .50 .20
❑ 415 Larry Luebbers RC .15 .05
❑ 416 Kevin Mitchell .15 .05
❑ 417 Hal Morris .15 .05
❑ 418 Joe Oliver .15 .05
❑ 419 Tim Pugh .15 .05
❑ 420 Jeff Reardon .30 .10
❑ 421 Jose Rijo .15 .05
❑ 422 Bip Roberts .15 .05
❑ 423 John Roper .15 .05
❑ 424 Johnny Ruffin .15 .05
❑ 425 Chris Sabo .15 .05
❑ 426 Juan Samuel .15 .05
❑ 427 Reggie Sanders .30 .10
❑ 428 Scott Service .15 .05
❑ 429 John Smiley .15 .05
❑ 430 Jerry Spradlin RC .15 .05
❑ 431 Kevin Wickander .15 .05
❑ 432 Freddie Benavides .15 .05
❑ 433 Dante Bichette .30 .10
❑ 434 Willie Blair .15 .05
❑ 435 Daryl Boston .15 .05
❑ 436 Kent Bottenfield .15 .05
❑ 437 Vinny Castilla .30 .10
❑ 438 Jerald Clark .15 .05
❑ 439 Alex Cole .15 .05
❑ 440 Andres Galarraga .30 .10
❑ 441 Joe Girardi .15 .05
❑ 442 Greg W. Harris .15 .05
❑ 443 Charlie Hayes .15 .05
❑ 444 Darren Holmes .15 .05
❑ 445 Chris Jones .15 .05
❑ 446 Roberto Mejia .15 .05
❑ 447 David Nied .15 .05
❑ 448 Jayhawk Owens .15 .05
❑ 449 Jeff Parrett .15 .05
❑ 450 Steve Reed .15 .05
❑ 451 Armando Reynoso .15 .05
❑ 452 Bruce Ruffin .15 .05
❑ 453 Mo Sanford .15 .05
❑ 454 Danny Sheaffer .15 .05
❑ 455 Jim Tatum .15 .05
❑ 456 Gary Wayne .15 .05
❑ 457 Eric Young .15 .05
❑ 458 Luis Aquino .15 .05
❑ 459 Alex Arias .15 .05
❑ 460 Jack Armstrong .15 .05
❑ 461 Bret Barberie .15 .05
❑ 462 Ryan Bowen .15 .05
❑ 463 Chuck Carr .15 .05
❑ 464 Jeff Conine .30 .10
❑ 465 Henry Cotto .15 .05
❑ 466 Orestes Destrade .15 .05
❑ 467 Chris Hammond .15 .05
❑ 468 Bryan Harvey .15 .05
❑ 469 Charlie Hough .30 .10
❑ 470 Joe Klink .15 .05

471	Richie Lewis	.15	.05
472	Bob Natal	.15	.05
473	Pat Rapp	.15	.05
474	Rich Renteria	.15	.05
475	Rich Rodriguez	.15	.05
476	Benito Santiago	.30	.10
477	Gary Sheffield	.30	.10
478	Matt Turner	.15	.05
479	David Weathers	.15	.05
480	Walt Weiss	.15	.05
481	Darrell Whitmore	.15	.05
482	Eric Anthony	.15	.05
483	Jeff Bagwell	.50	.20
484	Kevin Bass	.15	.05
485	Craig Biggio	.50	.20
486	Ken Caminiti	.30	.10
487	Andujar Cedeno	.15	.05
488	Chris Donnels	.15	.05
489	Doug Drabek	.15	.05
490	Steve Finley	.30	.10
491	Luis Gonzalez	.30	.10
492	Pete Harnisch	.15	.05
493	Xavier Hernandez	.15	.05
494	Doug Jones	.15	.05
495	Todd Jones	.15	.05
496	Darryl Kile	.30	.10
497	Al Osuna	.15	.05
498	Mark Portugal	.15	.05
499	Scott Servais	.15	.05
500	Greg Swindell	.15	.05
501	Eddie Taubensee	.15	.05
502	Jose Uribe	.15	.05
503	Brian Williams	.15	.05
504	Billy Ashley	.15	.05
505	Pedro Astacio	.15	.05
506	Brett Butler	.30	.10
507	Tom Candiotti	.15	.05
508	Omar Daal	.15	.05
509	Jim Gott	.15	.05
510	Kevin Gross	.15	.05
511	Dave Hansen	.15	.05
512	Carlos Hernandez	.15	.05
513	Orel Hershiser	.30	.10
514	Eric Karros	.30	.10
515	Pedro Martinez	.75	.30
516	Ramon Martinez	.15	.05
517	Roger McDowell	.15	.05
518	Raul Mondesi	.30	.10
519	Jose Offerman	.15	.05
520	Mike Piazza	1.50	.60
521	Jody Reed	.15	.05
522	Henry Rodriguez	.15	.05
523	Mike Sharperson	.15	.05
524	Cory Snyder	.15	.05
525	Darryl Strawberry	.30	.10
526	Rick Trlicek	.15	.05
527	Tim Wallach	.15	.05
528	Mitch Webster	.15	.05
529	Steve Wilson	.15	.05
530	Todd Worrell	.15	.05
531	Moises Alou	.30	.10
532	Brian Barnes	.15	.05
533	Sean Berry	.15	.05
534	Greg Colbrunn	.15	.05
535	Delino DeShields	.15	.05
536	Jeff Fassero	.15	.05
537	Darrin Fletcher	.15	.05
538	Cliff Floyd	.30	.10
539	Lou Frazier	.15	.05
540	Marquis Grissom	.30	.10
541	Butch Henry	.15	.05
542	Ken Hill	.15	.05
543	Mike Lansing	.15	.05
544	Brian Looney RC	.15	.05
545	Dennis Martinez	.30	.10
546	Chris Nabholz	.15	.05
547	Randy Ready	.15	.05
548	Mel Rojas	.15	.05
549	Kirk Rueter	.15	.05
550	Tim Scott	.15	.05
551	Jeff Shaw	.15	.05
552	Tim Spehr	.15	.05
553	John Vander Wal	.15	.05
554	Larry Walker	.30	.10
555	John Wetteland	.30	.10
556	Rondell White	.30	.10

557	Tim Bogar	.15	.05
558	Bobby Bonilla	.30	.10
559	Jeromy Burnitz	.30	.10
560	Sid Fernandez	.15	.05
561	John Franco	.30	.10
562	Dave Gallagher	.15	.05
563	Dwight Gooden	.30	.10
564	Eric Hillman	.15	.05
565	Todd Hundley	.15	.05
566	Jeff Innis	.15	.05
567	Darrin Jackson	.15	.05
568	Howard Johnson	.15	.05
569	Bobby Jones	.15	.05
570	Jeff Kent	.50	.20
571	Mike Maddux	.15	.05
572	Jeff McKnight	.15	.05
573	Eddie Murray	.75	.30
574	Charlie O'Brien	.15	.05
575	Joe Orsulak	.15	.05
576	Bret Saberhagen	.30	.10
577	Pete Schourek	.15	.05
578	Dave Telgheder	.15	.05
579	Ryan Thompson	.15	.05
580	Anthony Young	.15	.05
581	Ruben Amaro	.15	.05
582	Larry Andersen	.15	.05
583	Kim Batiste	.15	.05
584	Wes Chamberlain	.15	.05
585	Darren Daulton	.30	.10
586	Mariano Duncan	.15	.05
587	Lenny Dykstra	.30	.10
588	Jim Eisenreich	.15	.05
589	Tommy Greene	.15	.05
590	Dave Hollins	.15	.05
591	Pete Incaviglia	.15	.05
592	Danny Jackson	.15	.05
593	Ricky Jordan	.15	.05
594	John Kruk	.30	.10
595	Roger Mason	.15	.05
596	Mickey Morandini	.15	.05
597	Terry Mulholland	.15	.05
598	Todd Pratt	.15	.05
599	Ben Rivera	.15	.05
600	Curt Schilling	.30	.10
601	Kevin Stocker	.15	.05
602	Milt Thompson	.15	.05
603	David West	.15	.05
604	Mitch Williams	.15	.05
605	Jay Bell	.30	.10
606	Dave Clark	.15	.05
607	Steve Cooke	.15	.05
608	Tom Foley	.15	.05
609	Carlos Garcia	.15	.05
610	Joel Johnston	.15	.05
611	Jeff King	.15	.05
612	Al Martin	.15	.05
613	Lloyd McClendon	.15	.05
614	Orlando Merced	.15	.05
615	Blas Minor	.15	.05
616	Denny Neagle	.30	.10
617	Mark Petkovsek RC	.15	.05
618	Tom Prince	.15	.05
619	Don Slaught	.15	.05
620	Zane Smith	.15	.05
621	Randy Tomlin	.15	.05
622	Andy Van Slyke	.50	.20
623	Paul Wagner	.15	.05
624	Tim Wakefield	.50	.20
625	Bob Walk	.15	.05
626	Kevin Young	.15	.05
627	Luis Alicea	.15	.05
628	Rene Arocha	.15	.05
629	Rod Brewer	.15	.05
630	Rheal Cormier	.15	.05
631	Bernard Gilkey	.15	.05
632	Lee Guetterman	.15	.05
633	Gregg Jefferies	.15	.05
634	Brian Jordan	.30	.10
635	Les Lancaster	.15	.05
636	Ray Lankford	.30	.10
637	Rob Murphy	.15	.05
638	Omar Olivares	.15	.05
639	Jose Oquendo	.15	.05
640	Donovan Osborne	.15	.05
641	Tom Pagnozzi	.15	.05
642	Erik Pappas	.15	.05

643	Geronimo Pena	.15	.05
644	Mike Perez	.15	.05
645	Gerald Perry	.15	.05
646	Ozzie Smith	1.25	.50
647	Bob Tewksbury	.15	.05
648	Allen Watson	.15	.05
649	Mark Whiten	.15	.05
650	Tracy Woodson	.15	.05
651	Todd Zeile	.15	.05
652	Andy Ashby	.15	.05
653	Brad Ausmus	.50	.20
654	Billy Bean	.15	.05
655	Derek Bell	.15	.05
656	Andy Benes	.15	.05
657	Doug Brocail	.15	.05
658	Jarvis Brown	.15	.05
659	Archi Cianfrocco	.15	.05
660	Phil Clark	.15	.05
661	Mark Davis	.15	.05
662	Jeff Gardner	.15	.05
663	Pat Gomez	.15	.05
664	Ricky Gutierrez	.15	.05
665	Tony Gwynn	1.00	.40
666	Gene Harris	.15	.05
667	Kevin Higgins	.15	.05
668	Trevor Hoffman	.50	.20
669	Pedro A.Martinez RC	.15	.05
670	Tim Mauser	.15	.05
671	Melvin Nieves	.15	.05
672	Phil Plantier	.15	.05
673	Frank Seminara	.15	.05
674	Craig Shipley	.15	.05
675	Kerry Taylor	.15	.05
676	Tim Teufel	.15	.05
677	Guillermo Velasquez	.15	.05
678	Wally Whitehurst	.15	.05
679	Tim Worrell	.15	.05
680	Rod Beck	.15	.05
681	Mike Benjamin	.15	.05
682	Todd Benzinger	.15	.05
683	Bud Black	.15	.05
684	Barry Bonds	2.00	.75
685	Jeff Brantley	.15	.05
686	Dave Burba	.15	.05
687	John Burkett	.15	.05
688	Mark Carreon	.15	.05
689	Will Clark	.50	.20
690	Royce Clayton	.15	.05
691	Bryan Hickerson	.15	.05
692	Mike Jackson	.15	.05
693	Darren Lewis	.15	.05
694	Kirt Manwaring	.15	.05
695	Dave Martinez	.15	.05
696	Willie McGee	.30	.10
697	John Patterson	.15	.05
698	Jeff Reed	.15	.05
699	Kevin Rogers	.15	.05
700	Scott Sanderson	.15	.05
701	Steve Scarsone	.15	.05
702	Billy Swift	.15	.05
703	Robby Thompson	.15	.05
704	Matt Williams	.30	.10
705	Trevor Wilson	.15	.05
706	McGriff/Gant/Justice	.30	.10
707	J.Olerud/P.Molitor	.30	.10
708	M.Mussina/J.McDowell	.30	.10
709	L.Whitaker/A.Trammell	.30	.10
710	R.Palmeiro/J.Gonzalez	.30	.10
711	B.Butler/T.Gwynn	.50	.20
712	K.Puckett/C.Knoblauch	.50	.20
713	M.Piazza/E.Karros	.75	.30
714	Checklist 1	.15	.05
715	Checklist 2	.15	.05
716	Checklist 3	.15	.05
717	Checklist 4	.15	.05
718	Checklist 5	.15	.05
719	Checklist 6	.15	.05
720	Checklist 7	.15	.05
P69	Tim Salmon Promo	1.00	.40

1995 Fleer

	COMPLETE SET (600)	50.00	20.00
1	Brady Anderson	.30	.10
2	Harold Baines	.30	.10
3	Damon Buford	.15	.05
4	Mike Devereaux	.15	.05

❑	5 Mark Eichhorn	.15	.05
❑	6 Sid Fernandez	.15	.05
❑	7 Leo Gomez	.15	.05
❑	8 Jeffrey Hammonds	.15	.05
❑	9 Chris Hoiles	.15	.05
❑	10 Rick Krivda	.15	.05
❑	11 Ben McDonald	.15	.05
❑	12 Mark McLemore	.15	.05
❑	13 Alan Mills	.15	.05
❑	14 Jamie Moyer	.30	.10
❑	15 Mike Mussina	.50	.20
❑	16 Mike Oquist	.15	.05
❑	17 Rafael Palmeiro	.50	.20
❑	18 Arthur Rhodes	.15	.05
❑	19 Cal Ripken	2.50	1.00
❑	20 Chris Sabo	.15	.05
❑	21 Lee Smith	.30	.10
❑	22 Jack Voigt	.15	.05
❑	23 Damon Berryhill	.15	.05
❑	24 Tom Brunansky	.15	.05
❑	25 Wes Chamberlain	.15	.05
❑	26 Roger Clemens	1.50	.60
❑	27 Scott Cooper	.15	.05
❑	28 Andre Dawson	.30	.10
❑	29 Gar Finnvold	.15	.05
❑	30 Tony Fossas	.15	.05
❑	31 Mike Greenwell	.15	.05
❑	32 Joe Hesketh	.15	.05
❑	33 Chris Howard	.15	.05
❑	34 Chris Nabholz	.15	.05
❑	35 Tim Naehring	.15	.05
❑	36 Otis Nixon	.15	.05
❑	37 Carlos Rodriguez	.15	.05
❑	38 Rich Rowland	.15	.05
❑	39 Ken Ryan	.15	.05
❑	40 Aaron Sele	.15	.05
❑	41 John Valentin	.15	.05
❑	42 Mo Vaughn	.30	.10
❑	43 Frank Viola	.30	.10
❑	44 Danny Bautista	.15	.05
❑	45 Joe Boever	.15	.05
❑	46 Milt Cuyler	.15	.05
❑	47 Storm Davis	.15	.05
❑	48 John Doherty	.15	.05
❑	49 Junior Felix	.15	.05
❑	50 Cecil Fielder	.30	.10
❑	51 Travis Fryman	.30	.10
❑	52 Mike Gardiner	.15	.05
❑	53 Kirk Gibson	.30	.10
❑	54 Chris Gomez	.15	.05
❑	55 Buddy Groom	.15	.05
❑	56 Mike Henneman	.15	.05
❑	57 Chad Kreuter	.15	.05
❑	58 Mike Moore	.15	.05
❑	59 Tony Phillips	.15	.05
❑	60 Juan Samuel	.15	.05
❑	61 Mickey Tettleton	.15	.05
❑	62 Alan Trammell	.30	.10
❑	63 David Wells	.30	.10
❑	64 Lou Whitaker	.30	.10
❑	65 Jim Abbott	.50	.20
❑	66 Joe Ausanio	.15	.05
❑	67 Wade Boggs	.50	.20
❑	68 Mike Gallego	.15	.05
❑	69 Xavier Hernandez	.15	.05
❑	70 Sterling Hitchcock	.15	.05
❑	71 Steve Howe	.15	.05
❑	72 Scott Kamieniecki	.15	.05
❑	73 Pat Kelly	.15	.05
❑	74 Jimmy Key	.30	.10
❑	75 Jim Leyritz	.15	.05
❑	76 Don Mattingly	2.00	.75
❑	77 Terry Mulholland	.15	.05
❑	78 Paul O'Neill	.50	.20
❑	79 Melido Perez	.15	.05
❑	80 Luis Polonia	.15	.05
❑	81 Mike Stanley	.15	.05
❑	82 Danny Tartabull	.15	.05
❑	83 Randy Velarde	.15	.05
❑	84 Bob Wickman	.15	.05
❑	85 Bernie Williams	.50	.20
❑	86 Gerald Williams	.15	.05
❑	87 Roberto Alomar	.50	.20
❑	88 Pat Borders	.15	.05
❑	89 Joe Carter	.30	.10
❑	90 Tony Castillo	.15	.05
❑	91 Brad Cornett RC	.15	.05
❑	92 Carlos Delgado	.30	.10
❑	93 Alex Gonzalez	.15	.05
❑	94 Shawn Green	.30	.10
❑	95 Juan Guzman	.15	.05
❑	96 Darren Hall	.15	.05
❑	97 Pat Hentgen	.15	.05
❑	98 Mike Huff	.15	.05
❑	99 Randy Knorr	.15	.05
❑	100 Al Leiter	.30	.10
❑	101 Paul Molitor	.30	.10
❑	102 John Olerud	.30	.10
❑	103 Dick Schofield	.15	.05
❑	104 Ed Sprague	.15	.05
❑	105 Dave Stewart	.30	.10
❑	106 Todd Stottlemyre	.15	.05
❑	107 Devon White	.30	.10
❑	108 Woody Williams	.15	.05
❑	109 Wilson Alvarez	.15	.05
❑	110 Paul Assenmacher	.15	.05
❑	111 Jason Bere	.15	.05
❑	112 Dennis Cook	.15	.05
❑	113 Joey Cora	.15	.05
❑	114 Jose DeLeon	.15	.05
❑	115 Alex Fernandez	.15	.05
❑	116 Julio Franco	.30	.10
❑	117 Craig Grebeck	.15	.05
❑	118 Ozzie Guillen	.30	.10
❑	119 Roberto Hernandez	.15	.05
❑	120 Darrin Jackson	.15	.05
❑	121 Lance Johnson	.15	.05
❑	122 Ron Karkovice	.15	.05
❑	123 Mike LaValliere	.15	.05
❑	124 Norberto Martin	.15	.05
❑	125 Kirk McCaskill	.15	.05
❑	126 Jack McDowell	.15	.05
❑	127 Tim Raines	.30	.10
❑	128 Frank Thomas	.75	.30
❑	129 Robin Ventura	.30	.10
❑	130 Sandy Alomar Jr.	.15	.05
❑	131 Carlos Baerga	.15	.05
❑	132 Albert Belle	.30	.10
❑	133 Mark Clark	.15	.05
❑	134 Alvaro Espinoza	.15	.05
❑	135 Jason Grimsley	.15	.05
❑	136 Wayne Kirby	.15	.05
❑	137 Kenny Lofton	.30	.10
❑	138 Albie Lopez	.15	.05
❑	139 Dennis Martinez	.30	.10
❑	140 Jose Mesa	.15	.05
❑	141 Eddie Murray	.75	.30
❑	142 Charles Nagy	.15	.05
❑	143 Tony Pena	.15	.05
❑	144 Eric Plunk	.15	.05
❑	145 Manny Ramirez	.50	.20
❑	146 Jeff Russell	.15	.05
❑	147 Paul Shuey	.15	.05
❑	148 Paul Sorrento	.15	.05
❑	149 Jim Thome	.50	.20
❑	150 Omar Vizquel	.50	.20
❑	151 Dave Winfield	.30	.10
❑	152 Kevin Appier	.30	.10
❑	153 Billy Brewer	.15	.05
❑	154 Vince Coleman	.15	.05
❑	155 David Cone	.30	.10
❑	156 Gary Gaetti	.30	.10
❑	157 Greg Gagne	.15	.05
❑	158 Tom Gordon	.15	.05
❑	159 Mark Gubicza	.15	.05
❑	160 Bob Hamelin	.15	.05
❑	161 Dave Henderson	.15	.05
❑	162 Felix Jose	.15	.05
❑	163 Wally Joyner	.30	.10
❑	164 Jose Lind	.15	.05
❑	165 Mike Macfarlane	.15	.05
❑	166 Mike Magnante	.15	.05
❑	167 Brent Mayne	.15	.05
❑	168 Brian McRae	.15	.05
❑	169 Rusty Meacham	.15	.05
❑	170 Jeff Montgomery	.15	.05
❑	171 Hipolito Pichardo	.15	.05
❑	172 Terry Shumpert	.15	.05
❑	173 Michael Tucker	.15	.05
❑	174 Ricky Bones	.15	.05
❑	175 Jeff Cirillo	.15	.05
❑	176 Alex Diaz	.15	.05
❑	177 Cal Eldred	.15	.05
❑	178 Mike Fetters	.15	.05
❑	179 Darryl Hamilton	.15	.05
❑	180 Brian Harper	.15	.05
❑	181 John Jaha	.15	.05
❑	182 Pat Listach	.15	.05
❑	183 Graeme Lloyd	.15	.05
❑	184 Jose Mercedes	.15	.05
❑	185 Matt Mieske	.15	.05
❑	186 Dave Nilsson	.15	.05
❑	187 Jody Reed	.15	.05
❑	188 Bob Scanlan	.15	.05
❑	189 Kevin Seitzer	.15	.05
❑	190 Bill Spiers	.15	.05
❑	191 B.J. Surhoff	.30	.10
❑	192 Jose Valentin	.15	.05
❑	193 Greg Vaughn	.15	.05
❑	194 Turner Ward	.15	.05
❑	195 Bill Wegman	.15	.05
❑	196 Rick Aguilera	.15	.05
❑	197 Rich Becker	.15	.05
❑	198 Alex Cole	.15	.05
❑	199 Marty Cordova	.15	.05
❑	200 Steve Dunn	.15	.05
❑	201 Scott Erickson	.15	.05
❑	202 Mark Guthrie	.15	.05
❑	203 Chip Hale	.15	.05
❑	204 LaTroy Hawkins	.15	.05
❑	205 Denny Hocking	.15	.05
❑	206 Chuck Knoblauch	.30	.10
❑	207 Scott Leius	.15	.05
❑	208 Shane Mack	.15	.05
❑	209 Pat Mahomes	.15	.05
❑	210 Pat Meares	.15	.05
❑	211 Pedro Munoz	.15	.05
❑	212 Kirby Puckett	.75	.30
❑	213 Jeff Reboulet	.15	.05
❑	214 Dave Stevens	.15	.05
❑	215 Kevin Tapani	.15	.05
❑	216 Matt Walbeck	.15	.05
❑	217 Carl Willis	.15	.05
❑	218 Brian Anderson	.15	.05
❑	219 Chad Curtis	.15	.05
❑	220 Chili Davis	.30	.10
❑	221 Gary DiSarcina	.15	.05
❑	222 Damion Easley	.15	.05
❑	223 Jim Edmonds	.50	.20
❑	224 Chuck Finley	.30	.10
❑	225 Joe Grahe	.15	.05
❑	226 Rex Hudler	.15	.05
❑	227 Bo Jackson	.75	.30
❑	228 Mark Langston	.15	.05
❑	229 Phil Leftwich	.15	.05
❑	230 Mark Leiter	.15	.05
❑	231 Spike Owen	.15	.05
❑	232 Bob Patterson	.15	.05
❑	233 Troy Percival	.30	.10
❑	234 Eduardo Perez	.15	.05
❑	235 Tim Salmon	.50	.20
❑	236 J.T. Snow	.30	.10
❑	237 Chris Turner	.15	.05
❑	238 Mark Acre	.15	.05
❑	239 Geronimo Berroa	.15	.05
❑	240 Mike Bordick	.15	.05
❑	241 John Briscoe	.15	.05
❑	242 Scott Brosius	.30	.10
❑	243 Ron Darling	.15	.05
❑	244 Dennis Eckersley	.30	.10

❑ 245 Brent Gates .15 .05
❑ 246 Rickey Henderson .75 .30
❑ 247 Stan Javier .15 .05
❑ 248 Steve Karsay .15 .05
❑ 249 Mark McGwire 2.00 .75
❑ 250 Troy Neel .15 .05
❑ 251 Steve Ontiveros .15 .05
❑ 252 Carlos Reyes .15 .05
❑ 253 Ruben Sierra .30 .10
❑ 254 Terry Steinbach .15 .05
❑ 255 Bill Taylor .15 .05
❑ 256 Todd Van Poppel .15 .05
❑ 257 Bobby Witt .15 .05
❑ 258 Rich Amaral .15 .05
❑ 259 Eric Anthony .15 .05
❑ 260 Bobby Ayala .15 .05
❑ 261 Mike Blowers .15 .05
❑ 262 Chris Bosio .15 .05
❑ 263 Jay Buhner .30 .10
❑ 264 John Cummings .15 .05
❑ 265 Tim Davis .15 .05
❑ 266 Felix Fermin .15 .05
❑ 267 Dave Fleming .15 .05
❑ 268 Goose Gossage .30 .10
❑ 269 Ken Griffey Jr. 1.25 .50
❑ 270 Reggie Jefferson .15 .05
❑ 271 Randy Johnson .75 .30
❑ 272 Edgar Martinez .50 .20
❑ 273 Tino Martinez .50 .20
❑ 274 Greg Pirkl .15 .05
❑ 275 Bill Risley .15 .05
❑ 276 Roger Salkeld .15 .05
❑ 277 Luis Sojo .15 .05
❑ 278 Mac Suzuki .15 .05
❑ 279 Dan Wilson .15 .05
❑ 280 Kevin Brown .30 .10
❑ 281 Jose Canseco .60 .20
❑ 282 Cris Carpenter .15 .05
❑ 283 Will Clark .50 .20
❑ 284 Jeff Frye .15 .05
❑ 285 Juan Gonzalez .30 .10
❑ 286 Rick Helling .15 .05
❑ 287 Tom Henke .15 .05
❑ 288 David Hulse .15 .05
❑ 289 Chris James .15 .05
❑ 290 Manuel Lee .15 .05
❑ 291 Oddibe McDowell .15 .05
❑ 292 Dean Palmer .30 .10
❑ 293 Roger Pavlik .15 .05
❑ 294 Bill Ripken .15 .05
❑ 295 Ivan Rodriguez .50 .20
❑ 296 Kenny Rogers .30 .10
❑ 297 Doug Strange .15 .05
❑ 298 Matt Whiteside .15 .05
❑ 299 Steve Avery .15 .05
❑ 300 Steve Bedrosian .15 .05
❑ 301 Rafael Belliard .15 .05
❑ 302 Jeff Blauser .15 .05
❑ 303 Dave Gallagher .15 .05
❑ 304 Tom Glavine .50 .20
❑ 305 David Justice .30 .10
❑ 306 Mike Kelly .15 .05
❑ 307 Roberto Kelly .15 .05
❑ 308 Ryan Klesko .30 .10
❑ 309 Mark Lemke .15 .05
❑ 310 Javier Lopez .30 .10
❑ 311 Greg Maddux 1.25 .50
❑ 312 Fred McGriff .50 .20
❑ 313 Greg McMichael .15 .05
❑ 314 Kent Mercker .15 .05
❑ 315 Charlie O'Brien .15 .05
❑ 316 Jose Oliva .15 .05
❑ 317 Terry Pendleton .30 .10
❑ 318 John Smoltz .50 .20
❑ 319 Mike Stanton .15 .05
❑ 320 Tony Tarasco .15 .05
❑ 321 Terrell Wade .15 .05
❑ 322 Mark Wohlers .15 .05
❑ 323 Kurt Abbott .15 .05
❑ 324 Luis Aquino .15 .05
❑ 325 Bret Barberie .15 .05
❑ 326 Ryan Bowen .15 .05
❑ 327 Jerry Browne .15 .05
❑ 328 Chuck Carr .15 .05
❑ 329 Matias Carrillo .15 .05
❑ 330 Greg Colbrunn .15 .05
❑ 331 Jeff Conine .30 .10
❑ 332 Mark Gardner .15 .05
❑ 333 Chris Hammond .15 .05
❑ 334 Bryan Harvey .15 .05
❑ 335 Richie Lewis .15 .05
❑ 336 Dave Magadan .15 .05
❑ 337 Terry Mathews .15 .05
❑ 338 Robb Nen .30 .10
❑ 339 Yorkis Perez .15 .05
❑ 340 Pat Rapp .15 .05
❑ 341 Benito Santiago .30 .10
❑ 342 Gary Sheffield .30 .10
❑ 343 Dave Weathers .15 .05
❑ 344 Moises Alou .30 .10
❑ 345 Sean Berry .15 .05
❑ 346 Wil Cordero .15 .05
❑ 347 Joey Eischen .15 .05
❑ 348 Jeff Fassero .15 .05
❑ 349 Darrin Fletcher .15 .05
❑ 350 Cliff Floyd .30 .10
❑ 351 Marquis Grissom .30 .10
❑ 352 Butch Henry .15 .05
❑ 353 Gil Heredia .15 .05
❑ 354 Ken Hill .15 .05
❑ 355 Mike Lansing .15 .05
❑ 356 Pedro Martinez .60 .20
❑ 357 Mel Rojas .15 .05
❑ 358 Kirk Rueter .15 .05
❑ 359 Tim Scott .15 .05
❑ 360 Jeff Shaw .15 .05
❑ 361 Larry Walker .30 .10
❑ 362 Lenny Webster .15 .05
❑ 363 John Wetteland .30 .10
❑ 364 Rondell White .30 .10
❑ 365 Bobby Bonilla .30 .10
❑ 366 Rico Brogna .15 .05
❑ 367 Jeromy Burnitz .30 .10
❑ 368 John Franco .30 .10
❑ 369 Dwight Gooden .30 .10
❑ 370 Todd Hundley .15 .05
❑ 371 Jason Jacome .15 .05
❑ 372 Bobby Jones .15 .05
❑ 373 Jeff Kent .30 .10
❑ 374 Jim Lindeman .15 .05
❑ 375 Josias Manzanillo .15 .05
❑ 376 Roger Mason .15 .05
❑ 377 Kevin McReynolds .15 .05
❑ 378 Joe Orsulak .15 .05
❑ 379 Bill Pulsipher .15 .05
❑ 380 Bret Saberhagen .30 .10
❑ 381 David Segui .15 .05
❑ 382 Pete Smith .15 .05
❑ 383 Kelly Stinnett .15 .05
❑ 384 Ryan Thompson .15 .05
❑ 385 Jose Vizcaino .15 .05
❑ 386 Toby Borland .15 .05
❑ 387 Ricky Bottalico .15 .05
❑ 388 Darren Daulton .30 .10
❑ 389 Mariano Duncan .15 .05
❑ 390 Lenny Dykstra .30 .10
❑ 391 Jim Eisenreich .15 .05
❑ 392 Tommy Greene .15 .05
❑ 393 Dave Hollins .15 .05
❑ 394 Pete Incaviglia .15 .05
❑ 395 Danny Jackson .15 .05
❑ 396 Doug Jones .15 .05
❑ 397 Ricky Jordan .15 .05
❑ 398 John Kruk .30 .10
❑ 399 Mike Lieberthal .30 .10
❑ 400 Tony Longmire .15 .05
❑ 401 Mickey Morandini .15 .05
❑ 402 Bobby Munoz .15 .05
❑ 403 Curt Schilling .30 .10
❑ 404 Heathcliff Slocumb .15 .05
❑ 405 Kevin Stocker .15 .05
❑ 406 Fernando Valenzuela .30 .10
❑ 407 David West .15 .05
❑ 408 Willie Banks .15 .05
❑ 409 Jose Bautista .15 .05
❑ 410 Steve Buechele .15 .05
❑ 411 Jim Bullinger .15 .05
❑ 412 Chuck Crim .15 .05
❑ 413 Shawon Dunston .15 .05
❑ 414 Kevin Foster .15 .05
❑ 415 Mark Grace .50 .20
❑ 416 Jose Hernandez .15 .05
❑ 417 Glenallen Hill .15 .05
❑ 418 Brooks Kieschnick .15 .05
❑ 419 Derrick May .15 .05
❑ 420 Randy Myers .15 .05
❑ 421 Dan Plesac .15 .05
❑ 422 Karl Rhodes .15 .05
❑ 423 Rey Sanchez .15 .05
❑ 424 Sammy Sosa .75 .30
❑ 425 Steve Trachsel .15 .05
❑ 426 Rick Wilkins .15 .05
❑ 427 Anthony Young .15 .05
❑ 428 Eddie Zambrano .15 .05
❑ 429 Bret Boone .30 .10
❑ 430 Jeff Branson .15 .05
❑ 431 Jeff Brantley .15 .05
❑ 432 Hector Carrasco .15 .05
❑ 433 Brian Dorsett .15 .05
❑ 434 Tony Fernandez .15 .05
❑ 435 Tim Fortugno .15 .05
❑ 436 Erik Hanson .15 .05
❑ 437 Thomas Howard .15 .05
❑ 438 Kevin Jarvis .15 .05
❑ 439 Barry Larkin .50 .20
❑ 440 Chuck McElroy .15 .05
❑ 441 Kevin Mitchell .15 .05
❑ 442 Hal Morris .15 .05
❑ 443 Jose Rijo .15 .05
❑ 444 John Roper .15 .05
❑ 445 Johnny Ruffin .15 .05
❑ 446 Deion Sanders .50 .20
❑ 447 Reggie Sanders .30 .10
❑ 448 Pete Schourek .15 .05
❑ 449 John Smiley .15 .05
❑ 450 Eddie Taubensee .15 .05
❑ 451 Jeff Bagwell .50 .20
❑ 452 Kevin Bass .15 .05
❑ 453 Craig Biggio .50 .20
❑ 454 Ken Caminiti .30 .10
❑ 455 Andujar Cedeno .15 .05
❑ 456 Doug Drabek .15 .05
❑ 457 Tony Eusebio .15 .05
❑ 458 Mike Felder .15 .05
❑ 459 Steve Finley .30 .10
❑ 460 Luis Gonzalez .30 .10
❑ 461 Mike Hampton .30 .10
❑ 462 Pete Harnisch .15 .05
❑ 463 John Hudek .15 .05
❑ 464 Todd Jones .15 .05
❑ 465 Darryl Kile .30 .10
❑ 466 James Mouton .15 .05
❑ 467 Shane Reynolds .15 .05
❑ 468 Scott Servais .15 .05
❑ 469 Greg Swindell .15 .05
❑ 470 Dave Veres RC .40 .15
❑ 471 Brian Williams .15 .05
❑ 472 Jay Bell .30 .10
❑ 473 Jacob Brumfield .15 .05
❑ 474 Dave Clark .15 .05
❑ 475 Steve Cooke .15 .05
❑ 476 Midre Cummings .15 .05
❑ 477 Mark Dewey .15 .05
❑ 478 Tom Foley .15 .05
❑ 479 Carlos Garcia .15 .05
❑ 480 Jeff King .15 .05
❑ 481 Jon Lieber .15 .05
❑ 482 Ravelo Manzanillo .15 .05
❑ 483 Al Martin .15 .05
❑ 484 Orlando Merced .15 .05
❑ 485 Danny Miceli .15 .05
❑ 486 Denny Neagle .30 .10
❑ 487 Lance Parrish .30 .10
❑ 488 Don Slaught .15 .05
❑ 489 Zane Smith .15 .05
❑ 490 Andy Van Slyke .50 .20
❑ 491 Paul Wagner .15 .05
❑ 492 Rick White .15 .05
❑ 493 Luis Alicea .15 .05
❑ 494 Rene Arocha .15 .05
❑ 495 Rheal Cormier .15 .05
❑ 496 Bryan Eversgerd .15 .05
❑ 497 Bernard Gilkey .15 .05
❑ 498 John Habyan .15 .05
❑ 499 Gregg Jefferies .15 .05
❑ 500 Brian Jordan .30 .10
❑ 501 Ray Lankford .30 .10
❑ 502 John Mabry .15 .05

❑ 503 Terry McGriff .15 .05
❑ 504 Tom Pagnozzi .15 .05
❑ 505 Vicente Palacios .15 .05
❑ 506 Geronimo Pena .15 .05
❑ 507 Gerald Perry .15 .05
❑ 508 Rich Rodriguez .15 .05
❑ 509 Ozzie Smith 1.25 .50
❑ 510 Bob Tewksbury .15 .05
❑ 511 Allen Watson .15 .05
❑ 512 Mark Whiten .15 .05
❑ 513 Todd Zeile .15 .05
❑ 514 Dante Bichette .30 .10
❑ 515 Willie Blair .15 .05
❑ 516 Ellis Burks .30 .10
❑ 517 Marvin Freeman .15 .05
❑ 518 Andres Galarraga .30 .10
❑ 519 Joe Girardi .15 .05
❑ 520 Greg W. Harris .15 .05
❑ 521 Charlie Hayes .15 .05
❑ 522 Mike Kingery .15 .05
❑ 523 Nelson Liriano .15 .05
❑ 524 Mike Munoz .15 .05
❑ 525 David Nied .15 .05
❑ 526 Steve Reed .15 .05
❑ 527 Kevin Ritz .15 .05
❑ 528 Bruce Ruffin .15 .05
❑ 529 John Vander Wal .15 .05
❑ 530 Walt Weiss .15 .05
❑ 531 Eric Young .15 .05
❑ 532 Billy Ashley .15 .05
❑ 533 Pedro Astacio .15 .05
❑ 534 Rafael Bournigal .15 .05
❑ 535 Brett Butler .30 .10
❑ 536 Tom Candiotti .15 .05
❑ 537 Omar Daal .15 .05
❑ 538 Delino DeShields .15 .05
❑ 539 Darren Dreifort .15 .05
❑ 540 Kevin Gross .15 .05
❑ 541 Orel Hershiser .30 .10
❑ 542 Garey Ingram .15 .05
❑ 543 Eric Karros .30 .10
❑ 544 Ramon Martinez .15 .05
❑ 545 Raul Mondesi .30 .10
❑ 546 Chan Ho Park .30 .10
❑ 547 Mike Piazza 1.25 .50
❑ 548 Henry Rodriguez .15 .05
❑ 549 Rudy Seanez .15 .05
❑ 550 Ismael Valdes .15 .05
❑ 551 Tim Wallach .15 .05
❑ 552 Todd Worrell .15 .05
❑ 553 Andy Ashby .15 .05
❑ 554 Brad Ausmus .30 .10
❑ 555 Derek Bell .15 .05
❑ 556 Andy Benes .15 .05
❑ 557 Phil Clark .15 .05
❑ 558 Donnie Elliott .15 .05
❑ 559 Ricky Gutierrez .15 .05
❑ 560 Tony Gwynn 1.00 .40
❑ 561 Joey Hamilton .15 .05
❑ 562 Trevor Hoffman .30 .10
❑ 563 Luis Lopez .15 .05
❑ 564 Pedro A. Martinez .15 .05
❑ 565 Tim Mauser .15 .05
❑ 566 Phil Plantier .15 .05
❑ 567 Bip Roberts .15 .05
❑ 568 Scott Sanders .15 .05
❑ 569 Craig Shipley .15 .05
❑ 570 Jeff Tabaka .15 .05
❑ 571 Eddie Williams .15 .05
❑ 572 Rod Beck .15 .05
❑ 573 Mike Benjamin .15 .05
❑ 574 Barry Bonds 2.00 .75
❑ 575 Dave Burba .15 .05
❑ 576 John Burkett .15 .05
❑ 577 Mark Carreon .15 .05
❑ 578 Royce Clayton .15 .05
❑ 579 Steve Frey .15 .05
❑ 580 Bryan Hickerson .15 .05
❑ 581 Mike Jackson .15 .05
❑ 582 Darren Lewis .15 .05
❑ 583 Kirt Manwaring .15 .05
❑ 584 Rich Monteleone .15 .05
❑ 585 John Patterson .15 .05
❑ 586 J.R. Phillips .15 .05
❑ 587 Mark Portugal .15 .05
❑ 588 Joe Rosselli .15 .05
❑ 589 Darryl Strawberry .30 .10
❑ 590 Bill Swift .15 .05
❑ 591 Robby Thompson .15 .05
❑ 592 William VanLandingham .15 .05
❑ 593 Matt Williams .30 .10
❑ 594 Checklist .15 .05
❑ 595 Checklist .15 .05
❑ 596 Checklist .15 .05
❑ 597 Checklist .15 .05
❑ 598 Checklist .15 .05
❑ 599 Checklist .15 .05
❑ 600 Checklist .15 .05

1996 Fleer

❑ COMPLETE SET (600) 80.00 40.00
❑ 1 Manny Alexander .30 .10
❑ 2 Brady Anderson .30 .10
❑ 3 Harold Baines .30 .10
❑ 4 Armando Benitez .30 .10
❑ 5 Bobby Bonilla .30 .10
❑ 6 Kevin Brown .30 .10
❑ 7 Scott Erickson .30 .10
❑ 8 Curtis Goodwin .30 .10
❑ 9 Jeffrey Hammonds .30 .10
❑ 10 Jimmy Haynes .30 .10
❑ 11 Chris Hoiles .30 .10
❑ 12 Doug Jones .30 .10
❑ 13 Rick Krivda .30 .10
❑ 14 Jeff Manto .30 .10
❑ 15 Ben McDonald .30 .10
❑ 16 Jamie Moyer .30 .10
❑ 17 Mike Mussina .50 .20
❑ 18 Jesse Orosco .30 .10
❑ 19 Rafael Palmeiro .50 .20
❑ 20 Cal Ripken 2.50 1.00
❑ 21 Rick Aguilera .30 .10
❑ 22 Luis Alicea .30 .10
❑ 23 Stan Belinda .30 .10
❑ 24 Jose Canseco .50 .20
❑ 25 Roger Clemens 1.50 .60
❑ 26 Vaughn Eshelman .30 .10
❑ 27 Mike Greenwell .30 .10
❑ 28 Erik Hanson .30 .10
❑ 29 Dwayne Hosey .30 .10
❑ 30 Mike Macfarlane UER .30 .10
❑ 31 Tim Naehring .30 .10
❑ 32 Troy O'Leary .30 .10
❑ 33 Aaron Sele .30 .10
❑ 34 Zane Smith .30 .10
❑ 35 Jeff Suppan .30 .10
❑ 36 Lee Tinsley .30 .10
❑ 37 John Valentin .30 .10
❑ 38 Mo Vaughn .30 .10
❑ 39 Tim Wakefield .30 .10
❑ 40 Jim Abbott .50 .20
❑ 41 Brian Anderson .30 .10
❑ 42 Garret Anderson .30 .10
❑ 43 Chili Davis .30 .10
❑ 44 Gary DiSarcina .30 .10
❑ 45 Damion Easley .30 .10
❑ 46 Jim Edmonds .30 .10
❑ 47 Chuck Finley .30 .10
❑ 48 Todd Greene .30 .10
❑ 49 Mike Harkey .30 .10
❑ 50 Mike James .30 .10
❑ 51 Mark Langston .30 .10
❑ 52 Greg Myers .30 .10
❑ 53 Orlando Palmeiro .30 .10
❑ 54 Bob Patterson .30 .10
❑ 55 Troy Percival .30 .10
❑ 56 Tony Phillips .30 .10
❑ 57 Tim Salmon .50 .20
❑ 58 Lee Smith .30 .10
❑ 59 J.T. Snow .30 .10
❑ 60 Randy Velarde .30 .10
❑ 61 Wilson Alvarez .30 .10
❑ 62 Luis Andujar .30 .10
❑ 63 Jason Bere .30 .10
❑ 64 Ray Durham .30 .10
❑ 65 Alex Fernandez .30 .10
❑ 66 Ozzie Guillen .30 .10
❑ 67 Roberto Hernandez .30 .10
❑ 68 Lance Johnson .30 .10
❑ 69 Matt Karchner .30 .10
❑ 70 Ron Karkovice .30 .10
❑ 71 Norberto Martin .30 .10
❑ 72 Dave Martinez .30 .10
❑ 73 Kirk McCaskill .30 .10
❑ 74 Lyle Mouton .30 .10
❑ 75 Tim Raines .30 .10
❑ 76 Mike Sirotka RC .30 .10
❑ 77 Frank Thomas .75 .30
❑ 78 Larry Thomas .30 .10
❑ 79 Robin Ventura .30 .10
❑ 80 Sandy Alomar Jr. .30 .10
❑ 81 Paul Assenmacher .30 .10
❑ 82 Carlos Baerga .30 .10
❑ 83 Albert Belle .30 .10
❑ 84 Mark Clark .30 .10
❑ 85 Alan Embree .30 .10
❑ 86 Alvaro Espinoza .30 .10
❑ 87 Orel Hershiser .30 .10
❑ 88 Ken Hill .30 .10
❑ 89 Kenny Lofton .30 .10
❑ 90 Dennis Martinez .30 .10
❑ 91 Jose Mesa .30 .10
❑ 92 Eddie Murray .75 .30
❑ 93 Charles Nagy .30 .10
❑ 94 Chad Ogea .30 .10
❑ 95 Tony Pena .30 .10
❑ 96 Herb Perry .30 .10
❑ 97 Eric Plunk .30 .10
❑ 98 Jim Poole .30 .10
❑ 99 Manny Ramirez .50 .20
❑ 100 Paul Sorrento .30 .10
❑ 101 Julian Tavarez .30 .10
❑ 102 Jim Thome .50 .20
❑ 103 Omar Vizquel .50 .20
❑ 104 Dave Winfield .30 .10
❑ 105 Danny Bautista .30 .10
❑ 106 Joe Boever .30 .10
❑ 107 Chad Curtis .30 .10
❑ 108 John Doherty .30 .10
❑ 109 Cecil Fielder .30 .10
❑ 110 John Flaherty .30 .10
❑ 111 Travis Fryman .30 .10
❑ 112 Chris Gomez .30 .10
❑ 113 Bob Higginson .30 .10
❑ 114 Mark Lewis .30 .10
❑ 115 Jose Lima .30 .10
❑ 116 Felipe Lira .30 .10
❑ 117 Brian Maxcy .30 .10
❑ 118 C.J. Nitkowski .30 .10
❑ 119 Phil Plantier .30 .10
❑ 120 Clint Sodowsky .30 .10
❑ 121 Alan Trammell .30 .10
❑ 122 Lou Whitaker .30 .10
❑ 123 Kevin Appier .30 .10
❑ 124 Johnny Damon .50 .20
❑ 125 Gary Gaetti .30 .10
❑ 126 Tom Goodwin .30 .10
❑ 127 Tom Gordon .30 .10
❑ 128 Mark Gubicza .30 .10
❑ 129 Bob Hamelin .30 .10
❑ 130 David Howard .30 .10
❑ 131 Jason Jacome .30 .10
❑ 132 Wally Joyner .30 .10
❑ 133 Keith Lockhart .30 .10
❑ 134 Brent Mayne .30 .10
❑ 135 Jeff Montgomery .30 .10
❑ 136 Jon Nunnally .30 .10
❑ 137 Juan Samuel .30 .10
❑ 138 Mike Sweeney RC 1.00 .40
❑ 139 Michael Tucker .30 .10

❑ 140 Joe Vitiello .30 .10
❑ 141 Ricky Bones .30 .10
❑ 142 Chuck Carr .30 .10
❑ 143 Jeff Cirillo .30 .10
❑ 144 Mike Fetters .30 .10
❑ 145 Darryl Hamilton .30 .10
❑ 146 David Hulse .30 .10
❑ 147 John Jaha .30 .10
❑ 148 Scott Karl .30 .10
❑ 149 Mark Kiefer .30 .10
❑ 150 Pat Listach .30 .10
❑ 151 Mark Loretta .30 .10
❑ 152 Mike Matheny .30 .10
❑ 153 Matt Mieske .30 .10
❑ 154 Dave Nilsson .30 .10
❑ 155 Joe Oliver .30 .10
❑ 156 Al Reyes .30 .10
❑ 157 Kevin Seitzer .30 .10
❑ 158 Steve Sparks .30 .10
❑ 159 B.J. Surhoff .30 .10
❑ 160 Jose Valentin .30 .10
❑ 161 Greg Vaughn .30 .10
❑ 162 Fernando Vina .30 .10
❑ 163 Rich Becker .30 .10
❑ 164 Ron Coomer .30 .10
❑ 165 Marty Cordova .30 .10
❑ 166 Chuck Knoblauch .30 .10
❑ 167 Matt Lawton RC .50 .20
❑ 168 Pat Meares .30 .10
❑ 169 Paul Molitor .30 .10
❑ 170 Pedro Munoz .30 .10
❑ 171 Jose Parra .30 .10
❑ 172 Kirby Puckett .75 .30
❑ 173 Brad Radke .30 .10
❑ 174 Jeff Reboulet .30 .10
❑ 175 Rich Robertson .30 .10
❑ 176 Frank Rodriguez .30 .10
❑ 177 Scott Stahoviak .30 .10
❑ 178 Dave Stevens .30 .10
❑ 179 Matt Walbeck .30 .10
❑ 180 Wade Boggs .50 .20
❑ 181 David Cone .30 .10
❑ 182 Tony Fernandez .30 .10
❑ 183 Joe Girardi .30 .10
❑ 184 Derek Jeter 2.00 .75
❑ 185 Scott Kamieniecki .30 .10
❑ 186 Pat Kelly .30 .10
❑ 187 Jim Leyritz .30 .10
❑ 188 Tino Martinez .50 .20
❑ 189 Don Mattingly 2.00 .75
❑ 190 Jack McDowell .30 .10
❑ 191 Jeff Nelson .30 .10
❑ 192 Paul O'Neill .50 .20
❑ 193 Melido Perez .30 .10
❑ 194 Andy Pettitte .50 .20
❑ 195 Mariano Rivera .75 .30
❑ 196 Ruben Sierra .30 .10
❑ 197 Mike Stanley .30 .10
❑ 198 Darryl Strawberry .30 .10
❑ 199 John Wetteland .30 .10
❑ 200 Bob Wickman .30 .10
❑ 201 Bernie Williams .50 .20
❑ 202 Mark Acre .30 .10
❑ 203 Geronimo Berroa .30 .10
❑ 204 Mike Bordick .30 .10
❑ 205 Scott Brosius .30 .10
❑ 206 Dennis Eckersley .30 .10
❑ 207 Brent Gates .30 .10
❑ 208 Jason Giambi .30 .10
❑ 209 Rickey Henderson .75 .30
❑ 210 Jose Herrera .30 .10
❑ 211 Stan Javier .30 .10
❑ 212 Doug Johns .30 .10
❑ 213 Mark McGwire 2.00 .75
❑ 214 Steve Ontiveros .30 .10
❑ 215 Craig Paquette .30 .10
❑ 216 Ariel Prieto .30 .10
❑ 217 Carlos Reyes .30 .10
❑ 218 Terry Steinbach .30 .10
❑ 219 Todd Stottlemyre .30 .10
❑ 220 Danny Tartabull .30 .10
❑ 221 Todd Van Poppel .30 .10
❑ 222 John Wasdin .30 .10
❑ 223 George Williams .30 .10
❑ 224 Steve Wojciechowski .30 .10
❑ 225 Rich Amaral .30 .10
❑ 226 Bobby Ayala .30 .10
❑ 227 Tim Belcher .30 .10
❑ 228 Andy Benes .30 .10
❑ 229 Chris Bosio .30 .10
❑ 230 Darren Bragg .30 .10
❑ 231 Jay Buhner .30 .10
❑ 232 Norm Charlton .30 .10
❑ 233 Vince Coleman .30 .10
❑ 234 Joey Cora .30 .10
❑ 235 Russ Davis .30 .10
❑ 236 Alex Diaz .30 .10
❑ 237 Felix Fermin .30 .10
❑ 238 Ken Griffey Jr. 1.25 .50
❑ 239 Sterling Hitchcock .30 .10
❑ 240 Randy Johnson .75 .30
❑ 241 Edgar Martinez .50 .20
❑ 242 Bill Risley .30 .10
❑ 243 Alex Rodriguez 1.50 .60
❑ 244 Luis Sojo .30 .10
❑ 245 Dan Wilson .30 .10
❑ 246 Bob Wolcott .30 .10
❑ 247 Will Clark .50 .20
❑ 248 Jeff Frye .30 .10
❑ 249 Benji Gil .30 .10
❑ 250 Juan Gonzalez .30 .10
❑ 251 Rusty Greer .30 .10
❑ 252 Kevin Gross .30 .10
❑ 253 Roger McDowell .30 .10
❑ 254 Mark McLemore .30 .10
❑ 255 Otis Nixon .30 .10
❑ 256 Luis Ortiz .30 .10
❑ 257 Mike Pagliarulo .30 .10
❑ 258 Dean Palmer .30 .10
❑ 259 Roger Pavlik .30 .10
❑ 260 Ivan Rodriguez .50 .20
❑ 261 Kenny Rogers .30 .10
❑ 262 Jeff Russell .30 .10
❑ 263 Mickey Tettleton .30 .10
❑ 264 Bob Tewksbury .30 .10
❑ 265 Dave Valle .30 .10
❑ 266 Matt Whiteside .30 .10
❑ 267 Roberto Alomar .50 .20
❑ 268 Joe Carter .30 .10
❑ 269 Tony Castillo .30 .10
❑ 270 Domingo Cedeno .30 .10
❑ 271 Tim Crabtree UER .30 .10
❑ 272 Carlos Delgado .30 .10
❑ 273 Alex Gonzalez .30 .10
❑ 274 Shawn Green .30 .10
❑ 275 Juan Guzman .30 .10
❑ 276 Pat Hentgen .30 .10
❑ 277 Al Leiter .30 .10
❑ 278 Sandy Martinez .30 .10
❑ 279 Paul Menhart .30 .10
❑ 280 John Olerud .30 .10
❑ 281 Paul Quantrill .30 .10
❑ 282 Ken Robinson .30 .10
❑ 283 Ed Sprague .30 .10
❑ 284 Mike Timlin .30 .10
❑ 285 Steve Avery .30 .10
❑ 286 Rafael Belliard .30 .10
❑ 287 Jeff Blauser .30 .10
❑ 288 Pedro Borbon .30 .10
❑ 289 Brad Clontz .30 .10
❑ 290 Mike Devereaux .30 .10
❑ 291 Tom Glavine .50 .20
❑ 292 Marquis Grissom .30 .10
❑ 293 Chipper Jones .75 .30
❑ 294 David Justice .30 .10
❑ 295 Mike Kelly .30 .10
❑ 296 Ryan Klesko .30 .10
❑ 297 Mark Lemke .30 .10
❑ 298 Javier Lopez .30 .10
❑ 299 Greg Maddux 1.25 .50
❑ 300 Fred McGriff .50 .20
❑ 301 Greg McMichael .30 .10
❑ 302 Kent Mercker .30 .10
❑ 303 Mike Mordecai .30 .10
❑ 304 Charlie O'Brien .30 .10
❑ 305 Eduardo Perez .30 .10
❑ 306 Luis Polonia .30 .10
❑ 307 Jason Schmidt .50 .20
❑ 308 John Smoltz .50 .20
❑ 309 Terrell Wade .30 .10
❑ 310 Mark Wohlers .30 .10
❑ 311 Scott Bullett .30 .10
❑ 312 Jim Bullinger .30 .10
❑ 313 Larry Casian .30 .10
❑ 314 Frank Castillo .30 .10
❑ 315 Shawon Dunston .30 .10
❑ 316 Kevin Foster .30 .10
❑ 317 Matt Franco .30 .10
❑ 318 Luis Gonzalez .30 .10
❑ 319 Mark Grace .50 .20
❑ 320 Jose Hernandez .30 .10
❑ 321 Mike Hubbard .30 .10
❑ 322 Brian McRae .30 .10
❑ 323 Randy Myers .30 .10
❑ 324 Jaime Navarro .30 .10
❑ 325 Mark Parent .30 .10
❑ 326 Mike Perez .30 .10
❑ 327 Rey Sanchez .30 .10
❑ 328 Ryne Sandberg 1.25 .50
❑ 329 Scott Servais .30 .10
❑ 330 Sammy Sosa .75 .30
❑ 331 Ozzie Timmons .30 .10
❑ 332 Steve Trachsel .30 .10
❑ 333 Todd Zeile .30 .10
❑ 334 Bret Boone .30 .10
❑ 335 Jeff Branson .30 .10
❑ 336 Jeff Brantley .30 .10
❑ 337 Dave Burba .30 .10
❑ 338 Hector Carrasco .30 .10
❑ 339 Mariano Duncan .30 .10
❑ 340 Ron Gant .30 .10
❑ 341 Lenny Harris .30 .10
❑ 342 Xavier Hernandez .30 .10
❑ 343 Thomas Howard .30 .10
❑ 344 Mike Jackson .30 .10
❑ 345 Barry Larkin .50 .20
❑ 346 Darren Lewis .30 .10
❑ 347 Hal Morris .30 .10
❑ 348 Eric Owens .30 .10
❑ 349 Mark Portugal .30 .10
❑ 350 Jose Rijo .30 .10
❑ 351 Reggie Sanders .30 .10
❑ 352 Benito Santiago .30 .10
❑ 353 Pete Schourek .30 .10
❑ 354 John Smiley .30 .10
❑ 355 Eddie Taubensee .30 .10
❑ 356 Jerome Walton .30 .10
❑ 357 David Wells .30 .10
❑ 358 Roger Bailey .30 .10
❑ 359 Jason Bates .30 .10
❑ 360 Dante Bichette .30 .10
❑ 361 Ellis Burks .30 .10
❑ 362 Vinny Castilla .30 .10
❑ 363 Andres Galarraga .30 .10
❑ 364 Darren Holmes .30 .10
❑ 365 Mike Kingery .30 .10
❑ 366 Curt Leskanic .30 .10
❑ 367 Quinton McCracken .30 .10
❑ 368 Mike Munoz .30 .10
❑ 369 David Nied .30 .10
❑ 370 Steve Reed .30 .10
❑ 371 Bryan Rekar .30 .10
❑ 372 Kevin Ritz .30 .10
❑ 373 Bruce Ruffin .30 .10
❑ 374 Bret Saberhagen .30 .10
❑ 375 Bill Swift .30 .10
❑ 376 John Vander Wal .30 .10
❑ 377 Larry Walker .30 .10
❑ 378 Walt Weiss .30 .10
❑ 379 Eric Young .30 .10
❑ 380 Kurt Abbott .30 .10
❑ 381 Alex Arias .30 .10
❑ 382 Jerry Browne .30 .10
❑ 383 John Burkett .30 .10
❑ 384 Greg Colbrunn .30 .10
❑ 385 Jeff Conine .30 .10
❑ 386 Andre Dawson .30 .10
❑ 387 Chris Hammond .30 .10
❑ 388 Charles Johnson .30 .10
❑ 389 Terry Mathews .30 .10
❑ 390 Robb Nen .30 .10
❑ 391 Joe Orsulak .30 .10
❑ 392 Terry Pendleton .30 .10
❑ 393 Pat Rapp .30 .10
❑ 394 Gary Sheffield .30 .10
❑ 395 Jesus Tavarez .30 .10
❑ 396 Marc Valdes .30 .10
❑ 397 Quilvio Veras .30 .10

❑ 398 Randy Veres .30 .10
❑ 399 Devon White .30 .10
❑ 400 Jeff Bagwell .50 .20
❑ 401 Derek Bell .30 .10
❑ 402 Craig Biggio .50 .20
❑ 403 John Cangelosi .30 .10
❑ 404 Jim Dougherty .30 .10
❑ 405 Doug Drabek .30 .10
❑ 406 Tony Eusebio .30 .10
❑ 407 Ricky Gutierrez .30 .10
❑ 408 Mike Hampton .30 .10
❑ 409 Dean Hartgraves .30 .10
❑ 410 John Hudek .30 .10
❑ 411 Brian Hunter .30 .10
❑ 412 Todd Jones .30 .10
❑ 413 Darryl Kile .30 .10
❑ 414 Dave Magadan .30 .10
❑ 415 Derrick May .30 .10
❑ 416 Orlando Miller .30 .10
❑ 417 James Mouton .30 .10
❑ 418 Shane Reynolds .30 .10
❑ 419 Greg Swindell .30 .10
❑ 420 Jeff Tabaka .30 .10
❑ 421 Dave Veres .30 .10
❑ 422 Billy Wagner .30 .10
❑ 423 Donne Wall .30 .10
❑ 424 Rick Wilkins .30 .10
❑ 425 Billy Ashley .30 .10
❑ 426 Mike Blowers .30 .10
❑ 427 Brett Butler .30 .10
❑ 428 Tom Candiotti .30 .10
❑ 429 Juan Castro .30 .10
❑ 430 John Cummings .30 .10
❑ 431 Delino DeShields .30 .10
❑ 432 Joey Eischen .30 .10
❑ 433 Chad Fonville .30 .10
❑ 434 Greg Gagne .30 .10
❑ 435 Dave Hansen .30 .10
❑ 436 Carlos Hernandez .30 .10
❑ 437 Todd Hollandsworth .30 .10
❑ 438 Eric Karros .30 .10
❑ 439 Roberto Kelly .30 .10
❑ 440 Ramon Martinez .30 .10
❑ 441 Raul Mondesi .30 .10
❑ 442 Hideo Nomo .75 .30
❑ 443 Antonio Osuna .30 .10
❑ 444 Chan Ho Park .30 .10
❑ 445 Mike Piazza 1.25 .50
❑ 446 Felix Rodriguez .30 .10
❑ 447 Kevin Tapani .30 .10
❑ 448 Ismael Valdes .30 .10
❑ 449 Todd Worrell .30 .10
❑ 450 Moises Alou .30 .10
❑ 451 Shane Andrews .30 .10
❑ 452 Yamil Benitez .30 .10
❑ 453 Sean Berry .30 .10
❑ 454 Wil Cordero .30 .10
❑ 455 Jeff Fassero .30 .10
❑ 456 Darrin Fletcher .30 .10
❑ 457 Cliff Floyd .30 .10
❑ 458 Mark Grudzielanek .30 .10
❑ 459 Gil Heredia .30 .10
❑ 460 Tim Laker .30 .10
❑ 461 Mike Lansing .30 .10
❑ 462 Pedro Martinez .50 .20
❑ 463 Carlos Perez .30 .10
❑ 464 Curtis Pride .30 .10
❑ 465 Mel Rojas .30 .10
❑ 466 Kirk Rueter .30 .10
❑ 467 F.P. Santangelo .30 .10
❑ 468 Tim Scott .30 .10
❑ 469 David Segui .30 .10
❑ 470 Tony Tarasco .30 .10
❑ 471 Rondell White .30 .10
❑ 472 Edgardo Alfonzo .30 .10
❑ 473 Tim Bogar .30 .10
❑ 474 Rico Brogna .30 .10
❑ 475 Damon Buford .30 .10
❑ 476 Paul Byrd .30 .10
❑ 477 Carl Everett .30 .10
❑ 478 John Franco .30 .10
❑ 479 Todd Hundley .30 .10
❑ 480 Butch Huskey .30 .10
❑ 481 Jason Isringhausen .30 .10
❑ 482 Bobby Jones .30 .10
❑ 483 Chris Jones .30 .10
❑ 484 Jeff Kent .30 .10
❑ 485 Dave Mlicki .30 .10
❑ 486 Robert Person .30 .10
❑ 487 Bill Pulsipher .30 .10
❑ 488 Kelly Stinnett .30 .10
❑ 489 Ryan Thompson .30 .10
❑ 490 Jose Vizcaino .30 .10
❑ 491 Howard Battle .30 .10
❑ 492 Toby Borland .30 .10
❑ 493 Ricky Bottalico .30 .10
❑ 494 Darren Daulton .30 .10
❑ 495 Lenny Dykstra .30 .10
❑ 496 Jim Eisenreich .30 .10
❑ 497 Sid Fernandez .30 .10
❑ 498 Tyler Green .30 .10
❑ 499 Charlie Hayes .30 .10
❑ 500 Gregg Jefferies .30 .10
❑ 501 Kevin Jordan .30 .10
❑ 502 Tony Longmire .30 .10
❑ 503 Tom Marsh .30 .10
❑ 504 Michael Mimbs .30 .10
❑ 505 Mickey Morandini .30 .10
❑ 506 Gene Schall .30 .10
❑ 507 Curt Schilling .30 .10
❑ 508 Heathcliff Slocumb .30 .10
❑ 509 Kevin Stocker .30 .10
❑ 510 Andy Van Slyke .50 .20
❑ 511 Lenny Webster .30 .10
❑ 512 Mark Whiten .30 .10
❑ 513 Mike Williams .30 .10
❑ 514 Jay Bell .30 .10
❑ 515 Jacob Brumfield .30 .10
❑ 516 Jason Christiansen .30 .10
❑ 517 Dave Clark .30 .10
❑ 518 Midre Cummings .30 .10
❑ 519 Angelo Encarnacion .30 .10
❑ 520 John Ericks .30 .10
❑ 521 Carlos Garcia .30 .10
❑ 522 Mark Johnson .30 .10
❑ 523 Jeff King .30 .10
❑ 524 Nelson Liriano .30 .10
❑ 525 Esteban Loaiza .30 .10
❑ 526 Al Martin .30 .10
❑ 527 Orlando Merced .30 .10
❑ 528 Dan Miceli .30 .10
❑ 529 Ramon Morel .30 .10
❑ 530 Denny Neagle .30 .10
❑ 531 Steve Parris .30 .10
❑ 532 Dan Plesac .30 .10
❑ 533 Don Slaught .30 .10
❑ 534 Paul Wagner .30 .10
❑ 535 John Wehner .30 .10
❑ 536 Kevin Young .30 .10
❑ 537 Allen Battle .30 .10
❑ 538 David Bell .30 .10
❑ 539 Alan Benes .30 .10
❑ 540 Scott Cooper .30 .10
❑ 541 Tripp Cromer .30 .10
❑ 542 Tony Fossas .30 .10
❑ 543 Bernard Gilkey .30 .10
❑ 544 Tom Henke .30 .10
❑ 545 Brian Jordan .30 .10
❑ 546 Ray Lankford .30 .10
❑ 547 John Mabry .30 .10
❑ 548 T.J. Mathews .30 .10
❑ 549 Mike Morgan .30 .10
❑ 550 Jose Oliva .30 .10
❑ 551 Jose Oquendo .30 .10
❑ 552 Donovan Osborne .30 .10
❑ 553 Tom Pagnozzi .30 .10
❑ 554 Mark Petkovsek .30 .10
❑ 555 Danny Sheaffer .30 .10
❑ 556 Ozzie Smith 1.25 .50
❑ 557 Mark Sweeney .30 .10
❑ 558 Allen Watson .30 .10
❑ 559 Andy Ashby .30 .10
❑ 560 Brad Ausmus .30 .10
❑ 561 Willie Blair .30 .10
❑ 562 Ken Caminiti .30 .10
❑ 563 Andujar Cedeno .30 .10
❑ 564 Glenn Dishman .30 .10
❑ 565 Steve Finley .30 .10
❑ 566 Bryce Florie .30 .10
❑ 567 Tony Gwynn 1.00 .40
❑ 568 Joey Hamilton .30 .10
❑ 569 Dustin Hermanson UER .30 .10
❑ 570 Trevor Hoffman .30 .10
❑ 571 Brian Johnson .30 .10
❑ 572 Marc Kroon .30 .10
❑ 573 Scott Livingstone .30 .10
❑ 574 Marc Newfield .30 .10
❑ 575 Melvin Nieves .30 .10
❑ 576 Jody Reed .30 .10
❑ 577 Bip Roberts .30 .10
❑ 578 Scott Sanders .30 .10
❑ 579 Fernando Valenzuela .30 .10
❑ 580 Eddie Williams .30 .10
❑ 581 Rod Beck .30 .10
❑ 582 Marvin Benard RC .30 .10
❑ 583 Barry Bonds 2.00 .75
❑ 584 Jamie Brewington RC .30 .10
❑ 585 Mark Carreon .30 .10
❑ 586 Royce Clayton .30 .10
❑ 587 Shawn Estes .30 .10
❑ 588 Glenallen Hill .30 .10
❑ 589 Mark Leiter .30 .10
❑ 590 Kirt Manwaring .30 .10
❑ 591 David McCarty .30 .10
❑ 592 Terry Mulholland .30 .10
❑ 593 John Patterson .30 .10
❑ 594 J.R. Phillips .30 .10
❑ 595 Deion Sanders .50 .20
❑ 596 Steve Scarsone .30 .10
❑ 597 Robby Thompson .30 .10
❑ 598 Sergio Valdez .30 .10
❑ 599 William Van Landingham .30 .10
❑ 600 Matt Williams .30 .10
❑ P20 Cal Ripken
Promo 3.00 1.25

1997 Fleer

❑ COMPLETE SET (761) 140.00 70.00
❑ COMPLETE SERIES 1 (500) 60.00 30.00
❑ COMPLETE SERIES 2 (261) 80.00 40.00
❑ COMMON CARD (1-750) .30 .10
❑ COMMON CARD (751-761) .50 .20
❑ 1 Roberto Alomar .50 .20
❑ 2 Brady Anderson .30 .10
❑ 3 Bobby Bonilla .30 .10
❑ 4 Rocky Coppinger .30 .10
❑ 5 Cesar Devarez .30 .10
❑ 6 Scott Erickson .30 .10
❑ 7 Jeffrey Hammonds .30 .10
❑ 8 Chris Hoiles .30 .10
❑ 9 Eddie Murray .75 .30
❑ 10 Mike Mussina .50 .20
❑ 11 Randy Myers .30 .10
❑ 12 Rafael Palmeiro .50 .20
❑ 13 Cal Ripken 2.50 1.00
❑ 14 B.J. Surhoff .30 .10
❑ 15 David Wells .30 .10
❑ 16 Todd Zeile .30 .10
❑ 17 Darren Bragg .30 .10
❑ 18 Jose Canseco .50 .20
❑ 19 Roger Clemens 1.50 .60
❑ 20 Wil Cordero .30 .10
❑ 21 Jeff Frye .30 .10
❑ 22 Nomar Garciaparra 1.25 .50
❑ 23 Tom Gordon .30 .10
❑ 24 Mike Greenwell .30 .10
❑ 25 Reggie Jefferson .30 .10
❑ 26 Jose Malave .30 .10
❑ 27 Tim Naehring .30 .10
❑ 28 Troy O'Leary .30 .10

❑ 29 Heathcliff Slocumb .30 .10
❑ 30 Mike Stanley .30 .10
❑ 31 John Valentin .30 .10
❑ 32 Mo Vaughn .30 .10
❑ 33 Tim Wakefield .30 .10
❑ 34 Garret Anderson .30 .10
❑ 35 George Arias .30 .10
❑ 36 Shawn Boskie .30 .10
❑ 37 Chili Davis .30 .10
❑ 38 Jason Dickson .30 .10
❑ 39 Gary DiSarcina .30 .10
❑ 40 Jim Edmonds .30 .10
❑ 41 Darin Erstad .30 .10
❑ 42 Jorge Fabregas .30 .10
❑ 43 Chuck Finley .30 .10
❑ 44 Todd Greene .30 .10
❑ 45 Mike Holtz .30 .10
❑ 46 Rex Hudler .30 .10
❑ 47 Mike James .30 .10
❑ 48 Mark Langston .30 .10
❑ 49 Troy Percival .30 .10
❑ 50 Tim Salmon .50 .20
❑ 51 Jeff Schmidt .30 .10
❑ 52 J.T. Snow .30 .10
❑ 53 Randy Velarde .30 .10
❑ 54 Wilson Alvarez .30 .10
❑ 55 Harold Baines .30 .10
❑ 56 James Baldwin .30 .10
❑ 57 Jason Bere .30 .10
❑ 58 Mike Cameron .30 .10
❑ 59 Ray Durham .30 .10
❑ 60 Alex Fernandez .30 .10
❑ 61 Ozzie Guillen .30 .10
❑ 62 Roberto Hernandez .30 .10
❑ 63 Ron Karkovice .30 .10
❑ 64 Darren Lewis .30 .10
❑ 65 Dave Martinez .30 .10
❑ 66 Lyle Mouton .30 .10
❑ 67 Greg Norton .30 .10
❑ 68 Tony Phillips .30 .10
❑ 69 Chris Snopek .30 .10
❑ 70 Kevin Tapani .30 .10
❑ 71 Danny Tartabull .30 .10
❑ 72 Frank Thomas .75 .30
❑ 73 Robin Ventura .30 .10
❑ 74 Sandy Alomar Jr. .30 .10
❑ 75 Albert Belle .30 .10
❑ 76 Mark Carreon .30 .10
❑ 77 Julio Franco .30 .10
❑ 78 Brian Giles RC 1.50 .60
❑ 79 Orel Hershiser .30 .10
❑ 80 Kenny Lofton .30 .10
❑ 81 Dennis Martinez .30 .10
❑ 82 Jack McDowell .30 .10
❑ 83 Jose Mesa .30 .10
❑ 84 Charles Nagy .30 .10
❑ 85 Chad Ogea .30 .10
❑ 86 Eric Plunk .30 .10
❑ 87 Manny Ramirez .50 .20
❑ 88 Kevin Seitzer .30 .10
❑ 89 Julian Tavarez .30 .10
❑ 90 Jim Thome .50 .20
❑ 91 Jose Vizcaino .30 .10
❑ 92 Omar Vizquel .50 .20
❑ 93 Brad Ausmus .30 .10
❑ 94 Kimera Bartee .30 .10
❑ 95 Raul Casanova .30 .10
❑ 96 Tony Clark .30 .10
❑ 97 John Cummings .30 .10
❑ 98 Travis Fryman .30 .10
❑ 99 Bob Higginson .30 .10
❑ 100 Mark Lewis .30 .10
❑ 101 Felipe Lira .30 .10
❑ 102 Phil Nevin .30 .10
❑ 103 Melvin Nieves .30 .10
❑ 104 Curtis Pride .30 .10
❑ 105 A.J. Sager .30 .10
❑ 106 Ruben Sierra .30 .10
❑ 107 Justin Thompson .30 .10
❑ 108 Alan Trammell .30 .10
❑ 109 Kevin Appier .30 .10
❑ 110 Tim Belcher .30 .10
❑ 111 Jaime Bluma .30 .10
❑ 112 Johnny Damon .50 .20
❑ 113 Tom Goodwin .30 .10
❑ 114 Chris Haney .30 .10
❑ 115 Keith Lockhart .30 .10
❑ 116 Mike Macfarlane .30 .10
❑ 117 Jeff Montgomery .30 .10
❑ 118 Jose Offerman .30 .10
❑ 119 Craig Paquette .30 .10
❑ 120 Joe Randa .30 .10
❑ 121 Bip Roberts .30 .10
❑ 122 Jose Rosado .30 .10
❑ 123 Mike Sweeney .30 .10
❑ 124 Michael Tucker .30 .10
❑ 125 Jeromy Burnitz .30 .10
❑ 126 Jeff Cirillo .30 .10
❑ 127 Jeff D'Amico .30 .10
❑ 128 Mike Fetters .30 .10
❑ 129 John Jaha .30 .10
❑ 130 Scott Karl .30 .10
❑ 131 Jesse Levis .30 .10
❑ 132 Mark Loretta .30 .10
❑ 133 Mike Matheny .30 .10
❑ 134 Ben McDonald .30 .10
❑ 135 Matt Mieske .30 .10
❑ 136 Marc Newfield .30 .10
❑ 137 Dave Nilsson .30 .10
❑ 138 Jose Valentin .30 .10
❑ 139 Fernando Vina .30 .10
❑ 140 Bob Wickman .30 .10
❑ 141 Gerald Williams .30 .10
❑ 142 Rick Aguilera .30 .10
❑ 143 Rich Becker .30 .10
❑ 144 Ron Coomer .30 .10
❑ 145 Marty Cordova .30 .10
❑ 146 Roberto Kelly .30 .10
❑ 147 Chuck Knoblauch .30 .10
❑ 148 Matt Lawton .30 .10
❑ 149 Pat Meares .30 .10
❑ 150 Travis Miller .30 .10
❑ 151 Paul Molitor .30 .10
❑ 152 Greg Myers .30 .10
❑ 153 Dan Naulty .30 .10
❑ 154 Kirby Puckett .75 .30
❑ 155 Brad Radke .30 .10
❑ 156 Frank Rodriguez .30 .10
❑ 157 Scott Stahoviak .30 .10
❑ 158 Dave Stevens .30 .10
❑ 159 Matt Walbeck .30 .10
❑ 160 Todd Walker .30 .10
❑ 161 Wade Boggs .50 .20
❑ 162 David Cone .30 .10
❑ 163 Mariano Duncan .30 .10
❑ 164 Cecil Fielder .30 .10
❑ 165 Joe Girardi .30 .10
❑ 166 Dwight Gooden .30 .10
❑ 167 Charlie Hayes .30 .10
❑ 168 Derek Jeter 2.00 .75
❑ 169 Jimmy Key .30 .10
❑ 170 Jim Leyritz .30 .10
❑ 171 Tino Martinez .50 .20
❑ 172 Ramiro Mendoza RC .30 .10
❑ 173 Jeff Nelson .30 .10
❑ 174 Paul O'Neill .50 .20
❑ 175 Andy Pettitte .50 .20
❑ 176 Mariano Rivera .75 .30
❑ 177 Ruben Rivera .30 .10
❑ 178 Kenny Rogers .30 .10
❑ 179 Darryl Strawberry .30 .10
❑ 180 John Wetteland .30 .10
❑ 181 Bernie Williams .50 .20
❑ 182 Willie Adams .30 .10
❑ 183 Tony Batista .30 .10
❑ 184 Geronimo Berroa .30 .10
❑ 185 Mike Bordick .30 .10
❑ 186 Scott Brosius .30 .10
❑ 187 Bobby Chouinard .30 .10
❑ 188 Jim Corsi .30 .10
❑ 189 Brent Gates .30 .10
❑ 190 Jason Giambi .30 .10
❑ 191 Jose Herrera .30 .10
❑ 192 Damon Mashore .30 .10
❑ 193 Mark McGwire 2.00 .75
❑ 194 Mike Mohler .30 .10
❑ 195 Scott Spiezio .30 .10
❑ 196 Terry Steinbach .30 .10
❑ 197 Bill Taylor .30 .10
❑ 198 John Wasdin .30 .10
❑ 199 Steve Wojciechowski .30 .10
❑ 200 Ernie Young .30 .10
❑ 201 Rich Amaral .30 .10
❑ 202 Jay Buhner .30 .10
❑ 203 Norm Charlton .30 .10
❑ 204 Joey Cora .30 .10
❑ 205 Russ Davis .30 .10
❑ 206 Ken Griffey Jr. 1.25 .50
❑ 207 Sterling Hitchcock .30 .10
❑ 208 Brian Hunter .30 .10
❑ 209 Raul Ibanez .30 .10
❑ 210 Randy Johnson .75 .30
❑ 211 Edgar Martinez .50 .20
❑ 212 Jamie Moyer .30 .10
❑ 213 Alex Rodriguez 1.25 .50
❑ 214 Paul Sorrento .30 .10
❑ 215 Matt Wagner .30 .10
❑ 216 Bob Wells .30 .10
❑ 217 Dan Wilson .30 .10
❑ 218 Damon Buford .30 .10
❑ 219 Will Clark .50 .20
❑ 220 Kevin Elster .30 .10
❑ 221 Juan Gonzalez .30 .10
❑ 222 Rusty Greer .30 .10
❑ 223 Kevin Gross .30 .10
❑ 224 Darryl Hamilton .30 .10
❑ 225 Mike Henneman .30 .10
❑ 226 Ken Hill .30 .10
❑ 227 Mark McLemore .30 .10
❑ 228 Darren Oliver .30 .10
❑ 229 Dean Palmer .30 .10
❑ 230 Roger Pavlik .30 .10
❑ 231 Ivan Rodriguez .50 .20
❑ 232 Mickey Tettleton .30 .10
❑ 233 Bobby Witt .30 .10
❑ 234 Jacob Brumfield .30 .10
❑ 235 Joe Carter .30 .10
❑ 236 Tim Crabtree .30 .10
❑ 237 Carlos Delgado .30 .10
❑ 238 Huck Flener .30 .10
❑ 239 Alex Gonzalez .30 .10
❑ 240 Shawn Green .30 .10
❑ 241 Juan Guzman .30 .10
❑ 242 Pat Hentgen .30 .10
❑ 243 Marty Janzen .30 .10
❑ 244 Sandy Martinez .30 .10
❑ 245 Otis Nixon .30 .10
❑ 246 Charlie O'Brien .30 .10
❑ 247 John Olerud .30 .10
❑ 248 Robert Perez .30 .10
❑ 249 Ed Sprague .30 .10
❑ 250 Mike Timlin .30 .10
❑ 251 Steve Avery .30 .10
❑ 252 Jeff Blauser .30 .10
❑ 253 Brad Clontz .30 .10
❑ 254 Jermaine Dye .30 .10
❑ 255 Tom Glavine .50 .20
❑ 256 Marquis Grissom .30 .10
❑ 257 Andruw Jones .50 .20
❑ 258 Chipper Jones .75 .30
❑ 259 David Justice .30 .10
❑ 260 Ryan Klesko .30 .10
❑ 261 Mark Lemke .30 .10
❑ 262 Javier Lopez .30 .10
❑ 263 Greg Maddux 1.25 .50
❑ 264 Fred McGriff .50 .20
❑ 265 Greg McMichael .30 .10
❑ 266 Denny Neagle .30 .10
❑ 267 Terry Pendleton .30 .10
❑ 268 Eddie Perez .30 .10
❑ 269 John Smoltz .50 .20
❑ 270 Terrell Wade .30 .10
❑ 271 Mark Wohlers .30 .10
❑ 272 Terry Adams .30 .10
❑ 273 Brant Brown .30 .10
❑ 274 Leo Gomez .30 .10
❑ 275 Luis Gonzalez .30 .10
❑ 276 Mark Grace .50 .20
❑ 277 Tyler Houston .30 .10
❑ 278 Robin Jennings .30 .10
❑ 279 Brooks Kieschnick .30 .10
❑ 280 Brian McRae .30 .10
❑ 281 Jaime Navarro .30 .10
❑ 282 Ryne Sandberg 1.25 .50
❑ 283 Scott Servais .30 .10
❑ 284 Sammy Sosa .75 .30
❑ 285 Dave Swartzbaugh .30 .10
❑ 286 Amaury Telemaco .30 .10

❑	287	Steve Trachsel	.30	.10
❑	288	Pedro Valdes	.30	.10
❑	289	Turk Wendell	.30	.10
❑	290	Bret Boone	.30	.10
❑	291	Jeff Branson	.30	.10
❑	292	Jeff Brantley	.30	.10
❑	293	Eric Davis	.30	.10
❑	294	Willie Greene	.30	.10
❑	295	Thomas Howard	.30	.10
❑	296	Barry Larkin	.50	.20
❑	297	Kevin Mitchell	.30	.10
❑	298	Hal Morris	.30	.10
❑	299	Chad Mottola	.30	.10
❑	300	Joe Oliver	.30	.10
❑	301	Mark Portugal	.30	.10
❑	302	Roger Salkeld	.30	.10
❑	303	Reggie Sanders	.30	.10
❑	304	Pete Schourek	.30	.10
❑	305	John Smiley	.30	.10
❑	306	Eddie Taubensee	.30	.10
❑	307	Dante Bichette	.30	.10
❑	308	Ellis Burks	.30	.10
❑	309	Vinny Castilla	.30	.10
❑	310	Andres Galarraga	.30	.10
❑	311	Curt Leskanic	.30	.10
❑	312	Quinton McCracken	.30	.10
❑	313	Neifi Perez	.30	.10
❑	314	Jeff Reed	.30	.10
❑	315	Steve Reed	.30	.10
❑	316	Armando Reynoso	.30	.10
❑	317	Kevin Ritz	.30	.10
❑	318	Bruce Ruffin	.30	.10
❑	319	Larry Walker	.30	.10
❑	320	Walt Weiss	.30	.10
❑	321	Jamey Wright	.30	.10
❑	322	Eric Young	.30	.10
❑	323	Kurt Abbott	.30	.10
❑	324	Alex Arias	.30	.10
❑	325	Kevin Brown	.30	.10
❑	326	Luis Castillo	.30	.10
❑	327	Greg Colbrunn	.30	.10
❑	328	Jeff Conine	.30	.10
❑	329	Andre Dawson	.30	.10
❑	330	Charles Johnson	.30	.10
❑	331	Al Leiter	.30	.10
❑	332	Ralph Milliard	.30	.10
❑	333	Robb Nen	.30	.10
❑	334	Pat Rapp	.30	.10
❑	335	Edgar Renteria	.30	.10
❑	336	Gary Sheffield	.30	.10
❑	337	Devon White	.30	.10
❑	338	Bob Abreu	.50	.20
❑	339	Jeff Bagwell	.50	.20
❑	340	Derek Bell	.30	.10
❑	341	Sean Berry	.30	.10
❑	342	Craig Biggio	.50	.20
❑	343	Doug Drabek	.30	.10
❑	344	Tony Eusebio	.30	.10
❑	345	Ricky Gutierrez	.30	.10
❑	346	Mike Hampton	.30	.10
❑	347	Brian Hunter	.30	.10
❑	348	Todd Jones	.30	.10
❑	349	Darryl Kile	.30	.10
❑	350	Derrick May	.30	.10
❑	351	Orlando Miller	.30	.10
❑	352	James Mouton	.30	.10
❑	353	Shane Reynolds	.30	.10
❑	354	Billy Wagner	.30	.10
❑	355	Donne Wall	.30	.10
❑	356	Mike Blowers	.30	.10
❑	357	Brett Butler	.30	.10
❑	358	Roger Cedeno	.30	.10
❑	359	Chad Curtis	.30	.10
❑	360	Delino DeShields	.30	.10
❑	361	Greg Gagne	.30	.10
❑	362	Karim Garcia	.30	.10
❑	363	Wilton Guerrero	.30	.10
❑	364	Todd Hollandsworth	.30	.10
❑	365	Eric Karros	.30	.10
❑	366	Ramon Martinez	.30	.10
❑	367	Raul Mondesi	.30	.10
❑	368	Hideo Nomo	.75	.30
❑	369	Antonio Osuna	.30	.10
❑	370	Chan Ho Park	.30	.10
❑	371	Mike Piazza	1.25	.50
❑	372	Ismael Valdes	.30	.10
❑	373	Todd Worrell	.30	.10
❑	374	Moises Alou	.30	.10
❑	375	Shane Andrews	.30	.10
❑	376	Yamil Benitez	.30	.10
❑	377	Jeff Fassero	.30	.10
❑	378	Darrin Fletcher	.30	.10
❑	379	Cliff Floyd	.30	.10
❑	380	Mark Grudzielanek	.30	.10
❑	381	Mike Lansing	.30	.10
❑	382	Barry Manuel	.30	.10
❑	383	Pedro Martinez	.50	.20
❑	384	Henry Rodriguez	.30	.10
❑	385	Mel Rojas	.30	.10
❑	386	F.P. Santangelo	.30	.10
❑	387	David Segui	.30	.10
❑	388	Ugueth Urbina	.30	.10
❑	389	Rondell White	.30	.10
❑	390	Edgardo Alfonzo	.30	.10
❑	391	Carlos Baerga	.30	.10
❑	392	Mark Clark	.30	.10
❑	393	Alvaro Espinoza	.30	.10
❑	394	John Franco	.30	.10
❑	395	Bernard Gilkey	.30	.10
❑	396	Pete Harnisch	.30	.10
❑	397	Todd Hundley	.30	.10
❑	398	Butch Huskey	.30	.10
❑	399	Jason Isringhausen	.30	.10
❑	400	Lance Johnson	.30	.10
❑	401	Bobby Jones	.30	.10
❑	402	Alex Ochoa	.30	.10
❑	403	Rey Ordonez	.30	.10
❑	404	Robert Person	.30	.10
❑	405	Paul Wilson	.30	.10
❑	406	Matt Beech	.30	.10
❑	407	Ron Blazier	.30	.10
❑	408	Ricky Bottalico	.30	.10
❑	409	Lenny Dykstra	.30	.10
❑	410	Jim Eisenreich	.30	.10
❑	411	Bobby Estalella	.30	.10
❑	412	Mike Grace	.30	.10
❑	413	Gregg Jefferies	.30	.10
❑	414	Mike Lieberthal	.30	.10
❑	415	Wendell Magee	.30	.10
❑	416	Mickey Morandini	.30	.10
❑	417	Ricky Otero	.30	.10
❑	418	Scott Rolen	.50	.20
❑	419	Ken Ryan	.30	.10
❑	420	Benito Santiago	.30	.10
❑	421	Curt Schilling	.30	.10
❑	422	Kevin Sefcik	.30	.10
❑	423	Jermaine Allensworth	.30	.10
❑	424	Trey Beamon	.30	.10
❑	425	Jay Bell	.30	.10
❑	426	Francisco Cordova	.30	.10
❑	427	Carlos Garcia	.30	.10
❑	428	Mark Johnson	.30	.10
❑	429	Jason Kendall	.30	.10
❑	430	Jeff King	.30	.10
❑	431	Jon Lieber	.30	.10
❑	432	Al Martin	.30	.10
❑	433	Orlando Merced	.30	.10
❑	434	Ramon Morel	.30	.10
❑	435	Matt Ruebel	.30	.10
❑	436	Jason Schmidt	.30	.10
❑	437	Marc Wilkins	.30	.10
❑	438	Alan Benes	.30	.10
❑	439	Andy Benes	.30	.10
❑	440	Royce Clayton	.30	.10
❑	441	Dennis Eckersley	.30	.10
❑	442	Gary Gaetti	.30	.10
❑	443	Ron Gant	.30	.10
❑	444	Aaron Holbert	.30	.10
❑	445	Brian Jordan	.30	.10
❑	446	Ray Lankford	.30	.10
❑	447	John Mabry	.30	.10
❑	448	T.J. Mathews	.30	.10
❑	449	Willie McGee	.30	.10
❑	450	Donovan Osborne	.30	.10
❑	451	Tom Pagnozzi	.30	.10
❑	452	Ozzie Smith	1.25	.50
❑	453	Todd Stottlemyre	.30	.10
❑	454	Mark Sweeney	.30	.10
❑	455	Dmitri Young	.30	.10
❑	456	Andy Ashby	.30	.10
❑	457	Ken Caminiti	.30	.10
❑	458	Archi Cianfrocco	.30	.10
❑	459	Steve Finley	.30	.10
❑	460	John Flaherty	.30	.10
❑	461	Chris Gomez	.30	.10
❑	462	Tony Gwynn	1.00	.40
❑	463	Joey Hamilton	.30	.10
❑	464	Rickey Henderson	.75	.30
❑	465	Trevor Hoffman	.30	.10
❑	466	Brian Johnson	.30	.10
❑	467	Wally Joyner	.30	.10
❑	468	Jody Reed	.30	.10
❑	469	Scott Sanders	.30	.10
❑	470	Bob Tewksbury	.30	.10
❑	471	Fernando Valenzuela	.30	.10
❑	472	Greg Vaughn	.30	.10
❑	473	Tim Worrell	.30	.10
❑	474	Rich Aurilia	.30	.10
❑	475	Rod Beck	.30	.10
❑	476	Marvin Benard	.30	.10
❑	477	Barry Bonds	2.00	.75
❑	478	Jay Canizaro	.30	.10
❑	479	Shawon Dunston	.30	.10
❑	480	Shawn Estes	.30	.10
❑	481	Mark Gardner	.30	.10
❑	482	Glenallen Hill	.30	.10
❑	483	Stan Javier	.30	.10
❑	484	Marcus Jensen	.30	.10
❑	485	Bill Mueller RC	1.25	.50
❑	486	Wm. VanLandingham	.30	.10
❑	487	Allen Watson	.30	.10
❑	488	Rick Wilkins	.30	.10
❑	489	Matt Williams	.30	.10
❑	490	Desi Wilson	.30	.10
❑	491	Albert Belle CL	.30	.10
❑	492	Ken Griffey Jr. CL	.75	.30
❑	493	Andruw Jones CL	.30	.10
❑	494	Chipper Jones CL	.50	.20
❑	495	Mark McGwire CL	1.00	.40
❑	496	Paul Molitor CL	.30	.10
❑	497	Mike Piazza CL	.75	.30
❑	498	Cal Ripken CL	1.25	.50
❑	499	Alex Rodriguez CL	.75	.30
❑	500	Frank Thomas CL	.50	.20
❑	501	Kenny Lofton	.30	.10
❑	502	Carlos Perez	.30	.10
❑	503	Tim Raines	.30	.10
❑	504	Danny Patterson	.30	.10
❑	505	Derrick May	.30	.10
❑	506	Dave Hollins	.30	.10
❑	507	Felipe Crespo	.30	.10
❑	508	Brian Banks	.30	.10
❑	509	Jeff Kent	.30	.10
❑	510	Bubba Trammell RC	.40	.15
❑	511	Robert Person	.30	.10
❑	512	David Arias-Ortiz RC	40.00	15.00
❑	513	Ryan Jones	.30	.10
❑	514	David Justice	.30	.10
❑	515	Will Cunnane	.30	.10
❑	516	Russ Johnson	.30	.10
❑	517	John Burkett	.30	.10
❑	518	Robinson Checo RC	.30	.10
❑	519	Ricardo Rincon RC	.30	.10
❑	520	Woody Williams	.30	.10
❑	521	Rick Helling	.30	.10
❑	522	Jorge Posada	.50	.20
❑	523	Kevin Orie	.30	.10
❑	524	Fernando Tatis RC	.30	.10
❑	525	Jermaine Dye	.30	.10
❑	526	Brian Hunter	.30	.10
❑	527	Greg McMichael	.30	.10
❑	528	Matt Wagner	.30	.10
❑	529	Richie Sexson	.30	.10
❑	530	Scott Ruffcorn	.30	.10
❑	531	Luis Gonzalez	.30	.10
❑	532	Mike Johnson RC	.30	.10
❑	533	Mark Petkovsek	.30	.10
❑	534	Doug Drabek	.30	.10
❑	535	Jose Canseco	.50	.20
❑	536	Bobby Bonilla	.30	.10
❑	537	J.T. Snow	.30	.10
❑	538	Shawon Dunston	.30	.10
❑	539	John Ericks	.30	.10
❑	540	Terry Steinbach	.30	.10
❑	541	Jay Bell	.30	.10
❑	542	Joe Borowski RC	.40	.15
❑	543	David Wells	.30	.10
❑	544	Justin Towle RC	.30	.10

	Card		
❑	545 Mike Blowers	.30	.10
❑	546 Shannon Stewart	.30	.10
❑	547 Rudy Pemberton	.30	.10
❑	548 Bill Swift	.30	.10
❑	549 Osvaldo Fernandez	.30	.10
❑	550 Eddie Murray	.75	.30
❑	551 Don Wengert	.30	.10
❑	552 Brad Ausmus	.30	.10
❑	553 Carlos Garcia	.30	.10
❑	554 Jose Guillen	.30	.10
❑	555 Rheal Cormier	.30	.10
❑	556 Doug Brocail	.30	.10
❑	557 Rex Hudler	.30	.10
❑	558 Armando Benitez	.30	.10
❑	559 Eli Marrero	.30	.10
❑	560 Ricky Ledee RC	.40	.15
❑	561 Bartolo Colon	.30	.10
❑	562 Quilvio Veras	.30	.10
❑	563 Alex Fernandez	.30	.10
❑	564 Darren Dreifort	.30	.10
❑	565 Benji Gil	.30	.10
❑	566 Kent Mercker	.30	.10
❑	567 Glendon Rusch	.30	.10
❑	568 Ramon Tatis RC	.30	.10
❑	569 Roger Clemens	1.50	.60
❑	570 Mark Lewis	.30	.10
❑	571 Emil Brown RC	.30	.10
❑	572 Jaime Navarro	.30	.10
❑	573 Sherman Obando	.30	.10
❑	574 John Wasdin	.30	.10
❑	575 Calvin Maduro	.30	.10
❑	576 Todd Jones	.30	.10
❑	577 Orlando Merced	.30	.10
❑	578 Cal Eldred	.30	.10
❑	579 Mark Gubicza	.30	.10
❑	580 Michael Tucker	.30	.10
❑	581 Tony Saunders RC	.30	.10
❑	582 Garvin Alston	.30	.10
❑	583 Joe Roa	.30	.10
❑	584 Brady Raggio RC	.30	.10
❑	585 Jimmy Key	.30	.10
❑	586 Marc Sagmoen RC	.30	.10
❑	587 Jim Bullinger	.30	.10
❑	588 Yorkis Perez	.30	.10
❑	589 Jose Cruz Jr. RC	.40	.15
❑	590 Mike Stanton	.30	.10
❑	591 Deivi Cruz RC	.40	.15
❑	592 Steve Karsay	.30	.10
❑	593 Mike Trombley	.30	.10
❑	594 Doug Glanville	.30	.10
❑	595 Scott Sanders	.30	.10
❑	596 Thomas Howard	.30	.10
❑	597 T.J. Staton RC	.30	.10
❑	598 Garrett Stephenson	.30	.10
❑	599 Rico Brogna	.30	.10
❑	600 Albert Belle	.30	.10
❑	601 Jose Vizcaino	.30	.10
❑	602 Chili Davis	.30	.10
❑	603 Shane Mack	.30	.10
❑	604 Jim Eisenreich	.30	.10
❑	605 Todd Zeile	.30	.10
❑	606 Brian Boehringer RC	.30	.10
❑	607 Paul Shuey	.30	.10
❑	608 Kevin Tapani	.30	.10
❑	609 John Wetteland	.30	.10
❑	610 Jim Leyritz	.30	.10
❑	611 Ray Montgomery RC	.30	.10
❑	612 Doug Bochtler	.30	.10
❑	613 Wady Almonte RC	.30	.10
❑	614 Danny Tartabull	.30	.10
❑	615 Orlando Miller	.30	.10
❑	616 Bobby Ayala	.30	.10
❑	617 Tony Graffanino	.30	.10
❑	618 Marc Valdes	.30	.10
❑	619 Ron Villone	.30	.10
❑	620 Derrek Lee	.50	.20
❑	621 Greg Colbrunn	.30	.10
❑	622 Felix Heredia RC	.40	.15
❑	623 Carl Everett	.30	.10
❑	624 Mark Thompson	.30	.10
❑	625 Jeff Granger	.30	.10
❑	626 Damian Jackson	.30	.10
❑	627 Mark Leiter	.30	.10
❑	628 Chris Holt	.30	.10
❑	629 Dario Veras RC	.30	.10
❑	630 Dave Burba	.30	.10
❑	631 Darryl Hamilton	.30	.10
❑	632 Mark Acre	.30	.10
❑	633 Fernando Hernandez RC	.30	.10
❑	634 Terry Mulholland	.30	.10
❑	635 Dustin Hermanson	.30	.10
❑	636 Delino DeShields	.30	.10
❑	637 Steve Avery	.30	.10
❑	638 Tony Womack RC	.40	.15
❑	639 Mark Whiten	.30	.10
❑	640 Marquis Grissom	.30	.10
❑	641 Xavier Hernandez	.30	.10
❑	642 Eric Davis	.30	.10
❑	643 Bob Tewksbury	.30	.10
❑	644 Dante Powell	.30	.10
❑	645 Carlos Castillo RC	.30	.10
❑	646 Chris Widger	.30	.10
❑	647 Moises Alou	.30	.10
❑	648 Pat Listach	.30	.10
❑	649 Edgar Ramos RC	.30	.10
❑	650 Deion Sanders	.50	.20
❑	651 John Olerud	.30	.10
❑	652 Todd Dunwoody	.30	.10
❑	653 Randall Simon RC	.40	.15
❑	654 Dan Carlson	.30	.10
❑	655 Matt Williams	.30	.10
❑	656 Jeff King	.30	.10
❑	657 Luis Alicea	.30	.10
❑	658 Brian Moehler RC	.40	.15
❑	659 Ariel Prieto	.30	.10
❑	660 Kevin Elster	.30	.10
❑	661 Mark Hutton	.30	.10
❑	662 Aaron Sele	.30	.10
❑	663 Graeme Lloyd	.30	.10
❑	664 John Burke	.30	.10
❑	665 Mel Rojas	.30	.10
❑	666 Sid Fernandez	.30	.10
❑	667 Pedro Astacio	.30	.10
❑	668 Jeff Abbott	.30	.10
❑	669 Darren Daulton	.30	.10
❑	670 Mike Bordick	.30	.10
❑	671 Sterling Hitchcock	.30	.10
❑	672 Damion Easley	.30	.10
❑	673 Armando Reynoso	.30	.10
❑	674 Pat Cline	.30	.10
❑	675 Orlando Cabrera RC	.75	.30
❑	676 Alan Embree	.30	.10
❑	677 Brian Bevil	.30	.10
❑	678 David Weathers	.30	.10
❑	679 Cliff Floyd	.30	.10
❑	680 Joe Randa	.30	.10
❑	681 Bill Haselman	.30	.10
❑	682 Jeff Fassero	.30	.10
❑	683 Matt Morris	.30	.10
❑	684 Mark Portugal	.30	.10
❑	685 Lee Smith	.30	.10
❑	686 Pokey Reese	.30	.10
❑	687 Benito Santiago	.30	.10
❑	688 Brian Johnson	.30	.10
❑	689 Brent Brede RC	.30	.10
❑	690 Shigetoshi Hasegawa RC	.50	.20
❑	691 Julio Santana	.30	.10
❑	692 Steve Kline	.30	.10
❑	693 Julian Tavarez	.30	.10
❑	694 John Hudek	.30	.10
❑	695 Manny Alexander	.30	.10
❑	696 Roberto Alomar ENC	.30	.10
❑	697 Jeff Bagwell ENC	.30	.10
❑	698 Barry Bonds ENC	1.00	.40
❑	699 Ken Caminiti ENC	.30	.10
❑	700 Juan Gonzalez ENC	.30	.10
❑	701 Ken Griffey Jr. ENC	.75	.30
❑	702 Tony Gwynn ENC	.50	.20
❑	703 Derek Jeter ENC	1.00	.40
❑	704 Andruw Jones ENC	.50	.20
❑	705 Chipper Jones ENC	.50	.20
❑	706 Barry Larkin ENC	.30	.10
❑	707 Greg Maddux ENC	.75	.30
❑	708 Mark McGwire ENC	1.00	.40
❑	709 Paul Molitor ENC	.30	.10
❑	710 Hideo Nomo ENC	.30	.10
❑	711 Andy Pettitte ENC	.30	.10
❑	712 Mike Piazza ENC	.75	.30
❑	713 Manny Ramirez ENC	.50	.20
❑	714 Cal Ripken ENC	1.25	.50
❑	715 Alex Rodriguez ENC	.75	.30
❑	716 Ryne Sandberg ENC	.75	.30
❑	717 John Smoltz ENC	.30	.10
❑	718 Frank Thomas ENC	.50	.20
❑	719 Mo Vaughn ENC	.30	.10
❑	720 Bernie Williams ENC	.30	.10
❑	721 Tim Salmon CL	.30	.10
❑	722 Greg Maddux CL	.75	.30
❑	723 Cal Ripken CL	1.25	.50
❑	724 Mo Vaughn CL	.30	.10
❑	725 Ryne Sandberg CL	.75	.30
❑	726 Frank Thomas CL	.50	.20
❑	727 Barry Larkin CL	.30	.10
❑	728 Manny Ramirez CL	.30	.10
❑	729 Andres Galarraga CL	.30	.10
❑	730 Tony Clark CL	.30	.10
❑	731 Gary Sheffield CL	.30	.10
❑	732 Jeff Bagwell CL	.30	.10
❑	733 Kevin Appier CL	.30	.10
❑	734 Mike Piazza CL	.75	.30
❑	735 Jeff Cirillo CL	.30	.10
❑	736 Paul Molitor CL	.30	.10
❑	737 Henry Rodriguez CL	.30	.10
❑	738 Todd Hundley CL	.30	.10
❑	739 Derek Jeter CL	1.00	.40
❑	740 Mark McGwire CL	1.00	.40
❑	741 Curt Schilling CL	.30	.10
❑	742 Jason Kendall CL	.30	.10
❑	743 Tony Gwynn CL	.50	.20
❑	744 Barry Bonds CL	1.00	.40
❑	745 Ken Griffey Jr. CL	.75	.30
❑	746 Brian Jordan CL	.30	.10
❑	747 Juan Gonzalez CL	.30	.10
❑	748 Joe Carter CL	.30	.10
❑	749 Arizona Diamondbacks CL	.30	.10
❑	750 Tampa Bay Devil Rays CL	.30	.10
❑	751 Hideki Irabu RC	.75	.30
❑	752 Jeremi Gonzalez RC	.50	.20
❑	753 Mario Valdez RC	.50	.20
❑	754 Aaron Boone	.75	.30
❑	755 Brett Tomko	.50	.20
❑	756 Jaret Wright RC	.75	.30
❑	757 Ryan McGuire	.50	.20
❑	758 Jason McDonald	.50	.20
❑	759 Adrian Brown RC	.50	.20
❑	760 Keith Foulke RC	2.00	.75
❑	761 Bonus Checklist (751-761)	.50	.20
❑	P489 Matt Williams Promo	1.00	.40
❑	NNO A.Jones Circa AU/200	25.00	10.00

2002 Fleer

	Card		
❑	COMPLETE SET (540)	80.00	30.00
❑	COMMON CARD (1-540)	.25	.08
❑	COMMON CARD (492-531)	.50	.20
❑	1 Darin Erstad FP	.25	.08
❑	2 Randy Johnson FP	.60	.25
❑	3 Chipper Jones FP	.60	.25
❑	4 Jay Gibbons FP	.25	.08
❑	5 Nomar Garciaparra FP	1.00	.40
❑	6 Sammy Sosa FP	.60	.25
❑	7 Frank Thomas FP	.60	.25
❑	8 Ken Griffey Jr. FP	1.00	.40
❑	9 Jim Thome FP	.40	.15
❑	10 Todd Helton FP	.40	.15
❑	11 Jeff Weaver FP	.25	.08
❑	12 Cliff Floyd FP	.25	.08
❑	13 Jeff Bagwell FP	.40	.15
❑	14 Mike Sweeney FP	.25	.08
❑	15 Adrian Beltre FP	.25	.08
❑	16 Richie Sexson FP	.25	.08

	No.	Player		
❑	17	Brad Radke FP	.25	.08
❑	18	Vladimir Guerrero FP	.60	.25
❑	19	Mike Piazza FP	1.00	.40
❑	20	Derek Jeter FP	1.25	.50
❑	21	Eric Chavez FP	.25	.08
❑	22	Pat Burrell FP	.25	.08
❑	23	Brian Giles FP	.25	.08
❑	24	Trevor Hoffman FP	.25	.08
❑	25	Barry Bonds FP	1.00	.40
❑	26	Ichiro Suzuki FP	1.00	.40
❑	27	Albert Pujols FP	1.00	.40
❑	28	Ben Grieve FP	.25	.08
❑	29	Alex Rodriguez FP	1.00	.40
❑	30	Carlos Delgado FP	.25	.08
❑	31	Miguel Tejada	.40	.15
❑	32	Todd Hollandsworth	.25	.08
❑	33	Marlon Anderson	.25	.08
❑	34	Kerry Robinson	.25	.08
❑	35	Chris Richard	.25	.08
❑	36	Jamey Wright	.25	.08
❑	37	Ray Lankford	.40	.15
❑	38	Mike Bordick	.40	.15
❑	39	Danny Graves	.25	.08
❑	40	A.J. Pierzynski	.40	.15
❑	41	Shannon Stewart	.40	.15
❑	42	Tony Armas Jr.	.25	.08
❑	43	Brad Ausmus	.40	.15
❑	44	Alfonso Soriano	.40	.15
❑	45	Junior Spivey	.25	.08
❑	46	Brent Mayne	.25	.08
❑	47	Jim Thome	.60	.25
❑	48	Dan Wilson	.25	.08
❑	49	Geoff Jenkins	.25	.08
❑	50	Kris Benson	.25	.08
❑	51	Rafael Furcal	.40	.15
❑	52	Wiki Gonzalez	.25	.08
❑	53	Jeff Kent	.40	.15
❑	54	Curt Schilling	.40	.15
❑	55	Ken Harvey	.25	.08
❑	56	Roosevelt Brown	.25	.08
❑	57	David Segui	.25	.08
❑	58	Mario Valdez	.25	.08
❑	59	Adam Dunn	.40	.15
❑	60	Bob Howry	.25	.08
❑	61	Michael Barrett	.25	.08
❑	62	Garret Anderson	.40	.15
❑	63	Kelvim Escobar	.25	.08
❑	64	Ben Grieve	.25	.08
❑	65	Randy Johnson	1.00	.40
❑	66	Jose Offerman	.25	.08
❑	67	Jason Kendall	.40	.15
❑	68	Joel Pineiro	.25	.08
❑	69	Alex Escobar	.25	.08
❑	70	Chris George	.25	.08
❑	71	Bobby Higginson	.40	.15
❑	72	Nomar Garciaparra	1.50	.60
❑	73	Pat Burrell	.40	.15
❑	74	Lee Stevens	.25	.08
❑	75	Felipe Lopez	.25	.08
❑	76	Al Leiter	.40	.15
❑	77	Jim Edmonds	.40	.15
❑	78	Al Levine	.25	.08
❑	79	Raul Mondesi	.40	.15
❑	80	Jose Valentin	.25	.08
❑	81	Matt Clement	.40	.15
❑	82	Richard Hidalgo	.25	.08
❑	83	Jamie Moyer	.40	.15
❑	84	Brian Schneider	.25	.08
❑	85	John Franco	.40	.15
❑	86	Brian Buchanan	.25	.08
❑	87	Roy Oswalt	.40	.15
❑	88	Johnny Estrada	.25	.08
❑	89	Marcus Giles	.40	.15
❑	90	Carlos Valderrama	.25	.08
❑	91	Mark Mulder	.40	.15
❑	92	Mark Grace	.60	.25
❑	93	Andy Ashby	.25	.08
❑	94	Woody Williams	.25	.08
❑	95	Ben Petrick	.25	.08
❑	96	Roy Halladay	.40	.15
❑	97	Fred McGriff	.60	.25
❑	98	Shawn Green	.40	.15
❑	99	Todd Hundley	.25	.08
❑	100	Carlos Febles	.25	.08
❑	101	Jason Marquis	.25	.08
❑	102	Mike Redmond	.25	.08
❑	103	Shane Halter	.25	.08
❑	104	Trot Nixon	.40	.15
❑	105	Jeremy Giambi	.25	.08
❑	106	Carlos Delgado	.40	.15
❑	107	Richie Sexson	.40	.15
❑	108	Russ Ortiz	.25	.08
❑	109	David Ortiz	1.00	.40
❑	110	Curtis Leskanic	.25	.08
❑	111	Jay Payton	.25	.08
❑	112	Travis Phelps	.25	.08
❑	113	J.T. Snow	.40	.15
❑	114	Edgar Renteria	.40	.15
❑	115	Freddy Garcia	.40	.15
❑	116	Cliff Floyd	.40	.15
❑	117	Charles Nagy	.25	.08
❑	118	Tony Batista	.25	.08
❑	119	Rafael Palmeiro	.60	.25
❑	120	Darren Dreifort	.25	.08
❑	121	Warren Morris	.25	.08
❑	122	Augie Ojeda	.25	.08
❑	123	Rusty Greer	.40	.15
❑	124	Esteban Yan	.25	.08
❑	125	Corey Patterson	.25	.08
❑	126	Matt Ginter	.25	.08
❑	127	Matt Lawton	.25	.08
❑	128	Miguel Batista	.25	.08
❑	129	Randy Winn	.25	.08
❑	130	Eric Milton	.25	.08
❑	131	Jack Wilson	.25	.08
❑	132	Sean Casey	.40	.15
❑	133	Mike Sweeney	.40	.15
❑	134	Jason Tyner	.25	.08
❑	135	Carlos Hernandez	.25	.08
❑	136	Shea Hillenbrand	.40	.15
❑	137	Shawn Wooten	.25	.08
❑	138	Peter Bergeron	.25	.08
❑	139	Travis Lee	.25	.08
❑	140	Craig Wilson	.25	.08
❑	141	Carlos Guillen	.40	.15
❑	142	Chipper Jones	1.00	.40
❑	143	Gabe Kapler	.40	.15
❑	144	Raul Ibanez	.25	.08
❑	145	Eric Chavez	.40	.15
❑	146	D'Angelo Jimenez	.25	.08
❑	147	Chad Hermansen	.25	.08
❑	148	Joe Kennedy	.25	.08
❑	149	Mariano Rivera	1.00	.40
❑	150	Jeff Bagwell	.60	.25
❑	151	Joe McEwing	.25	.08
❑	152	Ronnie Belliard	.25	.08
❑	153	Desi Relaford	.25	.08
❑	154	Vinny Castilla	.40	.15
❑	155	Tim Hudson	.40	.15
❑	156	Wilton Guerrero	.25	.08
❑	157	Raul Casanova	.25	.08
❑	158	Edgardo Alfonzo	.25	.08
❑	159	Derrek Lee	.60	.25
❑	160	Phil Nevin	.40	.15
❑	161	Roger Clemens	2.00	.75
❑	162	Jason LaRue	.25	.08
❑	163	Brian Lawrence	.25	.08
❑	164	Adrian Beltre	.40	.15
❑	165	Troy Glaus	.40	.15
❑	166	Jeff Weaver	.25	.08
❑	167	B.J. Surhoff	.40	.15
❑	168	Eric Byrnes	.25	.08
❑	169	Mike Sirotka	.25	.08
❑	170	Bill Haselman	.25	.08
❑	171	Javier Vazquez	.40	.15
❑	172	Sidney Ponson	.25	.08
❑	173	Adam Everett	.25	.08
❑	174	Bubba Trammell	.25	.08
❑	175	Robb Nen	.40	.15
❑	176	Barry Larkin	.60	.25
❑	177	Tony Graffanino	.25	.08
❑	178	Rich Garces	.25	.08
❑	179	Juan Uribe	.25	.08
❑	180	Tom Glavine	.60	.25
❑	181	Eric Karros	.40	.15
❑	182	Michael Cuddyer	.25	.08
❑	183	Wade Miller	.25	.08
❑	184	Matt Williams	.40	.15
❑	185	Matt Morris	.40	.15
❑	186	Rickey Henderson	1.00	.40
❑	187	Trevor Hoffman	.40	.15
❑	188	Wilson Betemit	.25	.08
❑	189	Steve Karsay	.25	.08
❑	190	Frank Catalanotto	.25	.08
❑	191	Jason Schmidt	.40	.15
❑	192	Roger Cedeno	.25	.08
❑	193	Magglio Ordonez	.40	.15
❑	194	Pat Hentgen	.25	.08
❑	195	Mike Lieberthal	.40	.15
❑	196	Andy Pettitte	.60	.25
❑	197	Jay Gibbons	.25	.08
❑	198	Rolando Arrojo	.25	.08
❑	199	Joe Mays	.25	.08
❑	200	Aubrey Huff	.40	.15
❑	201	Nelson Figueroa	.25	.08
❑	202	Paul Konerko	.40	.15
❑	203	Ken Griffey Jr.	1.50	.60
❑	204	Brandon Duckworth	.25	.08
❑	205	Sammy Sosa	1.00	.40
❑	206	Carl Everett	.40	.15
❑	207	Scott Rolen	.60	.25
❑	208	Orlando Hernandez	.40	.15
❑	209	Todd Helton	.60	.25
❑	210	Preston Wilson	.40	.15
❑	211	Gil Meche	.25	.08
❑	212	Bill Mueller	.40	.15
❑	213	Craig Biggio	.60	.25
❑	214	Dean Palmer	.40	.15
❑	215	Randy Wolf	.25	.08
❑	216	Jeff Suppan	.25	.08
❑	217	Jimmy Rollins	.40	.15
❑	218	Alexis Gomez	.25	.08
❑	219	Ellis Burks	.40	.15
❑	220	Ramon E. Martinez	.25	.08
❑	221	Ramiro Mendoza	.25	.08
❑	222	Einar Diaz	.25	.08
❑	223	Brent Abernathy	.25	.08
❑	224	Darin Erstad	.40	.15
❑	225	Reggie Taylor	.25	.08
❑	226	Jason Jennings	.25	.08
❑	227	Ray Durham	.40	.15
❑	228	John Parrish	.25	.08
❑	229	Kevin Young	.25	.08
❑	230	Xavier Nady	.25	.08
❑	231	Juan Cruz	.25	.08
❑	232	Greg Norton	.25	.08
❑	233	Barry Bonds	2.50	1.00
❑	234	Kip Wells	.25	.08
❑	235	Paul LoDuca	.40	.15
❑	236	Javy Lopez	.40	.15
❑	237	Luis Castillo	.25	.08
❑	238	Tom Gordon	.25	.08
❑	239	Mike Mordecai	.25	.08
❑	240	Damian Rolls	.25	.08
❑	241	Julio Lugo	.25	.08
❑	242	Ichiro Suzuki	2.00	.75
❑	243	Tony Womack	.25	.08
❑	244	Matt Anderson	.25	.08
❑	245	Carlos Lee	.40	.15
❑	246	Alex Rodriguez	1.50	.60
❑	247	Bernie Williams	.60	.25
❑	248	Scott Sullivan	.25	.08
❑	249	Mike Hampton	.40	.15
❑	250	Orlando Cabrera	.40	.15
❑	251	Benito Santiago	.40	.15
❑	252	Steve Finley	.40	.15
❑	253	Dave Williams	.25	.08
❑	254	Adam Kennedy	.25	.08
❑	255	Omar Vizquel	.60	.25
❑	256	Garrett Stephenson	.25	.08
❑	257	Fernando Tatis	.25	.08
❑	258	Mike Piazza	1.50	.60
❑	259	Scott Spiezio	.25	.08
❑	260	Jacque Jones	.40	.15
❑	261	Russell Branyan	.25	.08
❑	262	Mark McLemore	.25	.08
❑	263	Mitch Meluskey	.25	.08
❑	264	Marlon Byrd	.25	.08
❑	265	Kyle Farnsworth	.25	.08
❑	266	Billy Sylvester	.25	.08
❑	267	C.C. Sabathia	.40	.15
❑	268	Mark Buehrle	.40	.15
❑	269	Geoff Blum	.25	.08
❑	270	Bret Prinz	.25	.08
❑	271	Placido Polanco	.25	.08
❑	272	John Olerud	.40	.15
❑	273	Pedro Martinez	.60	.25
❑	274	Doug Mientkiewicz	.40	.15

❑ 275 Jason Bere .25 .08
❑ 276 Bud Smith .25 .08
❑ 277 Terrence Long .25 .08
❑ 278 Troy Percival .40 .15
❑ 279 Derek Jeter 2.50 1.00
❑ 280 Eric Owens .25 .08
❑ 281 Jay Bell .40 .15
❑ 282 Mike Cameron .25 .08
❑ 283 Joe Randa .40 .15
❑ 284 Brian Roberts .40 .15
❑ 285 Ryan Klesko .40 .15
❑ 286 Ryan Dempster .25 .08
❑ 287 Cristian Guzman .25 .08
❑ 288 Tim Salmon .60 .25
❑ 289 Mark Johnson .25 .08
❑ 290 Brian Giles .40 .15
❑ 291 Jon Lieber .25 .08
❑ 292 Fernando Vina .25 .08
❑ 293 Mike Mussina .60 .25
❑ 294 Juan Pierre .40 .15
❑ 295 Carlos Beltran .40 .15
❑ 296 Vladimir Guerrero 1.00 .40
❑ 297 Orlando Merced .25 .08
❑ 298 Jose Hernandez .25 .08
❑ 299 Mike Lamb .25 .08
❑ 300 David Eckstein .40 .15
❑ 301 Mark Loretta .25 .08
❑ 302 Greg Vaughn .25 .08
❑ 303 Jose Vidro .25 .08
❑ 304 Jose Ortiz .25 .08
❑ 305 Mark Grudzielanek .25 .08
❑ 306 Rob Bell .25 .08
❑ 307 Elmer Dessens .25 .08
❑ 308 Tomas Perez .25 .08
❑ 309 Jerry Hairston Jr. .25 .08
❑ 310 Mike Stanton .25 .08
❑ 311 Todd Walker .25 .08
❑ 312 Jason Varitek 1.00 .40
❑ 313 Masato Yoshii .25 .08
❑ 314 Ben Sheets .40 .15
❑ 315 Roberto Hernandez .25 .08
❑ 316 Eli Marrero .25 .08
❑ 317 Josh Beckett .40 .15
❑ 318 Robert Fick .25 .08
❑ 319 Aramis Ramirez .40 .15
❑ 320 Bartolo Colon .40 .15
❑ 321 Kenny Kelly .25 .08
❑ 322 Luis Gonzalez .40 .15
❑ 323 John Smoltz .60 .25
❑ 324 Homer Bush .25 .08
❑ 325 Kevin Millwood .40 .15
❑ 326 Manny Ramirez .60 .25
❑ 327 Armando Benitez .25 .08
❑ 328 Luis Alicea .25 .08
❑ 329 Mark Kotsay .40 .15
❑ 330 Felix Rodriguez .25 .08
❑ 331 Eddie Taubensee .25 .08
❑ 332 John Burkett .25 .08
❑ 333 Ramon Ortiz .25 .08
❑ 334 Daryle Ward .25 .08
❑ 335 Jarrod Washburn .25 .08
❑ 336 Benji Gil .25 .08
❑ 337 Mike Lowell .40 .15
❑ 338 Larry Walker .40 .15
❑ 339 Andruw Jones .60 .25
❑ 340 Scott Elarton .25 .08
❑ 341 Tony McKnight .25 .08
❑ 342 Frank Thomas 1.00 .40
❑ 343 Kevin Brown .40 .15
❑ 344 Jermaine Dye .40 .15
❑ 345 Luis Rivas .25 .08
❑ 346 Jeff Conine .40 .15
❑ 347 Bobby Kielty .25 .08
❑ 348 Jeffrey Hammonds .25 .08
❑ 349 Keith Foulke .40 .15
❑ 350 Dave Martinez .25 .08
❑ 351 Adam Eaton .25 .08
❑ 352 Brandon Inge .25 .08
❑ 353 Tyler Houston .25 .08
❑ 354 Bobby Abreu .40 .15
❑ 355 Ivan Rodriguez .60 .25
❑ 356 Doug Glanville .25 .08
❑ 357 Jorge Julio .25 .08
❑ 358 Kerry Wood .40 .15
❑ 359 Eric Munson .25 .08
❑ 360 Joe Crede .40 .15
❑ 361 Denny Neagle .25 .08
❑ 362 Vance Wilson .25 .08
❑ 363 Neifi Perez .25 .08
❑ 364 Darryl Kile .40 .15
❑ 365 Jose Macias .25 .08
❑ 366 Michael Coleman .25 .08
❑ 367 Erubiel Durazo .25 .08
❑ 368 Darrin Fletcher .25 .08
❑ 369 Matt White .25 .08
❑ 370 Marvin Benard .25 .08
❑ 371 Brad Penny .25 .08
❑ 372 Chuck Finley .40 .15
❑ 373 Delino DeShields .25 .08
❑ 374 Adrian Brown .25 .08
❑ 375 Corey Koskie .25 .08
❑ 376 Kazuhiro Sasaki .40 .15
❑ 377 Brent Butler .25 .08
❑ 378 Paul Wilson .25 .08
❑ 379 Scott Williamson .25 .08
❑ 380 Mike Young 1.00 .40
❑ 381 Toby Hall .25 .08
❑ 382 Shane Reynolds .25 .08
❑ 383 Tom Goodwin .25 .08
❑ 384 Seth Etherton .25 .08
❑ 385 Billy Wagner .40 .15
❑ 386 Josh Phelps .25 .08
❑ 387 Kyle Lohse .25 .08
❑ 388 Jeremy Fikac .25 .08
❑ 389 Jorge Posada .60 .25
❑ 390 Bret Boone .40 .15
❑ 391 Angel Berroa .25 .08
❑ 392 Matt Mantei .25 .08
❑ 393 Alex Gonzalez .25 .08
❑ 394 Scott Strickland .25 .08
❑ 395 Charles Johnson .40 .15
❑ 396 Ramon Hernandez .25 .08
❑ 397 Damian Jackson .25 .08
❑ 398 Albert Pujols 2.00 .75
❑ 399 Gary Bennett .25 .08
❑ 400 Edgar Martinez .60 .25
❑ 401 Carl Pavano .40 .15
❑ 402 Chris Gomez .25 .08
❑ 403 Jaret Wright .25 .08
❑ 404 Lance Berkman .40 .15
❑ 405 Robert Person .25 .08
❑ 406 Brook Fordyce .25 .08
❑ 407 Adam Pettyjohn .25 .08
❑ 408 Chris Carpenter .40 .15
❑ 409 Rey Ordonez .25 .08
❑ 410 Eric Gagne .40 .15
❑ 411 Damion Easley .25 .08
❑ 412 A.J. Burnett .40 .15
❑ 413 Aaron Boone .40 .15
❑ 414 J.D. Drew .40 .15
❑ 415 Kelly Stinnett .25 .08
❑ 416 Mark Quinn .25 .08
❑ 417 Brad Radke .40 .15
❑ 418 Jose Cruz Jr. .25 .08
❑ 419 Greg Maddux 1.50 .60
❑ 420 Steve Cox .25 .08
❑ 421 Torii Hunter .40 .15
❑ 422 Sandy Alomar Jr. .25 .08
❑ 423 Barry Zito .40 .15
❑ 424 Bill Hall .40 .15
❑ 425 Marquis Grissom .40 .15
❑ 426 Rich Aurilia .25 .08
❑ 427 Royce Clayton .25 .08
❑ 428 Travis Fryman .40 .15
❑ 429 Pablo Ozuna .25 .08
❑ 430 David Dellucci .25 .08
❑ 431 Vernon Wells .40 .15
❑ 432 Gregg Zaun CP .25 .08
❑ 433 Alex Gonzalez CP .25 .08
❑ 434 Hideo Nomo CP 1.00 .40
❑ 435 Jeromy Burnitz CP .40 .15
❑ 436 Gary Sheffield CP .40 .15
❑ 437 Tino Martinez CP .60 .25
❑ 438 Tsuyoshi Shinjo CP .40 .15
❑ 439 Chan Ho Park CP .40 .15
❑ 440 Tony Clark CP .25 .08
❑ 441 Brad Fullmer CP .25 .08
❑ 442 Jason Giambi CP .25 .08
❑ 443 Billy Koch CP .25 .08
❑ 444 Mo Vaughn CP .40 .15
❑ 445 Alex Ochoa CP .25 .08
❑ 446 Darren Lewis CP .25 .08
❑ 447 John Rocker CP .40 .15
❑ 448 Scott Hatteberg CP .25 .08
❑ 449 Brady Anderson CP .40 .15
❑ 450 Chuck Knoblauch CP .40 .15
❑ 451 Pokey Reese CP .25 .08
❑ 452 Brian Jordan CP .40 .15
❑ 453 Albie Lopez CP .25 .08
❑ 454 David Bell CP .25 .08
❑ 455 Juan Gonzalez CP .40 .15
❑ 456 Terry Adams CP .25 .08
❑ 457 Kenny Lofton CP .40 .15
❑ 458 Shawn Estes CP .25 .08
❑ 459 Josh Fogg CP .25 .08
❑ 460 Dmitri Young CP .40 .15
❑ 461 Johnny Damon Sox CP .60 .25
❑ 462 Chris Singleton CP .25 .08
❑ 463 Ricky Ledee CP .25 .08
❑ 464 Dustin Hermanson CP .25 .08
❑ 465 Aaron Sele CP .25 .08
❑ 466 Chris Stynes CP .25 .08
❑ 467 Matt Stairs CP .25 .08
❑ 468 Kevin Appier CP .40 .15
❑ 469 Omar Daal CP .25 .08
❑ 470 Moises Alou CP .40 .15
❑ 471 Juan Encarnacion CP .25 .08
❑ 472 Robin Ventura CP .40 .15
❑ 473 Eric Hinske CP .25 .08
❑ 474 Rondell White CP .40 .15
❑ 475 Carlos Pena CP .25 .08
❑ 476 Craig Paquette CP .25 .08
❑ 477 Marty Cordova CP .25 .08
❑ 478 Brett Tomko CP .25 .08
❑ 479 Reggie Sanders CP .25 .08
❑ 480 Roberto Alomar CP .60 .25
❑ 481 Jeff Cirillo CP .25 .08
❑ 482 Todd Zeile CP .40 .15
❑ 483 John Vander Wal CP .25 .08
❑ 484 Rick Helling CP .25 .08
❑ 485 Jeff D'Amico CP .25 .08
❑ 486 David Justice CP .40 .15
❑ 487 Jason Isringhausen CP .40 .15
❑ 488 Shigetoshi Hasegawa CP .40 .15
❑ 489 Eric Young CP .25 .08
❑ 490 David Wells CP .40 .15
❑ 491 Ruben Sierra CP .25 .08
❑ 492 Aaron Cook FF RC .75 .30
❑ 493 Takahito Nomura FF RC .75 .30
❑ 494 Austin Kearns FF .50 .20
❑ 495 Kazuhisa Ishii FF RC 1.25 .50
❑ 496 Mark Teixeira FF 2.00 .75
❑ 497 Rene Reyes FF RC .75 .30
❑ 498 Tim Spooneybarger FF .50 .20
❑ 499 Ben Broussard FF .50 .20
❑ 500 Eric Oyr FF .50 .20
❑ 501 Anastacio Martinez FF RC .75 .30
❑ 502 Morgan Ensberg FF .75 .30
❑ 503 Steve Kent FF RC .75 .30
❑ 504 Franklin Nunez FF RC .75 .30
❑ 505 Adam Walker FF RC .75 .30
❑ 506 Anderson Machado FF RC .75 .30
❑ 507 Ryan Drese FF .50 .20
❑ 508 Luis Ugueto FF RC .75 .30
❑ 509 Jorge Nunez FF RC .75 .30
❑ 510 Colby Lewis FF .50 .20
❑ 511 Ron Calloway FF RC .75 .30
❑ 512 Hansel Izquierdo FF RC .75 .30
❑ 513 Jason Lane FF .75 .30
❑ 514 Rafael Soriano FF .50 .20
❑ 515 Jackson Melian FF .50 .20
❑ 516 Edwin Almonte FF RC .75 .30
❑ 517 Satoru Komiyama FF RC .75 .30
❑ 518 Corey Thurman FF RC .75 .30
❑ 519 Jorge De La Rosa FF RC .75 .30
❑ 520 Victor Martinez FF 2.00 .75
❑ 521 Dewon Brazelton FF .50 .20
❑ 522 Marlon Byrd FF .50 .20
❑ 523 Jae Seo FF .50 .20
❑ 524 Orlando Hudson FF .50 .20
❑ 525 Sean Burroughs FF .50 .20
❑ 526 Ryan Langerhans FF .75 .30
❑ 527 David Kelton FF .50 .20
❑ 528 So Taguchi FF RC 1.25 .50
❑ 529 Tyler Walker FF .50 .20
❑ 530 Hank Blalock FF 1.25 .50
❑ 531 Mark Prior FF 1.25 .50
❑ 532 Yankee Stadium CL .40 .15

❑ 533 Fenway Park CL .40 .15
❑ 534 Wrigley Field CL .40 .15
❑ 535 Dodger Stadium CL .40 .15
❑ 536 Camden Yards CL .40 .15
❑ 537 PacBell Park CL .25 .08
❑ 538 Jacobs Field CL .25 .08
❑ 539 SAFECO Field CL .25 .08
❑ 540 Miller Field CL .25 .08
❑ P279 Derek Jeter Promo

2006 Fleer

❑ Alay Soler RC
❑ COMP.FACT.SET (430) 50.00 20.00
❑ COMPLETE SET (400) 40.00 15.00
❑ COMMON CARD (1-400) .40 .15
❑ COMMON ROOKIE .50 .20
❑ COMMON ROOKIE (401-430) .60 .25
❑ 401-430 AVAIL. IN FLEER FACT.SET
❑ 1 Adam Kennedy .40 .15
❑ 2 Bartolo Colon .40 .15
❑ 3 Bengie Molina .40 .15
❑ 4 Chone Figgins .40 .15
❑ 5 Dallas McPherson .40 .15
❑ 6 Darin Erstad .40 .15
❑ 7 Francisco Rodriguez .40 .15
❑ 8 Garret Anderson .40 .15
❑ 9 Jarrod Washburn .40 .15
❑ 10 John Lackey .40 .15
❑ 11 Orlando Cabrera .40 .15
❑ 12 Ryan Theriot RC .50 .20
❑ 13 Steve Finley .40 .15
❑ 14 Vladimir Guerrero 1.00 .40
❑ 15 Adam Everett .40 .15
❑ 16 Andy Pettitte .60 .25
❑ 17 Charlton Jimerson (RC) .50 .20
❑ 18 Brad Lidge .40 .15
❑ 19 Chris Burke .40 .15
❑ 20 Craig Biggio .60 .25
❑ 21 Jason Lane .40 .15
❑ 22 Jeff Bagwell .60 .25
❑ 23 Lance Berkman .40 .15
❑ 24 Morgan Ensberg .40 .15
❑ 25 Roger Clemens 2.00 .75
❑ 26 Roy Oswalt .40 .15
❑ 27 Willy Taveras .40 .15
❑ 28 Barry Zito .40 .15
❑ 29 Bobby Crosby .40 .15
❑ 30 Bobby Kielty .40 .15
❑ 31 Dan Johnson .40 .15
❑ 32 Danny Haren .40 .15
❑ 33 Eric Chavez .40 .15
❑ 34 Huston Street .40 .15
❑ 35 Jason Kendall .40 .15
❑ 36 Jay Payton .40 .15
❑ 37 Joe Blanton .40 .15
❑ 38 Mark Kotsay .40 .15
❑ 39 Nick Swisher .40 .15
❑ 40 Rich Harden .40 .15
❑ 41 Ron Flores RC .50 .20
❑ 42 Alex Rios .40 .15
❑ 43 John-Ford Griffin (RC) .50 .20
❑ 44 Dave Bush .40 .15
❑ 45 Eric Hinske .40 .15
❑ 46 Frank Catalanotto .40 .15
❑ 47 Gustavo Chacin .40 .15
❑ 48 Josh Towers .40 .15
❑ 49 Miguel Batista .40 .15
❑ 50 Orlando Hudson .40 .15
❑ 51 Roy Halladay .40 .15
❑ 52 Shea Hillenbrand .40 .15
❑ 53 Shaun Marcum (RC) .50 .20
❑ 54 Vernon Wells .40 .15
❑ 55 Adam LaRoche .40 .15
❑ 56 Andruw Jones .60 .25
❑ 57 Chipper Jones 1.00 .40
❑ 58 Anthony Lerew (RC) .50 .20
❑ 59 Jeff Francoeur 1.00 .40
❑ 60 John Smoltz .60 .25
❑ 61 Johnny Estrada .40 .15
❑ 62 Julio Franco .40 .15
❑ 63 Joey Devine RC .50 .20
❑ 64 Marcus Giles .40 .15
❑ 65 Mike Hampton .40 .15
❑ 66 Rafael Furcal .40 .15
❑ 67 Chuck James (RC) .75 .30
❑ 68 Tim Hudson .40 .15
❑ 69 Ben Sheets .40 .15
❑ 70 Bill Hall .40 .15
❑ 71 Brady Clark .40 .15
❑ 72 Carlos Lee .40 .15
❑ 73 Chris Capuano .40 .15
❑ 74 Nelson Cruz (RC) .50 .20
❑ 75 Derrick Turnbow .40 .15
❑ 76 Doug Davis .40 .15
❑ 77 Geoff Jenkins .40 .15
❑ 78 J.J. Hardy .40 .15
❑ 79 Lyle Overbay .40 .15
❑ 80 Prince Fielder 1.50 .60
❑ 81 Rickie Weeks .40 .15
❑ 82 Albert Pujols 2.00 .75
❑ 83 Chris Carpenter .40 .15
❑ 84 David Eckstein .40 .15
❑ 85 Jason Isringhausen .40 .15
❑ 86 Tyler Johnson (RC) .50 .20
❑ 87 Adam Wainwright (RC) .50 .20
❑ 88 Jim Edmonds .60 .25
❑ 89 Chris Duncan (RC) .50 .20
❑ 90 Mark Grudzielanek .40 .15
❑ 91 Mark Mulder .40 .15
❑ 92 Matt Morris .40 .15
❑ 93 Reggie Sanders .40 .15
❑ 94 Scott Rolen .60 .25
❑ 95 Yadier Molina .40 .15
❑ 96 Aramis Ramirez .40 .15
❑ 97 Carlos Zambrano .40 .15
❑ 98 Corey Patterson .40 .15
❑ 99 Derrek Lee .40 .15
❑ 100 Glendon Rusch .40 .15
❑ 101 Greg Maddux 1.50 .60
❑ 102 Jeromy Burnitz .40 .15
❑ 103 Kerry Wood .40 .15
❑ 104 Mark Prior .60 .25
❑ 105 Michael Barrett .40 .15
❑ 106 Geovany Soto (RC) .50 .20
❑ 107 Nomar Garciaparra 1.00 .40
❑ 108 Ryan Dempster .40 .15
❑ 109 Todd Walker .40 .15
❑ 110 Alex S. Gonzalez .40 .15
❑ 111 Aubrey Huff .40 .15
❑ 112 Victor Diaz .40 .15
❑ 113 Carl Crawford .40 .15
❑ 114 Danys Baez .40 .15
❑ 115 Joey Gathright .40 .15
❑ 116 Jonny Gomes .40 .15
❑ 117 Jorge Cantu .40 .15
❑ 118 Julio Lugo .40 .15
❑ 119 Rocco Baldelli .40 .15
❑ 120 Scott Kazmir .60 .25
❑ 121 Toby Hall .40 .15
❑ 122 Tim Corcoran RC .50 .20
❑ 123 Alex Cintron .40 .15
❑ 124 Brandon Webb .40 .15
❑ 125 Chad Tracy .40 .15
❑ 126 Dustin Nippert (RC) .50 .20
❑ 127 Claudio Vargas .40 .15
❑ 128 Craig Counsell .40 .15
❑ 129 Javier Vazquez .40 .15
❑ 130 Jose Valverde .40 .15
❑ 131 Luis Gonzalez .40 .15
❑ 132 Royce Clayton .40 .15
❑ 133 Russ Ortiz .40 .15
❑ 134 Shawn Green .40 .15
❑ 135 Tony Clark .40 .15
❑ 136 Troy Glaus .40 .15
❑ 137 Brad Penny .40 .15
❑ 138 Cesar Izturis .40 .15
❑ 139 Derek Lowe .40 .15
❑ 140 Eric Gagne .40 .15
❑ 141 Hee Seop Choi .40 .15
❑ 142 J.D. Drew .40 .15
❑ 143 Jason Phillips .40 .15
❑ 144 Jayson Werth .40 .15
❑ 145 Jeff Kent .40 .15
❑ 146 Jeff Weaver .40 .15
❑ 147 Milton Bradley .40 .15
❑ 148 Odalis Perez .40 .15
❑ 149 Hong-Chih Kuo (RC) 1.25 .50
❑ 150 Brian Myrow RC .50 .20
❑ 151 Armando Benitez .40 .15
❑ 152 Edgardo Alfonzo .40 .15
❑ 153 J.T. Snow .40 .15
❑ 154 Jason Schmidt .40 .15
❑ 155 Lance Niekro .40 .15
❑ 156 Doug Clark (RC) .50 .20
❑ 157 Dan Ortmeier (RC) .50 .20
❑ 158 Moises Alou .40 .15
❑ 159 Noah Lowry .40 .15
❑ 160 Omar Vizquel .60 .25
❑ 161 Pedro Feliz .40 .15
❑ 162 Randy Winn .40 .15
❑ 163 Jeremy Accardo RC .50 .20
❑ 164 Aaron Boone .40 .15
❑ 165 Ryan Garko (RC) .50 .20
❑ 166 C.C. Sabathia .40 .15
❑ 167 Casey Blake .40 .15
❑ 168 Cliff Lee .40 .15
❑ 169 Coco Crisp .40 .15
❑ 170 Grady Sizemore .60 .25
❑ 171 Jake Westbrook .40 .15
❑ 172 Jhonny Peralta .40 .15
❑ 173 Kevin Millwood .40 .15
❑ 174 Scott Elarton .40 .15
❑ 175 Travis Hafner .40 .15
❑ 176 Victor Martinez .40 .15
❑ 177 Adrian Beltre .40 .15
❑ 178 Eddie Guardado .40 .15
❑ 179 Felix Hernandez .60 .25
❑ 180 Gil Meche .40 .15
❑ 181 Ichiro Suzuki 1.50 .60
❑ 182 Jamie Moyer .40 .15
❑ 183 Jeremy Reed .40 .15
❑ 184 Jaime Bubela (RC) .40 .15
❑ 185 Raul Ibanez .40 .15
❑ 186 Richie Sexson .40 .15
❑ 187 Ryan Franklin .40 .15
❑ 188 Jeff Harris RC .40 .15
❑ 189 A.J. Burnett .40 .15
❑ 190 Josh Wilson (RC) .50 .20
❑ 191 Josh Johnson (RC) .75 .30
❑ 192 Carlos Delgado .40 .15
❑ 193 Dontrelle Willis .40 .15
❑ 194 Bernie Castro (RC) .50 .20
❑ 195 Josh Beckett .40 .15
❑ 196 Juan Encarnacion .40 .15
❑ 197 Juan Pierre .40 .15
❑ 198 Robert Andino RC .50 .20
❑ 199 Miguel Cabrera .60 .25
❑ 200 Ryan Jorgensen RC .50 .20
❑ 201 Paul Lo Duca .40 .15
❑ 202 Todd Jones .40 .15
❑ 203 Braden Looper .40 .15
❑ 204 Carlos Beltran .40 .15
❑ 205 Cliff Floyd .40 .15
❑ 206 David Wright 1.50 .60
❑ 207 Doug Mientkiewicz .40 .15
❑ 208 Jae Seo .40 .15
❑ 209 Jose Reyes 1.00 .40
❑ 210 Anderson Hernandez (RC) .50 .20
❑ 211 Miguel Cairo .40 .15
❑ 212 Mike Cameron .40 .15
❑ 213 Mike Piazza 1.00 .40
❑ 214 Pedro Martinez .60 .25
❑ 215 Tom Glavine .60 .25
❑ 216 Tim Hamulack (RC) .40 .15
❑ 217 Brad Wilkerson .40 .15
❑ 218 Darrell Rasner (RC) .40 .15
❑ 219 Chad Cordero .40 .15
❑ 220 Cristian Guzman .40 .15
❑ 221 Jason Bergmann RC .50 .20
❑ 222 John Patterson .40 .15

- ❑ 223 Jose Guillen .40 .15
- ❑ 224 Jose Vidro .40 .15
- ❑ 225 Livan Hernandez .40 .15
- ❑ 226 Nick Johnson .40 .15
- ❑ 227 Preston Wilson .40 .15
- ❑ 228 Ryan Zimmerman (RC) 3.00 1.25
- ❑ 229 Vinny Castilla .40 .15
- ❑ 230 B.J. Ryan .40 .15
- ❑ 231 B.J. Surhoff .40 .15
- ❑ 232 Brian Roberts .40 .15
- ❑ 233 Walter Young (RC) .50 .20
- ❑ 234 Daniel Cabrera .40 .15
- ❑ 235 Erik Bedard .40 .15
- ❑ 236 Javy Lopez .40 .15
- ❑ 237 Jay Gibbons .40 .15
- ❑ 238 Luis Matos .40 .15
- ❑ 239 Melvin Mora .40 .15
- ❑ 240 Miguel Tejada .40 .15
- ❑ 241 Rafael Palmeiro .60 .25
- ❑ 242 Alejandro Freire RC .40 .15
- ❑ 243 Sammy Sosa 1.00 .40
- ❑ 244 Adam Eaton .40 .15
- ❑ 245 Brian Giles .40 .15
- ❑ 246 Brian Lawrence .40 .15
- ❑ 247 Dave Roberts .40 .15
- ❑ 248 Jake Peavy .40 .15
- ❑ 249 Khalil Greene .60 .25
- ❑ 250 Mark Loretta .40 .15
- ❑ 251 Ramon Hernandez .40 .15
- ❑ 252 Ryan Klesko .40 .15
- ❑ 253 Trevor Hoffman .40 .15
- ❑ 254 Woody Williams .40 .15
- ❑ 255 Craig Breslow RC .50 .20
- ❑ 256 Billy Wagner .40 .15
- ❑ 257 Bobby Abreu .40 .15
- ❑ 258 Brett Myers .40 .15
- ❑ 259 Chase Utley 1.00 .40
- ❑ 260 David Bell .40 .15
- ❑ 261 Jim Thome .60 .25
- ❑ 262 Jimmy Rollins .40 .15
- ❑ 263 Jon Lieber .40 .15
- ❑ 264 Danny Sandoval RC .50 .20
- ❑ 265 Mike Lieberthal .40 .15
- ❑ 266 Pat Burrell .40 .15
- ❑ 267 Randy Wolf .40 .15
- ❑ 268 Ryan Howard 1.50 .60
- ❑ 269 J.J. Furmaniak (RC) .50 .20
- ❑ 270 Ronny Paulino (RC) .50 .20
- ❑ 271 Craig Wilson .40 .15
- ❑ 272 Bryan Bullington (RC) .50 .20
- ❑ 273 Jack Wilson .40 .15
- ❑ 274 Jason Bay .40 .15
- ❑ 275 Matt Capps (RC) .50 .20
- ❑ 276 Oliver Perez .40 .15
- ❑ 277 Rob Mackowiak .40 .15
- ❑ 278 Tom Gorzelanny (RC) .50 .20
- ❑ 279 Zach Duke .40 .15
- ❑ 280 Alfonso Soriano .40 .15
- ❑ 281 Chris R. Young .40 .15
- ❑ 282 David Dellucci .40 .15
- ❑ 283 Francisco Cordero .40 .15
- ❑ 284 Jason Botts (RC) UER .50 .20
- ❑ 285 Hank Blalock .40 .15
- ❑ 286 Josh Rupe (RC) .50 .20
- ❑ 287 Kevin Mench .40 .15
- ❑ 288 Laynce Nix .40 .15
- ❑ 289 Mark Teixeira .60 .25
- ❑ 290 Michael Young .40 .15
- ❑ 291 Richard Hidalgo .40 .15
- ❑ 292 Scott Feldman RC .50 .20
- ❑ 293 Bill Mueller .40 .15
- ❑ 294 Hanley Ramirez (RC) 1.25 .50
- ❑ 295 Curt Schilling .60 .25
- ❑ 296 David Ortiz 1.00 .40
- ❑ 297 Alejandro Machado (RC) .50 .20
- ❑ 298 Edgar Renteria .40 .15
- ❑ 299 Jason Varitek 1.00 .40
- ❑ 300 Johnny Damon .60 .25
- ❑ 301 Keith Foulke .40 .15
- ❑ 302 Manny Ramirez .60 .25
- ❑ 303 Matt Clement .40 .15
- ❑ 304 Craig Hansen RC 2.00 .75
- ❑ 305 Tim Wakefield .40 .15
- ❑ 306 Trot Nixon .40 .15
- ❑ 307 Aaron Harang .40 .15
- ❑ 308 Adam Dunn .40 .15
- ❑ 309 Austin Kearns .40 .15
- ❑ 310 Brandon Claussen .40 .15
- ❑ 311 Chris Booker (RC) .50 .20
- ❑ 312 Edwin Encarnacion .40 .15
- ❑ 313 Chris Denorfia (RC) .50 .20
- ❑ 314 Felipe Lopez .40 .15
- ❑ 315 Miguel Perez (RC) .50 .20
- ❑ 316 Ken Griffey Jr. 1.50 .60
- ❑ 317 Ryan Freel .40 .15
- ❑ 318 Sean Casey .40 .15
- ❑ 319 Wily Mo Pena .40 .15
- ❑ 320 Mike Esposito (RC) .50 .20
- ❑ 321 Aaron Miles .40 .15
- ❑ 322 Brad Hawpe .40 .15
- ❑ 323 Brian Fuentes .40 .15
- ❑ 324 Clint Barmes .40 .15
- ❑ 325 Cory Sullivan .40 .15
- ❑ 326 Garrett Atkins .40 .15
- ❑ 327 J.D. Closser .40 .15
- ❑ 328 Jeff Francis .40 .15
- ❑ 329 Luis Gonzalez .40 .15
- ❑ 330 Matt Holliday 1.00 .40
- ❑ 331 Todd Helton .60 .25
- ❑ 332 Angel Berroa .40 .15
- ❑ 333 David DeJesus .40 .15
- ❑ 334 Emil Brown .40 .15
- ❑ 335 Jeremy Affeldt .40 .15
- ❑ 336 Chris Demaria RC .50 .20
- ❑ 337 Mark Teahen .40 .15
- ❑ 338 Matt Stairs .40 .15
- ❑ 339 Steve Stemle RC .50 .20
- ❑ 340 Mike Sweeney .40 .15
- ❑ 341 Runelvys Hernandez .40 .15
- ❑ 342 Jonah Bayliss RC .50 .20
- ❑ 343 Zack Greinke .40 .15
- ❑ 344 Brandon Inge .40 .15
- ❑ 345 Carlos Guillen .40 .15
- ❑ 346 Carlos Pena .40 .15
- ❑ 347 Chris Shelton .40 .15
- ❑ 348 Craig Monroe .40 .15
- ❑ 349 Dmitri Young .40 .15
- ❑ 350 Ivan Rodriguez .60 .25
- ❑ 351 Jeremy Bonderman .40 .15
- ❑ 352 Magglio Ordonez .40 .15
- ❑ 353 Mark Woodyard (RC) .50 .20
- ❑ 354 Omar Infante .40 .15
- ❑ 355 Placido Polanco .40 .15
- ❑ 356 Rondell White .40 .15
- ❑ 357 Brad Radke .40 .15
- ❑ 358 Carlos Silva .40 .15
- ❑ 359 Jacque Jones .40 .15
- ❑ 360 Joe Mauer .60 .25
- ❑ 361 Chris Heintz RC .50 .20
- ❑ 362 Joe Nathan .40 .15
- ❑ 363 Johan Santana .60 .25
- ❑ 364 Justin Morneau .40 .15
- ❑ 365 Francisco Liriano (RC) 2.50 1.00
- ❑ 366 Travis Bowyer (RC) .50 .20
- ❑ 367 Michael Cuddyer .40 .15
- ❑ 368 Scott Baker .40 .15
- ❑ 369 Shannon Stewart .40 .15
- ❑ 370 Torii Hunter .40 .15
- ❑ 371 A.J. Pierzynski .40 .15
- ❑ 372 Aaron Rowand .40 .15
- ❑ 373 Carl Everett .40 .15
- ❑ 374 Dustin Hermanson .40 .15
- ❑ 375 Frank Thomas 1.00 .40
- ❑ 376 Freddy Garcia .40 .15
- ❑ 377 Jermaine Dye .40 .15
- ❑ 378 Joe Crede .40 .15
- ❑ 379 Jon Garland .40 .15
- ❑ 380 Jose Contreras .40 .15
- ❑ 381 Juan Uribe .40 .15
- ❑ 382 Mark Buehrle .40 .15
- ❑ 383 Orlando Hernandez .40 .15
- ❑ 384 Paul Konerko .40 .15
- ❑ 385 Scott Podsednik .40 .15
- ❑ 386 Tadahito Iguchi .40 .15
- ❑ 387 Alex Rodriguez 1.50 .60
- ❑ 388 Bernie Williams .60 .25
- ❑ 389 Chien-Ming Wang 1.50 .60
- ❑ 390 Derek Jeter 2.50 1.00
- ❑ 391 Gary Sheffield .40 .15
- ❑ 392 Hideki Matsui 1.50 .60
- ❑ 393 Jason Giambi .40 .15
- ❑ 394 Jorge Posada .60 .25
- ❑ 395 Mike Vento (RC) .50 .20
- ❑ 396 Mariano Rivera 1.00 .40
- ❑ 397 Mike Mussina .60 .25
- ❑ 398 Randy Johnson 1.00 .40
- ❑ 399 Robinson Cano .60 .25
- ❑ 400 Tino Martinez .40 .15
- ❑ 401 Alay Soler RC .60 .25
- ❑ 402 Boof Bonser (RC) 1.00 .40
- ❑ 403 Cole Hamels (RC) 1.50 .60
- ❑ 404 Ian Kinsler (RC) 1.00 .40
- ❑ 405 Jason Kubel (RC) .60 .25
- ❑ 406 Joel Zumaya (RC) 1.50 .60
- ❑ 407 Jonathan Papelbon (RC) 3.00 1.25
- ❑ 408 Jered Weaver (RC) 3.00 1.25
- ❑ 409 Kendry Morales (RC) 1.50 .60
- ❑ 410 Lastings Milledge (RC) 1.00 .40
- ❑ 411 Matt Kemp (RC) 1.00 .40
- ❑ 412 Taylor Buchholz (RC) 1.00 .40
- ❑ 413 Andre Ethier (RC) 1.50 .60
- ❑ 414 Dan Uggla (RC) 1.50 .60
- ❑ 415 Jeremy Sowers (RC) .60 .25
- ❑ 416 Chad Billingsley (RC) 1.00 .40
- ❑ 417 Josh Barfield (RC) .60 .25
- ❑ 418 Matt Cain (RC) 1.00 .40
- ❑ 419 Fausto Carmona (RC) .60 .25
- ❑ 420 Josh Willingham (RC) .60 .25
- ❑ 421 Jeremy Hermida (RC) .60 .25
- ❑ 422 Conor Jackson (RC) 1.00 .40
- ❑ 423 Dave Gassner (RC) .60 .25
- ❑ 424 Brian Bannister (RC) .60 .25
- ❑ 425 Fernando Nieve (RC) .60 .25
- ❑ 426 Justin Verlander (RC) 2.50 1.00
- ❑ 427 Scott Olsen (RC) .60 .25
- ❑ 428 Takashi Saito RC .60 .25
- ❑ 429 Willie Eyre (RC) .60 .25
- ❑ 430 Travis Ishikawa (RC) .60 .25

2007 Fleer

- ❑ COMPLETE SET (400) 60.00 30.00
- ❑ COMP.FACT.SET (430) 60.00 30.00
- ❑ COMMON CARD (1-430) .30 .12
- ❑ COMMON RC .60 .25
- ❑ 401-430 ISSUED IN FACT.SET
- ❑ OVERALL PRINTING PLATE ODDS 1:720
- ❑ PLATE PRINT RUN 1 SET PER COLOR
- ❑ BLACK-CYAN-MAGENTA-YELLOW ISSUED
- ❑ NO PLATE PRICING DUE TO SCARCITY
- ❑ 1 Chad Cordero .30 .12
- ❑ 2 Alfonso Soriano .30 .12
- ❑ 3 Nick Johnson .30 .12
- ❑ 4 Austin Kearns .30 .12
- ❑ 5 Ramon Ortiz .30 .12
- ❑ 6 Brian Schneider .30 .12
- ❑ 7 Ryan Zimmerman .75 .30
- ❑ 8 Jose Vidro .30 .12
- ❑ 9 Felipe Lopez .30 .12
- ❑ 10 Cristian Guzman .30 .12
- ❑ 11 B.J. Ryan .30 .12
- ❑ 12 Alex Rios .30 .12
- ❑ 13 Vernon Wells .30 .12
- ❑ 14 Roy Halladay .30 .12
- ❑ 15 A.J. Burnett .30 .12
- ❑ 16 Lyle Overbay .30 .12
- ❑ 17 Troy Glaus .30 .12
- ❑ 18 Bengie Molina .30 .12
- ❑ 19 Gustavo Chacin .30 .12
- ❑ 20 Aaron Hill .30 .12
- ❑ 21 Vicente Padilla .30 .12

❑ 22 Kevin Millwood .30 .12
❑ 23 Akinori Otsuka .30 .12
❑ 24 Adam Eaton .30 .12
❑ 25 Hank Blalock .30 .12
❑ 26 Mark Teixeira .50 .20
❑ 27 Michael Young .30 .12
❑ 28 Mark DeRosa .30 .12
❑ 29 Gary Matthews .30 .12
❑ 30 Ian Kinsler .30 .12
❑ 31 Carlos Lee .30 .12
❑ 32 James Shields .30 .12
❑ 33 Scott Kazmir .50 .20
❑ 34 Carl Crawford .30 .12
❑ 35 Jonny Gomes .30 .12
❑ 36 Tim Corcoran .30 .12
❑ 37 B.J. Upton .30 .12
❑ 38 Rocco Baldelli .30 .12
❑ 39 Jae Seo .30 .12
❑ 40 Jorge Cantu .30 .12
❑ 41 Ty Wigginton .30 .12
❑ 42 Chris Carpenter .30 .12
❑ 43 Albert Pujols 1.50 .60
❑ 44 Scott Rolen .50 .20
❑ 45 Jim Edmonds .50 .20
❑ 46 Jason Isringhausen .30 .12
❑ 47 Yadier Molina .30 .12
❑ 48 Adam Wainwright .30 .12
❑ 49 Mark Mulder .30 .12
❑ 50 Jason Marquis .30 .12
❑ 51 Juan Encarnacion .30 .12
❑ 52 Aaron Miles .30 .12
❑ 53 Ichiro Suzuki 1.25 .50
❑ 54 Felix Hernandez .50 .20
❑ 55 Kenji Johjima .75 .30
❑ 56 Richie Sexson .30 .12
❑ 57 Yuniesky Betancourt .30 .12
❑ 58 J.J. Putz .30 .12
❑ 59 Jarrod Washburn .30 .12
❑ 60 Ben Broussard .30 .12
❑ 61 Adrian Beltre .30 .12
❑ 62 Raul Ibanez .30 .12
❑ 63 Jose Lopez .30 .12
❑ 64 Matt Cain .50 .20
❑ 65 Noah Lowry .30 .12
❑ 66 Jason Schmidt .30 .12
❑ 67 Pedro Feliz .30 .12
❑ 68 Matt Morris .30 .12
❑ 69 Ray Durham .30 .12
❑ 70 Steve Finley .30 .12
❑ 71 Randy Winn .30 .12
❑ 72 Moises Alou .30 .12
❑ 73 Eliezer Alfonzo .30 .12
❑ 74 Armando Benitez .30 .12
❑ 75 Omar Vizquel .50 .20
❑ 76 Chris R. Young .30 .12
❑ 77 Adrian Gonzalez .30 .12
❑ 78 Khalil Greene .50 .20
❑ 79 Mike Piazza .75 .30
❑ 80 Josh Barfield .30 .12
❑ 81 Brian Giles .30 .12
❑ 82 Jake Peavy .30 .12
❑ 83 Trevor Hoffman .30 .12
❑ 84 Mike Cameron .30 .12
❑ 85 Dave Roberts .30 .12
❑ 86 David Wells .30 .12
❑ 87 Zach Duke .30 .12
❑ 88 Ian Snell .30 .12
❑ 89 Jason Bay .30 .12
❑ 90 Freddy Sanchez .30 .12
❑ 91 Jack Wilson .30 .12
❑ 92 Tom Gorzelanny .30 .12
❑ 93 Chris Duffy .30 .12
❑ 94 Jose Castillo .30 .12
❑ 95 Matt Capps .30 .12
❑ 96 Mike Gonzalez .30 .12
❑ 97 Chase Utley .75 .30
❑ 98 Jimmy Rollins .30 .12
❑ 99 Aaron Rowand .30 .12
❑ 100 Ryan Howard 1.25 .50
❑ 101 Cole Hamels .50 .20
❑ 102 Pat Burrell .30 .12
❑ 103 Shane Victorino .30 .12
❑ 104 Jamie Moyer .30 .12
❑ 105 Mike Lieberthal .30 .12
❑ 106 Tom Gordon .30 .12
❑ 107 Brett Myers .30 .12
❑ 108 Nick Swisher .30 .12
❑ 109 Barry Zito .30 .12
❑ 110 Jason Kendall .30 .12
❑ 111 Milton Bradley .30 .12
❑ 112 Bobby Crosby .30 .12
❑ 113 Huston Street .30 .12
❑ 114 Eric Chavez .30 .12
❑ 115 Frank Thomas .75 .30
❑ 116 Dan Haren .30 .12
❑ 117 Jay Payton .30 .12
❑ 118 Randy Johnson .75 .30
❑ 119 Mike Mussina .50 .20
❑ 120 Bobby Abreu .30 .12
❑ 121 Jason Giambi .30 .12
❑ 122 Derek Jeter 2.00 .75
❑ 123 Alex Rodriguez 1.25 .50
❑ 124 Jorge Posada .50 .20
❑ 125 Robinson Cano .50 .20
❑ 126 Mariano Rivera .75 .30
❑ 127 Chien-Ming Wang 1.25 .50
❑ 128 Hideki Matsui .75 .30
❑ 129 Gary Sheffield .30 .12
❑ 130 Lastings Milledge .50 .20
❑ 131 Tom Glavine .50 .20
❑ 132 Billy Wagner .30 .12
❑ 133 Pedro Martinez .50 .20
❑ 134 Paul LoDuca .30 .12
❑ 135 Carlos Delgado .30 .12
❑ 136 Carlos Beltran .30 .12
❑ 137 David Wright 1.25 .50
❑ 138 Jose Reyes .30 .12
❑ 139 Julio Franco .30 .12
❑ 140 Michael Cuddyer .30 .12
❑ 141 Justin Morneau .30 .12
❑ 142 Johan Santana .50 .20
❑ 143 Francisco Liriano .75 .30
❑ 144 Joe Mauer .50 .20
❑ 145 Torii Hunter .30 .12
❑ 146 Luis Castillo .30 .12
❑ 147 Joe Nathan .30 .12
❑ 148 Carlos Silva .30 .12
❑ 149 Boof Bonser .30 .12
❑ 150 Ben Sheets .30 .12
❑ 151 Prince Fielder .75 .30
❑ 152 Bill Hall .30 .12
❑ 153 Rickie Weeks .30 .12
❑ 154 Geoff Jenkins .30 .12
❑ 155 Kevin Mench .30 .12
❑ 156 Francisco Cordero .30 .12
❑ 157 Chris Capuano .30 .12
❑ 158 Brady Clark .30 .12
❑ 159 Tony Gwynn Jr. .30 .12
❑ 160 Chad Billingsley .30 .12
❑ 161 Russell Martin .30 .12
❑ 162 Wilson Betemit .30 .12
❑ 163 Nomar Garciaparra .75 .30
❑ 164 Kenny Lofton .30 .12
❑ 165 Rafael Furcal .30 .12
❑ 166 Julio Lugo .30 .12
❑ 167 Brad Penny .30 .12
❑ 168 Jeff Kent .30 .12
❑ 169 Greg Maddux 1.25 .50
❑ 170 Derek Lowe .30 .12
❑ 171 Andre Ethier .50 .20
❑ 172 Chone Figgins .30 .12
❑ 173 Francisco Rodriguez .30 .12
❑ 174 Garret Anderson .30 .12
❑ 175 Orlando Cabrera .30 .12
❑ 176 Adam Kennedy .30 .12
❑ 177 John Lackey .30 .12
❑ 178 Vladimir Guerrero .75 .30
❑ 179 Bartolo Colon .30 .12
❑ 180 Jered Weaver .50 .20
❑ 181 Juan Rivera .30 .12
❑ 182 Howie Kendrick .30 .12
❑ 183 Ervin Santana .30 .12
❑ 184 Mark Redman .30 .12
❑ 185 David DeJesus .30 .12
❑ 186 Joey Gathright .30 .12
❑ 187 Mike Sweeney .30 .12
❑ 188 Mark Teahen .30 .12
❑ 189 Angel Berroa .30 .12
❑ 190 Ambiorix Burgos .30 .12
❑ 191 Luke Hudson .30 .12
❑ 192 Mark Grudzielanek .30 .12
❑ 193 Roger Clemens 1.25 .50
❑ 194 Willy Taveras .30 .12
❑ 195 Craig Biggio .50 .20
❑ 196 Andy Pettitte .50 .20
❑ 197 Roy Oswalt .30 .12
❑ 198 Lance Berkman .30 .12
❑ 199 Morgan Ensberg .30 .12
❑ 200 Brad Lidge .30 .12
❑ 201 Chris Burke .30 .12
❑ 202 Miguel Cabrera .50 .20
❑ 203 Dontrelle Willis .30 .12
❑ 204 Josh Johnson .30 .12
❑ 205 Ricky Nolasco .30 .12
❑ 206 Dan Uggla .50 .20
❑ 207 Jeremy Hermida .30 .12
❑ 208 Scott Olsen .30 .12
❑ 209 Josh Willingham .30 .12
❑ 210 Joe Borowski .30 .12
❑ 211 Hanley Ramirez .50 .20
❑ 212 Mike Jacobs .30 .12
❑ 213 Kenny Rogers .30 .12
❑ 214 Justin Verlander .75 .30
❑ 215 Ivan Rodriguez .50 .20
❑ 216 Magglio Ordonez .30 .12
❑ 217 Todd Jones .30 .12
❑ 218 Joel Zumaya .50 .20
❑ 219 Jeremy Bonderman .30 .12
❑ 220 Nate Robertson .30 .12
❑ 221 Brandon Inge .30 .12
❑ 222 Craig Monroe .30 .12
❑ 223 Carlos Guillen .30 .12
❑ 224 Jeff Francis .30 .12
❑ 225 Brian Fuentes .30 .12
❑ 226 Todd Helton .50 .20
❑ 227 Matt Holliday .75 .30
❑ 228 Garrett Atkins .30 .12
❑ 229 Clint Barmes .30 .12
❑ 230 Jason Jennings .30 .12
❑ 231 Aaron Cook .30 .12
❑ 232 Brad Hawpe .30 .12
❑ 233 Cory Sullivan .30 .12
❑ 234 Aaron Boone .30 .12
❑ 235 C.C. Sabathia .30 .12
❑ 236 Grady Sizemore .50 .20
❑ 237 Travis Hafner .30 .12
❑ 238 Jhonny Peralta .30 .12
❑ 239 Jake Westbrook .30 .12
❑ 240 Jeremy Sowers .30 .12
❑ 241 Andy Marte .30 .12
❑ 242 Victor Martinez .30 .12
❑ 243 Jason Michaels .30 .12
❑ 244 Cliff Lee .30 .12
❑ 245 Bronson Arroyo .30 .12
❑ 246 Aaron Harang .30 .12
❑ 247 Ken Griffey Jr. 1.25 .50
❑ 248 Adam Dunn .30 .12
❑ 249 Rich Aurilia .30 .12
❑ 250 Eric Milton .30 .12
❑ 251 David Ross .30 .12
❑ 252 Brandon Phillips .30 .12
❑ 253 Ryan Freel .30 .12
❑ 254 Eddie Guardado .30 .12
❑ 255 Jose Contreras .30 .12
❑ 256 Freddy Garcia .30 .12
❑ 257 Jon Garland .30 .12
❑ 258 Mark Buehrle .30 .12
❑ 259 Bobby Jenks .30 .12
❑ 260 Paul Konerko .30 .12
❑ 261 Jermaine Dye .30 .12
❑ 262 Joe Crede .30 .12
❑ 263 Jim Thome .50 .20
❑ 264 Javier Vazquez .30 .12
❑ 265 A.J. Pierzynski .30 .12
❑ 266 Tadahito Iguchi .30 .12
❑ 267 Carlos Zambrano .30 .12
❑ 268 Derrek Lee .30 .12
❑ 269 Aramis Ramirez .30 .12
❑ 270 Ryan Theriot .30 .12
❑ 271 Juan Pierre .30 .12
❑ 272 Rich Hill .30 .12
❑ 273 Ryan Dempster .30 .12
❑ 274 Jacque Jones .30 .12
❑ 275 Mark Prior .50 .20
❑ 276 Kerry Wood .30 .12
❑ 277 Josh Beckett .50 .20
❑ 278 David Ortiz .75 .30
❑ 279 Kevin Youkilis .30 .12

❑ 280	Jason Varitek	.75	.30
❑ 281	Manny Ramirez	.50	.20
❑ 282	Curt Schilling	.50	.20
❑ 283	Jon Lester	.50	.20
❑ 284	Jonathan Papelbon	.75	.30
❑ 285	Alex Gonzalez	.30	.12
❑ 286	Mike Lowell	.30	.12
❑ 287	Kyle Snyder	.30	.12
❑ 288	Miguel Tejada	.30	.12
❑ 289	Erik Bedard	.30	.12
❑ 290	Ramon Hernandez	.30	.12
❑ 291	Melvin Mora	.30	.12
❑ 292	Nick Markakis	.50	.20
❑ 293	Brian Roberts	.30	.12
❑ 294	Corey Patterson	.30	.12
❑ 295	Kris Benson	.30	.12
❑ 296	Jay Gibbons	.30	.12
❑ 297	Rodrigo Lopez	.30	.12
❑ 298	Chris Ray	.30	.12
❑ 299	Andruw Jones	.50	.20
❑ 300	Brian McCann	.30	.12
❑ 301	Jeff Francoeur	.75	.30
❑ 302	Chuck James	.30	.12
❑ 303	John Smoltz	.50	.20
❑ 304	Bob Wickman	.30	.12
❑ 305	Edgar Renteria	.30	.12
❑ 306	Adam LaRoche	.30	.12
❑ 307	Marcus Giles	.30	.12
❑ 308	Tim Hudson	.30	.12
❑ 309	Chipper Jones	.75	.30
❑ 310	Miguel Batista	.30	.12
❑ 311	Claudio Vargas	.30	.12
❑ 312	Brandon Webb	.30	.12
❑ 313	Luis Gonzalez	.30	.12
❑ 314	Livan Hernandez	.30	.12
❑ 315	Stephen Drew	.50	.20
❑ 316	Johnny Estrada	.30	.12
❑ 317	Orlando Hudson	.30	.12
❑ 318	Conor Jackson	.30	.12
❑ 319	Chad Tracy	.30	.12
❑ 320	Carlos Quentin	.30	.12
❑ 321	Alvin Colina RC	1.50	.60
❑ 322	Miguel Montero (RC)	.60	.25
❑ 323	Jeff Fiorentino (RC)	.60	.25
❑ 324	Jeff Baker (RC)	.60	.25
❑ 325	Brian Burres (RC)	.60	.25
❑ 326	David Murphy (RC)	.60	.25
❑ 327	Francisco Cruceta (RC)	.60	.25
❑ 328	Beltran Perez (RC)	.60	.25
❑ 329	Scott Moore (RC)	.60	.25
❑ 330	Sean Henn (RC)	.60	.25
❑ 331	Ryan Sweeney (RC)	.60	.25
❑ 332	Josh Fields (RC)	.60	.25
❑ 333	Jerry Owens (RC)	.60	.25
❑ 334	Vinny Rottino (RC)	.60	.25
❑ 335	Kevin Kouzmanoff (RC)	.60	.25
❑ 336	Alexi Casilla RC	1.00	.40
❑ 337	Justin Hampson (RC)	.60	.25
❑ 338	Troy Tulowitzki (RC)	1.50	.60
❑ 339	Jose Garcia RC	.60	.25
❑ 340	Andrew Miller RC	4.00	1.50
❑ 341	Glen Perkins (RC)	.60	.25
❑ 342	Ubaldo Jimenez (RC)	.60	.25
❑ 343	Doug Slaten RC	.60	.25
❑ 344	Angel Sanchez RC	.60	.25
❑ 345	Mitch Maier RC	.60	.25
❑ 346	Ryan Braun RC	.60	.25
❑ 347	Joselo Diaz (RC)	.60	.25
❑ 348	Delwyn Young (RC)	.60	.25
❑ 349	Kevin Hooper (RC)	.60	.25
❑ 350	Dennis Sarfate (RC)	.60	.25
❑ 351	Andy Cannizaro RC	.60	.25
❑ 352	Devern Hansack RC	.60	.25
❑ 353	Michael Bourn (RC)	.60	.25
❑ 354	Carlos Maldonado (RC)	.60	.25
❑ 355	Shane Youman RC	.60	.25
❑ 356	Philip Humber (RC)	1.00	.40
❑ 357	Hector Gimenez (RC)	.60	.25
❑ 358	Fred Lewis (RC)	.60	.25
❑ 359	Ryan Feierabend (RC)	.60	.25
❑ 360	Juan Morillo (RC)	.60	.25
❑ 361	Travis Chick (RC)	.60	.25
❑ 362	Oswaldo Navarro RC	.60	.25
❑ 363	Cesar Jimenez RC	.60	.25
❑ 364	Brian Stokes (RC)	.60	.25
❑ 365	Delmon Young (RC)	1.50	.60
❑ 366	Juan Salas (RC)	.60	.25
❑ 367	Shawn Riggans (RC)	.60	.25
❑ 368	Adam Lind (RC)	.60	.25
❑ 369	Joaquin Arias (RC)	.60	.25
❑ 370	Eric Stults RC	.60	.25
❑ 371	Brandon Webb CL	.30	.12
❑ 372	John Smoltz CL	.50	.20
❑ 373	Miguel Tejada CL	.30	.12
❑ 374	David Ortiz CL	.75	.30
❑ 375	Carlos Zambrano CL	.30	.12
❑ 376	Jermaine Dye CL	.30	.12
❑ 377	Ken Griffey Jr. CL	1.25	.50
❑ 378	Victor Martinez CL	.30	.12
❑ 379	Todd Helton CL	.50	.20
❑ 380	Ivan Rodriguez CL	.50	.20
❑ 381	Miguel Cabrera CL	.50	.20
❑ 382	Lance Berkman CL	.30	.12
❑ 383	Mike Sweeney CL	.30	.12
❑ 384	Vladimir Guerrero CL	.75	.30
❑ 385	Derek Lowe CL	.30	.12
❑ 386	Bill Hall CL	.30	.12
❑ 387	Johan Santana CL	.50	.20
❑ 388	Carlos Beltran CL	.30	.12
❑ 389	Derek Jeter CL	2.00	.75
❑ 390	Nick Swisher CL	.30	.12
❑ 391	Ryan Howard CL	1.25	.50
❑ 392	Jason Bay CL	.30	.12
❑ 393	Trevor Hoffman CL	.30	.12
❑ 394	Omar Vizquel CL	.50	.20
❑ 395	Ichiro Suzuki CL	1.25	.50
❑ 396	Albert Pujols CL	1.50	.60
❑ 397	Carl Crawford CL	.30	.12
❑ 398	Mark Teixeira CL	.50	.20
❑ 399	Roy Halladay CL	.30	.12
❑ 400	Ryan Zimmerman CL	.75	.30
❑ 401	Mark Reynolds RC	2.50	1.00
❑ 402	Micah Owings (RC)	.60	.25
❑ 403	Jarrod Saltalamacchia (RC)	1.00	.40
❑ 406	Felix Pie (RC)	.60	.25
❑ 407	Mike Fontenot (RC)	.60	.25
❑ 408	John Danks RC	.60	.25
❑ 409	Josh Hamilton (RC)	1.50	.60
❑ 410	Homer Bailey (RC)	1.00	.40
❑ 411	Alejandro De Aza RC	1.00	.40
❑ 412	Matt Lindstrom (RC)	.60	.25
❑ 415	Billy Butler (RC)	1.00	.40
❑ 416	Brandon Wood (RC)	.60	.25
❑ 417	Andy LaRoche (RC)	.60	.25
❑ 419	Joe Smith RC	.60	.25
❑ 420	Carlos Gomez RC	1.00	.40
❑ 421	Tyler Clippard (RC)	1.00	.40
❑ 422	Matt DeSalvo (RC)	.60	.25
❑ 424	Kei Igawa RC	1.50	.60
❑ 425	Chase Wright RC	1.50	.60
❑ 426	Travis Buck (RC)	.60	.25
❑ 427	Zack Segovia (RC)	.60	.25
❑ 429	Elijah Dukes RC	1.00	.40
❑ 430	Akinori Iwamura RC	1.50	.60

1998 Fleer Tradition

❑	COMPLETE SET (600)	150.00	60.00
❑	COMPLETE SERIES 1 (350)	90.00	35.00
❑	COMPLETE SERIES 2 (250)	60.00	25.00
❑	COMMON CARD (1-600)	.30	.10
❑	COMMON GM (311-320)	.50	.20
❑	COMMON TT (321-340)	.60	.25
❑	COMMON UM (576-600)	.75	.30
❑ 1	Ken Griffey Jr.	1.25	.50
❑ 2	Derek Jeter	2.00	.75
❑ 3	Gerald Williams	.30	.10
❑ 4	Carlos Delgado	.30	.10
❑ 5	Nomar Garciaparra	1.25	.50
❑ 6	Gary Sheffield	.30	.10
❑ 7	Jeff King	.30	.10
❑ 8	Cal Ripken	2.50	1.00
❑ 9	Matt Williams	.30	.10
❑ 10	Chipper Jones	.75	.30
❑ 11	Chuck Knoblauch	.30	.10
❑ 12	Mark Grudzielanek	.30	.10
❑ 13	Edgardo Alfonzo	.30	.10
❑ 14	Andres Galarraga	.30	.10
❑ 15	Tim Salmon	.50	.20
❑ 16	Reggie Sanders	.30	.10
❑ 17	Tony Clark	.30	.10
❑ 18	Jason Kendall	.30	.10
❑ 19	Juan Gonzalez	.30	.10
❑ 20	Ben Grieve	.30	.10
❑ 21	Roger Clemens	1.50	.60
❑ 22	Raul Mondesi	.30	.10
❑ 23	Robin Ventura	.30	.10
❑ 24	Derrek Lee	.50	.20
❑ 25	Mark McGwire	2.00	.75
❑ 26	Luis Gonzalez	.30	.10
❑ 27	Kevin Brown	.50	.20
❑ 28	Kirk Rueter	.30	.10
❑ 29	Bobby Estalella	.30	.10
❑ 30	Shawn Green	.30	.10
❑ 31	Greg Maddux	1.25	.50
❑ 32	Jorge Velandia	.30	.10
❑ 33	Larry Walker	.30	.10
❑ 34	Joey Cora	.30	.10
❑ 35	Frank Thomas	.75	.30
❑ 36	Curtis King RC	.30	.10
❑ 37	Aaron Boone	.30	.10
❑ 38	Curt Schilling	.30	.10
❑ 39	Bruce Aven	.30	.10
❑ 40	Ben McDonald	.30	.10
❑ 41	Andy Ashby	.30	.10
❑ 42	Jason McDonald	.30	.10
❑ 43	Eric Davis	.30	.10
❑ 44	Mark Grace	.50	.20
❑ 45	Pedro Martinez	.50	.20
❑ 46	Lou Collier	.30	.10
❑ 47	Chan Ho Park	.30	.10
❑ 48	Shane Halter	.30	.10
❑ 49	Brian Hunter	.30	.10
❑ 50	Jeff Bagwell	.50	.20
❑ 51	Bernie Williams	.50	.20
❑ 52	J.T. Snow	.30	.10
❑ 53	Todd Greene	.30	.10
❑ 54	Shannon Stewart	.30	.10
❑ 55	Darren Bragg	.30	.10
❑ 56	Fernando Tatis	.30	.10
❑ 57	Darryl Kile	.30	.10
❑ 58	Chris Stynes	.30	.10
❑ 59	Javier Valentin	.30	.10
❑ 60	Brian McRae	.30	.10
❑ 61	Tom Evans	.30	.10
❑ 62	Randall Simon	.30	.10
❑ 63	Darrin Fletcher	.30	.10
❑ 64	Jaret Wright	.30	.10
❑ 65	Luis Ordaz	.30	.10
❑ 66	Jose Canseco	.50	.20
❑ 67	Edgar Renteria	.30	.10
❑ 68	Jay Buhner	.30	.10
❑ 69	Paul Konerko	.30	.10
❑ 70	Adrian Brown	.30	.10
❑ 71	Chris Carpenter	.30	.10
❑ 72	Mike Lieberthal	.30	.10
❑ 73	Dean Palmer	.30	.10
❑ 74	Jorge Fabregas	.30	.10
❑ 75	Stan Javier	.30	.10
❑ 76	Damion Easley	.30	.10
❑ 77	David Cone	.30	.10
❑ 78	Aaron Sele	.30	.10
❑ 79	Antonio Alfonseca	.30	.10
❑ 80	Bobby Jones	.30	.10
❑ 81	David Justice	.30	.10
❑ 82	Jeffrey Hammonds	.30	.10
❑ 83	Doug Glanville	.30	.10
❑ 84	Jason Dickson	.30	.10
❑ 85	Brad Radke	.30	.10
❑ 86	David Segui	.30	.10
❑ 87	Greg Vaughn	.30	.10

❑ 88 Mike Cather RC .30 .10
❑ 89 Alex Fernandez .30 .10
❑ 90 Billy Taylor .30 .10
❑ 91 Jason Schmidt .30 .10
❑ 92 Mike DeJean RC .40 .15
❑ 93 Domingo Cedeno .30 .10
❑ 94 Jeff Cirillo .30 .10
❑ 95 Manny Aybar RC .40 .15
❑ 96 Jaime Navarro .30 .10
❑ 97 Dennis Reyes .30 .10
❑ 98 Barry Larkin .50 .20
❑ 99 Troy O'Leary .30 .10
❑ 100 Alex Rodriguez 1.25 .50
❑ 101 Pat Hentgen .30 .10
❑ 102 Bubba Trammell .30 .10
❑ 103 Glendon Rusch .30 .10
❑ 104 Kenny Lofton .30 .10
❑ 105 Craig Biggio .50 .20
❑ 106 Kelvim Escobar .30 .10
❑ 107 Mark Kotsay .30 .10
❑ 108 Rondell White .30 .10
❑ 109 Darren Oliver .30 .10
❑ 110 Jim Thome .50 .20
❑ 111 Rich Becker .30 .10
❑ 112 Chad Curtis .30 .10
❑ 113 Dave Hollins .30 .10
❑ 114 Bill Mueller .30 .10
❑ 115 Antone Williamson .30 .10
❑ 116 Tony Womack .30 .10
❑ 117 Randy Myers .30 .10
❑ 118 Rico Brogna .30 .10
❑ 119 Pat Watkins .30 .10
❑ 120 Eli Marrero .30 .10
❑ 121 Jay Bell .30 .10
❑ 122 Kevin Tapani .30 .10
❑ 123 Todd Erdos RC .30 .10
❑ 124 Neifi Perez .30 .10
❑ 125 Todd Hundley .30 .10
❑ 126 Jeff Abbott .30 .10
❑ 127 Todd Zeile .30 .10
❑ 128 Travis Fryman .30 .10
❑ 129 Sandy Alomar Jr. .30 .10
❑ 130 Fred McGriff .50 .20
❑ 131 Richard Hidalgo .30 .10
❑ 132 Scott Spiezio .30 .10
❑ 133 John Valentin .30 .10
❑ 134 Quilvio Veras .30 .10
❑ 135 Mike Lansing .30 .10
❑ 136 Paul Molitor .30 .10
❑ 137 Randy Johnson .75 .30
❑ 138 Harold Baines .30 .10
❑ 139 Doug Jones .30 .10
❑ 140 Abraham Nunez .30 .10
❑ 141 Alan Benes .30 .10
❑ 142 Matt Perisho .30 .10
❑ 143 Chris Clemons .30 .10
❑ 144 Andy Pettitte .50 .20
❑ 145 Jason Giambi .30 .10
❑ 146 Moises Alou .30 .10
❑ 147 Chad Fox RC .30 .10
❑ 148 Felix Martinez .30 .10
❑ 149 Carlos Mendoza RC .30 .10
❑ 150 Scott Rolen .50 .20
❑ 151 Jose Cabrera RC .30 .10
❑ 152 Justin Thompson .30 .10
❑ 153 Ellis Burks .30 .10
❑ 154 Pokey Reese .30 .10
❑ 155 Bartolo Colon .30 .10
❑ 156 Ray Durham .30 .10
❑ 157 Ugueth Urbina .30 .10
❑ 158 Tom Goodwin .30 .10
❑ 159 Dave Dellucci RC .60 .25
❑ 160 Rod Beck .30 .10
❑ 161 Ramon Martinez .30 .10
❑ 162 Joe Carter .30 .10
❑ 163 Kevin Orie .30 .10
❑ 164 Trevor Hoffman .30 .10
❑ 165 Emil Brown .30 .10
❑ 166 Robb Nen .30 .10
❑ 167 Paul O'Neill .50 .20
❑ 168 Ryan Long .30 .10
❑ 169 Ray Lankford .30 .10
❑ 170 Ivan Rodriguez .50 .20
❑ 171 Rick Aguilera .30 .10
❑ 172 Deivi Cruz .30 .10
❑ 173 Ricky Bottalico .30 .10
❑ 174 Garret Anderson .30 .10
❑ 175 Jose Vizcaino .30 .10
❑ 176 Omar Vizquel .50 .20
❑ 177 Jeff Blauser .30 .10
❑ 178 Orlando Cabrera .30 .10
❑ 179 Russ Johnson .30 .10
❑ 180 Matt Stairs .30 .10
❑ 181 Will Cunnane .30 .10
❑ 182 Adam Riggs .30 .10
❑ 183 Matt Morris .30 .10
❑ 184 Mario Valdez .30 .10
❑ 185 Larry Sutton .30 .10
❑ 186 Marc Pisciotta RC .30 .10
❑ 187 Dan Wilson .30 .10
❑ 188 John Franco .30 .10
❑ 189 Darren Daulton .30 .10
❑ 190 Todd Helton .50 .20
❑ 191 Brady Anderson .30 .10
❑ 192 Ricardo Rincon .30 .10
❑ 193 Kevin Stocker .30 .10
❑ 194 Jose Valentin .30 .10
❑ 195 Ed Sprague .30 .10
❑ 196 Ryan McGuire .30 .10
❑ 197 Scott Eyre .30 .10
❑ 198 Steve Finley .30 .10
❑ 199 T.J. Mathews .30 .10
❑ 200 Mike Piazza 1.25 .50
❑ 201 Mark Wohlers .30 .10
❑ 202 Brian Giles .30 .10
❑ 203 Eduardo Perez .30 .10
❑ 204 Shigetoshi Hasegawa .30 .10
❑ 205 Mariano Rivera .75 .30
❑ 206 Jose Rosado .30 .10
❑ 207 Michael Coleman .30 .10
❑ 208 James Baldwin .30 .10
❑ 209 Russ Davis .30 .10
❑ 210 Billy Wagner .30 .10
❑ 211 Sammy Sosa .75 .30
❑ 212 Frank Catalanotto RC .60 .25
❑ 213 Delino DeShields .30 .10
❑ 214 John Olerud .30 .10
❑ 215 Heath Murray .30 .10
❑ 216 Jose Vidro .30 .10
❑ 217 Jim Edmonds .30 .10
❑ 218 Shawon Dunston .30 .10
❑ 219 Homer Bush .30 .10
❑ 220 Midre Cummings .30 .10
❑ 221 Tony Saunders .30 .10
❑ 222 Jeromy Burnitz .30 .10
❑ 223 Enrique Wilson .30 .10
❑ 224 Chili Davis .30 .10
❑ 225 Jerry DiPoto .30 .10
❑ 226 Dante Powell .30 .10
❑ 227 Javier Lopez .30 .10
❑ 228 Kevin Polcovich .30 .10
❑ 229 Deion Sanders .50 .20
❑ 230 Jimmy Key .30 .10
❑ 231 Rusty Greer .30 .10
❑ 232 Reggie Jefferson .30 .10
❑ 233 Ron Coomer .30 .10
❑ 234 Bobby Higginson .30 .10
❑ 235 Magglio Ordonez RC 2.50 1.00
❑ 236 Miguel Tejada .75 .30
❑ 237 Rick Gorecki .30 .10
❑ 238 Charles Johnson .30 .10
❑ 239 Lance Johnson .30 .10
❑ 240 Derek Bell .30 .10
❑ 241 Will Clark .50 .20
❑ 242 Brady Raggio .30 .10
❑ 243 Orel Hershiser .30 .10
❑ 244 Vladimir Guerrero .75 .30
❑ 245 John LeRoy .30 .10
❑ 246 Shawn Estes .30 .10
❑ 247 Brett Tomko .30 .10
❑ 248 Dave Nilsson .30 .10
❑ 249 Edgar Martinez .50 .20
❑ 250 Tony Gwynn 1.00 .40
❑ 251 Mark Bellhorn .30 .10
❑ 252 Jed Hansen .30 .10
❑ 253 Butch Huskey .30 .10
❑ 254 Eric Young .30 .10
❑ 255 Vinny Castilla .30 .10
❑ 256 Hideki Irabu .30 .10
❑ 257 Mike Cameron .30 .10
❑ 258 Juan Encarnacion .30 .10
❑ 259 Brian Rose .30 .10
❑ 260 Brad Ausmus .30 .10
❑ 261 Dan Serafini .30 .10
❑ 262 Willie Greene .30 .10
❑ 263 Troy Percival .30 .10
❑ 264 Jeff Wallace .30 .10
❑ 265 Richie Sexson .30 .10
❑ 266 Rafael Palmeiro .50 .20
❑ 267 Brad Fullmer .30 .10
❑ 268 Jeremi Gonzalez .30 .10
❑ 269 Rob Stanifer RC .30 .10
❑ 270 Mickey Morandini .30 .10
❑ 271 Andruw Jones .50 .20
❑ 272 Royce Clayton .30 .10
❑ 273 Takashi Kashiwada RC .40 .15
❑ 274 Steve Woodard .30 .10
❑ 275 Jose Cruz Jr. .30 .10
❑ 276 Keith Foulke .30 .10
❑ 277 Brad Rigby .30 .10
❑ 278 Tino Martinez .50 .20
❑ 279 Todd Jones .30 .10
❑ 280 John Wetteland .30 .10
❑ 281 Alex Gonzalez .30 .10
❑ 282 Ken Cloude .30 .10
❑ 283 Jose Guillen .30 .10
❑ 284 Danny Clyburn .30 .10
❑ 285 David Ortiz 1.00 .40
❑ 286 John Thomson .30 .10
❑ 287 Kevin Appier .30 .10
❑ 288 Ismael Valdes .30 .10
❑ 289 Gary DiSarcina .30 .10
❑ 290 Todd Dunwoody .30 .10
❑ 291 Wally Joyner .30 .10
❑ 292 Charles Nagy .30 .10
❑ 293 Jeff Shaw .30 .10
❑ 294 Kevin Millwood RC 1.00 .40
❑ 295 Rigo Beltran RC .30 .10
❑ 296 Jeff Frye .30 .10
❑ 297 Oscar Henriquez .30 .10
❑ 298 Mike Thurman .30 .10
❑ 299 Garrett Stephenson .30 .10
❑ 300 Barry Bonds 2.00 .75
❑ 301 Roger Clemens SH .75 .30
❑ 302 David Cone SH .30 .10
❑ 303 Hideki Irabu SH .30 .10
❑ 304 Randy Johnson SH .50 .20
❑ 305 Greg Maddux SH .75 .30
❑ 306 Pedro Martinez SH .50 .20
❑ 307 Mike Mussina SH .30 .10
❑ 308 Andy Pettitte SH .30 .10
❑ 309 Curt Schilling SH .30 .10
❑ 310 John Smoltz SH .30 .10
❑ 311 Roger Clemens GM 2.50 1.00
❑ 312 Jose Cruz JR. GM .50 .20
❑ 313 Nomar Garciaparra GM 2.00 .75
❑ 314 Ken Griffey Jr. GM 2.00 .75
❑ 315 Tony Gwynn GM 1.50 .60
❑ 316 Hideki Irabu GM .50 .20
❑ 317 Randy Johnson GM 1.25 .50
❑ 318 Mark McGwire GM 3.00 1.25
❑ 319 Curt Schilling GM .50 .20
❑ 320 Larry Walker GM .50 .20
❑ 321 Jeff Bagwell TT 1.00 .40
❑ 322 Albert Belle TT .60 .25
❑ 323 Barry Bonds TT 4.00 1.50
❑ 324 Jay Buhner TT .60 .25
❑ 325 Tony Clark TT .60 .25
❑ 326 Jose Cruz Jr. TT .60 .25
❑ 327 Andres Galarraga TT .60 .25
❑ 328 Juan Gonzalez TT .60 .25
❑ 329 Ken Griffey Jr. TT 2.50 1.00
❑ 330 Andruw Jones TT 1.00 .40
❑ 331 Tino Martinez TT 1.00 .40
❑ 332 Mark McGwire TT 4.00 1.50
❑ 333 Rafael Palmeiro TT 1.00 .40
❑ 334 Mike Piazza TT 2.50 1.00
❑ 335 Manny Ramirez TT 1.00 .40
❑ 336 Alex Rodriguez TT 2.50 1.00
❑ 337 Frank Thomas TT 1.50 .60
❑ 338 Jim Thome TT 1.00 .40
❑ 339 Mo Vaughn TT .60 .25
❑ 340 Larry Walker TT .60 .25
❑ 341 Jose Cruz Jr. CL .30 .10
❑ 342 Ken Griffey Jr. CL .75 .30
❑ 343 Derek Jeter CL 1.00 .40
❑ 344 Andruw Jones CL .30 .10
❑ 345 Chipper Jones CL .50 .20

❑ 346 Greg Maddux CL .75 .30
❑ 347 Mike Piazza CL .75 .30
❑ 348 Cal Ripken CL 1.25 .50
❑ 349 Alex Rodriguez CL .75 .30
❑ 350 Frank Thomas CL .50 .20
❑ 351 Mo Vaughn .30 .10
❑ 352 Andres Galarraga .30 .10
❑ 353 Roberto Alomar .50 .20
❑ 354 Darin Erstad .30 .10
❑ 355 Albert Belle .30 .10
❑ 356 Matt Williams .30 .10
❑ 357 Darryl Kile .30 .10
❑ 358 Kenny Lofton .30 .10
❑ 359 Orel Hershiser .30 .10
❑ 360 Bob Abreu .30 .10
❑ 361 Chris Widger .30 .10
❑ 362 Glenallen Hill .30 .10
❑ 363 Chili Davis .30 .10
❑ 364 Kevin Brown .50 .20
❑ 365 Marquis Grissom .30 .10
❑ 366 Livan Hernandez .30 .10
❑ 367 Moises Alou .30 .10
❑ 368 Matt Lawton .30 .10
❑ 369 Rey Ordonez .30 .10
❑ 370 Kenny Rogers .30 .10
❑ 371 Lee Stevens .30 .10
❑ 372 Wade Boggs .50 .20
❑ 373 Luis Gonzalez .30 .10
❑ 374 Jeff Conine .30 .10
❑ 375 Esteban Loaiza .30 .10
❑ 376 Jose Canseco .50 .20
❑ 377 Henry Rodriguez .30 .10
❑ 378 Dave Burba .30 .10
❑ 379 Todd Hollandsworth .30 .10
❑ 380 Ron Gant .30 .10
❑ 381 Pedro Martinez .50 .20
❑ 382 Ryan Klesko .30 .10
❑ 383 Derrek Lee .50 .20
❑ 384 Doug Glanville .30 .10
❑ 385 David Wells .30 .10
❑ 386 Ken Caminiti .30 .10
❑ 387 Damon Hollins .30 .10
❑ 388 Manny Ramirez .50 .20
❑ 389 Mike Mussina .50 .20
❑ 390 Jay Bell .30 .10
❑ 391 Mike Piazza 1.25 .50
❑ 392 Mike Lansing .30 .10
❑ 393 Mike Hampton .30 .10
❑ 394 Geoff Jenkins .30 .10
❑ 395 Jimmy Haynes .30 .10
❑ 396 Scott Servais .30 .10
❑ 397 Kent Mercker .30 .10
❑ 398 Jeff Kent .30 .10
❑ 399 Kevin Elster .30 .10
❑ 400 Masato Yoshii RC .40 .15
❑ 401 Jose Vizcaino .30 .10
❑ 402 Javier Martinez RC .30 .10
❑ 403 David Segui .30 .10
❑ 404 Tony Saunders .30 .10
❑ 405 Karim Garcia .30 .10
❑ 406 Armando Benitez .30 .10
❑ 407 Joe Randa .30 .10
❑ 408 Vic Darensbourg .30 .10
❑ 409 Sean Casey .30 .10
❑ 410 Eric Milton .30 .10
❑ 411 Trey Moore .30 .10
❑ 412 Mike Stanley .30 .10
❑ 413 Tom Gordon .30 .10
❑ 414 Hal Morris .30 .10
❑ 415 Braden Looper .30 .10
❑ 416 Mike Kelly .30 .10
❑ 417 John Smoltz .50 .20
❑ 418 Roger Cedeno .30 .10
❑ 419 Al Leiter .30 .10
❑ 420 Chuck Knoblauch .30 .10
❑ 421 Felix Rodriguez .30 .10
❑ 422 Bip Roberts .30 .10
❑ 423 Ken Hill .30 .10
❑ 424 Jermaine Allensworth .30 .10
❑ 425 Esteban Yan RC .40 .15
❑ 426 Scott Karl .30 .10
❑ 427 Sean Berry .30 .10
❑ 428 Rafael Medina .30 .10
❑ 429 Javier Vazquez .30 .10
❑ 430 Rickey Henderson .75 .30
❑ 431 Adam Butler .30 .10
❑ 432 Todd Stottlemyre .30 .10
❑ 433 Yamil Benitez .30 .10
❑ 434 Sterling Hitchcock .30 .10
❑ 435 Paul Sorrento .30 .10
❑ 436 Bobby Ayala .30 .10
❑ 437 Tim Raines .30 .10
❑ 438 Chris Hoiles .30 .10
❑ 439 Rod Beck .30 .10
❑ 440 Donnie Sadler .30 .10
❑ 441 Charles Johnson .30 .10
❑ 442 Russ Ortiz .30 .10
❑ 443 Pedro Astacio .30 .10
❑ 444 Wilson Alvarez .30 .10
❑ 445 Mike Blowers .30 .10
❑ 446 Todd Zeile .30 .10
❑ 447 Mel Rojas .30 .10
❑ 448 F.P. Santangelo .30 .10
❑ 449 Dmitri Young .30 .10
❑ 450 Brian Anderson .30 .10
❑ 451 Cecil Fielder .30 .10
❑ 452 Roberto Hernandez .30 .10
❑ 453 Todd Walker .30 .10
❑ 454 Tyler Green .30 .10
❑ 455 Jorge Posada .50 .20
❑ 456 Geronimo Berroa .30 .10
❑ 457 Jose Silva .30 .10
❑ 458 Bobby Bonilla .30 .10
❑ 459 Walt Weiss .30 .10
❑ 460 Darren Dreifort .30 .10
❑ 461 B.J. Surhoff .30 .10
❑ 462 Quinton McCracken .30 .10
❑ 463 Derek Lowe .30 .10
❑ 464 Jorge Fabregas .30 .10
❑ 465 Joey Hamilton .30 .10
❑ 466 Brian Jordan .30 .10
❑ 467 Allen Watson .30 .10
❑ 468 John Jaha .30 .10
❑ 469 Heathcliff Slocumb .30 .10
❑ 470 Gregg Jefferies .30 .10
❑ 471 Scott Brosius .30 .10
❑ 472 Chad Ogea .30 .10
❑ 473 A.J. Hinch .30 .10
❑ 474 Bobby Smith .30 .10
❑ 475 Brian Moehler .30 .10
❑ 476 DaRond Stovall .30 .10
❑ 477 Kevin Young .30 .10
❑ 478 Jeff Suppan .30 .10
❑ 479 Marty Cordova .30 .10
❑ 480 John Halama RC .40 .15
❑ 481 Bubba Trammell .30 .10
❑ 482 Mike Caruso .30 .10
❑ 483 Eric Karros .30 .10
❑ 484 Jamey Wright .30 .10
❑ 485 Mike Sweeney .30 .10
❑ 486 Aaron Sele .30 .10
❑ 487 Cliff Floyd .30 .10
❑ 488 Jeff Brantley .30 .10
❑ 489 Jim Leyritz .30 .10
❑ 490 Denny Neagle .30 .10
❑ 491 Travis Fryman .30 .10
❑ 492 Carlos Baerga .30 .10
❑ 493 Eddie Taubensee .30 .10
❑ 494 Darryl Strawberry .30 .10
❑ 495 Brian Johnson .30 .10
❑ 496 Randy Myers .30 .10
❑ 497 Jeff Blauser .30 .10
❑ 498 Jason Wood .30 .10
❑ 499 Rolando Arrojo RC .40 .15
❑ 500 Johnny Damon .50 .20
❑ 501 Jose Mercedes .30 .10
❑ 502 Tony Batista .30 .10
❑ 503 Mike Piazza Mets 1.25 .50
❑ 504 Hideo Nomo .75 .30
❑ 505 Chris Gomez .30 .10
❑ 506 Jesus Sanchez RC .30 .10
❑ 507 Al Martin .30 .10
❑ 508 Brian Edmondson .30 .10
❑ 509 Joe Girardi .30 .10
❑ 510 Shayne Bennett .30 .10
❑ 511 Joe Carter .30 .10
❑ 512 Dave Mlicki .30 .10
❑ 513 Rich Butler RC .30 .10
❑ 514 Dennis Eckersley .30 .10
❑ 515 Travis Lee .30 .10
❑ 516 John Mabry .30 .10
❑ 517 Jose Mesa .30 .10
❑ 518 Phil Nevin .30 .10
❑ 519 Raul Casanova .30 .10
❑ 520 Mike Fetters .30 .10
❑ 521 Gary Sheffield .30 .10
❑ 522 Terry Steinbach .30 .10
❑ 523 Steve Trachsel .30 .10
❑ 524 Josh Booty .30 .10
❑ 525 Darryl Hamilton .30 .10
❑ 526 Mark McLemore .30 .10
❑ 527 Kevin Stocker .30 .10
❑ 528 Bret Boone .30 .10
❑ 529 Shane Andrews .30 .10
❑ 530 Robb Nen .30 .10
❑ 531 Carl Everett .30 .10
❑ 532 LaTroy Hawkins .30 .10
❑ 533 Fernando Vina .30 .10
❑ 534 Michael Tucker .30 .10
❑ 535 Mark Langston .30 .10
❑ 536 Mickey Mantle 5.00 2.00
❑ 537 Bernard Gilkey .30 .10
❑ 538 Francisco Cordova .30 .10
❑ 539 Mike Bordick .30 .10
❑ 540 Fred McGriff .50 .20
❑ 541 Cliff Politte .30 .10
❑ 542 Jason Varitek .75 .30
❑ 543 Shawon Dunston .30 .10
❑ 544 Brian Meadows .30 .10
❑ 545 Pat Meares .30 .10
❑ 546 Carlos Perez .30 .10
❑ 547 Desi Relaford .30 .10
❑ 548 Antonio Osuna .30 .10
❑ 549 Devon White .30 .10
❑ 550 Sean Runyan .30 .10
❑ 551 Mickey Morandini .30 .10
❑ 552 Dave Martinez .30 .10
❑ 553 Jeff Fassero .30 .10
❑ 554 Ryan Jackson RC .30 .10
❑ 555 Stan Javier .30 .10
❑ 556 Jaime Navarro .30 .10
❑ 557 Jose Offerman .30 .10
❑ 558 Mike Lowell RC 1.50 .60
❑ 559 Darrin Fletcher .30 .10
❑ 560 Mark Lewis .30 .10
❑ 561 Dante Bichette .30 .10
❑ 562 Chuck Finley .30 .10
❑ 563 Kerry Wood .40 .15
❑ 564 Andy Benes .30 .10
❑ 565 Freddy Garcia .30 .10
❑ 566 Tom Glavine .50 .20
❑ 567 Jon Nunnally .30 .10
❑ 568 Miguel Cairo .30 .10
❑ 569 Shane Reynolds .30 .10
❑ 570 Roberto Kelly .30 .10
❑ 571 Jose Cruz Jr. CL .30 .10
❑ 572 Ken Griffey Jr. CL .75 .30
❑ 573 Mark McGwire CL 1.00 .40
❑ 574 Cal Ripken CL 1.25 .50
❑ 575 Frank Thomas CL .50 .20
❑ 576 Jeff Bagwell UM 1.25 .50
❑ 577 Barry Bonds UM 5.00 2.00
❑ 578 Tony Clark UM .75 .30
❑ 579 Roger Clemens UM 4.00 1.50
❑ 580 Jose Cruz Jr. UM .75 .30
❑ 581 Nomar Garciaparra UM 3.00 1.25
❑ 582 Juan Gonzalez UM .75 .30
❑ 583 Ben Grieve UM .75 .30
❑ 584 Ken Griffey Jr. UM 3.00 1.25
❑ 585 Tony Gwynn UM 2.50 1.00
❑ 586 Derek Jeter UM 5.00 2.00
❑ 587 Randy Johnson UM 2.00 .75
❑ 588 Chipper Jones UM 2.00 .75
❑ 589 Greg Maddux UM 3.00 1.25
❑ 590 Mark McGwire UM 5.00 2.00
❑ 591 Andy Pettitte UM 1.25 .50
❑ 592 Paul Molitor UM .75 .30
❑ 593 Cal Ripken UM 6.00 2.50
❑ 594 Alex Rodriguez UM 3.00 1.25
❑ 595 Scott Rolen UM 1.25 .50
❑ 596 Curt Schilling UM .75 .30
❑ 597 Frank Thomas UM 2.00 .75
❑ 598 Jim Thome UM 1.25 .50
❑ 599 Larry Walker UM .75 .30
❑ 600 Bernie Williams UM 1.25 .50
❑ P100 Alex Rodriguez Promo 1.50 .60

1999 Fleer Tradition

❑	COMPLETE SET (600)	60.00	30.00
❑ 1	Mark McGwire	2.00	.75
❑ 2	Sammy Sosa	.75	.30
❑ 3	Ken Griffey Jr.	1.25	.50
❑ 4	Kerry Wood	.30	.10
❑ 5	Derek Jeter	2.00	.75
❑ 6	Stan Musial	1.50	.60
❑ 7	J.D. Drew	.30	.10
❑ 8	Cal Ripken	2.50	1.00
❑ 9	Alex Rodriguez	1.25	.50
❑ 10	Travis Lee	.20	.07
❑ 11	Andres Galarraga	.30	.10
❑ 12	Nomar Garciaparra	1.25	.50
❑ 13	Albert Belle	.30	.10
❑ 14	Barry Larkin	.50	.20
❑ 15	Dante Bichette	.30	.10
❑ 16	Tony Clark	.20	.07
❑ 17	Moises Alou	.30	.10
❑ 18	Rafael Palmeiro	.50	.20
❑ 19	Raul Mondesi	.30	.10
❑ 20	Vladimir Guerrero	.75	.30
❑ 21	John Olerud	.30	.10
❑ 22	Bernie Williams	.50	.20
❑ 23	Ben Grieve	.20	.07
❑ 24	Scott Rolen	.50	.20
❑ 25	Jeromy Burnitz	.30	.10
❑ 26	Ken Caminiti	.30	.10
❑ 27	Barry Bonds	2.00	.75
❑ 28	Todd Helton	.50	.20
❑ 29	Juan Gonzalez	.30	.10
❑ 30	Roger Clemens	1.50	.60
❑ 31	Andruw Jones	.50	.20
❑ 32	Mo Vaughn	.30	.10
❑ 33	Larry Walker	.30	.10
❑ 34	Frank Thomas	.75	.30
❑ 35	Manny Ramirez	.50	.20
❑ 36	Randy Johnson	.75	.30
❑ 37	Vinny Castilla	.30	.10
❑ 38	Juan Encarnacion	.20	.07
❑ 39	Jeff Bagwell	.50	.20
❑ 40	Gary Sheffield	.30	.10
❑ 41	Mike Piazza	1.25	.50
❑ 42	Richie Sexson	.30	.10
❑ 43	Tony Gwynn	1.00	.40
❑ 44	Chipper Jones	.75	.30
❑ 45	Jim Thome	.50	.20
❑ 46	Craig Biggio	.50	.20
❑ 47	Carlos Delgado	.30	.10
❑ 48	Greg Vaughn	.20	.07
❑ 49	Greg Maddux	1.25	.50
❑ 50	Troy Glaus	.50	.20
❑ 51	Roberto Alomar	.50	.20
❑ 52	Dennis Eckersley	.30	.10
❑ 53	Mike Caruso	.20	.07
❑ 54	Bruce Chen	.20	.07
❑ 55	Aaron Boone	.30	.10
❑ 56	Bartolo Colon	.30	.10
❑ 57	Derrick Gibson	.20	.07
❑ 58	Brian Anderson	.20	.07
❑ 59	Gabe Alvarez	.20	.07
❑ 60	Todd Dunwoody	.20	.07
❑ 61	Rod Beck	.20	.07
❑ 62	Derek Bell	.20	.07
❑ 63	Francisco Cordova	.20	.07
❑ 64	Johnny Damon	.50	.20
❑ 65	Adrian Beltre	.30	.10
❑ 66	Garret Anderson	.30	.10
❑ 67	Armando Benitez	.20	.07
❑ 68	Edgardo Alfonzo	.20	.07
❑ 69	Ryan Bradley	.20	.07
❑ 70	Eric Chavez	.30	.10
❑ 71	Bobby Abreu	.30	.10
❑ 72	Andy Ashby	.20	.07
❑ 73	Ellis Burks	.30	.10
❑ 74	Jeff Cirillo	.20	.07
❑ 75	Jay Buhner	.30	.10
❑ 76	Ron Gant	.30	.10
❑ 77	Rolando Arrojo	.20	.07
❑ 78	Will Clark	.50	.20
❑ 79	Chris Carpenter	.30	.10
❑ 80	Jim Edmonds	.30	.10
❑ 81	Tony Batista	.20	.07
❑ 82	Shane Andrews	.20	.07
❑ 83	Mark DeRosa	.20	.07
❑ 84	Brady Anderson	.30	.10
❑ 85	Tom Gordon	.20	.07
❑ 86	Brant Brown	.20	.07
❑ 87	Ray Durham	.30	.10
❑ 88	Ron Coomer	.20	.07
❑ 89	Bret Boone	.30	.10
❑ 90	Travis Fryman	.30	.10
❑ 91	Darryl Kile	.30	.10
❑ 92	Paul Bako	.20	.07
❑ 93	Cliff Floyd	.30	.10
❑ 94	Scott Elarton	.20	.07
❑ 95	Jeremy Giambi	.20	.07
❑ 96	Darren Dreifort	.20	.07
❑ 97	Marquis Grissom	.30	.10
❑ 98	Marty Cordova	.20	.07
❑ 99	Fernando Seguignol	.20	.07
❑ 100	Orlando Hernandez	.30	.10
❑ 101	Jose Cruz Jr.	.20	.07
❑ 102	Jason Giambi	.30	.10
❑ 103	Damion Easley	.20	.07
❑ 104	Freddy Garcia	.20	.07
❑ 105	Marlon Anderson	.20	.07
❑ 106	Kevin Brown	.50	.20
❑ 107	Joe Carter	.30	.10
❑ 108	Russ Davis	.20	.07
❑ 109	Brian Jordan	.30	.10
❑ 110	Wade Boggs	.50	.20
❑ 111	Tom Goodwin	.20	.07
❑ 112	Scott Brosius	.30	.10
❑ 113	Darin Erstad	.30	.10
❑ 114	Jay Bell	.30	.10
❑ 115	Tom Glavine	.50	.20
❑ 116	Pedro Martinez	.50	.20
❑ 117	Mark Grace	.50	.20
❑ 118	Russ Ortiz	.20	.07
❑ 119	Magglio Ordonez	.30	.10
❑ 120	Sean Casey	.30	.10
❑ 121	Rafael Roque RC	.20	.07
❑ 122	Brian Giles	.30	.10
❑ 123	Mike Lansing	.20	.07
❑ 124	David Cone	.30	.10
❑ 125	Alex Gonzalez	.20	.07
❑ 126	Carl Everett	.30	.10
❑ 127	Jeff King	.20	.07
❑ 128	Charles Johnson	.30	.10
❑ 129	Geoff Jenkins	.20	.07
❑ 130	Corey Koskie	.20	.07
❑ 131	Brad Fullmer	.20	.07
❑ 132	Al Leiter	.30	.10
❑ 133	Rickey Henderson	.75	.30
❑ 134	Rico Brogna	.20	.07
❑ 135	Jose Guillen	.30	.10
❑ 136	Matt Clement	.30	.10
❑ 137	Carlos Guillen	.30	.10
❑ 138	Orel Hershiser	.30	.10
❑ 139	Ray Lankford	.30	.10
❑ 140	Miguel Cairo	.20	.07
❑ 141	Chuck Finley	.30	.10
❑ 142	Rusty Greer	.30	.10
❑ 143	Kelvim Escobar	.20	.07
❑ 144	Ryan Klesko	.30	.10
❑ 145	Andy Benes	.20	.07
❑ 146	Eric Davis	.30	.10
❑ 147	David Wells	.30	.10
❑ 148	Trot Nixon	.30	.10
❑ 149	Jose Hernandez	.20	.07
❑ 150	Mark Johnson	.20	.07
❑ 151	Mike Frank	.20	.07
❑ 152	Joey Hamilton	.20	.07
❑ 153	David Justice	.30	.10
❑ 154	Mike Mussina	.50	.20
❑ 155	Neifi Perez	.20	.07
❑ 156	Luis Gonzalez	.30	.10
❑ 157	Livan Hernandez	.30	.10
❑ 158	Dermal Brown	.20	.07
❑ 159	Jose Lima	.20	.07
❑ 160	Eric Karros	.30	.10
❑ 161	Ronnie Belliard	.20	.07
❑ 162	Matt Lawton	.20	.07
❑ 163	Dustin Hermanson	.20	.07
❑ 164	Brian McRae	.20	.07
❑ 165	Mike Kinkade	.20	.07
❑ 166	A.J. Hinch	.20	.07
❑ 167	Doug Glanville	.20	.07
❑ 168	Hideo Nomo	.75	.30
❑ 169	Jason Kendall	.30	.10
❑ 170	Steve Finley	.30	.10
❑ 171	Jeff Kent	.30	.10
❑ 172	Ben Davis	.20	.07
❑ 173	Edgar Martinez	.50	.20
❑ 174	Eli Marrero	.20	.07
❑ 175	Quinton McCracken	.20	.07
❑ 176	Rick Helling	.20	.07
❑ 177	Tom Evans	.20	.07
❑ 178	Carl Pavano	.30	.10
❑ 179	Todd Greene	.20	.07
❑ 180	Omar Daal	.20	.07
❑ 181	George Lombard	.20	.07
❑ 182	Ryan Minor	.20	.07
❑ 183	Troy O'Leary	.20	.07
❑ 184	Robb Nen	.30	.10
❑ 185	Mickey Morandini	.20	.07
❑ 186	Robin Ventura	.30	.10
❑ 187	Pete Harnisch	.20	.07
❑ 188	Kenny Lofton	.30	.10
❑ 189	Eric Milton	.20	.07
❑ 190	Bobby Higginson	.30	.10
❑ 191	Jamie Moyer	.30	.10
❑ 192	Mark Kotsay	.30	.10
❑ 193	Shane Reynolds	.20	.07
❑ 194	Carlos Febles	.20	.07
❑ 195	Jeff Kubenka	.20	.07
❑ 196	Chuck Knoblauch	.30	.10
❑ 197	Kenny Rogers	.30	.10
❑ 198	Bill Mueller	.30	.10
❑ 199	Shane Monahan	.20	.07
❑ 200	Matt Morris	.30	.10
❑ 201	Fred McGriff	.50	.20
❑ 202	Ivan Rodriguez	.50	.20
❑ 203	Kevin Witt	.20	.07
❑ 204	Troy Percival	.30	.10
❑ 205	David Dellucci	.20	.07
❑ 206	Kevin Millwood	.30	.10
❑ 207	Jerry Hairston Jr.	.20	.07
❑ 208	Mike Stanley	.20	.07
❑ 209	Henry Rodriguez	.20	.07
❑ 210	Trevor Hoffman	.30	.10
❑ 211	Craig Wilson	.20	.07
❑ 212	Reggie Sanders	.30	.10
❑ 213	Carlton Loewer	.20	.07
❑ 214	Omar Vizquel	.50	.20
❑ 215	Gabe Kapler	.30	.10
❑ 216	Derrek Lee	.50	.20
❑ 217	Billy Wagner	.30	.10
❑ 218	Dean Palmer	.30	.10
❑ 219	Chan Ho Park	.30	.10
❑ 220	Fernando Vina	.20	.07
❑ 221	Roy Halladay	.30	.10
❑ 222	Paul Molitor	.30	.10
❑ 223	Ugueth Urbina	.20	.07
❑ 224	Rey Ordonez	.20	.07
❑ 225	Ricky Ledee	.20	.07
❑ 226	Scott Spiezio	.20	.07
❑ 227	Wendell Magee	.20	.07
❑ 228	Aramis Ramirez	.30	.10
❑ 229	Brian Simmons	.20	.07
❑ 230	Fernando Tatis	.20	.07
❑ 231	Bobby Smith	.20	.07
❑ 232	Aaron Sele	.20	.07
❑ 233	Shawn Green	.30	.10
❑ 234	Mariano Rivera	.75	.30
❑ 235	Tim Salmon	.50	.20
❑ 236	Andy Fox	.20	.07
❑ 237	Denny Neagle	.20	.07

❑ 238 John Valentin .20 .07
❑ 239 Kevin Tapani .20 .07
❑ 240 Paul Konerko .30 .10
❑ 241 Robert Fick .20 .07
❑ 242 Edgar Renteria .30 .10
❑ 243 Brett Tomko .20 .07
❑ 244 Daryle Ward .20 .07
❑ 245 Carlos Beltran .50 .20
❑ 246 Angel Pena .20 .07
❑ 247 Steve Woodard .20 .07
❑ 248 David Ortiz .75 .30
❑ 249 Justin Thompson .20 .07
❑ 250 Rondell White .30 .10
❑ 251 Jaret Wright .20 .07
❑ 252 Ed Sprague .20 .07
❑ 253 Jay Payton .20 .07
❑ 254 Mike Lowell .30 .10
❑ 255 Orlando Cabrera .30 .10
❑ 256 Jason Schmidt .30 .10
❑ 257 David Segui .20 .07
❑ 258 Paul Sorrento .20 .07
❑ 259 John Wetteland .30 .10
❑ 260 Devon White .30 .10
❑ 261 Odalis Perez .20 .07
❑ 262 Calvin Pickering .20 .07
❑ 263 Tyler Green .20 .07
❑ 264 Preston Wilson .30 .10
❑ 265 Brad Radke .30 .10
❑ 266 Walt Weiss .20 .07
❑ 267 Tim Young .20 .07
❑ 268 Tino Martinez .50 .20
❑ 269 Matt Stairs .20 .07
❑ 270 Curt Schilling .30 .10
❑ 271 Tony Womack .20 .07
❑ 272 Ismael Valdes .20 .07
❑ 273 Wally Joyner .30 .10
❑ 274 Armando Rios .20 .07
❑ 275 Andy Pettitte .50 .20
❑ 276 Bubba Trammell .20 .07
❑ 277 Todd Zeile .30 .10
❑ 278 Shannon Stewart .30 .10
❑ 279 Matt Williams .30 .10
❑ 280 John Rocker .30 .10
❑ 281 B.J. Surhoff .30 .10
❑ 282 Eric Young .20 .07
❑ 283 Dmitri Young .30 .10
❑ 284 John Smoltz .50 .20
❑ 285 Todd Walker .20 .07
❑ 286 Paul O'Neill .50 .20
❑ 287 Blake Stein .20 .07
❑ 288 Kevin Young .30 .10
❑ 289 Quilvio Veras .20 .07
❑ 290 Kirk Rueter .20 .07
❑ 291 Randy Winn .20 .07
❑ 292 Miguel Tejada .30 .10
❑ 293 J.T. Snow .30 .10
❑ 294 Michael Tucker .20 .07
❑ 295 Jay Tessmer .20 .07
❑ 296 Scott Erickson .20 .07
❑ 297 Tim Wakefield .30 .10
❑ 298 Jeff Abbott .20 .07
❑ 299 Eddie Taubensee .20 .07
❑ 300 Darryl Hamilton .20 .07
❑ 301 Kevin Orie .20 .07
❑ 302 Jose Offerman .20 .07
❑ 303 Scott Karl .20 .07
❑ 304 Chris Widger .20 .07
❑ 305 Todd Hundley .20 .07
❑ 306 Desi Relaford .20 .07
❑ 307 Sterling Hitchcock .20 .07
❑ 308 Delino DeShields .20 .07
❑ 309 Alex Gonzalez .20 .07
❑ 310 Justin Baughman .20 .07
❑ 311 Jamey Wright .20 .07
❑ 312 Wes Helms .20 .07
❑ 313 Dante Powell .20 .07
❑ 314 Jim Abbott .50 .20
❑ 315 Manny Alexander .20 .07
❑ 316 Harold Baines .30 .10
❑ 317 Danny Graves .20 .07
❑ 318 Sandy Alomar Jr. .20 .07
❑ 319 Pedro Astacio .20 .07
❑ 320 Jermaine Allensworth .20 .07
❑ 321 Matt Anderson .20 .07
❑ 322 Chad Curtis .20 .07
❑ 323 Antonio Osuna .20 .07
❑ 324 Brad Ausmus .30 .10
❑ 325 Steve Trachsel .20 .07
❑ 326 Mike Blowers .20 .07
❑ 327 Brian Bohanon .20 .07
❑ 328 Chris Gomez .20 .07
❑ 329 Valerio De Los Santos .20 .07
❑ 330 Rich Aurilia .20 .07
❑ 331 Michael Barrett .20 .07
❑ 332 Rick Aguilera .20 .07
❑ 333 Adrian Brown .20 .07
❑ 334 Bill Spiers .20 .07
❑ 335 Matt Beech .20 .07
❑ 336 David Bell .20 .07
❑ 337 Juan Acevedo .20 .07
❑ 338 Jose Canseco .50 .20
❑ 339 Wilson Alvarez .20 .07
❑ 340 Luis Alicea .20 .07
❑ 341 Jason Dickson .20 .07
❑ 342 Mike Bordick .20 .07
❑ 343 Ben Ford .20 .07
❑ 344 Javy Lopez .30 .10
❑ 345 Jason Christiansen .20 .07
❑ 346 Darren Bragg .20 .07
❑ 347 Doug Brocail .20 .07
❑ 348 Jeff Blauser .20 .07
❑ 349 James Baldwin .20 .07
❑ 350 Jeffrey Hammonds .20 .07
❑ 351 Ricky Bottalico .20 .07
❑ 352 Russ Branyan .20 .07
❑ 353 Mark Brownson RC .20 .07
❑ 354 Dave Berg .20 .07
❑ 355 Sean Bergman .20 .07
❑ 356 Jeff Conine .30 .10
❑ 357 Shayne Bennett .20 .07
❑ 358 Bobby Bonilla .30 .10
❑ 359 Bob Wickman .20 .07
❑ 360 Carlos Baerga .20 .07
❑ 361 Chris Fussell .20 .07
❑ 362 Chili Davis .30 .10
❑ 363 Jerry Spradlin .20 .07
❑ 364 Carlos Hernandez .20 .07
❑ 365 Roberto Hernandez .20 .07
❑ 366 Marvin Benard .20 .07
❑ 367 Ken Cloude .20 .07
❑ 368 Tony Fernandez .20 .07
❑ 369 John Burkett .20 .07
❑ 370 Gary DiSarcina .20 .07
❑ 371 Alan Benes .20 .07
❑ 372 Karim Garcia .20 .07
❑ 373 Carlos Perez .20 .07
❑ 374 Damon Buford .20 .07
❑ 375 Mark Clark .20 .07
❑ 376 Edgard Clemente .20 .07
❑ 377 Chad Bradford RC .20 .07
❑ 378 Frank Catalanotto .20 .07
❑ 379 Vic Darensbourg .20 .07
❑ 380 Sean Berry .20 .07
❑ 381 Dave Burba .20 .07
❑ 382 Sal Fasano .20 .07
❑ 383 Steve Parris .20 .07
❑ 384 Roger Cedeno .20 .07
❑ 385 Chad Fox .20 .07
❑ 386 Wilton Guerrero .20 .07
❑ 387 Dennis Cook .20 .07
❑ 388 Joe Girardi .20 .07
❑ 389 LaTroy Hawkins .20 .07
❑ 390 Ryan Christenson .20 .07
❑ 391 Paul Byrd .20 .07
❑ 392 Lou Collier .20 .07
❑ 393 Jeff Fassero .20 .07
❑ 394 Jim Leyritz .20 .07
❑ 395 Shawn Estes .20 .07
❑ 396 Mike Kelly .20 .07
❑ 397 Rich Croushore .20 .07
❑ 398 Royce Clayton .20 .07
❑ 399 Rudy Seanez .20 .07
❑ 400 Darrin Fletcher .20 .07
❑ 401 Shigetoshi Hasegawa .30 .10
❑ 402 Bernard Gilkey .20 .07
❑ 403 Juan Guzman .20 .07
❑ 404 Jeff Frye .20 .07
❑ 405 Donovan Osborne .20 .07
❑ 406 Alex Fernandez .20 .07
❑ 407 Gary Gaetti .20 .07
❑ 408 Dan Miceli .20 .07
❑ 409 Mike Cameron .20 .07
❑ 410 Mike Remlinger .20 .07
❑ 411 Joey Cora .20 .07
❑ 412 Mark Gardner .20 .07
❑ 413 Aaron Ledesma .20 .07
❑ 414 Jerry Dipoto .20 .07
❑ 415 Ricky Gutierrez .20 .07
❑ 416 John Franco .30 .10
❑ 417 Mendy Lopez .20 .07
❑ 418 Hideki Irabu .20 .07
❑ 419 Mark Grudzielanek .20 .07
❑ 420 Bobby Hughes .20 .07
❑ 421 Pat Meares .20 .07
❑ 422 Jimmy Haynes .20 .07
❑ 423 Bob Henley .20 .07
❑ 424 Bobby Estalella .20 .07
❑ 425 Jon Lieber .20 .07
❑ 426 Giomar Guevara RC .20 .07
❑ 427 Jose Jimenez .20 .07
❑ 428 Deivi Cruz .20 .07
❑ 429 Jonathan Johnson .20 .07
❑ 430 Ken Hill .20 .07
❑ 431 Craig Grebeck .20 .07
❑ 432 Jose Rosado .20 .07
❑ 433 Danny Klassen .20 .07
❑ 434 Bobby Howry .20 .07
❑ 435 Gerald Williams .20 .07
❑ 436 Omar Olivares .20 .07
❑ 437 Chris Hoiles .20 .07
❑ 438 Seth Greisinger .20 .07
❑ 439 Scott Hatteberg .20 .07
❑ 440 Jeremi Gonzalez .20 .07
❑ 441 Wil Cordero .20 .07
❑ 442 Jeff Montgomery .20 .07
❑ 443 Chris Stynes .20 .07
❑ 444 Tony Saunders .20 .07
❑ 445 Einar Diaz .20 .07
❑ 446 Lariel Gonzalez .20 .07
❑ 447 Ryan Jackson .20 .07
❑ 448 Mike Hampton .30 .10
❑ 449 Todd Hollandsworth .20 .07
❑ 450 Gabe White .20 .07
❑ 451 John Jaha .20 .07
❑ 452 Bret Saberhagen .30 .10
❑ 453 Otis Nixon .20 .07
❑ 454 Steve Kline .20 .07
❑ 455 Butch Huskey .20 .07
❑ 456 Mike Jerzembeck .20 .07
❑ 457 Wayne Gomes .20 .07
❑ 458 Mike Macfarlane .20 .07
❑ 459 Jesus Sanchez .20 .07
❑ 460 Al Martin .20 .07
❑ 461 Dwight Gooden .30 .10
❑ 462 Ruben Rivera .20 .07
❑ 463 Pat Hentgen .20 .07
❑ 464 Jose Valentin .20 .07
❑ 465 Vladimir Nunez .20 .07
❑ 466 Charlie Hayes .20 .07
❑ 467 Jay Powell .20 .07
❑ 468 Raul Ibanez .20 .07
❑ 469 Kent Mercker .20 .07
❑ 470 John Mabry .20 .07
❑ 471 Woody Williams .20 .07
❑ 472 Roberto Kelly .20 .07
❑ 473 Jim Mecir .20 .07
❑ 474 Dave Hollins .20 .07
❑ 475 Rafael Medina .20 .07
❑ 476 Darren Lewis .20 .07
❑ 477 Felix Heredia .20 .07
❑ 478 Brian Hunter .20 .07
❑ 479 Matt Mantei .20 .07
❑ 480 Richard Hidalgo .20 .07
❑ 481 Bobby Jones .20 .07
❑ 482 Hal Morris .20 .07
❑ 483 Ramiro Mendoza .20 .07
❑ 484 Matt Luke .20 .07
❑ 485 Esteban Loaiza .20 .07
❑ 486 Mark Loretta .20 .07
❑ 487 A.J. Pierzynski .30 .10
❑ 488 Charles Nagy .20 .07
❑ 489 Kevin Sefcik .20 .07
❑ 490 Jason McDonald .20 .07
❑ 491 Jeremy Powell .20 .07
❑ 492 Scott Servais .20 .07
❑ 493 Abraham Nunez .20 .07
❑ 494 Stan Spencer .20 .07
❑ 495 Stan Javier .20 .07

❑ 496 Jose Paniagua .20 .07
❑ 497 Gregg Jefferies .20 .07
❑ 498 Gregg Olson .20 .07
❑ 499 Derek Lowe .30 .10
❑ 500 Willis Otanez .20 .07
❑ 501 Brian Moehler .20 .07
❑ 502 Glenallen Hill .20 .07
❑ 503 Bobby M. Jones .20 .07
❑ 504 Greg Norton .20 .07
❑ 505 Mike Jackson .20 .07
❑ 506 Kirt Manwaring .20 .07
❑ 507 Eric Weaver RC .20 .07
❑ 508 Mitch Meluskey .20 .07
❑ 509 Todd Jones .20 .07
❑ 510 Mike Matheny .20 .07
❑ 511 Benj Sampson .20 .07
❑ 512 Tony Phillips .20 .07
❑ 513 Mike Thurman .20 .07
❑ 514 Jorge Posada .50 .20
❑ 515 Bill Taylor .20 .07
❑ 516 Mike Sweeney .30 .10
❑ 517 Jose Silva .20 .07
❑ 518 Mark Lewis .20 .07
❑ 519 Chris Peters .20 .07
❑ 520 Brian Johnson .20 .07
❑ 521 Mike Timlin .20 .07
❑ 522 Mark McLemore .20 .07
❑ 523 Dan Plesac .20 .07
❑ 524 Kelly Stinnett .20 .07
❑ 525 Sidney Ponson .20 .07
❑ 526 Jim Parque .20 .07
❑ 527 Tyler Houston .20 .07
❑ 528 John Thomson .20 .07
❑ 529 Reggie Jefferson .20 .07
❑ 530 Robert Person .20 .07
❑ 531 Marc Newfield .20 .07
❑ 532 Javier Vazquez .30 .10
❑ 533 Terry Steinbach .20 .07
❑ 534 Turk Wendell .20 .07
❑ 535 Tim Raines .30 .10
❑ 536 Brian Meadows .20 .07
❑ 537 Mike Lieberthal .30 .10
❑ 538 Ricardo Rincon .20 .07
❑ 539 Dan Wilson .20 .07
❑ 540 John Johnstone .20 .07
❑ 541 Todd Stottlemyre .20 .07
❑ 542 Kevin Stocker .20 .07
❑ 543 Ramon Martinez .20 .07
❑ 544 Mike Simms .20 .07
❑ 545 Paul Quantrill .20 .07
❑ 546 Matt Walbeck .20 .07
❑ 547 Turner Ward .20 .07
❑ 548 Bill Pulsipher .20 .07
❑ 549 Donnie Sadler .20 .07
❑ 550 Lance Johnson .20 .07
❑ 551 Bill Simas .20 .07
❑ 552 Jeff Reed .20 .07
❑ 553 Jeff Shaw .20 .07
❑ 554 Joe Randa .30 .10
❑ 555 Paul Shuey .20 .07
❑ 556 Mike Redmond RC .20 .07
❑ 557 Sean Runyan .20 .07
❑ 558 Enrique Wilson .20 .07
❑ 559 Scott Radinsky .20 .07
❑ 560 Larry Sutton .20 .07
❑ 561 Masato Yoshii .20 .07
❑ 562 David Nilsson .20 .07
❑ 563 Mike Trombley .20 .07
❑ 564 Darryl Strawberry .30 .10
❑ 565 Dave Mlicki .20 .07
❑ 566 Placido Polanco .20 .07
❑ 567 Yorkis Perez .20 .07
❑ 568 Esteban Yan .20 .07
❑ 569 Lee Stevens .20 .07
❑ 570 Steve Sinclair .20 .07
❑ 571 Jarrod Washburn .20 .07
❑ 572 Lenny Webster .20 .07
❑ 573 Mike Sirotka .20 .07
❑ 574 Jason Varitek .75 .30
❑ 575 Terry Mulholland .20 .07
❑ 576 Adrian Beltre FF .20 .07
❑ 577 Eric Chavez FF .20 .07
❑ 578 J.D. Drew FF .20 .07
❑ 579 Juan Encarnacion FF .20 .07
❑ 580 Nomar Garciaparra FF .75 .30
❑ 581 Troy Glaus FF .30 .10
❑ 582 Ben Grieve FF .20 .07
❑ 583 Vladimir Guerrero FF .50 .20
❑ 584 Todd Helton FF .30 .10
❑ 585 Derek Jeter FF 1.00 .40
❑ 586 Travis Lee FF .20 .07
❑ 587 Alex Rodriguez FF .75 .30
❑ 588 Scott Rolen FF .30 .10
❑ 589 Richie Sexson FF .20 .07
❑ 590 Kerry Wood FF .20 .07
❑ 591 Ken Griffey Jr. CL .75 .30
❑ 592 Chipper Jones CL .50 .20
❑ 593 Alex Rodriguez CL .75 .30
❑ 594 Sammy Sosa CL .50 .20
❑ 595 Mark McGwire CL 1.00 .40
❑ 596 Cal Ripken CL 1.25 .50
❑ 597 Nomar Garciaparra CL .75 .30
❑ 598 Derek Jeter CL 1.00 .40
❑ 599 Kerry Wood CL .20 .07
❑ 600 J.D. Drew CL .20 .07
❑ P7 J.D. Drew Promo 1.00 .40

2000 Fleer Tradition

❑ COMPLETE SET (450) 50.00 20.00
❑ 1 AL Home Run LL .75 .30
❑ 2 NL Home Run LL .75 .30
❑ 3 AL RBI LL .30 .10
❑ 4 NL RBI LL .75 .30
❑ 5 AL Avg LL .75 .30
❑ 6 NL Avg LL .30 .10
❑ 7 AL Wins LL .30 .10
❑ 8 NL Wins LL .30 .10
❑ 9 AL ERA LL .30 .10
❑ 10 NL ERA LL .50 .20
❑ 11 Matt Mantei .30 .10
❑ 12 John Rocker .30 .10
❑ 13 Kyle Farnsworth .30 .10
❑ 14 Juan Guzman .30 .10
❑ 15 Manny Ramirez .50 .20
❑ 16 M.Riley/C.Pickering .30 .10
❑ 17 Tony Clark .30 .10
❑ 18 Brian Meadows .30 .10
❑ 19 Orber Moreno .30 .10
❑ 20 Eric Karros .30 .10
❑ 21 Steve Woodard .30 .10
❑ 22 Scott Brosius .30 .10
❑ 23 Gary Bennett .30 .10
❑ 24 J.Wood/D.Borkowski .30 .10
❑ 25 Joe McEwing .30 .10
❑ 26 Juan Gonzalez .30 .10
❑ 27 Roy Halladay .30 .10
❑ 28 Trevor Hoffman .30 .10
❑ 29 Arizona Diamondbacks .30 .10
❑ 30 Domingo Guzman RC .30 .10
❑ 31 Bret Boone .30 .10
❑ 32 Nomar Garciaparra 1.25 .50
❑ 33 Bo Porter .30 .10
❑ 34 Eddie Taubensee .30 .10
❑ 35 Pedro Astacio .30 .10
❑ 36 Derek Bell .30 .10
❑ 37 Jacque Jones .30 .10
❑ 38 Ricky Ledee .30 .10
❑ 39 Jeff Kent .30 .10
❑ 40 Matt Williams .30 .10
❑ 41 A.Soriano/D.Jimenez .75 .30
❑ 42 B.J. Surhoff .30 .10
❑ 43 Denny Neagle .30 .10
❑ 44 Omar Vizquel .50 .20
❑ 45 Jeff Bagwell .50 .20
❑ 46 Mark Grudzielanek .30 .10
❑ 47 LaTroy Hawkins .30 .10
❑ 48 Orlando Hernandez .30 .10
❑ 49 Checklist/K.Griffey Jr. .75 .30
❑ 50 Fernando Tatis .30 .10
❑ 51 Quilvio Veras .30 .10
❑ 52 Wayne Gomes .30 .10
❑ 53 Rick Helling .30 .10
❑ 54 Shannon Stewart .30 .10
❑ 55 D.Brown/M.Quinn .30 .10
❑ 56 Randy Johnson .75 .30
❑ 57 Greg Maddux 1.25 .50
❑ 58 Mike Cameron .30 .10
❑ 59 Matt Anderson .30 .10
❑ 60 Milwaukee Brewers .30 .10
❑ 61 Derrek Lee .50 .20
❑ 62 Mike Sweeney .30 .10
❑ 63 Fernando Vina .30 .10
❑ 64 Orlando Cabrera .30 .10
❑ 65 Doug Glanville .30 .10
❑ 66 Stan Spencer .30 .10
❑ 67 Ray Lankford .30 .10
❑ 68 Kelly Dransfeldt .30 .10
❑ 69 Alex Gonzalez .30 .10
❑ 70 R.Branyan/D.Peoples .30 .10
❑ 71 Jim Edmonds .30 .10
❑ 72 Brady Anderson .30 .10
❑ 73 Mike Stanley .30 .10
❑ 74 Travis Fryman .30 .10
❑ 75 Carlos Febles .30 .10
❑ 76 Bobby Higginson .30 .10
❑ 77 Carlos Perez .30 .10
❑ 78 S.Cox/A.Sanchez .30 .10
❑ 79 Dustin Hermanson .30 .10
❑ 80 Kenny Rogers .30 .10
❑ 81 Miguel Tejada .30 .10
❑ 82 Ben Davis .30 .10
❑ 83 Reggie Sanders .30 .10
❑ 84 Eric Davis .30 .10
❑ 85 J.D. Drew .30 .10
❑ 86 Ryan Rupe .30 .10
❑ 87 Bobby Smith .30 .10
❑ 88 Jose Cruz Jr. .30 .10
❑ 89 Carlos Delgado .30 .10
❑ 90 Toronto Blue Jays .30 .10
❑ 91 D.Stark RC/G.Meche .30 .10
❑ 92 Randy Velarde .30 .10
❑ 93 Aaron Boone .30 .10
❑ 94 Javy Lopez .30 .10
❑ 95 Johnny Damon .50 .20
❑ 96 Jon Lieber .30 .10
❑ 97 Montreal Expos .30 .10
❑ 98 Mark Kotsay .30 .10
❑ 99 Luis Gonzalez .30 .10
❑ 100 Larry Walker .30 .10
❑ 101 Adrian Beltre .30 .10
❑ 102 Alex Ochoa .30 .10
❑ 103 Michael Barrett .30 .10
❑ 104 Tampa Bay Devil Rays .30 .10
❑ 105 Rey Ordonez .30 .10
❑ 106 Derek Jeter 1.50 .60
❑ 107 Mike Lieberthal .30 .10
❑ 108 Ellis Burks .30 .10
❑ 109 Steve Finley .30 .10
❑ 110 Ryan Klesko .30 .10
❑ 111 Steve Avery .30 .10
❑ 112 Dave Veres .30 .10
❑ 113 Cliff Floyd .30 .10
❑ 114 Shane Reynolds .30 .10
❑ 115 Kevin Brown .50 .20
❑ 116 Dave Nilsson .30 .10
❑ 117 Mike Trombley .30 .10
❑ 118 Todd Walker .30 .10
❑ 119 John Olerud .30 .10
❑ 120 Chuck Knoblauch .30 .10
❑ 121 Checklist/N.Garciaparra .75 .30
❑ 122 Trot Nixon .30 .10
❑ 123 Erubiel Durazo .30 .10
❑ 124 Edwards Guzman .30 .10
❑ 125 Curt Schilling .30 .10
❑ 126 Brian Jordan .30 .10
❑ 127 Cleveland Indians .30 .10
❑ 128 Benito Santiago .30 .10
❑ 129 Frank Thomas .75 .30
❑ 130 Neifi Perez .30 .10
❑ 131 Alex Fernandez .30 .10

- ❑ 132 Jose Lima .30 .10
- ❑ 133 J.Toca/M.Mora .30 .10
- ❑ 134 Scott Karl .30 .10
- ❑ 135 Brad Radke .30 .10
- ❑ 136 Paul O'Neill .50 .20
- ❑ 137 Kris Benson .30 .10
- ❑ 138 Colorado Rockies .30 .10
- ❑ 139 Jason Phillips .30 .10
- ❑ 140 Robb Nen .30 .10
- ❑ 141 Ken Hill .30 .10
- ❑ 142 Charles Johnson .30 .10
- ❑ 143 Paul Konerko .30 .10
- ❑ 144 Dmitri Young .30 .10
- ❑ 145 Justin Thompson .30 .10
- ❑ 146 Mark Loretta .30 .10
- ❑ 147 Edgardo Alfonzo .30 .10
- ❑ 148 Armando Benitez .30 .10
- ❑ 149 Octavio Dotel .30 .10
- ❑ 150 Wade Boggs .50 .20
- ❑ 151 Ramon Hernandez .30 .10
- ❑ 152 Freddy Garcia .30 .10
- ❑ 153 Edgar Martinez .50 .20
- ❑ 154 Ivan Rodriguez .50 .20
- ❑ 155 Kansas City Royals .30 .10
- ❑ 156 C.Davidson/C.Guzman .30 .10
- ❑ 157 Andy Benes .30 .10
- ❑ 158 Todd Dunwoody .30 .10
- ❑ 159 Pedro Martinez .50 .20
- ❑ 160 Mike Caruso .30 .10
- ❑ 161 Mike Sirotka .30 .10
- ❑ 162 Houston Astros .30 .10
- ❑ 163 Darryl Kile .30 .10
- ❑ 164 Chipper Jones .75 .30
- ❑ 165 Carl Everett .30 .10
- ❑ 166 Geoff Jenkins .30 .10
- ❑ 167 Dan Perkins .30 .10
- ❑ 168 Andy Pettitte .50 .20
- ❑ 169 Francisco Cordova .30 .10
- ❑ 170 Jay Buhner .30 .10
- ❑ 171 Jay Bell .30 .10
- ❑ 172 Andruw Jones .50 .20
- ❑ 173 Bobby Howry .30 .10
- ❑ 174 Chris Singleton .30 .10
- ❑ 175 Todd Helton .50 .20
- ❑ 176 A.J. Burnett .30 .10
- ❑ 177 Marquis Grissom .30 .10
- ❑ 178 Eric Milton .30 .10
- ❑ 179 Los Angeles Dodgers .30 .10
- ❑ 180 Kevin Appier .30 .10
- ❑ 181 Brian Giles .30 .10
- ❑ 182 Tom Davey .30 .10
- ❑ 183 Mo Vaughn .30 .10
- ❑ 184 Jose Hernandez .30 .10
- ❑ 185 Jim Parque .30 .10
- ❑ 186 Derrick Gibson .30 .10
- ❑ 187 Bruce Aven .30 .10
- ❑ 188 Jeff Cirillo .30 .10
- ❑ 189 Doug Mientkiewicz .30 .10
- ❑ 190 Eric Chavez .30 .10
- ❑ 191 Al Martin .30 .10
- ❑ 192 Tom Glavine .50 .20
- ❑ 193 Butch Huskey .30 .10
- ❑ 194 Ray Durham .30 .10
- ❑ 195 Greg Vaughn .30 .10
- ❑ 196 Vinny Castilla .30 .10
- ❑ 197 Ken Caminiti .30 .10
- ❑ 198 Joe Mays .30 .10
- ❑ 199 Chicago White Sox .30 .10
- ❑ 200 Mariano Rivera .75 .30
- ❑ 201 Checklist/M.McGwire 1.00 .40
- ❑ 202 Pat Meares .30 .10
- ❑ 203 Andres Galarraga .30 .10
- ❑ 204 Tom Gordon .30 .10
- ❑ 205 Henry Rodriguez .30 .10
- ❑ 206 Brett Tomko .30 .10
- ❑ 207 Dante Bichette .30 .10
- ❑ 208 Craig Biggio .50 .20
- ❑ 209 Matt Lawton .30 .10
- ❑ 210 Tino Martinez .50 .20
- ❑ 211 A.Myette/J.Paul .30 .10
- ❑ 212 Warren Morris .30 .10
- ❑ 213 San Diego Padres .30 .10
- ❑ 214 Ramon E. Martinez .30 .10
- ❑ 215 Troy Percival .30 .10
- ❑ 216 Jason Johnson .30 .10
- ❑ 217 Carlos Lee .30 .10
- ❑ 218 Scott Williamson .30 .10
- ❑ 219 Jeff Weaver .30 .10
- ❑ 220 Ronnie Belliard .30 .10
- ❑ 221 Jason Giambi .30 .10
- ❑ 222 Ken Griffey Jr. 1.25 .50
- ❑ 223 John Halama .30 .10
- ❑ 224 Brett Hinchliffe .30 .10
- ❑ 225 Wilson Alvarez .30 .10
- ❑ 226 Rolando Arrojo .30 .10
- ❑ 227 Ruben Mateo .30 .10
- ❑ 228 Rafael Palmeiro .50 .20
- ❑ 229 David Wells .30 .10
- ❑ 230 E.Gagne RC/J.Williams RC .75 .30
- ❑ 231 Tim Salmon .50 .20
- ❑ 232 Mike Mussina .50 .20
- ❑ 233 Magglio Ordonez .30 .10
- ❑ 234 Ron Villone .30 .10
- ❑ 235 Antonio Alfonseca .30 .10
- ❑ 236 Jeromy Burnitz .30 .10
- ❑ 237 Ben Grieve .30 .10
- ❑ 238 Giomar Guevara .30 .10
- ❑ 239 Garret Anderson .30 .10
- ❑ 240 John Smoltz .50 .20
- ❑ 241 Mark Grace .50 .20
- ❑ 242 C.Liniak/J.Molina .30 .10
- ❑ 243 Damion Easley .30 .10
- ❑ 244 Jeff Montgomery .30 .10
- ❑ 245 Kenny Lofton .30 .10
- ❑ 246 Masato Yoshii .30 .10
- ❑ 247 Philadelphia Phillies .30 .10
- ❑ 248 Raul Mondesi .30 .10
- ❑ 249 Marlon Anderson .30 .10
- ❑ 250 Shawn Green .30 .10
- ❑ 251 Sterling Hitchcock .30 .10
- ❑ 252 R.Wolf/A.Shumaker .30 .10
- ❑ 253 Jeff Fassero .30 .10
- ❑ 254 Eli Marrero .30 .10
- ❑ 255 Cincinnati Reds .30 .10
- ❑ 256 Rick Ankiel .30 .10
- ❑ 257 Darin Erstad .30 .10
- ❑ 258 Albert Belle .30 .10
- ❑ 259 Bartolo Colon .30 .10
- ❑ 260 Bret Saberhagen .30 .10
- ❑ 261 Carlos Beltran .30 .10
- ❑ 262 Glenallen Hill .30 .10
- ❑ 263 Gregg Jefferies .30 .10
- ❑ 264 Matt Clement .30 .10
- ❑ 265 Miguel Del Toro .30 .10
- ❑ 266 R.Cancel/K.Barker .30 .10
- ❑ 267 San Francisco Giants .30 .10
- ❑ 268 Kent Bottenfield .30 .10
- ❑ 269 Fred McGriff .50 .20
- ❑ 270 Chris Carpenter .30 .10
- ❑ 271 Atlanta Braves .30 .10
- ❑ 272 Tomo Ohka RC .40 .15
- ❑ 273 Will Clark .50 .20
- ❑ 274 Troy O'Leary .30 .10
- ❑ 275 Checklist/S.Sosa .50 .20
- ❑ 276 Travis Lee .30 .10
- ❑ 277 Sean Casey .30 .10
- ❑ 278 Ron Gant .30 .10
- ❑ 279 Roger Clemens 1.50 .60
- ❑ 280 Phil Nevin .30 .10
- ❑ 281 Mike Piazza 1.25 .50
- ❑ 282 Mike Lowell .30 .10
- ❑ 283 Kevin Millwood .30 .10
- ❑ 284 Joe Randa .30 .10
- ❑ 285 Jeff Shaw .30 .10
- ❑ 286 Jason Varitek .75 .30
- ❑ 287 Harold Baines .30 .10
- ❑ 288 Gabe Kapler .30 .10
- ❑ 289 Chuck Finley .30 .10
- ❑ 290 Carl Pavano .30 .10
- ❑ 291 Brad Ausmus .30 .10
- ❑ 292 Brad Fullmer .30 .10
- ❑ 293 Boston Red Sox .30 .10
- ❑ 294 Bob Wickman .30 .10
- ❑ 295 Billy Wagner .30 .10
- ❑ 296 Shawn Estes .30 .10
- ❑ 297 Gary Sheffield .30 .10
- ❑ 298 Fernando Seguignol .30 .10
- ❑ 299 Omar Olivares .30 .10
- ❑ 300 Baltimore Orioles .30 .10
- ❑ 301 Matt Stairs .30 .10
- ❑ 302 Andy Ashby .30 .10
- ❑ 303 Todd Greene .30 .10
- ❑ 304 Jesse Garcia .30 .10
- ❑ 305 Kerry Wood .30 .10
- ❑ 306 Roberto Alomar .50 .20
- ❑ 307 New York Mets .30 .10
- ❑ 308 Dean Palmer .30 .10
- ❑ 309 Mike Hampton .30 .10
- ❑ 310 Devon White .30 .10
- ❑ 311 Mike Garcia RC .30 .10
- ❑ 312 Tim Hudson .30 .10
- ❑ 313 John Franco .30 .10
- ❑ 314 Jason Schmidt .30 .10
- ❑ 315 J.T. Snow .30 .10
- ❑ 316 Ed Sprague .30 .10
- ❑ 317 Chris Widger .30 .10
- ❑ 318 Luther Hackman RC .30 .10
- ❑ 319 Jose Mesa .30 .10
- ❑ 320 Jose Canseco .50 .20
- ❑ 321 John Wetteland .30 .10
- ❑ 322 Minnesota Twins .30 .10
- ❑ 323 Jeff DaVanon RC .40 .15
- ❑ 324 Tony Womack .30 .10
- ❑ 325 Rod Beck .30 .10
- ❑ 326 Mickey Morandini .30 .10
- ❑ 327 Pokey Reese .30 .10
- ❑ 328 Jaret Wright .30 .10
- ❑ 329 Glen Barker .30 .10
- ❑ 330 Darren Dreifort .30 .10
- ❑ 331 Torii Hunter .30 .10
- ❑ 332 T.Armas/P.Bergeron .30 .10
- ❑ 333 Hideki Irabu .30 .10
- ❑ 334 Desi Relaford .30 .10
- ❑ 335 Barry Bonds 2.00 .75
- ❑ 336 Gary DiSarcina .30 .10
- ❑ 337 Gerald Williams .30 .10
- ❑ 338 John Valentin .30 .10
- ❑ 339 David Justice .30 .10
- ❑ 340 Juan Encarnacion .30 .10
- ❑ 341 Jeremy Giambi .30 .10
- ❑ 342 Chan Ho Park .30 .10
- ❑ 343 Vladimir Guerrero .75 .30
- ❑ 344 Robin Ventura .50 .20
- ❑ 345 Bob Abreu .30 .10
- ❑ 346 Tony Gwynn 1.00 .40
- ❑ 347 Jose Jimenez .30 .10
- ❑ 348 Royce Clayton .30 .10
- ❑ 349 Kelvim Escobar .30 .10
- ❑ 350 Chicago Cubs .30 .10
- ❑ 351 T.Dawkins/J.LaRue .30 .10
- ❑ 352 Barry Larkin .50 .20
- ❑ 353 Cal Ripken 2.50 1.00
- ❑ 354 Checklist/A.Rodriguez .75 .30
- ❑ 355 Todd Stottlemyre .30 .10
- ❑ 356 Terry Adams .30 .10
- ❑ 357 Pittsburgh Pirates .30 .10
- ❑ 358 Jim Thome .50 .20
- ❑ 359 C.Lee/D.Davis .30 .10
- ❑ 360 Moises Alou .30 .10
- ❑ 361 Todd Hollandsworth .30 .10
- ❑ 362 Marty Cordova .30 .10
- ❑ 363 David Cone .30 .10
- ❑ 364 J.Nathan/W.Delgado .30 .10
- ❑ 365 Paul Byrd .30 .10
- ❑ 366 Edgar Renteria .30 .10
- ❑ 367 Rusty Greer .30 .10
- ❑ 368 David Segui .30 .10
- ❑ 369 New York Yankees .50 .20
- ❑ 370 D.Ward/C.Hernandez .30 .10
- ❑ 371 Troy Glaus .30 .10
- ❑ 372 Delino DeShields .30 .10
- ❑ 373 Jose Offerman .30 .10
- ❑ 374 Sammy Sosa .75 .30
- ❑ 375 Sandy Alomar Jr. .30 .10
- ❑ 376 Masao Kida .30 .10
- ❑ 377 Richard Hidalgo .30 .10
- ❑ 378 Ismael Valdes .30 .10
- ❑ 379 Ugueth Urbina .30 .10
- ❑ 380 Darryl Hamilton .30 .10
- ❑ 381 John Jaha .30 .10
- ❑ 382 St. Louis Cardinals .30 .10
- ❑ 383 Scott Sauerbeck .30 .10
- ❑ 384 Russ Ortiz .30 .10
- ❑ 385 Jamie Moyer .30 .10
- ❑ 386 Dave Martinez .30 .10
- ❑ 387 Todd Zeile .30 .10
- ❑ 388 Anaheim Angels .30 .10
- ❑ 389 R.Ryan/N.Bierbrodt .30 .10

390	Rickey Henderson	.75	.30
391	Alex Rodriguez	1.25	.50
392	Texas Rangers	.30	.10
393	Roberto Hernandez	.30	.10
394	Tony Batista	.30	.10
395	Oakland Athletics	.30	.10
396	Dave Cortes RC	.30	.10
397	Gregg Olson	.30	.10
398	Sidney Ponson	.30	.10
399	Micah Bowie	.30	.10
400	Mark McGwire	2.00	.75
401	Florida Marlins	.30	.10
402	Chad Allen	.30	.10
403	C.Blake/V.Wells	.30	.10
404	Pete Harnisch	.30	.10
405	Preston Wilson	.30	.10
406	Richie Sexson	.30	.10
407	Rico Brogna	.30	.10
408	Todd Hundley	.30	.10
409	Wally Joyner	.30	.10
410	Tom Goodwin	.30	.10
411	Joey Hamilton	.30	.10
412	Detroit Tigers	.30	.10
413	Michael Tejera RC	.30	.10
414	Alex Gonzalez	.30	.10
415	Jermaine Dye	.30	.10
416	Jose Rosada	.30	.10
417	Wilton Guerrero	.30	.10
418	Rondell White	.30	.10
419	Al Leiter	.30	.10
420	Bernie Williams	.50	.20
421	A.J. Hinch	.30	.10
422	Pat Burrell	.30	.10
423	Scott Rolen	.50	.20
424	Jason Kendall	.30	.10
425	Kevin Young	.30	.10
426	Eric Owens	.30	.10
427	Checklist/D.Jeter	.75	.30
428	Livan Hernandez	.30	.10
429	Russ Davis	.30	.10
430	Dan Wilson	.30	.10
431	Quinton McCracken	.30	.10
432	Homer Bush	.30	.10
433	Seattle Mariners	.30	.10
434	C.Harville/L.Vizcaino	.30	.10
435	Carlos Beltran AW	.30	.10
436	Scott Williamson AW	.30	.10
437	Pedro Martinez AW	.50	.20
438	Randy Johnson AW	.50	.20
439	Ivan Rodriguez AW	.30	.10
440	Chipper Jones AW	.50	.20
441	Bernie Williams DIV	.30	.10
442	Pedro Martinez DIV	.50	.20
443	Derek Jeter DIV	1.00	.40
444	Brian Jordan DIV	.30	.10
445	Todd Pratt DIV	.30	.10
446	Kevin Millwood DIV	.30	.10
447	Orlando Hernandez WS	.30	.10
448	Derek Jeter WS	1.00	.40
449	Chad Curtis WS	.30	.10
450	Roger Clemens WS	.75	.30
P353	Cal Ripken Promo	3.00	1.25

2001 Fleer Tradition

COMP.FACT.SET (485)	100.00	50.00
COMPLETE SET (450)	50.00	20.00
COMMON CARD (1-450)	.30	.10
COMMON CARD (451-485)	.50	.20

1	Andres Galarraga	.30	.10
2	Armando Rios	.30	.10
3	Julio Lugo	.30	.10
4	Darryl Hamilton	.30	.10
5	Dave Veres	.30	.10
6	Edgardo Alfonzo	.30	.10
7	Brook Fordyce	.30	.10
8	Eric Karros	.30	.10
9	Neifi Perez	.30	.10
10	Jim Edmonds	.30	.10
11	Barry Larkin	.50	.20
12	Trot Nixon	.30	.10
13	Andy Pettitte	.50	.20
14	Jose Guillen	.30	.10
15	David Wells	.30	.10
16	Magglio Ordonez	.30	.10
17	David Segui	.30	.10
17A	David Segui ERR Card has no number on the back	.30	.10
18	Juan Encarnacion	.30	.10
19	Robert Person	.30	.10
20	Quilvio Veras	.30	.10
21	Mo Vaughn	.30	.10
22	B.J. Surhoff	.30	.10
23	Ken Caminiti	.30	.10
24	Frank Catalanotto	.30	.10
25	Luis Gonzalez	.30	.10
26	Pete Harnisch	.30	.10
27	Alex Gonzalez	.30	.10
28	Mark Quinn	.30	.10
29	Luis Castillo	.30	.10
30	Rick Helling	.30	.10
31	Barry Bonds	2.00	.75
32	Warren Morris	.30	.10
33	Aaron Boone	.30	.10
34	Ricky Gutierrez	.30	.10
35	Preston Wilson	.30	.10
36	Erubiel Durazo	.30	.10
37	Jermaine Dye	.30	.10
38	John Rocker	.30	.10
39	Mark Grudzielanek	.30	.10
40	Pedro Martinez	.50	.20
41	Phil Nevin	.30	.10
42	Luis Matos	.30	.10
43	Orlando Hernandez	.30	.10
44	Steve Cox	.30	.10
45	James Baldwin	.30	.10
46	Rafael Furcal	.30	.10
47	Todd Zeile	.30	.10
48	Elmer Dessens	.30	.10
49	Russell Branyan	.30	.10
50	Juan Gonzalez	.30	.10
51	Mac Suzuki	.30	.10
52	Adam Kennedy	.30	.10
53	Randy Velarde	.30	.10
54	David Bell	.30	.10
55	Royce Clayton	.30	.10
56	Greg Colbrunn	.30	.10
57	Rey Ordonez	.30	.10
58	Kevin Millwood	.30	.10
59	Fernando Vina	.30	.10
60	Eddie Taubensee	.30	.10
61	Enrique Wilson	.30	.10
62	Jay Bell	.30	.10
63	Brian Moehler	.30	.10
64	Brad Fullmer	.30	.10
65	Ben Petrick	.30	.10
66	Orlando Cabrera	.30	.10
67	Shane Reynolds	.30	.10
68	Mitch Meluskey	.30	.10
69	Jeff Shaw	.30	.10
70	Chipper Jones	.75	.30
71	Tomo Ohka	.30	.10
72	Ruben Rivera	.30	.10
73	Mike Sirotka	.30	.10
74	Scott Rolen	.50	.20
75	Glendon Rusch	.30	.10
76	Miguel Tejada	.30	.10
77	Brady Anderson	.30	.10
78	Bartolo Colon	.30	.10
79	Ron Coomer	.30	.10
80	Gary DiSarcina	.30	.10
81	Geoff Jenkins	.30	.10
82	Billy Koch	.30	.10
83	Mike Lamb	.30	.10
84	Alex Rodriguez	1.25	.50
85	Denny Neagle	.30	.10
86	Michael Tucker	.30	.10
87	Edgar Renteria	.30	.10
88	Brian Anderson	.30	.10
89	Glenallen Hill	.30	.10
90	Aramis Ramirez	.30	.10
91	Rondell White	.30	.10
92	Tony Womack	.30	.10
93	Jeffrey Hammonds	.30	.10
94	Freddy Garcia	.30	.10
95	Bill Mueller	.30	.10
96	Mike Lieberthal	.30	.10
97	Michael Barrett	.30	.10
98	Derrek Lee	.50	.20
99	Bill Spiers	.30	.10
100	Derek Lowe	.30	.10
101	Javy Lopez	.30	.10
102	Adrian Beltre	.30	.10
103	Jim Parque	.30	.10
104	Marquis Grissom	.30	.10
105	Eric Chavez	.30	.10
106	Todd Jones	.30	.10
107	Eric Owens	.30	.10
108	Roger Clemens	1.50	.60
109	Denny Hocking	.30	.10
110	Roberto Hernandez	.30	.10
111	Albert Belle	.30	.10
112	Troy Glaus	.30	.10
113	Ivan Rodriguez	.50	.20
114	Carlos Guillen	.30	.10
115	Chuck Finley	.30	.10
116	Dmitri Young	.30	.10
117	Paul Konerko	.30	.10
118	Damon Buford	.30	.10
119	Fernando Tatis	.30	.10
120	Larry Walker	.30	.10
121	Jason Kendall	.30	.10
122	Matt Williams	.30	.10
123	Henry Rodriguez	.30	.10
124	Placido Polanco	.30	.10
125	Bobby Estalella	.30	.10
126	Pat Burrell	.30	.10
127	Mark Loretta	.30	.10
128	Moises Alou	.30	.10
129	Tino Martinez	.50	.20
130	Milton Bradley	.30	.10
131	Todd Hundley	.30	.10
132	Keith Foulke	.30	.10
133	Robert Fick	.30	.10
134	Cristian Guzman	.30	.10
135	Rusty Greer	.30	.10
136	John Olerud	.30	.10
137	Mariano Rivera	.75	.30
138	Jeromy Burnitz	.30	.10
139	Dave Burba	.30	.10
140	Ken Griffey Jr.	1.25	.50
141	Tony Gwynn	1.00	.40
142	Carlos Delgado	.30	.10
143	Edgar Martinez	.50	.20
144	Ramon Hernandez	.30	.10
145	Pedro Astacio	.30	.10
146	Ray Lankford	.30	.10
147	Mike Mussina	.50	.20
148	Ray Durham	.30	.10
149	Lee Stevens	.30	.10
150	Jay Canizaro	.30	.10
151	Adrian Brown	.30	.10
152	Mike Piazza	1.25	.50
153	Cliff Floyd	.30	.10
154	Jose Vidro	.30	.10
155	Jason Giambi	.30	.10
156	Andruw Jones	.50	.20
157	Robin Ventura	.30	.10
158	Gary Sheffield	.30	.10
159	Jeff D'Amico	.30	.10
160	Chuck Knoblauch	.30	.10
161	Roger Cedeno	.30	.10
162	Jim Thome	.50	.20
163	Peter Bergeron	.30	.10
164	Kerry Wood	.30	.10
165	Gabe Kapler	.30	.10
166	Corey Koskie	.30	.10
167	Doug Glanville	.30	.10
168	Brent Mayne	.30	.10
169	Scott Spiezio	.30	.10
170	Steve Karsay	.30	.10

❑ 171 Al Martin .30 .10
❑ 172 Fred McGriff .50 .20
❑ 173 Gabe White .30 .10
❑ 174 Alex Gonzalez .30 .10
❑ 175 Mike Darr .30 .10
❑ 176 Bengie Molina .30 .10
❑ 177 Ben Grieve .30 .10
❑ 178 Marlon Anderson .30 .10
❑ 179 Brian Giles .30 .10
❑ 180 Jose Valentin .30 .10
❑ 181 Brian Jordan .30 .10
❑ 182 Randy Johnson .75 .30
❑ 183 Ricky Ledee .30 .10
❑ 184 Russ Ortiz .30 .10
❑ 185 Mike Lowell .30 .10
❑ 186 Curtis Leskanic .30 .10
❑ 187 Bob Abreu .30 .10
❑ 188 Derek Jeter 2.00 .75
❑ 189 Lance Berkman .30 .10
❑ 190 Roberto Alomar .50 .20
❑ 191 Darin Erstad .30 .10
❑ 192 Richie Sexson .30 .10
❑ 193 Alex Ochoa .30 .10
❑ 194 Carlos Febles .30 .10
❑ 195 David Ortiz .75 .30
❑ 196 Shawn Green .30 .10
❑ 197 Mike Sweeney .30 .10
❑ 198 Vladimir Guerrero .75 .30
❑ 199 Jose Jimenez .30 .10
❑ 200 Travis Lee .30 .10
❑ 201 Rickey Henderson .75 .30
❑ 202 Bob Wickman .30 .10
❑ 203 Miguel Cairo .30 .10
❑ 204 Steve Finley .30 .10
❑ 205 Tony Batista .30 .10
❑ 206 Jamey Wright .30 .10
❑ 207 Terrence Long .30 .10
❑ 208 Trevor Hoffman .30 .10
❑ 209 John VanderWal .30 .10
❑ 210 Greg Maddux 1.25 .50
❑ 211 Tim Salmon .50 .20
❑ 212 Herbert Perry .30 .10
❑ 213 Marvin Benard .30 .10
❑ 214 Jose Offerman .30 .10
❑ 215 Jay Payton .30 .10
❑ 216 Jon Lieber .30 .10
❑ 217 Mark Kotsay .30 .10
❑ 218 Scott Brosius .30 .10
❑ 219 Scott Williamson .30 .10
❑ 220 Omar Vizquel .50 .20
❑ 221 Mike Hampton .30 .10
❑ 222 Richard Hidalgo .30 .10
❑ 223 Rey Sanchez .30 .10
❑ 224 Matt Lawton .30 .10
❑ 225 Bruce Chen .30 .10
❑ 226 Ryan Klesko .30 .10
❑ 227 Garret Anderson .30 .10
❑ 228 Kevin Brown .30 .10
❑ 229 Mike Cameron .30 .10
❑ 230 Tony Clark .30 .10
❑ 231 Curt Schilling .30 .10
❑ 232 Vinny Castilla .30 .10
❑ 233 Carl Pavano .30 .10
❑ 234 Eric Davis .30 .10
❑ 235 Darrin Fletcher .30 .10
❑ 236 Matt Stairs .30 .10
❑ 237 Octavio Dotel .30 .10
❑ 238 Mark Grace .50 .20
❑ 239 John Smoltz .50 .20
❑ 240 Matt Clement .30 .10
❑ 241 Ellis Burks .30 .10
❑ 242 Charles Johnson .30 .10
❑ 243 Jeff Bagwell .50 .20
❑ 244 Derek Bell .30 .10
❑ 245 Nomar Garciaparra 1.25 .50
❑ 246 Jorge Posada .50 .20
❑ 247 Ryan Dempster .30 .10
❑ 248 J.T. Snow .30 .10
❑ 249 Eric Young .30 .10
❑ 250 Daryle Ward .30 .10
❑ 251 Joe Randa .30 .10
❑ 252 Travis Fryman .30 .10
❑ 253 Mike Williams .30 .10
❑ 254 Jacque Jones .30 .10
❑ 255 Scott Elarton .30 .10
❑ 256 Mark McGwire 2.00 .75
❑ 257 Jay Buhner .30 .10
❑ 258 Randy Wolf .30 .10
❑ 259 Sammy Sosa .75 .30
❑ 260 Chan Ho Park .30 .10
❑ 261 Damion Easley .30 .10
❑ 262 Rick Ankiel .30 .10
❑ 263 Frank Thomas .75 .30
❑ 264 Kris Benson .30 .10
❑ 265 Luis Alicea .30 .10
❑ 266 Jeromy Burnitz .30 .10
❑ 267 Geoff Blum .30 .10
❑ 268 Joe Girardi .30 .10
❑ 269 Livan Hernandez .30 .10
❑ 270 Jeff Conine .30 .10
❑ 271 Danny Graves .30 .10
❑ 272 Craig Biggio .50 .20
❑ 273 Jose Canseco .50 .20
❑ 274 Tom Glavine .50 .20
❑ 275 Ruben Mateo .30 .10
❑ 276 Jeff Kent .30 .10
❑ 277 Kevin Young .30 .10
❑ 278 A.J. Burnett .30 .10
❑ 279 Dante Bichette .30 .10
❑ 280 Sandy Alomar Jr. .30 .10
❑ 281 John Wetteland .30 .10
❑ 282 Torii Hunter .30 .10
❑ 283 Jarrod Washburn .30 .10
❑ 284 Rich Aurilia .30 .10
❑ 285 Jeff Cirillo .30 .10
❑ 286 Fernando Seguignol .30 .10
❑ 287 Darren Dreifort .30 .10
❑ 288 Deivi Cruz .30 .10
❑ 289 Pokey Reese .30 .10
❑ 290 Garrett Stephenson .30 .10
❑ 291 Bret Boone .30 .10
❑ 292 Tim Hudson .30 .10
❑ 293 John Flaherty .30 .10
❑ 294 Shannon Stewart .30 .10
❑ 295 Shawn Estes .30 .10
❑ 296 Wilton Guerrero .30 .10
❑ 297 Delino DeShields .30 .10
❑ 298 David Justice .30 .10
❑ 299 Harold Baines .30 .10
❑ 300 Al Leiter .30 .10
❑ 301 Wil Cordero .30 .10
❑ 302 Antonio Alfonseca .30 .10
❑ 303 Sean Casey .30 .10
❑ 304 Carlos Beltran .30 .10
❑ 305 Brad Radke .30 .10
❑ 306 Jason Varitek .75 .30
❑ 307 Shigetoshi Hasegawa .30 .10
❑ 308 Todd Stottlemyre .30 .10
❑ 309 Raul Mondesi .30 .10
❑ 310 Mike Bordick .30 .10
❑ 311 Darryl Kile .30 .10
❑ 312 Dean Palmer .30 .10
❑ 313 Johnny Damon .50 .20
❑ 314 Todd Helton .50 .20
❑ 315 Chad Hermansen .30 .10
❑ 316 Kevin Appier .30 .10
❑ 317 Greg Vaughn .30 .10
❑ 318 Robb Nen .30 .10
❑ 319 Jose Cruz Jr. .30 .10
❑ 320 Ron Belliard .30 .10
❑ 321 Bernie Williams .50 .20
❑ 322 Melvin Mora .30 .10
❑ 323 Kenny Lofton .30 .10
❑ 324 Armando Benitez .30 .10
❑ 325 Carlos Lee .30 .10
❑ 326 Damian Jackson .30 .10
❑ 327 Eric Milton .30 .10
❑ 328 J.D. Drew .30 .10
❑ 329 Byung-Hyun Kim .30 .10
❑ 330 Chris Stynes .30 .10
❑ 331 Kazuhiro Sasaki .30 .10
❑ 332 Troy O'Leary .30 .10
❑ 333 Pat Hentgen .30 .10
❑ 334 Brad Ausmus .30 .10
❑ 335 Todd Walker .30 .10
❑ 336 Jason Isringhausen .30 .10
❑ 337 Gerald Williams .30 .10
❑ 338 Aaron Sele .30 .10
❑ 339 Paul O'Neill .50 .20
❑ 340 Cal Ripken 2.50 1.00
❑ 341 Manny Ramirez .50 .20
❑ 342 Will Clark .50 .20
❑ 343 Mark Redman .30 .10
❑ 344 Bubba Trammell .30 .10
❑ 345 Troy Percival .30 .10
❑ 346 Chris Singleton .30 .10
❑ 347 Rafael Palmeiro .50 .20
❑ 348 Carl Everett .30 .10
❑ 349 Andy Benes .30 .10
❑ 350 Bobby Higginson .30 .10
❑ 351 Alex Cabrera .30 .10
❑ 352 Barry Zito .50 .20
❑ 353 Jace Brewer .30 .10
❑ 354 Paxton Crawford .30 .10
❑ 355 Oswaldo Mairena .30 .10
❑ 356 Joe Crede .75 .30
❑ 357 A.J. Pierzynski .30 .10
❑ 358 Daniel Garibay .30 .10
❑ 359 Jason Tyner .30 .10
❑ 360 Nate Rolison .30 .10
❑ 361 Scott Downs .30 .10
❑ 362 Keith Ginter .30 .10
❑ 363 Juan Pierre .30 .10
❑ 364 Adam Bernero .30 .10
❑ 365 Chris Richard .30 .10
❑ 366 Joey Nation .30 .10
❑ 367 Aubrey Huff .30 .10
❑ 368 Adam Eaton .30 .10
❑ 369 Jose Ortiz .30 .10
❑ 370 Eric Munson .30 .10
❑ 371 Matt Kinney .30 .10
❑ 372 Eric Byrnes .30 .10
❑ 373 Keith McDonald .30 .10
❑ 374 Matt Wise .30 .10
❑ 375 Timo Perez .30 .10
❑ 376 Julio Zuleta .30 .10
❑ 377 Jimmy Rollins .30 .10
❑ 378 Xavier Nady .30 .10
❑ 379 Ryan Kohlmeier .30 .10
❑ 380 Corey Patterson .30 .10
❑ 381 Todd Helton LL .30 .10
❑ 382 Moises Alou LL .30 .10
❑ 383 Vladimir Guerrero LL .50 .20
❑ 384 Luis Castillo LL .30 .10
❑ 385 Jeffrey Hammonds LL .30 .10
❑ 386 Nomar Garciaparra LL .75 .30
❑ 387 Carlos Delgado LL .30 .10
❑ 388 Darin Erstad LL .30 .10
❑ 389 Manny Ramirez LL .30 .10
❑ 390 Mike Sweeney LL .30 .10
❑ 391 Sammy Sosa LL .50 .20
❑ 392 Barry Bonds LL 1.00 .40
❑ 393 Jeff Bagwell LL .30 .10
❑ 394 Richard Hidalgo LL .30 .10
❑ 395 Vladimir Guerrero LL .50 .20
❑ 396 Troy Glaus LL .30 .10
❑ 397 Frank Thomas LL .50 .20
❑ 398 Carlos Delgado LL .30 .10
❑ 399 David Justice LL .30 .10
❑ 400 Jason Giambi LL .30 .10
❑ 401 Randy Johnson LL .50 .20
❑ 402 Kevin Brown LL .30 .10
❑ 403 Greg Maddux LL .75 .30
❑ 404 Al Leiter LL .30 .10
❑ 405 Mike Hampton LL .30 .10
❑ 406 Pedro Martinez LL .50 .20
❑ 407 Roger Clemens LL .75 .30
❑ 408 Mike Sirotka LL .30 .10
❑ 409 Mike Mussina LL .30 .10
❑ 410 Bartolo Colon LL .30 .10
❑ 411 Subway Series WS .50 .20
❑ 412 Jose Vizcaino WS .50 .20
❑ 413 Jose Vizcaino WS .50 .20
❑ 414 Roger Clemens WS .75 .30
❑ 415 Benitez/Alfonzo/Perez WS .30 .10
❑ 416 Al Leiter WS .50 .20
❑ 417 Luis Sojo WS .50 .20
❑ 418 Yankees 3-Peat WS .75 .30
❑ 419 Derek Jeter WS 1.00 .40
❑ 420 Toast of the Town WS .50 .20
❑ 421 Atlanta Braves CL .30 .10
❑ 422 New York Mets CL .75 .30
❑ 423 Florida Marlins CL .30 .10
❑ 424 Philadelphia Phillies CL .30 .10
❑ 425 Montreal Expos CL .30 .10
❑ 426 St. Louis Cardinals CL .30 .10
❑ 427 Cincinnati Reds CL .30 .10
❑ 428 Chicago Cubs CL .50 .20

❑ 429 Milwaukee Brewers CL	.30	.10
❑ 430 Houston Astros CL	.30	.10
❑ 431 Pittsburgh Pirates CL	.50	.20
❑ 432 San Francisco Giants CL	.30	.10
❑ 433 Arizona Diamondbacks CL	.30	.10
❑ 434 Los Angeles Dodgers CL UER	.30	.10
❑ 435 Colorado Rockies CL UER	.30	.10
❑ 436 San Diego Padres CL	.30	.10
❑ 437 New York Yankees CL	.75	.30
❑ 438 Boston Red Sox CL	.50	.20
❑ 439 Baltimore Orioles CL	.30	.10
❑ 440 Toronto Blue Jays CL	.30	.10
❑ 441 Tampa Bay Devil Rays CL	.30	.10
❑ 442 Chicago White Sox CL	.50	.20
❑ 443 Cleveland Indians CL	.30	.10
❑ 444 Detoit Tigers CL	.30	.10
❑ 445 Kansas City Royals CL	.30	.10
❑ 446 Minnesota Twins CL	.30	.10
❑ 447 Seattle Mariners CL	.30	.10
❑ 448 Oakland Athletics CL	.30	.10
❑ 449 Anaheim Angels CL	.30	.10
❑ 450 Texas Rangers CL	.30	.10
❑ 451 Albert Pujols RC	50.00	20.00
❑ 452 Ichiro Suzuki RC	15.00	6.00
❑ 453 Tsuyoshi Shinjo RC	.75	.30
❑ 454 Johnny Estrada RC	.75	.30
❑ 455 Elpidio Guzman RC	.50	.20
❑ 456 Adrian Hernandez RC	.50	.20
❑ 457 Rafael Soriano RC	.50	.20
❑ 458 Drew Henson RC	.75	.30
❑ 459 Juan Uribe RC	.75	.30
❑ 460 Matt White RC	.50	.20
❑ 461 Endy Chavez RC	.50	.20
❑ 462 Bud Smith RC	.50	.20
❑ 463 Morgan Ensberg RC	2.50	1.00
❑ 464 Jay Gibbons RC	.75	.30
❑ 465 Jackson Melian RC	.50	.20
❑ 466 Junior Spivey RC	.75	.30
❑ 467 Juan Cruz RC	.50	.20
❑ 468 Wilson Betemit RC	2.50	1.00
❑ 469 Alexis Gomez RC	.50	.20
❑ 470 Mark Teixeira RC	10.00	4.00
❑ 471 Erick Almonte RC	.50	.20
❑ 472 Travis Hafner RC	8.00	3.00
❑ 473 Carlos Valderrama RC	.50	.20
❑ 474 Brandon Duckworth RC	.50	.20
❑ 475 Ryan Freel RC	1.50	.60
❑ 476 Wilkin Ruan RC	.50	.20
❑ 477 Andres Torres RC	.50	.20
❑ 478 Josh Towers RC	.75	.30
❑ 479 Kyle Lohse RC	.75	.30
❑ 480 Jason Michaels RC	.50	.20
❑ 481 Alfonso Soriano	.75	.30
❑ 482 C.C. Sabathia	.50	.20
❑ 483 Roy Oswalt	1.25	.50
❑ 484 Ben Sheets	.75	.30
❑ 485 Adam Dunn	.75	.30

2002 Fleer Tradition

Card		
❑ COMPLETE SET (500)	200.00	125.00
❑ COMP.SET w/o SP's (400)	50.00	20.00
❑ COMMON CARD (101-500)	.30	.10
❑ COMMON SP (1-100)	3.00	1.25
❑ COMMON CARD (436-470)	.50	.20
❑ 1 Barry Bonds SP	12.00	5.00
❑ 2 Cal Ripken SP	15.00	6.00
❑ 3 Tony Gwynn SP	6.00	2.50
❑ 4 Brad Radke SP	3.00	1.25
❑ 5 Jose Ortiz SP	3.00	1.25
❑ 6 Mark Mulder SP	3.00	1.25
❑ 7 Jon Lieber SP	3.00	1.25
❑ 8 John Olerud SP	3.00	1.25
❑ 9 Phil Nevin SP	3.00	1.25
❑ 10 Craig Biggio SP	3.00	1.25
❑ 11 Pedro Martinez SP	3.00	1.25
❑ 12 Fred McGriff SP	3.00	1.25
❑ 13 Vladimir Guerrero SP	5.00	2.00
❑ 14 Jason Giambi SP	3.00	1.25
❑ 15 Mark Kotsay SP	3.00	1.25
❑ 16 Bud Smith SP	3.00	1.25
❑ 17 Kevin Brown SP	3.00	1.25
❑ 18 Darin Erstad SP	3.00	1.25
❑ 19 Julio Franco SP	3.00	1.25
❑ 20 C.C. Sabathia SP	3.00	1.25
❑ 21 Larry Walker SP	3.00	1.25
❑ 22 Doug Mientkiewicz SP	3.00	1.25
❑ 23 Luis Gonzalez SP	3.00	1.25
❑ 24 Albert Pujols SP	10.00	4.00
❑ 25 Brian Lawrence SP	3.00	1.25
❑ 26 Al Leiter SP	3.00	1.25
❑ 27 Mike Sweeney SP	3.00	1.25
❑ 28 Jeff Weaver SP	3.00	1.25
❑ 29 Matt Morris SP	3.00	1.25
❑ 30 Hideo Nomo SP	5.00	2.00
❑ 31 Tom Glavine SP	3.00	1.25
❑ 32 Magglio Ordonez SP	3.00	1.25
❑ 33 Roberto Alomar SP	3.00	1.25
❑ 34 Roger Cedeno SP	3.00	1.25
❑ 35 Greg Vaughn SP	3.00	1.25
❑ 36 Chan Ho Park SP	3.00	1.25
❑ 37 Rich Aurilia SP	3.00	1.25
❑ 38 Tsuyoshi Shinjo SP	3.00	1.25
❑ 39 Eric Young SP	3.00	1.25
❑ 40 Bobby Higginson SP	3.00	1.25
❑ 41 Marlon Anderson SP	3.00	1.25
❑ 42 Mark Grace SP	3.00	1.25
❑ 43 Steve Cox SP	3.00	1.25
❑ 44 Cliff Floyd SP	3.00	1.25
❑ 45 Brian Roberts SP	3.00	1.25
❑ 46 Paul Konerko SP	3.00	1.25
❑ 47 Brandon Duckworth SP	3.00	1.25
❑ 48 Josh Beckett SP	3.00	1.25
❑ 49 David Ortiz SP	5.00	2.00
❑ 50 Geoff Jenkins SP	3.00	1.25
❑ 51 Ruben Sierra SP	3.00	1.25
❑ 52 John Franco SP	3.00	1.25
❑ 53 Einar Diaz SP	3.00	1.25
❑ 54 Luis Castillo SP	3.00	1.25
❑ 55 Mark Quinn SP	3.00	1.25
❑ 56 Shea Hillenbrand SP	3.00	1.25
❑ 57 Rafael Palmeiro SP	3.00	1.25
❑ 58 Paul O'Neill SP	3.00	1.25
❑ 59 Andruw Jones SP	3.00	1.25
❑ 60 Lance Berkman SP	3.00	1.25
❑ 61 Jimmy Rollins SP	3.00	1.25
❑ 62 Jose Hernandez SP	3.00	1.25
❑ 63 Rusty Greer SP	3.00	1.25
❑ 64 Wade Miller SP	3.00	1.25
❑ 65 David Eckstein SP	3.00	1.25
❑ 66 Jose Valentin SP	3.00	1.25
❑ 67 Javier Vazquez SP	3.00	1.25
❑ 68 Roger Clemens SP	10.00	4.00
❑ 69 Omar Vizquel SP	3.00	1.25
❑ 70 Roy Oswalt SP	3.00	1.25
❑ 71 Shannon Stewart SP	3.00	1.25
❑ 72 Byung-Hyun Kim SP	3.00	1.25
❑ 73 Jay Gibbons SP	3.00	1.25
❑ 74 Barry Larkin SP	3.00	1.25
❑ 75 Brian Giles SP	3.00	1.25
❑ 76 Andres Galarraga SP	3.00	1.25
❑ 77 Sammy Sosa SP	5.00	2.00
❑ 78 Manny Ramirez SP	3.00	1.25
❑ 79 Carlos Delgado SP	3.00	1.25
❑ 80 Jorge Posada SP	3.00	1.25
❑ 81 Todd Ritchie SP	3.00	1.25
❑ 82 Russ Ortiz SP	3.00	1.25
❑ 83 Brent Mayne SP	3.00	1.25
❑ 84 Mike Mussina SP	3.00	1.25
❑ 85 Raul Mondesi SP	3.00	1.25
❑ 86 Mark Loretta SP	3.00	1.25
❑ 87 Tim Raines SP	3.00	1.25
❑ 88 Ichiro Suzuki SP	10.00	4.00
❑ 89 Juan Pierre SP	3.00	1.25
❑ 90 Adam Dunn SP	3.00	1.25
❑ 91 Jason Tyner SP	3.00	1.25
❑ 92 Miguel Tejada SP	3.00	1.25
❑ 93 Elpidio Guzman SP	3.00	1.25
❑ 94 Freddy Garcia SP	3.00	1.25
❑ 95 Marcus Giles SP	3.00	1.25
❑ 96 Junior Spivey SP	3.00	1.25
❑ 97 Aramis Ramirez SP	3.00	1.25
❑ 98 Jose Rijo SP	3.00	1.25
❑ 99 Paul LoDuca SP	3.00	1.25
❑ 100 Mike Cameron SP	3.00	1.25
❑ 101 Alex Hernandez	.30	.10
❑ 102 Benji Gil	.30	.10
❑ 103 Benito Santiago	.30	.10
❑ 104 Bobby Abreu	.30	.10
❑ 105 Brad Penny	.30	.10
❑ 106 Calvin Murray	.30	.10
❑ 107 Chad Durbin	.30	.10
❑ 108 Chris Singleton	.30	.10
❑ 109 Chris Carpenter	.30	.10
❑ 110 David Justice	.30	.10
❑ 111 Eric Chavez	.30	.10
❑ 112 Fernando Tatis	.30	.10
❑ 113 Frank Castillo	.30	.10
❑ 114 Jason LaRue	.30	.10
❑ 115 Jim Edmonds	.30	.10
❑ 116 Joe Kennedy	.30	.10
❑ 117 Jose Jimenez	.30	.10
❑ 118 Josh Towers	.30	.10
❑ 119 Junior Herndon	.30	.10
❑ 120 Luke Prokopec	.30	.10
❑ 121 Mac Suzuki	.30	.10
❑ 122 Mark DeRosa	.30	.10
❑ 123 Marty Cordova	.30	.10
❑ 124 Michael Tucker	.30	.10
❑ 125 Michael Young	.75	.30
❑ 126 Robin Ventura	.30	.10
❑ 127 Shane Halter	.30	.10
❑ 128 Shane Reynolds	.30	.10
❑ 129 Tony Womack	.30	.10
❑ 130 A.J. Pierzynski	.30	.10
❑ 131 Aaron Rowand	.30	.10
❑ 132 Antonio Alfonseca	.30	.10
❑ 133 Arthur Rhodes	.30	.10
❑ 134 Bob Wickman	.30	.10
❑ 135 Brady Clark	.30	.10
❑ 136 Chad Hermansen	.30	.10
❑ 137 Marlon Byrd	.30	.10
❑ 138 Dan Wilson	.30	.10
❑ 139 David Cone	.30	.10
❑ 140 Dean Palmer	.30	.10
❑ 141 Denny Neagle	.30	.10
❑ 142 Derek Jeter	2.00	.75
❑ 143 Erubiel Durazo	.30	.10
❑ 144 Felix Rodriguez	.30	.10
❑ 145 Jason Hart	.30	.10
❑ 146 Jay Bell	.30	.10
❑ 147 Jeff Suppan	.30	.10
❑ 148 Jeff Zimmerman	.30	.10
❑ 149 Kerry Wood	.30	.10
❑ 150 Kerry Robinson	.30	.10
❑ 151 Kevin Appier	.30	.10
❑ 152 Michael Barrett	.30	.10
❑ 153 Mo Vaughn	.30	.10
❑ 154 Rafael Furcal	.30	.10
❑ 155 Sidney Ponson	.30	.10
❑ 156 Terry Adams	.30	.10
❑ 157 Tim Redding	.30	.10
❑ 158 Toby Hall	.30	.10
❑ 159 Aaron Sele	.30	.10
❑ 160 Bartolo Colon	.30	.10
❑ 161 Brad Ausmus	.30	.10
❑ 162 Carlos Pena	.30	.10
❑ 163 Jace Brewer	.30	.10
❑ 164 David Wells	.30	.10
❑ 165 David Segui	.30	.10
❑ 166 Derek Lowe	.30	.10
❑ 167 Derek Bell	.30	.10
❑ 168 Jason Grabowski	.30	.10
❑ 169 Johnny Damon	.50	.20
❑ 170 Jose Mesa	.30	.10
❑ 171 Juan Encarnacion	.30	.10
❑ 172 Ken Caminiti	.30	.10
❑ 173 Ken Griffey Jr.	1.25	.50
❑ 174 Luis Rivas	.30	.10
❑ 175 Mariano Rivera	.75	.30
❑ 176 Mark Grudzielanek	.30	.10

❑	177	Mark McGwire	2.00	.75
❑	178	Mike Bordick	.30	.10
❑	179	Mike Hampton	.30	.10
❑	180	Nick Bierbrodt	.30	.10
❑	181	Paul Byrd	.30	.10
❑	182	Robb Nen	.30	.10
❑	183	Ryan Dempster	.30	.10
❑	184	Ryan Klesko	.30	.10
❑	185	Scott Spiezio	.30	.10
❑	186	Scott Strickland	.30	.10
❑	187	Todd Zeile	.30	.10
❑	188	Tom Gordon	.30	.10
❑	189	Troy Glaus	.30	.10
❑	190	Matt Williams	.30	.10
❑	191	Wes Helms	.30	.10
❑	192	Jerry Hairston Jr.	.30	.10
❑	193	Brook Fordyce	.30	.10
❑	194	Nomar Garciaparra	1.25	.50
❑	195	Kevin Tapani	.30	.10
❑	196	Mark Buehrle	.30	.10
❑	197	Dmitri Young	.30	.10
❑	198	John Rocker	.30	.10
❑	199	Juan Uribe	.30	.10
❑	200	Matt Anderson	.30	.10
❑	201	Alex Gonzalez	.30	.10
❑	202	Julio Lugo	.30	.10
❑	203	Roberto Hernandez	.30	.10
❑	204	Richie Sexson	.30	.10
❑	205	Corey Koskie	.30	.10
❑	206	Tony Armas Jr.	.30	.10
❑	207	Rey Ordonez	.30	.10
❑	208	Orlando Hernandez	.30	.10
❑	209	Pokey Reese	.30	.10
❑	210	Mike Lieberthal	.30	.10
❑	211	Kris Benson	.30	.10
❑	212	Jermaine Dye	.30	.10
❑	213	Livan Hernandez	.30	.10
❑	214	Bret Boone	.30	.10
❑	215	Dustin Hermanson	.30	.10
❑	216	Placido Polanco	.30	.10
❑	217	Jesus Colome	.30	.10
❑	218	Alex Gonzalez	.30	.10
❑	219	Adam Everett	.30	.10
❑	220	Adam Piatt	.30	.10
❑	221	Brad Fullmer	.30	.10
❑	222	Brian Buchanan	.30	.10
❑	223	Chipper Jones	.75	.30
❑	224	Chuck Finley	.30	.10
❑	225	David Bell	.30	.10
❑	226	Jack Wilson	.30	.10
❑	227	Jason Bere	.30	.10
❑	228	Jeff Conine	.30	.10
❑	229	Jeff Bagwell	.50	.20
❑	230	Joe McEwing	.30	.10
❑	231	Kip Wells	.30	.10
❑	232	Mike Lansing	.30	.10
❑	233	Neifi Perez	.30	.10
❑	234	Omar Daal	.30	.10
❑	235	Reggie Sanders	.30	.10
❑	236	Shawn Wooten	.30	.10
❑	237	Shawn Chacon	.30	.10
❑	238	Shawn Estes	.30	.10
❑	239	Steve Sparks	.30	.10
❑	240	Steve Kline	.30	.10
❑	241	Tino Martinez	.50	.20
❑	242	Tyler Houston	.30	.10
❑	243	Xavier Nady	.30	.10
❑	244	Bengie Molina	.30	.10
❑	245	Ben Davis	.30	.10
❑	246	Casey Fossum	.30	.10
❑	247	Chris Stynes	.30	.10
❑	248	Danny Graves	.30	.10
❑	249	Pedro Feliz	.30	.10
❑	250	Darren Oliver	.30	.10
❑	251	Dave Veres	.30	.10
❑	252	Deivi Cruz	.30	.10
❑	253	Desi Relaford	.30	.10
❑	254	Devon White	.30	.10
❑	255	Edgar Martinez	.50	.20
❑	256	Eric Munson	.30	.10
❑	257	Eric Karros	.30	.10
❑	258	Homer Bush	.30	.10
❑	259	Jason Kendall	.30	.10
❑	260	Javy Lopez	.30	.10
❑	261	Keith Foulke	.30	.10
❑	262	Keith Ginter	.30	.10
❑	263	Nick Johnson	.30	.10
❑	264	Pat Burrell	.30	.10
❑	265	Ricky Gutierrez	.30	.10
❑	266	Russ Johnson	.30	.10
❑	267	Steve Finley	.30	.10
❑	268	Terrence Long	.30	.10
❑	269	Tony Batista	.30	.10
❑	270	Torii Hunter	.30	.10
❑	271	Vinny Castilla	.30	.10
❑	272	A.J. Burnett	.30	.10
❑	273	Adrian Beltre	.30	.10
❑	274	Alex Rodriguez	1.25	.50
❑	275	Armando Benitez	.30	.10
❑	276	Billy Koch	.30	.10
❑	277	Brady Anderson	.30	.10
❑	278	Brian Jordan	.30	.10
❑	279	Carlos Febles	.30	.10
❑	280	Daryle Ward	.30	.10
❑	281	Eli Marrero	.30	.10
❑	282	Garret Anderson	.30	.10
❑	283	Jack Cust	.30	.10
❑	284	Jacque Jones	.30	.10
❑	285	Jamie Moyer	.30	.10
❑	286	Jeffrey Hammonds	.30	.10
❑	287	Jim Thome	.50	.20
❑	288	Jon Garland	.30	.10
❑	289	Jose Offerman	.30	.10
❑	290	Matt Stairs	.30	.10
❑	291	Orlando Cabrera	.30	.10
❑	292	Ramiro Mendoza	.30	.10
❑	293	Ray Durham	.30	.10
❑	294	Rickey Henderson	.75	.30
❑	295	Rob Mackowiak	.30	.10
❑	296	Scott Rolen	.50	.20
❑	297	Tim Hudson	.30	.10
❑	298	Todd Helton	.50	.20
❑	299	Tony Clark	.30	.10
❑	300	B.J. Surhoff	.30	.10
❑	301	Bernie Williams	.50	.20
❑	302	Bill Mueller	.30	.10
❑	303	Chris Richard	.30	.10
❑	304	Craig Paquette	.30	.10
❑	305	Curt Schilling	.30	.10
❑	306	Damian Jackson	.30	.10
❑	307	Derrek Lee	.50	.20
❑	308	Eric Milton	.30	.10
❑	309	Frank Catalanotto	.30	.10
❑	310	J.T. Snow	.30	.10
❑	311	Jared Sandberg	.30	.10
❑	312	Jason Varitek	.75	.30
❑	313	Jeff Cirillo	.30	.10
❑	314	Jeromy Burnitz	.30	.10
❑	315	Joe Crede	.30	.10
❑	316	Joel Pineiro	.30	.10
❑	317	Jose Cruz Jr.	.30	.10
❑	318	Kevin Young	.30	.10
❑	319	Marquis Grissom	.30	.10
❑	320	Moises Alou	.30	.10
❑	321	Randall Simon	.30	.10
❑	322	Royce Clayton	.30	.10
❑	323	Tim Salmon	.50	.20
❑	324	Travis Fryman	.30	.10
❑	325	Travis Lee	.30	.10
❑	326	Vance Wilson	.30	.10
❑	327	Jarrod Washburn	.30	.10
❑	328	Ben Petrick	.30	.10
❑	329	Ben Grieve	.30	.10
❑	330	Carl Everett	.30	.10
❑	331	Eric Byrnes	.30	.10
❑	332	Doug Glanville	.30	.10
❑	333	Edgardo Alfonzo	.30	.10
❑	334	Ellis Burks	.30	.10
❑	335	Gabe Kapler	.30	.10
❑	336	Gary Sheffield	.30	.10
❑	337	Greg Maddux	1.25	.50
❑	338	J.D. Drew	.30	.10
❑	339	Jamey Wright	.30	.10
❑	340	Jeff Kent	.30	.10
❑	341	Jeremy Giambi	.30	.10
❑	342	Joe Randa	.30	.10
❑	343	Joe Mays	.30	.10
❑	344	Jose Macias	.30	.10
❑	345	Kazuhiro Sasaki	.30	.10
❑	346	Mike Kinkade	.30	.10
❑	347	Mike Lowell	.30	.10
❑	348	Randy Johnson	.75	.30
❑	349	Randy Wolf	.30	.10
❑	350	Richard Hidalgo	.30	.10
❑	351	Ron Coomer	.30	.10
❑	352	Sandy Alomar Jr.	.30	.10
❑	353	Sean Casey	.30	.10
❑	354	Trevor Hoffman	.30	.10
❑	355	Adam Eaton	.30	.10
❑	356	Alfonso Soriano	.30	.10
❑	357	Barry Zito	.30	.10
❑	358	Billy Wagner	.30	.10
❑	359	Brent Abernathy	.30	.10
❑	360	Bret Prinz	.30	.10
❑	361	Carlos Beltran	.30	.10
❑	362	Carlos Guillen	.30	.10
❑	363	Charles Johnson	.30	.10
❑	364	Cristian Guzman	.30	.10
❑	365	Damion Easley	.30	.10
❑	366	Darryl Kile	.30	.10
❑	367	Delino DeShields	.30	.10
❑	368	Eric Davis	.30	.10
❑	369	Frank Thomas	.75	.30
❑	370	Ivan Rodriguez	.50	.20
❑	371	Jay Payton	.30	.10
❑	372	Jeff D'Amico	.30	.10
❑	373	John Burkett	.30	.10
❑	374	Melvin Mora	.30	.10
❑	375	Ramon Ortiz	.30	.10
❑	376	Robert Person	.30	.10
❑	377	Russell Branyan	.30	.10
❑	378	Shawn Green	.30	.10
❑	379	Todd Hollandsworth	.30	.10
❑	380	Tony McKnight	.30	.10
❑	381	Trot Nixon	.30	.10
❑	382	Vernon Wells	.30	.10
❑	383	Troy Percival	.30	.10
❑	384	Albie Lopez	.30	.10
❑	385	Alex Ochoa	.30	.10
❑	386	Andy Pettitte	.50	.20
❑	387	Brandon Inge	.30	.10
❑	388	Bubba Trammell	.30	.10
❑	389	Corey Patterson	.30	.10
❑	390	Damian Rolls	.30	.10
❑	391	Dee Brown	.30	.10
❑	392	Edgar Renteria	.30	.10
❑	393	Eric Gagne	.30	.10
❑	394	Jason Johnson	.30	.10
❑	395	Jeff Nelson	.30	.10
❑	396	John Vander Wal	.30	.10
❑	397	Johnny Estrada	.30	.10
❑	398	Jose Canseco	.50	.20
❑	399	Juan Gonzalez	.30	.10
❑	400	Kevin Millwood	.30	.10
❑	401	Lee Stevens	.30	.10
❑	402	Matt Lawton	.30	.10
❑	403	Mike Lamb	.30	.10
❑	404	Octavio Dotel	.30	.10
❑	405	Ramon Hernandez	.30	.10
❑	406	Ruben Quevedo	.30	.10
❑	407	Todd Walker	.30	.10
❑	408	Troy O'Leary	.30	.10
❑	409	Wascar Serrano	.30	.10
❑	410	Aaron Boone	.30	.10
❑	411	Aubrey Huff	.30	.10
❑	412	Ben Sheets	.30	.10
❑	413	Carlos Lee	.30	.10
❑	414	Chuck Knoblauch	.30	.10
❑	415	Steve Karsay	.30	.10
❑	416	Dante Bichette	.30	.10
❑	417	David Dellucci	.30	.10
❑	418	Esteban Loaiza	.30	.10
❑	419	Fernando Vina	.30	.10
❑	420	Ismael Valdes	.30	.10
❑	421	Jason Isringhausen	.30	.10
❑	422	Jeff Shaw	.30	.10
❑	423	John Smoltz	.50	.20
❑	424	Jose Vidro	.30	.10
❑	425	Kenny Lofton	.30	.10
❑	426	Mark Little	.30	.10
❑	427	Mark McLemore	.30	.10
❑	428	Marvin Benard	.30	.10
❑	429	Mike Piazza	1.25	.50
❑	430	Pat Hentgen	.30	.10
❑	431	Preston Wilson	.30	.10
❑	432	Rick Helling	.30	.10
❑	433	Robert Fick	.30	.10
❑	434	Rondell White	.30	.10

Card	Hi	Lo
❑ 435 Adam Kennedy	.30	.10
❑ 436 David Espinosa PROS	.50	.20
❑ 437 Dewon Brazelton PROS	.50	.20
❑ 438 Drew Henson PROS	.50	.20
❑ 439 Juan Cruz PROS	.50	.20
❑ 440 Jason Jennings PROS	.50	.20
❑ 441 Carlos Garcia PROS	.50	.20
❑ 442 Carlos Hernandez PROS	.50	.20
❑ 443 Wilkin Ruan PROS	.50	.20
❑ 444 Wilson Betemit PROS	.50	.20
❑ 445 Horacio Ramirez PROS	.50	.20
❑ 446 Danys Baez PROS	.50	.20
❑ 447 Abraham Nunez PROS	.50	.20
❑ 448 Josh Hamilton PROS	1.00	.40
❑ 449 Chris George PROS	.50	.20
❑ 450 Rick Bauer PROS	.50	.20
❑ 451 Donnie Bridges PROS	.50	.20
❑ 452 Erick Almonte PROS	.50	.20
❑ 453 Cory Aldridge PROS	.50	.20
❑ 454 Ryan Drese PROS	.50	.20
❑ 455 Jason Romano PROS	.50	.20
❑ 456 Corky Miller PROS	.50	.20
❑ 457 Rafael Soriano PROS	.50	.20
❑ 458 Mark Prior PROS	1.25	.50
❑ 459 Mark Teixeira PROS	1.25	.50
❑ 460 Adrian Hernandez PROS	.50	.20
❑ 461 Tim Spooneybarger PROS	.50	.20
❑ 462 Bill Ortega PROS	.50	.20
❑ 463 D'Angelo Jimenez PROS	.50	.20
❑ 464 Andres Torres PROS	.50	.20
❑ 465 Alexis Gomez PROS	.50	.20
❑ 466 Angel Berroa PROS	.50	.20
❑ 467 Henry Mateo PROS	.50	.20
❑ 468 Endy Chavez PROS	.50	.20
❑ 469 Billy Sylvester PROS	.50	.20
❑ 470 Nate Frese PROS	.50	.20
❑ 471 Luis Gonzalez BNR	.30	.10
❑ 472 Barry Bonds BNR	2.00	.75
❑ 473 Rich Aurilia BNR	.30	.10
❑ 474 Albert Pujols BNR	1.50	.60
❑ 475 Todd Helton BNR	.50	.20
❑ 476 Moises Alou BNR	.30	.10
❑ 477 Lance Berkman BNR	.30	.10
❑ 478 Brian Giles BNR	.30	.10
❑ 479 Cliff Floyd BNR	.30	.10
❑ 480 Sammy Sosa BNR	.75	.30
❑ 481 Shawn Green BNR	.30	.10
❑ 482 Jon Lieber BNR	.30	.10
❑ 483 Matt Morris BNR	.30	.10
❑ 484 Curt Schilling BNR	.30	.10
❑ 485 Randy Johnson BNR	.50	.20
❑ 486 Manny Ramirez BNR	.50	.20
❑ 487 Ichiro Suzuki BNR	1.50	.60
❑ 488 Juan Gonzalez BNR	.30	.10
❑ 489 Derek Jeter BNR	2.00	.75
❑ 490 Alex Rodriguez BNR	1.25	.50
❑ 491 Bret Boone BNR	.30	.10
❑ 492 Roberto Alomar BNR	.50	.20
❑ 493 Jason Giambi BNR	.30	.10
❑ 494 Rafael Palmeiro BNR	.50	.20
❑ 495 Doug Mientkiewicz BNR	.30	.10
❑ 496 Jim Thome BNR	.30	.10
❑ 497 Freddy Garcia BNR	.30	.10
❑ 498 Mark Buehrle BNR	.30	.10
❑ 499 Mark Mulder BNR	.30	.10
❑ 500 Roger Clemens BNR	1.50	.60

2003 Fleer Tradition

Card	Hi	Lo
❑ COMPLETE SET (485)	150.00	75.00
❑ COMP.SET w/o SP's (385)	40.00	15.00
❑ COMMON CARD (1-30)	1.00	.40
❑ COMM.SP (31-66/86-100)	1.00	.40
❑ COMMON ML (67-85)	1.50	.60
❑ COMMON CARD (101-485)	.30	.10
❑ COMMON PR (426-460)	.30	.10
❑ 1 Wash/Glaus/And/Ortiz TL	1.00	.40
❑ 2 L.Gonzalez/R.Johnson TL	1.50	.60
❑ 3 Andruw/Chip/Glav/Mill TL	1.50	.60
❑ 4 T.Batista/R.Lopez TL	1.00	.40
❑ 5 Ram/Nomar/Lowe/Pedro TL	1.50	.60
❑ 6 Sosa/Clement/Wood TL	2.50	1.00
❑ 7 Buehrle/Magglio/Wright TL	1.00	.40
❑ 8 Dunn/Boone/Haynes TL	1.00	.40
❑ 9 C.Sabathia/J.Thome TL	1.00	.40
❑ 10 T.Helton/J.Jennings TL	1.00	.40
❑ 11 Simon/Sparks/Redman TL	1.00	.40
❑ 12 Lee/Lowell/Burnett TL	1.50	.60
❑ 13 L.Berkman/R.Oswalt TL	1.00	.40
❑ 14 P.Byrd/C.Beltran TL	1.00	.40
❑ 15 S.Green/H.Nomo TL	1.50	.60
❑ 16 R.Sexson/B.Sheets TL	1.00	.40
❑ 17 Hunter/Lohse/Santana TL	1.50	.60
❑ 18 Vladdie/Ohka/Vazquez TL	1.50	.60
❑ 19 M.Piazza/A.Leiter TL	2.50	1.00
❑ 20 Giambi/Wells/Clemens TL	2.50	1.00
❑ 21 Chavez/Tejada/Zito TL	1.00	.40
❑ 22 Burrell/Padilla/Wolf TL	1.00	.40
❑ 23 Giles/Fogg/Wells TL	1.00	.40
❑ 24 R.Klesko/B.Lawrence TL	1.00	.40
❑ 25 Bonds/Ortiz/Schmidt TL	2.50	1.00
❑ 26 Cameron/Boone/Garcia TL	1.00	.40
❑ 27 A.Pujols/M.Morris TL	2.50	1.00
❑ 28 Huff/Winn/Kenn/Sturtze TL	1.00	.40
❑ 29 A-Rod/Rogers/Park TL	2.50	1.00
❑ 30 C.Delgado/R.Halladay TL	1.00	.40
❑ 31 Greg Maddux SP	4.00	1.50
❑ 32 Nick Neugebauer SP	1.00	.40
❑ 33 Larry Walker SP	1.00	.40
❑ 34 Freddy Garcia SP	1.00	.40
❑ 35 Rich Aurilia SP	1.00	.40
❑ 36 Craig Wilson SP	1.00	.40
❑ 37 Jeff Suppan SP	1.00	.40
❑ 38 Joel Pineiro SP	1.00	.40
❑ 39 Pedro Feliz SP	1.00	.40
❑ 40 Bartolo Colon SP	1.00	.40
❑ 41 Pete Walker SP	1.00	.40
❑ 42 Mo Vaughn SP	1.00	.40
❑ 43 Sidney Ponson SP	1.00	.40
❑ 44 Jason Isringhausen SP	1.00	.40
❑ 45 Hideki Irabu SP	1.00	.40
❑ 46 Pedro Martinez SP	1.50	.60
❑ 47 Tom Glavine SP	1.50	.60
❑ 48 Matt Lawton SP	1.00	.40
❑ 49 Kyle Lohse SP	1.00	.40
❑ 50 Corey Patterson SP	1.00	.40
❑ 51 Ichiro Suzuki SP	5.00	2.00
❑ 52 Wade Miller SP	1.00	.40
❑ 53 Ben Diggins SP	1.00	.40
❑ 54 Jayson Werth SP	1.00	.40
❑ 55 Masato Yoshii SP	1.00	.40
❑ 56 Mark Buehrle SP	1.00	.40
❑ 57 Drew Henson SP	1.00	.40
❑ 58 Dave Williams SP	1.00	.40
❑ 59 Juan Rivera SP	1.00	.40
❑ 60 Scott Schoeneweis SP	1.00	.40
❑ 61 Josh Beckett SP	1.00	.40
❑ 62 Vinny Castilla SP	1.00	.40
❑ 63 Barry Zito SP	1.00	.40
❑ 64 Jose Valentin SP	1.00	.40
❑ 65 Jon Lieber SP	1.00	.40
❑ 66 Jorge Padilla SP	1.00	.40
❑ 67 Luis Aparicio ML SP	1.50	.60
❑ 68 Boog Powell ML SP	2.50	1.00
❑ 69 Dick Radatz ML SP	1.50	.60
❑ 70 Frank Malzone ML SP	1.50	.60
❑ 71 Lou Brock ML SP	2.50	1.00
❑ 72 Billy Williams ML SP	1.50	.60
❑ 73 Early Wynn ML SP	1.50	.60
❑ 74 Jim Bunning ML SP	2.50	1.00
❑ 75 Al Kaline ML SP	4.00	1.50
❑ 76 Eddie Mathews ML SP	4.00	1.50
❑ 77 Harmon Killebrew ML SP	4.00	1.50
❑ 78 Gil Hodges ML SP	2.50	1.00
❑ 79 Duke Snider ML SP	2.50	1.00

Card	Hi	Lo
❑ 80 Yogi Berra ML SP	4.00	1.50
❑ 81 Whitey Ford ML SP	2.50	1.00
❑ 82 Willie Stargell ML SP	2.50	1.00
❑ 83 Willie McCovey ML SP	1.50	.60
❑ 84 Gaylord Perry ML SP	1.50	.60
❑ 85 Red Schoendienst ML SP	1.50	.60
❑ 86 Luis Castillo SP	1.00	.40
❑ 87 Derek Jeter SP	6.00	2.50
❑ 88 Orlando Hudson SP	1.00	.40
❑ 89 Bobby Higginson SP	1.00	.40
❑ 90 Brent Butler SP	1.00	.40
❑ 91 Brad Wilkerson SP	1.00	.40
❑ 92 Craig Biggio SP	1.50	.60
❑ 93 Marlon Anderson SP	1.00	.40
❑ 94 Ty Wigginton SP	1.00	.40
❑ 95 Hideo Nomo SP	2.50	1.00
❑ 96 Barry Larkin SP	1.50	.60
❑ 97 Roberto Alomar SP	1.50	.60
❑ 98 Omar Vizquel SP	1.50	.60
❑ 99 Andres Galarraga SP	1.00	.40
❑ 100 Shawn Green SP	1.00	.40
❑ 101 Rafael Furcal	.30	.10
❑ 102 Bill Selby	.30	.10
❑ 103 Brent Abernathy	.30	.10
❑ 104 Nomar Garciaparra	1.25	.50
❑ 105 Michael Barrett	.30	.10
❑ 106 Travis Hafner	.30	.10
❑ 107 Carl Crawford	.30	.10
❑ 108 Jeff Cirillo	.30	.10
❑ 109 Mike Hampton	.30	.10
❑ 110 Kip Wells	.30	.10
❑ 111 Luis Alicea	.30	.10
❑ 112 Ellis Burks	.30	.10
❑ 113 Matt Anderson	.30	.10
❑ 114 Carlos Beltran	.30	.10
❑ 115 Paul Lo Duca	.30	.10
❑ 116 Lance Berkman	.30	.10
❑ 117 Moises Alou	.30	.10
❑ 118 Roger Cedeno	.30	.10
❑ 119 Brad Fullmer	.30	.10
❑ 120 Sean Burroughs	.30	.10
❑ 121 Eric Byrnes	.30	.10
❑ 122 Milton Bradley	.30	.10
❑ 123 Jason Giambi	.30	.10
❑ 124 Brook Fordyce	.30	.10
❑ 125 Kevin Appier	.30	.10
❑ 126 Steve Cox	.30	.10
❑ 127 Danny Bautista	.30	.10
❑ 128 Edgardo Alfonzo	.30	.10
❑ 129 Matt Clement	.30	.10
❑ 130 Robb Nen	.30	.10
❑ 131 Roy Halladay	.30	.10
❑ 132 Brian Jordan	.30	.10
❑ 133 A.J. Burnett	.30	.10
❑ 134 Aaron Cook	.30	.10
❑ 135 Paul Byrd	.30	.10
❑ 136 Ramon Ortiz	.30	.10
❑ 137 Adam Hyzdu	.30	.10
❑ 138 Rafael Soriano	.30	.10
❑ 139 Marty Cordova	.30	.10
❑ 140 Nelson Cruz	.30	.10
❑ 141 Jamie Moyer	.30	.10
❑ 142 Raul Mondesi	.30	.10
❑ 143 Josh Bard	.30	.10
❑ 144 Elmer Dessens	.30	.10
❑ 145 Rickey Henderson	.75	.30
❑ 146 Joe McEwing	.30	.10
❑ 147 Luis Rivas	.30	.10
❑ 148 Armando Benitez	.30	.10
❑ 149 Keith Foulke	.30	.10
❑ 150 Zach Day	.30	.10
❑ 151 Trey Lunsford	.30	.10
❑ 152 Bobby Abreu	.30	.10
❑ 153 Juan Cruz	.30	.10
❑ 154 Ramon Hernandez	.30	.10
❑ 155 Brandon Duckworth	.30	.10
❑ 156 Matt Ginter	.30	.10
❑ 157 Rob Mackowiak	.30	.10
❑ 158 Josh Pearce	.30	.10
❑ 159 Marlon Byrd	.30	.10
❑ 160 Todd Walker	.30	.10
❑ 161 Chad Hermansen	.30	.10
❑ 162 Felix Escalona	.30	.10
❑ 163 Ruben Mateo	.30	.10
❑ 164 Mark Johnson	.30	.10
❑ 165 Juan Pierre	.30	.10

❑ 166 Gary Sheffield .30 .10
❑ 167 Edgar Martinez .50 .20
❑ 168 Randy Winn .30 .10
❑ 169 Pokey Reese .30 .10
❑ 170 Kevin Mench .30 .10
❑ 171 Albert Pujols 1.50 .60
❑ 172 J.T. Snow .30 .10
❑ 173 Dean Palmer .30 .10
❑ 174 Jay Payton .30 .10
❑ 175 Abraham Nunez .30 .10
❑ 176 Richie Sexson .30 .10
❑ 177 Jose Vidro .30 .10
❑ 178 Geoff Jenkins .30 .10
❑ 179 Dan Wilson .30 .10
❑ 180 John Olerud .30 .10
❑ 181 Javy Lopez .30 .10
❑ 182 Carl Everett .30 .10
❑ 183 Vernon Wells .30 .10
❑ 184 Juan Gonzalez .30 .10
❑ 185 Jorge Posada .50 .20
❑ 186 Mike Sweeney .30 .10
❑ 187 Cesar Izturis .30 .10
❑ 188 Jason Schmidt .30 .10
❑ 189 Chris Richard .30 .10
❑ 190 Jason Phillips .30 .10
❑ 191 Fred McGriff .50 .20
❑ 192 Shea Hillenbrand .30 .10
❑ 193 Ivan Rodriguez .50 .20
❑ 194 Mike Lowell .30 .10
❑ 195 Neifi Perez .30 .10
❑ 196 Kenny Lofton .30 .10
❑ 197 A.J. Pierzynski .30 .10
❑ 198 Larry Bigbie .30 .10
❑ 199 Juan Uribe .30 .10
❑ 200 Jeff Bagwell .50 .20
❑ 201 Timo Perez .30 .10
❑ 202 Jeremy Giambi .30 .10
❑ 203 Deivi Cruz .30 .10
❑ 204 Marquis Grissom .30 .10
❑ 205 Chipper Jones .75 .30
❑ 206 Alex Gonzalez .30 .10
❑ 207 Steve Finley .30 .10
❑ 208 Ben Davis .30 .10
❑ 209 Mike Bordick .30 .10
❑ 210 Casey Fossum .30 .10
❑ 211 Aramis Ramirez .30 .10
❑ 212 Aaron Boone .30 .10
❑ 213 Orlando Cabrera .30 .10
❑ 214 Hee Seop Choi .30 .10
❑ 215 Jeromy Burnitz .30 .10
❑ 216 Todd Hollandsworth .30 .10
❑ 217 Rey Sanchez .30 .10
❑ 218 Jose Cruz .30 .10
❑ 219 Roosevelt Brown .30 .10
❑ 220 Odalis Perez .30 .10
❑ 221 Carlos Delgado .30 .10
❑ 222 Orlando Hernandez .30 .10
❑ 223 Adam Everett .30 .10
❑ 224 Adrian Beltre .30 .10
❑ 225 Ken Griffey Jr. 1.25 .50
❑ 226 Brad Penny .30 .10
❑ 227 Carlos Lee .30 .10
❑ 228 J.C. Romero .30 .10
❑ 229 Ramon Martinez .30 .10
❑ 230 Matt Morris .30 .10
❑ 231 Ben Howard .30 .10
❑ 232 Damon Minor .30 .10
❑ 233 Jason Marquis .30 .10
❑ 234 Paul Wilson .30 .10
❑ 235 Ryan Dempster .30 .10
❑ 236 Jeffrey Hammonds .30 .10
❑ 237 Jaret Wright .30 .10
❑ 238 Carlos Pena .30 .10
❑ 239 Toby Hall .30 .10
❑ 240 Rick Helling .30 .10
❑ 241 Alex Escobar .30 .10
❑ 242 Trevor Hoffman .30 .10
❑ 243 Bernie Williams .50 .20
❑ 244 Jorge Julio .30 .10
❑ 245 Byung-Hyun Kim .30 .10
❑ 246 Mike Redmond .30 .10
❑ 247 Tony Armas .30 .10
❑ 248 Aaron Rowand .30 .10
❑ 249 Rusty Greer .30 .10
❑ 250 Aaron Harang .30 .10
❑ 251 Jeremy Fikac .30 .10
❑ 252 Jay Gibbons .30 .10
❑ 253 Brandon Puffer .30 .10
❑ 254 Dewayne Wise .30 .10
❑ 255 Chan Ho Park .30 .10
❑ 256 David Bell .30 .10
❑ 257 Kenny Rogers .30 .10
❑ 258 Mark Quinn .30 .10
❑ 259 Greg LaRocca .30 .10
❑ 260 Reggie Taylor .30 .10
❑ 261 Brett Tomko .30 .10
❑ 262 Jack Wilson .30 .10
❑ 263 Billy Wagner .30 .10
❑ 264 Greg Norton .30 .10
❑ 265 Tim Salmon .50 .20
❑ 266 Joe Randa .30 .10
❑ 267 Geronimo Gil .30 .10
❑ 268 Johnny Damon 2.50 1.00
❑ 269 Robin Ventura .30 .10
❑ 270 Frank Thomas .75 .30
❑ 271 Terrence Long .30 .10
❑ 272 Mark Redman .30 .10
❑ 273 Mark Kotsay .30 .10
❑ 274 Ben Sheets .30 .10
❑ 275 Reggie Sanders .30 .10
❑ 276 Mark Grace .50 .20
❑ 277 Eddie Guardado .30 .10
❑ 278 Julio Mateo .30 .10
❑ 279 Bengie Molina .30 .10
❑ 280 Bill Hall .30 .10
❑ 281 Eric Chavez .30 .10
❑ 282 Joe Kennedy .30 .10
❑ 283 John Valentin .30 .10
❑ 284 Ray Durham .30 .10
❑ 285 Trot Nixon .30 .10
❑ 286 Rondell White .30 .10
❑ 287 Alex Gonzalez .30 .10
❑ 288 Tomas Perez .30 .10
❑ 289 Jared Sandberg .30 .10
❑ 290 Jacque Jones .30 .10
❑ 291 Cliff Floyd .30 .10
❑ 292 Ryan Klesko .30 .10
❑ 293 Morgan Ensberg .30 .10
❑ 294 Jerry Hairston .30 .10
❑ 295 Doug Mientkiewicz .30 .10
❑ 296 Darin Erstad .30 .10
❑ 297 Jeff Conine .30 .10
❑ 298 Johnny Estrada .30 .10
❑ 299 Mark Mulder .30 .10
❑ 300 Jeff Kent .30 .10
❑ 301 Roger Clemens 1.50 .60
❑ 302 Endy Chavez .30 .10
❑ 303 Joe Crede .30 .10
❑ 304 J.D. Drew .30 .10
❑ 305 David Dellucci .30 .10
❑ 306 Eli Marrero .30 .10
❑ 307 Josh Fogg .30 .10
❑ 308 Mike Crudale .30 .10
❑ 309 Bret Boone .30 .10
❑ 310 Mariano Rivera .75 .30
❑ 311 Mike Piazza 1.25 .50
❑ 312 Jason Jennings .30 .10
❑ 313 Jason Varitek .75 .30
❑ 314 Vicente Padilla .30 .10
❑ 315 Kevin Millwood .30 .10
❑ 316 Nick Johnson .30 .10
❑ 317 Shane Reynolds .30 .10
❑ 318 Joe Thurston .30 .10
❑ 319 Mike Lamb .30 .10
❑ 320 Aaron Sele .30 .10
❑ 321 Fernando Tatis .30 .10
❑ 322 Randy Wolf .30 .10
❑ 323 David Justice .30 .10
❑ 324 Andy Pettitte .50 .20
❑ 325 Freddy Sanchez .30 .10
❑ 326 Scott Spiezio .30 .10
❑ 327 Randy Johnson .75 .30
❑ 328 Karim Garcia .30 .10
❑ 329 Eric Milton .30 .10
❑ 330 Jermaine Dye .30 .10
❑ 331 Kevin Brown .30 .10
❑ 332 Adam Pettyjohn .30 .10
❑ 333 Jason Lane .30 .10
❑ 334 Mark Prior .50 .20
❑ 335 Mike Lieberthal .30 .10
❑ 336 Matt White .30 .10
❑ 337 John Patterson .30 .10
❑ 338 Marcus Giles .30 .10
❑ 339 Kazuhisa Ishii .30 .10
❑ 340 Willie Harris .30 .10
❑ 341 Travis Phelps .30 .10
❑ 342 Randall Simon .30 .10
❑ 343 Manny Ramirez .50 .20
❑ 344 Kerry Wood .30 .10
❑ 345 Shannon Stewart .30 .10
❑ 346 Mike Mussina .50 .20
❑ 347 Joe Borchard .30 .10
❑ 348 Tyler Walker .30 .10
❑ 349 Preston Wilson .30 .10
❑ 350 Damian Moss .30 .10
❑ 351 Eric Karros .30 .10
❑ 352 Bobby Kielty .30 .10
❑ 353 Jason LaRue .30 .10
❑ 354 Phil Nevin .30 .10
❑ 355 Tony Graffanino .30 .10
❑ 356 Antonio Alfonseca .30 .10
❑ 357 Eddie Taubensee .30 .10
❑ 358 Luis Ugueto .30 .10
❑ 359 Greg Vaughn .30 .10
❑ 360 Corey Thurman .30 .10
❑ 361 Omar Infante .30 .10
❑ 362 Alex Cintron .30 .10
❑ 363 Esteban Loaiza .30 .10
❑ 364 Tino Martinez .50 .20
❑ 365 David Eckstein .30 .10
❑ 366 Dave Pember RC .30 .10
❑ 367 Damian Rolls .30 .10
❑ 368 Richard Hidalgo .30 .10
❑ 369 Brad Radke .30 .10
❑ 370 Alex Sanchez .30 .10
❑ 371 Ben Grieve .30 .10
❑ 372 Brandon Inge .30 .10
❑ 373 Adam Platt .30 .10
❑ 374 Charles Johnson .30 .10
❑ 375 Rafael Palmeiro .50 .20
❑ 376 Joe Mays .30 .10
❑ 377 Derrek Lee .50 .20
❑ 378 Fernando Vina .30 .10
❑ 379 Andruw Jones .50 .20
❑ 380 Troy Glaus .30 .10
❑ 381 Bobby Hill .30 .10
❑ 382 C.C. Sabathia .30 .10
❑ 383 Jose Hernandez .30 .10
❑ 384 Al Leiter .30 .10
❑ 385 Jarrod Washburn .30 .10
❑ 386 Cody Ransom .30 .10
❑ 387 Matt Stairs .30 .10
❑ 388 Edgar Renteria .30 .10
❑ 389 Tsuyoshi Shinjo .30 .10
❑ 390 Matt Williams .30 .10
❑ 391 Bubba Trammell .30 .10
❑ 392 Jason Kendall .30 .10
❑ 393 Scott Rolen .50 .20
❑ 394 Chuck Knoblauch .30 .10
❑ 395 Jimmy Rollins .30 .10
❑ 396 Gary Bennett .30 .10
❑ 397 David Wells .30 .10
❑ 398 Ronnie Belliard .30 .10
❑ 399 Austin Kearns .30 .10
❑ 400 Tim Hudson .30 .10
❑ 401 Andy Van Hekken .30 .10
❑ 402 Ray Lankford .30 .10
❑ 403 Todd Helton .50 .20
❑ 404 Jeff Weaver .30 .10
❑ 405 Gabe Kapler .30 .10
❑ 406 Luis Gonzalez .30 .10
❑ 407 Sean Casey .30 .10
❑ 408 Kazuhiro Sasaki .30 .10
❑ 409 Mark Teixeira .50 .20
❑ 410 Brian Giles .30 .10
❑ 411 Robert Fick .30 .10
❑ 412 Wilkin Ruan .30 .10
❑ 413 Jose Rijo .30 .10
❑ 414 Ben Broussard .30 .10
❑ 415 Aubrey Huff .30 .10
❑ 416 Magglio Ordonez .30 .10
❑ 417 Barry Bonds AW 1.00 .40
❑ 418 Miguel Tejada AW .30 .10
❑ 419 Randy Johnson AW .50 .20
❑ 420 Barry Zito AW .30 .10
❑ 421 Jason Jennings AW .30 .10
❑ 422 Eric Hinske AW .30 .10
❑ 423 Benito Santiago AW .30 .10

❑ 424 Adam Kennedy AW .30 .10
❑ 425 Troy Glaus AW .30 .10
❑ 426 Brandon Phillips PR .30 .10
❑ 427 Jake Peavy PR .30 .10
❑ 428 Jason Romano PR .30 .10
❑ 429 Jeriome Robertson PR .30 .10
❑ 430 Aaron Guiel PR .30 .10
❑ 431 Hank Blalock PR .30 .10
❑ 432 Brad Lidge PR .30 .10
❑ 433 Francisco Rodriguez PR .30 .10
❑ 434 Jaime Cerda PR .30 .10
❑ 435 Jung Bong PR .30 .10
❑ 436 Reed Johnson PR .30 .10
❑ 437 Rene Reyes PR .30 .10
❑ 438 Chris Snelling PR .30 .10
❑ 439 Miguel Olivo PR .30 .10
❑ 440 Brian Banks PR .30 .10
❑ 441 Eric Junge PR .30 .10
❑ 442 Kirk Saarloos PR .30 .10
❑ 443 Jamey Carroll PR .30 .10
❑ 444 Josh Hancock PR .30 .10
❑ 445 Michael Restovich PR .30 .10
❑ 446 Willie Bloomquist PR .30 .10
❑ 447 John Lackey PR .30 .10
❑ 448 Marcus Thames PR .30 .10
❑ 449 Victor Martinez PR .50 .20
❑ 450 Brett Myers PR .30 .10
❑ 451 Wes Obermueller PR .30 .10
❑ 452 Hansel Izquierdo PR .30 .10
❑ 453 Brian Tallet PR .30 .10
❑ 454 Craig Monroe PR .30 .10
❑ 455 Doug Devore PR .30 .10
❑ 456 John Buck PR .30 .10
❑ 457 Tony Alvarez PR .30 .10
❑ 458 Wily Mo Pena PR .30 .10
❑ 459 John Stephens PR .30 .10
❑ 460 Tony Torcato PR .30 .10
❑ 461 Adam Kennedy BNR .30 .10
❑ 462 Alex Rodriguez BNR .75 .30
❑ 463 Derek Lowe BNR .30 .10
❑ 464 Garret Anderson BNR .30 .10
❑ 465 Pat Burrell BNR .30 .10
❑ 466 Eric Gagne BNR .30 .10
❑ 467 Tomo Ohka BNR .30 .10
❑ 468 Josh Phelps BNR .30 .10
❑ 469 Sammy Sosa BNR .75 .30
❑ 470 Jim Thome BNR .30 .10
❑ 471 Vladimir Guerrero BNR .50 .20
❑ 472 Jason Simontacchi BNR .30 .10
❑ 473 Adam Dunn BNR .30 .10
❑ 474 Jim Edmonds BNR .30 .10
❑ 475 Barry Bonds BNR 1.00 .40
❑ 476 Paul Konerko BNR .30 .10
❑ 477 Alfonso Soriano BNR .30 .10
❑ 478 Curt Schilling BNR .30 .10
❑ 479 John Smoltz BNR .30 .10
❑ 480 Torii Hunter BNR .30 .10
❑ 481 Rodrigo Lopez BNR .30 .10
❑ 482 Miguel Tejada BNR .30 .10
❑ 483 Eric Hinske BNR .30 .10
❑ 484 Roy Oswalt BNR .30 .10
❑ 485 Junior Spivey BNR .30 .10
❑ P1 Barry Bonds Pin 8.00 3.00
❑ P87 Derek Jeter Promo 2.00 .75

2004 Fleer Tradition

❑ COMPLETE SET (500) 150.00 75.00
❑ COMP.SET w/o SP's (400) 40.00 15.00
❑ COMMON CARD (1-400) .30 .10
❑ COMMON CARD (401-470) 1.00 .40
❑ COMMON CARD (471-500) 1.00 .40
❑ 401-445 STATED ODDS 1:2
❑ 446-461 STATED ODDS 1:6
❑ 462-470 STATED ODDS 1:9
❑ 471-500 STATED ODDS 1:3
❑ 1 Juan Pierre WS .30 .10
❑ 2 Josh Beckett WS .30 .10
❑ 3 Ivan Rodriguez WS .50 .20
❑ 4 Miguel Cabrera WS .50 .20
❑ 5 Dontrelle Willis WS .50 .20
❑ 6 Derek Jeter WS 1.50 .60
❑ 7 Jason Giambi WS .30 .10
❑ 8 Bernie Williams WS .50 .20
❑ 9 Alfonso Soriano WS .30 .10
❑ 10 Hideki Matsui WS 1.25 .50
❑ 11 Anderson/Ortiz/Lackey TL .30 .10
❑ 12 Gonzalez/Webb/Schilling TL .30 .10
❑ 13 Lopez/Sheffield/Ortiz TL .30 .10
❑ 14 Batista/Gibb/Ponson/John TL .30 .10
❑ 15 Manny/Nomar/Lowe/Pedro TL .50 .20
❑ 16 Sosa/Prior/Wood TL .50 .20
❑ 17 Thomas/Lee/Loaiza TL .50 .20
❑ 18 Dunn/Casey/Reit/Wilson TL .30 .10
❑ 19 Gerut/Sabathia TL .30 .10
❑ 20 Wilson/Oliver/Jennings TL .30 .10
❑ 21 Young/Maroth/Bonderman TL .30 .10
❑ 22 Lowell/Willis/Beckett TL .50 .20
❑ 23 Bagwell/Robertson/Miller TL .30 .10
❑ 24 Beltran/May TL .30 .10
❑ 25 Beltre/Green/Nomo/Brown TL .30 .10
❑ 26 Sexson/Sheets TL .30 .10
❑ 27 Hunter/Radke/Santana TL .50 .20
❑ 28 Vlad/Cabrera/Livan/Vazq TL .50 .20
❑ 29 Floyd/Wigg/Trach/Leiter TL .30 .10
❑ 30 Giambi/Pettitte/Mussina TL .50 .20
❑ 31 Chavez/Tejada/Hudson TL .30 .10
❑ 32 Thome/Wolf TL .30 .10
❑ 33 Sanders/Fogg/Wells TL .30 .10
❑ 34 Klesko/Loretta/Peavy TL .30 .10
❑ 35 Cruz Jr./Alfonzo/Schmidt TL .30 .10
❑ 36 Boone/Moyer/Pineiro TL .30 .10
❑ 37 Pujols/Williams TL .75 .30
❑ 38 Huff/Zambrano TL .30 .10
❑ 39 A.Rodriguez/Thomson TL .75 .30
❑ 40 Delgado/Halladay TL .30 .10
❑ 41 Greg Maddux 1.25 .50
❑ 42 Ben Grieve .30 .10
❑ 43 Darin Erstad .30 .10
❑ 44 Ruben Sierra .30 .10
❑ 45 Byung-Hyung Kim .30 .10
❑ 46 Freddy Garcia .30 .10
❑ 47 Richard Hidalgo .30 .10
❑ 48 Tike Redman .30 .10
❑ 49 Kevin Millwood .30 .10
❑ 50 Marquis Grissom .30 .10
❑ 51 Jae Weong Seo .30 .10
❑ 52 Wil Cordero .30 .10
❑ 53 LaTroy Hawkins .30 .10
❑ 54 Jolbert Cabrera .30 .10
❑ 55 Kevin Appier .30 .10
❑ 56 John Lackey .30 .10
❑ 57 Garret Anderson .30 .10
❑ 58 R.A. Dickey .30 .10
❑ 59 David Segui .30 .10
❑ 60 Erubiel Durazo .30 .10
❑ 61 Bobby Abreu .30 .10
❑ 62 Travis Hafner .30 .10
❑ 63 Victor Zambrano .30 .10
❑ 64 Randy Johnson .75 .30
❑ 65 Bernie Williams .50 .20
❑ 66 J.T. Snow .30 .10
❑ 67 Sammy Sosa .75 .30
❑ 68 Al Leiter .30 .10
❑ 69 Jason Jennings .30 .10
❑ 70 Matt Morris .30 .10
❑ 71 Mike Hampton .30 .10
❑ 72 Juan Encarnacion .30 .10
❑ 73 Alex Gonzalez .30 .10
❑ 74 Bartolo Colon .30 .10
❑ 75 Brett Myers .30 .10
❑ 76 Michael Young .30 .10
❑ 77 Ichiro Suzuki 1.50 .60
❑ 78 Jason Johnson .30 .10
❑ 79 Brad Ausmus .30 .10
❑ 80 Ted Lilly .30 .10
❑ 81 Ken Griffey Jr. 1.25 .50
❑ 82 Chone Figgins .30 .10
❑ 83 Edgar Martinez .50 .20
❑ 84 Adam Eaton .30 .10
❑ 85 Ken Harvey .30 .10
❑ 86 Francisco Rodriguez .30 .10
❑ 87 Bill Mueller .30 .10
❑ 88 Mike Maroth .30 .10
❑ 89 Charles Johnson .30 .10
❑ 90 Jhonny Peralta .30 .10
❑ 91 Kip Wells .30 .10
❑ 92 Cesar Izturis .30 .10
❑ 93 Matt Clement .30 .10
❑ 94 Lyle Overbay .30 .10
❑ 95 Kirk Rueter .30 .10
❑ 96 Cristian Guzman .30 .10
❑ 97 Garrett Stephenson .30 .10
❑ 98 Lance Berkman .30 .10
❑ 99 Brett Tomko .30 .10
❑ 100 Chris Stynes .30 .10
❑ 101 Nate Cornejo .30 .10
❑ 102 Aaron Rowand .30 .10
❑ 103 Javier Vazquez .30 .10
❑ 104 Jason Kendall .30 .10
❑ 105 Mark Redman .30 .10
❑ 106 Benito Santiago .30 .10
❑ 107 C.C. Sabathia .30 .10
❑ 108 David Wells .30 .10
❑ 109 Mark Ellis .30 .10
❑ 110 Casey Blake .30 .10
❑ 111 Sean Burroughs .30 .10
❑ 112 Carlos Beltran .30 .10
❑ 113 Ramon Hernandez .30 .10
❑ 114 Eric Hinske .30 .10
❑ 115 Luis Gonzalez .30 .10
❑ 116 Jarrod Washburn .30 .10
❑ 117 Ronnie Belliard .30 .10
❑ 118 Troy Percival .30 .10
❑ 119 Jose Valentin .30 .10
❑ 120 Chase Utley .50 .20
❑ 121 Odalis Perez .30 .10
❑ 122 Steve Finley .30 .10
❑ 123 Bret Boone .30 .10
❑ 124 Jeff Conine .30 .10
❑ 125 Josh Fogg .30 .10
❑ 126 Neifi Perez .30 .10
❑ 127 Ben Sheets .30 .10
❑ 128 Randy Winn .30 .10
❑ 129 Matt Stairs .30 .10
❑ 130 Carlos Delgado .30 .10
❑ 131 Morgan Ensberg .30 .10
❑ 132 Vinny Castilla .30 .10
❑ 133 Matt Mantei .30 .10
❑ 134 Alex Rodriguez 1.25 .50
❑ 135 Matthew LeCroy .30 .10
❑ 136 Woody Williams .30 .10
❑ 137 Frank Catalanotto .30 .10
❑ 138 Rondell White .30 .10
❑ 139 Scott Rolen .50 .20
❑ 140 Cliff Floyd .30 .10
❑ 141 Chipper Jones .75 .30
❑ 142 Robin Ventura .30 .10
❑ 143 Mariano Rivera .75 .30
❑ 144 Brady Clark .30 .10
❑ 145 Ramon Ortiz .30 .10
❑ 146 Omar Infante .30 .10
❑ 147 Mike Matheny .30 .10
❑ 148 Pedro Martinez .50 .20
❑ 149 Carlos Baerga .30 .10
❑ 150 Shannon Stewart .30 .10
❑ 151 Travis Lee .30 .10
❑ 152 Eric Byrnes .30 .10
❑ 153 Rafael Furcal .30 .10
❑ 154 B.J. Surhoff .30 .10
❑ 155 Zach Day .30 .10
❑ 156 Marlon Anderson .30 .10
❑ 157 Mark Hendrickson .30 .10
❑ 158 Mike Mussina .50 .20
❑ 159 Randall Simon .30 .10
❑ 160 Jeff DaVanon .30 .10
❑ 161 Joel Pineiro .30 .10
❑ 162 Vernon Wells .30 .10
❑ 163 Adam Kennedy .30 .10
❑ 164 Trot Nixon .30 .10
❑ 165 Rodrigo Lopez .30 .10

❑ 166 Curt Schilling .30 .10
❑ 167 Horacio Ramirez .30 .10
❑ 168 Jason Marquis .30 .10
❑ 169 Magglio Ordonez .30 .10
❑ 170 Scott Schoeneweis .30 .10
❑ 171 Andruw Jones .50 .20
❑ 172 Tino Martinez .50 .20
❑ 173 Moises Alou .30 .10
❑ 174 Kelvim Escobar .30 .10
❑ 175 Xavier Nady .30 .10
❑ 176 Ramon Martinez .30 .10
❑ 177 Pat Hentgen .30 .10
❑ 178 Austin Kearns .30 .10
❑ 179 D'Angelo Jimenez .30 .10
❑ 180 Deivi Cruz .30 .10
❑ 181 John Smoltz .50 .20
❑ 182 Toby Hall .30 .10
❑ 183 Mark Buehrle .30 .10
❑ 184 Howie Clark .30 .10
❑ 185 David Ortiz .75 .30
❑ 186 Raul Mondesi .30 .10
❑ 187 Milton Bradley .30 .10
❑ 188 Jorge Julio .30 .10
❑ 189 Victor Martinez .30 .10
❑ 190 Gabe Kapler .30 .10
❑ 191 Julio Franco .30 .10
❑ 192 Ryan Freel .30 .10
❑ 193 Brad Fullmer .30 .10
❑ 194 Joe Borowski .30 .10
❑ 195 Darren Oliver .30 .10
❑ 196 Jason Varitek .75 .30
❑ 197 Greg Myers .30 .10
❑ 198 Eric Munson .30 .10
❑ 199 Tim Wakefield .30 .10
❑ 200 Kyle Farnsworth .30 .10
❑ 201 Johnny Vander Wal .30 .10
❑ 202 Alex Escobar .30 .10
❑ 203 Sean Casey .30 .10
❑ 204 John Thomson .30 .10
❑ 205 Carlos Zambrano .30 .10
❑ 206 Kenny Lofton .30 .10
❑ 207 Marcus Giles .30 .10
❑ 208 Wade Miller .30 .10
❑ 209 Geoff Blum .30 .10
❑ 210 Jason LaRue .30 .10
❑ 211 Omar Vizquel .50 .20
❑ 212 Carlos Pena .30 .10
❑ 213 Adam Dunn .30 .10
❑ 214 Oscar Villarreal .30 .10
❑ 215 Paul Konerko .30 .10
❑ 216 Hideo Nomo .75 .30
❑ 217 Mike Sweeney .30 .10
❑ 218 Coco Crisp .30 .10
❑ 219 Shawn Chacon .30 .10
❑ 220 Brook Fordyce .30 .10
❑ 221 Josh Beckett .30 .10
❑ 222 Paul Wilson .30 .10
❑ 223 Josh Towers .30 .10
❑ 224 Geoff Jenkins .30 .10
❑ 225 Shawn Green .30 .10
❑ 226 Derrek Lee .50 .20
❑ 227 Karim Garcia .30 .10
❑ 228 Preston Wilson .30 .10
❑ 229 Dane Sardinha .30 .10
❑ 230 Aramis Ramirez .30 .10
❑ 231 Doug Mientkiewicz .30 .10
❑ 232 Jay Gibbons .30 .10
❑ 233 Adam Everett .30 .10
❑ 234 Brooks Kieschnick .30 .10
❑ 235 Dmitri Young .30 .10
❑ 236 Brad Penny .30 .10
❑ 237 Todd Zeile .30 .10
❑ 238 Eric Gagne .30 .10
❑ 239 Esteban Loaiza .30 .10
❑ 240 Billy Wagner .30 .10
❑ 241 Nomar Garciaparra 1.25 .50
❑ 242 Desi Relaford .30 .10
❑ 243 Luis Rivas .30 .10
❑ 244 Andy Pettitte .50 .20
❑ 245 Ty Wigginton .30 .10
❑ 246 Edgar Gonzalez .30 .10
❑ 247 Brian Anderson .30 .10
❑ 248 Richie Sexson .30 .10
❑ 249 Russell Branyan .30 .10
❑ 250 Jose Guillen .30 .10
❑ 251 Chin-Hui Tsao .30 .10
❑ 252 Jose Hernandez .30 .10
❑ 253 Kevin Brown .30 .10
❑ 254 Pete LaForest .30 .10
❑ 255 Adrian Beltre .30 .10
❑ 256 Jacque Jones .30 .10
❑ 257 Jimmy Rollins .30 .10
❑ 258 Brandon Phillips .30 .10
❑ 259 Derek Jeter 1.50 .60
❑ 260 Carl Everett .30 .10
❑ 261 Wes Helms .30 .10
❑ 262 Kyle Lohse .30 .10
❑ 263 Jason Phillips .30 .10
❑ 264 Jake Peavy .30 .10
❑ 265 Orlando Hernandez .30 .10
❑ 266 Keith Foulke .30 .10
❑ 267 Brad Wilkerson .30 .10
❑ 268 Corey Koskie .30 .10
❑ 269 Josh Hall .30 .10
❑ 270 Bobby Higginson .30 .10
❑ 271 Andres Galarraga .30 .10
❑ 272 Alfonso Soriano .30 .10
❑ 273 Carlos Rivera .30 .10
❑ 274 Steve Trachsel .30 .10
❑ 275 David Bell .30 .10
❑ 276 Endy Chavez .30 .10
❑ 277 Jay Payton .30 .10
❑ 278 Mark Mulder .30 .10
❑ 279 Terrence Long .30 .10
❑ 280 A.J. Burnett .30 .10
❑ 281 Pokey Reese .30 .10
❑ 282 Phil Nevin .30 .10
❑ 283 Jose Contreras .30 .10
❑ 284 Jim Thome .50 .20
❑ 285 Pat Burrell .30 .10
❑ 286 Luis Castillo .30 .10
❑ 287 Juan Uribe .30 .10
❑ 288 Raul Ibanez .30 .10
❑ 289 Sidney Ponson .30 .10
❑ 290 Scott Hatteberg .30 .10
❑ 291 Jack Wilson .30 .10
❑ 292 Reggie Sanders .30 .10
❑ 293 Brian Giles .30 .10
❑ 294 Craig Biggio .50 .20
❑ 295 Kazuhisa Ishii .30 .10
❑ 296 Jim Edmonds .30 .10
❑ 297 Trevor Hoffman .30 .10
❑ 298 Ray Durham .30 .10
❑ 299 Mike Lieberthal .30 .10
❑ 300 Tim Worrell .30 .10
❑ 301 Chris George .30 .10
❑ 302 Jamie Moyer .30 .10
❑ 303 Mike Cameron .30 .10
❑ 304 Matt Kinney .30 .10
❑ 305 Aubrey Huff .30 .10
❑ 306 Brian Lawrence .30 .10
❑ 307 Carlos Guillen .30 .10
❑ 308 J.D. Drew .30 .10
❑ 309 Paul Lo Duca .30 .10
❑ 310 Tim Salmon .50 .20
❑ 311 Jason Schmidt .30 .10
❑ 312 A.J. Pierzynski .30 .10
❑ 313 Lance Carter .30 .10
❑ 314 Julio Lugo .30 .10
❑ 315 Johan Santana .75 .30
❑ 316 Laynce Nix .30 .10
❑ 317 John Olerud .30 .10
❑ 318 Robb Quinlan .30 .10
❑ 319 Scott Spiezio .30 .10
❑ 320 Tony Clark .30 .10
❑ 321 Jose Vidro .30 .10
❑ 322 Shea Hillenbrand .30 .10
❑ 323 Doug Glanville .30 .10
❑ 324 Orlando Palmeiro .30 .10
❑ 325 Juan Gonzalez .30 .10
❑ 326 Jason Giambi .30 .10
❑ 327 Junior Spivey .30 .10
❑ 328 Tom Glavine .50 .20
❑ 329 Reed Johnson .30 .10
❑ 330 David Eckstein .30 .10
❑ 331 Damian Jackson .30 .10
❑ 332 Orlando Hudson .30 .10
❑ 333 Barry Zito .30 .10
❑ 334 Robert Fick .30 .10
❑ 335 Aaron Boone .30 .10
❑ 336 Rafael Palmeiro .50 .20
❑ 337 Bobby Kielty .30 .10
❑ 338 Tony Batista .30 .10
❑ 339 Ryan Dempster .30 .10
❑ 340 Derek Lowe .30 .10
❑ 341 Alex Cintron .30 .10
❑ 342 Jermaine Dye .30 .10
❑ 343 John Burkett .30 .10
❑ 344 Javy Lopez .30 .10
❑ 345 Eric Karros .30 .10
❑ 346 Corey Patterson .30 .10
❑ 347 Josh Phelps .30 .10
❑ 348 Ryan Klesko .30 .10
❑ 349 Craig Wilson .30 .10
❑ 350 Brian Roberts .30 .10
❑ 351 Roberto Alomar .50 .20
❑ 352 Frank Thomas .75 .30
❑ 353 Gary Sheffield .30 .10
❑ 354 Alex Gonzalez .30 .10
❑ 355 Jose Cruz Jr. .30 .10
❑ 356 Jerome Williams .30 .10
❑ 357 Mark Kotsay .30 .10
❑ 358 Chris Reitsma .30 .10
❑ 359 Carlos Lee .30 .10
❑ 360 Todd Helton .50 .20
❑ 361 Gil Meche .30 .10
❑ 362 Ryan Franklin .30 .10
❑ 363 Josh Bard .30 .10
❑ 364 Juan Pierre .30 .10
❑ 365 Barry Larkin .50 .20
❑ 366 Edgar Renteria .30 .10
❑ 367 Alex Sanchez .30 .10
❑ 368 Jeff Bagwell .50 .20
❑ 369 Ben Broussard .30 .10
❑ 370 Chan-Ho Park .30 .10
❑ 371 Darrell May .30 .10
❑ 372 Roy Oswalt .30 .10
❑ 373 Craig Monroe .30 .10
❑ 374 Fred McGriff .50 .20
❑ 375 Bengie Molina .30 .10
❑ 376 Aaron Guiel .30 .10
❑ 377 Jeriome Robertson .30 .10
❑ 378 Kenny Rogers .30 .10
❑ 379 Colby Lewis .30 .10
❑ 380 Jeromy Burnitz .30 .10
❑ 381 Orlando Cabrera .30 .10
❑ 382 Joe Randa .30 .10
❑ 383 Miguel Batista .30 .10
❑ 384 Brad Radke .30 .10
❑ 385 Jeremy Giambi .30 .10
❑ 386 Vladimir Guerrero .75 .30
❑ 387 Melvin Mora .30 .10
❑ 388 Royce Clayton .30 .10
❑ 389 Danny Garcia .30 .10
❑ 390 Manny Ramirez .50 .20
❑ 391 Dave McCarty .30 .10
❑ 392 Mark Grudzielanek .30 .10
❑ 393 Mike Piazza 1.25 .50
❑ 394 Jorge Posada .50 .20
❑ 395 Tim Hudson .30 .10
❑ 396 Placido Polanco .30 .10
❑ 397 Mark Loretta .30 .10
❑ 398 Jesse Foppert .30 .10
❑ 399 Albert Pujols 1.50 .60
❑ 400 Jeremi Gonzalez .30 .10
❑ 401 Paul Bako SP 1.00 .40
❑ 402 Luis Matos SP 1.00 .40
❑ 403 Johnny Damon SP 1.50 .60
❑ 404 Kerry Wood SP 1.00 .40
❑ 405 Joe Crede SP 1.00 .40
❑ 406 Jason Davis SP 1.00 .40
❑ 407 Larry Walker SP 1.00 .40
❑ 408 Ivan Rodriguez SP 1.50 .60
❑ 409 Nick Johnson SP 1.00 .40
❑ 410 Jose Lima SP 1.00 .40
❑ 411 Brian Jordan SP 1.00 .40
❑ 412 Eddie Guardado SP 1.00 .40
❑ 413 Ron Calloway SP 1.00 .40
❑ 414 Aaron Heilman SP 1.00 .40
❑ 415 Eric Chavez SP 1.00 .40
❑ 416 Randy Wolf SP 1.00 .40
❑ 417 Jason Bay SP 1.00 .40
❑ 418 Edgardo Alfonzo SP 1.00 .40
❑ 419 Kazuhiro Sasaki SP 1.00 .40
❑ 420 Eduardo Perez SP 1.00 .40
❑ 421 Carl Crawford SP 1.00 .40
❑ 422 Troy Glaus SP 1.00 .40
❑ 423 Joaquin Benoit SP 1.00 .40

❑ 424 Russ Ortiz SP 1.00 .40
❑ 425 Larry Bigbie SP 1.00 .40
❑ 426 Todd Walker SP 1.00 .40
❑ 427 Kris Benson SP 1.00 .40
❑ 428 Sandy Alomar Jr. SP 1.00 .40
❑ 429 Jody Gerut SP 1.00 .40
❑ 430 Rene Reyes SP 1.00 .40
❑ 431 Mike Lowell SP 1.00 .40
❑ 432 Jeff Kent SP 1.00 .40
❑ 433 Mike MacDougal SP 1.00 .40
❑ 434 Dave Roberts SP 1.00 .40
❑ 435 Torii Hunter SP 1.00 .40
❑ 436 Tomo Ohka SP 1.00 .40
❑ 437 Jeremy Griffiths SP 1.00 .40
❑ 438 Miguel Tejada SP 1.00 .40
❑ 439 Vicente Padilla SP 1.00 .40
❑ 440 Bobby Hill SP 1.00 .40
❑ 441 Rich Aurilia SP 1.00 .40
❑ 442 Shigetoshi Hasegawa SP 1.00 .40
❑ 443 So Taguchi SP 1.00 .40
❑ 444 Damian Rolls SP 1.00 .40
❑ 445 Roy Halladay SP 1.00 .40
❑ 446 Rocco Baldelli SO SP 1.00 .40
❑ 447 Dontrelle Willis SO SP 1.50 .60
❑ 448 Mark Prior SO SP 1.50 .60
❑ 449 Jason Lane SO SP 1.00 .40
❑ 450 Angel Berroa SO SP 1.00 .40
❑ 451 Jose Reyes SO SP 1.00 .40
❑ 452 Ryan Wagner SO SP 1.00 .40
❑ 453 Marlon Byrd SO SP 1.00 .40
❑ 454 Hee Seop Choi SO SP 1.00 .40
❑ 455 Brandon Webb SO SP 1.00 .40
❑ 456 Bo Hart SO SP 1.00 .40
❑ 457 Hank Blalock SO SP 1.00 .40
❑ 458 Mark Teixeira SO SP 1.50 .60
❑ 459 Hideki Matsui SO SP 4.00 1.50
❑ 460 Scott Podsednik SO SP 1.00 .40
❑ 461 Miguel Cabrera SO SP 1.50 .60
❑ 462 Josh Beckett AW SP 1.00 .40
❑ 463 Mariano Rivera AW SP 2.50 1.00
❑ 464 Ivan Rodriguez AW SP 1.50 .60
❑ 465 Alex Rodriguez AW SP 4.00 1.50
❑ 466 Albert Pujols AW SP 5.00 2.00
❑ 467 Roy Halladay AW SP 1.00 .40
❑ 468 Eric Gagne AW SP 1.00 .40
❑ 469 Angel Berroa AW SP 1.00 .40
❑ 470 Dontrelle Willis AW SP 1.50 .60
❑ 471 Boot/Gregorio/Fischer SP 1.00 .40
❑ 472 Kata/Olson/Hammock SP 1.00 .40
❑ 473 Hessman/Waters/Aquino SP 1.00 .40
❑ 474 Mendez/Cabrera/Guthrie SP 1.00 .40
❑ 475 Almonte/Seibel/Sanchez SP 1.00 .40
❑ 476 Wellemeyer/Leicester/Mitre SP 1.00 .40
❑ 477 Stewart/Cotts/Miles SP 1.00 .40
❑ 478 Sledge/Hall/Claussen SP 1.00 .40
❑ 479 Cruceta/Stanford/Betan SP 1.00 .40
❑ 480 Lopez/Atkins/Barmes SP 1.50 .60
❑ 481 Ledez/Logan/Bonderman SP 1.50 .60
❑ 482 Willingham/Hoop/Roberts SP 1.00 .40
❑ 483 Porter/Gallo/Matranga SP 1.00 .40
❑ 484 DeJesus/Gilfillan/Gobble SP 1.00 .40
❑ 485 Hill/Gonzalez/Brown SP 1.00 .40
❑ 486 Weeks/Liriano/Oberm SP 1.50 .60
❑ 487 Prieto/Ryan/Ford SP 1.00 .40
❑ 488 Manon/Ayala/Song SP 1.00 .40
❑ 489 Duncan/Redman/Brazell SP 1.50 .60
❑ 490 Wang/M.Hern/M.Gonz SP 5.00 2.00
❑ 491 Harden/Neu/Geary SP 1.50 .60
❑ 492 Markwell/Gaudin/Sanders SP 1.00 .40
❑ 493 Kemp/Nakamura/Carrasco SP 1.00 .40
❑ 494 Greene/Ojeda/Castro SP 2.50 1.00
❑ 495 Lowry/Linden/Correia SP 1.50 .60
❑ 496 Looper/Sweeney/R.John SP 1.00 .40
❑ 497 J.Gall RC/Haren/Ohme SP 2.50 1.00
❑ 498 Young/Waechter/Diaz SP 2.50 1.00
❑ 499 Laird/Garcia/Nivar SP 1.00 .40
❑ 500 Rios/Quiroz/Rosario SP 1.50 .60

2005 Fleer Tradition

❑ COMPLETE SET (350) 150.00 75.00
❑ COMP.SET w/o SP's (300) 40.00 15.00
❑ COMMON CARD (1-300) .30 .10
❑ COMMON CARD (301-330) 5.00 2.00
❑ COMMON CARD (331-350) 1.00 .40
❑ 301-350 STATED ODDS 1:2 H, 1:4 R
❑ 1 Johan/Schil/Westbrook SL .50 .20

❑ 2 Sheets/Peavy/Randy SL .50 .20
❑ 3 Johan/Colon/Schilling SL .30 .10
❑ 4 Pavanvo/Oswalt/Clemens SL .75 .30
❑ 5 Johan/Pedro/Schilling SL .30 .10
❑ 6 Schmidt/Randy/Sheets SL .50 .20
❑ 7 Mora/Guerrero/Ichiro SL .75 .30
❑ 8 Beltre/Helton/Loretta SL .30 .10
❑ 9 Manny/Konerko/Ortiz SL .50 .20
❑ 10 Pujols/Beltre/Dunn SL .75 .30
❑ 11 Ortiz/Manny/Tejada SL .50 .20
❑ 12 Pujols/Castilla/Rolen SL .50 .20
❑ 13 Jason Bay .30 .10
❑ 14 Greg Maddux 1.25 .50
❑ 15 Melvin Mora .30 .10
❑ 16 Matt Stairs .30 .10
❑ 17 Scott Podsednik .30 .10
❑ 18 Bartolo Colon .30 .10
❑ 19 Roger Clemens 1.25 .50
❑ 20 Eric Hinske .30 .10
❑ 21 Johnny Estrada .30 .10
❑ 22 Brett Tomko .30 .10
❑ 23 John Buck .30 .10
❑ 24 Nomar Garciaparra .75 .30
❑ 25 Milton Bradley .30 .10
❑ 26 Craig Biggio .50 .20
❑ 27 Kyle Denney .30 .10
❑ 28 Brad Penny .30 .10
❑ 29 Todd Helton .50 .20
❑ 30 Luis Gonzalez .30 .10
❑ 31 Bill Hall .30 .10
❑ 32 Ruben Sierra .30 .10
❑ 33 Zack Greinke .30 .10
❑ 34 Sandy Alomar Jr. .30 .10
❑ 35 Jason Giambi .30 .10
❑ 36 Ben Sheets .30 .10
❑ 37 Edgardo Alfonzo .30 .10
❑ 38 Kenny Rogers .30 .10
❑ 39 Coco Crisp .30 .10
❑ 40 Randy Choate .30 .10
❑ 41 Braden Looper .30 .10
❑ 42 Adam Dunn .30 .10
❑ 43 Adam Eaton .30 .10
❑ 44 Luis Castillo .30 .10
❑ 45 Casey Fossum .30 .10
❑ 46 Mike Piazza .75 .30
❑ 47 Juan Pierre .30 .10
❑ 48 Doug Davis .30 .10
❑ 49 Manny Ramirez .50 .20
❑ 50 Travis Hafner .30 .10
❑ 51 Jack Wilson .30 .10
❑ 52 Mike Maroth .30 .10
❑ 53 Ken Harvey .30 .10
❑ 54 Brooks Kieschnick .30 .10
❑ 55 Brad Fullmer .30 .10
❑ 56 Octavio Dotel .30 .10
❑ 57 Mike Matheny .30 .10
❑ 58 Andruw Jones .50 .20
❑ 59 Alfonso Soriano .30 .10
❑ 60 Royce Clayton .30 .10
❑ 61 Jon Garland .30 .10
❑ 62 John Mabry .30 .10
❑ 63 Rafael Palmeiro .50 .20
❑ 64 Garett Atkins .30 .10
❑ 65 Brian Meadows .30 .10
❑ 66 Tony Armas Jr. .30 .10
❑ 67 Toby Hall .30 .10
❑ 68 Carlos Baerga .30 .10
❑ 69 Barry Larkin .50 .20
❑ 70 Jody Gerut .30 .10
❑ 71 Brent Mayne .30 .10
❑ 72 Shigetoshi Hasegawa .30 .10
❑ 73 Jose Cruz Jr. .30 .10
❑ 74 Dan Wilson .30 .10
❑ 75 Sidney Ponson .30 .10
❑ 76 Jason Jennings .30 .10
❑ 77 A.J. Burnett .30 .10
❑ 78 Tony Batista .30 .10
❑ 79 Kris Benson .30 .10
❑ 80 Sean Burroughs .30 .10
❑ 81 Eric Young .30 .10
❑ 82 Casey Kotchman .30 .10
❑ 83 Derrek Lee .50 .20
❑ 84 Mariano Rivera .75 .30
❑ 85 Julio Franco .30 .10
❑ 86 Corey Patterson .30 .10
❑ 87 Carlos Beltran .30 .10
❑ 88 Trevor Hoffman .30 .10
❑ 89 Danny Garcia .30 .10
❑ 90 Marcos Scutaro .30 .10
❑ 91 Marquis Grissom .30 .10
❑ 92 Aubrey Huff .30 .10
❑ 93 Tony Womack .30 .10
❑ 94 Placido Polanco .30 .10
❑ 95 Bengie Molina .30 .10
❑ 96 Roger Cedeno .30 .10
❑ 97 Geoff Jenkins .30 .10
❑ 98 Kip Wells .30 .10
❑ 99 Derek Jeter 1.50 .60
❑ 100 Omar Infante .30 .10
❑ 101 Phil Nevin .30 .10
❑ 102 Edgar Renteria .30 .10
❑ 103 B.J. Surhoff .30 .10
❑ 104 David DeJesus .30 .10
❑ 105 Raul Ibanez .30 .10
❑ 106 Hank Blalock .30 .10
❑ 107 Shawn Estes .30 .10
❑ 108 Wily Mo Pena .30 .10
❑ 109 Shawn Green .30 .10
❑ 110 David Wright 2.00 .75
❑ 111 Kenny Lofton .30 .10
❑ 112 Matt Clement .30 .10
❑ 113 Cesar Izturis .30 .10
❑ 114 John Lackey .30 .10
❑ 115 Torii Hunter .30 .10
❑ 116 Charles Johnson .30 .10
❑ 117 Ray Durham .30 .10
❑ 118 Luke Hudson .30 .10
❑ 119 Jeremy Bonderman .30 .10
❑ 120 Sean Casey .30 .10
❑ 121 Johnny Damon .50 .20
❑ 122 Eric Milton .30 .10
❑ 123 Shea Hillenbrand .30 .10
❑ 124 Johan Santana .75 .30
❑ 125 Jim Edmonds .30 .10
❑ 126 Javier Vazquez .30 .10
❑ 127 Jon Adkins .30 .10
❑ 128 Mike Lowell .30 .10
❑ 129 Khalil Greene .50 .20
❑ 130 Quinton McCracken .30 .10
❑ 131 Edgar Martinez .50 .20
❑ 132 Matt Lawton .30 .10
❑ 133 Jeff Weaver .30 .10
❑ 134 Marlon Byrd .30 .10
❑ 135 John Smoltz .50 .20
❑ 136 Grady Sizemore .50 .20
❑ 137 Brian Roberts .30 .10
❑ 138 Dee Brown .30 .10
❑ 139 Joel Pineiro .30 .10
❑ 140 David Dellucci .30 .10
❑ 141 Bobby Higginson .30 .10
❑ 142 Ryan Madson .30 .10
❑ 143 Scott Hatteberg .30 .10
❑ 144 Greg Zaun .30 .10
❑ 145 Brian Jordan .30 .10
❑ 146 Jason Isringhausen .30 .10
❑ 147 Vinnie Chulk .30 .10
❑ 148 Al Leiter .30 .10
❑ 149 Pedro Martinez .50 .20
❑ 150 Carlos Guillen .30 .10
❑ 151 Randy Wolf .30 .10
❑ 152 Vernon Wells .30 .10
❑ 153 Barry Zito .30 .10
❑ 154 Pedro Feliz .30 .10
❑ 155 Omar Vizquel .50 .20

❑ 156 Chone Figgins .30 .10
❑ 157 David Ortiz .50 .20
❑ 158 Sunny Kim .30 .10
❑ 159 Adam Kennedy .30 .10
❑ 160 Carlos Lee .30 .10
❑ 161 Rick Ankiel .30 .10
❑ 162 Roy Oswalt .30 .10
❑ 163 Armando Benitez .30 .10
❑ 164 Erubiel Durazo .30 .10
❑ 165 Adam Hyzdu .30 .10
❑ 166 Esteban Yan .30 .10
❑ 167 Victor Santos .30 .10
❑ 168 Kevin Millwood .30 .10
❑ 169 Andy Pettitte .50 .20
❑ 170 Mike Cameron .30 .10
❑ 171 Scott Rolen .50 .20
❑ 172 Trot Nixon .30 .10
❑ 173 Eric Munson .30 .10
❑ 174 Roy Halladay .30 .10
❑ 175 Juan Encarnacion .30 .10
❑ 176 Eric Chavez .30 .10
❑ 177 Termel Sledge .30 .10
❑ 178 Jason Schmidt .30 .10
❑ 179 Endy Chavez .30 .10
❑ 180 Carlos Zambrano .30 .10
❑ 181 Carlos Delgado .30 .10
❑ 182 Dewon Brazelton .30 .10
❑ 183 J.D. Drew .30 .10
❑ 184 Orlando Cabrera .30 .10
❑ 185 Craig Wilson .30 .10
❑ 186 Chin-Hui Tsao .30 .10
❑ 187 Jolbert Cabrera .30 .10
❑ 188 Rod Barajas .30 .10
❑ 189 Craig Monroe .30 .10
❑ 190 Dave Berg .30 .10
❑ 191 Carlos Silva .30 .10
❑ 192 Eric Gagne .30 .10
❑ 193 Marcus Giles .30 .10
❑ 194 Nick Johnson .30 .10
❑ 195 Kelvim Escobar .30 .10
❑ 196 Wade Miller .30 .10
❑ 197 David Bell .30 .10
❑ 198 Rondell White .30 .10
❑ 199 Brian Giles .30 .10
❑ 200 Jeromy Burnitz .30 .10
❑ 201 Carl Pavano .30 .10
❑ 202 Alex Rios .30 .10
❑ 203 Ryan Freel .30 .10
❑ 204 R.A. Dickey .30 .10
❑ 205 Miguel Cairo .30 .10
❑ 206 Kerry Wood .30 .10
❑ 207 C.C. Sabathia .30 .10
❑ 208 Jaime Cerda .30 .10
❑ 209 Jerome Williams .30 .10
❑ 210 Ryan Wagner .30 .10
❑ 211 Javy Lopez .30 .10
❑ 212 Tike Redman .30 .10
❑ 213 Richie Sexson .30 .10
❑ 214 Shannon Stewart .30 .10
❑ 215 Ben Davis .30 .10
❑ 216 Jeff Bagwell .50 .20
❑ 217 David Wells .30 .10
❑ 218 Justin Leone .30 .10
❑ 219 Brad Radke .30 .10
❑ 220 Ramon Santiago .30 .10
❑ 221 Richard Hidalgo .30 .10
❑ 222 Aaron Miles .30 .10
❑ 223 Mark Loretta .30 .10
❑ 224 Aaron Boone .30 .10
❑ 225 Steve Trachsel .30 .10
❑ 226 Geoff Blum .30 .10
❑ 227 Shingo Takatsu .30 .10
❑ 228 Kevin Youkilis .30 .10
❑ 229 Laynce Nix .30 .10
❑ 230 Daniel Cabrera .30 .10
❑ 231 Kyle Lohse .30 .10
❑ 232 Todd Pratt .30 .10
❑ 233 Reed Johnson .30 .10
❑ 234 Lance Berkman .30 .10
❑ 235 Hideki Matsui 1.25 .50
❑ 236 Randy Winn .30 .10
❑ 237 Joe Randa .30 .10
❑ 238 Bob Howry .30 .10
❑ 239 Jason LaRue .30 .10
❑ 240 Jose Valentin .30 .10
❑ 241 Livan Hernandez .30 .10
❑ 242 Jamie Moyer .30 .10
❑ 243 Garret Anderson .30 .10
❑ 244 Brad Ausmus .30 .10
❑ 245 Russell Branyan .30 .10
❑ 246 Paul Wilson .30 .10
❑ 247 Tim Wakefield .30 .10
❑ 248 Roberto Alomar .50 .20
❑ 249 Kazuhisa Ishii .30 .10
❑ 250 Tino Martinez .50 .20
❑ 251 Tomo Ohka .30 .10
❑ 252 Mark Redman .30 .10
❑ 253 Paul Byrd .30 .10
❑ 254 Greg Aquino .30 .10
❑ 255 Adrian Beltre .30 .10
❑ 256 Ricky Ledee .30 .10
❑ 257 Josh Fogg .30 .10
❑ 258 Derek Lowe .30 .10
❑ 259 Lew Ford .30 .10
❑ 260 Bobby Crosby .30 .10
❑ 261 Jim Thome .50 .20
❑ 262 Jaret Wright .30 .10
❑ 263 Chin-Feng Chen .30 .10
❑ 264 Troy Glaus .30 .10
❑ 265 Jorge Sosa .30 .10
❑ 266 Mike Lamb .30 .10
❑ 267 Russ Ortiz .30 .10
❑ 268 Reggie Sanders .30 .10
❑ 269 Orlando Hudson .30 .10
❑ 270 Rodrigo Lopez .30 .10
❑ 271 Jose Vidro .30 .10
❑ 272 Akinori Otsuka .30 .10
❑ 273 Victor Martinez .30 .10
❑ 274 Carl Crawford .30 .10
❑ 275 Roberto Novoa .30 .10
❑ 276 Brian Lawrence .30 .10
❑ 277 Angel Berroa .30 .10
❑ 278 Josh Beckett .30 .10
❑ 279 Lyle Overbay .30 .10
❑ 280 Dustin Hermanson .30 .10
❑ 281 Jeff Conine .30 .10
❑ 282 Mark Prior .50 .20
❑ 283 Kevin Brown .30 .10
❑ 284 Magglio Ordonez .30 .10
❑ 285 Dontrelle Willis .30 .10
❑ 286 Dallas McPherson .30 .10
❑ 287 Rafael Furcal .30 .10
❑ 288 Ty Wigginton .30 .10
❑ 289 Moises Alou .30 .10
❑ 290 A.J. Pierzynski .30 .10
❑ 291 Todd Walker .30 .10
❑ 292 Hideo Nomo .75 .30
❑ 293 Larry Walker .50 .20
❑ 294 Choo Freeman .30 .10
❑ 295 Eduardo Perez .30 .10
❑ 296 Miguel Tejada .30 .10
❑ 297 Corey Koskie .30 .10
❑ 298 Jermaine Dye .30 .10
❑ 299 John Riedling .30 .10
❑ 300 John Olerud .30 .10
❑ 301 Bittner/Woods/Jenks TP 5.00 2.00
❑ 302 Kroeger/Daigle/Medders TP 5.00 2.00
❑ 303 K.Johnson/Thom/Meyer TP 5.00 2.00
❑ 304 E.Rod/Hannam/Maine TP 5.00 2.00
❑ 305 A.Mart/Gamble/Dinardo TP 5.00 2.00
❑ 306 Cedeno/Vasquez/Pinto TP 5.00 2.00
❑ 307 Munoz/Wing/Diaz TP 5.00 2.00
❑ 308 Bergolla/Olmedo/E.Enc TP 5.00 2.00
❑ 309 Gomez/Ochoa/Tadano TP 5.00 2.00
❑ 310 Miller/Baker/Holliday TP 6.00 2.50
❑ 311 Larris/Grander/Raburn TP 5.00 2.00
❑ 312 Wilson/Kensing/Cave TP 5.00 2.00
❑ 313 H.Gim/Taveras/Buch TP 5.00 2.00
❑ 314 Gotay/Bass/Blanco TP 5.00 2.00
❑ 315 Hanrahan/Aybar/Braz TP 5.00 2.00
❑ 316 Krynzel/Hendr/Hart TP 5.00 2.00
❑ 317 Miller/Kubel/Durbin TP 5.00 2.00
❑ 318 Izturis/Cordero/Watson TP 5.00 2.00
❑ 319 Diaz/Baldiris/Lydon TP 5.00 2.00
❑ 320 Sierra/Navarro/Henn TP 5.00 2.00
❑ 321 Swish/Blant/D.Johnson TP 5.00 2.00
❑ 322 Howard/Floyd/Bucktrot TP 5.00 2.00
❑ 323 Doumit/Burnett/Bradley TP 5.00 2.00
❑ 324 Germ/Tucker/Guzman TP 5.00 2.00
❑ 325 Aardsma/Knoedler/Simon TP 5.00 2.00
❑ 326 Lopez/Rivera/Baek TP 5.00 2.00
❑ 327 Molina/Rust/Wainwright TP 5.00 2.00
❑ 328 Cantu/Kazmir/Upton TP 5.00 2.00
❑ 329 Gonzalez/Nivar/Bourg TP 5.00 2.00
❑ 330 Adams/McGow/Chacin TP 5.00 2.00
❑ 331 Alfonso Soriano AW 1.00 .40
❑ 332 Albert Pujols AW 3.00 1.25
❑ 333 David Ortiz AW 1.50 .60
❑ 334 Manny Ramirez AW 1.50 .60
❑ 335 Jason Bay AW 1.00 .40
❑ 336 Bobby Crosby AW 1.00 .40
❑ 337 Roger Clemens AW 2.50 1.00
❑ 338 Johan Santana AW 1.50 .60
❑ 339 Jim Thome AW 1.50 .60
❑ 340 Vladimir Guerrero AW 1.50 .60
❑ 341 David Ortiz PS 1.50 .60
❑ 342 Alex Rodriguez PS 2.50 1.00
❑ 343 Albert Pujols PS 3.00 1.25
❑ 344 Carlos Beltran PS 1.00 .40
❑ 345 Johnny Damon PS 1.50 .60
❑ 346 Scott Rolen PS 1.50 .60
❑ 347 Larry Walker PS 1.50 .60
❑ 348 Curt Schilling PS 1.50 .60
❑ 349 Pedro Martinez PS 1.50 .60
❑ 350 David Ortiz PS 1.50 .60

2006 Fleer Tradition

❑ COMPLETE SET (200) 30.00 12.50
❑ COMMON CARD (1-200) .30 .12
❑ COMMON RC (1-200) .50 .20
❑ OVERALL PLATE ODDS 1:288 HOBBY
❑ PLATE PRINT RUN 1 SET PER COLOR
❑ BLACK-CYAN-MAGENTA-YELLOW ISSUED
❑ NO PLATE PRICING DUE TO SCARCITY
❑ EXQUISITE EXCH ODDS 1:864 HOBBY
❑ EXQUISITE EXCH DEADLINE 07/27/07
❑ 1 Andruw Jones .50 .20
❑ 2 Chipper Jones .75 .30
❑ 3 John Smoltz .50 .20
❑ 4 Tim Hudson .30 .12
❑ 5 Joey Devine RC .50 .20
❑ 6 Chuck James (RC) .75 .30
❑ 7 Alay Soler RC .50 .20
❑ 8 Conor Jackson (RC) .75 .30
❑ 9 Luis Gonzalez .30 .12
❑ 10 Brandon Webb .30 .12
❑ 11 Chad Tracy .30 .12
❑ 12 Orlando Hudson .30 .12
❑ 13 Shawn Green .30 .12
❑ 14 Vladimir Guerrero .75 .30
❑ 15 Bartolo Colon .30 .12
❑ 16 Chone Figgins .30 .12
❑ 17 Garret Anderson .30 .12
❑ 18 Francisco Rodriguez .30 .12
❑ 19 Casey Kotchman .30 .12
❑ 20 Lance Berkman .30 .12
❑ 21 Craig Biggio .50 .20
❑ 22 Andy Pettitte .50 .20
❑ 23 Morgan Ensberg .30 .12
❑ 24 Brad Lidge .30 .12
❑ 25 Jered Weaver (RC) 2.50 1.00
❑ 26 Roy Oswalt .30 .12
❑ 27 Eric Chavez .30 .12
❑ 28 Rich Harden .30 .12
❑ 29 Cole Hamels (RC) 1.25 .50
❑ 30 Huston Street .30 .12
❑ 31 Bobby Crosby .30 .12
❑ 32 Nick Swisher .30 .12
❑ 33 Vernon Wells .30 .12
❑ 34 Roy Halladay .30 .12

❑ 35 A.J. Burnett .30 .12
❑ 36 Troy Glaus .30 .12
❑ 37 B.J. Ryan .30 .12
❑ 38 Bengie Molina .30 .12
❑ 39 Alex Rios .30 .12
❑ 40 Prince Fielder (RC) 2.00 .75
❑ 41 Jose Capellan (RC) .50 .20
❑ 42 Rickie Weeks .30 .12
❑ 43 Ben Sheets .30 .12
❑ 44 Carlos Lee .30 .12
❑ 45 J.J. Hardy .30 .12
❑ 46 Albert Pujols 1.50 .60
❑ 47 Skip Schumaker (RC) .50 .20
❑ 48 Adam Wainwright (RC) .50 .20
❑ 49 Jim Edmonds .50 .20
❑ 50 Scott Rolen .50 .20
❑ 51 Chris Carpenter .30 .12
❑ 52 David Eckstein .30 .12
❑ 53 Derrek Lee .30 .12
❑ 54 Jon Lester RC 1.50 .60
❑ 55 Mark Prior .50 .20
❑ 56 Aramis Ramirez .30 .12
❑ 57 Juan Pierre .30 .12
❑ 58 Greg Maddux 1.25 .50
❑ 59 Michael Barrett .30 .12
❑ 60 Carl Crawford .30 .12
❑ 61 Scott Kazmir .50 .20
❑ 62 Jorge Cantu .30 .12
❑ 63 Jonny Gomes .30 .12
❑ 64 Julio Lugo .30 .12
❑ 65 Aubrey Huff .30 .12
❑ 66 Jeff Kent .30 .12
❑ 67 Nomar Garciaparra .75 .30
❑ 68 Rafael Furcal .30 .12
❑ 69 Tim Hamulack (RC) .50 .20
❑ 70 Chad Billingsley (RC) .75 .30
❑ 71 Hong-Chih Kuo (RC) 1.25 .50
❑ 72 J.D. Drew .30 .12
❑ 73 Moises Alou .30 .12
❑ 74 Randy Winn .30 .12
❑ 75 Jason Schmidt .30 .12
❑ 76 Jeremy Accardo RC .50 .20
❑ 77 Matt Cain (RC) .75 .30
❑ 78 Joel Zumaya (RC) 1.25 .50
❑ 79 Travis Hafner .30 .12
❑ 80 Victor Martinez .30 .12
❑ 81 Grady Sizemore .50 .20
❑ 82 C.C. Sabathia .30 .12
❑ 83 Jhonny Peralta .30 .12
❑ 84 Jason Michaels .30 .12
❑ 85 Jeremy Sowers (RC) .50 .20
❑ 86 Ichiro Suzuki 1.25 .50
❑ 87 Richie Sexson .30 .12
❑ 88 Adrian Beltre .30 .12
❑ 89 Felix Hernandez .50 .20
❑ 90 Kenji Johjima RC 2.50 1.00
❑ 91 Jeff Harris RC .50 .20
❑ 92 Taylor Buchholz (RC) .75 .30
❑ 93 Miguel Cabrera .50 .20
❑ 94 Dontrelle Willis .30 .12
❑ 95 Jeremy Hermida (RC) .50 .20
❑ 96 Mike Jacobs (RC) .50 .20
❑ 97 Josh Johnson (RC) .75 .30
❑ 98 Hanley Ramirez (RC) 1.25 .50
❑ 99 Josh Willingham (RC) .50 .20
❑ 100 Dan Uggla (RC) 1.25 .50
❑ 101 David Wright 1.25 .50
❑ 102 Jose Reyes .75 .30
❑ 103 Pedro Martinez .50 .20
❑ 104 Carlos Beltran .30 .12
❑ 105 Carlos Delgado .30 .12
❑ 106 Billy Wagner .30 .12
❑ 107 Lastings Milledge (RC) .75 .30
❑ 108 Alfonso Soriano .30 .12
❑ 109 Jose Vidro .30 .12
❑ 110 Livan Hernandez .30 .12
❑ 111 Matt Kemp (RC) .75 .30
❑ 112 Brandon Watson (RC) .50 .20
❑ 113 Ryan Zimmerman (RC) 3.00 1.25
❑ 114 Miguel Tejada .30 .12
❑ 115 Ramon Hernandez .30 .12
❑ 116 Brian Roberts .30 .12
❑ 117 Melvin Mora .30 .12
❑ 118 Erik Bedard .30 .12
❑ 119 Jay Gibbons .30 .12
❑ 120 Aaron Rakers (RC) .50 .20
❑ 121 Jake Peavy .30 .12
❑ 122 Brian Giles .30 .12
❑ 123 Khalil Greene .50 .20
❑ 124 Trevor Hoffman .30 .12
❑ 125 Josh Barfield (RC) .50 .20
❑ 126 Ben Johnson (RC) .50 .20
❑ 127 Ryan Howard 1.25 .50
❑ 128 Bobby Abreu .30 .12
❑ 129 Chase Utley .75 .30
❑ 130 Pat Burrell .30 .12
❑ 131 Jimmy Rollins .30 .12
❑ 132 Brett Myers .30 .12
❑ 133 Mike Thompson RC .50 .20
❑ 134 Jason Bay .30 .12
❑ 135 Oliver Perez .30 .12
❑ 136 Matt Capps (RC) .50 .20
❑ 137 Paul Maholm (RC) .50 .20
❑ 138 Nate McLouth (RC) .50 .20
❑ 139 John Van Benschoten (RC) .50 .20
❑ 140 Mark Teixeira .50 .20
❑ 141 Michael Young .30 .12
❑ 142 Hank Blalock .30 .12
❑ 143 Kevin Millwood .30 .12
❑ 144 Laynce Nix .30 .12
❑ 145 Francisco Cordero .30 .12
❑ 146 Ian Kinsler (RC) .75 .30
❑ 147 David Ortiz .75 .30
❑ 148 Manny Ramirez .50 .20
❑ 149 Jason Varitek .75 .30
❑ 150 Curt Schilling .50 .20
❑ 151 Josh Beckett .30 .12
❑ 152 Coco Crisp .30 .12
❑ 153 Jonathan Papelbon (RC) 2.50 1.00
❑ 154 Ken Griffey Jr. 1.25 .50
❑ 155 Adam Dunn .30 .12
❑ 156 Felipe Lopez .30 .12
❑ 157 Bronson Arroyo .30 .12
❑ 158 Ryan Freel .30 .12
❑ 159 Chris Denorfia (RC) .50 .20
❑ 160 Todd Helton .50 .20
❑ 161 Garrett Atkins .30 .12
❑ 162 Matt Holliday .75 .30
❑ 163 Clint Barmes .30 .12
❑ 164 Kendry Morales (RC) 1.25 .50
❑ 165 Ryan Shealy (RC) .50 .20
❑ 166 Josh Wilson (RC) .50 .20
❑ 167 Reggie Sanders .30 .12
❑ 168 Angel Berroa .30 .12
❑ 169 Mike Sweeney .30 .12
❑ 170 Mark Grudzielanek .30 .12
❑ 171 Jeremy Affeldt .30 .12
❑ 172 Steve Stemle RC .50 .20
❑ 173 Justin Verlander (RC) 2.00 .75
❑ 174 Ivan Rodriguez .50 .20
❑ 175 Chris Shelton .30 .12
❑ 176 Jeremy Bonderman .30 .12
❑ 177 Magglio Ordonez .30 .12
❑ 178 Carlos Guillen .30 .12
❑ 179 Placido Polanco .30 .12
❑ 180 Johan Santana .50 .20
❑ 181 Torii Hunter .30 .12
❑ 182 Joe Nathan .30 .12
❑ 183 Joe Mauer .50 .20
❑ 184 Dave Gassner (RC) .50 .20
❑ 185 Jason Kubel (RC) .50 .20
❑ 186 Francisco Liriano (RC) 2.50 1.00
❑ 187 Jim Thome .50 .20
❑ 188 Paul Konerko .30 .12
❑ 189 Scott Podsednik .30 .12
❑ 190 Tadahito Iguchi .30 .12
❑ 191 A.J. Pierzynski .30 .12
❑ 192 Jose Contreras .30 .12
❑ 193 Brian Anderson (RC) .50 .20
❑ 194 Hideki Matsui .75 .30
❑ 195 Wil Nieves (RC) .50 .20
❑ 196 Alex Rodriguez 1.25 .50
❑ 197 Gary Sheffield .30 .12
❑ 198 Randy Johnson .75 .30
❑ 199 Johnny Damon .50 .20
❑ 200 Derek Jeter 2.00 .75
❑ NNO Exquisite Redemption

1933 Goudey

❑ COMPLETE SET (239) 40000.00 25000.00
❑ COMMON CARD (1-52) 75.00 45.00
❑ COMMON (41/43/53-240) 60.00 35.00

❑ WRAPPER (1-CENT, BAT.) 100.00 75.00
❑ WRAPPER (1-CENT, AD) 175.00 150.00
❑ 1 Benny Bengough RC 1500.00 900.00
❑ 2 Dazzy Vance RC 200.00 125.00
❑ 3 Hugh Critz BAT RC 75.00 40.00
❑ 4 Heinie Schuble RC 75.00 45.00
❑ 5 Babe Herman RC 75.00 40.00
❑ 6 Jimmy Dykes RC 75.00 40.00
❑ 7 Ted Lyons RC 150.00 90.00
❑ 8 Roy Johnson RC 75.00 45.00
❑ 9 Dave Harris RC 75.00 45.00
❑ 10 Glenn Myatt RC 75.00 45.00
❑ 11 Billy Rogell RC 75.00 45.00
❑ 12 George Pipgras RC 75.00 45.00
❑ 13 Fresco Thompson RC 75.00 45.00
❑ 14 Henry Johnson RC 75.00 45.00
❑ 15 Victor Sorrell RC 75.00 45.00
❑ 16 George Blaeholder RC 75.00 45.00
❑ 17 Watson Clark RC 75.00 45.00
❑ 18 Muddy Ruel RC 75.00 45.00
❑ 19 Bill Dickey RC 350.00 200.00
❑ 20 Bill Terry THROW RC 250.00 150.00
❑ 21 Phil Collins RC 75.00 45.00
❑ 22 Pie Traynor RC 250.00 150.00
❑ 23 Kiki Cuyler RC 200.00 125.00
❑ 24 Horace Ford RC 75.00 45.00
❑ 25 Paul Waner RC 200.00 125.00
❑ 26 Bill Cissell RC 75.00 45.00
❑ 27 George Connally RC 75.00 45.00
❑ 28 Dick Bartell RC 75.00 40.00
❑ 29 Jimmie Foxx RC 600.00 350.00
❑ 30 Frank Hogan RC 75.00 45.00
❑ 31 Tony Lazzeri RC 400.00 250.00
❑ 32 Bud Clancy RC 75.00 40.00
❑ 33 Ralph Kress RC 75.00 45.00
❑ 34 Bob O'Farrell RC 75.00 45.00
❑ 35 Al Simmons RC 350.00 200.00
❑ 36 Tommy Thevenow RC 75.00 45.00
❑ 37 Jimmy Wilson RC 75.00 45.00
❑ 38 Fred Brickell RC 75.00 45.00
❑ 39 Mark Koenig RC 75.00 40.00
❑ 40 Taylor Douthit RC 75.00 45.00
❑ 41 Gus Mancuso CATCH 60.00 35.00
❑ 42 Eddie Collins RC 150.00 90.00
❑ 43 Lew Fonseca RC 60.00 35.00
❑ 44 Jim Bottomley RC 150.00 90.00
❑ 45 Larry Benton RC 75.00 45.00
❑ 46 Ethan Allen RC 75.00 40.00
❑ 47 Heinie Manush BAT RC 175.00 100.00
❑ 48 Marty McManus RC 75.00 45.00
❑ 49 Frankie Frisch RC 300.00 175.00
❑ 50 Ed Brandt RC 75.00 45.00
❑ 51 Charlie Grimm RC 75.00 40.00
❑ 52 Andy Cohen RC 75.00 45.00
❑ 53 Babe Ruth RC 8000.00 5000.00
❑ 54 Ray Kremer RC 60.00 35.00
❑ 55 Pat Malone RC 60.00 35.00
❑ 56 Red Ruffing RC 175.00 100.00
❑ 57 Earl Clark RC 60.00 35.00
❑ 58 Lefty O'Doul RC 125.00 75.00
❑ 59 Bing Miller RC 60.00 35.00
❑ 60 Waite Hoyt RC 125.00 75.00
❑ 61 Max Bishop RC 60.00 35.00
❑ 62 Pepper Martin RC 125.00 75.00
❑ 63 Joe Cronin BAT RC 150.00 90.00
❑ 64 Burleigh Grimes RC 250.00 150.00
❑ 65 Milt Gaston RC 60.00 35.00
❑ 66 George Grantham RC 60.00 35.00
❑ 67 Guy Bush RC 60.00 35.00
❑ 68 Horace Lisenbee RC 60.00 35.00

❑ 69 Randy Moore RC 60.00 35.00
❑ 70 Floyd (Pete) Scott RC 60.00 35.00
❑ 71 Robert J. Burke RC 60.00 35.00
❑ 72 Owen Carroll RC 60.00 35.00
❑ 73 Jesse Haines RC 125.00 75.00
❑ 74 Eppa Rixey RC 150.00 90.00
❑ 75 Willie Kamm RC 60.00 35.00
❑ 76 Mickey Cochrane RC 500.00 300.00
❑ 77 Adam Comorosky RC 60.00 35.00
❑ 78 Jack Quinn RC 60.00 35.00
❑ 79 Red Faber RC 125.00 75.00
❑ 80 Clyde Manion RC 60.00 35.00
❑ 81 Sam Jones RC 60.00 35.00
❑ 82 Dib Williams RC 60.00 35.00
❑ 83 Pete Jablonowski RC 60.00 35.00
❑ 84 Glenn Spencer RC 60.00 35.00
❑ 85 Heinie Sand RC 60.00 35.00
❑ 86 Phil Todt RC 60.00 35.00
❑ 87 Frank O'Rourke RC 60.00 35.00
❑ 88 Russell Rollings RC 60.00 35.00
❑ 89 Tris Speaker RFT 300.00 175.00
❑ 90 Jess Petty RC 60.00 35.00
❑ 91 Tom Zachary RC 60.00 35.00
❑ 92 Lou Gehrig RC 2500.001500.00
❑ 93 John Welch RC 60.00 35.00
❑ 94 Bill Walker RC 60.00 35.00
❑ 95 Alvin Crowder RC 60.00 35.00
❑ 96 Willis Hudlin RC 60.00 35.00
❑ 97 Joe Morrissey RC 60.00 35.00
❑ 98 Wally Berger RC 75.00 45.00
❑ 99 Tony Cuccinello RC 75.00 45.00
❑ 100 George Uhle RC 60.00 35.00
❑ 101 Richard Coffman RC 60.00 35.00
❑ 102 Travis Jackson RC 150.00 90.00
❑ 103 Earle Combs RC 125.00 75.00
❑ 104 Fred Marberry RC 60.00 35.00
❑ 105 Bernie Friberg RC 60.00 35.00
❑ 106 Napoleon Lajoie SP 25000.0015000.00
❑ 107 Heinie Manush RC 125.00 75.00
❑ 108 Joe Kuhel RC 60.00 35.00
❑ 109 Joe Cronin RC 300.00 175.00
❑ 110 Goose Goslin RC 250.00 150.00
❑ 111 Monte Weaver RC 60.00 35.00
❑ 112 Fred Schulte RC 60.00 35.00
❑ 113 Oswald Bluege POR RC 60.00 35.00
❑ 114 Luke Sewell FIELD RC 75.00 45.00
❑ 115 Cliff Heathcote RC 60.00 35.00
❑ 116 Eddie Morgan RC 60.00 35.00
❑ 117 Rabbit Maranville RC 125.00 75.00
❑ 118 Val Picinich RC 60.00 35.00
❑ 119 Rogers Hornsby Field RC 600.00 350.00
❑ 120 Carl Reynolds RC 60.00 35.00
❑ 121 Walter Stewart RC 60.00 35.00
❑ 122 Alvin Crowder RC 60.00 35.00
❑ 123 Jack Russell RC 60.00 35.00
❑ 124 Earl Whitehill RC 60.00 35.00
❑ 125 Bill Terry RC 250.00 150.00
❑ 126 Joe Moore BAT RC 60.00 35.00
❑ 127 Mel Ott RC 400.00 250.00
❑ 128 Chuck Klein RC 175.00 100.00
❑ 129 Hal Schumacher PIT RC 60.00 35.00
❑ 130 Fred Fitzsimmons POR RC 60.0035.00
❑ 131 Fred Frankhouse RC 60.00 35.00
❑ 132 Jim Elliott RC 60.00 35.00
❑ 133 Fred Lindstrom RC 125.00 75.00
❑ 134 Sam Rice RC 200.00 125.00
❑ 135 Woody English RC 60.00 35.00
❑ 136 Flint Rhem RC 60.00 35.00
❑ 137 Red Lucas RC 60.00 35.00
❑ 138 Herb Pennock RC 175.00 100.00
❑ 139 Ben Cantwell RC 60.00 35.00
❑ 140 Bump Hadley RC 60.00 35.00
❑ 141 Ray Benge RC 60.00 35.00
❑ 142 Paul Richards RC 75.00 45.00
❑ 143 Glenn Wright RC 60.00 35.00
❑ 144 Babe Ruth Bat DP RC 4000.002500.00
❑ 145 Rube Walberg RC 60.00 35.00
❑ 146 Walter Stewart PIT RC 60.00 35.00
❑ 147 Leo Durocher RC 200.00 125.00
❑ 148 Eddie Farrell RC 60.00 35.00
❑ 149 Babe Ruth RC 5000.003000.00
❑ 150 Ray Kolp RC 60.00 35.00
❑ 151 Jake Flowers RC 60.00 35.00
❑ 152 Zack Taylor RC 60.00 35.00
❑ 153 Buddy Myer RC 60.00 35.00
❑ 154 Jimmie Foxx RC 600.00 350.00
❑ 155 Joe Judge RC 60.00 35.00
❑ 156 Danny MacFayden RC 60.00 35.00
❑ 157 Sam Byrd RC 60.00 35.00
❑ 158 Moe Berg RC 400.00 250.00
❑ 159 Oswald Bluege FIELD RC 60.00 35.00
❑ 160 Lou Gehrig RC 3000.001800.00
❑ 161 Al Spohrer RC 60.00 35.00
❑ 162 Leo Mangum RC 60.00 35.00
❑ 163 Luke Sewell POR RC 75.00 45.00
❑ 164 Lloyd Waner RC 250.00 150.00
❑ 165 Joe Sewell RC 125.00 75.00
❑ 166 Sam West RC 60.00 35.00
❑ 167 Jack Russell RC 60.00 35.00
❑ 168 Goose Goslin RC 200.00 125.00
❑ 169 Al Thomas RC 60.00 35.00
❑ 170 Harry McCurdy RC 60.00 35.00
❑ 171 Charlie Jamieson RC 60.00 35.00
❑ 172 Billy Hargrave RC 60.00 35.00
❑ 173 Roscoe Holm RC 60.00 35.00
❑ 174 Warren (Curly) Ogden RC 60.00 35.00
❑ 175 Dan Howley MG RC 60.00 35.00
❑ 176 John Ogden RC 60.00 35.00
❑ 177 Walter French RC 60.00 35.00
❑ 178 Jackie Warner RC 60.00 35.00
❑ 179 Fred Leach RC 60.00 35.00
❑ 180 Eddie Moore RC 60.00 35.00
❑ 181 Babe Ruth RC 5000.003500.00
❑ 182 Andy High RC 60.00 35.00
❑ 183 Rube Walberg RC 60.00 35.00
❑ 184 Charley Berry RC 60.00 35.00
❑ 185 Bob Smith RC 60.00 35.00
❑ 186 John Schulte RC 60.00 35.00
❑ 187 Heinie Manush RC 150.00 90.00
❑ 188 Rogers Hornsby RC 600.00 350.00
❑ 189 Joe Cronin RC 200.00 125.00
❑ 190 Fred Schulte RC 60.00 35.00
❑ 191 Ben Chapman RC 75.00 45.00
❑ 192 Walter Brown RC 60.00 35.00
❑ 193 Lynford Lary RC 60.00 35.00
❑ 194 Earl Averill RC 200.00 125.00
❑ 195 Evar Swanson RC 60.00 35.00
❑ 196 Leroy Mahaffey RC 60.00 35.00
❑ 197 Rick Ferrell RC 125.00 75.00
❑ 198 Jack Burns RC 60.00 35.00
❑ 199 Tom Bridges RC 60.00 35.00
❑ 200 Bill Hallahan RC 60.00 35.00
❑ 201 Ernie Orsatti RC 60.00 35.00
❑ 202 Gabby Hartnett RC 250.00 150.00
❑ 203 Lon Warneke RC 60.00 35.00
❑ 204 Riggs Stephenson RC 60.00 35.00
❑ 205 Heinie Meine RC 60.00 35.00
❑ 206 Gus Suhr RC 60.00 35.00
❑ 207 Mel Ott Bat RC 400.00 250.00
❑ 208 Bernie James RC 60.00 35.00
❑ 209 Adolfo Luque RC 75.00 45.00
❑ 210 Spud Davis RC 60.00 35.00
❑ 211 Hack Wilson RC 400.00 250.00
❑ 212 Billy Urbanski RC 60.00 35.00
❑ 213 Earl Adams RC 60.00 35.00
❑ 214 John Kerr RC 60.00 35.00
❑ 215 Russ Van Atta RC 60.00 35.00
❑ 216 Lefty Gomez RC 300.00 175.00
❑ 217 Frank Crosetti RC 150.00 90.00
❑ 218 Wes Ferrell RC 75.00 45.00
❑ 219 Mule Haas UER RC 60.00 35.00
❑ 220 Lefty Grove RC 500.00 300.00
❑ 221 Dale Alexander RC 60.00 35.00
❑ 222 Charley Gehringer RC 400.00 250.00
❑ 223 Dizzy Dean RC 800.00 500.00
❑ 224 Frank Demaree RC 60.00 35.00
❑ 225 Bill Jurges RC 60.00 35.00
❑ 226 Charley Root RC 60.00 35.00
❑ 227 Billy Herman RC 150.00 90.00
❑ 228 Tony Piet RC 60.00 35.00
❑ 229 Arky Vaughan RC 150.00 90.00
❑ 230 Carl Hubbell PIT RC 400.00 250.00
❑ 231 Joe Moore FIELD RC 60.00 35.00
❑ 232 Lefty O'Doul RC 125.00 75.00
❑ 233 Johnny Vergez RC 60.00 35.00
❑ 234 Carl Hubbell RC 400.00 250.00
❑ 235 Fred Fitzsimmons PIT RC 60.00 35.00
❑ 236 George Davis RC 60.00 35.00
❑ 237 Gus Mancuso FIELD RC 60.00 35.00
❑ 238 Hugh Critz FIELD RC 60.00 35.00
❑ 239 Leroy Parmelee RC 60.00 35.00
❑ 240 Hal Schumacher RC 125.00 75.00

1934 Goudey

❑ COMPLETE SET (96) 16000.009000.00
❑ COMMON CARD (1-48) 50.00 30.00
❑ COMMON CARD (49-72) 75.00 40.00
❑ COMMON CARD (73-96) 175.00 100.00
❑ WRAPPER (1-CENT, WHT.) 100.00 75.00
❑ WRAPPER (1-CENT, CLR.) 100.00 75.00
❑ 1 Jimmie Foxx 750.00 450.00
❑ 2 Mickey Cochrane 175.00 100.00
❑ 3 Charlie Grimm 60.00 35.00
❑ 4 Woody English 50.00 30.00
❑ 5 Ed Brandt 50.00 30.00
❑ 6 Dizzy Dean 700.00 400.00
❑ 7 Leo Durocher 175.00 100.00
❑ 8 Tony Piet 60.00 30.00
❑ 9 Ben Chapman 60.00 35.00
❑ 10 Chuck Klein 150.00 90.00
❑ 11 Paul Waner 150.00 90.00
❑ 12 Carl Hubbell 175.00 100.00
❑ 13 Frankie Frisch 175.00 100.00
❑ 14 Willie Kamm 50.00 30.00
❑ 15 Alvin Crowder 50.00 30.00
❑ 16 Joe Kuhel 50.00 30.00
❑ 17 Hugh Critz 50.00 30.00
❑ 18 Heinie Manush 125.00 75.00
❑ 19 Lefty Grove 300.00 175.00
❑ 20 Frank Hogan 50.00 30.00
❑ 21 Bill Terry 200.00 125.00
❑ 22 Arky Vaughan 125.00 75.00
❑ 23 Charley Gehringer 200.00 125.00
❑ 24 Ray Benge 50.00 30.00
❑ 25 Roger Cramer RC 60.00 35.00
❑ 26 Gerald Walker RC 50.00 30.00
❑ 27 Luke Appling RC 150.00 90.00
❑ 28 Ed Coleman RC 50.00 30.00
❑ 29 Larry French RC 50.00 30.00
❑ 30 Julius Solters RC 50.00 30.00
❑ 31 Buck Jordan RC 50.00 30.00
❑ 32 Blondy Ryan RC 50.00 30.00
❑ 33 Don Hurst RC 50.00 30.00
❑ 34 Chick Hafey RC 125.00 75.00
❑ 35 Ernie Lombardi RC 150.00 90.00
❑ 36 Walter Betts RC 50.00 30.00
❑ 37 Lou Gehrig 3000.002000.00
❑ 38 Oral Hildebrand RC 50.00 30.00
❑ 39 Fred Walker RC 50.00 30.00
❑ 40 John Stone 50.00 30.00
❑ 41 George Earnshaw RC 50.00 30.00
❑ 42 John Allen RC 50.00 30.00
❑ 43 Dick Porter RC 50.00 30.00
❑ 44 Tom Bridges 60.00 35.00
❑ 45 Oscar Melillo RC 50.00 30.00
❑ 46 Joe Stripp RC 50.00 30.00
❑ 47 John Frederick RC 50.00 30.00
❑ 48 Tex Carleton RC 50.00 30.00
❑ 49 Sam Leslie RC 75.00 40.00
❑ 50 Walter Beck RC 75.00 40.00
❑ 51 Rip Collins RC 75.00 40.00
❑ 52 Herman Bell RC 75.00 40.00
❑ 53 George Watkins RC 75.00 40.00
❑ 54 Wesley Schulmerich RC 75.00 40.00
❑ 55 Ed Holley RC 75.00 40.00
❑ 56 Mark Koenig 100.00 60.00
❑ 57 Bill Swift RC 75.00 40.00
❑ 58 Earl Grace RC 75.00 40.00
❑ 59 Joe Mowry RC 75.00 40.00
❑ 60 Lynn Nelson RC 75.00 40.00

❑ 61 Lou Gehrig 3000.00 2000.00
❑ 62 Hank Greenberg RC 700.00 400.00
❑ 63 Minter Hayes RC 75.00 40.00
❑ 64 Frank Grube RC 75.00 40.00
❑ 65 Cliff Bolton RC 75.00 40.00
❑ 66 Mel Harder RC 100.00 60.00
❑ 67 Bob Weiland RC 75.00 40.00
❑ 68 Bob Johnson RC 100.00 60.00
❑ 69 John Marcum RC 75.00 40.00
❑ 70 Pete Fox RC 75.00 40.00
❑ 71 Lyle Tinning RC 75.00 40.00
❑ 72 Arndt Jorgens RC 75.00 40.00
❑ 73 Ed Wells RC 175.00 100.00
❑ 74 Bob Boken RC 175.00 100.00
❑ 75 Bill Werber RC 175.00 100.00
❑ 76 Hal Trosky RC 200.00 125.00
❑ 77 Joe Vosmik RC 175.00 100.00
❑ 78 Pinky Higgins RC 200.00 125.00
❑ 79 Eddie Durham RC 175.00 100.00
❑ 80 Marty McManus CK 175.00 100.00
❑ 81 Bob Brown CK RC 175.00 100.00
❑ 82 Bill Hallahan CK 175.00 100.00
❑ 83 Jim Mooney CK RC 175.00 100.00
❑ 84 Paul Derringer CK RC 225.00 125.00
❑ 85 Adam Comorosky CK 175.00 100.00
❑ 86 Lloyd Johnson CK RC 175.00 100.00
❑ 87 George Darrow CK RC 175.00 100.00
❑ 88 Homer Peel CK RC 175.00 100.00
❑ 89 Linus Frey CK RC 175.00 100.00
❑ 90 KiKi Cuyler CK 350.00 200.00
❑ 91 Dolph Camilli CK RC 200.00 125.00
❑ 92 Steve Larkin RC 175.00 100.00
❑ 93 Fred Ostermueller RC 175.00 100.00
❑ 94 Red Rolfe RC 200.00 125.00
❑ 95 Myril Hoag RC 175.00 100.00
❑ 96 James DeShong RC 500.00 300.00

1949 Leaf

❑ COMPLETE SET (98) 40000.00 25000.00
❑ COMMON CARD (1-168) 25.00 15.00
❑ COMMON SP's 300.00 200.00
❑ WRAPPER (1-CENT) 160.00 120.00
❑ 1 Joe DiMaggio 3000.00 1800.00
❑ 3 Babe Ruth 2500.00 1500.00
❑ 4 Stan Musial 1000.00 600.00
❑ 5 Virgil Trucks SP RC 400.00 250.00
❑ 8 S.Paige SP RC 15000.00 9000.00
❑ 10 Dizzy Trout 40.00 25.00
❑ 11 Phil Rizzuto 350.00 200.00
❑ 13 Cass Michaels SP RC 300.00 200.00
❑ 14 Billy Johnson 40.00 25.00
❑ 17 Frank Overmire RC 25.00 15.00
❑ 19 Johnny Wyrostek SP 300.00 200.00
❑ 20 Hank Sauer SP 400.00 250.00
❑ 22 Al Evans RC 25.00 15.00
❑ 26 Sam Chapman 40.00 25.00
❑ 27 Mickey Harris RC 25.00 15.00
❑ 28 Jim Hegan RC 40.00 25.00
❑ 29 Elmer Valo RC 40.00 25.00
❑ 30 Billy Goodman SP RC 400.00 250.00
❑ 31 Lou Brissie RC 25.00 15.00
❑ 32 Warren Spahn 350.00 200.00
❑ 33 Peanuts Lowrey SP RC 300.00 200.00
❑ 36 Al Zarilla SP 300.00 200.00
❑ 38 Ted Kluszewski RC 200.00 125.00
❑ 39 Ewell Blackwell 60.00 35.00
❑ 42A Kent Peterson RC 25.00 15.00
❑ 42B Kent Peterson Red Cap
❑ 43 Ed Stevens SP RC 300.00 200.00
❑ 45 Ken Keltner SP RC 300.00 200.00
❑ 46 Johnny Mize 100.00 60.00
❑ 47 George Vico RC 25.00 15.00
❑ 48 Johnny Schmitz SP RC 300.00 200.00
❑ 49 Del Ennis RC 60.00 35.00
❑ 50 Dick Wakefield RC 25.00 15.00
❑ 51 Alvin Dark SP RC 500.00 300.00
❑ 53 Johnny VanderMeer 100.00 60.00
❑ 54 Bobby Adams SP RC 300.00 200.00
❑ 55 Tommy Henrich SP 500.00 300.00
❑ 56 Larry Jansen 40.00 25.00
❑ 57 Bob McCall RC 25.00 15.00
❑ 59 Luke Appling 100.00 60.00
❑ 61 Jake Early RC 25.00 15.00
❑ 62 Eddie Joost SP 300.00 200.00
❑ 63 Barney McCosky SP 300.00 200.00
❑ 65 Bob Elliott UER 100.00 60.00
❑ 66 Orval Grove SP RC 300.00 200.00
❑ 68 Eddie Miller SP 300.00 200.00
❑ 70 Honus Wagner 350.00 200.00
❑ 72 Hank Edwards RC 25.00 15.00
❑ 73 Pat Seerey RC 25.00 15.00
❑ 75 Dom DiMaggio SP 600.00 350.00
❑ 76 Ted Williams 1200.00 700.00
❑ 77 Roy Smalley RC 25.00 15.00
❑ 78 Hoot Evers SP RC 300.00 200.00
❑ 79 Jackie Robinson RC 2000.00 1200.00
❑ 81 Whitey Kurowski SP RC 300.00 200.00
❑ 82 Johnny Lindell 40.00 25.00
❑ 83 Bobby Doerr 100.00 60.00
❑ 84 Sid Hudson 25.00 15.00
❑ 85 Dave Philley SP RC 400.00 250.00
❑ 86 Ralph Weigel RC 25.00 15.00
❑ 88 Frank Gustine SP RC 300.00 200.00
❑ 91 Ralph Kiner 200.00 125.00
❑ 93 Bob Feller SP 2000.00 1400.00
❑ 95 Snuffy Stirnweiss 40.00 25.00
❑ 97 Marty Marion 60.00 35.00
❑ 98 Hal Newhouser SP RC 600.00 350.00
❑ 102A G.Hermansk ERR 250.00 150.00
❑ 102B Gene Hermanski COR RC 40.00 25.00
❑ 104 Eddie Stewart SP RC 300.00 200.00
❑ 106 Lou Boudreau MG RC 100.00 60.00
❑ 108 Matt Batts SP RC 300.00 200.00
❑ 111 Jerry Priddy RC 25.00 15.00
❑ 113 Dutch Leonard SP 300.00 200.00
❑ 117 Joe Gordon RC 40.00 25.00
❑ 120 George Kell SP RC 600.00 350.00
❑ 121 Johnny Pesky SP RC 400.00 250.00
❑ 123 Cliff Fannin SP RC 300.00 200.00
❑ 125 Andy Pafko RC 25.00 15.00
❑ 127 Enos Slaughter SP 800.00 500.00
❑ 128 Buddy Rosar 25.00 15.00
❑ 129 Kirby Higbe SP 300.00 200.00
❑ 131 Sid Gordon SP 300.00 200.00
❑ 133 Tommy Holmes SP RC 500.00 300.00
❑ 136A C.Aberson Full Slv RC 25.00 15.00
❑ 136B C.Aberson Short Slv 250.00 150.00
❑ 137 Harry Walker SP RC 400.00 250.00
❑ 138 Larry Doby SP RC 700.00 400.00
❑ 139 Johnny Hopp RC 25.00 15.00
❑ 142 D.Murtaugh SP RC 400.00 250.00
❑ 143 Dick Sisler SP RC 300.00 200.00
❑ 144 Bob Dillinger SP RC 300.00 200.00
❑ 146 Pete Reiser SP 500.00 300.00
❑ 149 Hank Majeski SP RC 300.00 200.00
❑ 153 Floyd Baker SP RC 300.00 200.00
❑ 158 H.Brecheen SP RC 400.00 250.00
❑ 159 Mizell Platt RC 25.00 15.00
❑ 160 Bob Scheffing SP RC 300.00 200.00
❑ 161 V.Stephens SP RC 400.00 250.00
❑ 163 F.Hutchinson SP RC 400.00 250.00
❑ 165 Dale Mitchell SP RC 400.00 250.00
❑ 168 Phil Cavarretta SP RC 500.00 300.00
❑ NNO Album

1990 Leaf

❑ COMPLETE SET (528) 60.00 30.00
❑ COMPLETE SERIES 1 (264) 40.00 20.00
❑ COMPLETE SERIES 2 (264) 20.00 10.00
❑ COMP. BERRA PUZZLE 1.00 .40
❑ 1 Introductory Card .40 .15
❑ 2 Mike Henneman .40 .15
❑ 3 Steve Bedrosian .40 .15
❑ 4 Mike Scott .40 .15

❑ 5 Allan Anderson .40 .15
❑ 6 Rick Sutcliffe .60 .25
❑ 7 Gregg Olson .60 .25
❑ 8 Kevin Elster .40 .15
❑ 9 Pete O'Brien .40 .15
❑ 10 Carlton Fisk 1.00 .40
❑ 11 Joe Magrane .40 .15
❑ 12 Roger Clemens 4.00 1.50
❑ 13 Tom Glavine 1.00 .40
❑ 14 Tom Gordon .60 .25
❑ 15 Todd Benzinger .40 .15
❑ 16 Hubie Brooks .40 .15
❑ 17 Roberto Kelly .40 .15
❑ 18 Barry Larkin 1.00 .40
❑ 19 Mike Boddicker .40 .15
❑ 20 Roger McDowell .40 .15
❑ 21 Nolan Ryan 5.00 2.00
❑ 22 John Farrell .40 .15
❑ 23 Bruce Hurst .40 .15
❑ 24 Wally Joyner .60 .25
❑ 25 Greg Maddux 5.00 2.00
❑ 26 Chris Bosio .40 .15
❑ 27 John Cerutti .40 .15
❑ 28 Tim Burke .40 .15
❑ 29 Dennis Eckersley .60 .25
❑ 30 Glenn Davis .40 .15
❑ 31 Jim Abbott 1.00 .40
❑ 32 Mike LaValliere .40 .15
❑ 33 Andres Thomas .40 .15
❑ 34 Lou Whitaker .60 .25
❑ 35 Alvin Davis .40 .15
❑ 36 Melido Perez .40 .15
❑ 37 Craig Biggio 1.50 .60
❑ 38 Rick Aguilera .60 .25
❑ 39 Pete Harnisch .40 .15
❑ 40 David Cone .60 .25
❑ 41 Scott Garrelts .40 .15
❑ 42 Jay Howell .40 .15
❑ 43 Eric King .40 .15
❑ 44 Pedro Guerrero .40 .15
❑ 45 Mike Bielecki .40 .15
❑ 46 Bob Boone .60 .25
❑ 47 Kevin Brown .60 .25
❑ 48 Jerry Browne .40 .15
❑ 49 Mike Scioscia .40 .15
❑ 50 Chuck Cary .40 .15
❑ 51 Wade Boggs 1.00 .40
❑ 52 Von Hayes .40 .15
❑ 53 Tony Fernandez .40 .15
❑ 54 Dennis Martinez .60 .25
❑ 55 Tom Candiotti .40 .15
❑ 56 Andy Benes .60 .25
❑ 57 Rob Dibble .60 .25
❑ 58 Chuck Crim .40 .15
❑ 59 John Smoltz 1.50 .60
❑ 60 Mike Heath .40 .15
❑ 61 Kevin Gross .40 .15
❑ 62 Mark McGwire 4.00 1.50
❑ 63 Bert Blyleven .60 .25
❑ 64 Bob Walk .40 .15
❑ 65 Mickey Tettleton .40 .15
❑ 66 Sid Fernandez .40 .15
❑ 67 Terry Kennedy .40 .15
❑ 68 Fernando Valenzuela .60 .25
❑ 69 Don Mattingly 4.00 1.50
❑ 70 Paul O'Neill 1.00 .40
❑ 71 Robin Yount 2.50 1.00
❑ 72 Bret Saberhagen .60 .25

❑ 73 Geno Petralli .40 .15
❑ 74 Brook Jacoby .40 .15
❑ 75 Roberto Alomar 1.00 .40
❑ 76 Devon White .60 .25
❑ 77 Jose Lind .40 .15
❑ 78 Pat Combs .40 .15
❑ 79 Dave Stieb .60 .25
❑ 80 Tim Wallach .40 .15
❑ 81 Dave Stewart .60 .25
❑ 82 Eric Anthony RC .40 .15
❑ 83 Randy Bush .40 .15
❑ 84 Rickey Henderson CL .60 .25
❑ 85 Jaime Navarro .40 .15
❑ 86 Tommy Gregg .40 .15
❑ 87 Frank Tanana .40 .15
❑ 88 Omar Vizquel 1.50 .60
❑ 89 Ivan Calderon .40 .15
❑ 90 Vince Coleman .40 .15
❑ 91 Barry Bonds 5.00 2.00
❑ 92 Randy Milligan .40 .15
❑ 93 Frank Viola .40 .15
❑ 94 Matt Williams .60 .25
❑ 95 Alfredo Griffin .40 .15
❑ 96 Steve Sax .40 .15
❑ 97 Gary Gaetti .60 .25
❑ 98 Ryne Sandberg 3.00 1.25
❑ 99 Danny Tartabull .40 .15
❑ 100 Rafael Palmeiro 1.00 .40
❑ 101 Jesse Orosco .40 .15
❑ 102 Garry Templeton .40 .15
❑ 103 Frank DiPino .40 .15
❑ 104 Tony Pena .40 .15
❑ 105 Dickie Thon .40 .15
❑ 106 Kelly Gruber .40 .15
❑ 107 Marquis Grissom RC 2.00 .75
❑ 108 Jose Canseco 1.00 .40
❑ 109 Mike Blowers RC .40 .15
❑ 110 Tom Browning .40 .15
❑ 111 Greg Vaughn .40 .15
❑ 112 Oddibe McDowell .40 .15
❑ 113 Gary Ward .40 .15
❑ 114 Jay Buhner .60 .25
❑ 115 Eric Show .40 .15
❑ 116 Bryan Harvey .40 .15
❑ 117 Andy Van Slyke 1.00 .40
❑ 118 Jeff Ballard .40 .15
❑ 119 Barry Lyons .40 .15
❑ 120 Kevin Mitchell .40 .15
❑ 121 Mike Gallego .40 .15
❑ 122 Dave Smith .40 .15
❑ 123 Kirby Puckett 1.50 .60
❑ 124 Jerome Walton .40 .15
❑ 125 Bo Jackson 1.50 .60
❑ 126 Harold Baines .60 .25
❑ 127 Scott Bankhead .40 .15
❑ 128 Ozzie Guillen .60 .25
❑ 129 Jose Oquendo UER (League misspelled as Leque) .40 .15
❑ 130 John Dopson .40 .15
❑ 131 Charlie Hayes .40 .15
❑ 132 Fred McGriff 1.50 .60
❑ 133 Chet Lemon .40 .15
❑ 134 Gary Carter .60 .25
❑ 135 Rafael Ramirez .40 .15
❑ 136 Shane Mack .40 .15
❑ 137 Mark Grace 1.00 .40
❑ 138 Phil Bradley .40 .15
❑ 139 Dwight Gooden .60 .25
❑ 140 Harold Reynolds .60 .25
❑ 141 Scott Fletcher .40 .15
❑ 142 Ozzie Smith 2.50 1.00
❑ 143 Mike Greenwell .40 .15
❑ 144 Pete Smith .40 .15
❑ 145 Mark Gubicza .40 .15
❑ 146 Chris Sabo .40 .15
❑ 147 Ramon Martinez .40 .15
❑ 148 Tim Leary .40 .15
❑ 149 Randy Myers .60 .25
❑ 150 Jody Reed .40 .15
❑ 151 Bruce Ruffin .40 .15
❑ 152 Jeff Russell .40 .15
❑ 153 Doug Jones .40 .15
❑ 154 Tony Gwynn 2.00 .75
❑ 155 Mark Langston .40 .15
❑ 156 Mitch Williams .40 .15
❑ 157 Gary Sheffield 1.50 .60
❑ 158 Tom Henke .40 .15
❑ 159 Oil Can Boyd .40 .15
❑ 160 Rickey Henderson 1.50 .60
❑ 161 Bill Doran .40 .15
❑ 162 Chuck Finley .60 .25
❑ 163 Jeff King .40 .15
❑ 164 Nick Esasky .40 .15
❑ 165 Cecil Fielder .60 .25
❑ 166 Dave Valle .40 .15
❑ 167 Robin Ventura 1.50 .60
❑ 168 Jim Deshaies .40 .15
❑ 169 Juan Berenguer .40 .15
❑ 170 Craig Worthington .40 .15
❑ 171 Gregg Jefferies .60 .25
❑ 172 Will Clark 1.00 .40
❑ 173 Kirk Gibson .60 .25
❑ 174 Checklist 89-176 (Carlton Fisk) .60 .25
❑ 175 Bobby Thigpen .40 .15
❑ 176 John Tudor .40 .15
❑ 177 Andre Dawson .60 .25
❑ 178 George Brett 4.00 1.50
❑ 179 Steve Buechele .40 .15
❑ 180 Albert Belle 1.50 .60
❑ 181 Eddie Murray 1.50 .60
❑ 182 Bob Geren .40 .15
❑ 183 Rob Murphy .40 .15
❑ 184 Tom Herr .40 .15
❑ 185 George Bell .40 .15
❑ 186 Spike Owen .40 .15
❑ 187 Cory Snyder .40 .15
❑ 188 Fred Lynn .40 .15
❑ 189 Eric Davis .60 .25
❑ 190 Dave Parker .60 .25
❑ 191 Jeff Blauser .40 .15
❑ 192 Matt Nokes .40 .15
❑ 193 Delino DeShields RC 1.00 .40
❑ 194 Scott Sanderson .40 .15
❑ 195 Lance Parrish .40 .15
❑ 196 Bobby Bonilla .60 .25
❑ 197 Cal Ripken 5.00 2.00
❑ 198 Kevin McReynolds .40 .15
❑ 199 Robby Thompson .40 .15
❑ 200 Tim Belcher .40 .15
❑ 201 Jesse Barfield .40 .15
❑ 202 Mariano Duncan .40 .15
❑ 203 Bill Spiers .40 .15
❑ 204 Frank White .60 .25
❑ 205 Julio Franco .60 .25
❑ 206 Greg Swindell .40 .15
❑ 207 Benito Santiago .60 .25
❑ 208 Johnny Ray .40 .15
❑ 209 Gary Redus .40 .15
❑ 210 Jeff Parrett .40 .15
❑ 211 Jimmy Key .60 .25
❑ 212 Tim Raines .60 .25
❑ 213 Carney Lansford .60 .25
❑ 214 Gerald Young .40 .15
❑ 215 Gene Larkin .40 .15
❑ 216 Dan Plesac .40 .15
❑ 217 Lonnie Smith .40 .15
❑ 218 Alan Trammell .60 .25
❑ 219 Jeffrey Leonard .40 .15
❑ 220 Sammy Sosa RC 12.00 5.00
❑ 221 Todd Zeile .60 .25
❑ 222 Bill Landrum .40 .15
❑ 223 Mike Devereaux .40 .15
❑ 224 Mike Marshall .40 .15
❑ 225 Jose Uribe .40 .15
❑ 226 Juan Samuel .40 .15
❑ 227 Mel Hall .40 .15
❑ 228 Kent Hrbek .60 .25
❑ 229 Shawon Dunston .40 .15
❑ 230 Kevin Seitzer .40 .15
❑ 231 Pete Incaviglia .40 .15
❑ 232 Sandy Alomar Jr. .60 .25
❑ 233 Bip Roberts .40 .15
❑ 234 Scott Terry .40 .15
❑ 235 Dwight Evans 1.00 .40
❑ 236 Ricky Jordan .40 .15
❑ 237 John Olerud RC 3.00 1.25
❑ 238 Zane Smith .40 .15
❑ 239 Walt Weiss .40 .15
❑ 240 Alvaro Espinoza .40 .15
❑ 241 Billy Hatcher .40 .15
❑ 242 Paul Molitor .60 .25
❑ 243 Dale Murphy 1.00 .40
❑ 244 Dave Bergman .40 .15
❑ 245 Ken Griffey Jr. 5.00 2.00
❑ 246 Ed Whitson .40 .15
❑ 247 Kirk McCaskill .40 .15
❑ 248 Jay Bell .60 .25
❑ 249 Ben McDonald RC 1.00 .40
❑ 250 Darryl Strawberry .60 .25
❑ 251 Brett Butler .60 .25
❑ 252 Terry Steinbach .40 .15
❑ 253 Ken Caminiti .60 .25
❑ 254 Dan Gladden .40 .15
❑ 255 Dwight Smith .40 .15
❑ 256 Kurt Stillwell .40 .15
❑ 257 Ruben Sierra .60 .25
❑ 258 Mike Schooler .40 .15
❑ 259 Lance Johnson .40 .15
❑ 260 Terry Pendleton .60 .25
❑ 261 Ellis Burks 1.00 .40
❑ 262 Len Dykstra .60 .25
❑ 263 Mookie Wilson .60 .25
❑ 264 Nolan Ryan CL UER 1.50 .60
❑ 265 Nolan Ryan SPEC 2.50 1.00
❑ 266 Brian DuBois RC .40 .15
❑ 267 Don Robinson .40 .15
❑ 268 Glenn Wilson .40 .15
❑ 269 Kevin Tapani RC 1.00 .40
❑ 270 Marvell Wynne .40 .15
❑ 271 Bill Ripken .40 .15
❑ 272 Howard Johnson .40 .15
❑ 273 Brian Holman .40 .15
❑ 274 Dan Pasqua .40 .15
❑ 275 Ken Dayley .40 .15
❑ 276 Jeff Reardon .60 .25
❑ 277 Jim Presley .40 .15
❑ 278 Jim Eisenreich .40 .15
❑ 279 Danny Jackson .40 .15
❑ 280 Orel Hershiser .60 .25
❑ 281 Andy Hawkins .40 .15
❑ 282 Jose Rijo .40 .15
❑ 283 Luis Rivera .40 .15
❑ 284 John Kruk .60 .25
❑ 285 Jeff Huson RC .40 .15
❑ 286 Joel Skinner .40 .15
❑ 287 Jack Clark .60 .25
❑ 288 Chili Davis .60 .25
❑ 289 Joe Girardi 1.00 .40
❑ 290 B.J. Surhoff .60 .25
❑ 291 Luis Sojo RC .40 .15
❑ 292 Tom Foley .40 .15
❑ 293 Mike Moore .40 .15
❑ 294 Ken Oberkfell .40 .15
❑ 295 Luis Polonia .40 .15
❑ 296 Doug Drabek .40 .15
❑ 297 David Justice RC 3.00 1.25
❑ 298 Paul Gibson .40 .15
❑ 299 Edgar Martinez 1.00 .40
❑ 300 Frank Thomas RC 12.00 5.00
❑ 301 Eric Yelding RC .40 .15
❑ 302 Greg Gagne .40 .15
❑ 303 Brad Komminsk .40 .15
❑ 304 Ron Darling .40 .15
❑ 305 Kevin Bass .40 .15
❑ 306 Jeff Hamilton .40 .15
❑ 307 Ron Karkovice .40 .15
❑ 308 M.Thompson UER Lankford 1.00 .40
❑ 309 Mike Harkey .40 .15
❑ 310 Mel Stottlemyre Jr. .40 .15
❑ 311 Kenny Rogers .60 .25
❑ 312 Mitch Webster .40 .15
❑ 313 Kal Daniels .40 .15
❑ 314 Matt Nokes .40 .15
❑ 315 Dennis Lamp .40 .15
❑ 316 Ken Howell .40 .15
❑ 317 Glenallen Hill .40 .15
❑ 318 Dave Martinez .40 .15
❑ 319 Chris James .40 .15
❑ 320 Mike Pagliarulo .40 .15
❑ 321 Hal Morris .40 .15
❑ 322 Rob Deer .40 .15
❑ 323 Greg Olson (C) RC .40 .15
❑ 324 Tony Phillips .40 .15
❑ 325 Larry Walker RC 8.00 3.00
❑ 326 Ron Hassey .40 .15
❑ 327 Jack Howell .40 .15

- ❑ 328 John Smiley .40 .15
- ❑ 329 Steve Finley .60 .25
- ❑ 330 Dave Magadan .40 .15
- ❑ 331 Greg Litton .40 .15
- ❑ 332 Mickey Hatcher .40 .15
- ❑ 333 Lee Guetterman .40 .15
- ❑ 334 Norm Charlton .40 .15
- ❑ 335 Edgar Diaz RC .40 .15
- ❑ 336 Willie Wilson .40 .15
- ❑ 337 Bobby Witt .40 .15
- ❑ 338 Candy Maldonado .40 .15
- ❑ 339 Craig Lefferts .40 .15
- ❑ 340 Dante Bichette .60 .25
- ❑ 341 Wally Backman .40 .15
- ❑ 342 Dennis Cook .40 .15
- ❑ 343 Pat Borders .40 .15
- ❑ 344 Wallace Johnson .40 .15
- ❑ 345 Willie Randolph .60 .25
- ❑ 346 Danny Darwin .40 .15
- ❑ 347 Al Newman .40 .15
- ❑ 348 Mark Knudson .40 .15
- ❑ 349 Joe Boever .40 .15
- ❑ 350 Larry Sheets .40 .15
- ❑ 351 Mike Jackson .40 .15
- ❑ 352 Wayne Edwards RC .40 .15
- ❑ 353 Bernard Gilkey RC 1.00 .40
- ❑ 354 Don Slaught .40 .15
- ❑ 355 Joe Orsulak .40 .15
- ❑ 356 John Franco .60 .25
- ❑ 357 Jeff Brantley .40 .15
- ❑ 358 Mike Morgan .40 .15
- ❑ 359 Deion Sanders 1.50 .60
- ❑ 360 Terry Leach .40 .15
- ❑ 361 Les Lancaster .40 .15
- ❑ 362 Storm Davis .40 .15
- ❑ 363 Scott Coolbaugh RC .40 .15
- ❑ 364 Checklist 265-352 (Ozzie Smith) 1.00 .40
- ❑ 365 Cecilio Guante .40 .15
- ❑ 366 Joey Cora .60 .25
- ❑ 367 Willie McGee .60 .25
- ❑ 368 Jerry Reed .40 .15
- ❑ 369 Darren Daulton .60 .25
- ❑ 370 Manny Lee .40 .15
- ❑ 371 Mark Gardner RC .40 .15
- ❑ 372 Rick Honeycutt .40 .15
- ❑ 373 Steve Balboni .40 .15
- ❑ 374 Jack Armstrong .40 .15
- ❑ 375 Charlie O'Brien .40 .15
- ❑ 376 Ron Gant .60 .25
- ❑ 377 Lloyd Moseby .40 .15
- ❑ 378 Gene Harris .40 .15
- ❑ 379 Joe Carter .60 .25
- ❑ 380 Scott Bailes .40 .15
- ❑ 381 R.J. Reynolds .40 .15
- ❑ 382 Bob Melvin .40 .15
- ❑ 383 Tim Teufel .40 .15
- ❑ 384 John Burkett .40 .15
- ❑ 385 Felix Jose .40 .15
- ❑ 386 Larry Andersen .40 .15
- ❑ 387 David West .40 .15
- ❑ 388 Luis Salazar .40 .15
- ❑ 389 Mike Macfarlane .40 .15
- ❑ 390 Charlie Hough .60 .25
- ❑ 391 Greg Briley .40 .15
- ❑ 392 Donn Pall .40 .15
- ❑ 393 Bryn Smith .40 .15
- ❑ 394 Carlos Quintana .40 .15
- ❑ 395 Steve Lake .40 .15
- ❑ 396 Mark Whiten RC 1.00 .40
- ❑ 397 Edwin Nunez .40 .15
- ❑ 398 Rick Parker RC .40 .15
- ❑ 399 Mark Portugal .40 .15
- ❑ 400 Roy Smith .40 .15
- ❑ 401 Hector Villanueva RC .40 .15
- ❑ 402 Bob Milacki .40 .15
- ❑ 403 Alejandro Pena .40 .15
- ❑ 404 Scott Bradley .40 .15
- ❑ 405 Ron Kittle .40 .15
- ❑ 406 Bob Tewksbury .40 .15
- ❑ 407 Wes Gardner .40 .15
- ❑ 408 Ernie Whitt .40 .15
- ❑ 409 Terry Shumpert RC .40 .15
- ❑ 410 Tim Layana RC .40 .15
- ❑ 411 Chris Gwynn .40 .15
- ❑ 412 Jeff D. Robinson .40 .15
- ❑ 413 Scott Scudder .40 .15
- ❑ 414 Kevin Romine .40 .15
- ❑ 415 Jose DeJesus .40 .15
- ❑ 416 Mike Jeffcoat .40 .15
- ❑ 417 Rudy Seanez RC .40 .15
- ❑ 418 Mike Dunne .40 .15
- ❑ 419 Dick Schofield .40 .15
- ❑ 420 Steve Wilson .40 .15
- ❑ 421 Bill Krueger .40 .15
- ❑ 422 Junior Felix .40 .15
- ❑ 423 Drew Hall .40 .15
- ❑ 424 Curt Young .40 .15
- ❑ 425 Franklin Stubbs .40 .15
- ❑ 426 Dave Winfield .60 .25
- ❑ 427 Rick Reed RC 1.00 .40
- ❑ 428 Charlie Leibrandt .40 .15
- ❑ 429 Jeff M. Robinson .40 .15
- ❑ 430 Erik Hanson .40 .15
- ❑ 431 Barry Jones .40 .15
- ❑ 432 Alex Trevino .40 .15
- ❑ 433 John Moses .40 .15
- ❑ 434 Dave Wayne Johnson RC .40 .15
- ❑ 435 Mackey Sasser .40 .15
- ❑ 436 Rick Leach .40 .15
- ❑ 437 Lenny Harris .40 .15
- ❑ 438 Carlos Martinez .40 .15
- ❑ 439 Rex Hudler .40 .15
- ❑ 440 Domingo Ramos .40 .15
- ❑ 441 Gerald Perry .40 .15
- ❑ 442 Jeff Russell .40 .15
- ❑ 443 Carlos Baerga RC 1.00 .40
- ❑ 444 Will Clark CL .60 .25
- ❑ 445 Stan Javier .40 .15
- ❑ 446 Kevin Maas RC 1.00 .40
- ❑ 447 Tom Brunansky .40 .15
- ❑ 448 Carmelo Martinez .40 .15
- ❑ 449 Willie Blair RC .40 .15
- ❑ 450 Andres Galarraga .60 .25
- ❑ 451 Bud Black .40 .15
- ❑ 452 Greg W. Harris .40 .15
- ❑ 453 Joe Oliver .40 .15
- ❑ 454 Greg Brock .40 .15
- ❑ 455 Jeff Treadway .40 .15
- ❑ 456 Lance McCullers .40 .15
- ❑ 457 Dave Schmidt .40 .15
- ❑ 458 Todd Burns .40 .15
- ❑ 459 Max Venable .40 .15
- ❑ 460 Neal Heaton .40 .15
- ❑ 461 Mark Williamson .40 .15
- ❑ 462 Keith Miller .40 .15
- ❑ 463 Mike LaCoss .40 .15
- ❑ 464 Jose Offerman RC 1.00 .40
- ❑ 465 Jim Leyritz RC 2.00 .75
- ❑ 466 Glenn Braggs .40 .15
- ❑ 467 Ron Robinson .40 .15
- ❑ 468 Mark Davis .40 .15
- ❑ 469 Gary Pettis .40 .15
- ❑ 470 Keith Hernandez .60 .25
- ❑ 471 Dennis Rasmussen .40 .15
- ❑ 472 Mark Eichhorn .40 .15
- ❑ 473 Ted Power .40 .15
- ❑ 474 Terry Mulholland .40 .15
- ❑ 475 Todd Stottlemyre .60 .25
- ❑ 476 Jerry Goff RC .40 .15
- ❑ 477 Gene Nelson .40 .15
- ❑ 478 Rich Gedman .40 .15
- ❑ 479 Brian Harper .40 .15
- ❑ 480 Mike Felder .40 .15
- ❑ 481 Steve Avery .40 .15
- ❑ 482 Jack Morris .60 .25
- ❑ 483 Randy Johnson 3.00 1.25
- ❑ 484 Scott Radinsky RC .40 .15
- ❑ 485 Jose DeLeon .40 .15
- ❑ 486 Stan Belinda RC .40 .15
- ❑ 487 Brian Holton .40 .15
- ❑ 488 Mark Carreon .40 .15
- ❑ 489 Trevor Wilson .40 .15
- ❑ 490 Mike Sharperson .40 .15
- ❑ 491 Alan Mills RC .40 .15
- ❑ 492 John Candelaria .40 .15
- ❑ 493 Paul Assenmacher .40 .15
- ❑ 494 Steve Crawford .40 .15
- ❑ 495 Brad Arnsberg .40 .15
- ❑ 496 Sergio Valdez RC .40 .15
- ❑ 497 Mark Parent .40 .15
- ❑ 498 Tom Pagnozzi .40 .15
- ❑ 499 Greg A. Harris .40 .15
- ❑ 500 Randy Ready .40 .15
- ❑ 501 Duane Ward .40 .15
- ❑ 502 Nelson Santovenia .40 .15
- ❑ 503 Joe Klink RC .40 .15
- ❑ 504 Eric Plunk .40 .15
- ❑ 505 Jeff Reed .40 .15
- ❑ 506 Ted Higuera .40 .15
- ❑ 507 Joe Hesketh .40 .15
- ❑ 508 Dan Petry .40 .15
- ❑ 509 Matt Young .40 .15
- ❑ 510 Jerald Clark .40 .15
- ❑ 511 John Orton RC .40 .15
- ❑ 512 Scott Ruskin RC .40 .15
- ❑ 513 Chris Hoiles RC 1.00 .40
- ❑ 514 Daryl Boston .40 .15
- ❑ 515 Francisco Oliveras .40 .15
- ❑ 516 Ozzie Canseco .40 .15
- ❑ 517 Xavier Hernandez RC .40 .15
- ❑ 518 Fred Manrique .40 .15
- ❑ 519 Shawn Boskie RC .40 .15
- ❑ 520 Jeff Montgomery .60 .25
- ❑ 521 Jack Daugherty RC .40 .15
- ❑ 522 Keith Comstock .40 .15
- ❑ 523 Greg Hibbard RC .40 .15
- ❑ 524 Lee Smith .60 .25
- ❑ 525 Dana Kiecker RC .40 .15
- ❑ 526 Darrel Akerfelds .40 .15
- ❑ 527 Greg Myers .40 .15
- ❑ 528 Ryne Sandberg CL 1.50 .60

1939 Play Ball

- ❑ COMPLETE SET (161) 10000.00 6000.00
- ❑ COMMON CARD (1-115) 20.00 12.00
- ❑ COMMON CARD (116-162) 75.00 40.00
- ❑ WRAPPER (1-CENT) 200.00 150.00
- ❑ 1 Jake Powell RC 60.00 30.00
- ❑ 2 Lee Grissom RC 20.00 12.00
- ❑ 3 Red Ruffing 75.00 40.00
- ❑ 4 Eldon Auker RC 20.00 12.00
- ❑ 5 Luke Sewell 25.00 15.00
- ❑ 6 Leo Durocher 100.00 60.00
- ❑ 7 Bobby Doerr RC 75.00 40.00
- ❑ 8 Henry Pippen RC 20.00 12.00
- ❑ 9 James Tobin RC 20.00 12.00
- ❑ 10 James DeShong 20.00 12.00
- ❑ 11 Johnny Rizzo RC 20.00 12.00
- ❑ 12 Hershel Martin RC 20.00 12.00
- ❑ 13 Luke Hamlin RC 20.00 12.00
- ❑ 14 Jim Tabor RC 20.00 12.00
- ❑ 15 Paul Derringer 30.00 18.00
- ❑ 16 John Peacock RC 20.00 12.00
- ❑ 17 Emerson Dickman RC 20.00 12.00
- ❑ 18 Harry Danning RC 20.00 12.00
- ❑ 19 Paul Dean RC 40.00 25.00
- ❑ 20 Joe Heving RC 20.00 12.00
- ❑ 21 Dutch Leonard RC 30.00 18.00
- ❑ 22 Bucky Walters RC 30.00 18.00
- ❑ 23 Burgess Whitehead RC 20.00 12.00
- ❑ 24 Richard Coffman 20.00 12.00
- ❑ 25 George Selkirk RC 40.00 25.00
- ❑ 26 Joe DiMaggio RC 1400.00 900.00
- ❑ 27 Fred Ostermueller 20.00 12.00
- ❑ 28 Sylvester Johnson RC 20.00 12.00
- ❑ 29 John(Jack) Wilson RC 20.00 12.00
- ❑ 30 Bill Dickey 125.00 75.00
- ❑ 31 Sam West 20.00 12.00
- ❑ 32 Bob Seeds RC 20.00 12.00
- ❑ 33 Del Young RC 20.00 12.00
- ❑ 34 Frank Demaree 20.00 12.00

❑ 35 Bill Jurges 20.00 12.00
❑ 36 Frank McCormick RC 20.00 12.00
❑ 37 Virgil Davis 20.00 12.00
❑ 38 Billy Myers RC 20.00 12.00
❑ 39 Rick Ferrell 75.00 40.00
❑ 40 James Bagby Jr. RC 20.00 12.00
❑ 41 Lon Warneke 25.00 15.00
❑ 42 Arndt Jorgens 20.00 12.00
❑ 43 Melo Almada RC 25.00 15.00
❑ 44 Don Heffner RC 20.00 12.00
❑ 45 Merrill May RC 20.00 12.00
❑ 46 Morris Arnovich RC 20.00 12.00
❑ 47 Buddy Lewis RC 20.00 12.00
❑ 48 Lefty Gomez 125.00 75.00
❑ 49 Eddie Miller RC 20.00 12.00
❑ 50 Charley Gehringer 125.00 75.00
❑ 51 Mel Ott 125.00 75.00
❑ 52 Tommy Henrich RC 40.00 25.00
❑ 53 Carl Hubbell 125.00 75.00
❑ 54 Harry Gumpert RC 20.00 12.00
❑ 55 Arky Vaughan 75.00 40.00
❑ 56 Hank Greenberg 200.00 125.00
❑ 57 Buddy Hassett RC 20.00 12.00
❑ 58 Lou Chiozza RC 20.00 12.00
❑ 59 Ken Chase RC 20.00 12.00
❑ 60 Schoolboy Rowe RC 40.00 25.00
❑ 61 Tony Cuccinello 25.00 15.00
❑ 62 Tom Carey RC 20.00 12.00
❑ 63 Emmett Mueller RC 20.00 12.00
❑ 64 Wally Moses RC 25.00 15.00
❑ 65 Harry Craft RC 25.00 15.00
❑ 66 Jimmy Ripple RC 20.00 12.00
❑ 67 Ed Joost RC 25.00 15.00
❑ 68 Fred Sington RC 20.00 12.00
❑ 69 Elbie Fletcher RC 20.00 12.00
❑ 70 Fred Frankhouse 20.00 12.00
❑ 71 Monte Pearson RC 30.00 18.00
❑ 72 Debs Garms RC 20.00 12.00
❑ 73 Hal Schumacher 25.00 15.00
❑ 74 Cookie Lavagetto RC 25.00 15.00
❑ 75 Stan Bordagaray RC 20.00 12.00
❑ 76 Goody Rosen RC 20.00 12.00
❑ 77 Lew Riggs RC 20.00 12.00
❑ 78 Julius Solters 20.00 12.00
❑ 79 Jo Jo Moore 20.00 12.00
❑ 80 Pete Fox 20.00 12.00
❑ 81 Babe Dahlgren RC 30.00 18.00
❑ 82 Chuck Klein 100.00 60.00
❑ 83 Gus Suhr 20.00 12.00
❑ 84 Skeeter Newsom RC 20.00 12.00
❑ 85 Johnny Cooney RC 20.00 12.00
❑ 86 Dolph Camilli 25.00 15.00
❑ 87 Milburn Shoffner RC 20.00 12.00
❑ 88 Charlie Keller RC 40.00 25.00
❑ 89 Lloyd Waner 75.00 40.00
❑ 90 Robert Klinger RC 20.00 12.00
❑ 91 John Knott RC 20.00 12.00
❑ 92 Ted Williams RC 1800.00 1000.00
❑ 93 Charles Gelbert RC 20.00 12.00
❑ 94 Heinie Manush 75.00 40.00
❑ 95 Whit Wyatt RC 25.00 15.00
❑ 96 Babe Phelps RC 20.00 12.00
❑ 97 Bob Johnson 30.00 18.00
❑ 98 Pinky Whitney RC 20.00 12.00
❑ 99 Wally Berger 30.00 18.00
❑ 100 Buddy Myer 25.00 15.00
❑ 101 Roger Cramer 25.00 15.00
❑ 102 Lem (Pep) Young RC 20.00 12.00
❑ 103 Moe Berg 125.00 75.00
❑ 104 Tom Bridges 25.00 15.00
❑ 105 Rabbit McNair RC 20.00 12.00
❑ 106 Dolly Stark UMP 30.00 18.00
❑ 107 Joe Vosmik 20.00 12.00
❑ 108 Frank Hayes 20.00 12.00
❑ 109 Myril Hoag 20.00 12.00
❑ 110 Fred Fitzsimmons 25.00 15.00
❑ 111 Van Lingle Mungo RC 30.00 18.00
❑ 112 Paul Waner 100.00 60.00
❑ 113 Al Schacht 30.00 18.00
❑ 114 Cecil Travis RC 25.00 15.00
❑ 115 Ralph Kress 20.00 12.00
❑ 116 Gene Desautels RC 75.00 40.00
❑ 117 Wayne Ambler RC 75.00 40.00
❑ 118 Lynn Nelson 75.00 40.00
❑ 119 Will Hershberger RC 100.00 50.00
❑ 120 Rabbit Warstler RC 75.00 40.00
❑ 121 Bill Posedel RC 75.00 40.00
❑ 122 George McQuinn RC 75.00 40.00
❑ 123 Ray T. Davis RC 75.00 40.00
❑ 124 Walter Brown 75.00 40.00
❑ 125 Cliff Melton RC 75.00 40.00
❑ 126 Not issued
❑ 127 Gil Brack RC 75.00 40.00
❑ 128 Joe Bowman RC 75.00 40.00
❑ 129 Bill Swift 75.00 40.00
❑ 130 Bill Brubaker RC 75.00 40.00
❑ 131 Mort Cooper RC 100.00 50.00
❑ 132 Jim Brown RC 75.00 40.00
❑ 133 Lynn Myers RC 75.00 40.00
❑ 134 Tot Presnell RC 75.00 40.00
❑ 135 Mickey Owen RC 100.00 50.00
❑ 136 Roy Bell RC 75.00 40.00
❑ 137 Pete Appleton 75.00 40.00
❑ 138 George Case RC 100.00 50.00
❑ 139 Vito Tamulis RC 75.00 40.00
❑ 140 Ray Hayworth RC 75.00 40.00
❑ 141 Pete Coscarart RC 75.00 40.00
❑ 142 Ira Hutchinson RC 75.00 40.00
❑ 143 Earl Averill 175.00 100.00
❑ 144 Zeke Bonura RC 100.00 50.00
❑ 145 Hugh Mulcahy RC 75.00 40.00
❑ 146 Tom Sunkel RC 75.00 40.00
❑ 147 George Coffman RC 75.00 40.00
❑ 148 Bill Trotter RC 75.00 40.00
❑ 149 Max West RC 75.00 40.00
❑ 150 James Walkup RC 75.00 40.00
❑ 151 Hugh Casey RC 100.00 50.00
❑ 152 Roy Weatherly RC 75.00 40.00
❑ 153 Dizzy Trout RC 100.00 50.00
❑ 154 Johnny Hudson RC 75.00 40.00
❑ 155 Jimmy Outlaw RC 75.00 40.00
❑ 156 Ray Berres RC 75.00 40.00
❑ 157 Don Padgett RC 75.00 40.00
❑ 158 Bud Thomas RC 75.00 40.00
❑ 159 Red Evans RC 75.00 40.00
❑ 160 Gene Moore RC 75.00 40.00
❑ 161 Lonnie Frey 75.00 40.00
❑ 162 Whitey Moore RC 100.00 50.00

1940 Play Ball

❑ COMPLETE SET (240) 15000.00 10000.00
❑ COMMON CARD (1-120) 20.00 12.00
❑ COMMON CARD (121-180) 20.00 12.00
❑ COMMON CARD (181-240) 70.00 35.00
❑ WRAP.(1-CENT, DIFF. COL.) 800.00 700.00
❑ 1 Joe DiMaggio 2500.00 1500.00
❑ 2 Art Jorgens 25.00 15.00
❑ 3 Babe Dahlgren 25.00 15.00
❑ 4 Tommy Henrich 50.00 25.00
❑ 5 Monte Pearson 25.00 15.00
❑ 6 Lefty Gomez 150.00 90.00
❑ 7 Bill Dickey 175.00 100.00
❑ 8 George Selkirk 25.00 15.00
❑ 9 Charlie Keller 50.00 25.00
❑ 10 Red Ruffing 90.00 50.00
❑ 11 Jake Powell 25.00 15.00
❑ 12 Johnny Schulte 20.00 12.00
❑ 13 Jack Knott 20.00 12.00
❑ 14 Rabbit McNair 20.00 12.00
❑ 15 George Case 25.00 15.00
❑ 16 Cecil Travis 25.00 15.00
❑ 17 Buddy Myer 25.00 15.00
❑ 18 Charlie Gelbert 20.00 12.00
❑ 19 Ken Chase 20.00 12.00
❑ 20 Buddy Lewis 20.00 12.00
❑ 21 Rick Ferrell 80.00 45.00
❑ 22 Sammy West 20.00 12.00
❑ 23 Dutch Leonard 25.00 15.00
❑ 24 Frank Hayes 20.00 12.00
❑ 25 Bob Johnson 25.00 15.00
❑ 26 Wally Moses 25.00 15.00
❑ 27 Ted Williams 1200.00 800.00
❑ 28 Gene Desautels 20.00 12.00
❑ 29 Doc Cramer 25.00 15.00
❑ 30 Moe Berg 150.00 90.00
❑ 31 Jack Wilson 20.00 12.00
❑ 32 Jim Bagby 20.00 12.00
❑ 33 Fritz Ostermueller 20.00 12.00
❑ 34 John Peacock 20.00 12.00
❑ 35 Joe Heving 20.00 12.00
❑ 36 Jim Tabor 20.00 12.00
❑ 37 Emerson Dickman 20.00 12.00
❑ 38 Bobby Doerr 90.00 50.00
❑ 39 Tom Carey 20.00 12.00
❑ 40 Hank Greenberg 200.00 100.00
❑ 41 Charley Gehringer 150.00 90.00
❑ 42 Bud Thomas 20.00 12.00
❑ 43 Pete Fox 20.00 12.00
❑ 44 Dizzy Trout 25.00 15.00
❑ 45 Red Kress 20.00 12.00
❑ 46 Earl Averill 90.00 50.00
❑ 47 Oscar Vitt RC 20.00 12.00
❑ 48 Luke Sewell 25.00 15.00
❑ 49 Stormy Weatherly 20.00 12.00
❑ 50 Hal Trosky 25.00 15.00
❑ 51 Don Heffner 20.00 12.00
❑ 52 Myril Hoag 20.00 12.00
❑ 53 George McQuinn 25.00 15.00
❑ 54 Bill Trotter 20.00 12.00
❑ 55 Slick Coffman 20.00 12.00
❑ 56 Eddie Miller RC 25.00 15.00
❑ 57 Max West 20.00 12.00
❑ 58 Bill Posedel 20.00 12.00
❑ 59 Rabbit Warstler 20.00 12.00
❑ 60 John Cooney 20.00 12.00
❑ 61 Tony Cuccinello 25.00 15.00
❑ 62 Buddy Hassett 20.00 12.00
❑ 63 Pete Coscarart 20.00 12.00
❑ 64 Van Lingle Mungo 25.00 15.00
❑ 65 Fred Fitzsimmons 25.00 15.00
❑ 66 Babe Phelps 20.00 12.00
❑ 67 Whit Wyatt 25.00 15.00
❑ 68 Dolph Camilli 25.00 15.00
❑ 69 Cookie Lavagetto 25.00 15.00
❑ 70 Luke Hamlin (Hot Potato) 20.00 12.00
❑ 71 Mel Almada 20.00 12.00
❑ 72 Chuck Dressen RC 25.00 15.00
❑ 73 Bucky Walters 25.00 15.00
❑ 74 Paul(Duke) Derringer 25.00 15.00
❑ 75 Frank (Buck) McCormick 25.00 15.00
❑ 76 Lonny Frey 20.00 12.00
❑ 77 Willard Hershberger 25.00 15.00
❑ 78 Lew Riggs 20.00 12.00
❑ 79 Harry Craft 25.00 15.00
❑ 80 Billy Myers 20.00 12.00
❑ 81 Wally Berger 25.00 15.00
❑ 82 Hank Gowdy CO 25.00 15.00
❑ 83 Cliff Melton 20.00 12.00
❑ 84 Jo Jo Moore 20.00 12.00
❑ 85 Hal Schumacher 25.00 15.00
❑ 86 Harry Gumbert 20.00 12.00
❑ 87 Carl Hubbell 125.00 75.00
❑ 88 Mel Ott 175.00 100.00
❑ 89 Bill Jurges 20.00 12.00
❑ 90 Frank Demaree 20.00 12.00
❑ 91 Bob Seeds 20.00 12.00
❑ 92 Whitey Whitehead 20.00 12.00
❑ 93 Harry Danning 20.00 12.00
❑ 94 Gus Suhr 20.00 12.00
❑ 95 Hugh Mulcahy 20.00 12.00
❑ 96 Heinie Mueller 20.00 12.00
❑ 97 Morry Arnovich 20.00 12.00
❑ 98 Pinky May 20.00 12.00
❑ 99 Syl Johnson 20.00 12.00
❑ 100 Hersh Martin 20.00 12.00
❑ 101 Del Young 20.00 12.00
❑ 102 Chuck Klein 100.00 60.00
❑ 103 Elbie Fletcher 20.00 12.00
❑ 104 Paul Waner 90.00 50.00

❑ 105 Lloyd Waner 80.00 45.00
❑ 106 Pep Young 20.00 12.00
❑ 107 Arky Vaughan 80.00 45.00
❑ 108 Johnny Rizzo 20.00 12.00
❑ 109 Don Padgett 20.00 12.00
❑ 110 Tom Sunkel 20.00 12.00
❑ 111 Mickey Owen 25.00 15.00
❑ 112 Jimmy Brown 20.00 12.00
❑ 113 Mort Cooper 25.00 15.00
❑ 114 Lon Warneke 25.00 15.00
❑ 115 Mike Gonzalez CO 25.00 15.00
❑ 116 Al Schacht 25.00 15.00
❑ 117 Dolly Stark UMP 25.00 15.00
❑ 118 Waite Hoyt 90.00 50.00
❑ 119 Grover C. Alexander 175.00 100.00
❑ 120 Walter Johnson 200.00 100.00
❑ 121 Atley Donald RC 25.00 15.00
❑ 122 Sandy Sundra RC 25.00 15.00
❑ 123 Hildy Hildebrand 25.00 15.00
❑ 124 Earle Combs 100.00 60.00
❑ 125 Art Fletcher RC 25.00 15.00
❑ 126 Jake Solters 20.00 12.00
❑ 127 Muddy Ruel 20.00 12.00
❑ 128 Pete Appleton 20.00 12.00
❑ 129 Bucky Harris MG RC 80.00 45.00
❑ 130 Clyde Milan RC 25.00 15.00
❑ 131 Zeke Bonura 25.00 15.00
❑ 132 Connie Mack MG RC 150.00 75.00
❑ 133 Jimmie Foxx 200.00 100.00
❑ 134 Joe Cronin 100.00 60.00
❑ 135 Line Drive Nelson 20.00 12.00
❑ 136 Cotton Pippen 20.00 12.00
❑ 137 Bing Miller 20.00 12.00
❑ 138 Beau Bell 20.00 12.00
❑ 139 Elden Auker 20.00 12.00
❑ 140 Dick Coffman 20.00 12.00
❑ 141 Casey Stengel MG RC 175.00 100.00
❑ 142 George Kelly RC 90.00 50.00
❑ 143 Gene Moore 20.00 12.00
❑ 144 Joe Vosmik 20.00 12.00
❑ 145 Vito Tamulis 20.00 12.00
❑ 146 Tot Pressnell 20.00 12.00
❑ 147 Johnny Hudson 20.00 12.00
❑ 148 Hugh Casey 25.00 15.00
❑ 149 Pinky Shoffner 20.00 12.00
❑ 150 Whitey Moore 20.00 12.00
❑ 151 Edwin Joost 25.00 15.00
❑ 152 Jimmy Wilson 20.00 12.00
❑ 153 Bill McKechnie MG RC 80.00 45.00
❑ 154 Jumbo Brown 20.00 12.00
❑ 155 Ray Hayworth 20.00 12.00
❑ 156 Daffy Dean 50.00 25.00
❑ 157 Lou Chiozza 20.00 12.00
❑ 158 Travis Jackson 90.00 50.00
❑ 159 Pancho Snyder RC 20.00 12.00
❑ 160 Hans Lobert CO 20.00 12.00
❑ 161 Debs Garms 20.00 12.00
❑ 162 Joe Bowman 20.00 12.00
❑ 163 Spud Davis 20.00 12.00
❑ 164 Ray Berres 20.00 12.00
❑ 165 Bob Klinger 20.00 12.00
❑ 166 Bill Brubaker 20.00 12.00
❑ 167 Frankie Frisch MG 90.00 50.00
❑ 168 Honus Wagner CO 200.00 100.00
❑ 169 Gabby Street 20.00 12.00
❑ 170 Tris Speaker 175.00 100.00
❑ 171 Harry Heilmann 80.00 45.00
❑ 172 Chief Bender 80.00 45.00
❑ 173 Napoleon Lajoie 175.00 100.00
❑ 174 Johnny Evers 90.00 50.00
❑ 175 Christy Mathewson 250.00 150.00
❑ 176 Heinie Manush 90.00 50.00
❑ 177 Frank Baker 100.00 60.00
❑ 178 Max Carey 90.00 50.00
❑ 179 George Sisler 125.00 75.00
❑ 180 Mickey Cochrane 150.00 90.00
❑ 181 Spud Chandler RC 80.00 45.00
❑ 182 Knick Knickerbocker RC 70.00 35.00
❑ 183 Marvin Breuer RC 70.00 35.00
❑ 184 Mule Haas 70.00 35.00
❑ 185 Joe Kuhel 70.00 35.00
❑ 186 Taft Wright RC 70.00 35.00
❑ 187 Jimmy Dykes MG 80.00 45.00
❑ 188 Joe Krakauskas RC 70.00 35.00
❑ 189 Jim Bloodworth RC 70.00 35.00
❑ 190 Charley Berry 70.00 35.00
❑ 191 John Babich RC 70.00 35.00
❑ 192 Dick Siebert RC 70.00 35.00
❑ 193 Chubby Dean RC 70.00 35.00
❑ 194 Sam Chapman RC 70.00 35.00
❑ 195 Dee Miles RC 70.00 35.00
❑ 196 Red (Nonny) Nonnenkamp RC 70.00 35.00
❑ 197 Lou Finney RC 70.00 35.00
❑ 198 Denny Galehouse RC 70.00 35.00
❑ 199 Pinky Higgins 70.00 35.00
❑ 200 Soup Campbell RC 70.00 35.00
❑ 201 Barney McCosky RC 70.00 35.00
❑ 202 Al Milnar RC 70.00 35.00
❑ 203 Bad News Hale RC 70.00 35.00
❑ 204 Harry Eisenstat RC 70.00 35.00
❑ 205 Rollie Hemsley RC 70.00 35.00
❑ 206 Chet Laabs RC 70.00 35.00
❑ 207 Gus Mancuso 70.00 35.00
❑ 208 Lee Gamble RC 70.00 35.00
❑ 209 Hy Vandenberg RC 70.00 35.00
❑ 210 Bill Lohrman RC 70.00 35.00
❑ 211 Pop Joiner RC 70.00 35.00
❑ 212 Babe Young RC 70.00 35.00
❑ 213 John Rucker RC 70.00 35.00
❑ 214 Ken O'Dea RC 70.00 35.00
❑ 215 Johnnie McCarthy RC 70.00 35.00
❑ 216 Joe Marty RC 70.00 35.00
❑ 217 Walter Beck 70.00 35.00
❑ 218 Wally Millies RC 70.00 35.00
❑ 219 Russ Bauers RC 70.00 35.00
❑ 220 Mace Brown RC 70.00 35.00
❑ 221 Lee Handley RC 70.00 35.00
❑ 222 Max Butcher RC 70.00 35.00
❑ 223 Hughie Jennings 150.00 90.00
❑ 224 Pie Traynor 175.00 100.00
❑ 225 Joe Jackson 2500.001500.00
❑ 226 Harry Hooper 150.00 90.00
❑ 227 Jesse Haines 150.00 90.00
❑ 228 Charlie Grimm 80.00 45.00
❑ 229 Buck Herzog 70.00 35.00
❑ 230 Red Faber 175.00 100.00
❑ 231 Dolf Luque 100.00 60.00
❑ 232 Goose Goslin 150.00 90.00
❑ 233 George Earnshaw 80.00 45.00
❑ 234 Frank Chance 150.00 90.00
❑ 235 John McGraw 175.00 100.00
❑ 236 Jim Bottomley 150.00 90.00
❑ 237 Willie Keeler 175.00 100.00
❑ 238 Tony Lazzeri 175.00 100.00
❑ 239 George Uhle 70.00 35.00
❑ 240 Bill Atwood RC 100.00 60.00

1941 Play Ball

HARRY "GUNBOAT" GUMBERT

❑ COMPLETE SET (72) 10000.006000.00
❑ COMMON CARD (1-48) 40.00 20.00
❑ COMMON CARD (49-72) 60.00 30.00
❑ WRAPPER (1-CENT) 800.00 700.00
❑ 1 Eddie Miller 125.00 75.00
❑ 2 Max West 40.00 20.00
❑ 3 Bucky Walters 45.00 25.00
❑ 4 Paul Derringer 50.00 30.00
❑ 5 Frank (Buck) McCormick 45.00 25.00
❑ 6 Carl Hubbell 175.00 100.00
❑ 7 Harry Danning 40.00 20.00
❑ 8 Mel Ott 225.00 125.00
❑ 9 Pinky May 40.00 20.00
❑ 10 Arky Vaughan 100.00 60.00
❑ 11 Debs Garms 40.00 20.00
❑ 12 Jimmy Brown 40.00 20.00
❑ 13 Jimmie Foxx 300.00 175.00
❑ 14 Ted Williams 1500.00 900.00
❑ 15 Joe Cronin 125.00 75.00
❑ 16 Hal Trosky 45.00 25.00
❑ 17 Roy Weatherly 40.00 20.00
❑ 18 Hank Greenberg 300.00 175.00
❑ 19 Charley Gehringer 200.00 125.00
❑ 20 Red Ruffing 125.00 75.00
❑ 21 Charlie Keller 60.00 35.00
❑ 22 Bob Johnson 50.00 30.00
❑ 23 George McQuinn 40.00 20.00
❑ 24 Dutch Leonard 45.00 25.00
❑ 25 Gene Moore 40.00 20.00
❑ 26 Harry Gumpert 40.00 20.00
❑ 27 Babe Young 40.00 20.00
❑ 28 Joe Marty 40.00 20.00
❑ 29 Jack Wilson 40.00 20.00
❑ 30 Lou Finney 40.00 20.00
❑ 31 Joe Kuhel 40.00 20.00
❑ 32 Taft Wright 40.00 20.00
❑ 33 Al Milnar 40.00 20.00
❑ 34 Rollie Hemsley 40.00 20.00
❑ 35 Pinky Higgins 45.00 25.00
❑ 36 Barney McCosky 40.00 20.00
❑ 37 Bruce Campbell RC 40.00 20.00
❑ 38 Atley Donald 50.00 30.00
❑ 39 Tommy Henrich 60.00 35.00
❑ 40 John Babich 40.00 20.00
❑ 41 Frank (Blimp) Hayes 40.00 20.00
❑ 42 Wally Moses 45.00 25.00
❑ 43 Al Brancato RC 40.00 20.00
❑ 44 Sam Chapman 40.00 20.00
❑ 45 Eldon Auker 40.00 20.00
❑ 46 Sid Hudson RC 40.00 20.00
❑ 47 Buddy Lewis 40.00 20.00
❑ 48 Cecil Travis 45.00 25.00
❑ 49 Babe Dahlgren 65.00 35.00
❑ 50 Johnny Cooney 60.00 30.00
❑ 51 Dolph Camilli 65.00 35.00
❑ 52 Kirby Higbe RC 60.00 30.00
❑ 53 Luke Hamlin 60.00 30.00
❑ 54 Pee Wee Reese RC 600.00 350.00
❑ 55 Whit Wyatt 65.00 35.00
❑ 56 Johnny VanderMeer RC 100.00 60.00
❑ 57 Moe Arnovich 60.00 30.00
❑ 58 Frank Demaree 60.00 30.00
❑ 59 Bill Jurges 60.00 30.00
❑ 60 Chuck Klein 150.00 90.00
❑ 61 Vince DiMaggio RC 225.00 125.00
❑ 62 Elbie Fletcher 60.00 30.00
❑ 63 Dom DiMaggio RC 250.00 150.00
❑ 64 Bobby Doerr 175.00 100.00
❑ 65 Tommy Bridges 65.00 35.00
❑ 66 Harland Clift RC 60.00 30.00
❑ 67 Walt Judnich RC 60.00 30.00
❑ 68 John Knott 60.00 30.00
❑ 69 George Case 65.00 35.00
❑ 70 Bill Dickey 400.00 250.00
❑ 71 Joe DiMaggio 2500.001500.00
❑ 72 Lefty Gomez 475.00 275.00

1993 SP

❑ COMPLETE SET (290) 80.00 40.00
❑ COMMON CARD (1-270) .50 .20
❑ FOIL PROSPECTS (271-290) 1.00 .40
❑ 1 Roberto Alomar AS 1.25 .50
❑ 2 Wade Boggs AS 1.25 .50
❑ 3 Joe Carter AS .50 .20
❑ 4 Ken Griffey Jr. AS 3.00 1.25

❑ 5 Mark Langston AS .50 .20
❑ 6 John Olerud AS .75 .30
❑ 7 Kirby Puckett AS 2.00 .75
❑ 8 Cal Ripken AS 6.00 2.50
❑ 9 Ivan Rodriguez AS 1.25 .50
❑ 10 Barry Bonds AS 5.00 2.00
❑ 11 Darren Daulton AS .75 .30
❑ 12 Marquis Grissom AS .75 .30
❑ 13 David Justice AS .75 .30
❑ 14 John Kruk AS .75 .30
❑ 15 Barry Larkin AS 1.25 .50
❑ 16 Terry Mulholland AS .50 .20
❑ 17 Ryne Sandberg AS 3.00 1.25
❑ 18 Gary Sheffield AS .75 .30
❑ 19 Chad Curtis .50 .20
❑ 20 Chili Davis .75 .30
❑ 21 Gary DiSarcina .50 .20
❑ 22 Damion Easley .50 .20
❑ 23 Chuck Finley .75 .30
❑ 24 Luis Polonia .50 .20
❑ 25 Tim Salmon 1.25 .50
❑ 26 J.T.Snow RC 1.25 .50
❑ 27 Russ Springer .50 .20
❑ 28 Jeff Bagwell 1.25 .50
❑ 29 Craig Biggio 1.25 .50
❑ 30 Ken Caminiti .75 .30
❑ 31 Andujar Cedeno .50 .20
❑ 32 Doug Drabek .50 .20
❑ 33 Steve Finley .75 .30
❑ 34 Luis Gonzalez .75 .30
❑ 35 Pete Harnisch .50 .20
❑ 36 Darryl Kile .75 .30
❑ 37 Mike Bordick .50 .20
❑ 38 Dennis Eckersley .75 .30
❑ 39 Brent Gates .50 .20
❑ 40 Rickey Henderson 2.00 .75
❑ 41 Mark McGwire 5.00 2.00
❑ 42 Craig Paquette .50 .20
❑ 43 Ruben Sierra .75 .30
❑ 44 Terry Steinbach .50 .20
❑ 45 Todd Van Poppel .50 .20
❑ 46 Pat Borders .50 .20
❑ 47 Tony Fernandez .50 .20
❑ 48 Juan Guzman .50 .20
❑ 49 Pat Hentgen .50 .20
❑ 50 Paul Molitor .75 .30
❑ 51 Jack Morris .75 .30
❑ 52 Ed Sprague .50 .20
❑ 53 Duane Ward .50 .20
❑ 54 Devon White .75 .30
❑ 55 Steve Avery .50 .20
❑ 56 Jeff Blauser .50 .20
❑ 57 Ron Gant .75 .30
❑ 58 Tom Glavine 1.25 .50
❑ 59 Greg Maddux 3.00 1.25
❑ 60 Fred McGriff 1.25 .50
❑ 61 Terry Pendleton .75 .30
❑ 62 Deion Sanders 1.25 .50
❑ 63 John Smoltz 1.25 .50
❑ 64 Cal Eldred .50 .20
❑ 65 Darryl Hamilton .50 .20
❑ 66 John Jaha .50 .20
❑ 67 Pat Listach .50 .20
❑ 68 Jaime Navarro .50 .20
❑ 69 Kevin Reimer .50 .20
❑ 70 B.J. Surhoff .75 .30
❑ 71 Greg Vaughn .50 .20
❑ 72 Robin Yount 3.00 1.25
❑ 73 Rene Arocha RC .75 .30
❑ 74 Bernard Gilkey .50 .20
❑ 75 Gregg Jefferies .50 .20
❑ 76 Ray Lankford .75 .30
❑ 77 Tom Pagnozzi .50 .20
❑ 78 Lee Smith .75 .30
❑ 79 Ozzie Smith 3.00 1.25
❑ 80 Bob Tewksbury .50 .20
❑ 81 Mark Whiten .50 .20
❑ 82 Steve Buechele .50 .20
❑ 83 Mark Grace 1.25 .50
❑ 84 Jose Guzman .50 .20
❑ 85 Derrick May .50 .20
❑ 86 Mike Morgan .50 .20
❑ 87 Randy Myers .50 .20
❑ 88 Kevin Roberson RC .50 .20
❑ 89 Sammy Sosa 2.00 .75
❑ 90 Rick Wilkins .50 .20
❑ 91 Brett Butler .75 .30
❑ 92 Eric Davis .75 .30
❑ 93 Orel Hershiser .75 .30
❑ 94 Eric Karros .75 .30
❑ 95 Ramon Martinez .50 .20
❑ 96 Raul Mondesi .75 .30
❑ 97 Jose Offerman .50 .20
❑ 98 Mike Piazza 5.00 2.00
❑ 99 Darryl Strawberry .75 .30
❑ 100 Moises Alou .75 .30
❑ 101 Wil Cordero .50 .20
❑ 102 Delino DeShields .50 .20
❑ 103 Darrin Fletcher .50 .20
❑ 104 Ken Hill .50 .20
❑ 105 Mike Lansing RC .75 .30
❑ 106 Dennis Martinez .75 .30
❑ 107 Larry Walker .75 .30
❑ 108 John Wetteland .75 .30
❑ 109 Rod Beck .50 .20
❑ 110 John Burkett .50 .20
❑ 111 Will Clark 1.25 .50
❑ 112 Royce Clayton .50 .20
❑ 113 Darren Lewis .50 .20
❑ 114 Willie McGee .75 .30
❑ 115 Bill Swift .50 .20
❑ 116 Robby Thompson .50 .20
❑ 117 Matt Williams .75 .30
❑ 118 Sandy Alomar Jr. .50 .20
❑ 119 Carlos Baerga .50 .20
❑ 120 Albert Belle .75 .30
❑ 121 Reggie Jefferson .50 .20
❑ 122 Wayne Kirby .50 .20
❑ 123 Kenny Lofton .75 .30
❑ 124 Carlos Martinez .50 .20
❑ 125 Charles Nagy .50 .20
❑ 126 Paul Sorrento .50 .20
❑ 127 Rich Amaral .50 .20
❑ 128 Jay Buhner .75 .30
❑ 129 Norm Charlton .50 .20
❑ 130 Dave Fleming .50 .20
❑ 131 Erik Hanson .50 .20
❑ 132 Randy Johnson 2.00 .75
❑ 133 Edgar Martinez 1.25 .50
❑ 134 Tino Martinez 1.25 .50
❑ 135 Omar Vizquel 1.25 .50
❑ 136 Bret Barberie .50 .20
❑ 137 Chuck Carr .50 .20
❑ 138 Jeff Conine .75 .30
❑ 139 Orestes Destrade .50 .20
❑ 140 Chris Hammond .50 .20
❑ 141 Bryan Harvey .50 .20
❑ 142 Benito Santiago .75 .30
❑ 143 Walt Weiss .50 .20
❑ 144 Darrell Whitmore RC .50 .20
❑ 145 Tim Bogar RC .50 .20
❑ 146 Bobby Bonilla .75 .30
❑ 147 Jeromy Burnitz .75 .30
❑ 148 Vince Coleman .50 .20
❑ 149 Dwight Gooden .75 .30
❑ 150 Todd Hundley .50 .20
❑ 151 Howard Johnson .50 .20
❑ 152 Eddie Murray 2.00 .75
❑ 153 Bret Saberhagen .75 .30
❑ 154 Brady Anderson .75 .30
❑ 155 Mike Devereaux .50 .20
❑ 156 Jeffrey Hammonds .50 .20
❑ 157 Chris Hoiles .50 .20
❑ 158 Ben McDonald .50 .20
❑ 159 Mark McLemore .50 .20
❑ 160 Mike Mussina 1.25 .50
❑ 161 Gregg Olson .50 .20
❑ 162 David Segui .50 .20
❑ 163 Derek Bell .50 .20
❑ 164 Andy Benes .50 .20
❑ 165 Archi Cianfrocco .50 .20
❑ 166 Ricky Gutierrez .50 .20
❑ 167 Tony Gwynn 2.50 1.00
❑ 168 Gene Harris .50 .20
❑ 169 Trevor Hoffman 2.00 .75
❑ 170 Ray McDavid RC .50 .20
❑ 171 Phil Plantier .50 .20
❑ 172 Mariano Duncan .50 .20
❑ 173 Len Dykstra .75 .30
❑ 174 Tommy Greene .50 .20
❑ 175 Dave Hollins .50 .20
❑ 176 Pete Incaviglia .50 .20
❑ 177 Mickey Morandini .50 .20
❑ 178 Curt Schilling .75 .30
❑ 179 Kevin Stocker .50 .20
❑ 180 Mitch Williams .50 .20
❑ 181 Stan Belinda .50 .20
❑ 182 Jay Bell .75 .30
❑ 183 Steve Cooke .50 .20
❑ 184 Carlos Garcia .50 .20
❑ 185 Jeff King .50 .20
❑ 186 Orlando Merced .50 .20
❑ 187 Don Slaught .50 .20
❑ 188 Andy Van Slyke 1.25 .50
❑ 189 Kevin Young .75 .30
❑ 190 Kevin Brown .75 .30
❑ 191 Jose Canseco 1.25 .50
❑ 192 Julio Franco .75 .30
❑ 193 Benji Gil .50 .20
❑ 194 Juan Gonzalez .75 .30
❑ 195 Tom Henke .50 .20
❑ 196 Rafael Palmeiro 1.25 .50
❑ 197 Dean Palmer .75 .30
❑ 198 Nolan Ryan 8.00 3.00
❑ 199 Roger Clemens 4.00 1.50
❑ 200 Scott Cooper .50 .20
❑ 201 Andre Dawson .75 .30
❑ 202 Mike Greenwell .50 .20
❑ 203 Carlos Quintana .50 .20
❑ 204 Jeff Russell .50 .20
❑ 205 Aaron Sele .50 .20
❑ 206 Mo Vaughn .75 .30
❑ 207 Frank Viola .75 .30
❑ 208 Rob Dibble .75 .30
❑ 209 Roberto Kelly .50 .20
❑ 210 Kevin Mitchell .50 .20
❑ 211 Hal Morris .50 .20
❑ 212 Joe Oliver .50 .20
❑ 213 Jose Rijo .50 .20
❑ 214 Bip Roberts .50 .20
❑ 215 Chris Sabo .50 .20
❑ 216 Reggie Sanders .75 .30
❑ 217 Dante Bichette .75 .30
❑ 218 Jerald Clark .50 .20
❑ 219 Alex Cole .50 .20
❑ 220 Andres Galarraga .75 .30
❑ 221 Joe Girardi .50 .20
❑ 222 Charlie Hayes .50 .20
❑ 223 Roberto Mejia RC .50 .20
❑ 224 Armando Reynoso .50 .20
❑ 225 Eric Young .50 .20
❑ 226 Kevin Appier .75 .30
❑ 227 George Brett 5.00 2.00
❑ 228 David Cone .75 .30
❑ 229 Phil Hiatt .50 .20
❑ 230 Felix Jose .50 .20
❑ 231 Wally Joyner .75 .30
❑ 232 Mike Macfarlane .50 .20
❑ 233 Brian McRae .50 .20
❑ 234 Jeff Montgomery .50 .20
❑ 235 Rob Deer .50 .20
❑ 236 Cecil Fielder .75 .30
❑ 237 Travis Fryman .75 .30
❑ 238 Mike Henneman .50 .20
❑ 239 Tony Phillips .50 .20
❑ 240 Mickey Tettleton .50 .20
❑ 241 Alan Trammell .75 .30
❑ 242 David Wells .75 .30
❑ 243 Lou Whitaker .75 .30
❑ 244 Rick Aguilera .50 .20
❑ 245 Scott Erickson .50 .20
❑ 246 Brian Harper .50 .20
❑ 247 Kent Hrbek .75 .30
❑ 248 Chuck Knoblauch .75 .30
❑ 249 Shane Mack .50 .20
❑ 250 David McCarty .50 .20
❑ 251 Pedro Munoz .50 .20
❑ 252 Dave Winfield .75 .30
❑ 253 Alex Fernandez .50 .20
❑ 254 Ozzie Guillen .75 .30
❑ 255 Bo Jackson 2.00 .75
❑ 256 Lance Johnson .50 .20
❑ 257 Ron Karkovice .50 .20
❑ 258 Jack McDowell .50 .20
❑ 259 Tim Raines .75 .30
❑ 260 Frank Thomas 2.00 .75
❑ 261 Robin Ventura .75 .30
❑ 262 Jim Abbott 1.25 .50

Card		
❑ 263 Steve Farr	.50	.20
❑ 264 Jimmy Key	.75	.30
❑ 265 Don Mattingly	5.00	2.00
❑ 266 Paul O'Neill	1.25	.50
❑ 267 Mike Stanley	.50	.20
❑ 268 Danny Tartabull	.50	.20
❑ 269 Bob Wickman	.50	.20
❑ 270 Bernie Williams	1.25	.50
❑ 271 Jason Bere FOIL	1.00	.40
❑ 272 Roger Cedeno FOIL RC	1.50	.60
❑ 273 Johnny Damon FOIL RC	12.00	5.00
❑ 274 Russ Davis FOIL RC	1.50	.60
❑ 275 Carlos Delgado FOIL	4.00	1.50
❑ 276 Carl Everett FOIL	1.50	.60
❑ 277 Cliff Floyd FOIL	.75	.30
❑ 278 Alex Gonzalez FOIL	1.00	.40
❑ 279 Derek Jeter FOIL RC !	100.00	50.00
❑ 280 Chipper Jones FOIL	4.00	1.50
❑ 281 Javier Lopez FOIL	1.25	.50
❑ 282 Chad Mottola FOIL RC	1.00	.40
❑ 283 Marc Newfield FOIL	1.00	.40
❑ 284 Eduardo Perez FOIL	1.00	.40
❑ 285 Manny Ramirez FOIL	5.00	2.00
❑ 286 Todd Steverson FOIL RC	1.00	.40
❑ 287 Michael Tucker FOIL	1.00	.40
❑ 288 Allen Watson FOIL	1.00	.40
❑ 289 Rondell White FOIL	1.50	.60
❑ 290 Dmitri Young FOIL	1.50	.60

1994 SP

Card		
❑ COMPLETE SET (200)	150.00	75.00
❑ COMMON CARD (21-200)	.20	.07
❑ COMMON FOIL (1-20)	.50	.20
❑ 1 Mike Bell FOIL RC	.50	.20
❑ 2 D.J. Boston FOIL RC	.50	.20
❑ 3 Johnny Damon FOIL	2.00	.75
❑ 4 Brad Fullmer FOIL RC	1.00	.40
❑ 5 Joey Hamilton FOIL	.50	.20
❑ 6 Todd Hollandsworth FOIL	.50	.20
❑ 7 Brian L.Hunter FOIL	.50	.20
❑ 8 LaTroy Hawkins FOIL RC	1.00	.40
❑ 9 Brooks Kieschnick FOIL RC	.50	.20
❑ 10 Derrek Lee FOIL RC	10.00	4.00
❑ 11 Trot Nixon FOIL RC	4.00	1.50
❑ 12 Alex Ochoa FOIL	.50	.20
❑ 13 Chan Ho Park FOIL RC	2.00	.75
❑ 14 Kirk Presley FOIL RC	.50	.20
❑ 15 Alex Rodriguez FOIL RC	150.00	75.00
❑ 16 Jose Silva FOIL RC	.50	.20
❑ 17 Terrell Wade FOIL RC	.50	.20
❑ 18 Billy Wagner FOIL RC	4.00	1.50
❑ 19 Glenn Williams FOIL RC	.50	.20
❑ 20 Preston Wilson FOIL	1.00	.40
❑ 21 Brian Anderson RC	.40	.15
❑ 22 Chad Curtis	.20	.07
❑ 23 Chili Davis	.40	.15
❑ 24 Bo Jackson	1.00	.40
❑ 25 Mark Langston	.20	.07
❑ 26 Tim Salmon	.60	.25
❑ 27 Jeff Bagwell	.60	.25
❑ 28 Craig Biggio	.60	.25
❑ 29 Ken Caminiti	.40	.15
❑ 30 Doug Drabek	.20	.07
❑ 31 John Hudek RC	.20	.07
❑ 32 Greg Swindell	.20	.07
❑ 33 Brent Gates	.20	.07
❑ 34 Rickey Henderson	1.00	.40
❑ 35 Steve Karsay	.20	.07
❑ 36 Mark McGwire	2.50	1.00
❑ 37 Ruben Sierra	.40	.15
❑ 38 Terry Steinbach	.20	.07
❑ 39 Roberto Alomar	.60	.25
❑ 40 Joe Carter	.40	.15
❑ 41 Carlos Delgado	.60	.25
❑ 42 Alex Gonzalez	.20	.07
❑ 43 Juan Guzman	.20	.07
❑ 44 Paul Molitor	.40	.15
❑ 45 John Olerud	.40	.15
❑ 46 Devon White	.40	.15
❑ 47 Steve Avery	.20	.07
❑ 48 Jeff Blauser	.20	.07
❑ 49 Tom Glavine	.60	.25
❑ 50 David Justice	.40	.15
❑ 51 Roberto Kelly	.20	.07
❑ 52 Ryan Klesko	.40	.15
❑ 53 Javier Lopez	.40	.15
❑ 54 Greg Maddux	1.50	.60
❑ 55 Fred McGriff	.60	.25
❑ 56 Ricky Bones	.20	.07
❑ 57 Cal Eldred	.20	.07
❑ 58 Brian Harper	.20	.07
❑ 59 Pat Listach	.20	.07
❑ 60 B.J. Surhoff	.40	.15
❑ 61 Greg Vaughn	.20	.07
❑ 62 Bernard Gilkey	.20	.07
❑ 63 Gregg Jefferies	.20	.07
❑ 64 Ray Lankford	.40	.15
❑ 65 Ozzie Smith	1.50	.60
❑ 66 Bob Tewksbury	.20	.07
❑ 67 Mark Whiten	.20	.07
❑ 68 Todd Zeile	.20	.07
❑ 69 Mark Grace	.60	.25
❑ 70 Randy Myers	.20	.07
❑ 71 Ryne Sandberg	1.50	.60
❑ 72 Sammy Sosa	1.00	.40
❑ 73 Steve Trachsel	.20	.07
❑ 74 Rick Wilkins	.20	.07
❑ 75 Brett Butler	.40	.15
❑ 76 Delino DeShields	.20	.07
❑ 77 Orel Hershiser	.40	.15
❑ 78 Eric Karros	.40	.15
❑ 79 Raul Mondesi	.40	.15
❑ 80 Mike Piazza	2.00	.75
❑ 81 Tim Wallach	.20	.07
❑ 82 Moises Alou	.40	.15
❑ 83 Cliff Floyd	.40	.15
❑ 84 Marquis Grissom	.40	.15
❑ 85 Pedro Martinez	1.00	.40
❑ 86 Larry Walker	.40	.15
❑ 87 John Wetteland	.40	.15
❑ 88 Rondell White	.40	.15
❑ 89 Rod Beck	.20	.07
❑ 90 Barry Bonds	2.50	1.00
❑ 91 John Burkett	.20	.07
❑ 92 Royce Clayton	.20	.07
❑ 93 Billy Swift	.20	.07
❑ 94 Robby Thompson	.20	.07
❑ 95 Matt Williams	.40	.15
❑ 96 Carlos Baerga	.20	.07
❑ 97 Albert Belle	.40	.15
❑ 98 Kenny Lofton	.40	.15
❑ 99 Dennis Martinez	.40	.15
❑ 100 Eddie Murray	1.00	.40
❑ 101 Manny Ramirez	1.00	.40
❑ 102 Eric Anthony	.20	.07
❑ 103 Chris Bosio	.20	.07
❑ 104 Jay Buhner	.40	.15
❑ 105 Ken Griffey Jr.	1.50	.60
❑ 106 Randy Johnson	1.00	.40
❑ 107 Edgar Martinez	.60	.25
❑ 108 Chuck Carr	.20	.07
❑ 109 Jeff Conine	.40	.15
❑ 110 Carl Everett	.40	.15
❑ 111 Chris Hammond	.20	.07
❑ 112 Bryan Harvey	.20	.07
❑ 113 Charles Johnson	.40	.15
❑ 114 Gary Sheffield	.40	.15
❑ 115 Bobby Bonilla	.40	.15
❑ 116 Dwight Gooden	.40	.15
❑ 117 Todd Hundley	.20	.07
❑ 118 Bobby Jones	.20	.07
❑ 119 Jeff Kent	.60	.25
❑ 120 Bret Saberhagen	.40	.15
❑ 121 Jeffrey Hammonds	.20	.07
❑ 122 Chris Hoiles	.20	.07
❑ 123 Ben McDonald	.20	.07
❑ 124 Mike Mussina	.60	.25
❑ 125 Rafael Palmeiro	.60	.25
❑ 126 Cal Ripken	3.00	1.25
❑ 127 Lee Smith	.40	.15
❑ 128 Derek Bell	.20	.07
❑ 129 Andy Benes	.20	.07
❑ 130 Tony Gwynn	1.25	.50
❑ 131 Trevor Hoffman	.60	.25
❑ 132 Phil Plantier	.20	.07
❑ 133 Bip Roberts	.20	.07
❑ 134 Darren Daulton	.40	.15
❑ 135 Lenny Dykstra	.40	.15
❑ 136 Dave Hollins	.20	.07
❑ 137 Danny Jackson	.20	.07
❑ 138 John Kruk	.40	.15
❑ 139 Kevin Stocker	.20	.07
❑ 140 Jay Bell	.40	.15
❑ 141 Carlos Garcia	.20	.07
❑ 142 Jeff King	.20	.07
❑ 143 Orlando Merced	.20	.07
❑ 144 Andy Van Slyke	.60	.25
❑ 145 Rick White	.20	.07
❑ 146 Jose Canseco	.60	.25
❑ 147 Will Clark	.60	.25
❑ 148 Juan Gonzalez	.40	.15
❑ 149 Rick Helling	.20	.07
❑ 150 Dean Palmer	.40	.15
❑ 151 Ivan Rodriguez	.60	.25
❑ 152 Roger Clemens	2.00	.75
❑ 153 Scott Cooper	.20	.07
❑ 154 Andre Dawson	.40	.15
❑ 155 Mike Greenwell	.20	.07
❑ 156 Aaron Sele	.20	.07
❑ 157 Mo Vaughn	.40	.15
❑ 158 Bret Boone	.40	.15
❑ 159 Barry Larkin	.60	.25
❑ 160 Kevin Mitchell	.20	.07
❑ 161 Jose Rijo	.20	.07
❑ 162 Deion Sanders	.60	.25
❑ 163 Reggie Sanders	.40	.15
❑ 164 Dante Bichette	.40	.15
❑ 165 Ellis Burks	.40	.15
❑ 166 Andres Galarraga	.40	.15
❑ 167 Charlie Hayes	.20	.07
❑ 168 David Nied	.20	.07
❑ 169 Walt Weiss	.20	.07
❑ 170 Kevin Appier	.40	.15
❑ 171 David Cone	.40	.15
❑ 172 Jeff Granger	.20	.07
❑ 173 Felix Jose	.20	.07
❑ 174 Wally Joyner	.40	.15
❑ 175 Brian McRae	.20	.07
❑ 176 Cecil Fielder	.40	.15
❑ 177 Travis Fryman	.40	.15
❑ 178 Mike Henneman	.20	.07
❑ 179 Tony Phillips	.20	.07
❑ 180 Mickey Tettleton	.20	.07
❑ 181 Alan Trammell	.40	.15
❑ 182 Rick Aguilera	.20	.07
❑ 183 Rich Becker	.20	.07
❑ 184 Scott Erickson	.20	.07
❑ 185 Chuck Knoblauch	.40	.15
❑ 186 Kirby Puckett	1.00	.40
❑ 187 Dave Winfield	.40	.15
❑ 188 Wilson Alvarez	.20	.07
❑ 189 Jason Bere	.20	.07
❑ 190 Alex Fernandez	.20	.07
❑ 191 Julio Franco	.40	.15
❑ 192 Jack McDowell	.20	.07
❑ 193 Frank Thomas	1.00	.40
❑ 194 Robin Ventura	.40	.15
❑ 195 Jim Abbott	.60	.25
❑ 196 Wade Boggs	.60	.25
❑ 197 Jimmy Key	.40	.15
❑ 198 Don Mattingly	2.50	1.00
❑ 199 Paul O'Neill	.60	.25
❑ 200 Danny Tartabull	.20	.07
❑ P24 Ken Griffey Jr. Promo	2.00	.75

1995 SP

Card		
❑ COMPLETE SET (207)	40.00	15.00
❑ COMMON CARD (1-207)	.20	.07
❑ COMMON FOIL (5-24)	.50	.20
❑ GRIFFEY AU SENT TO DEALERS AS BONUS		

Card		
❑ 1 Cal Ripken Salute	3.00	1.25
❑ 2 Nolan Ryan Salute	4.00	1.50
❑ 3 George Brett Salute	2.50	1.00
❑ 4 Mike Schmidt Salute	1.50	.60
❑ 5 Dustin Hermanson FOIL	.50	.20
❑ 6 Antonio Osuna FOIL	.50	.20
❑ 7 Mark Grudzielanek FOIL RC	1.25	.50
❑ 8 Ray Durham FOIL	.75	.30
❑ 9 Ugueth Urbina FOIL	.50	.20
❑ 10 Ruben Rivera FOIL	.50	.20
❑ 11 Curtis Goodwin FOIL	.50	.20
❑ 12 Jimmy Hurst FOIL	.50	.20
❑ 13 Jose Malave FOIL	.50	.20
❑ 14 Hideo Nomo FOIL RC	4.00	1.50
❑ 15 Juan Acevedo RC FOIL	.50	.20
❑ 16 Tony Clark FOIL	.50	.20
❑ 17 Jim Pittsley FOIL	.50	.20
❑ 18 Freddy Adrian Garcia RC FOIL	.50	.20
❑ 19 Carlos Perez RC FOIL	.75	.30
❑ 20 Raul Casanova FOIL RC	.50	.20
❑ 21 Quilvio Veras FOIL	.50	.20
❑ 22 Edgardo Alfonzo FOIL	.50	.20
❑ 23 Marty Cordova FOIL	.50	.20
❑ 24 C.J. Nitkowski FOIL	.50	.20
❑ 25 Wade Boggs CL	.40	.15
❑ 26 Dave Winfield CL	.20	.07
❑ 27 Eddie Murray CL	.60	.25
❑ 28 David Justice	.40	.15
❑ 29 Marquis Grissom	.40	.15
❑ 30 Fred McGriff	.60	.25
❑ 31 Greg Maddux	1.50	.60
❑ 32 Tom Glavine	.60	.25
❑ 33 Steve Avery	.20	.07
❑ 34 Chipper Jones	1.00	.40
❑ 35 Sammy Sosa	1.00	.40
❑ 36 Jaime Navarro	.20	.07
❑ 37 Randy Myers	.20	.07
❑ 38 Mark Grace	.60	.25
❑ 39 Todd Zeile	.20	.07
❑ 40 Brian McRae	.20	.07
❑ 41 Reggie Sanders	.40	.15
❑ 42 Ron Gant	.40	.15
❑ 43 Deion Sanders	.60	.25
❑ 44 Bret Boone	.40	.15
❑ 45 Barry Larkin	.60	.25
❑ 46 Jose Rijo	.20	.07
❑ 47 Jason Bates	.20	.07
❑ 48 Andres Galarraga	.40	.15
❑ 49 Bill Swift	.20	.07
❑ 50 Larry Walker	.40	.15
❑ 51 Vinny Castilla	.40	.15
❑ 52 Dante Bichette	.40	.15
❑ 53 Jeff Conine	.40	.15
❑ 54 John Burkett	.20	.07
❑ 55 Gary Sheffield	.40	.15
❑ 56 Andre Dawson	.40	.15
❑ 57 Terry Pendleton	.40	.15
❑ 58 Charles Johnson	.40	.15
❑ 59 Brian L.Hunter	.20	.07
❑ 60 Jeff Bagwell	.60	.25
❑ 61 Craig Biggio	.60	.25
❑ 62 Phil Nevin	.40	.15
❑ 63 Doug Drabek	.20	.07
❑ 64 Derek Bell	.20	.07
❑ 65 Raul Mondesi	.40	.15
❑ 66 Eric Karros	.40	.15
❑ 67 Roger Cedeno	.20	.07
❑ 68 Delino DeShields	.20	.07
❑ 69 Ramon Martinez	.20	.07
❑ 70 Mike Piazza	1.50	.60
❑ 71 Billy Ashley	.20	.07
❑ 72 Jeff Fassero	.20	.07
❑ 73 Shane Andrews	.20	.07
❑ 74 Wil Cordero	.20	.07
❑ 75 Tony Tarasco	.20	.07
❑ 76 Rondell White	.40	.15
❑ 77 Pedro Martinez	.60	.25
❑ 78 Moises Alou	.40	.15
❑ 79 Rico Brogna	.20	.07
❑ 80 Bobby Bonilla	.40	.15
❑ 81 Jeff Kent	.40	.15
❑ 82 Brett Butler	.40	.15
❑ 83 Bobby Jones	.20	.07
❑ 84 Bill Pulsipher	.20	.07
❑ 85 Bret Saberhagen	.40	.15
❑ 86 Gregg Jefferies	.20	.07
❑ 87 Lenny Dykstra	.40	.15
❑ 88 Dave Hollins	.20	.07
❑ 89 Charlie Hayes	.20	.07
❑ 90 Darren Daulton	.40	.15
❑ 91 Curt Schilling	.40	.15
❑ 92 Heathcliff Slocumb	.20	.07
❑ 93 Carlos Garcia	.20	.07
❑ 94 Denny Neagle	.40	.15
❑ 95 Jay Bell	.40	.15
❑ 96 Orlando Merced	.20	.07
❑ 97 Dave Clark	.20	.07
❑ 98 Bernard Gilkey	.20	.07
❑ 99 Scott Cooper	.20	.07
❑ 100 Ozzie Smith	1.50	.60
❑ 101 Tom Henke	.20	.07
❑ 102 Ken Hill	.20	.07
❑ 103 Brian Jordan	.40	.15
❑ 104 Ray Lankford	.40	.15
❑ 105 Tony Gwynn	1.25	.50
❑ 106 Andy Benes	.20	.07
❑ 107 Ken Caminiti	.40	.15
❑ 108 Steve Finley	.40	.15
❑ 109 Joey Hamilton	.20	.07
❑ 110 Bip Roberts	.20	.07
❑ 111 Eddie Williams	.20	.07
❑ 112 Rod Beck	.20	.07
❑ 113 Matt Williams	.40	.15
❑ 114 Glenallen Hill	.20	.07
❑ 115 Barry Bonds	2.50	1.00
❑ 116 Robby Thompson	.20	.07
❑ 117 Mark Portugal	.20	.07
❑ 118 Brady Anderson	.40	.15
❑ 119 Mike Mussina	.60	.25
❑ 120 Rafael Palmeiro	.60	.25
❑ 121 Chris Hoiles	.20	.07
❑ 122 Harold Baines	.40	.15
❑ 123 Jeffrey Hammonds	.20	.07
❑ 124 Tim Naehring	.20	.07
❑ 125 Mo Vaughn	.40	.15
❑ 126 Mike Macfarlane	.20	.07
❑ 127 Roger Clemens	2.00	.75
❑ 128 John Valentin	.20	.07
❑ 129 Aaron Sele	.20	.07
❑ 130 Jose Canseco	.60	.25
❑ 131 J.T. Snow	.40	.15
❑ 132 Mark Langston	.20	.07
❑ 133 Chili Davis	.40	.15
❑ 134 Chuck Finley	.40	.15
❑ 135 Tim Salmon	.60	.25
❑ 136 Tony Phillips	.20	.07
❑ 137 Jason Bere	.20	.07
❑ 138 Robin Ventura	.40	.15
❑ 139 Tim Raines	.40	.15
❑ 140 Frank Thomas	1.00	.40
❑ 140A Frank Thomas ERR	1.00	.40
❑ 141 Alex Fernandez	.20	.07
❑ 142 Jim Abbott	.60	.25
❑ 143 Wilson Alvarez	.20	.07
❑ 144 Carlos Baerga	.20	.07
❑ 145 Albert Belle	.40	.15
❑ 146 Jim Thome	.60	.25
❑ 147 Dennis Martinez	.40	.15
❑ 148 Eddie Murray	1.00	.40
❑ 149 Dave Winfield	.40	.15
❑ 150 Kenny Lofton	.40	.15
❑ 151 Manny Ramirez	.60	.25
❑ 152 Chad Curtis	.20	.07
❑ 153 Lou Whitaker	.40	.15
❑ 154 Alan Trammell	.40	.15
❑ 155 Cecil Fielder	.40	.15
❑ 156 Kirk Gibson	.40	.15
❑ 157 Michael Tucker	.20	.07
❑ 158 Jon Nunnally	.20	.07
❑ 159 Wally Joyner	.40	.15
❑ 160 Kevin Appier	.40	.15
❑ 161 Jeff Montgomery	.20	.07
❑ 162 Greg Gagne	.20	.07
❑ 163 Ricky Bones	.20	.07
❑ 164 Cal Eldred	.20	.07
❑ 165 Greg Vaughn	.20	.07
❑ 166 Kevin Seitzer	.20	.07
❑ 167 Jose Valentin	.20	.07
❑ 168 Joe Oliver	.20	.07
❑ 169 Rick Aguilera	.20	.07
❑ 170 Kirby Puckett	1.00	.40
❑ 171 Scott Stahoviak	.20	.07
❑ 172 Kevin Tapani	.20	.07
❑ 173 Chuck Knoblauch	.40	.15
❑ 174 Rich Becker	.20	.07
❑ 175 Don Mattingly	2.50	1.00
❑ 176 Jack McDowell	.20	.07
❑ 177 Jimmy Key	.40	.15
❑ 178 Paul O'Neill	.60	.25
❑ 179 John Wetteland	.40	.15
❑ 180 Wade Boggs	.60	.25
❑ 181 Derek Jeter	2.50	1.00
❑ 182 Rickey Henderson	1.00	.40
❑ 183 Terry Steinbach	.20	.07
❑ 184 Ruben Sierra	.40	.15
❑ 185 Mark McGwire	2.50	1.00
❑ 186 Todd Stottlemyre	.20	.07
❑ 187 Dennis Eckersley	.40	.15
❑ 188 Alex Rodriguez	2.50	1.00
❑ 189 Randy Johnson	1.00	.40
❑ 190 Ken Griffey Jr.	1.50	.60
❑ 191 Tino Martinez	.60	.25
❑ 192 Jay Buhner	.40	.15
❑ 193 Edgar Martinez	.60	.25
❑ 194 Mickey Tettleton	.20	.07
❑ 195 Juan Gonzalez	.40	.15
❑ 196 Benji Gil	.20	.07
❑ 197 Dean Palmer	.40	.15
❑ 198 Ivan Rodriguez	.60	.25
❑ 199 Kenny Rogers	.40	.15
❑ 200 Will Clark	.60	.25
❑ 201 Roberto Alomar	.60	.25
❑ 202 David Cone	.40	.15
❑ 203 Paul Molitor	.40	.15
❑ 204 Shawn Green	.40	.15
❑ 205 Joe Carter	.40	.15
❑ 206 Alex Gonzalez	.20	.07
❑ 207 Pat Hentgen	.20	.07
❑ P100 Ken Griffey Jr. Promo	2.00	.75
❑ AU190 Ken Griffey Jr. AU	175.00	100.00

1996 SP

Card		
❑ COMPLETE SET (188)	40.00	15.00
❑ 1 Rey Ordonez FOIL	.40	.15
❑ 2 George Arias FOIL	.40	.15
❑ 3 Osvaldo Fernandez FOIL	.40	.15
❑ 4 Darin Erstad FOIL RC	5.00	2.00
❑ 5 Paul Wilson FOIL	.40	.15
❑ 6 Richard Hidalgo FOIL	.40	.15
❑ 7 Justin Thompson FOIL	.40	.15
❑ 8 Jimmy Haynes FOIL	.40	.15
❑ 9 Edgar Renteria FOIL	.40	.15

❑ 10 Ruben Rivera FOIL .40 .15
❑ 11 Chris Snopek FOIL .40 .15
❑ 12 Billy Wagner FOIL .40 .15
❑ 13 Mike Grace FOIL RC .40 .15
❑ 14 Todd Greene FOIL .40 .15
❑ 15 Karim Garcia FOIL .40 .15
❑ 16 John Wasdin FOIL .40 .15
❑ 17 Jason Kendall FOIL .40 .15
❑ 18 Bob Abreu FOIL 1.00 .40
❑ 19 Jermaine Dye FOIL .40 .15
❑ 20 Jason Schmidt FOIL .60 .25
❑ 21 Javy Lopez .40 .15
❑ 22 Ryan Klesko .40 .15
❑ 23 Tom Glavine .60 .25
❑ 24 John Smoltz .60 .25
❑ 25 Greg Maddux 1.50 .60
❑ 26 Chipper Jones 1.00 .40
❑ 27 Fred McGriff .60 .25
❑ 28 David Justice .40 .15
❑ 29 Roberto Alomar .60 .25
❑ 30 Cal Ripken 3.00 1.25
❑ 31 B.J. Surhoff .40 .15
❑ 32 Bobby Bonilla .40 .15
❑ 33 Mike Mussina .60 .25
❑ 34 Randy Myers .40 .15
❑ 35 Rafael Palmeiro .60 .25
❑ 36 Brady Anderson .40 .15
❑ 37 Tim Naehring .40 .15
❑ 38 Jose Canseco .60 .25
❑ 39 Roger Clemens 2.00 .75
❑ 40 Mo Vaughn .40 .15
❑ 41 John Valentin .40 .15
❑ 42 Kevin Mitchell .40 .15
❑ 43 Chili Davis .40 .15
❑ 44 Garret Anderson .40 .15
❑ 45 Tim Salmon .60 .25
❑ 46 Chuck Finley .40 .15
❑ 47 Troy Percival .40 .15
❑ 48 Jim Abbott .60 .25
❑ 49 J.T. Snow .40 .15
❑ 50 Jim Edmonds .40 .15
❑ 51 Sammy Sosa 1.00 .40
❑ 52 Brian McRae .40 .15
❑ 53 Ryne Sandberg 1.50 .60
❑ 54 Jaime Navarro .40 .15
❑ 55 Mark Grace .60 .25
❑ 56 Harold Baines .40 .15
❑ 57 Robin Ventura .40 .15
❑ 58 Tony Phillips .40 .15
❑ 59 Alex Fernandez .40 .15
❑ 60 Frank Thomas 1.00 .40
❑ 61 Ray Durham .40 .15
❑ 62 Bret Boone .40 .15
❑ 63 Reggie Sanders .40 .15
❑ 64 Pete Schourek .40 .15
❑ 65 Barry Larkin .60 .25
❑ 66 John Smiley .40 .15
❑ 67 Carlos Baerga .40 .15
❑ 68 Jim Thome .60 .25
❑ 69 Eddie Murray 1.00 .40
❑ 70 Albert Belle .40 .15
❑ 71 Dennis Martinez .40 .15
❑ 72 Jack McDowell .40 .15
❑ 73 Kenny Lofton .40 .15
❑ 74 Manny Ramirez .60 .25
❑ 75 Dante Bichette .40 .15
❑ 76 Vinny Castilla .40 .15
❑ 77 Andres Galarraga .40 .15
❑ 78 Walt Weiss .40 .15
❑ 79 Ellis Burks .40 .15
❑ 80 Larry Walker .40 .15
❑ 81 Cecil Fielder .40 .15
❑ 82 Melvin Nieves .40 .15
❑ 83 Travis Fryman .40 .15
❑ 84 Chad Curtis .40 .15
❑ 85 Alan Trammell .40 .15
❑ 86 Gary Sheffield .40 .15
❑ 87 Charles Johnson .40 .15
❑ 88 Andre Dawson .40 .15
❑ 89 Jeff Conine .40 .15
❑ 90 Greg Colbrunn .40 .15
❑ 91 Derek Bell .40 .15
❑ 92 Brian L.Hunter .40 .15
❑ 93 Doug Drabek .40 .15
❑ 94 Craig Biggio .60 .25
❑ 95 Jeff Bagwell .60 .25
❑ 96 Kevin Appier .40 .15
❑ 97 Jeff Montgomery .40 .15
❑ 98 Michael Tucker .40 .15
❑ 99 Bip Roberts .40 .15
❑ 100 Johnny Damon .60 .25
❑ 101 Eric Karros .40 .15
❑ 102 Raul Mondesi .40 .15
❑ 103 Ramon Martinez .40 .15
❑ 104 Ismael Valdes .40 .15
❑ 105 Mike Piazza 1.50 .60
❑ 106 Hideo Nomo 1.00 .40
❑ 107 Chan Ho Park .40 .15
❑ 108 Ben McDonald .40 .15
❑ 109 Kevin Seitzer .40 .15
❑ 110 Greg Vaughn .40 .15
❑ 111 Jose Valentin .40 .15
❑ 112 Rick Aguilera .40 .15
❑ 113 Marty Cordova .40 .15
❑ 114 Brad Radke .40 .15
❑ 115 Kirby Puckett 1.00 .40
❑ 116 Chuck Knoblauch .40 .15
❑ 117 Paul Molitor .40 .15
❑ 118 Pedro Martinez .60 .25
❑ 119 Mike Lansing .40 .15
❑ 120 Rondell White .40 .15
❑ 121 Moises Alou .40 .15
❑ 122 Mark Grudzielanek .40 .15
❑ 123 Jeff Fassero .40 .15
❑ 124 Rico Brogna .40 .15
❑ 125 Jason Isringhausen .40 .15
❑ 126 Jeff Kent .40 .15
❑ 127 Bernard Gilkey .40 .15
❑ 128 Todd Hundley .40 .15
❑ 129 David Cone .40 .15
❑ 130 Andy Pettitte .60 .25
❑ 131 Wade Boggs .60 .25
❑ 132 Paul O'Neill .60 .25
❑ 133 Ruben Sierra .40 .15
❑ 134 John Wetteland .40 .15
❑ 135 Derek Jeter 2.50 1.00
❑ 136 Geronimo Berroa .40 .15
❑ 137 Terry Steinbach .40 .15
❑ 138 Ariel Prieto .40 .15
❑ 139 Scott Brosius .40 .15
❑ 140 Mark McGwire 2.50 1.00
❑ 141 Lenny Dykstra .40 .15
❑ 142 Todd Zeile .40 .15
❑ 143 Benito Santiago .40 .15
❑ 144 Mickey Morandini .40 .15
❑ 145 Gregg Jefferies .40 .15
❑ 146 Denny Neagle .40 .15
❑ 147 Orlando Merced .40 .15
❑ 148 Charlie Hayes .40 .15
❑ 149 Carlos Garcia .40 .15
❑ 150 Jay Bell .40 .15
❑ 151 Ray Lankford .40 .15
❑ 152 Alan Benes/Andy Benes .40 .15
❑ 153 Dennis Eckersley .40 .15
❑ 154 Gary Gaetti .40 .15
❑ 155 Ozzie Smith 1.50 .60
❑ 156 Ron Gant .40 .15
❑ 157 Brian Jordan .40 .15
❑ 158 Ken Caminiti .40 .15
❑ 159 Rickey Henderson 1.00 .40
❑ 160 Tony Gwynn 1.25 .50
❑ 161 Wally Joyner .40 .15
❑ 162 Andy Ashby .40 .15
❑ 163 Steve Finley .40 .15
❑ 164 Glenallen Hill .40 .15
❑ 165 Matt Williams .40 .15
❑ 166 Barry Bonds 2.50 1.00
❑ 167 William Vanlandingham .40 .15
❑ 168 Rod Beck .40 .15
❑ 169 Randy Johnson 1.00 .40
❑ 170 Ken Griffey Jr. 1.50 .60
❑ 171 Alex Rodriguez 2.00 .75
❑ 172 Edgar Martinez .60 .25
❑ 173 Jay Buhner .40 .15
❑ 174 Russ Davis .40 .15
❑ 175 Juan Gonzalez .40 .15
❑ 176 Mickey Tettleton .40 .15
❑ 177 Will Clark .60 .25
❑ 178 Ken Hill .40 .15
❑ 179 Dean Palmer .40 .15
❑ 180 Ivan Rodriguez .60 .25
❑ 181 Carlos Delgado .40 .15
❑ 182 Alex Gonzalez .40 .15
❑ 183 Shawn Green .40 .15
❑ 184 Juan Guzman .40 .15
❑ 185 Joe Carter .40 .15
❑ 186 Hideo Nomo CL .60 .25
❑ 187 Cal Ripken CL 1.50 .60
❑ 188 Ken Griffey Jr. CL 1.00 .40

1997 SP

❑ COMPLETE SET (184) 40.00 15.00
❑ 1 Andruw Jones FOIL 1.00 .40
❑ 2 Kevin Orie FOIL .50 .20
❑ 3 Nomar Garciaparra FOIL 2.50 1.00
❑ 4 Jose Guillen FOIL .75 .30
❑ 5 Todd Walker FOIL .50 .20
❑ 6 Derrick Gibson FOIL .50 .20
❑ 7 Aaron Boone FOIL .75 .30
❑ 8 Bartolo Colon FOIL .75 .30
❑ 9 Derrek Lee FOIL 1.00 .40
❑ 10 Vladimir Guerrero FOIL 1.50 .60
❑ 11 Wilton Guerrero FOIL .50 .20
❑ 12 Luis Castillo FOIL .50 .20
❑ 13 Jason Dickson FOIL .50 .20
❑ 14 Bubba Trammell FOIL RC .75 .30
❑ 15 Jose Cruz Jr. FOIL RC .75 .30
❑ 16 Eddie Murray 1.00 .40
❑ 17 Darin Erstad .40 .15
❑ 18 Garret Anderson .40 .15
❑ 19 Jim Edmonds .40 .15
❑ 20 Tim Salmon .60 .25
❑ 21 Chuck Finley .40 .15
❑ 22 John Smoltz .60 .25
❑ 23 Greg Maddux 1.50 .60
❑ 24 Kenny Lofton .40 .15
❑ 25 Chipper Jones 1.00 .40
❑ 26 Ryan Klesko .40 .15
❑ 27 Javy Lopez .40 .15
❑ 28 Fred McGriff .60 .25
❑ 29 Roberto Alomar .60 .25
❑ 30 Rafael Palmeiro .60 .25
❑ 31 Mike Mussina .60 .25
❑ 32 Brady Anderson .40 .15
❑ 33 Rocky Coppinger .40 .15
❑ 34 Cal Ripken 3.00 1.25
❑ 35 Mo Vaughn .40 .15
❑ 36 Steve Avery .40 .15
❑ 37 Tom Gordon .40 .15
❑ 38 Tim Naehring .40 .15
❑ 39 Troy O'Leary .40 .15
❑ 40 Sammy Sosa 1.00 .40
❑ 41 Brian McRae .40 .15
❑ 42 Mel Rojas .40 .15
❑ 43 Ryne Sandberg 1.50 .60
❑ 44 Mark Grace .60 .25
❑ 45 Albert Belle .40 .15
❑ 46 Robin Ventura .40 .15
❑ 47 Roberto Hernandez .40 .15
❑ 48 Ray Durham .40 .15
❑ 49 Harold Baines .40 .15
❑ 50 Frank Thomas 1.00 .40
❑ 51 Bret Boone .40 .15
❑ 52 Reggie Sanders .40 .15
❑ 53 Deion Sanders .60 .25
❑ 54 Hal Morris .40 .15
❑ 55 Barry Larkin .60 .25
❑ 56 Jim Thome .60 .25
❑ 57 Marquis Grissom .40 .15
❑ 58 David Justice .40 .15

❑ 59 Charles Nagy	.40	.15
❑ 60 Manny Ramirez	.60	.25
❑ 61 Matt Williams	.40	.15
❑ 62 Jack McDowell	.40	.15
❑ 63 Vinny Castilla	.40	.15
❑ 64 Dante Bichette	.40	.15
❑ 65 Andres Galarraga	.40	.15
❑ 66 Ellis Burks	.40	.15
❑ 67 Larry Walker	.40	.15
❑ 68 Eric Young	.40	.15
❑ 69 Brian L. Hunter	.40	.15
❑ 70 Travis Fryman	.40	.15
❑ 71 Tony Clark	.40	.15
❑ 72 Bobby Higginson	.40	.15
❑ 73 Melvin Nieves	.40	.15
❑ 74 Jeff Conine	.40	.15
❑ 75 Gary Sheffield	.40	.15
❑ 76 Moises Alou	.40	.15
❑ 77 Edgar Renteria	.40	.15
❑ 78 Alex Fernandez	.40	.15
❑ 79 Charles Johnson	.40	.15
❑ 80 Bobby Bonilla	.40	.15
❑ 81 Darryl Kile	.40	.15
❑ 82 Derek Bell	.40	.15
❑ 83 Shane Reynolds	.40	.15
❑ 84 Craig Biggio	.60	.25
❑ 85 Jeff Bagwell	.60	.25
❑ 86 Billy Wagner	.40	.15
❑ 87 Chili Davis	.40	.15
❑ 88 Kevin Appier	.40	.15
❑ 89 Jay Bell	.40	.15
❑ 90 Johnny Damon	.60	.25
❑ 91 Jeff King	.40	.15
❑ 92 Hideo Nomo	1.00	.40
❑ 93 Todd Hollandsworth	.40	.15
❑ 94 Eric Karros	.40	.15
❑ 95 Mike Piazza	1.50	.60
❑ 96 Ramon Martinez	.40	.15
❑ 97 Todd Worrell	.40	.15
❑ 98 Raul Mondesi	.40	.15
❑ 99 Dave Nilsson	.40	.15
❑ 100 John Jaha	.40	.15
❑ 101 Jose Valentin	.40	.15
❑ 102 Jeff Cirillo	.40	.15
❑ 103 Jeff D'Amico	.40	.15
❑ 104 Ben McDonald	.40	.15
❑ 105 Paul Molitor	.40	.15
❑ 106 Rich Becker	.40	.15
❑ 107 Frank Rodriguez	.40	.15
❑ 108 Marty Cordova	.40	.15
❑ 109 Terry Steinbach	.40	.15
❑ 110 Chuck Knoblauch	.40	.15
❑ 111 Mark Grudzielanek	.40	.15
❑ 112 Mike Lansing	.40	.15
❑ 113 Pedro Martinez	.60	.25
❑ 114 Henry Rodriguez	.40	.15
❑ 115 Rondell White	.40	.15
❑ 116 Rey Ordonez	.40	.15
❑ 117 Carlos Baerga	.40	.15
❑ 118 Lance Johnson	.40	.15
❑ 119 Bernard Gilkey	.40	.15
❑ 120 Todd Hundley	.40	.15
❑ 121 John Franco	.40	.15
❑ 122 Bernie Williams	.60	.25
❑ 123 David Cone	.40	.15
❑ 124 Cecil Fielder	.40	.15
❑ 125 Derek Jeter	2.50	1.00
❑ 126 Tino Martinez	.60	.25
❑ 127 Mariano Rivera	1.00	.40
❑ 128 Andy Pettitte	.60	.25
❑ 129 Wade Boggs	.60	.25
❑ 130 Mark McGwire	2.50	1.00
❑ 131 Jose Canseco	.60	.25
❑ 132 Geronimo Berroa	.40	.15
❑ 133 Jason Giambi	.40	.15
❑ 134 Ernie Young	.40	.15
❑ 135 Scott Rolen	.60	.25
❑ 136 Ricky Bottalico	.40	.15
❑ 137 Curt Schilling	.40	.15
❑ 138 Gregg Jefferies	.40	.15
❑ 139 Mickey Morandini	.40	.15
❑ 140 Jason Kendall	.40	.15
❑ 141 Kevin Elster	.40	.15
❑ 142 Al Martin	.40	.15
❑ 143 Joe Randa	.40	.15
❑ 144 Jason Schmidt	.40	.15
❑ 145 Ray Lankford	.40	.15
❑ 146 Brian Jordan	.40	.15
❑ 147 Andy Benes	.40	.15
❑ 148 Alan Benes	.40	.15
❑ 149 Gary Gaetti	.40	.15
❑ 150 Ron Gant	.40	.15
❑ 151 Dennis Eckersley	.40	.15
❑ 152 Rickey Henderson	1.00	.40
❑ 153 Joey Hamilton	.40	.15
❑ 154 Ken Caminiti	.40	.15
❑ 155 Tony Gwynn	1.25	.50
❑ 156 Steve Finley	.40	.15
❑ 157 Trevor Hoffman	.40	.15
❑ 158 Greg Vaughn	.40	.15
❑ 159 J.T. Snow	.40	.15
❑ 160 Barry Bonds	2.50	1.00
❑ 161 Glenallen Hill	.40	.15
❑ 162 Bill Van Landingham	.40	.15
❑ 163 Jeff Kent	.40	.15
❑ 164 Jay Buhner	.40	.15
❑ 165 Ken Griffey Jr.	1.50	.60
❑ 166 Alex Rodriguez	1.50	.60
❑ 167 Randy Johnson	1.00	.40
❑ 168 Edgar Martinez	.60	.25
❑ 169 Dan Wilson	.40	.15
❑ 170 Ivan Rodriguez	.60	.25
❑ 171 Roger Pavlik	.40	.15
❑ 172 Will Clark	.60	.25
❑ 173 Dean Palmer	.40	.15
❑ 174 Rusty Greer	.40	.15
❑ 175 Juan Gonzalez	.40	.15
❑ 176 John Wetteland	.40	.15
❑ 177 Joe Carter	.40	.15
❑ 178 Ed Sprague	.40	.15
❑ 179 Carlos Delgado	.40	.15
❑ 180 Roger Clemens	2.00	.75
❑ 181 Juan Guzman	.40	.15
❑ 182 Pat Hentgen	.40	.15
❑ 183 Ken Griffey Jr. CL	1.00	.40
❑ 184 Hideki Irabu RC	.40	.15

1998 SP Authentic

❑ COMPLETE SET (198)	40.00	15.00
❑ 1 Travis Lee FOIL	.40	.15
❑ 2 Mike Caruso FOIL	.40	.15
❑ 3 Kerry Wood FOIL	.50	.20
❑ 4 Mark Kotsay FOIL	.40	.15
❑ 5 Magglio Ordonez FOIL RC	12.00	5.00
❑ 6 Scott Elarton FOIL	.40	.15
❑ 7 Carl Pavano FOIL	.40	.15
❑ 8 A.J. Hinch FOIL	.40	.15
❑ 9 Rolando Arrojo FOIL RC	.40	.15
❑ 10 Ben Grieve FOIL	.40	.15
❑ 11 Gabe Alvarez FOIL	.40	.15
❑ 12 Mike Kinkade FOIL RC	.40	.15
❑ 13 Bruce Chen FOIL	.40	.15
❑ 14 Juan Encarnacion FOIL	.40	.15
❑ 15 Todd Helton FOIL	.60	.25
❑ 16 Aaron Boone FOIL	.40	.15
❑ 17 Sean Casey FOIL	.40	.15
❑ 18 Ramon Hernandez FOIL	.40	.15
❑ 19 Daryle Ward FOIL	.40	.15
❑ 20 Paul Konerko FOIL	.40	.15
❑ 21 David Ortiz FOIL	1.25	.50
❑ 22 Derrek Lee FOIL	.60	.25
❑ 23 Brad Fullmer FOIL	.40	.15
❑ 24 Javier Vazquez FOIL	.40	.15
❑ 25 Miguel Tejada FOIL	1.00	.40
❑ 26 Dave Dellucci FOIL RC	.60	.25
❑ 27 Alex Gonzalez FOIL	.40	.15
❑ 28 Matt Clement FOIL	.40	.15
❑ 29 Masato Yoshii FOIL RC	.40	.15
❑ 30 Russell Branyan FOIL	.40	.15
❑ 31 Chuck Finley	.40	.15
❑ 32 Jim Edmonds	.40	.15
❑ 33 Darin Erstad	.40	.15
❑ 34 Jason Dickson	.40	.15
❑ 35 Tim Salmon	.60	.25
❑ 36 Cecil Fielder	.40	.15
❑ 37 Todd Greene	.40	.15
❑ 38 Andy Benes	.40	.15
❑ 39 Jay Bell	.40	.15
❑ 40 Matt Williams	.40	.15
❑ 41 Brian Anderson	.40	.15
❑ 42 Karim Garcia	.40	.15
❑ 43 Javy Lopez	.40	.15
❑ 44 Tom Glavine	.60	.25
❑ 45 Greg Maddux	1.50	.60
❑ 46 Andruw Jones	.60	.25
❑ 47 Chipper Jones	1.00	.40
❑ 48 Ryan Klesko	.40	.15
❑ 49 John Smoltz	.60	.25
❑ 50 Andres Galarraga	.40	.15
❑ 51 Rafael Palmeiro	.60	.25
❑ 52 Mike Mussina	.60	.25
❑ 53 Roberto Alomar	.60	.25
❑ 54 Joe Carter	.40	.15
❑ 55 Cal Ripken	3.00	1.25
❑ 56 Brady Anderson	.40	.15
❑ 57 Mo Vaughn	.40	.15
❑ 58 John Valentin	.40	.15
❑ 59 Dennis Eckersley	.40	.15
❑ 60 Nomar Garciaparra	1.50	.60
❑ 61 Pedro Martinez	.60	.25
❑ 62 Jeff Blauser	.40	.15
❑ 63 Kevin Orie	.40	.15
❑ 64 Henry Rodriguez	.40	.15
❑ 65 Mark Grace	.60	.25
❑ 66 Albert Belle	.40	.15
❑ 67 Mike Cameron	.40	.15
❑ 68 Robin Ventura	.40	.15
❑ 69 Frank Thomas	1.00	.40
❑ 70 Barry Larkin	.60	.25
❑ 71 Brett Tomko	.40	.15
❑ 72 Willie Greene	.40	.15
❑ 73 Reggie Sanders	.40	.15
❑ 74 Sandy Alomar Jr.	.40	.15
❑ 75 Kenny Lofton	.40	.15
❑ 76 Jaret Wright	.40	.15
❑ 77 David Justice	.40	.15
❑ 78 Omar Vizquel	.60	.25
❑ 79 Manny Ramirez	.60	.25
❑ 80 Jim Thome	.60	.25
❑ 81 Travis Fryman	.40	.15
❑ 82 Neifi Perez	.40	.15
❑ 83 Mike Lansing	.40	.15
❑ 84 Vinny Castilla	.40	.15
❑ 85 Larry Walker	.40	.15
❑ 86 Dante Bichette	.40	.15
❑ 87 Darryl Kile	.40	.15
❑ 88 Justin Thompson	.40	.15
❑ 89 Damion Easley	.40	.15
❑ 90 Tony Clark	.40	.15
❑ 91 Bobby Higginson	.40	.15
❑ 92 Brian Hunter	.40	.15
❑ 93 Edgar Renteria	.40	.15
❑ 94 Craig Counsell	.40	.15
❑ 95 Mike Piazza	1.50	.60
❑ 96 Livan Hernandez	.40	.15
❑ 97 Todd Zeile	.40	.15
❑ 98 Richard Hidalgo	.40	.15
❑ 99 Moises Alou	.40	.15
❑ 100 Jeff Bagwell	.60	.25
❑ 101 Mike Hampton	.40	.15
❑ 102 Craig Biggio	.60	.25
❑ 103 Dean Palmer	.40	.15
❑ 104 Tim Belcher	.40	.15
❑ 105 Jeff King	.40	.15
❑ 106 Jeff Conine	.40	.15
❑ 107 Johnny Damon	.60	.25
❑ 108 Hideo Nomo	1.00	.40
❑ 109 Raul Mondesi	.40	.15
❑ 110 Gary Sheffield	.40	.15
❑ 111 Ramon Martinez	.40	.15

Card		
112 Chan Ho Park	.40	.15
113 Eric Young	.40	.15
114 Charles Johnson	.40	.15
115 Eric Karros	.40	.15
116 Bobby Bonilla	.40	.15
117 Jeromy Burnitz	.40	.15
118 Cal Eldred	.40	.15
119 Jeff D'Amico	.40	.15
120 Marquis Grissom	.40	.15
121 Dave Nilsson	.40	.15
122 Brad Radke	.40	.15
123 Marty Cordova	.40	.15
124 Ron Coomer	.40	.15
125 Paul Molitor	.40	.15
126 Todd Walker	.40	.15
127 Rondell White	.40	.15
128 Mark Grudzielanek	.40	.15
129 Carlos Perez	.40	.15
130 Vladimir Guerrero	1.00	.40
131 Dustin Hermanson	.40	.15
132 Butch Huskey	.40	.15
133 John Franco	.40	.15
134 Rey Ordonez	.40	.15
135 Todd Hundley	.40	.15
136 Edgardo Alfonzo	.40	.15
137 Bobby Jones	.40	.15
138 John Olerud	.40	.15
139 Chili Davis	.40	.15
140 Tino Martinez	.60	.25
141 Andy Pettitte	.60	.25
142 Chuck Knoblauch	.40	.15
143 Bernie Williams	.60	.25
144 David Cone	.40	.15
145 Derek Jeter	2.50	1.00
146 Paul O'Neill	.60	.25
147 Rickey Henderson	1.00	.40
148 Jason Giambi	.40	.15
149 Kenny Rogers	.40	.15
150 Scott Rolen	.60	.25
151 Curt Schilling	.40	.15
152 Ricky Bottalico	.40	.15
153 Mike Lieberthal	.40	.15
154 Francisco Cordova	.40	.15
155 Jose Guillen	.40	.15
156 Jason Schmidt	.40	.15
157 Jason Kendall	.40	.15
158 Kevin Young	.40	.15
159 Delino DeShields	.40	.15
160 Mark McGwire	2.50	1.00
161 Ray Lankford	.40	.15
162 Brian Jordan	.40	.15
163 Ron Gant	.40	.15
164 Todd Stottlemyre	.40	.15
165 Ken Caminiti	.40	.15
166 Kevin Brown	.60	.25
167 Trevor Hoffman	.40	.15
168 Steve Finley	.40	.15
169 Wally Joyner	.40	.15
170 Tony Gwynn	1.25	.50
171 Shawn Estes	.40	.15
172 J.T. Snow	.40	.15
173 Jeff Kent	.40	.15
174 Robb Nen	.40	.15
175 Barry Bonds	2.50	1.00
176 Randy Johnson	1.00	.40
177 Edgar Martinez	.60	.25
178 Jay Buhner	.40	.15
179 Alex Rodriguez	1.50	.60
180 Ken Griffey Jr.	1.50	.60
181 Ken Cloude	.40	.15
182 Wade Boggs	.60	.25
183 Tony Saunders	.40	.15
184 Wilson Alvarez	.40	.15
185 Fred McGriff	.60	.25
186 Roberto Hernandez	.40	.15
187 Kevin Stocker	.40	.15
188 Fernando Tatis	.40	.15
189 Will Clark	.60	.25
190 Juan Gonzalez	.40	.15
191 Rusty Greer	.40	.15
192 Ivan Rodriguez	.60	.25
193 Jose Canseco	.60	.25
194 Carlos Delgado	.40	.15
195 Roger Clemens	2.00	.75
196 Pat Hentgen	.40	.15
197 Randy Myers	.40	.15
198 Ken Griffey Jr. CL	1.00	.40
S123 Ken Griffey Jr. Sample	2.00	.75

1999 SP Authentic

Card		
COMP.SET w/o SP's (90)	25.00	10.00
COMMON CARD (1-90)	.40	.15
COMMON FW (91-120)	10.00	4.00
COMMON STR (121-135)	3.00	1.25
1 Mo Vaughn	.40	.15
2 Jim Edmonds	.40	.15
3 Darin Erstad	.40	.15
4 Travis Lee	.40	.15
5 Matt Williams	.40	.15
6 Randy Johnson	1.00	.40
7 Chipper Jones	1.00	.40
8 Greg Maddux	1.50	.60
9 Andruw Jones	.60	.25
10 Andres Galarraga	.40	.15
11 Tom Glavine	.60	.25
12 Cal Ripken	3.00	1.25
13 Brady Anderson	.40	.15
14 Albert Belle	.40	.15
15 Nomar Garciaparra	1.50	.60
16 Donnie Sadler	.40	.15
17 Pedro Martinez	.60	.25
18 Sammy Sosa	1.00	.40
19 Kerry Wood	.40	.15
20 Mark Grace	.60	.25
21 Mike Caruso	.40	.15
22 Frank Thomas	1.00	.40
23 Paul Konerko	.40	.15
24 Sean Casey	.40	.15
25 Barry Larkin	.60	.25
26 Kenny Lofton	.40	.15
27 Manny Ramirez	.60	.25
28 Jim Thome	.60	.25
29 Bartolo Colon	.40	.15
30 Jaret Wright	.40	.15
31 Larry Walker	.40	.15
32 Todd Helton	.60	.25
33 Tony Clark	.40	.15
34 Dean Palmer	.40	.15
35 Mark Kotsay	.40	.15
36 Cliff Floyd	.40	.15
37 Ken Caminiti	.40	.15
38 Craig Biggio	.60	.25
39 Jeff Bagwell	.60	.25
40 Moises Alou	.40	.15
41 Johnny Damon	.60	.25
42 Larry Sutton	.40	.15
43 Kevin Brown	.60	.25
44 Gary Sheffield	.40	.15
45 Raul Mondesi	.40	.15
46 Jeromy Burnitz	.40	.15
47 Jeff Cirillo	.40	.15
48 Todd Walker	.40	.15
49 David Ortiz	1.00	.40
50 Brad Radke	.40	.15
51 Vladimir Guerrero	1.00	.40
52 Rondell White	.40	.15
53 Brad Fullmer	.40	.15
54 Mike Piazza	1.50	.60
55 Robin Ventura	.40	.15
56 John Olerud	.40	.15
57 Derek Jeter	2.50	1.00
58 Tino Martinez	.60	.25
59 Bernie Williams	.60	.25
60 Roger Clemens	2.00	.75
61 Ben Grieve	.40	.15
62 Miguel Tejada	.40	.15
63 A.J. Hinch	.40	.15
64 Scott Rolen	.60	.25
65 Curt Schilling	.40	.15
66 Doug Glanville	.40	.15
67 Aramis Ramirez	.40	.15
68 Tony Womack	.40	.15
69 Jason Kendall	.40	.15
70 Tony Gwynn	1.25	.50
71 Wally Joyner	.40	.15
72 Greg Vaughn	.40	.15
73 Barry Bonds	2.50	1.00
74 Ellis Burks	.40	.15
75 Jeff Kent	.40	.15
76 Ken Griffey Jr.	1.50	.60
77 Alex Rodriguez	1.50	.60
78 Edgar Martinez	.60	.25
79 Mark McGwire	2.50	1.00
80 Eli Marrero	.40	.15
81 Matt Morris	.40	.15
82 Rolando Arrojo	.40	.15
83 Quinton McCracken	.40	.15
84 Jose Canseco	.60	.25
85 Ivan Rodriguez	.60	.25
86 Juan Gonzalez	.40	.15
87 Royce Clayton	.40	.15
88 Shawn Green	.40	.15
89 Jose Cruz Jr.	.40	.15
90 Carlos Delgado	.40	.15
91 Troy Glaus FW	12.00	5.00
92 George Lombard FW	10.00	4.00
93 Ryan Minor FW	10.00	4.00
94 Calvin Pickering FW	10.00	4.00
95 Jin Ho Cho FW	10.00	4.00
96 Russ Branyan FW	10.00	4.00
97 Derrick Gibson FW	10.00	4.00
98 Gabe Kapler FW	10.00	4.00
99 Matt Anderson FW	10.00	4.00
100 Preston Wilson FW	10.00	4.00
101 Alex Gonzalez FW	10.00	4.00
102 Carlos Beltran FW	12.00	5.00
103 Dee Brown FW	10.00	4.00
104 Jeremy Giambi FW	10.00	4.00
105 Angel Pena FW	10.00	4.00
106 Geoff Jenkins FW	10.00	4.00
107 Corey Koskie FW	10.00	4.00
108 A.J. Pierzynski FW	10.00	4.00
109 Michael Barrett FW	10.00	4.00
110 Fernando Seguignol FW	10.00	4.00
111 Mike Kinkade FW	10.00	4.00
112 Ricky Ledee FW	10.00	4.00
113 Mike Lowell FW	10.00	4.00
114 Eric Chavez FW	10.00	4.00
115 Matt Clement FW	10.00	4.00
116 Shane Monahan FW	10.00	4.00
117 J.D. Drew FW	10.00	4.00
118 Bubba Trammell FW	10.00	4.00
119 Kevin Witt FW	10.00	4.00
120 Roy Halladay FW	10.00	4.00
121 Mark McGwire STR	12.00	5.00
122 M.McGwire/S.Sosa STR	10.00	4.00
123 Sammy Sosa STR	5.00	2.00
124 Ken Griffey Jr. STR	8.00	3.00
125 Cal Ripken STR	15.00	6.00
126 Juan Gonzalez STR	3.00	1.25
127 Kerry Wood STR	3.00	1.25
128 Trevor Hoffman STR	3.00	1.25
129 Barry Bonds STR	12.00	5.00
130 Alex Rodriguez STR	8.00	3.00
131 Ben Grieve STR	3.00	1.25
132 Tom Glavine STR	3.00	1.25
133 David Wells STR	3.00	1.25
134 Mike Piazza STR	8.00	3.00
135 Scott Brosius STR	3.00	1.25

2000 SP Authentic

Card		
COMP.BASIC w/o SP's (90)	25.00	10.00
COMP.UPDATE w/o SP'S (30)	10.00	4.00
COMMON CARD (1-90)	.40	.15
COMMON SUP (91-105)	3.00	1.25
COMMON FW (106-135)	5.00	2.00
COMMON FW (136-164)	5.00	2.00
COMMON CARD (166-195)	.60	.25
1 Mo Vaughn	.40	.15
2 Troy Glaus	.40	.15

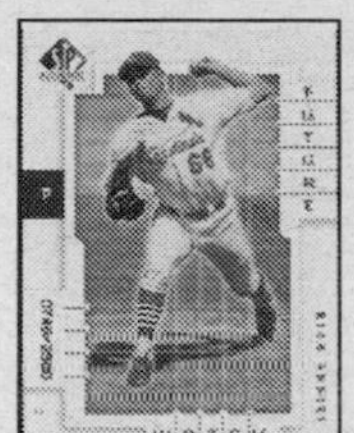

❑ 3 Jason Giambi .40 .15
❑ 4 Tim Hudson .40 .15
❑ 5 Eric Chavez .40 .15
❑ 6 Shannon Stewart .40 .15
❑ 7 Raul Mondesi .40 .15
❑ 8 Carlos Delgado .40 .15
❑ 9 Jose Canseco .60 .25
❑ 10 Vinny Castilla .40 .15
❑ 11 Greg Vaughn .40 .15
❑ 12 Manny Ramirez .60 .25
❑ 13 Roberto Alomar .60 .25
❑ 14 Jim Thome .60 .25
❑ 15 Richie Sexson .40 .15
❑ 16 Alex Rodriguez 1.50 .60
❑ 17 Freddy Garcia .40 .15
❑ 18 John Olerud .40 .15
❑ 19 Albert Belle .40 .15
❑ 20 Cal Ripken 3.00 1.25
❑ 21 Mike Mussina .60 .25
❑ 22 Ivan Rodriguez .60 .25
❑ 23 Gabe Kapler .40 .15
❑ 24 Rafael Palmeiro .60 .25
❑ 25 Nomar Garciaparra 1.50 .60
❑ 26 Pedro Martinez .60 .25
❑ 27 Carl Everett .40 .15
❑ 28 Carlos Beltran .40 .15
❑ 29 Jermaine Dye .40 .15
❑ 30 Juan Gonzalez .40 .15
❑ 31 Dean Palmer .40 .15
❑ 32 Corey Koskie .40 .15
❑ 33 Jacque Jones .40 .15
❑ 34 Frank Thomas 1.00 .40
❑ 35 Paul Konerko .40 .15
❑ 36 Magglio Ordonez .40 .15
❑ 37 Bernie Williams .60 .25
❑ 38 Derek Jeter 2.50 1.00
❑ 39 Roger Clemens 2.00 .75
❑ 40 Mariano Rivera 1.00 .40
❑ 41 Jeff Bagwell .60 .25
❑ 42 Craig Biggio .60 .25
❑ 43 Jose Lima .40 .15
❑ 44 Moises Alou .40 .15
❑ 45 Chipper Jones 1.00 .40
❑ 46 Greg Maddux 1.50 .60
❑ 47 Andruw Jones .60 .25
❑ 48 Andres Galarraga .40 .15
❑ 49 Jeromy Burnitz .40 .15
❑ 50 Geoff Jenkins .40 .15
❑ 51 Mark McGwire 2.50 1.00
❑ 52 Fernando Tatis .40 .15
❑ 53 J.D. Drew .40 .15
❑ 54 Sammy Sosa 1.00 .40
❑ 55 Kerry Wood .40 .15
❑ 56 Mark Grace .60 .25
❑ 57 Matt Williams .40 .15
❑ 58 Randy Johnson 1.00 .40
❑ 59 Erubiel Durazo .40 .15
❑ 60 Gary Sheffield .40 .15
❑ 61 Kevin Brown .60 .25
❑ 62 Shawn Green .40 .15
❑ 63 Vladimir Guerrero 1.00 .40
❑ 64 Michael Barrett .40 .15
❑ 65 Barry Bonds 2.50 1.00
❑ 66 Jeff Kent .40 .15
❑ 67 Russ Ortiz .40 .15
❑ 68 Preston Wilson .40 .15
❑ 69 Mike Lowell .40 .15
❑ 70 Mike Piazza 1.50 .60
❑ 71 Mike Hampton .40 .15
❑ 72 Robin Ventura .40 .15
❑ 73 Edgardo Alfonzo .40 .15
❑ 74 Tony Gwynn 1.25 .50
❑ 75 Ryan Klesko .40 .15
❑ 76 Trevor Hoffman .40 .15
❑ 77 Scott Rolen .60 .25
❑ 78 Bob Abreu .40 .15
❑ 79 Mike Lieberthal .40 .15
❑ 80 Curt Schilling .40 .15
❑ 81 Jason Kendall .40 .15
❑ 82 Brian Giles .40 .15
❑ 83 Kris Benson .40 .15
❑ 84 Ken Griffey Jr. 1.50 .60
❑ 85 Sean Casey .40 .15
❑ 86 Pokey Reese .40 .15
❑ 87 Barry Larkin .60 .25
❑ 88 Larry Walker .40 .15
❑ 89 Todd Helton .60 .25
❑ 90 Jeff Cirillo .40 .15
❑ 91 Ken Griffey Jr. SUP 8.00 3.00
❑ 92 Mark McGwire SUP 12.00 5.00
❑ 93 Chipper Jones SUP 5.00 2.00
❑ 94 Derek Jeter SUP 12.00 5.00
❑ 95 Shawn Green SUP 3.00 1.25
❑ 96 Pedro Martinez SUP 3.00 1.25
❑ 97 Mike Piazza SUP 8.00 3.00
❑ 98 Alex Rodriguez SUP 8.00 3.00
❑ 99 Jeff Bagwell SUP 3.00 1.25
❑ 100 Cal Ripken SUP 15.00 6.00
❑ 101 Sammy Sosa SUP 5.00 2.00
❑ 102 Barry Bonds SUP 12.00 5.00
❑ 103 Jose Canseco SUP 3.00 1.25
❑ 104 Nomar Garciaparra SUP 8.00 3.00
❑ 105 Ivan Rodriguez SUP 3.00 1.25
❑ 106 Rick Ankiel FW 8.00 3.00
❑ 107 Pat Burrell FW 3.00 1.25
❑ 108 Vernon Wells FW 5.00 2.00
❑ 109 Nick Johnson FW 5.00 2.00
❑ 110 Kip Wells FW 5.00 2.00
❑ 111 Matt Riley FW 5.00 2.00
❑ 112 Alfonso Soriano FW 8.00 3.00
❑ 113 Josh Beckett FW 8.00 3.00
❑ 114 Danys Baez FW RC 5.00 2.00
❑ 115 Travis Dawkins FW 5.00 2.00
❑ 116 Eric Gagne FW 8.00 3.00
❑ 117 Mike Lamb FW RC 8.00 3.00
❑ 118 Eric Munson FW 5.00 2.00
❑ 119 Wilfredo Rodriguez FW RC 5.00 2.00
❑ 120 Kazuhiro Sasaki FW RC 8.00 3.00
❑ 121 Chad Hutchinson FW 5.00 2.00
❑ 122 Peter Bergeron FW 5.00 2.00
❑ 123 Wascar Serrano FW RC 5.00 2.00
❑ 124 Tony Armas Jr. FW 5.00 2.00
❑ 125 Ramon Ortiz FW 5.00 2.00
❑ 126 Adam Kennedy FW 5.00 2.00
❑ 127 Joe Crede FW 10.00 4.00
❑ 128 Roosevelt Brown FW 5.00 2.00
❑ 129 Mark Mulder FW 5.00 2.00
❑ 130 Brad Penny FW 5.00 2.00
❑ 131 Terrence Long FW 5.00 2.00
❑ 132 Ruben Mateo FW 5.00 2.00
❑ 133 Wily Mo Pena FW 5.00 2.00
❑ 134 Rafael Furcal FW 5.00 2.00
❑ 135 Mario Encarnacion FW 5.00 2.00
❑ 136 Barry Zito FW RC 20.00 8.00
❑ 137 Aaron McNeal FW RC 5.00 2.00
❑ 138 Timo Perez FW RC 5.00 2.00
❑ 139 Sun Woo Kim FW RC 5.00 2.00
❑ 140 Xavier Nady FW RC 10.00 4.00
❑ 141 Matt Wheatland FW RC 5.00 2.00
❑ 142 Brent Abernathy FW RC 5.00 2.00
❑ 143 Cory Vance FW RC 5.00 2.00
❑ 144 Scott Heard FW RC 5.00 2.00
❑ 145 Mike Meyers FW RC 5.00 2.00
❑ 146 Ben Diggins FW RC 5.00 2.00
❑ 147 Luis Matos FW RC 5.00 2.00
❑ 148 Ben Sheets FW RC 12.00 5.00
❑ 149 Kurt Ainsworth FW RC 5.00 2.00
❑ 150 Dave Krynzel FW RC 5.00 2.00
❑ 151 Alex Cabrera FW RC 5.00 2.00
❑ 152 Mike Tonis FW RC 5.00 2.00
❑ 153 Dane Sardinha FW RC 5.00 2.00
❑ 154 Keith Ginter FW RC 5.00 2.00
❑ 155 David Espinosa FW RC 5.00 2.00
❑ 156 Joe Torres FW RC 5.00 2.00
❑ 157 Daylan Holt FW RC 5.00 2.00
❑ 158 Koyie Hill FW RC 5.00 2.00
❑ 159 Brad Wilkerson FW RC 8.00 3.00
❑ 160 Juan Pierre FW RC 8.00 3.00
❑ 161 Matt Ginter FW RC 5.00 2.00
❑ 162 Dane Artman FW RC 5.00 2.00
❑ 163 Jon Rauch FW RC 5.00 2.00
❑ 164 Sean Burnett FW RC 5.00 2.00
❑ 165 Does Not Exist
❑ 166 Darin Erstad .60 .25
❑ 167 Ben Grieve .60 .25
❑ 168 David Wells .60 .25
❑ 169 Fred McGriff 1.00 .40
❑ 170 Bob Wickman .60 .25
❑ 171 Al Martin .60 .25
❑ 172 Melvin Mora .60 .25
❑ 173 Ricky Ledee .60 .25
❑ 174 Dante Bichette .60 .25
❑ 175 Mike Sweeney .60 .25
❑ 176 Bobby Higginson .60 .25
❑ 177 Matt Lawton .60 .25
❑ 178 Charles Johnson .60 .25
❑ 179 David Justice .60 .25
❑ 180 Richard Hidalgo .60 .25
❑ 181 B.J. Surhoff .60 .25
❑ 182 Richie Sexson .60 .25
❑ 183 Jim Edmonds .60 .25
❑ 184 Rondell White .60 .25
❑ 185 Curt Schilling .60 .25
❑ 186 Tom Goodwin .60 .25
❑ 187 Jose Vidro .60 .25
❑ 188 Ellis Burks .60 .25
❑ 189 Henry Rodriguez .60 .25
❑ 190 Mike Bordick .60 .25
❑ 191 Eric Owens .60 .25
❑ 192 Travis Lee .60 .25
❑ 193 Kevin Young .60 .25
❑ 194 Aaron Boone .60 .25
❑ 195 Todd Hollandsworth .60 .25
❑ SPA Ken Griffey Jr. Sample 2.00 .75

2001 SP Authentic

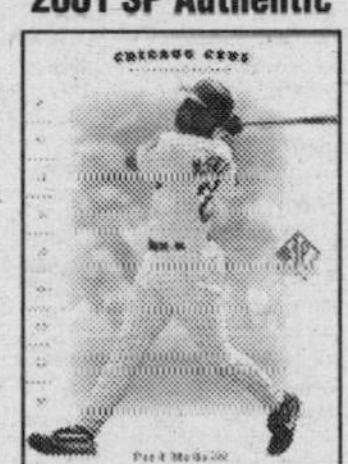

❑ COMP.BASIC w/o SP's (90) 25.00 10.00
❑ COMP.UPDATE w/o SP's (30) 10.00 4.00
❑ COMMON CARD (1-90) .40 .15
❑ COMMON FW (91-135) 8.00 3.00
❑ COMMON SS (136-180) 5.00 2.00
❑ COMMON CARD (181-210) .60 .25
❑ COMMON CARD (211-240) 0.00 2.50
❑ 1 Troy Glaus .40 .15
❑ 2 Darin Erstad .40 .15
❑ 3 Jason Giambi .40 .15
❑ 4 Tim Hudson .40 .15
❑ 5 Eric Chavez .40 .15
❑ 6 Miguel Tejada .40 .15
❑ 7 Jose Ortiz .40 .15
❑ 8 Carlos Delgado .40 .15
❑ 9 Tony Batista .40 .15
❑ 10 Raul Mondesi .40 .15
❑ 11 Aubrey Huff .40 .15
❑ 12 Greg Vaughn .40 .15
❑ 13 Roberto Alomar .60 .25
❑ 14 Juan Gonzalez .40 .15
❑ 15 Jim Thome .60 .25
❑ 16 Omar Vizquel .60 .25
❑ 17 Edgar Martinez .60 .25
❑ 18 Freddy Garcia .40 .15
❑ 19 Cal Ripken 3.00 1.25

Card		
20 Ivan Rodriguez	.60	.25
21 Rafael Palmeiro	.60	.25
22 Alex Rodriguez	1.50	.60
23 Manny Ramirez Sox	.60	.25
24 Pedro Martinez	.60	.25
25 Nomar Garciaparra	1.50	.60
26 Mike Sweeney	.40	.15
27 Jermaine Dye	.40	.15
28 Bobby Higginson	.40	.15
29 Dean Palmer	.40	.15
30 Matt Lawton	.40	.15
31 Eric Milton	.40	.15
32 Frank Thomas	1.00	.40
33 Magglio Ordonez	.40	.15
34 David Wells	.40	.15
35 Paul Konerko	.40	.15
36 Derek Jeter	2.50	1.00
37 Bernie Williams	.60	.25
38 Roger Clemens	2.00	.75
39 Mike Mussina	.60	.25
40 Jorge Posada	.60	.25
41 Jeff Bagwell	.60	.25
42 Richard Hidalgo	.40	.15
43 Craig Biggio	.60	.25
44 Greg Maddux	1.50	.60
45 Chipper Jones	1.00	.40
46 Andruw Jones	.60	.25
47 Rafael Furcal	.40	.15
48 Tom Glavine	.60	.25
49 Jeromy Burnitz	.40	.15
50 Jeffrey Hammonds	.40	.15
51 Mark McGwire	2.50	1.00
52 Jim Edmonds	.40	.15
53 Rick Ankiel	.40	.15
54 J.D. Drew	.40	.15
55 Sammy Sosa	1.00	.40
56 Corey Patterson	.40	.15
57 Kerry Wood	.40	.15
58 Randy Johnson	1.00	.40
59 Luis Gonzalez	.40	.15
60 Curt Schilling	.40	.15
61 Gary Sheffield	.40	.15
62 Shawn Green	.40	.15
63 Kevin Brown	.40	.15
64 Vladimir Guerrero	1.00	.40
65 Jose Vidro	.40	.15
66 Barry Bonds	2.50	1.00
67 Jeff Kent	.40	.15
68 Livan Hernandez	.40	.15
69 Preston Wilson	.40	.15
70 Charles Johnson	.40	.15
71 Ryan Dempster	.40	.15
72 Mike Piazza	1.50	.60
73 Al Leiter	.40	.15
74 Edgardo Alfonzo	.40	.15
75 Robin Ventura	.40	.15
76 Tony Gwynn	1.25	.50
77 Phil Nevin	.40	.15
78 Trevor Hoffman	.40	.15
79 Scott Rolen	.60	.25
80 Pat Burrell	.40	.15
81 Bob Abreu	.40	.15
82 Jason Kendall	.40	.15
83 Brian Giles	.40	.15
84 Kris Benson	.40	.15
85 Ken Griffey Jr.	1.50	.60
86 Barry Larkin	.60	.25
87 Sean Casey	.40	.15
88 Todd Helton	.60	.25
89 Mike Hampton	.40	.15
90 Larry Walker	.40	.15
91 Ichiro Suzuki FW RC	120.00	60.00
92 Wilson Betemit FW RC	15.00	6.00
93 Adrian Hernandez FW RC	8.00	3.00
94 Juan Uribe FW RC	10.00	4.00
95 Travis Hafner FW RC	50.00	20.00
96 Morgan Ensberg FW RC	15.00	6.00
97 Sean Douglass FW RC	8.00	3.00
98 Juan Diaz FW RC	8.00	3.00
99 Erick Almonte FW RC	8.00	3.00
100 Ryan Freel FW RC	8.00	3.00
101 Elpidio Guzman FW RC	8.00	3.00
102 Christian Parker FW RC	8.00	3.00
103 Josh Fogg FW RC	8.00	3.00
104 Bert Snow FW RC	8.00	3.00
105 Horacio Ramirez FW RC	10.00	4.00
106 Ricardo Rodriguez FW RC	8.00	3.00
107 Tyler Walker FW RC	8.00	3.00
108 Jose Mieses FW RC	8.00	3.00
109 Billy Sylvester FW RC	8.00	3.00
110 Martin Vargas FW RC	8.00	3.00
111 Andres Torres FW RC	8.00	3.00
112 Greg Miller FW RC	8.00	3.00
113 Alexis Gomez FW RC	8.00	3.00
114 Grant Balfour FW RC	8.00	3.00
115 Henry Mateo FW RC	8.00	3.00
116 Esix Snead FW RC	8.00	3.00
117 Jackson Melian FW RC	8.00	3.00
118 Nate Teut FW RC	8.00	3.00
119 Tsuyoshi Shinjo FW RC	10.00	4.00
120 Carlos Valderrama FW RC	8.00	3.00
121 Johnny Estrada FW RC	10.00	4.00
122 Jason Michaels FW RC	8.00	3.00
123 William Ortega FW RC	8.00	3.00
124 Jason Smith FW RC	8.00	3.00
125 Brian Lawrence FW RC	8.00	3.00
126 Albert Pujols FW RC	300.00	200.00
127 Wilkin Ruan FW RC	8.00	3.00
128 Josh Towers FW RC	10.00	4.00
129 Kris Keller FW RC	8.00	3.00
130 Nick Maness FW RC	8.00	3.00
131 Jack Wilson FW RC	10.00	4.00
132 Brandon Duckworth FW RC	8.00	3.00
133 Mike Penney FW RC	8.00	3.00
134 Jay Gibbons FW RC	10.00	4.00
135 Cesar Crespo FW RC	8.00	3.00
136 Ken Griffey Jr. SS	10.00	4.00
137 Mark McGwire SS	15.00	6.00
138 Derek Jeter SS	15.00	6.00
139 Alex Rodriguez SS	10.00	4.00
140 Sammy Sosa SS	6.00	2.50
141 Carlos Delgado SS	5.00	2.00
142 Cal Ripken SS	20.00	8.00
143 Pedro Martinez SS	5.00	2.00
144 Frank Thomas SS	6.00	2.50
145 Juan Gonzalez SS	5.00	2.00
146 Troy Glaus SS	5.00	2.00
147 Jason Giambi SS	5.00	2.00
148 Ivan Rodriguez SS	5.00	2.00
149 Chipper Jones SS	6.00	2.50
150 Vladimir Guerrero SS	6.00	2.50
151 Mike Piazza SS	10.00	4.00
152 Jeff Bagwell SS	5.00	2.00
153 Randy Johnson SS	6.00	2.50
154 Todd Helton SS	5.00	2.00
155 Gary Sheffield SS	5.00	2.00
156 Tony Gwynn SS	8.00	3.00
157 Barry Bonds SS	15.00	6.00
158 Nomar Garciaparra SS	10.00	4.00
159 Bernie Williams SS	5.00	2.00
160 Greg Vaughn SS	5.00	2.00
161 David Wells SS	5.00	2.00
162 Roberto Alomar SS	5.00	2.00
163 Jermaine Dye SS	5.00	2.00
164 Rafael Palmeiro SS	5.00	2.00
165 Andruw Jones SS	5.00	2.00
166 Preston Wilson SS	5.00	2.00
167 Edgardo Alfonzo SS	5.00	2.00
168 Pat Burrell SS	5.00	2.00
169 Jim Edmonds SS	5.00	2.00
170 Mike Hampton SS	5.00	2.00
171 Jeff Kent SS	5.00	2.00
172 Kevin Brown SS	5.00	2.00
173 Manny Ramirez Sox SS	5.00	2.00
174 Magglio Ordonez SS	5.00	2.00
175 Roger Clemens SS	12.00	5.00
176 Jim Thome SS	5.00	2.00
177 Barry Zito SS	5.00	2.00
178 Brian Giles SS	5.00	2.00
179 Rick Ankiel SS	5.00	2.00
180 Corey Patterson SS	5.00	2.00
181 Garret Anderson	.60	.25
182 Jermaine Dye	.60	.25
183 Shannon Stewart	.60	.25
184 Ben Grieve	.60	.25
185 Ellis Burks	.60	.25
186 John Olerud	.60	.25
187 Tony Batista	.60	.25
188 Ruben Sierra	.60	.25
189 Carl Everett	.60	.25
190 Neifi Perez	.60	.25
191 Tony Clark	.60	.25
192 Doug Mientkiewicz	.60	.25
193 Carlos Lee	.60	.25
194 Jorge Posada	1.00	.40
195 Lance Berkman	5.00	2.00
196 Ken Caminiti	.60	.25
197 Ben Sheets	1.00	.40
198 Matt Morris	.60	.25
199 Fred McGriff	1.00	.40
200 Mark Grace	1.00	.40
201 Paul LoDuca	.60	.25
202 Tony Armas Jr.	.60	.25
203 Andres Galarraga	.60	.25
204 Cliff Floyd	.60	.25
205 Matt Lawton	.60	.25
206 Ryan Klesko	.60	.25
207 Jimmy Rollins	.60	.25
208 Aramis Ramirez	.60	.25
209 Aaron Boone	.60	.25
210 Jose Ortiz	.60	.25
211 Mark Prior FW RC	40.00	15.00
212 Mark Teixeira FW RC	50.00	20.00
213 Bud Smith FW RC	6.00	2.50
214 Wilmy Caceres FW RC	6.00	2.50
215 Dave Williams FW RC	6.00	2.50
216 Delvin James FW RC	6.00	2.50
217 Endy Chavez FW RC	6.00	2.50
218 Doug Nickle FW RC	6.00	2.50
219 Bret Prinz FW RC	6.00	2.50
220 Troy Mattes FW RC	6.00	2.50
221 Duaner Sanchez FW RC	6.00	2.50
222 Dewon Brazelton FW RC	6.00	2.50
223 Brian Bowles FW RC	6.00	2.50
224 Donaldo Mendez FW RC	6.00	2.50
225 Jorge Julio FW RC	6.00	2.50
226 Matt White FW RC	6.00	2.50
227 Casey Fossum FW RC	6.00	2.50
228 Mike Rivera FW RC	6.00	2.50
229 Joe Kennedy FW RC	8.00	3.00
230 Kyle Lohse FW RC	8.00	3.00
231 Juan Cruz FW RC	6.00	2.50
232 Jeremy Affeldt FW RC	6.00	2.50
233 Brandon Lyon FW RC	6.00	2.50
234 Brian Roberts FW RC	20.00	8.00
235 Willie Harris FW RC	6.00	2.50
236 Pedro Santana FW RC	6.00	2.50
237 Rafael Soriano FW RC	6.00	2.50
238 Steve Green FW RC	6.00	2.50
239 Junior Spivey FW RC	8.00	3.00
240 Rob Mackowiak FW RC	8.00	3.00
NNO Ken Griffey Jr. Promo	2.00	.75

2002 SP Authentic

Card		
COMP.LOW w/o SP's (90)	15.00	6.00
COMP.UPDATE w/o SP's (30)	10.00	4.00
COMMON CARD (1-90)	.40	.15
COMMON (91-135/201-230)	5.00	2.00
COMMON CARD (136-170)	10.00	4.00
COMMON CARD (171-200)	.60	.25
1 Troy Glaus	.40	.15
2 Darin Erstad	.40	.15
3 Barry Zito	.40	.15
4 Eric Chavez	.40	.15
5 Tim Hudson	.40	.15
6 Miguel Tejada	.40	.15
7 Carlos Delgado	.40	.15
8 Shannon Stewart	.40	.15
9 Ben Grieve	.40	.15
10 Jim Thome	.60	.25

❑ 11 C.C. Sabathia .40 .15
❑ 12 Ichiro Suzuki 2.00 .75
❑ 13 Freddy Garcia .40 .15
❑ 14 Edgar Martinez .60 .25
❑ 15 Bret Boone .40 .15
❑ 16 Jeff Conine .40 .15
❑ 17 Alex Rodriguez 1.50 .60
❑ 18 Juan Gonzalez .40 .15
❑ 19 Ivan Rodriguez .60 .25
❑ 20 Rafael Palmeiro .60 .25
❑ 21 Hank Blalock .60 .25
❑ 22 Pedro Martinez .60 .25
❑ 23 Manny Ramirez .60 .25
❑ 24 Nomar Garciaparra 1.50 .60
❑ 25 Carlos Beltran .40 .15
❑ 26 Mike Sweeney .40 .15
❑ 27 Randall Simon .40 .15
❑ 28 Dmitri Young .40 .15
❑ 29 Bobby Higginson .40 .15
❑ 30 Corey Koskie .40 .15
❑ 31 Eric Milton .40 .15
❑ 32 Torii Hunter .40 .15
❑ 33 Joe Mays .40 .15
❑ 34 Frank Thomas 1.00 .40
❑ 35 Mark Buehrle .40 .15
❑ 36 Magglio Ordonez .40 .15
❑ 37 Kenny Lofton .40 .15
❑ 38 Roger Clemens 2.00 .75
❑ 39 Derek Jeter 2.50 1.00
❑ 40 Jason Giambi .40 .15
❑ 41 Bernie Williams .60 .25
❑ 42 Alfonso Soriano .40 .15
❑ 43 Lance Berkman .40 .15
❑ 44 Roy Oswalt .40 .15
❑ 45 Jeff Bagwell .60 .25
❑ 46 Craig Biggio .60 .25
❑ 47 Chipper Jones 1.00 .40
❑ 48 Greg Maddux 1.50 .60
❑ 49 Gary Sheffield .40 .15
❑ 50 Andruw Jones .60 .25
❑ 51 Ben Sheets .40 .15
❑ 52 Richie Sexson .40 .15
❑ 53 Albert Pujols 2.00 .75
❑ 54 Matt Morris .40 .15
❑ 55 J.D. Drew .40 .15
❑ 56 Sammy Sosa 1.00 .40
❑ 57 Kerry Wood .40 .15
❑ 58 Corey Patterson .40 .15
❑ 59 Mark Prior .60 .25
❑ 60 Randy Johnson 1.00 .40
❑ 61 Luis Gonzalez .40 .15
❑ 62 Curt Schilling .40 .15
❑ 63 Shawn Green .40 .15
❑ 64 Kevin Brown .40 .15
❑ 65 Hideo Nomo 1.00 .40
❑ 66 Vladimir Guerrero 1.00 .40
❑ 67 Jose Vidro .40 .15
❑ 68 Barry Bonds 2.50 1.00
❑ 69 Jeff Kent .40 .15
❑ 70 Rich Aurilia .40 .15
❑ 71 Preston Wilson .40 .15
❑ 72 Josh Beckett .40 .15
❑ 73 Mike Lowell .40 .15
❑ 74 Roberto Alomar .60 .25
❑ 75 Mo Vaughn .40 .15
❑ 76 Jeromy Burnitz .40 .15
❑ 77 Mike Piazza 1.50 .60
❑ 78 Sean Burroughs .40 .15
❑ 79 Phil Nevin .40 .15
❑ 80 Bobby Abreu .40 .15
❑ 81 Pat Burrell .40 .15
❑ 82 Scott Rolen .60 .25
❑ 83 Jason Kendall .40 .15
❑ 84 Brian Giles .40 .15
❑ 85 Ken Griffey Jr. 1.50 .60
❑ 86 Adam Dunn .40 .15
❑ 87 Sean Casey .40 .15
❑ 88 Todd Helton .60 .25
❑ 89 Larry Walker .40 .15
❑ 90 Mike Hampton .40 .15
❑ 91 Brandon Puffer FW RC 5.00 2.00
❑ 92 Tom Shearn FW RC 5.00 2.00
❑ 93 Chris Baker FW RC 5.00 2.00
❑ 94 Gustavo Chacin FW RC 8.00 3.00
❑ 95 Joe Orloski FW RC 5.00 2.00
❑ 96 Mike Smith FW RC 5.00 2.00
❑ 97 John Ennis FW RC 5.00 2.00
❑ 98 John Foster FW RC 5.00 2.00
❑ 99 Kevin Gryboski FW RC 5.00 2.00
❑ 100 Brian Mallette FW RC 5.00 2.00
❑ 101 Takahito Nomura FW RC 5.00 2.00
❑ 102 So Taguchi FW RC 8.00 3.00
❑ 103 Jeremy Lambert FW RC 5.00 2.00
❑ 104 Jason Simontacchi FW RC 5.00 2.00
❑ 105 Jorge Sosa FW RC 8.00 3.00
❑ 106 Brandon Backe FW RC 8.00 3.00
❑ 107 P.J. Bevis FW RC 5.00 2.00
❑ 108 Jeremy Ward FW RC 5.00 2.00
❑ 109 Doug Devore FW RC 5.00 2.00
❑ 110 Ron Chiavacci FW 5.00 2.00
❑ 111 Ron Calloway FW RC 5.00 2.00
❑ 112 Nelson Castro FW RC 5.00 2.00
❑ 113 Deivis Santos FW 5.00 2.00
❑ 114 Earl Snyder FW RC 5.00 2.00
❑ 115 Julio Mateo FW RC 5.00 2.00
❑ 116 J.J. Putz FW RC 5.00 2.00
❑ 117 Allan Simpson FW RC 5.00 2.00
❑ 118 Satoru Komiyama FW RC 5.00 2.00
❑ 119 Adam Walker FW RC 5.00 2.00
❑ 120 Oliver Perez FW RC 8.00 3.00
❑ 121 Cliff Bartosh FW RC 5.00 2.00
❑ 122 Todd Donovan FW RC 5.00 2.00
❑ 123 [illegible] FW RC 5.00 2.00
❑ 124 Pete Zamora FW RC 5.00 2.00
❑ 125 Mike Gonzalez FW RC 5.00 2.00
❑ 126 Travis Hughes FW RC 5.00 2.00
❑ 127 Jorge De La Rosa FW RC 5.00 2.00
❑ 128 Anastacio Martinez FW RC 5.00 2.00
❑ 129 Colin Young FW RC 5.00 2.00
❑ 130 Nate Field FW RC 5.00 2.00
❑ 131 Tim Kalita FW RC 5.00 2.00
❑ 132 Julius Matos FW RC 5.00 2.00
❑ 133 Terry Pearson FW RC 5.00 2.00
❑ 134 Kyle Kane FW RC 5.00 2.00
❑ 135 Mitch Wylie FW RC 5.00 2.00
❑ 136 Rodrigo Rosario AU RC 10.00 4.00
❑ 137 Franklyn German AU RC 10.00 4.00
❑ 138 Reed Johnson AU RC 20.00 8.00
❑ 139 Luis Martinez AU RC 10.00 4.00
❑ 140 Michael Crudale AU RC 10.00 4.00
❑ 141 Francis Beltran AU RC 10.00 4.00
❑ 142 Steve Kent AU RC 10.00 4.00
❑ 143 Felix Escalona AU RC 10.00 4.00
❑ 144 Jose Valverde AU RC 10.00 4.00
❑ 145 Victor Alvarez AU RC 10.00 4.00
❑ 146 Kazuhisa Ishii AU/249 RC 40.00 15.00
❑ 147 Jorge Nunez AU RC 10.00 4.00
❑ 148 Eric Good AU RC 10.00 4.00
❑ 149 Luis Ugueto AU RC 10.00 4.00
❑ 150 Matt Thornton AU RC 10.00 4.00
❑ 151 Wilson Valdez AU RC 10.00 4.00
❑ 152 Han Izquierdo AU/249 RC 40.00 15.00
❑ 153 Jaime Cerda AU RC 10.00 4.00
❑ 154 Mark Corey AU RC 10.00 4.00
❑ 155 Tyler Yates AU RC 10.00 4.00
❑ 156 Steve Bechler AU RC 10.00 4.00
❑ 157 Ben Howard AU/249 RC 40.00 15.00
❑ 158 Anderson Machado AU RC 10.00 4.00
❑ 159 Jorge Padilla AU RC 10.00 4.00
❑ 160 Eric Junge AU RC 10.00 4.00
❑ 161 Adrian Burnside AU RC 10.00 4.00
❑ 162 Josh Hancock AU RC 20.00 8.00
❑ 163 Chris Booker AU RC 10.00 4.00
❑ 164 Cam Esslinger AU RC 10.00 4.00
❑ 165 Rene Reyes AU RC 10.00 4.00
❑ 166 Aaron Cook AU RC 15.00 6.00
❑ 167 Juan Brito AU RC 10.00 4.00
❑ 168 Miguel Ascencio AU RC 10.00 4.00
❑ 169 Kevin Frederick AU RC 10.00 4.00
❑ 170 Edwin Almonte AU RC 10.00 4.00
❑ 171 Erubiel Durazo .60 .25
❑ 172 Junior Spivey .60 .25
❑ 173 Geronimo Gil .60 .25
❑ 174 Cliff Floyd .60 .25
❑ 175 Brandon Larson .60 .25
❑ 176 Aaron Boone .60 .25
❑ 177 Shawn Estes .60 .25
❑ 178 Austin Kearns .60 .25
❑ 179 Joe Borchard .60 .25
❑ 180 Russell Branyan .60 .25
❑ 181 Jay Payton .60 .25
❑ 182 Andres Torres .60 .25
❑ 183 Andy Van Hekken .60 .25
❑ 184 Alex Sanchez .60 .25
❑ 185 Endy Chavez .60 .25
❑ 186 Bartolo Colon .60 .25
❑ 187 Raul Mondesi .60 .25
❑ 188 Robin Ventura .60 .25
❑ 189 Mike Mussina 1.00 .40
❑ 190 Jorge Posada 1.00 .40
❑ 191 Ted Lilly .60 .25
❑ 192 Ray Durham .60 .25
❑ 193 Brett Myers .60 .25
❑ 194 Marlon Byrd .60 .25
❑ 195 Vicente Padilla .60 .25
❑ 196 Josh Fogg .60 .25
❑ 197 Kenny Lofton .60 .25
❑ 198 Scott Rolen 1.00 .40
❑ 199 Jason Lane .60 .25
❑ 200 Josh Phelps .60 .25
❑ 201 Travis Driskill FW RC 5.00 2.00
❑ 202 Howie Clark FW RC 5.00 2.00
❑ 203 Mike Mahoney FW 5.00 2.00
❑ 204 Brian Tallet FW RC 5.00 2.00
❑ 205 Kirk Saarloos FW RC 5.00 2.00
❑ 206 Barry Wesson FW RC 5.00 2.00
❑ 207 Aaron Guiel FW RC 5.00 2.00
❑ 208 Shawn Sedlacek FW RC 5.00 2.00
❑ 209 Jose Diaz FW RC 5.00 2.00
❑ 210 Jorge Nunez FW 5.00 2.00
❑ 211 Danny Mota FW RC 5.00 2.00
❑ 212 David Ross FW RC 8.00 3.00
❑ 213 Jayson Durocher FW RC 5.00 2.00
❑ 214 Shane Nance FW RC 5.00 2.00
❑ 215 Wil Nieves FW RC 5.00 2.00
❑ 216 Freddy Sanchez FW RC 10.00 4.00
❑ 217 Alex Pelaez FW RC 5.00 2.00
❑ 218 Jamey Carroll FW RC 8.00 3.00
❑ 219 J.J. Trujillo FW RC 5.00 2.00
❑ 220 Kevin Pickford FW RC 5.00 2.00
❑ 221 Clay Condrey FW RC 5.00 2.00
❑ 222 Chris Snelling FW RC 6.00 2.50
❑ 223 Cliff Lee FW RC 25.00 10.00
❑ 224 Jeremy Hill FW RC 5.00 2.00
❑ 225 Jose Rodriguez FW RC 5.00 2.00
❑ 226 Lance Carter FW RC 5.00 2.00
❑ 227 Ken Huckaby FW RC 5.00 2.00
❑ 228 Scott Wiggins FW RC 5.00 2.00
❑ 229 Corey Thurman FW RC 5.00 2.00
❑ 230 Kevin Cash FW RC 5.00 2.00
❑ RJ-D Joe DiMaggio AU Poster 200.00 125.00

2003 SP Authentic

❑ COMP.LO SET w/o SP's (90) 15.00 6.00
❑ COMMON CARD (1-90) .40 .15
❑ COMMON CARD (91-123) 3.00 1.25
❑ COMMON CARD (124-150) 3.00 1.25
❑ COMMON CARD (151-180) 5.00 2.00
❑ COMMON CARD (181-189) 15.00 6.00
❑ 91-189 RANDOM INSERTS IN PACKS
❑ COMMON CARD (190-239) 5.00 2.00
❑ 190-239 RANDOM IN 03 UD FINITE PACKS
❑ 190-239 PRINT RUN 699 SERIAL #'d SETS
❑ 1 Darin Erstad .40 .15
❑ 2 Garret Anderson .40 .15
❑ 3 Troy Glaus .40 .15
❑ 4 Eric Chavez .40 .15
❑ 5 Barry Zito .40 .15
❑ 6 Miguel Tejada .40 .15

Card		
❑ 7 Eric Hinske	.40	.15
❑ 8 Carlos Delgado	.40	.15
❑ 9 Josh Phelps	.40	.15
❑ 10 Ben Grieve	.40	.15
❑ 11 Carl Crawford	.40	.15
❑ 12 Omar Vizquel	.60	.25
❑ 13 Matt Lawton	.40	.15
❑ 14 C.C. Sabathia	.40	.15
❑ 15 Ichiro Suzuki	2.00	.75
❑ 16 John Olerud	.40	.15
❑ 17 Freddy Garcia	.40	.15
❑ 18 Jay Gibbons	.40	.15
❑ 19 Tony Batista	.40	.15
❑ 20 Melvin Mora	.40	.15
❑ 21 Alex Rodriguez	1.50	.60
❑ 22 Rafael Palmeiro	.60	.25
❑ 23 Hank Blalock	.40	.15
❑ 24 Nomar Garciaparra	1.50	.60
❑ 25 Pedro Martinez	.60	.25
❑ 26 Johnny Damon	.60	.25
❑ 27 Mike Sweeney	.40	.15
❑ 28 Carlos Febles	.40	.15
❑ 29 Carlos Beltran	.40	.15
❑ 30 Carlos Pena	.40	.15
❑ 31 Eric Munson	.40	.15
❑ 32 Bobby Higginson	.40	.15
❑ 33 Torii Hunter	.40	.15
❑ 34 Doug Mientkiewicz	.40	.15
❑ 35 Jacque Jones	.40	.15
❑ 36 Paul Konerko	.40	.15
❑ 37 Bartolo Colon	.40	.15
❑ 38 Magglio Ordonez	.40	.15
❑ 39 Derek Jeter	2.50	1.00
❑ 40 Bernie Williams	.60	.25
❑ 41 Jason Giambi	.40	.15
❑ 42 Alfonso Soriano	.40	.15
❑ 43 Roger Clemens	2.00	.75
❑ 44 Jeff Bagwell	.60	.25
❑ 45 Jeff Kent	.40	.15
❑ 46 Lance Berkman	.40	.15
❑ 47 Chipper Jones	1.00	.40
❑ 48 Andruw Jones	.60	.25
❑ 49 Gary Sheffield	.40	.15
❑ 50 Ben Sheets	.40	.15
❑ 51 Richie Sexson	.40	.15
❑ 52 Geoff Jenkins	.40	.15
❑ 53 Jim Edmonds	.40	.15
❑ 54 Albert Pujols	2.00	.75
❑ 55 Scott Rolen	.60	.25
❑ 56 Sammy Sosa	1.00	.40
❑ 57 Kerry Wood	.40	.15
❑ 58 Eric Karros	.40	.15
❑ 59 Luis Gonzalez	.40	.15
❑ 60 Randy Johnson	1.00	.40
❑ 61 Curt Schilling	.40	.15
❑ 62 Fred McGriff	.60	.25
❑ 63 Shawn Green	.40	.15
❑ 64 Paul Lo Duca	.40	.15
❑ 65 Vladimir Guerrero	1.00	.40
❑ 66 Jose Vidro	.40	.15
❑ 67 Barry Bonds	2.50	1.00
❑ 68 Rich Aurilia	.40	.15
❑ 69 Edgardo Alfonzo	.40	.15
❑ 70 Ivan Rodriguez	.60	.25
❑ 71 Mike Lowell	.40	.15
❑ 72 Derrek Lee	.60	.25
❑ 73 Tom Glavine	.60	.25
❑ 74 Mike Piazza	1.50	.60
❑ 75 Roberto Alomar	.60	.25
❑ 76 Ryan Klesko	.40	.15
❑ 77 Phil Nevin	.40	.15
❑ 78 Mark Kotsay	.40	.15
❑ 79 Jim Thome	.60	.25
❑ 80 Pat Burrell	.40	.15
❑ 81 Bobby Abreu	.40	.15
❑ 82 Jason Kendall	.40	.15
❑ 83 Brian Giles	.40	.15
❑ 84 Aramis Ramirez	.40	.15
❑ 85 Austin Kearns	.40	.15
❑ 86 Ken Griffey Jr.	1.50	.60
❑ 87 Adam Dunn	.40	.15
❑ 88 Larry Walker	.40	.15
❑ 89 Todd Helton	.60	.25
❑ 90 Preston Wilson	.40	.15
❑ 91 Derek Jeter RA	8.00	3.00
❑ 92 Johnny Damon RA	3.00	1.25
❑ 93 Chipper Jones RA	3.00	1.25
❑ 94 Manny Ramirez RA	3.00	1.25
❑ 95 Trot Nixon RA	3.00	1.25
❑ 96 Alex Rodriguez RA	5.00	2.00
❑ 97 Chan Ho Park RA	3.00	1.25
❑ 98 Brad Fullmer RA	3.00	1.25
❑ 99 Billy Wagner RA	3.00	1.25
❑ 100 Hideo Nomo RA	3.00	1.25
❑ 101 Freddy Garcia RA	3.00	1.25
❑ 102 Darin Erstad RA	3.00	1.25
❑ 103 Jose Cruz Jr. RA	3.00	1.25
❑ 104 Nomar Garciaparra RA	5.00	2.00
❑ 105 Magglio Ordonez RA	3.00	1.25
❑ 106 Kerry Wood RA	3.00	1.25
❑ 107 Troy Glaus RA	3.00	1.25
❑ 108 J.D. Drew RA	3.00	1.25
❑ 109 Alfonso Soriano RA	3.00	1.25
❑ 110 Danys Baez RA	3.00	1.25
❑ 111 Kazuhiro Sasaki RA	3.00	1.25
❑ 112 Barry Zito RA	3.00	1.25
❑ 113 Brent Abernathy RA	3.00	1.25
❑ 114 Ben Diggins RA	3.00	1.25
❑ 115 Ben Sheets RA	3.00	1.25
❑ 116 Brad Wilkerson RA	3.00	1.25
❑ 117 Juan Pierre RA	3.00	1.25
❑ 118 Jon Rauch RA	3.00	1.25
❑ 119 Ichiro Suzuki RA	6.00	2.50
❑ 120 Albert Pujols RA	6.00	2.50
❑ 121 Mark Prior RA	3.00	1.25
❑ 122 Mark Teixeira RA	3.00	1.25
❑ 123 Kazuhisa Ishii RA	3.00	1.25
❑ 124 Troy Glaus B93	3.00	1.25
❑ 125 Randy Johnson B93	3.00	1.25
❑ 126 Curt Schilling B93	3.00	1.25
❑ 127 Chipper Jones B93	3.00	1.25
❑ 128 Greg Maddux B93	5.00	2.00
❑ 129 Nomar Garciaparra B93	5.00	2.00
❑ 130 Pedro Martinez B93	3.00	1.25
❑ 131 Sammy Sosa B93	3.00	1.25
❑ 132 Mark Prior B93	3.00	1.25
❑ 133 Ken Griffey Jr. B93	5.00	2.00
❑ 134 Adam Dunn B93	3.00	1.25
❑ 135 Jeff Bagwell B93	3.00	1.25
❑ 136 Vladimir Guerrero B93	3.00	1.25
❑ 137 Mike Piazza B93	5.00	2.00
❑ 138 Tom Glavine B93	3.00	1.25
❑ 139 Derek Jeter B93	8.00	3.00
❑ 140 Roger Clemens B93	6.00	2.50
❑ 141 Jason Giambi B93	3.00	1.25
❑ 142 Alfonso Soriano B93	3.00	1.25
❑ 143 Miguel Tejada B93	3.00	1.25
❑ 144 Barry Zito B93	3.00	1.25
❑ 145 Jim Thome B93	3.00	1.25
❑ 146 Barry Bonds B93	8.00	3.00
❑ 147 Ichiro Suzuki B93	6.00	2.50
❑ 148 Albert Pujols B93	6.00	2.50
❑ 149 Alex Rodriguez B93	5.00	2.00
❑ 150 Carlos Delgado B93	3.00	1.25
❑ 151 Rich Fischer FW HC	5.00	2.00
❑ 152 Brandon Webb FW RC	25.00	10.00
❑ 153 Rob Hammock FW RC	5.00	2.00
❑ 154 Matt Kata FW RC	5.00	2.00
❑ 155 Tim Olson FW RC	5.00	2.00
❑ 156 Oscar Villarreal FW RC	5.00	2.00
❑ 157 Michael Hessman FW RC	5.00	2.00
❑ 158 Daniel Cabrera FW RC	8.00	3.00
❑ 159 Jon Leicester FW RC	5.00	2.00
❑ 160 Todd Wellemeyer FW RC	5.00	2.00
❑ 161 Felix Sanchez FW RC	5.00	2.00
❑ 162 David Sanders FW RC	5.00	2.00
❑ 163 Josh Stewart FW RC	5.00	2.00
❑ 164 Arnie Munoz FW RC	5.00	2.00
❑ 165 Ryan Cameron FW RC	5.00	2.00
❑ 166 Clint Barmes FW RC	5.00	2.00
❑ 167 Josh Willingham FW RC	10.00	4.00
❑ 169 Willie Eyre FW RC	5.00	2.00
❑ 170 Brent Hoard FW RC	5.00	2.00
❑ 171 Termel Sledge FW RC	5.00	2.00
❑ 172 Phil Seibel FW RC	5.00	2.00
❑ 173 Craig Brazell FW RC	5.00	2.00
❑ 174 Jeff Duncan FW RC	5.00	2.00
❑ 176 Bernie Castro FW RC	5.00	2.00
❑ 177 Mike Nicolas FW RC	5.00	2.00
❑ 178 Rett Johnson FW RC	5.00	2.00
❑ 179 Bobby Madritsch FW RC	5.00	2.00
❑ 180 Chris Capuano FW RC	25.00	10.00
❑ 181 Hid Matsui FW AU RC	300.00	175.00
❑ 182 Jose Contreras FW AU RC	30.0012.50	
❑ 183 Lew Ford FW AU RC	25.00	10.00
❑ 184 Jeremy Griffiths FW AU RC	15.00	6.00
❑ 185 G.Quiroz FW AU RC	15.00	6.00
❑ 186 Alej Machado FW AU RC	15.00	6.00
❑ 187 Fran Cruceta FW AU RC	15.00	6.00
❑ 188 Prentice Redman FW AU RC	15.006.00	
❑ 189 Shane Bazzell FW AU RC	15.00	6.00
❑ 190 Aaron Looper FW RC	5.00	2.00
❑ 191 Alex Prieto FW RC	5.00	2.00
❑ 192 Alfredo Gonzalez FW RC	5.00	2.00
❑ 193 Andrew Brown FW RC	8.00	3.00
❑ 194 Anthony Ferrari FW RC	5.00	2.00
❑ 195 Aquilino Lopez FW RC	5.00	2.00
❑ 196 Beau Kemp FW RC	5.00	2.00
❑ 197 Bo Hart FW RC	5.00	2.00
❑ 198 Chad Gaudin FW RC	5.00	2.00
❑ 199 Colin Porter FW RC	5.00	2.00
❑ 200 D.J. Carrasco FW RC	5.00	2.00
❑ 201 Dan Haren FW RC	8.00	3.00
❑ 202 Danny Garcia FW RC	5.00	2.00
❑ 203 Jon Switzer FW	5.00	2.00
❑ 204 Edwin Jackson FW RC	8.00	3.00
❑ 205 Fernando Cabrera FW RC	5.00	2.00
❑ 206 Garrett Atkins FW	5.00	2.00
❑ 207 Gerald Laird FW	5.00	2.00
❑ 208 Greg Jones FW RC	5.00	2.00
❑ 209 Ian Ferguson FW RC	5.00	2.00
❑ 210 Jason Roach FW RC	5.00	2.00
❑ 211 Jason Shiell FW RC	5.00	2.00
❑ 212 Jeremy Bonderman FW RC	25.0010.00	
❑ 213 Jeremy Wedel FW RC	5.00	2.00
❑ 214 Jhonny Peralta FW	8.00	3.00
❑ 215 Delmon Young FW RC	50.00	25.00
❑ 216 Jorge DePaula FW	5.00	2.00
❑ 217 Josh Hall FW RC	5.00	2.00
❑ 218 Julio Manon FW RC	5.00	2.00
❑ 219 Kevin Correia FW RC	5.00	2.00
❑ 220 Kevin Ohme FW RC	5.00	2.00
❑ 221 Kevin Tolar FW RC	5.00	2.00
❑ 222 Luis Ayala FW RC	5.00	2.00
❑ 223 Luis De Los Santos FW	5.00	2.00
❑ 224 Chad Cordero FW RC	10.00	4.00
❑ 225 Mark Malaska FW RC	5.00	2.00
❑ 226 Khalil Greene FW	8.00	3.00
❑ 227 Michael Nakamura FW RC	5.00	2.00
❑ 228 Michel Hernandez FW RC	5.00	2.00
❑ 229 Miguel Ojeda FW RC	5.00	2.00
❑ 230 Mike Neu FW RC	5.00	2.00
❑ 231 Nate Bland FW RC	5.00	2.00
❑ 232 Pete LaForest FW RC	5.00	2.00
❑ 233 Rickie Weeks FW RC	20.00	8.00
❑ 234 Rosman Garcia FW RC	5.00	2.00
❑ 235 Ryan Wagner FW RC	5.00	2.00
❑ 236 Lance Niekro FW	5.00	2.00
❑ 237 Tom Gregorio FW RC	5.00	2.00
❑ 238 Tommy Phelps FW	5.00	2.00
❑ 239 Wilfredo Ledezma FW RC	5.00	2.00

2004 SP Authentic

❑ COMP.SET w/o SP's (90)	15.00	6.00
❑ COMMON CARD (1-90)	.40	.15
❑ COMMON (91-132/178-191)	5.00	2.00

❑ 91-132/178-191 OVERALL FW ODDS 1:24
❑ 91-132/178-179/181-191 PRINT 704 #'d SETS
❑ 91-132/178-179/181-191 #'d FROM 296-999
❑ CARD 180 PRINT RUN 999 #'d COPIES

Card		
❑ CARD 180 #'d FROM 1-999		
❑ COMMON CARD (133-177)	3.00	1.25
❑ 133-177 STATED ODDS 1:24		
❑ 133-177 PRINT RUN 999 SERIAL #'d SETS		
❑ 1 Bret Boone	.40	.15
❑ 2 Gary Sheffield	.40	.15
❑ 3 Rafael Palmeiro	.60	.25
❑ 4 Jorge Posada	.60	.25
❑ 5 Derek Jeter	2.00	.75
❑ 6 Garret Anderson	.40	.15
❑ 7 Bartolo Colon	.40	.15
❑ 8 Kevin Brown	.40	.15
❑ 9 Shea Hillenbrand	.40	.15
❑ 10 Ryan Klesko	.40	.15
❑ 11 Bobby Abreu	.40	.15
❑ 12 Scott Rolen	.60	.25
❑ 13 Alfonso Soriano	.40	.15
❑ 14 Jason Giambi	.40	.15
❑ 15 Tom Glavine	.60	.25
❑ 16 Hideo Nomo	1.00	.40
❑ 17 Johan Santana	1.00	.40
❑ 18 Sammy Sosa	1.00	.40
❑ 19 Rickie Weeks	.40	.15
❑ 20 Barry Zito	.40	.15
❑ 21 Kerry Wood	.40	.15
❑ 22 Austin Kearns	.40	.15
❑ 23 Shawn Green	.40	.15
❑ 24 Miguel Cabrera	.60	.25
❑ 25 Richard Hidalgo	.40	.15
❑ 26 Andruw Jones	.60	.25
❑ 27 Randy Wolf	.40	.15
❑ 28 David Ortiz	1.00	.40
❑ 29 Roy Oswalt	.40	.15
❑ 30 Vernon Wells	.40	.15
❑ 31 Ben Sheets	.40	.15
❑ 32 Mike Lowell	.40	.15
❑ 33 Todd Helton	.60	.25
❑ 34 Jacque Jones	.40	.15
❑ 35 Mike Sweeney	.40	.15
❑ 36 Hank Blalock	.40	.15
❑ 37 Jason Schmidt	.40	.15
❑ 38 Jeff Kent	.40	.15
❑ 39 Josh Beckett	.40	.15
❑ 40 Manny Ramirez	.60	.25
❑ 41 Torii Hunter	.40	.15
❑ 42 Brian Giles	.40	.15
❑ 43 Javier Vazquez	.40	.15
❑ 44 Jim Edmonds	.40	.15
❑ 45 Dmitri Young	.40	.15
❑ 46 Preston Wilson	.40	.15
❑ 47 Jeff Bagwell	.60	.25
❑ 48 Pedro Martinez	.60	.25
❑ 49 Eric Chavez	.40	.15
❑ 50 Ken Griffey Jr.	1.50	.60
❑ 51 Shannon Stewart	.40	.15
❑ 52 Rafael Furcal	.40	.15
❑ 53 Brandon Webb	.40	.15
❑ 54 Juan Pierre	.40	.15
❑ 55 Roger Clemens	2.00	.75
❑ 56 Geoff Jenkins	.40	.15
❑ 57 Lance Berkman	.40	.15
❑ 58 Albert Pujols	2.00	.75
❑ 59 Frank Thomas	1.00	.40
❑ 60 Edgar Martinez	.60	.25
❑ 61 Tim Hudson	.40	.15
❑ 62 Eric Gagne	.40	.15
❑ 63 Richie Sexson	.40	.15
❑ 64 Corey Patterson	.40	.15
❑ 65 Nomar Garciaparra	1.50	.60
❑ 66 Hideki Matsui	1.50	.60
❑ 67 Mark Teixeira	.60	.25
❑ 68 Troy Glaus	.40	.15
❑ 69 Carlos Lee	.40	.15
❑ 70 Mike Mussina	.60	.25
❑ 71 Magglio Ordonez	.40	.15
❑ 72 Roy Halladay	.40	.15
❑ 73 Ichiro Suzuki	2.00	.75
❑ 74 Randy Johnson	1.00	.40
❑ 75 Luis Gonzalez	.40	.15
❑ 76 Mark Prior	.60	.25
❑ 77 Carlos Beltran	.40	.15
❑ 78 Ivan Rodriguez	.60	.25
❑ 79 Alex Rodriguez	1.50	.60
❑ 80 Dontrelle Willis	.60	.25
❑ 81 Mike Piazza	1.50	.60
❑ 82 Curt Schilling	.60	.25
❑ 83 Vladimir Guerrero	1.00	.40
❑ 84 Greg Maddux	1.50	.60
❑ 85 Jim Thome	.60	.25
❑ 86 Miguel Tejada	.40	.15
❑ 87 Carlos Delgado	.40	.15
❑ 88 Jose Reyes	.40	.15
❑ 89 Matt Morris	.40	.15
❑ 90 Mark Mulder	.40	.15
❑ 91 Angel Chavez FW RC	5.00	2.00
❑ 92 Brandon Medders FW RC	5.00	2.00
❑ 93 Carlos Vasquez FW RC	5.00	2.00
❑ 94 Chris Aguila FW RC	5.00	2.00
❑ 95 Colby Miller FW RC	5.00	2.00
❑ 96 Dave Crouthers FW RC	5.00	2.00
❑ 97 Dennis Sarfate FW RC	5.00	2.00
❑ 98 Donnie Kelly FW RC	5.00	2.00
❑ 99 Merkin Valdez FW RC	5.00	2.00
❑ 100 Eddy Rodriguez FW RC	5.00	2.00
❑ 101 Edwin Moreno FW RC	5.00	2.00
❑ 102 Enemencio Pacheco FW RC	5.00	2.00
❑ 103 Roberto Novoa FW RC	5.00	2.00
❑ 104 Greg Dobbs FW RC	5.00	2.00
❑ 105 Hector Gimenez FW RC	5.00	2.00
❑ 106 Ian Snell FW RC	8.00	3.00
❑ 107 Jake Woods FW RC	5.00	2.00
❑ 108 Jamie Brown FW RC	5.00	2.00
❑ 109 Jason Frasor FW RC	5.00	2.00
❑ 110 Jerome Gamble FW RC	5.00	2.00
❑ 111 Jerry Gil FW RC	5.00	2.00
❑ 112 Jesse Harper FW RC	5.00	2.00
❑ 113 Jorge Vasquez FW RC	5.00	2.00
❑ 114 Jose Capellan FW RC	5.00	2.00
❑ 115 Josh Labandeira FW RC	5.00	2.00
❑ 116 Justin Hampson FW RC	5.00	2.00
❑ 117 Justin Huisman FW RC	5.00	2.00
❑ 118 Justin Leone FW RC	5.00	2.00
❑ 119 Lincoln Holdzkom FW RC	5.00	2.00
❑ 120 Lino Urdaneta FW RC	5.00	2.00
❑ 121 Mike Gosling FW RC	5.00	2.00
❑ 122 Mike Johnston FW RC	5.00	2.00
❑ 123 Mike Rouse FW RC	5.00	2.00
❑ 124 Scott Proctor FW RC	5.00	2.00
❑ 125 Roman Colon FW RC	5.00	2.00
❑ 126 Ronny Cedeno FW RC	8.00	3.00
❑ 127 Ryan Meaux FW RC	5.00	2.00
❑ 128 Scott Dohmann FW RC	5.00	2.00
❑ 129 Sean Henn FW RC	5.00	2.00
❑ 130 Tim Bausher FW RC	5.00	2.00
❑ 131 Tim Bittner FW RC	5.00	2.00
❑ 132 William Bergolla FW RC	5.00	2.00
❑ 133 Rick Ferrell ASM	3.00	1.25
❑ 134 Joe DiMaggio ASM	5.00	2.00
❑ 135 Bob Feller ASM	3.00	1.25
❑ 136 Ted Williams ASM	8.00	3.00
❑ 137 Stan Musial ASM	5.00	2.00
❑ 138 Larry Doby ASM	3.00	1.25
❑ 139 Red Schoendienst ASM	3.00	1.25
❑ 140 Enos Slaughter ASM	3.00	1.25
❑ 141 Stan Musial ASM	5.00	2.00
❑ 142 Mickey Mantle ASM	10.00	4.00
❑ 143 Ted Williams ASM	8.00	3.00
❑ 144 Mickey Mantle ASM	10.00	4.00
❑ 145 Stan Musial ASM	5.00	2.00
❑ 146 Tom Seaver ASM	4.00	1.50
❑ 147 Willie McCovey ASM	4.00	1.50
❑ 148 Bob Gibson ASM	4.00	1.50
❑ 149 Frank Robinson ASM	3.00	1.25
❑ 150 Joe Morgan ASM	3.00	1.25
❑ 151 Billy Williams ASM	3.00	1.25
❑ 152 Catfish Hunter ASM	4.00	1.50
❑ 153 Joe Morgan ASM	3.00	1.25
❑ 154 Joe Morgan ASM	3.00	1.25
❑ 155 Mike Schmidt ASM	8.00	3.00
❑ 156 Tommy Lasorda ASM	3.00	1.25
❑ 157 Robin Yount ASM	4.00	1.50
❑ 158 Nolan Ryan ASM	10.00	4.00
❑ 159 John Franco ASM	3.00	1.25
❑ 160 Nolan Ryan ASM	10.00	4.00
❑ 161 Ken Griffey Jr. ASM	5.00	2.00
❑ 162 Cal Ripken ASM	10.00	4.00
❑ 163 Ken Griffey Jr. ASM	5.00	2.00
❑ 164 Gary Sheffield ASM	3.00	1.25
❑ 165 Fred McGriff ASM	4.00	1.50
❑ 166 Hideo Nomo ASM	4.00	1.50
❑ 167 Mike Piazza ASM	5.00	2.00
❑ 168 Sandy Alomar Jr. ASM	3.00	1.25
❑ 169 Roberto Alomar ASM	4.00	1.50
❑ 170 Ted Williams ASM	8.00	3.00
❑ 171 Pedro Martinez ASM	4.00	1.50
❑ 172 Derek Jeter ASM	6.00	2.50
❑ 173 Cal Ripken ASM	10.00	4.00
❑ 174 Torii Hunter ASM	3.00	1.25
❑ 175 Alfonso Soriano ASM	3.00	1.25
❑ 176 Hank Blalock ASM	3.00	1.25
❑ 177 Ichiro Suzuki ASM	6.00	2.50
❑ 178 Orlando Rodriguez FW RC	5.00	2.00
❑ 179 Ramon Ramirez FW RC	5.00	2.00
❑ 180 Kazuo Matsui FW RC	5.00	2.00
❑ 181 Kevin Cave FW RC	5.00	2.00
❑ 182 John Gall FW RC	5.00	2.00
❑ 183 Freddy Guzman FW RC	5.00	2.00
❑ 184 Chris Oxspring FW RC	5.00	2.00
❑ 185 Rusty Tucker FW RC	5.00	2.00
❑ 186 Jorge Sequea FW RC	5.00	2.00
❑ 187 Carlos Hines FW RC	5.00	2.00
❑ 188 Michael Vento FW RC	5.00	2.00
❑ 189 Ryan Wing FW RC	5.00	2.00
❑ 190 Jeff Bennett FW RC	5.00	2.00
❑ 191 Luis A. Gonzalez FW RC	5.00	2.00

2005 SP Authentic

Card		
❑ COMP.BASIC SET (100)	25.00	10.00
❑ COMMON CARD (1-100)	.40	.15
❑ COMMON RETIRED 1-100	.40	.15
❑ 1-100 ISSUED IN 05 SP COLLECTION PACKS		
❑ COMMON AUTO (101-186)	10.00	4.00
❑ 101-186 ODDS APPX 1:8 '05 UD UPDATE		
❑ 101-186 PRINT RUN 185 SERIAL #'d SETS		
❑ 105, 115, 118-119, 142, 154 DO NOT EXIST		
❑ 161, 180, 183, 186 DO NOT EXIST		
❑ 1 A.J. Burnett	.40	.15
❑ 2 Aaron Rowand	.40	.15
❑ 3 Adam Dunn	.40	.15
❑ 4 Adrian Beltre	.40	.15
❑ 5 Adrian Gonzalez	.40	.15
❑ 6 Akinori Otsuka	.40	.15
❑ 7 Albert Pujols	2.00	.75
❑ 8 Andre Dawson	.40	.15
❑ 9 Andruw Jones	.60	.25
❑ 10 Aramis Ramirez	.40	.15
❑ 11 Barry Larkin	.60	.25
❑ 12 Ben Sheets	.40	.15
❑ 13 Bo Jackson	1.00	.40
❑ 14 Bobby Abreu	.40	.15
❑ 15 Bobby Crosby	.40	.15
❑ 16 Bronson Arroyo	.40	.15
❑ 17 Cal Ripken	3.00	1.25
❑ 18 Carl Crawford	.40	.15
❑ 19 Carlos Zambrano	.40	.15
❑ 20 Casey Kotchman	.40	.15
❑ 21 Cesar Izturis	.40	.15
❑ 22 Chone Figgins	.40	.15
❑ 23 Corey Patterson	.40	.15
❑ 24 Craig Biggio	.60	.25
❑ 25 Dale Murphy	.60	.25
❑ 26 Dallas McPherson	.40	.15
❑ 27 Danny Haren	.40	.15
❑ 28 Darryl Strawberry	.40	.15
❑ 29 David Ortiz	.60	.25
❑ 30 David Wright	1.50	.60
❑ 31 Derek Jeter	2.00	.75
❑ 32 Derrek Lee	.60	.25
❑ 33 Don Mattingly	2.00	.75
❑ 34 Dwight Gooden	.40	.15

	Card		
❑	35 Edgar Renteria	.40	.15
❑	36 Eric Chavez	.40	.15
❑	37 Eric Gagne	.40	.15
❑	38 Gary Sheffield	.40	.15
❑	39 Gavin Floyd	.40	.15
❑	40 Pedro Martinez	.60	.25
❑	41 Greg Maddux	1.50	.60
❑	42 Hank Blalock	.40	.15
❑	43 Huston Street	.60	.25
❑	44 J.D. Drew	.40	.15
❑	45 Jake Peavy	.40	.15
❑	46 Jake Westbrook	.40	.15
❑	47 Jason Bay	.40	.15
❑	48 Austin Kearns	.40	.15
❑	49 Jeremy Reed	.40	.15
❑	50 Jim Rice	.40	.15
❑	51 Jimmy Rollins	.40	.15
❑	52 Joe Blanton	.40	.15
❑	53 Joe Mauer	1.00	.40
❑	54 Johan Santana	1.00	.40
❑	55 John Smoltz	.60	.25
❑	56 Johnny Estrada	.40	.15
❑	57 Jose Reyes	.40	.15
❑	58 Ken Griffey Jr.	1.50	.60
❑	59 Kerry Wood	.40	.15
❑	60 Khalil Greene	.60	.25
❑	61 Marcus Giles	.40	.15
❑	62 Melvin Mora	.40	.15
❑	63 Mark Grace	.60	.25
❑	64 Mark Mulder	.40	.15
❑	65 Mark Prior	.60	.25
❑	66 Mark Teixeria	.60	.25
❑	67 Matt Clement	.40	.15
❑	68 Michael Young	.40	.15
❑	69 Miguel Cabrera	.60	.25
❑	70 Miguel Tejada	.40	.15
❑	71 Mike Piazza	1.00	.40
❑	72 Mike Schmidt	2.00	.75
❑	73 Nolan Ryan	2.50	1.00
❑	74 Oliver Perez	.40	.15
❑	75 Nick Johnson	.40	.15
❑	76 Paul Molitor	.40	.15
❑	77 Rafael Palmeiro	.60	.25
❑	78 Randy Johnson	1.00	.40
❑	79 Reggie Jackson	.60	.25
❑	80 Rich Harden	.40	.15
❑	81 Rickie Weeks	.40	.15
❑	82 Robin Yount	1.00	.40
❑	83 Roger Clemens	1.50	.60
❑	84 Roy Oswalt	.40	.15
❑	85 Ryan Howard	2.50	1.00
❑	86 Ryne Sandberg	2.00	.75
❑	87 Scott Kazmir	.40	.15
❑	88 Scott Rolen	.60	.25
❑	89 Sean Burroughs	.40	.15
❑	90 Sean Casey	.40	.15
❑	91 Shingo Takatsu	.40	.15
❑	92 Tim Hudson	.40	.15
❑	93 Tony Gwynn	1.25	.50
❑	94 Torii Hunter	.40	.15
❑	95 Travis Hafner	.40	.15
❑	96 Victor Martinez	.40	.15
❑	97 Vladimir Guerrero	1.00	.40
❑	98 Wade Boggs	.60	.25
❑	99 Will Clark	.60	.25
❑	100 Yadier Molina	.40	.15
❑	101 Adam Shabala AU RC	10.00	4.00
❑	102 Ambiorix Burgos AU RC	10.00	4.00
❑	103 Ambiorix Concepcion AU RC	10.004.00	
❑	104 Anibal Sanchez AU RC	40.00	15.00
❑	106 Brandon McCarthy AU RC	40.00	15.00
❑	107 Brian Burres AU RC	10.00	4.00
❑	108 Carlos Ruiz AU RC	25.00	10.00
❑	109 Casey Rogowski AU RC	15.00	6.00
❑	110 Chad Orvella AU RC	10.00	4.00
❑	111 Chris Resop AU RC	15.00	6.00
❑	112 Chris Roberson AU RC	10.00	4.00
❑	113 Chris Seddon AU RC	10.00	4.00
❑	114 Colter Bean AU RC	15.00	6.00
❑	116 Dave Gassner AU RC	10.00	4.00
❑	117 Brian Anderson AU RC	40.00	15.00
❑	120 Devon Lowery AU RC	10.00	4.00
❑	121 Enrique Gonzalez AU RC	15.00	6.00
❑	122 Eude Brito AU RC	10.00	4.00
❑	123 Francisco Butto AU RC	10.00	4.00
❑	124 Franquelis Osoria AU RC	10.00	4.00
❑	125 Garrett Jones AU RC	10.00	4.00
❑	126 Geovany Soto AU RC	200.00	150.00
❑	127 Hayden Penn AU RC	25.00	10.00
❑	128 Ismael Ramirez AU RC	10.00	4.00
❑	129 Jared Gothreaux AU RC	10.00	4.00
❑	130 Jason Hammel AU RC	10.00	4.00
❑	131 Jeff Miller AU RC	10.00	4.00
❑	132 Jeff Niemann AU RC	30.00	12.50
❑	133 Joel Peralta AU RC	10.00	4.00
❑	134 John Hattig AU RC	10.00	4.00
❑	135 Jorge Campillo AU RC	10.00	4.00
❑	136 Juan Morillo AU RC	10.00	4.00
❑	137 Justin Verlander AU RC	150.00	90.00
❑	138 Ryan Garko AU RC	50.00	25.00
❑	139 Keiichi Yabu AU RC	15.00	6.00
❑	140 Kendry Morales AU RC	60.00	30.00
❑	141 Luis Hernandez AU RC	10.00	4.00
❑	143 Luis O.Rodriguez AU RC	10.00	4.00
❑	144 Luke Scott AU RC	60.00	30.00
❑	145 Marcos Carvajal AU RC	10.00	4.00
❑	146 Mark Woodyard AU RC	10.00	4.00
❑	147 Matt A.Smith AU RC	10.00	4.00
❑	148 Matthew Lindstrom AU RC	10.00	4.00
❑	149 Miguel Negron AU RC	15.00	6.00
❑	150 Mike Morse AU RC	20.00	8.00
❑	151 Nate McLouth AU RC	100.00	50.00
❑	152 Nelson Cruz AU RC	50.00	25.00
❑	153 Nick Masset AU RC	10.00	4.00
❑	155 Paulino Reynoso AU RC	10.00	4.00
❑	156 Pedro Lopez AU RC	10.00	4.00
❑	157 Pete Orr AU RC	10.00	4.00
❑	158 Philip Humber AU RC	30.00	12.50
❑	159 Prince Fielder AU RC	300.00	225.00
❑	160 Randy Messenger AU RC	10.00	4.00
❑	162 Raul Tablado AU RC	10.00	4.00
❑	163 Ronny Paulino AU RC	25.00	10.00
❑	164 Russ Rohlicek AU RC	10.00	4.00
❑	165 Russell Martin AU RC	120.00	60.00
❑	166 Scott Baker AU RC	15.00	6.00
❑	167 Scott Munter AU RC	10.00	4.00
❑	168 Sean Thompson AU RC	10.00	4.00
❑	169 Sean Tracey AU RC	10.00	4.00
❑	170 Shane Costa AU RC	10.00	4.00
❑	171 Stephen Drew AU RC	60.00	30.00
❑	172 Steve Schmoll AU RC	10.00	4.00
❑	173 Tadahito Iguchi AU RC	50.00	20.00
❑	174 Tony Giarratano AU RC	10.00	4.00
❑	175 Tony Pena AU RC	10.00	4.00
❑	176 Travis Bowyer AU RC	10.00	4.00
❑	177 Ubaldo Jimenez AU RC	50.00	20.00
❑	178 Wladimir Balentien AU RC	100.0050.00	
❑	179 Yorman Bazardo AU RC	10.00	4.00
❑	181 Ryan Zimmerman AU RC	225.00150.00	
❑	182 Chris Denorfia AU RC	25.00	10.00
❑	184 Jermaine Van Buren AU	10.00	4.00
❑	185 Mark McLemore AU RC	10.00	4.00

2006 SP Authentic

	Card		
❑	COMP.SET w/o SP's (100)	15.00	6.00
❑	1 Erik Bedard	.40	.15
❑	2 Corey Patterson	.40	.15
❑	3 Ramon Hernandez	.40	.15
❑	4 Kris Benson	.40	.15
❑	5 Miguel Batista	.40	.15
❑	6 Orlando Hudson	.40	.15
❑	7 Shawn Green	.40	.15
❑	8 Jeff Francoeur	1.00	.40
❑	9 Marcus Giles	.40	.15
❑	10 Edgar Renteria	.40	.15
❑	11 Tim Hudson	.40	.15
❑	12 Tim Wakefield	.40	.15
❑	13 Mark Loretta	.40	.15
❑	14 Kevin Youkilis	.40	.15
❑	15 Mike Lowell	.40	.15
❑	16 Coco Crisp	.40	.15
❑	17 Tadahito Iguchi	.40	.15
❑	18 Scott Podsednik	.40	.15
❑	19 Jermaine Dye	.40	.15
❑	20 Jose Contreras	.40	.15
❑	21 Carlos Zambrano	.40	.15
❑	22 Aramis Ramirez	.40	.15
❑	23 Jacque Jones	.40	.15
❑	24 Austin Kearns	.40	.15
❑	25 Felipe Lopez	.40	.15
❑	26 Brandon Phillips	.40	.15
❑	27 Aaron Harang	.40	.15
❑	28 Cliff Lee	.40	.15
❑	29 Jhonny Peralta	.40	.15
❑	30 Jason Michaels	.40	.15
❑	31 Clint Barmes	.40	.15
❑	32 Brad Hawpe	.40	.15
❑	33 Aaron Cook	.40	.15
❑	34 Kenny Rogers	.40	.15
❑	35 Carlos Guillen	.40	.15
❑	36 Brian Moehler	.40	.15
❑	37 Andy Pettitte	.60	.25
❑	38 Wandy Rodriguez	.40	.15
❑	39 Morgan Ensberg	.40	.15
❑	40 Preston Wilson	.40	.15
❑	41 Mark Grudzielanek	.40	.15
❑	42 Angel Berroa	.40	.15
❑	43 Jeremy Affeldt	.40	.15
❑	44 Zack Greinke	.40	.15
❑	45 Orlando Cabrera	.40	.15
❑	46 Garret Anderson	.40	.15
❑	47 Ervin Santana	.40	.15
❑	48 Derek Lowe	.40	.15
❑	49 Nomar Garciaparra	1.00	.40
❑	50 J.D. Drew	.40	.15
❑	51 Rafael Furcal	.40	.15
❑	52 Rickie Weeks	.40	.15
❑	53 Geoff Jenkins	.40	.15
❑	54 Bill Hall	.40	.15
❑	55 Chris Capuano	.40	.15
❑	56 Derrick Turnbow	.40	.15
❑	57 Justin Morneau	.40	.15
❑	58 Michael Cuddyer	.40	.15
❑	59 Luis Castillo	.40	.15
❑	60 Hideki Matsui	1.00	.40
❑	61 Jason Giambi	.40	.15
❑	62 Jorge Posada	.60	.25
❑	63 Mariano Rivera	1.00	.40
❑	64 Billy Wagner	.40	.15
❑	65 Carlos Delgado	.40	.15
❑	66 Jose Reyes	1.00	.40
❑	67 Nick Swisher	.40	.15
❑	68 Bobby Crosby	.40	.15
❑	69 Frank Thomas	1.00	.40
❑	70 Ryan Howard	1.50	.60
❑	71 Pat Burrell	.40	.15
❑	72 Jimmy Rollins	.40	.15
❑	73 Craig Wilson	.40	.15
❑	74 Freddy Sanchez	.40	.15
❑	75 Sean Casey	.40	.15
❑	76 Mike Piazza	1.00	.40
❑	77 Dave Roberts	.40	.15
❑	78 Chris Young	.40	.15
❑	79 Noah Lowry	.40	.15
❑	80 Armando Benitez	.40	.15
❑	81 Pedro Feliz	.40	.15
❑	82 Jose Lopez	.40	.15
❑	83 Adrian Beltre	.40	.15
❑	84 Jamie Moyer	.40	.15
❑	85 Jason Isringhausen	.40	.15
❑	86 Jason Marquis	.40	.15
❑	87 David Eckstein	.40	.15
❑	88 Juan Encarnacion	.40	.15
❑	89 Julio Lugo	.40	.15
❑	90 Ty Wigginton	.40	.15
❑	91 Jorge Cantu	.40	.15
❑	92 Akinori Otsuka	.40	.15
❑	93 Hank Blalock	.40	.15
❑	94 Kevin Mench	.40	.15
❑	95 Lyle Overbay	.40	.15

❑ 96 Shea Hillenbrand .40 .15
❑ 97 B.J. Ryan .40 .15
❑ 98 Tony Armas .40 .15
❑ 99 Chad Cordero .40 .15
❑ 100 Jose Guillen .40 .15
❑ 101 Miguel Tejada 4.00 1.50
❑ 102 Brian Roberts 4.00 1.50
❑ 103 Melvin Mora 4.00 1.50
❑ 104 Brandon Webb 4.00 1.50
❑ 105 Chad Tracy 4.00 1.50
❑ 106 Luis Gonzalez 4.00 1.50
❑ 107 Andruw Jones 5.00 2.00
❑ 108 Chipper Jones 5.00 2.00
❑ 109 John Smoltz 5.00 2.00
❑ 110 Curt Schilling 5.00 2.00
❑ 111 Josh Beckett 4.00 1.50
❑ 112 David Ortiz 5.00 2.00
❑ 113 Manny Ramirez 5.00 2.00
❑ 114 Jason Varitek 5.00 2.00
❑ 115 Jim Thome 5.00 2.00
❑ 116 Paul Konerko 4.00 1.50
❑ 117 Javier Vazquez 4.00 1.50
❑ 118 Mark Prior 4.00 1.50
❑ 119 Derrek Lee 4.00 1.50
❑ 120 Greg Maddux 8.00 3.00
❑ 121 Ken Griffey Jr. 8.00 3.00
❑ 122 Adam Dunn 4.00 1.50
❑ 123 Bronson Arroyo 5.00 2.00
❑ 124 Travis Hafner 4.00 1.50
❑ 125 Victor Martinez 4.00 1.50
❑ 126 Grady Sizemore 5.00 2.00
❑ 127 C.C. Sabathia 4.00 1.50
❑ 128 Todd Helton 5.00 2.00
❑ 129 Matt Holliday 5.00 2.00
❑ 130 Garrett Atkins 4.00 1.50
❑ 131 Jeff Francis 4.00 1.50
❑ 132 Jeremy Bonderman 4.00 1.50
❑ 133 Ivan Rodriguez 5.00 2.00
❑ 134 Chris Shelton 4.00 1.50
❑ 135 Magglio Ordonez 4.00 1.50
❑ 136 Dontrelle Willis 4.00 1.50
❑ 137 Miguel Cabrera 5.00 2.00
❑ 138 Roger Clemens 8.00 3.00
❑ 139 Roy Oswalt 4.00 1.50
❑ 140 Lance Berkman 4.00 1.50
❑ 141 Reggie Sanders 4.00 1.50
❑ 142 Vladimir Guerrero 5.00 2.00
❑ 143 Bartolo Colon 4.00 1.50
❑ 144 Chone Figgins 4.00 1.50
❑ 145 Francisco Rodriguez 4.00 1.50
❑ 146 Brad Penny 4.00 1.50
❑ 147 Jeff Kent 4.00 1.50
❑ 148 Eric Gagne 4.00 1.50
❑ 149 Carlos Lee 4.00 1.50
❑ 150 Ben Sheets 4.00 1.50
❑ 151 Johan Santana 5.00 2.00
❑ 152 Torii Hunter 4.00 1.50
❑ 153 Joe Nathan 4.00 1.50
❑ 154 Alex Rodriguez 8.00 3.00
❑ 155 Derek Jeter 10.00 4.00
❑ 156 Randy Johnson 5.00 2.00
❑ 157 Johnny Damon 5.00 2.00
❑ 158 Mike Mussina 5.00 2.00
❑ 159 Pedro Martinez 5.00 2.00
❑ 160 Tom Glavine 5.00 2.00
❑ 161 David Wright 8.00 3.00
❑ 162 Carlos Beltran 4.00 1.50
❑ 163 Rich Harden 4.00 1.50
❑ 164 Barry Zito 4.00 1.50
❑ 165 Eric Chavez 4.00 1.50
❑ 166 Huston Street 4.00 1.50
❑ 167 Bobby Abreu 4.00 1.50
❑ 168 Chase Utley 5.00 2.00
❑ 169 Brett Myers 4.00 1.50
❑ 170 Jason Bay 4.00 1.50
❑ 171 Zach Duke 4.00 1.50
❑ 172 Jake Peavy 4.00 1.50
❑ 173 Brian Giles 4.00 1.50
❑ 174 Khalil Greene 5.00 2.00
❑ 175 Trevor Hoffman 4.00 1.50
❑ 176 Jason Schmidt 4.00 1.50
❑ 177 Randy Winn 4.00 1.50
❑ 178 Omar Vizquel 5.00 2.00
❑ 179 Kenji Johjima 8.00 3.00
❑ 180 Ichiro Suzuki 8.00 3.00
❑ 181 Richie Sexson 4.00 1.50
❑ 182 Felix Hernandez 5.00 2.00
❑ 183 Albert Pujols 10.00 4.00
❑ 184 Chris Carpenter 5.00 2.00
❑ 185 Jim Edmonds 5.00 2.00
❑ 186 Scott Rolen 5.00 2.00
❑ 187 Carl Crawford 4.00 1.50
❑ 188 Scott Kazmir 4.00 1.50
❑ 189 Jonny Gomes 4.00 1.50
❑ 190 Mark Teixeira 5.00 2.00
❑ 191 Michael Young 4.00 1.50
❑ 192 Kevin Millwood 4.00 1.50
❑ 193 Vernon Wells 4.00 1.50
❑ 194 Troy Glaus 4.00 1.50
❑ 195 Roy Halladay 4.00 1.50
❑ 196 Alex Rios 4.00 1.50
❑ 197 Nick Johnson 4.00 1.50
❑ 198 Livan Hernandez 4.00 1.50
❑ 199 Alfonso Soriano 4.00 1.50
❑ 200 Jose Vidro 4.00 1.50
❑ 201 A.Rakers AU/399 (RC) 8.00 3.00
❑ 202 A.Pagan AU/399 (RC) 15.00 6.00
❑ 203 B.Hendrick AU/399 (RC) 8.00 3.00
❑ 204 B.Livingston AU/399 (RC) 8.00 3.00
❑ 205 D.Rasner AU/399 (RC) 8.00 3.00
❑ 206 B.Bannister AU/399 (RC) 30.00 12.50
❑ 207 B.Wilson AU/899 RC 8.00 3.00
❑ 208 B.Keppel AU/199 (RC) 15.00 6.00
❑ 209 C.Freeman AU/399 (RC) 8.00 3.00
❑ 210 C.Booker AU/899 (RC) 8.00 3.00
❑ 211 C.Britton AU/399 (RC) 10.00 4.00
❑ 212 C.Demaria AU/329 RC 10.00 4.00
❑ 213 C.Resop AU/899 (RC) 8.00 3.00
❑ 214 T.Gwynn Jr. AU/399 (RC) 60.00 30.00
❑ 215 E.Reed AU/399 (RC) 8.00 3.00
❑ 216 F.Castro AU/399 RC 20.00 8.00
❑ 217 F.Nieve AU/299 (RC) 10.00 4.00
❑ 218 F.Bynum AU/899 (RC) 8.00 3.00
❑ 219 G.Quiroz AU/399 (RC) 8.00 3.00
❑ 220 H.Kuo AU/899 (RC) 60.00 30.00
❑ 221 R.Theriot AU/399 RC 60.00 30.00
❑ 222 J.Taschner AU/899 (RC) 8.00 3.00
❑ 223 J.Bergmann AU/899 (RC) 8.00 3.00
❑ 224 J.Hammel AU/899 (RC) 8.00 3.00
❑ 225 J.Harris AU/399 RC 8.00 3.00
❑ 226 J.Accardo AU/399 RC 10.00 4.00
❑ 227 T.Taubenheim AU/399 RC 30.00 12.50
❑ 228 J.Zumaya AU/399 (RC) 40.00 15.00
❑ 229 J.Koronka AU/399 (RC) 8.00 3.00
❑ 230 E.Aybar AU/399 (RC) 8.00 3.00
❑ 231 J.Tata AU/399 RC 15.00 6.00
❑ 232 R.Martin AU/399 (RC) 40.00 15.00
❑ 233 J.Rupe AU/399 (RC) 8.00 3.00
❑ 234 K.Frandsen AU/399 (RC) 15.00 6.00
❑ 235 M.Prado AU/399 (RC) 15.00 6.00
❑ 236 M.Capps AU/399 (RC) 8.00 3.00
❑ 237 A.Montero AU/199 (RC) 10.00 4.00
❑ 238 M.Thompson AU/399 RC 8.00 3.00
❑ 239 N.McLouth AU/399 (RC) 20.00 8.00
❑ 240 P.Moylan AU/399 RC 8.00 3.00
❑ 241 R.Abercrom AU/399 (RC) 8.00 3.00
❑ 242 C.Quentin AU/399 (RC) 20.00 8.00
❑ 243 H.Flores AU/399 RC 8.00 3.00
❑ 244 R.Shealy AU/399 (RC) 20.00 8.00
❑ 245 M.Rouse AU/399 (RC) 8.00 3.00
❑ 246 S.Ramirez AU/399 (RC) 8.00 3.00
❑ 247 C.Hensley AU/899 (RC) 8.00 3.00
❑ 248 S.Schumaker AU/399 (RC) 10.00 4.00
❑ 249 E.Alfonzo AU/899 RC 8.00 3.00
❑ 250 S.Stemle AU/399 RC 8.00 3.00
❑ 251 T.Hamulack AU/399 (RC) 8.00 3.00
❑ 252 T.Pena Jr. AU/299 (RC) 10.00 4.00
❑ 253 E.Fruto AU/899 RC 8.00 3.00
❑ 254 W.Nieves AU/399 (RC) 10.00 4.00
❑ 255 J.Devine AU/399 RC 10.00 4.00
❑ 256 A.Wainwright AU/399 (RC) 25.00 10.00
❑ 257 A.Ethier AU/399 (RC) 25.00 10.00
❑ 258 B.Johnson AU/399 (RC) 8.00 3.00
❑ 259 B.Logan AU/399 RC 15.00 6.00
❑ 260 C.Denorfia AU/899 (RC) 10.00 4.00
❑ 261 A.Soler AU/299 RC 15.00 6.00
❑ 262 C.Ross AU/899 (RC) 8.00 3.00
❑ 263 D.Gassner AU/399 (RC) 8.00 3.00
❑ 264 F.Carmona AU/399 (RC) 40.00 15.00
❑ 265 J.Sowers AU/299 (RC) 25.00 10.00
❑ 266 J.Kubel AU/399 (RC) 10.00 4.00
❑ 267 J.VanBenSch AU/399 (RC) 8.00 3.00
❑ 268 J.Capellan AU/399 (RC) 8.00 3.00
❑ 269 J.Wilson AU/399 (RC) 8.00 3.00
❑ 270 K.Shoppach AU/399 (RC) 8.00 3.00
❑ 271 M.McBride AU/399 (RC) 10.00 4.00
❑ 272 M.Cain AU/399 (RC) 25.00 10.00
❑ 273 M.Jacobs AU/399 (RC) 15.00 6.00
❑ 274 P.Maholm AU/399 (RC) 10.00 4.00
❑ 275 C.Billingsley AU/399 (RC) 25.00 10.00
❑ 276 R.Lugo AU/399 (RC) 8.00 3.00
❑ 277 J.Lester AU/399 RC 50.00 20.00
❑ 278 S.Marshall AU/383 (RC) 25.00 10.00
❑ 279 Me.Cabrera AU/399 (RC) 40.00 15.00
❑ 280 Y.Petit AU/399 (RC) 10.00 4.00
❑ 281 A.Hernandez AU/299 (RC) 10.00 4.00
❑ 282 B.Anderson AU/699 (RC) 10.00 4.00
❑ 283 C.Hamels AU/299 (RC) 50.00 20.00
❑ 284 B.Bonser AU/299 (RC) 15.00 6.00
❑ 285 D.Uggla AU/199 (RC) 50.00 20.00
❑ 286 F.Liriano AU/299 (RC) 40.00 15.00
❑ 287 H.Ramirez AU/199 (RC) 60.00 30.00
❑ 288 I.Kinsler AU/299 (RC) 15.00 6.00
❑ 289 J.Hermida AU/299 (RC) 15.00 6.00
❑ 290 J.Papelbon AU/199 (RC) 60.00 30.00
❑ 291 J.Weaver AU/199 (RC) 40.00 15.00
❑ 292 J.Johnson AU/299 (RC) 15.00 6.00
❑ 293 J.Willingham AU/199 (RC) 15.00 6.00
❑ 294 J.Verlander AU/199 (RC) 80.00 40.00
❑ 295 S.Drew AU/299 (RC) 30.00 12.50
❑ 296 P.Fielder AU/125 (RC) 120.00 60.00
❑ 297 R.Zimmer AU/199 (RC) 70.00 40.00
❑ 298 T.Saito AU/283 RC 40.00 15.00
❑ 299 T.Buchholz AU/299 (RC) 10.00 4.00
❑ 300 Co.Jackson AU/299 (RC) 15.00 6.00

2007 SP Authentic

❑ COMP.SET w/o RCs (100) 15.00 6.00
❑ COMMON CARD (1-100) .40 .15
❑ COMMON AU RC (101-158) 12.00 5.00
❑ OVERALL BY THE LETTER AUTOS 1:12
❑ AU RC PRINT RUN B/WN 20-120 COPIES PER
❑ EXCHANGE DEADLINE 11/08/2008
❑ 1 Chipper Jones 1.00 .40
❑ 2 Andruw Jones .60 .25
❑ 3 John Smoltz .60 .25
❑ 4 Carlos Quentin .40 .15
❑ 5 Randy Johnson 1.00 .40
❑ 6 Brandon Webb .40 .15
❑ 7 Alfonso Soriano .40 .15
❑ 8 Derrek Lee .40 .15
❑ 9 Aramis Ramirez .40 .15
❑ 10 Carlos Zambrano .40 .15
❑ 11 Ken Griffey Jr. 1.50 .60
❑ 12 Adam Dunn .40 .15
❑ 13 Josh Hamilton 1.00 .40
❑ 14 Todd Helton .60 .25
❑ 15 Jeff Francis .40 .15
❑ 16 Matt Holliday 1.00 .40
❑ 17 Hanley Ramirez .60 .25
❑ 18 Dontrelle Willis .40 .15
❑ 19 Miguel Cabrera .60 .25
❑ 20 Lance Berkman .40 .15
❑ 21 Roy Oswalt .40 .15
❑ 22 Carlos Lee .40 .15
❑ 23 Nomar Garciaparra 1.00 .40
❑ 24 Derek Lowe .40 .15
❑ 25 Juan Pierre .40 .15
❑ 26 Rafael Furcal .40 .15
❑ 27 Rickie Weeks .40 .15

❑ 28 Prince Fielder 1.00 .40
❑ 29 Ben Sheets .40 .15
❑ 30 David Wright 1.50 .60
❑ 31 Jose Reyes 1.00 .40
❑ 32 Tom Glavine .60 .25
❑ 33 Carlos Beltran .40 .15
❑ 34 Cole Hamels .60 .25
❑ 35 Jimmy Rollins .40 .15
❑ 36 Ryan Howard 1.50 .60
❑ 37 Jason Bay .40 .15
❑ 38 Freddy Sanchez .40 .15
❑ 39 Ian Snell .40 .15
❑ 40 Jake Peavy .40 .15
❑ 41 Greg Maddux 1.50 .60
❑ 42 Trevor Hoffman .40 .15
❑ 43 Matt Cain .60 .25
❑ 44 Barry Zito .40 .15
❑ 45 Ray Durham .40 .15
❑ 46 Albert Pujols 2.00 .75
❑ 47 Chris Carpenter .40 .15
❑ 48 Jim Edmonds .60 .25
❑ 49 Scott Rolen .60 .25
❑ 50 Ryan Zimmerman 1.00 .40
❑ 51 Felipe Lopez .40 .15
❑ 52 Austin Kearns .40 .15
❑ 53 Miguel Tejada .40 .15
❑ 54 Erik Bedard .40 .15
❑ 55 Daniel Cabrera .40 .15
❑ 56 David Ortiz 1.00 .40
❑ 57 Curt Schilling .60 .25
❑ 58 Manny Ramirez .60 .25
❑ 59 Jonathan Papelbon 1.00 .40
❑ 60 Jim Thome .60 .25
❑ 61 Paul Konerko .40 .15
❑ 62 Bobby Jenks .40 .15
❑ 63 Grady Sizemore .60 .25
❑ 64 Victor Martinez .40 .15
❑ 65 Travis Hafner .40 .15
❑ 66 Ivan Rodriguez .60 .25
❑ 67 Justin Verlander 1.00 .40
❑ 68 Joel Zumaya .60 .25
❑ 69 Jeremy Bonderman .40 .15
❑ 70 Gil Meche .40 .15
❑ 71 Mike Sweeney .40 .15
❑ 72 Mark Teahen .40 .15
❑ 73 Vladimir Guerrero 1.00 .40
❑ 74 Howie Kendrick .40 .15
❑ 75 Francisco Rodriguez .40 .15
❑ 76 Johan Santana .60 .25
❑ 77 Justin Morneau .40 .15
❑ 78 Joe Mauer .60 .25
❑ 79 Joe Nathan .40 .15
❑ 80a Alex Rodriguez 1.50 .60
❑ 80b A.Rodriguez Angels
❑ 80c A.Rodriguez Cubs
❑ 80d A.Rodriguez Dodgers
❑ 80e A.Rodriguez Mets
❑ 80f A.Rodriguez Red Sox
❑ 81 Derek Jeter 2.50 1.00
❑ 82 Johnny Damon .60 .25
❑ 83 Chien-Ming Wang 1.50 .60
❑ 84 Rich Harden .40 .15
❑ 85 Mike Piazza 1.00 .40
❑ 86 Dan Haren .40 .15
❑ 87 Ichiro Suzuki 1.50 .60
❑ 88 Felix Hernandez .60 .25
❑ 89 Kenji Johjima 1.00 .40
❑ 90 Adrian Beltre .40 .15
❑ 91 Carl Crawford .40 .15
❑ 92 Scott Kazmir .60 .25
❑ 93 Delmon Young .60 .25
❑ 94 Michael Young .40 .15
❑ 95 Mark Teixeira .60 .25
❑ 96 Eric Gagne .40 .15
❑ 97 Hank Blalock .40 .15
❑ 98 Vernon Wells .40 .15
❑ 99 Roy Halladay .40 .15
❑ 100 Frank Thomas 1.00 .40
❑ 101 Joaquin Arias AU/75 (RC) 12.00 5.00
❑ 102 Jeff Baker AU (RC) EXCH 12.00 5.00
❑ 103 M.Bourn AU/75 (RC) 15.00 6.00
❑ 104 Brian Burres AU/75 (RC) 15.00 6.00
❑ 105 Jared Burton AU/75 RC 15.00 6.00
❑ 106 Ryan Braun AU/50 (RC) 150.00 60.00
❑ 109 Alex Gordon AU/50 RC 80.00 40.00
❑ 112 Sean Henn AU/75 (RC) 25.00 10.00
❑ 113 P.Hughes AU (RC) EXCH 80.00 40.00
❑ 114 Kei Igawa AU/25 RC 60.00 30.00
❑ 115 A.Iwamura AU/20 RC 80.00 40.00
❑ 119 Adam Lind AU/75 (RC) 25.00 10.00
❑ 123 Brad Salmon AU/75 RC 12.00 5.00
❑ 127 Cesar Jimenez AU RC EXCH 12.00 5.00
❑ 129 T.Tulowit AU (RC) EXCH 60.00 30.00
❑ 130 Chase Wright AU/75 RC 30.00 12.50
❑ 131 Delmon Young AU/20 (RC) 50.00 20.00
❑ 133 Brian Barden AU/75 RC 12.00 5.00
❑ 137 Billy Butler AU/75 (RC) 50.00 20.00
❑ 139 Kory Casto AU/75 (RC) 15.00 6.00
❑ 140 Matt Chico AU/75 (RC) 15.00 6.00
❑ 141 John Danks AU/75 RC 25.00 10.00
❑ 142 Andrew Miller AU/50 RC 50.00 20.00
❑ 145 D.Hansack AU RC EXCH 15.00 6.00
❑ 146 Mike Rabelo AU/75 RC 20.00 8.00
❑ 150 D.Matsuzaka AU RC 300.00 200.00
❑ 152 Micah Owings AU/75 (RC) 50.00 20.00
❑ 153 Hunter Pence AU/75 (RC) 80.00 40.00
❑ 156 Danny Putnam AU/75 (RC) 15.00 6.00
❑ 159 Doug Slaten AU/75 RC 15.00 6.00
❑ 160 Joe Smith AU/75 RC 20.00 8.00
❑ 161 Justin Upton AU/120 RC 100.00 50.00
❑ 162 J.Chamberlain AU/60 RC 200.00 100.00
❑ 107a Y.Gallardo AU/75 (RC) 50.00 20.00
❑ 107b Y.Gallardo AU/35 (RC) 60.00 30.00
❑ 108a H.Gimenez AU/75 (RC) 15.00 6.00
❑ 108b H.Gimenez AU/50 (RC) 15.00 6.00
❑ 110a J.Hamilton AU/50 (RC) 60.00 30.00
❑ 110b J.Hamilton AU/35 (RC) 80.00 40.00
❑ 111a Justin Hampson AU/75 (RC) 12.00 5.00
❑ 111b Justin Hampson AU/50 (RC) 12.00 5.00
❑ 116a M.Reynolds AU/75 RC 80.00 40.00
❑ 116b M.Reynolds AU/35 (RC) 100.00 50.00
❑ 117a Homer Bailey AU/75 (RC) 25.00 10.00
❑ 117b Homer Bailey AU/50 (RC) 25.00 10.00
❑ 118a K.Kouzmanoff AU/75 (RC) 20.00 8.00
❑ 118b K.Kouzmanoff AU/40 (RC) 20.00 8.00
❑ 120a Carlos Gomez AU/75 RC 50.00 20.00
❑ 120b Carlos Gomez AU/50 (RC) 50.00 20.00
❑ 121a Glen Perkins AU/75 (RC) 15.00 6.00
❑ 121b Glen Perkins AU/50 (RC) 15.00 6.00
❑ 122a R.Vanden Hurk AU/75 RC 25.00 10.00
❑ 122b R.Vanden Hurk AU/35 (RC) 30.00 12.50
❑ 124a Zack Segovia AU/75 (RC) 12.00 5.00
❑ 124b Zack Segovia AU/50 (RC) 12.00 5.00
❑ 125a Kurt Suzuki AU/75 (RC) 30.00 12.50
❑ 125b Kurt Suzuki AU/50 (RC) 30.00 12.50
❑ 126a Chris Stewart AU/75 RC 12.00 5.00
❑ 126b Chris Stewart AU/50 (RC) 12.00 5.00
❑ 128a Ryan Sweeney AU/50 (RC) 15.00 6.00
❑ 128b Ryan Sweeney AU/40 (RC) 15.00 6.00
❑ 132a Tony Abreu AU/75 RC 25.00 10.00
❑ 132b Tony Abreu AU/57 (RC) 25.00 10.00
❑ 132c Tony Abreu AU/50 (RC) 25.00 10.00
❑ 134a C.Thigpen AU/75 (RC) 25.00 10.00
❑ 134b C.Thigpen AU/40 (RC) 25.00 10.00
❑ 135a Jon Coutlangus AU/75 (RC) 12.00 5.00
❑ 135b Jon Coutlangus AU/55 (RC) 12.00 5.00
❑ 136a Kevin Cameron AU/75 RC 12.00 5.00
❑ 136b Kevin Cameron AU/50 (RC) 12.00 5.00
❑ 138a A.Casilla AU/75 RC 15.00 6.00
❑ 138b A.Casilla AU/50 (RC) 15.00 6.00
❑ 143a B.Francisco AU/75 (RC) 15.00 6.00
❑ 143b B.Francisco AU/40 (RC) 15.00 6.00
❑ 144a Andy Gonzalez AU/75 RC 12.00 5.00
❑ 144b Andy Gonzalez AU/50 RC 12.00 5.00
❑ 147a Tim Lincecum AU/50 RC 120.00 60.00
❑ 147b Tim Lincecum AU/25 (RC) 200.00 100.00
❑ 148a M.Lindstrom AU/75 (RC) 15.00 6.00
❑ 148b M.Lindstrom AU/40 (RC) 15.00 6.00
❑ 149a Jay Marshall AU/75 RC 12.00 5.00
❑ 149b Jay Marshall AU/50 (RC) 12.00 5.00
❑ 151a M.Montero AU/75 (RC) 15.00 6.00
❑ 151b M.Montero AU/60 (RC) 15.00 6.00
❑ 154a Brandon Wood AU/75 (RC) 15.00 6.00
❑ 155a Felix Pie AU/75 (RC) 30.00 12.50
❑ 155b Felix Pie AU/70 (RC) 30.00 12.50
❑ 157a Andy LaRoche AU/50 (RC) 15.00 6.00
❑ 157b Andy LaRoche AU/40 (RC) 15.00 6.00
❑ 158a J.Saltalamac AU/75 (RC) 25.00 10.00
❑ 158b J.Saltalamac AU/25 (RC) 30.00 12.50

2001 SP Legendary Cuts

❑ COMPLETE SET (90) 25.00 10.00
❑ 1 Al Simmons .30 .10
❑ 2 Jimmie Foxx .75 .30
❑ 3 Mickey Cochrane .50 .20
❑ 4 Phil Niekro .30 .10
❑ 5 Eddie Mathews .75 .30
❑ 6 Gary Matthews .30 .10
❑ 7 Hank Aaron 1.50 .60
❑ 8 Joe Adcock .30 .10
❑ 9 Warren Spahn .50 .20
❑ 10 George Sisler .30 .10
❑ 11 Stan Musial 1.25 .50
❑ 12 Dizzy Dean .75 .30
❑ 13 Frankie Frisch .30 .10
❑ 14 Harvey Haddix .30 .10
❑ 15 Johnny Mize .50 .20
❑ 16 Ken Boyer .30 .10
❑ 17 Rogers Hornsby .75 .30
❑ 18 Cap Anson .75 .30
❑ 19 Andre Dawson .30 .10
❑ 20 Billy Williams .30 .10
❑ 21 Billy Herman .30 .10
❑ 22 Hack Wilson .50 .20
❑ 23 Ron Santo .50 .20
❑ 24 Ryne Sandberg 1.25 .50
❑ 25 Ernie Banks .75 .30
❑ 26 Burleigh Grimes .30 .10
❑ 27 Don Drysdale .50 .20
❑ 28 Gil Hodges .75 .30
❑ 29 Jackie Robinson .75 .30
❑ 30 Tommy Lasorda .30 .10
❑ 31 Pee Wee Reese .75 .30
❑ 32 Roy Campanella .75 .30
❑ 33 Tommy Davis .30 .10
❑ 34 Branch Rickey .30 .10
❑ 35 Leo Durocher .50 .20
❑ 36 Walt Alston .30 .10
❑ 37 Bill Terry .30 .10
❑ 38 Carl Hubbell .50 .20
❑ 39 Eddie Stanky .30 .10
❑ 40 George Kelly .30 .10
❑ 41 Mel Ott .75 .30
❑ 42 Juan Marichal .30 .10
❑ 43 Rube Marquard .30 .10
❑ 44 Travis Jackson .30 .10
❑ 45 Bob Feller .30 .10
❑ 46 Earl Averill .30 .10
❑ 47 Elmer Flick .30 .10
❑ 48 Ken Keltner .30 .10
❑ 49 Lou Boudreau .50 .20
❑ 50 Early Wynn .50 .20
❑ 51 Satchel Paige .75 .30
❑ 52 Ron Hunt .30 .10
❑ 53 Tom Seaver .50 .20
❑ 54 Richie Ashburn .50 .20
❑ 55 Mike Schmidt 1.50 .60
❑ 56 Honus Wagner 1.00 .40
❑ 57 Lloyd Waner .50 .20
❑ 58 Max Carey .30 .10
❑ 59 Paul Waner .50 .20
❑ 60 Roberto Clemente 2.00 .75
❑ 61 Nolan Ryan 2.00 .75
❑ 62 Bobby Doerr .50 .20
❑ 63 Carlton Fisk .50 .20
❑ 64 Joe Cronin .30 .10
❑ 65 Joe Wood .50 .20

❑	66 Tony Conigliaro	.50	.20
❑	67 Edd Roush	.30	.10
❑	68 Johnny VanderMeer	.30	.10
❑	69 Walter Johnson	.75	.30
❑	70 Charlie Gehringer	.30	.10
❑	71 Al Kaline	.75	.30
❑	72 Ty Cobb	1.25	.50
❑	73 Tony Oliva	.30	.10
❑	74 Luke Appling	.30	.10
❑	75 Minnie Minoso	.30	.10
❑	76 Nellie Fox	.50	.20
❑	77 Joe Jackson	1.50	.60
❑	78 Babe Ruth	2.50	1.00
❑	79 Bill Dickey	.50	.20
❑	80 Elston Howard	.50	.20
❑	81 Joe DiMaggio	1.50	.60
❑	82 Lefty Gomez	.75	.30
❑	83 Lou Gehrig	1.50	.60
❑	84 Mickey Mantle	3.00	1.25
❑	85 Reggie Jackson	.50	.20
❑	86 Roger Maris	.75	.30
❑	87 Whitey Ford	.50	.20
❑	88 Waite Hoyt	.30	.10
❑	89 Yogi Berra	.75	.30
❑	90 Casey Stengel	.75	.30

2002 SP Legendary Cuts

❑	COMPLETE SET (90)	25.00	10.00
❑	1 Al Kaline	1.50	.60
❑	2 Alvin Dark	.60	.25
❑	3 Andre Dawson	.60	.25
❑	4 Babe Ruth	5.00	2.00
❑	5 Ernie Banks	1.50	.60
❑	6 Bob Lemon	1.00	.40
❑	7 Bobby Bonds	.60	.25
❑	8 Carl Erskine	.60	.25
❑	9 Carl Hubbell	1.00	.40
❑	10 Casey Stengel	1.50	.60
❑	11 Charlie Gehringer	1.00	.40
❑	12 Christy Mathewson	1.50	.60
❑	13 Dale Murphy	1.00	.40
❑	14 Dave Concepcion	.60	.25
❑	15 Dave Parker	.60	.25
❑	16 Dazzy Vance	.60	.25
❑	17 Dizzy Dean	1.00	.40
❑	18 Don Baylor	.60	.25
❑	19 Don Drysdale	1.00	.40
❑	20 Duke Snider	1.00	.40
❑	21 Earl Averill	.60	.25
❑	22 Early Wynn	.60	.25
❑	23 Edd Roush	.60	.25
❑	24 Elston Howard	.60	.25
❑	25 Ferguson Jenkins	.60	.25
❑	26 Frank Crosetti	.60	.25
❑	27 Frankie Frisch	.60	.25
❑	28 Gaylord Perry	.60	.25
❑	29 George Foster	.60	.25
❑	30 George Kell	.60	.25
❑	31 Gil Hodges	1.00	.40
❑	32 Hank Greenberg	1.50	.60
❑	33 Phil Niekro	.60	.25
❑	34 Harvey Haddix	.60	.25
❑	35 Harvey Kuenn	.60	.25
❑	36 Honus Wagner	2.50	1.00
❑	37 Jackie Robinson	1.50	.60
❑	38 Orlando Cepeda	.60	.25
❑	39 Joe Adcock	.60	.25
❑	40 Joe Cronin	.60	.25
❑	41 Joe DiMaggio	2.50	1.00
❑	42 Joe Morgan	.60	.25
❑	43 Johnny Mize	.60	.25
❑	44 Lefty Gomez	1.00	.40
❑	45 Lefty Grove	1.00	.40
❑	46 Jim Palmer	.60	.25
❑	47 Lou Boudreau	.60	.25
❑	48 Lou Gehrig	2.50	1.00
❑	49 Luke Appling	.60	.25
❑	50 Mark McGwire	5.00	2.00
❑	51 Mel Ott	1.50	.60
❑	52 Mickey Cochrane	1.00	.40
❑	53 Mickey Mantle	5.00	2.00
❑	54 Minnie Minoso	.60	.25
❑	55 Brooks Robinson	1.00	.40
❑	56 Nellie Fox	1.00	.40
❑	57 Nolan Ryan	4.00	1.50
❑	58 Rollie Fingers	.60	.25
❑	59 Pee Wee Reese	1.00	.40
❑	60 Phil Rizzuto	1.00	.40
❑	61 Ralph Kiner	.60	.25
❑	62 Ray Dandridge	.60	.25
❑	63 Richie Ashburn	1.00	.40
❑	64 Robin Yount	1.50	.60
❑	65 Rocky Colavito	1.00	.40
❑	66 Roger Maris	1.50	.60
❑	67 Rogers Hornsby	1.50	.60
❑	68 Ron Santo	.60	.25
❑	69 Ryne Sandberg	3.00	1.25
❑	70 Stan Musial	2.50	1.00
❑	71 Sam McDowell	.60	.25
❑	72 Satchel Paige	1.50	.60
❑	73 Willie McCovey	.60	.25
❑	74 Steve Garvey	.60	.25
❑	75 Ted Kluszewski	1.00	.40
❑	76 Catfish Hunter	1.00	.40
❑	77 Terry Moore	.40	.15
❑	78 Thurman Munson	1.50	.60
❑	79 Tom Seaver	1.00	.40
❑	80 Tommy John	.60	.25
❑	81 Tony Gwynn	2.00	.75
❑	82 Tony Kubek	1.00	.40
❑	83 Tony Lazzeri	.60	.25
❑	84 Ty Cobb	2.50	1.00
❑	85 Wade Boggs	1.00	.40
❑	86 Waite Hoyt	.60	.25
❑	87 Walter Johnson	1.50	.60
❑	88 Willie Stargell	1.00	.40
❑	89 Yogi Berra	1.50	.60
❑	90 Zack Wheat	.60	.25
❑	MM M.McGwire AU/100 EX		

2003 SP Legendary Cuts

❑	COMP.SET w/o SP's (100)	40.00	15.00
❑	COMMON CARD	.40	.15
❑	COMMON SP	8.00	3.00
❑	1 Luis Aparicio	.60	.25
❑	2 Al Barlick	.40	.15
❑	3 Al Lopez	.60	.25
❑	4 Ernie Banks	1.50	.60
❑	5 Alexander Cartwright	.60	.25
❑	6 Lou Brock	1.00	.40
❑	7 Babe Ruth/1299	15.00	6.00
❑	8 Bill Dickey	1.00	.40
❑	9 Bill Mazeroski	1.00	.40
❑	10 Bob Feller	.60	.25
❑	11 Billy Herman	.60	.25
❑	12 Billy Williams	.60	.25
❑	13 Bob Gibson/1299	10.00	4.00
❑	14 Bob Lemon	.60	.25
❑	15 Bobby Doerr	.60	.25
❑	16 Branch Rickey	.60	.25
❑	17 Gary Carter	.60	.25
❑	18 Burleigh Grimes	.60	.25
❑	19 Cap Anson	1.00	.40
❑	20 Carl Hubbell	1.00	.40
❑	21 Carlton Fisk	1.00	.40
❑	22 Casey Stengel	1.00	.40
❑	23 Charlie Gehringer	.60	.25
❑	24 Chief Bender	.60	.25
❑	25 Christy Mathewson/1299	10.00	4.00
❑	26 Cy Young	1.50	.60
❑	27 Dave Winfield	.60	.25
❑	28 Dazzy Vance	.60	.25
❑	29 Dizzy Dean/1299	10.00	4.00
❑	30 Don Drysdale/1299	10.00	4.00
❑	31 Duke Snider/1299	10.00	4.00
❑	32 Earl Averill	.60	.25
❑	33 Earle Combs	.60	.25
❑	34 Edd Roush	.60	.25
❑	35 Earl Weaver	.60	.25
❑	36 Eddie Collins	.60	.25
❑	37 Eddie Plank	.60	.25
❑	38 Elmer Flick	.60	.25
❑	39 Enos Slaughter	.60	.25
❑	40 Ernie Lombardi	.60	.25
❑	41 Ford Frick	.40	.15
❑	42 Jim Hunter	1.00	.40
❑	43 Frankie Frisch	.60	.25
❑	44 Gabby Hartnett	.60	.25
❑	45 George Kell	.60	.25
❑	46 Early Wynn	.60	.25
❑	47 Ferguson Jenkins	.60	.25
❑	48 Al Kaline	1.50	.60
❑	49 Harmon Killebrew	1.50	.60
❑	50 Hal Newhouser	.60	.25
❑	51 Hank Greenberg/1299	10.00	4.00
❑	52 Harry Caray	1.00	.40
❑	53 Tommy Lasorda	.60	.25
❑	54 Honus Wagner/1299	10.00	4.00
❑	55 Hoyt Wilhelm/1299	8.00	3.00
❑	56 Jackie Robinson/1299	10.00	4.00
❑	57 Jim Bottomley	.60	.25
❑	58 Jim Bunning/1299	10.00	4.00
❑	59 Jimmie Foxx/1299	10.00	4.00
❑	60 Eddie Mathews	1.50	.60
❑	61 Joe Cronin	.60	.25
❑	62 Joe DiMaggio/1299	10.00	4.00
❑	63 Joe McCarthy/1299	8.00	3.00
❑	64 Joe Morgan/1299	8.00	3.00
❑	65 Willie McCovey	.60	.25
❑	66 Joe Tinker	.60	.25
❑	67 Johnny Bench/1299	10.00	4.00
❑	68 Johnny Evers/1299	8.00	3.00
❑	69 Johnny Mize/1299	8.00	3.00
❑	70 Josh Gibson/1299	10.00	4.00
❑	71 Juan Marichal	.60	.25
❑	72 Judy Johnson	.60	.25
❑	73 Stan Musial	2.50	1.00
❑	74 Kiki Cuyler	.60	.25
❑	75 Larry Doby	.60	.25
❑	76 Nap Lajoie	1.00	.40
❑	77 Larry MacPhail	.40	.15
❑	78 Phil Niekro	.60	.25
❑	79 Lefty Gomez/1299	10.00	4.00
❑	80 Lefty Grove/1299	10.00	4.00
❑	81 Leo Durocher/1299	8.00	3.00
❑	82 Leon Day	.60	.25
❑	83 Gaylord Perry/1299	8.00	3.00
❑	84 Lou Boudreau	.60	.25
❑	85 Lou Gehrig	2.50	1.00
❑	86 Luke Appling	.60	.25
❑	87 Max Carey	.60	.25
❑	88 Mel Allen/1299	8.00	3.00
❑	89 Mel Ott/1299	10.00	4.00
❑	90 Mickey Cochrane	.60	.25
❑	91 Mickey Mantle	5.00	2.00
❑	92 Brooks Robinson	1.00	.40
❑	93 Monte Irvin	.60	.25
❑	94 Nellie Fox	1.00	.40
❑	95 Nolan Ryan/1299	12.00	5.00
❑	96 Ozzie Smith/1299	10.00	4.00
❑	97 Mike Schmidt	3.00	1.25
❑	98 Pee Wee Reese/1299	10.00	4.00

❑ 99 Phil Rizzuto	1.00	.40
❑ 100 Ralph Kiner	.60	.25
❑ 101 Ray Dandridge	.60	.25
❑ 102 Richie Ashburn	1.00	.40
❑ 103 Rick Ferrell	.60	.25
❑ 104 Roberto Clemente	4.00	1.50
❑ 105 Robin Roberts	.60	.25
❑ 106 Robin Yount	1.50	.60
❑ 107 Rogers Hornsby	1.50	.60
❑ 108 Rollie Fingers	.60	.25
❑ 109 Roy Campanella	1.50	.60
❑ 110 Rube Marquard	.60	.25
❑ 111 Sam Crawford	.60	.25
❑ 112 Steve Carlton	.60	.25
❑ 113 Satchel Paige/1299	10.00	4.00
❑ 114 Sparky Anderson	.60	.25
❑ 115 Stan Coveleski	.60	.25
❑ 116 Red Schoendienst	1.00	.40
❑ 117 Ted Williams	3.00	1.25
❑ 118 Tom Seaver	1.00	.40
❑ 119 Tom Yawkey	.40	.15
❑ 120 Tony Lazzeri	.60	.25
❑ 121 Tony Perez	.60	.25
❑ 122 Tris Speaker	1.50	.60
❑ 123 Ty Cobb	2.50	1.00
❑ 124 Waite Hoyt/1299	8.00	3.00
❑ 125 Walter Alston	.60	.25
❑ 126 Walter Johnson	1.50	.60
❑ 127 Warren Spahn	1.00	.40
❑ 128 Whitey Ford	1.00	.40
❑ 129 Willie Stargell	1.00	.40
❑ 130 Yogi Berra	1.50	.60

2004 SP Legendary Cuts

❑ COMPLETE SET (126)	40.00	15.00
❑ 1 Al Kaline	1.50	.60
❑ 2 Al Lopez	.60	.25
❑ 3 Alan Trammell	.60	.25
❑ 4 Andre Dawson	.60	.25
❑ 5 Babe Ruth	5.00	2.00
❑ 6 Bert Campaneris	.40	.15
❑ 7 Bill Mazeroski	1.00	.40
❑ 8 Bill Russell	.40	.15
❑ 9 Billy Williams	.60	.25
❑ 10 Bob Feller	1.00	.40
❑ 11 Bob Gibson	1.00	.40
❑ 12 Bob Lemon	.60	.25
❑ 13 Bobby Doerr	.60	.25
❑ 14 Brooks Robinson	1.00	.40
❑ 15 Cal Ripken	5.00	2.00
❑ 16 Carl Yastrzemski	2.50	1.00
❑ 17 Carlton Fisk	1.00	.40
❑ 18 Catfish Hunter	.60	.25
❑ 19 Dale Murphy	1.00	.40
❑ 20 Darryl Strawberry	.60	.25
❑ 21 Dave Concepcion	.60	.25
❑ 22 Dave Winfield	.60	.25
❑ 23 Dennis Eckersley	.60	.25
❑ 24 Denny McLain	.60	.25
❑ 25 Don Drysdale	1.00	.40
❑ 26 Don Larsen	.60	.25
❑ 27 Don Mattingly	3.00	1.25
❑ 28 Don Sutton	.60	.25
❑ 29 Duke Snider	1.00	.40
❑ 30 Dusty Baker	.60	.25
❑ 31 Dwight Gooden	.60	.25
❑ 32 Earl Weaver	.40	.15
❑ 33 Early Wynn	.60	.25
❑ 34 Eddie Mathews	1.50	.60
❑ 35 Eddie Murray	1.50	.60
❑ 36 Enos Slaughter	.60	.25
❑ 37 Ernie Banks	1.50	.60
❑ 38 Fergie Jenkins	.60	.25
❑ 39 Frank Robinson	.60	.25
❑ 40 Fred Lynn	.40	.15
❑ 41 Gary Carter	.60	.25
❑ 42 Gaylord Perry	.60	.25
❑ 43 George Brett	3.00	1.25
❑ 44 George Foster	.40	.15
❑ 45 George Kell	.60	.25
❑ 46 Greg Luzinski	.60	.25
❑ 47 Hal Newhouser	.60	.25
❑ 48 Hank Greenberg	1.50	.60
❑ 49 Harmon Killebrew	1.50	.60
❑ 50 Honus Wagner	1.50	.60
❑ 51 Hoyt Wilhelm	.60	.25
❑ 52 Jackie Robinson	1.50	.60
❑ 53 Jim Bunning	1.00	.40
❑ 54 Jim Palmer	.60	.25
❑ 55 Jimmie Foxx	1.50	.60
❑ 56 Joe Carter	.60	.25
❑ 57 Joe DiMaggio	2.50	1.00
❑ 58 Joe Morgan	.60	.25
❑ 59 Joe Torre	1.00	.40
❑ 60 Johnny Bench	1.50	.60
❑ 61 Johnny Podres	.60	.25
❑ 62 Johnny Roseboro	.40	.15
❑ 63 Johnny Sain	.60	.25
❑ 64 Juan Marichal	.60	.25
❑ 65 Keith Hernandez	.60	.25
❑ 66 Kirby Puckett	1.50	.60
❑ 67 Kirk Gibson	.60	.25
❑ 68 Will Clark	1.00	.40
❑ 69 Jim Rice	.60	.25
❑ 70 Larry Doby	.60	.25
❑ 71 Lou Boudreau	.60	.25
❑ 72 Lou Brock	1.00	.40
❑ 73 Lou Gehrig	2.50	1.00
❑ 74 Lou Piniella	.60	.25
❑ 75 Luis Aparicio	.60	.25
❑ 76 Mark Grace	1.00	.40
❑ 77 Mel Ott	1.50	.60
❑ 78 Mickey Lolich	.60	.25
❑ 79 Mickey Mantle	8.00	3.00
❑ 80 Mike Greenwell	.40	.15
❑ 81 Mike Schmidt	3.00	1.25
❑ 82 Monte Irvin	.60	.25
❑ 83 Nellie Fox	1.00	.40
❑ 84 Nolan Ryan	4.00	1.50
❑ 85 Orlando Cepeda	.60	.25
❑ 86 Ozzie Smith	2.50	1.00
❑ 87 Paul Molitor	.60	.25
❑ 88 Pee Wee Reese	1.00	.40
❑ 89 Phil Niekro	.60	.25
❑ 90 Phil Rizzuto	1.00	.40
❑ 91 Ralph Kiner	1.00	.40
❑ 92 Red Rolfe	.40	.15
❑ 93 Red Schoendienst	.60	.25
❑ 94 Reggie Smith	.40	.15
❑ 95 Rich Gossage	.60	.25
❑ 96 Richie Ashburn	1.00	.40
❑ 97 Rick Ferrell	.60	.25
❑ 98 Elston Howard	.60	.25
❑ 99 Roberto Clemente	4.00	1.50
❑ 100 Robin Roberts	.60	.25
❑ 101 Robin Yount	1.50	.60
❑ 102 Roger Maris	1.50	.60
❑ 103 Rollie Fingers	.60	.25
❑ 104 Ron Santo	1.00	.40
❑ 105 Roy Campanella	1.50	.60
❑ 106 Ryne Sandberg	3.00	1.25
❑ 107 Sparky Anderson	.60	.25
❑ 108 Sparky Lyle	.40	.15
❑ 109 Stan Musial	2.50	1.00
❑ 110 Steve Carlton	.60	.25
❑ 111 Steve Garvey	.60	.25
❑ 112 Ted Williams	3.00	1.25
❑ 113 Thurman Munson	1.50	.60
❑ 114 Tom Seaver	1.00	.40
❑ 115 Tommy Henrich	.60	.25
❑ 116 Tommy Lasorda	.60	.25
❑ 117 Tony Gwynn	2.00	.75
❑ 118 Tony Perez	.60	.25
❑ 119 Ty Cobb	2.00	.75
❑ 120 Wade Boggs	1.00	.40
❑ 121 Warren Spahn	1.00	.40
❑ 122 Whitey Ford	1.00	.40
❑ 123 Willie McCovey	1.00	.40
❑ 124 Willie Randolph	.60	.25
❑ 125 Willie Stargell	1.00	.40
❑ 126 Yogi Berra	1.50	.60

2005 SP Legendary Cuts

❑ COMPLETE SET (90)	25.00	10.00
❑ COMMON CARD (1-90)	.40	.15
❑ 1 Al Kaline	1.50	.60
❑ 2 Babe Ruth	5.00	2.00
❑ 3 Bill Mazeroski	1.00	.40
❑ 4 Billy Williams	.60	.25
❑ 5 Bob Feller	1.00	.40
❑ 6 Bob Gibson	1.00	.40
❑ 7 Bob Lemon	.60	.25
❑ 8 Bobby Doerr	.60	.25
❑ 9 Brooks Robinson	1.00	.40
❑ 10 Carl Yastrzemski	2.50	1.00
❑ 11 Carlton Fisk	1.00	.40
❑ 12 Casey Stengel	1.00	.40
❑ 13 Catfish Hunter	.60	.25
❑ 14 Christy Mathewson	1.50	.60
❑ 15 Cy Young	1.50	.60
❑ 16 Dennis Eckersley	.60	.25
❑ 17 Dizzy Dean	1.00	.40
❑ 18 Don Drysdale	1.00	.40
❑ 19 Don Sutton	.60	.25
❑ 20 Duke Snider	1.00	.40
❑ 21 Early Wynn	.60	.25
❑ 22 Eddie Mathews	1.50	.60
❑ 23 Eddie Murray	1.50	.60
❑ 24 Enos Slaughter	.60	.25
❑ 25 Ernie Banks	1.50	.60
❑ 26 Fergie Jenkins	.60	.25
❑ 27 Frank Robinson	.60	.25
❑ 28 Gary Carter	.60	.25
❑ 29 Gaylord Perry	.60	.25
❑ 30 Reggie Jackson	1.00	.40
❑ 31 George Kell	.60	.25
❑ 32 George Sisler	.60	.25
❑ 33 Hal Newhouser	.60	.25
❑ 34 Harmon Killebrew	1.50	.60
❑ 35 Honus Wagner	1.50	.60
❑ 36 Jackie Robinson	1.50	.60
❑ 37 Jim Bunning	1.00	.40
❑ 38 Jim Palmer	.60	.25
❑ 39 Jimmie Foxx	1.50	.60
❑ 40 Joe DiMaggio	2.50	1.00
❑ 41 Joe Morgan	.60	.25
❑ 42 Johnny Bench	1.50	.60
❑ 43 Johnny Mize	.60	.25
❑ 44 Juan Marichal	.60	.25
❑ 45 Kirby Puckett	1.50	.60
❑ 46 Larry Doby	.60	.25
❑ 47 Lefty Grove	1.00	.40
❑ 48 Lou Boudreau	.60	.25
❑ 49 Lou Brock	1.00	.40
❑ 50 Lou Gehrig	2.50	1.00
❑ 51 Luis Aparicio	.60	.25
❑ 52 Mel Ott	1.50	.60
❑ 53 Mickey Cochrane	.60	.25
❑ 54 Mickey Mantle	8.00	3.00
❑ 55 Mike Schmidt	3.00	1.25
❑ 56 Monte Irvin	.60	.25
❑ 57 Nolan Ryan	4.00	1.50

❑ 58 Orlando Cepeda .60 .25
❑ 59 Ozzie Smith 2.50 1.00
❑ 60 Paul Molitor .60 .25
❑ 61 Pee Wee Reese 1.00 .40
❑ 62 Phil Niekro .60 .25
❑ 63 Phil Rizzuto 1.00 .40
❑ 64 Ralph Kiner 1.00 .40
❑ 65 Red Schoendienst .60 .25
❑ 66 Richie Ashburn 1.00 .40
❑ 67 Rick Ferrell .60 .25
❑ 68 Robin Roberts .60 .25
❑ 69 Robin Yount 1.50 .60
❑ 70 Rod Carew 1.00 .40
❑ 71 Rogers Hornsby 1.00 .40
❑ 72 Rollie Fingers .60 .25
❑ 73 Roy Campanella 1.50 .60
❑ 74 Ryne Sandberg 3.00 1.25
❑ 75 Satchel Paige 1.50 .60
❑ 76 Stan Musial 2.50 1.00
❑ 77 Steve Carlton .60 .25
❑ 78 Ted Williams 3.00 1.25
❑ 79 Thurman Munson 1.50 .60
❑ 80 Tom Seaver 1.00 .40
❑ 81 Tony Gwynn 2.00 .75
❑ 82 Tony Perez .60 .25
❑ 83 Ty Cobb 2.00 .75
❑ 84 Wade Boggs 1.00 .40
❑ 85 Walter Johnson 1.50 .60
❑ 86 Warren Spahn 1.00 .40
❑ 87 Whitey Ford 1.00 .40
❑ 88 Willie McCovey 1.00 .40
❑ 89 Willie Stargell 1.00 .40
❑ 90 Yogi Berra 1.50 .60

2006 SP Legendary Cuts

❑ COMP.SET w/o SP's (100) 25.00 10.00
❑ COMMON CARD (1-100) .60 .25
❑ COMMON CARD (101-200) 5.00 2.00
❑ 101-200: ONE BASIC OR BRONZE PER BOX
❑ 101-200 PRINT RUN 550 SERIAL #'d SETS
❑ EXQUISITE EXCH ODDS 1:60
❑ EXQUISITE EXCH DEADLINE 07/27/07
❑ 1 Juan Marichal .60 .25
❑ 2 Monte Irvin .60 .25
❑ 3 Will Clark 1.00 .40
❑ 4 Willie McCovey 1.00 .40
❑ 5 Eddie Gaedel .60 .25
❑ 6 Ken Williams .60 .25
❑ 7 Earl Battey .60 .25
❑ 8 Rick Ferrell .60 .25
❑ 9 Bob Gibson 1.00 .40
❑ 10 Elmer Flick .60 .25
❑ 11 Joe Medwick .60 .25
❑ 12 Lou Brock 1.00 .40
❑ 13 Ozzie Smith 2.50 1.00
❑ 14 Red Schoendienst .60 .25
❑ 15 Stan Musial 2.50 1.00
❑ 16 Tony Oliva .60 .25
❑ 17 Phil Niekro .60 .25
❑ 18 Boog Powell .60 .25
❑ 19 Brooks Robinson 1.00 .40
❑ 20 Cal Ripken 6.00 2.50
❑ 21 Eddie Murray 1.50 .60
❑ 22 Frank Robinson .60 .25
❑ 23 Jim Palmer .60 .25
❑ 24 Jocko Conlon .60 .25
❑ 25 Carlton Fisk 1.00 .40
❑ 26 Dwight Evans .60 .25
❑ 27 Fred Lynn .60 .25
❑ 28 Jim Rice .60 .25
❑ 29 Ted Williams 4.00 1.50
❑ 30 Wade Boggs 1.00 .40
❑ 31 Hugh Duffy .60 .25
❑ 32 Kid Nichols .60 .25
❑ 33 Johnny Vander Meer .60 .25
❑ 34 Dolph Camilli .60 .25
❑ 35 Carl Yastrzemski 2.50 1.00
❑ 36 Chick Hafey .60 .25
❑ 37 Kirby Higbe .60 .25
❑ 38 Pee Wee Reese 1.00 .40
❑ 39 Pete Reiser .60 .25
❑ 40 Don Sutton .60 .25
❑ 41 Rod Carew 1.00 .40
❑ 42 Andre Dawson .60 .25
❑ 43 Billy Herman .60 .25
❑ 44 Billy Williams .60 .25
❑ 45 Charley Root .60 .25
❑ 46 Hack Wilson 1.00 .40
❑ 47 Ernie Banks 1.50 .60
❑ 48 Fergie Jenkins .60 .25
❑ 49 Gabby Hartnett .60 .25
❑ 50 Ken Hubbs .60 .25
❑ 51 Kiki Cuyler .60 .25
❑ 52 Mark Grace 1.00 .40
❑ 53 Ryne Sandberg 3.00 1.25
❑ 54 Harold Newhouser .60 .25
❑ 55 Charlie Robertson .60 .25
❑ 56 Harold Baines .60 .25
❑ 57 Luis Aparicio .60 .25
❑ 58 Luke Appling .60 .25
❑ 59 Nellie Fox 1.00 .40
❑ 60 Ray Schalk .60 .25
❑ 61 Red Faber .60 .25
❑ 62 Sloppy Thurston .60 .25
❑ 63 Freddie Lindstrom .60 .25
❑ 64 Vern Kennedy .60 .25
❑ 65 Barry Larkin 1.00 .40
❑ 66 Bucky Walters .60 .25
❑ 67 Dolf Luque .60 .25
❑ 68 Al Campanis .60 .25
❑ 69 Ernie Lombardi .60 .25
❑ 70 George Foster .60 .25
❑ 71 Joe Morgan .60 .25
❑ 72 Johnny Bench 1.50 .60
❑ 73 Ken Griffey Sr. .60 .25
❑ 74 Ted Kluszewski 1.00 .40
❑ 75 Tony Perez .60 .25
❑ 76 Wally Post .60 .25
❑ 77 Bob Feller .60 .25
❑ 78 Bob Lemon .60 .25
❑ 79 Earl Averill .60 .25
❑ 80 Joe Sewell .60 .25
❑ 81 Johnny Hodapp .60 .25
❑ 82 Larry Doby .60 .25
❑ 83 Lou Boudreau .60 .25
❑ 84 Rocky Colavito 1.00 .40
❑ 85 Stan Coveleski .60 .25
❑ 86 Nap Lajoie 1.00 .40
❑ 87 Al Kaline 1.50 .60
❑ 88 Alan Trammell .60 .25
❑ 89 Charlie Gehringer .60 .25
❑ 90 Denny McLain .60 .25
❑ 91 Hank Greenberg 1.50 .60
❑ 92 Jack Morris .60 .25
❑ 93 Mark Fidrych .60 .25
❑ 94 Ray Boone .60 .25
❑ 95 Rudy York .60 .25
❑ 96 Buck Leonard .60 .25
❑ 97 Bo Jackson 1.50 .60
❑ 98 Zoilo Versalles .60 .25
❑ 99 John Kruk .60 .25
❑ 100 Don Drysdale 1.00 .40
❑ 101 Cecil Cooper 5.00 2.00
❑ 102 Vic Wertz 5.00 2.00
❑ 103 Kirk Gibson 5.00 2.00
❑ 104 Maury Wills 5.00 2.00
❑ 105 Steve Garvey 5.00 2.00
❑ 106 Warren Spahn 8.00 3.00
❑ 107 Paul Molitor 5.00 2.00
❑ 108 Robin Yount 8.00 3.00
❑ 109 Rollie Fingers 5.00 2.00
❑ 110 Bob Allison 5.00 2.00
❑ 111 Kirby Puckett 8.00 3.00
❑ 112 Tim Raines 5.00 2.00
❑ 113 George Pipgras 5.00 2.00
❑ 114 Eddie Grant 5.00 2.00
❑ 115 Hoyt Wilhelm 5.00 2.00
❑ 116 Sal Maglie 5.00 2.00
❑ 117 Ron Santo 8.00 3.00
❑ 118 Wally Joyner 5.00 2.00
❑ 119 Tom Seaver 8.00 3.00
❑ 120 Tommie Agee 5.00 2.00
❑ 121 Harmon Killebrew 8.00 3.00
❑ 122 Bill Dickey 5.00 2.00
❑ 123 Early Wynn 5.00 2.00
❑ 124 Bobby Murcer 8.00 3.00
❑ 125 Bucky Dent 5.00 2.00
❑ 126 Dave Winfield 5.00 2.00
❑ 127 Don Larsen 5.00 2.00
❑ 128 Don Mattingly 10.00 4.00
❑ 129 Earle Combs 5.00 2.00
❑ 130 Ed Lopat 5.00 2.00
❑ 131 Elston Howard 5.00 2.00
❑ 132 Everett Scott 5.00 2.00
❑ 133 Goose Gossage 5.00 2.00
❑ 134 Graig Nettles 5.00 2.00
❑ 135 Joe DiMaggio 10.00 4.00
❑ 136 Lou Piniella 5.00 2.00
❑ 137 Bill Skowron 5.00 2.00
❑ 138 Phil Rizzuto 8.00 3.00
❑ 139 Red Ruffing 5.00 2.00
❑ 140 Reggie Jackson 8.00 3.00
❑ 141 Roger Maris 8.00 3.00
❑ 142 Ron Guidry 5.00 2.00
❑ 143 Tiny Bonham 5.00 2.00
❑ 144 Bruce Sutter 5.00 2.00
❑ 145 Tony Lazzeri 5.00 2.00
❑ 146 Waite Hoyt 5.00 2.00
❑ 147 Whitey Ford 8.00 3.00
❑ 148 Steve Sax 5.00 2.00
❑ 149 Yogi Berra 8.00 3.00
❑ 150 Enos Slaughter 5.00 2.00
❑ 151 Catfish Hunter 5.00 2.00
❑ 152 Dennis Eckersley 5.00 2.00
❑ 153 Jose Canseco 8.00 3.00
❑ 154 Al Rosen 5.00 2.00
❑ 155 Al Simmons 5.00 2.00
❑ 156 Chief Bender 5.00 2.00
❑ 157 Cy Williams 5.00 2.00
❑ 158 Mike Schmidt 10.00 4.00
❑ 159 Richie Ashburn 8.00 3.00
❑ 160 Robin Roberts 5.00 2.00
❑ 161 Steve Carlton 5.00 2.00
❑ 162 Judy Johnson 5.00 2.00
❑ 163 Al Oliver 5.00 2.00
❑ 164 Bill Mazeroski 8.00 3.00
❑ 165 Dave Parker 5.00 2.00
❑ 166 Max Carey 5.00 2.00
❑ 167 Pie Traynor 5.00 2.00
❑ 168 Ralph Kiner 5.00 2.00
❑ 169 Roberto Clemente 15.00 6.00
❑ 170 Willie Stargell 5.00 2.00
❑ 171 Gaylord Perry 5.00 2.00
❑ 172 Tony Gwynn 8.00 3.00
❑ 173 Nolan Ryan 10.00 4.00
❑ 174 Joe Carter 5.00 2.00
❑ 175 Frank Howard 5.00 2.00
❑ 176 George Kell 5.00 2.00
❑ 177 Heinie Manush 5.00 2.00
❑ 178 Sam Rice 5.00 2.00
❑ 179 Babe Ruth 15.00 6.00
❑ 180 Casey Stengel 8.00 3.00
❑ 181 Christy Mathewson 8.00 3.00
❑ 182 Cy Young 8.00 3.00
❑ 183 Dizzy Dean 8.00 3.00
❑ 184 Eddie Mathews 8.00 3.00
❑ 185 George Sisler 5.00 2.00
❑ 186 Honus Wagner 8.00 3.00
❑ 187 Jackie Robinson 8.00 3.00
❑ 188 Jimmie Foxx 8.00 3.00
❑ 189 Johnny Mize 5.00 2.00
❑ 190 Lefty Gomez 5.00 2.00
❑ 191 Lou Gehrig 10.00 4.00
❑ 192 Mel Ott 8.00 3.00
❑ 193 Mickey Cochrane 5.00 2.00
❑ 194 Rogers Hornsby 8.00 3.00
❑ 195 Roy Campanella 8.00 3.00
❑ 196 Satchel Paige 8.00 3.00
❑ 197 Thurman Munson 8.00 3.00
❑ 198 Ty Cobb 10.00 4.00

Card		
❑ 199 Walter Johnson	8.00	3.00
❑ 200 Lefty Grove	5.00	2.00
❑ NNO Exquisite Redemption		

2007 SP Legendary Cuts

Card		
❑ COMP.SET w/o SP's (100)	25.00	10.00
❑ COMMON CARD (1-100)	.60	.25
❑ COMMON CARD (101-200)	5.00	2.00
❑ 101-200 RANDOMLY INSERTED		
❑ 101-200 PRINT RUN 550 SERIAL #'d SETS		
❑ 1 Phil Niekro	.60	.25
❑ 2 Brooks Robinson	1.00	.40
❑ 3 Frank Robinson	.60	.25
❑ 4 Jim Palmer	.60	.25
❑ 5 Cal Ripken Jr.	6.00	2.50
❑ 6 Warren Spahn	1.00	.40
❑ 7 Cy Young	1.50	.60
❑ 8 Carl Yastrzemski	2.50	1.00
❑ 9 Wade Boggs	1.00	.40
❑ 10 Carlton Fisk	1.00	.40
❑ 11 Joe Cronin	.60	.25
❑ 12 Bobby Doerr	.60	.25
❑ 13 Roy Campanella	1.50	.60
❑ 14 Pee Wee Reese	1.00	.40
❑ 15 Rod Carew	1.00	.40
❑ 16 Ernie Banks	1.50	.60
❑ 17 Fergie Jenkins	.60	.25
❑ 18 Billy Williams	.60	.25
❑ 19 Gabby Hartnett	.60	.25
❑ 20 Luis Aparicio	.60	.25
❑ 21 Nellie Fox	1.00	.40
❑ 22 Luke Appling	.60	.25
❑ 23 Joe Morgan	.60	.25
❑ 24 Johnny Bench	1.50	.60
❑ 25 Tony Perez	.60	.25
❑ 26 George Foster	.60	.25
❑ 27 Johnny Vander Meer	.60	.25
❑ 28 Bob Feller	.60	.25
❑ 29 Bob Lemon	.60	.25
❑ 30 Lou Boudreau	.60	.25
❑ 31 Early Wynn	.60	.25
❑ 32 Charlie Gehringer	.60	.25
❑ 33 George Kell	.60	.25
❑ 34 Hal Newhouser	.60	.25
❑ 35 Al Kaline	1.50	.60
❑ 36 Ted Kluszewski	1.00	.40
❑ 37 Harvey Kuenn	.60	.25
❑ 38 Maury Wills	.60	.25
❑ 39 Don Drysdale	1.00	.40
❑ 40 Don Sutton	.60	.25
❑ 41 Eddie Mathews	1.50	.60
❑ 42 Joe Adcock	.60	.25
❑ 43 Paul Molitor	.60	.25
❑ 44 Kirby Puckett	1.50	.60
❑ 45 Harmon Killebrew	1.50	.60
❑ 46 Monte Irvin	.60	.25
❑ 47 Ralph Kiner	1.00	.40
❑ 48 Christy Mathewson	1.50	.60
❑ 49 Hoyt Wilhelm	.60	.25
❑ 50 Tom Seaver	1.00	.40
❑ 51 Allie Reynolds	.60	.25
❑ 52 Joe DiMaggio	3.00	1.25
❑ 53 Lou Gehrig	3.00	1.25
❑ 54 Babe Ruth	4.00	1.50
❑ 55 Casey Stengel	.60	.25
❑ 56 Phil Rizzuto	1.00	.40
❑ 57 Thurman Munson	1.50	.60
❑ 58 Johnny Mize	.60	.25
❑ 59 Yogi Berra	1.50	.60
❑ 60 Rube Marquard	.60	.25
❑ 61 Don Mattingly	3.00	1.25
❑ 62 Ray Dandridge	.60	.25
❑ 63 Rollie Fingers	.60	.25
❑ 64 Roberto Clemente	5.00	2.00
❑ 65 Reggie Jackson	1.00	.40
❑ 66 Dennis Eckersley	.60	.25
❑ 67 Robin Yount	1.50	.60
❑ 68 Jimmie Foxx	1.50	.60
❑ 69 Lefty Grove	.60	.25
❑ 70 Richie Ashburn	1.00	.40
❑ 71 Jim Bunning	.60	.25
❑ 72 Steve Carlton	.60	.25
❑ 73 Robin Roberts	.60	.25
❑ 74 Mike Schmidt	2.50	1.00
❑ 75 Willie Stargell	1.00	.40
❑ 76 Ozzie Smith	2.50	1.00
❑ 77 Bill Mazeroski	1.00	.40
❑ 78 Honus Wagner	1.50	.60
❑ 79 Pie Traynor	.60	.25
❑ 80 Tony Gwynn	1.50	.60
❑ 81 Willie McCovey	1.00	.40
❑ 82 Gaylord Perry	.60	.25
❑ 83 Juan Marichal	.60	.25
❑ 84 Orlando Cepeda	.60	.25
❑ 85 Satchel Paige	1.50	.60
❑ 86 George Sisler	.60	.25
❑ 87 Ken Boyer	.60	.25
❑ 88 Joe Medwick	.60	.25
❑ 89 Travis Jackson	.60	.25
❑ 90 Stan Musial	2.50	1.00
❑ 91 Dizzy Dean	1.00	.40
❑ 92 Bob Gibson	1.00	.40
❑ 93 Red Schoendienst	.60	.25
❑ 94 Lou Brock	1.00	.40
❑ 95 Enos Slaughter	.60	.25
❑ 96 Nolan Ryan	4.00	1.50
❑ 97 Smokey Burgess	.60	.25
❑ 98 Mickey Vernon	.60	.25
❑ 99 Vern Stephens	.60	.25
❑ 100 Rick Ferrell	.60	.25
❑ 101 Phil Niekro LL	5.00	2.00
❑ 102 Brooks Robinson LL	8.00	3.00
❑ 103 Frank Robinson LL	5.00	2.00
❑ 104 Jim Palmer LL	5.00	2.00
❑ 105 Cal Ripken Jr. LL	12.00	5.00
❑ 106 Warren Spahn LL	8.00	3.00
❑ 107 Cy Young LL	8.00	3.00
❑ 108 Nellie Fox LL	8.00	3.00
❑ 109 Carl Yastrzemski LL	8.00	3.00
❑ 110 Joe Sewell LL	5.00	2.00
❑ 111 Wade Boggs LL	8.00	3.00
❑ 112 Carlton Fisk LL	8.00	3.00
❑ 113 Jackie Robinson LL	8.00	3.00
❑ 114 Roy Campanella LL	8.00	3.00
❑ 115 Pee Wee Reese LL	8.00	3.00
❑ 116 Earl Averill LL	5.00	2.00
❑ 117 Rod Carew LL	8.00	3.00
❑ 118 Ernie Banks LL	8.00	3.00
❑ 119 Fergie Jenkins LL	5.00	2.00
❑ 120 Billy Williams LL	5.00	2.00
❑ 121 Al Lopez LL	5.00	2.00
❑ 122 Luis Aparicio LL	5.00	2.00
❑ 123 Luke Appling LL	5.00	2.00
❑ 124 Joe Morgan LL	5.00	2.00
❑ 125 Johnny Bench LL	8.00	3.00
❑ 126 Tony Perez LL	5.00	2.00
❑ 127 George Foster LL	5.00	2.00
❑ 128 Bob Feller LL	5.00	2.00
❑ 129 Bob Lemon LL	5.00	2.00
❑ 130 Larry Doby LL	5.00	2.00
❑ 131 Lou Boudreau LL	5.00	2.00
❑ 132 George Kell LL	5.00	2.00
❑ 133 Hal Newhouser LL	5.00	2.00
❑ 134 Al Kaline LL	8.00	3.00
❑ 135 Ty Cobb LL	10.00	4.00
❑ 136 Charlie Keller LL	5.00	2.00
❑ 137 Buck Leonard LL	5.00	2.00
❑ 138 Maury Wills LL	5.00	2.00
❑ 139 Don Drysdale LL	8.00	3.00
❑ 140 Don Sutton LL	5.00	2.00
❑ 141 Eddie Mathews LL	8.00	3.00
❑ 142 Paul Molitor LL	5.00	2.00
❑ 143 Kirby Puckett LL	10.00	4.00
❑ 144 Harmon Killebrew LL	8.00	3.00
❑ 145 Monte Irvin LL	5.00	2.00
❑ 146 Mel Ott LL	5.00	2.00
❑ 147 Charlie Gehringer LL	5.00	2.00
❑ 148 Hoyt Wilhelm LL	5.00	2.00
❑ 149 Tom Seaver LL	8.00	3.00
❑ 150 Ted Kluszewski LL	8.00	3.00
❑ 151 Joe DiMaggio LL	10.00	4.00
❑ 152 Lou Gehrig LL	10.00	4.00
❑ 153 Babe Ruth LL	12.00	5.00
❑ 154 Casey Stengel LL	5.00	2.00
❑ 155 Phil Rizzuto LL	8.00	3.00
❑ 156 Thurman Munson LL	8.00	3.00
❑ 157 Johnny Mize LL	5.00	2.00
❑ 158 Yogi Berra LL	8.00	3.00
❑ 159 Roger Maris LL	8.00	3.00
❑ 160 Early Wynn LL	5.00	2.00
❑ 161 Bobby Doerr LL	5.00	2.00
❑ 162 Joe Cronin LL	5.00	2.00
❑ 163 Don Mattingly LL	10.00	4.00
❑ 164 Ray Dandridge LL	5.00	2.00
❑ 165 Rollie Fingers LL	5.00	2.00
❑ 166 Christy Mathewson LL	8.00	3.00
❑ 167 Reggie Jackson LL	8.00	3.00
❑ 168 Dennis Eckersley LL	5.00	2.00
❑ 169 Mickey Cochrane LL	5.00	2.00
❑ 170 Jimmie Foxx LL	8.00	3.00
❑ 171 Lefty Gomez LL	5.00	2.00
❑ 172 Jim Bunning LL	5.00	2.00
❑ 173 Steve Carlton LL	5.00	2.00
❑ 174 Robin Roberts LL	5.00	2.00
❑ 175 Richie Ashburn LL	8.00	3.00
❑ 176 Mike Schmidt LL	8.00	3.00
❑ 177 Ralph Kiner LL	8.00	3.00
❑ 178 Willie Stargell LL	8.00	3.00
❑ 179 Roberto Clemente LL	15.00	6.00
❑ 180 Bill Mazeroski LL	8.00	3.00
❑ 181 Honus Wagner LL	8.00	3.00
❑ 182 Pie Traynor LL	5.00	2.00
❑ 183 Tony Gwynn LL	8.00	3.00
❑ 184 Willie McCovey LL	8.00	3.00
❑ 185 Gaylord Perry LL	5.00	2.00
❑ 186 Juan Marichal LL	5.00	2.00
❑ 187 Orlando Cepeda LL	5.00	2.00
❑ 188 Satchel Paige LL	8.00	3.00
❑ 189 George Sisler LL	5.00	2.00
❑ 190 Rogers Hornsby LL	8.00	3.00
❑ 191 Stan Musial LL	8.00	3.00
❑ 192 Dizzy Dean LL	8.00	3.00
❑ 193 Bob Gibson LL	8.00	3.00
❑ 194 Red Schoendienst LL	5.00	2.00
❑ 195 Lou Brock LL	8.00	3.00
❑ 196 Enos Slaughter LL	5.00	2.00
❑ 197 Nolan Ryan LL	12.00	5.00
❑ 198 Mickey Vernon LL	5.00	2.00
❑ 199 Walter Johnson LL	8.00	3.00
❑ 200 Rick Ferrell LL	5.00	2.00

2008 SP Legendary Cuts

Card		
❑ COMP.SET w/o SP's (100)	20.00	8.00
❑ COMMON CARD (1-100)	.50	.20
❑ COMMON CARD (101-146)	5.00	2.00
❑ COMMON CARD (147-200)	5.00	2.00
❑ 101-200 RANDOMLY INSERTED		
❑ 101-200 PRINT RUN 550 SERIAL #'d SETS		
❑ 1 Ken Griffey Jr.	2.00	.75
❑ 2 Derek Jeter	3.00	1.25
❑ 3 Albert Pujols	2.50	1.00
❑ 4 Ichiro Suzuki	2.00	.75

❑ 5 Ryan Braun 1.50 .60
❑ 6 Manny Ramirez 1.25 .50
❑ 7 David Ortiz 1.25 .50
❑ 8 Greg Maddux 1.50 .60
❑ 9 Roger Clemens 1.50 .60
❑ 10 Chase Utley 1.25 .50
❑ 11 Vladimir Guerrero 1.25 .50
❑ 12 Johan Santana 1.25 .50
❑ 13 Chipper Jones 1.50 .60
❑ 14 Tom Glavine .75 .30
❑ 15 Ryan Howard 1.50 .60
❑ 16 Hunter Pence 1.25 .50
❑ 17 Prince Fielder 1.25 .50
❑ 18 Jeff Francoeur .75 .30
❑ 19 David Wright 1.50 .60
❑ 20 Carlos Beltran .50 .20
❑ 21 Carlos Lee .50 .20
❑ 22 Cole Hamels .75 .30
❑ 23 Jered Weaver .50 .20
❑ 24 B.J. Upton .75 .30
❑ 25 Akinori Iwamura .50 .20
❑ 26 Daisuke Matsuzaka 2.00 .75
❑ 27 Curt Schilling .75 .30
❑ 28 Adam Dunn .50 .20
❑ 29 Jose Reyes .75 .30
❑ 30 Nomar Garciaparra 1.25 .50
❑ 31 Hideki Matsui 1.25 .50
❑ 32 Matt Holliday .75 .30
❑ 33 Jason Bay .50 .20
❑ 34 Grady Sizemore .75 .30
❑ 35 Travis Hafner .50 .20
❑ 36 Victor Martinez .50 .20
❑ 37 C.C. Sabathia .50 .20
❑ 38 Justin Morneau .75 .30
❑ 39 Torii Hunter .50 .20
❑ 40 Joe Mauer .75 .30
❑ 41 Russell Martin .50 .20
❑ 42 Frank Thomas 1.25 .50
❑ 43 Miguel Tejada .50 .20
❑ 44 Brian Roberts .75 .30
❑ 45 Justin Verlander .75 .30
❑ 46 Gary Sheffield .50 .20
❑ 47 Magglio Ordonez .75 .30
❑ 48 Alex Rodriguez 2.00 .75
❑ 49 Bobby Abreu .50 .20
❑ 50 Mark Teixeira .75 .30
❑ 51 Andruw Jones .50 .20
❑ 52 Derrek Lee .75 .30
❑ 53 Aramis Ramirez .50 .20
❑ 54 Carlos Zambrano .50 .20
❑ 55 Alfonso Soriano .75 .30
❑ 56 Omar Vizquel .50 .20
❑ 57 Lance Berkman .75 .30
❑ 58 Roy Oswalt .50 .20
❑ 59 Jake Peavy .50 .20
❑ 60 Chris B. Young .50 .20
❑ 61 Khalil Greene .75 .30
❑ 62 Troy Tulowitzki .75 .30
❑ 63 Todd Helton .75 .30
❑ 64 Josh Beckett .75 .30
❑ 65 Miguel Cabrera .75 .30
❑ 66 Hanley Ramirez 1.25 .50
❑ 67 Dan Uggla .75 .30
❑ 68 Scott Kazmir .75 .30
❑ 69 Delmon Young .75 .30
❑ 70 Erik Bedard .50 .20
❑ 71 Alex Gordon 1.25 .50
❑ 72 Felix Hernandez .75 .30
❑ 73 Kenji Johjima .50 .20
❑ 74 John Lackey .50 .20
❑ 75 Ryan Zimmerman .75 .30
❑ 76 Jeremy Bonderman .50 .20
❑ 77 Chien-Ming Wang 1.50 .60
❑ 78 Jim Thome .75 .30
❑ 79 Jimmy Rollins .75 .30
❑ 80 Mariano Rivera 1.25 .50
❑ 81 Curtis Granderson .75 .30
❑ 82 Nick Markakis .75 .30
❑ 83 Trevor Hoffman .50 .20
❑ 84 Barry Zito .50 .20
❑ 85 Yovani Gallardo .50 .20
❑ 86 Dan Haren .50 .20
❑ 87 Vernon Wells .50 .20
❑ 88 Ian Kennedy RC 1.50 .60
❑ 89 Phil Hughes 1.25 .50
❑ 90 Brian McCann .75 .30
❑ 91 J.J. Hardy .50 .20
❑ 92 Roy Halladay .50 .20
❑ 93 Mike Piazza 1.25 .50
❑ 94 Ivan Rodriguez .75 .30
❑ 95 Dontrelle Willis .50 .20
❑ 96 Brandon Webb .50 .20
❑ 97 Carl Crawford .50 .20
❑ 98 Tim Lincecum 1.25 .50
❑ 99 Jason Varitek 1.25 .50
❑ 100 Freddy Sanchez .50 .20
❑ 101 Abraham Lincoln 10.00 4.00
❑ 102 Ulysses S. Grant 8.00 3.00
❑ 103 Andrew Johnson 5.00 2.00
❑ 104 George Washington 8.00 3.00
❑ 105 Thomas Jefferson 5.00 2.00
❑ 106 Andrew Jackson 8.00 3.00
❑ 107 James Madison 5.00 2.00
❑ 108 James Monroe 5.00 2.00
❑ 109 Benjamin Franklin 6.00 2.50
❑ 110 Alexander Graham Bell 5.00 2.00
❑ 111 Thomas Edison 5.00 2.00
❑ 112 Red Baron 5.00 2.00
❑ 113 Robert E. Lee 8.00 3.00
❑ 114 Mark Twain 5.00 2.00
❑ 115 Arthur Conan Doyle 5.00 2.00
❑ 116 Bram Stoker 5.00 2.00
❑ 117 Jules Verne 5.00 2.00
❑ 118 Billy the Kid 6.00 2.50
❑ 119 Harriet Beecher Stowe 5.00 2.00
❑ 120 Andrew Carnegie 5.00 2.00
❑ 121 Lewis Carroll 5.00 2.00
❑ 122 Cornelius Vanderbilt 5.00 2.00
❑ 123 Brigham Young 5.00 2.00
❑ 124 Charles Dickens 5.00 2.00
❑ 125 Vincent Van Gogh 5.00 2.00
❑ 126 Claude Monet 5.00 2.00
❑ 127 Jesse James 6.00 2.50
❑ 128 John D. Rockefeller 5.00 2.00
❑ 129 Harry Longabaugh 5.00 2.00
❑ 130 John F. Kennedy 10.00 4.00
❑ 131 Richard Nixon 6.00 2.50
❑ 132 Lyndon B. Johnson 6.00 2.50
❑ 133 Dwight D. Eisenhower 5.00 2.00
❑ 134 Franklin D. Roosevelt 5.00 2.00
❑ 135 Harry Truman 5.00 2.00
❑ 136 Ronald Reagan 10.00 4.00
❑ 137 Bill Clinton 6.00 2.50
❑ 138 George H.W. Bush 6.00 2.50
❑ 139 Jimmy Carter 6.00 2.50
❑ 140 Gerald Ford 6.00 2.50
❑ 141 Herbert Hoover 5.00 2.00
❑ 142 Calvin Coolidge 5.00 2.00
❑ 143 Warren G. Harding 5.00 2.00
❑ 144 Woodrow Wilson 5.00 2.00
❑ 145 William Taft 5.00 2.00
❑ 146 Theodore Roosevelt 6.00 2.50
❑ 147 Phil Niekro 5.00 2.00
❑ 148 Brooks Robinson 8.00 3.00
❑ 149 Cal Ripken Jr. 15.00 6.00
❑ 150 Eddie Murray 8.00 3.00
❑ 151 Jim Palmer 5.00 2.00
❑ 152 Abner Doubleday 5.00 2.00
❑ 153 Wade Boggs 5.00 2.00
❑ 154 Carl Yastrzemski 12.00 5.00
❑ 155 Bobby Doerr 5.00 2.00
❑ 156 Carlton Fisk 8.00 3.00
❑ 157 Pee Wee Reese 8.00 3.00
❑ 158 Ernie Banks 8.00 3.00
❑ 159 Fergie Jenkins 5.00 2.00
❑ 160 Billy Williams 5.00 2.00
❑ 161 Ryne Sandberg 10.00 4.00
❑ 162 Luis Aparicio 5.00 2.00
❑ 163 Joe Morgan 5.00 2.00
❑ 164 Johnny Bench 8.00 3.00
❑ 165 Tony Perez 5.00 2.00
❑ 166 Bob Feller 5.00 2.00
❑ 167 Larry Doby 5.00 2.00
❑ 168 Bob Lemon 5.00 2.00
❑ 169 Al Kaline 8.00 3.00
❑ 170 Warren Spahn 8.00 3.00
❑ 171 Robin Yount 8.00 3.00
❑ 172 Rollie Fingers 5.00 2.00
❑ 173 Harmon Killebrew 8.00 3.00
❑ 174 Rod Carew 8.00 3.00
❑ 175 Babe Ruth 12.00 5.00
❑ 176 Monte Irvin 5.00 2.00
❑ 177 Tom Seaver 8.00 3.00
❑ 178 Phil Rizzuto 8.00 3.00
❑ 179 Jack Chesbro 5.00 2.00
❑ 180 Catfish Hunter 5.00 2.00
❑ 181 Babe Ruth 12.00 5.00
❑ 182 Reggie Jackson 8.00 3.00
❑ 183 Dennis Eckersley 5.00 2.00
❑ 184 Steve Carlton 5.00 2.00
❑ 185 Ed Delahanty 5.00 2.00
❑ 186 Mike Schmidt 10.00 4.00
❑ 187 Jim Bunning 5.00 2.00
❑ 188 Robin Roberts 5.00 2.00
❑ 189 Willie Stargell 8.00 3.00
❑ 190 Bill Mazeroski 8.00 3.00
❑ 191 Ralph Kiner 8.00 3.00
❑ 192 Tony Gwynn 15.00 6.00
❑ 193 Juan Marichal 5.00 2.00
❑ 194 Willie McCovey 8.00 3.00
❑ 195 Orlando Cepeda 5.00 2.00
❑ 196 Stan Musial 10.00 4.00
❑ 197 Ozzie Smith 10.00 4.00
❑ 198 Bob Gibson 8.00 3.00
❑ 199 Bruce Sutter 5.00 2.00
❑ 200 Nolan Ryan 12.00 5.00

1996 SPx

❑ COMPLETE SET (60) 50.00 20.00
❑ 1 Greg Maddux 3.00 1.25
❑ 2 Chipper Jones 2.00 .75
❑ 3 Fred McGriff 1.25 .50
❑ 4 Tom Glavine 1.25 .50
❑ 5 Cal Ripken 6.00 2.50
❑ 6 Roberto Alomar 1.25 .50
❑ 7 Rafael Palmeiro 1.25 .50
❑ 8 Jose Canseco 1.25 .50
❑ 9 Roger Clemens 4.00 1.50
❑ 10 Mo Vaughn .75 .30
❑ 11 Jim Edmonds .75 .30
❑ 12 Tim Salmon 1.25 .50
❑ 13 Sammy Sosa 2.00 .75
❑ 14 Ryne Sandberg 3.00 1.25
❑ 15 Mark Grace 1.25 .50
❑ 16 Frank Thomas 2.00 .75
❑ 17 Barry Larkin 1.25 .50
❑ 18 Kenny Lofton .75 .30
❑ 19 Albert Belle .75 .30
❑ 20 Eddie Murray 2.00 .75
❑ 21 Manny Ramirez 1.25 .50
❑ 22 Dante Bichette .75 .30
❑ 23 Larry Walker .75 .30
❑ 24 Vinny Castilla .75 .30
❑ 25 Andres Galarraga .75 .30
❑ 26 Cecil Fielder .75 .30
❑ 27 Gary Sheffield .75 .30
❑ 28 Craig Biggio 1.25 .50
❑ 29 Jeff Bagwell 1.25 .50
❑ 30 Derek Bell .75 .30
❑ 31 Johnny Damon 1.25 .50
❑ 32 Eric Karros .75 .30
❑ 33 Mike Piazza 3.00 1.25
❑ 34 Raul Mondesi .75 .30
❑ 35 Hideo Nomo 2.00 .75
❑ 36 Kirby Puckett 2.00 .75
❑ 37 Paul Molitor .75 .30
❑ 38 Marty Cordova .75 .30
❑ 39 Rondell White .75 .30
❑ 40 Jason Isringhausen .75 .30
❑ 41 Paul Wilson .75 .30

❑ 42	Rey Ordonez	.75	.30
❑ 43	Derek Jeter	5.00	2.00
❑ 44	Wade Boggs	1.25	.50
❑ 45	Mark McGwire	5.00	2.00
❑ 46	Jason Kendall	.75	.30
❑ 47	Ron Gant	.75	.30
❑ 48	Ozzie Smith	3.00	1.25
❑ 49	Tony Gwynn	2.50	1.00
❑ 50	Ken Caminiti	.75	.30
❑ 51	Barry Bonds	5.00	2.00
❑ 52	Matt Williams	.75	.30
❑ 53	Osvaldo Fernandez	.75	.30
❑ 54	Jay Buhner	.75	.30
❑ 55	Ken Griffey Jr.	3.00	1.25
❑ 56	Randy Johnson	2.00	.75
❑ 57	Alex Rodriguez	4.00	1.50
❑ 58	Juan Gonzalez	.75	.30
❑ 59	Joe Carter	.75	.30
❑ 60	Carlos Delgado	.75	.30
❑ KG1	Ken Griffey Jr. Comm.	5.00	2.00
❑ MP1	Mike Piazza Trib.	5.00	2.00
❑ KGA1	Ken Griffey Jr. Auto.	250.00	150.00
❑ MPA1	Mike Piazza Auto.	200.00	125.00

1997 SPx

❑	COMPLETE SET (50)	60.00	25.00
❑ 1	Eddie Murray	1.50	.60
❑ 2	Darin Erstad	.60	.25
❑ 3	Tim Salmon	1.00	.40
❑ 4	Andruw Jones	1.00	.40
❑ 5	Chipper Jones	1.50	.60
❑ 6	John Smoltz	1.00	.40
❑ 7	Greg Maddux	2.50	1.00
❑ 8	Kenny Lofton	.60	.25
❑ 9	Roberto Alomar	1.00	.40
❑ 10	Rafael Palmeiro	1.00	.40
❑ 11	Brady Anderson	.60	.25
❑ 12	Cal Ripken	5.00	2.00
❑ 13	Nomar Garciaparra	2.50	1.00
❑ 14	Mo Vaughn	.60	.25
❑ 15	Ryne Sandberg	2.50	1.00
❑ 16	Sammy Sosa	1.50	.60
❑ 17	Frank Thomas	1.50	.60
❑ 18	Albert Belle	.60	.25
❑ 19	Barry Larkin	1.00	.40
❑ 20	Deion Sanders	1.00	.40
❑ 21	Manny Ramirez	1.00	.40
❑ 22	Jim Thome	1.00	.40
❑ 23	Dante Bichette	.60	.25
❑ 24	Andres Galarraga	.60	.25
❑ 25	Larry Walker	.60	.25
❑ 26	Gary Sheffield	.60	.25
❑ 27	Jeff Bagwell	1.00	.40
❑ 28	Raul Mondesi	.60	.25
❑ 29	Hideo Nomo	1.50	.60
❑ 30	Mike Piazza	2.50	1.00
❑ 31	Paul Molitor	.60	.25
❑ 32	Todd Walker	.60	.25
❑ 33	Vladimir Guerrero	1.50	.60
❑ 34	Todd Hundley	.60	.25
❑ 35	Andy Pettitte	1.00	.40
❑ 36	Derek Jeter	4.00	1.50
❑ 37	Jose Canseco	1.00	.40
❑ 38	Mark McGwire	4.00	1.50
❑ 39	Scott Rolen	1.00	.40
❑ 40	Ron Gant	.60	.25
❑ 41	Ken Caminiti	.60	.25
❑ 42	Tony Gwynn	2.00	.75
❑ 43	Barry Bonds	4.00	1.50
❑ 44	Jay Buhner	.60	.25
❑ 45	Ken Griffey Jr.	2.50	1.00
❑ 46	Alex Rodriguez	2.50	1.00
❑ 47	Jose Cruz Jr. RC	1.00	.40
❑ 48	Juan Gonzalez	.60	.25
❑ 49	Ivan Rodriguez	1.00	.40
❑ 50	Roger Clemens	3.00	1.25
❑ S45	Ken Griffey Jr. Sample	2.00	.75

1998 SPx Finite

❑	COMP.YM SER.1 (30)	40.00	15.00
❑	COMMON YM (1-30)	1.50	.60
❑	COMP.PE SER.1 (20)	120.00	50.00
❑	COMMON PE (31-50)	2.50	1.00
❑	COMP.BASIC SER.1 (90)	80.00	30.00
❑	COMMON CARD (51-140)	1.00	.40
❑	COMP.SF SER.1 (30)	100.00	40.00
❑	COMMON SF (141-170)	1.25	.50
❑	COMP.HG SER.1 (10)	150.00	60.00
❑	COMMON HG (171-180)	4.00	1.50
❑	COMP.YM SER.2 (30)	60.00	25.00
❑	COMMON YM (181-210)	1.50	.60
❑	COMP.PP SER.2 (30)	80.00	30.00
❑	COMMON PP (211-240)	1.25	.50
❑	COMP.BASIC SER.2 (90)	50.00	20.00
❑	COMMON CARD (241-330)	1.00	.40
❑	COMP.TW SER.2 (20)	30.00	12.50
❑	COMMON TW (331-350)	2.50	1.00
❑	COMP.CG SER.2 (10)	150.00	60.00
❑	COMMON CG (351-360)	4.00	1.50
❑ 1	Nomar Garciaparra YM	6.00	2.50
❑ 2	Miguel Tejada YM	4.00	1.50
❑ 3	Mike Cameron YM	1.50	.60
❑ 4	Ken Cloude YM	1.50	.60
❑ 5	Jaret Wright YM	1.50	.60
❑ 6	Mark Kotsay YM	1.50	.60
❑ 7	Craig Counsell YM	1.50	.60
❑ 8	Jose Guillen YM	1.50	.60
❑ 9	Neifi Perez YM	1.50	.60
❑ 10	Jose Cruz Jr. YM	1.50	.60
❑ 11	Brett Tomko YM	1.50	.60
❑ 12	Matt Morris YM	1.50	.60
❑ 13	Justin Thompson YM	1.50	.60
❑ 14	Jeremi Gonzalez YM	1.50	.60
❑ 15	Scott Rolen YM	2.50	1.00
❑ 16	Vladimir Guerrero YM	4.00	1.50
❑ 17	Brad Fullmer YM	1.50	.60
❑ 18	Brian Giles YM	1.50	.60
❑ 19	Todd Dunwoody YM	1.50	.60
❑ 20	Ben Grieve YM	1.50	.60
❑ 21	Juan Encarnacion YM	1.50	.60
❑ 22	Aaron Boone YM	1.50	.60
❑ 23	Richie Sexson YM	1.50	.60
❑ 24	Richard Hidalgo YM	1.50	.60
❑ 25	Andruw Jones YM	2.50	1.00
❑ 26	Todd Helton YM	2.50	1.00
❑ 27	Paul Konerko YM	1.50	.60
❑ 28	Dante Powell YM	1.50	.60
❑ 29	Eli Marrero YM	1.50	.60
❑ 30	Derek Jeter YM	10.00	4.00
❑ 31	Mike Piazza PE	10.00	4.00
❑ 32	Tony Clark PE	2.50	1.00
❑ 33	Larry Walker PE	2.50	1.00
❑ 34	Jim Thome PE	4.00	1.50
❑ 35	Juan Gonzalez PE	5.00	2.00
❑ 36	Jeff Bagwell PE	4.00	1.50
❑ 37	Jay Buhner PE	2.50	1.00
❑ 38	Tim Salmon PE	4.00	1.50
❑ 39	Albert Belle PE	2.50	1.00
❑ 40	Mark McGwire PE	15.00	6.00
❑ 41	Sammy Sosa PE	6.00	2.50
❑ 42	Mo Vaughn PE	2.50	1.00
❑ 43	Manny Ramirez PE	4.00	1.50
❑ 44	Tino Martinez PE	4.00	1.50
❑ 45	Frank Thomas PE	6.00	2.50
❑ 46	Nomar Garciaparra PE	10.00	4.00
❑ 47	Alex Rodriguez PE	10.00	4.00
❑ 48	Chipper Jones PE	6.00	2.50
❑ 49	Barry Bonds PE	15.00	6.00
❑ 50	Ken Griffey Jr. PE	10.00	4.00
❑ 51	Jason Dickson	1.00	.40
❑ 52	Jim Edmonds	1.00	.40
❑ 53	Darin Erstad	1.00	.40
❑ 54	Tim Salmon	1.50	.60
❑ 55	Chipper Jones	2.50	1.00
❑ 56	Ryan Klesko	1.00	.40
❑ 57	Tom Glavine	1.50	.60
❑ 58	Denny Neagle	1.00	.40
❑ 59	John Smoltz	1.50	.60
❑ 60	Javy Lopez	1.00	.40
❑ 61	Roberto Alomar	1.50	.60
❑ 62	Rafael Palmeiro	1.50	.60
❑ 63	Mike Mussina	1.50	.60
❑ 64	Cal Ripken	8.00	3.00
❑ 65	Mo Vaughn	1.00	.40
❑ 66	Tim Naehring	1.00	.40
❑ 67	John Valentin	1.00	.40
❑ 68	Mark Grace	1.50	.60
❑ 69	Kevin Orie	1.00	.40
❑ 70	Sammy Sosa	2.50	1.00
❑ 71	Albert Belle	1.00	.40
❑ 72	Frank Thomas	2.50	1.00
❑ 73	Robin Ventura	1.00	.40
❑ 74	David Justice	1.00	.40
❑ 75	Kenny Lofton	1.00	.40
❑ 76	Omar Vizquel	1.50	.60
❑ 77	Manny Ramirez	1.50	.60
❑ 78	Jim Thome	1.50	.60
❑ 79	Dante Bichette	1.00	.40
❑ 80	Larry Walker	1.00	.40
❑ 81	Vinny Castilla	1.00	.40
❑ 82	Ellis Burks	1.00	.40
❑ 83	Bobby Higginson	1.00	.40
❑ 84	Brian Hunter	1.00	.40
❑ 85	Tony Clark	1.00	.40
❑ 86	Mike Hampton	1.00	.40
❑ 87	Jeff Bagwell	1.50	.60
❑ 88	Craig Biggio	1.50	.60
❑ 89	Derek Bell	1.00	.40
❑ 90	Mike Piazza	4.00	1.50
❑ 91	Ramon Martinez	1.00	.40
❑ 92	Raul Mondesi	1.00	.40
❑ 93	Hideo Nomo	2.50	1.00
❑ 94	Eric Karros	1.00	.40
❑ 95	Paul Molitor	1.00	.40
❑ 96	Marty Cordova	1.00	.40
❑ 97	Brad Radke	1.00	.40
❑ 98	Mark Grudzielanek	1.00	.40
❑ 99	Carlos Perez	1.00	.40
❑ 100	Rondell White	1.00	.40
❑ 101	Todd Hundley	1.00	.40
❑ 102	Edgardo Alfonzo	1.00	.40
❑ 103	John Franco	1.00	.40
❑ 104	John Olerud	1.00	.40
❑ 105	Tino Martinez	1.50	.60
❑ 106	David Cone	1.00	.40
❑ 107	Paul O'Neill	1.50	.60
❑ 108	Andy Pettitte	1.50	.60
❑ 109	Bernie Williams	1.50	.60
❑ 110	Rickey Henderson	4.00	1.50
❑ 111	Jason Giambi	1.00	.40
❑ 112	Matt Stairs	1.00	.40
❑ 113	Gregg Jefferies	1.00	.40
❑ 114	Rico Brogna	1.00	.40
❑ 115	Curt Schilling	1.00	.40
❑ 116	Jason Schmidt	1.00	.40
❑ 117	Jose Guillen	1.00	.40
❑ 118	Kevin Young	1.00	.40
❑ 119	Ray Lankford	1.00	.40
❑ 120	Mark McGwire	6.00	2.50
❑ 121	Delino DeShields	1.00	.40
❑ 122	Ken Caminiti	1.00	.40
❑ 123	Tony Gwynn	3.00	1.25

❑ 124 Trevor Hoffman 1.00 .40
❑ 125 Barry Bonds 6.00 2.50
❑ 126 Jeff Kent 1.00 .40
❑ 127 Shawn Estes 1.00 .40
❑ 128 J.T. Snow 1.00 .40
❑ 129 Jay Buhner 1.00 .40
❑ 130 Ken Griffey Jr. 4.00 1.50
❑ 131 Dan Wilson 1.00 .40
❑ 132 Edgar Martinez 1.50 .60
❑ 133 Alex Rodriguez 4.00 1.50
❑ 134 Rusty Greer 1.00 .40
❑ 135 Juan Gonzalez 1.00 .40
❑ 136 Fernando Tatis 1.00 .40
❑ 137 Ivan Rodriguez 1.50 .60
❑ 138 Carlos Delgado 1.00 .40
❑ 139 Pat Hentgen 1.00 .40
❑ 140 Roger Clemens 5.00 2.00
❑ 141 Chipper Jones SF 3.00 1.25
❑ 142 Greg Maddux SF 5.00 2.00
❑ 143 Rafael Palmeiro SF 2.00 .75
❑ 144 Mike Mussina SF 2.00 .75
❑ 145 Cal Ripken SF 10.00 4.00
❑ 146 Nomar Garciaparra SF 5.00 2.00
❑ 147 Mo Vaughn SF 1.25 .50
❑ 148 Sammy Sosa SF 3.00 1.25
❑ 149 Albert Belle SF 1.25 .50
❑ 150 Frank Thomas SF 3.00 1.25
❑ 151 Jim Thome SF 2.00 .75
❑ 152 Kenny Lofton SF 1.25 .50
❑ 153 Manny Ramirez SF 2.00 .75
❑ 154 Larry Walker SF 1.25 .50
❑ 155 Jeff Bagwell SF 2.00 .75
❑ 156 Craig Biggio SF 2.00 .75
❑ 157 Mike Piazza SF 5.00 2.00
❑ 158 Paul Molitor SF 1.25 .50
❑ 159 Derek Jeter SF 8.00 3.00
❑ 160 Tino Martinez SF 2.00 .75
❑ 161 Curt Schilling SF 1.25 .50
❑ 162 Mark McGwire SF 8.00 3.00
❑ 163 Tony Gwynn SF 4.00 1.50
❑ 164 Barry Bonds SF 8.00 3.00
❑ 165 Ken Griffey Jr. SF 5.00 2.00
❑ 166 Randy Johnson SF 3.00 1.25
❑ 167 Alex Rodriguez SF 5.00 2.00
❑ 168 Juan Gonzalez SF 1.25 .50
❑ 169 Ivan Rodriguez SF 2.00 .75
❑ 170 Roger Clemens SF 6.00 2.50
❑ 171 Greg Maddux HG 15.00 6.00
❑ 172 Cal Ripken HG 30.00 12.50
❑ 173 Frank Thomas HG 10.00 4.00
❑ 174 Jeff Bagwell HG 6.00 2.50
❑ 175 Mike Piazza HG 15.00 6.00
❑ 176 Mark McGwire HG 25.00 10.00
❑ 177 Barry Bonds HG 25.00 10.00
❑ 178 Ken Griffey Jr. HG 15.00 6.00
❑ 179 Alex Rodriguez HG 15.00 6.00
❑ 180 Roger Clemens HG 20.00 8.00
❑ 181 Mike Caruso YM 1.50 .60
❑ 182 David Ortiz YM 5.00 2.00
❑ 183 Gabe Alvarez YM 1.50 .60
❑ 184 Gary Matthews Jr. YM RC 2.50 1.00
❑ 185 Kerry Wood YM 2.00 .75
❑ 186 Carl Pavano YM 1.50 .60
❑ 187 Alex Gonzalez YM 1.50 .60
❑ 188 Masato Yoshii YM RC 1.50 .60
❑ 189 Larry Sutton YM 1.50 .60
❑ 190 Russell Branyan YM 1.50 .60
❑ 191 Bruce Chen YM 1.50 .60
❑ 192 Rolando Arrojo YM RC 1.50 .60
❑ 193 Ryan Christenson YM RC 1.50 .60
❑ 194 Cliff Politte YM 1.50 .60
❑ 195 A.J. Hinch YM 1.50 .60
❑ 196 Kevin Witt YM 1.50 .60
❑ 197 Daryle Ward YM 1.50 .60
❑ 198 Corey Koskie YM RC 2.50 1.00
❑ 199 Mike Lowell YM RC 10.00 4.00
❑ 200 Travis Lee YM 1.50 .60
❑ 201 Kevin Millwood YM RC 5.00 2.00
❑ 202 Robert Smith YM 1.50 .60
❑ 203 Magglio Ordonez YM RC 15.00 6.00
❑ 204 Eric Milton YM 1.50 .60
❑ 205 Geoff Jenkins YM 1.50 .60
❑ 206 Rich Butler YM RC 1.50 .60
❑ 207 Mike Kinkade YM RC 1.50 .60
❑ 208 Braden Looper YM 1.50 .60
❑ 209 Matt Clement YM 1.50 .60
❑ 210 Derrek Lee YM 2.50 1.00
❑ 211 Randy Johnson PP 3.00 1.25
❑ 212 John Smoltz PP 2.00 .75
❑ 213 Roger Clemens PP 6.00 2.50
❑ 214 Curt Schilling PP 1.25 .50
❑ 215 Pedro Martinez PP 2.00 .75
❑ 216 Vinny Castilla PP 1.25 .50
❑ 217 Jose Cruz Jr. PP 1.25 .50
❑ 218 Jim Thome PP 2.00 .75
❑ 219 Alex Rodriguez PP 5.00 2.00
❑ 220 Frank Thomas PP 3.00 1.25
❑ 221 Tim Salmon PP 2.00 .75
❑ 222 Larry Walker PP 1.25 .50
❑ 223 Albert Belle PP 1.25 .50
❑ 224 Manny Ramirez PP 2.00 .75
❑ 225 Mark McGwire PP 8.00 3.00
❑ 226 Mo Vaughn PP 1.25 .50
❑ 227 Andres Galarraga PP 1.25 .50
❑ 228 Scott Rolen PP 2.00 .75
❑ 229 Travis Lee PP 1.25 .50
❑ 230 Mike Piazza PP 5.00 2.00
❑ 231 Nomar Garciaparra PP 6.00 2.00
❑ 232 Andruw Jones PP 2.00 .75
❑ 233 Barry Bonds PP 8.00 3.00
❑ 234 Jeff Bagwell PP 2.00 .75
❑ 235 Juan Gonzalez PP 1.25 .50
❑ 236 Tino Martinez PP 2.00 .75
❑ 237 Vladimir Guerrero PP 3.00 1.25
❑ 238 Rafael Palmeiro PP 2.00 .75
❑ 239 Russell Branyan PP 1.25 .50
❑ 240 Ken Griffey Jr. PP 5.00 2.00
❑ 241 Cecil Fielder 1.00 .40
❑ 242 Chuck Finley 1.00 .40
❑ 243 Jay Bell 1.00 .40
❑ 244 Andy Benes 1.00 .40
❑ 245 Matt Williams 1.00 .40
❑ 246 Brian Anderson 1.00 .40
❑ 247 Dave Dellucci RC 1.50 .60
❑ 248 Andres Galarraga 1.00 .40
❑ 249 Andruw Jones 1.50 .60
❑ 250 Greg Maddux 4.00 1.50
❑ 251 Brady Anderson 1.00 .40
❑ 252 Joe Carter 1.00 .40
❑ 253 Eric Davis 1.00 .40
❑ 254 Pedro Martinez 1.50 .60
❑ 255 Nomar Garciaparra 4.00 1.50
❑ 256 Dennis Eckersley 1.00 .40
❑ 257 Henry Rodriguez 1.00 .40
❑ 258 Jeff Blauser 1.00 .40
❑ 259 Jaime Navarro 1.00 .40
❑ 260 Ray Durham 1.00 .40
❑ 261 Chris Stynes 1.00 .40
❑ 262 Willie Greene 1.00 .40
❑ 263 Reggie Sanders 1.00 .40
❑ 264 Bret Boone 1.00 .40
❑ 265 Barry Larkin 1.50 .60
❑ 266 Travis Fryman 1.00 .40
❑ 267 Charles Nagy 1.00 .40
❑ 268 Sandy Alomar Jr. 1.00 .40
❑ 269 Darryl Kile 1.00 .40
❑ 270 Mike Lansing 1.00 .40
❑ 271 Pedro Astacio 1.00 .40
❑ 272 Damion Easley 1.00 .40
❑ 273 Joe Randa 1.00 .40
❑ 274 Luis Gonzalez 1.00 .40
❑ 275 Mike Piazza 4.00 1.50
❑ 276 Todd Zeile 1.00 .40
❑ 277 Edgar Renteria 1.00 .40
❑ 278 Livan Hernandez 1.00 .40
❑ 279 Cliff Floyd 1.00 .40
❑ 280 Moises Alou 1.00 .40
❑ 281 Billy Wagner 1.00 .40
❑ 282 Jeff King 1.00 .40
❑ 283 Hal Morris 1.00 .40
❑ 284 Johnny Damon 1.50 .60
❑ 285 Dean Palmer 1.00 .40
❑ 286 Tim Belcher 1.00 .40
❑ 287 Eric Young 1.00 .40
❑ 288 Bobby Bonilla 1.00 .40
❑ 289 Gary Sheffield 1.00 .40
❑ 290 Chan Ho Park 1.00 .40
❑ 291 Charles Johnson 1.00 .40
❑ 292 Jeff Cirillo 1.00 .40
❑ 293 Jeromy Burnitz 1.00 .40
❑ 294 Jose Valentin 1.00 .40
❑ 295 Marquis Grissom 1.00 .40
❑ 296 Todd Walker 1.00 .40
❑ 297 Terry Steinbach 1.00 .40
❑ 298 Rick Aguilera 1.00 .40
❑ 299 Vladimir Guerrero 2.50 1.00
❑ 300 Rey Ordonez 1.00 .40
❑ 301 Butch Huskey 1.00 .40
❑ 302 Bernard Gilkey 1.00 .40
❑ 303 Mariano Rivera 2.50 1.00
❑ 304 Chuck Knoblauch 1.00 .40
❑ 305 Derek Jeter 6.00 2.50
❑ 306 Ricky Bottalico 1.00 .40
❑ 307 Bob Abreu 1.00 .40
❑ 308 Scott Rolen 1.50 .60
❑ 309 Al Martin 1.00 .40
❑ 310 Jason Kendall 1.00 .40
❑ 311 Brian Jordan 1.00 .40
❑ 312 Ron Gant 1.00 .40
❑ 313 Todd Stottlemyre 1.00 .40
❑ 314 Greg Vaughn 1.00 .40
❑ 315 Kevin Brown 1.50 .60
❑ 316 Wally Joyner 1.00 .40
❑ 317 Robb Nen 1.00 .40
❑ 318 Orel Hershiser 1.00 .40
❑ 319 Russ Davis 1.00 .40
❑ 320 Randy Johnson 2.50 1.00
❑ 321 Quinton McCracken 1.00 .40
❑ 322 Tony Saunders 1.00 .40
❑ 323 Wilson Alvarez 1.00 .40
❑ 324 Wade Boggs 1.50 .60
❑ 325 Fred McGriff 1.50 .60
❑ 326 Lee Stevens 1.00 .40
❑ 327 John Wetteland 1.00 .40
❑ 328 Jose Canseco 1.50 .60
❑ 329 Randy Myers 1.00 .40
❑ 330 Jose Cruz Jr. 1.00 .40
❑ 331 Matt Williams TW 2.50 1.00
❑ 332 Andres Galarraga TW 2.50 1.00
❑ 333 Walt Weiss TW 2.50 1.00
❑ 334 Joe Carter TW 2.50 1.00
❑ 335 Pedro Martinez TW 4.00 1.50
❑ 336 Henry Rodriguez TW 2.50 1.00
❑ 337 Travis Fryman TW 2.50 1.00
❑ 338 Darryl Kile TW 2.50 1.00
❑ 339 Mike Lansing TW 2.50 1.00
❑ 340 Mike Piazza TW 10.00 4.00
❑ 341 Moises Alou TW 2.50 1.00
❑ 342 Charles Johnson TW 2.50 1.00
❑ 343 Chuck Knoblauch TW 2.50 1.00
❑ 344 Rickey Henderson TW 6.00 2.50
❑ 345 Kevin Brown TW 4.00 1.50
❑ 346 Orel Hershiser TW 2.50 1.00
❑ 347 Wade Boggs TW 4.00 1.50
❑ 348 Fred McGriff TW 4.00 1.50
❑ 349 Jose Canseco TW 4.00 1.50
❑ 350 Gary Sheffield TW 2.50 1.00
❑ 351 Travis Lee CG 4.00 1.50
❑ 352 Nomar Garciaparra CG 15.00 6.00
❑ 353 Frank Thomas CG 10.00 4.00
❑ 354 Cal Ripken CG 30.00 12.50
❑ 355 Mark McGwire CG 25.00 10.00
❑ 356 Mike Piazza CG 15.00 6.00
❑ 357 Alex Rodriguez CG 15.00 6.00
❑ 358 Barry Bonds CG 25.00 10.00
❑ 359 Tony Gwynn CG 12.00 5.00
❑ 360 Ken Griffey Jr. CG 15.00 6.00

1999 SPx

❑ COMP.SET w/o SP's (80)	25.00	10.00
❑ COMMON MCGWIRE (1-10)	1.50	.60
❑ COMMON CARD (11-80)	.50	.20
❑ COMMON SP (81-120)	10.00	4.00
❑ 1 Mark McGwire 61	3.00	1.25
❑ 2 Mark McGwire 62	3.00	1.25
❑ 3 Mark McGwire 63	1.50	.60
❑ 4 Mark McGwire 64	1.50	.60
❑ 5 Mark McGwire 65	1.50	.60
❑ 6 Mark McGwire 66	1.50	.60
❑ 7 Mark McGwire 67	1.50	.60
❑ 8 Mark McGwire 68	1.50	.60
❑ 9 Mark McGwire 69	1.50	.60
❑ 10 Mark McGwire 70	4.00	1.50
❑ 11 Mo Vaughn	.50	.20
❑ 12 Darin Erstad	.50	.20
❑ 13 Travis Lee	.50	.20
❑ 14 Randy Johnson	1.25	.50
❑ 15 Matt Williams	.50	.20
❑ 16 Chipper Jones	1.25	.50
❑ 17 Greg Maddux	2.00	.75
❑ 18 Andruw Jones	.75	.30
❑ 19 Andres Galarraga	.50	.20
❑ 20 Cal Ripken	4.00	1.50
❑ 21 Albert Belle	.50	.20
❑ 22 Mike Mussina	.75	.30
❑ 23 Nomar Garciaparra	2.00	.75
❑ 24 Pedro Martinez	.75	.30
❑ 25 John Valentin	.50	.20
❑ 26 Kerry Wood	.50	.20
❑ 27 Sammy Sosa	1.25	.50
❑ 28 Mark Grace	.75	.30
❑ 29 Frank Thomas	1.25	.50
❑ 30 Mike Caruso	.50	.20
❑ 31 Barry Larkin	.75	.30
❑ 32 Sean Casey	.50	.20
❑ 33 Jim Thome	.75	.30
❑ 34 Kenny Lofton	.50	.20
❑ 35 Manny Ramirez	.75	.30
❑ 36 Larry Walker	.50	.20
❑ 37 Todd Helton	.75	.30
❑ 38 Vinny Castilla	.50	.20
❑ 39 Tony Clark	.50	.20
❑ 40 Derrek Lee	.75	.30
❑ 41 Mark Kotsay	.50	.20
❑ 42 Jeff Bagwell	.75	.30
❑ 43 Craig Biggio	.75	.30
❑ 44 Moises Alou	.50	.20
❑ 45 Larry Sutton	.50	.20
❑ 46 Johnny Damon	.75	.30
❑ 47 Gary Sheffield	.50	.20
❑ 48 Raul Mondesi	.50	.20
❑ 49 Jeromy Burnitz	.50	.20
❑ 50 Todd Walker	.50	.20
❑ 51 David Ortiz	1.25	.50
❑ 52 Vladimir Guerrero	1.25	.50
❑ 53 Rondell White	.50	.20
❑ 54 Mike Piazza	2.00	.75
❑ 55 Derek Jeter	3.00	1.25
❑ 56 Tino Martinez	.75	.30
❑ 57 Roger Clemens	2.50	1.00
❑ 58 Ben Grieve	.50	.20
❑ 59 A.J. Hinch	.50	.20
❑ 60 Scott Rolen	.75	.30
❑ 61 Doug Glanville	.50	.20
❑ 62 Aramis Ramirez	.50	.20
❑ 63 Jose Guillen	.50	.20
❑ 64 Tony Gwynn	1.50	.60
❑ 65 Greg Vaughn	.50	.20
❑ 66 Ruben Rivera	.50	.20
❑ 67 Barry Bonds	3.00	1.25
❑ 68 J.T. Snow	.50	.20
❑ 69 Alex Rodriguez	2.00	.75
❑ 70 Ken Griffey Jr.	2.00	.75
❑ 71 Jay Buhner	.50	.20
❑ 72 Mark McGwire	3.00	1.25
❑ 73 Fernando Tatis	.50	.20
❑ 74 Quinton McCracken	.50	.20
❑ 75 Wade Boggs	.75	.30
❑ 76 Ivan Rodriguez	.75	.30
❑ 77 Juan Gonzalez	.50	.20
❑ 78 Rafael Palmeiro	.75	.30
❑ 79 Jose Cruz Jr.	.50	.20
❑ 80 Carlos Delgado	.50	.20
❑ 81 Troy Glaus SP	15.00	6.00
❑ 82 Vladimir Nunez SP	10.00	4.00
❑ 83 George Lombard SP	10.00	4.00
❑ 84 Bruce Chen SP	10.00	4.00
❑ 85 Ryan Minor SP	10.00	4.00
❑ 86 Calvin Pickering SP	10.00	4.00
❑ 87 Jin Ho Cho SP	10.00	4.00
❑ 88 Russ Branyan SP	10.00	4.00
❑ 89 Derrick Gibson SP	10.00	4.00
❑ 90 Gabe Kapler SP AU	15.00	6.00
❑ 91 Matt Anderson SP	10.00	4.00
❑ 92 Robert Fick SP	10.00	4.00
❑ 93 Juan Encarnacion SP	10.00	4.00
❑ 94 Preston Wilson SP	10.00	4.00
❑ 95 Alex Gonzalez SP	10.00	4.00
❑ 96 Carlos Beltran SP	15.00	6.00
❑ 97 Jeremy Giambi SP	10.00	4.00
❑ 98 Dee Brown SP	10.00	4.00
❑ 99 Adrian Beltre SP	10.00	4.00
❑ 100 Alex Cora SP	10.00	4.00
❑ 101 Angel Pena SP	10.00	4.00
❑ 102 Geoff Jenkins SP	10.00	4.00
❑ 103 Ronnie Belliard SP	10.00	4.00
❑ 104 Corey Koskie SP	10.00	4.00
❑ 105 A.J. Pierzynski SP	10.00	4.00
❑ 106 Michael Barrett SP	10.00	4.00
❑ 107 Fernando Seguignol SP	10.00	4.00
❑ 108 Mike Kinkade SP	10.00	4.00
❑ 109 Mike Lowell SP	10.00	4.00
❑ 110 Ricky Ledee SP	10.00	4.00
❑ 111 Eric Chavez SP	10.00	4.00
❑ 112 Abraham Nunez SP	10.00	4.00
❑ 113 Matt Clement SP	10.00	4.00
❑ 114 Ben Davis SP	10.00	4.00
❑ 115 Mike Darr SP	10.00	4.00
❑ 116 Ramon E.Martinez SP RC	10.00	4.00
❑ 117 Carlos Guillen SP	10.00	4.00
❑ 118 Shane Monahan SP	10.00	4.00
❑ 119 J.D. Drew SP AU	15.00	6.00
❑ 120 Kevin Witt SP	10.00	4.00
❑ 24EAST Ken Griffey Jr. Sample	2.00	.75

2000 SPx

❑ COMP.BASIC w/o SP's (90)	25.00	10.00
❑ COMP.UPDATE w/o SP's (30)	10.00	4.00
❑ COMMON CARD (1-90)	.50	.20
❑ COMMON AU/1500 (91-120)	10.00	4.00
❑ COMMON (121-135/182-196)	8.00	3.00
❑ COMMON CARD (136-151)	10.00	4.00
❑ COMMON CARD (152-181)	.75	.30
❑ 1 Troy Glaus	.50	.20
❑ 2 Mo Vaughn	.50	.20
❑ 3 Ramon Ortiz	.50	.20
❑ 4 Jeff Bagwell	.75	.30
❑ 5 Moises Alou	.50	.20
❑ 6 Craig Biggio	.75	.30
❑ 7 Jose Lima	.50	.20
❑ 8 Jason Giambi	.50	.20
❑ 9 John Jaha	.50	.20
❑ 10 Matt Stairs	.50	.20
❑ 11 Chipper Jones	1.25	.50
❑ 12 Greg Maddux	2.00	.75
❑ 13 Andres Galarraga	.50	.20
❑ 14 Andruw Jones	.75	.30
❑ 15 Jeromy Burnitz	.50	.20
❑ 16 Ron Belliard	.50	.20
❑ 17 Carlos Delgado	.50	.20
❑ 18 David Wells	.50	.20
❑ 19 Tony Batista	.50	.20
❑ 20 Shannon Stewart	.50	.20
❑ 21 Sammy Sosa	1.25	.50
❑ 22 Mark Grace	.75	.30
❑ 23 Henry Rodriguez	.50	.20
❑ 24 Mark McGwire	3.00	1.25
❑ 25 J.D. Drew	.50	.20
❑ 26 Luis Gonzalez	.50	.20
❑ 27 Randy Johnson	1.25	.50
❑ 28 Matt Williams	.50	.20
❑ 29 Steve Finley	.50	.20
❑ 30 Shawn Green	.50	.20
❑ 31 Kevin Brown	.75	.30
❑ 32 Gary Sheffield	.50	.20
❑ 33 Jose Canseco	.75	.30
❑ 34 Greg Vaughn	.50	.20
❑ 35 Vladimir Guerrero	1.25	.50
❑ 36 Michael Barrett	.50	.20
❑ 37 Russ Ortiz	.50	.20
❑ 38 Barry Bonds	3.00	1.25
❑ 39 Jeff Kent	.50	.20
❑ 40 Richie Sexson	.50	.20
❑ 41 Manny Ramirez	.75	.30
❑ 42 Jim Thome	.75	.30
❑ 43 Roberto Alomar	.75	.30
❑ 44 Edgar Martinez	.75	.30
❑ 45 Alex Rodriguez	2.00	.75
❑ 46 John Olerud	.50	.20
❑ 47 Alex Gonzalez	.50	.20
❑ 48 Cliff Floyd	.50	.20
❑ 49 Mike Piazza	2.00	.75
❑ 50 Al Leiter	.50	.20
❑ 51 Robin Ventura	.75	.30
❑ 52 Edgardo Alfonzo	.50	.20
❑ 53 Albert Belle	.50	.20
❑ 54 Cal Ripken	4.00	1.50
❑ 55 B.J. Surhoff	.50	.20
❑ 56 Tony Gwynn	1.50	.60
❑ 57 Trevor Hoffman	.50	.20
❑ 58 Brian Giles	.50	.20
❑ 59 Jason Kendall	.50	.20
❑ 60 Kris Benson	.50	.20
❑ 61 Bob Abreu	.50	.20
❑ 62 Scott Rolen	.75	.30
❑ 63 Curt Schilling	.50	.20
❑ 64 Mike Lieberthal	.50	.20
❑ 65 Sean Casey	.50	.20
❑ 66 Dante Bichette	.50	.20
❑ 67 Ken Griffey Jr.	2.00	.75
❑ 68 Pokey Reese	.50	.20
❑ 69 Mike Sweeney	.50	.20
❑ 70 Carlos Febles	.50	.20
❑ 71 Ivan Rodriguez	.75	.30
❑ 72 Ruben Mateo	.50	.20
❑ 73 Rafael Palmeiro	.75	.30
❑ 74 Larry Walker	.50	.20
❑ 75 Todd Helton	.75	.30
❑ 76 Nomar Garciaparra	2.00	.75
❑ 77 Pedro Martinez	.75	.30
❑ 78 Troy O'Leary	.50	.20
❑ 79 Jacque Jones	.50	.20
❑ 80 Corey Koskie	.50	.20
❑ 81 Juan Gonzalez	.50	.20
❑ 82 Dean Palmer	.50	.20
❑ 83 Juan Encarnacion	.50	.20
❑ 84 Frank Thomas	1.25	.50
❑ 85 Magglio Ordonez	.50	.20
❑ 86 Paul Konerko	.50	.20
❑ 87 Bernie Williams	.75	.30
❑ 88 Derek Jeter	3.00	1.25
❑ 89 Roger Clemens	2.50	1.00
❑ 90 Orlando Hernandez	.50	.20
❑ 91 Vernon Wells AU/1500	25.00	10.00
❑ 92 Rick Ankiel AU/1500	80.00	40.00
❑ 93 Eric Chavez AU/1500	25.00	10.00
❑ 94 Alfonso Soriano AU/1500	60.00	30.00
❑ 95 Eric Gagne AU/1500	60.00	30.00
❑ 96 Rob Bell AU/1500	10.00	4.00
❑ 97 Matt Riley AU/1500	10.00	4.00
❑ 98 Josh Beckett AU/1500	100.00	50.00
❑ 99 Ben Petrick AU/1500	10.00	4.00
❑ 100 Rob Ramsay AU/1500	10.00	4.00
❑ 101 Scott Williamson AU/1500	10.00	4.00
❑ 102 Doug Davis AU/1500	15.00	6.00
❑ 103 Eric Munson AU/1500	10.00	4.00
❑ 104 Pat Burrell AU/500	60.00	30.00
❑ 105 Jim Morris AU/1500	25.00	10.00
❑ 106 Gabe Kapler AU/500	40.00	15.00

❑ 107 Lance Berkman/1000 8.00 3.00
❑ 108 Erubiel Durazo AU/1500 10.00 4.00
❑ 109 Tim Hudson AU/1500 40.00 15.00
❑ 110 Ben Davis AU/1500 10.00 4.00
❑ 111 Nick Johnson AU/1500 15.00 6.00
❑ 112 Octavio Dotel AU/1500 10.00 4.00
❑ 113 Jerry Hairston/1000 8.00 3.00
❑ 114 Ruben Mateo/1000 8.00 3.00
❑ 115 Chris Singleton/1000 8.00 3.00
❑ 116 Bruce Chen AU/1500 10.00 4.00
❑ 117 Derrick Gibson/1000 8.00 3.00
❑ 118 Carlos Beltran AU/500 125.00 75.00
❑ 119 Freddy Garcia AU/1500 15.00 6.00
❑ 120 Preston Wilson AU/1500 15.00 6.00
❑ 121 Brad Wilkerson/1600 RC 10.00 4.00
❑ 122 Roy Oswalt/1600 RC 120.00 60.00
❑ 123 Wascar Serrano/1600 RC 8.00 3.00
❑ 124 Sean Burnett/1600 RC 8.00 3.00
❑ 125 Alex Cabrera/1600 RC 8.00 3.00
❑ 126 Timo Perez/1600 RC 8.00 3.00
❑ 127 Juan Pierre/1600 RC 10.00 4.00
❑ 128 Daylan Holt/1600 RC 8.00 3.00
❑ 129 Tomokazu Ohka/1600 RC 8.00 3.00
❑ 130 Kazuhiro Sasaki/1600 RC 10.00 4.00
❑ 131 Kurt Ainsworth/1600 RC 8.00 3.00
❑ 132 Brent Abernathy/1600 RC 8.00 3.00
❑ 133 Danys Baez/1600 RC 8.00 3.00
❑ 134 Brad Cresse/1600 RC 8.00 3.00
❑ 135 Ryan Franklin/1600 RC 8.00 3.00
❑ 136 Mike Lamb AU/1500 RC 15.00 6.00
❑ 137 David Espinosa AU/1500 RC 10.004.00
❑ 138 Matt Wheatland AU/1500 RC 10.004.00
❑ 139 Xavier Nady AU/1500 RC 40.00 15.00
❑ 140 Scott Heard AU/1500 RC 10.00 4.00
❑ 141 P.Coco AU/1500 UER54 RC 10.004.00
❑ 142 Justin Miller AU/1500 RC 10.00 4.00
❑ 143 Dave Krynzel AU/1500 RC 10.00 4.00
❑ 144 Dane Sardinha AU/1500 RC 10.004.00
❑ 145 Ben Sheets AU/1500 RC 60.00 30.00
❑ 146 Luis Estrella AU/1500 RC 10.00 4.00
❑ 147 Ben Diggins AU/1500 RC 10.00 4.00
❑ 148 Barry Zito AU/1500 RC 50.00 20.00
❑ 149 Joe Torres AU/1500 RC 10.00 4.00
❑ 150 Mike Meyers AU/1500 RC 10.00 4.00
❑ 151 Kris Wilson AU/1500 RC 10.00 4.00
❑ 152 Darin Erstad .75 .30
❑ 153 Richard Hidalgo .75 .30
❑ 154 Eric Chavez .75 .30
❑ 155 B.J. Surhoff .75 .30
❑ 156 Richie Sexson .75 .30
❑ 157 Raul Mondesi .75 .30
❑ 158 Rondell White .75 .30
❑ 159 Jim Edmonds .75 .30
❑ 160 Curt Schilling .75 .30
❑ 161 Tom Goodwin .75 .30
❑ 162 Fred McGriff 1.25 .50
❑ 163 Jose Vidro .75 .30
❑ 164 Ellis Burks .75 .30
❑ 165 David Segui .75 .30
❑ 166 Aaron Sele .75 .30
❑ 167 Henry Rodriguez .75 .30
❑ 168 Mike Bordick .75 .30
❑ 169 Mike Mussina 1.25 .50
❑ 170 Ryan Klesko .75 .30
❑ 171 Kevin Young .75 .30
❑ 172 Travis Lee .75 .30
❑ 173 Aaron Boone .75 .30
❑ 174 Jermaine Dye .75 .30
❑ 175 Ricky Ledee .75 .30
❑ 176 Jeffrey Hammonds .75 .30
❑ 177 Carl Everett .75 .30
❑ 178 Matt Lawton .75 .30
❑ 179 Bobby Higginson .75 .30
❑ 180 Charles Johnson .75 .30
❑ 181 David Justice .75 .30
❑ 182 Joey Nation/1600 RC 8.00 3.00
❑ 183 Rico Washington/1600 RC 8.00 3.00
❑ 184 Luis Matos/1600 RC 8.00 3.00
❑ 185 Chris Wakeland/1600 RC 8.00 3.00
❑ 186 Sun Woo Kim/1600 RC 8.00 3.00
❑ 187 Keith Ginter/1600 RC 8.00 3.00
❑ 188 Geraldo Guzman/1600 RC 8.00 3.00
❑ 189 Jay Spurgeon/1600 RC 8.00 3.00
❑ 190 Jace Brewer/1600 RC 8.00 3.00
❑ 191 Juan Guzman/1600 RC 8.00 3.00
❑ 192 Ross Gload/1600 RC 8.00 3.00
❑ 193 Paxton Crawford/1600 RC 8.00 3.00
❑ 194 Ryan Kohlmeier/1600 RC 8.00 3.00
❑ 195 Julio Zuleta/1600 RC 8.00 3.00
❑ 196 Matt Ginter/1600 RC 8.00 3.00

2001 SPx

❑ COMP.BASIC w/o SP's (90) 25.00 10.00
❑ COMP.UPDATE w/o SP's (30) 10.00 4.00
❑ COMMON CARD (1-90) .50 .20
❑ COMMON YS (91-120) 5.00 2.00
❑ COMMON JSY (121-135) 8.00 3.00
❑ COMMON JSY AU (136-150) 15.00 6.00
❑ COMMON CARD (151-180) .75 .30
❑ COMMON CARD (181-205) 5.00 2.00
❑ 1 Darin Erstad .50 .20
❑ 2 Troy Glaus .50 .20
❑ 3 Mo Vaughn .50 .20
❑ 4 Johnny Damon .75 .30
❑ 5 Jason Giambi .50 .20
❑ 6 Tim Hudson .50 .20
❑ 7 Miguel Tejada .50 .20
❑ 8 Carlos Delgado .50 .20
❑ 9 Raul Mondesi .50 .20
❑ 10 Tony Batista .50 .20
❑ 11 Ben Grieve .50 .20
❑ 12 Greg Vaughn .50 .20
❑ 13 Juan Gonzalez .50 .20
❑ 14 Jim Thome .75 .30
❑ 15 Roberto Alomar .75 .30
❑ 16 John Olerud .50 .20
❑ 17 Edgar Martinez .75 .30
❑ 18 Albert Belle .50 .20
❑ 19 Cal Ripken 4.00 1.50
❑ 20 Ivan Rodriguez .75 .30
❑ 21 Rafael Palmeiro .75 .30
❑ 22 Alex Rodriguez 2.00 .75
❑ 23 Nomar Garciaparra 2.00 .75
❑ 24 Pedro Martinez .75 .30
❑ 25 Manny Ramirez Sox .75 .30
❑ 26 Jermaine Dye .50 .20
❑ 27 Mark Quinn .50 .20
❑ 28 Carlos Beltran .50 .20
❑ 29 Tony Clark .50 .20
❑ 30 Bobby Higginson .50 .20
❑ 31 Eric Milton .50 .20
❑ 32 Matt Lawton .50 .20
❑ 33 Frank Thomas 1.25 .50
❑ 34 Magglio Ordonez .50 .20
❑ 35 Ray Durham .50 .20
❑ 36 David Wells .50 .20
❑ 37 Derek Jeter 3.00 1.25
❑ 38 Bernie Williams .75 .30
❑ 39 Roger Clemens 2.50 1.00
❑ 40 David Justice .50 .20
❑ 41 Jeff Bagwell .75 .30
❑ 42 Richard Hidalgo .50 .20
❑ 43 Moises Alou .50 .20
❑ 44 Chipper Jones 1.25 .50
❑ 45 Andruw Jones .75 .30
❑ 46 Greg Maddux 2.00 .75
❑ 47 Rafael Furcal .50 .20
❑ 48 Jeromy Burnitz .50 .20
❑ 49 Geoff Jenkins .50 .20
❑ 50 Mark McGwire 3.00 1.25
❑ 51 Jim Edmonds .50 .20
❑ 52 Rick Ankiel .50 .20
❑ 53 Edgar Renteria .50 .20
❑ 54 Sammy Sosa 1.25 .50
❑ 55 Kerry Wood .50 .20
❑ 56 Rondell White .50 .20
❑ 57 Randy Johnson 1.25 .50
❑ 58 Steve Finley .50 .20
❑ 59 Matt Williams .50 .20
❑ 60 Luis Gonzalez .50 .20
❑ 61 Kevin Brown .50 .20
❑ 62 Gary Sheffield .50 .20
❑ 63 Shawn Green .50 .20
❑ 64 Vladimir Guerrero 1.25 .50
❑ 65 Jose Vidro .50 .20
❑ 66 Barry Bonds 3.00 1.25
❑ 67 Jeff Kent .50 .20
❑ 68 Livan Hernandez .50 .20
❑ 69 Preston Wilson .50 .20
❑ 70 Charles Johnson .50 .20
❑ 71 Cliff Floyd .50 .20
❑ 72 Mike Piazza 2.00 .75
❑ 73 Edgardo Alfonzo .50 .20
❑ 74 Jay Payton .50 .20
❑ 75 Robin Ventura .50 .20
❑ 76 Tony Gwynn 1.50 .60
❑ 77 Phil Nevin .50 .20
❑ 78 Ryan Klesko .50 .20
❑ 79 Scott Rolen .75 .30
❑ 80 Pat Burrell .50 .20
❑ 81 Bob Abreu .50 .20
❑ 82 Brian Giles .50 .20
❑ 83 Kris Benson .50 .20
❑ 84 Jason Kendall .50 .20
❑ 85 Ken Griffey Jr. 2.00 .75
❑ 86 Barry Larkin .75 .30
❑ 87 Sean Casey .50 .20
❑ 88 Todd Helton .75 .30
❑ 89 Larry Walker .50 .20
❑ 90 Mike Hampton .50 .20
❑ 91 Billy Sylvester YS RC 5.00 2.00
❑ 92 Josh Towers YS RC 8.00 3.00
❑ 93 Zach Day YS RC 5.00 2.00
❑ 94 Martin Vargas YS RC 5.00 2.00
❑ 95 Adam Pettyjohn YS RC 5.00 2.00
❑ 96 Andres Torres YS RC 5.00 2.00
❑ 97 Kris Keller YS RC 5.00 2.00
❑ 98 Blaine Neal YS RC 5.00 2.00
❑ 99 Kyle Kessel YS RC 5.00 2.00
❑ 100 Greg Miller YS RC 5.00 2.00
❑ 101 Shawn Sonnier YS 5.00 2.00
❑ 102 Alexis Gomez YS RC 5.00 2.00
❑ 103 Grant Balfour YS RC 5.00 2.00
❑ 104 Henry Mateo YS RC 5.00 2.00
❑ 105 Wilken Ruan YS RC 5.00 2.00
❑ 106 Nick Maness YS RC 5.00 2.00
❑ 107 Jason Michaels YS RC 5.00 2.00
❑ 108 Esix Snead YS RC 5.00 2.00
❑ 109 William Ortega YS RC 5.00 2.00
❑ 110 David Elder YS RC 5.00 2.00
❑ 111 Jackson Melian YS RC 5.00 2.00
❑ 112 Nate Teut YS RC 5.00 2.00
❑ 113 Jason Smith YS RC 5.00 2.00
❑ 114 Mike Penney YS RC 5.00 2.00
❑ 115 Jose Mieses YS RC 5.00 2.00
❑ 116 Juan Pena YS 5.00 2.00
❑ 117 Brian Lawrence YS RC 5.00 2.00
❑ 118 Jeremy Owens YS RC 5.00 2.00
❑ 119 Carlos Valderrama YS RC 5.00 2.00
❑ 120 Rafael Soriano YS RC 5.00 2.00
❑ 121 Horacio Ramirez JSY RC 10.00 4.00
❑ 122 Ricardo Rodriguez JSY RC 8.00 3.00
❑ 123 Juan Diaz JSY RC 8.00 3.00
❑ 124 Donnie Bridges JSY 8.00 3.00
❑ 125 Tyler Walker JSY RC 8.00 3.00
❑ 126 Erick Almonte JSY RC 8.00 3.00
❑ 127 Jesus Colome JSY 8.00 3.00
❑ 128 Ryan Freel JSY RC 10.00 4.00
❑ 129 Elpidio Guzman JSY RC 8.00 3.00
❑ 130 Jack Cust JSY 8.00 3.00
❑ 131 Eric Hinske JSY RC 10.00 4.00
❑ 132 Josh Fogg JSY RC 8.00 3.00
❑ 133 Juan Uribe JSY RC 10.00 4.00
❑ 134 Bert Snow JSY RC 8.00 3.00
❑ 135 Pedro Feliz JSY 8.00 3.00
❑ 136 Wilson Betemit JSY AU RC 40.0015.00
❑ 137 Sean Douglass JSY AU RC 15.00 6.00
❑ 138 Dernell Stenson JSY AU 15.00 6.00
❑ 139 Brandon Inge JSY AU 15.00 6.00
❑ 140 Mor.Ensberg JSY AU RC 40.00 15.00

❑ 141 Brian Cole JSY AU 15.00 6.00
❑ 142 A.Hernandez JSY AU RC 15.00 6.00
❑ 143 B.Duckworth JSY AU RC 15.00 6.00
❑ 144 Jack Wilson JSY AU RC 25.00 10.00
❑ 145 Travis Hafner JSY AU RC 80.00 40.00
❑ 146 Carlos Pena JSY AU 15.00 6.00
❑ 147 Corey Patterson JSY AU 15.00 6.00
❑ 148 Xavier Nady JSY AU 15.00 6.00
❑ 149 Jason Hart JSY AU 15.00 6.00
❑ 150 I.Suzuki JSY AU RC 800.00 600.00
❑ 151 Garret Anderson .75 .30
❑ 152 Jermaine Dye .75 .30
❑ 153 Shannon Stewart .75 .30
❑ 154 Toby Hall .75 .30
❑ 155 C.C. Sabathia .75 .30
❑ 156 Bret Boone .75 .30
❑ 157 Tony Batista .75 .30
❑ 158 Gabe Kapler .75 .30
❑ 159 Carl Everett .75 .30
❑ 160 Mike Sweeney .75 .30
❑ 161 Dean Palmer .75 .30
❑ 162 Doug Mientkiewicz .75 .30
❑ 163 Carlos Lee .75 .30
❑ 164 Mike Mussina 1.25 .50
❑ 165 Lance Berkman .75 .30
❑ 166 Ken Caminiti .75 .30
❑ 167 Ben Sheets 1.25 .50
❑ 168 Matt Morris .75 .30
❑ 169 Fred McGriff 1.25 .50
❑ 170 Curt Schilling .75 .30
❑ 171 Paul LoDuca .75 .30
❑ 172 Javier Vazquez .75 .30
❑ 173 Rich Aurilia .75 .30
❑ 174 A.J. Burnett .75 .30
❑ 175 Al Leiter .75 .30
❑ 176 Mark Kotsay .75 .30
❑ 177 Jimmy Rollins .75 .30
❑ 178 Aramis Ramirez .75 .30
❑ 179 Aaron Boone .75 .30
❑ 180 Jeff Cirillo .75 .30
❑ 181 Johnny Estrada YS RC 8.00 3.00
❑ 182 Dave Williams YS RC 5.00 2.00
❑ 183 Donaldo Mendez YS RC 5.00 2.00
❑ 184 Junior Spivey YS RC 8.00 3.00
❑ 185 Jay Gibbons YS RC 8.00 3.00
❑ 186 Kyle Lohse YS RC 8.00 3.00
❑ 187 Willie Harris YS RC 5.00 2.00
❑ 188 Juan Cruz YS RC 5.00 2.00
❑ 189 Joe Kennedy YS RC 8.00 3.00
❑ 190 Duaner Sanchez YS RC 5.00 2.00
❑ 191 Jorge Julio YS RC 5.00 2.00
❑ 192 Cesar Crespo YS RC 5.00 2.00
❑ 193 Casey Fossum YS RC 5.00 2.00
❑ 194 Brian Roberts YS RC 15.00 6.00
❑ 195 Troy Mattes YS RC 5.00 2.00
❑ 196 Rob Mackowiak YS RC 8.00 3.00
❑ 197 Tsuyoshi Shinjo YS RC 8.00 3.00
❑ 198 Nick Punto YS RC 5.00 2.00
❑ 199 Wilmy Caceres YS RC 5.00 2.00
❑ 200 Jeremy Affeldt YS RC 5.00 2.00
❑ 201 Bret Prinz YS RC 5.00 2.00
❑ 202 Delvin James YS RC 5.00 2.00
❑ 203 Luis Pineda YS RC 5.00 2.00
❑ 204 Matt White YS RC 5.00 2.00
❑ 205 Brandon Knight YS RC 5.00 2.00
❑ 206 Albert Pujols YS AU RC 500.00 300.00
❑ 207 Mark Teixeira YS AU RC 100.00 50.00
❑ 208 Mark Prior YS AU RC 60.00 30.00
❑ 209 Dewon Brazelton YS AU RC 15.00 6.00
❑ 210 Bud Smith YS AU RC 15.00 6.00

2002 SPx

❑ COMP.LOW w/o SP's (90) 25.00 10.00
❑ COMP.UPDATE w/o SP's (30) 10.00 4.00
❑ COMMON CARD (1-90) .50 .20
❑ COMMON CARD (91-120) 8.00 3.00
❑ COMMON CARD (121-150) 15.00 6.00
❑ COMMON CARD (151-190) 8.00 3.00
❑ COMMON CARD (191-220) .75 .30
❑ COMMON CARD (221-250) 10.00 4.00
❑ 1 Troy Glaus .50 .20
❑ 2 Darin Erstad .50 .20
❑ 3 David Justice .50 .20
❑ 4 Tim Hudson .50 .20
❑ 5 Miguel Tejada .50 .20
❑ 6 Barry Zito .50 .20

❑ 7 Carlos Delgado .50 .20
❑ 8 Shannon Stewart .50 .20
❑ 9 Greg Vaughn .50 .20
❑ 10 Toby Hall .50 .20
❑ 11 Jim Thome .75 .30
❑ 12 C.C. Sabathia .50 .20
❑ 13 Ichiro Suzuki 2.50 1.00
❑ 14 Edgar Martinez .75 .30
❑ 15 Freddy Garcia .50 .20
❑ 16 Mike Cameron .50 .20
❑ 17 Jeff Conine .50 .20
❑ 18 Tony Batista .50 .20
❑ 19 Alex Rodriguez 2.00 .75
❑ 20 Rafael Palmeiro .75 .30
❑ 21 Ivan Rodriguez .75 .30
❑ 22 Carl Everett .50 .20
❑ 23 Pedro Martinez .75 .30
❑ 24 Manny Ramirez .75 .30
❑ 25 Nomar Garciaparra 2.00 .75
❑ 26 Johnny Damon Sox .75 .30
❑ 27 Mike Sweeney .50 .20
❑ 28 Carlos Beltran .50 .20
❑ 29 Dmitri Young .50 .20
❑ 30 Joe Mays .50 .20
❑ 31 Doug Mientkiewicz .50 .20
❑ 32 Cristian Guzman .50 .20
❑ 33 Corey Koskie .50 .20
❑ 34 Frank Thomas 1.25 .50
❑ 35 Magglio Ordonez .50 .20
❑ 36 Mark Buehrle .50 .20
❑ 37 Bernie Williams .75 .30
❑ 38 Roger Clemens 2.50 1.00
❑ 39 Derek Jeter 3.00 1.25
❑ 40 Jason Giambi .50 .20
❑ 41 Mike Mussina .75 .30
❑ 42 Lance Berkman .50 .20
❑ 43 Jeff Bagwell .75 .30
❑ 44 Roy Oswalt .50 .20
❑ 45 Greg Maddux 2.00 .75
❑ 46 Chipper Jones 1.25 .50
❑ 47 Andruw Jones .75 .30
❑ 48 Gary Sheffield .50 .20
❑ 49 Geoff Jenkins .50 .20
❑ 50 Richie Sexson .50 .20
❑ 51 Ben Sheets .50 .20
❑ 52 Albert Pujols 2.50 1.00
❑ 53 J.D. Drew .50 .20
❑ 54 Jim Edmonds .50 .20
❑ 55 Sammy Sosa 1.25 .50
❑ 56 Moises Alou .50 .20
❑ 57 Kerry Wood .50 .20
❑ 58 Jon Lieber .50 .20
❑ 59 Fred McGriff .75 .30
❑ 60 Randy Johnson 1.25 .50
❑ 61 Luis Gonzalez .50 .20
❑ 62 Curt Schilling .50 .20
❑ 63 Kevin Brown .50 .20
❑ 64 Hideo Nomo 1.25 .50
❑ 65 Shawn Green .50 .20
❑ 66 Vladimir Guerrero 1.25 .50
❑ 67 Jose Vidro .50 .20
❑ 68 Barry Bonds 3.00 1.25
❑ 69 Jeff Kent .50 .20
❑ 70 Rich Aurilia .50 .20
❑ 71 Cliff Floyd .50 .20
❑ 72 Josh Beckett .50 .20
❑ 73 Preston Wilson .50 .20
❑ 74 Mike Piazza 2.00 .75
❑ 75 Mo Vaughn .50 .20
❑ 76 Jeromy Burnitz .50 .20
❑ 77 Roberto Alomar .75 .30
❑ 78 Phil Nevin .50 .20
❑ 79 Ryan Klesko .50 .20
❑ 80 Scott Rolen .75 .30
❑ 81 Bobby Abreu .50 .20
❑ 82 Jimmy Rollins .50 .20
❑ 83 Brian Giles .50 .20
❑ 84 Aramis Ramirez .50 .20
❑ 85 Ken Griffey Jr. 2.00 .75
❑ 86 Sean Casey .50 .20
❑ 87 Barry Larkin .75 .30
❑ 88 Mike Hampton .50 .20
❑ 89 Larry Walker .50 .20
❑ 90 Todd Helton .75 .30
❑ 91A Ron Calloway YS RC 8.00 3.00
❑ 91P Ron Calloway YS RC 8.00 3.00
❑ 92A Joe Orloski YS RC 8.00 3.00
❑ 92P Joe Orloski YS RC 8.00 3.00
❑ 93A Anderson Machado YS RC 8.00 3.00
❑ 93P Anderson Machado YS RC 8.00 3.00
❑ 94A Eric Good YS RC 8.00 3.00
❑ 94P Eric Good YS RC 8.00 3.00
❑ 95A Reed Johnson YS RC 10.00 4.00
❑ 95P Reed Johnson YS RC 10.00 4.00
❑ 96A Brendan Donnelly YS RC 8.00 3.00
❑ 96P Brendan Donnelly YS RC 8.00 3.00
❑ 97A Chris Baker YS RC 8.00 3.00
❑ 97P Chris Baker YS RC 8.00 3.00
❑ 98A Wilson Valdez YS RC 8.00 3.00
❑ 98P Wilson Valdez YS RC 8.00 3.00
❑ 99A Scotty Layfield YS RC 8.00 3.00
❑ 99P Scotty Layfield YS RC 8.00 3.00
❑ 100A P.J. Bevis YS RC 8.00 3.00
❑ 100P P.J. Bevis YS RC 8.00 3.00
❑ 101A Edwin Almonte YS RC 8.00 3.00
❑ 101P Edwin Almonte YS RC 8.00 3.00
❑ 102A Francis Beltran YS RC 8.00 3.00
❑ 102P Francis Beltran YS RC 8.00 3.00
❑ 103A Val Pascucci YS 8.00 3.00
❑ 103P Val Pascucci YS 8.00 3.00
❑ 104A Nelson Castro YS RC 8.00 3.00
❑ 104P Nelson Castro YS RC 8.00 3.00
❑ 105A Michael Crudale YS RC 8.00 3.00
❑ 105P Michael Crudale YS RC 8.00 3.00
❑ 106A Colin Young YS RC 8.00 3.00
❑ 106P Colin Young YS RC 8.00 3.00
❑ 107A Todd Donovan YS RC 8.00 3.00
❑ 107P Todd Donovan YS RC 8.00 3.00
❑ 108A Felix Escalona YS RC 8.00 3.00
❑ 108P Felix Escalona YS RC 8.00 3.00
❑ 109A Brandon Backe YS RC 10.00 4.00
❑ 109P Brandon Backe YS RC 10.00 4.00
❑ 110A Corey Thurman YS RC 8.00 3.00
❑ 110P Corey Thurman YS RC 8.00 3.00
❑ 111A Kyle Kane YS RC 8.00 3.00
❑ 111P Kyle Kane YS RC 8.00 3.00
❑ 112A Allan Simpson YS RC 8.00 3.00
❑ 112P Allan Simpson YS RC 8.00 3.00
❑ 113A Jose Valverde YS RC 8.00 3.00
❑ 113P Jose Valverde YS RC 8.00 3.00
❑ 114A Chris Booker YS RC 8.00 3.00
❑ 114P Chris Booker YS RC 8.00 3.00
❑ 115A Brandon Puffer YS RC 8.00 3.00
❑ 115P Brandon Puffer YS RC 8.00 3.00
❑ 116A John Foster YS RC 8.00 3.00
❑ 116P John Foster YS RC 8.00 3.00
❑ 117A Cliff Bartosh YS RC 8.00 3.00
❑ 117P Cliff Bartosh YS RC 8.00 3.00
❑ 118A Gustavo Chacin YS RC 10.00 4.00
❑ 118P Gustavo Chacin YS RC 10.00 4.00
❑ 119A Steve Kent YS RC 8.00 3.00
❑ 119P Steve Kent YS RC 8.00 3.00
❑ 120A Nate Field YS RC 8.00 3.00
❑ 120P Nate Field YS RC 8.00 3.00
❑ 121 Victor Alvarez AU RC 10.00 4.00
❑ 122 Steve Bechler AU RC 10.00 4.00
❑ 123 Adrian Burnside AU RC 10.00 4.00
❑ 124 Marlon Byrd AU 15.00 6.00
❑ 125 Jaime Cerda AU RC 10.00 4.00
❑ 126 Brandon Claussen AU 15.00 6.00
❑ 127 Mark Corey AU RC 10.00 4.00
❑ 128 Doug Devore AU RC 10.00 4.00
❑ 129 Kazuhisa Ishii AU SP RC 60.00 30.00
❑ 130 John Ennis AU RC 10.00 4.00

❑ 131	Kevin Frederick AU RC	10.00	4.00
❑ 132	Josh Hancock AU RC	20.00	8.00
❑ 133	Ben Howard AU RC	10.00	4.00
❑ 134	Orlando Hudson AU	15.00	6.00
❑ 135	Hansel Izquierdo AU RC	10.00	4.00
❑ 136	Eric Junge AU RC	10.00	4.00
❑ 137	Austin Kearns AU	15.00	6.00
❑ 138	Victor Martinez AU	25.00	10.00
❑ 139	Luis Martinez AU RC	10.00	4.00
❑ 140	Danny Mota AU RC	10.00	4.00
❑ 141	Jorge Padilla AU RC	10.00	4.00
❑ 142	Andy Pratt AU RC	10.00	4.00
❑ 143	Rene Reyes AU RC	10.00	4.00
❑ 144	Rodrigo Rosario AU RC	10.00	4.00
❑ 145	Tom Shearn AU RC	10.00	4.00
❑ 146	So Taguchi AU SP RC	25.00	10.00
❑ 147	Dennis Tankersley AU	15.00	6.00
❑ 148	Matt Thornton AU RC	10.00	4.00
❑ 149	Jeremy Ward AU RC	10.00	4.00
❑ 150	Mitch Wylie AU RC	10.00	4.00
❑ 151	Pedro Martinez JSY/800	10.00	4.00
❑ 152	Cal Ripken JSY/800	25.00	10.00
❑ 153	Roger Clemens JSY/800	15.00	6.00
❑ 154	Bernie Williams JSY/800	10.00	4.00
❑ 155	Jason Giambi JSY/700	8.00	3.00
❑ 156	Robin Ventura JSY/800	8.00	3.00
❑ 157	Carlos Delgado JSY/800	8.00	3.00
❑ 158	Frank Thomas JSY/800	10.00	4.00
❑ 159	Magglio Ordonez JSY/800	8.00	3.00
❑ 160	Jim Thome JSY/800	10.00	4.00
❑ 161	Darin Erstad JSY/800	8.00	3.00
❑ 162	Tim Salmon JSY/800	10.00	4.00
❑ 163	Tim Hudson JSY/800	8.00	3.00
❑ 164	Barry Zito JSY/800	8.00	3.00
❑ 165	Ichiro Suzuki JSY/800	25.00	10.00
❑ 166	Edgar Martinez JSY/800	10.00	4.00
❑ 167	Alex Rodriguez JSY/800	15.00	6.00
❑ 168	Ivan Rodriguez JSY/800	10.00	4.00
❑ 169	Juan Gonzalez JSY/800	8.00	3.00
❑ 170	Greg Maddux JSY/800	15.00	6.00
❑ 171	Chipper Jones JSY/800	10.00	4.00
❑ 172	Andruw Jones JSY/800	10.00	4.00
❑ 173	Tom Glavine JSY/800	10.00	4.00
❑ 174	Mike Piazza JSY/800	15.00	6.00
❑ 175	Roberto Alomar JSY/800	10.00	4.00
❑ 176	Scott Rolen JSY/800	10.00	4.00
❑ 177	Sammy Sosa JSY/800	10.00	4.00
❑ 178	Moises Alou JSY/800	8.00	3.00
❑ 179	Ken Griffey Jr. JSY/700	20.00	8.00
❑ 180	Jeff Bagwell JSY/800	10.00	4.00
❑ 181	Jim Edmonds JSY/800	8.00	3.00
❑ 182	J.D. Drew JSY/800	8.00	3.00
❑ 183	Brian Giles JSY/800	8.00	3.00
❑ 184	Randy Johnson JSY/800	10.00	4.00
❑ 185	Curt Schilling JSY/800	8.00	3.00
❑ 186	Luis Gonzalez JSY/800	8.00	3.00
❑ 187	Todd Helton JSY/800	10.00	4.00
❑ 188	Shawn Green JSY/800	8.00	3.00
❑ 189	David Wells JSY/800	8.00	3.00
❑ 190	Jeff Kent JSY/800	8.00	3.00
❑ 191	Tom Glavine	1.25	.50
❑ 192	Cliff Floyd	.75	.30
❑ 193	Mark Prior	1.25	.50
❑ 194	Corey Patterson	.75	.30
❑ 195	Paul Konerko	.75	.30
❑ 196	Adam Dunn	.75	.30
❑ 197	Joe Borchard	.75	.30
❑ 198	Carlos Pena	.75	.30
❑ 199	Juan Encarnacion	.75	.30
❑ 200	Luis Castillo	.75	.30
❑ 201	Torii Hunter	.75	.30
❑ 202	Hee Seop Choi	.75	.30
❑ 203	Bartolo Colon	.75	.30
❑ 204	Raul Mondesi	.75	.30
❑ 205	Jeff Weaver	.75	.30
❑ 206	Eric Munson	.75	.30
❑ 207	Alfonso Soriano	.75	.30
❑ 208	Ray Durham	.75	.30
❑ 209	Eric Chavez	.75	.30
❑ 210	Brett Myers	.75	.30
❑ 211	Jeremy Giambi	.75	.30
❑ 212	Vicente Padilla	.75	.30
❑ 213	Felipe Lopez	.75	.30
❑ 214	Sean Burroughs	.75	.30
❑ 215	Kenny Lofton	.75	.30
❑ 216	Scott Rolen	1.25	.50
❑ 217	Carl Crawford	.75	.30
❑ 218	Juan Gonzalez	.75	.30
❑ 219	Orlando Hudson	.75	.30
❑ 220	Eric Hinske	.75	.30
❑ 221	Adam Walker AU RC	10.00	4.00
❑ 222	Aaron Cook AU RC	15.00	6.00
❑ 223	Cam Esslinger AU RC	10.00	4.00
❑ 224	Kirk Saarloos AU RC	10.00	4.00
❑ 225	Jose Diaz AU RC	10.00	4.00
❑ 226	David Ross AU RC	25.00	10.00
❑ 227	Jayson Durocher AU RC	10.00	4.00
❑ 228	Brian Mallette AU RC	10.00	4.00
❑ 229	Aaron Guiel AU RC	10.00	4.00
❑ 230	Jorge Nunez AU RC	10.00	4.00
❑ 231	Satoru Komiyama AU RC	25.00	10.00
❑ 232	Tyler Yates AU RC	10.00	4.00
❑ 233	Pete Zamora AU RC	10.00	4.00
❑ 234	Mike Gonzalez AU RC	10.00	4.00
❑ 235	Oliver Perez AU RC	30.00	12.50
❑ 236	Julius Matos AU RC	10.00	4.00
❑ 237	Andy Shibilo AU RC	10.00	4.00
❑ 238	Jason Simontacchi AU RC	10.00	4.00
❑ 239	Ron Chiavacci AU	10.00	4.00
❑ 240	Deivis Santos AU	10.00	4.00
❑ 241	Travis Driskill AU RC	10.00	4.00
❑ 242	Jorge De La Rosa AU RC	10.00	4.00
❑ 243	Anastacio Martinez AU RC	10.00	4.00
❑ 244	Earl Snyder AU RC	10.00	4.00
❑ 245	Freddy Sanchez AU RC	30.00	12.50
❑ 246	Miguel Asencio AU RC	10.00	4.00
❑ 247	Juan Brito AU RC	10.00	4.00
❑ 248	Franklyn German AU RC	10.00	4.00
❑ 249	Chris Snelling AU RC	15.00	6.00
❑ 250	Ken Huckaby AU RC	10.00	4.00

2003 SPx

❑	COMP.LO SET w/o SP's (100)	25.00	10.00
❑	COMP.LO SET w/ SP's (125)	100.00	50.00
❑	COMMON CARD (1-125)	.50	.20
❑	COMMON SP (1-125)	4.00	1.50
❑	COMMON CARD (126-160)	8.00	3.00
❑	COMMON CARD (161-178)	15.00	6.00
❑	163-178 PRINT RUN 1224 SERIAL #'d SETS		
❑	126-178 RANDOM INSERTS IN SPx PACKS		
❑	COMMON CARD (179-193)	15.00	6.00
❑	COMMON CARD (381-387)	15.00	6.00
❑ 1	Darin Erstad	.50	.20
❑ 2	Garret Anderson	.50	.20
❑ 3	Tim Salmon	.75	.30
❑ 4	Troy Glaus SP	4.00	1.50
❑ 5	Luis Gonzalez	.50	.20
❑ 6	Randy Johnson	1.25	.50
❑ 7	Curt Schilling	.50	.20
❑ 8	Lyle Overbay	.50	.20
❑ 9	Andruw Jones SP	4.00	1.50
❑ 10	Gary Sheffield	.50	.20
❑ 11	Rafael Furcal	.50	.20
❑ 12	Greg Maddux	2.00	.75
❑ 13	Chipper Jones SP	5.00	2.00
❑ 14	Tony Batista	.50	.20
❑ 15	Rodrigo Lopez	.50	.20
❑ 16	Jay Gibbons	.50	.20
❑ 17	Byung-Hyun Kim	.50	.20
❑ 18	Johnny Damon	.75	.30
❑ 19	Derek Lowe	.50	.20
❑ 20	Nomar Garciaparra SP	8.00	3.00
❑ 21	Pedro Martinez	.75	.30
❑ 22	Manny Ramirez SP	4.00	1.50
❑ 23	Mark Prior	.75	.30
❑ 24	Kerry Wood	.50	.20
❑ 25	Corey Patterson	.50	.20
❑ 26	Sammy Sosa SP	5.00	2.00
❑ 27	Moises Alou	.50	.20
❑ 28	Magglio Ordonez	.50	.20
❑ 29	Frank Thomas	1.25	.50
❑ 30	Paul Konerko	.50	.20
❑ 31	Bartolo Colon	.50	.20
❑ 32	Adam Dunn	.50	.20
❑ 33	Austin Kearns	.50	.20
❑ 34	Aaron Boone	.50	.20
❑ 35	Ken Griffey Jr. SP	8.00	3.00
❑ 36	Omar Vizquel	.75	.30
❑ 37	C.C. Sabathia	.50	.20
❑ 38	Jason Davis	.50	.20
❑ 39	Travis Hafner	.50	.20
❑ 40	Brandon Phillips	.50	.20
❑ 41	Larry Walker	.50	.20
❑ 42	Preston Wilson	.50	.20
❑ 43	Jay Payton	.50	.20
❑ 44	Todd Helton	.75	.30
❑ 45	Carlos Pena	.50	.20
❑ 46	Eric Munson	.50	.20
❑ 47	Ivan Rodriguez	.75	.30
❑ 48	Josh Beckett	.50	.20
❑ 49	Alex Gonzalez	.50	.20
❑ 50	Roy Oswalt	.50	.20
❑ 51	Craig Biggio	.75	.30
❑ 52	Jeff Bagwell	.75	.30
❑ 53	Dontrelle Willis SP	5.00	2.00
❑ 54	Mike Sweeney	.50	.20
❑ 55	Carlos Beltran	.50	.20
❑ 56	Brent Mayne	.50	.20
❑ 57	Hideo Nomo	1.25	.50
❑ 58	Rickey Henderson	1.25	.50
❑ 59	Adrian Beltre	.50	.20
❑ 60	Miguel Cabrera SP	5.00	2.00
❑ 61	Kazuhisa Ishii	.50	.20
❑ 62	Ben Sheets	.50	.20
❑ 63	Richie Sexson	.50	.20
❑ 64	Torii Hunter SP	4.00	1.50
❑ 65	Jacque Jones	.50	.20
❑ 66	Joe Mays	.50	.20
❑ 67	Corey Koskie	.50	.20
❑ 68	A.J. Pierzynski	.50	.20
❑ 69	Jose Vidro	.50	.20
❑ 70	Vladimir Guerrero SP	5.00	2.00
❑ 71	Tom Glavine	.75	.30
❑ 72	Jose Reyes SP	4.00	1.50
❑ 73	Aaron Heilman	.50	.20
❑ 74	Mike Piazza	2.00	.75
❑ 75	Jorge Posada	.75	.30
❑ 76	Mike Mussina	.75	.30
❑ 77	Robin Ventura	.50	.20
❑ 78	Mariano Rivera	1.25	.50
❑ 79	Roger Clemens SP	10.00	4.00
❑ 80	Jason Giambi	.50	.20
❑ 81	Bernie Williams	.75	.30
❑ 82	Alfonso Soriano SP	4.00	1.50
❑ 83	Derek Jeter SP	12.00	5.00
❑ 84	Miguel Tejada SP	4.00	1.50
❑ 85	Eric Chavez	.50	.20
❑ 86	Tim Hudson	.50	.20
❑ 87	Barry Zito	.50	.20
❑ 88	Mark Mulder	.50	.20
❑ 89	Erubiel Durazo	.50	.20
❑ 90	Pat Burrell	.50	.20
❑ 91	Jim Thome SP	4.00	1.50
❑ 92	Bobby Abreu	.50	.20
❑ 93	Brian Giles	.50	.20
❑ 94	Reggie Sanders SP	4.00	1.50
❑ 95	Kenny Lofton	.50	.20
❑ 96	Ryan Klesko	.50	.20
❑ 97	Sean Burroughs	.50	.20
❑ 98	Edgardo Alfonzo	.50	.20
❑ 99	Rich Aurilia	.50	.20
❑ 100	Jose Cruz Jr.	.50	.20
❑ 101	Barry Bonds SP	12.00	5.00
❑ 102	Mike Cameron	.50	.20
❑ 103	Kazuhiro Sasaki	.50	.20
❑ 104	Bret Boone	.50	.20
❑ 105	Ichiro Suzuki SP	10.00	4.00
❑ 106	J.D. Drew	.50	.20
❑ 107	Jim Edmonds	.50	.20
❑ 108	Scott Rolen SP	4.00	1.50

❑ 109 Matt Morris .50 .20
❑ 110 Tino Martinez .75 .30
❑ 111 Albert Pujols SP 10.00 4.00
❑ 112 Damian Rolls .50 .20
❑ 113 Carl Crawford .50 .20
❑ 114 Rocco Baldelli SP 4.00 1.50
❑ 115 Hank Blalock .50 .20
❑ 116 Alex Rodriguez SP 8.00 3.00
❑ 117 Kevin Mench .50 .20
❑ 118 Rafael Palmeiro .75 .30
❑ 119 Mark Teixeira .75 .30
❑ 120 Shannon Stewart .50 .20
❑ 121 Vernon Wells .50 .20
❑ 122 Josh Phelps .50 .20
❑ 123 Eric Hinske .50 .20
❑ 124 Orlando Hudson .50 .20
❑ 125 Carlos Delgado SP 4.00 1.50
❑ 126 Jason Roach ROO RC 8.00 3.00
❑ 127 Dan Haren ROO RC 10.00 4.00
❑ 128 Luis Ayala ROO RC 8.00 3.00
❑ 129 Bo Hart ROO RC 8.00 3.00
❑ 130 Wilfredo Ledezma ROO RC 8.00 3.00
❑ 131 Rick Roberts ROO RC 8.00 3.00
❑ 132 Miguel Ojeda ROO RC 8.00 3.00
❑ 133 Aquilino Lopez ROO RC 8.00 3.00
❑ 134 Roger Deago ROO RC 8.00 3.00
❑ 135 Arnie Munoz ROO RC 8.00 3.00
❑ 136 Brent Hoard ROO RC 8.00 3.00
❑ 137 Terrmel Sledge ROO RC 8.00 3.00
❑ 138 Ryan Cameron ROO RC 8.00 3.00
❑ 139 Prentice Redman ROO RC 8.00 3.00
❑ 140 Clint Barmes ROO RC 6.00 2.50
❑ 141 Jeremy Griffiths ROO RC 8.00 3.00
❑ 142 Jon Leicester ROO RC 8.00 3.00
❑ 143 Brandon Webb ROO RC 12.00 5.00
❑ 144 Todd Wellemeyer ROO RC 8.00 3.00
❑ 145 Felix Sanchez ROO RC 8.00 3.00
❑ 146 Anthony Ferrari ROO RC 8.00 3.00
❑ 147 Ian Ferguson ROO RC 8.00 3.00
❑ 148 Michael Nakamura ROO RC 8.00 3.00
❑ 149 Lew Ford ROO RC 10.00 4.00
❑ 150 Nate Bland ROO RC 8.00 3.00
❑ 151 David Matranga ROO RC 8.00 3.00
❑ 152 Edgar Gonzalez ROO RC 8.00 3.00
❑ 153 Carlos Mendez ROO RC 8.00 3.00
❑ 154 Jason Gilfillan ROO RC 8.00 3.00
❑ 155 Mike Neu ROO RC 8.00 3.00
❑ 156 Jason Shiell ROO RC 8.00 3.00
❑ 157 Jeff Duncan ROO RC 8.00 3.00
❑ 158 Oscar Villarreal ROO RC 8.00 3.00
❑ 159 Diegomar Markwell ROO RC 8.00 3.00
❑ 160 Joe Valentine ROO RC 8.00 3.00
❑ 161 Hideki Matsui AU JSY RC 400.00 200.00
❑ 162 Jose Contreras AU RC 40.00 20.00
❑ 163 Willie Eyre AU JSY RC 15.00 6.00
❑ 164 Matt Bruback AU JSY RC 15.00 6.00
❑ 165 Rett Johnson AU JSY RC 15.00 6.00
❑ 166 Jeremy Griffiths AU JSY 15.00 6.00
❑ 167 Fran Cruceta AU JSY RC 15.00 6.00
❑ 168 Fern Cabrera AU JSY RC 15.00 6.00
❑ 169 Jhonny Peralta AU JSY 15.00 6.00
❑ 170 Shane Bazzell AU JSY RC 15.00 6.00
❑ 171 Bob Madritsch AU JSY RC 25.00 10.00
❑ 172 Phil Seibel AU JSY RC 15.00 6.00
❑ 173 J.Willingham AU JSY RC 50.00 25.00
❑ 174 Rob Hammock AU JSY RC 15.00 6.00
❑ 175 A.Machado AU JSY RC 15.00 6.00
❑ 176 David Sanders AU JSY RC 15.00 6.00
❑ 177 Matt Kata AU JSY RC 15.00 6.00
❑ 178 Heath Bell AU JSY RC 15.00 6.00
❑ 179 Chad Gaudin ROO RC 15.00 6.00
❑ 180 Chris Capuano ROO RC 25.00 10.00
❑ 181 Danny Garcia ROO RC 15.00 6.00
❑ 182 Delmon Young ROO 80.00 50.00
❑ 183 Edwin Jackson ROO RC 20.00 8.00
❑ 184 Greg Jones ROO RC 15.00 6.00
❑ 185 Jeremy Bonderman ROO RC 50.00 20.00
❑ 186 Jorge DePaula ROO 15.00 6.00
❑ 187 Khalil Greene ROO 20.00 8.00
❑ 188 Chad Cordero ROO RC 25.00 10.00
❑ 189 Miguel Cabrera ROO 20.00 8.00
❑ 190 Rich Harden ROO 20.00 8.00
❑ 191 Rickie Weeks ROO 40.00 15.00
❑ 192 Rosman Garcia ROO RC 15.00 6.00
❑ 193 Tom Gregorio ROO RC 15.00 6.00
❑ 381 Andrew Brown AU JSY RC 15.00 6.00
❑ 382 Delm Young AU JSY RC 450.00 350.00
❑ 383 Colin Porter AU JSY RC 15.00 6.00
❑ 385 Rick. Weeks AU JSY RC 80.00 40.00
❑ 386 David Matranga AU JSY RC 15.00 6.00
❑ 387 Bo Hart AU JSY 15.00 6.00

2004 SPx

❑ COMP.SET w/o SP's (100) 25.00 10.00
❑ COMMON CARD (1-100) .50 .20
❑ COMMON CARD (101-110) 8.00 3.00
❑ 101-110 STATED ODDS 1:18
❑ COMMON CARD (111-145) 5.00 2.00
❑ 111-145 PRINT RUN 1599 SERIAL #'d SETS
❑ COMMON CARD (146-154) 8.00 3.00
❑ 146-154 PRINT RUN 499 SERIAL #'d SETS
❑ COMMON CARD (155-160) 8.00 3.00
❑ 155-160 PRINT RUN 299 SERIAL #'d SETS
❑ 111-160 ODDS W/SPECTRUM 1:9
❑ 161-202 ODDS W/SPECTRUM 1:18
❑ 161-202 PRINT RUN 799 SERIAL #'d SETS
❑ EXCHANGE DEADLINE 12/03/07
❑ MASTER PLATE ODDS 1:2500
❑ MASTER PLATE PRINT RUN 1 #'d SET
❑ NO PLATE PRICING DUE TO SCARCITY
❑ 1 Alfonso Soriano .50 .20
❑ 2 Todd Helton .75 .30
❑ 3 Andruw Jones .75 .30
❑ 4 Eric Gagne .50 .20
❑ 5 Craig Wilson .50 .20
❑ 6 Brian Giles .50 .20
❑ 7 Miguel Tejada .50 .20
❑ 8 Kevin Brown .50 .20
❑ 9 Shawn Green .50 .20
❑ 10 Ben Sheets .50 .20
❑ 11 John Smoltz .75 .30
❑ 12 Tim Hudson .50 .20
❑ 13 Jason Schmidt .50 .20
❑ 14 Paul Konerko .50 .20
❑ 15 Randy Johnson 1.25 .50
❑ 16 Roy Oswalt .50 .20
❑ 17 Mike Lowell .50 .20
❑ 18 Carlos Lee .50 .20
❑ 19 Sean Burroughs .50 .20
❑ 20 Edgar Renteria .50 .20
❑ 21 Michael Young .50 .20
❑ 22 Jose Vidro .50 .20
❑ 23 Scott Rolen .75 .30
❑ 24 Rafael Furcal .50 .20
❑ 25 Tom Glavine .75 .30
❑ 26 Scott Podsednik .50 .20
❑ 27 Gary Sheffield .50 .20
❑ 28 Eric Chavez .50 .20
❑ 29 Mark Prior .75 .30
❑ 30 Chipper Jones 1.25 .50
❑ 31 Frank Thomas 1.25 .50
❑ 32 Victor Martinez .50 .20
❑ 33 Jake Peavy .50 .20
❑ 34 Carlos Beltran .50 .20
❑ 35 Roy Halladay .50 .20
❑ 36 Mark Teixeira .75 .30
❑ 37 Jacque Jones .50 .20
❑ 38 Mike Sweeney .50 .20
❑ 39 Troy Glaus .50 .20
❑ 40 Pat Burrell .50 .20
❑ 41 Ichiro Suzuki 2.50 1.00
❑ 42 Vladimir Guerrero 1.25 .50
❑ 43 Bobby Abreu .50 .20
❑ 44 Jim Edmonds .50 .20
❑ 45 Garret Anderson .50 .20
❑ 46 J.D. Drew .50 .20
❑ 47 C.C. Sabathia .50 .20
❑ 48 Joe Mauer 1.25 .50
❑ 49 Phil Nevin .50 .20
❑ 50 Hank Blalock .50 .20
❑ 51 Carlos Zambrano .50 .20
❑ 52 Mike Piazza 2.00 .75
❑ 53 Manny Ramirez .75 .30
❑ 54 Lance Berkman .50 .20
❑ 55 Delmon Young .75 .30
❑ 56 Nomar Garciaparra 2.00 .75
❑ 57 Alex Rodriguez 2.00 .75
❑ 58 Rickie Weeks .50 .20
❑ 59 Adrian Beltre .50 .20
❑ 60 Albert Pujols 2.50 1.00
❑ 61 Richie Sexson .50 .20
❑ 62 Magglio Ordonez .50 .20
❑ 63 Derrek Lee .75 .30
❑ 64 Sammy Sosa 1.25 .50
❑ 65 Jason Giambi .50 .20
❑ 66 Curt Schilling .75 .30
❑ 67 Jorge Posada .75 .30
❑ 68 Rafael Palmeiro .75 .30
❑ 69 Jeff Kent .50 .20
❑ 70 Jose Reyes .50 .20
❑ 71 David Ortiz 1.25 .50
❑ 72 Aubrey Huff .50 .20
❑ 73 Jim Thome .75 .30
❑ 74 Andy Pettitte .75 .30
❑ 75 Barry Zito .50 .20
❑ 76 Carlos Delgado .50 .20
❑ 77 Hideki Matsui 2.00 .75
❑ 78 Sean Casey .50 .20
❑ 79 Luis Gonzalez .50 .20
❑ 80 Marcus Giles .50 .20
❑ 81 Preston Wilson .50 .20
❑ 82 Javy Lopez .50 .20
❑ 83 Mark Mulder .50 .20
❑ 84 Derek Jeter 2.50 1.00
❑ 85 Miguel Cabrera .75 .30
❑ 86 Vernon Wells .50 .20
❑ 87 Roger Clemens 2.50 1.00
❑ 88 Lyle Overbay .50 .20
❑ 89 Bret Boone .50 .20
❑ 90 Melvin Mora .50 .20
❑ 91 Greg Maddux 2.00 .75
❑ 92 Kerry Wood .50 .20
❑ 93 Ivan Rodriguez .75 .30
❑ 94 Pedro Martinez .75 .30
❑ 95 Jeff Bagwell .75 .30
❑ 96 Torii Hunter .50 .20
❑ 97 Ken Griffey Jr. 2.00 .75
❑ 98 Mike Mussina .75 .30
❑ 99 Oliver Perez .50 .20
❑ 100 Josh Beckett .50 .20
❑ 101 Bob Gibson LGD 8.00 3.00
❑ 102 Cal Ripken LGD 15.00 6.00
❑ 103 Ted Williams LGD 8.00 3.00
❑ 104 Nolan Ryan LGD 10.00 4.00
❑ 105 Mickey Mantle LGD 15.00 6.00
❑ 106 Ernie Banks LGD 8.00 3.00
❑ 107 Joe DiMaggio LGD 8.00 3.00
❑ 108 Stan Musial LGD 8.00 3.00
❑ 109 Tom Seaver LGD 8.00 3.00
❑ 110 Mike Schmidt LGD 10.00 4.00
❑ 111 Jerry Gil T1 RC 5.00 2.00
❑ 112 Dioner Navarro T1 RC 8.00 3.00
❑ 113 Bartolome Fortunato T1 RC 5.00 2.00
❑ 114 Carlos Hines T1 RC 5.00 2.00
❑ 115 Franklyn Gracesqui T1 RC 5.00 2.00
❑ 116 Aarom Baldiris T1 RC 8.00 3.00
❑ 117 Casey Daigle T1 RC 5.00 2.00
❑ 118 Joey Gathright T1 RC 8.00 3.00
❑ 119 William Bergolla T1 RC 5.00 2.00
❑ 120 Jeff Bennett T1 RC 5.00 2.00
❑ 121 Lincoln Holdzkom T1 RC 5.00 2.00
❑ 122 Jorge Vasquez T1 RC 5.00 2.00
❑ 123 Donnie Kelly T1 RC 5.00 2.00
❑ 124 Yadier Molina T1 RC 8.00 3.00
❑ 125 Ryan Wing T1 RC 5.00 2.00
❑ 126 Justin Germano T1 RC 5.00 2.00
❑ 127 Freddy Guzman T1 RC 5.00 2.00
❑ 128 Onil Joseph T1 RC 5.00 2.00
❑ 129 Roman Colon T1 RC 5.00 2.00
❑ 130 Roberto Novoa T1 RC 8.00 3.00

131	Renyel Pinto T1 RC	8.00	3.00
132	Evan Rust T1 RC	5.00	2.00
133	Orlando Rodriguez T1 RC	5.00	2.00
134	Edwardo Sierra T1 RC	8.00	3.00
135	Mike Rose T1 RC	5.00	2.00
136	Phil Stockman T1 RC	5.00	2.00
137	Greg Dobbs T1 RC	5.00	2.00
138	Brad Halsey T1 RC	8.00	3.00
139	David Aardsma T1 RC	8.00	3.00
140	Joe Hietpas T1 RC	5.00	2.00
141	Josh Labandeira T1 RC	5.00	2.00
142	Mariano Gomez T1 RC	5.00	2.00
143	Jeff Bajenaru T1 RC	5.00	2.00
144	Travis Blackley T1 RC	5.00	2.00
145	Abe Alvarez T1 RC	8.00	3.00
146	Ramon Ramirez T2 RC	8.00	3.00
147	Edwin Moreno T2 RC	10.00	4.00
148	Ronny Cedeno T2 RC	10.00	4.00
149	Hector Gimenez T2 RC	8.00	3.00
150	Carlos Vasquez T2 RC	10.00	4.00
151	Jesse Crain T2 RC	15.00	6.00
152	Logan Kensing T2 RC	8.00	3.00
153	Sean Henn T2 RC	8.00	3.00
154	Rusty Tucker T2 RC	10.00	4.00
155	Justin Lehr T3 RC	8.00	3.00
156	Ian Snell T3 RC	10.00	4.00
157	Merkin Valdez T3 RC	8.00	3.00
158	Scott Proctor T3 RC	10.00	4.00
159	Jose Capellan T3 RC	10.00	4.00
160	Kazuo Matsui T3 RC	8.00	3.00
161	Chris Oxspring AU JSY RC	15.00	6.00
162	Jimmy Serrano AU JSY RC	15.00	6.00
163	Jeff Keppinger AU JSY RC	20.00	8.00
164	B.Medders AU JSY RC	15.00	6.00
165	Brian Dallimore AU JSY RC	15.00	6.00
166	Chad Bentz AU JSY RC	15.00	6.00
167	Chris Aguila AU JSY RC	15.00	6.00
168	Chris Saenz AU JSY RC	15.00	6.00
169	Frank Francisco AU JSY RC	15.00	6.00
170	Colby Miller AU JSY RC	15.00	6.00
171	D.Crouth AU JSY RC EXCH	15.00	6.00
172	Charles Thomas AU JSY RC	15.00	6.00
173	Dennis Sarfate AU JSY RC	15.00	6.00
174	Lance Cormier AU JSY RC	15.00	6.00
175	Joe Horgan AU JSY RC	15.00	6.00
176	Fernando Nieve AU JSY RC	15.00	6.00
177	Jake Woods AU JSY RC	15.00	6.00
178	Matt Treanor AU JSY RC	15.00	6.00
179	Jerome Gamble AU JSY RC	15.00	6.00
180	John Gall AU JSY RC	25.00	10.00
181	Jorge Sequea AU JSY RC	15.00	6.00
182	Justin Hampson AU JSY RC	15.00	6.00
183	Justin Huisman AU JSY RC	15.00	6.00
184	Justin Knoedler AU JSY RC	15.00	6.00
185	Justin Leone AU JSY RC	25.00	10.00
186	Scott Atchison AU JSY RC	15.00	6.00
187	Jon Knott AU JSY RC	15.00	6.00
188	Kevin Cave AU JSY RC	15.00	6.00
189	Jason Frasor AU JSY RC	15.00	6.00
190	George Sherrill AU JSY RC	15.00	6.00
191	Mike Gosling AU JSY RC	15.00	6.00
192	Mike Johnston AU JSY RC	15.00	6.00
193	Mike Rouse AU JSY RC	15.00	6.00
194	Nick Regilio AU JSY RC	15.00	6.00
195	Ryan Meaux AU JSY RC	15.00	6.00
196	Scott Dohmann AU JSY RC	15.00	6.00
197	Shawn Camp AU JSY RC	15.00	6.00
198	Shawn Hill AU JSY RC	15.00	6.00
199	Shingo Takatsu AU JSY RC	15.00	6.00
200	Tim Bausher AU JSY RC	15.00	6.00
201	Tim Bittner AU JSY RC	15.00	6.00
202	Scott Kazmir AU JSY RC	50.00	20.00

2005 SPx

	COMP.BASIC SET (100)	25.00	10.00
	COMMON CARD (1-100)	.40	.15
	COMMON RC (1-100)	.40	.15
	1-100 ISSUED IN 05 SP COLLECTION PACKS		
	COMMON AUTO (101-180)	10.00	4.00
	101-180 ODDS APPX 1:8 '05 UD UPDATE		
	101-180 PRINT RUN 185 SERIAL #'d SETS		
	105, 117, 139, 149, 155, 172 DO NOT EXIST		
	175, 178, 180 DO NOT EXIST		
1	Aaron Harang	.40	.15
2	Aaron Rowand	.40	.15
3	Aaron Miles	.40	.15

4	Adrian Gonzalez	.40	.15
5	Alex Rios	.40	.15
6	Angel Berroa	.40	.15
7	B.J. Upton	.40	.15
8	Brandon Claussen	.40	.15
9	Andy Marte	.40	.15
10	Brandon Webb	.40	.15
11	Bronson Arroyo	.40	.15
12	Casey Kotchman	.40	.15
13	Cesar Izturis	.40	.15
14	Chad Cordero	.40	.15
15	Chad Tracy	.40	.15
16	Charles Thomas	.40	.15
17	Chase Utley	.60	.25
18	Chone Figgins	.40	.15
19	Chris Burke	.40	.15
20	Cliff Lee	.40	.15
21	Clint Barmes	.40	.15
22	Coco Crisp	.40	.15
23	Bill Hall	.40	.15
24	Dallas McPherson	.40	.15
25	Brad Halsey	.40	.15
26	Daniel Cabrera	.40	.15
27	Danny Haren	.40	.15
28	Dave Bush	.40	.15
29	David DeJesus	.40	.15
30	D.J. Houlton RC	.60	.25
31	Derek Jeter	2.00	.75
32	Dewon Brazelton	.40	.15
33	Edwin Jackson	.40	.15
34	Brad Hawpe	.40	.15
35	Brandon Inge	.40	.15
36	Brett Myers	.40	.15
37	Garrett Atkins	.40	.15
38	Gavin Floyd	.40	.15
39	Grady Sizemore	.60	.25
40	Guillermo Mota	.40	.15
41	Carlos Guillen	.40	.15
42	Gustavo Chacin	.40	.15
43	Huston Street	.60	.25
44	Chris Duffy	.40	.15
45	J.D. Closser	.40	.15
46	J.J. Hardy	.40	.15
47	Jason Bartlett	.40	.15
48	Jason DuBois	.40	.15
49	Chris Shelton	.60	.25
50	Jason Lane	.40	.15
51	Jayson Werth	.40	.15
52	Jeff Baker	.40	.15
53	Jeff Francis	.40	.15
54	Jeremy Bonderman	.40	.15
55	Jeremy Reed	.40	.15
56	Jerome Williams	.40	.15
57	Jesse Crain	.40	.15
58	Chris Young	.40	.15
59	Jhonny Peralta	.40	.15
60	Joe Blanton	.40	.15
61	Joe Crede	.40	.15
62	Joel Pineiro	.40	.15
63	Joey Gathright	.40	.15
64	John Buck	.40	.15
65	Jonny Gomes	.40	.15
66	Jorge Cantu	.40	.15
67	Dan Johnson	.40	.15
68	Jose Valverde	.40	.15
69	Ervin Santana	.40	.15
70	Justin Morneau	.40	.15
71	Keiichi Yabu RC	.60	.25
72	Ken Griffey Jr.	1.50	.60
73	Jason Repko	.40	.15
74	Kevin Youkilis	.40	.15
75	Koyie Hill	.40	.15
76	Laynce Nix	.40	.15
77	Luke Scott RC	2.00	.75
78	Juan Rivera	.40	.15
79	Justin Duchscherer	.40	.15
80	Mark Teahen	.40	.15
81	Lance Niekro	.40	.15
82	Michael Cuddyer	.40	.15
83	Nick Swisher	.40	.15
84	Noah Lowry	.40	.15
85	Matt Holliday	.50	.20
86	Reed Johnson	.40	.15
87	Rich Harden	.40	.15
88	Robb Quinlan	.40	.15
89	Nick Johnson	.40	.15
90	Ryan Howard	2.50	1.00
91	Nook Logan	.40	.15
92	Steve Schmoll RC	.60	.25
93	Tadahito Iguchi RC	4.00	1.50
94	Willy Taveras	.40	.15
95	Wily Mo Pena	.40	.15
96	Xavier Nady	.40	.15
97	Yadier Molina	.40	.15
98	Yhency Brazoban	.40	.15
99	Ryan Freel	.40	.15
100	Zack Greinke	.40	.15
101	Adam Shabala AU RC	10.00	4.00
102	Ambiorix Burgos AU RC	10.00	4.00
103	Ambiorix Concepcion AU RC	10.00	4.00
104	Anibal Sanchez AU RC	40.00	15.00
106	Brandon McCarthy AU RC	30.00	12.50
107	Brian Burres AU RC	10.00	4.00
108	Carlos Ruiz AU RC	15.00	6.00
109	Casey Rogowski AU RC	15.00	6.00
110	Chad Orvella AU RC	10.00	4.00
111	Chris Resop AU RC	15.00	6.00
112	Chris Roberson AU RC	10.00	4.00
113	Chris Seddon AU RC	10.00	4.00
114	Colter Bean AU RC	15.00	6.00
115	Dave Gassner AU RC	10.00	4.00
116	Brian Anderson AU RC	40.00	15.00
118	Devon Lowery AU RC	10.00	4.00
119	Enrique Gonzalez AU RC	15.00	6.00
120	Eude Brito AU RC	10.00	4.00
121	Francisco Butto AU RC	10.00	4.00
122	Franquelis Osoria AU RC	10.00	4.00
123	Garrett Jones AU RC	10.00	4.00
124	Geovany Soto AU RC	175.00	125.00
125	Hayden Penn AU RC	20.00	8.00
126	Ismael Ramirez AU RC	10.00	4.00
127	Jared Gothreaux AU RC	10.00	4.00
128	Jason Hammel AU RC	10.00	4.00
129	Jeff Miller AU RC	10.00	4.00
130	Jeff Niemann AU RC	30.00	12.50
131	Joel Peralta AU RC	10.00	4.00
132	John Hattig AU RC	10.00	4.00
133	Jorge Campillo AU RC	10.00	4.00
134	Juan Morillo AU RC	10.00	4.00
135	Justin Verlander AU RC	200.00	125.00
136	Ryan Garko AU RC	40.00	15.00
137	Kendry Morales AU RC	60.00	30.00
138	Luis Hernandez AU RC	10.00	4.00
140	Luis O.Rodriguez AU RC	10.00	4.00
141	Mark Woodyard AU RC	10.00	4.00
142	Matt A.Smith AU RC	10.00	4.00
143	Matthew Lindstrom AU RC	10.00	4.00
144	Miguel Negron AU RC	15.00	6.00
145	Mike Morse AU RC	20.00	8.00
146	Nate McLouth AU RC	50.00	20.00
147	Nelson Cruz AU RC	40.00	15.00
148	Nick Masset AU RC	10.00	4.00
150	Paulino Reynoso AU RC	10.00	4.00
151	Pedro Lopez AU RC	10.00	4.00
152	Philip Humber AU RC	30.00	12.50
153	Prince Fielder AU RC	200.00	125.00
154	Randy Messenger AU RC	10.00	4.00
156	Raul Tablado AU RC	10.00	4.00
157	Ronny Paulino AU RC	15.00	6.00
158	Russ Rohlicek AU RC	10.00	4.00
159	Russell Martin AU RC	60.00	30.00
160	Scott Baker AU RC	15.00	6.00
161	Scott Munter AU RC	10.00	4.00
162	Sean Thompson AU RC	10.00	4.00

❑ 163 Sean Tracey AU RC 10.00 4.00
❑ 164 Shane Costa AU RC 10.00 4.00
❑ 165 Stephen Drew AU RC 60.00 30.00
❑ 166 Tony Giarratano AU RC 10.00 4.00
❑ 167 Tony Pena AU RC 10.00 4.00
❑ 168 Travis Bowyer AU RC 10.00 4.00
❑ 169 Ubaldo Jimenez AU RC 50.00 20.00
❑ 170 Wladimir Balentien AU RC 80.00 40.00
❑ 171 Yorman Bazardo AU RC 10.00 4.00
❑ 173 Ryan Zimmerman AU RC 150.00 75.00
❑ 174 Chris Denorfia AU RC 15.00 6.00
❑ 176 Jermaine Van Buren AU 10.00 4.00
❑ 177 Mark McLemore AU RC 10.00 4.00
❑ 179 Ryan Speier AU RC 10.00 4.00

2006 SPx

❑ COMP.BASIC SET (100) 25.00 10.00
❑ COMMON CARD (1-100) .40 .15
❑ COMMON AU p/r 659-999 10.00 4.00
❑ COMMON AU p/r 350-500 10.00 4.00
❑ OVERALL 101-161 AU ODDS 1:9
❑ 101-161 AU EXCH DEADLINE 09/07/08
❑ 101-161 AU PRINT RUN B/WN 190-999 PER
❑ 101-161 PRINTING PLATE ODDS 1:224
❑ 101-161 PLATES PRINT RUN 1 SET PER CLR
❑ 101-161 PLATES FEATURE AUTOS
❑ BLACK-CYAN-MAGENTA-YELLOW ISSUED
❑ NO PLATE PRICING DUE TO SCARCITY
❑ EXQUISITE EXCH ODDS 1:36
❑ EXQUISITE EXCH DEADLINE 07/27/07
❑ 1 Luis Gonzalez .40 .15
❑ 2 Chad Tracy .40 .15
❑ 3 Brandon Webb .40 .15
❑ 4 Andruw Jones .60 .25
❑ 5 Chipper Jones 1.00 .40
❑ 6 John Smoltz .60 .25
❑ 7 Tim Hudson .40 .15
❑ 8 Miguel Tejada .40 .15
❑ 9 Brian Roberts .40 .15
❑ 10 Ramon Hernandez .40 .15
❑ 11 Curt Schilling .60 .25
❑ 12 David Ortiz 1.00 .40
❑ 13 Manny Ramirez .60 .25
❑ 14 Jason Varitek 1.00 .40
❑ 15 Josh Beckett .40 .15
❑ 16 Greg Maddux 1.50 .60
❑ 17 Derrek Lee .40 .15
❑ 18 Mark Prior .60 .25
❑ 19 Aramis Ramirez .40 .15
❑ 20 Jim Thome .60 .25
❑ 21 Paul Konerko .40 .15
❑ 22 Scott Podsednik .40 .15
❑ 23 Jose Contreras .40 .15
❑ 24 Ken Griffey Jr. 1.50 .60
❑ 25 Adam Dunn .40 .15
❑ 26 Felipe Lopez .40 .15
❑ 27 Travis Hafner .40 .15
❑ 28 Victor Martinez .40 .15
❑ 29 Grady Sizemore .60 .25
❑ 30 Jhonny Peralta .40 .15
❑ 31 Todd Helton .60 .25
❑ 32 Garrett Atkins .40 .15
❑ 33 Clint Barmes .40 .15
❑ 34 Ivan Rodriguez .60 .25
❑ 35 Chris Shelton .40 .15
❑ 36 Jeremy Bonderman .40 .15
❑ 37 Miguel Cabrera .60 .25
❑ 38 Dontrelle Willis .40 .15
❑ 39 Lance Berkman .40 .15
❑ 40 Morgan Ensberg .40 .15
❑ 41 Roy Oswalt .40 .15
❑ 42 Reggie Sanders .40 .15
❑ 43 Mike Sweeney .40 .15
❑ 44 Vladimir Guerrero 1.00 .40
❑ 45 Bartolo Colon .40 .15
❑ 46 Chone Figgins .40 .15
❑ 47 Nomar Garciaparra 1.00 .40
❑ 48 Jeff Kent .40 .15
❑ 49 J.D. Drew .40 .15
❑ 50 Carlos Lee .40 .15
❑ 51 Ben Sheets .40 .15
❑ 52 Rickie Weeks .40 .15
❑ 53 Johan Santana .60 .25
❑ 54 Torii Hunter .40 .15
❑ 55 Joe Mauer .60 .25
❑ 56 Pedro Martinez .60 .25
❑ 57 David Wright 1.50 .60
❑ 58 Carlos Beltran .40 .15
❑ 59 Carlos Delgado .40 .15
❑ 60 Jose Reyes 1.00 .40
❑ 61 Derek Jeter 2.50 1.00
❑ 62 Alex Rodriguez 1.50 .60
❑ 63 Randy Johnson 1.00 .40
❑ 64 Hideki Matsui 1.00 .40
❑ 65 Gary Sheffield .40 .15
❑ 66 Rich Harden .40 .15
❑ 67 Eric Chavez .40 .15
❑ 68 Huston Street .40 .15
❑ 69 Bobby Crosby .40 .15
❑ 70 Bobby Abreu .40 .15
❑ 71 Ryan Howard 1.50 .60
❑ 72 Chase Utley 1.00 .40
❑ 73 Pat Burrell .40 .15
❑ 74 Jason Bay .40 .15
❑ 75 Sean Casey .40 .15
❑ 76 Mike Piazza 1.00 .40
❑ 77 Jake Peavy .40 .15
❑ 78 Brian Giles .40 .15
❑ 79 Milton Bradley .40 .15
❑ 80 Omar Vizquel .60 .25
❑ 81 Jason Schmidt .40 .15
❑ 82 Ichiro Suzuki 1.50 .60
❑ 83 Felix Hernandez .60 .25
❑ 84 Richie Sexson .40 .15
❑ 85 Albert Pujols 2.00 .75
❑ 86 Chris Carpenter .40 .15
❑ 87 Scott Rolen .60 .25
❑ 88 Jim Edmonds .60 .25
❑ 89 Carl Crawford .40 .15
❑ 90 Jonny Gomes .40 .15
❑ 91 Scott Kazmir .60 .25
❑ 92 Mark Teixeira .60 .25
❑ 93 Michael Young .40 .15
❑ 94 Phil Nevin .40 .15
❑ 95 Vernon Wells .40 .15
❑ 96 Roy Halladay .40 .15
❑ 97 Troy Glaus .40 .15
❑ 98 Alfonso Soriano .40 .15
❑ 99 Nick Johnson .40 .15
❑ 100 Jose Vidro .40 .15
❑ 101 Conor Jackson AU/999 (RC) 15.00 6.00
❑ 102 J.Weaver AU/299 (RC) EXCH 40.00 15.00
❑ 103 Macay McBride AU/999 (RC) 10.00 4.00
❑ 104 Aaron Rakers AU/499 (RC) 10.00 4.00
❑ 105 J.Papelbon AU/499 (RC) 30.00 12.50
❑ 106 J.Bergmann AU/999 RC 10.00 4.00
❑ 107 S.Drew AU/350 (RC) 30.00 12.50
❑ 108 Chris Denorfia AU/999 (RC) 10.00 4.00
❑ 109 Kelly Shoppach AU/999 (RC) 10.00 4.00
❑ 110 Ryan Shealy AU/999 (RC) 10.00 4.00
❑ 111 Josh Wilson AU/999 (RC) 10.00 4.00
❑ 112 Brian Anderson AU/999 (RC) 10.00 4.00
❑ 113 J.Verlander AU/749 (RC) 50.00 20.00
❑ 114 J.Hermida AU/999 (RC) 15.00 6.00
❑ 115 M.Jacobs AU/999 (RC) 15.00 6.00
❑ 116 Josh Johnson AU/999 (RC) 15.00 6.00
❑ 117 Hanley Ramirez AU/659 (RC) 50.00 20.00
❑ 118 Chris Resop AU/999 (RC) 10.00 4.00
❑ 119 J.Willingham AU/999 (RC) 10.00 4.00
❑ 120 Cole Hamels AU/499 (RC) 50.00 20.00
❑ 121 Matt Cain AU/999 (RC) 20.00 8.00
❑ 122 Steve Stemle AU/999 RC 10.00 4.00
❑ 123 Tim Hamulack AU/999 (RC) 10.00 4.00
❑ 124 Choo Freeman AU/999 (RC) 10.00 4.00
❑ 125 H.Kuo AU/999 (RC) 50.00 20.00
❑ 126 Cody Ross AU/999 (RC) 10.00 4.00
❑ 127 Jose Capellan AU/999 (RC) 10.00 4.00
❑ 128 Prince Fielder AU/190 (RC) 120.00 60.00
❑ 129 David Gassner AU/999 (RC) 10.00 4.00
❑ 130 Jason Kubel AU/999 (RC) 10.00 4.00
❑ 131 F.Liriano AU/299 (RC) 50.00 20.00
❑ 132 A.Hernandez AU/999 (RC) 15.00 6.00
❑ 133 Joey Devine AU/499 RC 10.00 4.00
❑ 134 Chris Booker AU/999 (RC) 10.00 4.00
❑ 135 Matt Capps AU/999 (RC) 10.00 4.00
❑ 136 Paul Maholm AU/999 (RC) 10.00 4.00
❑ 137 N.McLouth AU/999 (RC) 20.00 8.00
❑ 138 J.Van Benschoten AU/999 (RC) 10.00 4.00
❑ 139 Jeff Harris AU/999 RC 10.00 4.00
❑ 140 Ben Johnson AU/999 (RC) 10.00 4.00
❑ 141 Wil Nieves AU/999 (RC) 10.00 4.00
❑ 142 G.Quiroz AU/999 (RC) 10.00 4.00
❑ 143 Josh Rupe AU/500 (RC) 10.00 4.00
❑ 144 Skip Schumaker AU/999 (RC) 10.00 4.00
❑ 145 Jack Taschner AU/999 (RC) 10.00 4.00
❑ 146 A.Wainwright AU/999 (RC) 25.00 10.00
❑ 147 Alay Soler AU/499 RC 25.00 10.00
❑ 148 Kendry Morales AU/999 (RC) 15.00 6.00
❑ 149 Ian Kinsler AU/999 (RC) 20.00 8.00
❑ 150 Jason Hammel AU/999 (RC) 10.00 4.00
❑ 151 C.Billingsley AU/499 (RC) 25.00 10.00
❑ 152 Boof Bonser AU/999 (RC) 15.00 6.00
❑ 153 Peter Moylan AU/999 RC 10.00 4.00
❑ 154 Chris Britton AU/999 RC 10.00 4.00
❑ 155 Takashi Saito AU/999 RC 30.00 12.50
❑ 156 Scott Dunn AU/999 (RC) 10.00 4.00
❑ 157 J.Zumaya AU/299 (RC) EXCH 30.00 12.50
❑ 158 Dan Uggla AU/999 (RC) 25.00 10.00
❑ 159 Taylor Buchholz AU/999 (RC) 10.00 4.00
❑ 160 M.Cabrera AU/499 (RC) EXCH 40.00 15.00
❑ NNO Exquisite Redemption

2007 SPx

❑ COMMON CARD (1-100) .75 .30
❑ COMMON AU RC (101-150) 8.00 3.00
❑ OVERALL 101-150 AU RC ODDS 1:3
❑ 101-150 AU RC EXCH DEADLINE 05/10/2010
❑ ASTERISK EQUALS PARTIAL EXCH
❑ APPX.PRINTING PLATE ODDS 2 PER CASE
❑ PLATES PRINT RUN 1 SET PER COLOR
❑ BLACK-CYAN-MAGENTA-YELLOW ISSUED
❑ NO PLATE PRICING DUE TO SCARCITY
❑ 1 Miguel Tejada .75 .30
❑ 2 Brian Roberts .75 .30
❑ 3 Melvin Mora .75 .30
❑ 4 David Ortiz 2.00 .75
❑ 5 Manny Ramirez 1.25 .50
❑ 6 Jason Varitek 2.00 .75
❑ 7 Curt Schilling 1.25 .50
❑ 8 Jim Thome 1.25 .50
❑ 9 Paul Konerko .75 .30
❑ 10 Jermaine Dye .75 .30
❑ 11 Travis Hafner .75 .30
❑ 12 Victor Martinez .75 .30
❑ 13 Grady Sizemore 1.25 .50
❑ 14 C.C. Sabathia .75 .30
❑ 15 Ivan Rodriguez 1.25 .50
❑ 16 Magglio Ordonez .75 .30
❑ 17 Carlos Guillen .75 .30
❑ 18 Justin Verlander 2.00 .75
❑ 19 Shane Costa .75 .30
❑ 20 Emil Brown .75 .30

❑ 21	Mark Teahen	.75	.30
❑ 22	Vladimir Guerrero	2.00	.75
❑ 23	Jered Weaver	1.25	.50
❑ 24	Juan Rivera	.75	.30
❑ 25	Justin Morneau	.75	.30
❑ 26	Joe Mauer	1.25	.50
❑ 27	Torii Hunter	.75	.30
❑ 28	Johan Santana	1.25	.50
❑ 29	Derek Jeter	5.00	2.00
❑ 30	Alex Rodriguez	3.00	1.25
❑ 31	Johnny Damon	1.25	.50
❑ 32	Jason Giambi	.75	.30
❑ 33	Bobby Crosby	.75	.30
❑ 34	Nick Swisher	.75	.30
❑ 35	Eric Chavez	.75	.30
❑ 36	Ichiro Suzuki	3.00	1.25
❑ 37	Raul Ibanez	.75	.30
❑ 38	Richie Sexson	.75	.30
❑ 39	Carl Crawford	.75	.30
❑ 40	Rocco Baldelli	.75	.30
❑ 41	Scott Kazmir	1.25	.50
❑ 42	Michael Young	.75	.30
❑ 43	Mark Teixeira	1.25	.50
❑ 44	Ian Kinsler	.75	.30
❑ 45	Troy Glaus	.75	.30
❑ 46	Vernon Wells	.75	.30
❑ 47	Roy Halladay	.75	.30
❑ 48	Lyle Overbay	.75	.30
❑ 49	Brandon Webb	.75	.30
❑ 50	Conor Jackson	.75	.30
❑ 51	Stephen Drew	1.25	.50
❑ 52	Chipper Jones	2.00	.75
❑ 53	Andruw Jones	1.25	.50
❑ 54	Adam LaRoche	.75	.30
❑ 55	John Smoltz	1.25	.50
❑ 56	Derrek Lee	.75	.30
❑ 57	Aramis Ramirez	.75	.30
❑ 58	Carlos Zambrano	.75	.30
❑ 59	Ken Griffey Jr.	3.00	1.25
❑ 60	Adam Dunn	.75	.30
❑ 61	Aaron Harang	.75	.30
❑ 62	Todd Helton	1.25	.50
❑ 63	Matt Holliday	1.00	.40
❑ 64	Garrett Atkins	.75	.30
❑ 65	Miguel Cabrera	1.25	.50
❑ 66	Hanley Ramirez	1.25	.50
❑ 67	Dontrelle Willis	.75	.30
❑ 68	Lance Berkman	.75	.30
❑ 69	Roy Oswalt	.75	.30
❑ 70	Craig Biggio	1.25	.50
❑ 71	J.D. Drew	.75	.30
❑ 72	Nomar Garciaparra	2.00	.75
❑ 73	Rafael Furcal	.75	.30
❑ 74	Jeff Kent	.75	.30
❑ 75	Prince Fielder	2.00	.75
❑ 76	Bill Hall	.75	.30
❑ 77	Rickie Weeks	.75	.30
❑ 78	Jose Reyes	.75	.30
❑ 79	David Wright	3.00	1.25
❑ 80	Carlos Delgado	.75	.30
❑ 81	Carlos Beltran	.75	.30
❑ 82	Ryan Howard	3.00	1.25
❑ 83	Chase Utley	2.00	.75
❑ 84	Jimmy Rollins	.75	.30
❑ 85	Jason Bay	.75	.30
❑ 86	Freddy Sanchez	.75	.30
❑ 87	Zach Duke	.75	.30
❑ 88	Trevor Hoffman	.75	.30
❑ 89	Adrian Gonzalez	.75	.30
❑ 90	Chris Young	.75	.30
❑ 91	Ray Durham	.75	.30
❑ 92	Omar Vizquel	1.25	.50
❑ 93	Jason Schmidt	.75	.30
❑ 94	Albert Pujols	4.00	1.50
❑ 95	Scott Rolen	1.25	.50
❑ 96	Jim Edmonds	1.25	.50
❑ 97	Chris Carpenter	.75	.30
❑ 98	Alfonso Soriano	.75	.30
❑ 99	Ryan Zimmerman	2.00	.75
❑ 100	Nick Johnson	.75	.30
❑ 101	Delmon Young AU (RC)	25.00	10.00
❑ 102	A.Miller AU RC EXCH *	25.00	10.00
❑ 103	Troy Tulowitzki AU (RC)	30.00	12.50
❑ 104	Jeff Fiorentino AU (RC)	8.00	3.00
❑ 105	David Murphy AU (RC)	8.00	3.00
❑ 106	T.Lincecum AU RC	120.00	60.00
❑ 107	P.Hughes AU (RC) EXCH	100.00	50.00
❑ 108	K.Kouzmanoff AU (RC) EXCH	15.00	6.00
❑ 109	A.Lind AU (RC) EXCH *	15.00	6.00
❑ 110	M.Reynolds AU RC EXCH	50.00	20.00
❑ 111	Kevin Hooper AU (RC)	8.00	3.00
❑ 112	Mitch Maier AU RC	8.00	3.00
❑ 113	Homey Bailey AU (RC) EXCH	25.00	10.00
❑ 114	Dennis Sarfate AU (RC)	8.00	3.00
❑ 115	Drew Anderson AU RC	8.00	3.00
❑ 116	Miguel Montero AU (RC)	8.00	3.00
❑ 117	G.Perkins AU (RC) EXCH	8.00	3.00
❑ 118	Kevin Slowey AU (RC) EXCH	25.00	10.00
❑ 119	Tim Gradoville AU RC	8.00	3.00
❑ 120	Ryan Braun AU (RC)	100.00	50.00
❑ 121	Chris Narveson AU (RC)	8.00	3.00
❑ 122	P.Misch AU (RC) EXCH *	8.00	3.00
❑ 123	Juan Salas AU (RC)	8.00	3.00
❑ 124	Beltran Perez AU (RC)	8.00	3.00
❑ 125	Joaquin Arias AU (RC)	8.00	3.00
❑ 126	Philip Humber AU (RC)	15.00	6.00
❑ 127	Kei Igawa AU RC	60.00	30.00
❑ 128	Daisuke Matsuzaka AU RC	150.00	90.00
❑ 129	Andy Cannizaro AU RC	15.00	6.00
❑ 130	Ubaldo Jimenez AU (RC)	15.00	6.00
❑ 131	Fred Lewis AU (RC)	15.00	6.00
❑ 132	Ryan Sweeney AU (RC)	8.00	3.00
❑ 133	Jeff Baker AU (RC)	8.00	3.00
❑ 134	Michael Bourn AU (RC)	8.00	3.00
❑ 135	Akinori Iwamura AU RC	25.00	10.00
❑ 136	Oswaldo Navarro AU RC	8.00	3.00
❑ 137	Hunter Pence AU (RC)	40.00	15.00
❑ 138	Jon Knott AU (RC)	8.00	3.00
❑ 139	J.Hampson AU (RC) EXCH	8.00	3.00
❑ 140	J.Salazar AU (RC) EXCH	8.00	3.00
❑ 141	Juan Morillo AU (RC)	8.00	3.00
❑ 142	Delwyn Young AU (RC)	8.00	3.00
❑ 143	Brian Burres AU (RC)	12.00	5.00
❑ 144	Chris Stewart AU RC	8.00	3.00
❑ 145	Eric Stults AU RC	8.00	3.00
❑ 146	Carlos Maldonado AU (RC)	8.00	3.00
❑ 147	Angel Sanchez AU RC	8.00	3.00
❑ 148	Cesar Jimenez AU RC	8.00	3.00
❑ 149	Shawn Riggans AU (RC)	8.00	3.00
❑ 150	John Nelson AU (RC)	8.00	3.00

2008 SPx

❑	COMMON CARD (1-100)	.60	.25
❑	COMMON AU RC (101-150)	8.00	3.00
❑	OVERALL AU ODDS FOUR PER BOX		
❑ 1	Brandon Webb	.60	.25
❑ 2	Chris B. Young	.60	.25
❑ 3	Eric Byrnes	.60	.25
❑ 4	Dan Haren	.60	.25
❑ 5	Mark Teixeira	1.00	.40
❑ 6	Chipper Jones	2.00	.75
❑ 7	John Smoltz	1.50	.60
❑ 8	Erik Bedard	.60	.25
❑ 9	Nick Markakis	1.00	.40
❑ 10	Brian Roberts	1.00	.40
❑ 11	David Ortiz	1.50	.60
❑ 12	Curt Schilling	1.00	.40
❑ 13	Manny Ramirez	1.50	.60
❑ 14	Daisuke Matsuzaka	2.50	1.00
❑ 15	Josh Beckett	1.00	.40
❑ 16	Derrek Lee	1.00	.40
❑ 17	Alfonso Soriano	1.00	.40
❑ 18	Carlos Zambrano	.60	.25
❑ 19	Aramis Ramirez	.60	.25
❑ 20	Jermaine Dye	.60	.25
❑ 21	Jim Thome	1.00	.40
❑ 22	Nick Swisher	.60	.25
❑ 23	Ken Griffey Jr.	2.50	1.00
❑ 24	Adam Dunn	.60	.25
❑ 25	Brandon Phillips	.60	.25
❑ 26	Grady Sizemore	1.00	.40
❑ 27	Victor Martinez	.60	.25
❑ 28	C.C. Sabathia	.60	.25
❑ 29	Travis Hafner	.60	.25
❑ 30	Matt Holliday	1.00	.40
❑ 31	Todd Helton	1.00	.40
❑ 32	Troy Tulowitzki	1.00	.40
❑ 33	Magglio Ordonez	1.00	.40
❑ 34	Gary Sheffield	.60	.25
❑ 35	Justin Verlander	1.00	.40
❑ 36	Curtis Granderson	1.00	.40
❑ 37	Miguel Cabrera	1.00	.40
❑ 38	Hanley Ramirez	1.50	.60
❑ 39	Dan Uggla	1.00	.40
❑ 40	Miguel Tejada	.60	.25
❑ 41	Lance Berkman	1.00	.40
❑ 42	Hunter Pence	1.50	.60
❑ 43	Carlos Lee	.60	.25
❑ 44	Alex Gordon	1.50	.60
❑ 45	David DeJesus	.60	.25
❑ 46	Vladimir Guerrero	1.50	.60
❑ 47	Jered Weaver	.60	.25
❑ 48	Torii Hunter	.60	.25
❑ 49	Andruw Jones	.60	.25
❑ 50	Rafael Furcal	.60	.25
❑ 51	Russell Martin	.60	.25
❑ 52	Brad Penny	.60	.25
❑ 53	Ryan Braun	2.00	.75
❑ 54	Prince Fielder	1.50	.60
❑ 55	J.J. Hardy	.60	.25
❑ 56	Justin Morneau	.60	.25
❑ 57	Johan Santana	1.50	.60
❑ 58	Joe Mauer	1.00	.40
❑ 59	Delmon Young	1.00	.40
❑ 60	Jose Reyes	1.00	.40
❑ 61	David Wright	2.00	.75
❑ 62	Carlos Beltran	.60	.25
❑ 63	Pedro Martinez	1.00	.40
❑ 64	Chien-Ming Wang	2.50	1.00
❑ 65	Alex Rodriguez	2.50	1.00
❑ 66	Derek Jeter	4.00	1.50
❑ 67	Robinson Cano	1.00	.40
❑ 68	Hideki Matsui	1.50	.60
❑ 69	Joe Blanton	.60	.25
❑ 70	Jack Cust	.60	.25
❑ 71	Cole Hamels	1.00	.40
❑ 72	Jimmy Rollins	1.00	.40
❑ 73	Ryan Howard	2.00	.75
❑ 74	Chase Utley	1.50	.60
❑ 75	Jason Bay	.60	.25
❑ 76	Freddy Sanchez	.60	.25
❑ 77	Jake Peavy	.60	.25
❑ 78	Greg Maddux	2.00	.75
❑ 79	Adrian Gonzalez	1.00	.40
❑ 80	Barry Zito	.60	.25
❑ 81	Omar Vizquel	.60	.25
❑ 82	Tim Lincecum	1.50	.60
❑ 83	Ichiro Suzuki	2.50	1.00
❑ 84	Felix Hernandez	1.00	.40
❑ 85	Kenji Johjima	.60	.25
❑ 86	Albert Pujols	3.00	1.25
❑ 87	Scott Rolen	1.00	.40
❑ 88	Chris Carpenter	.60	.25
❑ 89	Rick Ankiel	.60	.25
❑ 90	Scott Kazmir	1.00	.40
❑ 91	Carl Crawford	.60	.25
❑ 92	B.J. Upton	1.00	.40
❑ 93	Michael Young	.60	.25
❑ 94	Josh Hamilton	2.00	.75
❑ 95	Hank Blalock	.60	.25
❑ 96	Roy Halladay	.60	.25
❑ 97	Vernon Wells	.60	.25
❑ 98	Alex Rios	.60	.25
❑ 99	Ryan Zimmerman	1.00	.40
❑ 100	Dmitri Young	.60	.25
❑ 101	Bill Murphy AU (RC)	8.00	3.00
❑ 102	Emilio Bonifacio AU RC	8.00	3.00
❑ 103	Brandon Jones AU RC	8.00	3.00
❑ 104	Clint Sammons AU (RC)	8.00	3.00
❑ 105	Clay Buchholz AU (RC)	25.00	10.00

❑ 106 Kevin Hart AU (RC) 8.00 3.00
❑ 107 Donny Lucy AU (RC) 8.00 3.00
❑ 108 Lance Broadway AU (RC) 8.00 3.00
❑ 109 Joey Votto AU (RC) 25.00 10.00
❑ 110 Ryan Hanigan AU RC 8.00 3.00
❑ 111 Joe Koshansky AU (RC) 8.00 3.00
❑ 112 Josh Newman AU RC 8.00 3.00
❑ 113 Seth Smith AU (RC) 8.00 3.00
❑ 114 Chris Seddon AU (RC) 8.00 3.00
❑ 115 Harvey Garcia AU (RC) 8.00 3.00
❑ 116 Felipe Paulino AU RC 8.00 3.00
❑ 117 J.R. Towles AU RC 10.00 4.00
❑ 118 Josh Anderson AU (RC) 8.00 3.00
❑ 119 Troy Patton AU (RC) 8.00 3.00
❑ 120 Billy Buckner AU (RC) 8.00 3.00
❑ 121 Luke Hochevar AU RC 8.00 3.00
❑ 122 Chin-Lung Hu AU (RC) 15.00 6.00
❑ 123 Jonathan Meloan AU RC
❑ 124 Jose Morales AU (RC) 15.00 6.00
❑ 125 Carlos Muniz AU RC
❑ 126 Alberto Gonzalez AU RC 8.00 3.00
❑ 127 Bronson Sardinha AU (RC) 8.00 3.00
❑ 128 Ian Kennedy AU RC 25.00 10.00
❑ 129 Ross Ohlendorf AU RC 8.00 3.00
❑ 130 Daric Barton AU (RC) 15.00 6.00
❑ 131 Jerry Blevins AU RC 8.00 3.00
❑ 132 Dave Davidson AU RC 8.00 3.00
❑ 133 Nyjer Morgan AU (RC) 8.00 3.00
❑ 134 Steve Pearce AU RC 8.00 3.00
❑ 135 Colt Morton AU RC 8.00 3.00
❑ 136 Eugenio Velez AU RC 8.00 3.00
❑ 137 Jeff Clement AU (RC)
❑ 138 Rob Johnson AU (RC) 8.00 3.00
❑ 139 Wladimir Balentien AU (RC) 8.00 3.00
❑ 140 Justin Ruggiano AU RC 8.00 3.00
❑ 141 Bill White AU RC 8.00 3.00
❑ 142 Luis Mendoza AU (RC) 8.00 3.00
❑ 143 Jonathan Albaladejo AU RC 8.00 3.00
❑ 144 Justin Maxwell AU RC
❑ 145 Ross Detwiler AU RC 15.00 6.00
❑ 146 J.Bruce AU (RC) EXCH
❑ 147 C.Gonzalez AU (RC) EXCH
❑ 148 E.Longoria AU RC EXCH
❑ 149 Collin Balester AU (RC)
❑ 150 Kosuke Fukudome AU RC
❑ 151 C.Kershaw AU RC EXCH

2001 Sweet Spot

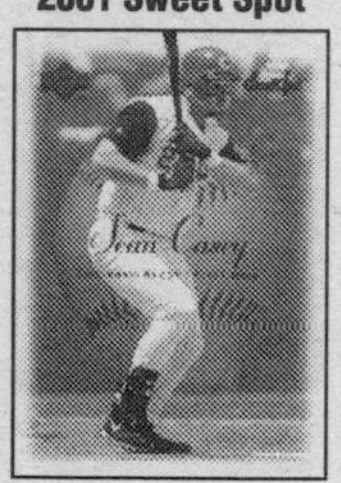

❑ COMP.BASIC w/o SP's (60) 20.00 8.00
❑ COMP.UPDATE w/o SP's (30) 10.00 4.00
❑ COMMON CARD (1-60) .40 .15
❑ COMMON CARD (61-90) 10.00 4.00
❑ COMMON CARD (91-120) .60 .25
❑ COMMON CARD (121-150) 5.00 2.00
❑ 1 Troy Glaus .40 .15
❑ 2 Darin Erstad .40 .15
❑ 3 Jason Giambi .40 .15
❑ 4 Tim Hudson .40 .15
❑ 5 Ben Grieve .40 .15
❑ 6 Carlos Delgado .40 .15
❑ 7 David Wells .40 .15
❑ 8 Greg Vaughn .40 .15
❑ 9 Roberto Alomar .60 .25
❑ 10 Jim Thome .60 .25
❑ 11 John Olerud .40 .15
❑ 12 Edgar Martinez .60 .25
❑ 13 Cal Ripken 3.00 1.25
❑ 14 Albert Belle .40 .15
❑ 15 Ivan Rodriguez .60 .25
❑ 16 Alex Rodriguez Rangers 3.00 1.25
❑ 17 Pedro Martinez .60 .25
❑ 18 Nomar Garciaparra 1.50 .60
❑ 19 Manny Ramirez .60 .25
❑ 20 Jermaine Dye .40 .15
❑ 21 Juan Gonzalez .40 .15
❑ 22 Dean Palmer .40 .15
❑ 23 Matt Lawton .40 .15
❑ 24 Eric Milton .40 .15
❑ 25 Frank Thomas 1.00 .40
❑ 26 Magglio Ordonez .40 .15
❑ 27 Derek Jeter 2.50 1.00
❑ 28 Bernie Williams .60 .25
❑ 29 Roger Clemens 2.00 .75
❑ 30 Jeff Bagwell .60 .25
❑ 31 Richard Hidalgo .40 .15
❑ 32 Chipper Jones 1.00 .40
❑ 33 Greg Maddux 1.50 .60
❑ 34 Richie Sexson .40 .15
❑ 35 Jeromy Burnitz .40 .15
❑ 36 Mark McGwire 2.50 1.00
❑ 37 Jim Edmonds .40 .15
❑ 38 Sammy Sosa 1.00 .40
❑ 39 Randy Johnson 1.00 .40
❑ 40 Steve Finley .40 .15
❑ 41 Gary Sheffield .40 .15
❑ 42 Shawn Green .40 .15
❑ 43 Vladimir Guerrero 1.00 .40
❑ 44 Jose Vidro .40 .15
❑ 45 Barry Bonds 2.50 1.00
❑ 46 Jeff Kent .40 .15
❑ 47 Preston Wilson .40 .15
❑ 48 Luis Castillo .40 .15
❑ 49 Mike Piazza 1.50 .60
❑ 50 Edgardo Alfonzo .40 .15
❑ 51 Tony Gwynn 1.25 .50
❑ 52 Ryan Klesko .40 .15
❑ 53 Scott Rolen .60 .25
❑ 54 Bob Abreu .40 .15
❑ 55 Jason Kendall .40 .15
❑ 56 Brian Giles .40 .15
❑ 57 Ken Griffey Jr. 1.50 .60
❑ 58 Barry Larkin .60 .25
❑ 59 Todd Helton .60 .25
❑ 60 Mike Hampton UER .40 .15
❑ 61 Corey Patterson SB 10.00 4.00
❑ 62 Ichiro Suzuki SB RC 200.00 125.00
❑ 63 Jason Grilli SB 10.00 4.00
❑ 64 Brian Cole SB 10.00 4.00
❑ 65 Juan Pierre SB 10.00 4.00
❑ 66 Matt Ginter SB 10.00 4.00
❑ 67 Jimmy Rollins SB 10.00 4.00
❑ 68 Jason Smith SB RC 10.00 4.00
❑ 69 Israel Alcantara SB 10.00 4.00
❑ 70 Adam Pettyjohn SB RC 10.00 4.00
❑ 71 Luke Prokopec SB 10.00 4.00
❑ 72 Barry Zito SB 12.00 5.00
❑ 73 Keith Ginter SB 10.00 4.00
❑ 74 Sun Woo Kim SB 10.00 4.00
❑ 75 Ross Gload SB 10.00 4.00
❑ 76 Matt Wise SB 10.00 4.00
❑ 77 Aubrey Huff SB 10.00 4.00
❑ 78 Ryan Franklin SB 10.00 4.00
❑ 79 Brandon Inge SB 10.00 4.00
❑ 80 Wes Helms SB 10.00 4.00
❑ 81 Junior Spivey SB RC 12.00 5.00
❑ 82 Ryan Vogelsong SB 10.00 4.00
❑ 83 John Parrish SB 10.00 4.00
❑ 84 Joe Crede SB 12.00 5.00
❑ 85 Damian Rolls SB 10.00 4.00
❑ 86 Esix Snead SB RC 10.00 4.00
❑ 87 Rocky Biddle SB 10.00 4.00
❑ 88 Brady Clark SB 10.00 4.00
❑ 89 Timo Perez SB 10.00 4.00
❑ 90 Jay Spurgeon SB 10.00 4.00
❑ 91 Garret Anderson .60 .25
❑ 92 Jermaine Dye .60 .25
❑ 93 Shannon Stewart .60 .25
❑ 94 Ben Grieve .60 .25
❑ 95 Juan Gonzalez .60 .25
❑ 96 Brett Boone .60 .25
❑ 97 Tony Batista .60 .25
❑ 98 Rafael Palmeiro 1.00 .40
❑ 99 Carl Everett .60 .25
❑ 100 Mike Sweeney .60 .25
❑ 101 Tony Clark .60 .25
❑ 102 Doug Mientkiewicz .60 .25
❑ 103 Jose Canseco 1.00 .40
❑ 104 Mike Mussina 1.00 .40
❑ 105 Lance Berkman .60 .25
❑ 106 Andruw Jones 1.00 .40
❑ 107 Geoff Jenkins .60 .25
❑ 108 Matt Morris .60 .25
❑ 109 Fred McGriff 1.00 .40
❑ 110 Luis Gonzalez .60 .25
❑ 111 Kevin Brown .60 .25
❑ 112 Tony Armas Jr. .60 .25
❑ 113 John Vander Wal .60 .25
❑ 114 Cliff Floyd .60 .25
❑ 115 Matt Lawton .60 .25
❑ 116 Phil Nevin .60 .25
❑ 117 Pat Burrell .60 .25
❑ 118 Aramis Ramirez .60 .25
❑ 119 Sean Casey .60 .25
❑ 120 Larry Walker .60 .25
❑ 121 Albert Pujols SB RC 200.00 100.00
❑ 122 Johnny Estrada SB RC 5.00 2.00
❑ 123 Wilson Betemit SB RC 8.00 3.00
❑ 124 Adrian Hernandez SB RC 5.00 2.00
❑ 125 Morgan Ensberg SB RC 8.00 3.00
❑ 126 Horacio Ramirez SB RC 5.00 2.00
❑ 127 Josh Towers SB RC 5.00 2.00
❑ 128 Juan Uribe SB RC 5.00 2.00
❑ 129 Wilken Ruan SB RC 5.00 2.00
❑ 130 Andres Torres SB RC 5.00 2.00
❑ 131 Brian Lawrence SB RC 5.00 2.00
❑ 132 Ryan Freel SB RC 5.00 2.00
❑ 133 Brandon Duckworth SB RC 5.00 2.00
❑ 134 Juan Diaz SB RC 5.00 2.00
❑ 135 Rafael Soriano SB RC 5.00 2.00
❑ 136 Ricardo Rodriguez SB RC 5.00 2.00
❑ 137 Bud Smith SB RC 5.00 2.00
❑ 138 Mark Teixeira SB RC 30.00 12.50
❑ 139 Mark Prior SB RC 15.00 6.00
❑ 140 Jackson Melian SB RC 5.00 2.00
❑ 141 Dewon Brazelton SB RC 5.00 2.00
❑ 142 Greg Miller SB RC 5.00 2.00
❑ 143 Billy Sylvester SB RC 5.00 2.00
❑ 144 Elpidio Guzman SB RC 5.00 2.00
❑ 145 Jack Wilson SB RC 5.00 2.00
❑ 146 Jose Mieses SB RC 5.00 2.00
❑ 147 Brandon Lyon SB RC 5.00 2.00
❑ 148 Tsuyoshi Shinjo SB RC 5.00 2.00
❑ 149 Juan Cruz SB RC 5.00 2.00
❑ 150 Jay Gibbons SB RC 5.00 2.00

2002 Sweet Spot

❑ COMP.SET w/o SP's (90) 20.00 8.00
❑ COMMON CARD (1-90) .40 .15
❑ COMMON CARD (91-130) 4.00 1.50
❑ COMMON TIER 1 AU (131-145) 15.00 6.00
❑ COMMON TIER 2 AU (131-145) 25.00 10.00
❑ COMMON CARD (146-175) 10.00 4.00
❑ MCGWIRE AU EXCH.RANDOM IN PACKS
❑ 1 Troy Glaus .40 .15
❑ 2 Darin Erstad .40 .15
❑ 3 Tim Hudson .40 .15
❑ 4 Eric Chavez .40 .15
❑ 5 Barry Zito .40 .15
❑ 6 Miguel Tejada .40 .15
❑ 7 Carlos Delgado .40 .15
❑ 8 Eric Hinske .40 .15
❑ 9 Ben Grieve .40 .15

Card		
❑ 10 Jim Thome	.60	.25
❑ 11 C.C. Sabathia	.40	.15
❑ 12 Omar Vizquel	.60	.25
❑ 13 Ichiro Suzuki	2.00	.75
❑ 14 Edgar Martinez	.60	.25
❑ 15 Bret Boone	.40	.15
❑ 16 Freddy Garcia	.40	.15
❑ 17 Tony Batista	.40	.15
❑ 18 Geronimo Gil	.40	.15
❑ 19 Alex Rodriguez	1.50	.60
❑ 20 Rafael Palmeiro	.60	.25
❑ 21 Ivan Rodriguez	.60	.25
❑ 22 Hank Blalock	.60	.25
❑ 23 Juan Gonzalez	.40	.15
❑ 24 Nomar Garciaparra	1.50	.60
❑ 25 Pedro Martinez	.60	.25
❑ 26 Manny Ramirez	.60	.25
❑ 27 Mike Sweeney	.40	.15
❑ 28 Carlos Beltran	.40	.15
❑ 29 Dmitri Young	.40	.15
❑ 30 Torii Hunter	.40	.15
❑ 31 Eric Milton	.40	.15
❑ 32 Corey Koskie	.40	.15
❑ 33 Frank Thomas	1.00	.40
❑ 34 Mark Buehrle	.40	.15
❑ 35 Magglio Ordonez	.40	.15
❑ 36 Roger Clemens	2.00	.75
❑ 37 Derek Jeter	2.50	1.00
❑ 38 Jason Giambi	.40	.15
❑ 39 Alfonso Soriano	.40	.15
❑ 40 Bernie Williams	.60	.25
❑ 41 Jeff Bagwell	.60	.25
❑ 42 Roy Oswalt	.40	.15
❑ 43 Lance Berkman	.40	.15
❑ 44 Greg Maddux	1.50	.60
❑ 45 Chipper Jones	1.00	.40
❑ 46 Gary Sheffield	.40	.15
❑ 47 Andruw Jones	.60	.25
❑ 48 Richie Sexson	.40	.15
❑ 49 Ben Sheets	.40	.15
❑ 50 Albert Pujols	2.00	.75
❑ 51 Matt Morris	.40	.15
❑ 52 J.D. Drew	.40	.15
❑ 53 Sammy Sosa	1.00	.40
❑ 54 Kerry Wood	.40	.15
❑ 55 Mark Prior	.60	.25
❑ 56 Moises Alou	.40	.15
❑ 57 Corey Patterson	.40	.15
❑ 58 Randy Johnson	1.00	.40
❑ 59 Luis Gonzalez	.40	.15
❑ 60 Curt Schilling	.40	.15
❑ 61 Shawn Green	.40	.15
❑ 62 Kevin Brown	.40	.15
❑ 63 Paul Lo Duca	.40	.15
❑ 64 Adrian Beltre	.40	.15
❑ 65 Vladimir Guerrero	1.00	.40
❑ 66 Jose Vidro	.40	.15
❑ 67 Javier Vazquez	.40	.15
❑ 68 Barry Bonds	2.50	1.00
❑ 69 Jeff Kent	.40	.15
❑ 70 Rich Aurilia	.40	.15
❑ 71 Mike Lowell	.40	.15
❑ 72 Josh Beckett	.40	.15
❑ 73 Brad Penny	.40	.15
❑ 74 Roberto Alomar	.60	.25
❑ 75 Mike Piazza	1.50	.60
❑ 76 Jeromy Burnitz	.40	.15
❑ 77 Mo Vaughn	.40	.15
❑ 78 Phil Nevin	.40	.15
❑ 79 Sean Burroughs	.40	.15
❑ 80 Jeremy Giambi	.40	.15
❑ 81 Bobby Abreu	.40	.15
❑ 82 Jimmy Rollins	.40	.15
❑ 83 Pat Burrell	.40	.15
❑ 84 Brian Giles	.40	.15
❑ 85 Aramis Ramirez	.40	.15
❑ 86 Ken Griffey Jr.	1.50	.60
❑ 87 Adam Dunn	.40	.15
❑ 88 Austin Kearns	.40	.15
❑ 89 Todd Helton	.60	.25
❑ 90 Larry Walker	.40	.15
❑ 91 Earl Snyder SB RC	4.00	1.50
❑ 92 Jorge Padilla SB RC	4.00	1.50
❑ 93 Felix Escalona SB RC	4.00	1.50
❑ 94 John Foster SB RC	4.00	1.50
❑ 95 Brandon Puffer SB RC	4.00	1.50
❑ 96 Steve Bechler SB RC	4.00	1.50
❑ 97 Hansel Izquierdo SB RC	4.00	1.50
❑ 98 Chris Baker SB RC	4.00	1.50
❑ 99 Jeremy Ward SB RC	4.00	1.50
❑ 100 Kevin Frederick SB RC	4.00	1.50
❑ 101 Josh Hancock SB RC	5.00	2.00
❑ 102 Allan Simpson SB RC	4.00	1.50
❑ 103 Mitch Wylie SB RC	4.00	1.50
❑ 104 Mark Corey SB RC	4.00	1.50
❑ 105 Victor Alvarez SB RC	4.00	1.50
❑ 106 Todd Donovan SB RC	4.00	1.50
❑ 107 Nelson Castro SB RC	4.00	1.50
❑ 108 Chris Booker SB RC	4.00	1.50
❑ 109 Corey Thurman SB RC	4.00	1.50
❑ 110 Kirk Saarloos SB RC	4.00	1.50
❑ 111 Michael Crudale SB RC	4.00	1.50
❑ 112 Jason Simontacchi SB RC	4.00	1.50
❑ 113 Ron Calloway SB RC	4.00	1.50
❑ 114 Brandon Backe SB RC	5.00	2.00
❑ 115 Tom Shearn SB RC	4.00	1.50
❑ 116 Oliver Perez SB RC	5.00	2.00
❑ 117 Kyle Kane SB RC	4.00	1.50
❑ 118 Francis Beltran SB RC	4.00	1.50
❑ 119 So Taguchi SB RC	5.00	2.00
❑ 120 Doug Devore SB RC	4.00	1.50
❑ 121 Juan Brito SB RC	4.00	1.50
❑ 122 Cliff Bartosh SB RC	4.00	1.50
❑ 123 Eric Junge SB RC	4.00	1.50
❑ 124 Joe Orloski SB RC	4.00	1.50
❑ 125 Scotty Layfield SB RC	4.00	1.50
❑ 126 Jorge Sosa SB RC	5.00	2.00
❑ 127 Satoru Komiyama SB RC	4.00	1.50
❑ 128 Edwin Almonte SB RC	4.00	1.50
❑ 129 Takahito Nomura SB RC	4.00	1.50
❑ 130 John Ennis SB RC	4.00	1.50
❑ 131 Kazuhisa Ishii T2 AU RC	80.00	40.00
❑ 132 Ben Howard T2 AU RC	25.00	10.00
❑ 133 Aaron Cook T1 AU RC	20.00	8.00
❑ 134 Andy Machado T1 AU RC	15.00	6.00
❑ 135 Luis Ugueto T1 AU RC	15.00	6.00
❑ 136 Tyler Yates T1 AU RC	15.00	6.00
❑ 137 Rodrigo Rosario T1 AU RC	15.00	6.00
❑ 138 Jaime Cerda T1 AU RC	15.00	6.00
❑ 139 Luis Martinez T1 AU RC	15.00	6.00
❑ 140 Rene Reyes T1 AU RC	15.00	6.00
❑ 141 Eric Good T1 AU RC	15.00	6.00
❑ 142 Matt Thornton T2 AU RC	25.00	10.00
❑ 143 Steve Kent T1 AU RC	15.00	6.00
❑ 144 Jose Valverde T1 AU RC	15.00	6.00
❑ 145 Adrian Burnside T1 AU RC	15.00	6.00
❑ 146 Barry Bonds GF	25.00	10.00
❑ 147 Ken Griffey Jr. GF	15.00	6.00
❑ 148 Alex Rodriguez GF	15.00	6.00
❑ 149 Jason Giambi GF	4.00	1.50
❑ 150 Chipper Jones GF	10.00	4.00
❑ 151 Nomar Garciaparra GF	15.00	6.00
❑ 152 Mike Piazza GF	15.00	6.00
❑ 153 Sammy Sosa GF	10.00	4.00
❑ 154 Derek Jeter GF	25.00	10.00
❑ 155 Jeff Bagwell GF	10.00	4.00
❑ 156 Albert Pujols GF	15.00	6.00
❑ 157 Ichiro Suzuki GF	15.00	6.00
❑ 158 Randy Johnson GF	10.00	4.00
❑ 159 Frank Thomas GF	10.00	4.00
❑ 160 Greg Maddux GF	15.00	6.00
❑ 161 Jim Thome GF	10.00	4.00
❑ 162 Scott Rolen GF	10.00	4.00
❑ 163 Shawn Green GF	10.00	4.00
❑ 164 Vladimir Guerrero GF	10.00	4.00
❑ 165 Troy Glaus GF	10.00	4.00
❑ 166 Carlos Delgado GF	10.00	4.00
❑ 167 Luis Gonzalez GF	10.00	4.00
❑ 168 Roger Clemens GF	20.00	8.00
❑ 169 Todd Helton GF	10.00	4.00
❑ 170 Eric Chavez GF	10.00	4.00
❑ 171 Rafael Palmeiro GF	10.00	4.00
❑ 172 Pedro Martinez GF	10.00	4.00
❑ 173 Lance Berkman GF	10.00	4.00
❑ 174 Josh Beckett GF	10.00	4.00
❑ 175 Sean Burroughs GF	10.00	4.00
❑ MM Mark McGwire AU EXCH/100		

2003 Sweet Spot

Card		
❑ COMP.SET w/o SP's (100)	20.00	8.00
❑ COMP.SET w/SP's (130)	120.00	60.00
❑ COMMON CARD (1-130)	.50	.20
❑ COMMON SP (1-130)	3.00	1.25
❑ COMMON CARD (131-190)	3.00	1.25
❑ 131-190 PRINT RUN 2003 SERIAL #'d SETS		
❑ COMMON P1 (191-232)	4.00	1.50
❑ P1 191-232 PRINT RUN 500 SERIAL #'d SETS		
❑ COMMON P2-P3 (191-232)	3.00	1.25
❑ P2 191-232 PRINT RUN 1200 SERIAL #'d SETS		
❑ P3 191-232 PRINT RUN 1400 SERIAL #'d SETS		
❑ 1 Darin Erstad	.50	.20
❑ 2 Garret Anderson	.50	.20
❑ 3 Tim Salmon	.75	.30
❑ 4 Troy Glaus	.50	.20
❑ 5 Luis Gonzalez	.50	.20
❑ 6 Randy Johnson	1.25	.50
❑ 7 Curt Schilling	.50	.20
❑ 8 Lyle Overbay	.50	.20
❑ 9 Andruw Jones SP	4.00	1.50
❑ 10 Gary Sheffield SP	3.00	1.25
❑ 11 Rafael Furcal SP	3.00	1.25
❑ 12 Greg Maddux SP	6.00	2.50
❑ 13 Chipper Jones SP	4.00	1.50
❑ 14 Tony Batista	.50	.20
❑ 15 Rodrigo Lopez	.50	.20
❑ 16 Jay Gibbons	.50	.20
❑ 17 Jason Johnson	.50	.20
❑ 18 Byung-Hyun Kim SP	3.00	1.25
❑ 19 Johnny Damon SP	4.00	1.50
❑ 20 Derek Lowe SP	3.00	1.25
❑ 21 Nomar Garciaparra SP	6.00	2.50
❑ 22 Pedro Martinez SP	4.00	1.50
❑ 23 Manny Ramirez SP	4.00	1.50
❑ 24 Mark Prior	.75	.30
❑ 25 Kerry Wood	.50	.20
❑ 26 Corey Patterson	.50	.20
❑ 27 Sammy Sosa	1.25	.50
❑ 28 Moises Alou	.50	.20
❑ 29 Magglio Ordonez	.50	.20
❑ 30 Frank Thomas	1.25	.50
❑ 31 Paul Konerko	.50	.20
❑ 32 Roberto Alomar	.75	.30
❑ 33 Adam Dunn	.50	.20
❑ 34 Austin Kearns	.50	.20
❑ 35 Ryan Wagner RC	.50	.20
❑ 36 Ken Griffey Jr.	2.00	.75
❑ 37 Sean Casey	.50	.20
❑ 38 Omar Vizquel	.75	.30
❑ 39 C.C. Sabathia	.50	.20
❑ 40 Jason Davis	.50	.20
❑ 41 Travis Hafner	.50	.20
❑ 42 Brandon Phillips	.50	.20
❑ 43 Larry Walker	.50	.20
❑ 44 Preston Wilson	.50	.20
❑ 45 Jay Payton	.50	.20
❑ 46 Todd Helton	.75	.30
❑ 47 Carlos Pena	.50	.20
❑ 48 Eric Munson	.50	.20
❑ 49 Ivan Rodriguez	.75	.30
❑ 50 Josh Beckett	.50	.20
❑ 51 Alex Gonzalez	.50	.20
❑ 52 Roy Oswalt	.50	.20
❑ 53 Craig Biggio	.75	.30
❑ 54 Jeff Bagwell	.75	.30
❑ 55 Lance Berkman	.50	.20
❑ 56 Mike Sweeney	.50	.20
❑ 57 Carlos Beltran	.50	.20
❑ 58 Brent Mayne	.50	.20
❑ 59 Mike MacDougal	.50	.20
❑ 60 Hideo Nomo	1.25	.50

❑ 61	Dave Roberts	.50	.20
❑ 62	Adrian Beltre	.50	.20
❑ 63	Shawn Green	.50	.20
❑ 64	Kazuhisa Ishii	.50	.20
❑ 65	Rickey Henderson	1.25	.50
❑ 66	Richie Sexson	.50	.20
❑ 67	Torii Hunter	.50	.20
❑ 68	Jacque Jones	.50	.20
❑ 69	Joe Mays	.50	.20
❑ 70	Corey Koskie	.50	.20
❑ 71	A.J. Pierzynski	.50	.20
❑ 72	Jose Vidro	.50	.20
❑ 73	Vladimir Guerrero	1.25	.50
❑ 74	Tom Glavine	.75	.30
❑ 75	Mike Piazza	2.00	.75
❑ 76	Jose Reyes	.50	.20
❑ 77	Jae Weong Seo	.50	.20
❑ 78	Jorge Posada SP	4.00	1.50
❑ 79	Mike Mussina SP	4.00	1.50
❑ 80	Robin Ventura SP	3.00	1.25
❑ 81	Mariano Rivera SP	4.00	1.50
❑ 82	Roger Clemens SP	8.00	3.00
❑ 83	Jason Giambi SP	3.00	1.25
❑ 84	Bernie Williams SP	4.00	1.50
❑ 85	Alfonso Soriano SP	3.00	1.25
❑ 86	Derek Jeter	3.00	1.25
❑ 87	Miguel Tejada	.50	.20
❑ 88	Eric Chavez	.50	.20
❑ 89	Tim Hudson	.50	.20
❑ 90	Barry Zito	.50	.20
❑ 91	Mark Mulder	.50	.20
❑ 92	Erubiel Durazo	.50	.20
❑ 93	Pat Burrell	.50	.20
❑ 94	Jim Thome	.75	.30
❑ 95	Bobby Abreu	.50	.20
❑ 96	Brian Giles	.50	.20
❑ 97	Reggie Sanders	.50	.20
❑ 98	Jose Hernandez	.50	.20
❑ 99	Ryan Klesko	.50	.20
❑ 100	Sean Burroughs	.50	.20
❑ 101	Edgardo Alfonzo SP	3.00	1.25
❑ 102	Rich Aurilia SP	3.00	1.25
❑ 103	Jose Cruz Jr. SP	3.00	1.25
❑ 104	Barry Bonds SP	10.00	4.00
❑ 105	Andres Galarraga SP	3.00	1.25
❑ 106	Mike Cameron	.50	.20
❑ 107	Kazuhiro Sasaki	.50	.20
❑ 108	Bret Boone	.50	.20
❑ 109	Ichiro Suzuki	2.50	1.00
❑ 110	John Olerud	.50	.20
❑ 111	J.D. Drew SP	3.00	1.25
❑ 112	Jim Edmonds SP	3.00	1.25
❑ 113	Scott Rolen SP	4.00	1.50
❑ 114	Matt Morris SP	3.00	1.25
❑ 115	Tino Martinez SP	4.00	1.50
❑ 116	Albert Pujols SP	8.00	3.00
❑ 117	Jared Sandberg	.50	.20
❑ 118	Carl Crawford	.50	.20
❑ 119	Rafael Palmeiro	.75	.30
❑ 120	Hank Blalock	.50	.20
❑ 121	Alex Rodriguez SP	6.00	2.50
❑ 122	Kevin Mench	.50	.20
❑ 123	Juan Gonzalez	.50	.20
❑ 124	Mark Teixeira	.75	.30
❑ 125	Shannon Stewart	.50	.20
❑ 126	Vernon Wells	.50	.20
❑ 127	Josh Phelps	.50	.20
❑ 128	Eric Hinske	.50	.20
❑ 129	Orlando Hudson	.50	.20
❑ 130	Carlos Delgado	.50	.20
❑ 131	Jason Shiell SB RC	3.00	1.25
❑ 132	Kevin Tolar SB RC	3.00	1.25
❑ 133	Nathan Bland SB RC	3.00	1.25
❑ 134	Brent Hoard SB RC	3.00	1.25
❑ 135	Jon Pridie SB RC	3.00	1.25
❑ 136	Mike Ryan SB RC	3.00	1.25
❑ 137	Francisco Rosario SB RC	3.00	1.25
❑ 138	Runelvys Hernandez SB	3.00	1.25
❑ 139	Guillermo Quiroz SB RC	3.00	1.25
❑ 140	Chin-Hui Tsao SB	3.00	1.25
❑ 141	Rett Johnson SB RC	3.00	1.25
❑ 142	Colin Porter SB RC	3.00	1.25
❑ 143	Jose Castillo SB	3.00	1.25
❑ 144	Chris Waters SB RC	3.00	1.25
❑ 145	Jeremy Guthrie SB	3.00	1.25
❑ 146	Pedro Liriano SB	3.00	1.25

❑ 147	Joe Borowski SB	3.00	1.25
❑ 148	Felix Sanchez SB RC	3.00	1.25
❑ 149	Todd Wellemeyer SB RC	3.00	1.25
❑ 150	Gerald Laird SB	3.00	1.25
❑ 151	Brandon Webb SB RC	8.00	3.00
❑ 152	Tommy Whiteman SB	3.00	1.25
❑ 153	Carlos Rivera SB	3.00	1.25
❑ 154	Rick Roberts SB RC	3.00	1.25
❑ 155	Terrmel Sledge SB RC	3.00	1.25
❑ 156	Jeff Duncan SB RC	3.00	1.25
❑ 157	Craig Brazell SB RC	3.00	1.25
❑ 158	Bernie Castro SB RC	3.00	1.25
❑ 159	Cory Stewart SB RC	3.00	1.25
❑ 160	Brandon Villafuerte SB	3.00	1.25
❑ 161	Tommy Phelps SB	3.00	1.25
❑ 162	Josh Hall SB RC	3.00	1.25
❑ 163	Ryan Cameron SB RC	3.00	1.25
❑ 164	Garret Atkins SB	3.00	1.25
❑ 165	Brian Stokes SB RC	3.00	1.25
❑ 166	Rafael Betancourt SB RC	4.00	1.50
❑ 167	Jaime Cerda SB	3.00	1.25
❑ 168	D.J. Carrasco SB RC	3.00	1.25
❑ 169	Ian Ferguson SB RC	3.00	1.25
❑ 170	Jorge Cordova SB RC	3.00	1.25
❑ 171	Eric Munson SB	3.00	1.25
❑ 172	Nook Logan SB RC	4.00	1.50
❑ 173	Jeremy Bonderman SB RC	12.00	5.00
❑ 174	Kyle Snyder SB	3.00	1.25
❑ 175	Rich Harden SB	4.00	1.50
❑ 176	Kevin Ohme SB RC	3.00	1.25
❑ 177	Roger Deago SB RC	3.00	1.25
❑ 178	Marlon Byrd SB	3.00	1.25
❑ 179	Dontrelle Willis SB	4.00	1.50
❑ 180	Bobby Hill SB	3.00	1.25
❑ 181	Jesse Foppert SB	3.00	1.25
❑ 182	Andrew Good SB	3.00	1.25
❑ 183	Chase Utley SB	4.00	1.50
❑ 184	Bo Hart SB RC	3.00	1.25
❑ 185	Dan Haren SB RC	4.00	1.50
❑ 186	Tim Olson SB RC	3.00	1.25
❑ 187	Joe Thurston SB	3.00	1.25
❑ 188	Jason Anderson SB	3.00	1.25
❑ 189	Jason Gilfillan SB RC	3.00	1.25
❑ 190	Rickie Weeks SB RC	8.00	3.00
❑ 191	Hideki Matsui SB P1 RC	25.00	10.00
❑ 192	Jose Contreras SB P3 RC	4.00	1.50
❑ 193	Willie Eyre SB P3 RC	3.00	1.25
❑ 194	Matt Bruback SB P3 RC	3.00	1.25
❑ 195	Heath Bell SB P3 RC	3.00	1.25
❑ 196	Lew Ford SB P3 RC	4.00	1.50
❑ 197	Jeremy Griffiths SB P3 RC	3.00	1.25
❑ 198	Oscar Villarreal SB P1 RC	4.00	1.50
❑ 199	Francisco Cruceta SB P3 RC	3.00	1.25
❑ 200	Fern Cabrera SB P3 RC	3.00	1.25
❑ 201	Jhonny Peralta SB P3	4.00	1.50
❑ 202	Shane Bazzell SB P3 RC	3.00	1.25
❑ 203	Bobby Madritsch SB P1 RC	4.00	1.50
❑ 204	Phil Seibel SB P3 RC	3.00	1.25
❑ 205	Josh Willingham SB P3 RC	5.00	2.00
❑ 206	Rob Hammock SB P1 RC	4.00	1.50
❑ 207	Alejandro Machado SB P3 RC	3.00	1.25
❑ 208	David Sanders SB P3 RC	3.00	1.25
❑ 209	Mike Neu SB P1 RC	4.00	1.50
❑ 210	Andrew Brown SB P3 RC	4.00	1.50
❑ 211	Nate Robertson SB P3 RC	5.00	2.00
❑ 212	Miguel Ojeda SB P3 RC	3.00	1.25
❑ 213	Beau Kemp SB P3 RC	3.00	1.25
❑ 214	Aaron Looper SB P3 RC	3.00	1.25
❑ 215	Alfredo Gonzalez SB P3 RC	3.00	1.25
❑ 216	Rich Fischer SB P1 RC	4.00	1.50
❑ 218	Jeremy Wedel SB P3 RC	3.00	1.25
❑ 219	Prentice Redman SB P3 RC	3.00	1.25
❑ 220	Michel Hernandez SB P3 RC	3.00	1.25
❑ 221	Rocco Baldelli SB P1	4.00	1.50
❑ 222	Luis Ayala SB P3 RC	3.00	1.25
❑ 223	Arnaldo Munoz SB P3 RC	3.00	1.25
❑ 224	Wilfredo Ledezma SB P3 RC	3.00	1.25
❑ 225	Chris Capuano SB P3 RC	4.00	1.50
❑ 226	Aquilino Lopez SB P3 RC	3.00	1.25
❑ 227	Joe Valentine SB P1 RC	4.00	1.50
❑ 228	Matt Kata SB P2 RC	3.00	1.25
❑ 229	Diegomar Markwell SB P2 RC	3.00	1.25
❑ 230	Clint Barmes SB P2 RC	3.00	1.25
❑ 231	Mike Nicolas SB P1 RC	4.00	1.50
❑ 232	Jon Leicester SB P2 RC	3.00	1.25

2004 Sweet Spot

❑ COMP.SET w/o SP's (90)	20.00	8.00
❑ COMMON CARD (1-90)	.50	.20
❑ COMMON (91-170/261-262)	4.00	1.50
❑ 91-170/261-262 STATED ODDS 1:12		
❑ 91-170/261-262 PRINT RUN 799 #'d SETS		
❑ COMMON CARD (171-230)	4.00	1.50
❑ 171-230 PRINT RUN 399 SERIAL #'d SETS		
❑ COMMON CARD (231-250)	4.00	1.50
❑ 231-250 PRINT RUN 299 SERIAL #'d SETS		
❑ COMMON CARD (251-260)	6.00	2.50
❑ 251-260 PRINT RUN 199 SERIAL #'d SETS		
❑ 171-260/Ltd 10/W99 OVERALL ODDS 1:12		
❑ OVERALL PLATES ODDS 1:360 HOBBY		
❑ PLATES PRINT RUN 1 SET PER COLOR		
❑ BLACK-CYAN-MAGENTA-YELLOW ISSUED		
❑ NO PLATES PRICING DUE TO SACRCITY		

❑ 1	Albert Pujols	2.50	1.00
❑ 2	Alex Rodriguez	2.00	.75
❑ 3	Alfonso Soriano	.50	.20
❑ 4	Andruw Jones	.75	.30
❑ 5	Andy Pettitte	.75	.30
❑ 6	Aubrey Huff	.50	.20
❑ 7	Austin Kearns	.50	.20
❑ 8	Barry Zito	.50	.20
❑ 9	Bobby Abreu	.50	.20
❑ 10	Brandon Webb	.50	.20
❑ 11	Bret Boone	.50	.20
❑ 12	Brian Giles	.50	.20
❑ 13	C.C. Sabathia	.50	.20
❑ 14	Carlos Beltran	.50	.20
❑ 15	Carlos Delgado	.50	.20
❑ 16	Chipper Jones	1.25	.50
❑ 17	Cliff Floyd	.50	.20
❑ 18	Curt Schilling	.75	.30
❑ 19	Delmon Young	.75	.30
❑ 20	Derek Jeter	2.50	1.00
❑ 21	Dontrelle Willis	.75	.30
❑ 22	Edgar Martinez	.75	.30
❑ 23	Edgar Renteria	.50	.20
❑ 24	Eric Chavez	.50	.20
❑ 25	Eric Gagne	.50	.20
❑ 26	Frank Thomas	1.25	.50
❑ 27	Garret Anderson	.50	.20
❑ 28	Gary Sheffield	.50	.20
❑ 29	Geoff Jenkins	.50	.20
❑ 30	Greg Maddux	2.00	.75
❑ 31	Hank Blalock	.50	.20
❑ 32	Hideo Nomo	1.25	.50
❑ 33	Ichiro Suzuki	2.50	1.00
❑ 34	Ivan Rodriguez	.75	.30
❑ 35	Jacque Jones	.50	.20
❑ 36	Jason Giambi	.50	.20
❑ 37	Jason Schmidt	.50	.20
❑ 38	Javier Vazquez	.50	.20
❑ 39	Javy Lopez	.50	.20
❑ 40	Jeff Bagwell	.75	.30
❑ 41	Jim Edmonds	.50	.20
❑ 42	Jim Thome	.75	.30
❑ 43	Joe Mauer	1.25	.50
❑ 44	John Smoltz	.50	.20
❑ 45	Jose Cruz Jr.	.50	.20
❑ 46	Jose Reyes	.50	.20
❑ 47	Jose Vidro	.50	.20
❑ 48	Josh Beckett	.50	.20
❑ 49	Ken Griffey Jr.	2.00	.75
❑ 50	Kerry Wood	.50	.20

	Card		
❑ 51	Kevin Brown	.50	.20
❑ 52	Larry Walker	.50	.20
❑ 53	Magglio Ordonez	.50	.20
❑ 54	Manny Ramirez	.75	.30
❑ 55	Mark Mulder	.50	.20
❑ 56	Mark Prior	.75	.30
❑ 57	Mark Teixeira	.75	.30
❑ 58	Miguel Cabrera	.75	.30
❑ 59	Miguel Tejada	.50	.20
❑ 60	Mike Lowell	.50	.20
❑ 61	Mike Mussina	.75	.30
❑ 62	Mike Piazza	2.00	.75
❑ 63	Nomar Garciaparra	2.00	.75
❑ 64	Orlando Cabrera	.50	.20
❑ 65	Pat Burrell	.50	.20
❑ 66	Pedro Martinez	.75	.30
❑ 67	Phil Nevin	.50	.20
❑ 68	Preston Wilson	.50	.20
❑ 69	Rafael Furcal	.50	.20
❑ 70	Rafael Palmeiro	.75	.30
❑ 71	Randy Johnson	1.25	.50
❑ 72	Craig Wilson	.50	.20
❑ 73	Rich Harden	.50	.20
❑ 74	Richie Sexson	.50	.20
❑ 75	Rickie Weeks	.50	.20
❑ 76	Rocco Baldelli	.50	.20
❑ 77	Roger Clemens	2.50	1.00
❑ 78	Roy Halladay	.50	.20
❑ 79	Roy Oswalt	.50	.20
❑ 80	Ryan Klesko	.50	.20
❑ 81	Sammy Sosa	1.25	.50
❑ 82	Scott Podsednik	.50	.20
❑ 83	Scott Rolen	.75	.30
❑ 84	Shawn Green	.50	.20
❑ 85	Tim Hudson	.50	.20
❑ 86	Todd Helton	.75	.30
❑ 87	Torii Hunter	.50	.20
❑ 88	Troy Glaus	.50	.20
❑ 89	Vernon Wells	.50	.20
❑ 90	Vladimir Guerrero	1.25	.50
❑ 91	Aarom Baldiris SB RC	5.00	2.00
❑ 92	Akinori Otsuka SB RC	4.00	1.50
❑ 93	Andres Blanco SB RC	4.00	1.50
❑ 94	Angel Chavez SB RC	4.00	1.50
❑ 95	Brian Dallimore SB RC	4.00	1.50
❑ 96	Carlos Hines SB RC	4.00	1.50
❑ 97	Carlos Vasquez SB RC	5.00	2.00
❑ 98	Casey Daigle SB RC	4.00	1.50
❑ 99	Chad Bentz SB RC	4.00	1.50
❑ 100	Chris Aguila SB RC	4.00	1.50
❑ 101	Chris Oxspring SB RC	4.00	1.50
❑ 102	Chris Saenz SB RC	4.00	1.50
❑ 103	Chris Shelton SB RC	5.00	2.00
❑ 104	Colby Miller SB RC	4.00	1.50
❑ 105	Dave Crouthers SB RC	4.00	1.50
❑ 106	David Aardsma SB RC	5.00	2.00
❑ 107	Dennis Sarfate SB RC	4.00	1.50
❑ 108	Donnie Kelly SB RC	4.00	1.50
❑ 109	Eddy Rodriguez SB RC	5.00	2.00
❑ 110	Eduardo Villacis SB RC	4.00	1.50
❑ 111	Edwin Moreno SB RC	5.00	2.00
❑ 112	Enemencio Pacheco SB RC	4.00	1.50
❑ 113	Fernando Nieve SB RC	5.00	2.00
❑ 114	Franklyn Gracesqui SB RC	4.00	1.50
❑ 115	Freddy Guzman SB RC	4.00	1.50
❑ 116	Greg Dobbs SB RC	4.00	1.50
❑ 117	Hector Gimenez SB RC	4.00	1.50
❑ 118	Ian Snell SB RC	5.00	2.00
❑ 119	Ivan Ochoa SB RC	4.00	1.50
❑ 120	Jake Woods SB RC	4.00	1.50
❑ 121	Jamie Brown SB RC	4.00	1.50
❑ 122	Jason Bartlett SB RC	5.00	2.00
❑ 123	Jason Frasor SB RC	4.00	1.50
❑ 124	Jeff Bennett SB RC	4.00	1.50
❑ 125	Jerome Gamble SB RC	4.00	1.50
❑ 126	Jerry Gil SB RC	4.00	1.50
❑ 127	Brandon Medders SB RC	4.00	1.50
❑ 128	Ryan Meaux SB RC	4.00	1.50
❑ 129	John Gall SB RC	5.00	2.00
❑ 130	Jorge Sequea SB RC	4.00	1.50
❑ 131	Jorge Vasquez SB RC	4.00	1.50
❑ 132	Jose Capellan SB RC	5.00	2.00
❑ 133	Josh Labandeira SB RC	4.00	1.50
❑ 134	Justin Germano SB RC	4.00	1.50
❑ 135	Justin Hampson SB RC	4.00	1.50
❑ 136	Justin Huisman SB RC	4.00	1.50
❑ 137	Justin Knoedler SB RC	4.00	1.50
❑ 138	Justin Leone SB RC	5.00	2.00
❑ 139	Kazuhito Tadano SB RC	5.00	2.00
❑ 140	Kazuo Matsui SB RC	5.00	2.00
❑ 141	Kevin Cave SB RC	4.00	1.50
❑ 142	Lincoln Holdzkom SB RC	4.00	1.50
❑ 143	Lino Urdaneta SB RC	4.00	1.50
❑ 144	Luis A. Gonzalez SB RC	4.00	1.50
❑ 145	Mariano Gomez SB RC	4.00	1.50
❑ 146	Merkin Valdez SB RC	5.00	2.00
❑ 147	Michael Vento SB RC	5.00	2.00
❑ 148	Michael Wuertz SB RC	5.00	2.00
❑ 149	Mike Gosling SB RC	4.00	1.50
❑ 150	Mike Johnston SB RC	4.00	1.50
❑ 151	Mike House SB RC	4.00	1.50
❑ 152	Nick Regilio SB RC	4.00	1.50
❑ 153	Onil Joseph SB RC	4.00	1.50
❑ 154	Orlando Rodriguez SB RC	4.00	1.50
❑ 155	Ramon Ramirez SB RC	4.00	1.50
❑ 156	Renyel Pinto SB RC	5.00	2.00
❑ 157	Roberto Novoa SB RC	5.00	2.00
❑ 158	Roman Colon SB RC	4.00	1.50
❑ 159	Ronald Belisario SB RC	4.00	1.50
❑ 160	Ronny Cedeno SB RC	5.00	2.00
❑ 161	Rusty Tucker SB RC	5.00	2.00
❑ 162	Ryan Wing SB RC	4.00	1.50
❑ 163	Scott Dohmann SB RC	4.00	1.50
❑ 164	Scott Proctor SB RC	5.00	2.00
❑ 165	Sean Henn SB RC	4.00	1.50
❑ 166	Shawn Camp SB RC	4.00	1.50
❑ 167	Shawn Hill SB RC	4.00	1.50
❑ 168	Shingo Takatsu SB RC	5.00	2.00
❑ 169	Tim Hamulack SB RC	4.00	1.50
❑ 170	William Bergolla SB RC	4.00	1.50
❑ 171	Adam Dunn SF	4.00	1.50
❑ 172	Albert Pujols SF	10.00	4.00
❑ 173	Alex Rodriguez SF	8.00	3.00
❑ 174	Alfonso Soriano SF	4.00	1.50
❑ 175	Andruw Jones SF	5.00	2.00
❑ 176	Bret Boone SF	4.00	1.50
❑ 177	Brian Giles SF	4.00	1.50
❑ 178	Carlos Delgado SF	4.00	1.50
❑ 179	Derrek Lee SF	5.00	2.00
❑ 180	Eric Chavez SF	4.00	1.50
❑ 181	Frank Thomas SF	5.00	2.00
❑ 182	Garret Anderson SF	4.00	1.50
❑ 183	Gary Sheffield SF	4.00	1.50
❑ 184	Hank Blalock SF	4.00	1.50
❑ 185	Jason Giambi SF	4.00	1.50
❑ 186	Javy Lopez SF	4.00	1.50
❑ 187	Jeff Bagwell SF	5.00	2.00
❑ 188	Jim Edmonds SF	4.00	1.50
❑ 189	Jim Thome SF	5.00	2.00
❑ 190	Ken Griffey Jr. SF	8.00	3.00
❑ 191	Lance Berkman SF	4.00	1.50
❑ 192	Magglio Ordonez SF	4.00	1.50
❑ 193	Manny Ramirez SF	5.00	2.00
❑ 194	Mike Lowell SF	4.00	1.50
❑ 195	Mike Piazza SF	8.00	3.00
❑ 196	Preston Wilson SF	4.00	1.50
❑ 197	Rafael Palmeiro SF	5.00	2.00
❑ 198	Richie Sexson SF	4.00	1.50
❑ 199	Sammy Sosa SF	5.00	2.00
❑ 200	Scott Rolen SF	5.00	2.00
❑ 201	Shawn Green SF	4.00	1.50
❑ 202	Todd Helton SF	5.00	2.00
❑ 203	Troy Glaus SF	4.00	1.50
❑ 204	Vernon Wells SF	4.00	1.50
❑ 205	Vladimir Guerrero SF	5.00	2.00
❑ 206	G.Anderson/V.Guerrero SL	5.00	2.00
❑ 207	L.Gonzalez/R.Sexson SL	4.00	1.50
❑ 208	A.Jones/C.Jones SL	5.00	2.00
❑ 209	J.Lopez/M.Tejada SL	4.00	1.50
❑ 210	M.Ramirez/D.Ortiz SL	5.00	2.00
❑ 211	D.Lee/S.Sosa SL	5.00	2.00
❑ 212	F.Thomas/M.Ordonez SL	5.00	2.00
❑ 213	A.Kearns/K.Griffey Jr. SL	8.00	3.00
❑ 214	P.Wilson/T.Helton SL	5.00	2.00
❑ 215	D.Young/I.Rodriguez SL	5.00	2.00
❑ 216	M.Cabrera/M.Lowell SL	5.00	2.00
❑ 217	J.Bagwell/L.Berkman SL	5.00	2.00
❑ 218	L.Overbay/G.Jenkins SL	4.00	1.50
❑ 219	A.Beltre/S.Green SL	4.00	1.50
❑ 220	J.Jones/T.Hunter SL	4.00	1.50
❑ 221	J.Vidro/N.Johnson SL	4.00	1.50
❑ 222	K.Matsui/M.Piazza SL	8.00	3.00
❑ 223	A.Rodriguez/J.Giambi SL	8.00	3.00
❑ 224	E.Chavez/J.Dye SL	4.00	1.50
❑ 225	J.Thome/P.Burrell SL	5.00	2.00
❑ 226	B.Giles/P.Nevin SL	4.00	1.50
❑ 227	B.Boone/I.Suzuki SL	10.00	4.00
❑ 228	A.Pujols/S.Rolen SL	10.00	4.00
❑ 229	H.Blalock/M.Teixeira SL	5.00	2.00
❑ 230	C.Delgado/V.Wells SL	4.00	1.50
❑ 231	Albert Pujols PD	10.00	4.00
❑ 232	Alex Rodriguez PD	8.00	3.00
❑ 233	Chipper Jones PD	5.00	2.00
❑ 234	Craig Biggio PD	5.00	2.00
❑ 235	Curt Schilling PD	5.00	2.00
❑ 236	Derek Jeter PD	10.00	4.00
❑ 237	Ivan Rodriguez PD	5.00	2.00
❑ 238	Jeff Bagwell PD	5.00	2.00
❑ 239	Jim Edmonds PD	4.00	1.50
❑ 240	Jim Thome PD	5.00	2.00
❑ 241	Josh Beckett PD	4.00	1.50
❑ 242	Kerry Wood PD	4.00	1.50
❑ 243	Kevin Brown PD	4.00	1.50
❑ 244	Mark Prior PD	5.00	2.00
❑ 245	Miguel Tejada PD	4.00	1.50
❑ 246	Mike Mussina PD	5.00	2.00
❑ 247	Nomar Garciaparra PD	8.00	3.00
❑ 248	Pedro Martinez PD	5.00	2.00
❑ 249	Randy Johnson PD	5.00	2.00
❑ 250	Roger Clemens PD	10.00	4.00
❑ 251	A.Rodriguez/D.Jeter DD	15.00	6.00
❑ 252	A.Soriano/H.Blalock DD	6.00	2.50
❑ 253	B.Abreu/P.Burrell DD	6.00	2.50
❑ 254	E.Renteria/S.Rolen DD	8.00	3.00
❑ 255	G.Anderson/V.Guerrero DD	8.00	3.00
❑ 256	J.Bagwell/J.Kent DD	8.00	3.00
❑ 257	J.Reyes/K.Matsui DD	8.00	3.00
❑ 258	K.Greene/S.Burroughs DD	8.00	3.00
❑ 259	M.Giles/R.Furcal DD	6.00	2.50
❑ 260	M.Ramirez/J.Damon DD	8.00	3.00
❑ 261	Tim Bausher SB RC	4.00	1.50
❑ 262	Tim Bittner SB RC	4.00	1.50

2005 Sweet Spot

	Card		
❑	COMP.BASIC SET (90)	20.00	8.00
❑	COMP.UPDATE SET (84)	25.00	10.00
❑	COMMON CARD (1-90)	.50	.20
❑	COMMON CARD (91-174)	1.00	.40
❑	91-174 ONE PER '05 UD UPDATE PACK		
❑ 1	Magglio Ordonez	.50	.20
❑ 2	Craig Biggio	.75	.30
❑ 3	Hank Blalock	.50	.20
❑ 4	Nomar Garciaparra	1.25	.50
❑ 5	Ken Griffey Jr.	2.00	.75
❑ 6	Khalil Greene	.75	.30
❑ 7	Andruw Jones	.75	.30
❑ 8	Ichiro Suzuki	2.50	1.00
❑ 9	Philip Humber RC	1.25	.50
❑ 10	Vladimir Guerrero	1.25	.50
❑ 11	Carlos Delgado	.50	.20
❑ 12	Jeff Niemann RC	1.25	.50
❑ 13	Chipper Jones	1.25	.50
❑ 14	Jose Vidro	.50	.20
❑ 15	Miguel Cabrera	.75	.30
❑ 16	Albert Pujols	2.50	1.00
❑ 17	Tadahito Iguchi RC	2.00	.75
❑ 18	Norihiro Nakamura RC	1.50	.60
❑ 19	Jeff Bagwell	.75	.30
❑ 20	Troy Glaus	.50	.20
❑ 21	Scott Rolen	.75	.30

❑	22	Derek Lowe	.50	.20
❑	23	Mark Prior	.75	.30
❑	24	Bobby Abreu	.50	.20
❑	25	David Wright	2.00	.75
❑	26	Barry Zito	.50	.20
❑	27	Livan Hernandez	.50	.20
❑	28	Mark Teixeira	.75	.30
❑	29	Manny Ramirez	.75	.30
❑	30	Paul Konerko	.50	.20
❑	31	Victor Martinez	.50	.20
❑	32	Greg Maddux	2.00	.75
❑	33	Jim Thome	.75	.30
❑	34	Miguel Tejada	.50	.20
❑	35	Ivan Rodriguez	.75	.30
❑	36	Carlos Beltran	.50	.20
❑	37	Steve Finley	.50	.20
❑	38	Torii Hunter	.50	.20
❑	39	Bobby Crosby	.50	.20
❑	40	Jorge Posada	.75	.30
❑	41	Ben Sheets	.50	.20
❑	42	Mike Piazza	1.25	.50
❑	43	Luis Gonzalez	.50	.20
❑	44	Joe Mauer	1.25	.50
❑	45	Shawn Green	.50	.20
❑	46	Eric Gagne	.50	.20
❑	47	Kerry Wood	.50	.20
❑	48	Derek Jeter	3.00	1.25
❑	49	Josh Beckett	.50	.20
❑	50	Alex Rodriguez	2.00	.75
❑	51	Aubrey Huff	.50	.20
❑	52	Eric Chavez	.50	.20
❑	53	Sammy Sosa	1.25	.50
❑	54	Roger Clemens	2.00	.75
❑	55	Mike Mussina	.75	.30
❑	56	Mike Sweeney	.50	.20
❑	57	Oliver Perez	.50	.20
❑	58	Tim Hudson	.50	.20
❑	59	Justin Verlander RC	4.00	1.50
❑	60	Johan Santana	1.25	.50
❑	61	Hideki Matsui	2.00	.75
❑	62	Mark Mulder	.50	.20
❑	63	Jake Peavy	.50	.20
❑	64	Adam Dunn	.50	.20
❑	65	Dallas McPherson	.50	.20
❑	66	Jeff Kent	.50	.20
❑	67	Pedro Martinez	.75	.30
❑	68	J.D. Drew	.50	.20
❑	69	Frank Thomas	1.25	.50
❑	70	Kazuo Matsui	.50	.20
❑	71	Travis Hafner	.50	.20
❑	72	John Smoltz	.75	.30
❑	73	Jason Schmidt	.50	.20
❑	74	Carlos Lee	.50	.20
❑	75	Todd Helton	.75	.30
❑	76	David Ortiz	1.25	.50
❑	77	Roy Oswalt	.50	.20
❑	78	Brian Giles	.50	.20
❑	79	Gary Sheffield	.50	.20
❑	80	Jason Bay	.50	.20
❑	81	Alfonso Soriano	.50	.20
❑	82	Randy Johnson	1.25	.50
❑	83	Tom Glavine	.75	.30
❑	84	Richie Sexson	.50	.20
❑	85	Curt Schilling	.75	.30
❑	86	Adrian Beltre	.50	.20
❑	87	Jim Edmonds	.50	.20
❑	88	Roy Halladay	.50	.20
❑	89	Johnny Damon	.75	.30
❑	90	Lance Berkman	.50	.20
❑	91	Adam Shabala SB RC	1.00	.40
❑	92	Ambiorix Burgos SB RC	1.00	.40
❑	93	Ambiorix Concepcion SB RC	1.00	.40
❑	94	Anibal Sanchez SB RC	3.00	1.25
❑	95	Bill McCarthy SB RC	1.00	.40
❑	96	Brandon McCarthy SB RC	1.50	.60
❑	97	Brian Burres SB RC	1.00	.40
❑	98	Carlos Ruiz SB RC	1.00	.40
❑	99	Casey Rogowski SB RC	1.25	.50
❑	100	Chad Orvella SB RC	1.00	.40
❑	101	Chris Resop SB RC	1.00	.40
❑	102	Chris Roberson SB RC	1.00	.40
❑	103	Chris Seddon SB RC	1.00	.40
❑	104	Colter Bean SB RC	1.00	.40
❑	105	Dae-Sung Koo SB RC	1.00	.40
❑	106	Ryan Zimmerman SB RC	8.00	3.00
❑	107	Dave Gassner SB RC	1.00	.40
❑	108	Brian Anderson SB RC	1.50	.60
❑	109	D.J. Houlton SB RC	1.00	.40
❑	110	Derek Wathan SB RC	1.00	.40
❑	111	Devon Lowery SB RC	1.00	.40
❑	112	Enrique Gonzalez SB RC	1.00	.40
❑	113	Chris Denorfia SB RC	1.25	.50
❑	114	Eude Brito SB RC	1.00	.40
❑	115	Francisco Butto SB RC	1.00	.40
❑	116	Franquelis Osoria SB RC	1.00	.40
❑	117	Garrett Jones SB RC	1.00	.40
❑	118	Geovany Soto SB RC	4.00	1.50
❑	119	Hayden Penn SB RC	1.25	.50
❑	120	Ismael Ramirez SB RC	1.00	.40
❑	121	Jared Gothreaux SB RC	1.00	.40
❑	122	Jason Hammel SB RC	1.00	.40
❑	123	Dana Eveland SB RC	1.00	.40
❑	124	Jeff Miller SB RC	1.00	.40
❑	125	Jermaine Van Buren SB	1.00	.40
❑	126	Joel Peralta SB RC	1.00	.40
❑	127	John Hattig SB RC	1.00	.40
❑	128	Jorge Campillo SB RC	1.00	.40
❑	129	Juan Morillo SB RC	1.00	.40
❑	130	Ryan Garko SB RC	2.00	.75
❑	131	Keiichi Yabu SB RC	1.00	.40
❑	132	Kendry Morales SB RC	2.50	1.00
❑	133	Luis Hernandez SB RC	1.00	.40
❑	134	Mark McLemore SB RC	1.00	.40
❑	135	Luis Pena SB RC	1.00	.40
❑	136	Luis O.Rodriguez SB RC	1.00	.40
❑	137	Luke Scott SB RC	2.00	.75
❑	138	Marcos Carvajal SB RC	1.00	.40
❑	139	Mark Woodyard SB RC	1.00	.40
❑	140	Matt A.Smith SB RC	1.00	.40
❑	141	Matthew Lindstrom SB RC	1.00	.40
❑	142	Miguel Negron SB RC	1.25	.50
❑	143	Mike Morse SB RC	1.00	.40
❑	144	Nate McLouth SB RC	1.25	.50
❑	145	Nelson Cruz SB RC	2.00	.75
❑	146	Nick Masset SB RC	1.00	.40
❑	147	Ryan Spilborghs SB RC	1.25	.50
❑	148	Oscar Robles SB RC	1.00	.40
❑	149	Paulino Reynoso SB RC	1.00	.40
❑	150	Pedro Lopez SB RC	1.00	.40
❑	151	Pete Orr SB RC	1.00	.40
❑	152	Prince Fielder SB RC	4.00	1.50
❑	153	Randy Messenger SB RC	1.00	.40
❑	154	Randy Williams SB RC	1.00	.40
❑	155	Raul Tablado SB RC	1.00	.40
❑	156	Ronny Paulino SB RC	1.25	.50
❑	157	Russ Rohlicek SB RC	1.00	.40
❑	158	Russell Martin SB RC	2.00	.75
❑	159	Scott Baker SB RC	1.25	.50
❑	160	Scott Munter SB RC	1.00	.40
❑	161	Sean Thompson SB RC	1.00	.40
❑	162	Sean Tracey SB RC	1.00	.40
❑	163	Shane Costa SB RC	1.00	.40
❑	164	Stephen Drew SB RC	5.00	2.00
❑	165	Steve Schmoll SB RC	1.00	.40
❑	166	Ryan Speier SB RC	1.00	.40
❑	167	Tadahito Iguchi SB	2.00	.75
❑	168	Tony Giarratano SB RC	1.00	.40
❑	169	Tony Pena SB RC	1.00	.40
❑	170	Travis Bowyer SB RC	1.00	.40
❑	171	Ubaldo Jimenez SB RC	2.00	.75
❑	172	Wladimir Balentien SB RC	1.25	.50
❑	173	Yorman Bazardo SB RC	1.00	.40
❑	174	Yuniesky Betancourt SB RC	2.00	.75

2006 Sweet Spot

❑		COMP.SET w/o AU's (100)	25.00	10.00
❑		COMMON CARD (1-100)	.50	.20
❑		OVERALL AU ODDS 1:12		
❑		AU PRINT RUNS B/WN 45-275 PER		
❑		EXCHANGE DEADLINE 05/25/08		
❑		ASTERISK = PARTIAL EXCHANGE		
❑	1	Bartolo Colon	.50	.20
❑	2	Garret Anderson	.50	.20
❑	3	Francisco Rodriguez	.50	.20
❑	4	Dallas McPherson	.50	.20
❑	5	Andy Pettitte	.75	.30
❑	6	Lance Berkman	.50	.20
❑	7	Willy Taveras	.50	.20
❑	8	Bobby Crosby	.50	.20
❑	9	Dan Haren	.50	.20
❑	10	Nick Swisher	.50	.20
❑	11	Vernon Wells	.50	.20
❑	12	Orlando Hudson	.50	.20
❑	13	Roy Halladay	.50	.20
❑	14	Andruw Jones	.75	.30
❑	15	Chipper Jones	1.25	.50
❑	16	Jeff Francoeur	1.25	.50
❑	17	John Smoltz	.75	.30
❑	18	Carlos Lee	.50	.20
❑	19	Rickie Weeks	.50	.20
❑	20	Bill Hall	.50	.20
❑	21	Jim Edmonds	.75	.30
❑	22	David Eckstein	.50	.20
❑	23	Mark Mulder	.50	.20
❑	24	Aramis Ramirez	.50	.20
❑	25	Greg Maddux	2.00	.75
❑	26	Nomar Garciaparra	1.25	.50
❑	27	Carlos Zambrano	.50	.20
❑	28	Scott Kazmir	.75	.30
❑	29	Jorge Cantu	.50	.20
❑	30	Carl Crawford	.50	.20
❑	31	Luis Gonzalez	.50	.20
❑	32	Troy Glaus	.50	.20
❑	33	Shawn Green	.50	.20
❑	34	Jeff Kent	.50	.20
❑	35	Milton Bradley	.50	.20
❑	36	Cesar Izturis	.50	.20
❑	37	Omar Vizquel	.75	.30
❑	38	Moises Alou	.50	.20
❑	39	Randy Winn	.50	.20
❑	40	Jason Schmidt	.50	.20
❑	41	Coco Crisp	.50	.20
❑	42	C.C. Sabathia	.50	.20
❑	43	Cliff Lee	.50	.20
❑	44	Ichiro Suzuki	2.00	.75
❑	45	Richie Sexson	.50	.20
❑	46	Jeremy Reed	.50	.20
❑	47	Carlos Delgado	.50	.20
❑	48	Miguel Cabrera	.75	.30
❑	49	Luis Castillo	.50	.20
❑	50	Carlos Beltran	.50	.20
❑	51	Tom Glavine	.75	.30
❑	52	David Wright	2.00	.75
❑	53	Cliff Floyd	.50	.20
❑	54	Chad Cordero	.50	.20
❑	55	Jose Vidro	.50	.20
❑	56	Jose Guillen	.50	.20
❑	57	Nick Johnson	.50	.20
❑	58	Miguel Tejada	.50	.20
❑	59	Melvin Mora	.50	.20
❑	60	Javy Lopez	.50	.20
❑	61	Khalil Greene	.75	.30
❑	62	Brian Giles	.50	.20
❑	63	Trevor Hoffman	.50	.20
❑	64	Bobby Abreu	.50	.20
❑	65	Jimmy Rollins	.50	.20
❑	66	Pat Burrell	.50	.20
❑	67	Billy Wagner	.50	.20
❑	68	Jack Wilson	.50	.20
❑	69	Zach Duke	.50	.20
❑	70	Craig Wilson	.50	.20
❑	71	Mark Teixeira	.75	.30
❑	72	Hank Blalock	.50	.20
❑	73	David Dellucci	.50	.20
❑	74	Manny Ramirez	.75	.30
❑	75	Johnny Damon	.75	.30
❑	76	Jason Varitek	1.25	.50
❑	77	Trot Nixon	.50	.20
❑	78	Adam Dunn	.50	.20
❑	79	Felipe Lopez	.50	.20

❑ 80 Brandon Claussen .50 .20
❑ 81 Sean Casey .50 .20
❑ 82 Todd Helton .75 .30
❑ 83 Clint Barmes .50 .20
❑ 84 Matt Holliday 1.25 .50
❑ 85 Mike Sweeney .50 .20
❑ 86 Zack Greinke .50 .20
❑ 87 David DeJesus .50 .20
❑ 88 Ivan Rodriguez .75 .30
❑ 89 Jeremy Bonderman .50 .20
❑ 90 Magglio Ordonez .50 .20
❑ 91 Torii Hunter .50 .20
❑ 92 Joe Nathan .50 .20
❑ 93 Michael Cuddyer .50 .20
❑ 94 Paul Konerko .50 .20
❑ 95 Jermaine Dye .50 .20
❑ 96 Jon Garland .50 .20
❑ 97 Alex Rodriguez 2.00 .75
❑ 98 Hideki Matsui 1.25 .50
❑ 99 Jason Giambi .50 .20
❑ 100 Mariano Rivera 1.25 .50
❑ 101 Adrian Beltre AU/99 40.00 15.00
❑ 102 Matt Cain AU/275 (RC) 40.00 15.00
❑ 103 Craig Biggio AU/99 60.00 30.00
❑ 104 Eric Chavez AU/99 30.00 12.50
❑ 105 J.D. Drew AU/99 30.00 12.50
❑ 106 Eric Gagne AU/99 50.00 20.00
❑ 107 Tim Hudson AU/99 40.00 15.00
❑ 108 Tom Glavine AU/275 50.00 20.00
❑ 109 David Ortiz AU/99 80.00 40.00
❑ 110 Scott Rolen AU/275 40.00 15.00
❑ 111 Johan Santana AU/99 50.00 20.00
❑ 112 Curt Schilling AU/96 80.00 40.00
❑ 113 John Smoltz AU/99 60.00 30.00
❑ 114 Alfonso Soriano AU/99 60.00 30.00
❑ 115 Kerry Wood AU/99 30.00 12.50
❑ 116 Edwin Jackson AU/99 20.00 8.00
❑ 117 Felix Hernandez AU/125 50.00 20.00
❑ 118 Prince Fielder AU/99 (RC) 120.00 60.00
❑ 119 Vladimir Guerrero AU/86 60.00 30.00
❑ 120 Roger Clemens AU/99 150.00 75.00
❑ 121 Albert Pujols AU/45 300.00 175.00
❑ 122 Chris Carpenter AU/99 50.00 20.00
❑ 123 Derrek Lee AU/99 40.00 15.00
❑ 124 Dontrelle Willis AU/99 30.00 12.50
❑ 125 Roy Oswalt AU/99 40.00 15.00
❑ 126 Ryan Garko AU/275 (RC) 25.00 10.00
❑ 127 Tadahito Iguchi AU/275 50.00 20.00
❑ 128 Mark Loretta AU/275 25.00 10.00
❑ 129 Joe Mauer AU/275 50.00 20.00
❑ 130 Victor Martinez AU/275 25.00 10.00
❑ 131 Wily Mo Pena AU/275 25.00 10.00
❑ 132 Oliver Perez AU/274 15.00 6.00
❑ 133 C.Patterson AU/275 EXCH 25.00 10.00
❑ 134 Ben Sheets AU/275 25.00 10.00
❑ 135 Michael Young AU/275 25.00 10.00
❑ 136 Jonny Gomes AU/275 15.00 6.00
❑ 137 Derek Jeter AU/99 200.00 125.00
❑ 138 K.Griffey Jr. AU/275 EXCH * 80.00 40.00
❑ 139 R.Zimmerman AU/275 (RC) 60.00 30.00
❑ 140 Scott Baker AU/275 (RC) 15.00 6.00
❑ 141 Huston Street AU/275 25.00 10.00
❑ 142 Jason Bay AU/275 EXCH 25.00 10.00
❑ 143 Ryan Howard AU/275 80.00 40.00
❑ 145 Travis Hafner AU/275 25.00 10.00
❑ 146 Brian Myrow AU/275 RC 15.00 6.00
❑ 147 Scott Podsednik AU/275 25.00 10.00
❑ 148 Brian Roberts AU/275 25.00 10.00
❑ 149 Grady Sizemore AU/135 40.00 15.00
❑ 150 Chris Demaria AU/275 RC 15.00 6.00
❑ 151 Jonah Bayliss AU/275 RC 15.00 6.00
❑ 152 Geovany Soto AU/275 (RC) 25.00 10.00
❑ 153 Lyle Overbay AU/275 15.00 6.00
❑ 154 Joey Devine AU/275 RC 15.00 6.00
❑ 155 A.Freire AU/275 RC 15.00 6.00
❑ 156 Conor Jackson AU/275 (RC) 25.00 10.00
❑ 157 Danny Sandoval AU/275 RC 15.00 6.00
❑ 158 Chase Utley AU/275 50.00 20.00
❑ 159 Jeff Harris AU/275 RC 15.00 6.00
❑ 160 Ron Flores AU/275 RC 15.00 6.00
❑ 161 Scott Feldman AU/275 RC 15.00 6.00
❑ 162 Yadier Molina AU/275 25.00 10.00
❑ 163 Tim Corcoran AU/275 RC 15.00 6.00
❑ 164 Craig Hansen AU/275 RC 40.00 15.00
❑ 165 Jason Bergmann AU/275 RC 15.00 6.00
❑ 166 Craig Breslow AU/275 RC 15.00 6.00
❑ 167 Jhonny Peralta AU/275 15.00 6.00
❑ 168 J.Hermida AU/275 (RC) 25.00 10.00
❑ 169 Scott Kazmir AU/275 25.00 10.00
❑ 170 Bobby Crosby AU/99 30.00 12.50
❑ 171 Rich Harden AU/275 15.00 6.00
❑ 172 Casey Kotchman AU/275 15.00 6.00
❑ 173 Tim Hamulack AU/275 (RC) 15.00 6.00
❑ 174 Justin Morneau AU/275 25.00 10.00
❑ 175 Jake Peavy AU/275 25.00 10.00
❑ 176 Y.Betancourt AU/275 25.00 10.00
❑ 177 Jeremy Accardo AU/275 RC 15.00 6.00
❑ 178 Jorge Cantu AU/200 25.00 10.00
❑ 179 Marlon Byrd AU/275 15.00 6.00
❑ 180 R.Jorgensen AU/275 RC 15.00 6.00
❑ 181 C.Denorfia AU/275 (RC) 15.00 6.00
❑ 182 Steve Stemle AU/275 RC 15.00 6.00
❑ 183 Robert Andino AU/275 RC 15.00 6.00
❑ 184 Chris Heintz AU/275 RC 15.00 6.00

2007 Sweet Spot

❑ COMMON CARD (1-100) 2.00 .75
❑ STATED PRINT RUN 850 SER.#'d SETS
❑ TWO BASE CARDS PER TIN
❑ COMMON AU RC (101-142) 8.00 3.00
❑ OVERALL AU ODDS ONE PER TIN
❑ EXCHANGE DEADLINE 11/9/2009
❑ 1 Adam Dunn 2.00 .75
❑ 2 Adrian Beltre 2.00 .75
❑ 3 Albert Pujols 10.00 4.00
❑ 4 Alex Rios 2.00 .75
❑ 5 Alex Rodriguez 8.00 3.00
❑ 6 Alfonso Soriano 2.00 .75
❑ 7 Andruw Jones 3.00 1.25
❑ 8 Aramis Ramirez 2.00 .75
❑ 9 B.J. Upton 2.00 .75
❑ 10 Barry Zito 2.00 .75
❑ 11 Bartolo Colon 2.00 .75
❑ 12 Ben Sheets 2.00 .75
❑ 13 Bill Hall 2.00 .75
❑ 14 Brad Penny 2.00 .75
❑ 15 Brandon Webb 2.00 .75
❑ 16 C.C. Sabathia 2.00 .75
❑ 17 Carl Crawford 2.00 .75
❑ 18 Carlos Beltran 2.00 .75
❑ 19 Carlos Guillen 2.00 .75
❑ 20 Carlos Lee 2.00 .75
❑ 21 Chase Utley 5.00 2.00
❑ 22 Chien-Ming Wang 8.00 3.00
❑ 23 Chipper Jones 5.00 2.00
❑ 24 Chris Carpenter 2.00 .75
❑ 25 Cole Hamels 3.00 1.25
❑ 26 Craig Biggio 3.00 1.25
❑ 27 Curt Schilling 3.00 1.25
❑ 28 Dan Haren 2.00 .75
❑ 29 David Ortiz 5.00 2.00
❑ 30 David Wright 8.00 3.00
❑ 31 Delmon Young 3.00 1.25
❑ 32 Derek Jeter 12.00 5.00
❑ 33 Derrek Lee 2.00 .75
❑ 34 Dontrelle Willis 2.00 .75
❑ 35 Felix Hernandez 3.00 1.25
❑ 36 Frank Thomas 5.00 2.00
❑ 37 Gil Meche 2.00 .75
❑ 38 Grady Sizemore 3.00 1.25
❑ 39 Greg Maddux 8.00 3.00
❑ 40 Ian Kinsler 2.00 .75
❑ 41 Ichiro Suzuki 8.00 3.00
❑ 42 Ivan Rodriguez 3.00 1.25
❑ 43 Jake Peavy 2.00 .75
❑ 44 Jason Bay 2.00 .75
❑ 45 Jason Varitek 5.00 2.00
❑ 46 Jeff Kent 2.00 .75
❑ 47 Jermaine Dye 2.00 .75
❑ 48 Jim Edmonds 3.00 1.25
❑ 49 Jim Thome 3.00 1.25
❑ 50 Jimmy Rollins 2.00 .75
❑ 51 Joe Mauer 3.00 1.25
❑ 52 Johan Santana 3.00 1.25
❑ 53 John Smoltz 3.00 1.25
❑ 54 Jonathan Papelbon 5.00 2.00
❑ 55 Jorge Posada 3.00 1.25
❑ 56 Jose Reyes 5.00 2.00
❑ 57 Josh Beckett 3.00 1.25
❑ 58 Justin Morneau 2.00 .75
❑ 59 Justin Verlander 5.00 2.00
❑ 60 Ken Griffey Jr. 8.00 3.00
❑ 61 Kenji Johjima 5.00 2.00
❑ 62 Lance Berkman 2.00 .75
❑ 63 Magglio Ordonez 2.00 .75
❑ 64 Manny Ramirez 0.00 1.25
❑ 65 Mariano Rivera 5.00 2.00
❑ 66 Mark Buehrle 2.00 .75
❑ 67 Mark Teixeira 3.00 1.25
❑ 68 Matt Holliday 5.00 2.00
❑ 69 Matt Morris 2.00 .75
❑ 70 Melvin Mora 2.00 .75
❑ 71 Michael Young 2.00 .75
❑ 72 Miguel Cabrera 3.00 1.25
❑ 73 Miguel Tejada 2.00 .75
❑ 74 Mike Lowell 2.00 .75
❑ 75 Mike Mussina 3.00 1.25
❑ 76 Mike Piazza 5.00 2.00
❑ 77 Nick Swisher 2.00 .75
❑ 78 Orlando Hudson 2.00 .75
❑ 79 Paul Konerko 2.00 .75
❑ 80 Paul Lo Duca 2.00 .75
❑ 81 Pedro Martinez 3.00 1.25
❑ 82 Prince Fielder 5.00 2.00
❑ 83 Randy Johnson 5.00 2.00
❑ 84 Rickie Weeks 2.00 .75
❑ 85 Roger Clemens 8.00 3.00
❑ 86 Roy Halladay 2.00 .75
❑ 87 Roy Oswalt 2.00 .75
❑ 88 Russell Martin 2.00 .75
❑ 89 Ryan Howard 8.00 3.00
❑ 90 Ryan Zimmerman 5.00 2.00
❑ 91 Sammy Sosa 5.00 2.00
❑ 92 Scott Rolen 3.00 1.25
❑ 93 Shawn Green 2.00 .75
❑ 94 Todd Helton 3.00 1.25
❑ 95 Tom Glavine 3.00 1.25
❑ 96 Torii Hunter 2.00 .75
❑ 97 Travis Hafner 2.00 .75
❑ 98 Vernon Wells 2.00 .75
❑ 99 Victor Martinez 2.00 .75
❑ 100 Vladimir Guerrero 5.00 2.00
❑ 101 Adam Lind AU (RC) 8.00 3.00
❑ 102 Akinori Iwamura AU SP RC 40.00 15.00
❑ 103 Alex Gordon AU RC 80.00 40.00
❑ 104 Alexi Casilla AU RC 15.00 6.00
❑ 105 Andy LaRoche AU (RC) 15.00 6.00
❑ 106 Billy Butler AU (RC) 15.00 6.00
❑ 107 Ryan Rowland-Smith AU RC 8.00 3.00
❑ 108 Brandon Wood AU (RC) 15.00 6.00
❑ 109 Brian Burres AU (RC) 8.00 3.00
❑ 110 Chase Wright AU RC 10.00 4.00
❑ 111 Chris Stewart AU RC 8.00 3.00
❑ 112 Daisuke Matsuzaka AU SP RC 250.00 150.00
❑ 113 Delmon Young AU SP (RC) 15.00 6.00
❑ 114 Andy Sonnanstine AU RC 8.00 3.00
❑ 115 Andrew Miller AU RC
❑ 116 Fred Lewis AU (RC) 10.00 4.00
❑ 117 Glen Perkins AU SP (RC) 25.00 10.00
❑ 118 David Murphy AU (RC) 8.00 3.00
❑ 119 Hunter Pence AU (RC) 30.00 12.50
❑ 120 Jarrod Saltalamacchia AU (RC) 15.00 6.00
❑ 121 Jeff Baker AU SP (RC) 10.00 4.00
❑ 122 Jesus Flores AU SP RC 25.00 10.00
❑ 123 Joakim Soria AU SP RC 25.00 10.00
❑ 124 Joe Smith AU RC 10.00 4.00
❑ 125 Jon Knott AU (RC) 8.00 3.00
❑ 126 Josh Hamilton AU (RC) 40.00 15.00
❑ 127 Justin Hampson AU (RC) 8.00 3.00
❑ 128 Kei Igawa AU SP RC 25.00 10.00

❑ 129 Kevin Cameron AU RC 8.00 3.00
❑ 130 Matt Chico AU (RC) 10.00 4.00
❑ 131 Matt DeSalvo AU (RC) 10.00 4.00
❑ 132 Micah Owings AU SP (RC) 25.00 10.00
❑ 133 Michael Bourn AU (RC) 10.00 4.00
❑ 134 Miguel Montero AU (RC) 8.00 3.00
❑ 135 Phil Hughes AU SP (RC) 50.00 20.00
❑ 136 Rick Vanden Hurk AU RC 8.00 3.00
❑ 137 Ryan Sweeney AU SP (RC)
❑ 138 Tim Lincecum AU RC
❑ 139 Travis Buck AU (RC) 10.00 4.00
❑ 140 Troy Tulowitzki AU SP (RC) 50.00 20.00
❑ 141 Sean Henn AU (RC) 10.00 4.00
❑ 142 Zack Segovia AU (RC) 10.00 4.00
❑ NNO Michael Buysner 40.00 15.00

2007 Sweet Spot Classic

❑ COMMON CARD 1.50 .60
❑ STATED PRINT RUN 575 SER.#'d SETS
❑ 1 Phil Niekro 1.50 .60
❑ 2 Fred McGriff 2.50 1.00
❑ 3 Bob Horner 1.50 .60
❑ 4 Earl Weaver 1.50 .60
❑ 5 Boog Powell 1.50 .60
❑ 6 Eddie Murray 4.00 1.50
❑ 7 Fred Lynn 1.50 .60
❑ 8 Dwight Evans 1.50 .60
❑ 9 Jim Rice 1.50 .60
❑ 10 Carlton Fisk 2.50 1.00
❑ 11 Luis Tiant 1.50 .60
❑ 12 Robin Yount 4.00 1.50
❑ 13 Bobby Doerr 1.50 .60
❑ 14 Ryne Sandberg 8.00 3.00
❑ 15 Billy Williams 1.50 .60
❑ 16 Andre Dawson 1.50 .60
❑ 17 Mark Grace 2.50 1.00
❑ 18 Ron Santo 2.50 1.00
❑ 19 Shawon Dunston 1.50 .60
❑ 20 Harold Baines 1.50 .60
❑ 21 Carlton Fisk 2.50 1.00
❑ 22 Sparky Anderson 1.50 .60
❑ 23 George Foster 1.50 .60
❑ 24 Dave Parker 1.50 .60
❑ 25 Ken Griffey Sr. 1.50 .60
❑ 26 Dave Concepcion 1.50 .60
❑ 27 Rafael Palmeiro 2.50 1.00
❑ 28 Al Rosen 1.50 .60
❑ 29 Kirk Gibson 1.50 .60
❑ 30 Alan Trammell 1.50 .60
❑ 31 Jack Morris 1.50 .60
❑ 32 Willie Horton 1.50 .60
❑ 33 JR Richard 1.50 .60
❑ 34 Jose Cruz 1.50 .60
❑ 36 Willie Wilson 1.50 .60
❑ 37 Bo Jackson 4.00 1.50
❑ 38 Nolan Ryan 10.00 4.00
❑ 39 Don Baylor 1.50 .60
❑ 40 Maury Wills 1.50 .60
❑ 41 Tommy John 1.50 .60
❑ 42 Ron Cey 1.50 .60
❑ 43 Davey Lopes 1.50 .60
❑ 44 Tommy Lasorda 1.50 .60
❑ 45 Burt Hooton 1.50 .60
❑ 46 Reggie Smith 1.50 .60
❑ 47 Rollie Fingers 1.50 .60
❑ 48 Cecil Cooper 1.50 .60
❑ 49 Paul Molitor 1.50 .60
❑ 50 Vern Stephens 1.50 .60
❑ 51 Tony Oliva 1.50 .60
❑ 52 Andres Galarraga 1.50 .60
❑ 53 Tim Raines 1.50 .60
❑ 54 Dennis Martinez 1.50 .60
❑ 55 Lee Mazzilli 1.50 .60
❑ 56 Rusty Staub 1.50 .60
❑ 57 David Cone 1.50 .60
❑ 58 Reggie Jackson 2.50 1.00
❑ 59 Ron Guidry 1.50 .60
❑ 60 Tino Martinez 1.50 .60
❑ 61 Don Mattingly 8.00 3.00
❑ 62 Chris Chambliss 1.50 .60
❑ 63 Sparky Lyle 1.50 .60
❑ 64 Goose Gossage 1.50 .60
❑ 65 Dave Righetti 1.50 .60
❑ 66 Phil Garner 1.50 .60
❑ 67 Bill Madlock 1.50 .60
❑ 68 Kent Hrbek 1.50 .60
❑ 69 Al Oliver 1.50 .60
❑ 70 John Kruk 1.50 .60
❑ 71 Greg Luzinski 1.50 .60
❑ 72 Dick Allen 1.50 .60
❑ 73 Richie Ashburn 2.50 1.00
❑ 74 Gary Matthews 1.50 .60
❑ 76 Mike Schmidt 6.00 2.50
❑ 77 Waite Hoyt 1.50 .60
❑ 78 Bruce Sutter 1.50 .60
❑ 79 Roger Maris 4.00 1.50
❑ 80 Joe Torre 2.50 1.00
❑ 81 Kevin Mitchell 1.50 .60
❑ 82 John Montefusco 1.50 .60
❑ 83 Rick Reuschel 1.50 .60
❑ 84 Will Clark 2.50 1.00
❑ 85 Jack Clark 1.50 .60
❑ 86 Matt Williams 1.50 .60
❑ 87 Steve Garvey 1.50 .60
❑ 88 Dave Winfield 1.50 .60
❑ 89 Jay Buhner 1.50 .60
❑ 90 Edgar Martinez 2.50 1.00
❑ 91 Carney Lansford 1.50 .60
❑ 92 Sal Bando 1.50 .60
❑ 93 Dave Stewart 1.50 .60
❑ 94 Dennis Eckersley 1.50 .60
❑ 95 Jose Canseco 2.50 1.00
❑ 96 Dennis Eckersley 1.50 .60
❑ 97 Roberto Alomar 2.50 1.00
❑ 98 George Bell 1.50 .60
❑ 99 Joe Carter 1.50 .60
❑ 100 Frank Howard 1.50 .60
❑ 101 Brooks Robinson 2.50 1.00
❑ 102 Frank Robinson 1.50 .60
❑ 103 Jim Palmer 1.50 .60
❑ 104 Cal Ripken Jr. 15.00 6.00
❑ 105 Warren Spahn 2.50 1.00
❑ 106 Cy Young 4.00 1.50
❑ 107 Waite Hoyt 1.50 .60
❑ 108 Carl Yastrzemski 6.00 2.50
❑ 109 Johnny Pesky 1.50 .60
❑ 110 Wade Boggs 2.50 1.00
❑ 111 Jackie Robinson 4.00 1.50
❑ 112 Roy Campanella 4.00 1.50
❑ 113 Pee Wee Reese 2.50 1.00
❑ 114 Don Newcombe 1.50 .60
❑ 115 Rod Carew 2.50 1.00
❑ 116 Ernie Banks 4.00 1.50
❑ 117 Fergie Jenkins 1.50 .60
❑ 118 Al Lopez 1.50 .60
❑ 119 Luis Aparicio 1.50 .60
❑ 120 Toby Harrah 1.50 .60
❑ 121 Joe Morgan 1.50 .60
❑ 122 Johnny Bench 4.00 1.50
❑ 123 Tony Perez 1.50 .60
❑ 124 Ted Kluszewski 2.50 1.00
❑ 125 Bob Feller 1.50 .60
❑ 126 Bob Lemon 1.50 .60
❑ 127 Larry Doby 1.50 .60
❑ 128 Lou Boudreau 1.50 .60
❑ 129 George Kell 1.50 .60
❑ 130 Hal Newhouser 1.50 .60
❑ 131 Al Kaline 4.00 1.50
❑ 132 Ty Cobb 6.00 2.50
❑ 133 Denny McLain 1.50 .60
❑ 134 Buck Leonard 1.50 .60
❑ 135 Dean Chance 1.50 .60
❑ 136 Don Drysdale 2.50 1.00
❑ 137 Don Sutton 1.50 .60
❑ 138 Eddie Mathews 4.00 1.50
❑ 139 Paul Molitor 1.50 .60
❑ 140 Kirby Puckett 4.00 1.50
❑ 141 Rod Carew 2.50 1.00
❑ 142 Harmon Killebrew 4.00 1.50
❑ 143 Monte Irvin 1.50 .60
❑ 144 Mel Ott 1.50 .60
❑ 145 Christy Mathewson 4.00 1.50
❑ 146 Hoyt Wilhelm 1.50 .60
❑ 147 Tom Seaver 2.50 1.00
❑ 148 Joe McCarthy 1.50 .60
❑ 149 Joe DiMaggio 8.00 3.00
❑ 150 Lou Gehrig 8.00 3.00
❑ 151 Babe Ruth 10.00 4.00
❑ 152 Casey Stengel 1.50 .60
❑ 153 Phil Rizzuto 2.50 1.00
❑ 154 Thurman Munson 4.00 1.50
❑ 155 Johnny Mize 1.50 .60
❑ 156 Yogi Berra 4.00 1.50
❑ 157 Roger Maris 4.00 1.50
❑ 158 Don Larsen 1.50 .60
❑ 159 Bill Skowron 1.50 .60
❑ 160 Lou Piniella 1.50 .60
❑ 161 Joe Pepitone 1.50 .60
❑ 162 Ray Dandridge 1.50 .60
❑ 163 Rollie Fingers 1.50 .60
❑ 165 Reggie Jackson 2.50 1.00
❑ 166 Mickey Cochrane 1.50 .60
❑ 167 Jimmie Foxx 4.00 1.50
❑ 168 Lefty Grove 1.50 .60
❑ 169 Gus Zernial 1.50 .60
❑ 170 Jim Bunning 1.50 .60
❑ 171 Steve Carlton 1.50 .60
❑ 172 Robin Roberts 1.50 .60
❑ 173 Ralph Kiner 2.50 1.00
❑ 174 Willie Stargell 2.50 1.00
❑ 175 Roberto Clemente 12.00 5.00
❑ 176 Bill Mazeroski 2.50 1.00
❑ 177 Honus Wagner 4.00 1.50
❑ 178 Pie Traynor 1.50 .60
❑ 179 Elroy Face 1.50 .60
❑ 180 Dick Groat 1.50 .60
❑ 181 Tony Gwynn 4.00 1.50
❑ 182 Willie McCovey 2.50 1.00
❑ 183 Gaylord Perry 1.50 .60
❑ 184 Juan Marichal 1.50 .60
❑ 185 Orlando Cepeda 1.50 .60
❑ 186 Satchel Paige 4.00 1.50
❑ 187 George Sisler 1.50 .60
❑ 188 Rogers Hornsby 2.50 1.00
❑ 189 Stan Musial 6.00 2.50
❑ 190 Dizzy Dean 2.50 1.00
❑ 191 Bob Gibson 2.50 1.00
❑ 192 Red Schoendienst 1.50 .60
❑ 193 Lou Brock 2.50 1.00
❑ 194 Enos Slaughter 1.50 .60
❑ 195 Nolan Ryan 10.00 4.00
❑ 196 Mickey Vernon 1.50 .60
❑ 197 Walter Johnson 4.00 1.50
❑ 198 Rick Ferrell 1.50 .60
❑ 199 Roy Sievers 1.50 .60
❑ 200 Judy Johnson 1.50 .60

2006 Sweet Spot Update

❑ COMP.SET w/o AU's (100) 25.00 10.00
❑ COMMON CARD (1-100) .50 .20
❑ COMMON AU p/r 399-499 8.00 3.00
❑ COMMON AU p/r 150-240 10.00 4.00

Card		
❑ COMMON AU p/r 98-125	10.00	4.00
❑ OVERALL AU ODDS 1:6		
❑ AU PRINT RUNS B/WN 98-499 PER		
❑ EXCHANGE DEADLINE 12/19/09		
❑ 1 Luis Gonzalez	.50	.20
❑ 2 Chad Tracy	.50	.20
❑ 3 Brandon Webb	.50	.20
❑ 4 Andruw Jones	.75	.30
❑ 5 Chipper Jones	1.25	.50
❑ 6 John Smoltz	.75	.30
❑ 7 Tim Hudson	.50	.20
❑ 8 Miguel Tejada	.50	.20
❑ 9 Brian Roberts	.50	.20
❑ 10 Ramon Hernandez	.50	.20
❑ 11 Curt Schilling	.75	.30
❑ 12 David Ortiz	1.25	.50
❑ 13 Manny Ramirez	.75	.30
❑ 14 Jason Varitek	1.25	.50
❑ 15 Josh Beckett	.50	.20
❑ 16 Greg Maddux	2.00	.75
❑ 17 Derrek Lee	.50	.20
❑ 18 Mark Prior	.75	.30
❑ 19 Aramis Ramirez	.50	.20
❑ 20 Jim Thome	.75	.00
❑ 21 Paul Konerko	.50	.20
❑ 22 Scott Podsednik	.50	.20
❑ 23 Jose Contreras	.50	.20
❑ 24 Ken Griffey Jr.	2.00	.75
❑ 25 Adam Dunn	.50	.20
❑ 26 Felipe Lopez	.50	.20
❑ 27 Travis Hafner	.50	.20
❑ 28 Victor Martinez	.50	.20
❑ 29 Grady Sizemore	.75	.30
❑ 30 Jhonny Peralta	.50	.20
❑ 31 Todd Helton	.75	.30
❑ 32 Garrett Atkins	.50	.20
❑ 33 Clint Barmes	.50	.20
❑ 34 Ivan Rodriguez	.75	.30
❑ 35 Chris Shelton	.50	.20
❑ 36 Jeremy Bonderman	.50	.20
❑ 37 Miguel Cabrera	.75	.30
❑ 38 Dontrelle Willis	.50	.20
❑ 39 Lance Berkman	.50	.20
❑ 40 Morgan Ensberg	.50	.20
❑ 41 Roy Oswalt	.50	.20
❑ 42 Reggie Sanders	.50	.20
❑ 43 Mike Sweeney	.50	.20
❑ 44 Vladimir Guerrero	1.25	.50
❑ 45 Bartolo Colon	.50	.20
❑ 46 Chone Figgins	.50	.20
❑ 47 Nomar Garciaparra	1.25	.50
❑ 48 Jeff Kent	.50	.20
❑ 49 J.D. Drew	.50	.20
❑ 50 Carlos Lee	.50	.20
❑ 51 Ben Sheets	.50	.20
❑ 52 Rickie Weeks	.50	.20
❑ 53 Johan Santana	.75	.30
❑ 54 Torii Hunter	.50	.20
❑ 55 Joe Mauer	.75	.30
❑ 56 Pedro Martinez	.75	.30
❑ 57 David Wright	2.00	.75
❑ 58 Carlos Beltran	.50	.20
❑ 59 Carlos Delgado	.50	.20
❑ 60 Jose Reyes	1.25	.50
❑ 61 Derek Jeter	3.00	1.25
❑ 62 Alex Rodriguez	2.00	.75
❑ 63 Randy Johnson	1.25	.50
❑ 64 Hideki Matsui	1.25	.50
❑ 65 Gary Sheffield	.50	.20
❑ 66 Rich Harden	.50	.20
❑ 67 Eric Chavez	.50	.20
❑ 68 Huston Street	.50	.20
❑ 69 Bobby Crosby	.50	.20
❑ 70 Bobby Abreu	.50	.20
❑ 71 Ryan Howard	2.00	.75
❑ 72 Chase Utley	1.25	.50
❑ 73 Pat Burrell	.50	.20
❑ 74 Jason Bay	.50	.20
❑ 75 Sean Casey	.50	.20
❑ 76 Mike Piazza	1.25	.50
❑ 77 Jake Peavy	.50	.20
❑ 78 Brian Giles	.50	.20
❑ 79 Milton Bradley	.50	.20
❑ 80 Omar Vizquel	.75	.30
❑ 81 Jason Schmidt	.50	.20
❑ 82 Ichiro Suzuki	2.00	.75
❑ 83 Felix Hernandez	.75	.30
❑ 84 Kenji Johjima RC	2.50	1.00
❑ 85 Albert Pujols	2.50	1.00
❑ 86 Chris Carpenter	.50	.20
❑ 87 Scott Rolen	.75	.30
❑ 88 Jim Edmonds	.75	.30
❑ 89 Carl Crawford	.50	.20
❑ 90 Jonny Gomes	.50	.20
❑ 91 Scott Kazmir	.75	.30
❑ 92 Mark Teixeira	.75	.30
❑ 93 Michael Young	.50	.20
❑ 94 Phil Nevin	.50	.20
❑ 95 Vernon Wells	.50	.20
❑ 96 Roy Halladay	.50	.20
❑ 97 Troy Glaus	.50	.20
❑ 98 Alfonso Soriano	.50	.20
❑ 99 Nick Johnson	.50	.20
❑ 100 Jose Vidro	.50	.20
❑ 101 A.Wainwright AU/100 (RC)	40.00	15.00
❑ 102 A.Hernandez AU/100 (RC) EXCH	15.00	6.00
❑ 103 A.Ethier AU/150 (RC)	30.00	12.50
❑ 104 J.Botts AU/100 (RC) EXCH	15.00	6.00
❑ 105 B.Johnson AU/400 (RC)	8.00	3.00
❑ 106 B.Bonser AU/100 (RC)	15.00	6.00
❑ 107 B.Logan AU/200 RC	10.00	4.00
❑ 108 B.Anderson AU/200 (RC)	10.00	4.00
❑ 109 B.Bannister AU/100 (RC)	20.00	8.00
❑ 110 C.Denorfia AU/100 (RC)	10.00	4.00
❑ 111 A.Montero AU/100 (RC)	15.00	6.00
❑ 112 C.Ross AU/100 (RC)	10.00	4.00
❑ 113 C.Hamels AU/399 (RC)	40.00	15.00
❑ 114 C.Jackson AU/400 (RC)	10.00	4.00
❑ 115 D.Uggla AU/125 (RC)	30.00	12.50
❑ 116 D.Gassner AU/100 (RC)	10.00	4.00
❑ 117 C.Wilson AU/150 (RC)	10.00	4.00
❑ 118 E.Reed AU/150 (RC)	10.00	4.00
❑ 119 F.Carmona AU/99 (RC)	25.00	10.00
❑ 120 F.Nieve AU/100 (RC)	10.00	4.00
❑ 121 F.Liriano AU/499 (RC)	25.00	10.00
❑ 122 F.Bynum AU/100 (RC)	10.00	4.00
❑ 123 H.Ramirez AU/100 (RC)	40.00	15.00
❑ 124 H.Kuo AU/100 (RC)	150.00	75.00
❑ 125 I.Kinsler AU/100 (RC)	15.00	6.00
❑ 126 C.Marmol AU/100 RC	15.00	6.00
❑ 127 B.Keppel AU/200 (RC)	10.00	4.00
❑ 128 J.Kubel AU/100 (RC)	15.00	6.00
❑ 129 J.Harris AU/100 RC	10.00	4.00
❑ 130 A.Soler AU/100 RC	15.00	6.00
❑ 131 J.Weaver AU/100 (RC) EXCH	25.00	10.00
❑ 132 C.Quentin AU/100 (RC)	30.00	12.50
❑ 133 J.Hermida AU/100 (RC)	15.00	6.00
❑ 134 J.Zumaya AU/100 (RC)	50.00	20.00
❑ 135 J.Devine AU/100 RC	15.00	6.00
❑ 136 J.Koronka AU/98 (RC)	10.00	4.00
❑ 137 J.Papelbon AU/399 (RC)	40.00	15.00
❑ 138 J.Capellan AU/240 (RC)	10.00	4.00
❑ 139 J.Johnson AU/100 (RC)	15.00	0.00
❑ 140 J.Rupe AU/100 (RC) EXCH	10.00	4.00
❑ 141 J.Willingham AU/100 (RC)	10.00	4.00
❑ 143 J.Verlander AU/100 (RC)	40.00	15.00
❑ 144 K.Shoppach AU/100 (RC)	15.00	6.00
❑ 145 K.Morales AU/100 (RC) EXCH	10.00	4.00
❑ 146 K.Thompson AU/100 (RC)	10.00	4.00
❑ 147 M.McBride AU/100 (RC)	10.00	4.00
❑ 148 M.Prado AU/100 (RC) EXCH	10.00	4.00
❑ 149 M.Cain AU/150 (RC) EXCH	15.00	6.00
❑ 150 C.Hensley AU/100 (RC)	10.00	4.00
❑ 151 T.Taubenheim AU/100 RC	25.00	10.00
❑ 152 M.Jacobs AU/200 (RC)	10.00	4.00
❑ 153 S.Rivera AU/100 (RC)	10.00	4.00
❑ 154 M.Thompson AU/100 RC	10.00	4.00
❑ 155 N.McLouth AU/100 (RC)	25.00	10.00
❑ 156 M.Vento AU/100 (RC)	10.00	4.00
❑ 157 P.Maholm AU/200 (RC)	10.00	4.00
❑ 159 R.Abercrombie AU/100 (RC)	10.00	4.00
❑ 160 M.Rouse AU/100 (RC)	10.00	4.00
❑ 161 K.Ray AU/100 (RC)	10.00	4.00
❑ 162 R.Flores AU/100 RC	10.00	4.00
❑ 163 R.Zimmerman AU/100 (RC)	60.00	30.00
❑ 164 E.Aybar AU/100 (RC)	15.00	6.00
❑ 165 S.Marshall AU/150 (RC)	20.00	8.00
❑ 166 T.Saito AU/100 RC EXCH		
❑ 167 T.Buchholz AU/100 (RC)	10.00	4.00
❑ 168 M.Murton AU/100 (RC)	30.00	12.50
❑ 169 L.Figueroa AU/100 RC EXCH	15.00	6.00
❑ 170 W.Nieves AU/100 (RC)	15.00	6.00
❑ 171 J.Shields AU/100 RC	15.00	6.00
❑ 172 J.Lester AU/399 RC	50.00	20.00
❑ 173 C.Hansen AU/100 RC EXCH	30.00	12.50
❑ 174 A.Rakers AU/100 (RC)	10.00	4.00
❑ 175 B.Livingston AU/100 (RC)	15.00	6.00
❑ 176 B.Harris AU/100 (RC)	10.00	4.00
❑ 177 Z.Jackson AU/100 (RC)	15.00	6.00
❑ 178 C.Britton AU/100 RC	10.00	4.00
❑ 179 H.Kendrick AU/399 (RC)	25.00	10.00
❑ 180 Z.Miner AU/100 (RC)	15.00	6.00
❑ 181 K.Frandsen AU/100 (RC)	10.00	4.00
❑ 182 M.Capps AU/100 (RC)	10.00	4.00
❑ 183 P.Moylan AU/100 RC	10.00	4.00
❑ 184 M.Cabrera AU/100 (RC) EXCH	50.00	20.00

1911 T205 Gold Border

Card		
❑ COMPLETE SET (218)	50000.00	25000.00
❑ COMMON MAJOR (1-186)	150.00	90.00
❑ COM. MINOR (187-198)	300.00	150.00
❑ 1 Ed Abbaticchio	100.00	60.00
❑ 2 Merle (Doc) Adkins	200.00	125.00
❑ 3 Red Ames	100.00	60.00
❑ 4 Jimmy Archer	100.00	60.00
❑ 5 Jimmy Austin	100.00	60.00
❑ 6 Bill Bailey	100.00	60.00
❑ 7 Frank Baker	300.00	175.00
❑ 8 Neal Ball	100.00	60.00
❑ 9 Cy Barger Full B	100.00	60.00
❑ 10 Cy Barger Part B	400.00	250.00
❑ 11 Jack Barry	100.00	60.00
❑ 12 Emil Batch	200.00	125.00
❑ 13 Johnny Bates	100.00	60.00
❑ 14 Fred Beck	100.00	60.00
❑ 15 Beals Becker	100.00	60.00
❑ 16 George Bell	100.00	60.00
❑ 17 Chief Bender	300.00	175.00
❑ 18 Bill Bergen	100.00	60.00
❑ 19 Bob Bescher	100.00	60.00
❑ 20 Joe Birmingham	100.00	60.00
❑ 21 Russ Blackburne	100.00	60.00
❑ 22 Kitty Bransfield	100.00	60.00
❑ 23 R.Bresnahan Closed	300.00	175.00
❑ 24 R.Bresnahan Open	500.00	300.00
❑ 25 Al Bridwell	100.00	60.00
❑ 26 Mordecai Brown	300.00	175.00
❑ 27 Bobby Byrne	100.00	60.00
❑ 28 Hick Cady	250.00	150.00
❑ 29 Howie Camnitz	100.00	60.00
❑ 30 Bill Carrigan	100.00	60.00
❑ 31 Frank Chance	300.00	175.00
❑ 32A Hal Chase Both - Ends	200.00	125.00
❑ 32B Hal Chase Both - Extends	200.00	125.00
❑ 33 Hal Chase Left Ear	500.00	300.00
❑ 34 Eddie Cicotte	400.00	250.00
❑ 35 Fred Clarke	250.00	150.00
❑ 36 Ty Cobb	4000.00	2500.00
❑ 37 E.Collins Mouth Closed	300.00	175.00
❑ 38 E.Collins Mouth Open	600.00	350.00
❑ 39 Jimmy Collins	400.00	250.00
❑ 40 Frank Corridon	100.00	60.00
❑ 41A Otis Crandall (Otis)	250.00	150.00
❑ 41B Otis Crandall (Olis)	150.00	90.00
❑ 42 Lou Criger	100.00	60.00
❑ 43 Bill Dahlen	400.00	250.00
❑ 44 Jake Daubert	100.00	60.00
❑ 45 Jim Delahanty	100.00	60.00
❑ 46 Art Devlin	100.00	60.00

❑ 47 Josh Devore 100.00 60.00
❑ 48 Walt Dickson 100.00 60.00
❑ 49 Jiggs Donohue 400.00 250.00
❑ 50 Red Dooin 100.00 60.00
❑ 51 Mickey Doolan 100.00 60.00
❑ 52A Patsy Dougherty Red 250.00 150.00
❑ 52B Patsy Dougherty White 250.00 150.00
❑ 53 Tom Downey 100.00 60.00
❑ 54 Larry Doyle 100.00 60.00
❑ 55 Hugh Duffy 300.00 175.00
❑ 56 Jack Dunn 300.00 175.00
❑ 57 Jimmy Dygert 100.00 60.00
❑ 58 Dick Egan 100.00 60.00
❑ 59 Kid Elberfeld 100.00 60.00
❑ 60 Clyde Engle 100.00 60.00
❑ 61 Steve Evans 100.00 60.00
❑ 62 Johnny Evers 500.00 300.00
❑ 63 Bob Ewing 100.00 60.00
❑ 64 George Ferguson 100.00 60.00
❑ 65 Ray Fisher 300.00 175.00
❑ 66 Art Fletcher 100.00 60.00
❑ 67 John Flynn 100.00 60.00
❑ 68 Russ Ford Dark Cap 100.00 60.00
❑ 69 Russ Ford Light Cap 400.00 250.00
❑ 70 Bill Foxen 100.00 60.00
❑ 71 James Frick 250.00 150.00
❑ 72 Art Fromme 100.00 60.00
❑ 73 Earl Gardner 100.00 60.00
❑ 74 Harry Gaspar 100.00 60.00
❑ 75 George Gibson 100.00 60.00
❑ 76 Wilbur Good 100.00 60.00
❑ 77 P.Graham Cubs 400.00 250.00
❑ 78 P.Graham Rustlers 100.00 60.00
❑ 79 Eddie Grant 400.00 250.00
❑ 80A Dolly Gray w/o Stats 250.00 150.00
❑ 80B Dolly Gray w/Stats 1000.00 600.00
❑ 81 Clark Griffith 300.00 175.00
❑ 82 Bob Groom 100.00 60.00
❑ 83 Charles Hanford 250.00 150.00
❑ 84 Bob Harmon Both Ears 100.00 60.00
❑ 85 Bob Harmon Left Ear 400.00 250.00
❑ 86 Topsy Hartsel 100.00 60.00
❑ 87 Arnold Hauser 100.00 60.00
❑ 88 Charlie Hemphill 100.00 60.00
❑ 89 Buck Herzog 100.00 60.00
❑ 90A D.Hoblitzell No Stats 12000.007000.00
❑ 90B D.Hoblitzell w/CIN 150.00 90.00
❑ 90C D.Hoblitzell (Hoblitzel) 600.00 350.00
❑ 90D D.Hoblitzell w/o CIN 600.00 350.00
❑ 91 Danny Hoffman 100.00 60.00
❑ 92 Miller Huggins 300.00 175.00
❑ 93 John Hummell 100.00 60.00
❑ 94 Fred Jacklitsch 100.00 60.00
❑ 95 Hughie Jennings 300.00 175.00
❑ 96 Walter Johnson 1800.001000.00
❑ 97 Davy Jones 100.00 60.00
❑ 98 Tom Jones 100.00 60.00
❑ 99 Addie Joss 1500.00 900.00
❑ 100 Ed Karger 400.00 250.00
❑ 101 Ed Killian 100.00 60.00
❑ 102 Red Kleinow 400.00 250.00
❑ 103 John Kling 100.00 60.00
❑ 104 John Knight 100.00 60.00
❑ 105 Ed Konetchy 100.00 60.00
❑ 106 Harry Krause 100.00 60.00
❑ 107 Rube Kroh 100.00 60.00
❑ 108 Frank Lang 100.00 60.00
❑ 109 Frank LaPorte 100.00 60.00
❑ 110A Arlie Latham (A.) 200.00 125.00
❑ 110B Arlie Latham (W.A.) 400.00 250.00
❑ 111 Tommy Leach 100.00 60.00
❑ 112 Wyatt Lee 150.00 90.00
❑ 113 Sam Leever 100.00 60.00
❑ 114A Lefty Leifield (A.) 250.00 150.00
❑ 114B Lefty Leifield (A.P.) 400.00 250.00
❑ 115 Ed Lennox 100.00 60.00
❑ 116 Paddy Livingston 100.00 60.00
❑ 117 Hans Lobert 100.00 60.00
❑ 118 Bris Lord 100.00 60.00
❑ 119 Harry Lord 100.00 60.00
❑ 120 John Lush 100.00 60.00
❑ 121 Nick Maddox 100.00 60.00
❑ 122 Sherry Magee 100.00 60.00
❑ 123 Rube Marquard 300.00 175.00
❑ 124 Christy Mathewson 1800.001000.00
❑ 125 Al Mattern 100.00 60.00

❑ 126 Lewis McAllister 150.00 90.00
❑ 127 George McBride 100.00 60.00
❑ 128 Amby McConnell 100.00 60.00
❑ 129 Pryor McElveen 100.00 60.00
❑ 130 John McGraw MG 300.00 175.00
❑ 131 Harry McIntire 100.00 60.00
❑ 132 Matty McIntyre 100.00 60.00
❑ 133 Larry McLean 100.00 60.00
❑ 134 Fred Merkle 100.00 60.00
❑ 135 George Merritt 250.00 150.00
❑ 136 Chief Meyers 100.00 60.00
❑ 137 Clyde Milan 100.00 60.00
❑ 138 Dots Miller 100.00 60.00
❑ 139 Mike Mitchell 100.00 60.00
❑ 140A Pat Moran Extra Stat 1500.00 900.00
❑ 140B Pat Moran 100.00 60.00
❑ 141 George Moriarty 100.00 60.00
❑ 142 George Mullin 100.00 60.00
❑ 143 Danny Murphy 100.00 60.00
❑ 144 Red Murray 100.00 60.00
❑ 145 John Nee 250.00 150.00
❑ 146 Tom Needham 100.00 60.00
❑ 147 Rebel Oakes 100.00 60.00
❑ 148 Rube Oldring 100.00 60.00
❑ 149 Charley O'Leary 100.00 60.00
❑ 150 Fred Olmstead 100.00 60.00
❑ 151 Orval Overall 100.00 60.00
❑ 152 Freddy Parent 100.00 60.00
❑ 153 Dode Paskert 100.00 60.00
❑ 154 Fred Payne 100.00 60.00
❑ 155 Barney Pelty 100.00 60.00
❑ 156 Jack Pfiester 100.00 60.00
❑ 157 James Phelan 250.00 150.00
❑ 158 Ed Phelps 100.00 60.00
❑ 159 Decon Phillippe 100.00 60.00
❑ 160 Jack Quinn 100.00 60.00
❑ 161 Bugs Raymond 400.00 250.00
❑ 162 Ed Reulbach 100.00 60.00
❑ 163 Lewis Richie 100.00 60.00
❑ 164 Jack Rowan 300.00 175.00
❑ 165 Nap Rucker 100.00 60.00
❑ 166 Doc Scanlan 400.00 250.00
❑ 167 Germany Schaefer 100.00 60.00
❑ 168 Admiral Schlei 100.00 60.00
❑ 169 Boss Schmidt 100.00 60.00
❑ 170 Wildfire Schulte 100.00 60.00
❑ 171 Jim Scott 100.00 60.00
❑ 172 Bayard Sharpe 100.00 60.00
❑ 173 David Shean Cubs 300.00 175.00
❑ 174 David Shean Rustlers 100.00 60.00
❑ 175 Jimmy Sheckard 100.00 60.00
❑ 176 Hack Simmons 100.00 60.00
❑ 177 Tony Smith 100.00 60.00
❑ 178 Fred Snodgrass 100.00 60.00
❑ 179 Tris Speaker 800.00 500.00
❑ 180 Jake Stahl 100.00 60.00
❑ 181 Oscar Stanage 100.00 60.00
❑ 182 Harry Steinfeldt 100.00 60.00
❑ 183 George Stone 100.00 60.00
❑ 184 George Stovall 100.00 60.00
❑ 185 Gabby Street 100.00 60.00
❑ 186 George Suggs 400.00 250.00
❑ 187 Ed Summers 100.00 60.00
❑ 188 Jeff Sweeney 400.00 250.00
❑ 189 Lee Tannehill 100.00 60.00
❑ 190 Ira Thomas 100.00 60.00
❑ 191 Joe Tinker 300.00 175.00
❑ 192 John Titus 100.00 60.00
❑ 193 Terry Turner 400.00 250.00
❑ 194 Hippo Vaughn 500.00 300.00
❑ 195 Heinie Wagner 300.00 175.00
❑ 196 B.Wallace w/cap 250.00 150.00
❑ 197A B.Wallace w/o Cap 1 Line 2000.00 1200.00
❑ 197B B.Wallace w/o Cap 2 Lines 1200.00 700.00
❑ 198 Ed Walsh 800.00 500.00
❑ 199 Zach Wheat 300.00 175.00
❑ 200 Doc White 100.00 60.00
❑ 201 Kirby White 400.00 250.00
❑ 202A Irvin K. Wilhelm 600.00 350.00
❑ 202B Irvin K. Wilhelm Missing Letter 300.00 175.00
❑ 203 Ed Willett 100.00 60.00
❑ 204 Owen Wilson 100.00 60.00
❑ 205 H.Wiltse Both Ears 100.00 60.00
❑ 206 H.Wiltse Right Ear 400.00 250.00
❑ 207 Harry Wolter 100.00 60.00
❑ 208 Cy Young 1800.001000.00

1909-11 T206

❑ COMPLETE SET (520) 55000.0030000.00
❑ COMMON MAJOR (1-389) 100.00 50.00
❑ COMMON MINOR (390-475) 100.00 50.00
❑ COM. SO. LEA. (476-523) 250.00 125.00
❑ CARDS PRICED IN EXMT CONDITION
❑ HONUS WAGNER PRICED IN GOOD CONDITION
❑ 1 Ed Abbaticchio Blue 135.00 85.00
❑ 2 Ed Abbaticchio Brown 135.00 85.00
❑ 3 Fred Abbott 100.00 60.00
❑ 4 Bill Abstein 100.00 60.00
❑ 5 Doc Adkins 200.00 125.00
❑ 6 Whitey Alperman 100.00 60.00
❑ 7 Red Ames Hands at 250.00 150.00
❑ 8 Red Ames Hands over 100.00 60.00
❑ 9 Red Ames Portrait 100.00 60.00
❑ 10 John Anderson 100.00 60.00
❑ 11 Frank Arellanes 100.00 60.00
❑ 12 Herman Armbruster 100.00 60.00
❑ 13 Harry Arndt 120.00 70.00
❑ 14 Jake Atz 100.00 60.00
❑ 15 Home Run Baker 400.00 250.00
❑ 16 Neal Ball Cleveland 100.00 60.00
❑ 17 Neal Ball New York 100.00 60.00
❑ 18 Jap Barbeau 100.00 60.00
❑ 19 Cy Barger 100.00 60.00
❑ 20 Jack Barry 100.00 60.00
❑ 21 Shad Barry 100.00 60.00
❑ 22 Jack Bastian 300.00 175.00
❑ 23 Emil Batch 100.00 60.00
❑ 24 Johnny Bates 100.00 60.00
❑ 25 Harry Bay 300.00 175.00
❑ 26 Ginger Beaumont 100.00 60.00
❑ 27 Fred Beck 100.00 60.00
❑ 28 Beals Becker 100.00 60.00
❑ 29 Jake Beckley 300.00 175.00
❑ 30 George Bell Follow 100.00 60.00
❑ 31 George Bell Hands above 100.00 60.00
❑ 32 Chief Bender Pitching 400.00 250.00
❑ 33 Chief Bender Pitching Trees 400.00 250.00
❑ 34 Chief Bender Portrait 500.00 300.00
❑ 35 Bill Bergen Batting 100.00 60.00
❑ 36 Bill Bergen Catching 100.00 60.00
❑ 37 Heinie Berger 100.00 60.00
❑ 38 Bill Bernhard 300.00 175.00
❑ 39 Bob Bescher Hands 100.00 60.00
❑ 40 Bob Bescher Portrait 100.00 60.00
❑ 41 Joe Birmingham 150.00 90.00
❑ 42 Lena Blackburne 100.00 60.00
❑ 43 Jack Bliss 100.00 60.00
❑ 44 Frank Bowerman 100.00 60.00
❑ 45 Bill Bradley with Bat 100.00 60.00
❑ 46 Bill Bradley Portrait 100.00 60.00
❑ 47 David Brain 100.00 60.00
❑ 48 Kitty Bransfield 100.00 60.00
❑ 49 Roy Brashear 100.00 60.00
❑ 50 Ted Breitenstein 300.00 175.00
❑ 51 Roger Bresnahan Portrait 300.00175.00
❑ 52 Roger Bresnahan with Bat 300.00175.00
❑ 53 Al Bridwell No Cap 100.00 60.00
❑ 54 Al Bridwell with Cap 100.00 60.00
❑ 55 George Brown Chicago 200.00 125.00
❑ 56 George Brown Washington 500.00 300.00
❑ 57 Mordecai Brown Chicago 350.00 200.00
❑ 58 Mordecai Brown Cubs 600.00 350.00
❑ 59 Mordecai Brown Portrait 500.00 300.00
❑ 60 Al Burch Batting 200.00 125.00

❑ 61	Al Burch Fielding	100.00	60.00
❑ 62	Fred Burchell	100.00	60.00
❑ 63	Jimmy Burke	100.00	60.00
❑ 64	Bill Burns	100.00	60.00
❑ 65	Donie Bush	100.00	60.00
❑ 66	John Butler	100.00	60.00
❑ 67	Bobby Byrne	100.00	60.00
❑ 68	Howie Camnitz Arm at Side	100.00	60.00
❑ 69	Howie Camnitz Folded	100.00	60.00
❑ 70	Howie Camnitz Hands	100.00	60.00
❑ 71	Billy Campbell	100.00	60.00
❑ 72	Scoops Carey	300.00	175.00
❑ 73	Charley Carr	100.00	60.00
❑ 74	Bill Carrigan	100.00	60.00
❑ 75	Doc Casey	100.00	60.00
❑ 76	Peter Cassidy	100.00	60.00
❑ 77	Frank Chance Batting	400.00	250.00
❑ 78	F.Chance Portrait Red	500.00	300.00
❑ 79	F.Chance Portrait Yel	400.00	250.00
❑ 80	Bill Chappelle	100.00	60.00
❑ 81	Chappie Charles	100.00	60.00
❑ 82	Hal Chase Dark Cap	150.00	90.00
❑ 83	Hal Chase Holding Trophy	250.00	150.00
❑ 84	Hal Chase Portrait Blue	150.00	90.00
❑ 85	Hal Chase Portrait Pink	400.00	250.00
❑ 86	Hal Chase White Cap	200.00	125.00
❑ 87	Jack Chesbro	400.00	250.00
❑ 88	Ed Cicotte	300.00	175.00
❑ 89	Bill Clancy (Clancey)	100.00	60.00
❑ 90	Fred Clarke Holding Bat	400.00	250.00
❑ 91	Fred Clarke Portrait	400.00	250.00
❑ 92	Josh Clark (Clarke) ML	100.00	60.00
❑ 93	J.J. (Nig) Clarke	100.00	60.00
❑ 94	Bill Clymer	100.00	60.00
❑ 95	Ty Cobb Bat off Shoulder	2500.00	1500.00
❑ 96	Ty Cobb Bat on Shoulder	2500.00	1500.00
❑ 97	Ty Cobb Portrait Green	5000.00	3500.00
❑ 98	Ty Cobb Portrait Red	2000.00	1200.00
❑ 99	Cad Coles	300.00	175.00
❑ 100	Eddie Collins	350.00	200.00
❑ 101	Jimmy Collins	300.00	175.00
❑ 102	Bunk Congalton	100.00	60.00
❑ 103	Wid Conroy Fielding	100.00	60.00
❑ 104	Wid Conroy with Bat	100.00	60.00
❑ 105	Harry Covaleski (Coveleski)	100.00	60.00
❑ 106	Doc Crandall No Cap	100.00	60.00
❑ 107	Doc Crandall with Cap	100.00	60.00
❑ 108	Bill Cranston	300.00	175.00
❑ 109	Gavvy Cravath	100.00	60.00
❑ 110	Sam Crawford Throwing	400.00	250.00
❑ 111	Sam Crawford with Bat	400.00	250.00
❑ 112	Birdie Cree	100.00	60.00
❑ 113	Lou Criger	100.00	60.00
❑ 114	Dode Criss	100.00	60.00
❑ 115	Monte Cross	100.00	60.00
❑ 116	Bill Dahlen Boston	150.00	90.00
❑ 117	Bill Dahlen Brooklyn	500.00	300.00
❑ 118	Paul Davidson	100.00	60.00
❑ 119	George Davis	300.00	175.00
❑ 120	Harry Davis (Davis on Front)	100.00	60.00
❑ 121	Harry Davis (H.Davis on Front)	100.00	60.00
❑ 122	Frank Delehanty	100.00	60.00
❑ 123	Jim Delehanty	100.00	60.00
❑ 124	Ray Demmitt New York	120.00	70.00
❑ 125	Ray Demmitt St. Louis	10000.00	6000.00
❑ 126	Rube Dessau	135.00	85.00
❑ 127	Art Devlin	100.00	60.00
❑ 128	Josh Devore	100.00	60.00
❑ 129	Bill Dineen	100.00	60.00
❑ 130	Mike Donlin Fielding	200.00	125.00
❑ 131	Mike Donlin Sitting	100.00	60.00
❑ 132	Mike Donlin with Bat	100.00	60.00
❑ 133	Jiggs Donahue (Donohue)	100.00	60.00
❑ 134	Wild Bill Donovan Portrait	100.00	60.00
❑ 135	Wild Bill Donovan Throwing	100.00	60.00
❑ 136	Red Dooin	100.00	60.00
❑ 137	Mickey Doolan Batting	100.00	60.00
❑ 138	Mickey Doolan Fielding	100.00	60.00
❑ 139	Mickey Doolin (Doolan)	100.00	60.00
❑ 140	Gus Dorner	100.00	60.00
❑ 141	Patsy Dougherty Arm in Air	100.00	60.00
❑ 142	Patsy Dougherty Portrait	100.00	60.00
❑ 143	Tom Downey Batting	100.00	60.00
❑ 144	Tom Downey Fielding	100.00	60.00
❑ 145	Jerry Downs	100.00	60.00
❑ 146	Joe Doyle	600.00	350.00
❑ 147	Joe Doyle Nat'l		
❑ 148	Larry Doyle Portrait	100.00	60.00
❑ 149	Larry Doyle Throwing	100.00	60.00
❑ 150	Larry Doyle with Bat	100.00	60.00
❑ 151	Jean Dubuc	100.00	60.00
❑ 152	Hugh Duffy	300.00	175.00
❑ 153	Jack Dunn Baltimore	100.00	60.00
❑ 154	Joe Dunn Brooklyn	100.00	60.00
❑ 155	Bull Durham	100.00	60.00
❑ 156	Jimmy Dygert	100.00	60.00
❑ 157	Ted Easterly	100.00	60.00
❑ 158	Dick Egan	150.00	90.00
❑ 159	Kid Elberfeld Fielding	100.00	60.00
❑ 160	Kid Elberfeld Port NY	100.00	60.00
❑ 161	Kid Elberfeld Port Wash	3000.00	1800.00
❑ 162	Roy Ellam	300.00	175.00
❑ 163	Clyde Engle	100.00	60.00
❑ 164	Steve Evans	100.00	60.00
❑ 165	J.Evers Portrait	600.00	350.00
❑ 166	J.Evers Chi Shirt	400.00	250.00
❑ 167	J.Evers Cubs Shirt	800.00	500.00
❑ 168	Bob Ewing	100.00	60.00
❑ 169	Cecil Ferguson	100.00	60.00
❑ 170	Hobe Ferris	100.00	60.00
❑ 171	Lou Fiene Portrait	100.00	60.00
❑ 172	Lou Fiene Throwing	100.00	60.00
❑ 173	Steamer Flanagan	100.00	60.00
❑ 174	Art Fletcher	100.00	60.00
❑ 175	Elmer Flick	300.00	175.00
❑ 176	Russ Ford	100.00	60.00
❑ 177	Ed Foster	300.00	175.00
❑ 178	Jerry Freeman	100.00	60.00
❑ 179	John Frill	100.00	60.00
❑ 180	Charlie Fritz	300.00	175.00
❑ 181	Art Fromme	100.00	60.00
❑ 182	Chick Gandil	300.00	175.00
❑ 183	Bob Ganley	100.00	60.00
❑ 184	John Ganzel	100.00	60.00
❑ 185	Harry Gasper (Gaspar)	100.00	60.00
❑ 186	Rube Geyer	100.00	60.00
❑ 187	George Gibson	100.00	60.00
❑ 188	Billy Gilbert	100.00	60.00
❑ 189	Wilbur Goode (Good)	100.00	60.00
❑ 190	Bill Graham St. Louis	100.00	60.00
❑ 191	Peaches Graham	120.00	70.00
❑ 192	Dolly Gray	100.00	60.00
❑ 193	Ed Greminger	300.00	175.00
❑ 194	Clark Griffith Batting	300.00	175.00
❑ 195	Clark Griffith Portrait	300.00	175.00
❑ 196	Moose Grimshaw	100.00	60.00
❑ 197	Bob Groom	100.00	60.00
❑ 198	Tom Guiheen	300.00	175.00
❑ 199	Ed Hahn	100.00	60.00
❑ 200	Bob Hall	100.00	60.00
❑ 201	Bill Hallman	100.00	60.00
❑ 202	Jack Hannifan (Hannifin)	100.00	60.00
❑ 203	Bill Hart Little Rock	300.00	175.00
❑ 204	Jimmy Hart Montgomery	300.00	175.00
❑ 205	Topsy Hartsel	100.00	60.00
❑ 206	Jack Hayden	100.00	60.00
❑ 207	J.Ross Helm	300.00	175.00
❑ 208	Charlie Hemphill	100.00	60.00
❑ 209	Buck Herzog Boston	100.00	60.00
❑ 210	Buck Herzog New York	100.00	60.00
❑ 211	Gordon Hickman	300.00	175.00
❑ 212	Bill Hinchman	100.00	60.00
❑ 213	Harry Hinchman	100.00	60.00
❑ 214	Doc Hoblitzell	100.00	60.00
❑ 215	Danny Hoffman St. Louis	100.00	60.00
❑ 216	Izzy Hoffman Providence	100.00	60.00
❑ 217	Solly Hofman	100.00	60.00
❑ 218	Buck Hooker	300.00	175.00
❑ 219	Del Howard Chicago	100.00	60.00
❑ 220	Ernie Howard Savannah	300.00	175.00
❑ 221	Harry Howell Hand at Waist	100.00	60.00
❑ 222	Harry Howell Portrait	100.00	60.00
❑ 223	M.Huggins Mouth	300.00	175.00
❑ 224	M.Huggins Portrait	300.00	175.00
❑ 225	Rudy Hulswitt	100.00	60.00
❑ 226	John Hummel	100.00	60.00
❑ 227	George Hunter	100.00	60.00
❑ 228	Frank Isbell	100.00	60.00
❑ 229	Fred Jacklitsch	100.00	60.00
❑ 230	Jimmy Jackson	100.00	60.00
❑ 231	H.Jennings Both	300.00	175.00
❑ 232	H.Jennings One	300.00	175.00
❑ 233	H.Jennings Portrait	300.00	175.00
❑ 234	Walter Johnson Hands	1200.00	700.00
❑ 235	Walter Johnson Port	1800.00	1000.00
❑ 236	Davy Jones Detroit	100.00	60.00
❑ 237	Fielder Jones Hands at Hips	100.00	60.00
❑ 238	Fielder Jones Portrait	100.00	60.00
❑ 239	Tom Jones St. Louis	100.00	60.00
❑ 240	Dutch Jordan Atlanta	300.00	175.00
❑ 241	Tim Jordan Batting	100.00	60.00
❑ 242	Tim Jordan Portrait	100.00	60.00
❑ 243	Addie Joss Pitching	300.00	175.00
❑ 244	Addie Joss Portrait	400.00	250.00
❑ 245	Ed Karger	100.00	60.00
❑ 246	Willie Keeler Portrait	600.00	350.00
❑ 247	Willie Keeler Batting	600.00	350.00
❑ 248	Joe Kelley	250.00	150.00
❑ 249	J.F. Kiernan	500.00	300.00
❑ 250	Ed Killian Pitching	100.00	60.00
❑ 251	Ed Killian Portrait	100.00	60.00
❑ 252	Frank King	300.00	175.00
❑ 253	Rube Kisinger (Kissinger)	100.00	60.00
❑ 254	Red Kleinow Boston	500.00	300.00
❑ 255	Red Kleinow NY Catch	100.00	60.00
❑ 256	Red Kleinow NY Bat	100.00	60.00
❑ 257	Johnny Kling	100.00	60.00
❑ 258	Otto Knabe	100.00	60.00
❑ 259	Jack Knight Portrait	100.00	60.00
❑ 260	Jack Knight with Bat	100.00	60.00
❑ 261	Ed Konetchy Glove Lo	100.00	60.00
❑ 262	Ed Konetchy Glove Hi	100.00	60.00
❑ 263	Harry Krause Pitching	100.00	60.00
❑ 264	Harry Krause Portrait	100.00	60.00
❑ 265	Rube Kroh	100.00	60.00
❑ 266	Otto Kruger (Krueger)	100.00	60.00
❑ 267	James LaFitte	300.00	175.00
❑ 268	Nap Lajoie Portrait	800.00	500.00
❑ 269	Nap Lajoie Throwing	700.00	400.00
❑ 270	Nap Lajoie with Bat	700.00	400.00
❑ 271	Joe Lake NY	100.00	60.00
❑ 272	Joe Lake Stl No Ball	100.00	60.00
❑ 273	Joe Lake Stl with Ball	100.00	60.00
❑ 274	Frank LaPorte	100.00	60.00
❑ 275	Arlie Latham	100.00	60.00
❑ 276	Bill Lattimore	100.00	60.00
❑ 277	Jimmy Lavender	100.00	60.00
❑ 278	Tommy Leach Bending Over	100.00	60.00
❑ 279	Tommy Leach Portrait	100.00	60.00
❑ 280	Lefty Leifield Batting	100.00	60.00
❑ 281	Lefty Leifield Pitching	100.00	60.00
❑ 282	Ed Lennox	100.00	60.00
❑ 283	Harry Lentz (Sentz) SL	400.00	250.00
❑ 284	Glenn Liebhardt	100.00	60.00
❑ 285	Vive Lindaman	100.00	60.00
❑ 286	Perry Lipe	300.00	175.00
❑ 287	Paddy Livingstone (Livingston)	100.00	60.00
❑ 288	Hans Lobert	100.00	60.00
❑ 289	Harry Lord	100.00	60.00
❑ 290	Harry Lumley	100.00	60.00
❑ 291	Carl Lundgren Chicago	800.00	500.00
❑ 292	Carl Lundgren Kansas City	200.00	125.00
❑ 293	Nick Maddox	100.00	60.00
❑ 294	Sherry Magee with Bat	100.00	60.00
❑ 295	Sherry Magee Portrait	250.00	150.00
❑ 296	Sherry Magie Portrait EHH	25000.00	15000.00
❑ 297	Bill Malarkey	100.00	60.00
❑ 298	Bill Maloney	100.00	60.00
❑ 299	George Manion	300.00	175.00
❑ 300	Rube Manning Batting	100.00	60.00
❑ 301	Rube Manning Pitching	100.00	60.00
❑ 302	R.Marquard Follow	300.00	175.00
❑ 303	R.Marquard Hands	300.00	175.00
❑ 304	R.Marquard Portrait	350.00	200.00
❑ 305	Doc Marshall	100.00	60.00
❑ 306	C.Mathewson Drk Cap	1200.00	700.00
❑ 307	C.Mathewson Portrait	1500.00	900.00
❑ 308	C.Mathewson Wht Cap	1500.00	900.00
❑ 309	Al Mattern	100.00	60.00
❑ 310	John McAleese	100.00	60.00
❑ 311	George McBride	100.00	60.00
❑ 312	Pat McCauley	300.00	175.00
❑ 313	Moose McCormick	100.00	60.00
❑ 314	Pryor McElveen	100.00	60.00
❑ 315	Dennis McGann	100.00	60.00
❑ 316	Jim McGinley	100.00	60.00
❑ 317	Iron Man McGinnity	300.00	175.00
❑ 318	Stoney McGlynn	100.00	60.00

Card		
❑ 319 J.McGraw Finger	400.00	250.00
❑ 320 J.McGraw Glove-Hip	400.00	250.00
❑ 321 J.McGraw w/o Cap	400.00	250.00
❑ 322 J.McGraw w/Cap	400.00	250.00
❑ 323 Harry McIntyre Brooklyn	100.00	60.00
❑ 324 Harry McIntyre Brooklyn-Chicago	100.00	60.00
❑ 325 Matty McIntyre Detroit	100.00	60.00
❑ 326 Larry McLean	100.00	60.00
❑ 327 George McQuillan Ball in Hand	100.00	60.00
❑ 328 George McQuillan with Bat	100.00	60.00
❑ 329 Fred Merkle Portrait	120.00	70.00
❑ 330 Fred Merkle Throwing	150.00	90.00
❑ 331 George Merritt	100.00	60.00
❑ 332 Chief Meyers	100.00	60.00
❑ 333 Chief Myers Batting (Meyers)	120.00	70.00
❑ 334 Chief Myers Fielding (Meyers)	100.00	60.00
❑ 335 Clyde Milan	100.00	60.00
❑ 336 Molly Miller Dallas	300.00	175.00
❑ 337 Dots Miller Pittsburgh	100.00	60.00
❑ 338 Bill Milligan	100.00	60.00
❑ 339 Fred Mitchell Toronto	100.00	60.00
❑ 340 Mike Mitchell Cincinnati	100.00	60.00
❑ 341 Dan Moeller	100.00	60.00
❑ 342 Carleton Molesworth	300.00	175.00
❑ 343 Herbie Moran Providence	100.00	60.00
❑ 344 Pat Moran Chicago	100.00	60.00
❑ 345 George Moriarty	100.00	60.00
❑ 346 Mike Mowrey	100.00	60.00
❑ 347 Dom Mullaney	300.00	175.00
❑ 348 George Mullen (Mullin)	100.00	60.00
❑ 349 George Mullin with Bat	100.00	60.00
❑ 350 George Mullin Throwing	100.00	60.00
❑ 351 Danny Murphy Batting	100.00	60.00
❑ 352 Danny Murphy Throwing	100.00	60.00
❑ 353 Red Murray Batting	100.00	60.00
❑ 354 Red Murray Portrait	100.00	60.00
❑ 355 Billy Nattress	100.00	60.00
❑ 356 Tom Needham	100.00	60.00
❑ 357 Simon Nicholls Hands on Knees	100.00	60.00
❑ 358 Simon Nichols Batting (Nicholls)	100.00	60.00
❑ 359 Harry Niles	100.00	60.00
❑ 360 Rebel Oakes	100.00	60.00
❑ 361 Frank Oberlin	100.00	60.00
❑ 362 Peter O'Brien	100.00	60.00
❑ 363 Bill O'Hara NY	100.00	60.00
❑ 364 Bill O'Hara Stl	10000.00	6000.00
❑ 365 Rube Oldring Batting	100.00	60.00
❑ 366 Rube Oldring Fielding	100.00	60.00
❑ 367 Charley O'Leary Hands on Knees	100.00	60.00
❑ 368 Charley O'Leary Portrait	100.00	60.00
❑ 369 William O'Neil	250.00	150.00
❑ 370 Albert Orth	300.00	175.00
❑ 371 William Otey	300.00	175.00
❑ 372 Orval Overall Hand at Face	100.00	60.00
❑ 373 Orval Overall Hands at Waist	100.00	60.00
❑ 374 Orval Overall Portrait	100.00	60.00
❑ 375 Frank Owen (Owens)	100.00	60.00
❑ 376 George Paige	300.00	175.00
❑ 377 Fred Parent	100.00	60.00
❑ 378 Dode Paskert	100.00	60.00
❑ 379 Jim Pastorius	100.00	60.00
❑ 380 Harry Pattee	100.00	60.00
❑ 381 Fred Payne	100.00	60.00
❑ 382 Barney Pelty Horizontal	100.00	60.00
❑ 383 Barney Pelty Vertical	100.00	60.00
❑ 384 Hub Perdue	300.00	175.00
❑ 385 George Perring	100.00	60.00
❑ 386 Arch Persons	300.00	175.00
❑ 387 Francis Pfeffer	100.00	60.00
❑ 388 Jake Pfeister Seated (Pfiester)	100.00	60.00
❑ 389 Jake Pfeister Throwing (Pfiester)	100.00	60.00
❑ 390 Jimmy Phelan	100.00	60.00
❑ 391 Eddie Phelps	100.00	60.00
❑ 392 Deacon Phillippe	100.00	60.00
❑ 393 Ollie Pickering	100.00	60.00
❑ 394 Eddie Plank	60000.00	45000.00
❑ 395 Phil Poland	100.00	60.00
❑ 396 Jack Powell	100.00	60.00
❑ 397 Mike Powers	100.00	60.00
❑ 398 Billy Purtell	100.00	60.00
❑ 399 Ambrose Puttman (Puttmann)	135.00	85.00
❑ 400 Lee Quillen (Quillin)	100.00	60.00
❑ 401 Jack Quinn	100.00	60.00
❑ 402 Newt Randall	100.00	60.00
❑ 403 Bugs Raymond	100.00	60.00
❑ 404 Ed Reagan	300.00	175.00
❑ 405 Ed Reulbach Glove	100.00	60.00
❑ 406 Ed Reulbach No Glove	120.00	70.00
❑ 407 Dutch Revelle	300.00	175.00
❑ 408 Bob Rhoades Hands	100.00	60.00
❑ 409 Bob Rhoades Right	100.00	60.00
❑ 410 Charlie Rhodes	100.00	60.00
❑ 411 Claude Ritchey	100.00	60.00
❑ 412 Lou Ritter	100.00	60.00
❑ 413 Ike Rockenfeld	300.00	175.00
❑ 414 Claude Rossman	100.00	60.00
❑ 415 Nap Rucker Portrait	100.00	60.00
❑ 416 Nap Rucker Throwing	100.00	60.00
❑ 417 Dick Rudolph	100.00	60.00
❑ 418 Ray Ryan	300.00	175.00
❑ 419 Germany Schaefer Det	100.00	60.00
❑ 420 Germany Schaefer Wash	100.00	60.00
❑ 421 George Schirm	135.00	85.00
❑ 422 Larry Schlafly	100.00	60.00
❑ 423 Admiral Schlei Batting	100.00	60.00
❑ 424 Admiral Schlei Catching	100.00	60.00
❑ 425 Admiral Schlei Portrait	100.00	60.00
❑ 426 Boss Schmidt Portrait	100.00	60.00
❑ 427 Boss Schmidt Throwing	100.00	60.00
❑ 428 Ossee Schreck (Schreckengost)	120.00	70.00
❑ 429 Wildfire Schulte Back View	100.00	60.00
❑ 430 Wildfire Schulte Front View	300.00	175.00
❑ 431 Jim Scott	100.00	60.00
❑ 432 Charles Seitz	300.00	175.00
❑ 433 Cy Seymour Batting	100.00	60.00
❑ 434 Cy Seymour Portrait	100.00	60.00
❑ 435 Cy Seymour Throwing	100.00	60.00
❑ 436 Spike Shannon	100.00	60.00
❑ 437 Bud Sharpe	100.00	60.00
❑ 437B Bud Shappe ERR (Sharpe) ML		
❑ 438 Shag Shaughnessy	300.00	175.00
❑ 439 Al Shaw St. Louis	100.00	60.00
❑ 440 Hunky Shaw Providence	100.00	60.00
❑ 441 Jimmy Sheckard Glove	100.00	60.00
❑ 442 Jimmy Sheckard No Glove	100.00	60.00
❑ 443 Bill Shipke	100.00	60.00
❑ 444 Jimmy Slagle	100.00	60.00
❑ 445 Carlos Smith Shreveport	300.00	175.00
❑ 446 Frank Smith Chi-Bos	600.00	350.00
❑ 447 Frank Smith Chi F.Smith	100.00	60.00
❑ 448 Frank Smith Chi Whit Cap	100.00	60.00
❑ 449 Heinie Smith Buffalo	100.00	60.00
❑ 450 Happy Smith Brooklyn	100.00	60.00
❑ 451 Sid Smith Atlanta	300.00	175.00
❑ 452 F.Snodgrass Batting	100.00	60.00
❑ 452B F.nodgrass Batting ERR		
❑ 453 F.Snodgrass Catching	100.00	60.00
❑ 454 Bob Spade	100.00	60.00
❑ 455 Tris Speaker	1000.00	600.00
❑ 456 Tubby Spencer	100.00	60.00
❑ 457 Jake Stahl Glove	135.00	85.00
❑ 458 Jake Stahl No Glove	100.00	60.00
❑ 459 Oscar Stanage	100.00	60.00
❑ 460 Dolly Stark	300.00	175.00
❑ 461 Charlie Starr	100.00	60.00
❑ 462 Harry Steinfeldt with Bat	100.00	60.00
❑ 463 Harry Steinfeldt Portrait	100.00	60.00
❑ 464 Jim Stephens	100.00	60.00
❑ 465 George Stone	100.00	60.00
❑ 466 George Stovall Batting	100.00	60.00
❑ 467 George Stovall Portrait	100.00	60.00
❑ 468 Sam Strang	100.00	60.00
❑ 469 Gabby Street Catching	100.00	60.00
❑ 470 Gabby Street Portrait	100.00	60.00
❑ 471 Billy Sullivan	100.00	60.00
❑ 472 Ed Summers	100.00	60.00
❑ 473 Bill Sweeney Boston	100.00	60.00
❑ 474 Jeff Sweeney New York	100.00	60.00
❑ 475 Jesse Tannehill Washington	100.00	60.00
❑ 476 Lee Tannehill Chi L.Tannehill	100.00	60.00
❑ 477 Lee Tannehill Chi Tannehill	100.00	60.00
❑ 478 Dummy Taylor	100.00	60.00
❑ 479 Fred Tenney	100.00	60.00
❑ 480 Tony Thebo	300.00	175.00
❑ 481 Jake Thielman	150.00	90.00
❑ 482 Ira Thomas	100.00	60.00
❑ 483 Woodie Thornton	300.00	175.00
❑ 484 J.Tinker Bat off Shldr	400.00	250.00
❑ 485 J.Tinker Bat on Shldr	400.00	400.00
❑ 486 J.Tinker Hand-Knee	600.00	350.00
❑ 487 J.Tinker Portrait	600.00	350.00
❑ 488 John Titus	100.00	60.00
❑ 489 Terry Turner	100.00	60.00
❑ 490 Bob Unglaub	100.00	60.00
❑ 491 Juan Violat (Viola)	300.00	175.00
❑ 492 R.Waddell Portrait	400.00	250.00
❑ 493 R.Waddell Throwing	400.00	250.00
❑ 494 Heinie Wagner on Left	100.00	60.00
❑ 495 Heinie Wagner on Right	100.00	60.00
❑ 496 Honus Wagner	300000.00	200000.00
❑ 497 Bobby Wallace	300.00	175.00
❑ 498 Ed Walsh	400.00	250.00
❑ 499 Jack Warhop	100.00	60.00
❑ 500 Jake Weimer	100.00	60.00
❑ 501 James Westlake	300.00	175.00
❑ 502 Zack Wheat	350.00	200.00
❑ 503 Doc White Pitching	100.00	60.00
❑ 504 Doc White Portrait	100.00	60.00
❑ 505 Foley White Houston	300.00	175.00
❑ 506 Jack White Buffalo	100.00	60.00
❑ 507 Kaiser Wilhelm Hands	100.00	60.00
❑ 508 Kaiser Wilhelm with Bat	100.00	60.00
❑ 509 Ed Willett with Bat	100.00	60.00
❑ 510 Ed Willetts Throwing (Willett)	100.00	60.00
❑ 511 Jimmy Williams	100.00	60.00
❑ 512 Vic Willis Pitt	350.00	200.00
❑ 513 Vic Willis Stl Throw	300.00	175.00
❑ 514 Vic Willis Stl Bat	300.00	175.00
❑ 515 Owen Wilson	100.00	60.00
❑ 516 Hooks Wiltse Pitching	100.00	60.00
❑ 517 Hooks Wiltse Portrait	100.00	60.00
❑ 518 Hooks Wiltse Sweater	100.00	60.00
❑ 519 Lucky Wright	100.00	60.00
❑ 520 Cy Young Bare Hand	1200.00	700.00
❑ 521 Cy Young w/Glove	1200.00	700.00
❑ 522 Cy Young Portrait	1800.00	1000.00
❑ 523 Irv Young Minneapolis	120.00	70.00
❑ 524 Heinie Zimmerman	100.00	60.00

1952 Topps

Card		
❑ COMP.MASTER SET (487)	80000.00	40000.00
❑ COMPLETE SET (407)	65000.00	40000.00
❑ COMMON CARD (1-80)	60.00	35.00
❑ COMMON CARD (81-250)	40.00	20.00
❑ COMMON CARD (251-310)	50.00	30.00
❑ COMMON CARD (311-407)	250.00	150.00
❑ WRAPPER (1-CENT)	250.00	200.00
❑ WRAPPER (5-CENT)	100.00	75.00
❑ 1 Andy Pafko	5000.00	3000.00
❑ 1A Andy Pafko Black	3000.00	1800.00
❑ 2 Pete Runnels RC	250.00	150.00
❑ 2A Pete Runnels Black	250.00	150.00
❑ 3 Hank Thompson	70.00	40.00
❑ 3A Hank Thompson Black	70.00	40.00
❑ 4 Don Lenhardt	60.00	35.00
❑ 4A Don Lenhardt Black	60.00	35.00
❑ 5 Larry Jansen	70.00	40.00
❑ 5A Larry Jansen Black	70.00	40.00
❑ 6 Grady Hatton	60.00	35.00
❑ 6A Grady Hatton Black	60.00	35.00
❑ 7 Wayne Terwilliger	60.00	35.00
❑ 7A Wayne Terwilliger Black	60.00	35.00
❑ 8 Fred Marsh RC	60.00	35.00
❑ 8A Fred Marsh Black	60.00	35.00
❑ 9 Robert Hogue RC	60.00	35.00
❑ 9A Robert Hogue Black	60.00	35.00
❑ 10 Al Rosen	70.00	40.00

❑ 10A Al Rosen Black 70.00 40.00
❑ 11 Phil Rizzuto 400.00 250.00
❑ 11A Phil Rizzuto Black 350.00 200.00
❑ 12 Monty Basgall RC 60.00 35.00
❑ 12A Monty Basgall Black 60.00 35.00
❑ 13 Johnny Wyrostek 60.00 35.00
❑ 13A Johnny Wyrostek Black 60.00 35.00
❑ 14 Bob Elliott 70.00 40.00
❑ 14A Bob Elliott Black 70.00 40.00
❑ 15 Johnny Pesky 70.00 40.00
❑ 15A Johnny Pesky Black 70.00 40.00
❑ 16 Gene Hermanski 60.00 35.00
❑ 16A Gene Hermanski Black 60.00 35.00
❑ 17 Jim Hegan 70.00 40.00
❑ 17A Jim Hegan Black 70.00 40.00
❑ 18 Merrill Combs RC 60.00 35.00
❑ 18A Merrill Combs Black 60.00 35.00
❑ 19 Johnny Bucha RC 60.00 35.00
❑ 19A Johnny Bucha Black 60.00 35.00
❑ 20 Billy Loes SP RC 150.00 90.00
❑ 20A Billy Loes Black 150.00 90.00
❑ 21 Ferris Fain 70.00 40.00
❑ 21A Ferris Fain Black 70.00 40.00
❑ 22 Dom DiMaggio 125.00 75.00
❑ 22A Dom DiMaggio Black 100.00 60.00
❑ 23 Billy Goodman 70.00 40.00
❑ 23A Billy Goodman Black 70.00 40.00
❑ 24 Luke Easter 80.00 50.00
❑ 24A Luke Easter Black 80.00 50.00
❑ 25 Johnny Groth 60.00 35.00
❑ 25A Johnny Groth Black 60.00 35.00
❑ 26 Monte Irvin 150.00 90.00
❑ 26A Monte Irvin Black 150.00 90.00
❑ 27 Sam Jethroe 70.00 40.00
❑ 27A Sam Jethroe Black 70.00 40.00
❑ 28 Jerry Priddy 60.00 35.00
❑ 28A Jerry Priddy Black 60.00 35.00
❑ 29 Ted Kluszewski 125.00 75.00
❑ 29A Ted Kluszewski Black 125.00 75.00
❑ 30 Mel Parnell 70.00 40.00
❑ 30A Mel Parnell Black 70.00 40.00
❑ 31 Gus Zernial Baseballs 80.00 50.00
❑ 31A Gus Zernial Black 80.00 50.00
❑ 32 Eddie Robinson 60.00 35.00
❑ 32A Eddie Robinson Black 60.00 35.00
❑ 33 Warren Spahn 300.00 175.00
❑ 33A Warren Spahn Black 300.00 175.00
❑ 34 Elmer Valo 60.00 35.00
❑ 34A Elmer Valo Black 60.00 35.00
❑ 35 Hank Sauer 70.00 40.00
❑ 35A Hank Sauer Black 70.00 40.00
❑ 36 Gil Hodges 300.00 175.00
❑ 36A Gil Hodges Black 300.00 175.00
❑ 37 Duke Snider 500.00 300.00
❑ 37A Duke Snider Black 500.00 300.00
❑ 38 Wally Westlake 60.00 35.00
❑ 38A Wally Westlake Black 60.00 35.00
❑ 39 Dizzy Trout 70.00 40.00
❑ 39A Dizzy Trout Black 70.00 40.00
❑ 40 Irv Noren 70.00 40.00
❑ 40A Irv Noren Black 70.00 40.00
❑ 41 Bob Wellman RC 60.00 35.00
❑ 41A Bob Wellman Black 60.00 35.00
❑ 42 Lou Kretlow RC 60.00 35.00
❑ 42A Lou Kretlow Black 60.00 35.00
❑ 43 Ray Scarborough 60.00 35.00
❑ 43A Ray Scarborough Black 60.00 35.00
❑ 44 Con Dempsey RC 60.00 35.00
❑ 44A Con Dempsey Black 60.00 35.00
❑ 45 Eddie Joost 60.00 35.00
❑ 45A Eddie Joost Black 60.00 35.00
❑ 46 Gordon Goldsberry RC 60.00 35.00
❑ 46A Gordon Goldsberry Black 60.00 35.00
❑ 47 Willie Jones 70.00 40.00
❑ 47A Willie Jones Black 70.00 40.00
❑ 48A Joe Page ERR BLA 400.00 250.00
❑ 48B Joe Page COR BLA 125.00 75.00
❑ 48C Joe Page COR Red 125.00 75.00
❑ 49A John Sain ERR BLA 400.00 250.00
❑ 49B John Sain COR BLA 125.00 75.00
❑ 49C Joe Page COR Red 125.00 75.00
❑ 50 Marv Rickert RC 60.00 35.00
❑ 50A Marv Rickert Black 60.00 35.00
❑ 51 Jim Russell 60.00 35.00
❑ 51A Jim Russell Black 60.00 35.00
❑ 52 Don Mueller 70.00 40.00
❑ 52A Don Mueller Black 70.00 40.00
❑ 53 Chris Van Cuyk RC 60.00 35.00
❑ 53A Chris Van Cuyk Black 60.00 35.00
❑ 54 Leo Kiely RC 60.00 35.00
❑ 54A Leo Kiely Black 60.00 35.00
❑ 55 Ray Boone 80.00 50.00
❑ 55A Ray Boone Black 80.00 50.00
❑ 56 Tommy Glaviano 60.00 35.00
❑ 56A Tommy Glaviano Black 60.00 35.00
❑ 57 Ed Lopat 100.00 60.00
❑ 57A Ed Lopat Black 100.00 60.00
❑ 58 Bob Mahoney RC 60.00 35.00
❑ 58A Bob Mahoney Black 60.00 35.00
❑ 59 Robin Roberts 175.00 100.00
❑ 59A Robin Roberts Black 175.00 100.00
❑ 60 Sid Hudson 60.00 35.00
❑ 60A Sid Hudson Black 60.00 35.00
❑ 61 Tookie Gilbert 60.00 35.00
❑ 61A Tookie Gilbert Black 60.00 35.00
❑ 62 Chuck Stobbs RC 60.00 35.00
❑ 62A Chuck Stobbs Black 60.00 35.00
❑ 63 Howie Pollet 60.00 35.00
❑ 63A Howie Pollet Black 60.00 35.00
❑ 64 Roy Sievers 70.00 40.00
❑ 64A Roy Sievers Black 70.00 40.00
❑ 65 Enos Slaughter 175.00 100.00
❑ 65A Enos Slaughter Black 175.00 100.00
❑ 66 Preacher Roe 100.00 60.00
❑ 66A Preacher Roe Black 100.00 60.00
❑ 67 Allie Reynolds 125.00 75.00
❑ 67A Allie Reynolds Black 125.00 75.00
❑ 68 Cliff Chambers 60.00 35.00
❑ 68A Cliff Chambers Black 60.00 35.00
❑ 69 Virgil Stallcup 60.00 35.00
❑ 69A Virgil Stallcup Black 60.00 35.00
❑ 70 Al Zarilla 60.00 35.00
❑ 70A Al Zarilla Black 60.00 35.00
❑ 71 Tom Upton RC 60.00 35.00
❑ 71A Tom Upton Black 60.00 35.00
❑ 72 Karl Olson RC 60.00 35.00
❑ 72A Karl Olson Black 60.00 35.00
❑ 73 Bill Werle 60.00 35.00
❑ 73A Bill Werle Black 60.00 35.00
❑ 74 Andy Hansen RC 60.00 35.00
❑ 74A Andy Hansen Black 60.00 35.00
❑ 75 Wes Westrum 70.00 40.00
❑ 75A Wes Westrum Black 70.00 40.00
❑ 76 Eddie Stanky 70.00 40.00
❑ 76A Eddie Stanky Black 70.00 40.00
❑ 77 Bob Kennedy 70.00 40.00
❑ 77A Bob Kennedy Black 70.00 40.00
❑ 78 Ellis Kinder 60.00 35.00
❑ 78A Ellis Kinder Black 60.00 35.00
❑ 79 Gerry Staley 60.00 35.00
❑ 79A Gerry Staley Black 60.00 35.00
❑ 80 Herman Wehmeier 80.00 50.00
❑ 80A Herman Wehmeier Black 80.00 50.00
❑ 81 Vern Law 80.00 50.00
❑ 82 Duane Pillette 40.00 20.00
❑ 83 Billy Johnson 40.00 20.00
❑ 84 Vern Stephens 50.00 30.00
❑ 85 Bob Kuzava 50.00 30.00
❑ 86 Ted Gray 40.00 20.00
❑ 87 Dale Coogan 40.00 20.00
❑ 88 Bob Feller 250.00 150.00
❑ 89 Johnny Lipon 40.00 20.00
❑ 90 Mickey Grasso 40.00 20.00
❑ 91 Red Schoendienst 150.00 90.00
❑ 92 Dale Mitchell 50.00 30.00
❑ 93 Al Sima RC 40.00 20.00
❑ 94 Sam Mele 40.00 20.00
❑ 95 Ken Holcombe 40.00 20.00
❑ 96 Willard Marshall 40.00 20.00
❑ 97 Earl Torgeson 40.00 20.00
❑ 98 Billy Pierce 50.00 30.00
❑ 99 Gene Woodling 60.00 35.00
❑ 100 Del Rice 40.00 20.00
❑ 101 Max Lanier 40.00 20.00
❑ 102 Bill Kennedy 40.00 20.00
❑ 103 Cliff Mapes 40.00 20.00
❑ 104 Don Kolloway 40.00 20.00
❑ 105 Johnny Pramesa 40.00 20.00
❑ 106 Mickey Vernon 60.00 35.00
❑ 107 Connie Ryan 40.00 20.00
❑ 108 Jim Konstanty 60.00 35.00
❑ 109 Ted Wilks 40.00 20.00
❑ 110 Dutch Leonard 40.00 20.00
❑ 111 Peanuts Lowrey 40.00 20.00
❑ 112 Hank Majeski 40.00 20.00
❑ 113 Dick Sisler 50.00 30.00
❑ 114 Willard Ramsdell 40.00 20.00
❑ 115 George Munger 40.00 20.00
❑ 116 Carl Scheib 40.00 20.00
❑ 117 Sherm Lollar 50.00 30.00
❑ 118 Ken Raffensberger 40.00 20.00
❑ 119 Mickey McDermott 40.00 20.00
❑ 120 Bob Chakales RC 40.00 20.00
❑ 121 Gus Niarhos 40.00 20.00
❑ 122 Jackie Jensen 80.00 50.00
❑ 123 Eddie Yost 50.00 30.00
❑ 124 Monte Kennedy 40.00 20.00
❑ 125 Bill Rigney 40.00 20.00
❑ 126 Fred Hutchinson 50.00 30.00
❑ 127 Paul Minner RC 40.00 20.00
❑ 128 Don Bollweg RC 40.00 20.00
❑ 129 Johnny Mize 150.00 90.00
❑ 130 Sheldon Jones 40.00 20.00
❑ 131 Morrie Martin RC 40.00 20.00
❑ 132 Clyde Kluttz RC 40.00 20.00
❑ 133 Al Widmar 40.00 20.00
❑ 134 Joe Tipton 40.00 20.00
❑ 135 Dixie Howell 40.00 20.00
❑ 136 Johnny Schmitz 40.00 20.00
❑ 137 Roy McMillan RC 50.00 30.00
❑ 138 Bill MacDonald 40.00 20.00
❑ 139 Ken Wood 40.00 20.00
❑ 140 Johnny Antonelli 60.00 35.00
❑ 141 Clint Hartung 40.00 20.00
❑ 142 Harry Perkowski RC 40.00 20.00
❑ 143 Les Moss 40.00 20.00
❑ 144 Ed Blake RC 40.00 20.00
❑ 145 Joe Haynes 40.00 20.00
❑ 146 Frank House RC 40.00 20.00
❑ 147 Bob Young RC 40.00 20.00
❑ 148 Johnny Klippstein 40.00 20.00
❑ 149 Dick Kryhoski 40.00 20.00
❑ 150 Ted Beard 40.00 20.00
❑ 151 Wally Post RC 50.00 30.00
❑ 152 Al Evans 40.00 20.00
❑ 153 Bob Rush 40.00 20.00
❑ 154 Joe Muir RC 40.00 20.00
❑ 155 Frank Overmire 40.00 20.00
❑ 156 Frank Hiller RC 40.00 20.00
❑ 157 Bob Usher 40.00 20.00
❑ 158 Eddie Waitkus 40.00 20.00
❑ 159 Saul Rogovin RC 40.00 20.00
❑ 160 Owen Friend 40.00 20.00
❑ 161 Bud Byerly RC 40.00 20.00
❑ 162 Del Crandall 50.00 30.00
❑ 163 Stan Rojek 40.00 20.00
❑ 164 Walt Dubiel 40.00 20.00
❑ 165 Eddie Kazak 40.00 20.00
❑ 166 Paul LaPalme RC 40.00 20.00
❑ 167 Bill Howerton 40.00 20.00
❑ 168 Charlie Silvera RC 60.00 35.00
❑ 169 Howie Judson 40.00 20.00
❑ 170 Gus Bell 50.00 30.00
❑ 171 Ed Erautt RC 40.00 20.00
❑ 172 Eddie Miksis 40.00 20.00
❑ 173 Roy Smalley 40.00 20.00
❑ 174 Clarence Marshall RC 60.00 35.00
❑ 175 Billy Martin RC 500.00 300.00
❑ 176 Hank Edwards 40.00 20.00
❑ 177 Bill Wight 40.00 20.00
❑ 178 Cass Michaels 40.00 20.00
❑ 179 Frank Smith RC 40.00 20.00
❑ 180 Charlie Maxwell RC 50.00 30.00
❑ 181 Bob Swift 40.00 20.00
❑ 182 Billy Hitchcock 40.00 20.00
❑ 183 Erv Dusak 40.00 20.00
❑ 184 Bob Ramazzotti 40.00 20.00
❑ 185 Bill Nicholson 50.00 30.00
❑ 186 Walt Masterson 40.00 20.00
❑ 187 Bob Miller 40.00 20.00
❑ 188 Clarence Podbielan RC 40.00 20.00
❑ 189 Pete Reiser 60.00 35.00
❑ 190 Don Johnson RC 40.00 20.00
❑ 191 Yogi Berra 800.00 500.00
❑ 192 Myron Ginsberg RC 40.00 20.00
❑ 193 Harry Simpson RC 50.00 30.00
❑ 194 Joe Hatton 40.00 20.00
❑ 195 Minnie Minoso RC 150.00 90.00

	No.	Player	Price 1	Price 2
❑	196	Solly Hemus RC	60.00	35.00
❑	197	George Strickland RC	40.00	20.00
❑	198	Phil Haugstad RC	40.00	20.00
❑	199	George Zuverink RC	40.00	20.00
❑	200	Ralph Houk RC	80.00	50.00
❑	201	Alex Kellner	40.00	20.00
❑	202	Joe Collins RC	60.00	35.00
❑	203	Curt Simmons	60.00	35.00
❑	204	Ron Northey	40.00	20.00
❑	205	Clyde King	60.00	35.00
❑	206	Joe Ostrowski RC	40.00	20.00
❑	207	Mickey Harris	40.00	20.00
❑	208	Marlin Stuart RC	40.00	20.00
❑	209	Howie Fox	40.00	20.00
❑	210	Dick Fowler	40.00	20.00
❑	211	Ray Coleman	40.00	20.00
❑	212	Ned Garver	40.00	20.00
❑	213	Nippy Jones	40.00	20.00
❑	214	Johnny Hopp	50.00	30.00
❑	215	Hank Bauer	100.00	60.00
❑	216	Richie Ashburn	250.00	150.00
❑	217	Snuffy Stirnweiss	50.00	30.00
❑	218	Clyde McCullough	40.00	20.00
❑	219	Bobby Shantz	60.00	35.00
❑	220	Joe Presko RC	40.00	20.00
❑	221	Granny Hamner	40.00	20.00
❑	222	Hoot Evers	40.00	20.00
❑	223	Del Ennis	50.00	30.00
❑	224	Bruce Edwards	40.00	20.00
❑	225	Frank Baumholtz	40.00	20.00
❑	226	Dave Philley	40.00	20.00
❑	227	Joe Garagiola	80.00	50.00
❑	228	Al Brazle	40.00	20.00
❑	229	Gene Bearden UER	40.00	20.00
❑	230	Matt Batts	40.00	20.00
❑	231	Sam Zoldak	40.00	20.00
❑	232	Billy Cox	50.00	30.00
❑	233	Bob Friend RC	80.00	50.00
❑	234	Steve Souchock RC	40.00	20.00
❑	235	Walt Dropo	40.00	20.00
❑	236	Ed Fitzgerald	40.00	20.00
❑	237	Jerry Coleman	60.00	35.00
❑	238	Art Houtteman	40.00	20.00
❑	239	Rocky Bridges RC	50.00	30.00
❑	240	Jack Phillips RC	40.00	20.00
❑	241	Tommy Byrne	40.00	20.00
❑	242	Tom Poholsky RC	40.00	20.00
❑	243	Larry Doby	80.00	50.00
❑	244	Vic Wertz	40.00	20.00
❑	245	Sherry Robertson	40.00	20.00
❑	246	George Kell	80.00	50.00
❑	247	Randy Gumpert	40.00	20.00
❑	248	Frank Shea	40.00	20.00
❑	249	Bobby Adams	40.00	20.00
❑	250	Carl Erskine	100.00	60.00
❑	251	Chico Carrasquel	50.00	30.00
❑	252	Vern Bickford	50.00	30.00
❑	253	John Berardino	100.00	60.00
❑	254	Joe Dobson	50.00	30.00
❑	255	Clyde Vollmer	50.00	30.00
❑	256	Pete Suder	50.00	30.00
❑	257	Bobby Avila	60.00	35.00
❑	258	Steve Gromek	60.00	35.00
❑	259	Bob Addis RC	50.00	30.00
❑	260	Pete Castiglione	50.00	30.00
❑	261	Willie Mays	3000.00	2000.00
❑	262	Virgil Trucks	60.00	35.00
❑	263	Harry Brecheen	60.00	35.00
❑	264	Roy Hartsfield	50.00	30.00
❑	265	Chuck Diering	50.00	30.00
❑	266	Murry Dickson	50.00	30.00
❑	267	Sid Gordon	60.00	35.00
❑	268	Bob Lemon	150.00	90.00
❑	269	Willard Nixon	50.00	30.00
❑	270	Lou Brissie	50.00	30.00
❑	271	Jim Delsing	60.00	35.00
❑	272	Mike Garcia	80.00	50.00
❑	273	Erv Palica	50.00	30.00
❑	274	Ralph Branca	125.00	75.00
❑	275	Pat Mullin	50.00	30.00
❑	276	Jim Wilson RC	50.00	30.00
❑	277	Early Wynn	175.00	100.00
❑	278	Allie Clark	50.00	30.00
❑	279	Eddie Stewart	50.00	30.00
❑	280	Cloyd Boyer	80.00	50.00
❑	281	Tommy Brown SP	80.00	50.00
❑	282	Birdie Tebbetts SP	80.00	50.00
❑	283	Phil Masi SP	60.00	35.00
❑	284	Hank Arft SP	60.00	35.00
❑	285	Cliff Fannin SP	60.00	35.00
❑	286	Joe DeMaestri SP RC	60.00	35.00
❑	287	Steve Bilko SP	60.00	35.00
❑	288	Chet Nichols SP RC	80.00	50.00
❑	289	Tommy Holmes MG	100.00	60.00
❑	290	Joe Astroth SP	60.00	35.00
❑	291	Gil Coan SP	60.00	35.00
❑	292	Floyd Baker SP	60.00	35.00
❑	293	Sibby Sisti SP	60.00	35.00
❑	294	Walker Cooper SP	60.00	35.00
❑	295	Phil Cavarretta	80.00	50.00
❑	296	Red Rolfe MG	60.00	35.00
❑	297	Andy Seminick SP	60.00	35.00
❑	298	Bob Ross SP RC	60.00	35.00
❑	299	Ray Murray SP RC	80.00	50.00
❑	300	Barney McCosky SP	80.00	50.00
❑	301	Bob Porterfield	50.00	30.00
❑	302	Max Surkont RC	50.00	30.00
❑	303	Harry Dorish	50.00	30.00
❑	304	Sam Dente	50.00	30.00
❑	305	Paul Richards MG	60.00	35.00
❑	306	Lou Sleater RC	50.00	30.00
❑	307	Frank Campos RC	50.00	30.00
❑	307A	Frank Campos Star		
❑	308	Luis Aloma	50.00	30.00
❑	309	Jim Busby	60.00	35.00
❑	310	George Metkovich	100.00	60.00
❑	311	Mickey Mantle DP	30000.00	18000.00
❑	311B	Mickey Mantle DP	30000.00	18000.00
❑	312	Jackie Robinson DP	2500.00	1500.00
❑	312B	Jackie Robinson Stitch	2500.00	1500.00
❑	313	Bobby Thomson DP	350.00	200.00
❑	313B	Bobby Thomson Stitch	350.00	200.00
❑	314	Roy Campanella	2500.00	1500.00
❑	315	Leo Durocher MG	600.00	350.00
❑	316	Dave Williams RC	300.00	175.00
❑	317	Conrado Marrero	300.00	175.00
❑	318	Harold Gregg RC	300.00	175.00
❑	319	Rube Walker RC	250.00	150.00
❑	320	John Rutherford RC	300.00	175.00
❑	321	Joe Black RC	500.00	350.00
❑	322	Randy Jackson RC	300.00	175.00
❑	323	Bubba Church	250.00	150.00
❑	324	Warren Hacker	250.00	150.00
❑	325	Bill Serena	300.00	175.00
❑	326	George Shuba RC	500.00	350.00
❑	327	Al Wilson RC	250.00	150.00
❑	328	Bob Borkowski RC	300.00	175.00
❑	329	Ike Delock RC	300.00	175.00
❑	330	Turk Lown RC	300.00	175.00
❑	331	Tom Morgan RC	300.00	175.00
❑	332	Tony Bartirome RC	300.00	175.00
❑	333	Pee Wee Reese	1800.00	1000.00
❑	334	Wilmer Mizell RC	300.00	175.00
❑	335	Ted Lepcio RC	250.00	150.00
❑	336	Dave Koslo	250.00	150.00
❑	337	Jim Hearn	300.00	175.00
❑	338	Sal Yvars RC	300.00	175.00
❑	339	Russ Meyer	300.00	175.00
❑	340	Bob Hooper	300.00	175.00
❑	341	Hal Jeffcoat	300.00	175.00
❑	342	Clem Labine RC	500.00	350.00
❑	343	Dick Gernert RC	250.00	150.00
❑	344	Ewell Blackwell	300.00	175.00
❑	345	Sammy White RC	250.00	150.00
❑	346	George Spencer RC	250.00	150.00
❑	347	Joe Adcock	400.00	250.00
❑	348	Robert Kelly RC	250.00	150.00
❑	349	Bob Cain	300.00	175.00
❑	350	Cal Abrams	300.00	175.00
❑	351	Alvin Dark	300.00	175.00
❑	352	Karl Drews	300.00	175.00
❑	353	Bobby Del Greco RC	300.00	175.00
❑	354	Fred Hatfield RC	300.00	175.00
❑	355	Bobby Morgan	300.00	175.00
❑	356	Toby Atwell RC	300.00	175.00
❑	357	Smoky Burgess	300.00	175.00
❑	358	John Kucab RC	300.00	175.00
❑	359	Dee Fondy RC	250.00	150.00
❑	360	George Crowe RC	300.00	175.00
❑	361	Bill Posedel CO	250.00	150.00
❑	362	Ken Heintzelman	300.00	175.00
❑	363	Dick Rozek RC	300.00	175.00
❑	364	Clyde Sukeforth CO RC	300.00	175.00
❑	365	Cookie Lavagetto CO	400.00	250.00
❑	366	Dave Madison RC	250.00	150.00
❑	367	Ben Thorpe RC	300.00	175.00
❑	368	Ed Wright RC	300.00	175.00
❑	369	Dick Groat RC	500.00	350.00
❑	370	Billy Hoeft RC	300.00	175.00
❑	371	Bobby Hofman	250.00	150.00
❑	372	Gil McDougald RC	500.00	300.00
❑	373	Jim Turner CO RC	400.00	250.00
❑	374	Al Benton RC	250.00	150.00
❑	375	John Merson RC	250.00	150.00
❑	376	Faye Throneberry RC	250.00	150.00
❑	377	Chuck Dressen MG	400.00	250.00
❑	378	Leroy Fusselman RC	300.00	175.00
❑	379	Joe Rossi RC	250.00	150.00
❑	380	Clem Koshorek RC	250.00	150.00
❑	381	Milton Stock CO RC	300.00	175.00
❑	382	Sam Jones RC	350.00	200.00
❑	383	Del Wilber RC	250.00	150.00
❑	384	Frank Crosetti CO	500.00	300.00
❑	385	Herman Franks CO RC	250.00	150.00
❑	386	Ed Yuhas RC	300.00	175.00
❑	387	Billy Meyer MG	250.00	150.00
❑	388	Bob Chipman	250.00	150.00
❑	389	Ben Wade RC	300.00	175.00
❑	390	Rocky Nelson RC	300.00	175.00
❑	391	Ben Chapman CO UER	250.00	150.00
❑	392	Hoyt Wilhelm RC	1000.00	600.00
❑	393	Ebba St.Claire RC	300.00	175.00
❑	394	Billy Herman CO	600.00	350.00
❑	395	Jake Pitler CO	300.00	175.00
❑	396	Dick Williams RC	500.00	300.00
❑	397	Forrest Main RC	250.00	150.00
❑	398	Hal Rice	250.00	150.00
❑	399	Jim Fridley RC	250.00	150.00
❑	400	Bill Dickey CO	1800.00	1000.00
❑	401	Bob Schultz RC	300.00	175.00
❑	402	Earl Harrist RC	300.00	175.00
❑	403	Bill Miller RC	300.00	175.00
❑	404	Dick Brodowski RC	300.00	175.00
❑	405	Eddie Pellagrini	300.00	175.00
❑	406	Joe Nuxhall RC	400.00	250.00
❑	407	Eddie Mathews RC	10000.00	6000.00

1953 Topps

	No.	Item	Price 1	Price 2
❑		COMPLETE SET (274)	15000.00	9000.00
❑		COMMON CARD (1-165)	30.00	15.00
❑		COMMON DP (1-165)	15.00	7.50
❑		COMMON CARD (166-220)	25.00	12.50
❑		COMMON CARD (221-280)	100.00	50.00
❑		NOT ISSUED (253/261/267)		
❑		NOT ISSUED (268/271/275)		
❑		WRAP.(1-CENT, DATED)	200.00	150.00
❑		WRAP.(1-CENT,NO DATE)	300.00	250.00
❑		WRAP.(5-CENT, DATED)	400.00	300.00
❑		WRAP.(5-CENT,NO DATE)	350.00	275.00
❑	1	Jackie Robinson DP	800.00	500.00
❑	2	Luke Easter DP	20.00	10.00
❑	3	George Crowe	40.00	25.00
❑	4	Ben Wade	30.00	15.00
❑	5	Joe Dobson	30.00	15.00
❑	6	Sam Jones	40.00	25.00
❑	7	Bob Borkowski DP	15.00	7.50
❑	8	Clem Koshorek DP	15.00	7.50
❑	9	Joe Collins	60.00	35.00
❑	10	Smoky Burgess SP	80.00	50.00
❑	11	Sal Yvars	30.00	15.00

❑ 12	Howie Judson DP	15.00	7.50
❑ 13	Conrado Marrero DP	15.00	7.50
❑ 14	Clem Labine DP	20.00	10.00
❑ 15	Bobo Newsom DP RC	20.00	10.00
❑ 16	Peanuts Lowrey DP	15.00	7.50
❑ 17	Billy Hitchcock	30.00	15.00
❑ 18	Ted Lepcio DP	15.00	7.50
❑ 19	Mel Parnell DP	20.00	10.00
❑ 20	Hank Thompson	40.00	25.00
❑ 21	Billy Johnson	30.00	15.00
❑ 22	Howie Fox	30.00	15.00
❑ 23	Toby Atwell DP	15.00	7.50
❑ 24	Ferris Fain	40.00	25.00
❑ 25	Ray Boone	40.00	25.00
❑ 26	Dale Mitchell DP	20.00	10.00
❑ 27	Roy Campanella DP	300.00	175.00
❑ 28	Eddie Pellagrini	30.00	15.00
❑ 29	Hal Jeffcoat	30.00	15.00
❑ 30	Willard Nixon	30.00	15.00
❑ 31	Ewell Blackwell	60.00	35.00
❑ 32	Clyde Vollmer	30.00	15.00
❑ 33	Bob Kennedy DP	15.00	7.50
❑ 34	George Shuba	40.00	25.00
❑ 35	Irv Noren DP	15.00	7.50
❑ 36	Johnny Groth DP	15.00	7.50
❑ 37	Eddie Mathews DP	250.00	150.00
❑ 38	Jim Hearn DP	15.00	7.50
❑ 39	Eddie Miksis	30.00	15.00
❑ 40	John Lipon	30.00	15.00
❑ 41	Enos Slaughter	80.00	50.00
❑ 42	Gus Zernial DP	20.00	10.00
❑ 43	Gil McDougald	60.00	35.00
❑ 44	Ellis Kinder SP	60.00	35.00
❑ 45	Grady Hatton DP	15.00	7.50
❑ 46	Johnny Klippstein DP	15.00	7.50
❑ 47	Bubba Church DP	15.00	7.50
❑ 48	Bob Del Greco DP	15.00	7.50
❑ 49	Faye Throneberry DP	15.00	7.50
❑ 50	Chuck Dressen DP	20.00	10.00
❑ 51	Frank Campos DP	15.00	7.50
❑ 52	Ted Gray DP	15.00	7.50
❑ 53	Sherm Lollar DP	20.00	10.00
❑ 54	Bob Feller DP	150.00	90.00
❑ 55	Maurice McDermott DP	15.00	7.50
❑ 56	Gerry Staley DP	15.00	7.50
❑ 57	Carl Scheib	30.00	15.00
❑ 58	George Metkovich	30.00	15.00
❑ 59	Karl Drews DP	15.00	7.50
❑ 60	Cloyd Boyer DP	15.00	7.50
❑ 61	Early Wynn SP	125.00	75.00
❑ 62	Monte Irvin DP	40.00	25.00
❑ 63	Gus Niarhos DP	15.00	7.50
❑ 64	Dave Philley	30.00	15.00
❑ 65	Earl Harrist	30.00	15.00
❑ 66	Minnie Minoso	60.00	35.00
❑ 67	Roy Sievers DP	20.00	10.00
❑ 68	Del Rice	30.00	15.00
❑ 69	Dick Brodowski	30.00	15.00
❑ 70	Ed Yuhas	30.00	15.00
❑ 71	Tony Bartirome	30.00	15.00
❑ 72	Fred Hutchinson SP	60.00	35.00
❑ 73	Eddie Robinson	30.00	15.00
❑ 74	Joe Rossi	30.00	15.00
❑ 75	Mike Garcia	40.00	25.00
❑ 76	Pee Wee Reese	175.00	100.00
❑ 77	Johnny Mize DP	80.00	50.00
❑ 78	Red Schoendienst	80.00	50.00
❑ 79	Johnny Wyrostek	30.00	15.00
❑ 80	Jim Hegan	40.00	25.00
❑ 81	Joe Black SP	80.00	50.00
❑ 82	Mickey Mantle	3000.00	2000.00
❑ 83	Howie Pollet	30.00	15.00
❑ 84	Bob Hooper DP	15.00	7.50
❑ 85	Bobby Morgan DP	15.00	7.50
❑ 86	Billy Martin	125.00	75.00
❑ 87	Ed Lopat	60.00	35.00
❑ 88	Willie Jones DP	15.00	7.50
❑ 89	Chuck Stobbs DP	15.00	7.50
❑ 90	Hank Edwards DP	15.00	7.50
❑ 91	Ebba St.Claire DP	15.00	7.50
❑ 92	Paul Minner DP	15.00	7.50
❑ 93	Hal Rice DP	15.00	7.50
❑ 94	Bill Kennedy DP	15.00	7.50
❑ 95	Willard Marshall DP	15.00	7.50
❑ 96	Virgil Trucks	40.00	25.00
❑ 97	Don Kolloway DP	15.00	7.50
❑ 98	Cal Abrams DP	15.00	7.50
❑ 99	Dave Madison	30.00	15.00
❑ 100	Bill Miller	30.00	15.00
❑ 101	Ted Wilks	30.00	15.00
❑ 102	Connie Ryan DP	15.00	7.50
❑ 103	Joe Astroth DP	15.00	7.50
❑ 104	Yogi Berra	400.00	250.00
❑ 105	Joe Nuxhall DP	20.00	10.00
❑ 106	Johnny Antonelli	40.00	25.00
❑ 107	Danny O'Connell DP	15.00	7.50
❑ 108	Bob Porterfield DP	15.00	7.50
❑ 109	Alvin Dark	60.00	35.00
❑ 110	Herman Wehmeier DP	15.00	7.50
❑ 111	Hank Sauer DP	15.00	7.50
❑ 112	Ned Garver DP	15.00	7.50
❑ 113	Jerry Priddy	30.00	15.00
❑ 114	Phil Rizzuto	250.00	150.00
❑ 115	George Spencer	30.00	15.00
❑ 116	Frank Smith DP	15.00	7.50
❑ 117	Sid Gordon DP	15.00	7.50
❑ 118	Gus Bell DP	20.00	10.00
❑ 119	Johnny Sain SP	60.00	35.00
❑ 120	Davey Williams	40.00	25.00
❑ 121	Walt Dropo	40.00	25.00
❑ 122	Elmer Valo	30.00	15.00
❑ 123	Tommy Byrne DP	15.00	7.50
❑ 124	Sibby Sisti DP	15.00	7.50
❑ 125	Dick Williams DP	20.00	10.00
❑ 126	Bill Connelly DP RC	15.00	7.50
❑ 127	Clint Courtney DP RC	15.00	7.50
❑ 128	Wilmer Mizell DP	20.00	10.00
❑ 129	Keith Thomas RC	30.00	15.00
❑ 130	Turk Lown DP	15.00	7.50
❑ 131	Harry Byrd DP RC	15.00	7.50
❑ 132	Tom Morgan	30.00	15.00
❑ 133	Gil Coan	30.00	15.00
❑ 134	Rube Walker	40.00	25.00
❑ 135	Al Rosen DP	20.00	10.00
❑ 136	Ken Heintzelman DP	15.00	7.50
❑ 137	John Rutherford DP	15.00	7.50
❑ 138	George Kell	80.00	50.00
❑ 139	Sammy White	30.00	15.00
❑ 140	Tommy Glaviano	30.00	15.00
❑ 141	Allie Reynolds DP	15.00	7.50
❑ 142	Vic Wertz	40.00	25.00
❑ 143	Billy Pierce	60.00	35.00
❑ 144	Bob Schultz DP	15.00	7.50
❑ 145	Harry Dorish DP	15.00	7.50
❑ 146	Granny Hamner	30.00	15.00
❑ 147	Warren Spahn	175.00	100.00
❑ 148	Mickey Grasso	30.00	15.00
❑ 149	Dom DiMaggio DP	15.00	7.50
❑ 150	Harry Simpson DP	15.00	7.50
❑ 151	Hoyt Wilhelm	100.00	60.00
❑ 152	Bob Adams DP	15.00	7.50
❑ 153	Andy Seminick DP	15.00	7.50
❑ 154	Dick Groat	40.00	25.00
❑ 155	Dutch Leonard	30.00	15.00
❑ 156	Jim Rivera DP RC	20.00	10.00
❑ 157	Bob Addis DP	15.00	7.50
❑ 158	Johnny Logan RC	40.00	25.00
❑ 159	Wayne Terwilliger DP	15.00	7.50
❑ 160	Bob Young	30.00	15.00
❑ 161	Vern Bickford DP	15.00	7.50
❑ 162	Ted Kluszewski	60.00	35.00
❑ 163	Fred Hatfield DP	15.00	7.50
❑ 164	Frank Shea DP	15.00	7.50
❑ 165	Billy Hoeft	30.00	15.00
❑ 166	Billy Hunter RC	25.00	12.50
❑ 167	Art Schult RC	25.00	12.50
❑ 168	Willard Schmidt RC	25.00	12.50
❑ 169	Dizzy Trout	30.00	15.00
❑ 170	Bill Werle	25.00	12.50
❑ 171	Bill Glynn RC	25.00	12.50
❑ 172	Rip Repulski RC	25.00	12.50
❑ 173	Preston Ward	25.00	12.50
❑ 174	Billy Loes	30.00	15.00
❑ 175	Ron Kline RC	25.00	12.50
❑ 176	Don Hoak RC	40.00	25.00
❑ 177	Jim Dyck RC	25.00	12.50
❑ 178	Jim Waugh RC	25.00	12.50
❑ 179	Gene Hermanski	25.00	12.50
❑ 180	Virgil Stallcup	25.00	12.50
❑ 181	Al Zarilla	25.00	12.50
❑ 182	Bobby Hofman	25.00	12.50
❑ 183	Stu Miller RC	40.00	25.00
❑ 184	Hal Brown RC	25.00	12.50
❑ 185	Jim Pendleton RC	25.00	12.50
❑ 186	Charlie Bishop RC	25.00	12.50
❑ 187	Jim Fridley	25.00	12.50
❑ 188	Andy Carey RC	40.00	25.00
❑ 189	Ray Jablonski RC	25.00	12.50
❑ 190	Dixie Walker CO	30.00	15.00
❑ 191	Ralph Kiner	80.00	50.00
❑ 192	Wally Westlake	25.00	12.50
❑ 193	Mike Clark RC	25.00	12.50
❑ 194	Eddie Kazak	25.00	12.50
❑ 195	Ed McGhee RC	25.00	12.50
❑ 196	Bob Keegan RC	25.00	12.50
❑ 197	Del Crandall	40.00	25.00
❑ 198	Forrest Main	25.00	12.50
❑ 199	Marion Fricano RC	25.00	12.50
❑ 200	Gordon Goldsberry	25.00	12.50
❑ 201	Paul LaPalme	25.00	12.50
❑ 202	Carl Sawatski RC	25.00	12.50
❑ 203	Cliff Fannin	25.00	12.50
❑ 204	Dick Bokelman RC	25.00	12.50
❑ 205	Vern Benson RC	25.00	12.50
❑ 206	Ed Bailey RC	30.00	15.00
❑ 207	Whitey Ford	300.00	175.00
❑ 208	Jim Wilson	25.00	12.50
❑ 209	Jim Greengrass RC	25.00	12.50
❑ 210	Bob Cerv RC	40.00	25.00
❑ 211	J.W. Porter RC	25.00	12.50
❑ 212	Jack Dittmer RC	25.00	12.50
❑ 213	Ray Scarborough	25.00	12.50
❑ 214	Bill Bruton RC	40.00	25.00
❑ 215	Gene Conley RC	30.00	15.00
❑ 216	Jim Hughes RC	25.00	12.50
❑ 217	Murray Wall RC	25.00	12.50
❑ 218	Les Fusselman	25.00	12.50
❑ 219	Pete Runnels UER (Photo actually Don Johnson)	30.00	15.00
❑ 220	Satchel Paige UER	600.00	350.00
❑ 221	Bob Milliken RC	100.00	50.00
❑ 222	Vic Janowicz DP RC	50.00	25.00
❑ 223	Johnny O'Brien DP RC	50.00	25.00
❑ 224	Lou Sleater DP	50.00	25.00
❑ 225	Bobby Shantz	125.00	75.00
❑ 226	Ed Erautt	100.00	50.00
❑ 227	Morrie Martin	100.00	50.00
❑ 228	Hal Newhouser	150.00	90.00
❑ 229	Rocky Krsnich RC	100.00	50.00
❑ 230	Johnny Lindell DP	50.00	25.00
❑ 231	Solly Hemus DP	50.00	25.00
❑ 232	Dick Kokos	100.00	50.00
❑ 233	Al Aber RC	100.00	50.00
❑ 234	Ray Murray DP	50.00	25.00
❑ 235	John Hetki DP RC	50.00	25.00
❑ 236	Harry Perkowski DP	50.00	25.00
❑ 237	Bud Podbielan DP	50.00	25.00
❑ 238	Cal Hogue DP RC	50.00	25.00
❑ 239	Jim Delsing	100.00	50.00
❑ 240	Fred Marsh	100.00	50.00
❑ 241	Al Sima DP	50.00	25.00
❑ 242	Charlie Silvera	125.00	75.00
❑ 243	Carlos Bernier DP RC	50.00	25.00
❑ 244	Willie Mays	2500.00	1500.00
❑ 245	Bill Norman CO	100.00	50.00
❑ 246	Roy Face RC DP RC	80.00	50.00
❑ 247	Mike Sandlock DP RC	50.00	25.00
❑ 248	Gene Stephens DP RC	50.00	25.00
❑ 249	Eddie O'Brien RC	100.00	50.00
❑ 250	Bob Wilson RC	100.00	50.00
❑ 251	Sid Hudson	100.00	50.00
❑ 252	Hank Foiles RC	100.00	50.00
❑ 253	Does not exist		
❑ 254	Preacher Roe DP	80.00	50.00
❑ 255	Dixie Howell	100.00	50.00
❑ 256	Les Peden RC	100.00	50.00
❑ 257	Bob Boyd RC	100.00	50.00
❑ 258	Jim Gilliam RC	400.00	250.00
❑ 259	Roy McMillan DP	50.00	25.00
❑ 260	Sam Calderone RC	100.00	50.00
❑ 261	Does not exist		
❑ 262	Bob Oldis RC	100.00	50.00
❑ 263	Johnny Podres RC	300.00	175.00
❑ 264	Gene Woodling DP	60.00	30.00
❑ 265	Jackie Jensen	125.00	75.00
❑ 266	Bob Cain	100.00	50.00
❑ 267	Does not exist		

❑ 268 Does not exist		
❑ 269 Duane Pillette	100.00	50.00
❑ 270 Vern Stephens	125.00	75.00
❑ 271 Does not exist		
❑ 272 Bill Antonello RC	100.00	50.00
❑ 273 Harvey Haddix RC	150.00	90.00
❑ 274 John Riddle CO	100.00	50.00
❑ 275 Does not exist		
❑ 276 Ken Raffensberger	100.00	50.00
❑ 277 Don Lund RC	100.00	50.00
❑ 278 Willie Miranda RC	100.00	50.00
❑ 279 Joe Coleman DP	50.00	25.00
❑ 280 Milt Bolling RC	350.00	200.00

1954 Topps

❑ COMPLETE SET (250)	8000.00	5000.00
❑ COMMON (1-50/76-250)	15.00	7.50
❑ COMMON CARD (51-75)	25.00	12.50
❑ WRAP.(1-CENT, DATED)	200.00	150.00
❑ WRAP.(1-CENT, UNDAT)	150.00	100.00
❑ WRAP.(5-CENT, DATED)	300.00	250.00
❑ WRAP.(5-CENT, UNDAT)	250.00	200.00
❑ 1 Ted Williams	800.00	500.00
❑ 2 Gus Zernial	25.00	12.50
❑ 3 Monte Irvin	50.00	25.00
❑ 4 Hank Sauer	25.00	12.50
❑ 5 Ed Lopat	25.00	12.50
❑ 6 Pete Runnels	25.00	12.50
❑ 7 Ted Kluszewski	50.00	25.00
❑ 8 Bob Young	15.00	7.50
❑ 9 Harvey Haddix	25.00	12.50
❑ 10 Jackie Robinson	400.00	250.00
❑ 11 Paul Leslie Smith RC	15.00	7.50
❑ 12 Del Crandall	25.00	12.50
❑ 13 Billy Martin	100.00	60.00
❑ 14 Preacher Roe UER	25.00	12.50
❑ 15 Al Rosen	25.00	12.50
❑ 16 Vic Janowicz	25.00	12.50
❑ 17 Phil Rizzuto	125.00	75.00
❑ 18 Walt Dropo	25.00	12.50
❑ 19 Johnny Lipon	15.00	7.50
❑ 20 Warren Spahn	125.00	75.00
❑ 21 Bobby Shantz	25.00	12.50
❑ 22 Jim Greengrass	15.00	7.50
❑ 23 Luke Easter	25.00	12.50
❑ 24 Granny Hamner	15.00	7.50
❑ 25 Harvey Kuenn RC	40.00	20.00
❑ 26 Ray Jablonski	15.00	7.50
❑ 27 Ferris Fain	25.00	12.50
❑ 28 Paul Minner	15.00	7.50
❑ 29 Jim Hegan	25.00	12.50
❑ 30 Eddie Mathews	100.00	60.00
❑ 31 Johnny Klippstein	15.00	7.50
❑ 32 Duke Snider	200.00	125.00
❑ 33 Johnny Schmitz	15.00	7.50
❑ 34 Jim Rivera	15.00	7.50
❑ 35 Junior Gilliam	50.00	25.00
❑ 36 Hoyt Wilhelm	50.00	25.00
❑ 37 Whitey Ford	200.00	125.00
❑ 38 Eddie Stanky MG	25.00	12.50
❑ 39 Sherm Lollar	25.00	12.50
❑ 40 Mel Parnell	25.00	12.50
❑ 41 Willie Jones	15.00	7.50
❑ 42 Don Mueller	25.00	12.50
❑ 43 Dick Groat	25.00	12.50
❑ 44 Ned Garver	15.00	7.50
❑ 45 Richie Ashburn	80.00	50.00
❑ 46 Ken Raffensberger	15.00	7.50
❑ 47 Ellis Kinder	15.00	7.50
❑ 48 Billy Hunter	25.00	12.50
❑ 49 Ray Murray	15.00	7.50
❑ 50 Yogi Berra	300.00	175.00
❑ 51 Johnny Lindell	25.00	12.50
❑ 52 Vic Power RC	30.00	15.00
❑ 53 Jack Dittmer	25.00	12.50
❑ 54 Vern Stephens	30.00	15.00
❑ 55 Phil Cavarretta MG	30.00	15.00
❑ 56 Willie Miranda	25.00	12.50
❑ 57 Luis Aloma	25.00	12.50
❑ 58 Bob Wilson	25.00	12.50
❑ 59 Gene Conley	30.00	15.00
❑ 60 Frank Baumholtz	25.00	12.50
❑ 61 Bob Cain	25.00	12.50
❑ 62 Eddie Robinson	25.00	12.50
❑ 63 Johnny Pesky	30.00	15.00
❑ 64 Hank Thompson	25.00	12.50
❑ 65 Bob Swift CO	25.00	12.50
❑ 66 Ted Lepcio	25.00	12.50
❑ 67 Jim Willis RC	25.00	12.50
❑ 68 Sam Calderone	25.00	12.50
❑ 69 Bud Podbielan	25.00	12.50
❑ 70 Larry Doby	60.00	30.00
❑ 71 Frank Smith	25.00	12.50
❑ 72 Preston Ward	25.00	12.50
❑ 73 Wayne Terwilliger	25.00	12.50
❑ 74 Bill Taylor RC	25.00	12.50
❑ 75 Fred Haney MG RC	25.00	12.50
❑ 76 Bob Scheffing CO	15.00	7.50
❑ 77 Ray Boone	25.00	12.50
❑ 78 Ted Kazanski RC	15.00	7.50
❑ 79 Andy Pafko	25.00	12.50
❑ 80 Jackie Jensen	25.00	12.50
❑ 81 Dave Hoskins RC	15.00	7.50
❑ 82 Milt Bolling	15.00	7.50
❑ 83 Joe Collins	25.00	12.50
❑ 84 Dick Cole RC	15.00	7.50
❑ 85 Bob Turley RC	40.00	20.00
❑ 86 Billy Herman CO	25.00	12.50
❑ 87 Roy Face	25.00	12.50
❑ 88 Matt Batts	15.00	7.50
❑ 89 Howie Pollet	15.00	7.50
❑ 90 Willie Mays	800.00	500.00
❑ 91 Bob Oldis	15.00	7.50
❑ 92 Wally Westlake	15.00	7.50
❑ 93 Sid Hudson	15.00	7.50
❑ 94 Ernie Banks RC	1500.00	900.00
❑ 95 Hal Rice	15.00	7.50
❑ 96 Charlie Silvera	25.00	12.50
❑ 97 Jerald Hal Lane RC	15.00	7.50
❑ 98 Joe Black	40.00	20.00
❑ 99 Bobby Hofman	15.00	7.50
❑ 100 Bob Keegan	15.00	7.50
❑ 101 Gene Woodling	25.00	12.50
❑ 102 Gil Hodges	80.00	50.00
❑ 103 Jim Lemon RC	15.00	7.50
❑ 104 Mike Sandlock	15.00	7.50
❑ 105 Andy Carey	25.00	12.50
❑ 106 Dick Kokos	15.00	7.50
❑ 107 Duane Pillette	15.00	7.50
❑ 108 Thornton Kipper RC	15.00	7.50
❑ 109 Bill Bruton	25.00	12.50
❑ 110 Harry Dorish	15.00	7.50
❑ 111 Jim Delsing	15.00	7.50
❑ 112 Bill Renna RC	15.00	7.50
❑ 113 Bob Boyd	15.00	7.50
❑ 114 Dean Stone RC	15.00	7.50
❑ 115 Rip Repulski	15.00	7.50
❑ 116 Steve Bilko	15.00	7.50
❑ 117 Solly Hemus	15.00	7.50
❑ 118 Carl Scheib	15.00	7.50
❑ 119 Johnny Antonelli	25.00	12.50
❑ 120 Roy McMillan	25.00	12.50
❑ 121 Clem Labine	25.00	12.50
❑ 122 Johnny Logan	25.00	12.50
❑ 123 Bobby Adams	15.00	7.50
❑ 124 Marion Fricano	15.00	7.50
❑ 125 Harry Perkowski	15.00	7.50
❑ 126 Ben Wade	15.00	7.50
❑ 127 Steve O'Neill MG	15.00	7.50
❑ 128 Hank Aaron RC	1800.00	1000.00
❑ 129 Forrest Jacobs RC	15.00	7.50
❑ 130 Hank Bauer	25.00	12.50
❑ 131 Reno Bertoia RC	25.00	12.50
❑ 132 Tommy Lasorda RC	250.00	150.00
❑ 133 Del Baker CO	15.00	7.50
❑ 134 Cal Hogue	15.00	7.50
❑ 135 Joe Presko	15.00	7.50
❑ 136 Connie Ryan	15.00	7.50
❑ 137 Wally Moon RC	40.00	20.00
❑ 138 Bob Borkowski	15.00	7.50
❑ 139 J.O'Brien/E.O'Brien	50.00	25.00
❑ 140 Tom Wright	15.00	7.50
❑ 141 Joey Jay RC	25.00	12.50
❑ 142 Tom Poholsky	15.00	7.50
❑ 143 Rollie Hemsley CO	15.00	7.50
❑ 144 Bill Werle	15.00	7.50
❑ 145 Elmer Valo	15.00	7.50
❑ 146 Don Johnson	15.00	7.50
❑ 147 Johnny Riddle CO	15.00	7.50
❑ 148 Bob Trice RC	15.00	7.50
❑ 149 Al Robertson	15.00	7.50
❑ 150 Dick Kryhoski	15.00	7.50
❑ 151 Alex Grammas RC	15.00	7.50
❑ 152 Michael Blyzka RC	15.00	7.50
❑ 153 Al Walker	25.00	12.50
❑ 154 Mike Fornieles RC	15.00	7.50
❑ 155 Bob Kennedy	25.00	12.50
❑ 156 Joe Coleman	25.00	12.50
❑ 157 Don Lenhardt	25.00	12.50
❑ 158 Peanuts Lowrey	15.00	7.50
❑ 159 Dave Philley	15.00	7.50
❑ 160 Ralph Kress CO	15.00	7.50
❑ 161 John Hetki	15.00	7.50
❑ 162 Herman Wehmeier	15.00	7.50
❑ 163 Frank House	15.00	7.50
❑ 164 Stu Miller	25.00	12.50
❑ 165 Jim Pendleton	15.00	7.50
❑ 166 Johnny Podres	40.00	20.00
❑ 167 Don Lund	15.00	7.50
❑ 168 Morrie Martin	25.00	12.50
❑ 169 Jim Hughes	40.00	20.00
❑ 170 Dusty Rhodes RC	25.00	12.50
❑ 171 Leo Kiely	15.00	7.50
❑ 172 Harold Brown RC	15.00	7.50
❑ 173 Jack Harshman RC	15.00	7.50
❑ 174 Tom Qualters RC	15.00	7.50
❑ 175 Frank Leja RC	25.00	12.50
❑ 176 Robert Keely CO	15.00	7.50
❑ 177 Bob Milliken	15.00	7.50
❑ 178 Bill Glynn UER	15.00	7.50
❑ 179 Gair Allie RC	15.00	7.50
❑ 180 Wes Westrum	25.00	12.50
❑ 181 Mel Roach RC	15.00	7.50
❑ 182 Chuck Harmon RC	15.00	7.50
❑ 183 Earle Combs CO	25.00	12.50
❑ 184 Ed Bailey	15.00	7.50
❑ 185 Chuck Stobbs	15.00	7.50
❑ 186 Karl Olson	15.00	7.50
❑ 187 Heinie Manush CO	25.00	12.50
❑ 188 Dave Jolly RC	15.00	7.50
❑ 189 Bob Ross	15.00	7.50
❑ 190 Ray Herbert RC	15.00	7.50
❑ 191 Dick Schofield RC	25.00	12.50
❑ 192 Ellis Deal CO	15.00	7.50
❑ 193 Johnny Hopp CO	25.00	12.50
❑ 194 Bill Sarni RC	15.00	7.50
❑ 195 Billy Consolo RC	15.00	7.50
❑ 196 Stan Jok RC	15.00	7.50
❑ 197 Lynwood Rowe CO	25.00	12.50
❑ 198 Carl Sawatski	15.00	7.50
❑ 199 Glenn (Rocky) Nelson	15.00	7.50
❑ 200 Larry Jansen	25.00	12.50
❑ 201 Al Kaline RC	700.00	400.00
❑ 202 Bob Purkey RC	25.00	12.50
❑ 203 Harry Brecheen CO	25.00	12.50
❑ 204 Angel Scull RC	15.00	7.50
❑ 205 Johnny Sain	40.00	20.00
❑ 206 Ray Crone RC	15.00	7.50
❑ 207 Tom Oliver CO RC	15.00	7.50
❑ 208 Grady Hatton	15.00	7.50
❑ 209 Chuck Thompson RC	15.00	7.50
❑ 210 Bob Buhl RC	25.00	12.50
❑ 211 Don Hoak	25.00	12.50
❑ 212 Bob Micelotta RC	15.00	7.50
❑ 213 Johnny Fitzpatrick CO RC	15.00	7.50
❑ 214 Arnie Portocarrero RC	15.00	7.50
❑ 215 Ed McGhee	25.00	12.50
❑ 216 Al Sima	15.00	7.50
❑ 217 Paul Schreiber CO RC	15.00	7.50
❑ 218 Fred Marsh	15.00	7.50

Card		
❑ 219 Chuck Kress RC	15.00	7.50
❑ 220 Ruben Gomez RC	25.00	12.50
❑ 221 Dick Brodowski	15.00	7.50
❑ 222 Bill Wilson RC	15.00	7.50
❑ 223 Joe Haynes CO	15.00	7.50
❑ 224 Dick Weik RC	15.00	7.50
❑ 225 Don Liddle RC	15.00	7.50
❑ 226 Jehosie Heard RC	25.00	12.50
❑ 227 Buster Mills CO RC	15.00	7.50
❑ 228 Gene Hermanski	15.00	7.50
❑ 229 Bob Talbot RC	15.00	7.50
❑ 230 Bob Kuzava	25.00	12.50
❑ 231 Roy Smalley	15.00	7.50
❑ 232 Lou Limmer RC	15.00	7.50
❑ 233 Augie Galan CO	15.00	7.50
❑ 234 Jerry Lynch RC	15.00	7.50
❑ 235 Vern Law	25.00	12.50
❑ 236 Paul Penson RC	15.00	7.50
❑ 237 Mike Ryba CO RC	15.00	7.50
❑ 238 Al Aber	15.00	7.50
❑ 239 Bill Skowron RC	100.00	60.00
❑ 240 Sam Mele	25.00	12.50
❑ 241 Robert Miller RC	15.00	7.50
❑ 242 Curt Roberts RC	15.00	7.50
❑ 243 Ray Blades CO RC	15.00	7.50
❑ 244 Leroy Wheat RC	15.00	7.50
❑ 245 Roy Sievers	25.00	12.50
❑ 246 Howie Fox	15.00	7.50
❑ 247 Ed Mayo CO	15.00	7.50
❑ 248 Al Smith RC	25.00	12.50
❑ 249 Wilmer Mizell	25.00	12.50
❑ 250 Ted Williams	1000.00	500.00

1955 Topps

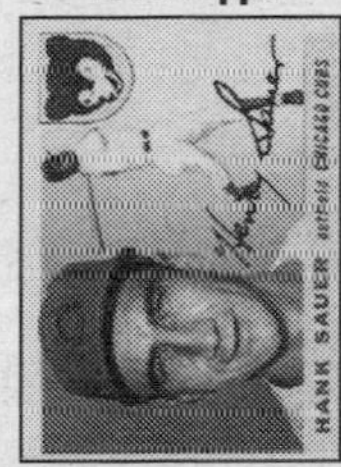

Card		
❑ COMPLETE SET (206)	8000.00	5000.00
❑ COMMON CARD (1-150)	12.00	6.00
❑ COMMON CARD (151-160)	20.00	10.00
❑ COMMON CARD (161-210)	30.00	15.00
❑ NOT ISSUED (175/186/203/209)		
❑ WRAP.(1-CENT, DATED)	150.00	100.00
❑ WRAP.(1-CENT, UNDAT)	50.00	40.00
❑ WRAP.(5-CENT, DATED)	150.00	100.00
❑ WRAP.(5-CENT, UNDAT)	100.00	75.00
❑ 1 Dusty Rhodes	125.00	75.00
❑ 2 Ted Williams	700.00	400.00
❑ 3 Art Fowler RC	15.00	7.50
❑ 4 Al Kaline	150.00	90.00
❑ 5 Jim Gilliam	40.00	20.00
❑ 6 Stan Hack MG RC	25.00	12.50
❑ 7 Jim Hegan	15.00	7.50
❑ 8 Harold Smith RC	12.00	6.00
❑ 9 Robert Miller	12.00	6.00
❑ 10 Bob Keegan	12.00	6.00
❑ 11 Ferris Fain	15.00	7.50
❑ 12 Vernon (Jake) Thies RC	12.00	6.00
❑ 13 Fred Marsh	12.00	6.00
❑ 14 Jim Finigan RC	12.00	6.00
❑ 15 Jim Pendleton	12.00	6.00
❑ 16 Roy Sievers	15.00	7.50
❑ 17 Bobby Hofman	12.00	6.00
❑ 18 Russ Kemmerer RC	12.00	6.00
❑ 19 Billy Herman CO	15.00	7.50
❑ 20 Andy Carey	15.00	7.50
❑ 21 Alex Grammas	12.00	6.00
❑ 22 Bill Skowron	40.00	20.00
❑ 23 Jack Parks RC	12.00	6.00
❑ 24 Hal Newhouser	40.00	20.00
❑ 25 Johnny Podres	25.00	12.50
❑ 26 Dick Groat	15.00	7.50
❑ 27 Billy Gardner RC	15.00	7.50
❑ 28 Ernie Banks	200.00	125.00
❑ 29 Herman Wehmeier	12.00	6.00
❑ 30 Vic Power	15.00	7.50
❑ 31 Warren Spahn	100.00	60.00
❑ 32 Warren McGhee RC	12.00	6.00
❑ 33 Tom Qualters	12.00	6.00
❑ 34 Wayne Terwilliger	12.00	6.00
❑ 35 Dave Jolly	12.00	6.00
❑ 36 Leo Kiely	12.00	6.00
❑ 37 Joe Cunningham RC	15.00	7.50
❑ 38 Bob Turley	15.00	7.50
❑ 39 Bill Glynn	12.00	6.00
❑ 40 Don Hoak	15.00	7.50
❑ 41 Chuck Stobbs	12.00	6.00
❑ 42 John (Windy) McCall RC	12.00	6.00
❑ 43 Harvey Haddix	15.00	7.50
❑ 44 Harold Valentine RC	12.00	6.00
❑ 45 Hank Sauer	15.00	7.50
❑ 46 Ted Kazanski	12.00	6.00
❑ 47 Hank Aaron	400.00	250.00
❑ 48 Bob Kennedy	15.00	7.50
❑ 49 J.W. Porter	12.00	6.00
❑ 50 Jackie Robinson	500.00	300.00
❑ 51 Jim Hughes	15.00	7.50
❑ 52 Bill Tremel RC	12.00	6.00
❑ 53 Bill Taylor	12.00	6.00
❑ 54 Lou Limmer	12.00	6.00
❑ 55 Rip Repulski	12.00	6.00
❑ 56 Ray Jablonski	12.00	6.00
❑ 57 Billy O'Dell RC	12.00	6.00
❑ 58 Jim Rivera	12.00	6.00
❑ 59 Gair Allie	12.00	6.00
❑ 60 Dean Stone	12.00	6.00
❑ 61 Forrest Jacobs	12.00	6.00
❑ 62 Thornton Kipper	12.00	6.00
❑ 63 Joe Collins	15.00	7.50
❑ 64 Gus Triandos RC	15.00	7.50
❑ 65 Ray Boone	15.00	7.50
❑ 66 Ron Jackson RC	12.00	6.00
❑ 67 Wally Moon	15.00	7.50
❑ 68 Jim Davis RC	12.00	6.00
❑ 69 Ed Bailey	15.00	7.50
❑ 70 Al Rosen	15.00	7.50
❑ 71 Ruben Gomez	12.00	6.00
❑ 72 Karl Olson	12.00	6.00
❑ 73 Jack Shepard RC	12.00	6.00
❑ 74 Bob Borkowski	12.00	6.00
❑ 75 Sandy Amoros RC	40.00	20.00
❑ 76 Howie Pollet	12.00	6.00
❑ 77 Arnie Portocarrero	12.00	6.00
❑ 78 Gordon Jones RC	12.00	6.00
❑ 79 Clyde (Danny) Schell RC	12.00	6.00
❑ 80 Bob Grim RC	15.00	7.50
❑ 81 Gene Conley	15.00	7.50
❑ 82 Chuck Harmon	12.00	6.00
❑ 83 Tom Brewer RC	12.00	6.00
❑ 84 Camilo Pascual RC	15.00	7.50
❑ 85 Don Mossi RC	25.00	12.50
❑ 86 Bill Wilson	12.00	6.00
❑ 87 Frank House	12.00	6.00
❑ 88 Bob Skinner RC	15.00	7.50
❑ 89 Joe Frazier RC	15.00	7.50
❑ 90 Karl Spooner RC	15.00	7.50
❑ 91 Milt Bolling	12.00	6.00
❑ 92 Don Zimmer RC	25.00	12.50
❑ 93 Steve Bilko	12.00	6.00
❑ 94 Reno Bertoia	12.00	6.00
❑ 95 Preston Ward	12.00	6.00
❑ 96 Chuck Bishop	12.00	6.00
❑ 97 Carlos Paula RC	12.00	6.00
❑ 98 John Riddle CO	12.00	6.00
❑ 99 Frank Leja	12.00	6.00
❑ 100 Monte Irvin	40.00	20.00
❑ 101 Johnny Gray RC	12.00	6.00
❑ 102 Wally Westlake	12.00	6.00
❑ 103 Chuck White RC	12.00	6.00
❑ 104 Jack Harshman	12.00	6.00
❑ 105 Chuck Diering	12.00	6.00
❑ 106 Frank Sullivan RC	12.00	6.00
❑ 107 Curt Roberts	12.00	6.00
❑ 108 Rube Walker	15.00	7.50
❑ 109 Ed Lopat	15.00	7.50
❑ 110 Gus Zernial	15.00	7.50
❑ 111 Bob Milliken	15.00	7.50
❑ 112 Nelson King RC	12.00	6.00
❑ 113 Harry Brecheen CO	15.00	7.50
❑ 114 Louis Ortiz RC	12.00	6.00
❑ 115 Ellis Kinder	12.00	6.00
❑ 116 Tom Hurd RC	12.00	6.00
❑ 117 Mel Roach	12.00	6.00
❑ 118 Bob Purkey	12.00	6.00
❑ 119 Bob Lennon RC	12.00	6.00
❑ 120 Ted Kluszewski	80.00	50.00
❑ 121 Bill Renna	12.00	6.00
❑ 122 Carl Sawatski	12.00	6.00
❑ 123 Sandy Koufax RC	1200.00	700.00
❑ 124 Harmon Killebrew RC	250.00	150.00
❑ 125 Ken Boyer RC	80.00	50.00
❑ 126 Dick Hall RC	12.00	6.00
❑ 127 Dale Long RC	15.00	7.50
❑ 128 Ted Lepcio	12.00	6.00
❑ 129 Elvin Tappe	15.00	7.50
❑ 130 Mayo Smith MG RC	12.00	6.00
❑ 131 Grady Hatton	12.00	6.00
❑ 132 Bob Trice	12.00	6.00
❑ 133 Dave Hoskins	12.00	6.00
❑ 134 Joey Jay	15.00	7.50
❑ 135 Johnny O'Brien	15.00	7.50
❑ 136 Veston (Bunky) Stewart RC	12.00	6.00
❑ 137 Harry Elliott RC	12.00	6.00
❑ 138 Ray Herbert	12.00	6.00
❑ 139 Steve Kraly RC	12.00	6.00
❑ 140 Mel Parnell	15.00	7.50
❑ 141 Tom Wright	12.00	6.00
❑ 142 Jerry Lynch	15.00	7.50
❑ 143 John Schofield	15.00	7.50
❑ 144 Joe Amalfitano RC	12.00	6.00
❑ 145 Elmer Valo	12.00	6.00
❑ 146 Dick Donovan RC	12.00	6.00
❑ 147 Hugh Pepper RC	12.00	6.00
❑ 148 Hector Brown	12.00	6.00
❑ 149 Ray Crone	12.00	6.00
❑ 150 Mike Higgins MG	12.00	6.00
❑ 151 Ralph Kress CO	20.00	10.00
❑ 152 Harry Agganis RC	100.00	60.00
❑ 153 Bud Podbielan	25.00	12.50
❑ 154 Willie Miranda	20.00	10.00
❑ 155 Eddie Mathews	200.00	125.00
❑ 156 Joe Black	50.00	30.00
❑ 157 Robert Miller	20.00	10.00
❑ 158 Tommy Carroll RC	25.00	12.50
❑ 159 Johnny Schmitz	20.00	10.00
❑ 160 Ray Narleski RC	20.00	10.00
❑ 161 Chuck Tanner RC	40.00	20.00
❑ 162 Joe Coleman	30.00	15.00
❑ 163 Faye Throneberry	30.00	15.00
❑ 164 Roberto Clemente RC	2200.00	1400.00
❑ 165 Don Johnson	30.00	15.00
❑ 166 Hank Bauer	80.00	50.00
❑ 167 Tom Casagrande RC	30.00	15.00
❑ 168 Duane Pillette	30.00	15.00
❑ 169 Bob Oldis	40.00	20.00
❑ 170 Jim Pearce DP RC	15.00	7.50
❑ 171 Dick Brodowski	30.00	15.00
❑ 172 Frank Baumholtz DP	15.00	7.50
❑ 173 Bob Kline RC	30.00	15.00
❑ 174 Rudy Minarcin RC	30.00	15.00
❑ 175 Does not exist		
❑ 176 Norm Zauchin RC	30.00	15.00
❑ 177 Al Robertson	30.00	15.00
❑ 178 Bobby Adams	30.00	15.00
❑ 179 Jim Bolger RC	30.00	15.00
❑ 180 Clem Labine	60.00	30.00
❑ 181 Roy McMillan	40.00	20.00
❑ 182 Humberto Robinson RC	30.00	15.00
❑ 183 Anthony Jacobs RC	30.00	15.00
❑ 184 Harry Perkowski DP	15.00	7.50
❑ 185 Don Ferrarese RC	30.00	15.00
❑ 186 Does not exist		
❑ 187 Gil Hodges	175.00	100.00
❑ 188 Charlie Silvera DP	15.00	7.50
❑ 189 Phil Rizzuto	175.00	100.00
❑ 190 Gene Woodling	40.00	20.00
❑ 191 Eddie Stanky MG	40.00	20.00
❑ 192 Jim Delsing	40.00	20.00
❑ 193 Johnny Sain	60.00	30.00
❑ 194 Willie Mays	600.00	350.00
❑ 195 Ed Roebuck RC	60.00	30.00
❑ 196 Gale Wade RC	30.00	15.00
❑ 197 Al Smith	60.00	30.00

❑ 198	Yogi Berra	300.00	175.00
❑ 199	Bert Hamric RC	40.00	20.00
❑ 200	Jackie Jensen	60.00	30.00
❑ 201	Sherman Lollar	40.00	20.00
❑ 202	Jim Owens RC	30.00	15.00
❑ 203	Does not exist		
❑ 204	Frank Smith	30.00	15.00
❑ 205	Gene Freese RC	40.00	20.00
❑ 206	Pete Daley RC	30.00	15.00
❑ 207	Billy Consolo	30.00	15.00
❑ 208	Ray Moore RC	40.00	20.00
❑ 209	Does not exist		
❑ 210	Duke Snider	600.00	350.00

1956 Topps

❑	COMPLETE SET (340)	8000.00	5000.00
❑	COMMON CARD (1-100)	10.00	5.00
❑	COMMON CARD (101-180)	12.00	6.00
❑	COMMON CARD (261-340)	12.00	6.00
❑	COMMON CARD (181-260)	15.00	7.50
❑	WRAP.(1-CENT)	250.00	200.00
❑	WRAP.(1-CENT, REPEAT)	100.00	75.00
❑	WRAPPER (5-CENT)	200.00	150.00
❑ 1	Will Harridge PRES	125.00	75.00
❑ 2	Warren Giles PRES DP	50.00	30.00
❑ 3	Elmer Valo	15.00	7.50
❑ 4	Carlos Paula	15.00	7.50
❑ 5	Ted Williams	500.00	300.00
❑ 6	Ray Boone	25.00	15.00
❑ 7	Ron Negray RC	10.00	5.00
❑ 8	Walter Alston MG RC	40.00	25.00
❑ 9	Ruben Gomez DP	10.00	5.00
❑ 10	Warren Spahn	120.00	70.00
❑ 11A	Chicago Cubs TC Center	30.00	15.00
❑ 11B	Chicago Cubs TC D'55	80.00	50.00
❑ 11C	Chicago Cubs TC Left	30.00	15.00
❑ 12	Andy Carey	15.00	7.50
❑ 13	Roy Face	15.00	7.50
❑ 14	Ken Boyer DP	15.00	7.50
❑ 15	Ernie Banks DP	100.00	60.00
❑ 16	Hector Lopez RC	15.00	7.50
❑ 17	Gene Conley	15.00	7.50
❑ 18	Dick Donovan	10.00	5.00
❑ 19	Chuck Diering DP	10.00	5.00
❑ 20	Al Kaline	125.00	75.00
❑ 21	Joe Collins DP	15.00	7.50
❑ 22	Jim Finigan	10.00	5.00
❑ 23	Fred Marsh	10.00	5.00
❑ 24	Dick Groat	15.00	7.50
❑ 25	Ted Kluszewski	80.00	50.00
❑ 25A	Ted Kluszewski GB		
❑ 26	Grady Hatton	10.00	5.00
❑ 27	Nelson Burbrink DP RC	10.00	5.00
❑ 28	Bobby Hofman	10.00	5.00
❑ 29	Jack Harshman	10.00	5.00
❑ 30	Jackie Robinson DP	250.00	150.00
❑ 31	Hank Aaron UER DP	350.00	200.00
❑ 32	Frank House	10.00	5.00
❑ 33	Roberto Clemente	400.00	250.00
❑ 34	Tom Brewer DP	10.00	5.00
❑ 35	Al Rosen	15.00	7.50
❑ 36	Rudy Minarcin	15.00	7.50
❑ 37	Alex Grammas	10.00	5.00
❑ 38	Bob Kennedy	15.00	7.50
❑ 39	Don Mossi	15.00	7.50
❑ 40	Bob Turley	15.00	7.50
❑ 41	Hank Sauer	15.00	7.50
❑ 42	Sandy Amoros	25.00	15.00
❑ 43	Ray Moore	10.00	5.00
❑ 44	Windy McCall	10.00	5.00
❑ 45	Gus Zernial	15.00	7.50
❑ 46	Gene Freese DP	10.00	5.00
❑ 47	Art Fowler	10.00	5.00
❑ 48	Jim Hegan	15.00	7.50
❑ 49	Pedro Ramos RC	10.00	5.00
❑ 50	Dusty Rhodes DP	15.00	7.50
❑ 51	Ernie Oravetz RC	10.00	5.00
❑ 52	Bob Grim DP	15.00	7.50
❑ 53	Arnie Portocarrero	10.00	5.00
❑ 54	Bob Keegan	10.00	5.00
❑ 55	Wally Moon	15.00	7.50
❑ 56	Dale Long	15.00	7.50
❑ 57	Duke Maas RC	10.00	5.00
❑ 58	Ed Roebuck	25.00	15.00
❑ 59	Jose Santiago RC	10.00	5.00
❑ 60	Mayo Smith MG DP	10.00	5.00
❑ 61	Bill Skowron	25.00	15.00
❑ 62	Hal Smith	15.00	7.50
❑ 63	Roger Craig RC	40.00	25.00
❑ 64	Luis Arroyo RC	10.00	5.00
❑ 65	Johnny O'Brien	15.00	7.50
❑ 66	Bob Speake DP RC	10.00	5.00
❑ 67	Vic Power	15.00	7.50
❑ 68	Chuck Stobbs	10.00	5.00
❑ 69	Chuck Tanner	15.00	7.50
❑ 70	Jim Rivera	10.00	5.00
❑ 71	Frank Sullivan	10.00	5.00
❑ 72A	Philadelphia Phillies TC Center	30.00	15.00
❑ 72B	Philadelphia Phillies TC D'55	80.00	50.00
❑ 72C	Philadelphia Phillies TC Left DP	30.00	15.00
❑ 73	Wayne Terwilliger	10.00	5.00
❑ 74	Jim King RC	10.00	5.00
❑ 75	Roy Sievers DP	15.00	7.50
❑ 76	Ray Crone	10.00	5.00
❑ 77	Harvey Haddix	15.00	7.50
❑ 78	Herman Wehmeier	10.00	5.00
❑ 79	Sandy Koufax	350.00	200.00
❑ 80	Gus Triandos DP	10.00	5.00
❑ 81	Wally Westlake	10.00	5.00
❑ 82	Bill Renna DP	10.00	5.00
❑ 83	Karl Spooner	15.00	7.50
❑ 84	Babe Birrer RC	10.00	5.00
❑ 85A	Cleveland Indians TC Center	30.00	15.00
❑ 85B	Cleveland Indians TC D'55	80.00	50.00
❑ 85C	Cleveland Indians TC Left	30.00	15.00
❑ 86	Ray Jablonski DP	10.00	5.00
❑ 87	Dean Stone	10.00	5.00
❑ 88	Johnny Kucks RC	15.00	7.50
❑ 89	Norm Zauchin	10.00	5.00
❑ 90A	Cincinnati Redlegs TC Center	30.00	15.00
❑ 90B	Cincinnati Reds TC D'55	80.00	50.00
❑ 90C	Cincinnati Reds TC Left	30.00	15.00
❑ 91	Gail Harris RC	10.00	5.00
❑ 92	Bob (Red) Wilson	10.00	5.00
❑ 93	George Susce	10.00	5.00
❑ 94	Ron Kline	10.00	5.00
❑ 95A	Milwaukee Braves TC Center	40.00	20.00
❑ 95B	Milwaukee Braves TC D'55	80.00	50.00
❑ 95C	Milwaukee Braves TC Left	40.00	20.00
❑ 96	Bill Tremel	10.00	5.00
❑ 97	Jerry Lynch	15.00	7.50
❑ 98	Camilo Pascual	15.00	7.50
❑ 99	Don Zimmer	25.00	15.00
❑ 100A	Baltimore Orioles TC Center	40.00	20.00
❑ 100B	Baltimore Orioles TC D'55	80.00	50.00
❑ 100C	Baltimore Orioles TC Left	40.00	20.00
❑ 101	Roy Campanella	150.00	90.00
❑ 102	Jim Davis	12.00	6.00
❑ 103	Willie Miranda	12.00	6.00
❑ 104	Bob Lennon	12.00	6.00
❑ 105	Al Smith	12.00	6.00
❑ 106	Joe Astroth	12.00	6.00
❑ 107	Eddie Mathews	100.00	60.00
❑ 108	Laurin Pepper	12.00	6.00
❑ 109	Enos Slaughter	40.00	25.00
❑ 110	Yogi Berra	175.00	100.00
❑ 111	Boston Red Sox TC	40.00	20.00
❑ 112	Dee Fondy	12.00	6.00
❑ 113	Phil Rizzuto	150.00	90.00
❑ 114	Jim Owens	15.00	7.50
❑ 115	Jackie Jensen	15.00	7.50
❑ 116	Eddie O'Brien	12.00	6.00
❑ 117	Virgil Trucks	15.00	7.50
❑ 118	Nellie Fox	80.00	50.00
❑ 119	Larry Jackson RC	15.00	7.50
❑ 120	Richie Ashburn	60.00	35.00
❑ 121	Pittsburgh Pirates TC	40.00	20.00
❑ 122	Willard Nixon	12.00	6.00
❑ 123	Roy McMillan	15.00	7.50
❑ 124	Don Kaiser	12.00	6.00
❑ 125	Minnie Minoso	40.00	25.00
❑ 126	Jim Brady RC	12.00	6.00
❑ 127	Willie Jones	15.00	7.50
❑ 128	Eddie Yost	15.00	7.50
❑ 129	Jake Martin RC	12.00	6.00
❑ 130	Willie Mays	300.00	175.00
❑ 131	Bob Roselli RC	12.00	6.00
❑ 132	Bobby Avila	12.00	6.00
❑ 133	Ray Narleski	12.00	6.00
❑ 134	St. Louis Cardinals TC	40.00	20.00
❑ 135	Mickey Mantle	1500.00	900.00
❑ 136	Johnny Logan	15.00	7.50
❑ 137	Al Silvera RC	12.00	6.00
❑ 138	Johnny Antonelli	15.00	7.50
❑ 139	Tommy Carroll	15.00	7.50
❑ 140	Herb Score RC	60.00	35.00
❑ 141	Joe Frazier	12.00	6.00
❑ 142	Gene Baker	12.00	6.00
❑ 143	Jim Piersall	15.00	7.50
❑ 144	Leroy Powell RC	12.00	6.00
❑ 145	Gil Hodges	60.00	35.00
❑ 146	Washington Nationals TC	40.00	20.00
❑ 147	Earl Torgeson	12.00	6.00
❑ 148	Alvin Dark	15.00	7.50
❑ 149	Dixie Howell	12.00	6.00
❑ 150	Duke Snider	125.00	75.00
❑ 151	Spook Jacobs	15.00	7.50
❑ 152	Billy Hoeft	15.00	7.50
❑ 153	Frank Thomas	15.00	7.50
❑ 154	Dave Pope	12.00	6.00
❑ 155	Harvey Kuenn	15.00	7.50
❑ 156	Wes Westrum	15.00	7.50
❑ 157	Dick Brodowski	12.00	6.00
❑ 158	Wally Post	15.00	7.50
❑ 159	Clint Courtney	12.00	6.00
❑ 160	Billy Pierce	15.00	7.50
❑ 161	Joe DeMaestri	12.00	6.00
❑ 162	Dave (Gus) Bell	15.00	7.50
❑ 163	Gene Woodling	15.00	7.50
❑ 164	Harmon Killebrew	100.00	60.00
❑ 165	Red Schoendienst	40.00	25.00
❑ 166	Brooklyn Dodgers TC	200.00	125.00
❑ 167	Harry Dorish	12.00	6.00
❑ 168	Sammy White	12.00	6.00
❑ 169	Bob Nelson RC	12.00	6.00
❑ 170	Bill Virdon	15.00	7.50
❑ 171	Jim Wilson	12.00	6.00
❑ 172	Frank Torre RC	15.00	7.50
❑ 173	Johnny Podres	25.00	15.00
❑ 174	Glen Gorbous RC	12.00	6.00
❑ 175	Del Crandall	15.00	7.50
❑ 176	Alex Kellner	12.00	6.00
❑ 177	Hank Bauer	25.00	15.00
❑ 178	Joe Black	15.00	7.50
❑ 179	Harry Chiti	12.00	6.00
❑ 180	Robin Roberts	50.00	30.00
❑ 181	Billy Martin	125.00	75.00
❑ 182	Paul Minner	15.00	7.50
❑ 183	Stan Lopata	20.00	10.00
❑ 184	Don Bessent RC	20.00	10.00
❑ 185	Bill Bruton	20.00	10.00
❑ 186	Ron Jackson	15.00	7.50
❑ 187	Early Wynn	50.00	30.00
❑ 188	Chicago White Sox TC	50.00	30.00
❑ 189	Ned Garver	15.00	7.50
❑ 190	Carl Furillo	30.00	18.00
❑ 191	Frank Lary	20.00	10.00
❑ 192	Smoky Burgess	20.00	10.00
❑ 193	Wilmer Mizell	20.00	10.00
❑ 194	Monte Irvin	30.00	18.00
❑ 195	George Kell	30.00	18.00
❑ 196	Tom Poholsky	15.00	7.50
❑ 197	Granny Hamner	15.00	7.50
❑ 198	Ed Fitzgerald	15.00	7.50
❑ 199	Hank Thompson	20.00	10.00
❑ 200	Bob Feller	125.00	75.00
❑ 201	Rip Repulski	15.00	7.50
❑ 202	Jim Hearn	15.00	7.50
❑ 203	Bill Tuttle	15.00	7.50
❑ 204	Art Swanson RC	15.00	7.50

❑ 205 Whitey Lockman 20.00 10.00
❑ 206 Erv Palica 15.00 7.50
❑ 207 Jim Small RC 15.00 7.50
❑ 208 Elston Howard 60.00 35.00
❑ 209 Max Surkont 15.00 7.50
❑ 210 Mike Garcia 20.00 10.00
❑ 211 Murry Dickson 15.00 7.50
❑ 212 Johnny Temple 15.00 7.50
❑ 213 Detroit Tigers TC 60.00 35.00
❑ 214 Bob Rush 15.00 7.50
❑ 215 Tommy Byrne 20.00 10.00
❑ 216 Jerry Schoonmaker RC 15.00 7.50
❑ 217 Billy Klaus 15.00 7.50
❑ 218 Joe Nuxhall UER 20.00 10.00
❑ 219 Lew Burdette 20.00 10.00
❑ 220 Del Ennis 20.00 10.00
❑ 221 Bob Friend 20.00 10.00
❑ 222 Dave Philley 15.00 7.50
❑ 223 Randy Jackson 15.00 7.50
❑ 224 Bud Podbielan 15.00 7.50
❑ 225 Gil McDougald 50.00 30.00
❑ 226 New York Giants TC 80.00 50.00
❑ 227 Russ Meyer 15.00 7.50
❑ 228 Mickey Vernon 20.00 10.00
❑ 229 Harry Brecheen CO 20.00 10.00
❑ 230 Chico Carrasquel 15.00 7.50
❑ 231 Bob Hale RC 15.00 7.50
❑ 232 Toby Atwell 15.00 7.50
❑ 233 Carl Erskine 30.00 18.00
❑ 234 Pete Runnels 15.00 7.50
❑ 235 Don Newcombe 50.00 30.00
❑ 236 Kansas City Athletics TC 40.00 20.00
❑ 237 Jose Valdivielso RC 15.00 7.50
❑ 238 Walt Dropo 20.00 10.00
❑ 239 Harry Simpson 15.00 7.50
❑ 240 Whitey Ford 125.00 75.00
❑ 241 Don Mueller UER 20.00 10.00
❑ 242 Hershell Freeman 15.00 7.50
❑ 243 Sherm Lollar 20.00 10.00
❑ 244 Bob Buhl 30.00 18.00
❑ 245 Billy Goodman 20.00 10.00
❑ 246 Tom Gorman 15.00 7.50
❑ 247 Bill Sarni 15.00 7.50
❑ 248 Bob Porterfield 15.00 7.50
❑ 249 Johnny Klippstein 15.00 7.50
❑ 250 Larry Doby 30.00 18.00
❑ 251 New York Yankees TC UER 250.00 150.00
❑ 252 Vern Law 20.00 10.00
❑ 253 Irv Noren 30.00 18.00
❑ 254 George Crowe 15.00 7.50
❑ 255 Bob Lemon 50.00 30.00
❑ 256 Tom Hurd 15.00 7.50
❑ 257 Bobby Thomson 30.00 18.00
❑ 258 Art Ditmar 15.00 7.50
❑ 259 Sam Jones 20.00 10.00
❑ 260 Pee Wee Reese 150.00 90.00
❑ 261 Bobby Shantz 15.00 7.50
❑ 262 Howie Pollet 12.00 6.00
❑ 263 Bob Miller 12.00 6.00
❑ 264 Ray Monzant RC 12.00 6.00
❑ 265 Sandy Consuegra 12.00 6.00
❑ 266 Don Ferrarese 12.00 6.00
❑ 267 Bob Nieman 12.00 6.00
❑ 268 Dale Mitchell 15.00 7.50
❑ 269 Jack Meyer RC 12.00 6.00
❑ 270 Billy Loes 15.00 7.50
❑ 271 Foster Castleman RC 12.00 6.00
❑ 272 Danny O'Connell 12.00 6.00
❑ 273 Walker Cooper 12.00 6.00
❑ 274 Frank Baumholtz 12.00 6.00
❑ 275 Jim Greengrass 12.00 6.00
❑ 276 George Zuverink 12.00 6.00
❑ 277 Daryl Spencer 12.00 6.00
❑ 278 Chet Nichols 12.00 6.00
❑ 279 Johnny Groth 12.00 6.00
❑ 280 Jim Gilliam 40.00 25.00
❑ 281 Art Houtteman 12.00 6.00
❑ 282 Warren Hacker 12.00 6.00
❑ 283 Hal R.Smith RC 15.00 7.50
❑ 284 Ike Delock 12.00 6.00
❑ 285 Eddie Miksis 12.00 6.00
❑ 286 Bill Wight 12.00 6.00
❑ 287 Bobby Adams 12.00 6.00
❑ 288 Bob Cerv 40.00 25.00
❑ 289 Hal Jeffcoat 12.00 6.00
❑ 290 Curt Simmons 15.00 7.50
❑ 291 Frank Kellert RC 12.00 6.00
❑ 292 Luis Aparicio RC 150.00 90.00
❑ 293 Stu Miller 25.00 15.00
❑ 294 Ernie Johnson 15.00 7.50
❑ 295 Clem Labine 15.00 7.50
❑ 296 Andy Seminick 12.00 6.00
❑ 297 Bob Skinner 15.00 7.50
❑ 298 Johnny Schmitz 12.00 6.00
❑ 299 Charlie Neal 40.00 25.00
❑ 300 Vic Wertz 15.00 7.50
❑ 301 Marv Grissom 12.00 6.00
❑ 302 Eddie Robinson 12.00 6.00
❑ 303 Jim Dyck 12.00 6.00
❑ 304 Frank Malzone 15.00 7.50
❑ 305 Brooks Lawrence 12.00 6.00
❑ 306 Curt Roberts 12.00 6.00
❑ 307 Hoyt Wilhelm 40.00 25.00
❑ 308 Chuck Harmon 12.00 6.00
❑ 309 Don Blasingame RC 15.00 7.50
❑ 310 Steve Gromek 12.00 6.00
❑ 311 Hal Naragon 12.00 6.00
❑ 312 Andy Pafko 15.00 7.50
❑ 313 Gene Stephens 12.00 6.00
❑ 314 Hobie Landrith 12.00 6.00
❑ 315 Milt Bolling 12.00 6.00
❑ 316 Jerry Coleman 15.00 7.50
❑ 317 Al Aber 12.00 6.00
❑ 318 Fred Hatfield 12.00 6.00
❑ 319 Jack Crimian RC 12.00 6.00
❑ 320 Joe Adcock 15.00 7.50
❑ 321 Jim Konstanty 15.00 7.50
❑ 322 Karl Olson 12.00 6.00
❑ 323 Willard Schmidt 12.00 6.00
❑ 324 Rocky Bridges 15.00 7.50
❑ 325 Don Liddle 12.00 6.00
❑ 326 Connie Johnson RC 12.00 6.00
❑ 327 Bob Wiesler RC 12.00 6.00
❑ 328 Preston Ward 12.00 6.00
❑ 329 Lou Berberet RC 12.00 6.00
❑ 330 Jim Busby 15.00 7.50
❑ 331 Dick Hall 12.00 6.00
❑ 332 Don Larsen 60.00 35.00
❑ 333 Rube Walker 12.00 6.00
❑ 334 Bob Miller 15.00 7.50
❑ 335 Don Hoak 15.00 7.50
❑ 336 Ellis Kinder 12.00 6.00
❑ 337 Bobby Morgan 12.00 6.00
❑ 338 Jim Delsing 12.00 6.00
❑ 339 Rance Pless RC 12.00 6.00
❑ 340 Mickey McDermott 60.00 35.00
❑ CL1 Checklist 1/3 300.00 175.00
❑ CL2 Checklist 2/4 300.00 175.00

1957 Topps

❑ COMPLETE SET (407) 10000.00 7000.00
❑ COMMON CARD (1-88) 10.00 5.00
❑ COMMON CARD (89-176) 8.00 4.00
❑ COMMON CARD (177-264) 8.00 4.00
❑ COMMON CARD (265-352) 20.00 10.00
❑ COMMON CARD (353-407) 8.00 4.00
❑ COMMON DP (265-352) 12.00 6.00
❑ WRAPPER (1-CENT) 300.00 250.00
❑ WRAPPER (5-CENT) 200.00 150.00
❑ 1 Ted Williams 600.00 350.00
❑ 2 Yogi Berra 200.00 125.00
❑ 3 Dale Long 20.00 10.00
❑ 4 Johnny Logan 20.00 10.00
❑ 5 Sal Maglie 20.00 10.00
❑ 6 Hector Lopez 15.00 7.50
❑ 7 Luis Aparicio 30.00 15.00
❑ 8 Don Mossi 15.00 7.50
❑ 9 Johnny Temple 15.00 7.50
❑ 10 Willie Mays 400.00 250.00
❑ 11 George Zuverink 10.00 5.00
❑ 12 Dick Groat 20.00 10.00
❑ 13 Wally Burnette RC 10.00 5.00
❑ 14 Bob Nieman 10.00 5.00
❑ 15 Robin Roberts 30.00 15.00
❑ 16 Walt Moryn 10.00 5.00
❑ 17 Billy Gardner 10.00 5.00
❑ 18 Don Drysdale RC 250.00 150.00
❑ 19 Bob Wilson 10.00 5.00
❑ 20 Hank Aaron UER 300.00 175.00
❑ 21 Frank Sullivan 10.00 5.00
❑ 22 Jerry Snyder UER 10.00 5.00
❑ 23 Sherm Lollar 15.00 7.50
❑ 24 Bill Mazeroski RC 80.00 50.00
❑ 25 Whitey Ford 175.00 100.00
❑ 26 Bob Boyd 10.00 5.00
❑ 27 Ted Kazanski 10.00 5.00
❑ 28 Gene Conley 15.00 7.50
❑ 29 Whitey Herzog RC 30.00 15.00
❑ 30 Pee Wee Reese 80.00 50.00
❑ 31 Ron Northey 10.00 5.00
❑ 32 Hershell Freeman 10.00 5.00
❑ 33 Jim Small 10.00 5.00
❑ 34 Tom Sturdivant RC 15.00 7.50
❑ 35 Frank Robinson RC 300.00 175.00
❑ 36 Bob Grim 10.00 5.00
❑ 37 Frank Torre 15.00 7.50
❑ 38 Nellie Fox 50.00 30.00
❑ 39 Al Worthington RC 10.00 5.00
❑ 40 Early Wynn 30.00 15.00
❑ 41 Hal W. Smith 10.00 5.00
❑ 42 Dee Fondy 10.00 5.00
❑ 43 Connie Johnson 10.00 5.00
❑ 44 Joe DeMaestri 10.00 5.00
❑ 45 Carl Furillo 30.00 15.00
❑ 46 Robert J. Miller 10.00 5.00
❑ 47 Don Blasingame 10.00 5.00
❑ 48 Bill Bruton 15.00 7.50
❑ 49 Daryl Spencer 10.00 5.00
❑ 50 Herb Score 30.00 15.00
❑ 51 Clint Courtney 10.00 5.00
❑ 52 Lee Walls 10.00 5.00
❑ 53 Clem Labine 20.00 10.00
❑ 54 Elmer Valo 10.00 5.00
❑ 55 Ernie Banks 125.00 75.00
❑ 56 Dave Sisler RC 10.00 5.00
❑ 57 Jim Lemon 15.00 7.50
❑ 58 Ruben Gomez 10.00 5.00
❑ 59 Dick Williams 15.00 7.50
❑ 60 Billy Hoeft 15.00 7.50
❑ 61 Dusty Rhodes 15.00 7.50
❑ 62 Billy Martin 60.00 35.00
❑ 63 Ike Delock 10.00 5.00
❑ 64 Pete Runnels 15.00 7.50
❑ 65 Wally Moon 15.00 7.50
❑ 66 Brooks Lawrence 10.00 5.00
❑ 67 Chico Carrasquel 10.00 5.00
❑ 68 Ray Crone 10.00 5.00
❑ 69 Roy McMillan 15.00 7.50
❑ 70 Richie Ashburn 50.00 30.00
❑ 71 Murry Dickson 10.00 5.00
❑ 72 Bill Tuttle 10.00 5.00
❑ 73 George Crowe 10.00 5.00
❑ 74 Vito Valentinetti RC 10.00 5.00
❑ 75 Jimmy Piersall 15.00 7.50
❑ 76 Roberto Clemente 300.00 175.00
❑ 77 Paul Foytack RC 10.00 5.00
❑ 78 Vic Wertz 15.00 7.50
❑ 79 Lindy McDaniel RC 15.00 7.50
❑ 80 Gil Hodges 50.00 30.00
❑ 81 Herman Wehmeier 10.00 5.00
❑ 82 Elston Howard 30.00 15.00
❑ 83 Lou Skizas RC 10.00 5.00
❑ 84 Moe Drabowsky RC 15.00 7.50
❑ 85 Larry Doby 30.00 15.00
❑ 86 Bill Sarni 10.00 5.00
❑ 87 Tom Gorman 10.00 5.00
❑ 88 Harvey Kuenn 15.00 7.50
❑ 89 Roy Sievers 15.00 7.50
❑ 90 Warren Spahn 80.00 50.00
❑ 91 Mack Burk RC 8.00 4.00

- ❑ 92 Mickey Vernon 15.00 7.50
- ❑ 93 Hal Jeffcoat 8.00 4.00
- ❑ 94 Bobby Del Greco 8.00 4.00
- ❑ 95 Mickey Mantle 1200.00 700.00
- ❑ 96 Hank Aguirre RC 8.00 4.00
- ❑ 97 New York Yankees TC 100.00 60.00
- ❑ 98 Alvin Dark 15.00 7.50
- ❑ 99 Bob Keegan 8.00 4.00
- ❑ 100 W.Giles/W.Harridge 15.00 7.50
- ❑ 101 Chuck Stobbs 8.00 4.00
- ❑ 102 Ray Boone 15.00 7.50
- ❑ 103 Joe Nuxhall 15.00 7.50
- ❑ 104 Hank Foiles 8.00 4.00
- ❑ 105 Johnny Antonelli 15.00 7.50
- ❑ 106 Ray Moore 8.00 4.00
- ❑ 107 Jim Rivera 8.00 4.00
- ❑ 108 Tommy Byrne 15.00 7.50
- ❑ 109 Hank Thompson 8.00 4.00
- ❑ 110 Bill Virdon 15.00 7.50
- ❑ 111 Hal R. Smith 8.00 4.00
- ❑ 112 Tom Brewer 8.00 4.00
- ❑ 113 Wilmer Mizell 15.00 7.50
- ❑ 114 Milwaukee Braves TC 20.00 10.00
- ❑ 115 Jim Gilliam 15.00 7.50
- ❑ 116 Mike Fornieles 8.00 4.00
- ❑ 117 Joe Adcock 20.00 10.00
- ❑ 118 Bob Porterfield 8.00 4.00
- ❑ 119 Stan Lopata 8.00 4.00
- ❑ 120 Bob Lemon 30.00 15.00
- ❑ 121 Clete Boyer RC 30.00 15.00
- ❑ 122 Ken Boyer 20.00 10.00
- ❑ 123 Steve Ridzik 8.00 4.00
- ❑ 124 Dave Philley 8.00 4.00
- ❑ 125 Al Kaline 100.00 60.00
- ❑ 126 Bob Wiesler 8.00 4.00
- ❑ 127 Bob Buhl 15.00 7.50
- ❑ 128 Ed Bailey 15.00 7.50
- ❑ 129 Saul Rogovin 8.00 4.00
- ❑ 130 Don Newcombe 20.00 10.00
- ❑ 131 Milt Bolling 8.00 4.00
- ❑ 132 Art Ditmar 15.00 7.50
- ❑ 133 Del Crandall 15.00 7.50
- ❑ 134 Don Kaiser 8.00 4.00
- ❑ 135 Bill Skowron 20.00 10.00
- ❑ 136 Jim Hegan 15.00 7.50
- ❑ 137 Bob Rush 8.00 4.00
- ❑ 138 Minnie Minoso 20.00 10.00
- ❑ 139 Lou Kretlow 8.00 4.00
- ❑ 140 Frank Thomas 15.00 7.50
- ❑ 141 Al Aber 8.00 4.00
- ❑ 142 Charley Thompson 8.00 4.00
- ❑ 143 Andy Pafko 15.00 7.50
- ❑ 144 Ray Narleski 8.00 4.00
- ❑ 145 Al Smith 8.00 4.00
- ❑ 146 Don Ferrarese 8.00 4.00
- ❑ 147 Al Walker 8.00 4.00
- ❑ 148 Don Mueller 15.00 7.50
- ❑ 149 Bob Kennedy 15.00 7.50
- ❑ 150 Bob Friend 15.00 7.50
- ❑ 151 Willie Miranda 8.00 4.00
- ❑ 152 Jack Harshman 8.00 4.00
- ❑ 153 Karl Olson 8.00 4.00
- ❑ 154 Red Schoendienst 30.00 15.00
- ❑ 155 Jim Brosnan 15.00 7.50
- ❑ 156 Gus Triandos 15.00 7.50
- ❑ 157 Wally Post 15.00 7.50
- ❑ 158 Curt Simmons 15.00 7.50
- ❑ 159 Solly Drake RC 8.00 4.00
- ❑ 160 Billy Pierce 15.00 7.50
- ❑ 161 Pittsburgh Pirates TC 15.00 7.50
- ❑ 162 Jack Meyer 8.00 4.00
- ❑ 163 Sammy White 8.00 4.00
- ❑ 164 Tommy Carroll 8.00 4.00
- ❑ 165 Ted Kluszewski 100.00 60.00
- ❑ 166 Roy Face 15.00 7.50
- ❑ 167 Vic Power 15.00 7.50
- ❑ 168 Frank Lary 15.00 7.50
- ❑ 169 Herb Plews RC 8.00 4.00
- ❑ 170 Duke Snider 125.00 75.00
- ❑ 171 Boston Red Sox TC 15.00 7.50
- ❑ 172 Gene Woodling 15.00 7.50
- ❑ 173 Roger Craig 15.00 7.50
- ❑ 174 Willie Jones 8.00 4.00
- ❑ 175 Don Larsen 30.00 15.00
- ❑ 176A Gene Bakep ERR 350.00 200.00
- ❑ 176B Gene Baker COR 15.00 7.50
- ❑ 177 Eddie Yost 15.00 7.50
- ❑ 178 Don Bessent 8.00 4.00
- ❑ 179 Ernie Oravetz 8.00 4.00
- ❑ 180 Gus Bell 15.00 7.50
- ❑ 181 Dick Donovan 8.00 4.00
- ❑ 182 Hobie Landrith 8.00 4.00
- ❑ 183 Chicago Cubs TC 15.00 7.50
- ❑ 184 Tito Francona RC 8.00 4.00
- ❑ 185 Johnny Kucks 15.00 7.50
- ❑ 186 Jim King 15.00 7.50
- ❑ 187 Virgil Trucks 15.00 7.50
- ❑ 188 Felix Mantilla RC 15.00 7.50
- ❑ 189 Willard Nixon 8.00 4.00
- ❑ 190 Randy Jackson 8.00 4.00
- ❑ 191 Joe Margoneri RC 8.00 4.00
- ❑ 192 Jerry Coleman 15.00 7.50
- ❑ 193 Del Rice 8.00 4.00
- ❑ 194 Hal Brown 8.00 4.00
- ❑ 195 Bobby Avila 8.00 4.00
- ❑ 196 Larry Jackson 15.00 7.50
- ❑ 197 Hank Sauer 15.00 7.50
- ❑ 198 Detroit Tigers TC 15.00 7.50
- ❑ 199 Vern Law 15.00 7.50
- ❑ 200 Gil McDougald 15.00 7.50
- ❑ 201 Sandy Amoros 15.00 7.50
- ❑ 202 Dick Gernert 8.00 4.00
- ❑ 203 Hoyt Wilhelm 30.00 15.00
- ❑ 204 Kansas City Athletics TC 15.00 7.50
- ❑ 205 Charlie Maxwell 15.00 7.50
- ❑ 206 Willard Schmidt 8.00 4.00
- ❑ 207 Gordon (Billy) Hunter 8.00 4.00
- ❑ 208 Lew Burdette 15.00 7.50
- ❑ 209 Bob Skinner 15.00 7.50
- ❑ 210 Roy Campanella 150.00 90.00
- ❑ 211 Camilo Pascual 15.00 7.50
- ❑ 212 Rocky Colavito RC 125.00 75.00
- ❑ 213 Les Moss 8.00 4.00
- ❑ 214 Philadelphia Phillies TC 15.00 7.50
- ❑ 215 Enos Slaughter 30.00 15.00
- ❑ 216 Marv Grissom 8.00 4.00
- ❑ 217 Gene Stephens 8.00 4.00
- ❑ 218 Ray Jablonski 8.00 4.00
- ❑ 219 Tom Acker RC 8.00 4.00
- ❑ 220 Jackie Jensen 20.00 10.00
- ❑ 221 Dixie Howell 8.00 4.00
- ❑ 222 Alex Grammas 8.00 4.00
- ❑ 223 Frank House 8.00 4.00
- ❑ 224 Marv Blaylock 8.00 4.00
- ❑ 225 Harry Simpson 8.00 4.00
- ❑ 226 Preston Ward 8.00 4.00
- ❑ 227 Gerry Staley 8.00 4.00
- ❑ 228 Smoky Burgess UER 15.00 7.50
- ❑ 229 George Susce 8.00 4.00
- ❑ 230 George Kell 30.00 15.00
- ❑ 231 Solly Hemus 8.00 4.00
- ❑ 232 Whitey Lockman 15.00 7.50
- ❑ 233 Art Fowler 8.00 4.00
- ❑ 234 Dick Cole 8.00 4.00
- ❑ 235 Tom Poholsky 8.00 4.00
- ❑ 236 Joe Ginsberg 8.00 4.00
- ❑ 237 Foster Castleman 8.00 4.00
- ❑ 238 Eddie Robinson 8.00 4.00
- ❑ 239 Tom Morgan 8.00 4.00
- ❑ 240 Hank Bauer 15.00 7.50
- ❑ 241 Joe Lonnett RC 8.00 4.00
- ❑ 242 Charlie Neal 15.00 7.50
- ❑ 243 St. Louis Cardinals TC 15.00 7.50
- ❑ 244 Billy Loes 15.00 7.50
- ❑ 245 Rip Repulski 8.00 4.00
- ❑ 246 Jose Valdivielso 8.00 4.00
- ❑ 247 Turk Lown 8.00 4.00
- ❑ 248 Jim Finigan 8.00 4.00
- ❑ 249 Dave Pope 8.00 4.00
- ❑ 250 Eddie Mathews 50.00 30.00
- ❑ 251 Baltimore Orioles TC 15.00 7.50
- ❑ 252 Carl Erskine 15.00 7.50
- ❑ 253 Gus Zernial 15.00 7.50
- ❑ 254 Ron Negray 8.00 4.00
- ❑ 255 Charlie Silvera 15.00 7.50
- ❑ 256 Ron Kline 8.00 4.00
- ❑ 257 Walt Dropo 8.00 4.00
- ❑ 258 Steve Gromek 8.00 4.00
- ❑ 259 Eddie O'Brien 8.00 4.00
- ❑ 260 Del Ennis 15.00 7.50
- ❑ 261 Bob Chakales 8.00 4.00
- ❑ 262 Bobby Thomson 15.00 7.50
- ❑ 263 George Strickland 8.00 4.00
- ❑ 264 Bob Turley 15.00 7.50
- ❑ 265 Harvey Haddix DP 12.00 6.00
- ❑ 266 Ken Kuhn DP RC 12.00 6.00
- ❑ 267 Danny Kravitz RC 20.00 10.00
- ❑ 268 Jack Collum 20.00 10.00
- ❑ 269 Bob Cerv 30.00 15.00
- ❑ 270 Washington Senators TC 60.00 35.00
- ❑ 271 Danny O'Connell DP 12.00 6.00
- ❑ 272 Bobby Shantz 30.00 15.00
- ❑ 273 Jim Davis 20.00 10.00
- ❑ 274 Don Hoak 15.00 7.50
- ❑ 275 Cleveland Indians TC UER 60.0035.00
- ❑ 276 Jim Pyburn RC 20.00 10.00
- ❑ 277 Johnny Podres DP 40.00 20.00
- ❑ 278 Fred Hatfield DP 12.00 6.00
- ❑ 279 Bob Thurman RC 20.00 10.00
- ❑ 280 Alex Kellner 20.00 10.00
- ❑ 281 Gail Harris 20.00 10.00
- ❑ 282 Jack Dittmer DP 12.00 6.00
- ❑ 283 Wes Covington DP RC 12.00 6.00
- ❑ 284 Don Zimmer 40.00 20.00
- ❑ 285 Ned Garver 20.00 10.00
- ❑ 286 Bobby Richardson RC 125.00 75.00
- ❑ 287 Sam Jones 20.00 10.00
- ❑ 288 Ted Lepcio 20.00 10.00
- ❑ 289 Jim Bolger DP 12.00 6.00
- ❑ 290 Andy Carey DP 40.00 20.00
- ❑ 291 Windy McCall 20.00 10.00
- ❑ 292 Billy Klaus 20.00 10.00
- ❑ 293 Ted Abernathy RC 20.00 10.00
- ❑ 294 Rocky Bridges DP 12.00 6.00
- ❑ 295 Joe Collins DP 40.00 20.00
- ❑ 296 Johnny Klippstein 20.00 10.00
- ❑ 297 Jack Crimian 20.00 10.00
- ❑ 298 Irv Noren DP 12.00 6.00
- ❑ 299 Chuck Harmon 20.00 10.00
- ❑ 300 Mike Garcia 30.00 15.00
- ❑ 301 Sammy Esposito DP RC 20.00 10.00
- ❑ 302 Sandy Koufax DP 350.00 200.00
- ❑ 303 Billy Goodman 30.00 15.00
- ❑ 304 Joe Cunningham 30.00 15.00
- ❑ 305 Chico Fernandez 20.00 10.00
- ❑ 306 Darrell Johnson DP RC 12.00 6.00
- ❑ 307 Jack D. Phillips DP 12.00 6.00
- ❑ 308 Dick Hall 20.00 10.00
- ❑ 309 Jim Busby DP 12.00 6.00
- ❑ 310 Max Surkont DP 12.00 6.00
- ❑ 311 Al Pilarcik DP RC 12.00 6.00
- ❑ 312 Tony Kubek DP RC 100.00 60.00
- ❑ 313 Mel Parnell 15.00 7.50
- ❑ 314 Ed Bouchee DP RC 12.00 6.00
- ❑ 315 Lou Berberet DP 12.00 6.00
- ❑ 316 Billy O'Dell 20.00 10.00
- ❑ 317 New York Giants TC 80.00 50.00
- ❑ 318 Mickey McDermott 20.00 10.00
- ❑ 319 Gino Cimoli RC 20.00 10.00
- ❑ 320 Neil Chrisley RC 20.00 10.00
- ❑ 321 John (Red) Murff RC 20.00 10.00
- ❑ 322 Cincinnati Reds TC 80.00 50.00
- ❑ 323 Wes Westrum 30.00 15.00
- ❑ 324 Brooklyn Dodgers TC 150.00 90.00
- ❑ 325 Frank Bolling 20.00 10.00
- ❑ 326 Pedro Ramos 20.00 10.00
- ❑ 327 Jim Pendleton 20.00 10.00
- ❑ 328 Brooks Robinson RC 400.00 250.00
- ❑ 329 Chicago White Sox TC 60.00 35.00
- ❑ 330 Jim Wilson 20.00 10.00
- ❑ 331 Ray Katt 20.00 10.00
- ❑ 332 Bob Bowman RC 20.00 10.00
- ❑ 333 Ernie Johnson 20.00 10.00
- ❑ 334 Jerry Schoonmaker 20.00 10.00
- ❑ 335 Granny Hamner 20.00 10.00
- ❑ 336 Haywood Sullivan RC 40.00 20.00
- ❑ 337 Rene Valdes RC 20.00 10.00
- ❑ 338 Jim Bunning RC 150.00 90.00
- ❑ 339 Bob Speake 20.00 10.00
- ❑ 340 Bill Wight 20.00 10.00
- ❑ 341 Don Gross RC 20.00 10.00
- ❑ 342 Gene Mauch 30.00 15.00
- ❑ 343 Taylor Phillips RC 15.00 7.50
- ❑ 344 Paul LaPalme 20.00 10.00
- ❑ 345 Paul Smith 20.00 10.00
- ❑ 346 Dick Littlefield 20.00 10.00
- ❑ 347 Hal Naragon 20.00 10.00
- ❑ 348 Jim Hearn 20.00 10.00

❑ 349 Nellie King	20.00	10.00
❑ 350 Eddie Miksis	20.00	10.00
❑ 351 Dave Hillman RC	20.00	10.00
❑ 352 Ellis Kinder	20.00	10.00
❑ 353 Cal Neeman RC	8.00	4.00
❑ 354 Rip Coleman RC	8.00	4.00
❑ 355 Frank Malzone	15.00	7.50
❑ 356 Faye Throneberry	8.00	4.00
❑ 357 Earl Torgeson	8.00	4.00
❑ 358 Jerry Lynch	15.00	7.50
❑ 359 Tom Cheney RC	8.00	4.00
❑ 360 Johnny Groth	8.00	4.00
❑ 361 Curt Barclay RC	8.00	4.00
❑ 362 Roman Mejias RC	15.00	7.50
❑ 363 Eddie Kasko RC	8.00	4.00
❑ 364 Cal McLish RC	15.00	7.50
❑ 365 Ozzie Virgil RC	8.00	4.00
❑ 366 Ken Lehman	8.00	4.00
❑ 367 Ed Fitzgerald	8.00	4.00
❑ 368 Bob Purkey	8.00	4.00
❑ 369 Milt Graff RC	8.00	4.00
❑ 370 Warren Hacker	8.00	4.00
❑ 371 Bob Lennon	8.00	4.00
❑ 372 Norm Zauchin	8.00	4.00
❑ 373 Pete Whisenant RC	8.00	4.00
❑ 374 Don Cardwell RC	8.00	4.00
❑ 375 Jim Landis RC	15.00	7.50
❑ 376 Don Elston RC	8.00	4.00
❑ 377 Andre Rodgers RC	8.00	4.00
❑ 378 Elmer Singleton	8.00	4.00
❑ 379 Don Lee RC	8.00	4.00
❑ 380 Walker Cooper	8.00	4.00
❑ 381 Dean Stone	8.00	4.00
❑ 382 Jim Brideweser	8.00	4.00
❑ 383 Juan Pizarro RC	8.00	4.00
❑ 384 Bobby G. Smith RC	8.00	4.00
❑ 385 Art Houtteman	8.00	4.00
❑ 386 Lyle Luttrell RC	8.00	4.00
❑ 387 Jack Sanford RC	15.00	7.50
❑ 388 Pete Daley	8.00	4.00
❑ 389 Dave Jolly	8.00	4.00
❑ 390 Reno Bertoia	8.00	4.00
❑ 391 Ralph Terry RC	15.00	7.50
❑ 392 Chuck Tanner	15.00	7.50
❑ 393 Raul Sanchez RC	8.00	4.00
❑ 394 Luis Arroyo	15.00	7.50
❑ 395 Bubba Phillips	8.00	4.00
❑ 396 Casey Wise RC	8.00	4.00
❑ 397 Roy Smalley	8.00	4.00
❑ 398 Al Cicotte RC	15.00	7.50
❑ 399 Billy Consolo	8.00	4.00
❑ 400 Fur/Hodges/Campy/Snider	250.00	150.00
❑ 401 Earl Battey RC	15.00	7.50
❑ 402 Jim Pisoni RC	8.00	4.00
❑ 403 Dick Hyde RC	8.00	4.00
❑ 404 Harry Anderson RC	8.00	4.00
❑ 405 Duke Maas	8.00	4.00
❑ 406 Bob Hale	8.00	4.00
❑ 407 Y.Berra/M.Mantle	600.00	350.00
❑ CC1 Contest May 4	100.00	60.00
❑ CC2 Contest May 25	100.00	60.00
❑ CC3 Contest June 22	125.00	75.00
❑ CC4 Contest July 19	125.00	75.00
❑ NNO Checklist 1/2 Bazooka	250.00	150.00
❑ NNO Checklist 1/2 Blony	250.00	150.00
❑ NNO Checklist 2/3 Bazooka	400.00	250.00
❑ NNO Checklist 2/3 Blony	400.00	250.00
❑ NNO Checklist 3/4 Bazooka	800.00	500.00
❑ NNO Checklist 3/4 Blony	600.00	350.00
❑ NNO Checklist 4/5 Bazooka	1000.00	600.00
❑ NNO Checklist 4/5 Blony	800.00	500.00
❑ NNO Lucky Penny Card	100.00	60.00

1958 Topps

❑ COMP. MASTER SET (534)	12000.00	8000.00
❑ COMPLETE SET (494)	6000.00	4000.00
❑ COMMON CARD (1-110)	12.00	6.00
❑ COMMON CARD (111-495)	8.00	4.00
❑ WRAPPER (1-CENT)	100.00	75.00
❑ WRAPPER (5-CENT)	125.00	100.00
❑ 1 Ted Williams	600.00	350.00
❑ 2A Bob Lemon	30.00	15.00
❑ 2B Bob Lemon YT	60.00	35.00
❑ 3 Alex Kellner	12.00	6.00
❑ 4 Hank Foiles	12.00	6.00
❑ 5 Willie Mays	300.00	175.00

❑ 6 George Zuverink	12.00	6.00
❑ 7 Dale Long	15.00	7.50
❑ 8A Eddie Kasko	12.00	6.00
❑ 8B Eddie Kasko YN	40.00	20.00
❑ 9 Hank Bauer	20.00	10.00
❑ 10 Lew Burdette	20.00	10.00
❑ 11A Jim Rivera	12.00	6.00
❑ 11B Jim Rivera YT	40.00	20.00
❑ 12 George Crowe	12.00	6.00
❑ 13A Billy Hoeft	12.00	6.00
❑ 13B Billy Hoeft YN	40.00	20.00
❑ 14 Rip Repulski	12.00	6.00
❑ 15 Jim Lemon	15.00	7.50
❑ 16 Charlie Neal	15.00	7.50
❑ 17 Felix Mantilla	12.00	6.00
❑ 18 Frank Sullivan	12.00	6.00
❑ 19 San Francisco Giants TC	40.00	20.00
❑ 20A Gil McDougald	20.00	10.00
❑ 20B Gil McDougald YN	60.00	35.00
❑ 21 Curt Barclay	12.00	6.00
❑ 22 Hal Naragon	12.00	6.00
❑ 23A Bill Tuttle	12.00	6.00
❑ 23B Bill Tuttle YN	40.00	20.00
❑ 24A Hobie Landrith	12.00	6.00
❑ 24B Hobie Landrith YN	40.00	20.00
❑ 25 Don Drysdale	100.00	60.00
❑ 26 Ron Jackson	12.00	6.00
❑ 27 Bud Freeman	12.00	6.00
❑ 28 Jim Busby	12.00	6.00
❑ 29 Ted Lepcio	12.00	6.00
❑ 30A Hank Aaron	200.00	125.00
❑ 30B Hank Aaron YN	600.00	350.00
❑ 31 Tex Clevenger RC	12.00	6.00
❑ 32A J.W. Porter	12.00	6.00
❑ 32B J.W. Porter YN	40.00	20.00
❑ 33A Cal Neeman	12.00	6.00
❑ 33B Cal Neeman YT	40.00	20.00
❑ 34 Bob Thurman	12.00	6.00
❑ 35A Don Mossi	15.00	7.50
❑ 35B Don Mossi YT	40.00	20.00
❑ 36 Ted Kazanski	12.00	6.00
❑ 37 Mike McCormick UER RC	15.00	7.50
❑ 38 Dick Gernert	12.00	6.00
❑ 39 Bob Martyn RC	12.00	6.00
❑ 40 George Kell	30.00	15.00
❑ 41 Dave Hillman	12.00	6.00
❑ 42 John Roseboro RC	30.00	15.00
❑ 43 Sal Maglie	15.00	7.50
❑ 44 Washington Senators TC	20.00	10.00
❑ 45 Dick Groat	15.00	7.50
❑ 46A Lou Sleater	12.00	6.00
❑ 46B Lou Sleater YN	40.00	20.00
❑ 47 Roger Maris RC	500.00	300.00
❑ 48 Chuck Harmon	12.00	6.00
❑ 49 Smoky Burgess	15.00	7.50
❑ 50A Billy Pierce	15.00	7.50
❑ 50B Billy Pierce YT	40.00	20.00
❑ 51 Del Rice	12.00	6.00
❑ 52A Roberto Clemente	300.00	175.00
❑ 52B Roberto Clemente YT	500.00	300.00
❑ 53A Morrie Martin	12.00	6.00
❑ 53B Morrie Martin YN	40.00	20.00
❑ 54 Norm Siebern RC	20.00	10.00
❑ 55 Chico Carrasquel	12.00	6.00
❑ 56 Bill Fischer RC	12.00	6.00
❑ 57A Tim Thompson	12.00	6.00
❑ 57B Tim Thompson YN	40.00	20.00
❑ 58A Art Schult	12.00	6.00
❑ 58B Art Schult YT	40.00	20.00
❑ 59 Dave Sisler	12.00	6.00
❑ 60A Del Ennis	15.00	7.50
❑ 60B Del Ennis YN	40.00	20.00
❑ 61A Darrell Johnson	12.00	6.00
❑ 61B Darrell Johnson YN	40.00	20.00
❑ 62 Joe DeMaestri	12.00	6.00
❑ 63 Joe Nuxhall	15.00	7.50
❑ 64 Joe Lonnett	12.00	6.00
❑ 65A Von McDaniel RC	12.00	6.00
❑ 65B Von McDaniel YN	40.00	20.00
❑ 66 Lee Walls	12.00	6.00
❑ 67 Joe Ginsberg	12.00	6.00
❑ 68 Daryl Spencer	12.00	6.00
❑ 69 Wally Burnette	12.00	6.00
❑ 70A Al Kaline	100.00	60.00
❑ 70B Al Kaline YN	250.00	150.00
❑ 71 Los Angeles Dodgers TC	60.00	35.00
❑ 72 Bud Byerly UER	12.00	6.00
❑ 73 Pete Daley	12.00	6.00
❑ 74 Roy Face	15.00	7.50
❑ 75 Gus Bell	15.00	7.50
❑ 76A Dick Farrell RC	12.00	6.00
❑ 76B Dick Farrell YT	40.00	20.00
❑ 77A Don Zimmer	15.00	7.50
❑ 77B Don Zimmer YT	40.00	20.00
❑ 78A Ernie Johnson	15.00	7.50
❑ 78B Ernie Johnson YN	40.00	20.00
❑ 79A Dick Williams	15.00	7.50
❑ 79B Dick Williams YT	40.00	20.00
❑ 80 Dick Drott RC	12.00	6.00
❑ 81A Steve Boros RC	12.00	6.00
❑ 81B Steve Boros YT	40.00	20.00
❑ 82 Ron Kline	12.00	6.00
❑ 83 Bob Hazle RC	12.00	6.00
❑ 84 Billy O'Dell	12.00	6.00
❑ 85A Luis Aparicio	30.00	15.00
❑ 85B Luis Aparicio YT	80.00	50.00
❑ 86 Valmy Thomas RC	12.00	6.00
❑ 87 Johnny Kucks	12.00	6.00
❑ 88 Duke Snider	80.00	50.00
❑ 89 Billy Klaus	12.00	6.00
❑ 90 Robin Roberts	30.00	15.00
❑ 91 Chuck Tanner	15.00	7.50
❑ 92A Clint Courtney	12.00	6.00
❑ 92B Clint Courtney YN	40.00	20.00
❑ 93 Sandy Amoros	15.00	7.50
❑ 94 Bob Skinner	15.00	7.50
❑ 95 Frank Bolling	12.00	6.00
❑ 96 Joe Durham RC	12.00	6.00
❑ 97A Larry Jackson	12.00	6.00
❑ 97B Larry Jackson YN	40.00	20.00
❑ 98A Billy Hunter	12.00	6.00
❑ 98B Billy Hunter YN	40.00	20.00
❑ 99 Bobby Adams	12.00	6.00
❑ 100A Early Wynn	30.00	15.00
❑ 100B Early Wynn YT	80.00	50.00
❑ 101A Bobby Richardson	30.00	15.00
❑ 101B B.Richardson YN	60.00	35.00
❑ 102 George Strickland	12.00	6.00
❑ 103 Jerry Lynch	15.00	7.50
❑ 104 Jim Pendleton	12.00	6.00
❑ 105 Billy Gardner	12.00	6.00
❑ 106 Dick Schofield	15.00	7.50
❑ 107 Ossie Virgil	12.00	6.00
❑ 108A Jim Landis	12.00	6.00
❑ 108B Jim Landis YT	40.00	20.00
❑ 109 Herb Plews	12.00	6.00
❑ 110 Johnny Logan	15.00	7.50
❑ 111 Stu Miller	10.00	5.00
❑ 112 Gus Zernial	10.00	5.00
❑ 113 Jerry Walker RC	8.00	4.00
❑ 114 Irv Noren	10.00	5.00
❑ 115 Jim Bunning	30.00	15.00
❑ 116 Dave Philley	8.00	4.00
❑ 117 Frank Torre	10.00	5.00
❑ 118 Harvey Haddix	10.00	5.00
❑ 119 Harry Chiti	8.00	4.00
❑ 120 Johnny Podres	10.00	5.00
❑ 121 Eddie Miksis	8.00	4.00
❑ 122 Walt Moryn	8.00	4.00
❑ 123 Dick Tomanek RC	8.00	4.00
❑ 124 Bobby Usher	8.00	4.00
❑ 125 Alvin Dark	10.00	5.00
❑ 126 Stan Palys RC	8.00	4.00
❑ 127 Tom Sturdivant	10.00	5.00

❑ 128 Willie Kirkland RC 8.00 4.00
❑ 129 Jim Derrington RC 8.00 4.00
❑ 130 Jackie Jensen 10.00 5.00
❑ 131 Bob Henrich RC 8.00 4.00
❑ 132 Vern Law 10.00 5.00
❑ 133 Russ Nixon RC 8.00 4.00
❑ 134 Philadelphia Phillies TC 15.00 7.50
❑ 135 Mike (Moe)Drabowsky 10.00 5.00
❑ 136 Jim Finigan 8.00 4.00
❑ 137 Russ Kemmerer 8.00 4.00
❑ 138 Earl Torgeson 8.00 4.00
❑ 139 George Brunet RC 8.00 4.00
❑ 140 Wes Covington 10.00 5.00
❑ 141 Ken Lehman 8.00 4.00
❑ 142 Enos Slaughter 25.00 12.50
❑ 143 Billy Muffett RC 8.00 4.00
❑ 144 Bobby Morgan 8.00 4.00
❑ 145 Never issued
❑ 146 Dick Gray RC 8.00 4.00
❑ 147 Don McMahon RC 8.00 4.00
❑ 148 Billy Consolo 8.00 4.00
❑ 149 Tom Acker 8.00 4.00
❑ 150 Mickey Mantle 1000.00 600.00
❑ 151 Buddy Pritchard RC 8.00 4.00
❑ 152 Johnny Antonelli 10.00 5.00
❑ 153 Les Moss 8.00 4.00
❑ 154 Harry Byrd 8.00 4.00
❑ 155 Hector Lopez 10.00 5.00
❑ 156 Dick Hyde 8.00 4.00
❑ 157 Dee Fondy 8.00 4.00
❑ 158 Cleveland Indians TC 15.00 7.50
❑ 159 Taylor Phillips 8.00 4.00
❑ 160 Don Hoak 10.00 5.00
❑ 161 Don Larsen 15.00 7.50
❑ 162 Gil Hodges 40.00 20.00
❑ 163 Jim Wilson 8.00 4.00
❑ 164 Bob Taylor RC 8.00 4.00
❑ 165 Bob Nieman 8.00 4.00
❑ 166 Danny O'Connell 8.00 4.00
❑ 167 Frank Baumann RC 8.00 4.00
❑ 168 Joe Cunningham 8.00 4.00
❑ 169 Ralph Terry 10.00 5.00
❑ 170 Vic Wertz 10.00 5.00
❑ 171 Harry Anderson 8.00 4.00
❑ 172 Don Gross 8.00 4.00
❑ 173 Eddie Yost 8.00 4.00
❑ 174 Kansas City Athletics TC 15.00 7.50
❑ 175 Marv Throneberry RC 15.00 7.50
❑ 176 Bob Buhl 10.00 5.00
❑ 177 Al Smith 8.00 4.00
❑ 178 Ted Kluszewski 25.00 12.50
❑ 179 Willie Miranda 8.00 4.00
❑ 180 Lindy McDaniel 10.00 5.00
❑ 181 Willie Jones 8.00 4.00
❑ 182 Joe Caffie RC 8.00 4.00
❑ 183 Dave Jolly 8.00 4.00
❑ 184 Elvin Tappe 8.00 4.00
❑ 185 Ray Boone 10.00 5.00
❑ 186 Jack Meyer 8.00 4.00
❑ 187 Sandy Koufax 250.00 150.00
❑ 188 Milt Bolling UER 8.00 4.00
❑ 189 George Susce 8.00 4.00
❑ 190 Red Schoendienst 25.00 12.50
❑ 191 Art Ceccarelli RC 8.00 4.00
❑ 192 Milt Graff 8.00 4.00
❑ 193 Jerry Lumpe RC 8.00 4.00
❑ 194 Roger Craig 10.00 5.00
❑ 195 Whitey Lockman 10.00 5.00
❑ 196 Mike Garcia 10.00 5.00
❑ 197 Haywood Sullivan 10.00 5.00
❑ 198 Bill Virdon 10.00 5.00
❑ 199 Don Blasingame 8.00 4.00
❑ 200 Bob Keegan 8.00 4.00
❑ 201 Jim Bolger 8.00 4.00
❑ 202 Woody Held RC 8.00 4.00
❑ 203 Al Walker 8.00 4.00
❑ 204 Leo Kiely 8.00 4.00
❑ 205 Johnny Temple 10.00 5.00
❑ 206 Bob Shaw RC 8.00 4.00
❑ 207 Solly Hemus 8.00 4.00
❑ 208 Cal McLish 8.00 4.00
❑ 209 Bob Anderson RC 8.00 4.00
❑ 210 Wally Moon 10.00 5.00
❑ 211 Pete Burnside RC 8.00 4.00
❑ 212 Bubba Phillips 8.00 4.00
❑ 213 Red Wilson 8.00 4.00
❑ 214 Willard Schmidt 8.00 4.00
❑ 215 Jim Gilliam 15.00 7.50
❑ 216 St. Louis Cardinals TC 15.00 7.50
❑ 217 Jack Harshman 8.00 4.00
❑ 218 Dick Rand RC 8.00 4.00
❑ 219 Camilo Pascual 10.00 5.00
❑ 220 Tom Brewer 8.00 4.00
❑ 221 Jerry Kindall RC 8.00 4.00
❑ 222 Bud Daley RC 8.00 4.00
❑ 223 Andy Pafko 10.00 5.00
❑ 224 Bob Grim 10.00 5.00
❑ 225 Billy Goodman 10.00 5.00
❑ 226 Bob Smith RC 8.00 4.00
❑ 227 Gene Stephens 8.00 4.00
❑ 228 Duke Maas 8.00 4.00
❑ 229 Frank Zupo RC 8.00 4.00
❑ 230 Richie Ashburn 40.00 20.00
❑ 231 Lloyd Merritt RC 8.00 4.00
❑ 232 Reno Bertoia 8.00 4.00
❑ 233 Mickey Vernon 10.00 5.00
❑ 234 Carl Sawatski 8.00 4.00
❑ 235 Tom Gorman 8.00 4.00
❑ 236 Ed Fitzgerald 8.00 4.00
❑ 237 Bill Wight 8.00 4.00
❑ 238 Bill Mazeroski 30.00 15.00
❑ 239 Chuck Stobbs 8.00 4.00
❑ 240 Bill Skowron 25.00 12.50
❑ 241 Dick Littlefield 8.00 4.00
❑ 242 Johnny Klippstein 8.00 4.00
❑ 243 Larry Raines RC 8.00 4.00
❑ 244 Don Demeter RC 8.00 4.00
❑ 245 Frank Lary 10.00 5.00
❑ 246 New York Yankees TC 100.00 60.00
❑ 247 Casey Wise 8.00 4.00
❑ 248 Herman Wehmeier 8.00 4.00
❑ 249 Ray Moore 8.00 4.00
❑ 250 Roy Sievers 10.00 5.00
❑ 251 Warren Hacker 8.00 4.00
❑ 252 Bob Trowbridge RC 8.00 4.00
❑ 253 Don Mueller 10.00 5.00
❑ 254 Alex Grammas 8.00 4.00
❑ 255 Bob Turley 10.00 5.00
❑ 256 Chicago White Sox TC 15.00 7.50
❑ 257 Hal Smith 8.00 4.00
❑ 258 Carl Erskine 15.00 7.50
❑ 259 Al Pilarcik 8.00 4.00
❑ 260 Frank Malzone 10.00 5.00
❑ 261 Turk Lown 8.00 4.00
❑ 262 Johnny Groth 8.00 4.00
❑ 263 Eddie Bressoud RC 10.00 5.00
❑ 264 Jack Sanford 10.00 5.00
❑ 265 Pete Runnels 10.00 5.00
❑ 266 Connie Johnson 8.00 4.00
❑ 267 Sherm Lollar 10.00 5.00
❑ 268 Granny Hamner 8.00 4.00
❑ 269 Paul Smith 8.00 4.00
❑ 270 Warren Spahn 60.00 35.00
❑ 271 Billy Martin 40.00 20.00
❑ 272 Ray Crone 8.00 4.00
❑ 273 Hal Smith 8.00 4.00
❑ 274 Rocky Bridges 8.00 4.00
❑ 275 Elston Howard 15.00 7.50
❑ 276 Bobby Avila 8.00 4.00
❑ 277 Virgil Trucks 10.00 5.00
❑ 278 Mack Burk 8.00 4.00
❑ 279 Bob Boyd 8.00 4.00
❑ 280 Jim Piersall 10.00 5.00
❑ 281 Sammy Taylor RC 8.00 4.00
❑ 282 Paul Foytack 8.00 4.00
❑ 283 Ray Shearer RC 8.00 4.00
❑ 284 Ray Katt 8.00 4.00
❑ 285 Frank Robinson 100.00 60.00
❑ 286 Gino Cimoli 8.00 4.00
❑ 287 Sam Jones 10.00 5.00
❑ 288 Harmon Killebrew 100.00 60.00
❑ 289 B.Shantz/L.Burdette 10.00 5.00
❑ 290 Dick Donovan 8.00 4.00
❑ 291 Don Landrum RC 8.00 4.00
❑ 292 Ned Garver 8.00 4.00
❑ 293 Gene Freese 8.00 4.00
❑ 294 Hal Jeffcoat 8.00 4.00
❑ 295 Minnie Minoso 25.00 12.50
❑ 296 Ryne Duren RC 15.00 7.50
❑ 297 Don Buddin RC 8.00 4.00
❑ 298 Jim Hearn 8.00 4.00
❑ 299 Harry Simpson 8.00 4.00
❑ 300 W.Harridge/W.Giles 15.00 7.50
❑ 301 Randy Jackson 8.00 4.00
❑ 302 Mike Baxes RC 8.00 4.00
❑ 303 Neil Chrisley 8.00 4.00
❑ 304 H.Kuenn/A.Kaline 25.00 12.50
❑ 305 Clem Labine 10.00 5.00
❑ 306 Whammy Douglas RC 8.00 4.00
❑ 307 Brooks Robinson 100.00 60.00
❑ 308 Paul Giel 10.00 5.00
❑ 309 Gail Harris 8.00 4.00
❑ 310 Ernie Banks 100.00 60.00
❑ 311 Bob Purkey 8.00 4.00
❑ 312 Boston Red Sox TC 15.00 7.50
❑ 313 Bob Rush 8.00 4.00
❑ 314 D.Snider/W.Alston 50.00 30.00
❑ 315 Bob Friend 10.00 5.00
❑ 316 Tito Francona 10.00 5.00
❑ 317 Albie Pearson RC 10.00 5.00
❑ 318 Frank House 8.00 4.00
❑ 319 Lou Skizas 8.00 4.00
❑ 320 Whitey Ford 60.00 35.00
❑ 321 T.Kluszewski/T.Williams 100.00 60.00
❑ 322 Harding Peterson RC 10.00 5.00
❑ 323 Elmer Valo 8.00 4.00
❑ 324 Hoyt Wilhelm 25.00 12.50
❑ 325 Joe Adcock 10.00 5.00
❑ 326 Bob Miller 8.00 4.00
❑ 327 Chicago Cubs TC 15.00 7.50
❑ 328 Ike Delock 8.00 4.00
❑ 329 Bob Cerv 10.00 5.00
❑ 330 Ed Bailey 10.00 5.00
❑ 331 Pedro Ramos 8.00 4.00
❑ 332 Jim King 8.00 4.00
❑ 333 Andy Carey 10.00 5.00
❑ 334 B.Friend/B.Pierce 10.00 5.00
❑ 335 Ruben Gomez 8.00 4.00
❑ 336 Bert Hamric 8.00 4.00
❑ 337 Hank Aguirre 8.00 4.00
❑ 338 Walt Dropo 10.00 5.00
❑ 339 Fred Hatfield 8.00 4.00
❑ 340 Don Newcombe 15.00 7.50
❑ 341 Pittsburgh Pirates TC 15.00 7.50
❑ 342 Jim Brosnan 10.00 5.00
❑ 343 Orlando Cepeda RC 100.00 60.00
❑ 344 Bob Porterfield 8.00 4.00
❑ 345 Jim Hegan 10.00 5.00
❑ 346 Steve Bilko 8.00 4.00
❑ 347 Don Rudolph RC 8.00 4.00
❑ 348 Chico Fernandez 8.00 4.00
❑ 349 Murry Dickson 8.00 4.00
❑ 350 Ken Boyer 25.00 12.50
❑ 351 Cran/Math/Aaron/Adcock 40.00 20.00
❑ 352 Herb Score 15.00 7.50
❑ 353 Stan Lopata 8.00 4.00
❑ 354 Art Ditmar 10.00 5.00
❑ 355 Bill Bruton 10.00 5.00
❑ 356 Bob Malkmus RC 8.00 4.00
❑ 357 Danny McDevitt RC 8.00 4.00
❑ 358 Gene Baker 8.00 4.00
❑ 359 Billy Loes 10.00 5.00
❑ 360 Roy McMillan 10.00 5.00
❑ 361 Mike Fornieles 8.00 4.00
❑ 362 Ray Jablonski 8.00 4.00
❑ 363 Don Elston 8.00 4.00
❑ 364 Earl Battey 8.00 4.00
❑ 365 Tom Morgan 8.00 4.00
❑ 366 Gene Green RC 8.00 4.00
❑ 367 Jack Urban RC 8.00 4.00
❑ 368 Rocky Colavito 50.00 30.00
❑ 369 Ralph Lumenti RC 8.00 4.00
❑ 370 Yogi Berra 100.00 60.00
❑ 371 Marty Keough RC 8.00 4.00
❑ 372 Don Cardwell 8.00 4.00
❑ 373 Joe Pignatano RC 8.00 4.00
❑ 374 Brooks Lawrence 8.00 4.00
❑ 375 Pee Wee Reese 80.00 50.00
❑ 376 Charley Rabe RC 8.00 4.00
❑ 377A Milwaukee Braves TC Alpha 15.00 7.50
❑ 377B Milwaukee Braves TC Num 100.00 60.00
❑ 378 Hank Sauer 10.00 5.00
❑ 379 Ray Herbert 8.00 4.00
❑ 380 Charlie Maxwell 10.00 5.00
❑ 381 Hal Brown 8.00 4.00
❑ 382 Al Cicotte 8.00 4.00
❑ 383 Lou Berberet 8.00 4.00
❑ 384 John Goryl RC 8.00 4.00

❑ 385 Wilmer Mizell 10.00 5.00
❑ 386 Bailey/Tebbets/F.Rob 15.00 7.50
❑ 387 Wally Post 10.00 5.00
❑ 388 Billy Moran RC 8.00 4.00
❑ 389 Bill Taylor 8.00 4.00
❑ 390 Del Crandall 10.00 5.00
❑ 391 Dave Melton RC 8.00 4.00
❑ 392 Bennie Daniels RC 8.00 4.00
❑ 393 Tony Kubek 30.00 15.00
❑ 394 Jim Grant RC 8.00 4.00
❑ 395 Willard Nixon 8.00 4.00
❑ 396 Dutch Dotterer RC 8.00 4.00
❑ 397A Detroit Tigers TC Alpha 15.00 7.50
❑ 397B Detroit Tigers TC Num 100.00 60.00
❑ 398 Gene Woodling 10.00 5.00
❑ 399 Marv Grissom 8.00 4.00
❑ 400 Nellie Fox 40.00 20.00
❑ 401 Don Bessent 8.00 4.00
❑ 402 Bobby Gene Smith 8.00 4.00
❑ 403 Steve Korcheck RC 8.00 4.00
❑ 404 Curt Simmons 10.00 5.00
❑ 405 Ken Aspromonte RC 8.00 4.00
❑ 406 Vic Power 10.00 5.00
❑ 407 Carlton Willey RC 10.00 5.00
❑ 408A Baltimore Orioles TC Alpha 15.00 7.50
❑ 408B Baltimore Orioles TC Num 100.00 60.00
❑ 409 Frank Thomas 10.00 5.00
❑ 410 Murray Wall 8.00 4.00
❑ 411 Tony Taylor RC 10.00 5.00
❑ 412 Gerry Staley 8.00 4.00
❑ 413 Jim Davenport RC 8.00 4.00
❑ 414 Sammy White 8.00 4.00
❑ 415 Bob Bowman 8.00 4.00
❑ 416 Foster Castleman 8.00 4.00
❑ 417 Carl Furillo 15.00 7.50
❑ 418 M.Mantle/H.Aaron 400.00 250.00
❑ 419 Bobby Shantz 10.00 5.00
❑ 420 Vada Pinson RC 40.00 20.00
❑ 421 Dixie Howell 8.00 4.00
❑ 422 Norm Zauchin 8.00 4.00
❑ 423 Phil Clark RC 8.00 4.00
❑ 424 Larry Doby 25.00 12.50
❑ 425 Sammy Esposito 8.00 4.00
❑ 426 Johnny O'Brien 10.00 5.00
❑ 427 Al Worthington 8.00 4.00
❑ 428A Cincinnati Reds TC Alpha 15.00 7.50
❑ 428B Cincinnati Reds TC Num 100.00 60.00
❑ 429 Gus Triandos 10.00 5.00
❑ 430 Bobby Thomson 10.00 5.00
❑ 431 Gene Conley 10.00 5.00
❑ 432 John Powers RC 8.00 4.00
❑ 433A Pancho Herrera COR 10.00 5.00
❑ 433B Pancho Herrer ERR (No a) 600.00 350.00
❑ 434 Harvey Kuenn 10.00 5.00
❑ 435 Ed Roebuck 10.00 5.00
❑ 436 W.Mays/D.Snider 100.00 60.00
❑ 437 Bob Speake 8.00 4.00
❑ 438 Whitey Herzog 10.00 5.00
❑ 439 Ray Narleski 8.00 4.00
❑ 440 Eddie Mathews 80.00 50.00
❑ 441 Jim Marshall RC 10.00 5.00
❑ 442 Phil Paine RC 8.00 4.00
❑ 443 Billy Harrell SP RC 20.00 10.00
❑ 444 Danny Kravitz 8.00 4.00
❑ 445 Bob Smith RC 8.00 4.00
❑ 446 Carroll Hardy SP RC 20.00 10.00
❑ 447 Ray Monzant 8.00 4.00
❑ 448 Charley Lau RC 10.00 5.00
❑ 449 Gene Fodge RC 8.00 4.00
❑ 450 Preston Ward SP 20.00 10.00
❑ 451 Joe Taylor RC 8.00 4.00
❑ 452 Roman Mejias 8.00 4.00
❑ 453 Tom Qualters 8.00 4.00
❑ 454 Harry Hanebrink RC 8.00 4.00
❑ 455 Hal Griggs RC 8.00 4.00
❑ 456 Dick Brown RC 8.00 4.00
❑ 457 Milt Pappas RC 10.00 5.00
❑ 458 Julio Becquer RC 8.00 4.00
❑ 459 Ron Blackburn RC 8.00 4.00
❑ 460 Chuck Essegian RC 8.00 4.00
❑ 461 Ed Mayer RC 8.00 4.00
❑ 462 Gary Geiger SP RC 20.00 10.00
❑ 463 Vito Valentinetti 8.00 4.00
❑ 464 Curt Flood RC 30.00 15.00
❑ 465 Arnie Portocarrero 8.00 4.00
❑ 466 Pete Whisenant 8.00 4.00
❑ 467 Glen Hobbie RC 8.00 4.00
❑ 468 Bob Schmidt RC 8.00 4.00
❑ 469 Don Ferrarese 8.00 4.00
❑ 470 R.C. Stevens RC 8.00 4.00
❑ 471 Lenny Green RC 8.00 4.00
❑ 472 Joey Jay 10.00 5.00
❑ 473 Bill Renna 8.00 4.00
❑ 474 Roman Semproch RC 8.00 4.00
❑ 475 F.Haney/C.Stengel AS 25.00 12.50
❑ 476 Stan Musial AS TP 50.00 30.00
❑ 477 Bill Skowron AS 10.00 5.00
❑ 478 Johnny Temple AS UER 8.00 4.00
❑ 479 Nellie Fox AS 15.00 7.50
❑ 480 Eddie Mathews AS 30.00 15.00
❑ 481 Frank Malzone AS 8.00 4.00
❑ 482 Ernie Banks AS 40.00 20.00
❑ 483 Luis Aparicio AS 15.00 7.50
❑ 484 Frank Robinson AS 40.00 20.00
❑ 485 Ted Williams AS 150.00 90.00
❑ 486 Willie Mays AS 60.00 35.00
❑ 487 Mickey Mantle AS TP 200.00 125.00
❑ 488 Hank Aaron AS 60.00 35.00
❑ 489 Jackie Jensen AS 10.00 5.00
❑ 490 Ed Bailey AS 8.00 4.00
❑ 491 Sherm Lollar AS 8.00 4.00
❑ 492 Bob Friend AS 8.00 4.00
❑ 493 Bob Turley AS 10.00 5.00
❑ 494 Warren Spahn AS 25.00 12.50
❑ 495 Herb Score AS 15.00 7.50
❑ NNO Contest Cards 40.00 20.00
❑ NNO Felt Emblem Insert

1959 Topps

❑ COMPLETE SET (572) 8000.00 5000.00
❑ COMMON CARD (1-110) 6.00 3.00
❑ COMMON CARD (111-506) 4.00 2.00
❑ COMMON CARD (507-572) 15.00 7.50
❑ WRAPPER (1 CENT) 125.00 100.00
❑ WRAPPER (5-CENT) 100.00 75.00
❑ 1 Ford Frick COMM 60.00 35.00
❑ 2 Eddie Yost 8.00 4.00
❑ 3 Don McMahon 8.00 4.00
❑ 4 Albie Pearson 8.00 4.00
❑ 5 Dick Donovan 8.00 4.00
❑ 6 Alex Grammas 6.00 3.00
❑ 7 Al Pilarcik 6.00 3.00
❑ 8 Philadelphia Phillies CL 80.00 50.00
❑ 9 Paul Giel 8.00 4.00
❑ 10 Mickey Mantle 1000.00 600.00
❑ 11 Billy Hunter 8.00 4.00
❑ 12 Vern Law 8.00 4.00
❑ 13 Dick Gernert 6.00 3.00
❑ 14 Pete Whisenant 6.00 3.00
❑ 15 Dick Drott 6.00 3.00
❑ 16 Joe Pignatano 6.00 3.00
❑ 17 Thomas/Murtaugh/Klusz 8.00 4.00
❑ 18 Jack Urban 6.00 3.00
❑ 19 Eddie Bressoud 6.00 3.00
❑ 20 Duke Snider 60.00 35.00
❑ 21 Connie Johnson 6.00 3.00
❑ 22 Al Smith 8.00 4.00
❑ 23 Murry Dickson 8.00 4.00
❑ 24 Red Wilson 6.00 3.00
❑ 25 Don Hoak 8.00 4.00
❑ 26 Chuck Stobbs 6.00 3.00
❑ 27 Andy Pafko 8.00 4.00
❑ 28 Al Worthington 6.00 3.00
❑ 29 Jim Bolger 6.00 3.00
❑ 30 Nellie Fox 30.00 15.00
❑ 31 Ken Lehman 6.00 3.00
❑ 32 Don Buddin 6.00 3.00
❑ 33 Ed Fitzgerald 6.00 3.00
❑ 34 Al Kaline/C.Maxwell 20.00 10.00
❑ 35 Ted Kluszewski 12.00 6.00
❑ 36 Hank Aguirre 6.00 3.00
❑ 37 Gene Green 6.00 3.00
❑ 38 Morrie Martin 6.00 3.00
❑ 39 Ed Bouchee 6.00 3.00
❑ 40A Warren Spahn ERR 80.00 50.00
❑ 40B Warren Spahn ERR 100.00 60.00
❑ 40C Warren Spahn COR 60.00 35.00
❑ 41 Bob Martyn 6.00 3.00
❑ 42 Murray Wall 6.00 3.00
❑ 43 Steve Bilko 6.00 3.00
❑ 44 Vito Valentinetti 6.00 3.00
❑ 45 Andy Carey 8.00 4.00
❑ 46 Bill R. Henry 6.00 3.00
❑ 47 Jim Finigan 6.00 3.00
❑ 48 Baltimore Orioles CL 25.00 12.50
❑ 49 Bill Hall RC 6.00 3.00
❑ 50 Willie Mays 175.00 100.00
❑ 51 Rip Coleman 6.00 3.00
❑ 52 Coot Veal RC 6.00 3.00
❑ 53 Stan Williams RC 8.00 4.00
❑ 54 Mel Roach 6.00 3.00
❑ 55 Tom Brewer 6.00 3.00
❑ 56 Carl Sawatski 6.00 3.00
❑ 57 Al Cicotte 6.00 3.00
❑ 58 Eddie Miksis 6.00 3.00
❑ 59 Irv Noren 8.00 4.00
❑ 60 Bob Turley 8.00 4.00
❑ 61 Dick Brown 6.00 3.00
❑ 62 Tony Taylor 8.00 4.00
❑ 63 Jim Hearn 6.00 3.00
❑ 64 Joe DeMaestri 6.00 3.00
❑ 65 Frank Torre 8.00 4.00
❑ 66 Joe Ginsberg 6.00 3.00
❑ 67 Brooks Lawrence 6.00 3.00
❑ 68 Dick Schofield 8.00 4.00
❑ 69 San Francisco Giants CL 25.00 12.50
❑ 70 Harvey Kuenn 8.00 4.00
❑ 71 Don Bessent 6.00 3.00
❑ 72 Bill Renna 6.00 3.00
❑ 73 Ron Jackson 8.00 4.00
❑ 74 Lemon/Lavagetto/Sievers 8.00 4.00
❑ 75 Sam Jones 8.00 4.00
❑ 76 Bobby Richardson 20.00 10.00
❑ 77 John Goryl 6.00 3.00
❑ 78 Pedro Ramos 6.00 3.00
❑ 79 Harry Chiti 6.00 3.00
❑ 80 Minnie Minoso 12.00 6.00
❑ 81 Hal Jeffcoat 6.00 3.00
❑ 82 Bob Boyd 6.00 3.00
❑ 83 Bob Smith 6.00 3.00
❑ 84 Reno Bertoia 6.00 3.00
❑ 85 Harry Anderson 6.00 3.00
❑ 86 Bob Keegan 8.00 4.00
❑ 87 Danny O'Connell 6.00 3.00
❑ 88 Herb Score 12.00 6.00
❑ 89 Billy Gardner 6.00 3.00
❑ 90 Bill Skowron 12.00 6.00
❑ 91 Herb Moford RC 6.00 3.00
❑ 92 Dave Philley 6.00 3.00
❑ 93 Julio Becquer 6.00 3.00
❑ 94 Chicago White Sox CL 40.00 20.00
❑ 95 Carl Willey 6.00 3.00
❑ 96 Lou Berberet 6.00 3.00
❑ 97 Jerry Lynch 8.00 4.00
❑ 98 Arnie Portocarrero 6.00 3.00
❑ 99 Ted Kazanski 6.00 3.00
❑ 100 Bob Cerv 8.00 4.00
❑ 101 Alex Kellner 6.00 3.00
❑ 102 Felipe Alou RC 30.00 15.00
❑ 103 Billy Goodman 8.00 4.00
❑ 104 Del Rice 8.00 4.00
❑ 105 Lee Walls 6.00 3.00
❑ 106 Hal Woodeshick RC 6.00 3.00
❑ 107 Norm Larker RC 8.00 4.00
❑ 108 Zack Monroe RC 8.00 4.00
❑ 109 Bob Schmidt 6.00 3.00
❑ 110 George Witt RC 8.00 4.00
❑ 111 Cincinnati Redlegs CL 15.00 7.50
❑ 112 Billy Consolo 4.00 2.00
❑ 113 Taylor Phillips 4.00 2.00

❑ 114 Earl Battey 8.00 4.00
❑ 115 Mickey Vernon 8.00 4.00
❑ 116 Bob Allison RS RC 12.00 6.00
❑ 117 John Blanchard RS RC 12.00 6.00
❑ 118 John Buzhardt RS RC 5.00 2.50
❑ 119 Johnny Callison RS RC 12.00 6.00
❑ 120 Chuck Coles RS RC 5.00 2.50
❑ 121 Bob Conley RS RC 5.00 2.50
❑ 122 Bennie Daniels RS 5.00 2.50
❑ 123 Don Dillard RS RC 5.00 2.50
❑ 124 Dan Dobbek RS RC 5.00 2.50
❑ 125 Ron Fairly RS RC 12.00 6.00
❑ 126 Eddie Haas RS RC 5.00 2.50
❑ 127 Kent Hadley RS RC 5.00 2.50
❑ 128 Bob Hartman RS RC 5.00 2.50
❑ 129 Frank Herrera RS 5.00 2.50
❑ 130 Lou Jackson RS RC 5.00 2.50
❑ 131 Deron Johnson RS RC 12.00 6.00
❑ 132 Don Lee RS 5.00 2.50
❑ 133 Bob Lillis RS RC 5.00 2.50
❑ 134 Jim McDaniel RS RC 5.00 2.50
❑ 135 Gene Oliver RS RC 5.00 2.50
❑ 136 Jim O'Toole RS RC 5.00 2.50
❑ 137 Dick Ricketts RS RC 5.00 2.50
❑ 138 John Romano RS RC 5.00 2.50
❑ 139 Ed Sadowski RS RC 5.00 2.50
❑ 140 Charlie Secrest RS RC 5.00 2.50
❑ 141 Joe Shipley RS RC 5.00 2.50
❑ 142 Dick Stigman RS RC 5.00 2.50
❑ 143 Willie Tasby RS RC 5.00 2.50
❑ 144 Jerry Walker RS 5.00 2.50
❑ 145 Dom Zanni RS RC 5.00 2.50
❑ 146 Jerry Zimmerman RS RC 5.00 2.50
❑ 147 Long/Banks/Moryn 30.00 15.00
❑ 148 Mike McCormick 8.00 4.00
❑ 149 Jim Bunning 20.00 10.00
❑ 150 Stan Musial 120.00 60.00
❑ 151 Bob Malkmus 4.00 2.00
❑ 152 Johnny Klippstein 4.00 2.00
❑ 153 Jim Marshall 4.00 2.00
❑ 154 Ray Herbert 4.00 2.00
❑ 155 Enos Slaughter 20.00 10.00
❑ 156 B.Pierce/R.Roberts 12.00 6.00
❑ 157 Felix Mantilla 4.00 2.00
❑ 158 Walt Dropo 4.00 2.00
❑ 159 Bob Shaw 8.00 4.00
❑ 160 Dick Groat 8.00 4.00
❑ 161 Frank Baumann 4.00 2.00
❑ 162 Bobby G. Smith 4.00 2.00
❑ 163 Sandy Koufax 150.00 90.00
❑ 164 Johnny Groth 4.00 2.00
❑ 165 Bill Bruton 4.00 2.00
❑ 166 Minoso/Colavito/Doby 30.00 15.00
❑ 167 Duke Maas 4.00 2.00
❑ 168 Carroll Hardy 4.00 2.00
❑ 169 Ted Abernathy 4.00 2.00
❑ 170 Gene Woodling 8.00 4.00
❑ 171 Willard Schmidt 4.00 2.00
❑ 172 Kansas City Athletics CL 15.00 7.50
❑ 173 Bill Monbouquette RC 8.00 4.00
❑ 174 Jim Pendleton 4.00 2.00
❑ 175 Dick Farrell 8.00 4.00
❑ 176 Preston Ward 4.00 2.00
❑ 177 John Briggs RC 4.00 2.00
❑ 178 Ruben Amaro RC 12.00 6.00
❑ 179 Don Rudolph 4.00 2.00
❑ 180 Yogi Berra 80.00 50.00
❑ 181 Bob Porterfield 4.00 2.00
❑ 182 Milt Graff 4.00 2.00
❑ 183 Stu Miller 8.00 4.00
❑ 184 Harvey Haddix 8.00 4.00
❑ 185 Jim Busby 4.00 2.00
❑ 186 Mudcat Grant 8.00 4.00
❑ 187 Bubba Phillips 8.00 4.00
❑ 188 Juan Pizarro 4.00 2.00
❑ 189 Neil Chrisley 4.00 2.00
❑ 190 Bill Virdon 8.00 4.00
❑ 191 Russ Kemmerer 4.00 2.00
❑ 192 Charlie Beamon RC 4.00 2.00
❑ 193 Sammy Taylor 4.00 2.00
❑ 194 Jim Brosnan 8.00 4.00
❑ 195 Rip Repulski 4.00 2.00
❑ 196 Billy Moran 4.00 2.00
❑ 197 Ray Semproch 4.00 2.00
❑ 198 Jim Davenport 8.00 4.00
❑ 199 Leo Kiely 4.00 2.00
❑ 200 W.Giles NL PRES 8.00 4.00
❑ 201 Tom Acker 4.00 2.00
❑ 202 Roger Maris 125.00 75.00
❑ 203 Ossie Virgil 4.00 2.00
❑ 204 Casey Wise 4.00 2.00
❑ 205 Don Larsen 8.00 4.00
❑ 206 Carl Furillo 12.00 6.00
❑ 207 George Strickland 4.00 2.00
❑ 208 Willie Jones 4.00 2.00
❑ 209 Lenny Green 4.00 2.00
❑ 210 Ed Bailey 4.00 2.00
❑ 211 Bob Blaylock RC 4.00 2.00
❑ 212 H.Aaron/E.Mathews 80.00 50.00
❑ 213 Jim Rivera 8.00 4.00
❑ 214 Marcelino Solis RC 4.00 2.00
❑ 215 Jim Lemon 8.00 4.00
❑ 216 Andre Rodgers 4.00 2.00
❑ 217 Carl Erskine 12.00 6.00
❑ 218 Roman Mejias 4.00 2.00
❑ 219 George Zuverink 4.00 2.00
❑ 220 Frank Malzone 8.00 4.00
❑ 221 Bob Bowman 4.00 2.00
❑ 222 Bobby Shantz 8.00 4.00
❑ 223 St. Louis Cardinals CL 15.00 7.50
❑ 224 Claude Osteen RC 8.00 4.00
❑ 225 Johnny Logan 8.00 4.00
❑ 226 Art Ceccarelli 4.00 2.00
❑ 227 Hal W. Smith 4.00 2.00
❑ 228 Don Gross 4.00 2.00
❑ 229 Vic Power 8.00 4.00
❑ 230 Bill Fischer 4.00 2.00
❑ 231 Ellis Burton RC 4.00 2.00
❑ 232 Eddie Kasko 4.00 2.00
❑ 233 Paul Foytack 4.00 2.00
❑ 234 Chuck Tanner 8.00 4.00
❑ 235 Valmy Thomas 4.00 2.00
❑ 236 Ted Bowsfield RC 4.00 2.00
❑ 237 McDougald/Turley/B.Rich 12.00 6.00
❑ 238 Gene Baker 4.00 2.00
❑ 239 Bob Trowbridge 4.00 2.00
❑ 240 Hank Bauer 12.00 6.00
❑ 241 Billy Muffett 4.00 2.00
❑ 242 Ron Samford RC 4.00 2.00
❑ 243 Marv Grissom 4.00 2.00
❑ 244 Ted Gray 4.00 2.00
❑ 245 Ned Garver 4.00 2.00
❑ 246 J.W. Porter 4.00 2.00
❑ 247 Don Ferrarese 4.00 2.00
❑ 248 Boston Red Sox CL 15.00 7.50
❑ 249 Bobby Adams 4.00 2.00
❑ 250 Billy O'Dell 4.00 2.00
❑ 251 Clete Boyer 12.00 6.00
❑ 252 Ray Boone 8.00 4.00
❑ 253 Seth Morehead RC 4.00 2.00
❑ 254 Zeke Bella RC 4.00 2.00
❑ 255 Del Ennis 8.00 4.00
❑ 256 Jerry Davie RC 4.00 2.00
❑ 257 Leon Wagner RC 8.00 4.00
❑ 258 Fred Kipp RC 4.00 2.00
❑ 259 Jim Pisoni 4.00 2.00
❑ 260 Early Wynn UER 20.00 10.00
❑ 261 Gene Stephens 4.00 2.00
❑ 262 Podres/Labine/Drysdale 12.00 6.00
❑ 263 Bud Daley 4.00 2.00
❑ 264 Chico Carrasquel 4.00 2.00
❑ 265 Ron Kline 4.00 2.00
❑ 266 Woody Held 4.00 2.00
❑ 267 John Romonosky RC 4.00 2.00
❑ 268 Tito Francona 8.00 4.00
❑ 269 Jack Meyer 4.00 2.00
❑ 270 Gil Hodges 30.00 15.00
❑ 271 Orlando Pena RC 4.00 2.00
❑ 272 Jerry Lumpe 4.00 2.00
❑ 273 Joey Jay 8.00 4.00
❑ 274 Jerry Kindall 8.00 4.00
❑ 275 Jack Sanford 8.00 4.00
❑ 276 Pete Daley 4.00 2.00
❑ 277 Turk Lown 8.00 4.00
❑ 278 Chuck Essegian 4.00 2.00
❑ 279 Ernie Johnson 4.00 2.00
❑ 280 Frank Bolling 4.00 2.00
❑ 281 Walt Craddock RC 4.00 2.00
❑ 282 R.C. Stevens 4.00 2.00
❑ 283 Russ Heman RC 4.00 2.00
❑ 284 Steve Korcheck 4.00 2.00
❑ 285 Joe Cunningham 4.00 2.00
❑ 286 Dean Stone 4.00 2.00
❑ 287 Don Zimmer 12.00 6.00
❑ 288 Dutch Dotterer 4.00 2.00
❑ 289 Johnny Kucks 8.00 4.00
❑ 290 Wes Covington 4.00 2.00
❑ 291 P.Ramos/C.Pascual 4.00 2.00
❑ 292 Dick Williams 8.00 4.00
❑ 293 Ray Moore 4.00 2.00
❑ 294 Hank Foiles 4.00 2.00
❑ 295 Billy Martin 30.00 15.00
❑ 296 Ernie Broglio RC 4.00 2.00
❑ 297 Jackie Brandt RC 4.00 2.00
❑ 298 Tex Clevenger 4.00 2.00
❑ 299 Billy Klaus 4.00 2.00
❑ 300 Richie Ashburn 30.00 15.00
❑ 301 Earl Averill Jr. RC 4.00 2.00
❑ 302 Don Mossi 8.00 4.00
❑ 303 Marty Keough 4.00 2.00
❑ 304 Chicago Cubs CL 15.00 7.50
❑ 305 Curt Raydon RC 4.00 2.00
❑ 306 Jim Gilliam 8.00 4.00
❑ 307 Curt Barclay 4.00 2.00
❑ 308 Norm Siebern 4.00 2.00
❑ 309 Sal Maglie 8.00 4.00
❑ 310 Luis Aparicio 20.00 10.00
❑ 311 Norm Zauchin 4.00 2.00
❑ 312 Don Newcombe 8.00 4.00
❑ 313 Frank House 4.00 2.00
❑ 314 Don Cardwell 4.00 2.00
❑ 315 Joe Adcock 8.00 4.00
❑ 316A Ralph Lumenti UER 4.00 2.00
❑ 316B Ralph Lumenti UER 80.00 50.00
❑ 317 R.Ashburn/W.Mays 80.00 50.00
❑ 318 Rocky Bridges 4.00 2.00
❑ 319 Dave Hillman 4.00 2.00
❑ 320 Bob Skinner 8.00 4.00
❑ 321A Bob Giallombardo RC 8.00 4.00
❑ 321B Bob Giallombardo ERR 80.00 50.00
❑ 322A Harry Hanebrink TR 8.00 4.00
❑ 322B H.Hanebrink ERR 80.00 50.00
❑ 323 Frank Sullivan 4.00 2.00
❑ 324 Don Demeter 4.00 2.00
❑ 325 Ken Boyer 12.00 6.00
❑ 326 Marv Throneberry 8.00 4.00
❑ 327 Gary Bell RC 4.00 2.00
❑ 328 Lou Skizas 4.00 2.00
❑ 329 Detroit Tigers CL 15.00 7.50
❑ 330 Gus Triandos 8.00 4.00
❑ 331 Steve Boros 4.00 2.00
❑ 332 Ray Monzant 4.00 2.00
❑ 333 Harry Simpson 4.00 2.00
❑ 334 Glen Hobbie 4.00 2.00
❑ 335 Johnny Temple 8.00 4.00
❑ 336A Billy Loes TR 8.00 4.00
❑ 336B Billy Loes ERR 80.00 50.00
❑ 337 George Crowe 4.00 2.00
❑ 338 Sparky Anderson RC 60.00 35.00
❑ 339 Roy Face 8.00 4.00
❑ 340 Roy Sievers 8.00 4.00
❑ 341 Tom Qualters 4.00 2.00
❑ 342 Ray Jablonski 4.00 2.00
❑ 343 Billy Hoeft 4.00 2.00
❑ 344 Russ Nixon 4.00 2.00
❑ 345 Gil McDougald 12.00 6.00
❑ 346 D.Sisler/T.Brewer 4.00 2.00
❑ 347 Bob Buhl 4.00 2.00
❑ 348 Ted Lepcio 4.00 2.00
❑ 349 Hoyt Wilhelm 20.00 10.00
❑ 350 Ernie Banks 80.00 50.00
❑ 351 Earl Torgeson 4.00 2.00
❑ 352 Robin Roberts 20.00 10.00
❑ 353 Curt Flood 8.00 4.00
❑ 354 Pete Burnside 4.00 2.00
❑ 355 Jimmy Piersall 8.00 4.00
❑ 356 Bob Mabe RC 4.00 2.00
❑ 357 Dick Stuart RC 8.00 4.00
❑ 358 Ralph Terry 8.00 4.00
❑ 359 Bill White RC 20.00 10.00
❑ 360 Al Kaline 60.00 35.00
❑ 361 Willard Nixon 4.00 2.00
❑ 362A Dolan Nichols RC 4.00 2.00
❑ 362B Dolan Nichols ERR 80.00 50.00
❑ 363 Bobby Avila 4.00 2.00
❑ 364 Danny McDevitt 4.00 2.00
❑ 365 Gus Bell 8.00 4.00
❑ 366 Humberto Robinson 4.00 2.00

❑	367 Cal Neeman	4.00	2.00
❑	368 Don Mueller	8.00	4.00
❑	369 Dick Tomanek	4.00	2.00
❑	370 Pete Runnels	8.00	4.00
❑	371 Dick Brodowski	4.00	2.00
❑	372 Jim Hegan	8.00	4.00
❑	373 Herb Plews	4.00	2.00
❑	374 Art Ditmar	8.00	4.00
❑	375 Bob Nieman	4.00	2.00
❑	376 Hal Naragon	4.00	2.00
❑	377 John Antonelli	8.00	4.00
❑	378 Gail Harris	4.00	2.00
❑	379 Bob Miller	4.00	2.00
❑	380 Hank Aaron	150.00	90.00
❑	381 Mike Baxes	4.00	2.00
❑	382 Curt Simmons	8.00	4.00
❑	383 D.Larsen/C.Stengel	12.00	6.00
❑	384 Dave Sisler	4.00	2.00
❑	385 Sherm Lollar	8.00	4.00
❑	386 Jim Delsing	4.00	2.00
❑	387 Don Drysdale	50.00	30.00
❑	388 Bob Will RC	4.00	2.00
❑	389 Joe Nuxhall	8.00	4.00
❑	390 Orlando Cepeda	20.00	10.00
❑	391 Milt Pappas	8.00	4.00
❑	392 Whitey Herzog	8.00	4.00
❑	393 Frank Lary	8.00	4.00
❑	394 Randy Jackson	4.00	2.00
❑	395 Elston Howard	12.00	6.00
❑	396 Bob Rush	4.00	2.00
❑	397 Washington Senators CL	15.00	7.50
❑	398 Wally Post	8.00	4.00
❑	399 Larry Jackson	4.00	2.00
❑	400 Jackie Jensen	8.00	4.00
❑	401 Ron Blackburn	4.00	2.00
❑	402 Hector Lopez	8.00	4.00
❑	403 Clem Labine	8.00	4.00
❑	404 Hank Sauer	8.00	4.00
❑	405 Roy McMillan	8.00	4.00
❑	406 Solly Drake	4.00	2.00
❑	407 Moe Drabowsky	8.00	4.00
❑	408 N.Fox/L.Aparicio	40.00	20.00
❑	409 Gus Zernial	8.00	4.00
❑	410 Billy Pierce	8.00	4.00
❑	411 Whitey Lockman	8.00	4.00
❑	412 Stan Lopata	4.00	2.00
❑	413 Camilo Pascual UER	8.00	4.00
❑	414 Dale Long	8.00	4.00
❑	415 Bill Mazeroski	12.00	6.00
❑	416 Haywood Sullivan	8.00	4.00
❑	417 Virgil Trucks	8.00	4.00
❑	418 Gino Cimoli	4.00	2.00
❑	419 Milwaukee Braves CL	15.00	7.50
❑	420 Rocky Colavito	30.00	15.00
❑	421 Herman Wehmeier	4.00	2.00
❑	422 Hobie Landrith	4.00	2.00
❑	423 Bob Grim	8.00	4.00
❑	424 Ken Aspromonte	4.00	2.00
❑	425 Del Crandall	8.00	4.00
❑	426 Gerry Staley	8.00	4.00
❑	427 Charlie Neal	8.00	4.00
❑	428 Kline/Friend/Law/Face	4.00	2.00
❑	429 Bobby Thomson	8.00	4.00
❑	430 Whitey Ford	60.00	35.00
❑	431 Whammy Douglas	4.00	2.00
❑	432 Smoky Burgess	8.00	4.00
❑	433 Billy Harrell	4.00	2.00
❑	434 Hal Griggs	4.00	2.00
❑	435 Frank Robinson	50.00	30.00
❑	436 Granny Hamner	4.00	2.00
❑	437 Ike Delock	4.00	2.00
❑	438 Sammy Esposito	4.00	2.00
❑	439 Brooks Robinson	50.00	30.00
❑	440 Lew Burdette UER	8.00	4.00
❑	441 John Roseboro	8.00	4.00
❑	442 Ray Narleski	4.00	2.00
❑	443 Daryl Spencer	4.00	2.00
❑	444 Ron Hansen RC	8.00	4.00
❑	445 Cal McLish	4.00	2.00
❑	446 Rocky Nelson	4.00	2.00
❑	447 Bob Anderson	4.00	2.00
❑	448 Vada Pinson UER	12.00	6.00
❑	449 Tom Gorman	4.00	2.00
❑	450 Eddie Mathews	40.00	20.00
❑	451 Jimmy Constable RC	4.00	2.00
❑	452 Chico Fernandez	4.00	2.00
❑	453 Les Moss	4.00	2.00
❑	454 Phil Clark	4.00	2.00
❑	455 Larry Doby	12.00	6.00
❑	456 Jerry Casale RC	4.00	2.00
❑	457 Los Angeles Dodgers CL	30.00	15.00
❑	458 Gordon Jones	4.00	2.00
❑	459 Bill Tuttle	4.00	2.00
❑	460 Bob Friend	8.00	4.00
❑	461 Mickey Mantle BT	125.00	75.00
❑	462 Rocky Colavito BT	12.00	6.00
❑	463 Al Kaline BT	30.00	15.00
❑	464 Willie Mays BT	40.00	20.00
❑	465 Roy Sievers BT	8.00	4.00
❑	466 Billy Pierce BT	8.00	4.00
❑	467 Hank Aaron BT	40.00	20.00
❑	468 Duke Snider BT	20.00	10.00
❑	469 Ernie Banks BT	20.00	10.00
❑	470 Stan Musial BT	30.00	15.00
❑	471 Tom Sturdivant	4.00	2.00
❑	472 Gene Freese	4.00	2.00
❑	473 Mike Fornieles	4.00	2.00
❑	474 Moe Thacker RC	4.00	2.00
❑	475 Jack Harshman	4.00	2.00
❑	476 Cleveland Indians CL	15.00	7.50
❑	477 Barry Latman RC	4.00	2.00
❑	478 Roberto Clemente	175.00	100.00
❑	479 Lindy McDaniel	8.00	4.00
❑	480 Red Schoendienst	12.00	6.00
❑	481 Charlie Maxwell	8.00	4.00
❑	482 Russ Meyer	4.00	2.00
❑	483 Clint Courtney	4.00	2.00
❑	484 Willie Kirkland	4.00	2.00
❑	485 Ryne Duren	8.00	4.00
❑	486 Sammy White	4.00	2.00
❑	487 Hal Brown	4.00	2.00
❑	488 Walt Moryn	4.00	2.00
❑	489 John Powers	4.00	2.00
❑	490 Frank Thomas	8.00	4.00
❑	491 Don Blasingame	4.00	2.00
❑	492 Gene Conley	8.00	4.00
❑	493 Jim Landis	8.00	4.00
❑	494 Don Pavletich RC	4.00	2.00
❑	495 Johnny Podres	12.00	6.00
❑	496 Wayne Terwilliger UER	4.00	2.00
❑	497 Hal R. Smith	4.00	2.00
❑	498 Dick Hyde	4.00	2.00
❑	499 Johnny O'Brien	8.00	4.00
❑	500 Vic Wertz	8.00	4.00
❑	501 Bob Tiefenauer RC	4.00	2.00
❑	502 Alvin Dark	8.00	4.00
❑	503 Jim Owens	4.00	2.00
❑	504 Ossie Alvarez RC	4.00	2.00
❑	505 Tony Kubek	12.00	6.00
❑	506 Bob Purkey	4.00	2.00
❑	507 Bob Hale	15.00	7.50
❑	508 Art Fowler	15.00	7.50
❑	509 Norm Cash RC	80.00	60.00
❑	510 New York Yankees CL	125.00	75.00
❑	511 George Susce	15.00	7.50
❑	512 George Altman RC	15.00	7.50
❑	513 Tommy Carroll	15.00	7.50
❑	514 Bob Gibson RC	300.00	175.00
❑	515 Harmon Killebrew	125.00	75.00
❑	516 Mike Garcia	20.00	10.00
❑	517 Joe Koppe RC	15.00	7.50
❑	518 Mike Cuellar UER RC	30.00	18.00
❑	519 Runnels/Gernert/Malzone	20.00	10.00
❑	520 Don Elston	15.00	7.50
❑	521 Gary Geiger	15.00	7.50
❑	522 Gene Snyder RC	15.00	7.50
❑	523 Harry Bright RC	15.00	7.50
❑	524 Larry Osborne RC	15.00	7.50
❑	525 Jim Coates RC	20.00	10.00
❑	526 Bob Speake	15.00	7.50
❑	527 Solly Hemus	15.00	7.50
❑	528 Pittsburgh Pirates CL	80.00	50.00
❑	529 George Bamberger RC	20.00	10.00
❑	530 Wally Moon	20.00	10.00
❑	531 Ray Webster RC	15.00	7.50
❑	532 Mark Freeman RC	15.00	7.50
❑	533 Darrell Johnson	20.00	10.00
❑	534 Faye Throneberry	15.00	7.50
❑	535 Ruben Gomez	15.00	7.50
❑	536 Danny Kravitz	15.00	7.50
❑	537 Rudolph Arias RC	15.00	7.50
❑	538 Chick King	15.00	7.50
❑	539 Gary Blaylock RC	15.00	7.50
❑	540 Willie Miranda	15.00	7.50
❑	541 Bob Thurman	15.00	7.50
❑	542 Jim Perry RC	30.00	18.00
❑	543 Skinner/Virdon/Clemente	125.00	75.00
❑	544 Lee Tate RC	15.00	7.50
❑	545 Tom Morgan	15.00	7.50
❑	546 Al Schroll	15.00	7.50
❑	547 Jim Baxes RC	15.00	7.50
❑	548 Elmer Singleton	15.00	7.50
❑	549 Howie Nunn RC	15.00	7.50
❑	550 R.Campanella Courage	150.00	90.00
❑	551 Fred Haney AS MG	15.00	7.50
❑	552 Casey Stengel AS	30.00	18.00
❑	553 Orlando Cepeda AS	30.00	18.00
❑	554 Bill Skowron AS	20.00	10.00
❑	555 Bill Mazeroski AS	30.00	18.00
❑	556 Nellie Fox AS	40.00	20.00
❑	557 Ken Boyer AS	30.00	18.00
❑	558 Frank Malzone AS	15.00	7.50
❑	559 Ernie Banks AS	60.00	35.00
❑	560 Luis Aparicio AS	40.00	25.00
❑	561 Hank Aaron AS	125.00	75.00
❑	562 Al Kaline AS	60.00	35.00
❑	563 Willie Mays AS	125.00	75.00
❑	564 Mickey Mantle AS	300.00	175.00
❑	565 Wes Covington AS	20.00	10.00
❑	566 Roy Sievers AS	15.00	7.50
❑	567 Del Crandall AS	15.00	7.50
❑	568 Gus Triandos AS	15.00	7.50
❑	569 Bob Friend AS	15.00	7.50
❑	570 Bob Turley AS	15.00	7.50
❑	571 Warren Spahn AS	50.00	30.00
❑	572 Billy Pierce AS	40.00	25.00

1960 Topps

❑	COMPLETE SET (572)	5000.00	2500.00
❑	COMMON CARD (1-440)	4.00	1.50
❑	COMMON CARD (441-506)	8.00	3.00
❑	COMMON CARD (507-572)	15.00	6.00
❑	WRAPPER (1-CENT)	1000.00	500.00
❑	WRAP. (1-CENT REPEAT)	500.00	250.00
❑	WRAPPER (5-CENT)	40.00	15.00
❑	1 Early Wynn	40.00	15.00
❑	2 Roman Mejias	4.00	1.50
❑	3 Joe Adcock	6.00	2.50
❑	4 Bob Purkey	4.00	1.50
❑	5 Wally Moon	6.00	2.50
❑	6 Lou Berberet	4.00	1.50
❑	7 W.Mays/B.Rigney	25.00	10.00
❑	8 Bud Daley	4.00	1.50
❑	9 Faye Throneberry	4.00	1.50
❑	10 Ernie Banks	50.00	20.00
❑	11 Norm Siebern	4.00	1.50
❑	12 Milt Pappas	6.00	2.50
❑	13 Wally Post	6.00	2.50
❑	14 Jim Grant	6.00	2.50
❑	15 Pete Runnels	6.00	2.50
❑	16 Ernie Broglio	6.00	2.50
❑	17 Johnny Callison	6.00	2.50
❑	18 Los Angeles Dodgers CL	50.00	20.00
❑	19 Felix Mantilla	4.00	1.50
❑	20 Roy Face	6.00	2.50
❑	21 Dutch Dotterer	4.00	1.50
❑	22 Rocky Bridges	4.00	1.50
❑	23 Eddie Fisher RC	4.00	1.50
❑	24 Dick Gray	4.00	1.50
❑	25 Roy Sievers	6.00	2.50

❑ 26 Wayne Terwilliger 4.00 1.50
❑ 27 Dick Drott 4.00 1.50
❑ 28 Brooks Robinson 50.00 20.00
❑ 29 Clem Labine 6.00 2.50
❑ 30 Tito Francona 4.00 1.50
❑ 31 Sammy Esposito 4.00 1.50
❑ 32 J.O'Toole/V.Pinson 4.00 1.50
❑ 33 Tom Morgan 4.00 1.50
❑ 34 Sparky Anderson 15.00 6.00
❑ 35 Whitey Ford 50.00 20.00
❑ 36 Russ Nixon 4.00 1.50
❑ 37 Bill Bruton 4.00 1.50
❑ 38 Jerry Casale 4.00 1.50
❑ 39 Earl Averill Jr. 4.00 1.50
❑ 40 Joe Cunningham 4.00 1.50
❑ 41 Barry Latman 4.00 1.50
❑ 42 Hobie Landrith 4.00 1.50
❑ 43 Washington Senators CL 10.00 4.00
❑ 44 Bobby Locke RC 4.00 1.50
❑ 45 Roy McMillan 6.00 2.50
❑ 46 Jack Fisher RC 4.00 1.50
❑ 47 Don Zimmer 6.00 2.50
❑ 48 Hal W. Smith 4.00 1.50
❑ 49 Curt Raydon 4.00 1.50
❑ 50 Al Kaline 50.00 20.00
❑ 51 Jim Coates 6.00 2.50
❑ 52 Dave Philley 4.00 1.50
❑ 53 Jackie Brandt 4.00 1.50
❑ 54 Mike Fornieles 4.00 1.50
❑ 55 Bill Mazeroski 15.00 6.00
❑ 56 Steve Korcheck 4.00 1.50
❑ 57 T.Lown/G.Staley 4.00 1.50
❑ 58 Gino Cimoli 4.00 1.50
❑ 58A Gino Cimoli Cards
❑ 59 Juan Pizarro 4.00 1.50
❑ 60 Gus Triandos 6.00 2.50
❑ 61 Eddie Kasko 4.00 1.50
❑ 62 Roger Craig 6.00 2.50
❑ 63 George Strickland 4.00 1.50
❑ 64 Jack Meyer 4.00 1.50
❑ 65 Elston Howard 6.00 2.50
❑ 66 Bob Trowbridge 4.00 1.50
❑ 67 Jose Pagan RC 4.00 1.50
❑ 68 Dave Hillman 4.00 1.50
❑ 69 Billy Goodman 6.00 2.50
❑ 70 Lew Burdette UER 6.00 2.50
❑ 71 Marty Keough 4.00 1.50
❑ 72 Detroit Tigers CL 25.00 10.00
❑ 73 Bob Gibson 50.00 20.00
❑ 74 Walt Moryn 4.00 1.50
❑ 75 Vic Power 6.00 2.50
❑ 76 Bill Fischer 4.00 1.50
❑ 77 Hank Foiles 4.00 1.50
❑ 78 Bob Grim 4.00 1.50
❑ 79 Walt Dropo 4.00 1.50
❑ 80 Johnny Antonelli 6.00 2.50
❑ 81 Russ Snyder RC 4.00 1.50
❑ 82 Ruben Gomez 4.00 1.50
❑ 83 Tony Kubek 15.00 6.00
❑ 84 Hal R. Smith 4.00 1.50
❑ 85 Frank Lary 6.00 2.50
❑ 86 Dick Gernert 4.00 1.50
❑ 87 John Romonosky 4.00 1.50
❑ 88 John Roseboro 6.00 2.50
❑ 89 Hal Brown 4.00 1.50
❑ 90 Bobby Avila 4.00 1.50
❑ 91 Bennie Daniels 4.00 1.50
❑ 92 Whitey Herzog 6.00 2.50
❑ 93 Art Schult 4.00 1.50
❑ 94 Leo Kiely 4.00 1.50
❑ 95 Frank Thomas 6.00 2.50
❑ 96 Ralph Terry 6.00 2.50
❑ 97 Ted Lepcio 4.00 1.50
❑ 98 Gordon Jones 4.00 1.50
❑ 99 Lenny Green 4.00 1.50
❑ 100 Nellie Fox 20.00 8.00
❑ 101 Bob Miller RC 4.00 1.50
❑ 102 Kent Hadley 4.00 1.50
❑ 102A Kent Hadley A's
❑ 103 Dick Farrell 6.00 2.50
❑ 104 Dick Schofield 6.00 2.50
❑ 105 Larry Sherry RC 6.00 2.50
❑ 106 Billy Gardner 4.00 1.50
❑ 107 Carlton Willey 4.00 1.50
❑ 108 Pete Daley 4.00 1.50
❑ 109 Clete Boyer 15.00 6.00
❑ 110 Cal McLish 4.00 1.50
❑ 111 Vic Wertz 6.00 2.50
❑ 112 Jack Harshman 4.00 1.50
❑ 113 Bob Skinner 4.00 1.50
❑ 114 Ken Aspromonte 4.00 1.50
❑ 115 R.Face/H.Wilhelm 6.00 2.50
❑ 116 Jim Rivera 4.00 1.50
❑ 117 Tom Borland RS 4.00 1.50
❑ 118 Bob Bruce RS RC 4.00 1.50
❑ 119 Chico Cardenas RS RC 6.00 2.50
❑ 120 Duke Carmel RS RC 4.00 1.50
❑ 121 Camilo Carreon RS RC 4.00 1.50
❑ 122 Don Dillard RS 4.00 1.50
❑ 123 Dan Dobbek RS 4.00 1.50
❑ 124 Jim Donohue RS RC 4.00 1.50
❑ 125 Dick Ellsworth RS RC 6.00 2.50
❑ 126 Chuck Estrada RS RC 4.00 1.50
❑ 127 Ron Hansen RS 6.00 2.50
❑ 128 Bill Harris RS RC 4.00 1.50
❑ 129 Bob Hartman RS 4.00 1.50
❑ 130 Frank Herrera RS 4.00 1.50
❑ 131 Ed Hobaugh RS RC 4.00 1.50
❑ 132 Frank Howard RS RC 25.00 10.00
❑ 133 Julian Javier RS RC 6.00 2.50
❑ 134 Deron Johnson RS 6.00 2.50
❑ 135 Ken Johnson RS RC 4.00 1.50
❑ 136 Jim Kaat RS RC 40.00 15.00
❑ 137 Lou Klimchock RS RC 4.00 1.50
❑ 138 Art Mahaffey RS RC 6.00 2.50
❑ 139 Carl Mathias RS RC 4.00 1.50
❑ 140 Julio Navarro RS RC 4.00 1.50
❑ 141 Jim Proctor RS RC 4.00 1.50
❑ 142 Bill Short RS RC 4.00 1.50
❑ 143 Al Spangler RS RC 4.00 1.50
❑ 144 Al Stieglitz RS RC 4.00 1.50
❑ 145 Jim Umbricht RS RC 4.00 1.50
❑ 146 Ted Wieand RS RC 4.00 1.50
❑ 147 Bob Will RS 4.00 1.50
❑ 148 C.Yastrzemski RS RC 200.00 100.00
❑ 149 Bob Nieman 4.00 1.50
❑ 150 Billy Pierce 6.00 2.50
❑ 151 San Francisco Giants CL 10.00 4.00
❑ 152 Gail Harris 4.00 1.50
❑ 153 Bobby Thomson 6.00 2.50
❑ 154 Jim Davenport 6.00 2.50
❑ 155 Charlie Neal 6.00 2.50
❑ 156 Art Ceccarelli 4.00 1.50
❑ 157 Rocky Nelson 6.00 2.50
❑ 158 Wes Covington 6.00 2.50
❑ 159 Jim Piersall 6.00 2.50
❑ 160 M.Mantle/K.Boyer 120.00 60.00
❑ 161 Ray Narleski 4.00 1.50
❑ 162 Sammy Taylor 4.00 1.50
❑ 163 Hector Lopez 6.00 2.50
❑ 164 Cincinnati Reds CL 10.00 4.00
❑ 165 Jack Sanford 6.00 2.50
❑ 166 Chuck Essegian 4.00 1.50
❑ 167 Valmy Thomas 4.00 1.50
❑ 168 Alex Grammas 4.00 1.50
❑ 169 Jake Striker RC 4.00 1.50
❑ 170 Del Crandall 6.00 2.50
❑ 171 Johnny Groth 4.00 1.50
❑ 172 Willie Kirkland 4.00 1.50
❑ 173 Billy Martin 20.00 8.00
❑ 174 Cleveland Indians CL 10.00 4.00
❑ 175 Pedro Ramos 4.00 1.50
❑ 176 Vada Pinson 6.00 2.50
❑ 177 Johnny Kucks 4.00 1.50
❑ 178 Woody Held 4.00 1.50
❑ 179 Rip Coleman 4.00 1.50
❑ 180 Harry Simpson 4.00 1.50
❑ 181 Billy Loes 6.00 2.50
❑ 182 Glen Hobbie 4.00 1.50
❑ 183 Eli Grba RC 4.00 1.50
❑ 184 Gary Geiger 4.00 1.50
❑ 185 Jim Owens 4.00 1.50
❑ 186 Dave Sisler 4.00 1.50
❑ 187 Jay Hook RC 4.00 1.50
❑ 188 Dick Williams 6.00 2.50
❑ 189 Don McMahon 4.00 1.50
❑ 190 Gene Woodling 6.00 2.50
❑ 191 Johnny Klippstein 4.00 1.50
❑ 192 Danny O'Connell 4.00 1.50
❑ 193 Dick Hyde 4.00 1.50
❑ 194 Bobby Gene Smith 4.00 1.50
❑ 195 Lindy McDaniel 6.00 2.50
❑ 196 Andy Carey 6.00 2.50
❑ 197 Ron Kline 4.00 1.50
❑ 198 Jerry Lynch 6.00 2.50
❑ 199 Dick Donovan 6.00 2.50
❑ 200 Willie Mays 120.00 60.00
❑ 201 Larry Osborne 4.00 1.50
❑ 202 Fred Kipp 4.00 1.50
❑ 203 Sammy White 4.00 1.50
❑ 204 Ryne Duren 6.00 2.50
❑ 205 Johnny Logan 6.00 2.50
❑ 206 Claude Osteen 6.00 2.50
❑ 207 Bob Boyd 4.00 1.50
❑ 208 Chicago White Sox CL 10.00 4.00
❑ 209 Ron Blackburn 4.00 1.50
❑ 210 Harmon Killebrew 40.00 15.00
❑ 211 Taylor Phillips 4.00 1.50
❑ 212 Walter Alston MG 10.00 4.00
❑ 213 Chuck Dressen MG 6.00 2.50
❑ 214 Jimmy Dykes MG 6.00 2.50
❑ 215 Bob Elliott MG 6.00 2.50
❑ 216 Joe Gordon MG 6.00 2.50
❑ 217 Charlie Grimm MG 6.00 2.50
❑ 218 Solly Hemus MG 4.00 1.50
❑ 219 Fred Hutchinson MG 6.00 2.50
❑ 220 Billy Jurges MG 4.00 1.50
❑ 221 Cookie Lavagetto MG 4.00 1.50
❑ 222 Al Lopez MG 10.00 4.00
❑ 223 Danny Murtaugh MG 6.00 2.50
❑ 224 Paul Richards MG 6.00 2.50
❑ 225 Bill Rigney MG 4.00 1.50
❑ 226 Eddie Sawyer MG 4.00 1.50
❑ 227 Casey Stengel MG 15.00 6.00
❑ 228 Ernie Johnson 6.00 2.50
❑ 229 Joe M. Morgan RC 4.00 1.50
❑ 230 Burdette/Spahn/Buhl 10.00 4.00
❑ 231 Hal Naragon 4.00 1.50
❑ 232 Jim Busby 4.00 1.50
❑ 233 Don Elston 4.00 1.50
❑ 234 Don Demeter 4.00 1.50
❑ 235 Gus Bell 6.00 2.50
❑ 236 Dick Ricketts 4.00 1.50
❑ 237 Elmer Valo 4.00 1.50
❑ 238 Danny Kravitz 4.00 1.50
❑ 239 Joe Shipley 4.00 1.50
❑ 240 Luis Aparicio 15.00 6.00
❑ 241 Albie Pearson 6.00 2.50
❑ 242 St. Louis Cardinals CL 10.00 4.00
❑ 243 Bubba Phillips 4.00 1.50
❑ 244 Hal Griggs 4.00 1.50
❑ 245 Eddie Yost 6.00 2.50
❑ 246 Lee Maye RC 6.00 2.50
❑ 247 Gil McDougald 10.00 4.00
❑ 248 Del Rice 4.00 1.50
❑ 249 Earl Wilson RC 6.00 2.50
❑ 250 Stan Musial 100.00 50.00
❑ 251 Bob Malkmus 4.00 1.50
❑ 252 Ray Herbert 4.00 1.50
❑ 253 Eddie Bressoud 4.00 1.50
❑ 254 Arnie Portocarrero 4.00 1.50
❑ 255 Jim Gilliam 6.00 2.50
❑ 256 Dick Brown 4.00 1.50
❑ 257 Gordy Coleman RC 4.00 1.50
❑ 258 Dick Groat 6.00 2.50
❑ 259 George Altman 4.00 1.50
❑ 260 R.Colavito/T.Francona 15.00 6.00
❑ 261 Pete Burnside 4.00 1.50
❑ 262 Hank Bauer 6.00 2.50
❑ 263 Darrell Johnson 4.00 1.50
❑ 264 Robin Roberts 15.00 6.00
❑ 265 Rip Repulski 4.00 1.50
❑ 266 Joey Jay 6.00 2.50
❑ 267 Jim Marshall 4.00 1.50
❑ 268 Al Worthington 4.00 1.50
❑ 269 Gene Green 4.00 1.50
❑ 270 Bob Turley 6.00 2.50
❑ 271 Julio Becquer 4.00 1.50
❑ 272 Fred Green RC 6.00 2.50
❑ 273 Neil Chrisley 4.00 1.50
❑ 274 Tom Acker 4.00 1.50
❑ 275 Curt Flood 6.00 2.50
❑ 276 Ken McBride RC 4.00 1.50
❑ 277 Harry Bright 4.00 1.50
❑ 278 Stan Williams 6.00 2.50
❑ 279 Chuck Tanner 6.00 2.50
❑ 280 Frank Sullivan 4.00 1.50
❑ 281 Ray Boone 6.00 2.50

❑ 282 Joe Nuxhall 6.00 2.50
❑ 283 Johnny Blanchard 6.00 2.50
❑ 284 Don Gross 4.00 1.50
❑ 285 Harry Anderson 4.00 1.50
❑ 286 Ray Semproch 4.00 1.50
❑ 287 Felipe Alou 6.00 2.50
❑ 288 Bob Mabe 4.00 1.50
❑ 289 Willie Jones 4.00 1.50
❑ 290 Jerry Lumpe 4.00 1.50
❑ 291 Bob Keegan 4.00 1.50
❑ 292 J.Pignatano/J.Roseboro 6.00 2.50
❑ 293 Gene Conley 6.00 2.50
❑ 294 Tony Taylor 6.00 2.50
❑ 295 Gil Hodges 25.00 10.00
❑ 296 Nelson Chittum RC 4.00 1.50
❑ 297 Reno Bertoia 4.00 1.50
❑ 298 George Witt 4.00 1.50
❑ 299 Earl Torgeson 4.00 1.50
❑ 300 Hank Aaron 120.00 60.00
❑ 301 Jerry Davie 4.00 1.50
❑ 302 Philadelphia Phillies CL 10.00 4.00
❑ 303 Billy O'Dell 4.00 1.50
❑ 304 Joe Ginsberg 4.00 1.50
❑ 305 Richie Ashburn 20.00 8.00
❑ 306 Frank Baumann 4.00 1.50
❑ 307 Gene Oliver 4.00 1.50
❑ 308 Dick Hall 4.00 1.50
❑ 309 Bob Hale 4.00 1.50
❑ 310 Frank Malzone 6.00 2.50
❑ 311 Raul Sanchez 4.00 1.50
❑ 312 Charley Lau 6.00 2.50
❑ 313 Turk Lown 4.00 1.50
❑ 314 Chico Fernandez 4.00 1.50
❑ 315 Bobby Shantz 10.00 4.00
❑ 316 W.McCovey ASR RC 120.00 60.00
❑ 317 Pumpsie Green ASR RC 6.00 2.50
❑ 318 Jim Baxes ASR 6.00 2.50
❑ 319 Joe Koppe ASR 6.00 2.50
❑ 320 Bob Allison ASR 6.00 2.50
❑ 321 Ron Fairly ASR 6.00 2.50
❑ 322 Willie Tasby ASR 6.00 2.50
❑ 323 John Romano ASR 6.00 2.50
❑ 324 Jim Perry ASR 6.00 2.50
❑ 325 Jim O'Toole ASR 6.00 2.50
❑ 326 Roberto Clemente 200.00 100.00
❑ 327 Ray Sadecki RC 4.00 1.50
❑ 328 Earl Battey 4.00 1.50
❑ 329 Zack Monroe 4.00 1.50
❑ 330 Harvey Kuenn 6.00 2.50
❑ 331 Henry Mason RC 4.00 1.50
❑ 332 New York Yankees CL 80.00 40.00
❑ 333 Danny McDevitt 4.00 1.50
❑ 334 Ted Abernathy 4.00 1.50
❑ 335 Red Schoendienst 15.00 6.00
❑ 336 Ike Delock 4.00 1.50
❑ 337 Cal Neeman 4.00 1.50
❑ 338 Ray Monzant 4.00 1.50
❑ 339 Harry Chiti 4.00 1.50
❑ 340 Harvey Haddix 6.00 2.50
❑ 341 Carroll Hardy 4.00 1.50
❑ 342 Casey Wise 4.00 1.50
❑ 343 Sandy Koufax 120.00 60.00
❑ 344 Clint Courtney 4.00 1.50
❑ 345 Don Newcombe 6.00 2.50
❑ 346 J.C. Martin UER RC 6.00 2.50
❑ 347 Ed Bouchee 4.00 1.50
❑ 348 Barry Shetrone RC 4.00 1.50
❑ 349 Moe Drabowsky 6.00 2.50
❑ 350 Mickey Mantle 600.00 300.00
❑ 351 Don Nottebart RC 4.00 1.50
❑ 352 Bell/F.Robinson/Lynch 10.00 4.00
❑ 353 Don Larsen 6.00 2.50
❑ 354 Bob Lillis 4.00 1.50
❑ 355 Bill White 6.00 2.50
❑ 356 Joe Amalfitano 4.00 1.50
❑ 357 Al Schroll 4.00 1.50
❑ 358 Joe DeMaestri 4.00 1.50
❑ 359 Buddy Gilbert RC 4.00 1.50
❑ 360 Herb Score 6.00 2.50
❑ 361 Bob Oldis 6.00 2.50
❑ 362 Russ Kemmerer 4.00 1.50
❑ 363 Gene Stephens 4.00 1.50
❑ 364 Paul Foytack 4.00 1.50
❑ 365 Minnie Minoso 10.00 4.00
❑ 366 Dallas Green RC 10.00 4.00
❑ 367 Bill Tuttle 4.00 1.50
❑ 368 Daryl Spencer 4.00 1.50
❑ 369 Billy Hoeft 4.00 1.50
❑ 370 Bill Skowron 10.00 4.00
❑ 371 Bud Byerly 4.00 1.50
❑ 372 Frank House 4.00 1.50
❑ 373 Don Hoak 6.00 2.50
❑ 374 Bob Buhl 6.00 2.50
❑ 375 Dale Long 10.00 4.00
❑ 376 John Briggs 4.00 1.50
❑ 377 Roger Maris 100.00 50.00
❑ 378 Stu Miller 6.00 2.50
❑ 379 Red Wilson 4.00 1.50
❑ 380 Bob Shaw 4.00 1.50
❑ 381 Milwaukee Braves CL 10.00 4.00
❑ 382 Ted Bowsfield 4.00 1.50
❑ 383 Leon Wagner 4.00 1.50
❑ 384 Don Cardwell 4.00 1.50
❑ 385 Charlie Neal WS1 8.00 3.00
❑ 386 Charlie Neal WS2 8.00 3.00
❑ 387 Carl Furillo WS3 8.00 3.00
❑ 388 Gil Hodges WS4 10.00 4.00
❑ 389 L.Aparicio WS5 w/M.Wills 10.00 4.00
❑ 390 Scrambling After Ball WS6 8.00 3.00
❑ 391 Champs Celebrate WS 8.00 3.00
❑ 392 Tex Clevenger 4.00 1.50
❑ 393 Smoky Burgess 6.00 2.50
❑ 394 Norm Larker 6.00 2.50
❑ 395 Hoyt Wilhelm 15.00 6.00
❑ 396 Steve Bilko 4.00 1.50
❑ 397 Don Blasingame 4.00 1.50
❑ 398 Mike Cuellar 6.00 2.50
❑ 399 Pappas/Fisher/Walker 6.00 2.50
❑ 400 Rocky Colavito 20.00 8.00
❑ 401 Bob Duliba RC 4.00 1.50
❑ 402 Dick Stuart 15.00 6.00
❑ 403 Ed Sadowski 4.00 1.50
❑ 404 Bob Rush 4.00 1.50
❑ 405 Bobby Richardson 15.00 6.00
❑ 406 Billy Klaus 4.00 1.50
❑ 407 Gary Peters UER RC 6.00 2.50
❑ 408 Carl Furillo 10.00 4.00
❑ 409 Ron Samford 4.00 1.50
❑ 410 Sam Jones 6.00 2.50
❑ 411 Ed Bailey 4.00 1.50
❑ 412 Bob Anderson 4.00 1.50
❑ 413 Kansas City Athletics CL 10.00 4.00
❑ 414 Don Williams RC 4.00 1.50
❑ 415 Bob Cerv 4.00 1.50
❑ 416 Humberto Robinson 4.00 1.50
❑ 417 Chuck Cottier RC 4.00 1.50
❑ 418 Don Mossi 6.00 2.50
❑ 419 George Crowe 4.00 1.50
❑ 420 Eddie Mathews 40.00 15.00
❑ 421 Duke Maas 4.00 1.50
❑ 422 John Powers 4.00 1.50
❑ 423 Ed Fitzgerald 4.00 1.50
❑ 424 Pete Whisenant 4.00 1.50
❑ 425 Johnny Podres 6.00 2.50
❑ 426 Ron Jackson 4.00 1.50
❑ 427 Al Grunwald RC 4.00 1.50
❑ 428 Al Smith 4.00 1.50
❑ 429 Nellie Fox/H.Kuenn 10.00 4.00
❑ 430 Art Ditmar 4.00 1.50
❑ 431 Andre Rodgers 4.00 1.50
❑ 432 Chuck Stobbs 4.00 1.50
❑ 433 Irv Noren 4.00 1.50
❑ 434 Brooks Lawrence 6.00 2.50
❑ 435 Gene Freese 4.00 1.50
❑ 436 Marv Throneberry 6.00 2.50
❑ 437 Bob Friend 6.00 2.50
❑ 438 Jim Coker RC 4.00 1.50
❑ 439 Tom Brewer 4.00 1.50
❑ 440 Jim Lemon 6.00 2.50
❑ 441 Gary Bell 10.00 4.00
❑ 442 Joe Pignatano 8.00 3.00
❑ 443 Charlie Maxwell 8.00 3.00
❑ 444 Jerry Kindall 8.00 3.00
❑ 445 Warren Spahn 50.00 20.00
❑ 446 Ellis Burton 8.00 3.00
❑ 447 Ray Moore 8.00 3.00
❑ 448 Jim Gentile RC 15.00 6.00
❑ 449 Jim Brosnan 8.00 3.00
❑ 450 Orlando Cepeda 25.00 10.00
❑ 451 Curt Simmons 8.00 3.00
❑ 452 Ray Webster 8.00 3.00
❑ 453 Vern Law 25.00 10.00
❑ 454 Hal Woodeshick 8.00 3.00
❑ 455 Baltimore Coaches 8.00 3.00
❑ 456 Red Sox Coaches 10.00 4.00
❑ 457 Cubs Coaches 8.00 3.00
❑ 458 White Sox Coaches 8.00 3.00
❑ 459 Reds Coaches 8.00 3.00
❑ 460 Indians Coaches 15.00 6.00
❑ 461 Tigers Coaches 10.00 4.00
❑ 462 Athletics Coaches 8.00 3.00
❑ 463 Dodgers Coaches 8.00 3.00
❑ 464 Braves Coaches 8.00 3.00
❑ 465 Yankees Coaches 25.00 10.00
❑ 466 Phillies Coaches 8.00 3.00
❑ 467 Pirates Coaches 8.00 3.00
❑ 468 Cardinals Coaches 8.00 3.00
❑ 469 Giants Coaches 8.00 3.00
❑ 470 Senators Coaches 8.00 3.00
❑ 471 Ned Garver 8.00 3.00
❑ 472 Alvin Dark 8.00 3.00
❑ 473 Al Cicotte 8.00 3.00
❑ 474 Haywood Sullivan 8.00 3.00
❑ 475 Don Drysdale 40.00 15.00
❑ 476 Lou Johnson RC 8.00 3.00
❑ 477 Don Ferrarese 8.00 3.00
❑ 478 Frank Torre 8.00 3.00
❑ 479 Georges Maranda RC 8.00 3.00
❑ 480 Yogi Berra 80.00 40.00
❑ 481 Wes Stock RC 8.00 3.00
❑ 482 Frank Bolling 8.00 3.00
❑ 483 Camilo Pascual 8.00 3.00
❑ 484 Pittsburgh Pirates CL 40.00 15.00
❑ 485 Ken Boyer 15.00 6.00
❑ 486 Bobby Del Greco 8.00 3.00
❑ 487 Tom Sturdivant 8.00 3.00
❑ 488 Norm Cash 25.00 10.00
❑ 489 Steve Ridzik 8.00 3.00
❑ 490 Frank Robinson 50.00 20.00
❑ 491 Mel Roach 8.00 3.00
❑ 492 Larry Jackson 8.00 3.00
❑ 493 Duke Snider 50.00 20.00
❑ 494 Baltimore Orioles CL 25.00 10.00
❑ 495 Sherm Lollar 8.00 3.00
❑ 496 Bill Virdon 10.00 4.00
❑ 497 John Tsitouris 8.00 3.00
❑ 498 Al Pilarcik 8.00 3.00
❑ 499 Johnny James RC 10.00 4.00
❑ 500 Johnny Temple 8.00 3.00
❑ 501 Bob Schmidt 8.00 3.00
❑ 502 Jim Bunning 25.00 10.00
❑ 503 Don Lee 8.00 3.00
❑ 504 Seth Morehead 8.00 3.00
❑ 505 Ted Kluszewski 25.00 10.00
❑ 506 Lee Walls 8.00 3.00
❑ 507 Dick Stigman 15.00 6.00
❑ 508 Billy Consolo 15.00 6.00
❑ 509 Tommy Davis RC 25.00 10.00
❑ 510 Gerry Staley 15.00 6.00
❑ 511 Ken Walters RC 15.00 6.00
❑ 512 Joe Gibbon RC 15.00 6.00
❑ 513 Chicago Cubs CL 30.00 12.50
❑ 514 Steve Barber RC 15.00 6.00
❑ 515 Stan Lopata 15.00 6.00
❑ 516 Marty Kutyna RC 15.00 6.00
❑ 517 Charlie James RC 25.00 10.00
❑ 518 Tony Gonzalez RC 15.00 6.00
❑ 519 Ed Roebuck 15.00 6.00
❑ 520 Don Buddin 15.00 6.00
❑ 521 Mike Lee RC 15.00 6.00
❑ 522 Ken Hunt RC 30.00 12.50
❑ 523 Clay Dalrymple RC 15.00 6.00
❑ 524 Bill Henry 15.00 6.00
❑ 525 Marv Breeding RC 15.00 6.00
❑ 526 Paul Giel 25.00 10.00
❑ 527 Jose Valdivielso 25.00 10.00
❑ 528 Ben Johnson RC 15.00 6.00
❑ 529 Norm Sherry RC 20.00 8.00
❑ 530 Mike McCormick 15.00 6.00
❑ 531 Sandy Amoros 20.00 8.00
❑ 532 Mike Garcia 20.00 8.00
❑ 533 Lu Clinton RC 15.00 6.00
❑ 534 Ken MacKenzie RC 15.00 6.00
❑ 535 Whitey Lockman 15.00 6.00
❑ 536 Wynn Hawkins RC 15.00 6.00
❑ 537 Boston Red Sox CL 30.00 12.50
❑ 538 Frank Barnes RC 15.00 6.00
❑ 539 Gene Baker 15.00 6.00

❑ 540 Jerry Walker 15.00 6.00
❑ 541 Tony Curry RC 15.00 6.00
❑ 542 Ken Hamlin RC 15.00 6.00
❑ 543 Elio Chacon RC 15.00 6.00
❑ 544 Bill Monbouquette 20.00 8.00
❑ 545 Carl Sawatski 15.00 6.00
❑ 546 Hank Aguirre 15.00 6.00
❑ 547 Bob Aspromonte RC 20.00 8.00
❑ 548 Don Mincher RC 15.00 6.00
❑ 549 John Buzhardt 15.00 6.00
❑ 550 Jim Landis 15.00 6.00
❑ 551 Ed Rakow RC 15.00 6.00
❑ 552 Walt Bond RC 15.00 6.00
❑ 553 Bill Skowron AS 20.00 8.00
❑ 554 Willie McCovey AS 40.00 15.00
❑ 555 Nellie Fox AS 30.00 12.50
❑ 556 Charlie Neal AS 15.00 6.00
❑ 557 Frank Malzone AS 15.00 6.00
❑ 558 Eddie Mathews AS 40.00 15.00
❑ 559 Luis Aparicio AS 30.00 12.50
❑ 560 Ernie Banks AS 60.00 30.00
❑ 561 Al Kaline AS 60.00 30.00
❑ 562 Joe Cunningham AS 15.00 6.00
❑ 563 Mickey Mantle AS 250.00 125.00
❑ 564 Willie Mays AS 100.00 50.00
❑ 565 Roger Maris AS 100.00 50.00
❑ 566 Hank Aaron AS 100.00 50.00
❑ 567 Sherm Lollar AS 15.00 6.00
❑ 568 Del Crandall AS 15.00 6.00
❑ 569 Camilo Pascual AS 15.00 6.00
❑ 570 Don Drysdale AS 40.00 15.00
❑ 571 Billy Pierce AS 15.00 6.00
❑ 572 Johnny Antonelli AS 30.00 12.50
❑ NNO Iron-on team transfer 5.00 2.00

1961 Topps

❑ COMPLETE SET (587) 7000.00 3500.00
❑ COMMON CARD (1-370) 3.00 1.25
❑ COMMON CARD (371-446) 4.00 1.50
❑ COMMON CARD (447-522) 8.00 3.00
❑ COMMON CARD (523-589) 30.00 12.50
❑ NOT ISSUED (587/588)
❑ WRAPPER (1-CENT) 200.00 100.00
❑ WRAP.(1-CENT, REPEAT) 100.00 50.00
❑ WRAPPER (5-CENT) 40.00 15.00
❑ 1 Dick Groat 30.00 12.50
❑ 2 Roger Maris 250.00 125.00
❑ 3 John Buzhardt 3.00 1.25
❑ 4 Lenny Green 3.00 1.25
❑ 5 John Romano 3.00 1.25
❑ 6 Ed Roebuck 3.00 1.25
❑ 7 Chicago White Sox TC 8.00 3.00
❑ 8 Dick Williams 6.00 2.50
❑ 9 Bob Purkey 3.00 1.25
❑ 10 Brooks Robinson 50.00 20.00
❑ 11 Curt Simmons 6.00 2.50
❑ 12 Moe Thacker 3.00 1.25
❑ 13 Chuck Cottier 3.00 1.25
❑ 14 Don Mossi 6.00 2.50
❑ 15 Willie Kirkland 3.00 1.25
❑ 16 Billy Muffett 3.00 1.25
❑ 17 Checklist 1 10.00 4.00
❑ 18 Jim Grant 6.00 2.50
❑ 19 Clete Boyer 8.00 3.00
❑ 20 Robin Roberts 15.00 6.00
❑ 21 Zoilo Versalles UER RC 8.00 3.00
❑ 22 Clem Labine 6.00 2.50
❑ 23 Don Demeter 3.00 1.25
❑ 24 Ken Johnson 6.00 2.50
❑ 25 Pinson/Bell/F.Robinson 8.00 3.00
❑ 26 Wes Stock 3.00 1.25
❑ 27 Jerry Kindall 3.00 1.25
❑ 28 Hector Lopez 6.00 2.50
❑ 29 Don Nottebart 3.00 1.25
❑ 30 Nellie Fox 15.00 6.00
❑ 31 Bob Schmidt 3.00 1.25
❑ 32 Ray Sadecki 3.00 1.25
❑ 33 Gary Geiger 3.00 1.25
❑ 34 Wynn Hawkins 3.00 1.25
❑ 35 Ron Santo RC 40.00 15.00
❑ 36 Jack Kralick RC 3.00 1.25
❑ 37 Charley Maxwell 6.00 2.50
❑ 38 Bob Lillis 3.00 1.25
❑ 39 Leo Posada RC 3.00 1.25
❑ 40 Bob Turley 6.00 2.50
❑ 41 Groat/Mays/Clemente LL 40.00 15.00
❑ 42 Runnels/Minoso/Skow LL 8.00 3.00
❑ 43 Banks/Aaron/Mathews LL 30.00 12.50
❑ 44 Mante/Maris/Colavito LL 80.00 40.00
❑ 45 McCormick/Drysdale LL 8.00 3.00
❑ 46 Baumann/Bunning/Dit LL 8.00 3.00
❑ 47 Broglio/Spahn/Burdette LL 8.00 3.00
❑ 48 Estrada/Perry/Daley LL 8.00 3.00
❑ 49 Drysdale/Koufax LL 20.00 8.00
❑ 50 Bunning/Ramos/Wynn LL 8.00 3.00
❑ 51 Detroit Tigers TC 8.00 3.00
❑ 52 George Crowe 3.00 1.25
❑ 53 Russ Nixon 3.00 1.50
❑ 54 Earl Francis RC 3.00 1.25
❑ 55 Jim Davenport 6.00 2.50
❑ 56 Russ Kemmerer 3.00 1.25
❑ 57 Marv Throneberry 6.00 2.50
❑ 58 Joe Schaffernoth RC 3.00 1.25
❑ 59 Jim Woods 3.00 1.25
❑ 60 Woody Held 3.00 1.25
❑ 61 Ron Piche RC 3.00 1.25
❑ 62 Al Pilarcik 3.00 1.25
❑ 63 Jim Kaat 8.00 3.00
❑ 64 Alex Grammas 3.00 1.25
❑ 65 Ted Kluszewski 8.00 3.00
❑ 66 Bill Henry 3.00 1.25
❑ 67 Ossie Virgil 3.00 1.25
❑ 68 Deron Johnson 6.00 2.50
❑ 69 Earl Wilson 6.00 2.50
❑ 70 Bill Virdon 6.00 2.50
❑ 71 Jerry Adair 3.00 1.25
❑ 72 Stu Miller 6.00 2.50
❑ 73 Al Spangler 3.00 1.25
❑ 74 Joe Pignatano 3.00 1.25
❑ 75 L.McDaniel/L.Jackson 6.00 2.50
❑ 76 Harry Anderson 3.00 1.25
❑ 77 Dick Stigman 3.00 1.25
❑ 78 Lee Walls 6.00 2.50
❑ 79 Joe Ginsberg 3.00 1.25
❑ 80 Harmon Killebrew 20.00 8.00
❑ 81 Tracy Stallard RC 3.00 1.25
❑ 82 Joe Christopher RC 3.00 1.25
❑ 83 Bob Bruce 3.00 1.25
❑ 84 Lee Maye 3.00 1.25
❑ 85 Jerry Walker 3.00 1.25
❑ 86 Los Angeles Dodgers TC 8.00 3.00
❑ 87 Joe Amalfitano 3.00 1.25
❑ 88 Richie Ashburn 15.00 6.00
❑ 89 Billy Martin 15.00 6.00
❑ 90 Gerry Staley 3.00 1.25
❑ 91 Walt Moryn 3.00 1.25
❑ 92 Hal Naragon 3.00 1.25
❑ 93 Tony Gonzalez 3.00 1.25
❑ 94 Johnny Kucks 3.00 1.25
❑ 95 Norm Cash 8.00 3.00
❑ 96 Billy O'Dell 3.00 1.25
❑ 97 Jerry Lynch 6.00 2.50
❑ 98A Checklist 2 Red 10.00 4.00
❑ 98B Checklist 2 Yellow B/W 10.00 4.00
❑ 98C Checklist 2 Yellow W/B 10.00 4.00
❑ 99 Don Buddin UER 3.00 1.25
❑ 100 Harvey Haddix 6.00 2.50
❑ 101 Bubba Phillips 3.00 1.25
❑ 102 Gene Stephens 3.00 1.25
❑ 103 Ruben Amaro 3.00 1.25
❑ 104 John Blanchard 8.00 3.00
❑ 105 Carl Willey 3.00 1.25
❑ 106 Whitey Herzog 3.00 1.25
❑ 107 Seth Morehead 3.00 1.25
❑ 108 Dan Dobbek 3.00 1.25
❑ 109 Johnny Podres 8.00 3.00
❑ 110 Vada Pinson 8.00 3.00
❑ 111 Jack Meyer 3.00 1.25
❑ 112 Chico Fernandez 3.00 1.25
❑ 113 Mike Fornieles 3.00 1.25
❑ 114 Hobie Landrith 3.00 1.25
❑ 115 Johnny Antonelli 6.00 2.50
❑ 116 Joe DeMaestri 3.00 1.25
❑ 117 Dale Long 6.00 2.50
❑ 118 Chris Cannizzaro RC 3.00 1.25
❑ 119 Siebern/Bauer/Lumpe 6.00 2.50
❑ 120 Eddie Mathews 30.00 12.50
❑ 121 Eli Grba 6.00 2.50
❑ 122 Chicago Cubs TC 8.00 3.00
❑ 123 Billy Gardner 3.00 1.25
❑ 124 J.C. Martin 3.00 1.25
❑ 125 Steve Barber 3.00 1.25
❑ 126 Dick Stuart 6.00 2.50
❑ 127 Ron Kline 3.00 1.25
❑ 128 Rip Repulski 3.00 1.25
❑ 129 Ed Hobaugh 3.00 1.25
❑ 130 Norm Larker 3.00 1.25
❑ 131 Paul Richards MG 6.00 2.50
❑ 132 Al Lopez MG 8.00 3.00
❑ 133 Ralph Houk MG 6.00 2.50
❑ 134 Mickey Vernon MG 6.00 2.50
❑ 135 Fred Hutchinson MG 6.00 2.50
❑ 136 Walter Alston MG 8.00 3.00
❑ 137 Chuck Dressen MG 6.00 2.50
❑ 138 Danny Murtaugh MG 6.00 2.50
❑ 139 Solly Hemus MG 6.00 2.50
❑ 140 Gus Triandos 6.00 2.50
❑ 141 Billy Williams RC 60.00 30.00
❑ 142 Luis Arroyo 6.00 2.50
❑ 143 Russ Snyder 3.00 1.25
❑ 144 Jim Coker 3.00 1.25
❑ 145 Bob Buhl 6.00 2.50
❑ 146 Marty Keough 3.00 1.25
❑ 147 Ed Rakow 3.00 1.25
❑ 148 Julian Javier 6.00 2.50
❑ 149 Bob Oldis 3.00 1.25
❑ 150 Willie Mays 100.00 50.00
❑ 151 Jim Donohue 3.00 1.25
❑ 152 Earl Torgeson 3.00 1.25
❑ 153 Don Lee 3.00 1.25
❑ 154 Bobby Del Greco 3.00 1.25
❑ 155 Johnny Temple 6.00 2.50
❑ 156 Ken Hunt 6.00 2.50
❑ 157 Cal McLish 3.00 1.25
❑ 158 Pete Daley 3.00 1.25
❑ 159 Baltimore Orioles TC 8.00 3.00
❑ 160 Whitey Ford UER 50.00 20.00
❑ 161 Sherman Jones UER RC 3.00 1.25
❑ 162 Jay Hook 3.00 1.25
❑ 163 Ed Sadowski 3.00 1.25
❑ 164 Felix Mantilla 3.00 1.25
❑ 165 Gino Cimoli 3.00 1.25
❑ 166 Danny Kravitz 3.00 1.25
❑ 167 San Francisco Giants TC 8.00 3.00
❑ 168 Tommy Davis 8.00 3.00
❑ 169 Don Elston 3.00 1.25
❑ 170 Al Smith 3.00 1.25
❑ 171 Paul Foytack 3.00 1.25
❑ 172 Don Dillard 3.00 1.25
❑ 173 Malzone/Wertz/Jensen 6.00 2.50
❑ 174 Ray Semproch 3.00 1.25
❑ 175 Gene Freese 3.00 1.25
❑ 176 Ken Aspromonte 3.00 1.25
❑ 177 Don Larsen 6.00 2.50
❑ 178 Bob Nieman 3.00 1.25
❑ 179 Joe Koppe 3.00 1.25
❑ 180 Bobby Richardson 12.00 5.00
❑ 181 Fred Green 3.00 1.25
❑ 182 Dave Nicholson RC 3.00 1.25
❑ 183 Andre Rodgers 3.00 1.25
❑ 184 Steve Bilko 6.00 2.50
❑ 185 Herb Score 6.00 2.50
❑ 186 Elmer Valo 6.00 2.50
❑ 187 Billy Klaus 3.00 1.25
❑ 188 Jim Marshall 3.00 1.25
❑ 189A Checklist 3 Copyright 263 10.00 4.00
❑ 189B Checklist 3 Copyright 264 10.00 4.00
❑ 190 Stan Williams 6.00 2.50
❑ 191 Mike de la Hoz RC 3.00 1.25
❑ 192 Dick Brown 3.00 1.25

❑ 193	Gene Conley	6.00	2.50
❑ 194	Gordy Coleman	6.00	2.50
❑ 195	Jerry Casale	3.00	1.25
❑ 196	Ed Bouchee	3.00	1.25
❑ 197	Dick Hall	3.00	1.25
❑ 198	Carl Sawatski	3.00	1.25
❑ 199	Bob Boyd	3.00	1.25
❑ 200	Warren Spahn	40.00	15.00
❑ 201	Pete Whisenant	3.00	1.25
❑ 202	Al Neiger RC	3.00	1.25
❑ 203	Eddie Bressoud	3.00	1.25
❑ 204	Bob Skinner	6.00	2.50
❑ 205	Billy Pierce	6.00	2.50
❑ 206	Gene Green	3.00	1.25
❑ 207	S.Koufax/J.Podres	30.00	12.50
❑ 208	Larry Osborne	3.00	1.25
❑ 209	Ken McBride	3.00	1.25
❑ 210	Pete Runnels	6.00	2.50
❑ 211	Bob Gibson	40.00	15.00
❑ 212	Haywood Sullivan	6.00	2.50
❑ 213	Bill Stafford RC	3.00	1.25
❑ 214	Danny Murphy RC	6.00	2.50
❑ 215	Gus Bell	6.00	2.50
❑ 216	Ted Bowsfield	3.00	1.25
❑ 217	Mel Roach	3.00	1.25
❑ 218	Hal Brown	3.00	1.25
❑ 219	Gene Mauch MG	6.00	2.50
❑ 220	Alvin Dark MG	6.00	2.50
❑ 221	Mike Higgins MG	3.00	1.25
❑ 222	Jimmy Dykes MG	6.00	2.50
❑ 223	Bob Scheffing MG	3.00	1.25
❑ 224	Joe Gordon MG	6.00	2.50
❑ 225	Bill Rigney MG	6.00	2.50
❑ 226	Cookie Lavagetto MG	6.00	2.50
❑ 227	Juan Pizarro	3.00	1.25
❑ 228	New York Yankees TC	60.00	30.00
❑ 229	Rudy Hernandez RC	3.00	1.25
❑ 230	Don Hoak	6.00	2.50
❑ 231	Dick Drott	3.00	1.25
❑ 232	Bill White	6.00	2.50
❑ 233	Joey Jay	6.00	2.50
❑ 234	Ted Lepcio	3.00	1.25
❑ 235	Camilo Pascual	6.00	2.50
❑ 236	Don Gile RC	3.00	1.25
❑ 237	Billy Loes	6.00	2.50
❑ 238	Jim Gilliam	6.00	2.50
❑ 239	Dave Sisler	3.00	1.25
❑ 240	Ron Hansen	3.00	1.25
❑ 241	Al Cicotte	3.00	1.25
❑ 242	Hal Smith	3.00	1.25
❑ 243	Frank Lary	6.00	2.50
❑ 244	Chico Cardenas	6.00	2.50
❑ 245	Joe Adcock	6.00	2.50
❑ 246	Bob Davis RC	3.00	1.25
❑ 247	Billy Goodman	6.00	2.50
❑ 248	Ed Keegan RC	3.00	1.25
❑ 249	Cincinnati Reds TC	8.00	3.00
❑ 250	V.Law/R.Face	6.00	2.50
❑ 251	Bill Bruton	3.00	1.25
❑ 252	Bill Short	3.00	1.25
❑ 253	Sammy Taylor	3.00	1.25
❑ 254	Ted Sadowski RC	6.00	2.50
❑ 255	Vic Power	6.00	2.50
❑ 256	Billy Hoeft	3.00	1.25
❑ 257	Carroll Hardy	3.00	1.25
❑ 258	Jack Sanford	6.00	2.50
❑ 259	John Schaive RC	3.00	1.25
❑ 260	Don Drysdale	30.00	12.50
❑ 261	Charlie Lau	6.00	2.50
❑ 262	Tony Curry	3.00	1.25
❑ 263	Ken Hamlin	3.00	1.25
❑ 264	Glen Hobbie	3.00	1.25
❑ 265	Tony Kubek	12.00	5.00
❑ 266	Lindy McDaniel	6.00	2.50
❑ 267	Norm Siebern	3.00	1.25
❑ 268	Ike Delock	3.00	1.25
❑ 269	Harry Chiti	3.00	1.25
❑ 270	Bob Friend	6.00	2.50
❑ 271	Jim Landis	3.00	1.25
❑ 272	Tom Morgan	3.00	1.25
❑ 273A	Checklist 4 Copyright 336	15.00	6.00
❑ 273B	Checklist 4 Copyright 339	10.00	4.00
❑ 274	Gary Bell	3.00	1.25
❑ 275	Gene Woodling	6.00	2.50
❑ 276	Ray Rippelmeyer RC	3.00	1.25
❑ 277	Hank Foiles	3.00	1.25
❑ 278	Don McMahon	3.00	1.25
❑ 279	Jose Pagan	3.00	1.25
❑ 280	Frank Howard	8.00	3.00
❑ 281	Frank Sullivan	3.00	1.25
❑ 282	Faye Throneberry	3.00	1.25
❑ 283	Bob Anderson	3.00	1.25
❑ 284	Dick Gernert	3.00	1.25
❑ 285	Sherm Lollar	6.00	2.50
❑ 286	George Witt	3.00	1.25
❑ 287	Carl Yastrzemski	50.00	20.00
❑ 288	Albie Pearson	6.00	2.50
❑ 289	Ray Moore	3.00	1.25
❑ 290	Stan Musial	100.00	50.00
❑ 291	Tex Clevenger	3.00	1.25
❑ 292	Jim Baumer RC	3.00	1.25
❑ 293	Tom Sturdivant	3.00	1.25
❑ 294	Don Blasingame	3.00	1.25
❑ 295	Milt Pappas	6.00	2.50
❑ 296	Wes Covington	6.00	2.50
❑ 297	Kansas City Athletics TC	8.00	3.00
❑ 298	Jim Golden RC	3.00	1.25
❑ 299	Clay Dalrymple	3.00	1.25
❑ 300	Mickey Mantle	600.00	300.00
❑ 301	Chet Nichols	3.00	1.25
❑ 302	Al Heist RC	3.00	1.25
❑ 303	Gary Peters	6.00	2.50
❑ 304	Rocky Nelson	3.00	1.25
❑ 305	Mike McCormick	6.00	2.50
❑ 306	Bill Virdon WS1	10.00	4.00
❑ 307	Mickey Mantle WS2	80.00	40.00
❑ 308	Bobby Richardson WS3	12.00	5.00
❑ 309	Gino Cimoli WS4	10.00	4.00
❑ 310	Roy Face WS5	10.00	4.00
❑ 311	Whitey Ford WS6	15.00	6.00
❑ 312	Bill Mazeroski WS7	20.00	8.00
❑ 313	Pirates Celebrate WS	15.00	6.00
❑ 314	Bob Miller	3.00	1.25
❑ 315	Earl Battey	6.00	2.50
❑ 316	Bobby Gene Smith	3.00	1.25
❑ 317	Jim Brewer RC	3.00	1.25
❑ 318	Danny O'Connell	3.00	1.25
❑ 319	Valmy Thomas	3.00	1.25
❑ 320	Lou Burdette	6.00	2.50
❑ 321	Marv Breeding	3.00	1.25
❑ 322	Bill Kunkel RC	6.00	2.50
❑ 323	Sammy Esposito	3.00	1.25
❑ 324	Hank Aguirre	3.00	1.25
❑ 325	Wally Moon	6.00	2.50
❑ 326	Dave Hillman	3.00	1.25
❑ 327	Matty Alou RC	12.00	5.00
❑ 328	Jim O'Toole	6.00	2.50
❑ 329	Julio Becquer	3.00	1.25
❑ 330	Rocky Colavito	20.00	8.00
❑ 331	Ned Garver	3.00	1.25
❑ 332	Dutch Dotterer UER	3.00	1.25
❑ 333	Fritz Brickell RC	3.00	1.25
❑ 334	Walt Bond	3.00	1.25
❑ 335	Frank Bolling	3.00	1.25
❑ 336	Don Mincher	6.00	2.50
❑ 337	Wynn/Lopez/Score	8.00	3.00
❑ 338	Don Landrum	3.00	1.25
❑ 339	Gene Baker	3.00	1.25
❑ 340	Vic Wertz	6.00	2.50
❑ 341	Jim Owens	3.00	1.25
❑ 342	Clint Courtney	3.00	1.25
❑ 343	Earl Robinson RC	3.00	1.25
❑ 344	Sandy Koufax	100.00	50.00
❑ 345	Jimmy Piersall	8.00	3.00
❑ 346	Howie Nunn	3.00	1.25
❑ 347	St. Louis Cardinals TC	8.00	3.00
❑ 348	Steve Boros	3.00	1.25
❑ 349	Danny McDevitt	3.00	1.25
❑ 350	Ernie Banks	40.00	15.00
❑ 351	Jim King	3.00	1.25
❑ 352	Bob Shaw	3.00	1.25
❑ 353	Howie Bedell RC	3.00	1.25
❑ 354	Billy Harrell	6.00	2.50
❑ 355	Bob Allison	8.00	3.00
❑ 356	Ryne Duren	3.00	1.25
❑ 357	Daryl Spencer	3.00	1.25
❑ 358	Earl Averill Jr.	6.00	2.50
❑ 359	Dallas Green	3.00	1.25
❑ 360	Frank Robinson	40.00	15.00
❑ 361A	Checklist 5 No Ad on Back	15.00	6.00
❑ 361B	Checklist 5 Ad on Back	15.00	6.00
❑ 362	Frank Funk RC	3.00	1.25
❑ 363	John Roseboro	6.00	2.50
❑ 364	Moe Drabowsky	6.00	2.50
❑ 365	Jerry Lumpe	3.00	1.25
❑ 366	Eddie Fisher	3.00	1.25
❑ 367	Jim Rivera	3.00	1.25
❑ 368	Bennie Daniels	3.00	1.25
❑ 369	Dave Philley	3.00	1.25
❑ 370	Roy Face	6.00	2.50
❑ 371	Bill Skowron SP	50.00	20.00
❑ 372	Bob Hendley RC	4.00	1.50
❑ 373	Boston Red Sox TC	8.00	3.00
❑ 374	Paul Giel	4.00	1.50
❑ 375	Ken Boyer	12.00	5.00
❑ 376	Mike Roarke RC	6.00	2.50
❑ 377	Ruben Gomez	4.00	1.50
❑ 378	Wally Post	6.00	2.50
❑ 379	Bobby Shantz	4.00	1.50
❑ 380	Minnie Minoso	8.00	3.00
❑ 381	Dave Wickersham RC	4.00	1.50
❑ 382	Frank Thomas	6.00	2.50
❑ 383	McCormick/Sanford/O'Dell	6.00	2.50
❑ 384	Chuck Essegian	4.00	1.50
❑ 385	Jim Perry	6.00	2.50
❑ 386	Joe Hicks	4.00	1.50
❑ 387	Duke Maas	4.00	1.50
❑ 388	Roberto Clemente	120.00	60.00
❑ 389	Ralph Terry	6.00	2.50
❑ 390	Del Crandall	8.00	3.00
❑ 391	Winston Brown RC	4.00	1.50
❑ 392	Reno Bertoia	4.00	1.50
❑ 393	D.Cardwell/G.Hobbie	4.00	1.50
❑ 394	Ken Walters	4.00	1.50
❑ 395	Chuck Estrada	6.00	2.50
❑ 396	Bob Aspromonte	4.00	1.50
❑ 397	Hal Woodeshick	4.00	1.50
❑ 398	Hank Bauer	6.00	2.50
❑ 399	Cliff Cook RC	4.00	1.50
❑ 400	Vern Law	6.00	2.50
❑ 401	Babe Ruth 60th HR	60.00	30.00
❑ 402	Don Larsen Perfect SP	25.00	10.00
❑ 403	26 Inning Tie/Oeschger/Cadore	8.00	3.00
❑ 404	Rogers Hornsby .424	12.00	5.00
❑ 405	Lou Gehrig Streak	80.00	40.00
❑ 406	Mickey Mantle 565 HR	100.00	50.00
❑ 407	Jack Chesbro Wins 41	8.00	3.00
❑ 408	Christy Mathewson K's SP	20.00	8.00
❑ 409	Walter Johnson Shutout	12.00	5.00
❑ 410	Harvey Haddix 12 Perfect	8.00	3.00
❑ 411	Tony Taylor	6.00	2.50
❑ 412	Larry Sherry	6.00	2.50
❑ 413	Eddie Yost	6.00	2.50
❑ 414	Dick Donovan	6.00	2.50
❑ 415	Hank Aaron	120.00	60.00
❑ 416	Dick Howser RC	8.00	3.00
❑ 417	Juan Marichal SP RC	100.00	50.00
❑ 418	Ed Bailey	6.00	2.50
❑ 419	Tom Borland	4.00	1.50
❑ 420	Ernie Broglio	6.00	2.50
❑ 421	Ty Cline SP RC	20.00	8.00
❑ 422	Bud Daley	4.00	1.50
❑ 423	Charlie Neal SP	20.00	8.00
❑ 424	Turk Lown	4.00	1.50
❑ 425	Yogi Berra	80.00	40.00
❑ 426	Milwaukee Braves TC UER	12.00	5.00
❑ 427	Dick Ellsworth	6.00	2.50
❑ 428	Ray Barker SP RC	20.00	8.00
❑ 429	Al Kaline	50.00	20.00
❑ 430	Bill Mazeroski SP	50.00	20.00
❑ 431	Chuck Stobbs	4.00	1.50
❑ 432	Coot Veal	6.00	2.50
❑ 433	Art Mahaffey	4.00	1.50
❑ 434	Tom Brewer	4.00	1.50
❑ 435	Orlando Cepeda UER	12.00	5.00
❑ 436	Jim Maloney SP RC	20.00	8.00
❑ 437A	Checklist 6 440 Louis	15.00	6.00
❑ 437B	Checklist 6 440 Luis	15.00	6.00
❑ 438	Curt Flood	8.00	3.00
❑ 439	Phil Regan RC	6.00	2.50
❑ 440	Luis Aparicio	12.00	5.00
❑ 441	Dick Bertell RC	4.00	1.50
❑ 442	Gordon Jones	4.00	1.50
❑ 443	Duke Snider	50.00	20.00
❑ 444	Joe Nuxhall	6.00	2.50
❑ 445	Frank Malzone	6.00	2.50
❑ 446	Bob Taylor	4.00	1.50
❑ 447	Harry Bright	8.00	3.00

❑ 448 Del Rice 15.00 6.00
❑ 449 Bob Bolin RC 8.00 3.00
❑ 450 Jim Lemon 8.00 3.00
❑ 451 Spencer/White/Broglio 8.00 3.00
❑ 452 Bob Allen RC 8.00 3.00
❑ 453 Dick Schofield 8.00 3.00
❑ 454 Pumpsie Green 8.00 3.00
❑ 455 Early Wynn 15.00 6.00
❑ 456 Hal Bevan 8.00 3.00
❑ 457 Johnny James 8.00 3.00
❑ 458 Willie Tasby 8.00 3.00
❑ 459 Terry Fox RC 10.00 4.00
❑ 460 Gil Hodges 25.00 10.00
❑ 461 Smoky Burgess 15.00 6.00
❑ 462 Lou Klimchock 8.00 3.00
❑ 463 Jack Fisher See 426 8.00 3.00
❑ 464 Lee Thomas RC 10.00 4.00
❑ 465 Roy McMillan 15.00 6.00
❑ 466 Ron Moeller RC 8.00 3.00
❑ 467 Cleveland Indians TC 12.00 5.00
❑ 468 John Callison 10.00 4.00
❑ 469 Ralph Lumenti 8.00 3.00
❑ 470 Roy Sievers 10.00 4.00
❑ 471 Phil Rizzuto MVP 25.00 10.00
❑ 472 Yogi Berra MVP SP 50.00 20.00
❑ 473 Bob Shantz MVP 8.00 3.00
❑ 474 Al Rosen MVP 10.00 4.00
❑ 475 Mickey Mantle MVP 200.00 100.00
❑ 476 Jackie Jensen MVP 10.00 4.00
❑ 477 Nellie Fox MVP 15.00 6.00
❑ 478 Roger Maris MVP 60.00 30.00
❑ 479 Jim Konstanty MVP 8.00 3.00
❑ 480 Roy Campanella MVP 40.00 15.00
❑ 481 Hank Sauer MVP 8.00 3.00
❑ 482 Willie Mays MVP 50.00 20.00
❑ 483 Don Newcombe MVP 10.00 4.00
❑ 484 Hank Aaron MVP 50.00 20.00
❑ 485 Ernie Banks MVP 40.00 15.00
❑ 486 Dick Groat MVP 10.00 4.00
❑ 487 Gene Oliver 8.00 3.00
❑ 488 Joe McClain RC 10.00 4.00
❑ 489 Walt Dropo 8.00 3.00
❑ 490 Jim Bunning 25.00 10.00
❑ 491 Philadelphia Phillies TC 12.00 5.00
❑ 492 Ron Fairly 10.00 4.00
❑ 493 Don Zimmer UER 10.00 4.00
❑ 494 Tom Cheney 15.00 6.00
❑ 495 Elston Howard 10.00 4.00
❑ 496 Ken MacKenzie 8.00 3.00
❑ 497 Willie Jones 8.00 3.00
❑ 498 Ray Herbert 8.00 3.00
❑ 499 Chuck Schilling RC 8.00 3.00
❑ 500 Harvey Kuenn 10.00 4.00
❑ 501 John DeMerit RC 8.00 3.00
❑ 502 Choo Choo Coleman RC 10.00 4.00
❑ 503 Tito Francona 8.00 3.00
❑ 504 Billy Consolo 8.00 3.00
❑ 505 Red Schoendienst 15.00 6.00
❑ 506 Willie Davis RC 15.00 6.00
❑ 507 Pete Burnside 8.00 3.00
❑ 508 Rocky Bridges 8.00 3.00
❑ 509 Camilo Carreon 8.00 3.00
❑ 510 Art Ditmar 8.00 3.00
❑ 511 Joe M. Morgan 8.00 3.00
❑ 512 Bob Will 8.00 3.00
❑ 513 Jim Brosnan 8.00 3.00
❑ 514 Jake Wood RC 8.00 3.00
❑ 515 Jackie Brandt 8.00 3.00
❑ 516 Checklist 7 15.00 6.00
❑ 517 Willie McCovey 40.00 15.00
❑ 518 Andy Carey 8.00 3.00
❑ 519 Jim Pagliaroni RC 8.00 3.00
❑ 520 Joe Cunningham 8.00 3.00
❑ 521 N.Sherry/L.Sherry 8.00 3.00
❑ 522 Dick Farrell UER 15.00 6.00
❑ 523 Joe Gibbon 30.00 12.50
❑ 524 Johnny Logan 30.00 12.50
❑ 525 Ron Perranoski RC 60.00 30.00
❑ 526 R.C. Stevens 30.00 12.50
❑ 527 Gene Leek RC 30.00 12.50
❑ 528 Pedro Ramos 30.00 12.50
❑ 529 Bob Roselli 30.00 12.50
❑ 530 Bob Malkmus 30.00 12.50
❑ 531 Jim Coates 50.00 20.00
❑ 532 Bob Hale 30.00 12.50
❑ 533 Jack Curtis RC 30.00 12.50
❑ 534 Eddie Kasko 40.00 15.00
❑ 535 Larry Jackson 30.00 12.50
❑ 536 Bill Tuttle 30.00 12.50
❑ 537 Bobby Locke 30.00 12.50
❑ 538 Chuck Hiller RC 30.00 12.50
❑ 539 Johnny Klippstein 30.00 12.50
❑ 540 Jackie Jensen 40.00 15.00
❑ 541 Rollie Sheldon RC 50.00 20.00
❑ 542 Minnesota Twins TC 60.00 30.00
❑ 543 Roger Craig 40.00 15.00
❑ 544 George Thomas RC 50.00 20.00
❑ 545 Hoyt Wilhelm 60.00 30.00
❑ 546 Marty Kutyna 30.00 12.50
❑ 547 Leon Wagner 30.00 12.50
❑ 548 Ted Wills 30.00 12.50
❑ 549 Hal R. Smith 30.00 12.50
❑ 550 Frank Baumann 30.00 12.50
❑ 551 George Altman 40.00 15.00
❑ 552 Jim Archer RC 30.00 12.50
❑ 553 Bill Fischer 30.00 12.50
❑ 554 Pittsburgh Pirates TC 80.00 40.00
❑ 555 Sam Jones 30.00 12.50
❑ 556 Ken R. Hunt RC 30.00 12.50
❑ 557 Jose Valdivielso 30.00 12.50
❑ 558 Don Ferrarese 30.00 12.50
❑ 559 Jim Gentile 60.00 30.00
❑ 560 Barry Latman 40.00 15.00
❑ 561 Charley James 30.00 12.50
❑ 562 Bill Monbouquette 30.00 12.50
❑ 563 Bob Cerv 60.00 30.00
❑ 564 Don Cardwell 30.00 12.50
❑ 565 Felipe Alou 50.00 20.00
❑ 566 Paul Richards AS MG 30.00 12.50
❑ 567 Danny Murtaugh AS MG 30.00 12.50
❑ 568 Bill Skowron AS 50.00 20.00
❑ 569 Frank Herrera AS 40.00 15.00
❑ 570 Nellie Fox AS 60.00 30.00
❑ 571 Bill Mazeroski AS 60.00 30.00
❑ 572 Brooks Robinson AS 80.00 40.00
❑ 573 Ken Boyer AS 50.00 20.00
❑ 574 Luis Aparicio AS 60.00 30.00
❑ 575 Ernie Banks AS 80.00 40.00
❑ 576 Roger Maris AS 200.00 100.00
❑ 577 Hank Aaron AS 150.00 75.00
❑ 578 Mickey Mantle AS 500.00 250.00
❑ 579 Willie Mays AS 150.00 75.00
❑ 580 Al Kaline AS 80.00 40.00
❑ 581 Frank Robinson AS 80.00 40.00
❑ 582 Earl Battey AS 30.00 12.50
❑ 583 Del Crandall AS 30.00 12.50
❑ 584 Jim Perry AS 30.00 12.50
❑ 585 Bob Friend AS 30.00 12.50
❑ 586 Whitey Ford AS 100.00 50.00
❑ 589 Warren Spahn AS 100.00 50.00

1962 Topps

❑ COMP. MASTER SET (689) 10000.00 5000.00
❑ COMPLETE SET (598) 8000.00 4000.00
❑ COMMON CARD (1-370) 5.00 2.00
❑ COMMON CARD (371-446) 6.00 2.50
❑ COMMON CARD (447-522) 12.00 5.00
❑ COMMON CARD (523-598) 20.00 8.00
❑ WRAPPER (1-CENT) 100.00 50.00
❑ WRAPPER (5-CENT) 30.00 12.50
❑ 1 Roger Maris 500.00 250.00
❑ 2 Jim Brosnan 5.00 2.00
❑ 3 Pete Runnels 5.00 2.00
❑ 4 John DeMerit 8.00 3.00
❑ 5 Sandy Koufax UER 150.00 75.00
❑ 6 Marv Breeding 5.00 2.00
❑ 7 Frank Thomas 10.00 4.00
❑ 8 Ray Herbert 5.00 2.00
❑ 9 Jim Davenport 8.00 3.00
❑ 10 Roberto Clemente 200.00 100.00
❑ 11 Tom Morgan 5.00 2.00
❑ 12 Harry Craft MG 8.00 3.00
❑ 13 Dick Howser 8.00 3.00
❑ 14 Bill White 8.00 3.00
❑ 15 Dick Donovan 5.00 2.00
❑ 16 Darrell Johnson 5.00 2.00
❑ 17 Johnny Callison 8.00 3.00
❑ 18 M.Mantle/W.Mays 200.00 100.00
❑ 19 Ray Washburn RC 5.00 2.00
❑ 20 Rocky Colavito 15.00 6.00
❑ 21 Jim Kaat 8.00 3.00
❑ 22A Checklist 1 ERR 12.00 5.00
❑ 22B Checklist 1 COR 12.00 5.00
❑ 23 Norm Larker 5.00 2.00
❑ 24 Detroit Tigers TC 10.00 4.00
❑ 25 Ernie Banks 50.00 20.00
❑ 26 Chris Cannizzaro 8.00 3.00
❑ 27 Chuck Cottier 5.00 2.00
❑ 28 Minnie Minoso 10.00 4.00
❑ 29 Casey Stengel MG 20.00 8.00
❑ 30 Eddie Mathews 40.00 15.00
❑ 31 Tom Tresh RC 15.00 6.00
❑ 32 John Roseboro 8.00 3.00
❑ 33 Don Larsen 8.00 3.00
❑ 34 Johnny Temple 8.00 3.00
❑ 35 Don Schwall RC 10.00 4.00
❑ 36 Don Leppert RC 5.00 2.00
❑ 37 Latman/Stigman/Perry 5.00 2.00
❑ 38 Gene Stephens 5.00 2.00
❑ 39 Joe Koppe 5.00 2.00
❑ 40 Orlando Cepeda 15.00 6.00
❑ 41 Cliff Cook 5.00 2.00
❑ 42 Jim King 5.00 2.00
❑ 43 Los Angeles Dodgers TC 10.00 4.00
❑ 44 Don Taussig RC 5.00 2.00
❑ 45 Brooks Robinson 50.00 20.00
❑ 46 Jack Baldschun RC 5.00 2.00
❑ 47 Bob Will 5.00 2.00
❑ 48 Ralph Terry 8.00 3.00
❑ 49 Hal Jones RC 5.00 2.00
❑ 50 Stan Musial 100.00 50.00
❑ 51 Cash/Kaline/Howard LL 8.00 3.00
❑ 52 Clemente/Pins/Boyer LL 20.00 8.00
❑ 53 Maris/Mantle/Kill LL 100.00 50.00
❑ 54 Cepeda/Mays/F.Rob LL 20.00 8.00
❑ 55 Donovan/Staff/Mossi LL 8.00 3.00
❑ 56 Spahn/O'Toole/Simm LL 8.00 3.00
❑ 57 Ford/Lary/Bunning LL 8.00 3.00
❑ 58 Spahn/Jay/O'Toole LL 8.00 3.00
❑ 59 Pascual/Ford/Bunning LL 8.00 3.00
❑ 60 Koufax/Will/Drysdale LL 20.00 8.00
❑ 61 St. Louis Cardinals TC 10.00 4.00
❑ 62 Steve Boros 5.00 2.00
❑ 63 Tony Cloninger RC 8.00 3.00
❑ 64 Russ Snyder 5.00 2.00
❑ 65 Bobby Richardson 10.00 4.00
❑ 66 Cuno Barragan RC 5.00 2.00
❑ 67 Harvey Haddix 8.00 3.00
❑ 68 Ken Hunt 5.00 2.00
❑ 69 Phil Ortega RC 5.00 2.00
❑ 70 Harmon Killebrew 25.00 10.00
❑ 71 Dick LeMay RC 5.00 2.00
❑ 72 Boros/Scheffing/Wood 5.00 2.00
❑ 73 Nellie Fox 20.00 8.00
❑ 74 Bob Lillis 8.00 3.00
❑ 75 Milt Pappas 8.00 3.00
❑ 76 Howie Bedell 5.00 2.00
❑ 77 Tony Taylor 8.00 3.00
❑ 78 Gene Green 5.00 2.00
❑ 79 Ed Hobaugh 5.00 2.00
❑ 80 Vada Pinson 8.00 3.00
❑ 81 Jim Pagliaroni 5.00 2.00
❑ 82 Deron Johnson 8.00 3.00
❑ 83 Larry Jackson 5.00 2.00
❑ 84 Lenny Green 5.00 2.00
❑ 85 Gil Hodges 20.00 8.00
❑ 86 Donn Clendenon RC 8.00 3.00
❑ 87 Mike Roarke 5.00 2.00
❑ 88 Ralph Houk MG 8.00 3.00
❑ 89 Barney Schultz RC 5.00 2.00

❑ 90 Jimmy Piersall 8.00 3.00
❑ 91 J.C. Martin 5.00 2.00
❑ 92 Sam Jones 5.00 2.00
❑ 93 John Blanchard 8.00 3.00
❑ 94 Jay Hook 8.00 3.00
❑ 95 Don Hoak 8.00 3.00
❑ 96 Eli Grba 5.00 2.00
❑ 97 Tito Francona 5.00 2.00
❑ 98 Checklist 2 12.00 5.00
❑ 99 Boog Powell RC 30.00 12.50
❑ 100 Warren Spahn 40.00 15.00
❑ 101 Carroll Hardy 5.00 2.00
❑ 102 Al Schroll 5.00 2.00
❑ 103 Don Blasingame 5.00 2.00
❑ 104 Ted Savage RC 5.00 2.00
❑ 105 Don Mossi 8.00 3.00
❑ 106 Carl Sawatski 5.00 2.00
❑ 107 Mike McCormick 8.00 3.00
❑ 108 Willie Davis 8.00 3.00
❑ 109 Bob Shaw 5.00 2.00
❑ 110 Bill Skowron 8.00 3.00
❑ 110A Bill Skowron Green Tint 8.00 3.00
❑ 111 Dallas Green 8.00 3.00
❑ 111A Dallas Green Green Tint 8.00 3.00
❑ 112 Hank Foiles 5.00 2.00
❑ 112A Hank Foiles Green Tint 5.00 2.00
❑ 113 Chicago White Sox TC 10.00 4.00
❑ 113A Chicago White Sox TC Green Tint 10.00 4.00
❑ 114 Howie Koplitz RC 5.00 2.00
❑ 114A Howie Koplitz Green Tint 5.00 2.00
❑ 115 Bob Skinner 8.00 3.00
❑ 115A Bob Skinner Green Tint 8.00 3.00
❑ 116 Herb Score 8.00 3.00
❑ 116A Herb Score Green Tint 8.00 3.00
❑ 117 Gary Geiger 8.00 3.00
❑ 117A Gary Geiger Green Tint 8.00 3.00
❑ 118 Julian Javier 8.00 3.00
❑ 118A Julian Javier Green Tint 8.00 3.00
❑ 119 Danny Murphy 5.00 2.00
❑ 119A Danny Murphy Green Tint 5.00 2.00
❑ 120 Bob Purkey 5.00 2.00
❑ 120A Bob Purkey Green Tint 5.00 2.00
❑ 121 Billy Hitchcock MG 5.00 2.00
❑ 121A Billy Hitchcock Green Tint 5.00 2.00
❑ 122 Norm Bass RC 5.00 2.00
❑ 122A Norm Bass Green Tint 5.00 2.00
❑ 123 Mike de la Hoz 5.00 2.00
❑ 123A Mike de la Hoz Green Tint 5.00 2.00
❑ 124 Bill Pleis RC 5.00 2.00
❑ 124A Bill Pleis Green Tint 5.00 2.00
❑ 125 Gene Woodling 8.00 3.00
❑ 125A Gene Woodling Green Tint 8.00 3.00
❑ 126 Al Cicotte 5.00 2.00
❑ 126A Al Cicotte Green Tint 5.00 2.00
❑ 127 Siebern/Bauer/Lumpe 5.00 2.00
❑ 127A Siebern/Bauer/Lumpe Green Tint 5.00 2.00
❑ 128 Art Fowler 5.00 2.00
❑ 128A Art Fowler Green Tint 5.00 2.00
❑ 129A Lee Walls Facing Right 5.00 2.00
❑ 129B Lee Walls Facing Left 30.00 12.50
❑ 130 Frank Bolling 5.00 2.00
❑ 130A Frank Bolling Green Tint 5.00 2.00
❑ 131 Pete Richert RC 5.00 2.00
❑ 131A Pete Richert Green Tint 5.00 2.00
❑ 132A Los Angeles Angels TC w/o Photo 10.00 4.00
❑ 132B Los Angeles Angels TC w/Photo 30.00 12.50
❑ 133 Felipe Alou 8.00 3.00
❑ 133A Felipe Alou Green Tint 8.00 3.00
❑ 134A Billy Hoeft Blue Sky 5.00 2.00
❑ 134B Billy Hoeft Green Sky 30.00 12.50
❑ 135 Babe as a Boy 20.00 8.00
❑ 135A Babe as a Boy Green 20.00 8.00
❑ 136 Babe Joins Yanks 20.00 8.00
❑ 136A Babe Joins Yanks Green 20.00 8.00
❑ 137 Babe with Mgr. Huggins 20.00 8.00
❑ 137A Babe with Mgr. Huggins Green 20.00 8.00
❑ 138 The Famous Slugger 20.00 8.00
❑ 138A The Famous Slugger Green 20.00 8.00
❑ 139A1 Babe Hits 60 (Pole) 30.00 12.50
❑ 139B Hal Reniff Portrait 15.00 6.00
❑ 139C Hal Reniff Pitching 60.00 30.00
❑ 140 Gehrig and Ruth 60.00 30.00
❑ 140A Gehrig and Ruth Green 60.00 30.00
❑ 141 Twilight Years 20.00 8.00
❑ 141A Twilight Years Green 20.00 8.00
❑ 142 Coaching the Dodgers 20.00 8.00
❑ 142A Coaching the Dodgers Green 20.00 8.00
❑ 143 Greatest Sports Hero 20.00 8.00
❑ 143A Greatest Sports Hero Green 20.00 8.00
❑ 144 Farewell Speech 20.00 8.00
❑ 144A Farewell Speech Green 20.00 8.00
❑ 145 Barry Latman 5.00 2.00
❑ 145A Barry Latman Green Tint 5.00 2.00
❑ 146 Don Demeter 5.00 2.00
❑ 146A Don Demeter Green Tint 5.00 2.00
❑ 147A Bill Kunkel Portrait 5.00 2.00
❑ 147B Bill Kunkel Pitching 30.00 12.50
❑ 148 Wally Post 5.00 2.00
❑ 148A Wally Post Green Tint 5.00 2.00
❑ 149 Bob Duliba 5.00 2.00
❑ 149A Bob Duliba Green Tint 5.00 2.00
❑ 150 Al Kaline 50.00 20.00
❑ 150A Al Kaline Green Tint 50.00 20.00
❑ 151 Johnny Klippstein 5.00 2.00
❑ 151A Johnny Klippstei Green Tint 5.00 2.00
❑ 152 Mickey Vernon MG 8.00 3.00
❑ 152A Mickey Vernon MG Green Tint 8.00 3.00
❑ 153 Pumpsie Green 6.00 2.50
❑ 153A Pumpsie Green Green Tint 6.00 2.50
❑ 154 Lee Thomas 6.00 2.50
❑ 154A Lee Thomas Green Tint 6.00 2.50
❑ 155 Stu Miller 6.00 2.50
❑ 155A Stu Miller Green Tint 6.00 2.50
❑ 156 Merritt Ranew RC 5.00 2.00
❑ 156A Merritt Ranew Green Tint 5.00 2.00
❑ 157 Wes Covington 8.00 3.00
❑ 157A Wes Covington Green Tint 8.00 3.00
❑ 158 Milwaukee Braves TC 10.00 4.00
❑ 158A Milwaukee Braves TC Green Tint 15.00 6.00
❑ 159 Hal Reniff RC 8.00 3.00
❑ 160 Dick Stuart 8.00 3.00
❑ 160A Dick Stuart Green Tint 8.00 3.00
❑ 161 Frank Baumann 5.00 2.00
❑ 161A Frank Baumann Green Tint 5.00 2.00
❑ 162 Sammy Drake RC 5.00 2.00
❑ 162A Sammy Drake Green Tint 5.00 2.00
❑ 163 B.Gardner/C.Boyer 8.00 3.00
❑ 163A B.Gardner/C.Boyer Green Tint 8.00 3.00
❑ 164 Hal Naragon 5.00 2.00
❑ 164A Hal Naragon Green Tint 5.00 2.00
❑ 165 Jackie Brandt 5.00 2.00
❑ 165A Jackie Brandt Green Tint 5.00 2.00
❑ 166 Don Lee 5.00 2.00
❑ 166A Don Lee Green Tint 5.00 2.00
❑ 167 Tim McCarver RC 30.00 12.50
❑ 167A Tim McCarver Green Tint 30.00 12.50
❑ 168 Leo Posada 5.00 2.00
❑ 168A Leo Posada Green Tint 5.00 2.00
❑ 169 Bob Cerv 10.00 4.00
❑ 169A Bob Cerv Green Tint 10.00 4.00
❑ 170 Ron Santo 15.00 6.00
❑ 170A Ron Santo Green Tint 15.00 6.00
❑ 171 Dave Sisler 5.00 2.00
❑ 171A Dave Sisler Green Tint 5.00 2.00
❑ 172 Fred Hutchinson MG 8.00 3.00
❑ 172A Fred Hutchinson MG Green Tint 8.00 3.00
❑ 173 Chico Fernandez 5.00 2.00
❑ 173A Chico Fernandez Green Tint 5.00 2.00
❑ 174A Carl Willey w/o Cap 5.00 2.00
❑ 174B Carl Willey w/Cap 30.00 12.50
❑ 175 Frank Howard 10.00 4.00
❑ 175A Frank Howard Green Tint 10.00 4.00
❑ 176A Eddie Yost Portrait 5.00 2.00
❑ 176B Eddie Yost Batting 30.00 12.50
❑ 177 Bobby Shantz 8.00 3.00
❑ 177A Bobby Shantz Green Tint 8.00 3.00
❑ 178 Camilo Carreon 5.00 2.00
❑ 178A Camilo Carreon Green Tint 5.00 2.00
❑ 179 Tom Sturdivant 5.00 2.00
❑ 179A Tom Sturdivant Green Tint 5.00 2.00
❑ 180 Bob Allison 10.00 4.00
❑ 180A Bob Allison Green Tint 10.00 4.00
❑ 181 Paul Brown RC 5.00 2.00
❑ 181A Paul Brown Green Tint 5.00 2.00
❑ 182 Bob Nieman 5.00 2.00
❑ 182A Bob Nieman Green Tint 5.00 2.00
❑ 183 Roger Craig 8.00 3.00
❑ 183A Roger Craig Green Tint 8.00 3.00
❑ 184 Haywood Sullivan 8.00 3.00
❑ 184A Haywood Sullivan Green Tint 8.00 3.00
❑ 185 Roland Sheldon 10.00 4.00
❑ 185A Roland Sheldon Green Tint 10.00 4.00
❑ 186 Mack Jones RC 5.00 2.00
❑ 186A Mack Jones Green Tint 5.00 2.00
❑ 187 Gene Conley 5.00 2.00
❑ 187A Gene Conley Green Tint 5.00 2.00
❑ 188 Chuck Hiller 5.00 2.00
❑ 188A Chuck Hiller Green Tint 5.00 2.00
❑ 189 Dick Hall 5.00 2.00
❑ 189A Dick Hall Green Tint 5.00 2.00
❑ 190A Wally Moon Portrait 8.00 3.00
❑ 190B Wally Moon Batting 30.00 12.50
❑ 191 Jim Brewer 5.00 2.00
❑ 191A Jim Brewer Green Tint 5.00 2.00
❑ 192A Checklist 3 w/o Comma 12.00 5.00
❑ 192B Checklist 3 w/Comma 15.00 6.00
❑ 193 Eddie Kasko 5.00 2.00
❑ 193A Eddie Kasko Green Tint 5.00 2.00
❑ 194 Dean Chance RC 8.00 3.00
❑ 194A Dean Chance Green Tint 8.00 3.00
❑ 195 Joe Cunningham 5.00 2.00
❑ 195A Joe Cunningham Green Tint 5.00 2.00
❑ 196 Terry Fox 5.00 2.00
❑ 196A Terry Fox Green Tint 5.00 2.00
❑ 197 Daryl Spencer 5.00 2.00
❑ 198 Johnny Keane MG 5.00 2.00
❑ 199 Gaylord Perry RC 80.00 40.00
❑ 200 Mickey Mantle 600.00 300.00
❑ 201 Ike Delock 5.00 2.00
❑ 202 Carl Warwick RC 5.00 2.00
❑ 203 Jack Fisher 5.00 2.00
❑ 204 Johnny Weekly RC 5.00 2.00
❑ 205 Gene Freese 5.00 2.00
❑ 206 Washington Senators TC 10.00 4.00
❑ 207 Pete Burnside 5.00 2.00
❑ 208 Billy Martin 20.00 8.00
❑ 209 Jim Fregosi RC 15.00 6.00
❑ 210 Roy Face 8.00 3.00
❑ 211 F.Bolling/R.McMillan 5.00 2.00
❑ 212 Jim Owens 5.00 2.00
❑ 213 Richie Ashburn 20.00 8.00
❑ 214 Dom Zanni 5.00 2.00
❑ 215 Woody Held 5.00 2.00
❑ 216 Ron Kline 5.00 2.00
❑ 217 Walter Alston MG 10.00 4.00
❑ 218 Joe Torre RC 40.00 15.00
❑ 219 Al Downing RC 8.00 3.00
❑ 220 Roy Sievers 8.00 3.00
❑ 221 Bill Short 5.00 2.00
❑ 222 Jerry Zimmerman 5.00 2.00
❑ 223 Alex Grammas 5.00 2.00
❑ 224 Don Rudolph 5.00 2.00
❑ 225 Frank Malzone 8.00 3.00
❑ 226 San Francisco Giants TC 10.00 4.00
❑ 227 Bob Tiefenauer 5.00 2.00
❑ 228 Dale Long 10.00 4.00
❑ 229 Jesus McFarlane RC 5.00 2.00
❑ 230 Camilo Pascual 8.00 3.00
❑ 231 Ernie Bowman RC 5.00 2.00
❑ 232 Yanks Win Opener WS1 10.00 4.00
❑ 233 Joey Jay WS2 10.00 4.00
❑ 234 Roger Maris WS3 25.00 10.00
❑ 235 Whitey Ford WS4 15.00 6.00
❑ 236 Yanks Crush Reds WS5 10.00 4.00
❑ 237 Yanks Celebrate WS 10.00 4.00
❑ 238 Norm Sherry 5.00 2.00
❑ 239 Cecil Butler RC 5.00 2.00
❑ 240 George Altman 5.00 2.00
❑ 241 Johnny Kucks 5.00 2.00
❑ 242 Mel McGaha MG RC 5.00 2.00
❑ 243 Robin Roberts 15.00 6.00
❑ 244 Don Gile 5.00 2.00
❑ 245 Ron Hansen 5.00 2.00
❑ 246 Art Ditmar 5.00 2.00
❑ 247 Joe Pignatano 5.00 2.00
❑ 248 Bob Aspromonte 8.00 3.00
❑ 249 Ed Keegan 5.00 2.00
❑ 250 Norm Cash 10.00 4.00
❑ 251 New York Yankees TC 50.00 20.00
❑ 252 Earl Francis 5.00 2.00

❑ 253 Harry Chiti CO 5.00 2.00
❑ 254 Gordon Windhorn RC 5.00 2.00
❑ 255 Juan Pizarro 5.00 2.00
❑ 256 Elio Chacon 8.00 3.00
❑ 257 Jack Spring RC 5.00 2.00
❑ 258 Marty Keough 5.00 2.00
❑ 259 Lou Klimchock 5.00 2.00
❑ 260 Billy Pierce 8.00 3.00
❑ 261 George Alusik RC 5.00 2.00
❑ 262 Bob Schmidt 5.00 2.00
❑ 263 Purkey/Turner/Jay 5.00 2.00
❑ 264 Dick Ellsworth 8.00 3.00
❑ 265 Joe Adcock 8.00 3.00
❑ 266 John Anderson RC 5.00 2.00
❑ 267 Dan Dobbek 5.00 2.00
❑ 268 Ken McBride 5.00 2.00
❑ 269 Bob Oldis 5.00 2.00
❑ 270 Dick Groat 8.00 3.00
❑ 271 Ray Rippelmeyer 5.00 2.00
❑ 272 Earl Robinson 5.00 2.00
❑ 273 Gary Bell 5.00 2.00
❑ 274 Sammy Taylor 5.00 2.00
❑ 275 Norm Siebern 5.00 2.00
❑ 276 Hal Kolstad RC 5.00 2.00
❑ 277 Checklist 4 15.00 6.00
❑ 278 Ken Johnson 8.00 3.00
❑ 279 Hobie Landrith UER 8.00 3.00
❑ 280 Johnny Podres 8.00 3.00
❑ 281 Jake Gibbs RC 10.00 4.00
❑ 282 Dave Hillman 5.00 2.00
❑ 283 Charlie Smith RC 5.00 2.00
❑ 284 Ruben Amaro 5.00 2.00
❑ 285 Curt Simmons 8.00 3.00
❑ 286 Al Lopez MG 10.00 4.00
❑ 287 George Witt 5.00 2.00
❑ 288 Billy Williams 30.00 12.50
❑ 289 Mike Krsnich RC 5.00 2.00
❑ 290 Jim Gentile 8.00 3.00
❑ 291 Hal Stowe RC 5.00 2.00
❑ 292 Jerry Kindall 5.00 2.00
❑ 293 Bob Miller 8.00 3.00
❑ 294 Philadelphia Phillies TC 10.00 4.00
❑ 295 Vern Law 8.00 3.00
❑ 296 Ken Hamlin 5.00 2.00
❑ 297 Ron Perranoski 8.00 3.00
❑ 298 Bill Tuttle 5.00 2.00
❑ 299 Don Wert RC 5.00 2.00
❑ 300 Willie Mays 250.00 125.00
❑ 301 Galen Cisco RC 5.00 2.00
❑ 302 Johnny Edwards RC 5.00 2.00
❑ 303 Frank Torre 8.00 3.00
❑ 304 Dick Farrell 8.00 3.00
❑ 305 Jerry Lumpe 5.00 2.00
❑ 306 L.McDaniel/L.Jackson 5.00 2.00
❑ 307 Jim Grant 8.00 3.00
❑ 308 Neil Chrisley 8.00 3.00
❑ 309 Moe Morhardt RC 5.00 2.00
❑ 310 Whitey Ford 50.00 20.00
❑ 311 Tony Kubek IA 8.00 3.00
❑ 312 Warren Spahn IA 15.00 6.00
❑ 313 Roger Maris IA 80.00 40.00
❑ 314 Rocky Colavito IA 8.00 3.00
❑ 315 Whitey Ford IA 15.00 6.00
❑ 316 Harmon Killebrew IA 15.00 6.00
❑ 317 Stan Musial IA 20.00 8.00
❑ 318 Mickey Mantle IA 150.00 75.00
❑ 319 Mike McCormick IA 5.00 2.00
❑ 320 Hank Aaron 150.00 75.00
❑ 321 Lee Stange RC 5.00 2.00
❑ 322 Alvin Dark MG 8.00 3.00
❑ 323 Don Landrum 5.00 2.00
❑ 324 Joe McClain 5.00 2.00
❑ 325 Luis Aparicio 15.00 6.00
❑ 326 Tom Parsons RC 5.00 2.00
❑ 327 Ozzie Virgil 5.00 2.00
❑ 328 Ken Walters 5.00 2.00
❑ 329 Bob Bolin 5.00 2.00
❑ 330 John Romano 5.00 2.00
❑ 331 Moe Drabowsky 8.00 3.00
❑ 332 Don Buddin 5.00 2.00
❑ 333 Frank Cipriani RC 5.00 2.00
❑ 334 Boston Red Sox TC 10.00 4.00
❑ 335 Bill Bruton 5.00 2.00
❑ 336 Billy Muffett 5.00 2.00
❑ 337 Jim Marshall 8.00 3.00
❑ 338 Billy Gardner 5.00 2.00
❑ 339 Jose Valdivielso 5.00 2.00
❑ 340 Don Drysdale 50.00 20.00
❑ 341 Mike Hershberger RC 5.00 2.00
❑ 342 Ed Rakow 5.00 2.00
❑ 343 Albie Pearson 8.00 3.00
❑ 344 Ed Bauta RC 5.00 2.00
❑ 345 Chuck Schilling 5.00 2.00
❑ 346 Jack Kralick 5.00 2.00
❑ 347 Chuck Hinton RC 5.00 2.00
❑ 348 Larry Burright RC 8.00 3.00
❑ 349 Paul Foytack 5.00 2.00
❑ 350 Frank Robinson 50.00 20.00
❑ 351 J.Torre/D.Crandall 8.00 3.00
❑ 352 Frank Sullivan 5.00 2.00
❑ 353 Bill Mazeroski 15.00 6.00
❑ 354 Roman Mejias 8.00 3.00
❑ 355 Steve Barber 5.00 2.00
❑ 356 Tom Haller RC 5.00 2.00
❑ 357 Jerry Walker 5.00 2.00
❑ 358 Tommy Davis 8.00 3.00
❑ 359 Bobby Locke 5.00 2.00
❑ 360 Yogi Berra 80.00 40.00
❑ 361 Bob Hendley 5.00 2.00
❑ 362 Ty Cline 5.00 2.00
❑ 363 Bob Roselli 5.00 2.00
❑ 364 Ken Hunt 5.00 2.00
❑ 365 Charlie Neal 8.00 3.00
❑ 366 Phil Regan 8.00 3.00
❑ 367 Checklist 5 15.00 6.00
❑ 368 Bob Tillman RC 5.00 2.00
❑ 369 Ted Bowsfield 5.00 2.00
❑ 370 Ken Boyer 10.00 4.00
❑ 371 Earl Battey 6.00 2.50
❑ 372 Jack Curtis 6.00 2.50
❑ 373 Al Heist 6.00 2.50
❑ 374 Gene Mauch MG 10.00 4.00
❑ 375 Ron Fairly 10.00 4.00
❑ 376 Bud Daley 8.00 3.00
❑ 377 John Orsino RC 6.00 2.50
❑ 378 Bennie Daniels 6.00 2.50
❑ 379 Chuck Essegian 6.00 2.50
❑ 380 Lew Burdette 10.00 4.00
❑ 381 Chico Cardenas 10.00 4.00
❑ 382 Dick Williams 8.00 3.00
❑ 383 Ray Sadecki 6.00 2.50
❑ 384 Kansas City Athletics TC 10.00 4.00
❑ 385 Early Wynn 15.00 6.00
❑ 386 Don Mincher 8.00 3.00
❑ 387 Lou Brock RC 120.00 60.00
❑ 388 Ryne Duren 8.00 3.00
❑ 389 Smoky Burgess 10.00 4.00
❑ 390 Orlando Cepeda AS 10.00 4.00
❑ 391 Bill Mazeroski AS 10.00 4.00
❑ 392 Ken Boyer AS UER 8.00 3.00
❑ 393 Roy McMillan AS 6.00 2.50
❑ 394 Hank Aaron AS 50.00 20.00
❑ 395 Willie Mays AS 50.00 20.00
❑ 396 Frank Robinson AS 15.00 6.00
❑ 397 John Roseboro AS 6.00 2.50
❑ 398 Don Drysdale AS 15.00 6.00
❑ 399 Warren Spahn AS 15.00 6.00
❑ 400 Elston Howard 10.00 4.00
❑ 401 O.Cepeda/R.Maris 60.00 30.00
❑ 402 Gino Cimoli 6.00 2.50
❑ 403 Chet Nichols 6.00 2.50
❑ 404 Tim Harkness RC 8.00 3.00
❑ 405 Jim Perry 8.00 3.00
❑ 406 Bob Taylor 6.00 2.50
❑ 407 Hank Aguirre 6.00 2.50
❑ 408 Gus Bell 8.00 3.00
❑ 409 Pittsburgh Pirates TC 10.00 4.00
❑ 410 Al Smith 6.00 2.50
❑ 411 Danny O'Connell 6.00 2.50
❑ 412 Charlie James 6.00 2.50
❑ 413 Matty Alou 10.00 4.00
❑ 414 Joe Gaines RC 6.00 2.50
❑ 415 Bill Virdon 10.00 4.00
❑ 416 Bob Scheffing MG 6.00 2.50
❑ 417 Joe Azcue RC 6.00 2.50
❑ 418 Andy Carey 6.00 2.50
❑ 419 Bob Bruce 8.00 3.00
❑ 420 Gus Triandos 8.00 3.00
❑ 421 Ken MacKenzie 8.00 3.00
❑ 422 Steve Bilko 6.00 2.50
❑ 423 R.Face/H.Wilhelm 10.00 4.00
❑ 424 Al McBean RC 6.00 2.50
❑ 425 Carl Yastrzemski 120.00 60.00
❑ 426 Bob Farley RC 6.00 2.50
❑ 427 Jake Wood 6.00 2.50
❑ 428 Joe Hicks 6.00 2.50
❑ 429 Billy O'Dell 6.00 2.50
❑ 430 Tony Kubek 15.00 6.00
❑ 431 Bob (Buck) Rodgers RC 8.00 3.00
❑ 432 Jim Pendleton 6.00 2.50
❑ 433 Jim Archer 6.00 2.50
❑ 434 Clay Dalrymple 6.00 2.50
❑ 435 Larry Sherry 8.00 3.00
❑ 436 Felix Mantilla 8.00 3.00
❑ 437 Ray Moore 6.00 2.50
❑ 438 Dick Brown 6.00 2.50
❑ 439 Jerry Buchek RC 6.00 2.50
❑ 440 Joey Jay 6.00 2.50
❑ 441 Checklist 6 15.00 6.00
❑ 442 Wes Stock 6.00 2.50
❑ 443 Del Crandall 8.00 3.00
❑ 444 Ted Wills 6.00 2.50
❑ 445 Vic Power 8.00 3.00
❑ 446 Don Elston 6.00 2.50
❑ 447 Willie Kirkland 12.00 5.00
❑ 448 Joe Gibbon 12.00 5.00
❑ 449 Jerry Adair 12.00 5.00
❑ 450 Jim O'Toole 15.00 6.00
❑ 451 Jose Tartabull RC 15.00 6.00
❑ 452 Earl Averill Jr. 12.00 5.00
❑ 453 Cal McLish 12.00 5.00
❑ 454 Floyd Robinson RC 12.00 5.00
❑ 455 Luis Arroyo 15.00 6.00
❑ 456 Joe Amalfitano 15.00 6.00
❑ 457 Lou Clinton 12.00 5.00
❑ 458A Bob Buhl Emblem 15.00 6.00
❑ 458B Bob Buhl No Emblem 50.00 20.00
❑ 459 Ed Bailey 12.00 5.00
❑ 460 Jim Bunning 20.00 8.00
❑ 461 Ken Hubbs RC 30.00 12.50
❑ 462A Willie Tasby Emblem 12.00 5.00
❑ 462B Willie Tasby No Emblem 50.00 20.00
❑ 463 Hank Bauer MG 15.00 6.00
❑ 464 Al Jackson RC 12.00 5.00
❑ 465 Cincinnati Reds TC 20.00 8.00
❑ 466 Norm Cash AS 15.00 6.00
❑ 467 Chuck Schilling AS 12.00 5.00
❑ 468 Brooks Robinson AS 25.00 10.00
❑ 469 Luis Aparicio AS 15.00 6.00
❑ 470 Al Kaline AS 25.00 10.00
❑ 471 Mickey Mantle AS 200.00 100.00
❑ 472 Rocky Colavito AS 15.00 6.00
❑ 473 Elston Howard AS 15.00 6.00
❑ 474 Frank Lary AS 12.00 5.00
❑ 475 Whitey Ford AS 20.00 8.00
❑ 476 Baltimore Orioles TC 20.00 8.00
❑ 477 Andre Rodgers 12.00 5.00
❑ 478 Don Zimmer 20.00 8.00
❑ 479 Joel Horlen RC 12.00 5.00
❑ 480 Harvey Kuenn 15.00 6.00
❑ 481 Vic Wertz 15.00 6.00
❑ 482 Sam Mele MG 12.00 5.00
❑ 483 Don McMahon 12.00 5.00
❑ 484 Dick Schofield 12.00 5.00
❑ 485 Pedro Ramos 12.00 5.00
❑ 486 Jim Gilliam 15.00 6.00
❑ 487 Jerry Lynch 12.00 5.00
❑ 488 Hal Brown 12.00 5.00
❑ 489 Julio Gotay RC 12.00 5.00
❑ 490 Clete Boyer UER 15.00 6.00
❑ 491 Leon Wagner 12.00 5.00
❑ 492 Hal W. Smith 15.00 6.00
❑ 493 Danny McDevitt 12.00 5.00
❑ 494 Sammy White 12.00 5.00
❑ 495 Don Cardwell 12.00 5.00
❑ 496 Wayne Causey RC 12.00 5.00
❑ 497 Ed Bouchee 15.00 6.00
❑ 498 Jim Donohue 12.00 5.00
❑ 499 Zoilo Versalles 15.00 6.00
❑ 500 Duke Snider 60.00 30.00
❑ 501 Claude Osteen 15.00 6.00
❑ 502 Hector Lopez 15.00 6.00
❑ 503 Danny Murtaugh MG 15.00 6.00
❑ 504 Eddie Bressoud 12.00 5.00
❑ 505 Juan Marichal 40.00 15.00
❑ 506 Charlie Maxwell 15.00 6.00
❑ 507 Ernie Broglio 15.00 6.00
❑ 508 Gordy Coleman 15.00 6.00

Card		
❑ 509 Dave Giusti RC	15.00	6.00
❑ 510 Jim Lemon	12.00	5.00
❑ 511 Bubba Phillips	12.00	5.00
❑ 512 Mike Fornieles	12.00	5.00
❑ 513 Whitey Herzog	15.00	6.00
❑ 514 Sherm Lollar	15.00	6.00
❑ 515 Stan Williams	15.00	6.00
❑ 516A Checklist 7 White	15.00	6.00
❑ 516B Checklist 7 Yellow	15.00	6.00
❑ 517 Dave Wickersham	12.00	5.00
❑ 518 Lee Maye	12.00	5.00
❑ 519 Bob Johnson RC	12.00	5.00
❑ 520 Bob Friend	15.00	6.00
❑ 521 Jacke Davis UER RC	12.00	5.00
❑ 522 Lindy McDaniel	15.00	6.00
❑ 523 Russ Nixon SP	30.00	12.50
❑ 524 Howie Nunn SP	30.00	12.50
❑ 525 George Thomas	20.00	8.00
❑ 526 Hal Woodeshick SP	30.00	12.50
❑ 527 Dick McAuliffe RC	30.00	12.50
❑ 528 Turk Lown	20.00	8.00
❑ 529 John Schaive SP	30.00	12.50
❑ 530 Bob Gibson SP	120.00	60.00
❑ 531 Bobby G. Smith	20.00	8.00
❑ 532 Dick Stigman	20.00	8.00
❑ 533 Charley Lau SP	30.00	12.50
❑ 534 Tony Gonzalez SP	30.00	12.50
❑ 535 Ed Roebuck	20.00	8.00
❑ 536 Dick Gernert	20.00	8.00
❑ 537 Cleveland Indians TC	50.00	20.00
❑ 538 Jack Sanford	20.00	8.00
❑ 539 Billy Moran	20.00	8.00
❑ 540 Jim Landis SP	30.00	12.50
❑ 541 Don Nottebart SP	30.00	12.50
❑ 542 Dave Philley	20.00	8.00
❑ 543 Bob Allen SP	30.00	12.50
❑ 544 Willie McCovey SP	120.00	60.00
❑ 545 Hoyt Wilhelm SP	50.00	20.00
❑ 546 Moe Thacker SP	30.00	12.50
❑ 547 Don Ferrarese	20.00	8.00
❑ 548 Bobby Del Greco	20.00	8.00
❑ 549 Bill Rigney MG SP	30.00	12.50
❑ 550 Art Mahaffey SP	30.00	12.50
❑ 551 Harry Bright	20.00	8.00
❑ 552 Chicago Cubs TC SP	50.00	20.00
❑ 553 Jim Coates	30.00	12.50
❑ 554 Bubba Morton SP RC	30.00	12.50
❑ 555 John Buzhardt SP	30.00	12.50
❑ 556 Al Spangler	20.00	8.00
❑ 557 Bob Anderson SP	30.00	12.50
❑ 558 John Goryl	20.00	8.00
❑ 559 Mike Higgins MG	20.00	8.00
❑ 560 Chuck Estrada SP	30.00	12.50
❑ 561 Gene Oliver SP	30.00	12.50
❑ 562 Bill Henry	20.00	8.00
❑ 563 Ken Aspromonte	20.00	8.00
❑ 564 Bob Grim	20.00	8.00
❑ 565 Jose Pagan	20.00	8.00
❑ 566 Marty Kutyna SP	30.00	12.50
❑ 567 Tracy Stallard SP	30.00	12.50
❑ 568 Jim Golden	20.00	8.00
❑ 569 Ed Sadowski SP	30.00	12.50
❑ 570 Bill Stafford SP	30.00	12.50
❑ 571 Billy Klaus SP	30.00	12.50
❑ 572 Bob G.Miller SP	30.00	12.50
❑ 573 Johnny Logan	20.00	8.00
❑ 574 Dean Stone	20.00	8.00
❑ 575 Red Schoendienst SP	50.00	20.00
❑ 576 Russ Kemmerer SP	30.00	12.50
❑ 577 Dave Nicholson SP	30.00	12.50
❑ 578 Jim Duffalo RC	20.00	8.00
❑ 579 Jim Schaffer SP RC	30.00	12.50
❑ 580 Bill Monbouquette	20.00	8.00
❑ 581 Mel Roach	20.00	8.00
❑ 582 Ron Piche	20.00	8.00
❑ 583 Larry Osborne	20.00	8.00
❑ 584 Minnesota Twins TC SP	60.00	30.00
❑ 585 Glen Hobbie SP	30.00	12.50
❑ 586 Sammy Esposito SP	30.00	12.50
❑ 587 Frank Funk SP	30.00	12.50
❑ 588 Birdie Tebbetts MG	20.00	8.00
❑ 589 Bob Turley	30.00	12.50
❑ 590 Curt Flood	30.00	12.50
❑ 591 Sam McDowell SP RC	80.00	40.00
❑ 592 Jim Bouton SP RC	80.00	40.00
❑ 593 Rookie Pitchers SP	50.00	20.00
❑ 594 Bob Uecker SP RC	80.00	40.00
❑ 595 Rookie Infielders SP	50.00	20.00
❑ 596 Joe Pepitone SP RC	80.00	40.00
❑ 597 Rookie Infield SP	50.00	20.00
❑ 598 Rookie Outfielders SP	80.00	40.00

1963 Topps

Card		
❑ COMPLETE SET (576)	6000.00	3000.00
❑ COMMON CARD (1-196)	4.00	1.50
❑ COMMON CARD (197-283)	5.00	2.00
❑ COMMON CARD (284-370)	5.00	2.00
❑ COMMON CARD (371-446)	5.00	2.00
❑ COMMON CARD (447-522)	25.00	10.00
❑ COMMON CARD (523-576)	15.00	6.00
❑ WRAPPER (1-CENT)	40.00	15.00
❑ WRAPPER (5-CENT)	30.00	12.50
❑ 1 F.Rob/Musial/Aaron LL	40.00	15.00
❑ 2 Runnels/Mantle/Rob LL	50.00	20.00
❑ 3 Mays/Aaron/Rob/Cep/Banks LL	40.00	15.00
❑ 4 Kill/Cash/Colav/Maris LL	20.00	8.00
❑ 5 Koufax/Gibson/Drysdale LL	25.00	10.00
❑ 6 Aguirre/Roberts/Ford LL	10.00	4.00
❑ 7 Drysdale/Sanf/Purk LL	10.00	4.00
❑ 8 Terry/Donovan/Bunning LL	8.00	3.00
❑ 9 Drysdale/Koufax/Gibson LL	30.00	12.50
❑ 10 Pascual/Bunning/Kaat LL	8.00	3.00
❑ 11 Lee Walls	4.00	1.50
❑ 12 Steve Barber	4.00	1.50
❑ 13 Philadelphia Phillies TC	8.00	3.00
❑ 14 Pedro Ramos	4.00	1.50
❑ 15 Ken Hubbs UER NPO	10.00	4.00
❑ 16 Al Smith	4.00	1.50
❑ 17 Ryne Duren	8.00	3.00
❑ 18 Burg/Stu/Clemente/Skin	80.00	40.00
❑ 19 Pete Burnside	4.00	1.50
❑ 20 Tony Kubek	10.00	4.00
❑ 21 Marty Keough	4.00	1.50
❑ 22 Curt Simmons	8.00	3.00
❑ 23 Ed Lopat MG	8.00	3.00
❑ 24 Bob Bruce	4.00	1.50
❑ 25 Al Kaline	50.00	20.00
❑ 26 Ray Moore	4.00	1.50
❑ 27 Choo Choo Coleman	8.00	3.00
❑ 28 Mike Fornieles	4.00	1.50
❑ 29A Rookie Stars 1962	10.00	4.00
❑ 29B Rookie Stars 1963	4.00	1.50
❑ 30 Harvey Kuenn	8.00	3.00
❑ 31 Cal Koonce RC	4.00	1.50
❑ 32 Tony Gonzalez	4.00	1.50
❑ 33 Bo Belinsky	8.00	3.00
❑ 34 Dick Schofield	4.00	1.50
❑ 35 John Buzhardt	4.00	1.50
❑ 36 Jerry Kindall	4.00	1.50
❑ 37 Jerry Lynch	4.00	1.50
❑ 38 Bud Daley	8.00	3.00
❑ 39 Los Angeles Angels TC	8.00	3.00
❑ 40 Vic Power	8.00	3.00
❑ 41 Charley Lau	8.00	3.00
❑ 42 Stan Williams	8.00	3.00
❑ 43 C.Stengel/G.Woodling	8.00	3.00
❑ 44 Terry Fox	4.00	1.50
❑ 45 Bob Aspromonte	4.00	1.50
❑ 46 Tommie Aaron RC	8.00	3.00
❑ 47 Don Lock RC	4.00	1.50
❑ 48 Birdie Tebbetts MG	8.00	3.00
❑ 49 Dal Maxvill RC	8.00	3.00
❑ 50 Billy Pierce	8.00	3.00
❑ 51 George Alusik	4.00	1.50
❑ 52 Chuck Schilling	4.00	1.50
❑ 53 Joe Moeller RC	8.00	3.00
❑ 54A Dave DeBusschere 62	15.00	6.00
❑ 54B Dave DeBusschere 63 RC	8.00	3.00
❑ 55 Bill Virdon	8.00	3.00
❑ 56 Dennis Bennett RC	4.00	1.50
❑ 57 Billy Moran	4.00	1.50
❑ 58 Bob Will	4.00	1.50
❑ 59 Craig Anderson	4.00	1.50
❑ 60 Elston Howard	8.00	3.00
❑ 61 Ernie Bowman	4.00	1.50
❑ 62 Bob Hendley	4.00	1.50
❑ 63 Cincinnati Reds TC	8.00	3.00
❑ 64 Dick McAuliffe	8.00	3.00
❑ 65 Jackie Brandt	4.00	1.50
❑ 66 Mike Joyce RC	4.00	1.50
❑ 67 Ed Charles	4.00	1.50
❑ 68 G.Hodges/D.Snider	25.00	10.00
❑ 69 Bud Zipfel RC	4.00	1.50
❑ 70 Jim O'Toole	8.00	3.00
❑ 71 Bobby Wine RC	8.00	3.00
❑ 72 Johnny Romano	4.00	1.50
❑ 73 Bobby Bragan MG RC	8.00	3.00
❑ 74 Denny Lemaster RC	4.00	1.50
❑ 75 Bob Allison	8.00	3.00
❑ 76 Earl Wilson	8.00	3.00
❑ 77 Al Spangler	4.00	1.50
❑ 78 Marv Throneberry	8.00	3.00
❑ 79 Checklist 1	12.00	5.00
❑ 80 Jim Gilliam	8.00	3.00
❑ 81 Jim Schaffer	4.00	1.50
❑ 82 Ed Rakow	4.00	1.50
❑ 83 Charley James	4.00	1.50
❑ 84 Ron Kline	4.00	1.50
❑ 85 Tom Haller	8.00	3.00
❑ 86 Charley Maxwell	8.00	3.00
❑ 87 Bob Veale	8.00	3.00
❑ 88 Ron Hansen	4.00	1.50
❑ 89 Dick Stigman	4.00	1.50
❑ 90 Gordy Coleman	8.00	3.00
❑ 91 Dallas Green	8.00	3.00
❑ 92 Hector Lopez	8.00	3.00
❑ 93 Galen Cisco	4.00	1.50
❑ 94 Bob Schmidt	4.00	1.50
❑ 95 Larry Jackson	4.00	1.50
❑ 96 Lou Clinton	4.00	1.50
❑ 97 Bob Duliba	4.00	1.50
❑ 98 George Thomas	4.00	1.50
❑ 99 Jim Umbricht	4.00	1.50
❑ 100 Joe Cunningham	4.00	1.50
❑ 101 Joe Gibbon	4.00	1.50
❑ 102A Checklist 2 Red/Yellow	12.00	5.00
❑ 102B Checklist 2 White/Red	12.00	5.00
❑ 103 Chuck Essegian	4.00	1.50
❑ 104 Lew Krausse RC	4.00	1.50
❑ 105 Ron Fairly	8.00	3.00
❑ 106 Bobby Bolin	4.00	1.50
❑ 107 Jim Hickman	8.00	3.00
❑ 108 Hoyt Wilhelm	10.00	4.00
❑ 109 Lee Maye	4.00	1.50
❑ 110 Rich Rollins	8.00	3.00
❑ 111 Al Jackson	4.00	1.50
❑ 112 Dick Brown	4.00	1.50
❑ 113 Don Landrum UER	4.00	1.50
❑ 114 Dan Osinski RC	4.00	1.50
❑ 115 Carl Yastrzemski	40.00	15.00
❑ 116 Jim Brosnan	8.00	3.00
❑ 117 Jacke Davis	4.00	1.50
❑ 118 Sherm Lollar	4.00	1.50
❑ 119 Bob Lillis	4.00	1.50
❑ 120 Roger Maris	80.00	40.00
❑ 121 Jim Hannan RC	4.00	1.50
❑ 122 Julio Gotay	4.00	1.50
❑ 123 Frank Howard	8.00	3.00
❑ 124 Dick Howser	8.00	3.00
❑ 125 Robin Roberts	15.00	6.00
❑ 126 Bob Uecker	15.00	6.00
❑ 127 Bill Tuttle	4.00	1.50
❑ 128 Matty Alou	8.00	3.00
❑ 129 Gary Bell	4.00	1.50
❑ 130 Dick Groat	8.00	3.00
❑ 131 Washington Senators TC	8.00	3.00
❑ 132 Jack Hamilton	4.00	1.50
❑ 133 Gene Freese	4.00	1.50
❑ 134 Bob Scheffing MG	4.00	1.50
❑ 135 Richie Ashburn	20.00	8.00

❑	136	Ike Delock	4.00	1.50
❑	137	Mack Jones	4.00	1.50
❑	138	W.Mays/S.Musial	80.00	40.00
❑	139	Earl Averill Jr.	4.00	1.50
❑	140	Frank Lary	8.00	3.00
❑	141	Manny Mota RC	8.00	3.00
❑	142	Whitey Ford WS1	10.00	4.00
❑	143	Jack Sanford WS2	8.00	3.00
❑	144	Roger Maris WS3	15.00	6.00
❑	145	Chuck Hiller WS4	8.00	3.00
❑	146	Tom Tresh WS5	8.00	3.00
❑	147	Billy Pierce WS6	8.00	3.00
❑	148	Ralph Terry WS7	8.00	3.00
❑	149	Marv Breeding	4.00	1.50
❑	150	Johnny Podres	8.00	3.00
❑	151	Pittsburgh Pirates TC	8.00	3.00
❑	152	Ron Nischwitz	4.00	1.50
❑	153	Hal Smith	4.00	1.50
❑	154	Walter Alston MG	8.00	3.00
❑	155	Bill Stafford	4.00	1.50
❑	156	Roy McMillan	8.00	3.00
❑	157	Diego Segui RC	8.00	3.00
❑	158	Tommy Harper RC	8.00	3.00
❑	159	Jim Pagliaroni	4.00	1.50
❑	160	Juan Pizarro	4.00	1.50
❑	161	Frank Torre	8.00	3.00
❑	162	Minnesota Twins TC	8.00	3.00
❑	163	Don Larsen	8.00	3.00
❑	164	Bubba Morton	4.00	1.50
❑	165	Jim Kaat	8.00	3.00
❑	166	Johnny Keane MG	4.00	1.50
❑	167	Jim Fregosi	8.00	3.00
❑	168	Russ Nixon	4.00	1.50
❑	169	Gaylord Perry	25.00	10.00
❑	170	Joe Adcock	8.00	3.00
❑	171	Steve Hamilton RC	4.00	1.50
❑	172	Gene Oliver	4.00	1.50
❑	173	Tresh/Mantle/Richardson	150.00	75.00
❑	174	Larry Burright	4.00	1.50
❑	175	Bob Buhl	8.00	3.00
❑	176	Jim King	4.00	1.50
❑	177	Bubba Phillips	4.00	1.50
❑	178	Johnny Edwards	4.00	1.50
❑	179	Ron Piche	4.00	1.50
❑	180	Bill Skowron	8.00	3.00
❑	181	Sammy Esposito	4.00	1.50
❑	182	Albie Pearson	8.00	3.00
❑	183	Joe Pepitone	8.00	3.00
❑	184	Vern Law	8.00	3.00
❑	185	Chuck Hiller	4.00	1.50
❑	186	Jerry Zimmerman	4.00	1.50
❑	187	Willie Kirkland	4.00	1.50
❑	188	Eddie Bressoud	4.00	1.50
❑	189	Dave Giusti	8.00	3.00
❑	190	Minnie Minoso	8.00	3.00
❑	191	Checklist 3	12.00	5.00
❑	192	Clay Dalrymple	4.00	1.50
❑	193	Andre Rodgers	4.00	1.50
❑	194	Joe Nuxhall	8.00	3.00
❑	195	Manny Jimenez	4.00	1.50
❑	196	Doug Camilli	4.00	1.50
❑	197	Roger Craig	8.00	3.00
❑	198	Lenny Green	5.00	2.00
❑	199	Joe Amalfitano	5.00	2.00
❑	200	Mickey Mantle	600.00	300.00
❑	201	Cecil Butler	5.00	2.00
❑	202	Boston Red Sox TC	8.00	3.00
❑	203	Chico Cardenas	8.00	3.00
❑	204	Don Nottebart	5.00	2.00
❑	205	Luis Aparicio	15.00	6.00
❑	206	Ray Washburn	5.00	2.00
❑	207	Ken Hunt	5.00	2.00
❑	208	Rookie Stars	5.00	2.00
❑	209	Hobie Landrith	5.00	2.00
❑	210	Sandy Koufax	150.00	75.00
❑	211	Fred Whitfield RC	5.00	2.00
❑	212	Glen Hobbie	5.00	2.00
❑	213	Billy Hitchcock MG	5.00	2.00
❑	214	Orlando Pena	5.00	2.00
❑	215	Bob Skinner	8.00	3.00
❑	216	Gene Conley	8.00	3.00
❑	217	Joe Christopher	5.00	2.00
❑	218	Lary/Mossi/Bunning	8.00	3.00
❑	219	Chuck Cottier	5.00	2.00
❑	220	Camilo Pascual	8.00	3.00
❑	221	Cookie Rojas RC	8.00	3.00
❑	222	Chicago Cubs TC	8.00	3.00
❑	223	Eddie Fisher	5.00	2.00
❑	224	Mike Roarke	5.00	2.00
❑	225	Joey Jay	5.00	2.00
❑	226	Julian Javier	8.00	3.00
❑	227	Jim Grant	8.00	3.00
❑	228	Tony Oliva RC	50.00	20.00
❑	229	Willie Davis	8.00	3.00
❑	230	Pete Runnels	8.00	3.00
❑	231	Eli Grba UER	5.00	2.00
❑	232	Frank Malzone	8.00	3.00
❑	233	Casey Stengel MG	20.00	8.00
❑	234	Dave Nicholson	5.00	2.00
❑	235	Billy O'Dell	5.00	2.00
❑	236	Bill Bryan RC	5.00	2.00
❑	237	Jim Coates	8.00	3.00
❑	238	Lou Johnson	5.00	2.00
❑	239	Harvey Haddix	8.00	3.00
❑	240	Rocky Colavito	15.00	6.00
❑	241	Billy Smith RC	5.00	2.00
❑	242	E.Banks/H.Aaron	60.00	30.00
❑	243	Don Leppert	5.00	2.00
❑	244	John Tsitouris	5.00	2.00
❑	245	Gil Hodges	20.00	8.00
❑	246	Lee Stange	5.00	2.00
❑	247	New York Yankees TC	50.00	20.00
❑	248	Tito Francona	5.00	2.00
❑	249	Leo Burke RC	5.00	2.00
❑	250	Stan Musial	100.00	50.00
❑	251	Jack Lamabe	5.00	2.00
❑	252	Ron Santo	10.00	4.00
❑	253	Rookie Stars	5.00	2.00
❑	254	Mike Hershberger	5.00	2.00
❑	255	Bob Shaw	5.00	2.00
❑	256	Jerry Lumpe	5.00	2.00
❑	257	Hank Aguirre	5.00	2.00
❑	258	Alvin Dark MG	8.00	3.00
❑	259	Johnny Logan	8.00	3.00
❑	260	Jim Gentile	8.00	3.00
❑	261	Bob Miller	5.00	2.00
❑	262	Ellis Burton	5.00	2.00
❑	263	Dave Stenhouse	5.00	2.00
❑	264	Phil Linz	5.00	2.00
❑	265	Vada Pinson	8.00	3.00
❑	266	Bob Allen	5.00	2.00
❑	267	Carl Sawatski	5.00	2.00
❑	268	Don Demeter	5.00	2.00
❑	269	Don Mincher	5.00	2.00
❑	270	Felipe Alou	8.00	3.00
❑	271	Dean Stone	5.00	2.00
❑	272	Danny Murphy	5.00	2.00
❑	273	Sammy Taylor	5.00	2.00
❑	274	Checklist 4	12.00	5.00
❑	275	Eddie Mathews	30.00	12.50
❑	276	Barry Shetrone	5.00	2.00
❑	277	Dick Farrell	5.00	2.00
❑	278	Chico Fernandez	5.00	2.00
❑	279	Wally Moon	8.00	3.00
❑	280	Bob (Buck) Rodgers	5.00	2.00
❑	281	Tom Sturdivant	5.00	2.00
❑	282	Bobby Del Greco	5.00	2.00
❑	283	Roy Sievers	8.00	3.00
❑	284	Dave Sisler	5.00	2.00
❑	285	Dick Stuart	8.00	3.00
❑	286	Stu Miller	8.00	3.00
❑	287	Dick Bertell	5.00	2.00
❑	288	Chicago White Sox TC	10.00	4.00
❑	289	Hal Brown	5.00	2.00
❑	290	Bill White	8.00	3.00
❑	291	Don Rudolph	5.00	2.00
❑	292	Pumpsie Green	8.00	3.00
❑	293	Bill Pleis	5.00	2.00
❑	294	Bill Rigney MG	5.00	2.00
❑	295	Ed Roebuck	5.00	2.00
❑	296	Doc Edwards	5.00	2.00
❑	297	Jim Golden	5.00	2.00
❑	298	Don Dillard	5.00	2.00
❑	299	Rookie Stars	8.00	3.00
❑	300	Willie Mays	150.00	75.00
❑	301	Bill Fischer	5.00	2.00
❑	302	Whitey Herzog	8.00	3.00
❑	303	Earl Francis	5.00	2.00
❑	304	Harry Bright	5.00	2.00
❑	305	Don Hoak	5.00	2.00
❑	306	E.Battey/E.Howard	10.00	4.00
❑	307	Chet Nichols	5.00	2.00
❑	308	Camilo Carreon	5.00	2.00
❑	309	Jim Brewer	5.00	2.00
❑	310	Tommy Davis	8.00	3.00
❑	311	Joe McClain	5.00	2.00
❑	312	Houston Colts TC	25.00	10.00
❑	313	Ernie Broglio	5.00	2.00
❑	314	John Goryl	5.00	2.00
❑	315	Ralph Terry	8.00	3.00
❑	316	Norm Sherry	8.00	3.00
❑	317	Sam McDowell	8.00	3.00
❑	318	Gene Mauch MG	8.00	3.00
❑	319	Joe Gaines	5.00	2.00
❑	320	Warren Spahn	60.00	30.00
❑	321	Gino Cimoli	5.00	2.00
❑	322	Bob Turley	8.00	3.00
❑	323	Bill Mazeroski	15.00	6.00
❑	324	Vic Davalillo RC	8.00	3.00
❑	325	Jack Sanford	5.00	2.00
❑	326	Hank Foiles	5.00	2.00
❑	327	Paul Foytack	5.00	2.00
❑	328	Dick Williams	8.00	3.00
❑	329	Lindy McDaniel	8.00	3.00
❑	330	Chuck Hinton	5.00	2.00
❑	331	Stafford/Pierce	8.00	3.00
❑	332	Joel Horlen	8.00	3.00
❑	333	Carl Warwick	5.00	2.00
❑	334	Wynn Hawkins	5.00	2.00
❑	335	Leon Wagner	5.00	2.00
❑	336	Ed Bauta	5.00	2.00
❑	337	Los Angeles Dodgers TC	25.00	10.00
❑	338	Russ Kemmerer	5.00	2.00
❑	339	Ted Bowsfield	5.00	2.00
❑	340	Yogi Berra P/CO	100.00	50.00
❑	341	Jack Baldschun	5.00	2.00
❑	342	Gene Woodling	8.00	3.00
❑	343	Johnny Pesky MG	8.00	3.00
❑	344	Don Schwall	5.00	2.00
❑	345	Brooks Robinson	60.00	30.00
❑	346	Billy Hoeft	5.00	2.00
❑	347	Joe Torre	15.00	6.00
❑	348	Vic Wertz	8.00	3.00
❑	349	Zoilo Versalles	8.00	3.00
❑	350	Bob Purkey	5.00	2.00
❑	351	Al Luplow	5.00	2.00
❑	352	Ken Johnson	5.00	2.00
❑	353	Billy Williams	30.00	12.50
❑	354	Dom Zanni	5.00	2.00
❑	355	Dean Chance	8.00	3.00
❑	356	John Schaive	5.00	2.00
❑	357	George Altman	5.00	2.00
❑	358	Milt Pappas	8.00	3.00
❑	359	Haywood Sullivan	8.00	3.00
❑	360	Don Drysdale	60.00	30.00
❑	361	Clete Boyer	10.00	4.00
❑	362	Checklist 5	12.00	5.00
❑	363	Dick Radatz	8.00	3.00
❑	364	Howie Goss	5.00	2.00
❑	365	Jim Bunning	20.00	8.00
❑	366	Tony Taylor	8.00	3.00
❑	367	Tony Cloninger	5.00	2.00
❑	368	Ed Bailey	5.00	2.00
❑	369	Jim Lemon	5.00	2.00
❑	370	Dick Donovan	5.00	2.00
❑	371	Rod Kanehl	8.00	3.00
❑	372	Don Lee	5.00	2.00
❑	373	Jim Campbell RC	5.00	2.00
❑	374	Claude Osteen	8.00	3.00
❑	375	Ken Boyer	15.00	6.00
❑	376	John Wyatt RC	5.00	2.00
❑	377	Baltimore Orioles TC	10.00	4.00
❑	378	Bill Henry	5.00	2.00
❑	379	Bob Anderson	5.00	2.00
❑	380	Ernie Banks UER	100.00	50.00
❑	381	Frank Baumann	5.00	2.00
❑	382	Ralph Houk MG	10.00	4.00
❑	383	Pete Richert	5.00	2.00
❑	384	Bob Tillman	5.00	2.00
❑	385	Art Mahaffey	5.00	2.00
❑	386	Rookie Stars	5.00	2.00
❑	387	Al McBean	5.00	2.00
❑	388	Jim Davenport	8.00	3.00
❑	389	Frank Sullivan	5.00	2.00
❑	390	Hank Aaron	200.00	100.00
❑	391	Bill Dailey RC	5.00	2.00
❑	392	Romano/Francona	5.00	2.00
❑	393	Ken MacKenzie	8.00	3.00

❑	394 Tim McCarver	15.00	6.00
❑	395 Don McMahon	5.00	2.00
❑	396 Joe Koppe	5.00	2.00
❑	397 Kansas City Athletics TC	10.00	4.00
❑	398 Boog Powell	25.00	10.00
❑	399 Dick Ellsworth	5.00	2.00
❑	400 Frank Robinson	60.00	30.00
❑	401 Jim Bouton	15.00	6.00
❑	402 Mickey Vernon MG	8.00	3.00
❑	403 Ron Perranoski	8.00	3.00
❑	404 Bob Oldis	5.00	2.00
❑	405 Floyd Robinson	5.00	2.00
❑	406 Howie Koplitz	5.00	2.00
❑	407 Rookie Stars	8.00	3.00
❑	408 Billy Gardner	5.00	2.00
❑	409 Roy Face	8.00	3.00
❑	410 Earl Battey	5.00	2.00
❑	411 Jim Constable	5.00	2.00
❑	412 Podres/Drysdale/Koufax	50.00	20.00
❑	413 Jerry Walker	5.00	2.00
❑	414 Ty Cline	5.00	2.00
❑	415 Bob Gibson	[illegible]	[illegible]
❑	416 Alex Grammas	5.00	2.00
❑	417 San Francisco Giants TC	10.00	4.00
❑	418 John Orsino	5.00	2.00
❑	419 Tracy Stallard	5.00	2.00
❑	420 Bobby Richardson	15.00	6.00
❑	421 Tom Morgan	5.00	2.00
❑	422 Fred Hutchinson MG	8.00	3.00
❑	423 Ed Hobaugh	5.00	2.00
❑	424 Charlie Smith	5.00	2.00
❑	425 Smoky Burgess	8.00	3.00
❑	426 Barry Latman	5.00	2.00
❑	427 Bernie Allen	5.00	2.00
❑	428 Carl Boles RC	5.00	2.00
❑	429 Lew Burdette	8.00	3.00
❑	430 Norm Siebern	5.00	2.00
❑	431A Checklist 6 White/Red	12.00	5.00
❑	431B Checklist 6 Black/Orange	30.00	12.50
❑	432 Roman Mejias	5.00	2.00
❑	433 Denis Menke	5.00	2.00
❑	434 John Callison	8.00	3.00
❑	435 Woody Held	5.00	2.00
❑	436 Tim Harkness	8.00	3.00
❑	437 Bill Bruton	5.00	2.00
❑	438 Wes Stock	5.00	2.00
❑	439 Don Zimmer	8.00	3.00
❑	440 Juan Marichal	30.00	12.50
❑	441 Lee Thomas	8.00	3.00
❑	442 J.C. Hartman RC	5.00	2.00
❑	443 Jimmy Piersall	8.00	3.00
❑	444 Jim Maloney	8.00	3.00
❑	445 Norm Cash	10.00	4.00
❑	446 Whitey Ford	60.00	30.00
❑	447 Felix Mantilla	25.00	10.00
❑	448 Jack Kralick	25.00	10.00
❑	449 Jose Tartabull	25.00	10.00
❑	450 Bob Friend	30.00	12.50
❑	451 Cleveland Indians TC	40.00	15.00
❑	452 Barney Schultz	25.00	10.00
❑	453 Jake Wood	25.00	10.00
❑	454A Art Fowler White	25.00	10.00
❑	454B Art Fowler Orange	30.00	12.50
❑	455 Ruben Amaro	25.00	10.00
❑	456 Jim Coker	25.00	10.00
❑	457 Tex Clevenger	25.00	10.00
❑	458 Al Lopez MG	30.00	12.50
❑	459 Dick LeMay	25.00	10.00
❑	460 Del Crandall	30.00	12.50
❑	461 Norm Bass	25.00	10.00
❑	462 Wally Post	25.00	10.00
❑	463 Joe Schaffernoth	25.00	10.00
❑	464 Ken Aspromonte	25.00	10.00
❑	465 Chuck Estrada	25.00	10.00
❑	466 Bill Freehan SP RC	60.00	30.00
❑	467 Phil Ortega	25.00	10.00
❑	468 Carroll Hardy	30.00	12.50
❑	469 Jay Hook	30.00	12.50
❑	470 Tom Tresh SP	60.00	30.00
❑	471 Ken Retzer	25.00	10.00
❑	472 Lou Brock	80.00	40.00
❑	473 New York Mets TC	100.00	50.00
❑	474 Jack Fisher	25.00	10.00
❑	475 Gus Triandos	30.00	12.50
❑	476 Frank Funk	25.00	10.00
❑	477 Donn Clendenon	30.00	12.50
❑	478 Paul Brown	25.00	10.00
❑	479 Ed Brinkman RC	25.00	10.00
❑	480 Bill Monbouquette	25.00	10.00
❑	481 Bob Taylor	25.00	10.00
❑	482 Felix Torres	25.00	10.00
❑	483 Jim Owens UER	25.00	10.00
❑	484 Dale Long SP	30.00	12.50
❑	485 Jim Landis	25.00	10.00
❑	486 Ray Sadecki	25.00	10.00
❑	487 John Roseboro	30.00	12.50
❑	488 Jerry Adair	25.00	10.00
❑	489 Paul Toth RC	25.00	10.00
❑	490 Willie McCovey	100.00	50.00
❑	491 Harry Craft MG	25.00	10.00
❑	492 Dave Wickersham	25.00	10.00
❑	493 Walt Bond	25.00	10.00
❑	494 Phil Regan	25.00	10.00
❑	495 Frank Thomas SP	30.00	12.50
❑	496 Rookie Stars	30.00	12.50
❑	497 Bennie Daniels	25.00	10.00
❑	498 Eddie Kasko	25.00	10.00
❑	499 J.C. Martin	25.00	10.00
❑	500 Harmon Killebrew SP	150.00	75.00
❑	501 Joe Azcue	25.00	10.00
❑	502 Daryl Spencer	25.00	10.00
❑	503 Milwaukee Braves TC	40.00	15.00
❑	504 Bob Johnson	25.00	10.00
❑	505 Curt Flood	40.00	15.00
❑	506 Gene Green	25.00	10.00
❑	507 Roland Sheldon	30.00	12.50
❑	508 Ted Savage	25.00	10.00
❑	509A Checklist 7 Centered	30.00	12.50
❑	509B Checklist 7 Right	30.00	12.50
❑	510 Ken McBride	25.00	10.00
❑	511 Charlie Neal	30.00	12.50
❑	512 Cal McLish	25.00	10.00
❑	513 Gary Geiger	25.00	10.00
❑	514 Larry Osborne	25.00	10.00
❑	515 Don Elston	25.00	10.00
❑	516 Purnell Goldy RC	25.00	10.00
❑	517 Hal Woodeshick	25.00	10.00
❑	518 Don Blasingame	25.00	10.00
❑	519 Claude Raymond RC	25.00	10.00
❑	520 Orlando Cepeda	40.00	15.00
❑	521 Dan Pfister	25.00	10.00
❑	522 Rookie Stars	30.00	12.50
❑	523 Bill Kunkel	15.00	6.00
❑	524 St. Louis Cardinals TC	30.00	12.50
❑	525 Nellie Fox	50.00	20.00
❑	526 Dick Hall	15.00	6.00
❑	527 Ed Sadowski	15.00	6.00
❑	528 Carl Willey	15.00	6.00
❑	529 Wes Covington	15.00	6.00
❑	530 Don Mossi	20.00	8.00
❑	531 Sam Mele MG	15.00	6.00
❑	532 Steve Boros	15.00	6.00
❑	533 Bobby Shantz	20.00	8.00
❑	534 Ken Walters	15.00	6.00
❑	535 Jim Perry	20.00	8.00
❑	536 Norm Larker	15.00	6.00
❑	537 Pete Rose RC	1000.00	500.00
❑	538 George Brunet	15.00	6.00
❑	539 Wayne Causey	15.00	6.00
❑	540 Roberto Clemente	250.00	125.00
❑	541 Ron Moeller	15.00	6.00
❑	542 Lou Klimchock	15.00	6.00
❑	543 Russ Snyder	15.00	6.00
❑	544 Rusty Staub RC	50.00	20.00
❑	545 Jose Pagan	15.00	6.00
❑	546 Hal Reniff	20.00	8.00
❑	547 Gus Bell	15.00	6.00
❑	548 Tom Satriano RC	15.00	6.00
❑	549 Rookie Stars	15.00	6.00
❑	550 Duke Snider	80.00	40.00
❑	551 Billy Klaus	15.00	6.00
❑	552 Detroit Tigers TC	50.00	20.00
❑	553 Willie Stargell RC	120.00	60.00
❑	554 Hank Fischer RC	15.00	6.00
❑	555 John Blanchard	20.00	8.00
❑	556 Al Worthington	15.00	6.00
❑	557 Cuno Barragan	15.00	6.00
❑	558 Ron Hunt RC	20.00	8.00
❑	559 Danny Murtaugh MG	15.00	6.00
❑	560 Ray Herbert	15.00	6.00
❑	561 Mike De La Hoz	15.00	6.00
❑	562 Dave McNally RC	30.00	12.50
❑	563 Mike McCormick	15.00	6.00
❑	564 George Banks RC	15.00	6.00
❑	565 Larry Sherry	15.00	6.00
❑	566 Cliff Cook	15.00	6.00
❑	567 Jim Duffalo	15.00	6.00
❑	568 Bob Sadowski	15.00	6.00
❑	569 Luis Arroyo	20.00	8.00
❑	570 Frank Bolling	15.00	6.00
❑	571 Johnny Klippstein	15.00	6.00
❑	572 Jack Spring	15.00	6.00
❑	573 Coot Veal	15.00	6.00
❑	574 Hal Kolstad	15.00	6.00
❑	575 Don Cardwell	15.00	6.00
❑	576 Johnny Temple	30.00	12.50

1964 Topps

❑	COMPLETE SET (587)	3500.00	2750.00
❑	COMMON CARD (1-196)	3.00	1.25
❑	COMMON CARD (197-370)	4.00	1.50
❑	COMMON CARD (371-522)	8.00	3.00
❑	COMMON CARD (523-587)	15.00	6.00
❑	WRAPPER (1-CENT)	100.00	50.00
❑	WRAP.(1-CENT, REPEAT)	120.00	60.00
❑	WRAPPER (5-CENT)	30.00	12.50
❑	WRAPPER (5-CENT, COIN)	40.00	15.00
❑	1 Koufax/Ellis/Friend LL	30.00	12.50
❑	2 Peters/Pizarro/Pascual LL	8.00	3.00
❑	3 Koufax/Marichal/Spahn LL	20.00	8.00
❑	4 Ford/Pascual/Bouton LL	8.00	3.00
❑	5 Koufax/Malon/Drysdale LL	15.00	6.00
❑	6 Pascual/Bunning/Stigman LL	8.00	3.00
❑	7 Clemente/Groat/Aaron LL	20.00	8.00
❑	8 Yaz/Kaline/Rollins LL	15.00	6.00
❑	9 Aaron/McCov/Mays/Cep LL	30.00	12.50
❑	10 Killebrew/Stuart/Allison LL	8.00	3.00
❑	11 Aaron/Boyer/White LL	15.00	6.00
❑	12 Stuart/Kaline/Killebrew LL	8.00	3.00
❑	13 Hoyt Wilhelm	12.00	5.00
❑	14 D.Nen RC/N.Willhite RC	3.00	1.25
❑	15 Zoilo Versalles	6.00	2.50
❑	16 John Boozer	3.00	1.25
❑	17 Willie Kirkland	3.00	1.25
❑	18 Billy O'Dell	3.00	1.25
❑	19 Don Wert	3.00	1.25
❑	20 Bob Friend	6.00	2.50
❑	21 Yogi Berra MG	40.00	15.00
❑	22 Jerry Adair	3.00	1.25
❑	23 Chris Zachary RC	3.00	1.25
❑	24 Carl Sawatski	3.00	1.25
❑	25 Bill Monbouquette	3.00	1.25
❑	26 Gino Cimoli	3.00	1.25
❑	27 New York Mets TC	8.00	3.00
❑	28 Claude Osteen	6.00	2.50
❑	29 Lou Brock	40.00	15.00
❑	30 Ron Perranoski	6.00	2.50
❑	31 Dave Nicholson	3.00	1.25
❑	32 Dean Chance	6.00	2.50
❑	33 S.Ellis/M.Queen	6.00	2.50
❑	34 Jim Perry	6.00	2.50
❑	35 Eddie Mathews	20.00	8.00
❑	36 Hal Reniff	3.00	1.25
❑	37 Smoky Burgess	6.00	2.50
❑	38 Jim Wynn RC	8.00	3.00
❑	39 Hank Aguirre	3.00	1.25
❑	40 Dick Groat	6.00	2.50
❑	41 W.McCovey/L.Wagner	8.00	3.00
❑	42 Moe Drabowsky	6.00	2.50
❑	43 Roy Sievers	6.00	2.50

44	Duke Carmel	3.00	1.25
45	Milt Pappas	6.00	2.50
46	Ed Brinkman	3.00	1.25
47	J.Alou RC/R.Herbel	6.00	2.50
48	Bob Perry RC	3.00	1.25
49	Bill Henry	3.00	1.25
50	Mickey Mantle	500.00	250.00
51	Pete Richert	3.00	1.25
52	Chuck Hinton	3.00	1.25
53	Denis Menke	3.00	1.25
54	Sam Mele MG	3.00	1.25
55	Ernie Banks	40.00	15.00
56	Hal Brown	3.00	1.25
57	Tim Harkness	6.00	2.50
58	Don Demeter	6.00	2.50
59	Ernie Broglio	3.00	1.25
60	Frank Malzone	6.00	2.50
61	B.Rodgers/E.Sadowski	6.00	2.50
62	Ted Savage	3.00	1.25
63	John Orsino	3.00	1.25
64	Ted Abernathy	3.00	1.25
65	Felipe Alou	6.00	2.50
66	Eddie Fisher	3.00	1.25
67	Detroit Tigers TC	6.00	2.50
68	Willie Davis	6.00	2.50
69	Clete Boyer	6.00	2.50
70	Joe Torre	8.00	3.00
71	Jack Spring	3.00	1.25
72	Chico Cardenas	6.00	2.50
73	Jimmie Hall RC	8.00	3.00
74	B.Priddy RC/T.Butters	3.00	1.25
75	Wayne Causey	3.00	1.25
76	Checklist 1	10.00	4.00
77	Jerry Walker	3.00	1.25
78	Merritt Ranew	3.00	1.25
79	Bob Heffner RC	3.00	1.25
80	Vada Pinson	8.00	3.00
81	N.Fox/H.Killebrew	12.00	5.00
82	Jim Davenport	6.00	2.50
83	Gus Triandos	6.00	2.50
84	Carl Willey	3.00	1.25
85	Pete Ward	3.00	1.25
86	Al Downing	6.00	2.50
87	St. Louis Cardinals TC	6.00	2.50
88	John Roseboro	6.00	2.50
89	Boog Powell	6.00	2.50
90	Earl Battey	3.00	1.25
91	Bob Bailey	6.00	2.50
92	Steve Ridzik	3.00	1.25
93	Gary Geiger	3.00	1.25
94	J.Britton RC/L.Maxie RC	3.00	1.25
95	George Altman	3.00	1.25
96	Bob Buhl	6.00	2.50
97	Jim Fregosi	6.00	2.50
98	Bill Bruton	3.00	1.25
99	Al Stanek RC	3.00	1.25
100	Elston Howard	6.00	2.50
101	Walt Alston MG	8.00	3.00
102	Checklist 2	10.00	4.00
103	Curt Flood	6.00	2.50
104	Art Mahaffey	6.00	2.50
105	Woody Held	3.00	1.25
106	Joe Nuxhall	6.00	2.50
107	B.Howard RC/F.Kruetzer RC	3.00	1.25
108	John Wyatt	3.00	1.25
109	Rusty Staub	6.00	2.50
110	Albie Pearson	6.00	2.50
111	Don Elston	3.00	1.25
112	Bob Tillman	3.00	1.25
113	Grover Powell RC	6.00	2.50
114	Don Lock	3.00	1.25
115	Frank Bolling	3.00	1.25
116	J.Ward RC/T.Oliva	12.00	5.00
117	Earl Francis	3.00	1.25
118	John Blanchard	6.00	2.50
119	Gary Kolb RC	3.00	1.25
120	Don Drysdale	20.00	8.00
121	Pete Runnels	6.00	2.50
122	Don McMahon	3.00	1.25
123	Jose Pagan	3.00	1.25
124	Orlando Pena	3.00	1.25
125	Pete Rose UER	250.00	125.00
126	Russ Snyder	3.00	1.25
127	A.Gatewood RC/D.Simpson	3.00	1.25
128	Mickey Lolich RC	20.00	8.00
129	Amado Samuel	3.00	1.25
130	Gary Peters	6.00	2.50
131	Steve Boros	3.00	1.25
132	Milwaukee Braves TC	6.00	2.50
133	Jim Grant	6.00	2.50
134	Don Zimmer	6.00	2.50
135	Johnny Callison	6.00	2.50
136	Sandy Koufax WS1	20.00	8.00
137	Willie Davis WS2	8.00	3.00
138	Ron Fairly WS3	8.00	3.00
139	Frank Howard WS4	8.00	3.00
140	Dodgers Celebrate WS	8.00	3.00
141	Danny Murtaugh MG	6.00	2.50
142	John Bateman	3.00	1.25
143	Bubba Phillips	3.00	1.25
144	Al Worthington	3.00	1.25
145	Norm Siebern	3.00	1.25
146	T.John RC/B.Chance RC	30.00	12.50
147	Ray Sadecki	3.00	1.25
148	J.C. Martin	3.00	1.25
149	Paul Foytack	3.00	1.25
150	Willie Mays	120.00	60.00
151	Kansas City Athletics TC	6.00	2.50
152	Denny Lemaster	3.00	1.25
153	Dick Williams	6.00	2.50
154	Dick Tracewski RC	6.00	2.50
155	Duke Snider	30.00	12.50
156	Bill Dailey	3.00	1.25
157	Gene Mauch MG	6.00	2.50
158	Ken Johnson	3.00	1.25
159	Charlie Dees RC	3.00	1.25
160	Ken Boyer	6.00	2.50
161	Dave McNally	6.00	2.50
162	D.Sisler/V.Pinson	6.00	2.50
163	Donn Clendenon	6.00	2.50
164	Bud Daley	3.00	1.25
165	Jerry Lumpe	3.00	1.25
166	Marty Keough	3.00	1.25
167	M.Brumley RC/L.Piniella RC	30.00	12.50
168	Al Weis	3.00	1.25
169	Del Crandall	6.00	2.50
170	Dick Radatz	6.00	2.50
171	Ty Cline	3.00	1.25
172	Cleveland Indians TC	6.00	2.50
173	Ryne Duren	6.00	2.50
174	Doc Edwards	3.00	1.25
175	Billy Williams	12.00	5.00
176	Tracy Stallard	3.00	1.25
177	Harmon Killebrew	20.00	8.00
178	Hank Bauer MG	6.00	2.50
179	Carl Warwick	3.00	1.25
180	Tommy Davis	6.00	2.50
181	Dave Wickersham	3.00	1.25
182	C.Yastrzemski/C.Schilling	15.00	6.00
183	Ron Taylor	3.00	1.25
184	Al Luplow	3.00	1.25
185	Jim O'Toole	6.00	2.50
186	Roman Mejias	3.00	1.25
187	Ed Roebuck	3.00	1.25
188	Checklist 3	10.00	4.00
189	Bob Hendley	3.00	1.25
190	Bobby Richardson	8.00	3.00
191	Clay Dalrymple	6.00	2.50
192	J.Boccabella RC/B.Cowan RC	3.00	1.25
193	Jerry Lynch	3.00	1.25
194	John Goryl	3.00	1.25
195	Floyd Robinson	3.00	1.25
196	Jim Gentile	3.00	1.25
197	Frank Lary	6.00	2.50
198	Len Gabrielson	4.00	1.50
199	Joe Azcue	4.00	1.50
200	Sandy Koufax	120.00	60.00
201	S.Bowens RC/W.Bunker RC	6.00	2.50
202	Galen Cisco	6.00	2.50
203	John Kennedy RC	6.00	2.50
204	Matty Alou	6.00	2.50
205	Nellie Fox	12.00	5.00
206	Steve Hamilton	6.00	2.50
207	Fred Hutchinson MG	6.00	2.50
208	Wes Covington	6.00	2.50
209	Bob Allen	4.00	1.50
210	Carl Yastrzemski	40.00	15.00
211	Jim Coker	4.00	1.50
212	Pete Lovrich	4.00	1.50
213	Los Angeles Angels TC	6.00	2.50
214	Ken McMullen	6.00	2.50
215	Ray Herbert	4.00	1.50
216	Mike de la Hoz	4.00	1.50
217	Jim King	4.00	1.50
218	Hank Fischer	4.00	1.50
219	A.Downing/J.Bouton	6.00	2.50
220	Dick Ellsworth	6.00	2.50
221	Bob Saverine	4.00	1.50
222	Billy Pierce	6.00	2.50
223	George Banks	4.00	1.50
224	Tommie Sisk	4.00	1.50
225	Roger Maris	60.00	30.00
226	J.Grote RC/L.Yellen RC	6.00	2.50
227	Barry Latman	4.00	1.50
228	Felix Mantilla	4.00	1.50
229	Charley Lau	6.00	2.50
230	Brooks Robinson	40.00	15.00
231	Dick Calmus RC	4.00	1.50
232	Al Lopez MG	8.00	3.00
233	Hal Smith	4.00	1.50
234	Gary Bell	4.00	1.50
235	Ron Hunt	4.00	1.50
236	Bill Faul	4.00	1.50
237	Chicago Cubs TC	6.00	2.50
238	Roy McMillan	6.00	2.50
239	Herm Starrette RC	4.00	1.50
240	Bill White	6.00	2.50
241	Jim Owens	4.00	1.50
242	Harvey Kuenn	6.00	2.50
243	R.Allen RC/J.Hernstein	30.00	12.50
244	Tony LaRussa RC	30.00	12.50
245	Dick Stigman	4.00	1.50
246	Manny Mota	6.00	2.50
247	Dave DeBusschere	6.00	2.50
248	Johnny Pesky MG	6.00	2.50
249	Doug Camilli	4.00	1.50
250	Al Kaline	40.00	15.00
251	Choo Choo Coleman	6.00	2.50
252	Ken Aspromonte	4.00	1.50
253	Wally Post	6.00	2.50
254	Don Hoak	6.00	2.50
255	Lee Thomas	6.00	2.50
256	Johnny Weekly	4.00	1.50
257	San Francisco Giants TC	6.00	2.50
258	Garry Roggenburk	4.00	1.50
259	Harry Bright	4.00	1.50
260	Frank Robinson	40.00	15.00
261	Jim Hannan	4.00	1.50
262	M.Shannon RC/H.Fanok	8.00	3.00
263	Chuck Estrada	4.00	1.50
264	Jim Landis	4.00	1.50
265	Jim Bunning	12.00	5.00
266	Gene Freese	4.00	1.50
267	Wilbur Wood RC	6.00	2.50
268	D.Murtaugh/B.Virdon	6.00	2.50
269	Ellis Burton	4.00	1.50
270	Rich Rollins	6.00	2.50
271	Bob Sadowski	4.00	1.50
272	Jake Wood	4.00	1.50
273	Mel Nelson	4.00	1.50
274	Checklist 4	10.00	4.00
275	John Tsitouris	4.00	1.50
276	Jose Tartabull	6.00	2.50
277	Ken Retzer	4.00	1.50
278	Bobby Shantz	6.00	2.50
279	Joe Koppe	4.00	1.50
280	Juan Marichal	15.00	6.00
281	J.,Gibbs/T.Metclaf RC	6.00	2.50
282	Bob Bruce	4.00	1.50
283	Tom McCraw RC	4.00	1.50
284	Dick Schofield	4.00	1.50
285	Robin Roberts	15.00	6.00
286	Don Landrum	4.00	1.50
287	T.Conig.RC/B.Spans.RC	50.00	20.00
288	Al Moran	4.00	1.50
289	Frank Funk	4.00	1.50
290	Bob Allison	6.00	2.50
291	Phil Ortega	4.00	1.50
292	Mike Roarke	4.00	1.50
293	Philadelphia Phillies TC	6.00	2.50
294	Ken L. Hunt	4.00	1.50
295	Roger Craig	6.00	2.50
296	Ed Kirkpatrick	4.00	1.50
297	Ken MacKenzie	4.00	1.50
298	Harry Craft MG	4.00	1.50
299	Bill Stafford	4.00	1.50
300	Hank Aaron	100.00	50.00
301	Larry Brown RC	4.00	1.50

302	Dan Pfister	4.00	1.50
303	Jim Campbell	4.00	1.50
304	Bob Johnson	4.00	1.50
305	Jack Lamabe	4.00	1.50
306	Willie Mays/O.Cepeda	40.00	15.00
307	Joe Gibbon	4.00	1.50
308	Gene Stephens	4.00	1.50
309	Paul Toth	4.00	1.50
310	Jim Gilliam	6.00	2.50
311	Tom W. Brown RC	6.00	2.50
312	F.Fisher RC/F.Gladding RC	4.00	1.50
313	Chuck Hiller	4.00	1.50
314	Jerry Buchek	4.00	1.50
315	Bo Belinsky	6.00	2.50
316	Gene Oliver	4.00	1.50
317	Al Smith	4.00	1.50
318	Minnesota Twins TC	6.00	2.50
319	Paul Brown	4.00	1.50
320	Rocky Colavito	12.00	5.00
321	Bob Lillis	4.00	1.50
322	George Brunet	4.00	1.50
323	John Buzhardt	4.00	1.50
324	Casey Stengel MG	15.00	6.00
325	Hector Lopez	6.00	2.50
326	Ron Brand RC	4.00	1.50
327	Don Blasingame	4.00	1.50
328	Bob Shaw	4.00	1.50
329	Russ Nixon	4.00	1.50
330	Tommy Harper	6.00	2.50
331	Maris/Cash/Mantle/Kaline	150.00	75.00
332	Ray Washburn	4.00	1.50
333	Billy Moran	4.00	1.50
334	Lew Krausse	4.00	1.50
335	Don Mossi	6.00	2.50
336	Andre Rodgers	4.00	1.50
337	A.Ferrara RC/J.Torborg RC	6.00	2.50
338	Jack Kralick	4.00	1.50
339	Walt Bond	4.00	1.50
340	Joe Cunningham	4.00	1.50
341	Jim Roland	4.00	1.50
342	Willie Stargell	30.00	12.50
343	Washington Senators TC	6.00	2.50
344	Phil Linz	6.00	2.50
345	Frank Thomas	8.00	3.00
346	Joey Jay	4.00	1.50
347	Bobby Wine	6.00	2.50
348	Ed Lopat MG	6.00	2.50
349	Art Fowler	4.00	1.50
350	Willie McCovey	25.00	10.00
351	Dan Schneider	4.00	1.50
352	Eddie Bressoud	4.00	1.50
353	Wally Moon	6.00	2.50
354	Dave Giusti	4.00	1.50
355	Vic Power	6.00	2.50
356	B.McCool RC/C.Ruiz	6.00	2.50
357	Charley James	4.00	1.50
358	Ron Kline	4.00	1.50
359	Jim Schaffer	4.00	1.50
360	Joe Pepitone	12.00	5.00
361	Jay Hook	4.00	1.50
362	Checklist 5	10.00	4.00
363	Dick McAuliffe	6.00	2.50
364	Joe Gaines	4.00	1.50
365	Cal McLish	6.00	2.50
366	Nelson Mathews	4.00	1.50
367	Fred Whitfield	4.00	1.50
368	F.Ackley RC/D.Buford RC	6.00	2.50
369	Jerry Zimmerman	4.00	1.50
370	Hal Woodeshick	4.00	1.50
371	Frank Howard	8.00	3.00
372	Howie Koplitz	8.00	3.00
373	Pittsburgh Pirates TC	12.00	5.00
374	Bobby Bolin	8.00	3.00
375	Ron Santo	10.00	4.00
376	Dave Morehead	8.00	3.00
377	Bob Skinner	8.00	3.00
378	W.Woodward RC/J.Smith	10.00	4.00
379	Tony Gonzalez	8.00	3.00
380	Whitey Ford	40.00	15.00
381	Bob Taylor	8.00	3.00
382	Wes Stock	8.00	3.00
383	Bill Rigney MG	8.00	3.00
384	Ron Hansen	8.00	3.00
385	Curt Simmons	10.00	4.00
386	Lenny Green	8.00	3.00
387	Terry Fox	8.00	3.00
388	J.O'Donoghue RC/G.Williams	10.00	4.00
389	Jim Umbricht	10.00	4.00
390	Orlando Cepeda	25.00	10.00
391	Sam McDowell	10.00	4.00
392	Jim Pagliaroni	8.00	3.00
393	C.Stengel/E.Kranepool	15.00	6.00
394	Bob Miller	8.00	3.00
395	Tom Tresh	10.00	4.00
396	Dennis Bennett	8.00	3.00
397	Chuck Cottier	8.00	3.00
398	B.Haas/D.Smith	10.00	4.00
399	Jackie Brandt	8.00	3.00
400	Warren Spahn	40.00	15.00
401	Charlie Maxwell	8.00	3.00
402	Tom Sturdivant	8.00	3.00
403	Cincinnati Reds TC	12.00	5.00
404	Tony Martinez	8.00	3.00
405	Ken McBride	8.00	3.00
406	Al Spangler	8.00	3.00
407	Bill Freehan	10.00	4.00
408	J.Stewart RC/F.Burdette RC	8.00	3.00
409	Bill Fischer	0.00	0.00
410	Dick Stuart	10.00	4.00
411	Lee Walls	8.00	3.00
412	Ray Culp	10.00	4.00
413	Johnny Keane MG	8.00	3.00
414	Jack Sanford	8.00	3.00
415	Tony Kubek	15.00	6.00
416	Lee Maye	8.00	3.00
417	Don Cardwell	8.00	3.00
418	D.Knowles RC/B.Narum RC	10.00	4.00
419	Ken Harrelson RC	15.00	6.00
420	Jim Maloney	10.00	4.00
421	Camilo Carreon	8.00	3.00
422	Jack Fisher	8.00	3.00
423	H.Aaron/W.Mays	120.00	60.00
424	Dick Bertell	8.00	3.00
425	Norm Cash	10.00	4.00
426	Bob Rodgers	8.00	3.00
427	Don Rudolph	8.00	3.00
428	A.Skeen RC/P.Smith RC	8.00	3.00
429	Tim McCarver	10.00	4.00
430	Juan Pizarro	8.00	3.00
431	George Alusik	8.00	3.00
432	Ruben Amaro	10.00	4.00
433	New York Yankees TC	40.00	15.00
434	Don Nottebart	8.00	3.00
435	Vic Davalillo	8.00	3.00
436	Charlie Neal	10.00	4.00
437	Ed Bailey	8.00	3.00
438	Checklist 6	15.00	6.00
439	Harvey Haddix	10.00	4.00
440	Roberto Clemente UER	200.00	100.00
441	Bob Duliba	8.00	3.00
442	Pumpsie Green	10.00	4.00
443	Chuck Dressen MG	10.00	4.00
444	Larry Jackson	8.00	3.00
445	Bill Skowron	10.00	4.00
446	Julian Javier	15.00	6.00
447	Ted Bowsfield	8.00	3.00
448	Cookie Rojas	10.00	4.00
449	Deron Johnson	10.00	4.00
450	Steve Barber	8.00	3.00
451	Joe Amalfitano	8.00	3.00
452	G.Garrido RC/J.Hart RC	10.00	4.00
453	Frank Baumann	8.00	3.00
454	Tommie Aaron	10.00	4.00
455	Bernie Allen	8.00	3.00
456	W.Parker RC/J.Werhas RC	10.00	4.00
457	Jesse Gonder	8.00	3.00
458	Ralph Terry	10.00	4.00
459	P.Charton RC/D.Jones RC	8.00	3.00
460	Bob Gibson	40.00	15.00
461	George Thomas	8.00	3.00
462	Birdie Tebbetts MG	8.00	3.00
463	Don Leppert	8.00	3.00
464	Dallas Green	15.00	6.00
465	Mike Hershberger	8.00	3.00
466	D.Green RC/A.Monteagudo RC	10.00	4.00
467	Bob Aspromonte	8.00	3.00
468	Gaylord Perry	40.00	15.00
469	F.Norman RC/S.Slaughter RC	10.00	4.00
470	Jim Bouton	10.00	4.00
471	Gates Brown RC	10.00	4.00
472	Vern Law	10.00	4.00
473	Baltimore Orioles TC	12.00	5.00
474	Larry Sherry	10.00	4.00
475	Ed Charles	8.00	3.00
476	R.Carty RC/D.Kelley RC	15.00	6.00
477	Mike Joyce	8.00	3.00
478	Dick Howser	10.00	4.00
479	D.Bakenhaster RC/J.Lewis RC	8.00	3.00
480	Bob Purkey	8.00	3.00
481	Chuck Schilling	8.00	3.00
482	J.Briggs RC/D.Cater RC	10.00	4.00
483	Fred Valentine RC	8.00	3.00
484	Bill Pleis	8.00	3.00
485	Tom Haller	8.00	3.00
486	Bob Kennedy MG	8.00	3.00
487	Mike McCormick	10.00	4.00
488	P.Mikkelsen RC/B.Meyer RC	15.00	6.00
489	Julio Navarro	8.00	3.00
490	Ron Fairly	10.00	4.00
491	Ed Rakow	8.00	3.00
492	J.Beauchamp RC/M.White RC	8.00	3.00
493	Don Lee	8.00	3.00
494	Al Jackson	8.00	3.00
495	Bill Virdon	10.00	4.00
496	Chicago White Sox TC	12.00	5.00
497	Jeoff Long RC	8.00	3.00
498	Dave Stenhouse	8.00	3.00
499	C.Slamon RC/G.Seyfried RC	8.00	3.00
500	Camilo Pascual	10.00	4.00
501	Bob Veale	10.00	4.00
502	B.Knoop RC/B.Lee RC	8.00	3.00
503	Earl Wilson	8.00	3.00
504	Claude Raymond	8.00	3.00
505	Stan Williams	8.00	3.00
506	Bobby Bragan MG	8.00	3.00
507	Johnny Edwards	8.00	3.00
508	Diego Segui	8.00	3.00
509	G.Alley RC/O.McFarlane RC	10.00	4.00
510	Lindy McDaniel	10.00	4.00
511	Lou Jackson	10.00	4.00
512	W.Horton RC/J.Sparma RC	15.00	6.00
513	Don Larsen	10.00	4.00
514	Jim Hickman	10.00	4.00
515	Johnny Romano	8.00	3.00
516	J.Arrigo RC/D.Siebler RC	8.00	3.00
517A	Checklist 7 ERR	25.00	10.00
517B	Checklist 7 COR	15.00	6.00
518	Carl Bouldin	8.00	3.00
519	Charlie Smith	8.00	3.00
520	Jack Baldschun	10.00	4.00
521	Tom Satriano	8.00	3.00
522	Bob Tiefenauer	8.00	3.00
523	Lou Burdette UER	20.00	8.00
524	J.Dickson RC/B.Klaus RC	15.00	6.00
525	Al McBean	15.00	6.00
526	Lou Clinton	15.00	6.00
527	Larry Bearnarth	15.00	6.00
528	D.Duncan RC/T.Reynolds RC	20.00	8.00
529	Alvin Dark MG	20.00	8.00
530	Leon Wagner	15.00	6.00
531	Los Angeles Dodgers TC	25.00	10.00
532	B.Bloomfield RC/J.Nossek RC	15.00	6.00
533	Johnny Klippstein	15.00	6.00
534	Gus Bell	15.00	6.00
535	Phil Regan	15.00	6.00
536	L.Elliot/J.Stephenson RC	15.00	6.00
537	Dan Osinski	15.00	6.00
538	Minnie Minoso	20.00	8.00
539	Roy Face	20.00	8.00
540	Luis Aparicio	40.00	15.00
541	P.Roof/P.Niekro RC	80.00	40.00
542	Don Mincher	15.00	6.00
543	Bob Uecker	40.00	15.00
544	S.Hertz RC/J.Hoerner RC	15.00	6.00
545	Max Alvis	15.00	6.00
546	Joe Christopher	15.00	6.00
547	Gil Hodges MG	30.00	12.50
548	W.Schurr RC/P.Speckenbach RC	20.00	8.00
549	Joe Moeller	15.00	6.00
550	Ken Hubbs MEM	40.00	15.00
551	Billy Hoeft	15.00	6.00
552	T.Kelley RC/S.Siebert RC	15.00	6.00
553	Jim Brewer	15.00	6.00
554	Hank Foiles	15.00	6.00
555	Lee Stange	15.00	6.00
556	S.Dillon RC/R.Locke RC	15.00	6.00
557	Leo Burke	15.00	6.00
558	Don Schwall	15.00	6.00

❑ 559 Dick Phillips 15.00 6.00
❑ 560 Dick Farrell 15.00 6.00
❑ 561 D.Bennett RC/R.Wise RC 20.00 8.00
❑ 562 Pedro Ramos 15.00 6.00
❑ 563 Dal Maxvill 20.00 8.00
❑ 564 J.McCabe RC/J.McNertney RC 20.00 8.00
❑ 565 Stu Miller 15.00 6.00
❑ 566 Ed Kranepool 20.00 8.00
❑ 567 Jim Kaat 20.00 8.00
❑ 568 P.Gagliano RC/C.Peterson RC 15.00 6.00
❑ 569 Fred Newman 15.00 6.00
❑ 570 Bill Mazeroski 40.00 15.00
❑ 571 Gene Conley 15.00 6.00
❑ 572 D.Gray RC/D.Egan 15.00 6.00
❑ 573 Jim Duffalo 15.00 6.00
❑ 574 Manny Jimenez 15.00 6.00
❑ 575 Tony Cloninger 15.00 6.00
❑ 576 J.Hinsley RC/B.Wakefield RC 15.00 6.00
❑ 577 Gordy Coleman 15.00 6.00
❑ 578 Glen Hobbie 15.00 6.00
❑ 579 Boston Red Sox TC 25.00 10.00
❑ 580 Johnny Podres 20.00 8.00
❑ 581 P.Gonzalez/A.Moore RC 20.00 8.00
❑ 582 Rod Kanehl 20.00 8.00
❑ 583 Tito Francona 15.00 6.00
❑ 584 Joel Horlen 15.00 6.00
❑ 585 Tony Taylor 20.00 8.00
❑ 586 Jimmy Piersall 20.00 8.00
❑ 587 Bennie Daniels 20.00 8.00

1965 Topps

❑ COMPLETE SET (598) 5000.00 2500.00
❑ COMMON CARD (1-196) 2.00 .75
❑ COMMON CARD (197-283) 2.50 1.00
❑ COMMON CARD (284-370) 4.00 1.50
❑ COMMON CARD (371-598) 8.00 3.00
❑ WRAPPER (1-CENT) 120.00 60.00
❑ WRAPPER (5-CENT) 100.00 50.00
❑ 1 Oliva/Howard/Brooks LL 20.00 8.00
❑ 2 Clemente/Aaron/Carty LL 25.00 10.00
❑ 3 Killebrew/Mantle/Powell LL 50.00 20.00
❑ 4 Mays/B.Will/Cepeda LL 15.00 6.00
❑ 5 Brooks/Kill/Mantle LL 40.00 15.00
❑ 6 Boyer/Mays Santo LL 12.00 5.00
❑ 7 D.Chance/J.Horlen LL 5.00 2.00
❑ 8 S.Koufax/D.Drysdale LL 20.00 8.00
❑ 9 Chance/Peters/Wick LL 5.00 2.00
❑ 10 Jackson/Sad/Marichal LL 5.00 2.00
❑ 11 Downing/Chance/Pascual LL 5.00 2.00
❑ 12 Veale/Drysdale/Gibson LL 10.00 4.00
❑ 13 Pedro Ramos 4.00 1.50
❑ 14 Len Gabrielson 2.00 .75
❑ 15 Robin Roberts 10.00 4.00
❑ 16 Joe Morgan RC DP 60.00 30.00
❑ 17 Johnny Romano 2.00 .75
❑ 18 Bill McCool 2.00 .75
❑ 19 Gates Brown 4.00 1.50
❑ 20 Jim Bunning 10.00 4.00
❑ 21 Don Blasingame 2.00 .75
❑ 22 Charlie Smith 2.00 .75
❑ 23 Bob Tiefenauer 2.00 .75
❑ 24 Minnesota Twins TC 6.00 2.50
❑ 25 Al McBean 2.00 .75
❑ 26 Bobby Knoop 2.00 .75
❑ 27 Dick Bertell 2.00 .75
❑ 28 Barney Schultz 2.00 .75
❑ 29 Felix Mantilla 2.00 .75
❑ 30 Jim Bouton 6.00 2.50
❑ 31 Mike White 2.00 .75
❑ 32 Herman Franks MG 2.00 .75
❑ 33 Jackie Brandt 2.00 .75
❑ 34 Cal Koonce 2.00 .75
❑ 35 Ed Charles 2.00 .75
❑ 36 Bobby Wine 2.00 .75
❑ 37 Fred Gladding 2.00 .75
❑ 38 Jim King 2.00 .75
❑ 39 Gerry Arrigo 2.00 .75
❑ 40 Frank Howard 6.00 2.50
❑ 41 B.Howard/M.Staehle RC 2.00 .75
❑ 42 Earl Wilson 4.00 1.50
❑ 43 Mike Shannon 4.00 1.50
❑ 44 Wade Blasingame RC 2.00 .75
❑ 45 Roy McMillan 4.00 1.50
❑ 46 Bob Lee 2.00 .75
❑ 47 Tommy Harper 4.00 1.50
❑ 48 Claude Raymond 4.00 1.50
❑ 49 C.Blefary RC/J.Miller 4.00 1.50
❑ 50 Juan Marichal 10.00 4.00
❑ 51 Bill Bryan 2.00 .75
❑ 52 Ed Roebuck 2.00 .75
❑ 53 Dick McAuliffe 4.00 1.50
❑ 54 Joe Gibbon 2.00 .75
❑ 55 Tony Conigliaro 15.00 6.00
❑ 56 Ron Kline 2.00 .75
❑ 57 St. Louis Cardinals TC 6.00 2.50
❑ 58 Fred Talbot RC 2.00 .75
❑ 59 Nate Oliver 2.00 .75
❑ 60 Jim O'Toole 4.00 1.50
❑ 61 Chris Cannizzaro 2.00 .75
❑ 62 Jim Kaat UER DP 6.00 2.50
❑ 63 Ty Cline 2.00 .75
❑ 64 Lou Burdette 4.00 1.50
❑ 65 Tony Kubek 10.00 4.00
❑ 66 Bill Rigney MG 2.00 .75
❑ 67 Harvey Haddix 4.00 1.50
❑ 68 Del Crandall 4.00 1.50
❑ 69 Bill Virdon 4.00 1.50
❑ 70 Bill Skowron 6.00 2.50
❑ 71 John O'Donoghue 2.00 .75
❑ 72 Tony Gonzalez 2.00 .75
❑ 73 Dennis Ribant RC 2.00 .75
❑ 74 R.Petrocelli RC/J.Steph RC 10.00 4.00
❑ 75 Deron Johnson 4.00 1.50
❑ 76 Sam McDowell 6.00 2.50
❑ 77 Doug Camilli 2.00 .75
❑ 78 Dal Maxvill 2.00 .75
❑ 79A Checklist 1 Cannizzaro 10.00 4.00
❑ 79B Checklist 1 C.Cannizzaro 10.00 4.00
❑ 80 Turk Farrell 2.00 .75
❑ 81 Don Buford 4.00 1.50
❑ 82 S.Alomar RC/J.Braun RC 6.00 2.50
❑ 83 George Thomas 2.00 .75
❑ 84 Ron Herbel 2.00 .75
❑ 85 Willie Smith RC 2.00 .75
❑ 86 Buster Narum 2.00 .75
❑ 87 Nelson Mathews 2.00 .75
❑ 88 Jack Lamabe 2.00 .75
❑ 89 Mike Hershberger 2.00 .75
❑ 90 Rich Rollins 4.00 1.50
❑ 91 Chicago Cubs TC 6.00 2.50
❑ 92 Dick Howser 4.00 1.50
❑ 93 Jack Fisher 2.00 .75
❑ 94 Charlie Lau 4.00 1.50
❑ 95 Bill Mazeroski DP 6.00 2.50
❑ 96 Sonny Siebert 4.00 1.50
❑ 97 Pedro Gonzalez 2.00 .75
❑ 98 Bob Miller 2.00 .75
❑ 99 Gil Hodges MG 6.00 2.50
❑ 100 Ken Boyer 10.00 4.00
❑ 101 Fred Newman 2.00 .75
❑ 102 Steve Boros 2.00 .75
❑ 103 Harvey Kuenn 4.00 1.50
❑ 104 Checklist 2 10.00 4.00
❑ 105 Chico Salmon 2.00 .75
❑ 106 Gene Oliver 2.00 .75
❑ 107 P.Corrales RC/C.Shockley RC 4.00 1.50
❑ 108 Don Mincher 2.00 .75
❑ 109 Walt Bond 2.00 .75
❑ 110 Ron Santo 6.00 2.50
❑ 111 Lee Thomas 4.00 1.50
❑ 112 Derrell Griffith RC 2.00 .75
❑ 113 Steve Barber 2.00 .75
❑ 114 Jim Hickman 4.00 1.50
❑ 115 Bobby Richardson 10.00 4.00
❑ 116 D.Dowling RC/B.Tolan RC 4.00 1.50
❑ 117 Wes Stock 2.00 .75
❑ 118 Hal Lanier RC 4.00 1.50
❑ 119 John Kennedy 2.00 .75
❑ 120 Frank Robinson 40.00 15.00
❑ 121 Gene Alley 4.00 1.50
❑ 122 Bill Pleis 2.00 .75
❑ 123 Frank Thomas 4.00 1.50
❑ 124 Tom Satriano 2.00 .75
❑ 125 Juan Pizarro 2.00 .75
❑ 126 Los Angeles Dodgers TC 6.00 2.50
❑ 127 Frank Lary 2.00 .75
❑ 128 Vic Davalillo 2.00 .75
❑ 129 Bennie Daniels 2.00 .75
❑ 130 Al Kaline 40.00 15.00
❑ 131 Johnny Keane MG 2.00 .75
❑ 132 Cards Take Opener WS1 10.00 4.00
❑ 133 Mel Stottlemyre WS2 6.00 2.50
❑ 134 Mickey Mantle WS3 80.00 40.00
❑ 135 Ken Boyer WS4 10.00 4.00
❑ 136 Tim McCarver WS5 6.00 2.50
❑ 137 Jim Bouton WS6 6.00 2.50
❑ 138 Bob Gibson WS7 12.00 5.00
❑ 139 Cards Celebrate WS 6.00 2.50
❑ 140 Dean Chance 4.00 1.50
❑ 141 Charlie James 2.00 .75
❑ 142 Bill Monbouquette 2.00 .75
❑ 143 J.Gelnar RC/J.May RC 2.00 .75
❑ 144 Ed Kranepool 4.00 1.50
❑ 145 Luis Tiant RC 10.00 4.00
❑ 146 Ron Hansen 2.00 .75
❑ 147 Dennis Bennett 2.00 .75
❑ 148 Willie Kirkland 2.00 .75
❑ 149 Wayne Schurr 2.00 .75
❑ 150 Brooks Robinson 40.00 15.00
❑ 151 Kansas City Athletics TC 6.00 2.50
❑ 152 Phil Ortega 2.00 .75
❑ 153 Norm Cash 6.00 2.50
❑ 154 Bob Humphreys RC 2.00 .75
❑ 155 Roger Maris 60.00 30.00
❑ 156 Bob Sadowski 2.00 .75
❑ 157 Zoilo Versalles 4.00 1.50
❑ 158 Dick Sisler 2.00 .75
❑ 159 Jim Duffalo 2.00 .75
❑ 160 Roberto Clemente UER 200.00 100.00
❑ 161 Frank Baumann 2.00 .75
❑ 162 Russ Nixon 2.00 .75
❑ 163 Johnny Briggs 2.00 .75
❑ 164 Al Spangler 2.00 .75
❑ 165 Dick Ellsworth 2.00 .75
❑ 166 G.Culver RC/T.Agee RC 4.00 1.50
❑ 167 Bill Wakefield 2.00 .75
❑ 168 Dick Green 2.00 .75
❑ 169 Dave Vineyard RC 2.00 .75
❑ 170 Hank Aaron 150.00 75.00
❑ 171 Jim Roland 2.00 .75
❑ 172 Jimmy Piersall 6.00 2.50
❑ 173 Detroit Tigers TC 6.00 2.50
❑ 174 Joey Jay 2.00 .75
❑ 175 Bob Aspromonte 2.00 .75
❑ 176 Willie McCovey 20.00 8.00
❑ 177 Pete Mikkelsen 2.00 .75
❑ 178 Dalton Jones 2.00 .75
❑ 179 Hal Woodeshick 2.00 .75
❑ 180 Bob Allison 4.00 1.50
❑ 181 D.Loun RC/J.McCabe 2.00 .75
❑ 182 Mike de la Hoz 2.00 .75
❑ 183 Dave Nicholson 2.00 .75
❑ 184 John Boozer 2.00 .75
❑ 185 Max Alvis 2.00 .75
❑ 186 Billy Cowan 2.00 .75
❑ 187 Casey Stengel MG 15.00 6.00
❑ 188 Sam Bowens 2.00 .75
❑ 189 Checklist 3 10.00 4.00
❑ 190 Bill White 6.00 2.50
❑ 191 Phil Regan 4.00 1.50
❑ 192 Jim Coker 2.00 .75
❑ 193 Gaylord Perry 15.00 6.00
❑ 194 B.Kelso RC/R.Reichardt RC 2.00 .75
❑ 195 Bob Veale 4.00 1.50
❑ 196 Ron Fairly 4.00 1.50
❑ 197 Diego Segui 2.50 1.00
❑ 198 Smoky Burgess 4.00 1.50
❑ 199 Bob Heffner 2.50 1.00
❑ 200 Joe Torre 6.00 2.50
❑ 201 S.Valdespino RC/C.Tovar RC 4.00 1.50

❑ 202 Leo Burke 2.50 1.00
❑ 203 Dallas Green 4.00 1.50
❑ 204 Russ Snyder 2.50 1.00
❑ 205 Warren Spahn 30.00 12.50
❑ 206 Willie Horton 4.00 1.50
❑ 207 Pete Rose 200.00 100.00
❑ 208 Tommy John 6.00 2.50
❑ 209 Pittsburgh Pirates TC 6.00 2.50
❑ 210 Jim Fregosi 4.00 1.50
❑ 211 Steve Ridzik 2.50 1.00
❑ 212 Ron Brand 2.50 1.00
❑ 213 Jim Davenport 2.50 1.00
❑ 214 Bob Purkey 2.50 1.00
❑ 215 Pete Ward 2.50 1.00
❑ 216 Al Worthington 2.50 1.00
❑ 217 Walter Alston MG 6.00 2.50
❑ 218 Dick Schofield 2.50 1.00
❑ 219 Bob Meyer 2.50 1.00
❑ 220 Billy Williams 10.00 4.00
❑ 221 John Tsitouris 2.50 1.00
❑ 222 Bob Tillman 2.50 1.00
❑ 223 Dan Osinski 2.50 1.00
❑ 224 Bob Chance 2.50 1.00
❑ 225 Bo Belinsky 4.00 1.50
❑ 226 E.Jimenez RC/J.Gibbs 6.00 2.50
❑ 227 Bobby Klaus 2.50 1.00
❑ 228 Jack Sanford 2.50 1.00
❑ 229 Lou Clinton 2.50 1.00
❑ 230 Ray Sadecki 2.50 1.00
❑ 231 Jerry Adair 2.50 1.00
❑ 232 Steve Blass RC 4.00 1.50
❑ 233 Don Zimmer 4.00 1.50
❑ 234 Chicago White Sox TC 6.00 2.50
❑ 235 Chuck Hinton 2.50 1.00
❑ 236 Denny McLain RC 25.00 10.00
❑ 237 Bernie Allen 2.50 1.00
❑ 238 Joe Moeller 2.50 1.00
❑ 239 Doc Edwards 2.50 1.00
❑ 240 Bob Bruce 2.50 1.00
❑ 241 Mack Jones 2.50 1.00
❑ 242 George Brunet 2.50 1.00
❑ 243 T.Davidson RC/T.Helms RC 4.00 1.50
❑ 244 Lindy McDaniel 4.00 1.50
❑ 245 Joe Pepitone 6.00 2.50
❑ 246 Tom Butters 4.00 1.50
❑ 247 Wally Moon 4.00 1.50
❑ 248 Gus Triandos 4.00 1.50
❑ 249 Dave McNally 4.00 1.50
❑ 250 Willie Mays 150.00 75.00
❑ 251 Billy Herman MG 4.00 1.50
❑ 252 Pete Richert 2.50 1.00
❑ 253 Danny Cater 2.50 1.00
❑ 254 Roland Sheldon 2.50 1.00
❑ 255 Camilo Pascual 4.00 1.50
❑ 256 Tito Francona 2.50 1.00
❑ 257 Jim Wynn 4.00 1.50
❑ 258 Larry Bearnarth 2.50 1.00
❑ 259 J.Northrup RC/R.Oyler RC 6.00 2.50
❑ 260 Don Drysdale 20.00 8.00
❑ 261 Duke Carmel 2.50 1.00
❑ 262 Bud Daley 2.50 1.00
❑ 263 Marty Keough 2.50 1.00
❑ 264 Bob Buhl 4.00 1.50
❑ 265 Jim Pagliaroni 2.50 1.00
❑ 266 Bert Campaneris RC 10.00 4.00
❑ 267 Washington Senators TC 6.00 2.50
❑ 268 Ken McBride 2.50 1.00
❑ 269 Frank Bolling 2.50 1.00
❑ 270 Milt Pappas 4.00 1.50
❑ 271 Don Wert 4.00 1.50
❑ 272 Chuck Schilling 2.50 1.00
❑ 273 Checklist 4 10.00 4.00
❑ 274 Lum Harris MG RC 2.50 1.00
❑ 275 Dick Groat 6.00 2.50
❑ 276 Hoyt Wilhelm 10.00 4.00
❑ 277 Johnny Lewis 2.50 1.00
❑ 278 Ken Retzer 2.50 1.00
❑ 279 Dick Tracewski 2.50 1.00
❑ 280 Dick Stuart 4.00 1.50
❑ 281 Bill Stafford 2.50 1.00
❑ 282 D.Est RC/M.Murakami RC 40.00 15.00
❑ 283 Fred Whitfield 2.50 1.00
❑ 284 Nick Willhite 4.00 1.50
❑ 285 Ron Hunt 4.00 1.50
❑ 286 J.Dickson/A.Monteagudo 4.00 1.50
❑ 287 Gary Kolb 4.00 1.50
❑ 288 Jack Hamilton 4.00 1.50
❑ 289 Gordy Coleman 6.00 2.50
❑ 290 Wally Bunker 6.00 2.50
❑ 291 Jerry Lynch 4.00 1.50
❑ 292 Larry Yellen 4.00 1.50
❑ 293 Los Angeles Angels TC 6.00 2.50
❑ 294 Tim McCarver 10.00 4.00
❑ 295 Dick Radatz 6.00 2.50
❑ 296 Tony Taylor 6.00 2.50
❑ 297 Dave DeBusschere 10.00 4.00
❑ 298 Jim Stewart 4.00 1.50
❑ 299 Jerry Zimmerman 4.00 1.50
❑ 300 Sandy Koufax 100.00 50.00
❑ 301 Birdie Tebbetts MG 6.00 2.50
❑ 302 Al Stanek 4.00 1.50
❑ 303 John Orsino 4.00 1.50
❑ 304 Dave Stenhouse 4.00 1.50
❑ 305 Rico Carty 6.00 2.50
❑ 306 Bubba Phillips 4.00 1.50
❑ 307 Barry Latman 4.00 1.50
❑ 308 C.Jones RC/T.Parsons 6.00 2.50
❑ 309 Steve Hamilton 6.00 2.50
❑ 310 Johnny Callison 6.00 2.50
❑ 311 Orlando Pena 4.00 1.50
❑ 312 Joe Nuxhall 4.00 1.50
❑ 313 Jim Schaffer 4.00 1.50
❑ 314 Sterling Slaughter 4.00 1.50
❑ 315 Frank Malzone 6.00 2.50
❑ 316 Cincinnati Reds TC 6.00 2.50
❑ 317 Don McMahon 4.00 1.50
❑ 318 Matty Alou 6.00 2.50
❑ 319 Ken McMullen 4.00 1.50
❑ 320 Bob Gibson 50.00 20.00
❑ 321 Rusty Staub 10.00 4.00
❑ 322 Rick Wise 6.00 2.50
❑ 323 Hank Bauer MG 6.00 2.50
❑ 324 Bobby Locke 4.00 1.50
❑ 325 Donn Clendenon 6.00 2.50
❑ 326 Dwight Siebler 4.00 1.50
❑ 327 Denis Menke 4.00 1.50
❑ 328 Eddie Fisher 4.00 1.50
❑ 329 Hawk Taylor RC 4.00 1.50
❑ 330 Whitey Ford 40.00 15.00
❑ 331 A.Ferrara/J.Purdin RC 6.00 2.50
❑ 332 Ted Abernathy 4.00 1.50
❑ 333 Tom Reynolds 4.00 1.50
❑ 334 Vic Roznovsky RC 4.00 1.50
❑ 335 Mickey Lolich 6.00 2.50
❑ 336 Woody Held 4.00 1.50
❑ 337 Mike Cuellar 6.00 2.50
❑ 338 Philadelphia Phillies TC 6.00 2.50
❑ 339 Ryne Duren 6.00 2.50
❑ 340 Tony Oliva 20.00 8.00
❑ 341 Bob Bolin 4.00 1.50
❑ 342 Bob Rodgers 6.00 2.50
❑ 343 Mike McCormick 6.00 2.50
❑ 344 Wes Parker 6.00 2.50
❑ 345 Floyd Robinson 4.00 1.50
❑ 346 Bobby Bragan MG 4.00 1.50
❑ 347 Roy Face 6.00 2.50
❑ 348 George Banks 4.00 1.50
❑ 349 Larry Miller RC 4.00 1.50
❑ 350 Mickey Mantle 600.00 300.00
❑ 351 Jim Perry 6.00 2.50
❑ 352 Alex Johnson RC 6.00 2.50
❑ 353 Jerry Lumpe 4.00 1.50
❑ 354 B.Ott RC/J.Warner RC 4.00 1.50
❑ 355 Vada Pinson 10.00 4.00
❑ 356 Bill Spanswick 4.00 1.50
❑ 357 Carl Warwick 4.00 1.50
❑ 358 Albie Pearson 6.00 2.50
❑ 359 Ken Johnson 4.00 1.50
❑ 360 Orlando Cepeda 15.00 6.00
❑ 361 Checklist 5 12.00 5.00
❑ 362 Don Schwall 4.00 1.50
❑ 363 Bob Johnson 4.00 1.50
❑ 364 Galen Cisco 4.00 1.50
❑ 365 Jim Gentile 6.00 2.50
❑ 366 Dan Schneider 4.00 1.50
❑ 367 Leon Wagner 4.00 1.50
❑ 368 K.Berry RC/J.Gibson RC 6.00 2.50
❑ 369 Phil Linz 6.00 2.50
❑ 370 Tommy Davis 6.00 2.50
❑ 371 Frank Kreutzer 8.00 3.00
❑ 372 Clay Dalrymple 8.00 3.00
❑ 373 Curt Simmons 8.00 3.00
❑ 374 J.Cardenal RC/D.Simpson 8.00 3.00
❑ 375 Dave Wickersham 8.00 3.00
❑ 376 Jim Landis 8.00 3.00
❑ 377 Willie Stargell 25.00 10.00
❑ 378 Chuck Estrada 8.00 3.00
❑ 379 San Francisco Giants TC 8.00 3.00
❑ 380 Rocky Colavito 25.00 10.00
❑ 381 Al Jackson 8.00 3.00
❑ 382 J.C. Martin 8.00 3.00
❑ 383 Felipe Alou 15.00 6.00
❑ 384 Johnny Klippstein 8.00 3.00
❑ 385 Carl Yastrzemski 60.00 30.00
❑ 386 P.Jaeckel RC/F.Norman 8.00 3.00
❑ 387 Johnny Podres 15.00 6.00
❑ 388 John Blanchard 15.00 6.00
❑ 389 Don Larsen 15.00 6.00
❑ 390 Bill Freehan 15.00 6.00
❑ 391 Mel McGaha MG 8.00 3.00
❑ 392 Bob Friend 15.00 6.00
❑ 393 Ed Kirkpatrick 8.00 3.00
❑ 394 Jim Hannan 8.00 3.00
❑ 395 Jim Ray Hart 8.00 3.00
❑ 396 Frank Bertaina RC 8.00 3.00
❑ 397 Jerry Buchek 8.00 3.00
❑ 398 D.Neville RC/A.Shamsky RC 15.00 6.00
❑ 399 Ray Herbert 8.00 3.00
❑ 400 Harmon Killebrew 50.00 20.00
❑ 401 Carl Willey 8.00 3.00
❑ 402 Joe Amalfitano 8.00 3.00
❑ 403 Boston Red Sox TC 8.00 3.00
❑ 404 Stan Williams 8.00 3.00
❑ 405 John Roseboro 20.00 8.00
❑ 406 Ralph Terry 15.00 6.00
❑ 407 Lee Maye 8.00 3.00
❑ 408 Larry Sherry 8.00 3.00
❑ 409 J.Beauchamp RC/L.Dierker RC 15.00 6.00
❑ 410 Luis Aparicio 25.00 10.00
❑ 411 Roger Craig 15.00 6.00
❑ 412 Bob Bailey 8.00 3.00
❑ 413 Hal Reniff 8.00 3.00
❑ 414 Al Lopez MG 15.00 6.00
❑ 415 Curt Flood 15.00 6.00
❑ 416 Jim Brewer 8.00 3.00
❑ 417 Ed Brinkman 8.00 3.00
❑ 418 Johnny Edwards 8.00 3.00
❑ 419 Ruben Amaro 8.00 3.00
❑ 420 Larry Jackson 8.00 3.00
❑ 421 G.Dotter RC/J.Ward 8.00 3.00
❑ 422 Aubrey Gatewood 8.00 3.00
❑ 423 Jesse Gonder 8.00 3.00
❑ 424 Gary Bell 8.00 3.00
❑ 425 Wayne Causey 8.00 3.00
❑ 426 Milwaukee Braves TC 8.00 3.00
❑ 427 Bob Saverine 8.00 3.00
❑ 428 Bob Shaw 8.00 3.00
❑ 429 Don Demeter 8.00 3.00
❑ 430 Gary Peters 8.00 3.00
❑ 431 N.Briles RC/W.Spiezio RC 15.00 6.00
❑ 432 Jim Grant 15.00 6.00
❑ 433 John Bateman 8.00 3.00
❑ 434 Dave Morehead 8.00 3.00
❑ 435 Willie Davis 15.00 6.00
❑ 436 Don Elston 8.00 3.00
❑ 437 Chico Cardenas 15.00 6.00
❑ 438 Harry Walker MG 8.00 3.00
❑ 439 Moe Drabowsky 15.00 6.00
❑ 440 Tom Tresh 15.00 6.00
❑ 441 Denny Lemaster 8.00 3.00
❑ 442 Vic Power 8.00 3.00
❑ 443 Checklist 6 12.00 5.00
❑ 444 Bob Hendley 8.00 3.00
❑ 445 Don Lock 8.00 3.00
❑ 446 Art Mahaffey 8.00 3.00
❑ 447 Julian Javier 15.00 6.00
❑ 448 Lee Stange 8.00 3.00
❑ 449 J.Hinsley/G.Kroll RC 15.00 6.00
❑ 450 Elston Howard 15.00 6.00
❑ 451 Jim Owens 8.00 3.00
❑ 452 Gary Geiger 8.00 3.00
❑ 453 W.Crawford RC/J.Werhas 15.00 6.00
❑ 454 Ed Rakow 8.00 3.00
❑ 455 Norm Siebern 8.00 3.00
❑ 456 Bill Henry 8.00 3.00
❑ 457 Bob Kennedy MG 15.00 6.00
❑ 458 John Buzhardt 8.00 3.00
❑ 459 Frank Kostro 8.00 3.00

	Card	NRMT	VG-E
❑	460 Richie Allen	40.00	15.00
❑	461 C.Carroll RC/P.Niekro	50.00	20.00
❑	462 Lew Krausse UER	8.00	3.00
❑	463 Manny Mota	15.00	6.00
❑	464 Ron Piche	8.00	3.00
❑	465 Tom Haller	15.00	6.00
❑	466 P.Craig RC/D.Nen	8.00	3.00
❑	467 Ray Washburn	8.00	3.00
❑	468 Larry Brown	8.00	3.00
❑	469 Don Nottebart	8.00	3.00
❑	470 Yogi Berra P/CO	50.00	20.00
❑	471 Billy Hoeft	8.00	3.00
❑	472 Don Pavletich	8.00	3.00
❑	473 P.Blair RC/D.Johnson RC	15.00	6.00
❑	474 Cookie Rojas	15.00	6.00
❑	475 Clete Boyer	15.00	6.00
❑	476 Billy O'Dell	8.00	3.00
❑	477 Steve Carlton RC	200.00	100.00
❑	478 Wilbur Wood	15.00	6.00
❑	479 Ken Harrelson	15.00	6.00
❑	480 Joel Horlen	8.00	3.00
❑	481 Cleveland Indians TC	10.00	4.00
❑	482 Bob Priddy	8.00	3.00
❑	483 George Smith RC	8.00	3.00
❑	484 Ron Perranoski	20.00	8.00
❑	485 Nellie Fox	25.00	10.00
❑	486 T.Egan/P.Rogan RC	8.00	3.00
❑	487 Woody Woodward	15.00	6.00
❑	488 Ted Wills	8.00	3.00
❑	489 Gene Mauch MG	15.00	6.00
❑	490 Earl Battey	8.00	3.00
❑	491 Tracy Stallard	8.00	3.00
❑	492 Gene Freese	8.00	3.00
❑	493 B.Roman RC/B.Brubaker RC	8.00	3.00
❑	494 Jay Ritchie RC	8.00	3.00
❑	495 Joe Christopher	8.00	3.00
❑	496 Joe Cunningham	8.00	3.00
❑	497 K.Henderson RC/J.Hiatt RC	15.00	6.00
❑	498 Gene Stephens	8.00	3.00
❑	499 Stu Miller	15.00	6.00
❑	500 Eddie Mathews	40.00	15.00
❑	501 R.Gagliano RC/J.Rittwage RC	8.00	3.00
❑	502 Don Cardwell	8.00	3.00
❑	503 Phil Gagliano	8.00	3.00
❑	504 Jerry Grote	15.00	6.00
❑	505 Ray Culp	8.00	3.00
❑	506 Sam Mele MG	8.00	3.00
❑	507 Sammy Ellis	8.00	3.00
❑	508 Checklist 7	12.00	5.00
❑	509 B.Guindon RC/G.Vezendy RC	8.00	3.00
❑	510 Ernie Banks	80.00	40.00
❑	511 Ron Locke	8.00	3.00
❑	512 Cap Peterson	8.00	3.00
❑	513 New York Yankees TC	40.00	15.00
❑	514 Joe Azcue	8.00	3.00
❑	515 Vern Law	15.00	6.00
❑	516 Al Weis	8.00	3.00
❑	517 P.Schaal RC/J.Warner	15.00	6.00
❑	518 Ken Rowe	8.00	3.00
❑	519 Bob Uecker UER	30.00	12.50
❑	520 Tony Cloninger	8.00	3.00
❑	521 D.Bennett/M.Stevens RC	8.00	3.00
❑	522 Hank Aguirre	8.00	3.00
❑	523 Mike Brumley SP	12.00	5.00
❑	524 Dave Giusti SP	12.00	5.00
❑	525 Eddie Bressoud	8.00	3.00
❑	526 J.Odom/J.Hunter SP RC	80.00	40.00
❑	527 Jeff Torborg SP	12.00	5.00
❑	528 George Altman	8.00	3.00
❑	529 Jerry Fosnow SP RC	12.00	5.00
❑	530 Jim Maloney	15.00	6.00
❑	531 Chuck Hiller	8.00	3.00
❑	532 Hector Lopez	15.00	6.00
❑	533 R.Swob/T.McGraw SP RC	25.00	10.00
❑	534 John Herrnstein	8.00	3.00
❑	535 Jack Kralick SP	12.00	5.00
❑	536 Andre Rodgers SP	12.00	5.00
❑	537 Lopez/Roof/May RC	8.00	3.00
❑	538 Chuck Dressen MG SP	12.00	5.00
❑	539 Herm Starrette	8.00	3.00
❑	540 Lou Brock SP	50.00	20.00
❑	541 G.Bollo RC/B.Locker RC	8.00	3.00
❑	542 Lou Klimchock	8.00	3.00
❑	543 Ed Connolly SP RC	12.00	5.00
❑	544 Howie Reed RC	8.00	3.00
❑	545 Jesus Alou SP	15.00	6.00
❑	546 Davis/Hed/Bark/Weav RC	8.00	3.00
❑	547 Jake Wood SP	12.00	5.00
❑	548 Dick Stigman	8.00	3.00
❑	549 R.Pena RC/G.Beckert RC	20.00	8.00
❑	550 Mel Stottlemyre SP RC	30.00	12.50
❑	551 New York Mets TC SP	30.00	12.50
❑	552 Julio Gotay	8.00	3.00
❑	553 Coombs/Ratliff/McClure RC	8.00	3.00
❑	554 Chico Ruiz SP	12.00	5.00
❑	555 Jack Baldschun SP	12.00	5.00
❑	556 R.Schoendienst SP	25.00	10.00
❑	557 Jose Santiago RC	8.00	3.00
❑	558 Tommie Sisk	8.00	3.00
❑	559 Ed Bailey SP	12.00	5.00
❑	560 Boog Powell SP	25.00	10.00
❑	561 Dab/Kek/Valle/Lefebvre RC	15.00	6.00
❑	562 Billy Moran	8.00	3.00
❑	563 Julio Navarro	8.00	3.00
❑	564 Mel Nelson	8.00	3.00
❑	565 Ernie Broglio SP	12.00	5.00
❑	566 Blanco/Moschitto/Lopez RC	12.00	5.00
❑	567 Tommie Aaron	8.00	3.00
❑	568 Ron Taylor SP	12.00	5.00
❑	569 Gino Cimoli SP	12.00	5.00
❑	570 Claude Osteen SP	15.00	6.00
❑	571 Ossie Virgil SP	12.00	5.00
❑	572 Baltimore Orioles TC SP	25.00	10.00
❑	573 Jim Lonborg SP RC	25.00	10.00
❑	574 Roy Sievers	15.00	6.00
❑	575 Jose Pagan	8.00	3.00
❑	576 Terry Fox SP	12.00	5.00
❑	577 Knowles/Busch/Schein RC	12.00	5.00
❑	578 Camilo Carreon SP	12.00	5.00
❑	579 Dick Smith SP	12.00	5.00
❑	580 Jimmie Hall SP	12.00	5.00
❑	581 Tony Perez SP RC	80.00	40.00
❑	582 Bob Schmidt SP	12.00	5.00
❑	583 Wes Covington SP	12.00	5.00
❑	584 Harry Bright	15.00	6.00
❑	585 Hank Fischer	8.00	3.00
❑	586 Tom McCraw SP	12.00	5.00
❑	587 Joe Sparma	8.00	3.00
❑	588 Lenny Green	8.00	3.00
❑	589 F.Linzy RC/B.Schroder RC	12.00	5.00
❑	590 John Wyatt	8.00	3.00
❑	591 Bob Skinner SP	12.00	5.00
❑	592 Frank Bork SP RC	12.00	5.00
❑	593 J.Sullivan RC/J.Moore RC SP	12.00	5.00
❑	594 Joe Gaines	8.00	3.00
❑	595 Don Lee	8.00	3.00
❑	596 Don Landrum SP	12.00	5.00
❑	597 Nossek/Sevcik/Reese RC	8.00	3.00
❑	598 Al Downing SP	25.00	10.00

1966 Topps

	Card	NRMT	VG-E
❑	COMPLETE SET (598)	4000.00	2500.00
❑	COMMON CARD (1-109)	1.50	.60
❑	COMMON CARD (110-283)	2.00	.75
❑	COMMON CARD (284-370)	3.00	1.25
❑	COMMON CARD (371-446)	5.00	2.00
❑	COMMON CARD (447-522)	10.00	4.00
❑	COMMON CARD (523-598)	15.00	6.00
❑	COMMON SP (523-598)	30.00	12.50
❑	WRAPPER (5-CENT)	25.00	10.00
❑	1 Willie Mays	250.00	125.00
❑	2 Ted Abernathy	1.50	.60
❑	3 Sam Mele MG	1.50	.60
❑	4 Ray Culp	1.50	.60
❑	5 Jim Fregosi	2.00	.75
❑	6 Chuck Schilling	1.50	.60
❑	7 Tracy Stallard	1.50	.60
❑	8 Floyd Robinson	1.50	.60
❑	9 Clete Boyer	2.00	.75
❑	10 Tony Cloninger	1.50	.60
❑	11 B.Alyea RC/P.Craig	1.50	.60
❑	12 John Tsitouris	1.50	.60
❑	13 Lou Johnson	2.00	.75
❑	14 Norm Siebern	1.50	.60
❑	15 Vern Law	2.00	.75
❑	16 Larry Brown	1.50	.60
❑	17 John Stephenson	1.50	.60
❑	18 Roland Sheldon	1.50	.60
❑	19 San Francisco Giants TC	5.00	2.00
❑	20 Willie Horton	2.00	.75
❑	21 Don Nottebart	1.50	.60
❑	22 Joe Nossek	1.50	.60
❑	23 Jack Sanford	1.50	.60
❑	24 Don Kessinger RC	4.00	1.50
❑	25 Pete Ward	1.50	.60
❑	26 Ray Sadecki	1.50	.60
❑	27 D.Knowles/A.Etchebarren RC	1.50	.60
❑	28 Phil Niekro	20.00	8.00
❑	29 Mike Brumley	1.50	.60
❑	30 Pete Rose UER DP	100.00	50.00
❑	31 Jack Cullen	2.00	.75
❑	32 Adolfo Phillips RC	1.50	.60
❑	33 Jim Pagliaroni	1.50	.60
❑	34 Checklist 1	8.00	3.00
❑	35 Ron Swoboda	4.00	1.50
❑	36 Jim Hunter UER DP	20.00	8.00
❑	37 Billy Herman MG	2.00	.75
❑	38 Ron Nischwitz	1.50	.60
❑	39 Ken Henderson	1.50	.60
❑	40 Jim Grant	1.50	.60
❑	41 Don LeJohn RC	1.50	.60
❑	42 Aubrey Gatewood	1.50	.60
❑	43A D.Landrum Dark Button	2.00	.75
❑	43B D.Landrum Airbrush Button	20.00	8.00
❑	43C D.Landrum No Button	2.00	.75
❑	44 B.Davis/T.Kelley	1.50	.60
❑	45 Jim Gentile	2.00	.75
❑	46 Howie Koplitz	1.50	.60
❑	47 J.C. Martin	1.50	.60
❑	48 Paul Blair	2.00	.75
❑	49 Woody Woodward	2.00	.75
❑	50 Mickey Mantle DP	350.00	175.00
❑	51 Gordon Richardson RC	1.50	.60
❑	52 W.Covington/J.Callison	4.00	1.50
❑	53 Bob Duliba	1.50	.60
❑	54 Jose Pagan	1.50	.60
❑	55 Ken Harrelson	2.00	.75
❑	56 Sandy Valdespino	1.50	.60
❑	57 Jim Lefebvre	2.00	.75
❑	58 Dave Wickersham	1.50	.60
❑	59 Cincinnati Reds TC	5.00	2.00
❑	60 Curt Flood	4.00	1.50
❑	61 Bob Bolin	1.50	.60
❑	62A Merritt Ranew Sold Line	2.00	.75
❑	62B Merritt Ranew NTR	30.00	12.50
❑	63 Jim Stewart	1.50	.60
❑	64 Bob Bruce	1.50	.60
❑	65 Leon Wagner	1.50	.60
❑	66 Al Weis	1.50	.60
❑	67 C.Jones/D.Selma RC	4.00	1.50
❑	68 Hal Reniff	1.50	.60
❑	69 Ken Hamlin	1.50	.60
❑	70 Carl Yastrzemski	30.00	12.50
❑	71 Frank Carpin RC	1.50	.60
❑	72 Tony Perez	25.00	10.00
❑	73 Jerry Zimmerman	1.50	.60
❑	74 Don Mossi	2.00	.75
❑	75 Tommy Davis	2.00	.75
❑	76 Red Schoendienst MG	4.00	1.50
❑	77 John Orsino	1.50	.60
❑	78 Frank Linzy	1.50	.60
❑	79 Joe Pepitone	4.00	1.50
❑	80 Richie Allen	6.00	2.50
❑	81 Ray Oyler	1.50	.60
❑	82 Bob Hendley	1.50	.60
❑	83 Albie Pearson	2.00	.75
❑	84 J.Beauchamp/D.Kelley	1.50	.60
❑	85 Eddie Fisher	1.50	.60
❑	86 John Bateman	1.50	.60
❑	87 Dan Napoleon	1.50	.60

❑ 88 Fred Whitfield 1.50 .60
❑ 89 Ted Davidson 1.50 .60
❑ 90 Luis Aparicio DP 8.00 3.00
❑ 91A Bob Uecker TR 10.00 4.00
❑ 91B Bob Uecker NTR 40.00 15.00
❑ 92 New York Yankees TC 15.00 6.00
❑ 93 Jim Lonborg DP 2.00 .75
❑ 94 Matty Alou 2.00 .75
❑ 95 Pete Richert 1.50 .60
❑ 96 Felipe Alou 4.00 1.50
❑ 97 Jim Merritt RC 1.50 .60
❑ 98 Don Demeter 1.50 .60
❑ 99 W.Stargell/D.Clendenon 6.00 2.50
❑ 100 Sandy Koufax DP 100.00 50.00
❑ 101A Checklist 2 Spahn ERR 15.00 6.00
❑ 101B Cheklist 2 Henry COR 10.00 4.00
❑ 102 Ed Kirkpatrick 1.50 .60
❑ 103A Dick Groat TR 2.00 .75
❑ 103B Dick Groat NTR 40.00 15.00
❑ 104A Alex Johnson TR 2.00 .75
❑ 104B Alex Johnson NTR 30.00 12.50
❑ 105 Milt Pappas 2.00 .75
❑ 106 Rusty Staub 4.00 1.50
❑ 107 L.Stahl RC/R.Tompkins RC 1.50 .60
❑ 108 Bobby Klaus 1.50 .60
❑ 109 Ralph Terry 2.00 .75
❑ 110 Ernie Banks 30.00 12.50
❑ 111 Gary Peters 2.00 .75
❑ 112 Manny Mota 4.00 1.50
❑ 113 Hank Aguirre 2.00 .75
❑ 114 Jim Gosger 2.00 .75
❑ 115 Bill Henry 2.00 .75
❑ 116 Walter Alston MG 6.00 2.50
❑ 117 Jake Gibbs 2.00 .75
❑ 118 Mike McCormick 2.00 .75
❑ 119 Art Shamsky 2.00 .75
❑ 120 Harmon Killebrew 15.00 6.00
❑ 121 Ray Herbert 2.00 .75
❑ 122 Joe Gaines 2.00 .75
❑ 123 F.Bork/J.May 2.00 .75
❑ 124 Tug McGraw 4.00 1.50
❑ 125 Lou Brock 20.00 8.00
❑ 126 Jim Palmer UER RC 100.00 50.00
❑ 127 Ken Berry 2.00 .75
❑ 128 Jim Landis 2.00 .75
❑ 129 Jack Kralick 2.00 .75
❑ 130 Joe Torre 6.00 2.50
❑ 131 California Angels TC 5.00 2.00
❑ 132 Orlando Cepeda 8.00 3.00
❑ 133 Don McMahon 2.00 .75
❑ 134 Wes Parker 4.00 1.50
❑ 135 Dave Morehead 2.00 .75
❑ 136 Woody Held 2.00 .75
❑ 137 Pat Corrales 2.00 .75
❑ 138 Roger Repoz RC 2.00 .75
❑ 139 B.Browne RC/D.Young RC 2.00 .75
❑ 140 Jim Maloney 4.00 1.50
❑ 141 Tom McCraw 2.00 .75
❑ 142 Don Dennis RC 2.00 .75
❑ 143 Jose Tartabull 4.00 1.50
❑ 144 Don Schwall 2.00 .75
❑ 145 Bill Freehan 4.00 1.50
❑ 146 George Altman 2.00 .75
❑ 147 Lum Harris MG 2.00 .75
❑ 148 Bob Johnson 2.00 .75
❑ 149 Dick Nen 2.00 .75
❑ 150 Rocky Colavito 8.00 3.00
❑ 151 Gary Wagner RC 2.00 .75
❑ 152 Frank Malzone 4.00 1.50
❑ 153 Rico Carty 4.00 1.50
❑ 154 Chuck Hiller 2.00 .75
❑ 155 Marcelino Lopez 2.00 .75
❑ 156 D.Schofield/H.Lanier 2.00 .75
❑ 157 Rene Lachemann 2.00 .75
❑ 158 Jim Brewer 2.00 .75
❑ 159 Chico Ruiz 2.00 .75
❑ 160 Whitey Ford 30.00 12.50
❑ 161 Jerry Lumpe 2.00 .75
❑ 162 Lee Maye 2.00 .75
❑ 163 Tito Francona 2.00 .75
❑ 164 T.Agee/M.Staehle 4.00 1.50
❑ 165 Don Lock 2.00 .75
❑ 166 Chris Krug RC 2.00 .75
❑ 167 Boog Powell 6.00 2.50
❑ 168 Dan Osinski 2.00 .75
❑ 169 Duke Sims RC 2.00 .75
❑ 170 Cookie Rojas 4.00 1.50
❑ 171 Nick Willhite 2.00 .75
❑ 172 New York Mets TC 5.00 2.00
❑ 173 Al Spangler 2.00 .75
❑ 174 Ron Taylor 2.00 .75
❑ 175 Bert Campaneris 4.00 1.50
❑ 176 Jim Davenport 2.00 .75
❑ 177 Hector Lopez 2.00 .75
❑ 178 Bob Tillman 2.00 .75
❑ 179 D.Aust RC/B.Tolan 4.00 1.50
❑ 180 Vada Pinson 4.00 1.50
❑ 181 Al Worthington 2.00 .75
❑ 182 Jerry Lynch 2.00 .75
❑ 183A Checklist 3 Large Print 8.00 3.00
❑ 183B Checklist 3 Small Print 8.00 3.00
❑ 184 Denis Menke 2.00 .75
❑ 185 Bob Buhl 4.00 1.50
❑ 186 Ruben Amaro 2.00 .75
❑ 187 Chuck Dressen MG 4.00 1.50
❑ 188 Al Luplow 2.00 .75
❑ 189 John Roseboro 4.00 1.50
❑ 190 Jimmie Hall 2.00 .75
❑ 191 Darrell Sutherland RC 2.00 .75
❑ 192 Vic Power 4.00 1.50
❑ 193 Dave McNally 4.00 1.50
❑ 194 Washington Senators TC 5.00 2.00
❑ 195 Joe Morgan 15.00 6.00
❑ 196 Don Pavletich 2.00 .75
❑ 197 Sonny Siebert 2.00 .75
❑ 198 Mickey Stanley RC 6.00 2.50
❑ 199 Skowron/Romano/Robinson 4.00 1.50
❑ 200 Eddie Mathews 15.00 6.00
❑ 201 Jim Dickson 2.00 .75
❑ 202 Clay Dalrymple 2.00 .75
❑ 203 Jose Santiago 2.00 .75
❑ 204 Chicago Cubs TC 5.00 2.00
❑ 205 Tom Tresh 4.00 1.50
❑ 206 Al Jackson 2.00 .75
❑ 207 Frank Quilici RC 2.00 .75
❑ 208 Bob Miller 2.00 .75
❑ 209 F.Fisher/J.Hiller RC 4.00 1.50
❑ 210 Bill Mazeroski 8.00 3.00
❑ 211 Frank Kreutzer 2.00 .75
❑ 212 Ed Kranepool 4.00 1.50
❑ 213 Fred Newman 2.00 .75
❑ 214 Tommy Harper 4.00 1.50
❑ 215 Clemente/Aaron/Mays LL 50.00 20.00
❑ 216 Oliva/Yaz/Davalillo LL 5.00 2.00
❑ 217 Mays/McCovey/B.Will LL 20.00 8.00
❑ 218 Conigliaro/Cash/Horton LL 5.00 2.00
❑ 219 Johnson/F.Rob/Mays LL 12.00 5.00
❑ 220 Colavito/Horton/Oliva LL 5.00 2.00
❑ 221 Koufax/Marichal/Law LL 12.00 5.00
❑ 222 McDowell/Fisher/Siebert LL 5.00 2.00
❑ 223 Koufax/Clon/Drysdale LL 12.00 5.00
❑ 224 Grant/Stottlemyre/Kaat LL 5.00 2.00
❑ 225 Koufax/Veale/Gibson LL 12.00 5.00
❑ 226 McDowell/Lolich/McLain LL 5.00 2.00
❑ 227 Russ Nixon 2.00 .75
❑ 228 Larry Dierker 4.00 1.50
❑ 229 Hank Bauer MG 4.00 1.50
❑ 230 Johnny Callison 4.00 1.50
❑ 231 Floyd Weaver 2.00 .75
❑ 232 Glenn Beckert 4.00 1.50
❑ 233 Dom Zanni 2.00 .75
❑ 234 R.Beck RC/R.White RC 8.00 3.00
❑ 235 Don Cardwell 2.00 .75
❑ 236 Mike Hershberger 2.00 .75
❑ 237 Billy O'Dell 2.00 .75
❑ 238 Los Angeles Dodgers TC 5.00 2.00
❑ 239 Orlando Pena 2.00 .75
❑ 240 Earl Battey 2.00 .75
❑ 241 Dennis Ribant 2.00 .75
❑ 242 Jesus Alou 2.00 .75
❑ 243 Nelson Briles 4.00 1.50
❑ 244 C.Harrison RC//S.Jackson 2.00 .75
❑ 245 John Buzhardt 2.00 .75
❑ 246 Ed Bailey 2.00 .75
❑ 247 Carl Warwick 2.00 .75
❑ 248 Pete Mikkelsen 2.00 .75
❑ 249 Bill Rigney MG 2.00 .75
❑ 250 Sammy Ellis 2.00 .75
❑ 251 Ed Brinkman 2.00 .75
❑ 252 Denny Lemaster 2.00 .75
❑ 253 Don Wert 2.00 .75
❑ 254 Fergie Jenkins RC 60.00 30.00
❑ 255 Willie Stargell 20.00 8.00
❑ 256 Lew Krausse 2.00 .75
❑ 257 Jeff Torborg 4.00 1.50
❑ 258 Dave Giusti 2.00 .75
❑ 259 Boston Red Sox TC 5.00 2.00
❑ 260 Bob Shaw 2.00 .75
❑ 261 Ron Hansen 2.00 .75
❑ 262 Jack Hamilton 2.00 .75
❑ 263 Tom Egan 2.00 .75
❑ 264 A.Kosco RC/T.Uhlaender RC 2.00 .75
❑ 265 Stu Miller 4.00 1.50
❑ 266 Pedro Gonzalez UER 2.00 .75
❑ 267 Joe Sparma 2.00 .75
❑ 268 John Blanchard 2.00 .75
❑ 269 Don Heffner MG 2.00 .75
❑ 270 Claude Osteen 4.00 1.50
❑ 271 Hal Lanier 2.00 .75
❑ 272 Jack Baldschun 2.00 .75
❑ 273 B.Aspromonte/R.Staub 4.00 1.50
❑ 274 Buster Narum 2.00 .75
❑ 275 Tim McCarver 4.00 1.50
❑ 276 Jim Bouton 4.00 1.50
❑ 277 George Thomas 2.00 .75
❑ 278 Cal Koonce 2.00 .75
❑ 279A Checklist 4 Black Cap 8.00 3.00
❑ 279B Checklist 4 Red Cap 8.00 3.00
❑ 280 Bobby Knoop 2.00 .75
❑ 281 Bruce Howard 2.00 .75
❑ 282 Johnny Lewis 2.00 .75
❑ 283 Jim Perry 4.00 1.50
❑ 284 Bobby Wine 3.00 1.25
❑ 285 Luis Tiant 5.00 2.00
❑ 286 Gary Geiger 3.00 1.25
❑ 287 Jack Aker RC 3.00 1.25
❑ 288 D.Sutton RC/B.Singer RC 60.00 30.00
❑ 289 Larry Sherry 3.00 1.25
❑ 290 Ron Santo 5.00 2.00
❑ 291 Moe Drabowsky 5.00 2.00
❑ 292 Jim Coker 3.00 1.25
❑ 293 Mike Shannon 5.00 2.00
❑ 294 Steve Ridzik 3.00 1.25
❑ 295 Jim Ray Hart 5.00 2.00
❑ 296 Johnny Keane MG 5.00 2.00
❑ 297 Jim Owens 3.00 1.25
❑ 298 Rico Petrocelli 5.00 2.00
❑ 299 Lou Burdette 5.00 2.00
❑ 300 Roberto Clemente 150.00 75.00
❑ 301 Greg Bollo 3.00 1.25
❑ 302 Ernie Bowman 3.00 1.25
❑ 303 Cleveland Indians TC 5.00 2.00
❑ 304 John Herrnstein 3.00 1.25
❑ 305 Camilo Pascual 5.00 2.00
❑ 306 Ty Cline 3.00 1.25
❑ 307 Clay Carroll 5.00 2.00
❑ 308 Tom Haller 5.00 2.00
❑ 309 Diego Segui 3.00 1.25
❑ 310 Frank Robinson 40.00 15.00
❑ 311 T.Helms/D.Simpson 5.00 2.00
❑ 312 Bob Saverine 3.00 1.25
❑ 313 Chris Zachary 3.00 1.25
❑ 314 Hector Valle 3.00 1.25
❑ 315 Norm Cash 5.00 2.00
❑ 316 Jack Fisher 3.00 1.25
❑ 317 Dalton Jones 3.00 1.25
❑ 318 Harry Walker MG 3.00 1.25
❑ 319 Gene Freese 3.00 1.25
❑ 320 Bob Gibson 25.00 10.00
❑ 321 Rick Reichardt 3.00 1.25
❑ 322 Bill Faul 3.00 1.25
❑ 323 Ray Barker 3.00 1.25
❑ 324 John Boozer 3.00 1.25
❑ 325 Vic Davalillo 3.00 1.25
❑ 326 Atlanta Braves TC 5.00 2.00
❑ 327 Bernie Allen 3.00 1.25
❑ 328 Jerry Grote 5.00 2.00
❑ 329 Pete Charton 3.00 1.25
❑ 330 Ron Fairly 5.00 2.00
❑ 331 Ron Herbel 3.00 1.25
❑ 332 Bill Bryan 3.00 1.25
❑ 333 J.Coleman RC/J.French RC 3.00 1.25
❑ 334 Marty Keough 3.00 1.25
❑ 335 Juan Pizarro 3.00 1.25
❑ 336 Gene Alley 5.00 2.00
❑ 337 Fred Gladding 3.00 1.25
❑ 338 Dal Maxvill 3.00 1.25
❑ 339 Del Crandall 5.00 2.00

❑ 340 Dean Chance 5.00 2.00
❑ 341 Wes Westrum MG 5.00 2.00
❑ 342 Bob Humphreys 3.00 1.25
❑ 343 Joe Christopher 3.00 1.25
❑ 344 Steve Blass 5.00 2.00
❑ 345 Bob Allison 5.00 2.00
❑ 346 Mike de la Hoz 3.00 1.25
❑ 347 Phil Regan 5.00 2.00
❑ 348 Baltimore Orioles TC 8.00 3.00
❑ 349 Cap Peterson 3.00 1.25
❑ 350 Mel Stottlemyre 8.00 3.00
❑ 351 Fred Valentine 3.00 1.25
❑ 352 Bob Aspromonte 3.00 1.25
❑ 353 Al McBean 3.00 1.25
❑ 354 Smoky Burgess 5.00 2.00
❑ 355 Wade Blasingame 3.00 1.25
❑ 356 O.Johnson RC/K.Sanders RC 3.00 1.25
❑ 357 Gerry Arrigo 3.00 1.25
❑ 358 Charlie Smith 3.00 1.25
❑ 359 Johnny Briggs 3.00 1.25
❑ 360 Ron Hunt 3.00 1.25
❑ 361 Tom Satriano 3.00 1.25
❑ 362 Gates Brown 5.00 2.00
❑ 363 Checklist 5 10.00 4.00
❑ 364 Nate Oliver 3.00 1.25
❑ 365 Roger Maris UER 50.00 20.00
❑ 366 Wayne Causey 3.00 1.25
❑ 367 Mel Nelson 3.00 1.25
❑ 368 Charlie Lau 5.00 2.00
❑ 369 Jim King 3.00 1.25
❑ 370 Chico Cardenas 3.00 1.25
❑ 371 Lee Stange 5.00 2.00
❑ 372 Harvey Kuenn 8.00 3.00
❑ 373 J.Hiatt/D.Estelle 8.00 3.00
❑ 374 Bob Locker 5.00 2.00
❑ 375 Donn Clendenon 8.00 3.00
❑ 376 Paul Schaal 5.00 2.00
❑ 377 Turk Farrell 5.00 2.00
❑ 378 Dick Tracewski 5.00 2.00
❑ 379 St. Louis Cardinals TC 10.00 4.00
❑ 380 Tony Conigliaro 10.00 4.00
❑ 381 Hank Fischer 5.00 2.00
❑ 382 Phil Roof 5.00 2.00
❑ 383 Jackie Brandt 5.00 2.00
❑ 384 Al Downing 8.00 3.00
❑ 385 Ken Boyer 10.00 4.00
❑ 386 Gil Hodges MG 8.00 3.00
❑ 387 Howie Reed 5.00 2.00
❑ 388 Don Mincher 5.00 2.00
❑ 389 Jim O'Toole 8.00 3.00
❑ 390 Brooks Robinson 50.00 20.00
❑ 391 Chuck Hinton 5.00 2.00
❑ 392 B.Hands RC/R.Hundley RC 8.00 3.00
❑ 393 George Brunet 5.00 2.00
❑ 394 Ron Brand 5.00 2.00
❑ 395 Len Gabrielson 5.00 2.00
❑ 396 Jerry Stephenson 5.00 2.00
❑ 397 Bill White 8.00 3.00
❑ 398 Danny Cater 5.00 2.00
❑ 399 Ray Washburn 5.00 2.00
❑ 400 Zoilo Versalles 8.00 3.00
❑ 401 Ken McMullen 5.00 2.00
❑ 402 Jim Hickman 5.00 2.00
❑ 403 Fred Talbot 5.00 2.00
❑ 404 Pittsburgh Pirates TC 10.00 4.00
❑ 405 Elston Howard 8.00 3.00
❑ 406 Joey Jay 5.00 2.00
❑ 407 John Kennedy 5.00 2.00
❑ 408 Lee Thomas 8.00 3.00
❑ 409 Billy Hoeft 5.00 2.00
❑ 410 Al Kaline 40.00 15.00
❑ 411 Gene Mauch MG 5.00 2.00
❑ 412 Sam Bowens 5.00 2.00
❑ 413 Johnny Romano 5.00 2.00
❑ 414 Dan Coombs 5.00 2.00
❑ 415 Max Alvis 5.00 2.00
❑ 416 Phil Ortega 5.00 2.00
❑ 417 J.McGlothlin RC/E.Sukla RC 5.00 2.00
❑ 418 Phil Gagliano 5.00 2.00
❑ 419 Mike Ryan 5.00 2.00
❑ 420 Juan Marichal 15.00 6.00
❑ 421 Roy McMillan 8.00 3.00
❑ 422 Ed Charles 5.00 2.00
❑ 423 Ernie Broglio 5.00 2.00
❑ 424 L.May RC/D.Osteen RC 10.00 4.00
❑ 425 Bob Veale 8.00 3.00
❑ 426 Chicago White Sox TC 10.00 4.00
❑ 427 John Miller 5.00 2.00
❑ 428 Sandy Alomar 5.00 2.00
❑ 429 Bill Monbouquette 5.00 2.00
❑ 430 Don Drysdale 20.00 8.00
❑ 431 Walt Bond 5.00 2.00
❑ 432 Bob Heffner 5.00 2.00
❑ 433 Alvin Dark MG 8.00 3.00
❑ 434 Willie Kirkland 5.00 2.00
❑ 435 Jim Bunning 15.00 6.00
❑ 436 Julian Javier 8.00 3.00
❑ 437 Al Stanek 5.00 2.00
❑ 438 Willie Smith 5.00 2.00
❑ 439 Pedro Ramos 5.00 2.00
❑ 440 Deron Johnson 8.00 3.00
❑ 441 Tommie Sisk 5.00 2.00
❑ 442 E.Barnowski RC/E.Watt RC 5.00 2.00
❑ 443 Bill Wakefield 3.00 1.25
❑ 444 Checklist 6 10.00 4.00
❑ 445 Jim Kaat 10.00 4.00
❑ 446 Mack Jones 5.00 2.00
❑ 447 D.Ellsw UER Hubbs 15.00 6.00
❑ 448 Eddie Stanky MG 10.00 4.00
❑ 449 Joe Moeller 10.00 4.00
❑ 450 Tony Oliva 15.00 6.00
❑ 451 Barry Latman 10.00 4.00
❑ 452 Joe Azcue 10.00 4.00
❑ 453 Ron Kline 10.00 4.00
❑ 454 Jerry Buchek 10.00 4.00
❑ 455 Mickey Lolich 15.00 6.00
❑ 456 D.Brandon RC/J.Foy RC 10.00 4.00
❑ 457 Joe Gibbon 10.00 4.00
❑ 458 Manny Jiminez 10.00 4.00
❑ 459 Bill McCool 10.00 4.00
❑ 460 Curt Blefary 10.00 4.00
❑ 461 Roy Face 15.00 6.00
❑ 462 Bob Rodgers 10.00 4.00
❑ 463 Philadelphia Phillies TC 15.00 6.00
❑ 464 Larry Bearnarth 10.00 4.00
❑ 465 Don Buford 10.00 4.00
❑ 466 Ken Johnson 10.00 4.00
❑ 467 Vic Roznovsky 10.00 4.00
❑ 468 Johnny Podres 15.00 6.00
❑ 469 B.Murcer RC/D.Womack RC 30.00 12.50
❑ 470 Sam McDowell 15.00 6.00
❑ 471 Bob Skinner 10.00 4.00
❑ 472 Terry Fox 10.00 4.00
❑ 473 Rich Rollins 10.00 4.00
❑ 474 Dick Schofield 10.00 4.00
❑ 475 Dick Radatz 10.00 4.00
❑ 476 Bobby Bragan MG 10.00 4.00
❑ 477 Steve Barber 10.00 4.00
❑ 478 Tony Gonzalez 10.00 4.00
❑ 479 Jim Hannan 10.00 4.00
❑ 480 Dick Stuart 10.00 4.00
❑ 481 Bob Lee 10.00 4.00
❑ 482 J.Boccabella/D.Dowling 10.00 4.00
❑ 483 Joe Nuxhall 10.00 4.00
❑ 484 Wes Covington 10.00 4.00
❑ 485 Bob Bailey 10.00 4.00
❑ 486 Tommy John 15.00 6.00
❑ 487 Al Ferrara 10.00 4.00
❑ 488 George Banks 10.00 4.00
❑ 489 Curt Simmons 10.00 4.00
❑ 490 Bobby Richardson 25.00 10.00
❑ 491 Dennis Bennett 10.00 4.00
❑ 492 Kansas City Athletics TC 15.00 6.00
❑ 493 Johnny Klippstein 10.00 4.00
❑ 494 Gordy Coleman 10.00 4.00
❑ 495 Dick McAuliffe 15.00 6.00
❑ 496 Lindy McDaniel 10.00 4.00
❑ 497 Chris Cannizzaro 10.00 4.00
❑ 498 L.Walker RC/W.Fryman RC 10.00 4.00
❑ 499 Wally Bunker 10.00 4.00
❑ 500 Hank Aaron 120.00 60.00
❑ 501 John O'Donoghue 10.00 4.00
❑ 502 Lenny Green UER 10.00 4.00
❑ 503 Steve Hamilton 15.00 6.00
❑ 504 Grady Hatton MG 10.00 4.00
❑ 505 Jose Cardenal 10.00 4.00
❑ 506 Bo Belinsky 15.00 6.00
❑ 507 Johnny Edwards 10.00 4.00
❑ 508 Steve Hargan RC 15.00 6.00
❑ 509 Jake Wood 10.00 4.00
❑ 510 Hoyt Wilhelm 25.00 10.00
❑ 511 B.Barton RC/T.Fuentes RC 10.00 4.00
❑ 512 Dick Stigman 10.00 4.00
❑ 513 Camilo Carreon 10.00 4.00
❑ 514 Hal Woodeshick 10.00 4.00
❑ 515 Frank Howard 15.00 6.00
❑ 516 Eddie Bressoud 10.00 4.00
❑ 517A Checklist 7 White Sox 15.00 6.00
❑ 517B Checklist 7 W.Sox 15.00 6.00
❑ 518 H.Hippauf RC/A.Umbach RC 10.00 4.00
❑ 519 Bob Friend 15.00 6.00
❑ 520 Jim Wynn 15.00 6.00
❑ 521 John Wyatt 10.00 4.00
❑ 522 Phil Linz 10.00 4.00
❑ 523 Bob Sadowski 10.00 4.00
❑ 524 O.Brown RC/D.Mason RC SP 30.00 12.50
❑ 525 Gary Bell SP 30.00 12.50
❑ 526 Minnesota Twins TC SP 100.00 50.00
❑ 527 Julio Navarro 15.00 6.00
❑ 528 Jesse Gonder SP 30.00 12.50
❑ 529 Elia/Higgins/Voss RC 15.00 6.00
❑ 530 Robin Roberts 50.00 20.00
❑ 531 Joe Cunningham 15.00 6.00
❑ 532 A.Monteagudo SP 30.00 12.50
❑ 533 Jerry Adair SP 30.00 12.50
❑ 534 D.Eilers RC/R.Gardner RC 15.00 6.00
❑ 535 Willie Davis SP 40.00 15.00
❑ 536 Dick Egan 15.00 6.00
❑ 537 Herman Franks MG 15.00 6.00
❑ 538 Bob Allen SP 30.00 12.50
❑ 539 B.Heath RC/C.Sembera RC 25.00 10.00
❑ 540 Denny McLain SP 60.00 30.00
❑ 541 Gene Oliver SP 30.00 12.50
❑ 542 George Smith 15.00 6.00
❑ 543 Roger Craig SP 30.00 12.50
❑ 544 Hoerner/Kernek/Williams RC SP 30.00 12.50
❑ 545 Dick Green SP 30.00 12.50
❑ 546 Dwight Siebler 25.00 10.00
❑ 547 Horace Clarke SP RC 40.00 15.00
❑ 548 Gary Kroll SP 30.00 12.50
❑ 549 A.Closter RC/C.Cox RC 15.00 6.00
❑ 550 Willie McCovey SP 100.00 50.00
❑ 551 Bob Purkey SP 30.00 12.50
❑ 552 B.Tebbetts MG SP 30.00 12.50
❑ 553 P.Garrett RC/J.Warner 15.00 6.00
❑ 554 Jim Northrup SP 30.00 12.50
❑ 555 Ron Perranoski SP 30.00 12.50
❑ 556 Mel Queen SP 30.00 12.50
❑ 557 Felix Mantilla SP 30.00 12.50
❑ 558 Grilli/Magrini/Scott RC 20.00 8.00
❑ 559 Roberto Pena SP 30.00 12.50
❑ 560 Joel Horlen 15.00 6.00
❑ 561 Choo Choo Coleman SP 30.00 12.50
❑ 562 Russ Snyder 25.00 10.00
❑ 563 P.Cimino RC/C.Tovar RC 15.00 6.00
❑ 564 Bob Chance SP 30.00 12.50
❑ 565 Jimmy Piersall SP 40.00 15.00
❑ 566 Mike Cuellar SP 30.00 12.50
❑ 567 Dick Howser SP 40.00 15.00
❑ 568 P.Lindblad RC/R.Stone RC 15.00 6.00
❑ 569 Orlando McFarlane SP 30.00 12.50
❑ 570 Art Mahaffey SP 30.00 12.50
❑ 571 Dave Roberts SP 30.00 12.50
❑ 572 Bob Priddy 15.00 6.00
❑ 573 Derrell Griffith 15.00 6.00
❑ 574 B.Hepler RC/B.Murphy RC 15.00 6.00
❑ 575 Earl Wilson 15.00 6.00
❑ 576 Dave Nicholson SP 30.00 12.50
❑ 577 Jack Lamabe SP 30.00 12.50
❑ 578 Chi Chi Olivo SP RC 30.00 12.50
❑ 579 Bertaina/Brabender/Johnson RC 20.00 8.00
❑ 580 Billy Williams SP 60.00 30.00
❑ 581 Tony Martinez 15.00 6.00
❑ 582 Garry Roggenburk 15.00 6.00
❑ 583 Detroit Tigers TC SP 120.00 60.00
❑ 584 F.Fernandez RC/F.Peterson RC 15.00 6.00
❑ 585 Tony Taylor 25.00 10.00
❑ 586 Claude Raymond SP 30.00 12.50
❑ 587 Dick Bertell 15.00 6.00
❑ 588 C.Dobson RC/K.Suarez RC 15.00 6.00
❑ 589 Lou Klimchock SP 30.00 12.50
❑ 590 Bill Skowron SP 40.00 15.00
❑ 591 B.Shirley RC/G.Jackson RC SP 40.00 15.00
❑ 592 Andre Rodgers 15.00 6.00
❑ 593 Doug Camilli SP 30.00 12.50
❑ 594 Chico Salmon 15.00 6.00
❑ 595 Larry Jackson 15.00 6.00
❑ 596 N.Colbert RC/G.Sims RC SP 30.00 12.50

❑ 597 John Sullivan 15.00 6.00
❑ 598 Gaylord Perry SP 200.00 100.00

1967 Topps

❑ COMPLETE SET (609) 5000.00 2500.00
❑ COMMON CARD (1-109) 1.50 .60
❑ COMMON CARD (110-283) 2.00 .75
❑ COMMON CARD (284-370) 2.50 1.00
❑ COMMON CARD (371-457) 4.00 1.50
❑ COMMON CARD (458-533) 6.00 2.50
❑ COMMON CARD (534-609) 15.00 6.00
❑ COMMON DP (534-609) 8.00 3.00
❑ WRAPPER (5-CENT) 25.00 10.00
❑ 1 Robinson/Bauer/Robinson DP 25.00 10.00
❑ 2 Jack Hamilton 1.50 .60
❑ 3 Duke Sims 1.50 .60
❑ 4 Hal Lanier 1.50 .60
❑ 5 Whitey Ford UER 20.00 8.00
❑ 6 Dick Simpson 1.50 .60
❑ 7 Don McMahon 1.50 .60
❑ 8 Chuck Harrison 1.50 .60
❑ 9 Ron Hansen 1.50 .60
❑ 10 Matty Alou 4.00 1.50
❑ 11 Barry Moore RC 1.50 .60
❑ 12 J.Campanis RC/B.Singer 4.00 1.50
❑ 13 Joe Sparma 1.50 .60
❑ 14 Phil Linz 4.00 1.50
❑ 15 Earl Battey 1.50 .60
❑ 16 Bill Hands 1.50 .60
❑ 17 Jim Gosger 1.50 .60
❑ 18 Gene Oliver 1.50 .60
❑ 19 Jim McGlothlin 1.50 .60
❑ 20 Orlando Cepeda 8.00 3.00
❑ 21 Dave Bristol MG RC 1.50 .60
❑ 22 Gene Brabender 1.50 .60
❑ 23 Larry Elliot 1.50 .60
❑ 24 Bob Allen 1.50 .60
❑ 25 Elston Howard 4.00 1.50
❑ 26A Bob Priddy NTR 30.00 12.50
❑ 26B Bob Priddy TR 4.00 1.50
❑ 27 Bob Saverine 1.50 .60
❑ 28 Barry Latman 1.50 .60
❑ 29 Tom McCraw 1.50 .60
❑ 30 Al Kaline DP 20.00 8.00
❑ 31 Jim Brewer 1.50 .60
❑ 32 Bob Bailey 4.00 1.50
❑ 33 S.Bando RC/R.Schwartz RC 6.00 2.50
❑ 34 Pete Cimino 1.50 .60
❑ 35 Rico Carty 4.00 1.50
❑ 36 Bob Tillman 1.50 .60
❑ 37 Rick Wise 4.00 1.50
❑ 38 Bob Johnson 1.50 .60
❑ 39 Curt Simmons 4.00 1.50
❑ 40 Rick Reichardt 1.50 .60
❑ 41 Joe Hoerner 1.50 .60
❑ 42 New York Mets TC 10.00 4.00
❑ 43 Chico Salmon 1.50 .60
❑ 44 Joe Nuxhall 4.00 1.50
❑ 45 Roger Maris 50.00 20.00
❑ 45A R.Maris Yanks/Blank Back 1500.00 900.00
❑ 46 Lindy McDaniel 4.00 1.50
❑ 47 Ken McMullen 1.50 .60
❑ 48 Bill Freehan 4.00 1.50
❑ 49 Roy Face 4.00 1.50
❑ 50 Tony Oliva 6.00 2.50
❑ 51 D.Adlesh RC/W.Bales RC 1.50 .60
❑ 52 Dennis Higgins 1.50 .60
❑ 53 Clay Dalrymple 1.50 .60
❑ 54 Dick Green 1.50 .60
❑ 55 Don Drysdale 15.00 6.00
❑ 56 Jose Tartabull 4.00 1.50
❑ 57 Pat Jarvis RC 4.00 1.50
❑ 58A Paul Schaal Green Bat 20.00 8.00
❑ 58B P.Schaal Normal Bat 1.50 .60
❑ 59 Ralph Terry 4.00 1.50
❑ 60 Luis Aparicio 8.00 3.00
❑ 61 Gordy Coleman 1.50 .60
❑ 62 Frank Robinson CL1 8.00 3.00
❑ 63 L.Brock/C.Flood 8.00 3.00
❑ 64 Fred Valentine 1.50 .60
❑ 65 Tom Haller 4.00 1.50
❑ 66 Manny Mota 4.00 1.50
❑ 67 Ken Berry 1.50 .60
❑ 68 Bob Buhl 4.00 1.50
❑ 69 Vic Davalillo 1.50 .60
❑ 70 Ron Santo 6.00 2.50
❑ 71 Camilo Pascual 4.00 1.50
❑ 72 G.Korince ERR RC/T.Matchick RC 1.50 .60
❑ 73 Rusty Staub 6.00 2.50
❑ 74 Wes Stock 1.50 .60
❑ 75 George Scott 4.00 1.50
❑ 76 Jim Barbieri RC 1.50 .60
❑ 77 Dooley Womack 4.00 1.50
❑ 78 Pat Corrales 1.50 .60
❑ 79 Bubba Morton 1.50 .60
❑ 80 Jim Maloney 4.00 1.50
❑ 81 Eddie Stanky MG 4.00 1.50
❑ 82 Steve Barber 1.50 .60
❑ 83 Ollie Brown 1.50 .60
❑ 84 Tommie Sisk 1.50 .60
❑ 85 Johnny Callison 4.00 1.50
❑ 86A Mike McCormick NTR 30.00 12.50
❑ 86B Mike McCormick TR 4.00 1.50
❑ 87 George Altman 1.50 .60
❑ 88 Mickey Lolich 4.00 1.50
❑ 89 Felix Millan RC 4.00 1.50
❑ 90 Jim Nash RC 1.50 .60
❑ 91 Johnny Lewis 1.50 .60
❑ 92 Ray Washburn 1.50 .60
❑ 93 S.Bahnsen RC/B.Murcer 4.00 1.50
❑ 94 Ron Fairly 4.00 1.50
❑ 95 Sonny Siebert 1.50 .60
❑ 96 Art Shamsky 1.50 .60
❑ 97 Mike Cuellar 4.00 1.50
❑ 98 Rich Rollins 1.50 .60
❑ 99 Lee Stange 1.50 .60
❑ 100 Frank Robinson DP 15.00 6.00
❑ 101 Ken Johnson 1.50 .60
❑ 102 Philadelphia Phillies TC 4.00 1.50
❑ 103A Mickey Mantle CL2 DP D.Mc 20.00 8.00
❑ 104 Minnie Rojas RC 1.50 .60
❑ 105 Ken Boyer 6.00 2.50
❑ 106 Randy Hundley 4.00 1.50
❑ 107 Joel Horlen 1.50 .60
❑ 108 Alex Johnson 4.00 1.50
❑ 109 R.Colavito/L.Wagner 6.00 2.50
❑ 110 Jack Aker 4.00 1.50
❑ 111 John Kennedy 2.00 .75
❑ 112 Dave Wickersham 2.00 .75
❑ 113 Dave Nicholson 2.00 .75
❑ 114 Jack Baldschun 2.00 .75
❑ 115 Paul Casanova RC 2.00 .75
❑ 116 Herman Franks MG 2.00 .75
❑ 117 Darrell Brandon 2.00 .75
❑ 118 Bernie Allen 2.00 .75
❑ 119 Wade Blasingame 2.00 .75
❑ 120 Floyd Robinson 2.00 .75
❑ 121 Eddie Bressoud 2.00 .75
❑ 122 George Brunet 2.00 .75
❑ 123 J.Price RC/L.Walker 4.00 1.50
❑ 124 Jim Stewart 2.00 .75
❑ 125 Moe Drabowsky 4.00 1.50
❑ 126 Tony Taylor 2.00 .75
❑ 127 John O'Donoghue 2.00 .75
❑ 128 Ed Spiezio RC 2.00 .75
❑ 129 Phil Roof 2.00 .75
❑ 130 Phil Regan 4.00 1.50
❑ 131 New York Yankees TC 10.00 4.00
❑ 132 Ozzie Virgil 2.00 .75
❑ 133 Ron Kline 2.00 .75
❑ 134 Gates Brown 6.00 2.50
❑ 135 Deron Johnson 4.00 1.50
❑ 136 Carroll Sembera 2.00 .75
❑ 137 R.Clark RC/J.Ollum 2.00 .75
❑ 138 Dick Kelley 2.00 .75
❑ 139 Dalton Jones 4.00 1.50
❑ 140 Willie Stargell 20.00 8.00
❑ 141 John Miller 2.00 .75
❑ 142 Jackie Brandt 2.00 .75
❑ 143 P.Ward/D.Buford 2.00 .75
❑ 144 Bill Hepler 2.00 .75
❑ 145 Larry Brown 2.00 .75
❑ 146 Steve Carlton 50.00 20.00
❑ 147 Tom Egan 2.00 .75
❑ 148 Adolfo Phillips 2.00 .75
❑ 149 Joe Moeller 2.00 .75
❑ 150 Mickey Mantle 350.00 175.00
❑ 151 Moe Drabowsky WS1 5.00 2.00
❑ 152 Jim Palmer WS2 8.00 3.00
❑ 153 Paul Blair WS3 5.00 2.00
❑ 154 Robinson/McNally WS4 5.00 2.00
❑ 155 Orioles Celebrate WS 5.00 2.00
❑ 156 Ron Herbel 2.00 .75
❑ 157 Danny Cater 2.00 .75
❑ 158 Jimmie Coker 2.00 .75
❑ 159 Bruce Howard 2.00 .75
❑ 160 Willie Davis 4.00 1.50
❑ 161 Dick Williams MG 4.00 1.50
❑ 162 Billy O'Dell 2.00 .75
❑ 163 Vic Roznovsky 2.00 .75
❑ 164 Dwight Siebler UER 2.00 .75
❑ 165 Cleon Jones 4.00 1.50
❑ 166 Eddie Mathews 15.00 6.00
❑ 167 J.Coleman RC/T.Cullen RC 2.00 .75
❑ 168 Ray Culp 2.00 .75
❑ 169 Horace Clarke 4.00 1.50
❑ 170 Dick McAuliffe 4.00 1.50
❑ 171 Cal Koonce 2.00 .75
❑ 172 Bill Heath 2.00 .75
❑ 173 St. Louis Cardinals TC 4.00 1.50
❑ 174 Dick Radatz 4.00 1.50
❑ 175 Bobby Knoop 2.00 .75
❑ 176 Sammy Ellis 2.00 .75
❑ 177 Tito Fuentes 1.50 .60
❑ 178 John Buzhardt 2.00 .75
❑ 179 C.Vaughan RC/C.Epshaw RC 4.00 1.50
❑ 180 Curt Blefary 2.00 .75
❑ 181 Terry Fox 2.00 .75
❑ 182 Ed Charles 2.00 .75
❑ 183 Jim Pagliaroni 2.00 .75
❑ 184 George Thomas 2.00 .75
❑ 185 Ken Holtzman RC 4.00 1.50
❑ 186 E.Kranepool/R.Swoboda 4.00 1.50
❑ 187 Pedro Ramos 2.00 .75
❑ 188 Ken Harrelson 4.00 1.50
❑ 189 Chuck Hinton 2.00 .75
❑ 190 Turk Farrell 2.00 .75
❑ 191A W.Mays CL3 214 Tom 10.00 4.00
❑ 191B W.Mays CL3 214 Dick 12.00 5.00
❑ 192 Fred Gladding 2.00 .75
❑ 193 Jose Cardenal 4.00 1.50
❑ 194 Bob Allison 4.00 1.50
❑ 195 Al Jackson 2.00 .75
❑ 196 Johnny Romano 2.00 .75
❑ 197 Ron Perranoski 4.00 1.50
❑ 198 Chuck Hiller 2.00 .75
❑ 199 Billy Hitchcock MG 2.00 .75
❑ 200 Willie Mays UER 100.00 50.00
❑ 201 Hal Reniff 4.00 1.50
❑ 202 Johnny Edwards 2.00 .75
❑ 203 Al McBean 2.00 .75
❑ 204 M.Epstein RC/T.Phoebus RC 6.00 2.50
❑ 205 Dick Groat 4.00 1.50
❑ 206 Dennis Bennett 2.00 .75
❑ 207 John Orsino 2.00 .75
❑ 208 Jack Lamabe 2.00 .75
❑ 209 Joe Nossek 2.00 .75
❑ 210 Bob Gibson 20.00 8.00
❑ 211 Minnesota Twins TC 4.00 1.50
❑ 212 Chris Zachary 2.00 .75
❑ 213 Jay Johnstone RC 4.00 1.50
❑ 214 Dick Kelley 2.00 .75
❑ 215 Ernie Banks 20.00 8.00
❑ 216 A.Kaline/N.Cash 8.00 3.00
❑ 217 Rob Gardner 2.00 .75
❑ 218 Wes Parker 4.00 1.50
❑ 219 Clay Carroll 4.00 1.50
❑ 220 Jim Ray Hart 4.00 1.50
❑ 221 Woody Fryman 4.00 1.50
❑ 222 D.Osteen/L.May 4.00 1.50

❑ 223 Mike Ryan 4.00 1.50
❑ 224 Walt Bond 2.00 .75
❑ 225 Mel Stottlemyre 6.00 2.50
❑ 226 Julian Javier 4.00 1.50
❑ 227 Paul Lindblad 2.00 .75
❑ 228 Gil Hodges MG 6.00 2.50
❑ 229 Larry Jackson 2.00 .75
❑ 230 Boog Powell 6.00 2.50
❑ 231 John Bateman 2.00 .75
❑ 232 Don Buford 2.00 .75
❑ 233 Peters/Horlen/Hargan LL 4.00 1.50
❑ 234 Koufax/Cuellar/Marichal LL 15.00 6.00
❑ 235 Kaat/McLain/Wilson LL 6.00 2.50
❑ 236 Koufax/Mari/Gibs/Perry LL 25.00 10.00
❑ 237 McDowell/Kaat/Wilson LL 6.00 2.50
❑ 238 Koufax/Bunning/Veale LL 12.00 5.00
❑ 239 F.Rob/Oliva/Kaline LL 10.00 4.00
❑ 240 Alou/Alou/Carty LL 6.00 2.50
❑ 241 F.Rob/Killebrew/Powell LL 10.00 4.00
❑ 242 Aaron/Clemente/Allen LL 25.00 10.00
❑ 243 F.Rob/Killebrew/Powell LL 10.00 4.00
❑ 244 Aaron/Allen/Mays LL 20.00 8.00
❑ 245 Curt Flood 6.00 2.50
❑ 246 Jim Perry 4.00 1.50
❑ 247 Jerry Lumpe 2.00 .75
❑ 248 Gene Mauch MG 4.00 1.50
❑ 249 Nick Willhite 2.00 .75
❑ 250 Hank Aaron UER 80.00 40.00
❑ 251 Woody Held 2.00 .75
❑ 252 Bob Bolin 2.00 .75
❑ 253 B.Davis/G.Gil RC 2.00 .75
❑ 254 Milt Pappas 4.00 1.50
❑ 255 Frank Howard 4.00 1.50
❑ 256 Bob Hendley 2.00 .75
❑ 257 Charlie Smith 2.00 .75
❑ 258 Lee Maye 2.00 .75
❑ 259 Don Dennis 2.00 .75
❑ 260 Jim Lefebvre 4.00 1.50
❑ 261 John Wyatt 2.00 .75
❑ 262 Kansas City Athletics TC 4.00 1.50
❑ 263 Hank Aguirre 2.00 .75
❑ 264 Ron Swoboda 4.00 1.50
❑ 265 Lou Burdette 4.00 1.50
❑ 266 W.Stargell/D.Clendenon 4.00 1.50
❑ 267 Don Schwall 2.00 .75
❑ 268 Johnny Briggs 2.00 .75
❑ 269 Don Nottebart 2.00 .75
❑ 270 Zoilo Versalles 2.00 .75
❑ 271 Eddie Watt 2.00 .75
❑ 272 B.Connors RC/D.Dowling 4.00 1.50
❑ 273 Dick Lines RC 2.00 .75
❑ 274 Bob Aspromonte 2.00 .75
❑ 275 Fred Whitfield 2.00 .75
❑ 276 Bruce Brubaker 2.00 .75
❑ 277 Steve Whitaker RC 6.00 2.50
❑ 278 Jim Kaat CL4 8.00 3.00
❑ 279 Frank Linzy 2.00 .75
❑ 280 Tony Conigliaro 8.00 3.00
❑ 281 Bob Rodgers 2.00 .75
❑ 282 John Odom 2.00 .75
❑ 283 Gene Alley 4.00 1.50
❑ 284 Johnny Podres 4.00 1.50
❑ 285 Lou Brock 20.00 8.00
❑ 286 Wayne Causey 2.50 1.00
❑ 287 G.Goosen RC/B.Shirley 2.50 1.00
❑ 288 Denny Lemaster 2.50 1.00
❑ 289 Tom Tresh 5.00 2.00
❑ 290 Bill White 5.00 2.00
❑ 291 Jim Hannan 2.50 1.00
❑ 292 Don Pavletich 2.50 1.00
❑ 293 Ed Kirkpatrick 2.50 1.00
❑ 294 Walter Alston MG 8.00 3.00
❑ 295 Sam McDowell 5.00 2.00
❑ 296 Glenn Beckert 5.00 2.00
❑ 297 Dave Morehead 5.00 2.00
❑ 298 Ron Davis RC 2.50 1.00
❑ 299 Norm Siebern 2.50 1.00
❑ 300 Jim Kaat 5.00 2.00
❑ 301 Jesse Gonder 2.50 1.00
❑ 302 Baltimore Orioles TC 8.00 3.00
❑ 303 Gil Blanco 2.50 1.00
❑ 304 Phil Gagliano 2.50 1.00
❑ 305 Earl Wilson 5.00 2.00
❑ 306 Bud Harrelson RC 5.00 2.00
❑ 307 Jim Beauchamp 2.50 1.00
❑ 308 Al Downing 5.00 2.00
❑ 309 J.Callison/R.Allen 5.00 2.00
❑ 310 Gary Peters 2.50 1.00
❑ 311 Ed Brinkman 2.50 1.00
❑ 312 Don Mincher 2.50 1.00
❑ 313 Bob Lee 2.50 1.00
❑ 314 M.Andrews RC/R.Smith RC 8.00 3.00
❑ 315 Billy Williams 15.00 6.00
❑ 316 Jack Kralick 2.50 1.00
❑ 317 Cesar Tovar 2.50 1.00
❑ 318 Dave Giusti 2.50 1.00
❑ 319 Paul Blair 5.00 2.00
❑ 320 Gaylord Perry 15.00 6.00
❑ 321 Mayo Smith MG 2.50 1.00
❑ 322 Jose Pagan 2.50 1.00
❑ 323 Mike Hershberger 2.50 1.00
❑ 324 Hal Woodeshick 2.50 1.00
❑ 325 Chico Cardenas 5.00 2.00
❑ 326 Bob Uecker 10.00 4.00
❑ 327 California Angels TC 8.00 3.00
❑ 328 Clete Boyer UER 5.00 2.00
❑ 329 Charlie Lau 5.00 2.00
❑ 330 Claude Osteen 5.00 2.00
❑ 331 Joe Foy 5.00 2.00
❑ 332 Jesus Alou 2.50 1.00
❑ 333 Fergie Jenkins 20.00 8.00
❑ 334 H.Killebrew/B.Allison 10.00 4.00
❑ 335 Bob Veale 5.00 2.00
❑ 336 Joe Azcue 2.50 1.00
❑ 337 Joe Morgan 15.00 6.00
❑ 338 Bob Locker 2.50 1.00
❑ 339 Chico Ruiz 2.50 1.00
❑ 340 Joe Pepitone 8.00 3.00
❑ 341 D.Dietz RC/B.Sorrell 2.50 1.00
❑ 342 Hank Fischer 2.50 1.00
❑ 343 Tom Satriano 2.50 1.00
❑ 344 Ossie Chavarria RC 2.50 1.00
❑ 345 Stu Miller 5.00 2.00
❑ 346 Jim Hickman 2.50 1.00
❑ 347 Grady Hatton MG 2.50 1.00
❑ 348 Tug McGraw 5.00 2.00
❑ 349 Bob Chance 2.50 1.00
❑ 350 Joe Torre 8.00 3.00
❑ 351 Vern Law 5.00 2.00
❑ 352 Ray Oyler 2.50 1.00
❑ 353 Bill McCool 2.50 1.00
❑ 354 Chicago Cubs TC 8.00 3.00
❑ 355 Carl Yastrzemski 60.00 30.00
❑ 356 Larry Jaster RC 2.50 1.00
❑ 357 Bill Skowron 5.00 2.00
❑ 358 Ruben Amaro 2.50 1.00
❑ 359 Dick Ellsworth 2.50 1.00
❑ 360 Leon Wagner 2.50 1.00
❑ 361 Roberto Clemente CL5 15.00 6.00
❑ 362 Darold Knowles 2.50 1.00
❑ 363 Davey Johnson 5.00 2.00
❑ 364 Claude Raymond 2.50 1.00
❑ 365 John Roseboro 5.00 2.00
❑ 366 Andy Kosco 2.50 1.00
❑ 367 B.Kelso/D.Wallace RC 2.50 1.00
❑ 368 Jack Hiatt 2.50 1.00
❑ 369 Jim Hunter 15.00 6.00
❑ 370 Tommy Davis 5.00 2.00
❑ 371 Jim Lonborg 8.00 3.00
❑ 372 Mike de la Hoz 4.00 1.50
❑ 373 D.Josephson RC/F.Klages RC DP 4.00 1.50
❑ 374A Mel Queen ERR 20.00 8.00
❑ 374B Mel Queen COR DP 4.00 1.50
❑ 375 Jake Gibbs 8.00 3.00
❑ 376 Don Lock DP 4.00 1.50
❑ 377 Luis Tiant 8.00 3.00
❑ 378 Detroit Tigers TC UER 8.00 3.00
❑ 379 Jerry May DP 4.00 1.50
❑ 380 Dean Chance DP 4.00 1.50
❑ 381 Dick Schofield DP 4.00 1.50
❑ 382 Dave McNally 8.00 3.00
❑ 383 Ken Henderson DP 4.00 1.50
❑ 384 J.Cosman RC/D.Hughes RC 4.00 1.50
❑ 385 Jim Fregosi 8.00 3.00
❑ 386 Dick Selma DP 4.00 1.50
❑ 387 Cap Peterson DP 4.00 1.50
❑ 388 Arnold Earley DP 4.00 1.50
❑ 389 Alvin Dark MG DP 8.00 3.00
❑ 390 Jim Wynn DP 8.00 3.00
❑ 391 Wilbur Wood DP 8.00 3.00
❑ 392 Tommy Harper DP 8.00 3.00
❑ 393 Jim Bouton DP 8.00 3.00
❑ 394 Jake Wood DP 4.00 1.50
❑ 395 Chris Short RC 8.00 3.00
❑ 396 D.Menke/T.Cloninger 4.00 1.50
❑ 397 Willie Smith DP 4.00 1.50
❑ 398 Jeff Torborg 8.00 3.00
❑ 399 Al Worthington DP 4.00 1.50
❑ 400 Roberto Clemente DP 120.00 60.00
❑ 401 Jim Coates 4.00 1.50
❑ 402A G.Jackson/B.Wilson Stat Line 20.00 8.00
❑ 402B G.Jackson/B.Wilson RC DP 8.00 3.00
❑ 403 Dick Nen 4.00 1.50
❑ 404 Nelson Briles 8.00 3.00
❑ 405 Russ Snyder 4.00 1.50
❑ 406 Lee Elia DP 4.00 1.50
❑ 407 Cincinnati Reds TC 8.00 3.00
❑ 408 Jim Northrup DP 8.00 3.00
❑ 409 Ray Sadecki 4.00 1.50
❑ 410 Lou Johnson DP 4.00 1.50
❑ 411 Dick Howser DP 4.00 1.50
❑ 412 N.Miller RC/D.Rader RC 8.00 3.00
❑ 413 Jerry Grote 4.00 1.50
❑ 414 Casey Cox 4.00 1.50
❑ 415 Sonny Jackson 4.00 1.50
❑ 416 Roger Repoz 4.00 1.50
❑ 417A Bob Bruce ERR 30.00 12.50
❑ 417B Bob Bruce COR DP 4.00 1.50
❑ 418 Sam Mele MG 4.00 1.50
❑ 419 Don Kessinger DP 8.00 4.00
❑ 420 Denny McLain 12.00 5.00
❑ 421 Dal Maxvill DP 4.00 1.50
❑ 422 Hoyt Wilhelm 15.00 6.00
❑ 423 W.Mays/W.McCovey DP 25.00 10.00
❑ 424 Pedro Gonzalez 4.00 1.50
❑ 425 Pete Mikkelsen 4.00 1.50
❑ 426 Lou Clinton 4.00 1.50
❑ 427A Ruben Gomez ERR 20.00 8.00
❑ 427B Ruben Gomez COR DP 4.00 1.50
❑ 428 T.Hutton RC/G.Michael RC DP 8.00 3.00
❑ 429 Garry Roggenburk DP 4.00 1.50
❑ 430 Pete Rose 100.00 50.00
❑ 431 Ted Uhlaender 4.00 1.50
❑ 432 Jimmie Hall DP 4.00 1.50
❑ 433 Al Luplow DP 4.00 1.50
❑ 434 Eddie Fisher DP 4.00 1.50
❑ 435 Mack Jones DP 4.00 1.50
❑ 436 Pete Ward 4.00 1.50
❑ 437 Washington Senators TC 8.00 3.00
❑ 438 Chuck Dobson 4.00 1.50
❑ 439 Byron Browne 4.00 1.50
❑ 440 Steve Hargan 4.00 1.50
❑ 441 Jim Davenport 4.00 1.50
❑ 442 B.Robinson RC/J.Verbanic RC DP 8.00 3.00
❑ 443 Tito Francona DP 4.00 1.50
❑ 444 George Smith 4.00 1.50
❑ 445 Don Sutton 25.00 10.00
❑ 446 Russ Nixon DP 4.00 1.50
❑ 447A Bo Belinsky ERR DP 4.00 1.50
❑ 447B Bo Belinsky COR 8.00 3.00
❑ 448 Harry Walker MG DP 4.00 1.50
❑ 449 Orlando Pena 4.00 1.50
❑ 450 Richie Allen 8.00 3.00
❑ 451 Fred Newman DP 4.00 1.50
❑ 452 Ed Kranepool 8.00 3.00
❑ 453 Aurelio Monteagudo DP 4.00 1.50
❑ 454A J.Marichal CL6 No Ear DP 12.00 5.00
❑ 454B Juan Marichal CL6 w/Ear DP 12.00 5.00
❑ 455 Tommie Agee 8.00 3.00
❑ 456 Phil Niekro 15.00 6.00
❑ 457 Andy Etchebarren DP 8.00 3.00
❑ 458 Lee Thomas 6.00 2.50
❑ 459 D.Bosman RC/P.Craig 6.00 2.50
❑ 460 Harmon Killebrew 60.00 30.00
❑ 461 Bob Miller 12.00 5.00
❑ 462 Bob Barton 6.00 2.50
❑ 463 S.McDowell/S.Siebert 12.00 5.00
❑ 464 Dan Coombs 6.00 2.50
❑ 465 Willie Horton 12.00 5.00
❑ 466 Bobby Wine 6.00 2.50
❑ 467 Jim O'Toole 6.00 2.50
❑ 468 Ralph Houk MG 6.00 2.50
❑ 469 Len Gabrielson 6.00 2.50
❑ 470 Bob Shaw 6.00 2.50
❑ 471 Rene Lachemann 6.00 2.50
❑ 472 J.Gelnar/G.Spriggs RC 6.00 2.50
❑ 473 Jose Santiago 6.00 2.50
❑ 474 Bob Tolan 6.00 2.50

- ❑ 475 Jim Palmer 80.00 40.00
- ❑ 476 Tony Perez SP 60.00 30.00
- ❑ 477 Atlanta Braves TC 15.00 6.00
- ❑ 478 Bob Humphreys 6.00 2.50
- ❑ 479 Gary Bell 6.00 2.50
- ❑ 480 Willie McCovey 40.00 15.00
- ❑ 481 Leo Durocher MG 20.00 8.00
- ❑ 482 Bill Monbouquette 6.00 2.50
- ❑ 483 Jim Landis 6.00 2.50
- ❑ 484 Jerry Adair 6.00 2.50
- ❑ 485 Tim McCarver 25.00 10.00
- ❑ 486 R.Reese RC/B.Whitby RC 6.00 2.50
- ❑ 487 Tommie Reynolds 0.00 2.50
- ❑ 488 Gerry Arrigo 6.00 2.50
- ❑ 489 Doug Clemens RC 6.00 2.50
- ❑ 490 Tony Cloninger 6.00 2.50
- ❑ 491 Sam Bowens 6.00 2.50
- ❑ 492 Pittsburgh Pirates TC 15.00 6.00
- ❑ 493 Phil Ortega 6.00 2.50
- ❑ 494 Bill Rigney MG 6.00 2.50
- ❑ 495 Fritz Peterson 6.00 2.50
- ❑ 496 Orlando McFarlane 6.00 2.50
- ❑ 497 Ron Campbell RC 0.00 2.50
- ❑ 498 Larry Dierker 12.00 5.00
- ❑ 499 G.Culver/J.Vidal RC 6.00 2.50
- ❑ 500 Juan Marichal 25.00 10.00
- ❑ 501 Jerry Zimmerman 6.00 2.50
- ❑ 502 Derrell Griffith 6.00 2.50
- ❑ 503 Los Angeles Dodgers TC 20.00 8.00
- ❑ 504 Orlando Martinez RC 6.00 2.50
- ❑ 505 Tommy Helms 12.00 5.00
- ❑ 506 Smoky Burgess 6.00 2.50
- ❑ 507 E.Barnowski/L.Haney RC 6.00 2.50
- ❑ 508 Dick Hall 6.00 2.50
- ❑ 509 Jim King 6.00 2.50
- ❑ 510 Bill Mazeroski 25.00 10.00
- ❑ 511 Don Wert 6.00 2.50
- ❑ 512 Red Schoendienst MG 25.00 10.00
- ❑ 513 Marcelino Lopez 6.00 2.50
- ❑ 514 John Werhas 6.00 2.50
- ❑ 515 Bert Campaneris 12.00 5.00
- ❑ 516 San Francisco Giants TC 15.00 0.00
- ❑ 517 Fred Talbot 12.00 5.00
- ❑ 518 Denis Menke 6.00 2.50
- ❑ 519 Ted Davidson 6.00 2.50
- ❑ 520 Max Alvis 6.00 2.50
- ❑ 521 B.Powell/C.Bletary 12.00 5.00
- ❑ 522 John Stephenson 6.00 2.50
- ❑ 523 Jim Merritt 6.00 2.50
- ❑ 524 Felix Mantilla 6.00 2.50
- ❑ 525 Ron Hunt 6.00 2.50
- ❑ 526 P.Dobson RC/G.Korince RC 6.00 2.50
- ❑ 527 Dennis Ribant 6.00 2.50
- ❑ 528 Rico Petrocelli 20.00 8.00
- ❑ 529 Gary Wagner 6.00 2.50
- ❑ 530 Felipe Alou 12.00 5.00
- ❑ 531 B.Robinson CL7 DP 15.00 6.00
- ❑ 532 Jim Hicks RC 6.00 2.50
- ❑ 533 Jack Fisher 6.00 2.50
- ❑ 534 Hank Bauer MG DP 8.00 3.00
- ❑ 535 Donn Clendenon 25.00 10.00
- ❑ 536 J.Niekro RC/P.Popovich RC 50.00 20.00
- ❑ 537 Chuck Estrada DP 8.00 3.00
- ❑ 538 J.C. Martin 15.00 6.00
- ❑ 539 Dick Egan DP 8.00 3.00
- ❑ 540 Norm Cash 50.00 20.00
- ❑ 541 Joe Gibbon 15.00 6.00
- ❑ 542 R.Monday RC/T.Pierce RC DP 15.00 6.00
- ❑ 543 Dan Schneider 15.00 6.00
- ❑ 544 Cleveland Indians TC 30.00 12.50
- ❑ 545 Jim Grant 25.00 10.00
- ❑ 546 Woody Woodward 25.00 10.00
- ❑ 547 R.Gibson RC/B.Rohr RC DP 8.00 3.00
- ❑ 548 Tony Gonzalez DP 8.00 3.00
- ❑ 549 Jack Sanford 15.00 6.00
- ❑ 550 Vada Pinson DP 10.00 4.00
- ❑ 551 Doug Camilli DP 8.00 3.00
- ❑ 552 Ted Savage 25.00 10.00
- ❑ 553 M.Hegan RC/T.Tillotson 40.00 15.00
- ❑ 554 Andre Rodgers DP 8.00 3.00
- ❑ 555 Don Cardwell 25.00 10.00
- ❑ 556 Al Weis DP 8.00 3.00
- ❑ 557 Al Ferrara 25.00 10.00
- ❑ 558 M.Belanger RC/B.Dillman RC 50.00 20.00
- ❑ 559 Dick Tracewski DP 8.00 3.00
- ❑ 560 Jim Bunning 60.00 30.00
- ❑ 561 Sandy Alomar 40.00 15.00
- ❑ 562 Steve Blass DP 8.00 3.00
- ❑ 563 Joe Adcock MG 40.00 15.00
- ❑ 564 A.Harris RC/A.Pointer RC DP 8.00 3.00
- ❑ 565 Lew Krausse 25.00 10.00
- ❑ 566 Gary Geiger DP 8.00 3.00
- ❑ 567 Steve Hamilton 40.00 15.00
- ❑ 568 John Sullivan 40.00 15.00
- ❑ 569 Rod Carew RC DP 300.00 150.00
- ❑ 570 Maury Wills 80.00 40.00
- ❑ 571 Larry Sherry 25.00 10.00
- ❑ 572 Don Demeter 25.00 10.00
- ❑ 573 Chicago White Sox TC 30.00 12.50
- ❑ 574 Jerry Buchek 25.00 10.00
- ❑ 575 Dave Boswell RC 15.00 6.00
- ❑ 576 R.Hernandez RC/N.Gigon RC 40.00 15.00
- ❑ 577 Bill Short 15.00 6.00
- ❑ 578 John Boccabella 15.00 6.00
- ❑ 579 Bill Henry 15.00 6.00
- ❑ 580 Rocky Colavito 150.00 75.00
- ❑ 581 Tom Seaver RC 600.00 300.00
- ❑ 582 Jim Owens DP 8.00 3.00
- ❑ 583 Ray Barker 40.00 15.00
- ❑ 584 Jimmy Piersall 40.00 15.00
- ❑ 585 Wally Bunker 25.00 10.00
- ❑ 586 Manny Jimenez 15.00 6.00
- ❑ 587 D.Shaw RC/G.Sutherland RC 40.00 15.00
- ❑ 588 Johnny Klippstein DP 8.00 3.00
- ❑ 589 Dave Ricketts DP 8.00 3.00
- ❑ 590 Pete Richert 15.00 6.00
- ❑ 591 Ty Cline 25.00 10.00
- ❑ 592 J.Shellenback RC/R.Willis RC 25.00 10.00
- ❑ 593 Wes Westrum MG 50.00 20.00
- ❑ 594 Dan Osinski 40.00 15.00
- ❑ 595 Cookie Rojas 25.00 10.00
- ❑ 596 Galen Cisco DP 8.00 3.00
- ❑ 597 Ted Abernathy 15.00 6.00
- ❑ 598 W.Williams RC/E.Stroud RC 25.00 10.00
- ❑ 599 Bob Duliba DP 8.00 3.00
- ❑ 600 Brooks Robinson 250.00 125.00
- ❑ 601 Bill Bryan DP 8.00 3.00
- ❑ 602 Juan Pizarro 40.00 15.00
- ❑ 603 T.Talton RC/R.Webster RC 25.00 10.00
- ❑ 604 Boston Red Sox TC 120.00 60.00
- ❑ 605 Mike Shannon 50.00 20.00
- ❑ 606 Ron Taylor 25.00 10.00
- ❑ 607 Mickey Stanley 50.00 20.00
- ❑ 608 R.Nye RC/J.Upham RC DP 8.00 3.00
- ❑ 609 Tommy John 80.00 40.00

1968 Topps

- ❑ COMPLETE SET (598) 3000.00 1500.00
- ❑ COMMON CARD (1-457) 2.00 .75
- ❑ COMMON CARD (458-598) 4.00 1.50
- ❑ WRAPPER (5-CENT) 25.00 10.00
- ❑ 1 Clemente/Gonz/Alou LL 30.00 12.50
- ❑ 2 Yaz/F.Rob/Kaline LL 15.00 6.00
- ❑ 3 Cep/Clemente/Aaron LL 20.00 8.00
- ❑ 4 Yaz/Killebrew/F.Rob LL 15.00 6.00
- ❑ 5 Aaron/Santo/McCovey LL 8.00 3.00
- ❑ 6 Yaz/Killebrew/Howard LL 8.00 3.00
- ❑ 7 Niekro/Bunning/Short LL 4.00 1.50
- ❑ 8 Horlen/Peters/Siebert LL 4.00 1.50
- ❑ 9 McCor/Jenkins/Bunning LL 4.00 1.50
- ❑ 10A Lonb/Wils/Chance LL ERR 4.00 1.50
- ❑ 10B Lonb/Wils/Chance LL COR 4.00 1.50
- ❑ 11 Bunning/jenkins/Perry LL 6.00 2.50
- ❑ 12 Lonborg/McDow/Chance LL 4.00 1.50
- ❑ 13 Chuck Hartenstein RC 2.00 .75
- ❑ 14 Jerry McNertney 2.00 .75
- ❑ 15 Ron Hunt 2.00 .75
- ❑ 16 L.Piniella/R.Scheinblum 6.00 2.50
- ❑ 17 Dick Hall 2.00 .75
- ❑ 18 Mike Hershberger 2.00 .75
- ❑ 19 Juan Pizarro 2.00 .75
- ❑ 20 Brooks Robinson 25.00 10.00
- ❑ 21 Ron Davis 2.00 .75
- ❑ 22 Pat Dobson 4.00 1.50
- ❑ 23 Chico Cardenas 4.00 1.50
- ❑ 24 Bobby Locke 2.00 .75
- ❑ 25 Julian Javier 4.00 1.50
- ❑ 26 Darrell Brandon 2.00 .75
- ❑ 27 Gil Hodges MG 0.00 3.00
- ❑ 28 Ted Uhlaender 2.00 .75
- ❑ 29 Joe Verbanic 2.00 .75
- ❑ 30 Joe Torre 6.00 2.50
- ❑ 31 Ed Stroud 2.00 .75
- ❑ 32 Joe Gibbon 2.00 .75
- ❑ 33 Pete Ward 2.00 .75
- ❑ 34 Al Ferrara 2.00 .75
- ❑ 35 Steve Hargan 2.00 .75
- ❑ 36 B.Moose RC/B.Robertson RC 4.00 1.50
- ❑ 37 Billy Williams 0.00 3.00
- ❑ 38 Tony Pierce 2.00 .75
- ❑ 39 Cookie Rojas 2.00 .75
- ❑ 40 Denny McLain 8.00 3.00
- ❑ 41 Julio Gotay 2.00 .75
- ❑ 42 Larry Haney 2.00 .75
- ❑ 43 Gary Bell 2.00 .75
- ❑ 44 Frank Kostro 2.00 .75
- ❑ 45 Tom Seaver DP 50.00 20.00
- ❑ 46 Dave Ricketts 2.00 .75
- ❑ 47 Ralph Houk MG 4.00 1.50
- ❑ 48 Ted Davidson 2.00 .75
- ❑ 49A E.Brinkman White 2.00 .75
- ❑ 49B E.Brinkman Yellow Tm 50.00 20.00
- ❑ 50 Willie Mays 60.00 30.00
- ❑ 51 Bob Locker 2.00 .75
- ❑ 52 Hawk Taylor 2.00 .75
- ❑ 53 Gene Alley 4.00 1.50
- ❑ 54 Stan Williams 2.00 .75
- ❑ 55 Felipe Alou 4.00 1.50
- ❑ 56 D.Leonhard RC/D.May RC 2.00 .75
- ❑ 57 Dan Schneider 2.00 .75
- ❑ 58 Eddie Mathews 15.00 6.00
- ❑ 59 Don Lock 2.00 .75
- ❑ 60 Ken Holtzman 4.00 1.50
- ❑ 61 Reggie Smith 4.00 1.50
- ❑ 62 Chuck Dobson 2.00 .75
- ❑ 63 Dick Kenworthy RC 2.00 .75
- ❑ 64 Jim Merritt 2.00 .75
- ❑ 65 John Roseboro 4.00 1.50
- ❑ 66A Casey Cox White 2.00 .75
- ❑ 66B C.Cox Yellow Tm 100.00 50.00
- ❑ 67 Checklist 1/Kaat 6.00 2.50
- ❑ 68 Ron Willis 2.00 .75
- ❑ 69 Tom Tresh 4.00 1.50
- ❑ 70 Bob Veale 4.00 1.50
- ❑ 71 Vern Fuller RC 2.00 .75
- ❑ 72 Tommy John 6.00 2.50
- ❑ 73 Jim Ray Hart 4.00 1.50
- ❑ 74 Milt Pappas 4.00 1.50
- ❑ 75 Don Mincher 2.00 .75
- ❑ 76 J.Britton/R.Reed RC 4.00 1.50
- ❑ 77 Don Wilson RC 4.00 1.50
- ❑ 78 Jim Northrup 6.00 2.50
- ❑ 79 Ted Kubiak RC 2.00 .75
- ❑ 80 Rod Carew 50.00 20.00
- ❑ 81 Larry Jackson 2.00 .75
- ❑ 82 Sam Bowens 2.00 .75
- ❑ 83 John Stephenson 2.00 .75
- ❑ 84 Bob Tolan 2.00 .75
- ❑ 85 Gaylord Perry 8.00 3.00
- ❑ 86 Willie Stargell 8.00 3.00
- ❑ 87 Dick Williams MG 4.00 1.50
- ❑ 88 Phil Regan 4.00 1.50
- ❑ 89 Jake Gibbs 4.00 1.50
- ❑ 90 Vada Pinson 4.00 1.50
- ❑ 91 Jim Ollom RC 2.00 .75
- ❑ 92 Ed Kranepool 4.00 1.50
- ❑ 93 Tony Cloninger 2.00 .75
- ❑ 94 Lee Maye 2.00 .75
- ❑ 95 Bob Aspromonte 2.00 .75
- ❑ 96 F.Coggins RC/D.Nold 2.00 .75

❑ 97	Tom Phoebus	2.00	.75
❑ 98	Gary Sutherland	2.00	.75
❑ 99	Rocky Colavito	8.00	3.00
❑ 100	Bob Gibson	25.00	10.00
❑ 101	Glenn Beckert	4.00	1.50
❑ 102	Jose Cardenal	4.00	1.50
❑ 103	Don Sutton	8.00	3.00
❑ 104	Dick Dietz	2.00	.75
❑ 105	Al Downing	4.00	1.50
❑ 106	Dalton Jones	2.00	.75
❑ 107A	Checklist 2/Marichal Wide	6.00	2.50
❑ 107B	Checklist 2/J.Marichal Fine	6.00	2.50
❑ 108	Don Pavletich	2.00	.75
❑ 109	Bert Campaneris	4.00	1.50
❑ 110	Hank Aaron	60.00	30.00
❑ 111	Rich Reese	2.00	.75
❑ 112	Woody Fryman	2.00	.75
❑ 113	T.Matchick/D.Patterson RC	4.00	1.50
❑ 114	Ron Swoboda	4.00	1.50
❑ 115	Sam McDowell	4.00	1.50
❑ 116	Ken McMullen	2.00	.75
❑ 117	Larry Jaster	2.00	.75
❑ 118	Mark Belanger	4.00	1.50
❑ 119	Ted Savage	2.00	.75
❑ 120	Mel Stottlemyre	4.00	1.50
❑ 121	Jimmie Hall	2.00	.75
❑ 122	Gene Mauch MG	4.00	1.50
❑ 123	Jose Santiago	2.00	.75
❑ 124	Nate Oliver	2.00	.75
❑ 125	Joel Horlen	2.00	.75
❑ 126	Bobby Etheridge RC	2.00	.75
❑ 127	Paul Lindblad	2.00	.75
❑ 128	T.Dukes RC/A.Harris	2.00	.75
❑ 129	Mickey Stanley	6.00	2.50
❑ 130	Tony Perez	8.00	3.00
❑ 131	Frank Bertaina	2.00	.75
❑ 132	Bud Harrelson	4.00	1.50
❑ 133	Fred Whitfield	2.00	.75
❑ 134	Pat Jarvis	2.00	.75
❑ 135	Paul Blair	4.00	1.50
❑ 136	Randy Hundley	4.00	1.50
❑ 137	Minnesota Twins TC	4.00	1.50
❑ 138	Ruben Amaro	2.00	.75
❑ 139	Chris Short	2.00	.75
❑ 140	Tony Conigliaro	8.00	3.00
❑ 141	Dal Maxvill	2.00	.75
❑ 142	B.Bradford RC/B.Voss	2.00	.75
❑ 143	Pete Cimino	2.00	.75
❑ 144	Joe Morgan	12.00	5.00
❑ 145	Don Drysdale	12.00	5.00
❑ 146	Sal Bando	4.00	1.50
❑ 147	Frank Linzy	2.00	.75
❑ 148	Dave Bristol MG	2.00	.75
❑ 149	Bob Saverine	2.00	.75
❑ 150	Roberto Clemente	80.00	40.00
❑ 151	Lou Brock WS1	10.00	4.00
❑ 152	Carl Yastrzemski WS2	10.00	4.00
❑ 153	Nelson Briles WS3	5.00	2.00
❑ 154	Bob Gibson WS4	10.00	4.00
❑ 155	Jim Lonborg WS5	5.00	2.00
❑ 156	Rico Petrocelli WS6	5.00	2.00
❑ 157	St. Louis Wins It WS7	5.00	2.00
❑ 158	Cardinals Celebrate WS	5.00	2.00
❑ 159	Don Kessinger	4.00	1.50
❑ 160	Earl Wilson	4.00	1.50
❑ 161	Norm Miller	2.00	.75
❑ 162	H.Gilson RC/M.Torrez RC	4.00	1.50
❑ 163	Gene Brabender	2.00	.75
❑ 164	Ramon Webster	2.00	.75
❑ 165	Tony Oliva	6.00	2.50
❑ 166	Claude Raymond	2.00	.75
❑ 167	Elston Howard	6.00	2.50
❑ 168	Los Angeles Dodgers TC	4.00	1.50
❑ 169	Bob Bolin	2.00	.75
❑ 170	Jim Fregosi	4.00	1.50
❑ 171	Don Nottebart	2.00	.75
❑ 172	Walt Williams	2.00	.75
❑ 173	John Boozer	2.00	.75
❑ 174	Bob Tillman	2.00	.75
❑ 175	Maury Wills	6.00	2.50
❑ 176	Bob Allen	2.00	.75
❑ 177	N.Ryan RC/J.Koosman RC	500.00	250.00
❑ 178	Don Wert	4.00	1.50
❑ 179	Bill Stoneman RC	2.00	.75
❑ 180	Curt Flood	6.00	2.50
❑ 181	Jerry Zimmerman	2.00	.75
❑ 182	Dave Giusti	2.00	.75
❑ 183	Bob Kennedy MG	4.00	1.50
❑ 184	Lou Johnson	2.00	.75
❑ 185	Tom Haller	2.00	.75
❑ 186	Eddie Watt	2.00	.75
❑ 187	Sonny Jackson	2.00	.75
❑ 188	Cap Peterson	2.00	.75
❑ 189	Bill Landis RC	2.00	.75
❑ 190	Bill White	4.00	1.50
❑ 191	Dan Frisella RC	2.00	.75
❑ 192A	Checklist 3/Yaz Ball	8.00	3.00
❑ 192B	Checklist 3/Yaz Game	8.00	3.00
❑ 193	Jack Hamilton	2.00	.75
❑ 194	Don Buford	2.00	.75
❑ 195	Joe Pepitone	4.00	1.50
❑ 196	Gary Nolan RC	4.00	1.50
❑ 197	Larry Brown	2.00	.75
❑ 198	Roy Face	4.00	1.50
❑ 199	R.Rodriguez RC/D.Osteen	2.00	.75
❑ 200	Orlando Cepeda	8.00	3.00
❑ 201	Mike Marshall RC	4.00	1.50
❑ 202	Adolfo Phillips	2.00	.75
❑ 203	Dick Kelley	2.00	.75
❑ 204	Andy Etchebarren	2.00	.75
❑ 205	Juan Marichal	8.00	3.00
❑ 206	Cal Ermer MG RC	2.00	.75
❑ 207	Carroll Sembera	2.00	.75
❑ 208	Willie Davis	4.00	1.50
❑ 209	Tim Cullen	2.00	.75
❑ 210	Gary Peters	2.00	.75
❑ 211	J.C. Martin	2.00	.75
❑ 212	Dave Morehead	2.00	.75
❑ 213	Chico Ruiz	2.00	.75
❑ 214	S.Bahnsen/F.Fernandez	4.00	1.50
❑ 215	Jim Bunning	8.00	3.00
❑ 216	Bubba Morton	2.00	.75
❑ 217	Dick Farrell	2.00	.75
❑ 218	Ken Suarez	2.00	.75
❑ 219	Rob Gardner	2.00	.75
❑ 220	Harmon Killebrew	15.00	6.00
❑ 221	Atlanta Braves TC	4.00	1.50
❑ 222	Jim Hardin RC	2.00	.75
❑ 223	Ollie Brown	2.00	.75
❑ 224	Jack Aker	2.00	.75
❑ 225	Richie Allen	6.00	2.50
❑ 226	Jimmie Price	2.00	.75
❑ 227	Joe Hoerner	2.00	.75
❑ 228	J.Billingham RC/J.Fairey RC	4.00	1.50
❑ 229	Fred Klages	2.00	.75
❑ 230	Pete Rose	60.00	30.00
❑ 231	Dave Baldwin RC	2.00	.75
❑ 232	Denis Menke	2.00	.75
❑ 233	George Scott	4.00	1.50
❑ 234	Bill Monbouquette	2.00	.75
❑ 235	Ron Santo	8.00	3.00
❑ 236	Tug McGraw	6.00	2.50
❑ 237	Alvin Dark MG	4.00	1.50
❑ 238	Tom Satriano	2.00	.75
❑ 239	Bill Henry	2.00	.75
❑ 240	Al Kaline	40.00	15.00
❑ 241	Felix Millan	2.00	.75
❑ 242	Moe Drabowsky	4.00	1.50
❑ 243	Rich Rollins	2.00	.75
❑ 244	John Donaldson RC	2.00	.75
❑ 245	Tony Gonzalez	2.00	.75
❑ 246	Fritz Peterson	4.00	1.50
❑ 247	Johnny Bench RC	120.00	60.00
❑ 248	Fred Valentine	2.00	.75
❑ 249	Bill Singer	2.00	.75
❑ 250	Carl Yastrzemski	30.00	12.50
❑ 251	Manny Sanguillen RC	6.00	2.50
❑ 252	California Angels TC	4.00	1.50
❑ 253	Dick Hughes	2.00	.75
❑ 254	Cleon Jones	4.00	1.50
❑ 255	Dean Chance	4.00	1.50
❑ 256	Norm Cash	6.00	2.50
❑ 257	Phil Niekro	8.00	3.00
❑ 258	J.Arcia RC/B.Schlesinger	2.00	.75
❑ 259	Ken Boyer	6.00	2.50
❑ 260	Jim Wynn	4.00	1.50
❑ 261	Dave Duncan	4.00	1.50
❑ 262	Rick Wise	4.00	1.50
❑ 263	Horace Clarke	4.00	1.50
❑ 264	Ted Abernathy	2.00	.75
❑ 265	Tommy Davis	4.00	1.50
❑ 266	Paul Popovich	2.00	.75
❑ 267	Herman Franks MG	2.00	.75
❑ 268	Bob Humphreys	2.00	.75
❑ 269	Bob Tiefenauer	2.00	.75
❑ 270	Matty Alou	4.00	1.50
❑ 271	Bobby Knoop	2.00	.75
❑ 272	Ray Culp	2.00	.75
❑ 273	Dave Johnson	4.00	1.50
❑ 274	Mike Cuellar	4.00	1.50
❑ 275	Tim McCarver	6.00	2.50
❑ 276	Jim Roland	2.00	.75
❑ 277	Jerry Buchek	2.00	.75
❑ 278	Checklist 4/Cepeda	6.00	2.50
❑ 279	Bill Hands	2.00	.75
❑ 280	Mickey Mantle	350.00	175.00
❑ 281	Jim Campanis	2.00	.75
❑ 282	Rick Monday	4.00	1.50
❑ 283	Mel Queen	2.00	.75
❑ 284	Johnny Briggs	2.00	.75
❑ 285	Dick McAuliffe	6.00	2.50
❑ 286	Cecil Upshaw	2.00	.75
❑ 287	M.Abarbanel RC/C.Carlos RC	2.00	.75
❑ 288	Dave Wickersham	2.00	.75
❑ 289	Woody Held	2.00	.75
❑ 290	Willie McCovey	12.00	5.00
❑ 291	Dick Lines	2.00	.75
❑ 292	Art Shamsky	2.00	.75
❑ 293	Bruce Howard	2.00	.75
❑ 294	Red Schoendienst MG	6.00	2.50
❑ 295	Sonny Siebert	2.00	.75
❑ 296	Byron Browne	2.00	.75
❑ 297	Russ Gibson	2.00	.75
❑ 298	Jim Brewer	2.00	.75
❑ 299	Gene Michael	4.00	1.50
❑ 300	Rusty Staub	4.00	1.50
❑ 301	G.Mitterwald RC/R.Renick RC	2.00	.75
❑ 302	Gerry Arrigo	2.00	.75
❑ 303	Dick Green	4.00	1.50
❑ 304	Sandy Valdespino	2.00	.75
❑ 305	Minnie Rojas	2.00	.75
❑ 306	Mike Ryan	2.00	.75
❑ 307	John Hiller	4.00	1.50
❑ 308	Pittsburgh Pirates TC	4.00	1.50
❑ 309	Ken Henderson	2.00	.75
❑ 310	Luis Aparicio	8.00	3.00
❑ 311	Jack Lamabe	2.00	.75
❑ 312	Curt Blefary	2.00	.75
❑ 313	Al Weis	2.00	.75
❑ 314	B.Rohr/G.Spriggs	2.00	.75
❑ 315	Zoilo Versalles	2.00	.75
❑ 316	Steve Barber	2.00	.75
❑ 317	Ron Brand	2.00	.75
❑ 318	Chico Salmon	2.00	.75
❑ 319	George Culver	2.00	.75
❑ 320	Frank Howard	4.00	1.50
❑ 321	Leo Durocher MG	6.00	2.50
❑ 322	Dave Boswell	2.00	.75
❑ 323	Deron Johnson	4.00	1.50
❑ 324	Jim Nash	2.00	.75
❑ 325	Manny Mota	4.00	1.50
❑ 326	Dennis Ribant	2.00	.75
❑ 327	Tony Taylor	4.00	1.50
❑ 328	C.Vinson RC/J.Weaver RC	2.00	.75
❑ 329	Duane Josephson	2.00	.75
❑ 330	Roger Maris	50.00	20.00
❑ 331	Dan Osinski	2.00	.75
❑ 332	Doug Rader	4.00	1.50
❑ 333	Ron Herbel	2.00	.75
❑ 334	Baltimore Orioles TC	4.00	1.50
❑ 335	Bob Allison	4.00	1.50
❑ 336	John Purdin	2.00	.75
❑ 337	Bill Robinson	4.00	1.50
❑ 338	Bob Johnson	2.00	.75
❑ 339	Rich Nye	2.00	.75
❑ 340	Max Alvis	2.00	.75
❑ 341	Jim Lemon MG	2.00	.75
❑ 342	Ken Johnson	2.00	.75
❑ 343	Jim Gosger	2.00	.75
❑ 344	Donn Clendenon	4.00	1.50
❑ 345	Bob Hendley	2.00	.75
❑ 346	Jerry Adair	2.00	.75
❑ 347	George Brunet	2.00	.75
❑ 348	L.Colton RC/D.Thoenen RC	2.00	.75
❑ 349	Ed Spiezio	4.00	1.50
❑ 350	Hoyt Wilhelm	8.00	3.00
❑ 351	Bob Barton	2.00	.75
❑ 352	Jackie Hernandez RC	2.00	.75

❑ 353 Mack Jones 2.00 .75
❑ 354 Pete Richert 2.00 .75
❑ 355 Ernie Banks 25.00 10.00
❑ 356A Checklist 5/Holtzman Center 6.00 2.50
❑ 356B Checklist 5/Holtzman Right 6.00 2.50
❑ 357 Len Gabrielson 2.00 .75
❑ 358 Mike Epstein 2.00 .75
❑ 359 Joe Moeller 2.00 .75
❑ 360 Willie Horton 6.00 2.50
❑ 361 Harmon Killebrew AS 8.00 3.00
❑ 362 Orlando Cepeda AS 6.00 2.50
❑ 363 Rod Carew AS 8.00 3.00
❑ 364 Joe Morgan AS 8.00 3.00
❑ 365 Brooks Robinson AS 8.00 3.00
❑ 366 Ron Santo AS 6.00 2.50
❑ 367 Jim Fregosi AS 4.00 1.50
❑ 368 Gene Alley AS 4.00 1.50
❑ 369 Carl Yastrzemski AS 10.00 4.00
❑ 370 Hank Aaron AS 20.00 8.00
❑ 371 Tony Oliva AS 6.00 2.50
❑ 372 Lou Brock AS 8.00 3.00
❑ 373 Frank Robinson AS 8.00 3.00
❑ 374 Roberto Clemente AS 30.00 12.50
❑ 375 Bill Freehan AS 4.00 1.50
❑ 376 Tim McCarver AS 4.00 1.50
❑ 377 Joel Horlen AS 4.00 1.50
❑ 378 Bob Gibson AS 8.00 3.00
❑ 379 Gary Peters AS 4.00 1.50
❑ 380 Ken Holtzman AS 4.00 1.50
❑ 381 Boog Powell 4.00 1.50
❑ 382 Ramon Hernandez 2.00 .75
❑ 383 Steve Whitaker 2.00 .75
❑ 384 B.Henry/H.McRae RC 6.00 2.50
❑ 385 Jim Hunter 10.00 4.00
❑ 386 Greg Goossen 2.00 .75
❑ 387 Joe Foy 2.00 .75
❑ 388 Ray Washburn 2.00 .75
❑ 389 Jay Johnstone 4.00 1.50
❑ 390 Bill Mazeroski 8.00 3.00
❑ 391 Bob Priddy 2.00 .75
❑ 392 Grady Hatton MG 2.00 .75
❑ 393 Jim Perry 4.00 1.50
❑ 394 Tommie Aaron 6.00 2.50
❑ 395 Camilo Pascual 4.00 1.50
❑ 396 Bobby Wine 2.00 .75
❑ 397 Vic Davalillo 2.00 .75
❑ 398 Jim Grant 2.00 .75
❑ 399 Ray Oyler 4.00 1.50
❑ 400A Mike McCormick YT 4.00 1.50
❑ 400B M.McCormick White Tm 150.00 75.00
❑ 401 Mets Team 4.00 1.50
❑ 402 Mike Hegan 4.00 1.50
❑ 403 John Buzhardt 2.00 .75
❑ 404 Floyd Robinson 2.00 .75
❑ 405 Tommy Helms 4.00 1.50
❑ 406 Dick Ellsworth 2.00 .75
❑ 407 Gary Kolb 2.00 .75
❑ 408 Steve Carlton 30.00 12.50
❑ 409 F.Peters RC/R.Stone 2.00 .75
❑ 410 Ferguson Jenkins 10.00 4.00
❑ 411 Ron Hansen 2.00 .75
❑ 412 Clay Carroll 4.00 1.50
❑ 413 Tom McCraw 2.00 .75
❑ 414 Mickey Lolich 8.00 3.00
❑ 415 Johnny Callison 4.00 1.50
❑ 416 Bill Rigney MG 2.00 .75
❑ 417 Willie Crawford 2.00 .75
❑ 418 Eddie Fisher 2.00 .75
❑ 419 Jack Hiatt 2.00 .75
❑ 420 Cesar Tovar 2.00 .75
❑ 421 Ron Taylor 2.00 .75
❑ 422 Rene Lachemann 2.00 .75
❑ 423 Fred Gladding 2.00 .75
❑ 424 Chicago White Sox TC 4.00 1.50
❑ 425 Jim Maloney 4.00 1.50
❑ 426 Hank Allen 2.00 .75
❑ 427 Dick Calmus 2.00 .75
❑ 428 Vic Roznovsky 2.00 .75
❑ 429 Tommie Sisk 2.00 .75
❑ 430 Rico Petrocelli 4.00 1.50
❑ 431 Dooley Womack 2.00 .75
❑ 432 B.Davis/J.Vidal 2.00 .75
❑ 433 Bob Rodgers 2.00 .75
❑ 434 Ricardo Joseph RC 2.00 .75
❑ 435 Ron Perranoski 4.00 1.50
❑ 436 Hal Lanier 2.00 .75
❑ 437 Don Cardwell 2.00 .75
❑ 438 Lee Thomas 4.00 1.50
❑ 439 Lum Harris MG 2.00 .75
❑ 440 Claude Osteen 4.00 1.50
❑ 441 Alex Johnson 4.00 1.50
❑ 442 Dick Bosman 2.00 .75
❑ 443 Joe Azcue 2.00 .75
❑ 444 Jack Fisher 2.00 .75
❑ 445 Mike Shannon 4.00 1.50
❑ 446 Ron Kline 2.00 .75
❑ 447 G.Korince/F.Lasher RC 4.00 1.50
❑ 448 Gary Wagner 2.00 .75
❑ 449 Gene Oliver 2.00 .75
❑ 450 Jim Kaat 6.00 2.50
❑ 451 Al Spangler 2.00 .75
❑ 452 Jesus Alou 2.00 .75
❑ 453 Sammy Ellis 2.00 .75
❑ 454A Checklist 6/F.Rob Complete 8.00 3.00
❑ 454B Checklist 6/F.Rob Partial 8.00 3.00
❑ 455 Rico Carty 4.00 1.50
❑ 456 John O'Donoghue 2.00 .75
❑ 457 Jim Lefebvre 4.00 1.50
❑ 458 Lew Krausse 6.00 2.50
❑ 459 Dick Simpson 4.00 1.50
❑ 460 Jim Lonborg 6.00 2.50
❑ 461 Chuck Hiller 4.00 1.50
❑ 462 Barry Moore 4.00 1.50
❑ 463 Jim Schaffer 4.00 1.50
❑ 464 Don McMahon 4.00 1.50
❑ 465 Tommie Agee 10.00 4.00
❑ 466 Bill Dillman 4.00 1.50
❑ 467 Dick Howser 10.00 4.00
❑ 468 Larry Sherry 4.00 1.50
❑ 469 Ty Cline 4.00 1.50
❑ 470 Bill Freehan 10.00 4.00
❑ 471 Orlando Pena 4.00 1.50
❑ 472 Walter Alston MG 6.00 2.50
❑ 473 Al Worthington 4.00 1.50
❑ 474 Paul Schaal 4.00 1.50
❑ 475 Joe Niekro 6.00 2.50
❑ 476 Woody Woodward 4.00 1.50
❑ 477 Philadelphia Phillies TC 8.00 3.00
❑ 478 Dave McNally 6.00 2.50
❑ 479 Phil Gagliano 6.00 2.50
❑ 480 Oliva/Chico/Clemente 80.00 40.00
❑ 481 John Wyatt 4.00 1.50
❑ 482 Jose Pagan 4.00 1.50
❑ 483 Darold Knowles 4.00 1.50
❑ 484 Phil Roof 4.00 1.50
❑ 485 Ken Berry 6.00 2.50
❑ 486 Cal Koonce 4.00 1.50
❑ 487 Lee May 10.00 4.00
❑ 488 Dick Tracewski 6.00 2.50
❑ 489 Wally Bunker 4.00 1.50
❑ 490 Kill/Mays/Mantle 150.00 75.00
❑ 491 Denny Lemaster 4.00 1.50
❑ 492 Jeff Torborg 6.00 2.50
❑ 493 Jim McGlothlin 4.00 1.50
❑ 494 Ray Sadecki 4.00 1.50
❑ 495 Leon Wagner 4.00 1.50
❑ 496 Steve Hamilton 6.00 2.50
❑ 497 St. Louis Cardinals TC 8.00 3.00
❑ 498 Bill Bryan 6.00 2.50
❑ 499 Steve Blass 6.00 2.50
❑ 500 Frank Robinson 30.00 12.50
❑ 501 John Odom 6.00 2.50
❑ 502 Mike Andrews 4.00 1.50
❑ 503 Al Jackson 6.00 2.50
❑ 504 Russ Snyder 4.00 1.50
❑ 505 Joe Sparma 10.00 4.00
❑ 506 Clarence Jones RC 4.00 1.50
❑ 507 Wade Blasingame 4.00 1.50
❑ 508 Duke Sims 4.00 1.50
❑ 509 Dennis Higgins 4.00 1.50
❑ 510 Ron Fairly 10.00 4.00
❑ 511 Bill Kelso 4.00 1.50
❑ 512 Grant Jackson 4.00 1.50
❑ 513 Hank Bauer MG 6.00 2.50
❑ 514 Al McBean 4.00 1.50
❑ 515 Russ Nixon 4.00 1.50
❑ 516 Pete Mikkelsen 4.00 1.50
❑ 517 Diego Segui 6.00 2.50
❑ 518A Checklist 7/Boyer ERR 12.00 5.00
❑ 518B Checklist 7/Boyer COR 12.00 5.00
❑ 519 Jerry Stephenson 4.00 1.50
❑ 520 Lou Brock 25.00 10.00
❑ 521 Don Shaw 4.00 1.50
❑ 522 Wayne Causey 4.00 1.50
❑ 523 John Tsitouris 4.00 1.50
❑ 524 Andy Kosco 6.00 2.50
❑ 525 Jim Davenport 4.00 1.50
❑ 526 Bill Denehy 4.00 1.50
❑ 527 Tito Francona 4.00 1.50
❑ 528 Detroit Tigers TC 60.00 30.00
❑ 529 Bruce Von Hoff RC 4.00 1.50
❑ 530 B.Robinson/F.Robinson 40.00 15.00
❑ 531 Chuck Hinton 4.00 1.50
❑ 532 Luis Tiant 6.00 2.50
❑ 533 Wes Parker 6.00 2.50
❑ 534 Bob Miller 6.00 2.50
❑ 535 Danny Cater 6.00 2.50
❑ 536 Bill Short 4.00 1.50
❑ 537 Norm Siebern 6.00 2.50
❑ 538 Manny Jimenez 6.00 2.50
❑ 539 J.Ray RC/M.Ferraro RC 4.00 1.50
❑ 540 Nelson Briles 6.00 2.50
❑ 541 Candy Alomar 6.00 2.50
❑ 542 John Boccabella 4.00 1.50
❑ 543 Bob Lee 4.00 1.50
❑ 544 Mayo Smith MG 12.00 5.00
❑ 545 Lindy McDaniel 6.00 2.50
❑ 546 Roy White 6.00 2.50
❑ 547 Dan Coombs 4.00 1.50
❑ 548 Bernie Allen 4.00 1.50
❑ 549 C.Motton RC/R.Nelson RC 4.00 1.50
❑ 550 Clete Boyer 6.00 2.50
❑ 551 Darrell Sutherland 4.00 1.50
❑ 552 Ed Kirkpatrick 4.00 1.50
❑ 553 Hank Aguirre 4.00 1.50
❑ 554 Oakland Athletics TC 10.00 4.00
❑ 555 Jose Tartabull 6.00 2.50
❑ 556 Dick Selma 4.00 1.50
❑ 557 Frank Quilici 6.00 2.50
❑ 558 Johnny Edwards 4.00 1.50
❑ 559 C.Taylor RC/L.Walker 4.00 1.50
❑ 560 Paul Casanova 4.00 1.50
❑ 561 Lee Elia 4.00 1.50
❑ 562 Jim Bouton 6.00 2.50
❑ 563 Ed Charles 4.00 1.50
❑ 564 Eddie Stanky MG 6.00 2.50
❑ 565 Larry Dierker 6.00 2.50
❑ 566 Ken Harrelson 6.00 2.50
❑ 567 Clay Dalrymple 4.00 1.50
❑ 568 Willie Smith 4.00 1.50
❑ 569 I.Murrell RC/L.Rohr RC 4.00 1.50
❑ 570 Rick Reichardt 4.00 1.50
❑ 571 Tony LaRussa 12.00 5.00
❑ 572 Don Bosch RC 4.00 1.50
❑ 573 Joe Coleman 4.00 1.50
❑ 574 Cincinnati Reds TC 10.00 4.00
❑ 575 Jim Palmer 40.00 15.00
❑ 576 Dave Adlesh 4.00 1.50
❑ 577 Fred Talbot 4.00 1.50
❑ 578 Orlando Martinez 4.00 1.50
❑ 579 L.Hisle RC/M.Lum RC 10.00 4.00
❑ 580 Bob Bailey 4.00 1.50
❑ 581 Garry Roggenburk 4.00 1.50
❑ 582 Jerry Grote 10.00 4.00
❑ 583 Gates Brown 10.00 4.00
❑ 584 Larry Shepard MG RC 4.00 1.50
❑ 585 Wilbur Wood 6.00 2.50
❑ 586 Jim Pagliaroni 6.00 2.50
❑ 587 Roger Repoz 4.00 1.50
❑ 588 Dick Schofield 4.00 1.50
❑ 589 R.Clark/M.Ogier RC 4.00 1.50
❑ 590 Tommy Harper 6.00 2.50
❑ 591 Dick Nen 4.00 1.50
❑ 592 John Bateman 4.00 1.50
❑ 593 Lee Stange 4.00 1.50
❑ 594 Phil Linz 6.00 2.50
❑ 595 Phil Ortega 4.00 1.50
❑ 596 Charlie Smith 4.00 1.50
❑ 597 Bill McCool 4.00 1.50
❑ 598 Jerry May 6.00 2.50

1969 Topps

❑ COMP. MASTER SET (695) 5000.00 2500.00
❑ COMPLETE SET (664) 3000.00 1500.00
❑ COMMON (1-218/328-512) 1.50 .60
❑ COMMON CARD (219-327) 2.50 1.00
❑ COMMON CARD (513-588) 2.00 .75
❑ COMMON CARD (589-664) 3.00 1.25

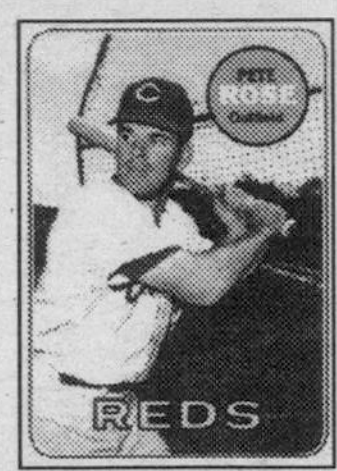

❑ WRAPPER (5-CENT) 20.00 8.00
❑ 1 Yaz/Cater/Oliva LL 15.00 6.00
❑ 2 Rose/Alou/Alou LL 8.00 3.00
❑ 3 Harrelson/Howard/North LL 4.00 1.50
❑ 4 McCovey/Santo/B.Will LL 6.00 2.50
❑ 5 Howard/Horton/Harrelson LL 4.00 1.50
❑ 6 McCovey/Allen/Banks LL 6.00 2.50
❑ 7 Tiant/McDow/McNally LL 4.00 1.50
❑ 8 Gibson/Bolin/Veale LL 6.00 2.50
❑ 9 McLain/McNal/Tiant/Stott LL 4.00 1.50
❑ 10 Marichal/Gibson/Jenkins LL 8.00 3.00
❑ 11 McDowell/McLain/Tiant LL 4.00 1.50
❑ 12 Gibson/Jenkins/Singer LL 4.00 1.50
❑ 13 Mickey Stanley 2.50 1.00
❑ 14 Al McBean 1.50 .60
❑ 15 Boog Powell 4.00 1.50
❑ 16 C.Gutierrez RC/R.Robertson RC 1.50 .60
❑ 17 Mike Marshall 2.50 1.00
❑ 18 Dick Schofield 1.50 .60
❑ 19 Ken Suarez 1.50 .60
❑ 20 Ernie Banks 20.00 8.00
❑ 21 Jose Santiago 1.50 .60
❑ 22 Jesus Alou 2.50 1.00
❑ 23 Lew Krausse 1.50 .60
❑ 24 Walt Alston MG 4.00 1.50
❑ 25 Roy White 2.50 1.00
❑ 26 Clay Carroll 2.50 1.00
❑ 27 Bernie Allen 1.50 .60
❑ 28 Mike Ryan 1.50 .60
❑ 29 Dave Morehead 1.50 .60
❑ 30 Bob Allison 2.50 1.00
❑ 31 G.Gentry RC/A.Otis RC 2.50 1.00
❑ 32 Sammy Ellis 1.50 .60
❑ 33 Wayne Causey 1.50 .60
❑ 34 Gary Peters 1.50 .60
❑ 35 Joe Morgan 10.00 4.00
❑ 36 Luke Walker 1.50 .60
❑ 37 Curt Motton 1.50 .60
❑ 38 Zoilo Versalles 2.50 1.00
❑ 39 Dick Hughes 1.50 .60
❑ 40 Mayo Smith MG 1.50 .60
❑ 41 Bob Barton 1.50 .60
❑ 42 Tommy Harper 2.50 1.00
❑ 43 Joe Niekro 2.50 1.00
❑ 44 Danny Cater 1.50 .60
❑ 45 Maury Wills 2.50 1.00
❑ 46 Fritz Peterson 2.50 1.00
❑ 47A P.Popovich Thick Airbrush 2.50 1.00
❑ 47B P.Popovich Light Airbrush 2.50 1.00
❑ 47C P.Popovich C on Helmet 25.00 10.00
❑ 48 Brant Alyea 1.50 .60
❑ 49A S.Jones/E.Rodriguez ERR 25.00 10.00
❑ 49B S.Jones RC/E.Rodriguez RC 1.50 .60
❑ 50 Roberto Clemente UER 60.00 30.00
❑ 51 Woody Fryman 2.50 1.00
❑ 52 Mike Andrews 1.50 .60
❑ 53 Sonny Jackson 1.50 .60
❑ 54 Cisco Carlos 1.50 .60
❑ 55 Jerry Grote 2.50 1.00
❑ 56 Rich Reese 1.50 .60
❑ 57 Checklist 1/McLain 6.00 2.50
❑ 58 Fred Gladding 1.50 .60
❑ 59 Jay Johnstone 2.50 1.00
❑ 60 Nelson Briles 2.50 1.00
❑ 61 Jimmie Hall 1.50 .60
❑ 62 Chico Salmon 1.50 .60
❑ 63 Jim Hickman 2.50 1.00
❑ 64 Bill Monbouquette 1.50 .60
❑ 65 Willie Davis 2.50 1.00
❑ 66 M.Adamson RC/M.Rettenmund RC 1.50 .60
❑ 67 Bill Stoneman 2.50 1.00
❑ 68 Dave Duncan 2.50 1.00
❑ 69 Steve Hamilton 2.50 1.00
❑ 70 Tommy Helms 2.50 1.00
❑ 71 Steve Whitaker 2.50 1.00
❑ 72 Ron Taylor 1.50 .60
❑ 73 Johnny Briggs 1.50 .60
❑ 74 Preston Gomez MG 2.50 1.00
❑ 75 Luis Aparicio 6.00 2.50
❑ 76 Norm Miller 1.50 .60
❑ 77A R.Perranoski No LA 2.50 1.00
❑ 77B R.Perranoski LA Cap 25.00 10.00
❑ 78 Tom Satriano 1.50 .60
❑ 79 Milt Pappas 2.50 1.00
❑ 80 Norm Cash 2.50 1.00
❑ 81 Mel Queen 1.50 .60
❑ 82 R.Hebner RC/A.Oliver RC 8.00 3.00
❑ 83 Mike Ferraro 2.50 1.00
❑ 84 Bob Humphreys 1.50 .60
❑ 85 Lou Brock 20.00 8.00
❑ 86 Pete Richert 1.50 .60
❑ 87 Horace Clarke 2.50 1.00
❑ 88 Rich Nye 1.50 .60
❑ 89 Russ Gibson 1.50 .60
❑ 90 Jerry Koosman 2.50 1.00
❑ 91 Alvin Dark MG 2.50 1.00
❑ 92 Jack Billingham 2.50 1.00
❑ 93 Joe Foy 2.50 1.00
❑ 94 Hank Aguirre 1.50 .60
❑ 95 Johnny Bench 50.00 20.00
❑ 96 Denny Lemaster 1.50 .60
❑ 97 Buddy Bradford 1.50 .60
❑ 98 Dave Giusti 1.50 .60
❑ 99A D.Morris RC/G.Nettles RC 15.00 6.00
❑ 99B D.Morris/G.Nettles ERR 15.00 6.00
❑ 100 Hank Aaron 50.00 20.00
❑ 101 Daryl Patterson 1.50 .60
❑ 102 Jim Davenport 1.50 .60
❑ 103 Roger Repoz 1.50 .60
❑ 104 Steve Blass 1.50 .60
❑ 105 Rick Monday 2.50 1.00
❑ 106 Jim Hannan 1.50 .60
❑ 107A Checklist 2/Gibson ERR 6.00 2.50
❑ 107B Checklist 2/Gibson COR 8.00 3.00
❑ 108 Tony Taylor 2.50 1.00
❑ 109 Jim Lonborg 2.50 1.00
❑ 110 Mike Shannon 2.50 1.00
❑ 111 John Morris RC 1.50 .60
❑ 112 J.C. Martin 2.50 1.00
❑ 113 Dave May 1.50 .60
❑ 114 A.Closter/J.Cumberland RC 2.50 1.00
❑ 115 Bill Hands 1.50 .60
❑ 116 Chuck Harrison 1.50 .60
❑ 117 Jim Fairey 2.50 1.00
❑ 118 Stan Williams 1.50 .60
❑ 119 Doug Rader 2.50 1.00
❑ 120 Pete Rose 50.00 20.00
❑ 121 Joe Grzenda RC 1.50 .60
❑ 122 Ron Fairly 2.50 1.00
❑ 123 Wilbur Wood 2.50 1.00
❑ 124 Hank Bauer MG 2.50 1.00
❑ 125 Ray Sadecki 1.50 .60
❑ 126 Dick Tracewski 1.50 .60
❑ 127 Kevin Collins 2.50 1.00
❑ 128 Tommie Aaron 2.50 1.00
❑ 129 Bill McCool 1.50 .60
❑ 130 Carl Yastrzemski 20.00 8.00
❑ 131 Chris Cannizzaro 1.50 .60
❑ 132 Dave Baldwin 1.50 .60
❑ 133 Johnny Callison 2.50 1.00
❑ 134 Jim Weaver 1.50 .60
❑ 135 Tommy Davis 2.50 1.00
❑ 136 S.Huntz RC/M.Torrez 1.50 .60
❑ 137 Wally Bunker 1.50 .60
❑ 138 John Bateman 1.50 .60
❑ 139 Andy Kosco 1.50 .60
❑ 140 Jim Lefebvre 2.50 1.00
❑ 141 Bill Dillman 1.50 .60
❑ 142 Woody Woodward 1.50 .60
❑ 143 Joe Nossek 1.50 .60
❑ 144 Bob Hendley 2.50 1.00
❑ 145 Max Alvis 1.50 .60
❑ 146 Jim Perry 2.50 1.00
❑ 147 Leo Durocher MG 4.00 1.50
❑ 148 Lee Stange 1.50 .60
❑ 149 Ollie Brown 2.50 1.00
❑ 150 Denny McLain 4.00 1.50
❑ 151A C.Dalrymple Portrait 1.50 .60
❑ 151B C.Dalrymple Catch 15.00 6.00
❑ 152 Tommie Sisk 1.50 .60
❑ 153 Ed Brinkman 1.50 .60
❑ 154 Jim Britton 1.50 .60
❑ 155 Pete Ward 1.50 .60
❑ 156 H.Gilson/L.McFadden RC 1.50 .60
❑ 157 Bob Rodgers 2.50 1.00
❑ 158 Joe Gibbon 1.50 .60
❑ 159 Jerry Adair 1.50 .60
❑ 160 Vada Pinson 2.50 1.00
❑ 161 John Purdin 1.50 .60
❑ 162 Bob Gibson WS1 8.00 3.00
❑ 163 Willie Horton WS2 6.00 2.50
❑ 164 T.McCarv w/Maris WS3 12.00 5.00
❑ 165 Lou Brock WS4 8.00 3.00
❑ 166 Al Kaline WS5 8.00 3.00
❑ 167 Jim Northrup WS6 6.00 2.50
❑ 168 M.Lolich/B.Gibson WS7 8.00 3.00
❑ 169 Tigers Celebrate WS 6.00 2.50
❑ 170 Frank Howard 2.50 1.00
❑ 171 Glenn Beckert 2.50 1.00
❑ 172 Jerry Stephenson 1.50 .60
❑ 173 B.Christian RC/G.Nyman RC 1.50 .60
❑ 174 Grant Jackson 1.50 .60
❑ 175 Jim Bunning 6.00 2.50
❑ 176 Joe Azcue 1.50 .60
❑ 177 Ron Reed 1.50 .60
❑ 178 Ray Oyler 2.50 1.00
❑ 179 Don Pavletich 1.50 .60
❑ 180 Willie Horton 2.50 1.00
❑ 181 Mel Nelson 1.50 .60
❑ 182 Bill Rigney MG 1.50 .60
❑ 183 Don Shaw 2.50 1.00
❑ 184 Roberto Pena 1.50 .60
❑ 185 Tom Phoebus 1.50 .60
❑ 186 Johnny Edwards 1.50 .60
❑ 187 Leon Wagner 1.50 .60
❑ 188 Rick Wise 2.50 1.00
❑ 189 J.Lahoud RC/J.Thibodeau RC 1.50 .60
❑ 190 Willie Mays 80.00 40.00
❑ 191 Lindy McDaniel 2.50 1.00
❑ 192 Jose Pagan 1.50 .60
❑ 193 Don Cardwell 2.50 1.00
❑ 194 Ted Uhlaender 1.50 .60
❑ 195 John Odom 1.50 .60
❑ 196 Lum Harris MG 1.50 .60
❑ 197 Dick Selma 1.50 .60
❑ 198 Willie Smith 1.50 .60
❑ 199 Jim French 1.50 .60
❑ 200 Bob Gibson 12.00 5.00
❑ 201 Russ Snyder 1.50 .60
❑ 202 Don Wilson 2.50 1.00
❑ 203 Dave Johnson 2.50 1.00
❑ 204 Jack Hiatt 1.50 .60
❑ 205 Rick Reichardt 1.50 .60
❑ 206 L.Hisle/B.Lersch RC 2.50 1.00
❑ 207 Roy Face 2.50 1.00
❑ 208A D.Clendenon Houston 2.50 1.00
❑ 208B D.Clendenon Expos 15.00 6.00
❑ 209 Larry Haney UER 1.50 .60
❑ 210 Felix Millan 1.50 .60
❑ 211 Galen Cisco 1.50 .60
❑ 212 Tom Tresh 2.50 1.00
❑ 213 Gerry Arrigo 1.50 .60
❑ 214 Checklist 3 6.00 2.50
❑ 215 Rico Petrocelli 2.50 1.00
❑ 216 Don Sutton DP 6.00 2.50
❑ 217 John Donaldson 1.50 .60
❑ 218 John Roseboro 2.50 1.00
❑ 219 Fred Patek RC 4.00 1.50
❑ 220 Sam McDowell 4.00 1.50
❑ 221 Art Shamsky 4.00 1.50
❑ 222 Duane Josephson 2.50 1.00
❑ 223 Tom Dukes 4.00 1.50
❑ 224 B.Harrelson RC/S.Kealey RC 2.50 1.00
❑ 225 Don Kessinger 4.00 1.50
❑ 226 Bruce Howard 2.50 1.00
❑ 227 Frank Johnson RC 2.50 1.00
❑ 228 Dave Leonhard 2.50 1.00
❑ 229 Don Lock 2.50 1.00
❑ 230 Rusty Staub UER 4.00 1.50
❑ 231 Pat Dobson 4.00 1.50

❑ 232 Dave Ricketts 2.50 1.00
❑ 233 Steve Barber 4.00 1.50
❑ 234 Dave Bristol MG 2.50 1.00
❑ 235 Jim Hunter 10.00 4.00
❑ 236 Manny Mota 4.00 1.50
❑ 237 Bobby Cox RC 10.00 4.00
❑ 238 Ken Johnson 2.50 1.00
❑ 239 Bob Taylor 4.00 1.50
❑ 240 Ken Harrelson 4.00 1.50
❑ 241 Jim Brewer 2.50 1.00
❑ 242 Frank Kostro 2.50 1.00
❑ 243 Ron Kline 2.50 1.00
❑ 244 R.Fosse RC/G.Woodson RC 4.00 1.50
❑ 245 Ed Charles 4.00 1.50
❑ 246 Joe Coleman 2.50 1.00
❑ 247 Gene Oliver 2.50 1.00
❑ 248 Bob Priddy 2.50 1.00
❑ 249 Ed Spiezio 4.00 1.50
❑ 250 Frank Robinson 20.00 8.00
❑ 251 Ron Herbel 2.50 1.00
❑ 252 Chuck Cottier 2.50 1.00
❑ 253 Jerry Johnson RC 2.50 1.00
❑ 254 Joe Schultz MG RC 4.00 1.50
❑ 255 Steve Carlton 30.00 12.50
❑ 256 Gates Brown 4.00 1.50
❑ 257 Jim Ray 2.50 1.00
❑ 258 Jackie Hernandez 4.00 1.50
❑ 259 Bill Short 2.50 1.00
❑ 260 Reggie Jackson RC 300.00 150.00
❑ 261 Bob Johnson 2.50 1.00
❑ 262 Mike Kekich 4.00 1.50
❑ 263 Jerry May 2.50 1.00
❑ 264 Bill Landis 2.50 1.00
❑ 265 Chico Cardenas 4.00 1.50
❑ 266 T.Hutton/A.Foster RC 4.00 1.50
❑ 267 Vicente Romo RC 2.50 1.00
❑ 268 Al Spangler 2.50 1.00
❑ 269 Al Weis 4.00 1.50
❑ 270 Mickey Lolich 4.00 1.50
❑ 271 Larry Stahl 4.00 1.50
❑ 272 Ed Stroud 2.50 1.00
❑ 273 Ron Willis 2.50 1.00
❑ 274 Clyde King MG 2.50 1.00
❑ 275 Vic Davalillo 2.50 1.00
❑ 276 Gary Wagner 2.50 1.00
❑ 277 Elrod Hendricks RC 2.50 1.00
❑ 278 Gary Geiger UER 2.50 1.00
❑ 279 Roger Nelson 4.00 1.50
❑ 280 Alex Johnson 4.00 1.50
❑ 281 Ted Kubiak 2.50 1.00
❑ 282 Pat Jarvis 2.50 1.00
❑ 283 Sandy Alomar 4.00 1.50
❑ 284 J.Robertson RC/M.Wegener RC 4.00 1.50
❑ 285 Don Mincher 4.00 1.50
❑ 286 Dock Ellis RC 4.00 1.50
❑ 287 Jose Tartabull 4.00 1.50
❑ 288 Ken Holtzman 4.00 1.50
❑ 289 Bart Shirley 2.50 1.00
❑ 290 Jim Kaat 4.00 1.50
❑ 291 Vern Fuller 2.50 1.00
❑ 292 Al Downing 4.00 1.50
❑ 293 Dick Dietz 2.50 1.00
❑ 294 Jim Lemon MG 2.50 1.00
❑ 295 Tony Perez 12.00 5.00
❑ 296 Andy Messersmith RC 4.00 1.50
❑ 297 Deron Johnson 2.50 1.00
❑ 298 Dave Nicholson 4.00 1.50
❑ 299 Mark Belanger 4.00 1.50
❑ 300 Felipe Alou 4.00 1.50
❑ 301 Darrell Brandon 4.00 1.50
❑ 302 Jim Pagliaroni 2.50 1.00
❑ 303 Cal Koonce 4.00 1.50
❑ 304 B.Davis/C.Gaston RC 6.00 2.50
❑ 305 Dick McAuliffe 4.00 1.50
❑ 306 Jim Grant 4.00 1.50
❑ 307 Gary Kolb 2.50 1.00
❑ 308 Wade Blasingame 2.50 1.00
❑ 309 Walt Williams 2.50 1.00
❑ 310 Tom Haller 2.50 1.00
❑ 311 Sparky Lyle RC 10.00 4.00
❑ 312 Lee Elia 2.50 1.00
❑ 313 Bill Robinson 4.00 1.50
❑ 314 Checklist 4/Drysdale 6.00 2.50
❑ 315 Eddie Fisher 2.50 1.00
❑ 316 Hal Lanier 2.50 1.00
❑ 317 Bruce Look RC 2.50 1.00
❑ 318 Jack Fisher 2.50 1.00
❑ 319 Ken McMullen UER 2.50 1.00
❑ 320 Dal Maxvill 2.50 1.00
❑ 321 Jim McAndrew RC 4.00 1.50
❑ 322 Jose Vidal 4.00 1.50
❑ 323 Larry Miller 2.50 1.00
❑ 324 L.Cain RC/D.Campbell RC 4.00 1.50
❑ 325 Jose Cardenal 4.00 1.50
❑ 326 Gary Sutherland 4.00 1.50
❑ 327 Willie Crawford 2.50 1.00
❑ 328 Joel Horlen 1.50 .60
❑ 329 Rick Joseph 1.50 .60
❑ 330 Tony Conigliaro 4.00 1.50
❑ 331 G.Garrido/T.House RC 2.50 1.00
❑ 332 Fred Talbot 1.50 .60
❑ 333 Ivan Murrell 1.50 .60
❑ 334 Phil Roof 1.50 .60
❑ 335 Bill Mazeroski 6.00 2.50
❑ 336 Jim Roland 1.50 .60
❑ 337 Marty Martinez RC 1.50 .60
❑ 338 Del Unser RC 1.50 .60
❑ 339 S.Mingori RC/J.Pena RC 1.50 .60
❑ 340 Dave McNally 2.50 1.00
❑ 341 Dave Adlesh 1.50 .60
❑ 342 Bubba Morton 1.50 .60
❑ 343 Dan Frisella 1.50 .60
❑ 344 Tom Matchick 1.50 .60
❑ 345 Frank Linzy 1.50 .60
❑ 346 Wayne Comer RC 1.50 .60
❑ 347 Randy Hundley 2.50 1.00
❑ 348 Steve Hargan 1.50 .60
❑ 349 Dick Williams MG 2.50 1.00
❑ 350 Richie Allen 4.00 1.50
❑ 351 Carroll Sembera 1.50 .60
❑ 352 Paul Schaal 2.50 1.00
❑ 353 Jeff Torborg 2.50 1.00
❑ 354 Nate Oliver 1.50 .60
❑ 355 Phil Niekro 6.00 2.50
❑ 356 Frank Quilici 1.50 .60
❑ 357 Carl Taylor 1.50 .60
❑ 358 G.Lauzerique RC/R.Rodriguez 1.50 .60
❑ 359 Dick Kelley 1.50 .60
❑ 360 Jim Wynn 2.50 1.00
❑ 361 Gary Holman RC 1.50 .60
❑ 362 Jim Maloney 2.50 1.00
❑ 363 Russ Nixon 1.50 .60
❑ 364 Tommie Agee 4.00 1.50
❑ 365 Jim Fregosi 2.50 1.00
❑ 366 Bo Belinsky 2.50 1.00
❑ 367 Lou Johnson 2.50 1.00
❑ 368 Vic Roznovsky 1.50 .60
❑ 369 Bob Skinner MG 2.50 1.00
❑ 370 Juan Marichal 8.00 3.00
❑ 371 Sal Bando 2.50 1.00
❑ 372 Adolfo Phillips 1.50 .60
❑ 373 Fred Lasher 1.50 .60
❑ 374 Bob Tillman 1.50 .60
❑ 375 Harmon Killebrew 15.00 6.00
❑ 376 M.Fiore RC/J.Rooker RC 1.50 .60
❑ 377 Gary Bell 2.50 1.00
❑ 378 Jose Herrera RC 1.50 .60
❑ 379 Ken Boyer 2.50 1.00
❑ 380 Stan Bahnsen 2.50 1.00
❑ 381 Ed Kranepool 2.50 1.00
❑ 382 Pat Corrales 2.50 1.00
❑ 383 Casey Cox 1.50 .60
❑ 384 Larry Shepard MG 1.50 .60
❑ 385 Orlando Cepeda 6.00 2.50
❑ 386 Jim McGlothlin 1.50 .60
❑ 387 Bobby Klaus 1.50 .60
❑ 388 Tom McCraw 1.50 .60
❑ 389 Dan Coombs 1.50 .60
❑ 390 Bill Freehan 2.50 1.00
❑ 391 Ray Culp 1.50 .60
❑ 392 Bob Burda RC 1.50 .60
❑ 393 Gene Brabender 2.50 1.00
❑ 394 L.Piniella/M.Staehle 6.00 2.50
❑ 395 Chris Short 1.50 .60
❑ 396 Jim Campanis 1.50 .60
❑ 397 Chuck Dobson 1.50 .60
❑ 398 Tito Francona 1.50 .60
❑ 399 Bob Bailey 2.50 1.00
❑ 400 Don Drysdale 15.00 6.00
❑ 401 Jake Gibbs 2.50 1.00
❑ 402 Ken Boswell RC 2.50 1.00
❑ 403 Bob Miller 1.50 .60
❑ 404 V.LaRose RC/G.Ross RC 2.50 1.00
❑ 405 Lee May 2.50 1.00
❑ 406 Phil Ortega 1.50 .60
❑ 407 Tom Egan 1.50 .60
❑ 408 Nate Colbert 1.50 .60
❑ 409 Bob Moose 1.50 .60
❑ 410 Al Kaline 25.00 10.00
❑ 411 Larry Dierker 2.50 1.00
❑ 412 Checklist 5/Mantle DP 15.00 6.00
❑ 413 Roland Sheldon 2.50 1.00
❑ 414 Duke Sims 1.50 .60
❑ 415 Ray Washburn 1.50 .60
❑ 416 Willie McCovey AS 8.00 3.00
❑ 417 Ken Harrelson AS 3.00 1.25
❑ 418 Tommy Helms AS 3.00 1.25
❑ 419 Rod Carew AS 10.00 4.00
❑ 420 Ron Santo AS 4.00 1.50
❑ 421 Brooks Robinson AS 8.00 3.00
❑ 422 Don Kessinger AS 3.00 1.25
❑ 423 Bert Campaneris AS 4.00 1.50
❑ 424 Pete Rose AS 15.00 6.00
❑ 425 Carl Yastrzemski AS 10.00 4.00
❑ 426 Curt Flood AS 4.00 1.50
❑ 427 Tony Oliva AS 4.00 1.50
❑ 428 Lou Brock AS 6.00 2.50
❑ 429 Willie Horton AS 3.00 1.25
❑ 430 Johnny Bench AS 10.00 4.00
❑ 431 Bill Freehan AS 4.00 1.50
❑ 432 Bob Gibson AS 6.00 2.50
❑ 433 Denny McLain AS 3.00 1.25
❑ 434 Jerry Koosman AS 3.00 1.25
❑ 435 Sam McDowell AS 2.50 1.00
❑ 436 Gene Alley 2.50 1.00
❑ 437 Luis Alcaraz RC 1.50 .60
❑ 438 Gary Waslewski RC 1.50 .60
❑ 439 E.Herrmann RC/D.Lazar RC 1.50 .60
❑ 440A Willie McCovey 15.00 6.00
❑ 440B Willie McCovey WL 100.00 50.00
❑ 441A Dennis Higgins 1.50 .60
❑ 441B Dennis Higgins WL
❑ 442 Ty Cline 1.50 .60
❑ 443 Don Wert 1.50 .60
❑ 444A Joe Moeller 1.50 .60
❑ 444B Joe Moeller WL
❑ 445 Bobby Knoop 1.50 .60
❑ 446 Claude Raymond 1.50 .60
❑ 447A Ralph Houk MG 2.50 1.00
❑ 447B Ralph Houk MG WL
❑ 448 Bob Tolan 2.50 1.00
❑ 449 Paul Lindblad 1.50 .60
❑ 450 Billy Williams 8.00 3.00
❑ 451A Rich Rollins 2.50 1.00
❑ 451B Rich Rollins WL
❑ 452A Al Ferrara 1.50 .60
❑ 452B Al Ferrara WL
❑ 453 Mike Cuellar 2.50 1.00
❑ 454A L.Colton/D.Money RC 2.50 1.00
❑ 454B L.Colton/D.Money WL
❑ 455 Sonny Siebert 1.50 .60
❑ 456 Bud Harrelson 2.50 1.00
❑ 457 Dalton Jones 1.50 .60
❑ 458 Curt Blefary 1.50 .60
❑ 459 Dave Boswell 1.50 .60
❑ 460 Joe Torre 4.00 1.50
❑ 461A Mike Epstein 1.50 .60
❑ 461B Mike Epstein WL
❑ 462 R.Schoendienst MG 2.50 1.00
❑ 463 Dennis Ribant 1.50 .60
❑ 464A Dave Marshall RC 1.50 .60
❑ 464B Dave Marshall WL
❑ 465 Tommy John 4.00 1.50
❑ 466 John Boccabella 2.50 1.00
❑ 467 Tommie Reynolds 1.50 .60
❑ 468A B.Dal Canton RC/B.Robertson 1.50 .60
❑ 468B B.Dal Canton/B.Robertson WL
❑ 469 Chico Ruiz 1.50 .60
❑ 470A Mel Stottlemyre 2.50 1.00
❑ 470B Mel Stottlemyre WL 30.00 12.50
❑ 471A Ted Savage 1.50 .60
❑ 471B Ted Savage WL
❑ 472 Jim Price 1.50 .60
❑ 473A Jose Arcia 1.50 .60
❑ 473B Jose Arcia WL
❑ 474 Tom Murphy RC 1.50 .60
❑ 475 Tim McCarver 4.00 1.50
❑ 476A K.Brett RC/G.Moses 2.50 1.00

❑ 476B K.Brett/G.Moses WL 30.00 12.50
❑ 477 Jeff James RC 1.50 .60
❑ 478 Don Buford 1.50 .60
❑ 479 Richie Scheinblum 1.50 .60
❑ 480 Tom Seaver 80.00 40.00
❑ 481 Bill Melton RC 2.50 1.00
❑ 482A Jim Gosger 1.50 .60
❑ 482B Jim Gosger WL
❑ 483 Ted Abernathy 1.50 .60
❑ 484 Joe Gordon MG 2.50 1.00
❑ 485A Gaylord Perry 10.00 4.00
❑ 485B Gaylord Perry WL 80.00 40.00
❑ 486A Paul Casanova 1.50 .60
❑ 486B Paul Casanova WL
❑ 487 Denis Menke 1.50 .60
❑ 488 Joe Sparma 1.50 .60
❑ 489 Clete Boyer 2.50 1.00
❑ 490 Matty Alou 2.50 1.00
❑ 491A J.Crider RC/G.Mitterwald 1.50 .60
❑ 491B J.Crider/G.Mitterwald WL
❑ 492 Tony Cloninger 1.50 .60
❑ 493A Wes Parker 2.50 1.00
❑ 493B Wes Parker WL
❑ 494 Ken Berry 1.50 .60
❑ 495 Bert Campaneris 2.50 1.00
❑ 496 Larry Jaster 1.50 .60
❑ 497 Julian Javier 2.50 1.00
❑ 498 Juan Pizarro 2.50 1.00
❑ 499 D.Bryant RC/S.Shea RC 1.50 .60
❑ 500A Mickey Mantle UER 350.00 175.00
❑ 500B Mickey Mantle UER WL 2000.00 1000.00
❑ 501A Tony Gonzalez 2.50 1.00
❑ 501B Tony Gonzalez WL
❑ 502 Minnie Rojas 1.50 .60
❑ 503 Larry Brown 1.50 .60
❑ 504 Checklist 6/B.Robinson 8.00 3.00
❑ 505A Bobby Bolin 1.50 .60
❑ 505B Bobby Bolin WL
❑ 506 Paul Blair 2.50 1.00
❑ 507 Cookie Rojas 2.50 1.00
❑ 508 Moe Drabowsky 2.50 1.00
❑ 509 Manny Sanguillen 2.50 1.00
❑ 510 Rod Carew 40.00 15.00
❑ 511A Diego Segui 2.50 1.00
❑ 511B Diego Segui WL
❑ 512 Cleon Jones 2.50 1.00
❑ 513 Camilo Pascual 3.00 1.25
❑ 514 Mike Lum 2.00 .75
❑ 515 Dick Green 2.00 .75
❑ 516 Earl Weaver MG RC 20.00 8.00
❑ 517 Mike McCormick 3.00 1.25
❑ 518 Fred Whitfield 2.00 .75
❑ 519 J.Kenney RC/L.Boehmer RC 2.00 .75
❑ 520 Bob Veale 3.00 1.25
❑ 521 George Thomas 2.00 .75
❑ 522 Joe Hoerner 2.00 .75
❑ 523 Bob Chance 2.00 .75
❑ 524 J.Laboy RC/F.Wicker RC 3.00 1.25
❑ 525 Earl Wilson 3.00 1.25
❑ 526 Hector Torres RC 2.00 .75
❑ 527 Al Lopez MG 5.00 2.00
❑ 528 Claude Osteen 3.00 1.25
❑ 529 Ed Kirkpatrick 3.00 1.25
❑ 530 Cesar Tovar 2.00 .75
❑ 531 Dick Farrell 2.00 .75
❑ 532 Phoeb/Hard/McNally/Cuellar 3.00 1.25
❑ 533 Nolan Ryan 200.00 100.00
❑ 534 Jerry McNertney 3.00 1.25
❑ 535 Phil Regan 3.00 1.25
❑ 536 D.Breeden RC/D.Roberts RC 2.00 .75
❑ 537 Mike Paul RC 2.00 .75
❑ 538 Charlie Smith 2.00 .75
❑ 539 T.Williams/M.Epstein 12.00 5.00
❑ 540 Curt Flood 3.00 1.25
❑ 541 Joe Verbanic 2.00 .75
❑ 542 Bob Aspromonte 2.00 .75
❑ 543 Fred Newman 2.00 .75
❑ 544 M.Kilkenny RC/R.Woods RC 2.00 .75
❑ 545 Willie Stargell 12.00 5.00
❑ 546 Jim Nash 2.00 .75
❑ 547 Billy Martin MG 5.00 2.00
❑ 548 Bob Locker 2.00 .75
❑ 549 Ron Brand 2.00 .75
❑ 550 Brooks Robinson 30.00 12.50
❑ 551 Wayne Granger RC 2.00 .75
❑ 552 T.Sizemore RC/B.Sudakis RC 3.00 1.25
❑ 553 Ron Davis 2.00 .75
❑ 554 Frank Bertaina 2.00 .75
❑ 555 Jim Ray Hart 3.00 1.25
❑ 556 Bando/Campaneris/Cater 3.00 1.25
❑ 557 Frank Fernandez 2.00 .75
❑ 558 Tom Burgmeier RC 3.00 1.25
❑ 559 J.Hague RC/J.Hicks 2.00 .75
❑ 560 Luis Tiant 3.00 1.25
❑ 561 Ron Clark 2.00 .75
❑ 562 Bob Watson RC 8.00 3.00
❑ 563 Marty Pattin RC 3.00 1.25
❑ 564 Gil Hodges MG 10.00 4.00
❑ 565 Hoyt Wilhelm 8.00 3.00
❑ 566 Ron Hansen 2.00 .75
❑ 567 E.Jimenez/J.Shellenback 2.00 .75
❑ 568 Cecil Upshaw 2.00 .75
❑ 569 Billy Harris 1.50 .60
❑ 570 Ron Santo 8.00 3.00
❑ 571 Cap Peterson 2.00 .75
❑ 572 W.McCovey/J.Marichal 15.00 6.00
❑ 573 Jim Palmer 30.00 12.50
❑ 574 George Scott 3.00 1.25
❑ 575 Bill Singer 3.00 1.25
❑ 576 R.Stone/B.Wilson 2.00 .75
❑ 577 Mike Hegan 3.00 1.25
❑ 578 Don Bosch 2.00 .75
❑ 579 Dave Nelson RC 2.00 .75
❑ 580 Jim Northrup 3.00 1.25
❑ 581 Gary Nolan 3.00 1.25
❑ 582A Checklist 7/Oliva White 6.00 2.50
❑ 582B Checklist 7/Oliva Red 8.00 3.00
❑ 583 Clyde Wright RC 2.00 .75
❑ 584 Don Mason 2.00 .75
❑ 585 Ron Swoboda 3.00 1.25
❑ 586 Tim Cullen 2.00 .75
❑ 587 Joe Rudi RC 8.00 3.00
❑ 588 Bill White 3.00 1.25
❑ 589 Joe Pepitone 5.00 2.00
❑ 590 Rico Carty 5.00 2.00
❑ 591 Mike Hedlund 3.00 1.25
❑ 592 R.Robles RC/A.Santorini RC 5.00 2.00
❑ 593 Don Nottebart 3.00 1.25
❑ 594 Dooley Womack 3.00 1.25
❑ 595 Lee Maye 3.00 1.25
❑ 596 Chuck Hartenstein 3.00 1.25
❑ 597 Rollie Fingers RC 40.00 15.00
❑ 598 Ruben Amaro 3.00 1.25
❑ 599 John Boozer 3.00 1.25
❑ 600 Tony Oliva 8.00 3.00
❑ 601 Tug McGraw SP 8.00 3.00
❑ 602 Distaso/Young/Qualls RC 5.00 2.00
❑ 603 Joe Keough RC 3.00 1.25
❑ 604 Bobby Etheridge 3.00 1.25
❑ 605 Dick Ellsworth 3.00 1.25
❑ 606 Gene Mauch MG 5.00 2.00
❑ 607 Dick Bosman 3.00 1.25
❑ 608 Dick Simpson 3.00 1.25
❑ 609 Phil Gagliano 3.00 1.25
❑ 610 Jim Hardin 3.00 1.25
❑ 611 Didier/Hriniak/Niebauer RC 5.00 2.00
❑ 612 Jack Aker 5.00 2.00
❑ 613 Jim Beauchamp 3.00 1.25
❑ 614 T.Griffin RC/S.Guinn RC 3.00 1.25
❑ 615 Len Gabrielson 3.00 1.25
❑ 616 Don McMahon 3.00 1.25
❑ 617 Jesse Gonder 3.00 1.25
❑ 618 Ramon Webster 3.00 1.25
❑ 619 Butler/Kelly/Rios RC 5.00 2.00
❑ 620 Dean Chance 5.00 2.00
❑ 621 Bill Voss 3.00 1.25
❑ 622 Dan Osinski 3.00 1.25
❑ 623 Hank Allen 3.00 1.25
❑ 624 Chaney/Dyer/Harmon RC 5.00 2.00
❑ 625 Mack Jones UER 5.00 2.00
❑ 626 Gene Michael 5.00 2.00
❑ 627 George Stone RC 3.00 1.25
❑ 628 Conigliaro/O'Brien/Wenz RC 5.00 2.00
❑ 629 Jack Hamilton 3.00 1.25
❑ 630 Bobby Bonds RC 30.00 12.50
❑ 631 John Kennedy 5.00 2.00
❑ 632 Jon Warden RC 3.00 1.25
❑ 633 Harry Walker MG 3.00 1.25
❑ 634 Andy Etchebarren 3.00 1.25
❑ 635 George Culver 3.00 1.25
❑ 636 Woody Held 3.00 1.25
❑ 637 DaVanon/Reberger/Kirby RC 5.00 2.00
❑ 638 Ed Sprague RC 3.00 1.25
❑ 639 Barry Moore 3.00 1.25
❑ 640 Ferguson Jenkins 20.00 8.00
❑ 641 Darwin/Miller/Dean RC 5.00 2.00
❑ 642 John Hiller 3.00 1.25
❑ 643 Billy Cowan 3.00 1.25
❑ 644 Chuck Hinton 3.00 1.25
❑ 645 George Brunet 3.00 1.25
❑ 646 D.McGinn RC/C.Morton RC 5.00 2.00
❑ 647 Dave Wickersham 3.00 1.25
❑ 648 Bobby Wine 5.00 2.00
❑ 649 Al Jackson 3.00 1.25
❑ 650 Ted Williams MG 20.00 8.00
❑ 651 Gus Gil 5.00 2.00
❑ 652 Eddie Watt 3.00 1.25
❑ 653 Aurelio Rodriguez UER RC 5.00 2.00
❑ 654 May/Secrist/Morales RC 5.00 2.00
❑ 655 Mike Hershberger 3.00 1.25
❑ 656 Dan Schneider 3.00 1.25
❑ 657 Bobby Murcer 8.00 3.00
❑ 658 Hall/Burbach/Miles RC 3.00 1.25
❑ 659 Johnny Podres 5.00 2.00
❑ 660 Reggie Smith 5.00 2.00
❑ 661 Jim Merritt 3.00 1.25
❑ 662 Drago/Spriggs/Oliver RC 5.00 2.00
❑ 663 Dick Radatz 5.00 2.00
❑ 664 Ron Hunt 5.00 2.00

1970 Topps

❑ COMPLETE SET (720) 2000.00 1000.00
❑ COMMON CARD (1-132) .75 .30
❑ COMMON CARD (133-372) 1.00 .40
❑ COMMON CARD (373-459) 1.50 .60
❑ COMMON CARD (460-546) 2.00 .75
❑ COMMON CARD (547-633) 4.00 1.50
❑ COMMON CARD (634-720) 10.00 4.00
❑ WRAPPER (10-CENT) 20.00 8.00
❑ 1 New York Mets TC 30.00 12.50
❑ 2 Diego Segui 1.00 .40
❑ 3 Darrel Chaney .75 .30
❑ 4 Tom Egan .75 .30
❑ 5 Wes Parker 1.00 .40
❑ 6 Grant Jackson .75 .30
❑ 7 G.Boyd RC/R.Nagelson RC .75 .30
❑ 8 Jose Martinez RC .75 .30
❑ 9 Checklist 1 12.00 5.00
❑ 10 Carl Yastrzemski 20.00 8.00
❑ 11 Nate Colbert .75 .30
❑ 12 John Hiller .75 .30
❑ 13 Jack Hiatt .75 .30
❑ 14 Hank Allen .75 .30
❑ 15 Larry Dierker .75 .30
❑ 16 Charlie Metro MG RC .75 .30
❑ 17 Hoyt Wilhelm 4.00 1.50
❑ 18 Carlos May 1.00 .40
❑ 19 John Boccabella .75 .30
❑ 20 Dave McNally 1.00 .40
❑ 21 V.Blue RC/G.Tenace RC 4.00 1.50
❑ 22 Ray Washburn .75 .30
❑ 23 Bill Robinson 1.00 .40
❑ 24 Dick Selma .75 .30
❑ 25 Cesar Tovar .75 .30
❑ 26 Tug McGraw 2.00 .75
❑ 27 Chuck Hinton .75 .30
❑ 28 Billy Wilson .75 .30
❑ 29 Sandy Alomar 1.00 .40
❑ 30 Matty Alou 1.00 .40

❑ 31	Marty Pattin	1.00	.40
❑ 32	Harry Walker MG	.75	.30
❑ 33	Don Wert	.75	.30
❑ 34	Willie Crawford	.75	.30
❑ 35	Joel Horlen	.75	.30
❑ 36	D.Breeden/B.Carbo RC	1.00	.40
❑ 37	Dick Drago	.75	.30
❑ 38	Mack Jones	.75	.30
❑ 39	Mike Nagy RC	.75	.30
❑ 40	Richie Allen	2.00	.75
❑ 41	George Lauzerique	.75	.30
❑ 42	Tito Fuentes	.75	.30
❑ 43	Jack Aker	.75	.30
❑ 44	Roberto Pena	.75	.30
❑ 45	Dave Johnson	1.00	.40
❑ 46	Ken Rudolph RC	.75	.30
❑ 47	Bob Miller	.75	.30
❑ 48	Gil Garrido	.75	.30
❑ 49	Tim Cullen	.75	.30
❑ 50	Tommie Agee	1.00	.40
❑ 51	Bob Christian	.75	.30
❑ 52	Bruce Dal Canton	.75	.30
❑ 53	John Kennedy	.75	.30
❑ 54	Jeff Torborg	1.00	.40
❑ 55	John Odom	.75	.30
❑ 56	J.Lis RC/S.Reid RC	.75	.30
❑ 57	Pat Kelly	.75	.30
❑ 58	Dave Marshall	.75	.30
❑ 59	Dick Ellsworth	.75	.30
❑ 60	Jim Wynn	1.00	.40
❑ 61	Rose/Clemente/Jones LL	12.00	5.00
❑ 62	Carew/Smith/Oliva LL	2.00	.75
❑ 63	McCovey/Santo/Perez LL	2.00	.75
❑ 64	Kill/Powell/Jackson LL	4.00	1.50
❑ 65	McCovey/Aaron/May LL	4.00	1.50
❑ 66	Kill/Howard/Jackson LL	4.00	1.50
❑ 67	Marichal/Carlton/Gibson LL	4.00	1.50
❑ 68	Bosman/Palmer/Cuellar LL	1.00	.40
❑ 69	Seav/Niek/Jenk/Mari LL	4.00	1.50
❑ 70	McLain/Cuellar/Boswell LL	1.00	.40
❑ 71	Jenkins/Gibson/Singer LL	2.00	.75
❑ 72	McDowell/Lolich/Mess LL	1.00	.40
❑ 73	Wayne Granger	.75	.30
❑ 74	G.Washburn RC/W.Wolf	.75	.30
❑ 75	Jim Kaat	1.00	.40
❑ 76	Carl Taylor	.75	.30
❑ 77	Frank Linzy	.75	.30
❑ 78	Joe Lahoud	.75	.30
❑ 79	Clay Kirby	.75	.30
❑ 80	Don Kessinger	1.00	.40
❑ 81	Dave May	.75	.30
❑ 82	Frank Fernandez	.75	.30
❑ 83	Don Cardwell	.75	.30
❑ 84	Paul Casanova	.75	.30
❑ 85	Max Alvis	.75	.30
❑ 86	Lum Harris MG	.75	.30
❑ 87	Steve Renko RC	.75	.30
❑ 88	M.Fuentes RC/D.Baney RC	1.00	.40
❑ 89	Juan Rios	.75	.30
❑ 90	Tim McCarver	1.00	.40
❑ 91	Rich Morales	.75	.30
❑ 92	George Culver	.75	.30
❑ 93	Rick Renick	.75	.30
❑ 94	Freddie Patek	1.00	.40
❑ 95	Earl Wilson	1.00	.40
❑ 96	L.Lee RC/J.Reuss RC	1.00	.40
❑ 97	Joe Moeller	.75	.30
❑ 98	Gates Brown	1.00	.40
❑ 99	Bobby Pfeil RC	.75	.30
❑ 100	Mel Stottlemyre	1.00	.40
❑ 101	Bobby Floyd	.75	.30
❑ 102	Joe Rudi	1.00	.40
❑ 103	Frank Reberger	.75	.30
❑ 104	Gerry Moses	.75	.30
❑ 105	Tony Gonzalez	.75	.30
❑ 106	Darold Knowles	.75	.30
❑ 107	Bobby Etheridge	.75	.30
❑ 108	Tom Burgmeier	.75	.30
❑ 109	G.Jestadt RC/C.Morton	.75	.30
❑ 110	Bob Moose	.75	.30
❑ 111	Mike Hegan	1.00	.40
❑ 112	Dave Nelson	.75	.30
❑ 113	Jim Ray	.75	.30
❑ 114	Gene Michael	1.00	.40
❑ 115	Alex Johnson	1.00	.40
❑ 116	Sparky Lyle	1.00	.40
❑ 117	Don Young	.75	.30
❑ 118	George Mitterwald	.75	.30
❑ 119	Chuck Taylor RC	.75	.30
❑ 120	Sal Bando	1.00	.40
❑ 121	F.Beene RC/T.Crowley RC	.75	.30
❑ 122	George Stone	.75	.30
❑ 123	Don Gutteridge MG RC	.75	.30
❑ 124	Larry Jaster	.75	.30
❑ 125	Deron Johnson	.75	.30
❑ 126	Marty Martinez	.75	.30
❑ 127	Joe Coleman	.75	.30
❑ 128A	Checklist 2 R Perranoski	6.00	2.50
❑ 128B	Checklist 2 R. Perranoski	6.00	2.50
❑ 129	Jimmie Price	.75	.30
❑ 130	Ollie Brown	.75	.30
❑ 131	R.Lamb RC/B.Stinson RC	.75	.30
❑ 132	Jim McGlothlin	.75	.30
❑ 133	Clay Carroll	1.00	.40
❑ 134	Danny Walton RC	1.00	.40
❑ 135	Dick Dietz	1.00	.40
❑ 136	Steve Hargan	1.00	.40
❑ 137	Art Shamsky	1.00	.40
❑ 138	Joe Foy	1.00	.40
❑ 139	Rich Nye	1.00	.40
❑ 140	Reggie Jackson	50.00	20.00
❑ 141	D.Cash RC/J.Jeter RC	1.50	.60
❑ 142	Fritz Peterson	1.00	.40
❑ 143	Phil Gagliano	1.00	.40
❑ 144	Ray Culp	1.00	.40
❑ 145	Rico Carty	1.50	.60
❑ 146	Danny Murphy	1.00	.40
❑ 147	Angel Hermoso RC	1.00	.40
❑ 148	Earl Weaver MG	3.00	1.25
❑ 149	Billy Champion RC	1.00	.40
❑ 150	Harmon Killebrew	8.00	3.00
❑ 151	Dave Roberts	1.00	.40
❑ 152	Ike Brown RC	1.00	.40
❑ 153	Gary Gentry	1.00	.40
❑ 154	J.Miles/J.Dukes RC	1.00	.40
❑ 155	Denis Menke	1.00	.40
❑ 156	Eddie Fisher	1.00	.40
❑ 157	Manny Mota	1.50	.60
❑ 158	Jerry McNertney	1.50	.60
❑ 159	Tommy Helms	1.50	.60
❑ 160	Phil Niekro	5.00	2.00
❑ 161	Richie Scheinblum	1.00	.40
❑ 162	Jerry Johnson	1.00	.40
❑ 163	Syd O'Brien	1.00	.40
❑ 164	Ty Cline	1.00	.40
❑ 165	Ed Kirkpatrick	1.00	.40
❑ 166	Al Oliver	3.00	1.25
❑ 167	Bill Burbach	1.00	.40
❑ 168	Dave Watkins RC	1.00	.40
❑ 169	Tom Hall	1.00	.40
❑ 170	Billy Williams	5.00	2.00
❑ 171	Jim Nash	1.00	.40
❑ 172	G.Hill RC/R.Garr RC	1.50	.60
❑ 173	Jim Hicks	1.00	.40
❑ 174	Ted Sizemore	1.50	.60
❑ 175	Dick Bosman	1.00	.40
❑ 176	Jim Ray Hart	1.50	.60
❑ 177	Jim Northrup	1.50	.60
❑ 178	Denny Lemaster	1.00	.40
❑ 179	Ivan Murrell	1.00	.40
❑ 180	Tommy John	1.50	.60
❑ 181	Sparky Anderson MG	5.00	2.00
❑ 182	Dick Hall	1.00	.40
❑ 183	Jerry Grote	1.50	.60
❑ 184	Ray Fosse	1.00	.40
❑ 185	Don Mincher	1.50	.60
❑ 186	Rick Joseph	1.00	.40
❑ 187	Mike Hedlund	1.00	.40
❑ 188	Manny Sanguillen	1.50	.60
❑ 189	Thurman Munson RC	100.00	50.00
❑ 190	Joe Torre	3.00	1.25
❑ 191	Vicente Romo	1.00	.40
❑ 192	Jim Qualls	1.00	.40
❑ 193	Mike Wegener	1.00	.40
❑ 194	Chuck Manuel RC	1.00	.40
❑ 195	Tom Seaver NLCS1	15.00	6.00
❑ 196	Ken Boswell NLCS2	2.00	.75
❑ 197	Nolan Ryan NLCS3	30.00	12.50
❑ 198	Mets Celebrate/w/Ryan	15.00	6.00
❑ 199	Mike Cuellar ALCS1	2.00	.75
❑ 200	Boog Powell ALCS2	3.00	1.25
❑ 201	B.Powell/A.Etch ALCS3	2.00	.75
❑ 202	Orioles Celebrate ALCS	2.00	.75
❑ 203	Rudy May	1.00	.40
❑ 204	Len Gabrielson	1.00	.40
❑ 205	Bert Campaneris	1.50	.60
❑ 206	Clete Boyer	1.50	.60
❑ 207	N.McRae RC/B.Reed RC	1.00	.40
❑ 208	Fred Gladding	1.00	.40
❑ 209	Ken Suarez	1.00	.40
❑ 210	Juan Marichal	5.00	2.00
❑ 211	Ted Williams MG UER	15.00	6.00
❑ 212	Al Santorini	1.00	.40
❑ 213	Andy Etchebarren	1.00	.40
❑ 214	Ken Boswell	1.00	.40
❑ 215	Reggie Smith	1.50	.60
❑ 216	Chuck Hartenstein	1.00	.40
❑ 217	Ron Hansen	1.00	.40
❑ 218	Ron Stone	1.00	.40
❑ 219	Jerry Kenney	1.00	.40
❑ 220	Steve Carlton	15.00	6.00
❑ 221	Ron Brand	1.00	.40
❑ 222	Jim Rooker	1.00	.40
❑ 223	Nate Oliver	1.00	.40
❑ 224	Steve Barber	1.50	.60
❑ 225	Lee May	1.50	.60
❑ 226	Ron Perranoski	1.00	.40
❑ 227	J.Mayberry RC/B.Watkins RC	1.50	.60
❑ 228	Aurelio Rodriguez	1.00	.40
❑ 229	Rich Robertson	1.00	.40
❑ 230	Brooks Robinson	15.00	6.00
❑ 231	Luis Tiant	1.50	.60
❑ 232	Bob Didier	1.00	.40
❑ 233	Lew Krausse	1.00	.40
❑ 234	Tommy Dean	1.00	.40
❑ 235	Mike Epstein	1.00	.40
❑ 236	Bob Veale	1.00	.40
❑ 237	Russ Gibson	1.00	.40
❑ 238	Jose Laboy	1.00	.40
❑ 239	Ken Berry	1.00	.40
❑ 240	Ferguson Jenkins	5.00	2.00
❑ 241	A.Fitzmorris RC/S.Northey RC	1.00	.40
❑ 242	Walt Alston MG	3.00	1.25
❑ 243	Joe Sparma	1.00	.40
❑ 244A	Checklist 3 Red Bat	6.00	2.50
❑ 244B	Checklist 3 Brown Bat	6.00	2.50
❑ 245	Leo Cardenas	1.00	.40
❑ 246	Jim McAndrew	1.00	.40
❑ 247	Lou Klimchock	1.00	.40
❑ 248	Jesus Alou	1.00	.40
❑ 249	Bob Locker	1.00	.40
❑ 250	Willie McCovey UER	10.00	4.00
❑ 251	Dick Schofield	1.00	.40
❑ 252	Lowell Palmer RC	1.00	.40
❑ 253	Ron Woods	1.00	.40
❑ 254	Camilo Pascual	1.00	.40
❑ 255	Jim Spencer RC	1.00	.40
❑ 256	Vic Davalillo	1.00	.40
❑ 257	Dennis Higgins	1.00	.40
❑ 258	Paul Popovich	1.00	.40
❑ 259	Tommie Reynolds	1.00	.40
❑ 260	Claude Osteen	1.00	.40
❑ 261	Curt Motton	1.00	.40
❑ 262	J.Morales RC/J.Williams RC	1.00	.40
❑ 263	Duane Josephson	1.00	.40
❑ 264	Rich Hebner	1.00	.40
❑ 265	Randy Hundley	1.00	.40
❑ 266	Wally Bunker	1.00	.40
❑ 267	H.Hill RC/P.Ratliff	1.00	.40
❑ 268	Claude Raymond	1.00	.40
❑ 269	Cesar Gutierrez	1.00	.40
❑ 270	Chris Short	1.00	.40
❑ 271	Greg Goossen	1.50	.60
❑ 272	Hector Torres	1.00	.40
❑ 273	Ralph Houk MG	1.50	.60
❑ 274	Gerry Arrigo	1.00	.40
❑ 275	Duke Sims	1.00	.40
❑ 276	Ron Hunt	1.00	.40
❑ 277	Paul Doyle RC	1.00	.40
❑ 278	Tommie Aaron	1.00	.40
❑ 279	Bill Lee RC	1.50	.60
❑ 280	Donn Clendenon	1.50	.60
❑ 281	Casey Cox	1.00	.40
❑ 282	Steve Huntz	1.00	.40
❑ 283	Angel Bravo RC	1.00	.40
❑ 284	Jack Baldschun	1.00	.40
❑ 285	Paul Blair	1.50	.60
❑ 286	J.Jenkins RC/B.Buckner RC	5.00	2.00

❑ 287 Fred Talbot 1.00 .40
❑ 288 Larry Hisle 1.50 .60
❑ 289 Gene Brabender 1.00 .40
❑ 290 Rod Carew 15.00 6.00
❑ 291 Leo Durocher MG 3.00 1.25
❑ 292 Eddie Leon RC 1.00 .40
❑ 293 Bob Bailey 1.50 .60
❑ 294 Jose Azcue 1.00 .40
❑ 295 Cecil Upshaw 1.00 .40
❑ 296 Woody Woodward 1.00 .40
❑ 297 Curt Blefary 1.00 .40
❑ 298 Ken Henderson 1.00 .40
❑ 299 Buddy Bradford 1.00 .40
❑ 300 Tom Seaver 30.00 12.50
❑ 301 Chico Salmon 1.00 .40
❑ 302 Jeff James 1.00 .40
❑ 303 Brant Alyea 1.00 .40
❑ 304 Bill Russell RC 5.00 2.00
❑ 305 Don Buford WS1 4.00 1.50
❑ 306 Donn Clendenon WS2 4.00 1.50
❑ 307 Tommie Agee WS3 4.00 1.50
❑ 308 J.C. Martin WS4 4.00 1.50
❑ 309 Jerry Koosman WS5 4.00 1.50
❑ 310 Mets Celebrate WS 5.00 2.00
❑ 311 Dick Green 1.00 .40
❑ 312 Mike Torrez 1.00 .40
❑ 313 Mayo Smith MG 1.00 .40
❑ 314 Bill McCool 1.00 .40
❑ 315 Luis Aparicio 5.00 2.00
❑ 316 Skip Guinn 1.00 .40
❑ 317 B.Conigliaro/L.Alvarado RC 1.50 .60
❑ 318 Willie Smith 1.00 .40
❑ 319 Clay Dalrymple 1.00 .40
❑ 320 Jim Maloney 1.50 .60
❑ 321 Lou Piniella 1.50 .60
❑ 322 Luke Walker 1.00 .40
❑ 323 Wayne Comer 1.00 .40
❑ 324 Tony Taylor 1.50 .60
❑ 325 Dave Boswell 1.00 .40
❑ 326 Bill Voss 1.00 .40
❑ 327 Hal King RC 1.00 .40
❑ 328 George Brunet 1.00 .40
❑ 329 Chris Cannizzaro 1.00 .40
❑ 330 Lou Brock 10.00 4.00
❑ 331 Chuck Dobson 1.00 .40
❑ 332 Bobby Wine 1.00 .40
❑ 333 Bobby Murcer 1.50 .60
❑ 334 Phil Regan 1.00 .40
❑ 335 Bill Freehan 1.50 .60
❑ 336 Del Unser 1.00 .40
❑ 337 Mike McCormick 1.50 .60
❑ 338 Paul Schaal 1.00 .40
❑ 339 Johnny Edwards 1.00 .40
❑ 340 Tony Conigliaro 3.00 1.25
❑ 341 Bill Sudakis 1.00 .40
❑ 342 Wilbur Wood 1.50 .60
❑ 343A Checklist 4 Red Bat 6.00 2.50
❑ 343B Checklist 4 Brown Bat 6.00 2.50
❑ 344 Marcelino Lopez 1.00 .40
❑ 345 Al Ferrara 1.00 .40
❑ 346 Red Schoendienst MG 1.50 .60
❑ 347 Russ Snyder 1.00 .40
❑ 348 M.Jorgensen RC/J.Hudson RC 1.50 .60
❑ 349 Steve Hamilton 1.00 .40
❑ 350 Roberto Clemente 60.00 30.00
❑ 351 Tom Murphy 1.00 .40
❑ 352 Bob Barton 1.00 .40
❑ 353 Stan Williams 1.00 .40
❑ 354 Amos Otis 1.50 .60
❑ 355 Doug Rader 1.00 .40
❑ 356 Fred Lasher 1.00 .40
❑ 357 Bob Burda 1.00 .40
❑ 358 Pedro Borbon RC 1.50 .60
❑ 359 Phil Roof 1.00 .40
❑ 360 Curt Flood 1.50 .60
❑ 361 Ray Jarvis 1.00 .40
❑ 362 Joe Hague 1.00 .40
❑ 363 Tom Shopay RC 1.00 .40
❑ 364 Dan McGinn 1.00 .40
❑ 365 Zoilo Versalles 1.00 .40
❑ 366 Barry Moore 1.00 .40
❑ 367 Mike Lum 1.00 .40
❑ 368 Ed Herrmann 1.00 .40
❑ 369 Alan Foster 1.00 .40
❑ 370 Tommy Harper 1.50 .60
❑ 371 Rod Gaspar RC 1.00 .40
❑ 372 Dave Giusti 1.00 .40
❑ 373 Roy White 2.00 .75
❑ 374 Tommie Sisk 1.50 .60
❑ 375 Johnny Callison 2.00 .75
❑ 376 Lefty Phillips MG RC 1.50 .60
❑ 377 Bill Butler 1.50 .60
❑ 378 Jim Davenport 1.50 .60
❑ 379 Tom Tischinski RC 1.50 .60
❑ 380 Tony Perez 6.00 2.50
❑ 381 B.Brooks RC/M.Olivo RC 1.50 .60
❑ 382 Jack DiLauro RC 1.50 .60
❑ 383 Mickey Stanley 2.00 .75
❑ 384 Gary Neibauer 1.50 .60
❑ 385 George Scott 2.00 .75
❑ 386 Bill Dillman 1.50 .60
❑ 387 Baltimore Orioles TC 3.00 1.25
❑ 388 Byron Browne 1.50 .60
❑ 389 Jim Shellenback 1.50 .60
❑ 390 Willie Davis 2.00 .75
❑ 391 Larry Brown 1.50 .60
❑ 392 Walt Hriniak 2.00 .75
❑ 393 John Gelnar 1.50 .60
❑ 394 Gil Hodges MG 4.00 1.50
❑ 395 Walt Williams 1.50 .60
❑ 396 Steve Blass 2.00 .75
❑ 397 Roger Repoz 1.50 .60
❑ 398 Bill Stoneman 1.50 .60
❑ 399 New York Yankees TC 3.00 1.25
❑ 400 Denny McLain 4.00 1.50
❑ 401 J.Harrell RC/B.Williams RC 1.50 .60
❑ 402 Ellie Rodriguez 1.50 .60
❑ 403 Jim Bunning 6.00 2.50
❑ 404 Rich Reese 1.50 .60
❑ 405 Bill Hands 1.50 .60
❑ 406 Mike Andrews 1.50 .60
❑ 407 Bob Watson 2.00 .75
❑ 408 Paul Lindblad 1.50 .60
❑ 409 Bob Tolan 1.50 .60
❑ 410 Boog Powell 4.00 1.50
❑ 411 Los Angeles Dodgers TC 3.00 1.25
❑ 412 Larry Burchart 1.50 .60
❑ 413 Sonny Jackson 1.50 .60
❑ 414 Paul Edmondson RC 1.50 .60
❑ 415 Julian Javier 2.00 .75
❑ 416 Joe Verbanic 1.50 .60
❑ 417 John Bateman 1.50 .60
❑ 418 John Donaldson 1.50 .60
❑ 419 Ron Taylor 1.50 .60
❑ 420 Ken McMullen 2.00 .75
❑ 421 Pat Dobson 2.00 .75
❑ 422 Kansas City Royals TC 3.00 1.25
❑ 423 Jerry May 1.50 .60
❑ 424 Mike Kilkenny 1.50 .60
❑ 425 Bobby Bonds 6.00 2.50
❑ 426 Bill Rigney MG 1.50 .60
❑ 427 Fred Norman 1.50 .60
❑ 428 Don Buford 1.50 .60
❑ 429 R.Bobb RC/J.Cosman 1.50 .60
❑ 430 Andy Messersmith 2.00 .75
❑ 431 Ron Swoboda 2.00 .75
❑ 432A Checklist 5 Yellow Ltr 6.00 2.50
❑ 432B Checklist 5 White Ltr 6.00 2.50
❑ 433 Ron Bryant RC 1.50 .60
❑ 434 Felipe Alou 2.00 .75
❑ 435 Nelson Briles 2.00 .75
❑ 436 Philadelphia Phillies TC 3.00 1.25
❑ 437 Danny Cater 1.50 .60
❑ 438 Pat Jarvis 1.50 .60
❑ 439 Lee Maye 1.50 .60
❑ 440 Bill Mazeroski 6.00 2.50
❑ 441 John O'Donoghue 1.50 .60
❑ 442 Gene Mauch MG 2.00 .75
❑ 443 Al Jackson 1.50 .60
❑ 444 B.Farmer RC/J.Matias RC 1.50 .60
❑ 445 Vada Pinson 2.00 .75
❑ 446 Billy Grabarkewitz RC 1.50 .60
❑ 447 Lee Stange 1.50 .60
❑ 448 Houston Astros TC 3.00 1.25
❑ 449 Jim Palmer 12.00 5.00
❑ 450 Willie McCovey AS 6.00 2.50
❑ 451 Boog Powell AS 4.00 1.50
❑ 452 Felix Millan AS 2.00 .75
❑ 453 Rod Carew AS 6.00 2.50
❑ 454 Ron Santo AS 4.00 1.50
❑ 455 Brooks Robinson AS 6.00 2.50
❑ 456 Don Kessinger AS 2.00 .75
❑ 457 Rico Petrocelli AS 4.00 1.50
❑ 458 Pete Rose AS 15.00 6.00
❑ 459 Reggie Jackson AS 12.00 5.00
❑ 460 Matty Alou AS 3.00 1.25
❑ 461 Carl Yastrzemski AS 10.00 4.00
❑ 462 Hank Aaron AS 15.00 6.00
❑ 463 Frank Robinson AS 8.00 3.00
❑ 464 Johnny Bench AS 15.00 6.00
❑ 465 Bill Freehan AS 3.00 1.25
❑ 466 Juan Marichal AS 5.00 2.00
❑ 467 Denny McLain AS 3.00 1.25
❑ 468 Jerry Koosman AS 3.00 1.25
❑ 469 Sam McDowell AS 3.00 1.25
❑ 470 Willie Stargell 10.00 4.00
❑ 471 Chris Zachary 2.00 .75
❑ 472 Atlanta Braves TC 4.00 1.50
❑ 473 Don Bryant 2.00 .75
❑ 474 Dick Kelley 2.00 .75
❑ 475 Dick McAuliffe 3.00 1.25
❑ 476 Don Shaw 2.00 .75
❑ 477 A.Severinsen RC/R.Freed RC 2.00 .75
❑ 478 Bobby Heise RC 2.00 .75
❑ 479 Dick Woodson RC 2.00 .75
❑ 480 Glenn Beckert 3.00 1.25
❑ 481 Jose Tartabull 2.00 .75
❑ 482 Tom Hilgendorf RC 2.00 .75
❑ 483 Gail Hopkins RC 2.00 .75
❑ 484 Gary Nolan 3.00 1.25
❑ 485 Jay Johnstone 3.00 1.25
❑ 486 Terry Harmon 2.00 .75
❑ 487 Cisco Carlos 2.00 .75
❑ 488 J.C. Martin 2.00 .75
❑ 489 Eddie Kasko MG 2.00 .75
❑ 490 Bill Singer 3.00 1.25
❑ 491 Graig Nettles 5.00 2.00
❑ 492 K.Lampard RC/S.Spinks RC 2.00 .75
❑ 493 Lindy McDaniel 3.00 1.25
❑ 494 Larry Stahl 2.00 .75
❑ 495 Dave Morehead 2.00 .75
❑ 496 Steve Whitaker 2.00 .75
❑ 497 Eddie Watt 2.00 .75
❑ 498 Al Weis 2.00 .75
❑ 499 Skip Lockwood 3.00 1.25
❑ 500 Hank Aaron 50.00 20.00
❑ 501 Chicago White Sox TC 4.00 1.50
❑ 502 Rollie Fingers 10.00 4.00
❑ 503 Dal Maxvill 2.00 .75
❑ 504 Don Pavletich 2.00 .75
❑ 505 Ken Holtzman 3.00 1.25
❑ 506 Ed Stroud 2.00 .75
❑ 507 Pat Corrales 2.00 .75
❑ 508 Joe Niekro 3.00 1.25
❑ 509 Montreal Expos TC 4.00 1.50
❑ 510 Tony Oliva 5.00 2.00
❑ 511 Joe Hoerner 2.00 .75
❑ 512 Billy Harris 2.00 .75
❑ 513 Preston Gomez MG 2.00 .75
❑ 514 Steve Hovley RC 2.00 .75
❑ 515 Don Wilson 3.00 1.25
❑ 516 J.Ellis RC/J.Lyttle RC 2.00 .75
❑ 517 Joe Gibbon 2.00 .75
❑ 518 Bill Melton 2.00 .75
❑ 519 Don McMahon 2.00 .75
❑ 520 Willie Horton 3.00 1.25
❑ 521 Cal Koonce 2.00 .75
❑ 522 California Angels TC 4.00 1.50
❑ 523 Jose Pena 2.00 .75
❑ 524 Alvin Dark MG 3.00 1.25
❑ 525 Jerry Adair 2.00 .75
❑ 526 Ron Herbel 2.00 .75
❑ 527 Don Bosch 2.00 .75
❑ 528 Elrod Hendricks 2.00 .75
❑ 529 Bob Aspromonte 2.00 .75
❑ 530 Bob Gibson 15.00 6.00
❑ 531 Ron Clark 2.00 .75
❑ 532 Danny Murtaugh MG 3.00 1.25
❑ 533 Buzz Stephen RC 2.00 .75
❑ 534 Minnesota Twins TC 4.00 1.50
❑ 535 Andy Kosco 2.00 .75
❑ 536 Mike Kekich 2.00 .75
❑ 537 Joe Morgan 10.00 4.00
❑ 538 Bob Humphreys 2.00 .75
❑ 539 D.Doyle RC/L.Bowa RC 8.00 3.00
❑ 540 Gary Peters 2.00 .75
❑ 541 Bill Heath 2.00 .75
❑ 542A Checklist 6 Brown Bat 6.00 2.50

❑ 543 Clyde Wright 2.00 .75
❑ 544 Cincinnati Reds TC 4.00 1.50
❑ 545 Ken Harrelson 3.00 1.25
❑ 546 Ron Reed 2.00 .75
❑ 547 Rick Monday 6.00 2.50
❑ 548 Howie Reed 4.00 1.50
❑ 549 St. Louis Cardinals TC 6.00 2.50
❑ 550 Frank Howard 6.00 2.50
❑ 551 Dock Ellis 6.00 2.50
❑ 552 O'Riley/Paepke/Rico RC 4.00 1.50
❑ 553 Jim Lefebvre 6.00 2.50
❑ 554 Tom Timmermann RC 4.00 1.50
❑ 555 Orlando Cepeda 12.00 5.00
❑ 556 Dave Bristol MG 6.00 2.50
❑ 557 Ed Kranepool 6.00 2.50
❑ 558 Vern Fuller 4.00 1.50
❑ 559 Tommy Davis 6.00 2.50
❑ 560 Gaylord Perry 12.00 5.00
❑ 561 Tom McCraw 4.00 1.50
❑ 562 Ted Abernathy 4.00 1.50
❑ 563 Boston Red Sox TC 6.00 2.50
❑ 564 Johnny Briggs 4.00 1.50
❑ 565 Jim Hunter 12.00 5.00
❑ 566 Gene Alley 6.00 2.50
❑ 567 Bob Oliver 4.00 1.50
❑ 568 Stan Bahnsen 6.00 2.50
❑ 569 Cookie Rojas 6.00 2.50
❑ 570 Jim Fregosi 6.00 2.50
❑ 571 Jim Brewer 4.00 1.50
❑ 572 Frank Quilici 4.00 1.50
❑ 573 Corkins/Robles/Slocum RC 4.00 1.50
❑ 574 Bobby Bolin 6.00 2.50
❑ 575 Cleon Jones 6.00 2.50
❑ 576 Milt Pappas 6.00 2.50
❑ 577 Bernie Allen 4.00 1.50
❑ 578 Tom Griffin 4.00 1.50
❑ 579 Detroit Tigers TC 6.00 2.50
❑ 580 Pete Rose 60.00 30.00
❑ 581 Tom Satriano 4.00 1.50
❑ 582 Mike Paul 4.00 1.50
❑ 583 Hal Lanier 4.00 1.50
❑ 584 Al Downing 6.00 2.50
❑ 585 Rusty Staub 8.00 3.00
❑ 586 Rickey Clark RC 4.00 1.50
❑ 587 Jose Arcia 4.00 1.50
❑ 588A Checklist 7 Adolfo 8.00 3.00
❑ 588B Checklist 7 Adolpho 6.00 2.50
❑ 589 Joe Keough 4.00 1.50
❑ 590 Mike Cuellar 6.00 2.50
❑ 591 Mike Ryan UER 4.00 1.50
❑ 592 Daryl Patterson 4.00 1.50
❑ 593 Chicago Cubs TC 8.00 3.00
❑ 594 Jake Gibbs 4.00 1.50
❑ 595 Maury Wills 8.00 3.00
❑ 596 Mike Hershberger 6.00 2.50
❑ 597 Sonny Siebert 4.00 1.50
❑ 598 Joe Pepitone 6.00 2.50
❑ 599 Stelmaszek/Martin/Such RC 4.00 1.50
❑ 600 Willie Mays 80.00 40.00
❑ 601 Pete Richert 4.00 1.50
❑ 602 Ted Savage 4.00 1.50
❑ 603 Ray Oyler 4.00 1.50
❑ 604 Cito Gaston 6.00 2.50
❑ 605 Rick Wise 6.00 2.50
❑ 606 Chico Ruiz 4.00 1.50
❑ 607 Gary Waslewski 4.00 1.50
❑ 608 Pittsburgh Pirates TC 6.00 2.50
❑ 609 Buck Martinez RC 6.00 2.50
❑ 610 Jerry Koosman 8.00 3.00
❑ 611 Norm Cash 6.00 2.50
❑ 612 Jim Hickman 6.00 2.50
❑ 613 Dave Baldwin 6.00 2.50
❑ 614 Mike Shannon 6.00 2.50
❑ 615 Mark Belanger 6.00 2.50
❑ 616 Jim Merritt 4.00 1.50
❑ 617 Jim French 4.00 1.50
❑ 618 Billy Wynne RC 4.00 1.50
❑ 619 Norm Miller 4.00 1.50
❑ 620 Jim Perry 6.00 2.50
❑ 621 McQueen/Evans/Kester RC 12.00 5.00
❑ 622 Don Sutton 12.00 5.00
❑ 623 Horace Clarke 6.00 2.50
❑ 624 Clyde King MG 4.00 1.50
❑ 625 Dean Chance 4.00 1.50
❑ 626 Dave Ricketts 4.00 1.50
❑ 627 Gary Wagner 4.00 1.50
❑ 628 Wayne Garrett RC 4.00 1.50
❑ 629 Merv Rettenmund 4.00 1.50
❑ 630 Ernie Banks 50.00 20.00
❑ 631 Oakland Athletics TC 6.00 2.50
❑ 632 Gary Sutherland 4.00 1.50
❑ 633 Roger Nelson 4.00 1.50
❑ 634 Bud Harrelson 15.00 6.00
❑ 635 Bob Allison 15.00 6.00
❑ 636 Jim Stewart 10.00 4.00
❑ 637 Cleveland Indians TC 12.00 5.00
❑ 638 Frank Bertaina 10.00 4.00
❑ 639 Dave Campbell 15.00 6.00
❑ 640 Al Kaline 50.00 20.00
❑ 641 Al McBean 10.00 4.00
❑ 642 Garrett/Lund/Tatum RC 10.00 4.00
❑ 643 Jose Pagan 10.00 4.00
❑ 644 Gerry Nyman 10.00 4.00
❑ 645 Don Money 15.00 6.00
❑ 646 Jim Britton 10.00 4.00
❑ 647 Tom Matchick 10.00 4.00
❑ 648 Larry Haney 10.00 4.00
❑ 649 Jimmie Hall 10.00 4.00
❑ 650 Sam McDowell 15.00 6.00
❑ 651 Jim Gosger 10.00 4.00
❑ 652 Rich Rollins 15.00 6.00
❑ 653 Moe Drabowsky 10.00 4.00
❑ 654 Gamble/Day/Mangual RC 15.00 6.00
❑ 655 John Roseboro 15.00 6.00
❑ 656 Jim Hardin 10.00 4.00
❑ 657 San Diego Padres TC 12.00 5.00
❑ 658 Ken Tatum RC 10.00 4.00
❑ 659 Pete Ward 10.00 4.00
❑ 660 Johnny Bench 80.00 40.00
❑ 661 Jerry Robertson 10.00 4.00
❑ 662 Frank Lucchesi MG RC 10.00 4.00
❑ 663 Tito Francona 10.00 4.00
❑ 664 Bob Robertson 10.00 4.00
❑ 665 Jim Lonborg 15.00 6.00
❑ 666 Adolpho Phillips 10.00 4.00
❑ 667 Bob Meyer 15.00 6.00
❑ 668 Bob Tillman 10.00 4.00
❑ 669 Johnson/Lazar/Scott RC 10.00 4.00
❑ 670 Ron Santo 15.00 6.00
❑ 671 Jim Campanis 10.00 4.00
❑ 672 Leon McFadden 10.00 4.00
❑ 673 Ted Uhlaender 10.00 4.00
❑ 674 Dave Leonhard 10.00 4.00
❑ 675 Jose Cardenal 15.00 6.00
❑ 676 Washington Senators TC 12.00 5.00
❑ 677 Woodie Fryman 10.00 4.00
❑ 678 Dave Duncan 15.00 6.00
❑ 679 Ray Sadecki 10.00 4.00
❑ 680 Rico Petrocelli 15.00 6.00
❑ 681 Bob Garibaldi RC 10.00 4.00
❑ 682 Dalton Jones 10.00 4.00
❑ 683 Geishart/McRae/Simpson RC 15.00 6.00
❑ 684 Jack Fisher 10.00 4.00
❑ 685 Tom Haller 10.00 4.00
❑ 686 Jackie Hernandez 10.00 4.00
❑ 687 Bob Priddy 10.00 4.00
❑ 688 Ted Kubiak 15.00 6.00
❑ 689 Frank Tepedino RC 15.00 6.00
❑ 690 Ron Fairly 15.00 6.00
❑ 691 Joe Grzenda 10.00 4.00
❑ 692 Duffy Dyer 10.00 4.00
❑ 693 Bob Johnson 10.00 4.00
❑ 694 Gary Ross 10.00 4.00
❑ 695 Bobby Knoop 10.00 4.00
❑ 696 San Francisco Giants TC 12.00 5.00
❑ 697 Jim Hannan 10.00 4.00
❑ 698 Tom Tresh 15.00 6.00
❑ 699 Hank Aguirre 10.00 4.00
❑ 700 Frank Robinson 50.00 20.00
❑ 701 Jack Billingham 10.00 4.00
❑ 702 Johnson/Klimkowski/Zepp RC 10.00 4.00
❑ 703 Lou Marone RC 10.00 4.00
❑ 704 Frank Baker RC 10.00 4.00
❑ 705 Tony Cloninger UER 10.00 4.00
❑ 706 John McNamara MG RC 10.00 4.00
❑ 707 Kevin Collins 10.00 4.00
❑ 708 Jose Santiago 10.00 4.00
❑ 709 Mike Fiore 10.00 4.00
❑ 710 Felix Millan 10.00 4.00
❑ 711 Ed Brinkman 10.00 4.00
❑ 712 Nolan Ryan 200.00 100.00
❑ 713 Seattle Pilots TC 25.00 10.00
❑ 714 Al Spangler 10.00 4.00
❑ 715 Mickey Lolich 15.00 6.00
❑ 716 Campisi/Cleveland/Guzman RC 15.00 6.00
❑ 717 Tom Phoebus 10.00 4.00
❑ 718 Ed Spiezio 10.00 4.00
❑ 719 Jim Roland 10.00 4.00
❑ 720 Rick Reichardt 15.00 6.00

1971 Topps

❑ COMPLETE SET (752) 2500.00 1250.00
❑ COMMON CARD (1-393) 1.50 .60
❑ COMMON CARD (394-523) 2.50 1.00
❑ COMMON CARD (524-643) 4.00 1.50
❑ COMMON CARD (644-752) 8.00 3.00
❑ COMMON SP (644-752) 12.00 5.00
❑ WRAPPER (10-CENT) 15.00 6.00
❑ 1 Baltimore Orioles TC 20.00 8.00
❑ 2 Dock Ellis 1.50 .60
❑ 3 Dick McAuliffe 2.00 .75
❑ 4 Vic Davalillo 1.50 .60
❑ 5 Thurman Munson 120.00 60.00
❑ 6 Ed Spiezio 1.50 .60
❑ 7 Jim Holt RC 1.50 .60
❑ 8 Mike McQueen 1.50 .60
❑ 9 George Scott 2.00 .75
❑ 10 Claude Osteen 2.00 .75
❑ 11 Elliott Maddox RC 1.50 .60
❑ 12 Johnny Callison 2.00 .75
❑ 13 C.Brinkman RC/D.Moloney RC 1.50 .60
❑ 14 Dave Concepcion RC 15.00 6.00
❑ 15 Andy Messersmith 2.00 .75
❑ 16 Ken Singleton RC 4.00 1.50
❑ 17 Billy Sorrell 1.50 .60
❑ 18 Norm Miller 1.50 .60
❑ 19 Skip Pitlock RC 1.50 .60
❑ 20 Reggie Jackson 50.00 20.00
❑ 21 Dan McGinn 1.50 .60
❑ 22 Phil Roof 1.50 .60
❑ 23 Oscar Gamble 1.50 .60
❑ 24 Rich Hand RC 1.50 .60
❑ 25 Cito Gaston 2.00 .75
❑ 26 Bert Blyleven RC 20.00 8.00
❑ 27 F.Cambria RC/G.Clines RC 1.50 .60
❑ 28 Ron Klimkowski 1.50 .60
❑ 29 Don Buford 1.50 .60
❑ 30 Phil Niekro 6.00 2.50
❑ 31 Eddie Kasko MG 1.50 .60
❑ 32 Jerry DaVanon 1.50 .60
❑ 33 Del Unser 1.50 .60
❑ 34 Sandy Vance RC 1.50 .60
❑ 35 Lou Piniella 2.00 .75
❑ 36 Dean Chance 2.00 .75
❑ 37 Rich McKinney RC 1.50 .60
❑ 38 Jim Colborn RC 1.50 .60
❑ 39 L.LaGrow RC/G.Lamont RC 2.00 .75
❑ 40 Lee May 2.00 .75
❑ 41 Rick Austin RC 1.50 .60
❑ 42 Boots Day 1.50 .60
❑ 43 Steve Kealey 1.50 .60
❑ 44 Johnny Edwards 1.50 .60
❑ 45 Jim Hunter 6.00 2.50
❑ 46 Dave Campbell 2.00 .75
❑ 47 Johnny Jeter 1.50 .60
❑ 48 Dave Baldwin 1.50 .60
❑ 49 Don Money 1.50 .60
❑ 50 Willie McCovey 10.00 4.00
❑ 51 Steve Kline RC 1.50 .60
❑ 52 O.Brown RC/E.Williams RC 1.50 .60

53	Paul Blair	2.00	.75
54	Checklist 1	10.00	4.00
55	Steve Carlton	20.00	8.00
56	Duane Josephson	1.50	.60
57	Von Joshua RC	1.50	.60
58	Bill Lee	2.00	.75
59	Gene Mauch MG	2.00	.75
60	Dick Bosman	1.50	.60
61	Johnson/Yaz/Oliva LL	4.00	1.50
62	Carty/Torre/Sang LL	2.00	.75
63	Howard/Conig/Powell LL	4.00	1.50
64	Bench/Perez/B.Will LL	6.00	2.50
65	Howard/Killebrew/Yaz LL	4.00	1.50
66	Bench/B.Will/Perez LL	6.00	2.50
67	Segui/Palmer/Wright LL	4.00	1.50
68	Seaver/Simp/Walk LL	4.00	1.50
69	Cuellar/McNally/Perry LL	2.00	.75
70	Gibson/Perry/Jenkins LL	6.00	2.50
71	McDowell/Lolich/John LL	2.00	.75
72	Seaver/Gibson/Jenkins LL	6.00	2.50
73	George Brunet	1.50	.60
74	P.Hamm RC/J.Nettles RC	1.50	.60
75	Gary Nolan	2.00	.75
76	Ted Savage	1.50	.60
77	Mike Compton RC	1.50	.60
78	Jim Spencer	1.50	.60
79	Wade Blasingame	1.50	.60
80	Bill Melton	1.50	.60
81	Felix Millan	1.50	.60
82	Casey Cox	1.50	.60
83	T.Foli RC/R.Bobb	2.00	.75
84	Marcel Lachemann RC	1.50	.60
85	Billy Grabarkewitz	1.50	.60
86	Mike Kilkenny	1.50	.60
87	Jack Heidemann RC	1.50	.60
88	Hal King	1.50	.60
89	Ken Brett	1.50	.60
90	Joe Pepitone	2.00	.75
91	Bob Lemon MG	2.00	.75
92	Fred Wenz	1.50	.60
93	N.McRae/D.Riddleberger	1.50	.60
94	Don Hahn RC	1.50	.60
95	Luis Tiant	2.00	.75
96	Joe Hague	1.50	.60
97	Floyd Wicker	1.50	.60
98	Joe Decker RC	1.50	.60
99	Mark Belanger	2.00	.75
100	Pete Rose	80.00	40.00
101	Les Cain	1.50	.60
102	K.Forsch RC/L.Howard RC	2.00	.75
103	Rich Severson RC	1.50	.60
104	Dan Frisella	1.50	.60
105	Tony Conigliaro	2.00	.75
106	Tom Dukes	1.50	.60
107	Roy Foster RC	1.50	.60
108	John Cumberland	1.50	.60
109	Steve Hovley	1.50	.60
110	Bill Mazeroski	6.00	2.50
111	L.Colson RC/B.Mitchell RC	1.50	.60
112	Manny Mota	2.00	.75
113	Jerry Crider	1.50	.60
114	Billy Conigliaro	2.00	.75
115	Donn Clendenon	2.00	.75
116	Ken Sanders	1.50	.60
117	Ted Simmons RC	8.00	3.00
118	Cookie Rojas	2.00	.75
119	Frank Lucchesi MG	1.50	.60
120	Willie Horton	2.00	.75
121	J.Dunegan/R.Skidmore RC	1.50	.60
122	Eddie Watt	1.50	.60
123A	Checklist 2 Right	10.00	4.00
123B	Checklist 2 Centered	10.00	4.00
124	Don Gullett RC	2.00	.75
125	Ray Fosse	1.50	.60
126	Danny Coombs	1.50	.60
127	Danny Thompson RC	2.00	.75
128	Frank Johnson	1.50	.60
129	Aurelio Monteagudo	1.50	.60
130	Denis Menke	1.50	.60
131	Curt Blefary	1.50	.60
132	Jose Laboy	1.50	.60
133	Mickey Lolich	2.00	.75
134	Jose Arcia	1.50	.60
135	Rick Monday	2.00	.75
136	Duffy Dyer	1.50	.60
137	Marcelino Lopez	1.50	.60
138	J.Lis/W.Montanez RC	2.00	.75
139	Paul Casanova	1.50	.60
140	Gaylord Perry	6.00	2.50
141	Frank Quilici	1.50	.60
142	Mack Jones	1.50	.60
143	Steve Blass	2.00	.75
144	Jackie Hernandez	1.50	.60
145	Bill Singer	2.00	.75
146	Ralph Houk MG	2.00	.75
147	Bob Priddy	1.50	.60
148	John Mayberry	2.00	.75
149	Mike Hershberger	1.50	.60
150	Sam McDowell	2.00	.75
151	Tommy Davis	2.00	.75
152	L.Allen RC/W.Llenas RC	1.50	.60
153	Gary Ross	1.50	.60
154	Cesar Gutierrez	1.50	.60
155	Ken Henderson	1.50	.60
156	Bart Johnson	1.50	.60
157	Bob Bailey	2.00	.75
158	Jerry Reuss	2.00	.75
159	Jarvis Tatum	1.50	.60
160	Tom Seaver	30.00	12.50
161	Coin Checklist	10.00	4.00
162	Jack Billingham	1.50	.60
163	Buck Martinez	2.00	.75
164	F.Duffy RC/M.Wilcox RC	2.00	.75
165	Cesar Tovar	1.50	.60
166	Joe Hoerner	1.50	.60
167	Tom Grieve RC	2.00	.75
168	Bruce Dal Canton	1.50	.60
169	Ed Herrmann	1.50	.60
170	Mike Cuellar	2.00	.75
171	Bobby Wine	1.50	.60
172	Duke Sims	1.50	.60
173	Gil Garrido	1.50	.60
174	Dave LaRoche RC	1.50	.60
175	Jim Hickman	1.50	.60
176	B.Montgomery RC/D.Griffin RC	2.00	.75
177	Hal McRae	2.00	.75
178	Dave Duncan	2.00	.75
179	Mike Corkins	1.50	.60
180	Al Kaline UER	20.00	8.00
181	Hal Lanier	1.50	.60
182	Al Downing	2.00	.75
183	Gil Hodges MG	4.00	1.50
184	Stan Bahnsen	1.50	.60
185	Julian Javier	1.50	.60
186	Bob Spence RC	1.50	.60
187	Ted Abernathy	1.50	.60
188	B.Valentine RC/M.Strahler RC	6.00	2.50
189	George Mitterwald	1.50	.60
190	Bob Tolan	1.50	.60
191	Mike Andrews	1.50	.60
192	Billy Wilson	1.50	.60
193	Bob Grich RC	4.00	1.50
194	Mike Lum	1.50	.60
195	Boog Powell ALCS	2.00	.75
196	Dave McNally ALCS	2.00	.75
197	Jim Palmer ALCS	4.00	1.50
198	Orioles Celebrate ALCS	2.00	.75
199	Ty Cline NLCS	2.00	.75
200	Bobby Tolan NLCS	2.00	.75
201	Ty Cline NLCS	2.00	.75
202	Reds Celebrate NLCS	2.00	.75
203	Larry Gura RC	2.00	.75
204	B.Smith RC/G.Kopacz RC	1.50	.60
205	Gerry Moses	1.50	.60
206	Checklist 3	10.00	4.00
207	Alan Foster	1.50	.60
208	Billy Martin MG	4.00	1.50
209	Steve Renko	1.50	.60
210	Rod Carew	15.00	6.00
211	Phil Hennigan RC	1.50	.60
212	Rich Hebner	2.00	.75
213	Frank Baker RC	1.50	.60
214	Al Ferrara	1.50	.60
215	Diego Segui	1.50	.60
216	R.Cleveland/L.Melendez RC	1.50	.60
217	Ed Stroud	1.50	.60
218	Tony Cloninger	1.50	.60
219	Elrod Hendricks	1.50	.60
220	Ron Santo	4.00	1.50
221	Dave Morehead	1.50	.60
222	Bob Watson	2.00	.75
223	Cecil Upshaw	1.50	.60
224	Alan Gallagher RC	1.50	.60
225	Gary Peters	1.50	.60
226	Bill Russell	2.00	.75
227	Floyd Weaver	1.50	.60
228	Wayne Garrett	1.50	.60
229	Jim Hannan	1.50	.60
230	Willie Stargell	15.00	6.00
231	V.Colbert RC/J.Lowenstein RC	2.00	.75
232	John Strohmayer RC	1.50	.60
233	Larry Bowa	2.00	.75
234	Jim Lyttle	1.50	.60
235	Nate Colbert	1.50	.60
236	Bob Humphreys	1.50	.60
237	Cesar Cedeno RC	2.00	.75
238	Chuck Dobson	1.50	.60
239	Red Schoendienst MG	2.00	.75
240	Clyde Wright	1.50	.60
241	Dave Nelson	1.50	.60
242	Jim Ray	1.50	.60
243	Carlos May	1.50	.60
244	Bob Tillman	1.50	.60
245	Jim Kaat	2.00	.75
246	Tony Taylor	1.50	.60
247	J.Cram RC/P.Splittorff RC	2.00	.75
248	Hoyt Wilhelm	6.00	2.50
249	Chico Salmon	1.50	.60
250	Johnny Bench	50.00	20.00
251	Frank Reberger	1.50	.60
252	Eddie Leon	1.50	.60
253	Bill Sudakis	1.50	.60
254	Cal Koonce	1.50	.60
255	Bob Robertson	2.00	.75
256	Tony Gonzalez	1.50	.60
257	Nelson Briles	2.00	.75
258	Dick Green	1.50	.60
259	Dave Marshall	1.50	.60
260	Tommy Harper	2.00	.75
261	Darold Knowles	1.50	.60
262	J.Williams/D.Robinson RC	1.50	.60
263	John Ellis	1.50	.60
264	Joe Morgan	8.00	3.00
265	Jim Northrup	2.00	.75
266	Bill Stoneman	1.50	.60
267	Rich Morales	1.50	.60
268	Philadelphia Phillies TC	4.00	1.50
269	Gail Hopkins	1.50	.60
270	Rico Carty	2.00	.75
271	Bill Zepp	1.50	.60
272	Tommy Helms	2.00	.75
273	Pete Richert	1.50	.60
274	Ron Slocum	1.50	.60
275	Vada Pinson	2.00	.75
276	M.Davison RC/G.Foster RC	8.00	3.00
277	Gary Waslewski	1.50	.60
278	Jerry Grote	2.00	.75
279	Lefty Phillips MG	1.50	.60
280	Ferguson Jenkins	6.00	2.50
281	Danny Walton	1.50	.60
282	Jose Pagan	1.50	.60
283	Dick Such	1.50	.60
284	Jim Gosger	1.50	.60
285	Sal Bando	2.00	.75
286	Jerry McNertney	1.50	.60
287	Mike Fiore	1.50	.60
288	Joe Moeller	1.50	.60
289	Chicago White Sox TC	4.00	1.50
290	Tony Oliva	4.00	1.50
291	George Culver	1.50	.60
292	Jay Johnstone	2.00	.75
293	Pat Corrales	2.00	.75
294	Steve Dunning RC	1.50	.60
295	Bobby Bonds	4.00	1.50
296	Tom Timmermann	1.50	.60
297	Johnny Briggs	1.50	.60
298	Jim Nelson RC	1.50	.60
299	Ed Kirkpatrick	1.50	.60
300	Brooks Robinson	20.00	8.00
301	Earl Wilson	1.50	.60
302	Phil Gagliano	1.50	.60
303	Lindy McDaniel	2.00	.75
304	Ron Brand	1.50	.60
305	Reggie Smith	2.00	.75
306	Jim Nash	1.50	.60
307	Don Wert	1.50	.60
308	St. Louis Cardinals TC	4.00	1.50
309	Dick Ellsworth	1.50	.60

❑	310	Tommie Agee	2.00	.75
❑	311	Lee Stange	1.50	.60
❑	312	Harry Walker MG	1.50	.60
❑	313	Tom Hall	1.50	.60
❑	314	Jeff Torborg	2.00	.75
❑	315	Ron Fairly	2.00	.75
❑	316	Fred Scherman RC	1.50	.60
❑	317	J.Driscoll RC/A.Mangual	1.50	.60
❑	318	Rudy May	1.50	.60
❑	319	Ty Cline	1.50	.60
❑	320	Dave McNally	2.00	.75
❑	321	Tom Matchick	1.50	.60
❑	322	Jim Beauchamp	1.50	.60
❑	323	Billy Champion	1.50	.60
❑	324	Graig Nettles	2.00	.75
❑	325	Juan Marichal	8.00	3.00
❑	326	Richie Scheinblum	1.50	.60
❑	327	Boog Powell WS	2.00	.75
❑	328	Don Buford WS	2.00	.75
❑	329	Frank Robinson WS	4.00	1.50
❑	330	Reds Stay Alive WS	2.00	.75
❑	331	Brooks Robinson WS	[illegible]	[illegible]
❑	332	Orioles Celebrate WS	2.00	.75
❑	333	Clay Kirby	1.50	.60
❑	334	Roberto Pena	1.50	.60
❑	335	Jerry Koosman	2.00	.75
❑	336	Detroit Tigers TC	4.00	1.50
❑	337	Jesus Alou	1.50	.60
❑	338	Gene Tenace	2.00	.75
❑	339	Wayne Simpson	1.50	.60
❑	340	Rico Petrocelli	2.00	.75
❑	341	Steve Garvey RC	40.00	12.50
❑	342	Frank Tepedino	2.00	.75
❑	343	E.Acosta RC/M.May RC	2.00	.75
❑	344	Ellie Rodriguez	1.50	.60
❑	345	Joel Horlen	1.50	.60
❑	346	Lum Harris MG	1.50	.60
❑	347	Ted Uhlaender	1.50	.60
❑	348	Fred Norman	1.50	.60
❑	349	Rich Reese	1.50	.60
❑	350	Billy Williams	6.00	2.50
❑	351	Jim Shellenback	1.50	.60
❑	352	Denny Doyle	1.50	.60
❑	353	Carl Taylor	1.50	.60
❑	354	Don McMahon	1.50	.60
❑	355	Bud Harrelson w/Ryan	4.00	1.50
❑	356	Bob Locker	1.50	.60
❑	357	Cincinnati Reds TC	4.00	1.50
❑	358	Danny Cater	1.50	.60
❑	359	Ron Reed	1.50	.60
❑	360	Jim Fregosi	2.00	.75
❑	361	Don Sutton	6.00	2.50
❑	362	M.Adamson/R.Freed	1.50	.60
❑	363	Mike Nagy	1.50	.60
❑	364	Tommy Dean	1.50	.60
❑	365	Bob Johnson	1.50	.60
❑	366	Ron Stone	1.50	.60
❑	367	Dalton Jones	1.50	.60
❑	368	Bob Veale	2.00	.75
❑	369	Checklist 4	10.00	4.00
❑	370	Joe Torre	4.00	1.50
❑	371	Jack Hiatt	1.50	.60
❑	372	Lew Krausse	1.50	.60
❑	373	Tom McCraw	1.50	.60
❑	374	Clete Boyer	2.00	.75
❑	375	Steve Hargan	1.50	.60
❑	376	C.Mashore RC/E.McAnally RC	1.50	.60
❑	377	Greg Garrett	1.50	.60
❑	378	Tito Fuentes	1.50	.60
❑	379	Wayne Granger	1.50	.60
❑	380	Ted Williams MG	12.00	5.00
❑	381	Fred Gladding	1.50	.60
❑	382	Jake Gibbs	1.50	.60
❑	383	Rod Gaspar	1.50	.60
❑	384	Rollie Fingers	6.00	2.50
❑	385	Maury Wills	4.00	1.50
❑	386	Boston Red Sox TC	2.00	.75
❑	387	Ron Herbel	1.50	.60
❑	388	Al Oliver	4.00	1.50
❑	389	Ed Brinkman	1.50	.60
❑	390	Glenn Beckert	2.00	.75
❑	391	S.Brye RC/C.Nash RC	2.00	.75
❑	392	Grant Jackson	1.50	.60
❑	393	Merv Rettenmund	2.00	.75
❑	394	Clay Carroll	2.50	1.00
❑	395	Roy White	4.00	1.50
❑	396	Dick Schofield	2.50	1.00
❑	397	Alvin Dark MG	4.00	1.50
❑	398	Howie Reed	2.50	1.00
❑	399	Jim French	2.50	1.00
❑	400	Hank Aaron	60.00	30.00
❑	401	Tom Murphy	2.50	1.00
❑	402	Los Angeles Dodgers TC	6.00	2.50
❑	403	Joe Coleman	2.50	1.00
❑	404	B.Harris RC/R.Metzger RC	2.50	1.00
❑	405	Leo Cardenas	2.50	1.00
❑	406	Ray Sadecki	2.50	1.00
❑	407	Joe Rudi	4.00	1.50
❑	408	Rafael Robles	2.50	1.00
❑	409	Don Pavletich	2.50	1.00
❑	410	Ken Holtzman	4.00	1.50
❑	411	George Spriggs	2.50	1.00
❑	412	Jerry Johnson	2.50	1.00
❑	413	Pat Kelly	2.50	1.00
❑	414	Woodie Fryman	2.50	1.00
❑	415	Mike Hegan	2.50	1.00
❑	416	Gene Alley	2.50	1.00
❑	417	Dick Hall	2.50	1.00
❑	418	Adolfo Phillips	2.50	1.00
❑	419	Ron Hansen	2.50	1.00
❑	420	Jim Merritt	2.50	1.00
❑	421	John Stephenson	2.50	1.00
❑	422	Frank Bertaina	2.50	1.00
❑	423	D.Saunders/T.Marting RC	2.50	1.00
❑	424	Roberto Rodriquez	2.50	1.00
❑	425	Doug Rader	4.00	1.50
❑	426	Chris Cannizzaro	2.50	1.00
❑	427	Bernie Allen	2.50	1.00
❑	428	Jim McAndrew	2.50	1.00
❑	429	Chuck Hinton	2.50	1.00
❑	430	Wes Parker	4.00	1.50
❑	431	Tom Burgmeier	2.50	1.00
❑	432	Bob Didier	2.50	1.00
❑	433	Skip Lockwood	2.50	1.00
❑	434	Gary Sutherland	2.50	1.00
❑	435	Jose Cardenal	4.00	1.50
❑	436	Wilbur Wood	4.00	1.50
❑	437	Danny Murtaugh MG	4.00	1.50
❑	438	Mike McCormick	4.00	1.50
❑	439	G.Luzinski RC/S.Reid	6.00	2.50
❑	440	Bert Campaneris	4.00	1.50
❑	441	Milt Pappas	4.00	1.50
❑	442	California Angels TC	4.00	1.50
❑	443	Rich Robertson	2.50	1.00
❑	444	Jimmie Price	2.50	1.00
❑	445	Art Shamsky	2.50	1.00
❑	446	Bobby Bolin	2.50	1.00
❑	447	Cesar Geronimo RC	4.00	1.50
❑	448	Dave Roberts	2.50	1.00
❑	449	Brant Alyea	2.50	1.00
❑	450	Bob Gibson	15.00	6.00
❑	451	Joe Keough	2.50	1.00
❑	452	John Boccabella	2.50	1.00
❑	453	Terry Crowley	2.50	1.00
❑	454	Mike Paul	2.50	1.00
❑	455	Don Kessinger	4.00	1.50
❑	456	Bob Meyer	2.50	1.00
❑	457	Willie Smith	2.50	1.00
❑	458	R.Lolich RC/D.Lemonds RC	2.50	1.00
❑	459	Jim Lefebvre	2.50	1.00
❑	460	Fritz Peterson	2.50	1.00
❑	461	Jim Ray Hart	2.50	1.00
❑	462	Washington Senators TC	6.00	2.50
❑	463	Tom Kelley	2.50	1.00
❑	464	Aurelio Rodriguez	2.50	1.00
❑	465	Tim McCarver	6.00	2.50
❑	466	Ken Berry	2.50	1.00
❑	467	Al Santorini	2.50	1.00
❑	468	Frank Fernandez	2.50	1.00
❑	469	Bob Aspromonte	2.50	1.00
❑	470	Bob Oliver	2.50	1.00
❑	471	Tom Griffin	2.50	1.00
❑	472	Ken Rudolph	2.50	1.00
❑	473	Gary Wagner	2.50	1.00
❑	474	Jim Fairey	2.50	1.00
❑	475	Ron Perranoski	2.50	1.00
❑	476	Dal Maxvill	2.50	1.00
❑	477	Earl Weaver MG	6.00	2.50
❑	478	Bernie Carbo	2.50	1.00
❑	479	Dennis Higgins	2.50	1.00
❑	480	Manny Sanguillen	4.00	1.50
❑	481	Daryl Patterson	2.50	1.00
❑	482	San Diego Padres TC	6.00	2.50
❑	483	Gene Michael	2.50	1.00
❑	484	Don Wilson	2.50	1.00
❑	485	Ken McMullen	2.50	1.00
❑	486	Steve Huntz	2.50	1.00
❑	487	Paul Schaal	2.50	1.00
❑	488	Jerry Stephenson	2.50	1.00
❑	489	Luis Alvarado	2.50	1.00
❑	490	Deron Johnson	2.50	1.00
❑	491	Jim Hardin	2.50	1.00
❑	492	Ken Boswell	2.50	1.00
❑	493	Dave May	2.50	1.00
❑	494	R.Garr/R.Kester	4.00	1.50
❑	495	Felipe Alou	4.00	1.50
❑	496	Woody Woodward	2.50	1.00
❑	497	Horacio Pina RC	2.50	1.00
❑	498	John Kennedy	2.50	1.00
❑	499	Checklist 5	10.00	4.00
❑	500	Jim Perry	4.00	1.50
❑	501	Andy Etchebarren	2.50	1.00
❑	502	Chicago Cubs TC	6.00	2.50
❑	503	Gates Brown	4.00	1.50
❑	504	Ken Wright RC	2.50	1.00
❑	505	Ollie Brown	2.50	1.00
❑	506	Bobby Knoop	2.50	1.00
❑	507	George Stone	2.50	1.00
❑	508	Roger Repoz	2.50	1.00
❑	509	Jim Grant	2.50	1.00
❑	510	Ken Harrelson	4.00	1.50
❑	511	Chris Short w/Rose	4.00	1.50
❑	512	D.Mills RC/M.Garman RC	2.50	1.00
❑	513	Nolan Ryan	150.00	75.00
❑	514	Ron Woods	2.50	1.00
❑	515	Carl Morton	2.50	1.00
❑	516	Ted Kubiak	2.50	1.00
❑	517	Charlie Fox MG RC	2.50	1.00
❑	518	Joe Grzenda	2.50	1.00
❑	519	Willie Crawford	2.50	1.00
❑	520	Tommy John	6.00	2.50
❑	521	Leron Lee	2.50	1.00
❑	522	Minnesota Twins TC	6.00	2.50
❑	523	John Odom	2.50	1.00
❑	524	Mickey Stanley	6.00	2.50
❑	525	Ernie Banks	50.00	20.00
❑	526	Ray Jarvis	4.00	1.50
❑	527	Cleon Jones	6.00	2.50
❑	528	Wally Bunker	4.00	1.50
❑	529	Hernandez/Bucker/Perez RC	6.00	2.50
❑	530	Carl Yastrzemski	30.00	12.50
❑	531	Mike Torrez	4.00	1.50
❑	532	Bill Rigney MG	4.00	1.50
❑	533	Mike Ryan	4.00	1.50
❑	534	Luke Walker	4.00	1.50
❑	535	Curt Flood	6.00	2.50
❑	536	Claude Raymond	4.00	1.50
❑	537	Tom Egan	4.00	1.50
❑	538	Angel Bravo	4.00	1.50
❑	539	Larry Brown	4.00	1.50
❑	540	Larry Dierker	6.00	2.50
❑	541	Bob Burda	4.00	1.50
❑	542	Bob Miller	4.00	1.50
❑	543	New York Yankees TC	10.00	4.00
❑	544	Vida Blue	6.00	2.50
❑	545	Dick Dietz	4.00	1.50
❑	546	John Matias	4.00	1.50
❑	547	Pat Dobson	6.00	2.50
❑	548	Don Mason	4.00	1.50
❑	549	Jim Brewer	6.00	2.50
❑	550	Harmon Killebrew	25.00	10.00
❑	551	Frank Linzy	4.00	1.50
❑	552	Buddy Bradford	4.00	1.50
❑	553	Kevin Collins	4.00	1.50
❑	554	Lowell Palmer	4.00	1.50
❑	555	Walt Williams	4.00	1.50
❑	556	Jim McGlothlin	4.00	1.50
❑	557	Tom Satriano	4.00	1.50
❑	558	Hector Torres	4.00	1.50
❑	559	Cox/Gogolewski/Jones RC	4.00	1.50
❑	560	Rusty Staub	6.00	2.50
❑	561	Syd O'Brien	4.00	1.50
❑	562	Dave Giusti	4.00	1.50
❑	563	San Francisco Giants TC	8.00	3.00
❑	564	Al Fitzmorris	4.00	1.50
❑	565	Jim Wynn	6.00	2.50
❑	566	Tim Cullen	4.00	1.50
❑	567	Walt Alston MG	8.00	3.00

❑ 568 Sal Campisi 4.00 1.50
❑ 569 Ivan Murrell 4.00 1.50
❑ 570 Jim Palmer 30.00 12.50
❑ 571 Ted Sizemore 4.00 1.50
❑ 572 Jerry Kenney 4.00 1.50
❑ 573 Ed Kranepool 6.00 2.50
❑ 574 Jim Bunning 8.00 3.00
❑ 575 Bill Freehan 6.00 2.50
❑ 576 Garrett/Davis/Jestadt RC 4.00 1.50
❑ 577 Jim Lonborg 6.00 2.50
❑ 578 Ron Hunt 4.00 1.50
❑ 579 Marty Pattin 4.00 1.50
❑ 580 Tony Perez 20.00 8.00
❑ 581 Roger Nelson 4.00 1.50
❑ 582 Dave Cash 6.00 2.50
❑ 583 Ron Cook RC 4.00 1.50
❑ 584 Cleveland Indians TC 8.00 3.00
❑ 585 Willie Davis 6.00 2.50
❑ 586 Dick Woodson 4.00 1.50
❑ 587 Sonny Jackson 4.00 1.50
❑ 588 Tom Bradley RC 4.00 1.50
❑ 589 Bob Barton 4.00 1.50
❑ 590 Alex Johnson 6.00 2.50
❑ 591 Jackie Brown RC 4.00 1.50
❑ 592 Randy Hundley 6.00 2.50
❑ 593 Jack Aker 4.00 1.50
❑ 594 Chlupsa/Stinson/Hrabosky RC 6.00 2.50
❑ 595 Dave Johnson 6.00 2.50
❑ 596 Mike Jorgensen 4.00 1.50
❑ 597 Ken Suarez 4.00 1.50
❑ 598 Rick Wise 6.00 2.50
❑ 599 Norm Cash 6.00 2.50
❑ 600 Willie Mays 100.00 50.00
❑ 601 Ken Tatum 4.00 1.50
❑ 602 Marty Martinez 4.00 1.50
❑ 603 Pittsburgh Pirates TC 8.00 3.00
❑ 604 John Gelnar 4.00 1.50
❑ 605 Orlando Cepeda 8.00 3.00
❑ 606 Chuck Taylor 4.00 1.50
❑ 607 Paul Ratliff 4.00 1.50
❑ 608 Mike Wegener 4.00 1.50
❑ 609 Leo Durocher MG 8.00 3.00
❑ 610 Amos Otis 6.00 2.50
❑ 611 Tom Phoebus 4.00 1.50
❑ 612 Camilli/Ford/Mingori RC 4.00 1.50
❑ 613 Pedro Borbon 4.00 1.50
❑ 614 Billy Cowan 4.00 1.50
❑ 615 Mel Stottlemyre 6.00 2.50
❑ 616 Larry Hisle 6.00 2.50
❑ 617 Clay Dalrymple 4.00 1.50
❑ 618 Tug McGraw 6.00 2.50
❑ 619A Checklist 6 ERR w/o Copy 10.00 4.00
❑ 619B Checklist 6 COR w/Copy 6.00 2.50
❑ 620 Frank Howard 6.00 2.50
❑ 621 Ron Bryant 4.00 1.50
❑ 622 Joe Lahoud 4.00 1.50
❑ 623 Pat Jarvis 4.00 1.50
❑ 624 Oakland Athletics TC 8.00 3.00
❑ 625 Lou Brock 30.00 12.50
❑ 626 Freddie Patek 6.00 2.50
❑ 627 Steve Hamilton 4.00 1.50
❑ 628 John Bateman 4.00 1.50
❑ 629 John Hiller 6.00 2.50
❑ 630 Roberto Clemente 150.00 75.00
❑ 631 Eddie Fisher 4.00 1.50
❑ 632 Darrel Chaney 4.00 1.50
❑ 633 Brooks/Koegel/Northey RC 4.00 1.50
❑ 634 Phil Regan 4.00 1.50
❑ 635 Bobby Murcer 6.00 2.50
❑ 636 Denny Lemaster 4.00 1.50
❑ 637 Dave Bristol MG 4.00 1.50
❑ 638 Stan Williams 4.00 1.50
❑ 639 Tom Haller 4.00 1.50
❑ 640 Frank Robinson 40.00 12.50
❑ 641 New York Mets TC 15.00 6.00
❑ 642 Jim Roland 4.00 1.50
❑ 643 Rick Reichardt 4.00 1.50
❑ 644 Jim Stewart SP 12.00 5.00
❑ 645 Jim Maloney SP 15.00 6.00
❑ 646 Bobby Floyd SP 12.00 5.00
❑ 647 Juan Pizarro 8.00 3.00
❑ 648 Folkers/Martinez/Matlack SP RC 25.00 10.00
❑ 649 Sparky Lyle SP 15.00 6.00
❑ 650 Richie Allen SP 30.00 12.50
❑ 651 Jerry Robertson SP 12.00 5.00
❑ 652 Atlanta Braves TC 12.00 5.00
❑ 653 Russ Snyder SP 12.00 5.00
❑ 654 Don Shaw SP 12.00 5.00
❑ 655 Mike Epstein SP 12.00 5.00
❑ 656 Gerry Nyman SP 12.00 5.00
❑ 657 Jose Azcue 8.00 3.00
❑ 658 Paul Lindblad SP 12.00 5.00
❑ 659 Byron Browne SP 12.00 5.00
❑ 660 Ray Culp 8.00 3.00
❑ 661 Chuck Tanner MG SP 15.00 6.00
❑ 662 Mike Hedlund SP 12.00 5.00
❑ 663 Marv Staehle 8.00 3.00
❑ 664 Reynolds/Reynolds /Reynolds SP RC 12.00 5.00
❑ 665 Ron Swoboda SP 15.00 6.00
❑ 666 Gene Brabender SP 12.00 5.00
❑ 667 Pete Ward 8.00 3.00
❑ 668 Gary Neibauer 8.00 3.00
❑ 669 Ike Brown SP 12.00 5.00
❑ 670 Bill Hands 8.00 3.00
❑ 671 Bill Voss SP 12.00 5.00
❑ 672 Ed Crosby SP RC 12.00 5.00
❑ 673 Gerry Janeski SP RC 12.00 5.00
❑ 674 Montreal Expos TC 12.00 5.00
❑ 675 Dave Boswell 8.00 3.00
❑ 676 Tommie Reynolds 8.00 3.00
❑ 677 Jack DiLauro SP 12.00 5.00
❑ 678 George Thomas 8.00 3.00
❑ 679 Don O'Riley 8.00 3.00
❑ 680 Don Mincher SP 12.00 5.00
❑ 681 Bill Butler 8.00 3.00
❑ 682 Terry Harmon 8.00 3.00
❑ 683 Bill Burbach SP 12.00 5.00
❑ 684 Curt Motton 8.00 3.00
❑ 685 Moe Drabowsky 8.00 3.00
❑ 686 Chico Ruiz SP 12.00 5.00
❑ 687 Ron Taylor SP 12.00 5.00
❑ 688 S.Anderson MG SP 30.00 12.50
❑ 689 Frank Baker 8.00 3.00
❑ 690 Bob Moose 8.00 3.00
❑ 691 Bobby Heise 8.00 3.00
❑ 692 Haydel/Moret/Twitchell SP RC 12.00 5.00
❑ 693 Jose Pena SP 12.00 5.00
❑ 694 Rick Renick SP 12.00 5.00
❑ 695 Joe Niekro 12.00 5.00
❑ 696 Jerry Morales 8.00 3.00
❑ 697 Rickey Clark SP 12.00 5.00
❑ 698 Milwaukee Brewers TC SP 20.00 8.00
❑ 699 Jim Britton 8.00 3.00
❑ 700 Boog Powell SP 25.00 10.00
❑ 701 Bob Garibaldi 8.00 3.00
❑ 702 Milt Ramirez RC 8.00 3.00
❑ 703 Mike Kekich 8.00 3.00
❑ 704 J.C. Martin SP 12.00 5.00
❑ 705 Dick Selma SP 12.00 5.00
❑ 706 Joe Foy SP 12.00 5.00
❑ 707 Fred Lasher 8.00 3.00
❑ 708 Russ Nagelson SP 12.00 5.00
❑ 709 Baker/Baylor/Pac SP RC 80.00 40.00
❑ 710 Sonny Siebert 8.00 3.00
❑ 711 Larry Stahl SP 12.00 5.00
❑ 712 Jose Martinez 8.00 3.00
❑ 713 Mike Marshall SP 15.00 6.00
❑ 714 Dick Williams MG SP 15.00 6.00
❑ 715 Horace Clarke SP 15.00 6.00
❑ 716 Dave Leonhard 8.00 3.00
❑ 717 Tommie Aaron SP 12.00 5.00
❑ 718 Billy Wynne 8.00 3.00
❑ 719 Jerry May SP 12.00 5.00
❑ 720 Matty Alou 12.00 5.00
❑ 721 John Morris 8.00 3.00
❑ 722 Houston Astros TC SP 20.00 8.00
❑ 723 Vicente Romo SP 12.00 5.00
❑ 724 Tom Tischinski SP 12.00 5.00
❑ 725 Gary Gentry SP 12.00 5.00
❑ 726 Paul Popovich 8.00 3.00
❑ 727 Ray Lamb SP 12.00 5.00
❑ 728 Redmond/Lampard/Williams RC 8.00 3.00
❑ 729 Dick Billings RC 8.00 3.00
❑ 730 Jim Rooker 8.00 3.00
❑ 731 Jim Qualls SP 12.00 5.00
❑ 732 Bob Reed 8.00 3.00
❑ 733 Lee Maye SP 12.00 5.00
❑ 734 Rob Gardner SP 12.00 5.00
❑ 735 Mike Shannon SP 15.00 6.00
❑ 736 Mel Queen SP 12.00 5.00
❑ 737 Preston Gomez MG SP 12.00 5.00
❑ 738 Russ Gibson SP 12.00 5.00
❑ 739 Barry Lersch SP 12.00 5.00
❑ 740 Luis Aparicio SP 30.00 12.50
❑ 741 Skip Guinn 8.00 3.00
❑ 742 Kansas City Royals TC 12.00 5.00
❑ 743 John O'Donoghue SP 12.00 5.00
❑ 744 Chuck Manuel SP 12.00 5.00
❑ 745 Sandy Alomar SP 12.00 5.00
❑ 746 Andy Kosco 8.00 3.00
❑ 747 Severinsen/Spinks/Moore RC 8.00 3.00
❑ 748 John Purdin SP 12.00 5.00
❑ 749 Ken Szotkiewicz RC 8.00 3.00
❑ 750 Denny McLain SP 25.00 10.00
❑ 751 Al Weis SP 15.00 6.00
❑ 752 Dick Drago 12.00 5.00

1972 Topps

❑ COMPLETE SET (787) 1500.00 750.00
❑ COMMON CARD (1-132) .60 .25
❑ COMMON CARD (133-263) 1.00 .40
❑ COMMON CARD (264-394) 1.25 .50
❑ COMMON CARD (395-525) 1.50 .60
❑ COMMON CARD (526-656) 4.00 1.50
❑ COMMON CARD (657-787) 12.00 5.00
❑ WRAPPER (10-CENT) 15.00 6.00
❑ 1 Pittsburgh Pirates TC 8.00 3.00
❑ 2 Ray Culp .60 .25
❑ 3 Bob Tolan .60 .25
❑ 4 Checklist 1-132 6.00 2.50
❑ 5 John Bateman .60 .25
❑ 6 Fred Scherman .60 .25
❑ 7 Enzo Hernandez .60 .25
❑ 8 Ron Swoboda 1.25 .50
❑ 9 Stan Williams .60 .25
❑ 10 Amos Otis 1.25 .50
❑ 11 Bobby Valentine 1.25 .50
❑ 12 Jose Cardenal .60 .25
❑ 13 Joe Grzenda .60 .25
❑ 14 Koegel/Anderson/Twitchell RC .60 .25
❑ 15 Walt Williams .60 .25
❑ 16 Mike Jorgensen .60 .25
❑ 17 Dave Duncan 1.25 .50
❑ 18A Juan Pizarro Yellow .60 .25
❑ 18B Juan Pizarro Green 5.00 2.00
❑ 19 Billy Cowan .60 .25
❑ 20 Don Wilson .60 .25
❑ 21 Atlanta Braves TC 1.50 .60
❑ 22 Rob Gardner .60 .25
❑ 23 Ted Kubiak .60 .25
❑ 24 Ted Ford .60 .25
❑ 25 Bill Singer .60 .25
❑ 26 Andy Etchebarren .60 .25
❑ 27 Bob Johnson .60 .25
❑ 28 Gebhard/Brye Haydel RC .60 .25
❑ 29A Bill Bonham Yellow RC .60 .25
❑ 29B Bill Bonham Green 5.00 2.00
❑ 30 Rico Petrocelli 1.25 .50
❑ 31 Cleon Jones 1.25 .50
❑ 32 Cleon Jones IA .60 .25
❑ 33 Billy Martin MG 4.00 1.50
❑ 34 Billy Martin IA 2.50 1.00
❑ 35 Jerry Johnson .60 .25
❑ 36 Jerry Johnson IA .60 .25
❑ 37 Carl Yastrzemski 10.00 4.00
❑ 38 Carl Yastrzemski IA 8.00 3.00
❑ 39 Bob Barton .60 .25
❑ 40 Bob Barton IA .60 .25
❑ 41 Tommy Davis 1.25 .50

❑ 42 Tommy Davis IA .60 .25
❑ 43 Rick Wise 1.25 .50
❑ 44 Rick Wise IA .60 .25
❑ 45A Glenn Beckert Yellow 1.25 .50
❑ 45B Glenn Beckert Green 5.00 2.00
❑ 46 Glenn Beckert IA .60 .25
❑ 47 John Ellis .60 .25
❑ 48 John Ellis IA .60 .25
❑ 49 Willie Mays 40.00 12.50
❑ 50 Willie Mays IA 20.00 8.00
❑ 51 Harmon Killebrew 8.00 3.00
❑ 52 Harmon Killebrew IA 4.00 1.50
❑ 53 Bud Harrelson 1.25 .50
❑ 54 Bud Harrelson IA .60 .25
❑ 55 Clyde Wright .60 .25
❑ 56 Rich Chiles RC .60 .25
❑ 57 Bob Oliver .60 .25
❑ 58 Ernie McAnally .60 .25
❑ 59 Fred Stanley RC .60 .25
❑ 60 Manny Sanguillen 1.25 .50
❑ 61 Hooten/Hisler/Stephenson RC 1.25 .50
❑ 62 Angel Mangual .60 .25
❑ 63 Duke Sims .60 .25
❑ 64 Pete Broberg RC .60 .25
❑ 65 Cesar Cedeno 1.25 .50
❑ 66 Ray Corbin RC .60 .25
❑ 67 Red Schoendienst MG 2.50 1.00
❑ 68 Jim York RC .60 .25
❑ 69 Roger Freed .60 .25
❑ 70 Mike Cuellar 1.25 .50
❑ 71 California Angels TC 1.50 .60
❑ 72 Bruce Kison RC .60 .25
❑ 73 Steve Huntz .60 .25
❑ 74 Cecil Upshaw .60 .25
❑ 75 Bert Campaneris 1.25 .50
❑ 76 Don Carrithers RC .60 .25
❑ 77 Ron Theobald RC .60 .25
❑ 78 Steve Arlin RC .60 .25
❑ 79 C.Fisk RC/C.Cooper RC 50.00 20.00
❑ 80 Tony Perez 4.00 1.50
❑ 81 Mike Hedlund .60 .25
❑ 82 Ron Woods .60 .25
❑ 83 Dalton Jones .60 .25
❑ 84 Vince Colbert .60 .25
❑ 85 Torre/Garr/Beckert LL 2.50 1.00
❑ 86 Oliva/Murcer/Rett LL 2.50 1.00
❑ 87 Torre/Stargell/Aaron LL 4.00 1.50
❑ 88 Kill/F.Rob/Smith LL 4.00 1.50
❑ 89 Stargell/Aaron/May LL 2.50 1.00
❑ 90 Melton/Cash/Jackson LL 2.50 1.00
❑ 91 Seaver/Roberts/Wilson LL 2.50 1.00
❑ 92 Blue/Wood/Palmer LL 2.50 1.00
❑ 93 Jenkins/Carlton/Seaver LL 4.00 1.50
❑ 94 Lolich/Blue/Wood LL 2.50 1.00
❑ 95 Seaver/Jenkins/Stone LL 4.00 1.50
❑ 96 Lolich/Blue/Coleman LL 2.50 1.00
❑ 97 Tom Kelley .60 .25
❑ 98 Chuck Tanner MG 1.25 .50
❑ 99 Ross Grimsley RC .60 .25
❑ 100 Frank Robinson 8.00 3.00
❑ 101 Grief/Richard/Busse RC 2.50 1.00
❑ 102 Lloyd Allen .60 .25
❑ 103 Checklist 133-263 6.00 2.50
❑ 104 Toby Harrah RC 1.25 .50
❑ 105 Gary Gentry .60 .25
❑ 106 Milwaukee Brewers TC 1.50 .60
❑ 107 Jose Cruz RC 1.25 .50
❑ 108 Gary Waslewski .60 .25
❑ 109 Jerry May .60 .25
❑ 110 Ron Hunt .60 .25
❑ 111 Jim Grant .60 .25
❑ 112 Greg Luzinski 1.25 .50
❑ 113 Rogelio Moret .60 .25
❑ 114 Bill Buckner 1.25 .50
❑ 115 Jim Fregosi 1.25 .50
❑ 116 Ed Farmer RC .60 .25
❑ 117A Cleo James Yellow RC .60 .25
❑ 117B Cleo James Green 5.00 2.00
❑ 118 Skip Lockwood .60 .25
❑ 119 Marty Perez .60 .25
❑ 120 Bill Freehan 1.25 .50
❑ 121 Ed Sprague .60 .25
❑ 122 Larry Biittner RC .60 .25
❑ 123 Ed Acosta .60 .25
❑ 124 Closter/Torres/Hambright RC .60 .25
❑ 125 Dave Cash 1.25 .50
❑ 126 Bart Johnson .60 .25
❑ 127 Duffy Dyer .60 .25
❑ 128 Eddie Watt .60 .25
❑ 129 Charlie Fox MG .60 .25
❑ 130 Bob Gibson 8.00 3.00
❑ 131 Jim Nettles .60 .25
❑ 132 Joe Morgan 6.00 2.50
❑ 133 Joe Keough 1.00 .40
❑ 134 Carl Morton 1.00 .40
❑ 135 Vada Pinson 2.00 .75
❑ 136 Darrel Chaney 1.00 .40
❑ 137 Dick Williams MG 2.00 .75
❑ 138 Mike Kekich 1.00 .40
❑ 139 Tim McCarver 2.00 .75
❑ 140 Pat Dobson 2.00 .75
❑ 141 Capra/Stanton/Matlack RC 2.00 .75
❑ 142 Chris Chambliss RC 4.00 1.50
❑ 143 Garry Jestadt 1.00 .40
❑ 144 Marty Pattin 1.00 .40
❑ 145 Don Kessinger 2.00 .75
❑ 146 Steve Kealey 1.00 .40
❑ 147 Dave Kingman RC 6.00 2.50
❑ 148 Dick Billings 1.00 .40
❑ 149 Gary Neibauer 1.00 .40
❑ 150 Norm Cash 2.00 .75
❑ 151 Jim Brewer 1.00 .40
❑ 152 Gene Clines 1.00 .40
❑ 153 Rick Auerbach RC 1.00 .40
❑ 154 Ted Simmons 4.00 1.50
❑ 155 Larry Dierker 1.00 .40
❑ 156 Minnesota Twins TC 2.00 .75
❑ 157 Don Gullett 1.00 .40
❑ 158 Jerry Kenney 1.00 .40
❑ 159 John Boccabella 1.00 .40
❑ 160 Andy Messersmith 2.00 .75
❑ 161 Brock Davis 1.00 .40
❑ 162 Bell/Porter/Reynolds RC 2.00 .75
❑ 163 Tug McGraw 4.00 1.50
❑ 164 Tug McGraw IA 2.00 .75
❑ 165 Chris Speier RC 2.00 .75
❑ 166 Chris Speier IA 1.00 .40
❑ 167 Deron Johnson 1.00 .40
❑ 168 Deron Johnson IA 1.00 .40
❑ 169 Vida Blue 4.00 1.50
❑ 170 Vida Blue IA 2.00 .75
❑ 171 Darrell Evans 4.00 1.50
❑ 172 Darrell Evans IA 2.00 .75
❑ 173 Clay Kirby 1.00 .40
❑ 174 Clay Kirby IA 1.00 .40
❑ 175 Tom Haller 1.00 .40
❑ 176 Tom Haller IA 1.00 .40
❑ 177 Paul Schaal 1.00 .40
❑ 178 Paul Schaal IA 1.00 .40
❑ 179 Dock Ellis 1.00 .40
❑ 180 Dock Ellis IA 1.00 .40
❑ 181 Ed Kranepool 2.00 .75
❑ 182 Ed Kranepool IA 1.00 .40
❑ 183 Bill Melton 1.00 .40
❑ 184 Bill Melton IA 1.00 .40
❑ 185 Ron Bryant 1.00 .40
❑ 186 Ron Bryant IA 1.00 .40
❑ 187 Gates Brown 1.00 .40
❑ 188 Frank Lucchesi MG 1.00 .40
❑ 189 Gene Tenace 2.00 .75
❑ 190 Dave Giusti 1.00 .40
❑ 191 Jeff Burroughs RC 4.00 1.50
❑ 192 Chicago Cubs TC 2.00 .75
❑ 193 Kurt Bevacqua RC 1.00 .40
❑ 194 Fred Norman 1.00 .40
❑ 195 Orlando Cepeda 6.00 2.50
❑ 196 Mel Queen 1.00 .40
❑ 197 Johnny Briggs 1.00 .40
❑ 198 Hough/O'Brien/Strahler RC 6.00 2.50
❑ 199 Mike Fiore 1.00 .40
❑ 200 Lou Brock 8.00 3.00
❑ 201 Phil Roof 1.00 .40
❑ 202 Scipio Spinks 1.00 .40
❑ 203 Ron Blomberg RC 1.00 .40
❑ 204 Tommy Helms 1.00 .40
❑ 205 Dick Drago 1.00 .40
❑ 206 Dal Maxvill 1.00 .40
❑ 207 Tom Egan 1.00 .40
❑ 208 Milt Pappas 2.00 .75
❑ 209 Joe Rudi 2.00 .75
❑ 210 Denny McLain 2.00 .75
❑ 211 Gary Sutherland 1.00 .40
❑ 212 Grant Jackson 1.00 .40
❑ 213 Parker/Kusnyer/Silverio RC 1.00 .40
❑ 214 Mike McQueen 1.00 .40
❑ 215 Alex Johnson 2.00 .75
❑ 216 Joe Niekro 2.00 .75
❑ 217 Roger Metzger 1.00 .40
❑ 218 Eddie Kasko MG 1.00 .40
❑ 219 Rennie Stennett RC 2.00 .75
❑ 220 Jim Perry 2.00 .75
❑ 221 NL Playoffs Bucs 2.00 .75
❑ 222 AL Playoffs B.Robinson 4.00 1.50
❑ 223 Dave McNally WS 2.00 .75
❑ 224 D.Johnson/M.Belanger WS 2.00 .75
❑ 225 Manny Sanguillen WS 2.00 .75
❑ 226 Roberto Clemente WS 8.00 3.00
❑ 227 Nellie Briles WS 2.00 .75
❑ 228 F.Robinson/M.Sanguillen WS 2.00 .75
❑ 229 Steve Blass WS 2.00 .75
❑ 230 Pirates Celebrate WS 2.00 .75
❑ 231 Casey Cox 1.00 .40
❑ 232 Arnold/Barr/Rader RC 1.00 .40
❑ 233 Jay Johnstone 2.00 .75
❑ 234 Ron Taylor 1.00 .40
❑ 235 Merv Rettenmund 1.00 .40
❑ 236 Jim McGlothlin 1.00 .40
❑ 237 New York Yankees TC 2.00 .75
❑ 238 Leron Lee 1.00 .40
❑ 239 Tom Timmermann 1.00 .40
❑ 240 Richie Allen 2.00 .75
❑ 241 Rollie Fingers 6.00 2.50
❑ 242 Don Mincher 1.00 .40
❑ 243 Frank Linzy 1.00 .40
❑ 244 Steve Braun RC 1.00 .40
❑ 245 Tommie Agee 2.00 .75
❑ 246 Tom Burgmeier 1.00 .40
❑ 247 Milt May 1.00 .40
❑ 248 Tom Bradley 1.00 .40
❑ 249 Harry Walker MG 1.00 .40
❑ 250 Boog Powell 2.00 .75
❑ 251 Checklist 264-394 6.00 2.50
❑ 252 Ken Reynolds 1.00 .40
❑ 253 Sandy Alomar 2.00 .75
❑ 254 Boots Day 1.00 .40
❑ 255 Jim Lonborg 2.00 .75
❑ 256 George Foster 2.00 .75
❑ 257 Foor/Hosley/Jata RC 1.00 .40
❑ 258 Randy Hundley 1.00 .40
❑ 259 Sparky Lyle 2.00 .75
❑ 260 Ralph Garr 2.00 .75
❑ 261 Steve Mingori 1.00 .40
❑ 262 San Diego Padres TC 2.00 .75
❑ 263 Felipe Alou 2.00 .75
❑ 264 Tommy John 2.00 .75
❑ 265 Wes Parker 2.00 .75
❑ 266 Bobby Bolin 1.25 .50
❑ 267 Dave Concepcion 4.00 1.50
❑ 268 D.Anderson RC/C.Floethe RC 1.25 .50
❑ 269 Don Hahn 1.25 .50
❑ 270 Jim Palmer 8.00 3.00
❑ 271 Ken Rudolph 1.25 .50
❑ 272 Mickey Rivers RC 2.00 .75
❑ 273 Bobby Floyd 1.25 .50
❑ 274 Al Severinsen 1.25 .50
❑ 275 Cesar Tovar 1.25 .50
❑ 276 Gene Mauch MG 2.00 .75
❑ 277 Elliott Maddox 1.25 .50
❑ 278 Dennis Higgins 1.25 .50
❑ 279 Larry Brown 1.25 .50
❑ 280 Willie McCovey 6.00 2.50
❑ 281 Bill Parsons RC 1.25 .50
❑ 282 Houston Astros TC 2.00 .75
❑ 283 Darrell Brandon 1.25 .50
❑ 284 Ike Brown 1.25 .50
❑ 285 Gaylord Perry 6.00 2.50
❑ 286 Gene Alley 1.25 .50
❑ 287 Jim Hardin 1.25 .50
❑ 288 Johnny Jeter 1.25 .50
❑ 289 Syd O'Brien 1.25 .50
❑ 290 Sonny Siebert 1.25 .50
❑ 291 Hal McRae 2.00 .75
❑ 292 Hal McRae IA 1.25 .50
❑ 293 Dan Frisella 1.25 .50
❑ 294 Dan Frisella IA 1.25 .50
❑ 295 Dick Dietz 1.25 .50
❑ 296 Dick Dietz IA 1.25 .50
❑ 297 Claude Osteen 2.00 .75

❑ 298 Claude Osteen IA 1.25 .50
❑ 299 Hank Aaron 40.00 12.50
❑ 300 Hank Aaron IA 20.00 8.00
❑ 301 George Mitterwald 1.25 .50
❑ 302 George Mitterwald IA 1.25 .50
❑ 303 Joe Pepitone 2.00 .75
❑ 304 Joe Pepitone IA 1.25 .50
❑ 305 Ken Boswell 1.25 .50
❑ 306 Ken Boswell IA 1.25 .50
❑ 307 Steve Renko 1.25 .50
❑ 308 Steve Renko IA 1.25 .50
❑ 309 Roberto Clemente 50.00 20.00
❑ 310 Roberto Clemente IA 25.00 10.00
❑ 311 Clay Carroll 1.25 .50
❑ 312 Clay Carroll IA 1.25 .50
❑ 313 Luis Aparicio 6.00 2.50
❑ 314 Luis Aparicio IA 2.00 .75
❑ 315 Paul Splittorff 1.25 .50
❑ 316 Bibby/Roque/Guzman RC 2.00 .75
❑ 317 Rich Hand 1.25 .50
❑ 318 Sonny Jackson 1.25 .50
❑ 319 Aurelio Rodriguez 1.25 .50
❑ 320 Steve Blass 2.00 .75
❑ 321 Joe Lahoud 1.25 .50
❑ 322 Jose Pena 1.25 .50
❑ 323 Earl Weaver MG 4.00 1.50
❑ 324 Mike Ryan 1.25 .50
❑ 325 Mel Stottlemyre 2.00 .75
❑ 326 Pat Kelly 1.25 .50
❑ 327 Steve Stone RC 2.00 .75
❑ 328 Boston Red Sox TC 2.00 .75
❑ 329 Roy Foster 1.25 .50
❑ 330 Jim Hunter 6.00 2.50
❑ 331 Stan Swanson RC 1.25 .50
❑ 332 Buck Martinez 1.25 .50
❑ 333 Steve Barber 1.25 .50
❑ 334 Fahey/Mason Ragland RC 1.25 .50
❑ 335 Bill Hands 1.25 .50
❑ 336 Marty Martinez 1.25 .50
❑ 337 Mike Kilkenny 1.25 .50
❑ 338 Bob Grich 2.00 .75
❑ 339 Ron Cook 1.25 .50
❑ 340 Roy White 2.00 .75
❑ 341 Joe Torre KP 1.25 .50
❑ 342 Wilbur Wood KP 1.25 .50
❑ 343 Willie Stargell KP 2.00 .75
❑ 344 Dave McNally KP 1.25 .50
❑ 345 Rick Wise KP 1.25 .50
❑ 346 Jim Fregosi KP 1.25 .50
❑ 347 Tom Seaver KP 4.00 1.50
❑ 348 Sal Bando KP 1.25 .50
❑ 349 Al Fitzmorris 1.25 .50
❑ 350 Frank Howard 2.00 .75
❑ 351 House/Kester/Britton 2.00 .75
❑ 352 Dave LaRoche 1.25 .50
❑ 353 Art Shamsky 1.25 .50
❑ 354 Tom Murphy 1.25 .50
❑ 355 Bob Watson 2.00 .75
❑ 356 Gerry Moses 1.25 .50
❑ 357 Woody Fryman 1.25 .50
❑ 358 Sparky Anderson MG 4.00 1.50
❑ 359 Don Pavletich 1.25 .50
❑ 360 Dave Roberts 1.25 .50
❑ 361 Mike Andrews 1.25 .50
❑ 362 New York Mets TC 2.00 .75
❑ 363 Ron Klimkowski 1.25 .50
❑ 364 Johnny Callison 2.00 .75
❑ 365 Dick Bosman 2.00 .75
❑ 366 Jimmy Rosario RC 1.25 .50
❑ 367 Ron Perranoski 1.25 .50
❑ 368 Danny Thompson 1.25 .50
❑ 369 Jim Lefebvre 2.00 .75
❑ 370 Don Buford 1.25 .50
❑ 371 Denny Lemaster 1.25 .50
❑ 372 L.Clemons RC/M.Montgomery RC 1.25 .50
❑ 373 John Mayberry 2.00 .75
❑ 374 Jack Heidemann 1.25 .50
❑ 375 Reggie Cleveland 1.25 .50
❑ 376 Andy Kosco 1.25 .50
❑ 377 Terry Harmon 1.25 .50
❑ 378 Checklist 395-525 6.00 2.50
❑ 379 Ken Berry 1.25 .50
❑ 380 Earl Williams 1.25 .50
❑ 381 Chicago White Sox TC 2.00 .75
❑ 382 Joe Gibbon 1.25 .50
❑ 383 Brant Alyea 1.25 .50
❑ 384 Dave Campbell 2.00 .75
❑ 385 Mickey Stanley 2.00 .75
❑ 386 Jim Colborn 1.25 .50
❑ 387 Horace Clarke 2.00 .75
❑ 388 Charlie Williams RC 1.25 .50
❑ 389 Bill Rigney MG 1.25 .50
❑ 390 Willie Davis 2.00 .75
❑ 391 Ken Sanders 1.25 .50
❑ 392 F.Cambria/R.Zisk RC 2.00 .75
❑ 393 Curt Motton 1.25 .50
❑ 394 Ken Forsch 2.00 .75
❑ 395 Matty Alou 2.00 .75
❑ 396 Paul Lindblad 1.50 .60
❑ 397 Philadelphia Phillies TC 2.00 .75
❑ 398 Larry Hisle 2.00 .75
❑ 399 Milt Wilcox 2.00 .75
❑ 400 Tony Oliva 4.00 1.50
❑ 401 Jim Nash 1.50 .60
❑ 402 Bobby Heise 1.50 .60
❑ 403 John Cumberland 1.50 .60
❑ 404 Jeff Torborg 2.00 .75
❑ 405 Ron Fairly 2.00 .75
❑ 406 George Hendrick RC 2.00 .75
❑ 407 Chuck Taylor 1.50 .60
❑ 408 Jim Northrup 2.00 .75
❑ 409 Frank Baker 1.50 .60
❑ 410 Ferguson Jenkins 6.00 2.50
❑ 411 Bob Montgomery 1.50 .60
❑ 412 Dick Kelley 1.50 .60
❑ 413 D.Eddy RC/D.Lemonds 1.50 .60
❑ 414 Bob Miller 1.50 .60
❑ 415 Cookie Rojas 2.00 .75
❑ 416 Johnny Edwards 1.50 .60
❑ 417 Tom Hall 1.50 .60
❑ 418 Tom Shopay 1.50 .60
❑ 419 Jim Spencer 1.50 .60
❑ 420 Steve Carlton 20.00 8.00
❑ 421 Ellie Rodriguez 1.50 .60
❑ 422 Ray Lamb 1.50 .60
❑ 423 Oscar Gamble 2.00 .75
❑ 424 Bill Gogolewski 1.50 .60
❑ 425 Ken Singleton 2.00 .75
❑ 426 Ken Singleton IA 1.50 .60
❑ 427 Tito Fuentes 1.50 .60
❑ 428 Tito Fuentes IA 1.50 .60
❑ 429 Bob Robertson 1.50 .60
❑ 430 Bob Robertson IA 1.50 .60
❑ 431 Cito Gaston 2.00 .75
❑ 432 Cito Gaston IA 2.00 .75
❑ 433 Johnny Bench 25.00 10.00
❑ 434 Johnny Bench IA 15.00 6.00
❑ 435 Reggie Jackson 30.00 12.50
❑ 436 Reggie Jackson IA 12.00 5.00
❑ 437 Maury Wills 2.00 .75
❑ 438 Maury Wills IA 2.00 .75
❑ 439 Billy Williams 6.00 2.50
❑ 440 Billy Williams IA 4.00 1.50
❑ 441 Thurman Munson 15.00 6.00
❑ 442 Thurman Munson IA 8.00 3.00
❑ 443 Ken Henderson 1.50 .60
❑ 444 Ken Henderson IA 1.50 .60
❑ 445 Tom Seaver 30.00 12.50
❑ 446 Tom Seaver IA 15.00 6.00
❑ 447 Willie Stargell 8.00 3.00
❑ 448 Willie Stargell IA 4.00 1.50
❑ 449 Bob Lemon MG 2.00 .75
❑ 450 Mickey Lolich 2.00 .75
❑ 451 Tony LaRussa 4.00 1.50
❑ 452 Ed Herrmann 1.50 .60
❑ 453 Barry Lersch 1.50 .60
❑ 454 Oakland Athletics TC 2.00 .75
❑ 455 Tommy Harper 2.00 .75
❑ 456 Mark Belanger 2.00 .75
❑ 457 Fast/Thomas/Ivie RC 1.50 .60
❑ 458 Aurelio Monteagudo 1.50 .60
❑ 459 Rick Renick 1.50 .60
❑ 460 Al Downing 1.50 .60
❑ 461 Tim Cullen 1.50 .60
❑ 462 Rickey Clark 1.50 .60
❑ 463 Bernie Carbo 1.50 .60
❑ 464 Jim Roland 1.50 .60
❑ 465 Gil Hodges MG 4.00 1.50
❑ 466 Norm Miller 1.50 .60
❑ 467 Steve Kline 1.50 .60
❑ 468 Richie Scheinblum 1.50 .60
❑ 469 Ron Herbel 1.50 .60
❑ 470 Ray Fosse 1.50 .60
❑ 471 Luke Walker 1.50 .60
❑ 472 Phil Gagliano 1.50 .60
❑ 473 Dan McGinn 1.50 .60
❑ 474 Baylor/Harrison/Oates RC 15.00 6.00
❑ 475 Gary Nolan 2.00 .75
❑ 476 Lee Richard RC 1.50 .60
❑ 477 Tom Phoebus 1.50 .60
❑ 478 Checklist 526-656 6.00 2.50
❑ 479 Don Shaw 1.50 .60
❑ 480 Lee May 2.00 .75
❑ 481 Billy Conigliaro 2.00 .75
❑ 482 Joe Hoerner 1.50 .60
❑ 483 Ken Suarez 1.50 .60
❑ 484 Lum Harris MG 1.50 .60
❑ 485 Phil Regan 2.00 .75
❑ 486 John Lowenstein 1.50 .60
❑ 487 Detroit Tigers TC 2.00 .75
❑ 488 Mike Nagy 1.50 .60
❑ 489 T.Humphrey RC/K.Lampard 1.50 .60
❑ 490 Dave McNally 2.00 .75
❑ 491 Lou Piniella KP 2.00 .75
❑ 492 Mel Stottlemyre KP 2.00 .75
❑ 493 Bob Bailey KP 2.00 .75
❑ 494 Willie Horton KP 2.00 .75
❑ 495 Bill Melton KP 2.00 .75
❑ 496 Bud Harrelson KP 2.00 .75
❑ 497 Jim Perry KP 2.00 .75
❑ 498 Brooks Robinson KP 4.00 1.50
❑ 499 Vicente Romo 1.50 .60
❑ 500 Joe Torre 4.00 1.50
❑ 501 Pete Hamm 1.50 .60
❑ 502 Jackie Hernandez 1.50 .60
❑ 503 Gary Peters 1.50 .60
❑ 504 Ed Spiezio 1.50 .60
❑ 505 Mike Marshall 2.00 .75
❑ 506 Ley/Moyer/Tidrow RC 1.50 .60
❑ 507 Fred Gladding 1.50 .60
❑ 508 Elrod Hendricks 1.50 .60
❑ 509 Don McMahon 1.50 .60
❑ 510 Ted Williams MG 12.00 5.00
❑ 511 Tony Taylor 2.00 .75
❑ 512 Paul Popovich 1.50 .60
❑ 513 Lindy McDaniel 2.00 .75
❑ 514 Ted Sizemore 1.50 .60
❑ 515 Bert Blyleven 4.00 1.50
❑ 516 Oscar Brown 1.50 .60
❑ 517 Ken Brett 1.50 .60
❑ 518 Wayne Garrett 1.50 .60
❑ 519 Ted Abernathy 1.50 .60
❑ 520 Larry Bowa 2.00 .75
❑ 521 Alan Foster 1.50 .60
❑ 522 Los Angeles Dodgers TC 2.00 .75
❑ 523 Chuck Dobson 1.50 .60
❑ 524 E.Armbrister RC/M.Behney RC 1.50 .60
❑ 525 Carlos May 2.00 .75
❑ 526 Bob Bailey 6.00 2.50
❑ 527 Dave Leonhard 4.00 1.50
❑ 528 Ron Stone 4.00 1.50
❑ 529 Dave Nelson 6.00 2.50
❑ 530 Don Sutton 12.00 5.00
❑ 531 Freddie Patek 6.00 2.50
❑ 532 Fred Kendall RC 4.00 1.50
❑ 533 Ralph Houk MG 6.00 2.50
❑ 534 Jim Hickman 6.00 2.50
❑ 535 Ed Brinkman 4.00 1.50
❑ 536 Doug Rader 6.00 2.50
❑ 537 Bob Locker 4.00 1.50
❑ 538 Charlie Sands RC 4.00 1.50
❑ 539 Terry Forster RC 6.00 2.50
❑ 540 Felix Millan 4.00 1.50
❑ 541 Roger Repoz 4.00 1.50
❑ 542 Jack Billingham 4.00 1.50
❑ 543 Duane Josephson 4.00 1.50
❑ 544 Ted Martinez 4.00 1.50
❑ 545 Wayne Granger 4.00 1.50
❑ 546 Joe Hague 4.00 1.50
❑ 547 Cleveland Indians TC 8.00 3.00
❑ 548 Frank Reberger 4.00 1.50
❑ 549 Dave May 4.00 1.50
❑ 550 Brooks Robinson 25.00 10.00
❑ 551 Ollie Brown 4.00 1.50
❑ 552 Ollie Brown IA 4.00 1.50
❑ 553 Wilbur Wood 6.00 2.50
❑ 554 Wilbur Wood IA 4.00 1.50
❑ 555 Ron Santo 8.00 3.00

❑ 556 Ron Santo IA 6.00 2.50
❑ 557 John Odom 4.00 1.50
❑ 558 John Odom IA 4.00 1.50
❑ 559 Pete Rose 50.00 20.00
❑ 560 Pete Rose IA 25.00 10.00
❑ 561 Leo Cardenas 4.00 1.50
❑ 562 Leo Cardenas IA 4.00 1.50
❑ 563 Ray Sadecki 4.00 1.50
❑ 564 Ray Sadecki IA 4.00 1.50
❑ 565 Reggie Smith 6.00 2.50
❑ 566 Reggie Smith IA 4.00 1.50
❑ 567 Juan Marichal 12.00 5.00
❑ 568 Juan Marichal IA 6.00 2.50
❑ 569 Ed Kirkpatrick 4.00 1.50
❑ 570 Ed Kirkpatrick IA 4.00 1.50
❑ 571 Nate Colbert 4.00 1.50
❑ 572 Nate Colbert IA 4.00 1.50
❑ 573 Fritz Peterson 4.00 1.50
❑ 574 Fritz Peterson IA 4.00 1.50
❑ 575 Al Oliver 8.00 3.00
❑ 576 Leo Durocher MG 6.00 2.50
❑ 577 Mike Paul 6.00 2.50
❑ 578 Billy Grabarkewitz 4.00 1.50
❑ 579 Doyle Alexander RC 6.00 2.50
❑ 580 Lou Piniella 6.00 2.50
❑ 581 Wade Blasingame 4.00 1.50
❑ 582 Montreal Expos TC 8.00 3.00
❑ 583 Darold Knowles 4.00 1.50
❑ 584 Jerry McNertney 4.00 1.50
❑ 585 George Scott 6.00 2.50
❑ 586 Denis Menke 4.00 1.50
❑ 587 Billy Wilson 4.00 1.50
❑ 588 Jim Holt 4.00 1.50
❑ 589 Hal Lanier 4.00 1.50
❑ 590 Graig Nettles 8.00 3.00
❑ 591 Paul Casanova 4.00 1.50
❑ 592 Lew Krausse 4.00 1.50
❑ 593 Rich Morales 4.00 1.50
❑ 594 Jim Beauchamp 4.00 1.50
❑ 595 Nolan Ryan 100.00 50.00
❑ 596 Manny Mota 6.00 2.50
❑ 597 Jim Magnuson RC 4.00 1.50
❑ 598 Hal King 6.00 2.50
❑ 599 Billy Champion 4.00 1.50
❑ 600 Al Kaline 25.00 10.00
❑ 601 George Stone 4.00 1.50
❑ 602 Dave Bristol MG 4.00 1.50
❑ 603 Jim Ray 4.00 1.50
❑ 604A Checklist 657-787 Right Copy 12.00 5.00
❑ 604B Checklist 657-787 Left Copy 12.00 5.00
❑ 605 Nelson Briles 6.00 2.50
❑ 606 Luis Melendez 4.00 1.50
❑ 607 Frank Duffy 4.00 1.50
❑ 608 Mike Corkins 4.00 1.50
❑ 609 Tom Grieve 6.00 2.50
❑ 610 Bill Stoneman 6.00 2.50
❑ 611 Rich Reese 4.00 1.50
❑ 612 Joe Decker 4.00 1.50
❑ 613 Mike Ferraro 4.00 1.50
❑ 614 Ted Uhlaender 4.00 1.50
❑ 615 Steve Hargan 4.00 1.50
❑ 616 Joe Ferguson RC 6.00 2.50
❑ 617 Kansas City Royals TC 8.00 3.00
❑ 618 Rich Robertson 4.00 1.50
❑ 619 Rich McKinney 4.00 1.50
❑ 620 Phil Niekro 12.00 5.00
❑ 621 Commish Award 8.00 3.00
❑ 622 MVP Award 8.00 3.00
❑ 623 Cy Young Award 8.00 3.00
❑ 624 Minor Lg POY Award 8.00 3.00
❑ 625 Rookie of the Year 8.00 3.00
❑ 626 Babe Ruth Award 8.00 3.00
❑ 627 Moe Drabowsky 4.00 1.50
❑ 628 Terry Crowley 4.00 1.50
❑ 629 Paul Doyle 4.00 1.50
❑ 630 Rich Hebner 6.00 2.50
❑ 631 John Strohmayer 4.00 1.50
❑ 632 Mike Hegan 4.00 1.50
❑ 633 Jack Hiatt 4.00 1.50
❑ 634 Dick Woodson 4.00 1.50
❑ 635 Don Money 6.00 2.50
❑ 636 Bill Lee 6.00 2.50
❑ 637 Preston Gomez MG 4.00 1.50
❑ 638 Ken Wright 4.00 1.50
❑ 639 J.C. Martin 4.00 1.50
❑ 640 Joe Coleman 4.00 1.50
❑ 641 Mike Lum 4.00 1.50
❑ 642 Dennis Riddleberger RC 4.00 1.50
❑ 643 Russ Gibson 4.00 1.50
❑ 644 Bernie Allen 4.00 1.50
❑ 645 Jim Maloney 6.00 2.50
❑ 646 Chico Salmon 4.00 1.50
❑ 647 Bob Moose 4.00 1.50
❑ 648 Jim Lyttle 4.00 1.50
❑ 649 Pete Richert 4.00 1.50
❑ 650 Sal Bando 6.00 2.50
❑ 651 Cincinnati Reds TC 8.00 3.00
❑ 652 Marcelino Lopez 4.00 1.50
❑ 653 Jim Fairey 4.00 1.50
❑ 654 Horacio Pina 6.00 2.50
❑ 655 Jerry Grote 4.00 1.50
❑ 656 Rudy May 4.00 1.50
❑ 657 Bobby Wine 12.00 5.00
❑ 658 Steve Dunning 12.00 5.00
❑ 659 Bob Aspromonte 12.00 5.00
❑ 660 Paul Blair 15.00 6.00
❑ 661 Bill Virdon MG 12.00 5.00
❑ 662 Stan Bahnsen 12.00 5.00
❑ 663 Fran Healy RC 15.00 6.00
❑ 664 Bobby Knoop 12.00 5.00
❑ 665 Chris Short 12.00 5.00
❑ 666 Hector Torres 12.00 5.00
❑ 667 Ray Newman RC 12.00 5.00
❑ 668 Texas Rangers TC 30.00 12.50
❑ 669 Willie Crawford 12.00 5.00
❑ 670 Ken Holtzman 15.00 6.00
❑ 671 Donn Clendenon 15.00 6.00
❑ 672 Archie Reynolds 12.00 5.00
❑ 673 Dave Marshall 12.00 5.00
❑ 674 John Kennedy 12.00 5.00
❑ 675 Pat Jarvis 12.00 5.00
❑ 676 Danny Cater 12.00 5.00
❑ 677 Ivan Murrell 12.00 5.00
❑ 678 Steve Luebber RC 12.00 5.00
❑ 679 B.Fenwick RC/B.Stinson 12.00 5.00
❑ 680 Dave Johnson 15.00 6.00
❑ 681 Bobby Pfeil 12.00 5.00
❑ 682 Mike McCormick 15.00 6.00
❑ 683 Steve Hovley 12.00 5.00
❑ 684 Hal Breeden RC 12.00 5.00
❑ 685 Joel Horlen 12.00 5.00
❑ 686 Steve Garvey 40.00 12.50
❑ 687 Del Unser 12.00 5.00
❑ 688 St. Louis Cardinals TC 20.00 8.00
❑ 689 Eddie Fisher 12.00 5.00
❑ 690 Willie Montanez 15.00 6.00
❑ 691 Curt Blefary 12.00 5.00
❑ 692 Curt Blefary IA 12.00 5.00
❑ 693 Alan Gallagher 12.00 5.00
❑ 694 Alan Gallagher IA 12.00 5.00
❑ 695 Rod Carew 50.00 20.00
❑ 696 Rod Carew IA 30.00 12.50
❑ 697 Jerry Koosman 15.00 6.00
❑ 698 Jerry Koosman IA 15.00 6.00
❑ 699 Bobby Murcer 15.00 6.00
❑ 700 Bobby Murcer IA 15.00 6.00
❑ 701 Jose Pagan 12.00 5.00
❑ 702 José Pagan IA 12.00 5.00
❑ 703 Doug Griffin 12.00 5.00
❑ 704 Doug Griffin IA 12.00 5.00
❑ 705 Pat Corrales 15.00 6.00
❑ 706 Pat Corrales IA 12.00 5.00
❑ 707 Tim Foli 12.00 5.00
❑ 708 Tim Foli IA 12.00 5.00
❑ 709 Jim Kaat 15.00 6.00
❑ 710 Jim Kaat IA 15.00 6.00
❑ 711 Bobby Bonds 20.00 8.00
❑ 712 Bobby Bonds IA 15.00 6.00
❑ 713 Gene Michael 20.00 8.00
❑ 714 Gene Michael IA 15.00 6.00
❑ 715 Mike Epstein 12.00 5.00
❑ 716 Jesus Alou 12.00 5.00
❑ 717 Bruce Dal Canton 12.00 5.00
❑ 718 Del Rice MG 12.00 5.00
❑ 719 Cesar Geronimo 12.00 5.00
❑ 720 Sam McDowell 15.00 6.00
❑ 721 Eddie Leon 12.00 5.00
❑ 722 Bill Sudakis 12.00 5.00
❑ 723 Al Santorini 12.00 5.00
❑ 724 Curtis/Hinton/Scott RC 12.00 5.00
❑ 725 Dick McAuliffe 15.00 6.00
❑ 726 Dick Selma 12.00 5.00
❑ 727 Jose Laboy 12.00 5.00
❑ 728 Gail Hopkins 12.00 5.00
❑ 729 Bob Veale 15.00 6.00
❑ 730 Rick Monday 15.00 6.00
❑ 731 Baltimore Orioles TC 20.00 8.00
❑ 732 George Culver 12.00 5.00
❑ 733 Jim Ray Hart 15.00 6.00
❑ 734 Bob Burda 12.00 5.00
❑ 735 Diego Segui 12.00 5.00
❑ 736 Bill Russell 15.00 6.00
❑ 737 Len Randle RC 15.00 6.00
❑ 738 Jim Merritt 12.00 5.00
❑ 739 Don Mason 12.00 5.00
❑ 740 Rico Carty 15.00 6.00
❑ 741 Hutton/Milner/Miller RC 15.00 6.00
❑ 742 Jim Rooker 12.00 5.00
❑ 743 Cesar Gutierrez 12.00 5.00
❑ 744 Jim Slaton RC 12.00 5.00
❑ 745 Julian Javier 15.00 6.00
❑ 746 Lowell Palmer 12.00 5.00
❑ 747 Jim Stewart 12.00 5.00
❑ 748 Phil Hennigan 12.00 5.00
❑ 749 Walt Alston MG 20.00 8.00
❑ 750 Willie Horton 15.00 6.00
❑ 751 Steve Carlton TR 40.00 12.50
❑ 752 Joe Morgan TR 40.00 12.50
❑ 753 Denny McLain TR 20.00 8.00
❑ 754 Frank Robinson TR 40.00 12.50
❑ 755 Jim Fregosi TR 15.00 6.00
❑ 756 Rick Wise TR 15.00 6.00
❑ 757 Jose Cardenal TR 15.00 6.00
❑ 758 Gil Garrido 12.00 5.00
❑ 759 Chris Cannizzaro 12.00 5.00
❑ 760 Bill Mazeroski 25.00 10.00
❑ 761 Oglivie/Cey/Williams RC 25.00 10.00
❑ 762 Wayne Simpson 12.00 5.00
❑ 763 Ron Hansen 12.00 5.00
❑ 764 Dusty Baker 20.00 8.00
❑ 765 Ken McMullen 12.00 5.00
❑ 766 Steve Hamilton 12.00 5.00
❑ 767 Tom McCraw 15.00 6.00
❑ 768 Denny Doyle 12.00 5.00
❑ 769 Jack Aker 12.00 5.00
❑ 770 Jim Wynn 15.00 6.00
❑ 771 San Francisco Giants TC 20.00 8.00
❑ 772 Ken Tatum 12.00 5.00
❑ 773 Ron Brand 12.00 5.00
❑ 774 Luis Alvarado 12.00 5.00
❑ 775 Jerry Reuss 15.00 6.00
❑ 776 Bill Voss 12.00 5.00
❑ 777 Hoyt Wilhelm 25.00 10.00
❑ 778 Albury/Dempsey/Strickland RC 20.00 8.00
❑ 779 Tony Cloninger 12.00 5.00
❑ 780 Dick Green 12.00 5.00
❑ 781 Jim McAndrew 12.00 5.00
❑ 782 Larry Stahl 12.00 5.00
❑ 783 Les Cain 12.00 5.00
❑ 784 Ken Aspromonte 12.00 5.00
❑ 785 Vic Davalillo 12.00 5.00
❑ 786 Chuck Brinkman 12.00 5.00
❑ 787 Ron Reed 15.00 6.00

1973 Topps

❑ COMPLETE SET (660) 700.00 350.00
❑ COMMON CARD (1-264) .50 .20
❑ COMMON CARD (265-396) .75 .30
❑ COMMON CARD (397-528) 1.25 .50
❑ COMMON CARD (529-660) 3.00 1.25

Card	NRMT	VG-E
❑ WRAPPER (10-CENT, BAT)	15.00	6.00
❑ WRAPPER (10-CENT)	15.00	6.00
❑ 1 Ruth/Aaron/Mays HR	40.00	12.50
❑ 2 Rich Hebner	1.50	.60
❑ 3 Jim Lonborg	1.50	.60
❑ 4 John Milner	.50	.20
❑ 5 Ed Brinkman	.50	.20
❑ 6 Mac Scarce RC	.50	.20
❑ 7 Texas Rangers TC	2.00	.75
❑ 8 Tom Hall	.50	.20
❑ 9 Johnny Oates	1.50	.60
❑ 10 Don Sutton	4.00	1.50
❑ 11 Chris Chambliss UER	1.50	.60
❑ 12A Don Zimmer MG w/o Ear	3.00	1.25
❑ 12B Don Zimmer MG w/Ear	.75	.30
❑ 13 George Hendrick	1.50	.60
❑ 14 Sonny Siebert	.50	.20
❑ 15 Ralph Garr	1.50	.60
❑ 16 Steve Braun	.50	.20
❑ 17 Fred Gladding	.50	.20
❑ 18 Leroy Stanton	.50	.20
❑ 19 Tim Foli	.50	.20
❑ 20 Stan Bahnsen	.50	.20
❑ 21 Randy Hundley	1.50	.60
❑ 22 Ted Abernathy	.50	.20
❑ 23 Dave Kingman	1.50	.60
❑ 24 Al Santorini	.50	.20
❑ 25 Roy White	1.50	.60
❑ 26 Pittsburgh Pirates TC	2.00	.75
❑ 27 Bill Gogolewski	.50	.20
❑ 28 Hal McRae	1.50	.60
❑ 29 Tony Taylor	1.50	.60
❑ 30 Tug McGraw	1.50	.60
❑ 31 Buddy Bell RC	2.50	1.00
❑ 32 Fred Norman	.50	.20
❑ 33 Jim Breazeale RC	.50	.20
❑ 34 Pat Dobson	.50	.20
❑ 35 Willie Davis	1.50	.60
❑ 36 Steve Barber	.50	.20
❑ 37 Bill Robinson	1.50	.60
❑ 38 Mike Epstein	.50	.20
❑ 39 Dave Roberts	.50	.20
❑ 40 Reggie Smith	1.50	.60
❑ 41 Tom Walker RC	.50	.20
❑ 42 Mike Andrews	.50	.20
❑ 43 Randy Moffitt RC	.50	.20
❑ 44 Rick Monday	1.50	.60
❑ 45 Ellie Rodriguez UER	.50	.20
❑ 46 Lindy McDaniel	1.50	.60
❑ 47 Luis Melendez	.50	.20
❑ 48 Paul Splittorff	.50	.20
❑ 49A Frank Quilici MG Solid	3.00	1.25
❑ 49B Frank Quilici MG Natural	.75	.30
❑ 50 Roberto Clemente	40.00	12.50
❑ 51 Chuck Seelbach RC	.50	.20
❑ 52 Denis Menke	.50	.20
❑ 53 Steve Dunning	.50	.20
❑ 54 Checklist 1-132	3.00	1.25
❑ 55 Jon Matlack	1.50	.60
❑ 56 Merv Rettenmund	.50	.20
❑ 57 Derrel Thomas	.50	.20
❑ 58 Mike Paul	.50	.20
❑ 59 Steve Yeager RC	1.50	.60
❑ 60 Ken Holtzman	1.50	.60
❑ 61 B.Williams/R.Carew LL	2.50	1.00
❑ 62 J.Bench/D.Allen LL	2.50	1.00
❑ 63 J.Bench/D.Allen LL	2.50	1.00
❑ 64 L.Brock/Campaneris LL	1.50	.60
❑ 65 S.Carlton/L.Tiant LL	1.50	.60
❑ 66 Carlton/Perry/Wood LL	1.50	.60
❑ 67 S.Carlton/N.Ryan LL	25.00	10.00
❑ 68 C.Carroll/S.Lyle LL	1.50	.60
❑ 69 Phil Gagliano	.50	.20
❑ 70 Milt Pappas	1.50	.60
❑ 71 Johnny Briggs	.50	.20
❑ 72 Ron Reed	.50	.20
❑ 73 Ed Herrmann	.50	.20
❑ 74 Billy Champion	.50	.20
❑ 75 Vada Pinson	1.50	.60
❑ 76 Doug Rader	.50	.20
❑ 77 Mike Torrez	1.50	.60
❑ 78 Richie Scheinblum	.50	.20
❑ 79 Jim Willoughby RC	.50	.20
❑ 80 Tony Oliva UER	2.50	1.00
❑ 81A W.Lockman MG w/Banks Solid	1.50	.60
❑ 81B W.Lockman MG w/Banks Natural	1.50	.60
❑ 82 Fritz Peterson	.50	.20
❑ 83 Leron Lee	.50	.20
❑ 84 Rollie Fingers	4.00	1.50
❑ 85 Ted Simmons	1.50	.60
❑ 86 Tom McCraw	.50	.20
❑ 87 Ken Boswell	.50	.20
❑ 88 Mickey Stanley	1.50	.60
❑ 89 Jack Billingham	.50	.20
❑ 90 Brooks Robinson	8.00	3.00
❑ 91 Los Angeles Dodgers TC	2.00	.75
❑ 92 Jerry Bell	.50	.20
❑ 93 Jesus Alou	.50	.20
❑ 94 Dick Billings	.50	.20
❑ 95 Steve Blass	1.50	.60
❑ 96 Doug Griffin	.50	.20
❑ 97 Willie Montanez	1.50	.60
❑ 98 Dick Woodson	.50	.20
❑ 99 Carl Taylor	.50	.20
❑ 100 Hank Aaron	40.00	12.50
❑ 101 Ken Henderson	.50	.20
❑ 102 Rudy May	.50	.20
❑ 103 Celerino Sanchez RC	.50	.20
❑ 104 Reggie Cleveland	.50	.20
❑ 105 Carlos May	.50	.20
❑ 106 Terry Humphrey	.50	.20
❑ 107 Phil Hennigan	.50	.20
❑ 108 Bill Russell	1.50	.60
❑ 109 Doyle Alexander	1.50	.60
❑ 110 Bob Watson	1.50	.60
❑ 111 Dave Nelson	.50	.20
❑ 112 Gary Ross	.50	.20
❑ 113 Jerry Grote	1.50	.60
❑ 114 Lynn McGlothen RC	.50	.20
❑ 115 Ron Santo	1.50	.60
❑ 116A Ralph Houk MG Solid	3.00	1.25
❑ 116B Ralph Houk MG Natural	.75	.30
❑ 117 Ramon Hernandez	.50	.20
❑ 118 John Mayberry	1.50	.60
❑ 119 Larry Bowa	1.50	.60
❑ 120 Joe Coleman	.50	.20
❑ 121 Dave Rader	.50	.20
❑ 122 Jim Strickland	.50	.20
❑ 123 Sandy Alomar	1.50	.60
❑ 124 Jim Hardin	.50	.20
❑ 125 Ron Fairly	1.50	.60
❑ 126 Jim Brewer	.50	.20
❑ 127 Milwaukee Brewers TC	2.00	.75
❑ 128 Ted Sizemore	.50	.20
❑ 129 Terry Forster	1.50	.60
❑ 130 Pete Rose	30.00	12.50
❑ 131A Eddie Kasko MG w/oEar	3.00	1.25
❑ 131B Eddie Kasko MG w/Ear	1.50	.60
❑ 132 Matty Alou	1.50	.60
❑ 133 Dave Roberts RC	.50	.20
❑ 134 Milt Wilcox	.50	.20
❑ 135 Lee May UER	1.50	.60
❑ 136A Earl Weaver MG Orange	1.50	.60
❑ 136B Earl Weaver MG Pale	3.00	1.25
❑ 137 Jim Beauchamp	.50	.20
❑ 138 Horacio Pina	.50	.20
❑ 139 Carmen Fanzone RC	.50	.20
❑ 140 Lou Piniella	2.50	1.00
❑ 141 Bruce Kison	.50	.20
❑ 142 Thurman Munson	8.00	3.00
❑ 143 John Curtis	.50	.20
❑ 144 Marty Perez	.50	.20
❑ 145 Bobby Bonds	2.50	1.00
❑ 146 Woodie Fryman	.50	.20
❑ 147 Mike Anderson	.50	.20
❑ 148 Dave Goltz RC	.50	.20
❑ 149 Ron Hunt	.50	.20
❑ 150 Wilbur Wood	1.50	.60
❑ 151 Wes Parker	1.50	.60
❑ 152 Dave May	.50	.20
❑ 153 Al Hrabosky	1.50	.60
❑ 154 Jeff Torborg	1.50	.60
❑ 155 Sal Bando	1.50	.60
❑ 156 Cesar Geronimo	.50	.20
❑ 157 Denny Riddleberger	.50	.20
❑ 158 Houston Astros TC	2.00	.75
❑ 159 Cito Gaston	1.50	.60
❑ 160 Jim Palmer	6.00	2.50
❑ 161 Ted Martinez	.50	.20
❑ 162 Pete Broberg	.50	.20
❑ 163 Vic Davalillo	.50	.20
❑ 164 Monty Montgomery	.50	.20
❑ 165 Luis Aparicio	4.00	1.50
❑ 166 Terry Harmon	.50	.20
❑ 167 Steve Stone	1.50	.60
❑ 168 Jim Northrup	1.50	.60
❑ 169 Ron Schueler RC	1.50	.60
❑ 170 Harmon Killebrew	5.00	2.00
❑ 171 Bernie Carbo	.50	.20
❑ 172 Steve Kline	.50	.20
❑ 173 Hal Breeden	.50	.20
❑ 174 Goose Gossage RC	6.00	2.50
❑ 175 Frank Robinson	6.00	2.50
❑ 176 Chuck Taylor	.50	.20
❑ 177 Bill Plummer RC	.50	.20
❑ 178 Don Rose RC	.50	.20
❑ 179A Dick Williams w/Ear	4.00	1.50
❑ 179B Dick Williams w/o Ear	1.50	.60
❑ 180 Ferguson Jenkins	4.00	1.50
❑ 181 Jack Brohamer RC	.50	.20
❑ 182 Mike Caldwell RC	1.50	.60
❑ 183 Don Buford	.50	.20
❑ 184 Jerry Koosman	1.50	.60
❑ 185 Jim Wynn	1.50	.60
❑ 186 Bill Fahey	.50	.20
❑ 187 Luke Walker	.50	.20
❑ 188 Cookie Rojas	1.50	.60
❑ 189 Greg Luzinski	2.50	1.00
❑ 190 Bob Gibson	8.00	3.00
❑ 191 Detroit Tigers TC	2.50	1.00
❑ 192 Pat Jarvis	.50	.20
❑ 193 Carlton Fisk	10.00	4.00
❑ 194 Jorge Orta RC	.50	.20
❑ 195 Clay Carroll	.50	.20
❑ 196 Ken McMullen	.50	.20
❑ 197 Ed Goodson RC	.50	.20
❑ 198 Horace Clarke	.50	.20
❑ 199 Bert Blyleven	2.50	1.00
❑ 200 Billy Williams	4.00	1.50
❑ 201 George Hendrick ALCS	1.50	.60
❑ 202 George Foster NLCS	1.50	.60
❑ 203 Gene Tenace WS	1.50	.60
❑ 204 A's Two Straight WS	1.50	.60
❑ 205 Tony Perez WS	2.50	1.00
❑ 206 Gene Tenace WS	1.50	.60
❑ 207 Blue Moon Odom WS	1.50	.60
❑ 208 Johnny Bench WS	5.00	2.00
❑ 209 Bert Campaneris WS	1.50	.60
❑ 210 A's Win WS	.50	.20
❑ 211 Balor Moore	.50	.20
❑ 212 Joe Lahoud	.50	.20
❑ 213 Steve Garvey	5.00	2.00
❑ 214 Dave Hamilton RC	.50	.20
❑ 215 Dusty Baker	2.50	1.00
❑ 216 Toby Harrah	1.50	.60
❑ 217 Don Wilson	.50	.20
❑ 218 Aurelio Rodriguez	.50	.20
❑ 219 St. Louis Cardinals TC	2.50	1.00
❑ 220 Nolan Ryan	50.00	20.00
❑ 221 Fred Kendall	.50	.20
❑ 222 Rob Gardner	.50	.20
❑ 223 Bud Harrelson	1.50	.60
❑ 224 Bill Lee	1.50	.60
❑ 225 Al Oliver	1.50	.60
❑ 226 Ray Fosse	.50	.20
❑ 227 Wayne Twitchell	.50	.20
❑ 228 Bobby Darwin	.50	.20
❑ 229 Roric Harrison	.50	.20
❑ 230 Joe Morgan	6.00	2.50
❑ 231 Bill Parsons	.50	.20
❑ 232 Ken Singleton	1.50	.60
❑ 233 Ed Kirkpatrick	.50	.20
❑ 234 Bill North RC	.50	.20
❑ 235 Jim Hunter	4.00	1.50
❑ 236 Tito Fuentes	.50	.20
❑ 237A Eddie Mathews MG w/Ear	1.50	.60
❑ 237B Eddie Mathews MG w/o Ear	3.00	1.25
❑ 238 Tony Muser RC	.50	.20
❑ 239 Pete Richert	.50	.20
❑ 240 Bobby Murcer	1.50	.60
❑ 241 Dwain Anderson	.50	.20
❑ 242 George Culver	.50	.20
❑ 243 California Angels TC	2.50	1.00
❑ 244 Ed Acosta	.50	.20
❑ 245 Carl Yastrzemski	10.00	4.00
❑ 246 Ken Sanders	.50	.20
❑ 247 Del Unser	.50	.20
❑ 248 Jerry Johnson	.50	.20

❑	249	Larry Biittner	.50	.20
❑	250	Manny Sanguillen	1.50	.60
❑	251	Roger Nelson	.50	.20
❑	252A	Charlie Fox MG Orange	4.00	1.50
❑	252B	Charlie Fox MG Pale	1.50	.60
❑	253	Mark Belanger	1.50	.60
❑	254	Bill Stoneman	.50	.20
❑	255	Reggie Jackson	15.00	6.00
❑	256	Chris Zachary	.50	.20
❑	257A	Yogi Berra MG Orange	3.00	1.25
❑	257B	Yogi Berra MG Pale	5.00	2.00
❑	258	Tommy John	1.50	.60
❑	259	Jim Holt	.50	.20
❑	260	Gary Nolan	1.50	.60
❑	261	Pat Kelly	.50	.20
❑	262	Jack Aker	.50	.20
❑	263	George Scott	1.50	.60
❑	264	Checklist 133-264	3.00	1.25
❑	265	Gene Michael	1.50	.60
❑	266	Mike Lum	.75	.30
❑	267	Lloyd Allen	.75	.30
❑	268	Jerry Morales	.75	.30
❑	269	Tim McCarver	1.50	.60
❑	270	Luis Tiant	1.50	.60
❑	271	Tom Hutton	.75	.30
❑	272	Ed Farmer	.75	.30
❑	273	Chris Speier	.75	.30
❑	274	Darold Knowles	.75	.30
❑	275	Tony Perez	4.00	1.50
❑	276	Joe Lovitto RC	.75	.30
❑	277	Bob Miller	.75	.30
❑	278	Baltimore Orioles TC	1.50	.60
❑	279	Mike Strahler	.75	.30
❑	280	Al Kaline	8.00	3.00
❑	281	Mike Jorgensen	.75	.30
❑	282	Steve Hovley	.75	.30
❑	283	Ray Sadecki	.75	.30
❑	284	Glenn Borgmann RC	.75	.30
❑	285	Don Kessinger	1.50	.60
❑	286	Frank Linzy	.75	.30
❑	287	Eddie Leon	.75	.30
❑	288	Gary Gentry	.75	.30
❑	289	Bob Oliver	.75	.30
❑	290	Cesar Cedeno	1.50	.60
❑	291	Rogelio Moret	.75	.30
❑	292	Jose Cruz	1.50	.60
❑	293	Bernie Allen	.75	.30
❑	294	Steve Arlin	.75	.30
❑	295	Bert Campaneris	1.50	.60
❑	296	Sparky Anderson MG	2.50	1.00
❑	297	Walt Williams	.75	.30
❑	298	Ron Bryant	.75	.30
❑	299	Ted Ford	.75	.30
❑	300	Steve Carlton	10.00	4.00
❑	301	Billy Grabarkewitz	.75	.30
❑	302	Terry Crowley	.75	.30
❑	303	Nelson Briles	.75	.30
❑	304	Duke Sims	.75	.30
❑	305	Willie Mays	40.00	12.50
❑	306	Tom Burgmeier	.75	.30
❑	307	Boots Day	.75	.30
❑	308	Skip Lockwood	.75	.30
❑	309	Paul Popovich	.75	.30
❑	310	Dick Allen	1.50	.60
❑	311	Joe Decker	.75	.30
❑	312	Oscar Brown	.75	.30
❑	313	Jim Ray	.75	.30
❑	314	Ron Swoboda	1.50	.60
❑	315	John Odom	.75	.30
❑	316	San Diego Padres TC	1.50	.60
❑	317	Danny Cater	.75	.30
❑	318	Jim McGlothlin	.75	.30
❑	319	Jim Spencer	.75	.30
❑	320	Lou Brock	8.00	3.00
❑	321	Rich Hinton	.75	.30
❑	322	Garry Maddox RC	1.50	.60
❑	323	Billy Martin MG	1.50	.60
❑	324	Al Downing	.75	.30
❑	325	Boog Powell	1.50	.60
❑	326	Darrell Brandon	.75	.30
❑	327	John Lowenstein	.75	.30
❑	328	Bill Bonham	.75	.30
❑	329	Ed Kranepool	1.50	.60
❑	330	Rod Carew	8.00	3.00
❑	331	Carl Morton	.75	.30
❑	332	John Felske RC	.75	.30
❑	333	Gene Clines	.75	.30
❑	334	Freddie Patek	.75	.30
❑	335	Bob Tolan	.75	.30
❑	336	Tom Bradley	.75	.30
❑	337	Dave Duncan	1.50	.60
❑	338	Checklist 265-396	3.00	1.25
❑	339	Dick Tidrow	.75	.30
❑	340	Nate Colbert	.75	.30
❑	341	Jim Palmer KP	2.50	1.00
❑	342	Sam McDowell KP	.75	.30
❑	343	Bobby Murcer KP	.75	.30
❑	344	Jim Hunter KP	2.50	1.00
❑	345	Chris Speier KP	.75	.30
❑	346	Gaylord Perry KP	1.50	.60
❑	347	Kansas City Royals TC	1.50	.60
❑	348	Rennie Stennett	.75	.30
❑	349	Dick McAuliffe	.75	.30
❑	350	Tom Seaver	12.00	5.00
❑	351	Jimmy Stewart	.75	.30
❑	352	Don Stanhouse RC	.75	.30
❑	353	Steve Brye	.75	.30
❑	354	Billy Parker	.75	.30
❑	355	Mike Marshall	1.50	.60
❑	356	Chuck Tanner MG	4.00	1.50
❑	357	Ross Grimsley	.75	.30
❑	358	Jim Nettles	.75	.30
❑	359	Cecil Upshaw	.75	.30
❑	360	Joe Rudi UER	1.50	.60
❑	361	Fran Healy	.75	.30
❑	362	Eddie Watt	.75	.30
❑	363	Jackie Hernandez	.75	.30
❑	364	Rick Wise	.75	.30
❑	365	Rico Petrocelli	1.50	.60
❑	366	Brock Davis	.75	.30
❑	367	Burt Hooton	1.50	.60
❑	368	Bill Buckner	1.50	.60
❑	369	Lerrin LaGrow	.75	.30
❑	370	Willie Stargell	5.00	2.00
❑	371	Mike Kekich	.75	.30
❑	372	Oscar Gamble	.75	.30
❑	373	Clyde Wright	.75	.30
❑	374	Darrell Evans	1.50	.60
❑	375	Larry Dierker	1.50	.60
❑	376	Frank Duffy	.75	.30
❑	377	Gene Mauch MG	4.00	1.50
❑	378	Len Randle	.75	.30
❑	379	Cy Acosta RC	.75	.30
❑	380	Johnny Bench	12.00	5.00
❑	381	Vicente Romo	.75	.30
❑	382	Mike Hegan	.75	.30
❑	383	Diego Segui	.75	.30
❑	384	Don Baylor	4.00	1.50
❑	385	Jim Perry	1.50	.60
❑	386	Don Money	.75	.30
❑	387	Jim Barr	.75	.30
❑	388	Ben Oglivie	1.50	.60
❑	389	New York Mets TC	4.00	1.50
❑	390	Mickey Lolich	1.50	.60
❑	391	Lee Lacy RC	1.50	.60
❑	392	Dick Drago	.75	.30
❑	393	Jose Cardenal	.75	.30
❑	394	Sparky Lyle	1.50	.60
❑	395	Roger Metzger	.75	.30
❑	396	Grant Jackson	.75	.30
❑	397	Dave Cash	1.25	.50
❑	398	Rich Hand	1.25	.50
❑	399	George Foster	2.00	.75
❑	400	Gaylord Perry	5.00	2.00
❑	401	Clyde Mashore	1.25	.50
❑	402	Jack Hiatt	1.25	.50
❑	403	Sonny Jackson	1.25	.50
❑	404	Chuck Brinkman	1.25	.50
❑	405	Cesar Tovar	1.25	.50
❑	406	Paul Lindblad	1.25	.50
❑	407	Felix Millan	1.25	.50
❑	408	Jim Colborn	1.25	.50
❑	409	Ivan Murrell	1.25	.50
❑	410	Willie McCovey	6.00	2.50
❑	411	Ray Corbin	1.25	.50
❑	412	Manny Mota	2.00	.75
❑	413	Tom Timmermann	1.25	.50
❑	414	Ken Rudolph	1.25	.50
❑	415	Marty Pattin	1.25	.50
❑	416	Paul Schaal	1.25	.50
❑	417	Scipio Spinks	1.25	.50
❑	418	Bob Grich	2.00	.75
❑	419	Casey Cox	1.25	.50
❑	420	Tommie Agee	1.25	.50
❑	421A	B.Winkles MG RC Orange	1.50	.60
❑	421B	Bobby Winkles MG Pale	3.00	1.25
❑	422	Bob Robertson	1.25	.50
❑	423	Johnny Jeter	1.25	.50
❑	424	Denny Doyle	1.25	.50
❑	425	Alex Johnson	1.25	.50
❑	426	Dave LaRoche	1.25	.50
❑	427	Rick Auerbach	1.25	.50
❑	428	Wayne Simpson	1.25	.50
❑	429	Jim Fairey	1.25	.50
❑	430	Vida Blue	2.00	.75
❑	431	Gerry Moses	1.25	.50
❑	432	Dan Frisella	1.25	.50
❑	433	Willie Horton	2.00	.75
❑	434	San Francisco Giants TC	3.00	1.25
❑	435	Rico Carty	2.00	.75
❑	436	Jim McAndrew	1.25	.50
❑	437	John Kennedy	1.25	.50
❑	438	Enzo Hernandez	1.25	.50
❑	439	Eddie Fisher	1.25	.50
❑	440	Glenn Beckert	1.25	.50
❑	441	Gail Hopkins	1.25	.50
❑	442	Dick Dietz	1.25	.50
❑	443	Danny Thompson	1.25	.50
❑	444	Ken Brett	1.25	.50
❑	445	Ken Berry	1.25	.50
❑	446	Jerry Reuss	2.00	.75
❑	447	Joe Hague	1.25	.50
❑	448	John Hiller	1.25	.50
❑	449A	K.Aspro MG w/Spahn Point	4.00	1.50
❑	449B	K.Aspro MG w/Spahn Round	4.00	1.50
❑	450	Joe Torre	3.00	1.25
❑	451	John Vukovich RC	1.25	.50
❑	452	Paul Casanova	1.25	.50
❑	453	Checklist 397-528	3.00	1.25
❑	454	Tom Haller	1.25	.50
❑	455	Bill Melton	1.25	.50
❑	456	Dick Green	1.25	.50
❑	457	John Strohmayer	1.25	.50
❑	458	Jim Mason	1.25	.50
❑	459	Jimmy Howarth RC	1.25	.50
❑	460	Bill Freehan	2.00	.75
❑	461	Mike Corkins	1.25	.50
❑	462	Ron Blomberg	1.25	.50
❑	463	Ken Tatum	1.25	.50
❑	464	Chicago Cubs TC	3.00	1.25
❑	465	Dave Giusti	1.25	.50
❑	466	Jose Arcia	1.25	.50
❑	467	Mike Ryan	1.25	.50
❑	468	Tom Griffin	1.25	.50
❑	469	Dan Monzon RC	1.25	.50
❑	470	Mike Cuellar	2.00	.75
❑	471	Ty Cobb LDR	10.00	4.00
❑	472	Lou Gehrig LDR	15.00	6.00
❑	473	Hank Aaron LDR	10.00	4.00
❑	474	Babe Ruth LDR	20.00	8.00
❑	475	Ty Cobb LDR	8.00	3.00
❑	476	Walter Johnson LDR	3.00	1.25
❑	477	Cy Young LDR	3.00	1.25
❑	478	Walter Johnson LDR	3.00	1.25
❑	479	Hal Lanier	1.25	.50
❑	480	Juan Marichal	5.00	2.00
❑	481	Chicago White Sox TC	3.00	1.25
❑	482	Rick Reuschel RC	3.00	1.25
❑	483	Dal Maxvill	1.25	.50
❑	484	Ernie McAnally	1.25	.50
❑	485	Norm Cash	2.00	.75
❑	486A	D.Ozark MG RC Orange	1.50	.60
❑	486B	Danny Ozark MG Pale	3.00	1.25
❑	487	Bruce Dal Canton	1.25	.50
❑	488	Dave Campbell	2.00	.75
❑	489	Jeff Burroughs	2.00	.75
❑	490	Claude Osteen	2.00	.75
❑	491	Bob Montgomery	1.25	.50
❑	492	Pedro Borbon	1.25	.50
❑	493	Duffy Dyer	1.25	.50
❑	494	Rich Morales	1.25	.50
❑	495	Tommy Helms	1.25	.50
❑	496	Ray Lamb	1.25	.50
❑	497A	R.Schoen MG Orange	2.00	.75
❑	497B	R.Schoen MG Pale	3.00	1.25
❑	498	Graig Nettles	3.00	1.25
❑	499	Bob Moose	1.25	.50
❑	500	Oakland Athletics TC	3.00	1.25

❑ 501 Larry Gura 1.25 .50
❑ 502 Bobby Valentine 3.00 1.25
❑ 503 Phil Niekro 5.00 2.00
❑ 504 Earl Williams 1.25 .50
❑ 505 Bob Bailey 1.25 .50
❑ 506 Bart Johnson 1.25 .50
❑ 507 Darrel Chaney 1.25 .50
❑ 508 Gates Brown 1.25 .50
❑ 509 Jim Nash 1.25 .50
❑ 510 Amos Otis 2.00 .75
❑ 511 Sam McDowell 2.00 .75
❑ 512 Dalton Jones 1.25 .50
❑ 513 Dave Marshall 1.25 .50
❑ 514 Jerry Kenney 1.25 .50
❑ 515 Andy Messersmith 2.00 .75
❑ 516 Danny Walton 1.25 .50
❑ 517A Bill Virdon MG w/o Ear 1.50 .60
❑ 517B Bill Virdon MG w/Ear 3.00 1.25
❑ 518 Bob Veale 1.25 .50
❑ 519 Johnny Edwards 1.25 .50
❑ 520 Mel Stottlemyre 2.00 .75
❑ 521 Atlanta Braves TC 3.00 1.25
❑ 522 Leo Cardenas 1.25 .50
❑ 523 Wayne Granger 1.25 .50
❑ 524 Gene Tenace 2.00 .75
❑ 525 Jim Fregosi 2.00 .75
❑ 526 Ollie Brown 1.25 .50
❑ 527 Dan McGinn 1.25 .50
❑ 528 Paul Blair 1.25 .50
❑ 529 Milt May 3.00 1.25
❑ 530 Jim Kaat 5.00 2.00
❑ 531 Ron Woods 3.00 1.25
❑ 532 Steve Mingori 3.00 1.25
❑ 533 Larry Stahl 3.00 1.25
❑ 534 Dave Lemonds 3.00 1.25
❑ 535 Johnny Callison 5.00 2.00
❑ 536 Philadelphia Phillies TC 6.00 2.50
❑ 537 Bill Slayback RC 3.00 1.25
❑ 538 Jim Ray Hart 5.00 2.00
❑ 539 Tom Murphy 3.00 1.25
❑ 540 Cleon Jones 5.00 2.00
❑ 541 Bob Bolin 3.00 1.25
❑ 542 Pat Corrales 5.00 2.00
❑ 543 Alan Foster 3.00 1.25
❑ 544 Von Joshua 3.00 1.25
❑ 545 Orlando Cepeda 8.00 3.00
❑ 546 Jim York 3.00 1.25
❑ 547 Bobby Heise 3.00 1.25
❑ 548 Don Durham RC 3.00 1.25
❑ 549 Whitey Herzog MG 5.00 2.00
❑ 550 Dave Johnson 5.00 2.00
❑ 551 Mike Kilkenny 3.00 1.25
❑ 552 J.C. Martin 3.00 1.25
❑ 553 Mickey Scott 3.00 1.25
❑ 554 Dave Concepcion 5.00 2.00
❑ 555 Bill Hands 3.00 1.25
❑ 556 New York Yankees TC 8.00 3.00
❑ 557 Bernie Williams 3.00 1.25
❑ 558 Jerry May 3.00 1.25
❑ 559 Barry Lersch 3.00 1.25
❑ 560 Frank Howard 5.00 2.00
❑ 561 Jim Geddes RC 3.00 1.25
❑ 562 Wayne Garrett 3.00 1.25
❑ 563 Larry Haney 3.00 1.25
❑ 564 Mike Thompson RC 3.00 1.25
❑ 565 Jim Hickman 3.00 1.25
❑ 566 Lew Krausse 3.00 1.25
❑ 567 Bob Fenwick 3.00 1.25
❑ 568 Ray Newman 3.00 1.25
❑ 569 Walt Alston MG 8.00 3.00
❑ 570 Bill Singer 5.00 2.00
❑ 571 Rusty Torres 3.00 1.25
❑ 572 Gary Sutherland 3.00 1.25
❑ 573 Fred Beene 3.00 1.25
❑ 574 Bob Didier 3.00 1.25
❑ 575 Dock Ellis 3.00 1.25
❑ 576 Montreal Expos TC 6.00 2.50
❑ 577 Eric Soderholm RC 3.00 1.25
❑ 578 Ken Wright 3.00 1.25
❑ 579 Tom Grieve 5.00 2.00
❑ 580 Joe Pepitone 5.00 2.00
❑ 581 Steve Kealey 3.00 1.25
❑ 582 Darrell Porter 5.00 2.00
❑ 583 Bill Greif 3.00 1.25
❑ 584 Chris Arnold 3.00 1.25
❑ 585 Joe Niekro 5.00 2.00
❑ 586 Bill Sudakis 3.00 1.25
❑ 587 Rich McKinney 3.00 1.25
❑ 588 Checklist 529-660 20.00 8.00
❑ 589 Ken Forsch 3.00 1.25
❑ 590 Deron Johnson 3.00 1.25
❑ 591 Mike Hedlund 3.00 1.25
❑ 592 John Boccabella 3.00 1.25
❑ 593 Jack McKeon MG RC 4.00 1.50
❑ 594 Vic Harris RC 3.00 1.25
❑ 595 Don Gullett 5.00 2.00
❑ 596 Boston Red Sox TC 6.00 2.50
❑ 597 Mickey Rivers 5.00 2.00
❑ 598 Phil Roof 3.00 1.25
❑ 599 Ed Crosby 3.00 1.25
❑ 600 Dave McNally 5.00 2.00
❑ 601 Robles/Pena/Stelmaszek RC 5.00 2.00
❑ 602 Behney/Garcia/Rau RC 5.00 2.00
❑ 603 Hughes/McNulty/Reitz RC 5.00 2.00
❑ 604 Jefferson/O'Toole/Stampe RC 5.00 2.00
❑ 605 Cabell/Bourque/Marquez RC 5.00 2.00
❑ 606 Matthews/Pac/Roque RC 5.00 2.00
❑ 607 Frias/Busse/Guerrero RC 5.00 2.00
❑ 608 Busby/Colpaert/Medich RC 5.00 2.00
❑ 609 Blanks/Garcia/Lopes RC 5.00 2.00
❑ 610 Freeman/Hough/Webb RC 5.00 2.00
❑ 611 Coggins/Wohlford/Zisk RC 5.00 2.00
❑ 612 Lawson/Reynolds/Strom RC 5.00 2.00
❑ 613 Boone/Jutze/Ivie RC 15.00 6.00
❑ 614 Bumbry/Evans/Spikes RC 20.00 8.00
❑ 615 Mike Schmidt RC 150.00 75.00
❑ 616 Angelini/Blateric/Garman RC 5.00 2.00
❑ 617 Rich Chiles 3.00 1.25
❑ 618 Andy Etchebarren 3.00 1.25
❑ 619 Billy Wilson 3.00 1.25
❑ 620 Tommy Harper 5.00 2.00
❑ 621 Joe Ferguson 5.00 2.00
❑ 622 Larry Hisle 5.00 2.00
❑ 623 Steve Renko 3.00 1.25
❑ 624 Leo Durocher MG 5.00 2.00
❑ 625 Angel Mangual 3.00 1.25
❑ 626 Bob Barton 3.00 1.25
❑ 627 Luis Alvarado 3.00 1.25
❑ 628 Jim Slaton 3.00 1.25
❑ 629 Cleveland Indians TC 6.00 2.50
❑ 630 Denny McLain 8.00 3.00
❑ 631 Tom Matchick 3.00 1.25
❑ 632 Dick Selma 3.00 1.25
❑ 633 Ike Brown 3.00 1.25
❑ 634 Alan Closter 3.00 1.25
❑ 635 Gene Alley 5.00 2.00
❑ 636 Rickey Clark 3.00 1.25
❑ 637 Norm Miller 3.00 1.25
❑ 638 Ken Reynolds 3.00 1.25
❑ 639 Willie Crawford 3.00 1.25
❑ 640 Dick Bosman 3.00 1.25
❑ 641 Cincinnati Reds TC 6.00 2.50
❑ 642 Jose Laboy 3.00 1.25
❑ 643 Al Fitzmorris 3.00 1.25
❑ 644 Jack Heidemann 3.00 1.25
❑ 645 Bob Locker 3.00 1.25
❑ 646 Del Crandall MG 4.00 1.50
❑ 647 George Stone 3.00 1.25
❑ 648 Tom Egan 3.00 1.25
❑ 649 Rich Folkers 3.00 1.25
❑ 650 Felipe Alou 5.00 2.00
❑ 651 Don Carrithers 3.00 1.25
❑ 652 Ted Kubiak 3.00 1.25
❑ 653 Joe Hoerner 3.00 1.25
❑ 654 Minnesota Twins TC 6.00 2.50
❑ 655 Clay Kirby 3.00 1.25
❑ 656 John Ellis 3.00 1.25
❑ 657 Bob Johnson 3.00 1.25
❑ 658 Elliott Maddox 3.00 1.25
❑ 659 Jose Pagan 3.00 1.25
❑ 660 Fred Scherman 5.00 2.00

1974 Topps

❑ COMPLETE SET (660) 400.00 200.00
❑ COMP.FACT.SET (660) 600.00 300.00
❑ WRAPPERS (10-CENTS) 10.00 4.00
❑ 1 Hank Aaron 715 50.00 20.00
❑ 2 Aaron Special 54-57 8.00 3.00
❑ 3 Aaron Special 58-61 8.00 3.00
❑ 4 Aaron Special 62-65 8.00 3.00
❑ 5 Aaron Special 66-69 8.00 3.00
❑ 6 Aaron Special 70-73 8.00 3.00

❑ 7 Jim Hunter 4.00 1.50
❑ 8 George Theodore RC .50 .20
❑ 9 Mickey Lolich 1.00 .40
❑ 10 Johnny Bench 15.00 6.00
❑ 11 Jim Bibby .50 .20
❑ 12 Dave May .50 .20
❑ 13 Tom Hilgendorf .50 .20
❑ 14 Paul Popovich .50 .20
❑ 15 Joe Torre 2.00 .75
❑ 16 Baltimore Orioles TC 1.00 .40
❑ 17 Doug Bird RC .50 .20
❑ 18 Gary Thomasson RC .50 .20
❑ 19 Gerry Moses .50 .20
❑ 20 Nolan Ryan 40.00 12.50
❑ 21 Bob Gallagher RC .50 .20
❑ 22 Cy Acosta .50 .20
❑ 23 Craig Robinson RC .50 .20
❑ 24 John Hiller 1.00 .40
❑ 25 Ken Singleton 1.00 .40
❑ 26 Bill Campbell RC .50 .20
❑ 27 George Scott 1.00 .40
❑ 28 Manny Sanguillen 1.00 .40
❑ 29 Phil Niekro 3.00 1.25
❑ 30 Bobby Bonds 2.00 .75
❑ 31 Preston Gomez MG 1.00 .40
❑ 32A Johnny Grubb SD RC 1.00 .40
❑ 32B Johnny Grubb WASH 4.00 1.50
❑ 33 Don Newhauser RC .50 .20
❑ 34 Andy Kosco .50 .20
❑ 35 Gaylord Perry 3.00 1.25
❑ 36 St. Louis Cardinals TC 1.00 .40
❑ 37 Dave Sells RC .50 .20
❑ 38 Don Kessinger 1.00 .40
❑ 39 Ken Suarez .50 .20
❑ 40 Jim Palmer 8.00 3.00
❑ 41 Bobby Floyd .50 .20
❑ 42 Claude Osteen 1.00 .40
❑ 43 Jim Wynn 1.00 .40
❑ 44 Mel Stottlemyre 1.00 .40
❑ 45 Dave Johnson 1.00 .40
❑ 46 Pat Kelly .50 .20
❑ 47 Dick Ruthven RC .50 .20
❑ 48 Dick Sharon RC .50 .20
❑ 49 Steve Renko .50 .20
❑ 50 Rod Carew 8.00 3.00
❑ 51 Bobby Heise .50 .20
❑ 52 Al Oliver 1.00 .40
❑ 53A Fred Kendall SD 1.00 .40
❑ 53B Fred Kendall WASH 4.00 1.50
❑ 54 Elias Sosa RC .50 .20
❑ 55 Frank Robinson 8.00 3.00
❑ 56 New York Mets TC 1.00 .40
❑ 57 Darold Knowles .50 .20
❑ 58 Charlie Spikes .50 .20
❑ 59 Ross Grimsley .50 .20
❑ 60 Lou Brock 6.00 2.50
❑ 61 Luis Aparicio 3.00 1.25
❑ 62 Bob Locker .50 .20
❑ 63 Bill Sudakis .50 .20
❑ 64 Doug Rau .50 .20
❑ 65 Amos Otis 1.00 .40
❑ 66 Sparky Lyle 1.00 .40
❑ 67 Tommy Helms .50 .20
❑ 68 Grant Jackson .50 .20
❑ 69 Del Unser .50 .20
❑ 70 Dick Allen 2.00 .75
❑ 71 Dan Frisella .50 .20
❑ 72 Aurelio Rodriguez .50 .20

Card		
❑ 73 Mike Marshall	2.00	.75
❑ 74 Minnesota Twins TC	1.00	.40
❑ 75 Jim Colborn	.50	.20
❑ 76 Mickey Rivers	1.00	.40
❑ 77A Rich Troedson SD	1.00	.40
❑ 77B Rich Troedson WASH	4.00	1.50
❑ 78 Charlie Fox MG	1.00	.40
❑ 79 Gene Tenace	1.00	.40
❑ 80 Tom Seaver	12.00	5.00
❑ 81 Frank Duffy	.50	.20
❑ 82 Dave Giusti	.50	.20
❑ 83 Orlando Cepeda	3.00	1.25
❑ 84 Rick Wise	.50	.20
❑ 85 Joe Morgan	8.00	3.00
❑ 86 Joe Ferguson	1.00	.40
❑ 87 Fergie Jenkins	3.00	1.25
❑ 88 Freddie Patek	1.00	.40
❑ 89 Jackie Brown	.50	.20
❑ 90 Bobby Murcer	1.00	.40
❑ 91 Ken Forsch	.50	.20
❑ 92 Paul Blair	1.00	.40
❑ 93 Rod Gilbreath RC	.50	.20
❑ 94 Detroit Tigers TC	1.00	.40
❑ 95 Steve Carlton	8.00	3.00
❑ 96 Jerry Hairston RC	.50	.20
❑ 97 Bob Bailey	.50	.20
❑ 98 Bert Blyleven	2.00	.75
❑ 99 Del Crandall MG	1.00	.40
❑ 100 Willie Stargell	6.00	2.50
❑ 101 Bobby Valentine	1.00	.40
❑ 102A Bill Greif SD	1.00	.40
❑ 102B Bill Greif WASH	4.00	1.50
❑ 103 Sal Bando	1.00	.40
❑ 104 Ron Bryant	.50	.20
❑ 105 Carlton Fisk	12.00	5.00
❑ 106 Harry Parker RC	.50	.20
❑ 107 Alex Johnson	.50	.20
❑ 108 Al Hrabosky	1.00	.40
❑ 109 Bob Grich	1.00	.40
❑ 110 Billy Williams	3.00	1.25
❑ 111 Clay Carroll	.50	.20
❑ 112 Davey Lopes	2.00	.75
❑ 113 Dick Drago	.50	.20
❑ 114 California Angels TC	1.00	.40
❑ 115 Willie Horton	1.00	.40
❑ 116 Jerry Reuss	1.00	.40
❑ 117 Ron Blomberg	.50	.20
❑ 118 Bill Lee	1.00	.40
❑ 119 Danny Ozark MG	1.00	.40
❑ 120 Wilbur Wood	.50	.20
❑ 121 Larry Lintz RC	.50	.20
❑ 122 Jim Holt	.50	.20
❑ 123 Nelson Briles	1.00	.40
❑ 124 Bobby Coluccio RC	.50	.20
❑ 125A Nate Colbert SD	1.00	.40
❑ 125B Nate Colbert WASH	4.00	1.50
❑ 126 Checklist 1-132	3.00	1.25
❑ 127 Tom Paciorek	1.00	.40
❑ 128 John Ellis	.50	.20
❑ 129 Chris Speier	.50	.20
❑ 130 Reggie Jackson	15.00	6.00
❑ 131 Bob Boone	2.00	.75
❑ 132 Felix Millan	.50	.20
❑ 133 David Clyde RC	1.00	.40
❑ 134 Denis Menke	.50	.20
❑ 135 Roy White	1.00	.40
❑ 136 Rick Reuschel	1.00	.40
❑ 137 Al Bumbry	1.00	.40
❑ 138 Eddie Brinkman	.50	.20
❑ 139 Aurelio Monteagudo	.50	.20
❑ 140 Darrell Evans	2.00	.75
❑ 141 Pat Bourque	.50	.20
❑ 142 Pedro Garcia	.50	.20
❑ 143 Dick Woodson	.50	.20
❑ 144 Walter Alston MG	3.00	1.25
❑ 145 Dock Ellis	.50	.20
❑ 146 Ron Fairly	1.00	.40
❑ 147 Bart Johnson	.50	.20
❑ 148A Dave Hilton SD	1.00	.40
❑ 148B Dave Hilton WASH	4.00	1.50
❑ 149 Mac Scarce	.50	.20
❑ 150 John Mayberry	1.00	.40
❑ 151 Diego Segui	.50	.20
❑ 152 Oscar Gamble	1.00	.40
❑ 153 Jon Matlack	1.00	.40
❑ 154 Houston Astros TC	1.00	.40
❑ 155 Bert Campaneris	1.00	.40
❑ 156 Randy Moffitt	.50	.20
❑ 157 Vic Harris	.50	.20
❑ 158 Jack Billingham	.50	.20
❑ 159 Jim Ray Hart	.50	.20
❑ 160 Brooks Robinson	8.00	3.00
❑ 161 Ray Burris UER RC	1.00	.40
❑ 162 Bill Freehan	1.00	.40
❑ 163 Ken Berry	.50	.20
❑ 164 Tom House	.50	.20
❑ 165 Willie Davis	1.00	.40
❑ 166 Jack McKeon MG	1.00	.40
❑ 167 Luis Tiant	2.00	.75
❑ 168 Danny Thompson	.50	.20
❑ 169 Steve Rogers RC	2.00	.75
❑ 170 Bill Melton	.50	.20
❑ 171 Eduardo Rodriguez RC	.50	.20
❑ 172 Gene Clines	.50	.20
❑ 173A Randy Jones SD RC	2.00	.75
❑ 173B Randy Jones WASH	5.00	2.00
❑ 174 Bill Robinson	1.00	.40
❑ 175 Reggie Cleveland	.50	.20
❑ 176 John Lowenstein	.50	.20
❑ 177 Dave Roberts	.50	.20
❑ 178 Garry Maddox	1.00	.40
❑ 179 Yogi Berra MG	5.00	2.00
❑ 180 Ken Holtzman	1.00	.40
❑ 181 Cesar Geronimo	.50	.20
❑ 182 Lindy McDaniel	1.00	.40
❑ 183 Johnny Oates	1.00	.40
❑ 184 Texas Rangers TC	1.00	.40
❑ 185 Jose Cardenal	.50	.20
❑ 186 Fred Scherman	.50	.20
❑ 187 Don Baylor	2.00	.75
❑ 188 Rudy Meoli RC	.50	.20
❑ 189 Jim Brewer	.50	.20
❑ 190 Tony Oliva	2.00	.75
❑ 191 Al Fitzmorris	.50	.20
❑ 192 Mario Guerrero	.50	.20
❑ 193 Tom Walker	.50	.20
❑ 194 Darrell Porter	1.00	.40
❑ 195 Carlos May	.50	.20
❑ 196 Jim Fregosi	1.00	.40
❑ 197A Vicente Romo SD	1.00	.40
❑ 197B Vicente Romo WASH	4.00	1.50
❑ 198 Dave Cash	.50	.20
❑ 199 Mike Kekich	.50	.20
❑ 200 Cesar Cedeno	1.00	.40
❑ 201 R.Carew/P.Rose LL	6.00	2.50
❑ 202 R.Jackson/W.Stargell LL	5.00	2.00
❑ 203 R.Jackson/W.Stargell LL	5.00	2.00
❑ 204 T.Harper/L.Brock LL	2.00	.75
❑ 205 W.Wood/R.Bryant LL	1.00	.40
❑ 206 J.Palmer/T.Seaver LL	5.00	2.00
❑ 207 N.Ryan/T.Seaver LL	12.00	5.00
❑ 208 J.Hiller/M.Marshall LL	1.00	.40
❑ 209 Ted Sizemore	.50	.20
❑ 210 Bill Singer	.50	.20
❑ 211 Chicago Cubs TC	1.00	.40
❑ 212 Rollie Fingers	3.00	1.25
❑ 213 Dave Rader	.50	.20
❑ 214 Billy Grabarkewitz	.50	.20
❑ 215 Al Kaline UER	10.00	4.00
❑ 216 Ray Sadecki	.50	.20
❑ 217 Tim Foli	.50	.20
❑ 218 Johnny Briggs	.50	.20
❑ 219 Doug Griffin	.50	.20
❑ 220 Don Sutton	3.00	1.25
❑ 221 Chuck Tanner MG	1.00	.40
❑ 222 Ramon Hernandez	.50	.20
❑ 223 Jeff Burroughs	2.00	.75
❑ 224 Roger Metzger	.50	.20
❑ 225 Paul Splittorff	.50	.20
❑ 226A San Diego Padres TC SD	2.00	.75
❑ 226B San Diego Padres TC WASH	8.00	3.00
❑ 227 Mike Lum	.50	.20
❑ 228 Ted Kubiak	.50	.20
❑ 229 Fritz Peterson	.50	.20
❑ 230 Tony Perez	4.00	1.50
❑ 231 Dick Tidrow	.50	.20
❑ 232 Steve Brye	.50	.20
❑ 233 Jim Barr	.50	.20
❑ 234 John Milner	.50	.20
❑ 235 Dave McNally	1.00	.40
❑ 236 Red Schoendienst MG	3.00	1.25
❑ 237 Ken Brett	.50	.20
❑ 238 F.Healy w/Munson	.50	.20
❑ 239 Bill Russell	1.00	.40
❑ 240 Joe Coleman	.50	.20
❑ 241A Glenn Beckert SD	1.00	.40
❑ 241B Glenn Beckert WASH	4.00	1.50
❑ 242 Bill Gogolewski	.50	.20
❑ 243 Bob Oliver	.50	.20
❑ 244 Carl Morton	.50	.20
❑ 245 Cleon Jones	.50	.20
❑ 246 Oakland Athletics TC	2.00	.75
❑ 247 Rick Miller	.50	.20
❑ 248 Tom Hall	.50	.20
❑ 249 George Mitterwald	.50	.20
❑ 250A Willie McCovey SD	8.00	3.00
❑ 250B Willie McCovey WASH	25.00	10.00
❑ 251 Graig Nettles	2.00	.75
❑ 252 Dave Parker RC	10.00	4.00
❑ 253 John Boccabella	.50	.20
❑ 254 Stan Bahnsen	.50	.20
❑ 255 Larry Bowa	1.00	.40
❑ 256 Tom Griffin	.50	.20
❑ 257 Buddy Bell	2.00	.75
❑ 258 Jerry Morales	.50	.20
❑ 259 Bob Reynolds	.50	.20
❑ 260 Ted Simmons	2.00	.75
❑ 261 Jerry Bell	.50	.20
❑ 262 Ed Kirkpatrick	.50	.20
❑ 263 Checklist 133-264	3.00	1.25
❑ 264 Joe Rudi	1.00	.40
❑ 265 Tug McGraw	2.00	.75
❑ 266 Jim Northrup	1.00	.40
❑ 267 Andy Messersmith	1.00	.40
❑ 268 Tom Grieve	1.00	.40
❑ 269 Bob Johnson	.50	.20
❑ 270 Ron Santo	2.00	.75
❑ 271 Bill Hands	.50	.20
❑ 272 Paul Casanova	.50	.20
❑ 273 Checklist 265-396	3.00	1.25
❑ 274 Fred Beene	.50	.20
❑ 275 Ron Hunt	.50	.20
❑ 276 Bobby Winkles MG	1.00	.40
❑ 277 Gary Nolan	1.00	.40
❑ 278 Cookie Rojas	1.00	.40
❑ 279 Jim Crawford RC	.50	.20
❑ 280 Carl Yastrzemski	12.00	5.00
❑ 281 San Francisco Giants TC	1.00	.40
❑ 282 Doyle Alexander	1.00	.40
❑ 283 Mike Schmidt	20.00	8.00
❑ 284 Dave Duncan	1.00	.40
❑ 285 Reggie Smith	1.00	.40
❑ 286 Tony Muser	.50	.20
❑ 287 Clay Kirby	.50	.20
❑ 288 Gorman Thomas RC	2.00	.75
❑ 289 Rick Auerbach	.50	.20
❑ 290 Vida Blue	1.00	.40
❑ 291 Don Hahn	.50	.20
❑ 292 Chuck Seelbach	.50	.20
❑ 293 Milt May	.50	.20
❑ 294 Steve Foucault RC	.50	.20
❑ 295 Rick Monday	1.00	.40
❑ 296 Ray Corbin	.50	.20
❑ 297 Hal Breeden	.50	.20
❑ 298 Roric Harrison	.50	.20
❑ 299 Gene Michael	.50	.20
❑ 300 Pete Rose	25.00	10.00
❑ 301 Bob Montgomery	.50	.20
❑ 302 Rudy May	.50	.20
❑ 303 George Hendrick	1.00	.40
❑ 304 Don Wilson	.50	.20
❑ 305 Tito Fuentes	.50	.20
❑ 306 Earl Weaver MG	3.00	1.25
❑ 307 Luis Melendez	.50	.20
❑ 308 Bruce Dal Canton	.50	.20
❑ 309A Dave Roberts SD	1.00	.40
❑ 309B Dave Roberts WASH	6.00	2.50
❑ 310 Terry Forster	1.00	.40
❑ 311 Jerry Grote	1.00	.40
❑ 312 Deron Johnson	.50	.20
❑ 313 Barry Lersch	.50	.20
❑ 314 Milwaukee Brewers TC	1.00	.40
❑ 315 Ron Cey	2.00	.75
❑ 316 Jim Perry	1.00	.40
❑ 317 Richie Zisk	1.00	.40
❑ 318 Jim Merritt	.50	.20
❑ 319 Randy Hundley	.50	.20
❑ 320 Dusty Baker	2.00	.75

❑ 321	Steve Braun	.50	.20
❑ 322	Ernie McAnally	.50	.20
❑ 323	Richie Scheinblum	.50	.20
❑ 324	Steve Kline	.50	.20
❑ 325	Tommy Harper	1.00	.40
❑ 326	Sparky Anderson MG	3.00	1.25
❑ 327	Tom Timmermann	.50	.20
❑ 328	Skip Jutze	.50	.20
❑ 329	Mark Belanger	1.00	.40
❑ 330	Juan Marichal	5.00	2.00
❑ 331	C.Fisk/J.Bench AS	5.00	2.00
❑ 332	D.Allen/H.Aaron AS	8.00	3.00
❑ 333	R.Carew/J.Morgan AS	4.00	1.50
❑ 334	B.Robinson/R.Santo AS	2.00	.75
❑ 335	B.Campaneris/C.Speier AS	1.00	.40
❑ 336	B.Murcer/P.Rose AS	5.00	2.00
❑ 337	A.Otis/C.Cedeno AS	1.00	.40
❑ 338	R.Jackson/B.Williams AS	5.00	2.00
❑ 339	J.Hunter/R.Wise AS	3.00	1.25
❑ 340	Thurman Munson	8.00	3.00
❑ 341	Dan Driessen RC	1.00	.40
❑ 342	Jim Lonborg	1.00	.40
❑ 343	Kansas City Royals TC	1.00	.40
❑ 344	Mike Caldwell	.50	.20
❑ 345	Bill North	.50	.20
❑ 346	Ron Reed	.50	.20
❑ 347	Sandy Alomar	1.00	.40
❑ 348	Pete Richert	.50	.20
❑ 349	John Vukovich	.50	.20
❑ 350	Bob Gibson	8.00	3.00
❑ 351	Dwight Evans	3.00	1.25
❑ 352	Bill Stoneman	.50	.20
❑ 353	Rich Coggins	.50	.20
❑ 354	Whitey Lockman MG	1.00	.40
❑ 355	Dave Nelson	.50	.20
❑ 356	Jerry Koosman	1.00	.40
❑ 357	Buddy Bradford	.50	.20
❑ 358	Dal Maxvill	.50	.20
❑ 359	Brent Strom	.50	.20
❑ 360	Greg Luzinski	2.00	.75
❑ 361	Don Carrithers	.50	.20
❑ 362	Hal King	.50	.20
❑ 363	New York Yankees TC	2.00	.75
❑ 364A	Cito Gaston SD	2.00	.75
❑ 364B	Cito Gaston WASH	8.00	3.00
❑ 365	Steve Busby	1.00	.40
❑ 366	Larry Hisle	1.00	.40
❑ 367	Norm Cash	2.00	.75
❑ 368	Manny Mota	1.00	.40
❑ 369	Paul Lindblad	.50	.20
❑ 370	Bob Watson	1.00	.40
❑ 371	Jim Slaton	.50	.20
❑ 372	Ken Reitz	.50	.20
❑ 373	John Curtis	.50	.20
❑ 374	Marty Perez	.50	.20
❑ 375	Earl Williams	.50	.20
❑ 376	Jorge Orta	.50	.20
❑ 377	Ron Woods	.50	.20
❑ 378	Burt Hooton	1.00	.40
❑ 379	Billy Martin MG	2.00	.75
❑ 380	Bud Harrelson	1.00	.40
❑ 381	Charlie Sands	.50	.20
❑ 382	Bob Moose	.50	.20
❑ 383	Philadelphia Phillies TC	1.00	.40
❑ 384	Chris Chambliss	1.00	.40
❑ 385	Don Gullett	1.00	.40
❑ 386	Gary Matthews	2.00	.75
❑ 387A	Rich Morales SD	1.00	.40
❑ 387B	Rich Morales WASH	6.00	2.50
❑ 388	Phil Roof	.50	.20
❑ 389	Gates Brown	.50	.20
❑ 390	Lou Piniella	2.00	.75
❑ 391	Billy Champion	.50	.20
❑ 392	Dick Green	.50	.20
❑ 393	Orlando Pena	.50	.20
❑ 394	Ken Henderson	.50	.20
❑ 395	Doug Rader	.50	.20
❑ 396	Tommy Davis	1.00	.40
❑ 397	George Stone	.50	.20
❑ 398	Duke Sims	.50	.20
❑ 399	Mike Paul	.50	.20
❑ 400	Harmon Killebrew	6.00	2.50
❑ 401	Elliott Maddox	.50	.20
❑ 402	Jim Rooker	.50	.20
❑ 403	Darrell Johnson MG	1.00	.40
❑ 404	Jim Howarth	.50	.20
❑ 405	Ellie Rodriguez	.50	.20
❑ 406	Steve Arlin	.50	.20
❑ 407	Jim Wohlford	.50	.20
❑ 408	Charlie Hough	1.00	.40
❑ 409	Ike Brown	.50	.20
❑ 410	Pedro Borbon	.50	.20
❑ 411	Frank Baker	.50	.20
❑ 412	Chuck Taylor	.50	.20
❑ 413	Don Money	1.00	.40
❑ 414	Checklist 397-528	3.00	1.25
❑ 415	Gary Gentry	.50	.20
❑ 416	Chicago White Sox TC	1.00	.40
❑ 417	Rich Folkers	.50	.20
❑ 418	Walt Williams	.50	.20
❑ 419	Wayne Twitchell	.50	.20
❑ 420	Ray Fosse	.50	.20
❑ 421	Dan Fife RC	.50	.20
❑ 422	Gonzalo Marquez	.50	.20
❑ 423	Fred Stanley	.50	.20
❑ 424	Jim Beauchamp	.50	.20
❑ 425	Pete Broberg	.50	.20
❑ 426	Rennie Stennett	.50	.20
❑ 427	Bobby Bolin	.50	.20
❑ 428	Gary Sutherland	.50	.20
❑ 429	Dick Lange RC	.50	.20
❑ 430	Matty Alou	1.00	.40
❑ 431	Gene Garber RC	1.00	.40
❑ 432	Chris Arnold	.50	.20
❑ 433	Lerrin LaGrow	.50	.20
❑ 434	Ken McMullen	.50	.20
❑ 435	Dave Concepcion	2.00	.75
❑ 436	Don Hood RC	.50	.20
❑ 437	Jim Lyttle	.50	.20
❑ 438	Ed Herrmann	.50	.20
❑ 439	Norm Miller	.50	.20
❑ 440	Jim Kaat	2.00	.75
❑ 441	Tom Ragland	.50	.20
❑ 442	Alan Foster	.50	.20
❑ 443	Tom Hutton	.50	.20
❑ 444	Vic Davalillo	.50	.20
❑ 445	George Medich	.50	.20
❑ 446	Len Randle	.50	.20
❑ 447	Frank Quilici MG	1.00	.40
❑ 448	Ron Hodges RC	.50	.20
❑ 449	Tom McCraw	.50	.20
❑ 450	Rich Hebner	1.00	.40
❑ 451	Tommy John	2.00	.75
❑ 452	Gene Hiser	.50	.20
❑ 453	Balor Moore	.50	.20
❑ 454	Kurt Bevacqua	.50	.20
❑ 455	Tom Bradley	.50	.20
❑ 456	Dave Winfield RC	50.00	20.00
❑ 457	Chuck Goggin RC	.50	.20
❑ 458	Jim Ray	.50	.20
❑ 459	Cincinnati Reds TC	2.00	.75
❑ 460	Boog Powell	2.00	.75
❑ 461	John Odom	.50	.20
❑ 462	Luis Alvarado	.50	.20
❑ 463	Pat Dobson	.50	.20
❑ 464	Jose Cruz	2.00	.75
❑ 465	Dick Bosman	.50	.20
❑ 466	Dick Billings	.50	.20
❑ 467	Winston Llenas	.50	.20
❑ 468	Pepe Frias	.50	.20
❑ 469	Joe Decker	.50	.20
❑ 470	Reggie Jackson ALCS	5.00	2.00
❑ 471	Jon Matlack NLCS	1.00	.40
❑ 472	Darold Knowles WS1	1.00	.40
❑ 473	Willie Mays WS	8.00	3.00
❑ 474	Bert Campaneris WS3	1.00	.40
❑ 475	Rusty Staub WS4	1.00	.40
❑ 476	Cleon Jones WS5	1.00	.40
❑ 477	Reggie Jackson WS	5.00	2.00
❑ 478	Bert Campaneris WS7	1.00	.40
❑ 479	A's Celebrate WS	1.00	.40
❑ 480	Willie Crawford	.50	.20
❑ 481	Jerry Terrell RC	.50	.20
❑ 482	Bob Didier	.50	.20
❑ 483	Atlanta Braves TC	1.00	.40
❑ 484	Carmen Fanzone	.50	.20
❑ 485	Felipe Alou	2.00	.75
❑ 486	Steve Stone	1.00	.40
❑ 487	Ted Martinez	.50	.20
❑ 488	Andy Etchebarren	.50	.20
❑ 489	Danny Murtaugh MG	1.00	.40
❑ 490	Vada Pinson	2.00	.75
❑ 491	Roger Nelson	.50	.20
❑ 492	Mike Rogodzinski RC	.50	.20
❑ 493	Joe Hoerner	.50	.20
❑ 494	Ed Goodson	.50	.20
❑ 495	Dick McAuliffe	1.00	.40
❑ 496	Tom Murphy	.50	.20
❑ 497	Bobby Mitchell	.50	.20
❑ 498	Pat Corrales	.50	.20
❑ 499	Rusty Torres	.50	.20
❑ 500	Lee May	1.00	.40
❑ 501	Eddie Leon	.50	.20
❑ 502	Dave LaRoche	.50	.20
❑ 503	Eric Soderholm	.50	.20
❑ 504	Joe Niekro	1.00	.40
❑ 505	Bill Buckner	1.00	.40
❑ 506	Ed Farmer	.50	.20
❑ 507	Larry Stahl	.50	.20
❑ 508	Montreal Expos TC	1.00	.40
❑ 509	Jesse Jefferson	.50	.20
❑ 510	Wayne Garrett	.50	.20
❑ 511	Toby Harrah	1.00	.40
❑ 512	Joe Lahoud	.50	.20
❑ 513	Jim Campanis	.50	.20
❑ 514	Paul Schaal	.50	.20
❑ 515	Willie Montanez	.50	.20
❑ 516	Horacio Pina	.50	.20
❑ 517	Mike Hegan	.50	.20
❑ 518	Derrel Thomas	.50	.20
❑ 519	Bill Sharp RC	.50	.20
❑ 520	Tim McCarver	2.00	.75
❑ 521	Ken Aspromonte MG	1.00	.40
❑ 522	J.R. Richard	2.00	.75
❑ 523	Cecil Cooper	2.00	.75
❑ 524	Bill Plummer	.50	.20
❑ 525	Clyde Wright	.50	.20
❑ 526	Frank Tepedino	1.00	.40
❑ 527	Bobby Darwin	.50	.20
❑ 528	Bill Bonham	.50	.20
❑ 529	Horace Clarke	1.00	.40
❑ 530	Mickey Stanley	1.00	.40
❑ 531	Gene Mauch MG	1.00	.40
❑ 532	Skip Lockwood	.50	.20
❑ 533	Mike Phillips RC	.50	.20
❑ 534	Eddie Watt	.50	.20
❑ 535	Bob Tolan	.50	.20
❑ 536	Duffy Dyer	.50	.20
❑ 537	Steve Mingori	.50	.20
❑ 538	Cesar Tovar	.50	.20
❑ 539	Lloyd Allen	.50	.20
❑ 540	Bob Robertson	.50	.20
❑ 541	Cleveland Indians TC	1.00	.40
❑ 542	Goose Gossage	2.00	.75
❑ 543	Danny Cater	.50	.20
❑ 544	Ron Schueler	.50	.20
❑ 545	Billy Conigliaro	1.00	.40
❑ 546	Mike Corkins	.50	.20
❑ 547	Glenn Borgmann	.50	.20
❑ 548	Sonny Siebert	.50	.20
❑ 549	Mike Jorgensen	.50	.20
❑ 550	Sam McDowell	1.00	.40
❑ 551	Von Joshua	.50	.20
❑ 552	Denny Doyle	.50	.20
❑ 553	Jim Willoughby	.50	.20
❑ 554	Tim Johnson RC	.50	.20
❑ 555	Woodie Fryman	.50	.20
❑ 556	Dave Campbell	1.00	.40
❑ 557	Jim McGlothlin	.50	.20
❑ 558	Bill Fahey	.50	.20
❑ 559	Darrel Chaney	.50	.20
❑ 560	Mike Cuellar	1.00	.40
❑ 561	Ed Kranepool	1.00	.40
❑ 562	Jack Aker	.50	.20
❑ 563	Hal McRae	1.00	.40
❑ 564	Mike Ryan	.50	.20
❑ 565	Milt Wilcox	.50	.20
❑ 566	Jackie Hernandez	.50	.20
❑ 567	Boston Red Sox TC	1.00	.40
❑ 568	Mike Torrez	1.00	.40
❑ 569	Rick Dempsey	1.00	.40
❑ 570	Ralph Garr	1.00	.40
❑ 571	Rich Hand	.50	.20
❑ 572	Enzo Hernandez	.50	.20
❑ 573	Mike Adams RC	.50	.20
❑ 574	Bill Parsons	.50	.20
❑ 575	Steve Garvey	3.00	1.25
❑ 576	Scipio Spinks	.50	.20

❑ 577 Mike Sadek RC .50 .20
❑ 578 Ralph Houk MG 1.00 .40
❑ 579 Cecil Upshaw .50 .20
❑ 580 Jim Spencer .50 .20
❑ 581 Fred Norman .50 .20
❑ 582 Bucky Dent RC 5.00 2.00
❑ 583 Marty Pattin .50 .20
❑ 584 Ken Rudolph .50 .20
❑ 585 Merv Rettenmund .50 .20
❑ 586 Jack Brohamer .50 .20
❑ 587 Larry Christenson RC .50 .20
❑ 588 Hal Lanier .50 .20
❑ 589 Boots Day .50 .20
❑ 590 Roger Moret .50 .20
❑ 591 Sonny Jackson .50 .20
❑ 592 Ed Bane RC .50 .20
❑ 593 Steve Yeager 1.00 .40
❑ 594 Leroy Stanton .50 .20
❑ 595 Steve Blass 1.00 .40
❑ 596 Gar/Hold/Lit/Pole RC .50 .20
❑ 597 Chalk/Gam/Mac/Trillo RC 1.00 .40
❑ 598 Ken Griffey RC 12.00 5.00
❑ 599A Dior/Freis/Ric/Shan Wash 2.00 .75
❑ 599B Dior/Freis/Ric/Shan Lg 15.00 6.00
❑ 599C Dior/Freis/Ric/Shan Sm 6.00 2.50
❑ 600 Cash/Cox/Madlock/Sand RC 5.00 2.00
❑ 601 Arm/Bladt/Downing/McBride RC 3.00 1.25
❑ 602 Abb/Henn/Swan/Voss RC 1.00 .40
❑ 603 Foote/Lund/Moore/Robles RC 1.00 .40
❑ 604 Hugh/Knox/Thornton/White RC 5.00 2.00
❑ 605 Alb/Frail/Kob/Tanana RC 4.00 1.50
❑ 606 Fuller/Howard/Smith/Velez RC 1.00 .40
❑ 607 Fost/Hein/Ros/Taveras RC 1.00 .40
❑ 608A Apod/Ban/D'Acq/Wall ERR 2.00 .75
❑ 608B Apod/Ban/D'Acq/Wall RC 1.00 .40
❑ 609 Rico Petrocelli 1.00 .40
❑ 610 Dave Kingman 2.00 .75
❑ 611 Rich Stelmaszek .50 .20
❑ 612 Luke Walker .50 .20
❑ 613 Dan Monzon .50 .20
❑ 614 Adrian Devine RC .50 .20
❑ 615 Johnny Jeter UER .50 .20
❑ 616 Larry Gura .50 .20
❑ 617 Ted Ford .50 .20
❑ 618 Jim Mason .50 .20
❑ 619 Mike Anderson .50 .20
❑ 620 Al Downing .50 .20
❑ 621 Bernie Carbo .50 .20
❑ 622 Phil Gagliano .50 .20
❑ 623 Celerino Sanchez .50 .20
❑ 624 Bob Miller .50 .20
❑ 625 Ollie Brown .50 .20
❑ 626 Pittsburgh Pirates TC 1.00 .40
❑ 627 Carl Taylor .50 .20
❑ 628 Ivan Murrell .50 .20
❑ 629 Rusty Staub 2.00 .75
❑ 630 Tommie Agee 1.00 .40
❑ 631 Steve Barber .50 .20
❑ 632 George Culver .50 .20
❑ 633 Dave Hamilton .50 .20
❑ 634 Eddie Mathews MG 3.00 1.25
❑ 635 Johnny Edwards .50 .20
❑ 636 Dave Goltz .50 .20
❑ 637 Checklist 529-660 3.00 1.25
❑ 638 Ken Sanders .50 .20
❑ 639 Joe Lovitto .50 .20
❑ 640 Milt Pappas 1.00 .40
❑ 641 Chuck Brinkman .50 .20
❑ 642 Terry Harmon .50 .20
❑ 643 Los Angeles Dodgers TC 1.00 .40
❑ 644 Wayne Granger .50 .20
❑ 645 Ken Boswell .50 .20
❑ 646 George Foster 2.00 .75
❑ 647 Juan Beniquez RC .50 .20
❑ 648 Terry Crowley .50 .20
❑ 649 Fernando Gonzalez RC .50 .20
❑ 650 Mike Epstein .50 .20
❑ 651 Leron Lee .50 .20
❑ 652 Gail Hopkins .50 .20
❑ 653 Bob Stinson .50 .20
❑ 654A Jesus Alou NPOF 4.00 1.50
❑ 654B Jesus Alou COR 1.00 .40
❑ 655 Mike Tyson RC .50 .20
❑ 656 Adrian Garrett .50 .20
❑ 657 Jim Shellenback .50 .20
❑ 658 Lee Lacy .50 .20
❑ 659 Joe Lis .50 .20
❑ 660 Larry Dierker 2.00 .75

1975 Topps

❑ COMPLETE SET (660) 600.00 300.00
❑ WRAPPER (15 CENT) 8.00 3.00
❑ 1 Hank Aaron HL 30.00 12.50
❑ 2 Lou Brock HL 3.00 1.25
❑ 3 Bob Gibson HL 3.00 1.25
❑ 4 Al Kaline HL 6.00 2.50
❑ 5 Nolan Ryan HL 15.00 6.00
❑ 6 Mike Marshall HL 1.00 .40
❑ 7 Ryan/Busby/Bosman HL 8.00 3.00
❑ 8 Rogelio Moret .50 .20
❑ 9 Frank Tepedino 1.00 .40
❑ 10 Willie Davis 1.00 .40
❑ 11 Bill Melton .50 .20
❑ 12 David Clyde .50 .20
❑ 13 Gene Locklear RC 1.00 .40
❑ 14 Milt Wilcox .50 .20
❑ 15 Jose Cardenal 1.00 .40
❑ 16 Frank Tanana 2.00 .75
❑ 17 Dave Concepcion 2.00 .75
❑ 18 Detroit Tigers CL/Houk 2.00 .75
❑ 19 Jerry Koosman 1.00 .40
❑ 20 Thurman Munson 8.00 3.00
❑ 21 Rollie Fingers 3.00 1.25
❑ 22 Dave Cash .50 .20
❑ 23 Bill Russell 1.00 .40
❑ 24 Al Fitzmorris .50 .20
❑ 25 Lee May 1.00 .40
❑ 26 Dave McNally 1.00 .40
❑ 27 Ken Reitz .50 .20
❑ 28 Tom Murphy .50 .20
❑ 29 Dave Parker 3.00 1.25
❑ 30 Bert Blyleven 2.00 .75
❑ 31 Dave Rader .50 .20
❑ 32 Reggie Cleveland .50 .20
❑ 33 Dusty Baker 2.00 .75
❑ 34 Steve Renko .50 .20
❑ 35 Ron Santo 1.00 .40
❑ 36 Joe Lovitto .50 .20
❑ 37 Dave Freisleben .50 .20
❑ 38 Buddy Bell 2.00 .75
❑ 39 Andre Thornton 1.00 .40
❑ 40 Bill Singer .50 .20
❑ 41 Cesar Geronimo 1.00 .40
❑ 42 Joe Coleman .50 .20
❑ 43 Cleon Jones 1.00 .40
❑ 44 Pat Dobson .50 .20
❑ 45 Joe Rudi 1.00 .40
❑ 46 Philadelphia Phillies CL/Ozark 2.00 .75
❑ 47 Tommy John 2.00 .75
❑ 48 Freddie Patek 1.00 .40
❑ 49 Larry Dierker 1.00 .40
❑ 50 Brooks Robinson 8.00 3.00
❑ 51 Bob Forsch RC 1.00 .40
❑ 52 Darrell Porter 1.00 .40
❑ 53 Dave Giusti .50 .20
❑ 54 Eric Soderholm .50 .20
❑ 55 Bobby Bonds 2.00 .75
❑ 56 Rick Wise 1.00 .40
❑ 57 Dave Johnson 1.00 .40
❑ 58 Chuck Taylor .50 .20
❑ 59 Ken Henderson .50 .20
❑ 60 Fergie Jenkins 3.00 1.25
❑ 61 Dave Winfield 15.00 6.00
❑ 62 Fritz Peterson .50 .20
❑ 63 Steve Swisher RC .50 .20
❑ 64 Dave Chalk .50 .20
❑ 65 Don Gullett 1.00 .40
❑ 66 Willie Horton 1.00 .40
❑ 67 Tug McGraw 1.00 .40
❑ 68 Ron Blomberg .50 .20
❑ 69 John Odom .50 .20
❑ 70 Mike Schmidt 20.00 8.00
❑ 71 Charlie Hough 1.00 .40
❑ 72 Kansas City Royals CL/McKeon 2.00 .75
❑ 73 J.R. Richard 1.00 .40
❑ 74 Mark Belanger 1.00 .40
❑ 75 Ted Simmons 2.00 .75
❑ 76 Ed Sprague .50 .20
❑ 77 Richie Zisk 1.00 .40
❑ 78 Ray Corbin .50 .20
❑ 79 Gary Matthews 1.00 .40
❑ 80 Carlton Fisk 8.00 3.00
❑ 81 Ron Reed .50 .20
❑ 82 Pat Kelly .50 .20
❑ 83 Jim Merritt .50 .20
❑ 84 Enzo Hernandez .50 .20
❑ 85 Bill Bonham .50 .20
❑ 86 Joe Lis .50 .20
❑ 87 George Foster 2.00 .75
❑ 88 Tom Egan .50 .20
❑ 89 Jim Ray .50 .20
❑ 90 Rusty Staub 2.00 .75
❑ 91 Dick Green .50 .20
❑ 92 Cecil Upshaw .50 .20
❑ 93 Davey Lopes 2.00 .75
❑ 94 Jim Lonborg 1.00 .40
❑ 95 John Mayberry 1.00 .40
❑ 96 Mike Cosgrove RC .50 .20
❑ 97 Earl Williams .50 .20
❑ 98 Rich Folkers .50 .20
❑ 99 Mike Hegan .50 .20
❑ 100 Willie Stargell 4.00 1.50
❑ 101 Montreal Expos CL/Mauch 2.00 .75
❑ 102 Joe Decker .50 .20
❑ 103 Rick Miller .50 .20
❑ 104 Bill Madlock 2.00 .75
❑ 105 Buzz Capra .50 .20
❑ 106 Mike Hargrove UER RC 3.00 1.25
❑ 107 Jim Barr .50 .20
❑ 108 Tom Hall .50 .20
❑ 109 George Hendrick 1.00 .40
❑ 110 Wilbur Wood .50 .20
❑ 111 Wayne Garrett .50 .20
❑ 112 Larry Hardy RC .50 .20
❑ 113 Elliott Maddox .50 .20
❑ 114 Dick Lange .50 .20
❑ 115 Joe Ferguson .50 .20
❑ 116 Lerrin LaGrow .50 .20
❑ 117 Baltimore Orioles CL/Weaver 3.00 1.25
❑ 118 Mike Anderson .50 .20
❑ 119 Tommy Helms .50 .20
❑ 120 Steve Busby UER 1.00 .40
❑ 121 Bill North .50 .20
❑ 122 Al Hrabosky 1.00 .40
❑ 123 Johnny Briggs .50 .20
❑ 124 Jerry Reuss 1.00 .40
❑ 125 Ken Singleton 1.00 .40
❑ 126 Checklist 1-132 3.00 1.25
❑ 127 Glenn Borgmann .50 .20
❑ 128 Bill Lee 1.00 .40
❑ 129 Rick Monday 1.00 .40
❑ 130 Phil Niekro 3.00 1.25
❑ 131 Toby Harrah 1.00 .40
❑ 132 Randy Moffitt .50 .20
❑ 133 Dan Driessen 1.00 .40
❑ 134 Ron Hodges .50 .20
❑ 135 Charlie Spikes .50 .20
❑ 136 Jim Mason .50 .20
❑ 137 Terry Forster 1.00 .40
❑ 138 Del Unser .50 .20
❑ 139 Horacio Pina .50 .20
❑ 140 Steve Garvey 3.00 1.25
❑ 141 Mickey Stanley 1.00 .40
❑ 142 Bob Reynolds .50 .20
❑ 143 Cliff Johnson RC 1.00 .40
❑ 144 Jim Wohlford .50 .20
❑ 145 Ken Holtzman 1.00 .40
❑ 146 San Diego Padres CL/McNamara 2.00 .75
❑ 147 Pedro Garcia .50 .20
❑ 148 Jim Rooker .50 .20

❑ 149 Tim Foli .50 .20
❑ 150 Bob Gibson 6.00 2.50
❑ 151 Steve Brye .50 .20
❑ 152 Mario Guerrero .50 .20
❑ 153 Rick Reuschel 1.00 .40
❑ 154 Mike Lum .50 .20
❑ 155 Jim Bibby .50 .20
❑ 156 Dave Kingman 2.00 .75
❑ 157 Pedro Borbon 1.00 .40
❑ 158 Jerry Grote .50 .20
❑ 159 Steve Arlin .50 .20
❑ 160 Graig Nettles 2.00 .75
❑ 161 Stan Bahnsen .50 .20
❑ 162 Willie Montanez .50 .20
❑ 163 Jim Brewer .50 .20
❑ 164 Mickey Rivers 1.00 .40
❑ 165 Doug Rader 1.00 .40
❑ 166 Woodie Fryman .50 .20
❑ 167 Rich Coggins .50 .20
❑ 168 Bill Greif .50 .20
❑ 169 Cookie Rojas .50 .20
❑ 170 Bert Campaneris 1.00 .40
❑ 171 Ed Kirkpatrick .50 .20
❑ 172 Boston Red Sox CL/Johnson 3.00 1.25
❑ 173 Steve Rogers 1.00 .40
❑ 174 Bake McBride 1.00 .40
❑ 175 Don Money 1.00 .40
❑ 176 Burt Hooton 1.00 .40
❑ 177 Vic Correll RC .50 .20
❑ 178 Cesar Tovar .50 .20
❑ 179 Tom Bradley .50 .20
❑ 180 Joe Morgan 6.00 2.50
❑ 181 Fred Beene .50 .20
❑ 182 Don Hahn .50 .20
❑ 183 Mel Stottlemyre 1.00 .40
❑ 184 Jorge Orta .50 .20
❑ 185 Steve Carlton 8.00 3.00
❑ 186 Willie Crawford .50 .20
❑ 187 Denny Doyle .50 .20
❑ 188 Tom Griffin .50 .20
❑ 189 Y.Berra/Campanella MVP 4.00 1.50
❑ 190 B.Shantz/H.Sauer MVP 2.00 .75
❑ 191 Al Rosen/Campanella MVP 2.00 .75
❑ 192 Y.Berra/W.Mays MVP 4.00 1.50
❑ 193 Y.Berra/Campanella MVP 3.00 1.25
❑ 194 M.Mantle/D.Newcombe MVP 10.004.00
❑ 195 M.Mantle/H.Aaron MVP 12.00 5.00
❑ 196 J.Jensen/E.Banks MVP 3.00 1.25
❑ 197 N.Fox/E.Banks MVP 2.00 .75
❑ 198 R.Maris/D.Groat MVP 2.00 .75
❑ 199 R.Maris/F.Robinson MVP 3.00 1.25
❑ 200 M.Mantle/M.Wills MVP 10.00 4.00
❑ 201 E.Howard/S.Koufax MVP 2.00 .75
❑ 202 B.Robinson/K.Boyer MVP 1.00 .40
❑ 203 Z.Versailes/W.Mays MVP 2.00 .75
❑ 204 F.Robinson/B.Clemente MVP 6.002.50
❑ 205 C.Yastrzemski/O.Cepeda MVP 2.00 .75
❑ 206 D.McLain/B.Gibson MVP 2.00 .75
❑ 207 H.Killebrew/W.McCovey MVP 1.00 .40
❑ 208 B.Powell/J.Bench MVP 2.00 .75
❑ 209 V.Blue/J.Torre MVP 2.00 .75
❑ 210 R.Allen/J.Bench MVP 2.00 .75
❑ 211 R.Jackson/P.Rose MVP 5.00 2.00
❑ 212 J.Burroughs/S.Garvey MVP 2.00 .75
❑ 213 Oscar Gamble 1.00 .40
❑ 214 Harry Parker .50 .20
❑ 215 Bobby Valentine 1.00 .40
❑ 216 San Francisco Giants CL/Westrum 2.00 .75
❑ 217 Lou Piniella 2.00 .75
❑ 218 Jerry Johnson .50 .20
❑ 219 Ed Herrmann .50 .20
❑ 220 Don Sutton 3.00 1.25
❑ 221 Aurelio Rodriguez .50 .20
❑ 222 Dan Spillner RC .50 .20
❑ 223 Robin Yount RC 50.00 20.00
❑ 224 Ramon Hernandez .50 .20
❑ 225 Bob Grich 1.00 .40
❑ 226 Bill Campbell .50 .20
❑ 227 Bob Watson 1.00 .40
❑ 228 George Brett RC 80.00 40.00
❑ 229 Barry Foote .50 .20
❑ 230 Jim Hunter 4.00 1.50
❑ 231 Mike Tyson .50 .20
❑ 232 Diego Segui .50 .20
❑ 233 Billy Grabarkewitz .50 .20
❑ 234 Tom Grieve 1.00 .40
❑ 235 Jack Billingham 1.00 .40
❑ 236 California Angels CL/Williams 2.00 .75
❑ 237 Carl Morton 1.00 .40
❑ 238 Dave Duncan 1.00 .40
❑ 239 George Stone .50 .20
❑ 240 Garry Maddox 1.00 .40
❑ 241 Dick Tidrow .50 .20
❑ 242 Jay Johnstone 1.00 .40
❑ 243 Jim Kaat 2.00 .75
❑ 244 Bill Buckner 1.00 .40
❑ 245 Mickey Lolich 2.00 .75
❑ 246 St. Louis Cardinals CL/Schoen 2.00 .75
❑ 247 Enos Cabell .50 .20
❑ 248 Randy Jones 2.00 .75
❑ 249 Danny Thompson .50 .20
❑ 250 Ken Brett .50 .20
❑ 251 Fran Healy .50 .20
❑ 252 Fred Scherman .50 .20
❑ 253 Jesus Alou .50 .20
❑ 254 Mike Torrez 1.00 .40
❑ 255 Dwight Evans 2.00 .75
❑ 256 Billy Champion .50 .20
❑ 257 Checklist: 133-264 3.00 1.25
❑ 258 Dave LaRoche .50 .20
❑ 259 Len Randle .50 .20
❑ 260 Johnny Bench 15.00 6.00
❑ 261 Andy Hassler RC .50 .20
❑ 262 Rowland Office RC .50 .20
❑ 263 Jim Perry 1.00 .40
❑ 264 John Milner .50 .20
❑ 265 Ron Bryant .50 .20
❑ 266 Sandy Alomar 1.00 .40
❑ 267 Dick Ruthven .50 .20
❑ 268 Hal McRae 1.00 .40
❑ 269 Doug Rau .50 .20
❑ 270 Ron Fairly 1.00 .40
❑ 271 Gerry Moses .50 .20
❑ 272 Lynn McGlothen .50 .20
❑ 273 Steve Braun .50 .20
❑ 274 Vicente Romo .50 .20
❑ 275 Paul Blair 1.00 .40
❑ 276 Chicago White Sox CL/Tanner 2.00 .75
❑ 277 Frank Taveras .50 .20
❑ 278 Paul Lindblad .50 .20
❑ 279 Milt May .50 .20
❑ 280 Carl Yastrzemski 12.00 5.00
❑ 281 Jim Slaton .50 .20
❑ 282 Jerry Morales .50 .20
❑ 283 Steve Foucault .50 .20
❑ 284 Ken Griffey Sr. 4.00 1.50
❑ 285 Ellie Rodriguez .50 .20
❑ 286 Mike Jorgensen .50 .20
❑ 287 Roric Harrison .50 .20
❑ 288 Bruce Ellingsen RC .50 .20
❑ 289 Ken Rudolph .50 .20
❑ 290 Jon Matlack .50 .20
❑ 291 Bill Sudakis .50 .20
❑ 292 Ron Schueler .50 .20
❑ 293 Dick Sharon .50 .20
❑ 294 Geoff Zahn RC .50 .20
❑ 295 Vada Pinson 2.00 .75
❑ 296 Alan Foster .50 .20
❑ 297 Craig Kusick RC .50 .20
❑ 298 Johnny Grubb .50 .20
❑ 299 Bucky Dent 2.00 .75
❑ 300 Reggie Jackson 15.00 6.00
❑ 301 Dave Roberts .50 .20
❑ 302 Rick Burleson RC 1.00 .40
❑ 303 Grant Jackson .50 .20
❑ 304 Pittsburgh Pirates CL/Murtaugh 2.00 .75
❑ 305 Jim Colborn .50 .20
❑ 306 R.Carew/R.Garr LL 2.00 .75
❑ 307 D.Allen/M.Schmidt LL 4.00 1.50
❑ 308 J.Burroughs/J.Bench LL 2.00 .75
❑ 309 B.North/L.Brock LL 2.00 .75
❑ 310 Hunter/Jenk/Mess/Niek LL 2.00 .75
❑ 311 J.Hunter/B.Capra LL 2.00 .75
❑ 312 N.Ryan/S.Carlton LL 12.00 5.00
❑ 313 T.Forster/M.Marshall LL 1.00 .40
❑ 314 Buck Martinez .50 .20
❑ 315 Don Kessinger 1.00 .40
❑ 316 Jackie Brown .50 .20
❑ 317 Joe Lahoud .50 .20
❑ 318 Ernie McAnally .50 .20
❑ 319 Johnny Oates 1.00 .40
❑ 320 Pete Rose 30.00 12.50
❑ 321 Rudy May .50 .20
❑ 322 Ed Goodson .50 .20
❑ 323 Fred Holdsworth .50 .20
❑ 324 Ed Kranepool 1.00 .40
❑ 325 Tony Oliva 2.00 .75
❑ 326 Wayne Twitchell .50 .20
❑ 327 Jerry Hairston .50 .20
❑ 328 Sonny Siebert .50 .20
❑ 329 Ted Kubiak .50 .20
❑ 330 Mike Marshall 1.00 .40
❑ 331 Cleveland Indians CL/Robinson 2.00 .75
❑ 332 Fred Kendall .50 .20
❑ 333 Dick Drago .50 .20
❑ 334 Greg Gross RC .50 .20
❑ 335 Jim Palmer 6.00 2.50
❑ 336 Rennie Stennett .50 .20
❑ 337 Kevin Kobel .50 .20
❑ 338 Rich Stelmaszek .50 .20
❑ 339 Jim Fregosi 1.00 .40
❑ 340 Paul Splittorff .50 .20
❑ 341 Hal Breeden .50 .20
❑ 342 Leroy Stanton .50 .20
❑ 343 Danny Frisella .50 .20
❑ 344 Ben Oglivie 1.00 .40
❑ 345 Clay Carroll 1.00 .40
❑ 346 Bobby Darwin .50 .20
❑ 347 Mike Caldwell .50 .20
❑ 348 Tony Muser .50 .20
❑ 349 Ray Sadecki .50 .20
❑ 350 Bobby Murcer 1.00 .40
❑ 351 Bob Boone 2.00 .75
❑ 352 Darold Knowles .50 .20
❑ 353 Luis Melendez .50 .20
❑ 354 Dick Bosman .50 .20
❑ 355 Chris Cannizzaro .50 .20
❑ 356 Rico Petrocelli 1.00 .40
❑ 357 Ken Forsch UER .50 .20
❑ 358 Al Bumbry 1.00 .40
❑ 359 Paul Popovich .50 .20
❑ 360 George Scott 1.00 .40
❑ 361 Los Angeles Dodgers CL/Alston 2.00 .75
❑ 362 Steve Hargan .50 .20
❑ 363 Carmen Fanzone .50 .20
❑ 364 Doug Bird .50 .20
❑ 365 Bob Bailey .50 .20
❑ 366 Ken Sanders .50 .20
❑ 367 Craig Robinson .50 .20
❑ 368 Vic Albury .50 .20
❑ 369 Merv Rettenmund .50 .20
❑ 370 Tom Seaver 12.00 5.00
❑ 371 Gates Brown .50 .20
❑ 372 John D'Acquisto .50 .20
❑ 373 Bill Sharp .50 .20
❑ 374 Eddie Watt .50 .20
❑ 375 Roy White 1.00 .40
❑ 376 Steve Yeager 1.00 .40
❑ 377 Tom Hilgendorf .50 .20
❑ 378 Derrel Thomas .50 .20
❑ 379 Bernie Carbo .50 .20
❑ 380 Sal Bando 1.00 .40
❑ 381 John Curtis .50 .20
❑ 382 Don Baylor 2.00 .75
❑ 383 Jim York .50 .20
❑ 384 Milwaukee Brewers CL/Crandall 2.00 .75
❑ 385 Dock Ellis .50 .20
❑ 386 Checklist: 265-396 UER 3.00 1.25
❑ 387 Jim Spencer .50 .20
❑ 388 Steve Stone 1.00 .40
❑ 389 Tony Solaita RC .50 .20
❑ 390 Ron Cey 2.00 .75
❑ 391 Don DeMola RC .50 .20
❑ 392 Bruce Bochte RC 1.00 .40
❑ 393 Gary Gentry .50 .20
❑ 394 Larvell Blanks .50 .20
❑ 395 Bud Harrelson 1.00 .40
❑ 396 Fred Norman 1.00 .40
❑ 397 Bill Freehan 1.00 .40
❑ 398 Elias Sosa .50 .20
❑ 399 Terry Harmon .50 .20
❑ 400 Dick Allen 2.00 .75
❑ 401 Mike Wallace .50 .20
❑ 402 Bob Tolan .50 .20
❑ 403 Tom Buskey RC .50 .20
❑ 404 Ted Sizemore .50 .20
❑ 405 John Montague RC .50 .20
❑ 406 Bob Gallagher .50 .20

❑ 407 Herb Washington RC 2.00 .75
❑ 408 Clyde Wright UER .50 .20
❑ 409 Bob Robertson .50 .20
❑ 410 Mike Cuellar UER 1.00 .40
❑ 411 George Mitterwald .50 .20
❑ 412 Bill Hands .50 .20
❑ 413 Marty Pattin .50 .20
❑ 414 Manny Mota 1.00 .40
❑ 415 John Hiller 1.00 .40
❑ 416 Larry Lintz .50 .20
❑ 417 Skip Lockwood .50 .20
❑ 418 Leo Foster .50 .20
❑ 419 Dave Goltz .50 .20
❑ 420 Larry Bowa 2.00 .75
❑ 421 New York Mets CL/Berra 3.00 1.25
❑ 422 Brian Downing 1.00 .40
❑ 423 Clay Kirby .50 .20
❑ 424 John Lowenstein .50 .20
❑ 425 Tito Fuentes .50 .20
❑ 426 George Medich .50 .20
❑ 427 Clarence Gaston 1.00 .40
❑ 428 Dave Hamilton .50 .20
❑ 429 Jim Dwyer RC .50 .20
❑ 430 Luis Tiant 2.00 .75
❑ 431 Rod Gilbreath .50 .20
❑ 432 Ken Berry .50 .20
❑ 433 Larry Demery RC .50 .20
❑ 434 Bob Locker .50 .20
❑ 435 Dave Nelson .50 .20
❑ 436 Ken Frailing .50 .20
❑ 437 Al Cowens RC 1.00 .40
❑ 438 Don Carrithers .50 .20
❑ 439 Ed Brinkman .50 .20
❑ 440 Andy Messersmith 1.00 .40
❑ 441 Bobby Heise .50 .20
❑ 442 Maximino Leon RC .50 .20
❑ 443 Minnesota Twins CL/Quilici 2.00 .75
❑ 444 Gene Garber 1.00 .40
❑ 445 Felix Millan .50 .20
❑ 446 Bart Johnson .50 .20
❑ 447 Terry Crowley .50 .20
❑ 448 Frank Duffy .50 .20
❑ 449 Charlie Williams .50 .20
❑ 450 Willie McCovey 6.00 2.50
❑ 451 Rick Dempsey 1.00 .40
❑ 452 Angel Mangual .50 .20
❑ 453 Claude Osteen 1.00 .40
❑ 454 Doug Griffin .50 .20
❑ 455 Don Wilson .50 .20
❑ 456 Bob Coluccio .50 .20
❑ 457 Mario Mendoza RC .50 .20
❑ 458 Ross Grimsley .50 .20
❑ 459 1974 AL Championships 1.00 .40
❑ 460 1974 NL Championships 2.00 .75
❑ 461 Reggie Jackson WS1 5.00 2.00
❑ 462 W.Alston/J.Ferguson WS2 1.00 .40
❑ 463 Rollie Fingers WS3 2.00 .75
❑ 464 A's Batter WS4 1.00 .40
❑ 465 Joe Rudi WS5 1.00 .40
❑ 466 A's Do it Again WS 2.00 .75
❑ 467 Ed Halicki RC .50 .20
❑ 468 Bobby Mitchell .50 .20
❑ 469 Tom Dettore RC .50 .20
❑ 470 Jeff Burroughs 1.00 .40
❑ 471 Bob Stinson .50 .20
❑ 472 Bruce Dal Canton .50 .20
❑ 473 Ken McMullen .50 .20
❑ 474 Luke Walker .50 .20
❑ 475 Darrell Evans 1.00 .40
❑ 476 Ed Figueroa RC .50 .20
❑ 477 Tom Hutton .50 .20
❑ 478 Tom Burgmeier .50 .20
❑ 479 Ken Boswell .50 .20
❑ 480 Carlos May .50 .20
❑ 481 Will McEnaney RC 1.00 .40
❑ 482 Tom McCraw .50 .20
❑ 483 Steve Ontiveros .50 .20
❑ 484 Glenn Beckert 1.00 .40
❑ 485 Sparky Lyle 1.00 .40
❑ 486 Ray Fosse .50 .20
❑ 487 Houston Astros CL/Gomez 2.00 .75
❑ 488 Bill Travers RC .50 .20
❑ 489 Cecil Cooper 2.00 .75
❑ 490 Reggie Smith 1.00 .40
❑ 491 Doyle Alexander 1.00 .40
❑ 492 Rich Hebner 1.00 .40
❑ 493 Don Stanhouse .50 .20
❑ 494 Pete LaCock RC .50 .20
❑ 495 Nelson Briles 1.00 .40
❑ 496 Pepe Frias .50 .20
❑ 497 Jim Nettles .50 .20
❑ 498 Al Downing .50 .20
❑ 499 Marty Perez .50 .20
❑ 500 Nolan Ryan 50.00 20.00
❑ 501 Bill Robinson 1.00 .40
❑ 502 Pat Bourque .50 .20
❑ 503 Fred Stanley .50 .20
❑ 504 Buddy Bradford .50 .20
❑ 505 Chris Speier .50 .20
❑ 506 Leron Lee .50 .20
❑ 507 Tom Carroll RC .50 .20
❑ 508 Bob Hansen RC .50 .20
❑ 509 Dave Hilton .50 .20
❑ 510 Vida Blue 1.00 .40
❑ 511 Texas Rangers CL/Martin 2.00 .75
❑ 512 Larry Milbourne RC .50 .20
❑ 513 Dick Pole .50 .20
❑ 514 Jose Cruz 2.00 .75
❑ 515 Manny Sanguillen 1.00 .40
❑ 516 Don Hood .50 .20
❑ 517 Checklist: 397-528 3.00 1.25
❑ 518 Leo Cardenas .50 .20
❑ 519 Jim Todd RC .50 .20
❑ 520 Amos Otis 1.00 .40
❑ 521 Dennis Blair RC .50 .20
❑ 522 Gary Sutherland .50 .20
❑ 523 Tom Paciorek 1.00 .40
❑ 524 John Doherty RC .50 .20
❑ 525 Tom House .50 .20
❑ 526 Larry Hisle 1.00 .40
❑ 527 Mac Scarce .50 .20
❑ 528 Eddie Leon .50 .20
❑ 529 Gary Thomasson .50 .20
❑ 530 Gaylord Perry 3.00 1.25
❑ 531 Cincinnati Reds CL/Anderson 5.00 2.00
❑ 532 Gorman Thomas 1.00 .40
❑ 533 Rudy Meoli .50 .20
❑ 534 Alex Johnson .50 .20
❑ 535 Gene Tenace 1.00 .40
❑ 536 Bob Moose .50 .20
❑ 537 Tommy Harper 1.00 .40
❑ 538 Duffy Dyer .50 .20
❑ 539 Jesse Jefferson .50 .20
❑ 540 Lou Brock 6.00 2.50
❑ 541 Roger Metzger .50 .20
❑ 542 Pete Broberg .50 .20
❑ 543 Larry Biittner .50 .20
❑ 544 Steve Mingori .50 .20
❑ 545 Billy Williams 3.00 1.25
❑ 546 John Knox .50 .20
❑ 547 Von Joshua .50 .20
❑ 548 Charlie Sands .50 .20
❑ 549 Bill Butler .50 .20
❑ 550 Ralph Garr 1.00 .40
❑ 551 Larry Christenson .50 .20
❑ 552 Jack Brohamer .50 .20
❑ 553 John Boccabella .50 .20
❑ 554 Goose Gossage 2.00 .75
❑ 555 Al Oliver 1.00 .40
❑ 556 Tim Johnson .50 .20
❑ 557 Larry Gura .50 .20
❑ 558 Dave Roberts .50 .20
❑ 559 Bob Montgomery .50 .20
❑ 560 Tony Perez 4.00 1.50
❑ 561 Oakland Athletics CL/Dark 2.00 .75
❑ 562 Gary Nolan 1.00 .40
❑ 563 Wilbur Howard .50 .20
❑ 564 Tommy Davis 1.00 .40
❑ 565 Joe Torre 2.00 .75
❑ 566 Ray Burris .50 .20
❑ 567 Jim Sundberg RC 2.00 .75
❑ 568 Dale Murray RC .50 .20
❑ 569 Frank White 1.00 .40
❑ 570 Jim Wynn 1.00 .40
❑ 571 Dave Lemanczyk RC .50 .20
❑ 572 Roger Nelson .50 .20
❑ 573 Orlando Pena .50 .20
❑ 574 Tony Taylor .50 .20
❑ 575 Gene Clines .50 .20
❑ 576 Phil Roof .50 .20
❑ 577 John Morris .50 .20
❑ 578 Dave Tomlin RC .50 .20
❑ 579 Skip Pitlock .50 .20
❑ 580 Frank Robinson 6.00 2.50
❑ 581 Darrel Chaney .50 .20
❑ 582 Eduardo Rodriguez .50 .20
❑ 583 Andy Etchebarren .50 .20
❑ 584 Mike Garman .50 .20
❑ 585 Chris Chambliss 1.00 .40
❑ 586 Tim McCarver 2.00 .75
❑ 587 Chris Ward RC .50 .20
❑ 588 Rick Auerbach .50 .20
❑ 589 Atlanta Braves CL/King 2.00 .75
❑ 590 Cesar Cedeno 1.00 .40
❑ 591 Glenn Abbott .50 .20
❑ 592 Balor Moore .50 .20
❑ 593 Gene Lamont .50 .20
❑ 594 Jim Fuller .50 .20
❑ 595 Joe Niekro 1.00 .40
❑ 596 Ollie Brown .50 .20
❑ 597 Winston Llenas .50 .20
❑ 598 Bruce Kison .50 .20
❑ 599 Nate Colbert .50 .20
❑ 600 Rod Carew 8.00 3.00
❑ 601 Juan Beniquez .50 .20
❑ 602 John Vukovich .50 .20
❑ 603 Lew Krausse .50 .20
❑ 604 Oscar Zamora RC .50 .20
❑ 605 John Ellis .50 .20
❑ 606 Bruce Miller RC .50 .20
❑ 607 Jim Holt .50 .20
❑ 608 Gene Michael .50 .20
❑ 609 Elrod Hendricks .50 .20
❑ 610 Ron Hunt .50 .20
❑ 611 New York Yankees CL/Virdon 2.00 .75
❑ 612 Terry Hughes .50 .20
❑ 613 Bill Parsons .50 .20
❑ 614 Kuc/Mill/Ruhle/Sieb RC 1.00 .40
❑ 615 Darcy/Leonard/Und/Webb RC 2.00 .75
❑ 616 Jim Rice RC 15.00 6.00
❑ 617 Cubb/DeCinces/Sand/Trillo RC 2.00 .75
❑ 618 East/John/McGregor/Rhoden RC 1.00 .40
❑ 619 Ayala/Nyman/Smith Turner RC 1.00 .40
❑ 620 Gary Carter RC 15.00 6.00
❑ 621 Denny/Eastwick/Kern/Vein RC 2.00 .75
❑ 622 Fred Lynn RC 8.00 3.00
❑ 623 K.Hern RC/P.Garner RC 10.00 4.00
❑ 624 Kon/Lavelle/Otten/Sol RC 1.00 .40
❑ 625 Boog Powell 2.00 .75
❑ 626 Larry Haney UER .50 .20
❑ 627 Tom Walker .50 .20
❑ 628 Ron LeFlore RC 1.00 .40
❑ 629 Joe Hoerner .50 .20
❑ 630 Greg Luzinski 2.00 .75
❑ 631 Lee Lacy .50 .20
❑ 632 Morris Nettles RC .50 .20
❑ 633 Paul Casanova .50 .20
❑ 634 Cy Acosta .50 .20
❑ 635 Chuck Dobson .50 .20
❑ 636 Charlie Moore .50 .20
❑ 637 Ted Martinez .50 .20
❑ 638 Chicago Cubs CL/Marshall 2.00 .75
❑ 639 Steve Kline .50 .20
❑ 640 Harmon Killebrew 6.00 2.50
❑ 641 Jim Northrup 1.00 .40
❑ 642 Mike Phillips .50 .20
❑ 643 Brent Strom .50 .20
❑ 644 Bill Fahey .50 .20
❑ 645 Danny Cater .50 .20
❑ 646 Checklist: 529-660 3.00 1.25
❑ 647 Claudell Washington RC 2.00 .75
❑ 648 Dave Pagan RC .50 .20
❑ 649 Jack Heidemann .50 .20
❑ 650 Dave May .50 .20
❑ 651 John Morlan RC .50 .20
❑ 652 Lindy McDaniel 1.00 .40
❑ 653 Lee Richard UER .50 .20
❑ 654 Jerry Terrell .50 .20
❑ 655 Rico Carty 1.00 .40
❑ 656 Bill Plummer .50 .20
❑ 657 Bob Oliver .50 .20
❑ 658 Vic Harris .50 .20
❑ 659 Bob Apodaca .50 .20
❑ 660 Hank Aaron 30.00 12.50

1976 Topps

❑ COMPLETE SET (660)	250.00	125.00
❑ 1 Hank Aaron RB	15.00	6.00
❑ 2 Bobby Bonds RB	1.50	.60
❑ 3 Mickey Lolich RB	.75	.30
❑ 4 Dave Lopes RB	.75	.30
❑ 5 Tom Seaver RB	5.00	2.00
❑ 6 Rennie Stennett RB	.75	.30
❑ 7 Jim Umbarger RC	.40	.15
❑ 8 Tito Fuentes	.40	.15
❑ 9 Paul Lindblad	.40	.15
❑ 10 Lou Brock	5.00	2.00
❑ 11 Jim Hughes	.40	.15
❑ 12 Richie Zisk	.75	.30
❑ 13 John Wockenfuss RC	.40	.15
❑ 14 Gene Garber	.75	.30
❑ 15 George Scott	.75	.30
❑ 16 Bob Apodaca	.40	.15
❑ 17 New York Yankees CL/Martin	1.50	.60
❑ 18 Dale Murray	.40	.15
❑ 19 George Brett	30.00	12.50
❑ 20 Bob Watson	.75	.30
❑ 21 Dave LaRoche	.40	.15
❑ 22 Bill Russell	.75	.30
❑ 23 Brian Downing	.40	.15
❑ 24 Cesar Geronimo	.75	.30
❑ 25 Mike Torrez	.75	.30
❑ 26 Andre Thornton	.75	.30
❑ 27 Ed Figueroa	.40	.15
❑ 28 Dusty Baker	1.50	.60
❑ 29 Rick Burleson	.75	.30
❑ 30 John Montefusco RC	.75	.30
❑ 31 Len Randle	.40	.15
❑ 32 Danny Frisella	.40	.15
❑ 33 Bill North	.40	.15
❑ 34 Mike Garman	.40	.15
❑ 35 Tony Oliva	1.50	.60
❑ 36 Frank Taveras	.40	.15
❑ 37 John Hiller	.75	.30
❑ 38 Garry Maddox	.75	.30
❑ 39 Pete Broberg	.40	.15
❑ 40 Dave Kingman	1.50	.60
❑ 41 Tippy Martinez RC	.75	.30
❑ 42 Barry Foote	.40	.15
❑ 43 Paul Splittorff	.40	.15
❑ 44 Doug Rader	.75	.30
❑ 45 Boog Powell	1.50	.60
❑ 46 Los Angeles Dodgers CL/Alston	1.50	.60
❑ 47 Jesse Jefferson	.40	.15
❑ 48 Dave Concepcion	1.50	.60
❑ 49 Dave Duncan	.75	.30
❑ 50 Fred Lynn	1.50	.60
❑ 51 Ray Burris	.40	.15
❑ 52 Dave Chalk	.40	.15
❑ 53 Mike Beard RC	.40	.15
❑ 54 Dave Rader	.40	.15
❑ 55 Gaylord Perry	2.50	1.00
❑ 56 Bob Tolan	.40	.15
❑ 57 Phil Garner	.75	.30
❑ 58 Ron Reed	.40	.15
❑ 59 Larry Hisle	.75	.30
❑ 60 Jerry Reuss	.75	.30
❑ 61 Ron LeFlore	.75	.30
❑ 62 Johnny Oates	.75	.30
❑ 63 Bobby Darwin	.40	.15
❑ 64 Jerry Koosman	.75	.30
❑ 65 Chris Chambliss	.75	.30
❑ 66 Gus/Buddy Bell FS	.75	.30
❑ 67 Bob/Ray Boone FS	.75	.30
❑ 68 Joe/Joe Jr. Coleman FS	.40	.15
❑ 69 Jim/Mike Hegan FS	.40	.15
❑ 70 Roy/Roy Jr. Smalley FS	.75	.30
❑ 71 Steve Rogers	.75	.30
❑ 72 Hal McRae	.75	.30
❑ 73 Baltimore Orioles CL/Weaver	1.50	.60
❑ 74 Oscar Gamble	.75	.30
❑ 75 Larry Dierker	.75	.30
❑ 76 Willie Crawford	.40	.15
❑ 77 Pedro Borbon	.75	.30
❑ 78 Cecil Cooper	.75	.30
❑ 79 Jerry Morales	.40	.15
❑ 80 Jim Kaat	1.50	.60
❑ 81 Darrell Evans	.75	.30
❑ 82 Von Joshua	.40	.15
❑ 83 Jim Spencer	.40	.15
❑ 84 Brent Strom	.40	.15
❑ 85 Mickey Rivers	.75	.30
❑ 86 Mike Tyson	.40	.15
❑ 87 Tom Burgmeier	.40	.15
❑ 88 Duffy Dyer	.40	.15
❑ 89 Vern Ruhle	.40	.15
❑ 90 Sal Bando	.75	.30
❑ 91 Tom Hutton	.40	.15
❑ 92 Eduardo Rodriguez	.40	.15
❑ 93 Mike Phillips	.40	.15
❑ 94 Jim Dwyer	.40	.15
❑ 95 Brooks Robinson	6.00	2.50
❑ 96 Doug Bird	.40	.15
❑ 97 Wilbur Howard	.40	.15
❑ 98 Dennis Eckersley RC	30.00	12.50
❑ 99 Lee Lacy	.40	.15
❑ 100 Jim Hunter	3.00	1.25
❑ 101 Pete LaCock	.40	.15
❑ 102 Jim Willoughby	.40	.15
❑ 103 Biff Pocoroba RC	.40	.15
❑ 104 Cincinnati Reds CL/Anderson	2.50	1.00
❑ 105 Gary Lavelle	.40	.15
❑ 106 Tom Grieve	.75	.30
❑ 107 Dave Roberts	.40	.15
❑ 108 Don Kirkwood RC	.40	.15
❑ 109 Larry Lintz	.40	.15
❑ 110 Carlos May	.40	.15
❑ 111 Danny Thompson	.40	.15
❑ 112 Kent Tekulve RC	1.50	.60
❑ 113 Gary Sutherland	.40	.15
❑ 114 Jay Johnstone	.75	.30
❑ 115 Ken Holtzman	.75	.30
❑ 116 Charlie Moore	.40	.15
❑ 117 Mike Jorgensen	.40	.15
❑ 118 Boston Red Sox CL/Johnson	1.50	.60
❑ 119 Checklist 1-132	1.50	.60
❑ 120 Rusty Staub	.75	.30
❑ 121 Tony Solaita	.40	.15
❑ 122 Mike Cosgrove	.40	.15
❑ 123 Walt Williams	.40	.15
❑ 124 Doug Rau	.40	.15
❑ 125 Don Baylor	1.50	.60
❑ 126 Tom Dettore	.40	.15
❑ 127 Larvell Blanks	.40	.15
❑ 128 Ken Griffey Sr.	2.50	1.00
❑ 129 Andy Etchebarren	.40	.15
❑ 130 Luis Tiant	1.50	.60
❑ 131 Bill Stein RC	.40	.15
❑ 132 Don Hood	.40	.15
❑ 133 Gary Matthews	.75	.30
❑ 134 Mike Ivie	.40	.15
❑ 135 Bake McBride	.75	.30
❑ 136 Dave Goltz	.40	.15
❑ 137 Bill Robinson	.75	.30
❑ 138 Lerrin LaGrow	.40	.15
❑ 139 Gorman Thomas	.75	.30
❑ 140 Vida Blue	.75	.30
❑ 141 Larry Parrish RC	1.50	.60
❑ 142 Dick Drago	.40	.15
❑ 143 Jerry Grote	.40	.15
❑ 144 Al Fitzmorris	.40	.15
❑ 145 Larry Bowa	.75	.30
❑ 146 George Medich	.40	.15
❑ 147 Houston Astros CL/Virdon	1.50	.60
❑ 148 Stan Thomas RC	.40	.15
❑ 149 Tommy Davis	.75	.30
❑ 150 Steve Garvey	2.50	1.00
❑ 151 Bill Bonham	.40	.15
❑ 152 Leroy Stanton	.40	.15
❑ 153 Buzz Capra	.40	.15
❑ 154 Bucky Dent	.75	.30
❑ 155 Jack Billingham	.75	.30
❑ 156 Rico Carty	.75	.30
❑ 157 Mike Caldwell	.40	.15
❑ 158 Ken Reitz	.40	.15
❑ 159 Jerry Terrell	.40	.15
❑ 160 Dave Winfield	10.00	4.00
❑ 161 Bruce Kison	.40	.15
❑ 162 Jack Pierce RC	.40	.15
❑ 163 Jim Slaton	.40	.15
❑ 164 Pepe Mangual	.40	.15
❑ 165 Gene Tenace	.75	.30
❑ 166 Skip Lockwood	.40	.15
❑ 167 Freddie Patek	.75	.30
❑ 168 Tom Hilgendorf	.40	.15
❑ 169 Graig Nettles	1.50	.60
❑ 170 Rick Wise	.40	.15
❑ 171 Greg Gross	.40	.15
❑ 172 Texas Rangers CL/Lucchesi	1.50	.60
❑ 173 Steve Swisher	.40	.15
❑ 174 Charlie Hough	.75	.30
❑ 175 Ken Singleton	.75	.30
❑ 176 Dick Lange	.40	.15
❑ 177 Marty Perez	.40	.15
❑ 178 Tom Buskey	.40	.15
❑ 179 George Foster	1.50	.60
❑ 180 Goose Gossage	1.50	.60
❑ 181 Willie Montanez	.40	.15
❑ 182 Harry Rasmussen	.40	.15
❑ 183 Steve Braun	.40	.15
❑ 184 Bill Greif	.40	.15
❑ 185 Dave Parker	1.50	.60
❑ 186 Tom Walker	.40	.15
❑ 187 Pedro Garcia	.40	.15
❑ 188 Fred Scherman	.40	.15
❑ 189 Claudell Washington	.75	.30
❑ 190 Jon Matlack	.40	.15
❑ 191 Madlock/Simm/Mang LL	.75	.30
❑ 192 Carew/Lynn/Munson LL	2.50	1.00
❑ 193 Schmidt/King/Luz LL	3.00	1.25
❑ 194 Reggie/Scott/Mayb LL	3.00	1.25
❑ 195 Luz/Bench/Perez LL	1.50	.60
❑ 196 Scott/Mayb/Lynn LL	.75	.30
❑ 197 Lopes/Morgan/Brock LL	1.50	.60
❑ 198 Rivers/Wash/Otis LL	.75	.30
❑ 199 Seaver/Jones/Mess LL	2.50	1.00
❑ 200 Hunter/Palmer/Blue LL	1.50	.60
❑ 201 Jones/Mess/Seaver LL	1.50	.60
❑ 202 Palmer/Hunter/Eck LL	3.00	1.25
❑ 203 Seaver/Mont/Mess LL	2.50	1.00
❑ 204 Tanana/Blyleven/Perry LL	.75	.30
❑ 205 A.Hrabosky/G.Gossage LL	.75	.30
❑ 206 Manny Trillo	.40	.15
❑ 207 Andy Hassler	.40	.15
❑ 208 Mike Lum	.40	.15
❑ 209 Alan Ashby RC	.40	.15
❑ 210 Lee May	.75	.30
❑ 211 Clay Carroll	.75	.30
❑ 212 Pat Kelly	.40	.15
❑ 213 Dave Heaverlo RC	.40	.15
❑ 214 Eric Soderholm	.40	.15
❑ 215 Reggie Smith	.75	.30
❑ 216 Montreal Expos CL/Kuehl	1.50	.60
❑ 217 Dave Freisleben	.40	.15
❑ 218 John Knox	.40	.15
❑ 219 Tom Murphy	.40	.15
❑ 220 Manny Sanguillen	.75	.30
❑ 221 Jim Todd	.40	.15
❑ 222 Wayne Garrett	.40	.15
❑ 223 Ollie Brown	.40	.15
❑ 224 Jim York	.40	.15
❑ 225 Roy White	.75	.30
❑ 226 Jim Sundberg	.75	.30
❑ 227 Oscar Zamora	.40	.15
❑ 228 John Hale RC	.40	.15
❑ 229 Jerry Remy RC	.40	.15
❑ 230 Carl Yastrzemski	10.00	4.00
❑ 231 Tom House	.40	.15
❑ 232 Frank Duffy	.40	.15
❑ 233 Grant Jackson	.40	.15
❑ 234 Mike Sadek	.40	.15
❑ 235 Bert Blyleven	1.50	.60
❑ 236 Kansas City Royals CL/Herzog	1.50	.60
❑ 237 Dave Hamilton	.40	.15

❑ 238 Larry Biittner .40 .15
❑ 239 John Curtis .40 .15
❑ 240 Pete Rose 25.00 10.00
❑ 241 Hector Torres .40 .15
❑ 242 Dan Meyer .40 .15
❑ 243 Jim Rooker .40 .15
❑ 244 Bill Sharp .40 .15
❑ 245 Felix Millan .40 .15
❑ 246 Cesar Tovar .40 .15
❑ 247 Terry Harmon .40 .15
❑ 248 Dick Tidrow .40 .15
❑ 249 Cliff Johnson .75 .30
❑ 250 Fergie Jenkins 2.50 1.00
❑ 251 Rick Monday .75 .30
❑ 252 Tim Nordbrook RC .40 .15
❑ 253 Bill Buckner .75 .30
❑ 254 Rudy Meoli .40 .15
❑ 255 Fritz Peterson .40 .15
❑ 256 Rowland Office .40 .15
❑ 257 Ross Grimsley .40 .15
❑ 258 Nyls Nyman .40 .15
❑ 259 Darrel Chaney .40 .15
❑ 260 Steve Busby .40 .15
❑ 261 Gary Thomasson .40 .15
❑ 262 Checklist 133-264 1.50 .60
❑ 263 Lyman Bostock RC 1.50 .60
❑ 264 Steve Henko .40 .15
❑ 265 Willie Davis .75 .30
❑ 266 Alan Foster .40 .15
❑ 267 Aurelio Rodriguez .40 .15
❑ 268 Del Unser .40 .15
❑ 269 Rick Austin .40 .15
❑ 270 Willie Stargell 3.00 1.25
❑ 271 Jim Lonborg .75 .30
❑ 272 Rick Dempsey .75 .30
❑ 273 Joe Niekro .75 .30
❑ 274 Tommy Harper .75 .30
❑ 275 Rick Manning RC .40 .15
❑ 276 Mickey Scott .40 .15
❑ 277 Chicago Cubs CL/Marshall 1.50 .60
❑ 278 Bernie Carbo .40 .15
❑ 279 Roy Howell RC .40 .15
❑ 280 Burt Hooton .75 .30
❑ 281 Dave May .40 .15
❑ 282 Dan Osborn RC .40 .15
❑ 283 Merv Rettenmund .40 .15
❑ 284 Steve Ontiveros .40 .15
❑ 285 Mike Cuellar .75 .30
❑ 286 Jim Wohlford .40 .15
❑ 287 Pete Mackanin .40 .15
❑ 288 Bill Campbell .40 .15
❑ 289 Enzo Hernandez .40 .15
❑ 290 Ted Simmons .75 .30
❑ 291 Ken Sanders .40 .15
❑ 292 Leon Roberts .40 .15
❑ 293 Bill Castro RC .40 .15
❑ 294 Ed Kirkpatrick .40 .15
❑ 295 Dave Cash .40 .15
❑ 296 Pat Dobson .40 .15
❑ 297 Roger Metzger .40 .15
❑ 298 Dick Bosman .40 .15
❑ 299 Champ Summers RC .40 .15
❑ 300 Johnny Bench 12.00 5.00
❑ 301 Jackie Brown .40 .15
❑ 302 Rick Miller .40 .15
❑ 303 Steve Foucault .40 .15
❑ 304 California Angels CL/Williams 1.50 .60
❑ 305 Andy Messersmith .75 .30
❑ 306 Rod Gilbreath .40 .15
❑ 307 Al Bumbry .75 .30
❑ 308 Jim Barr .40 .15
❑ 309 Bill Melton .40 .15
❑ 310 Randy Jones .75 .30
❑ 311 Cookie Rojas .40 .15
❑ 312 Don Carrithers .40 .15
❑ 313 Dan Ford RC .40 .15
❑ 314 Ed Kranepool .40 .15
❑ 315 Al Hrabosky .75 .30
❑ 316 Robin Yount 15.00 6.00
❑ 317 John Candelaria RC 1.50 .60
❑ 318 Bob Boone 1.50 .60
❑ 319 Larry Gura .40 .15
❑ 320 Willie Horton .75 .30
❑ 321 Jose Cruz 1.50 .60
❑ 322 Glenn Abbott .40 .15
❑ 323 Rob Sperring RC .40 .15
❑ 324 Jim Bibby .40 .15
❑ 325 Tony Perez 3.00 1.25
❑ 326 Dick Pole .40 .15
❑ 327 Dave Moates RC .40 .15
❑ 328 Carl Morton .40 .15
❑ 329 Joe Ferguson .40 .15
❑ 330 Nolan Ryan 25.00 10.00
❑ 331 San Diego Padres CL/McNamara 1.50 .60
❑ 332 Charlie Williams .40 .15
❑ 333 Bob Coluccio .40 .15
❑ 334 Dennis Leonard .75 .30
❑ 335 Bob Grich .75 .30
❑ 336 Vic Albury .40 .15
❑ 337 Bud Harrelson .75 .30
❑ 338 Bob Bailey .40 .15
❑ 339 John Denny .75 .30
❑ 340 Jim Rice 4.00 1.50
❑ 341 Lou Gehrig ATG 12.00 5.00
❑ 342 Rogers Hornsby ATG 3.00 1.25
❑ 343 Pie Traynor ATG 1.50 .60
❑ 344 Honus Wagner ATG 5.00 2.00
❑ 345 Babe Ruth ATG 15.00 6.00
❑ 346 Ty Cobb ATG 12.00 5.00
❑ 347 Ted Williams ATG 12.00 5.00
❑ 348 Mickey Cochrane ATG 1.50 .60
❑ 349 Walter Johnson ATG 5.00 2.00
❑ 350 Lefty Grove ATG 1.50 .60
❑ 351 Randy Hundley .75 .30
❑ 352 Dave Giusti .40 .15
❑ 353 Sixto Lezcano RC .75 .30
❑ 354 Ron Blomberg .40 .15
❑ 355 Steve Carlton 6.00 2.50
❑ 356 Ted Martinez .40 .15
❑ 357 Ken Forsch .40 .15
❑ 358 Buddy Bell .75 .30
❑ 359 Rick Reuschel .75 .30
❑ 360 Jeff Burroughs .75 .30
❑ 361 Detroit Tigers CL/Houk 1.50 .60
❑ 362 Will McEnaney .75 .30
❑ 363 Dave Collins RC .75 .30
❑ 364 Elias Sosa .40 .15
❑ 365 Carlton Fisk 6.00 2.50
❑ 366 Bobby Valentine .75 .30
❑ 367 Bruce Miller .40 .15
❑ 368 Wilbur Wood .40 .15
❑ 369 Frank White .75 .30
❑ 370 Ron Cey .75 .30
❑ 371 Elrod Hendricks .40 .15
❑ 372 Rick Baldwin RC .40 .15
❑ 373 Johnny Briggs .40 .15
❑ 374 Dan Warthen RC .40 .15
❑ 375 Ron Fairly .75 .30
❑ 376 Rich Hebner .75 .30
❑ 377 Mike Hegan .40 .15
❑ 378 Steve Stone .75 .30
❑ 379 Ken Boswell .40 .15
❑ 380 Bobby Bonds 1.50 .60
❑ 381 Denny Doyle .40 .15
❑ 382 Matt Alexander RC .40 .15
❑ 383 John Ellis .40 .15
❑ 384 Philadelphia Phillies CL/Ozark 1.50 .60
❑ 385 Mickey Lolich .75 .30
❑ 386 Ed Goodson .40 .15
❑ 387 Mike Miley RC .40 .15
❑ 388 Stan Perzanowski RC .40 .15
❑ 389 Glenn Adams RC .40 .15
❑ 390 Don Gullett .75 .30
❑ 391 Jerry Hairston .40 .15
❑ 392 Checklist 265-396 1.50 .60
❑ 393 Paul Mitchell RC .40 .15
❑ 394 Fran Healy .40 .15
❑ 395 Jim Wynn .75 .30
❑ 396 Bill Lee .40 .15
❑ 397 Tim Foli .40 .15
❑ 398 Dave Tomlin .40 .15
❑ 399 Luis Melendez .40 .15
❑ 400 Rod Carew 6.00 2.50
❑ 401 Ken Brett .40 .15
❑ 402 Don Money .75 .30
❑ 403 Geoff Zahn .40 .15
❑ 404 Enos Cabell .40 .15
❑ 405 Rollie Fingers 2.50 1.00
❑ 406 Ed Herrmann .40 .15
❑ 407 Tom Underwood .40 .15
❑ 408 Charlie Spikes .40 .15
❑ 409 Dave Lemanczyk .40 .15
❑ 410 Ralph Garr .75 .30
❑ 411 Bill Singer .40 .15
❑ 412 Toby Harrah .75 .30
❑ 413 Pete Varney RC .40 .15
❑ 414 Wayne Garland .40 .15
❑ 415 Vada Pinson 1.50 .60
❑ 416 Tommy John 1.50 .60
❑ 417 Gene Clines .40 .15
❑ 418 Jose Morales RC .40 .15
❑ 419 Reggie Cleveland .40 .15
❑ 420 Joe Morgan 5.00 2.00
❑ 421 Oakland Athletics CL 1.50 .60
❑ 422 Johnny Grubb .40 .15
❑ 423 Ed Halicki .40 .15
❑ 424 Phil Roof .40 .15
❑ 425 Rennie Stennett .40 .15
❑ 426 Bob Forsch .40 .15
❑ 427 Kurt Bevacqua .40 .15
❑ 428 Jim Crawford .40 .15
❑ 429 Fred Stanley .40 .15
❑ 430 Jose Cardenal .75 .30
❑ 431 Dick Ruthven .40 .15
❑ 432 Tom Veryzer .40 .15
❑ 433 Rick Waits RC .40 .15
❑ 434 Morris Nettles .40 .15
❑ 435 Phil Niekro 2.50 1.00
❑ 436 Bill Fahey .40 .15
❑ 437 Terry Forster .40 .15
❑ 438 Doug DeCinces .75 .30
❑ 439 Rick Rhoden .75 .30
❑ 440 John Mayberry .75 .30
❑ 441 Gary Carter 4.00 1.50
❑ 442 Hank Webb .40 .15
❑ 443 San Francisco Giants CL 1.50 .60
❑ 444 Gary Nolan .75 .30
❑ 445 Rico Petrocelli .75 .30
❑ 446 Larry Haney .40 .15
❑ 447 Gene Locklear .75 .30
❑ 448 Tom Johnson .40 .15
❑ 449 Bob Robertson .40 .15
❑ 450 Jim Palmer 5.00 2.00
❑ 451 Buddy Bradford .40 .15
❑ 452 Tom Hausman RC .40 .15
❑ 453 Lou Piniella 1.50 .60
❑ 454 Tom Griffin .40 .15
❑ 455 Dick Allen 1.50 .60
❑ 456 Joe Coleman .40 .15
❑ 457 Ed Crosby .40 .15
❑ 458 Earl Williams .40 .15
❑ 459 Jim Brewer .40 .15
❑ 460 Cesar Cedeno .75 .30
❑ 461 NL/AL Champs .75 .30
❑ 462 1975 WS/Reds Champs .75 .30
❑ 463 Steve Hargan .40 .15
❑ 464 Ken Henderson .40 .15
❑ 465 Mike Marshall .75 .30
❑ 466 Bob Stinson .40 .15
❑ 467 Woodie Fryman .40 .15
❑ 468 Jesus Alou .40 .15
❑ 469 Rawly Eastwick .75 .30
❑ 470 Bobby Murcer .75 .30
❑ 471 Jim Burton .40 .15
❑ 472 Bob Davis RC .40 .15
❑ 473 Paul Blair .75 .30
❑ 474 Ray Corbin .40 .15
❑ 475 Joe Rudi .75 .30
❑ 476 Bob Moose .40 .15
❑ 477 Cleveland Indians CL/Robinson 1.50 .60
❑ 478 Lynn McGlothen .40 .15
❑ 479 Bobby Mitchell .40 .15
❑ 480 Mike Schmidt 15.00 6.00
❑ 481 Rudy May .40 .15
❑ 482 Tim Hosley .40 .15
❑ 483 Mickey Stanley .40 .15
❑ 484 Eric Raich RC .40 .15
❑ 485 Mike Hargrove .75 .30
❑ 486 Bruce Dal Canton .40 .15
❑ 487 Leron Lee .40 .15
❑ 488 Claude Osteen .75 .30
❑ 489 Skip Jutze .40 .15
❑ 490 Frank Tanana .75 .30
❑ 491 Terry Crowley .40 .15
❑ 492 Marty Pattin .40 .15
❑ 493 Derrel Thomas .40 .15
❑ 494 Craig Swan .75 .30
❑ 495 Nate Colbert .40 .15

❑ 496 Juan Beniquez .40 .15
❑ 497 Joe McIntosh RC .40 .15
❑ 498 Glenn Borgmann .40 .15
❑ 499 Mario Guerrero .40 .15
❑ 500 Reggie Jackson 12.00 5.00
❑ 501 Billy Champion .40 .15
❑ 502 Tim McCarver 1.50 .60
❑ 503 Elliott Maddox .40 .15
❑ 504 Pittsburgh Pirates CL/Murtaugh 1.50 .60
❑ 505 Mark Belanger .75 .30
❑ 506 George Mitterwald .40 .15
❑ 507 Ray Bare RC .40 .15
❑ 508 Duane Kuiper RC .40 .15
❑ 509 Bill Hands .40 .15
❑ 510 Amos Otis .75 .30
❑ 511 Jamie Easterley .40 .15
❑ 512 Ellie Rodriguez .40 .15
❑ 513 Bart Johnson .40 .15
❑ 514 Dan Driessen .75 .30
❑ 515 Steve Yeager .75 .30
❑ 516 Wayne Granger .40 .15
❑ 517 John Milner .40 .15
❑ 518 Doug Flynn RC .40 .15
❑ 519 Steve Brye .40 .15
❑ 520 Willie McCovey 5.00 2.00
❑ 521 Jim Colborn .40 .15
❑ 522 Ted Sizemore .40 .15
❑ 523 Bob Montgomery .40 .15
❑ 524 Pete Falcone RC .40 .15
❑ 525 Billy Williams 2.50 1.00
❑ 526 Checklist 397-528 1.50 .60
❑ 527 Mike Anderson .40 .15
❑ 528 Dock Ellis .40 .15
❑ 529 Deron Johnson .40 .15
❑ 530 Don Sutton 2.50 1.00
❑ 531 New York Mets CL/Frazier 1.50 .60
❑ 532 Milt May .40 .15
❑ 533 Lee Richard .40 .15
❑ 534 Stan Bahnsen .40 .15
❑ 535 Dave Nelson .40 .15
❑ 536 Mike Thompson .40 .15
❑ 537 Tony Muser .40 .15
❑ 538 Pat Darcy .40 .15
❑ 539 John Balaz RC .40 .15
❑ 540 Bill Freehan .75 .30
❑ 541 Steve Mingori .40 .15
❑ 542 Keith Hernandez .75 .30
❑ 543 Wayne Twitchell .40 .15
❑ 544 Pepe Frias .40 .15
❑ 545 Sparky Lyle .75 .30
❑ 546 Dave Rosello .40 .15
❑ 547 Roric Harrison .40 .15
❑ 548 Manny Mota .75 .30
❑ 549 Randy Tate RC .40 .15
❑ 550 Hank Aaron 25.00 10.00
❑ 551 Jerry DaVanon .40 .15
❑ 552 Terry Humphrey .40 .15
❑ 553 Randy Moffitt .40 .15
❑ 554 Ray Fosse .40 .15
❑ 555 Dyar Miller .40 .15
❑ 556 Minnesota Twins CL/Mauch 1.50 .60
❑ 557 Dan Spillner .40 .15
❑ 558 Clarence Gaston .75 .30
❑ 559 Clyde Wright .40 .15
❑ 560 Jorge Orta .40 .15
❑ 561 Tom Carroll .40 .15
❑ 562 Adrian Garrett .40 .15
❑ 563 Larry Demery .40 .15
❑ 564 Kurt Bevacqua GUM 1.50 .60
❑ 565 Tug McGraw .75 .30
❑ 566 Ken McMullen .40 .15
❑ 567 George Stone .40 .15
❑ 568 Rob Andrews RC .40 .15
❑ 569 Nelson Briles .75 .30
❑ 570 George Hendrick .75 .30
❑ 571 Don DeMola .40 .15
❑ 572 Rich Coggins .40 .15
❑ 573 Bill Travers .40 .15
❑ 574 Don Kessinger .75 .30
❑ 575 Dwight Evans 1.50 .60
❑ 576 Maximino Leon .40 .15
❑ 577 Marc Hill .40 .15
❑ 578 Ted Kubiak .40 .15
❑ 579 Clay Kirby .40 .15
❑ 580 Bert Campaneris .75 .30
❑ 581 St. Louis Cardinals
CL/Schoendienst 1.50 .60
❑ 582 Mike Kekich .40 .15
❑ 583 Tommy Helms .40 .15
❑ 584 Stan Wall RC .40 .15
❑ 585 Joe Torre 1.50 .60
❑ 586 Ron Schueler .40 .15
❑ 587 Leo Cardenas .40 .15
❑ 588 Kevin Kobel .40 .15
❑ 589 Alc/Flanagan/Pac/Torr RC 1.50 .60
❑ 590 Cruz/Lemon/Valen/Whit RC .75 .30
❑ 591 Grilli/Mitch/Sosa/Throop RC .75 .30
❑ 592 Randolph/McK/Roy/Sta RC 5.00 2.00
❑ 593 And/Crosby/Litell/Metzger RC .75 .30
❑ 594 Mer/Ott/Still/White RC .75 .30
❑ 595 DeFil/Lerch/Monge/Barr RC .75 .30
❑ 596 Rey/John/LeMas/Manuel RC .75 .30
❑ 597 Aase/Kucek/LaCorte/Pazik RC .75 .30
❑ 598 Cruz/Quirk/Turner/Wallis RC .75 .30
❑ 599 Dres/Guidry/McCl/Zach RC 8.00 3.00
❑ 600 Tom Seaver 10.00 4.00
❑ 601 Ken Rudolph .40 .15
❑ 602 Doug Konieczny .40 .15
❑ 603 Jim Holt .40 .15
❑ 604 Joe Lovitto .40 .15
❑ 605 Al Downing .40 .15
❑ 606 Milwaukee Brewers CL/Grammas 1.50 .60
❑ 607 Rich Hinton .40 .15
❑ 608 Vic Correll .40 .15
❑ 609 Fred Norman .40 .15
❑ 610 Greg Luzinski 1.50 .60
❑ 611 Rich Folkers .40 .15
❑ 612 Joe Lahoud .40 .15
❑ 613 Tim Johnson .40 .15
❑ 614 Fernando Arroyo RC .40 .15
❑ 615 Mike Cubbage .40 .15
❑ 616 Buck Martinez .40 .15
❑ 617 Darold Knowles .40 .15
❑ 618 Jack Brohamer .40 .15
❑ 619 Bill Butler .40 .15
❑ 620 Al Oliver .75 .30
❑ 621 Tom Hall .40 .15
❑ 622 Rick Auerbach .40 .15
❑ 623 Bob Allietta RC .40 .15
❑ 624 Tony Taylor .40 .15
❑ 625 J.R. Richard .75 .30
❑ 626 Bob Sheldon .40 .15
❑ 627 Bill Plummer .40 .15
❑ 628 John D'Acquisto .40 .15
❑ 629 Sandy Alomar .75 .30
❑ 630 Chris Speier .40 .15
❑ 631 Atlanta Braves CL/Bristol 1.50 .60
❑ 632 Rogelio Moret .40 .15
❑ 633 John Stearns RC .75 .30
❑ 634 Larry Christenson .40 .15
❑ 635 Jim Fregosi .75 .30
❑ 636 Joe Decker .40 .15
❑ 637 Bruce Bochte .40 .15
❑ 638 Doyle Alexander .75 .30
❑ 639 Fred Kendall .40 .15
❑ 640 Bill Madlock 1.50 .60
❑ 641 Tom Paciorek .75 .30
❑ 642 Dennis Blair .40 .15
❑ 643 Checklist 529-660 1.50 .60
❑ 644 Tom Bradley .40 .15
❑ 645 Darrell Porter .75 .30
❑ 646 John Lowenstein .40 .15
❑ 647 Ramon Hernandez .40 .15
❑ 648 Al Cowens .75 .30
❑ 649 Dave Roberts .40 .15
❑ 650 Thurman Munson 6.00 2.50
❑ 651 John Odom .40 .15
❑ 652 Ed Armbrister .40 .15
❑ 653 Mike Norris RC .75 .30
❑ 654 Doug Griffin .40 .15
❑ 655 Mike Vail RC .40 .15
❑ 656 Chicago White Sox CL/Tanner 1.50 .60
❑ 657 Roy Smalley RC .75 .30
❑ 658 Jerry Johnson .40 .15
❑ 659 Ben Oglivie .75 .30
❑ 660 Davey Lopes 1.50 .60

1977 Topps

❑ COMPLETE SET (660) 250.00 125.00
❑ 1 G.Brett/B.Madlock LL 8.00 3.00
❑ 2 G.Nettles/M.Schmidt LL 2.50 1.00
❑ 3 L.May/G.Foster LL 1.50 .60

❑ 4 B.North/D.Lopes LL .75 .30
❑ 5 J.Palmer/R.Jones LL 1.50 .60
❑ 6 N.Ryan/T.Seaver LL 15.00 6.00
❑ 7 M.Fidrych/J.Denny LL .75 .30
❑ 8 B.Campbell/R.Eastwick LL .75 .30
❑ 9 Doug Rader .30 .12
❑ 10 Reggie Jackson 10.00 4.00
❑ 11 Rob Dressler .30 .12
❑ 12 Larry Haney .30 .12
❑ 13 Luis Gomez RC .30 .12
❑ 14 Tommy Smith .30 .12
❑ 15 Don Gullett .75 .30
❑ 16 Bob Jones RC .30 .12
❑ 17 Steve Stone .75 .30
❑ 18 Cleveland Indians CL/Robinson 1.50 .60
❑ 19 John D'Acquisto .30 .12
❑ 20 Graig Nettles 1.50 .60
❑ 21 Ken Forsch .30 .12
❑ 22 Bill Freehan .75 .30
❑ 23 Dan Driessen .30 .12
❑ 24 Carl Morton .30 .12
❑ 25 Dwight Evans 1.50 .60
❑ 26 Ray Sadecki .30 .12
❑ 27 Bill Buckner .75 .30
❑ 28 Woodie Fryman .30 .12
❑ 29 Bucky Dent .75 .30
❑ 30 Greg Luzinski 1.50 .60
❑ 31 Jim Todd .30 .12
❑ 32 Checklist 1-132 1.50 .60
❑ 33 Wayne Garland .30 .12
❑ 34 California Angels CL/Sherry 1.50 .60
❑ 35 Rennie Stennett .30 .12
❑ 36 John Ellis .30 .12
❑ 37 Steve Hargan .30 .12
❑ 38 Craig Kusick .30 .12
❑ 39 Tom Griffin .30 .12
❑ 40 Bobby Murcer .75 .30
❑ 41 Jim Kern .30 .12
❑ 42 Jose Cruz .75 .30
❑ 43 Ray Bare .30 .12
❑ 44 Bud Harrelson .75 .30
❑ 45 Rawly Eastwick .30 .12
❑ 46 Buck Martinez .30 .12
❑ 47 Lynn McGlothen .30 .12
❑ 48 Tom Paciorek .75 .30
❑ 49 Grant Jackson .30 .12
❑ 50 Ron Cey .75 .30
❑ 51 Milwaukee Brewers CL/Grammas 1.50 .60
❑ 52 Ellis Valentine .30 .12
❑ 53 Paul Mitchell .30 .12
❑ 54 Sandy Alomar .75 .30
❑ 55 Jeff Burroughs .75 .30
❑ 56 Rudy May .30 .12
❑ 57 Marc Hill .30 .12
❑ 58 Chet Lemon .75 .30
❑ 59 Larry Christenson .30 .12
❑ 60 Jim Rice 2.50 1.00
❑ 61 Manny Sanguillen .75 .30
❑ 62 Eric Raich .30 .12
❑ 63 Tito Fuentes .30 .12
❑ 64 Larry Biittner .30 .12
❑ 65 Skip Lockwood .30 .12
❑ 66 Roy Smalley .75 .30
❑ 67 Joaquin Andujar RC .75 .30
❑ 68 Bruce Bochte .30 .12
❑ 69 Jim Crawford .30 .12
❑ 70 Johnny Bench 10.00 4.00
❑ 71 Dock Ellis .30 .12

❑ 72 Mike Anderson .30 .12
❑ 73 Charlie Williams .30 .12
❑ 74 Oakland Athletics CL/McKeon 1.50 .60
❑ 75 Dennis Leonard .75 .30
❑ 76 Tim Foli .30 .12
❑ 77 Dyar Miller .30 .12
❑ 78 Bob Davis .30 .12
❑ 79 Don Money .75 .30
❑ 80 Andy Messersmith .75 .30
❑ 81 Juan Beniquez .30 .12
❑ 82 Jim Rooker .30 .12
❑ 83 Kevin Bell RC .30 .12
❑ 84 Ollie Brown .30 .12
❑ 85 Duane Kuiper .30 .12
❑ 86 Pat Zachry .30 .12
❑ 87 Glenn Borgmann .30 .12
❑ 88 Stan Wall .30 .12
❑ 89 Butch Hobson RC .75 .30
❑ 90 Cesar Cedeno .75 .30
❑ 91 John Verhoeven RC .30 .12
❑ 92 Dave Rosello .30 .12
❑ 93 Tom Poquette .30 .12
❑ 94 Craig Swan .30 .12
❑ 95 Keith Hernandez .75 .30
❑ 96 Lou Piniella .75 .30
❑ 97 Dave Heaverlo .30 .12
❑ 98 Milt May .30 .12
❑ 99 Tom Hausman .30 .12
❑ 100 Joe Morgan 4.00 1.50
❑ 101 Dick Bosman .30 .12
❑ 102 Jose Morales .30 .12
❑ 103 Mike Bacsik RC .30 .12
❑ 104 Omar Moreno RC .75 .30
❑ 105 Steve Yeager .75 .30
❑ 106 Mike Flanagan .75 .30
❑ 107 Bill Melton .30 .12
❑ 108 Alan Foster .30 .12
❑ 109 Jorge Orta .30 .12
❑ 110 Steve Carlton 5.00 2.00
❑ 111 Rico Petrocelli .75 .30
❑ 112 Bill Greif .30 .12
❑ 113 Toronto Blue Jays CL/Hartsfield 1.50 .60
❑ 114 Bruce Dal Canton .30 .12
❑ 115 Rick Manning .30 .12
❑ 116 Joe Niekro .75 .30
❑ 117 Frank White .75 .30
❑ 118 Rick Jones RC .30 .12
❑ 119 John Stearns .30 .12
❑ 120 Rod Carew 5.00 2.00
❑ 121 Gary Nolan .30 .12
❑ 122 Ben Oglivie .75 .30
❑ 123 Fred Stanley .30 .12
❑ 124 George Mitterwald .30 .12
❑ 125 Bill Travers .30 .12
❑ 126 Rod Gilbreath .30 .12
❑ 127 Ron Fairly .75 .30
❑ 128 Tommy John 1.50 .60
❑ 129 Mike Sadek .30 .12
❑ 130 Al Oliver .75 .30
❑ 131 Orlando Ramirez RC .30 .12
❑ 132 Chip Lang RC .30 .12
❑ 133 Ralph Garr .75 .30
❑ 134 San Diego Padres CL/McNamara 1.50 .60
❑ 135 Mark Belanger .75 .30
❑ 136 Jerry Mumphrey RC .75 .30
❑ 137 Jeff Terpko RC .30 .12
❑ 138 Bob Stinson .30 .12
❑ 139 Fred Norman .30 .12
❑ 140 Mike Schmidt 12.00 5.00
❑ 141 Mark Littell .30 .12
❑ 142 Steve Dillard RC .30 .12
❑ 143 Ed Herrmann .30 .12
❑ 144 Bruce Sutter RC 15.00 6.00
❑ 145 Tom Veryzer .30 .12
❑ 146 Dusty Baker 1.50 .60
❑ 147 Jackie Brown .30 .12
❑ 148 Fran Healy .30 .12
❑ 149 Mike Cubbage .30 .12
❑ 150 Tom Seaver 8.00 3.00
❑ 151 Johnny LeMaster .30 .12
❑ 152 Gaylord Perry 2.50 1.00
❑ 153 Ron Jackson RC .30 .12
❑ 154 Dave Giusti .30 .12
❑ 155 Joe Rudi .75 .30
❑ 156 Pete Mackanin .30 .12
❑ 157 Ken Brett .30 .12
❑ 158 Ted Kubiak .30 .12
❑ 159 Bernie Carbo .30 .12
❑ 160 Will McEnaney .30 .12
❑ 161 Garry Templeton RC 1.50 .60
❑ 162 Mike Cuellar .75 .30
❑ 163 Dave Hilton .30 .12
❑ 164 Tug McGraw .75 .30
❑ 165 Jim Wynn .75 .30
❑ 166 Bill Campbell .30 .12
❑ 167 Rich Hebner .75 .30
❑ 168 Charlie Spikes .30 .12
❑ 169 Darold Knowles .30 .12
❑ 170 Thurman Munson 5.00 2.00
❑ 171 Ken Sanders .30 .12
❑ 172 John Milner .30 .12
❑ 173 Chuck Scrivener RC .30 .12
❑ 174 Nelson Briles .75 .30
❑ 175 Butch Wynegar RC .75 .30
❑ 176 Bob Robertson .30 .12
❑ 177 Bart Johnson .30 .12
❑ 178 Bombo Rivera RC .30 .12
❑ 179 Paul Hartzell RC .30 .12
❑ 180 Dave Lopes .75 .30
❑ 181 Ken McMullen .30 .12
❑ 182 Dan Spillner .30 .12
❑ 183 St.Louis Cardinals CL/V.Rapp 1.50 .60
❑ 184 Bo McLaughlin RC .30 .12
❑ 185 Sixto Lezcano .30 .12
❑ 186 Doug Flynn .30 .12
❑ 187 Dick Pole .30 .12
❑ 188 Bob Tolan .30 .12
❑ 189 Rick Dempsey .75 .30
❑ 190 Ray Burris .30 .12
❑ 191 Doug Griffin .30 .12
❑ 192 Clarence Gaston .75 .30
❑ 193 Larry Gura .30 .12
❑ 194 Gary Matthews .75 .30
❑ 195 Ed Figueroa .30 .12
❑ 196 Len Randle .30 .12
❑ 197 Ed Ott .30 .12
❑ 198 Wilbur Wood .30 .12
❑ 199 Pepe Frias .30 .12
❑ 200 Frank Tanana .75 .30
❑ 201 Ed Kranepool .30 .12
❑ 202 Tom Johnson .30 .12
❑ 203 Ed Armbrister .30 .12
❑ 204 Jeff Newman RC .30 .12
❑ 205 Pete Falcone .30 .12
❑ 206 Boog Powell 1.50 .60
❑ 207 Glenn Abbott .30 .12
❑ 208 Checklist 133-264 1.50 .60
❑ 209 Rob Andrews .30 .12
❑ 210 Fred Lynn .75 .30
❑ 211 San Francisco Giants CL/Altobelli 1.50 .60
❑ 212 Jim Mason .30 .12
❑ 213 Maximino Leon .30 .12
❑ 214 Darrell Porter .75 .30
❑ 215 Butch Metzger .30 .12
❑ 216 Doug DeCinces .75 .30
❑ 217 Tom Underwood .30 .12
❑ 218 John Wathan RC .75 .30
❑ 219 Joe Coleman .30 .12
❑ 220 Chris Chambliss .75 .30
❑ 221 Bob Bailey .30 .12
❑ 222 Francisco Barrios RC .30 .12
❑ 223 Earl Williams .30 .12
❑ 224 Rusty Torres .30 .12
❑ 225 Bob Apodaca .30 .12
❑ 226 Leroy Stanton .75 .30
❑ 227 Joe Sambito RC .30 .12
❑ 228 Minnesota Twins CL/Mauch 1.50 .60
❑ 229 Don Kessinger .75 .30
❑ 230 Vida Blue .75 .30
❑ 231 George Brett RB 8.00 3.00
❑ 232 Minnie Minoso RB .75 .30
❑ 233 Jose Morales RB .30 .12
❑ 234 Nolan Ryan RB 15.00 6.00
❑ 235 Cecil Cooper .75 .30
❑ 236 Tom Buskey .30 .12
❑ 237 Gene Clines .30 .12
❑ 238 Tippy Martinez .30 .12
❑ 239 Bill Plummer .30 .12
❑ 240 Ron LeFlore .75 .30
❑ 241 Dave Tomlin .30 .12
❑ 242 Ken Henderson .30 .12
❑ 243 Ron Reed .30 .12
❑ 244 John Mayberry .75 .30
❑ 245 Rick Rhoden .75 .30
❑ 246 Mike Vail .30 .12
❑ 247 Chris Knapp RC .30 .12
❑ 248 Wilbur Howard .30 .12
❑ 249 Pete Redfern RC .30 .12
❑ 250 Bill Madlock .75 .30
❑ 251 Tony Muser .30 .12
❑ 252 Dale Murray .30 .12
❑ 253 John Hale .30 .12
❑ 254 Doyle Alexander .30 .12
❑ 255 George Scott .75 .30
❑ 256 Joe Hoerner .30 .12
❑ 257 Mike Miley .30 .12
❑ 258 Luis Tiant .75 .30
❑ 259 New York Mets CL/Frazier 1.50 .60
❑ 260 J.R. Richard .75 .30
❑ 261 Phil Garner .75 .30
❑ 262 Al Cowens .75 .30
❑ 263 Mike Marshall .75 .30
❑ 264 Tom Hutton .30 .12
❑ 265 Mark Fidrych RC 3.00 1.25
❑ 266 Derrel Thomas .30 .12
❑ 267 Ray Fosse .30 .12
❑ 268 Rick Sawyer RC .30 .12
❑ 269 Joe Lis .30 .12
❑ 270 Dave Parker 1.50 .60
❑ 271 Terry Forster .30 .12
❑ 272 Lee Lacy .30 .12
❑ 273 Eric Soderholm .30 .12
❑ 274 Don Stanhouse .30 .12
❑ 275 Mike Hargrove .75 .30
❑ 276 Chris Chambliss ALCS 1.50 .60
❑ 277 Pete Rose NLCS 5.00 2.00
❑ 278 Danny Frisella .30 .12
❑ 279 Joe Wallis .30 .12
❑ 280 Jim Hunter 2.50 1.00
❑ 281 Roy Staiger .30 .12
❑ 282 Sid Monge .30 .12
❑ 283 Jerry DaVanon .30 .12
❑ 284 Mike Norris .30 .12
❑ 285 Brooks Robinson 5.00 2.00
❑ 286 Johnny Grubb .30 .12
❑ 287 Cincinnati Reds CL/Anderson 1.50 .60
❑ 288 Bob Montgomery .30 .12
❑ 289 Gene Garber .75 .30
❑ 290 Amos Otis .75 .30
❑ 291 Jason Thompson RC .75 .30
❑ 292 Rogelio Moret .30 .12
❑ 293 Jack Brohamer .30 .12
❑ 294 George Medich .30 .12
❑ 295 Gary Carter 2.50 1.00
❑ 296 Don Hood .30 .12
❑ 297 Ken Reitz .30 .12
❑ 298 Charlie Hough .75 .30
❑ 299 Otto Velez .75 .30
❑ 300 Jerry Koosman .75 .30
❑ 301 Toby Harrah .75 .30
❑ 302 Mike Garman .30 .12
❑ 303 Gene Tenace .75 .30
❑ 304 Jim Hughes .30 .12
❑ 305 Mickey Rivers .75 .30
❑ 306 Rick Waits .30 .12
❑ 307 Gary Sutherland .30 .12
❑ 308 Gene Pentz RC .30 .12
❑ 309 Boston Red Sox CL/Zimmer 1.50 .60
❑ 310 Larry Bowa .75 .30
❑ 311 Vern Ruhle .30 .12
❑ 312 Rob Belloir RC .30 .12
❑ 313 Paul Blair .75 .30
❑ 314 Steve Mingori .30 .12
❑ 315 Dave Chalk .30 .12
❑ 316 Steve Rogers .30 .12
❑ 317 Kurt Bevacqua .30 .12
❑ 318 Duffy Dyer .30 .12
❑ 319 Goose Gossage 1.50 .60
❑ 320 Ken Griffey Sr. 1.50 .60
❑ 321 Dave Goltz .30 .12
❑ 322 Bill Russell .75 .30
❑ 323 Larry Lintz .30 .12
❑ 324 John Curtis .30 .12
❑ 325 Mike Ivie .30 .12
❑ 326 Jesse Jefferson .30 .12
❑ 327 Houston Astros CL/Virdon 1.50 .60
❑ 328 Tommy Boggs RC .30 .12
❑ 329 Ron Hodges .30 .12

❑ 330 George Hendrick .75 .30
❑ 331 Jim Colborn .30 .12
❑ 332 Elliott Maddox .30 .12
❑ 333 Paul Reuschel RC .30 .12
❑ 334 Bill Stein .30 .12
❑ 335 Bill Robinson .75 .30
❑ 336 Denny Doyle .30 .12
❑ 337 Ron Schueler .30 .12
❑ 338 Dave Duncan .75 .30
❑ 339 Adrian Devine .30 .12
❑ 340 Hal McRae .75 .30
❑ 341 Joe Kerrigan RC .30 .12
❑ 342 Jerry Remy .30 .12
❑ 343 Ed Halicki .30 .12
❑ 344 Brian Downing .75 .30
❑ 345 Reggie Smith .75 .30
❑ 346 Bill Singer .30 .12
❑ 347 George Foster 1.50 .60
❑ 348 Brent Strom .30 .12
❑ 349 Jim Holt .30 .12
❑ 350 Larry Dierker .75 .30
❑ 351 Jim Sundberg .75 .30
❑ 352 Mike Phillips .30 .12
❑ 353 Stan Thomas .30 .12
❑ 354 Pittsburgh Pirates CL/Tanner 1.50 .60
❑ 355 Lou Brock 4.00 1.50
❑ 356 Checklist 265-396 1.50 .60
❑ 357 Tim McCarver 1.50 .60
❑ 358 Tom House .30 .12
❑ 359 Willie Randolph 1.50 .60
❑ 360 Rick Monday .75 .30
❑ 361 Eduardo Rodriguez .30 .12
❑ 362 Tommy Davis .75 .30
❑ 363 Dave Roberts .30 .12
❑ 364 Vic Correll .30 .12
❑ 365 Mike Torrez .75 .30
❑ 366 Ted Sizemore .30 .12
❑ 367 Dave Hamilton .30 .12
❑ 368 Mike Jorgensen .30 .12
❑ 369 Terry Humphrey .30 .12
❑ 370 John Montefusco .30 .12
❑ 371 Kansas City Royals CL/Herzog 1.50 .60
❑ 372 Rich Folkers .30 .12
❑ 373 Bert Campaneris .75 .30
❑ 374 Kent Tekulve .75 .30
❑ 375 Larry Hisle .75 .30
❑ 376 Nino Espinosa RC .30 .12
❑ 377 Dave McKay .30 .12
❑ 378 Jim Umbarger .30 .12
❑ 379 Larry Cox RC .30 .12
❑ 380 Lee May .75 .30
❑ 381 Bob Forsch .30 .12
❑ 382 Charlie Moore .30 .12
❑ 383 Stan Bahnsen .30 .12
❑ 384 Darrel Chaney .30 .12
❑ 385 Dave LaRoche .30 .12
❑ 386 Manny Mota .75 .30
❑ 387 New York Yankees CL/Martin 2.50 1.00
❑ 388 Terry Harmon .30 .12
❑ 389 Ken Kravec RC .30 .12
❑ 390 Dave Winfield 6.00 2.50
❑ 391 Dan Warthen .30 .12
❑ 392 Phil Roof .30 .12
❑ 393 John Lowenstein .30 .12
❑ 394 Bill Laxton RC .30 .12
❑ 395 Manny Trillo .30 .12
❑ 396 Tom Murphy .30 .12
❑ 397 Larry Herndon RC .75 .30
❑ 398 Tom Burgmeier .30 .12
❑ 399 Bruce Boisclair RC .30 .12
❑ 400 Steve Garvey 2.50 1.00
❑ 401 Mickey Scott .30 .12
❑ 402 Tommy Helms .30 .12
❑ 403 Tom Grieve .75 .30
❑ 404 Eric Rasmussen RC .30 .12
❑ 405 Claudell Washington .75 .30
❑ 406 Tim Johnson .30 .12
❑ 407 Dave Freisleben .30 .12
❑ 408 Cesar Tovar .30 .12
❑ 409 Pete Broberg .30 .12
❑ 410 Willie Montanez .30 .12
❑ 411 J.Morgan/J.Bench WS 2.50 1.00
❑ 412 Johnny Bench WS 2.50 1.00
❑ 413 Cincy Wins WS .75 .30
❑ 414 Tommy Harper .75 .30
❑ 415 Jay Johnstone .75 .30
❑ 416 Chuck Hartenstein .30 .12
❑ 417 Wayne Garrett .30 .12
❑ 418 Chicago White Sox CL/Lemon 1.50 .60
❑ 419 Steve Swisher .30 .12
❑ 420 Rusty Staub 1.50 .60
❑ 421 Doug Rau .30 .12
❑ 422 Freddie Patek .75 .30
❑ 423 Gary Lavelle .30 .12
❑ 424 Steve Brye .30 .12
❑ 425 Joe Torre 1.50 .60
❑ 426 Dick Drago .30 .12
❑ 427 Dave Rader .30 .12
❑ 428 Texas Rangers CL/Lucchesi 1.50 .60
❑ 429 Ken Boswell .30 .12
❑ 430 Fergie Jenkins 2.50 1.00
❑ 431 Dave Collins UER .75 .30
❑ 432 Buzz Capra .30 .12
❑ 433 Nate Colbert TBC .30 .12
❑ 434 Carl Yastrzemski TBC 1.50 .60
❑ 435 Maury Wills TBC .75 .30
❑ 436 Bob Keegan TBC .30 .12
❑ 437 Ralph Kiner TBC 1.50 .60
❑ 438 Marty Perez .30 .12
❑ 439 Gorman Thomas .75 .30
❑ 440 Jon Matlack .30 .12
❑ 441 Larvell Blanks .30 .12
❑ 442 Atlanta Braves CL/Bristol 1.50 .60
❑ 443 Lamar Johnson .30 .12
❑ 444 Wayne Twitchell .30 .12
❑ 445 Ken Singleton .75 .30
❑ 446 Bill Bonham .30 .12
❑ 447 Jerry Turner .30 .12
❑ 448 Ellie Rodriguez .30 .12
❑ 449 Al Fitzmorris .30 .12
❑ 450 Pete Rose 20.00 8.00
❑ 451 Checklist 397-528 1.50 .60
❑ 452 Mike Caldwell .30 .12
❑ 453 Pedro Garcia .30 .12
❑ 454 Andy Etchebarren .30 .12
❑ 455 Rick Wise .30 .12
❑ 456 Leon Roberts .30 .12
❑ 457 Steve Luebber .30 .12
❑ 458 Leo Foster .30 .12
❑ 459 Steve Foucault .30 .12
❑ 460 Willie Stargell 2.50 1.00
❑ 461 Dick Tidrow .30 .12
❑ 462 Don Baylor 1.50 .60
❑ 463 Jamie Quirk .30 .12
❑ 464 Randy Moffitt .30 .12
❑ 465 Rico Carty .75 .30
❑ 466 Fred Holdsworth .30 .12
❑ 467 Philadelphia Phillies CL/Ozark 1.50 .60
❑ 468 Ramon Hernandez .30 .12
❑ 469 Pat Kelly .30 .12
❑ 470 Ted Simmons .75 .30
❑ 471 Del Unser .30 .12
❑ 472 Aase/McCl/Patt/Wehr RC .30 .12
❑ 473 Andre Dawson RC 20.00 8.00
❑ 474 Bailor/Gar/Reyn/Tav RC .75 .30
❑ 475 Batt/Camp/McGr/Sarm RC .75 .30
❑ 476 Dale Murphy RC 15.00 6.00
❑ 477 Ault/Dauer/Gonz/Mank RC .75 .30
❑ 478 Gid/Hoot/John/Lemong RC .75 .30
❑ 479 Assel/Gross/Mej/Woods RC .75 .30
❑ 480 Carl Yastrzemski 8.00 3.00
❑ 481 Roger Metzger .30 .12
❑ 482 Tony Solaita .30 .12
❑ 483 Richie Zisk .30 .12
❑ 484 Burt Hooton .75 .30
❑ 485 Roy White .75 .30
❑ 486 Ed Bane .30 .12
❑ 487 And/Glynn/Hend/Terl RC .75 .30
❑ 488 J.Clark/L.Mazzilli RC 3.00 1.25
❑ 489 Barker/Ler/Mint/Overy RC .75 .30
❑ 490 Almon/Klutts/McM/Wag RC .75 .30
❑ 491 Dennis Martinez RC 3.00 1.25
❑ 492 Armas/Kemp/Lop/Woods RC .75 .30
❑ 493 Krukow/Ott/Wheel/Will RC .75 .30
❑ 494 J.Gantner/B.Wills RC 1.50 .60
❑ 495 Al Hrabosky .75 .30
❑ 496 Gary Thomasson .30 .12
❑ 497 Clay Carroll .30 .12
❑ 498 Sal Bando .75 .30
❑ 499 Pablo Torrealba .30 .12
❑ 500 Dave Kingman 1.50 .60
❑ 501 Jim Bibby .30 .12
❑ 502 Randy Hundley .30 .12
❑ 503 Bill Lee .30 .12
❑ 504 Los Angeles Dodgers CL/Lasorda 1.50 .60
❑ 505 Oscar Gamble .75 .30
❑ 506 Steve Grilli .30 .12
❑ 507 Mike Hegan .30 .12
❑ 508 Dave Pagan .30 .12
❑ 509 Cookie Rojas .75 .30
❑ 510 John Candelaria .30 .12
❑ 511 Bill Fahey .30 .12
❑ 512 Jack Billingham .30 .12
❑ 513 Jerry Terrell .30 .12
❑ 514 Cliff Johnson .30 .12
❑ 515 Chris Speier .30 .12
❑ 516 Bake McBride .75 .30
❑ 517 Pete Vuckovich RC .75 .30
❑ 518 Chicago Cubs CL/Franks 1.50 .60
❑ 519 Don Kirkwood .30 .12
❑ 520 Garry Maddox .30 .12
❑ 521 Bob Grich .75 .30
❑ 522 Enzo Hernandez .30 .12
❑ 523 Rollie Fingers 2.50 1.00
❑ 524 Rowland Office .30 .12
❑ 525 Dennis Eckersley 5.00 2.00
❑ 526 Larry Parrish .75 .30
❑ 527 Dan Meyer .75 .30
❑ 528 Bill Castro .30 .12
❑ 529 Jim Essian RC .30 .12
❑ 530 Rick Reuschel .75 .30
❑ 531 Lyman Bostock .75 .30
❑ 532 Jim Willoughby .30 .12
❑ 533 Mickey Stanley .30 .12
❑ 534 Paul Splittorff .30 .12
❑ 535 Cesar Geronimo .30 .12
❑ 536 Vic Albury .30 .12
❑ 537 Dave Roberts .30 .12
❑ 538 Frank Taveras .30 .12
❑ 539 Mike Wallace .30 .12
❑ 540 Bob Watson .75 .30
❑ 541 John Denny .75 .30
❑ 542 Frank Duffy .30 .12
❑ 543 Ron Blomberg .30 .12
❑ 544 Gary Ross .30 .10
❑ 545 Bob Boone .75 .30
❑ 546 Baltimore Orioles CL/Weaver 1.50 .60
❑ 547 Willie McCovey 4.00 1.50
❑ 548 Joel Youngblood RC .30 .12
❑ 549 Jerry Royster .30 .12
❑ 550 Randy Jones .30 .12
❑ 551 Bill North .30 .12
❑ 552 Pepe Mangual .30 .12
❑ 553 Jack Heidemann .30 .12
❑ 554 Bruce Kimm RC .30 .12
❑ 555 Dan Ford .30 .12
❑ 556 Doug Bird .30 .12
❑ 557 Jerry White .30 .12
❑ 558 Elias Sosa .30 .12
❑ 559 Alan Bannister RC .30 .12
❑ 560 Dave Concepcion 1.50 .60
❑ 561 Pete LaCock .30 .12
❑ 562 Checklist 529-660 1.50 .60
❑ 563 Bruce Kison .30 .12
❑ 564 Alan Ashby .30 .12
❑ 565 Mickey Lolich .75 .30
❑ 566 Rick Miller .30 .12
❑ 567 Enos Cabell .30 .12
❑ 568 Carlos May .30 .12
❑ 569 Jim Lonborg .75 .30
❑ 570 Bobby Bonds 1.50 .60
❑ 571 Darrell Evans .75 .30
❑ 572 Ross Grimsley .30 .12
❑ 573 Joe Ferguson .30 .12
❑ 574 Aurelio Rodriguez .30 .12
❑ 575 Dick Ruthven .30 .12
❑ 576 Fred Kendall .30 .12
❑ 577 Jerry Augustine RC .30 .12
❑ 578 Bob Randall RC .30 .12
❑ 579 Don Carrithers .30 .12
❑ 580 George Brett 15.00 6.00
❑ 581 Pedro Borbon .30 .12
❑ 582 Ed Kirkpatrick .30 .12
❑ 583 Paul Lindblad .30 .12
❑ 584 Ed Goodson .30 .12
❑ 585 Rick Burleson .75 .30
❑ 586 Steve Renko .30 .12
❑ 587 Rick Baldwin .30 .12

❑ 588 Dave Moates .30 .12
❑ 589 Mike Cosgrove .30 .12
❑ 590 Buddy Bell .75 .30
❑ 591 Chris Arnold .30 .12
❑ 592 Dan Briggs RC .30 .12
❑ 593 Dennis Blair .30 .12
❑ 594 Biff Pocoroba .30 .12
❑ 595 John Hiller .30 .12
❑ 596 Jerry Martin RC .30 .12
❑ 597 Seattle Mariners CL/Johnson 1.50 .60
❑ 598 Sparky Lyle .75 .30
❑ 599 Mike Tyson .30 .12
❑ 600 Jim Palmer 4.00 1.50
❑ 601 Mike Lum .30 .12
❑ 602 Andy Hassler .30 .12
❑ 603 Willie Davis .75 .30
❑ 604 Jim Slaton .30 .12
❑ 605 Felix Millan .30 .12
❑ 606 Steve Braun .30 .12
❑ 607 Larry Demery .30 .12
❑ 608 Roy Howell .30 .12
❑ 609 Jim Barr .30 .12
❑ 610 Jose Cardenal .75 .30
❑ 611 Dave Lemanczyk .30 .12
❑ 612 Barry Foote .30 .12
❑ 613 Reggie Cleveland .30 .12
❑ 614 Greg Gross .30 .12
❑ 615 Phil Niekro 2.50 1.00
❑ 616 Tommy Sandt RC .30 .12
❑ 617 Bobby Darwin .30 .12
❑ 618 Pat Dobson .30 .12
❑ 619 Johnny Oates .75 .30
❑ 620 Don Sutton 2.50 1.00
❑ 621 Detroit Tigers CL/Houk 1.50 .60
❑ 622 Jim Wohlford .30 .12
❑ 623 Jack Kucek .30 .12
❑ 624 Hector Cruz .30 .12
❑ 625 Ken Holtzman .75 .30
❑ 626 Al Bumbry .75 .30
❑ 627 Bob Myrick RC .30 .12
❑ 628 Mario Guerrero .30 .12
❑ 629 Bobby Valentine .75 .30
❑ 630 Bert Blyleven 1.50 .60
❑ 631 Brett Brothers 6.00 2.50
❑ 632 Forsch Brothers .75 .30
❑ 633 May Brothers .75 .30
❑ 634 Reuschel Brothers UER .75 .30
❑ 635 Robin Yount 8.00 3.00
❑ 636 Santo Alcala .30 .12
❑ 637 Alex Johnson .30 .12
❑ 638 Jim Kaat 1.50 .60
❑ 639 Jerry Morales .30 .12
❑ 640 Carlton Fisk 5.00 2.00
❑ 641 Dan Larson RC .30 .12
❑ 642 Willie Crawford .30 .12
❑ 643 Mike Pazik .30 .12
❑ 644 Matt Alexander .30 .12
❑ 645 Jerry Reuss .75 .30
❑ 646 Andres Mora RC .30 .12
❑ 647 Montreal Expos CL/Williams 1.50 .60
❑ 648 Jim Spencer .30 .12
❑ 649 Dave Cash .30 .12
❑ 650 Nolan Ryan 30.00 12.50
❑ 651 Von Joshua .30 .12
❑ 652 Tom Walker .30 .12
❑ 653 Diego Segui .75 .30
❑ 654 Ron Pruitt RC .30 .12
❑ 655 Tony Perez 2.50 1.00
❑ 656 Ron Guidry 1.50 .60
❑ 657 Mick Kelleher RC .30 .12
❑ 658 Marty Pattin .30 .12
❑ 659 Merv Rettenmund .30 .12
❑ 660 Willie Horton 1.50 .60

1978 Topps

❑ COMPLETE SET (726) 200.00 100.00
❑ COMMON CARD (1-726) .25 .10
❑ COMMON CARD DP .20 .08
❑ 1 Lou Brock RB 3.00 1.25
❑ 2 Sparky Lyle RB .60 .25
❑ 3 Willie McCovey RB 2.50 1.00
❑ 4 Brooks Robinson RB 1.25 .50
❑ 5 Pete Rose RB 8.00 3.00
❑ 6 Nolan Ryan RB 15.00 6.00
❑ 7 Reggie Jackson RB 4.00 1.50
❑ 8 Mike Sadek .25 .10

❑ 9 Doug DeCinces .60 .25
❑ 10 Phil Niekro 2.50 1.00
❑ 11 Rick Manning .25 .10
❑ 12 Don Aase .25 .10
❑ 13 Art Howe RC .60 .25
❑ 14 Lerrin LaGrow .25 .10
❑ 15 Tony Perez DP 1.25 .50
❑ 16 Roy White .60 .25
❑ 17 Mike Krukow .25 .10
❑ 18 Bob Grich .60 .25
❑ 19 Darrell Porter .60 .25
❑ 20 Pete Rose DP 12.00 5.00
❑ 21 Steve Kemp .25 .10
❑ 22 Charlie Hough .60 .25
❑ 23 Bump Wills .25 .10
❑ 24 Don Money DP .20 .08
❑ 25 Jon Matlack .25 .10
❑ 26 Rich Hebner .60 .25
❑ 27 Geoff Zahn .25 .10
❑ 28 Ed Ott .25 .10
❑ 29 Bob Lacey RC .25 .10
❑ 30 George Hendrick .60 .25
❑ 31 Glenn Abbott .25 .10
❑ 32 Garry Templeton .60 .25
❑ 33 Dave Lemanczyk .25 .10
❑ 34 Willie McCovey 3.00 1.25
❑ 35 Sparky Lyle .60 .25
❑ 36 Eddie Murray RC 50.00 20.00
❑ 37 Rick Waits .25 .10
❑ 38 Willie Montanez .25 .10
❑ 39 Floyd Bannister RC .25 .10
❑ 40 Carl Yastrzemski 6.00 2.50
❑ 41 Burt Hooton .60 .25
❑ 42 Jorge Orta .25 .10
❑ 43 Bill Atkinson RC .25 .10
❑ 44 Toby Harrah .60 .25
❑ 45 Mark Fidrych 2.50 1.00
❑ 46 Al Cowens .60 .25
❑ 47 Jack Billingham .25 .10
❑ 48 Don Baylor 1.25 .50
❑ 49 Ed Kranepool .60 .25
❑ 50 Rick Reuschel .60 .25
❑ 51 Charlie Moore DP .20 .08
❑ 52 Jim Lonborg .60 .25
❑ 53 Phil Garner DP .25 .10
❑ 54 Tom Johnson .25 .10
❑ 55 Mitchell Page RC .25 .10
❑ 56 Randy Jones .25 .10
❑ 57 Dan Meyer .25 .10
❑ 58 Bob Forsch .25 .10
❑ 59 Otto Velez .25 .10
❑ 60 Thurman Munson 4.00 1.50
❑ 61 Larvell Blanks .25 .10
❑ 62 Jim Barr .25 .10
❑ 63 Don Zimmer MG .60 .25
❑ 64 Gene Pentz .25 .10
❑ 65 Ken Singleton .60 .25
❑ 66 Chicago White Sox CL 1.25 .50
❑ 67 Claudell Washington .60 .25
❑ 68 Steve Foucault DP .20 .08
❑ 69 Mike Vail .25 .10
❑ 70 Goose Gossage 1.25 .50
❑ 71 Terry Humphrey .25 .10
❑ 72 Andre Dawson 4.00 1.50
❑ 73 Andy Hassler .25 .10
❑ 74 Checklist 1-121 1.25 .50
❑ 75 Dick Ruthven .25 .10
❑ 76 Steve Ontiveros .25 .10
❑ 77 Ed Kirkpatrick .25 .10
❑ 78 Pablo Torrealba .25 .10
❑ 79 Darrell Johnson MG DP .20 .08
❑ 80 Ken Griffey Sr. 1.25 .50
❑ 81 Pete Redfern .25 .10
❑ 82 San Francisco Giants CL 1.25 .50
❑ 83 Bob Montgomery .25 .10
❑ 84 Kent Tekulve .60 .25
❑ 85 Ron Fairly .60 .25
❑ 86 Dave Tomlin .25 .10
❑ 87 John Lowenstein .25 .10
❑ 88 Mike Phillips .25 .10
❑ 89 Ken Clay RC .25 .10
❑ 90 Larry Bowa 1.25 .50
❑ 91 Oscar Zamora .25 .10
❑ 92 Adrian Devine .25 .10
❑ 93 Bobby Cox DP .20 .08
❑ 94 Chuck Scrivener .25 .10
❑ 95 Jamie Quirk .25 .10
❑ 96 Baltimore Orioles CL 1.25 .50
❑ 97 Stan Bahnsen .25 .10
❑ 98 Jim Essian .60 .25
❑ 99 Willie Hernandez RC 1.25 .50
❑ 100 George Brett 15.00 6.00
❑ 101 Sid Monge .25 .10
❑ 102 Matt Alexander .25 .10
❑ 103 Tom Murphy .25 .10
❑ 104 Lee Lacy .25 .10
❑ 105 Reggie Cleveland .25 .10
❑ 106 Bill Plummer .25 .10
❑ 107 Ed Halicki .25 .10
❑ 108 Von Joshua .25 .10
❑ 109 Joe Torre MG .60 .25
❑ 110 Richie Zisk .25 .10
❑ 111 Mike Tyson .25 .10
❑ 112 Houston Astros CL 1.25 .50
❑ 113 Don Carrithers .25 .10
❑ 114 Paul Blair .60 .25
❑ 115 Gary Nolan .25 .10
❑ 116 Tucker Ashford RC .25 .10
❑ 117 John Montague .25 .10
❑ 118 Terry Harmon .25 .10
❑ 119 Dennis Martinez 2.50 1.00
❑ 120 Gary Carter 2.50 1.00
❑ 121 Alvis Woods .25 .10
❑ 122 Dennis Eckersley 3.00 1.25
❑ 123 Manny Trillo .25 .10
❑ 124 Dave Rozema RC .25 .10
❑ 125 George Scott .60 .25
❑ 126 Paul Moskau RC .25 .10
❑ 127 Chet Lemon .60 .25
❑ 128 Bill Russell .60 .25
❑ 129 Jim Colborn .25 .10
❑ 130 Jeff Burroughs .60 .25
❑ 131 Bert Blyleven 1.25 .50
❑ 132 Enos Cabell .25 .10
❑ 133 Jerry Augustine .25 .10
❑ 134 Steve Henderson RC .25 .10
❑ 135 Ron Guidry DP 1.25 .50
❑ 136 Ted Sizemore .25 .10
❑ 137 Craig Kusick .25 .10
❑ 138 Larry Demery .25 .10
❑ 139 Wayne Gross .25 .10
❑ 140 Rollie Fingers 2.50 1.00
❑ 141 Ruppert Jones .25 .10
❑ 142 John Montefusco .25 .10
❑ 143 Keith Hernandez .60 .25
❑ 144 Jesse Jefferson .25 .10
❑ 145 Rick Monday .60 .25
❑ 146 Doyle Alexander .60 .25
❑ 147 Lee Mazzilli .25 .10
❑ 148 Andre Thornton .60 .25
❑ 149 Dale Murray .25 .10
❑ 150 Bobby Bonds 1.25 .50
❑ 151 Milt Wilcox .25 .10
❑ 152 Ivan DeJesus RC .25 .10
❑ 153 Steve Stone .60 .25
❑ 154 Cecil Cooper DP .25 .10
❑ 155 Butch Hobson .25 .10
❑ 156 Andy Messersmith .60 .25
❑ 157 Pete LaCock DP .20 .08
❑ 158 Joaquin Andujar .60 .25
❑ 159 Lou Piniella .60 .25
❑ 160 Jim Palmer 3.00 1.25
❑ 161 Bob Boone 1.25 .50
❑ 162 Paul Thormodsgard RC .25 .10

❑ 163 Bill North .25 .10
❑ 164 Bob Owchinko RC .25 .10
❑ 165 Rennie Stennett .25 .10
❑ 166 Carlos Lopez .25 .10
❑ 167 Tim Foli .25 .10
❑ 168 Reggie Smith .60 .25
❑ 169 Jerry Johnson .25 .10
❑ 170 Lou Brock 3.00 1.25
❑ 171 Pat Zachry .25 .10
❑ 172 Mike Hargrove .60 .25
❑ 173 Robin Yount UER 5.00 2.00
❑ 174 Wayne Garland .25 .10
❑ 175 Jerry Morales .25 .10
❑ 176 Milt May .25 .10
❑ 177 Gene Garber DP .25 .10
❑ 178 Dave Chalk .25 .10
❑ 179 Dick Tidrow .25 .10
❑ 180 Dave Concepcion 1.25 .50
❑ 181 Ken Forsch .25 .10
❑ 182 Jim Spencer .25 .10
❑ 183 Doug Bird .25 .10
❑ 184 Checklist 122-242 1.25 .50
❑ 185 Ellis Valentine .25 .10
❑ 186 Bob Stanley DP RC .20 .08
❑ 187 Jerry Royster DP .20 .08
❑ 188 Al Bumbry .60 .25
❑ 189 Tom Lasorda MG DP 2.50 1.00
❑ 190 John Candelaria .60 .25
❑ 191 Rodney Scott RC .25 .10
❑ 192 San Diego Padres CL 1.25 .50
❑ 193 Rich Chiles .25 .10
❑ 194 Derrel Thomas .25 .10
❑ 195 Larry Dierker .60 .25
❑ 196 Bob Bailor .25 .10
❑ 197 Nino Espinosa .25 .10
❑ 198 Ron Pruitt .25 .10
❑ 199 Craig Reynolds .25 .10
❑ 200 Reggie Jackson 8.00 3.00
❑ 201 D.Parker/R.Carew LL 1.25 .50
❑ 202 G.Foster/J.Rice LL DP .60 .25
❑ 203 G.Foster/L.Hisle LL .60 .25
❑ 204 F.Taveras/F.Patek LL DP .25 .10
❑ 205 Carlton/Gol/Leon/Palm LL 2.50 1.00
❑ 206 P.Niekro/N.Ryan LL DP 6.00 2.50
❑ 207 J.Cand/F.Tanana LL DP .60 .25
❑ 208 R.Fingers/B.Campbell LL 1.25 .50
❑ 209 Dock Ellis .25 .10
❑ 210 Jose Cardenal .25 .10
❑ 211 Earl Weaver MG DP 1.25 .50
❑ 212 Mike Caldwell .25 .10
❑ 213 Alan Bannister .25 .10
❑ 214 California Angels CL 1.25 .50
❑ 215 Darrell Evans .60 .25
❑ 216 Mike Paxton RC .25 .10
❑ 217 Rod Gilbreath .25 .10
❑ 218 Marty Pattin .25 .10
❑ 219 Mike Cubbage .25 .10
❑ 220 Pedro Borbon .25 .10
❑ 221 Chris Speier .25 .10
❑ 222 Jerry Martin .25 .10
❑ 223 Bruce Kison .25 .10
❑ 224 Jerry Tabb RC .25 .10
❑ 225 Don Gullett DP .25 .10
❑ 226 Joe Ferguson .25 .10
❑ 227 Al Fitzmorris .25 .10
❑ 228 Manny Mota DP .25 .10
❑ 229 Leo Foster .25 .10
❑ 230 Al Hrabosky .60 .25
❑ 231 Wayne Nordhagen RC .25 .10
❑ 232 Mickey Stanley .25 .10
❑ 233 Dick Pole .25 .10
❑ 234 Herman Franks MG .25 .10
❑ 235 Tim McCarver .60 .25
❑ 236 Terry Whitfield .25 .10
❑ 237 Rich Dauer .25 .10
❑ 238 Juan Beniquez .25 .10
❑ 239 Dyar Miller .25 .10
❑ 240 Gene Tenace .60 .25
❑ 241 Pete Vuckovich .60 .25
❑ 242 Barry Bonnell DP RC .20 .08
❑ 243 Bob McClure .25 .10
❑ 244 Montreal Expos CL DP .60 .25
❑ 245 Rick Burleson .60 .25
❑ 246 Dan Driessen .25 .10
❑ 247 Larry Christenson .25 .10
❑ 248 Frank White DP .60 .25
❑ 249 Dave Goltz DP .20 .08
❑ 250 Graig Nettles DP .60 .25
❑ 251 Don Kirkwood .25 .10
❑ 252 Steve Swisher DP .20 .08
❑ 253 Jim Kern .25 .10
❑ 254 Dave Collins .60 .25
❑ 255 Jerry Reuss .60 .25
❑ 256 Joe Altobelli MG RC .25 .10
❑ 257 Hector Cruz .25 .10
❑ 258 John Hiller .25 .10
❑ 259 Los Angeles Dodgers CL 1.25 .50
❑ 260 Bert Campaneris .60 .25
❑ 261 Tim Hosley .25 .10
❑ 262 Rudy May .25 .10
❑ 263 Danny Walton .25 .10
❑ 264 Jamie Easterly .25 .10
❑ 265 Sal Bando DP .60 .25
❑ 266 Bob Shirley RC .25 .10
❑ 267 Doug Ault .25 .10
❑ 268 Gil Flores RC .25 .10
❑ 269 Wayne Twitchell .25 .10
❑ 270 Carlton Fisk 4.00 1.50
❑ 271 Randy Lerch DP .20 .08
❑ 272 Royle Stillman .25 .10
❑ 273 Fred Norman .25 .10
❑ 274 Freddie Patek .60 .25
❑ 275 Dan Ford .25 .10
❑ 276 Bill Bonham DP .20 .08
❑ 277 Bruce Boisclair .25 .10
❑ 278 Enrique Romo RC .25 .10
❑ 279 Bill Virdon MG .25 .10
❑ 280 Buddy Bell .60 .25
❑ 281 Eric Rasmussen DP .20 .08
❑ 282 New York Yankees CL 2.50 1.00
❑ 283 Omar Moreno .25 .10
❑ 284 Randy Moffitt .25 .10
❑ 285 Steve Yeager DP .60 .25
❑ 286 Ben Oglivie .60 .25
❑ 287 Kiko Garcia .25 .10
❑ 288 Dave Hamilton .25 .10
❑ 289 Checklist 243-363 1.25 .50
❑ 290 Willie Horton .60 .25
❑ 291 Gary Ross .25 .10
❑ 292 Gene Richards .25 .10
❑ 293 Mike Willis .25 .10
❑ 294 Larry Parrish .60 .25
❑ 295 Bill Lee .25 .10
❑ 296 Biff Pocoroba .25 .10
❑ 297 Warren Brusstar DP RC .20 .08
❑ 298 Tony Armas .60 .25
❑ 299 Whitey Herzog MG .60 .25
❑ 300 Joe Morgan 3.00 1.25
❑ 301 Buddy Schultz RC .25 .10
❑ 302 Chicago Cubs CL 1.25 .50
❑ 303 Sam Hinds RC .25 .10
❑ 304 John Milner .25 .10
❑ 305 Rico Carty .60 .25
❑ 306 Joe Niekro .60 .25
❑ 307 Glenn Borgmann .25 .10
❑ 308 Jim Rooker .25 .10
❑ 309 Cliff Johnson .25 .10
❑ 310 Don Sutton 2.50 1.00
❑ 311 Jose Baez DP RC .20 .08
❑ 312 Greg Minton .25 .10
❑ 313 Andy Etchebarren .25 .10
❑ 314 Paul Lindblad .25 .10
❑ 315 Mark Belanger .60 .25
❑ 316 Henry Cruz DP .20 .08
❑ 317 Dave Johnson .25 .10
❑ 318 Tom Griffin .25 .10
❑ 319 Alan Ashby .25 .10
❑ 320 Fred Lynn .60 .25
❑ 321 Santo Alcala .25 .10
❑ 322 Tom Paciorek .60 .25
❑ 323 Jim Fregosi DP .25 .10
❑ 324 Vern Rapp MG RC .25 .10
❑ 325 Bruce Sutter 3.00 1.25
❑ 326 Mike Lum DP .20 .08
❑ 327 Rick Langford DP RC .20 .08
❑ 328 Milwaukee Brewers CL 1.25 .50
❑ 329 John Verhoeven .25 .10
❑ 330 Bob Watson .60 .25
❑ 331 Mark Littell .25 .10
❑ 332 Duane Kuiper .25 .10
❑ 333 Jim Todd .25 .10
❑ 334 John Stearns .25 .10
❑ 335 Bucky Dent .60 .25
❑ 336 Steve Busby .25 .10
❑ 337 Tom Grieve .60 .25
❑ 338 Dave Heaverlo .25 .10
❑ 339 Mario Guerrero .25 .10
❑ 340 Bake McBride .60 .25
❑ 341 Mike Flanagan .60 .25
❑ 342 Aurelio Rodriguez .25 .10
❑ 343 John Wathan DP .20 .08
❑ 344 Sam Ewing RC .25 .10
❑ 345 Luis Tiant .60 .25
❑ 346 Larry Biittner .25 .10
❑ 347 Terry Forster .25 .10
❑ 348 Del Unser .25 .10
❑ 349 Rick Camp DP .20 .08
❑ 350 Steve Garvey 2.50 1.00
❑ 351 Jeff Torborg .60 .25
❑ 352 Tony Scott RC .25 .10
❑ 353 Doug Bair RC .25 .10
❑ 354 Cesar Geronimo .25 .10
❑ 355 Bill Travers .25 .10
❑ 356 New York Mets CL 1.25 .50
❑ 357 Tom Poquette .25 .10
❑ 358 Mark Lemongello .25 .10
❑ 359 Marc Hill .25 .10
❑ 360 Mike Schmidt 10.00 4.00
❑ 361 Chris Knapp .25 .10
❑ 362 Dave May .25 .10
❑ 363 Bob Randall .25 .10
❑ 364 Jerry Turner .25 .10
❑ 365 Ed Figueroa .25 .10
❑ 366 Larry Milbourne DP .20 .08
❑ 367 Rick Dempsey .60 .25
❑ 368 Balor Moore .25 .10
❑ 369 Tim Nordbrook .25 .10
❑ 370 Rusty Staub 1.25 .50
❑ 371 Ray Burris .25 .10
❑ 372 Brian Asselstine .25 .10
❑ 373 Jim Willoughby .25 .10
❑ 374 Jose Morales .25 .10
❑ 375 Tommy John 1.25 .50
❑ 376 Jim Wohlford .25 .10
❑ 377 Manny Sarmiento .25 .10
❑ 378 Bobby Winkles MG .25 .10
❑ 379 Skip Lockwood .25 .10
❑ 380 Ted Simmons .60 .25
❑ 381 Philadelphia Phillies CL 1.25 .50
❑ 382 Joe Lahoud .25 .10
❑ 383 Mario Mendoza .25 .10
❑ 384 Jack Clark 1.25 .50
❑ 385 Tito Fuentes .25 .10
❑ 386 Bob Gorinski RC .25 .10
❑ 387 Ken Holtzman .60 .25
❑ 388 Bill Fahey DP .20 .08
❑ 389 Julio Gonzalez RC .25 .10
❑ 390 Oscar Gamble .60 .25
❑ 391 Larry Haney .25 .10
❑ 392 Billy Almon .25 .10
❑ 393 Tippy Martinez .60 .25
❑ 394 Roy Howell DP .20 .08
❑ 395 Jim Hughes .25 .10
❑ 396 Bob Stinson DP .20 .08
❑ 397 Greg Gross .25 .10
❑ 398 Don Hood .25 .10
❑ 399 Pete Mackanin .25 .10
❑ 400 Nolan Ryan 25.00 10.00
❑ 401 Sparky Anderson MG .60 .25
❑ 402 Dave Campbell .25 .10
❑ 403 Bud Harrelson .60 .25
❑ 404 Detroit Tigers CL 1.25 .50
❑ 405 Rawly Eastwick .25 .10
❑ 406 Mike Jorgensen .25 .10
❑ 407 Odell Jones RC .25 .10
❑ 408 Joe Zdeb RC .25 .10
❑ 409 Ron Schueler .25 .10
❑ 410 Bill Madlock .60 .25
❑ 411 Mickey Rivers ALCS .60 .25
❑ 412 Davey Lopes NLCS .60 .25
❑ 413 Reggie Jackson WS 4.00 1.50
❑ 414 Darold Knowles DP .20 .08
❑ 415 Ray Fosse .25 .10
❑ 416 Jack Brohamer .25 .10
❑ 417 Mike Garman DP .20 .08
❑ 418 Tony Muser .25 .10
❑ 419 Jerry Garvin RC .25 .10
❑ 420 Greg Luzinski 1.25 .50

❑	421	Junior Moore RC	.25	.10
❑	422	Steve Braun	.25	.10
❑	423	Dave Rosello	.25	.10
❑	424	Boston Red Sox CL	1.25	.50
❑	425	Steve Rogers DP	.25	.10
❑	426	Fred Kendall	.25	.10
❑	427	Mario Soto RC	.60	.25
❑	428	Joel Youngblood	.25	.10
❑	429	Mike Barlow RC	.25	.10
❑	430	Al Oliver	.60	.25
❑	431	Butch Metzger	.25	.10
❑	432	Terry Bulling RC	.25	.10
❑	433	Fernando Gonzalez	.25	.10
❑	434	Mike Norris	.25	.10
❑	435	Checklist 364-484	1.25	.50
❑	436	Vic Harris DP	.20	.08
❑	437	Bo McLaughlin	.25	.10
❑	438	John Ellis	.25	.10
❑	439	Ken Kravec	.25	.10
❑	440	Dave Lopes	.60	.25
❑	441	Larry Gura	.25	.10
❑	442	Elliott Maddox	.25	.10
❑	443	Darrel Chaney	.25	.10
❑	444	Roy Hartsfield MG	.25	.10
❑	445	Mike Ivie	.25	.10
❑	446	Tug McGraw	.60	.25
❑	447	Leroy Stanton	.25	.10
❑	448	Bill Castro	.25	.10
❑	449	Tim Blackwell DP RC	.20	.08
❑	450	Tom Seaver	6.00	2.50
❑	451	Minnesota Twins CL	1.25	.50
❑	452	Jerry Mumphrey	.25	.10
❑	453	Doug Flynn	.25	.10
❑	454	Dave LaRoche	.25	.10
❑	455	Bill Robinson	.60	.25
❑	456	Vern Ruhle	.25	.10
❑	457	Bob Bailey	.25	.10
❑	458	Jeff Newman	.25	.10
❑	459	Charlie Spikes	.25	.10
❑	460	Jim Hunter	2.50	1.00
❑	461	Rob Andrews DP	.20	.08
❑	462	Rogelio Moret	.25	.10
❑	463	Kevin Bell	.25	.10
❑	464	Jerry Grote	.25	.10
❑	465	Hal McRae	.60	.25
❑	466	Dennis Blair	.25	.10
❑	467	Alvin Dark MG	.60	.25
❑	468	Warren Cromartie RC	.60	.25
❑	469	Rick Cerone	.60	.25
❑	470	J.R. Richard	.60	.25
❑	471	Roy Smalley	.60	.25
❑	472	Ron Reed	.25	.10
❑	473	Bill Buckner	.60	.25
❑	474	Jim Slaton	.25	.10
❑	475	Gary Matthews	.60	.25
❑	476	Bill Stein	.25	.10
❑	477	Doug Capilla RC	.25	.10
❑	478	Jerry Remy	.25	.10
❑	479	St. Louis Cardinals CL	1.25	.50
❑	480	Ron LeFlore	.60	.25
❑	481	Jackson Todd RC	.25	.10
❑	482	Rick Miller	.25	.10
❑	483	Ken Macha RC	.25	.10
❑	484	Jim Norris RC	.25	.10
❑	485	Chris Chambliss	.60	.25
❑	486	John Curtis	.25	.10
❑	487	Jim Tyrone	.25	.10
❑	488	Dan Spillner	.25	.10
❑	489	Rudy Meoli	.25	.10
❑	490	Amos Otis	.60	.25
❑	491	Scott McGregor	.60	.25
❑	492	Jim Sundberg	.60	.25
❑	493	Steve Renko	.25	.10
❑	494	Chuck Tanner MG	.60	.25
❑	495	Dave Cash	.25	.10
❑	496	Jim Clancy DP RC	.20	.08
❑	497	Glenn Adams	.25	.10
❑	498	Joe Sambito	.25	.10
❑	499	Seattle Mariners CL	1.25	.50
❑	500	George Foster	1.25	.50
❑	501	Dave Roberts	.25	.10
❑	502	Pat Rockett RC	.25	.10
❑	503	Ike Hampton RC	.25	.10
❑	504	Roger Freed	.25	.10
❑	505	Felix Millan	.25	.10
❑	506	Ron Blomberg	.25	.10
❑	507	Willie Crawford	.25	.10
❑	508	Johnny Oates	.60	.25
❑	509	Brent Strom	.25	.10
❑	510	Willie Stargell	2.50	1.00
❑	511	Frank Duffy	.25	.10
❑	512	Larry Herndon	.25	.10
❑	513	Barry Foote	.25	.10
❑	514	Rob Sperring	.25	.10
❑	515	Tim Corcoran RC	.25	.10
❑	516	Gary Beare RC	.25	.10
❑	517	Andres Mora	.25	.10
❑	518	Tommy Boggs DP	.20	.08
❑	519	Brian Downing	.60	.25
❑	520	Larry Hisle	.25	.10
❑	521	Steve Staggs RC	.25	.10
❑	522	Dick Williams MG	.60	.25
❑	523	Donnie Moore RC	.25	.10
❑	524	Bernie Carbo	.25	.10
❑	525	Jerry Terrell	.25	.10
❑	526	Cincinnati Reds CL	1.25	.50
❑	527	Vic Correll	.25	.10
❑	528	Rob Picciolo RC	.25	.10
❑	529	Paul Hartzell	.25	.10
❑	530	Dave Winfield	4.00	1.50
❑	531	Tom Underwood	.25	.10
❑	532	Skip Jutze	.25	.10
❑	533	Sandy Alomar	.60	.25
❑	534	Wilbur Howard	.25	.10
❑	535	Checklist 485-605	1.25	.50
❑	536	Roric Harrison	.25	.10
❑	537	Bruce Bochte	.25	.10
❑	538	Johnny LeMaster	.25	.10
❑	539	Vic Davalillo DP	.20	.08
❑	540	Steve Carlton	4.00	1.50
❑	541	Larry Cox	.25	.10
❑	542	Tim Johnson	.25	.10
❑	543	Larry Harlow DP RC	.20	.08
❑	544	Len Randle DP	.20	.08
❑	545	Bill Campbell	.25	.10
❑	546	Ted Martinez	.25	.10
❑	547	John Scott	.25	.10
❑	548	Billy Hunter MG DP	.20	.08
❑	549	Joe Kerrigan	.25	.10
❑	550	John Mayberry	.60	.25
❑	551	Atlanta Braves CL	1.25	.50
❑	552	Francisco Barrios	.25	.10
❑	553	Terry Puhl RC	.60	.25
❑	554	Joe Coleman	.25	.10
❑	555	Butch Wynegar	.25	.10
❑	556	Ed Armbrister	.25	.10
❑	557	Tony Solaita	.25	.10
❑	558	Paul Mitchell	.25	.10
❑	559	Phil Mankowski	.25	.10
❑	560	Dave Parker	1.25	.50
❑	561	Charlie Williams	.25	.10
❑	562	Glenn Burke RC	.25	.10
❑	563	Dave Rader	.25	.10
❑	564	Mick Kelleher	.25	.10
❑	565	Jerry Koosman	.60	.25
❑	566	Merv Rettenmund	.25	.10
❑	567	Dick Drago	.25	.10
❑	568	Tom Hutton	.25	.10
❑	569	Lary Sorensen RC	.25	.10
❑	570	Dave Kingman	1.25	.50
❑	571	Buck Martinez	.25	.10
❑	572	Rick Wise	.25	.10
❑	573	Luis Gomez	.25	.10
❑	574	Bob Lemon MG	1.25	.50
❑	575	Pat Dobson	.25	.10
❑	576	Sam Mejias	.25	.10
❑	577	Oakland Athletics CL	1.25	.50
❑	578	Buzz Capra	.25	.10
❑	579	Rance Mulliniks RC	.25	.10
❑	580	Rod Carew	4.00	1.50
❑	581	Lynn McGlothen	.25	.10
❑	582	Fran Healy	.25	.10
❑	583	George Medich	.25	.10
❑	584	John Hale	.25	.10
❑	585	Woodie Fryman DP	.20	.08
❑	586	Ed Goodson	.25	.10
❑	587	John Urrea RC	.25	.10
❑	588	Jim Mason	.25	.10
❑	589	Bob Knepper RC	.25	.10
❑	590	Bobby Murcer	.60	.25
❑	591	George Zeber RC	.25	.10
❑	592	Bob Apodaca	.25	.10
❑	593	Dave Skaggs RC	.25	.10
❑	594	Dave Freisleben	.25	.10
❑	595	Sixto Lezcano	.25	.10
❑	596	Gary Wheelock	.25	.10
❑	597	Steve Dillard	.25	.10
❑	598	Eddie Solomon	.25	.10
❑	599	Gary Woods	.25	.10
❑	600	Frank Tanana	.60	.25
❑	601	Gene Mauch MG	.60	.25
❑	602	Eric Soderholm	.25	.10
❑	603	Will McEnaney	.25	.10
❑	604	Earl Williams	.25	.10
❑	605	Rick Rhoden	.60	.25
❑	606	Pittsburgh Pirates CL	1.25	.50
❑	607	Fernando Arroyo	.25	.10
❑	608	Johnny Grubb	.25	.10
❑	609	John Denny	.25	.10
❑	610	Garry Maddox	.60	.25
❑	611	Pat Scanlon RC	.25	.10
❑	612	Ken Henderson	.25	.10
❑	613	Marty Perez	.25	.10
❑	614	Joe Wallis	.25	.10
❑	615	Clay Carroll	.25	.10
❑	616	Pat Kelly	.25	.10
❑	617	Joe Nolan RC	.25	.10
❑	618	Tommy Helms	.25	.10
❑	619	Thad Bosley DP RC	.20	.08
❑	620	Willie Randolph	1.25	.50
❑	621	Craig Swan DP	.20	.08
❑	622	Champ Summers	.25	.10
❑	623	Eduardo Rodriguez	.25	.10
❑	624	Gary Alexander DP	.20	.08
❑	625	Jose Cruz	.60	.25
❑	626	Toronto Blue Jays CL DP	1.25	.50
❑	627	David Johnson	.25	.10
❑	628	Ralph Garr	.60	.25
❑	629	Don Stanhouse	.25	.10
❑	630	Ron Cey	1.25	.50
❑	631	Danny Ozark MG	.25	.10
❑	632	Rowland Office	.25	.10
❑	633	Tom Veryzer	.25	.10
❑	634	Len Barker	.25	.10
❑	635	Joe Rudi	.60	.25
❑	636	Jim Bibby	.25	.10
❑	637	Duffy Dyer	.25	.10
❑	638	Paul Splittorff	.25	.10
❑	639	Gene Clines	.25	.10
❑	640	Lee May DP	.25	.10
❑	641	Doug Rau	.25	.10
❑	642	Denny Doyle	.25	.10
❑	643	Tom House	.25	.10
❑	644	Jim Dwyer	.25	.10
❑	645	Mike Torrez	.60	.25
❑	646	Rick Auerbach DP	.20	.08
❑	647	Steve Dunning	.25	.10
❑	648	Gary Thomasson	.25	.10
❑	649	Moose Haas RC	.25	.10
❑	650	Cesar Cedeno	.60	.25
❑	651	Doug Rader	.25	.10
❑	652	Checklist 606-726	1.25	.50
❑	653	Ron Hodges DP	.20	.08
❑	654	Pepe Frias	.25	.10
❑	655	Lyman Bostock	.60	.25
❑	656	Dave Garcia MG RC	.25	.10
❑	657	Bombo Rivera	.25	.10
❑	658	Manny Sanguillen	.60	.25
❑	659	Texas Rangers CL	1.25	.50
❑	660	Jason Thompson	.60	.25
❑	661	Grant Jackson	.25	.10
❑	662	Paul Dade RC	.25	.10
❑	663	Paul Reuschel	.25	.10
❑	664	Fred Stanley	.25	.10
❑	665	Dennis Leonard	.60	.25
❑	666	Billy Smith RC	.25	.10
❑	667	Jeff Byrd RC	.25	.10
❑	668	Dusty Baker	1.25	.50
❑	669	Pete Falcone	.25	.10
❑	670	Jim Rice	1.25	.50
❑	671	Gary Lavelle	.25	.10
❑	672	Don Kessinger	.60	.25
❑	673	Steve Brye	.25	.10
❑	674	Ray Knight RC	2.50	1.00
❑	675	Jay Johnstone	.60	.25
❑	676	Bob Myrick	.25	.10
❑	677	Ed Herrmann	.25	.10
❑	678	Tom Burgmeier	.25	.10

❑ 679 Wayne Garrett .25 .10
❑ 680 Vida Blue .60 .25
❑ 681 Rob Belloir .25 .10
❑ 682 Ken Brett .25 .10
❑ 683 Mike Champion .25 .10
❑ 684 Ralph Houk MG .60 .25
❑ 685 Frank Taveras .25 .10
❑ 686 Gaylord Perry 2.50 1.00
❑ 687 Julio Cruz RC .25 .10
❑ 688 George Mitterwald .25 .10
❑ 689 Cleveland Indians CL 1.25 .50
❑ 690 Mickey Rivers .60 .25
❑ 691 Ross Grimsley .25 .10
❑ 692 Ken Reitz .25 .10
❑ 693 Lamar Johnson .25 .10
❑ 694 Elias Sosa .25 .10
❑ 695 Dwight Evans 1.25 .50
❑ 696 Steve Mingori .25 .10
❑ 697 Roger Metzger .25 .10
❑ 698 Juan Bernhardt .25 .10
❑ 699 Jackie Brown .25 .10
❑ 700 Johnny Bench 8.00 3.00
❑ 701 Hume/Land/McC/Tay RC .60 .25
❑ 702 Nah/Pas/Sweet/Wer RC .60 .25
❑ 703 Jack Morris DP RC 5.00 2.00
❑ 704 Lou Whitaker RC 8.00 3.00
❑ 705 Berg/Milone/Hurdle/Nor RC 1.25 .50
❑ 706 Cage/Cox/Put/Rev RC .60 .25
❑ 707 P.Molitor RC/A.Trammell RC 50.00 20.00
❑ 708 D.Murphy/L.Parrish RC 4.00 1.50
❑ 709 Burke/Keough/Rau/Schat RC .60 .25
❑ 710 Alston/Bos/Easler/Smith RC 1.25 .50
❑ 711 Camp/Lamp/Mit/Tho DP RC .25 .10
❑ 712 Bobby Valentine .60 .25
❑ 713 Bob Davis .25 .10
❑ 714 Mike Anderson .25 .10
❑ 715 Jim Kaat 1.25 .50
❑ 716 Clarence Gaston .60 .25
❑ 717 Nelson Briles .25 .10
❑ 718 Ron Jackson .25 .10
❑ 719 Randy Elliott RC .25 .10
❑ 720 Fergie Jenkins 2.50 1.00
❑ 721 Billy Martin MG 1.25 .50
❑ 722 Pete Broberg .25 .10
❑ 723 John Wockenfuss .25 .10
❑ 724 Kansas City Royals CL 1.25 .50
❑ 725 Kurt Bevacqua .25 .10
❑ 726 Wilbur Wood 1.25 .50

1979 Topps

❑ COMPLETE SET (726) 200.00 100.00
❑ COMMON CARD (1-726) .25 .10
❑ COMMON CARD DP .20 .08
❑ 1 R.Carew/D.Parker LL 2.50 1.00
❑ 2 J.Rice/G.Foster LL 1.50 .60
❑ 3 J.Rice/G.Foster LL 1.50 .60
❑ 4 R.LeFlore/O.Moreno LL .75 .30
❑ 5 R.Guidry/G.Perry LL .75 .30
❑ 6 N.Ryan/J.Richard LL 5.00 2.00
❑ 7 R.Guidry/C.Swan LL .75 .30
❑ 8 R.Gossage/R.Fingers LL 1.50 .60
❑ 9 Dave Campbell .25 .10
❑ 10 Lee May .75 .30
❑ 11 Marc Hill .25 .10
❑ 12 Dick Drago .25 .10
❑ 13 Paul Dade .25 .10
❑ 14 Rafael Landestoy RC .25 .10
❑ 15 Ross Grimsley .25 .10
❑ 16 Fred Stanley .25 .10
❑ 17 Donnie Moore .25 .10
❑ 18 Tony Solaita .25 .10
❑ 19 Larry Gura DP .20 .08
❑ 20 Joe Morgan DP 2.50 1.00
❑ 21 Kevin Kobel .25 .10
❑ 22 Mike Jorgensen .25 .10
❑ 23 Terry Forster .25 .10
❑ 24 Paul Molitor 10.00 4.00
❑ 25 Steve Carlton 3.00 1.25
❑ 26 Jamie Quirk .25 .10
❑ 27 Dave Goltz .25 .10
❑ 28 Steve Brye .25 .10
❑ 29 Rick Langford .25 .10
❑ 30 Dave Winfield 4.00 1.50
❑ 31 Tom House DP .20 .08
❑ 32 Jerry Mumphrey .25 .10
❑ 33 Dave Rozema .25 .10
❑ 34 Rob Andrews .25 .10
❑ 35 Ed Figueroa .25 .10
❑ 36 Alan Ashby .25 .10
❑ 37 Joe Kerrigan DP .20 .08
❑ 38 Bernie Carbo .25 .10
❑ 39 Dale Murphy 3.00 1.25
❑ 40 Dennis Eckersley 2.50 1.00
❑ 41 Minnesota Twins CL/Mauch 1.50 .60
❑ 42 Ron Blomberg .25 .10
❑ 43 Wayne Twitchell .25 .10
❑ 44 Kurt Bevacqua .25 .10
❑ 45 Al Hrabosky .75 .30
❑ 46 Ron Hodges .25 .10
❑ 47 Fred Norman .25 .10
❑ 48 Merv Rettenmund .25 .10
❑ 49 Vern Ruhle .25 .10
❑ 50 Steve Garvey DP 1.50 .60
❑ 51 Ray Fosse DP .20 .08
❑ 52 Randy Lerch .25 .10
❑ 53 Mick Kelleher .25 .10
❑ 54 Dell Alston DP .20 .08
❑ 55 Willie Stargell 2.50 1.00
❑ 56 John Hale .25 .10
❑ 57 Eric Rasmussen .25 .10
❑ 58 Bob Randall DP .20 .08
❑ 59 John Denny DP .25 .10
❑ 60 Mickey Rivers .75 .30
❑ 61 Bo Diaz .25 .10
❑ 62 Randy Moffitt .25 .10
❑ 63 Jack Brohamer .25 .10
❑ 64 Tom Underwood .25 .10
❑ 65 Mark Belanger .75 .30
❑ 66 Detroit Tigers CL/Moss 1.50 .60
❑ 67 Jim Mason DP .20 .08
❑ 68 Joe Niekro DP .25 .10
❑ 69 Elliott Maddox .25 .10
❑ 70 John Candelaria .75 .30
❑ 71 Brian Downing .75 .30
❑ 72 Steve Mingori .25 .10
❑ 73 Ken Henderson .25 .10
❑ 74 Shane Rawley RC .25 .10
❑ 75 Steve Yeager .75 .30
❑ 76 Warren Cromartie .75 .30
❑ 77 Dan Briggs DP .20 .08
❑ 78 Elias Sosa .25 .10
❑ 79 Ted Cox .25 .10
❑ 80 Jason Thompson .75 .30
❑ 81 Roger Erickson RC .25 .10
❑ 82 New York Mets CL/Torre 1.50 .60
❑ 83 Fred Kendall .25 .10
❑ 84 Greg Minton .25 .10
❑ 85 Gary Matthews .75 .30
❑ 86 Rodney Scott .25 .10
❑ 87 Pete Falcone .25 .10
❑ 88 Bob Molinaro RC .25 .10
❑ 89 Dick Tidrow .25 .10
❑ 90 Bob Boone 1.50 .60
❑ 91 Terry Crowley .25 .10
❑ 92 Jim Bibby .25 .10
❑ 93 Phil Mankowski .25 .10
❑ 94 Len Barker .25 .10
❑ 95 Robin Yount 5.00 2.00
❑ 96 Cleveland Indians CL/Torborg 1.50 .60
❑ 97 Sam Mejias .25 .10
❑ 98 Ray Burris .25 .10
❑ 99 John Wathan .75 .30
❑ 100 Tom Seaver DP 4.00 1.50
❑ 101 Roy Howell .25 .10
❑ 102 Mike Anderson .25 .10
❑ 103 Jim Todd .25 .10
❑ 104 Johnny Oates DP .25 .10
❑ 105 Rick Camp DP .20 .08
❑ 106 Frank Duffy .25 .10
❑ 107 Jesus Alou DP .20 .08
❑ 108 Eduardo Rodriguez .25 .10
❑ 109 Joel Youngblood .25 .10
❑ 110 Vida Blue .75 .30
❑ 111 Roger Freed .25 .10
❑ 112 Philadelphia Phillies CL/Ozark 1.50 .60
❑ 113 Pete Redfern .25 .10
❑ 114 Cliff Johnson .25 .10
❑ 115 Nolan Ryan 20.00 8.00
❑ 116 Ozzie Smith RC 60.00 30.00
❑ 117 Grant Jackson .25 .10
❑ 118 Bud Harrelson .75 .30
❑ 119 Don Stanhouse .25 .10
❑ 120 Jim Sundberg .75 .30
❑ 121 Checklist 1-121 DP .75 .30
❑ 122 Mike Paxton .25 .10
❑ 123 Lou Whitaker 2.50 1.00
❑ 124 Dan Schatzeder .25 .10
❑ 125 Rick Burleson .25 .10
❑ 126 Doug Bair .25 .10
❑ 127 Thad Bosley .25 .10
❑ 128 Ted Martinez .25 .10
❑ 129 Marty Pattin DP .20 .08
❑ 130 Bob Watson DP .25 .10
❑ 131 Jim Clancy .25 .10
❑ 132 Rowland Office .25 .10
❑ 133 Bill Castro .25 .10
❑ 134 Alan Bannister .25 .10
❑ 135 Bobby Murcer .75 .30
❑ 136 Jim Kaat .75 .30
❑ 137 Larry Wolfe DP RC .20 .08
❑ 138 Mark Lee RC .25 .10
❑ 139 Luis Pujols RC .25 .10
❑ 140 Don Gullett .75 .30
❑ 141 Tom Paciorek .75 .30
❑ 142 Charlie Williams .25 .10
❑ 143 Tony Scott .25 .10
❑ 144 Sandy Alomar .25 .10
❑ 145 Rick Rhoden .25 .10
❑ 146 Duane Kuiper .25 .10
❑ 147 Dave Hamilton .25 .10
❑ 148 Bruce Boisclair .25 .10
❑ 149 Manny Sarmiento .25 .10
❑ 150 Wayne Cage .25 .10
❑ 151 John Hiller .25 .10
❑ 152 Rick Cerone .25 .10
❑ 153 Dennis Lamp .25 .10
❑ 154 Jim Gantner DP .25 .10
❑ 155 Dwight Evans 1.50 .60
❑ 156 Buddy Solomon RC .25 .10
❑ 157 U.L. Washington UER .25 .10
❑ 158 Joe Sambito .25 .10
❑ 159 Roy White .75 .30
❑ 160 Mike Flanagan 1.50 .60
❑ 161 Barry Foote .25 .10
❑ 162 Tom Johnson .25 .10
❑ 163 Glenn Burke .25 .10
❑ 164 Mickey Lolich .75 .30
❑ 165 Frank Taveras .25 .10
❑ 166 Leon Roberts .25 .10
❑ 167 Roger Metzger DP .20 .08
❑ 168 Dave Freisleben .25 .10
❑ 169 Bill Nahorodny .25 .10
❑ 170 Don Sutton 2.50 1.00
❑ 171 Gene Clines .25 .10
❑ 172 Mike Bruhert RC .25 .10
❑ 173 John Lowenstein .25 .10
❑ 174 Rick Auerbach .25 .10
❑ 175 George Hendrick 1.50 .60
❑ 176 Aurelio Rodriguez .25 .10
❑ 177 Ron Reed .25 .10
❑ 178 Alvis Woods .25 .10
❑ 179 Jim Beattie DP RC .20 .08
❑ 180 Larry Hisle .25 .10
❑ 181 Mike Garman .25 .10
❑ 182 Tim Johnson .25 .10
❑ 183 Paul Splittorff .25 .10
❑ 184 Darrel Chaney .25 .10
❑ 185 Mike Torrez .75 .30
❑ 186 Eric Soderholm .25 .10
❑ 187 Mark Lemongello .25 .10

❑ 188 Pat Kelly .25 .10
❑ 189 Ed Whitson RC .25 .10
❑ 190 Ron Cey .75 .30
❑ 191 Mike Norris .25 .10
❑ 192 St. Louis Cardinals CL/Boyer 1.50 .60
❑ 193 Glenn Adams .25 .10
❑ 194 Randy Jones .25 .10
❑ 195 Bill Madlock .75 .30
❑ 196 Steve Kemp DP .25 .10
❑ 197 Bob Apodaca .25 .10
❑ 198 Johnny Grubb .25 .10
❑ 199 Larry Milbourne .25 .10
❑ 200 Johnny Bench DP 5.00 2.00
❑ 201 Mike Edwards RB .25 .10
❑ 202 Ron Guidry RB .75 .30
❑ 203 J.R. Richard RB .25 .10
❑ 204 Pete Rose RB 5.00 2.00
❑ 205 John Stearns RB .25 .10
❑ 206 Sammy Stewart RB .25 .10
❑ 207 Dave Lemanczyk .25 .10
❑ 208 Clarence Gaston .25 .10
❑ 209 Reggie Cleveland .25 .10
❑ 210 Larry Bowa .75 .30
❑ 211 Dennis Martinez 2.50 1.00
❑ 212 Carney Lansford RC 1.50 .60
❑ 213 Bill Travers .25 .10
❑ 214 Boston Red Sox CL/Zimmer 1.50 .60
❑ 215 Willie McCovey 2.50 1.00
❑ 216 Wilbur Wood .25 .10
❑ 217 Steve Dillard .25 .10
❑ 218 Dennis Leonard .75 .30
❑ 219 Roy Smalley .75 .30
❑ 220 Cesar Geronimo .25 .10
❑ 221 Jesse Jefferson .25 .10
❑ 222 Bob Beall RC .25 .10
❑ 223 Kent Tekulve .75 .30
❑ 224 Dave Revering .25 .10
❑ 225 Goose Gossage 1.50 .60
❑ 226 Ron Pruitt .25 .10
❑ 227 Steve Stone .75 .30
❑ 228 Vic Davalillo .25 .10
❑ 229 Doug Flynn .25 .10
❑ 230 Bob Forsch .25 .10
❑ 231 John Wockenfuss .25 .10
❑ 232 Jimmy Sexton RC .25 .10
❑ 233 Paul Mitchell .25 .10
❑ 234 Toby Harrah .75 .30
❑ 235 Steve Rogers .25 .10
❑ 236 Jim Dwyer .25 .10
❑ 237 Billy Smith .25 .10
❑ 238 Balor Moore .25 .10
❑ 239 Willie Horton .75 .30
❑ 240 Rick Reuschel .75 .30
❑ 241 Checklist 122-242 DP .75 .30
❑ 242 Pablo Torrealba .25 .10
❑ 243 Buck Martinez DP .20 .08
❑ 244 Pittsburgh Pirates CL/Tanner 1.50 .60
❑ 245 Jeff Burroughs .75 .30
❑ 246 Darrell Jackson RC .25 .10
❑ 247 Tucker Ashford DP .20 .08
❑ 248 Pete LaCock .25 .10
❑ 249 Paul Thormodsgard .25 .10
❑ 250 Willie Randolph .75 .30
❑ 251 Jack Morris 2.50 1.00
❑ 252 Bob Stinson .25 .10
❑ 253 Rick Wise .25 .10
❑ 254 Luis Gomez .25 .10
❑ 255 Tommy John 1.50 .60
❑ 256 Mike Sadek .25 .10
❑ 257 Adrian Devine .25 .10
❑ 258 Mike Phillips .25 .10
❑ 259 Cincinnati Reds CL/Anderson 1.50 .60
❑ 260 Richie Zisk .25 .10
❑ 261 Mario Guerrero .25 .10
❑ 262 Nelson Briles .25 .10
❑ 263 Oscar Gamble .75 .30
❑ 264 Don Robinson RC .25 .10
❑ 265 Don Money .25 .10
❑ 266 Jim Willoughby .25 .10
❑ 267 Joe Rudi .75 .30
❑ 268 Julio Gonzalez .25 .10
❑ 269 Woodie Fryman .25 .10
❑ 270 Butch Hobson .75 .30
❑ 271 Rawly Eastwick .25 .10
❑ 272 Tim Corcoran .25 .10
❑ 273 Jerry Terrell .25 .10
❑ 274 Willie Norwood .25 .10
❑ 275 Junior Moore .25 .10
❑ 276 Jim Colborn .25 .10
❑ 277 Tom Grieve .75 .30
❑ 278 Andy Messersmith .75 .30
❑ 279 Jerry Grote DP .20 .08
❑ 280 Andre Thornton .75 .30
❑ 281 Vic Correll DP .20 .08
❑ 282 Toronto Blue Jays CL/Hartsfield .75 .30
❑ 283 Ken Kravec .25 .10
❑ 284 Johnnie LeMaster .25 .10
❑ 285 Bobby Bonds 1.50 .60
❑ 286 Duffy Dyer .25 .10
❑ 287 Andres Mora .25 .10
❑ 288 Milt Wilcox .25 .10
❑ 289 Jose Cruz 1.50 .60
❑ 290 Dave Lopes .75 .30
❑ 291 Tom Griffin .25 .10
❑ 292 Don Reynolds RC .25 .10
❑ 293 Jerry Garvin .25 .10
❑ 294 Pepe Frias .25 .10
❑ 295 Mitchell Page .25 .10
❑ 296 Preston Hanna RC .25 .10
❑ 297 Ted Sizemore .25 .10
❑ 298 Rich Gale RC .25 .10
❑ 299 Steve Ontiveros .25 .10
❑ 300 Rod Carew 3.00 1.25
❑ 301 Tom Hume .25 .10
❑ 302 Atlanta Braves CL/Cox 1.50 .60
❑ 303 Lary Sorensen DP .20 .08
❑ 304 Steve Swisher .25 .10
❑ 305 Willie Montanez .25 .10
❑ 306 Floyd Bannister .25 .10
❑ 307 Larvell Blanks .25 .10
❑ 308 Bert Blyleven 1.50 .60
❑ 309 Ralph Garr .75 .30
❑ 310 Thurman Munson 3.00 1.25
❑ 311 Gary Lavelle .25 .10
❑ 312 Bob Robertson .25 .10
❑ 313 Dyar Miller .25 .10
❑ 314 Larry Harlow .25 .10
❑ 315 Jon Matlack .25 .10
❑ 316 Milt May .25 .10
❑ 317 Jose Cardenal .75 .30
❑ 318 Bob Welch RC 2.50 1.00
❑ 319 Wayne Garrett .25 .10
❑ 320 Carl Yastrzemski 5.00 2.00
❑ 321 Gaylord Perry 2.50 1.00
❑ 322 Danny Goodwin RC .25 .10
❑ 323 Lynn McGlothen .25 .10
❑ 324 Mike Tyson .25 .10
❑ 325 Cecil Cooper .75 .30
❑ 326 Pedro Borbon .25 .10
❑ 327 Art Howe DP .25 .10
❑ 328 Oakland Athletics CL/McKeon 1.50 .60
❑ 329 Joe Coleman .25 .10
❑ 330 George Brett 10.00 4.00
❑ 331 Mickey Mahler .25 .10
❑ 332 Gary Alexander .25 .10
❑ 333 Chet Lemon .75 .30
❑ 334 Craig Swan .25 .10
❑ 335 Chris Chambliss .75 .30
❑ 336 Bobby Thompson RC .25 .10
❑ 337 John Montague .25 .10
❑ 338 Vic Harris .25 .10
❑ 339 Ron Jackson .25 .10
❑ 340 Jim Palmer 2.50 1.00
❑ 341 Willie Upshaw RC .75 .30
❑ 342 Dave Roberts .25 .10
❑ 343 Ed Glynn .25 .10
❑ 344 Jerry Royster .25 .10
❑ 345 Tug McGraw .75 .30
❑ 346 Bill Buckner .75 .30
❑ 347 Doug Rau .25 .10
❑ 348 Andre Dawson 3.00 1.25
❑ 349 Jim Wright RC .25 .10
❑ 350 Garry Templeton .75 .30
❑ 351 Wayne Nordhagen DP .20 .08
❑ 352 Steve Renko .25 .10
❑ 353 Checklist 243-363 1.50 .60
❑ 354 Bill Bonham .25 .10
❑ 355 Lee Mazzilli .25 .10
❑ 356 San Francisco Giants CL/Altobelli 1.50 .60
❑ 357 Jerry Augustine .25 .10
❑ 358 Alan Trammell 3.00 1.25
❑ 359 Dan Spillner DP .20 .08
❑ 360 Amos Otis .75 .30
❑ 361 Tom Dixon RC .25 .10
❑ 362 Mike Cubbage .25 .10
❑ 363 Craig Skok RC .25 .10
❑ 364 Gene Richards .25 .10
❑ 365 Sparky Lyle .75 .30
❑ 366 Juan Bernhardt .25 .10
❑ 367 Dave Skaggs .25 .10
❑ 368 Don Aase .25 .10
❑ 369A Bump Wills ERR 3.00 1.25
❑ 369B Bump Wills COR 3.00 1.25
❑ 370 Dave Kingman 1.50 .60
❑ 371 Jeff Holly RC .25 .10
❑ 372 Lamar Johnson .25 .10
❑ 373 Lance Rautzhan .25 .10
❑ 374 Ed Herrmann .25 .10
❑ 375 Bill Campbell .25 .10
❑ 376 Gorman Thomas .75 .30
❑ 377 Paul Moskau .25 .10
❑ 378 Rob Picciolo DP .20 .08
❑ 379 Dale Murray .25 .10
❑ 380 John Mayberry .75 .30
❑ 381 Houston Astros CL/Virdon 1.50 .60
❑ 382 Jerry Martin .25 .10
❑ 383 Phil Garner .75 .30
❑ 384 Tommy Boggs .25 .10
❑ 385 Dan Ford .25 .10
❑ 386 Francisco Barrios .25 .10
❑ 387 Gary Thomasson .25 .10
❑ 388 Jack Billingham .25 .10
❑ 389 Joe Zdeb .25 .10
❑ 390 Rollie Fingers 2.50 1.00
❑ 391 Al Oliver .75 .30
❑ 392 Doug Ault .25 .10
❑ 393 Scott McGregor .75 .30
❑ 394 Randy Stein RC .25 .10
❑ 395 Dave Cash .25 .10
❑ 396 Bill Plummer .25 .10
❑ 397 Sergio Ferrer RC .25 .10
❑ 398 Ivan DeJesus .25 .10
❑ 399 David Clyde .25 .10
❑ 400 Jim Rice 1.50 .60
❑ 401 Ray Knight .75 .30
❑ 402 Paul Hartzell .25 .10
❑ 403 Tim Foli .25 .10
❑ 404 Chicago White Sox CL/Kessinger 1.50 .60
❑ 405 Butch Wynegar DP .20 .08
❑ 406 Joe Wallis DP .20 .08
❑ 407 Pete Vuckovich .75 .30
❑ 408 Charlie Moore DP .20 .08
❑ 409 Willie Wilson RC 1.50 .60
❑ 410 Darrell Evans 1.50 .60
❑ 411 G.Sisler/T.Cobb ATL 2.50 1.00
❑ 412 H.Wilson/H.Aaron ATL 2.50 1.00
❑ 413 R.Maris/H.Aaron ATL 4.00 1.50
❑ 414 R.Hornsby/T.Cobb ATL 2.50 1.00
❑ 415 L.Brock/L.Brock ATL 1.50 .60
❑ 416 J.Chesbro/C.Young ATL .75 .30
❑ 417 N.Ryan/W.Johnson ATL DP 5.00 2.00
❑ 418 D.Leonard/W.Johnson ATL DP .25 .10
❑ 419 Dick Ruthven .25 .10
❑ 420 Ken Griffey Sr. .75 .30
❑ 421 Doug DeCinces .75 .30
❑ 422 Ruppert Jones .25 .10
❑ 423 Bob Montgomery .25 .10
❑ 424 California Angels CL/Fregosi 1.50 .60
❑ 425 Rick Manning .25 .10
❑ 426 Chris Speier .25 .10
❑ 427 Andy Replogle RC .25 .10
❑ 428 Bobby Valentine .75 .30
❑ 429 John Urrea DP .20 .08
❑ 430 Dave Parker .75 .30
❑ 431 Glenn Borgmann .25 .10
❑ 432 Dave Heaverlo .25 .10
❑ 433 Larry Biittner .25 .10
❑ 434 Ken Clay .25 .10
❑ 435 Gene Tenace .75 .30
❑ 436 Hector Cruz .25 .10
❑ 437 Rick Williams RC .25 .10
❑ 438 Horace Speed RC .25 .10
❑ 439 Frank White .75 .30
❑ 440 Rusty Staub 1.50 .60
❑ 441 Lee Lacy .25 .10
❑ 442 Doyle Alexander .25 .10
❑ 443 Bruce Bochte .25 .10
❑ 444 Aurelio Lopez RC .25 .10

❑ 445 Steve Henderson	.25	.10
❑ 446 Jim Lonborg	.75	.30
❑ 447 Manny Sanguillen	.75	.30
❑ 448 Moose Haas	.25	.10
❑ 449 Bombo Rivera	.25	.10
❑ 450 Dave Concepcion	1.50	.60
❑ 451 Kansas City Royals CL/Herzog	1.50	.60
❑ 452 Jerry Morales	.25	.10
❑ 453 Chris Knapp	.25	.10
❑ 454 Len Randle	.25	.10
❑ 455 Bill Lee DP	.20	.08
❑ 456 Chuck Baker RC	.25	.10
❑ 457 Bruce Sutter	2.50	1.00
❑ 458 Jim Essian	.25	.10
❑ 459 Sid Monge	.25	.10
❑ 460 Graig Nettles	1.50	.60
❑ 461 Jim Barr DP	.20	.08
❑ 462 Otto Velez	.25	.10
❑ 463 Steve Comer RC	.25	.10
❑ 464 Joe Nolan	.25	.10
❑ 465 Reggie Smith	.75	.30
❑ 466 Mark Littell	.25	.10
❑ 467 Don Kessinger DP	.25	.10
❑ 468 Stan Bahnsen DP	.20	.08
❑ 469 Lance Parrish	1.50	.60
❑ 470 Garry Maddox DP	.25	.10
❑ 471 Joaquin Andujar	.75	.30
❑ 472 Craig Kusick	.25	.10
❑ 473 Dave Roberts	.25	.10
❑ 474 Dick Davis RC	.25	.10
❑ 475 Dan Driessen	.25	.10
❑ 476 Tom Poquette	.25	.10
❑ 477 Bob Grich	.75	.30
❑ 478 Juan Beniquez	.25	.10
❑ 479 San Diego Padres CL/Craig	1.50	.60
❑ 480 Fred Lynn	.75	.30
❑ 481 Skip Lockwood	.25	.10
❑ 482 Craig Reynolds	.25	.10
❑ 483 Checklist 364-484 DP	.75	.30
❑ 484 Rick Waits	.25	.10
❑ 485 Bucky Dent	.75	.30
❑ 486 Bob Knepper	.25	.10
❑ 487 Miguel Dilone	.25	.10
❑ 488 Bob Owchinko	.25	.10
❑ 489 Larry Cox UER	.25	.10
❑ 490 Al Cowens	.75	.30
❑ 491 Tippy Martinez	.25	.10
❑ 492 Bob Bailor	.25	.10
❑ 493 Larry Christenson	.25	.10
❑ 494 Jerry White	.25	.10
❑ 495 Tony Perez	2.50	1.00
❑ 496 Barry Bonnell DP	.20	.08
❑ 497 Glenn Abbott	.25	.10
❑ 498 Rich Chiles	.25	.10
❑ 499 Texas Rangers CL/Corrrales	1.50	.60
❑ 500 Ron Guidry	.75	.30
❑ 501 Junior Kennedy RC	.25	.10
❑ 502 Steve Braun	.25	.10
❑ 503 Terry Humphrey	.25	.10
❑ 504 Larry McWilliams RC	.25	.10
❑ 505 Ed Kranepool	.25	.10
❑ 506 John D'Acquisto	.25	.10
❑ 507 Tony Armas	.75	.30
❑ 508 Charlie Hough	.75	.30
❑ 509 Mario Mendoza UER	.25	.10
❑ 510 Ted Simmons	1.50	.60
❑ 511 Paul Reuschel DP	.20	.08
❑ 512 Jack Clark	.75	.30
❑ 513 Dave Johnson	.75	.30
❑ 514 Mike Proly RC	.25	.10
❑ 515 Enos Cabell	.25	.10
❑ 516 Champ Summers DP	.20	.08
❑ 517 Al Bumbry	.75	.30
❑ 518 Jim Umbarger	.25	.10
❑ 519 Ben Oglivie	.75	.30
❑ 520 Gary Carter	1.50	.60
❑ 521 Sam Ewing	.25	.10
❑ 522 Ken Holtzman	.75	.30
❑ 523 John Milner	.25	.10
❑ 524 Tom Burgmeier	.25	.10
❑ 525 Freddie Patek	.25	.10
❑ 526 Los Angeles Dodgers CL/Lasorda	1.50	.60
❑ 527 Lerrin LaGrow	.25	.10
❑ 528 Wayne Gross DP	.20	.08
❑ 529 Brian Asselstine	.25	.10
❑ 530 Frank Tanana	.75	.30

❑ 531 Fernando Gonzalez	.25	.10
❑ 532 Buddy Schultz	.25	.10
❑ 533 Leroy Stanton	.25	.10
❑ 534 Ken Forsch	.25	.10
❑ 535 Ellis Valentine	.25	.10
❑ 536 Jerry Reuss	.75	.30
❑ 537 Tom Veryzer	.25	.10
❑ 538 Mike Ivie DP	.20	.08
❑ 539 John Ellis	.25	.10
❑ 540 Greg Luzinski	.75	.30
❑ 541 Jim Slaton	.25	.10
❑ 542 Rick Bosetti	.25	.10
❑ 543 Kiko Garcia	.25	.10
❑ 544 Fergie Jenkins	2.50	1.00
❑ 545 John Stearns	.25	.10
❑ 546 Bill Russell	.75	.30
❑ 547 Clint Hurdle	.25	.10
❑ 548 Enrique Romo	.25	.10
❑ 549 Bob Bailey	.25	.10
❑ 550 Sal Bando	.75	.30
❑ 551 Chicago Cubs CL/Franks	1.50	.60
❑ 552 Jose Morales	.25	.10
❑ 553 Denny Walling	.25	.10
❑ 554 Matt Keough	.25	.10
❑ 555 Biff Pocoroba	.25	.10
❑ 556 Mike Lum	.25	.10
❑ 557 Ken Brett	.25	.10
❑ 558 Jay Johnstone	.75	.30
❑ 559 Greg Pryor RC	.25	.10
❑ 560 John Montefusco	.25	.10
❑ 561 Ed Ott	.25	.10
❑ 562 Dusty Baker	1.50	.60
❑ 563 Roy Thomas	.25	.10
❑ 564 Jerry Turner	.25	.10
❑ 565 Rico Carty	.75	.30
❑ 566 Nino Espinosa	.25	.10
❑ 567 Richie Hebner	.75	.30
❑ 568 Carlos Lopez	.25	.10
❑ 569 Bob Sykes	.25	.10
❑ 570 Cesar Cedeno	.75	.30
❑ 571 Darrell Porter	.75	.30
❑ 572 Rod Gilbreath	.25	.10
❑ 573 Jim Kern	.25	.10
❑ 574 Claudell Washington	.75	.30
❑ 575 Luis Tiant	.75	.30
❑ 576 Mike Parrott RC	.25	.10
❑ 577 Milwaukee Brewers CL/Bamberger	1.50	.60
❑ 578 Pete Broberg	.25	.10
❑ 579 Greg Gross	.25	.10
❑ 580 Ron Fairly	.75	.30
❑ 581 Darold Knowles	.25	.10
❑ 582 Paul Blair	.75	.30
❑ 583 Julio Cruz	.25	.10
❑ 584 Jim Rooker	.25	.10
❑ 585 Hal McRae	1.50	.60
❑ 586 Bob Horner RC	1.50	.60
❑ 587 Ken Reitz	.25	.10
❑ 588 Tom Murphy	.25	.10
❑ 589 Terry Whitfield	.25	.10
❑ 590 J.R. Richard	.75	.30
❑ 591 Mike Hargrove	.75	.30
❑ 592 Mike Krukow	.25	.10
❑ 593 Rick Dempsey	.75	.30
❑ 594 Bob Shirley	.25	.10
❑ 595 Phil Niekro	2.50	1.00
❑ 596 Jim Wohlford	.25	.10
❑ 597 Bob Stanley	.25	.10
❑ 598 Mark Wagner	.25	.10
❑ 599 Jim Spencer	.25	.10
❑ 600 George Foster	.75	.30
❑ 601 Dave LaRoche	.25	.10
❑ 602 Checklist 485-605	1.50	.60
❑ 603 Rudy May	.25	.10
❑ 604 Jeff Newman	.25	.10
❑ 605 Rick Monday DP	.25	.10
❑ 606 Montreal Expos CL/Williams	1.50	.60
❑ 607 Omar Moreno	.25	.10
❑ 608 Dave McKay	.25	.10
❑ 609 Silvio Martinez RC	.25	.10
❑ 610 Mike Schmidt	8.00	3.00
❑ 611 Jim Norris	.25	.10
❑ 612 Rick Honeycutt RC	.75	.30
❑ 613 Mike Edwards RC	.25	.10
❑ 614 Willie Hernandez	.75	.30
❑ 615 Ken Singleton	.75	.30
❑ 616 Billy Almon	.25	.10

❑ 617 Terry Puhl	.25	.10
❑ 618 Jerry Remy	.25	.10
❑ 619 Ken Landreaux RC	.75	.30
❑ 620 Bert Campaneris	.75	.30
❑ 621 Pat Zachry	.25	.10
❑ 622 Dave Collins	.75	.30
❑ 623 Bob McClure	.25	.10
❑ 624 Larry Herndon	.25	.10
❑ 625 Mark Fidrych	2.50	1.00
❑ 626 New York Yankees CL/Lemon	1.50	.60
❑ 627 Gary Serum RC	.25	.10
❑ 628 Del Unser	.25	.10
❑ 629 Gene Garber	.75	.30
❑ 630 Bake McBride	.75	.30
❑ 631 Jorge Orta	.25	.10
❑ 632 Don Kirkwood	.25	.10
❑ 633 Rob Wilfong DP RC	.20	.08
❑ 634 Paul Lindblad	.25	.10
❑ 635 Don Baylor	1.50	.60
❑ 636 Wayne Garland	.25	.10
❑ 637 Bill Robinson	.75	.30
❑ 638 Al Fitzmorris	.25	.10
❑ 639 Manny Trillo	.25	.10
❑ 640 Eddie Murray	12.00	5.00
❑ 641 Bobby Castillo RC	.25	.10
❑ 642 Wilbur Howard DP	.20	.08
❑ 643 Tom Hausman	.25	.10
❑ 644 Manny Mota	.75	.30
❑ 645 George Scott DP	.25	.10
❑ 646 Rick Sweet	.25	.10
❑ 647 Bob Lacey	.25	.10
❑ 648 Lou Piniella	.75	.30
❑ 649 John Curtis	.25	.10
❑ 650 Pete Rose	12.00	5.00
❑ 651 Mike Caldwell	.25	.10
❑ 652 Stan Papi RC	.25	.10
❑ 653 Warren Brusstar DP	.20	.08
❑ 654 Rick Miller	.25	.10
❑ 655 Jerry Koosman	.75	.30
❑ 656 Hosken Powell RC	.25	.10
❑ 657 George Medich	.25	.10
❑ 658 Taylor Duncan RC	.25	.10
❑ 659 Seattle Mariners CL/Johnson	1.50	.60
❑ 660 Ron LeFlore DP	.25	.10
❑ 661 Bruce Kison	.25	.10
❑ 662 Kevin Bell	.25	.10
❑ 663 Mike Vail	.25	.10
❑ 664 Doug Bird	.25	.10
❑ 665 Lou Brock	2.50	1.00
❑ 666 Rich Dauer	.25	.10
❑ 667 Don Hood	.25	.10
❑ 668 Bill North	.25	.10
❑ 669 Checklist 606-726	1.50	.60
❑ 670 Jim Hunter DP	1.50	.60
❑ 671 Joe Ferguson DP	.20	.08
❑ 672 Ed Halicki	.25	.10
❑ 673 Tom Hutton	.25	.10
❑ 674 Dave Tomlin	.25	.10
❑ 675 Tim McCarver	1.50	.60
❑ 676 Johnny Sutton RC	.25	.10
❑ 677 Larry Parrish	.75	.30
❑ 678 Geoff Zahn	.25	.10
❑ 679 Derrel Thomas	.25	.10
❑ 680 Carlton Fisk	3.00	1.25
❑ 681 John Henry Johnson RC	.25	.10
❑ 682 Dave Chalk	.25	.10
❑ 683 Dan Meyer DP	.20	.08
❑ 684 Jamie Easterly DP	.20	.08
❑ 685 Sixto Lezcano	.25	.10
❑ 686 Ron Schueler DP	.20	.08
❑ 687 Rennie Stennett	.25	.10
❑ 688 Mike Willis	.25	.10
❑ 689 Baltimore Orioles CL/Weaver	1.50	.60
❑ 690 Buddy Bell DP	.25	.10
❑ 691 Dock Ellis DP	.20	.08
❑ 692 Mickey Stanley	.25	.10
❑ 693 Dave Rader	.25	.10
❑ 694 Burt Hooton	.75	.30
❑ 695 Keith Hernandez	.75	.30
❑ 696 Andy Hassler	.25	.10
❑ 697 Dave Bergman	.25	.10
❑ 698 Bill Stein	.25	.10
❑ 699 Hal Dues RC	.25	.10
❑ 700 Reggie Jackson DP	5.00	2.00
❑ 701 Corey/Flinn/Stewart RC	.75	.30
❑ 702 Finch/Hancock/Ripley RC	.75	.30

❑ 703 Anderson/Frost/Slater RC .75 .30
❑ 704 Baumgarten/Colbern/Squires RC .75 .30
❑ 705 Griffin/Norrid/Oliver RC 1.50 .60
❑ 706 Stegman/Tobik/Young RC .75 .30
❑ 707 Bass/Gaudet/McGilberry RC 1.50 .60
❑ 708 Bass/Romero/Yost RC 1.50 .60
❑ 709 Perlozzo/Sofield/Stanfield RC .75 .30
❑ 710 Doyle/Heath/Rajisch RC .75 .30
❑ 711 Murphy/Robinson/Wirth RC 1.50 .60
❑ 712 Anderson/Biercevicz/McLaughlin RC .75 .30
❑ 713 Darwin/Putnam/Sample RC 1.50 .60
❑ 714 Cruz/Kelly/Whitt RC .75 .30
❑ 715 Benedict/Hubbard/Whisenton RC 1.50 .60
❑ 716 Geisel/Pagel/Thompson RC .75 .30
❑ 717 LaCoss/Oester/Spilman RC .75 .30
❑ 718 Bochy/Fischlin/Pisker RC .75 .30
❑ 719 Guerrero/Law/Simpson RC 1.50 .60
❑ 720 Fry/Pirtle/Sanderson RC 1.50 .60
❑ 721 Berenguer/Bernard/Norman RC .75 .30
❑ 722 Morrison/Smith/Wright RC 1.50 .60
❑ 723 Berra/Cotes/Wiltbank RC .75 .30
❑ 724 Bruno/Frazier/Kennedy RC 1.50 .60
❑ 725 Beswick/Mura/Perkins RC .75 .30
❑ 726 Johnston/Strain/Tamargo RC .75 .30

1980 Topps

❑ COMPLETE SET (726) 120.00 70.00
❑ COMMON CARD (1-726) .25 .08
❑ COMMON DP .25 .08
❑ 1 L.Brock/C.Yastrzemski HL 2.50 1.00
❑ 2 Willie McCovey HL .75 .30
❑ 3 Manny Mota HL .25 .08
❑ 4 Pete Rose HL 3.00 1.25
❑ 5 Garry Templeton HL .25 .08
❑ 6 Del Unser HL .25 .08
❑ 7 Mike Lum .25 .08
❑ 8 Craig Swan .25 .08
❑ 9 Steve Braun .25 .08
❑ 10 Dennis Martinez .75 .30
❑ 11 Jimmy Sexton .25 .08
❑ 12 John Curtis DP .25 .08
❑ 13 Ron Pruitt .25 .08
❑ 14 Dave Cash .75 .30
❑ 15 Bill Campbell .25 .08
❑ 16 Jerry Narron RC .25 .08
❑ 17 Bruce Sutter 1.50 .60
❑ 18 Ron Jackson .25 .08
❑ 19 Balor Moore .25 .08
❑ 20 Dan Ford .25 .08
❑ 21 Manny Sarmiento .25 .08
❑ 22 Pat Putnam .25 .08
❑ 23 Derrel Thomas .25 .08
❑ 24 Jim Slaton .25 .08
❑ 25 Lee Mazzilli .75 .30
❑ 26 Marty Pattin .25 .08
❑ 27 Del Unser .25 .08
❑ 28 Bruce Kison .25 .08
❑ 29 Mark Wagner .25 .08
❑ 30 Vida Blue .75 .30
❑ 31 Jay Johnstone .25 .08
❑ 32 Julio Cruz DP .25 .08
❑ 33 Tony Scott .25 .08
❑ 34 Jeff Newman DP .25 .08
❑ 35 Luis Tiant .75 .30
❑ 36 Rusty Torres .25 .08
❑ 37 Kiko Garcia .25 .08
❑ 38 Dan Spillner DP .25 .08
❑ 39 Rowland Office .25 .08
❑ 40 Carlton Fisk 2.50 1.00
❑ 41 Texas Rangers CL/Corrales .75 .30
❑ 42 David Palmer RC .25 .08
❑ 43 Bombo Rivera .25 .08
❑ 44 Bill Fahey .25 .08
❑ 45 Frank White .75 .30
❑ 46 Rico Carty .75 .30
❑ 47 Bill Bonham DP .25 .08
❑ 48 Rick Miller .25 .08
❑ 49 Mario Guerrero .25 .08
❑ 50 J.R. Richard .75 .30
❑ 51 Joe Ferguson DP .25 .08
❑ 52 Warren Brusstar .25 .08
❑ 53 Ben Oglivie .75 .30
❑ 54 Dennis Lamp .25 .08
❑ 55 Bill Madlock .75 .30
❑ 56 Bobby Valentine .75 .30
❑ 57 Pete Vuckovich .25 .08
❑ 58 Doug Flynn .25 .08
❑ 59 Eddy Putman RC .25 .08
❑ 60 Bucky Dent .75 .30
❑ 61 Gary Serum .25 .08
❑ 62 Mike Ivie .25 .08
❑ 63 Bob Stanley .25 .08
❑ 64 Joe Nolan .25 .08
❑ 65 Al Bumbry .75 .30
❑ 66 Kansas City Royals CL/Frey .75 .30
❑ 67 Doyle Alexander .25 .08
❑ 68 Larry Harlow .25 .08
❑ 69 Rick Williams .25 .08
❑ 70 Gary Carter 1.50 .60
❑ 71 John Milner DP .25 .08
❑ 72 Fred Howard DP RC .25 .08
❑ 73 Dave Collins .25 .08
❑ 74 Sid Monge .25 .08
❑ 75 Bill Russell .75 .30
❑ 76 John Stearns .25 .08
❑ 77 Dave Stieb RC 1.50 .60
❑ 78 Ruppert Jones .25 .08
❑ 79 Bob Owchinko .25 .08
❑ 80 Ron LeFlore .75 .30
❑ 81 Ted Sizemore .25 .08
❑ 82 Houston Astros CL/Virdon .75 .30
❑ 83 Steve Trout RC .25 .08
❑ 84 Gary Lavelle .25 .08
❑ 85 Ted Simmons .75 .30
❑ 86 Dave Hamilton .25 .08
❑ 87 Pepe Frias .25 .08
❑ 88 Ken Landreaux .25 .08
❑ 89 Don Hood .25 .08
❑ 90 Manny Trillo .75 .30
❑ 91 Rick Dempsey .75 .30
❑ 92 Rick Rhoden .25 .08
❑ 93 Dave Roberts DP .25 .08
❑ 94 Neil Allen RC .25 .08
❑ 95 Cecil Cooper .75 .30
❑ 96 Oakland Athletics CL/Marshall .75 .30
❑ 97 Bill Lee .75 .30
❑ 98 Jerry Terrell .25 .08
❑ 99 Victor Cruz .25 .08
❑ 100 Johnny Bench 3.00 1.25
❑ 101 Aurelio Lopez .25 .08
❑ 102 Rich Dauer .25 .08
❑ 103 Bill Caudill RC .25 .08
❑ 104 Manny Mota .75 .30
❑ 105 Frank Tanana .75 .30
❑ 106 Jeff Leonard RC 1.50 .60
❑ 107 Francisco Barrios .25 .08
❑ 108 Bob Horner .75 .30
❑ 109 Bill Travers .25 .08
❑ 110 Fred Lynn DP .50 .20
❑ 111 Bob Knepper .25 .08
❑ 112 Chicago White Sox CL/LaRussa .75 .30
❑ 113 Geoff Zahn .25 .08
❑ 114 Juan Beniquez .25 .08
❑ 115 Sparky Lyle .75 .30
❑ 116 Larry Cox .25 .08
❑ 117 Dock Ellis .75 .30
❑ 118 Phil Garner .75 .30
❑ 119 Sammy Stewart .25 .08
❑ 120 Greg Luzinski .75 .30
❑ 121 Checklist 1-121 .75 .30
❑ 122 Dave Rosello DP .25 .08
❑ 123 Lynn Jones RC .25 .08
❑ 124 Dave Lemanczyk .25 .08
❑ 125 Tony Perez .75 .30
❑ 126 Dave Tomlin .25 .08
❑ 127 Gary Thomasson .25 .08
❑ 128 Tom Burgmeier .25 .08
❑ 129 Craig Reynolds .25 .08
❑ 130 Amos Otis .75 .30
❑ 131 Paul Mitchell .25 .08
❑ 132 Biff Pocoroba .25 .08
❑ 133 Jerry Turner .25 .08
❑ 134 Matt Keough .25 .08
❑ 135 Bill Buckner .75 .30
❑ 136 Dick Ruthven .25 .08
❑ 137 John Castino RC .25 .08
❑ 138 Ross Baumgarten .25 .08
❑ 139 Dane Iorg RC .25 .08
❑ 140 Rich Gossage .75 .30
❑ 141 Gary Alexander .25 .08
❑ 142 Phil Huffman RC .25 .08
❑ 143 Bruce Bochte DP .25 .08
❑ 144 Steve Comer .25 .08
❑ 145 Darrell Evans .75 .30
❑ 146 Bob Welch .75 .30
❑ 147 Terry Puhl .25 .08
❑ 148 Manny Sanguillen .75 .30
❑ 149 Tom Hume .25 .08
❑ 150 Jason Thompson .25 .08
❑ 151 Tom Hausman DP .25 .08
❑ 152 John Fulgham RC .25 .08
❑ 153 Tim Blackwell .25 .08
❑ 154 Lary Sorensen .25 .08
❑ 155 Jerry Remy .25 .08
❑ 156 Tony Brizzolara RC .25 .08
❑ 157 Willie Wilson DP .50 .20
❑ 158 Rob Picciolo DP .25 .08
❑ 159 Ken Clay .25 .08
❑ 160 Eddie Murray 5.00 2.00
❑ 161 Larry Christenson .25 .08
❑ 162 Bob Randall .25 .08
❑ 163 Steve Swisher .25 .08
❑ 164 Greg Pryor .25 .08
❑ 165 Omar Moreno .25 .08
❑ 166 Glenn Abbott .25 .08
❑ 167 Jack Clark .75 .30
❑ 168 Rick Waits .25 .08
❑ 169 Luis Gomez .25 .08
❑ 170 Burt Hooton .75 .30
❑ 171 Fernando Gonzalez .25 .08
❑ 172 Ron Hodges .25 .08
❑ 173 John Henry Johnson .25 .08
❑ 174 Ray Knight .75 .30
❑ 175 Rick Reuschel .75 .30
❑ 176 Champ Summers .25 .08
❑ 177 Dave Heaverlo .25 .08
❑ 178 Tim McCarver .75 .30
❑ 179 Ron Davis RC .25 .08
❑ 180 Warren Cromartie .25 .08
❑ 181 Moose Haas .25 .08
❑ 182 Ken Reitz .25 .08
❑ 183 Jim Anderson DP .25 .08
❑ 184 Steve Renko DP .25 .08
❑ 185 Hal McRae .75 .30
❑ 186 Junior Moore .25 .08
❑ 187 Alan Ashby .25 .08
❑ 188 Terry Crowley .25 .08
❑ 189 Kevin Kobel .25 .08
❑ 190 Buddy Bell .75 .30
❑ 191 Ted Martinez .25 .08
❑ 192 Atlanta Braves CL/Cox .75 .30
❑ 193 Dave Goltz .25 .08
❑ 194 Mike Easler .25 .08
❑ 195 John Montefusco .75 .30
❑ 196 Lance Parrish .75 .30
❑ 197 Byron McLaughlin .25 .08
❑ 198 Dell Alston DP .25 .08
❑ 199 Mike LaCoss .25 .08
❑ 200 Jim Rice .75 .30
❑ 201 K.Hernandez/F.Lynn LL .75 .30
❑ 202 D.Kingman/G.Thomas LL 1.50 .60
❑ 203 D.Winfield/D.Baylor LL 1.50 .60
❑ 204 O.Moreno/W.Wilson LL .75 .30
❑ 205 Niekro/Niekro/Flan LL .75 .30
❑ 206 J.Richard/N.Ryan LL 5.00 2.00
❑ 207 J.Richard/R.Guidry LL .75 .30
❑ 208 Wayne Cage .25 .08
❑ 209 Von Joshua .25 .08
❑ 210 Steve Carlton 1.50 .60
❑ 211 Dave Skaggs DP .25 .08

	No.	Player	NrMt	VG-E
❑	212	Dave Roberts	.25	.08
❑	213	Mike Jorgensen DP	.25	.08
❑	214	California Angels CL/Fregosi	.75	.30
❑	215	Sixto Lezcano	.25	.08
❑	216	Phil Mankowski	.25	.08
❑	217	Ed Halicki	.25	.08
❑	218	Jose Morales	.25	.08
❑	219	Steve Mingori	.25	.08
❑	220	Dave Concepcion	.75	.30
❑	221	Joe Cannon RC	.25	.08
❑	222	Ron Hassey RC	.25	.08
❑	223	Bob Sykes	.25	.08
❑	224	Willie Montanez	.25	.08
❑	225	Lou Piniella	.75	.30
❑	226	Bill Stein	.25	.08
❑	227	Len Barker	.75	.30
❑	228	Johnny Oates	.75	.30
❑	229	Jim Bibby	.25	.08
❑	230	Dave Winfield	1.50	.60
❑	231	Steve McCatty	.25	.08
❑	232	Alan Trammell	1.50	.60
❑	233	LaRue Washington RC	.25	.08
❑	234	Vern Ruhle	.25	.08
❑	235	Andre Dawson	1.50	.60
❑	236	Marc Hill	.25	.08
❑	237	Scott McGregor	.75	.30
❑	238	Rob Wilfong	.25	.08
❑	239	Don Aase	.25	.08
❑	240	Dave Kingman	.75	.30
❑	241	Checklist 122-242	.75	.30
❑	242	Lamar Johnson	.25	.08
❑	243	Jerry Augustine	.25	.08
❑	244	St. Louis Cardinals CL/Boyer	.75	.30
❑	245	Phil Niekro	.75	.30
❑	246	Tim Foli DP	.25	.08
❑	247	Frank Riccelli	.25	.08
❑	248	Jamie Quirk	.25	.08
❑	249	Jim Clancy	.25	.08
❑	250	Jim Kaat	.75	.30
❑	251	Kip Young	.25	.08
❑	252	Ted Cox	.25	.08
❑	253	John Montague	.25	.08
❑	254	Paul Dade DP	.25	.08
❑	255	Dusty Baker DP	.50	.20
❑	256	Roger Erickson	.25	.08
❑	257	Larry Herndon	.25	.08
❑	258	Paul Moskau	.25	.08
❑	259	New York Mets CL/Torre	1.50	.60
❑	260	Al Oliver	.75	.30
❑	261	Dave Chalk	.25	.08
❑	262	Benny Ayala	.25	.08
❑	263	Dave LaRoche DP	.25	.08
❑	264	Bill Robinson	.25	.08
❑	265	Robin Yount	3.00	1.25
❑	266	Bernie Carbo	.25	.08
❑	267	Dan Schatzeder	.25	.08
❑	268	Rafael Landestoy	.25	.08
❑	269	Dave Tobik	.25	.08
❑	270	Mike Schmidt DP	3.00	1.25
❑	271	Dick Drago DP	.25	.08
❑	272	Ralph Garr	.75	.30
❑	273	Eduardo Rodriguez	.25	.08
❑	274	Dale Murphy	2.50	1.00
❑	275	Jerry Koosman	.75	.30
❑	276	Tom Veryzer	.25	.08
❑	277	Rick Bosetti	.25	.08
❑	278	Jim Spencer	.25	.08
❑	279	Rob Andrews	.25	.08
❑	280	Gaylord Perry	.75	.30
❑	281	Paul Blair	.75	.30
❑	282	Seattle Mariners CL/Johnson	.75	.30
❑	283	John Ellis	.25	.08
❑	284	Larry Murray DP RC	.25	.08
❑	285	Don Baylor	.75	.30
❑	286	Darold Knowles DP	.25	.08
❑	287	John Lowenstein	.25	.08
❑	288	Dave Rozema	.25	.08
❑	289	Bruce Bochy	.25	.08
❑	290	Steve Garvey	1.50	.60
❑	291	Randy Scarberry RC	.25	.08
❑	292	Dale Berra	.25	.08
❑	293	Elias Sosa	.25	.08
❑	294	Charlie Spikes	.25	.08
❑	295	Larry Gura	.25	.08
❑	296	Dave Rader	.25	.08
❑	297	Tim Johnson	.25	.08
❑	298	Ken Holtzman	.75	.30
❑	299	Steve Henderson	.25	.08
❑	300	Ron Guidry	.75	.30
❑	301	Mike Edwards	.25	.08
❑	302	Los Angeles Dodgers CL/Lasorda	1.50	.60
❑	303	Bill Castro	.25	.08
❑	304	Butch Wynegar	.25	.08
❑	305	Randy Jones	.75	.30
❑	306	Denny Walling	.25	.08
❑	307	Rick Honeycutt	.25	.08
❑	308	Mike Hargrove	.75	.30
❑	309	Larry McWilliams	.25	.08
❑	310	Dave Parker	.75	.30
❑	311	Roger Metzger	.25	.08
❑	312	Mike Barlow	.25	.08
❑	313	Johnny Grubb	.25	.08
❑	314	Tim Stoddard RC	.25	.08
❑	315	Steve Kemp	.75	.30
❑	316	Bob Lacey	.25	.08
❑	317	Mike Anderson DP	.25	.08
❑	318	Jerry Reuss	.75	.30
❑	319	Chris Speier	.25	.08
❑	320	Dennis Eckersley	1.50	.60
❑	321	Keith Hernandez	.75	.30
❑	322	Claudell Washington	.25	.08
❑	323	Mick Kelleher	.25	.08
❑	324	Tom Underwood	.25	.08
❑	325	Dan Driessen	.25	.08
❑	326	Bo McLaughlin	.25	.08
❑	327	Ray Fosse DP	.50	.20
❑	328	Minnesota Twins CL/Mauch	.75	.30
❑	329	Bert Roberge RC	.25	.08
❑	330	Al Cowens	.75	.30
❑	331	Richie Hebner	.25	.08
❑	332	Enrique Romo	.25	.08
❑	333	Jim Norris DP	.25	.08
❑	334	Jim Beattie	.25	.08
❑	335	Willie McCovey	1.50	.60
❑	336	George Medich	.25	.08
❑	337	Carney Lansford	.75	.30
❑	338	John Wockenfuss	.25	.08
❑	339	John D'Acquisto	.25	.08
❑	340	Ken Singleton	.75	.30
❑	341	Jim Essian	.25	.08
❑	342	Odell Jones	.25	.08
❑	343	Mike Vail	.25	.08
❑	344	Randy Lerch	.25	.08
❑	345	Larry Parrish	.75	.30
❑	346	Buddy Solomon	.25	.08
❑	347	Harry Chappas RC	.25	.08
❑	348	Checklist 243-363	.75	.30
❑	349	Jack Brohamer	.25	.08
❑	350	George Hendrick	.75	.30
❑	351	Bob Davis	.25	.08
❑	352	Dan Briggs	.25	.08
❑	353	Andy Hassler	.25	.08
❑	354	Rick Auerbach	.25	.08
❑	355	Gary Matthews	.75	.30
❑	356	San Diego Padres CL/Coleman	.75	.30
❑	357	Bob McClure	.25	.08
❑	358	Lou Whitaker	.75	.30
❑	359	Randy Moffitt	.25	.08
❑	360	Darrell Porter DP	.50	.20
❑	361	Wayne Garland	.25	.08
❑	362	Danny Goodwin	.25	.08
❑	363	Wayne Gross	.25	.08
❑	364	Ray Burris	.25	.08
❑	365	Bobby Murcer	.75	.30
❑	366	Rob Dressler	.25	.08
❑	367	Billy Smith	.25	.08
❑	368	Willie Aikens RC	.25	.08
❑	369	Jim Kern	.25	.08
❑	370	Cesar Cedeno	.75	.30
❑	371	Jack Morris	.75	.30
❑	372	Joel Youngblood	.25	.08
❑	373	Dan Petry DP RC	.75	.30
❑	374	Jim Gantner	.75	.30
❑	375	Ross Grimsley	.25	.08
❑	376	Gary Allenson RC	.25	.08
❑	377	Junior Kennedy	.25	.08
❑	378	Jerry Mumphrey	.25	.08
❑	379	Kevin Bell	.25	.08
❑	380	Garry Maddox	.75	.30
❑	381	Chicago Cubs CL/Gomez	.75	.30
❑	382	Dave Freisleben	.25	.08
❑	383	Ed Ott	.25	.08
❑	384	Joey McLaughlin RC	.25	.08
❑	385	Enos Cabell	.25	.08
❑	386	Darrell Jackson	.25	.08
❑	387A	F.Stanley Yellow	2.00	.75
❑	387B	F.Stanley Red Name	.25	.08
❑	388	Mike Paxton	.25	.08
❑	389	Pete LaCock	.25	.08
❑	390	Fergie Jenkins	.75	.30
❑	391	Tony Armas DP	.50	.20
❑	392	Milt Wilcox	.25	.08
❑	393	Ozzie Smith	10.00	4.00
❑	394	Reggie Cleveland	.25	.08
❑	395	Ellis Valentine	.25	.08
❑	396	Dan Meyer	.25	.08
❑	397	Roy Thomas DP	.25	.08
❑	398	Barry Foote	.25	.08
❑	399	Mike Proly DP	.25	.08
❑	400	George Foster	.75	.30
❑	401	Pete Falcone	.25	.08
❑	402	Merv Rettenmund	.25	.08
❑	403	Pete Redfern DP	.25	.08
❑	404	Baltimore Orioles CL/Weaver	.75	.30
❑	405	Dwight Evans	1.50	.60
❑	406	Paul Molitor	4.00	1.50
❑	407	Tony Solaita	.25	.08
❑	408	Bill North	.25	.08
❑	409	Paul Splittorff	.25	.08
❑	410	Bobby Bonds	.75	.30
❑	411	Frank LaCorte	.25	.08
❑	412	Thad Bosley	.25	.08
❑	413	Allen Ripley	.25	.08
❑	414	George Scott	.75	.30
❑	415	Bill Atkinson	.25	.08
❑	416	Tom Brookens RC	.25	.08
❑	417	Craig Chamberlain DP RC	.25	.08
❑	418	Roger Freed DP	.25	.08
❑	419	Vic Correll	.25	.08
❑	420	Butch Hobson	.25	.08
❑	421	Doug Bird	.25	.08
❑	422	Larry Milbourne	.25	.08
❑	423	Dave Frost	.25	.08
❑	424	New York Yankees CL/Howser	.75	.30
❑	424A	New York Yankees CL/Martin		
❑	425	Mark Belanger	.75	.30
❑	426	Grant Jackson	.25	.08
❑	427	Tom Hutton DP	.25	.08
❑	428	Pat Zachry	.25	.08
❑	429	Duane Kuiper	.25	.08
❑	430	Larry Hisle DP	.25	.08
❑	431	Mike Krukow	.25	.08
❑	432	Willie Norwood	.25	.08
❑	433	Rich Gale	.25	.08
❑	434	Johnnie LeMaster	.25	.08
❑	435	Don Gullett	.75	.30
❑	436	Billy Almon	.25	.08
❑	437	Joe Niekro	.75	.30
❑	438	Dave Revering	.25	.08
❑	439	Mike Phillips	.25	.08
❑	440	Don Sutton	.75	.30
❑	441	Eric Soderholm	.25	.08
❑	442	Jorge Orta	.25	.08
❑	443	Mike Parrott	.25	.08
❑	444	Alvis Woods	.25	.08
❑	445	Mark Fidrych	.75	.30
❑	446	Duffy Dyer	.25	.08
❑	447	Nino Espinosa	.25	.08
❑	448	Jim Wohlford	.25	.08
❑	449	Doug Bair	.25	.08
❑	450	George Brett	8.00	3.00
❑	451	Cleveland Indians CL/Garcia	.75	.30
❑	452	Steve Dillard	.25	.08
❑	453	Mike Bacsik	.25	.08
❑	454	Tom Donohue RC	.25	.08
❑	455	Mike Torrez	.75	.30
❑	456	Frank Taveras	.25	.08
❑	457	Bert Blyleven	.75	.30
❑	458	Billy Sample	.25	.08
❑	459	Mickey Lolich DP	.50	.20
❑	460	Willie Randolph	.75	.30
❑	461	Dwayne Murphy	.25	.08
❑	462	Mike Sadek DP	.25	.08
❑	463	Jerry Royster	.25	.08
❑	464	John Denny	.75	.30
❑	465	Rick Monday	.75	.30
❑	466	Mike Squires	.25	.08
❑	467	Jesse Jefferson	.25	.08

- ❑ 468 Aurelio Rodriguez .25 .08
- ❑ 469 Randy Niemann DP RC .25 .08
- ❑ 470 Bob Boone .75 .30
- ❑ 471 Hosken Powell DP .25 .08
- ❑ 472 Willie Hernandez .75 .30
- ❑ 473 Bump Wills .25 .08
- ❑ 474 Steve Busby .25 .08
- ❑ 475 Cesar Geronimo .75 .30
- ❑ 476 Bob Shirley .25 .08
- ❑ 477 Buck Martinez .25 .08
- ❑ 478 Gil Flores .25 .08
- ❑ 479 Montreal Expos CL/Williams .75 .30
- ❑ 480 Bob Watson .75 .30
- ❑ 481 Tom Paciorek .75 .30
- ❑ 482 Rickey Henderson RC 50.00 20.00
- ❑ 483 Bo Diaz .25 .08
- ❑ 484 Checklist 364-484 .75 .30
- ❑ 485 Mickey Rivers .75 .30
- ❑ 486 Mike Tyson DP .25 .08
- ❑ 487 Wayne Nordhagen .25 .08
- ❑ 488 Roy Howell .25 .08
- ❑ 489 Preston Hanna DP .25 .08
- ❑ 490 Lee May .75 .30
- ❑ 491 Steve Mura DP .25 .08
- ❑ 492 Todd Cruz RC .25 .08
- ❑ 493 Jerry Martin .25 .08
- ❑ 494 Craig Minetto RC .25 .08
- ❑ 495 Bake McBride .75 .30
- ❑ 496 Silvio Martinez .25 .08
- ❑ 497 Jim Mason .25 .08
- ❑ 498 Danny Darwin .25 .08
- ❑ 499 San Francisco Giants CL/Bristol .75 .30
- ❑ 500 Tom Seaver 3.00 1.25
- ❑ 501 Rennie Stennett .25 .08
- ❑ 502 Rich Wortham DP RC .25 .08
- ❑ 503 Mike Cubbage .25 .08
- ❑ 504 Gene Garber .25 .08
- ❑ 505 Bert Campaneris .75 .30
- ❑ 506 Tom Buskey .25 .08
- ❑ 507 Leon Roberts .25 .08
- ❑ 508 U.L. Washington .25 .08
- ❑ 509 Ed Glynn .25 .08
- ❑ 510 Ron Cey .75 .30
- ❑ 511 Eric Wilkins RC .25 .08
- ❑ 512 Jose Cardenal .25 .08
- ❑ 513 Tom Dixon DP .25 .08
- ❑ 514 Steve Ontiveros .25 .08
- ❑ 515 Mike Caldwell UER .25 .08
- ❑ 516 Hector Cruz .25 .08
- ❑ 517 Don Stanhouse .25 .08
- ❑ 518 Nelson Norman RC .25 .08
- ❑ 519 Steve Nicosia RC .25 .08
- ❑ 520 Steve Rogers .75 .30
- ❑ 521 Ken Brett .25 .08
- ❑ 522 Jim Morrison .25 .08
- ❑ 523 Ken Henderson .25 .08
- ❑ 524 Jim Wright DP .25 .08
- ❑ 525 Clint Hurdle .25 .08
- ❑ 526 Philadelphia Phillies CL/Green .75 .30
- ❑ 527 Doug Rau DP .25 .08
- ❑ 528 Adrian Devine .25 .08
- ❑ 529 Jim Barr .25 .08
- ❑ 530 Jim Sundberg DP .50 .20
- ❑ 531 Eric Rasmussen .25 .08
- ❑ 532 Willie Horton .75 .30
- ❑ 533 Checklist 485-605 .75 .30
- ❑ 534 Andre Thornton .75 .30
- ❑ 535 Bob Forsch .25 .08
- ❑ 536 Lee Lacy .25 .08
- ❑ 537 Alex Trevino RC .25 .08
- ❑ 538 Joe Strain .25 .08
- ❑ 539 Rudy May .25 .08
- ❑ 540 Pete Rose 8.00 3.00
- ❑ 541 Miguel Dilone .25 .08
- ❑ 542 Joe Coleman .25 .08
- ❑ 543 Pat Kelly .25 .08
- ❑ 544 Rick Sutcliffe RC 1.50 .60
- ❑ 545 Jeff Burroughs .75 .30
- ❑ 546 Rick Langford .25 .08
- ❑ 547 John Wathan .25 .08
- ❑ 548 Dave Rajsich .25 .08
- ❑ 549 Larry Wolfe .25 .08
- ❑ 550 Ken Griffey Sr. .75 .30
- ❑ 551 Pittsburgh Pirates CL/Tanner .75 .30
- ❑ 552 Bill Nahorodny .25 .08
- ❑ 553 Dick Davis .25 .08
- ❑ 554 Art Howe .75 .30
- ❑ 555 Ed Figueroa .25 .08
- ❑ 556 Joe Rudi .75 .30
- ❑ 557 Mark Lee .25 .08
- ❑ 558 Alfredo Griffin .25 .08
- ❑ 559 Dale Murray .25 .08
- ❑ 560 Dave Lopes .75 .30
- ❑ 561 Eddie Whitson .25 .08
- ❑ 562 Joe Wallis .25 .08
- ❑ 563 Will McEnaney .25 .08
- ❑ 564 Rick Manning .25 .08
- ❑ 565 Dennis Leonard .25 .08
- ❑ 566 Bud Harrelson .75 .30
- ❑ 567 Skip Lockwood .25 .08
- ❑ 568 Gary Roenicke RC .25 .08
- ❑ 569 Terry Kennedy .25 .08
- ❑ 570 Roy Smalley .75 .30
- ❑ 571 Joe Sambito .25 .08
- ❑ 572 Jerry Morales DP .25 .08
- ❑ 573 Kent Tekulve .75 .30
- ❑ 574 Scot Thompson .25 .08
- ❑ 575 Ken Kravec .25 .08
- ❑ 576 Jim Dwyer .25 .08
- ❑ 577 Toronto Blue Jays CL/Mattick .75 .30
- ❑ 578 Scott Sanderson .25 .08
- ❑ 579 Charlie Moore .25 .08
- ❑ 580 Nolan Ryan 15.00 6.00
- ❑ 581 Bob Bailor .25 .08
- ❑ 582 Brian Doyle .25 .08
- ❑ 583 Bob Stinson .25 .08
- ❑ 584 Kurt Bevacqua .25 .08
- ❑ 585 Al Hrabosky .75 .30
- ❑ 586 Mitchell Page .25 .08
- ❑ 587 Garry Templeton .75 .30
- ❑ 588 Greg Minton .25 .08
- ❑ 589 Chet Lemon .75 .30
- ❑ 590 Jim Palmer 1.50 .60
- ❑ 591 Rick Cerone .25 .08
- ❑ 592 Jon Matlack .75 .30
- ❑ 593 Jesus Alou .25 .08
- ❑ 594 Dick Tidrow .25 .08
- ❑ 595 Don Money .25 .08
- ❑ 596 Rick Matula RC .25 .08
- ❑ 597 Tom Poquette .25 .08
- ❑ 598 Fred Kendall DP .25 .08
- ❑ 599 Mike Norris .25 .08
- ❑ 600 Reggie Jackson 3.00 1.25
- ❑ 601 Buddy Schultz .25 .08
- ❑ 602 Brian Downing .75 .30
- ❑ 603 Jack Billingham DP .25 .08
- ❑ 604 Glenn Adams .25 .08
- ❑ 605 Terry Forster .75 .30
- ❑ 606 Cincinnati Reds CL/McNamara .75 .30
- ❑ 607 Woodie Fryman .25 .08
- ❑ 608 Alan Bannister .25 .08
- ❑ 609 Ron Reed .25 .08
- ❑ 610 Willie Stargell 1.50 .60
- ❑ 611 Jerry Garvin DP .25 .08
- ❑ 612 Cliff Johnson .25 .08
- ❑ 613 Randy Stein .25 .08
- ❑ 614 John Hiller .25 .08
- ❑ 615 Doug DeCinces .75 .30
- ❑ 616 Gene Richards .25 .08
- ❑ 617 Joaquin Andujar .75 .30
- ❑ 618 Bob Montgomery DP .25 .08
- ❑ 619 Sergio Ferrer .25 .08
- ❑ 620 Richie Zisk .75 .30
- ❑ 621 Bob Grich .75 .30
- ❑ 622 Mario Soto .75 .30
- ❑ 623 Gorman Thomas .75 .30
- ❑ 624 Lerrin LaGrow .25 .08
- ❑ 625 Chris Chambliss .75 .30
- ❑ 626 Detroit Tigers CL/Anderson .75 .30
- ❑ 627 Pedro Borbon .25 .08
- ❑ 628 Doug Capilla .25 .08
- ❑ 629 Jim Todd .25 .08
- ❑ 630 Larry Bowa .75 .30
- ❑ 631 Mark Littell .25 .08
- ❑ 632 Barry Bonnell .25 .08
- ❑ 633 Bob Apodaca .25 .08
- ❑ 634 Glenn Borgmann DP .25 .08
- ❑ 635 John Candelaria .75 .30
- ❑ 636 Toby Harrah .75 .30
- ❑ 637 Joe Simpson .25 .08
- ❑ 638 Mark Clear RC .25 .08
- ❑ 639 Larry Biittner .25 .08
- ❑ 640 Mike Flanagan .75 .30
- ❑ 641 Ed Kranepool .75 .30
- ❑ 642 Ken Forsch DP .25 .08
- ❑ 643 John Mayberry .75 .30
- ❑ 644 Charlie Hough .75 .30
- ❑ 645 Rick Burleson .75 .30
- ❑ 646 Checklist 606-726 .75 .30
- ❑ 647 Milt May .25 .08
- ❑ 648 Roy White .75 .30
- ❑ 649 Tom Griffin .25 .08
- ❑ 650 Joe Morgan 1.50 .60
- ❑ 651 Rollie Fingers .75 .30
- ❑ 652 Mario Mendoza .25 .08
- ❑ 653 Stan Bahnsen .25 .08
- ❑ 654 Bruce Boisclair DP .25 .08
- ❑ 655 Tug McGraw .75 .30
- ❑ 656 Larvell Blanks .25 .08
- ❑ 657 Dave Edwards RC .25 .08
- ❑ 658 Chris Knapp .25 .08
- ❑ 659 Milwaukee Brewers CL/Bamberger .75 .30
- ❑ 660 Rusty Staub .75 .30
- ❑ 661 Corey/Ford/Krenchiki RC .25 .08
- ❑ 662 Finch/O'Berry/Rainey RC .25 .08
- ❑ 663 Botting/Clark/Thon RC .75 .30
- ❑ 664 Colbern/Hoffman/Robinson RC .25 .08
- ❑ 665 Andersen/Cuellar/Wihtol RC .25 .08
- ❑ 666 Chris/Greene/Robbins RC .25 .08
- ❑ 667 Mart/Pasch/Quisenberry RC .75 .30
- ❑ 668 Boitano/Mueller/Sakata RC .25 .08
- ❑ 669 Graham/Sofield/Ward RC .75 .30
- ❑ 670 Brown/Gulden/Jones RC .25 .08
- ❑ 671 Bryant/Kingman/Morgan RC .75 .30
- ❑ 672 Beamon/Craig/Vasquez RC .25 .08
- ❑ 673 Allard/Gleaton/Mahlberg RC .25 .08
- ❑ 674 Edge/Kelly/Wilborn RC .25 .08
- ❑ 675 Benedict/Bradford/Miller RC .25 .08
- ❑ 676 Geisel/Macko/Pagel RC .25 .08
- ❑ 677 DeFreites/Pastore/Spilman RC .25 .08
- ❑ 678 Baldwin/Knicely/Ladd RC .25 .08
- ❑ 679 Beckwith/Hatcher/Patterson RC .75 .30
- ❑ 680 Bernazard/Miller/Tamargo RC .25 .08
- ❑ 681 Norman/Orosco/Scott RC 1.50 .60
- ❑ 682 Aviles/Noles/Saucier RC .25 .08
- ❑ 683 Boyland/Lois/Saferight RC .25 .08
- ❑ 684 Frazier/Herr/O'Brien RC .75 .30
- ❑ 685 Flannery/Greer/Wilhelm RC .25 .08
- ❑ 686 Johnston/Littlejohn/Nastu RC .25 .08
- ❑ 687 Mike Heath DP .25 .08
- ❑ 688 Steve Stone .75 .30
- ❑ 689 Boston Red Sox CL/Zimmer .75 .30
- ❑ 690 Tommy John .75 .30
- ❑ 691 Ivan DeJesus .25 .08
- ❑ 692 Rawly Eastwick DP .50 .20
- ❑ 693 Craig Kusick .25 .08
- ❑ 694 Jim Rooker .25 .08
- ❑ 695 Reggie Smith .75 .30
- ❑ 696 Julio Gonzalez .25 .08
- ❑ 697 David Clyde .25 .08
- ❑ 698 Oscar Gamble .75 .30
- ❑ 699 Floyd Bannister .25 .08
- ❑ 700 Rod Carew DP .75 .30
- ❑ 701 Ken Oberkfell RC .25 .08
- ❑ 702 Ed Farmer .25 .08
- ❑ 703 Otto Velez .25 .08
- ❑ 704 Gene Tenace .75 .30
- ❑ 705 Freddie Patek .75 .30
- ❑ 706 Tippy Martinez .25 .08
- ❑ 707 Elliott Maddox .25 .08
- ❑ 708 Bob Tolan .25 .08
- ❑ 709 Pat Underwood RC .25 .08
- ❑ 710 Graig Nettles .75 .30
- ❑ 711 Bob Galasso RC .25 .08
- ❑ 712 Rodney Scott .25 .08
- ❑ 713 Terry Whitfield .25 .08
- ❑ 714 Fred Norman .25 .08
- ❑ 715 Sal Bando .75 .30
- ❑ 716 Lynn McGlothen .25 .08
- ❑ 717 Mickey Klutts DP .25 .08
- ❑ 718 Greg Gross .25 .08
- ❑ 719 Don Robinson .75 .30
- ❑ 720 Carl Yastrzemski DP 2.00 .75
- ❑ 721 Paul Hartzell .25 .08
- ❑ 722 Jose Cruz .75 .30
- ❑ 723 Shane Rawley .25 .08
- ❑ 724 Jerry White .25 .08

❑ 725 Rick Wise .25 .08
❑ 726 Steve Yeager .75 .30

1981 Topps

❑ COMPLETE SET (726) 60.00 30.00
❑ COMMON CARD (1-726) .15 .05
❑ COMMON CARD DP .15 .05
❑ 1 G.Brett/B.Buckner LL 3.00 1.25
❑ 2 Reggie/Ogliv/Schmidt LL 1.50 .60
❑ 3 C.Cooper/M.Schmidt LL 1.50 .60
❑ 4 R.Henderson/LeFlore LL 3.00 1.25
❑ 5 S.Stone/S.Carlton LL .40 .15
❑ 6 Len Barker/S.Carlton LL .40 .15
❑ 7 R.May/D.Sutton LL .40 .15
❑ 8 Quis/Fingers/Hume LL .40 .15
❑ 9 Pete LaCock DP .15 .05
❑ 10 Mike Flanagan .15 .05
❑ 11 Jim Wohlford DP .15 .05
❑ 12 Mark Clear .15 .05
❑ 13 Joe Charboneau RC 1.50 .60
❑ 14 John Tudor RC 1.50 .60
❑ 15 Larry Parrish .15 .05
❑ 16 Ron Davis .15 .05
❑ 17 Cliff Johnson .15 .05
❑ 18 Glenn Adams .15 .05
❑ 19 Jim Clancy .15 .05
❑ 20 Jeff Burroughs .40 .15
❑ 21 Ron Oester .15 .05
❑ 22 Danny Darwin .15 .05
❑ 23 Alex Trevino .15 .05
❑ 24 Don Stanhouse .15 .05
❑ 25 Sixto Lezcano .15 .05
❑ 26 U.L. Washington .15 .05
❑ 27 Champ Summers DP .15 .05
❑ 28 Enrique Romo .15 .05
❑ 29 Gene Tenace .40 .15
❑ 30 Jack Clark .40 .15
❑ 31 Checklist 1-121 DP .25 .08
❑ 32 Ken Oberkfell .15 .05
❑ 33 Rick Honeycutt .15 .05
❑ 34 Aurelio Rodriguez .15 .05
❑ 35 Mitchell Page .15 .05
❑ 36 Ed Farmer .15 .05
❑ 37 Gary Roenicke .15 .05
❑ 38 Win Remmerswaal RC .15 .05
❑ 39 Tom Veryzer .15 .05
❑ 40 Tug McGraw .40 .15
❑ 41 Babcock/Butcher/Gleaton RC .25 .08
❑ 42 Jerry White DP .15 .05
❑ 43 Jose Morales .15 .05
❑ 44 Larry McWilliams .15 .05
❑ 45 Enos Cabell .15 .05
❑ 46 Rick Bosetti .15 .05
❑ 47 Ken Brett .15 .05
❑ 48 Dave Skaggs .15 .05
❑ 49 Bob Shirley .15 .05
❑ 50 Dave Lopes .40 .15
❑ 51 Bill Robinson DP .15 .05
❑ 52 Hector Cruz .15 .05
❑ 53 Kevin Saucier .15 .05
❑ 54 Ivan DeJesus .15 .05
❑ 55 Mike Norris .15 .05
❑ 56 Buck Martinez .15 .05
❑ 57 Dave Roberts .15 .05
❑ 58 Joel Youngblood .15 .05
❑ 59 Dan Petry .15 .05
❑ 60 Willie Randolph .40 .15
❑ 61 Butch Wynegar .15 .05
❑ 62 Joe Pettini RC .15 .05
❑ 63 Steve Renko DP .15 .05
❑ 64 Brian Asselstine .15 .05
❑ 65 Scott McGregor .15 .05
❑ 66 Castillo/Ireland/M.Jones RC .25 .08
❑ 67 Ken Kravec .15 .05
❑ 68 Matt Alexander DP .15 .05
❑ 69 Ed Halicki .15 .05
❑ 70 Al Oliver DP .25 .08
❑ 71 Hal Dues .15 .05
❑ 72 Barry Evans DP RC .15 .05
❑ 73 Doug Bair .15 .05
❑ 74 Mike Hargrove .15 .05
❑ 75 Reggie Smith .40 .15
❑ 76 Mario Mendoza .15 .05
❑ 77 Mike Barlow .15 .05
❑ 78 Steve Dillard .15 .05
❑ 79 Bruce Robbins .15 .05
❑ 80 Rusty Staub .40 .15
❑ 81 Dave Stapleton RC .15 .05
❑ 82 Heep/Knicely/Sprowl RC .25 .08
❑ 83 Mike Proly .15 .05
❑ 84 Johnnie LeMaster .15 .05
❑ 85 Mike Caldwell .15 .05
❑ 86 Wayne Gross .15 .05
❑ 87 Rick Camp .15 .05
❑ 88 Joe Lefebvre RC .15 .05
❑ 89 Darrell Jackson .15 .05
❑ 90 Bake McBride .40 .15
❑ 91 Tim Stoddard DP .15 .05
❑ 92 Mike Easler .15 .05
❑ 93 Ed Glynn DP .15 .05
❑ 94 Harry Spilman DP .15 .05
❑ 95 Jim Sundberg .40 .15
❑ 96 Beard/Camacho/Dempsey RC .25 .08
❑ 97 Chris Speier .15 .05
❑ 98 Clint Hurdle .15 .05
❑ 99 Eric Wilkins .15 .05
❑ 100 Rod Carew .75 .30
❑ 101 Benny Ayala .15 .05
❑ 102 Dave Tobik .15 .05
❑ 103 Jerry Martin .15 .05
❑ 104 Terry Forster .40 .15
❑ 105 Jose Cruz .40 .15
❑ 106 Don Money .15 .05
❑ 107 Rich Wortham .15 .05
❑ 108 Bruce Benedict .15 .05
❑ 109 Mike Scott .40 .15
❑ 110 Carl Yastrzemski 2.50 1.00
❑ 111 Greg Minton .15 .05
❑ 112 Kuntz/Mullins/Sutherland RC .25 .08
❑ 113 Mike Phillips .15 .05
❑ 114 Tom Underwood .15 .05
❑ 115 Roy Smalley .40 .15
❑ 116 Joe Simpson .15 .05
❑ 117 Pete Falcone .15 .05
❑ 118 Kurt Bevacqua .15 .05
❑ 119 Tippy Martinez .15 .05
❑ 120 Larry Bowa .40 .15
❑ 121 Larry Harlow .15 .05
❑ 122 John Denny .15 .05
❑ 123 Al Cowens .15 .05
❑ 124 Jerry Garvin .15 .05
❑ 125 Andre Dawson .75 .30
❑ 126 Charlie Leibrandt RC .75 .30
❑ 127 Rudy Law .15 .05
❑ 128 Gary Allenson DP .15 .05
❑ 129 Art Howe .15 .05
❑ 130 Larry Gura .15 .05
❑ 131 Keith Moreland RC .15 .05
❑ 132 Tommy Boggs .15 .05
❑ 133 Jeff Cox RC .15 .05
❑ 134 Steve Mura .15 .05
❑ 135 Gorman Thomas .40 .15
❑ 136 Doug Capilla .15 .05
❑ 137 Hosken Powell .15 .05
❑ 138 Rich Dotson DP RC .15 .05
❑ 139 Oscar Gamble .15 .05
❑ 140 Bob Forsch .15 .05
❑ 141 Miguel Dilone .15 .05
❑ 142 Jackson Todd .15 .05
❑ 143 Dan Meyer .15 .05
❑ 144 Allen Ripley .15 .05
❑ 145 Mickey Rivers .15 .05
❑ 146 Bobby Castillo .15 .05
❑ 147 Dale Berra .15 .05
❑ 148 Randy Niemann .15 .05
❑ 149 Joe Nolan RC .15 .05
❑ 150 Mark Fidrych .40 .15
❑ 151 Claudell Washington .15 .05
❑ 152 John Urrea .15 .05
❑ 153 Tom Poquette .15 .05
❑ 154 Rick Langford .15 .05
❑ 155 Chris Chambliss .40 .15
❑ 156 Bob McClure .15 .05
❑ 157 John Wathan .15 .05
❑ 158 Fergie Jenkins .40 .15
❑ 159 Brian Doyle .15 .05
❑ 160 Garry Maddox .15 .05
❑ 161 Dan Graham .15 .05
❑ 162 Doug Corbett RC .15 .05
❑ 163 Bill Almon RC .15 .05
❑ 164 LaMarr Hoyt RC .75 .30
❑ 165 Tony Scott .15 .05
❑ 166 Floyd Bannister .15 .05
❑ 167 Terry Whitfield .15 .05
❑ 168 Don Robinson DP .15 .05
❑ 169 John Mayberry .15 .05
❑ 170 Ross Grimsley .15 .05
❑ 171 Gene Richards .15 .05
❑ 172 Gary Woods .15 .05
❑ 173 Bump Wills .15 .05
❑ 174 Doug Rau .15 .05
❑ 175 Dave Collins .15 .05
❑ 176 Mike Krukow RC .15 .05
❑ 177 Rick Peters RC .15 .05
❑ 178 Jim Essian DP .15 .05
❑ 179 Rudy May .15 .05
❑ 180 Pete Rose 5.00 2.00
❑ 181 Elias Sosa .15 .05
❑ 182 Bob Grich .40 .15
❑ 183 Dick Davis DP .15 .05
❑ 184 Jim Dwyer .15 .05
❑ 185 Dennis Leonard .15 .05
❑ 186 Wayne Nordhagen .15 .05
❑ 187 Mike Parrott .15 .05
❑ 188 Doug DeCinces .15 .05
❑ 189 Craig Swan .15 .05
❑ 190 Cesar Cedeno .40 .15
❑ 191 Rick Sutcliffe .40 .15
❑ 192 Harper/Miller/Ramirez RC .25 .08
❑ 193 Pete Vuckovich .15 .05
❑ 194 Rod Scurry RC .15 .05
❑ 195 Rich Murray RC .15 .05
❑ 196 Duffy Dyer .15 .05
❑ 197 Jim Kern .15 .05
❑ 198 Jerry Dybzinski RC .15 .05
❑ 199 Chuck Rainey .15 .05
❑ 200 George Foster .40 .15
❑ 201 Johnny Bench RB .75 .30
❑ 202 Steve Carlton RB .40 .15
❑ 203 Bill Gullickson RB .15 .05
❑ 204 R.LeFlore/R.Scott RB .40 .15
❑ 205 Pete Rose RB 1.50 .60
❑ 206 Mike Schmidt RB 1.50 .60
❑ 207 Ozzie Smith RB 2.00 .75
❑ 208 Willie Wilson RB .15 .05
❑ 209 Dickie Thon DP .15 .05
❑ 210 Jim Palmer .75 .30
❑ 211 Derrel Thomas .15 .05
❑ 212 Steve Nicosia .15 .05
❑ 213 Al Holland RC .15 .05
❑ 214 Botting/Dorsey/J.Harris RC .25 .08
❑ 215 Larry Hisle .15 .05
❑ 216 John Henry Johnson .15 .05
❑ 217 Rich Hebner .15 .05
❑ 218 Paul Splittorff .15 .05
❑ 219 Ken Landreaux .15 .05
❑ 220 Tom Seaver 1.50 .60
❑ 221 Bob Davis .15 .05
❑ 222 Jorge Orta .15 .05
❑ 223 Roy Lee Jackson RC .15 .05
❑ 224 Pat Zachry .15 .05
❑ 225 Ruppert Jones .15 .05
❑ 226 Manny Sanguillen DP .25 .08
❑ 227 Fred Martinez RC .15 .05
❑ 228 Tom Paciorek .15 .05
❑ 229 Rollie Fingers .40 .15
❑ 230 George Hendrick .40 .15
❑ 231 Joe Beckwith .15 .05
❑ 232 Mickey Klutts .15 .05
❑ 233 Skip Lockwood .15 .05

❑ 234 Lou Whitaker .75 .30
❑ 235 Scott Sanderson .15 .05
❑ 236 Mike Ivie .15 .05
❑ 237 Charlie Moore .15 .05
❑ 238 Willie Hernandez .15 .05
❑ 239 Rick Miller DP .15 .05
❑ 240 Nolan Ryan 8.00 3.00
❑ 241 Checklist 122-242 DP .25 .08
❑ 242 Chet Lemon .40 .15
❑ 243 Sal Butera RC .15 .05
❑ 244 Landrum/Olmsted/Rincon RC .25 .08
❑ 245 Ed Figueroa .15 .05
❑ 246 Ed Ott DP .15 .05
❑ 247 Glenn Hubbard DP .15 .05
❑ 248 Joey McLaughlin .15 .05
❑ 249 Larry Cox .15 .05
❑ 250 Ron Guidry .40 .15
❑ 251 Tom Brookens .15 .05
❑ 252 Victor Cruz .15 .05
❑ 253 Dave Bergman .15 .05
❑ 254 Ozzie Smith 5.00 2.00
❑ 255 Mark Littell .15 .05
❑ 256 Bombo Rivera .15 .05
❑ 257 Rennie Stennett .15 .05
❑ 258 Joe Price RC .15 .05
❑ 259 M.Wilson/H.Brooks RC 5.00 2.00
❑ 260 Ron Cey .40 .15
❑ 261 Rickey Henderson 10.00 4.00
❑ 262 Sammy Stewart .15 .05
❑ 263 Brian Downing .40 .15
❑ 264 Jim Norris .15 .05
❑ 265 John Candelaria .40 .15
❑ 266 Tom Herr .15 .05
❑ 267 Stan Bahnsen .15 .05
❑ 268 Jerry Royster .15 .05
❑ 269 Ken Forsch .15 .05
❑ 270 Greg Luzinski .40 .15
❑ 271 Bill Castro .15 .05
❑ 272 Bruce Kimm .15 .05
❑ 273 Stan Papi .15 .05
❑ 274 Craig Chamberlain .15 .05
❑ 275 Dwight Evans .75 .30
❑ 276 Dan Spillner .15 .05
❑ 277 Alfredo Griffin .15 .05
❑ 278 Rick Sofield .15 .05
❑ 279 Bob Knepper .15 .05
❑ 280 Ken Griffey .40 .15
❑ 281 Fred Stanley .15 .05
❑ 282 Anderson/Biercevicz/Craig RC .25 .08
❑ 283 Billy Sample .15 .05
❑ 284 Brian Kingman .15 .05
❑ 285 Jerry Turner .15 .05
❑ 286 Dave Frost .15 .05
❑ 287 Lenn Sakata .15 .05
❑ 288 Bob Clark .15 .05
❑ 289 Mickey Hatcher .15 .05
❑ 290 Bob Boone DP .25 .08
❑ 291 Aurelio Lopez .15 .05
❑ 292 Mike Squires .15 .05
❑ 293 Charlie Lea RC .15 .05
❑ 294 Mike Tyson DP .15 .05
❑ 295 Hal McRae .40 .15
❑ 296 Bill Nahorodny DP .15 .05
❑ 297 Bob Bailor .15 .05
❑ 298 Buddy Solomon .15 .05
❑ 299 Elliott Maddox .15 .05
❑ 300 Paul Molitor 1.50 .60
❑ 301 Matt Keough .15 .05
❑ 302 F.Valenzuela/M.Scioscia RC 8.00 3.00
❑ 303 Johnny Oates .40 .15
❑ 304 John Castino .15 .05
❑ 305 Ken Clay .15 .05
❑ 306 Juan Beniquez DP .15 .05
❑ 307 Gene Garber .15 .05
❑ 308 Rick Manning .15 .05
❑ 309 Luis Salazar RC .75 .30
❑ 310 Vida Blue DP .25 .08
❑ 311 Freddie Patek .15 .05
❑ 312 Rick Rhoden .15 .05
❑ 313 Luis Pujols .15 .05
❑ 314 Rich Dauer .15 .05
❑ 315 Kirk Gibson RC 8.00 3.00
❑ 316 Craig Minetto .15 .05
❑ 317 Lonnie Smith .40 .15
❑ 318 Steve Yeager .40 .15
❑ 319 Rowland Office .15 .05
❑ 320 Tom Burgmeier .15 .05
❑ 321 Leon Durham RC .75 .30
❑ 322 Neil Allen .15 .05
❑ 323 Jim Morrison DP .15 .05
❑ 324 Mike Willis .15 .05
❑ 325 Ray Knight .40 .15
❑ 326 Biff Pocoroba .15 .05
❑ 327 Moose Haas .15 .05
❑ 328 Engle/Johnston/G.Ward .25 .08
❑ 329 Joaquin Andujar .40 .15
❑ 330 Frank White .40 .15
❑ 331 Dennis Lamp .15 .05
❑ 332 Lee Lacy DP .15 .05
❑ 333 Sid Monge .15 .05
❑ 334 Dane Iorg .15 .05
❑ 335 Rick Cerone .15 .05
❑ 336 Eddie Whitson .15 .05
❑ 337 Lynn Jones .15 .05
❑ 338 Checklist 243-363 .40 .15
❑ 339 John Ellis .15 .05
❑ 340 Bruce Kison .15 .05
❑ 341 Dwayne Murphy .15 .05
❑ 342 Eric Rasmussen DP .15 .05
❑ 343 Frank Taveras .15 .05
❑ 344 Byron McLaughlin .15 .05
❑ 345 Warren Cromartie .15 .05
❑ 346 Larry Christenson DP .15 .05
❑ 347 Harold Baines RC 3.00 1.25
❑ 348 Bob Sykes .15 .05
❑ 349 Glenn Hoffman RC .15 .05
❑ 350 J.R. Richard .40 .15
❑ 351 Otto Velez .15 .05
❑ 352 Dick Tidrow DP .15 .05
❑ 353 Terry Kennedy .15 .05
❑ 354 Mario Soto .40 .15
❑ 355 Bob Horner .40 .15
❑ 356 Stablein/Stimac/Tellmann RC .25 .08
❑ 357 Jim Slaton .15 .05
❑ 358 Mark Wagner .15 .05
❑ 359 Tom Hausman .15 .05
❑ 360 Willie Wilson .40 .15
❑ 361 Joe Strain .15 .05
❑ 362 Bo Diaz .15 .05
❑ 363 Geoff Zahn .15 .05
❑ 364 Mike Davis RC .25 .08
❑ 365 Graig Nettles DP .25 .08
❑ 366 Mike Ramsey RC .25 .08
❑ 367 Dennis Martinez .40 .15
❑ 368 Leon Roberts .15 .05
❑ 369 Frank Tanana .40 .15
❑ 370 Dave Winfield .75 .30
❑ 371 Charlie Hough .40 .15
❑ 372 Jay Johnstone .15 .05
❑ 373 Pat Underwood .15 .05
❑ 374 Tommy Hutton .15 .05
❑ 375 Dave Concepcion .40 .15
❑ 376 Ron Reed .15 .05
❑ 377 Jerry Morales .15 .05
❑ 378 Dave Rader .15 .05
❑ 379 Lary Sorensen .15 .05
❑ 380 Willie Stargell .75 .30
❑ 381 Lezcano/Macko/Martz RC .25 .08
❑ 382 Paul Mirabella RC .15 .05
❑ 383 Eric Soderholm DP .15 .05
❑ 384 Mike Sadek .15 .05
❑ 385 Joe Sambito .15 .05
❑ 386 Dave Edwards .15 .05
❑ 387 Phil Niekro .40 .15
❑ 388 Andre Thornton .40 .15
❑ 389 Marty Pattin .15 .05
❑ 390 Cesar Geronimo .15 .05
❑ 391 Dave Lemanczyk DP .15 .05
❑ 392 Lance Parrish .40 .15
❑ 393 Broderick Perkins .15 .05
❑ 394 Woodie Fryman .15 .05
❑ 395 Scot Thompson .15 .05
❑ 396 Bill Campbell .15 .05
❑ 397 Julio Cruz .15 .05
❑ 398 Ross Baumgarten .15 .05
❑ 399 Boddicker/Corey/Rayford RC .75 .30
❑ 400 Reggie Jackson 1.50 .60
❑ 401 George Brett ALCS 2.50 1.00
❑ 402 NL Champs .75 .30
❑ 403 Larry Bowa WS .75 .30
❑ 404 Tug McGraw WS .75 .30
❑ 405 Nino Espinosa .15 .05
❑ 406 Dickie Noles .15 .05
❑ 407 Ernie Whitt .15 .05
❑ 408 Fernando Arroyo .15 .05
❑ 409 Larry Herndon .15 .05
❑ 410 Bert Campaneris .40 .15
❑ 411 Terry Puhl .15 .05
❑ 412 Britt Burns RC .15 .05
❑ 413 Tony Bernazard .15 .05
❑ 414 John Pacella DP RC .15 .05
❑ 415 Ben Oglivie .40 .15
❑ 416 Gary Alexander .15 .05
❑ 417 Dan Schatzeder .15 .05
❑ 418 Bobby Brown .15 .05
❑ 419 Tom Hume .15 .05
❑ 420 Keith Hernandez .40 .15
❑ 421 Bob Stanley .15 .05
❑ 422 Dan Ford .15 .05
❑ 423 Shane Rawley .15 .05
❑ 424 Lollar/Robinson/Werth RC .25 .08
❑ 425 Al Bumbry .15 .05
❑ 426 Warren Brusstar .15 .05
❑ 427 John D'Acquisto .15 .05
❑ 428 John Stearns .15 .05
❑ 429 Mick Kelleher .15 .05
❑ 430 Jim Bibby .15 .05
❑ 431 Dave Roberts .15 .05
❑ 432 Len Barker .40 .15
❑ 433 Rance Mulliniks .15 .05
❑ 434 Roger Erickson .15 .05
❑ 435 Jim Spencer .15 .05
❑ 436 Gary Lucas RC .15 .05
❑ 437 Mike Heath DP .15 .05
❑ 438 John Montefusco .15 .05
❑ 439 Denny Walling .15 .05
❑ 440 Jerry Reuss .15 .05
❑ 441 Ken Reitz .15 .05
❑ 442 Ron Pruitt .15 .05
❑ 443 Jim Beattie DP .15 .05
❑ 444 Garth Iorg .15 .05
❑ 445 Ellis Valentine .15 .05
❑ 446 Checklist 364-484 .40 .15
❑ 447 Junior Kennedy DP .15 .05
❑ 448 Tim Corcoran .15 .05
❑ 449 Paul Mitchell .15 .05
❑ 450 Dave Kingman DP .25 .08
❑ 451 Bando/Brennan/Wihtol RC .25 .08
❑ 452 Renie Martin .15 .05
❑ 453 Rob Wilfong DP .15 .05
❑ 454 Andy Hassler .15 .05
❑ 455 Rick Burleson .15 .05
❑ 456 Jeff Reardon RC 1.50 .60
❑ 457 Mike Lum .15 .05
❑ 458 Randy Jones .40 .15
❑ 459 Greg Gross .15 .05
❑ 460 Rich Gossage .40 .15
❑ 461 Dave McKay RC .15 .05
❑ 462 Jack Brohamer .15 .05
❑ 463 Milt May .15 .05
❑ 464 Adrian Devine .15 .05
❑ 465 Bill Russell .40 .15
❑ 466 Bob Molinaro .15 .05
❑ 467 Dave Stieb .40 .15
❑ 468 John Wockenfuss .15 .05
❑ 469 Jeff Leonard .40 .15
❑ 470 Manny Trillo .15 .05
❑ 471 Mike Vail .15 .05
❑ 472 Dyar Miller DP .15 .05
❑ 473 Jose Cardenal .15 .05
❑ 474 Mike LaCoss .15 .05
❑ 475 Buddy Bell .40 .15
❑ 476 Jerry Koosman .40 .15
❑ 477 Luis Gomez .15 .05
❑ 478 Juan Eichelberger RC .15 .05
❑ 479 Tim Raines RC 4.00 1.50
❑ 480 Carlton Fisk .75 .30
❑ 481 Bob Lacey DP .15 .05
❑ 482 Jim Gantner .15 .05
❑ 483 Mike Griffin RC .25 .08
❑ 484 Max Venable DP RC .15 .05
❑ 485 Garry Templeton .40 .15
❑ 486 Marc Hill .15 .05
❑ 487 Dewey Robinson .15 .05
❑ 488 Damaso Garcia RC .15 .05
❑ 489 John Littlefield RC .15 .05
❑ 490 Eddie Murray 2.50 1.00
❑ 491 Gordy Pladson RC .15 .05

❑ 492 Barry Foote .15 .05
❑ 493 Dan Quisenberry .15 .05
❑ 494 Bob Walk RC .75 .30
❑ 495 Dusty Baker .40 .15
❑ 496 Paul Dade .15 .05
❑ 497 Fred Norman .15 .05
❑ 498 Pat Putnam .15 .05
❑ 499 Frank Pastore .15 .05
❑ 500 Jim Rice .40 .15
❑ 501 Tim Foli DP .15 .05
❑ 502 Bourjos/Hargesheimer/Rowland RC .25 .08
❑ 503 Steve McCatty .15 .05
❑ 504 Dale Murphy .75 .30
❑ 505 Jason Thompson .15 .05
❑ 506 Phil Huffman .15 .05
❑ 507 Jamie Quirk .15 .05
❑ 508 Rob Dressler .15 .05
❑ 509 Pete Mackanin .15 .05
❑ 510 Lee Mazzilli .40 .15
❑ 511 Wayne Garland .15 .05
❑ 512 Gary Thomasson .15 .05
❑ 513 Frank LaCorte .15 .05
❑ 514 George Riley RC .15 .05
❑ 515 Robin Yount 2.50 1.00
❑ 516 Doug Bird .15 .05
❑ 517 Richie Zisk .15 .05
❑ 518 Grant Jackson .15 .05
❑ 519 John Tamargo DP .15 .05
❑ 520 Steve Stone .15 .05
❑ 521 Sam Mejias .15 .05
❑ 522 Mike Colbern .15 .05
❑ 523 John Fulgham .15 .05
❑ 524 Willie Aikens .15 .05
❑ 525 Mike Torrez .15 .05
❑ 526 Bystrom/Loviglio/Wright RC .25 .08
❑ 527 Danny Goodwin .15 .05
❑ 528 Gary Matthews .40 .15
❑ 529 Dave LaRoche .15 .05
❑ 530 Steve Garvey .75 .30
❑ 531 John Curtis .15 .05
❑ 532 Bill Stein .15 .05
❑ 533 Jesus Figueroa RC .15 .05
❑ 534 Dave Smith RC .75 .30
❑ 535 Omar Moreno .15 .05
❑ 536 Bob Owchinko DP .15 .05
❑ 537 Ron Hodges .15 .05
❑ 538 Tom Griffin .15 .05
❑ 539 Rodney Scott .15 .05
❑ 540 Mike Schmidt DP 2.00 .75
❑ 541 Steve Swisher .15 .05
❑ 542 Larry Bradford DP .15 .05
❑ 543 Terry Crowley .15 .05
❑ 544 Rich Gale .15 .05
❑ 545 Johnny Grubb .15 .05
❑ 546 Paul Moskau .15 .05
❑ 547 Mario Guerrero .15 .05
❑ 548 Dave Goltz .15 .05
❑ 549 Jerry Remy .15 .05
❑ 550 Tommy John .40 .15
❑ 551 Law/Pena/Perez RC .75 .30
❑ 552 Steve Trout .15 .05
❑ 553 Tim Blackwell .15 .05
❑ 554 Bert Blyleven .40 .15
❑ 555 Cecil Cooper .40 .15
❑ 556 Jerry Mumphrey .15 .05
❑ 557 Chris Knapp .15 .05
❑ 558 Barry Bonnell .15 .05
❑ 559 Willie Montanez .15 .05
❑ 560 Joe Morgan .75 .30
❑ 561 Dennis Littlejohn .15 .05
❑ 562 Checklist 485-605 .40 .15
❑ 563 Jim Kaat .40 .15
❑ 564 Ron Hassey DP .15 .05
❑ 565 Burt Hooton .15 .05
❑ 566 Del Unser .15 .05
❑ 567 Mark Bomback RC .15 .05
❑ 568 Dave Revering .15 .05
❑ 569 Al Williams DP RC .15 .05
❑ 570 Ken Singleton .40 .15
❑ 571 Todd Cruz .15 .05
❑ 572 Jack Morris .75 .30
❑ 573 Phil Garner .40 .15
❑ 574 Bill Caudill .15 .05
❑ 575 Tony Perez .75 .30
❑ 576 Reggie Cleveland .15 .05
❑ 577 Leal/Milner/Schrom RC .25 .08
❑ 578 Bill Gullickson RC .75 .30
❑ 579 Tim Flannery .15 .05
❑ 580 Don Baylor .40 .15
❑ 581 Roy Howell .15 .05
❑ 582 Gaylord Perry .40 .15
❑ 583 Larry Milbourne .15 .05
❑ 584 Randy Lerch .15 .05
❑ 585 Amos Otis .40 .15
❑ 586 Silvio Martinez .15 .05
❑ 587 Jeff Newman .15 .05
❑ 588 Gary Lavelle .15 .05
❑ 589 Lamar Johnson .15 .05
❑ 590 Bruce Sutter .75 .30
❑ 591 John Lowenstein .15 .05
❑ 592 Steve Comer .15 .05
❑ 593 Steve Kemp .15 .05
❑ 594 Preston Hanna DP .15 .05
❑ 595 Butch Hobson .15 .05
❑ 596 Jerry Augustine .15 .05
❑ 597 Rafael Landestoy .15 .05
❑ 598 George Vukovich DP RC .15 .05
❑ 599 Dennis Kinney RC .15 .05
❑ 600 Johnny Bench 1.50 .60
❑ 601 Don Aase .15 .05
❑ 602 Bobby Murcer .40 .15
❑ 603 John Verhoeven .15 .05
❑ 604 Rob Picciolo .15 .05
❑ 605 Don Sutton .40 .15
❑ 606 Berenyi/Combe /Householder DP RC .25 .08
❑ 607 David Palmer .15 .05
❑ 608 Greg Pryor .15 .05
❑ 609 Lynn McGlothen .15 .05
❑ 610 Darrell Porter .15 .05
❑ 611 Rick Matula DP .15 .05
❑ 612 Duane Kuiper .15 .05
❑ 613 Jim Anderson .15 .05
❑ 614 Dave Rozema .15 .05
❑ 615 Rick Dempsey .15 .05
❑ 616 Rick Wise .15 .05
❑ 617 Craig Reynolds .15 .05
❑ 618 John Milner .15 .05
❑ 619 Steve Henderson .15 .05
❑ 620 Dennis Eckersley .75 .30
❑ 621 Tom Donohue .15 .05
❑ 622 Randy Moffitt .15 .05
❑ 623 Sal Bando .40 .15
❑ 624 Bob Welch .40 .15
❑ 625 Bill Buckner .40 .15
❑ 626 Steffen/Ujdur/Weaver RC .25 .08
❑ 627 Luis Tiant .40 .15
❑ 628 Vic Correll .15 .05
❑ 629 Tony Armas .40 .15
❑ 630 Steve Carlton .75 .30
❑ 631 Ron Jackson .15 .05
❑ 632 Alan Bannister .15 .05
❑ 633 Bill Lee .40 .15
❑ 634 Doug Flynn .15 .05
❑ 635 Bobby Bonds .40 .15
❑ 636 Al Hrabosky .40 .15
❑ 637 Jerry Narron .15 .05
❑ 638 Checklist 606-726 .40 .15
❑ 639 Carney Lansford .40 .15
❑ 640 Dave Parker .40 .15
❑ 641 Mark Belanger .15 .05
❑ 642 Vern Ruhle .15 .05
❑ 643 Lloyd Moseby RC .75 .30
❑ 644 Ramon Aviles DP .15 .05
❑ 645 Rick Reuschel .40 .15
❑ 646 Marvis Foley RC .15 .05
❑ 647 Dick Drago .15 .05
❑ 648 Darrell Evans .40 .15
❑ 649 Manny Sarmiento .15 .05
❑ 650 Bucky Dent .40 .15
❑ 651 Pedro Guerrero .40 .15
❑ 652 John Montague .15 .05
❑ 653 Bill Fahey .15 .05
❑ 654 Ray Burris .15 .05
❑ 655 Dan Driessen .15 .05
❑ 656 Jon Matlack .15 .05
❑ 657 Mike Cubbage DP .15 .05
❑ 658 Milt Wilcox .15 .05
❑ 659 Flinn/Romero/Yost .75 .30
❑ 660 Gary Carter .75 .30
❑ 661 Orioles Team CL Earl Weaver MG .40 .15
❑ 662 Red Sox Team CL Ralph Houk MG .40 .15
❑ 663 Angels Team CL Jim Fregosi MG .40 .15
❑ 664 White Sox Team/Mgr. Tony LaRussa (Checklist back .40 .15
❑ 665 Indians Team CL Dave Garcia MG .40 .15
❑ 666 Tigers Team/Mgr. Sparky Anderson (Checklist back .40 .15
❑ 667 Royals Team CL Jim Frey MG .40 .15
❑ 668 Brewers Team CL Bob Rodgers MG .40 .15
❑ 669 Twins Team CL. John Goryl MG .40 .15
❑ 670 Yankees Team CL Gene Michael MG .40 .15
❑ 671 A's Team CL Billy Martin MG .75 .30
❑ 672 Mariners Team CL Maury Wills MG .40 .15
❑ 673 Rangers Team CL Don Zimmer MG .40 .15
❑ 674 Blue Jays Team/Mgr. Bobby Mattick (Checklist bac .40 .15
❑ 675 Braves Team CL Bobby Cox MG .40 .15
❑ 676 Cubs Team CL Joe Amalfitano MG .40 .15
❑ 677 Reds Team CL John McNamara MG .40 .15
❑ 678 Astros Team CL Bill Virdon MG .40 .15
❑ 679 Dodgers Team CL Tom Lasorda MG .75 .30
❑ 680 Expos Team CL Dick Williams MG .40 .15
❑ 681 Mets Team CL Joe Torre MG .75 .30
❑ 682 Phillies Team CL Dallas Green MG .40 .15
❑ 683 Pirates Team CL Chuck Tanner MG .40 .15
❑ 684 Cardinals Team/Mgr. Whitey Herzog (Checklist bac .40 .15
❑ 685 Padres Team CL Frank Howard MG .40 .15
❑ 686 Giants Team CL Dave Bristol MG .40 .15
❑ 687 Jeff Jones RC .15 .05
❑ 688 Kiko Garcia .15 .05
❑ 689 Bruce Hurst RC .75 .30
❑ 690 Bob Watson .15 .05
❑ 691 Dick Ruthven .15 .05
❑ 692 Lenny Randle .15 .05
❑ 693 Steve Howe RC .25 .08
❑ 694 Bud Harrelson DP .25 .08
❑ 695 Kent Tekulve .15 .05
❑ 696 Alan Ashby .15 .05
❑ 697 Rick Waits .15 .05
❑ 698 Mike Jorgensen .15 .05
❑ 699 Glenn Abbott .15 .05
❑ 700 George Brett 4.00 1.50
❑ 701 Joe Rudi .40 .15
❑ 702 George Medich .15 .05
❑ 703 Alvis Woods .15 .05
❑ 704 Bill Travers DP .15 .05
❑ 705 Ted Simmons .40 .15
❑ 706 Dave Ford RC .15 .05
❑ 707 Dave Cash .15 .05
❑ 708 Doyle Alexander .15 .05
❑ 709 Alan Trammell DP .50 .20
❑ 710 Ron LeFlore DP .25 .08
❑ 711 Joe Ferguson .15 .05
❑ 712 Bill Bonham .15 .05
❑ 713 Bill North .15 .05
❑ 714 Pete Redfern .15 .05
❑ 715 Bill Madlock .40 .15
❑ 716 Glenn Borgmann .15 .05
❑ 717 Jim Barr DP .15 .05
❑ 718 Larry Biittner .15 .05

❑ 719 Sparky Lyle	.40	.15
❑ 720 Fred Lynn	.40	.15
❑ 721 Toby Harrah	.40	.15
❑ 722 Joe Niekro	.15	.05
❑ 723 Bruce Bochte	.15	.05
❑ 724 Lou Piniella	.40	.15
❑ 725 Steve Rogers	.40	.15
❑ 726 Rick Monday	.40	.15

1982 Topps

❑ COMPLETE SET (792)	80.00	40.00
❑ 1 Steve Carlton HL	.30	.10
❑ 2 Ron Davis HL		
Fans 8 straight		
in relief	.15	.05
❑ 3 Tim Raines HL	.30	.10
❑ 4 Pete Rose HL	.60	.25
❑ 5 Nolan Ryan HL	3.00	1.25
❑ 6 Fernando Valenzuela HL		
8 shutouts as rookie	.60	.25
❑ 7 Scott Sanderson	.15	.05
❑ 8 Rich Dauer	.15	.05
❑ 9 Ron Guidry	.30	.10
❑ 10 Ron Guidry SA	.15	.05
❑ 11 Gary Alexander	.15	.05
❑ 12 Moose Haas	.15	.05
❑ 13 Lamar Johnson	.15	.05
❑ 14 Steve Howe	.15	.05
❑ 15 Ellis Valentine	.15	.05
❑ 16 Steve Comer	.15	.05
❑ 17 Darrell Evans	.30	.10
❑ 18 Fernando Arroyo	.15	.05
❑ 19 Ernie Whitt	.15	.05
❑ 20 Garry Maddox	.15	.05
❑ 21 Cal Ripken RC	50.00	20.00
❑ 22 Jim Beattie	.15	.05
❑ 23 Willie Hernandez	.15	.05
❑ 24 Dave Frost	.15	.05
❑ 25 Jerry Remy	.15	.05
❑ 26 Jorge Orta	.15	.05
❑ 27 Tom Herr	.15	.05
❑ 28 John Urrea	.15	.05
❑ 29 Dwayne Murphy	.15	.05
❑ 30 Tom Seaver	1.25	.50
❑ 31 Tom Seaver SA	.30	.10
❑ 32 Gene Garber	.15	.05
❑ 33 Jerry Morales	.15	.05
❑ 34 Joe Sambito	.15	.05
❑ 35 Willie Aikens	.15	.05
❑ 36 Rangers TL		
BA: Al Oliver		
Pitching: Doc Medich	.60	.25
❑ 37 Dan Graham	.15	.05
❑ 38 Charlie Lea	.15	.05
❑ 39 Lou Whitaker	.30	.10
❑ 40 Dave Parker	.30	.10
❑ 41 Dave Parker SA	.15	.05
❑ 42 Rick Sofield	.15	.05
❑ 43 Mike Cubbage	.15	.05
❑ 44 Britt Burns	.15	.05
❑ 45 Rick Cerone	.15	.05
❑ 46 Jerry Augustine	.15	.05
❑ 47 Jeff Leonard	.15	.05
❑ 48 Bobby Castillo	.15	.05
❑ 49 Alvis Woods	.15	.05
❑ 50 Buddy Bell	.30	.10
❑ 51 Howell/Lezcano/Waller RC	.75	.30
❑ 52 Larry Andersen	.15	.05
❑ 53 Greg Gross	.15	.05
❑ 54 Ron Hassey	.15	.05
❑ 55 Rick Burleson	.15	.05
❑ 56 Mark Littell	.15	.05
❑ 57 Craig Reynolds	.15	.05
❑ 58 John D'Acquisto	.15	.05
❑ 59 Rich Gedman	.75	.30
❑ 60 Tony Armas	.30	.10
❑ 61 Tommy Boggs	.15	.05
❑ 62 Mike Tyson	.15	.05
❑ 63 Mario Soto	.30	.10
❑ 64 Lynn Jones	.15	.05
❑ 65 Terry Kennedy	.15	.05
❑ 66 Astros TL/Nolan Ryan	2.00	.75
❑ 67 Rich Gale	.15	.05
❑ 68 Roy Howell	.15	.05
❑ 69 Al Williams	.15	.05
❑ 70 Tim Raines	.60	.25
❑ 71 Roy Lee Jackson	.15	.05
❑ 72 Rick Auerbach	.15	.05
❑ 73 Buddy Solomon	.15	.05
❑ 74 Bob Clark	.15	.05
❑ 75 Tommy John	.30	.10
❑ 76 Greg Pryor	.15	.05
❑ 77 Miguel Dilone	.15	.05
❑ 78 George Medich	.15	.05
❑ 79 Bob Bailor	.15	.05
❑ 80 Jim Palmer	.30	.10
❑ 81 Jim Palmer SA	.15	.05
❑ 82 Bob Welch	.30	.10
❑ 83 Balboni/McGaf/Rob RC	.75	.30
❑ 84 Rennie Stennett	.15	.05
❑ 85 Lynn McGlothen	.15	.05
❑ 86 Dane Iorg	.15	.05
❑ 87 Matt Keough	.15	.05
❑ 88 Biff Pocoroba	.15	.05
❑ 89 Steve Henderson	.15	.05
❑ 90 Nolan Ryan	6.00	2.50
❑ 91 Carney Lansford	.30	.10
❑ 92 Brad Havens	.15	.05
❑ 93 Larry Hisle	.15	.05
❑ 94 Andy Hassler	.15	.05
❑ 95 Ozzie Smith	2.50	1.00
❑ 96 Royals TL/George Brett	1.25	.50
❑ 97 Paul Moskau	.15	.05
❑ 98 Terry Bulling	.15	.05
❑ 99 Barry Bonnell	.15	.05
❑ 100 Mike Schmidt	3.00	1.25
❑ 101 Mike Schmidt SA	1.25	.50
❑ 102 Dan Briggs	.15	.05
❑ 103 Bob Lacey	.15	.05
❑ 104 Rance Mulliniks	.15	.05
❑ 105 Kirk Gibson	1.25	.50
❑ 106 Enrique Romo	.15	.05
❑ 107 Wayne Krenchicki	.15	.05
❑ 108 Bob Sykes	.15	.05
❑ 109 Dave Revering	.15	.05
❑ 110 Carlton Fisk	.60	.25
❑ 111 Carlton Fisk SA	.30	.10
❑ 112 Billy Sample	.15	.05
❑ 113 Steve McCatty	.15	.05
❑ 114 Ken Landreaux	.15	.05
❑ 115 Gaylord Perry	.30	.10
❑ 116 Jim Wohlford	.15	.05
❑ 117 Rawly Eastwick	.30	.10
❑ 118 Francona/Mills/Smith RC	5.00	2.00
❑ 119 Joe Pittman	.15	.05
❑ 120 Gary Lucas	.15	.05
❑ 121 Ed Lynch	.15	.05
❑ 122 Jamie Easterly UER		
(Photo actually		
Reggie Cleveland)	.15	.05
❑ 123 Danny Goodwin	.15	.05
❑ 124 Reid Nichols	.15	.05
❑ 125 Danny Ainge	.30	.10
❑ 126 Braves TL		
BA: Claudell Washington		
Pitching: Rick	.60	.25
❑ 127 Lonnie Smith	.15	.05
❑ 128 Frank Pastore	.15	.05
❑ 129 Checklist 1-132	.30	.10
❑ 130 Julio Cruz	.15	.05
❑ 131 Stan Bahnsen	.15	.05
❑ 132 Lee May	.15	.05
❑ 133 Pat Underwood	.15	.05
❑ 134 Dan Ford	.15	.05
❑ 135 Andy Rincon	.15	.05
❑ 136 Lenn Sakata	.15	.05
❑ 137 George Cappuzzello	.15	.05
❑ 138 Tony Pena	.30	.10
❑ 139 Jeff Jones	.15	.05
❑ 140 Ron LeFlore	.30	.10
❑ 141 Bando/Brennan/Hayes RC	.75	.30
❑ 142 Dave LaRoche	.15	.05
❑ 143 Mookie Wilson	.30	.10
❑ 144 Fred Breining	.15	.05
❑ 145 Bob Horner	.30	.10
❑ 146 Mike Griffin	.15	.05
❑ 147 Denny Walling	.15	.05
❑ 148 Mickey Klutts	.15	.05
❑ 149 Pat Putnam	.15	.05
❑ 150 Ted Simmons	.30	.10
❑ 151 Dave Edwards	.15	.05
❑ 152 Ramon Aviles	.15	.05
❑ 153 Roger Erickson	.15	.05
❑ 154 Dennis Werth	.15	.05
❑ 155 Otto Velez	.15	.05
❑ 156 A's TL/Rickey Henderson	1.25	.50
❑ 157 Steve Crawford	.15	.05
❑ 158 Brian Downing	.30	.10
❑ 159 Larry Biittner	.15	.05
❑ 160 Luis Tiant	.30	.10
❑ 161 Bill Madlock		
Carney Lansford LL	.30	.10
❑ 162 Schmidt/Armas/Murray LL	1.25	.50
❑ 163 Mike Schmidt/E.Murray LL	1.25	.50
❑ 164 T.Raines/R.Henderson LL	1.25	.50
❑ 165 Seav/Martinez/Morris LL	.30	.10
❑ 166 Strikeout Leaders		
Fernando Valenzuela		
Len Barker	.30	.10
❑ 167 N.Ryan/S.McCatty LL	2.00	.75
❑ 168 B.Sutter/R.Fingers LL	.30	.10
❑ 169 Charlie Leibrandt	.15	.05
❑ 170 Jim Bibby	.15	.05
❑ 171 Brenly/Davis/Tufts RC	1.50	.60
❑ 172 Bill Gullickson	.15	.05
❑ 173 Jamie Quirk	.15	.05
❑ 174 Dave Ford	.15	.05
❑ 175 Jerry Mumphrey	.15	.05
❑ 176 Dewey Robinson	.15	.05
❑ 177 John Ellis	.15	.05
❑ 178 Dyar Miller	.15	.05
❑ 179 Steve Garvey	.30	.10
❑ 180 Steve Garvey SA	.15	.05
❑ 181 Silvio Martinez	.15	.05
❑ 182 Larry Herndon	.15	.05
❑ 183 Mike Proly	.15	.05
❑ 184 Mick Kelleher	.15	.05
❑ 185 Phil Niekro	.30	.10
❑ 186 Cardinals TL		
BA: Keith Hernandez		
Pitching: Bob F	.30	.10
❑ 187 Jeff Newman	.15	.05
❑ 188 Randy Martz	.15	.05
❑ 189 Glenn Hoffman	.15	.05
❑ 190 J.R. Richard	.30	.10
❑ 191 Tim Wallach RC	1.50	.60
❑ 192 Broderick Perkins	.15	.05
❑ 193 Darrell Jackson	.15	.05
❑ 194 Mike Vail	.15	.05
❑ 195 Paul Molitor	.30	.10
❑ 196 Willie Upshaw	.75	.30
❑ 197 Shane Rawley	.15	.05
❑ 198 Chris Speier	.15	.05
❑ 199 Don Aase	.15	.05
❑ 200 George Brett	3.00	1.25
❑ 201 George Brett SA	1.50	.60
❑ 202 Rick Manning	.15	.05
❑ 203 Barfield/Miln/Wells RC	1.50	.60
❑ 204 Gary Roenicke	.15	.05
❑ 205 Neil Allen	.15	.05
❑ 206 Tony Bernazard	.15	.05
❑ 207 Rod Scurry	.15	.05
❑ 208 Bobby Murcer	.30	.10
❑ 209 Gary Lavelle	.15	.05
❑ 210 Keith Hernandez	.30	.10
❑ 211 Dan Petry	.15	.05
❑ 212 Mario Mendoza	.15	.05
❑ 213 Dave Stewart RC	2.50	1.00
❑ 214 Brian Asselstine	.15	.05
❑ 215 Mike Krukow	.15	.05

❑ 216 White Sox TL BA: Chet Lemon Pitching: Dennis Lam .60 .25
❑ 217 Bo McLaughlin .15 .05
❑ 218 Dave Roberts .15 .05
❑ 219 John Curtis .15 .05
❑ 220 Manny Trillo .15 .05
❑ 221 Jim Slaton .15 .05
❑ 222 Butch Wynegar .15 .05
❑ 223 Lloyd Moseby .15 .05
❑ 224 Bruce Bochte .15 .05
❑ 225 Mike Torrez .15 .05
❑ 226 Checklist 133-264 .60 .25
❑ 227 Ray Burris .15 .05
❑ 228 Sam Mejias .15 .05
❑ 229 Geoff Zahn .15 .05
❑ 230 Willie Wilson .30 .10
❑ 231 Davis/Dernier/Virgil RC .75 .30
❑ 232 Terry Crowley .15 .05
❑ 233 Duane Kuiper .15 .05
❑ 234 Ron Hodges .15 .05
❑ 235 Mike Easler .15 .05
❑ 236 John Martin RC .25 .08
❑ 237 Rusty Kuntz .15 .05
❑ 238 Kevin Saucier .15 .05
❑ 239 Jon Matlack .15 .05
❑ 240 Bucky Dent .30 .10
❑ 241 Bucky Dent SA .15 .05
❑ 242 Milt May .15 .05
❑ 243 Bob Owchinko .15 .05
❑ 244 Rufino Linares .15 .05
❑ 245 Ken Reitz .15 .05
❑ 246 New York Mets TL BA: Hubie Brooks Pitching: Mike .60 .25
❑ 247 Pedro Guerrero .30 .10
❑ 248 Frank LaCorte .15 .05
❑ 249 Tim Flannery .15 .05
❑ 250 Tug McGraw .30 .10
❑ 251 Fred Lynn .30 .10
❑ 252 Fred Lynn SA .15 .05
❑ 253 Chuck Baker .15 .05
❑ 254 George Bell RC 1.50 .60
❑ 255 Tony Perez .60 .25
❑ 256 Tony Perez SA .30 .10
❑ 257 Larry Harlow .15 .05
❑ 258 Bo Diaz .15 .05
❑ 259 Rodney Scott .15 .05
❑ 260 Bruce Sutter .60 .25
❑ 261 Bailey/Castillo/Rucker RC .15 .05
❑ 262 Doug Bair .15 .05
❑ 263 Victor Cruz .15 .05
❑ 264 Dan Quisenberry .15 .05
❑ 265 Al Bumbry .15 .05
❑ 266 Rick Leach .15 .05
❑ 267 Kurt Bevacqua .15 .05
❑ 268 Rickey Keeton .15 .05
❑ 269 Jim Essian .15 .05
❑ 270 Rusty Staub .30 .10
❑ 271 Larry Bradford .15 .05
❑ 272 Bump Wills .15 .05
❑ 273 Doug Bird .15 .05
❑ 274 Bob Ojeda RC .75 .30
❑ 275 Bob Watson .15 .05
❑ 276 Angels TL/Rod Carew .60 .25
❑ 277 Terry Puhl .15 .05
❑ 278 John Littlefield .15 .05
❑ 279 Bill Russell .30 .10
❑ 280 Ben Oglivie .30 .10
❑ 281 John Verhoeven .15 .05
❑ 282 Ken Macha .15 .05
❑ 283 Brian Allard .15 .05
❑ 284 Bob Grich .30 .10
❑ 285 Sparky Lyle .30 .10
❑ 286 Bill Fahey .15 .05
❑ 287 Alan Bannister .15 .05
❑ 288 Garry Templeton .30 .10
❑ 289 Bob Stanley .15 .05
❑ 290 Ken Singleton .30 .10
❑ 291 Law/Long/Ray RC .30 .10
❑ 292 David Palmer .15 .05
❑ 293 Rob Picciolo .15 .05
❑ 294 Mike LaCoss .15 .05
❑ 295 Jason Thompson .15 .05
❑ 296 Bob Walk .15 .05
❑ 297 Clint Hurdle .15 .05
❑ 298 Danny Darwin .15 .05
❑ 299 Steve Trout .15 .05
❑ 300 Reggie Jackson .60 .25
❑ 301 Reggie Jackson SA .30 .10
❑ 302 Doug Flynn .15 .05
❑ 303 Bill Caudill .15 .05
❑ 304 Johnnie LeMaster .15 .05
❑ 305 Don Sutton .30 .10
❑ 306 Don Sutton SA .15 .05
❑ 307 Randy Bass .75 .30
❑ 308 Charlie Moore .15 .05
❑ 309 Pete Redfern .15 .05
❑ 310 Mike Hargrove .15 .05
❑ 311 Dusty Baker Burt Hooton TL .30 .10
❑ 312 Lenny Randle .15 .05
❑ 313 John Harris .15 .05
❑ 314 Buck Martinez .15 .05
❑ 315 Burt Hooton .15 .05
❑ 316 Steve Braun .15 .05
❑ 317 Dick Ruthven .15 .05
❑ 318 Mike Heath .15 .05
❑ 319 Dave Rozema .15 .05
❑ 320 Chris Chambliss .30 .10
❑ 321 Chris Chambliss SA .15 .05
❑ 322 Garry Hancock .15 .05
❑ 323 Bill Lee .30 .10
❑ 324 Steve Dillard .15 .05
❑ 325 Jose Cruz .30 .10
❑ 326 Pete Falcone .15 .05
❑ 327 Joe Nolan .15 .05
❑ 328 Ed Farmer .15 .05
❑ 329 U.L. Washington .15 .05
❑ 330 Rick Wise .15 .05
❑ 331 Benny Ayala .15 .05
❑ 332 Don Robinson .15 .05
❑ 333 DiPino/Edwards/Porter RC .15 .05
❑ 334 Aurelio Rodriguez .15 .05
❑ 335 Jim Sundberg .30 .10
❑ 336 Mariners TL BA: Tom Paciorek Pitching: Glenn Abb .60 .25
❑ 337 Pete Rose AS .60 .25
❑ 338 Dave Lopes AS .15 .05
❑ 339 Mike Schmidt AS 1.25 .50
❑ 340 Dave Concepcion AS .15 .05
❑ 341 Andre Dawson AS .15 .05
❑ 342A George Foster AS (With autograph) .30 .10
❑ 342B G.Foster AS ERR NO AU 1.25 .50
❑ 343 Dave Parker AS .15 .05
❑ 344 Gary Carter AS .15 .05
❑ 345 Fernando Valenzuela AS .60 .25
❑ 346 Tom Seaver AS .30 .10
❑ 346B Tom Seaver AS COR .30 .10
❑ 347 Bruce Sutter AS .30 .10
❑ 348 Derrel Thomas .15 .05
❑ 349 George Frazier .15 .05
❑ 350 Thad Bosley .15 .05
❑ 351 Brown/Comb/House RC .15 .05
❑ 352 Dick Davis .15 .05
❑ 353 Jack O'Connor .15 .05
❑ 354 Roberto Ramos .15 .05
❑ 355 Dwight Evans .60 .25
❑ 356 Denny Lewallyn .15 .05
❑ 357 Butch Hobson .15 .05
❑ 358 Mike Parrott .15 .05
❑ 359 Jim Dwyer .15 .05
❑ 360 Len Barker .15 .05
❑ 361 Rafael Landestoy .15 .05
❑ 362 Jim Wright UER (Wrong Jim Wright pictured) .15 .05
❑ 363 Bob Molinaro .15 .05
❑ 364 Doyle Alexander .15 .05
❑ 365 Bill Madlock .30 .10
❑ 366 Padres TL BA: Luis Salazar Pitching: Juan Eiche .60 .25
❑ 367 Jim Kaat .30 .10
❑ 368 Alex Trevino .15 .05
❑ 369 Champ Summers .15 .05
❑ 370 Mike Norris .15 .05
❑ 371 Jerry Don Gleaton .15 .05
❑ 372 Luis Gomez .15 .05
❑ 373 Gene Nelson .15 .05
❑ 374 Tim Blackwell .15 .05
❑ 375 Dusty Baker .30 .10
❑ 376 Chris Welsh .15 .05
❑ 377 Kiko Garcia .15 .05
❑ 378 Mike Caldwell .15 .05
❑ 379 Rob Wilfong .15 .05
❑ 380 Dave Stieb .30 .10
❑ 381 Bruce Hurst Dave Schmidt RC Julio Valdez RC .15 .05
❑ 382 Joe Simpson .15 .05
❑ 383A Pascual Perez ERR NPO 40.00 15.00
❑ 383B Pascual Perez COR .30 .10
❑ 384 Keith Moreland .15 .05
❑ 385 Ken Forsch .15 .05
❑ 386 Jerry White .15 .05
❑ 387 Tom Veryzer .15 .05
❑ 388 Joe Rudi .30 .10
❑ 389 George Vukovich .15 .05
❑ 390 Eddie Murray 1.25 .50
❑ 391 Dave Tobik .15 .05
❑ 392 Rick Bosetti .15 .05
❑ 393 Al Hrabosky .15 .05
❑ 394 Checklist 265-396 .60 .25
❑ 395 Omar Moreno .15 .05
❑ 396 Twins TL BA: John Castino Pitching: Fernando Ar .60 .25
❑ 397 Ken Brett .15 .05
❑ 398 Mike Squires .15 .05
❑ 399 Pat Zachry .15 .05
❑ 400 Johnny Bench 1.25 .50
❑ 401 Johnny Bench SA .60 .25
❑ 402 Bill Stein .15 .05
❑ 403 Jim Tracy .30 .10
❑ 404 Dickie Thon .15 .05
❑ 405 Rick Reuschel .30 .10
❑ 406 Al Holland .15 .05
❑ 407 Danny Boone .15 .05
❑ 408 Ed Romero .15 .05
❑ 409 Don Cooper .15 .05
❑ 410 Ron Cey .30 .10
❑ 411 Ron Cey SA .15 .05
❑ 412 Luis Leal .15 .05
❑ 413 Dan Meyer .15 .05
❑ 414 Elias Sosa .15 .05
❑ 415 Don Baylor .30 .10
❑ 416 Marty Bystrom .15 .05
❑ 417 Pat Kelly .15 .05
❑ 418 Butcher/John/Schmidt RC .15 .05
❑ 419 Steve Stone .15 .05
❑ 420 George Hendrick .30 .10
❑ 421 Mark Clear .15 .05
❑ 422 Cliff Johnson .15 .05
❑ 423 Stan Papi .15 .05
❑ 424 Bruce Benedict .15 .05
❑ 425 John Candelaria .15 .05
❑ 426 Orioles TL/Eddie Murray .60 .25
❑ 427 Ron Oester .15 .05
❑ 428 LaMarr Hoyt .15 .05
❑ 429 John Wathan .15 .05
❑ 430 Vida Blue .30 .10
❑ 431 Vida Blue SA .15 .05
❑ 432 Mike Scott .30 .10
❑ 433 Alan Ashby .15 .05
❑ 434 Joe Lefebvre .15 .05
❑ 435 Robin Yount 2.00 .75
❑ 436 Joe Strain .15 .05
❑ 437 Juan Berenguer .15 .05
❑ 438 Pete Mackanin .15 .05
❑ 439 Dave Righetti RC 2.50 1.00
❑ 440 Jeff Burroughs .15 .05
❑ 441 Heep/Smith/Sprowl RC .15 .05
❑ 442 Bruce Kison .15 .05
❑ 443 Mark Wagner .15 .05
❑ 444 Terry Forster .30 .10
❑ 445 Larry Parrish .15 .05
❑ 446 Wayne Garland .15 .05
❑ 447 Darrell Porter .15 .05
❑ 448 Darrell Porter SA .15 .05
❑ 449 Luis Aguayo .15 .05
❑ 450 Jack Morris .30 .10
❑ 451 Ed Miller .15 .05
❑ 452 Lee Smith RC 3.00 1.25

❑ 453	Art Howe	.15	.05
❑ 454	Rick Langford	.15	.05
❑ 455	Tom Burgmeier	.15	.05
❑ 456	Chicago Cubs TL		
	BA: Bill Buckner		
	Pitching: Randy	.30	.10
❑ 457	Tim Stoddard	.15	.05
❑ 458	Willie Montanez	.15	.05
❑ 459	Bruce Berenyi	.15	.05
❑ 460	Jack Clark	.30	.10
❑ 461	Rich Dotson	.15	.05
❑ 462	Dave Chalk	.15	.05
❑ 463	Jim Kern	.15	.05
❑ 464	Juan Bonilla RC	.25	.08
❑ 465	Lee Mazzilli	.30	.10
❑ 466	Randy Lerch	.15	.05
❑ 467	Mickey Hatcher	.15	.05
❑ 468	Floyd Bannister	.15	.05
❑ 469	Ed Ott	.15	.05
❑ 470	John Mayberry	.15	.05
❑ 471	Hammaker/Jones/Motley RC	.15	.05
❑ 472	Oscar Gamble	.15	.05
❑ 473	Mike Stanton	.15	.05
❑ 474	Ken Oberkfell	.15	.05
❑ 475	Alan Trammell	.30	.10
❑ 476	Brian Kingman	.15	.05
❑ 477	Steve Yeager	.30	.10
❑ 478	Ray Searage	.15	.05
❑ 479	Rowland Office	.15	.05
❑ 480	Steve Carlton	.60	.25
❑ 481	Steve Carlton SA	.30	.10
❑ 482	Glenn Hubbard	.15	.05
❑ 483	Gary Woods	.15	.05
❑ 484	Ivan DeJesus	.15	.05
❑ 485	Kent Tekulve	.15	.05
❑ 486	Yankees TL		
	BA: Jerry Mumphrey		
	Pitching: Tommy Jo	.30	.10
❑ 487	Bob McClure	.15	.05
❑ 488	Ron Jackson	.15	.05
❑ 489	Rick Dempsey	.15	.05
❑ 490	Dennis Eckersley	.60	.25
❑ 491	Checklist 397-528	.60	.25
❑ 492	Joe Price	.15	.05
❑ 493	Chet Lemon	.30	.10
❑ 494	Hubie Brooks	.15	.05
❑ 495	Dennis Leonard	.15	.05
❑ 496	Johnny Grubb	.15	.05
❑ 497	Jim Anderson	.15	.05
❑ 498	Dave Bergman	.15	.05
❑ 499	Paul Mirabella	.15	.05
❑ 500	Rod Carew	.60	.25
❑ 501	Rod Carew SA	.30	.10
❑ 502	Brett Butler RC	1.50	.60
❑ 503	Julio Gonzalez	.15	.05
❑ 504	Rick Peters	.15	.05
❑ 505	Graig Nettles	.30	.10
❑ 506	Graig Nettles SA	.15	.05
❑ 507	Terry Harper	.15	.05
❑ 508	Jody Davis	.15	.05
❑ 509	Harry Spilman	.15	.05
❑ 510	Fernando Valenzuela	1.25	.50
❑ 511	Ruppert Jones	.15	.05
❑ 512	Jerry Dybzinski	.15	.05
❑ 513	Rick Rhoden	.15	.05
❑ 514	Joe Ferguson	.15	.05
❑ 515	Larry Bowa	.30	.10
❑ 516	Larry Bowa SA	.15	.05
❑ 517	Mark Brouhard	.15	.05
❑ 518	Garth Iorg	.15	.05
❑ 519	Glenn Adams	.15	.05
❑ 520	Mike Flanagan	.15	.05
❑ 521	Bill Almon	.15	.05
❑ 522	Chuck Rainey	.15	.05
❑ 523	Gary Gray	.15	.05
❑ 524	Tom Hausman	.15	.05
❑ 525	Ray Knight	.30	.10
❑ 526	Expos TL		
	BA: Warren Cromartie		
	Pitching: Bill Gul	.60	.25
❑ 527	John Henry Johnson	.15	.05
❑ 528	Matt Alexander	.15	.05
❑ 529	Allen Ripley	.15	.05
❑ 530	Dickie Noles	.15	.05
❑ 531	Bordi/Budaska/Moore RC	.15	.05
❑ 532	Toby Harrah	.30	.10
❑ 533	Joaquin Andujar	.30	.10
❑ 534	Dave McKay	.15	.05
❑ 535	Lance Parrish	.30	.10
❑ 536	Rafael Ramirez	.15	.05
❑ 537	Doug Capilla	.15	.05
❑ 538	Lou Piniella	.30	.10
❑ 539	Vern Ruhle	.15	.05
❑ 540	Andre Dawson	.30	.10
❑ 541	Barry Evans	.15	.05
❑ 542	Ned Yost	.15	.05
❑ 543	Bill Robinson	.15	.05
❑ 544	Larry Christenson	.15	.05
❑ 545	Reggie Smith	.30	.10
❑ 546	Reggie Smith SA	.15	.05
❑ 547	Rod Carew AS	.30	.10
❑ 548	Willie Randolph AS	.15	.05
❑ 549	George Brett AS	1.50	.60
❑ 550	Bucky Dent AS	.15	.05
❑ 551	Reggie Jackson AS	.30	.10
❑ 552	Ken Singleton AS	.15	.05
❑ 553	Dave Winfield AS	.15	.05
❑ 554	Carlton Fisk AS	.30	.10
❑ 555	Scott McGregor AS	.15	.05
❑ 556	Jack Morris AS	.15	.05
❑ 557	Rich Gossage AS	.15	.05
❑ 558	John Tudor	.30	.10
❑ 559	Indians TL		
	BA: Mike Hargrove		
	Pitching: Bert Blyl	.30	.10
❑ 560	Doug Corbett	.15	.05
❑ 561	Brum/DeLeon/Roof RC	.15	.05
❑ 562	Mike O'Berry	.15	.05
❑ 563	Ross Baumgarten	.15	.05
❑ 564	Doug DeCinces	.15	.05
❑ 565	Jackson Todd	.15	.05
❑ 566	Mike Jorgensen	.15	.05
❑ 567	Bob Babcock	.15	.05
❑ 568	Joe Pettini	.15	.05
❑ 569	Willie Randolph	.30	.10
❑ 570	Willie Randolph SA	.15	.05
❑ 571	Glenn Abbott	.15	.05
❑ 572	Juan Beniquez	.15	.05
❑ 573	Rick Waits	.15	.05
❑ 574	Mike Ramsey	.15	.05
❑ 575	Al Cowens	.15	.05
❑ 576	Giants TL		
	BA: Milt May		
	Pitching: Vida Blue		
	(Che	.60	.25
❑ 577	Rick Monday	.30	.10
❑ 578	Shooty Babitt	.15	.05
❑ 579	Rick Mahler	.15	.05
❑ 580	Bobby Bonds	.30	.10
❑ 581	Ron Reed	.15	.05
❑ 582	Luis Pujols	.15	.05
❑ 583	Tippy Martinez	.15	.05
❑ 584	Hosken Powell	.15	.05
❑ 585	Rollie Fingers	.30	.10
❑ 586	Rollie Fingers SA	.15	.05
❑ 587	Tim Lollar	.15	.05
❑ 588	Dale Berra	.15	.05
❑ 589	Dave Stapleton	.15	.05
❑ 590	Al Oliver	.30	.10
❑ 591	Al Oliver SA	.15	.05
❑ 592	Craig Swan	.15	.05
❑ 593	Billy Smith	.15	.05
❑ 594	Renie Martin	.15	.05
❑ 595	Dave Collins	.15	.05
❑ 596	Damaso Garcia	.15	.05
❑ 597	Wayne Nordhagen	.15	.05
❑ 598	Bob Galasso	.15	.05
❑ 599	Lovig/Patt/Suth RC	.15	.05
❑ 600	Dave Winfield	.30	.10
❑ 601	Sid Monge	.15	.05
❑ 602	Freddie Patek	.15	.05
❑ 603	Rich Hebner	.15	.05
❑ 604	Orlando Sanchez	.15	.05
❑ 605	Steve Rogers	.30	.10
❑ 606	Blue Jays TL		
	BA: John Mayberry		
	Pitching: Dave St	.30	.10
❑ 607	Leon Durham	.15	.05
❑ 608	Jerry Royster	.15	.05
❑ 609	Rick Sutcliffe	.30	.10
❑ 610	Rickey Henderson	4.00	1.50
❑ 611	Joe Niekro	.15	.05
❑ 612	Gary Ward	.15	.05
❑ 613	Jim Gantner	.15	.05
❑ 614	Juan Eichelberger	.15	.05
❑ 615	Bob Boone	.30	.10
❑ 616	Bob Boone SA	.15	.05
❑ 617	Scott McGregor	.15	.05
❑ 618	Tim Foli	.15	.05
❑ 619	Bill Campbell	.15	.05
❑ 620	Ken Griffey	.30	.10
❑ 621	Ken Griffey SA	.15	.05
❑ 622	Dennis Lamp	.15	.05
❑ 623	Gardenhire/Leach/Leary RC	.75	.30
❑ 624	Fergie Jenkins	.30	.10
❑ 625	Hal McRae	.30	.10
❑ 626	Randy Jones	.15	.05
❑ 627	Enos Cabell	.15	.05
❑ 628	Bill Travers	.15	.05
❑ 629	John Wockenfuss	.15	.05
❑ 630	Joe Charboneau	.30	.10
❑ 631	Gene Tenace	.30	.10
❑ 632	Bryan Clark RC	.25	.08
❑ 633	Mitchell Page	.15	.05
❑ 634	Checklist 529-660	.60	.25
❑ 635	Ron Davis	.15	.05
❑ 636	Phillies TL/Rose/Carlton	1.25	.50
❑ 637	Rick Camp	.15	.05
❑ 638	John Milner	.15	.05
❑ 639	Ken Kravec	.15	.05
❑ 640	Cesar Cedeno	.30	.10
❑ 641	Steve Mura	.15	.05
❑ 642	Mike Scioscia	.30	.10
❑ 643	Pete Vuckovich	.15	.05
❑ 644	John Castino	.15	.05
❑ 645	Frank White	.30	.10
❑ 646	Frank White SA	.15	.05
❑ 647	Warren Brusstar	.15	.05
❑ 648	Jose Morales	.15	.05
❑ 649	Ken Clay	.15	.05
❑ 650	Carl Yastrzemski	2.00	.75
❑ 651	Carl Yastrzemski SA	1.25	.50
❑ 652	Steve Nicosia	.15	.05
❑ 653	Brunansky/Sanch/Scon RC	1.50	.60
❑ 654	Jim Morrison	.15	.05
❑ 655	Joel Youngblood	.15	.05
❑ 656	Eddie Whitson	.15	.05
❑ 657	Tom Poquette	.15	.05
❑ 658	Tito Landrum	.15	.05
❑ 659	Fred Martinez	.15	.05
❑ 660	Dave Concepcion	.30	.10
❑ 661	Dave Concepcion SA	.15	.05
❑ 662	Luis Salazar	.15	.05
❑ 663	Hector Cruz	.15	.05
❑ 664	Dan Spillner	.15	.05
❑ 665	Jim Clancy	.15	.05
❑ 666	Tigers TL		
	BA: Steve Kemp		
	Pitching: Dan Petry C	.60	.25
❑ 667	Jeff Reardon	.30	.10
❑ 668	Dale Murphy	.60	.25
❑ 669	Larry Milbourne	.15	.05
❑ 670	Steve Kemp	.15	.05
❑ 671	Mike Davis	.15	.05
❑ 672	Bob Knepper	.15	.05
❑ 673	Keith Drumwright	.15	.05
❑ 674	Dave Goltz	.15	.05
❑ 675	Cecil Cooper	.30	.10
❑ 676	Sal Butera	.15	.05
❑ 677	Alfredo Griffin	.15	.05
❑ 678	Tom Paciorek	.15	.05
❑ 679	Sammy Stewart	.15	.05
❑ 680	Gary Matthews	.30	.10
❑ 681	Marshall/Roen/Sax RC	1.50	.60
❑ 682	Jesse Jefferson	.15	.05
❑ 683	Phil Garner	.30	.10
❑ 684	Harold Baines	.30	.10
❑ 685	Bert Blyleven	.30	.10
❑ 686	Gary Allenson	.15	.05
❑ 687	Greg Minton	.15	.05
❑ 688	Leon Roberts	.15	.05
❑ 689	Lary Sorensen	.15	.05
❑ 690	Dave Kingman	.30	.10
❑ 691	Dan Schatzeder	.15	.05
❑ 692	Wayne Gross	.15	.05
❑ 693	Cesar Geronimo	.15	.05
❑ 694	Dave Wehrmeister	.15	.05
❑ 695	Warren Cromartie	.15	.05

❑ 696 Pirates TL
BA: Bill Madlock
Pitching: Eddie Solo .60 .25
❑ 697 John Montefusco .15 .05
❑ 698 Tony Scott .15 .05
❑ 699 Dick Tidrow .15 .05
❑ 700 George Foster .30 .10
❑ 701 George Foster SA .15 .05
❑ 702 Steve Renko .15 .05
❑ 703 Brewers TL
BA: Cecil Cooper
Pitching: Pete Vucko .60 .25
❑ 704 Mickey Rivers .15 .05
❑ 705 Mickey Rivers SA .15 .05
❑ 706 Barry Foote .15 .05
❑ 707 Mark Bomback .15 .05
❑ 708 Gene Richards .15 .05
❑ 709 Don Money .15 .05
❑ 710 Jerry Reuss .15 .05
❑ 711 Edler/Henderson/Walton RC .75 .30
❑ 712 Dennis Martinez .30 .10
❑ 713 Del Unser .15 .05
❑ 714 Jerry Koosman .30 .10
❑ 715 Willie Stargell .60 .25
❑ 716 Willie Stargell SA .30 .10
❑ 717 Rick Miller .15 .05
❑ 718 Charlie Hough .30 .10
❑ 719 Jerry Narron .15 .05
❑ 720 Greg Luzinski .30 .10
❑ 721 Greg Luzinski SA .15 .05
❑ 722 Jerry Martin .15 .05
❑ 723 Junior Kennedy .15 .05
❑ 724 Dave Rosello .15 .05
❑ 725 Amos Otis .30 .10
❑ 726 Amos Otis SA .15 .05
❑ 727 Sixto Lezcano .15 .05
❑ 728 Aurelio Lopez .15 .05
❑ 729 Jim Spencer .15 .05
❑ 730 Gary Carter .30 .10
❑ 731 Armstrong/Gwosdz/Kuhaulua RC .15 .05
❑ 732 Mike Lum .15 .05
❑ 733 Larry McWilliams .15 .05
❑ 734 Mike Ivie .15 .05
❑ 735 Rudy May .15 .05
❑ 736 Jerry Turner .15 .05
❑ 737 Reggie Cleveland .15 .05
❑ 738 Dave Engle .15 .05
❑ 739 Joey McLaughlin .15 .05
❑ 740 Dave Lopes .30 .10
❑ 741 Dave Lopes SA .15 .05
❑ 742 Dick Drago .15 .05
❑ 743 John Stearns .15 .05
❑ 744 Mike Witt .75 .30
❑ 745 Bake McBride .30 .10
❑ 746 Andre Thornton .15 .05
❑ 747 John Lowenstein .15 .05
❑ 748 Marc Hill .15 .05
❑ 749 Bob Shirley .15 .05
❑ 750 Jim Rice .30 .10
❑ 751 Rick Honeycutt .15 .05
❑ 752 Lee Lacy .15 .05
❑ 753 Tom Brookens .15 .05
❑ 754 Joe Morgan .30 .10
❑ 755 Joe Morgan SA .15 .05
❑ 756 Reds TL/Griffey/Seaver .30 .10
❑ 757 Tom Underwood .15 .05
❑ 758 Claudell Washington .15 .05
❑ 759 Paul Splittorff .15 .05
❑ 760 Bill Buckner .30 .10
❑ 761 Dave Smith .15 .05
❑ 762 Mike Phillips .15 .05
❑ 763 Tom Hume .15 .05
❑ 764 Steve Swisher .15 .05
❑ 765 Gorman Thomas .30 .10
❑ 766 Faedo/Hrbek/Laudner RC 1.50 .60
❑ 767 Roy Smalley .15 .05
❑ 768 Jerry Garvin .15 .05
❑ 769 Richie Zisk .15 .05
❑ 770 Rich Gossage .30 .10
❑ 771 Rich Gossage SA .15 .05
❑ 772 Bert Campaneris .30 .10
❑ 773 John Denny .15 .05
❑ 774 Jay Johnstone .15 .05
❑ 775 Bob Forsch .15 .05
❑ 776 Mark Belanger .15 .05
❑ 777 Tom Griffin .15 .05
❑ 778 Kevin Hickey RC .25 .08
❑ 779 Grant Jackson .15 .05
❑ 780 Pete Rose 4.00 1.50
❑ 781 Pete Rose SA 1.25 .50
❑ 782 Frank Taveras .15 .05
❑ 783 Greg Harris RC .25 .08
❑ 784 Milt Wilcox .15 .05
❑ 785 Dan Driessen .15 .05
❑ 786 Red Sox TL
BA: Carney Lansford
Pitching: Mike To .60 .25
❑ 787 Fred Stanley .15 .05
❑ 788 Woodie Fryman .15 .05
❑ 789 Checklist 661-792 .60 .25
❑ 790 Larry Gura .15 .05
❑ 791 Bobby Brown .15 .05
❑ 792 Frank Tanana .30 .10

1982 Topps Traded

❑ COMP.FACT.SET (132) 175.00 100.00
❑ 1T Doyle Alexander .50 .20
❑ 2T Jesse Barfield 3.00 1.25
❑ 3T Ross Baumgarten .50 .20
❑ 4T Steve Bedrosian 1.50 .60
❑ 5T Mark Belanger .50 .20
❑ 6T Kurt Bevacqua .50 .20
❑ 7T Tim Blackwell .50 .20
❑ 8T Vida Blue 1.00 .40
❑ 9T Bob Boone 1.00 .40
❑ 10T Larry Bowa 1.00 .40
❑ 11T Dan Briggs .50 .20
❑ 12T Bobby Brown .50 .20
❑ 13T Tom Brunansky 3.00 1.25
❑ 14T Jeff Burroughs .50 .20
❑ 15T Enos Cabell .50 .20
❑ 16T Bill Campbell .50 .20
❑ 17T Bobby Castillo .50 .20
❑ 18T Bill Caudill .50 .20
❑ 19T Cesar Cedeno 1.00 .40
❑ 20T Dave Collins .50 .20
❑ 21T Doug Corbett .50 .20
❑ 22T Al Cowens .50 .20
❑ 23T Chili Davis 3.00 1.25
❑ 24T Dick Davis .50 .20
❑ 25T Ron Davis .50 .20
❑ 26T Doug DeCinces .50 .20
❑ 27T Ivan DeJesus .50 .20
❑ 28T Bob Dernier .50 .20
❑ 29T Bo Diaz .50 .20
❑ 30T Roger Erickson .50 .20
❑ 31T Jim Essian .50 .20
❑ 32T Ed Farmer .50 .20
❑ 33T Doug Flynn .50 .20
❑ 34T Tim Foli .50 .20
❑ 35T Dan Ford .50 .20
❑ 36T George Foster 1.00 .40
❑ 37T Dave Frost .50 .20
❑ 38T Rich Gale .50 .20
❑ 39T Ron Gardenhire 1.50 .60
❑ 40T Ken Griffey 1.00 .40
❑ 41T Greg Harris .50 .20
❑ 42T Von Hayes 1.50 .60
❑ 43T Larry Herndon .50 .20
❑ 44T Kent Hrbek 3.00 1.25
❑ 45T Mike Ivie .50 .20
❑ 46T Grant Jackson .50 .20
❑ 47T Reggie Jackson 2.00 .75
❑ 48T Ron Jackson .50 .20
❑ 49T Fergie Jenkins 1.00 .40
❑ 50T Lamar Johnson .50 .20
❑ 51T Randy Johnson .50 .20
❑ 52T Jay Johnstone .50 .20
❑ 53T Mick Kelleher .50 .20
❑ 54T Steve Kemp .50 .20
❑ 55T Junior Kennedy .50 .20
❑ 56T Jim Kern .50 .20
❑ 57T Ray Knight 1.00 .40
❑ 58T Wayne Krenchicki .50 .20
❑ 59T Mike Krukow .50 .20
❑ 60T Duane Kuiper .50 .20
❑ 61T Mike LaCoss .50 .20
❑ 62T Chet Lemon 1.00 .40
❑ 63T Sixto Lezcano .50 .20
❑ 64T Dave Lopes 1.00 .40
❑ 65T Jerry Martin .50 .20
❑ 66T Renie Martin .50 .20
❑ 67T John Mayberry .50 .20
❑ 68T Lee Mazzilli 1.00 .40
❑ 69T Bake McBride 1.00 .40
❑ 70T Dan Meyer .50 .20
❑ 71T Larry Milbourne .50 .20
❑ 72T Eddie Milner .50 .20
❑ 73T Sid Monge .50 .20
❑ 74T John Montefusco .50 .20
❑ 75T Jose Morales .50 .20
❑ 76T Keith Moreland .50 .20
❑ 77T Jim Morrison .50 .20
❑ 78T Rance Mulliniks .50 .20
❑ 79T Steve Mura .50 .20
❑ 80T Gene Nelson .50 .20
❑ 81T Joe Nolan .50 .20
❑ 82T Dickie Noles .50 .20
❑ 83T Al Oliver 1.00 .40
❑ 84T Jorge Orta .50 .20
❑ 85T Tom Paciorek .50 .20
❑ 86T Larry Parrish .50 .20
❑ 87T Jack Perconte .50 .20
❑ 88T Gaylord Perry 1.00 .40
❑ 89T Rob Picciolo .50 .20
❑ 90T Joe Pittman .50 .20
❑ 91T Hosken Powell .50 .20
❑ 92T Mike Proly .50 .20
❑ 93T Greg Pryor .50 .20
❑ 94T Charlie Puleo .50 .20
❑ 95T Shane Rawley .50 .20
❑ 96T Johnny Ray 1.50 .60
❑ 97T Dave Revering .50 .20
❑ 98T Cal Ripken 150.00 90.00
❑ 99T Allen Ripley .50 .20
❑ 100T Bill Robinson .50 .20
❑ 101T Aurelio Rodriguez .50 .20
❑ 102T Joe Rudi 1.00 .40
❑ 103T Steve Sax 3.00 1.25
❑ 104T Dan Schatzeder .50 .20
❑ 105T Bob Shirley .50 .20
❑ 106T Eric Show XRC 1.50 .60
❑ 107T Roy Smalley .50 .20
❑ 108T Lonnie Smith .50 .20
❑ 109T Ozzie Smith 15.00 6.00
❑ 110T Reggie Smith 1.00 .40
❑ 111T Lary Sorensen .50 .20
❑ 112T Elias Sosa .50 .20
❑ 113T Mike Stanton .50 .20
❑ 114T Steve Stroughter .50 .20
❑ 115T Champ Summers .50 .20
❑ 116T Rick Sutcliffe 1.00 .40
❑ 117T Frank Tanana 1.00 .40
❑ 118T Frank Taveras .50 .20
❑ 119T Garry Templeton 1.00 .40
❑ 120T Alex Trevino .50 .20
❑ 121T Jerry Turner .50 .20
❑ 122T Ed VandeBerg .50 .20
❑ 123T Tom Veryzer .50 .20
❑ 124T Ron Washington .50 .20
❑ 125T Bob Watson .50 .20
❑ 126T Dennis Werth .50 .20
❑ 127T Eddie Whitson .50 .20
❑ 128T Rob Wilfong .50 .20
❑ 129T Bump Wills .50 .20
❑ 130T Gary Woods .50 .20
❑ 131T Butch Wynegar .50 .20
❑ 132T Checklist: 1-132 .50 .20

1983 Topps

❑ COMPLETE SET (792) 80.00 40.00
❑ 1 Tony Armas RB .30 .10
❑ 2 Rickey Henderson RB 1.25 .50
❑ 3 Greg Minton RB .15 .05
❑ 4 Lance Parrish RB .15 .05
❑ 5 Manny Trillo RB .15 .05
❑ 6 John Wathan RB .15 .05
❑ 7 Gene Richards .15 .05
❑ 8 Steve Balboni .15 .05
❑ 9 Joey McLaughlin .15 .05
❑ 10 Gorman Thomas .30 .10
❑ 11 Billy Gardner MG .15 .05
❑ 12 Paul Mirabella .15 .05
❑ 13 Larry Herndon .15 .05
❑ 14 Frank LaCorte .15 .05
❑ 15 Ron Cey .30 .10
❑ 16 George Vukovich .15 .05
❑ 17 Kent Tekulve .15 .05
❑ 18 Kent Tekulve SV .15 .05
❑ 19 Oscar Gamble .15 .05
❑ 20 Carlton Fisk .60 .25
❑ 21 Orioles TL/Murray/Palmer .60 .25
❑ 22 Randy Martz .15 .05
❑ 23 Mike Heath .15 .05
❑ 24 Steve Mura .15 .05
❑ 25 Hal McRae .30 .10
❑ 26 Jerry Royster .15 .05
❑ 27 Doug Corbett .15 .05
❑ 28 Bruce Bochte .15 .05
❑ 29 Randy Jones .15 .05
❑ 30 Jim Rice .30 .10
❑ 31 Bill Gullickson .15 .05
❑ 32 Dave Bergman .15 .05
❑ 33 Jack O'Connor .15 .05
❑ 34 Paul Householder .15 .05
❑ 35 Rollie Fingers .30 .10
❑ 36 Rollie Fingers SV .15 .05
❑ 37 Darrell Johnson MG .15 .05
❑ 38 Tim Flannery .15 .05
❑ 39 Terry Puhl .15 .05
❑ 40 Fernando Valenzuela .30 .10
❑ 41 Jerry Turner .15 .05
❑ 42 Dale Murray .15 .05
❑ 43 Bob Dernier .15 .05
❑ 44 Don Robinson .15 .05
❑ 45 John Mayberry .15 .05
❑ 46 Richard Dotson .15 .05
❑ 47 Dave McKay .15 .05
❑ 48 Lary Sorensen .15 .05
❑ 49 Willie McGee RC 2.50 1.00
❑ 50 Bob Horner UER .30 .10
❑ 51 Cubs TL/F.Jenkins .15 .05
❑ 52 Onix Concepcion .15 .05
❑ 53 Mike Witt .15 .05
❑ 54 Jim Maler .15 .05
❑ 55 Mookie Wilson .30 .10
❑ 56 Chuck Rainey .15 .05
❑ 57 Tim Blackwell .15 .05
❑ 58 Al Holland .15 .05
❑ 59 Benny Ayala .15 .05
❑ 60 Johnny Bench 1.25 .50
❑ 61 Johnny Bench SV .60 .25
❑ 62 Bob McClure .15 .05
❑ 63 Rick Monday .30 .10
❑ 64 Bill Stein .15 .05
❑ 65 Jack Morris .30 .10
❑ 66 Bob Lillis MG .15 .05
❑ 67 Sal Butera .15 .05
❑ 68 Eric Show RC .75 .30
❑ 69 Lee Lacy .15 .05
❑ 70 Steve Carlton .60 .25
❑ 71 Steve Carlton SV .30 .10
❑ 72 Tom Paciorek .15 .05
❑ 73 Allen Ripley .15 .05
❑ 74 Julio Gonzalez .15 .05
❑ 75 Amos Otis .30 .10
❑ 76 Rick Mahler .15 .05
❑ 77 Hosken Powell .15 .05
❑ 78 Bill Caudill .15 .05
❑ 79 Mick Kelleher .15 .05
❑ 80 George Foster .30 .10
❑ 81 J.Mumphrey/D.Righetti TL .30 .10
❑ 82 Bruce Hurst .15 .05
❑ 83 Ryne Sandberg RC 20.00 8.00
❑ 84 Milt May .15 .05
❑ 85 Ken Singleton .30 .10
❑ 86 Tom Hume .15 .05
❑ 87 Joe Rudi .30 .10
❑ 88 Jim Gantner .15 .05
❑ 89 Leon Roberts .15 .05
❑ 90 Jerry Reuss .15 .05
❑ 91 Larry Milbourne .15 .05
❑ 92 Mike LaCoss .15 .05
❑ 93 John Castino .15 .05
❑ 94 Dave Edwards .15 .05
❑ 95 Alan Trammell .30 .10
❑ 96 Dick Howser MG .15 .05
❑ 97 Ross Baumgarten .15 .05
❑ 98 Vance Law .15 .05
❑ 99 Dickie Noles .15 .05
❑ 100 Pete Rose 4.00 1.50
❑ 101 Pete Rose SV 1.25 .50
❑ 102 Dave Beard .15 .05
❑ 103 Darrell Porter .15 .05
❑ 104 Bob Walk .15 .05
❑ 105 Don Baylor .30 .10
❑ 106 Gene Nelson .15 .05
❑ 107 Mike Jorgensen .15 .05
❑ 108 Glenn Hoffman .15 .05
❑ 109 Luis Leal .15 .05
❑ 110 Ken Griffey .30 .10
❑ 111 Montreal Expos TL
BA: Al Oliver
ERA: Steve Roger .30 .10
❑ 112 Bob Shirley .15 .05
❑ 113 Ron Roenicke .15 .05
❑ 114 Jim Slaton .15 .05
❑ 115 Chili Davis .30 .10
❑ 116 Dave Schmidt .15 .05
❑ 117 Alan Knicely .15 .05
❑ 118 Chris Welsh .15 .05
❑ 119 Tom Brookens .15 .05
❑ 120 Len Barker .15 .05
❑ 121 Mickey Hatcher .15 .05
❑ 122 Jimmy Smith .15 .05
❑ 123 George Frazier .15 .05
❑ 124 Marc Hill .15 .05
❑ 125 Leon Durham .15 .05
❑ 126 Joe Torre MG .30 .10
❑ 127 Preston Hanna .15 .05
❑ 128 Mike Ramsey .15 .05
❑ 129 Checklist 1-132 .30 .10
❑ 130 Dave Stieb .30 .10
❑ 131 Ed Ott .15 .05
❑ 132 Todd Cruz .15 .05
❑ 133 Jim Barr .15 .05
❑ 134 Hubie Brooks .15 .05
❑ 135 Dwight Evans .60 .25
❑ 136 Willie Aikens .15 .05
❑ 137 Woodie Fryman .15 .05
❑ 138 Rick Dempsey .15 .05
❑ 139 Bruce Berenyi .15 .05
❑ 140 Willie Randolph .30 .10
❑ 141 Indians TL
BA: Toby Harrah
ERA: Rick Sutcliffe .30 .10
❑ 142 Mike Caldwell .15 .05
❑ 143 Joe Pettini .15 .05
❑ 144 Mark Wagner .15 .05
❑ 145 Don Sutton .30 .10
❑ 146 Don Sutton SV .15 .05
❑ 147 Rick Leach .15 .05
❑ 148 Dave Roberts .15 .05
❑ 149 Johnny Ray .15 .05
❑ 150 Bruce Sutter .60 .25
❑ 151 Bruce Sutter SV .30 .10
❑ 152 Jay Johnstone .15 .05
❑ 153 Jerry Koosman .30 .10
❑ 154 Johnnie LeMaster .15 .05
❑ 155 Dan Quisenberry .15 .05
❑ 156 Billy Martin MG .60 .25
❑ 157 Steve Bedrosian .15 .05
❑ 158 Rob Wilfong .15 .05
❑ 159 Mike Stanton .15 .05
❑ 160 Dave Kingman .30 .10
❑ 161 Dave Kingman SV .15 .05
❑ 162 Mark Clear .15 .05
❑ 163 Cal Ripken 10.00 4.00
❑ 164 David Palmer .15 .05
❑ 165 Dan Driessen .15 .05
❑ 166 John Pacella .15 .05
❑ 167 Mark Brouhard .15 .05
❑ 168 Juan Eichelberger .15 .05
❑ 169 Doug Flynn .15 .05
❑ 170 Steve Howe .15 .05
❑ 171 Giants TL/Joe Morgan .30 .10
❑ 172 Vern Ruhle .15 .05
❑ 173 Jim Morrison .15 .05
❑ 174 Jerry Ujdur .15 .05
❑ 175 Bo Diaz .15 .05
❑ 176 Dave Righetti .30 .10
❑ 177 Harold Baines .30 .10
❑ 178 Luis Tiant .30 .10
❑ 179 Luis Tiant SV .15 .05
❑ 180 Rickey Henderson 2.50 1.00
❑ 181 Terry Felton .15 .05
❑ 182 Mike Fischlin .15 .05
❑ 183 Ed VandeBerg .15 .05
❑ 184 Bob Clark .15 .05
❑ 185 Tim Lollar .15 .05
❑ 186 Whitey Herzog MG .30 .10
❑ 187 Terry Leach .15 .05
❑ 188 Rick Miller .15 .05
❑ 189 Dan Schatzeder .15 .05
❑ 190 Cecil Cooper .30 .10
❑ 191 Joe Price .15 .05
❑ 192 Floyd Rayford .15 .05
❑ 193 Harry Spilman .15 .05
❑ 194 Cesar Geronimo .15 .05
❑ 195 Bob Stoddard .15 .05
❑ 196 Bill Fahey .15 .05
❑ 197 Jim Eisenreich RC .75 .30
❑ 198 Kiko Garcia .15 .05
❑ 199 Marty Bystrom .15 .05
❑ 200 Rod Carew .60 .25
❑ 201 Rod Carew SV .30 .10
❑ 202 Blue Jays TL
BA: Damaso Garcia
ERA: Dave Stieb .30 .10
❑ 203 Mike Morgan .15 .05
❑ 204 Junior Kennedy .15 .05
❑ 205 Dave Parker .30 .10
❑ 206 Ken Oberkfell .15 .05
❑ 207 Rick Camp .15 .05
❑ 208 Dan Meyer .15 .05
❑ 209 Mike Moore RC .75 .30
❑ 210 Jack Clark .30 .10
❑ 211 John Denny .15 .05
❑ 212 John Stearns .15 .05
❑ 213 Tom Burgmeier .15 .05
❑ 214 Jerry White .15 .05
❑ 215 Mario Soto .30 .10
❑ 216 Tony LaRussa MG .30 .10
❑ 217 Tim Stoddard .15 .05
❑ 218 Roy Howell .15 .05
❑ 219 Mike Armstrong .15 .05
❑ 220 Dusty Baker .30 .10
❑ 221 Joe Niekro .15 .05
❑ 222 Damaso Garcia .15 .05
❑ 223 John Montefusco .15 .05
❑ 224 Mickey Rivers .15 .05
❑ 225 Enos Cabell .15 .05
❑ 226 Enrique Romo .15 .05
❑ 227 Chris Bando .15 .05
❑ 228 Joaquin Andujar .30 .10
❑ 229 Phillies TL/S.Carlton .15 .05
❑ 230 Fergie Jenkins .30 .10
❑ 231 Fergie Jenkins SV .15 .05

❑ 232	Tom Brunansky	.30	.10
❑ 233	Wayne Gross	.15	.05
❑ 234	Larry Andersen	.15	.05
❑ 235	Claudell Washington	.15	.05
❑ 236	Steve Renko	.15	.05
❑ 237	Dan Norman	.15	.05
❑ 238	Bud Black RC	.75	.30
❑ 239	Dave Stapleton	.15	.05
❑ 240	Rich Gossage	.30	.10
❑ 241	Rich Gossage SV	.15	.05
❑ 242	Joe Nolan	.15	.05
❑ 243	Duane Walker	.15	.05
❑ 244	Dwight Bernard	.15	.05
❑ 245	Steve Sax	.30	.10
❑ 246	George Bamberger MG	.15	.05
❑ 247	Dave Smith	.15	.05
❑ 248	Bake McBride	.30	.10
❑ 249	Checklist: 133-264	.30	.10
❑ 250	Bill Buckner	.30	.10
❑ 251	Alan Wiggins	.15	.05
❑ 252	Luis Aguayo	.15	.05
❑ 253	Larry McWilliams	.15	.05
❑ 254	Rick Cerone	.15	.05
❑ 255	Gene Garber	.15	.05
❑ 256	Gene Garber SV	.15	.05
❑ 257	Jesse Barfield	.30	.10
❑ 258	Manny Castillo	.15	.05
❑ 259	Jeff Jones	.15	.05
❑ 260	Steve Kemp	.15	.05
❑ 261	Tigers TL		
	BA: Larry Herndon		
	ERA: Dan Petry		
	(Che	.30	.10
❑ 262	Ron Jackson	.15	.05
❑ 263	Renie Martin	.15	.05
❑ 264	Jamie Quirk	.15	.05
❑ 265	Joel Youngblood	.15	.05
❑ 266	Paul Boris	.15	.05
❑ 267	Terry Francona	.30	.10
❑ 268	Storm Davis RC	.75	.30
❑ 269	Ron Oester	.15	.05
❑ 270	Dennis Eckersley	.60	.25
❑ 271	Ed Romero	.15	.05
❑ 272	Frank Tanana	.30	.10
❑ 273	Mark Belanger	.15	.05
❑ 274	Terry Kennedy	.15	.05
❑ 275	Ray Knight	.30	.10
❑ 276	Gene Mauch MG	.15	.05
❑ 277	Rance Mulliniks	.15	.05
❑ 278	Kevin Hickey	.15	.05
❑ 279	Greg Gross	.15	.05
❑ 280	Bert Blyleven	.30	.10
❑ 281	Andre Robertson	.15	.05
❑ 282	R.Smith w/Sandberg	1.25	.50
❑ 283	Reggie Smith SV	.15	.05
❑ 284	Jeff Lahti	.15	.05
❑ 285	Lance Parrish	.30	.10
❑ 286	Rick Langford	.15	.05
❑ 287	Bobby Brown	.15	.05
❑ 288	Joe Cowley	.15	.05
❑ 289	Jerry Dybzinski	.15	.05
❑ 290	Jeff Reardon	.30	.10
❑ 291	Bill Madlock		
	John Candelaria TL	.30	.10
❑ 292	Craig Swan	.15	.05
❑ 293	Glenn Gulliver	.15	.05
❑ 294	Dave Engle	.15	.05
❑ 295	Jerry Remy	.15	.05
❑ 296	Greg Harris	.15	.05
❑ 297	Ned Yost	.15	.05
❑ 298	Floyd Chiffer	.15	.05
❑ 299	George Wright RC	.75	.30
❑ 300	Mike Schmidt	3.00	1.25
❑ 301	Mike Schmidt SV	1.25	.50
❑ 302	Ernie Whitt	.15	.05
❑ 303	Miguel Dilone	.15	.05
❑ 304	Dave Rucker	.15	.05
❑ 305	Larry Bowa	.30	.10
❑ 306	Tom Lasorda MG	.60	.25
❑ 307	Lou Piniella	.30	.10
❑ 308	Jesus Vega	.15	.05
❑ 309	Jeff Leonard	.15	.05
❑ 310	Greg Luzinski	.30	.10
❑ 311	Glenn Brummer	.15	.05
❑ 312	Brian Kingman	.15	.05
❑ 313	Gary Gray	.15	.05
❑ 314	Ken Dayley	.15	.05
❑ 315	Rick Burleson	.15	.05
❑ 316	Paul Splittorff	.15	.05
❑ 317	Gary Rajsich	.15	.05
❑ 318	John Tudor	.30	.10
❑ 319	Lenn Sakata	.15	.05
❑ 320	Steve Rogers	.30	.10
❑ 321	Brewers TL/Robin Yount	1.25	.50
❑ 322	Dave Van Gorder	.15	.05
❑ 323	Luis DeLeon	.15	.05
❑ 324	Mike Marshall	.15	.05
❑ 325	Von Hayes	.15	.05
❑ 326	Garth Iorg	.15	.05
❑ 327	Bobby Castillo	.15	.05
❑ 328	Craig Reynolds	.15	.05
❑ 329	Randy Niemann	.15	.05
❑ 330	Buddy Bell	.30	.10
❑ 331	Mike Krukow	.15	.05
❑ 332	Glenn Wilson	.75	.30
❑ 333	Dave LaRoche	.15	.05
❑ 334	Dave LaRoche SV	.15	.05
❑ 335	Steve Henderson	.15	.05
❑ 336	Rene Lachemann MG	.15	.05
❑ 337	Tito Landrum	.15	.05
❑ 338	Bob Owchinko	.15	.05
❑ 339	Terry Harper	.15	.05
❑ 340	Larry Gura	.15	.05
❑ 341	Doug DeCinces	.15	.05
❑ 342	Atlee Hammaker	.15	.05
❑ 343	Bob Bailor	.15	.05
❑ 344	Roger LaFrancois	.15	.05
❑ 345	Jim Clancy	.15	.05
❑ 346	Joe Pittman	.15	.05
❑ 347	Sammy Stewart	.15	.05
❑ 348	Alan Bannister	.15	.05
❑ 349	Checklist: 265-396	.30	.10
❑ 350	Robin Yount	2.00	.75
❑ 351	Reds TL		
	BA: Cesar Cedeno		
	ERA: Mario Soto		
	(Check	.30	.10
❑ 352	Mike Scioscia	.30	.10
❑ 353	Steve Comer	.15	.05
❑ 354	Randy Johnson	.15	.05
❑ 355	Jim Bibby	.15	.05
❑ 356	Gary Woods	.15	.05
❑ 357	Len Matuszek	.15	.05
❑ 358	Jerry Garvin	.15	.05
❑ 359	Dave Collins	.15	.05
❑ 360	Nolan Ryan	6.00	2.50
❑ 361	Nolan Ryan SV	3.00	1.25
❑ 362	Bill Almon	.15	.05
❑ 363	John Stuper	.15	.05
❑ 364	Brett Butler	.30	.10
❑ 365	Dave Lopes	.30	.10
❑ 366	Dick Williams MG	.15	.05
❑ 367	Bud Anderson	.15	.05
❑ 368	Richie Zisk	.15	.05
❑ 369	Jesse Orosco	.15	.05
❑ 370	Gary Carter	.30	.10
❑ 371	Mike Richardt	.15	.05
❑ 372	Terry Crowley	.15	.05
❑ 373	Kevin Saucier	.15	.05
❑ 374	Wayne Krenchicki	.15	.05
❑ 375	Pete Vuckovich	.15	.05
❑ 376	Ken Landreaux	.15	.05
❑ 377	Lee May	.15	.05
❑ 378	Lee May SV	.15	.05
❑ 379	Guy Sularz	.15	.05
❑ 380	Ron Davis	.15	.05
❑ 381	Red Sox TL		
	BA: Jim Rice		
	ERA: Bob Stanley		
	(Check	.30	.10
❑ 382	Bob Knepper	.15	.05
❑ 383	Ozzie Virgil	.15	.05
❑ 384	Dave Dravecky RC	1.50	.60
❑ 385	Mike Easler	.15	.05
❑ 386	Rod Carew AS	.30	.10
❑ 387	Bob Grich AS	.15	.05
❑ 388	George Brett AS	1.50	.60
❑ 389	Robin Yount AS	1.25	.50
❑ 390	Reggie Jackson AS	.30	.10
❑ 391	Rickey Henderson AS	1.25	.50
❑ 392	Fred Lynn AS	.15	.05
❑ 393	Carlton Fisk AS	.30	.10
❑ 394	Pete Vuckovich AS	.15	.05
❑ 395	Larry Gura AS	.15	.05
❑ 396	Dan Quisenberry AS	.15	.05
❑ 397	Pete Rose AS	.60	.25
❑ 398	Manny Trillo AS	.15	.05
❑ 399	Mike Schmidt AS	1.25	.50
❑ 400	Dave Concepcion AS	.15	.05
❑ 401	Dale Murphy AS	.30	.10
❑ 402	Andre Dawson AS	.15	.05
❑ 403	Tim Raines AS	.15	.05
❑ 404	Gary Carter AS	.15	.05
❑ 405	Steve Rogers AS	.15	.05
❑ 406	Steve Carlton AS	.30	.10
❑ 407	Bruce Sutter AS	.30	.10
❑ 408	Rudy May	.15	.05
❑ 409	Marvis Foley	.15	.05
❑ 410	Phil Niekro	.30	.10
❑ 411	Phil Niekro SV	.15	.05
❑ 412	Rangers TL		
	BA: Buddy Bell		
	ERA: Charlie Hough (C	.30	.10
❑ 413	Matt Keough	.15	.05
❑ 414	Julio Cruz	.15	.05
❑ 415	Bob Forsch	.15	.05
❑ 416	Joe Ferguson	.15	.05
❑ 417	Tom Hausman	.15	.05
❑ 418	Greg Pryor	.15	.05
❑ 419	Steve Crawford	.15	.05
❑ 420	Al Oliver	.30	.10
❑ 421	Al Oliver SV	.15	.05
❑ 422	George Cappuzzello	.15	.05
❑ 423	Tom Lawless	.15	.05
❑ 424	Jerry Augustine	.15	.05
❑ 425	Pedro Guerrero	.30	.10
❑ 426	Earl Weaver MG	.30	.10
❑ 427	Roy Lee Jackson	.15	.05
❑ 428	Champ Summers	.15	.05
❑ 429	Eddie Whitson	.15	.05
❑ 430	Kirk Gibson	.30	.10
❑ 431	Gary Gaetti RC	1.50	.60
❑ 432	Porfirio Altamirano	.15	.05
❑ 433	Dale Berra	.15	.05
❑ 434	Dennis Lamp	.15	.05
❑ 435	Tony Armas	.30	.10
❑ 436	Bill Campbell	.15	.05
❑ 437	Rick Sweet	.15	.05
❑ 438	Dave LaPoint	.15	.05
❑ 439	Rafael Ramirez	.15	.05
❑ 440	Ron Guidry	.30	.10
❑ 441	Astros TL		
	BA: Ray Knight		
	ERA: Joe Niekro		
	(Check	.30	.10
❑ 442	Brian Downing	.30	.10
❑ 443	Don Hood	.15	.05
❑ 444	Wally Backman	.15	.05
❑ 445	Mike Flanagan	.15	.05
❑ 446	Reid Nichols	.15	.05
❑ 447	Bryn Smith	.15	.05
❑ 448	Darrell Evans	.30	.10
❑ 449	Eddie Milner	.15	.05
❑ 450	Ted Simmons	.30	.10
❑ 451	Ted Simmons SV	.15	.05
❑ 452	Lloyd Moseby	.15	.05
❑ 453	Lamar Johnson	.15	.05
❑ 454	Bob Welch	.30	.10
❑ 455	Sixto Lezcano	.15	.05
❑ 456	Lee Elia MG	.15	.05
❑ 457	Milt Wilcox	.15	.05
❑ 458	Ron Washington	.15	.05
❑ 459	Ed Farmer	.15	.05
❑ 460	Roy Smalley	.15	.05
❑ 461	Steve Trout	.15	.05
❑ 462	Steve Nicosia	.15	.05
❑ 463	Gaylord Perry	.30	.10
❑ 464	Gaylord Perry SV	.15	.05
❑ 465	Lonnie Smith	.15	.05
❑ 466	Tom Underwood	.15	.05
❑ 467	Rufino Linares	.15	.05
❑ 468	Dave Goltz	.15	.05
❑ 469	Ron Gardenhire	.15	.05
❑ 470	Greg Minton	.15	.05
❑ 471	Kansas City Royals TL		
	BA: Willie Wilson		
	ERA: Vid	.30	.10
❑ 472	Gary Allenson	.15	.05

❑ 473 John Lowenstein .15 .05
❑ 474 Ray Burris .15 .05
❑ 475 Cesar Cedeno .30 .10
❑ 476 Rob Picciolo .15 .05
❑ 477 Tom Niedenfuer .15 .05
❑ 478 Phil Garner .30 .10
❑ 479 Charlie Hough .30 .10
❑ 480 Toby Harrah .30 .10
❑ 481 Scot Thompson .15 .05
❑ 482 Tony Gwynn RC 30.00 12.50
❑ 483 Lynn Jones .15 .05
❑ 484 Dick Ruthven .15 .05
❑ 485 Omar Moreno .15 .05
❑ 486 Clyde King MG .15 .05
❑ 487 Jerry Hairston .15 .05
❑ 488 Alfredo Griffin .15 .05
❑ 489 Tom Herr .15 .05
❑ 490 Jim Palmer .30 .10
❑ 491 Jim Palmer SV .15 .05
❑ 492 Paul Serna .15 .05
❑ 493 Steve McCatty .15 .05
❑ 494 Bob Brenly .15 .05
❑ 495 Warren Cromartie .15 .05
❑ 496 Tom Veryzer .15 .05
❑ 497 Rick Sutcliffe .30 .10
❑ 498 Wade Boggs RC 15.00 6.00
❑ 499 Jeff Little .15 .05
❑ 500 Reggie Jackson .60 .25
❑ 501 Reggie Jackson SV .30 .10
❑ 502 Braves TL/Murphy/Niekro .60 .25
❑ 503 Moose Haas .15 .05
❑ 504 Don Werner .15 .05
❑ 505 Garry Templeton .30 .10
❑ 506 Jim Gott RC .75 .30
❑ 507 Tony Scott .15 .05
❑ 508 Tom Filer .15 .05
❑ 509 Lou Whitaker .30 .10
❑ 510 Tug McGraw .30 .10
❑ 511 Tug McGraw SV .15 .05
❑ 512 Doyle Alexander .15 .05
❑ 513 Fred Stanley .15 .05
❑ 514 Rudy Law .15 .05
❑ 515 Gene Tenace .30 .10
❑ 516 Bill Virdon MG .15 .05
❑ 517 Gary Ward .15 .05
❑ 518 Bill Laskey .15 .05
❑ 519 Terry Bulling .15 .05
❑ 520 Fred Lynn .30 .10
❑ 521 Bruce Benedict .15 .05
❑ 522 Pat Zachry .15 .05
❑ 523 Carney Lansford .30 .10
❑ 524 Tom Brennan .15 .05
❑ 525 Frank White .30 .10
❑ 526 Checklist: 397-528 .30 .10
❑ 527 Larry Biittner .15 .05
❑ 528 Jamie Easterly .15 .05
❑ 529 Tim Laudner .15 .05
❑ 530 Eddie Murray 1.25 .50
❑ 531 A's TL/Rickey Henderson 1.25 .50
❑ 532 Dave Stewart .30 .10
❑ 533 Luis Salazar .15 .05
❑ 534 John Butcher .15 .05
❑ 535 Manny Trillo .15 .05
❑ 536 John Wockenfuss .15 .05
❑ 537 Rod Scurry .15 .05
❑ 538 Danny Heep .15 .05
❑ 539 Roger Erickson .15 .05
❑ 540 Ozzie Smith 2.00 .75
❑ 541 Britt Burns .15 .05
❑ 542 Jody Davis .15 .05
❑ 543 Alan Fowlkes .15 .05
❑ 544 Larry Whisenton .15 .05
❑ 545 Floyd Bannister .15 .05
❑ 546 Dave Garcia MG .15 .05
❑ 547 Geoff Zahn .15 .05
❑ 548 Brian Giles .15 .05
❑ 549 Charlie Puleo .15 .05
❑ 550 Carl Yastrzemski 2.00 .75
❑ 551 Carl Yastrzemski SV 1.25 .50
❑ 552 Tim Wallach .30 .10
❑ 553 Dennis Martinez .30 .10
❑ 554 Mike Vail .15 .05
❑ 555 Steve Yeager .30 .10
❑ 556 Willie Upshaw .15 .05
❑ 557 Rick Honeycutt .15 .05
❑ 558 Dickie Thon .15 .05
❑ 559 Pete Redfern .15 .05
❑ 560 Ron LeFlore .30 .10
❑ 561 Cardinals TL
BA: Lonnie Smith
ERA: Joaquin Anduj .30 .10
❑ 562 Dave Rozema .15 .05
❑ 563 Juan Bonilla .15 .05
❑ 564 Sid Monge .15 .05
❑ 565 Bucky Dent .30 .10
❑ 566 Manny Sarmiento .15 .05
❑ 567 Joe Simpson .15 .05
❑ 568 Willie Hernandez .15 .05
❑ 569 Jack Perconte .15 .05
❑ 570 Vida Blue .30 .10
❑ 571 Mickey Klutts .15 .05
❑ 572 Bob Watson .15 .05
❑ 573 Andy Hassler .15 .05
❑ 574 Glenn Adams .15 .05
❑ 575 Neil Allen .15 .05
❑ 576 Frank Robinson MG .60 .25
❑ 577 Luis Aponte .15 .05
❑ 578 David Green RC .75 .30
❑ 579 Rich Dauer .15 .05
❑ 580 Tom Seaver 1.25 .50
❑ 581 Tom Seaver SV .30 .10
❑ 582 Marshall Edwards .15 .05
❑ 583 Terry Forster .30 .10
❑ 584 Dave Hostetler .15 .05
❑ 585 Jose Cruz .30 .10
❑ 586 Frank Viola RC 2.50 1.00
❑ 587 Ivan DeJesus .15 .05
❑ 588 Pat Underwood .15 .05
❑ 589 Alvis Woods .15 .05
❑ 590 Tony Pena .15 .05
❑ 591 White Sox TL
BA: Greg Luzinski
ERA: LaMarr Hoyt# .30 .10
❑ 592 Shane Rawley .15 .05
❑ 593 Broderick Perkins .15 .05
❑ 594 Eric Rasmussen .15 .05
❑ 595 Tim Raines .30 .10
❑ 596 Randy Johnson .15 .05
❑ 597 Mike Proly .15 .05
❑ 598 Dwayne Murphy .15 .05
❑ 599 Don Aase .15 .05
❑ 600 George Brett 3.00 1.25
❑ 601 Ed Lynch .15 .05
❑ 602 Rich Gedman .15 .05
❑ 603 Joe Morgan .30 .10
❑ 604 Joe Morgan SV .15 .05
❑ 605 Gary Roenicke .15 .05
❑ 606 Bobby Cox MG .30 .10
❑ 607 Charlie Leibrandt .15 .05
❑ 608 Don Money .15 .05
❑ 609 Danny Darwin .15 .05
❑ 610 Steve Garvey .30 .10
❑ 611 Bert Roberge .15 .05
❑ 612 Steve Swisher .15 .05
❑ 613 Mike Ivie .15 .05
❑ 614 Ed Glynn .15 .05
❑ 615 Garry Maddox .15 .05
❑ 616 Bill Nahorodny .15 .05
❑ 617 Butch Wynegar .15 .05
❑ 618 LaMarr Hoyt .15 .05
❑ 619 Keith Moreland .15 .05
❑ 620 Mike Norris .15 .05
❑ 621 New York Mets TL
BA: Mookie Wilson
ERA: Craig Sw .30 .10
❑ 622 Dave Edler .15 .05
❑ 623 Luis Sanchez .15 .05
❑ 624 Glenn Hubbard .15 .05
❑ 625 Ken Forsch .15 .05
❑ 626 Jerry Martin .15 .05
❑ 627 Doug Bair .15 .05
❑ 628 Julio Valdez .15 .05
❑ 629 Charlie Lea .15 .05
❑ 630 Paul Molitor .30 .10
❑ 631 Tippy Martinez .15 .05
❑ 632 Alex Trevino .15 .05
❑ 633 Vicente Romo .15 .05
❑ 634 Max Venable .15 .05
❑ 635 Graig Nettles .30 .10
❑ 636 Graig Nettles SV .15 .05
❑ 637 Pat Corrales MG .15 .05
❑ 638 Dan Petry .15 .05
❑ 639 Art Howe .15 .05
❑ 640 Andre Thornton .15 .05
❑ 641 Billy Sample .15 .05
❑ 642 Checklist: 529-660 .30 .10
❑ 643 Bump Wills .15 .05
❑ 644 Joe Lefebvre .15 .05
❑ 645 Bill Madlock .30 .10
❑ 646 Jim Essian .15 .05
❑ 647 Bobby Mitchell .15 .05
❑ 648 Jeff Burroughs .15 .05
❑ 649 Tommy Boggs .15 .05
❑ 650 George Hendrick .30 .10
❑ 651 Angels TL/Rod Carew .30 .10
❑ 652 Butch Hobson .15 .05
❑ 653 Ellis Valentine .15 .05
❑ 654 Bob Ojeda .15 .05
❑ 655 Al Bumbry .15 .05
❑ 656 Dave Frost .15 .05
❑ 657 Mike Gates .15 .05
❑ 658 Frank Pastore .15 .05
❑ 659 Charlie Moore .15 .05
❑ 660 Mike Hargrove .15 .05
❑ 661 Bill Russell .30 .10
❑ 662 Joe Sambito .15 .05
❑ 663 Tom O'Malley .15 .05
❑ 664 Bob Molinaro .15 .05
❑ 665 Jim Sundberg .30 .10
❑ 666 Sparky Anderson MG .30 .10
❑ 667 Dick Davis .15 .05
❑ 668 Larry Christenson .15 .05
❑ 669 Mike Squires .15 .05
❑ 670 Jerry Mumphrey .15 .05
❑ 671 Lenny Faedo .15 .05
❑ 672 Jim Kaat .30 .10
❑ 673 Jim Kaat SV .15 .05
❑ 674 Kurt Bevacqua .15 .05
❑ 675 Jim Beattie .15 .05
❑ 676 Biff Pocoroba .15 .05
❑ 677 Dave Revering .15 .05
❑ 678 Juan Beniquez .15 .05
❑ 679 Mike Scott .30 .10
❑ 680 Andre Dawson .30 .10
❑ 681 Dodgers Leaders
BA: Pedro Guerrero
ERA: Fernando .30 .10
❑ 682 Bob Stanley .15 .05
❑ 683 Dan Ford .15 .05
❑ 684 Rafael Landestoy .15 .05
❑ 685 Lee Mazzilli .30 .10
❑ 686 Randy Lerch .15 .05
❑ 687 U.L. Washington .15 .05
❑ 688 Jim Wohlford .15 .05
❑ 689 Ron Hassey .15 .05
❑ 690 Kent Hrbek .30 .10
❑ 691 Dave Tobik .15 .05
❑ 692 Denny Walling .15 .05
❑ 693 Sparky Lyle .30 .10
❑ 694 Sparky Lyle SV .15 .05
❑ 695 Ruppert Jones .15 .05
❑ 696 Chuck Tanner MG .15 .05
❑ 697 Barry Foote .15 .05
❑ 698 Tony Bernazard .15 .05
❑ 699 Lee Smith .60 .25
❑ 700 Keith Hernandez .30 .10
❑ 701 Willie Wilson
Al Oliver LL .30 .10
❑ 702 Reggie/Thomas/Kingman LL .30 .10
❑ 703 RBI Leaders
AL: Hal McRae
NL: Dale Murphy
NL: A .60 .25
❑ 704 R.Henderson/T.Raines LL 1.25 .50
❑ 705 L.Hoyt/S.Carlton LL .30 .10
❑ 706 F.Bannister/Carlton LL .30 .10
❑ 707 Rick Sutcliffe
Steve Rogers LL .30 .10
❑ 708 Leading Firemen
AL: Dan Quisenberry
NL: Bruce Su .30 .10
❑ 709 Jimmy Sexton .15 .05
❑ 710 Willie Wilson .30 .10
❑ 711 Mariners TL
BA: Bruce Bochte
ERA: Jim Beattie .30 .10
❑ 712 Bruce Kison .15 .05
❑ 713 Ron Hodges .15 .05

❑ 714 Wayne Nordhagen .15 .05
❑ 715 Tony Perez .60 .25
❑ 716 Tony Perez SV .30 .10
❑ 717 Scott Sanderson .15 .05
❑ 718 Jim Dwyer .15 .05
❑ 719 Rich Gale .15 .05
❑ 720 Dave Concepcion .30 .10
❑ 721 John Martin .15 .05
❑ 722 Jorge Orta .15 .05
❑ 723 Randy Moffitt .15 .05
❑ 724 Johnny Grubb .15 .05
❑ 725 Dan Spillner .15 .05
❑ 726 Harvey Kuenn MG .15 .05
❑ 727 Chet Lemon .30 .10
❑ 728 Ron Reed .15 .05
❑ 729 Jerry Morales .15 .05
❑ 730 Jason Thompson .15 .05
❑ 731 Al Williams .15 .05
❑ 732 Dave Henderson .15 .05
❑ 733 Buck Martinez .15 .05
❑ 734 Steve Braun .15 .05
❑ 735 Tommy John .30 .10
❑ 736 Tommy John SV .15 .05
❑ 737 Mitchell Page .15 .05
❑ 738 Tim Foli .15 .05
❑ 739 Rick Ownbey .15 .05
❑ 740 Rusty Staub .30 .10
❑ 741 Rusty Staub SV .15 .05
❑ 742 Padres TL
BA: Terry Kennedy
ERA: Tim Lollar
(Ch .30 .10
❑ 743 Mike Torrez .15 .05
❑ 744 Brad Mills .15 .05
❑ 745 Scott McGregor .15 .05
❑ 746 John Wathan .15 .05
❑ 747 Fred Breining .15 .05
❑ 748 Derrel Thomas .15 .05
❑ 749 Jon Matlack .15 .05
❑ 750 Ben Oglivie .30 .10
❑ 751 Brad Havens .15 .05
❑ 752 Luis Pujols .15 .05
❑ 753 Elias Sosa .15 .05
❑ 754 Bill Robinson .15 .05
❑ 755 John Candelaria .15 .05
❑ 756 Russ Nixon MG .15 .05
❑ 757 Rick Manning .15 .05
❑ 758 Aurelio Rodriguez .15 .05
❑ 759 Doug Bird .15 .05
❑ 760 Dale Murphy .60 .25
❑ 761 Gary Lucas .15 .05
❑ 762 Cliff Johnson .15 .05
❑ 763 Al Cowens .15 .05
❑ 764 Pete Falcone .15 .05
❑ 765 Bob Boone .30 .10
❑ 766 Barry Bonnell .15 .05
❑ 767 Duane Kuiper .15 .05
❑ 768 Chris Speier .15 .05
❑ 769 Checklist: 661-792 .30 .10
❑ 770 Dave Winfield .30 .10
❑ 771 Twins TL
BA: Kent Hrbek
ERA: Bobby Castillo
(Ch .30 .10
❑ 772 Jim Kern .15 .05
❑ 773 Larry Hisle .15 .05
❑ 774 Alan Ashby .15 .05
❑ 775 Burt Hooton .15 .05
❑ 776 Larry Parrish .15 .05
❑ 777 John Curtis .15 .05
❑ 778 Rich Hebner .15 .05
❑ 779 Rick Waits .15 .05
❑ 780 Gary Matthews .30 .10
❑ 781 Rick Rhoden .15 .05
❑ 782 Bobby Murcer .30 .10
❑ 783 Bobby Murcer SV .15 .05
❑ 784 Jeff Newman .15 .05
❑ 785 Dennis Leonard .15 .05
❑ 786 Ralph Houk MG .15 .05
❑ 787 Dick Tidrow .15 .05
❑ 788 Dane Iorg .15 .05
❑ 789 Bryan Clark .15 .05
❑ 790 Bob Grich .30 .10
❑ 791 Gary Lavelle .15 .05
❑ 792 Chris Chambliss .30 .10
❑ XX Game Insert Card .10 .02

1984 Topps

❑ COMPLETE SET (792) 50.00 20.00
❑ 1 Steve Carlton HL .25 .08
❑ 2 Rickey Henderson HL .60 .25
❑ 3 Dan Quisenberry HL
Sets save record .15 .05
❑ 4 N.Ryan/Carlton/Perry HL 1.00 .40
❑ 5 Dave Righetti&
Bob Forsch&
and Mike Warren HL .25 .08
❑ 6 J.Bench/G.Perry/C.Yaz HL .40 .15
❑ 7 Gary Lucas .15 .05
❑ 8 Don Mattingly RC 15.00 6.00
❑ 9 Jim Gott .15 .05
❑ 10 Robin Yount 1.00 .40
❑ 11 Minnesota Twins TL
Kent Hrbek
Ken Schrom
(Check .25 .08
❑ 12 Billy Sample .15 .05
❑ 13 Scott Holman .15 .05
❑ 14 Tom Brookens .25 .08
❑ 15 Burt Hooton .15 .05
❑ 16 Omar Moreno .15 .05
❑ 17 John Denny .15 .05
❑ 18 Dale Berra .15 .05
❑ 19 Ray Fontenot .15 .05
❑ 20 Greg Luzinski .25 .08
❑ 21 Joe Altobelli MG .15 .05
❑ 22 Bryan Clark .15 .05
❑ 23 Keith Moreland .15 .05
❑ 24 John Martin .15 .05
❑ 25 Glenn Hubbard .15 .05
❑ 26 Bud Black .15 .05
❑ 27 Daryl Sconiers .15 .05
❑ 28 Frank Viola .40 .15
❑ 29 Danny Heep .15 .05
❑ 30 Wade Boggs 1.50 .60
❑ 31 Andy McGaffigan .15 .05
❑ 32 Bobby Ramos .15 .05
❑ 33 Tom Burgmeier .15 .05
❑ 34 Eddie Milner .15 .05
❑ 35 Don Sutton .25 .08
❑ 36 Denny Walling .15 .05
❑ 37 Texas Rangers TL
Buddy Bell
Rick Honeycutt
(Che .25 .08
❑ 38 Luis DeLeon .15 .05
❑ 39 Garth Iorg .15 .05
❑ 40 Dusty Baker .25 .08
❑ 41 Tony Bernazard .15 .05
❑ 42 Johnny Grubb .15 .05
❑ 43 Ron Reed .15 .05
❑ 44 Jim Morrison .15 .05
❑ 45 Jerry Mumphrey .15 .05
❑ 46 Ray Smith .15 .05
❑ 47 Rudy Law .15 .05
❑ 48 Julio Franco .25 .08
❑ 49 John Stuper .15 .05
❑ 50 Chris Chambliss .25 .08
❑ 51 Jim Frey MG .15 .05
❑ 52 Paul Splittorff .15 .05
❑ 53 Juan Beniquez .15 .05
❑ 54 Jesse Orosco .15 .05
❑ 55 Dave Concepcion .25 .08
❑ 56 Gary Allenson .15 .05
❑ 57 Dan Schatzeder .15 .05
❑ 58 Max Venable .15 .05
❑ 59 Sammy Stewart .15 .05
❑ 60 Paul Molitor .25 .08
❑ 61 Chris Codiroli .15 .05
❑ 62 Dave Hostetler .15 .05
❑ 63 Ed VandeBerg .15 .05
❑ 64 Mike Scioscia .25 .08
❑ 65 Kirk Gibson .60 .25
❑ 66 Astros TL/Nolan Ryan 1.00 .40
❑ 67 Gary Ward .15 .05
❑ 68 Luis Salazar .15 .05
❑ 69 Rod Scurry .15 .05
❑ 70 Gary Matthews .25 .08
❑ 71 Leo Hernandez .15 .05
❑ 72 Mike Squires .15 .05
❑ 73 Jody Davis .15 .05
❑ 74 Jerry Martin .15 .05
❑ 75 Bob Forsch .15 .05
❑ 76 Alfredo Griffin .15 .05
❑ 77 Brett Butler .25 .08
❑ 78 Mike Torrez .15 .05
❑ 79 Rob Wilfong .15 .05
❑ 80 Steve Rogers .25 .08
❑ 81 Billy Martin MG .40 .15
❑ 82 Doug Bird .15 .05
❑ 83 Richie Zisk .15 .05
❑ 84 Lenny Faedo .15 .05
❑ 85 Atlee Hammaker .15 .05
❑ 86 John Shelby .15 .05
❑ 87 Frank Pastore .15 .05
❑ 88 Rob Picciolo .15 .05
❑ 89 Mike Smithson .15 .05
❑ 90 Pedro Guerrero .25 .08
❑ 91 Dan Spillner .15 .05
❑ 92 Lloyd Moseby .15 .05
❑ 93 Bob Knepper .15 .05
❑ 94 Mario Ramirez .15 .05
❑ 95 Aurelio Lopez .25 .08
❑ 96 Kansas City Royals TL
Hal McRae
Larry Gura
(Che .25 .08
❑ 97 LaMarr Hoyt .15 .05
❑ 98 Steve Nicosia .15 .05
❑ 99 Craig Lefferts RC .15 .05
❑ 100 Reggie Jackson .40 .15
❑ 101 Porfirio Altamirano .15 .05
❑ 102 Ken Oberkfell .15 .05
❑ 103 Dwayne Murphy .15 .05
❑ 104 Ken Dayley .15 .05
❑ 105 Tony Armas .25 .08
❑ 106 Tim Stoddard .15 .05
❑ 107 Ned Yost .15 .05
❑ 108 Randy Moffitt .15 .05
❑ 109 Brad Wellman .15 .05
❑ 110 Ron Guidry .25 .08
❑ 111 Bill Virdon MG .15 .05
❑ 112 Tom Niedenfuer .15 .05
❑ 113 Kelly Paris .15 .05
❑ 114 Checklist 1-132 .25 .08
❑ 115 Andre Thornton .15 .05
❑ 116 George Bjorkman .15 .05
❑ 117 Tom Veryzer .15 .05
❑ 118 Charlie Hough .25 .08
❑ 119 John Wockenfuss .15 .05
❑ 120 Keith Hernandez .25 .08
❑ 121 Pat Sheridan .15 .05
❑ 122 Cecilio Guante .15 .05
❑ 123 Butch Wynegar .15 .05
❑ 124 Damaso Garcia .15 .05
❑ 125 Britt Burns .15 .05
❑ 126 Braves TL/Dale Murphy .40 .15
❑ 127 Mike Madden .15 .05
❑ 128 Rick Manning .15 .05
❑ 129 Bill Laskey .15 .05
❑ 130 Ozzie Smith 1.00 .40
❑ 131 W.Boggs/B.Madlock LL .60 .25
❑ 132 Mike Schmidt/J.Rice LL .60 .25
❑ 133 D.Murphy/Coop/Rice LL .40 .15
❑ 134 T.Raines/R.Henderson LL .60 .25
❑ 135 John Denny
LaMarr Hoyt LL .60 .25
❑ 136 S.Carlton/J.Morris LL .25 .08
❑ 137 A.Hammaker/R.Honeycutt LL .25 .08
❑ 138 Al Holland

Dan Quisenberry LL .25 .08
❑ 139 Bert Campaneris .25 .08
❑ 140 Storm Davis .15 .05
❑ 141 Pat Corrales MG .15 .05
❑ 142 Rich Gale .15 .05
❑ 143 Jose Morales .15 .05
❑ 144 Brian Harper RC .40 .15
❑ 145 Gary Lavelle .15 .05
❑ 146 Ed Romero .15 .05
❑ 147 Dan Petry .25 .08
❑ 148 Joe Lefebvre .15 .05
❑ 149 Jon Matlack .15 .05
❑ 150 Dale Murphy .40 .15
❑ 151 Steve Trout .15 .05
❑ 152 Glenn Brummer .15 .05
❑ 153 Dick Tidrow .15 .05
❑ 154 Dave Henderson .25 .08
❑ 155 Frank White .25 .08
❑ 156 A's TL/Rickey Henderson .60 .25
❑ 157 Gary Gaetti .40 .15
❑ 158 John Curtis .15 .05
❑ 159 Darryl Cias .15 .05
❑ 160 Mario Soto .25 .08
❑ 161 Junior Ortiz .15 .05
❑ 162 Bob Ojeda .15 .05
❑ 163 Lorenzo Gray .15 .05
❑ 164 Scott Sanderson .15 .05
❑ 165 Ken Singleton .25 .08
❑ 166 Jamie Nelson .15 .05
❑ 167 Marshall Edwards .15 .05
❑ 168 Juan Bonilla .15 .05
❑ 169 Larry Parrish .15 .05
❑ 170 Jerry Reuss .15 .05
❑ 171 Frank Robinson MG .40 .15
❑ 172 Frank DiPino .15 .05
❑ 173 Marvell Wynne .40 .15
❑ 174 Juan Berenguer .15 .05
❑ 175 Graig Nettles .25 .08
❑ 176 Lee Smith .25 .08
❑ 177 Jerry Hairston .15 .05
❑ 178 Bill Krueger RC .15 .05
❑ 179 Buck Martinez .15 .05
❑ 180 Manny Trillo .15 .05
❑ 181 Roy Thomas .15 .05
❑ 182 Darryl Strawberry RC 3.00 1.25
❑ 183 Al Williams .15 .05
❑ 184 Mike O'Berry .15 .05
❑ 185 Sixto Lezcano .15 .05
❑ 186 Cardinal TL
Lonnie Smith
John Stuper
(Checklist .25 .08
❑ 187 Luis Aponte .15 .05
❑ 188 Bryan Little .15 .05
❑ 189 Tim Conroy .15 .05
❑ 190 Ben Oglivie .25 .08
❑ 191 Mike Boddicker .15 .05
❑ 192 Nick Esasky .15 .05
❑ 193 Darrell Brown .15 .05
❑ 194 Domingo Ramos .15 .05
❑ 195 Jack Morris .25 .08
❑ 196 Don Slaught .25 .08
❑ 197 Garry Hancock .15 .05
❑ 198 Bill Doran RC* .40 .15
❑ 199 Willie Hernandez .15 .05
❑ 200 Andre Dawson .25 .08
❑ 201 Bruce Kison .15 .05
❑ 202 Bobby Cox MG .25 .08
❑ 203 Matt Keough .15 .05
❑ 204 Bobby Meacham .15 .05
❑ 205 Greg Minton .15 .05
❑ 206 Andy Van Slyke RC 1.50 .60
❑ 207 Donnie Moore .15 .05
❑ 208 Jose Oquendo RC .40 .15
❑ 209 Manny Sarmiento .15 .05
❑ 210 Joe Morgan .25 .08
❑ 211 Rick Sweet .15 .05
❑ 212 Broderick Perkins .15 .05
❑ 213 Bruce Hurst .15 .05
❑ 214 Paul Householder .15 .05
❑ 215 Tippy Martinez .15 .05
❑ 216 White Sox TL/C.Fisk .25 .08
❑ 217 Alan Ashby .15 .05
❑ 218 Rick Waits .15 .05
❑ 219 Joe Simpson .15 .05
❑ 220 Fernando Valenzuela .25 .08
❑ 221 Cliff Johnson .15 .05
❑ 222 Rick Honeycutt .15 .05
❑ 223 Wayne Krenchicki .15 .05
❑ 224 Sid Monge .15 .05
❑ 225 Lee Mazzilli .25 .08
❑ 226 Juan Eichelberger .15 .05
❑ 227 Steve Braun .15 .05
❑ 228 John Rabb .15 .05
❑ 229 Paul Owens MG .15 .05
❑ 230 Rickey Henderson 1.00 .40
❑ 231 Gary Woods .15 .05
❑ 232 Tim Wallach .15 .05
❑ 233 Checklist 133-264 .25 .08
❑ 234 Rafael Ramirez .15 .05
❑ 235 Matt Young RC .40 .15
❑ 236 Ellis Valentine .15 .05
❑ 237 John Castino .15 .05
❑ 238 Reid Nichols .15 .05
❑ 239 Jay Howell .15 .05
❑ 240 Eddie Murray .60 .25
❑ 241 Bill Almon .15 .05
❑ 242 Alex Trevino .15 .05
❑ 243 Pete Ladd .15 .05
❑ 244 Candy Maldonado .15 .05
❑ 245 Rick Sutcliffe .25 .08
❑ 246 Mets TL/Tom Seaver .25 .08
❑ 247 Onix Concepcion .15 .05
❑ 248 Bill Dawley .15 .05
❑ 249 Jay Johnstone .15 .05
❑ 250 Bill Madlock .25 .08
❑ 251 Tony Gwynn 2.50 1.00
❑ 252 Larry Christenson .15 .05
❑ 253 Jim Wohlford .15 .05
❑ 254 Shane Rawley .15 .05
❑ 255 Bruce Benedict .15 .05
❑ 256 Dave Geisel .15 .05
❑ 257 Julio Cruz .15 .05
❑ 258 Luis Sanchez .15 .05
❑ 259 Sparky Anderson MG .25 .08
❑ 260 Scott McGregor .15 .05
❑ 261 Bobby Brown .15 .05
❑ 262 Tom Candiotti RC .75 .30
❑ 263 Jack Fimple .15 .05
❑ 264 Doug Frobel RC .15 .05
❑ 265 Donnie Hill .15 .05
❑ 266 Steve Lubratich .15 .05
❑ 267 Carmelo Martinez .15 .05
❑ 268 Jack O'Connor .15 .05
❑ 269 Aurelio Rodriguez .15 .05
❑ 270 Jeff Russell RC .40 .15
❑ 271 Moose Haas .15 .05
❑ 272 Rick Dempsey .15 .05
❑ 273 Charlie Puleo .15 .05
❑ 274 Rick Monday .25 .08
❑ 275 Len Matuszek .15 .05
❑ 276 Angels TL/Rod Carew .25 .08
❑ 277 Eddie Whitson .15 .05
❑ 278 George Bell .25 .08
❑ 279 Ivan DeJesus .15 .05
❑ 280 Floyd Bannister .15 .05
❑ 281 Larry Milbourne .15 .05
❑ 282 Jim Barr .15 .05
❑ 283 Larry Biittner .15 .05
❑ 284 Howard Bailey .15 .05
❑ 285 Darrell Porter .15 .05
❑ 286 Lary Sorensen .15 .05
❑ 287 Warren Cromartie .15 .05
❑ 288 Jim Beattie .15 .05
❑ 289 Randy Johnson .15 .05
❑ 290 Dave Dravecky .15 .05
❑ 291 Chuck Tanner MG .15 .05
❑ 292 Tony Scott .15 .05
❑ 293 Ed Lynch .15 .05
❑ 294 U.L. Washington .15 .05
❑ 295 Mike Flanagan .15 .05
❑ 296 Jeff Newman .15 .05
❑ 297 Bruce Berenyi .15 .05
❑ 298 Jim Gantner .15 .05
❑ 299 John Butcher .15 .05
❑ 300 Pete Rose 2.00 .75
❑ 301 Frank LaCorte .15 .05
❑ 302 Barry Bonnell .15 .05
❑ 303 Marty Castillo .15 .05
❑ 304 Warren Brusstar .15 .05
❑ 305 Roy Smalley .15 .05
❑ 306 Dodgers TL
Pedro Guerrero
Bob Welch
(Checklist .25 .08
❑ 307 Bobby Mitchell .15 .05
❑ 308 Ron Hassey .15 .05
❑ 309 Tony Phillips RC .75 .30
❑ 310 Willie McGee .25 .08
❑ 311 Jerry Koosman .25 .08
❑ 312 Jorge Orta .15 .05
❑ 313 Mike Jorgensen .15 .05
❑ 314 Orlando Mercado .15 .05
❑ 315 Bob Grich .25 .08
❑ 316 Mark Bradley .15 .05
❑ 317 Greg Pryor .15 .05
❑ 318 Bill Gullickson .15 .05
❑ 319 Al Bumbry .15 .05
❑ 320 Bob Stanley .15 .05
❑ 321 Harvey Kuenn MG .15 .05
❑ 322 Ken Schrom .15 .05
❑ 323 Alan Knicely .15 .05
❑ 324 Alejandro Pena RC* .75 .30
❑ 325 Darrell Evans .25 .08
❑ 326 Bob Kearney .15 .05
❑ 327 Ruppert Jones .15 .05
❑ 328 Vern Ruhle .15 .05
❑ 329 Pat Tabler .15 .05
❑ 330 John Candelaria .15 .05
❑ 331 Bucky Dent .25 .08
❑ 332 Kevin Gross RC .40 .15
❑ 333 Larry Herndon .25 .08
❑ 334 Chuck Rainey .15 .05
❑ 335 Don Baylor .25 .08
❑ 336 Seattle Mariners TL
Pat Putnam
Matt Young
(Chec .25 .08
❑ 337 Kevin Hagen .15 .05
❑ 338 Mike Warren .15 .05
❑ 339 Roy Lee Jackson .15 .05
❑ 340 Hal McRae .25 .08
❑ 341 Dave Tobik .15 .05
❑ 342 Tim Foli .15 .05
❑ 343 Mark Davis .15 .05
❑ 344 Rick Miller .15 .05
❑ 345 Kent Hrbek .25 .08
❑ 346 Kurt Bevacqua .15 .05
❑ 347 Allan Ramirez .15 .05
❑ 348 Toby Harrah .25 .08
❑ 349 Bob L. Gibson RC .15 .05
❑ 350 George Foster .25 .08
❑ 351 Russ Nixon MG .15 .05
❑ 352 Dave Stewart .25 .08
❑ 353 Jim Anderson .15 .05
❑ 354 Jeff Burroughs .15 .05
❑ 355 Jason Thompson .15 .05
❑ 356 Glenn Abbott .15 .05
❑ 357 Ron Cey .25 .08
❑ 358 Bob Dernier .15 .05
❑ 359 Jim Acker .15 .05
❑ 360 Willie Randolph .25 .08
❑ 361 Dave Smith .15 .05
❑ 362 David Green .15 .05
❑ 363 Tim Laudner .15 .05
❑ 364 Scott Fletcher .15 .05
❑ 365 Steve Bedrosian .15 .05
❑ 366 Padres TL
Terry Kennedy
Dave Dravecky
(Checklis .25 .08
❑ 367 Jamie Easterly .15 .05
❑ 368 Hubie Brooks .15 .05
❑ 369 Steve McCatty .15 .05
❑ 370 Tim Raines .25 .08
❑ 371 Dave Gumpert .15 .05
❑ 372 Gary Roenicke .15 .05
❑ 373 Bill Scherrer .15 .05
❑ 374 Don Money .15 .05
❑ 375 Dennis Leonard .15 .05
❑ 376 Dave Anderson RC .15 .05
❑ 377 Danny Darwin .15 .05
❑ 378 Bob Brenly .15 .05
❑ 379 Checklist 265-396 .25 .08
❑ 380 Steve Garvey .25 .08
❑ 381 Ralph Houk MG .15 .05
❑ 382 Chris Nyman .15 .05
❑ 383 Terry Puhl .15 .05

❑ 384 Lee Tunnell .15 .05
❑ 385 Tony Perez .40 .15
❑ 386 George Hendrick AS .15 .05
❑ 387 Johnny Ray AS .15 .05
❑ 388 Mike Schmidt AS .60 .25
❑ 389 Ozzie Smith AS .60 .25
❑ 390 Tim Raines AS .15 .05
❑ 391 Dale Murphy AS .25 .08
❑ 392 Andre Dawson AS .15 .05
❑ 393 Gary Carter AS .15 .05
❑ 394 Steve Rogers AS .15 .05
❑ 395 Steve Carlton AS .25 .08
❑ 396 Jesse Orosco AS .15 .05
❑ 397 Eddie Murray AS .40 .15
❑ 398 Lou Whitaker AS .15 .05
❑ 399 George Brett AS .60 .25
❑ 400 Cal Ripken AS 2.00 .75
❑ 401 Jim Rice AS .15 .05
❑ 402 Dave Winfield AS .15 .05
❑ 403 Lloyd Moseby AS .15 .05
❑ 404 Ted Simmons AS .15 .05
❑ 405 LaMarr Hoyt AS .15 .05
❑ 406 Ron Guidry AS .15 .05
❑ 407 Dan Quisenberry AS .15 .05
❑ 408 Lou Piniella .25 .08
❑ 409 Juan Agosto .15 .05
❑ 410 Claudell Washington .15 .05
❑ 411 Houston Jimenez .15 .05
❑ 412 Doug Rader MG .15 .05
❑ 413 Spike Owen RC .40 .15
❑ 414 Mitchell Page .15 .05
❑ 415 Tommy John .25 .08
❑ 416 Dane Iorg .15 .05
❑ 417 Mike Armstrong .15 .05
❑ 418 Ron Hodges .15 .05
❑ 419 John Henry Johnson .15 .05
❑ 420 Cecil Cooper .25 .08
❑ 421 Charlie Lea .15 .05
❑ 422 Jose Cruz .25 .08
❑ 423 Mike Morgan .15 .05
❑ 424 Dann Bilardello .15 .05
❑ 425 Steve Howe .15 .05
❑ 426 Orioles TL/Cal Ripken 1.50 .60
❑ 427 Rick Leach .15 .05
❑ 428 Fred Breining .15 .05
❑ 429 Randy Bush .15 .05
❑ 430 Rusty Staub .25 .08
❑ 431 Chris Bando .15 .05
❑ 432 Charles Hudson .15 .05
❑ 433 Rich Hebner .15 .05
❑ 434 Harold Baines .25 .08
❑ 435 Neil Allen .15 .05
❑ 436 Rick Peters .15 .05
❑ 437 Mike Proly .15 .05
❑ 438 Biff Pocoroba .15 .05
❑ 439 Bob Stoddard .15 .05
❑ 440 Steve Kemp .15 .05
❑ 441 Bob Lillis MG .15 .05
❑ 442 Byron McLaughlin .15 .05
❑ 443 Benny Ayala .15 .05
❑ 444 Steve Renko .15 .05
❑ 445 Jerry Remy .15 .05
❑ 446 Luis Pujols .15 .05
❑ 447 Tom Brunansky .15 .05
❑ 448 Ben Hayes .15 .05
❑ 449 Joe Pettini .15 .05
❑ 450 Gary Carter .25 .08
❑ 451 Bob Jones .15 .05
❑ 452 Chuck Porter .15 .05
❑ 453 Willie Upshaw .15 .05
❑ 454 Joe Beckwith .15 .05
❑ 455 Terry Kennedy .15 .05
❑ 456 Cubs TL/F.Jenkins .15 .05
❑ 457 Dave Rozema .15 .05
❑ 458 Kiko Garcia .15 .05
❑ 459 Kevin Hickey .15 .05
❑ 460 Dave Winfield .25 .08
❑ 461 Jim Maler .15 .05
❑ 462 Lee Lacy .15 .05
❑ 463 Dave Engle .15 .05
❑ 464 Jeff A. Jones .15 .05
❑ 465 Mookie Wilson .25 .08
❑ 466 Gene Garber .15 .05
❑ 467 Mike Ramsey .15 .05
❑ 468 Geoff Zahn .15 .05
❑ 469 Tom O'Malley .15 .05
❑ 470 Nolan Ryan 3.00 1.25
❑ 471 Dick Howser MG .15 .05
❑ 472 Mike G. Brown RC .15 .05
❑ 473 Jim Dwyer .15 .05
❑ 474 Greg Bargar .15 .05
❑ 475 Gary Redus RC* .40 .15
❑ 476 Tom Tellmann .15 .05
❑ 477 Rafael Landestoy .15 .05
❑ 478 Alan Bannister .15 .05
❑ 479 Frank Tanana .25 .08
❑ 480 Ron Kittle .15 .05
❑ 481 Mark Thurmond .15 .05
❑ 482 Enos Cabell .15 .05
❑ 483 Fergie Jenkins .25 .08
❑ 484 Ozzie Virgil .15 .05
❑ 485 Rick Rhoden .15 .05
❑ 486 D.Baylor/R.Guidry TL .25 .08
❑ 487 Ricky Adams .15 .05
❑ 488 Jesse Barfield .25 .08
❑ 489 Dave Von Ohlen .15 .05
❑ 490 Cal Ripken 4.00 1.50
❑ 491 Bobby Castillo .15 .05
❑ 492 Tucker Ashford .15 .05
❑ 493 Mike Norris .15 .05
❑ 494 Chili Davis .25 .08
❑ 495 Rollie Fingers .25 .08
❑ 496 Terry Francona .25 .08
❑ 497 Bud Anderson .15 .05
❑ 498 Rich Gedman .15 .05
❑ 499 Mike Witt .15 .05
❑ 500 George Brett 1.50 .60
❑ 501 Steve Henderson .15 .05
❑ 502 Joe Torre MG .25 .08
❑ 503 Elias Sosa .15 .05
❑ 504 Mickey Rivers .15 .05
❑ 505 Pete Vuckovich .15 .05
❑ 506 Ernie Whitt .15 .05
❑ 507 Mike LaCoss .15 .05
❑ 508 Mel Hall .25 .08
❑ 509 Brad Havens .15 .05
❑ 510 Alan Trammell .25 .08
❑ 511 Marty Bystrom .15 .05
❑ 512 Oscar Gamble .15 .05
❑ 513 Dave Beard .15 .05
❑ 514 Floyd Rayford .15 .05
❑ 515 Gorman Thomas .25 .08
❑ 516 Montreal Expos TL
Al Oliver
Charlie Lea
(Checkl .25 .08
❑ 517 John Moses .15 .05
❑ 518 Greg Walker .40 .15
❑ 519 Ron Davis .15 .05
❑ 520 Bob Boone .25 .08
❑ 521 Pete Falcone .15 .05
❑ 522 Dave Bergman .15 .05
❑ 523 Glenn Hoffman .15 .05
❑ 524 Carlos Diaz .15 .05
❑ 525 Willie Wilson .25 .08
❑ 526 Ron Oester .15 .05
❑ 527 Checklist 397-528 .25 .08
❑ 528 Mark Brouhard .15 .05
❑ 529 Keith Atherton .15 .05
❑ 530 Dan Ford .15 .05
❑ 531 Steve Boros MG .15 .05
❑ 532 Eric Show .15 .05
❑ 533 Ken Landreaux .15 .05
❑ 534 Pete O'Brien RC* .40 .15
❑ 535 Bo Diaz .15 .05
❑ 536 Doug Bair .15 .05
❑ 537 Johnny Ray .15 .05
❑ 538 Kevin Bass .15 .05
❑ 539 George Frazier .15 .05
❑ 540 George Hendrick .25 .08
❑ 541 Dennis Lamp .15 .05
❑ 542 Duane Kuiper .15 .05
❑ 543 Craig McMurtry .15 .05
❑ 544 Cesar Geronimo .15 .05
❑ 545 Bill Buckner .25 .08
❑ 546 Indians TL
Mike Hargrove
Lary Sorensen
(Checkli .25 .08
❑ 547 Mike Moore .15 .05
❑ 548 Ron Jackson .15 .05
❑ 549 Walt Terrell .15 .05
❑ 550 Jim Rice .25 .08
❑ 551 Scott Ullger .15 .05
❑ 552 Ray Burris .15 .05
❑ 553 Joe Nolan .15 .05
❑ 554 Ted Power .15 .05
❑ 555 Greg Brock .15 .05
❑ 556 Joey McLaughlin .15 .05
❑ 557 Wayne Tolleson .15 .05
❑ 558 Mike Davis .15 .05
❑ 559 Mike Scott .25 .08
❑ 560 Carlton Fisk .40 .15
❑ 561 Whitey Herzog MG .25 .08
❑ 562 Manny Castillo .15 .05
❑ 563 Glenn Wilson .25 .08
❑ 564 Al Holland .15 .05
❑ 565 Leon Durham .15 .05
❑ 566 Jim Bibby .15 .05
❑ 567 Mike Heath .15 .05
❑ 568 Pete Filson .15 .05
❑ 569 Bake McBride .25 .08
❑ 570 Dan Quisenberry .15 .05
❑ 571 Bruce Bochy .15 .05
❑ 572 Jerry Royster .15 .05
❑ 573 Dave Kingman .25 .08
❑ 574 Brian Downing .25 .08
❑ 575 Jim Clancy .15 .05
❑ 576 Giants TL
Jeff Leonard
Atlee Hammaker
(Checklis .25 .08
❑ 577 Mark Clear .15 .05
❑ 578 Lenn Sakata .15 .05
❑ 579 Bob James .15 .05
❑ 580 Lonnie Smith .15 .05
❑ 581 Jose DeLeon RC .40 .15
❑ 582 Bob McClure .15 .05
❑ 583 Derrel Thomas .15 .05
❑ 584 Dave Schmidt .15 .05
❑ 585 Dan Driessen .15 .05
❑ 586 Joe Niekro .15 .05
❑ 587 Von Hayes .15 .05
❑ 588 Milt Wilcox .15 .05
❑ 589 Mike Easler .15 .05
❑ 590 Dave Stieb .25 .08
❑ 591 Tony LaRussa MG .25 .08
❑ 592 Andre Robertson .15 .05
❑ 593 Jeff Lahti .15 .05
❑ 594 Gene Richards .15 .05
❑ 595 Jeff Reardon .25 .08
❑ 596 Ryne Sandberg 2.50 1.00
❑ 597 Rick Camp .15 .05
❑ 598 Rusty Kuntz .15 .05
❑ 599 Doug Sisk .15 .05
❑ 600 Rod Carew .40 .15
❑ 601 John Tudor .25 .08
❑ 602 John Wathan .15 .05
❑ 603 Renie Martin .15 .05
❑ 604 John Lowenstein .15 .05
❑ 605 Mike Caldwell .15 .05
❑ 606 Blue Jays TL
Lloyd Moseby
Dave Stieb
(Checklist .25 .08
❑ 607 Tom Hume .15 .05
❑ 608 Bobby Johnson .15 .05
❑ 609 Dan Meyer .15 .05
❑ 610 Steve Sax .15 .05
❑ 611 Chet Lemon .25 .08
❑ 612 Harry Spilman .15 .05
❑ 613 Greg Gross .15 .05
❑ 614 Len Barker .15 .05
❑ 615 Garry Templeton .25 .08
❑ 616 Don Robinson .15 .05
❑ 617 Rick Cerone .15 .05
❑ 618 Dickie Noles .15 .05
❑ 619 Jerry Dybzinski .15 .05
❑ 620 Al Oliver .25 .08
❑ 621 Frank Howard MG .25 .08
❑ 622 Al Cowens .15 .05
❑ 623 Ron Washington .15 .05
❑ 624 Terry Harper .15 .05
❑ 625 Larry Gura .15 .05
❑ 626 Bob Clark .15 .05
❑ 627 Dave LaPoint .15 .05
❑ 628 Ed Jurak .15 .05
❑ 629 Rick Langford .15 .05

❑ 630 Ted Simmons .25 .08
❑ 631 Dennis Martinez .25 .08
❑ 632 Tom Foley .15 .05
❑ 633 Mike Krukow .15 .05
❑ 634 Mike Marshall .15 .05
❑ 635 Dave Righetti .25 .08
❑ 636 Pat Putnam .15 .05
❑ 637 Phillies TL
Gary Matthews
John Denny
(Checklist .25 .08
❑ 638 George Vukovich .15 .05
❑ 639 Rick Lysander .15 .05
❑ 640 Lance Parrish .40 .15
❑ 641 Mike Richardt .15 .05
❑ 642 Tom Underwood .15 .05
❑ 643 Mike C. Brown .15 .05
❑ 644 Tim Lollar .15 .05
❑ 645 Tony Pena .15 .05
❑ 646 Checklist 529-660 .25 .08
❑ 647 Ron Roenicke .15 .05
❑ 648 Len Whitehouse .15 .05
❑ 649 Tom Herr .15 .05
❑ 650 Phil Niekro .25 .08
❑ 651 John McNamara MG .15 .05
❑ 652 Rudy May .15 .05
❑ 653 Dave Stapleton .15 .05
❑ 654 Bob Bailor .15 .05
❑ 655 Amos Otis .25 .08
❑ 656 Bryn Smith .15 .05
❑ 657 Thad Bosley .15 .05
❑ 658 Jerry Augustine .15 .05
❑ 659 Duane Walker .15 .05
❑ 660 Ray Knight .25 .08
❑ 661 Steve Yeager .25 .08
❑ 662 Tom Brennan .15 .05
❑ 663 Johnnie LeMaster .15 .05
❑ 664 Dave Stegman .15 .05
❑ 665 Buddy Bell .25 .08
❑ 666 Tigers TL/Morris/Whitak .25 .08
❑ 667 Vance Law .15 .05
❑ 668 Larry McWilliams .15 .05
❑ 669 Dave Lopes .25 .08
❑ 670 Rich Gossage .25 .08
❑ 671 Jamie Quirk .15 .05
❑ 672 Ricky Nelson .15 .05
❑ 673 Mike Walters .15 .05
❑ 674 Tim Flannery .15 .05
❑ 675 Pascual Perez .15 .05
❑ 676 Brian Giles .15 .05
❑ 677 Doyle Alexander .15 .05
❑ 678 Chris Speier .15 .05
❑ 679 Art Howe .15 .05
❑ 680 Fred Lynn .25 .08
❑ 681 Tom Lasorda MG .40 .15
❑ 682 Dan Morogiello .15 .05
❑ 683 Marty Barrett RC .40 .15
❑ 684 Bob Shirley .15 .05
❑ 685 Willie Aikens .15 .05
❑ 686 Joe Price .15 .05
❑ 687 Roy Howell .15 .05
❑ 688 George Wright .15 .05
❑ 689 Mike Fischlin .15 .05
❑ 690 Jack Clark .25 .08
❑ 691 Steve Lake .15 .05
❑ 692 Dickie Thon .15 .05
❑ 693 Alan Wiggins .15 .05
❑ 694 Mike Stanton .15 .05
❑ 695 Lou Whitaker .25 .08
❑ 696 Pirates TL
Bill Madlock
Rick Rhoden
(Checklist .25 .08
❑ 697 Dale Murray .15 .05
❑ 698 Marc Hill .15 .05
❑ 699 Dave Rucker .15 .05
❑ 700 Mike Schmidt 1.50 .60
❑ 701 Madlock/Rose/Parker LL .60 .25
❑ 702 Rose/Staub/Perez LL .60 .25
❑ 703 Schmidt/Perez/Kingm LL .60 .25
❑ 704 Tony Perez
Rusty Staub
Al Oliver LL .25 .08
❑ 705 Morgan/Cedeno/Bowa LL .40 .15
❑ 706 S.Carlton/Jenk/Seaver LL .25 .08
❑ 707 N.Ryan/Seaver/Carlton LL 1.50 .60
❑ 708 Seaver/Carlton/Rog LL .25 .08
❑ 709 NL Active Save
Bruce Sutter
Tug McGraw
Gene Gar .25 .08
❑ 710 Carew/Brett/Cooper LL .40 .15
❑ 711 Carew/Camp/Reggie LL .25 .08
❑ 712 Reggie/Nettles/Luz LL .25 .08
❑ 713 Reggie/Simmons/Nett LL .25 .08
❑ 714 AL Active Steals
Bert Campaneris
Dave Lopes
Oma .25 .08
❑ 715 Palmer/Sutton/John LL .25 .08
❑ 716 AL Active Strikeout
Don Sutton
Bert Blyleven
Jo .40 .15
❑ 717 Jim Palmer/Fingers LL .25 .08
❑ 718 Fingers/Goose/Quis LL .25 .08
❑ 719 Andy Hassler .15 .05
❑ 720 Dwight Evans .40 .15
❑ 721 Del Crandall MG .15 .05
❑ 722 Bob Welch .25 .08
❑ 723 Rich Dauer .15 .05
❑ 724 Eric Rasmussen .15 .05
❑ 725 Cesar Cedeno .25 .08
❑ 726 Brewers TL
Ted Simmons
Moose Haas
(Checklist on .25 .08
❑ 727 Joel Youngblood .15 .05
❑ 728 Tug McGraw .25 .08
❑ 729 Gene Tenace .25 .08
❑ 730 Bruce Sutter .40 .15
❑ 731 Lynn Jones .15 .05
❑ 732 Terry Crowley .15 .05
❑ 733 Dave Collins .15 .05
❑ 734 Odell Jones .15 .05
❑ 735 Rick Burleson .15 .05
❑ 736 Dick Ruthven .15 .05
❑ 737 Jim Essian .15 .05
❑ 738 Bill Schroeder .15 .05
❑ 739 Bob Watson .15 .05
❑ 740 Tom Seaver .60 .25
❑ 741 Wayne Gross .15 .05
❑ 742 Dick Williams MG .15 .05
❑ 743 Don Hood .15 .05
❑ 744 Jamie Allen .15 .05
❑ 745 Dennis Eckersley .40 .15
❑ 746 Mickey Hatcher .15 .05
❑ 747 Pat Zachry .15 .05
❑ 748 Jeff Leonard .15 .05
❑ 749 Doug Flynn .15 .05
❑ 750 Jim Palmer .25 .08
❑ 751 Charlie Moore .15 .05
❑ 752 Phil Garner .25 .08
❑ 753 Doug Gwosdz .15 .05
❑ 754 Kent Tekulve .15 .05
❑ 755 Garry Maddox .15 .05
❑ 756 Reds TL
Ron Oester
Mario Soto
(Checklist on bac .25 .08
❑ 757 Larry Bowa .25 .08
❑ 758 Bill Stein .15 .05
❑ 759 Richard Dotson .15 .05
❑ 760 Bob Horner .25 .08
❑ 761 John Montefusco .15 .05
❑ 762 Rance Mulliniks .15 .05
❑ 763 Craig Swan .15 .05
❑ 764 Mike Hargrove .15 .05
❑ 765 Ken Forsch .15 .05
❑ 766 Mike Vail .15 .05
❑ 767 Carney Lansford .25 .08
❑ 768 Champ Summers .15 .05
❑ 769 Bill Caudill .15 .05
❑ 770 Ken Griffey .25 .08
❑ 771 Billy Gardner MG .15 .05
❑ 772 Jim Slaton .15 .05
❑ 773 Todd Cruz .15 .05
❑ 774 Tom Gorman .15 .05
❑ 775 Dave Parker .25 .08
❑ 776 Craig Reynolds .15 .05
❑ 777 Tom Paciorek .15 .05
❑ 778 Andy Hawkins .15 .05
❑ 779 Jim Sundberg .25 .08
❑ 780 Steve Carlton .40 .15
❑ 781 Checklist 661-792 .25 .08
❑ 782 Steve Balboni .15 .05
❑ 783 Luis Leal .15 .05
❑ 784 Leon Roberts .15 .05
❑ 785 Joaquin Andujar .25 .08
❑ 786 Red Sox TL/Boggs/Ojeda .40 .15
❑ 787 Bill Campbell .15 .05
❑ 788 Milt May .15 .05
❑ 789 Bert Blyleven .25 .08
❑ 790 Doug DeCinces .15 .05
❑ 791 Terry Forster .25 .08
❑ 792 Bill Russell .25 .08

1985 Topps

❑ COMPLETE SET (792) 80.00 40.00
❑ COMP.FACT.SET (792) 175.00 100.00
❑ 1 Carlton Fisk RB .25 .08
❑ 2 Steve Garvey RB .15 .05
❑ 3 Dwight Gooden RB .60 .25
❑ 4 Cliff Johnson RB .15 .05
❑ 5 Joe Morgan RB .15 .05
❑ 6 Pete Rose RB .40 .15
❑ 7 Nolan Ryan RB 1.50 .60
❑ 8 Juan Samuel RB .15 .05
❑ 9 Bruce Sutter RB .15 .05
❑ 10 Don Sutton RB .15 .05
❑ 11 Ralph Houk MG .15 .05
❑ 12 Dave Lopes .25 .08
❑ 13 Tim Lollar .15 .05
❑ 14 Chris Bando .15 .05
❑ 15 Jerry Koosman .25 .08
❑ 16 Bobby Meacham .15 .05
❑ 17 Mike Scott .25 .08
❑ 18 Mickey Hatcher .15 .05
❑ 19 George Frazier .15 .05
❑ 20 Chet Lemon .25 .08
❑ 21 Lee Tunnell .15 .05
❑ 22 Duane Kuiper .15 .05
❑ 23 Bret Saberhagen RC 1.00 .40
❑ 24 Jesse Barfield .25 .08
❑ 25 Steve Bedrosian .15 .05
❑ 26 Roy Smalley .15 .05
❑ 27 Bruce Berenyi .15 .05
❑ 28 Dann Bilardello .15 .05
❑ 29 Odell Jones .15 .05
❑ 30 Cal Ripken 2.50 1.00
❑ 31 Terry Whitfield .15 .05
❑ 32 Chuck Porter .15 .05
❑ 33 Tito Landrum .15 .05
❑ 34 Ed Nunez .15 .05
❑ 35 Graig Nettles .25 .08
❑ 36 Fred Breining .15 .05
❑ 37 Reid Nichols .15 .05
❑ 38 Jackie Moore MG .15 .05
❑ 39 John Wockenfuss .15 .05
❑ 40 Phil Niekro .25 .08
❑ 41 Mike Fischlin .15 .05
❑ 42 Luis Sanchez .15 .05
❑ 43 Andre David .15 .05
❑ 44 Dickie Thon .15 .05
❑ 45 Greg Minton .15 .05
❑ 46 Gary Woods .15 .05
❑ 47 Dave Rozema .15 .05
❑ 48 Tony Fernandez .25 .08
❑ 49 Butch Davis .15 .05
❑ 50 John Candelaria .15 .05

❑ 51	Bob Watson	.15	.05
❑ 52	Jerry Dybzinski	.15	.05
❑ 53	Tom Gorman	.15	.05
❑ 54	Cesar Cedeno	.25	.08
❑ 55	Frank Tanana	.25	.08
❑ 56	Jim Dwyer	.15	.05
❑ 57	Pat Zachry	.15	.05
❑ 58	Orlando Mercado	.15	.05
❑ 59	Rick Waits	.15	.05
❑ 60	George Hendrick	.25	.08
❑ 61	Curt Kaufman	.15	.05
❑ 62	Mike Ramsey	.15	.05
❑ 63	Steve McCatty	.15	.05
❑ 64	Mark Bailey	.15	.05
❑ 65	Bill Buckner	.25	.08
❑ 66	Dick Williams MG	.15	.05
❑ 67	Rafael Santana	.15	.05
❑ 68	Von Hayes	.15	.05
❑ 69	Jim Winn	.15	.05
❑ 70	Don Baylor	.25	.08
❑ 71	Tim Laudner	.15	.05
❑ 72	Rick Sutcliffe	.25	.08
❑ 73	Rusty Kuntz	.15	.05
❑ 74	Mike Krukow	.15	.05
❑ 75	Willie Upshaw	.15	.05
❑ 76	Alan Bannister	.15	.05
❑ 77	Joe Beckwith	.15	.05
❑ 78	Scott Fletcher	.15	.05
❑ 79	Rick Mahler	.15	.05
❑ 80	Keith Hernandez	.25	.08
❑ 81	Lenn Sakata	.15	.05
❑ 82	Joe Price	.15	.05
❑ 83	Charlie Moore	.15	.05
❑ 84	Spike Owen	.15	.05
❑ 85	Mike Marshall	.15	.05
❑ 86	Don Aase	.15	.05
❑ 87	David Green	.15	.05
❑ 88	Bryn Smith	.15	.05
❑ 89	Jackie Gutierrez	.15	.05
❑ 90	Rich Gossage	.25	.08
❑ 91	Jeff Burroughs	.15	.05
❑ 92	Paul Owens MG	.15	.05
❑ 93	Don Schulze	.15	.05
❑ 94	Toby Harrah	.25	.08
❑ 95	Jose Cruz	.25	.08
❑ 96	Johnny Ray	.15	.05
❑ 97	Pete Filson	.15	.05
❑ 98	Steve Lake	.15	.05
❑ 99	Milt Wilcox	.15	.05
❑ 100	George Brett	1.50	.60
❑ 101	Jim Acker	.15	.05
❑ 102	Tommy Dunbar	.15	.05
❑ 103	Randy Lerch	.15	.05
❑ 104	Mike Fitzgerald	.15	.05
❑ 105	Ron Kittle	.15	.05
❑ 106	Pascual Perez	.15	.05
❑ 107	Tom Foley	.15	.05
❑ 108	Darnell Coles	.15	.05
❑ 109	Gary Roenicke	.15	.05
❑ 110	Alejandro Pena	.15	.05
❑ 111	Doug DeCinces	.15	.05
❑ 112	Tom Tellmann	.15	.05
❑ 113	Tom Herr	.15	.05
❑ 114	Bob James	.15	.05
❑ 115	Rickey Henderson	.75	.30
❑ 116	Dennis Boyd	.15	.05
❑ 117	Greg Gross	.15	.05
❑ 118	Eric Show	.15	.05
❑ 119	Pat Corrales MG	.15	.05
❑ 120	Steve Kemp	.15	.05
❑ 121	Checklist: 1-132	.15	.05
❑ 122	Tom Brunansky	.15	.05
❑ 123	Dave Smith	.15	.05
❑ 124	Rich Hebner	.15	.05
❑ 125	Kent Tekulve	.15	.05
❑ 126	Ruppert Jones	.15	.05
❑ 127	Mark Gubicza RC*	.40	.15
❑ 128	Ernie Whitt	.15	.05
❑ 129	Gene Garber	.15	.05
❑ 130	Al Oliver	.25	.08
❑ 131	Buddy/Gus Bell FS	.25	.08
❑ 132	Yogi/Dale Berra FS	.60	.25
❑ 133	Bob/Ray Boone FS	.15	.05
❑ 134	Terry/Tito Francona FS	.25	.08
❑ 135	Terry/Bob Kennedy FS	.15	.05
❑ 136	Jeff/Bill Kunkel FS	.15	.05
❑ 137	Vance/Vern Law FS	.25	.08
❑ 138	Dick/Dick Schofield FS	.15	.05
❑ 139	Joel/Bob Skinner FS	.15	.05
❑ 140	Roy/Roy Smalley FS	.15	.05
❑ 141	Mike/Dave Stenhouse FS	.15	.05
❑ 142	Steve/Dizzy Trout FS	.15	.05
❑ 143	Ozzie/Ossie Virgil FS	.15	.05
❑ 144	Ron Gardenhire	.15	.05
❑ 145	Alvin Davis RC*	.40	.15
❑ 146	Gary Redus	.15	.05
❑ 147	Bill Swaggerty	.15	.05
❑ 148	Steve Yeager	.25	.08
❑ 149	Dickie Noles	.15	.05
❑ 150	Jim Rice	.25	.08
❑ 151	Moose Haas	.15	.05
❑ 152	Steve Braun	.15	.05
❑ 153	Frank LaCorte	.15	.05
❑ 154	Angel Salazar	.15	.05
❑ 155	Yogi Berra MG/TC	.60	.25
❑ 156	Craig Reynolds	.15	.05
❑ 157	Tug McGraw	.25	.08
❑ 158	Pat Tabler	.15	.05
❑ 159	Carlos Diaz	.15	.05
❑ 160	Lance Parrish	.25	.08
❑ 161	Ken Schrom	.15	.05
❑ 162	Benny Distefano	.15	.05
❑ 163	Dennis Eckersley	.40	.15
❑ 164	Jorge Orta	.15	.05
❑ 165	Dusty Baker	.25	.08
❑ 166	Keith Atherton	.15	.05
❑ 167	Rufino Linares	.15	.05
❑ 168	Garth Iorg	.15	.05
❑ 169	Dan Spillner	.15	.05
❑ 170	George Foster	.25	.08
❑ 171	Bill Stein	.15	.05
❑ 172	Jack Perconte	.15	.05
❑ 173	Mike Young	.15	.05
❑ 174	Rick Honeycutt	.15	.05
❑ 175	Dave Parker	.25	.08
❑ 176	Bill Schroeder	.15	.05
❑ 177	Dave Von Ohlen	.15	.05
❑ 178	Miguel Dilone	.15	.05
❑ 179	Tommy John	.25	.08
❑ 180	Dave Winfield	.25	.08
❑ 181	Roger Clemens RC	20.00	8.00
❑ 182	Tim Flannery	.15	.05
❑ 183	Larry McWilliams	.15	.05
❑ 184	Carmen Castillo	.15	.05
❑ 185	Al Holland	.15	.05
❑ 186	Bob Lillis MG	.15	.05
❑ 187	Mike Walters	.15	.05
❑ 188	Greg Pryor	.15	.05
❑ 189	Warren Brusstar	.15	.05
❑ 190	Rusty Staub	.25	.08
❑ 191	Steve Nicosia	.15	.05
❑ 192	Howard Johnson	.25	.08
❑ 193	Jimmy Key RC	.75	.30
❑ 194	Dave Stegman	.15	.05
❑ 195	Glenn Hubbard	.15	.05
❑ 196	Pete O'Brien	.15	.05
❑ 197	Mike Warren	.15	.05
❑ 198	Eddie Milner	.15	.05
❑ 199	Dennis Martinez	.25	.08
❑ 200	Reggie Jackson	.40	.15
❑ 201	Burt Hooton	.15	.05
❑ 202	Gorman Thomas	.25	.08
❑ 203	Bob McClure	.15	.05
❑ 204	Art Howe	.15	.05
❑ 205	Steve Rogers	.25	.08
❑ 206	Phil Garner	.25	.08
❑ 207	Mark Clear	.15	.05
❑ 208	Champ Summers	.15	.05
❑ 209	Bill Campbell	.15	.05
❑ 210	Gary Matthews	.25	.08
❑ 211	Clay Christiansen	.15	.05
❑ 212	George Vukovich	.15	.05
❑ 213	Billy Gardner MG	.15	.05
❑ 214	John Tudor	.25	.08
❑ 215	Bob Brenly	.15	.05
❑ 216	Jerry Don Gleaton	.15	.05
❑ 217	Leon Roberts	.15	.05
❑ 218	Doyle Alexander	.15	.05
❑ 219	Gerald Perry	.15	.05
❑ 220	Fred Lynn	.25	.08
❑ 221	Ron Reed	.15	.05
❑ 222	Hubie Brooks	.15	.05
❑ 223	Tom Hume	.15	.05
❑ 224	Al Cowens	.15	.05
❑ 225	Mike Boddicker	.15	.05
❑ 226	Juan Beniquez	.15	.05
❑ 227	Danny Darwin	.15	.05
❑ 228	Dion James	.15	.05
❑ 229	Dave LaPoint	.15	.05
❑ 230	Gary Carter	.25	.08
❑ 231	Dwayne Murphy	.15	.05
❑ 232	Dave Beard	.15	.05
❑ 233	Ed Jurak	.15	.05
❑ 234	Jerry Narron	.15	.05
❑ 235	Garry Maddox	.15	.05
❑ 236	Mark Thurmond	.15	.05
❑ 237	Julio Franco	.25	.08
❑ 238	Jose Rijo RC	.75	.30
❑ 239	Tim Teufel	.15	.05
❑ 240	Dave Stieb	.25	.08
❑ 241	Jim Frey MG	.15	.05
❑ 242	Greg Harris	.15	.05
❑ 243	Barbaro Garbey	.15	.05
❑ 244	Mike Jones	.15	.05
❑ 245	Chili Davis	.25	.08
❑ 246	Mike Norris	.15	.05
❑ 247	Wayne Tolleson	.15	.05
❑ 248	Terry Forster	.25	.08
❑ 249	Harold Baines	.25	.08
❑ 250	Jesse Orosco	.15	.05
❑ 251	Brad Gulden	.15	.05
❑ 252	Dan Ford	.15	.05
❑ 253	Sid Bream RC	.40	.15
❑ 254	Pete Vuckovich	.15	.05
❑ 255	Lonnie Smith	.15	.05
❑ 256	Mike Stanton	.15	.05
❑ 257	Bryan Little	.15	.05
❑ 258	Mike C. Brown	.15	.05
❑ 259	Gary Allenson	.15	.05
❑ 260	Dave Righetti	.25	.08
❑ 261	Checklist: 133-264	.15	.05
❑ 262	Greg Booker	.15	.05
❑ 263	Mel Hall	.15	.05
❑ 264	Joe Sambito	.15	.05
❑ 265	Juan Samuel	.15	.05
❑ 266	Frank Viola	.25	.08
❑ 267	Henry Cotto RC	.15	.05
❑ 268	Chuck Tanner MG	.15	.05
❑ 269	Doug Baker	.15	.05
❑ 270	Dan Quisenberry	.15	.05
❑ 271	Tim Foli FDP	.15	.05
❑ 272	Jeff Burroughs FDP	.15	.05
❑ 273	Bill Almon FDP	.15	.05
❑ 274	Floyd Bannister FDP	.15	.05
❑ 275	Harold Baines FDP	.15	.05
❑ 276	Bob Horner FDP	.15	.05
❑ 277	Al Chambers FDP	.15	.05
❑ 278	Darryl Strawberry FDP	.40	.15
❑ 279	Mike Moore FDP	.15	.05
❑ 280	Shawon Dunston FDP RC	.75	.30
❑ 281	Tim Belcher FDP RC	.40	.15
❑ 282	Shawn Abner FDP RC	.15	.05
❑ 283	Fran Mullins	.15	.05
❑ 284	Marty Bystrom	.15	.05
❑ 285	Dan Driessen	.15	.05
❑ 286	Rudy Law	.15	.05
❑ 287	Walt Terrell	.15	.05
❑ 288	Jeff Kunkel	.15	.05
❑ 289	Tom Underwood	.15	.05
❑ 290	Cecil Cooper	.25	.08
❑ 291	Bob Welch	.25	.08
❑ 292	Brad Komminsk	.15	.05
❑ 293	Curt Young	.15	.05
❑ 294	Tom Nieto	.15	.05
❑ 295	Joe Niekro	.15	.05
❑ 296	Ricky Nelson	.15	.05
❑ 297	Gary Lucas	.15	.05
❑ 298	Marty Barrett	.15	.05
❑ 299	Andy Hawkins	.15	.05
❑ 300	Rod Carew	.40	.15
❑ 301	John Montefusco	.15	.05
❑ 302	Tim Corcoran	.15	.05
❑ 303	Mike Jeffcoat	.15	.05
❑ 304	Gary Gaetti	.25	.08
❑ 305	Dale Berra	.15	.05
❑ 306	Rick Reuschel	.25	.08
❑ 307	Sparky Anderson MG	.25	.08
❑ 308	John Wathan	.15	.05

❑ 309 Mike Witt .15 .05
❑ 310 Manny Trillo .15 .05
❑ 311 Jim Gott .15 .05
❑ 312 Marc Hill .15 .05
❑ 313 Dave Schmidt .15 .05
❑ 314 Ron Oester .15 .05
❑ 315 Doug Sisk .15 .05
❑ 316 John Lowenstein .15 .05
❑ 317 Jack Lazorko .15 .05
❑ 318 Ted Simmons .25 .08
❑ 319 Jeff Jones .15 .05
❑ 320 Dale Murphy .40 .15
❑ 321 Ricky Horton .15 .05
❑ 322 Dave Stapleton .15 .05
❑ 323 Andy McGaffigan .15 .05
❑ 324 Bruce Bochy .15 .05
❑ 325 John Denny .15 .05
❑ 326 Kevin Bass .15 .05
❑ 327 Brook Jacoby .15 .05
❑ 328 Bob Shirley .15 .05
❑ 329 Ron Washington .15 .05
❑ 330 Leon Durham .15 .05
❑ 331 Bill Laskey .15 .05
❑ 332 Brian Harper .15 .05
❑ 333 Willie Hernandez .15 .05
❑ 334 Dick Howser MG .15 .05
❑ 335 Bruce Benedict .15 .05
❑ 336 Rance Mulliniks .15 .05
❑ 337 Billy Sample .15 .05
❑ 338 Britt Burns .15 .05
❑ 339 Danny Heep .15 .05
❑ 340 Robin Yount 1.00 .40
❑ 341 Floyd Rayford .15 .05
❑ 342 Ted Power .15 .05
❑ 343 Bill Russell .25 .08
❑ 344 Dave Henderson .15 .05
❑ 345 Charlie Lea .15 .05
❑ 346 Terry Pendleton RC .75 .30
❑ 347 Rick Langford .15 .05
❑ 348 Bob Boone .25 .08
❑ 349 Domingo Ramos .15 .05
❑ 350 Wade Boggs .60 .25
❑ 351 Juan Agosto .15 .05
❑ 352 Joe Morgan .25 .08
❑ 353 Julio Solano .15 .05
❑ 354 Andre Robertson .15 .05
❑ 355 Bert Blyleven .25 .08
❑ 356 Dave Meier .15 .05
❑ 357 Rich Bordi .15 .05
❑ 358 Tony Pena .15 .05
❑ 359 Pat Sheridan .15 .05
❑ 360 Steve Carlton .25 .08
❑ 361 Alfredo Griffin .15 .05
❑ 362 Craig McMurtry .15 .05
❑ 363 Ron Hodges .15 .05
❑ 364 Richard Dotson .15 .05
❑ 365 Danny Ozark MG .15 .05
❑ 366 Todd Cruz .15 .05
❑ 367 Keefe Cato .15 .05
❑ 368 Dave Bergman .15 .05
❑ 369 R.J. Reynolds .15 .05
❑ 370 Bruce Sutter .25 .08
❑ 371 Mickey Rivers .15 .05
❑ 372 Roy Howell .15 .05
❑ 373 Mike Moore .15 .05
❑ 374 Brian Downing .25 .08
❑ 375 Jeff Reardon .25 .08
❑ 376 Jeff Newman .15 .05
❑ 377 Checklist: 265-396 .15 .05
❑ 378 Alan Wiggins .15 .05
❑ 379 Charles Hudson .15 .05
❑ 380 Ken Griffey .25 .08
❑ 381 Roy Smith .15 .05
❑ 382 Denny Walling .15 .05
❑ 383 Rick Lysander .15 .05
❑ 384 Jody Davis .15 .05
❑ 385 Jose DeLeon .15 .05
❑ 386 Dan Gladden RC .40 .15
❑ 387 Buddy Biancalana .15 .05
❑ 388 Bert Roberge .15 .05
❑ 389 Rod Dedeaux OLY CO RC .25 .08
❑ 390 Sid Akins OLY RC .15 .05
❑ 391 Flavio Alfaro OLY RC .15 .05
❑ 392 Don August OLY RC .15 .05
❑ 393 Scott Bankhead OLY RC .15 .05
❑ 394 Bob Caffrey OLY RC .15 .05
❑ 395 Mike Dunne OLY RC .15 .05
❑ 396 Gary Green OLY RC .15 .05
❑ 397 John Hoover OLY RC .15 .05
❑ 398 Shane Mack OLY RC .40 .15
❑ 399 John Marzano OLY RC .15 .05
❑ 400 Oddibe McDowell OLY RC .40 .15
❑ 401 Mark McGwire OLY RC 30.00 12.50
❑ 402 Pat Pacillo OLY RC .15 .05
❑ 403 Cory Snyder OLY RC .75 .30
❑ 404 Bill Swift OLY RC .40 .15
❑ 405 Tom Veryzer .15 .05
❑ 406 Len Whitehouse .15 .05
❑ 407 Bobby Ramos .15 .05
❑ 408 Sid Monge .15 .05
❑ 409 Brad Wellman .15 .05
❑ 410 Bob Horner .25 .08
❑ 411 Bobby Cox MG .25 .08
❑ 412 Bud Black .15 .05
❑ 413 Vance Law .15 .05
❑ 414 Gary Ward .15 .05
❑ 415 Ron Darling UER .25 .08
❑ 416 Wayne Gross .15 .05
❑ 417 John Franco RC .75 .30
❑ 418 Ken Landreaux .15 .05
❑ 419 Mike Caldwell .15 .05
❑ 420 Andre Dawson .25 .08
❑ 421 Dave Rucker .15 .05
❑ 422 Carney Lansford .25 .08
❑ 423 Barry Bonnell .15 .05
❑ 424 Al Nipper .15 .05
❑ 425 Mike Hargrove .15 .05
❑ 426 Vern Ruhle .15 .05
❑ 427 Mario Ramirez .15 .05
❑ 428 Larry Andersen .15 .05
❑ 429 Rick Cerone .15 .05
❑ 430 Ron Davis .15 .05
❑ 431 U.L. Washington .15 .05
❑ 432 Thad Bosley .15 .05
❑ 433 Jim Morrison .15 .05
❑ 434 Gene Richards .15 .05
❑ 435 Dan Petry .15 .05
❑ 436 Willie Aikens .15 .05
❑ 437 Al Jones .15 .05
❑ 438 Joe Torre MG .25 .08
❑ 439 Junior Ortiz .15 .05
❑ 440 Fernando Valenzuela .25 .08
❑ 441 Duane Walker .15 .05
❑ 442 Ken Forsch .15 .05
❑ 443 George Wright .15 .05
❑ 444 Tony Phillips .15 .05
❑ 445 Tippy Martinez .15 .05
❑ 446 Jim Sundberg .25 .08
❑ 447 Jeff Lahti .15 .05
❑ 448 Derrel Thomas .15 .05
❑ 449 Phil Bradley .40 .15
❑ 450 Steve Garvey .25 .08
❑ 451 Bruce Hurst .15 .05
❑ 452 John Castino .15 .05
❑ 453 Tom Waddell .15 .05
❑ 454 Glenn Wilson .15 .05
❑ 455 Bob Knepper .15 .05
❑ 456 Tim Foli .15 .05
❑ 457 Cecilio Guante .15 .05
❑ 458 Randy Johnson .15 .05
❑ 459 Charlie Leibrandt .15 .05
❑ 460 Ryne Sandberg 1.25 .50
❑ 461 Marty Castillo .15 .05
❑ 462 Gary Lavelle .15 .05
❑ 463 Dave Collins .15 .05
❑ 464 Mike Mason RC .15 .05
❑ 465 Bob Grich .25 .08
❑ 466 Tony LaRussa MG .25 .08
❑ 467 Ed Lynch .15 .05
❑ 468 Wayne Krenchicki .15 .05
❑ 469 Sammy Stewart .15 .05
❑ 470 Steve Sax .15 .05
❑ 471 Pete Ladd .15 .05
❑ 472 Jim Essian .15 .05
❑ 473 Tim Wallach .15 .05
❑ 474 Kurt Kepshire .15 .05
❑ 475 Andre Thornton .15 .05
❑ 476 Jeff Stone RC .15 .05
❑ 477 Bob Ojeda .15 .05
❑ 478 Kurt Bevacqua .15 .05
❑ 479 Mike Madden .15 .05
❑ 480 Lou Whitaker .25 .08
❑ 481 Dale Murray .15 .05
❑ 482 Harry Spilman .15 .05
❑ 483 Mike Smithson .15 .05
❑ 484 Larry Bowa .25 .08
❑ 485 Matt Young .15 .05
❑ 486 Steve Balboni .15 .05
❑ 487 Frank Williams .15 .05
❑ 488 Joel Skinner .15 .05
❑ 489 Bryan Clark .15 .05
❑ 490 Jason Thompson .15 .05
❑ 491 Rick Camp .15 .05
❑ 492 Dave Johnson MG .15 .05
❑ 493 Orel Hershiser RC 2.00 .75
❑ 494 Rich Dauer .15 .05
❑ 495 Mario Soto .25 .08
❑ 496 Donnie Scott .15 .05
❑ 497 Gary Pettis UER .15 .05
❑ 498 Ed Romero .15 .05
❑ 499 Danny Cox .15 .05
❑ 500 Mike Schmidt 1.50 .60
❑ 501 Dan Schatzeder .15 .05
❑ 502 Rick Miller .15 .05
❑ 503 Tim Conroy .15 .05
❑ 504 Jerry Willard .15 .05
❑ 505 Jim Beattie .15 .05
❑ 506 Franklin Stubbs .15 .05
❑ 507 Ray Fontenot .15 .05
❑ 508 John Shelby .15 .05
❑ 509 Milt May .15 .05
❑ 510 Kent Hrbek .25 .08
❑ 511 Lee Smith .25 .08
❑ 512 Tom Brookens .15 .05
❑ 513 Lynn Jones .15 .05
❑ 514 Jeff Cornell .15 .05
❑ 515 Dave Concepcion .25 .08
❑ 516 Roy Lee Jackson .15 .05
❑ 517 Jerry Martin .15 .05
❑ 518 Chris Chambliss .25 .08
❑ 519 Doug Rader MG .15 .05
❑ 520 LaMarr Hoyt .15 .05
❑ 521 Rick Dempsey .15 .05
❑ 522 Paul Molitor .25 .08
❑ 523 Candy Maldonado .15 .05
❑ 524 Rob Wilfong .15 .05
❑ 525 Darrell Porter .15 .05
❑ 526 David Palmer .15 .05
❑ 527 Checklist: 397-528 .15 .05
❑ 528 Bill Krueger .15 .05
❑ 529 Rich Gedman .15 .05
❑ 530 Dave Dravecky .15 .05
❑ 531 Joe Lefebvre .15 .05
❑ 532 Frank DiPino .15 .05
❑ 533 Tony Bernazard .15 .05
❑ 534 Brian Dayett .15 .05
❑ 535 Pat Putnam .15 .05
❑ 536 Kirby Puckett RC 12.00 5.00
❑ 537 Don Robinson .15 .05
❑ 538 Keith Moreland .15 .05
❑ 539 Aurelio Lopez .15 .05
❑ 540 Claudell Washington .15 .05
❑ 541 Mark Davis .15 .05
❑ 542 Don Slaught .15 .05
❑ 543 Mike Squires .15 .05
❑ 544 Bruce Kison .15 .05
❑ 545 Lloyd Moseby .15 .05
❑ 546 Brent Gaff .15 .05
❑ 547 Pete Rose MG/TC .40 .15
❑ 548 Larry Parrish .15 .05
❑ 549 Mike Scioscia .25 .08
❑ 550 Scott McGregor .15 .05
❑ 551 Andy Van Slyke .40 .15
❑ 552 Chris Codiroli .15 .05
❑ 553 Bob Clark .15 .05
❑ 554 Doug Flynn .15 .05
❑ 555 Bob Stanley .15 .05
❑ 556 Sixto Lezcano .15 .05
❑ 557 Len Barker .15 .05
❑ 558 Carmelo Martinez .15 .05
❑ 559 Jay Howell .15 .05
❑ 560 Bill Madlock .25 .08
❑ 561 Darryl Motley .15 .05
❑ 562 Houston Jimenez .15 .05
❑ 563 Dick Ruthven .15 .05
❑ 564 Alan Ashby .15 .05
❑ 565 Kirk Gibson .25 .08
❑ 566 Ed VandeBerg .15 .05

❑ 567	Joel Youngblood	.15	.05
❑ 568	Cliff Johnson	.15	.05
❑ 569	Ken Oberkfell	.15	.05
❑ 570	Darryl Strawberry	.60	.25
❑ 571	Charlie Hough	.25	.08
❑ 572	Tom Paciorek	.15	.05
❑ 573	Jay Tibbs	.15	.05
❑ 574	Joe Altobelli MG	.15	.05
❑ 575	Pedro Guerrero	.25	.08
❑ 576	Jaime Cocanower	.15	.05
❑ 577	Chris Speier	.15	.05
❑ 578	Terry Francona	.25	.08
❑ 579	Ron Romanick	.15	.05
❑ 580	Dwight Evans	.40	.15
❑ 581	Mark Wagner	.15	.05
❑ 582	Ken Phelps	.15	.05
❑ 583	Bobby Brown	.15	.05
❑ 584	Kevin Gross	.15	.05
❑ 585	Butch Wynegar	.15	.05
❑ 586	Bill Scherrer	.15	.05
❑ 587	Doug Frobel	.15	.05
❑ 588	Bobby Castillo	.15	.05
❑ 589	Bob Dernier	.15	.05
❑ 590	Ray Knight	.25	.08
❑ 591	Larry Herndon	.15	.05
❑ 592	Jeff D. Robinson	.15	.05
❑ 593	Rick Leach	.15	.05
❑ 594	Curt Wilkerson	.15	.05
❑ 595	Larry Gura	.15	.05
❑ 596	Jerry Hairston	.15	.05
❑ 597	Brad Lesley	.15	.05
❑ 598	Jose Oquendo	.15	.05
❑ 599	Storm Davis	.15	.05
❑ 600	Pete Rose	1.50	.60
❑ 601	Tom Lasorda MG	.40	.15
❑ 602	Jeff Dedmon	.15	.05
❑ 603	Rick Manning	.15	.05
❑ 604	Daryl Sconiers	.15	.05
❑ 605	Ozzie Smith	1.00	.40
❑ 606	Rich Gale	.15	.05
❑ 607	Bill Almon	.15	.05
❑ 608	Craig Lefferts	.15	.05
❑ 609	Broderick Perkins	.15	.05
❑ 610	Jack Morris	.25	.08
❑ 611	Ozzie Virgil	.15	.05
❑ 612	Mike Armstrong	.15	.05
❑ 613	Terry Puhl	.15	.05
❑ 614	Al Williams	.15	.05
❑ 615	Marvell Wynne	.15	.05
❑ 616	Scott Sanderson	.15	.05
❑ 617	Willie Wilson	.25	.08
❑ 618	Pete Falcone	.15	.05
❑ 619	Jeff Leonard	.15	.05
❑ 620	Dwight Gooden RC	2.00	.75
❑ 621	Marvis Foley	.15	.05
❑ 622	Luis Leal	.15	.05
❑ 623	Greg Walker	.15	.05
❑ 624	Benny Ayala	.15	.05
❑ 625	Mark Langston RC	.75	.30
❑ 626	German Rivera	.15	.05
❑ 627	Eric Davis RC	2.00	.75
❑ 628	Rene Lachemann MG	.15	.05
❑ 629	Dick Schofield	.15	.05
❑ 630	Tim Raines	.25	.08
❑ 631	Bob Forsch	.15	.05
❑ 632	Bruce Bochte	.15	.05
❑ 633	Glenn Hoffman	.15	.05
❑ 634	Bill Dawley	.15	.05
❑ 635	Terry Kennedy	.15	.05
❑ 636	Shane Rawley	.15	.05
❑ 637	Brett Butler	.25	.08
❑ 638	Mike Pagliarulo	.15	.05
❑ 639	Ed Hodge	.15	.05
❑ 640	Steve Henderson	.15	.05
❑ 641	Rod Scurry	.15	.05
❑ 642	Dave Owen	.15	.05
❑ 643	Johnny Grubb	.15	.05
❑ 644	Mark Huismann	.15	.05
❑ 645	Damaso Garcia	.15	.05
❑ 646	Scot Thompson	.15	.05
❑ 647	Rafael Ramirez	.15	.05
❑ 648	Bob Jones	.15	.05
❑ 649	Sid Fernandez	.25	.08
❑ 650	Greg Luzinski	.25	.08
❑ 651	Jeff Russell	.15	.05
❑ 652	Joe Nolan	.15	.05
❑ 653	Mark Brouhard	.15	.05
❑ 654	Dave Anderson	.15	.05
❑ 655	Joaquin Andujar	.25	.08
❑ 656	Chuck Cottier MG	.15	.05
❑ 657	Jim Slaton	.15	.05
❑ 658	Mike Stenhouse	.15	.05
❑ 659	Checklist: 529-660	.15	.05
❑ 660	Tony Gwynn	1.25	.50
❑ 661	Steve Crawford	.15	.05
❑ 662	Mike Heath	.15	.05
❑ 663	Luis Aguayo	.15	.05
❑ 664	Steve Farr RC	.40	.15
❑ 665	Don Mattingly	2.50	1.00
❑ 666	Mike LaCoss	.15	.05
❑ 667	Dave Engle	.15	.05
❑ 668	Steve Trout	.15	.05
❑ 669	Lee Lacy	.15	.05
❑ 670	Tom Seaver	.40	.15
❑ 671	Dane Iorg	.15	.05
❑ 672	Juan Berenguer	.15	.05
❑ 673	Buck Martinez	.15	.05
❑ 674	Atlee Hammaker	.15	.05
❑ 675	Tony Perez	.40	.15
❑ 676	Albert Hall	.15	.05
❑ 677	Wally Backman	.15	.05
❑ 678	Joey McLaughlin	.15	.05
❑ 679	Bob Kearney	.15	.05
❑ 680	Jerry Reuss	.15	.05
❑ 681	Ben Oglivie	.25	.08
❑ 682	Doug Corbett	.15	.05
❑ 683	Whitey Herzog MG	.25	.08
❑ 684	Bill Doran	.15	.05
❑ 685	Bill Caudill	.15	.05
❑ 686	Mike Easler	.15	.05
❑ 687	Bill Gullickson	.15	.05
❑ 688	Len Matuszek	.15	.05
❑ 689	Luis DeLeon	.15	.05
❑ 690	Alan Trammell	.25	.08
❑ 691	Dennis Rasmussen	.15	.05
❑ 692	Randy Bush	.15	.05
❑ 693	Tim Stoddard	.15	.05
❑ 694	Joe Carter	.60	.25
❑ 695	Rick Rhoden	.15	.05
❑ 696	John Rabb	.15	.05
❑ 697	Onix Concepcion	.15	.05
❑ 698	George Bell	.25	.08
❑ 699	Donnie Moore	.15	.05
❑ 700	Eddie Murray	.60	.25
❑ 701	Eddie Murray AS	.40	.15
❑ 702	Damaso Garcia AS	.15	.05
❑ 703	George Brett AS	.60	.25
❑ 704	Cal Ripken AS	1.50	.60
❑ 705	Dave Winfield AS	.15	.05
❑ 706	Rickey Henderson AS	.40	.15
❑ 707	Tony Armas AS	.15	.05
❑ 708	Lance Parrish AS	.15	.05
❑ 709	Mike Boddicker AS	.15	.05
❑ 710	Frank Viola AS	.15	.05
❑ 711	Dan Quisenberry AS	.15	.05
❑ 712	Keith Hernandez AS	.15	.05
❑ 713	Ryne Sandberg AS	.60	.25
❑ 714	Mike Schmidt AS	.60	.25
❑ 715	Ozzie Smith AS	.60	.25
❑ 716	Dale Murphy AS	.25	.08
❑ 717	Tony Gwynn AS	1.00	.40
❑ 718	Jeff Leonard AS	.15	.05
❑ 719	Gary Carter AS	.15	.05
❑ 720	Rick Sutcliffe AS	.15	.05
❑ 721	Bob Knepper AS	.15	.05
❑ 722	Bruce Sutter AS	.15	.05
❑ 723	Dave Stewart	.25	.08
❑ 724	Oscar Gamble	.15	.05
❑ 725	Floyd Bannister	.15	.05
❑ 726	Al Bumbry	.15	.05
❑ 727	Frank Pastore	.15	.05
❑ 728	Bob Bailor	.15	.05
❑ 729	Don Sutton	.25	.08
❑ 730	Dave Kingman	.25	.08
❑ 731	Neil Allen	.15	.05
❑ 732	John McNamara MG	.15	.05
❑ 733	Tony Scott	.15	.05
❑ 734	John Henry Johnson	.15	.05
❑ 735	Garry Templeton	.25	.08
❑ 736	Jerry Mumphrey	.15	.05
❑ 737	Bo Diaz	.15	.05
❑ 738	Omar Moreno	.15	.05
❑ 739	Ernie Camacho	.15	.05
❑ 740	Jack Clark	.25	.08
❑ 741	John Butcher	.15	.05
❑ 742	Ron Hassey	.15	.05
❑ 743	Frank White	.25	.08
❑ 744	Doug Bair	.15	.05
❑ 745	Buddy Bell	.25	.08
❑ 746	Jim Clancy	.15	.05
❑ 747	Alex Trevino	.15	.05
❑ 748	Lee Mazzilli	.25	.08
❑ 749	Julio Cruz	.15	.05
❑ 750	Rollie Fingers	.25	.08
❑ 751	Kelvin Chapman	.15	.05
❑ 752	Bob Owchinko	.15	.05
❑ 753	Greg Brock	.15	.05
❑ 754	Larry Milbourne	.15	.05
❑ 755	Ken Singleton	.25	.08
❑ 756	Rob Picciolo	.15	.05
❑ 757	Willie McGee	.25	.08
❑ 758	Ray Burris	.15	.05
❑ 759	Jim Fanning MG	.15	.05
❑ 760	Nolan Ryan	3.00	1.25
❑ 761	Jerry Remy	.15	.05
❑ 762	Eddie Whitson	.15	.05
❑ 763	Kiko Garcia	.15	.05
❑ 764	Jamie Easterly	.15	.05
❑ 765	Willie Randolph	.25	.08
❑ 766	Paul Mirabella	.15	.05
❑ 767	Darrell Brown	.15	.05
❑ 768	Ron Cey	.25	.08
❑ 769	Joe Cowley	.15	.05
❑ 770	Carlton Fisk	.40	.15
❑ 771	Geoff Zahn	.15	.05
❑ 772	Johnnie LeMaster	.15	.05
❑ 773	Hal McRae	.25	.08
❑ 774	Dennis Lamp	.15	.05
❑ 775	Mookie Wilson	.25	.08
❑ 776	Jerry Royster	.15	.05
❑ 777	Ned Yost	.15	.05
❑ 778	Mike Davis	.15	.05
❑ 779	Nick Esasky	.15	.05
❑ 780	Mike Flanagan	.15	.05
❑ 781	Jim Gantner	.15	.05
❑ 782	Tom Niedenfuer	.15	.05
❑ 783	Mike Jorgensen	.15	.05
❑ 784	Checklist: 661-792	.15	.05
❑ 785	Tony Armas	.25	.08
❑ 786	Enos Cabell	.15	.05
❑ 787	Jim Wohlford	.15	.05
❑ 788	Steve Comer	.15	.05
❑ 789	Luis Salazar	.15	.05
❑ 790	Ron Guidry	.25	.08
❑ 791	Ivan DeJesus	.15	.05
❑ 792	Darrell Evans	.25	.08

1986 Topps

❑	COMPLETE SET (792)	25.00	10.00
❑	COMP.X-MAS.SET (792)	150.00	75.00
❑ 1	Pete Rose	2.00	.75
❑ 2	Rose Special: '63-'66	.25	.08
❑ 3	Rose Special: '67-'70	.25	.08
❑ 4	Rose Special: '71-'74	.25	.08
❑ 5	Rose Special: '75-'78	.25	.08
❑ 6	Rose Special: '79-'82	.25	.08
❑ 7	Rose Special: '83-'85	.25	.08
❑ 8	Dwayne Murphy	.10	.02
❑ 9	Roy Smith	.10	.02
❑ 10	Tony Gwynn	.60	.25

Card	NRMT	VG-E
❑ 11 Bob Ojeda	.10	.02
❑ 12 Jose Uribe	.10	.02
❑ 13 Bob Kearney	.10	.02
❑ 14 Julio Cruz	.10	.02
❑ 15 Eddie Whitson	.10	.02
❑ 16 Rick Schu	.10	.02
❑ 17 Mike Stenhouse	.10	.02
❑ 18 Brent Gaff	.10	.02
❑ 19 Rich Hebner	.10	.02
❑ 20 Lou Whitaker	.15	.05
❑ 21 George Bamberger MG	.10	.02
❑ 22 Duane Walker	.10	.02
❑ 23 Manuel Lee RC*	.10	.02
❑ 24 Len Barker	.10	.02
❑ 25 Willie Wilson	.15	.05
❑ 26 Frank DiPino	.10	.02
❑ 27 Ray Knight	.15	.05
❑ 28 Eric Davis	.40	.15
❑ 29 Tony Phillips	.10	.02
❑ 30 Eddie Murray	.40	.15
❑ 31 Jamie Easterly	.10	.02
❑ 32 Steve Yeager	.15	.05
❑ 33 Jeff Lahti	.10	.02
❑ 34 Ken Phelps	.10	.02
❑ 35 Jeff Reardon	.15	.05
❑ 36 Tigers Leaders		
Lance Parrish	.15	.05
❑ 37 Mark Thurmond	.10	.02
❑ 38 Glenn Hoffman	.10	.02
❑ 39 Dave Rucker	.10	.02
❑ 40 Ken Griffey	.15	.05
❑ 41 Brad Wellman	.10	.02
❑ 42 Geoff Zahn	.10	.02
❑ 43 Dave Engle	.10	.02
❑ 44 Lance McCullers	.10	.02
❑ 45 Damaso Garcia	.10	.02
❑ 46 Billy Hatcher	.10	.02
❑ 47 Juan Berenguer	.10	.02
❑ 48 Bill Almon	.10	.02
❑ 49 Rick Manning	.10	.02
❑ 50 Dan Quisenberry	.10	.02
❑ 51 Bobby Wine MG ERR		
(Checklist back)		
(Number of ca	.10	.02
❑ 52 Chris Welsh	.10	.02
❑ 53 Len Dykstra RC	.75	.30
❑ 54 John Franco	.15	.05
❑ 55 Fred Lynn	.15	.05
❑ 56 Tom Niedenfuer	.10	.02
❑ 57 Bill Doran		
(See also 51)	.10	.02
❑ 58 Bill Krueger	.10	.02
❑ 59 Andre Thornton	.10	.02
❑ 60 Dwight Evans	.25	.08
❑ 61 Karl Best	.10	.02
❑ 62 Bob Boone	.15	.05
❑ 63 Ron Roenicke	.10	.02
❑ 64 Floyd Bannister	.10	.02
❑ 65 Dan Driessen	.10	.02
❑ 66 Cardinals Leaders		
Bob Forsch	.10	.02
❑ 67 Carmelo Martinez	.10	.02
❑ 68 Ed Lynch	.10	.02
❑ 69 Luis Aguayo	.10	.02
❑ 70 Dave Winfield	.15	.05
❑ 71 Ken Schrom	.10	.02
❑ 72 Shawon Dunston	.15	.05
❑ 73 Randy O'Neal	.10	.02
❑ 74 Rance Mulliniks	.10	.02
❑ 75 Jose DeLeon	.10	.02
❑ 76 Dion James	.10	.02
❑ 77 Charlie Leibrandt	.10	.02
❑ 78 Bruce Benedict	.10	.02
❑ 79 Dave Schmidt	.10	.02
❑ 80 Darryl Strawberry	.25	.08
❑ 81 Gene Mauch MG	.10	.02
❑ 82 Tippy Martinez	.10	.02
❑ 83 Phil Garner	.15	.05
❑ 84 Curt Young	.10	.02
❑ 85 Tony Perez w/E.Davis	.15	.05
❑ 86 Tom Waddell	.10	.02
❑ 87 Candy Maldonado	.10	.02
❑ 88 Tom Nieto	.10	.02
❑ 89 Randy St.Claire	.10	.02
❑ 90 Garry Templeton	.15	.05
❑ 91 Steve Crawford	.10	.02
❑ 92 Al Cowens	.10	.02
❑ 93 Scot Thompson	.10	.02
❑ 94 Rich Bordi	.10	.02
❑ 95 Ozzie Virgil	.10	.02
❑ 96 Blue Jays Leaders		
Jim Clancy	.10	.02
❑ 97 Gary Gaetti	.15	.05
❑ 98 Dick Ruthven	.10	.02
❑ 99 Buddy Biancalana	.10	.02
❑ 100 Nolan Ryan	2.00	.75
❑ 101 Dave Bergman	.10	.02
❑ 102 Joe Orsulak RC*	.25	.08
❑ 103 Luis Salazar	.10	.02
❑ 104 Sid Fernandez	.10	.02
❑ 105 Gary Ward	.10	.02
❑ 106 Ray Burris	.10	.02
❑ 107 Rafael Ramirez	.10	.02
❑ 108 Ted Power	.10	.02
❑ 109 Len Matuszek	.10	.02
❑ 110 Scott McGregor	.10	.02
❑ 111 Roger Craig MG	.15	.05
❑ 112 Bill Campbell	.10	.02
❑ 113 U.L. Washington	.10	.02
❑ 114 Mike C. Brown	.10	.02
❑ 115 Jay Howell	.10	.02
❑ 116 Brook Jacoby	.10	.02
❑ 117 Bruce Kison	.10	.02
❑ 118 Jerry Royster	.10	.02
❑ 119 Barry Bonnell	.10	.02
❑ 120 Steve Carlton	.15	.05
❑ 121 Nelson Simmons	.10	.02
❑ 122 Pete Filson	.10	.02
❑ 123 Greg Walker	.10	.02
❑ 124 Luis Sanchez	.10	.02
❑ 125 Dave Lopes	.15	.05
❑ 126 Mets Leaders		
Mookie Wilson	.10	.02
❑ 127 Jack Howell	.10	.02
❑ 128 John Wathan	.10	.02
❑ 129 Jeff Dedmon	.10	.02
❑ 130 Alan Trammell	.15	.05
❑ 131 Checklist: 1-132	.15	.05
❑ 132 Razor Shines	.10	.02
❑ 133 Andy McGaffigan	.10	.02
❑ 134 Carney Lansford	.15	.05
❑ 135 Joe Niekro	.10	.02
❑ 136 Mike Hargrove	.10	.02
❑ 137 Charlie Moore	.10	.02
❑ 138 Mark Davis	.10	.02
❑ 139 Daryl Boston	.10	.02
❑ 140 John Candelaria	.10	.02
❑ 141 Chuck Cottier MG		
See also 171	.10	.02
❑ 142 Bob Jones	.10	.02
❑ 143 Dave Van Gorder	.10	.02
❑ 144 Doug Sisk	.10	.02
❑ 145 Pedro Guerrero	.15	.05
❑ 146 Jack Perconte	.10	.02
❑ 147 Larry Sheets	.10	.02
❑ 148 Mike Heath	.10	.02
❑ 149 Brett Butler	.15	.05
❑ 150 Joaquin Andujar	.15	.05
❑ 151 Dave Stapleton	.10	.02
❑ 152 Mike Morgan	.10	.02
❑ 153 Ricky Adams	.10	.02
❑ 154 Bert Roberge	.10	.02
❑ 155 Bob Grich	.15	.05
❑ 156 White Sox Leaders		
Richard Dotson	.10	.02
❑ 157 Ron Hassey	.10	.02
❑ 158 Derrel Thomas	.10	.02
❑ 159 Orel Hershiser UER	.40	.15
❑ 160 Chet Lemon	.15	.05
❑ 161 Lee Tunnell	.10	.02
❑ 162 Greg Gagne	.10	.02
❑ 163 Pete Ladd	.10	.02
❑ 164 Steve Balboni	.10	.02
❑ 165 Mike Davis	.10	.02
❑ 166 Dickie Thon	.10	.02
❑ 167 Zane Smith	.10	.02
❑ 168 Jeff Burroughs	.10	.02
❑ 169 George Wright	.10	.02
❑ 170 Gary Carter	.15	.05
❑ 171 Bob Rodgers MG ERR		
(Checklist back)		
(Number of c	.10	.02
❑ 172 Jerry Reed	.10	.02
❑ 173 Wayne Gross	.10	.02
❑ 174 Brian Snyder	.10	.02
❑ 175 Steve Sax	.10	.02
❑ 176 Jay Tibbs	.10	.02
❑ 177 Joel Youngblood	.10	.02
❑ 178 Ivan DeJesus	.10	.02
❑ 179 Stu Cliburn	.10	.02
❑ 180 Don Mattingly	1.25	.50
❑ 181 Al Nipper	.10	.02
❑ 182 Bobby Brown	.10	.02
❑ 183 Larry Andersen	.10	.02
❑ 184 Tim Laudner	.10	.02
❑ 185 Rollie Fingers	.15	.05
❑ 186 Astros Leaders		
Jose Cruz	.10	.02
❑ 187 Scott Fletcher	.10	.02
❑ 188 Bob Dernier	.10	.02
❑ 189 Mike Mason	.10	.02
❑ 190 George Hendrick	.15	.05
❑ 191 Wally Backman	.10	.02
❑ 192 Milt Wilcox	.10	.02
❑ 193 Daryl Sconiers	.10	.02
❑ 194 Craig McMurtry	.10	.02
❑ 195 Dave Concepcion	.15	.05
❑ 196 Doyle Alexander	.10	.02
❑ 197 Enos Cabell	.10	.02
❑ 198 Ken Dixon	.10	.02
❑ 199 Dick Howser MG	.10	.02
❑ 200 Mike Schmidt	1.00	.40
❑ 201 Vince Coleman RB		
Most stolen bases&		
season& rook	.15	.05
❑ 202 Dwight Gooden RB	.25	.08
❑ 203 Keith Hernandez RB	.10	.02
❑ 204 Phil Niekro RB		
Oldest shutout pitcher	.15	.05
❑ 205 Tony Perez RB		
Oldest grand slammer	.15	.05
❑ 206 Pete Rose RB	.40	.15
❑ 207 Fernando Valenzuela RB		
Most cons. innings&		
start	.10	.02
❑ 208 Ramon Romero	.10	.02
❑ 209 Randy Ready	.10	.02
❑ 210 Calvin Schiraldi	.10	.02
❑ 211 Ed Wojna	.10	.02
❑ 212 Chris Speier	.10	.02
❑ 213 Bob Shirley	.10	.02
❑ 214 Randy Bush	.10	.02
❑ 215 Frank White	.15	.05
❑ 216 A's Leaders		
Dwayne Murphy	.10	.02
❑ 217 Bill Scherrer	.10	.02
❑ 218 Randy Hunt	.10	.02
❑ 219 Dennis Lamp	.10	.02
❑ 220 Bob Horner	.15	.05
❑ 221 Dave Henderson	.10	.02
❑ 222 Craig Gerber	.10	.02
❑ 223 Atlee Hammaker	.10	.02
❑ 224 Cesar Cedeno	.15	.05
❑ 225 Ron Darling	.15	.05
❑ 226 Lee Lacy	.10	.02
❑ 227 Al Jones	.10	.02
❑ 228 Tom Lawless	.10	.02
❑ 229 Bill Gullickson	.10	.02
❑ 230 Terry Kennedy	.10	.02
❑ 231 Jim Frey MG	.10	.02
❑ 232 Rick Rhoden	.10	.02
❑ 233 Steve Lyons	.10	.02
❑ 234 Doug Corbett	.10	.02
❑ 235 Butch Wynegar	.10	.02
❑ 236 Frank Eufemia	.10	.02
❑ 237 Ted Simmons	.15	.05
❑ 238 Larry Parrish	.10	.02
❑ 239 Joel Skinner	.10	.02
❑ 240 Tommy John	.15	.05
❑ 241 Tony Fernandez	.10	.02
❑ 242 Rich Thompson	.10	.02
❑ 243 Johnny Grubb	.10	.02
❑ 244 Craig Lefferts	.10	.02
❑ 245 Jim Sundberg	.15	.05
❑ 246 Steve Carlton TL	.10	.02
❑ 247 Terry Harper	.10	.02
❑ 248 Spike Owen	.10	.02
❑ 249 Rob Deer	.10	.02

❑ 250 Dwight Gooden .40 .15
❑ 251 Rich Dauer .10 .02
❑ 252 Bobby Castillo .10 .02
❑ 253 Dann Bilardello .10 .02
❑ 254 Ozzie Guillen RC 1.50 .60
❑ 255 Tony Armas .15 .05
❑ 256 Kurt Kepshire .10 .02
❑ 257 Doug DeCinces .10 .02
❑ 258 Tim Burke .10 .02
❑ 259 Dan Pasqua .10 .02
❑ 260 Tony Pena .10 .02
❑ 261 Bobby Valentine MG .15 .05
❑ 262 Mario Ramirez .10 .02
❑ 263 Checklist: 133-264 .15 .05
❑ 264 Darren Daulton RC .50 .20
❑ 265 Ron Davis .10 .02
❑ 266 Keith Moreland .10 .02
❑ 267 Paul Molitor .15 .05
❑ 268 Mike Scott .15 .05
❑ 269 Dane Iorg .10 .02
❑ 270 Jack Morris .15 .05
❑ 271 Dave Collins .10 .02
❑ 272 Tim Tolman .10 .02
❑ 273 Jerry Willard .10 .02
❑ 274 Ron Gardenhire .10 .02
❑ 275 Charlie Hough .15 .05
❑ 276 Yankees Leaders
Willie Randolph .15 .05
❑ 277 Jaime Cocanower .10 .02
❑ 278 Sixto Lezcano .10 .02
❑ 279 Al Pardo .10 .02
❑ 280 Tim Raines .15 .05
❑ 281 Steve Mura .10 .02
❑ 282 Jerry Mumphrey .10 .02
❑ 283 Mike Fischlin .10 .02
❑ 284 Brian Dayett .10 .02
❑ 285 Buddy Bell .15 .05
❑ 286 Luis DeLeon .10 .02
❑ 287 John Christensen .10 .02
❑ 288 Don Aase .10 .02
❑ 289 Johnnie LeMaster .10 .02
❑ 290 Carlton Fisk .25 .08
❑ 291 Tom Lasorda MG .25 .08
❑ 292 Chuck Porter .10 .02
❑ 293 Chris Chambliss .15 .05
❑ 294 Danny Cox .10 .02
❑ 295 Kirk Gibson .15 .05
❑ 296 Geno Petralli .10 .02
❑ 297 Tim Lollar .10 .02
❑ 298 Craig Reynolds .10 .02
❑ 299 Bryn Smith .10 .02
❑ 300 George Brett 1.00 .40
❑ 301 Dennis Rasmussen .10 .02
❑ 302 Greg Gross .10 .02
❑ 303 Curt Wardle .10 .02
❑ 304 Mike Gallego RC .10 .02
❑ 305 Phil Bradley .10 .02
❑ 306 Padres Leaders
Terry Kennedy .10 .02
❑ 307 Dave Sax .10 .02
❑ 308 Ray Fontenot .10 .02
❑ 309 John Shelby .10 .02
❑ 310 Greg Minton .10 .02
❑ 311 Dick Schofield .10 .02
❑ 312 Tom Filer .10 .02
❑ 313 Joe DeSa .10 .02
❑ 314 Frank Pastore .10 .02
❑ 315 Mookie Wilson .15 .05
❑ 316 Sammy Khalifa .10 .02
❑ 317 Ed Romero .10 .02
❑ 318 Terry Whitfield .10 .02
❑ 319 Rick Camp .10 .02
❑ 320 Jim Rice .15 .05
❑ 321 Earl Weaver MG .15 .05
❑ 322 Bob Forsch .10 .02
❑ 323 Jerry Davis .10 .02
❑ 324 Dan Schatzeder .10 .02
❑ 325 Juan Beniquez .10 .02
❑ 326 Kent Tekulve .10 .02
❑ 327 Mike Pagliarulo .10 .02
❑ 328 Pete O'Brien .10 .02
❑ 329 Kirby Puckett 1.00 .40
❑ 330 Rick Sutcliffe .15 .05
❑ 331 Alan Ashby .10 .02
❑ 332 Darryl Motley .10 .02
❑ 333 Tom Henke .15 .05
❑ 334 Ken Oberkfell .10 .02
❑ 335 Don Sutton .15 .05
❑ 336 Indians Leaders
Andre Thornton .15 .05
❑ 337 Darnell Coles .10 .02
❑ 338 Jorge Bell .15 .05
❑ 339 Bruce Berenyi .10 .02
❑ 340 Cal Ripken 1.50 .60
❑ 341 Frank Williams .10 .02
❑ 342 Gary Redus .10 .02
❑ 343 Carlos Diaz .10 .02
❑ 344 Jim Wohlford .10 .02
❑ 345 Donnie Moore .10 .02
❑ 346 Bryan Little .10 .02
❑ 347 Teddy Higuera RC* .25 .08
❑ 348 Cliff Johnson .10 .02
❑ 349 Mark Clear .10 .02
❑ 350 Jack Clark .15 .05
❑ 351 Chuck Tanner MG .10 .02
❑ 352 Harry Spilman .10 .02
❑ 353 Keith Atherton .10 .02
❑ 354 Tony Bernazard .10 .02
❑ 355 Lee Smith .15 .05
❑ 356 Mickey Hatcher .10 .02
❑ 357 Ed VandeBerg .10 .02
❑ 358 Rick Dempsey .10 .02
❑ 359 Mike LaCoss .10 .02
❑ 360 Lloyd Moseby .10 .02
❑ 361 Shane Rawley .10 .02
❑ 362 Tom Paciorek .10 .02
❑ 363 Terry Forster .15 .05
❑ 364 Reid Nichols .10 .02
❑ 365 Mike Flanagan .10 .02
❑ 366 Reds Leaders
Dave Concepcion .15 .05
❑ 367 Aurelio Lopez .10 .02
❑ 368 Greg Brock .10 .02
❑ 369 Al Holland .10 .02
❑ 370 Vince Coleman RC .50 .20
❑ 371 Bill Stein .10 .02
❑ 372 Ben Oglivie .15 .05
❑ 373 Urbano Lugo .10 .02
❑ 374 Terry Francona .15 .05
❑ 375 Rich Gedman .10 .02
❑ 376 Bill Dawley .10 .02
❑ 377 Joe Carter .15 .05
❑ 378 Bruce Bochte .10 .02
❑ 379 Bobby Meacham .10 .02
❑ 380 LaMarr Hoyt .10 .02
❑ 381 Ray Miller MG .10 .02
❑ 382 Ivan Calderon RC* .25 .08
❑ 383 Chris Brown RC .10 .02
❑ 384 Steve Trout .10 .02
❑ 385 Cecil Cooper .15 .05
❑ 386 Cecil Fielder RC 1.00 .40
❑ 387 Steve Kemp .10 .02
❑ 388 Dickie Noles .10 .02
❑ 389 Glenn Davis .10 .02
❑ 390 Tom Seaver .25 .08
❑ 391 Julio Franco .15 .05
❑ 392 John Russell .10 .02
❑ 393 Chris Pittaro .10 .02
❑ 394 Checklist: 265-396 .15 .05
❑ 395 Scott Garrelts .10 .02
❑ 396 Red Sox Leaders
Dwight Evans .25 .08
❑ 397 Steve Buechele RC .25 .08
❑ 398 Earnie Riles .10 .02
❑ 399 Bill Swift .10 .02
❑ 400 Rod Carew .25 .08
❑ 401 Fernando Valenzuela
TBC '81 .10 .02
❑ 402 Tom Seaver TBC .15 .05
❑ 403 Willie Mays TBC .40 .15
❑ 404 Frank Robinson TBC .15 .05
❑ 405 Roger Maris TBC .40 .15
❑ 406 Scott Sanderson .10 .02
❑ 407 Sal Butera .10 .02
❑ 408 Dave Smith .10 .02
❑ 409 Paul Runge RC .10 .02
❑ 410 Dave Kingman .15 .05
❑ 411 Sparky Anderson MG .15 .05
❑ 412 Jim Clancy .10 .02
❑ 413 Tim Flannery .10 .02
❑ 414 Tom Gorman .10 .02
❑ 415 Hal McRae .15 .05
❑ 416 Dennis Martinez .15 .05
❑ 417 R.J. Reynolds .10 .02
❑ 418 Alan Knicely .10 .02
❑ 419 Frank Wills .10 .02
❑ 420 Von Hayes .10 .02
❑ 421 David Palmer .10 .02
❑ 422 Mike Jorgensen .10 .02
❑ 423 Dan Spillner .10 .02
❑ 424 Rick Miller .10 .02
❑ 425 Larry McWilliams .10 .02
❑ 426 Brewers Leaders
Charlie Moore .10 .02
❑ 427 Joe Cowley .10 .02
❑ 428 Max Venable .10 .02
❑ 429 Greg Booker .10 .02
❑ 430 Kent Hrbek .15 .05
❑ 431 George Frazier .10 .02
❑ 432 Mark Bailey .10 .02
❑ 433 Chris Codiroli .10 .02
❑ 434 Curt Wilkerson .10 .02
❑ 435 Bill Caudill .10 .02
❑ 436 Doug Flynn .10 .02
❑ 437 Rick Mahler .10 .02
❑ 438 Clint Hurdle .10 .02
❑ 439 Rick Honeycutt .10 .02
❑ 440 Alvin Davis .10 .02
❑ 441 Whitey Herzog MG .25 .08
❑ 442 Ron Robinson .10 .02
❑ 443 Bill Buckner .15 .05
❑ 444 Alex Trevino .10 .02
❑ 445 Bert Blyleven .15 .05
❑ 446 Lenn Sakata .10 .02
❑ 447 Jerry Don Gleaton .10 .02
❑ 448 Herm Winningham .10 .02
❑ 449 Rod Scurry .10 .02
❑ 450 Graig Nettles .15 .05
❑ 451 Mark Brown .10 .02
❑ 452 Bob Clark .10 .02
❑ 453 Steve Jeltz .10 .02
❑ 454 Burt Hooton .10 .02
❑ 455 Willie Randolph .15 .05
❑ 456 Braves Leaders
Dale Murphy .25 .08
❑ 457 Mickey Tettleton RC .25 .08
❑ 458 Kevin Bass .10 .02
❑ 459 Luis Leal .10 .02
❑ 460 Leon Durham .10 .02
❑ 461 Walt Terrell .10 .02
❑ 462 Domingo Ramos .10 .02
❑ 463 Jim Gott .10 .02
❑ 464 Ruppert Jones .10 .02
❑ 465 Jesse Orosco .10 .02
❑ 466 Tom Foley .10 .02
❑ 467 Bob James .10 .02
❑ 468 Mike Scioscia .15 .05
❑ 469 Storm Davis .10 .02
❑ 470 Bill Madlock .15 .05
❑ 471 Bobby Cox MG .15 .05
❑ 472 Joe Hesketh .10 .02
❑ 473 Mark Brouhard .10 .02
❑ 474 John Tudor .15 .05
❑ 475 Juan Samuel .10 .02
❑ 476 Ron Mathis .10 .02
❑ 477 Mike Easler .10 .02
❑ 478 Andy Hawkins .10 .02
❑ 479 Bob Melvin .10 .02
❑ 480 Oddibe McDowell .10 .02
❑ 481 Scott Bradley .10 .02
❑ 482 Rick Lysander .10 .02
❑ 483 George Vukovich .10 .02
❑ 484 Donnie Hill .10 .02
❑ 485 Gary Matthews .15 .05
❑ 486 Angels Leaders
Bobby Grich .10 .02
❑ 487 Bret Saberhagen .15 .05
❑ 488 Lou Thornton .10 .02
❑ 489 Jim Winn .10 .02
❑ 490 Jeff Leonard .10 .02
❑ 491 Pascual Perez .10 .02
❑ 492 Kelvin Chapman .10 .02
❑ 493 Gene Nelson .10 .02
❑ 494 Gary Roenicke .10 .02
❑ 495 Mark Langston .15 .05
❑ 496 Jay Johnstone .10 .02
❑ 497 John Stuper .10 .02
❑ 498 Tito Landrum .10 .02

❑ 499 Bob L. Gibson .10 .02
❑ 500 Rickey Henderson .40 .15
❑ 501 Dave Johnson MG .10 .02
❑ 502 Glen Cook .10 .02
❑ 503 Mike Fitzgerald .10 .02
❑ 504 Denny Walling .10 .02
❑ 505 Jerry Koosman .15 .05
❑ 506 Bill Russell .15 .05
❑ 507 Steve Ontiveros RC .10 .02
❑ 508 Alan Wiggins .10 .02
❑ 509 Ernie Camacho .10 .02
❑ 510 Wade Boggs .25 .08
❑ 511 Ed Nunez .10 .02
❑ 512 Thad Bosley .10 .02
❑ 513 Ron Washington .10 .02
❑ 514 Mike Jones .10 .02
❑ 515 Darrell Evans .15 .05
❑ 516 Giants Leaders
Greg Minton .10 .02
❑ 517 Milt Thompson RC .25 .08
❑ 518 Buck Martinez .10 .02
❑ 519 Danny Darwin .10 .02
❑ 520 Keith Hernandez .15 .05
❑ 521 Nate Snell .10 .02
❑ 522 Bob Dailor .10 .02
❑ 523 Joe Price .10 .02
❑ 524 Darrell Miller .10 .02
❑ 525 Marvell Wynne .10 .02
❑ 526 Charlie Lea .10 .02
❑ 527 Checklist: 397-528 .15 .05
❑ 528 Terry Pendleton .15 .05
❑ 529 Marc Sullivan .10 .02
❑ 530 Rich Gossage .15 .05
❑ 531 Tony LaRussa MG .15 .05
❑ 532 Don Carman .10 .02
❑ 533 Billy Sample .10 .02
❑ 534 Jeff Calhoun .10 .02
❑ 535 Toby Harrah .15 .05
❑ 536 Jose Rijo .15 .05
❑ 537 Mark Salas .10 .02
❑ 538 Dennis Eckersley .25 .08
❑ 539 Glenn Hubbard .10 .02
❑ 540 Dan Petry .10 .02
❑ 541 Jorge Orta .10 .02
❑ 542 Don Schulze .10 .02
❑ 543 Jerry Narron .10 .02
❑ 544 Eddie Milner .10 .02
❑ 545 Jimmy Key .15 .05
❑ 546 Mariners Leaders
Dave Henderson .10 .02
❑ 547 Roger McDowell RC* .25 .08
❑ 548 Mike Young .10 .02
❑ 549 Bob Welch .15 .05
❑ 550 Tom Herr .10 .02
❑ 551 Dave LaPoint .10 .02
❑ 552 Marc Hill .10 .02
❑ 553 Jim Morrison .10 .02
❑ 554 Paul Householder .10 .02
❑ 555 Hubie Brooks .10 .02
❑ 556 John Denny .10 .02
❑ 557 Gerald Perry .10 .02
❑ 558 Tim Stoddard .10 .02
❑ 559 Tommy Dunbar .10 .02
❑ 560 Dave Righetti .15 .05
❑ 561 Bob Lillis MG .10 .02
❑ 562 Joe Beckwith .10 .02
❑ 563 Alejandro Sanchez .10 .02
❑ 564 Warren Brusstar .10 .02
❑ 565 Tom Brunansky .10 .02
❑ 566 Alfredo Griffin .10 .02
❑ 567 Jeff Barkley .10 .02
❑ 568 Donnie Scott .10 .02
❑ 569 Jim Acker .10 .02
❑ 570 Rusty Staub .15 .05
❑ 571 Mike Jeffcoat .10 .02
❑ 572 Paul Zuvella .10 .02
❑ 573 Tom Hume .10 .02
❑ 574 Ron Kittle .10 .02
❑ 575 Mike Boddicker .10 .02
❑ 576 Andre Dawson TL .10 .02
❑ 577 Jerry Reuss .10 .02
❑ 578 Lee Mazzilli .15 .05
❑ 579 Jim Slaton .10 .02
❑ 580 Willie McGee .15 .05
❑ 581 Bruce Hurst .10 .02
❑ 582 Jim Gantner .10 .02
❑ 583 Al Bumbry .10 .02
❑ 584 Brian Fisher RC .10 .02
❑ 585 Garry Maddox .10 .02
❑ 586 Greg Harris .10 .02
❑ 587 Rafael Santana .10 .02
❑ 588 Steve Lake .10 .02
❑ 589 Sid Bream .10 .02
❑ 590 Bob Knepper .10 .02
❑ 591 Jackie Moore MG .10 .02
❑ 592 Frank Tanana .15 .05
❑ 593 Jesse Barfield .15 .05
❑ 594 Chris Bando .10 .02
❑ 595 Dave Parker .15 .05
❑ 596 Onix Concepcion .10 .02
❑ 597 Sammy Stewart .10 .02
❑ 598 Jim Presley .10 .02
❑ 599 Rick Aguilera RC .25 .08
❑ 600 Dale Murphy .25 .08
❑ 601 Gary Lucas .10 .02
❑ 602 Mariano Duncan RC .25 .08
❑ 603 Bill Laskey .10 .02
❑ 604 Gary Pettis .10 .02
❑ 605 Dennis Boyd .10 .02
❑ 606 Royals Leaders
Hal McRae .15 .05
❑ 607 Ken Dayley .10 .02
❑ 608 Bruce Bochy .10 .02
❑ 609 Barbaro Garbey .10 .02
❑ 610 Ron Guidry .15 .05
❑ 611 Gary Woods .10 .02
❑ 612 Richard Dotson .10 .02
❑ 613 Roy Smalley .10 .02
❑ 614 Rick Waits .10 .02
❑ 615 Johnny Ray .10 .02
❑ 616 Glenn Brummer .10 .02
❑ 617 Lonnie Smith .10 .02
❑ 618 Jim Pankovits .10 .02
❑ 619 Danny Heep .10 .02
❑ 620 Bruce Sutter .15 .05
❑ 621 John Felske MG .10 .02
❑ 622 Gary Lavelle .10 .02
❑ 623 Floyd Rayford .10 .02
❑ 624 Steve McCatty .10 .02
❑ 625 Bob Brenly .10 .02
❑ 626 Roy Thomas .10 .02
❑ 627 Ron Oester .10 .02
❑ 628 Kirk McCaskill RC .25 .08
❑ 629 Mitch Webster .10 .02
❑ 630 Fernando Valenzuela .15 .05
❑ 631 Steve Braun .10 .02
❑ 632 Dave Von Ohlen .10 .02
❑ 633 Jackie Gutierrez .10 .02
❑ 634 Roy Lee Jackson .10 .02
❑ 635 Jason Thompson .10 .02
❑ 636 Lee Smith TL .10 .02
❑ 637 Rudy Law .10 .02
❑ 638 John Butcher .10 .02
❑ 639 Bo Diaz .10 .02
❑ 640 Jose Cruz .15 .05
❑ 641 Wayne Tolleson .10 .02
❑ 642 Ray Searage .10 .02
❑ 643 Tom Brookens .10 .02
❑ 644 Mark Gubicza .10 .02
❑ 645 Dusty Baker .15 .05
❑ 646 Mike Moore .10 .02
❑ 647 Mel Hall .10 .02
❑ 648 Steve Bedrosian .10 .02
❑ 649 Ronn Reynolds .10 .02
❑ 650 Dave Stieb .15 .05
❑ 651 Billy Martin MG/TC .25 .08
❑ 652 Tom Browning .10 .02
❑ 653 Jim Dwyer .10 .02
❑ 654 Ken Howell .10 .02
❑ 655 Manny Trillo .10 .02
❑ 656 Brian Harper .10 .02
❑ 657 Juan Agosto .10 .02
❑ 658 Rob Wilfong .10 .02
❑ 659 Checklist: 529-660 .15 .05
❑ 660 Steve Garvey .15 .05
❑ 661 Roger Clemens 4.00 1.50
❑ 662 Bill Schroeder .10 .02
❑ 663 Neil Allen .10 .02
❑ 664 Tim Corcoran .10 .02
❑ 665 Alejandro Pena .10 .02
❑ 666 Rangers Leaders
Charlie Hough .15 .05
❑ 667 Tim Teufel .10 .02
❑ 668 Cecilio Guante .10 .02
❑ 669 Ron Cey .15 .05
❑ 670 Willie Hernandez .10 .02
❑ 671 Lynn Jones .10 .02
❑ 672 Rob Picciolo .10 .02
❑ 673 Ernie Whitt .10 .02
❑ 674 Pat Tabler .10 .02
❑ 675 Claudell Washington .10 .02
❑ 676 Matt Young .10 .02
❑ 677 Nick Esasky .10 .02
❑ 678 Dan Gladden .10 .02
❑ 679 Britt Burns .10 .02
❑ 680 George Foster .15 .05
❑ 681 Dick Williams MG .10 .02
❑ 682 Junior Ortiz .10 .02
❑ 683 Andy Van Slyke .25 .08
❑ 684 Bob McClure .10 .02
❑ 685 Tim Wallach .10 .02
❑ 686 Jeff Stone .10 .02
❑ 687 Mike Trujillo .10 .02
❑ 688 Larry Herndon .10 .02
❑ 689 Dave Stewart .15 .05
❑ 690 Ryne Sandberg .75 .30
❑ 691 Mike Madden .10 .02
❑ 692 Dale Berra .10 .02
❑ 693 Tom Tellmann .10 .02
❑ 694 Garth Iorg .10 .02
❑ 695 Mike Smithson .10 .02
❑ 696 Dodgers Leaders
Bill Russell .15 .05
❑ 697 Bud Black .10 .02
❑ 698 Brad Komminsk .10 .02
❑ 699 Pat Corrales MG .10 .02
❑ 700 Reggie Jackson .25 .08
❑ 701 Keith Hernandez AS .10 .02
❑ 702 Tom Herr AS .10 .02
❑ 703 Tim Wallach AS .10 .02
❑ 704 Ozzie Smith AS .40 .15
❑ 705 Dale Murphy AS .15 .05
❑ 706 Pedro Guerrero AS .10 .02
❑ 707 Willie McGee AS .10 .02
❑ 708 Gary Carter AS .10 .02
❑ 709 Dwight Gooden AS .25 .08
❑ 710 John Tudor AS .10 .02
❑ 711 Jeff Reardon AS .10 .02
❑ 712 Don Mattingly AS .60 .25
❑ 713 Damaso Garcia AS .10 .02
❑ 714 George Brett AS .40 .15
❑ 715 Cal Ripken AS .40 .15
❑ 716 Rickey Henderson AS .25 .08
❑ 717 Dave Winfield AS .10 .02
❑ 718 George Bell AS .10 .02
❑ 719 Carlton Fisk AS .15 .05
❑ 720 Bret Saberhagen AS .10 .02
❑ 721 Ron Guidry AS .10 .02
❑ 722 Dan Quisenberry AS .10 .02
❑ 723 Marty Bystrom .10 .02
❑ 724 Tim Hulett .10 .02
❑ 725 Mario Soto .15 .05
❑ 726 Orioles Leaders
Rick Dempsey .15 .05
❑ 727 David Green .10 .02
❑ 728 Mike Marshall .10 .02
❑ 729 Jim Beattie .10 .02
❑ 730 Ozzie Smith .60 .25
❑ 731 Don Robinson .10 .02
❑ 732 Floyd Youmans .10 .02
❑ 733 Ron Romanick .10 .02
❑ 734 Marty Barrett .10 .02
❑ 735 Dave Dravecky .10 .02
❑ 736 Glenn Wilson .10 .02
❑ 737 Pete Vuckovich .10 .02
❑ 738 Andre Robertson .10 .02
❑ 739 Dave Rozema .10 .02
❑ 740 Lance Parrish .15 .05
❑ 741 Pete Rose MG/TC .40 .15
❑ 742 Frank Viola .15 .05
❑ 743 Pat Sheridan .10 .02
❑ 744 Lary Sorensen .10 .02
❑ 745 Willie Upshaw .10 .02
❑ 746 Denny Gonzalez .10 .02
❑ 747 Rick Cerone .10 .02
❑ 748 Steve Henderson .10 .02
❑ 749 Ed Jurak .10 .02
❑ 750 Gorman Thomas .15 .05

❑ 751 Howard Johnson .15 .05
❑ 752 Mike Krukow .10 .02
❑ 753 Dan Ford .10 .02
❑ 754 Pat Clements .10 .02
❑ 755 Harold Baines .15 .05
❑ 756 Pirates Leaders
Rick Rhoden .10 .02
❑ 757 Darrell Porter .10 .02
❑ 758 Dave Anderson .10 .02
❑ 759 Moose Haas .10 .02
❑ 760 Andre Dawson .15 .05
❑ 761 Don Slaught .10 .02
❑ 762 Eric Show .10 .02
❑ 763 Terry Puhl .10 .02
❑ 764 Kevin Gross .10 .02
❑ 765 Don Baylor .15 .05
❑ 766 Rick Langford .10 .02
❑ 767 Jody Davis .10 .02
❑ 768 Vern Ruhle .10 .02
❑ 769 Harold Reynolds RC .75 .30
❑ 770 Vida Blue .15 .05
❑ 771 John McNamara MG .10 .02
❑ 772 Brian Downing .15 .05
❑ 773 Greg Pryor .10 .02
❑ 774 Terry Leach .10 .02
❑ 775 Al Oliver .15 .05
❑ 776 Gene Garber .10 .02
❑ 777 Wayne Krenchicki .10 .02
❑ 778 Jerry Hairston .10 .02
❑ 779 Rick Reuschel .15 .05
❑ 780 Robin Yount .60 .25
❑ 781 Joe Nolan .10 .02
❑ 782 Ken Landreaux .10 .02
❑ 783 Ricky Horton .10 .02
❑ 784 Alan Bannister .10 .02
❑ 785 Bob Stanley .10 .02
❑ 786 Twins Leaders
Mickey Hatcher .10 .02
❑ 787 Vance Law .10 .02
❑ 788 Marty Castillo .10 .02
❑ 789 Kurt Bevacqua .10 .02
❑ 790 Phil Niekro .15 .05
❑ 791 Checklist: 661-792 .15 .05
❑ 792 Charles Hudson .10 .02

1987 Topps

❑ COMPLETE SET (792) 25.00 10.00
❑ COMP.FACT SET (792) 40.00 15.00
❑ COMP.HOBBY SET (792) 40.00 15.00
❑ COMP.X-MAS.SET (792) 40.00 15.00
❑ 1 Roger Clemens RB 1.00 .40
❑ 2 Jim Deshaies RB
Most cons. K's&
start of game .05 .01
❑ 3 Dwight Evans RB
Earliest home run&
season .15 .05
❑ 4 Davey Lopes RB
Most steals& season&
40-year-old .05 .01
❑ 5 Dave Righetti RB
Most saves& season .05 .01
❑ 6 Ruben Sierra RB .25 .08
❑ 7 Todd Worrell RB
Most saves&
season& rookie .05 .01
❑ 8 Terry Pendleton .10 .02
❑ 9 Jay Tibbs .05 .01
❑ 10 Cecil Cooper .10 .02
❑ 11 Indians Team
(Mound conference) .05 .01
❑ 12 Jeff Sellers .05 .01
❑ 13 Nick Esasky .05 .01
❑ 14 Dave Stewart .10 .02
❑ 15 Claudell Washington .05 .01
❑ 16 Pat Clements .05 .01
❑ 17 Pete O'Brien .05 .01
❑ 18 Dick Howser MG .05 .01
❑ 19 Matt Young .05 .01
❑ 20 Gary Carter .10 .02
❑ 21 Mark Davis .05 .01
❑ 22 Doug DeCinces .05 .01
❑ 23 Lee Smith .10 .02
❑ 24 Tony Walker .05 .01
❑ 25 Bert Blyleven .10 .02
❑ 26 Greg Brock .05 .01
❑ 27 Joe Cowley .05 .01
❑ 28 Rick Dempsey .05 .01
❑ 29 Jimmy Key .10 .02
❑ 30 Tim Raines .10 .02
❑ 31 Braves Team
(Glenn Hubbard and
Rafael Ramirez) .05 .01
❑ 32 Tim Leary .05 .01
❑ 33 Andy Van Slyke .15 .05
❑ 34 Jose Rijo .10 .02
❑ 35 Sid Bream .05 .01
❑ 36 Eric King .05 .01
❑ 37 Marvell Wynne .05 .01
❑ 38 Dennis Leonard .05 .01
❑ 39 Marty Barrett .05 .01
❑ 40 Dave Righetti .10 .02
❑ 41 Bo Diaz .05 .01
❑ 42 Gary Redus .05 .01
❑ 43 Gene Michael MG .05 .01
❑ 44 Greg Harris .05 .01
❑ 45 Jim Presley .05 .01
❑ 46 Dan Gladden .05 .01
❑ 47 Dennis Powell .05 .01
❑ 48 Wally Backman .05 .01
❑ 49 Terry Harper .05 .01
❑ 50 Dave Smith .05 .01
❑ 51 Mel Hall .05 .01
❑ 52 Keith Atherton .05 .01
❑ 53 Ruppert Jones .05 .01
❑ 54 Bill Dawley .05 .01
❑ 55 Tim Wallach .05 .01
❑ 56 Brewers Team
(Mound conference) .10 .02
❑ 57 Scott Nielsen .05 .01
❑ 58 Thad Bosley .05 .01
❑ 59 Ken Dayley .05 .01
❑ 60 Tony Pena .05 .01
❑ 61 Bobby Thigpen RC .25 .08
❑ 62 Bobby Meacham .05 .01
❑ 63 Fred Toliver .05 .01
❑ 64 Harry Spilman .05 .01
❑ 65 Tom Browning .05 .01
❑ 66 Marc Sullivan .05 .01
❑ 67 Bill Swift .05 .01
❑ 68 Tony LaRussa MG .10 .02
❑ 69 Lonnie Smith .05 .01
❑ 70 Charlie Hough .10 .02
❑ 71 Mike Aldrete .05 .01
❑ 72 Walt Terrell .05 .01
❑ 73 Dave Anderson .05 .01
❑ 74 Dan Pasqua .05 .01
❑ 75 Ron Darling .10 .02
❑ 76 Rafael Ramirez .05 .01
❑ 77 Bryan Oelkers .05 .01
❑ 78 Tom Foley .05 .01
❑ 79 Juan Nieves .05 .01
❑ 80 Wally Joyner RC .40 .15
❑ 81 Padres Team
(Andy Hawkins and
Terry Kennedy) .05 .01
❑ 82 Rob Murphy .05 .01
❑ 83 Mike Davis .05 .01
❑ 84 Steve Lake .05 .01
❑ 85 Kevin Bass .05 .01
❑ 86 Nate Snell .05 .01
❑ 87 Mark Salas .05 .01
❑ 88 Ed Wojna .05 .01
❑ 89 Ozzie Guillen .15 .05
❑ 90 Dave Stieb .10 .02
❑ 91 Harold Reynolds .10 .02
❑ 92A Urbano Lugo
ERR (no trademark) .15 .05
❑ 92B Urbano Lugo COR .05 .01
❑ 93 Jim Leyland MG/TC RC * .25 .08
❑ 94 Calvin Schiraldi .05 .01
❑ 95 Oddibe McDowell .05 .01
❑ 96 Frank Williams .05 .01
❑ 97 Glenn Wilson .05 .01
❑ 98 Bill Scherrer .05 .01
❑ 99 Darryl Motley
(Now with Braves
on card front) .05 .01
❑ 100 Steve Garvey .10 .02
❑ 101 Carl Willis RC .10 .02
❑ 102 Paul Zuvella .05 .01
❑ 103 Rick Aguilera .05 .01
❑ 104 Billy Sample .05 .01
❑ 105 Floyd Youmans .05 .01
❑ 106 Blue Jays Team
(George Bell and
Jesse Barfield) .05 .01
❑ 107 John Butcher .05 .01
❑ 108 Jim Gantner UER
(Brewers logo
reversed) .05 .01
❑ 109 R.J. Reynolds .05 .01
❑ 110 John Tudor .10 .02
❑ 111 Alfredo Griffin .05 .01
❑ 112 Alan Ashby .05 .01
❑ 113 Neil Allen .05 .01
❑ 114 Billy Beane .10 .02
❑ 115 Donnie Moore .05 .01
❑ 116 Bill Russell .10 .02
❑ 117 Jim Beattie .05 .01
❑ 118 Bobby Valentine MG .10 .02
❑ 119 Ron Robinson .05 .01
❑ 120 Eddie Murray .25 .08
❑ 121 Kevin Romine .05 .01
❑ 122 Jim Clancy .05 .01
❑ 123 John Kruk RC .50 .20
❑ 124 Ray Fontenot .05 .01
❑ 125 Bob Brenly .05 .01
❑ 126 Mike Loynd RC .10 .02
❑ 127 Vance Law .05 .01
❑ 128 Checklist 1-132 .05 .01
❑ 129 Rick Cerone .05 .01
❑ 130 Dwight Gooden .15 .05
❑ 131 Pirates Team
(Sid Bream and
Tony Pena) .05 .01
❑ 132 Paul Assenmacher .25 .08
❑ 133 Jose Oquendo .05 .01
❑ 134 Rich Yett .05 .01
❑ 135 Mike Easler .05 .01
❑ 136 Ron Romanick .05 .01
❑ 137 Jerry Willard .05 .01
❑ 138 Roy Lee Jackson .05 .01
❑ 139 Devon White RC .40 .15
❑ 140 Bret Saberhagen .10 .02
❑ 141 Herm Winningham .05 .01
❑ 142 Rick Sutcliffe .10 .02
❑ 143 Steve Boros MG .05 .01
❑ 144 Mike Scioscia .10 .02
❑ 145 Charlie Kerfeld .05 .01
❑ 146 Tracy Jones .05 .01
❑ 147 Randy Niemann .05 .01
❑ 148 Dave Collins .05 .01
❑ 149 Ray Searage .05 .01
❑ 150 Wade Boggs .15 .05
❑ 151 Mike LaCoss .05 .01
❑ 152 Toby Harrah .10 .02
❑ 153 Duane Ward RC * .25 .08
❑ 154 Tom O'Malley .05 .01
❑ 155 Eddie Whitson .05 .01
❑ 156 Mariners Team
(Mound conference) .05 .01
❑ 157 Danny Darwin .05 .01
❑ 158 Tim Teufel .05 .01
❑ 159 Ed Olwine .05 .01
❑ 160 Julio Franco .10 .02
❑ 161 Steve Ontiveros .05 .01
❑ 162 Mike LaValliere RC * .25 .08
❑ 163 Kevin Gross .05 .01
❑ 164 Sammy Khalifa .05 .01

❑ 165 Jeff Reardon .10 .02
❑ 166 Bob Boone .10 .02
❑ 167 Jim Deshaies RC * .10 .02
❑ 168 Lou Piniella MG .10 .02
❑ 169 Ron Washington .05 .01
❑ 170 Bo Jackson RC 3.00 1.25
❑ 171 Chuck Cary .05 .01
❑ 172 Ron Oester .05 .01
❑ 173 Alex Trevino .05 .01
❑ 174 Henry Cotto .05 .01
❑ 175 Bob Stanley .05 .01
❑ 176 Steve Buechele .05 .01
❑ 177 Keith Moreland .05 .01
❑ 178 Cecil Fielder .10 .02
❑ 179 Bill Wegman .05 .01
❑ 180 Chris Brown .05 .01
❑ 181 Cardinals Team
(Mound conference) .05 .01
❑ 182 Lee Lacy .05 .01
❑ 183 Andy Hawkins .05 .01
❑ 184 Bobby Bonilla RC .40 .15
❑ 185 Roger McDowell .05 .01
❑ 186 Bruce Benedict .05 .01
❑ 187 Mark Huismann .05 .01
❑ 188 Tony Phillips .05 .01
❑ 189 Joe Hesketh .05 .01
❑ 190 Jim Sundberg .10 .02
❑ 191 Charles Hudson .05 .01
❑ 192 Cory Snyder .05 .01
❑ 193 Roger Craig MG .10 .02
❑ 194 Kirk McCaskill .05 .01
❑ 195 Mike Pagliarulo .05 .01
❑ 196 Randy O'Neal UER
(Wrong ML career
W-L totals) .05 .01
❑ 197 Mark Bailey .05 .01
❑ 198 Lee Mazzilli .10 .02
❑ 199 Mariano Duncan .05 .01
❑ 200 Pete Rose .60 .25
❑ 201 John Cangelosi .05 .01
❑ 202 Ricky Wright .05 .01
❑ 203 Mike Kingery RC .10 .02
❑ 204 Sammy Stewart .05 .01
❑ 205 Graig Nettles .10 .02
❑ 206 Twins Team
(Frank Viola and
Tim Laudner) .05 .01
❑ 207 George Frazier .05 .01
❑ 208 John Shelby .05 .01
❑ 209 Rick Schu .05 .01
❑ 210 Lloyd Moseby .05 .01
❑ 211 John Morris .05 .01
❑ 212 Mike Fitzgerald .05 .01
❑ 213 Randy Myers RC .40 .15
❑ 214 Omar Moreno .05 .01
❑ 215 Mark Langston .05 .01
❑ 216 B.J. Surhoff RC .40 .15
❑ 217 Chris Codiroli .05 .01
❑ 218 Sparky Anderson MG .10 .02
❑ 219 Cecilio Guante .05 .01
❑ 220 Joe Carter .10 .02
❑ 221 Vern Ruhle .05 .01
❑ 222 Denny Walling .05 .01
❑ 223 Charlie Leibrandt .05 .01
❑ 224 Wayne Tolleson .05 .01
❑ 225 Mike Smithson .05 .01
❑ 226 Max Venable .05 .01
❑ 227 Jamie Moyer RC .50 .20
❑ 228 Curt Wilkerson .05 .01
❑ 229 Mike Birkbeck .10 .02
❑ 230 Don Baylor .10 .02
❑ 231 Giants Team
(Bob Brenly and
Jim Gott) .05 .01
❑ 232 Reggie Williams .05 .01
❑ 233 Russ Morman .05 .01
❑ 234 Pat Sheridan .05 .01
❑ 235 Alvin Davis .05 .01
❑ 236 Tommy John .10 .02
❑ 237 Jim Morrison .05 .01
❑ 238 Bill Krueger .05 .01
❑ 239 Juan Espino .05 .01
❑ 240 Steve Balboni .05 .01
❑ 241 Danny Heep .05 .01
❑ 242 Rick Mahler .05 .01
❑ 243 Whitey Herzog MG .10 .02
❑ 244 Dickie Noles .05 .01
❑ 245 Willie Upshaw .05 .01
❑ 246 Jim Dwyer .05 .01
❑ 247 Jeff Reed .05 .01
❑ 248 Gene Walter .05 .01
❑ 249 Jim Pankovits .05 .01
❑ 250 Teddy Higuera .05 .01
❑ 251 Rob Wilfong .05 .01
❑ 252 Dennis Martinez .10 .02
❑ 253 Eddie Milner .05 .01
❑ 254 Bob Tewksbury RC * .25 .08
❑ 255 Juan Samuel .05 .01
❑ 256 Royals TL/George Brett .15 .05
❑ 257 Bob Forsch .05 .01
❑ 258 Steve Yeager .10 .02
❑ 259 Mike Greenwell RC .25 .08
❑ 260 Vida Blue .10 .02
❑ 261 Ruben Sierra RC .50 .20
❑ 262 Jim Winn .05 .01
❑ 263 Stan Javier .05 .01
❑ 264 Checklist 133-264 .05 .01
❑ 265 Darrell Evans .10 .02
❑ 266 Jeff Hamilton .05 .01
❑ 267 Howard Johnson .10 .02
❑ 268 Pat Corrales MG .05 .01
❑ 269 Cliff Speck .05 .01
❑ 270 Jody Davis .05 .01
❑ 271 Mike G. Brown .05 .01
❑ 272 Andres Galarraga .10 .02
❑ 273 Gene Nelson .05 .01
❑ 274 Jeff Hearron UER
(Duplicate 1986
stat line on ba .05 .01
❑ 275 LaMarr Hoyt .05 .01
❑ 276 Jackie Gutierrez .05 .01
❑ 277 Juan Agosto .05 .01
❑ 278 Gary Pettis .05 .01
❑ 279 Dan Plesac .05 .01
❑ 280 Jeff Leonard .05 .01
❑ 281 Reds TL/Rose .25 .08
❑ 282 Jeff Calhoun .05 .01
❑ 283 Doug Drabek RC .40 .15
❑ 284 John Moses .05 .01
❑ 285 Dennis Boyd .05 .01
❑ 286 Mike Woodard .05 .01
❑ 287 Dave Von Ohlen .05 .01
❑ 288 Tito Landrum .05 .01
❑ 289 Bob Kipper .05 .01
❑ 290 Leon Durham .05 .01
❑ 291 Mitch Williams RC * .25 .08
❑ 292 Franklin Stubbs .05 .01
❑ 293 Bob Rodgers MG
(Checklist back&
inconsistent des .05 .01
❑ 294 Steve Jeltz .05 .01
❑ 295 Len Dykstra .10 .02
❑ 296 Andres Thomas .05 .01
❑ 297 Don Schulze .05 .01
❑ 298 Larry Herndon .05 .01
❑ 299 Joel Davis .05 .01
❑ 300 Reggie Jackson .15 .05
❑ 301 Luis Aquino UER
(No trademark
never corrected) .05 .01
❑ 302 Bill Schroeder .05 .01
❑ 303 Juan Berenguer .05 .01
❑ 304 Phil Garner .10 .02
❑ 305 John Franco .10 .02
❑ 306 Red Sox TL/Seaver .10 .02
❑ 307 Lee Guetterman .05 .01
❑ 308 Don Slaught .05 .01
❑ 309 Mike Young .05 .01
❑ 310 Frank Viola .10 .02
❑ 311 Rickey Henderson TBC .15 .05
❑ 312 Reggie Jackson TBC .10 .02
❑ 313 Roberto Clemente TBC .25 .08
❑ 314 Carl Yastrzemski TBC .25 .08
❑ 315 Maury Wills TBC '62 .10 .02
❑ 316 Brian Fisher .05 .01
❑ 317 Clint Hurdle .05 .01
❑ 318 Jim Fregosi MG .05 .01
❑ 319 Greg Swindell RC .25 .08
❑ 320 Barry Bonds RC 10.00 4.00
❑ 321 Mike Laga .05 .01
❑ 322 Chris Bando .05 .01
❑ 323 Al Newman RC .05 .01
❑ 324 David Palmer .05 .01
❑ 325 Garry Templeton .10 .02
❑ 326 Mark Gubicza .05 .01
❑ 327 Dale Sveum .05 .01
❑ 328 Bob Welch .10 .02
❑ 329 Ron Roenicke .05 .01
❑ 330 Mike Scott .10 .02
❑ 331 Mets TL/Carter/Straw .10 .02
❑ 332 Joe Price .05 .01
❑ 333 Ken Phelps .05 .01
❑ 334 Ed Correa .05 .01
❑ 335 Candy Maldonado .05 .01
❑ 336 Allan Anderson RC .05 .01
❑ 337 Darrell Miller .05 .01
❑ 338 Tim Conroy .05 .01
❑ 339 Donnie Hill .05 .01
❑ 340 Roger Clemens 1.50 .60
❑ 341 Mike C. Brown .05 .01
❑ 342 Bob James .05 .01
❑ 343 Hal Lanier MG .05 .01
❑ 344A Joe Niekro
(Copyright inside
righthand border) .05 .01
❑ 344B Joe Niekro
(Copyright outside
righthand border) .05 .01
❑ 345 Andre Dawson .10 .02
❑ 346 Shawon Dunston .05 .01
❑ 347 Mickey Brantley .05 .01
❑ 348 Carmelo Martinez .05 .01
❑ 349 Storm Davis .05 .01
❑ 350 Keith Hernandez .10 .02
❑ 351 Gene Garber .05 .01
❑ 352 Mike Felder .05 .01
❑ 353 Ernie Camacho .05 .01
❑ 354 Jamie Quirk .05 .01
❑ 355 Don Carman .05 .01
❑ 356 White Sox Team
(Mound conference) .05 .01
❑ 357 Steve Fireovid .05 .01
❑ 358 Sal Butera .05 .01
❑ 359 Doug Corbett .05 .01
❑ 360 Pedro Guerrero .10 .02
❑ 361 Mark Thurmond .05 .01
❑ 362 Luis Quinones .05 .01
❑ 363 Jose Guzman .05 .01
❑ 364 Randy Bush .05 .01
❑ 365 Rick Rhoden .05 .01
❑ 366 Mark McGwire 4.00 1.50
❑ 367 Jeff Lahti .05 .01
❑ 368 John McNamara MG .05 .01
❑ 369 Brian Dayett .05 .01
❑ 370 Fred Lynn .10 .02
❑ 371 Mark Eichhorn .05 .01
❑ 372 Jerry Mumphrey .05 .01
❑ 373 Jeff Dedmon .05 .01
❑ 374 Glenn Hoffman .05 .01
❑ 375 Ron Guidry .10 .02
❑ 376 Scott Bradley .05 .01
❑ 377 John Henry Johnson .05 .01
❑ 378 Rafael Santana .05 .01
❑ 379 John Russell .05 .01
❑ 380 Rich Gossage .10 .02
❑ 381 Expos Team
(Mound conference) .05 .01
❑ 382 Rudy Law .05 .01
❑ 383 Ron Davis .05 .01
❑ 384 Johnny Grubb .05 .01
❑ 385 Orel Hershiser .15 .05
❑ 386 Dickie Thon .05 .01
❑ 387 T.R. Bryden .05 .01
❑ 388 Geno Petralli .05 .01
❑ 389 Jeff D. Robinson .05 .01
❑ 390 Gary Matthews .10 .02
❑ 391 Jay Howell .05 .01
❑ 392 Checklist 265-396 .05 .01
❑ 393 Pete Rose MG/TC .15 .05
❑ 394 Mike Bielecki .05 .01
❑ 395 Damaso Garcia .05 .01
❑ 396 Tim Lollar .05 .01
❑ 397 Greg Walker .05 .01
❑ 398 Brad Havens .05 .01
❑ 399 Curt Ford .05 .01
❑ 400 George Brett .60 .25
❑ 401 Billy Joe Robidoux .05 .01
❑ 402 Mike Trujillo .05 .01

Card		
❑ 403 Jerry Royster	.05	.01
❑ 404 Doug Sisk	.05	.01
❑ 405 Brook Jacoby	.05	.01
❑ 406 Yankees TL/Hend/Matt	.50	.20
❑ 407 Jim Acker	.05	.01
❑ 408 John Mizerock	.05	.01
❑ 409 Milt Thompson	.05	.01
❑ 410 Fernando Valenzuela	.10	.02
❑ 411 Darnell Coles	.05	.01
❑ 412 Eric Davis	.15	.05
❑ 413 Moose Haas	.05	.01
❑ 414 Joe Orsulak	.05	.01
❑ 415 Bobby Witt RC	.25	.08
❑ 416 Tom Nieto	.05	.01
❑ 417 Pat Perry	.05	.01
❑ 418 Dick Williams MG	.05	.01
❑ 419 Mark Portugal RC *	.25	.08
❑ 420 Will Clark RC	1.00	.40
❑ 421 Jose DeLeon	.05	.01
❑ 422 Jack Howell	.05	.01
❑ 423 Jaime Cocanower	.05	.01
❑ 424 Chris Speier	.05	.01
❑ 425 Tom Seaver	.15	.05
❑ 426 Floyd Rayford	.05	.01
❑ 427 Edwin Nunez	.05	.01
❑ 428 Bruce Bochy	.05	.01
❑ 429 Tim Pyznarski	.05	.01
❑ 430 Mike Schmidt	.50	.20
❑ 431 Dodgers Team (Mound conference)	.05	.01
❑ 432 Jim Slaton	.05	.01
❑ 433 Ed Hearn RC	.05	.01
❑ 434 Mike Fischlin	.05	.01
❑ 435 Bruce Sutter	.10	.02
❑ 436 Andy Allanson RC	.05	.01
❑ 437 Ted Power	.05	.01
❑ 438 Kelly Downs RC	.10	.02
❑ 439 Karl Best	.05	.01
❑ 440 Willie McGee	.10	.02
❑ 441 Dave Leiper	.05	.01
❑ 442 Mitch Webster	.05	.01
❑ 443 John Felske MG	.05	.01
❑ 444 Jeff Russell	.05	.01
❑ 445 Dave Lopes	.10	.02
❑ 446 Chuck Finley RC	.40	.15
❑ 447 Bill Almon	.05	.01
❑ 448 Chris Bosio RC	.25	.08
❑ 449 Pat Dodson	.10	.02
❑ 450 Kirby Puckett	.50	.20
❑ 451 Joe Sambito	.05	.01
❑ 452 Dave Henderson	.05	.01
❑ 453 Scott Terry RC	.10	.02
❑ 454 Luis Salazar	.05	.01
❑ 455 Mike Boddicker	.05	.01
❑ 456 A's Team (Mound conference)	.05	.01
❑ 457 Len Matuszek	.05	.01
❑ 458 Kelly Gruber	.05	.01
❑ 459 Dennis Eckersley	.15	.05
❑ 460 Darryl Strawberry	.10	.02
❑ 461 Craig McMurtry	.05	.01
❑ 462 Scott Fletcher	.05	.01
❑ 463 Tom Candiotti	.05	.01
❑ 464 Butch Wynegar	.05	.01
❑ 465 Todd Worrell	.05	.01
❑ 466 Kal Daniels	.05	.01
❑ 467 Randy St.Claire	.05	.01
❑ 468 George Bamberger MG	.05	.01
❑ 469 Mike Diaz	.05	.01
❑ 470 Dave Dravecky	.05	.01
❑ 471 Ronn Reynolds	.05	.01
❑ 472 Bill Doran	.05	.01
❑ 473 Steve Farr	.05	.01
❑ 474 Jerry Narron	.05	.01
❑ 475 Scott Garrelts	.05	.01
❑ 476 Danny Tartabull	.05	.01
❑ 477 Ken Howell	.05	.01
❑ 478 Tim Laudner	.05	.01
❑ 479 Bob Sebra	.05	.01
❑ 480 Jim Rice	.10	.02
❑ 481 Phillies Team (Glenn Wilson& Juan Samuel& and V	.05	.01
❑ 482 Daryl Boston	.05	.01
❑ 483 Dwight Lowry	.05	.01
❑ 484 Jim Traber	.05	.01
❑ 485 Tony Fernandez	.05	.01
❑ 486 Otis Nixon	.05	.01
❑ 487 Dave Gumpert	.05	.01
❑ 488 Ray Knight	.10	.02
❑ 489 Bill Gullickson	.05	.01
❑ 490 Dale Murphy	.15	.05
❑ 491 Ron Karkovice RC	.25	.08
❑ 492 Mike Heath	.05	.01
❑ 493 Tom Lasorda MG	.15	.05
❑ 494 Barry Jones	.05	.01
❑ 495 Gorman Thomas	.10	.02
❑ 496 Bruce Bochte	.05	.01
❑ 497 Dale Mohorcic	.05	.01
❑ 498 Bob Kearney	.05	.01
❑ 499 Bruce Ruffin RC	.10	.02
❑ 500 Don Mattingly	.60	.25
❑ 501 Craig Lefferts	.05	.01
❑ 502 Dick Schofield	.05	.01
❑ 503 Larry Andersen	.05	.01
❑ 504 Mickey Hatcher	.05	.01
❑ 505 Bryn Smith	.05	.01
❑ 506 Orioles Team (Mound conference)	.05	.01
❑ 507 Dave L. Stapleton	.05	.01
❑ 508 Scott Bankhead	.05	.01
❑ 509 Enos Cabell	.05	.01
❑ 510 Tom Henke	.05	.01
❑ 511 Steve Lyons	.05	.01
❑ 512 Dave Magadan RC	.25	.08
❑ 513 Carmen Castillo	.05	.01
❑ 514 Orlando Mercado	.05	.01
❑ 515 Willie Hernandez	.05	.01
❑ 516 Ted Simmons	.10	.02
❑ 517 Mario Soto	.10	.02
❑ 518 Gene Mauch MG	.05	.01
❑ 519 Curt Young	.05	.01
❑ 520 Jack Clark	.10	.02
❑ 521 Rick Reuschel	.10	.02
❑ 522 Checklist 397-528	.05	.01
❑ 523 Earnie Riles	.05	.01
❑ 524 Bob Shirley	.05	.01
❑ 525 Phil Bradley	.05	.01
❑ 526 Roger Mason	.05	.01
❑ 527 Jim Wohlford	.05	.01
❑ 528 Ken Dixon	.05	.01
❑ 529 Alvaro Espinoza RC	.10	.02
❑ 530 Tony Gwynn	.30	.10
❑ 531 Astros TL/Y.Berra	.10	.02
❑ 532 Jeff Stone	.05	.01
❑ 533 Angel Salazar	.05	.01
❑ 534 Scott Sanderson	.05	.01
❑ 535 Tony Armas	.10	.02
❑ 536 Terry Mulholland RC	.25	.08
❑ 537 Rance Mulliniks	.05	.01
❑ 538 Tom Niedenfuer	.05	.01
❑ 539 Reid Nichols	.05	.01
❑ 540 Terry Kennedy	.05	.01
❑ 541 Rafael Belliard RC	.25	.08
❑ 542 Ricky Horton	.05	.01
❑ 543 Dave Johnson MG	.05	.01
❑ 544 Zane Smith	.05	.01
❑ 545 Buddy Bell	.10	.02
❑ 546 Mike Morgan	.05	.01
❑ 547 Rob Deer	.05	.01
❑ 548 Bill Mooneyham	.05	.01
❑ 549 Bob Melvin	.05	.01
❑ 550 Pete Incaviglia RC *	.25	.08
❑ 551 Frank Wills	.05	.01
❑ 552 Larry Sheets	.05	.01
❑ 553 Mike Maddux RC	.05	.01
❑ 554 Buddy Biancalana	.05	.01
❑ 555 Dennis Rasmussen	.05	.01
❑ 556 Angels Team (Rene Lachemann CO& Mike Witt& and	.05	.01
❑ 557 John Cerutti	.05	.01
❑ 558 Greg Gagne	.05	.01
❑ 559 Lance McCullers	.05	.01
❑ 560 Glenn Davis	.05	.01
❑ 561 Rey Quinones	.05	.01
❑ 562 Bryan Clutterbuck	.05	.01
❑ 563 John Stefero	.05	.01
❑ 564 Larry McWilliams	.05	.01
❑ 565 Dusty Baker	.10	.02
❑ 566 Tim Hulett	.05	.01
❑ 567 Greg Mathews	.05	.01
❑ 568 Earl Weaver MG	.10	.02
❑ 569 Wade Rowdon	.05	.01
❑ 570 Sid Fernandez	.05	.01
❑ 571 Ozzie Virgil	.05	.01
❑ 572 Pete Ladd	.05	.01
❑ 573 Hal McRae	.10	.02
❑ 574 Manny Lee	.05	.01
❑ 575 Pat Tabler	.05	.01
❑ 576 Frank Pastore	.05	.01
❑ 577 Dann Bilardello	.05	.01
❑ 578 Billy Hatcher	.05	.01
❑ 579 Rick Burleson	.05	.01
❑ 580 Mike Krukow	.05	.01
❑ 581 Cubs Team (Ron Cey and Steve Trout)	.05	.01
❑ 582 Bruce Berenyi	.05	.01
❑ 583 Junior Ortiz	.05	.01
❑ 584 Ron Kittle	.05	.01
❑ 585 Scott Bailes	.05	.01
❑ 586 Ben Oglivie	.10	.02
❑ 587 Eric Plunk	.05	.01
❑ 588 Wallace Johnson	.05	.01
❑ 589 Steve Crawford	.05	.01
❑ 590 Vince Coleman	.05	.01
❑ 591 Spike Owen	.05	.01
❑ 592 Chris Welsh	.05	.01
❑ 593 Chuck Tanner MG	.05	.01
❑ 594 Rick Anderson	.05	.01
❑ 595 Keith Hernandez AS	.05	.01
❑ 596 Steve Sax AS	.05	.01
❑ 597 Mike Schmidt AS	.25	.08
❑ 598 Ozzie Smith AS	.25	.08
❑ 599 Tony Gwynn AS	.15	.05
❑ 600 Dave Parker AS	.05	.01
❑ 601 Darryl Strawberry AS	.05	.01
❑ 602 Gary Carter AS	.05	.01
❑ 603A Dwight Gooden AS NoTM	.10	.02
❑ 603B Dwight Gooden AS TM	.10	.02
❑ 604 Fernando Valenzuela AS	.05	.01
❑ 605 Todd Worrell AS	.05	.01
❑ 606 Don Mattingly AS	.30	.10
❑ 606A Don Mattingly AS NoTM	1.00	.40
❑ 607 Tony Bernazard AS	.05	.01
❑ 608 Wade Boggs AS	.10	.02
❑ 609 Cal Ripken AS	.25	.08
❑ 610 Jim Rice AS	.05	.01
❑ 611 Kirby Puckett AS	.25	.08
❑ 612 George Bell AS	.05	.01
❑ 613 Lance Parrish AS UER (Pitcher heading on back)	.05	.01
❑ 614 Roger Clemens AS	1.00	.40
❑ 615 Teddy Higuera AS	.05	.01
❑ 616 Dave Righetti AS	.05	.01
❑ 617 Al Nipper	.05	.01
❑ 618 Tom Kelly MG	.05	.01
❑ 619 Jerry Reed	.05	.01
❑ 620 Jose Canseco	1.00	.40
❑ 621 Danny Cox	.05	.01
❑ 622 Glenn Braggs RC	.10	.02
❑ 623 Kurt Stillwell	.05	.01
❑ 624 Tim Burke	.05	.01
❑ 625 Mookie Wilson	.10	.02
❑ 626 Joel Skinner	.05	.01
❑ 627 Ken Oberkfell	.05	.01
❑ 628 Bob Walk	.05	.01
❑ 629 Larry Parrish	.05	.01
❑ 630 John Candelaria	.05	.01
❑ 631 Tigers Team (Mound conference)	.05	.01
❑ 632 Rob Woodward	.05	.01
❑ 633 Jose Uribe	.05	.01
❑ 634 Rafael Palmeiro RC	1.50	.60
❑ 635 Ken Schrom	.05	.01
❑ 636 Darren Daulton	.10	.02
❑ 637 Bip Roberts RC	.25	.08
❑ 638 Rich Bordi	.05	.01
❑ 639 Gerald Perry	.05	.01
❑ 640 Mark Clear	.05	.01
❑ 641 Domingo Ramos	.05	.01
❑ 642 Al Pulido	.05	.01
❑ 643 Ron Shepherd	.05	.01
❑ 644 John Denny	.05	.01
❑ 645 Dwight Evans	.15	.05
❑ 646 Mike Mason	.05	.01

❑ 647 Tom Lawless .05 .01
❑ 648 Barry Larkin RC 1.00 .40
❑ 649 Mickey Tettleton .05 .01
❑ 650 Hubie Brooks .05 .01
❑ 651 Benny Distefano .05 .01
❑ 652 Terry Forster .10 .02
❑ 653 Kevin Mitchell RC * .40 .15
❑ 654 Checklist 529-660 .10 .02
❑ 655 Jesse Barfield .10 .02
❑ 656 Rangers Team
(Bobby Valentine MG
and Ricky Wrigh .05 .01
❑ 657 Tom Waddell .05 .01
❑ 658 Robby Thompson RC * .25 .08
❑ 659 Aurelio Lopez .05 .01
❑ 660 Bob Horner .10 .02
❑ 661 Lou Whitaker .10 .02
❑ 662 Frank DiPino .05 .01
❑ 663 Cliff Johnson .05 .01
❑ 664 Mike Marshall .05 .01
❑ 665 Rod Scurry .05 .01
❑ 666 Von Hayes .05 .01
❑ 667 Ron Hassey .05 .01
❑ 668 Juan Bonilla .05 .01
❑ 669 Bud Black .05 .01
❑ 670 Jose Cruz .10 .02
❑ 671A Ray Soff ERR
(No D* before
copyright line) .05 .01
❑ 671B Ray Soff COR
(D* before
copyright line) .05 .01
❑ 672 Chili Davis .10 .02
❑ 673 Don Sutton .10 .02
❑ 674 Bill Campbell .05 .01
❑ 675 Ed Romero .05 .01
❑ 676 Charlie Moore .05 .01
❑ 677 Bob Grich .10 .02
❑ 678 Carney Lansford .10 .02
❑ 679 Kent Hrbek .10 .02
❑ 680 Ryne Sandberg .40 .15
❑ 681 George Bell .10 .02
❑ 682 Jerry Reuss .05 .01
❑ 683 Gary Roenicke .05 .01
❑ 684 Kent Tekulve .05 .01
❑ 685 Jerry Hairston .05 .01
❑ 686 Doyle Alexander .05 .01
❑ 687 Alan Trammell .10 .02
❑ 688 Juan Beniquez .05 .01
❑ 689 Darrell Porter .05 .01
❑ 690 Dane Iorg .05 .01
❑ 691 Dave Parker .10 .02
❑ 692 Frank White .10 .02
❑ 693 Terry Puhl .05 .01
❑ 694 Phil Niekro .10 .02
❑ 695 Chico Walker .05 .01
❑ 696 Gary Lucas .05 .01
❑ 697 Ed Lynch .05 .01
❑ 698 Ernie Whitt .05 .01
❑ 699 Ken Landreaux .05 .01
❑ 700 Dave Bergman .05 .01
❑ 701 Willie Randolph .10 .02
❑ 702 Greg Gross .05 .01
❑ 703 Dave Schmidt .05 .01
❑ 704 Jesse Orosco .05 .01
❑ 705 Bruce Hurst .05 .01
❑ 706 Rick Manning .05 .01
❑ 707 Bob McClure .05 .01
❑ 708 Scott McGregor .05 .01
❑ 709 Dave Kingman .10 .02
❑ 710 Gary Gaetti .10 .02
❑ 711 Ken Griffey .10 .02
❑ 712 Don Robinson .05 .01
❑ 713 Tom Brookens .05 .01
❑ 714 Dan Quisenberry .05 .01
❑ 715 Bob Dernier .05 .01
❑ 716 Rick Leach .05 .01
❑ 717 Ed VandeBerg .05 .01
❑ 718 Steve Carlton .10 .02
❑ 719 Tom Hume .05 .01
❑ 720 Richard Dotson .05 .01
❑ 721 Tom Herr .05 .01
❑ 722 Bob Knepper .05 .01
❑ 723 Brett Butler .10 .02
❑ 724 Greg Minton .05 .01
❑ 725 George Hendrick .10 .02
❑ 726 Frank Tanana .10 .02
❑ 727 Mike Moore .05 .01
❑ 728 Tippy Martinez .05 .01
❑ 729 Tom Paciorek .05 .01
❑ 730 Eric Show .05 .01
❑ 731 Dave Concepcion .10 .02
❑ 732 Manny Trillo .05 .01
❑ 733 Bill Caudill .05 .01
❑ 734 Bill Madlock .10 .02
❑ 735 Rickey Henderson .25 .08
❑ 736 Steve Bedrosian .05 .01
❑ 737 Floyd Bannister .05 .01
❑ 738 Jorge Orta .05 .01
❑ 739 Chet Lemon .10 .02
❑ 740 Rich Gedman .05 .01
❑ 741 Paul Molitor .10 .02
❑ 742 Andy McGaffigan .05 .01
❑ 743 Dwayne Murphy .05 .01
❑ 744 Roy Smalley .05 .01
❑ 745 Glenn Hubbard .05 .01
❑ 746 Bob Ojeda .05 .01
❑ 747 Johnny Ray .05 .01
❑ 748 Mike Flanagan .05 .01
❑ 749 Ozzie Smith .40 .15
❑ 750 Steve Trout .05 .01
❑ 751 Garth Iorg .05 .01
❑ 752 Dan Petry .05 .01
❑ 753 Rick Honeycutt .05 .01
❑ 754 Dave LaPoint .05 .01
❑ 755 Luis Aguayo .05 .01
❑ 756 Carlton Fisk .15 .05
❑ 757 Nolan Ryan 1.00 .40
❑ 758 Tony Bernazard .05 .01
❑ 759 Joel Youngblood .05 .01
❑ 760 Mike Witt .05 .01
❑ 761 Greg Pryor .05 .01
❑ 762 Gary Ward .05 .01
❑ 763 Tim Flannery .05 .01
❑ 764 Bill Buckner .10 .02
❑ 765 Kirk Gibson .10 .02
❑ 766 Don Aase .05 .01
❑ 767 Ron Cey .10 .02
❑ 768 Dennis Lamp .05 .01
❑ 769 Steve Sax .05 .01
❑ 770 Dave Winfield .10 .02
❑ 771 Shane Rawley .05 .01
❑ 772 Harold Baines .10 .02
❑ 773 Robin Yount .40 .15
❑ 774 Wayne Krenchicki .05 .01
❑ 775 Joaquin Andujar .10 .02
❑ 776 Tom Brunansky .05 .01
❑ 777 Chris Chambliss .10 .02
❑ 778 Jack Morris .10 .02
❑ 779 Craig Reynolds .05 .01
❑ 780 Andre Thornton .05 .01
❑ 781 Atlee Hammaker .05 .01
❑ 782 Brian Downing .10 .02
❑ 783 Willie Wilson .10 .02
❑ 784 Cal Ripken .75 .30
❑ 785 Terry Francona .10 .02
❑ 786 Jimy Williams MG .05 .01
❑ 787 Alejandro Pena .05 .01
❑ 788 Tim Stoddard .05 .01
❑ 789 Dan Schatzeder .05 .01
❑ 790 Julio Cruz .05 .01
❑ 791 Lance Parrish UER
(No trademark&
never corrected .10 .02
❑ 792 Checklist 661-792 .05 .01

1988 Topps

❑ COMPLETE SET (792) 15.00 6.00
❑ COMP.FACT SET (792) 15.00 6.00
❑ COMP.X-MAS.SET (792) 40.00 15.00
❑ 1 Vince Coleman RB
100 Steals for
Third Cons. Seas .05 .01
❑ 2 Don Mattingly RB .30 .10
❑ 3 Mark McGwire RB .75 .30
❑ 3A Mark McGwire ERR RB .75 .30
❑ 4 Eddie Murray RB .15 .05
❑ 4A Eddie Murray ERR RB .50 .20
❑ 5 Phil Niekro
Joe Niekro RB
Brothers Win Record .10 .02
❑ 6 Nolan Ryan RB .40 .15
❑ 7 Benito Santiago RB .05 .01
❑ 8 Kevin Elster .05 .01
❑ 9 Andy Hawkins .05 .01
❑ 10 Ryne Sandberg .40 .15
❑ 11 Mike Young .05 .01
❑ 12 Bill Schroeder .05 .01
❑ 13 Andres Thomas .05 .01
❑ 14 Sparky Anderson MG .10 .02
❑ 15 Chili Davis .10 .02
❑ 16 Kirk McCaskill .05 .01
❑ 17 Ron Oester .05 .01
❑ 18A Al Leiter ERR RC .50 .20
❑ 18B Al Leiter RC .50 .20
❑ 19 Mark Davidson .05 .01
❑ 20 Kevin Gross .05 .01
❑ 21 Wade Boggs
Spike Owen TL .10 .02
❑ 22 Greg Swindell .05 .01
❑ 23 Ken Landreaux .05 .01
❑ 24 Jim Deshaies .05 .01
❑ 25 Andres Galarraga .10 .02
❑ 26 Mitch Williams .05 .01
❑ 27 R.J. Reynolds .05 .01
❑ 28 Jose Nunez .05 .01
❑ 29 Angel Salazar .05 .01
❑ 30 Sid Fernandez .05 .01
❑ 31 Bruce Bochy .05 .01
❑ 32 Mike Morgan .05 .01
❑ 33 Rob Deer .05 .01
❑ 34 Ricky Horton .05 .01
❑ 35 Harold Baines .10 .02
❑ 36 Jamie Moyer .10 .02
❑ 37 Ed Romero .05 .01
❑ 38 Jeff Calhoun .05 .01
❑ 39 Gerald Perry .05 .01
❑ 40 Orel Hershiser .10 .02
❑ 41 Bob Melvin .05 .01
❑ 42 Bill Landrum .05 .01
❑ 43 Dick Schofield .05 .01
❑ 44 Lou Piniella MG .10 .02
❑ 45 Kent Hrbek .10 .02
❑ 46 Darnell Coles .05 .01
❑ 47 Joaquin Andujar .10 .02
❑ 48 Alan Ashby .05 .01
❑ 49 Dave Clark .05 .01
❑ 50 Hubie Brooks .05 .01
❑ 51 C.Ripken/E.Murray TL .40 .15
❑ 52 Don Robinson .05 .01
❑ 53 Curt Wilkerson .05 .01
❑ 54 Jim Clancy .05 .01
❑ 55 Phil Bradley .05 .01
❑ 56 Ed Hearn .05 .01
❑ 57 Tim Crews RC .25 .08
❑ 58 Dave Magadan .05 .01
❑ 59 Danny Cox .05 .01
❑ 60 Rickey Henderson .20 .07
❑ 61 Mark Knudson .05 .01
❑ 62 Jeff Hamilton .05 .01
❑ 63 Jimmy Jones .05 .01
❑ 64 Ken Caminiti RC 2.00 .75
❑ 65 Leon Durham .05 .01
❑ 66 Shane Rawley .05 .01
❑ 67 Ken Oberkfell .05 .01
❑ 68 Dave Dravecky .05 .01
❑ 69 Mike Hart .05 .01
❑ 70 Roger Clemens 1.00 .40
❑ 71 Gary Pettis .05 .01
❑ 72 Dennis Eckersley .15 .05

❑ 73 Randy Bush .05 .01
❑ 74 Tom Lasorda MG .15 .05
❑ 75 Joe Carter .10 .02
❑ 76 Dennis Martinez .10 .02
❑ 77 Tom O'Malley .05 .01
❑ 78 Dan Petry .05 .01
❑ 79 Ernie Whitt .05 .01
❑ 80 Mark Langston .05 .01
❑ 81 Ron Robinson
John Franco TL .05 .01
❑ 82 Darrel Akerfelds .05 .01
❑ 83 Jose Oquendo .05 .01
❑ 84 Cecilio Guante .05 .01
❑ 85 Howard Johnson .10 .02
❑ 86 Ron Karkovice .05 .01
❑ 87 Mike Mason .05 .01
❑ 88 Earnie Riles .05 .01
❑ 89 Gary Thurman .05 .01
❑ 90 Dale Murphy .15 .05
❑ 91 Joey Cora RC .25 .08
❑ 92 Len Matuszek .05 .01
❑ 93 Bob Sebra .05 .01
❑ 94 Chuck Jackson .05 .01
❑ 95 Lance Parrish .10 .02
❑ 96 Todd Benzinger RC* .25 .08
❑ 97 Scott Garrelts .05 .01
❑ 98 Rene Gonzales RC .10 .02
❑ 99 Chuck Finley .10 .02
❑ 100 Jack Clark .10 .02
❑ 101 Allan Anderson .05 .01
❑ 102 Barry Larkin .15 .05
❑ 103 Curt Young .05 .01
❑ 104 Dick Williams MG .05 .01
❑ 105 Jesse Orosco .05 .01
❑ 106 Jim Walewander .05 .01
❑ 107 Scott Bailes .05 .01
❑ 108 Steve Lyons .05 .01
❑ 109 Joel Skinner .05 .01
❑ 110 Teddy Higuera .05 .01
❑ 111 Hubie Brooks
Vance Law TL .05 .01
❑ 112 Les Lancaster .05 .01
❑ 113 Kelly Gruber .05 .01
❑ 114 Jeff Russell .05 .01
❑ 115 Johnny Ray .05 .01
❑ 116 Jerry Don Gleaton .05 .01
❑ 117 James Steels .05 .01
❑ 118 Bob Welch .10 .02
❑ 119 Robbie Wine .05 .01
❑ 120 Kirby Puckett .20 .07
❑ 121 Checklist 1-132 .05 .01
❑ 122 Tony Bernazard .05 .01
❑ 123 Tom Candiotti .05 .01
❑ 124 Ray Knight .10 .02
❑ 125 Bruce Hurst .05 .01
❑ 126 Steve Jeltz .05 .01
❑ 127 Jim Gott .05 .01
❑ 128 Johnny Grubb .05 .01
❑ 129 Greg Minton .05 .01
❑ 130 Buddy Bell .10 .02
❑ 131 Don Schulze .05 .01
❑ 132 Donnie Hill .05 .01
❑ 133 Greg Mathews .05 .01
❑ 134 Chuck Tanner MG .05 .01
❑ 135 Dennis Rasmussen .05 .01
❑ 136 Brian Dayett .05 .01
❑ 137 Chris Bosio .05 .01
❑ 138 Mitch Webster .05 .01
❑ 139 Jerry Browne .05 .01
❑ 140 Jesse Barfield .10 .02
❑ 141 G.Brett/B.Saberhagen TL .20 .07
❑ 142 Andy Van Slyke .15 .05
❑ 143 Mickey Tettleton .05 .01
❑ 144 Don Gordon .05 .01
❑ 145 Bill Madlock .10 .02
❑ 146 Donell Nixon .05 .01
❑ 147 Bill Buckner .10 .02
❑ 148 Carmelo Martinez .05 .01
❑ 149 Ken Howell .05 .01
❑ 150 Eric Davis .10 .02
❑ 151 Bob Knepper .05 .01
❑ 152 Jody Reed RC .25 .08
❑ 153 John Habyan .05 .01
❑ 154 Jeff Stone .05 .01
❑ 155 Bruce Sutter .10 .02
❑ 156 Gary Matthews .10 .02
❑ 157 Atlee Hammaker .05 .01
❑ 158 Tim Hulett .05 .01
❑ 159 Brad Arnsberg .05 .01
❑ 160 Willie McGee .10 .02
❑ 161 Bryn Smith .05 .01
❑ 162 Mark McLemore .05 .01
❑ 163 Dale Mohorcic .05 .01
❑ 164 Dave Johnson MG .05 .01
❑ 165 Robin Yount .30 .10
❑ 166 Rick Rodriquez .05 .01
❑ 167 Rance Mulliniks .05 .01
❑ 168 Barry Jones .05 .01
❑ 169 Ross Jones .05 .01
❑ 170 Rich Gossage .10 .02
❑ 171 Shawon Dunston
Manny Trillo TL .05 .01
❑ 172 Lloyd McClendon RC .25 .08
❑ 173 Eric Plunk .05 .01
❑ 174 Phil Garner .10 .02
❑ 175 Kevin Bass .05 .01
❑ 176 Jeff Reed .05 .01
❑ 177 Frank Tanana .10 .02
❑ 178 Dwayne Henry .05 .01
❑ 179 Charlie Puleo .05 .01
❑ 180 Terry Kennedy .05 .01
❑ 181 David Cone .10 .02
❑ 182 Ken Phelps .05 .01
❑ 183 Tom Lawless .05 .01
❑ 184 Ivan Calderon .05 .01
❑ 185 Rick Rhoden .05 .01
❑ 186 Rafael Palmeiro .40 .15
❑ 187 Steve Kiefer .05 .01
❑ 188 John Russell .05 .01
❑ 189 Wes Gardner .05 .01
❑ 190 Candy Maldonado .05 .01
❑ 191 John Cerutti .05 .01
❑ 192 Devon White .10 .02
❑ 193 Brian Fisher .05 .01
❑ 194 Tom Kelly MG .05 .01
❑ 195 Dan Quisenberry .05 .01
❑ 196 Dave Engle .05 .01
❑ 197 Lance McCullers .05 .01
❑ 198 Franklin Stubbs .05 .01
❑ 199 Dave Meads .05 .01
❑ 200 Wade Boggs .15 .05
❑ 201 Rangers TL
Bobby Valentine MG&
Pete O'Brien&
Pe .05 .01
❑ 202 Glenn Hoffman .05 .01
❑ 203 Fred Toliver .05 .01
❑ 204 Paul O'Neill .15 .05
❑ 205 Nelson Liriano .05 .01
❑ 206 Domingo Ramos .05 .01
❑ 207 John Mitchell RC .10 .02
❑ 208 Steve Lake .05 .01
❑ 209 Richard Dotson .05 .01
❑ 210 Willie Randolph .10 .02
❑ 211 Frank DiPino .05 .01
❑ 212 Greg Brock .05 .01
❑ 213 Albert Hall .05 .01
❑ 214 Dave Schmidt .05 .01
❑ 215 Von Hayes .05 .01
❑ 216 Jerry Reuss .05 .01
❑ 217 Harry Spilman .05 .01
❑ 218 Dan Schatzeder .05 .01
❑ 219 Mike Stanley .05 .01
❑ 220 Tom Henke .05 .01
❑ 221 Rafael Belliard .05 .01
❑ 222 Steve Farr .05 .01
❑ 223 Stan Jefferson .05 .01
❑ 224 Tom Trebelhorn MG .05 .01
❑ 225 Mike Scioscia .10 .02
❑ 226 Dave Lopes .10 .02
❑ 227 Ed Correa .05 .01
❑ 228 Wallace Johnson .05 .01
❑ 229 Jeff Musselman .05 .01
❑ 230 Pat Tabler .05 .01
❑ 231 B.Bonds/B.Bonilla TL 1.00 .40
❑ 232 Bob James .05 .01
❑ 233 Rafael Santana .05 .01
❑ 234 Ken Dayley .05 .01
❑ 235 Gary Ward .05 .01
❑ 236 Ted Power .05 .01
❑ 237 Mike Heath .05 .01
❑ 238 Luis Polonia RC* .25 .08
❑ 239 Roy Smalley .05 .01
❑ 240 Lee Smith .10 .02
❑ 241 Damaso Garcia .05 .01
❑ 242 Tom Niedenfuer .05 .01
❑ 243 Mark Ryal .05 .01
❑ 244 Jeff D. Robinson .05 .01
❑ 245 Rich Gedman .05 .01
❑ 246 Mike Campbell .05 .01
❑ 247 Thad Bosley .05 .01
❑ 248 Storm Davis .05 .01
❑ 249 Mike Marshall .05 .01
❑ 250 Nolan Ryan 1.00 .40
❑ 251 Tom Foley .05 .01
❑ 252 Bob Brower .05 .01
❑ 253 Checklist 133-264 .05 .01
❑ 254 Lee Elia MG .05 .01
❑ 255 Mookie Wilson .10 .02
❑ 256 Ken Schrom .05 .01
❑ 257 Jerry Royster .05 .01
❑ 258 Ed Nunez .05 .01
❑ 259 Ron Kittle .05 .01
❑ 260 Vince Coleman .05 .01
❑ 261 Giants TL
(Five players) .05 .01
❑ 262 Drew Hall .05 .01
❑ 263 Glenn Braggs .05 .01
❑ 264 Les Straker .05 .01
❑ 265 Bo Diaz .05 .01
❑ 266 Paul Assenmacher .05 .01
❑ 267 Billy Bean RC .10 .02
❑ 268 Bruce Ruffin .05 .01
❑ 269 Ellis Burks RC .40 .15
❑ 270 Mike Witt .05 .01
❑ 271 Ken Gerhart .05 .01
❑ 272 Steve Ontiveros .05 .01
❑ 273 Garth Iorg .05 .01
❑ 274 Junior Ortiz .05 .01
❑ 275 Kevin Seitzer .05 .01
❑ 276 Luis Salazar .05 .01
❑ 277 Alejandro Pena .05 .01
❑ 278 Jose Cruz .10 .02
❑ 279 Randy St.Claire .05 .01
❑ 280 Pete Incaviglia .05 .01
❑ 281 Jerry Hairston .05 .01
❑ 282 Pat Perry .05 .01
❑ 283 Phil Lombardi .05 .01
❑ 284 Larry Bowa MG .10 .02
❑ 285 Jim Presley .05 .01
❑ 286 Chuck Crim .05 .01
❑ 287 Manny Trillo .05 .01
❑ 288 Pat Pacillo .05 .01
❑ 289 Dave Bergman .05 .01
❑ 290 Tony Fernandez .05 .01
❑ 291 Billy Hatcher
Kevin Bass TL .05 .01
❑ 292 Carney Lansford .10 .02
❑ 293 Doug Jones RC .25 .08
❑ 294 Al Pedrique .05 .01
❑ 295 Bert Blyleven .10 .02
❑ 296 Floyd Rayford .05 .01
❑ 297 Zane Smith .05 .01
❑ 298 Milt Thompson .05 .01
❑ 299 Steve Crawford .05 .01
❑ 300 Don Mattingly .60 .25
❑ 301 Bud Black .05 .01
❑ 302 Jose Uribe .05 .01
❑ 303 Eric Show .05 .01
❑ 304 George Hendrick .10 .02
❑ 305 Steve Sax .05 .01
❑ 306 Billy Hatcher .05 .01
❑ 307 Mike Trujillo .05 .01
❑ 308 Lee Mazzilli .10 .02
❑ 309 Bill Long .05 .01
❑ 310 Tom Herr .05 .01
❑ 311 Scott Sanderson .05 .01
❑ 312 Joey Meyer .05 .01
❑ 313 Bob McClure .05 .01
❑ 314 Jimy Williams MG .05 .01
❑ 315 Dave Parker .10 .02
❑ 316 Jose Rijo .10 .02
❑ 317 Tom Nieto .05 .01
❑ 318 Mel Hall .05 .01
❑ 319 Mike Loynd .05 .01
❑ 320 Alan Trammell .10 .02
❑ 321 Harold Baines
Carlton Fisk TL .10 .02

No.	Player		
❑ 322	Vicente Palacios	.05	.01
❑ 323	Rick Leach	.05	.01
❑ 324	Danny Jackson	.05	.01
❑ 325	Glenn Hubbard	.05	.01
❑ 326	Al Nipper	.05	.01
❑ 327	Larry Sheets	.05	.01
❑ 328	Greg Cadaret	.05	.01
❑ 329	Chris Speier	.05	.01
❑ 330	Eddie Whitson	.05	.01
❑ 331	Brian Downing	.10	.02
❑ 332	Jerry Reed	.05	.01
❑ 333	Wally Backman	.05	.01
❑ 334	Dave LaPoint	.05	.01
❑ 335	Claudell Washington	.05	.01
❑ 336	Ed Lynch	.05	.01
❑ 337	Jim Gantner	.05	.01
❑ 338	Brian Holton UER (1987 ERA .389& should be 3.89)	.05	.01
❑ 339	Kurt Stillwell	.05	.01
❑ 340	Jack Morris	.10	.02
❑ 341	Carmen Castillo	.05	.01
❑ 342	Larry Andersen	.05	.01
❑ 343	Greg Gagne	.05	.01
❑ 344	Tony LaRussa MG	.10	.02
❑ 345	Scott Fletcher	.05	.01
❑ 346	Vance Law	.05	.01
❑ 347	Joe Johnson	.05	.01
❑ 348	Jim Eisenreich	.05	.01
❑ 349	Bob Walk	.05	.01
❑ 350	Will Clark	.20	.07
❑ 351	Red Schoendienst CO Tony Pena TL	.10	.02
❑ 352	Bill Ripken RC*	.05	.01
❑ 353	Ed Olwine	.05	.01
❑ 354	Marc Sullivan	.05	.01
❑ 355	Roger McDowell	.05	.01
❑ 356	Luis Aguayo	.05	.01
❑ 357	Floyd Bannister	.05	.01
❑ 358	Rey Quinones	.05	.01
❑ 359	Tim Stoddard	.05	.01
❑ 360	Tony Gwynn	.30	.10
❑ 361	Greg Maddux	1.00	.40
❑ 362	Juan Castillo	.05	.01
❑ 363	Willie Fraser	.05	.01
❑ 364	Nick Esasky	.05	.01
❑ 365	Floyd Youmans	.05	.01
❑ 366	Chet Lemon	.10	.02
❑ 367	Tim Leary	.05	.01
❑ 368	Gerald Young	.05	.01
❑ 369	Greg Harris	.05	.01
❑ 370	Jose Canseco	.50	.20
❑ 371	Joe Hesketh	.05	.01
❑ 372	Matt Williams RC	.75	.30
❑ 373	Checklist 265-396	.05	.01
❑ 374	Doc Edwards MG	.05	.01
❑ 375	Tom Brunansky	.05	.01
❑ 376	Bill Wilkinson	.05	.01
❑ 377	Sam Horn RC	.10	.02
❑ 378	Todd Frohwirth	.05	.01
❑ 379	Rafael Ramirez	.05	.01
❑ 380	Joe Magrane RC*	.05	.01
❑ 381	Wally Joyner Jack Howell TL	.10	.02
❑ 382	Keith Miller RC	.25	.08
❑ 383	Eric Bell	.05	.01
❑ 384	Neil Allen	.05	.01
❑ 385	Carlton Fisk	.15	.05
❑ 386	Don Mattingly AS	.30	.10
❑ 387	Willie Randolph AS	.05	.01
❑ 388	Wade Boggs AS	.10	.02
❑ 389	Alan Trammell AS	.05	.01
❑ 390	George Bell AS	.05	.01
❑ 391	Kirby Puckett AS	.15	.05
❑ 392	Dave Winfield AS	.05	.01
❑ 393	Matt Nokes AS	.05	.01
❑ 394	Roger Clemens AS	.50	.20
❑ 395	Jimmy Key AS	.05	.01
❑ 396	Tom Henke AS	.05	.01
❑ 397	Jack Clark AS	.05	.01
❑ 398	Juan Samuel AS	.05	.01
❑ 399	Tim Wallach AS	.05	.01
❑ 400	Ozzie Smith AS	.20	.07
❑ 401	Andre Dawson AS	.05	.01
❑ 402	Tony Gwynn AS	.15	.05
❑ 403	Tim Raines AS	.05	.01
❑ 404	Benny Santiago AS	.05	.01
❑ 405	Dwight Gooden AS	.05	.01
❑ 406	Shane Rawley AS	.05	.01
❑ 407	Steve Bedrosian AS	.05	.01
❑ 408	Dion James	.05	.01
❑ 409	Joel McKeon	.05	.01
❑ 410	Tony Pena	.05	.01
❑ 411	Wayne Tolleson	.05	.01
❑ 412	Randy Myers	.10	.02
❑ 413	John Christensen	.05	.01
❑ 414	John McNamara MG	.05	.01
❑ 415	Don Carman	.05	.01
❑ 416	Keith Moreland	.05	.01
❑ 417	Mark Ciardi	.05	.01
❑ 418	Joel Youngblood	.05	.01
❑ 419	Scott McGregor	.05	.01
❑ 420	Wally Joyner	.10	.02
❑ 421	Ed VandeBerg	.05	.01
❑ 422	Dave Concepcion	.10	.02
❑ 423	John Smiley RC*	.25	.08
❑ 424	Dwayne Murphy	.05	.01
❑ 425	Jeff Reardon	.10	.02
❑ 426	Randy Ready	.05	.01
❑ 427	Paul Kilgus	.05	.01
❑ 428	John Shelby	.05	.01
❑ 429	A.Trammell/K.Gibson TL	.10	.02
❑ 430	Glenn Davis	.05	.01
❑ 431	Casey Candaele	.05	.01
❑ 432	Mike Moore	.05	.01
❑ 433	Bill Pecota RC*	.05	.01
❑ 434	Rick Aguilera	.05	.01
❑ 435	Mike Pagliarulo	.05	.01
❑ 436	Mike Bielecki	.05	.01
❑ 437	Fred Manrique	.05	.01
❑ 438	Rob Ducey	.05	.01
❑ 439	Dave Martinez	.05	.01
❑ 440	Steve Bedrosian	.05	.01
❑ 441	Rick Manning	.05	.01
❑ 442	Tom Bolton	.05	.01
❑ 443	Ken Griffey	.10	.02
❑ 444	Cal Ripken& Sr. MG (Checklist back) UER (two cop	.05	.01
❑ 445	Mike Krukow	.05	.01
❑ 446	Doug DeCinces (Now with Cardinals on card front)	.05	.01
❑ 447	Jeff Montgomery RC	.25	.08
❑ 448	Mike Davis	.05	.01
❑ 449	Jeff M. Robinson	.05	.01
❑ 450	Barry Bonds	2.00	.75
❑ 451	Keith Atherton	.05	.01
❑ 452	Willie Wilson	.10	.02
❑ 453	Dennis Powell	.05	.01
❑ 454	Marvell Wynne	.05	.01
❑ 455	Shawn Hillegas	.05	.01
❑ 456	Dave Anderson	.05	.01
❑ 457	Terry Leach	.05	.01
❑ 458	Ron Hassey	.05	.01
❑ 459	Dave Winfield Willie Randolph TL	.05	.01
❑ 460	Ozzie Smith	.30	.10
❑ 461	Danny Darwin	.05	.01
❑ 462	Don Slaught	.05	.01
❑ 463	Fred McGriff	.20	.07
❑ 464	Jay Tibbs	.05	.01
❑ 465	Paul Molitor	.10	.02
❑ 466	Jerry Mumphrey	.05	.01
❑ 467	Don Aase	.05	.01
❑ 468	Darren Daulton	.10	.02
❑ 469	Jeff Dedmon	.05	.01
❑ 470	Dwight Evans	.15	.05
❑ 471	Donnie Moore	.05	.01
❑ 472	Robby Thompson	.05	.01
❑ 473	Joe Niekro	.05	.01
❑ 474	Tom Brookens	.05	.01
❑ 475	Pete Rose MG/TC	.50	.20
❑ 476	Dave Stewart	.10	.02
❑ 477	Jamie Quirk	.05	.01
❑ 478	Sid Bream	.05	.01
❑ 479	Brett Butler	.10	.02
❑ 480	Dwight Gooden	.10	.02
❑ 481	Mariano Duncan	.05	.01
❑ 482	Mark Davis	.05	.01
❑ 483	Rod Booker	.05	.01
❑ 484	Pat Clements	.05	.01
❑ 485	Harold Reynolds	.10	.02
❑ 486	Pat Keedy	.05	.01
❑ 487	Jim Pankovits	.05	.01
❑ 488	Andy McGaffigan	.05	.01
❑ 489	Dodgers TL Pedro Guerrero and Fernando Valenzuel	.05	.01
❑ 490	Larry Parrish	.05	.01
❑ 491	B.J. Surhoff	.10	.02
❑ 492	Doyle Alexander	.05	.01
❑ 493	Mike Greenwell	.05	.01
❑ 494	Wally Ritchie	.05	.01
❑ 495	Eddie Murray	.20	.07
❑ 496	Guy Hoffman	.05	.01
❑ 497	Kevin Mitchell	.10	.02
❑ 498	Bob Boone	.10	.02
❑ 499	Eric King	.05	.01
❑ 500	Andre Dawson	.10	.02
❑ 501	Tim Birtsas	.05	.01
❑ 502	Dan Gladden	.05	.01
❑ 503	Junior Noboa	.05	.01
❑ 504	Bob Rodgers MG	.05	.01
❑ 505	Willie Upshaw	.05	.01
❑ 506	John Cangelosi	.05	.01
❑ 507	Mark Gubicza	.05	.01
❑ 508	Tim Teufel	.05	.01
❑ 509	Bill Dawley	.05	.01
❑ 510	Dave Winfield	.10	.02
❑ 511	Joel Davis	.05	.01
❑ 512	Alex Trevino	.05	.01
❑ 513	Tim Flannery	.05	.01
❑ 514	Pat Sheridan	.05	.01
❑ 515	Juan Nieves	.05	.01
❑ 516	Jim Sundberg	.10	.02
❑ 517	Ron Robinson	.05	.01
❑ 518	Greg Gross	.05	.01
❑ 519	Harold Reynolds Phil Bradley TL	.05	.01
❑ 520	Dave Smith	.05	.01
❑ 521	Jim Dwyer	.05	.01
❑ 522	Bob Patterson	.05	.01
❑ 523	Gary Roenicke	.05	.01
❑ 524	Gary Lucas	.05	.01
❑ 525	Marty Barrett	.05	.01
❑ 526	Juan Berenguer	.05	.01
❑ 527	Steve Henderson	.05	.01
❑ 528A	Checklist 397-528 ERR (455 S. Carlton)	.15	.05
❑ 528B	Checklist 397-528 COR (455 S. Hillegas)	.10	.02
❑ 529	Tim Burke	.05	.01
❑ 530	Gary Carter	.10	.02
❑ 531	Rich Yett	.05	.01
❑ 532	Mike Kingery	.05	.01
❑ 533	John Farrell RC	.10	.02
❑ 534	John Wathan MG	.05	.01
❑ 535	Ron Guidry	.10	.02
❑ 536	John Morris	.05	.01
❑ 537	Steve Buechele	.05	.01
❑ 538	Bill Wegman	.05	.01
❑ 539	Mike LaValliere	.05	.01
❑ 540	Bret Saberhagen	.10	.02
❑ 541	Juan Beniquez	.05	.01
❑ 542	Paul Noce	.05	.01
❑ 543	Kent Tekulve	.05	.01
❑ 544	Jim Traber	.05	.01
❑ 545	Don Baylor	.10	.02
❑ 546	John Candelaria	.05	.01
❑ 547	Felix Fermin	.05	.01
❑ 548	Shane Mack	.05	.01
❑ 549	Braves TL Albert Hall& Dale Murphy& Ken Griffey	.10	.02
❑ 550	Pedro Guerrero	.10	.02
❑ 551	Terry Steinbach	.10	.02
❑ 552	Mark Thurmond	.05	.01
❑ 553	Tracy Jones	.05	.01
❑ 554	Mike Smithson	.05	.01
❑ 555	Brook Jacoby	.05	.01
❑ 556	Stan Clarke	.05	.01
❑ 557	Craig Reynolds	.05	.01
❑ 558	Bob Ojeda	.05	.01
❑ 559	Ken Williams	.05	.01
❑ 560	Tim Wallach	.05	.01
❑ 561	Rick Cerone	.05	.01

❑ 562 Jim Lindeman .05 .01
❑ 563 Jose Guzman .05 .01
❑ 564 Frank Lucchesi MG .05 .01
❑ 565 Lloyd Moseby .05 .01
❑ 566 Charlie O'Brien .05 .01
❑ 567 Mike Diaz .05 .01
❑ 568 Chris Brown .05 .01
❑ 569 Charlie Leibrandt .05 .01
❑ 570 Jeffrey Leonard .05 .01
❑ 571 Mark Williamson .05 .01
❑ 572 Chris James .05 .01
❑ 573 Bob Stanley .05 .01
❑ 574 Graig Nettles .10 .02
❑ 575 Don Sutton .10 .02
❑ 576 Tommy Hinzo .05 .01
❑ 577 Tom Browning .05 .01
❑ 578 Gary Gaetti .10 .02
❑ 579 Gary Carter
Kevin McReynolds TL .05 .01
❑ 580 Mark McGwire 1.50 .60
❑ 581 Tito Landrum .05 .01
❑ 582 Mike Henneman RC* .25 .08
❑ 583 Dave Valle .05 .01
❑ 584 Steve Trout .05 .01
❑ 585 Ozzie Guillen .10 .02
❑ 586 Bob Forsch .05 .01
❑ 587 Terry Puhl .05 .01
❑ 588 Jeff Parrett .05 .01
❑ 589 Geno Petralli .05 .01
❑ 590 George Bell .10 .02
❑ 591 Doug Drabek .05 .01
❑ 592 Dale Sveum .05 .01
❑ 593 Bob Tewksbury .05 .01
❑ 594 Bobby Valentine MG .10 .02
❑ 595 Frank White .10 .02
❑ 596 John Kruk .10 .02
❑ 597 Gene Garber .05 .01
❑ 598 Lee Lacy .05 .01
❑ 599 Calvin Schiraldi .05 .01
❑ 600 Mike Schmidt .50 .20
❑ 601 Jack Lazorko .05 .01
❑ 602 Mike Aldrete .05 .01
❑ 603 Rob Murphy .05 .01
❑ 604 Chris Bando .05 .01
❑ 605 Kirk Gibson .20 .07
❑ 606 Moose Haas .05 .01
❑ 607 Mickey Hatcher .05 .01
❑ 608 Charlie Kerfeld .05 .01
❑ 609 Gary Gaetti
Kent Hrbek TL .10 .02
❑ 610 Keith Hernandez .10 .02
❑ 611 Tommy John .10 .02
❑ 612 Curt Ford .05 .01
❑ 613 Bobby Thigpen .05 .01
❑ 614 Herm Winningham .05 .01
❑ 615 Jody Davis .05 .01
❑ 616 Jay Aldrich .05 .01
❑ 617 Oddibe McDowell .05 .01
❑ 618 Cecil Fielder .10 .02
❑ 619 Mike Dunne
(Inconsistent design&
black name on f .05 .01
❑ 620 Cory Snyder .05 .01
❑ 621 Gene Nelson .05 .01
❑ 622 Kal Daniels .05 .01
❑ 623 Mike Flanagan .05 .01
❑ 624 Jim Leyland MG .10 .02
❑ 625 Frank Viola .10 .02
❑ 626 Glenn Wilson .05 .01
❑ 627 Joe Boever .05 .01
❑ 628 Dave Henderson .05 .01
❑ 629 Kelly Downs .05 .01
❑ 630 Darrell Evans .10 .02
❑ 631 Jack Howell .05 .01
❑ 632 Steve Shields .05 .01
❑ 633 Barry Lyons .05 .01
❑ 634 Jose DeLeon .05 .01
❑ 635 Terry Pendleton .10 .02
❑ 636 Charles Hudson .05 .01
❑ 637 Jay Bell RC .40 .15
❑ 638 Steve Balboni .05 .01
❑ 639 Glenn Braggs
Tony Muser CO TL .05 .01
❑ 640 Garry Templeton
(Inconsistent design&
green bord .10 .02

❑ 641 Rick Honeycutt .05 .01
❑ 642 Bob Dernier .05 .01
❑ 643 Rocky Childress .05 .01
❑ 644 Terry McGriff .05 .01
❑ 645 Matt Nokes RC* .25 .08
❑ 646 Checklist 529-660 .05 .01
❑ 647 Pascual Perez .05 .01
❑ 648 Al Newman .05 .01
❑ 649 DeWayne Buice .05 .01
❑ 650 Cal Ripken .75 .30
❑ 651 Mike Jackson RC* .25 .08
❑ 652 Bruce Benedict .05 .01
❑ 653 Jeff Sellers .05 .01
❑ 654 Roger Craig MG .10 .02
❑ 655 Len Dykstra .10 .02
❑ 656 Lee Guetterman .05 .01
❑ 657 Gary Redus .05 .01
❑ 658 Tim Conroy
(Inconsistent design,
name in white) .05 .01
❑ 659 Bobby Meacham .05 .01
❑ 660 Rick Reuschel .10 .02
❑ 661 Nolan Ryan TBC .50 .20
❑ 662 Jim Rice TBC .05 .01
❑ 663 Ron Blomberg TBC .05 .01
❑ 664 Bob Gibson TBC .25 .08
❑ 665 Stan Musial TBC .20 .07
❑ 666 Mario Soto .10 .02
❑ 667 Luis Quinones .05 .01
❑ 668 Walt Terrell .05 .01
❑ 669 Lance Parrish
Mike Ryan CO TL .05 .01
❑ 670 Dan Plesac .05 .01
❑ 671 Tim Laudner .05 .01
❑ 672 John Davis .05 .01
❑ 673 Tony Phillips .05 .01
❑ 674 Mike Fitzgerald .05 .01
❑ 675 Jim Rice .10 .02
❑ 676 Ken Dixon .05 .01
❑ 677 Eddie Milner .05 .01
❑ 678 Jim Acker .05 .01
❑ 679 Darrell Miller .05 .01
❑ 680 Charlie Hough .10 .02
❑ 681 Bobby Bonilla .10 .02
❑ 682 Jimmy Key .10 .02
❑ 683 Julio Franco .10 .02
❑ 684 Hal Lanier MG .05 .01
❑ 685 Ron Darling .10 .02
❑ 686 Terry Francona .10 .02
❑ 687 Mickey Brantley .05 .01
❑ 688 Jim Winn .05 .01
❑ 689 Tom Pagnozzi RC .10 .02
❑ 690 Jay Howell .05 .01
❑ 691 Dan Pasqua .05 .01
❑ 692 Mike Birkbeck .05 .01
❑ 693 Benito Santiago .10 .02
❑ 694 Eric Nolte .05 .01
❑ 695 Shawon Dunston .05 .01
❑ 696 Duane Ward .05 .01
❑ 697 Steve Lombardozzi .05 .01
❑ 698 Brad Havens .05 .01
❑ 699 B.Santiago/T.Gwynn TL .10 .02
❑ 700 George Brett .50 .20
❑ 701 Sammy Stewart .05 .01
❑ 702 Mike Gallego .05 .01
❑ 703 Bob Brenly .05 .01
❑ 704 Dennis Boyd .05 .01
❑ 705 Juan Samuel .05 .01
❑ 706 Rick Mahler .05 .01
❑ 707 Fred Lynn .10 .02
❑ 708 Gus Polidor .05 .01
❑ 709 George Frazier .05 .01
❑ 710 Darryl Strawberry .10 .02
❑ 711 Bill Gullickson .05 .01
❑ 712 John Moses .05 .01
❑ 713 Willie Hernandez .05 .01
❑ 714 Jim Fregosi MG .05 .01
❑ 715 Todd Worrell .05 .01
❑ 716 Lenn Sakata .05 .01
❑ 717 Jay Baller .05 .01
❑ 718 Mike Felder .05 .01
❑ 719 Denny Walling .05 .01
❑ 720 Tim Raines .10 .02
❑ 721 Pete O'Brien .05 .01
❑ 722 Manny Lee .05 .01
❑ 723 Bob Kipper .05 .01

❑ 724 Danny Tartabull .05 .01
❑ 725 Mike Boddicker .05 .01
❑ 726 Alfredo Griffin .05 .01
❑ 727 Greg Booker .05 .01
❑ 728 Andy Allanson .05 .01
❑ 729 G.Bell/F.McGriff TL .10 .02
❑ 730 John Franco .10 .02
❑ 731 Rick Schu .05 .01
❑ 732 David Palmer .05 .01
❑ 733 Spike Owen .05 .01
❑ 734 Craig Lefferts .05 .01
❑ 735 Kevin McReynolds .05 .01
❑ 736 Matt Young .05 .01
❑ 737 Butch Wynegar .05 .01
❑ 738 Scott Bankhead .05 .01
❑ 739 Daryl Boston .05 .01
❑ 740 Rick Sutcliffe .10 .02
❑ 741 Mike Easler .05 .01
❑ 742 Mark Clear .05 .01
❑ 743 Larry Herndon .05 .01
❑ 744 Whitey Herzog MG .10 .02
❑ 745 Bill Doran .05 .01
❑ 746 Gene Larkin RC* .25 .08
❑ 747 Bobby Witt .05 .01
❑ 748 Reid Nichols .05 .01
❑ 749 Mark Eichhorn .05 .01
❑ 750 Bo Jackson .20 .07
❑ 751 Jim Morrison .05 .01
❑ 752 Mark Grant .05 .01
❑ 753 Danny Heep .05 .01
❑ 754 Mike LaCoss .05 .01
❑ 755 Ozzie Virgil .05 .01
❑ 756 Mike Maddux .05 .01
❑ 757 John Marzano .05 .01
❑ 758 Eddie Williams RC .10 .02
❑ 759 M.McGwire/J.Canseco TL 1.00 .40
❑ 760 Mike Scott .10 .02
❑ 761 Tony Armas .10 .02
❑ 762 Scott Bradley .05 .01
❑ 763 Doug Sisk .05 .01
❑ 764 Greg Walker .05 .01
❑ 765 Neal Heaton .05 .01
❑ 766 Henry Cotto .05 .01
❑ 767 Jose Lind RC .25 .08
❑ 768 Dickie Noles
(Now with Tigers
on card front) .05 .01
❑ 769 Cecil Cooper .10 .02
❑ 770 Lou Whitaker .10 .02
❑ 771 Ruben Sierra .10 .02
❑ 772 Sal Butera .05 .01
❑ 773 Frank Williams .05 .01
❑ 774 Gene Mauch MG .05 .01
❑ 775 Dave Stieb .10 .02
❑ 776 Checklist 661-792 .05 .01
❑ 777 Lonnie Smith .05 .01
❑ 778A Keith Comstock ERR WL 2.00 .75
❑ 778B Keith Comstock COR
(Blue Padres) .05 .01
❑ 779 Tom Glavine RC 2.50 1.00
❑ 780 Fernando Valenzuela .10 .02
❑ 781 Keith Hughes .05 .01
❑ 782 Jeff Ballard .05 .01
❑ 783 Ron Roenicke .05 .01
❑ 784 Joe Sambito .05 .01
❑ 785 Alvin Davis .05 .01
❑ 786 Joe Price
(Inconsistent design&
orange team name .05 .01
❑ 787 Bill Almon .05 .01
❑ 788 Ray Searage .05 .01
❑ 789 Joe Carter TL .05 .01
❑ 790 Dave Righetti .10 .02
❑ 791 Ted Simmons .10 .02
❑ 792 John Tudor .10 .02

1989 Topps

❑ COMPLETE SET (792) 20.00 8.00
❑ COMP.FACT SET (792) 25.00 10.00
❑ COMP.X-MAS.SET (792) 25.00 10.00
❑ FS SUBSET VARIATIONS EXIST
❑ FS PHOTOS ARE PLACED HIGHER/LOWER
❑ 1 George Bell RB .05 .01
❑ 2 Wade Boggs RB .10 .02
❑ 3 Gary Carter RB .05 .01
❑ 4 Andre Dawson RB .05 .01

❑ 5 Orel Hershiser RB .05 .01
❑ 6 Doug Jones RB UER .05 .01
❑ 7 Kevin McReynolds RB .05 .01
❑ 8 Dave Eiland .05 .01
❑ 9 Tim Teufel .05 .01
❑ 10 Andre Dawson .10 .02
❑ 11 Bruce Sutter .10 .02
❑ 12 Dale Sveum .05 .01
❑ 13 Doug Sisk .05 .01
❑ 14 Tom Kelly MG .05 .01
❑ 15 Robby Thompson .05 .01
❑ 16 Ron Robinson .05 .01
❑ 17 Brian Downing .10 .02
❑ 18 Rick Rhoden .05 .01
❑ 19 Greg Gagne .05 .01
❑ 20 Steve Bedrosian .05 .01
❑ 21 Greg Walker TL .05 .01
❑ 22 Tim Crews .05 .01
❑ 23 Mike Fitzgerald .05 .01
❑ 24 Larry Andersen .05 .01
❑ 25 Frank White .10 .02
❑ 26 Dale Mohorcic .05 .01
❑ 27A Orestes Destrade RC * .10 .02
❑ 27B Orestes Destrade VAR .10 .02
❑ 28 Mike Moore .05 .01
❑ 29 Kelly Gruber .05 .01
❑ 30 Dwight Gooden .10 .02
❑ 31 Terry Francona .10 .02
❑ 32 Dennis Rasmussen .05 .01
❑ 33 B.J. Surhoff .10 .02
❑ 34 Ken Williams .05 .01
❑ 35 John Tudor UER
(With Red Sox in '84,should be Pir .10 .02
❑ 36 Mitch Webster .05 .01
❑ 37 Bob Stanley .05 .01
❑ 38 Paul Runge .05 .01
❑ 39 Mike Maddux .05 .01
❑ 40 Steve Sax .05 .01
❑ 41 Terry Mulholland .05 .01
❑ 42 Jim Eppard .05 .01
❑ 43 Guillermo Hernandez .05 .01
❑ 44 Jim Snyder MG .05 .01
❑ 45 Kal Daniels .05 .01
❑ 46 Mark Portugal .05 .01
❑ 47 Carney Lansford .10 .02
❑ 48 Tim Burke .05 .01
❑ 49 Craig Biggio RC 3.00 1.25
❑ 50 George Bell .10 .02
❑ 51 Mark McLemore TL .05 .01
❑ 52 Bob Brenly .05 .01
❑ 53 Ruben Sierra .10 .02
❑ 54 Steve Trout .05 .01
❑ 55 Julio Franco .10 .02
❑ 56 Pat Tabler .05 .01
❑ 57 Alejandro Pena .05 .01
❑ 58 Lee Mazzilli .10 .02
❑ 59 Mark Davis .05 .01
❑ 60 Tom Brunansky .05 .01
❑ 61 Neil Allen .05 .01
❑ 62 Alfredo Griffin .05 .01
❑ 63 Mark Clear .05 .01
❑ 64 Alex Trevino .05 .01
❑ 65 Rick Reuschel .10 .02
❑ 66 Manny Trillo .05 .01
❑ 67 Dave Palmer .05 .01
❑ 68 Darrell Miller .05 .01
❑ 69 Jeff Ballard .05 .01
❑ 70 Mark McGwire 1.00 .40
❑ 71 Mike Boddicker .05 .01
❑ 72 John Moses .05 .01
❑ 73 Pascual Perez .05 .01
❑ 74 Nick Leyva MG .05 .01
❑ 75 Tom Henke .05 .01
❑ 76 Terry Blocker .05 .01
❑ 77 Doyle Alexander .05 .01
❑ 78 Jim Sundberg .10 .02
❑ 79 Scott Bankhead .05 .01
❑ 80 Cory Snyder .05 .01
❑ 81 Tim Raines TL .05 .01
❑ 82 Dave Leiper .05 .01
❑ 83 Jeff Blauser .05 .01
❑ 84 Bill Bene FDP .05 .01
❑ 85 Kevin McReynolds .05 .01
❑ 86 Al Nipper .05 .01
❑ 87 Larry Owen .05 .01
❑ 88 Darryl Hamilton RC * .25 .08
❑ 89 Dave LaPoint .05 .01
❑ 90 Vince Coleman UER
(Wrong birth year) .05 .01
❑ 91 Floyd Youmans .05 .01
❑ 92 Jeff Kunkel .05 .01
❑ 93 Ken Howell .05 .01
❑ 94 Chris Speier .05 .01
❑ 95 Gerald Young .05 .01
❑ 96 Rick Cerone .05 .01
❑ 97 Greg Mathews .05 .01
❑ 98 Larry Sheets .05 .01
❑ 99 Sherman Corbett .05 .01
❑ 100 Mike Schmidt .50 .20
❑ 101 Les Straker .05 .01
❑ 102 Mike Gallego .05 .01
❑ 103 Tim Birtsas .05 .01
❑ 104 Dallas Green MG .05 .01
❑ 105 Ron Darling .10 .02
❑ 106 Willie Upshaw .05 .01
❑ 107 Jose DeLeon .05 .01
❑ 108 Fred Manrique .05 .01
❑ 109 Hipolito Pena .05 .01
❑ 110 Paul Molitor .10 .02
❑ 111 Eric Davis TL .05 .01
❑ 112 Jim Presley .05 .01
❑ 113 Lloyd Moseby .05 .01
❑ 114 Bob Kipper .05 .01
❑ 115 Jody Davis .05 .01
❑ 116 Jeff Montgomery .05 .01
❑ 117 Dave Anderson .05 .01
❑ 118 Checklist 1-132 .05 .01
❑ 119 Terry Puhl .05 .01
❑ 120 Frank Viola .10 .02
❑ 121 Garry Templeton .10 .02
❑ 122 Lance Johnson .05 .01
❑ 123 Spike Owen .05 .01
❑ 124 Jim Traber .05 .01
❑ 125 Mike Krukow .05 .01
❑ 126 Sid Bream .05 .01
❑ 127 Walt Terrell .05 .01
❑ 128 Milt Thompson .05 .01
❑ 129 Terry Clark .05 .01
❑ 130 Gerald Perry .05 .01
❑ 131 Dave Otto .05 .01
❑ 132 Curt Ford .05 .01
❑ 133 Bill Long .05 .01
❑ 134 Don Zimmer MG .10 .02
❑ 135 Jose Rijo .10 .02
❑ 136 Joey Meyer .05 .01
❑ 137 Geno Petralli .05 .01
❑ 138 Wallace Johnson .05 .01
❑ 139 Mike Flanagan .05 .01
❑ 140 Shawon Dunston .05 .01
❑ 141 Brook Jacoby TL .05 .01
❑ 142 Mike Diaz .05 .01
❑ 143 Mike Campbell .05 .01
❑ 144 Jay Bell .10 .02
❑ 145 Dave Stewart .10 .02
❑ 146 Gary Pettis .05 .01
❑ 147 DeWayne Buice .05 .01
❑ 148 Bill Pecota .05 .01
❑ 149 Doug Dascenzo .05 .01
❑ 150 Fernando Valenzuela .10 .02
❑ 151 Terry McGriff .05 .01
❑ 152 Mark Thurmond .05 .01
❑ 153 Jim Pankovits .05 .01
❑ 154 Don Carman .05 .01
❑ 155 Marty Barrett .05 .01
❑ 156 Dave Gallagher .05 .01
❑ 157 Tom Glavine .25 .08
❑ 158 Mike Aldrete .05 .01
❑ 159 Pat Clements .05 .01
❑ 160 Jeffrey Leonard .05 .01
❑ 161 Gregg Olson UER RC .25 .08
❑ 162 John Davis .05 .01
❑ 163 Bob Forsch .05 .01
❑ 164 Hal Lanier MG .05 .01
❑ 165 Mike Dunne .05 .01
❑ 166 Doug Jennings .05 .01
❑ 167 Steve Searcy FS .05 .01
❑ 168 Willie Wilson .10 .02
❑ 169 Mike Jackson .05 .01
❑ 170 Tony Fernandez .05 .01
❑ 171 Andres Thomas TL .05 .01
❑ 172 Frank Williams .05 .01
❑ 173 Mel Hall .05 .01
❑ 174 Todd Burns .05 .01
❑ 175 John Shelby .05 .01
❑ 176 Jeff Parrett .05 .01
❑ 177 Monty Fariss FDP .05 .01
❑ 178 Mark Grant .05 .01
❑ 179 Ozzie Virgil .05 .01
❑ 180 Mike Scott .10 .02
❑ 181 Craig Worthington .05 .01
❑ 182 Bob McClure .05 .01
❑ 183 Oddibe McDowell .05 .01
❑ 184 John Costello .05 .01
❑ 185 Claudell Washington .05 .01
❑ 186 Pat Perry .05 .01
❑ 187 Darren Daulton .10 .02
❑ 188 Dennis Lamp .05 .01
❑ 189 Kevin Mitchell .10 .02
❑ 190 Mike Witt .05 .01
❑ 191 Sil Campusano .05 .01
❑ 192 Paul Mirabella .05 .01
❑ 193 Sparky Anderson MG
(Team checklist back)
UER (55 .10 .02
❑ 194 Greg W.Harris RC .10 .02
❑ 195 Ozzie Guillen .10 .02
❑ 196 Denny Walling .05 .01
❑ 197 Neal Heaton .05 .01
❑ 198 Danny Heep .05 .01
❑ 199 Mike Schooler RC * .10 .02
❑ 200 George Brett .60 .25
❑ 201 Kelly Gruber TL .05 .01
❑ 202 Brad Moore .05 .01
❑ 203 Rob Ducey .05 .01
❑ 204 Brad Havens .05 .01
❑ 205 Dwight Evans .15 .05
❑ 206 Roberto Alomar .25 .08
❑ 207 Terry Leach .05 .01
❑ 208 Tom Pagnozzi .05 .01
❑ 209 Jeff Bittiger .05 .01
❑ 210 Dale Murphy .15 .05
❑ 211 Mike Pagliarulo .05 .01
❑ 212 Scott Sanderson .05 .01
❑ 213 Rene Gonzales .05 .01
❑ 214 Charlie O'Brien .05 .01
❑ 215 Kevin Gross .05 .01
❑ 216 Jack Howell .05 .01
❑ 217 Joe Price .05 .01
❑ 218 Mike LaValliere .05 .01
❑ 219 Jim Clancy .05 .01
❑ 220 Gary Gaetti .10 .02
❑ 221 Cecil Espy .05 .01
❑ 222 Mark Lewis RC .25 .08
❑ 223 Jay Buhner .10 .02
❑ 224 Tony LaRussa MG .10 .02
❑ 225 Ramon Martinez RC .25 .08
❑ 226 Bill Doran .05 .01
❑ 227 John Farrell .05 .01
❑ 228 Nelson Santovenia .05 .01
❑ 229 Jimmy Key .10 .02
❑ 230 Ozzie Smith .40 .15
❑ 231 Padres TL/R.Alomar .25 .08
❑ 232 Ricky Horton .05 .01
❑ 233 Gregg Jefferies .05 .01
❑ 234 Tom Browning .05 .01
❑ 235 John Kruk .10 .02
❑ 236 Charles Hudson .05 .01
❑ 237 Glenn Hubbard .05 .01
❑ 238 Eric King .05 .01
❑ 239 Tim Laudner .05 .01

❑	240	Greg Maddux	.50	.20
❑	241	Brett Butler	.10	.02
❑	242	Ed VandeBerg	.05	.01
❑	243	Bob Boone	.10	.02
❑	244	Jim Acker	.05	.01
❑	245	Jim Rice	.10	.02
❑	246	Rey Quinones	.05	.01
❑	247	Shawn Hillegas	.05	.01
❑	248	Tony Phillips	.05	.01
❑	249	Tim Leary	.05	.01
❑	250	Cal Ripken	.75	.30
❑	251	John Dopson	.05	.01
❑	252	Billy Hatcher	.05	.01
❑	253	Jose Alvarez RC	.10	.02
❑	254	Tom Lasorda MG	.15	.05
❑	255	Ron Guidry	.10	.02
❑	256	Benny Santiago	.10	.02
❑	257	Rick Aguilera	.05	.01
❑	258	Checklist 133-264	.05	.01
❑	259	Larry McWilliams	.05	.01
❑	260	Dave Winfield	.10	.02
❑	261	St.Louis Cardinals TL Tom Brunansky (With Luis A	.05	.01
❑	262	Jeff Pico	.05	.01
❑	263	Mike Felder	.05	.01
❑	264	Rob Dibble RC	.40	.15
❑	265	Kent Hrbek	.10	.02
❑	266	Luis Aquino	.05	.01
❑	267	Jeff M. Robinson	.05	.01
❑	268	Keith Miller RC	.25	.08
❑	269	Tom Bolton	.05	.01
❑	270	Wally Joyner	.10	.02
❑	271	Jay Tibbs	.05	.01
❑	272	Ron Hassey	.05	.01
❑	273	Jose Lind	.05	.01
❑	274	Mark Eichhorn	.05	.01
❑	275	Danny Tartabull UER (Born San Juan& PR should be	.05	.01
❑	276	Paul Kilgus	.05	.01
❑	277	Mike Davis	.05	.01
❑	278	Andy McGaffigan	.05	.01
❑	279	Scott Bradley	.05	.01
❑	280	Bob Knepper	.05	.01
❑	281	Gary Redus	.05	.01
❑	282	Cris Carpenter RC *	.10	.02
❑	283	Andy Allanson	.05	.01
❑	284	Jim Leyland MG	.10	.02
❑	285	John Candelaria	.05	.01
❑	286	Darrin Jackson	.10	.02
❑	287	Juan Nieves	.05	.01
❑	288	Pat Sheridan	.05	.01
❑	289	Ernie Whitt	.05	.01
❑	290	John Franco	.10	.02
❑	291	New York Mets TL Darryl Strawberry (With Keith H	.05	.01
❑	292	Jim Corsi	.05	.01
❑	293	Glenn Wilson	.05	.01
❑	294	Juan Berenguer	.05	.01
❑	295	Scott Fletcher	.05	.01
❑	296	Ron Gant	.10	.02
❑	297	Oswald Peraza	.05	.01
❑	298	Chris James	.05	.01
❑	299	Steve Ellsworth	.05	.01
❑	300	Darryl Strawberry	.10	.02
❑	301	Charlie Leibrandt	.05	.01
❑	302	Gary Ward	.05	.01
❑	303	Felix Fermin	.05	.01
❑	304	Joel Youngblood	.05	.01
❑	305	Dave Smith	.05	.01
❑	306	Tracy Woodson	.05	.01
❑	307	Lance McCullers	.05	.01
❑	308	Ron Karkovice	.05	.01
❑	309	Mario Diaz	.05	.01
❑	310	Rafael Palmeiro	.25	.08
❑	311	Chris Bosio	.05	.01
❑	312	Tom Lawless	.05	.01
❑	313	Dennis Martinez	.10	.02
❑	314	Bobby Valentine MG	.10	.02
❑	315	Greg Swindell	.05	.01
❑	316	Walt Weiss	.05	.01
❑	317	Jack Armstrong RC *	.25	.08
❑	318	Gene Larkin	.05	.01
❑	319	Greg Booker	.05	.01
❑	320	Lou Whitaker	.10	.02
❑	321	Jody Reed TL	.05	.01
❑	322	John Smiley	.05	.01
❑	323	Gary Thurman	.05	.01
❑	324	Bob Milacki	.05	.01
❑	325	Jesse Barfield	.10	.02
❑	326	Dennis Boyd	.05	.01
❑	327	Mark Lemke RC	.40	.15
❑	328	Rick Honeycutt	.05	.01
❑	329	Bob Melvin	.05	.01
❑	330	Eric Davis	.10	.02
❑	331	Curt Wilkerson	.05	.01
❑	332	Tony Armas	.10	.02
❑	333	Bob Ojeda	.05	.01
❑	334	Steve Lyons	.05	.01
❑	335	Dave Righetti	.10	.02
❑	336	Steve Balboni	.05	.01
❑	337	Calvin Schiraldi	.05	.01
❑	338	Jim Adduci	.05	.01
❑	339	Scott Bailes	.05	.01
❑	340	Kirk Gibson	.10	.02
❑	341	Jim Deshaies	.05	.01
❑	342	Tom Brookens	.05	.01
❑	343	Gary Sheffield RC	1.50	.60
❑	344	Tom Trebelhorn MG	.05	.01
❑	345	Charlie Hough	.10	.02
❑	346	Rex Hudler	.05	.01
❑	347	John Cerutti	.05	.01
❑	348	Ed Hearn	.05	.01
❑	349	Ron Jones	.10	.02
❑	350	Andy Van Slyke	.15	.05
❑	351	San Fran. Giants TL Bob Melvin (With Bill Fahey	.05	.01
❑	352	Rick Schu	.05	.01
❑	353	Marvell Wynne	.05	.01
❑	354	Larry Parrish	.05	.01
❑	355	Mark Langston	.05	.01
❑	356	Kevin Elster	.05	.01
❑	357	Jerry Reuss	.05	.01
❑	358	Ricky Jordan RC *	.25	.08
❑	359	Tommy John	.10	.02
❑	360	Ryne Sandberg	.40	.15
❑	361	Kelly Downs	.05	.01
❑	362	Jack Lazorko	.05	.01
❑	363	Rich Yett	.05	.01
❑	364	Rob Deer	.05	.01
❑	365	Mike Henneman	.05	.01
❑	366	Herm Winningham	.05	.01
❑	367	Johnny Paredes	.05	.01
❑	368	Brian Holton	.05	.01
❑	369	Ken Caminiti	.15	.05
❑	370	Dennis Eckersley	.15	.05
❑	371	Manny Lee	.05	.01
❑	372	Craig Lefferts	.05	.01
❑	373	Tracy Jones	.05	.01
❑	374	John Wathan MG	.05	.01
❑	375	Terry Pendleton	.10	.02
❑	376	Steve Lombardozzi	.05	.01
❑	377	Mike Smithson	.05	.01
❑	378	Checklist 265-396	.05	.01
❑	379	Tim Flannery	.05	.01
❑	380	Rickey Henderson	.25	.08
❑	381	Larry Sheets TL	.05	.01
❑	382	John Smoltz RC	1.50	.60
❑	383	Howard Johnson	.10	.02
❑	384	Mark Salas	.05	.01
❑	385	Von Hayes	.05	.01
❑	386	Andres Galarraga AS	.05	.01
❑	387	Ryne Sandberg AS	.25	.08
❑	388	Bobby Bonilla AS	.05	.01
❑	389	Ozzie Smith AS	.25	.08
❑	390	Darryl Strawberry AS	.05	.01
❑	391	Andre Dawson AS	.05	.01
❑	392	Andy Van Slyke AS	.10	.02
❑	393	Gary Carter AS	.05	.01
❑	394	Orel Hershiser AS	.05	.01
❑	395	Danny Jackson AS	.05	.01
❑	396	Kirk Gibson AS	.10	.02
❑	397	Don Mattingly AS	.30	.10
❑	398	Julio Franco AS	.05	.01
❑	399	Wade Boggs AS	.10	.02
❑	400	Alan Trammell AS	.05	.01
❑	401	Jose Canseco AS	.15	.05
❑	402	Mike Greenwell AS	.05	.01
❑	403	Kirby Puckett AS	.15	.05
❑	404	Bob Boone AS	.05	.01
❑	405	Roger Clemens AS	.50	.20
❑	406	Frank Viola AS	.05	.01
❑	407	Dave Winfield AS	.05	.01
❑	408	Greg Walker	.05	.01
❑	409	Ken Dayley	.05	.01
❑	410	Jack Clark	.10	.02
❑	411	Mitch Williams	.05	.01
❑	412	Barry Lyons	.05	.01
❑	413	Mike Kingery	.05	.01
❑	414	Jim Fregosi MG	.05	.01
❑	415	Rich Gossage	.10	.02
❑	416	Fred Lynn	.10	.02
❑	417	Mike LaCoss	.05	.01
❑	418	Bob Dernier	.05	.01
❑	419	Tom Filer	.05	.01
❑	420	Joe Carter	.10	.02
❑	421	Kirk McCaskill	.05	.01
❑	422	Bo Diaz	.05	.01
❑	423	Brian Fisher	.05	.01
❑	424	Luis Polonia UER (Wrong birthdate)	.05	.01
❑	425	Jay Howell	.05	.01
❑	426	Dan Gladden	.05	.01
❑	427	Eric Show	.05	.01
❑	428	Craig Reynolds	.05	.01
❑	429	Minnesota Twins TL Greg Gagne (Taking throw at 2	.05	.01
❑	430	Mark Gubicza	.05	.01
❑	431	Luis Rivera	.05	.01
❑	432	Chad Kreuter RC	.25	.08
❑	433	Albert Hall	.05	.01
❑	434	Ken Patterson	.05	.01
❑	435	Len Dykstra	.10	.02
❑	436	Bobby Meacham	.05	.01
❑	437	Andy Benes RC *	.40	.15
❑	438	Greg Gross	.05	.01
❑	439	Frank DiPino	.05	.01
❑	440	Bobby Bonilla	.10	.02
❑	441	Jerry Reed	.05	.01
❑	442	Jose Oquendo	.05	.01
❑	443	Rod Nichols	.05	.01
❑	444	Moose Stubing MG	.05	.01
❑	445	Matt Nokes	.05	.01
❑	446	Rob Murphy	.05	.01
❑	447	Donell Nixon	.05	.01
❑	448	Eric Plunk	.05	.01
❑	449	Carmelo Martinez	.05	.01
❑	450	Roger Clemens	1.00	.40
❑	451	Mark Davidson	.05	.01
❑	452	Israel Sanchez	.05	.01
❑	453	Tom Prince	.05	.01
❑	454	Paul Assenmacher	.05	.01
❑	455	Johnny Ray	.05	.01
❑	456	Tim Belcher	.05	.01
❑	457	Mackey Sasser	.05	.01
❑	458	Donn Pall	.05	.01
❑	459	Dave Valle TL	.05	.01
❑	460	Dave Stieb	.10	.02
❑	461	Buddy Bell	.10	.02
❑	462	Jose Guzman	.05	.01
❑	463	Steve Lake	.05	.01
❑	464	Bryn Smith	.05	.01
❑	465	Mark Grace	.25	.08
❑	466	Chuck Crim	.05	.01
❑	467	Jim Walewander	.05	.01
❑	468	Henry Cotto	.05	.01
❑	469	Jose Bautista RC	.10	.02
❑	470	Lance Parrish	.10	.02
❑	471	Steve Curry	.05	.01
❑	472	Brian Harper	.05	.01
❑	473	Don Robinson	.05	.01
❑	474	Bob Rodgers MG	.05	.01
❑	475	Dave Parker	.10	.02
❑	476	Jon Perlman	.05	.01
❑	477	Dick Schofield	.05	.01
❑	478	Doug Drabek	.05	.01
❑	479	Mike Macfarlane RC *	.25	.08
❑	480	Keith Hernandez	.10	.02
❑	481	Chris Brown	.05	.01
❑	482	Steve Peters	.05	.01
❑	483	Mickey Hatcher	.05	.01
❑	484	Steve Shields	.05	.01
❑	485	Hubie Brooks	.05	.01
❑	486	Jack McDowell	.10	.02

❑ 487 Scott Lusader .05 .01
❑ 488 Kevin Coffman
(%%Now with Cubs~) .05 .01
❑ 489 Phillies TL/M.Schmidt .15 .05
❑ 490 Chris Sabo RC * .40 .15
❑ 491 Mike Birkbeck .05 .01
❑ 492 Alan Ashby .05 .01
❑ 493 Todd Benzinger .05 .01
❑ 494 Shane Rawley .05 .01
❑ 495 Candy Maldonado .05 .01
❑ 496 Dwayne Henry .05 .01
❑ 497 Pete Stanicek .05 .01
❑ 498 Dave Valle .05 .01
❑ 499 Don Heinkel .05 .01
❑ 500 Jose Canseco .25 .08
❑ 501 Vance Law .05 .01
❑ 502 Duane Ward .05 .01
❑ 503 Al Newman .05 .01
❑ 504 Bob Walk .05 .01
❑ 505 Pete Rose MG/TC .50 .20
❑ 506 Kirt Manwaring .05 .01
❑ 507 Steve Farr .05 .01
❑ 508 Wally Backman .05 .01
❑ 509 Bud Black .05 .01
❑ 510 Bob Horner .10 .02
❑ 511 Richard Dotson .05 .01
❑ 512 Donnie Hill .05 .01
❑ 513 Jesse Orosco .05 .01
❑ 514 Chet Lemon .10 .02
❑ 515 Barry Larkin .15 .05
❑ 516 Eddie Whitson .05 .01
❑ 517 Greg Brock .05 .01
❑ 518 Bruce Ruffin .05 .01
❑ 519 Willie Randolph TL .05 .01
❑ 520 Rick Sutcliffe .10 .02
❑ 521 Mickey Tettleton .05 .01
❑ 522 Randy Kramer .05 .01
❑ 523 Andres Thomas .05 .01
❑ 524 Checklist 397-528 .05 .01
❑ 525 Chili Davis .10 .02
❑ 526 Wes Gardner .05 .01
❑ 527 Dave Henderson .05 .01
❑ 528 Luis Medina
(Lower left front
has white triangle .05 .01
❑ 529 Tom Foley .05 .01
❑ 530 Nolan Ryan 1.00 .40
❑ 531 Dave Hengel .05 .01
❑ 532 Jerry Browne .05 .01
❑ 533 Andy Hawkins .05 .01
❑ 534 Doc Edwards MG .05 .01
❑ 535 Todd Worrell UER
(4 wins in '88&
should be 5) .05 .01
❑ 536 Joel Skinner .05 .01
❑ 537 Pete Smith .05 .01
❑ 538 Juan Castillo .05 .01
❑ 539 Barry Jones .05 .01
❑ 540 Bo Jackson .25 .08
❑ 541 Cecil Fielder .10 .02
❑ 542 Todd Frohwirth .05 .01
❑ 543 Damon Berryhill .05 .01
❑ 544 Jeff Sellers .05 .01
❑ 545 Mookie Wilson .10 .02
❑ 546 Mark Williamson .05 .01
❑ 547 Mark McLemore .05 .01
❑ 548 Bobby Witt .05 .01
❑ 549 Jamie Moyer TL .05 .01
❑ 550 Orel Hershiser .10 .02
❑ 551 Randy Ready .05 .01
❑ 552 Greg Cadaret .05 .01
❑ 553 Luis Salazar .05 .01
❑ 554 Nick Esasky .05 .01
❑ 555 Bert Blyleven .10 .02
❑ 556 Bruce Fields .05 .01
❑ 557 Keith A. Miller .05 .01
❑ 558 Dan Pasqua .05 .01
❑ 559 Juan Agosto .05 .01
❑ 560 Tim Raines .10 .02
❑ 561 Luis Aguayo .05 .01
❑ 562 Danny Cox .05 .01
❑ 563 Bill Schroeder .05 .01
❑ 564 Russ Nixon MG .05 .01
❑ 565 Jeff Russell .05 .01
❑ 566 Al Pedrique .05 .01
❑ 567 David Wells UER .10 .02
❑ 568 Mickey Brantley .05 .01
❑ 569 German Jimenez .05 .01
❑ 570 Tony Gwynn .30 .10
❑ 571 Billy Ripken .05 .01
❑ 572 Atlee Hammaker .05 .01
❑ 573 Jim Abbott RC 1.00 .40
❑ 574 Dave Clark .05 .01
❑ 575 Juan Samuel .05 .01
❑ 576 Greg Minton .05 .01
❑ 577 Randy Bush .05 .01
❑ 578 John Morris .05 .01
❑ 579 Glenn Davis TL .05 .01
❑ 580 Harold Reynolds .10 .02
❑ 581 Gene Nelson .05 .01
❑ 582 Mike Marshall .05 .01
❑ 583 Paul Gibson .05 .01
❑ 584 Randy Velarde UER
(Signed 1935&
should be 1985) .05 .01
❑ 585 Harold Baines .10 .02
❑ 586 Joe Boever .05 .01
❑ 587 Mike Stanley .05 .01
❑ 588 Luis Alicea RC * .25 .08
❑ 589 Dave Meads .05 .01
❑ 590 Andres Galarraga .10 .02
❑ 591 Jeff Musselman .05 .01
❑ 592 John Cangelosi .05 .01
❑ 593 Drew Hall .05 .01
❑ 594 Jimy Williams MG .05 .01
❑ 595 Teddy Higuera .05 .01
❑ 596 Kurt Stillwell .05 .01
❑ 597 Terry Taylor RC .10 .02
❑ 598 Ken Gerhart .05 .01
❑ 599 Tom Candiotti .05 .01
❑ 600 Wade Boggs .15 .05
❑ 601 Dave Dravecky .05 .01
❑ 602 Devon White .10 .02
❑ 603 Frank Tanana .10 .02
❑ 604 Paul O'Neill .15 .05
❑ 605A Bob Welch ML Line ERR 10.00 4.00
❑ 605B Bob Welch COR .10 .02
❑ 606 Rick Dempsey .05 .01
❑ 607 Willie Ansley RC .10 .02
❑ 608 Phil Bradley .05 .01
❑ 609 Detroit Tigers TL
Frank Tanana
(With Alan Tramme .05 .01
❑ 610 Randy Myers .10 .02
❑ 611 Don Slaught .05 .01
❑ 612 Dan Quisenberry .05 .01
❑ 613 Gary Varsho .05 .01
❑ 614 Joe Hesketh .05 .01
❑ 615 Robin Yount .40 .15
❑ 616 Steve Rosenberg .05 .01
❑ 617 Mark Parent .05 .01
❑ 618 Rance Mulliniks .05 .01
❑ 619 Checklist 529-660 .05 .01
❑ 620 Barry Bonds 1.50 .60
❑ 621 Rick Mahler .05 .01
❑ 622 Stan Javier .05 .01
❑ 623 Fred Toliver .05 .01
❑ 624 Jack McKeon MG .10 .02
❑ 625 Eddie Murray .25 .08
❑ 626 Jeff Reed .05 .01
❑ 627 Greg A. Harris .05 .01
❑ 628 Matt Williams .25 .08
❑ 629 Pete O'Brien .05 .01
❑ 630 Mike Greenwell .05 .01
❑ 631 Dave Bergman .05 .01
❑ 632 Bryan Harvey RC * .25 .08
❑ 633 Daryl Boston .05 .01
❑ 634 Marvin Freeman .05 .01
❑ 635 Willie Randolph .10 .02
❑ 636 Bill Wilkinson .05 .01
❑ 637 Carmen Castillo .05 .01
❑ 638 Floyd Bannister .05 .01
❑ 639 Walt Weiss TL .05 .01
❑ 640 Willie McGee .10 .02
❑ 641 Curt Young .05 .01
❑ 642 Angel Salazar .05 .01
❑ 643 Louie Meadows .05 .01
❑ 644 Lloyd McClendon .05 .01
❑ 645 Jack Morris .10 .02
❑ 646 Kevin Bass .05 .01
❑ 647 Randy Johnson RC 2.00 .75
❑ 648 Sandy Alomar Jr. RC .40 .15
❑ 649 Stu Cliburn .05 .01
❑ 650 Kirby Puckett .25 .08
❑ 651 Tom Niedenfuer .05 .01
❑ 652 Rich Gedman .05 .01
❑ 653 Tommy Barrett .05 .01
❑ 654 Whitey Herzog MG .10 .02
❑ 655 Dave Magadan .05 .01
❑ 656 Ivan Calderon .05 .01
❑ 657 Joe Magrane .05 .01
❑ 658 R.J. Reynolds .05 .01
❑ 659 Al Leiter .25 .08
❑ 660 Will Clark .15 .05
❑ 661 Dwight Gooden TBC 84 .05 .01
❑ 662 Lou Brock TBC .10 .02
❑ 663 Hank Aaron TBC .25 .08
❑ 664 Gil Hodges TBC 69 .10 .02
❑ 665A T.Oliva TBC Copyright ERR
❑ 665B Tony Oliva TBC 64
COR (fabricated
card) .10 .02
❑ 666 Randy St.Claire .05 .01
❑ 667 Dwayne Murphy .05 .01
❑ 668 Mike Bielecki .05 .01
❑ 669 L.A. Dodgers TL
Orel Hershiser
(Mound conference .10 .02
❑ 670 Kevin Seitzer .05 .01
❑ 671 Jim Gantner .05 .01
❑ 672 Allan Anderson .05 .01
❑ 673 Don Baylor .10 .02
❑ 674 Otis Nixon .05 .01
❑ 675 Bruce Hurst .05 .01
❑ 676 Ernie Riles .05 .01
❑ 677 Dave Schmidt .05 .01
❑ 678 Dion James .05 .01
❑ 679 Willie Fraser .05 .01
❑ 680 Gary Carter .10 .02
❑ 681 Jeff D. Robinson .05 .01
❑ 682 Rick Leach .05 .01
❑ 683 Jose Cecena .05 .01
❑ 684 Dave Johnson MG .05 .01
❑ 685 Jeff Treadway .05 .01
❑ 686 Scott Terry .05 .01
❑ 687 Alvin Davis .05 .01
❑ 688 Zane Smith .05 .01
❑ 689A Stan Jefferson Pink ERR 10.00 4.00
❑ 689B Stan Jefferson
(Violet triangle on
front bottom .05 .01
❑ 690 Doug Jones .05 .01
❑ 691 Roberto Kelly UER .05 .01
❑ 692 Steve Ontiveros .05 .01
❑ 693 Pat Borders RC * .25 .08
❑ 694 Les Lancaster .05 .01
❑ 695 Carlton Fisk .15 .05
❑ 696 Don August .05 .01
❑ 697A Franklin Stubbs White ERR 10.00 4.00
❑ 697B Franklin Stubbs
(Team name on front
in gray) .05 .01
❑ 698 Keith Atherton .05 .01
❑ 699 Pittsburgh Pirates TL
Al Pedrique
(Tony Gwynn sl .05 .01
❑ 700 Don Mattingly .60 .25
❑ 701 Storm Davis .05 .01
❑ 702 Jamie Quirk .05 .01
❑ 703 Scott Garrelts .05 .01
❑ 704 Carlos Quintana RC .10 .02
❑ 705 Terry Kennedy .05 .01
❑ 706 Pete Incaviglia .05 .01
❑ 707 Steve Jeltz .05 .01
❑ 708 Chuck Finley .10 .02
❑ 709 Tom Herr .05 .01
❑ 710 David Cone .10 .02
❑ 711 Candy Sierra .05 .01
❑ 712 Bill Swift .05 .01
❑ 713 Ty Griffin FDP .05 .01
❑ 714 Joe Morgan MG .10 .02
❑ 715 Tony Pena .05 .01
❑ 716 Wayne Tolleson .05 .01
❑ 717 Jamie Moyer .10 .02
❑ 718 Glenn Braggs .05 .01
❑ 719 Danny Darwin .05 .01
❑ 720 Tim Wallach .05 .01
❑ 721 Ron Tingley .05 .01

❑ 722 Todd Stottlemyre	.05	.01
❑ 723 Rafael Belliard	.05	.01
❑ 724 Jerry Don Gleaton	.05	.01
❑ 725 Terry Steinbach	.10	.02
❑ 726 Dickie Thon	.05	.01
❑ 727 Joe Orsulak	.05	.01
❑ 728 Charlie Puleo	.05	.01
❑ 729 Texas Rangers TL Steve Buechele (Inconsistent de	.05	.01
❑ 730 Danny Jackson	.05	.01
❑ 731 Mike Young	.05	.01
❑ 732 Steve Buechele	.05	.01
❑ 733 Randy Bockus	.05	.01
❑ 734 Jody Reed	.05	.01
❑ 735 Roger McDowell	.05	.01
❑ 736 Jeff Hamilton	.05	.01
❑ 737 Norm Charlton RC	.25	.08
❑ 738 Darnell Coles	.05	.01
❑ 739 Brook Jacoby	.05	.01
❑ 740 Dan Plesac	.05	.01
❑ 741 Ken Phelps	.05	.01
❑ 742 Mike Harkey RC	.10	.02
❑ 743 Mike Heath	.05	.01
❑ 744 Roger Craig MG	.10	.02
❑ 745 Fred McGriff	.15	.05
❑ 746 German Gonzalez UER (Wrong birthdate)	.05	.01
❑ 747 Wil Tejada	.05	.01
❑ 748 Jimmy Jones	.05	.01
❑ 749 Rafael Ramirez	.05	.01
❑ 750 Bret Saberhagen	.10	.02
❑ 751 Ken Oberkfell	.05	.01
❑ 752 Jim Gott	.05	.01
❑ 753 Jose Uribe	.05	.01
❑ 754 Bob Brower	.05	.01
❑ 755 Mike Scioscia	.10	.02
❑ 756 Scott Medvin	.05	.01
❑ 757 Brady Anderson RC	.40	.15
❑ 758 Gene Walter	.05	.01
❑ 759 Milwaukee Brewers TL Rob Deer	.05	.01
❑ 760 Lee Smith	.10	.02
❑ 761 Dante Bichette RC	.40	.15
❑ 762 Bobby Thigpen	.05	.01
❑ 763 Dave Martinez	.05	.01
❑ 764 Robin Ventura RC	.75	.30
❑ 765 Glenn Davis	.05	.01
❑ 766 Cecilio Guante	.05	.01
❑ 767 Mike Capel	.05	.01
❑ 768 Bill Wegman	.05	.01
❑ 769 Junior Ortiz	.05	.01
❑ 770 Alan Trammell	.10	.02
❑ 771 Ron Kittle	.05	.01
❑ 772 Ron Oester	.05	.01
❑ 773 Keith Moreland	.05	.01
❑ 774 Frank Robinson MG/TC	.15	.05
❑ 775 Jeff Reardon	.10	.02
❑ 776 Nelson Liriano	.05	.01
❑ 777 Ted Power	.05	.01
❑ 778 Bruce Benedict	.05	.01
❑ 779 Craig McMurtry	.05	.01
❑ 780 Pedro Guerrero	.10	.02
❑ 781 Greg Briley	.10	.02
❑ 782 Checklist 661-792	.05	.01
❑ 783 Trevor Wilson RC	.10	.02
❑ 784 Steve Avery RC	.25	.08
❑ 785 Ellis Burks	.10	.02
❑ 786 Melido Perez	.05	.01
❑ 787 Dave West RC	.10	.02
❑ 788 Mike Morgan	.05	.01
❑ 789 Royals TL/Bo Jackson	.25	.08
❑ 790 Sid Fernandez	.05	.01
❑ 791 Jim Lindeman	.05	.01
❑ 792 Rafael Santana	.05	.01

1990 Topps

❑ COMPLETE SET (792)	20.00	8.00
❑ COMP.FACT.SET (792)	25.00	10.00
❑ COMP.X-MAS.SET (792)	40.00	15.00
❑ 1 Nolan Ryan	1.00	.40
❑ 2 Nolan Ryan Salute New York Mets	.50	.20
❑ 3 Nolan Ryan Salute California Angels	.50	.20
❑ 4 Nolan Ryan Salute Houston Astros	.50	.20
❑ 5 Nolan Ryan Salute Texas Rangers UER (Says Texas	.50	.20
❑ 6 Vince Coleman RB (50 consecutive stolen bases)	.05	.01
❑ 7 Rickey Henderson RB	.15	.05
❑ 8 Cal Ripken RB	.25	.08
❑ 9 Eric Plunk	.05	.01
❑ 10 Barry Larkin	.15	.05
❑ 11 Paul Gibson	.05	.01
❑ 12 Joe Girardi	.15	.05
❑ 13 Mark Williamson	.05	.01
❑ 14 Mike Fetters RC	.25	.08
❑ 15 Teddy Higuera	.05	.01
❑ 16 Kent Anderson	.05	.01
❑ 17 Kelly Downs	.05	.01
❑ 18 Carlos Quintana	.05	.01
❑ 19 Al Newman	.05	.01
❑ 20 Mark Gubicza	.05	.01
❑ 21 Jeff Torborg MG	.05	.01
❑ 22 Bruce Ruffin	.05	.01
❑ 23 Randy Velarde	.05	.01
❑ 24 Joe Hesketh	.05	.01
❑ 25 Willie Randolph	.10	.02
❑ 26 Don Slaught	.05	.01
❑ 27 Rick Leach	.05	.01
❑ 28 Duane Ward	.05	.01
❑ 29 John Cangelosi	.05	.01
❑ 30 David Cone	.10	.02
❑ 31 Henry Cotto	.05	.01
❑ 32 John Farrell	.05	.01
❑ 33 Greg Walker	.05	.01
❑ 34 Tony Fossas RC	.05	.01
❑ 35 Benito Santiago	.10	.02
❑ 36 John Costello	.05	.01
❑ 37 Domingo Ramos	.05	.01
❑ 38 Wes Gardner	.05	.01
❑ 39 Curt Ford	.05	.01
❑ 40 Jay Howell	.05	.01
❑ 41 Matt Williams	.10	.02
❑ 42 Jeff M. Robinson	.05	.01
❑ 43 Dante Bichette	.10	.02
❑ 44 Roger Salkeld FDP RC	.10	.02
❑ 45 Dave Parker UER	.10	.02
❑ 46 Rob Dibble	.10	.02
❑ 47 Brian Harper	.05	.01
❑ 48 Zane Smith	.05	.01
❑ 49 Tom Lawless	.05	.01
❑ 50 Glenn Davis	.05	.01
❑ 51 Doug Rader MG	.05	.01
❑ 52 Jack Daugherty RC	.05	.01
❑ 53 Mike LaCoss	.05	.01
❑ 54 Joel Skinner	.05	.01
❑ 55 Darrell Evans UER (HR total should be 414& not 4	.10	.02
❑ 56 Franklin Stubbs	.05	.01
❑ 57 Greg Vaughn	.05	.01
❑ 58 Keith Miller	.05	.01
❑ 59 Ted Power	.05	.01
❑ 60 George Brett	.60	.25
❑ 61 Deion Sanders	.25	.08
❑ 62 Ramon Martinez	.05	.01
❑ 63 Mike Pagliarulo	.05	.01
❑ 64 Danny Darwin	.05	.01
❑ 65 Devon White	.10	.02
❑ 66 Greg Litton	.05	.01
❑ 67 Scott Sanderson	.05	.01
❑ 68 Dave Henderson	.05	.01
❑ 69 Todd Frohwirth	.05	.01
❑ 70 Mike Greenwell	.05	.01
❑ 71 Allan Anderson	.05	.01
❑ 72 Jeff Huson RC	.10	.02
❑ 73 Bob Milacki	.05	.01
❑ 74 Jeff Jackson FDP RC	.10	.02
❑ 75 Doug Jones	.05	.01
❑ 76 Dave Valle	.05	.01
❑ 77 Dave Bergman	.05	.01
❑ 78 Mike Flanagan	.05	.01
❑ 79 Ron Kittle	.05	.01
❑ 80 Jeff Russell	.05	.01
❑ 81 Bob Rodgers MG	.05	.01
❑ 82 Scott Terry	.05	.01
❑ 83 Hensley Meulens	.05	.01
❑ 84 Ray Searage	.05	.01
❑ 85 Juan Samuel	.05	.01
❑ 86 Paul Kilgus	.05	.01
❑ 87 Rick Luecken RC	.05	.01
❑ 88 Glenn Braggs	.05	.01
❑ 89 Clint Zavaras RC	.05	.01
❑ 90 Jack Clark	.10	.02
❑ 91 Steve Frey RC	.05	.01
❑ 92 Mike Stanley	.05	.01
❑ 93 Shawn Hillegas	.05	.01
❑ 94 Herm Winningham	.05	.01
❑ 95 Todd Worrell	.05	.01
❑ 96 Jody Reed	.05	.01
❑ 97 Curt Schilling	1.00	.40
❑ 98 Jose Gonzalez	.05	.01
❑ 99 Rich Monteleone	.05	.01
❑ 100 Will Clark	.15	.05
❑ 101 Shane Rawley	.05	.01
❑ 102 Stan Javier	.05	.01
❑ 103 Marvin Freeman	.05	.01
❑ 104 Bob Knepper	.05	.01
❑ 105 Randy Myers	.10	.02
❑ 106 Charlie O'Brien	.05	.01
❑ 107 Fred Lynn	.05	.01
❑ 108 Rod Nichols	.05	.01
❑ 109 Roberto Kelly	.05	.01
❑ 110 Tommy Helms MG	.05	.01
❑ 111 Ed Whited RC	.05	.01
❑ 112 Glenn Wilson	.05	.01
❑ 113 Manny Lee	.05	.01
❑ 114 Mike Bielecki	.05	.01
❑ 115 Tony Pena	.05	.01
❑ 116 Floyd Bannister	.05	.01
❑ 117 Mike Sharperson	.05	.01
❑ 118 Erik Hanson	.05	.01
❑ 119 Billy Hatcher	.05	.01
❑ 120 John Franco	.10	.02
❑ 121 Robin Ventura	.25	.08
❑ 122 Shawn Abner	.05	.01
❑ 123 Rich Gedman	.05	.01
❑ 124 Dave Dravecky	.10	.02
❑ 125 Kent Hrbek	.10	.02
❑ 126 Randy Kramer	.05	.01
❑ 127 Mike Devereaux	.05	.01
❑ 128 Checklist 1	.05	.01
❑ 129 Ron Jones	.05	.01
❑ 130 Bert Blyleven	.10	.02
❑ 131 Matt Nokes	.05	.01
❑ 132 Lance Blankenship	.05	.01
❑ 133 Ricky Horton	.05	.01
❑ 134 Earl Cunningham FDP RC	.10	.02
❑ 135 Dave Magadan	.05	.01
❑ 136 Kevin Brown	.10	.02
❑ 137 Marty Pevey RC	.05	.01
❑ 138 Al Leiter	.25	.08
❑ 139 Greg Brock	.05	.01
❑ 140 Andre Dawson	.10	.02
❑ 141 John Hart MG RC	.05	.01
❑ 142 Jeff Wetherby RC	.05	.01
❑ 143 Rafael Belliard	.05	.01
❑ 144 Bud Black	.05	.01
❑ 145 Terry Steinbach	.05	.01
❑ 146 Rob Richie RC	.05	.01
❑ 147 Chuck Finley	.10	.02
❑ 148 Edgar Martinez	.15	.05
❑ 149 Steve Farr	.05	.01
❑ 150 Kirk Gibson	.10	.02
❑ 151 Rick Mahler	.05	.01

	No.	Player		
❑	152	Lonnie Smith	.05	.01
❑	153	Randy Milligan	.05	.01
❑	154	Mike Maddux	.05	.01
❑	155	Ellis Burks	.15	.05
❑	156	Ken Patterson	.05	.01
❑	157	Craig Biggio	.25	.08
❑	158	Craig Lefferts	.05	.01
❑	159	Mike Felder	.05	.01
❑	160	Dave Righetti	.05	.01
❑	161	Harold Reynolds	.10	.02
❑	162	Todd Zeile	.10	.02
❑	163	Phil Bradley	.05	.01
❑	164	Jeff Juden FDP RC	.10	.02
❑	165	Walt Weiss	.05	.01
❑	166	Bobby Witt	.05	.01
❑	167	Kevin Appier	.10	.02
❑	168	Jose Lind	.05	.01
❑	169	Richard Dotson	.05	.01
❑	170	George Bell	.05	.01
❑	171	Russ Nixon MG	.05	.01
❑	172	Tom Lampkin	.05	.01
❑	173	Tim Belcher	.05	.01
❑	174	Jeff Kunkel	.05	.01
❑	175	Mike Moore	.05	.01
❑	176	Luis Quinones	.05	.01
❑	177	Mike Henneman	.05	.01
❑	178	Chris James	.05	.01
❑	179	Brian Holton	.05	.01
❑	180	Tim Raines	.10	.02
❑	181	Juan Agosto	.05	.01
❑	182	Mookie Wilson	.10	.02
❑	183	Steve Lake	.05	.01
❑	184	Danny Cox	.05	.01
❑	185	Ruben Sierra	.10	.02
❑	186	Dave LaPoint	.05	.01
❑	187	Rick Wrona	.05	.01
❑	188	Mike Smithson	.05	.01
❑	189	Dick Schofield	.05	.01
❑	190	Rick Reuschel	.05	.01
❑	191	Pat Borders	.05	.01
❑	192	Don August	.05	.01
❑	193	Andy Benes	.10	.02
❑	194	Glenallen Hill	.05	.01
❑	195	Tim Burke	.05	.01
❑	196	Gerald Young	.05	.01
❑	197	Doug Drabek	.05	.01
❑	198	Mike Marshall	.05	.01
❑	199	Sergio Valdez RC	.05	.01
❑	200	Don Mattingly	.60	.25
❑	201	Cito Gaston MG	.05	.01
❑	202	Mike Macfarlane	.05	.01
❑	203	Mike Roesler RC	.05	.01
❑	204	Bob Dernier	.05	.01
❑	205	Mark Davis	.05	.01
❑	206	Nick Esasky	.05	.01
❑	207	Bob Ojeda	.05	.01
❑	208	Brook Jacoby	.05	.01
❑	209	Greg Mathews	.05	.01
❑	210	Ryne Sandberg	.40	.15
❑	211	John Cerutti	.05	.01
❑	212	Joe Orsulak	.05	.01
❑	213	Scott Bankhead	.05	.01
❑	214	Terry Francona	.10	.02
❑	215	Kirk McCaskill	.05	.01
❑	216	Ricky Jordan	.05	.01
❑	217	Don Robinson	.05	.01
❑	218	Wally Backman	.05	.01
❑	219	Donn Pall	.05	.01
❑	220	Barry Bonds	1.00	.40
❑	221	Gary Mielke RC	.05	.01
❑	222	Kurt Stillwell UER (Graduate misspelled as gradu	.05	.01
❑	223	Tommy Gregg	.05	.01
❑	224	Delino DeShields RC	.25	.08
❑	225	Jim Deshaies	.05	.01
❑	226	Mickey Hatcher	.05	.01
❑	227	Kevin Tapani RC	.25	.08
❑	228	Dave Martinez	.05	.01
❑	229	David Wells	.10	.02
❑	230	Keith Hernandez	.10	.02
❑	231	Jack McKeon MG	.05	.01
❑	232	Darnell Coles	.05	.01
❑	233	Ken Hill	.10	.02
❑	234	Mariano Duncan	.05	.01
❑	235	Jeff Reardon	.10	.02
❑	236	Hal Morris	.05	.01
❑	237	Kevin Ritz RC	.05	.01
❑	238	Felix Jose	.05	.01
❑	239	Eric Show	.05	.01
❑	240	Mark Grace	.15	.05
❑	241	Mike Krukow	.05	.01
❑	242	Fred Manrique	.05	.01
❑	243	Barry Jones	.05	.01
❑	244	Bill Schroeder	.05	.01
❑	245	Roger Clemens	1.00	.40
❑	246	Jim Eisenreich	.05	.01
❑	247	Jerry Reed	.05	.01
❑	248	Dave Anderson	.05	.01
❑	249	Mike (Texas) Smith RC	.05	.01
❑	250	Jose Canseco	.15	.05
❑	251	Jeff Blauser	.05	.01
❑	252	Otis Nixon	.05	.01
❑	253	Mark Portugal	.05	.01
❑	254	Francisco Cabrera	.05	.01
❑	255	Bobby Thigpen	.05	.01
❑	256	Marvell Wynne	.05	.01
❑	257	Jose DeLeon	.05	.01
❑	258	Barry Lyons	.05	.01
❑	259	Lance McCullers	.05	.01
❑	260	Eric Davis	.10	.02
❑	261	Whitey Herzog MG	.10	.02
❑	262	Checklist 2	.05	.01
❑	263	Mel Stottlemyre Jr.	.05	.01
❑	264	Bryan Clutterbuck	.05	.01
❑	265	Pete O'Brien	.05	.01
❑	266	German Gonzalez	.05	.01
❑	267	Mark Davidson	.05	.01
❑	268	Rob Murphy	.05	.01
❑	269	Dickie Thon	.05	.01
❑	270	Dave Stewart	.10	.02
❑	271	Chet Lemon	.05	.01
❑	272	Bryan Harvey	.05	.01
❑	273	Bobby Bonilla	.10	.02
❑	274	Mauro Gozzo RC	.05	.01
❑	275	Mickey Tettleton	.05	.01
❑	276	Gary Thurman	.05	.01
❑	277	Lenny Harris	.05	.01
❑	278	Pascual Perez	.05	.01
❑	279	Steve Buechele	.05	.01
❑	280	Lou Whitaker	.10	.02
❑	281	Kevin Bass	.05	.01
❑	282	Derek Lilliquist	.05	.01
❑	283	Albert Belle	.25	.08
❑	284	Mark Gardner RC	.10	.02
❑	285	Willie McGee	.10	.02
❑	286	Lee Guetterman	.05	.01
❑	287	Vance Law	.05	.01
❑	288	Greg Briley	.05	.01
❑	289	Norm Charlton	.05	.01
❑	290	Robin Yount	.40	.15
❑	291	Dave Johnson MG	.10	.02
❑	292	Jim Gott	.05	.01
❑	293	Mike Gallego	.05	.01
❑	294	Craig McMurtry	.05	.01
❑	295	Fred McGriff	.25	.08
❑	296	Jeff Ballard	.05	.01
❑	297	Tommy Herr	.05	.01
❑	298	Dan Gladden	.05	.01
❑	299	Adam Peterson	.05	.01
❑	300	Bo Jackson	.25	.08
❑	301	Don Aase	.05	.01
❑	302	Marcus Lawton RC	.05	.01
❑	303	Rick Cerone	.05	.01
❑	304	Marty Clary	.05	.01
❑	305	Eddie Murray	.25	.08
❑	306	Tom Niedenfuer	.05	.01
❑	307	Bip Roberts	.05	.01
❑	308	Jose Guzman	.05	.01
❑	309	Eric Yelding RC	.05	.01
❑	310	Steve Bedrosian	.05	.01
❑	311	Dwight Smith	.05	.01
❑	312	Dan Quisenberry	.05	.01
❑	313	Gus Polidor	.05	.01
❑	314	Donald Harris FDP RC	.05	.01
❑	315	Bruce Hurst	.05	.01
❑	316	Carney Lansford	.10	.02
❑	317	Mark Guthrie RC	.05	.01
❑	318	Wallace Johnson	.05	.01
❑	319	Dion James	.05	.01
❑	320	Dave Stieb	.10	.02
❑	321	Joe Morgan MG	.05	.01
❑	322	Junior Ortiz	.05	.01
❑	323	Willie Wilson	.05	.01
❑	324	Pete Harnisch	.05	.01
❑	325	Robby Thompson	.05	.01
❑	326	Tom McCarthy	.05	.01
❑	327	Ken Williams	.05	.01
❑	328	Curt Young	.05	.01
❑	329	Oddibe McDowell	.05	.01
❑	330	Ron Darling	.05	.01
❑	331	Juan Gonzalez RC	1.00	.40
❑	332	Paul O'Neill	.15	.05
❑	333	Bill Wegman	.05	.01
❑	334	Johnny Ray	.05	.01
❑	335	Andy Hawkins	.05	.01
❑	336	Ken Griffey Jr.	.75	.30
❑	337	Lloyd McClendon	.05	.01
❑	338	Dennis Lamp	.05	.01
❑	339	Dave Clark	.05	.01
❑	340	Fernando Valenzuela	.10	.02
❑	341	Tom Foley	.05	.01
❑	342	Alex Trevino	.05	.01
❑	343	Frank Tanana	.05	.01
❑	344	George Canale RC	.05	.01
❑	345	Harold Baines	.10	.02
❑	346	Jim Presley	.05	.01
❑	347	Junior Felix	.05	.01
❑	348	Gary Wayne	.05	.01
❑	349	Steve Finley	.10	.02
❑	350	Bret Saberhagen	.10	.02
❑	351	Roger Craig MG	.05	.01
❑	352	Bryn Smith	.05	.01
❑	353	Sandy Alomar Jr. (Not listed as Jr. on card fron	.10	.02
❑	354	Stan Belinda RC	.10	.02
❑	355	Marty Barrett	.05	.01
❑	356	Randy Ready	.05	.01
❑	357	Dave West	.05	.01
❑	358	Andres Thomas	.05	.01
❑	359	Jimmy Jones	.05	.01
❑	360	Paul Molitor	.10	.02
❑	361	Randy McCament RC	.05	.01
❑	362	Damon Berryhill	.05	.01
❑	363	Dan Petry	.05	.01
❑	364	Rolando Roomes	.05	.01
❑	365	Ozzie Guillen	.10	.02
❑	366	Mike Heath	.05	.01
❑	367	Mike Morgan	.05	.01
❑	368	Bill Doran	.05	.01
❑	369	Todd Burns	.05	.01
❑	370	Tim Wallach	.05	.01
❑	371	Jimmy Key	.10	.02
❑	372	Terry Kennedy	.05	.01
❑	373	Alvin Davis	.05	.01
❑	374	Steve Cummings RC	.05	.01
❑	375	Dwight Evans	.15	.05
❑	376	Checklist 3 UER (Higuera misalphabetized in Br	.05	.01
❑	377	Mickey Weston RC	.05	.01
❑	378	Luis Salazar	.05	.01
❑	379	Steve Rosenberg	.05	.01
❑	380	Dave Winfield	.10	.02
❑	381	Frank Robinson MG	.15	.05
❑	382	Jeff Musselman	.05	.01
❑	383	John Morris	.05	.01
❑	384	Pat Combs	.05	.01
❑	385	Fred McGriff AS	.10	.02
❑	386	Julio Franco AS	.05	.01
❑	387	Wade Boggs AS	.10	.02
❑	388	Cal Ripken AS	.40	.15
❑	389	Robin Yount AS	.25	.08
❑	390	Ruben Sierra AS	.05	.01
❑	391	Kirby Puckett AS	.15	.05
❑	392	Carlton Fisk AS	.10	.02
❑	393	Bret Saberhagen AS	.05	.01
❑	394	Jeff Ballard AS	.05	.01
❑	395	Jeff Russell AS	.05	.01
❑	396	Bart Giamatti MEM	.25	.08
❑	397	Will Clark AS	.10	.02
❑	398	Ryne Sandberg AS	.25	.08
❑	399	Howard Johnson AS	.05	.01
❑	400	Ozzie Smith AS	.25	.08
❑	401	Kevin Mitchell AS	.05	.01
❑	402	Eric Davis AS	.05	.01
❑	403	Tony Gwynn AS	.15	.05

❑ 404 Craig Biggio AS .25 .08
❑ 405 Mike Scott AS .05 .01
❑ 406 Joe Magrane AS .05 .01
❑ 407 Mark Davis AS .05 .01
❑ 408 Trevor Wilson .05 .01
❑ 409 Tom Brunansky .05 .01
❑ 410 Joe Boever .05 .01
❑ 411 Ken Phelps .05 .01
❑ 412 Jamie Moyer .10 .02
❑ 413 Brian DuBois RC .05 .01
❑ 414A FrankThomas NNOF ! 700.00 400.00
❑ 414B Frank Thomas RC 2.00 .75
❑ 415 Shawon Dunston .05 .01
❑ 416 Dave Wayne Johnson RC .05 .01
❑ 417 Jim Gantner .05 .01
❑ 418 Tom Browning .05 .01
❑ 419 Beau Allred RC .05 .01
❑ 420 Carlton Fisk .15 .05
❑ 421 Greg Minton .05 .01
❑ 422 Pat Sheridan .05 .01
❑ 423 Fred Toliver .05 .01
❑ 424 Jerry Reuss .05 .01
❑ 425 Bill Landrum .05 .01
❑ 426 Jeff Hamilton UER (Stats say he fanned 197 times .05 .01
❑ 427 Carmen Castillo .05 .01
❑ 428 Steve Davis RC .05 .01
❑ 429 Tom Kelly MG .05 .01
❑ 430 Pete Incaviglia .05 .01
❑ 431 Randy Johnson .50 .20
❑ 432 Damaso Garcia .05 .01
❑ 433 Steve Olin RC .25 .08
❑ 434 Mark Carreon .05 .01
❑ 435 Kevin Seitzer .05 .01
❑ 436 Mel Hall .05 .01
❑ 437 Les Lancaster .05 .01
❑ 438 Greg Myers .05 .01
❑ 439 Jeff Parrett .05 .01
❑ 440 Alan Trammell .10 .02
❑ 441 Bob Kipper .05 .01
❑ 442 Jerry Browne .05 .01
❑ 443 Cris Carpenter .05 .01
❑ 444 Kyle Abbott FDP RC .05 .01
❑ 445 Danny Jackson .05 .01
❑ 446 Dan Pasqua .05 .01
❑ 447 Atlee Hammaker .05 .01
❑ 448 Greg Gagne .05 .01
❑ 449 Dennis Rasmussen .05 .01
❑ 450 Rickey Henderson .25 .08
❑ 451 Mark Lemke .05 .01
❑ 452 Luis DeLosSantos .05 .01
❑ 453 Jody Davis .05 .01
❑ 454 Jeff King .05 .01
❑ 455 Jeffrey Leonard .05 .01
❑ 456 Chris Gwynn .05 .01
❑ 457 Gregg Jefferies .10 .02
❑ 458 Bob McClure .05 .01
❑ 459 Jim Lefebvre MG .05 .01
❑ 460 Mike Scott .05 .01
❑ 461 Carlos Martinez .05 .01
❑ 462 Denny Walling .05 .01
❑ 463 Drew Hall .05 .01
❑ 464 Jerome Walton .05 .01
❑ 465 Kevin Gross .05 .01
❑ 466 Rance Mulliniks .05 .01
❑ 467 Juan Nieves .05 .01
❑ 468 Bill Ripken .05 .01
❑ 469 John Kruk .10 .02
❑ 470 Frank Viola .05 .01
❑ 471 Mike Brumley .05 .01
❑ 472 Jose Uribe .05 .01
❑ 473 Joe Price .05 .01
❑ 474 Rich Thompson .05 .01
❑ 475 Bob Welch .05 .01
❑ 476 Brad Komminsk .05 .01
❑ 477 Willie Fraser .05 .01
❑ 478 Mike LaValliere .05 .01
❑ 479 Frank White .10 .02
❑ 480 Sid Fernandez .05 .01
❑ 481 Garry Templeton .05 .01
❑ 482 Steve Carter .05 .01
❑ 483 Alejandro Pena .05 .01
❑ 484 Mike Fitzgerald .05 .01
❑ 485 John Candelaria .05 .01
❑ 486 Jeff Treadway .05 .01
❑ 487 Steve Searcy .05 .01
❑ 488 Ken Oberkfell .05 .01
❑ 489 Nick Leyva MG .05 .01
❑ 490 Dan Plesac .05 .01
❑ 491 Dave Cochrane RC .05 .01
❑ 492 Ron Oester .05 .01
❑ 493 Jason Grimsley RC .10 .02
❑ 494 Terry Puhl .05 .01
❑ 495 Lee Smith .10 .02
❑ 496 Cecil Espy UER ('88 stats have 3 SB's& should be .05 .01
❑ 497 Dave Schmidt .05 .01
❑ 498 Rick Schu .05 .01
❑ 499 Bill Long .05 .01
❑ 500 Kevin Mitchell .05 .01
❑ 501 Matt Young .05 .01
❑ 502 Mitch Webster .05 .01
❑ 503 Randy St.Claire .05 .01
❑ 504 Tom O'Malley .05 .01
❑ 505 Kelly Gruber .05 .01
❑ 506 Tom Glavine .15 .05
❑ 507 Gary Redus .05 .01
❑ 508 Terry Leach .05 .01
❑ 509 Tom Pagnozzi .05 .01
❑ 510 Dwight Gooden .10 .02
❑ 511 Clay Parker .05 .01
❑ 512 Gary Pettis .05 .01
❑ 513 Mark Eichhorn .05 .01
❑ 514 Andy Allanson .05 .01
❑ 515 Len Dykstra .10 .02
❑ 516 Tim Leary .05 .01
❑ 517 Roberto Alomar .15 .05
❑ 518 Bill Krueger .05 .01
❑ 519 Bucky Dent MG .05 .01
❑ 520 Mitch Williams .05 .01
❑ 521 Craig Worthington .05 .01
❑ 522 Mike Dunne .05 .01
❑ 523 Jay Bell .10 .02
❑ 524 Daryl Boston .05 .01
❑ 525 Wally Joyner .10 .02
❑ 526 Checklist 4 .05 .01
❑ 527 Ron Hassey .05 .01
❑ 528 Kevin Wickander UER (Monthly scoreboard strikeou .05 .01
❑ 529 Greg A. Harris .05 .01
❑ 530 Mark Langston .05 .01
❑ 531 Ken Caminiti .10 .02
❑ 532 Cecilio Guante .05 .01
❑ 533 Tim Jones .05 .01
❑ 534 Louie Meadows .05 .01
❑ 535 John Smoltz .25 .08
❑ 536 Bob Geren .05 .01
❑ 537 Mark Grant .05 .01
❑ 538 Bill Spiers UER (Photo actually George Canale) .05 .01
❑ 539 Neal Heaton .05 .01
❑ 540 Danny Tartabull .05 .01
❑ 541 Pat Perry .05 .01
❑ 542 Darren Daulton .10 .02
❑ 543 Nelson Liriano .05 .01
❑ 544 Dennis Boyd .05 .01
❑ 545 Kevin McReynolds .05 .01
❑ 546 Kevin Hickey .05 .01
❑ 547 Jack Howell .05 .01
❑ 548 Pat Clements .05 .01
❑ 549 Don Zimmer MG .05 .01
❑ 550 Julio Franco .10 .02
❑ 551 Tim Crews .05 .01
❑ 552 Mike (Miss.) Smith RC .05 .01
❑ 553 Scott Scudder UER (Cedar Rap1ds) .05 .01
❑ 554 Jay Buhner .10 .02
❑ 555 Jack Morris .10 .02
❑ 556 Gene Larkin .05 .01
❑ 557 Jeff Innis RC .05 .01
❑ 558 Rafael Ramirez .05 .01
❑ 559 Andy McGaffigan .05 .01
❑ 560 Steve Sax .05 .01
❑ 561 Ken Dayley .05 .01
❑ 562 Chad Kreuter .05 .01
❑ 563 Alex Sanchez .05 .01
❑ 564 Tyler Houston FDP RC .25 .08
❑ 565 Scott Fletcher .05 .01
❑ 566 Mark Knudson .05 .01
❑ 567 Ron Gant .10 .02
❑ 568 John Smiley .05 .01
❑ 569 Ivan Calderon .05 .01
❑ 570 Cal Ripken .75 .30
❑ 571 Brett Butler .10 .02
❑ 572 Greg W. Harris .05 .01
❑ 573 Danny Heep .05 .01
❑ 574 Bill Swift .05 .01
❑ 575 Lance Parrish .05 .01
❑ 576 Mike Dyer RC .05 .01
❑ 577 Charlie Hayes .05 .01
❑ 578 Joe Magrane .05 .01
❑ 579 Art Howe MG .05 .01
❑ 580 Joe Carter .10 .02
❑ 581 Ken Griffey Sr. .10 .02
❑ 582 Rick Honeycutt .05 .01
❑ 583 Bruce Benedict .05 .01
❑ 584 Phil Stephenson .05 .01
❑ 585 Kal Daniels .05 .01
❑ 586 Edwin Nunez .05 .01
❑ 587 Lance Johnson .05 .01
❑ 588 Rick Rhoden .05 .01
❑ 589 Mike Aldrete .05 .01
❑ 590 Ozzie Smith .40 .15
❑ 591 Todd Stottlemyre .10 .02
❑ 592 R.J. Reynolds .05 .01
❑ 593 Scott Bradley .05 .01
❑ 594 Luis Sojo RC .05 .01
❑ 595 Greg Swindell .05 .01
❑ 596 Jose DeJesus .05 .01
❑ 597 Chris Bosio .05 .01
❑ 598 Brady Anderson .10 .02
❑ 599 Frank Williams .05 .01
❑ 600 Darryl Strawberry .10 .02
❑ 601 Luis Rivera .05 .01
❑ 602 Scott Garrelts .05 .01
❑ 603 Tony Armas .05 .01
❑ 604 Ron Robinson .05 .01
❑ 605 Mike Scioscia .05 .01
❑ 606 Storm Davis .05 .01
❑ 607 Steve Jeltz .05 .01
❑ 608 Eric Anthony RC .10 .02
❑ 609 Sparky Anderson MG .10 .02
❑ 610 Pedro Guerrero .05 .01
❑ 611 Walt Terrell .05 .01
❑ 612 Dave Gallagher .05 .01
❑ 613 Jeff Pico .05 .01
❑ 614 Nelson Santovenia .05 .01
❑ 615 Rob Deer .05 .01
❑ 616 Brian Holman .05 .01
❑ 617 Geronimo Berroa .05 .01
❑ 618 Ed Whitson .05 .01
❑ 619 Rob Ducey .05 .01
❑ 620 Tony Castillo .05 .01
❑ 621 Melido Perez .05 .01
❑ 622 Sid Bream .05 .01
❑ 623 Jim Corsi .05 .01
❑ 624 Darrin Jackson .05 .01
❑ 625 Roger McDowell .05 .01
❑ 626 Bob Melvin .05 .01
❑ 627 Jose Rijo .05 .01
❑ 628 Candy Maldonado .05 .01
❑ 629 Eric Hetzel .05 .01
❑ 630 Gary Gaetti .10 .02
❑ 631 John Wetteland .25 .08
❑ 632 Scott Lusader .05 .01
❑ 633 Dennis Cook .05 .01
❑ 634 Luis Polonia .05 .01
❑ 635 Brian Downing .05 .01
❑ 636 Jesse Orosco .05 .01
❑ 637 Craig Reynolds .05 .01
❑ 638 Jeff Montgomery .10 .02
❑ 639 Tony LaRussa MG .10 .02
❑ 640 Rick Sutcliffe .10 .02
❑ 641 Doug Strange RC .05 .01
❑ 642 Jack Armstrong .05 .01
❑ 643 Alfredo Griffin .05 .01
❑ 644 Paul Assenmacher .05 .01
❑ 645 Jose Oquendo .05 .01
❑ 646 Checklist 5 .05 .01
❑ 647 Rex Hudler .05 .01
❑ 648 Jim Clancy .05 .01
❑ 649 Dan Murphy RC .10 .02
❑ 650 Mike Witt .05 .01
❑ 651 Rafael Santana .05 .01

❑ 652 Mike Boddicker .05 .01
❑ 653 John Moses .05 .01
❑ 654 Paul Coleman FDP RC .10 .02
❑ 655 Gregg Olson .10 .02
❑ 656 Mackey Sasser .05 .01
❑ 657 Terry Mulholland .05 .01
❑ 658 Donell Nixon .05 .01
❑ 659 Greg Cadaret .05 .01
❑ 660 Vince Coleman .05 .01
❑ 661 Dick Howser TBC'85 UER (Seaver's 300th on 7/11/8 .05 .01
❑ 662 Mike Schmidt TBC .25 .08
❑ 663 Fred Lynn TBC'75 .05 .01
❑ 664 Johnny Bench TBC .15 .05
❑ 665 Sandy Koufax TBC .50 .20
❑ 666 Brian Fisher .05 .01
❑ 667 Curt Wilkerson .05 .01
❑ 668 Joe Oliver .05 .01
❑ 669 Tom Lasorda MG .25 .08
❑ 670 Dennis Eckersley .10 .02
❑ 671 Bob Boone .10 .02
❑ 672 Roy Smith .05 .01
❑ 673 Joey Meyer .05 .01
❑ 674 Spike Owen .05 .01
❑ 675 Jim Abbott .15 .05
❑ 676 Randy Kutcher .05 .01
❑ 677 Jay Tibbs .05 .01
❑ 678 Kirt Manwaring UER ('88 Phoenix stats repeated) .05 .01
❑ 679 Gary Ward .05 .01
❑ 680 Howard Johnson .05 .01
❑ 681 Mike Schooler .05 .01
❑ 682 Dann Bilardello .05 .01
❑ 683 Kenny Rogers .10 .02
❑ 684 Julio Machado RC .05 .01
❑ 685 Tony Fernandez .05 .01
❑ 686 Carmelo Martinez .05 .01
❑ 687 Tim Birtsas .05 .01
❑ 688 Milt Thompson .05 .01
❑ 689 Rich Yett .05 .01
❑ 690 Mark McGwire .60 .25
❑ 691 Chuck Cary .05 .01
❑ 692 Sammy Sosa RC 2.50 1.00
❑ 693 Calvin Schiraldi .05 .01
❑ 694 Mike Stanton RC .25 .08
❑ 695 Tom Henke .05 .01
❑ 696 B.J. Surhoff .10 .02
❑ 697 Mike Davis .05 .01
❑ 698 Omar Vizquel .25 .08
❑ 699 Jim Leyland MG .05 .01
❑ 700 Kirby Puckett .25 .08
❑ 701 Bernie Williams RC 1.50 .60
❑ 702 Tony Phillips .05 .01
❑ 703 Jeff Brantley .05 .01
❑ 704 Chip Hale RC .05 .01
❑ 705 Claudell Washington .05 .01
❑ 706 Geno Petralli .05 .01
❑ 707 Luis Aquino .05 .01
❑ 708 Larry Sheets .05 .01
❑ 709 Juan Berenguer .05 .01
❑ 710 Von Hayes .05 .01
❑ 711 Rick Aguilera .10 .02
❑ 712 Todd Benzinger .05 .01
❑ 713 Tim Drummond RC .05 .01
❑ 714 Marquis Grissom RC .40 .15
❑ 715 Greg Maddux .40 .15
❑ 716 Steve Balboni .05 .01
❑ 717 Ron Karkovice .05 .01
❑ 718 Gary Sheffield .25 .08
❑ 719 Wally Whitehurst .05 .01
❑ 720 Andres Galarraga .10 .02
❑ 721 Lee Mazzilli .05 .01
❑ 722 Felix Fermin .05 .01
❑ 723 Jeff D. Robinson .05 .01
❑ 724 Juan Bell .05 .01
❑ 725 Terry Pendleton .10 .02
❑ 726 Gene Nelson .05 .01
❑ 727 Pat Tabler .05 .01
❑ 728 Jim Acker .05 .01
❑ 729 Bobby Valentine MG .05 .01
❑ 730 Tony Gwynn .30 .10
❑ 731 Don Carman .05 .01
❑ 732 Ernest Riles .05 .01
❑ 733 John Dopson .05 .01
❑ 734 Kevin Elster .05 .01
❑ 735 Charlie Hough .10 .02
❑ 736 Rick Dempsey .05 .01
❑ 737 Chris Sabo .05 .01
❑ 738 Gene Harris .05 .01
❑ 739 Dale Sveum .05 .01
❑ 740 Jesse Barfield .05 .01
❑ 741 Steve Wilson .05 .01
❑ 742 Ernie Whitt .05 .01
❑ 743 Tom Candiotti .05 .01
❑ 744 Kelly Mann RC .05 .01
❑ 745 Hubie Brooks .05 .01
❑ 746 Dave Smith .05 .01
❑ 747 Randy Bush .05 .01
❑ 748 Doyle Alexander .05 .01
❑ 749 Mark Parent UER ('87 BA .80, should be .080) .05 .01
❑ 750 Dale Murphy .15 .05
❑ 751 Steve Lyons .05 .01
❑ 752 Tom Gordon .10 .02
❑ 753 Chris Speier .05 .01
❑ 754 Bob Walk .05 .01
❑ 755 Rafael Palmeiro .15 .05
❑ 756 Ken Howell .05 .01
❑ 757 Larry Walker RC 1.00 .40
❑ 758 Mark Thurmond .05 .01
❑ 759 Tom Trebelhorn MG .05 .01
❑ 760 Wade Boggs .15 .05
❑ 761 Mike Jackson .05 .01
❑ 762 Doug Dascenzo .05 .01
❑ 763 Dennis Martinez .10 .02
❑ 764 Tim Teufel .05 .01
❑ 765 Chili Davis .10 .02
❑ 766 Brian Meyer .05 .01
❑ 767 Tracy Jones .05 .01
❑ 768 Chuck Crim .05 .01
❑ 769 Greg Hibbard RC .10 .02
❑ 770 Cory Snyder .05 .01
❑ 771 Pete Smith .05 .01
❑ 772 Jeff Reed .05 .01
❑ 773 Dave Leiper .05 .01
❑ 774 Ben McDonald RC .25 .08
❑ 775 Andy Van Slyke .15 .05
❑ 776 Charlie Leibrandt .05 .01
❑ 777 Tim Laudner .05 .01
❑ 778 Mike Jeffcoat .05 .01
❑ 779 Lloyd Moseby .05 .01
❑ 780 Orel Hershiser .10 .02
❑ 781 Mario Diaz .05 .01
❑ 782 Jose Alvarez .05 .01
❑ 783 Checklist 6 .05 .01
❑ 784 Scott Bailes .05 .01
❑ 785 Jim Rice .10 .02
❑ 786 Eric King .05 .01
❑ 787 Rene Gonzales .05 .01
❑ 788 Frank DiPino .05 .01
❑ 789 John Wathan MG .05 .01
❑ 790 Gary Carter .10 .02
❑ 791 Alvaro Espinoza .05 .01
❑ 792 Gerald Perry .05 .01
❑ NNO George Bush PRES

1991 Topps

❑ COMPLETE SET (792) 20.00 8.00
❑ COMP.FACT.SET (792) 25.00 10.00
❑ 1 Nolan Ryan 1.50 .60
❑ 2 George Brett RB .30 .10
❑ 3 Carlton Fisk RB .10 .02
❑ 4 Kevin Maas RB .05 .01
❑ 5 Cal Ripken RB .40 .15
❑ 6 Nolan Ryan RB .50 .20
❑ 7 Ryne Sandberg RB .25 .08
❑ 8 Bobby Thigpen RB .05 .01
❑ 9 Darrin Fletcher .05 .01
❑ 10 Gregg Olson .05 .01
❑ 11 Roberto Kelly .05 .01
❑ 12 Paul Assenmacher .05 .01
❑ 13 Mariano Duncan .05 .01
❑ 14 Dennis Lamp .05 .01
❑ 15 Von Hayes .05 .01
❑ 16 Mike Heath .05 .01
❑ 17 Jeff Brantley .05 .01
❑ 18 Nelson Liriano .05 .01
❑ 19 Jeff D. Robinson .05 .01
❑ 20 Pedro Guerrero .10 .02
❑ 21 Joe Morgan MG .05 .01
❑ 22 Storm Davis .05 .01
❑ 23 Jim Gantner .05 .01
❑ 24 Dave Martinez .05 .01
❑ 25 Tim Belcher .05 .01
❑ 26 Luis Sojo UER (Born in Barquisimento& not Carqui .05 .01
❑ 27 Bobby Witt .05 .01
❑ 28 Alvaro Espinoza .05 .01
❑ 29 Bob Walk .05 .01
❑ 30 Gregg Jefferies .05 .01
❑ 31 Colby Ward RC .05 .01
❑ 32 Mike Simms RC .05 .01
❑ 33 Barry Jones .05 .01
❑ 34 Atlee Hammaker .05 .01
❑ 35 Greg Maddux .40 .15
❑ 36 Donnie Hill .05 .01
❑ 37 Tom Bolton .05 .01
❑ 38 Scott Bradley .05 .01
❑ 39 Jim Neidlinger RC .05 .01
❑ 40 Kevin Mitchell .05 .01
❑ 41 Ken Dayley .05 .01
❑ 42 Chris Hoiles .05 .01
❑ 43 Roger McDowell .05 .01
❑ 44 Mike Felder .05 .01
❑ 45 Chris Sabo .05 .01
❑ 46 Tim Drummond .05 .01
❑ 47 Brook Jacoby .05 .01
❑ 48 Dennis Boyd .05 .01
❑ 49A Pat Borders ERR (40 steals at Kinston in '86) .25 .08
❑ 49B Pat Borders COR (0 steals at Kinston in '86) .05 .01
❑ 50 Bob Welch .05 .01
❑ 51 Art Howe MG .05 .01
❑ 52 Francisco Oliveras .05 .01
❑ 53 Mike Sharperson UER (Born in 1961, not 1960) .05 .01
❑ 54 Gary Mielke .05 .01
❑ 55 Jeffrey Leonard .05 .01
❑ 56 Jeff Parrett .05 .01
❑ 57 Jack Howell .05 .01
❑ 58 Mel Stottlemyre Jr. .05 .01
❑ 59 Eric Yelding .05 .01
❑ 60 Frank Viola .10 .02
❑ 61 Stan Javier .05 .01
❑ 62 Lee Guetterman .05 .01
❑ 63 Milt Thompson .05 .01
❑ 64 Tom Herr .05 .01
❑ 65 Bruce Hurst .05 .01
❑ 66 Terry Kennedy .05 .01
❑ 67 Rick Honeycutt .05 .01
❑ 68 Gary Sheffield .10 .02
❑ 69 Steve Wilson .05 .01
❑ 70 Ellis Burks .10 .02
❑ 71 Jim Acker .05 .01
❑ 72 Junior Ortiz .05 .01
❑ 73 Craig Worthington .05 .01
❑ 74 Shane Andrews RC .25 .08
❑ 75 Jack Morris .10 .02
❑ 76 Jerry Browne .05 .01
❑ 77 Drew Hall .05 .01
❑ 78 Geno Petralli .05 .01
❑ 79 Frank Thomas .25 .08
❑ 80A Fernando Valenzuela ERR .40 .15

❑ 80B Fernando Valenzuela COR .10 .02
❑ 81 Cito Gaston MG .05 .01
❑ 82 Tom Glavine .15 .05
❑ 83 Daryl Boston .05 .01
❑ 84 Bob McClure .05 .01
❑ 85 Jesse Barfield .05 .01
❑ 86 Les Lancaster .05 .01
❑ 87 Tracy Jones .05 .01
❑ 88 Bob Tewksbury .05 .01
❑ 89 Darren Daulton .10 .02
❑ 90 Danny Tartabull .05 .01
❑ 91 Greg Colbrunn RC .25 .08
❑ 92 Danny Jackson .05 .01
❑ 93 Ivan Calderon .05 .01
❑ 94 John Dopson .05 .01
❑ 95 Paul Molitor .10 .02
❑ 96 Trevor Wilson .05 .01
❑ 97A Brady Anderson ERR .40 .15
❑ 97B Brady Anderson COR .10 .02
❑ 98 Sergio Valdez .05 .01
❑ 99 Chris Gwynn .05 .01
❑ 100 Don Mattingly .60 .25
❑ 100A Don Mattingly ERR 2.00 .75
❑ 101 Rob Ducey .05 .01
❑ 102 Gene Larkin .05 .01
❑ 103 Tim Costo RC .05 .01
❑ 104 Don Robinson .05 .01
❑ 105 Kevin McReynolds .05 .01
❑ 106 Ed Nunez .05 .01
❑ 107 Luis Polonia .05 .01
❑ 108 Matt Young .05 .01
❑ 109 Greg Riddoch MG .05 .01
❑ 110 Tom Henke .05 .01
❑ 111 Andres Thomas .05 .01
❑ 112 Frank DiPino .05 .01
❑ 113 Carl Everett RC .50 .20
❑ 114 Lance Dickson RC .10 .02
❑ 115 Hubie Brooks .05 .01
❑ 116 Mark Davis .05 .01
❑ 117 Dion James .05 .01
❑ 118 Tom Edens RC .05 .01
❑ 119 Carl Nichols .05 .01
❑ 120 Joe Carter .10 .02
❑ 121 Eric King .05 .01
❑ 122 Paul O'Neill .15 .05
❑ 123 Greg A. Harris .05 .01
❑ 124 Randy Bush .05 .01
❑ 125 Steve Bedrosian .05 .01
❑ 126 Bernard Gilkey .05 .01
❑ 127 Joe Price .05 .01
❑ 128 Travis Fryman .10 .02
❑ 129 Mark Eichhorn .05 .01
❑ 130 Ozzie Smith .40 .15
❑ 131A Checklist 1 ERR
727 Phil Bradley .25 .08
❑ 131B Checklist 1 COR
717 Phil Bradley .05 .01
❑ 132 Jamie Quirk .05 .01
❑ 133 Greg Briley .05 .01
❑ 134 Kevin Elster .05 .01
❑ 135 Jerome Walton .05 .01
❑ 136 Dave Schmidt .05 .01
❑ 137 Randy Ready .05 .01
❑ 138 Jamie Moyer .10 .02
❑ 139 Jeff Treadway .05 .01
❑ 140 Fred McGriff .15 .05
❑ 141 Nick Leyva MG .05 .01
❑ 142 Curt Wilkerson .05 .01
❑ 143 John Smiley .05 .01
❑ 144 Dave Henderson .05 .01
❑ 145 Lou Whitaker .10 .02
❑ 146 Dan Plesac .05 .01
❑ 147 Carlos Baerga .05 .01
❑ 148 Rey Palacios .05 .01
❑ 149 Al Osuna UER RC .10 .02
❑ 150 Cal Ripken .75 .30
❑ 151 Tom Browning .05 .01
❑ 152 Mickey Hatcher .05 .01
❑ 153 Bryan Harvey .05 .01
❑ 154 Jay Buhner .10 .02
❑ 155A Dwight Evans ERR .50 .20
❑ 155B Dwight Evans COR .15 .05
❑ 156 Carlos Martinez .05 .01
❑ 157 John Smoltz .15 .05
❑ 158 Jose Uribe .05 .01
❑ 159 Joe Boever .05 .01
❑ 160 Vince Coleman UER
(Wrong birth year&
born 9/22/6 .05 .01
❑ 161 Tim Leary .05 .01
❑ 162 Ozzie Canseco .05 .01
❑ 163 Dave Johnson .05 .01
❑ 164 Edgar Diaz .05 .01
❑ 165 Sandy Alomar Jr. .05 .01
❑ 166 Harold Baines .10 .02
❑ 167A Randy Tomlin ERR .25 .08
❑ 167B Randy Tomlin COR RC .10 .02
❑ 168 John Olerud .10 .02
❑ 169 Luis Aquino .05 .01
❑ 170 Carlton Fisk .15 .05
❑ 171 Tony LaRussa MG .10 .02
❑ 172 Pete Incaviglia .05 .01
❑ 173 Jason Grimsley .05 .01
❑ 174 Ken Caminiti .10 .02
❑ 175 Jack Armstrong .05 .01
❑ 176 John Orton .05 .01
❑ 177 Reggie Harris .05 .01
❑ 178 Dave Valle .05 .01
❑ 179 Pete Harnisch .05 .01
❑ 180 Tony Gwynn .30 .10
❑ 181 Duane Ward .05 .01
❑ 182 Junior Noboa .05 .01
❑ 183 Clay Parker .05 .01
❑ 184 Gary Green .05 .01
❑ 185 Joe Magrane .05 .01
❑ 186 Rod Booker .05 .01
❑ 187 Greg Cadaret .05 .01
❑ 188 Damon Berryhill .05 .01
❑ 189 Daryl Irvine RC .05 .01
❑ 190 Matt Williams .10 .02
❑ 191 Willie Blair .05 .01
❑ 192 Rob Deer .05 .01
❑ 193 Felix Fermin .05 .01
❑ 194 Xavier Hernandez .05 .01
❑ 195 Wally Joyner .10 .02
❑ 196 Jim Vatcher RC .05 .01
❑ 197 Chris Nabholz .05 .01
❑ 198 R.J. Reynolds .05 .01
❑ 199 Mike Hartley .05 .01
❑ 200 Darryl Strawberry .10 .02
❑ 201 Tom Kelly MG .05 .01
❑ 202 Jim Leyritz .05 .01
❑ 203 Gene Harris .05 .01
❑ 204 Herm Winningham .05 .01
❑ 205 Mike Perez RC .10 .02
❑ 206 Carlos Quintana .05 .01
❑ 207 Gary Wayne .05 .01
❑ 208 Willie Wilson .05 .01
❑ 209 Ken Howell .05 .01
❑ 210 Lance Parrish .10 .02
❑ 211 Brian Barnes RC .05 .01
❑ 212 Steve Finley .10 .02
❑ 213 Frank Wills .05 .01
❑ 214 Joe Girardi .05 .01
❑ 215 Dave Smith .05 .01
❑ 216 Greg Gagne .05 .01
❑ 217 Chris Bosio .05 .01
❑ 218 Rick Parker .05 .01
❑ 219 Jack McDowell .05 .01
❑ 220 Tim Wallach .05 .01
❑ 221 Don Slaught .05 .01
❑ 222 Brian McRae RC .25 .08
❑ 223 Allan Anderson .05 .01
❑ 224 Juan Gonzalez .25 .08
❑ 225 Randy Johnson .30 .10
❑ 226 Alfredo Griffin .05 .01
❑ 227 Steve Avery UER .05 .01
❑ 228 Rex Hudler .05 .01
❑ 229 Rance Mulliniks .05 .01
❑ 230 Sid Fernandez .05 .01
❑ 231 Doug Rader MG .05 .01
❑ 232 Jose DeJesus .05 .01
❑ 233 Al Leiter .10 .02
❑ 234 Scott Erickson .05 .01
❑ 235 Dave Parker .10 .02
❑ 236A Frank Tanana ERR
(Tied for lead with
269 K's in .25 .08
❑ 236B Frank Tanana COR
(Led league with
269 K's in '75 .05 .01
❑ 237 Rick Cerone .05 .01
❑ 238 Mike Dunne .05 .01
❑ 239 Darren Lewis FTC .05 .01
❑ 240 Mike Scott .05 .01
❑ 241 Dave Clark UER
(Career totals 19 HR
and 5 3B& sh .05 .01
❑ 242 Mike LaCoss .05 .01
❑ 243 Lance Johnson .05 .01
❑ 244 Mike Jeffcoat .05 .01
❑ 245 Kal Daniels .05 .01
❑ 246 Kevin Wickander .05 .01
❑ 247 Jody Reed .05 .01
❑ 248 Tom Gordon .05 .01
❑ 249 Bob Melvin .05 .01
❑ 250 Dennis Eckersley .10 .02
❑ 251 Mark Lemke .05 .01
❑ 252 Mel Rojas .05 .01
❑ 253 Garry Templeton .05 .01
❑ 254 Shawn Boskie .05 .01
❑ 255 Brian Downing .05 .01
❑ 256 Greg Hibbard .05 .01
❑ 257 Tom O'Malley .05 .01
❑ 258 Chris Hammond FTC .05 .01
❑ 259 Hensley Meulens .05 .01
❑ 260 Harold Reynolds .10 .02
❑ 261 Bud Harrelson MG .05 .01
❑ 262 Tim Jones .05 .01
❑ 263 Checklist 2 .05 .01
❑ 264 Dave Hollins .05 .01
❑ 265 Mark Gubicza .05 .01
❑ 266 Carmelo Castillo .05 .01
❑ 267 Mark Knudson .05 .01
❑ 268 Tom Brookens .05 .01
❑ 269 Joe Hesketh .05 .01
❑ 270 Mark McGwire .75 .30
❑ 270A Mark McGwire ERR 2.00 .75
❑ 271 Omar Olivares RC .10 .02
❑ 272 Jeff King .05 .01
❑ 273 Johnny Ray .05 .01
❑ 274 Ken Williams .05 .01
❑ 275 Alan Trammell .10 .02
❑ 276 Bill Swift .05 .01
❑ 277 Scott Coolbaugh .05 .01
❑ 278 Alex Fernandez UER .05 .01
❑ 279A Jose Gonzalez ERR
(Photo actually
Billy Bean) .25 .08
❑ 279B Jose Gonzalez COR .05 .01
❑ 280 Bret Saberhagen .10 .02
❑ 281 Larry Sheets .05 .01
❑ 282 Don Carman .05 .01
❑ 283 Marquis Grissom .10 .02
❑ 284 Billy Spiers .05 .01
❑ 285 Jim Abbott .15 .05
❑ 286 Ken Oberkfell .05 .01
❑ 287 Mark Grant .05 .01
❑ 288 Derrick May .05 .01
❑ 289 Tim Birtsas .05 .01
❑ 290 Steve Sax .05 .01
❑ 291 John Wathan MG .05 .01
❑ 292 Bud Black .05 .01
❑ 293 Jay Bell .10 .02
❑ 294 Mike Moore .05 .01
❑ 295 Rafael Palmeiro .15 .05
❑ 296 Mark Williamson .05 .01
❑ 297 Manny Lee .05 .01
❑ 298 Omar Vizquel .15 .05
❑ 299 Scott Radinsky .05 .01
❑ 300 Kirby Puckett .25 .08
❑ 301 Steve Farr .05 .01
❑ 302 Tim Teufel .05 .01
❑ 303 Mike Boddicker .05 .01
❑ 304 Kevin Reimer .05 .01
❑ 305 Mike Scioscia .05 .01
❑ 306A Lonnie Smith ERR
(136 games in '90) .40 .15
❑ 306B Lonnie Smith COR
(135 games in '90) .05 .01
❑ 307 Andy Benes .05 .01
❑ 308 Tom Pagnozzi .05 .01
❑ 309 Norm Charlton .05 .01
❑ 310 Gary Carter .10 .02
❑ 311 Jeff Pico .05 .01
❑ 312 Charlie Hayes .05 .01
❑ 313 Ron Robinson .05 .01
❑ 314 Gary Pettis .05 .01

❑ 315 Roberto Alomar .15 .05
❑ 316 Gene Nelson .05 .01
❑ 317 Mike Fitzgerald .05 .01
❑ 318 Rick Aguilera .10 .02
❑ 319 Jeff McKnight .05 .01
❑ 320 Tony Fernandez .05 .01
❑ 321 Bob Rodgers MG .05 .01
❑ 322 Terry Shumpert .05 .01
❑ 323 Cory Snyder .05 .01
❑ 324A Ron Kittle ERR (Set another standard ...) .40 .15
❑ 324B Ron Kittle COR (Tied another standard ...) .05 .01
❑ 325 Brett Butler .10 .02
❑ 326 Ken Patterson .05 .01
❑ 327 Ron Hassey .05 .01
❑ 328 Walt Terrell .05 .01
❑ 329 David Justice UER .10 .02
❑ 330 Dwight Gooden .10 .02
❑ 331 Eric Anthony .05 .01
❑ 332 Kenny Rogers .10 .02
❑ 333 Chipper Jones RC 4.00 1.50
❑ 334 Todd Benzinger .05 .01
❑ 335 Mitch Williams .05 .01
❑ 336 Matt Nokes .05 .01
❑ 337A Keith Comstock ERR (Cubs logo on front) .25 .08
❑ 337B Keith Comstock COR (Mariners logo on front) .05 .01
❑ 338 Luis Rivera .05 .01
❑ 339 Larry Walker .25 .08
❑ 340 Ramon Martinez .05 .01
❑ 341 John Moses .05 .01
❑ 342 Mickey Morandini .05 .01
❑ 343 Jose Oquendo .05 .01
❑ 344 Jeff Russell .05 .01
❑ 345 Len Dykstra .10 .02
❑ 346 Jesse Orosco .05 .01
❑ 347 Greg Vaughn .05 .01
❑ 348 Todd Stottlemyre .05 .01
❑ 349 Dave Gallagher .05 .01
❑ 350 Glenn Davis .05 .01
❑ 351 Joe Torre MG .10 .02
❑ 352 Frank White .10 .02
❑ 353 Tony Castillo .05 .01
❑ 354 Sid Bream .05 .01
❑ 355 Chili Davis .10 .02
❑ 356 Mike Marshall .05 .01
❑ 357 Jack Savage .05 .01
❑ 358 Mark Parent .05 .01
❑ 359 Chuck Cary .05 .01
❑ 360 Tim Raines .10 .02
❑ 361 Scott Garrelts .05 .01
❑ 362 Hector Villenueva .05 .01
❑ 363 Rick Mahler .05 .01
❑ 364 Dan Pasqua .05 .01
❑ 365 Mike Schooler .05 .01
❑ 366A Checklist 3 ERR 19 Carl Nichols .25 .08
❑ 366B Checklist 3 COR 119 Carl Nichols .05 .01
❑ 367 Dave Walsh RC .05 .01
❑ 368 Felix Jose .05 .01
❑ 369 Steve Searcy .05 .01
❑ 370 Kelly Gruber .05 .01
❑ 371 Jeff Montgomery .05 .01
❑ 372 Spike Owen .05 .01
❑ 373 Darrin Jackson .05 .01
❑ 374 Larry Casian RC .05 .01
❑ 375 Tony Pena .05 .01
❑ 376 Mike Harkey .05 .01
❑ 377 Rene Gonzales .05 .01
❑ 378A Wilson Alvarez ERR .25 .08
❑ 378B Wilson Alvarez FTC COR .05 .01
❑ 379 Randy Velarde .05 .01
❑ 380 Willie McGee .10 .02
❑ 381 Jim Leyland MG .05 .01
❑ 382 Mackey Sasser .05 .01
❑ 383 Pete Smith .05 .01
❑ 384 Gerald Perry .05 .01
❑ 385 Mickey Tettleton .05 .01
❑ 386 Cecil Fielder AS .05 .01
❑ 387 Julio Franco AS .05 .01
❑ 388 Kelly Gruber AS .05 .01
❑ 389 Alan Trammell AS .10 .02
❑ 390 Jose Canseco AS .10 .02
❑ 391 Rickey Henderson AS .15 .05
❑ 392 Ken Griffey Jr. AS .40 .15
❑ 393 Carlton Fisk AS .10 .02
❑ 394 Bob Welch AS .05 .01
❑ 395 Chuck Finley AS .05 .01
❑ 396 Bobby Thigpen AS .05 .01
❑ 397 Eddie Murray AS .15 .05
❑ 398 Ryne Sandberg AS .25 .08
❑ 399 Matt Williams AS .05 .01
❑ 400 Barry Larkin AS .10 .02
❑ 401 Barry Bonds AS .50 .20
❑ 402 Darryl Strawberry AS .05 .01
❑ 403 Bobby Bonilla AS .05 .01
❑ 404 Mike Scioscia AS .05 .01
❑ 405 Doug Drabek AS .05 .01
❑ 406 Frank Viola AS .05 .01
❑ 407 John Franco AS .05 .01
❑ 408 Earnest Riles .05 .01
❑ 409 Mike Stanley .05 .01
❑ 410 Dave Righetti .10 .02
❑ 411 Lance Blankenship .05 .01
❑ 412 Dave Bergman .05 .01
❑ 413 Terry Mulholland .05 .01
❑ 414 Sammy Sosa .25 .08
❑ 415 Rick Sutcliffe .10 .02
❑ 416 Randy Milligan .05 .01
❑ 417 Bill Krueger .05 .01
❑ 418 Nick Esasky .05 .01
❑ 419 Jeff Reed .05 .01
❑ 420 Bobby Thigpen .05 .01
❑ 421 Alex Cole .05 .01
❑ 422 Rick Reuschel .05 .01
❑ 423 Rafael Ramirez UER (Born 1959, not 1958) .05 .01
❑ 424 Calvin Schiraldi .05 .01
❑ 425 Andy Van Slyke .15 .05
❑ 426 Joe Grahe RC .10 .02
❑ 427 Rick Dempsey .05 .01
❑ 428 John Barfield .05 .01
❑ 429 Stump Merrill MG .05 .01
❑ 430 Gary Gaetti .10 .02
❑ 431 Paul Gibson .05 .01
❑ 432 Delino DeShields .10 .02
❑ 433 Pat Tabler .05 .01
❑ 434 Julio Machado .05 .01
❑ 435 Kevin Maas .05 .01
❑ 436 Scott Bankhead .05 .01
❑ 437 Doug Dascenzo .05 .01
❑ 438 Vicente Palacios .05 .01
❑ 439 Dickie Thon .05 .01
❑ 440 George Bell .05 .01
❑ 441 Zane Smith .05 .01
❑ 442 Charlie O'Brien .05 .01
❑ 443 Jeff Innis .05 .01
❑ 444 Glenn Braggs .05 .01
❑ 445 Greg Swindell .05 .01
❑ 446 Craig Grebeck .05 .01
❑ 447 John Burkett .05 .01
❑ 448 Craig Lefferts .05 .01
❑ 449 Juan Berenguer .05 .01
❑ 450 Wade Boggs .15 .05
❑ 451 Neal Heaton .05 .01
❑ 452 Bill Schroeder .05 .01
❑ 453 Lenny Harris .05 .01
❑ 454A Kevin Appier ERR .40 .15
❑ 454B Kevin Appier COR .10 .02
❑ 455 Walt Weiss .05 .01
❑ 456 Charlie Leibrandt .05 .01
❑ 457 Todd Hundley .05 .01
❑ 458 Brian Holman .05 .01
❑ 459 Tom Trebelhorn MG UER (Pitching and batting colu .05 .01
❑ 460 Dave Stieb .05 .01
❑ 461 Robin Ventura .10 .02
❑ 462 Steve Frey .05 .01
❑ 463 Dwight Smith .05 .01
❑ 464 Steve Buechele .05 .01
❑ 465 Ken Griffey Sr. .10 .02
❑ 466 Charles Nagy .05 .01
❑ 467 Dennis Cook .05 .01
❑ 468 Tim Hulett .05 .01
❑ 469 Chet Lemon .05 .01
❑ 470 Howard Johnson .05 .01
❑ 471 Mike Lieberthal RC .40 .15
❑ 472 Kirt Manwaring .05 .01
❑ 473 Curt Young .05 .01
❑ 474 Phil Plantier RC .10 .02
❑ 475 Ted Higuera .05 .01
❑ 476 Glenn Wilson .05 .01
❑ 477 Mike Fetters .05 .01
❑ 478 Kurt Stillwell .05 .01
❑ 479 Bob Patterson UER (Has a decimal point between 7 .05 .01
❑ 480 Dave Magadan .05 .01
❑ 481 Eddie Whitson .05 .01
❑ 482 Tino Martinez .25 .08
❑ 483 Mike Aldrete .05 .01
❑ 484 Dave LaPoint .05 .01
❑ 485 Terry Pendleton .10 .02
❑ 486 Tommy Greene .05 .01
❑ 487 Rafael Belliard .05 .01
❑ 488 Jeff Manto .05 .01
❑ 489 Bobby Valentine MG .05 .01
❑ 490 Kirk Gibson .10 .02
❑ 491 Kurt Miller RC .05 .01
❑ 492 Ernie Whitt .05 .01
❑ 493 Jose Rijo .05 .01
❑ 494 Chris James .05 .01
❑ 495 Charlie Hough .10 .02
❑ 496 Marty Barrett .05 .01
❑ 497 Ben McDonald .05 .01
❑ 498 Mark Salas .05 .01
❑ 499 Melido Perez .05 .01
❑ 500 Will Clark .15 .05
❑ 501 Mike Bielecki .05 .01
❑ 502 Carney Lansford .10 .02
❑ 503 Roy Smith .05 .01
❑ 504 Julio Valera .05 .01
❑ 505 Chuck Finley .10 .02
❑ 506 Darnell Coles .05 .01
❑ 507 Steve Jeltz .05 .01
❑ 508 Mike York RC .05 .01
❑ 509 Glenallen Hill .05 .01
❑ 510 John Franco .10 .02
❑ 511 Steve Balboni .05 .01
❑ 512 Jose Mesa .05 .01
❑ 513 Jerald Clark .05 .01
❑ 514 Mike Stanton .05 .01
❑ 515 Alvin Davis .05 .01
❑ 516 Karl Rhodes .05 .01
❑ 517 Joe Oliver .05 .01
❑ 518 Cris Carpenter .05 .01
❑ 519 Sparky Anderson MG .10 .02
❑ 520 Mark Grace .15 .05
❑ 521 Joe Orsulak .05 .01
❑ 522 Stan Belinda .05 .01
❑ 523 Rodney McCray RC .05 .01
❑ 524 Darrel Akerfelds .05 .01
❑ 525 Willie Randolph .10 .02
❑ 526A Moises Alou ERR .40 .15
❑ 526B Moises Alou COR .10 .02
❑ 527A Checklist 4 ERR 105 Keith Miller 719 Kevin McRey .25 .08
❑ 527B Checklist 4 COR 105 Kevin McReynolds 719 Keith M .05 .01
❑ 528 Dennis Martinez .10 .02
❑ 529 Marc Newfield RC .10 .02
❑ 530 Roger Clemens .75 .30
❑ 531 Dave Rohde .05 .01
❑ 532 Kirk McCaskill .05 .01
❑ 533 Oddibe McDowell .05 .01
❑ 534 Mike Jackson .05 .01
❑ 535 Ruben Sierra UER .10 .02
❑ 536 Mike Witt .05 .01
❑ 537 Jose Lind .05 .01
❑ 538 Bip Roberts .05 .01
❑ 539 Scott Terry .05 .01
❑ 540 George Brett .60 .25
❑ 541 Domingo Ramos .05 .01
❑ 542 Rob Murphy .05 .01
❑ 543 Junior Felix .05 .01
❑ 544 Alejandro Pena .05 .01
❑ 545 Dale Murphy .15 .05
❑ 546 Jeff Ballard .05 .01
❑ 547 Mike Pagliarulo .05 .01
❑ 548 Jaime Navarro .05 .01

❑ 549 John McNamara MG .05 .01
❑ 550 Eric Davis .10 .02
❑ 551 Bob Kipper .05 .01
❑ 552 Jeff Hamilton .05 .01
❑ 553 Joe Klink .05 .01
❑ 554 Brian Harper .05 .01
❑ 555 Turner Ward RC .10 .02
❑ 556 Gary Ward .05 .01
❑ 557 Wally Whitehurst .05 .01
❑ 558 Otis Nixon .05 .01
❑ 559 Adam Peterson .05 .01
❑ 560 Greg Smith .05 .01
❑ 561 Tim McIntosh .05 .01
❑ 562 Jeff Kunkel .05 .01
❑ 563 Brent Knackert .05 .01
❑ 564 Dante Bichette .10 .02
❑ 565 Craig Biggio .15 .05
❑ 566 Craig Wilson RC .05 .01
❑ 567 Dwayne Henry .05 .01
❑ 568 Ron Karkovice .05 .01
❑ 569 Curt Schilling .25 .08
❑ 570 Barry Bonds 1.00 .40
❑ 571 Pat Combs .05 .01
❑ 572 Dave Anderson .05 .01
❑ 573 Rich Rodriguez UER RC .05 .01
❑ 574 John Marzano .05 .01
❑ 575 Robin Yount .40 .15
❑ 576 Jeff Kaiser .05 .01
❑ 577 Bill Doran .05 .01
❑ 578 Dave West .05 .01
❑ 579 Roger Craig MG .05 .01
❑ 580 Dave Stewart .10 .02
❑ 581 Luis Quinones .05 .01
❑ 582 Marty Clary .05 .01
❑ 583 Tony Phillips .05 .01
❑ 584 Kevin Brown .10 .02
❑ 585 Pete O'Brien .05 .01
❑ 586 Fred Lynn .05 .01
❑ 587 Jose Offerman UER .05 .01
❑ 588 Mark Whiten FTC .05 .01
❑ 589 Scott Ruskin .05 .01
❑ 590 Eddie Murray .25 .08
❑ 591 Ken Hill .05 .01
❑ 592 B.J. Surhoff .10 .02
❑ 593A Mike Walker ERR
('90 Canton-Akron
stat line omit .25 .08
❑ 593B Mike Walker COR .05 .01
❑ 594 Rich Garces RC .10 .02
❑ 595 Bill Landrum .05 .01
❑ 596 Ronnie Walden RC .10 .02
❑ 597 Jerry Don Gleaton .05 .01
❑ 598 Sam Horn .05 .01
❑ 599A Greg Myers ERR
('90 Syracuse
stat line omitted) .25 .08
❑ 599B Greg Myers COR .05 .01
❑ 600 Bo Jackson .25 .08
❑ 601 Bob Ojeda .05 .01
❑ 602 Casey Candaele .05 .01
❑ 603A Wes Chamberlain ERR .40 .15
❑ 603B Wes Chamberlain COR RC .10 .02
❑ 604 Billy Hatcher .05 .01
❑ 605 Jeff Reardon .10 .02
❑ 606 Jim Gott .05 .01
❑ 607 Edgar Martinez .15 .05
❑ 608 Todd Burns .05 .01
❑ 609 Jeff Torborg MG .05 .01
❑ 610 Andres Galarraga .10 .02
❑ 611 Dave Eiland .05 .01
❑ 612 Steve Lyons .05 .01
❑ 613 Eric Show .05 .01
❑ 614 Luis Salazar .05 .01
❑ 615 Bert Blyleven .10 .02
❑ 616 Todd Zeile .05 .01
❑ 617 Bill Wegman .05 .01
❑ 618 Sil Campusano .05 .01
❑ 619 David Wells .10 .02
❑ 620 Ozzie Guillen .10 .02
❑ 621 Ted Power .05 .01
❑ 622 Jack Daugherty .05 .01
❑ 623 Jeff Blauser .05 .01
❑ 624 Tom Candiotti .05 .01
❑ 625 Terry Steinbach .05 .01
❑ 626 Gerald Young .05 .01
❑ 627 Tim Layana .05 .01
❑ 628 Greg Litton .05 .01
❑ 629 Wes Gardner .05 .01
❑ 630 Dave Winfield .10 .02
❑ 631 Mike Morgan .05 .01
❑ 632 Lloyd Moseby .05 .01
❑ 633 Kevin Tapani .05 .01
❑ 634 Henry Cotto .05 .01
❑ 635 Andy Hawkins .05 .01
❑ 636 Geronimo Pena .05 .01
❑ 637 Bruce Ruffin .05 .01
❑ 638 Mike Macfarlane .05 .01
❑ 639 Frank Robinson MG .15 .05
❑ 640 Andre Dawson .10 .02
❑ 641 Mike Henneman .05 .01
❑ 642 Hal Morris .05 .01
❑ 643 Jim Presley .05 .01
❑ 644 Chuck Crim .05 .01
❑ 645 Juan Samuel .05 .01
❑ 646 Andujar Cedeno .05 .01
❑ 647 Mark Portugal .05 .01
❑ 648 Lee Stevens .05 .01
❑ 649 Bill Sampen .05 .01
❑ 650 Jack Clark .10 .02
❑ 651 Alan Mills .05 .01
❑ 652 Kevin Romine .05 .01
❑ 653 Anthony Telford RC .05 .01
❑ 654 Paul Sorrento .05 .01
❑ 655 Erik Hanson .05 .01
❑ 656A Checklist 5 ERR
348 Vicente Palacios
381 Jose Li .25 .08
❑ 656B Checklist 5 ERR
433 Vicente Palacios
(Palacios s .25 .08
❑ 656C Checklist 5 COR
438 Vicente Palacios
537 Jose Li .05 .01
❑ 657 Mike Kingery .05 .01
❑ 658 Scott Aldred .05 .01
❑ 659 Oscar Azocar .05 .01
❑ 660 Lee Smith .10 .02
❑ 661 Steve Lake .05 .01
❑ 662 Ron Dibble .10 .02
❑ 663 Greg Brock .05 .01
❑ 664 John Farrell .05 .01
❑ 665 Mike LaValliere .05 .01
❑ 666 Danny Darwin .05 .01
❑ 667 Kent Anderson .05 .01
❑ 668 Bill Long .05 .01
❑ 669 Lou Piniella MG .10 .02
❑ 670 Rickey Henderson .25 .08
❑ 671 Andy McGaffigan .05 .01
❑ 672 Shane Mack .05 .01
❑ 673 Greg Olson UER
(6 RBI in '88 at Tide-
water and .05 .01
❑ 674A Kevin Gross ERR
(89 BB with Phillies
in '88 tied .25 .08
❑ 674B Kevin Gross COR
(89 BB with Phillies
in '88 led .05 .01
❑ 675 Tom Brunansky .05 .01
❑ 676 Scott Chiamparino .05 .01
❑ 677 Billy Ripken .05 .01
❑ 678 Mark Davidson .05 .01
❑ 679 Bill Bathe .05 .01
❑ 680 David Cone .10 .02
❑ 681 Jeff Schaefer .05 .01
❑ 682 Ray Lankford .10 .02
❑ 683 Derek Lilliquist .05 .01
❑ 684 Milt Cuyler .05 .01
❑ 685 Doug Drabek .05 .01
❑ 686 Mike Gallego .05 .01
❑ 687A John Cerutti ERR
(4.46 ERA in '90) .25 .08
❑ 687B John Cerutti COR
(4.76 ERA in '90) .05 .01
❑ 688 Rosario Rodriguez RC .05 .01
❑ 689 John Kruk .10 .02
❑ 690 Orel Hershiser .10 .02
❑ 691 Mike Blowers .05 .01
❑ 692A Efrain Valdez ERR .25 .08
❑ 692B Efrain Valdez COR RC .05 .01
❑ 693 Francisco Cabrera .05 .01
❑ 694 Randy Veres .05 .01
❑ 695 Kevin Seitzer .05 .01
❑ 696 Steve Olin .05 .01
❑ 697 Shawn Abner .05 .01
❑ 698 Mark Guthrie .05 .01
❑ 699 Jim Lefebvre MG .05 .01
❑ 700 Jose Canseco .15 .05
❑ 701 Pascual Perez .05 .01
❑ 702 Tim Naehring .05 .01
❑ 703 Juan Agosto .05 .01
❑ 704 Devon White .10 .02
❑ 705 Robby Thompson .05 .01
❑ 706A Brad Arnsberg ERR .25 .08
❑ 706B Brad Arnsberg COR .05 .01
❑ 707 Jim Eisenreich .05 .01
❑ 708 John Mitchell .05 .01
❑ 709 Matt Sinatro .05 .01
❑ 710 Kent Hrbek .10 .02
❑ 711 Jose DeLeon .05 .01
❑ 712 Ricky Jordan .05 .01
❑ 713 Scott Scudder .05 .01
❑ 714 Marvell Wynne .05 .01
❑ 715 Tim Burke .05 .01
❑ 716 Bob Geren .05 .01
❑ 717 Phil Bradley .05 .01
❑ 718 Steve Crawford .05 .01
❑ 719 Keith Miller .05 .01
❑ 720 Cecil Fielder .10 .02
❑ 721 Mark Lee RC .05 .01
❑ 722 Wally Backman .05 .01
❑ 723 Candy Maldonado .05 .01
❑ 724 David Segui .05 .01
❑ 725 Ron Gant .10 .02
❑ 726 Phil Stephenson .05 .01
❑ 727 Mookie Wilson .10 .02
❑ 728 Scott Sanderson .05 .01
❑ 729 Don Zimmer MG .10 .02
❑ 730 Barry Larkin .15 .05
❑ 731 Jeff Gray RC .05 .01
❑ 732 Franklin Stubbs .05 .01
❑ 733 Kelly Downs .05 .01
❑ 734 John Russell .05 .01
❑ 735 Ron Darling .05 .01
❑ 736 Dick Schofield .05 .01
❑ 737 Tim Crews .05 .01
❑ 738 Mel Hall .05 .01
❑ 739 Russ Swan .05 .01
❑ 740 Ryne Sandberg .40 .15
❑ 741 Jimmy Key .10 .02
❑ 742 Tommy Gregg .05 .01
❑ 743 Bryn Smith .05 .01
❑ 744 Nelson Santovenia .05 .01
❑ 745 Doug Jones .05 .01
❑ 746 John Shelby .05 .01
❑ 747 Tony Fossas .05 .01
❑ 748 Al Newman .05 .01
❑ 749 Greg W. Harris .05 .01
❑ 750 Bobby Bonilla .10 .02
❑ 751 Wayne Edwards .05 .01
❑ 752 Kevin Bass .05 .01
❑ 753 Paul Marak UER RC .05 .01
❑ 754 Bill Pecota .05 .01
❑ 755 Mark Langston .05 .01
❑ 756 Jeff Huson .05 .01
❑ 757 Mark Gardner .05 .01
❑ 758 Mike Devereaux .05 .01
❑ 759 Bobby Cox MG .05 .01
❑ 760 Benny Santiago .10 .02
❑ 761 Larry Andersen .05 .01
❑ 762 Mitch Webster .05 .01
❑ 763 Dana Kiecker .05 .01
❑ 764 Mark Carreon .05 .01
❑ 765 Shawon Dunston .05 .01
❑ 766 Jeff Robinson .05 .01
❑ 767 Dan Wilson RC .25 .08
❑ 768 Don Pall .05 .01
❑ 769 Tim Sherrill .05 .01
❑ 770 Jay Howell .05 .01
❑ 771 Gary Redus UER
(Born in Tanner&
should say Athen .05 .01
❑ 772 Kent Mercker
(Born in Indianapolis&
should say D .05 .01
❑ 773 Tom Foley .05 .01
❑ 774 Dennis Rasmussen .05 .01
❑ 775 Julio Franco .10 .02

❑ 776 Brent Mayne .05 .01
❑ 777 John Candelaria .05 .01
❑ 778 Dan Gladden .05 .01
❑ 779 Carmelo Martinez .05 .01
❑ 780A Randy Myers ERR
(15 career losses) .40 .15
❑ 780B Randy Myers COR
(19 career losses) .05 .01
❑ 781 Darryl Hamilton .05 .01
❑ 782 Jim Deshaies .05 .01
❑ 783 Joel Skinner .05 .01
❑ 784 Willie Fraser .05 .01
❑ 785 Scott Fletcher .05 .01
❑ 786 Eric Plunk .05 .01
❑ 787 Checklist 6 .05 .01
❑ 788 Bob Milacki .05 .01
❑ 789 Tom Lasorda MG .25 .08
❑ 790 Ken Griffey Jr. .75 .30
❑ 791 Mike Benjamin .05 .01
❑ 792 Mike Greenwell .05 .01

1992 Topps

❑ COMPLETE SET (792) 25.00 10.00
❑ COMP.FACT.SET (802) 25.00 10.00
❑ COMP.HOLIDAY SET (811) 40.00 15.00
❑ 1 Nolan Ryan 1.00 .40
❑ 2 Rickey Henderson RB .15 .05
❑ 3 Jeff Reardon RB .05 .01
❑ 4 Nolan Ryan RB .50 .20
❑ 5 Dave Winfield RB .05 .01
❑ 6 Brien Taylor RC .25 .08
❑ 7 Jim Olander .05 .01
❑ 8 Bryan Hickerson RC .10 .02
❑ 9 Jon Farrell RC .10 .02
❑ 10 Wade Boggs .15 .05
❑ 11 Jack McDowell .05 .01
❑ 12 Luis Gonzalez .10 .02
❑ 13 Mike Scioscia .05 .01
❑ 14 Wes Chamberlain .05 .01
❑ 15 Dennis Martinez .10 .02
❑ 16 Jeff Montgomery .05 .01
❑ 17 Randy Milligan .05 .01
❑ 18 Greg Cadaret .05 .01
❑ 19 Jamie Quirk .05 .01
❑ 20 Bip Roberts .05 .01
❑ 21 Buck Rodgers MG .05 .01
❑ 22 Bill Wegman .05 .01
❑ 23 Chuck Knoblauch .10 .02
❑ 24 Randy Myers .05 .01
❑ 25 Ron Gant .10 .02
❑ 26 Mike Bielecki .05 .01
❑ 27 Juan Gonzalez .15 .05
❑ 28 Mike Schooler .05 .01
❑ 29 Mickey Tettleton .05 .01
❑ 30 John Kruk .10 .02
❑ 31 Bryn Smith .05 .01
❑ 32 Chris Nabholz .05 .01
❑ 33 Carlos Baerga .05 .01
❑ 34 Jeff Juden .05 .01
❑ 35 Dave Righetti .10 .02
❑ 36 Scott Ruffcorn RC .10 .02
❑ 37 Luis Polonia .05 .01
❑ 38 Tom Candiotti .05 .01
❑ 39 Greg Olson .05 .01
❑ 40 Cal Ripken/Gehrig 2.00 .75
❑ 41 Craig Lefferts .05 .01
❑ 42 Mike Macfarlane .05 .01
❑ 43 Jose Lind .05 .01
❑ 44 Rick Aguilera .10 .02
❑ 45 Gary Carter .10 .02
❑ 46 Steve Farr .05 .01
❑ 47 Rex Hudler .05 .01
❑ 48 Scott Scudder .05 .01
❑ 49 Damon Berryhill .05 .01
❑ 50 Ken Griffey Jr. .40 .15
❑ 51 Tom Runnells MG .05 .01
❑ 52 Juan Bell .05 .01
❑ 53 Tommy Gregg .05 .01
❑ 54 David Wells .10 .02
❑ 55 Rafael Palmeiro .15 .05
❑ 56 Charlie O'Brien .05 .01
❑ 57 Donn Pall .05 .01
❑ 58 Brad Ausmus RC 1.50 .60
❑ 59 Mo Vaughn .10 .02
❑ 60 Tony Fernandez .05 .01
❑ 61 Paul O'Neill .15 .05
❑ 62 Gene Nelson .05 .01
❑ 63 Randy Ready .05 .01
❑ 64 Bob Kipper .05 .01
❑ 65 Willie McGee .10 .02
❑ 66 Scott Stahoviak RC .10 .02
❑ 67 Luis Salazar .05 .01
❑ 68 Marvin Freeman .05 .01
❑ 69 Kenny Lofton .15 .05
❑ 70 Gary Gaetti .10 .02
❑ 71 Erik Hanson .05 .01
❑ 72 Eddie Zosky .05 .01
❑ 73 Brian Barnes .05 .01
❑ 74 Scott Leius .05 .01
❑ 75 Bret Saberhagen .10 .02
❑ 76 Mike Gallego .05 .01
❑ 77 Jack Armstrong .05 .01
❑ 78 Ivan Rodriguez .25 .08
❑ 79 Jesse Orosco .05 .01
❑ 80 David Justice .10 .02
❑ 81 Ced Landrum .05 .01
❑ 82 Doug Simons .05 .01
❑ 83 Tommy Greene .05 .01
❑ 84 Leo Gomez .05 .01
❑ 85 Jose DeLeon .05 .01
❑ 86 Steve Finley .10 .02
❑ 87 Bob MacDonald .05 .01
❑ 88 Darrin Jackson .05 .01
❑ 89 Neal Heaton .05 .01
❑ 90 Robin Yount .40 .15
❑ 91 Jeff Reed .05 .01
❑ 92 Lenny Harris .05 .01
❑ 93 Reggie Jefferson .05 .01
❑ 94 Sammy Sosa .25 .08
❑ 95 Scott Bailes .05 .01
❑ 96 Tom McKinnon RC .10 .02
❑ 97 Luis Rivera .05 .01
❑ 98 Mike Harkey .05 .01
❑ 99 Jeff Treadway .05 .01
❑ 100 Jose Canseco .15 .05
❑ 101 Omar Vizquel .15 .05
❑ 102 Scott Kamieniecki .05 .01
❑ 103 Ricky Jordan .05 .01
❑ 104 Jeff Ballard .05 .01
❑ 105 Felix Jose .05 .01
❑ 106 Mike Boddicker .05 .01
❑ 107 Dan Pasqua .05 .01
❑ 108 Mike Timlin .05 .01
❑ 109 Roger Craig MG .05 .01
❑ 110 Ryne Sandberg .40 .15
❑ 111 Mark Carreon .05 .01
❑ 112 Oscar Azocar .05 .01
❑ 113 Mike Greenwell .05 .01
❑ 114 Mark Portugal .05 .01
❑ 115 Terry Pendleton .10 .02
❑ 116 Willie Randolph .10 .02
❑ 117 Scott Terry .05 .01
❑ 118 Chili Davis .10 .02
❑ 119 Mark Gardner .05 .01
❑ 120 Alan Trammell .10 .02
❑ 121 Derek Bell .10 .02
❑ 122 Gary Varsho .05 .01
❑ 123 Bob Ojeda .05 .01
❑ 124 Shawn Livsey RC .10 .02
❑ 125 Chris Hoiles .05 .01
❑ 126 Klesko/Jaha/Brogna/Staton .25 .08
❑ 127 Carlos Quintana .05 .01
❑ 128 Kurt Stillwell .05 .01
❑ 129 Melido Perez .05 .01
❑ 130 Alvin Davis .05 .01
❑ 131 Checklist 1-132 .05 .01
❑ 132 Eric Show .05 .01
❑ 133 Rance Mulliniks .05 .01
❑ 134 Darryl Kile .10 .02
❑ 135 Von Hayes .05 .01
❑ 136 Bill Doran .05 .01
❑ 137 Jeff D. Robinson .05 .01
❑ 138 Monty Fariss .05 .01
❑ 139 Jeff Innis .05 .01
❑ 140 Mark Grace UER .15 .05
❑ 141 Jim Leyland MG UER
(No closed parenthesis
after .10 .02
❑ 142 Todd Van Poppel .05 .01
❑ 143 Paul Gibson .05 .01
❑ 144 Bill Swift .05 .01
❑ 145 Danny Tartabull .05 .01
❑ 146 Al Newman .05 .01
❑ 147 Cris Carpenter .05 .01
❑ 148 Anthony Young .05 .01
❑ 149 Brian Bohanon .05 .01
❑ 150 Roger Clemens .50 .20
❑ 151 Jeff Hamilton .05 .01
❑ 152 Charlie Leibrandt .05 .01
❑ 153 Ron Karkovice .05 .01
❑ 154 Hensley Meulens .05 .01
❑ 155 Scott Bankhead .05 .01
❑ 156 Manny Ramirez RC 5.00 2.00
❑ 157 Keith Miller .05 .01
❑ 158 Todd Frohwirth .05 .01
❑ 159 Darrin Fletcher .05 .01
❑ 160 Bobby Bonilla .10 .02
❑ 161 Casey Candaele .05 .01
❑ 162 Paul Faries .05 .01
❑ 163 Dana Kiecker .05 .01
❑ 164 Shane Mack .05 .01
❑ 165 Mark Langston .05 .01
❑ 166 Geronimo Pena .05 .01
❑ 167 Andy Allanson .05 .01
❑ 168 Dwight Smith .05 .01
❑ 169 Chuck Crim .05 .01
❑ 170 Alex Cole .05 .01
❑ 171 Bill Plummer MG .05 .01
❑ 172 Juan Berenguer .05 .01
❑ 173 Brian Downing .05 .01
❑ 174 Steve Frey .05 .01
❑ 175 Orel Hershiser .10 .02
❑ 176 Ramon Garcia .05 .01
❑ 177 Dan Gladden .05 .01
❑ 178 Jim Acker .05 .01
❑ 179 DeJard/Bern/Moreno/Stank .05 .01
❑ 180 Kevin Mitchell .05 .01
❑ 181 Hector Villanueva .05 .01
❑ 182 Jeff Reardon .10 .02
❑ 183 Brent Mayne .05 .01
❑ 184 Jimmy Jones .05 .01
❑ 185 Benito Santiago .10 .02
❑ 186 Cliff Floyd RC .75 .30
❑ 187 Ernie Riles .05 .01
❑ 188 Jose Guzman .05 .01
❑ 189 Junior Felix .05 .01
❑ 190 Glenn Davis .05 .01
❑ 191 Charlie Hough .10 .02
❑ 192 Dave Fleming .05 .01
❑ 193 Omar Olivares .05 .01
❑ 194 Eric Karros .10 .02
❑ 195 David Cone .10 .02
❑ 196 Frank Castillo .05 .01
❑ 197 Glenn Braggs .05 .01
❑ 198 Scott Aldred .05 .01
❑ 199 Jeff Blauser .05 .01
❑ 200 Len Dykstra .10 .02
❑ 201 Buck Showalter MG RC .25 .08
❑ 202 Rick Honeycutt .05 .01
❑ 203 Greg Myers .05 .01
❑ 204 Trevor Wilson .05 .01
❑ 205 Jay Howell .05 .01
❑ 206 Luis Sojo .05 .01
❑ 207 Jack Clark .10 .02
❑ 208 Julio Machado .05 .01
❑ 209 Lloyd McClendon .05 .01
❑ 210 Ozzie Guillen .10 .02
❑ 211 Jeremy Hernandez RC .10 .02
❑ 212 Randy Velarde .05 .01
❑ 213 Les Lancaster .05 .01

No.	Player		
❑ 214	Andy Mota	.05	.01
❑ 215	Rich Gossage	.10	.02
❑ 216	Brent Gates RC	.10	.02
❑ 217	Brian Harper	.05	.01
❑ 218	Mike Flanagan	.05	.01
❑ 219	Jerry Browne	.05	.01
❑ 220	Jose Rijo	.05	.01
❑ 221	Skeeter Barnes	.05	.01
❑ 222	Jaime Navarro	.05	.01
❑ 223	Mel Hall	.05	.01
❑ 224	Bret Barberie	.05	.01
❑ 225	Roberto Alomar	.15	.05
❑ 226	Pete Smith	.05	.01
❑ 227	Daryl Boston	.05	.01
❑ 228	Eddie Whitson	.05	.01
❑ 229	Shawn Boskie	.05	.01
❑ 230	Dick Schofield	.05	.01
❑ 231	Brian Drahman	.05	.01
❑ 232	John Smiley	.05	.01
❑ 233	Mitch Webster	.05	.01
❑ 234	Terry Steinbach	.05	.01
❑ 235	Jack Morris	.10	.02
❑ 236	Bill Pecota	.05	.01
❑ 237	Jose Hernandez RC	.25	.08
❑ 238	Greg Litton	.05	.01
❑ 239	Brian Holman	.05	.01
❑ 240	Andres Galarraga	.10	.02
❑ 241	Gerald Young	.05	.01
❑ 242	Mike Mussina	.25	.08
❑ 243	Alvaro Espinoza	.05	.01
❑ 244	Darren Daulton	.10	.02
❑ 245	John Smoltz	.15	.05
❑ 246	Jason Pruitt RC	.10	.02
❑ 247	Chuck Finley	.10	.02
❑ 248	Jim Gantner	.05	.01
❑ 249	Tony Fossas	.05	.01
❑ 250	Ken Griffey Sr.	.10	.02
❑ 251	Kevin Elster	.05	.01
❑ 252	Dennis Rasmussen	.05	.01
❑ 253	Terry Kennedy	.05	.01
❑ 254	Ryan Bowen	.05	.01
❑ 255	Robin Ventura	.10	.02
❑ 256	Mike Aldrete	.05	.01
❑ 257	Jeff Russell	.05	.01
❑ 258	Jim Lindeman	.05	.01
❑ 259	Ron Darling	.05	.01
❑ 260	Devon White	.10	.02
❑ 261	Tom Lasorda MG	.10	.02
❑ 262	Terry Lee	.05	.01
❑ 263	Bob Patterson	.05	.01
❑ 264	Checklist 133-264	.05	.01
❑ 265	Teddy Higuera	.05	.01
❑ 266	Roberto Kelly	.05	.01
❑ 267	Steve Bedrosian	.05	.01
❑ 268	Brady Anderson	.10	.02
❑ 269	Ruben Amaro	.05	.01
❑ 270	Tony Gwynn	.30	.10
❑ 271	Tracy Jones	.05	.01
❑ 272	Jerry Don Gleaton	.05	.01
❑ 273	Craig Grebeck	.05	.01
❑ 274	Bob Scanlan	.05	.01
❑ 275	Todd Zeile	.05	.01
❑ 276	Shawn Green RC	1.00	.40
❑ 277	Scott Chiamparino	.05	.01
❑ 278	Darryl Hamilton	.05	.01
❑ 279	Jim Clancy	.05	.01
❑ 280	Carlos Martinez	.05	.01
❑ 281	Kevin Appier	.10	.02
❑ 282	John Wehner	.05	.01
❑ 283	Reggie Sanders	.10	.02
❑ 284	Gene Larkin	.05	.01
❑ 285	Bob Welch	.05	.01
❑ 286	Gilberto Reyes	.05	.01
❑ 287	Pete Schourek	.05	.01
❑ 288	Andujar Cedeno	.05	.01
❑ 289	Mike Morgan	.05	.01
❑ 290	Bo Jackson	.25	.08
❑ 291	Phil Garner MG	.10	.02
❑ 292	Ray Lankford	.10	.02
❑ 293	Mike Henneman	.05	.01
❑ 294	Dave Valle	.05	.01
❑ 295	Alonzo Powell	.05	.01
❑ 296	Tom Brunansky	.05	.01
❑ 297	Kevin Brown	.10	.02
❑ 298	Kelly Gruber	.05	.01
❑ 299	Charles Nagy	.05	.01
❑ 300	Don Mattingly	.60	.25
❑ 301	Kirk McCaskill	.05	.01
❑ 302	Joey Cora	.05	.01
❑ 303	Dan Plesac	.05	.01
❑ 304	Joe Oliver	.05	.01
❑ 305	Tom Glavine	.15	.05
❑ 306	Al Shirley RC	.10	.02
❑ 307	Bruce Ruffin	.05	.01
❑ 308	Craig Shipley	.05	.01
❑ 309	Dave Martinez	.05	.01
❑ 310	Jose Mesa	.05	.01
❑ 311	Henry Cotto	.05	.01
❑ 312	Mike LaValliere	.05	.01
❑ 313	Kevin Tapani	.05	.01
❑ 314	Jeff Huson	.05	.01
❑ 315	Juan Samuel	.05	.01
❑ 316	Curt Schilling	.15	.05
❑ 317	Mike Bordick	.05	.01
❑ 318	Steve Howe	.05	.01
❑ 319	Tony Phillips	.05	.01
❑ 320	George Bell	.05	.01
❑ 321	Lou Piniella MG	.10	.02
❑ 322	Tim Burke	.05	.01
❑ 323	Milt Thompson	.05	.01
❑ 324	Danny Darwin	.05	.01
❑ 325	Joe Orsulak	.05	.01
❑ 326	Eric King	.05	.01
❑ 327	Jay Buhner	.10	.02
❑ 328	Joel Johnston	.05	.01
❑ 329	Franklin Stubbs	.05	.01
❑ 330	Will Clark	.15	.05
❑ 331	Steve Lake	.05	.01
❑ 332	Chris Jones	.05	.01
❑ 333	Pat Tabler	.05	.01
❑ 334	Kevin Gross	.05	.01
❑ 335	Dave Henderson	.05	.01
❑ 336	Greg Anthony RC	.10	.02
❑ 337	Alejandro Pena	.05	.01
❑ 338	Shawn Abner	.05	.01
❑ 339	Tom Browning	.05	.01
❑ 340	Otis Nixon	.05	.01
❑ 341	Bob Geren	.05	.01
❑ 342	Tim Spehr	.05	.01
❑ 343	John Vander Wal	.05	.01
❑ 344	Jack Daugherty	.05	.01
❑ 345	Zane Smith	.05	.01
❑ 346	Rheal Cormier	.05	.01
❑ 347	Kent Hrbek	.10	.02
❑ 348	Rick Wilkins	.05	.01
❑ 349	Steve Lyons	.05	.01
❑ 350	Gregg Olson	.05	.01
❑ 351	Greg Riddoch MG	.05	.01
❑ 352	Ed Nunez	.05	.01
❑ 353	Braulio Castillo	.05	.01
❑ 354	Dave Bergman	.05	.01
❑ 355	Warren Newson	.05	.01
❑ 356	Luis Quinones	.05	.01
❑ 357	Mike Witt	.05	.01
❑ 358	Ted Wood	.05	.01
❑ 359	Mike Moore	.05	.01
❑ 360	Lance Parrish	.10	.02
❑ 361	Barry Jones	.05	.01
❑ 362	Javier Ortiz	.05	.01
❑ 363	John Candelaria	.05	.01
❑ 364	Glenallen Hill	.05	.01
❑ 365	Duane Ward	.05	.01
❑ 366	Checklist 265-396	.05	.01
❑ 367	Rafael Belliard	.05	.01
❑ 368	Bill Krueger	.05	.01
❑ 369	Steve Whitaker RC	.10	.02
❑ 370	Shawon Dunston	.05	.01
❑ 371	Dante Bichette	.10	.02
❑ 372	Kip Gross	.05	.01
❑ 373	Don Robinson	.05	.01
❑ 374	Bernie Williams	.15	.05
❑ 375	Bert Blyleven	.10	.02
❑ 376	Chris Donnels	.05	.01
❑ 377	Bob Zupcic RC	.10	.02
❑ 378	Joel Skinner	.05	.01
❑ 379	Steve Chitren	.05	.01
❑ 380	Barry Bonds	1.00	.40
❑ 381	Sparky Anderson MG	.10	.02
❑ 382	Sid Fernandez	.05	.01
❑ 383	Dave Hollins	.05	.01
❑ 384	Mark Lee	.05	.01
❑ 385	Tim Wallach	.05	.01
❑ 386	Will Clark AS	.10	.02
❑ 387	Ryne Sandberg AS	.25	.08
❑ 388	Howard Johnson AS	.05	.01
❑ 389	Barry Larkin AS	.10	.02
❑ 390	Barry Bonds AS	.50	.20
❑ 391	Ron Gant AS	.05	.01
❑ 392	Bobby Bonilla AS	.05	.01
❑ 393	Craig Biggio AS	.10	.02
❑ 394	Dennis Martinez AS	.05	.01
❑ 395	Tom Glavine AS	.10	.02
❑ 396	Lee Smith AS	.05	.01
❑ 397	Cecil Fielder AS	.05	.01
❑ 398	Julio Franco AS	.05	.01
❑ 399	Wade Boggs AS	.10	.02
❑ 400	Cal Ripken AS	.40	.15
❑ 401	Jose Canseco AS	.15	.05
❑ 402	Joe Carter AS	.05	.01
❑ 403	Ruben Sierra AS	.05	.01
❑ 404	Matt Nokes AS	.05	.01
❑ 405	Roger Clemens AS	.25	.08
❑ 406	Jim Abbott AS	.10	.02
❑ 407	Bryan Harvey AS	.05	.01
❑ 408	Bob Milacki	.05	.01
❑ 409	Geno Petralli	.05	.01
❑ 410	Dave Stewart	.10	.02
❑ 411	Mike Jackson	.05	.01
❑ 412	Luis Aquino	.05	.01
❑ 413	Tim Teufel	.05	.01
❑ 414	Jeff Ware	.05	.01
❑ 415	Jim Deshaies	.05	.01
❑ 416	Ellis Burks	.10	.02
❑ 417	Allan Anderson	.05	.01
❑ 418	Alfredo Griffin	.05	.01
❑ 419	Wally Whitehurst	.05	.01
❑ 420	Sandy Alomar Jr.	.05	.01
❑ 421	Juan Agosto	.05	.01
❑ 422	Sam Horn	.05	.01
❑ 423	Jeff Fassero	.05	.01
❑ 424	Paul McClellan	.05	.01
❑ 425	Cecil Fielder	.10	.02
❑ 426	Tim Raines	.10	.02
❑ 427	Eddie Taubensee RC	.25	.08
❑ 428	Dennis Boyd	.05	.01
❑ 429	Tony LaRussa MG	.10	.02
❑ 430	Steve Sax	.05	.01
❑ 431	Tom Gordon	.05	.01
❑ 432	Billy Hatcher	.05	.01
❑ 433	Cal Eldred	.05	.01
❑ 434	Wally Backman	.05	.01
❑ 435	Mark Eichhorn	.05	.01
❑ 436	Mookie Wilson	.10	.02
❑ 437	Scott Servais	.05	.01
❑ 438	Mike Maddux	.05	.01
❑ 439	Chico Walker	.05	.01
❑ 440	Doug Drabek	.05	.01
❑ 441	Rob Deer	.05	.01
❑ 442	Dave West	.05	.01
❑ 443	Spike Owen	.05	.01
❑ 444	Tyrone Hill RC	.10	.02
❑ 445	Matt Williams	.10	.02
❑ 446	Mark Lewis	.05	.01
❑ 447	David Segui	.05	.01
❑ 448	Tom Pagnozzi	.05	.01
❑ 449	Jeff Johnson	.05	.01
❑ 450	Mark McGwire	.60	.25
❑ 451	Tom Henke	.05	.01
❑ 452	Wilson Alvarez	.05	.01
❑ 453	Gary Redus	.05	.01
❑ 454	Darren Holmes	.05	.01
❑ 455	Pete O'Brien	.05	.01
❑ 456	Pat Combs	.05	.01
❑ 457	Hubie Brooks	.05	.01
❑ 458	Frank Tanana	.05	.01
❑ 459	Tom Kelly MG	.05	.01
❑ 460	Andre Dawson	.10	.02
❑ 461	Doug Jones	.05	.01
❑ 462	Rich Rodriguez	.05	.01
❑ 463	Mike Simms	.05	.01
❑ 464	Mike Jeffcoat	.05	.01
❑ 465	Barry Larkin	.15	.05
❑ 466	Stan Belinda	.05	.01
❑ 467	Lonnie Smith	.05	.01
❑ 468	Greg Harris	.05	.01
❑ 469	Jim Eisenreich	.05	.01
❑ 470	Pedro Guerrero	.10	.02
❑ 471	Jose DeJesus	.05	.01

❑ 472 Rich Rowland RC .10 .02
❑ 473 Bolick/Paquette/Red/Russo .05 .01
❑ 474 Mike Rossiter RC .10 .02
❑ 475 Robby Thompson .05 .01
❑ 476 Randy Bush .05 .01
❑ 477 Greg Hibbard .05 .01
❑ 478 Dale Sveum .05 .01
❑ 479 Chito Martinez .05 .01
❑ 480 Scott Sanderson .05 .01
❑ 481 Tino Martinez .15 .05
❑ 482 Jimmy Key .10 .02
❑ 483 Terry Shumpert .05 .01
❑ 484 Mike Hartley .05 .01
❑ 485 Chris Sabo .05 .01
❑ 486 Bob Walk .05 .01
❑ 487 John Cerutti .05 .01
❑ 488 Scott Cooper .05 .01
❑ 489 Bobby Cox MG .10 .02
❑ 490 Julio Franco .10 .02
❑ 491 Jeff Brantley .05 .01
❑ 492 Mike Devereaux .05 .01
❑ 493 Jose Offerman .05 .01
❑ 494 Gary Thurman .05 .01
❑ 495 Carney Lansford .10 .02
❑ 496 Joe Grahe .05 .01
❑ 497 Andy Ashby .05 .01
❑ 498 Gerald Perry .05 .01
❑ 499 Dave Otto .05 .01
❑ 500 Vince Coleman .05 .01
❑ 501 Rob Mallicoat .05 .01
❑ 502 Greg Briley .05 .01
❑ 503 Pascual Perez .05 .01
❑ 504 Aaron Sele RC .25 .08
❑ 505 Bobby Thigpen .05 .01
❑ 506 Todd Benzinger .05 .01
❑ 507 Candy Maldonado .05 .01
❑ 508 Bill Gullickson .05 .01
❑ 509 Doug Dascenzo .05 .01
❑ 510 Frank Viola .10 .02
❑ 511 Kenny Rogers .10 .02
❑ 512 Mike Heath .05 .01
❑ 513 Kevin Bass .05 .01
❑ 514 Kim Batiste .05 .01
❑ 515 Delino DeShields .05 .01
❑ 516 Ed Sprague .05 .01
❑ 517 Jim Gott .05 .01
❑ 518 Jose Melendez .05 .01
❑ 519 Hal McRae MG .10 .02
❑ 520 Jeff Bagwell .25 .08
❑ 521 Joe Hesketh .05 .01
❑ 522 Milt Cuyler .05 .01
❑ 523 Shawn Hillegas .05 .01
❑ 524 Don Slaught .05 .01
❑ 525 Randy Johnson .25 .08
❑ 526 Doug Piatt .05 .01
❑ 527 Checklist 397-528 .05 .01
❑ 528 Steve Foster .05 .01
❑ 529 Joe Girardi .05 .01
❑ 530 Jim Abbott .15 .05
❑ 531 Larry Walker .15 .05
❑ 532 Mike Huff .05 .01
❑ 533 Mackey Sasser .05 .01
❑ 534 Benji Gil RC .25 .08
❑ 535 Dave Stieb .05 .01
❑ 536 Willie Wilson .05 .01
❑ 537 Mark Leiter .05 .01
❑ 538 Jose Uribe .05 .01
❑ 539 Thomas Howard .05 .01
❑ 540 Ben McDonald .05 .01
❑ 541 Jose Tolentino .05 .01
❑ 542 Keith Mitchell .05 .01
❑ 543 Jerome Walton .05 .01
❑ 544 Cliff Brantley .05 .01
❑ 545 Andy Van Slyke .15 .05
❑ 546 Paul Sorrento .05 .01
❑ 547 Herm Winningham .05 .01
❑ 548 Mark Guthrie .05 .01
❑ 549 Joe Torre MG .10 .02
❑ 550 Darryl Strawberry .10 .02
❑ 551 Chipper Jones .25 .08
❑ 552 Dave Gallagher .05 .01
❑ 553 Edgar Martinez .15 .05
❑ 554 Donald Harris .05 .01
❑ 555 Frank Thomas .25 .08
❑ 556 Storm Davis .05 .01
❑ 557 Dickie Thon .05 .01
❑ 558 Scott Garrelts .05 .01
❑ 559 Steve Olin .05 .01
❑ 560 Rickey Henderson .25 .08
❑ 561 Jose Vizcaino .05 .01
❑ 562 Wade Taylor .05 .01
❑ 563 Pat Borders .05 .01
❑ 564 Jimmy Gonzalez RC .10 .02
❑ 565 Lee Smith .10 .02
❑ 566 Bill Sampen .05 .01
❑ 567 Dean Palmer .10 .02
❑ 568 Bryan Harvey .05 .01
❑ 569 Tony Pena .05 .01
❑ 570 Lou Whitaker .10 .02
❑ 571 Randy Tomlin .05 .01
❑ 572 Greg Vaughn .05 .01
❑ 573 Kelly Downs .05 .01
❑ 574 Steve Avery UER .05 .01
❑ 575 Kirby Puckett .25 .08
❑ 576 Heathcliff Slocumb .05 .01
❑ 577 Kevin Seitzer .05 .01
❑ 578 Lee Guetterman .05 .01
❑ 579 Johnny Oates MG .05 .01
❑ 580 Greg Maddux .40 .15
❑ 581 Stan Javier .05 .01
❑ 582 Vicente Palacios .05 .01
❑ 583 Mel Hojas .05 .01
❑ 584 Wayne Rosenthal RC .10 .02
❑ 585 Lenny Webster .05 .01
❑ 586 Rod Nichols .05 .01
❑ 587 Mickey Morandini .05 .01
❑ 588 Russ Swan .05 .01
❑ 589 Mariano Duncan .05 .01
❑ 590 Howard Johnson .05 .01
❑ 591 Burnitz/Brum/Coc/Dozier .10 .02
❑ 592 Denny Neagle .10 .02
❑ 593 Steve Decker .05 .01
❑ 594 Brian Barber RC .10 .02
❑ 595 Bruce Hurst .05 .01
❑ 596 Kent Mercker .05 .01
❑ 597 Mike Magnante RC .10 .02
❑ 598 Jody Reed .05 .01
❑ 599 Steve Searcy .05 .01
❑ 600 Paul Molitor .10 .02
❑ 601 Dave Smith .05 .01
❑ 602 Mike Fetters .05 .01
❑ 603 Luis Mercedes .05 .01
❑ 604 Chris Gwynn .05 .01
❑ 605 Scott Erickson .05 .01
❑ 606 Brook Jacoby .05 .01
❑ 607 Todd Stottlemyre .05 .01
❑ 608 Scott Bradley .05 .01
❑ 609 Mike Hargrove MG .10 .02
❑ 610 Eric Davis .10 .02
❑ 611 Brian Hunter .05 .01
❑ 612 Pat Kelly .05 .01
❑ 613 Pedro Munoz .05 .01
❑ 614 Al Osuna .05 .01
❑ 615 Matt Merullo .05 .01
❑ 616 Larry Andersen .05 .01
❑ 617 Junior Ortiz .05 .01
❑ 618 Hern/Hosey/McNeely/Pelt .05 .01
❑ 619 Danny Jackson .05 .01
❑ 620 George Brett .60 .25
❑ 621 Dan Gakeler .05 .01
❑ 622 Steve Buechele .05 .01
❑ 623 Bob Tewksbury .05 .01
❑ 624 Shawn Estes RC .25 .08
❑ 625 Kevin McReynolds .05 .01
❑ 626 Chris Haney .05 .01
❑ 627 Mike Sharperson .05 .01
❑ 628 Mark Williamson .05 .01
❑ 629 Wally Joyner .10 .02
❑ 630 Carlton Fisk .15 .05
❑ 631 Armando Reynoso RC .25 .08
❑ 632 Felix Fermin .05 .01
❑ 633 Mitch Williams .05 .01
❑ 634 Manuel Lee .05 .01
❑ 635 Harold Baines .10 .02
❑ 636 Greg Harris .05 .01
❑ 637 Orlando Merced .05 .01
❑ 638 Chris Bosio .05 .01
❑ 639 Wayne Housie .05 .01
❑ 640 Xavier Hernandez .05 .01
❑ 641 David Howard .05 .01
❑ 642 Tim Crews .05 .01
❑ 643 Rick Cerone .05 .01
❑ 644 Terry Leach .05 .01
❑ 645 Deion Sanders .15 .05
❑ 646 Craig Wilson .05 .01
❑ 647 Marquis Grissom .10 .02
❑ 648 Scott Fletcher .05 .01
❑ 649 Norm Charlton .05 .01
❑ 650 Jesse Barfield .05 .01
❑ 651 Joe Slusarski .05 .01
❑ 652 Bobby Rose .05 .01
❑ 653 Dennis Lamp .05 .01
❑ 654 Allen Watson RC .10 .02
❑ 655 Brett Butler .10 .02
❑ 656 Pem/H.Rod/Tinsley/G.Will .10 .02
❑ 657 Dave Johnson .05 .01
❑ 658 Checklist 529-660 .05 .01
❑ 659 Brian McRae .05 .01
❑ 660 Fred McGriff .15 .05
❑ 661 Bill Landrum .05 .01
❑ 662 Juan Guzman .05 .01
❑ 663 Greg Gagne .05 .01
❑ 664 Ken Hill .05 .01
❑ 665 Dave Haas .05 .01
❑ 666 Tom Foley .05 .01
❑ 667 Roberto Hernandez .05 .01
❑ 668 Dwayne Henry .05 .01
❑ 669 Jim Fregosi MG .05 .01
❑ 670 Harold Reynolds .10 .02
❑ 671 Mark Whiten .05 .01
❑ 672 Eric Plunk .05 .01
❑ 673 Todd Hundley .05 .01
❑ 674 Mo Sanford .05 .01
❑ 675 Bobby Witt .05 .01
❑ 676 Mil/Mahomes/Wendell/Salk .25 .08
❑ 677 John Marzano .05 .01
❑ 678 Joe Klink .05 .01
❑ 679 Pete Incaviglia .05 .01
❑ 680 Dale Murphy .15 .05
❑ 681 Rene Gonzales .05 .01
❑ 682 Andy Benes .05 .01
❑ 683 Jim Poole .05 .01
❑ 684 Trever Miller RC .10 .02
❑ 685 Scott Livingstone .05 .01
❑ 686 Rich DeLucia .05 .01
❑ 687 Harvey Pulliam .05 .01
❑ 688 Tim Belcher .05 .01
❑ 689 Mark Lemke .05 .01
❑ 690 John Franco .10 .02
❑ 691 Walt Weiss .05 .01
❑ 692 Scott Ruskin .05 .01
❑ 693 Jeff King .05 .01
❑ 694 Mike Gardiner .05 .01
❑ 695 Gary Sheffield .10 .02
❑ 696 Joe Boever .05 .01
❑ 697 Mike Felder .05 .01
❑ 698 John Habyan .05 .01
❑ 699 Cito Gaston MG .05 .01
❑ 700 Ruben Sierra .10 .02
❑ 701 Scott Radinsky .05 .01
❑ 702 Lee Stevens .05 .01
❑ 703 Mark Wohlers .05 .01
❑ 704 Curt Young .05 .01
❑ 705 Dwight Evans .15 .05
❑ 706 Rob Murphy .05 .01
❑ 707 Gregg Jefferies .05 .01
❑ 708 Tom Bolton .05 .01
❑ 709 Chris James .05 .01
❑ 710 Kevin Maas .05 .01
❑ 711 Ricky Bones .05 .01
❑ 712 Curt Wilkerson .05 .01
❑ 713 Roger McDowell .05 .01
❑ 714 Pokey Reese RC .25 .08
❑ 715 Craig Biggio .15 .05
❑ 716 Kirk Dressendorfer .05 .01
❑ 717 Ken Dayley .05 .01
❑ 718 B.J. Surhoff .10 .02
❑ 719 Terry Mulholland .05 .01
❑ 720 Kirk Gibson .10 .02
❑ 721 Mike Pagliarulo .05 .01
❑ 722 Walt Terrell .05 .01
❑ 723 Jose Oquendo .05 .01
❑ 724 Kevin Morton .05 .01
❑ 725 Dwight Gooden .10 .02
❑ 726 Kirt Manwaring .05 .01
❑ 727 Chuck McElroy .05 .01
❑ 728 Dave Burba .05 .01
❑ 729 Art Howe MG .05 .01

❑ 730 Ramon Martinez .05 .01
❑ 731 Donnie Hill .05 .01
❑ 732 Nelson Santovenia .05 .01
❑ 733 Bob Melvin .05 .01
❑ 734 Scott Hatteberg RC .25 .08
❑ 735 Greg Swindell .05 .01
❑ 736 Lance Johnson .05 .01
❑ 737 Kevin Reimer .05 .01
❑ 738 Dennis Eckersley .10 .02
❑ 739 Rob Ducey .05 .01
❑ 740 Ken Caminiti .10 .02
❑ 741 Mark Gubicza .05 .01
❑ 742 Bill Spiers .05 .01
❑ 743 Darren Lewis .05 .01
❑ 744 Chris Hammond .05 .01
❑ 745 Dave Magadan .05 .01
❑ 746 Bernard Gilkey .05 .01
❑ 747 Willie Banks .05 .01
❑ 748 Matt Nokes .05 .01
❑ 749 Jerald Clark .05 .01
❑ 750 Travis Fryman .10 .02
❑ 751 Steve Wilson .05 .01
❑ 752 Billy Ripken .05 .01
❑ 753 Paul Assenmacher .05 .01
❑ 754 Charlie Hayes .05 .01
❑ 755 Alex Fernandez .05 .01
❑ 756 Gary Pettis .05 .01
❑ 757 Rob Dibble .10 .02
❑ 758 Tim Naehring .05 .01
❑ 759 Jeff Torborg MG .05 .01
❑ 760 Ozzie Smith .40 .15
❑ 761 Mike Fitzgerald .05 .01
❑ 762 John Burkett .05 .01
❑ 763 Kyle Abbott .05 .01
❑ 764 Tyler Green RC .10 .02
❑ 765 Pete Harnisch .05 .01
❑ 766 Mark Davis .05 .01
❑ 767 Kal Daniels .05 .01
❑ 768 Jim Thome .25 .08
❑ 769 Jack Howell .05 .01
❑ 770 Sid Bream .05 .01
❑ 771 Arthur Rhodes .05 .01
❑ 772 Garry Templeton UER
(Stat heading in for pitchers .05 .01
❑ 773 Hal Morris .05 .01
❑ 774 Bud Black .05 .01
❑ 775 Ivan Calderon .05 .01
❑ 776 Doug Henry RC .10 .02
❑ 777 John Olerud .10 .02
❑ 778 Tim Leary .05 .01
❑ 779 Jay Bell .10 .02
❑ 780 Eddie Murray .25 .08
❑ 781 Paul Abbott .05 .01
❑ 782 Phil Plantier .05 .01
❑ 783 Joe Magrane .05 .01
❑ 784 Ken Patterson .05 .01
❑ 785 Albert Belle .10 .02
❑ 786 Royce Clayton .05 .01
❑ 787 Checklist 661-792 .05 .01
❑ 788 Mike Stanton .05 .01
❑ 789 Bobby Valentine MG .05 .01
❑ 790 Joe Carter .10 .02
❑ 791 Danny Cox .05 .01
❑ 792 Dave Winfield .10 .02

1993 Topps

❑ COMPLETE SET (825) 50.00 20.00
❑ COMP.HOBBY.SET (847) 60.00 30.00
❑ COMP.RETAIL.SET (838) 50.00 20.00
❑ COMPLETE SERIES 1 (396) 25.00 10.00
❑ COMPLETE SERIES 2 (429) 25.00 10.00
❑ 1 Robin Yount .75 .30
❑ 2 Barry Bonds 1.50 .60
❑ 3 Ryne Sandberg .75 .30
❑ 4 Roger Clemens 1.00 .40
❑ 5 Tony Gwynn .60 .25
❑ 6 Jeff Tackett .10 .02
❑ 7 Pete Incaviglia .10 .02
❑ 8 Mark Wohlers .10 .02
❑ 9 Kent Hrbek .20 .07
❑ 10 Will Clark .30 .10
❑ 11 Eric Karros .20 .07
❑ 12 Lee Smith .20 .07
❑ 13 Esteban Beltre .10 .02
❑ 14 Greg Briley .10 .02
❑ 15 Marquis Grissom .20 .07
❑ 16 Dan Plesac .10 .02
❑ 17 Dave Hollins .10 .02
❑ 18 Terry Steinbach .10 .02
❑ 19 Ed Nunez .10 .02
❑ 20 Tim Salmon .30 .10
❑ 21 Luis Salazar .10 .02
❑ 22 Jim Eisenreich .10 .02
❑ 23 Todd Stottlemyre .10 .02
❑ 24 Tim Naehring .10 .02
❑ 25 John Franco .20 .07
❑ 26 Skeeter Barnes .10 .02
❑ 27 Carlos Garcia .10 .02
❑ 28 Joe Orsulak .10 .02
❑ 29 Dwayne Henry .10 .02
❑ 30 Fred McGriff .30 .10
❑ 31 Derek Lilliquist .10 .02
❑ 32 Don Mattingly 1.25 .50
❑ 33 B.J.Wallace .10 .02
❑ 34 Juan Gonzalez .20 .07
❑ 35 John Smoltz .30 .10
❑ 36 Scott Servais .10 .02
❑ 37 Lenny Webster .10 .02
❑ 38 Chris James .10 .02
❑ 39 Roger McDowell .10 .02
❑ 40 Ozzie Smith .75 .30
❑ 41 Alex Fernandez .10 .02
❑ 42 Spike Owen .10 .02
❑ 43 Ruben Amaro .10 .02
❑ 44 Kevin Seitzer .10 .02
❑ 45 Dave Fleming .10 .02
❑ 46 Eric Fox .10 .02
❑ 47 Bob Scanlan .10 .02
❑ 48 Bert Blyleven .20 .07
❑ 49 Brian McRae .10 .02
❑ 50 Roberto Alomar .30 .10
❑ 51 Mo Vaughn .20 .07
❑ 52 Bobby Bonilla .20 .07
❑ 53 Frank Tanana .10 .02
❑ 54 Mike LaValliere .10 .02
❑ 55 Mark McLemore .10 .02
❑ 56 Chad Mottola RC .10 .02
❑ 57 Norm Charlton .10 .02
❑ 58 Jose Melendez .10 .02
❑ 59 Carlos Martinez .10 .02
❑ 60 Roberto Kelly .10 .02
❑ 61 Gene Larkin .10 .02
❑ 62 Rafael Belliard .10 .02
❑ 63 Al Osuna .10 .02
❑ 64 Scott Chiamparino .10 .02
❑ 65 Brett Butler .20 .07
❑ 66 John Burkett .10 .02
❑ 67 Felix Jose .10 .02
❑ 68 Omar Vizquel .30 .10
❑ 69 John Vander Wal .10 .02
❑ 70 Roberto Hernandez .10 .02
❑ 71 Ricky Bones .10 .02
❑ 72 Jeff Grotewold .10 .02
❑ 73 Mike Moore .10 .02
❑ 74 Steve Buechele .10 .02
❑ 75 Juan Guzman .10 .02
❑ 76 Kevin Appier .20 .07
❑ 77 Junior Felix .10 .02
❑ 78 Greg W. Harris .10 .02
❑ 79 Dick Schofield .10 .02
❑ 80 Cecil Fielder .20 .07
❑ 81 Lloyd McClendon .10 .02
❑ 82 David Segui .10 .02
❑ 83 Reggie Sanders .20 .07
❑ 84 Kurt Stillwell .10 .02
❑ 85 Sandy Alomar Jr. .10 .02
❑ 86 John Habyan .10 .02
❑ 87 Kevin Reimer .10 .02
❑ 88 Mike Stanton .10 .02
❑ 89 Eric Anthony .10 .02
❑ 90 Scott Erickson .10 .02
❑ 91 Craig Colbert .10 .02
❑ 92 Tom Pagnozzi .10 .02
❑ 93 Pedro Astacio .10 .02
❑ 94 Lance Johnson .10 .02
❑ 95 Larry Walker .20 .07
❑ 96 Russ Swan .10 .02
❑ 97 Scott Fletcher .10 .02
❑ 98 Derek Jeter RC 12.00 5.00
❑ 99 Mike Williams .10 .02
❑ 100 Mark McGwire 1.25 .50
❑ 101 Jim Bullinger .10 .02
❑ 102 Brian Hunter .10 .02
❑ 103 Jody Reed .10 .02
❑ 104 Mike Butcher .10 .02
❑ 105 Gregg Jefferies .10 .02
❑ 106 Howard Johnson .10 .02
❑ 107 John Kiely .10 .02
❑ 108 Jose Lind .10 .02
❑ 109 Sam Horn .10 .02
❑ 110 Barry Larkin .30 .10
❑ 111 Bruce Hurst .10 .02
❑ 112 Brian Barnes .10 .02
❑ 113 Thomas Howard .10 .02
❑ 114 Mel Hall .10 .02
❑ 115 Robby Thompson .10 .02
❑ 116 Mark Lemke .10 .02
❑ 117 Eddie Taubensee .10 .02
❑ 118 David Hulse RC .10 .02
❑ 119 Pedro Munoz .10 .02
❑ 120 Ramon Martinez .10 .02
❑ 121 Todd Worrell .10 .02
❑ 122 Joey Cora .10 .02
❑ 123 Moises Alou .20 .07
❑ 124 Franklin Stubbs .10 .02
❑ 125 Pete O'Brien .10 .02
❑ 126 Bob Ayrault .10 .02
❑ 127 Carney Lansford .20 .07
❑ 128 Kal Daniels .10 .02
❑ 129 Joe Grahe .10 .02
❑ 130 Jeff Montgomery .10 .02
❑ 131 Dave Winfield .20 .07
❑ 132 Preston Wilson RC .75 .30
❑ 133 Steve Wilson .10 .02
❑ 134 Lee Guetterman .10 .02
❑ 135 Mickey Tettleton .10 .02
❑ 136 Jeff King .10 .02
❑ 137 Alan Mills .10 .02
❑ 138 Joe Oliver .10 .02
❑ 139 Gary Gaetti .20 .07
❑ 140 Gary Sheffield .20 .07
❑ 141 Dennis Cook .10 .02
❑ 142 Charlie Hayes .10 .02
❑ 143 Jeff Huson .10 .02
❑ 144 Kent Mercker .10 .02
❑ 145 Eric Young .10 .02
❑ 146 Scott Leius .10 .02
❑ 147 Bryan Hickerson .10 .02
❑ 148 Steve Finley .20 .07
❑ 149 Rheal Cormier .10 .02
❑ 150 Frank Thomas .50 .20
❑ 151 Archi Cianfrocco .10 .02
❑ 152 Rich DeLucia .10 .02
❑ 153 Greg Vaughn .10 .02
❑ 154 Wes Chamberlain .10 .02
❑ 155 Dennis Eckersley .20 .07
❑ 156 Sammy Sosa .50 .20
❑ 157 Gary DiSarcina .10 .02
❑ 158 Kevin Koslofski .10 .02
❑ 159 Doug Linton .10 .02
❑ 160 Lou Whitaker .20 .07
❑ 161 Chad McConnell .10 .02
❑ 162 Joe Hesketh .10 .02
❑ 163 Tim Wakefield .50 .20
❑ 164 Leo Gomez .10 .02
❑ 165 Jose Rijo .10 .02
❑ 166 Tim Scott .10 .02
❑ 167 Steve Olin UER .10 .02
❑ 168 Kevin Maas .10 .02
❑ 169 Kenny Rogers .20 .07

❑ 170 David Justice .20 .07
❑ 171 Doug Jones .10 .02
❑ 172 Jeff Reboulet .10 .02
❑ 173 Andres Galarraga .20 .07
❑ 174 Randy Velarde .10 .02
❑ 175 Kirk McCaskill .10 .02
❑ 176 Darren Lewis .10 .02
❑ 177 Lenny Harris .10 .02
❑ 178 Jeff Fassero .10 .02
❑ 179 Ken Griffey Jr. .75 .30
❑ 180 Darren Daulton .20 .07
❑ 181 John Jaha .10 .02
❑ 182 Ron Darling .10 .02
❑ 183 Greg Maddux .75 .30
❑ 184 Damion Easley .10 .02
❑ 185 Jack Morris .20 .07
❑ 186 Mike Magnante .10 .02
❑ 187 John Dopson .10 .02
❑ 188 Sid Fernandez .10 .02
❑ 189 Tony Phillips .10 .02
❑ 190 Doug Drabek .10 .02
❑ 191 Sean Lowe RC .10 .02
❑ 192 Bob Milacki .10 .02
❑ 193 Steve Foster .10 .02
❑ 194 Jerald Clark .10 .02
❑ 195 Pete Harnisch .10 .02
❑ 196 Pat Kelly .10 .02
❑ 197 Jeff Frye .10 .02
❑ 198 Alejandro Pena .10 .02
❑ 199 Junior Ortiz .10 .02
❑ 200 Kirby Puckett .50 .20
❑ 201 Jose Uribe .10 .02
❑ 202 Mike Scioscia .10 .02
❑ 203 Bernard Gilkey .10 .02
❑ 204 Dan Pasqua .10 .02
❑ 205 Gary Carter .20 .07
❑ 206 Henry Cotto .10 .02
❑ 207 Paul Molitor .20 .07
❑ 208 Mike Hartley .10 .02
❑ 209 Jeff Parrett .10 .02
❑ 210 Mark Langston .10 .02
❑ 211 Doug Dascenzo .10 .02
❑ 212 Rick Reed .10 .02
❑ 213 Candy Maldonado .10 .02
❑ 214 Danny Darwin .10 .02
❑ 215 Pat Howell .10 .02
❑ 216 Mark Leiter .10 .02
❑ 217 Kevin Mitchell .10 .02
❑ 218 Ben McDonald .10 .02
❑ 219 Bip Roberts .10 .02
❑ 220 Benny Santiago .20 .07
❑ 221 Carlos Baerga .10 .02
❑ 222 Bernie Williams .30 .10
❑ 223 Roger Pavlik .10 .02
❑ 224 Sid Bream .10 .02
❑ 225 Matt Williams .20 .07
❑ 226 Willie Banks .10 .02
❑ 227 Jeff Bagwell .30 .10
❑ 228 Tom Goodwin .10 .02
❑ 229 Mike Perez .10 .02
❑ 230 Carlton Fisk .30 .10
❑ 231 John Wetteland .20 .07
❑ 232 Tino Martinez .30 .10
❑ 233 Rick Greene .10 .02
❑ 234 Tim McIntosh .10 .02
❑ 235 Mitch Williams .10 .02
❑ 236 Kevin Campbell .10 .02
❑ 237 Jose Vizcaino .10 .02
❑ 238 Chris Donnels .10 .02
❑ 239 Mike Boddicker .10 .02
❑ 240 John Olerud .20 .07
❑ 241 Mike Gardiner .10 .02
❑ 242 Charlie O'Brien .10 .02
❑ 243 Rob Deer .10 .02
❑ 244 Denny Neagle .20 .07
❑ 245 Chris Sabo .10 .02
❑ 246 Gregg Olson .10 .02
❑ 247 Frank Seminara UER .10 .02
❑ 248 Scott Scudder .10 .02
❑ 249 Tim Burke .10 .02
❑ 250 Chuck Knoblauch .20 .07
❑ 251 Mike Bielecki .10 .02
❑ 252 Xavier Hernandez .10 .02
❑ 253 Jose Guzman .10 .02
❑ 254 Cory Snyder .10 .02
❑ 255 Orel Hershiser .20 .07
❑ 256 Wil Cordero .10 .02
❑ 257 Luis Alicea .10 .02
❑ 258 Mike Schooler .10 .02
❑ 259 Craig Grebeck .10 .02
❑ 260 Duane Ward .10 .02
❑ 261 Bill Wegman .10 .02
❑ 262 Mickey Morandini .10 .02
❑ 263 Vince Horsman .10 .02
❑ 264 Paul Sorrento .10 .02
❑ 265 Andre Dawson .20 .07
❑ 266 Rene Gonzales .10 .02
❑ 267 Keith Miller .10 .02
❑ 268 Derek Bell .10 .02
❑ 269 Todd Steverson RC .10 .02
❑ 270 Frank Viola .20 .07
❑ 271 Wally Whitehurst .10 .02
❑ 272 Kurt Knudsen .10 .02
❑ 273 Dan Walters .10 .02
❑ 274 Rick Sutcliffe .20 .07
❑ 275 Andy Van Slyke .30 .10
❑ 276 Paul O'Neill .30 .10
❑ 277 Mark Whiten .10 .02
❑ 278 Chris Nabholz .10 .02
❑ 279 Todd Burns .10 .02
❑ 280 Tom Glavine .30 .10
❑ 281 Butch Henry .10 .02
❑ 282 Shane Mack .10 .02
❑ 283 Mike Jackson .10 .02
❑ 284 Henry Rodriguez .10 .02
❑ 285 Bob Tewksbury .10 .02
❑ 286 Ron Karkovice .10 .02
❑ 287 Mike Gallego .10 .02
❑ 288 Dave Cochrane .10 .02
❑ 289 Jesse Orosco .10 .02
❑ 290 Dave Stewart .20 .07
❑ 291 Tommy Greene .10 .02
❑ 292 Rey Sanchez .10 .02
❑ 293 Rob Ducey .10 .02
❑ 294 Brent Mayne .10 .02
❑ 295 Dave Stieb .10 .02
❑ 296 Luis Rivera .10 .02
❑ 297 Jeff Innis .10 .02
❑ 298 Scott Livingstone .10 .02
❑ 299 Bob Patterson .10 .02
❑ 300 Cal Ripken 1.50 .60
❑ 301 Cesar Hernandez .10 .02
❑ 302 Randy Myers .10 .02
❑ 303 Brook Jacoby .10 .02
❑ 304 Melido Perez .10 .02
❑ 305 Rafael Palmeiro .30 .10
❑ 306 Damon Berryhill .10 .02
❑ 307 Dan Serafini RC .10 .02
❑ 308 Darryl Kile .20 .07
❑ 309 J.T. Bruett .10 .02
❑ 310 Dave Righetti .20 .07
❑ 311 Jay Howell .10 .02
❑ 312 Geronimo Pena .10 .02
❑ 313 Greg Hibbard .10 .02
❑ 314 Mark Gardner .10 .02
❑ 315 Edgar Martinez .30 .10
❑ 316 Dave Nilsson .10 .02
❑ 317 Kyle Abbott .10 .02
❑ 318 Willie Wilson .10 .02
❑ 319 Paul Assenmacher .10 .02
❑ 320 Tim Fortugno .10 .02
❑ 321 Rusty Meacham .10 .02
❑ 322 Pat Borders .10 .02
❑ 323 Mike Greenwell .10 .02
❑ 324 Willie Randolph .20 .07
❑ 325 Bill Gullickson .10 .02
❑ 326 Gary Varsho .10 .02
❑ 327 Tim Hulett .10 .02
❑ 328 Scott Ruskin .10 .02
❑ 329 Mike Maddux .10 .02
❑ 330 Danny Tartabull .10 .02
❑ 331 Kenny Lofton .20 .07
❑ 332 Geno Petralli .10 .02
❑ 333 Otis Nixon .10 .02
❑ 334 Jason Kendall RC 1.00 .40
❑ 335 Mark Portugal .10 .02
❑ 336 Mike Pagliarulo .10 .02
❑ 337 Kirt Manwaring .10 .02
❑ 338 Bob Ojeda .10 .02
❑ 339 Mark Clark .10 .02
❑ 340 John Kruk .20 .07
❑ 341 Mel Rojas .10 .02
❑ 342 Erik Hanson .10 .02
❑ 343 Doug Henry .10 .02
❑ 344 Jack McDowell .10 .02
❑ 345 Harold Baines .20 .07
❑ 346 Chuck McElroy .10 .02
❑ 347 Luis Sojo .10 .02
❑ 348 Andy Stankiewicz .10 .02
❑ 349 Hipolito Pichardo .10 .02
❑ 350 Joe Carter .20 .07
❑ 351 Ellis Burks .20 .07
❑ 352 Pete Schourek .10 .02
❑ 353 Buddy Groom .10 .02
❑ 354 Jay Bell .20 .07
❑ 355 Brady Anderson .20 .07
❑ 356 Freddie Benavides .10 .02
❑ 357 Phil Stephenson .10 .02
❑ 358 Kevin Wickander .10 .02
❑ 359 Mike Stanley .10 .02
❑ 360 Ivan Rodriguez .30 .10
❑ 361 Scott Bankhead .10 .02
❑ 362 Luis Gonzalez .20 .07
❑ 363 John Smiley .10 .02
❑ 364 Trevor Wilson .10 .02
❑ 365 Tom Candiotti .10 .02
❑ 366 Craig Wilson .10 .02
❑ 367 Steve Sax .10 .02
❑ 368 Delino DeShields .10 .02
❑ 369 Jaime Navarro .10 .02
❑ 370 Dave Valle .10 .02
❑ 371 Mariano Duncan .10 .02
❑ 372 Rod Nichols .10 .02
❑ 373 Mike Morgan .10 .02
❑ 374 Julio Valera .10 .02
❑ 375 Wally Joyner .20 .07
❑ 376 Tom Henke .10 .02
❑ 377 Herm Winningham .10 .02
❑ 378 Orlando Merced .10 .02
❑ 379 Mike Munoz .10 .02
❑ 380 Todd Hundley .10 .02
❑ 381 Mike Flanagan .10 .02
❑ 382 Tim Belcher .10 .02
❑ 383 Jerry Browne .10 .02
❑ 384 Mike Benjamin .10 .02
❑ 385 Jim Leyritz .10 .02
❑ 386 Ray Lankford .20 .07
❑ 387 Devon White .20 .07
❑ 388 Jeremy Hernandez .10 .02
❑ 389 Brian Harper .10 .02
❑ 390 Wade Boggs .30 .10
❑ 391 Derrick May .10 .02
❑ 392 Travis Fryman .20 .07
❑ 393 Ron Gant .20 .07
❑ 394 Checklist 1-132 .10 .02
❑ 395 Checklist 133-264 UER .10 .02
❑ 396 Checklist 265-396 .10 .02
❑ 397 George Brett 1.25 .50
❑ 398 Bobby Witt .10 .02
❑ 399 Daryl Boston .10 .02
❑ 400 Bo Jackson .50 .20
❑ 401 F.McGriff/F.Thomas AS .30 .10
❑ 402 R.Sandberg/C.Baerga AS .50 .20
❑ 403 G.Sheffield/E.Martinez AS .20 .07
❑ 404 B.Larkin/T.Fryman AS .20 .07
❑ 405 K.Griffey Jr./A.Van Slyke AS .50 .20
❑ 406 L.Walker/K.Puckett AS .30 .10
❑ 407 B.Bonds/J.Carter AS .75 .30
❑ 408 D.Daulton/B.Harper AS .20 .07
❑ 409 G.Maddux/R.Clemens AS .50 .20
❑ 410 T.Glavine/D.Fleming AS .20 .07
❑ 411 L.Smith/D.Eckersley AS .20 .07
❑ 412 Jamie McAndrew .10 .02
❑ 413 Pete Smith .10 .02
❑ 414 Juan Guerrero .10 .02
❑ 415 Todd Frohwirth .10 .02
❑ 416 Randy Tomlin .10 .02
❑ 417 B.J. Surhoff .20 .07
❑ 418 Jim Gott .10 .02
❑ 419 Mark Thompson RC .10 .02
❑ 420 Kevin Tapani .10 .02
❑ 421 Curt Schilling .20 .07
❑ 422 J.T.Snow RC .50 .20
❑ 423 Ryan Klesko .20 .07
❑ 424 John Valentin .10 .02
❑ 425 Joe Girardi .10 .02
❑ 426 Nigel Wilson .10 .02
❑ 427 Bob MacDonald .10 .02

No.	Player		
428	Todd Zeile	.10	.02
429	Milt Cuyler	.10	.02
430	Eddie Murray	.50	.20
431	Rich Amaral	.10	.02
432	Pete Young	.10	.02
433	Tom Schmidt RC	.10	.02
434	Jack Armstrong	.10	.02
435	Willie McGee	.20	.07
436	Greg W. Harris	.10	.02
437	Chris Hammond	.10	.02
438	Ritchie Moody RC	.10	.02
439	Bryan Harvey	.10	.02
440	Ruben Sierra	.20	.07
441	Todd Pridy RC	.10	.02
442	Kevin McReynolds	.10	.02
443	Terry Leach	.10	.02
444	David Nied	.10	.02
445	Dale Murphy	.30	.10
446	Luis Mercedes	.10	.02
447	Keith Shepherd RC	.10	.02
448	Ken Caminiti	.20	.07
449	Jim Austin	.10	.02
450	Darryl Strawberry	.20	.07
451	Quinton McCracken RC	.25	.08
452	Bob Wickman	.10	.02
453	Victor Cole	.10	.02
454	John Johnstone RC	.10	.02
455	Chili Davis	.20	.07
456	Scott Taylor	.10	.02
457	Tracy Woodson	.10	.02
458	David Wells	.20	.07
459	Derek Wallace RC	.10	.02
460	Randy Johnson	.50	.20
461	Steve Reed RC	.10	.02
462	Felix Fermin	.10	.02
463	Scott Aldred	.10	.02
464	Greg Colbrunn	.10	.02
465	Tony Fernandez	.10	.02
466	Mike Felder	.10	.02
467	Lee Stevens	.10	.02
468	Matt Whiteside RC	.10	.02
469	Dave Hansen	.10	.02
470	Rob Dibble	.20	.07
471	Dave Gallagher	.10	.02
472	Chris Gwynn	.10	.02
473	Dave Henderson	.10	.02
474	Ozzie Guillen	.20	.07
475	Jeff Reardon	.20	.07
476	Will Scalzitti RC	.10	.02
477	Jimmy Jones	.10	.02
478	Greg Cadaret	.10	.02
479	Todd Pratt RC	.10	.02
480	Pat Listach	.10	.02
481	Ryan Luzinski RC	.10	.02
482	Darren Reed	.10	.02
483	Brian Griffiths RC	.10	.02
484	John Wehner	.10	.02
485	Glenn Davis	.10	.02
486	Eric Wedge RC	.10	.02
487	Jesse Hollins	.10	.02
488	Manuel Lee	.10	.02
489	Scott Fredrickson RC	.10	.02
490	Omar Olivares	.10	.02
491	Shawn Hare	.10	.02
492	Tom Lampkin	.10	.02
493	Jeff Nelson	.10	.02
494	L.Lucca RC/E.Perez	.10	.02
495	Ken Hill	.10	.02
496	Reggie Jefferson	.10	.02
497	Willie Brown RC	.10	.02
498	Bud Black	.10	.02
499	Chuck Crim	.10	.02
500	Jose Canseco	.30	.10
501	Johnny Oates MG		
	Bobby Cox MG	.20	.07
502	Butch Hobson MG		
	Jim Lefebvre MG	.10	.02
503	Buck Rodgers MG		
	Tony Perez MG	.20	.07
504	Gene Lamont MG		
	Don Baylor MG	.20	.07
505	Mike Hargrove MG		
	Rene Lachemann MG	.20	.07
506	Sparky Anderson MG		
	Art Howe MG	.20	.07
507	Hal McRae MG		
	Tom Lasorda MG	.20	.07
508	Phil Garner MG		
	Felipe Alou MG	.20	.07
509	Tom Kelly MG		
	Jeff Torborg MG	.10	.02
510	Buck Showalter MG		
	Jim Fregosi MG	.20	.07
511	Tony LaRussa MG		
	Jim Leyland MG	.20	.07
512	Lou Piniella MG		
	Joe Torre MG	.20	.07
513	Kevin Kennedy MG		
	Jim Riggleman MG	.10	.02
514	Cito Gaston MG		
	Dusty Baker MG	.20	.07
515	Greg Swindell	.10	.02
516	Alex Arias	.10	.02
517	Bill Pecota	.10	.02
518	Benji Grigsby RC	.10	.02
519	David Howard	.10	.02
520	Charlie Hough	.20	.07
521	Kevin Flora	.10	.02
522	Shane Reynolds	.10	.02
523	Doug Bochtler RC	.10	.02
524	Chris Hoiles	.10	.02
525	Scott Sanderson	.10	.02
526	Mike Sharperson	.10	.02
527	Mike Fetters	.10	.02
528	Paul Quantrill	.10	.02
529	Chipper Jones	.50	.20
530	Sterling Hitchcock RC	.25	.08
531	Joe Millette	.10	.02
532	Tom Brunansky	.10	.02
533	Frank Castillo	.10	.02
534	Randy Knorr	.10	.02
535	Jose Oquendo	.10	.02
536	Dave Haas	.10	.02
537	Jason Hutchins RC	.10	.02
538	Jimmy Baron RC	.10	.02
539	Kerry Woodson	.10	.02
540	Ivan Calderon	.10	.02
541	Denis Boucher	.10	.02
542	Royce Clayton	.10	.02
543	Reggie Williams	.10	.02
544	Steve Decker	.10	.02
545	Dean Palmer	.20	.07
546	Hal Morris	.10	.02
547	Ryan Thompson	.10	.02
548	Lance Blankenship	.10	.02
549	Hensley Meulens	.10	.02
550	Scott Radinsky	.10	.02
551	Eric Young	.10	.02
552	Jeff Blauser	.10	.02
553	Andujar Cedeno	.10	.02
554	Arthur Rhodes	.10	.02
555	Terry Mulholland	.10	.02
556	Darryl Hamilton	.10	.02
557	Pedro Martinez	1.00	.40
558	Ryan Whitman RC	.10	.02
559	Jamie Arnold RC	.10	.02
560	Zane Smith	.10	.02
561	Matt Nokes	.10	.02
562	Bob Zupcic	.10	.02
563	Shawn Boskie	.10	.02
564	Mike Timlin	.10	.02
565	Jerald Clark	.10	.02
566	Rod Brewer	.10	.02
567	Mark Carreon	.10	.02
568	Andy Benes	.10	.02
569	Shawn Barton RC	.10	.02
570	Tim Wallach	.10	.02
571	Dave Mlicki	.10	.02
572	Trevor Hoffman	.50	.20
573	John Patterson	.10	.02
574	DeShawn Warren RC	.10	.02
575	Monty Fariss	.10	.02
576	Cliff Floyd	.20	.07
577	Tim Costo	.10	.02
578	Dave Magadan	.10	.02
579	Jason Bates RC	.10	.02
580	Walt Weiss	.10	.02
581	Chris Haney	.10	.02
582	Shawn Abner	.10	.02
583	Marvin Freeman	.10	.02
584	Casey Candaele	.10	.02
585	Ricky Jordan	.10	.02
586	Jeff Tabaka RC	.10	.02
587	Manny Alexander	.10	.02
588	Mike Trombley	.10	.02
589	Carlos Hernandez	.10	.02
590	Cal Eldred	.10	.02
591	Alex Cole	.10	.02
592	Phil Plantier	.10	.02
593	Brett Merriman RC	.10	.02
594	Jerry Nielsen	.10	.02
595	Shawon Dunston	.10	.02
596	Jimmy Key	.20	.07
597	Gerald Perry	.10	.02
598	Rico Brogna	.10	.02
599	Clemente Nunez	.10	.02
600	Bret Saberhagen	.20	.07
601	Craig Shipley	.10	.02
602	Henry Mercedes	.10	.02
603	Jim Thome	.30	.10
604	Rod Beck	.10	.02
605	Chuck Finley	.20	.07
606	Jayhawk Owens RC	.10	.02
607	Dan Smith	.10	.02
608	Bill Doran	.10	.02
609	Lance Parrish	.20	.07
610	Dennis Martinez	.20	.07
611	Tom Gordon	.10	.02
612	Byron Mathews RC	.10	.02
613	Joel Adamson RC	.10	.02
614	Brian Williams	.10	.02
615	Steve Avery	.10	.02
616	Midre Cummings RC	.10	.02
617	Craig Lefferts	.10	.02
618	Tony Pena	.10	.02
619	Billy Spiers	.10	.02
620	Todd Benzinger	.10	.02
621	Greg Boyd RC	.10	.02
622	Ben Rivera	.10	.02
623	Al Martin	.10	.02
624	Sam Militello UER	.10	.02
625	Rick Aguilera	.10	.02
626	Dan Gladden	.10	.02
627	Andres Berumen RC	.10	.02
628	Kelly Gruber	.10	.02
629	Cris Carpenter	.10	.02
630	Mark Grace	.30	.10
631	Jeff Brantley	.10	.02
632	Chris Widger RC	.25	.08
633	Three Russians	.10	.02
634	Mo Sanford	.10	.02
635	Albert Belle	.20	.07
636	Tim Teufel	.10	.02
637	Greg Myers	.10	.02
638	Brian Bohanon	.10	.02
639	Mike Bordick	.10	.02
640	Dwight Gooden	.20	.07
641	P.Leahy/G.Baugh RC	.10	.02
642	Milt Hill	.10	.02
643	Luis Aquino	.10	.02
644	Dante Bichette	.20	.07
645	Bobby Thigpen	.10	.02
646	Rich Scheid RC	.10	.02
647	Brian Sackinsky RC	.10	.02
648	Ryan Hawblitzel	.10	.02
649	Tom Marsh	.10	.02
650	Terry Pendleton	.20	.07
651	Rafael Bournigal	.10	.02
652	Dave West	.10	.02
653	Steve Hosey	.10	.02
654	Gerald Williams	.10	.02
655	Scott Cooper	.10	.02
656	Gary Scott	.10	.02
657	Mike Harkey	.10	.02
658	J.Burnitz/S.Walker RC	.20	.07
659	Ed Sprague	.10	.02
660	Alan Trammell	.20	.07
661	Garvin Alston RC	.10	.02
662	Donovan Osborne	.10	.02
663	Jeff Gardner	.10	.02
664	Calvin Jones	.10	.02
665	Darrin Fletcher	.10	.02
666	Glenallen Hill	.10	.02
667	Jim Rosenbohm RC	.10	.02
668	Scott Lewis	.10	.02
669	Kip Yaughn RC	.10	.02
670	Julio Franco	.20	.07
671	Dave Martinez	.10	.02

❑ 672 Kevin Bass .10 .02
❑ 673 Todd Van Poppel .10 .02
❑ 674 Mark Gubicza .10 .02
❑ 675 Tim Raines .20 .07
❑ 676 Rudy Seanez .10 .02
❑ 677 Charlie Leibrandt .10 .02
❑ 678 Randy Milligan .10 .02
❑ 679 Kim Batiste .10 .02
❑ 680 Craig Biggio .30 .10
❑ 681 Darren Holmes .10 .02
❑ 682 John Candelaria .10 .02
❑ 683 Eddie Christian RC .10 .02
❑ 684 Pat Mahomes .10 .02
❑ 685 Bob Walk .10 .02
❑ 686 Russ Springer .10 .02
❑ 687 Tony Sheffield RC .10 .02
❑ 688 Dwight Smith .10 .02
❑ 689 Eddie Zosky .10 .02
❑ 690 Bien Figueroa .10 .02
❑ 691 Jim Tatum RC .10 .02
❑ 692 Chad Kreuter .10 .02
❑ 693 Rich Rodriguez .10 .02
❑ 694 Shane Turner .10 .02
❑ 695 Kent Bottenfield .10 .02
❑ 696 Jose Mesa .10 .02
❑ 697 Darrell Whitmore RC .10 .02
❑ 698 Ted Wood .10 .02
❑ 699 Chad Curtis .10 .02
❑ 700 Nolan Ryan 2.00 .75
❑ 701 M.Piazza/C.Delgado 3.00 1.25
❑ 702 Tim Pugh RC .10 .02
❑ 703 Jeff Kent .50 .20
❑ 704 J.Goodrich/D.Figueroa RC .10 .02
❑ 705 Bob Welch .10 .02
❑ 706 Sherard Clinkscales RC .10 .02
❑ 707 Donn Pall .10 .02
❑ 708 Greg Olson .10 .02
❑ 709 Jeff Juden .10 .02
❑ 710 Mike Mussina .30 .10
❑ 711 Scott Chiamparino .10 .02
❑ 712 Stan Javier .10 .02
❑ 713 John Doherty .10 .02
❑ 714 Kevin Gross .10 .02
❑ 715 Greg Gagne .10 .02
❑ 716 Steve Cooke .10 .02
❑ 717 Steve Farr .10 .02
❑ 718 Jay Buhner .20 .07
❑ 719 Butch Henry .10 .02
❑ 720 David Cone .20 .07
❑ 721 Rick Wilkins .10 .02
❑ 722 Chuck Carr .10 .02
❑ 723 Kenny Felder RC .10 .02
❑ 724 Guillermo Velasquez .10 .02
❑ 725 Billy Hatcher .10 .02
❑ 726 Mike Veneziale RC .10 .02
❑ 727 Jonathan Hurst .10 .02
❑ 728 Steve Frey .10 .02
❑ 729 Mark Leonard .10 .02
❑ 730 Charles Nagy .10 .02
❑ 731 Donald Harris .10 .02
❑ 732 Travis Buckley RC .10 .02
❑ 733 Tom Browning .10 .02
❑ 734 Anthony Young .10 .02
❑ 735 Steve Shifflett .10 .02
❑ 736 Jeff Russell .10 .02
❑ 737 Wilson Alvarez .10 .02
❑ 738 Lance Painter RC .10 .02
❑ 739 Dave Weathers .10 .02
❑ 740 Len Dykstra .20 .07
❑ 741 Mike Devereaux .10 .02
❑ 742 R.Arocha RC/A.Embree .25 .08
❑ 743 Dave Landaker RC .10 .02
❑ 744 Chris George .10 .02
❑ 745 Eric Davis .20 .07
❑ 746 Lamar Rogers RC .10 .02
❑ 747 Carl Willis .10 .02
❑ 748 Stan Belinda .10 .02
❑ 749 Scott Kamieniecki .10 .02
❑ 750 Rickey Henderson .50 .20
❑ 751 Eric Hillman .10 .02
❑ 752 Pat Hentgen .10 .02
❑ 753 Jim Corsi .10 .02
❑ 754 Brian Jordan .20 .07
❑ 755 Bill Swift .10 .02
❑ 756 Mike Henneman .10 .02
❑ 757 Harold Reynolds .20 .07
❑ 758 Sean Berry .10 .02
❑ 759 Charlie Hayes .10 .02
❑ 760 Luis Polonia .10 .02
❑ 761 Darrin Jackson .10 .02
❑ 762 Mark Lewis .10 .02
❑ 763 Rob Maurer .10 .02
❑ 764 Willie Greene .10 .02
❑ 765 Vince Coleman .10 .02
❑ 766 Todd Revenig .10 .02
❑ 767 Rich Ireland RC .10 .02
❑ 768 Mike Macfarlane .10 .02
❑ 769 Francisco Cabrera .10 .02
❑ 770 Robin Ventura .20 .07
❑ 771 Kevin Ritz .10 .02
❑ 772 Chito Martinez .10 .02
❑ 773 Cliff Brantley .10 .02
❑ 774 Curt Leskanic RC .25 .08
❑ 775 Chris Bosio .10 .02
❑ 776 Jose Offerman .10 .02
❑ 777 Mark Guthrie .10 .02
❑ 778 Don Slaught .10 .02
❑ 779 Rich Monteleone .10 .02
❑ 780 Jim Abbott .30 .10
❑ 781 Jack Clark .20 .07
❑ 782 R.Mendoza/D.Roman RC .10 .02
❑ 783 Heathcliff Slocumb .10 .02
❑ 784 Jeff Branson .10 .02
❑ 785 Kevin Brown .20 .07
❑ 786 K.Ryan/Gandarillas RC .10 .02
❑ 787 Mike Matthews RC .10 .02
❑ 788 Mackey Sasser .10 .02
❑ 789 Jeff Conine UER .20 .07
❑ 790 George Bell .10 .02
❑ 791 Pat Rapp .10 .02
❑ 792 Joe Boever .10 .02
❑ 793 Jim Poole .10 .02
❑ 794 Andy Ashby .10 .02
❑ 795 Deion Sanders .30 .10
❑ 796 Scott Brosius .20 .07
❑ 797 Brad Pennington .10 .02
❑ 798 Greg Blosser .10 .02
❑ 799 Jim Edmonds RC 2.00 .75
❑ 800 Shawn Jeter .10 .02
❑ 801 Jesse Levis .10 .02
❑ 802 Phil Clark UER .10 .02
❑ 803 Eddie Pierce RC .10 .02
❑ 804 Jose Valentin RC .25 .08
❑ 805 Terry Jorgensen .10 .02
❑ 806 Mark Hutton .10 .02
❑ 807 Troy Neel .10 .02
❑ 808 Bret Boone .20 .07
❑ 809 Cris Colon .10 .02
❑ 810 Domingo Martinez RC .10 .02
❑ 811 Javier Lopez .30 .10
❑ 812 Matt Walbeck RC .10 .02
❑ 813 Dan Wilson .20 .07
❑ 814 Scooter Tucker .10 .02
❑ 815 Billy Ashley .10 .02
❑ 816 Tim Laker RC .10 .02
❑ 817 Bobby Jones .20 .07
❑ 818 Brad Brink .10 .02
❑ 819 William Pennyfeather .10 .02
❑ 820 Stan Royer .10 .02
❑ 821 Doug Brocail .10 .02
❑ 822 Kevin Rogers .10 .02
❑ 823 Checklist 397-540 .10 .02
❑ 824 Checklist 541-691 .10 .02
❑ 825 Checklist 692-825 .10 .02

1994 Topps

❑ COMPLETE SET (792) 50.00 20.00
❑ COMP.FACT.SET (808) 80.00 40.00
❑ COMP.BAKER SET (817) 80.00 40.00
❑ COMPLETE SERIES 1 (396) 25.00 10.00
❑ COMPLETE SERIES 2 (396) 25.00 10.00
❑ 1 Mike Piazza 1.00 .40
❑ 2 Bernie Williams .30 .10
❑ 3 Kevin Rogers .10 .02
❑ 4 Paul Carey .10 .02
❑ 5 Ozzie Guillen .20 .07
❑ 6 Derrick May .10 .02
❑ 7 Jose Mesa .10 .02
❑ 8 Todd Hundley .10 .02
❑ 9 Chris Haney .10 .02
❑ 10 John Olerud .20 .07
❑ 11 Andujar Cedeno .10 .02

❑ 12 John Smiley .10 .02
❑ 13 Phil Plantier .10 .02
❑ 14 Willie Banks .10 .02
❑ 15 Jay Bell .20 .07
❑ 16 Doug Henry .10 .02
❑ 17 Lance Blankenship .10 .02
❑ 18 Greg W. Harris .10 .02
❑ 19 Scott Livingstone .10 .02
❑ 20 Bryan Harvey .10 .02
❑ 21 Wil Cordero .10 .02
❑ 22 Roger Pavlik .10 .02
❑ 23 Mark Lemke .10 .02
❑ 24 Jeff Nelson .10 .02
❑ 25 Todd Zeile .10 .02
❑ 26 Billy Hatcher .10 .02
❑ 27 Joe Magrane .10 .02
❑ 28 Tony Longmire .10 .02
❑ 29 Omar Daal .10 .02
❑ 30 Kirt Manwaring .10 .02
❑ 31 Melido Perez .10 .02
❑ 32 Tim Hulett .10 .02
❑ 33 Jeff Schwarz .10 .02
❑ 34 Nolan Ryan 2.00 .75
❑ 35 Jose Guzman .10 .02
❑ 36 Felix Fermin .10 .02
❑ 37 Jeff Innis .10 .02
❑ 38 Brett Mayne .10 .02
❑ 39 Huck Flener RC .10 .02
❑ 40 Jeff Bagwell .30 .10
❑ 41 Kevin Wickander .10 .02
❑ 42 Ricky Gutierrez .10 .02
❑ 43 Pat Mahomes .10 .02
❑ 44 Jeff King .10 .02
❑ 45 Cal Eldred .10 .02
❑ 46 Craig Paquette .10 .02
❑ 47 Richie Lewis .10 .02
❑ 48 Tony Phillips .10 .02
❑ 49 Armando Reynoso .10 .02
❑ 50 Moises Alou .20 .07
❑ 51 Manuel Lee .10 .02
❑ 52 Otis Nixon .10 .02
❑ 53 Billy Ashley .10 .02
❑ 54 Mark Whiten .10 .02
❑ 55 Jeff Russell .10 .02
❑ 56 Chad Curtis .10 .02
❑ 57 Kevin Stocker .10 .02
❑ 58 Mike Jackson .10 .02
❑ 59 Matt Nokes .10 .02
❑ 60 Chris Bosio .10 .02
❑ 61 Damon Buford .10 .02
❑ 62 Tim Belcher .10 .02
❑ 63 Glenallen Hill .10 .02
❑ 64 Bill Wertz .10 .02
❑ 65 Eddie Murray .50 .20
❑ 66 Tom Gordon .10 .02
❑ 67 Alex Gonzalez .10 .02
❑ 68 Eddie Taubensee .10 .02
❑ 69 Jacob Brumfield .10 .02
❑ 70 Andy Benes .10 .02
❑ 71 Rich Becker .10 .02
❑ 72 Steve Cooke .10 .02
❑ 73 Billy Spiers .10 .02
❑ 74 Scott Brosius .20 .07
❑ 75 Alan Trammell .20 .07
❑ 76 Luis Aquino .10 .02
❑ 77 Jerald Clark .10 .02
❑ 78 Mel Rojas .10 .02
❑ 79 Craig McClure RC .10 .02

Card	Player	Price 1	Price 2
❑ 80	Jose Canseco	.30	.10
❑ 81	Greg McMichael	.10	.02
❑ 82	Brian Turang RC	.10	.02
❑ 83	Tom Urbani	.10	.02
❑ 84	Garret Anderson	.50	.20
❑ 85	Tony Pena	.10	.02
❑ 86	Ricky Jordan	.10	.02
❑ 87	Jim Gott	.10	.02
❑ 88	Pat Kelly	.10	.02
❑ 89	Bud Black	.10	.02
❑ 90	Robin Ventura	.20	.07
❑ 91	Rick Sutcliffe	.20	.07
❑ 92	Jose Bautista	.10	.02
❑ 93	Bob Ojeda	.10	.02
❑ 94	Phil Hiatt	.10	.02
❑ 95	Tim Pugh	.10	.02
❑ 96	Randy Knorr	.10	.02
❑ 97	Todd Jones	.10	.02
❑ 98	Ryan Thompson	.10	.02
❑ 99	Tim Mauser	.10	.02
❑ 100	Kirby Puckett	.50	.20
❑ 101	Mark Dewey	.10	.02
❑ 102	B.J. Surhoff	.20	.07
❑ 103	Sterling Hitchcock	.10	.02
❑ 104	Alex Arias	.10	.02
❑ 105	David Wells	.20	.07
❑ 106	Daryl Boston	.10	.02
❑ 107	Mike Stanton	.10	.02
❑ 108	Gary Redus	.10	.02
❑ 109	Delino DeShields	.10	.02
❑ 110	Lee Smith	.20	.07
❑ 111	Greg Litton	.10	.02
❑ 112	Frankie Rodriguez	.10	.02
❑ 113	Russ Springer	.10	.02
❑ 114	Mitch Williams	.10	.02
❑ 115	Eric Karros	.20	.07
❑ 116	Jeff Brantley	.10	.02
❑ 117	Jack Voigt	.10	.02
❑ 118	Jason Bere	.10	.02
❑ 119	Kevin Roberson	.10	.02
❑ 120	Jimmy Key	.20	.07
❑ 121	Reggie Jefferson	.10	.02
❑ 122	Jeromy Burnitz	.20	.07
❑ 123	Billy Brewer	.10	.02
❑ 124	Willie Canate	.10	.02
❑ 125	Greg Swindell	.10	.02
❑ 126	Hal Morris	.10	.02
❑ 127	Brad Ausmus	.30	.10
❑ 128	George Tsamis	.10	.02
❑ 129	Denny Neagle	.20	.07
❑ 130	Pat Listach	.10	.02
❑ 131	Steve Karsay	.10	.02
❑ 132	Bret Barberie	.10	.02
❑ 133	Mark Leiter	.10	.02
❑ 134	Greg Colbrunn	.10	.02
❑ 135	David Nied	.10	.02
❑ 136	Dean Palmer	.20	.07
❑ 137	Steve Avery	.10	.02
❑ 138	Bill Haselman	.10	.02
❑ 139	Tripp Cromer	.10	.02
❑ 140	Frank Viola	.20	.07
❑ 141	Rene Gonzales	.10	.02
❑ 142	Curt Schilling	.20	.07
❑ 143	Tim Wallach	.10	.02
❑ 144	Bobby Munoz	.10	.02
❑ 145	Brady Anderson	.20	.07
❑ 146	Rod Beck	.10	.02
❑ 147	Mike LaValliere	.10	.02
❑ 148	Greg Hibbard	.10	.02
❑ 149	Kenny Lofton	.20	.07
❑ 150	Dwight Gooden	.20	.07
❑ 151	Greg Gagne	.10	.02
❑ 152	Ray McDavid	.10	.02
❑ 153	Chris Donnels	.10	.02
❑ 154	Dan Wilson	.10	.02
❑ 155	Todd Stottlemyre	.10	.02
❑ 156	David McCarty	.10	.02
❑ 157	Paul Wagner	.10	.02
❑ 158	Derek Jeter	1.50	.60
❑ 159	Mike Fetters	.10	.02
❑ 160	Scott Lydy	.10	.02
❑ 161	Darrell Whitmore	.10	.02
❑ 162	Bob MacDonald	.10	.02
❑ 163	Vinny Castilla	.20	.07
❑ 164	Denis Boucher	.10	.02
❑ 165	Ivan Rodriguez	.30	.10
❑ 166	Ron Gant	.20	.07
❑ 167	Tim Davis	.10	.02
❑ 168	Steve Dixon	.10	.02
❑ 169	Scott Fletcher	.10	.02
❑ 170	Terry Mulholland	.10	.02
❑ 171	Greg Myers	.10	.02
❑ 172	Brett Butler	.20	.07
❑ 173	Bob Wickman	.10	.02
❑ 174	Dave Martinez	.10	.02
❑ 175	Fernando Valenzuela	.20	.07
❑ 176	Craig Grebeck	.10	.02
❑ 177	Shawn Boskie	.10	.02
❑ 178	Albie Lopez	.10	.02
❑ 179	Butch Huskey	.10	.02
❑ 180	George Brett	1.25	.50
❑ 181	Juan Guzman	.10	.02
❑ 182	Eric Anthony	.10	.02
❑ 183	Rob Dibble	.20	.07
❑ 184	Craig Shipley	.10	.02
❑ 185	Kevin Tapani	.10	.02
❑ 186	Marcus Moore	.10	.02
❑ 187	Graeme Lloyd	.10	.02
❑ 188	Mike Bordick	.10	.02
❑ 189	Chris Hammond	.10	.02
❑ 190	Cecil Fielder	.20	.07
❑ 191	Curt Leskanic	.10	.02
❑ 192	Lou Frazier	.10	.02
❑ 193	Steve Dreyer RC	.10	.02
❑ 194	Javier Lopez	.20	.07
❑ 195	Edgar Martinez	.30	.10
❑ 196	Allen Watson	.10	.02
❑ 197	John Flaherty	.10	.02
❑ 198	Kurt Stillwell	.10	.02
❑ 199	Danny Jackson	.10	.02
❑ 200	Cal Ripken	1.50	.60
❑ 201	Mike Bell RC	.10	.02
❑ 202	Alan Benes RC	.25	.08
❑ 203	Matt Farner RC	.10	.02
❑ 204	Jeff Granger	.10	.02
❑ 205	Brooks Kieschnick RC	.10	.02
❑ 206	Jeremy Lee RC	.10	.02
❑ 207	Charles Peterson RC	.10	.02
❑ 208	Andy Rice RC	.10	.02
❑ 209	Billy Wagner RC	1.50	.60
❑ 210	Kelly Wunsch RC	.25	.08
❑ 211	Tom Candiotti	.10	.02
❑ 212	Domingo Jean	.10	.02
❑ 213	John Burkett	.10	.02
❑ 214	George Bell	.10	.02
❑ 215	Dan Plesac	.10	.02
❑ 216	Manny Ramirez	.50	.20
❑ 217	Mike Maddux	.10	.02
❑ 218	Kevin McReynolds	.10	.02
❑ 219	Pat Borders	.10	.02
❑ 220	Doug Drabek	.10	.02
❑ 221	Larry Luebbers RC	.10	.02
❑ 222	Trevor Hoffman	.30	.10
❑ 223	Pat Meares	.10	.02
❑ 224	Danny Miceli	.10	.02
❑ 225	Greg Vaughn	.10	.02
❑ 226	Scott Hemond	.10	.02
❑ 227	Pat Rapp	.10	.02
❑ 228	Kirk Gibson	.20	.07
❑ 229	Lance Painter	.10	.02
❑ 230	Larry Walker	.20	.07
❑ 231	Benji Gil	.10	.02
❑ 232	Mark Wohlers	.10	.02
❑ 233	Rich Amaral	.10	.02
❑ 234	Eric Pappas	.10	.02
❑ 235	Scott Cooper	.10	.02
❑ 236	Mike Butcher	.10	.02
❑ 237	Pride RC/Green/Sweeney RC	.50	.20
❑ 238	Kim Batiste	.10	.02
❑ 239	Paul Assenmacher	.10	.02
❑ 240	Will Clark	.30	.10
❑ 241	Jose Offerman	.10	.02
❑ 242	Todd Frohwirth	.10	.02
❑ 243	Tim Raines	.20	.07
❑ 244	Rick Wilkins	.10	.02
❑ 245	Bret Saberhagen	.20	.07
❑ 246	Thomas Howard	.10	.02
❑ 247	Stan Belinda	.10	.02
❑ 248	Rickey Henderson	.50	.20
❑ 249	Brian Williams	.10	.02
❑ 250	Barry Larkin	.30	.10
❑ 251	Jose Valentin	.10	.02
❑ 252	Lenny Webster	.10	.02
❑ 253	Blas Minor	.10	.02
❑ 254	Tim Teufel	.10	.02
❑ 255	Bobby Witt	.10	.02
❑ 256	Walt Weiss	.10	.02
❑ 257	Chad Kreuter	.10	.02
❑ 258	Roberto Mejia	.10	.02
❑ 259	Cliff Floyd	.20	.07
❑ 260	Julio Franco	.20	.07
❑ 261	Rafael Belliard	.10	.02
❑ 262	Marc Newfield	.10	.02
❑ 263	Gerald Perry	.10	.02
❑ 264	Ken Ryan	.10	.02
❑ 265	Chili Davis	.20	.07
❑ 266	Dave West	.10	.02
❑ 267	Royce Clayton	.10	.02
❑ 268	Pedro Martinez	.50	.20
❑ 269	Mark Hutton	.10	.02
❑ 270	Frank Thomas	.50	.20
❑ 271	Brad Pennington	.10	.02
❑ 272	Mike Harkey	.10	.02
❑ 273	Sandy Alomar Jr.	.10	.02
❑ 274	Dave Gallagher	.10	.02
❑ 275	Wally Joyner	.20	.07
❑ 276	Ricky Trlicek	.10	.02
❑ 277	Al Osuna	.10	.02
❑ 278	Pokey Reese	.10	.02
❑ 279	Kevin Higgins	.10	.02
❑ 280	Rick Aguilera	.10	.02
❑ 281	Orlando Merced	.10	.02
❑ 282	Mike Mohler	.10	.02
❑ 283	John Jaha	.10	.02
❑ 284	Robb Nen	.20	.07
❑ 285	Travis Fryman	.20	.07
❑ 286	Mark Thompson	.10	.02
❑ 287	Mike Lansing	.10	.02
❑ 288	Craig Lefferts	.10	.02
❑ 289	Damon Berryhill	.10	.02
❑ 290	Randy Johnson	.50	.20
❑ 291	Jeff Reed	.10	.02
❑ 292	Danny Darwin	.10	.02
❑ 293	J.T.Snow	.20	.07
❑ 294	Tyler Green	.10	.02
❑ 295	Chris Hoiles	.10	.02
❑ 296	Roger McDowell	.10	.02
❑ 297	Spike Owen	.10	.02
❑ 298	Salomon Torres	.10	.02
❑ 299	Wilson Alvarez	.10	.02
❑ 300	Ryne Sandberg	.75	.30
❑ 301	Derek Lilliquist	.10	.02
❑ 302	Howard Johnson	.10	.02
❑ 303	Greg Cadaret	.10	.02
❑ 304	Pat Hentgen	.10	.02
❑ 305	Craig Biggio	.30	.10
❑ 306	Scott Service	.10	.02
❑ 307	Melvin Nieves	.10	.02
❑ 308	Mike Trombley	.10	.02
❑ 309	Carlos Garcia	.10	.02
❑ 310	Robin Yount	.75	.30
❑ 311	Marcos Armas	.10	.02
❑ 312	Rich Rodriguez	.10	.02
❑ 313	Justin Thompson	.10	.02
❑ 314	Danny Sheaffer	.10	.02
❑ 315	Ken Hill	.10	.02
❑ 316	Terrell Wade RC	.10	.02
❑ 317	Cris Carpenter	.10	.02
❑ 318	Jeff Blauser	.10	.02
❑ 319	Ted Power	.10	.02
❑ 320	Ozzie Smith	.75	.30
❑ 321	John Dopson	.10	.02
❑ 322	Chris Turner	.10	.02
❑ 323	Pete Incaviglia	.10	.02
❑ 324	Alan Mills	.10	.02
❑ 325	Jody Reed	.10	.02
❑ 326	Rich Monteleone	.10	.02
❑ 327	Mark Carreon	.10	.02
❑ 328	Donn Pall	.10	.02
❑ 329	Matt Walbeck	.10	.02
❑ 330	Charley Nagy	.10	.02
❑ 331	Jeff McKnight	.10	.02
❑ 332	Jose Lind	.10	.02
❑ 333	Mike Timlin	.10	.02
❑ 334	Doug Jones	.10	.02
❑ 335	Kevin Mitchell	.10	.02
❑ 336	Luis Lopez	.10	.02
❑ 337	Shane Mack	.10	.02

❑ 338 Randy Tomlin .10 .02
❑ 339 Matt Mieske .10 .02
❑ 340 Mark McGwire 1.25 .50
❑ 341 Nigel Wilson .10 .02
❑ 342 Danny Gladden .10 .02
❑ 343 Mo Sanford .10 .02
❑ 344 Sean Berry .10 .02
❑ 345 Kevin Brown .20 .07
❑ 346 Greg Olson .10 .02
❑ 347 Dave Magadan .10 .02
❑ 348 Rene Arocha .10 .02
❑ 349 Carlos Quintana .10 .02
❑ 350 Jim Abbott .30 .10
❑ 351 Gary DiSarcina .10 .02
❑ 352 Ben Rivera .10 .02
❑ 353 Carlos Hernandez .10 .02
❑ 354 Darren Lewis .10 .02
❑ 355 Harold Reynolds .20 .07
❑ 356 Scott Ruffcorn .10 .02
❑ 357 Mark Gubicza .10 .02
❑ 358 Paul Sorrento .10 .02
❑ 359 Anthony Young .10 .02
❑ 360 Mark Grace .30 .10
❑ 361 Rob Butler .10 .02
❑ 362 Kevin Bass .10 .02
❑ 363 Eric Helfand .10 .02
❑ 364 Derek Bell .10 .02
❑ 365 Scott Erickson .10 .02
❑ 366 Al Martin .10 .02
❑ 367 Ricky Bones .10 .02
❑ 368 Jeff Branson .10 .02
❑ 369 J.Giambi/D.Bell RC .50 .20
❑ 370 Benito Santiago .20 .07
❑ 371 John Doherty .10 .02
❑ 372 Joe Girardi .10 .02
❑ 373 Tim Scott .10 .02
❑ 374 Marvin Freeman .10 .02
❑ 375 Deion Sanders .30 .10
❑ 376 Roger Salkeld .10 .02
❑ 377 Bernard Gilkey .10 .02
❑ 378 Tony Fossas .10 .02
❑ 379 Mark McLemore UER .10 .02
❑ 380 Darren Daulton .20 .07
❑ 381 Chuck Finley .20 .07
❑ 382 Mitch Webster .10 .02
❑ 383 Gerald Williams .10 .02
❑ 384 F.Thomas/F.McGriff AS .30 .10
❑ 385 R.Alomar/R.Thompson AS .20 .07
❑ 386 W.Boggs/M.Williams AS .20 .07
❑ 387 C.Ripken/J.Blauser AS .50 .20
❑ 388 K.Griffey/L.Dykstra AS .50 .20
❑ 389 J.Gonzalez/D.Justice AS .20 .07
❑ 390 A.Belle/B.Bonds AS .75 .30
❑ 391 M.Stanley/M.Piazza AS .50 .20
❑ 392 J.McDowell/G.Maddux AS .30 .10
❑ 393 J.Key/T.Glavine AS .20 .07
❑ 394 J.Montgomery/R.Myers AS .10 .02
❑ 395 Checklist 1-198 .10 .02
❑ 396 Checklist 199-396 .10 .02
❑ 397 Tim Salmon .30 .10
❑ 398 Todd Benzinger .10 .02
❑ 399 Frank Castillo .10 .02
❑ 400 Ken Griffey Jr. .75 .30
❑ 401 John Kruk .20 .07
❑ 402 Dave Telgheder .10 .02
❑ 403 Gary Gaetti .20 .07
❑ 404 Jim Edmonds .50 .20
❑ 405 Don Slaught .10 .02
❑ 406 Jose Oquendo .10 .02
❑ 407 Bruce Ruffin .10 .02
❑ 408 Phil Clark .10 .02
❑ 409 Joe Klink .10 .02
❑ 410 Lou Whitaker .20 .07
❑ 411 Kevin Seitzer .10 .02
❑ 412 Darrin Fletcher .10 .02
❑ 413 Kenny Rogers .20 .07
❑ 414 Bill Pecota .10 .02
❑ 415 Dave Fleming .10 .02
❑ 416 Luis Alicea .10 .02
❑ 417 Paul Quantrill .10 .02
❑ 418 Damion Easley .10 .02
❑ 419 Wes Chamberlain .10 .02
❑ 420 Harold Baines .20 .07
❑ 421 Scott Radinsky .10 .02
❑ 422 Rey Sanchez .10 .02
❑ 423 Junior Ortiz .10 .02
❑ 424 Jeff Kent .30 .10
❑ 425 Brian McRae .10 .02
❑ 426 Ed Sprague .10 .02
❑ 427 Tom Edens .10 .02
❑ 428 Willie Greene .10 .02
❑ 429 Bryan Hickerson .10 .02
❑ 430 Dave Winfield .20 .07
❑ 431 Pedro Astacio .10 .02
❑ 432 Mike Gallego .10 .02
❑ 433 Dave Burba .10 .02
❑ 434 Bob Walk .10 .02
❑ 435 Darryl Hamilton .10 .02
❑ 436 Vince Horsman .10 .02
❑ 437 Bob Natal .10 .02
❑ 438 Mike Henneman .10 .02
❑ 439 Willie Blair .10 .02
❑ 440 Dennis Martinez .20 .07
❑ 441 Dan Peltier .10 .02
❑ 442 Tony Tarasco .10 .02
❑ 443 John Cummings .10 .02
❑ 444 Geronimo Pena .10 .02
❑ 445 Aaron Sele .10 .02
❑ 446 Stan Javier .10 .02
❑ 447 Mike Williams .10 .02
❑ 448 D.J. Boston RC .10 .02
❑ 449 Jim Poole .10 .02
❑ 450 Carlos Baerga .10 .02
❑ 451 Bob Scanlan .10 .02
❑ 452 Lance Johnson .10 .02
❑ 453 Eric Hillman .10 .02
❑ 454 Keith Miller .10 .02
❑ 455 Dave Stewart .20 .07
❑ 456 Pete Harnisch .10 .02
❑ 457 Roberto Kelly .10 .02
❑ 458 Tim Worrell .10 .02
❑ 459 Pedro Munoz .10 .02
❑ 460 Orel Hershiser .20 .07
❑ 461 Randy Velarde .10 .02
❑ 462 Trevor Wilson .10 .02
❑ 463 Jerry Goff .10 .02
❑ 464 Bill Wegman .10 .02
❑ 465 Dennis Eckersley .20 .07
❑ 466 Jeff Conine .20 .07
❑ 467 Joe Boever .10 .02
❑ 468 Dante Bichette .20 .07
❑ 469 Jeff Shaw .10 .02
❑ 470 Rafael Palmeiro .30 .10
❑ 471 Phil Leftwich RC .10 .02
❑ 472 Jay Buhner .20 .07
❑ 473 Bob Tewksbury .10 .02
❑ 474 Tim Naehring .10 .02
❑ 475 Tom Glavine .30 .10
❑ 476 Dave Hollins .10 .02
❑ 477 Arthur Rhodes .10 .02
❑ 478 Joey Cora .10 .02
❑ 479 Mike Morgan .10 .02
❑ 480 Albert Belle .20 .07
❑ 481 John Franco .20 .07
❑ 482 Hipolito Pichardo .10 .02
❑ 483 Duane Ward .10 .02
❑ 484 Luis Gonzalez .20 .07
❑ 485 Joe Oliver .10 .02
❑ 486 Wally Whitehurst .10 .02
❑ 487 Mike Benjamin .10 .02
❑ 488 Eric Davis .20 .07
❑ 489 Scott Kamieniecki .10 .02
❑ 490 Kent Hrbek .20 .07
❑ 491 John Hope RC .10 .02
❑ 492 Jesse Orosco .10 .02
❑ 493 Troy Neel .10 .02
❑ 494 Ryan Bowen .10 .02
❑ 495 Mickey Tettleton .10 .02
❑ 496 Chris Jones .10 .02
❑ 497 John Wetteland .20 .07
❑ 498 David Hulse .10 .02
❑ 499 Greg Maddux .75 .30
❑ 500 Bo Jackson .50 .20
❑ 501 Donovan Osborne .10 .02
❑ 502 Mike Greenwell .10 .02
❑ 503 Steve Frey .10 .02
❑ 504 Jim Eisenreich .10 .02
❑ 505 Robby Thompson .10 .02
❑ 506 Leo Gomez .10 .02
❑ 507 Dave Staton .10 .02
❑ 508 Wayne Kirby .10 .02
❑ 509 Tim Bogar .10 .02
❑ 510 David Cone .20 .07
❑ 511 Devon White .20 .07
❑ 512 Xavier Hernandez .10 .02
❑ 513 Tim Costo .10 .02
❑ 514 Gene Harris .10 .02
❑ 515 Jack McDowell .10 .02
❑ 516 Kevin Gross .10 .02
❑ 517 Scott Leius .10 .02
❑ 518 Lloyd McClendon .10 .02
❑ 519 Alex Diaz RC .10 .02
❑ 520 Wade Boggs .30 .10
❑ 521 Bob Welch .10 .02
❑ 522 Henry Cotto .10 .02
❑ 523 Mike Moore .10 .02
❑ 524 Tim Laker .10 .02
❑ 525 Andres Galarraga .20 .07
❑ 526 Jamie Moyer .20 .07
❑ 527 J.Hardtke RC/C.Sexton RC .10 .02
❑ 528 Sid Bream .10 .02
❑ 529 Erik Hanson .10 .02
❑ 530 Ray Lankford .20 .07
❑ 531 Rob Deer .10 .02
❑ 532 Rod Correia .10 .02
❑ 533 Roger Mason .10 .02
❑ 534 Mike Devereaux .10 .02
❑ 535 Jeff Montgomery .10 .02
❑ 536 Dwight Smith .10 .02
❑ 537 Jeremy Hernandez .10 .02
❑ 538 Ellis Burks .20 .07
❑ 539 Bobby Jones .10 .02
❑ 540 Paul Molitor .20 .07
❑ 541 Jeff Juden .10 .02
❑ 542 Chris Sabo .10 .02
❑ 543 Larry Casian .10 .02
❑ 544 Jeff Gardner .10 .02
❑ 545 Ramon Martinez .10 .02
❑ 546 Paul O'Neill .30 .10
❑ 547 Steve Hosey .10 .02
❑ 548 Dave Nilsson .10 .02
❑ 549 Ron Darling .10 .02
❑ 550 Matt Williams .20 .07
❑ 551 Jack Armstrong .10 .02
❑ 552 Bill Krueger .10 .02
❑ 553 Freddie Benavides .10 .02
❑ 554 Jeff Fassero .10 .02
❑ 555 Chuck Knoblauch .20 .07
❑ 556 Guillermo Velasquez .10 .02
❑ 557 Joel Johnston .10 .02
❑ 558 Tom Lampkin .10 .02
❑ 559 Todd Van Poppel .10 .02
❑ 560 Gary Sheffield .20 .07
❑ 561 Skeeter Barnes .10 .02
❑ 562 Darren Holmes .10 .02
❑ 563 John Vander Wal .10 .02
❑ 564 Mike Ignasiak .10 .02
❑ 565 Fred McGriff .30 .10
❑ 566 Luis Polonia .10 .02
❑ 567 Mike Perez .10 .02
❑ 568 John Valentin .10 .02
❑ 569 Mike Felder .10 .02
❑ 570 Tommy Greene .10 .02
❑ 571 David Segui .10 .02
❑ 572 Roberto Hernandez .10 .02
❑ 573 Steve Wilson .10 .02
❑ 574 Willie McGee .20 .07
❑ 575 Randy Myers .10 .02
❑ 576 Darrin Jackson .10 .02
❑ 577 Eric Plunk .10 .02
❑ 578 Mike Macfarlane .10 .02
❑ 579 Doug Brocail .10 .02
❑ 580 Steve Finley .20 .07
❑ 581 John Roper .10 .02
❑ 582 Danny Cox .10 .02
❑ 583 Chip Hale .10 .02
❑ 584 Scott Bullett .10 .02
❑ 585 Kevin Reimer .10 .02
❑ 586 Brent Gates .10 .02
❑ 587 Matt Turner .10 .02
❑ 588 Rich Rowland .10 .02
❑ 589 Kent Bottenfield .10 .02
❑ 590 Marquis Grissom .20 .07
❑ 591 Doug Strange .10 .02
❑ 592 Jay Howell .10 .02
❑ 593 Omar Vizquel .30 .10
❑ 594 Rheal Cormier .10 .02
❑ 595 Andre Dawson .20 .07

	No.	Player		
❑	596	Hilly Hathaway	.10	.02
❑	597	Todd Pratt	.10	.02
❑	598	Mike Mussina	.30	.10
❑	599	Alex Fernandez	.10	.02
❑	600	Don Mattingly	1.25	.50
❑	601	Frank Thomas MOG	.30	.10
❑	602	Ryne Sandberg MOG	.50	.20
❑	603	Wade Boggs MOG	.20	.07
❑	604	Cal Ripken MOG	.75	.30
❑	605	Barry Bonds MOG	.75	.30
❑	606	Ken Griffey Jr. MOG	.50	.20
❑	607	Kirby Puckett MOG	.30	.10
❑	608	Darren Daulton MOG	.10	.02
❑	609	Paul Molitor MOG	.10	.02
❑	610	Terry Steinbach	.10	.02
❑	611	Todd Worrell	.10	.02
❑	612	Jim Thome	.30	.10
❑	613	Chuck McElroy	.10	.02
❑	614	John Habyan	.10	.02
❑	615	Sid Fernandez	.10	.02
❑	616	Jermaine Allensworth RC	.10	.02
❑	617	Steve Bedrosian	.10	.02
❑	618	Rob Ducey	.10	.02
❑	619	Tom Browning	.10	.02
❑	620	Tony Gwynn	.60	.25
❑	621	Carl Willis	.10	.02
❑	622	Kevin Young	.10	.02
❑	623	Rafael Novoa	.10	.02
❑	624	Jerry Browne	.10	.02
❑	625	Charlie Hough	.20	.07
❑	626	Chris Gomez	.10	.02
❑	627	Steve Reed	.10	.02
❑	628	Kirk Rueter	.10	.02
❑	629	Matt Whiteside	.10	.02
❑	630	David Justice	.20	.07
❑	631	Brad Holman	.10	.02
❑	632	Brian Jordan	.20	.07
❑	633	Scott Bankhead	.10	.02
❑	634	Torey Lovullo	.10	.02
❑	635	Len Dykstra	.20	.07
❑	636	Ben McDonald	.10	.02
❑	637	Steve Howe	.10	.02
❑	638	Jose Vizcaino	.10	.02
❑	639	Bill Swift	.10	.02
❑	640	Darryl Strawberry	.20	.07
❑	641	Steve Farr	.10	.02
❑	642	Tom Kramer	.10	.02
❑	643	Joe Orsulak	.10	.02
❑	644	Tom Henke	.10	.02
❑	645	Joe Carter	.20	.07
❑	646	Ken Caminiti	.20	.07
❑	647	Reggie Sanders	.20	.07
❑	648	Andy Ashby	.10	.02
❑	649	Derek Parks	.10	.02
❑	650	Andy Van Slyke	.30	.10
❑	651	Juan Bell	.10	.02
❑	652	Roger Smithberg	.10	.02
❑	653	Chuck Carr	.10	.02
❑	654	Bill Gullickson	.10	.02
❑	655	Charlie Hayes	.10	.02
❑	656	Chris Nabholz	.10	.02
❑	657	Karl Rhodes	.10	.02
❑	658	Pete Smith	.10	.02
❑	659	Bret Boone	.20	.07
❑	660	Gregg Jefferies	.10	.02
❑	661	Bob Zupcic	.10	.02
❑	662	Steve Sax	.10	.02
❑	663	Mariano Duncan	.10	.02
❑	664	Jeff Tackett	.10	.02
❑	665	Mark Langston	.10	.02
❑	666	Steve Buechele	.10	.02
❑	667	Candy Maldonado	.10	.02
❑	668	Woody Williams	.20	.07
❑	669	Tim Wakefield	.30	.10
❑	670	Danny Tartabull	.10	.02
❑	671	Charlie O'Brien	.10	.02
❑	672	Felix Jose	.10	.02
❑	673	Bobby Ayala	.10	.02
❑	674	Scott Servais	.10	.02
❑	675	Roberto Alomar	.30	.10
❑	676	Pedro A.Martinez RC	.10	.02
❑	677	Eddie Guardado	.20	.07
❑	678	Mark-Lewis	.10	.02
❑	679	Jaime Navarro	.10	.02
❑	680	Ruben Sierrra	.20	.07
❑	681	Rick Renteria	.10	.02
❑	682	Storm Davis	.10	.02
❑	683	Cory Snyder	.10	.02
❑	684	Ron Karkovice	.10	.02
❑	685	Juan Gonzalez	.20	.07
❑	686	Carlos Delgado	.30	.10
❑	687	John Smoltz	.30	.10
❑	688	Brian Dorsett	.10	.02
❑	689	Omar Olivares	.10	.02
❑	690	Mo Vaughn	.20	.07
❑	691	Joe Grahe	.10	.02
❑	692	Mickey Morandini	.10	.02
❑	693	Tino Martinez	.30	.10
❑	694	Brian Barnes	.10	.02
❑	695	Mike Stanley	.10	.02
❑	696	Mark Clark	.10	.02
❑	697	Dave Hansen	.10	.02
❑	698	Willie Wilson	.10	.02
❑	699	Pete Schourek	.10	.02
❑	700	Barry Bonds	1.50	.60
❑	701	Kevin Appier	.20	.07
❑	702	Tony Fernandez	.10	.02
❑	703	Darryl Kile	.20	.07
❑	704	Archi Cianfrocco	.10	.02
❑	705	Jose Rijo	.10	.02
❑	706	Brian Harper	.10	.02
❑	707	Zane Smith	.10	.02
❑	708	Dave Henderson	.10	.02
❑	709	Angel Miranda UER	.10	.02
❑	710	Orestes Destrade	.10	.02
❑	711	Greg Gohr	.10	.02
❑	712	Eric Young	.10	.02
❑	713	Bullinger/Will/Wat/Welch	.10	.02
❑	714	Tim Spehr	.10	.02
❑	715	Hank Aaron 715 HR	.50	.20
❑	716	Nate Minchey	.10	.02
❑	717	Mike Blowers	.10	.02
❑	718	Kent Mercker	.10	.02
❑	719	Tom Pagnozzi	.10	.02
❑	720	Roger Clemens	1.00	.40
❑	721	Eduardo Perez	.10	.02
❑	722	Milt Thompson	.10	.02
❑	723	Gregg Olson	.10	.02
❑	724	Kirk McCaskill	.10	.02
❑	725	Sammy Sosa	.50	.20
❑	726	Alvaro Espinoza	.10	.02
❑	727	Henry Rodriguez	.10	.02
❑	728	Jim Leyritz	.10	.02
❑	729	Steve Scarsone	.10	.02
❑	730	Bobby Bonilla	.20	.07
❑	731	Chris Gwynn	.10	.02
❑	732	Al Leiter	.20	.07
❑	733	Bip Roberts	.10	.02
❑	734	Mark Portugal	.10	.02
❑	735	Terry Pendleton	.20	.07
❑	736	Dave Valle	.10	.02
❑	737	Paul Kilgus	.10	.02
❑	738	Greg A. Harris	.10	.02
❑	739	Jon Ratliff RC	.10	.02
❑	740	Kirk Presley RC	.10	.02
❑	741	Josue Estrada RC	.10	.02
❑	742	Wayne Gomes RC	.10	.02
❑	743	Pat Watkins RC	.10	.02
❑	744	Jamey Wright RC	.25	.08
❑	745	Jay Powell RC	.10	.02
❑	746	Ryan McGuire RC	.10	.02
❑	747	Marc Barcelo RC	.10	.02
❑	748	Sloan Smith RC	.10	.02
❑	749	John Wasdin RC	.10	.02
❑	750	Marc Valdes	.10	.02
❑	751	Dan Ehler RC	.10	.02
❑	752	Andre King RC	.10	.02
❑	753	Greg Keagle RC	.10	.02
❑	754	Jason Myers RC	.10	.02
❑	755	Dax Winslett RC	.10	.02
❑	756	Casey Whitten RC	.10	.02
❑	757	Tony Fuduric RC	.10	.02
❑	758	Greg Norton RC	.25	.08
❑	759	Jeff D'Amico RC	.10	.02
❑	760	Ryan Hancock RC	.10	.02
❑	761	David Cooper RC	.10	.02
❑	762	Kevin Orie RC	.10	.02
❑	763	J.O'Donoghue/M.Oquist	.10	.02
❑	764	C.Bailey RC/S.Hatteberg	.10	.02
❑	765	M.Holzemer/P.Swingle RC	.10	.02
❑	766	J.Baldwin/R.Bolton	.10	.02
❑	767	J.Tavarez RC/J.DiPoto	.25	.08
❑	768	D.Bautista/S.Bergman	.10	.02
❑	769	B.Hamelin/J.Vitiello	.10	.02
❑	770	M.Kiefer/T.O'Leary	.10	.02
❑	771	D.Hocking/O.Munoz RC	.10	.02
❑	772	Russ Davis/B.Taylor	.10	.02
❑	773	K.Abbott/M.Jimenez	.25	.08
❑	774	K.King RC/Plantenberg RC	.10	.02
❑	775	J.Shave/D.Wilson	.10	.02
❑	776	D.Cedeno/P.Spoljaric	.10	.02
❑	777	C.Jones/R.Klesko	.50	.20
❑	778	S.Trachsel/T.Wendell	.10	.02
❑	779	J.Spradlin RC/J.Ruffin	.10	.02
❑	780	J.Bates/J.Burke	.10	.02
❑	781	C.Everett/D.Weathers	.20	.07
❑	782	J.Mouton/G.Mota	.10	.02
❑	783	R.Mondesi/B.Van Ryn	.20	.07
❑	784	R.White/G.White	.20	.07
❑	785	B.Pulsipher/B.Fordyce	.20	.07
❑	786	K.Foster RC/G.Schall	.10	.02
❑	787	Rich Aude RC/M.Cummings	.10	.02
❑	788	B.Barber/R.Batchelor	.10	.02
❑	789	B.Johnson RC/S.Sanders	.10	.02
❑	790	J.Phillips/R.Faneyte	.10	.02
❑	791	Checklist 3	.10	.02
❑	792	Checklist 4	.10	.02

1995 Topps

	No.	Player		
❑		COMPLETE SET (660)	80.00	50.00
❑		COMP.HOBBY SET (677)	120.00	60.00
❑		COMP.RETAIL SET (677)	120.00	60.00
❑		COMPLETE SERIES 1 (396)	40.00	25.00
❑		COMPLETE SERIES 2 (264)	40.00	25.00
❑	1	Frank Thomas	.75	.30
❑	2	Mickey Morandini	.15	.05
❑	3	Babe Ruth 100th B-Day	2.00	.75
❑	4	Scott Cooper	.15	.05
❑	5	David Cone	.30	.10
❑	6	Jacob Shumate	.15	.05
❑	7	Trevor Hoffman	.30	.10
❑	8	Shane Mack	.15	.05
❑	9	Delino DeShields	.15	.05
❑	10	Matt Williams	.30	.10
❑	11	Sammy Sosa	.75	.30
❑	12	Gary DiSarcina	.15	.05
❑	13	Kenny Rogers	.30	.10
❑	14	Jose Vizcaino	.15	.05
❑	15	Lou Whitaker	.30	.10
❑	16	Ron Darling	.15	.05
❑	17	Dave Nilsson	.15	.05
❑	18	Chris Hammond	.15	.05
❑	19	Sid Bream	.15	.05
❑	20	Denny Martinez	.30	.10
❑	21	Orlando Merced	.15	.05
❑	22	John Wetteland	.30	.10
❑	23	Mike Devereaux	.15	.05
❑	24	Rene Arocha	.15	.05
❑	25	Jay Buhner	.30	.10
❑	26	Darren Holmes	.15	.05
❑	27	Hal Morris	.15	.05
❑	28	Brian Buchanan RC	.15	.05
❑	29	Keith Miller	.15	.05
❑	30	Paul Molitor	.30	.10
❑	31	Dave West	.15	.05
❑	32	Tony Tarasco	.15	.05
❑	33	Scott Sanders	.15	.05
❑	34	Eddie Zambrano	.15	.05
❑	35	Ricky Bones	.15	.05
❑	36	John Valentin	.15	.05

❑ 37	Kevin Tapani	.15	.05
❑ 38	Tim Wallach	.15	.05
❑ 39	Darren Lewis	.15	.05
❑ 40	Travis Fryman	.30	.10
❑ 41	Mark Leiter	.15	.05
❑ 42	Jose Bautista	.15	.05
❑ 43	Pete Smith	.15	.05
❑ 44	Bret Barberie	.15	.05
❑ 45	Dennis Eckersley	.30	.10
❑ 46	Ken Hill	.15	.05
❑ 47	Chad Ogea	.15	.05
❑ 48	Pete Harnisch	.15	.05
❑ 49	James Baldwin	.15	.05
❑ 50	Mike Mussina	.50	.20
❑ 51	Al Martin	.15	.05
❑ 52	Mark Thompson	.15	.05
❑ 53	Matt Smith	.15	.05
❑ 54	Joey Hamilton	.15	.05
❑ 55	Edgar Martinez	.50	.20
❑ 56	John Smiley	.15	.05
❑ 57	Rey Sanchez	.15	.05
❑ 58	Mike Timlin	.15	.05
❑ 59	Ricky Bottalico	.15	.05
❑ 60	Jim Abbott	.50	.20
❑ 61	Mike Kelly	.15	.05
❑ 62	Brian Jordan	.30	.10
❑ 63	Ken Ryan	.15	.05
❑ 64	Matt Mieske	.15	.05
❑ 65	Rick Aguilera	.15	.05
❑ 66	Ismael Valdes	.15	.05
❑ 67	Royce Clayton	.15	.05
❑ 68	Junior Felix	.15	.05
❑ 69	Harold Reynolds	.30	.10
❑ 70	Juan Gonzalez	.30	.10
❑ 71	Kelly Stinnett	.15	.05
❑ 72	Carlos Reyes	.15	.05
❑ 73	Dave Weathers	.15	.05
❑ 74	Mel Rojas	.15	.05
❑ 75	Doug Drabek	.15	.05
❑ 76	Charles Nagy	.15	.05
❑ 77	Tim Raines	.30	.10
❑ 78	Midre Cummings	.15	.05
❑ 79	Ray Brown RC	.15	.05
❑ 80	Rafael Palmeiro	.50	.20
❑ 81	Charlie Hayes	.15	.05
❑ 82	Ray Lankford	.30	.10
❑ 83	Tim Davis	.15	.05
❑ 84	C.J. Nitkowski	.15	.05
❑ 85	Andy Ashby	.15	.05
❑ 86	Gerald Williams	.15	.05
❑ 87	Terry Shumpert	.15	.05
❑ 88	Heathcliff Slocumb	.15	.05
❑ 89	Domingo Cedeno	.15	.05
❑ 90	Mark Grace	.50	.20
❑ 91	Brad Woodall RC	.15	.05
❑ 92	Gar Finnvold	.15	.05
❑ 93	Jaime Navarro	.15	.05
❑ 94	Carlos Hernandez	.15	.05
❑ 95	Mark Langston	.15	.05
❑ 96	Chuck Carr	.15	.05
❑ 97	Mike Gardiner	.15	.05
❑ 98	Dave McCarty	.15	.05
❑ 99	Cris Carpenter	.15	.05
❑ 100	Barry Bonds	2.00	.75
❑ 101	David Segui	.15	.05
❑ 102	Scott Brosius	.30	.10
❑ 103	Mariano Duncan	.15	.05
❑ 104	Kenny Lofton	.30	.10
❑ 105	Ken Caminiti	.30	.10
❑ 106	Darrin Jackson	.15	.05
❑ 107	Jim Poole	.15	.05
❑ 108	Wil Cordero	.15	.05
❑ 109	Danny Miceli	.15	.05
❑ 110	Walt Weiss	.15	.05
❑ 111	Tom Pagnozzi	.15	.05
❑ 112	Terrence Long	.15	.05
❑ 113	Bret Boone	.30	.10
❑ 114	Daryl Boston	.15	.05
❑ 115	Wally Joyner	.30	.10
❑ 116	Rob Butler	.15	.05
❑ 117	Rafael Belliard	.15	.05
❑ 118	Luis Lopez	.15	.05
❑ 119	Tony Fossas	.15	.05
❑ 120	Len Dykstra	.30	.10
❑ 121	Mike Morgan	.15	.05
❑ 122	Denny Hocking	.15	.05
❑ 123	Kevin Gross	.15	.05
❑ 124	Todd Benzinger	.15	.05
❑ 125	John Doherty	.15	.05
❑ 126	Eduardo Perez	.15	.05
❑ 127	Dan Smith	.15	.05
❑ 128	Joe Orsulak	.15	.05
❑ 129	Brent Gates	.15	.05
❑ 130	Jeff Conine	.30	.10
❑ 131	Doug Henry	.15	.05
❑ 132	Paul Sorrento	.15	.05
❑ 133	Mike Hampton	.30	.10
❑ 134	Tim Spehr	.15	.05
❑ 135	Julio Franco	.30	.10
❑ 136	Mike Dyer	.15	.05
❑ 137	Chris Sabo	.15	.05
❑ 138	Rheal Cormier	.15	.05
❑ 139	Paul Konerko	1.00	.40
❑ 140	Dante Bichette	.30	.10
❑ 141	Chuck McElroy	.15	.05
❑ 142	Mike Stanley	.15	.05
❑ 143	Bob Hamelin	.15	.05
❑ 144	Tommy Greene	.15	.05
❑ 145	John Smoltz	.50	.20
❑ 146	Ed Sprague	.15	.05
❑ 147	Ray McDavid	.15	.05
❑ 148	Otis Nixon	.15	.05
❑ 149	Turk Wendell	.15	.05
❑ 150	Chris James	.15	.05
❑ 151	Derek Parks	.15	.05
❑ 152	Jose Offerman	.15	.05
❑ 153	Tony Clark	.15	.05
❑ 154	Chad Curtis	.15	.05
❑ 155	Mark Portugal	.15	.05
❑ 156	Bill Pulsipher	.15	.05
❑ 157	Troy Neel	.15	.05
❑ 158	Dave Winfield	.30	.10
❑ 159	Bill Wegman	.15	.05
❑ 160	Benito Santiago	.30	.10
❑ 161	Jose Mesa	.15	.05
❑ 162	Luis Gonzalez	.30	.10
❑ 163	Alex Fernandez	.15	.05
❑ 164	Freddie Benavides	.15	.05
❑ 165	Ben McDonald	.15	.05
❑ 166	Blas Minor	.15	.05
❑ 167	Bret Wagner	.15	.05
❑ 168	Mac Suzuki	.15	.05
❑ 169	Roberto Mejia	.15	.05
❑ 170	Wade Boggs	.50	.20
❑ 171	Pokey Reese	.15	.05
❑ 172	Hipolito Pichardo	.15	.05
❑ 173	Kim Batiste	.15	.05
❑ 174	Darren Hall	.15	.05
❑ 175	Tom Glavine	.50	.20
❑ 176	Phil Plantier	.15	.05
❑ 177	Chris Howard	.15	.05
❑ 178	Karl Rhodes	.15	.05
❑ 179	LaTroy Hawkins	.15	.05
❑ 180	Raul Mondesi	.30	.10
❑ 181	Jeff Reed	.15	.05
❑ 182	Milt Cuyler	.15	.05
❑ 183	Jim Edmonds	.50	.20
❑ 184	Hector Fajardo	.15	.05
❑ 185	Jeff Kent	.30	.10
❑ 186	Wilson Alvarez	.15	.05
❑ 187	Geronimo Berroa	.15	.05
❑ 188	Billy Spiers	.15	.05
❑ 189	Derek Lilliquist	.15	.05
❑ 190	Craig Biggio	.50	.20
❑ 191	Roberto Hernandez	.15	.05
❑ 192	Bob Natal	.15	.05
❑ 193	Bobby Ayala	.15	.05
❑ 194	Travis Miller RC	.15	.05
❑ 195	Bob Tewksbury	.15	.05
❑ 196	Rondell White	.30	.10
❑ 197	Steve Cooke	.15	.05
❑ 198	Jeff Branson	.15	.05
❑ 199	Derek Jeter	2.00	.75
❑ 200	Tim Salmon	.50	.20
❑ 201	Steve Frey	.15	.05
❑ 202	Kent Mercker	.15	.05
❑ 203	Randy Johnson	.75	.30
❑ 204	Todd Worrell	.15	.05
❑ 205	Mo Vaughn	.30	.10
❑ 206	Howard Johnson	.15	.05
❑ 207	John Wasdin	.15	.05
❑ 208	Eddie Williams	.15	.05
❑ 209	Tim Belcher	.15	.05
❑ 210	Jeff Montgomery	.15	.05
❑ 211	Kirt Manwaring	.15	.05
❑ 212	Ben Grieve	.15	.05
❑ 213	Pat Hentgen	.15	.05
❑ 214	Shawon Dunston	.15	.05
❑ 215	Mike Greenwell	.15	.05
❑ 216	Alex Diaz	.15	.05
❑ 217	Pat Mahomes	.15	.05
❑ 218	Dave Hansen	.15	.05
❑ 219	Kevin Rogers	.15	.05
❑ 220	Cecil Fielder	.30	.10
❑ 221	Andrew Lorraine	.15	.05
❑ 222	Jack Armstrong	.15	.05
❑ 223	Todd Hundley	.15	.05
❑ 224	Mark Acre	.15	.05
❑ 225	Darrell Whitmore	.15	.05
❑ 226	Randy Milligan	.15	.05
❑ 227	Wayne Kirby	.15	.05
❑ 228	Darryl Kile	.30	.10
❑ 229	Bob Zupcic	.15	.05
❑ 230	Jay Bell	.30	.10
❑ 231	Dustin Hermanson	.15	.05
❑ 232	Harold Baines	.30	.10
❑ 233	Alan Benes	.15	.05
❑ 234	Felix Fermin	.15	.05
❑ 235	Ellis Burks	.30	.10
❑ 236	Jeff Brantley	.15	.05
❑ 237	Karim Garcia RC	.15	.05
❑ 238	Matt Nokes	.15	.05
❑ 239	Ben Rivera	.15	.05
❑ 240	Joe Carter	.30	.10
❑ 241	Jeff Granger	.15	.05
❑ 242	Terry Pendleton	.30	.10
❑ 243	Melvin Nieves	.15	.05
❑ 244	Frankie Rodriguez	.15	.05
❑ 245	Darryl Hamilton	.15	.05
❑ 246	Brooks Kieschnick	.15	.05
❑ 247	Todd Hollandsworth	.15	.05
❑ 248	Joe Rosselli	.15	.05
❑ 249	Bill Gullickson	.15	.05
❑ 250	Chuck Knoblauch	.30	.10
❑ 251	Kurt Miller	.15	.05
❑ 252	Bobby Jones	.15	.05
❑ 253	Lance Blankenship	.15	.05
❑ 254	Matt Whiteside	.15	.05
❑ 255	Darrin Fletcher	.15	.05
❑ 256	Eric Plunk	.15	.05
❑ 257	Shane Reynolds	.15	.05
❑ 258	Norberto Martin	.15	.05
❑ 259	Mike Thurman	.15	.05
❑ 260	Andy Van Slyke	.50	.20
❑ 261	Dwight Smith	.15	.05
❑ 262	Allen Watson	.15	.05
❑ 263	Dan Wilson	.15	.05
❑ 264	Brent Mayne	.15	.05
❑ 265	Bip Roberts	.15	.05
❑ 266	Sterling Hitchcock	.15	.05
❑ 267	Alex Gonzalez	.15	.05
❑ 268	Greg Harris	.15	.05
❑ 269	Ricky Jordan	.15	.05
❑ 270	Johnny Ruffin	.15	.05
❑ 271	Mike Stanton	.15	.05
❑ 272	Rich Rowland	.15	.05
❑ 273	Steve Trachsel	.15	.05
❑ 274	Pedro Munoz	.15	.05
❑ 275	Ramon Martinez	.15	.05
❑ 276	Dave Henderson	.15	.05
❑ 277	Chris Gomez	.15	.05
❑ 278	Joe Grahe	.15	.05
❑ 279	Rusty Greer	.30	.10
❑ 280	John Franco	.30	.10
❑ 281	Mike Bordick	.15	.05
❑ 282	Jeff D'Amico	.15	.05
❑ 283	Dave Magadan	.15	.05
❑ 284	Tony Pena	.15	.05
❑ 285	Greg Swindell	.15	.05
❑ 286	Doug Million	.15	.05
❑ 287	Gabe White	.15	.05
❑ 288	Trey Beamon	.15	.05
❑ 289	Arthur Rhodes	.15	.05
❑ 290	Juan Guzman	.15	.05
❑ 291	Jose Oquendo	.15	.05
❑ 292	Willie Blair	.15	.05
❑ 293	Eddie Taubensee	.15	.05
❑ 294	Steve Howe	.15	.05

❑	295	Greg Maddux	1.25	.50
❑	296	Mike Macfarlane	.15	.05
❑	297	Curt Schilling	.30	.10
❑	298	Phil Clark	.15	.05
❑	299	Woody Williams	.15	.05
❑	300	Jose Canseco	.50	.20
❑	301	Aaron Sele	.15	.05
❑	302	Carl Willis	.15	.05
❑	303	Steve Buechele	.15	.05
❑	304	Dave Burba	.15	.05
❑	305	Orel Hershiser	.30	.10
❑	306	Damion Easley	.15	.05
❑	307	Mike Henneman	.15	.05
❑	308	Josias Manzanillo	.15	.05
❑	309	Kevin Seitzer	.15	.05
❑	310	Ruben Sierra	.30	.10
❑	311	Bryan Harvey	.15	.05
❑	312	Jim Thome	.50	.20
❑	313	Ramon Castro RC	.40	.15
❑	314	Lance Johnson	.15	.05
❑	315	Marquis Grissom	.30	.10
❑	316	Eddie Priest RC	.15	.05
❑	317	Paul Wagner	.15	.05
❑	318	Jamie Moyer	.30	.10
❑	319	Todd Zeile	.15	.05
❑	320	Chris Bosio	.15	.05
❑	321	Steve Reed	.15	.05
❑	322	Erik Hanson	.15	.05
❑	323	Luis Polonia	.15	.05
❑	324	Ryan Klesko	.30	.10
❑	325	Kevin Appier	.30	.10
❑	326	Jim Eisenreich	.15	.05
❑	327	Randy Knorr	.15	.05
❑	328	Craig Shipley	.15	.05
❑	329	Tim Naehring	.15	.05
❑	330	Randy Myers	.15	.05
❑	331	Alex Cole	.15	.05
❑	332	Jim Gott	.15	.05
❑	333	Mike Jackson	.15	.05
❑	334	John Flaherty	.15	.05
❑	335	Chili Davis	.30	.10
❑	336	Benji Gil	.15	.05
❑	337	Jason Jacome	.15	.05
❑	338	Stan Javier	.15	.05
❑	339	Mike Fetters	.15	.05
❑	340	Rich Renteria	.15	.05
❑	341	Kevin Witt	.15	.05
❑	342	Scott Servais	.15	.05
❑	343	Craig Grebeck	.15	.05
❑	344	Kirk Rueter	.15	.05
❑	345	Don Slaught	.15	.05
❑	346	Armando Benitez	.15	.05
❑	347	Ozzie Smith	1.25	.50
❑	348	Mike Blowers	.15	.05
❑	349	Armando Reynoso	.15	.05
❑	350	Barry Larkin	.50	.20
❑	351	Mike Williams	.15	.05
❑	352	Scott Kamieniecki	.15	.05
❑	353	Gary Gaetti	.30	.10
❑	354	Todd Stottlemyre	.15	.05
❑	355	Fred McGriff	.50	.20
❑	356	Tim Mauser	.15	.05
❑	357	Chris Gwynn	.15	.05
❑	358	Frank Castillo	.15	.05
❑	359	Jeff Reboulet	.15	.05
❑	360	Roger Clemens	1.50	.60
❑	361	Mark Carreon	.15	.05
❑	362	Chad Kreuter	.15	.05
❑	363	Mark Farris	.15	.05
❑	364	Bob Welch	.15	.05
❑	365	Dean Palmer	.30	.10
❑	366	Jeromy Burnitz	.30	.10
❑	367	B.J. Surhoff	.30	.10
❑	368	Mike Butcher	.15	.05
❑	369	B.Buckles RC/B.Clontz	.15	.05
❑	370	Eddie Murray	.75	.30
❑	371	Orlando Miller	.15	.05
❑	372	Ron Karkovice	.15	.05
❑	373	Richie Lewis	.15	.05
❑	374	Lenny Webster	.15	.05
❑	375	Jeff Tackett	.15	.05
❑	376	Tom Urbani	.15	.05
❑	377	Tino Martinez	.50	.20
❑	378	Mark Dewey	.15	.05
❑	379	Charles O'Brien	.15	.05
❑	380	Terry Mulholland	.15	.05
❑	381	Thomas Howard	.15	.05
❑	382	Chris Haney	.15	.05
❑	383	Billy Hatcher	.15	.05
❑	384	F.Thomas/J.Bagwell AS	.50	.20
❑	385	B.Boone/C.Baerga AS	.30	.10
❑	386	M.Williams/W.Boggs AS	.30	.10
❑	387	C.Ripken/W.Cordero AS	.75	.30
❑	388	K.Griffey Jr./B.Bonds AS	1.00	.40
❑	389	T.Gwynn/A.Belle AS	.30	.10
❑	390	D.Bichette/K.Puckett AS	.50	.20
❑	391	M.Piazza/M.Stanley AS	.75	.30
❑	392	G.Maddux/D.Cone AS	.75	.30
❑	393	D.Jackson/J.Key AS	.15	.05
❑	394	J.Franco/L.Smith AS	.15	.05
❑	395	Checklist 1-198	.15	.05
❑	396	Checklist 199-396	.15	.05
❑	397	Ken Griffey Jr.	1.25	.50
❑	398	Rick Heiserman RC	.15	.05
❑	399	Don Mattingly	2.00	.75
❑	400	Henry Rodriguez	.15	.05
❑	401	Lenny Harris	.15	.05
❑	402	Ryan Thompson	.15	.05
❑	403	Darren Oliver	.15	.05
❑	404	Omar Vizquel	.50	.20
❑	405	Jeff Bagwell	.50	.20
❑	406	Doug Webb RC	.15	.05
❑	407	Todd Van Poppel	.15	.05
❑	408	Leo Gomez	.15	.05
❑	409	Mark Whiten	.15	.05
❑	410	Pedro A.Martinez	.15	.05
❑	411	Reggie Sanders	.30	.10
❑	412	Kevin Foster	.15	.05
❑	413	Danny Tartabull	.15	.05
❑	414	Jeff Blauser	.15	.05
❑	415	Mike Magnante	.15	.05
❑	416	Tom Candiotti	.15	.05
❑	417	Rod Beck	.15	.05
❑	418	Jody Reed	.15	.05
❑	419	Vince Coleman	.15	.05
❑	420	Danny Jackson	.15	.05
❑	421	Ryan Nye RC	.15	.05
❑	422	Larry Walker	.30	.10
❑	423	Russ Johnson DP	.15	.05
❑	424	Pat Borders	.15	.05
❑	425	Lee Smith	.30	.10
❑	426	Paul O'Neill	.50	.20
❑	427	Devon White	.30	.10
❑	428	Jim Bullinger	.15	.05
❑	429	Rob Welch RC	.15	.05
❑	430	Steve Avery	.15	.05
❑	431	Tony Gwynn	1.00	.40
❑	432	Pat Meares	.15	.05
❑	433	Bill Swift	.15	.05
❑	434	David Wells	.30	.10
❑	435	John Briscoe	.15	.05
❑	436	Roger Pavlik	.15	.05
❑	437	Jayson Peterson RC	.15	.05
❑	438	Roberto Alomar	.50	.20
❑	439	Billy Brewer	.15	.05
❑	440	Gary Sheffield	.30	.10
❑	441	Lou Frazier	.15	.05
❑	442	Terry Steinbach	.15	.05
❑	443	Jay Payton RC	.75	.30
❑	444	Jason Bere	.15	.05
❑	445	Denny Neagle	.30	.10
❑	446	Andres Galarraga	.30	.10
❑	447	Hector Carrasco	.15	.05
❑	448	Bill Risley	.15	.05
❑	449	Andy Benes	.15	.05
❑	450	Jim Leyritz	.15	.05
❑	451	Jose Oliva	.15	.05
❑	452	Greg Vaughn	.15	.05
❑	453	Rich Monteleone	.15	.05
❑	454	Tony Eusebio	.15	.05
❑	455	Chuck Finley	.30	.10
❑	456	Kevin Brown	.30	.10
❑	457	Joe Boever	.15	.05
❑	458	Bobby Munoz	.15	.05
❑	459	Bret Saberhagen	.30	.10
❑	460	Kurt Abbott	.15	.05
❑	461	Bobby Witt	.15	.05
❑	462	Cliff Floyd	.30	.10
❑	463	Mark Clark	.15	.05
❑	464	Andujar Cedeno	.15	.05
❑	465	Marvin Freeman	.15	.05
❑	466	Mike Piazza	1.25	.50
❑	467	Willie Greene	.15	.05
❑	468	Pat Kelly	.15	.05
❑	469	Carlos Delgado	.30	.10
❑	470	Willie Banks	.15	.05
❑	471	Matt Walbeck	.15	.05
❑	472	Mark McGwire	2.00	.75
❑	473	McKay Christensen RC	.15	.05
❑	474	Alan Trammell	.30	.10
❑	475	Tom Gordon	.15	.05
❑	476	Greg Colbrunn	.15	.05
❑	477	Darren Daulton	.30	.10
❑	478	Albie Lopez	.15	.05
❑	479	Robin Ventura	.30	.10
❑	480	Eddie Perez RC	.40	.15
❑	481	Bryan Eversgerd	.15	.05
❑	482	Dave Fleming	.15	.05
❑	483	Scott Livingstone	.15	.05
❑	484	Pete Schourek	.15	.05
❑	485	Bernie Williams	.50	.20
❑	486	Mark Lemke	.15	.05
❑	487	Eric Karros	.30	.10
❑	488	Scott Ruffcorn	.15	.05
❑	489	Billy Ashley	.15	.05
❑	490	Rico Brogna	.15	.05
❑	491	John Burkett	.15	.05
❑	492	Cade Gaspar RC	.15	.05
❑	493	Jorge Fabregas	.15	.05
❑	494	Greg Gagne	.15	.05
❑	495	Doug Jones	.15	.05
❑	496	Troy O'Leary	.15	.05
❑	497	Pat Rapp	.15	.05
❑	498	Butch Henry	.15	.05
❑	499	John Olerud	.30	.10
❑	500	John Hudek	.15	.05
❑	501	Jeff King	.15	.05
❑	502	Bobby Bonilla	.30	.10
❑	503	Albert Belle	.30	.10
❑	504	Rick Wilkins	.15	.05
❑	505	John Jaha	.15	.05
❑	506	Nigel Wilson	.15	.05
❑	507	Sid Fernandez	.15	.05
❑	508	Deion Sanders	.50	.20
❑	509	Gil Heredia	.15	.05
❑	510	Scott Elarton RC	.40	.15
❑	511	Melido Perez	.15	.05
❑	512	Greg McMichael	.15	.05
❑	513	Rusty Meacham	.15	.05
❑	514	Shawn Green	.30	.10
❑	515	Carlos Garcia	.15	.05
❑	516	Dave Stevens	.15	.05
❑	517	Eric Young	.15	.05
❑	518	Omar Daal	.15	.05
❑	519	Kirk Gibson	.30	.10
❑	520	Spike Owen	.15	.05
❑	521	Jacob Cruz RC	.30	.10
❑	522	Sandy Alomar Jr.	.15	.05
❑	523	Steve Bedrosian	.15	.05
❑	524	Ricky Gutierrez	.15	.05
❑	525	Dave Veres	.15	.05
❑	526	Gregg Jefferies	.15	.05
❑	527	Jose Valentin	.15	.05
❑	528	Robb Nen	.30	.10
❑	529	Jose Rijo	.15	.05
❑	530	Sean Berry	.15	.05
❑	531	Mike Gallego	.15	.05
❑	532	Roberto Kelly	.15	.05
❑	533	Kevin Stocker	.15	.05
❑	534	Kirby Puckett	.75	.30
❑	535	Chipper Jones	.75	.30
❑	536	Russ Davis	.15	.05
❑	537	Jon Lieber	.15	.05
❑	538	Trey Moore RC	.15	.05
❑	539	Joe Girardi	.15	.05
❑	540	Miguel Cairo RC	.15	.05
❑	541	Tony Phillips	.15	.05
❑	542	Brian Anderson	.15	.05
❑	543	Ivan Rodriguez	.50	.20
❑	544	Jeff Cirillo	.15	.05
❑	545	Joey Cora	.15	.05
❑	546	Chris Hoiles	.15	.05
❑	547	Bernard Gilkey	.15	.05
❑	548	Mike Lansing	.15	.05
❑	549	Jimmy Key	.30	.10
❑	550	Mark Wohlers	.15	.05
❑	551	Chris Clemons RC	.15	.05
❑	552	Vinny Castilla	.30	.10

❑ 553 Mark Guthrie .15 .05
❑ 554 Mike Lieberthal .30 .10
❑ 555 Tommy Davis RC .15 .05
❑ 556 Robby Thompson .15 .05
❑ 557 Danny Bautista .15 .05
❑ 558 Will Clark .50 .20
❑ 559 Rickey Henderson .75 .30
❑ 560 Todd Jones .15 .05
❑ 561 Jack McDowell .15 .05
❑ 562 Carlos Rodriguez .15 .05
❑ 563 Mark Eichhorn .15 .05
❑ 564 Jeff Nelson .15 .05
❑ 565 Eric Anthony .15 .05
❑ 566 Randy Velarde .15 .05
❑ 567 Javier Lopez .30 .10
❑ 568 Kevin Mitchell .15 .05
❑ 569 Steve Karsay .15 .05
❑ 570 Brian Meadows RC .15 .05
❑ 571 Rey Ordonez RC .75 .30
❑ 572 John Kruk .30 .10
❑ 573 Scott Leius .15 .05
❑ 574 John Patterson .15 .05
❑ 575 Kevin Brown .30 .10
❑ 576 Mike Moore .15 .05
❑ 577 Manny Ramirez .50 .20
❑ 578 Jose Lind .15 .05
❑ 579 Derrick May .15 .05
❑ 580 Cal Eldred .15 .05
❑ 581 A.Boone RC/D.Bell .75 .30
❑ 582 J.T. Snow .30 .10
❑ 583 Luis Sojo .15 .05
❑ 584 Moises Alou .30 .10
❑ 585 Dave Clark .15 .05
❑ 586 Dave Hollins .15 .05
❑ 587 Nomar Garciaparra 2.00 .75
❑ 588 Cal Ripken 2.50 1.00
❑ 589 Pedro Astacio .15 .05
❑ 590 J.R. Phillips .15 .05
❑ 591 Jeff Frye .15 .05
❑ 592 Bo Jackson .75 .30
❑ 593 Steve Ontiveros .15 .05
❑ 594 David Nied .15 .05
❑ 595 Brad Ausmus .30 .10
❑ 596 Carlos Baerga .15 .05
❑ 597 James Mouton .15 .05
❑ 598 Ozzie Guillen .30 .10
❑ 599 Johnny Damon .75 .30
❑ 600 Yorkis Perez .15 .05
❑ 601 Rich Rodriguez .15 .05
❑ 602 Mark McLemore .15 .05
❑ 603 Jeff Fassero .15 .05
❑ 604 John Roper .15 .05
❑ 605 Mark Johnson RC .40 .15
❑ 606 Wes Chamberlain .15 .05
❑ 607 Felix Jose .15 .05
❑ 608 Tony Longmire .15 .05
❑ 609 Duane Ward .15 .05
❑ 610 Brett Butler .30 .10
❑ 611 William VanLandingham .15 .05
❑ 612 Mickey Tettleton .15 .05
❑ 613 Brady Anderson .30 .10
❑ 614 Reggie Jefferson .15 .05
❑ 615 Mike Kingery .15 .05
❑ 616 Derek Bell .15 .05
❑ 617 Scott Erickson .15 .05
❑ 618 Bob Wickman .15 .05
❑ 619 Phil Leftwich .15 .05
❑ 620 David Justice .30 .10
❑ 621 Paul Wilson .15 .05
❑ 622 Pedro Martinez .50 .20
❑ 623 Terry Mathews .15 .05
❑ 624 Brian McRae .15 .05
❑ 625 Bruce Ruffin .15 .05
❑ 626 Steve Finley .30 .10
❑ 627 Ron Gant .30 .10
❑ 628 Rafael Bournigal .15 .05
❑ 629 Darryl Strawberry .30 .10
❑ 630 Luis Alicea .15 .05
❑ 631 Mark Smith .15 .05
❑ 632 C.Bailey/S.Hatteberg .15 .05
❑ 633 Todd Greene .30 .10
❑ 634 Rod Bolton .15 .05
❑ 635 Herbert Perry .15 .05
❑ 636 Sean Bergman .15 .05
❑ 637 J.Randa/J.Vitiello .30 .10
❑ 638 Jose Mercedes .15 .05
❑ 639 Marty Cordova .15 .05
❑ 640 R.Rivera/A.Pettitte .30 .10
❑ 641 W.Adams/S.Spiezio .15 .05
❑ 642 Eddy Diaz RC .15 .05
❑ 643 Jon Shave .15 .05
❑ 644 Paul Spoljaric .15 .05
❑ 645 Damon Hollins .15 .05
❑ 646 Doug Glanville .15 .05
❑ 647 Tim Belk .15 .05
❑ 648 Rod Pedraza .15 .05
❑ 649 Marc Valdes .15 .05
❑ 650 Rick Huisman .15 .05
❑ 651 Ron Coomer RC .15 .05
❑ 652 Carlos Perez RC .40 .15
❑ 653 Jason Isringhausen .30 .10
❑ 654 Kevin Jordan .15 .05
❑ 655 Esteban Loaiza .15 .05
❑ 656 John Frascatore .15 .05
❑ 657 Bryce Florie .15 .05
❑ 658 Keith Williams .15 .05
❑ 659 Checklist .15 .05
❑ 660 Checklist .15 .05

1995 Topps Traded

❑ COMPLETE SET (165) 40.00 15.00
❑ 1T Frank Thomas AB .60 .25
❑ 2T Ken Griffey Jr. AB 1.00 .40
❑ 3T Barry Bonds AB 1.25 .50
❑ 4T Albert Belle AB .40 .15
❑ 5T Cal Ripken AB 1.50 .60
❑ 6T Mike Piazza AB 1.00 .40
❑ 7T Tony Gwynn AB .60 .25
❑ 8T Jeff Bagwell AB .40 .15
❑ 9T Mo Vaughn AB .20 .07
❑ 10T Matt Williams AB .20 .07
❑ 11T Ray Durham .40 .15
❑ 12T J.LeBron RC UER Beltran 6.00 2.50
❑ 13T Shawn Green .40 .15
❑ 14T Kevin Gross .20 .07
❑ 15T Jon Nunnally .20 .07
❑ 16T Brian Maxcy RC .25 .08
❑ 17T Mark Kiefer .20 .07
❑ 18T C.Beltran RC UER LeBron 15.00 6.00
❑ 19T Michael Mimbs RC .25 .08
❑ 20T Larry Walker .40 .15
❑ 21T Chad Curtis .20 .07
❑ 22T Jeff Barry .20 .07
❑ 23T Joe Oliver .20 .07
❑ 24T Tomas Perez RC .25 .08
❑ 25T Michael Barrett RC 1.00 .40
❑ 26T Brian McRae .20 .07
❑ 27T Derek Bell .20 .07
❑ 28T Ray Durham .40 .15
❑ 29T Todd Williams .20 .07
❑ 30T Ryan Jaroncyk RC .25 .08
❑ 31T Todd Steverson .20 .07
❑ 32T Mike Devereaux .20 .07
❑ 33T Rheal Cormier .20 .07
❑ 34T Benny Santiago .40 .15
❑ 35T Bob Higginson RC 1.00 .40
❑ 36T Jack McDowell .20 .07
❑ 37T Mike MacFarlane .20 .07
❑ 38T Tony McKnight RC .25 .08
❑ 39T Brian L.Hunter .20 .07
❑ 40T Hideo Nomo RC 4.00 1.50
❑ 41T Brett Butler .40 .15
❑ 42T Donovan Osborne .20 .07
❑ 43T Scott Karl .20 .07
❑ 44T Tony Phillips .20 .07
❑ 45T Marty Cordova .20 .07
❑ 46T Dave Mlicki .20 .07
❑ 47T Bronson Arroyo RC 6.00 2.50
❑ 48T John Burkett .20 .07
❑ 49T J.D.Smart RC .25 .08
❑ 50T Mickey Tettleton .20 .07
❑ 51T Todd Stottlemyre .20 .07
❑ 52T Mike Perez .20 .07
❑ 53T Terry Mulholland .20 .07
❑ 54T Edgardo Alfonzo .20 .07
❑ 55T Zane Smith .20 .07
❑ 56T Jacob Brumfield .20 .07
❑ 57T Andujar Cedeno .20 .07
❑ 58T Jose Parra .20 .07
❑ 59T Manny Alexander .20 .07
❑ 60T Tony Tarasco .20 .07
❑ 61T Orel Hershiser .40 .15
❑ 62T Tim Scott .20 .07
❑ 63T Felix Rodriguez RC .25 .08
❑ 64T Ken Hill .20 .07
❑ 65T Marquis Grissom .40 .15
❑ 66T Lee Smith .40 .15
❑ 67T Jason Bates .20 .07
❑ 68T Felipe Lira .20 .07
❑ 69T Alex Hernandez RC .25 .08
❑ 70T Tony Fernandez .20 .07
❑ 71T Scott Radinsky .20 .07
❑ 72T Jose Canseco .60 .25
❑ 73T Mark Grudzielanek RC 1.00 .40
❑ 74T Ben Davis RC .25 .08
❑ 75T Jim Abbott .60 .25
❑ 76T Roger Bailey .20 .07
❑ 77T Gregg Jefferies .20 .07
❑ 78T Erik Hanson .20 .07
❑ 79T Brad Radke RC 1.00 .40
❑ 80T Jaime Navarro .20 .07
❑ 81T John Wetteland .40 .15
❑ 82T Chad Fonville RC .25 .08
❑ 83T John Mabry .20 .07
❑ 84T Glenallen Hill .20 .07
❑ 85T Ken Caminiti .40 .15
❑ 86T Tom Goodwin .20 .07
❑ 87T Darren Bragg .20 .07
❑ 88T Robbie Bell RC .25 .08
❑ 89T Jeff Russell .20 .07
❑ 90T Dave Gallagher .20 .07
❑ 91T Steve Finley .40 .15
❑ 92T Vaughn Eshelman .20 .07
❑ 93T Kevin Jarvis .20 .07
❑ 94T Mark Gubicza .20 .07
❑ 95T Tim Wakefield .40 .15
❑ 96T Bob Tewksbury .20 .07
❑ 97T Sid Roberson RC .25 .08
❑ 98T Tom Henke .20 .07
❑ 99T Michael Tucker .20 .07
❑ 100T Jason Bates .20 .07
❑ 101T Otis Nixon .20 .07
❑ 102T Mark Whiten .20 .07
❑ 103T Dilson Torres RC .25 .08
❑ 104T Melvin Bunch RC .25 .08
❑ 105T Terry Pendleton .40 .15
❑ 106T Corey Jenkins RC .25 .08
❑ 107T Glenn Dishman RC .25 .08
❑ 108T Reggie Taylor RC .25 .08
❑ 109T Curtis Goodwin .20 .07
❑ 110T David Cone .40 .15
❑ 111T Antonio Osuna .20 .07
❑ 112T Paul Shuey .20 .07
❑ 113T Doug Jones .20 .07
❑ 114T Mark McLemore .20 .07
❑ 115T Kevin Ritz .20 .07
❑ 116T John Kruk .40 .15
❑ 117T Trevor Wilson .20 .07
❑ 118T Jerald Clark .20 .07
❑ 119T Julian Tavarez .20 .07
❑ 120T Tim Pugh .20 .07
❑ 121T Todd Zeile .20 .07
❑ 122T R.Sexson/B.Schneider RC 4.00 1.50
❑ 123T Bobby Witt .20 .07
❑ 124T Hideo Nomo ROY 1.50 .60
❑ 125T Joey Cora .20 .07
❑ 126T Jim Scharrer RC .25 .08
❑ 127T Paul Quantrill .20 .07
❑ 128T Chipper Jones ROY .60 .25
❑ 129T Kenny James RC .25 .08

❑ 130T Mariano Rivera 1.25 .50
❑ 131T Tyler Green .20 .07
❑ 132T Brad Clontz .20 .07
❑ 133T Jon Nunnally .20 .07
❑ 134T Dave Magadan .20 .07
❑ 135T Al Leiter .40 .15
❑ 136T Bret Barberie .20 .07
❑ 137T Bill Swift .20 .07
❑ 138T Scott Cooper .20 .07
❑ 139T Roberto Kelly .20 .07
❑ 140T Charlie Hayes .20 .07
❑ 141T Pete Harnisch .20 .07
❑ 142T Rich Amaral .20 .07
❑ 143T Rudy Seanez .20 .07
❑ 144T Pat Listach .20 .07
❑ 145T Quilvio Veras .20 .07
❑ 146T Jose Olmeda RC .25 .08
❑ 147T Roberto Petagine .20 .07
❑ 148T Kevin Brown .40 .15
❑ 149T Phil Plantier .20 .07
❑ 150T Carlos Perez .40 .15
❑ 151T Pat Borders .20 .07
❑ 152T Tyler Green .20 .07
❑ 153T Stan Belinda .20 .07
❑ 154T Dave Stewart .40 .15
❑ 155T Andre Dawson .40 .15
❑ 156T F.Thomas/F.McGriff AS .60 .25
❑ 157T C.Baerga/C.Biggio AS .40 .15
❑ 158T W.Boggs/M.Williams AS .40 .15
❑ 159T C.Ripken/O.Smith AS 1.00 .40
❑ 160T K.Griffey/T.Gwynn AS 1.00 .40
❑ 161T A.Belle/B.Bonds AS 1.25 .50
❑ 162T K.Puckett/L.Dykstra AS .60 .25
❑ 163T I.Rodriguez/M.Piazza AS 1.00 .40
❑ 164T H.Nomo/R.Johnson AS 1.50 .60
❑ 165T Checklist .20 .07

1996 Topps

❑ COMPLETE SET (440) 40.00 15.00
❑ COMP.HOBBY SET (449) 40.00 15.00
❑ COMP.CEREAL SET (444) 50.00 25.00
❑ COMPLETE SERIES 1 (220) 20.00 8.00
❑ COMPLETE SERIES 2 (220) 20.00 8.00
❑ COMMON CARD (1-440) .20 .07
❑ COMMON RC .25 .08
❑ 1 Tony Gwynn STP .30 .10
❑ 2 Mike Piazza STP .50 .20
❑ 3 Greg Maddux STP .50 .20
❑ 4 Jeff Bagwell STP .20 .07
❑ 5 Larry Walker STP .20 .07
❑ 6 Barry Larkin STP .20 .07
❑ 7 Mickey Mantle 4.00 1.50
❑ 8 Tom Glavine STP .20 .07
❑ 9 Craig Biggio STP .20 .07
❑ 10 Barry Bonds STP .75 .30
❑ 11 Heathcliff Slocumb STP .20 .07
❑ 12 Matt Williams STP .20 .07
❑ 13 Todd Helton 1.00 .40
❑ 14 Mark Redman .25 .08
❑ 15 Michael Barrett .25 .08
❑ 16 Ben Davis .25 .08
❑ 17 Juan LeBron .25 .08
❑ 18 Tony McKnight .25 .08
❑ 19 Ryan Jaroncyk .25 .08
❑ 20 Corey Jenkins .25 .08
❑ 21 Jim Scharrer .25 .08
❑ 22 Mark Belhorn RC 1.00 .40
❑ 23 Jarrod Washburn RC .75 .30
❑ 24 Geoff Jenkins RC .75 .30
❑ 25 Sean Casey RC 4.00 1.50
❑ 26 Brett Tomko RC .40 .15
❑ 27 Tony Fernandez .20 .07
❑ 28 Rich Becker .20 .07
❑ 29 Andujar Cedeno .20 .07
❑ 30 Paul Molitor .20 .07
❑ 31 Brent Gates .20 .07
❑ 32 Glenallen Hill .20 .07
❑ 33 Mike Macfarlane .20 .07
❑ 34 Manny Alexander .20 .07
❑ 35 Todd Zeile .20 .07
❑ 36 Joe Girardi .20 .07
❑ 37 Tony Tarasco .20 .07
❑ 38 Tim Belcher .20 .07
❑ 39 Tom Goodwin .20 .07
❑ 40 Orel Hershiser .20 .07
❑ 41 Tripp Cromer .20 .07
❑ 42 Sean Bergman .20 .07
❑ 43 Troy Percival .20 .07
❑ 44 Kevin Stocker .20 .07
❑ 45 Albert Belle .20 .07
❑ 46 Tony Eusebio .20 .07
❑ 47 Sid Roberson .20 .07
❑ 48 Todd Hollandsworth .20 .07
❑ 49 Mark Wohlers .20 .07
❑ 50 Kirby Puckett .50 .20
❑ 51 Darren Holmes .20 .07
❑ 52 Ron Karkovice .20 .07
❑ 53 Al Martin .20 .07
❑ 54 Pat Rapp .20 .07
❑ 55 Mark Grace .30 .10
❑ 56 Greg Gagne .20 .07
❑ 57 Stan Javier .20 .07
❑ 58 Scott Sanders .20 .07
❑ 59 J.T. Snow .20 .07
❑ 60 David Justice .20 .07
❑ 61 Royce Clayton .20 .07
❑ 62 Kevin Foster .20 .07
❑ 63 Tim Naehring .20 .07
❑ 64 Orlando Miller .20 .07
❑ 65 Mike Mussina .30 .10
❑ 66 Jim Eisenreich .20 .07
❑ 67 Felix Fermin .20 .07
❑ 68 Bernie Williams .30 .10
❑ 69 Robb Nen .20 .07
❑ 70 Ron Gant .20 .07
❑ 71 Felipe Lira .20 .07
❑ 72 Jacob Brumfield .20 .07
❑ 73 John Mabry .20 .07
❑ 74 Mark Carreon .20 .07
❑ 75 Carlos Baerga .20 .07
❑ 76 Jim Dougherty .20 .07
❑ 77 Ryan Thompson .20 .07
❑ 78 Scott Leius .20 .07
❑ 79 Roger Pavlik .20 .07
❑ 80 Gary Sheffield .20 .07
❑ 81 Julian Tavarez .20 .07
❑ 82 Andy Ashby .20 .07
❑ 83 Mark Lemke .20 .07
❑ 84 Omar Vizquel .30 .10
❑ 85 Darren Daulton .20 .07
❑ 86 Mike Lansing .20 .07
❑ 87 Rusty Greer .20 .07
❑ 88 Dave Stevens .20 .07
❑ 89 Jose Offerman .20 .07
❑ 90 Tom Henke .20 .07
❑ 91 Troy O'Leary .20 .07
❑ 92 Michael Tucker .20 .07
❑ 93 Marvin Freeman .20 .07
❑ 94 Alex Diaz .20 .07
❑ 95 John Wetteland .20 .07
❑ 96 Cal Ripken 2131 2.00 .75
❑ 97 Mike Mimbs .20 .07
❑ 98 Bobby Higginson .20 .07
❑ 99 Edgardo Alfonzo .20 .07
❑ 100 Frank Thomas .50 .20
❑ 101 Bob Abreu .50 .20
❑ 102 B.Givens/T.J.Mathews .25 .08
❑ 103 C.Pritchett/T.Hubbard .25 .08
❑ 104 E.Owens/B.Huskey .25 .08
❑ 105 Doug Drabek .20 .07
❑ 106 Tomas Perez .20 .07
❑ 107 Mark Leiter .20 .07
❑ 108 Joe Oliver .20 .07
❑ 109 Tony Castillo .20 .07
❑ 110 Checklist (1-110) .20 .07
❑ 111 Kevin Seitzer .20 .07
❑ 112 Pete Schourek .20 .07
❑ 113 Sean Berry .20 .07
❑ 114 Todd Stottlemyre .20 .07
❑ 115 Joe Carter .20 .07
❑ 116 Jeff King .20 .07
❑ 117 Dan Wilson .20 .07
❑ 118 Kurt Abbott .20 .07
❑ 119 Lyle Mouton .20 .07
❑ 120 Jose Rijo .20 .07
❑ 121 Curtis Goodwin .20 .07
❑ 122 Jose Valentin .20 .07
❑ 123 Ellis Burks .20 .07
❑ 124 David Cone .20 .07
❑ 125 Eddie Murray .50 .20
❑ 126 Brian Jordan .20 .07
❑ 127 Darrin Fletcher .20 .07
❑ 128 Curt Schilling .20 .07
❑ 129 Ozzie Guillen .20 .07
❑ 130 Kenny Rogers .20 .07
❑ 131 Tom Pagnozzi .20 .07
❑ 132 Garret Anderson .20 .07
❑ 133 Bobby Jones .20 .07
❑ 134 Chris Gomez .20 .07
❑ 135 Mike Stanley .20 .07
❑ 136 Hideo Nomo .50 .20
❑ 137 Jon Nunnally .20 .07
❑ 138 Tim Wakefield .20 .07
❑ 139 Steve Finley .20 .07
❑ 140 Ivan Rodriguez .30 .10
❑ 141 Quilvio Veras .20 .07
❑ 142 Mike Fetters .20 .07
❑ 143 Mike Greenwell .20 .07
❑ 144 Bill Pulsipher .20 .07
❑ 145 Mark McGwire 1.25 .50
❑ 146 Frank Castillo .20 .07
❑ 147 Greg Vaughn .20 .07
❑ 148 Pat Hentgen .20 .07
❑ 149 Walt Weiss .20 .07
❑ 150 Randy Johnson .50 .20
❑ 151 David Segui .20 .07
❑ 152 Benji Gil .20 .07
❑ 153 Tom Candiotti .20 .07
❑ 154 Geronimo Berroa .20 .07
❑ 155 John Franco .20 .07
❑ 156 Jay Bell .20 .07
❑ 157 Mark Gubicza .20 .07
❑ 158 Hal Morris .20 .07
❑ 159 Wilson Alvarez .20 .07
❑ 160 Derek Bell .20 .07
❑ 161 Ricky Bottalico .20 .07
❑ 162 Bret Boone .20 .07
❑ 163 Brad Radke .20 .07
❑ 164 John Valentin .20 .07
❑ 165 Steve Avery .20 .07
❑ 166 Mark McLemore .20 .07
❑ 167 Danny Jackson .20 .07
❑ 168 Tino Martinez .30 .10
❑ 169 Shane Reynolds .20 .07
❑ 170 Terry Pendleton .20 .07
❑ 171 Jim Edmonds .20 .07
❑ 172 Esteban Loaiza .20 .07
❑ 173 Ray Durham .20 .07
❑ 174 Carlos Perez .20 .07
❑ 175 Raul Mondesi .20 .07
❑ 176 Steve Ontiveros .20 .07
❑ 177 Chipper Jones .50 .20
❑ 178 Otis Nixon .20 .07
❑ 179 John Burkett .20 .07
❑ 180 Gregg Jefferies .20 .07
❑ 181 Denny Martinez .20 .07
❑ 182 Ken Caminiti .20 .07
❑ 183 Doug Jones .20 .07
❑ 184 Brian McRae .20 .07
❑ 185 Don Mattingly 1.25 .50
❑ 186 Mel Rojas .20 .07
❑ 187 Marty Cordova .20 .07
❑ 188 Vinny Castilla .20 .07
❑ 189 John Smoltz .30 .10
❑ 190 Travis Fryman .20 .07
❑ 191 Chris Hoiles .20 .07
❑ 192 Chuck Finley .20 .07
❑ 193 Ryan Klesko .20 .07
❑ 194 Alex Fernandez .20 .07
❑ 195 Dante Bichette .20 .07

❑ 196	Eric Karros	.20	.07
❑ 197	Roger Clemens	1.00	.40
❑ 198	Randy Myers	.20	.07
❑ 199	Tony Phillips	.20	.07
❑ 200	Cal Ripken	1.50	.60
❑ 201	Rod Beck	.20	.07
❑ 202	Chad Curtis	.20	.07
❑ 203	Jack McDowell	.20	.07
❑ 204	Gary Gaetti	.20	.07
❑ 205	Ken Griffey Jr.	.75	.30
❑ 206	Ramon Martinez	.20	.07
❑ 207	Jeff Kent	.20	.07
❑ 208	Brad Ausmus	.20	.07
❑ 209	Devon White	.20	.07
❑ 210	Jason Giambi	.20	.07
❑ 211	Nomar Garciaparra	.75	.30
❑ 212	Billy Wagner	.20	.07
❑ 213	Todd Greene	.20	.07
❑ 214	Paul Wilson	.20	.07
❑ 215	Johnny Damon	.30	.10
❑ 216	Alan Benes	.20	.07
❑ 217	Karim Garcia	.20	.07
❑ 218	Dustin Hermanson	.20	.07
❑ 219	Derek Jeter	1.25	.50
❑ 220	Checklist (111-220)	.20	.07
❑ 221	Kirby Puckett STP	.30	.10
❑ 222	Cal Ripken STP	.75	.30
❑ 223	Albert Belle STP	.20	.07
❑ 224	Randy Johnson STP	.30	.10
❑ 225	Wade Boggs STP	.20	.07
❑ 226	Carlos Baerga STP	.20	.07
❑ 227	Ivan Rodriguez STP	.20	.07
❑ 228	Mike Mussina STP	.20	.07
❑ 229	Frank Thomas STP	.30	.10
❑ 230	Ken Griffey Jr. STP	.50	.20
❑ 231	Jose Mesa STP	.20	.07
❑ 232	Matt Morris RC	1.50	.60
❑ 233	Craig Wilson RC	.75	.30
❑ 234	Alvie Shepherd	.25	.08
❑ 235	Randy Winn RC	.75	.30
❑ 236	David Yocum RC	.25	.08
❑ 237	Jason Brester RC	.25	.08
❑ 238	Shane Monahan RC	.25	.08
❑ 239	Brian McNichol RC	.25	.08
❑ 240	Reggie Taylor	.25	.08
❑ 241	Garrett Long	.25	.08
❑ 242	Jonathan Johnson	.25	.08
❑ 243	Jeff Liefer RC	.25	.08
❑ 244	Brian Powell	.25	.08
❑ 245	Brian Buchanan RC	.25	.08
❑ 246	Mike Piazza	.75	.30
❑ 247	Edgar Martinez	.30	.10
❑ 248	Chuck Knoblauch	.20	.07
❑ 249	Andres Galarraga	.20	.07
❑ 250	Tony Gwynn	.60	.25
❑ 251	Lee Smith	.20	.07
❑ 252	Sammy Sosa	.50	.20
❑ 253	Jim Thome	.30	.10
❑ 254	Frank Rodriguez	.20	.07
❑ 255	Charlie Hayes	.20	.07
❑ 256	Bernard Gilkey	.20	.07
❑ 257	John Smiley	.20	.07
❑ 258	Brady Anderson	.20	.07
❑ 259	Rico Brogna	.20	.07
❑ 260	Kirt Manwaring	.20	.07
❑ 261	Len Dykstra	.20	.07
❑ 262	Tom Glavine	.30	.10
❑ 263	Vince Coleman	.20	.07
❑ 264	John Olerud	.20	.07
❑ 265	Orlando Merced	.20	.07
❑ 266	Kent Mercker	.20	.07
❑ 267	Terry Steinbach	.20	.07
❑ 268	Brian L. Hunter	.20	.07
❑ 269	Jeff Fassero	.20	.07
❑ 270	Jay Buhner	.20	.07
❑ 271	Jeff Brantley	.20	.07
❑ 272	Tim Raines	.20	.07
❑ 273	Jimmy Key	.20	.07
❑ 274	Mo Vaughn	.20	.07
❑ 275	Andre Dawson	.20	.07
❑ 276	Jose Mesa	.20	.07
❑ 277	Brett Butler	.20	.07
❑ 278	Luis Gonzalez	.20	.07
❑ 279	Steve Sparks	.20	.07
❑ 280	Chili Davis	.20	.07
❑ 281	Carl Everett	.20	.07
❑ 282	Jeff Cirillo	.20	.07
❑ 283	Thomas Howard	.20	.07
❑ 284	Paul O'Neill	.30	.10
❑ 285	Pat Meares	.20	.07
❑ 286	Mickey Tettleton	.20	.07
❑ 287	Rey Sanchez	.20	.07
❑ 288	Bip Roberts	.20	.07
❑ 289	Roberto Alomar	.30	.10
❑ 290	Ruben Sierra	.20	.07
❑ 291	John Flaherty	.20	.07
❑ 292	Bret Saberhagen	.20	.07
❑ 293	Barry Larkin	.30	.10
❑ 294	Sandy Alomar Jr.	.20	.07
❑ 295	Ed Sprague	.20	.07
❑ 296	Gary DiSarcina	.20	.07
❑ 297	Marquis Grissom	.20	.07
❑ 298	John Frascatore	.20	.07
❑ 299	Will Clark	.30	.10
❑ 300	Barry Bonds	1.50	.60
❑ 301	Ozzie Smith	.75	.30
❑ 302	Dave Nilsson	.20	.07
❑ 303	Pedro Martinez	.30	.10
❑ 304	Joey Cora	.20	.07
❑ 305	Rick Aguilera	.20	.07
❑ 306	Craig Biggio	.30	.10
❑ 307	Jose Vizcaino	.20	.07
❑ 308	Jeff Montgomery	.20	.07
❑ 309	Moises Alou	.20	.07
❑ 310	Robin Ventura	.20	.07
❑ 311	David Wells	.20	.07
❑ 312	Delino DeShields	.20	.07
❑ 313	Trevor Hoffman	.20	.07
❑ 314	Andy Benes	.20	.07
❑ 315	Deion Sanders	.30	.10
❑ 316	Jim Bullinger	.20	.07
❑ 317	John Jaha	.20	.07
❑ 318	Greg Maddux	.75	.30
❑ 319	Tim Salmon	.30	.10
❑ 320	Ben McDonald	.20	.07
❑ 321	Sandy Martinez	.20	.07
❑ 322	Dan Miceli	.20	.07
❑ 323	Wade Boggs	.30	.10
❑ 324	Ismael Valdes	.20	.07
❑ 325	Juan Gonzalez	.20	.07
❑ 326	Charles Nagy	.20	.07
❑ 327	Ray Lankford	.20	.07
❑ 328	Mark Portugal	.20	.07
❑ 329	Bobby Bonilla	.20	.07
❑ 330	Reggie Sanders	.20	.07
❑ 331	Jamie Brewington RC	.25	.08
❑ 332	Aaron Sele	.20	.07
❑ 333	Pete Harnisch	.20	.07
❑ 334	Cliff Floyd	.20	.07
❑ 335	Cal Eldred	.20	.07
❑ 336	Jason Bates	.20	.07
❑ 337	Tony Clark	.20	.07
❑ 338	Jose Herrera	.20	.07
❑ 339	Alex Ochoa	.20	.07
❑ 340	Mark Loretta	.20	.07
❑ 341	Donne Wall	.20	.07
❑ 342	Jason Kendall	.20	.07
❑ 343	Shannon Stewart	.20	.07
❑ 344	Brooks Kieschnick	.20	.07
❑ 345	Chris Snopek	.20	.07
❑ 346	Ruben Rivera	.20	.07
❑ 347	Jeff Suppan	.20	.07
❑ 348	Phil Nevin	.20	.07
❑ 349	John Wasdin	.20	.07
❑ 350	Jay Payton	.20	.07
❑ 351	Tim Crabtree	.20	.07
❑ 352	Rick Krivda	.20	.07
❑ 353	Bob Wolcott	.20	.07
❑ 354	Jimmy Haynes	.20	.07
❑ 355	Herb Perry	.20	.07
❑ 356	Ryne Sandberg	.75	.30
❑ 357	Harold Baines	.20	.07
❑ 358	Chad Ogea	.20	.07
❑ 359	Lee Tinsley	.20	.07
❑ 360	Matt Williams	.20	.07
❑ 361	Randy Velarde	.20	.07
❑ 362	Jose Canseco	.30	.10
❑ 363	Larry Walker	.20	.07
❑ 364	Kevin Appier	.20	.07
❑ 365	Darryl Hamilton	.20	.07
❑ 366	Jose Lima	.20	.07
❑ 367	Javy Lopez	.20	.07
❑ 368	Dennis Eckersley	.20	.07
❑ 369	Jason Isringhausen	.20	.07
❑ 370	Mickey Morandini	.20	.07
❑ 371	Scott Cooper	.20	.07
❑ 372	Jim Abbott	.30	.10
❑ 373	Paul Sorrento	.20	.07
❑ 374	Chris Hammond	.20	.07
❑ 375	Lance Johnson	.20	.07
❑ 376	Kevin Brown	.20	.07
❑ 377	Luis Alicea	.20	.07
❑ 378	Andy Pettitte	.30	.10
❑ 379	Dean Palmer	.20	.07
❑ 380	Jeff Bagwell	.30	.10
❑ 381	Jaime Navarro	.20	.07
❑ 382	Rondell White	.20	.07
❑ 383	Erik Hanson	.20	.07
❑ 384	Pedro Munoz	.20	.07
❑ 385	Heathcliff Slocumb	.20	.07
❑ 386	Wally Joyner	.20	.07
❑ 387	Bob Tewksbury	.20	.07
❑ 388	David Bell	.20	.07
❑ 389	Fred McGriff	.30	.10
❑ 390	Mike Henneman	.20	.07
❑ 391	Robby Thompson	.20	.07
❑ 392	Norm Charlton	.20	.07
❑ 393	Cecil Fielder	.20	.07
❑ 394	Benito Santiago	.20	.07
❑ 395	Rafael Palmeiro	.30	.10
❑ 396	Ricky Bones	.20	.07
❑ 397	Rickey Henderson	.50	.20
❑ 398	C.J. Nitkowski	.20	.07
❑ 399	Shawon Dunston	.20	.07
❑ 400	Manny Ramirez	.30	.10
❑ 401	Bill Swift	.20	.07
❑ 402	Chad Fonville	.20	.07
❑ 403	Joey Hamilton	.20	.07
❑ 404	Alex Gonzalez	.20	.07
❑ 405	Roberto Hernandez	.20	.07
❑ 406	Jeff Blauser	.20	.07
❑ 407	LaTroy Hawkins	.20	.07
❑ 408	Greg Colbrunn	.20	.07
❑ 409	Todd Hundley	.20	.07
❑ 410	Glenn Dishman	.20	.07
❑ 411	Joe Vitiello	.20	.07
❑ 412	Todd Worrell	.20	.07
❑ 413	Wil Cordero	.20	.07
❑ 414	Ken Hill	.20	.07
❑ 415	Carlos Garcia	.20	.07
❑ 416	Bryan Rekar	.20	.07
❑ 417	Shawn Green	.20	.07
❑ 418	Tyler Green	.20	.07
❑ 419	Mike Blowers	.20	.07
❑ 420	Kenny Lofton	.20	.07
❑ 421	Denny Neagle	.20	.07
❑ 422	Jeff Conine	.20	.07
❑ 423	Mark Langston	.20	.07
❑ 424	Ron Wright RC/D.Lee	.75	.30
❑ 425	D.Ward RC/R.Sexson	1.00	.40
❑ 426	Adam Riggs RC	.25	.08
❑ 427	N.Perez/E.Wilson	.25	.08
❑ 428	Bartolo Colon	.50	.20
❑ 429	Marty Janzen RC	.25	.08
❑ 430	Rich Hunter RC	.25	.08
❑ 431	Dave Coggin RC	.25	.08
❑ 432	R.Ibanez RC/P.Konerko	1.50	.60
❑ 433	Marc Kroon	.20	.07
❑ 434	S.Rolen/S.Spiezio	.50	.20
❑ 435	V.Guerrero/A.Jones	2.50	1.00
❑ 436	Shane Spencer RC	.40	.15
❑ 437	A.French/D.Stovall RC	.25	.08
❑ 438	M.Coleman RC/R.Hidalgo	.25	.08
❑ 439	Jermaine Dye	.20	.07
❑ 440	Checklist	.20	.07
❑ F7	Mickey Mantle Last Day	5.00	2.00
❑ NNO	Mickey Mantle Tribute Card, promotes the Mantle F	3.00	1.25

1997 Topps

❑	COMPLETE SET (495)	80.00	40.00
❑	COMPLETE SERIES 1 (276)	40.00	20.00
❑	COMPLETE SERIES 2 (220)	40.00	20.00
❑ 1	Barry Bonds	1.50	.60
❑ 2	Tom Pagnozzi	.20	.07
❑ 3	Terrell Wade	.20	.07
❑ 4	Jose Valentin	.20	.07
❑ 5	Mark Clark	.20	.07

❑ 6 Brady Anderson .20 .07
❑ 8 Wade Boggs .30 .10
❑ 9 Scott Stahoviak .20 .07
❑ 10 Andres Galarraga .20 .07
❑ 11 Steve Avery .20 .07
❑ 12 Rusty Greer .20 .07
❑ 13 Derek Jeter 1.25 .50
❑ 14 Ricky Bottalico .20 .07
❑ 15 Andy Ashby .20 .07
❑ 16 Paul Shuey .20 .07
❑ 17 F.P. Santangelo .20 .07
❑ 18 Royce Clayton .20 .07
❑ 19 Mike Mohler .20 .07
❑ 20 Mike Piazza .75 .30
❑ 21 Jaime Navarro .20 .07
❑ 22 Billy Wagner .20 .07
❑ 23 Mike Timlin .20 .07
❑ 24 Garret Anderson .20 .07
❑ 25 Ben McDonald .20 .07
❑ 26 Mel Rojas .20 .07
❑ 27 John Burkett .20 .07
❑ 28 Jeff King .20 .07
❑ 29 Reggie Jefferson .20 .07
❑ 30 Kevin Appier .20 .07
❑ 31 Felipe Lira .20 .07
❑ 32 Kevin Tapani .20 .07
❑ 33 Mark Portugal .20 .07
❑ 34 Carlos Garcia .20 .07
❑ 35 Joey Cora .20 .07
❑ 36 David Segui .20 .07
❑ 37 Mark Grace .30 .10
❑ 38 Erik Hanson .20 .07
❑ 39 Jeff D'Amico .20 .07
❑ 40 Jay Buhner .20 .07
❑ 41 B.J. Surhoff .20 .07
❑ 42 Jackie Robinson TRIB .50 .20
❑ 43 Roger Pavlik .20 .07
❑ 44 Hal Morris .20 .07
❑ 45 Mariano Duncan .20 .07
❑ 46 Harold Baines .20 .07
❑ 47 Jorge Fabregas .20 .07
❑ 48 Jose Herrera .20 .07
❑ 49 Jeff Cirillo .20 .07
❑ 50 Tom Glavine .30 .10
❑ 51 Pedro Astacio .20 .07
❑ 52 Mark Gardner .20 .07
❑ 53 Arthur Rhodes .20 .07
❑ 54 Troy O'Leary .20 .07
❑ 55 Bip Roberts .20 .07
❑ 56 Mike Lieberthal .20 .07
❑ 57 Shane Andrews .20 .07
❑ 58 Scott Karl .20 .07
❑ 59 Gary DiSarcina .20 .07
❑ 60 Andy Pettitte .30 .10
❑ 61 Kevin Elster .20 .07
❑ 61B Mike Fetters UER .20 .07
❑ 62 Mark McGwire 1.25 .50
❑ 63 Dan Wilson .20 .07
❑ 64 Mickey Morandini .20 .07
❑ 65 Chuck Knoblauch .20 .07
❑ 66 Tim Wakefield .20 .07
❑ 67 Raul Mondesi .20 .07
❑ 68 Todd Jones .20 .07
❑ 69 Albert Belle .20 .07
❑ 70 Trevor Hoffman .20 .07
❑ 71 Eric Young .20 .07
❑ 72 Robert Perez .20 .07
❑ 73 Butch Huskey .20 .07
❑ 74 Brian McRae .20 .07
❑ 75 Jim Edmonds .20 .07
❑ 76 Mike Henneman .20 .07
❑ 77 Frank Rodriguez .20 .07
❑ 78 Danny Tartabull .20 .07
❑ 79 Robb Nen .20 .07
❑ 80 Reggie Sanders .20 .07
❑ 81 Ron Karkovice .20 .07
❑ 82 Benito Santiago .20 .07
❑ 83 Mike Lansing .20 .07
❑ 85 Craig Biggio .30 .10
❑ 86 Mike Bordick .20 .07
❑ 87 Ray Lankford .20 .07
❑ 88 Charles Nagy .20 .07
❑ 89 Paul Wilson .20 .07
❑ 90 John Wetteland .20 .07
❑ 91 Tom Candiotti .20 .07
❑ 92 Carlos Delgado .20 .07
❑ 93 Derek Bell .20 .07
❑ 94 Mark Lemke .20 .07
❑ 95 Edgar Martinez .30 .10
❑ 96 Rickey Henderson .50 .20
❑ 97 Greg Myers .20 .07
❑ 98 Jim Leyritz .20 .07
❑ 99 Mark Johnson .20 .07
❑ 100 Dwight Gooden HL .20 .07
❑ 101 Al Leiter HL .20 .07
❑ 102 John Mabry HL .20 .07
❑ 103 Alex Ochoa HL .20 .07
❑ 104 Mike Piazza HL .50 .20
❑ 105 Jim Thome .30 .10
❑ 106 Ricky Otero .20 .07
❑ 107 Jamey Wright .20 .07
❑ 108 Frank Thomas .50 .20
❑ 109 Jody Reed .20 .07
❑ 110 Orel Hershiser .20 .07
❑ 111 Terry Steinbach .20 .07
❑ 112 Mark Loretta .20 .07
❑ 113 Turk Wendell .20 .07
❑ 114 Marvin Benard .20 .07
❑ 115 Kevin Brown .20 .07
❑ 116 Robert Person .20 .07
❑ 117 Joey Hamilton .20 .07
❑ 118 Francisco Cordova .20 .07
❑ 119 John Smiley .20 .07
❑ 120 Travis Fryman .20 .07
❑ 121 Jimmy Key .20 .07
❑ 122 Tom Goodwin .20 .07
❑ 123 Mike Greenwell .20 .07
❑ 124 Juan Gonzalez .20 .07
❑ 125 Pete Harnisch .20 .07
❑ 126 Roger Cedeno .20 .07
❑ 127 Ron Gant .20 .07
❑ 128 Mark Langston .20 .07
❑ 129 Tim Crabtree .20 .07
❑ 130 Greg Maddux .75 .30
❑ 131 William VanLandingham .20 .07
❑ 132 Wally Joyner .20 .07
❑ 133 Randy Myers .20 .07
❑ 134 John Valentin .20 .07
❑ 135 Bret Boone .20 .07
❑ 136 Bruce Ruffin .20 .07
❑ 137 Chris Snopek .20 .07
❑ 138 Paul Molitor .20 .07
❑ 139 Mark McLemore .20 .07
❑ 140 Rafael Palmeiro .30 .10
❑ 141 Herb Perry .20 .07
❑ 142 Luis Gonzalez .20 .07
❑ 143 Doug Drabek .20 .07
❑ 144 Ken Ryan .20 .07
❑ 145 Todd Hundley .20 .07
❑ 146 Ellis Burks .20 .07
❑ 147 Ozzie Guillen .20 .07
❑ 148 Rich Becker .20 .07
❑ 149 Sterling Hitchcock .20 .07
❑ 150 Bernie Williams .30 .10
❑ 151 Mike Stanley .20 .07
❑ 152 Roberto Alomar .30 .10
❑ 153 Jose Mesa .20 .07
❑ 154 Steve Trachsel .20 .07
❑ 155 Alex Gonzalez .20 .07
❑ 156 Troy Percival .20 .07
❑ 157 John Smoltz .30 .10
❑ 158 Pedro Martinez .30 .10
❑ 159 Jeff Conine .20 .07
❑ 160 Bernard Gilkey .20 .07
❑ 161 Jim Eisenreich .20 .07
❑ 162 Mickey Tettleton .20 .07
❑ 163 Justin Thompson .20 .07
❑ 164 Jose Offerman .20 .07
❑ 165 Tony Phillips .20 .07
❑ 166 Ismael Valdes .20 .07
❑ 167 Ryne Sandberg .75 .30
❑ 168 Matt Mieske .20 .07
❑ 169 Geronimo Berroa .20 .07
❑ 170 Otis Nixon .20 .07
❑ 171 John Mabry .20 .07
❑ 172 Shawon Dunston .20 .07
❑ 173 Omar Vizquel .30 .10
❑ 174 Chris Hoiles .20 .07
❑ 175 Dwight Gooden .20 .07
❑ 176 Wilson Alvarez .20 .07
❑ 177 Todd Hollandsworth .20 .07
❑ 178 Roger Salkeld .20 .07
❑ 179 Rey Sanchez .20 .07
❑ 180 Rey Ordonez .20 .07
❑ 181 Denny Martinez .20 .07
❑ 182 Ramon Martinez .20 .07
❑ 183 Dave Nilsson .20 .07
❑ 184 Marquis Grissom .20 .07
❑ 185 Randy Velarde .20 .07
❑ 186 Ron Coomer .20 .07
❑ 187 Tino Martinez .30 .10
❑ 188 Jeff Brantley .20 .07
❑ 189 Steve Finley .20 .07
❑ 190 Andy Benes .20 .07
❑ 191 Terry Adams .20 .07
❑ 192 Mike Blowers .20 .07
❑ 193 Russ Davis .20 .07
❑ 194 Darryl Hamilton .20 .07
❑ 195 Jason Kendall .20 .07
❑ 196 Johnny Damon .30 .10
❑ 197 Dave Martinez .20 .07
❑ 198 Mike Macfarlane .20 .07
❑ 199 Norm Charlton .20 .07
❑ 200 Damian Moss .25 .08
❑ 201 Jenkins/Ibanez/Cameron .20 .07
❑ 202 Sean Casey .30 .10
❑ 203 J.Hansen/H.Bush/F.Crespo .20 .07
❑ 204 K.Orie/G.Alvarez/A.Boone .20 .07
❑ 205 B.Davis/K.Brown/B.Estalella .20 .07
❑ 206 Bubba Trammell RC .40 .15
❑ 207 Jarrod Washburn .20 .07
❑ 208 Brian Hunter .20 .07
❑ 209 Jason Giambi .20 .07
❑ 210 Henry Rodriguez .20 .07
❑ 211 Edgar Renteria .20 .07
❑ 212 Edgardo Alfonzo .20 .07
❑ 213 Fernando Vina .20 .07
❑ 214 Shawn Green .20 .07
❑ 215 Ray Durham .20 .07
❑ 216 Joe Randa .20 .07
❑ 217 Armando Reynoso .20 .07
❑ 218 Eric Davis .20 .07
❑ 219 Bob Tewksbury .20 .07
❑ 220 Jacob Cruz .20 .07
❑ 221 Glenallen Hill .20 .07
❑ 222 Gary Gaetti .20 .07
❑ 223 Donne Wall .20 .07
❑ 224 Brad Clontz .20 .07
❑ 225 Marty Janzen .20 .07
❑ 226 Todd Worrell .20 .07
❑ 227 John Franco .20 .07
❑ 228 David Wells .20 .07
❑ 229 Gregg Jefferies .20 .07
❑ 230 Tim Naehring .20 .07
❑ 231 Thomas Howard .20 .07
❑ 232 Roberto Hernandez .20 .07
❑ 233 Kevin Ritz .20 .07
❑ 234 Julian Tavarez .20 .07
❑ 235 Ken Hill .20 .07
❑ 236 Greg Gagne .20 .07
❑ 237 Bobby Chouinard .20 .07
❑ 238 Joe Carter .20 .07
❑ 239 Jermaine Dye .20 .07
❑ 240 Antonio Osuna .20 .07
❑ 241 Julio Franco .20 .07
❑ 242 Mike Grace .20 .07
❑ 243 Aaron Sele .20 .07
❑ 244 David Justice .20 .07
❑ 245 Sandy Alomar Jr. .20 .07
❑ 246 Jose Canseco .30 .10

❑ 247 Paul O'Neill .30 .10
❑ 248 Sean Berry .20 .07
❑ 249 N.Bierbrodt/K.Sweeney RC .25 .08
❑ 250 Vladimir Nunez RC .25 .08
❑ 251 R.Hartman/D.Hayman RC .25 .08
❑ 252 A.Sanchez/M.Quatraro RC .40 .15
❑ 253 Ronni Seberino RC .25 .08
❑ 254 Rex Hudler .20 .07
❑ 255 Orlando Miller .20 .07
❑ 256 Mariano Rivera .50 .20
❑ 257 Brad Radke .20 .07
❑ 258 Bobby Higginson .20 .07
❑ 259 Jay Bell .20 .07
❑ 260 Mark Grudzielanek .20 .07
❑ 261 Lance Johnson .20 .07
❑ 262 Ken Caminiti .20 .07
❑ 263 J.T. Snow .20 .07
❑ 264 Gary Sheffield .20 .07
❑ 265 Darrin Fletcher .20 .07
❑ 266 Eric Owens .20 .07
❑ 267 Luis Castillo .20 .07
❑ 268 Scott Rolen .30 .10
❑ 269 T.Noel/J.Oliver RC .25 .08
❑ 270 Robert Stratton RC .40 .15
❑ 271 Gil Meche RC 1.00 .40
❑ 272 E.Milton RC/D.Brown RC .40 .15
❑ 273 Chris Reitsma RC .40 .15
❑ 274 J.Marquis/A.J.Zapp RC .50 .20
❑ 275 Checklist .20 .07
❑ 276 Checklist .20 .07
❑ 277 Chipper Jones UER276 .50 .20
❑ 278 Orlando Merced .20 .07
❑ 279 Ariel Prieto .20 .07
❑ 280 Al Leiter .20 .07
❑ 281 Pat Meares .20 .07
❑ 282 Darryl Strawberry .20 .07
❑ 283 Jamie Moyer .20 .07
❑ 284 Scott Servais .20 .07
❑ 285 Delino DeShields .20 .07
❑ 286 Danny Graves .20 .07
❑ 287 Gerald Williams .20 .07
❑ 288 Todd Greene .20 .07
❑ 289 Rico Brogna .20 .07
❑ 290 Derrick Gibson .20 .07
❑ 291 Joe Girardi .20 .07
❑ 292 Darren Lewis .20 .07
❑ 293 Nomar Garciaparra .75 .30
❑ 294 Greg Colbrunn .20 .07
❑ 295 Jeff Bagwell .30 .10
❑ 296 Brent Gates .20 .07
❑ 297 Jose Vizcaino .20 .07
❑ 298 Alex Ochoa .20 .07
❑ 299 Sid Fernandez .20 .07
❑ 300 Ken Griffey Jr. .75 .30
❑ 301 Chris Gomez .20 .07
❑ 302 Wendell Magee .20 .07
❑ 303 Darren Oliver .20 .07
❑ 304 Mel Nieves .20 .07
❑ 305 Sammy Sosa .50 .20
❑ 306 George Arias .20 .07
❑ 307 Jack McDowell .20 .07
❑ 308 Stan Javier .20 .07
❑ 309 Kimera Bartee .20 .07
❑ 310 James Baldwin .20 .07
❑ 311 Rocky Coppinger .20 .07
❑ 312 Keith Lockhart .20 .07
❑ 313 C.J. Nitkowski .20 .07
❑ 314 Allen Watson .20 .07
❑ 315 Darryl Kile .20 .07
❑ 316 Amaury Telemaco .20 .07
❑ 317 Jason Isringhausen .20 .07
❑ 318 Manny Ramirez .30 .10
❑ 319 Terry Pendleton .20 .07
❑ 320 Tim Salmon .30 .10
❑ 321 Eric Karros .20 .07
❑ 322 Mark Whiten .20 .07
❑ 323 Rick Krivda .20 .07
❑ 324 Brett Butler .20 .07
❑ 325 Randy Johnson .50 .20
❑ 326 Eddie Taubensee .20 .07
❑ 327 Mark Leiter .20 .07
❑ 328 Kevin Gross .20 .07
❑ 329 Ernie Young .20 .07
❑ 330 Pat Hentgen .20 .07
❑ 331 Rondell White .20 .07
❑ 332 Bobby Witt .20 .07
❑ 333 Eddie Murray .50 .20
❑ 334 Tim Raines .20 .07
❑ 335 Jeff Fassero .20 .07
❑ 336 Chuck Finley .20 .07
❑ 337 Willie Adams .20 .07
❑ 338 Chan Ho Park .20 .07
❑ 339 Jay Powell .20 .07
❑ 340 Ivan Rodriguez .30 .10
❑ 341 Jermaine Allensworth .20 .07
❑ 342 Jay Payton .20 .07
❑ 343 T.J. Mathews .20 .07
❑ 344 Tony Batista .20 .07
❑ 345 Ed Sprague .20 .07
❑ 346 Jeff Kent .20 .07
❑ 347 Scott Erickson .20 .07
❑ 348 Jeff Suppan .20 .07
❑ 349 Pete Schourek .20 .07
❑ 350 Kenny Lofton .20 .07
❑ 351 Alan Benes .20 .07
❑ 352 Fred McGriff .30 .10
❑ 353 Charlie O'Brien .20 .07
❑ 354 Darren Bragg .20 .07
❑ 355 Alex Fernandez .20 .07
❑ 356 Al Martin .20 .07
❑ 357 Bob Wells .20 .07
❑ 358 Chad Mottola .20 .07
❑ 359 Devon White .20 .07
❑ 360 David Cone .20 .07
❑ 361 Bobby Jones .20 .07
❑ 362 Scott Sanders .20 .07
❑ 363 Karim Garcia .20 .07
❑ 364 Kirt Manwaring .20 .07
❑ 365 Chili Davis .20 .07
❑ 366 Mike Hampton .20 .07
❑ 367 Chad Ogea .20 .07
❑ 368 Curt Schilling .20 .07
❑ 369 Phil Nevin .20 .07
❑ 370 Roger Clemens 1.00 .40
❑ 371 Willie Greene .20 .07
❑ 372 Kenny Rogers .20 .07
❑ 373 Jose Rijo .20 .07
❑ 374 Bobby Bonilla .20 .07
❑ 375 Mike Mussina .30 .10
❑ 376 Curtis Pride .20 .07
❑ 377 Todd Walker .20 .07
❑ 378 Jason Bere .20 .07
❑ 379 Heathcliff Slocumb .20 .07
❑ 380 Dante Bichette .20 .07
❑ 381 Carlos Baerga .20 .07
❑ 382 Livan Hernandez .20 .07
❑ 383 Jason Schmidt .20 .07
❑ 384 Kevin Stocker .20 .07
❑ 385 Matt Williams .20 .07
❑ 386 Bartolo Colon .20 .07
❑ 387 Will Clark .30 .10
❑ 388 Dennis Eckersley .20 .07
❑ 389 Brooks Kieschnick .20 .07
❑ 390 Ryan Klesko .20 .07
❑ 391 Mark Carreon .20 .07
❑ 392 Tim Worrell .20 .07
❑ 393 Dean Palmer .20 .07
❑ 394 Wil Cordero .20 .07
❑ 395 Javy Lopez .20 .07
❑ 396 Rich Aurilia .20 .07
❑ 397 Greg Vaughn .20 .07
❑ 398 Vinny Castilla .20 .07
❑ 399 Jeff Montgomery .20 .07
❑ 400 Cal Ripken 1.50 .60
❑ 401 Walt Weiss .20 .07
❑ 402 Brad Ausmus .20 .07
❑ 403 Ruben Rivera .20 .07
❑ 404 Mark Wohlers .20 .07
❑ 405 Rick Aguilera .20 .07
❑ 406 Tony Clark .20 .07
❑ 407 Lyle Mouton .20 .07
❑ 408 Bill Pulsipher .20 .07
❑ 409 Jose Rosado .20 .07
❑ 410 Tony Gwynn .60 .25
❑ 411 Cecil Fielder .20 .07
❑ 412 John Flaherty .20 .07
❑ 413 Lenny Dykstra .20 .07
❑ 414 Ugueth Urbina .20 .07
❑ 415 Brian Jordan .20 .07
❑ 416 Bob Abreu .30 .10
❑ 417 Craig Paquette .20 .07
❑ 418 Sandy Martinez .20 .07
❑ 419 Jeff Blauser .20 .07
❑ 420 Barry Larkin .30 .10
❑ 421 Kevin Seitzer .20 .07
❑ 422 Tim Belcher .20 .07
❑ 423 Paul Sorrento .20 .07
❑ 424 Cal Eldred .20 .07
❑ 425 Robin Ventura .20 .07
❑ 426 John Olerud .20 .07
❑ 427 Bob Wolcott .20 .07
❑ 428 Matt Lawton .20 .07
❑ 429 Rod Beck .20 .07
❑ 430 Shane Reynolds .20 .07
❑ 431 Mike James .20 .07
❑ 432 Steve Wojciechowski .20 .07
❑ 433 Vladimir Guerrero .50 .20
❑ 434 Dustin Hermanson .20 .07
❑ 435 Marty Cordova .20 .07
❑ 436 Marc Newfield .20 .07
❑ 437 Todd Stottlemyre .20 .07
❑ 438 Jeffrey Hammonds .20 .07
❑ 439 Dave Stevens .20 .07
❑ 440 Hideo Nomo .50 .20
❑ 441 Mark Thompson .20 .07
❑ 442 Mark Lewis .20 .07
❑ 443 Quinton McCracken .20 .07
❑ 444 Cliff Floyd .20 .07
❑ 445 Denny Neagle .20 .07
❑ 446 John Jaha .20 .07
❑ 447 Mike Sweeney .20 .07
❑ 448 John Wasdin .20 .07
❑ 449 Chad Curtis .20 .07
❑ 450 Mo Vaughn .20 .07
❑ 451 Donovan Osborne .20 .07
❑ 452 Ruben Sierra .20 .07
❑ 453 Michael Tucker .20 .07
❑ 454 Kurt Abbott .20 .07
❑ 455 Andruw Jones UER .30 .10
❑ 456 Shannon Stewart .20 .07
❑ 457 Scott Brosius .20 .07
❑ 458 Juan Guzman .20 .07
❑ 459 Ron Villone .20 .07
❑ 460 Moises Alou .20 .07
❑ 461 Larry Walker .20 .07
❑ 462 Eddie Murray SH .30 .10
❑ 463 Paul Molitor SH .20 .07
❑ 464 Hideo Nomo SH .20 .07
❑ 465 Barry Bonds SH .75 .30
❑ 466 Todd Hundley SH .20 .07
❑ 467 Rheal Cormier .20 .07
❑ 468 J.Sandoval/J.Conti RC .25 .08
❑ 469 R.Barajas/J.Rexrode RC 1.50 .60
❑ 470 Jared Sandberg RC .25 .08
❑ 471 P.Wilder/C.Gunner RC .25 .08
❑ 472 M.DeCelle/M.McCain RC .25 .08
❑ 473 Todd Zeile .20 .07
❑ 474 Neifi Perez .20 .07
❑ 475 Jeromy Burnitz .20 .07
❑ 476 Trey Beamon .20 .07
❑ 477 J.Patterson/B.Looper RC .75 .30
❑ 478 Jake Westbrook RC .50 .20
❑ 479 E.Chavez/A.Eaton RC 2.00 .75
❑ 480 P.Tucci/J.Lawrence RC .25 .08
❑ 481 K.Benson/B.Koch RC .50 .20
❑ 482 J.Nicholson/A.Prater RC .25 .08
❑ 483 M.Kotsay/M.Johnson RC .75 .30
❑ 484 Armando Benitez .20 .07
❑ 485 Mike Matheny .20 .07
❑ 486 Jeff Reed .20 .07
❑ 487 M.Bellhorn/R.Johnson/E.Wilson .20 .07
❑ 488 R.Hidalgo/B.Grieve .20 .07
❑ 489 Konerko/D.Lee/Wright .30 .10
❑ 490 Bill Mueller RC 1.25 .50
❑ 491 J.Abbott/S.Monahan/E.Velazquez .20 .07
❑ 492 Jimmy Anderson RC .25 .08
❑ 493 Carl Pavano .20 .07
❑ 494 Nelson Figueroa RC .25 .08
❑ 495 Checklist (277-400) .20 .07
❑ 496 Checklist (401-496) .20 .07
❑ NNO Derek Jeter AU 150.00 75.00

1998 Topps

❑ COMPLETE SET (503) 80.00 40.00
❑ COMP.HOBBY SET (511) 120.00 60.00
❑ COMP.RETAIL SET (511) 120.00 60.00
❑ COMPLETE SERIES 1 (282) 40.00 20.00
❑ COMPLETE SERIES 2 (221) 40.00 20.00

❑ 1 Tony Gwynn .60 .25
❑ 2 Larry Walker .20 .07
❑ 3 Billy Wagner .20 .07
❑ 4 Denny Neagle .20 .07
❑ 5 Vladimir Guerrero .50 .20
❑ 6 Kevin Brown .30 .10
❑ 8 Mariano Rivera .50 .20
❑ 9 Tony Clark .20 .07
❑ 10 Deion Sanders .30 .10
❑ 11 Francisco Cordova .20 .07
❑ 12 Matt Williams .20 .07
❑ 13 Carlos Baerga .20 .07
❑ 14 Mo Vaughn .20 .07
❑ 15 Bobby Witt .20 .07
❑ 16 Matt Stairs .20 .07
❑ 17 Chan Ho Park .20 .07
❑ 18 Mike Bordick .20 .07
❑ 19 Michael Tucker .20 .07
❑ 20 Frank Thomas .50 .20
❑ 21 Roberto Clemente 1.00 .40
❑ 22 Dmitri Young .20 .07
❑ 23 Steve Trachsel .20 .07
❑ 24 Jeff Kent .20 .07
❑ 25 Scott Rolen .30 .10
❑ 26 John Thomson .20 .07
❑ 27 Joe Vitiello .20 .07
❑ 28 Eddie Guardado .20 .07
❑ 29 Charlie Hayes .20 .07
❑ 30 Juan Gonzalez .20 .07
❑ 31 Garret Anderson .20 .07
❑ 32 John Jaha .20 .07
❑ 33 Omar Vizquel .30 .10
❑ 34 Brian Hunter .20 .07
❑ 35 Jeff Bagwell .30 .10
❑ 36 Mark Lemke .20 .07
❑ 37 Doug Glanville .20 .07
❑ 38 Dan Wilson .20 .07
❑ 39 Steve Cooke .20 .07
❑ 40 Chili Davis .20 .07
❑ 41 Mike Cameron .20 .07
❑ 42 F.P. Santangelo .20 .07
❑ 43 Brad Ausmus .20 .07
❑ 44 Gary DiSarcina .20 .07
❑ 45 Pat Hentgen .20 .07
❑ 46 Wilton Guerrero .20 .07
❑ 47 Devon White .20 .07
❑ 48 Danny Patterson .20 .07
❑ 49 Pat Meares .20 .07
❑ 50 Rafael Palmeiro .30 .10
❑ 51 Mark Gardner .20 .07
❑ 52 Jeff Blauser .20 .07
❑ 53 Dave Hollins .20 .07
❑ 54 Carlos Garcia .20 .07
❑ 55 Ben McDonald .20 .07
❑ 56 John Mabry .20 .07
❑ 57 Trevor Hoffman .20 .07
❑ 58 Tony Fernandez .20 .07
❑ 59 Rich Loiselle .20 .07
❑ 60 Mark Leiter .20 .07
❑ 61 Pat Kelly .20 .07
❑ 62 John Flaherty .20 .07
❑ 63 Roger Bailey .20 .07
❑ 64 Tom Gordon .20 .07
❑ 65 Ryan Klesko .20 .07
❑ 66 Darryl Hamilton .20 .07
❑ 67 Jim Eisenreich .20 .07
❑ 68 Butch Huskey .20 .07
❑ 69 Mark Grudzielanek .20 .07
❑ 70 Marquis Grissom .20 .07
❑ 71 Mark McLemore .20 .07
❑ 72 Gary Gaetti .20 .07
❑ 73 Greg Gagne .20 .07
❑ 74 Lyle Mouton .20 .07
❑ 75 Jim Edmonds .20 .07
❑ 76 Shawn Green .20 .07
❑ 77 Greg Vaughn .20 .07
❑ 78 Terry Adams .20 .07
❑ 79 Kevin Polcovich .20 .07
❑ 80 Troy O'Leary .20 .07
❑ 81 Jeff Shaw .20 .07
❑ 82 Rich Becker .20 .07
❑ 83 David Wells .20 .07
❑ 84 Steve Karsay .20 .07
❑ 85 Charles Nagy .20 .07
❑ 86 B.J. Surhoff .20 .07
❑ 87 Jamey Wright .20 .07
❑ 88 James Baldwin .20 .07
❑ 89 Edgardo Alfonzo .20 .07
❑ 90 Jay Buhner .20 .07
❑ 91 Brady Anderson .20 .07
❑ 92 Scott Servais .20 .07
❑ 93 Edgar Renteria .20 .07
❑ 94 Mike Lieberthal .20 .07
❑ 95 Rick Aguilera .20 .07
❑ 96 Walt Weiss .20 .07
❑ 97 Deivi Cruz .20 .07
❑ 98 Kurt Abbott .20 .07
❑ 99 Henry Rodriguez .20 .07
❑ 100 Mike Piazza .75 .30
❑ 101 Bill Taylor .20 .07
❑ 102 Todd Zeile .20 .07
❑ 103 Rey Ordonez .20 .07
❑ 104 Willie Greene .20 .07
❑ 105 Tony Womack .20 .07
❑ 106 Mike Sweeney .20 .07
❑ 107 Jeffrey Hammonds .20 .07
❑ 108 Kevin Orie .20 .07
❑ 109 Alex Gonzalez .20 .07
❑ 110 Jose Canseco .30 .10
❑ 111 Paul Sorrento .20 .07
❑ 112 Joey Hamilton .20 .07
❑ 113 Brad Radke .20 .07
❑ 114 Steve Avery .20 .07
❑ 115 Esteban Loaiza .20 .07
❑ 116 Stan Javier .20 .07
❑ 117 Chris Gomez .20 .07
❑ 118 Royce Clayton .20 .07
❑ 119 Orlando Merced .20 .07
❑ 120 Kevin Appier .20 .07
❑ 121 Mel Nieves .20 .07
❑ 122 Joe Girardi .20 .07
❑ 123 Rico Brogna .20 .07
❑ 124 Kent Mercker .20 .07
❑ 125 Manny Ramirez .30 .10
❑ 126 Jeromy Burnitz .20 .07
❑ 127 Kevin Foster .20 .07
❑ 128 Matt Morris .20 .07
❑ 129 Jason Dickson .20 .07
❑ 130 Tom Glavine .30 .10
❑ 131 Wally Joyner .20 .07
❑ 132 Rick Reed .20 .07
❑ 133 Todd Jones .20 .07
❑ 134 Dave Martinez .20 .07
❑ 135 Sandy Alomar Jr. .20 .07
❑ 136 Mike Lansing .20 .07
❑ 137 Sean Berry .20 .07
❑ 138 Doug Jones .20 .07
❑ 139 Todd Stottlemyre .20 .07
❑ 140 Jay Bell .20 .07
❑ 141 Jaime Navarro .20 .07
❑ 142 Chris Hoiles .20 .07
❑ 143 Joey Cora .20 .07
❑ 144 Scott Spiezio .20 .07
❑ 145 Joe Carter .20 .07
❑ 146 Jose Guillen .20 .07
❑ 147 Damion Easley .20 .07
❑ 148 Lee Stevens .20 .07
❑ 149 Alex Fernandez .20 .07
❑ 150 Randy Johnson .50 .20
❑ 151 J.T. Snow .20 .07
❑ 152 Chuck Finley .20 .07
❑ 153 Bernard Gilkey .20 .07
❑ 154 David Segui .20 .07
❑ 155 Dante Bichette .20 .07
❑ 156 Kevin Stocker .20 .07
❑ 157 Carl Everett .20 .07
❑ 158 Jose Valentin .20 .07
❑ 159 Pokey Reese .20 .07
❑ 160 Derek Jeter 1.25 .50
❑ 161 Roger Pavlik .20 .07
❑ 162 Mark Wohlers .20 .07
❑ 163 Ricky Bottalico .20 .07
❑ 164 Ozzie Guillen .20 .07
❑ 165 Mike Mussina .30 .10
❑ 166 Gary Sheffield .20 .07
❑ 167 Hideo Nomo .50 .20
❑ 168 Mark Grace .30 .10
❑ 169 Aaron Sele .20 .07
❑ 170 Darryl Kile .20 .07
❑ 171 Shawn Estes .20 .07
❑ 172 Vinny Castilla .20 .07
❑ 173 Ron Coomer .20 .07
❑ 174 Jose Rosado .20 .07
❑ 175 Kenny Lofton .20 .07
❑ 176 Jason Giambi .20 .07
❑ 177 Hal Morris .20 .07
❑ 178 Darren Bragg .20 .07
❑ 179 Orel Hershiser .20 .07
❑ 180 Ray Lankford .20 .07
❑ 181 Hideki Irabu .20 .07
❑ 182 Kevin Young .20 .07
❑ 183 Javy Lopez .20 .07
❑ 184 Jeff Montgomery .20 .07
❑ 185 Mike Holtz .20 .07
❑ 186 George Williams .20 .07
❑ 187 Cal Eldred .20 .07
❑ 188 Tom Candiotti .20 .07
❑ 189 Glenallen Hill .20 .07
❑ 190 Brian Giles .20 .07
❑ 191 Dave Mlicki .20 .07
❑ 192 Garrett Stephenson .20 .07
❑ 193 Jeff Frye .20 .07
❑ 194 Joe Oliver .20 .07
❑ 195 Bob Hamelin .20 .07
❑ 196 Luis Sojo .20 .07
❑ 197 LaTroy Hawkins .20 .07
❑ 198 Kevin Elster .20 .07
❑ 199 Jeff Reed .20 .07
❑ 200 Dennis Eckersley .20 .07
❑ 201 Bill Mueller .20 .07
❑ 202 Russ Davis .20 .07
❑ 203 Armando Benitez .20 .07
❑ 204 Quilvio Veras .20 .07
❑ 205 Tim Naehring .20 .07
❑ 206 Quinton McCracken .20 .07
❑ 207 Raul Casanova .20 .07
❑ 208 Matt Lawton .20 .07
❑ 209 Luis Alicea .20 .07
❑ 210 Luis Gonzalez .20 .07
❑ 211 Allen Watson .20 .07
❑ 212 Gerald Williams .20 .07
❑ 213 David Bell .20 .07
❑ 214 Todd Hollandsworth .20 .07
❑ 215 Wade Boggs .30 .10
❑ 216 Jose Mesa .20 .07
❑ 217 Jamie Moyer .20 .07
❑ 218 Darren Daulton .20 .07
❑ 219 Mickey Morandini .20 .07
❑ 220 Rusty Greer .20 .07
❑ 221 Jim Bullinger .20 .07
❑ 222 Jose Offerman .20 .07
❑ 223 Matt Karchner .20 .07
❑ 224 Woody Williams .20 .07
❑ 225 Mark Loretta .20 .07
❑ 226 Mike Hampton .20 .07
❑ 227 Willie Adams .20 .07
❑ 228 Scott Hatteberg .20 .07
❑ 229 Rich Amaral .20 .07
❑ 230 Terry Steinbach .20 .07
❑ 231 Glendon Rusch .20 .07
❑ 232 Bret Boone .20 .07
❑ 233 Robert Person .20 .07
❑ 234 Jose Hernandez .20 .07
❑ 235 Doug Drabek .20 .07
❑ 236 Jason McDonald .20 .07
❑ 237 Chris Widger .20 .07
❑ 238 Tom Martin .20 .07
❑ 239 Dave Burba .20 .07
❑ 240 Pete Rose Jr. .20 .07
❑ 241 Bobby Ayala .20 .07

	No.	Player		
❑	242	Tim Wakefield	.20	.07
❑	243	Dennis Springer	.20	.07
❑	244	Tim Belcher	.20	.07
❑	245	J.Garland/G.Goetz	.30	.10
❑	246	L.Berkman/G.Davis	.30	.10
❑	247	V.Wells/A.Akin	.30	.10
❑	248	A.Kennedy/J.Romano	.20	.07
❑	249	J.Dellaero/T.Cameron	.20	.07
❑	250	J.Sandberg/A.Sanchez	.20	.07
❑	251	P.Ortega/J.Manias	.20	.07
❑	252	Mike Stoner RC	.20	.07
❑	253	J.Patterson/L.Rodriguez	.20	.07
❑	254	R.Minor RC/A.Beltre	.30	.10
❑	255	B.Grieve/D.Brown	.20	.07
❑	256	Wood/Pavano/Meche	.30	.10
❑	257	D.Ortiz/Sexson/Ward	2.50	1.00
❑	258	J.Encarn/Winn/Vessel	.20	.07
❑	259	Bens/T.Smith RC/C.Dunc RC	.20	.07
❑	260	Warren Morris RC	.20	.07
❑	261	R.Hernandez/B.Davis/E.Marrero	.20	.07
❑	262	E.Chavez/R.Branyan	.30	.10
❑	263	Ryan Jackson RC	.20	.07
❑	264	B.Fuentes RC/Clement/Halladay	.30	.10
❑	265	Randy Johnson SH	.30	.10
❑	266	Kevin Brown SH	.20	.07
❑	267	R.Rincon/F.Cordova SH	.20	.07
❑	268	Nomar Garciaparra SH	.50	.20
❑	269	Tino Martinez SH	.20	.07
❑	270	Chuck Knoblauch IL	.20	.07
❑	271	Pedro Martinez IL	.30	.10
❑	272	Denny Neagle IL	.20	.07
❑	273	Juan Gonzalez IL	.20	.07
❑	274	Andres Galarraga IL	.20	.07
❑	275	Checklist (1-195)	.20	.07
❑	276	Checklist (196-283/inserts)	.20	.07
❑	277	Moises Alou WS	.20	.07
❑	278	Sandy Alomar Jr. WS	.20	.07
❑	279	Gary Sheffield WS	.20	.07
❑	280	Matt Williams WS	.20	.07
❑	281	Livan Hernandez WS	.20	.07
❑	282	Chad Ogea WS	.20	.07
❑	283	Marlins Champs	.20	.07
❑	284	Tino Martinez	.30	.10
❑	285	Roberto Alomar	.30	.10
❑	286	Jeff King	.20	.07
❑	287	Brian Jordan	.20	.07
❑	288	Darin Erstad	.20	.07
❑	289	Ken Caminiti	.20	.07
❑	290	Jim Thome	.30	.10
❑	291	Paul Molitor	.20	.07
❑	292	Ivan Rodriguez	.30	.10
❑	293	Bernie Williams	.30	.10
❑	294	Todd Hundley	.20	.07
❑	295	Andres Galarraga	.20	.07
❑	296	Greg Maddux	.75	.30
❑	297	Edgar Martinez	.30	.10
❑	298	Ron Gant	.20	.07
❑	299	Derek Bell	.20	.07
❑	300	Roger Clemens	1.00	.40
❑	301	Rondell White	.20	.07
❑	302	Barry Larkin	.30	.10
❑	303	Robin Ventura	.20	.07
❑	304	Jason Kendall	.20	.07
❑	305	Chipper Jones	.50	.20
❑	306	John Franco	.20	.07
❑	307	Sammy Sosa	.50	.20
❑	308	Troy Percival	.20	.07
❑	309	Chuck Knoblauch	.20	.07
❑	310	Ellis Burks	.20	.07
❑	311	Al Martin	.20	.07
❑	312	Tim Salmon	.30	.10
❑	313	Moises Alou	.20	.07
❑	314	Lance Johnson	.20	.07
❑	315	Justin Thompson	.20	.07
❑	316	Will Clark	.30	.10
❑	317	Barry Bonds	1.50	.60
❑	318	Craig Biggio	.30	.10
❑	319	John Smoltz	.30	.10
❑	320	Cal Ripken	1.50	.60
❑	321	Ken Griffey Jr.	.75	.30
❑	322	Paul O'Neill	.30	.10
❑	323	Todd Helton	.30	.10
❑	324	John Olerud	.20	.07
❑	325	Mark McGwire	1.25	.50
❑	326	Jose Cruz Jr.	.20	.07
❑	327	Jeff Cirillo	.20	.07
❑	328	Dean Palmer	.20	.07
❑	329	John Wetteland	.20	.07
❑	330	Steve Finley	.20	.07
❑	331	Albert Belle	.20	.07
❑	332	Curt Schilling	.20	.07
❑	333	Raul Mondesi	.20	.07
❑	334	Andruw Jones	.30	.10
❑	335	Nomar Garciaparra	.75	.30
❑	336	David Justice	.20	.07
❑	337	Andy Pettitte	.30	.10
❑	338	Pedro Martinez	.30	.10
❑	339	Travis Miller	.20	.07
❑	340	Chris Stynes	.20	.07
❑	341	Gregg Jefferies	.20	.07
❑	342	Jeff Fassero	.20	.07
❑	343	Craig Counsell	.20	.07
❑	344	Wilson Alvarez	.20	.07
❑	345	Bip Roberts	.20	.07
❑	346	Kelvim Escobar	.20	.07
❑	347	Mark Bellhorn	.20	.07
❑	348	Cory Lidle RC	1.50	.60
❑	349	Fred McGriff	.30	.10
❑	350	Chuck Carr	.20	.07
❑	351	Bob Abreu	.20	.07
❑	352	Juan Guzman	.20	.07
❑	353	Fernando Vina	.20	.07
❑	354	Andy Benes	.20	.07
❑	355	Dave Nilsson	.20	.07
❑	356	Bobby Bonilla	.20	.07
❑	357	Ismael Valdes	.20	.07
❑	358	Carlos Perez	.20	.07
❑	359	Kirk Rueter	.20	.07
❑	360	Bartolo Colon	.20	.07
❑	361	Mel Rojas	.20	.07
❑	362	Johnny Damon	.30	.10
❑	363	Geronimo Berroa	.20	.07
❑	364	Reggie Sanders	.20	.07
❑	365	Jermaine Allensworth	.20	.07
❑	366	Orlando Cabrera	.20	.07
❑	367	Jorge Fabregas	.20	.07
❑	368	Scott Stahoviak	.20	.07
❑	369	Ken Cloude	.20	.07
❑	370	Donovan Osborne	.20	.07
❑	371	Roger Cedeno	.20	.07
❑	372	Neifi Perez	.20	.07
❑	373	Chris Holt	.20	.07
❑	374	Cecil Fielder	.20	.07
❑	375	Marty Cordova	.20	.07
❑	376	Tom Goodwin	.20	.07
❑	377	Jeff Suppan	.20	.07
❑	378	Jeff Brantley	.20	.07
❑	379	Mark Langston	.20	.07
❑	380	Shane Reynolds	.20	.07
❑	381	Mike Fetters	.20	.07
❑	382	Todd Greene	.20	.07
❑	383	Ray Durham	.20	.07
❑	384	Carlos Delgado	.20	.07
❑	385	Jeff D'Amico	.20	.07
❑	386	Brian McRae	.20	.07
❑	387	Alan Benes	.20	.07
❑	388	Heathcliff Slocumb	.20	.07
❑	389	Eric Young	.20	.07
❑	390	Travis Fryman	.20	.07
❑	391	David Cone	.20	.07
❑	392	Otis Nixon	.20	.07
❑	393	Jeremi Gonzalez	.20	.07
❑	394	Jeff Juden	.20	.07
❑	395	Jose Vizcaino	.20	.07
❑	396	Ugueth Urbina	.20	.07
❑	397	Ramon Martinez	.20	.07
❑	398	Robb Nen	.20	.07
❑	399	Harold Baines	.20	.07
❑	400	Delino DeShields	.20	.07
❑	401	John Burkett	.20	.07
❑	402	Sterling Hitchcock	.20	.07
❑	403	Mark Clark	.20	.07
❑	404	Terrell Wade	.20	.07
❑	405	Scott Brosius	.20	.07
❑	406	Chad Curtis	.20	.07
❑	407	Brian Johnson	.20	.07
❑	408	Roberto Kelly	.20	.07
❑	409	Dave Dellucci RC	.40	.15
❑	410	Michael Tucker	.20	.07
❑	411	Mark Kotsay	.20	.07
❑	412	Mark Lewis	.20	.07
❑	413	Ryan McGuire	.20	.07
❑	414	Shawon Dunston	.20	.07
❑	415	Brad Rigby	.20	.07
❑	416	Scott Erickson	.20	.07
❑	417	Bobby Jones	.20	.07
❑	418	Darren Oliver	.20	.07
❑	419	John Smiley	.20	.07
❑	420	T.J. Mathews	.20	.07
❑	421	Dustin Hermanson	.20	.07
❑	422	Mike Timlin	.20	.07
❑	423	Willie Blair	.20	.07
❑	424	Manny Alexander	.20	.07
❑	425	Bob Tewksbury	.20	.07
❑	426	Pete Schourek	.20	.07
❑	427	Reggie Jefferson	.20	.07
❑	428	Ed Sprague	.20	.07
❑	429	Jeff Conine	.20	.07
❑	430	Roberto Hernandez	.20	.07
❑	431	Tom Pagnozzi	.20	.07
❑	432	Jaret Wright	.20	.07
❑	433	Livan Hernandez	.20	.07
❑	434	Andy Ashby	.20	.07
❑	435	Todd Dunn	.20	.07
❑	436	Bobby Higginson	.20	.07
❑	437	Rod Beck	.20	.07
❑	438	Jim Leyritz	.20	.07
❑	439	Matt Williams	.20	.07
❑	440	Brett Tomko	.20	.07
❑	441	Joe Randa	.20	.07
❑	442	Chris Carpenter	.20	.07
❑	443	Dennis Reyes	.20	.07
❑	444	Al Leiter	.20	.07
❑	445	Jason Schmidt	.20	.07
❑	446	Ken Hill	.20	.07
❑	447	Shannon Stewart	.20	.07
❑	448	Enrique Wilson	.20	.07
❑	449	Fernando Tatis	.20	.07
❑	450	Jimmy Key	.20	.07
❑	451	Darrin Fletcher	.20	.07
❑	452	John Valentin	.20	.07
❑	453	Kevin Tapani	.20	.07
❑	454	Eric Karros	.20	.07
❑	455	Jay Bell	.20	.07
❑	456	Walt Weiss	.20	.07
❑	457	Devon White	.20	.07
❑	458	Carl Pavano	.20	.07
❑	459	Mike Lansing	.20	.07
❑	460	John Flaherty	.20	.07
❑	461	Richard Hidalgo	.20	.07
❑	462	Quinton McCracken	.20	.07
❑	463	Karim Garcia	.20	.07
❑	464	Miguel Cairo	.20	.07
❑	465	Edwin Diaz	.20	.07
❑	466	Bobby Smith	.20	.07
❑	467	Yamil Benitez	.20	.07
❑	468	Rich Butler	.20	.07
❑	469	Ben Ford RC	.20	.07
❑	470	Bubba Trammell	.20	.07
❑	471	Brent Brede	.20	.07
❑	472	Brooks Kieschnick	.20	.07
❑	473	Carlos Castillo	.20	.07
❑	474	Brad Radke SH	.20	.07
❑	475	Roger Clemens SH	.50	.20
❑	476	Curt Schilling SH	.20	.07
❑	477	John Olerud SH	.20	.07
❑	478	Mark McGwire SH	.60	.25
❑	479	M.Piazza/K.Griffey Jr. IL	.50	.20
❑	480	J.Bagwell/F.Thomas IL	.30	.10
❑	481	C.Jones/N.Garciaparra IL	.30	.10
❑	482	L.Walker/J.Gonzalez IL	.20	.07
❑	483	G.Sheffield/T.Martinez IL	.20	.07
❑	484	D.Gib/M.Colem/Hutchins	.20	.07
❑	485	B.Rose/Looper/Politte	.20	.07
❑	486	E.Milton/Marquis/C.Lee	.20	.07
❑	487	Robert Fick RC	.30	.10
❑	488	A.Ramirez/A.Gonz/Casey	.30	.10
❑	489	D.Bridges/T.Drew RC	.20	.07
❑	490	D.McDonald/N.Ndungidi RC	.20	.07
❑	491	Ryan Anderson RC	.20	.07
❑	492	Troy Glaus RC	1.25	.50
❑	493	J.Werth/D.Reichert RC	.20	.07
❑	494	Michael Cuddyer RC	.75	.30
❑	495	Jack Cust RC	.50	.20
❑	496	Brian Anderson	.20	.07
❑	497	Tony Saunders	.20	.07
❑	498	J.Sandoval/V.Nunez	.20	.07
❑	499	B.Penny/N.Bierbrodt	.30	.10

❑ 500 D.Carr/L.Cruz RC .20 .07
❑ 501 C.Bowers/M.McCain .20 .07
❑ 502 Checklist .20 .07
❑ 503 Checklist .20 .07
❑ 504 Alex Rodriguez 2.00 .75

1999 Topps

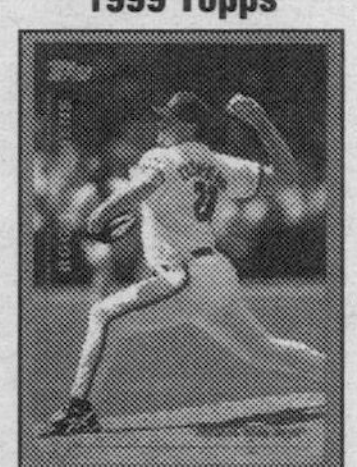

❑ COMPLETE SET (462) 80.00 30.00
❑ COMP.HOBBY SET (462) 80.00 40.00
❑ COMP.X-MAS SET (463) 80.00 40.00
❑ COMPLETE SERIES 1 (241) 40.00 15.00
❑ COMPLETE SERIES 2 (221) 40.00 15.00
❑ COMP.MAC HR SET (70) 500.00 250.00
❑ COMP.SOSA HR SET (66) 250.00 100.00
❑ 1 Roger Clemens 1.00 .40
❑ 2 Andres Galarraga .20 .07
❑ 3 Scott Brosius .20 .07
❑ 4 John Flaherty .20 .07
❑ 5 Jim Leyritz .20 .07
❑ 6 Ray Durham .20 .07
❑ 8 Jose Vizcaino .20 .07
❑ 9 Will Clark .30 .10
❑ 10 David Wells .20 .07
❑ 11 Jose Guillen .20 .07
❑ 12 Scott Hatteberg .20 .07
❑ 13 Edgardo Alfonzo .20 .07
❑ 14 Mike Bordick .20 .07
❑ 15 Manny Ramirez .30 .10
❑ 16 Greg Maddux .75 .30
❑ 17 David Segui .20 .07
❑ 18 Darryl Strawberry .20 .07
❑ 19 Brad Radke .20 .07
❑ 20 Kerry Wood .20 .07
❑ 21 Matt Anderson .20 .07
❑ 22 Derrek Lee .30 .10
❑ 23 Mickey Morandini .20 .07
❑ 24 Paul Konerko .20 .07
❑ 25 Travis Lee .20 .07
❑ 26 Ken Hill .20 .07
❑ 27 Kenny Rogers .20 .07
❑ 28 Paul Sorrento .20 .07
❑ 29 Quilvio Veras .20 .07
❑ 30 Todd Walker .20 .07
❑ 31 Ryan Jackson .20 .07
❑ 32 John Olerud .20 .07
❑ 33 Doug Glanville .20 .07
❑ 34 Nolan Ryan 2.00 .75
❑ 35 Ray Lankford .20 .07
❑ 36 Mark Loretta .20 .07
❑ 37 Jason Dickson .20 .07
❑ 38 Sean Bergman .20 .07
❑ 39 Quinton McCracken .20 .07
❑ 40 Bartolo Colon .20 .07
❑ 41 Brady Anderson .20 .07
❑ 42 Chris Stynes .20 .07
❑ 43 Jorge Posada .30 .10
❑ 44 Justin Thompson .20 .07
❑ 45 Johnny Damon .30 .10
❑ 46 Armando Benitez .20 .07
❑ 47 Brant Brown .20 .07
❑ 48 Charlie Hayes .20 .07
❑ 49 Darren Dreifort .20 .07
❑ 50 Juan Gonzalez .20 .07
❑ 51 Chuck Knoblauch .20 .07
❑ 52 Todd Helton .30 .10
❑ 53 Rick Reed .20 .07
❑ 54 Chris Gomez .20 .07
❑ 55 Gary Sheffield .20 .07
❑ 56 Rod Beck .20 .07
❑ 57 Rey Sanchez .20 .07
❑ 58 Garret Anderson .20 .07
❑ 59 Jimmy Haynes .20 .07
❑ 60 Steve Woodard .20 .07
❑ 61 Rondell White .20 .07
❑ 62 Vladimir Guerrero .50 .20
❑ 63 Eric Karros .20 .07
❑ 64 Russ Davis .20 .07
❑ 65 Mo Vaughn .20 .07
❑ 66 Sammy Sosa .50 .20
❑ 67 Troy Percival .20 .07
❑ 68 Kenny Lofton .20 .07
❑ 69 Bill Taylor .20 .07
❑ 70 Mark McGwire 1.25 .50
❑ 71 Roger Cedeno .20 .07
❑ 72 Javy Lopez .20 .07
❑ 73 Damion Easley .20 .07
❑ 74 Andy Pettitte .30 .10
❑ 75 Tony Gwynn .60 .25
❑ 76 Ricardo Rincon .20 .07
❑ 77 F.P. Santangelo .20 .07
❑ 78 Jay Bell .20 .07
❑ 79 Scott Servais .20 .07
❑ 80 Jose Canseco .30 .10
❑ 81 Roberto Hernandez .20 .07
❑ 82 Todd Dunwoody .20 .07
❑ 83 John Wetteland .20 .07
❑ 84 Mike Caruso .20 .07
❑ 85 Derek Jeter 1.25 .50
❑ 86 Aaron Sele .20 .07
❑ 87 Jose Lima .20 .07
❑ 88 Ryan Christenson .20 .07
❑ 89 Jeff Cirillo .20 .07
❑ 90 Jose Hernandez .20 .07
❑ 91 Mark Kotsay .20 .07
❑ 92 Darren Bragg .20 .07
❑ 93 Albert Belle .20 .07
❑ 94 Matt Lawton .20 .07
❑ 95 Pedro Martinez .30 .10
❑ 96 Greg Vaughn .20 .07
❑ 97 Neifi Perez .20 .07
❑ 98 Gerald Williams .20 .07
❑ 99 Derek Bell .20 .07
❑ 100 Ken Griffey Jr. .75 .30
❑ 101 David Cone .20 .07
❑ 102 Brian Johnson .20 .07
❑ 103 Dean Palmer .20 .07
❑ 104 Javier Valentin .20 .07
❑ 105 Trevor Hoffman .20 .07
❑ 106 Butch Huskey .20 .07
❑ 107 Dave Martinez .20 .07
❑ 108 Billy Wagner .20 .07
❑ 109 Shawn Green .20 .07
❑ 110 Ben Grieve .20 .07
❑ 111 Tom Goodwin .20 .07
❑ 112 Jaret Wright .20 .07
❑ 113 Aramis Ramirez .20 .07
❑ 114 Dmitri Young .20 .07
❑ 115 Hideki Irabu .20 .07
❑ 116 Roberto Kelly .20 .07
❑ 117 Jeff Fassero .20 .07
❑ 118 Mark Clark .20 .07
❑ 119 Jason McDonald .20 .07
❑ 120 Matt Williams .20 .07
❑ 121 Dave Burba .20 .07
❑ 122 Bret Saberhagen .20 .07
❑ 123 Deivi Cruz .20 .07
❑ 124 Chad Curtis .20 .07
❑ 125 Scott Rolen .30 .10
❑ 126 Lee Stevens .20 .07
❑ 127 J.T. Snow .20 .07
❑ 128 Rusty Greer .20 .07
❑ 129 Brian Meadows .20 .07
❑ 130 Jim Edmonds .20 .07
❑ 131 Ron Gant .20 .07
❑ 132 A.J. Hinch .20 .07
❑ 133 Shannon Stewart .20 .07
❑ 134 Brad Fullmer .20 .07
❑ 135 Cal Eldred .20 .07
❑ 136 Matt Walbeck .20 .07
❑ 137 Carl Everett .20 .07
❑ 138 Walt Weiss .20 .07
❑ 139 Fred McGriff .30 .10
❑ 140 Darin Erstad .20 .07
❑ 141 Dave Nilsson .20 .07
❑ 142 Eric Young .20 .07
❑ 143 Dan Wilson .20 .07
❑ 144 Jeff Reed .20 .07
❑ 145 Brett Tomko .20 .07
❑ 146 Terry Steinbach .20 .07
❑ 147 Seth Greisinger .20 .07
❑ 148 Pat Meares .20 .07
❑ 149 Livan Hernandez .20 .07
❑ 150 Jeff Bagwell .30 .10
❑ 151 Bob Wickman .20 .07
❑ 152 Omar Vizquel .30 .10
❑ 153 Eric Davis .20 .07
❑ 154 Larry Sutton .20 .07
❑ 155 Magglio Ordonez .20 .07
❑ 156 Eric Milton .20 .07
❑ 157 Darren Lewis .20 .07
❑ 158 Rick Aguilera .20 .07
❑ 159 Mike Lieberthal .20 .07
❑ 160 Robb Nen .20 .07
❑ 161 Brian Giles .20 .07
❑ 162 Jeff Brantley .20 .07
❑ 163 Gary DiSarcina .20 .07
❑ 164 John Valentin .20 .07
❑ 165 David Dellucci .20 .07
❑ 166 Chan Ho Park .20 .07
❑ 167 Masato Yoshii .20 .07
❑ 168 Jason Schmidt .20 .07
❑ 169 LaTroy Hawkins .20 .07
❑ 170 Bret Boone .20 .07
❑ 171 Jerry DiPoto .20 .07
❑ 172 Mariano Rivera .50 .20
❑ 173 Mike Cameron .20 .07
❑ 174 Scott Erickson .20 .07
❑ 175 Charles Johnson .20 .07
❑ 176 Bobby Jones .20 .07
❑ 177 Francisco Cordova .20 .07
❑ 178 Todd Jones .20 .07
❑ 179 Jeff Montgomery .20 .07
❑ 180 Mike Mussina .30 .10
❑ 181 Bob Abreu .20 .07
❑ 182 Ismael Valdes .20 .07
❑ 183 Andy Fox .20 .07
❑ 184 Woody Williams .20 .07
❑ 185 Denny Neagle .20 .07
❑ 186 Jose Valentin .20 .07
❑ 187 Darrin Fletcher .20 .07
❑ 188 Gabe Alvarez .20 .07
❑ 189 Eddie Taubensee .20 .07
❑ 190 Edgar Martinez .30 .10
❑ 191 Jason Kendall .20 .07
❑ 192 Darryl Kile .20 .07
❑ 193 Jeff King .20 .07
❑ 194 Rey Ordonez .20 .07
❑ 195 Andruw Jones .30 .10
❑ 196 Tony Fernandez .20 .07
❑ 197 Jamey Wright .20 .07
❑ 198 B.J. Surhoff .20 .07
❑ 199 Vinny Castilla .20 .07
❑ 200 David Wells HL .20 .07
❑ 201 Mark McGwire HL .60 .25
❑ 202 Sammy Sosa HL .30 .10
❑ 203 Roger Clemens HL .50 .20
❑ 204 Kerry Wood HL .20 .07
❑ 205 L.Berkman/G.Kapler .40 .15
❑ 206 Alex Escobar RC .40 .15
❑ 207 Peter Bergeron RC .25 .08
❑ 208 M.Barrett/B.Davis/R.Fick .25 .08
❑ 209 P.Cline/R.Hernandez/J.Werth .25 .08
❑ 210 R.Anderson/Chen/Enochs .25 .08
❑ 211 B.Penny/Dotel/Lincoln .25 .08
❑ 212 Chuck Abbott RC .25 .08
❑ 213 C.Jones/J.Urban RC .25 .08
❑ 214 T.Torcato/A.McDowell RC .25 .08
❑ 215 J.Tyner/J.McKinley RC .25 .08
❑ 216 M.Burch/S.Etherton RC .25 .08
❑ 217 R.Elder/M.Tucker RC .25 .08
❑ 218 J.M.Gold/R.Mills RC .25 .08
❑ 219 A.Brown/C.Freeman RC .25 .08
❑ 220A Mark McGwire HR 1 40.00 15.00
❑ 220B Mark McGwire HR 2 15.00 6.00
❑ 220C Mark McGwire HR 3 15.00 6.00
❑ 220D Mark McGwire HR 4 15.00 6.00
❑ 220E Mark McGwire HR 5 15.00 6.00
❑ 220F Mark McGwire HR 6 15.00 6.00
❑ 220G Mark McGwire HR 7 15.00 6.00
❑ 220H Mark McGwire HR 8 15.00 6.00

No.	Player	Mint	Nrmt
❑ 220I	Mark McGwire HR 9	15.00	6.00
❑ 220J	Mark McGwire HR 10	15.00	6.00
❑ 220K	Mark McGwire HR 11	15.00	6.00
❑ 220L	Mark McGwire HR 12	15.00	6.00
❑ 220M	Mark McGwire HR 13	15.00	6.00
❑ 220N	Mark McGwire HR 14	15.00	6.00
❑ 220O	Mark McGwire HR 15	15.00	6.00
❑ 220P	Mark McGwire HR 16	15.00	6.00
❑ 220Q	Mark McGwire HR 17	15.00	6.00
❑ 220R	Mark McGwire HR 18	15.00	6.00
❑ 220S	Mark McGwire HR 19	15.00	6.00
❑ 220T	Mark McGwire HR 20	15.00	6.00
❑ 220U	Mark McGwire HR 21	15.00	6.00
❑ 220V	Mark McGwire HR 22	15.00	6.00
❑ 220W	Mark McGwire HR 23	15.00	6.00
❑ 220X	Mark McGwire HR 24	15.00	6.00
❑ 220Y	Mark McGwire HR 25	15.00	6.00
❑ 220Z	Mark McGwire HR 26	15.00	6.00
❑ 220AA	Mark McGwire HR 27	15.00	6.00
❑ 220AB	Mark McGwire HR 28	15.00	6.00
❑ 220AC	Mark McGwire HR 29	15.00	6.00
❑ 220AD	Mark McGwire HR 30	15.00	6.00
❑ 220AE	Mark McGwire HR 31	15.00	6.00
❑ 220AF	Mark McGwire HR 32	15.00	6.00
❑ 220AG	Mark McGwire HR 33	15.00	6.00
❑ 220AH	Mark McGwire HR 34	15.00	6.00
❑ 220AI	Mark McGwire HR 35	15.00	6.00
❑ 220AJ	Mark McGwire HR 36	15.00	6.00
❑ 220AK	Mark McGwire HR 37	15.00	6.00
❑ 220AL	Mark McGwire HR 38	15.00	6.00
❑ 220AM	Mark McGwire HR 39	15.00	6.00
❑ 220AN	Mark McGwire HR 40	15.00	6.00
❑ 220AO	Mark McGwire HR 41	15.00	6.00
❑ 220AP	Mark McGwire HR 42	15.00	6.00
❑ 220AQ	Mark McGwire HR 43	15.00	6.00
❑ 220AR	Mark McGwire HR 44	15.00	6.00
❑ 220AS	Mark McGwire HR 45	15.00	6.00
❑ 220AT	Mark McGwire HR 46	15.00	6.00
❑ 220AU	Mark McGwire HR 47	15.00	6.00
❑ 220AV	Mark McGwire HR 48	15.00	6.00
❑ 220AW	Mark McGwire HR 49	15.00	6.00
❑ 220AX	Mark McGwire HR 50	15.00	6.00
❑ 220AY	Mark McGwire HR 51	15.00	6.00
❑ 220AZ	Mark McGwire HR 52	15.00	6.00
❑ 220BB	Mark McGwire HR 53	15.00	6.00
❑ 220CC	Mark McGwire HR 54	15.00	6.00
❑ 220DD	Mark McGwire HR 55	15.00	6.00
❑ 220EE	Mark McGwire HR 56	15.00	6.00
❑ 220FF	Mark McGwire HR 57	15.00	6.00
❑ 220GG	Mark McGwire HR 58	15.00	6.00
❑ 220HH	Mark McGwire HR 59	15.00	6.00
❑ 220II	Mark McGwire HR 60	15.00	6.00
❑ 220JJ	Mark McGwire HR 61	30.00	12.50
❑ 220KK	Mark McGwire HR 62	40.00	15.00
❑ 220LL	Mark McGwire HR 63	15.00	6.00
❑ 220MM	Mark McGwire HR 64	15.00	6.00
❑ 220NN	Mark McGwire HR 65	15.00	6.00
❑ 220OO	Mark McGwire HR 66	15.00	6.00
❑ 220PP	Mark McGwire HR 67	15.00	6.00
❑ 220QQ	Mark McGwire HR 68	15.00	6.00
❑ 220RR	Mark McGwire HR 69	15.00	6.00
❑ 220SS	Mark McGwire HR 70	100.00	50.00
❑ 221	Larry Walker LL	.20	.07
❑ 222	Bernie Williams LL	.20	.07
❑ 223	Mark McGwire LL	.60	.25
❑ 224	Ken Griffey Jr. LL	.50	.20
❑ 225	Sammy Sosa LL	.30	.10
❑ 226	Juan Gonzalez LL	.20	.07
❑ 227	Dante Bichette LL	.20	.07
❑ 228	Alex Rodriguez LL	.50	.20
❑ 229	Sammy Sosa LL	.30	.10
❑ 230	Derek Jeter LL	.60	.25
❑ 231	Greg Maddux LL	.50	.20
❑ 232	Roger Clemens LL	.50	.20
❑ 233	Ricky Ledee WS	.20	.07
❑ 234	Chuck Knoblauch WS	.20	.07
❑ 235	Bernie Williams WS	.20	.07
❑ 236	Tino Martinez WS	.20	.07
❑ 237	Orlando Hernandez WS	.20	.07
❑ 238	Scott Brosius WS	.20	.07
❑ 239	Andy Pettitte WS	.20	.07
❑ 240	Mariano Rivera WS	.30	.10
❑ 241	Checklist 1	.20	.07
❑ 242	Checklist 2	.20	.07
❑ 243	Tom Glavine	.30	.10
❑ 244	Andy Benes	.20	.07
❑ 245	Sandy Alomar Jr.	.20	.07
❑ 246	Wilton Guerrero	.20	.07
❑ 247	Alex Gonzalez	.20	.07
❑ 248	Roberto Alomar	.30	.10
❑ 249	Ruben Rivera	.20	.07
❑ 250	Eric Chavez	.20	.07
❑ 251	Ellis Burks	.20	.07
❑ 252	Richie Sexson	.20	.07
❑ 253	Steve Finley	.20	.07
❑ 254	Dwight Gooden	.20	.07
❑ 255	Dustin Hermanson	.20	.07
❑ 256	Kirk Rueter	.20	.07
❑ 257	Steve Trachsel	.20	.07
❑ 258	Gregg Jefferies	.20	.07
❑ 259	Matt Stairs	.20	.07
❑ 260	Shane Reynolds	.20	.07
❑ 261	Gregg Olson	.20	.07
❑ 262	Kevin Tapani	.20	.07
❑ 263	Matt Morris	.20	.07
❑ 264	Carl Pavano	.20	.07
❑ 265	Nomar Garciaparra	.75	.30
❑ 266	Kevin Young	.20	.07
❑ 267	Rick Helling	.20	.07
❑ 268	Matt Franco	.20	.07
❑ 269	Brian McRae	.20	.07
❑ 270	Cal Ripken	1.50	.60
❑ 271	Jeff Abbott	.20	.07
❑ 272	Tony Batista	.20	.07
❑ 273	Bill Simas	.20	.07
❑ 274	Brian Hunter	.20	.07
❑ 275	John Franco	.20	.07
❑ 276	Devon White	.20	.07
❑ 277	Rickey Henderson	.50	.20
❑ 278	Chuck Finley	.20	.07
❑ 279	Mike Blowers	.20	.07
❑ 280	Mark Grace	.30	.10
❑ 281	Randy Winn	.20	.07
❑ 282	Bobby Bonilla	.20	.07
❑ 283	David Justice	.20	.07
❑ 284	Shane Monahan	.20	.07
❑ 285	Kevin Brown	.30	.10
❑ 286	Todd Zeile	.20	.07
❑ 287	Al Martin	.20	.07
❑ 288	Troy O'Leary	.20	.07
❑ 289	Darryl Hamilton	.20	.07
❑ 290	Tino Martinez	.30	.10
❑ 291	David Ortiz	.50	.20
❑ 292	Tony Clark	.20	.07
❑ 293	Ryan Minor	.20	.07
❑ 294	Mark Leiter	.20	.07
❑ 295	Wally Joyner	.20	.07
❑ 296	Cliff Floyd	.20	.07
❑ 297	Shawn Estes	.20	.07
❑ 298	Pat Hentgen	.20	.07
❑ 299	Scott Elarton	.20	.07
❑ 300	Alex Rodriguez	.75	.30
❑ 301	Ozzie Guillen	.20	.07
❑ 302	Hideo Nomo	.50	.20
❑ 303	Ryan McGuire	.20	.07
❑ 304	Brad Ausmus	.20	.07
❑ 305	Alex Gonzalez	.20	.07
❑ 306	Brian Jordan	.20	.07
❑ 307	John Jaha	.20	.07
❑ 308	Mark Grudzielanek	.20	.07
❑ 309	Juan Guzman	.20	.07
❑ 310	Tony Womack	.20	.07
❑ 311	Dennis Reyes	.20	.07
❑ 312	Marty Cordova	.20	.07
❑ 313	Ramiro Mendoza	.20	.07
❑ 314	Robin Ventura	.20	.07
❑ 315	Rafael Palmeiro	.30	.10
❑ 316	Ramon Martinez	.20	.07
❑ 317	Pedro Astacio	.20	.07
❑ 318	Dave Hollins	.20	.07
❑ 319	Tom Candiotti	.20	.07
❑ 320	Al Leiter	.20	.07
❑ 321	Rico Brogna	.20	.07
❑ 322	Reggie Jefferson	.20	.07
❑ 323	Bernard Gilkey	.20	.07
❑ 324	Jason Giambi	.20	.07
❑ 325	Craig Biggio	.30	.10
❑ 326	Troy Glaus	.30	.10
❑ 327	Delino DeShields	.20	.07
❑ 328	Fernando Vina	.20	.07
❑ 329	John Smoltz	.30	.10
❑ 330	Jeff Kent	.20	.07
❑ 331	Roy Halladay	.20	.07
❑ 332	Andy Ashby	.20	.07
❑ 333	Tim Wakefield	.20	.07
❑ 334	Roger Clemens	1.00	.40
❑ 335	Bernie Williams	.30	.10
❑ 336	Desi Relaford	.20	.07
❑ 337	John Burkett	.20	.07
❑ 338	Mike Hampton	.20	.07
❑ 339	Royce Clayton	.20	.07
❑ 340	Mike Piazza	.75	.30
❑ 341	Jeremi Gonzalez	.20	.07
❑ 342	Mike Lansing	.20	.07
❑ 343	Jamie Moyer	.20	.07
❑ 344	Ron Coomer	.20	.07
❑ 345	Barry Larkin	.30	.10
❑ 346	Fernando Tatis	.20	.07
❑ 347	Chili Davis	.20	.07
❑ 348	Bobby Higginson	.20	.07
❑ 349	Hal Morris	.20	.07
❑ 350	Larry Walker	.20	.07
❑ 351	Carlos Guillen	.20	.07
❑ 352	Miguel Tejada	.20	.07
❑ 353	Travis Fryman	.20	.07
❑ 354	Jarrod Washburn	.20	.07
❑ 355	Chipper Jones	.50	.20
❑ 356	Todd Stottlemyre	.20	.07
❑ 357	Henry Rodriguez	.20	.07
❑ 358	Eli Marrero	.20	.07
❑ 359	Alan Benes	.20	.07
❑ 360	Tim Salmon	.30	.10
❑ 361	Luis Gonzalez	.20	.07
❑ 362	Scott Spiezio	.20	.07
❑ 363	Chris Carpenter	.20	.07
❑ 364	Bobby Howry	.20	.07
❑ 365	Raul Mondesi	.20	.07
❑ 366	Ugueth Urbina	.20	.07
❑ 367	Tom Evans	.20	.07
❑ 368	Kerry Ligtenberg RC	.25	.08
❑ 369	Adrian Beltre	.20	.07
❑ 370	Ryan Klesko	.20	.07
❑ 371	Wilson Alvarez	.20	.07
❑ 372	John Thomson	.20	.07
❑ 373	Tony Saunders	.20	.07
❑ 374	Dave Mlicki	.20	.07
❑ 375	Ken Caminiti	.20	.07
❑ 376	Jay Buhner	.20	.07
❑ 377	Bill Mueller	.20	.07
❑ 378	Jeff Blauser	.20	.07
❑ 379	Edgar Renteria	.20	.07
❑ 380	Jim Thome	.30	.10
❑ 381	Joey Hamilton	.20	.07
❑ 382	Calvin Pickering	.20	.07
❑ 383	Marquis Grissom	.20	.07
❑ 384	Omar Daal	.20	.07
❑ 385	Curt Schilling	.20	.07
❑ 386	Jose Cruz Jr.	.20	.07
❑ 387	Chris Widger	.20	.07
❑ 388	Pete Harnisch	.20	.07
❑ 389	Charles Nagy	.20	.07
❑ 390	Tom Gordon	.20	.07
❑ 391	Bobby Smith	.20	.07
❑ 392	Derrick Gibson	.20	.07
❑ 393	Jeff Conine	.20	.07
❑ 394	Carlos Perez	.20	.07
❑ 395	Barry Bonds	1.50	.60
❑ 396	Mark McLemore	.20	.07
❑ 397	Juan Encarnacion	.20	.07
❑ 398	Wade Boggs	.30	.10
❑ 399	Ivan Rodriguez	.30	.10
❑ 400	Moises Alou	.20	.07
❑ 401	Jeromy Burnitz	.20	.07
❑ 402	Sean Casey	.20	.07
❑ 403	Jose Offerman	.20	.07
❑ 404	Joe Fontenot	.20	.07
❑ 405	Kevin Millwood	.20	.07
❑ 406	Lance Johnson	.20	.07
❑ 407	Richard Hidalgo	.20	.07
❑ 408	Mike Jackson	.20	.07
❑ 409	Brian Anderson	.20	.07
❑ 410	Jeff Shaw	.20	.07
❑ 411	Preston Wilson	.20	.07
❑ 412	Todd Hundley	.20	.07
❑ 413	Jim Parque	.20	.07
❑ 414	Justin Baughman	.20	.07
❑ 415	Dante Bichette	.20	.07
❑ 416	Paul O'Neill	.30	.10

❑ 417 Miguel Cairo .20 .07
❑ 418 Randy Johnson .50 .20
❑ 419 Jesus Sanchez .20 .07
❑ 420 Carlos Delgado .20 .07
❑ 421 Ricky Ledee .20 .07
❑ 422 Orlando Hernandez .20 .07
❑ 423 Frank Thomas .50 .20
❑ 424 Pokey Reese .20 .07
❑ 425 C.Lee/M.Lowell .40 .15
❑ 426 M.Cuddyer/DeRosa/Hairston .25 .08
❑ 427 M.Anderson/Belliard/Cabrera .40 .15
❑ 428 M.Bowie/P.Norton RC/Wolf .25 .08
❑ 429 J.Cressend RC/Rocker .40 .15
❑ 430 R.Mateo/M.Zywica RC .25 .08
❑ 431 J.LaRue/LeCroy/Meluskey .25 .08
❑ 432 Gabe Kapler .40 .15
❑ 433 A.Kennedy/M.Lopez RC .25 .08
❑ 434 Jose Fernandez RC/C.Truby .25 .08
❑ 435 Doug Mientkiewicz RC .50 .20
❑ 436 R.Brown RC/V.Wells .25 .08
❑ 437 A.J. Burnett RC .75 .30
❑ 438 M.Belisle/M.Roney RC .25 .08
❑ 439 A.Kearns/C.George RC 1.50 .60
❑ 440 N.Cornejo/N.Bump RC .25 .08
❑ 441 B.Lidge/M.Nannini RC 1.50 .60
❑ 442 M.Holliday/J.Winchester RC 4.00 1.50
❑ 443 A.Everett/C.Ambres RC .50 .20
❑ 444 P.Burrell/E.Valent RC 1.50 .60
❑ 445 Roger Clemens SK .50 .20
❑ 446 Kerry Wood SK .20 .07
❑ 447 Curt Schilling SK .20 .07
❑ 448 Randy Johnson SK .30 .10
❑ 449 Pedro Martinez SK .30 .10
❑ 450 Bagwell/Galar/McGwire AT .50 .20
❑ 451 Olerud/Thome/Martinez AT .20 .07
❑ 452 ARod/Nomar/Jeter AT .60 .25
❑ 453 Castilla/Jones/Rolen AT .30 .10
❑ 454 Sosa/Griffey/Gonzalez AT .50 .20
❑ 455 Bonds/Ramirez/Walker AT .75 .30
❑ 456 Thomas/Salmon/Justice AT .50 .20
❑ 457 Lee/Helton/Grieve AT .20 .07
❑ 458 Guerrero/Vaughn/B.Will AT .20 .07
❑ 459 Piazza/IRod/Kendall AT .50 .20
❑ 460 Clemens/Wood/Maddux AT .50 .20
❑ 461A Sammy Sosa HR 1 15.00 6.00
❑ 461B Sammy Sosa HR 2 6.00 2.50
❑ 461C Sammy Sosa HR 3 6.00 2.50
❑ 461D Sammy Sosa HR 4 6.00 2.50
❑ 461E Sammy Sosa HR 5 6.00 2.50
❑ 461F Sammy Sosa HR 6 6.00 2.50
❑ 461G Sammy Sosa HR 7 6.00 2.50
❑ 461H Sammy Sosa HR 8 6.00 2.50
❑ 461I Sammy Sosa HR 9 6.00 2.50
❑ 461J Sammy Sosa HR 10 6.00 2.50
❑ 461K Sammy Sosa HR 11 6.00 2.50
❑ 461L Sammy Sosa HR 12 6.00 2.50
❑ 461M Sammy Sosa HR 13 6.00 2.50
❑ 461N Sammy Sosa HR 14 6.00 2.50
❑ 461O Sammy Sosa HR 15 6.00 2.50
❑ 461P Sammy Sosa HR 16 6.00 2.50
❑ 461Q Sammy Sosa HR 17 6.00 2.50
❑ 461R Sammy Sosa HR 18 6.00 2.50
❑ 461S Sammy Sosa HR 19 6.00 2.50
❑ 461T Sammy Sosa HR 20 6.00 2.50
❑ 461U Sammy Sosa HR 21 6.00 2.50
❑ 461V Sammy Sosa HR 22 6.00 2.50
❑ 461W Sammy Sosa HR 23 6.00 2.50
❑ 461X Sammy Sosa HR 24 6.00 2.50
❑ 461Y Sammy Sosa HR 25 6.00 2.50
❑ 461Z Sammy Sosa HR 26 6.00 2.50
❑ 461AA Sammy Sosa HR 27 6.00 2.50
❑ 461AB Sammy Sosa HR 28 6.00 2.50
❑ 461AC Sammy Sosa HR 29 6.00 2.50
❑ 461AD Sammy Sosa HR 30 6.00 2.50
❑ 461AE Sammy Sosa HR 31 6.00 2.50
❑ 461AF Sammy Sosa HR 32 6.00 2.50
❑ 461AG Sammy Sosa HR 33 6.00 2.50
❑ 461AH Sammy Sosa HR 34 6.00 2.50
❑ 461AI Sammy Sosa HR 35 6.00 2.50
❑ 461AJ Sammy Sosa HR 36 6.00 2.50
❑ 461AK Sammy Sosa HR 37 6.00 2.50
❑ 461AL Sammy Sosa HR 38 6.00 2.50
❑ 461AM Sammy Sosa HR 39 6.00 2.50
❑ 461AN Sammy Sosa HR 40 6.00 2.50
❑ 461AO Sammy Sosa HR 41 6.00 2.50
❑ 461AP Sammy Sosa HR 42 6.00 2.50
❑ 461AR Sammy Sosa HR 43 6.00 2.50
❑ 461AS Sammy Sosa HR 44 6.00 2.50
❑ 461AT Sammy Sosa HR 45 6.00 2.50
❑ 461AU Sammy Sosa HR 46 6.00 2.50
❑ 461AV Sammy Sosa HR 47 6.00 2.50
❑ 461AW Sammy Sosa HR 48 6.00 2.50
❑ 461AX Sammy Sosa HR 49 6.00 2.50
❑ 461AY Sammy Sosa HR 50 6.00 2.50
❑ 461AZ Sammy Sosa HR 51 6.00 2.50
❑ 461BB Sammy Sosa HR 52 6.00 2.50
❑ 461CC Sammy Sosa HR 53 6.00 2.50
❑ 461DD Sammy Sosa HR 54 6.00 2.50
❑ 461EE Sammy Sosa HR 55 6.00 2.50
❑ 461FF Sammy Sosa HR 56 6.00 2.50
❑ 461GG Sammy Sosa HR 57 6.00 2.50
❑ 461HH Sammy Sosa HR 58 6.00 2.50
❑ 461II Sammy Sosa HR 59 6.00 2.50
❑ 461JJ Sammy Sosa HR 60 6.00 2.50
❑ 461KK Sammy Sosa HR 61 15.00 6.00
❑ 461LL Sammy Sosa HR 62 20.00 8.00
❑ 461MM Sammy Sosa HR 63 8.00 3.00
❑ 461NN Sammy Sosa HR 64 8.00 3.00
❑ 461OO Sammy Sosa HR 65 8.00 3.00
❑ 461PP Sammy Sosa HR 66 25.00 10.00
❑ 462 Checklist .20 .07
❑ 463 Checklist .20 .07

1999 Topps Traded

❑ COMP.FACT.SET (122) 50.00 20.00
❑ COMPLETE SET (121) 30.00 12.50
❑ T1 Seth Etherton .20 .07
❑ T2 Mark Harriger RC .25 .08
❑ T3 Matt Wise RC .25 .08
❑ T4 Carlos Eduardo Hernandez RC .40 .15
❑ T5 Julio Lugo RC .75 .30
❑ T6 Mike Nannini .20 .07
❑ T7 Justin Bowles RC .25 .08
❑ T8 Mark Mulder RC 1.50 .60
❑ T9 Roberto Vaz RC .25 .08
❑ T10 Felipe Lopez RC 1.50 .60
❑ T11 Matt Belisle .50 .20
❑ T12 Micah Bowie .20 .07
❑ T13 Ruben Quevedo RC .25 .08
❑ T14 Jose Garcia RC .25 .08
❑ T15 David Kelton RC .25 .08
❑ T16 Phil Norton .20 .07
❑ T17 Corey Patterson RC 1.00 .40
❑ T18 Ron Walker RC .25 .08
❑ T19 Paul Hoover RC .25 .08
❑ T20 Ryan Rupe RC .25 .08
❑ T21 J.D. Closser RC .40 .15
❑ T22 Rob Ryan RC .25 .08
❑ T23 Steve Colyer RC .25 .08
❑ T24 Bubba Crosby RC .60 .25
❑ T25 Luke Prokopec RC .25 .08
❑ T26 Matt Blank RC .25 .08
❑ T27 Josh McKinley .20 .07
❑ T28 Nate Bump .20 .07
❑ T29 Giuseppe Chiaramonte RC .25 .08
❑ T30 Arturo McDowell .20 .07
❑ T31 Tony Torcato .20 .07
❑ T32 Dave Roberts RC .60 .25
❑ T33 C.C. Sabathia RC 2.00 .75
❑ T34 Sean Spencer RC .25 .08
❑ T35 Chip Ambres .20 .07
❑ T36 A.J. Burnett 1.00 .40
❑ T37 Mo Bruce RC .25 .08
❑ T38 Jason Tyner .20 .07
❑ T39 Mamon Tucker .20 .07
❑ T40 Sean Burroughs RC .60 .25
❑ T41 Kevin Eberwein RC .25 .08
❑ T42 Junior Herndon RC .25 .08
❑ T43 Bryan Wolff RC .25 .08
❑ T44 Pat Burrell 1.25 .50
❑ T45 Eric Valent .20 .07
❑ T46 Carlos Pena RC .50 .20
❑ T47 Mike Zywica .20 .07
❑ T48 Adam Everett .30 .10
❑ T49 Juan Pena RC .40 .15
❑ T50 Adam Dunn RC 4.00 1.50
❑ T51 Austin Kearns 1.25 .50
❑ T52 Jacobo Sequea RC .25 .08
❑ T53 Choo Freeman .20 .07
❑ T54 Jeff Winchester .20 .07
❑ T55 Matt Burch .20 .07
❑ T56 Chris George .20 .07
❑ T57 Scott Mullen RC .25 .08
❑ T58 Kit Pellow .20 .07
❑ T59 Mark Quinn RC .25 .08
❑ T60 Nate Cornejo .25 .08
❑ T61 Ryan Mills .20 .07
❑ T62 Kevin Beirne RC .25 .08
❑ T63 Kip Wells RC .40 .15
❑ T64 Juan Rivera RC 1.00 .40
❑ T65 Alfonso Soriano RC 5.00 2.00
❑ T66 Josh Hamilton RC 10.00 4.00
❑ T67 Josh Girdley RC .25 .08
❑ T68 Kyle Snyder RC .25 .08
❑ T69 Mike Paradis RC .25 .08
❑ T70 Jason Jennings RC .60 .25
❑ T71 David Walling RC .25 .08
❑ T72 Omar Ortiz RC .25 .08
❑ T73 Jay Gehrke RC .40 .15
❑ T74 Casey Burns RC .40 .15
❑ T75 Carl Crawford RC 4.00 1.50
❑ T76 Reggie Sanders .20 .07
❑ T77 Will Clark .30 .10
❑ T78 David Wells .20 .07
❑ T79 Paul Konerko .20 .07
❑ T80 Armando Benitez .20 .07
❑ T81 Brant Brown .20 .07
❑ T82 Mo Vaughn .20 .07
❑ T83 Jose Canseco .30 .10
❑ T84 Albert Belle .20 .07
❑ T85 Dean Palmer .20 .07
❑ T86 Greg Vaughn .20 .07
❑ T87 Mark Clark .20 .07
❑ T88 Pat Meares .20 .07
❑ T89 Eric Davis .20 .07
❑ T90 Brian Giles .20 .07
❑ T91 Jeff Brantley .20 .07
❑ T92 Bret Boone .20 .07
❑ T93 Ron Gant .20 .07
❑ T94 Mike Cameron .20 .07
❑ T95 Charles Johnson .20 .07
❑ T96 Denny Neagle .20 .07
❑ T97 Brian Hunter .20 .07
❑ T98 Jose Hernandez .20 .07
❑ T99 Rick Aguilera .20 .07
❑ T100 Tony Batista .20 .07
❑ T101 Roger Cedeno .20 .07
❑ T102 Creighton Gubanich RC .25 .08
❑ T103 Tim Belcher .20 .07
❑ T104 Bruce Aven .20 .07
❑ T105 Brian Daubach RC .40 .15
❑ T106 Ed Sprague .20 .07
❑ T107 Michael Tucker .20 .07
❑ T108 Homer Bush .20 .07
❑ T109 Armando Reynoso .20 .07
❑ T110 Brook Fordyce .20 .07
❑ T111 Matt Mantei .20 .07
❑ T112 Dave Mlicki .20 .07
❑ T113 Kenny Rogers .20 .07
❑ T114 Livan Hernandez .20 .07
❑ T115 Butch Huskey .20 .07
❑ T116 David Segui .20 .07
❑ T117 Darryl Hamilton .20 .07
❑ T118 Terry Mulholland .20 .07
❑ T119 Randy Velarde .20 .07
❑ T120 Bill Taylor .20 .07
❑ T121 Kevin Appier .20 .07

2000 Topps

- ❑ COMPLETE SET (478) 50.00 20.00
- ❑ COMP.HOBBY SET (478) 60.00 30.00
- ❑ COMPLETE SERIES 1 (239) 25.00 10.00
- ❑ COMPLETE SERIES 2 (240) 25.00 10.00
- ❑ MCGWIRE MM SET (5) 12.00 5.00
- ❑ AARON MM SET (5) 10.00 4.00
- ❑ RIPKEN MM SET (5) 15.00 6.00
- ❑ BOGGS MM SET (5) 3.00 1.25
- ❑ GWYNN MM SET (5) 6.00 2.50
- ❑ GRIFFEY MM SET (5) 8.00 3.00
- ❑ BONDS MM SET (5) 12.00 5.00
- ❑ SOSA MM SET (5) 8.00 3.00
- ❑ JETER MM SET (5) 12.00 5.00
- ❑ A.ROD MM SET (5) 8.00 3.00
- ❑ 1 Mark McGwire 1.25 .50
- ❑ 2 Tony Gwynn .60 .25
- ❑ 3 Wade Boggs .30 .10
- ❑ 4 Cal Ripken 1.50 .60
- ❑ 5 Matt Williams .20 .07
- ❑ 6 Jay Buhner .20 .07
- ❑ 8 Jeff Conine .20 .07
- ❑ 9 Todd Greene .20 .07
- ❑ 10 Mike Lieberthal .20 .07
- ❑ 11 Steve Avery .20 .07
- ❑ 12 Bret Saberhagen .20 .07
- ❑ 13 Magglio Ordonez .20 .07
- ❑ 14 Brad Radke .20 .07
- ❑ 15 Derek Jeter 1.25 .50
- ❑ 16 Javy Lopez .20 .07
- ❑ 17 Russ Davis .20 .07
- ❑ 18 Armando Benitez .20 .07
- ❑ 19 B.J. Surhoff .20 .07
- ❑ 20 Darryl Kile .20 .07
- ❑ 21 Mark Lewis .20 .07
- ❑ 22 Mike Williams .20 .07
- ❑ 23 Mark McLemore .20 .07
- ❑ 24 Sterling Hitchcock .20 .07
- ❑ 25 Darin Erstad .20 .07
- ❑ 26 Ricky Gutierrez .20 .07
- ❑ 27 John Jaha .20 .07
- ❑ 28 Homer Bush .20 .07
- ❑ 29 Darrin Fletcher .20 .07
- ❑ 30 Mark Grace .30 .10
- ❑ 31 Fred McGriff .30 .10
- ❑ 32 Omar Daal .20 .07
- ❑ 33 Eric Karros .20 .07
- ❑ 34 Orlando Cabrera .20 .07
- ❑ 35 J.T. Snow .20 .07
- ❑ 36 Luis Castillo .20 .07
- ❑ 37 Rey Ordonez .20 .07
- ❑ 38 Bob Abreu .20 .07
- ❑ 39 Warren Morris .20 .07
- ❑ 40 Juan Gonzalez .20 .07
- ❑ 41 Mike Lansing .20 .07
- ❑ 42 Chili Davis .20 .07
- ❑ 43 Dean Palmer .20 .07
- ❑ 44 Hank Aaron .75 .30
- ❑ 45 Jeff Dagwell .00 .10
- ❑ 46 Jose Valentin .20 .07
- ❑ 47 Shannon Stewart .20 .07
- ❑ 48 Kent Bottenfield .20 .07
- ❑ 49 Jeff Shaw .20 .07
- ❑ 50 Sammy Sosa .50 .20
- ❑ 51 Randy Johnson .50 .20
- ❑ 52 Benny Agbayani .20 .07
- ❑ 53 Dante Bichette .20 .07
- ❑ 54 Pete Harnisch .20 .07
- ❑ 55 Frank Thomas .50 .20
- ❑ 56 Jorge Posada .30 .10
- ❑ 57 Todd Walker .20 .07
- ❑ 58 Juan Encarnacion .20 .07
- ❑ 59 Mike Sweeney .20 .07
- ❑ 60 Pedro Martinez .30 .10
- ❑ 61 Lee Stevens .20 .07
- ❑ 62 Brian Giles .20 .07
- ❑ 63 Chad Ogea .20 .07
- ❑ 64 Ivan Rodriguez .30 .10
- ❑ 65 Roger Cedeno .20 .07
- ❑ 66 David Justice .20 .07
- ❑ 67 Steve Trachsel .20 .07
- ❑ 68 Eli Marrero .20 .07
- ❑ 69 Dave Nilsson .20 .07
- ❑ 70 Ken Caminiti .20 .07
- ❑ 71 Tim Raines .20 .07
- ❑ 72 Brian Jordan .20 .07
- ❑ 73 Jeff Blauser .20 .07
- ❑ 74 Bernard Gilkey .20 .07
- ❑ 75 John Flaherty .20 .07
- ❑ 76 Brent Mayne .20 .07
- ❑ 77 Jose Vidro .20 .07
- ❑ 78 David Bell .20 .07
- ❑ 79 Bruce Aven .20 .07
- ❑ 80 John Olerud .20 .07
- ❑ 81 Pokey Reese .20 .07
- ❑ 82 Woody Williams .20 .07
- ❑ 83 Ed Sprague .20 .07
- ❑ 84 Joe Girardi .20 .07
- ❑ 85 Barry Larkin .30 .10
- ❑ 86 Mike Caruso .20 .07
- ❑ 87 Bobby Higginson .20 .07
- ❑ 88 Roberto Kelly .20 .07
- ❑ 89 Edgar Martinez .30 .10
- ❑ 90 Mark Kotsay .20 .07
- ❑ 91 Paul Sorrento .20 .07
- ❑ 92 Eric Young .20 .07
- ❑ 93 Carlos Delgado .20 .07
- ❑ 94 Troy Glaus .20 .07
- ❑ 95 Ben Grieve .20 .07
- ❑ 96 Jose Lima .20 .07
- ❑ 97 Garret Anderson .20 .07
- ❑ 98 Luis Gonzalez .20 .07
- ❑ 99 Carl Pavano .20 .07
- ❑ 100 Alex Rodriguez .75 .30
- ❑ 101 Preston Wilson .20 .07
- ❑ 102 Ron Gant .20 .07
- ❑ 103 Brady Anderson .20 .07
- ❑ 104 Rickey Henderson .50 .20
- ❑ 105 Gary Sheffield .20 .07
- ❑ 106 Mickey Morandini .20 .07
- ❑ 107 Jim Edmonds .20 .07
- ❑ 108 Kris Benson .20 .07
- ❑ 109 Adrian Beltre .20 .07
- ❑ 110 Alex Fernandez .20 .07
- ❑ 111 Dan Wilson .20 .07
- ❑ 112 Mark Clark .20 .07
- ❑ 113 Greg Vaughn .20 .07
- ❑ 114 Neifi Perez .20 .07
- ❑ 115 Paul O'Neill .30 .10
- ❑ 116 Jermaine Dye .20 .07
- ❑ 117 Todd Jones .20 .07
- ❑ 118 Terry Steinbach .20 .07
- ❑ 119 Greg Norton .20 .07
- ❑ 120 Curt Schilling .20 .07
- ❑ 121 Todd Zeile .20 .07
- ❑ 122 Edgardo Alfonzo .20 .07
- ❑ 123 Ryan McGuire .20 .07
- ❑ 124 Rich Aurilia .20 .07
- ❑ 125 John Smoltz .30 .10
- ❑ 126 Bob Wickman .20 .07
- ❑ 127 Richard Hidalgo .20 .07
- ❑ 128 Chuck Finley .20 .07
- ❑ 129 Billy Wagner .20 .07
- ❑ 130 Todd Hundley .20 .07
- ❑ 131 Dwight Gooden .20 .07
- ❑ 132 Russ Ortiz .20 .07
- ❑ 133 Mike Lowell .20 .07
- ❑ 134 Reggie Sanders .20 .07
- ❑ 135 John Valentin .20 .07
- ❑ 136 Brad Ausmus .20 .07
- ❑ 137 Chad Kreuter .20 .07
- ❑ 138 David Cone .20 .07
- ❑ 139 Brook Fordyce .20 .07
- ❑ 140 Roberto Alomar .30 .10
- ❑ 141 Charles Nagy .20 .07
- ❑ 142 Brian Hunter .20 .07
- ❑ 143 Mike Mussina .30 .10
- ❑ 144 Robin Ventura .30 .10
- ❑ 145 Kevin Brown .30 .10
- ❑ 146 Pat Hentgen .20 .07
- ❑ 147 Ryan Klesko .20 .07
- ❑ 148 Derek Bell .20 .07
- ❑ 149 Andy Sheets .20 .07
- ❑ 150 Larry Walker .20 .07
- ❑ 151 Scott Williamson .20 .07
- ❑ 152 Jose Offerman .20 .07
- ❑ 153 Doug Mientkiewicz .20 .07
- ❑ 154 John Snyder RC .40 .15
- ❑ 155 Sandy Alomar Jr. .20 .07
- ❑ 156 Joe Nathan .20 .07
- ❑ 157 Lance Johnson .20 .07
- ❑ 158 Odalis Perez .20 .07
- ❑ 159 Hideo Nomo .50 .20
- ❑ 160 Steve Finley .20 .07
- ❑ 161 Dave Martinez .20 .07
- ❑ 162 Matt Walbeck .20 .07
- ❑ 163 Bill Spiers .20 .07
- ❑ 164 Fernando Tatis .20 .07
- ❑ 165 Kenny Lofton .20 .07
- ❑ 166 Paul Byrd .20 .07
- ❑ 167 Aaron Sele .20 .07
- ❑ 168 Eddie Taubensee .20 .07
- ❑ 169 Reggie Jefferson .20 .07
- ❑ 170 Roger Clemens 1.00 .40
- ❑ 171 Francisco Cordova .20 .07
- ❑ 172 Mike Bordick .20 .07
- ❑ 173 Wally Joyner .20 .07
- ❑ 174 Marvin Benard .20 .07
- ❑ 175 Jason Kendall .20 .07
- ❑ 176 Mike Stanley .20 .07
- ❑ 177 Chad Allen .20 .07
- ❑ 178 Carlos Beltran .20 .07
- ❑ 179 Deivi Cruz .20 .07
- ❑ 180 Chipper Jones .50 .20
- ❑ 181 Vladimir Guerrero .50 .20
- ❑ 182 Dave Burba .20 .07
- ❑ 183 Tom Goodwin .20 .07
- ❑ 184 Brian Daubach .20 .07
- ❑ 185 Jay Bell .20 .07
- ❑ 186 Roy Halladay .20 .07
- ❑ 187 Miguel Tejada .20 .07
- ❑ 188 Armando Rios .20 .07
- ❑ 189 Fernando Vina .20 .07
- ❑ 190 Eric Davis .20 .07
- ❑ 191 Henry Rodriguez .20 .07
- ❑ 192 Joe McEwing .20 .07
- ❑ 193 Jeff Kent .20 .07
- ❑ 194 Mike Jackson .20 .07
- ❑ 195 Mike Morgan .20 .07
- ❑ 196 Jeff Montgomery .20 .07
- ❑ 197 Jeff Zimmerman .20 .07
- ❑ 198 Tony Fernandez .20 .07
- ❑ 199 Jason Giambi .20 .07
- ❑ 200 Jose Canseco .30 .10
- ❑ 201 Alex Gonzalez .20 .07
- ❑ 202 J.Cust/Colangelo/D.Brown .40 .15
- ❑ 203 A.Soriano/F.Lopez .50 .20
- ❑ 204 Durazo/Burrell/Johnson .40 .15
- ❑ 205 John Sneed RC/K.Wells .40 .15
- ❑ 206 Kalinowski/Tejera/Mears RC .40 .15
- ❑ 207 L.Berkman/C.Patterson .40 .15
- ❑ 208 K.Pellow/K.Barker/R.Branyan .40 .15
- ❑ 209 B.Garbe/L.Bigbie RC .50 .20
- ❑ 210 B.Bradley RC/E.Munson .40 .15
- ❑ 211 J.Girdley/K.Snyder .40 .15
- ❑ 212 Chance Caple RC/J.Jennings .40 .15
- ❑ 213 B.Myers/R.Christianson RC 1.00 .40
- ❑ 214 J.Stumm/R.Purvis RC .40 .15
- ❑ 215 D.Walling/M.Paradis .40 .15
- ❑ 216 O.Ortiz/J.Gehrke .40 .15
- ❑ 217 David Cone HL .20 .07
- ❑ 218 Jose Jimenez HL .20 .07
- ❑ 219 Chris Singleton HL .20 .07
- ❑ 220 Fernando Tatis HL .20 .07
- ❑ 221 Todd Helton HL .20 .07
- ❑ 222 Kevin Millwood DIV .20 .07
- ❑ 223 Todd Pratt DIV .20 .07
- ❑ 224 Orlando Hernandez DIV .20 .07
- ❑ 225 Pedro Martinez DIV .30 .10
- ❑ 226 Tom Glavine LCS .20 .07
- ❑ 227 Bernie Williams LCS .20 .07
- ❑ 228 Mariano Rivera WS .30 .10
- ❑ 229 Tony Gwynn 20CB .60 .25
- ❑ 230 Wade Boggs 20CB .30 .10
- ❑ 231 Lance Johnson CB .20 .07
- ❑ 232 Mark McGwire 20CB 1.25 .50
- ❑ 233 Rickey Henderson 20CB .50 .20
- ❑ 234 Rickey Henderson 20CB .50 .20
- ❑ 235 Roger Clemens 20CB 1.00 .40
- ❑ 236A M.McGwire MM 1st HR 2.00 .75
- ❑ 236B M.McGwire MM 1987 ROY 2.00 .75
- ❑ 236C M.McGwire MM 62nd HR 2.00 .75
- ❑ 236D M.McGwire MM 70th HR 2.00 .75
- ❑ 236E M.McGwire MM 500th HR 2.00 .75
- ❑ 237A H.Aaron MM 1st Career HR 2.00 .75
- ❑ 237B H.Aaron MM 1957 MVP 2.00 .75

❑ 237C H.Aaron MM 3000th Hit 2.00 .75
❑ 237D H.Aaron MM 715th HR 2.00 .75
❑ 237E H.Aaron MM 755th HR 2.00 .75
❑ 238A C.Ripken MM 1982 ROY 4.00 1.50
❑ 238B C.Ripken MM 1991 MVP 4.00 1.50
❑ 238C C.Ripken MM 2131 Game 4.00 1.50
❑ 238D C.Ripken MM Streak Ends 4.00 1.50
❑ 238E C.Ripken MM 400th HR 4.00 1.50
❑ 239A W.Boggs MM 1983 Batting .75 .30
❑ 239B W.Boggs MM 1988 Batting .75 .30
❑ 239C W.Boggs MM 2000th Hit .75 .30
❑ 239D W.Boggs MM 1996 Champs .75 .30
❑ 239E W.Boggs MM 3000th Hit .75 .30
❑ 240A T.Gwynn MM 1984 Batting 1.50 .60
❑ 240B T.Gwynn MM 1984 NLCS 1.50 .60
❑ 240C T.Gwynn MM 1995 Batting 1.50 .60
❑ 240D T.Gwynn MM 1998 NLCS 1.50 .60
❑ 240E T.Gwynn MM 3000th Hit 1.50 .60
❑ 241 Tom Glavine .30 .10
❑ 242 David Wells .20 .07
❑ 243 Kevin Appier .20 .07
❑ 244 Troy Percival .20 .07
❑ 245 Ray Lankford .20 .07
❑ 246 Marquis Grissom .20 .07
❑ 247 Randy Winn .20 .07
❑ 248 Miguel Batista .20 .07
❑ 249 Darren Dreifort .20 .07
❑ 250 Barry Bonds 1.50 .60
❑ 251 Harold Baines .20 .07
❑ 252 Cliff Floyd .20 .07
❑ 253 Freddy Garcia .20 .07
❑ 254 Kenny Rogers .20 .07
❑ 255 Ben Davis .20 .07
❑ 256 Charles Johnson .20 .07
❑ 257 Bubba Trammell .20 .07
❑ 258 Desi Relaford .20 .07
❑ 259 Al Martin .20 .07
❑ 260 Andy Pettitte .30 .10
❑ 261 Carlos Lee .20 .07
❑ 262 Matt Lawton .20 .07
❑ 263 Andy Fox .20 .07
❑ 264 Chan Ho Park .20 .07
❑ 265 Billy Koch .20 .07
❑ 266 Dave Roberts .20 .07
❑ 267 Carl Everett .20 .07
❑ 268 Orel Hershiser .20 .07
❑ 269 Trot Nixon .20 .07
❑ 270 Rusty Greer .20 .07
❑ 271 Will Clark .30 .10
❑ 272 Quilvio Veras .20 .07
❑ 273 Rico Brogna .20 .07
❑ 274 Devon White .20 .07
❑ 275 Tim Hudson .20 .07
❑ 276 Mike Hampton .20 .07
❑ 277 Miguel Cairo .20 .07
❑ 278 Darren Oliver .20 .07
❑ 279 Jeff Cirillo .20 .07
❑ 280 Al Leiter .20 .07
❑ 281 Shane Andrews .20 .07
❑ 282 Carlos Febles .20 .07
❑ 283 Pedro Astacio .20 .07
❑ 284 Juan Guzman .20 .07
❑ 285 Orlando Hernandez .20 .07
❑ 286 Paul Konerko .20 .07
❑ 287 Tony Clark .20 .07
❑ 288 Aaron Boone .20 .07
❑ 289 Ismael Valdes .20 .07
❑ 290 Moises Alou .20 .07
❑ 291 Kevin Tapani .20 .07
❑ 292 John Franco .20 .07
❑ 293 Todd Zeile .20 .07
❑ 294 Jason Schmidt .20 .07
❑ 295 Johnny Damon .30 .10
❑ 296 Scott Brosius .20 .07
❑ 297 Travis Fryman .20 .07
❑ 298 Jose Vizcaino .20 .07
❑ 299 Eric Chavez .20 .07
❑ 300 Mike Piazza .75 .30
❑ 301 Matt Clement .20 .07
❑ 302 Cristian Guzman .20 .07
❑ 303 C.J. Nitkowski .20 .07
❑ 304 Michael Tucker .20 .07
❑ 305 Brett Tomko .20 .07
❑ 306 Mike Lansing .20 .07
❑ 307 Eric Owens .20 .07
❑ 308 Livan Hernandez .20 .07
❑ 309 Rondell White .20 .07
❑ 310 Todd Stottlemyre .20 .07
❑ 311 Chris Carpenter .20 .07
❑ 312 Ken Hill .20 .07
❑ 313 Mark Loretta .20 .07
❑ 314 John Rocker .20 .07
❑ 315 Richie Sexson .20 .07
❑ 316 Ruben Mateo .20 .07
❑ 317 Joe Randa .20 .07
❑ 318 Mike Sirotka .20 .07
❑ 319 Jose Rosado .20 .07
❑ 320 Matt Mantei .20 .07
❑ 321 Kevin Millwood .20 .07
❑ 322 Gary Disarcina .20 .07
❑ 323 Dustin Hermanson .20 .07
❑ 324 Mike Stanton .20 .07
❑ 325 Kirk Rueter .20 .07
❑ 326 Damian Miller RC .40 .15
❑ 327 Doug Glanville .20 .07
❑ 328 Scott Rolen .30 .10
❑ 329 Ray Durham .20 .07
❑ 330 Butch Huskey .20 .07
❑ 331 Mariano Rivera .50 .20
❑ 332 Darren Lewis .20 .07
❑ 333 Mike Timlin .20 .07
❑ 334 Mark Grudzielanek .20 .07
❑ 335 Mike Cameron .20 .07
❑ 336 Kelvim Escobar .20 .07
❑ 337 Bret Boone .20 .07
❑ 338 Mo Vaughn .20 .07
❑ 339 Craig Biggio .30 .10
❑ 340 Michael Barrett .20 .07
❑ 341 Marlon Anderson .20 .07
❑ 342 Bobby Jones .20 .07
❑ 343 John Halama .20 .07
❑ 344 Todd Ritchie .20 .07
❑ 345 Chuck Knoblauch .20 .07
❑ 346 Rick Reed .20 .07
❑ 347 Kelly Stinnett .20 .07
❑ 348 Tim Salmon .30 .10
❑ 349 A.J. Hinch .20 .07
❑ 350 Jose Cruz Jr. .20 .07
❑ 351 Roberto Hernandez .20 .07
❑ 352 Edgar Renteria .20 .07
❑ 353 Jose Hernandez .20 .07
❑ 354 Brad Fullmer .20 .07
❑ 355 Trevor Hoffman .20 .07
❑ 356 Troy O'Leary .20 .07
❑ 357 Justin Thompson .20 .07
❑ 358 Kevin Young .20 .07
❑ 359 Hideki Irabu .20 .07
❑ 360 Jim Thome .30 .10
❑ 361 Steve Karsay .20 .07
❑ 362 Octavio Dotel .20 .07
❑ 363 Omar Vizquel .30 .10
❑ 364 Raul Mondesi .20 .07
❑ 365 Shane Reynolds .20 .07
❑ 366 Bartolo Colon .20 .07
❑ 367 Chris Widger .20 .07
❑ 368 Gabe Kapler .20 .07
❑ 369 Bill Simas .20 .07
❑ 370 Tino Martinez .30 .10
❑ 371 John Thomson .20 .07
❑ 372 Delino Deshields .20 .07
❑ 373 Carlos Perez .20 .07
❑ 374 Eddie Perez .20 .07
❑ 375 Jeromy Burnitz .20 .07
❑ 376 Jimmy Haynes .20 .07
❑ 377 Travis Lee .20 .07
❑ 378 Darryl Hamilton .20 .07
❑ 379 Jamie Moyer .20 .07
❑ 380 Alex Gonzalez .20 .07
❑ 381 John Wetteland .20 .07
❑ 382 Vinny Castilla .20 .07
❑ 383 Jeff Suppan .20 .07
❑ 384 Jim Leyritz .20 .07
❑ 385 Robb Nen .20 .07
❑ 386 Wilson Alvarez .20 .07
❑ 387 Andres Galarraga .20 .07
❑ 388 Mike Remlinger .20 .07
❑ 389 Geoff Jenkins .20 .07
❑ 390 Matt Stairs .20 .07
❑ 391 Bill Mueller .20 .07
❑ 392 Mike Lowell .20 .07
❑ 393 Andy Ashby .20 .07
❑ 394 Ruben Rivera .20 .07
❑ 395 Todd Helton .30 .10
❑ 396 Bernie Williams .30 .10
❑ 397 Royce Clayton .20 .07
❑ 398 Manny Ramirez .30 .10
❑ 399 Kerry Wood .20 .07
❑ 400 Ken Griffey Jr. .75 .30
❑ 401 Enrique Wilson .20 .07
❑ 402 Joey Hamilton .20 .07
❑ 403 Shawn Estes .20 .07
❑ 404 Ugueth Urbina .20 .07
❑ 405 Albert Belle .20 .07
❑ 406 Rick Helling .20 .07
❑ 407 Steve Parris .20 .07
❑ 408 Eric Milton .20 .07
❑ 409 Dave Mlicki .20 .07
❑ 410 Shawn Green .20 .07
❑ 411 Jaret Wright .20 .07
❑ 412 Tony Womack .20 .07
❑ 413 Vernon Wells .20 .07
❑ 414 Ron Belliard .20 .07
❑ 415 Ellis Burks .20 .07
❑ 416 Scott Erickson .20 .07
❑ 417 Rafael Palmeiro .30 .10
❑ 418 Damion Easley .20 .07
❑ 419 Jamey Wright .20 .07
❑ 420 Corey Koskie .20 .07
❑ 421 Bobby Howry .20 .07
❑ 422 Ricky Ledee .20 .07
❑ 423 Dmitri Young .20 .07
❑ 424 Sidney Ponson .20 .07
❑ 425 Greg Maddux .75 .30
❑ 426 Jose Guillen .20 .07
❑ 427 Jon Lieber .20 .07
❑ 428 Andy Benes .20 .07
❑ 429 Randy Velarde .20 .07
❑ 430 Sean Casey .20 .07
❑ 431 Torii Hunter .20 .07
❑ 432 Ryan Rupe .20 .07
❑ 433 David Segui .20 .07
❑ 434 Todd Pratt .20 .07
❑ 435 Nomar Garciaparra .75 .30
❑ 436 Denny Neagle .20 .07
❑ 437 Ron Coomer .20 .07
❑ 438 Chris Singleton .20 .07
❑ 439 Tony Batista .20 .07
❑ 440 Andruw Jones .30 .10
❑ 441 Burroughs/Piatt/Huff .20 .07
❑ 442 Rafael Furcal .40 .15
❑ 443 M.Lamb RC/J.Crede 1.00 .40
❑ 444 Julio Zuleta RC .40 .15
❑ 445 Garry Maddox Jr. RC .40 .15
❑ 446 Riley/Sabathia/Mulder .40 .15
❑ 447 Scott Downs RC .40 .15
❑ 448 D.Mirabelli/B.Petrick/J.Werth .40 .15
❑ 449 C.Myers RC/J.Hamilton .50 .20
❑ 450 B.Christensen/R.Stahl RC .40 .15
❑ 451 B.Zito/B.Sheets RC 2.50 1.00
❑ 452 K.Ainsworth/Howington RC .40 .15
❑ 453 R.Asadoorian/V.Faison RC .40 .15
❑ 454 K.Reed/J.Heaverlo RC .40 .15
❑ 455 M.MacDougal/B.Baker RC .40 .15
❑ 456 Mark McGwire SH .60 .25
❑ 457 Cal Ripken SH .75 .30
❑ 458 Wade Boggs SH .20 .07
❑ 459 Tony Gwynn SH .30 .10
❑ 460 Jesse Orosco SH .20 .07
❑ 461 L.Walker/N.Garciaparra LL .30 .10
❑ 462 K.Griffey Jr./M.McGwire LL .50 .20
❑ 463 M.Ramirez/M.McGwire LL .50 .20
❑ 464 P.Martinez/R.Johnson LL .30 .10
❑ 465 P.Martinez/R.Johnson LL .30 .10
❑ 466 D.Jeter/L.Gonzalez LL .50 .20
❑ 467 L.Walker/M.Ramirez LL .30 .10
❑ 468 Tony Gwynn 20CB .60 .25
❑ 469 Mark McGwire 20CB 1.25 .50
❑ 470 Frank Thomas 20CB .30 .10
❑ 471 Harold Baines 20CB .20 .07
❑ 472 Roger Clemens 20CB 1.00 .40
❑ 473 John Franco 20CB .20 .07
❑ 474 John Franco 20CB .20 .07
❑ 475A K.Griffey Jr. MM 350th HR 2.00 .75
❑ 475B K.Griffey Jr. MM 1997 MVP 2.00 .75
❑ 475C K.Griffey Jr. MM HR Dad 2.00 .75
❑ 475D K.Griffey Jr. MM 1992 AS MVP 2.00 .75
❑ 475E K.Griffey Jr. MM 50 HR 1997 2.00 .75
❑ 476A B.Bonds MM 400HR/400SB 3.00 1.25

❑ 476B B.Bonds MM 40HR/40SB	3.00	1.25
❑ 476C B.Bonds MM 1993 MVP	3.00	1.25
❑ 476D B.Bonds MM 1990 MVP	3.00	1.25
❑ 476E B.Bonds MM 1992 MVP	3.00	1.25
❑ 477A S.Sosa MM 20 HR June	2.00	.75
❑ 477B S.Sosa MM 66 HR 1998	2.00	.75
❑ 477C S.Sosa MM 60 HR 1999	2.00	.75
❑ 477D S.Sosa MM 1998 MVP	2.00	.75
❑ 477E S.Sosa MM HR's 61/62	2.00	.75
❑ 478A D.Jeter MM 1996 ROY	3.00	1.25
❑ 478B D.Jeter MM Wins 1999 WS	3.00	1.25
❑ 478C D.Jeter MM Wins 1998 WS	3.00	1.25
❑ 478D D.Jeter MM Wins 1996 WS	3.00	1.25
❑ 478E D.Jeter MM 17 GM Hit Streak	3.00	1.25
❑ 479A A.Rodriguez MM 40HR/40SB	2.00	.75
❑ 479B A.Rodriguez MM 100th HR	2.00	.75
❑ 479C A.Rodriguez MM 1996 POY	2.00	.75
❑ 479D A.Rodriguez MM Wins 1 Million	2.00	.75
❑ 479E A.Rodriguez MM 1996 Batting Leader	2.00	.75
❑ NNO M.McGwire 85 Reprint	5.00	2.00

2000 Topps Traded

❑ COMP.FACT.SET (136)	40.00	25.00
❑ COMPLETE SET (135)	30.00	15.00
❑ FACT.SET PRICE IS FOR SEALED SETS		
❑ T1 Mike MacDougal	.30	.10
❑ T2 Andy Tracy RC	.30	.10
❑ T3 Brandon Phillips RC	1.00	.40
❑ T4 Brandon Inge RC	2.00	.75
❑ T5 Robbie Morrison RC	.30	.10
❑ T6 Josh Pressley RC	.30	.10
❑ T7 Todd Moser RC	.30	.10
❑ T8 Rob Purvis	.30	.10
❑ T9 Chance Caple	.20	.07
❑ T10 Ben Sheets	1.00	.40
❑ T11 Russ Jacobson RC	.30	.10
❑ T12 Brian Cole RC	.30	.10
❑ T13 Brad Baker	.20	.07
❑ T14 Alex Cintron RC	.30	.10
❑ T15 Lyle Overbay RC	.75	.30
❑ T16 Mike Edwards RC	.30	.10
❑ T17 Sean McGowan RC	.30	.10
❑ T18 Jose Molina	.20	.07
❑ T19 Marcos Castillo RC	.30	.10
❑ T20 Josue Espada RC	.30	.10
❑ T21 Alex Gordon RC	.30	.10
❑ T22 Rob Pugmire RC	.30	.10
❑ T23 Jason Stumm	.20	.07
❑ T24 Ty Howington	.20	.07
❑ T25 Brett Myers	.60	.25
❑ T26 Maicer Izturis RC	.30	.10
❑ T27 John McDonald	.20	.07
❑ T28 Wilfredo Rodriguez RC	.30	.10
❑ T29 Carlos Zambrano RC	4.00	1.50
❑ T30 Alejandro Diaz RC	.30	.10
❑ T31 Geraldo Guzman RC	.30	.10
❑ T32 J.R. House RC	.30	.10
❑ T33 Elvin Nina RC	.30	.10
❑ T34 Juan Pierre RC	.60	.25
❑ T35 Ben Johnson RC	1.25	.50
❑ T36 Jeff Bailey RC	.30	.10
❑ T37 Miguel Olivo RC	.50	.20
❑ T38 Francisco Rodriguez RC	1.50	.60
❑ T39 Tony Pena Jr. RC	.30	.10
❑ T40 Miguel Cabrera RC	15.00	6.00
❑ T41 Asdrubal Oropeza RC	.30	.10
❑ T42 Junior Zamora RC	.30	.10
❑ T43 Jovanny Cedeno RC	.30	.10
❑ T44 John Sneed	.30	.10
❑ T45 Josh Kalinowski	.30	.10
❑ T46 Mike Young RC	4.00	1.50
❑ T47 Rico Washington RC	.30	.10
❑ T48 Chad Durbin RC	.30	.10
❑ T49 Junior Brignac RC	.30	.10
❑ T50 Carlos Hernandez RC	.30	.10
❑ T51 Cesar Izturis RC	.50	.20
❑ T52 Oscar Salazar RC	.30	.10
❑ T53 Pat Strange RC	.30	.10
❑ T54 Rick Asadoorian	.30	.10
❑ T55 Keith Reed	.20	.07
❑ T56 Leo Estrella RC	.30	.10
❑ T57 Wascar Serrano RC	.30	.10
❑ T58 Richard Gomez RC	.30	.10
❑ T59 Ramon Santiago RC	.30	.10
❑ T60 Jovanny Sosa RC	.30	.10
❑ T61 Aaron Rowand RC	1.25	.50
❑ T62 Junior Guerrero RC	.30	.10
❑ T63 Luis Terrero RC	.30	.10
❑ T64 Brian Sanches RC	.30	.10
❑ T65 Scott Sobkowiak RC	.30	.10
❑ T66 Gary Majewski RC	.30	.10
❑ T67 Barry Zito	1.25	.50
❑ T68 Ryan Christianson	.20	.07
❑ T69 Cristian Guerrero RC	.30	.10
❑ T70 Tomas De La Rosa RC	.30	.10
❑ T71 Andrew Beinbrink RC	.30	.10
❑ T72 Ryan Knox RC	.30	.10
❑ T73 Alex Graman RC	.30	.10
❑ T74 Juan Guzman RC	.30	.10
❑ T75 Ruben Salazar RC	.30	.10
❑ T76 Luis Matos RC	.30	.10
❑ T77 Tony Mota RC	.30	.10
❑ T78 Doug Davis	.30	.10
❑ T79 Ben Christensen	.20	.07
❑ T80 Mike Lamb	.50	.20
❑ T81 Adrian Gonzalez RC	2.50	1.00
❑ T82 Mike Stodolka RC	.30	.10
❑ T83 Adam Johnson RC	.30	.10
❑ T84 Matt Wheatland RC	.30	.10
❑ T85 Corey Smith RC	.30	.10
❑ T86 Rocco Baldelli RC	1.25	.50
❑ T87 Keith Bucktrot RC	.30	.10
❑ T88 Adam Wainwright RC	1.00	.40
❑ T89 Scott Thorman RC	.75	.30
❑ T90 Tripper Johnson RC	.30	.10
❑ T91 Jim Edmonds Cards	.30	.10
❑ T92 Masato Yoshii	.20	.07
❑ T93 Adam Kennedy	.20	.07
❑ T94 Darryl Kile	.30	.10
❑ T95 Mark McLemore	.20	.07
❑ T96 Ricky Gutierrez	.20	.07
❑ T97 Juan Gonzalez	.30	.10
❑ T98 Melvin Mora	.30	.10
❑ T99 Dante Bichette	.30	.10
❑ T100 Lee Stevens	.20	.07
❑ T101 Roger Cedeno	.20	.07
❑ T102 John Olerud	.30	.10
❑ T103 Eric Young	.20	.07
❑ T104 Mickey Morandini	.20	.07
❑ T105 Travis Lee	.20	.07
❑ T106 Greg Vaughn	.20	.07
❑ T107 Todd Zeile	.30	.10
❑ T108 Chuck Finley	.30	.10
❑ T109 Ismael Valdes	.20	.07
❑ T110 Reggie Sanders	.30	.10
❑ T111 Pat Hentgen	.20	.07
❑ T112 Ryan Klesko	.30	.10
❑ T113 Derek Bell	.20	.07
❑ T114 Hideo Nomo	.75	.30
❑ T115 Aaron Sele	.20	.07
❑ T116 Fernando Vina	.20	.07
❑ T117 Wally Joyner	.30	.10
❑ T118 Brian Hunter	.20	.07
❑ T119 Joe Girardi	.20	.07
❑ T120 Omar Daal	.20	.07
❑ T121 Brook Fordyce	.20	.07
❑ T122 Jose Valentin	.20	.07
❑ T123 Curt Schilling	.30	.10
❑ T124 B.J. Surhoff	.30	.10
❑ T125 Henry Rodriguez	.20	.07
❑ T126 Mike Bordick	.20	.07
❑ T127 David Justice	.30	.10
❑ T128 Charles Johnson	.30	.10
❑ T129 Will Clark	.50	.20
❑ T130 Dwight Gooden	.30	.10
❑ T131 David Segui	.20	.07
❑ T132 Denny Neagle	.30	.10
❑ T133 Jose Canseco	.50	.20
❑ T134 Bruce Chen	.20	.07
❑ T135 Jason Bere	.20	.07

2001 Topps

❑ COMPLETE SET (790)	80.00	40.00
❑ COMP.FACT.BLUE SET (795)	120.00	60.00
❑ COMPLETE SERIES 1 (405)	40.00	20.00
❑ COMPLETE SERIES 2 (385)	40.00	20.00
❑ COMMON CARD (1-6/8-791)	.20	.07
❑ COMMON (352-376/727-751)	.25	.08
❑ 1 Cal Ripken	1.50	.60
❑ 2 Chipper Jones	.50	.20
❑ 3 Roger Cedeno	.20	.07
❑ 4 Garret Anderson	.20	.07
❑ 5 Robin Ventura	.20	.07
❑ 6 Daryle Ward	.20	.07
❑ 7 Does Not Exist		
❑ 8 Craig Paquette	.20	.07
❑ 9 Phil Nevin	.20	.07
❑ 10 Jermaine Dye	.20	.07
❑ 11 Chris Singleton	.20	.07
❑ 12 Mike Stanton	.20	.07
❑ 13 Brian Hunter	.20	.07
❑ 14 Mike Redmond	.20	.07
❑ 15 Jim Thome	.30	.10
❑ 16 Brian Jordan	.20	.07
❑ 17 Joe Girardi	.20	.07
❑ 18 Steve Woodard	.20	.07
❑ 19 Dustin Hermanson	.20	.07
❑ 20 Shawn Green	.20	.07
❑ 21 Todd Stottlemyre	.20	.07
❑ 22 Dan Wilson	.20	.07
❑ 23 Todd Pratt	.20	.07
❑ 24 Derek Lowe	.20	.07
❑ 25 Juan Gonzalez	.20	.07
❑ 26 Clay Bellinger	.20	.07
❑ 27 Jeff Fassero	.20	.07
❑ 28 Pat Meares	.20	.07
❑ 29 Eddie Taubensee	.20	.07
❑ 30 Paul O'Neill	.30	.10
❑ 31 Jeffrey Hammonds	.20	.07
❑ 32 Pokey Reese	.20	.07
❑ 33 Mike Mussina	.30	.10
❑ 34 Rico Brogna	.20	.07
❑ 35 Jay Buhner	.20	.07
❑ 36 Steve Cox	.20	.07
❑ 37 Quilvio Veras	.20	.07
❑ 38 Marquis Grissom	.20	.07
❑ 39 Shigetoshi Hasegawa	.20	.07
❑ 40 Shane Reynolds	.20	.07
❑ 41 Adam Piatt	.20	.07
❑ 42 Luis Polonia	.20	.07
❑ 43 Brook Fordyce	.20	.07
❑ 44 Preston Wilson	.20	.07
❑ 45 Ellis Burks	.20	.07
❑ 46 Armando Rios	.20	.07
❑ 47 Chuck Finley	.20	.07
❑ 48 Dan Plesac	.20	.07
❑ 49 Shannon Stewart	.20	.07
❑ 50 Mark McGwire	1.25	.50
❑ 51 Mark Loretta	.20	.07
❑ 52 Gerald Williams	.20	.07
❑ 53 Eric Young	.20	.07

No.	Player		
54	Peter Bergeron	.20	.07
55	Dave Hansen	.20	.07
56	Arthur Rhodes	.20	.07
57	Bobby Jones	.20	.07
58	Matt Clement	.20	.07
59	Mike Benjamin	.20	.07
60	Pedro Martinez	.30	.10
61	Jose Canseco	.30	.10
62	Matt Anderson	.20	.07
63	Torii Hunter	.20	.07
64	Carlos Lee	.20	.07
65	David Cone	.20	.07
66	Rey Sanchez	.20	.07
67	Eric Chavez	.20	.07
68	Rick Helling	.20	.07
69	Manny Alexander	.20	.07
70	John Franco	.20	.07
71	Mike Bordick	.20	.07
72	Andres Galarraga	.20	.07
73	Jose Cruz Jr.	.20	.07
74	Mike Matheny	.20	.07
75	Randy Johnson	.50	.20
76	Richie Sexson	.20	.07
77	Vladimir Nunez	.20	.07
78	Harold Baines	.20	.07
79	Aaron Boone	.20	.07
80	Darin Erstad	.20	.07
81	Alex Gonzalez	.20	.07
82	Gil Heredia	.20	.07
83	Shane Andrews	.20	.07
84	Todd Hundley	.20	.07
85	Bill Mueller	.20	.07
86	Mark McLemore	.20	.07
87	Scott Spiezio	.20	.07
88	Kevin McGlinchy	.20	.07
89	Bubba Trammell	.20	.07
90	Manny Ramirez	.30	.10
91	Mike Lamb	.20	.07
92	Scott Karl	.20	.07
93	Brian Buchanan	.20	.07
94	Chris Turner	.20	.07
95	Mike Sweeney	.20	.07
96	John Wetteland	.20	.07
97	Rob Bell	.20	.07
98	Pat Rapp	.20	.07
99	John Burkett	.20	.07
100	Derek Jeter	1.25	.50
101	J.D. Drew	.20	.07
102	Jose Offerman	.20	.07
103	Rick Reed	.20	.07
104	Will Clark	.30	.10
105	Rickey Henderson	.50	.20
106	Dave Berg	.20	.07
107	Kirk Rueter	.20	.07
108	Lee Stevens	.20	.07
109	Jay Bell	.20	.07
110	Fred McGriff	.30	.10
111	Julio Zuleta	.20	.07
112	Brian Anderson	.20	.07
113	Orlando Cabrera	.20	.07
114	Alex Fernandez	.20	.07
115	Derek Bell	.20	.07
116	Eric Owens	.20	.07
117	Brian Bohanon	.20	.07
118	Dennys Reyes	.20	.07
119	Mike Stanley	.20	.07
120	Jorge Posada	.30	.10
121	Rich Becker	.20	.07
122	Paul Konerko	.20	.07
123	Mike Remlinger	.20	.07
124	Travis Lee	.20	.07
125	Ken Caminiti	.20	.07
126	Kevin Barker	.20	.07
127	Paul Quantrill	.20	.07
128	Ozzie Guillen	.20	.07
129	Kevin Tapani	.20	.07
130	Mark Johnson	.20	.07
131	Randy Wolf	.20	.07
132	Michael Tucker	.20	.07
133	Darren Lewis	.20	.07
134	Joe Randa	.20	.07
135	Jeff Cirillo	.20	.07
136	David Ortiz	.50	.20
137	Herb Perry	.20	.07
138	Jeff Nelson	.20	.07
139	Chris Stynes	.20	.07
140	Johnny Damon	.30	.10
141	Jeff Reboulet	.20	.07
142	Jason Schmidt	.20	.07
143	Charles Johnson	.20	.07
144	Pat Burrell	.20	.07
145	Gary Sheffield	.20	.07
146	Tom Glavine	.30	.10
147	Jason Isringhausen	.20	.07
148	Chris Carpenter	.20	.07
149	Jeff Suppan	.20	.07
150	Ivan Rodriguez	.30	.10
151	Luis Sojo	.20	.07
152	Ron Villone	.20	.07
153	Mike Sirotka	.20	.07
154	Chuck Knoblauch	.20	.07
155	Jason Kendall	.20	.07
156	Dennis Cook	.20	.07
157	Bobby Estalella	.20	.07
158	Jose Guillen	.20	.07
159	Thomas Howard	.20	.07
160	Carlos Delgado	.20	.07
161	Benji Gil	.20	.07
162	Tim Bogar	.20	.07
163	Kevin Elster	.20	.07
164	Einar Diaz	.20	.07
165	Andy Benes	.20	.07
166	Adrian Beltre	.20	.07
167	David Bell	.20	.07
168	Turk Wendell	.20	.07
169	Pete Harnisch	.20	.07
170	Roger Clemens	1.00	.40
171	Scott Williamson	.20	.07
172	Kevin Jordan	.20	.07
173	Brad Penny	.20	.07
174	John Flaherty	.20	.07
175	Troy Glaus	.20	.07
176	Kevin Appier	.20	.07
177	Walt Weiss	.20	.07
178	Tyler Houston	.20	.07
179	Michael Barrett	.20	.07
180	Mike Hampton	.20	.07
181	Francisco Cordova	.20	.07
182	Mike Jackson	.20	.07
183	David Segui	.20	.07
184	Carlos Febles	.20	.07
185	Roy Halladay	.20	.07
186	Seth Etherton	.20	.07
187	Charlie Hayes	.20	.07
188	Fernando Tatis	.20	.07
189	Steve Trachsel	.20	.07
190	Livan Hernandez	.20	.07
191	Joe Oliver	.20	.07
192	Stan Javier	.20	.07
193	B.J. Surhoff	.20	.07
194	Rob Ducey	.20	.07
195	Barry Larkin	.30	.10
196	Danny Patterson	.20	.07
197	Bobby Howry	.20	.07
198	Dmitri Young	.20	.07
199	Brian Hunter	.20	.07
200	Alex Rodriguez	.75	.30
201	Hideo Nomo	.50	.20
202	Luis Alicea	.20	.07
203	Warren Morris	.20	.07
204	Antonio Alfonseca	.20	.07
205	Edgardo Alfonzo	.20	.07
206	Mark Grudzielanek	.20	.07
207	Fernando Vina	.20	.07
208	Willie Greene	.20	.07
209	Homer Bush	.20	.07
210	Jason Giambi	.20	.07
211	Mike Morgan	.20	.07
212	Steve Karsay	.20	.07
213	Matt Lawton	.20	.07
214	Wendell Magee Jr.	.20	.07
215	Rusty Greer	.20	.07
216	Keith Lockhart	.20	.07
217	Billy Koch	.20	.07
218	Todd Hollandsworth	.20	.07
219	Raul Ibanez	.20	.07
220	Tony Gwynn	.60	.25
221	Carl Everett	.20	.07
222	Hector Carrasco	.20	.07
223	Jose Valentin	.20	.07
224	Deivi Cruz	.20	.07
225	Bret Boone	.20	.07
226	Kurt Abbott	.20	.07
227	Melvin Mora	.20	.07
228	Danny Graves	.20	.07
229	Jose Jimenez	.20	.07
230	James Baldwin	.20	.07
231	C.J. Nitkowski	.20	.07
232	Jeff Zimmerman	.20	.07
233	Mike Lowell	.20	.07
234	Hideki Irabu	.20	.07
235	Greg Vaughn	.20	.07
236	Omar Daal	.20	.07
237	Darren Dreifort	.20	.07
238	Gil Meche	.20	.07
239	Damian Jackson	.20	.07
240	Frank Thomas	.50	.20
241	Travis Miller	.20	.07
242	Jeff Frye	.20	.07
243	Dave Magadan	.20	.07
244	Luis Castillo	.20	.07
245	Bartolo Colon	.20	.07
246	Steve Kline	.20	.07
247	Shawon Dunston	.20	.07
248	Rick Aguilera	.20	.07
249	Omar Olivares	.20	.07
250	Craig Biggio	.30	.10
251	Scott Schoeneweis	.20	.07
252	Dave Veres	.20	.07
253	Ramon Martinez	.20	.07
254	Jose Vidro	.20	.07
255	Todd Helton	.30	.10
256	Greg Norton	.20	.07
257	Jacque Jones	.20	.07
258	Jason Grimsley	.20	.07
259	Dan Reichert	.20	.07
260	Robb Nen	.20	.07
261	Mark Clark	.20	.07
262	Scott Hatteberg	.20	.07
263	Doug Brocail	.20	.07
264	Mark Johnson	.20	.07
265	Eric Davis	.20	.07
266	Terry Shumpert	.20	.07
267	Kevin Millar	.20	.07
268	Ismael Valdes	.20	.07
269	Richard Hidalgo	.20	.07
270	Randy Velarde	.20	.07
271	Bengie Molina	.20	.07
272	Tony Womack	.20	.07
273	Enrique Wilson	.20	.07
274	Jeff Brantley	.20	.07
275	Rick Ankiel	.20	.07
276	Terry Mulholland	.20	.07
277	Ron Belliard	.20	.07
278	Terrence Long	.20	.07
279	Alberto Castillo	.20	.07
280	Royce Clayton	.20	.07
281	Joe McEwing	.20	.07
282	Jason McDonald	.20	.07
283	Ricky Bottalico	.20	.07
284	Keith Foulke	.20	.07
285	Brad Radke	.20	.07
286	Gabe Kapler	.20	.07
287	Pedro Astacio	.20	.07
288	Armando Reynoso	.20	.07
289	Darryl Kile	.20	.07
290	Reggie Sanders	.20	.07
291	Esteban Yan	.20	.07
292	Joe Nathan	.20	.07
293	Jay Payton	.20	.07
294	Francisco Cordero	.20	.07
295	Gregg Jefferies	.20	.07
296	LaTroy Hawkins	.20	.07
297	Jeff Tam RC	.40	.15
298	Jacob Cruz	.20	.07
299	Chris Holt	.20	.07
300	Vladimir Guerrero	.50	.20
301	Marvin Benard	.20	.07
302	Alex Ramirez	.20	.07
303	Mike Williams	.20	.07
304	Sean Bergman	.20	.07
305	Juan Encarnacion	.20	.07
306	Russ Davis	.20	.07
307	Hanley Frias	.20	.07
308	Ramon Hernandez	.20	.07
309	Matt Walbeck	.20	.07
310	Bill Spiers	.20	.07
311	Bob Wickman	.20	.07

No.	Player		
312	Sandy Alomar Jr.	.20	.07
313	Eddie Guardado	.20	.07
314	Shane Halter	.20	.07
315	Geoff Jenkins	.20	.07
316	Brian Meadows	.20	.07
317	Damian Miller	.20	.07
318	Darrin Fletcher	.20	.07
319	Rafael Furcal	.20	.07
320	Mark Grace	.30	.10
321	Mark Mulder	.20	.07
322	Joe Torre MG	.30	.10
323	Bobby Cox MG	.20	.07
324	Mike Scioscia MG	.20	.07
325	Mike Hargrove MG	.20	.07
326	Jimy Williams MG	.20	.07
327	Jerry Manuel MG	.20	.07
328	Buck Showalter MG	.20	.07
329	Charlie Manuel MG	.20	.07
330	Don Baylor MG	.20	.07
331	Phil Garner MG	.20	.07
332	Jack McKeon MG	.20	.07
333	Tony Muser MG	.20	.07
334	Buddy Bell MG	.20	.07
335	Tom Kelly MG	.20	.07
336	John Boles MG	.20	.07
337	Art Howe MG	.20	.07
338	Larry Dierker MG	.20	.07
339	Lou Piniella MG	.20	.07
340	Davey Johnson MG	.20	.07
341	Larry Rothschild MG	.20	.07
342	Davey Lopes MG	.20	.07
343	Johnny Oates MG	.20	.07
344	Felipe Alou MG	.20	.07
345	Jim Fregosi MG	.20	.07
346	Bobby Valentine MG	.20	.07
347	Terry Francona MG	.20	.07
348	Gene Lamont MG	.20	.07
349	Tony LaRussa MG	.20	.07
350	Bruce Bochy MG	.20	.07
351	Dusty Baker MG	.20	.07
352	A.Gonzalez/A.Johnson	.25	.08
353	M.Wheatland/B.Digby	.25	.08
354	T.Johnson/S.Thorman	.25	.08
355	P.Dumatrait/A.Wainwright	.25	.08
356	David Parrish RC	.25	.08
357	M.Folsom RC/R.Baldelli	.40	.15
358	Dominic Rich RC	.25	.08
359	M.Stodolka/S.Burnett	.25	.08
360	D.Thompson/C.Smith	.25	.08
361	D.Borrell RC/J.Bourgeois RC	.25	.08
362	Chen/Patterson/Hamilton	.50	.20
363	B.Zito/C.Sabathia	.50	.20
364	Ben Sheets	.50	.20
365	Howington/Kalinowski/Girdley	.25	.08
366	Hee Seop Choi RC	.50	.20
367	Bradley/Ainsworth/Tsao	.40	.15
368	Glendenning/Kelly/Silvestre	.25	.08
369	J.R. House	.25	.08
370	Rafael Soriano RC	.40	.15
371	T.Hafner RC/B.Jacobsen	4.00	1.50
372	Conti/Wakeland/Cole	.25	.08
373	Seabol/Huff/Crede	.75	.30
374	Everett/Ortiz/Ginter	.25	.08
375	Hernandez/Guzman/Eaton	.25	.08
376	Kielty/Bradley/J.Rivera	.40	.15
377	Mark McGwire GM	.60	.25
378	Don Larsen GM	.20	.07
379	Bobby Thomson GM	.20	.07
380	Bill Mazeroski GM	.20	.07
381	Reggie Jackson GM	.30	.10
382	Kirk Gibson GM	.20	.07
383	Roger Maris GM	.30	.10
384	Cal Ripken GM	.75	.30
385	Hank Aaron GM	.50	.20
386	Joe Carter GM	.20	.07
387	Cal Ripken SH	1.50	.60
388	Randy Johnson SH	.30	.10
389	Ken Griffey Jr. SH	.75	.30
390	Troy Glaus SH	.20	.07
391	Kazuhiro Sasaki SH	.20	.07
392	S.Sosa/T.Glaus LL	.30	.10
393	T.Helton/E.Martinez LL	.20	.07
394	T.Helton/N.Garicaparra LL	.50	.20
395	B.Bonds/J.Giambi LL	.75	.30
396	T.Helton/M.Ramirez LL	.20	.07
397	T.Helton/D.Erstad LL	.20	.07
398	K.Brown/P.Martinez LL	.30	.10
399	R.Johnson/P.Martinez LL	.30	.10
400	Will Clark HL	.30	.10
401	New York Mets HL	.50	.20
402	New York Yankees HL	.75	.30
403	Seattle Mariners HL	.20	.07
404	Mike Hampton HL	.20	.07
405	New York Yankees HL	1.00	.40
406	New York Yankees Champs	2.00	.75
407	Jeff Bagwell	.30	.10
408	Brant Brown	.20	.07
409	Brad Fullmer	.20	.07
410	Dean Palmer	.20	.07
411	Greg Zaun	.20	.07
412	Jose Vizcaino	.20	.07
413	Jeff Abbott	.20	.07
414	Travis Fryman	.20	.07
415	Mike Cameron	.20	.07
416	Matt Mantei	.20	.07
417	Alan Benes	.20	.07
418	Mickey Morandini	.20	.07
419	Troy Percival	.20	.07
420	Eddie Perez	.20	.07
421	Vernon Wells	.20	.07
422	Ricky Gutierrez	.20	.07
423	Carlos Hernandez	.20	.07
424	Chan Ho Park	.20	.07
425	Armando Benitez	.20	.07
426	Sidney Ponson	.20	.07
427	Adrian Brown	.20	.07
428	Ruben Mateo	.20	.07
429	Alex Ochoa	.20	.07
430	Jose Rosado	.20	.07
431	Masato Yoshii	.20	.07
432	Corey Koskie	.20	.07
433	Andy Pettitte	.30	.10
434	Brian Daubach	.20	.07
435	Sterling Hitchcock	.20	.07
436	Timo Perez	.20	.07
437	Shawn Estes	.20	.07
438	Tony Armas Jr.	.20	.07
439	Danny Bautista	.20	.07
440	Randy Winn	.20	.07
441	Wilson Alvarez	.20	.07
442	Rondell White	.20	.07
443	Jeromy Burnitz	.20	.07
444	Kelvim Escobar	.20	.07
445	Paul Bako	.20	.07
446	Javier Vazquez	.20	.07
447	Eric Gagne	.20	.07
448	Kenny Lofton	.20	.07
449	Mark Kotsay	.20	.07
450	Jamie Moyer	.20	.07
451	Delino DeShields	.20	.07
452	Rey Ordonez	.20	.07
453	Russ Ortiz	.20	.07
454	Dave Burba	.20	.07
455	Eric Karros	.20	.07
456	Felix Martinez	.20	.07
457	Tony Batista	.20	.07
458	Bobby Higginson	.20	.07
459	Jeff D'Amico	.20	.07
460	Shane Spencer	.20	.07
461	Brent Mayne	.20	.07
462	Glendon Rusch	.20	.07
463	Chris Gomez	.20	.07
464	Jeff Shaw	.20	.07
465	Damon Buford	.20	.07
466	Mike DiFelice	.20	.07
467	Jimmy Haynes	.20	.07
468	Billy Wagner	.20	.07
469	A.J. Hinch	.20	.07
470	Gary DiSarcina	.20	.07
471	Tom Lampkin	.20	.07
472	Adam Eaton	.20	.07
473	Brian Giles	.20	.07
474	John Thomson	.20	.07
475	Cal Eldred	.20	.07
476	Ramiro Mendoza	.20	.07
477	Scott Sullivan	.20	.07
478	Scott Rolen	.30	.10
479	Todd Ritchie	.20	.07
480	Pablo Ozuna	.20	.07
481	Carl Pavano	.20	.07
482	Matt Morris	.20	.07
483	Matt Stairs	.20	.07
484	Tim Belcher	.20	.07
485	Lance Berkman	.20	.07
486	Brian Meadows	.20	.07
487	Bob Abreu	.20	.07
488	John VanderWal	.20	.07
489	Donnie Sadler	.20	.07
490	Damion Easley	.20	.07
491	David Justice	.20	.07
492	Ray Durham	.20	.07
493	Todd Zeile	.20	.07
494	Desi Relaford	.20	.07
495	Cliff Floyd	.20	.07
496	Scott Downs	.20	.07
497	Barry Bonds	1.25	.50
498	Jeff D'Amico	.20	.07
499	Octavio Dotel	.20	.07
500	Kent Mercker	.20	.07
501	Craig Grebeck	.20	.07
502	Roberto Hernandez	.20	.07
503	Matt Williams	.20	.07
504	Bruce Aven	.20	.07
505	Brett Tomko	.20	.07
506	Kris Benson	.20	.07
507	Neifi Perez	.20	.07
508	Alfonso Soriano	.30	.10
509	Keith Osik	.20	.07
510	Matt Franco	.20	.07
511	Steve Finley	.20	.07
512	Olmedo Saenz	.20	.07
513	Esteban Loaiza	.20	.07
514	Adam Kennedy	.20	.07
515	Scott Elarton	.20	.07
516	Moises Alou	.20	.07
517	Bryan Rekar	.20	.07
518	Darryl Hamilton	.20	.07
519	Osvaldo Fernandez	.20	.07
520	Kip Wells	.20	.07
521	Bernie Williams	.30	.10
522	Mike Darr	.20	.07
523	Marlon Anderson	.20	.07
524	Derrek Lee	.30	.10
525	Ugueth Urbina	.20	.07
526	Vinny Castilla	.20	.07
527	David Wells	.20	.07
528	Jason Marquis	.20	.07
529	Orlando Palmeiro	.20	.07
530	Carlos Perez	.20	.07
531	J.T. Snow	.20	.07
532	Al Leiter	.20	.07
533	Jimmy Anderson	.20	.07
534	Brett Laxton	.20	.07
535	Butch Huskey	.20	.07
536	Orlando Hernandez	.20	.07
537	Magglio Ordonez	.20	.07
538	Willie Blair	.20	.07
539	Kevin Sefcik	.20	.07
540	Chad Curtis	.20	.07
541	John Halama	.20	.07
542	Andy Fox	.20	.07
543	Juan Guzman	.20	.07
544	Frank Menechino RC	.20	.07
545	Raul Mondesi	.20	.07
546	Tim Salmon	.30	.10
547	Ryan Rupe	.20	.07
548	Jeff Reed	.20	.07
549	Mike Mordecai	.20	.07
550	Jeff Kent	.20	.07
551	Wiki Gonzalez	.20	.07
552	Kenny Rogers	.20	.07
553	Kevin Young	.20	.07
554	Brian Johnson	.20	.07
555	Tom Goodwin	.20	.07
556	Tony Clark	.20	.07
557	Mac Suzuki	.20	.07
558	Brian Moehler	.20	.07
559	Jim Parque	.20	.07
560	Mariano Rivera	.50	.20
561	Trot Nixon	.20	.07
562	Mike Mussina	.30	.10
563	Nelson Figueroa	.20	.07
564	Alex Gonzalez	.20	.07
565	Benny Agbayani	.20	.07
566	Ed Sprague	.20	.07
567	Scott Erickson	.20	.07
568	Abraham Nunez	.20	.07
569	Jerry DiPoto	.20	.07

❑ 570 Sean Casey .20 .07
❑ 571 Wilton Veras .20 .07
❑ 572 Joe Mays .20 .07
❑ 573 Bill Simas .20 .07
❑ 574 Doug Glanville .20 .07
❑ 575 Scott Sauerbeck .20 .07
❑ 576 Ben Davis .20 .07
❑ 577 Jesus Sanchez .20 .07
❑ 578 Ricardo Rincon .20 .07
❑ 579 John Olerud .20 .07
❑ 580 Curt Schilling .20 .07
❑ 581 Alex Cora .20 .07
❑ 582 Pat Hentgen .20 .07
❑ 583 Javy Lopez .20 .07
❑ 584 Ben Grieve .20 .07
❑ 585 Frank Castillo .20 .07
❑ 586 Kevin Stocker .20 .07
❑ 587 Mark Sweeney .20 .07
❑ 588 Ray Lankford .20 .07
❑ 589 Turner Ward .20 .07
❑ 590 Felipe Crespo .20 .07
❑ 591 Omar Vizquel .30 .10
❑ 592 Mike Lieberthal .20 .07
❑ 593 Ken Griffey Jr. .75 .30
❑ 594 Troy O'Leary .20 .07
❑ 595 Dave Mlicki .20 .07
❑ 596 Manny Ramirez Sox .30 .10
❑ 597 Mike Lansing .20 .07
❑ 598 Rich Aurilia .20 .07
❑ 599 Russell Branyan .20 .07
❑ 600 Russ Johnson .20 .07
❑ 601 Greg Colbrunn .20 .07
❑ 602 Andruw Jones .30 .10
❑ 603 Henry Blanco .20 .07
❑ 604 Jarrod Washburn .20 .07
❑ 605 Tony Eusebio .20 .07
❑ 606 Aaron Sele .20 .07
❑ 607 Charles Nagy .20 .07
❑ 608 Ryan Klesko .20 .07
❑ 609 Dante Bichette .20 .07
❑ 610 Bill Haselman .20 .07
❑ 611 Jerry Spradlin .20 .07
❑ 612 Alex Rodriguez Rangers .75 .30
❑ 613 Jose Silva .20 .07
❑ 614 Darren Oliver .20 .07
❑ 615 Pat Mahomes .20 .07
❑ 616 Roberto Alomar .30 .10
❑ 617 Edgar Renteria .20 .07
❑ 618 Jon Lieber .20 .07
❑ 619 John Rocker .20 .07
❑ 620 Miguel Tejada .20 .07
❑ 621 Mo Vaughn .20 .07
❑ 622 Jose Lima .20 .07
❑ 623 Kerry Wood .20 .07
❑ 624 Mike Timlin .20 .07
❑ 625 Wil Cordero .20 .07
❑ 626 Albert Belle .20 .07
❑ 627 Bobby Jones .20 .07
❑ 628 Doug Mirabelli .20 .07
❑ 629 Jason Tyner .20 .07
❑ 630 Andy Ashby .20 .07
❑ 631 Jose Hernandez .20 .07
❑ 632 Devon White .20 .07
❑ 633 Ruben Rivera .20 .07
❑ 634 Steve Parris .20 .07
❑ 635 David McCarty .20 .07
❑ 636 Jose Canseco .30 .10
❑ 637 Todd Walker .20 .07
❑ 638 Stan Spencer .20 .07
❑ 639 Wayne Gomes .20 .07
❑ 640 Freddy Garcia .20 .07
❑ 641 Jeremy Giambi .20 .07
❑ 642 Luis Lopez .20 .07
❑ 643 John Smoltz .30 .10
❑ 644 Kelly Stinnett .20 .07
❑ 645 Kevin Brown .20 .07
❑ 646 Wilton Guerrero .20 .07
❑ 647 Al Martin .20 .07
❑ 648 Woody Williams .20 .07
❑ 649 Brian Rose .20 .07
❑ 650 Rafael Palmeiro .30 .10
❑ 651 Pete Schourek .20 .07
❑ 652 Kevin Jarvis .20 .07
❑ 653 Mark Redman .20 .07
❑ 654 Ricky Ledee .20 .07
❑ 655 Larry Walker .20 .07
❑ 656 Paul Byrd .20 .07
❑ 657 Jason Bere .20 .07
❑ 658 Rick White .20 .07
❑ 659 Calvin Murray .20 .07
❑ 660 Greg Maddux .75 .30
❑ 661 Ron Gant .20 .07
❑ 662 Eli Marrero .20 .07
❑ 663 Graeme Lloyd .20 .07
❑ 664 Trevor Hoffman .20 .07
❑ 665 Nomar Garciaparra .75 .30
❑ 666 Glenallen Hill .20 .07
❑ 667 Matt LeCroy .20 .07
❑ 668 Justin Thompson .20 .07
❑ 669 Brady Anderson .20 .07
❑ 670 Miguel Batista .20 .07
❑ 671 Erubiel Durazo .20 .07
❑ 672 Kevin Millwood .20 .07
❑ 673 Mitch Meluskey .20 .07
❑ 674 Luis Gonzalez .20 .07
❑ 675 Edgar Martinez .30 .10
❑ 676 Robert Person .20 .07
❑ 677 Benito Santiago .20 .07
❑ 678 Todd Jones .20 .07
❑ 679 Tino Martinez .30 .10
❑ 680 Carlos Beltran .20 .07
❑ 681 Gabe White .20 .07
❑ 682 Bret Saberhagen .20 .07
❑ 683 Jeff Conine .20 .07
❑ 684 Jaret Wright .20 .07
❑ 685 Bernard Gilkey .20 .07
❑ 686 Garrett Stephenson .20 .07
❑ 687 Jamey Wright .20 .07
❑ 688 Sammy Sosa .50 .20
❑ 689 John Jaha .20 .07
❑ 690 Ramon Martinez .20 .07
❑ 691 Robert Fick .20 .07
❑ 692 Eric Milton .20 .07
❑ 693 Denny Neagle .20 .07
❑ 694 Ron Coomer .20 .07
❑ 695 John Valentin .20 .07
❑ 696 Placido Polanco .20 .07
❑ 697 Tim Hudson .20 .07
❑ 698 Marty Cordova .20 .07
❑ 699 Chad Kreuter .20 .07
❑ 700 Frank Catalanotto .20 .07
❑ 701 Tim Wakefield .20 .07
❑ 702 Jim Edmonds .20 .07
❑ 703 Michael Tucker .20 .07
❑ 704 Cristian Guzman .20 .07
❑ 705 Joey Hamilton .20 .07
❑ 706 Mike Piazza .75 .30
❑ 707 Dave Martinez .20 .07
❑ 708 Mike Hampton .20 .07
❑ 709 Bobby Bonilla .20 .07
❑ 710 Juan Pierre .20 .07
❑ 711 John Parrish .20 .07
❑ 712 Kory DeHaan .20 .07
❑ 713 Brian Tollberg .20 .07
❑ 714 Chris Truby .20 .07
❑ 715 Emil Brown .20 .07
❑ 716 Ryan Dempster .20 .07
❑ 717 Rich Garces .20 .07
❑ 718 Mike Myers .20 .07
❑ 719 Luis Ordaz .20 .07
❑ 720 Kazuhiro Sasaki .20 .07
❑ 721 Mark Quinn .20 .07
❑ 722 Ramon Ortiz .20 .07
❑ 723 Kerry Ligtenberg .20 .07
❑ 724 Rolando Arrojo .20 .07
❑ 725 Tsuyoshi Shinjo RC .50 .20
❑ 726 Ichiro Suzuki RC 12.00 5.00
❑ 727 Oswalt/Strange/Rauch .75 .30
❑ 728 Jake Peavy RC 4.00 1.40
❑ 729 S.Smyth RC/Bynum/Haynes .25 .08
❑ 730 Cuddyer/Lawrence/Freeman .25 .08
❑ 731 C.Pena/Barnes/Wise .25 .08
❑ 732 Dawkins/Almonte/Lopez .25 .08
❑ 733 Escobar/Valent/Wilkerson .25 .08
❑ 734 Hall/Barajas/Goldbach .25 .08
❑ 735 Romano/Giles/Ozuna .40 .15
❑ 736 D.Brown/Cust/V.Wells .25 .08
❑ 737 L.Montanez RC/D.Espinosa .25 .08
❑ 738 J.Wayne RC/A.Pluta RC .25 .08
❑ 739 J.Axelson RC/C.Cali RC .25 .08
❑ 740 S.Boyd RC/C.Morris RC .25 .08
❑ 741 T.Arko RC/D.Moylan RC .25 .08
❑ 742 L.Cotto RC/L.Escobar .25 .08
❑ 743 B.Mims RC/B.Williams RC .25 .08
❑ 744 C.Russ RC/B.Edwards .25 .08
❑ 745 J.Torres/B.Diggins .25 .08
❑ 746 Edwin Encarnacion RC 3.00 1.25
❑ 747 B.Bass RC/O.Ayala RC .25 .08
❑ 748 M.Matthews RC/J.Kaanoi .25 .08
❑ 749 S.McFarland RC/A.Sterrett RC .25 .08
❑ 750 D.Krynzel/G.Sizemore 1.50 .60
❑ 751 K.Bucktrot/D.Sardinha .25 .08
❑ 752 Anaheim Angels TC .20 .07
❑ 753 Arizona Diamondbacks TC .20 .07
❑ 754 Atlanta Braves TC .20 .07
❑ 755 Baltimore Orioles TC .20 .07
❑ 756 Boston Red Sox TC .20 .07
❑ 757 Chicago Cubs TC .20 .07
❑ 758 Chicago White Sox TC .20 .07
❑ 759 Cincinnati Reds TC .20 .07
❑ 760 Cleveland Indians TC .20 .07
❑ 761 Colorado Rockies TC .20 .07
❑ 762 Detroit Tigers TC .20 .07
❑ 763 Florida Marlins TC .20 .07
❑ 764 Houston Astros TC .20 .07
❑ 765 Kansas City Royals TC .20 .07
❑ 766 Los Angeles Dodgers TC .20 .07
❑ 767 Milwaukee Brewers TC .20 .07
❑ 768 Minnesota Twins TC .20 .07
❑ 769 Montreal Expos TC .20 .07
❑ 770 New York Mets TC .20 .07
❑ 771 New York Yankees TC 1.00 .40
❑ 772 Oakland Athletics TC .20 .07
❑ 773 Philadelphia Phillies TC .20 .07
❑ 774 Pittsburgh Pirates TC .20 .07
❑ 775 San Diego Padres TC .20 .07
❑ 776 San Francisco Giants TC .20 .07
❑ 777 Seattle Mariners TC .20 .07
❑ 778 St. Louis Cardinals TC .20 .07
❑ 779 Tampa Bay Devil Rays TC .20 .07
❑ 780 Texas Rangers TC .20 .07
❑ 781 Toronto Blue Jays TC .20 .07
❑ 782 Bucky Dent GM .20 .07
❑ 783 Jackie Robinson GM .50 .20
❑ 784 Roberto Clemente GM .60 .25
❑ 785 Nolan Ryan GM .75 .30
❑ 786 Kerry Wood GM .20 .07
❑ 787 Rickey Henderson GM .20 .07
❑ 788 Lou Brock GM .30 .10
❑ 789 David Wells GM .20 .07
❑ 790 Andruw Jones GM .20 .07
❑ 791 Carlton Fisk GM .20 .07
❑ TK B.Jackson/D.Sanders Bat 120.00 60.00
❑ NNO B.Thomson/R.Branca AU 60.00 30.00

2001 Topps Traded

❑ COMPLETE SET (265) 175.00 100.00
❑ COMMON CARD (1-99/145-265) .40 .15
❑ COMMON REPRINT (100-144) 1.00 .40
❑ T1 Sandy Alomar Jr. .40 .15
❑ T2 Kevin Appier .50 .20
❑ T3 Brad Ausmus .50 .20
❑ T4 Derek Bell .40 .15
❑ T5 Bret Boone .50 .20
❑ T6 Rico Brogna .40 .15
❑ T7 Ellis Burks .50 .20
❑ T8 Ken Caminiti .50 .20
❑ T9 Roger Cedeno .40 .15
❑ T10 Royce Clayton .40 .15
❑ T11 Enrique Wilson .40 .15

❑ T12	Rheal Cormier	.40	.15
❑ T13	Eric Davis	.50	.20
❑ T14	Shawon Dunston	.40	.15
❑ T15	Andres Galarraga	.50	.20
❑ T16	Tom Gordon	.40	.15
❑ T17	Mark Grace	.75	.30
❑ T18	Jeffrey Hammonds	.40	.15
❑ T19	Dustin Hermanson	.40	.15
❑ T20	Quinton McCracken	.40	.15
❑ T21	Todd Hundley	.40	.15
❑ T22	Charles Johnson	.50	.20
❑ T23	Marquis Grissom	.50	.20
❑ T24	Jose Mesa	.40	.15
❑ T25	Brian Boehringer	.40	.15
❑ T26	John Rocker	.50	.20
❑ T27	Jeff Frye	.40	.15
❑ T28	Reggie Sanders	.50	.20
❑ T29	David Segui	.40	.15
❑ T30	Mike Sirotka	.40	.15
❑ T31	Fernando Tatis	.40	.15
❑ T32	Steve Trachsel	.40	.15
❑ T33	Ismael Valdes	.40	.15
❑ T34	Randy Velarde	.40	.15
❑ T35	Ryan Kohlmeier	.40	.15
❑ T36	Mike Bordick	.50	.20
❑ T37	Kent Bottenfield	.40	.15
❑ T38	Pat Rapp	.40	.15
❑ T39	Jeff Nelson	.40	.15
❑ T40	Ricky Bottalico	.40	.15
❑ T41	Luke Prokopec	.40	.15
❑ T42	Hideo Nomo	1.25	.50
❑ T43	Bill Mueller	.50	.20
❑ T44	Roberto Kelly	.40	.15
❑ T45	Chris Holt	.40	.15
❑ T46	Mike Jackson	.40	.15
❑ T47	Devon White	.50	.20
❑ T48	Gerald Williams	.40	.15
❑ T49	Eddie Taubensee	.40	.15
❑ T50	Brian Hunter	.40	.15
❑ T51	Nelson Cruz	.40	.15
❑ T52	Jeff Fassero	.40	.15
❑ T53	Bubba Trammell	.40	.15
❑ T54	Bo Porter	.40	.15
❑ T55	Greg Norton	.40	.15
❑ T56	Benito Santiago	.50	.20
❑ T57	Ruben Rivera	.40	.15
❑ T58	Dee Brown	.40	.15
❑ T59	Jose Canseco	.75	.30
❑ T60	Chris Michalak	.40	.15
❑ T61	Tim Worrell	.40	.15
❑ T62	Matt Clement	.50	.20
❑ T63	Bill Pulsipher	.40	.15
❑ T64	Troy Brohawn RC	.40	.15
❑ T65	Mark Kotsay	.50	.20
❑ T66	Jimmy Rollins	.50	.20
❑ T67	Shea Hillenbrand	.50	.20
❑ T68	Ted Lilly	.40	.15
❑ T69	Jermaine Dye	.50	.20
❑ T70	Jerry Hairston Jr.	.40	.15
❑ T71	John Mabry	.40	.15
❑ T72	Kurt Abbott	.40	.15
❑ T73	Eric Owens	.40	.15
❑ T74	Jeff Brantley	.40	.15
❑ T75	Roy Oswalt	1.25	.50
❑ T76	Doug Mientkiewicz	.50	.20
❑ T77	Rickey Henderson	1.25	.50
❑ T78	Jason Grimsley	.40	.15
❑ T79	Christian Parker RC	.40	.15
❑ T80	Donne Wall	.40	.15
❑ T81	Alex Arias	.40	.15
❑ T82	Willis Roberts	.40	.15
❑ T83	Ryan Minor	.40	.15
❑ T84	Jason LaRue	.40	.15
❑ T85	Ruben Sierra	.50	.20
❑ T86	Johnny Damon	.75	.30
❑ T87	Juan Gonzalez	.50	.20
❑ T88	C.C. Sabathia	.50	.20
❑ T89	Tony Batista	.40	.15
❑ T90	Jay Witasick	.40	.15
❑ T91	Brent Abernathy	.40	.15
❑ T92	Paul LoDuca	.50	.20
❑ T93	Wes Helms	.40	.15
❑ T94	Mark Wohlers	.40	.15
❑ T95	Rob Bell	.40	.15
❑ T96	Tim Redding	.40	.15
❑ T97	Bud Smith RC	.40	.15
❑ T98	Adam Dunn	.75	.30
❑ T99	I.Suzuki/A.Pujols ROY	20.00	8.00
❑ T100	Carlton Fisk 81	1.25	.50
❑ T101	Tim Raines 81	1.00	.40
❑ T102	Juan Marichal 74	1.00	.40
❑ T103	Dave Winfield 81	1.00	.40
❑ T104	Reggie Jackson 82	1.25	.50
❑ T105	Cal Ripken 82	6.00	2.50
❑ T106	Ozzie Smith 82	3.00	1.25
❑ T107	Tom Seaver 83	1.25	.50
❑ T108	Lou Piniella 74	1.00	.40
❑ T109	Dwight Gooden 84	1.00	.40
❑ T110	Bret Saberhagen 84	1.00	.40
❑ T111	Gary Carter 85	1.00	.40
❑ T112	Jack Clark 85	1.00	.40
❑ T113	Rickey Henderson 85	2.00	.75
❑ T114	Barry Bonds 86	5.00	2.00
❑ T115	Bobby Bonilla 86	1.00	.40
❑ T116	Jose Canseco 86	1.25	.50
❑ T117	Will Clark 86	1.25	.50
❑ T118	Andres Galarraga 86	1.00	.40
❑ T119	Bo Jackson 86	2.00	.75
❑ T120	Wally Joyner 86	1.00	.40
❑ T121	Ellis Burks 87	1.00	.40
❑ T122	David Cone 87	1.00	.40
❑ T123	Greg Maddux 87	3.00	1.25
❑ T124	Willie Randolph 76	1.00	.40
❑ T125	Dennis Eckersley 87	1.00	.40
❑ T126	Matt Williams 87	1.00	.40
❑ T127	Joe Morgan 81	1.00	.40
❑ T128	Fred McGriff 87	1.25	.50
❑ T129	Roberto Alomar 88	1.25	.50
❑ T130	Lee Smith 88	1.00	.40
❑ T131	David Wells 88	1.00	.40
❑ T132	Ken Griffey Jr. 89	3.00	1.25
❑ T133	Deion Sanders 89	1.25	.50
❑ T134	Nolan Ryan 89	4.00	1.50
❑ T135	David Justice 90	1.00	.40
❑ T136	Joe Carter 91	1.00	.40
❑ T137	Jack Morris 92	1.00	.40
❑ T138	Mike Piazza 93	3.00	1.25
❑ T139	Barry Bonds 93	5.00	2.00
❑ T140	Terrence Long 94	1.00	.40
❑ T141	Ben Grieve 94	1.00	.40
❑ T142	Richie Sexson 95	1.00	.40
❑ T143	Sean Burroughs 99	1.00	.40
❑ T144	Alfonso Soriano 99	1.25	.50
❑ T145	Bob Boone MG	.50	.20
❑ T146	Larry Bowa MG	.50	.20
❑ T147	Bob Brenly MG	.40	.15
❑ T148	Buck Martinez MG	.40	.15
❑ T149	Lloyd McClendon MG	.40	.15
❑ T150	Jim Tracy MG	.40	.15
❑ T151	Jared Abruzzo RC	.40	.15
❑ T152	Kurt Ainsworth	.40	.15
❑ T153	Willie Bloomquist	.50	.20
❑ T154	Ben Broussard	.40	.15
❑ T155	Bobby Bradley	.40	.15
❑ T156	Mike Bynum	.40	.15
❑ T157	A.J. Hinch	.40	.15
❑ T158	Ryan Christianson	.40	.15
❑ T159	Carlos Silva	.40	.15
❑ T160	Joe Crede	1.25	.50
❑ T161	Jack Cust	.40	.15
❑ T162	Ben Diggins	.40	.15
❑ T163	Phil Dumatrait	.40	.15
❑ T164	Alex Escobar	.40	.15
❑ T165	Miguel Olivo	.40	.15
❑ T166	Chris George	.40	.15
❑ T167	Marcus Giles	.50	.20
❑ T168	Keith Ginter	.40	.15
❑ T169	Josh Girdley	.40	.15
❑ T170	Tony Alvarez	.40	.15
❑ T171	Scott Seabol	.40	.15
❑ T172	Josh Hamilton	.75	.30
❑ T173	Jason Hart	.40	.15
❑ T174	Israel Alcantara	.40	.15
❑ T175	Jake Peavy	2.00	.75
❑ T176	Stubby Clapp RC	.40	.15
❑ T177	D'Angelo Jimenez	.40	.15
❑ T178	Nick Johnson	.50	.20
❑ T179	Ben Johnson	.50	.20
❑ T180	Larry Bigbie	.40	.15
❑ T181	Allen Levrault	.40	.15
❑ T182	Felipe Lopez	.50	.20
❑ T183	Sean Burnett	.40	.15
❑ T184	Nick Neugebauer	.40	.15
❑ T185	Austin Kearns	.50	.20
❑ T186	Corey Patterson	.40	.15
❑ T187	Carlos Pena	.40	.15
❑ T188	Ricardo Rodriguez RC	.40	.15
❑ T189	Juan Rivera	.40	.15
❑ T190	Grant Roberts	.40	.15
❑ T191	Adam Pettyjohn RC	.40	.15
❑ T192	Jared Sandberg	.40	.15
❑ T193	Xavier Nady	.40	.15
❑ T194	Dane Sardinha	.40	.15
❑ T195	Shawn Sonnier	.40	.15
❑ T196	Rafael Soriano	.40	.15
❑ T197	Brian Specht RC	.40	.15
❑ T198	Aaron Myette	.40	.15
❑ T199	Juan Uribe RC	.50	.20
❑ T200	Jayson Werth	.40	.15
❑ T201	Brad Wilkerson	.40	.15
❑ T202	Horacio Estrada	.40	.15
❑ T203	Joel Pineiro	.50	.20
❑ T204	Matt LeCroy	.40	.15
❑ T205	Michael Coleman	.40	.15
❑ T206	Ben Sheets	.75	.30
❑ T207	Eric Byrnes	.40	.15
❑ T208	Sean Burroughs	.40	.15
❑ T209	Ken Harvey	.40	.15
❑ T210	Travis Hafner	4.00	1.50
❑ T211	Erick Almonte	.40	.15
❑ T212	Jason Belcher RC	.40	.15
❑ T213	Wilson Betemit RC	1.50	.60
❑ T214	Hank Blalock RC	2.50	1.00
❑ T215	Danny Borrell	.40	.15
❑ T216	John Buck RC	.50	.20
❑ T217	Freddie Bynum RC	.40	.15
❑ T218	Noel Devarez RC	.40	.15
❑ T219	Juan Diaz RC	.40	.15
❑ T220	Felix Diaz RC	.40	.15
❑ T221	Josh Fogg RC	.40	.15
❑ T222	Matt Ford RC	.40	.15
❑ T223	Scott Heard	.40	.15
❑ T224	Ben Hendrickson RC	.40	.15
❑ T225	Cody Ross RC	.40	.15
❑ T226	Adrian Hernandez RC	.40	.15
❑ T227	Alfredo Amezaga RC	.40	.15
❑ T228	Bob Keppel RC	.40	.15
❑ T229	Ryan Madson RC	.75	.30
❑ T230	Octavio Martinez RC	.40	.15
❑ T231	Hee Seop Choi	.50	.20
❑ T232	Thomas Mitchell	.40	.15
❑ T233	Luis Montanez	.40	.15
❑ T234	Andy Morales RC	.40	.15
❑ T235	Justin Morneau RC	8.00	3.00
❑ T236	Toe Nash RC	.40	.15
❑ T237	Valentino Pascucci RC	.40	.15
❑ T238	Roy Smith RC	.40	.15
❑ T239	Antonio Perez RC	.50	.20
❑ T240	Chad Petty RC	.40	.15
❑ T241	Steve Smyth	.40	.15
❑ T242	Jose Reyes RC	15.00	6.00
❑ T243	Eric Reynolds RC	.40	.15
❑ T244	Dominic Rich	.40	.15
❑ T245	Jason Richardson RC	.40	.15
❑ T246	Ed Rogers RC	.40	.15
❑ T247	Albert Pujols RC	50.00	20.00
❑ T248	Esix Snead RC	.40	.15
❑ T249	Luis Torres RC	.40	.15
❑ T250	Matt White RC	.40	.15
❑ T251	Blake Williams	.40	.15
❑ T252	Chris Russ	.40	.15
❑ T253	Joe Kennedy RC	.50	.20
❑ T254	Jeff Randazzo RC	.40	.15
❑ T255	Beau Hale RC	.40	.15
❑ T256	Brad Hennessey RC	1.25	.50
❑ T257	Jake Gautreau RC	.40	.15
❑ T258	Jeff Mathis RC	.50	.20
❑ T259	Aaron Heilman RC	.50	.20
❑ T260	Bronson Sardinha RC	.40	.15
❑ T261	Irvin Guzman RC	4.00	1.50
❑ T262	Gabe Gross RC	.50	.20
❑ T263	J.D. Martin RC	.40	.15
❑ T264	Chris Smith RC	.40	.15
❑ T265	Kenny Baugh RC	.40	.15

2002 Topps

Card		
❑ COMPLETE SET (718)	80.00	30.00
❑ COMP.FACT.BROWN SET (723)	80.00	40.00
❑ COMP.FACT.GREEN SET (723)	80.00	40.00
❑ COMPLETE SERIES 1 (364)	40.00	15.00
❑ COMPLETE SERIES 2 (354)	40.00	15.00
❑ COMMON CARD (1-6/8-719)	.20	.07
❑ COMMON (307-331/671-695)	.50	.20
❑ COMMON CARD (332-364)	.50	.20
❑ 1 Pedro Martinez	.30	.10
❑ 2 Mike Stanton	.20	.07
❑ 3 Brad Penny	.20	.07
❑ 4 Mike Matheny	.20	.07
❑ 5 Johnny Damon	.30	.10
❑ 6 Bret Boone	.20	.07
❑ 7 Does Not Exist		
❑ 8 Chris Truby	.20	.07
❑ 9 B.J. Surhoff	.20	.07
❑ 10 Mike Hampton	.20	.07
❑ 11 Juan Pierre	.20	.07
❑ 12 Mark Buehrle	.20	.07
❑ 13 Bob Abreu	.20	.07
❑ 14 David Cone	.20	.07
❑ 15 Aaron Sele	.20	.07
❑ 16 Fernando Tatis	.20	.07
❑ 17 Bobby Jones	.20	.07
❑ 18 Rick Helling	.20	.07
❑ 19 Dmitri Young	.20	.07
❑ 20 Mike Mussina	.30	.10
❑ 21 Mike Sweeney	.20	.07
❑ 22 Cristian Guzman	.20	.07
❑ 23 Ryan Kohlmeier	.20	.07
❑ 24 Adam Kennedy	.20	.07
❑ 25 Larry Walker	.20	.07
❑ 26 Eric Davis	.20	.07
❑ 27 Jason Tyner	.20	.07
❑ 28 Eric Young	.20	.07
❑ 29 Jason Marquis	.20	.07
❑ 30 Luis Gonzalez	.20	.07
❑ 31 Kevin Tapani	.20	.07
❑ 32 Orlando Cabrera	.20	.07
❑ 33 Marty Cordova	.20	.07
❑ 34 Brad Ausmus	.20	.07
❑ 35 Livan Hernandez	.20	.07
❑ 36 Alex Gonzalez	.20	.07
❑ 37 Edgar Renteria	.20	.07
❑ 38 Bengie Molina	.20	.07
❑ 39 Frank Menechino	.20	.07
❑ 40 Rafael Palmeiro	.30	.10
❑ 41 Brad Fullmer	.20	.07
❑ 42 Julio Zuleta	.20	.07
❑ 43 Darren Dreifort	.20	.07
❑ 44 Trot Nixon	.20	.07
❑ 45 Trevor Hoffman	.20	.07
❑ 46 Vladimir Nunez	.20	.07
❑ 47 Mark Kotsay	.20	.07
❑ 48 Kenny Rogers	.20	.07
❑ 49 Ben Petrick	.20	.07
❑ 50 Jeff Bagwell	.30	.10
❑ 51 Juan Encarnacion	.20	.07
❑ 52 Ramiro Mendoza	.20	.07
❑ 53 Brian Meadows	.20	.07
❑ 54 Chad Curtis	.20	.07
❑ 55 Aramis Ramirez	.20	.07
❑ 56 Mark McLemore	.20	.07
❑ 57 Dante Bichette	.20	.07
❑ 58 Scott Schoeneweis	.20	.07
❑ 59 Jose Cruz Jr.	.20	.07
❑ 60 Roger Clemens	1.00	.40
❑ 61 Jose Guillen	.20	.07
❑ 62 Darren Oliver	.20	.07
❑ 63 Chris Reitsma	.20	.07
❑ 64 Jeff Abbott	.20	.07
❑ 65 Robin Ventura	.20	.07
❑ 66 Denny Neagle	.20	.07
❑ 67 Al Martin	.20	.07
❑ 68 Benito Santiago	.20	.07
❑ 69 Roy Oswalt	.20	.07
❑ 70 Juan Gonzalez	.20	.07
❑ 71 Garret Anderson	.20	.07
❑ 72 Bobby Bonilla	.20	.07
❑ 73 Danny Bautista	.20	.07
❑ 74 J.T. Snow	.20	.07
❑ 75 Derek Jeter	1.25	.50
❑ 76 John Olerud	.20	.07
❑ 77 Kevin Appier	.20	.07
❑ 78 Phil Nevin	.20	.07
❑ 79 Sean Casey	.20	.07
❑ 80 Troy Glaus	.20	.07
❑ 81 Joe Randa	.20	.07
❑ 82 Jose Valentin	.20	.07
❑ 83 Ricky Bottalico	.20	.07
❑ 84 Todd Zeile	.20	.07
❑ 85 Barry Larkin	.30	.10
❑ 86 Bob Wickman	.20	.07
❑ 87 Jeff Shaw	.20	.07
❑ 88 Greg Vaughn	.20	.07
❑ 89 Fernando Vina	.20	.07
❑ 90 Mark Mulder	.20	.07
❑ 91 Paul Bako	.20	.07
❑ 92 Aaron Boone	.20	.07
❑ 93 Esteban Loaiza	.20	.07
❑ 94 Richie Sexson	.20	.07
❑ 95 Alfonso Soriano	.20	.07
❑ 96 Tony Womack	.20	.07
❑ 97 Paul Shuey	.20	.07
❑ 98 Melvin Mora	.20	.07
❑ 99 Tony Gwynn	.60	.25
❑ 100 Vladimir Guerrero	.50	.20
❑ 101 Keith Osik	.20	.07
❑ 102 Bud Smith	.20	.07
❑ 103 Scott Williamson	.20	.07
❑ 104 Daryle Ward	.20	.07
❑ 105 Doug Mientkiewicz	.20	.07
❑ 106 Stan Javier	.20	.07
❑ 107 Russ Ortiz	.20	.07
❑ 108 Wade Miller	.20	.07
❑ 109 Luke Prokopec	.20	.07
❑ 110 Andruw Jones	.30	.10
❑ 111 Ron Coomer	.20	.07
❑ 112 Dan Wilson	.20	.07
❑ 113 Luis Castillo	.20	.07
❑ 114 Derek Bell	.20	.07
❑ 115 Gary Sheffield	.20	.07
❑ 116 Ruben Rivera	.20	.07
❑ 117 Paul O'Neill	.30	.10
❑ 118 Craig Paquette	.20	.07
❑ 119 Kelvin Escobar	.20	.07
❑ 120 Brad Radke	.20	.07
❑ 121 Jorge Fabregas	.20	.07
❑ 122 Randy Winn	.20	.07
❑ 123 Tom Goodwin	.20	.07
❑ 124 Jaret Wright	.20	.07
❑ 125 Manny Ramirez	.30	.10
❑ 126 Al Leiter	.20	.07
❑ 127 Ben Davis	.20	.07
❑ 128 Frank Catalanotto	.20	.07
❑ 129 Jose Cabrera	.20	.07
❑ 130 Magglio Ordonez	.20	.07
❑ 131 Jose Macias	.20	.07
❑ 132 Ted Lilly	.20	.07
❑ 133 Chris Holt	.20	.07
❑ 134 Eric Milton	.20	.07
❑ 135 Shannon Stewart	.20	.07
❑ 136 Omar Olivares	.20	.07
❑ 137 David Segui	.20	.07
❑ 138 Jeff Nelson	.20	.07
❑ 139 Matt Williams	.20	.07
❑ 140 Ellis Burks	.20	.07
❑ 141 Jason Bere	.20	.07
❑ 142 Jimmy Haynes	.20	.07
❑ 143 Ramon Hernandez	.20	.07
❑ 144 Craig Counsell	.20	.07
❑ 145 John Smoltz	.30	.10
❑ 146 Homer Bush	.20	.07
❑ 147 Quilvio Veras	.20	.07
❑ 148 Esteban Yan	.20	.07
❑ 149 Ramon Ortiz	.20	.07
❑ 150 Carlos Delgado	.20	.07
❑ 151 Lee Stevens	.20	.07
❑ 152 Wil Cordero	.20	.07
❑ 153 Mike Bordick	.20	.07
❑ 154 John Flaherty	.20	.07
❑ 155 Omar Daal	.20	.07
❑ 156 Todd Ritchie	.20	.07
❑ 157 Carl Everett	.20	.07
❑ 158 Scott Sullivan	.20	.07
❑ 159 Deivi Cruz	.20	.07
❑ 160 Albert Pujols	1.00	.40
❑ 160A Albert Pujols COR		
❑ 161 Royce Clayton	.20	.07
❑ 162 Jeff Suppan	.20	.07
❑ 163 C.C. Sabathia	.20	.07
❑ 164 Jimmy Rollins	.20	.07
❑ 165 Rickey Henderson	.50	.20
❑ 166 Rey Ordonez	.20	.07
❑ 167 Shawn Estes	.20	.07
❑ 168 Reggie Sanders	.20	.07
❑ 169 Jon Lieber	.20	.07
❑ 170 Armando Benitez	.20	.07
❑ 171 Mike Remlinger	.20	.07
❑ 172 Billy Wagner	.20	.07
❑ 173 Troy Percival	.20	.07
❑ 174 Devon White	.20	.07
❑ 175 Ivan Rodriguez	.30	.10
❑ 176 Dustin Hermanson	.20	.07
❑ 177 Brian Anderson	.20	.07
❑ 178 Graeme Lloyd	.20	.07
❑ 179 Russell Branyan	.20	.07
❑ 180 Bobby Higginson	.20	.07
❑ 181 Alex Gonzalez	.20	.07
❑ 182 John Franco	.20	.07
❑ 183 Sidney Ponson	.20	.07
❑ 184 Jose Mesa	.20	.07
❑ 185 Todd Hollandsworth	.20	.07
❑ 186 Kevin Young	.20	.07
❑ 187 Tim Wakefield	.20	.07
❑ 188 Craig Biggio	.30	.10
❑ 189 Jason Isringhausen	.20	.07
❑ 190 Mark Quinn	.20	.07
❑ 191 Glendon Rusch	.20	.07
❑ 192 Damian Miller	.20	.07
❑ 193 Sandy Alomar Jr.	.20	.07
❑ 194 Scott Brosius	.20	.07
❑ 195 Dave Martinez	.20	.07
❑ 196 Danny Graves	.20	.07
❑ 197 Shea Hillenbrand	.20	.07
❑ 198 Jimmy Anderson	.20	.07
❑ 199 Travis Lee	.20	.07
❑ 200 Randy Johnson	.50	.20
❑ 201 Carlos Beltran	.20	.07
❑ 202 Jerry Hairston	.20	.07
❑ 203 Jesus Sanchez	.20	.07
❑ 204 Eddie Taubensee	.20	.07
❑ 205 David Wells	.20	.07
❑ 206 Russ Davis	.20	.07
❑ 207 Michael Barrett	.20	.07
❑ 208 Marquis Grissom	.20	.07
❑ 209 Byung-Hyun Kim	.20	.07
❑ 210 Hideo Nomo	.50	.20
❑ 211 Ryan Rupe	.20	.07
❑ 212 Ricky Gutierrez	.20	.07
❑ 213 Darryl Kile	.20	.07
❑ 214 Rico Brogna	.20	.07
❑ 215 Terrence Long	.20	.07
❑ 216 Mike Jackson	.20	.07
❑ 217 Jamey Wright	.20	.07
❑ 218 Adrian Beltre	.20	.07
❑ 219 Benny Agbayani	.20	.07
❑ 220 Chuck Knoblauch	.20	.07
❑ 221 Randy Wolf	.20	.07
❑ 222 Andy Ashby	.20	.07
❑ 223 Corey Koskie	.20	.07
❑ 224 Roger Cedeno	.20	.07
❑ 225 Ichiro Suzuki	1.00	.40
❑ 226 Keith Foulke	.20	.07
❑ 227 Ryan Minor	.20	.07
❑ 228 Shawon Dunston	.20	.07
❑ 229 Alex Cora	.20	.07

❑	230	Jeromy Burnitz	.20	.07
❑	231	Mark Grace	.30	.10
❑	232	Aubrey Huff	.20	.07
❑	233	Jeffrey Hammonds	.20	.07
❑	234	Olmedo Saenz	.20	.07
❑	235	Brian Jordan	.20	.07
❑	236	Jeremy Giambi	.20	.07
❑	237	Joe Girardi	.20	.07
❑	238	Eric Gagne	.20	.07
❑	239	Masato Yoshii	.20	.07
❑	240	Greg Maddux	.75	.30
❑	241	Bryan Rekar	.20	.07
❑	242	Ray Durham	.20	.07
❑	243	Torii Hunter	.20	.07
❑	244	Derrek Lee	.30	.10
❑	245	Jim Edmonds	.20	.07
❑	246	Einar Diaz	.20	.07
❑	247	Brian Bohanon	.20	.07
❑	248	Ron Belliard	.20	.07
❑	249	Mike Lowell	.20	.07
❑	250	Sammy Sosa	.50	.20
❑	251	Richard Hidalgo	.20	.07
❑	252	Bartolo Colon	.20	.07
❑	253	Jorge Posada	.30	.10
❑	254	LaTroy Hawkins	.20	.07
❑	255	Paul LoDuca	.20	.07
❑	256	Carlos Febles	.20	.07
❑	257	Nelson Cruz	.20	.07
❑	258	Edgardo Alfonzo	.20	.07
❑	259	Joey Hamilton	.20	.07
❑	260	Cliff Floyd	.20	.07
❑	261	Wes Helms	.20	.07
❑	262	Jay Bell	.20	.07
❑	263	Mike Cameron	.20	.07
❑	264	Paul Konerko	.20	.07
❑	265	Jeff Kent	.20	.07
❑	266	Robert Fick	.20	.07
❑	267	Allen Levrault	.20	.07
❑	268	Placido Polanco	.20	.07
❑	269	Marlon Anderson	.20	.07
❑	270	Mariano Rivera	.50	.20
❑	271	Chan Ho Park	.20	.07
❑	272	Jose Vizcaino	.20	.07
❑	273	Jeff D'Amico	.20	.07
❑	274	Mark Gardner	.20	.07
❑	275	Travis Fryman	.20	.07
❑	276	Darren Lewis	.20	.07
❑	277	Bruce Bochy MG	.20	.07
❑	278	Jerry Manuel MG	.20	.07
❑	279	Bob Brenly MG	.20	.07
❑	280	Don Baylor MG	.20	.07
❑	281	Davey Lopes MG	.20	.07
❑	282	Jerry Narron MG	.20	.07
❑	283	Tony Muser MG	.20	.07
❑	284	Hal McRae MG	.20	.07
❑	285	Bobby Cox MG	.20	.07
❑	286	Larry Dierker MG	.20	.07
❑	287	Phil Garner MG	.20	.07
❑	288	Joe Kerrigan MG	.20	.07
❑	289	Bobby Valentine MG	.20	.07
❑	290	Dusty Baker MG	.20	.07
❑	291	Lloyd McClendon MG	.20	.07
❑	292	Mike Scioscia MG	.20	.07
❑	293	Buck Martinez MG	.20	.07
❑	294	Larry Bowa MG	.20	.07
❑	295	Tony LaRussa MG	.20	.07
❑	296	Jeff Torborg MG	.20	.07
❑	297	Tom Kelly MG	.20	.07
❑	298	Mike Hargrove MG	.20	.07
❑	299	Art Howe MG	.20	.07
❑	300	Lou Piniella MG	.20	.07
❑	301	Charlie Manuel MG	.20	.07
❑	302	Buddy Bell MG	.20	.07
❑	303	Tony Perez MG	.20	.07
❑	304	Bob Boone MG	.20	.07
❑	305	Joe Torre MG	.30	.10
❑	306	Jim Tracy MG	.20	.07
❑	307	Jason Lane PROS	.50	.20
❑	308	Chris George PROS	.50	.20
❑	309	Hank Blalock PROS	1.00	.40
❑	310	Joe Borchard PROS	.50	.20
❑	311	Marlon Byrd PROS	.50	.20
❑	312	Raymond Cabrera PROS RC	.50	.20
❑	313	Freddy Sanchez PROS RC	2.00	.75
❑	314	Scott Wiggins PROS RC	.50	.20
❑	315	Jason Maule PROS RC	.50	.20
❑	316	Dionys Cesar PROS RC	.50	.20
❑	317	Boof Bonser PROS	.50	.20
❑	318	Juan Tolentino PROS RC	.50	.20
❑	319	Earl Snyder PROS RC	.50	.20
❑	320	Travis Wade PROS RC	.50	.20
❑	321	Napoleon Calzado PROS RC	.50	.20
❑	322	Eric Glaser PROS RC	.50	.20
❑	323	Craig Kuzmic PROS RC	.50	.20
❑	324	Nic Jackson PROS RC	.50	.20
❑	325	Mike Rivera PROS	.50	.20
❑	326	Jason Bay PROS RC	4.00	1.50
❑	327	Chris Smith DP	.50	.20
❑	328	Jake Gautreau DP	.50	.20
❑	329	Gabe Gross DP	.50	.20
❑	330	Kenny Baugh DP	.50	.20
❑	331	J.D. Martin DP	.50	.20
❑	332	Barry Bonds HL	1.25	.50
❑	333	Rickey Henderson HL	.50	.20
❑	334	Bud Smith HL	.50	.20
❑	335	Rickey Henderson HL	.50	.20
❑	336	Barry Bonds HL	1.25	.50
❑	337	Ichiro/Giambi/Alomar LL	.50	.20
❑	338	A.Rod/Ichiro/Boone LL	.50	.20
❑	339	A.Rod/Thome/Palmeiro LL	.50	.20
❑	340	Boone/J.Gonz/A.Rod LL	.50	.20
❑	341	Garcia/Mussina/Mays LL	.50	.20
❑	342	Nomo/Mussina/Clemens LL	.50	.20
❑	343	Walker/Helton/Alou/Berk LL	.50	.20
❑	344	Sosa/Helton/Bonds LL	.75	.30
❑	345	Bonds/Sosa/L.Gonz LL	.75	.30
❑	346	Sosa/Helton/L.Gonz LL	.50	.20
❑	347	R.John/Schilling/Burkett LL	.50	.20
❑	348	R.John/Schilling/Park LL	.50	.20
❑	349	Seattle Mariners PB	.50	.20
❑	350	Oakland Athletics PB	.50	.20
❑	351	New York Yankees PB	.50	.20
❑	352	Cleveland Indians PB	.50	.20
❑	353	Arizona Diamondbacks PB	.50	.20
❑	354	Atlanta Braves PB	.50	.20
❑	355	St. Louis Cardinals PB	.50	.20
❑	356	Houston Astros PB	.50	.20
❑	357	Diamondbacks-Astros UWS	.50	.20
❑	358	Mike Piazza UWS	.50	.20
❑	359	Braves-Phillies UWS	.50	.20
❑	360	Curt Schilling UWS	.50	.20
❑	361	R.Clemens/L.Mazzilli UWS	.50	.20
❑	362	Sammy Sosa UWS	.30	.10
❑	363	Lampkin/Ichiro/Boone UWS	.50	.20
❑	364	B.Bonds/J.Bagwell UWS	.75	.30
❑	365	Barry Bonds HR 1	15.00	6.00
❑	365	Barry Bonds HR 2	10.00	4.00
❑	365	Barry Bonds HR 3	10.00	4.00
❑	365	Barry Bonds HR 4	10.00	4.00
❑	365	Barry Bonds HR 5	10.00	4.00
❑	365	Barry Bonds HR 6	10.00	4.00
❑	365	Barry Bonds HR 7	10.00	4.00
❑	365	Barry Bonds HR 8	10.00	4.00
❑	365	Barry Bonds HR 9	10.00	4.00
❑	365	Barry Bonds HR 10	10.00	4.00
❑	365	Barry Bonds HR 11	10.00	4.00
❑	365	Barry Bonds HR 12	10.00	4.00
❑	365	Barry Bonds HR 13	10.00	4.00
❑	365	Barry Bonds HR 14	10.00	4.00
❑	365	Barry Bonds HR 15	10.00	4.00
❑	365	Barry Bonds HR 16	10.00	4.00
❑	365	Barry Bonds HR 17	10.00	4.00
❑	365	Barry Bonds HR 18	10.00	4.00
❑	365	Barry Bonds HR 19	10.00	4.00
❑	365	Barry Bonds HR 20	10.00	4.00
❑	365	Barry Bonds HR 21	10.00	4.00
❑	365	Barry Bonds HR 22	10.00	4.00
❑	365	Barry Bonds HR 23	10.00	4.00
❑	365	Barry Bonds HR 24	10.00	4.00
❑	365	Barry Bonds HR 25	10.00	4.00
❑	365	Barry Bonds HR 26	10.00	4.00
❑	365	Barry Bonds HR 27	10.00	4.00
❑	365	Barry Bonds HR 28	10.00	4.00
❑	365	Barry Bonds HR 29	10.00	4.00
❑	365	Barry Bonds HR 30	10.00	4.00
❑	365	Barry Bonds HR 31	10.00	4.00
❑	365	Barry Bonds HR 32	10.00	4.00
❑	365	Barry Bonds HR 33	10.00	4.00
❑	365	Barry Bonds HR 34	10.00	4.00
❑	365	Barry Bonds HR 35	10.00	4.00
❑	365	Barry Bonds HR 36	10.00	4.00
❑	365	Barry Bonds HR 37	10.00	4.00
❑	365	Barry Bonds HR 38	10.00	4.00
❑	365	Barry Bonds HR 39	10.00	4.00
❑	365	Barry Bonds HR 40	10.00	4.00
❑	365	Barry Bonds HR 41	10.00	4.00
❑	365	Barry Bonds HR 42	10.00	4.00
❑	365	Barry Bonds HR 43	10.00	4.00
❑	365	Barry Bonds HR 44	10.00	4.00
❑	365	Barry Bonds HR 45	10.00	4.00
❑	365	Barry Bonds HR 46	10.00	4.00
❑	365	Barry Bonds HR 47	10.00	4.00
❑	365	Barry Bonds HR 48	10.00	4.00
❑	365	Barry Bonds HR 49	10.00	4.00
❑	365	Barry Bonds HR 50	10.00	4.00
❑	365	Barry Bonds HR 51	10.00	4.00
❑	365	Barry Bonds HR 52	10.00	4.00
❑	365	Barry Bonds HR 53	10.00	4.00
❑	365	Barry Bonds HR 54	10.00	4.00
❑	365	Barry Bonds HR 55	10.00	4.00
❑	365	Barry Bonds HR 56	10.00	4.00
❑	365	Barry Bonds HR 57	10.00	4.00
❑	365	Barry Bonds HR 58	10.00	4.00
❑	365	Barry Bonds HR 59	10.00	4.00
❑	365	Barry Bonds HR 60	10.00	4.00
❑	365	Barry Bonds HR 61	15.00	6.00
❑	365	Barry Bonds HR 62	10.00	4.00
❑	365	Barry Bonds HR 63	10.00	4.00
❑	365	Barry Bonds HR 64	10.00	4.00
❑	365	Barry Bonds HR 65	10.00	4.00
❑	365	Barry Bonds HR 66	10.00	4.00
❑	365	Barry Bonds HR 67	10.00	4.00
❑	365	Barry Bonds HR 68	10.00	4.00
❑	365	Barry Bonds HR 69	10.00	4.00
❑	365	Barry Bonds HR 70	15.00	6.00
❑	365	Barry Bonds HR 71	10.00	4.00
❑	365	Barry Bonds HR 72	10.00	4.00
❑	365	Barry Bonds HR 73	50.00	20.00
❑	366	Pat Meares	.20	.07
❑	367	Mike Lieberthal	.20	.07
❑	368	Larry Bigbie	.20	.07
❑	369	Ron Gant	.20	.07
❑	370	Moises Alou	.20	.07
❑	371	Chad Kreuter	.20	.07
❑	372	Willis Roberts	.20	.07
❑	373	Toby Hall	.20	.07
❑	374	Miguel Batista	.20	.07
❑	375	John Burkett	.20	.07
❑	376	Cory Lidle	.20	.07
❑	377	Nick Neugebauer	.20	.07
❑	378	Jay Payton	.20	.07
❑	379	Steve Karsay	.20	.07
❑	380	Eric Chavez	.20	.07
❑	381	Kelly Stinnett	.20	.07
❑	382	Jarrod Washburn	.20	.07
❑	383	Rick White	.20	.07
❑	384	Jeff Conine	.20	.07
❑	385	Fred McGriff	.30	.10
❑	386	Marvin Benard	.20	.07
❑	387	Joe Crede	.20	.07
❑	388	Dennis Cook	.20	.07
❑	389	Rick Reed	.20	.07
❑	390	Tom Glavine	.30	.10
❑	391	Rondell White	.20	.07
❑	392	Matt Morris	.20	.07
❑	393	Pat Rapp	.20	.07
❑	394	Robert Person	.20	.07
❑	395	Omar Vizquel	.30	.10
❑	396	Jeff Cirillo	.20	.07
❑	397	Dave Mlicki	.20	.07
❑	398	Jose Ortiz	.20	.07
❑	399	Ryan Dempster	.20	.07
❑	400	Curt Schilling	.20	.07
❑	401	Peter Bergeron	.20	.07
❑	402	Kyle Lohse	.20	.07
❑	403	Craig Wilson	.20	.07
❑	404	David Justice	.20	.07
❑	405	Darin Erstad	.20	.07
❑	406	Jose Mercedes	.20	.07
❑	407	Carl Pavano	.20	.07
❑	408	Albie Lopez	.20	.07
❑	409	Alex Ochoa	.20	.07
❑	410	Chipper Jones	.50	.20
❑	411	Tyler Houston	.20	.07
❑	412	Dean Palmer	.20	.07
❑	413	Damian Jackson	.20	.07
❑	414	Josh Towers	.20	.07
❑	415	Rafael Furcal	.20	.07

❑ 416 Mike Morgan .20 .07
❑ 417 Herb Perry .20 .07
❑ 418 Mike Sirotka .20 .07
❑ 419 Mark Wohlers .20 .07
❑ 420 Nomar Garciaparra .75 .30
❑ 421 Felipe Lopez .20 .07
❑ 422 Joe McEwing .20 .07
❑ 423 Jacque Jones .20 .07
❑ 424 Julio Franco .20 .07
❑ 425 Frank Thomas .50 .20
❑ 426 So Taguchi RC .75 .30
❑ 427 Kazuhisa Ishii RC .50 .20
❑ 428 D'Angelo Jimenez .20 .07
❑ 429 Chris Stynes .20 .07
❑ 430 Kerry Wood .20 .07
❑ 431 Chris Singleton .20 .07
❑ 432 Erubiel Durazo .20 .07
❑ 433 Matt Lawton .20 .07
❑ 434 Bill Mueller .20 .07
❑ 435 Jose Canseco .30 .10
❑ 436 Ben Grieve .20 .07
❑ 437 Terry Mulholland .20 .07
❑ 438 David Bell .20 .07
❑ 439 A.J. Pierzynski .20 .07
❑ 440 Adam Dunn .20 .07
❑ 441 Jon Garland .20 .07
❑ 442 Jeff Fassero .20 .07
❑ 443 Julio Lugo .20 .07
❑ 444 Carlos Guillen .20 .07
❑ 445 Orlando Hernandez .20 .07
❑ 446 M.Loretta UER Leskanic .20 .07
❑ 447 Scott Spiezio .20 .07
❑ 448 Kevin Millwood .20 .07
❑ 449 Jamie Moyer .20 .07
❑ 450 Todd Helton .30 .10
❑ 451 Todd Walker .20 .07
❑ 452 Jose Lima .20 .07
❑ 453 Brook Fordyce .20 .07
❑ 454 Aaron Rowand .20 .07
❑ 455 Barry Zito .20 .07
❑ 456 Eric Owens .20 .07
❑ 457 Charles Nagy .20 .07
❑ 458 Raul Ibanez .20 .07
❑ 459 Joe Mays .20 .07
❑ 460 Jim Thome .30 .10
❑ 461 Adam Eaton .20 .07
❑ 462 Felix Martinez .20 .07
❑ 463 Vernon Wells .20 .07
❑ 464 Donnie Sadler .20 .07
❑ 465 Tony Clark .20 .07
❑ 466 Jose Hernandez .20 .07
❑ 467 Ramon Martinez .20 .07
❑ 468 Rusty Greer .20 .07
❑ 469 Rod Barajas .20 .07
❑ 470 Lance Berkman .20 .07
❑ 471 Brady Anderson .20 .07
❑ 472 Pedro Astacio .20 .07
❑ 473 Shane Halter .20 .07
❑ 474 Bret Prinz .20 .07
❑ 475 Edgar Martinez .30 .10
❑ 476 Steve Trachsel .20 .07
❑ 477 Gary Matthews Jr. .20 .07
❑ 478 Ismael Valdes .20 .07
❑ 479 Juan Uribe .20 .07
❑ 480 Shawn Green .20 .07
❑ 481 Kirk Rueter .20 .07
❑ 482 Damion Easley .20 .07
❑ 483 Chris Carpenter .20 .07
❑ 484 Kris Benson .20 .07
❑ 485 Antonio Alfonseca .20 .07
❑ 486 Kyle Farnsworth .20 .07
❑ 487 Brandon Lyon .20 .07
❑ 488 Hideki Irabu .20 .07
❑ 489 David Ortiz .50 .20
❑ 490 Mike Piazza .75 .30
❑ 491 Derek Lowe .20 .07
❑ 492 Chris Gomez .20 .07
❑ 493 Mark Johnson .20 .07
❑ 494 John Rocker .20 .07
❑ 495 Eric Karros .20 .07
❑ 496 Bill Haselman .20 .07
❑ 497 Dave Veres .20 .07
❑ 498 Pete Harnisch .20 .07
❑ 499 Tomokazu Ohka .20 .07
❑ 500 Barry Bonds 1.25 .50
❑ 501 David Dellucci .20 .07
❑ 502 Wendell Magee .20 .07
❑ 503 Tom Gordon .20 .07
❑ 504 Javier Vazquez .20 .07
❑ 505 Ben Sheets .20 .07
❑ 506 Wilton Guerrero .20 .07
❑ 507 John Halama .20 .07
❑ 508 Mark Redman .20 .07
❑ 509 Jack Wilson .20 .07
❑ 510 Bernie Williams .30 .10
❑ 511 Miguel Cairo .20 .07
❑ 512 Denny Hocking .20 .07
❑ 513 Tony Batista .20 .07
❑ 514 Mark Grudzielanek .20 .07
❑ 515 Jose Vidro .20 .07
❑ 516 Sterling Hitchcock .20 .07
❑ 517 Billy Koch .20 .07
❑ 518 Matt Clement .20 .07
❑ 519 Bruce Chen .20 .07
❑ 520 Roberto Alomar .30 .10
❑ 521 Orlando Palmeiro .20 .07
❑ 522 Steve Finley .20 .07
❑ 523 Danny Patterson .20 .07
❑ 524 Terry Adams .20 .07
❑ 525 Tino Martinez .30 .10
❑ 526 Tony Armas Jr. .20 .07
❑ 527 Geoff Jenkins .20 .07
❑ 528 Kerry Robinson .20 .07
❑ 529 Corey Patterson .20 .07
❑ 530 Brian Giles .20 .07
❑ 531 Jose Jimenez .20 .07
❑ 532 Joe Kennedy .20 .07
❑ 533 Armando Rios .20 .07
❑ 534 Osvaldo Fernandez .20 .07
❑ 535 Ruben Sierra .20 .07
❑ 536 Octavio Dotel .20 .07
❑ 537 Luis Sojo .20 .07
❑ 538 Brent Butler .20 .07
❑ 539 Pablo Ozuna .20 .07
❑ 540 Freddy Garcia .20 .07
❑ 541 Chad Durbin .20 .07
❑ 542 Orlando Merced .20 .07
❑ 543 Michael Tucker .20 .07
❑ 544 Roberto Hernandez .20 .07
❑ 545 Pat Burrell .20 .07
❑ 546 A.J. Burnett .20 .07
❑ 547 Bubba Trammell .20 .07
❑ 548 Scott Elarton .20 .07
❑ 549 Mike Darr .20 .07
❑ 550 Ken Griffey Jr. .75 .30
❑ 551 Ugueth Urbina .20 .07
❑ 552 Todd Jones .20 .07
❑ 553 Delino Deshields .20 .07
❑ 554 Adam Piatt .20 .07
❑ 555 Jason Kendall .20 .07
❑ 556 Hector Ortiz .20 .07
❑ 557 Turk Wendell .20 .07
❑ 558 Rob Bell .20 .07
❑ 559 Sun Woo Kim .20 .07
❑ 560 Raul Mondesi .20 .07
❑ 561 Brent Abernathy .20 .07
❑ 562 Seth Etherton .20 .07
❑ 563 Shawn Wooten .20 .07
❑ 564 Jay Buhner .20 .07
❑ 565 Andres Galarraga .20 .07
❑ 566 Shane Reynolds .20 .07
❑ 567 Rod Beck .20 .07
❑ 568 Dee Brown .20 .07
❑ 569 Pedro Feliz .20 .07
❑ 570 Ryan Klesko .20 .07
❑ 571 John Vander Wal .20 .07
❑ 572 Nick Bierbrodt .20 .07
❑ 573 Joe Nathan .20 .07
❑ 574 James Baldwin .20 .07
❑ 575 J.D. Drew .20 .07
❑ 576 Greg Colbrunn .20 .07
❑ 577 Doug Glanville .20 .07
❑ 578 Brandon Duckworth .20 .07
❑ 579 Shawn Chacon .20 .07
❑ 580 Rich Aurilia .20 .07
❑ 581 Chuck Finley .20 .07
❑ 582 Abraham Nunez .20 .07
❑ 583 Kenny Lofton .20 .07
❑ 584 Brian Daubach .20 .07
❑ 585 Miguel Tejada .20 .07
❑ 586 Nate Cornejo .20 .07
❑ 587 Kazuhiro Sasaki .20 .07
❑ 588 Chris Richard .20 .07
❑ 589 Armando Reynoso .20 .07
❑ 590 Tim Hudson .20 .07
❑ 591 Neifi Perez .20 .07
❑ 592 Steve Cox .20 .07
❑ 593 Henry Blanco .20 .07
❑ 594 Ricky Ledee .20 .07
❑ 595 Tim Salmon .30 .10
❑ 596 Luis Rivas .20 .07
❑ 597 Jeff Zimmerman .20 .07
❑ 598 Matt Stairs .20 .07
❑ 599 Preston Wilson .20 .07
❑ 600 Mark McGwire 1.25 .50
❑ 601 Timo Perez .20 .07
❑ 602 Matt Anderson .20 .07
❑ 603 Todd Hundley .20 .07
❑ 604 Rick Ankiel .20 .07
❑ 605 Tsuyoshi Shinjo .20 .07
❑ 606 Woody Williams .20 .07
❑ 607 Jason LaRue .20 .07
❑ 608 Carlos Lee .20 .07
❑ 609 Russ Johnson .20 .07
❑ 610 Scott Rolen .30 .10
❑ 611 Brent Mayne .20 .07
❑ 612 Darrin Fletcher .20 .07
❑ 613 Ray Lankford .20 .07
❑ 614 Troy O'Leary .20 .07
❑ 615 Javier Lopez .20 .07
❑ 616 Randy Velarde .20 .07
❑ 617 Vinny Castilla .20 .07
❑ 618 Milton Bradley .20 .07
❑ 619 Ruben Mateo .20 .07
❑ 620 Jason Giambi Yankees .20 .07
❑ 621 Andy Benes .20 .07
❑ 622 Joe Mauer RC 10.00 4.00
❑ 623 Andy Pettitte .30 .10
❑ 624 Jose Offerman .20 .07
❑ 625 Mo Vaughn .20 .07
❑ 626 Steve Sparks .20 .07
❑ 627 Mike Matthews .20 .07
❑ 628 Robb Nen .20 .07
❑ 629 Kip Wells .20 .07
❑ 630 Kevin Brown .20 .07
❑ 631 Arthur Rhodes .20 .07
❑ 632 Gabe Kapler .20 .07
❑ 633 Jermaine Dye .20 .07
❑ 634 Josh Beckett .20 .07
❑ 635 Pokey Reese .20 .07
❑ 636 Benji Gil .20 .07
❑ 637 Marcus Giles .20 .07
❑ 638 Julian Tavarez .20 .07
❑ 639 Jason Schmidt .20 .07
❑ 640 Alex Rodriguez .75 .30
❑ 641 Anaheim Angels TC .20 .07
❑ 642 Arizona Diamondbacks TC .30 .10
❑ 643 Atlanta Braves TC .20 .07
❑ 644 Baltimore Orioles TC .20 .07
❑ 645 Boston Red Sox TC .20 .07
❑ 646 Chicago Cubs TC .20 .07
❑ 647 Chicago White Sox TC .20 .07
❑ 648 Cincinnati Reds TC .20 .07
❑ 649 Cleveland Indians TC .20 .07
❑ 650 Colorado Rockies TC .20 .07
❑ 651 Detroit Tigers TC .20 .07
❑ 652 Florida Marlins TC .20 .07
❑ 653 Houston Astros TC .20 .07
❑ 654 Kansas City Royals TC .20 .07
❑ 655 Los Angeles Dodgers TC .20 .07
❑ 656 Milwaukee Brewers TC .20 .07
❑ 657 Minnesota Twins TC .20 .07
❑ 658 Montreal Expos TC .20 .07
❑ 659 New York Mets TC .20 .07
❑ 660 New York Yankees TC .50 .20
❑ 661 Oakland Athletics TC .20 .07
❑ 662 Philadelphia Phillies TC .20 .07
❑ 663 Pittsburgh Pirates TC .20 .07
❑ 664 San Diego Padres TC .20 .07
❑ 665 San Francisco Giants TC .20 .07
❑ 666 Seattle Mariners TC .30 .10
❑ 667 St. Louis Cardinals TC .20 .07
❑ 668 Tampa Bay Devil Rays TC .20 .07
❑ 669 Texas Rangers TC .20 .07
❑ 670 Toronto Blue Jays TC .20 .07
❑ 671 Juan Cruz PROS .50 .20
❑ 672 Kevin Cash PROS RC .50 .20
❑ 673 Jimmy Gobble PROS RC .50 .20

❑ 674	Mike Hill PROS RC	.50	.20
❑ 675	Taylor Buchholz PROS RC	.50	.20
❑ 676	Bill Hall PROS	.50	.20
❑ 677	Brett Roneberg PROS RC	.50	.20
❑ 678	Royce Huffman PROS RC	.50	.20
❑ 679	Chris Tritle PROS RC	.50	.20
❑ 680	Nate Espy PROS RC	.50	.20
❑ 681	Nick Alvarez PROS RC	.50	.20
❑ 682	Jason Botts PROS RC	.50	.20
❑ 683	Ryan Gripp PROS RC	.50	.20
❑ 684	Dan Phillips PROS RC	.50	.20
❑ 685	Pablo Arias PROS RC	.50	.20
❑ 686	John Rodriguez PROS RC	.50	.20
❑ 687	Rich Harden PROS RC	3.00	1.25
❑ 688	Neal Frendling PROS RC	.50	.20
❑ 689	Rich Thompson PROS RC	.50	.20
❑ 690	Greg Montalbano PROS RC	.50	.20
❑ 691	Len Dinardo DP RC	.50	.20
❑ 692	Ryan Raburn DP RC	.50	.20
❑ 693	Josh Barfield DP RC	2.50	1.00
❑ 694	David Bacani DP RC	.50	.20
❑ 695	Dan Johnson DP RC	1.00	.40
❑ 696	Mike Mussina GG	.20	.07
❑ 697	Ivan Rodriguez GG	.30	.10
❑ 698	Doug Mientkiewicz GG	.20	.07
❑ 699	Roberto Alomar GG	.20	.07
❑ 700	Eric Chavez GG	.20	.07
❑ 701	Omar Vizquel GG	.20	.07
❑ 702	Mike Cameron GG	.20	.07
❑ 703	Torii Hunter GG	.20	.07
❑ 704	Ichiro Suzuki GG	.50	.20
❑ 705	Greg Maddux GG	.50	.20
❑ 706	Brad Ausmus GG	.20	.07
❑ 707	Todd Helton GG	.20	.07
❑ 708	Fernando Vina GG	.20	.07
❑ 709	Scott Rolen GG	.20	.07
❑ 710	Orlando Cabrera GG	.20	.07
❑ 711	Andruw Jones GG	.20	.07
❑ 712	Jim Edmonds GG	.20	.07
❑ 713	Larry Walker GG	.20	.07
❑ 714	Roger Clemens CY	.50	.20
❑ 715	Randy Johnson CY	.30	.10
❑ 716	Ichiro Suzuki MVP	.50	.20
❑ 717	Barry Bonds MVP	.75	.30
❑ 718	Ichiro Suzuki ROY	.50	.20
❑ 719	Albert Pujols ROY	.50	.20

2002 Topps Traded

❑	COMPLETE SET (275)	200.00	100.00
❑	COMMON CARD (T1-T110)	2.00	.75
❑	COMMON CARD (T111-T275)	.40	.15
❑ T1	Jeff Weaver	2.00	.75
❑ T2	Jay Powell	2.00	.75
❑ T3	Alex Gonzalez	2.00	.75
❑ T4	Jason Isringhausen	2.00	.75
❑ T5	Tyler Houston	2.00	.75
❑ T6	Ben Broussard	2.00	.75
❑ T7	Chuck Knoblauch	2.00	.75
❑ T8	Brian L. Hunter	2.00	.75
❑ T9	Dustan Mohr	2.00	.75
❑ T10	Eric Hinske	2.00	.75
❑ T11	Roger Cedeno	2.00	.75
❑ T12	Eddie Perez	2.00	.75
❑ T13	Jeromy Burnitz	2.00	.75
❑ T14	Bartolo Colon	2.00	.75
❑ T15	Rick Helling	2.00	.75
❑ T16	Dan Plesac	2.00	.75
❑ T17	Scott Strickland	2.00	.75
❑ T18	Antonio Alfonseca	2.00	.75
❑ T19	Ricky Gutierrez	2.00	.75
❑ T20	John Valentin	2.00	.75
❑ T21	Raul Mondesi	2.00	.75
❑ T22	Ben Davis	2.00	.75
❑ T23	Nelson Figueroa	2.00	.75
❑ T24	Earl Snyder	2.00	.75
❑ T25	Robin Ventura	2.00	.75
❑ T26	Jimmy Haynes	2.00	.75
❑ T27	Kenny Kelly	2.00	.75
❑ T28	Morgan Ensberg	1.00	.40
❑ T29	Reggie Sanders	2.00	.75
❑ T30	Shigetoshi Hasegawa	2.00	.75
❑ T31	Mike Timlin	2.00	.75
❑ T32	Russell Branyan	2.00	.75
❑ T33	Alan Embree	2.00	.75
❑ T34	D'Angelo Jimenez	2.00	.75
❑ T35	Kent Mercker	2.00	.75
❑ T36	Jesse Orosco	2.00	.75
❑ T37	Gregg Zaun	2.00	.75
❑ T38	Reggie Taylor	2.00	.75
❑ T39	Andres Galarraga	2.00	.75
❑ T40	Chris Truby	2.00	.75
❑ T41	Bruce Chen	2.00	.75
❑ T42	Darren Lewis	2.00	.75
❑ T43	Ryan Kohlmeier	2.00	.75
❑ T44	John McDonald	2.00	.75
❑ T45	Omar Daal	2.00	.75
❑ T46	Matt Clement	2.00	.75
❑ T47	Glendon Rusch	2.00	.75
❑ T48	Chan Ho Park	2.00	.75
❑ T49	Benny Agbayani	2.00	.75
❑ T50	Juan Gonzalez	2.00	.75
❑ T51	Carlos Baerga	2.00	.75
❑ T52	Tim Raines	2.00	.75
❑ T53	Kevin Appier	2.00	.75
❑ T54	Marty Cordova	2.00	.75
❑ T55	Jeff D'Amico	2.00	.75
❑ T56	Dmitri Young	2.00	.75
❑ T57	Roosevelt Brown	2.00	.75
❑ T58	Dustin Hermanson	2.00	.75
❑ T59	Jose Rijo	2.00	.75
❑ T60	Todd Ritchie	2.00	.75
❑ T61	Lee Stevens	2.00	.75
❑ T62	Placido Polanco	2.00	.75
❑ T63	Eric Young	2.00	.75
❑ T64	Chuck Finley	2.00	.75
❑ T65	Dicky Gonzalez	2.00	.75
❑ T66	Jose Macias	2.00	.75
❑ T67	Gabe Kapler	2.00	.75
❑ T68	Sandy Alomar Jr.	2.00	.75
❑ T69	Henry Blanco	2.00	.75
❑ T70	Julian Tavarez	2.00	.75
❑ T71	Paul Bako	2.00	.75
❑ T72	Scott Rolen	3.00	1.25
❑ T73	Brian Jordan	2.00	.75
❑ T74	Rickey Henderson	4.00	1.50
❑ T75	Kevin Mench	2.00	.75
❑ T76	Hideo Nomo	4.00	1.50
❑ T77	Jeremy Giambi	2.00	.75
❑ T78	Brad Fullmer	2.00	.75
❑ T79	Carl Everett	2.00	.75
❑ T80	David Wells	2.00	.75
❑ T81	Aaron Sele	2.00	.75
❑ T82	Todd Hollandsworth	2.00	.75
❑ T83	Vicente Padilla	2.00	.75
❑ T84	Kenny Lofton	2.00	.75
❑ T85	Corky Miller	2.00	.75
❑ T86	Josh Fogg	2.00	.75
❑ T87	Cliff Floyd	2.00	.75
❑ T88	Craig Paquette	2.00	.75
❑ T89	Jay Payton	2.00	.75
❑ T90	Carlos Pena	2.00	.75
❑ T91	Juan Encarnacion	2.00	.75
❑ T92	Rey Sanchez	2.00	.75
❑ T93	Ryan Dempster	2.00	.75
❑ T94	Mario Encarnacion	2.00	.75
❑ T95	Jorge Julio	2.00	.75
❑ T96	John Mabry	2.00	.75
❑ T97	Todd Zeile	2.00	.75
❑ T98	Johnny Damon Sox	3.00	1.25
❑ T99	Deivi Cruz	2.00	.75
❑ T100	Gary Sheffield	2.00	.75
❑ T101	Ted Lilly	2.00	.75
❑ T102	Todd Van Poppel	2.00	.75
❑ T103	Shawn Estes	2.00	.75
❑ T104	Cesar Izturis	2.00	.75
❑ T105	Ron Coomer	2.00	.75
❑ T106	Grady Little MG RC	2.00	.75
❑ T107	Jimy Williams MG	2.00	.75
❑ T108	Tony Pena MG	2.00	.75
❑ T109	Frank Robinson MG	3.00	1.25
❑ T110	Ron Gardenhire MG	2.00	.75
❑ T111	Dennis Tankersley	.40	.15
❑ T112	Alejandro Cadena RC	.40	.15
❑ T113	Justin Reid RC	.40	.15
❑ T114	Nate Field RC	.40	.15
❑ T115	Rene Reyes RC	.40	.15
❑ T116	Nelson Castro RC	.40	.15
❑ T117	Miguel Olivo	.40	.15
❑ T118	David Espinosa	.40	.15
❑ T119	Chris Bootcheck RC	.40	.15
❑ T120	Rob Henkel RC	.40	.15
❑ T121	Steve Bechler RC	.40	.15
❑ T122	Mark Outlaw RC	.40	.15
❑ T123	Henry Pichardo RC	.40	.15
❑ T124	Michael Floyd RC	.40	.15
❑ T125	Richard Lane RC	.40	.15
❑ T126	Pete Zamora RC	.40	.15
❑ T127	Javier Colina	.40	.15
❑ T128	Greg Sain RC	.40	.15
❑ T129	Ronnie Merrill	.40	.15
❑ T130	Gavin Floyd RC	1.00	.40
❑ T131	Josh Bonifay RC	.40	.15
❑ T132	Tommy Marx RC	.40	.15
❑ T133	Gary Cates Jr. RC	.40	.15
❑ T134	Neal Cotts RC	1.00	.40
❑ T135	Angel Berroa	.40	.15
❑ T136	Elio Serrano RC	.40	.15
❑ T137	J.J. Putz RC	.50	.20
❑ T138	Ruben Gotay RC	.50	.20
❑ T139	Eddie Rogers	.40	.15
❑ T140	Wily Mo Pena	.40	.15
❑ T141	Tyler Yates RC	.40	.15
❑ T142	Colin Young RC	.40	.15
❑ T143	Chance Caple	.40	.15
❑ T144	Ben Howard RC	.40	.15
❑ T145	Ryan Bukvich RC	.40	.15
❑ T146	Cliff Bartosh RC	.40	.15
❑ T147	Brandon Claussen	.40	.15
❑ T148	Cristian Guerrero	.40	.15
❑ T149	Derrick Lewis	.40	.15
❑ T150	Eric Miller RC	.40	.15
❑ T151	Justin Huber RC	.75	.30
❑ T152	Adrian Gonzalez	.40	.15
❑ T153	Brian West RC	.40	.15
❑ T154	Chris Baker RC	.40	.15
❑ T155	Drew Henson	.40	.15
❑ T156	Scott Hairston RC	.50	.20
❑ T157	Jason Simontacchi RC	.40	.15
❑ T158	Jason Arnold RC	.40	.15
❑ T159	Brandon Phillips	.40	.15
❑ T160	Adam Roller RC	.40	.15
❑ T161	Scotty Layfield RC	.40	.15
❑ T162	Freddie Money RC	.40	.15
❑ T163	Noochie Varner RC	.40	.15
❑ T164	Terrance Hill RC	.40	.15
❑ T165	Jeremy Hill RC	.40	.15
❑ T166	Carlos Cabrera RC	.40	.15
❑ T167	Jose Morban RC	.40	.15
❑ T168	Kevin Frederick RC	.40	.15
❑ T169	Mark Teixeira	1.50	.60
❑ T170	Brian Rogers	.40	.15
❑ T171	Anastacio Martinez RC	.40	.15
❑ T172	Bobby Jenks RC	1.50	.60
❑ T173	David Gil RC	.40	.15
❑ T174	Andres Torres	.40	.15
❑ T175	James Barrett RC	.40	.15
❑ T176	Jimmy Journell	.40	.15
❑ T177	Brett Kay RC	.40	.15
❑ T178	Jason Young RC	.40	.15
❑ T179	Mark Hamilton RC	.40	.15
❑ T180	Jose Bautista RC	1.00	.40
❑ T181	Blake McGinley RC	.40	.15
❑ T182	Ryan Mottl RC	.40	.15
❑ T183	Jeff Austin RC	.40	.15
❑ T184	Xavier Nady	.40	.15
❑ T185	Kyle Kane RC	.40	.15
❑ T186	Travis Foley RC	.40	.15
❑ T187	Nathan Kaup RC	.40	.15
❑ T188	Eric Cyr	.40	.15
❑ T189	Josh Cisneros RC	.40	.15

❑ T190	Brad Nelson RC	.40	.15
❑ T191	Clint Weibl RC	.40	.15
❑ T192	Ron Calloway RC	.40	.15
❑ T193	Jung Bong	.40	.15
❑ T194	Rolando Viera RC	.40	.15
❑ T195	Jason Bulger RC	.40	.15
❑ T196	Chone Figgins RC	1.50	.60
❑ T197	Jimmy Alvarez RC	.40	.15
❑ T198	Joel Crump RC	.40	.15
❑ T199	Ryan Doumit RC	.60	.25
❑ T200	Demetrius Heath RC	.40	.15
❑ T201	John Ennis RC	.40	.15
❑ T202	Doug Sessions RC	.40	.15
❑ T203	Clinton Hosford RC	.40	.15
❑ T204	Chris Narveson RC	.40	.15
❑ T205	Ross Peeples RC	.40	.15
❑ T206	Alex Requena RC	.40	.15
❑ T207	Matt Erickson RC	.40	.15
❑ T208	Brian Forystek RC	.40	.15
❑ T209	Dewon Brazelton	.40	.15
❑ T210	Nathan Haynes	.40	.15
❑ T211	Jack Cust	.40	.15
❑ T212	Jesse Foppert RC	.50	.20
❑ T213	Jesus Cota RC	.40	.15
❑ T214	Juan M. Gonzalez RC	.40	.15
❑ T215	Tim Kalita RC	.40	.15
❑ T216	Manny Delcarmen RC	.50	.20
❑ T217	Jim Kavourias RC	.40	.15
❑ T218	C.J. Wilson RC	.40	.15
❑ T219	Edwin Yan RC	.40	.15
❑ T220	Andy Van Hekken	.40	.15
❑ T221	Michael Cuddyer	.40	.15
❑ T222	Jeff Verplancke RC	.40	.15
❑ T223	Mike Wilson RC	.40	.15
❑ T224	Corwin Malone RC	.40	.15
❑ T225	Chris Snelling RC	.60	.25
❑ T226	Joe Rogers RC	.40	.15
❑ T227	Jason Bay	4.00	1.50
❑ T228	Ezequiel Astacio RC	.40	.15
❑ T229	Joey Hammond RC	.40	.15
❑ T230	Chris Duffy RC	.50	.20
❑ T231	Mark Prior	1.50	.60
❑ T232	Hansel Izquierdo RC	.40	.15
❑ T233	Franklyn German RC	.40	.15
❑ T234	Alexis Gomez	.40	.15
❑ T235	Jorge Padilla RC	.40	.15
❑ T236	Ryan Snare RC	.40	.15
❑ T237	Deivis Santos	.40	.15
❑ T238	Taggert Bozied RC	.50	.20
❑ T239	Mike Peeples RC	.40	.15
❑ T240	Ronald Acuna RC	.40	.15
❑ T241	Koyie Hill	.40	.15
❑ T242	Garrett Guzman RC	.40	.15
❑ T243	Ryan Church RC	1.00	.40
❑ T244	Tony Fontana RC	.40	.15
❑ T245	Keto Anderson RC	.40	.15
❑ T246	Brad Bouras RC	.40	.15
❑ T247	Jason Dubois RC	.50	.20
❑ T248	Angel Guzman RC	.75	.30
❑ T249	Joel Hanrahan RC	.40	.15
❑ T250	Joe Jiannetti RC	.40	.15
❑ T251	Sean Pierce RC	.40	.15
❑ T252	Jake Mauer RC	.40	.15
❑ T253	Marshall McDougall RC	.40	.15
❑ T254	Edwin Almonte RC	.40	.15
❑ T255	Shawn Riggans RC	.40	.15
❑ T256	Steven Shell RC	.40	.15
❑ T257	Kevin Hooper RC	.40	.15
❑ T258	Michael Frick RC	.40	.15
❑ T259	Travis Chapman RC	.40	.15
❑ T260	Tim Hummel RC	.40	.15
❑ T261	Adam Morrissey RC	.40	.15
❑ T262	Dontrelle Willis RC	5.00	2.00
❑ T263	Justin Sherrod RC	.40	.15
❑ T264	Gerald Smiley RC	.40	.15
❑ T265	Tony Miller RC	.40	.15
❑ T266	Nolan Ryan WW	2.50	1.00
❑ T267	Reggie Jackson WW	.60	.25
❑ T268	Steve Garvey WW	.40	.15
❑ T269	Wade Boggs WW	.60	.25
❑ T270	Sammy Sosa WW	1.00	.40
❑ T271	Curt Schilling WW	.40	.15
❑ T272	Mark Grace WW	.60	.25
❑ T273	Jason Giambi WW	.40	.15
❑ T274	Ken Griffey Jr. WW	1.50	.60
❑ T275	Roberto Alomar WW	.60	.25

2003 Topps

❑	COMPLETE SET (720)	80.00	40.00
❑	COMPLETE SERIES 1 (366)	40.00	20.00
❑	COMPLETE SERIES 2 (354)	40.00	20.00
❑	COMMON CARD (1-6/8-721)	.20	.07
❑	COMMON (292-331/660-684)	.50	.20
❑ 1	Alex Rodriguez	.75	.30
❑ 2	Dan Wilson	.20	.07
❑ 3	Jimmy Rollins	.20	.07
❑ 4	Jermaine Dye	.20	.07
❑ 5	Steve Karsay	.20	.07
❑ 6	Timo Perez	.20	.07
❑ 8	Jose Vidro	.20	.07
❑ 9	Eddie Guardado	.20	.07
❑ 10	Mark Prior	.30	.10
❑ 11	Curt Schilling	.20	.07
❑ 12	Dennis Cook	.20	.07
❑ 13	Andruw Jones	.30	.10
❑ 14	David Segui	.20	.07
❑ 15	Trot Nixon	.20	.07
❑ 16	Kerry Wood	.20	.07
❑ 17	Magglio Ordonez	.20	.07
❑ 18	Jason LaRue	.20	.07
❑ 19	Danys Baez	.20	.07
❑ 20	Todd Helton	.30	.10
❑ 21	Denny Neagle	.20	.07
❑ 22	Dave Mlicki	.20	.07
❑ 23	Roberto Hernandez	.20	.07
❑ 24	Odalis Perez	.20	.07
❑ 25	Nick Neugebauer	.20	.07
❑ 26	David Ortiz	.50	.20
❑ 27	Andres Galarraga	.20	.07
❑ 28	Edgardo Alfonzo	.20	.07
❑ 29	Chad Bradford	.20	.07
❑ 30	Jason Giambi	.20	.07
❑ 31	Brian Giles	.20	.07
❑ 32	Deivi Cruz	.20	.07
❑ 33	Robb Nen	.20	.07
❑ 34	Jeff Nelson	.20	.07
❑ 35	Edgar Renteria	.20	.07
❑ 36	Aubrey Huff	.20	.07
❑ 37	Brandon Duckworth	.20	.07
❑ 38	Juan Gonzalez	.20	.07
❑ 39	Sidney Ponson	.20	.07
❑ 40	Eric Hinske	.20	.07
❑ 41	Kevin Appier	.20	.07
❑ 42	Danny Bautista	.20	.07
❑ 43	Javier Lopez	.20	.07
❑ 44	Jeff Conine	.20	.07
❑ 45	Carlos Baerga	.20	.07
❑ 46	Ugueth Urbina	.20	.07
❑ 47	Mark Buehrle	.20	.07
❑ 48	Aaron Boone	.20	.07
❑ 49	Jason Simontacchi	.20	.07
❑ 50	Sammy Sosa	.50	.20
❑ 51	Jose Jimenez	.20	.07
❑ 52	Bobby Higginson	.20	.07
❑ 53	Luis Castillo	.20	.07
❑ 54	Orlando Merced	.20	.07
❑ 55	Brian Jordan	.20	.07
❑ 56	Eric Young	.20	.07
❑ 57	Bobby Kielty	.20	.07
❑ 58	Luis Rivas	.20	.07
❑ 59	Brad Wilkerson	.20	.07
❑ 60	Roberto Alomar	.30	.10
❑ 61	Roger Clemens	1.00	.40
❑ 62	Scott Hatteberg	.20	.07

❑ 63	Andy Ashby	.20	.07
❑ 64	Mike Williams	.20	.07
❑ 65	Ron Gant	.20	.07
❑ 66	Benito Santiago	.20	.07
❑ 67	Bret Boone	.20	.07
❑ 68	Matt Morris	.20	.07
❑ 69	Troy Glaus	.20	.07
❑ 70	Austin Kearns	.20	.07
❑ 71	Jim Thome	.30	.10
❑ 72	Rickey Henderson	.50	.20
❑ 73	Luis Gonzalez	.20	.07
❑ 74	Brad Fullmer	.20	.07
❑ 75	Herbert Perry	.20	.07
❑ 76	Randy Wolf	.20	.07
❑ 77	Miguel Tejada	.20	.07
❑ 78	Jimmy Anderson	.20	.07
❑ 79	Ramon Martinez	.20	.07
❑ 80	Ivan Rodriguez	.30	.10
❑ 81	John Flaherty	.20	.07
❑ 82	Shannon Stewart	.20	.07
❑ 83	Orlando Palmeiro	.20	.07
❑ 84	Rafael Furcal	.20	.07
❑ 85	Kenny Rogers	.20	.07
❑ 86	Terry Adams	.20	.07
❑ 87	Mo Vaughn	.20	.07
❑ 88	Jose Cruz Jr.	.20	.07
❑ 89	Mike Matheny	.20	.07
❑ 90	Alfonso Soriano	.20	.07
❑ 91	Orlando Cabrera	.20	.07
❑ 92	Jeffrey Hammonds	.20	.07
❑ 93	Hideo Nomo	.50	.20
❑ 94	Carlos Febles	.20	.07
❑ 95	Billy Wagner	.20	.07
❑ 96	Alex Gonzalez	.20	.07
❑ 97	Todd Zeile	.20	.07
❑ 98	Omar Vizquel	.30	.10
❑ 99	Jose Rijo	.20	.07
❑ 100	Ichiro Suzuki	1.00	.40
❑ 101	Steve Cox	.20	.07
❑ 102	Hideki Irabu	.20	.07
❑ 103	Roy Halladay	.20	.07
❑ 104	David Eckstein	.20	.07
❑ 105	Greg Maddux	.75	.30
❑ 106	Jay Gibbons	.20	.07
❑ 107	Travis Driskill	.20	.07
❑ 108	Fred McGriff	.30	.10
❑ 109	Frank Thomas	.50	.20
❑ 110	Shawn Green	.20	.07
❑ 111	Ruben Quevedo	.20	.07
❑ 112	Jacque Jones	.20	.07
❑ 113	Tomo Ohka	.20	.07
❑ 114	Joe McEwing	.20	.07
❑ 115	Ramiro Mendoza	.20	.07
❑ 116	Mark Mulder	.20	.07
❑ 117	Mike Lieberthal	.20	.07
❑ 118	Jack Wilson	.20	.07
❑ 119	Randall Simon	.20	.07
❑ 120	Bernie Williams	.30	.10
❑ 121	Marvin Benard	.20	.07
❑ 122	Jamie Moyer	.20	.07
❑ 123	Andy Benes	.20	.07
❑ 124	Tino Martinez	.30	.10
❑ 125	Esteban Yan	.20	.07
❑ 126	Juan Uribe	.20	.07
❑ 127	Jason Isringhausen	.20	.07
❑ 128	Chris Carpenter	.20	.07
❑ 129	Mike Cameron	.20	.07
❑ 130	Gary Sheffield	.20	.07
❑ 131	Geronimo Gil	.20	.07
❑ 132	Brian Daubach	.20	.07
❑ 133	Corey Patterson	.20	.07
❑ 134	Aaron Rowand	.20	.07
❑ 135	Chris Reitsma	.20	.07
❑ 136	Bob Wickman	.20	.07
❑ 137	Cesar Izturis	.20	.07
❑ 138	Jason Jennings	.20	.07
❑ 139	Brandon Inge	.20	.07
❑ 140	Larry Walker	.20	.07
❑ 141	Ramon Santiago	.20	.07
❑ 142	Vladimir Nunez	.20	.07
❑ 143	Jose Vizcaino	.20	.07
❑ 144	Mark Quinn	.20	.07
❑ 145	Michael Tucker	.20	.07
❑ 146	Darren Dreifort	.20	.07
❑ 147	Ben Sheets	.20	.07
❑ 148	Corey Koskie	.20	.07

❑ 149	Tony Armas Jr.	.20	.07
❑ 150	Kazuhisa Ishii	.20	.07
❑ 151	Al Leiter	.20	.07
❑ 152	Steve Trachsel	.20	.07
❑ 153	Mike Stanton	.20	.07
❑ 154	David Justice	.20	.07
❑ 155	Marlon Anderson	.20	.07
❑ 156	Jason Kendall	.20	.07
❑ 157	Brian Lawrence	.20	.07
❑ 158	J.T. Snow	.20	.07
❑ 159	Edgar Martinez	.30	.10
❑ 160	Pat Burrell	.20	.07
❑ 161	Kerry Robinson	.20	.07
❑ 162	Greg Vaughn	.20	.07
❑ 163	Carl Everett	.20	.07
❑ 164	Vernon Wells	.20	.07
❑ 165	Jose Mesa	.20	.07
❑ 166	Troy Percival	.20	.07
❑ 167	Erubiel Durazo	.20	.07
❑ 168	Jason Marquis	.20	.07
❑ 169	Jerry Hairston Jr.	.20	.07
❑ 170	Vladimir Guerrero	.50	.20
❑ 171	Byung-Hyun Kim	.20	.07
❑ 172	Marcus Giles	.20	.07
❑ 173	Johnny Damon	.30	.10
❑ 174	Jon Lieber	.20	.07
❑ 175	Terrence Long	.20	.07
❑ 176	Sean Casey	.20	.07
❑ 177	Adam Dunn	.20	.07
❑ 178	Juan Pierre	.20	.07
❑ 179	Wendell Magee	.20	.07
❑ 180	Barry Zito	.20	.07
❑ 181	Aramis Ramirez	.20	.07
❑ 182	Pokey Reese	.20	.07
❑ 183	Jeff Kent	.20	.07
❑ 184	Russ Ortiz	.20	.07
❑ 185	Ruben Sierra	.20	.07
❑ 186	Brent Abernathy	.20	.07
❑ 187	Ismael Valdes	.20	.07
❑ 188	Tom Wilson	.20	.07
❑ 189	Craig Counsell	.20	.07
❑ 190	Mike Mussina	.30	.10
❑ 191	Ramon Hernandez	.20	.07
❑ 192	Adam Kennedy	.20	.07
❑ 193	Tony Womack	.20	.07
❑ 194	Wes Helms	.20	.07
❑ 195	Tony Batista	.20	.07
❑ 196	Rolando Arrojo	.20	.07
❑ 197	Kyle Farnsworth	.20	.07
❑ 198	Gary Bennett	.20	.07
❑ 199	Scott Sullivan	.20	.07
❑ 200	Albert Pujols	1.00	.40
❑ 201	Kirk Rueter	.20	.07
❑ 202	Phil Nevin	.20	.07
❑ 203	Kip Wells	.20	.07
❑ 204	Ron Coomer	.20	.07
❑ 205	Jeromy Burnitz	.20	.07
❑ 206	Kyle Lohse	.20	.07
❑ 207	Mike DeJean	.20	.07
❑ 208	Paul Lo Duca	.20	.07
❑ 209	Carlos Beltran	.20	.07
❑ 210	Roy Oswalt	.20	.07
❑ 211	Mike Lowell	.20	.07
❑ 212	Robert Fick	.20	.07
❑ 213	Todd Jones	.20	.07
❑ 214	C.C. Sabathia	.20	.07
❑ 215	Danny Graves	.20	.07
❑ 216	Todd Hundley	.20	.07
❑ 217	Tim Wakefield	.20	.07
❑ 218	Derek Lowe	.20	.07
❑ 219	Kevin Millwood	.20	.07
❑ 220	Jorge Posada	.30	.10
❑ 221	Bobby J. Jones	.20	.07
❑ 222	Carlos Guillen	.20	.07
❑ 223	Fernando Vina	.20	.07
❑ 224	Ryan Rupe	.20	.07
❑ 225	Kelvim Escobar	.20	.07
❑ 226	Ramon Ortiz	.20	.07
❑ 227	Junior Spivey	.20	.07
❑ 228	Juan Cruz	.20	.07
❑ 229	Melvin Mora	.20	.07
❑ 230	Lance Berkman	.20	.07
❑ 231	Brent Butler	.20	.07
❑ 232	Shane Halter	.20	.07
❑ 233	Derrek Lee	.30	.10
❑ 234	Matt Lawton	.20	.07
❑ 235	Chuck Knoblauch	.20	.07
❑ 236	Eric Gagne	.20	.07
❑ 237	Alex Sanchez	.20	.07
❑ 238	Denny Hocking	.20	.07
❑ 239	Eric Milton	.20	.07
❑ 240	Rey Ordonez	.20	.07
❑ 241	Orlando Hernandez	.20	.07
❑ 242	Robert Person	.20	.07
❑ 243	Sean Burroughs	.20	.07
❑ 244	Jeff Cirillo	.20	.07
❑ 245	Mike Lamb	.20	.07
❑ 246	Jose Valentin	.20	.07
❑ 247	Ellis Burks	.20	.07
❑ 248	Shawn Chacon	.20	.07
❑ 249	Josh Beckett	.20	.07
❑ 250	Nomar Garciaparra	.75	.30
❑ 251	Craig Biggio	.30	.10
❑ 252	Joe Randa	.20	.07
❑ 253	Mark Grudzielanek	.20	.07
❑ 254	Glendon Rusch	.20	.07
❑ 255	Michael Barrett	.20	.07
❑ 256	Omar Daal	.20	.07
❑ 257	Elmer Dessens	.20	.07
❑ 258	Wade Miller	.20	.07
❑ 259	Adrian Beltre	.20	.07
❑ 260	Vicente Padilla	.20	.07
❑ 261	Kazuhiro Sasaki	.20	.07
❑ 262	Mike Scioscia MG	.20	.07
❑ 263	Bobby Cox MG	.20	.07
❑ 264	Mike Hargrove MG	.20	.07
❑ 265	Grady Little MG RC	.20	.07
❑ 266	Alex Gonzalez	.20	.07
❑ 267	Jerry Manuel MG	.20	.07
❑ 268	Bob Boone MG	.20	.07
❑ 269	Joel Skinner MG	.20	.07
❑ 270	Clint Hurdle MG	.20	.07
❑ 271	Miguel Batista	.20	.07
❑ 272	Bob Brenly MG	.20	.07
❑ 273	Jeff Torborg MG	.20	.07
❑ 274	Jimy Williams MG	.20	.07
❑ 275	Tony Pena MG	.20	.07
❑ 276	Jim Tracy MG	.20	.07
❑ 277	Jerry Royster MG	.20	.07
❑ 278	Ron Gardenhire MG	.20	.07
❑ 279	Frank Robinson MG	.30	.10
❑ 280	John Halama	.20	.07
❑ 281	Joe Torre MG	.30	.10
❑ 282	Art Howe MG	.20	.07
❑ 283	Larry Bowa MG	.20	.07
❑ 284	Lloyd McClendon MG	.20	.07
❑ 285	Bruce Bochy MG	.20	.07
❑ 286	Dusty Baker MG	.20	.07
❑ 287	Lou Piniella MG	.20	.07
❑ 288	Tony LaRussa MG	.20	.07
❑ 289	Todd Walker	.20	.07
❑ 290	Jerry Narron MG	.20	.07
❑ 291	Carlos Tosca MG	.20	.07
❑ 292	Chris Duncan FY RC	5.00	2.00
❑ 293	Franklin Gutierrez FY RC	1.00	.40
❑ 294	Adam LaRoche FY	.50	.20
❑ 295	Manuel Ramirez FY RC	.50	.20
❑ 296	Il Kim FY RC	.50	.20
❑ 297	Wayne Lydon FY RC	.50	.20
❑ 298	Daryl Clark FY RC	.50	.20
❑ 299	Sean Pierce FY	.50	.20
❑ 300	Andy Marte FY RC	3.00	1.25
❑ 301	Matthew Peterson FY RC	.50	.20
❑ 302	Gonzalo Lopez FY RC	.50	.20
❑ 303	Bernie Castro FY RC	.50	.20
❑ 304	Cliff Lee FY	.50	.20
❑ 305	Jason Perry FY RC	.50	.20
❑ 306	Jaime Bubela FY RC	.50	.20
❑ 307	Alexis Rios FY	1.00	.40
❑ 308	Brendan Harris FY RC	.50	.20
❑ 309	Ramon Nivar-Martinez FY RC	.50	.20
❑ 310	Terry Tiffee FY RC	.50	.20
❑ 311	Kevin Youkilis FY RC	2.00	.75
❑ 312	Ruddy Lugo FY RC	.50	.20
❑ 313	C.J. Wilson FY	.50	.20
❑ 314	Mike McNutt FY RC	.50	.20
❑ 315	Jeff Clark FY RC	.50	.20
❑ 316	Mark Malaska FY RC	.50	.20
❑ 317	Doug Waechter FY RC	.50	.20
❑ 318	Derell McCall FY RC	.50	.20
❑ 319	Scott Tyler FY RC	.50	.20
❑ 320	Craig Brazell FY RC	.50	.20
❑ 321	Walter Young FY	.50	.20
❑ 322	M.Byrd/J.Padilla FS	.50	.20
❑ 323	C.Snelling/S.Choo FS	.50	.20
❑ 324	H.Blalock/M.Teixeira FS	.50	.20
❑ 325	J.Hamilton/C.Crawford FS	1.00	.40
❑ 326	O.Hudson/J.Phelps FS	.50	.20
❑ 327	J.Cust/R.Reyes FS	.50	.20
❑ 328	A.Berroa/A.Gomez FS	.50	.20
❑ 329	M.Cuddyer/M.Restovich FS	.50	.20
❑ 330	J.Rivera/M.Thames FS	.50	.20
❑ 331	B.Puffer/J.Bong FS	.50	.20
❑ 332	Mike Cameron SH	.20	.07
❑ 333	Shawn Green SH	.20	.07
❑ 334	Oakland A's SH	.20	.07
❑ 335	Jason Giambi SH	.20	.07
❑ 336	Derek Lowe SH	.20	.07
❑ 337	AL Batting Average LL	.30	.10
❑ 338	AL Runs Scored LL	.20	.07
❑ 339	AL Home Runs LL	.30	.10
❑ 340	AL RBI's LL	.50	.20
❑ 341	AL ERA LL	.20	.07
❑ 342	AL Strikeouts LL	.30	.10
❑ 343	NL Batting Average LL	.50	.20
❑ 344	NL Runs Scored LL	.50	.20
❑ 345	NL Home Runs LL	.50	.20
❑ 346	NL RBI's LL	.20	.07
❑ 347	NL ERA LL	.30	.10
❑ 348	NL Strikeouts LL	.30	.10
❑ 349	AL Division Angels	.20	.07
❑ 350	AL/NL Division Twins/Cards	.30	.10
❑ 351	AL/NL Division Angels/Giants	.30	.10
❑ 352	NL Division Cardinals	.30	.10
❑ 353	Adam Kennedy ALCS	.20	.07
❑ 354	J.T. Snow WS	.30	.10
❑ 355	David Bell NLCS	.30	.10
❑ 356	Jason Giambi AS	.20	.07
❑ 357	Alfonso Soriano AS	.20	.07
❑ 358	Alex Rodriguez AS	.50	.20
❑ 359	Eric Chavez AS	.20	.07
❑ 360	Torii Hunter AS	.20	.07
❑ 361	Bernie Williams AS	.20	.07
❑ 362	Garret Anderson AS	.20	.07
❑ 363	Jorge Posada AS	.20	.07
❑ 364	Derek Lowe AS	.20	.07
❑ 365	Barry Zito AS	.20	.07
❑ 366	Manny Ramirez AS	.30	.10
❑ 367	Mike Scioscia AS	.20	.07
❑ 368	Francisco Rodriguez	.20	.07
❑ 369	Chris Hammond	.20	.07
❑ 370	Chipper Jones	.50	.20
❑ 371	Chris Singleton	.20	.07
❑ 372	Cliff Floyd	.20	.07
❑ 373	Bobby Hill	.20	.07
❑ 374	Antonio Osuna	.20	.07
❑ 375	Barry Larkin	.30	.10
❑ 376	Charles Nagy	.20	.07
❑ 377	Denny Stark	.20	.07
❑ 378	Dean Palmer	.20	.07
❑ 379	Eric Owens	.20	.07
❑ 380	Randy Johnson	.50	.20
❑ 381	Jeff Suppan	.20	.07
❑ 382	Eric Karros	.20	.07
❑ 383	Luis Vizcaino	.20	.07
❑ 384	Johan Santana	.75	.30
❑ 385	Javier Vazquez	.20	.07
❑ 386	John Thomson	.20	.07
❑ 387	Nick Johnson	.20	.07
❑ 388	Mark Ellis	.20	.07
❑ 389	Doug Glanville	.20	.07
❑ 390	Ken Griffey Jr.	.75	.30
❑ 391	Bubba Trammell	.20	.07
❑ 392	Livan Hernandez	.20	.07
❑ 393	Desi Relaford	.20	.07
❑ 394	Eli Marrero	.20	.07
❑ 395	Jared Sandberg	.20	.07
❑ 396	Barry Bonds	1.25	.50
❑ 397	Esteban Loaiza	.20	.07
❑ 398	Aaron Sele	.20	.07
❑ 399	Geoff Blum	.20	.07
❑ 400	Derek Jeter	1.25	.50
❑ 401	Eric Byrnes	.20	.07
❑ 402	Mike Timlin	.20	.07
❑ 403	Mark Kotsay	.20	.07
❑ 404	Rich Aurilia	.20	.07
❑ 405	Joel Pineiro	.20	.07
❑ 406	Chuck Finley	.20	.07

❑ 407 Bengie Molina .20 .07
❑ 408 Steve Finley .20 .07
❑ 409 Julio Franco .20 .07
❑ 410 Marty Cordova .20 .07
❑ 411 Shea Hillenbrand .20 .07
❑ 412 Mark Bellhorn .20 .07
❑ 413 Jon Garland .20 .07
❑ 414 Reggie Taylor .20 .07
❑ 415 Milton Bradley .20 .07
❑ 416 Carlos Pena .20 .07
❑ 417 Andy Fox .20 .07
❑ 418 Brad Ausmus .20 .07
❑ 419 Brent Mayne .20 .07
❑ 420 Paul Quantrill .20 .07
❑ 421 Carlos Delgado .20 .07
❑ 422 Kevin Mench .20 .07
❑ 423 Joe Kennedy .20 .07
❑ 424 Mike Crudale .20 .07
❑ 425 Mark McLemore .20 .07
❑ 426 Bill Mueller .20 .07
❑ 427 Rob Mackowiak .20 .07
❑ 428 Ricky Ledee .20 .07
❑ 429 Ted Lilly .20 .07
❑ 430 Sterling Hitchcock .20 .07
❑ 431 Scott Strickland .20 .07
❑ 432 Damion Easley .20 .07
❑ 433 Torii Hunter .20 .07
❑ 434 Brad Radke .20 .07
❑ 435 Geoff Jenkins .20 .07
❑ 436 Paul Byrd .20 .07
❑ 437 Morgan Ensberg .20 .07
❑ 438 Mike Maroth .20 .07
❑ 439 Mike Hampton .20 .07
❑ 440 Adam Hyzdu .20 .07
❑ 441 Vance Wilson .20 .07
❑ 442 Todd Ritchie .20 .07
❑ 443 Tom Gordon .20 .07
❑ 444 John Burkett .20 .07
❑ 445 Rodrigo Lopez .20 .07
❑ 446 Tim Spooneybarger .20 .07
❑ 447 Quinton Mccracken .20 .07
❑ 448 Tim Salmon .30 .10
❑ 449 Jarrod Washburn .20 .07
❑ 450 Pedro Martinez .30 .10
❑ 451 Dustan Mohr .20 .07
❑ 452 Julio Lugo .20 .07
❑ 453 Scott Stewart .20 .07
❑ 454 Armando Benitez .20 .07
❑ 455 Raul Mondesi .20 .07
❑ 456 Robin Ventura .20 .07
❑ 457 Bobby Abreu .20 .07
❑ 458 Josh Fogg .20 .07
❑ 459 Ryan Klesko .20 .07
❑ 460 Tsuyoshi Shinjo .20 .07
❑ 461 Jim Edmonds .20 .07
❑ 462 Cliff Politte .20 .07
❑ 463 Chan Ho Park .20 .07
❑ 464 John Mabry .20 .07
❑ 465 Woody Williams .20 .07
❑ 466 Jason Michaels .20 .07
❑ 467 Scott Schoeneweis .20 .07
❑ 468 Brian Anderson .20 .07
❑ 469 Brett Tomko .20 .07
❑ 470 Scott Erickson .20 .07
❑ 471 Kevin Millar Sox .20 .07
❑ 472 Danny Wright .20 .07
❑ 473 Jason Schmidt .20 .07
❑ 474 Scott Williamson .20 .07
❑ 475 Einar Diaz .20 .07
❑ 476 Jay Payton .20 .07
❑ 477 Juan Acevedo .20 .07
❑ 478 Ben Grieve .20 .07
❑ 479 Raul Ibanez .20 .07
❑ 480 Richie Sexson .20 .07
❑ 481 Rick Reed .20 .07
❑ 482 Pedro Astacio .20 .07
❑ 483 Adam Piatt .20 .07
❑ 484 Bud Smith .20 .07
❑ 485 Tomas Perez .20 .07
❑ 486 Adam Eaton .20 .07
❑ 487 Rafael Palmeiro .30 .10
❑ 488 Jason Tyner .20 .07
❑ 489 Scott Rolen .30 .10
❑ 490 Randy Winn .20 .07
❑ 491 Ryan Jensen .20 .07
❑ 492 Trevor Hoffman .20 .07
❑ 493 Craig Wilson .20 .07
❑ 494 Jeremy Giambi .20 .07
❑ 495 Daryle Ward .20 .07
❑ 496 Shane Spencer .20 .07
❑ 497 Andy Pettitte .30 .10
❑ 498 John Franco .20 .07
❑ 499 Felipe Lopez .20 .07
❑ 500 Mike Piazza .75 .30
❑ 501 Cristian Guzman .20 .07
❑ 502 Jose Hernandez .20 .07
❑ 503 Octavio Dotel .20 .07
❑ 504 Brad Penny .20 .07
❑ 505 Dave Veres .20 .07
❑ 506 Ryan Dempster .20 .07
❑ 507 Joe Crede .20 .07
❑ 508 Chad Hermansen .20 .07
❑ 509 Gary Matthews Jr. .20 .07
❑ 510 Matt Franco .20 .07
❑ 511 Ben Weber .20 .07
❑ 512 Dave Berg .20 .07
❑ 513 Michael Young .30 .10
❑ 514 Frank Catalanotto .20 .07
❑ 515 Darin Erstad .20 .07
❑ 516 Matt Williams .20 .07
❑ 517 B.J. Surhoff .20 .07
❑ 518 Kerry Ligtenberg .20 .07
❑ 519 Mike Bordick .20 .07
❑ 520 Arthur Rhodes .20 .07
❑ 521 Joe Girardi .20 .07
❑ 522 D'Angelo Jimenez .20 .07
❑ 523 Paul Konerko .20 .07
❑ 524 Jose Macias .20 .07
❑ 525 Joe Mays .20 .07
❑ 526 Marquis Grissom .20 .07
❑ 527 Neifi Perez .20 .07
❑ 528 Preston Wilson .20 .07
❑ 529 Jeff Weaver .20 .07
❑ 530 Eric Chavez .20 .07
❑ 531 Placido Polanco .20 .07
❑ 532 Matt Mantei .20 .07
❑ 533 James Baldwin .20 .07
❑ 534 Toby Hall .20 .07
❑ 535 Brendan Donnelly .20 .07
❑ 536 Benji Gil .20 .07
❑ 537 Damian Moss .20 .07
❑ 538 Jorge Julio .20 .07
❑ 539 Matt Clement .20 .07
❑ 540 Brian Moehler .20 .07
❑ 541 Lee Stevens .20 .07
❑ 542 Jimmy Haynes .20 .07
❑ 543 Terry Mulholland .20 .07
❑ 544 Dave Roberts .20 .07
❑ 545 J.C. Romero .20 .07
❑ 546 Bartolo Colon .20 .07
❑ 547 Roger Cedeno .20 .07
❑ 548 Mariano Rivera .50 .20
❑ 549 Billy Koch .20 .07
❑ 550 Manny Ramirez .30 .10
❑ 551 Travis Lee .20 .07
❑ 552 Oliver Perez .20 .07
❑ 553 Tim Worrell .20 .07
❑ 554 Rafael Soriano .20 .07
❑ 555 Damian Miller .20 .07
❑ 556 John Smoltz .30 .10
❑ 557 Willis Roberts .20 .07
❑ 558 Tim Hudson .20 .07
❑ 559 Moises Alou .20 .07
❑ 560 Gary Glover .20 .07
❑ 561 Corky Miller .20 .07
❑ 562 Ben Broussard .20 .07
❑ 563 Gabe Kapler .20 .07
❑ 564 Chris Woodward .20 .07
❑ 565 Paul Wilson .20 .07
❑ 566 Todd Hollandsworth .20 .07
❑ 567 So Taguchi .20 .07
❑ 568 John Olerud .20 .07
❑ 569 Reggie Sanders .20 .07
❑ 570 Jake Peavy .20 .07
❑ 571 Kris Benson .20 .07
❑ 572 Todd Pratt .20 .07
❑ 573 Ray Durham .20 .07
❑ 574 Boomer Wells .20 .07
❑ 575 Chris Widger .20 .07
❑ 576 Shawn Wooten .20 .07
❑ 577 Tom Glavine .30 .10
❑ 578 Antonio Alfonseca .20 .07
❑ 579 Keith Foulke .20 .07
❑ 580 Shawn Estes .20 .07
❑ 581 Mark Grace .30 .10
❑ 582 Dmitri Young .20 .07
❑ 583 A.J. Burnett .20 .07
❑ 584 Richard Hidalgo .20 .07
❑ 585 Mike Sweeney .20 .07
❑ 586 Alex Cora .20 .07
❑ 587 Matt Stairs .20 .07
❑ 588 Doug Mientkiewicz .20 .07
❑ 589 Fernando Tatis .20 .07
❑ 590 David Weathers .20 .07
❑ 591 Cory Lidle .20 .07
❑ 592 Dan Plesac .20 .07
❑ 593 Jeff Bagwell .30 .10
❑ 594 Steve Sparks .20 .07
❑ 595 Sandy Alomar Jr. .20 .07
❑ 596 John Lackey .20 .07
❑ 597 Rick Helling .20 .07
❑ 598 Mark DeRosa .20 .07
❑ 599 Carlos Lee .20 .07
❑ 600 Garret Anderson .20 .07
❑ 601 Vinny Castilla .20 .07
❑ 602 Ryan Drese .20 .07
❑ 603 LaTroy Hawkins .20 .07
❑ 604 David Bell .20 .07
❑ 605 Freddy Garcia .20 .07
❑ 606 Miguel Cairo .20 .07
❑ 607 Scott Spiezio .20 .07
❑ 608 Mike Remlinger .20 .07
❑ 609 Tony Graffanino .20 .07
❑ 610 Russell Branyan .20 .07
❑ 611 Chris Magruder .20 .07
❑ 612 Jose Contreras RC 1.00 .40
❑ 613 Carl Pavano .20 .07
❑ 614 Kevin Brown .20 .07
❑ 615 Tyler Houston .20 .07
❑ 616 A.J. Pierzynski .20 .07
❑ 617 Tony Fiore .20 .07
❑ 618 Peter Bergeron .20 .07
❑ 619 Rondell White .20 .07
❑ 620 Brett Myers .20 .07
❑ 621 Kevin Young .20 .07
❑ 622 Kenny Lofton .20 .07
❑ 623 Ben Davis .20 .07
❑ 624 J.D. Drew .20 .07
❑ 625 Chris Gomez .20 .07
❑ 626 Karim Garcia .20 .07
❑ 627 Ricky Gutierrez .20 .07
❑ 628 Mark Redman .20 .07
❑ 629 Juan Encarnacion .20 .07
❑ 630 Anaheim Angels TC .30 .10
❑ 631 Arizona Diamondbacks TC .20 .07
❑ 632 Atlanta Braves TC .20 .07
❑ 633 Baltimore Orioles TC .20 .07
❑ 634 Boston Red Sox TC .20 .07
❑ 635 Chicago Cubs TC .20 .07
❑ 636 Chicago White Sox TC .20 .07
❑ 637 Cincinnati Reds TC .20 .07
❑ 638 Cleveland Indians TC .20 .07
❑ 639 Colorado Rockies TC .20 .07
❑ 640 Detroit Tigers TC .20 .07
❑ 641 Florida Marlins TC .20 .07
❑ 642 Houston Astros TC .20 .07
❑ 643 Kansas City Royals TC .20 .07
❑ 644 Los Angeles Dodgers TC .20 .07
❑ 645 Milwaukee Brewers TC .20 .07
❑ 646 Minnesota Twins TC .20 .07
❑ 647 Montreal Expos TC .20 .07
❑ 648 New York Mets TC .20 .07
❑ 649 New York Yankees TC .30 .10
❑ 650 Oakland Athletics TC .20 .07
❑ 651 Philadelphia Phillies TC .20 .07
❑ 652 Pittsburgh Pirates TC .20 .07
❑ 653 San Diego Padres TC .20 .07
❑ 654 San Francisco Giants TC .20 .07
❑ 655 Seattle Mariners TC .20 .07
❑ 656 St. Louis Cardinals TC .20 .07
❑ 657 Tampa Bay Devil Rays TC .20 .07
❑ 658 Texas Rangers TC .20 .07
❑ 659 Toronto Blue Jays TC .20 .07
❑ 660 Bryan Bullington DP RC .50 .20
❑ 661 Jeremy Guthrie DP .50 .20
❑ 662 Joey Gomes DP RC .50 .20
❑ 663 Evel Bastida-Martinez DP RC .50 .20
❑ 664 Brian Wright DP RC .50 .20

❑ 665 B.J. Upton DP .75 .30
❑ 666 Jeff Francis DP .50 .20
❑ 667 Drew Meyer DP .50 .20
❑ 668 Jeremy Hermida DP .75 .30
❑ 669 Khalil Greene DP .75 .30
❑ 670 Darrell Rasner DP RC .50 .20
❑ 671 Cole Hamels DP 2.00 .75
❑ 672 James Loney DP .60 .25
❑ 673 Sergio Santos DP .50 .20
❑ 674 Jason Pridie DP .50 .20
❑ 675 B.Phillips/V.Martinez .50 .20
❑ 676 H.Choi/N.Jackson .50 .20
❑ 677 D.Willis/J.Stokes .75 .30
❑ 678 C.Tracy/L.Overbay .50 .20
❑ 679 J.Borchard/C.Malone .50 .20
❑ 680 J.Mauer/J.Morneau .75 .30
❑ 681 D.Henson/B.Claussen .50 .20
❑ 682 C.Utley/G.Floyd .75 .30
❑ 683 T.Bozied/X.Nady .50 .20
❑ 684 A.Heilman/J.Reyes .50 .20
❑ 685 Kenny Rogers AW .20 .07
❑ 686 Bengie Molina AW .20 .07
❑ 687 John Olerud AW .20 .07
❑ 688 Bret Boone AW .20 .07
❑ 689 Eric Chavez AW .20 .07
❑ 690 Alex Rodriguez AW .50 .20
❑ 691 Darin Erstad AW .20 .07
❑ 692 Ichiro Suzuki AW .50 .20
❑ 693 Torii Hunter AW .20 .07
❑ 694 Greg Maddux AW .50 .20
❑ 695 Brad Ausmus AW .20 .07
❑ 696 Todd Helton AW .20 .07
❑ 697 Fernando Vina AW .20 .07
❑ 698 Scott Rolen AW .20 .07
❑ 699 Edgar Renteria AW .20 .07
❑ 700 Andruw Jones AW .20 .07
❑ 701 Larry Walker AW .20 .07
❑ 702 Jim Edmonds AW .20 .07
❑ 703 Barry Zito AW .20 .07
❑ 704 Randy Johnson AW .30 .10
❑ 705 Miguel Tejada AW .20 .07
❑ 706 Barry Bonds AW .75 .30
❑ 707 Eric Hinske AW .20 .07
❑ 708 Jason Jennings AW .20 .07
❑ 709 Todd Helton AS .20 .07
❑ 710 Jeff Kent AS .20 .07
❑ 711 Edgar Renteria AS .20 .07
❑ 712 Scott Rolen AS .20 .07
❑ 713 Barry Bonds AS .75 .30
❑ 714 Sammy Sosa AS .30 .10
❑ 715 Vladimir Guerrero AS .30 .10
❑ 716 Mike Piazza AS .50 .20
❑ 717 Curt Schilling AS .20 .07
❑ 718 Randy Johnson AS .30 .10
❑ 719 Bobby Cox AS .20 .07
❑ 720 Anaheim Angels WS .30 .10
❑ 721 Anaheim Angels WS .50 .20

2003 Topps Traded

❑ COMPLETE SET (275) 50.00 20.00
❑ COMMON CARD (T1-T120) .20 .07
❑ COMMON CARD (121-165) .40 .15
❑ T1 Juan Pierre .20 .07
❑ T2 Mark Grudzielanek .20 .07
❑ T3 Tanyon Sturtze .20 .07
❑ T4 Greg Vaughn .20 .07
❑ T5 Greg Myers .20 .07
❑ T6 Randall Simon .20 .07
❑ T7 Todd Hundley .20 .07
❑ T8 Marlon Anderson .20 .07
❑ T9 Jeff Reboulet .20 .07
❑ T10 Alex Sanchez .20 .07
❑ T11 Mike Rivera .20 .07
❑ T12 Todd Walker .20 .07
❑ T13 Ray King .20 .07
❑ T14 Shawn Estes .20 .07
❑ T15 Gary Matthews Jr. .20 .07
❑ T16 Jaret Wright .20 .07
❑ T17 Edgardo Alfonzo .20 .07
❑ T18 Omar Daal .20 .07
❑ T19 Ryan Rupe .20 .07
❑ T20 Tony Clark .20 .07
❑ T21 Jeff Suppan .20 .07
❑ T22 Mike Stanton .20 .07
❑ T23 Ramon Martinez .20 .07
❑ T24 Armando Rios .20 .07
❑ T25 Johnny Estrada .20 .07
❑ T26 Joe Girardi .20 .07
❑ T27 Ivan Rodriguez .30 .10
❑ T28 Robert Fick .20 .07
❑ T29 Rick White .20 .07
❑ T30 Robert Person .20 .07
❑ T31 Alan Benes .20 .07
❑ T32 Chris Carpenter .20 .07
❑ T33 Chris Widger .20 .07
❑ T34 Travis Hafner .20 .07
❑ T35 Mike Venafro .20 .07
❑ T36 Jon Lieber .20 .07
❑ T37 Orlando Hernandez .20 .07
❑ T38 Aaron Myette .20 .07
❑ T39 Paul Bako .20 .07
❑ T40 Erubiel Durazo .20 .07
❑ T41 Mark Guthrie .20 .07
❑ T42 Steve Avery .20 .07
❑ T43 Damian Jackson .20 .07
❑ T44 Rey Ordonez .20 .07
❑ T45 John Flaherty .20 .07
❑ T46 Byung-Hyun Kim .20 .07
❑ T47 Tom Goodwin .20 .07
❑ T48 Elmer Dessens .20 .07
❑ T49 Al Martin .20 .07
❑ T50 Gene Kingsale .20 .07
❑ T51 Lenny Harris .20 .07
❑ T52 David Ortiz Sox .50 .20
❑ T53 Jose Lima .20 .07
❑ T54 Mike Difelice .20 .07
❑ T55 Jose Hernandez .20 .07
❑ T56 Todd Zeile .20 .07
❑ T57 Roberto Hernandez .20 .07
❑ T58 Albie Lopez .20 .07
❑ T59 Roberto Alomar .30 .10
❑ T60 Russ Ortiz .20 .07
❑ T61 Brian Daubach .20 .07
❑ T62 Carl Everett .20 .07
❑ T63 Jeromy Burnitz .20 .07
❑ T64 Mark Bellhorn .20 .07
❑ T65 Ruben Sierra .20 .07
❑ T66 Mike Fetters .20 .07
❑ T67 Armando Benitez .20 .07
❑ T68 Deivi Cruz .20 .07
❑ T69 Jose Cruz Jr. .20 .07
❑ T70 Jeremy Fikac .20 .07
❑ T71 Jeff Kent .20 .07
❑ T72 Andres Galarraga .20 .07
❑ T73 Rickey Henderson .50 .20
❑ T74 Royce Clayton .20 .07
❑ T75 Troy O'Leary .20 .07
❑ T76 Ron Coomer .20 .07
❑ T77 Greg Colbrunn .20 .07
❑ T78 Wes Helms .20 .07
❑ T79 Kevin Millwood .20 .07
❑ T80 Damion Easley .20 .07
❑ T81 Bobby Kielty .20 .07
❑ T82 Keith Osik .20 .07
❑ T83 Ramiro Mendoza .20 .07
❑ T84 Shea Hillenbrand .20 .07
❑ T85 Shannon Stewart .20 .07
❑ T86 Eddie Perez .20 .07
❑ T87 Ugueth Urbina .20 .07
❑ T88 Orlando Palmeiro .20 .07
❑ T89 Graeme Lloyd .20 .07
❑ T90 John Vander Wal .20 .07
❑ T91 Gary Bennett .20 .07
❑ T92 Shane Reynolds .20 .07
❑ T93 Steve Parris .20 .07
❑ T94 Julio Lugo .20 .07
❑ T95 John Halama .20 .07
❑ T96 Carlos Baerga .20 .07
❑ T97 Jim Parque .20 .07
❑ T98 Mike Williams .20 .07
❑ T99 Fred McGriff .30 .10
❑ T100 Kenny Rogers .20 .07
❑ T101 Matt Herges .20 .07
❑ T102 Jay Bell .20 .07
❑ T103 Esteban Yan .20 .07
❑ T104 Eric Owens .20 .07
❑ T105 Aaron Fultz .20 .07
❑ T106 Rey Sanchez .20 .07
❑ T107 Jim Thome .30 .10
❑ T108 Aaron Boone .20 .07
❑ T109 Raul Mondesi .20 .07
❑ T110 Kenny Lofton .20 .07
❑ T111 Jose Guillen .20 .07
❑ T112 Aramis Ramirez .20 .07
❑ T113 Sidney Ponson .20 .07
❑ T114 Scott Williamson .20 .07
❑ T115 Robin Ventura .20 .07
❑ T116 Dusty Baker MG .20 .07
❑ T117 Felipe Alou MG .20 .07
❑ T118 Buck Showalter MG .20 .07
❑ T119 Jack McKeon MG .20 .07
❑ T120 Art Howe MG .20 .07
❑ T121 Bobby Crosby PROS .40 .15
❑ T122 Adrian Gonzalez PROS .40 .15
❑ T123 Kevin Cash PROS .40 .15
❑ T124 Shin-Soo Choo PROS .40 .15
❑ T125 Chin-Feng Chen PROS 1.00 .40
❑ T126 Miguel Cabrera PROS 1.00 .40
❑ T127 Jason Young PROS .40 .15
❑ T128 Alex Herrera PROS .40 .15
❑ T129 Jason Dubois PROS .40 .15
❑ T130 Jeff Mathis PROS .40 .15
❑ T131 Casey Kotchman PROS .40 .15
❑ T132 Ed Rogers PROS .40 .15
❑ T133 Wilson Betemit PROS .40 .15
❑ T134 Jim Kavourias PROS .40 .15
❑ T135 Taylor Buchholz PROS .40 .15
❑ T136 Adam LaRoche PROS .40 .15
❑ T137 Dallas McPherson PROS .40 .15
❑ T138 Jesus Cota PROS .40 .15
❑ T139 Clint Nageotte PROS .40 .15
❑ T140 Boof Bonser PROS .40 .15
❑ T141 Walter Young PROS .40 .15
❑ T142 Joe Crede PROS .40 .15
❑ T143 Denny Bautista PROS .40 .15
❑ T144 Victor Diaz PROS .40 .15
❑ T145 Chris Narveson PROS .40 .15
❑ T146 Gabe Gross PROS .40 .15
❑ T147 Jimmy Journell PROS .40 .15
❑ T148 Rafael Soriano PROS .40 .15
❑ T149 Jerome Williams PROS .40 .15
❑ T150 Aaron Cook PROS .40 .15
❑ T151 Anastacio Martinez PROS .40 .15
❑ T152 Scott Hairston PROS .40 .15
❑ T153 John Buck PROS .40 .15
❑ T154 Ryan Ludwick PROS .40 .15
❑ T155 Chris Bootcheck PROS .40 .15
❑ T156 John Rheinecker PROS .40 .15
❑ T157 Jason Lane PROS .40 .15
❑ T159 Adam Wainwright PROS .40 .15
❑ T160 Jason Arnold PROS .40 .15
❑ T161 Jonny Gomes PROS .60 .25
❑ T162 James Loney PROS .50 .20
❑ T163 Mike Fontenot PROS .40 .15
❑ T164 Khalil Greene PROS 1.00 .40
❑ T165 Sean Burnett PROS .40 .15
❑ T166 David Martinez FY RC .40 .15
❑ T167 Felix Pie FY RC 4.00 1.50
❑ T168 Joe Valentine FY RC .40 .15
❑ T169 Brandon Webb FY RC 3.00 1.25
❑ T170 Matt Diaz FY RC .75 .30
❑ T171 Lew Ford FY RC .50 .20
❑ T172 Jeremy Griffiths FY RC .40 .15
❑ T173 Matt Hensley FY RC .40 .15
❑ T174 Charlie Manning FY RC .40 .15
❑ T175 Elizardo Ramirez FY RC .50 .20
❑ T176 Greg Aquino FY RC .40 .15
❑ T177 Felix Sanchez FY RC .40 .15
❑ T178 Kelly Shoppach FY RC .75 .30
❑ T179 Bubba Nelson FY RC .50 .20

❑ T180 Mike O'Keefe FY RC .40 .15
❑ T181 Hanley Ramirez FY RC 5.00 2.00
❑ T182 Todd Wellemeyer FY RC .40 .15
❑ T183 Dustin Moseley FY RC .40 .15
❑ T184 Eric Crozier FY RC .50 .20
❑ T185 Ryan Shealy FY RC 2.50 1.00
❑ T186 Jeremy Bonderman FY RC 3.00 1.25
❑ T187 T.Story-Harden FY RC .40 .15
❑ T188 Dusty Brown FY RC .40 .15
❑ T189 Rob Hammock FY RC .40 .15
❑ T190 Jorge Piedra FY RC .50 .20
❑ T191 Chris De La Cruz FY RC .40 .15
❑ T192 Eli Whiteside FY RC .40 .15
❑ T193 Jason Kubel FY RC 1.00 .40
❑ T194 Jon Schuerholz FY RC .40 .15
❑ T195 Stephen Randolph FY RC .40 .15
❑ T196 Andy Sisco FY RC .40 .15
❑ T197 Sean Smith FY RC .50 .20
❑ T198 Jon-Mark Sprowl FY RC .40 .15
❑ T199 Matt Kata FY RC .40 .15
❑ T200 Robinson Cano FY RC 8.00 3.00
❑ T201 Nook Logan FY RC .50 .20
❑ T202 Ben Francisco FY RC .40 .15
❑ T203 Arnie Munoz FY RC .40 .15
❑ T204 Ozzie Chavez FY RC .40 .15
❑ T205 Eric Riggs FY RC .50 .20
❑ T206 Beau Kemp FY RC .40 .15
❑ T207 Travis Wong FY RC .50 .20
❑ T208 Dustin Yount FY RC .50 .20
❑ T209 Brian McCann FY RC 6.00 2.50
❑ T210 Wilton Reynolds FY RC .50 .20
❑ T211 Matt Bruback FY RC .40 .15
❑ T212 Andrew Brown FY RC .50 .20
❑ T213 Edgar Gonzalez FY RC .40 .15
❑ T214 Eider Torres FY RC .40 .15
❑ T215 Aquilino Lopez FY RC .40 .15
❑ T216 Bobby Basham FY RC .40 .15
❑ T217 Tim Olson FY RC .40 .15
❑ T218 Nathan Panther FY RC .40 .15
❑ T219 Bryan Grace FY RC .40 .15
❑ T220 Dusty Gomon FY RC .50 .20
❑ T221 Wil Ledezma FY RC .40 .15
❑ T222 Josh Willingham FY RC 1.00 .40
❑ T223 David Cash FY RC .40 .15
❑ T224 Oscar Villarreal FY RC .40 .15
❑ T225 Jeff Duncan FY RC .40 .15
❑ T226 Kade Johnson FY RC .40 .15
❑ T227 Luke Steidlmayer FY RC .40 .15
❑ T228 Brandon Watson FY RC .40 .15
❑ T229 Jose Morales FY RC .40 .15
❑ T230 Mike Gallo FY RC .40 .15
❑ T231 Tyler Adamczyk FY RC .40 .15
❑ T232 Adam Stern FY RC .40 .15
❑ T233 Brennan King FY RC .40 .15
❑ T234 Dan Haren FY RC .75 .30
❑ T235 Michel Hernandez FY RC .40 .15
❑ T236 Ben Fritz FY RC .40 .15
❑ T237 Clay Hensley FY RC .40 .15
❑ T238 Tyler Johnson FY RC .40 .15
❑ T239 Pete LaForest FY RC .40 .15
❑ T240 Tyler Martin FY RC .40 .15
❑ T241 J.D. Durbin FY RC .40 .15
❑ T242 Shane Victorino FY RC .75 .30
❑ T243 Rajai Davis FY RC .40 .15
❑ T244 Ismael Castro FY RC .40 .15
❑ T245 Chien-Ming Wang FY RC 6.00 2.50
❑ T246 Travis Ishikawa FY RC .75 .30
❑ T247 Corey Shafer FY RC .40 .15
❑ T248 Gary Schneidmiller FY RC .40 .15
❑ T249 Dave Pember FY RC .40 .15
❑ T250 Keith Stamler FY RC .40 .15
❑ T251 Tyson Graham FY RC .40 .15
❑ T252 Ryan Cameron FY RC .40 .15
❑ T253 Eric Eckenstahler FY .40 .15
❑ T254 Matthew Peterson FY RC .40 .15
❑ T255 Dustin McGowan FY RC .50 .20
❑ T256 Prentice Redman FY RC .40 .15
❑ T257 Haj Turay FY RC .40 .15
❑ T258 Carlos Guzman FY RC .50 .20
❑ T259 Matt DeMarco FY RC .40 .15
❑ T260 Derek Michaelis FY RC .40 .15
❑ T261 Brian Burgamy FY RC .40 .15
❑ T262 Jay Sitzman FY RC .40 .15
❑ T263 Chris Fallon FY RC .40 .15
❑ T264 Mike Adams FY RC .40 .15
❑ T265 Clint Barmes FY RC 1.00 .40
❑ T266 Eric Reed FY RC .40 .15
❑ T267 Willie Eyre FY RC .40 .15
❑ T268 Carlos Duran FY RC .40 .15
❑ T269 Nick Trzesniak FY RC .40 .15
❑ T270 Ferdin Tejeda FY RC .40 .15
❑ T271 Michael Garciaparra FY RC .40 .15
❑ T272 Michael Hinckley FY RC .50 .20
❑ T273 Branden Florence FY RC .40 .15
❑ T274 Trent Oeltjen FY RC .50 .20
❑ T275 Mike Neu FY RC .40 .15

2004 Topps

❑ COMP.HOBBY SET (737) 80.00 40.00
❑ COMP.HOLIDAY SET (742) 80.00 40.00
❑ COMP.RETAIL SET (737) 80.00 40.00
❑ COMP.ASTROS SET (737) 80.00 40.00
❑ COMP.CUBS SET (737) 80.00 40.00
❑ COMP.RED SOX SET (737) 80.00 40.00
❑ COMP.YANKEES SET (737) 80.00 40.00
❑ COMPLETE SET (732) 80.00 30.00
❑ COMPLETE SERIES 1 (366) 40.00 15.00
❑ COMPLETE SERIES 2 (366) 40.00 15.00
❑ COMMON CARD (1-6/8-732) .20 .07
❑ COMMON (297-326/668-687) .50 .20
❑ COMMON (327-331/688-692) .50 .20
❑ 1 Jim Thome .30 .10
❑ 2 Reggie Sanders .20 .07
❑ 3 Mark Kotsay .20 .07
❑ 4 Edgardo Alfonzo .20 .07
❑ 5 Ben Davis .20 .07
❑ 6 Mike Matheny .20 .07
❑ 8 Marlon Anderson .20 .07
❑ 9 Chan Ho Park .20 .07
❑ 10 Ichiro Suzuki 1.00 .40
❑ 11 Kevin Millwood .20 .07
❑ 12 Bengie Molina .20 .07
❑ 13 Tom Glavine .30 .10
❑ 14 Junior Spivey .20 .07
❑ 15 Marcus Giles .20 .07
❑ 16 David Segui .20 .07
❑ 17 Kevin Millar .20 .07
❑ 18 Corey Patterson .20 .07
❑ 19 Aaron Rowand .20 .07
❑ 20 Derek Jeter 1.00 .40
❑ 21 Jason LaRue .20 .07
❑ 22 Chris Hammond .20 .07
❑ 23 Jay Payton .20 .07
❑ 24 Bobby Higginson .20 .07
❑ 25 Lance Berkman .20 .07
❑ 26 Juan Pierre .20 .07
❑ 27 Brent Mayne .20 .07
❑ 28 Fred McGriff .30 .10
❑ 29 Richie Sexson .20 .07
❑ 30 Tim Hudson .20 .07
❑ 31 Mike Piazza .75 .30
❑ 32 Brad Radke .20 .07
❑ 33 Jeff Weaver .20 .07
❑ 34 Ramon Hernandez .20 .07
❑ 35 David Bell .20 .07
❑ 36 Craig Wilson .20 .07
❑ 37 Jake Peavy .20 .07
❑ 38 Tim Worrell .20 .07
❑ 39 Gil Meche .20 .07
❑ 40 Albert Pujols 1.00 .40
❑ 41 Michael Young .20 .07
❑ 42 Josh Phelps .20 .07
❑ 43 Brendan Donnelly .20 .07
❑ 44 Steve Finley .20 .07
❑ 45 John Smoltz .30 .10
❑ 46 Jay Gibbons .20 .07
❑ 47 Trot Nixon .20 .07
❑ 48 Carl Pavano .20 .07
❑ 49 Frank Thomas .50 .20
❑ 50 Mark Prior .30 .10
❑ 51 Danny Graves .20 .07
❑ 52 Milton Bradley UER .20 .07
❑ 53 Jose Jimenez .20 .07
❑ 54 Shane Halter .20 .07
❑ 55 Mike Lowell .20 .07
❑ 56 Geoff Blum .20 .07
❑ 57 Michael Tucker UER .20 .07
❑ 58 Paul Lo Duca .20 .07
❑ 59 Vicente Padilla .20 .07
❑ 60 Jacque Jones .20 .07
❑ 61 Fernando Tatis .20 .07
❑ 62 Ty Wigginton .20 .07
❑ 63 Pedro Astacio .20 .07
❑ 64 Andy Pettitte .30 .10
❑ 65 Terrence Long .20 .07
❑ 66 Cliff Floyd .20 .07
❑ 67 Mariano Rivera .50 .20
❑ 68 Carlos Silva .20 .07
❑ 69 Marlon Byrd .20 .07
❑ 70 Mark Mulder .20 .07
❑ 71 Kerry Ligtenberg .20 .07
❑ 72 Carlos Guillen .20 .07
❑ 73 Fernando Vina .20 .07
❑ 74 Lance Carter .20 .07
❑ 75 Hank Blalock .20 .07
❑ 76 Jimmy Rollins .20 .07
❑ 77 Francisco Rodriguez .20 .07
❑ 78 Javy Lopez .20 .07
❑ 79 Jerry Hairston Jr. .20 .07
❑ 80 Andruw Jones .30 .10
❑ 81 Rodrigo Lopez .20 .07
❑ 82 Johnny Damon .30 .10
❑ 83 Hee Seop Choi .20 .07
❑ 84 Miguel Olivo .20 .07
❑ 85 Jon Garland .20 .07
❑ 86 Matt Lawton .20 .07
❑ 87 Juan Uribe .20 .07
❑ 88 Steve Sparks .20 .07
❑ 89 Tim Spooneybarger .20 .07
❑ 90 Jose Vidro .20 .07
❑ 91 Luis Rivas .20 .07
❑ 92 Hideo Nomo .50 .20
❑ 93 Javier Vazquez .20 .07
❑ 94 Al Leiter .20 .07
❑ 95 Darren Dreifort .20 .07
❑ 96 Alex Cintron .20 .07
❑ 97 Zach Day .20 .07
❑ 98 Jorge Posada .30 .10
❑ 99 John Halama .20 .07
❑ 100 Alex Rodriguez .75 .30
❑ 101 Orlando Palmeiro .20 .07
❑ 102 Dave Berg .20 .07
❑ 103 Brad Fullmer .20 .07
❑ 104 Mike Hampton .20 .07
❑ 105 Willis Roberts .20 .07
❑ 106 Ramiro Mendoza .20 .07
❑ 107 Juan Cruz .20 .07
❑ 108 Esteban Loaiza .20 .07
❑ 109 Russell Branyan .20 .07
❑ 110 Todd Helton .30 .10
❑ 111 Braden Looper .20 .07
❑ 112 Octavio Dotel .20 .07
❑ 113 Mike MacDougal .20 .07
❑ 114 Cesar Izturis .20 .07
❑ 115 Johan Santana .50 .20
❑ 116 Jose Contreras .20 .07
❑ 117 Placido Polanco .20 .07
❑ 118 Jason Phillips .20 .07
❑ 119 Adam Eaton .20 .07
❑ 120 Vernon Wells .20 .07
❑ 121 Ben Grieve .20 .07
❑ 122 Randy Winn .20 .07
❑ 123 Ismael Valdes .20 .07
❑ 124 Eric Owens .20 .07
❑ 125 Curt Schilling .20 .07
❑ 126 Russ Ortiz .20 .07
❑ 127 Mark Buehrle .20 .07
❑ 128 Danys Baez .20 .07
❑ 129 Dmitri Young .20 .07
❑ 130 Kazuhisa Ishii .20 .07

❑ 131 A.J. Pierzynski .20 .07
❑ 132 Michael Barrett .20 .07
❑ 133 Joe McEwing .20 .07
❑ 134 Alex Cora .20 .07
❑ 135 Tom Wilson .20 .07
❑ 136 Carlos Zambrano .20 .07
❑ 137 Brett Tomko .20 .07
❑ 138 Shigetoshi Hasegawa .20 .07
❑ 139 Jarrod Washburn .20 .07
❑ 140 Greg Maddux .75 .30
❑ 141 Craig Counsell .20 .07
❑ 142 Reggie Taylor .20 .07
❑ 143 Omar Vizquel .30 .10
❑ 144 Alex Gonzalez .20 .07
❑ 145 Billy Wagner .20 .07
❑ 146 Brian Jordan .20 .07
❑ 147 Wes Helms .20 .07
❑ 148 Kyle Lohse .20 .07
❑ 149 Timo Perez .20 .07
❑ 150 Jason Giambi .20 .07
❑ 151 Erubiel Durazo .20 .07
❑ 152 Mike Lieberthal .20 .07
❑ 153 Jason Kendall .20 .07
❑ 154 Xavier Nady .20 .07
❑ 155 Kirk Rueter .20 .07
❑ 156 Mike Cameron .20 .07
❑ 157 Miguel Cairo .20 .07
❑ 158 Woody Williams .20 .07
❑ 159 Toby Hall .20 .07
❑ 160 Bernie Williams .30 .10
❑ 161 Darin Erstad .20 .07
❑ 162 Matt Mantei .20 .07
❑ 163 Geronimo Gil .20 .07
❑ 164 Bill Mueller .20 .07
❑ 165 Damian Miller .20 .07
❑ 166 Tony Graffanino .20 .07
❑ 167 Sean Casey .20 .07
❑ 168 Brandon Phillips .20 .07
❑ 169 Mike Remlinger .20 .07
❑ 170 Adam Dunn .20 .07
❑ 171 Carlos Lee .20 .07
❑ 172 Juan Encarnacion .20 .07
❑ 173 Angel Berroa .20 .07
❑ 174 Desi Relaford .20 .07
❑ 175 Paul Quantrill .20 .07
❑ 176 Ben Sheets .20 .07
❑ 177 Eddie Guardado .20 .07
❑ 178 Rocky Biddle .20 .07
❑ 179 Mike Stanton .20 .07
❑ 180 Eric Chavez .20 .07
❑ 181 Jason Michaels .20 .07
❑ 182 Terry Adams .20 .07
❑ 183 Kip Wells .20 .07
❑ 184 Brian Lawrence .20 .07
❑ 185 Bret Boone .20 .07
❑ 186 Tino Martinez .30 .10
❑ 187 Aubrey Huff .20 .07
❑ 188 Kevin Mench .20 .07
❑ 189 Tim Salmon .30 .10
❑ 190 Carlos Delgado .20 .07
❑ 191 John Lackey .20 .07
❑ 192 Oscar Villarreal .20 .07
❑ 193 Luis Matos .20 .07
❑ 194 Derek Lowe .20 .07
❑ 195 Mark Grudzielanek .20 .07
❑ 196 Tom Gordon .20 .07
❑ 197 Matt Clement .20 .07
❑ 198 Byung-Hyun Kim .20 .07
❑ 199 Brandon Inge .20 .07
❑ 200 Nomar Garciaparra .75 .30
❑ 201 Antonio Osuna .20 .07
❑ 202 Jose Mesa .20 .07
❑ 203 Bo Hart .20 .07
❑ 204 Jack Wilson .20 .07
❑ 205 Ray Durham .20 .07
❑ 206 Freddy Garcia .20 .07
❑ 207 J.D. Drew .20 .07
❑ 208 Einar Diaz .20 .07
❑ 209 Roy Halladay .20 .07
❑ 210 David Eckstein UER .20 .07
❑ 211 Jason Marquis .20 .07
❑ 212 Jorge Julio .20 .07
❑ 213 Tim Wakefield .20 .07
❑ 214 Moises Alou .20 .07
❑ 215 Bartolo Colon .20 .07
❑ 216 Jimmy Haynes .20 .07
❑ 217 Preston Wilson .20 .07
❑ 218 Luis Castillo .20 .07
❑ 219 Richard Hidalgo .20 .07
❑ 220 Manny Ramirez .30 .10
❑ 221 Mike Mussina .30 .10
❑ 222 Randy Wolf .20 .07
❑ 223 Kris Benson .20 .07
❑ 224 Ryan Klesko .20 .07
❑ 225 Rich Aurilia .20 .07
❑ 226 Kelvim Escobar .20 .07
❑ 227 Francisco Cordero .20 .07
❑ 228 Kazuhiro Sasaki .20 .07
❑ 229 Danny Bautista .20 .07
❑ 230 Rafael Furcal .20 .07
❑ 231 Travis Driskill .20 .07
❑ 232 Kyle Farnsworth .20 .07
❑ 233 Jose Valentin .20 .07
❑ 234 Felipe Lopez .20 .07
❑ 235 C.C. Sabathia .20 .07
❑ 236 Brad Penny .20 .07
❑ 237 Brad Ausmus .20 .07
❑ 238 Raul Ibanez .20 .07
❑ 239 Adrian Beltre .20 .07
❑ 240 Rocco Baldelli .20 .07
❑ 241 Orlando Hudson .20 .07
❑ 242 Dave Roberts .20 .07
❑ 243 Doug Mientkiewicz .20 .07
❑ 244 Brad Wilkerson .20 .07
❑ 245 Scott Strickland .20 .07
❑ 246 Ryan Franklin .20 .07
❑ 247 Chad Bradford .20 .07
❑ 248 Gary Bennett .20 .07
❑ 249 Jose Cruz Jr. .20 .07
❑ 250 Jeff Kent .20 .07
❑ 251 Josh Beckett .20 .07
❑ 252 Ramon Ortiz .20 .07
❑ 253 Miguel Batista .20 .07
❑ 254 Jung Bong .20 .07
❑ 255 Deivi Cruz .20 .07
❑ 256 Alex Gonzalez .20 .07
❑ 257 Shawn Chacon .20 .07
❑ 258 Runelvys Hernandez .20 .07
❑ 259 Joe Mays .20 .07
❑ 260 Eric Gagne .20 .07
❑ 261 Dustan Mohr .20 .07
❑ 262 Tomokazu Ohka .20 .07
❑ 263 Eric Byrnes .20 .07
❑ 264 Frank Catalanotto .20 .07
❑ 265 Cristian Guzman .20 .07
❑ 266 Orlando Cabrera .20 .07
❑ 267A Juan Castro .20 .07
❑ 267B Mike Scioscia MG UER 274 .20 .07
❑ 268 Bob Brenly MG .20 .07
❑ 269 Bobby Cox MG .20 .07
❑ 270 Mike Hargrove MG .20 .07
❑ 271 Grady Little MG .20 .07
❑ 272 Dusty Baker MG .20 .07
❑ 273 Jerry Manuel MG .20 .07
❑ 275 Eric Wedge MG .20 .07
❑ 276 Clint Hurdle MG .20 .07
❑ 277 Alan Trammell MG .20 .07
❑ 278 Jack McKeon MG .20 .07
❑ 279 Jimy Williams MG .20 .07
❑ 280 Tony Pena MG .20 .07
❑ 281 Jim Tracy MG .20 .07
❑ 282 Ned Yost MG .20 .07
❑ 283 Ron Gardenhire MG .20 .07
❑ 284 Frank Robinson MG .20 .07
❑ 285 Art Howe MG .20 .07
❑ 286 Joe Torre MG .30 .10
❑ 287 Ken Macha MG .20 .07
❑ 288 Larry Bowa MG .20 .07
❑ 289 Lloyd McClendon MG .20 .07
❑ 290 Bruce Bochy MG .20 .07
❑ 291 Felipe Alou MG .20 .07
❑ 292 Bob Melvin MG .20 .07
❑ 293 Tony LaRussa MG .20 .07
❑ 294 Lou Piniella MG .20 .07
❑ 295 Buck Showalter MG .20 .07
❑ 296 Carlos Tosca MG .20 .07
❑ 297 Anthony Acevedo FY RC .50 .20
❑ 298 Anthony Lerew FY RC .75 .30
❑ 299 Blake Hawksworth FY RC .50 .20
❑ 300 Brayan Pena FY RC .50 .20
❑ 301 Casey Myers FY RC .50 .20
❑ 302 Craig Ansman FY RC .50 .20
❑ 303 David Murphy FY RC .75 .30
❑ 304 Dave Crouthers FY RC .50 .20
❑ 305 Dioner Navarro FY RC .75 .30
❑ 306 Donald Levinski FY RC .50 .20
❑ 307 Jesse Roman FY RC .50 .20
❑ 308 Sung Jung FY RC .50 .20
❑ 309 Jon Knott FY RC .50 .20
❑ 310 Josh Labandeira FY RC .50 .20
❑ 311 Kenny Perez FY RC .50 .20
❑ 312 Khalid Ballouli FY RC .50 .20
❑ 313 Kyle Davies FY RC 2.50 1.00
❑ 314 Marcus McBeth FY RC .50 .20
❑ 315 Matt Creighton FY RC .50 .20
❑ 316 Chris O'Riordan FY RC .50 .20
❑ 317 Mike Gosling FY RC .50 .20
❑ 318 Nic Ungs FY RC .50 .20
❑ 319 Omar Falcon FY RC .50 .20
❑ 320 Rodney Choy Foo FY RC .50 .20
❑ 321 Tim Frend FY RC .50 .20
❑ 322 Todd Self FY RC .50 .20
❑ 323 Tydus Meadows FY RC .50 .20
❑ 324 Yadier Molina FY RC 2.00 .75
❑ 325 Zach Duke FY RC 2.00 .75
❑ 326 Zach Miner FY RC 1.25 .50
❑ 327 B.Castro/K.Greene FS .50 .20
❑ 328 R.Madson/E.Ramirez FS .50 .20
❑ 329 R.Harden/B.Crosby FS .50 .20
❑ 330 Z.Greinke/J.Gobble FS .50 .20
❑ 331 B.Jenks/C.Kotchman FS .50 .20
❑ 332 Sammy Sosa HL .30 .10
❑ 333 Kevin Millwood HL .20 .07
❑ 334 Rafael Palmeiro HL .20 .07
❑ 335 Roger Clemens HL .50 .20
❑ 336 Eric Gagne HL .20 .07
❑ 337 Mueller/Manny/Jeter LL .30 .10
❑ 338 V.Wells/Ichiro/M.Young LL .50 .20
❑ 339 A-Rod/Thomas/Delgado LL .50 .20
❑ 340 Delgado/A-Rod/Boone LL .50 .20
❑ 341 Pedro/Hudson/Loaiza LL .30 .10
❑ 342 Loaiza/Pedro/Halladay LL .30 .10
❑ 343 Pujols/Helton/Renteria LL .50 .20
❑ 344 Pujols/Helton/Pierre LL .50 .20
❑ 345 Thome/Sexson/J.Lopez LL .20 .07
❑ 346 P.Wilson/Sheff/Thome LL .20 .07
❑ 347 Schmidt/K.Brown/Prior LL .30 .10
❑ 348 Wood/Prior/Vazquez LL .30 .10
❑ 349 R.Clemens/D.Wells ALDS .50 .20
❑ 350 K.Wood/M.Prior NLDS .30 .10
❑ 351 Beckett/Cabrera/I.Rod NLCS .50 .20
❑ 352 Giambi/Rivera/Boone ALCS .50 .20
❑ 353 D.Lowe/I.Rod AL/NLDS .50 .20
❑ 354 Pedro/Posa/Clemens ALCS .50 .20
❑ 355 Juan Pierre WS .20 .07
❑ 356 Carlos Delgado AS .20 .07
❑ 357 Bret Boone AS .20 .07
❑ 358 Alex Rodriguez AS .50 .20
❑ 359 Bill Mueller AS .20 .07
❑ 360 Vernon Wells AS .20 .07
❑ 361 Garret Anderson AS .20 .07
❑ 362 Magglio Ordonez AS .20 .07
❑ 363 Jorge Posada AS .20 .07
❑ 364 Roy Halladay AS .20 .07
❑ 365 Andy Pettitte AS .20 .07
❑ 366 Frank Thomas AS .30 .10
❑ 367 Jody Gerut AS .20 .07
❑ 368 Sammy Sosa .50 .20
❑ 369 Joe Crede .20 .07
❑ 370 Gary Sheffield .20 .07
❑ 371 Coco Crisp .20 .07
❑ 372 Torii Hunter .20 .07
❑ 373 Derrek Lee .30 .10
❑ 374 Adam Everett .20 .07
❑ 375 Miguel Tejada .20 .07
❑ 376 Jeremy Affeldt .20 .07
❑ 377 Robin Ventura .20 .07
❑ 378 Scott Podsednik .20 .07
❑ 379 Matthew LeCroy .20 .07
❑ 380 Vladimir Guerrero .50 .20
❑ 381 Tike Redman .20 .07
❑ 382 Jeff Nelson .20 .07
❑ 383 Cliff Lee .20 .07
❑ 384 Bobby Abreu .20 .07
❑ 385 Josh Fogg .20 .07
❑ 386 Trevor Hoffman .20 .07
❑ 387 Jesse Foppert .20 .07
❑ 388 Edgar Martinez .30 .10

No.	Player		
389	Edgar Renteria	.20	.07
390	Chipper Jones	.50	.20
391	Eric Munson	.20	.07
392	Dewon Brazelton	.20	.07
393	John Thomson	.20	.07
394	Chris Woodward	.20	.07
395	Adam LaRoche	.20	.07
396	Elmer Dessens	.20	.07
397	Johnny Estrada	.20	.07
398	Damian Moss	.20	.07
399	Gabe Kapler	.20	.07
400	Dontrelle Willis	.30	.10
401	Troy Glaus	.20	.07
402	Raul Mondesi	.20	.07
403	Shane Reynolds	.20	.07
404	Kurt Ainsworth	.20	.07
405	Pedro Martinez	.30	.10
406	Eric Karros	.20	.07
407	Billy Koch	.20	.07
408	Scott Schoeneweis	.20	.07
409	Paul Wilson	.20	.07
410	Mike Sweeney	.20	.07
411	Jason Bay	.20	.07
412	Mark Redman	.20	.07
413	Jason Jennings	.20	.07
414	Rondell White	.20	.07
415	Todd Hundley	.20	.07
416	Shannon Stewart	.20	.07
417	Jae Weong Seo	.20	.07
418	Livan Hernandez	.20	.07
419	Mark Ellis	.20	.07
420	Pat Burrell	.20	.07
421	Mark Loretta	.20	.07
422	Robb Nen	.20	.07
423	Joel Pineiro	.20	.07
424	Jason Simontacchi	.20	.07
425	Sterling Hitchcock	.20	.07
426	Rey Ordonez	.20	.07
427	Greg Myers	.20	.07
428	Shane Spencer	.20	.07
429	Carlos Baerga	.20	.07
430	Garret Anderson	.20	.07
431	Horacio Ramirez	.20	.07
432	Brian Roberts	.20	.07
433	Damian Jackson	.20	.07
434	Doug Glanville	.20	.07
435	Brian Daubach	.20	.07
436	Alex Escobar	.20	.07
437	Alex Sanchez	.20	.07
438	Jeff Bagwell	.30	.10
439	Darrell May	.20	.07
440	Shawn Green	.20	.07
441	Geoff Jenkins	.20	.07
442	Endy Chavez	.20	.07
443	Nick Johnson	.20	.07
444	Jose Guillen	.20	.07
445	Tomas Perez	.20	.07
446	Phil Nevin	.20	.07
447	Jason Schmidt	.20	.07
448	Julio Mateo	.20	.07
449	So Taguchi	.20	.07
450	Randy Johnson	.50	.20
451	Paul Byrd	.20	.07
452	Chone Figgins	.20	.07
453	Larry Bigbie	.20	.07
454	Scott Williamson	.20	.07
455	Ramon Martinez	.20	.07
456	Roberto Alomar	.30	.10
457	Ryan Dempster	.20	.07
458	Ryan Ludwick	.20	.07
459	Ramon Santiago	.20	.07
460	Jeff Conine	.20	.07
461	Brad Lidge	.20	.07
462	Ken Harvey	.20	.07
463	Guillermo Mota	.20	.07
464	Rick Reed	.20	.07
465	Joey Eischen	.20	.07
466	Wade Miller	.20	.07
467	Steve Karsay	.20	.07
468	Chase Utley	.30	.10
469	Matt Stairs	.20	.07
470	Yorvit Torrealba	.20	.07
471	Joe Kennedy	.20	.07
472	Reed Johnson	.20	.07
473	Victor Zambrano	.20	.07
474	Jeff Davanon	.20	.07
475	Luis Gonzalez	.20	.07
476	Eli Marrero	.20	.07
477	Ray King	.20	.07
478	Jack Cust	.20	.07
479	Omar Daal	.20	.07
480	Todd Walker	.20	.07
481	Shawn Estes	.20	.07
482	Chris Reitsma	.20	.07
483	Jake Westbrook	.20	.07
484	Jeremy Bonderman	.20	.70
485	A.J. Burnett	.20	.07
486	Roy Oswalt	.20	.07
487	Kevin Brown	.20	.07
488	Eric Milton	.20	.07
489	Claudio Vargas	.20	.07
490	Roger Cedeno	.20	.07
491	David Wells	.20	.07
492	Scott Hatteberg	.20	.07
493	Ricky Ledee	.20	.07
494	Eric Young	.20	.07
495	Armando Benitez	.20	.07
496	Dan Haren	.20	.07
497	Carl Crawford	.20	.07
498	Laynce Nix	.20	.07
499	Eric Hinske	.20	.07
500	Ivan Rodriguez	.30	.10
501	Scot Shields	.20	.07
502	Brandon Webb	.20	.07
503	Mark DeRosa	.20	.07
504	Jhonny Peralta	.20	.07
505	Adam Kennedy	.20	.07
506	Tony Batista	.20	.07
507	Jeff Suppan	.20	.07
508	Kenny Lofton	.20	.07
509	Scott Sullivan	.20	.07
510	Ken Griffey Jr.	.75	.30
511	Billy Traber	.20	.07
512	Larry Walker	.20	.07
513	Mike Maroth	.20	.07
514	Todd Hollandsworth	.20	.07
515	Kirk Saarloos	.20	.07
516	Carlos Beltran	.20	.07
517	Juan Rivera	.20	.07
518	Roger Clemens	1.00	.40
519	Karim Garcia	.20	.07
520	Jose Reyes	.20	.07
521	Brandon Duckworth	.20	.07
522	Brian Giles	.20	.07
523	J.T. Snow	.20	.07
524	Jamie Moyer	.20	.07
525	Jason Isringhausen	.20	.07
526	Julio Lugo	.20	.07
527	Mark Teixeira	.30	.10
528	Cory Lidle	.20	.07
529	Lyle Overbay	.20	.07
530	Troy Percival	.20	.07
531	Robby Hammock	.20	.07
532	Robert Fick	.20	.07
533	Jason Johnson	.20	.07
534	Brandon Lyon	.20	.07
535	Antonio Alfonseca	.20	.07
536	Tom Goodwin	.20	.07
537	Paul Konerko	.20	.07
538	D'Angelo Jimenez	.20	.07
539	Ben Broussard	.20	.07
540	Magglio Ordonez	.20	.07
541	Ellis Burks	.20	.07
542	Carlos Pena	.20	.07
543	Chad Fox	.20	.07
544	Jeriome Robertson	.20	.07
545	Travis Hafner	.20	.07
546	Joe Randa	.20	.07
547	Wil Cordero	.20	.07
548	Brady Clark	.20	.07
549	Ruben Sierra	.20	.07
550	Barry Zito	.20	.07
551	Brett Myers	.20	.07
552	Oliver Perez	.20	.07
553	Trey Hodges	.20	.07
554	Benito Santiago	.20	.07
555	David Ross	.20	.07
556	Ramon Vazquez	.20	.07
557	Joe Nathan	.20	.07
558	Dan Wilson	.20	.07
559	Joe Mauer	.50	.20
560	Jim Edmonds	.20	.07
561	Shawn Wooten	.20	.07
562	Matt Kata	.20	.07
563	Vinny Castilla	.20	.07
564	Marty Cordova	.20	.07
565	Aramis Ramirez	.20	.07
566	Carl Everett	.20	.07
567	Ryan Freel	.20	.07
568	Jason Davis	.20	.07
569	Mark Bellhorn Sox	.20	.07
570	Craig Monroe	.20	.07
571	Roberto Hernandez	.20	.07
572	Tim Redding	.20	.07
573	Kevin Appier	.20	.07
574	Jeromy Burnitz	.20	.07
575	Miguel Cabrera	.30	.10
576	Ramon Nivar	.20	.07
577	Casey Blake	.20	.07
578	Aaron Boone	.20	.07
579	Jermaine Dye	.20	.07
580	Jerome Williams	.20	.07
581	John Olerud	.20	.07
582	Scott Rolen	.30	.10
583	Bobby Kielty	.20	.07
584	Travis Lee	.20	.07
585	Jeff Cirillo	.20	.07
586	Scott Spiezio	.20	.07
587	Stephen Randolph	.20	.07
588	Melvin Mora	.20	.07
589	Mike Timlin	.20	.07
590	Kerry Wood	.20	.07
591	Tony Womack	.20	.07
592	Jody Gerut	.20	.07
593	Franklyn German	.20	.07
594	Morgan Ensberg	.20	.07
595	Odalis Perez	.20	.07
596	Michael Cuddyer	.20	.07
597	Jon Lieber	.20	.07
598	Mike Williams	.20	.07
599	Jose Hernandez	.20	.07
600	Alfonso Soriano	.20	.07
601	Marquis Grissom	.20	.07
602	Matt Morris	.20	.07
603	Damian Rolls	.20	.07
604	Juan Gonzalez	.20	.07
605	Aquilino Lopez	.20	.07
606	Jose Valverde	.20	.07
607	Kenny Rogers	.20	.07
608	Joe Borowski	.20	.07
609	Josh Bard	.20	.07
610	Austin Kearns	.20	.07
611	Chin-Hui Tsao	.20	.07
612	Wil Ledezma	.20	.07
613	Aaron Guiel	.20	.07
614	LaTroy Hawkins	.20	.07
615	Tony Armas Jr.	.20	.07
616	Steve Trachsel	.20	.07
617	Ted Lilly	.20	.07
618	Todd Pratt	.20	.07
619	Sean Burroughs	.20	.07
620	Rafael Palmeiro	.30	.10
621	Jeremi Gonzalez	.20	.07
622	Quinton McCracken	.20	.07
623	David Ortiz	.50	.20
624	Randall Simon	.20	.07
625	Wily Mo Pena	.20	.07
626	Nate Cornejo	.20	.07
627	Brian Anderson	.20	.07
628	Corey Koskie	.20	.07
629	Keith Foulke Sox	.20	.07
630	Rheal Cormier	.20	.07
631	Sidney Ponson	.20	.07
632	Gary Matthews Jr.	.20	.07
633	Herbert Perry	.20	.07
634	Shea Hillenbrand	.20	.07
635	Craig Biggio	.30	.10
636	Barry Larkin	.30	.10
637	Arthur Rhodes	.20	.07
638	Anaheim Angels TC	.20	.07
639	Arizona Diamondbacks TC	.20	.07
640	Atlanta Braves TC	.20	.07
641	Baltimore Orioles TC	.20	.07
642	Boston Red Sox TC	.30	.10
643	Chicago Cubs TC	.20	.07
644	Chicago White Sox TC	.20	.07
645	Cincinnati Reds TC	.20	.07
646	Cleveland Indians TC	.20	.07

- ❑ 647 Colorado Rockies TC .20 .07
- ❑ 648 Detroit Tigers TC .20 .07
- ❑ 649 Florida Marlins TC .20 .07
- ❑ 650 Houston Astros TC .20 .07
- ❑ 651 Kansas City Royals TC .20 .07
- ❑ 652 Los Angeles Dodgers TC .20 .07
- ❑ 653 Milwaukee Brewers TC .20 .07
- ❑ 654 Minnesota Twins TC .20 .07
- ❑ 655 Montreal Expos TC .20 .07
- ❑ 656 New York Mets TC .20 .07
- ❑ 657 New York Yankees TC .50 .20
- ❑ 658 Oakland Athletics TC .20 .07
- ❑ 659 Philadelphia Phillies TC .20 .07
- ❑ 660 Pittsburgh Pirates TC .20 .07
- ❑ 661 San Diego Padres TC .20 .07
- ❑ 662 San Francisco Giants TC .20 .07
- ❑ 663 Seattle Mariners TC .20 .07
- ❑ 664 St. Louis Cardinals TC .20 .07
- ❑ 665 Tampa Bay Devil Rays TC .20 .07
- ❑ 666 Texas Rangers TC .20 .07
- ❑ 667 Toronto Blue Jays TC .20 .07
- ❑ 668 Kyle Sleeth DP RC .50 .20
- ❑ 669 Bradley Sullivan DP RC .50 .20
- ❑ 670 Carlos Quentin DP RC 2.50 1.00
- ❑ 671 Conor Jackson DP RC 3.00 1.25
- ❑ 672 Jeffrey Allison DP RC .50 .20
- ❑ 673 Matthew Moses DP RC 1.00 .40
- ❑ 674 Tim Stauffer DP RC .75 .30
- ❑ 675 Estee Harris DP RC .50 .20
- ❑ 676 David Aardsma DP RC .50 .20
- ❑ 677 Omar Quintanilla DP RC .50 .20
- ❑ 678 Aaron Hill DP .50 .20
- ❑ 679 Tony Richie DP RC .50 .20
- ❑ 680 Lastings Milledge DP RC 4.00 1.50
- ❑ 681 Brad Snyder DP RC 1.00 .40
- ❑ 682 Jason Hirsh DP RC 1.50 .60
- ❑ 683 Logan Kensing DP RC .50 .20
- ❑ 684 Chris Lubanski DP .50 .20
- ❑ 685 Ryan Harvey DP .50 .20
- ❑ 686 Ryan Wagner DP .50 .20
- ❑ 687 Rickie Weeks DP .50 .20
- ❑ 688 G.Sizemore/J.Guthrie .50 .20
- ❑ 689 E.Jackson/G.Miller .50 .20
- ❑ 690 J.Reed/N.Cotts .50 .20
- ❑ 691 A.Loewen/N.Markakis .50 .20
- ❑ 692 B.Upton/D.Young .50 .20
- ❑ 693 A.Rodriguez/D.Jeter 1.50 .60
- ❑ 694 I.Suzuki/A.Pujols 1.00 .40
- ❑ 695 J.Thome/M.Schmidt 1.00 .40
- ❑ 696 Mike Mussina GG .20 .07
- ❑ 697 Bengie Molina GG .20 .07
- ❑ 698 John Olerud GG .20 .07
- ❑ 699 Bret Boone GG .20 .07
- ❑ 700 Eric Chavez GG .20 .07
- ❑ 701 Alex Rodriguez GG .50 .20
- ❑ 702 Mike Cameron GG .20 .07
- ❑ 703 Ichiro Suzuki GG .50 .20
- ❑ 704 Torii Hunter GG .20 .07
- ❑ 705 Mike Hampton GG .20 .07
- ❑ 706 Mike Matheny GG .20 .07
- ❑ 707 Derrek Lee GG .20 .07
- ❑ 708 Luis Castillo GG .20 .07
- ❑ 709 Scott Rolen GG .20 .07
- ❑ 710 Edgar Renteria GG .20 .07
- ❑ 711 Andruw Jones GG .20 .07
- ❑ 712 Jose Cruz Jr. GG .20 .07
- ❑ 713 Jim Edmonds GG .20 .07
- ❑ 714 Roy Halladay CY .20 .07
- ❑ 715 Eric Gagne CY .20 .07
- ❑ 716 Alex Rodriguez MVP .50 .20
- ❑ 717 Angel Berroa ROY .20 .07
- ❑ 718 Dontrelle Willis ROY .20 .07
- ❑ 719 Todd Helton AS .20 .07
- ❑ 720 Marcus Giles AS .20 .07
- ❑ 721 Edgar Renteria AS .20 .07
- ❑ 722 Scott Rolen AS .20 .07
- ❑ 723 Albert Pujols AS .50 .20
- ❑ 724 Gary Sheffield AS .20 .07
- ❑ 725 Javy Lopez AS .20 .07
- ❑ 726 Eric Gagne AS .20 .07
- ❑ 727 Randy Wolf AS .20 .07
- ❑ 728 Bobby Cox AS .20 .07
- ❑ 729 Scott Podsednik AS .20 .07
- ❑ 730 Alex Gonzalez WS .30 .10
- ❑ 731 Brad Penny WS .30 .10
- ❑ 732 Beckett/I.Rod/A.Gonz WS .30 .10
- ❑ 733 Josh Beckett WS MVP .30 .10

2004 Topps Traded

- ❑ COMPLETE SET (220) 50.00 20.00
- ❑ COMMON CARD (1-70) .20 .07
- ❑ COMMON CARD (71-90) .50 .20
- ❑ COMMON CARD (91-110) .40 .15
- ❑ COMMON CARD (111-220) .40 .15
- ❑ BONDS AVAIL VIA HTA SHOP EXCHANGE
- ❑ PLATE ODDS 1:1151 H, 1:1173 R, 1:327 HTA
- ❑ PLATE PRINT RUN 1 SET PER COLOR
- ❑ BLACK CYAN MAGENTA YELLOW ISSUED
- ❑ NO PLATE PRICING DUE TO SCARCITY
- ❑ T1 Pokey Reese .20 .07
- ❑ T2 Tony Womack .20 .07
- ❑ T3 Richard Hidalgo .20 .07
- ❑ T4 Juan Uribe .20 .07
- ❑ T5 J.D. Drew .20 .07
- ❑ T6 Alex Gonzalez .20 .07
- ❑ T7 Carlos Guillen .20 .07
- ❑ T8 Doug Mientkiewicz .20 .07
- ❑ T9 Fernando Vina .20 .07
- ❑ T10 Milton Bradley .20 .07
- ❑ T11 Kelvim Escobar .20 .07
- ❑ T12 Ben Grieve .20 .07
- ❑ T13 Brian Jordan .20 .07
- ❑ T14 A.J. Pierzynski .20 .07
- ❑ T15 Billy Wagner .20 .07
- ❑ T16 Terrence Long .20 .07
- ❑ T17 Carlos Beltran .20 .07
- ❑ T18 Carl Everett .20 .07
- ❑ T19 Reggie Sanders .20 .07
- ❑ T20 Javy Lopez .20 .07
- ❑ T21 Jay Payton .20 .07
- ❑ T22 Octavio Dotel .20 .07
- ❑ T23 Eddie Guardado .20 .07
- ❑ T24 Andy Pettitte .30 .10
- ❑ T25 Richie Sexson .20 .07
- ❑ T26 Ronnie Belliard .20 .07
- ❑ T27 Michael Tucker .20 .07
- ❑ T28 Brad Fullmer .20 .07
- ❑ T29 Freddy Garcia .20 .07
- ❑ T30 Bartolo Colon .20 .07
- ❑ T31 Larry Walker Cards .30 .10
- ❑ T32 Mark Kotsay .20 .07
- ❑ T33 Jason Marquis .20 .07
- ❑ T34 Dustan Mohr .20 .07
- ❑ T35 Javier Vazquez .20 .07
- ❑ T36 Nomar Garciaparra .75 .30
- ❑ T37 Tino Martinez .30 .10
- ❑ T38 Hee Seop Choi .20 .07
- ❑ T39 Damian Miller .20 .07
- ❑ T40 Jose Lima .20 .07
- ❑ T41 Ty Wigginton .20 .07
- ❑ T42 Raul Ibanez .20 .07
- ❑ T43 Danys Baez .20 .07
- ❑ T44 Tony Clark .20 .07
- ❑ T45 Greg Maddux .75 .30
- ❑ T46 Victor Zambrano .20 .07
- ❑ T47 Orlando Cabrera Sox .20 .07
- ❑ T48 Jose Cruz Jr. .20 .07
- ❑ T49 Kris Benson .20 .07
- ❑ T50 Alex Rodriguez 1.00 .40
- ❑ T51 Steve Finley .20 .07
- ❑ T52 Ramon Hernandez .20 .07
- ❑ T53 Esteban Loaiza .20 .07
- ❑ T54 Ugueth Urbina .20 .07
- ❑ T55 Jeff Weaver .20 .07
- ❑ T56 Flash Gordon .20 .07
- ❑ T57 Jose Contreras .20 .07
- ❑ T58 Paul Lo Duca .20 .07
- ❑ T59 Junior Spivey .20 .07
- ❑ T60 Curt Schilling .30 .10
- ❑ T61 Brad Penny .20 .07
- ❑ T62 Braden Looper .20 .07
- ❑ T63 Miguel Cairo .20 .07
- ❑ T64 Juan Encarnacion .20 .07
- ❑ T65 Miguel Batista .20 .07
- ❑ T66 Terry Francona MG .20 .07
- ❑ T67 Lee Mazzilli MG .20 .07
- ❑ T68 Al Pedrique MG .20 .07
- ❑ T69 Ozzie Guillen MG .50 .20
- ❑ T70 Phil Garner MG .20 .07
- ❑ T71 Matt Bush DP RC 1.50 .60
- ❑ T72 Homer Bailey DP RC 3.00 1.25
- ❑ T73 Greg Golson DP RC 1.50 .60
- ❑ T74 Kyle Waldrop DP RC 1.25 .50
- ❑ T75 Richie Robnett DP RC 1.25 .50
- ❑ T76 Jay Rainville DP RC 1.50 .60
- ❑ T77 Bill Bray DP RC .50 .20
- ❑ T78 Philip Hughes DP RC 8.00 3.00
- ❑ T79 Scott Elbert DP RC 1.25 .50
- ❑ T80 Josh Fields DP RC 2.00 .75
- ❑ T81 Justin Orenduff DP RC .75 .30
- ❑ T82 Dan Putnam DP RC .75 .30
- ❑ T83 Chris Nelson DP RC 2.00 .75
- ❑ T84 Blake DeWitt DP RC 2.00 .75
- ❑ T85 J.P. Howell DP RC 1.25 .50
- ❑ T86 Huston Street DP RC 2.00 .75
- ❑ T87 Kurt Suzuki DP RC 1.25 .50
- ❑ T88 Erick San Pedro DP RC .50 .20
- ❑ T89 Matt Tuiasosopo DP RC 2.00 .75
- ❑ T90 Matt Macri DP RC 1.00 .40
- ❑ T91 Chad Tracy PROS .40 .15
- ❑ T92 Scott Hairston PROS .40 .15
- ❑ T93 Jonny Gomes PROS .40 .15
- ❑ T94 Chin-Feng Chen PROS .40 .15
- ❑ T95 Chien-Ming Wang PROS .75 .30
- ❑ T96 Dustin McGowan PROS .40 .15
- ❑ T97 Chris Burke PROS .40 .15
- ❑ T98 Denny Bautista PROS .40 .15
- ❑ T99 Preston Larrison PROS .40 .15
- ❑ T100 Kevin Youkilis PROS .40 .15
- ❑ T101 John Maine PROS .40 .15
- ❑ T102 Guillermo Quiroz PROS .40 .15
- ❑ T103 Dave Krynzel PROS .40 .15
- ❑ T104 David Kelton PROS .40 .15
- ❑ T105 Edwin Encarnacion PROS .40 .15
- ❑ T106 Chad Gaudin PROS .40 .15
- ❑ T107 Sergio Mitre PROS .40 .15
- ❑ T108 Laynce Nix PROS .40 .15
- ❑ T109 David Parrish PROS .40 .15
- ❑ T110 Brandon Claussen PROS .40 .15
- ❑ T111 Frank Francisco FY RC .40 .15
- ❑ T112 Brian Dallimore FY RC .40 .15
- ❑ T113 Jim Crowell FY RC .50 .20
- ❑ T114 Andres Blanco FY RC .40 .15
- ❑ T115 Eduardo Villacis FY RC .40 .15
- ❑ T116 Kazuhito Tadano FY RC .50 .20
- ❑ T117 Aarom Baldiris FY RC .50 .20
- ❑ T118 Justin Germano FY RC .40 .15
- ❑ T119 Joey Gathright FY RC 1.25 .50
- ❑ T120 Franklyn Gracesqui FY RC .40 .15
- ❑ T121 Chin-Lung Hu FY RC 1.25 .50
- ❑ T122 Scott Olsen FY RC 1.50 .60
- ❑ T123 Tyler Davidson FY RC .50 .20
- ❑ T124 Fausto Carmona FY RC 1.50 .60
- ❑ T125 Tim Hutting FY RC .40 .15
- ❑ T126 Ryan Meaux FY RC .40 .15
- ❑ T127 Jon Connolly FY RC 1.00 .40
- ❑ T128 Hector Made FY RC .75 .30
- ❑ T129 Jamie Brown FY RC .40 .15
- ❑ T130 Paul McAnulty FY RC .75 .30
- ❑ T131 Chris Saenz FY RC .40 .15
- ❑ T132 Marland Williams FY RC .50 .20
- ❑ T133 Mike Huggins FY RC .40 .15
- ❑ T134 Jesse Crain FY RC .75 .30
- ❑ T135 Chad Bentz FY RC .40 .15
- ❑ T136 Kazuo Matsui FY RC .75 .30
- ❑ T137 Paul Maholm FY RC 1.25 .50
- ❑ T138 Brock Jacobsen FY RC .40 .15
- ❑ T139 Casey Daigle FY RC .40 .15
- ❑ T140 Nyjer Morgan FY RC .40 .15

❑ T141 Tom Mastny FY RC .40 .15
❑ T142 Kody Kirkland FY RC .50 .20
❑ T143 Jose Capellan FY RC .50 .20
❑ T144 Felix Hernandez FY RC 8.00 3.00
❑ T145 Shawn Hill FY RC .40 .15
❑ T146 Danny Gonzalez FY RC .40 .15
❑ T147 Scott Dohmann FY RC .40 .15
❑ T148 Tommy Murphy FY RC .40 .15
❑ T149 Akinori Otsuka FY RC .40 .15
❑ T150 Miguel Perez FY RC .40 .15
❑ T151 Mike Rouse FY RC .40 .15
❑ T152 Ramon Ramirez FY RC .40 .15
❑ T153 Luke Hughes FY RC .40 .15
❑ T154 Howie Kendrick FY RC 10.00 4.00
❑ T155 Ryan Budde FY RC .40 .15
❑ T156 Charlie Zink FY RC .40 .15
❑ T157 Warner Madrigal FY RC .75 .30
❑ T158 Jason Szuminski FY RC .40 .15
❑ T159 Chad Chop FY RC .40 .15
❑ T160 Shingo Takatsu FY RC .75 .30
❑ T161 Matt Lemanczyk FY RC .40 .15
❑ T162 Wardell Starling FY RC .40 .15
❑ T163 Nick Gorneault FY RC .50 .20
❑ T164 Scott Proctor FY RC .50 .20
❑ T165 Brooks Conrad FY RC .50 .20
❑ T166 Hector Gimenez FY RC .40 .15
❑ T167 Kevin Howard FY RC .50 .20
❑ T168 Vince Perkins FY RC .50 .20
❑ T169 Brock Peterson FY RC .40 .15
❑ T170 Chris Shelton FY RC 1.25 .50
❑ T171 Erick Aybar FY RC .75 .30
❑ T172 Paul Bacot FY RC .50 .20
❑ T173 Matt Capps FY RC .40 .15
❑ T174 Kory Casto FY RC .50 .20
❑ T175 Juan Cedeno FY RC .40 .15
❑ T176 Vito Chiaravalloti FY RC .40 .15
❑ T177 Alec Zumwalt FY RC .40 .15
❑ T178 J.J. Furmaniak FY RC .75 .30
❑ T179 Lee Gwaltney FY RC .40 .15
❑ T180 Donald Kelly FY RC .40 .15
❑ T181 Benji DeQuin FY RC .40 .15
❑ T182 Brant Colamarino FY RC .75 .30
❑ T183 Juan Gutierrez FY RC .40 .15
❑ T184 Carl Loadenthal FY RC .50 .20
❑ T185 Ricky Nolasco FY RC 1.50 .60
❑ T186 Jeff Salazar FY RC 1.00 .40
❑ T187 Rob Tejeda FY RC .75 .30
❑ T188 Alex Romero FY RC .40 .15
❑ T189 Yoann Torrealba FY RC .40 .15
❑ T190 Carlos Sosa FY RC .40 .15
❑ T191 Tim Bittner FY RC .40 .15
❑ T192 Chris Aguila FY RC .40 .15
❑ T193 Jason Frasor FY RC .40 .15
❑ T194 Reid Gorecki FY RC .40 .15
❑ T195 Dustin Nippert FY RC .50 .20
❑ T196 Javier Guzman FY RC .50 .20
❑ T197 Harvey Garcia FY RC .40 .15
❑ T198 Ivan Ochoa FY RC .40 .15
❑ T199 David Wallace FY RC .50 .20
❑ T200 Joel Zumaya FY RC 4.00 1.50
❑ T201 Casey Kopitzke FY RC .40 .15
❑ T202 Lincoln Holdzkom FY RC .40 .15
❑ T203 Chad Santos FY RC .40 .15
❑ T204 Brian Pilkington FY RC .40 .15
❑ T205 Terry Jones FY RC .50 .20
❑ T206 Jerome Gamble FY RC .40 .15
❑ T207 Brad Eldred FY RC .50 .20
❑ T208 David Pauley FY RC 1.50 .60
❑ T209 Kevin Davidson FY RC .40 .15
❑ T210 Damaso Espino FY RC .40 .15
❑ T211 Tom Farmer FY RC .40 .15
❑ T212 Michael Mooney FY RC .40 .15
❑ T213 James Tomlin FY RC .40 .15
❑ T214 Greg Thissen FY RC .40 .15
❑ T215 Calvin Hayes FY RC .50 .20
❑ T216 Fernando Cortez FY RC .40 .15
❑ T217 Sergio Silva FY RC .40 .15
❑ T218 Jon de Vries FY RC .40 .15
❑ T219 Don Sutton FY RC 1.00 .40
❑ T220 Leo Nunez FY RC .40 .15
❑ T221 Barry Bonds HTA EXCH 8.00 3.00

2005 Topps

❑ COMP.HOBBY SET (737) 80.00 40.00
❑ COMP.HOLIDAY SET (742) 80.00 40.00
❑ COMP.CUBS SET (737) 80.00 40.00
❑ COMP.GIANTS SET (737) 80.00 40.00
❑ COMP.NATIONALS SET (737) 80.00 40.00
❑ COMP.RED SOX SET (737) 80.00 40.00
❑ COMP.TIGERS SET (737) 80.00 40.00
❑ COMP.YANKEES SET (737) 80.00 40.00
❑ COMPLETE SET (732) 80.00 40.00
❑ COMPLETE SERIES 1 (366) 40.00 20.00
❑ COMPLETE SERIES 2 (366) 40.00 20.00
❑ COMMON CARD (1-6/8-734) .20 .07
❑ COMMON (297-326/668-687) .50 .20
❑ COMMON (327-331/688-692) .50 .20
❑ COM (349-355/368/731-734) 1.00 .40
❑ CARD NUMBER 7 DOES NOT EXIST
❑ OVERALL PLATE SER.1 ODDS 1:154 HTA
❑ OVERALL PLATE SER.2 ODDS 1:112 HTA
❑ PLATE PRINT RUN 1 SET PER COLOR
❑ BLACK-CYAN-MAGENTA-YELLOW ISSUED
❑ NO PLATE PRICING DUE TO SCARCITY
❑ 1 Alex Rodriguez 1.00 .40
❑ 2 Placido Polanco .20 .07
❑ 3 Torii Hunter .20 .07
❑ 4 Lyle Overbay .20 .07
❑ 5 Johnny Damon .30 .10
❑ 6 Johnny Estrada .20 .07
❑ 8 Francisco Rodriguez .20 .07
❑ 9 Jason LaRue .20 .07
❑ 10 Sammy Sosa .50 .20
❑ 11 Randy Wolf .20 .07
❑ 12 Jason Bay .20 .07
❑ 13 Tom Glavine .30 .10
❑ 14 Michael Tucker .20 .07
❑ 15 Brian Giles .20 .07
❑ 16 Dan Wilson .20 .07
❑ 17 Jim Edmonds .20 .07
❑ 18 Danys Baez .20 .07
❑ 19 Roy Halladay .20 .07
❑ 20 Hank Blalock .20 .07
❑ 21 Darin Erstad .20 .07
❑ 22 Robby Hammock .20 .07
❑ 23 Mike Hampton .20 .07
❑ 24 Mark Bellhorn .20 .07
❑ 25 Jim Thome .30 .10
❑ 26 Scott Schoeneweis .20 .07
❑ 27 Jody Gerut .20 .07
❑ 28 Vinny Castilla .20 .07
❑ 29 Luis Castillo .20 .07
❑ 30 Ivan Rodriguez .30 .10
❑ 31 Craig Biggio .30 .10
❑ 32 Joe Randa .20 .07
❑ 33 Adrian Beltre .20 .07
❑ 34 Scott Podsednik .20 .07
❑ 35 Cliff Floyd .20 .07
❑ 36 Livan Hernandez .20 .07
❑ 37 Eric Byrnes .20 .07
❑ 38 Gabe Kapler .20 .07
❑ 39 Jack Wilson .20 .07
❑ 40 Gary Sheffield .20 .07
❑ 41 Chan Ho Park .20 .07
❑ 42 Carl Crawford .20 .07
❑ 43 Miguel Batista .20 .07
❑ 44 David Bell .20 .07
❑ 45 Jeff DaVanon .20 .07
❑ 46 Brandon Webb .20 .07
❑ 47 Bronson Arroyo .20 .07
❑ 48 Melvin Mora .20 .07
❑ 49 David Ortiz .50 .20
❑ 50 Andruw Jones .30 .10
❑ 51 Chone Figgins .20 .07
❑ 52 Danny Graves .20 .07
❑ 53 Preston Wilson .20 .07
❑ 54 Jeremy Bonderman .20 .07
❑ 55 Chad Fox .20 .07
❑ 56 Dan Miceli .20 .07
❑ 57 Jimmy Gobble .20 .07
❑ 58 Darren Dreifort .20 .07
❑ 59 Matt LeCroy .20 .07
❑ 60 Jose Vidro .20 .07
❑ 61 Al Leiter .20 .07
❑ 62 Javier Vazquez .20 .07
❑ 63 Erubiel Durazo .20 .07
❑ 64 Doug Glanville .20 .07
❑ 65 Scot Shields .20 .07
❑ 66 Edgardo Alfonzo .20 .07
❑ 67 Ryan Franklin .20 .07
❑ 68 Francisco Cordero .20 .07
❑ 69 Brett Myers .20 .07
❑ 70 Curt Schilling .30 .10
❑ 71 Matt Kata .20 .07
❑ 72 Mark DeRosa .20 .07
❑ 73 Rodrigo Lopez .20 .07
❑ 74 Tim Wakefield .30 .10
❑ 75 Frank Thomas .50 .20
❑ 76 Jimmy Rollins .20 .07
❑ 77 Barry Zito .20 .07
❑ 78 Hideo Nomo .50 .20
❑ 79 Brad Wilkerson .20 .07
❑ 80 Adam Dunn .20 .07
❑ 81 Billy Traber .20 .07
❑ 82 Fernando Vina .20 .07
❑ 83 Nate Robertson .20 .07
❑ 84 Brad Ausmus .20 .07
❑ 85 Mike Sweeney .20 .07
❑ 86 Kip Wells .20 .07
❑ 87 Chris Reitsma .20 .07
❑ 88 Zach Day .20 .07
❑ 89 Tony Clark .20 .07
❑ 90 Bret Boone .20 .07
❑ 91 Mark Loretta .20 .07
❑ 92 Jerome Williams .20 .07
❑ 93 Randy Winn .20 .07
❑ 94 Marlon Anderson .20 .07
❑ 95 Aubrey Huff .20 .07
❑ 96 Kevin Mench .20 .07
❑ 97 Frank Catalanotto .20 .07
❑ 98 Flash Gordon .20 .07
❑ 99 Scott Hatteberg .20 .07
❑ 100 Albert Pujols 1.00 .40
❑ 101 Jose/Bengie Molina .50 .20
❑ 102 Oscar Villarreal .20 .07
❑ 103 Jay Gibbons .20 .07
❑ 104 Byung-Hyun Kim .20 .07
❑ 105 Joe Borowski .20 .07
❑ 106 Mark Grudzielanek .20 .07
❑ 107 Mark Buehrle .20 .07
❑ 108 Paul Wilson .20 .07
❑ 109 Ronnie Belliard .20 .07
❑ 110 Reggie Sanders .20 .07
❑ 111 Tim Redding .20 .07
❑ 112 Brian Lawrence .20 .07
❑ 113 Darrell May .20 .07
❑ 114 Jose Hernandez .20 .07
❑ 115 Ben Sheets .20 .07
❑ 116 Johan Santana .50 .20
❑ 117 Billy Wagner .20 .07
❑ 118 Mariano Rivera .50 .20
❑ 119 Steve Trachsel .20 .07
❑ 120 Akinori Otsuka .20 .07
❑ 121 Bobby Kielty .20 .07
❑ 122 Orlando Hernandez .20 .07
❑ 123 Raul Ibanez .20 .07
❑ 124 Mike Matheny .20 .07
❑ 125 Vernon Wells .20 .07
❑ 126 Jason Isringhausen .20 .07
❑ 127 Jose Guillen .20 .07
❑ 128 Danny Bautista .20 .07
❑ 129 Marcus Giles .20 .07
❑ 130 Javy Lopez .20 .07
❑ 131 Kevin Millar .20 .07
❑ 132 Kyle Farnsworth .20 .07

❑ 133 Carl Pavano .20 .07
❑ 134 D'Angelo Jimenez .20 .07
❑ 135 Casey Blake .20 .07
❑ 136 Matt Holliday .25 .08
❑ 137 Bobby Higginson .20 .07
❑ 138 Nate Field .20 .07
❑ 139 Alex Gonzalez .20 .07
❑ 140 Jeff Kent .20 .07
❑ 141 Aaron Guiel .20 .07
❑ 142 Shawn Green .20 .07
❑ 143 Bill Hall .20 .07
❑ 144 Shannon Stewart .20 .07
❑ 145 Juan Rivera .20 .07
❑ 146 Coco Crisp .20 .07
❑ 147 Mike Mussina .30 .10
❑ 148 Eric Chavez .20 .07
❑ 149 Jon Lieber .20 .07
❑ 150 Vladimir Guerrero .50 .20
❑ 151 Alex Cintron .20 .07
❑ 152 Horacio Ramirez .20 .07
❑ 153 Sidney Ponson .20 .07
❑ 154 Trot Nixon .30 .10
❑ 155 Greg Maddux .75 .30
❑ 156 Edgar Renteria .20 .07
❑ 157 Ryan Freel .20 .07
❑ 158 Matt Lawton .20 .07
❑ 159 Shawn Chacon .20 .07
❑ 160 Josh Beckett .20 .07
❑ 161 Ken Harvey .20 .07
❑ 162 Juan Cruz .20 .07
❑ 163 Juan Encarnacion .20 .07
❑ 164 Wes Helms .20 .07
❑ 165 Brad Radke .20 .07
❑ 166 Claudio Vargas .20 .07
❑ 167 Mike Cameron .20 .07
❑ 168 Billy Koch .20 .07
❑ 169 Bobby Crosby .20 .07
❑ 170 Mike Lieberthal .20 .07
❑ 171 Rob Mackowiak .20 .07
❑ 172 Sean Burroughs .20 .07
❑ 173 J.T. Snow Jr. .20 .07
❑ 174 Paul Konerko .20 .07
❑ 175 Luis Gonzalez .20 .07
❑ 176 John Lackey .20 .07
❑ 177 Antonio Alfonseca .20 .07
❑ 178 Brian Roberts .20 .07
❑ 179 Bill Mueller .20 .07
❑ 180 Carlos Lee .20 .07
❑ 181 Corey Patterson .20 .07
❑ 182 Sean Casey .20 .07
❑ 183 Cliff Lee .20 .07
❑ 184 Jason Jennings .20 .07
❑ 185 Dmitri Young .20 .07
❑ 186 Juan Uribe .20 .07
❑ 187 Andy Pettitte .30 .10
❑ 188 Juan Gonzalez .20 .07
❑ 189 Pokey Reese .20 .07
❑ 190 Jason Phillips .20 .07
❑ 191 Rocky Biddle .20 .07
❑ 192 Lew Ford .20 .07
❑ 193 Mark Mulder .20 .07
❑ 194 Bobby Abreu .20 .07
❑ 195 Jason Kendall .20 .07
❑ 196 Terrence Long .20 .07
❑ 197 A.J. Pierzynski .20 .07
❑ 198 Eddie Guardado .20 .07
❑ 199 So Taguchi .20 .07
❑ 200 Jason Giambi .20 .07
❑ 201 Tony Batista .20 .07
❑ 202 Kyle Lohse .20 .07
❑ 203 Trevor Hoffman .20 .07
❑ 204 Tike Redman .20 .07
❑ 205 Matt Herges .20 .07
❑ 206 Gil Meche .20 .07
❑ 207 Chris Carpenter .20 .07
❑ 208 Ben Broussard .20 .07
❑ 209 Eric Young .20 .07
❑ 210 Doug Waechter .20 .07
❑ 211 Jarrod Washburn .20 .07
❑ 212 Chad Tracy .20 .07
❑ 213 John Smoltz .30 .10
❑ 214 Jorge Julio .20 .07
❑ 215 Todd Walker .20 .07
❑ 216 Shingo Takatsu .20 .07
❑ 217 Jose Acevedo .20 .07
❑ 218 David Riske .20 .07
❑ 219 Shawn Estes .20 .07
❑ 220 Lance Berkman .20 .07
❑ 221 Carlos Guillen .20 .07
❑ 222 Jeremy Affeldt .20 .07
❑ 223 Cesar Izturis .20 .07
❑ 224 Scott Sullivan .20 .07
❑ 225 Kazuo Matsui .20 .07
❑ 226 Josh Fogg .20 .07
❑ 227 Jason Schmidt .20 .07
❑ 228 Jason Marquis .20 .07
❑ 229 Scott Spiezio .20 .07
❑ 230 Miguel Tejada .20 .07
❑ 231 Bartolo Colon .20 .07
❑ 232 Jose Valverde .20 .07
❑ 233 Derrek Lee .30 .10
❑ 234 Scott Williamson .20 .07
❑ 235 Joe Crede .20 .07
❑ 236 John Thomson .20 .07
❑ 237 Mike MacDougal .20 .07
❑ 238 Eric Gagne .20 .07
❑ 239 Alex Sanchez .20 .07
❑ 240 Miguel Cabrera .30 .10
❑ 241 Luis Rivas .20 .07
❑ 242 Adam Everett .20 .07
❑ 243 Jason Johnson .20 .07
❑ 244 Travis Hafner .20 .07
❑ 245 Jose Valentin .20 .07
❑ 246 Stephen Randolph .20 .07
❑ 247 Rafael Furcal .20 .07
❑ 248 Adam Kennedy .20 .07
❑ 249 Luis Matos .20 .07
❑ 250 Mark Prior .30 .10
❑ 251 Angel Berroa .20 .07
❑ 252 Phil Nevin .20 .07
❑ 253 Oliver Perez .20 .07
❑ 254 Orlando Hudson .20 .07
❑ 255 Braden Looper .20 .07
❑ 256 Khalil Greene .30 .10
❑ 257 Tim Worrell .20 .07
❑ 258 Carlos Zambrano .20 .07
❑ 259 Odalis Perez .20 .07
❑ 260 Gerald Laird .20 .07
❑ 261 Jose Cruz Jr. .20 .07
❑ 262 Michael Barrett .20 .07
❑ 263 Michael Young UER .20 .07
❑ 264 Toby Hall .20 .07
❑ 265 Woody Williams .20 .07
❑ 266 Rich Harden .20 .07
❑ 267 Mike Scioscia MG .20 .07
❑ 268 Al Pedrique MG .20 .07
❑ 269 Bobby Cox MG .20 .07
❑ 270 Lee Mazzilli MG .20 .07
❑ 271 Terry Francona MG .30 .10
❑ 272 Dusty Baker MG .20 .07
❑ 273 Ozzie Guillen MG .50 .20
❑ 274 Dave Miley MG .20 .07
❑ 275 Eric Wedge MG .20 .07
❑ 276 Clint Hurdle MG .20 .07
❑ 277 Alan Trammell MG .20 .07
❑ 278 Jack McKeon MG .20 .07
❑ 279 Phil Garner MG .20 .07
❑ 280 Tony Pena MG .20 .07
❑ 281 Jim Tracy MG .20 .07
❑ 282 Ned Yost MG .20 .07
❑ 283 Ron Gardenhire MG .20 .07
❑ 284 Frank Robinson MG .20 .07
❑ 285 Art Howe MG .20 .07
❑ 286 Joe Torre MG .30 .10
❑ 287 Ken Macha MG .20 .07
❑ 288 Larry Bowa MG .20 .07
❑ 289 Lloyd McClendon MG .20 .07
❑ 290 Bruce Bochy MG .20 .07
❑ 291 Felipe Alou MG .20 .07
❑ 292 Bob Melvin MG .20 .07
❑ 293 Tony LaRussa MG .20 .07
❑ 294 Lou Piniella MG .20 .07
❑ 295 Buck Showalter MG .20 .07
❑ 296 John Gibbons MG .20 .07
❑ 297 Steve Doetsch FY RC .75 .30
❑ 298 Melky Cabrera FY RC 2.00 .75
❑ 299 Luis Ramirez FY RC .50 .20
❑ 300 Chris Seddon FY RC .50 .20
❑ 301 Nate Schierholtz FY .75 .30
❑ 302 Ian Kinsler FY RC 2.50 1.00
❑ 303 Brandon Moss FY RC 1.50 .60
❑ 304 Chadd Blasko FY RC .75 .30
❑ 305 Jeremy West FY RC .75 .30
❑ 306 Sean Marshall FY RC 1.50 .60
❑ 307 Matt DeSalvo FY RC .75 .30
❑ 308 Ryan Sweeney FY RC 1.00 .40
❑ 309 Matthew Lindstrom FY RC .50 .20
❑ 310 Ryan Goleski FY RC .75 .30
❑ 311 Brett Harper FY RC .75 .30
❑ 312 Chris Roberson FY RC .50 .20
❑ 313 Andre Ethier FY RC 5.00 2.00
❑ 314 Chris Denorfia FY RC 1.00 .40
❑ 315 Ian Bladergroen FY RC .75 .30
❑ 316 Darren Fenster FY RC .50 .20
❑ 317 Kevin West FY RC .50 .20
❑ 318 Chaz Lytle FY RC .75 .30
❑ 319 James Jurries FY RC .75 .30
❑ 320 Matt Rogelstad FY RC .50 .20
❑ 321 Wade Robinson FY RC .50 .20
❑ 322 Jake Dittler FY .50 .20
❑ 323 Brian Stavisky FY RC .50 .20
❑ 324 Kole Strayhorn FY RC .50 .20
❑ 325 Jose Vaquedano FY RC .50 .20
❑ 326 Elvys Quezada FY RC .50 .20
❑ 327 J.Maine/V.Majewski FS .50 .20
❑ 328 R.Weeks/J.Hardy FS .50 .20
❑ 329 G.Gross/G.Quiroz FS .50 .20
❑ 330 D.Wright/C.Brazell FS 3.00 1.25
❑ 331 D.McPherson/J.Mathis FS .50 .20
❑ 332 Randy Johnson SH .30 .10
❑ 333 Randy Johnson SH .30 .10
❑ 334 Ichiro Suzuki SH .50 .20
❑ 335 Ken Griffey Jr. SH .50 .20
❑ 336 Greg Maddux SH .50 .20
❑ 337 Ichiro/Mora/Guerrero LL .50 .20
❑ 338 Ichiro/Young/Guerrero LL .50 .20
❑ 339 Manny/Konerko/Ortiz LL .30 .10
❑ 340 Tejada/Ortiz/Manny LL .30 .10
❑ 341 Johan/Schill/West LL .30 .10
❑ 342 Johan/Pedro/Schill LL .30 .10
❑ 343 Helton/Loretta/Beltre LL .20 .07
❑ 344 Pierre/Loretta/Wilson LL .20 .07
❑ 345 Beltre/Dunn/Pujols LL .50 .20
❑ 346 Castilla/Rolen/Pujols LL .50 .20
❑ 347 Peavy/Johnson/Sheets LL .30 .10
❑ 348 Johnson/Sheets/Schmidt LL .30 .10
❑ 349 A.Rodriguez/R.Sierra ALDS 1.00 .40
❑ 350 L.Walker/A.Pujols NLDS 1.00 .40
❑ 351 C.Schilling/D.Ortiz ALDS 1.00 .40
❑ 352 Curt Schilling WS2 1.00 .40
❑ 353 Sox Celeb/Ortiz-Schil ALCS 1.00 .40
❑ 354 Cards Celeb/Puj-Edm NLCS 1.00 .40
❑ 355 Mark Bellhorn WS1 1.00 .40
❑ 356 Paul Konerko AS .20 .07
❑ 357 Alfonso Soriano AS .20 .07
❑ 358 Miguel Tejada AS .20 .07
❑ 359 Melvin Mora AS .20 .07
❑ 360 Vladimir Guerrero AS .30 .10
❑ 361 Ichiro Suzuki AS .50 .20
❑ 362 Manny Ramirez AS .30 .10
❑ 363 Ivan Rodriguez AS .20 .07
❑ 364 Johan Santana AS .30 .10
❑ 365 Paul Konerko AS .20 .07
❑ 366 David Ortiz AS .30 .10
❑ 367 Bobby Crosby AS .20 .07
❑ 368 Sox Celeb/Ram-Lowe WS4 1.50 .60
❑ 369 Garret Anderson .20 .07
❑ 370 Randy Johnson .50 .20
❑ 371 Charles Thomas .20 .07
❑ 372 Rafael Palmeiro .30 .10
❑ 373 Kevin Youkilis .20 .07
❑ 374 Freddy Garcia .20 .07
❑ 375 Magglio Ordonez .20 .07
❑ 376 Aaron Harang .20 .07
❑ 377 Grady Sizemore .30 .10
❑ 378 Chin-Hui Tsao .20 .07
❑ 379 Eric Munson .20 .07
❑ 380 Juan Pierre .20 .07
❑ 381 Brad Lidge .20 .07
❑ 382 Brian Anderson .20 .07
❑ 383 Alex Cora .20 .07
❑ 384 Brady Clark .20 .07
❑ 385 Todd Helton .30 .10
❑ 386 Chad Cordero .20 .07
❑ 387 Kris Benson .20 .07
❑ 388 Brad Halsey .20 .07
❑ 389 Jermaine Dye .20 .07
❑ 390 Manny Ramirez .30 .10

❑ 391 Daryle Ward .20 .07
❑ 392 Adam Eaton .20 .07
❑ 393 Brett Tomko .20 .07
❑ 394 Bucky Jacobsen .20 .07
❑ 395 Dontrelle Willis .20 .07
❑ 396 B.J. Upton .20 .07
❑ 397 Rocco Baldelli .20 .07
❑ 398 Ted Lilly .20 .07
❑ 399 Ryan Drese .20 .07
❑ 400 Ichiro Suzuki 1.00 .40
❑ 401 Brendan Donnelly .20 .07
❑ 402 Brandon Lyon .20 .07
❑ 403 Nick Green .20 .07
❑ 404 Jerry Hairston Jr. .20 .07
❑ 405 Mike Lowell .20 .07
❑ 406 Kerry Wood .20 .07
❑ 407 Carl Everett .20 .07
❑ 408 Hideki Matsui .75 .30
❑ 409 Omar Vizquel .30 .10
❑ 410 Joe Kennedy .20 .07
❑ 411 Carlos Pena .20 .07
❑ 412 Armando Benitez .20 .07
❑ 413 Carlos Beltran .20 .07
❑ 414 Kevin Appier .20 .07
❑ 415 Jeff Weaver .20 .07
❑ 416 Chad Moeller .20 .07
❑ 417 Joe Mays .20 .07
❑ 418 Termel Sledge .20 .07
❑ 419 Richard Hidalgo .20 .07
❑ 420 Kenny Lofton .20 .07
❑ 421 Justin Duchscherer .20 .07
❑ 422 Eric Milton .20 .07
❑ 423 Jose Mesa .20 .07
❑ 424 Ramon Hernandez .20 .07
❑ 425 Jose Reyes .20 .07
❑ 426 Joel Pineiro .20 .07
❑ 427 Matt Morris .20 .07
❑ 428 John Halama .20 .07
❑ 429 Gary Matthews Jr. .20 .07
❑ 430 Ryan Madson .20 .07
❑ 431 Mark Kotsay .20 .07
❑ 432 Carlos Delgado .20 .07
❑ 433 Casey Kotchman .20 .07
❑ 434 Greg Aquino .20 .07
❑ 435 Eli Marrero .20 .07
❑ 436 David Newhan .20 .07
❑ 437 Mike Timlin .20 .07
❑ 438 LaTroy Hawkins .20 .07
❑ 439 Jose Contreras .20 .07
❑ 440 Ken Griffey Jr. .75 .30
❑ 441 C.C. Sabathia .20 .07
❑ 442 Brandon Inge .20 .07
❑ 443 Pete Munro .20 .07
❑ 444 John Buck .20 .07
❑ 445 Hee Seop Choi .20 .07
❑ 446 Chris Capuano .20 .07
❑ 447 Jesse Crain .20 .07
❑ 448 Geoff Jenkins .20 .07
❑ 449 Brian Schneider .20 .07
❑ 450 Mike Piazza .50 .20
❑ 451 Jorge Posada .30 .10
❑ 452 Nick Swisher .20 .07
❑ 453 Kevin Millwood .20 .07
❑ 454 Mike Gonzalez .20 .07
❑ 455 Jake Peavy .20 .07
❑ 456 Dustin Hermanson .20 .07
❑ 457 Jeremy Reed .20 .07
❑ 458 Julian Tavarez .20 .07
❑ 459 Geoff Blum .20 .07
❑ 460 Alfonso Soriano .20 .07
❑ 461 Alexis Rios .20 .07
❑ 462 David Eckstein .20 .07
❑ 463 Shea Hillenbrand .20 .07
❑ 464 Russ Ortiz .20 .07
❑ 465 Kurt Ainsworth .20 .07
❑ 466 Orlando Cabrera .20 .07
❑ 467 Carlos Silva .20 .07
❑ 468 Ross Gload .20 .07
❑ 469 Josh Phelps .20 .07
❑ 470 Marquis Grissom .20 .07
❑ 471 Mike Maroth .20 .07
❑ 472 Guillermo Mota .20 .07
❑ 473 Chris Burke .20 .07
❑ 474 David DeJesus .20 .07
❑ 475 Jose Lima .20 .07
❑ 476 Cristian Guzman .20 .07
❑ 477 Nick Johnson .20 .07
❑ 478 Victor Zambrano .20 .07
❑ 479 Rod Barajas .20 .07
❑ 480 Damian Miller .20 .07
❑ 481 Chase Utley .30 .10
❑ 482 Todd Pratt .20 .07
❑ 483 Sean Burnett .20 .07
❑ 484 Boomer Wells .20 .07
❑ 485 Dustan Mohr .20 .07
❑ 486 Bobby Madritsch .20 .07
❑ 487 Ray King .20 .07
❑ 488 Reed Johnson .20 .07
❑ 489 R.A. Dickey .20 .07
❑ 490 Scott Kazmir .20 .07
❑ 491 Tony Womack .20 .07
❑ 492 Tomas Perez .20 .07
❑ 493 Esteban Loaiza .20 .07
❑ 494 Tomo Ohka .20 .07
❑ 495 Mike Lamb .20 .07
❑ 496 Ramon Ortiz .20 .07
❑ 497 Richie Sexson .20 .07
❑ 498 J.D. Drew .20 .07
❑ 499 David Segui .20 .07
❑ 500 Barry Bonds 2.00 .75
❑ 501 Aramis Ramirez .20 .07
❑ 502 Wily Mo Pena .20 .07
❑ 503 Jeromy Burnitz .20 .07
❑ 504 Craig Monroe .20 .07
❑ 505 Nomar Garciaparra .50 .20
❑ 506 Brandon Backe .20 .07
❑ 507 Marcus Thames .20 .07
❑ 508 Derek Lowe .20 .07
❑ 509 Doug Davis .20 .07
❑ 510 Joe Mauer .50 .20
❑ 511 Endy Chavez .20 .07
❑ 512 Bernie Williams .30 .10
❑ 513 Mark Redman .20 .07
❑ 514 Jason Michaels .20 .07
❑ 515 Craig Wilson .20 .07
❑ 516 Ryan Klesko .20 .07
❑ 517 Ray Durham .20 .07
❑ 518 Jose Lopez .20 .07
❑ 519 Jeff Suppan .20 .07
❑ 520 Julio Lugo .20 .07
❑ 521 Mike Wood .20 .07
❑ 522 David Bush .20 .07
❑ 523 Juan Rincon .20 .07
❑ 524 Paul Quantrill .20 .07
❑ 525 Marlon Byrd .20 .07
❑ 526 Roy Oswalt .20 .07
❑ 527 Rondell White .20 .07
❑ 528 Troy Glaus .20 .07
❑ 529 Scott Hairston .20 .07
❑ 530 Chipper Jones .50 .20
❑ 531 Daniel Cabrera .20 .07
❑ 532 Doug Mientkiewicz .20 .07
❑ 533 Glendon Rusch .20 .07
❑ 534 Jon Garland .20 .07
❑ 535 Austin Kearns .20 .07
❑ 536 Jake Westbrook .20 .07
❑ 537 Aaron Miles .20 .07
❑ 538 Omar Infante .20 .07
❑ 539 Paul Lo Duca .20 .07
❑ 540 Morgan Ensberg .20 .07
❑ 541 Tony Graffanino .20 .07
❑ 542 Milton Bradley .20 .07
❑ 543 Keith Ginter .20 .07
❑ 544 Justin Morneau .20 .07
❑ 545 Tony Armas Jr. .20 .07
❑ 546 Mike Stanton .20 .07
❑ 547 Kevin Brown .20 .07
❑ 548 Marco Scutaro .20 .07
❑ 549 Tim Hudson .20 .07
❑ 550 Pat Burrell .20 .07
❑ 551 Ty Wigginton .20 .07
❑ 552 Jeff Cirillo .20 .07
❑ 553 Jim Brower .20 .07
❑ 554 Jamie Moyer .20 .07
❑ 555 Larry Walker .30 .10
❑ 556 Dewon Brazelton .20 .07
❑ 557 Brian Jordan .20 .07
❑ 558 Josh Towers .20 .07
❑ 559 Shigetoshi Hasegawa .20 .07
❑ 560 Octavio Dotel .20 .07
❑ 561 Travis Lee .20 .07
❑ 562 Michael Cuddyer .20 .07
❑ 563 Junior Spivey .20 .07
❑ 564 Zack Greinke .20 .07
❑ 565 Roger Clemens .75 .30
❑ 566 Chris Shelton .30 .10
❑ 567 Ugueth Urbina .20 .07
❑ 568 Rafael Betancourt .20 .07
❑ 569 Willie Harris .20 .07
❑ 570 Todd Hollandsworth .20 .07
❑ 571 Keith Foulke .20 .07
❑ 572 Larry Bigbie .20 .07
❑ 573 Paul Byrd .20 .07
❑ 574 Troy Percival .20 .07
❑ 575 Pedro Martinez .30 .10
❑ 576 Matt Clement .20 .07
❑ 577 Ryan Wagner .20 .07
❑ 578 Jeff Francis .20 .07
❑ 579 Jeff Conine .20 .07
❑ 580 Wade Miller .20 .07
❑ 581 Matt Stairs .20 .07
❑ 582 Gavin Floyd .20 .07
❑ 583 Kazuhisa Ishii .20 .07
❑ 584 Victor Santos .20 .07
❑ 585 Jacque Jones .20 .07
❑ 586 Sunny Kim .20 .07
❑ 587 Dan Kolb .20 .07
❑ 588 Cory Lidle .20 .07
❑ 589 Jose Castillo .20 .07
❑ 590 Alex Gonzalez .20 .07
❑ 591 Kirk Rueter .20 .07
❑ 592 Jolbert Cabrera .20 .07
❑ 593 Erik Bedard .20 .07
❑ 594 Ben Grieve .20 .07
❑ 595 Ricky Ledee .20 .07
❑ 596 Mark Hendrickson .20 .07
❑ 597 Laynce Nix .20 .07
❑ 598 Jason Frasor .20 .07
❑ 599 Kevin Gregg .20 .07
❑ 600 Derek Jeter 1.00 .40
❑ 601 Luis Terrero .20 .07
❑ 602 Jaret Wright .20 .07
❑ 603 Edwin Jackson .20 .07
❑ 604 Dave Roberts .20 .07
❑ 605 Moises Alou .20 .07
❑ 606 Aaron Rowand .20 .07
❑ 607 Kazuhito Tadano .20 .07
❑ 608 Luis A. Gonzalez .20 .07
❑ 609 A.J. Burnett .20 .07
❑ 610 Jeff Bagwell .30 .10
❑ 611 Brad Penny .20 .07
❑ 612 Craig Counsell .20 .07
❑ 613 Corey Koskie .20 .07
❑ 614 Mark Ellis .20 .07
❑ 615 Felix Rodriguez .20 .07
❑ 616 Jay Payton .20 .07
❑ 617 Hector Luna .20 .07
❑ 618 Miguel Olivo .20 .07
❑ 619 Rob Bell .20 .07
❑ 620 Scott Rolen .30 .10
❑ 621 Ricardo Rodriguez .20 .07
❑ 622 Eric Hinske .20 .07
❑ 623 Tim Salmon .30 .10
❑ 624 Adam LaRoche .20 .07
❑ 625 B.J. Ryan .20 .07
❑ 626 Roberto Alomar .30 .10
❑ 627 Steve Finley .20 .07
❑ 628 Joe Nathan .20 .07
❑ 629 Scott Linebrink .20 .07
❑ 630 Vicente Padilla .20 .07
❑ 631 Raul Mondesi .20 .07
❑ 632 Yadier Molina .20 .07
❑ 633 Tino Martinez .30 .10
❑ 634 Mark Teixeira .30 .10
❑ 635 Kelvim Escobar .20 .07
❑ 636 Pedro Feliz .20 .07
❑ 637 Rich Aurilia .20 .07
❑ 638 Los Angeles Angels TC .20 .07
❑ 639 Arizona Diamondbacks TC .20 .07
❑ 640 Atlanta Braves TC .30 .10
❑ 641 Baltimore Orioles TC .20 .07
❑ 642 Boston Red Sox TC .50 .20
❑ 643 Chicago Cubs TC .30 .10
❑ 644 Chicago White Sox TC .20 .07
❑ 645 Cincinnati Reds TC .20 .07
❑ 646 Cleveland Indians TC .20 .07
❑ 647 Colorado Rockies TC .20 .07
❑ 648 Detroit Tigers TC .20 .07

- ❑ 649 Florida Marlins TC .20 .07
- ❑ 650 Houston Astros TC .20 .07
- ❑ 651 Kansas City Royals TC .20 .07
- ❑ 652 Los Angeles Dodgers TC .20 .07
- ❑ 653 Milwaukee Brewers TC .20 .07
- ❑ 654 Minnesota Twins TC .20 .07
- ❑ 655 Montreal Expos TC .20 .07
- ❑ 656 New York Mets TC .20 .07
- ❑ 657 New York Yankees TC .50 .20
- ❑ 658 Oakland Athletics TC .20 .07
- ❑ 659 Philadelphia Phillies TC .20 .07
- ❑ 660 Pittsburgh Pirates TC .20 .07
- ❑ 661 San Diego Padres TC .20 .07
- ❑ 662 San Francisco Giants TC .20 .07
- ❑ 663 Seattle Mariners TC .20 .07
- ❑ 664 St. Louis Cardinals TC .30 .10
- ❑ 665 Tampa Bay Devil Rays TC .20 .07
- ❑ 666 Texas Rangers TC .20 .07
- ❑ 667 Toronto Blue Jays TC .20 .07
- ❑ 668 Billy Butler FY RC 4.00 1.50
- ❑ 669 Wes Swackhamer FY RC .50 .20
- ❑ 670 Matt Campbell FY RC .50 .20
- ❑ 671 Ryan Webb FY .50 .20
- ❑ 672 Glen Perkins FY RC .75 .30
- ❑ 673 Michael Rogers FY RC .50 .20
- ❑ 674 Kevin Melillo FY RC .75 .30
- ❑ 675 Erik Cordier FY RC .50 .20
- ❑ 676 Landon Powell FY RC .75 .30
- ❑ 677 Justin Verlander FY RC 4.00 1.50
- ❑ 678 Eric Nielsen FY RC .50 .20
- ❑ 679 Alexander Smit FY RC .50 .20
- ❑ 680 Ryan Garko FY RC 1.50 .60
- ❑ 681 Bobby Livingston FY RC .50 .20
- ❑ 682 Jeff Niemann FY RC .75 .30
- ❑ 683 Wladimir Balentien FY RC .75 .30
- ❑ 684 Chip Cannon FY RC .75 .30
- ❑ 685 Yorman Bazardo FY RC .50 .20
- ❑ 686 Mike Bourn FY RC .75 .30
- ❑ 687 Andy LaRoche FY RC 3.00 1.25
- ❑ 688 F.Hernandez/J.Leone .50 .20
- ❑ 689 R.Howard/C.Hamels 5.00 2.00
- ❑ 690 M.Cain/M.Valdez 1.00 .40
- ❑ 691 A.Marte/J.Francoeur 2.00 .75
- ❑ 692 C.Billingsley/J.Guzman .50 .20
- ❑ 693 J.Hairston Jr./S.Hairston .20 .07
- ❑ 694 M.Tejada/L.Berkman .30 .10
- ❑ 695 Kenny Rogers GG .20 .07
- ❑ 696 Ivan Rodriguez GG .20 .07
- ❑ 697 Darin Erstad GG .20 .07
- ❑ 698 Bret Boone GG .20 .07
- ❑ 699 Eric Chavez GG .20 .07
- ❑ 700 Derek Jeter GG .50 .20
- ❑ 701 Vernon Wells GG .20 .07
- ❑ 702 Ichiro Suzuki GG .50 .20
- ❑ 703 Torii Hunter GG .20 .07
- ❑ 704 Greg Maddux GG .50 .20
- ❑ 705 Mike Matheny GG .20 .07
- ❑ 706 Todd Helton GG .20 .07
- ❑ 707 Luis Castillo GG .20 .07
- ❑ 708 Scott Rolen GG .20 .07
- ❑ 709 Cesar Izturis GG .20 .07
- ❑ 710 Jim Edmonds GG .20 .07
- ❑ 711 Andruw Jones GG .20 .07
- ❑ 712 Steve Finley GG .20 .07
- ❑ 713 Johan Santana CY .30 .10
- ❑ 714 Roger Clemens CY .50 .20
- ❑ 715 Vladimir Guerrero MVP .30 .10
- ❑ 716 Barry Bonds MVP 1.00 .40
- ❑ 717 Bobby Crosby ROY .20 .07
- ❑ 718 Jason Bay ROY .20 .07
- ❑ 719 Albert Pujols AS .50 .20
- ❑ 720 Mark Loretta AS .20 .07
- ❑ 721 Edgar Renteria AS .20 .07
- ❑ 722 Scott Rolen AS .20 .07
- ❑ 723 J.D. Drew AS .20 .07
- ❑ 724 Jim Edmonds AS .20 .07
- ❑ 725 Johnny Estrada AS .20 .07
- ❑ 726 Jason Schmidt AS .20 .07
- ❑ 727 Chris Carpenter AS .20 .07
- ❑ 728 Eric Gagne AS .20 .07
- ❑ 729 Jason Bay AS .20 .07
- ❑ 730 Bobby Cox MG AS .20 .07
- ❑ 731 D.Ortiz/M.Bellhorn WS1 1.00 .40
- ❑ 732 Curt Schilling WS2 1.00 .40
- ❑ 733 M.Ramirez/P.Martinez WS3 1.00 .40
- ❑ 734 Sox Win Damon/Lowe WS4 1.50 .60

2005 Topps Update

- ❑ COMPLETE SET (330) 40.00 15.00
- ❑ COMP.FACT.SET (330) 40.00 25.00
- ❑ COMMON CARD (1-330) .20 .07
- ❑ COM (90-110/203-220) .50 .20
- ❑ COMMON (116-134) .50 .20
- ❑ COM (14/66/221-310) .50 .20
- ❑ COMMON (311-330) .50 .20
- ❑ PLATE ODDS 1:2009 H, 1:582 HTA, 1:2009 R
- ❑ PLATE PRINT RUN 1 SET PER COLOR
- ❑ BLACK-CYAN-MAGENTA-YELLOW ISSUED
- ❑ NO PLATE PRICING DUE TO SCARCITY
- ❑ 1 Sammy Sosa .50 .20
- ❑ 2 Jeff Francoeur 1.50 .60
- ❑ 3 Tony Clark .20 .07
- ❑ 4 Michael Tucker .20 .07
- ❑ 5 Mike Matheny .20 .07
- ❑ 6 Eric Young .20 .07
- ❑ 7 Jose Valentin .20 .07
- ❑ 8 Matt Lawton .20 .07
- ❑ 9 Juan Rivera .20 .07
- ❑ 10 Shawn Green .20 .07
- ❑ 11 Aaron Boone .20 .07
- ❑ 12 Woody Williams .20 .07
- ❑ 13 Brad Wilkerson .20 .07
- ❑ 14 Anthony Reyes RC 1.00 .40
- ❑ 15 Russ Adams .20 .07
- ❑ 16 Gustavo Chacin .20 .07
- ❑ 17 Michael Restovich .20 .07
- ❑ 18 Humberto Quintero .20 .07
- ❑ 19 Matt Ginter .20 .07
- ❑ 20 Scott Podsednik .20 .07
- ❑ 21 Byung-Hyun Kim .20 .07
- ❑ 22 Orlando Hernandez .20 .07
- ❑ 23 Mark Grudzielanek .20 .07
- ❑ 24 Jody Gerut .20 .07
- ❑ 25 Adrian Beltré .20 .07
- ❑ 26 Scott Schoeneweis .20 .07
- ❑ 27 Marlon Anderson .20 .07
- ❑ 28 Jason Vargas .20 .07
- ❑ 29 Claudio Vargas .20 .07
- ❑ 30 Jason Kendall .20 .07
- ❑ 31 Aaron Small .20 .07
- ❑ 32 Juan Cruz .20 .07
- ❑ 33 Placido Polanco .20 .07
- ❑ 34 Jorge Sosa .20 .07
- ❑ 35 John Olerud .20 .07
- ❑ 36 Ryan Langerhans .20 .07
- ❑ 37 Randy Winn .20 .07
- ❑ 38 Zach Duke .30 .10
- ❑ 39 Garrett Atkins .20 .07
- ❑ 40 Al Leiter .20 .07
- ❑ 41 Shawn Chacon .20 .07
- ❑ 42 Mark DeRosa .20 .07
- ❑ 43 Miguel Ojeda .20 .07
- ❑ 44 A.J. Pierzynski .20 .07
- ❑ 45 Carlos Lee .20 .07
- ❑ 46 LaTroy Hawkins .20 .07
- ❑ 47 Nick Green .20 .07
- ❑ 48 Shawn Estes .20 .07
- ❑ 49 Eli Marrero .20 .07
- ❑ 50 Jeff Kent .20 .07
- ❑ 51 Joe Randa .20 .07
- ❑ 52 Jose Hernandez .20 .07
- ❑ 53 Joe Blanton .20 .07
- ❑ 54 Huston Street .30 .10
- ❑ 55 Marlon Byrd .20 .07
- ❑ 56 Alex Sanchez .20 .07
- ❑ 57 Livan Hernandez .20 .07
- ❑ 58 Chris Young .20 .07
- ❑ 59 Brad Eldred .20 .07
- ❑ 60 Terrence Long .20 .07
- ❑ 61 Phil Nevin .20 .07
- ❑ 62 Kyle Farnsworth .20 .07
- ❑ 63 Jon Lieber .20 .07
- ❑ 64 Antonio Alfonseca .20 .07
- ❑ 65 Tony Graffanino .20 .07
- ❑ 66 Tadahito Iguchi RC 1.50 .60
- ❑ 67 Brad Thompson .20 .07
- ❑ 68 Jose Vidro .20 .07
- ❑ 69 Jason Phillips .20 .07
- ❑ 70 Carl Pavano .20 .07
- ❑ 71 Pokey Reese .20 .07
- ❑ 72 Jerome Williams .20 .07
- ❑ 73 Kazuhisa Ishii .20 .07
- ❑ 74 Zach Day .20 .07
- ❑ 75 Edgar Renteria .20 .07
- ❑ 76 Mike Myers .20 .07
- ❑ 77 Jeff Cirillo .20 .07
- ❑ 78 Endy Chavez .20 .07
- ❑ 79 Jose Guillen .20 .07
- ❑ 80 Ugueth Urbina .20 .07
- ❑ 81 Vinny Castilla .20 .07
- ❑ 82 Javier Vazquez .20 .07
- ❑ 83 Willy Taveras .20 .07
- ❑ 84 Mark Mulder .20 .07
- ❑ 85 Mike Hargrove MG .20 .07
- ❑ 86 Buddy Bell MG .20 .07
- ❑ 87 Charlie Manuel MG .20 .07
- ❑ 88 Willie Randolph MG .20 .07
- ❑ 89 Bob Melvin MG .20 .07
- ❑ 90 Chris Lambert PROS .50 .20
- ❑ 91 Homer Bailey PROS .50 .20
- ❑ 92 Ervin Santana PROS .50 .20
- ❑ 93 Bill Bray PROS .50 .20
- ❑ 94 Thomas Diamond PROS .50 .20
- ❑ 95 Trevor Plouffe PROS .50 .20
- ❑ 96 James Houser PROS .50 .20
- ❑ 97 Jake Stevens PROS .50 .20
- ❑ 98 Anthony Whittington PROS .50 .20
- ❑ 99 Philip Hughes PROS .50 .20
- ❑ 100 Greg Golson PROS .50 .20
- ❑ 101 Paul Maholm PROS .50 .20
- ❑ 102 Carlos Quentin PROS .50 .20
- ❑ 103 Dan Johnson PROS .50 .20
- ❑ 104 Mark Rogers PROS .50 .20
- ❑ 105 Neil Walker PROS .50 .20
- ❑ 106 Omar Quintanilla PROS .50 .20
- ❑ 107 Blake DeWitt PROS .50 .20
- ❑ 108 Taylor Tankersley PROS .50 .20
- ❑ 109 David Murphy PROS .50 .20
- ❑ 110 Felix Hernandez PROS 1.00 .40
- ❑ 111 Craig Biggio HL .20 .07
- ❑ 112 Greg Maddux HL .50 .20
- ❑ 113 Bobby Abreu HL .20 .07
- ❑ 114 Alex Rodriguez HL .50 .20
- ❑ 115 Trevor Hoffman HL .20 .07
- ❑ 116 A.Pierzynski/T.Iguchi ALDS .50 .20
- ❑ 117 Reggie Sanders NLDS .50 .20
- ❑ 118 B.Molina/E.Santana ALDS .50 .20
- ❑ 119 Burke/Berkman/LaR NLDS .50 .20
- ❑ 120 Garret Anderson ALCS .50 .20
- ❑ 121 A.J. Pierzynski ALCS .50 .20
- ❑ 122 Paul Konerko ALCS .50 .20
- ❑ 123 Joe Crede ALCS .50 .20
- ❑ 124 M.Buehrle/J.Garland ALCS .50 .20
- ❑ 125 F.Garcia/J.Contreras ALCS .50 .20
- ❑ 126 Reggie Sanders NLCS .50 .20
- ❑ 127 Roy Oswalt NLCS .50 .20
- ❑ 128 Roger Clemens NLCS 1.00 .40
- ❑ 129 Albert Pujols NLCS 1.00 .40
- ❑ 130 Roy Oswalt NLCS .50 .20
- ❑ 131 J.Crede/B.Jenks WS .75 .30
- ❑ 132 P.Konerko/S.Podsed WS .75 .30
- ❑ 133 Geoff Blum WS .50 .20
- ❑ 134 White Sox Sweep WS 1.00 .40
- ❑ 135 ARod/Ortiz/Manny AL HR .50 .20
- ❑ 136 Young/ARod/Vlad AL BA .30 .10
- ❑ 137 Ortiz/Teix/Manny AL RBI .30 .10
- ❑ 138 Colon/Garland/Lee AL W .20 .07
- ❑ 139 Mill/Johan/Buehrle AL ERA .30 .10
- ❑ 140 Johan/Randy/Lackey AL K .30 .10
- ❑ 141 Andruw/Lee/Pujols NL HR .50 .20

❑ 142 Lee/Pujols/Cabrera NL BA .50 .20
❑ 143 Andruw/Pujols/Burr NL RBI .50 .20
❑ 144 Willis/Carp/Oswalt NL W .20 .07
❑ 145 Roger/Andy/Willis NL ERA .50 .20
❑ 146 Peavy/Carp/Pedro NL K .20 .07
❑ 147 Mark Teixeira AS .20 .07
❑ 148 Brian Roberts AS .20 .07
❑ 149 Michael Young AS .20 .07
❑ 150 Alex Rodriguez AS .50 .20
❑ 151 Johnny Damon AS .20 .07
❑ 152 Vladimir Guerrero AS .30 .10
❑ 153 Manny Ramirez AS .20 .07
❑ 154 David Ortiz AS .30 .10
❑ 155 Mariano Rivera AS .30 .10
❑ 156 Joe Nathan AS .20 .07
❑ 157 Albert Pujols AS .50 .20
❑ 158 Jeff Kent AS .20 .07
❑ 159 Felipe Lopez AS .20 .07
❑ 160 Morgan Ensberg AS .20 .07
❑ 161 Miguel Cabrera AS .20 .07
❑ 162 Ken Griffey Jr. AS .50 .20
❑ 163 Andruw Jones AS .20 .07
❑ 164 Paul Lo Duca AS .20 .07
❑ 165 Chad Cordero AS .20 .07
❑ 166 Ken Griffey Jr. Comeback .50 .20
❑ 167 Jason Giambi Comeback .20 .07
❑ 168 Willy Taveras ROY .20 .07
❑ 169 Huston Street ROY .20 .07
❑ 170 Chris Carpenter AS .20 .07
❑ 171 Bartolo Colon AS .20 .07
❑ 172 Bobby Cox AS MG .20 .07
❑ 173 Ozzie Guillen AS MG .50 .20
❑ 174 Andruw Jones POY .20 .07
❑ 175 Johnny Damon AS .20 .07
❑ 176 Alex Rodriguez AS .50 .20
❑ 177 David Ortiz AS .30 .10
❑ 178 Manny Ramirez AS .20 .07
❑ 179 Miguel Tejada AS .20 .07
❑ 180 Vladimir Guerrero AS .30 .10
❑ 181 Mark Teixeira AS .20 .07
❑ 182 Ivan Rodriguez AS .20 .07
❑ 183 Brian Roberts AS .20 .07
❑ 184 Mark Buehrle AS .20 .07
❑ 185 Bobby Abreu AS .20 .07
❑ 186 Carlos Beltran AS .20 .07
❑ 187 Albert Pujols AS .50 .20
❑ 188 Derrek Lee AS .20 .07
❑ 189 Jim Edmonds AS .20 .07
❑ 190 Aramis Ramirez AS .20 .07
❑ 191 Mike Piazza AS .30 .10
❑ 192 Jeff Kent AS .20 .07
❑ 193 David Eckstein AS .20 .07
❑ 194 Chris Carpenter AS .20 .07
❑ 195 Bobby Abreu HR .20 .07
❑ 196 Ivan Rodriguez HR .20 .07
❑ 197 Carlos Lee HR .20 .07
❑ 198 David Ortiz HR .30 .10
❑ 199 Hee-Seop Choi HR .20 .07
❑ 200 Andruw Jones HR .20 .07
❑ 201 Mark Teixeira HR .20 .07
❑ 202 Jason Bay HR .20 .07
❑ 203 Hanley Ramirez FUT .50 .20
❑ 204 Shin-Soo Choo FUT .50 .20
❑ 205 Justin Huber FUT .50 .20
❑ 206 Nelson Cruz FUT RC 1.25 .50
❑ 207 Edwin Encarnacion FUT .50 .20
❑ 208 Miguel Montero FUT RC 1.25 .50
❑ 209 William Bergolla FUT .50 .20
❑ 210 Luis Montanez FUT .50 .20
❑ 211 Francisco Liriano FUT 1.50 .60
❑ 212 Kevin Thompson FUT .50 .20
❑ 213 B.J. Upton FUT .50 .20
❑ 214 Conor Jackson FUT .50 .20
❑ 215 Delmon Young FUT .50 .20
❑ 216 Andy LaRoche FUT 1.00 .40
❑ 217 Ryan Garko FUT 1.25 .50
❑ 218 Josh Barfield FUT .50 .20
❑ 219 Chris B.Young FUT .50 .20
❑ 220 Justin Verlander FUT 1.50 .60
❑ 221 Drew Anderson FY RC .50 .20
❑ 222 Luis Hernandez FY RC .50 .20
❑ 223 Jim Burt FY RC .50 .20
❑ 224 Mike Morse FY RC .50 .20
❑ 225 Elliot Johnson FY RC .50 .20
❑ 226 C.J. Smith FY RC .50 .20
❑ 227 Casey McGehee FY RC .50 .20
❑ 228 Brian Miller FY RC .50 .20
❑ 229 Chris Vines FY RC .50 .20
❑ 230 D.J. Houlton FY RC .50 .20
❑ 231 Chuck Tiffany FY RC 1.00 .40
❑ 232 Humberto Sanchez FY RC 2.00 .75
❑ 233 Baltazar Lopez FY RC .50 .20
❑ 234 Russ Martin FY RC 2.50 1.00
❑ 235 Dana Eveland FY RC .50 .20
❑ 236 Johan Silva FY RC .50 .20
❑ 237 Adam Harben FY RC .75 .30
❑ 238 Brian Bannister FY RC 1.00 .40
❑ 239 Adam Boeve FY RC .50 .20
❑ 240 Thomas Oldham FY RC .50 .20
❑ 241 Cody Haerther FY RC .50 .20
❑ 242 Dan Santin FY RC .50 .20
❑ 243 Daniel Haigwood FY RC .75 .30
❑ 244 Craig Tatum FY RC .50 .20
❑ 245 Martin Prado FY RC .50 .20
❑ 246 Errol Simonitsch FY RC .75 .30
❑ 247 Lorenzo Scott FY RC .50 .20
❑ 248 Hayden Penn FY RC .75 .30
❑ 249 Heath Totten FY RC .50 .20
❑ 250 Nick Masset FY RC .50 .20
❑ 251 Pedro Lopez FY RC .50 .20
❑ 252 Ben Harrison FY .50 .20
❑ 253 Mike Spidale FY RC .50 .20
❑ 254 Jeremy Harts FY RC .50 .20
❑ 255 Danny Zell FY RC .50 .20
❑ 256 Kevin Collins FY RC .50 .20
❑ 257 Tony Americh FY RC .50 .20
❑ 258 Matt Albers FY RC 1.25 .50
❑ 259 Ricky Barrett FY RC .50 .20
❑ 260 Hernan Iribarren FY RC .75 .30
❑ 261 Sean Tracey FY RC .50 .20
❑ 262 Jerry Owens FY RC .75 .30
❑ 263 Steve Nelson FY RC .50 .20
❑ 264 Brandon McCarthy FY RC 1.00 .40
❑ 265 David Shepard FY RC .50 .20
❑ 266 Steven Bondurant FY RC .50 .20
❑ 267 Billy Sadler FY RC .50 .20
❑ 268 Ryan Feierabend FY RC .50 .20
❑ 269 Stuart Pomeranz FY RC .50 .20
❑ 270 Shaun Marcum FY .50 .20
❑ 271 Erik Schindewolf FY RC .50 .20
❑ 272 Stefan Bailie FY RC .50 .20
❑ 273 Mike Esposito FY RC .50 .20
❑ 274 Buck Coats FY RC .50 .20
❑ 275 Andy Sides FY RC .50 .20
❑ 276 Micah Schnurstein FY RC .50 .20
❑ 277 Jesse Gutierrez FY RC .50 .20
❑ 278 Jake Postlewait FY RC .50 .20
❑ 279 Willy Mota FY RC .50 .20
❑ 280 Ryan Speier FY RC .50 .20
❑ 281 Frank Mata FY RC .50 .20
❑ 282 Jair Jurrjens FY RC 1.50 .60
❑ 283 Nick Touchstone FY RC .50 .20
❑ 284 Matthew Kemp FY RC 3.00 1.25
❑ 285 Vinny Rottino FY RC .50 .20
❑ 286 J.B. Thurmond FY RC .50 .20
❑ 287 Kelvin Pichardo FY RC .50 .20
❑ 288 Scott Mitchinson FY RC .50 .20
❑ 289 Darwinson Salazar FY RC .50 .20
❑ 290 George Kottaras FY RC .75 .30
❑ 291 Kenny Durost FY RC .50 .20
❑ 292 Jonathan Sanchez FY RC 1.25 .50
❑ 293 Brandon Moorhead FY RC .50 .20
❑ 294 Kennard Bibbs FY RC .50 .20
❑ 295 David Gassner FY RC .50 .20
❑ 296 Micah Furtado FY RC .50 .20
❑ 297 Ismael Ramirez FY RC .50 .20
❑ 298 Carlos Gonzalez FY RC 1.50 1.00
❑ 299 Brandon Sing FY RC .75 .30
❑ 300 Jason Motte FY RC .50 .20
❑ 301 Chuck James FY RC 1.25 .50
❑ 302 Andy Santana FY RC .50 .20
❑ 303 Manny Parra FY RC .40 .15
❑ 304 Chris B.Young FY RC 1.25 .50
❑ 305 Juan Senreiso FY RC .50 .20
❑ 306 Franklin Morales FY RC .75 .30
❑ 307 Jared Gothreaux FY RC .50 .20
❑ 308 Jayce Tingler FY RC .50 .20
❑ 309 Matt Brown FY RC .50 .20
❑ 310 Frank Diaz FY RC .50 .20
❑ 311 Stephen Drew DP RC 4.00 1.50
❑ 312 Jered Weaver DP RC 4.00 1.50
❑ 313 Ryan Braun DP RC 12.00 5.00
❑ 314 John Mayberry Jr. DP RC 1.00 .40
❑ 315 Aaron Thompson DP RC .75 .30
❑ 316 Cesar Carrillo DP RC 1.00 .40
❑ 317 Jacoby Ellsbury DP RC 15.00 6.00
❑ 318 Matt Garza DP RC 2.00 .75
❑ 319 Cliff Pennington DP RC .75 .30
❑ 320 Colby Rasmus DP RC 6.00 2.50
❑ 321 Chris Volstad DP RC 1.00 .40
❑ 322 Ricky Romero DP RC .75 .30
❑ 323 Ryan Zimmerman DP RC 5.00 2.00
❑ 324 C.J. Henry DP RC 1.50 .60
❑ 325 Jay Bruce DP RC 12.00 5.00
❑ 326 Beau Jones DP RC 1.00 .40
❑ 327 Mark McCormick DP RC .75 .30
❑ 328 Eli Iorg DP RC .75 .30
❑ 329 Andrew McCutchen DP RC 2.00 .75
❑ 330 Mike Costanzo DP RC 1.25 .50

2006 Topps

❑ COMP.HOBBY SET (664) 80.00 50.00
❑ COMP.HOLIDAY SET (659) 80.00 50.00
❑ COMP.CARDINALS SET (664) 80.00 50.00
❑ COMP.CUBS SET (664) 80.00 50.00
❑ COMP.PIRATES SET (664) 80.00 50.00
❑ COMP.RED SOX SET (664) 80.00 50.00
❑ COMP.YANKEES SET (664) 80.00 50.00
❑ COMPLETE SET (659) 80.00 30.00
❑ COMPLETE SERIES 1 (329) 40.00 15.00
❑ COMPLETE SERIES 2 (330) 40.00 15.00
❑ COMMON CARD (1-660) .20 .07
❑ COMP.SER.1 SET EXCLUDES CARD 297
❑ CARD 297 NOT INTENDED FOR RELEASE
❑ CARDS 287b AND 312b ISSUED IN FACT.SET
❑ 2 TICKETS EXCH.CARD RANDOM IN PACKS
❑ OVERALL PLATE SER.1 ODDS 1:246 HTA
❑ OVERALL PLATE SER.2 ODDS 1:193 HTA
❑ PLATE PRINT RUN 1 SET PER COLOR
❑ BLACK-CYAN-MAGENTA-YELLOW ISSUED
❑ NO PLATE PRICING DUE TO SCARCITY
❑ 1 Alex Rodriguez .75 .30
❑ 2 Jose Valentin .20 .07
❑ 3 Garrett Atkins .20 .07
❑ 4 Scott Hatteberg .20 .07
❑ 5 Carl Crawford .20 .07
❑ 6 Armando Benitez .20 .07
❑ 7 Mickey Mantle 8.00 3.00
❑ 8 Mike Morse .20 .07
❑ 9 Damian Miller .20 .07
❑ 10 Clint Barmes .20 .07
❑ 11 Michael Barrett .20 .07
❑ 12 Coco Crisp .20 .07
❑ 13 Tadahito Iguchi .20 .07
❑ 14 Chris Snyder .20 .07
❑ 15 Brian Roberts .20 .07
❑ 16 David Wright .75 .30
❑ 17 Victor Santos .20 .07
❑ 18 Trevor Hoffman .20 .07
❑ 19 Jeremy Reed .20 .07
❑ 20 Bobby Abreu .20 .07
❑ 21 Lance Berkman .20 .07
❑ 22 Zach Day .20 .07
❑ 23 Jonny Gomes .20 .07
❑ 24 Jason Marquis .20 .07
❑ 25 Chipper Jones .50 .20
❑ 26 Scott Hairston .20 .07
❑ 27 Ryan Dempster .20 .07
❑ 28 Brandon Inge .20 .07
❑ 29 Aaron Harang .20 .07

❑ 30 Jon Garland .20 .07
❑ 31 Pokey Reese .20 .07
❑ 32 Mike MacDougal .20 .07
❑ 33 Mike Lieberthal .20 .07
❑ 34 Cesar Izturis .20 .07
❑ 35 Brad Wilkerson .20 .07
❑ 36 Jeff Suppan .20 .07
❑ 37 Adam Everett .20 .07
❑ 38 Bengie Molina .20 .07
❑ 39 Rickie Weeks .20 .07
❑ 40 Jorge Posada .30 .10
❑ 41 Rheal Cormier .20 .07
❑ 42 Reed Johnson .20 .07
❑ 43 Laynce Nix .20 .07
❑ 44 Carl Everett .20 .07
❑ 45 Greg Maddux .75 .30
❑ 46 Jeff Francis .20 .07
❑ 47 Felipe Lopez .20 .07
❑ 48 Dan Johnson .20 .07
❑ 49 Humberto Cota .20 .07
❑ 50 Manny Ramirez .30 .10
❑ 51 Juan Uribe .20 .07
❑ 52 Jaret Wright .20 .07
❑ 53 Tomo Ohka .20 .07
❑ 54 Mike Matheny .20 .07
❑ 55 Joe Mauer .50 .20
❑ 56 Jarrod Washburn .20 .07
❑ 57 Randy Winn .20 .07
❑ 58 Pedro Feliz .20 .07
❑ 59 Kenny Rogers .20 .07
❑ 60 Rocco Baldelli .20 .07
❑ 61 Eric Hinske .20 .07
❑ 62 Damaso Marte .20 .07
❑ 63 Desi Relaford .20 .07
❑ 64 Juan Encarnacion .20 .07
❑ 65 Nomar Garciaparra .50 .20
❑ 66 Shawn Estes .20 .07
❑ 67 Brian Jordan .20 .07
❑ 68 Steve Kline .20 .07
❑ 69 Braden Looper .20 .07
❑ 70 Carlos Lee .20 .07
❑ 71 Tom Glavine .30 .10
❑ 72 Craig Biggio .30 .10
❑ 73 Steve Finley .20 .07
❑ 74 David Newhan .20 .07
❑ 75 Eric Gagne .20 .07
❑ 76 Tony Graffanino .20 .07
❑ 77 Dallas McPherson .20 .07
❑ 78 Nick Punto .20 .07
❑ 79 Mark Kotsay .20 .07
❑ 80 Kerry Wood .20 .07
❑ 81 Kyle Farnsworth .20 .07
❑ 82 Huston Street .20 .07
❑ 83 Endy Chavez .20 .07
❑ 84 So Taguchi .20 .07
❑ 85 Hank Blalock .20 .07
❑ 86 Brad Radke .20 .07
❑ 87 Chien-Ming Wang .75 .30
❑ 88 B.J. Surhoff .20 .07
❑ 89 Glendon Rusch .20 .07
❑ 90 Mark Buehrle .20 .07
❑ 91 Rafael Betancourt .20 .07
❑ 92 Lance Cormier .20 .07
❑ 93 Alex Gonzalez .20 .07
❑ 94 Matt Stairs .20 .07
❑ 95 Andy Pettitte .30 .10
❑ 96 Jesse Crain .20 .07
❑ 97 Kenny Lofton .20 .07
❑ 98 Geoff Blum .20 .07
❑ 99 Mark Redman .20 .07
❑ 100 Barry Bonds 1.00 .40
❑ 101 Chad Orvella .20 .07
❑ 102 Xavier Nady .20 .07
❑ 103 Junior Spivey .20 .07
❑ 104 Bernie Williams .30 .10
❑ 105 Victor Martinez .20 .07
❑ 106 Nook Logan .20 .07
❑ 107 Mark Teahen .20 .07
❑ 108 Mike Lamb .20 .07
❑ 109 Jayson Werth .20 .07
❑ 110 Mariano Rivera .50 .20
❑ 111 Erubiel Durazo .20 .07
❑ 112 Ryan Vogelsong .20 .07
❑ 113 Bobby Madritsch .20 .07
❑ 114 Travis Lee .20 .07
❑ 115 Adam Dunn .20 .07
❑ 116 David Riske .20 .07
❑ 117 Troy Percival .20 .07
❑ 118 Chad Tracy .20 .07
❑ 119 Andy Marte .20 .07
❑ 120 Edgar Renteria .20 .07
❑ 121 Jason Giambi .20 .07
❑ 122 Justin Morneau .20 .07
❑ 123 J.T. Snow .20 .07
❑ 124 Danys Baez .20 .07
❑ 125 Carlos Delgado .20 .07
❑ 126 John Buck .20 .07
❑ 127 Shannon Stewart .20 .07
❑ 128 Mike Cameron .20 .07
❑ 129 Joe McEwing .20 .07
❑ 130 Richie Sexson .20 .07
❑ 131 Rod Barajas .20 .07
❑ 132 Russ Adams .20 .07
❑ 133 J.D. Closser .20 .07
❑ 134 Ramon Ortiz .20 .07
❑ 135 Josh Beckett .20 .07
❑ 136 Ryan Freel .20 .07
❑ 137 Victor Zambrano .20 .07
❑ 138 Ronnie Belliard .20 .07
❑ 139 Jason Michaels .20 .07
❑ 140 Brian Giles .20 .07
❑ 141 Randy Wolf .20 .07
❑ 142 Robinson Cano .30 .10
❑ 143 Joe Blanton .20 .07
❑ 144 Esteban Loaiza .20 .07
❑ 145 Troy Glaus .20 .07
❑ 146 Matt Clement .20 .07
❑ 147 Geoff Jenkins .20 .07
❑ 148 John Thomson .20 .07
❑ 149 A.J. Pierzynski .20 .07
❑ 150 Pedro Martinez .30 .10
❑ 151 Roger Clemens 1.00 .40
❑ 152 Jack Wilson .20 .07
❑ 153 Ray King .20 .07
❑ 154 Ryan Church .20 .07
❑ 155 Paul Lo Duca .20 .07
❑ 156 Dan Wheeler .20 .07
❑ 157 Carlos Zambrano .20 .07
❑ 158 Mike Timlin .20 .07
❑ 159 Brandon Claussen .20 .07
❑ 160 Travis Hafner .20 .07
❑ 161 Chris Shelton .20 .07
❑ 162 Rafael Furcal .20 .07
❑ 163 Tom Gordon .20 .07
❑ 164 Noah Lowry .20 .07
❑ 165 Larry Walker .30 .10
❑ 166 Dave Roberts .20 .07
❑ 167 Scott Schoeneweis .20 .07
❑ 168 Julian Tavarez .20 .07
❑ 169 Jhonny Peralta .20 .07
❑ 170 Vernon Wells .20 .07
❑ 171 Jorge Cantu .20 .07
❑ 172 Todd Greene .20 .07
❑ 173 Willy Taveras .20 .07
❑ 174 Corey Patterson .20 .07
❑ 175 Ivan Rodriguez .30 .10
❑ 176 Bobby Kielty .20 .07
❑ 177 Jose Reyes .20 .07
❑ 178 Barry Zito .20 .07
❑ 179 Deivi Cruz .20 .07
❑ 180 Mark Teixeira .30 .10
❑ 181 Chone Figgins .20 .07
❑ 182 Aaron Rowand .20 .07
❑ 183 Tim Wakefield .20 .07
❑ 184 Mike Maroth .20 .07
❑ 185 Johnny Damon .30 .10
❑ 186 Vicente Padilla .20 .07
❑ 187 Ryan Klesko .20 .07
❑ 188 Gary Matthews .20 .07
❑ 189 Jose Mesa .20 .07
❑ 190 Nick Johnson .20 .07
❑ 191 Freddy Garcia .20 .07
❑ 192 Larry Bigbie .20 .07
❑ 193 Chris Ray .20 .07
❑ 194 Torii Hunter .20 .07
❑ 195 Mike Sweeney .20 .07
❑ 196 Brad Penny .20 .07
❑ 197 Jason Frasor .20 .07
❑ 198 Kevin Mench .20 .07
❑ 199 Adam Kennedy .20 .07
❑ 200 Albert Pujols 1.00 .40
❑ 201 Jody Gerut .20 .07
❑ 202 Luis Gonzalez .20 .07
❑ 203 Zack Greinke .20 .07
❑ 204 Miguel Cairo .20 .07
❑ 205 Jimmy Rollins .20 .07
❑ 206 Edgardo Alfonzo .20 .07
❑ 207 Billy Wagner .20 .07
❑ 208 B.J. Ryan .20 .07
❑ 209 Orlando Hudson .20 .07
❑ 210 Preston Wilson .20 .07
❑ 211 Melvin Mora .20 .07
❑ 212 Bill Mueller .20 .07
❑ 213 Javy Lopez .20 .07
❑ 214 Wilson Betemit .20 .07
❑ 215 Garret Anderson .20 .07
❑ 216 Russell Branyan .20 .07
❑ 217 Jeff Weaver .20 .07
❑ 218 Doug Mientkiewicz .20 .07
❑ 219 Mark Ellis .20 .07
❑ 220 Jason Bay .20 .07
❑ 221 Adam LaRoche .20 .07
❑ 222 C.C. Sabathia .20 .07
❑ 223 Humberto Quintero .20 .07
❑ 224 Bartolo Colon .20 .07
❑ 225 Ichiro Suzuki .75 .30
❑ 226 Brett Tomko .20 .07
❑ 227 Corey Koskie .20 .07
❑ 228 David Eckstein .20 .07
❑ 229 Cristian Guzman .20 .07
❑ 230 Jeff Kent .20 .07
❑ 231 Chris Capuano .20 .07
❑ 232 Rodrigo Lopez .20 .07
❑ 233 Jason Phillips .20 .07
❑ 234 Luis Rivas .20 .07
❑ 235 Cliff Floyd .20 .07
❑ 236 Gil Meche .20 .07
❑ 237 Adam Eaton .20 .07
❑ 238 Matt Morris .20 .07
❑ 239 Kyle Davies .20 .07
❑ 240 David Wells .20 .07
❑ 241 John Smoltz .30 .10
❑ 242 Felix Hernandez .50 .20
❑ 243 Kenny Rogers GG .20 .07
❑ 244 Mark Teixeira GG .20 .07
❑ 245 Orlando Hudson GG .20 .07
❑ 246 Derek Jeter GG .50 .20
❑ 247 Eric Chavez GG .20 .07
❑ 248 Torii Hunter GG .20 .07
❑ 249 Vernon Wells GG .20 .07
❑ 250 Ichiro Suzuki GG .50 .20
❑ 251 Greg Maddux GG .50 .20
❑ 252 Mike Matheny GG .20 .07
❑ 253 Derrek Lee GG .20 .07
❑ 254 Luis Castillo GG .20 .07
❑ 255 Omar Vizquel GG .20 .07
❑ 256 Mike Lowell GG .20 .07
❑ 257 Andruw Jones GG .20 .07
❑ 258 Jim Edmonds GG .20 .07
❑ 259 Bobby Abreu GG .20 .07
❑ 260 Bartolo Colon CY .20 .07
❑ 261 Chris Carpenter CY .20 .07
❑ 262 Alex Rodriguez MVP .50 .20
❑ 263 Albert Pujols MVP .50 .20
❑ 264 Huston Street ROY .20 .07
❑ 265 Ryan Howard ROY .40 .15
❑ 266 Bob Melvin MG .20 .07
❑ 267 Bobby Cox MG .20 .07
❑ 268 Baltimore Orioles TC .20 .07
❑ 269 Boston Red Sox TC .50 .20
❑ 270 Chicago White Sox TC .50 .20
❑ 271 Dusty Baker MG .20 .07
❑ 272 Jerry Narron MG .20 .07
❑ 273 Cleveland Indians TC .20 .07
❑ 274 Clint Hurdle MG .20 .07
❑ 275 Detroit Tigers TC .20 .07
❑ 276 Jack McKeon MG .20 .07
❑ 277 Phil Garner MG .20 .07
❑ 278 Kansas City Royals TC .20 .07
❑ 279 Jim Tracy MG .20 .07
❑ 280 Los Angeles Angels TC .20 .07
❑ 281 Milwaukee Brewers TC .20 .07
❑ 282 Minnesota Twins TC .20 .07
❑ 283 Willie Randolph MG .20 .07
❑ 284 New York Yankees TC .50 .20
❑ 285 Oakland Athletics TC .20 .07
❑ 286 Charlie Manuel MG .20 .07
❑ 287a Pete Mackanin MG ERR .20 .07

❑	287b	Pete Mackanin MG COR	.20	.07
❑	288	Bruce Bochy MG	.20	.07
❑	289	Felipe Alou MG	.20	.07
❑	290	Seattle Mariners TC	.20	.07
❑	291	Tony LaRussa MG	.20	.07
❑	292	Tampa Bay Devil Rays TC	.20	.07
❑	293	Texas Rangers TC	.20	.07
❑	294	Toronto Blue Jays TC	.20	.07
❑	295	Frank Robinson MG	.30	.10
❑	296	Anderson Hernandez (RC)	.50	.20
❑	297A	Alex Gordon (RC) Full	800.00	500.00
❑	297B	Alex Gordon Cut Out	120.00	60.00
❑	297C	Alex Gordon Blank Gold	150.00	75.00
❑	297D	Alex Gordon Blank Silver		
❑	298	Jason Botts (RC)	.50	.20
❑	299	Jeff Mathis (RC)	.50	.20
❑	300	Ryan Garko (RC)	.50	.20
❑	301	Charlton Jimerson (RC)	.50	.20
❑	302	Chris Denorfia (RC)	.50	.20
❑	303	Anthony Reyes (RC)	.50	.20
❑	304	Bryan Bullington (RC)	.50	.20
❑	305	Chuck James (RC)	.50	.20
❑	306	Danny Sandoval RC	.50	.20
❑	307	Walter Young (RC)	.50	.20
❑	308	Fausto Carmona (RC)	.50	.20
❑	309	Francisco Liriano (RC)	2.00	.75
❑	310	Hong-Chih Kuo (RC)	1.00	.40
❑	311	Joe Saunders (RC)	.50	.20
❑	312a	John Koronka Cubs (RC)	.50	.20
❑	312b	John Koronka Rangers (RC)	.50	.20
❑	313	Robert Andino RC	.50	.20
❑	314	Shaun Marcum (RC)	.50	.20
❑	315	Tom Gorzelanny (RC)	.50	.20
❑	316	Craig Breslow RC	.50	.20
❑	317	Chris DeMaria RC	.50	.20
❑	318	Brayan Pena (RC)	.50	.20
❑	319	Rich Hill (RC)	.50	.20
❑	320	Rick Short (RC)	.50	.20
❑	321	C.J. Wilson (RC)	.50	.20
❑	322	Marshall McDougall (RC)	.50	.20
❑	323	Darrell Rasner (RC)	.50	.20
❑	324	Brandon Watson (RC)	.50	.20
❑	325	Paul McAnulty (RC)	.50	.20
❑	326	D.Jeter/A.Rodriguez TS	1.00	.40
❑	327	M.Tejada/M.Mora TS	.20	.07
❑	328	M.Giles/C.Jones TS	.30	.10
❑	329	M.Ramirez/D.Ortiz TS	.50	.20
❑	330	M.Barrett/G.Maddux TS	.50	.20
❑	331	Matt Holliday	.25	.08
❑	332	Orlando Cabrera	.20	.07
❑	333	Ryan Langerhans	.20	.07
❑	334	Lew Ford	.20	.07
❑	335	Mark Prior	.30	.10
❑	336	Ted Lilly	.20	.07
❑	337	Michael Young	.20	.07
❑	338	Livan Hernandez	.20	.07
❑	339	Yadier Molina	.20	.07
❑	340	Eric Chavez	.20	.07
❑	341	Miguel Batista	.20	.07
❑	342	Bruce Chen	.20	.07
❑	343	Sean Casey	.20	.07
❑	344	Doug Davis	.20	.07
❑	345	Andruw Jones	.30	.10
❑	346	Hideki Matsui	.50	.20
❑	347	Joe Randa	.20	.07
❑	348	Reggie Sanders	.20	.07
❑	349	Jason Jennings	.20	.07
❑	350	Joe Nathan	.20	.07
❑	351	Jose Lopez	.20	.07
❑	352	John Lackey	.20	.07
❑	353	Claudio Vargas	.20	.07
❑	354	Grady Sizemore	.30	.10
❑	355	Jon Papelbon (RC)	2.00	.75
❑	356	Luis Matos	.20	.07
❑	357	Orlando Hernandez	.20	.07
❑	358	Jamie Moyer	.20	.07
❑	359	Chase Utley	.50	.20
❑	360	Moises Alou	.20	.07
❑	361	Chad Cordero	.20	.07
❑	362	Brian McCann	.20	.07
❑	363	Jermaine Dye	.20	.07
❑	364	Ryan Madson	.20	.07
❑	365	Aramis Ramirez	.20	.07
❑	366	Matt Treanor	.20	.07
❑	367	Ray Durham	.20	.07
❑	368	Khalil Greene	.30	.10
❑	369	Mike Hampton	.20	.07
❑	370	Mike Mussina	.30	.10
❑	371	Brad Hawpe	.20	.07
❑	372	Marlon Byrd	.20	.07
❑	373	Woody Williams	.20	.07
❑	374	Victor Diaz	.20	.07
❑	375	Brady Clark	.20	.07
❑	376	Luis Gonzalez	.20	.07
❑	377	Raul Ibanez	.20	.07
❑	378	Tony Clark	.20	.07
❑	379	Shawn Chacon	.20	.07
❑	380	Marcus Giles	.20	.07
❑	381	Odalis Perez	.20	.07
❑	382	Steve Trachsel	.20	.07
❑	383	Russ Ortiz	.20	.07
❑	384	Toby Hall	.20	.07
❑	385	Bill Hall	.20	.07
❑	386	Luke Hudson	.20	.07
❑	387	Ken Griffey Jr.	.75	.30
❑	388	Tim Hudson	.20	.07
❑	389	Brian Moehler	.20	.07
❑	390	Jake Peavy	.20	.07
❑	391	Casey Blake	.20	.07
❑	392	Sidney Ponson	.20	.07
❑	393	Brian Schneider	.20	.07
❑	394	J.J. Hardy	.20	.07
❑	395	Austin Kearns	.20	.07
❑	396	Pat Burrell	.20	.07
❑	397	Jason Vargas	.20	.07
❑	398	Ryan Howard	.75	.30
❑	399	Joe Crede	.20	.07
❑	400	Vladimir Guerrero	.50	.20
❑	401	Roy Halladay	.20	.07
❑	402	David Dellucci	.20	.07
❑	403	Brandon Webb	.20	.07
❑	404	Marlon Anderson	.20	.07
❑	405	Miguel Tejada	.20	.07
❑	406	Ryan Doumit	.20	.07
❑	407	Kevin Youkilis	.20	.07
❑	408	Jon Lieber	.20	.07
❑	409	Edwin Encarnacion	.20	.07
❑	410	Miguel Cabrera	.30	.10
❑	411	A.J. Burnett	.20	.07
❑	412	David Bell	.20	.07
❑	413	Gregg Zaun	.20	.07
❑	414	Lance Niekro	.20	.07
❑	415	Shawn Green	.20	.07
❑	416	Roberto Hernandez	.20	.07
❑	417	Jay Gibbons	.20	.07
❑	418	Johnny Estrada	.20	.07
❑	419	Omar Vizquel	.30	.10
❑	420	Gary Sheffield	.20	.07
❑	421	Brad Halsey	.20	.07
❑	422	Aaron Cook	.20	.07
❑	423	David Ortiz	.50	.20
❑	424	Tony Womack	.20	.07
❑	425	Joe Kennedy	.20	.07
❑	426	Dustin McGowan	.20	.07
❑	427	Carl Pavano	.20	.07
❑	428	Nick Green	.20	.07
❑	429	Francisco Cordero	.20	.07
❑	430	Octavio Dotel	.20	.07
❑	431	Julio Franco	.20	.07
❑	432	Brett Myers	.20	.07
❑	433	Casey Kotchman	.20	.07
❑	434	Frank Catalanotto	.20	.07
❑	435	Paul Konerko	.20	.07
❑	436	Keith Foulke	.20	.07
❑	437	Juan Rivera	.20	.07
❑	438	Todd Pratt	.20	.07
❑	439	Ben Broussard	.20	.07
❑	440	Scott Kazmir	.30	.10
❑	441	Rich Aurilia	.20	.07
❑	442	Craig Monroe	.20	.07
❑	443	Danny Kolb	.20	.07
❑	444	Curtis Granderson	.20	.07
❑	445	Jeff Francoeur	.50	.20
❑	446	Dustin Hermanson	.20	.07
❑	447	Jacque Jones	.20	.07
❑	448	Bobby Crosby	.20	.07
❑	449	Jason LaRue	.20	.07
❑	450	Derrek Lee	.20	.07
❑	451	Curt Schilling	.30	.10
❑	452	Jake Westbrook	.20	.07
❑	453	Daniel Cabrera	.20	.07
❑	454	Bobby Jenks	.20	.07
❑	455	Dontrelle Willis	.20	.07
❑	456	Brad Lidge	.20	.07
❑	457	Shea Hillenbrand	.20	.07
❑	458	Luis Castillo	.20	.07
❑	459	Mark Hendrickson	.20	.07
❑	460	Randy Johnson	.50	.20
❑	461	Placido Polanco	.20	.07
❑	462	Aaron Boone	.20	.07
❑	463	Todd Walker	.20	.07
❑	464	Nick Swisher	.20	.07
❑	465	Joel Pineiro	.20	.07
❑	466	Jay Payton	.20	.07
❑	467	Cliff Lee	.20	.07
❑	468	Johan Santana	.30	.10
❑	469	Josh Willingham	.20	.07
❑	470	Jeremy Bonderman	.20	.07
❑	471	Runelvys Hernandez	.20	.07
❑	472	Duaner Sanchez	.20	.07
❑	473	Jason Lane	.20	.07
❑	474	Trot Nixon	.20	.07
❑	475	Ramon Hernandez	.20	.07
❑	476	Mike Lowell	.20	.07
❑	477	Chan Ho Park	.20	.07
❑	478	Doug Waechter	.20	.07
❑	479	Carlos Silva	.20	.07
❑	480	Jose Contreras	.20	.07
❑	481	Vinny Castilla	.20	.07
❑	482	Chris Reitsma	.20	.07
❑	483	Jose Guillen	.20	.07
❑	484	Aaron Hill	.20	.07
❑	485	Kevin Millwood	.20	.07
❑	486	Wily Mo Pena	.20	.07
❑	487	Rich Harden	.20	.07
❑	488	Chris Carpenter	.20	.07
❑	489	Jason Bartlett	.20	.07
❑	490	Magglio Ordonez	.20	.07
❑	491	John Rodriguez	.20	.07
❑	492	Bob Wickman	.20	.07
❑	493	Eddie Guardado	.20	.07
❑	494	Kip Wells	.20	.07
❑	495	Adrian Beltre	.20	.07
❑	496	Jose Capellan (RC)	.50	.20
❑	497	Scott Podsednik	.20	.07
❑	498	Brad Thompson	.20	.07
❑	499	Aaron Heilman	.20	.07
❑	500	Derek Jeter	1.25	.50
❑	501	Emil Brown	.20	.07
❑	502	Morgan Ensberg	.20	.07
❑	503	Nate Bump	.20	.07
❑	504	Phil Nevin	.20	.07
❑	505	Jason Schmidt	.20	.07
❑	506	Michael Cuddyer	.20	.07
❑	507	John Patterson	.20	.07
❑	508	Danny Haren	.20	.07
❑	509	Freddy Sanchez	.20	.07
❑	510	J.D. Drew	.20	.07
❑	511	Dmitri Young	.20	.07
❑	512	Eric Milton	.20	.07
❑	513	Ervin Santana	.20	.07
❑	514	Mark Loretta	.20	.07
❑	515	Mark Grudzielanek	.20	.07
❑	516	Derrick Turnbow	.20	.07
❑	517	Denny Bautista	.20	.07
❑	518	Lyle Overbay	.20	.07
❑	519	Julio Lugo	.20	.07
❑	520	Carlos Beltran	.20	.07
❑	521	Jose Cruz Jr.	.20	.07
❑	522	Jason Isringhausen	.20	.07
❑	523	Bronson Arroyo	.20	.07
❑	524	Ben Sheets	.20	.07
❑	525	Zach Duke	.20	.07
❑	526	Ryan Wagner	.20	.07
❑	527	Jose Vidro	.20	.07
❑	528	Doug Mirabelli	.20	.07
❑	529	Kris Benson	.20	.07
❑	530	Carlos Guillen	.20	.07
❑	531	Juan Pierre	.20	.07
❑	532	Scot Shields	.20	.07
❑	533	Scott Hatteberg	.20	.07
❑	534	Tim Stauffer	.20	.07
❑	535	Jim Edmonds	.30	.10
❑	536	Scot Eyre	.20	.07
❑	537	Ben Johnson	.20	.07
❑	538	Mark Mulder	.20	.07
❑	539	Juan Rincon	.20	.07
❑	540	Gustavo Chacin	.20	.07

Card	Player	Price	Price
541	Oliver Perez	.20	.07
542	Chris Young	.20	.07
543	Edinson Volquez	.20	.07
544	Mark Bellhorn	.20	.07
545	Kelvim Escobar	.20	.07
546	Andy Sisco	.20	.07
547	Derek Lowe	.20	.07
548	Sean Burroughs	.20	.07
549	Erik Bedard	.20	.07
550	Alfonso Soriano	.20	.07
551	Matt Murton	.20	.07
552	Eric Byrnes	.20	.07
553	Chris Duffy	.20	.07
554	Kazuo Matsui	.20	.07
555	Scott Rolen	.30	.10
556	Rob Mackowiak	.20	.07
557	Chris Burke	.20	.07
558	Jeromy Burnitz	.20	.07
559	Jerry Hairston Jr.	.20	.07
560	Jim Thome	.30	.10
561	Miguel Olivo	.20	.07
562	Jose Castillo	.20	.07
563	Brad Ausmus	.20	.07
564	Yorvit Torrealba	.20	.07
565	David DeJesus	.20	.07
566	Paul Byrd	.20	.07
567	Brandon Backe	.20	.07
568	Aubrey Huff	.20	.07
569	Mike Jacobs	.20	.07
570	Todd Helton	.30	.10
571	Angel Berroa	.20	.07
572	Todd Jones	.20	.07
573	Jeff Bagwell	.30	.10
574	Darin Erstad	.20	.07
575	Roy Oswalt	.20	.07
576	Rondell White	.20	.07
577	Alex Rios	.20	.07
578	Wes Helms	.20	.07
579	Javier Vazquez	.20	.07
580	Frank Thomas	.50	.20
581	Brian Fuentes	.20	.07
582	Francisco Rodriguez	.20	.07
583	Craig Counsell	.20	.07
584	Jorge Sosa	.20	.07
585	Mike Piazza	.50	.20
586	Mike Scioscia MG	.20	.07
587	Joe Torre MG	.30	.10
588	Ken Macha MG	.20	.07
589	John Gibbons MG	.20	.07
590	Joe Maddon MG	.20	.07
591	Eric Wedge MG	.20	.07
592	Mike Hargrove MG	.20	.07
593	Sam Perlozzo MG	.20	.07
594	Buck Showalter MG	.20	.07
595	Terry Francona MG	.20	.07
596	Buddy Bell MG	.20	.07
597	Jim Leyland MG	.20	.07
598	Ron Gardenhire MG	.20	.07
599	Ozzie Guillen MG	.20	.07
600	Ned Yost MG	.20	.07
601	Atlanta Braves TC	.30	.10
602	Philadelphia Phillies TC	.20	.07
603	New York Mets TC	.20	.07
604	Washington Nationals TC	.20	.07
605	Florida Marlins TC	.20	.07
606	Houston Astros TC	.20	.07
607	Chicago Cubs TC	.30	.10
608	St. Louis Cardinals TC	.30	.10
609	Pittsburgh Pirates TC	.20	.07
610	Cincinnati Reds TC	.20	.07
611	Colorado Rockies TC	.20	.07
612	Los Angeles Dodgers TC	.20	.07
613	San Francisco Giants TC	.20	.07
614	San Diego Padres TC	.20	.07
615	Arizona Diamondbacks TC	.20	.07
616	Kenji Johjima RC	2.00	.75
617	Ryan Zimmerman (RC)	2.50	1.00
618	Craig Hansen RC	1.50	.60
619	Joey Devine RC	.50	.20
620	Hanley Ramirez (RC)	.60	.25
621	Scott Olsen (RC)	.50	.20
622	Jason Bergmann RC	.50	.20
623	Geovany Soto (RC)	.50	.20
624	J.J. Furmaniak (RC)	.50	.20
625	Jeremy Accardo RC	.50	.20
626	Mark Woodyard (RC)	.50	.20

Card	Player	Price	Price
627	Matt Capps (RC)	.50	.20
628	Tim Corcoran RC	.50	.20
629	Ryan Jorgensen RC	.50	.20
630	Ronny Paulino (RC)	.50	.20
631	Dan Uggla (RC)	1.00	.40
632	Ian Kinsler (RC)	.60	.25
633	Josh Barfield (RC)	.50	.20
634	Reggie Abercrombie (RC)	.50	.20
635	Joel Zumaya (RC)	1.25	.50
636	Matt Cain (RC)	.75	.30
637	Conor Jackson (RC)	.75	.30
638	Brian Anderson (RC)	.50	.20
639	Prince Fielder (RC)	1.50	.60
640	Jeremy Hermida (RC)	.75	.30
641	Justin Verlander (RC)	1.50	.60
642	Brian Bannister (RC)	.50	.20
643	Willie Eyre (RC)	.50	.20
644	Ricky Nolasco (RC)	.50	.20
645	Paul Maholm (RC)	.50	.20
646	J.Damon/J.Giambi	.30	.10
647	R.White/L.Ford	.20	.07
648	O.Hernandez/O.Hudson	.20	.07
649	A.Dunn/K.Griffey Jr.	.75	.30
650	P.Burrell/M.Lieberthal	.20	.07
651	J.Reyes/K.Matsui	.20	.07
652	H.Blalock/M.Young	.20	.07
653	P.Fielder/R.Weeks	.75	.30
654	T.Lee/R.Baldelli	.20	.07
655	D.Lee/A.Ramirez	.20	.07
656	G.Sizemore/A.Boone	.30	.10
657	Gonzalez/Green/Hill	.20	.07
658	I.Rodriguez/C.Guillen	.30	.10
659	A.Rodriguez/G.Sheffield	.75	.30
660	E.Santana/F.Rodriguez	.20	.07
RC1	Alay Soler	60.00	30.00
NNO	2 Tickets EXCH	20.00	8.00

2006 Topps Update

Card	Player	Price	Price
	COMPLETE SET (330)	50.00	20.00
	COMMON CARD (1-102)	.20	.07
	SEMISTARS 1-132	.30	.12
	UNLISTED STARS 1-132	.50	.20
	COMMON ROOKIE (133-170)	.50	.20
	RC SEMIS 133-170	.75	.30
	RC UNLISTED 133-170	1.25	.50
	COMMON CARD (171-330)	.30	.12
	SEMISTARS 171-330	.50	.20
	UNLISTED STARS 171-330	.75	.30
	1-330 PLATE ODDS 1:85 HTA		
	PLATE PRINT RUN 1 SET PER COLOR		
	BLACK-CYAN-MAGENTA-YELLOW ISSUED		
	NO PLATE PRICING DUE TO SCARCITY		
1	Austin Kearns	.20	.07
2	Adam Eaton	.20	.07
3	Juan Encarnacion	.20	.07
4	Jarrod Washburn	.20	.07
5	Alex Gonzalez	.20	.07
6	Toby Hall	.20	.07
7	Preston Wilson	.20	.07
8	Ramon Ortiz	.20	.07
9	Jason Michaels	.20	.07
10	Jeff Weaver	.20	.07
11	Russell Branyan	.20	.07
12	Brett Tomko	.20	.07
13	Doug Mientkiewicz	.20	.07
14	David Wells	.20	.07
15	Corey Koskie	.20	.07
16	Russ Ortiz	.20	.07
17	Carlos Pena	.20	.07
18	Mark Hendrickson	.20	.07
19	Julian Tavarez	.20	.07
20	Jeff Conine	.20	.07
21	Dioner Navarro	.20	.07
22	Bob Wickman	.20	.07
23	Felipe Lopez	.20	.07
24	Eddie Guardado	.20	.07
25	David Dellucci	.20	.07
26	Ryan Wagner	.20	.07
27	Nick Green	.20	.07
28	Gary Majewski	.20	.07
29	Shea Hillenbrand	.20	.07
30	Jae Seo	.20	.07
31	Royce Clayton	.20	.07
32	Dave Riske	.20	.07
33	Joey Gathright	.20	.07
34	Robinson Tejada	.20	.07
35	Edwin Jackson	.20	.07
36	Aubrey Huff	.20	.07
37	Akinori Otsuka	.20	.07
38	Juan Castro	.20	.07
39	Zach Day	.20	.07
40	Jeremy Accardo	.20	.07
41	Shawn Green	.20	.07
42	Kazuo Matsui	.20	.07
43	J.J. Putz	.20	.07
44	David Ross	.20	.07
45	Scott Williamson	.20	.07
46	Joe Borchard	.20	.07
47	Elmer Dessens	.20	.07
48	Odalis Perez	.20	.07
49	Kelly Shoppach	.20	.07
50	Brandon Phillips	.20	.07
51	Guillermo Mota	.20	.07
52	Alex Cintron	.20	.07
53	Denny Bautista	.20	.07
54	Josh Bard	.20	.07
55	Julio Lugo	.20	.07
56	Doug Mirabelli	.20	.07
57	Kip Wells	.20	.07
58	Adrian Gonzalez	.20	.07
59	Shawn Chacon	.20	.07
60	Marcus Thames	.20	.07
61	Craig Wilson	.20	.07
62	Cory Sullivan	.20	.07
63	Ben Broussard	.20	.07
64	Todd Walker	.20	.07
65	Greg Maddux	.75	.30
66	Xavier Nady	.20	.07
67	Oliver Perez	.20	.07
68	Sean Casey	.20	.07
69	Kyle Lohse	.20	.07
70	Carlos Lee	.20	.07
71	Rheal Cormier	.20	.07
72	Ronnie Belliard	.20	.07
73	Cory Lidle	4.00	1.50
74	David Bell	.20	.07
75	Wilson Betemit	.20	.07
76	Danys Baez	.20	.07
77	Mike Stanton	.20	.07
78	Kevin Mench	.20	.07
79	Sandy Alomar Jr.	.20	.07
80	Cesar Izturis	.20	.07
81	Jeremy Affeldt	.20	.07
82	Matt Stairs	.20	.07
83	Hector Luna	.20	.07
84	Tony Graffanino	.20	.07
85	J.P Howell	.20	.07
86	Bengie Molina	.20	.07
87	Maicer Izturis	.20	.07
88	Marco Scutaro	.20	.07
89	Daryle Ward	.20	.07
90	Sal Fasano	.20	.07
91	Oscar Villarreal	.20	.07
92	Gabe Gross	.20	.07
93	Phil Nevin	.20	.07
94	Damon Hollins	.20	.07
95	Juan Cruz	.20	.07
96	Marlon Anderson	.20	.07
97	Jason Davis	.20	.07
98	Ryan Shealy	.20	.07
99	Francisco Cordero	.20	.07
100	Bobby Abreu	.20	.07
101	Roberto Hernandez	.20	.07
102	Gary Bennett	.20	.07

	No.	Player		
❑	103	Aaron Sele	.20	.07
❑	104	Nook Logan	.20	.07
❑	105	Alfredo Amezaga	.20	.07
❑	106	Chris Woodward	.20	.07
❑	107	Kevin Jarvis	.20	.07
❑	108	B.J. Upton	.20	.07
❑	109	Alan Embree	.20	.07
❑	110	Milton Bradley	.20	.07
❑	111	Pete Orr	.20	.07
❑	112	Jeff Cirillo	.20	.07
❑	113	Corey Patterson	.20	.07
❑	114	Josh Paul	.20	.07
❑	115	Fernando Rodney	.20	.07
❑	116	Jerry Hairston Jr.	.20	.07
❑	117	Scott Proctor	.20	.07
❑	118	Ambiorix Burgos	.20	.07
❑	119	Jose Bautista	.20	.07
❑	120	Livan Hernandez	.20	.07
❑	121	John McDonald	.20	.07
❑	122	Ronny Cedeno	.20	.07
❑	123	Nate Robertson	.20	.07
❑	124	Jamey Carroll	.20	.07
❑	125	Alex Escobar	.20	.07
❑	126	Endy Chavez	.20	.07
❑	127	Jorge Julio	.20	.07
❑	128	Kenny Lofton	.20	.07
❑	129	Matt Diaz	.20	.07
❑	130	Dave Bush	.20	.07
❑	131	Jose Molina	.20	.07
❑	132	Mike MacDougal	.20	.07
❑	133	Ben Zobrist (RC)	.75	.30
❑	134	Shane Komine RC	.75	.30
❑	135	Casey Janssen RC	.75	.30
❑	136	Kevin Frandsen (RC)	.75	.30
❑	137	John Rheinecker (RC)	.50	.20
❑	138	Matt Kemp (RC)	.75	.30
❑	139	Scott Mathieson (RC)	.50	.20
❑	140	Jered Weaver (RC)	2.50	1.00
❑	141	Joel Guzman (RC)	.50	.20
❑	142	Anibal Sanchez (RC)	.75	.30
❑	143	Melky Cabrera (RC)	.75	.30
❑	144	Howie Kendrick (RC)	2.50	1.00
❑	145	Cole Hamels (RC)	1.25	.50
❑	146	Willy Aybar (RC)	.50	.20
❑	147	Jamie Shields RC	.50	.20
❑	148	Kevin Thompson (RC)	.50	.20
❑	149	Jon Lester RC	1.50	.60
❑	150	Stephen Drew (RC)	1.25	.50
❑	151	Andre Ethier (RC)	1.25	.50
❑	152	Jordan Tata RC	.50	.20
❑	153	Mike Napoli RC	1.25	.50
❑	154	Kason Gabbard (RC)	.50	.20
❑	155	Lastings Milledge (RC)	.75	.30
❑	156	Erick Aybar (RC)	.50	.20
❑	157	Fausto Carmona (RC)	.50	.20
❑	158	Russ Martin (RC)	.75	.30
❑	159	David Pauley (RC)	.50	.20
❑	160	Andy Marte (RC)	.50	.20
❑	161	Carlos Quentin (RC)	.75	.30
❑	162	Franklin Gutierrez (RC)	.50	.20
❑	163	Taylor Buchholz (RC)	.75	.30
❑	164	Josh Johnson (RC)	.75	.30
❑	165	Chad Billingsley (RC)	.75	.30
❑	166	Kendry Morales (RC)	1.25	.50
❑	167	Adam Loewen (RC)	.75	.30
❑	168	Yusmeiro Petit (RC)	.50	.20
❑	169	Matt Albers (RC)	.50	.20
❑	170	John Maine (RC)	.75	.30
❑	171	Alex Rodriguez SH	1.25	.50
❑	172	Mike Piazza SH	.75	.30
❑	173	Cory Sullivan SH	.30	.12
❑	174	Anibal Sanchez SH	.30	.12
❑	175	Trevor Hoffman SH	.30	.12
❑	176	Barry Bonds SH	1.50	.60
❑	177	Derek Jeter SH	2.00	.75
❑	178	Jose Reyes SH	.75	.30
❑	179	Manny Ramirez SH	.50	.20
❑	180	Vladimir Guerrero SH	.75	.30
❑	181	Mariano Rivera SH	.75	.30
❑	182	Mark Kotsay PH	.30	.12
❑	183	Derek Jeter PH	2.00	.75
❑	184	Carlos Delgado PH	.30	.12
❑	185	Frank Thomas PH	.75	.30
❑	186	Albert Pujols PH	1.50	.60
❑	187	Magglio Ordonez PH	.30	.12
❑	188	Carlos Delgado PH	.30	.12
❑	189	Kenny Rogers PH	.30	.12
❑	190	Tom Glavine PH	.50	.20
❑	191	P.Polanco/J.Suppan PH	.30	.12
❑	192	Jose Reyes PH	.75	.30
❑	193	E.Chavez/Y.Molina PH	.30	.12
❑	194	Craig Monroe PH	.30	.12
❑	195	J.Verlander/J.Zumaya PH	1.25	.50
❑	196	P.LoDuca/C.Beltran PH	.30	.12
❑	197	A.Pujols/J.Edmonds/S.Rolen PH	1.50	.60
❑	198	Anthony Reyes PH	.30	.12
❑	199	Chris Carpenter PH	.30	.12
❑	200	David Eckstein PH	.30	.12
❑	201	Jered Weaver PH	1.50	.60
❑	202	D.Ortiz/J.Dye/T.Hafner LL	.75	.30
❑	203	J.Mauer/D.Jeter/R.Cano LL	2.00	.75
❑	204	D.Ortiz/J.Morneau/R.Ibanez LL	.75	.30
❑	205	Crawford/Figgins/Ichiro LL	1.25	.50
❑	206	J.Santana/C.Wang/J.Garland LL	1.25	.50
❑	207	J.Santana/R.Halladay /C.Sabathia LL	.50	.20
❑	208	J.Santana/J.Bonderman /J.Lackey LL	.50	.20
❑	209	F.Rodriguez/B.Jenks/B.Ryan LL	.30	.12
❑	210	R.Howard/A.Pujols/A.Soriano LL	1.50	.60
❑	211	Sanch./Cabrera/Pujols LL	1.50	.60
❑	212	Howard/Pujols/Berk.LL	1.50	.60
❑	213	J.Reyes/J.Pierre/H.Ramirez LL	.75	.30
❑	214	D.Lowe/B.Webb/C.Zambrano LL	.30	.12
❑	215	R.Oswalt/C.Carpenter/B.Webb LL	.30	.12
❑	216	A.Harang/J.Peavy/J.Smoltz LL	.50	.20
❑	217	T.Hoffman/B.Wagner/J.Borowski LL	.30	.12
❑	218	Ichiro Suzuki AS	1.25	.50
❑	219	Derek Jeter AS	2.00	.75
❑	220	Alex Rodriguez AS	1.25	.50
❑	221	David Ortiz AS	.75	.30
❑	222	Vladimir Guerrero AS	.75	.30
❑	223	Ivan Rodriguez AS	.50	.20
❑	224	Vernon Wells AS	.30	.12
❑	225	Mark Loretta AS	.30	.12
❑	226	Kenny Rogers AS	.30	.12
❑	227	Alfonso Soriano AS	.30	.12
❑	228	Carlos Beltran AS	.30	.12
❑	229	Albert Pujols AS	1.50	.60
❑	230	Jason Bay AS	.30	.12
❑	231	Edgar Renteria AS	.30	.12
❑	232	David Wright AS	1.25	.50
❑	233	Chase Utley AS	.75	.30
❑	234	Paul LoDuca AS	.30	.12
❑	235	Brad Penny AS	.30	.12
❑	236	Derrick Turnbow AS	.30	.12
❑	237	Mark Redman AS	.30	.12
❑	238	Francisco Liriano AS	.75	.30
❑	239	A.J. Pierzynski AS	.30	.12
❑	240	Grady Sizemore AS	.50	.20
❑	241	Jose Contreras AS	.30	.12
❑	242	Jermaine Dye AS	.30	.12
❑	243	Jason Schmidt AS	.30	.12
❑	244	Nomar Garciaparra AS	.75	.30
❑	245	Scott Kazmir AS	.50	.20
❑	246	Johan Santana AS	.50	.20
❑	247	Chris Capuano AS	.30	.12
❑	248	Magglio Ordonez AS	.30	.12
❑	249	Gary Matthews Jr. AS	.30	.12
❑	250	Carlos Lee AS	.30	.12
❑	251	David Eckstein AS	.30	.12
❑	252	Michael Young AS	.30	.12
❑	253	Matt Holliday AS	.75	.30
❑	254	Lance Berkman AS	.30	.12
❑	255	Scott Rolen AS	.50	.20
❑	256	Bronson Arroyo AS	.30	.12
❑	257	Barry Zito AS	.30	.12
❑	258	Brian McCann AS	.30	.12
❑	259	Jose Lopez AS	.30	.12
❑	260	Chris Carpenter AS	.30	.12
❑	261	Roy Halladay AS	.30	.12
❑	262	Jim Thome AS	.50	.20
❑	263	Dan Uggla AS	.75	.30
❑	264	Mariano Rivera AS	.75	.30
❑	265	Roy Oswalt AS	.30	.12
❑	266	Tom Gordon AS	.30	.12
❑	267	Troy Glaus AS	.30	.12
❑	268	Bobby Jenks AS	.30	.12
❑	269	Freddy Sanchez AS	.30	.12
❑	270	Paul Konerko AS	.30	.12
❑	271	Joe Mauer AS	.50	.20
❑	272	B.J. Ryan AS	.30	.12
❑	273	Ryan Howard AS	1.25	.50
❑	274	Brian Fuentes AS	.30	.12
❑	275	Miguel Cabrera AS	.50	.20
❑	276	Brandon Webb AS	.30	.12
❑	277	Mark Buehrle AS	.30	.12
❑	278	Trevor Hoffman AS	.30	.12
❑	279	Jonathan Papelbon AS	1.50	.60
❑	280	Andruw Jones AS	.50	.20
❑	281	Miguel Tejada AS	.30	.12
❑	282	Carlos Zambrano AS	.30	.12
❑	283	Ryan Howard HRD	1.25	.50
❑	284	David Wright HRD	1.25	.50
❑	285	Miguel Cabrera HRD	.50	.20
❑	286	David Ortiz HRD	.75	.30
❑	287	Jermaine Dye HRD	.30	.12
❑	288	Miguel Tejada HRD	.30	.12
❑	289	Lance Berkman HRD	.30	.12
❑	290	Troy Glaus HRD	.30	.12
❑	291	D.Wright/T.Glavine TL	1.25	.50
❑	292	R.Howard/T.Gordon TL	1.25	.50
❑	293	M.Cabrera/D.Willis TL	.50	.20
❑	294	A.Jones/J.Smoltz TL	.50	.20
❑	295	A.Soriano/A.Soriano TL	.30	.12
❑	296	A.Pujols/C.Carpenter TL	1.50	.60
❑	297	A.Dunn/B.Arroyo TL	.30	.12
❑	298	L.Berkman/R.Oswalt TL	.30	.12
❑	299	C.Capuano/P.Fielder TL	1.25	.50
❑	300	F.Sanchez/J.Bay TL	.30	.12
❑	301	C.Zambrano/J.Pierre TL	.30	.12
❑	302	A.Gonzalez/T.Hoffman TL	.30	.12
❑	303	D.Lowe/R.Furcal TL	.30	.12
❑	304	O.Vizquel/J.Schmidt TL	.50	.20
❑	305	B.Webb/C.Tracy TL	.30	.12
❑	306	M.Holliday/G.Atkins TL	.75	.30
❑	307	A.Rodriguez/C.Wang TL	1.25	.50
❑	308	C.Schilling/D.Ortiz TL	.75	.30
❑	309	R.Halladay/V.Wells TL	.30	.12
❑	310	M.Tejada/E.Bedard TL	.30	.12
❑	311	C.Crawford/S.Kazmir TL	.50	.20
❑	312	J.Bonderman/M.Ordonez TL	.30	.12
❑	313	J.Morneau/J.Santana TL	.50	.20
❑	314	J.Garland/J.Dye TL	.30	.12
❑	315	T.Hafner/C.Sabathia TL	.30	.12
❑	316	E.Brown/M.Grudzielanek TL	.30	.12
❑	317	F.Thomas/B.Zito TL	.75	.30
❑	318	J.Weaver/V.Guerrero TL	1.50	.60
❑	319	M.Young/G.Matthews TL	.30	.12
❑	320	I.Suzuki/J.Putz TL	1.25	.50
❑	321	D.Jeter/R.Cano CD	2.00	.75
❑	322	C.Carpenter/M.Mulder CD	.30	.12
❑	323	J.Schmidt/T.Hoffman CD	.30	.12
❑	324	D.Wright/P.LoDuca CD	1.25	.50
❑	325	L.Berkman/R.Oswalt CD	.30	.12
❑	326	D.Jeter/J.Reyes CD	.75	.30
❑	327	C.Floyd/D.Wright CD	1.25	.50
❑	328	F.Liriano/J.Santana CD	.75	.30
❑	329	J.Drew/S.Drew CD	.75	.30
❑	330	J.Weaver/J.Weaver CD	1.50	.60

2007 Topps

❑	COMP.HOBBY SET (661)	80.00	40.00
❑	COMP.HOLIDAY SET (661)	80.00	40.00
❑	COMP.CARDINALS SET (661)	80.00	40.00
❑	COMP.CUBS SET (661)	80.00	40.00
❑	COMP.DODGERS SET (661)	80.00	40.00
❑	COMP.RED SOX SET (661)	80.00	40.00
❑	COMP.YANKEES SET (661)	80.00	40.00
❑	COMP.SET w/o VAR. (661)	80.00	40.00

❑ COMPLETE SERIES 1 (330) 40.00 15.00
❑ COMP.SERIES 1 w/o #40 (329) 25.00 10.00
❑ COMPLETE SERIES 2 (331) 50.00 25.00
❑ COMMON CARD (1-330) .20 .07
❑ COMMON RC .50 .20
❑ SER.1 VAR. ODDS 1:3700 WAL-MART
❑ SER.2 VAR.ODDS 1:30 HOBBY
❑ NO SER.1 VAR.PRICING DUE TO SCARTIY
❑ OVERALL PLATE SER.1 ODDS 1:98 HTA
❑ OVERALL PLATE SER.2 ODDS 1:139 HTA
❑ PLATE PRINT RUN 1 SET PER COLOR
❑ BLACK-CYAN-MAGENTA-YELLOW ISSUED
❑ NO PLATE PRICING DUE TO SCARCITY
❑ 1 John Lackey .20 .07
❑ 2 Nick Swisher .20 .07
❑ 3 Brad Lidge .20 .07
❑ 4 Bengie Molina .20 .07
❑ 5 Bobby Abreu .20 .07
❑ 6 Edgar Renteria .20 .07
❑ 7 Mickey Mantle 2.50 1.00
❑ 8 Preston Wilson .20 .07
❑ 9 Ryan Dempster .20 .07
❑ 10 C.C. Sabathia .20 .07
❑ 11 Julio Lugo .20 .07
❑ 12 J.D. Drew .20 .07
❑ 13 Miguel Batista .20 .07
❑ 14 Eliezer Alfonzo .20 .07
❑ 15a Andrew Miller RC 3.00 1.25
❑ 15b A.Miller Posed RC 3.00 1.25
❑ 16 Jason Varitek .50 .20
❑ 17 Saul Rivera .20 .07
❑ 18 Orlando Hernandez .20 .07
❑ 19 Alfredo Amezaga .20 .07
❑ 20a D.Young Face Right (RC) 1.25 .50
❑ 20b D.Young Face Left (RC) 1.25 .50
❑ 21 Chris Britton .20 .07
❑ 22 Corey Patterson .20 .07
❑ 23 Josh Bard .20 .07
❑ 24 Tom Gordon .20 .07
❑ 25 Gary Matthews .20 .07
❑ 26 Jason Jennings .20 .07
❑ 27 Joey Gathright .20 .07
❑ 28 Brandon Inge .20 .07
❑ 29 Pat Neshek .75 .30
❑ 30 Bronson Arroyo .20 .07
❑ 31 Jay Payton .20 .07
❑ 32 Andy Pettitte .30 .12
❑ 33 Ervin Santana .20 .07
❑ 34 Paul Konerko .20 .07
❑ 35 Joel Zumaya .30 .12
❑ 36 Gregg Zaun .20 .07
❑ 37 Tony Gwynn Jr. .20 .07
❑ 38 Adam LaRoche .20 .07
❑ 39 Jim Edmonds .30 .12
❑ 40a D.Jeter w Mantle/Bush 15.00 6.00
❑ 40b Derek Jeter 1.25 .50
❑ 41 Rich Hill .20 .07
❑ 42 Livan Hernandez .20 .07
❑ 43 Aubrey Huff .20 .07
❑ 44 Todd Greene .20 .07
❑ 45 Andre Ethier .30 .12
❑ 46 Jeremy Sowers .20 .07
❑ 47 Ben Broussard .20 .07
❑ 48 Darren Oliver .20 .07
❑ 49 Nook Logan .20 .07
❑ 50 Miguel Cabrera .30 .12
❑ 51 Carlos Lee .20 .07
❑ 52 Jose Castillo .20 .07
❑ 53 Mike Piazza .50 .20
❑ 54 Daniel Cabrera .20 .07
❑ 55 Cole Hamels .30 .12
❑ 56 Mark Loretta .20 .07
❑ 57 Brian Fuentes .20 .07
❑ 58 Todd Coffey .20 .07
❑ 59 Brent Clevlen .20 .07
❑ 60 John Smoltz .30 .12
❑ 61 Jason Grilli .20 .07
❑ 62 Dan Wheeler .20 .07
❑ 63 Scott Proctor .20 .07
❑ 64 Bobby Kielty .20 .07
❑ 65 Dan Uggla .30 .12
❑ 66 Lyle Overbay .20 .07
❑ 67 Geoff Jenkins .20 .07
❑ 68 Michael Barrett .20 .07
❑ 69 Casey Fossum .20 .07
❑ 70 Ivan Rodriguez .30 .12
❑ 71 Jose Lopez .20 .07
❑ 72 Jake Westbrook .20 .07
❑ 73 Moises Alou .20 .07
❑ 74 Jose Valverde .20 .07
❑ 75 Jered Weaver .30 .12
❑ 76 Lastings Milledge .30 .12
❑ 77 Austin Kearns .20 .07
❑ 78 Adam Loewen .20 .07
❑ 79 Josh Barfield .20 .07
❑ 80 Johan Santana .30 .12
❑ 81 Ian Kinsler .20 .07
❑ 82 Ian Snell .20 .07
❑ 83 Mike Lowell .20 .07
❑ 84 Elizardo Ramirez .20 .07
❑ 85 Scott Rolen .30 .12
❑ 86 Shannon Stewart .20 .07
❑ 87 Alexis Gomez .20 .07
❑ 88 Jimmy Gobble .20 .07
❑ 89 Jamey Carroll .20 .07
❑ 90 Chipper Jones .50 .20
❑ 91 Carlos Silva .20 .07
❑ 92 Joe Crede .20 .07
❑ 93 Mike Napoli .20 .07
❑ 94 Willy Taveras .20 .07
❑ 95 Rafael Furcal .20 .07
❑ 96 Phil Nevin .20 .07
❑ 97 Dave Bush .20 .07
❑ 98 Marcus Giles .20 .07
❑ 99 Joe Blanton .20 .07
❑ 100 Dontrelle Willis .20 .07
❑ 101 Scott Kazmir .30 .12
❑ 102 Jeff Kent .20 .07
❑ 103 Pedro Feliz .20 .07
❑ 104 Johnny Estrada .20 .07
❑ 105 Travis Hafner .20 .07
❑ 106 Ryan Garko .20 .07
❑ 107 Rafael Soriano .20 .07
❑ 108 Wes Helms .20 .07
❑ 109 Billy Wagner .20 .07
❑ 110 Aaron Rowand .20 .07
❑ 111 Felipe Lopez .20 .07
❑ 112 Jeff Conine .20 .07
❑ 113 Nick Markakis .30 .12
❑ 114 John Koronka .20 .07
❑ 115 B.J. Ryan .20 .07
❑ 116 Tim Wakefield .20 .07
❑ 117 David Ross .20 .07
❑ 118 Emil Brown .20 .07
❑ 119 Michael Cuddyer .20 .07
❑ 120 Jason Giambi .20 .07
❑ 121 Alex Cintron .20 .07
❑ 122 Luke Scott .20 .07
❑ 123 Chone Figgins .20 .07
❑ 124 Huston Street .20 .07
❑ 125 Carlos Delgado .20 .07
❑ 126 Daryle Ward .20 .07
❑ 127 Chris Duncan .20 .07
❑ 128 Damian Miller .20 .07
❑ 129 Aramis Ramirez .20 .07
❑ 130 Albert Pujols 1.00 .40
❑ 131 Chris Snyder .20 .07
❑ 132 Ray Durham .20 .07
❑ 133 Gary Sheffield .20 .07
❑ 134 Mike Jacobs .20 .07
❑ 135a Troy Tulowitzki (RC) 1.25 .50
❑ 135b T.Tulowitzki Throw (RC) 1.25 .50
❑ 136 Jon Rauch .20 .07
❑ 137 Jay Gibbons .20 .07
❑ 138 Adrian Gonzalez .20 .07
❑ 139 Prince Fielder .50 .20
❑ 140 Freddy Sanchez .20 .07
❑ 141 Rich Aurilia .20 .07
❑ 142 Trot Nixon .20 .07
❑ 143 Vicente Padilla .20 .07
❑ 144 Jack Wilson .20 .07
❑ 145 Jake Peavy .20 .07
❑ 146 Luke Hudson .20 .07
❑ 147 Javier Vazquez .20 .07
❑ 148 Scott Podsednik .20 .07
❑ 149 M.Ordonez/I.Rodriguez CC .30 .12
❑ 150 Todd Helton .30 .12
❑ 151 Kendry Morales .30 .12
❑ 152 Adam Everett .20 .07
❑ 153 Bob Wickman .20 .07
❑ 154 Bill Hall .20 .07
❑ 155 Jeremy Bonderman .20 .07
❑ 156 Ryan Theriot .20 .07
❑ 157 Rocco Baldelli .20 .07
❑ 158 Noah Lowry .20 .07
❑ 159 Jason Michaels .20 .07
❑ 160 Justin Verlander .50 .20
❑ 161 Eduardo Perez .20 .07
❑ 162 Chris Ray .20 .07
❑ 163 Dave Roberts .20 .07
❑ 164 Zach Duke .20 .07
❑ 165 Mark Buehrle .20 .07
❑ 166 Hank Blalock .20 .07
❑ 167 Royce Clayton .20 .07
❑ 168 Mark Teahen .20 .07
❑ 169 Todd Jones .20 .07
❑ 170 Chien-Ming Wang .75 .30
❑ 171 Nick Punto .20 .07
❑ 172 Morgan Ensberg .20 .07
❑ 173 Rob Mackowiak .20 .07
❑ 174 Frank Catalanotto .20 .07
❑ 175 Matt Murton .20 .07
❑ 176 A.Soriano/C.Beltran CC .20 .07
❑ 177 Francisco Cordero .20 .07
❑ 178 Jason Marquis .20 .07
❑ 179 Joe Nathan .20 .07
❑ 180 Roy Halladay .20 .07
❑ 181 Melvin Mora .20 .07
❑ 182 Ramon Ortiz .20 .07
❑ 183 Jose Valentin .20 .07
❑ 184 Gil Meche .20 .07
❑ 185 B.J. Upton .20 .07
❑ 186 Grady Sizemore .30 .12
❑ 187 Matt Cain .30 .12
❑ 188 Eric Byrnes .20 .07
❑ 189 Carl Crawford .20 .07
❑ 190 J.J. Putz .20 .07
❑ 191 Cla Meredith .20 .07
❑ 192 Matt Capps .20 .07
❑ 193 Rod Barajas .20 .07
❑ 194 Edwin Encarnacion .20 .07
❑ 195 James Loney .30 .12
❑ 196 Johnny Damon .30 .12
❑ 197 Freddy Garcia .20 .07
❑ 198 Mike Redmond .20 .07
❑ 199 Ryan Shealy .20 .07
❑ 200 Carlos Beltran .20 .07
❑ 201 Chuck James .20 .07
❑ 202 Mark Ellis .20 .07
❑ 203 Brad Ausmus .20 .07
❑ 204 Juan Rivera .20 .07
❑ 205 Cory Sullivan .20 .07
❑ 206 Ben Sheets .20 .07
❑ 207 Mark Mulder .20 .07
❑ 208 Carlos Quentin .20 .07
❑ 209 Jonathan Broxton .20 .07
❑ 210 Kazuo Matsui .20 .07
❑ 211 Armando Benitez .20 .07
❑ 212 Richie Sexson .20 .07
❑ 213 Josh Johnson .20 .07
❑ 214 Brian Schneider .20 .07
❑ 215 Craig Monroe .20 .07
❑ 216 Chris Duffy .20 .07
❑ 217 Chris Coste .20 .07
❑ 218 Clay Hensley .20 .07
❑ 219 Chris Gomez .20 .07
❑ 220 Hideki Matsui .50 .20
❑ 221 Robinson Tejeda .20 .07
❑ 222 Scott Hatteberg .20 .07
❑ 223 Jeff Francis .20 .07
❑ 224 Matt Thornton .20 .07
❑ 225 Robinson Cano .30 .12
❑ 226 Chicago White Sox .20 .07
❑ 227 Oakland Athletics .20 .07
❑ 228 St. Louis Cardinals .20 .07
❑ 229 New York Mets .20 .07
❑ 230 Barry Zito .20 .07
❑ 231 Baltimore Orioles .20 .07
❑ 232 Seattle Mariners .20 .07
❑ 233 Houston Astros .20 .07
❑ 234 Pittsburgh Pirates .20 .07
❑ 235 Reed Johnson .20 .07
❑ 236 Boston Red Sox .75 .30
❑ 237 Cincinnati Reds .20 .07
❑ 238 Philadelphia Phillies .20 .07
❑ 239 New York Yankees .50 .20
❑ 240 Chris Carpenter .20 .07
❑ 241 Atlanta Braves .30 .12

❑ 242 San Francisco Giants .20 .07
❑ 243 Joe Torre MG .30 .12
❑ 244 Tampa Bay Devil Rays .20 .07
❑ 245 Chad Tracy .20 .07
❑ 246 Clint Hurdle MG .20 .07
❑ 247 Mike Scioscia MG .20 .07
❑ 248 Ron Gardenhire MG .20 .07
❑ 249 Tony LaRussa MG .20 .07
❑ 250 Anibal Sanchez .20 .07
❑ 251 Charlie Manuel MG .20 .07
❑ 252 John Gibbons MG .20 .07
❑ 253 Jim Tracy MG .20 .07
❑ 254 Jerry Narron MG .20 .07
❑ 255 Brad Penny .20 .07
❑ 256 Bobby Cox MG .20 .07
❑ 257 Bob Melvin MG .20 .07
❑ 258 Mike Hargrove MG .20 .07
❑ 259 Phil Garner MG .20 .07
❑ 260 David Wright .75 .30
❑ 261 Vinny Rottino (RC) .50 .20
❑ 262 Ryan Braun RC .50 .20
❑ 263 Kevin Kouzmanoff (RC) .50 .20
❑ 264 David Murphy (RC) .50 .20
❑ 265 Jimmy Rollins .20 .07
❑ 266 Joe Maddon MG .20 .07
❑ 267 Grady Little MG .20 .07
❑ 268 Ryan Sweeney (RC) .50 .20
❑ 269 Fred Lewis (RC) .50 .20
❑ 270 Alfonso Soriano .20 .07
❑ 271a Delwyn Young (RC) .50 .20
❑ 271b D.Young Swing (RC) .50 .20
❑ 272 Jeff Salazar (RC) .50 .20
❑ 273 Miguel Montero (RC) .50 .20
❑ 274 Shawn Riggans (RC) .50 .20
❑ 275 Greg Maddux .75 .30
❑ 276 Brian Stokes (RC) .50 .20
❑ 277 Philip Humber (RC) .50 .20
❑ 278 Scott Moore (RC) .50 .20
❑ 279 Adam Lind (RC) .50 .20
❑ 280 Curt Schilling .30 .12
❑ 281 Chris Narveson (RC) .50 .20
❑ 282 Oswaldo Navarro RC .50 .20
❑ 283 Drew Anderson RC .50 .20
❑ 284 Jerry Owens (RC) .50 .20
❑ 285 Stephen Drew .30 .12
❑ 286 Joaquin Arias (RC) .50 .20
❑ 287 Jose Garcia RC .50 .20
❑ 288 Shane Youman RC .50 .20
❑ 289 Brian Burres (RC) .50 .20
❑ 290 Matt Holliday .50 .20
❑ 291 Ryan Feierabend (RC) .50 .20
❑ 292a Josh Fields (RC) .50 .20
❑ 292b J.Fields Running (RC) .50 .20
❑ 293 Glen Perkins (RC) .50 .20
❑ 294 Mike Rabelo RC .50 .20
❑ 295 Jorge Posada .30 .12
❑ 296 Ubaldo Jimenez (RC) .50 .20
❑ 297 Brad Ausmus GG .20 .07
❑ 298 Eric Chavez GG .20 .07
❑ 299 Orlando Hudson GG .20 .07
❑ 300 Vladimir Guerrero .50 .20
❑ 301 Derek Jeter GG 1.25 .50
❑ 302 Scott Rolen GG .30 .12
❑ 303 Mark Grudzielanek GG .20 .07
❑ 304 Kenny Rogers GG .20 .07
❑ 305 Frank Thomas .50 .20
❑ 306 Mike Cameron GG .20 .07
❑ 307 Torii Hunter GG .20 .07
❑ 308 Albert Pujols GG 1.00 .40
❑ 309 Mark Teixeira GG .30 .12
❑ 310 Jonathan Papelbon .50 .20
❑ 311 Greg Maddux GG .75 .30
❑ 312 Carlos Beltran GG .20 .07
❑ 313 Ichiro Suzuki GG .75 .30
❑ 314 Andruw Jones GG .30 .12
❑ 315 Manny Ramirez .30 .12
❑ 316 Vernon Wells GG .20 .07
❑ 317 Omar Vizquel GG .30 .12
❑ 318 Ivan Rodriguez GG .30 .12
❑ 319 Brandon Webb CY .20 .07
❑ 320 Magglio Ordonez .20 .07
❑ 321 Johan Santana CY .30 .12
❑ 322 Ryan Howard MVP .75 .30
❑ 323 Justin Morneau MVP .20 .07
❑ 324 Hanley Ramirez ROY .30 .12
❑ 325 Joe Mauer .30 .12
❑ 326 Justin Verlander ROY .50 .20
❑ 327 B.Abreu/D.Jeter CC 1.25 .50
❑ 328 C.Delgado/D.Wright CC .75 .30
❑ 329 Y.Molina/A.Pujols CC 1.00 .40
❑ 330 Ryan Howard .75 .30
❑ 331 Kelly Johnson .20 .07
❑ 332 Chris Young .20 .07
❑ 333 Mark Kotsay .20 .07
❑ 334 A.J. Burnett .20 .07
❑ 335 Brian McCann .20 .07
❑ 336 Woody Williams .20 .07
❑ 337 Jason Isringhausen .20 .07
❑ 338 Juan Pierre .20 .07
❑ 339 Jonny Gomes .20 .07
❑ 340 Roger Clemens .75 .30
❑ 341 Akinori Iwamura RC 1.25 .50
❑ 342 Bengie Molina .20 .07
❑ 343 Shin-Soo Choo .30 .12
❑ 344 Kenji Johjima .50 .20
❑ 345 Joe Borowski .20 .07
❑ 346 Shawn Green .20 .07
❑ 347 Chicago Cubs .30 .12
❑ 348 Rodrigo Lopez .20 .07
❑ 349 Brian Giles .20 .07
❑ 350 Chase Utley .50 .20
❑ 351 Mark DeRosa .20 .07
❑ 352 Carl Pavano .20 .07
❑ 353 Kyle Lohse .20 .07
❑ 354 Chris Iannetta .20 .07
❑ 355 Oliver Perez .20 .07
❑ 356 Curtis Granderson .20 .07
❑ 357 Sean Casey .20 .07
❑ 358 Jason Tyner .20 .07
❑ 359 Jon Garland .20 .07
❑ 360 David Ortiz .50 .20
❑ 361 Adam Kennedy .20 .07
❑ 362 Chris Burke .20 .07
❑ 363 Bobby Crosby .20 .07
❑ 364 Conor Jackson .20 .07
❑ 365 Tim Hudson .20 .07
❑ 366 Rickie Weeks .20 .07
❑ 367 Cristian Guzman .20 .07
❑ 368 Mark Prior .30 .12
❑ 369 Ben Zobrist .20 .07
❑ 370 Troy Glaus .20 .07
❑ 371 Kenny Lofton .20 .07
❑ 372 Shane Victorino .20 .07
❑ 373 Cliff Lee .20 .07
❑ 374 Adrian Beltre .20 .07
❑ 375 Miguel Olivo .20 .07
❑ 376 Endy Chavez .20 .07
❑ 377 Zack Segovia (RC) .50 .20
❑ 378 Ramon Hernandez .20 .07
❑ 379 Chris Young .20 .07
❑ 380 Jason Schmidt .20 .07
❑ 381 Ronny Paulino .20 .07
❑ 382 Kevin Millwood .20 .07
❑ 383 Jon Lester .30 .12
❑ 384 Alex Gonzalez .20 .07
❑ 385 Brad Hawpe .20 .07
❑ 386 Placido Polanco .20 .07
❑ 387 Nate Robertson .20 .07
❑ 388 Torii Hunter .20 .07
❑ 389 Gavin Floyd .20 .07
❑ 390 Roy Oswalt .20 .07
❑ 391 Kelvim Escobar .20 .07
❑ 392 Craig Wilson .20 .07
❑ 393 Milton Bradley .20 .07
❑ 394 Aaron Hill .20 .07
❑ 395 Matt Diaz .20 .07
❑ 396 Chris Capuano .20 .07
❑ 397 Juan Encarnacion .20 .07
❑ 398 Jacque Jones .20 .07
❑ 399 James Shields .20 .07
❑ 400 Ichiro Suzuki .75 .30
❑ 401 Matt Kemp .20 .07
❑ 402 Matt Morris .20 .07
❑ 403 Casey Blake .20 .07
❑ 404 Corey Hart .20 .07
❑ 405 Josh Willingham .20 .07
❑ 406 Ryan Madson .20 .07
❑ 407 Nick Johnson .20 .07
❑ 408 Kevin Millar .20 .07
❑ 409 Khalil Greene .30 .12
❑ 410 Tom Glavine .30 .12
❑ 411a Jason Bay .20 .07
❑ 411b Jason Bay No Sig 5.00 2.00
❑ 412 Gerald Laird .20 .07
❑ 413 Coco Crisp .20 .07
❑ 414 Brandon Phillips .20 .07
❑ 415 Aaron Cook .20 .07
❑ 416 Mark Redman .20 .07
❑ 417 Mike Maroth .20 .07
❑ 418 Boof Bonser .20 .07
❑ 419 Jorge Cantu .20 .07
❑ 420 Jeff Weaver .20 .07
❑ 421 Melky Cabrera .20 .07
❑ 422 Francisco Rodriguez .20 .07
❑ 423 Mike Lamb .20 .07
❑ 424 Dan Haren .20 .07
❑ 425 Tomo Ohka .20 .07
❑ 426 Jeff Francoeur .50 .20
❑ 427 Randy Wolf .20 .07
❑ 428 So Taguchi .20 .07
❑ 429 Carlos Zambrano .20 .07
❑ 430 Justin Morneau .20 .07
❑ 431 Luis Gonzalez .20 .07
❑ 432 Takashi Saito .20 .07
❑ 433 Brandon Morrow RC 1.25 .50
❑ 434 Victor Martinez .20 .07
❑ 435 Felix Hernandez .30 .12
❑ 436 Ricky Nolasco .20 .07
❑ 437 Paul LoDuca .20 .07
❑ 437b Paul LoDuca No Sig 5.00 2.00
❑ 438 Chad Cordero .20 .07
❑ 439 Miguel Tejada .20 .07
❑ 440 Mark Teixeira .30 .12
❑ 441 Pat Burrell .20 .07
❑ 442 Paul Maholm .20 .07
❑ 443 Mike Cameron .20 .07
❑ 444 Josh Beckett .30 .12
❑ 445 Pablo Ozuna .20 .07
❑ 446 Jaret Wright .20 .07
❑ 447 Angel Berroa .20 .07
❑ 448 Fernando Rodney .20 .07
❑ 449 Francisco Liriano .50 .20
❑ 450 Ken Griffey Jr. .75 .30
❑ 451 Bobby Jenks .20 .07
❑ 452 Mike Mussina .30 .12
❑ 453 Howie Kendrick .20 .07
❑ 454 Milwaukee Brewers .20 .07
❑ 455 Dan Johnson .20 .07
❑ 456 Ted Lilly .20 .07
❑ 457 Mike Hampton .20 .07
❑ 458 J.J. Hardy .20 .07
❑ 459 Jeff Suppan .20 .07
❑ 460 Jose Reyes .20 .07
❑ 461 Jae Seo .20 .07
❑ 462 Edgar Gonzalez .20 .07
❑ 463 Russell Martin .20 .07
❑ 464 Omar Vizquel .30 .12
❑ 465 Jhonny Peralta .20 .07
❑ 466 Raul Ibanez .20 .07
❑ 467 Hanley Ramirez .30 .12
❑ 468 Kerry Wood .20 .07
❑ 469 Ryan Church .20 .07
❑ 470 Gary Sheffield .20 .07
❑ 471 David Wells .20 .07
❑ 472 David Dellucci .20 .07
❑ 473 Xavier Nady .20 .07
❑ 474 Michael Young .20 .07
❑ 475 Kevin Youkilis .20 .07
❑ 476 Aaron Harang .20 .07
❑ 477 Brian Lawrence .20 .07
❑ 478 Octavio Dotel .20 .07
❑ 479 Chris Shelton .20 .07
❑ 480 Matt Garza .20 .07
❑ 481a Jim Thome .30 .12
❑ 481b Jim Thome No Sig 5.00 2.00
❑ 482 Jose Contreras .20 .07
❑ 483 Kris Benson .20 .07
❑ 484 John Maine .20 .07
❑ 485 Tadahito Iguchi .20 .07
❑ 486 Wandy Rodriguez .20 .07
❑ 487 Eric Chavez .20 .07
❑ 488 Vernon Wells .20 .07
❑ 489 Doug Davis .20 .07
❑ 490 Andruw Jones .30 .12
❑ 491 David Eckstein .20 .07
❑ 492 Michael Barrett .20 .07
❑ 493 Greg Norton .20 .07
❑ 494 Orlando Hudson .20 .07

❑ 495 Wilson Betemit .20 .07
❑ 496 Ryan Klesko .20 .07
❑ 497 Fausto Carmona .20 .07
❑ 498 Jarrod Washburn .20 .07
❑ 499 Aaron Boone .20 .07
❑ 500 Pedro Martinez .30 .12
❑ 501 Mike O'Connor .20 .07
❑ 502 Brian Roberts .20 .07
❑ 503 Jeff Cirillo .20 .07
❑ 504 Brett Myers .20 .07
❑ 505 Jose Bautista .20 .07
❑ 506 Akinori Otsuka .20 .07
❑ 507 Shea Hillenbrand .20 .07
❑ 508 Ryan Langerhans .20 .07
❑ 509 Josh Fogg .20 .07
❑ 510 Alex Rodriguez .75 .30
❑ 511 Kenny Rogers .20 .07
❑ 512 Jason Kubel .20 .07
❑ 513 Jermaine Dye .20 .07
❑ 514 Mark Grudzielanek .20 .07
❑ 515 Josh Phelps .20 .07
❑ 516 Bartolo Colon .20 .07
❑ 517 Craig Biggio .30 .12
❑ 518 Esteban Loaiza .20 .07
❑ 519 Alex Rios .20 .07
❑ 520 Adam Dunn .20 .07
❑ 521 Derrick Turnbow .20 .07
❑ 522 Anthony Reyes .20 .07
❑ 523 Derrek Lee .20 .07
❑ 524 Ty Wigginton .20 .07
❑ 525 Jeremy Hermida .20 .07
❑ 526 Derek Lowe .20 .07
❑ 527 Randy Winn .20 .07
❑ 528 Paul Byrd .20 .07
❑ 529 Chris Snelling .20 .07
❑ 530 Brandon Webb .20 .07
❑ 531 Julio Franco .20 .07
❑ 532 Jose Vidro .20 .07
❑ 533 Erik Bedard .20 .07
❑ 534 Termel Sledge .20 .07
❑ 535 Jon Lieber .20 .07
❑ 536 Tom Gorzelanny .20 .07
❑ 537 Kip Wells .20 .07
❑ 538 Wily Mo Pena .20 .07
❑ 539 Eric Milton .20 .07
❑ 540 Chad Billingsley .20 .07
❑ 541 David DeJesus .20 .07
❑ 542 Omar Infante .20 .07
❑ 543 Rondell White .20 .07
❑ 544 Juan Uribe .20 .07
❑ 545 Miguel Cairo .20 .07
❑ 546 Orlando Cabrera .20 .07
❑ 547 Byung-Hyun Kim .20 .07
❑ 548 Jason Kendall .20 .07
❑ 549 Horacio Ramirez .20 .07
❑ 550 Trevor Hoffman .20 .07
❑ 551 Ronnie Belliard .20 .07
❑ 552 Chris Woodward .20 .07
❑ 553 Ramon Martinez .20 .07
❑ 554 Elizardo Ramirez .20 .07
❑ 555 Andy Marte .20 .07
❑ 556 John Patterson .20 .07
❑ 557 Scott Olsen .20 .07
❑ 558 Steve Trachsel .20 .07
❑ 559 Doug Mientkiewicz .20 .07
❑ 560 Randy Johnson .50 .20
❑ 561 Chan Ho Park .20 .07
❑ 562 Jamie Moyer .20 .07
❑ 563 Mike Gonzalez .20 .07
❑ 564 Nelson Cruz .20 .07
❑ 565 Alex Cora .20 .07
❑ 566 Ryan Freel .20 .07
❑ 567 Chris Stewart RC .50 .20
❑ 568 Carlos Guillen .20 .07
❑ 569 Jason Bartlett .20 .07
❑ 570 Mariano Rivera .50 .20
❑ 571 Norris Hopper .20 .07
❑ 572 Alex Escobar .20 .07
❑ 573 Gustavo Chacin .20 .07
❑ 574 Brandon McCarthy .20 .07
❑ 575 Seth McClung .20 .07
❑ 576 Yuniesky Betancourt .20 .07
❑ 577 Jason LaRue .20 .07
❑ 578 Dustin Pedroia .20 .07
❑ 579 Taylor Tankersley .20 .07
❑ 580 Garret Anderson .20 .07
❑ 581 Mike Sweeney .20 .07
❑ 582 Scott Thorman .20 .07
❑ 583 Joe Inglett .20 .07
❑ 584 Clint Barmes .20 .07
❑ 585 Willie Bloomquist .20 .07
❑ 586 Willy Aybar .20 .07
❑ 587 Brian Bannister .20 .07
❑ 588 Jose Guillen .20 .07
❑ 589 Brad Wilkerson .20 .07
❑ 590 Lance Berkman .20 .07
❑ 591 Toronto Blue Jays .20 .07
❑ 592 Florida Marlins .20 .07
❑ 593 Washington Nationals .20 .07
❑ 594 Los Angeles Angels .20 .07
❑ 595 Cleveland Indians .20 .07
❑ 596 Texas Rangers .20 .07
❑ 597 Detroit Tigers .20 .07
❑ 598 Arizona Diamondbacks .20 .07
❑ 599 Kansas City Royals .20 .07
❑ 600 Ryan Zimmerman .50 .20
❑ 601 Colorado Rockies .20 .07
❑ 602 Minnesota Twins .20 .07
❑ 603 Los Angeles Dodgers .20 .07
❑ 604 San Diego Padres .20 .07
❑ 605 Bruce Bochy MG .20 .07
❑ 606 Ron Washington MG .20 .07
❑ 607 Manny Acta MG .20 .07
❑ 608 Sam Perlozzo MG .20 .07
❑ 609 Terry Francona MG .20 .07
❑ 610 Jim Leyland MG .20 .07
❑ 611 Eric Wedge MG .20 .07
❑ 612 Ozzie Guillen MG .20 .07
❑ 613 Buddy Bell MG .20 .07
❑ 614 Bob Geren MG .20 .07
❑ 615 Lou Piniella MG .20 .07
❑ 616 Fredi Gonzalez MG .20 .07
❑ 617 Ned Yost MG .20 .07
❑ 618 Willie Randolph MG .20 .07
❑ 619 Bud Black MG .20 .07
❑ 620 Garrett Atkins .20 .07
❑ 621 Alexi Casilla RC .75 .30
❑ 622 Matt Chico (RC) .50 .20
❑ 623 Alejandro De Aza RC .50 .20
❑ 624 Jeremy Brown .20 .07
❑ 625 Josh Hamilton (RC) 1.25 .50
❑ 626 Doug Slaten RC .50 .20
❑ 627 Andy Cannizaro RC .50 .20
❑ 628 Juan Salas (RC) .50 .20
❑ 629 Levale Speigner RC .50 .20
❑ 630a D.Matsuzaka English RC 8.00 3.00
❑ 630b D.Matsuzaka Japanese 12.00 5.00
❑ 630c Daisuke Matsuzaka No Sig 12.005.00
❑ 631 Elijah Dukes RC .75 .30
❑ 632 Kevin Cameron RC .50 .20
❑ 633 Juan Perez RC .50 .20
❑ 634a Alex Gordon RC 3.00 1.25
❑ 634b A.Gordon No Sig 8.00 3.00
❑ 635 Juan Lara RC .50 .20
❑ 636 Mike Rabelo RC .50 .20
❑ 637 Justin Hampson (RC) .50 .20
❑ 638 Cesar Jimenez RC .50 .20
❑ 639 Joe Smith RC .50 .20
❑ 640 Kei Igawa RC 1.25 .50
❑ 641 Hideki Okajima RC 2.50 1.00
❑ 642 Sean Henn (RC) .50 .20
❑ 643 Jay Marshall RC .50 .20
❑ 644 Jared Burton RC .50 .20
❑ 645 Angel Sanchez RC .50 .20
❑ 646 Devern Hansack RC .50 .20
❑ 647 Juan Morillo (RC) .50 .20
❑ 648 Hector Gimenez (RC) .50 .20
❑ 649 Brian Barden RC .50 .20
❑ 650 A.Rodriguez/J.Giambi CC .75 .30
❑ 651 J.Michaels/T.Hafner CC .20 .07
❑ 652 J.Johnson/M.Olivo CC .20 .07
❑ 653 S.Casey/P.Polanco CC .20 .07
❑ 654 I.Rodriguez/F.Rodney CC .30 .12
❑ 655 D.Uggla/H.Ramirez CC .30 .12
❑ 656 C.Beltran/J.Reyes CC .20 .07
❑ 657 A.Rodriguez/D.Jeter CC 1.25 .50
❑ 658 A.Rowand/J.Rollins CC .20 .07
❑ 659 A.Berroa/A.Blanco CC .20 .07
❑ 660a Yadier Molina .20 .07
❑ 660b Yadier Molina No Sig 5.00 2.00
❑ 661 Barry Bonds 10.00 4.00

2007 Topps Update

❑ COMP.SET w/o SPs (330) 60.00 30.00
❑ COMMON CARD (1-330) .30 .12
❑ COMMON ROOKIE (1-330) .50 .20
❑ 1-330 PLATE ODDS 1:54 HTA
❑ PLATE PRINT RUN 1 SET PER COLOR
❑ BLACK-CYAN-MAGENTA-YELLOW ISSUED
❑ NO PLATE PRICING DUE TO SCARCITY
❑ 1 Tony Armas Jr. .30 .12
❑ 2 Shannon Stewart .30 .12
❑ 3 Jason Marquis .30 .12
❑ 4 Josh Wilson .30 .12
❑ 5 Steve Trachsel .30 .12
❑ 6 J.D. Drew .30 .12
❑ 7 Ronnie Belliard .30 .12
❑ 8 Trot Nixon .30 .12
❑ 9 Adam LaRoche .30 .12
❑ 10 Mark Loretta .30 .12
❑ 11 Matt Morris .30 .12
❑ 12 Marlon Anderson .30 .12
❑ 13 Jorge Julio .30 .12
❑ 14 Brady Clark .30 .12
❑ 15 David Wells .30 .12
❑ 16 Francisco Rosario .30 .12
❑ 17 Jason Ellison .30 .12
❑ 18 Adam Jones .30 .12
❑ 19 Russell Branyan .30 .12
❑ 20 Rob Bowen .30 .12
❑ 21 J.D. Durbin .30 .12
❑ 22 Jeff Salazar .30 .12
❑ 23 Tadahito Iguchi .30 .12
❑ 24 Brad Hennessey .30 .12
❑ 25 Mark Hendrickson .30 .12
❑ 26 Kameron Loe .30 .12
❑ 27 Yusmeiro Petit .30 .12
❑ 28 Olmedo Saenz .30 .12
❑ 29 Carlos Silva .30 .12
❑ 30 Kevin Frandsen .30 .12
❑ 31 Tony Pena .30 .12
❑ 32 Russ Ortiz .30 .12
❑ 33 Hong-Chih Kuo .30 .12
❑ 34 Paul McAnulty .30 .12
❑ 35 Hiram Bocachica .30 .12
❑ 36 Justin Germano .30 .12
❑ 37 Jason Simontacchi .30 .12
❑ 38 Jose Cruz .30 .12
❑ 39 Wilfredo Ledezma .30 .12
❑ 40 Chris Denorfia .30 .12
❑ 41 Ryan Langerhans .30 .12
❑ 42 Chris Snelling .30 .12
❑ 43 Ubaldo Jimenez .30 .12
❑ 44 Scott Spiezio .30 .12
❑ 45 Byung-Hyun Kim .30 .12
❑ 46 Brandon Lyon .30 .12
❑ 47 Scott Hairston .30 .12
❑ 48 Chad Durbin .30 .12
❑ 49 Sammy Sosa .75 .30
❑ 50 Jason Smith .30 .12
❑ 51 Zack Greinke .30 .12
❑ 52 Armando Benitez .30 .12
❑ 53 Randy Messenger .30 .12
❑ 54 Mark Teixeira .50 .20
❑ 55 Mike Maroth .30 .12
❑ 56 Jamie Burke .30 .12
❑ 57 Carlos Marmol .30 .12
❑ 58 David Weathers .30 .12
❑ 59 Ryan Doumit .30 .12

	Card		
❑	60 Michael Barrett	.30	.12
❑	61 Shawn Chacon	.30	.12
❑	62 Mike Fontenot	.30	.12
❑	63 Cesar Izturis	.30	.12
❑	64 Cliff Floyd	.30	.12
❑	65 Angel Pagan	.30	.12
❑	66 Aaron Miles	.30	.12
❑	67 Tony Graffanino	.30	.12
❑	68 Kevin Mench	.30	.12
❑	69 Claudio Vargas	.30	.12
❑	70 Jose Capellan	.30	.12
❑	71 A.J. Pierzynski	.30	.12
❑	72 Darin Erstad	.30	.12
❑	73 Boone Logan	.30	.12
❑	74 Luis Castillo	.30	.12
❑	75 Marcus Thames	.30	.12
❑	76 Neifi Perez	.30	.12
❑	77 Esteban German	.30	.12
❑	78 Tony Pena	.30	.12
❑	79 Adam Wainwright	.30	.12
❑	80 Reggie Sanders	.30	.12
❑	81 Kelly Shoppach	.30	.12
❑	82 Rafael Betancourt	.30	.12
❑	83 Tom Mastny	.30	.12
❑	84 Kyle Farnsworth	.30	.12
❑	85 Rick Ankiel	.50	.20
❑	86 Kevin Thompson	.30	.12
❑	87 Jeff Karstens	.30	.12
❑	88 Eric Hinske	.30	.12
❑	89 Doug Mirabelli	.30	.12
❑	90 Julian Tavarez	.30	.12
❑	91 Carlos Pena	.30	.12
❑	92 Brendan Harris	.30	.12
❑	93 Chris Sampson	.30	.12
❑	94 Al Reyes	.30	.12
❑	95 Dmitri Young	.30	.12
❑	96 Jason Bergmann	.30	.12
❑	97 Shawn Hill	.30	.12
❑	98 Greg Dobbs	.30	.12
❑	99 Carlos Ruiz	.30	.12
❑	100a Abraham Nunez	.30	.12
❑	100b Jacoby Ellsbury (RC)	120.00	60.00
❑	101 Jayson Werth	.30	.12
❑	102 Adam Eaton	.30	.12
❑	103 Antonio Alfonseca	.30	.12
❑	104 Jorge Sosa	.30	.12
❑	105 Ramon Castro	.30	.12
❑	106 Ruben Gotay	.30	.12
❑	107 Damion Easley	.30	.12
❑	108 David Newhan	.30	.12
❑	109 Jason Wood	.30	.12
❑	110 Reggie Abercrombie	.30	.12
❑	111 Kevin Gregg	.30	.12
❑	112 Henry Owens	.30	.12
❑	113 Willie Harris	.30	.12
❑	114 Pete Orr	.30	.12
❑	115 Casey Janssen	.30	.12
❑	116 Jason Frasor	.30	.12
❑	117 Jeremy Accardo	.30	.12
❑	118 John McDonald	.30	.12
❑	119 Matt Stairs	.30	.12
❑	120 Jason Phillips	.30	.12
❑	121 Justin Duchscherer	.30	.12
❑	122 Rich Harden	.30	.12
❑	123 Jack Cust	.30	.12
❑	124 Lenny DiNardo	.30	.12
❑	125 Joe Kennedy	.30	.12
❑	126 Chad Gaudin	.30	.12
❑	127 Marco Scutaro	.30	.12
❑	128 Brad Thompson	.30	.12
❑	129 Dustin Moseley	.30	.12
❑	130 Eric Gagne	.30	.12
❑	131 Marlon Byrd	.30	.12
❑	132 Scot Shields	.30	.12
❑	133 Victor Diaz	.30	.12
❑	134 Reggie Willits	.30	.12
❑	135 Jose Molina	.30	.12
❑	136 Ramon Vazquez	.30	.12
❑	137 Erick Aybar	.30	.12
❑	138 Sean Marshall	.30	.12
❑	139 Casey Kotchman	.30	.12
❑	140 Ryan Spilborghs	.30	.12
❑	141 Cameron Maybin RC	2.50	1.00
❑	142 Jeremy Guthrie	.30	.12
❑	143 Jeff Baker	.30	.12
❑	144 Edwin Jackson	.30	.12
❑	145 Macay McBride	.30	.12
❑	146 Freddie Bynum	.30	.12
❑	147 Eric Patterson	.30	.12
❑	148 Dustin McGowan	.30	.12
❑	149 Homer Bailey (RC)	.75	.30
❑	150 Ryan Braun (RC)	3.00	1.25
❑	151 Tony Abreu RC	1.25	.50
❑	152 Tyler Clippard (RC)	.75	.30
❑	153 Mark Reynolds RC	2.00	.75
❑	154 Jesse Litsch RC	.75	.30
❑	155 Carlos Gomez RC	.75	.30
❑	156 Matt DeSalvo (RC)	.50	.20
❑	157 Andy LaRoche (RC)	.50	.20
❑	158 Tim Lincecum RC	4.00	1.50
❑	159 Jarrod Saltalamacchia (RC)	.75	.30
❑	160 Hunter Pence (RC)	2.50	1.00
❑	161 Brandon Wood (RC)	.50	.20
❑	162 Phil Hughes (RC)	2.50	1.00
❑	163 Rocky Cherry RC	1.25	.50
❑	164 Chase Wright RC	1.25	.50
❑	165 Dallas Braden RC	.75	.30
❑	166 Felix Pie (RC)	.50	.20
❑	167 Zach McClellan RC	.50	.20
❑	168 Rick Vanden Hurk RC	.75	.30
❑	169 Micah Owings (RC)	.50	.20
❑	170 Jon Coutlangus (RC)	.50	.20
❑	171 Andy Sonnanstine RC	.50	.20
❑	172 Yunel Escobar (RC)	.50	.20
❑	173 Kevin Slowey (RC)	1.25	.50
❑	174 Curtis Thigpen (RC)	.50	.20
❑	175 Masumi Kuwata RC	4.00	1.50
❑	176 Kurt Suzuki (RC)	.50	.20
❑	177 Travis Buck (RC)	.50	.20
❑	178 Matt Lindstrom (RC)	.50	.20
❑	179 Jesus Flores RC	.50	.20
❑	180 Joakim Soria RC	.50	.20
❑	181 Nathan Haynes (RC)	.50	.20
❑	182 Matthew Brown RC	.50	.20
❑	183 Travis Metcalf RC	.75	.30
❑	184 Yovani Gallardo (RC)	1.50	.60
❑	185 Nate Schierholtz (RC)	.50	.20
❑	186 Kyle Kendrick RC	1.25	.50
❑	187 Kevin Melillo (RC)	.50	.20
❑	188 Ryan Rowland-Smith	.30	.12
❑	189 Lee Gronkiewicz RC	.50	.20
❑	190 Eulogio De La Cruz (RC)	.50	.20
❑	191 Brett Carroll RC	.50	.20
❑	192 Terry Evans RC	.50	.20
❑	193 Chase Headley (RC)	.50	.20
❑	194 Guillermo Rodriguez RC	.50	.20
❑	195 Marcus McBeth (RC)	.50	.20
❑	196 Brian Wolfe (RC)	.50	.20
❑	197 Troy Cate RC	.50	.20
❑	198 Mike Zagurski RC	.50	.20
❑	199 Yoel Hernandez RC	.30	.12
❑	200 Brad Salmon RC	.50	.20
❑	201 Alberto Arias RC	.50	.20
❑	202 Danny Putnam (RC)	.50	.20
❑	203 Jamie Vermilyea RC	.50	.20
❑	204 Kyle Lohse	.30	.12
❑	205 Sammy Sosa	.75	.30
❑	206 Tom Glavine	.50	.20
❑	207 Prince Fielder	.75	.30
❑	208 Mark Buehrle	.30	.12
❑	209 Troy Tulowitzki	.75	.30
❑	210 Daisuke Matsuzaka RC	5.00	2.00
❑	211 Randy Johnson	.75	.30
❑	212 Justin Verlander	.75	.30
❑	213 Trevor Hoffman	.30	.12
❑	214 Alex Rodriguez	1.25	.50
❑	215 Ivan Rodriguez	.50	.20
❑	216 David Ortiz	.75	.30
❑	217 Placido Polanco	.30	.12
❑	218 Derek Jeter	2.00	.75
❑	219 Alex Rodriguez	1.25	.50
❑	220 Vladimir Guerrero	.75	.30
❑	221 Magglio Ordonez	.30	.12
❑	222 Ichiro Suzuki	1.25	.50
❑	223 Russell Martin	.30	.12
❑	224 Prince Fielder	.75	.30
❑	225 Chase Utley	.75	.30
❑	226 Jose Reyes	.75	.30
❑	227 David Wright	1.25	.50
❑	228 Carlos Beltran	.30	.12
❑	229 Barry Bonds	1.50	.60
❑	230 Ken Griffey Jr.	1.25	.50
❑	231 Torii Hunter	.30	.12
❑	232 Jonathan Papelbon	.75	.30
❑	233 J.J. Putz	.30	.12
❑	234 Francisco Rodriguez	.30	.12
❑	235 C.C. Sabathia	.30	.12
❑	236 Johan Santana	.50	.20
❑	237 Justin Verlander	.75	.30
❑	238 Francisco Cordero	.30	.12
❑	239 Mike Lowell	.30	.12
❑	240 Cole Hamels	.50	.20
❑	241 Trevor Hoffman	.30	.12
❑	242 Manny Ramirez	.50	.20
❑	243 Jake Peavy	.30	.12
❑	244 Brad Penny	.30	.12
❑	245 Takashi Saito	.30	.12
❑	246 Ben Sheets	.30	.12
❑	247 Hideki Okajima	1.50	.60
❑	248 Roy Oswalt	.30	.12
❑	249 Billy Wagner	.30	.12
❑	250 Carl Crawford	.30	.12
❑	251 Chris Young	.30	.12
❑	252 Brian McCann	.30	.12
❑	253 Derrek Lee	.30	.12
❑	254 Albert Pujols	1.50	.60
❑	255 Dmitri Young	.30	.12
❑	256 Orlando Hudson	.30	.12
❑	257 J.J. Hardy	.30	.12
❑	258 Miguel Cabrera	.50	.20
❑	259 Freddy Sanchez	.30	.12
❑	260 Matt Holliday	.75	.30
❑	261 Carlos Lee	.30	.12
❑	262 Aaron Rowand	.30	.12
❑	263 Alfonso Soriano	.30	.12
❑	264 Victor Martinez	.30	.12
❑	265 Jorge Posada	.50	.20
❑	266 Justin Morneau	.30	.12
❑	267 Brian Roberts	.30	.12
❑	268 Carlos Guillen	.30	.12
❑	269 Grady Sizemore	.50	.20
❑	270 Josh Beckett	.50	.20
❑	271 Dan Haren	.30	.12
❑	272 Bobby Jenks	.30	.12
❑	273 John Lackey	.30	.12
❑	274 Gil Meche	.30	.12
❑	275 M.Fontenot/K.Greene	.30	.12
❑	276 A.Rodriguez/R.Martin	1.25	.50
❑	277 T.Tulowitzki/J.Reyes	.75	.30
❑	278 Posada/Jeter/ARod	2.00	.75
❑	279 C.Utley/Ichiro	1.25	.50
❑	280 C.Crawford/C.Guillen	.30	.12
❑	281 C.Hamels/R.Martin	.50	.20
❑	282 J.Papelbon/J.Posada	.75	.30
❑	283 C.Crawford/V.Martinez	.30	.12
❑	284 A.Soriano/J.Hardy	.30	.12
❑	285 Justin Morneau	.30	.12
❑	286 Prince Fielder	.75	.30
❑	287 Alex Rios	.30	.12
❑	288 Vladimir Guerrero	.75	.30
❑	289 Albert Pujols	1.50	.60
❑	290 Ryan Howard	1.25	.50
❑	291 Magglio Ordonez	.30	.12
❑	292 Matt Holliday	.75	.30
❑	293 Wilson Betemit	.30	.12
❑	294 Todd Wellemeyer	.30	.12
❑	295 Scott Baker	.30	.12
❑	296 Edgar Gonzalez	.30	.12
❑	297 J.P. Howell	.30	.12
❑	298 Shaun Marcum	.30	.12
❑	299 Edinson Volquez	.30	.12
❑	300 Kason Gabbard	.30	.12
❑	301 Bob Howry	.30	.12
❑	302 J.A. Happ	.30	.12
❑	303 Scott Feldman	.30	.12
❑	304 D'Angelo Jimenez	.30	.12
❑	305 Orlando Palmeiro	.30	.12
❑	306 Paul Bako	.30	.12
❑	307 Kyle Davies	.30	.12
❑	308 Gabe Gross	.30	.12
❑	309 John Wasdin	.30	.12
❑	310 Jon Knott	.30	.12
❑	311 Josh Phelps	.30	.12
❑	312a J.Chamberlain RC	10.00	4.00
❑	312b J.Chamberlain Rev.Neg	150.00	90.00
❑	312c J.Chamberlain Hou UER		
❑	313 Octavio Dotel	.30	.12
❑	314 Craig Monroe	.30	.12

❑ 315 Edward Mujica .30 .12
❑ 316 Brandon Watson .30 .12
❑ 317 Chris Schroder .30 .12
❑ 318 Scott Proctor .30 .12
❑ 319 Ty Wigginton .30 .12
❑ 320 Troy Percival .30 .12
❑ 321 Scott Linebrink .30 .12
❑ 322 David Murphy .30 .12
❑ 323 Jorge Cantu .30 .12
❑ 324 Dan Wheeler .30 .12
❑ 325 Jason Kendall .30 .12
❑ 326 Milton Bradley .30 .12
❑ 327 Justin Upton RC 3.00 1.25
❑ 328 Kenny Lofton .30 .12
❑ 329 Roger Clemens 1.25 .50
❑ 330 Brian Burres .30 .12
❑ SQ1 Poley Walnuts 30.00 12.50

2008 Topps

❑ COMP.SET w/o VAR (660) 100.00 40.00
❑ COMP.SERIES 1 (331) 50.00 20.00
❑ COMP.SERIES 2 (330) 50.00 20.00
❑ COMMON CARD (1-660) .30 .12
❑ COMMON RC (1-660) .60 .25
❑ SERIES 1 SET DOES NOT INCLUDE FS1
❑ SERIES 1 SET DOES NOT INCLUDE #234C
❑ SER.2 SET DOES NOT INCLUDE #661
❑ SER.2 SET DOES NOT INCLUDE NNO CARDS
❑ SER.1 PLATE ODDS 1:1348 HOBBY
❑ SER.2 PLATE ODDS 1:900 HOBBY
❑ PLATE PRINT RUN 1 SET PER COLOR
❑ BLACK-CYAN-MAGENTA-YELLOW ISSUED
❑ NO PLATE PRICING DUE TO SCARCITY
❑ 1 Alex Rodriguez 1.25 .50
❑ 2 Barry Zito .30 .12
❑ 3 Jeff Suppan .30 .12
❑ 4 Rick Ankiel .30 .12
❑ 5 Scott Kazmir .50 .20
❑ 6 Felix Pie .30 .12
❑ 7 Mickey Mantle 3.00 1.25
❑ 8 Stephen Drew .30 .12
❑ 9 Randy Wolf .30 .12
❑ 10 Miguel Cabrera .50 .20
❑ 11 Yorvit Torrealba .30 .12
❑ 12 Jason Bartlett .30 .12
❑ 13 Kendry Morales .30 .12
❑ 14 Lonny DiNardo .30 .12
❑ 15 Ordon/Suzuki/Polan 1.25 .50
❑ 16 Kevin Gregg .30 .12
❑ 17 Cristian Guzman .30 .12
❑ 18 J.D. Durbin .30 .12
❑ 19 Robinson Tejeda .30 .12
❑ 20 Daisuke Matsuzaka 1.25 .50
❑ 21 Edwin Encarnacion .30 .12
❑ 22 Ron Washington MG .30 .12
❑ 23 Chin-Lung Hu (RC) 1.00 .40
❑ 24 ARod/Ordon/Vlad .75 .30
❑ 25 Kaz Matsui .30 .12
❑ 26 Manny Ramirez .75 .30
❑ 27 Bob Melvin MG .30 .12
❑ 28 Kyle Kendrick .30 .12
❑ 29 Anibal Sanchez .30 .12
❑ 30 Jimmy Rollins .50 .20
❑ 31 Ronny Paulino .30 .12
❑ 32 Howie Kendrick .30 .12
❑ 33 Joe Mauer .50 .20
❑ 34 Aaron Cook .30 .12
❑ 35 Cole Hamels .50 .20
❑ 36 Brendan Harris .30 .12
❑ 37 Jason Marquis .30 .12
❑ 38 Preston Wilson .30 .12
❑ 39 Yovanni Gallardo .30 .12
❑ 40 Miguel Tejada .30 .12
❑ 41 Rich Aurilia .30 .12
❑ 42 Corey Hart .30 .12
❑ 43 Ryan Dempster .30 .12
❑ 44 Jonathan Broxton .30 .12
❑ 45 Dontrelle Willis .30 .12
❑ 46 Zack Greinke .30 .12
❑ 47 Orlando Cabrera .30 .12
❑ 48 Zach Duke .30 .12
❑ 49 Orlando Hernandez .30 .12
❑ 50 Jake Peavy .30 .12
❑ 51 Erik Bedard .30 .12
❑ 52 Trevor Hoffman .30 .12
❑ 53 Hank Blalock .30 .12
❑ 54 Victor Martinez .30 .12
❑ 55 Chris Young .30 .12
❑ 56 Seth Smith (RC) .60 .25
❑ 57 Wladimir Balentien (RC) .60 .25
❑ 58 Holliday/Howard/Mig.Cabrera 1.00 .40
❑ 59 Grady Sizemore .50 .20
❑ 60 Jose Reyes .50 .20
❑ 61 ARod/Pena/Ortiz 1.25 .50
❑ 62 Rich Thompson RC .60 .25
❑ 63 Jason Michaels .30 .12
❑ 64 Mike Lowell .30 .12
❑ 65 Billy Wagner .30 .12
❑ 66 Brad Wilkerson .30 .12
❑ 67 Wes Helms .30 .12
❑ 68 Kevin Millar .30 .12
❑ 69 Bobby Cox MG .30 .12
❑ 70 Dan Uggla .50 .20
❑ 71 Jarrod Washburn .30 .12
❑ 72 Mike Piazza .75 .30
❑ 73 Mike Napoli .30 .12
❑ 74 Garrett Atkins .30 .12
❑ 75 Felix Hernandez .50 .20
❑ 76 Ivan Rodriguez .50 .20
❑ 77 Angel Guzman .30 .12
❑ 78 Radhames Liz RC 1.00 .40
❑ 79 Omar Vizquel .30 .12
❑ 80 Alex Rios .30 .12
❑ 81 Ray Durham .30 .12
❑ 82 So Taguchi .30 .12
❑ 83 Mark Reynolds .30 .12
❑ 84 Brian Fuentes .30 .12
❑ 85 Jason Bay .30 .12
❑ 86 Scott Podsednik .30 .12
❑ 87 Maicer Izturis .30 .12
❑ 88 Jack Cust .30 .12
❑ 89 Josh Willingham .30 .12
❑ 90 Vladimir Guerrero .75 .30
❑ 91 Marcus Giles .30 .12
❑ 92 Ross Detwiler RC 1.50 .60
❑ 93 Kenny Lofton .30 .12
❑ 94 Bud Black MG .30 .12
❑ 95 John Lackey .30 .12
❑ 96 Sam Fuld (RC) .60 .25
❑ 97 Clint Sammons (RC) .60 .25
❑ 98 R.Howard/C.Utley .75 .30
❑ 99 D.Ortiz/M.Ramirez .75 .30
❑ 100 Ryan Howard 1.00 .40
❑ 101 Ryan Braun ROY 1.00 .40
❑ 102 Ross Ohlendorf RC 1.00 .40
❑ 103 Jonathan Albaladejo RC 1.00 .40
❑ 104 Kevin Youkilis .50 .20
❑ 105 Roger Clemens 1.00 .40
❑ 106 Josh Bard .30 .12
❑ 107 Shawn Green .30 .12
❑ 108 B.J. Ryan .30 .12
❑ 109 Joe Nathan .30 .12
❑ 110 Justin Morneau .50 .20
❑ 111 Ubaldo Jimenez .30 .12
❑ 112 Jacque Jones .30 .12
❑ 113 Kevin Frandsen .30 .12
❑ 114 Mike Fontenot .30 .12
❑ 115 Johan Santana .75 .30
❑ 116 Chuck James .30 .12
❑ 117 Boof Bonser .30 .12
❑ 118 Marco Scutaro .30 .12
❑ 119 Jeremy Hermida .30 .12
❑ 120 Andruw Jones .30 .12
❑ 121 Mike Cameron .30 .12
❑ 122 Jason Varitek .75 .30
❑ 123 Terry Francona MG .30 .12
❑ 124 Bob Geren MG .30 .12
❑ 125 Tim Hudson .30 .12
❑ 126 Brandon Jones RC 1.50 .60
❑ 127 Steve Pearce RC 1.00 .40
❑ 128 Kenny Lofton .30 .12
❑ 129 Kevin Hart (RC) .60 .25
❑ 130 Justin Upton .75 .30
❑ 131 Norris Hopper .30 .12
❑ 132 Ramon Vazquez .30 .12
❑ 133 Mike Bacsik .30 .12
❑ 134 Matt Stairs .30 .12
❑ 135 Brad Penny .30 .12
❑ 136 Robinson Cano .50 .20
❑ 137 Jamey Carroll .30 .12
❑ 138 Dan Wheeler .30 .12
❑ 139 Johnny Estrada .30 .12
❑ 140 Brandon Webb .30 .12
❑ 141 Ryan Klesko .30 .12
❑ 142 Chris Duncan .30 .12
❑ 143 Willie Harris .30 .12
❑ 144 Jerry Owens .30 .12
❑ 145 Magglio Ordonez .50 .20
❑ 146 Aaron Hill .30 .12
❑ 147 Marlon Anderson .30 .12
❑ 148 Gerald Laird .30 .12
❑ 149 Luke Hochevar RC 2.00 .75
❑ 150 Alfonso Soriano .50 .20
❑ 151 Adam Loewen .30 .12
❑ 152 Bronson Arroyo .30 .12
❑ 153 Luis Mendoza (RC) .60 .25
❑ 154 David Ross .30 .12
❑ 155 Carlos Zambrano .30 .12
❑ 156 Brandon McCarthy .30 .12
❑ 157 Tim Redding .30 .12
❑ 158 Jose Bautista .30 .12
❑ 159 Luke Scott .30 .12
❑ 160 Ben Sheets .50 .20
❑ 161 Matt Garza .30 .12
❑ 162 Andy Laroche .30 .12
❑ 163 Doug Davis .30 .12
❑ 164 Nate Schierholtz .30 .12
❑ 165 Tim Lincecum .75 .30
❑ 166 Andy Sonnanstine .30 .12
❑ 167 Jason Hirsh .30 .12
❑ 168 Phil Hughes .75 .30
❑ 169 Adam Lind .30 .12
❑ 170 Scott Rolen .50 .20
❑ 171 John Maine .30 .12
❑ 172 Chris Ray .30 .12
❑ 173 Jamie Moyer .30 .12
❑ 174 Julian Tavarez .30 .12
❑ 175 Delmon Young .50 .20
❑ 176 Troy Patton (RC) .60 .25
❑ 177 Josh Anderson (RC) .60 .25
❑ 178 Dustin Pedroia ROY .50 .20
❑ 179 Chris Young .30 .12
❑ 180 Jose Valverde .30 .12
❑ 181 Borowski/Jenks/Putz .30 .12
❑ 182 Billy Buckner (RC) .60 .25
❑ 183 Paul Byrd .30 .12
❑ 184 Tadahito Iguchi .30 .12
❑ 185 Yunel Escobar .30 .12
❑ 186 Lastings Milledge .30 .12
❑ 187 Dustin McGowan .30 .12
❑ 188 Kei Igawa .30 .12
❑ 189 Esteban German .30 .12
❑ 190 Russell Martin .30 .12
❑ 191 Orlando Hudson .30 .12
❑ 192 Jim Edmonds .50 .20
❑ 193 J.J. Hardy .30 .12
❑ 194 Chad Billingsley .30 .12
❑ 195 Todd Helton .50 .20
❑ 196 Ross Gload .30 .12
❑ 197 Melky Cabrera .30 .12
❑ 198 Shannon Stewart .30 .12
❑ 199 Adrian Beltre .30 .12
❑ 200 Manny Ramirez .75 .30
❑ 201 Matt Capps .30 .12
❑ 202 Mike Lamb .30 .12
❑ 203 Jason Tyner .30 .12
❑ 204 Rafael Furcal .30 .12
❑ 205 Gil Meche .30 .12
❑ 206 Geoff Jenkins .30 .12
❑ 207 Jeff Kent .30 .12

	No.	Player		
❑	208	David DeJesus	.30	.12
❑	209	Andy Phillips	.30	.12
❑	210	Mark Teahen	.30	.12
❑	211	Lyle Overbay	.30	.12
❑	212	Moises Alou	.30	.12
❑	213	Michael Barrett	.30	.12
❑	214	C.J. Wilson	.30	.12
❑	215	Bobby Jenks	.30	.12
❑	216	Ryan Garko	.30	.12
❑	217	Josh Beckett	.50	.20
❑	218	Clint Hurdle MG	.30	.12
❑	219	Kevin Kouzmanoff	.30	.12
❑	220	Roy Oswalt	.30	.12
❑	221	Ian Snell	.30	.12
❑	222	Mark Grudzielanek	.30	.12
❑	223	Odalis Perez	.30	.12
❑	224	Mark Buehrle	.30	.12
❑	225	Hunter Pence	.75	.30
❑	226	Kurt Suzuki	.30	.12
❑	227	Alfredo Amezaga	.30	.12
❑	228	Geoff Blum	.30	.12
❑	229	Dustin Pedroia	.50	.20
❑	230	Roy Halladay	.30	.12
❑	231	Casey Blake	.30	.12
❑	232	Clay Buchholz (RC)	1.50	.60
❑	233	Jimmy Rollins MVP	.50	.20
❑	234a	Boston Red Sox	1.25	.50
❑	234b	Red Sox w/Giuliani	8.00	3.00
❑	234c	Red Sox w/Giuliani Red	60.00	30.00
❑	235	Rich Harden	.30	.12
❑	236	Joe Koshansky (RC)	.60	.25
❑	237	Eric Wedge MG	.30	.12
❑	238	Shane Victorino	.30	.12
❑	239	Richie Sexson	.30	.12
❑	240	Jim Thome	.50	.20
❑	241	Ervin Santana	.30	.12
❑	242	Manny Acta	.30	.12
❑	243	Akinori Iwamura	.30	.12
❑	244	Adam Wainwright	.30	.12
❑	245	Dan Haren	.30	.12
❑	246	Jason Isringhausen	.30	.12
❑	247	Edgar Gonzalez	.30	.12
❑	248	Jose Contreras	.30	.12
❑	249	Chris Sampson	.30	.12
❑	250	Jonathan Papelbon	.50	.20
❑	251	Dan Johnson	.30	.12
❑	252	Dmitri Young	.30	.12
❑	253	Bronson Sardinha (RC)	.60	.25
❑	254	David Murphy	.30	.12
❑	255	Brandon Phillips	.30	.12
❑	256	A.Rodriguez MVP	1.25	.50
❑	257	A.Kearns/D.Young	.30	.12
❑	258	M.Ramirez/K.Youkilis	.50	.20
❑	259	Emilio Bonifacio RC	1.00	.40
❑	260	Chad Cordero	.30	.12
❑	261	Josh Barfield	.30	.12
❑	262	Brett Myers	.30	.12
❑	263	Nook Logan	.30	.12
❑	264	Byung-Hyun Kim	.30	.12
❑	265	Fredi Gonzalez	.30	.12
❑	266	Ryan Doumit	.30	.12
❑	267	Chris Burke	.30	.12
❑	268	Daric Barton (RC)	.60	.25
❑	269	James Loney	.50	.20
❑	270	C.C. Sabathia	.30	.12
❑	271	Chad Tracy	.30	.12
❑	272	Anthony Reyes	.30	.12
❑	273	Rafael Soriano	.30	.12
❑	274	Jermaine Dye	.30	.12
❑	275	C.C. Sabathia	.30	.12
❑	276	Brad Ausmus	.30	.12
❑	277	Aubrey Huff	.30	.12
❑	278	Xavier Nady	.30	.12
❑	279	Damion Easley	.30	.12
❑	280	Willie Randolph MG	.30	.12
❑	281	Carlos Ruiz	.30	.12
❑	282	Jon Lester	.50	.20
❑	283	Jorge Sosa	.30	.12
❑	284	Lance Broadway (RC)	.60	.25
❑	285	Tony LaRussa MG	.30	.12
❑	286	Jeff Clement (RC)	.60	.25
❑	287	Morneau/Santana/Mauer	.50	.20
❑	288	I.Rodriguez/J.Verlander	.50	.20
❑	289	Justin Ruggiano RC	1.00	.40
❑	290	Edgar Renteria	.30	.12
❑	291	Eugenio Velez RC	.60	.25
❑	292	Mark Loretta	.30	.12
❑	293	Gavin Floyd	.30	.12
❑	294	Brian McCann	.50	.20
❑	295	Tim Wakefield	.30	.12
❑	296	Paul Konerko	.30	.12
❑	297	Jorge Posada	.50	.20
❑	298	Fielder/Howard/Dunn	1.00	.40
❑	299	Cesar Izturis	.30	.12
❑	300	Chien-Ming Wang	1.00	.40
❑	301	Chris Duffy	.30	.12
❑	302	Horacio Ramirez	.30	.12
❑	303	Jose Lopez	.30	.12
❑	304	Jose Vidro	.30	.12
❑	305	Carlos Delgado	.30	.12
❑	306	Scott Olsen	.30	.12
❑	307	Shawn Hill	.30	.12
❑	308	Felipe Lopez	.30	.12
❑	309	Ryan Church	.30	.12
❑	310	Kelvim Escobar	.30	.12
❑	311	Jeremy Guthrie	.30	.12
❑	312	Ramon Hernandez	.30	.12
❑	313	Kameron Loe	.30	.12
❑	314	Ian Kinsler	.50	.20
❑	315	David Weathers	.30	.12
❑	316	Scott Hatteberg	.30	.12
❑	317	Cliff Lee	.30	.12
❑	318	Ned Yost MG	.30	.12
❑	319	Joey Votto (RC)	1.00	.40
❑	320	Ichiro Suzuki	1.25	.50
❑	321	J.R. Towles RC	1.50	.60
❑	322	Kazmir/Santana/Bedard	.50	.20
❑	323	Valverde/Cordero/Hoffman	.30	.12
❑	324	Jake Peavy	.30	.12
❑	325	Jim Leyland MG	.30	.12
❑	326	Holliday/Chipper/Hanley	1.00	.40
❑	327	Peavy/Harang/Smoltz	.30	.12
❑	328	Nyjer Morgan (RC)	.60	.25
❑	329	Lou Piniella MG	.30	.12
❑	330	Curtis Granderson	.50	.20
❑	331	Dave Roberts	.30	.12
❑	332	Grady Sizemore/Jhonny Peralta	.50	.20
❑	333	Jayson Nix (RC)	.60	.25
❑	334	Oliver Perez	.30	.12
❑	335	Eric Byrnes	.30	.12
❑	336	Jhonny Peralta	.30	.12
❑	337	Livan Hernandez	.30	.12
❑	338	Matt Diaz	.30	.12
❑	339	Troy Percival	.30	.12
❑	341	Daniel Cabrera	.30	.12
❑	342	Matt Belisle	.30	.12
❑	343	Kason Gabbard	.30	.12
❑	344	Mike Rabelo	.30	.12
❑	345	Carl Crawford	.30	.12
❑	346	Adam Everett	.30	.12
❑	347	Chris Capuano	.30	.12
❑	348	Craig Monroe	.30	.12
❑	349	Mike Mussina	.30	.12
❑	350	Mark Teixeira	.50	.20
❑	351	Bobby Crosby	.30	.12
❑	352	Miguel Batista	.30	.12
❑	353	Brendan Ryan	.30	.12
❑	354	Edwin Jackson	.30	.12
❑	355	Brian Roberts	.50	.20
❑	356	Manny Corpas	.30	.12
❑	357	Jeremy Accardo	.30	.12
❑	358	John Patterson	.30	.12
❑	359	Evan Meek RC	.60	.25
❑	360	David Ortiz	.75	.30
❑	361	Wesley Wright RC	.60	.25
❑	362	Fernando Hernandez RC	.60	.25
❑	363	Brian Barton RC	1.00	.40
❑	364	Al Reyes	.30	.12
❑	365	Derrek Lee	.50	.20
❑	366	Jeff Weaver	.30	.12
❑	367	Khalil Greene	.50	.20
❑	368	Michael Bourn	.30	.12
❑	369	Luis Castillo	.30	.12
❑	370	Adam Dunn	.30	.12
❑	371	Rickie Weeks	.30	.12
❑	372	Matt Kemp	.30	.12
❑	373	Casey Kotchman	.30	.12
❑	374	Jason Jennings	.30	.12
❑	375	Fausto Carmona	.30	.12
❑	376	Willy Taveras	.30	.12
❑	377	Jake Westbrook	.30	.12
❑	378	Ozzie Guillen	.30	.12
❑	379	Hideki Okajima	.30	.12
❑	380	Grady Sizemore	.50	.20
❑	381	Jeff Francoeur	.50	.20
❑	382	Micah Owings	.30	.12
❑	383	Jered Weaver	.30	.12
❑	384	Carlos Quentin	.30	.12
❑	385	Troy Tulowitzki	.50	.20
❑	386	Julio Lugo	.30	.12
❑	387	Sean Marshall	.30	.12
❑	388	Jorge Cantu	.30	.12
❑	389	Callix Crabbe (RC)	.60	.25
❑	390	Troy Glaus	.50	.20
❑	391	Nick Markakis	.50	.20
❑	392	Joey Gathright	.30	.12
❑	393	Michael Cuddyer	.30	.12
❑	394	Mark Ellis	.30	.12
❑	395	Lance Berkman	.50	.20
❑	396	Randy Johnson	.75	.30
❑	397	Brian Wilson	.30	.12
❑	398	Kenji Johjima	.30	.12
❑	399	Jarrod Saltalamacchia	.30	.12
❑	400	Matt Holliday	.50	.20
❑	401	Scott Hairston	.30	.12
❑	402	Taylor Buchholz	.30	.12
❑	403	Nate Robertson	.30	.12
❑	404	Cecil Cooper	.30	.12
❑	405	Travis Hafner	.30	.12
❑	406	Takashi Saito	.30	.12
❑	407	Johnny Damon	.50	.20
❑	408	Edinson Volquez	.30	.12
❑	409	Jason Giambi	.50	.20
❑	410	Alex Gordon	.75	.30
❑	411	Jason Kubel	.30	.12
❑	412	Joel Zumaya	.30	.12
❑	413	Wandy Rodriguez	.30	.12
❑	414	Andrew Miller	.50	.20
❑	415	Derek Lowe	.30	.12
❑	416	Elijah Dukes	.30	.12
❑	418	Dioner Navarro	.30	.12
❑	419	Bengie Molina	.30	.12
❑	420	Nick Swisher	.30	.12
❑	421	Brandon Backe	.30	.12
❑	422	Erick Aybar	.30	.12
❑	423	Mike Scioscia MG	.30	.12
❑	424	Aaron Harang	.30	.12
❑	425	Hanley Ramirez	.75	.30
❑	426	Franklin Gutierrez	.30	.12
❑	427	Carlos Guillen	.30	.12
❑	428	Jair Jurrjens	.30	.12
❑	429	Billy Butler	.30	.12
❑	431	Delwyn Young	.30	.12
❑	432	Jason Kendall	.30	.12
❑	433	Carlos Silva	.30	.12
❑	434	Ron Gardenhire MG	.30	.12
❑	435	Torii Hunter	.30	.12
❑	436	Joe Blanton	.30	.12
❑	437	Brandon Wood	.30	.12
❑	438	Jay Payton	.30	.12
❑	439	Josh Hamilton	1.00	.40
❑	440	Pedro Martinez	.50	.20
❑	441	Miguel Olivo	.30	.12
❑	442	Luis Gonzalez	.30	.12
❑	443	Greg Dobbs	.30	.12
❑	444	Jack Wilson	.30	.12
❑	445	Hideki Matsui	.75	.30
❑	446	Randor Bierd RC	.60	.25
❑	447	Chipper Jones/Mark Teixeira	1.00	.40
❑	448	Cameron Maybin	.75	.30
❑	449	Braden Looper	.30	.12
❑	450	Prince Fielder	.75	.30
❑	451	Brian Giles	.30	.12
❑	452	Kevin Slowey	.30	.12
❑	453	Josh Fogg	.30	.12
❑	454	Mike Hampton	.30	.12
❑	456	Chone Figgins	.30	.12
❑	457	Josh Fields	.30	.12
❑	458	Brad Hawpe	.30	.12
❑	459	Mike Sweeney	.30	.12
❑	460	Chase Utley	.75	.30
❑	462	Freddy Sanchez	.30	.12
❑	463	John McLaren	.30	.12
❑	464	Rocco Baldelli	.30	.12
❑	465	Huston Street	.30	.12
❑	466	Miguel Cabrera/Ivan Rodriguez	.50	.20
❑	467	Nick Blackburn RC	1.00	.40
❑	468	Gregor Blanco (RC)	.60	.25

❑ 469	Brian Bocock RC	.60	.25
❑ 470	Tom Gorzelanny	.30	.12
❑ 471	Brian Schneider	.30	.12
❑ 472	Shaun Marcum	.30	.12
❑ 473	Joe Maddon	.30	.12
❑ 474	Yuniesky Betancourt	.30	.12
❑ 475	Adrian Gonzalez	.50	.20
❑ 477	Ben Broussard	.30	.12
❑ 478	Geovany Soto	.30	.12
❑ 479	Bobby Abreu	.30	.12
❑ 480	Matt Cain	.30	.12
❑ 481	Manny Parra	.30	.12
❑ 483	Mike Jacobs	.30	.12
❑ 484	Todd Jones	.30	.12
❑ 485	J.J. Putz	.30	.12
❑ 486	Javier Vazquez	.30	.12
❑ 487	Corey Patterson	.30	.12
❑ 488	Mike Gonzalez	.30	.12
❑ 489	Joakim Soria	.30	.12
❑ 491	Cliff Floyd	.30	.12
❑ 492	Harvey Garcia (RC)	.60	.25
❑ 493	Steve Holm RC	.60	.25
❑ 494	Paul Maholm	.30	.12
❑ 495	James Shields	.30	.12
❑ 496	Brad Lidge	.30	.12
❑ 497	Cla Meredith	.30	.12
❑ 498	Matt Chico	.30	.12
❑ 499	Milton Bradley	.30	.12
❑ 500	Chipper Jones	1.00	.40
❑ 501	Elliot Johnson (RC)	.60	.25
❑ 502	Alex Cora	.30	.12
❑ 503	Jeremy Bonderman	.30	.12
❑ 504	Conor Jackson	.30	.12
❑ 505	B.J. Upton	.50	.20
❑ 506	Jay Gibbons	.30	.12
❑ 507	Mark DeRosa	.30	.12
❑ 508	John Danks	.30	.12
❑ 509	Alex Gonzalez	.30	.12
❑ 510	Justin Verlander	.50	.20
❑ 511	Jeff Francis	.30	.12
❑ 512	Placido Polanco	.30	.12
❑ 513	Rick Vanden Hurk	.30	.12
❑ 514	Tony Pena	.30	.12
❑ 515	A.J. Burnett	.30	.12
❑ 516	Jason Schmidt	.30	.12
❑ 517	Bill Hall	.30	.12
❑ 518	Ian Stewart	.30	.12
❑ 519	Travis Buck	.30	.12
❑ 520	Vernon Wells	.30	.12
❑ 521	Jayson Werth	.30	.12
❑ 522	Nate McLouth	.30	.12
❑ 523	Noah Lowry	.30	.12
❑ 524	Raul Ibanez	.30	.12
❑ 525	Gary Matthews	.30	.12
❑ 526	Juan Encarnacion	.30	.12
❑ 527	Marlon Byrd	.30	.12
❑ 528	Paul Lo Duca	.30	.12
❑ 530	Ryan Zimmerman	.50	.20
❑ 531	Hiroki Kuroda RC	1.00	.40
❑ 532	Tim Lahey RC	.60	.25
❑ 533	Kyle McClellan RC	.60	.25
❑ 534	Matt Tupman RC	.60	.25
❑ 535	Francisco Rodriguez	.30	.12
❑ 537	Scott Moore	.30	.12
❑ 538	Alex Romero (RC)	.60	.25
❑ 539	Clete Thomas RC	1.00	.40
❑ 540	John Smoltz	.75	.30
❑ 541	Adam Jones	.30	.12
❑ 542	Adam Kennedy	.30	.12
❑ 543	Carlos Lee	.30	.12
❑ 544	Chad Gaudin	.30	.12
❑ 545	Chris Young	.30	.12
❑ 546	Francisco Liriano	.50	.20
❑ 547	Fred Lewis	.30	.12
❑ 548	Garrett Olson	.30	.12
❑ 549	Gregg Zaun	.30	.12
❑ 550	Curt Schilling	.50	.20
❑ 551	Erick Threets (RC)	.60	.25
❑ 552	J.D. Drew	.30	.12
❑ 553	Jo-Jo Reyes	.30	.12
❑ 554	Joe Borowski	.30	.12
❑ 555	Josh Beckett	.50	.20
❑ 556	John Gibbons	.30	.12
❑ 557	John McDonald	.30	.12
❑ 558	John Russell	.30	.12
❑ 559	Jonny Gomes	.30	.12
❑ 560	Aramis Ramirez	.30	.12
❑ 562	Ronnie Belliard	.30	.12
❑ 563	Ramon Troncoso RC	.60	.25
❑ 564	Frank Catalanotto	.30	.12
❑ 565	A.J. Pierzynski	.30	.12
❑ 566	Kevin Millwood	.30	.12
❑ 567	David Eckstein	.30	.12
❑ 568	Jose Guillen	.30	.12
❑ 569	Brad Hennessey	.30	.12
❑ 570	Homer Bailey	.50	.20
❑ 571	Eric Gagne	.30	.12
❑ 572	Adam Eaton	.30	.12
❑ 573	Tom Gordon	.30	.12
❑ 574	Scott Baker	.30	.12
❑ 575	Ty Wigginton	.30	.12
❑ 576	Dave Bush	.30	.12
❑ 577	John Buck	.30	.12
❑ 578	Ricky Nolasco	.30	.12
❑ 579	Jesse Litsch	.30	.12
❑ 581	Kazuo Matsui	.30	.12
❑ 582	Dusty Baker	.30	.12
❑ 583	Nick Punto	.30	.12
❑ 584	Ryan Theriot	.30	.12
❑ 585	Brian Bannister	.30	.12
❑ 586	Coco Crisp	.30	.12
❑ 587	Chris Snyder	.30	.12
❑ 588	Tony Gwynn	.30	.12
❑ 589	Dave Trembley	.30	.12
❑ 590	Mariano Rivera	.75	.30
❑ 591	Rico Washington (RC)	.60	.25
❑ 592	Matt Morris	.30	.12
❑ 593	Randy Wells RC	.60	.25
❑ 594	Mike Morse	.30	.12
❑ 595	Francisco Cordero	.30	.12
❑ 597	Kyle Davies	.30	.12
❑ 598	Bruce Bochy	.30	.12
❑ 599	Austin Kearns	.30	.12
❑ 600	Tom Glavine	.50	.20
❑ 601	Felipe Paulino RC	1.00	.40
❑ 602	Lyle Overbay/Vernon Wells	.30	.12
❑ 604	Wily Mo Pena	.30	.12
❑ 605	Andre Ethier	.50	.20
❑ 606	Jason Bergmann	.30	.12
❑ 607	Ryan Spilborghs	.30	.12
❑ 608	Brian Burres	.30	.12
❑ 609	Ted Lilly	.30	.12
❑ 610	Carlos Beltran	.30	.12
❑ 611	Garret Anderson	.30	.12
❑ 612	Kelly Johnson	.30	.12
❑ 613	Melvin Mora	.30	.12
❑ 614	Rich Hill	.30	.12
❑ 615	Pat Burrell	.30	.12
❑ 616	Jon Garland	.30	.12
❑ 617	Asdrubal Cabrera	.30	.12
❑ 618	Pat Neshek	.30	.12
❑ 619	Sergio Mitre	.30	.12
❑ 620	Gary Sheffield	.30	.12
❑ 621	Denard Span	.30	.12
❑ 622	Jorge De La Rosa	.30	.12
❑ 623	Trey Hillman MG	.30	.12
❑ 624	Joe Torre MG	.50	.20
❑ 626	Mike Redmond	.30	.12
❑ 627	Mike Pelfrey	.30	.12
❑ 628	Andy Pettitte	.50	.20
❑ 629	Eric Chavez	.30	.12
❑ 630	Chris Carpenter	.30	.12
❑ 631	Joe Girardi MG	.30	.12
❑ 632	Charlie Manuel MG	.30	.12
❑ 633	Adam LaRoche	.30	.12
❑ 634	Kenny Rogers	.30	.12
❑ 635	Michael Young	.30	.12
❑ 636	Rafael Betancourt	.30	.12
❑ 637	Jose Castillo	.30	.12
❑ 638	Juan Pierre	.30	.12
❑ 639	Juan Uribe	.30	.12
❑ 640	Carlos Pena	.30	.12
❑ 641	Marcus Thames	.30	.12
❑ 642	Mark Kotsay	.30	.12
❑ 643	Matt Murton	.30	.12
❑ 644	Reggie Willits	.30	.12
❑ 645	Andy Marte	.30	.12
❑ 646	Rajai Davis	.30	.12
❑ 647	Randy Winn	.30	.12
❑ 648	Ryan Freel	.30	.12
❑ 649	Joe Crede	.30	.12
❑ 650	Frank Thomas	.75	.30
❑ 651	Martin Prado	.30	.12
❑ 652	Rod Barajas	.30	.12
❑ 653	Endy Chavez	.30	.12
❑ 654	Willy Aybar	.30	.12
❑ 655	Aaron Rowand	.30	.12
❑ 656	Darin Erstad	.30	.12
❑ 657	Jeff Keppinger	.30	.12
❑ 658	Kerry Wood	.30	.12
❑ 659	Vicente Padilla	.30	.12
❑ 660	Yadier Molina	.50	.20
❑ 661	Johan Santana NoNo	250.00	150.00
❑ FS1	Kazuo Uzuki	2.00	.75
❑ NNO	Alexei Ramirez	100.00	50.00
❑ NNO	Kosuke Fukudome	80.00	40.00
❑ NNO	Yasuhiko Yabuta	80.00	40.00

2003 Topps 205

❑	COMPLETE SERIES 1 (165)	40.00	15.00
❑	COMPLETE SERIES 2 (175)	125.00	75.00
❑	COMP.SERIES 2 w/o SP's (155)	40.00	15.00
❑	COM (1-130/161-169/193-315)	.50	.20
❑	COMMON (131-145/170-192)	.50	.20
❑	COMMON CARD (146-160)	1.00	.40
❑	COMMON SP	2.50	1.00
❑	SERIES 2 SP STATED ODDS 1:5		
❑ 1A	Barry Bonds w/Cap	3.00	1.25
❑ 1B	Barry Bonds w/Helmet	3.00	1.25
❑ 2	Bret Boone	.50	.20
❑ 3A	Albert Pujols Clear Logo	2.50	1.00
❑ 3B	Albert Pujols White Logo	2.50	1.00
❑ 4	Carl Crawford	.50	.20
❑ 5	Bartolo Colon	.50	.20
❑ 6	Cliff Floyd	.50	.20
❑ 7	John Olerud	.50	.20
❑ 8A	Jason Giambi Full Jkt	.50	.20
❑ 8B	Jason Giambi Partial Jkt	.50	.20
❑ 9	Edgardo Alfonzo	.50	.20
❑ 10	Ivan Rodriguez	.75	.30
❑ 11	Jim Edmonds	.50	.20
❑ 12A	Mike Piazza Orange	2.00	.75
❑ 12B	Mike Piazza Yellow	2.00	.75
❑ 13	Greg Maddux	2.00	.75
❑ 14	Jose Vidro	.50	.20
❑ 15A	Vlad Guerrero Clear Logo	1.25	.50
❑ 15B	Vlad Guerrero White Logo	1.25	.50
❑ 16	Bernie Williams	.75	.30
❑ 17	Roger Clemens	2.50	1.00
❑ 18A	Miguel Tejada Blue	.50	.20
❑ 18B	Miguel Tejada Green	.50	.20
❑ 19	Carlos Delgado	.50	.20
❑ 20A	Alfonso Soriano w/Bat	.50	.20
❑ 20B	Alfonso Soriano Sunglasses	.50	.20
❑ 21	Bobby Cox MG	.50	.20
❑ 22	Mike Scioscia	.50	.20
❑ 23	John Smoltz	.75	.30
❑ 24	Luis Gonzalez	.50	.20
❑ 25	Shawn Green	.50	.20
❑ 26	Raul Ibanez	.50	.20
❑ 27	Andruw Jones	.75	.30
❑ 28	Josh Beckett	.50	.20
❑ 29	Derek Lowe	.50	.20
❑ 30	Todd Helton	.75	.30
❑ 31	Barry Larkin	.75	.30
❑ 32	Jason Jennings	.50	.20
❑ 33	Darin Erstad	.50	.20
❑ 34	Magglio Ordonez	.50	.20
❑ 35	Mike Sweeney	.50	.20
❑ 36	Kazuhisa Ishii	.50	.20

❑ 37 Ron Gardenhire MG .50 .20
❑ 38 Tim Hudson .50 .20
❑ 39 Tim Salmon .75 .30
❑ 40A Pat Burrell Black Bat .50 .20
❑ 40B Pat Burrell Brown Bat .50 .20
❑ 41 Manny Ramirez .75 .30
❑ 42 Nick Johnson .50 .20
❑ 43 Tom Glavine .75 .30
❑ 44 Mark Mulder .50 .20
❑ 45 Brian Jordan .50 .20
❑ 46 Rafael Palmeiro .75 .30
❑ 47 Vernon Wells .50 .20
❑ 48 Bob Brenly MG .50 .20
❑ 49 C.C. Sabathia .50 .20
❑ 50A Alex Rodriguez Look Ahead 2.00 .75
❑ 50B Alex Rodriguez Look Away 2.00 .75
❑ 51A Sammy Sosa Head Duck 1.25 .50
❑ 51B Sammy Sosa Head Left 1.25 .50
❑ 52 Paul Konerko .50 .20
❑ 53 Craig Biggio .75 .30
❑ 54 Moises Alou .50 .20
❑ 55 Johnny Damon .75 .30
❑ 56 Torii Hunter .50 .20
❑ 57 Omar Vizquel .75 .30
❑ 58 Orlando Hernandez .50 .20
❑ 59 Barry Zito .50 .20
❑ 60 Lance Berkman .50 .20
❑ 61 Carlos Beltran .50 .20
❑ 62 Edgar Renteria .50 .20
❑ 63 Ben Sheets .50 .20
❑ 64 Doug Mientkiewicz .50 .20
❑ 65 Troy Glaus .50 .20
❑ 66 Preston Wilson .50 .20
❑ 67 Kerry Wood .50 .20
❑ 68 Frank Thomas 1.25 .50
❑ 69 Jimmy Rollins .50 .20
❑ 70 Brian Giles .50 .20
❑ 71 Bobby Higginson .50 .20
❑ 72 Larry Walker .50 .20
❑ 73 Randy Johnson 1.25 .50
❑ 74 Tony LaRussa MG .50 .20
❑ 75A Derek Jeter w/Gold Trim 3.00 1.25
❑ 75B Derek Jeter w/o Gold Trim 3.00 1.25
❑ 76 Bobby Abreu .50 .20
❑ 77A Adam Dunn Closed Mouth .50 .20
❑ 77B Adam Dunn Open Mouth .50 .20
❑ 78 Ryan Klesko .50 .20
❑ 79 Francisco Rodriguez .50 .20
❑ 80 Scott Rolen .75 .30
❑ 81 Roberto Alomar .75 .30
❑ 82 Joe Torre MG .75 .30
❑ 83 Jim Thome .75 .30
❑ 84 Kevin Millwood .50 .20
❑ 85 J.T. Snow .50 .20
❑ 86 Trevor Hoffman .50 .20
❑ 87 Jay Gibbons .50 .20
❑ 88A Mark Prior New Logo .75 .30
❑ 88B Mark Prior Old Logo .75 .30
❑ 89 Rich Aurilia .50 .20
❑ 90 Chipper Jones 1.25 .50
❑ 91 Richie Sexson .50 .20
❑ 92 Gary Sheffield .50 .20
❑ 93 Pedro Martinez .75 .30
❑ 94 Rodrigo Lopez .50 .20
❑ 95 Al Leiter .50 .20
❑ 96 Jorge Posada .75 .30
❑ 97 Luis Castillo .50 .20
❑ 98 Aubrey Huff .50 .20
❑ 99 A.J. Pierzynski .50 .20
❑ 100A Ichiro Suzuki Look Ahead 2.50 1.00
❑ 100B Ichiro Suzuki Look Right 2.50 1.00
❑ 101 Eric Chavez .50 .20
❑ 102 Brett Myers .50 .20
❑ 103 Jason Kendall .50 .20
❑ 104 Jeff Kent .50 .20
❑ 105 Eric Hinske .50 .20
❑ 106 Jacque Jones .50 .20
❑ 107 Phil Nevin .50 .20
❑ 108 Roy Oswalt .50 .20
❑ 109 Curt Schilling .50 .20
❑ 110A N.Garciaparra w/Gold Trim 2.00 .75
❑ 110B N.Garciaparra w/o Gold Trim 2.00 .75
❑ 111 Garret Anderson .50 .20
❑ 112 Eric Gagne .50 .20
❑ 113 Javier Vazquez .50 .20
❑ 114 Jeff Bagwell .75 .30
❑ 115 Mike Lowell .50 .20
❑ 116 Carlos Pena .50 .20
❑ 117 Ken Griffey Jr. 2.00 .75
❑ 118 Tony Batista .50 .20
❑ 119 Edgar Martinez .75 .30
❑ 120 Austin Kearns .50 .20
❑ 121 Jason Stokes PROS .50 .20
❑ 122 Jose Reyes PROS .50 .20
❑ 123 Rocco Baldelli PROS .50 .20
❑ 124 Joe Borchard PROS .50 .20
❑ 125 Joe Mauer PROS 1.25 .50
❑ 126 Gavin Floyd PROS .50 .20
❑ 127 Mark Teixeira PROS .75 .30
❑ 128 Jeremy Guthrie PROS .50 .20
❑ 129 B.J. Upton PROS 1.25 .50
❑ 130 Khalil Greene PROS 1.25 .50
❑ 131 Hanley Ramirez FY RC 5.00 2.00
❑ 132 Andy Marte FY RC 4.00 1.50
❑ 133 J.D. Durbin FY RC .50 .20
❑ 134 Jason Kubel FY RC 1.25 .50
❑ 135 Craig Brazell FY RC .50 .20
❑ 136 Bryan Bullington FY RC .50 .20
❑ 137 Jose Contreras FY RC 1.00 .40
❑ 138 Brian Burgamy FY RC .50 .20
❑ 139 Evel Bastida-Martinez FY RC .50 .20
❑ 140 Joey Gomes FY RC .50 .20
❑ 141 Ismael Castro FY RC .60 .25
❑ 142 Travis Wong FY RC .60 .25
❑ 143 Michael Garciaparra FY RC .50 .20
❑ 144 Arnaldo Munoz FY RC .50 .20
❑ 145 Louis Sockalexis FY XRC .50 .20
❑ 146 Richard Hoblitzell REP 1.00 .40
❑ 147 George Graham REP 1.00 .40
❑ 148 Hal Chase REP 1.00 .40
❑ 149 John McGraw REP 1.50 .60
❑ 150 Bobby Wallace REP 1.00 .40
❑ 151 David Shean REP 1.00 .40
❑ 152 Richard Hoblitzell REP SP 2.50 1.00
❑ 153 Hal Chase REP 1.00 .40
❑ 154 Hooks Wiltse REP 1.00 .40
❑ 155 George Brett RET 3.00 1.25
❑ 156 Willie Mays RET 3.00 1.25
❑ 157 Honus Wagner RET SP 10.00 4.00
❑ 158 Nolan Ryan RET 4.00 1.50
❑ 159 Reggie Jackson RET 1.50 .60
❑ 160 Mike Schmidt RET 3.00 1.25
❑ 161 Josh Barfield PROS .50 .20
❑ 162 Grady Sizemore PROS 1.25 .50
❑ 163 Justin Morneau PROS .50 .20
❑ 164 Laynce Nix PROS .50 .20
❑ 165 Zack Greinke PROS .50 .20
❑ 166 Victor Martinez PROS .75 .30
❑ 167 Jeff Mathis PROS .50 .20
❑ 168 Casey Kotchman PROS .50 .20
❑ 169 Gabe Gross PROS .50 .20
❑ 170 Edwin Jackson FY RC .60 .25
❑ 171 Delmon Young FY SP RC 10.00 4.00
❑ 172 Eric Duncan FY SP RC 6.00 2.50
❑ 173 Brian Snyder FY SP RC 5.00 2.00
❑ 174 Chris Lubanski FY SP RC 5.00 2.00
❑ 175 Ryan Harvey FY SP RC 6.00 2.50
❑ 176 Nick Markakis FY SP RC 8.00 3.00
❑ 177 Chad Billingsley FY SP RC 8.00 3.00
❑ 178 Elizardo Ramirez FY RC .60 .25
❑ 179 Ben Francisco FY RC .50 .20
❑ 180 Franklin Gutierrez FY SP RC 5.00 2.00
❑ 181 Aaron Hill FY SP RC 5.00 2.00
❑ 182 Kevin Correia FY RC .50 .20
❑ 183 Kelly Shoppach FY RC 1.00 .40
❑ 184 Felix Pie FY SP RC 8.00 3.00
❑ 185 Adam Loewen FY SP RC 5.00 2.00
❑ 186 Danny Garcia FY RC .50 .20
❑ 187 Rickie Weeks FY SP RC 8.00 3.00
❑ 188 Robby Hammock FY SP RC 4.00 1.50
❑ 189 Ryan Wagner FY SP RC 4.00 1.50
❑ 190 Matt Kata FY SP RC 4.00 1.50
❑ 191 Bo Hart FY SP RC 4.00 1.50
❑ 192 Brandon Webb FY SP RC 6.00 2.50
❑ 193 Bengie Molina .50 .20
❑ 194 Junior Spivey .50 .20
❑ 195 Gary Sheffield .50 .20
❑ 196 Jason Johnson .50 .20
❑ 197 David Ortiz 1.25 .50
❑ 198 Roberto Alomar .75 .30
❑ 199 Wily Mo Pena .50 .20
❑ 200 Sammy Sosa 1.25 .50
❑ 201 Jay Payton .50 .20
❑ 202 Dmitri Young .50 .20
❑ 203 Derrek Lee .75 .30
❑ 204A Jeff Bagwell w/Hat .75 .30
❑ 204B Jeff Bagwell w/o Hat .75 .30
❑ 205 Runelvys Hernandez .50 .20
❑ 206 Kevin Brown .50 .20
❑ 207 Wes Helms .50 .20
❑ 208 Eddie Guardado .50 .20
❑ 209 Orlando Cabrera .50 .20
❑ 210 Alfonso Soriano .50 .20
❑ 211 Ty Wigginton .50 .20
❑ 212A Rich Harden Look Left .75 .30
❑ 212B Rich Harden Look Right .75 .30
❑ 213 Mike Lieberthal .50 .20
❑ 214 Brian Giles .50 .20
❑ 215 Jason Schmidt .50 .20
❑ 216 Jamie Moyer .50 .20
❑ 217 Matt Morris .50 .20
❑ 218 Victor Zambrano .50 .20
❑ 219 Roy Halladay .50 .20
❑ 220 Mike Hampton .50 .20
❑ 221 Kevin Millar Sox .50 .20
❑ 222 Hideo Nomo 1.25 .50
❑ 223 Milton Bradley .50 .20
❑ 224 Jose Guillen .50 .20
❑ 225 Derek Jeter 3.00 1.25
❑ 226 Rondell White .50 .20
❑ 227A Hank Blalock Blue Jsy .50 .20
❑ 227B Hank Blalock White Jsy .50 .20
❑ 228 Shigetoshi Hasegawa .50 .20
❑ 229 Mike Mussina .75 .30
❑ 230 Cristian Guzman .50 .20
❑ 231A Todd Helton Blue .75 .30
❑ 231B Todd Helton Green .75 .30
❑ 232 Kenny Lofton .50 .20
❑ 233 Carl Everett .50 .20
❑ 234 Shea Hillenbrand .50 .20
❑ 235 Brad Fullmer .50 .20
❑ 236 Bernie Williams .75 .30
❑ 237 Vicente Padilla .50 .20
❑ 238 Tim Worrell .50 .20
❑ 239 Juan Gonzalez .50 .20
❑ 240 Ichiro Suzuki 2.50 1.00
❑ 241 Aaron Boone .50 .20
❑ 242 Shannon Stewart .50 .20
❑ 243A Barry Zito Blue .50 .20
❑ 243B Barry Zito Green .50 .20
❑ 244 Reggie Sanders .50 .20
❑ 245 Scott Podsednik .50 .20
❑ 246 Miguel Cabrera 1.25 .50
❑ 247 Angel Berroa .50 .20
❑ 248 Carlos Zambrano .50 .20
❑ 249 Marlon Byrd .50 .20
❑ 250 Mark Prior .75 .30
❑ 251 Esteban Loaiza .50 .20
❑ 252 David Eckstein .50 .20
❑ 253 Alex Cintron .50 .20
❑ 254 Melvin Mora .50 .20
❑ 255 Russ Ortiz .50 .20
❑ 256 Carlos Lee .50 .20
❑ 257 Tino Martinez .75 .30
❑ 258 Randy Wolf .50 .20
❑ 259 Jason Phillips .50 .20
❑ 260 Vladimir Guerrero 1.25 .50
❑ 261 Brad Wilkerson .50 .20
❑ 262 Ivan Rodriguez .75 .30
❑ 263 Matt Lawton .50 .20
❑ 264 Adam Dunn .50 .20
❑ 265 Joe Borowski .50 .20
❑ 266 Jody Gerut .50 .20
❑ 267 Alex Rodriguez 2.00 .75
❑ 268 Brendan Donnelly .50 .20
❑ 269A Randy Johnson Grey 1.25 .50
❑ 269B Randy Johnson Pink 1.25 .50
❑ 270 Nomar Garciaparra 2.00 .75
❑ 271 Javy Lopez .50 .20
❑ 272 Travis Hafner .50 .20
❑ 273 Juan Pierre .50 .20
❑ 274 Morgan Ensberg .50 .20
❑ 275 Albert Pujols 2.50 1.00
❑ 276 Jason LaRue .50 .20
❑ 277 Paul Lo Duca .50 .20
❑ 278 Andy Pettitte .75 .30
❑ 279 Mike Piazza 2.00 .75
❑ 280A Jim Thome Blue .75 .30

❑ 280B Jim Thome Green .75 .30
❑ 281 Marquis Grissom .50 .20
❑ 282 Woody Williams .50 .20
❑ 283A Curt Schilling Look Ahead .50 .20
❑ 283B Curt Schilling Look Right .50 .20
❑ 284A Chipper Jones Blue 1.25 .50
❑ 284B Chipper Jones Yellow 1.25 .50
❑ 285 Deivi Cruz .50 .20
❑ 286 Johnny Damon .75 .30
❑ 287 Chin-Hui Tsao .50 .20
❑ 288 Alex Gonzalez .50 .20
❑ 289 Billy Wagner .50 .20
❑ 290 Jason Giambi .50 .20
❑ 291 Keith Foulke .50 .20
❑ 292 Jerome Williams .50 .20
❑ 293 Livan Hernandez .50 .20
❑ 294 Aaron Guiel .50 .20
❑ 295 Randall Simon .50 .20
❑ 296 Byung-Hyun Kim .50 .20
❑ 297 Jorge Julio .50 .20
❑ 298 Miguel Batista .50 .20
❑ 299 Rafael Furcal .50 .20
❑ 300A Dontrelle Willis No Smile 1.25 .50
❑ 300B Dontrelle Willis Smile SP 4.00 1.50
❑ 301 Alex Sanchez .50 .20
❑ 302 Shawn Chacon .50 .20
❑ 303 Matt Clement .50 .20
❑ 304 Luis Matos .50 .20
❑ 305 Steve Finley .50 .20
❑ 306 Marcus Giles .50 .20
❑ 307 Boomer Wells .50 .20
❑ 308 Jeromy Burnitz .50 .20
❑ 309 Mike MacDougal .50 .20
❑ 310 Mariano Rivera 1.25 .50
❑ 311 Adrian Beltre .50 .20
❑ 312 Mark Loretta .50 .20
❑ 313 Ugueth Urbina .50 .20
❑ 314 Bill Mueller .50 .20
❑ 315 Johan Santana .75 .30
❑ NNO Vintage Buyback

2002 Topps 206

❑ COMPLETE SET (525) 220.00 110.00
❑ COMPLETE SERIES 1 (180) 60.00 25.00
❑ COMPLETE SERIES 2 (180) 60.00 25.00
❑ COMPLETE SERIES 3 (165) 100.00 50.00
❑ COM(1-140/181-270/308-418) .50 .20
❑ COMMON (141-155/271-285) .50 .20
❑ COMMON RC (308-418) .50 .20
❑ COMMON SP (308-398) 2.00 .75
❑ COMMON FYP SP (419-432) 1.00 .40
❑ COMMON RET SP (433-447) 2.00 .75
❑ 1 Vladimir Guerrero 1.25 .50
❑ 2 Sammy Sosa 1.25 .50
❑ 3 Garret Anderson .50 .20
❑ 4 Rafael Palmeiro .75 .30
❑ 5 Juan Gonzalez .50 .20
❑ 6 John Smoltz .75 .30
❑ 7 Mark Mulder .50 .20
❑ 8 Jon Lieber .50 .20
❑ 9 Greg Maddux 2.00 .75
❑ 10 Moises Alou .50 .20
❑ 11 Joe Randa .50 .20
❑ 12 Bobby Abreu .50 .20
❑ 13 Juan Pierre .50 .20
❑ 14 Kerry Wood .50 .20
❑ 15 Craig Biggio .75 .30
❑ 16 Curt Schilling .50 .20
❑ 17 Brian Jordan .50 .20
❑ 18 Edgardo Alfonzo .50 .20
❑ 19 Darren Dreifort .50 .20
❑ 20 Todd Helton .75 .30
❑ 21 Ramon Ortiz .50 .20
❑ 22 Ichiro Suzuki 2.50 1.00
❑ 23 Jimmy Rollins .50 .20
❑ 24 Darin Erstad .50 .20
❑ 25 Shawn Green .50 .20
❑ 26 Tino Martinez .75 .30
❑ 27 Bret Boone .50 .20
❑ 28 Alfonso Soriano .50 .20
❑ 29 Chan Ho Park .50 .20
❑ 30 Roger Clemens 2.50 1.00
❑ 31 Cliff Floyd .50 .20
❑ 32 Johnny Damon .75 .30
❑ 33 Frank Thomas 1.25 .50
❑ 34 Barry Bonds 3.00 1.25
❑ 35 Luis Gonzalez .50 .20
❑ 36 Carlos Lee .50 .20
❑ 37 Roberto Alomar .75 .30
❑ 38 Carlos Delgado .50 .20
❑ 39 Nomar Garciaparra 2.00 .75
❑ 40 Jason Kendall .50 .20
❑ 41 Scott Rolen .75 .30
❑ 42 Tom Glavine .75 .30
❑ 43 Ryan Klesko .50 .20
❑ 44 Brian Giles .50 .20
❑ 45 Bud Smith .50 .20
❑ 46 Charles Nagy .50 .20
❑ 47 Tony Gwynn 1.50 .60
❑ 48 C.C. Sabathia .50 .20
❑ 49 Frank Catalanotto .50 .20
❑ 50 Jerry Hairston .50 .20
❑ 51 Jeromy Burnitz .50 .20
❑ 52 David Justice .50 .20
❑ 53 Bartolo Colon .50 .20
❑ 54 Andres Galarraga .50 .20
❑ 55 Jeff Weaver .50 .20
❑ 56 Terrence Long .50 .20
❑ 57 Tsuyoshi Shinjo .50 .20
❑ 58 Barry Zito .50 .20
❑ 59 Mariano Rivera 1.25 .50
❑ 60 John Olerud .50 .20
❑ 61 Randy Johnson 1.25 .50
❑ 62 Kenny Lofton .50 .20
❑ 63 Jermaine Dye .50 .20
❑ 64 Troy Glaus .50 .20
❑ 65 Larry Walker .50 .20
❑ 66 Hideo Nomo 1.25 .50
❑ 67 Mike Mussina .75 .30
❑ 68 Paul LoDuca .50 .20
❑ 69 Magglio Ordonez .50 .20
❑ 70 Paul O'Neill .75 .30
❑ 71 Sean Casey .50 .20
❑ 72 Lance Berkman .50 .20
❑ 73 Adam Dunn .50 .20
❑ 74 Aramis Ramirez .50 .20
❑ 75 Rafael Furcal .50 .20
❑ 76 Gary Sheffield .50 .20
❑ 77 Todd Hollandsworth .50 .20
❑ 78 Chipper Jones 1.25 .50
❑ 79 Bernie Williams .75 .30
❑ 80 Richard Hidalgo .50 .20
❑ 81 Eric Chavez .50 .20
❑ 82 Mike Piazza 2.00 .75
❑ 83 J.D. Drew .50 .20
❑ 84 Ken Griffey Jr. 2.00 .75
❑ 85 Joe Kennedy .50 .20
❑ 86 Joel Pineiro .50 .20
❑ 87 Josh Towers .50 .20
❑ 88 Andruw Jones .75 .30
❑ 89 Carlos Beltran .50 .20
❑ 90 Mike Cameron .50 .20
❑ 91 Albert Pujols 2.50 1.00
❑ 92 Alex Rodriguez 2.00 .75
❑ 93 Omar Vizquel .75 .30
❑ 94 Juan Encarnacion .50 .20
❑ 95 Jeff Bagwell .75 .30
❑ 96 Jose Canseco .75 .30
❑ 97 Ben Sheets .50 .20
❑ 98 Mark Grace .75 .30
❑ 99 Mike Sweeney .50 .20
❑ 100 Mark McGwire 3.00 1.25
❑ 101 Ivan Rodriguez .75 .30
❑ 102 Rich Aurilia .50 .20
❑ 103 Cristian Guzman .50 .20
❑ 104 Roy Oswalt .50 .20
❑ 105 Tim Hudson .50 .20
❑ 106 Brent Abernathy .50 .20
❑ 107 Mike Hampton .50 .20
❑ 108 Miguel Tejada .50 .20
❑ 109 Bobby Higginson .50 .20
❑ 110 Edgar Martinez .75 .30
❑ 111 Jorge Posada .75 .30
❑ 112 Jason Giambi Yankees .50 .20
❑ 113 Pedro Astacio .50 .20
❑ 114 Kazuhiro Sasaki .50 .20
❑ 115 Preston Wilson .50 .20
❑ 116 Jason Bere .50 .20
❑ 117 Mark Quinn .50 .20
❑ 118 Pokey Reese .50 .20
❑ 119 Derek Jeter 3.00 1.25
❑ 120 Shannon Stewart .50 .20
❑ 121 Jeff Kent .50 .20
❑ 122 Jeremy Giambi .50 .20
❑ 123 Pat Burrell .50 .20
❑ 124 Jim Edmonds .50 .20
❑ 125 Mark Buehrle .50 .20
❑ 126 Kevin Brown .50 .20
❑ 127 Raul Mondesi .50 .20
❑ 128 Pedro Martinez .75 .30
❑ 129 Jim Thome .75 .30
❑ 130 Russ Ortiz .50 .20
❑ 131 Brandon Duckworth PROS .50 .20
❑ 132 Ryan Jamison PROS .50 .20
❑ 133 Brandon Inge PROS .50 .20
❑ 134 Felipe Lopez PROS .50 .20
❑ 135 Jason Lane PROS .50 .20
❑ 136 Forrest Johnson PROS RC .50 .20
❑ 137 Greg Nash PROS .50 .20
❑ 138 Covelli Crisp PROS 2.00 .75
❑ 139 Nick Neugebauer PROS .50 .20
❑ 140 Dustan Mohr PROS .50 .20
❑ 141 Freddy Sanchez FYP RC 2.00 .75
❑ 142 Justin Backsmeyer FYP RC .50 .20
❑ 143 Jorge Julio FYP .50 .20
❑ 144 Ryan Mottl FYP RC .50 .20
❑ 145 Chris Tritle FYP RC .50 .20
❑ 146 Noochie Varner FYP RC .50 .20
❑ 147 Brian Rogers FYP .50 .20
❑ 148 Michael Hill FYP RC .50 .20
❑ 149 Luis Pineda FYP .50 .20
❑ 150 Rich Thompson FYP RC .50 .20
❑ 151 Bill Hall FYP .50 .20
❑ 152 Juan Dominguez FYP RC .50 .20
❑ 153 Justin Woodrow FYP .50 .20
❑ 154 Nic Jackson FYP RC .50 .20
❑ 155 Laynce Nix FYP RC 1.50 .60
❑ 156 Hank Aaron RET 5.00 2.00
❑ 157 Ernie Banks RET 2.50 1.00
❑ 158 Johnny Bench RET 2.50 1.00
❑ 159 George Brett RET 5.00 2.00
❑ 160 Carlton Fisk RET 1.50 .60
❑ 161 Bob Gibson RET 1.50 .60
❑ 162 Reggie Jackson RET 1.50 .60
❑ 163 Don Mattingly RET 5.00 2.00
❑ 164 Kirby Puckett RET 2.50 1.00
❑ 165 Frank Robinson RET 1.50 .60
❑ 166 Nolan Ryan RET 6.00 2.50
❑ 167 Tom Seaver RET 1.50 .60
❑ 168 Mike Schmidt RET 5.00 2.00
❑ 169 Dave Winfield RET 1.00 .40
❑ 170 Carl Yastrzemski RET 3.00 1.25
❑ 171 Frank Chance REP 1.00 .40
❑ 172 Ty Cobb REP 5.00 2.00
❑ 173 Sam Crawford REP 1.00 .40
❑ 174 Johnny Evers REP 1.00 .40
❑ 175 John McGraw REP 1.50 .60
❑ 176 Eddie Plank REP 2.50 1.00
❑ 177 Tris Speaker REP 2.50 1.00
❑ 178 Joe Tinker REP 1.00 .40
❑ 179 H.Wagner Orange REP 8.00 3.00
❑ 180 Cy Young REP 2.50 1.00
❑ 181 Javier Vazquez .50 .20
❑ 182A Mark Mulder Green Jsy .50 .20
❑ 182B Mark Mulder White Jsy .50 .20
❑ 183A Roger Clemens Blue Jsy 2.50 1.00
❑ 183B Roger Clemens Pinstripes 2.50 1.00
❑ 184 Kazuhisa Ishii RC .75 .30
❑ 185 Roberto Alomar .75 .30
❑ 186 Lance Berkman .50 .20

❑ 187A Adam Dunn Arms Folded .50 .20
❑ 187B Adam Dunn w/Bat .50 .20
❑ 188A Aramis Ramirez w/Bat .50 .20
❑ 188B Aramis Ramirez w/o Bat .50 .20
❑ 189 Chuck Knoblauch .50 .20
❑ 190 Nomar Garciaparra 2.00 .75
❑ 191 Brad Penny .50 .20
❑ 192A Gary Sheffield w/Bat .50 .20
❑ 192B Gary Sheffield w/o Bat .50 .20
❑ 193 Alfonso Soriano .50 .20
❑ 194 Andruw Jones .75 .30
❑ 195A Randy Johnson Black Jsy 1.25 .50
❑ 195B Randy Johnson Purple Jsy 1.25 .50
❑ 196A Corey Patterson Blue Jsy .50 .20
❑ 196B Corey Patterson Pinstripes .50 .20
❑ 197 Milton Bradley .50 .20
❑ 198A J.Damon Blue Jsy/Cap .75 .30
❑ 198B J.Damon Blue Jsy/Hlmt .75 .30
❑ 198C J.Damon White Jsy .75 .30
❑ 199A Paul Lo Duca Blue Jsy .50 .20
❑ 199B Paul Lo Duca White Jsy .50 .20
❑ 200A Albert Pujols Red Jsy 2.50 1.00
❑ 200B Albert Pujols Running 2.50 1.00
❑ 200C Albert Pujols w/Bat 2.50 1.00
❑ 201 Scott Rolen .75 .30
❑ 202A J.D. Drew Running .50 .20
❑ 202B J.D. Drew w/Bat .50 .20
❑ 202C J.D. Drew White Jsy .50 .20
❑ 203 Vladimir Guerrero 1.25 .50
❑ 204A Jason Giambi Blue Jsy .50 .20
❑ 204B Jason Giambi Grey Jsy .50 .20
❑ 204C Jason Giambi Pinstripes .50 .20
❑ 205A Moises Alou Grey Jsy .50 .20
❑ 205B Moises Alou Pinstripes .50 .20
❑ 206A Magglio Ordonez Signing .50 .20
❑ 206B Magglio Ordonez w/Bat .50 .20
❑ 207 Carlos Febles .50 .20
❑ 208 So Taguchi RC .75 .30
❑ 209A Rafael Palmeiro One Hand .75 .30
❑ 209B Rafael Palmeiro Two Hands .75 .30
❑ 210 David Wells .50 .20
❑ 211 Orlando Cabrera .50 .20
❑ 212 Sammy Sosa 1.25 .50
❑ 213 Armando Benitez .50 .20
❑ 214 Wes Helms .50 .20
❑ 215A Mariano Rivera Arms Folded 1.25 .50
❑ 215B Mariano Rivera Holding Ball 1.25 .50
❑ 216 Jimmy Rollins .50 .20
❑ 217 Matt Lawton .50 .20
❑ 218A Shawn Green w/Bat .50 .20
❑ 218B Shawn Green w/o Bat .50 .20
❑ 219A Bernie Williams w/Bat .75 .30
❑ 219B Bernie Williams w/o Bat .75 .30
❑ 220A Bret Boone Blue Jsy .50 .20
❑ 220B Bret Boone White Jsy .50 .20
❑ 221A Alex Rodriguez Blue Jsy 2.00 .75
❑ 221B Alex Rodriguez One Hand 2.00 .75
❑ 221C Alex Rodriguez Two Hands 2.00 .75
❑ 222 Roger Cedeno .50 .20
❑ 223 Marty Cordova .50 .20
❑ 224 Fred McGriff .75 .30
❑ 225A Chipper Jones Batting 1.25 .50
❑ 225B Chipper Jones Running 1.25 .50
❑ 226 Kerry Wood .50 .20
❑ 227A Larry Walker Grey Jsy .50 .20
❑ 227B Larry Walker Purple Jsy .50 .20
❑ 228 Robin Ventura .50 .20
❑ 229 Robert Fick .50 .20
❑ 230A Tino Martinez Black Glove .75 .30
❑ 230B Tino Martinez Throwing .75 .30
❑ 230C Tino Martinez w/Bat .75 .30
❑ 231 Ben Petrick .50 .20
❑ 232 Neifi Perez .50 .20
❑ 233 Pedro Martinez .75 .30
❑ 234A Brian Jordan Grey Jsy .50 .20
❑ 234B Brian Jordan White Jsy .50 .20
❑ 235 Freddy Garcia .50 .20
❑ 236A Derek Jeter Batting 3.00 1.25
❑ 236B Derek Jeter Blue Jsy 3.00 1.25
❑ 236C Derek Jeter Kneeling 3.00 1.25
❑ 237 Ben Grieve .50 .20
❑ 238A Barry Bonds Black Jsy 3.00 1.25
❑ 238B Barry Bonds w/Wrist Band 3.00 1.25
❑ 238C B.Bonds w/o Wrist Band 3.00 1.25
❑ 239 Luis Gonzalez .50 .20
❑ 240 Shane Halter .50 .20
❑ 241A Brian Giles Black Jsy .50 .20
❑ 241B Brian Giles Grey Jsy .50 .20
❑ 242 Bud Smith .50 .20
❑ 243 Richie Sexson .50 .20
❑ 244A Barry Zito Green Jsy .50 .20
❑ 244B Barry Zito White Jsy .50 .20
❑ 245 Eric Milton .50 .20
❑ 246A Ivan Rodriguez Blue Jsy .75 .30
❑ 246B Ivan Rodriguez Grey Jsy .75 .30
❑ 246C Ivan Rodriguez White Jsy .75 .30
❑ 247 Toby Hall .50 .20
❑ 248A Mike Piazza Black Jsy 2.00 .75
❑ 248B Mike Piazza Grey Jsy 2.00 .75
❑ 249 Ruben Sierra .50 .20
❑ 250A Tsuyoshi Shinjo Cap .50 .20
❑ 250B Tsuyoshi Shinjo Helmet .50 .20
❑ 251A Jermaine Dye Green Jsy .50 .20
❑ 251B Jermaine Dye White Jsy .50 .20
❑ 252 Roy Oswalt .50 .20
❑ 253 Todd Helton .75 .30
❑ 254 Adrian Beltre .50 .20
❑ 255 Doug Mientkiewicz .50 .20
❑ 256A Ichiro Suzuki Blue Jsy 2.50 1.00
❑ 256B Ichiro Suzuki w/Bat 2.50 1.00
❑ 256C Ichiro Suzuki White Jsy 2.50 1.00
❑ 257A C.C. Sabathia Blue Jsy .50 .20
❑ 257B C.C. Sabathia White Jsy .50 .20
❑ 258 Paul Konerko .50 .20
❑ 259 Ken Griffey Jr. 2.00 .75
❑ 260A Jeromy Burnitz w/Bat .50 .20
❑ 260B Jeromy Burnitz w/o Bat .50 .20
❑ 261 Hank Blalock PROS .75 .30
❑ 262 Mark Prior PROS .75 .30
❑ 263 Josh Beckett PROS .50 .20
❑ 264 Carlos Pena PROS .50 .20
❑ 265 Sean Burroughs PROS .50 .20
❑ 266 Austin Kearns PROS .50 .20
❑ 267 Chin-Hui Tsao PROS .50 .20
❑ 268 Dewon Brazelton PROS .50 .20
❑ 269 J.D. Martin PROS .50 .20
❑ 270 Marlon Byrd PROS .50 .20
❑ 271 Joe Mauer FYP RC 10.00 4.00
❑ 272 Jason Botts FYP RC .50 .20
❑ 273 Mauricio Lara FYP RC .50 .20
❑ 274 Jonny Gomes FYP RC 2.50 1.00
❑ 275 Gavin Floyd FYP RC 1.00 .40
❑ 276 Alex Requena FYP RC .50 .20
❑ 277 Jimmy Gobble FYP RC .50 .20
❑ 278 Chris Duffy FYP RC .50 .20
❑ 279 Colt Griffin FYP RC .50 .20
❑ 280 Ryan Church FYP RC 1.00 .40
❑ 281 Beltran Perez FYP RC .50 .20
❑ 282 Clint Nageotte FYP RC .75 .30
❑ 283 Justin Schuda FYP RC .50 .20
❑ 284 Scott Hairston FYP RC .75 .30
❑ 285 Mario Ramos FYP RC .50 .20
❑ 286A Tom Seaver White Sox RET 1.50 .60
❑ 286B Tom Seaver Mets RET 1.50 .60
❑ 287A Hank Aaron White Jsy RET 5.00 2.00
❑ 287B Hank Aaron Blue Jsy RET 5.00 2.00
❑ 288 Mike Schmidt RET 5.00 2.00
❑ 289A Robin Yount Blue Jsy RET 2.50 1.00
❑ 289B Robin Yount P'stripes RET 2.50 1.00
❑ 290 Joe Morgan RET 1.00 .40
❑ 291 Frank Robinson RET 1.50 .60
❑ 292A Reggie Jackson A's RET 1.50 .60
❑ 292B Reggie Jackson Yanks RET 1.50 .60
❑ 293A Nolan Ryan Astros RET 6.00 2.50
❑ 293B Nolan Ryan Rangers RET 6.00 2.50
❑ 294 Dave Winfield RET 1.00 .40
❑ 295 Willie Mays RET 5.00 2.00
❑ 296 Brooks Robinson RET 1.50 .60
❑ 297A Mark McGwire A's RET 6.00 2.50
❑ 297B Mark McGwire Cards RET 6.00 2.50
❑ 298 Honus Wagner RET 2.50 1.00
❑ 299A Sherry Magee REP 1.00 .40
❑ 299B Sherry Magie UER REP 1.00 .40
❑ 300 Frank Chance REP 1.00 .40
❑ 301A Joe Doyle NY REP 1.00 .40
❑ 301B Joe Doyle NY Nat'l REP 1.00 .40
❑ 302 John McGraw REP 1.50 .60
❑ 303 Jimmy Collins REP 1.00 .40
❑ 304 Buck Herzog REP 1.00 .40
❑ 305 Sam Crawford REP 1.00 .40
❑ 306 Cy Young REP 2.50 1.00
❑ 307 Honus Wagner Blue REP 8.00 3.00
❑ 308A A.Rodriguez Blue Jsy SP 4.00 1.50
❑ 308B A.Rodriguez White Jsy 2.00 .75
❑ 309 Vernon Wells .50 .20
❑ 310A B.Bonds w/Elbow Pad 3.00 1.25
❑ 310B B.Bonds w/o Elbow Pad SP 6.00 2.50
❑ 311 Vicente Padilla .50 .20
❑ 312A A.Soriano w/Wristband .50 .20
❑ 312B A.Soriano w/o Wristband SP 2.00 .75
❑ 313 Mike Piazza 2.00 .75
❑ 314 Jacque Jones .50 .20
❑ 315 Shawn Green SP 2.00 .75
❑ 316 Paul Byrd .50 .20
❑ 317 Lance Berkman .50 .20
❑ 318 Larry Walker .50 .20
❑ 319 Ken Griffey Jr. SP 4.00 1.50
❑ 320 Shea Hillenbrand .50 .20
❑ 321 Jay Gibbons .50 .20
❑ 322 Andruw Jones .75 .30
❑ 323 Luis Gonzalez SP 2.00 .75
❑ 324 Garret Anderson .50 .20
❑ 325 Roy Halladay .50 .20
❑ 326 Randy Winn .50 .20
❑ 327 Matt Morris .50 .20
❑ 328 Robb Nen .50 .20
❑ 329 Trevor Hoffman .50 .20
❑ 330 Kip Wells .50 .20
❑ 331 Orlando Hernandez .50 .20
❑ 332 Rey Ordonez .50 .20
❑ 333 Torii Hunter .50 .20
❑ 334 Geoff Jenkins .50 .20
❑ 335 Eric Karros .50 .20
❑ 336 Mike Lowell .50 .20
❑ 337 Nick Johnson .50 .20
❑ 338 Randall Simon .50 .20
❑ 339 Ellis Burks .50 .20
❑ 340A Sammy Sosa Blue Jsy SP 2.50 1.00
❑ 340B Sammy Sosa White Jsy 1.25 .50
❑ 341 Pedro Martinez .75 .30
❑ 342 Junior Spivey .50 .20
❑ 343 Vinny Castilla .50 .20
❑ 344 Randy Johnson SP 2.50 1.00
❑ 345 Chipper Jones SP 2.50 1.00
❑ 346 Orlando Hudson .50 .20
❑ 347 Albert Pujols SP 5.00 2.00
❑ 348 Rondell White .50 .20
❑ 349 Vladimir Guerrero 1.25 .50
❑ 350A Mark Prior Red SP 1.50 .60
❑ 350B Mark Prior Yellow .75 .30
❑ 351 Eric Gagne .50 .20
❑ 352 Todd Zeile .50 .20
❑ 353 Manny Ramirez SP 2.00 .75
❑ 354 Kevin Millwood .50 .20
❑ 355 Troy Percival .50 .20
❑ 356A Jason Giambi Batting SP 2.00 .75
❑ 356B Jason Giambi Throwing .50 .20
❑ 357 Bartolo Colon .50 .20
❑ 358 Jeremy Giambi .50 .20
❑ 359 Jose Cruz Jr. .50 .20
❑ 360A I.Suzuki Blue Jsy SP 5.00 2.00
❑ 360B I.Suzuki White Jsy 2.50 1.00
❑ 361 Eddie Guardado .50 .20
❑ 362 Ivan Rodriguez .75 .30
❑ 363 Carl Crawford .50 .20
❑ 364 Jason Simontacchi RC .50 .20
❑ 365 Kenny Lofton .50 .20
❑ 366 Raul Mondesi .50 .20
❑ 367 A.J. Pierzynski .50 .20
❑ 368 Ugueth Urbina .50 .20
❑ 369 Rodrigo Lopez .50 .20
❑ 370A N.Garciaparra One Bat SP 4.00 1.50
❑ 370B N.Garciaparra Two Bats 2.00 .75
❑ 371 Craig Counsell .50 .20
❑ 372 Barry Larkin .75 .30
❑ 373 Carlos Pena .50 .20
❑ 374 Luis Castillo .50 .20
❑ 375 Raul Ibanez .50 .20
❑ 376 Kazuhisa Ishii SP 2.00 .75
❑ 377 Derek Lowe .50 .20
❑ 378 Curt Schilling .50 .20
❑ 379 Jim Thome Phillies .75 .30
❑ 380A Derek Jeter Blue SP 6.00 2.50
❑ 380B Derek Jeter Seats 3.00 1.25
❑ 381 Pat Burrell .50 .20
❑ 382 Jamie Moyer .50 .20
❑ 383 Eric Hinske .50 .20
❑ 384 Scott Rolen .75 .30

	Card	Player	Price	Price
❑	385	Miguel Tejada SP	2.00	.75
❑	386	Andy Pettitte	.75	.30
❑	387	Mike Lieberthal	.50	.20
❑	388	Al Leiter	.50	.20
❑	389	Todd Helton SP	2.00	.75
❑	390A	Adam Dunn Bat SP	2.00	.75
❑	390B	Adam Dunn Glove	.50	.20
❑	391	Cliff Floyd	.50	.20
❑	392	Tim Salmon	.75	.30
❑	393	Joe Torre MG	.75	.30
❑	394	Bobby Cox MG	.50	.20
❑	395	Tony LaRussa MG	.50	.20
❑	396	Art Howo MG	.50	.20
❑	397	Bob Brenly MG	.50	.20
❑	398	Ron Gardenhire MG	.50	.20
❑	399	Mike Cuddyer PROS	.50	.20
❑	400	Joe Mauer PROS	10.00	4.00
❑	401	Mark Teixeira PROS	1.25	.50
❑	402	Hee Seop Choi PROS	.50	.20
❑	403	Angel Berroa PROS	.50	.20
❑	404	Jesse Foppert PROS RC	.75	.30
❑	405	Bobby Crosby PROS	1.25	.50
❑	406	Jose Reyes PROS	.75	.30
❑	407	Casey Kotchman PROS RC	1.00	.40
❑	408	Aaron Heilman PROS	.50	.20
❑	409	Adrian Gonzalez PROS	.50	.20
❑	410	Delwyn Young PROS RC	1.00	.40
❑	411	Brett Myers PROS	.50	.20
❑	412	Justin Huber PROS RC	.75	.30
❑	413	Drew Henson PROS	.50	.20
❑	414	Taggert Bozied PROS RC	.75	.30
❑	415	Dontrelle Willis PROS RC	5.00	2.00
❑	416	Rocco Baldelli PROS	.50	.20
❑	417	Jason Stokes PROS RC	.50	.20
❑	418	Brandon Phillips PROS	.50	.20
❑	419	Jake Blalock FYP RC	.50	.20
❑	420	Micah Schilling FYP RC	1.00	.40
❑	421	Denard Span FYP RC	1.00	.40
❑	422A	J.Loney Red FYP RC	4.00	1.50
❑	422B	J.Loney w/Sky FYP RC	4.00	1.50
❑	423A	W.Bankston Blue FYP RC	2.00	.75
❑	423B	W.Bankston w/Sky FYP RC	2.00	.75
❑	424	Jeremy Hermida FYP RC	5.00	2.00
❑	425	Curtis Granderson FYP RC	3.00	1.25
❑	426A	J.Pridie Red FYP RC	1.00	.40
❑	426B	J.Pridie w/Sky FYP RC	1.00	.40
❑	427	Larry Broadway FYP RC	.50	.20
❑	428A	K.Greene Green FYP RC	8.00	3.00
❑	428B	K.Greene Red FYP RC	8.00	3.00
❑	429	Joey Votto FYP RC	3.00	1.25
❑	430A	B.Upton Grey FYP RC	5.00	2.00
❑	430B	B.Upton w/People FYP RC	5.00	2.00
❑	431A	S.Santos Gold FYP RC	1.00	.40
❑	431B	S.Santos Grey FYP RC	1.00	.40
❑	432	Brian Dopirak FYP RC	1.00	.40
❑	433	Ozzie Smith RET SP	4.00	1.50
❑	434	Wade Boggs RET SP	2.50	1.00
❑	435	Yogi Berra RET SP	4.00	1.50
❑	436	Al Kaline RET SP	4.00	1.50
❑	437	Robin Roberts RET SP	2.00	.75
❑	438	Roberto Clemente RET SP	8.00	3.00
❑	439	Gary Carter RET SP	2.00	.75
❑	440	Fergie Jenkins RET SP	2.00	.75
❑	441	Orlando Cepeda RET SP	2.00	.75
❑	442	Rod Carew RET SP	2.50	1.00
❑	443	Harmon Killebrew RET SP	4.00	1.50
❑	444	Duke Snider RET SP	2.50	1.00
❑	445	Stan Musial RET SP	6.00	2.50
❑	446	Hank Greenberg RET SP	4.00	1.50
❑	447	Lou Brock RET SP	2.50	1.00
❑	448	Jim Palmer RET	1.00	.40
❑	449	John McGraw REP	1.50	.60
❑	450	Mordecai Brown REP	1.00	.40
❑	451	Christy Mathewson REP	1.50	.60
❑	452	Sam Crawford REP	1.00	.40
❑	453	Bill O'Hara REP	1.00	.40
❑	454	Joe Tinker REP	1.00	.40
❑	455	Nap Lajoie REP	1.50	.60
❑	456	Honus Wagner Red REP	8.00	3.00
❑	NNO	Repurchased Tobacco Card		

2006 Topps 52

	Card	Player	Price	Price
❑		COMP.SET w/o SPs (275)	80.00	40.00
❑		COMMON CARD (1-275)	.50	.20
❑		COMMON LOGO VAR.	4.00	1.50
❑		LOGO VAR.STATED ODDS 1:5 H,1:5 R		
❑		COMMON SP	6.00	2.50
❑		SP STATED ODDS 1:5 H, 1:5 R		
❑	1	Howie Kendrick (RC)	1.25	.50
❑	2	Enrique Gonzalez (RC)	.50	.20
❑	3	Chuck James (RC)	.75	.30
❑	4	Chris Britton RC	.50	.20
❑	5	David Pauley (RC)	.50	.20
❑	6	Angel Pagan (RC)	.50	.20
❑	7	Pat Neshek RC	5.00	2.00
❑	8	Walter Young (RC)	.50	.20
❑	9	Chris Denorfia (RC)	.50	.20
❑	10	Rafael Perez RC	.50	.20
❑	11	Ryan Spilborghs (RC)	.75	.30
❑	12	Jon Huber RC	.50	.20
❑	13	Jordan Tata RC	.50	.20
❑	14	Eric Reed (RC)	.50	.20
❑	15	Norris Hopper RC	.50	.20
❑	16	Scott Olsen (RC)	.50	.20
❑	17	Fernando Nieve (RC)	.50	.20
❑	18	Chris Booker (RC)	.50	.20
❑	19	Chad Billingsley (RC)	.75	.30
❑	20	Carlos Villanueva RC	.50	.20
❑	21	Craig Hansen RC	2.00	.75
❑	22	Dave Gassner (RC)	.50	.20
❑	23	Mike Pelfrey RC	2.00	.75
❑	24	Matt Smith RC	.75	.30
❑	25	Chris Roberson (RC)	.50	.20
❑	26	John Van Benschoten (RC)	.50	.20
❑	27	Kevin Frandsen (RC)	.50	.20
❑	28	Les Walrond (RC)	.50	.20
❑	29	James Shields RC	.50	.20
❑	30	Russell Martin (RC)	.75	.30
❑	31	Ben Zobrist (RC)	.75	.30
❑	32	John Rheinecker (RC)	.50	.20
❑	33	Francisco Rosario (RC)	.50	.20
❑	34	Santiago Ramirez (RC)	.50	.20
❑	35	Mike Napoli RC	1.25	.50
❑	36	Tony Pena Jr. (RC)	.50	.20
❑	37A	Jeff Karstens RC	1.25	.50
❑	37B	Jeff Karstens 52 Logo	4.00	1.50
❑	38	Phil Stockman (RC)	.50	.20
❑	39	Kurt Birkins RC	.50	.20
❑	41	Buck Coats (RC)	.50	.20
❑	42	Jim Johnson RC	.50	.20
❑	43	Angel Guzman (RC)	.50	.20
❑	44	Kelly Shoppach (RC)	.50	.20
❑	45	Josh Wilson (RC)	.50	.20
❑	46	Jack Hannahan RC	.50	.20
❑	47	Ricky Nolasco (RC)	.50	.20
❑	48	T.J. Bohn (RC)	.50	.20
❑	49	Joel Zumaya (RC)	1.25	.50
❑	50	Phil Barzilla RC	.50	.20
❑	51	Justin Huber (RC)	.50	.20
❑	52A	Willy Aybar (RC)	.50	.20
❑	52B	Willy Aybar 52 Logo	4.00	1.50
❑	53	Tony Gwynn Jr. (RC)	1.25	.50
❑	54	Chris Barnwell RC	.50	.20
❑	55	Henry Owens RC	.75	.30
❑	56	Jeff Bajenaru (RC)	.50	.20
❑	57	Jonah Bayliss RC	.50	.20
❑	58	Josh Sharpless RC	.50	.20
❑	59	Eliezer Alfonzo RC	.50	.20

	Card	Player	Price	Price
❑	60	Bobby Livingston (RC)	.50	.20
❑	61	John Gall (RC)	.50	.20
❑	62	Ruddy Lugo (RC)	.50	.20
❑	63	Fabio Castro RC	.50	.20
❑	64	Casey Janssen RC	.75	.30
❑	65	Mike O'Connor RC	.50	.20
❑	66	Kendry Morales (RC)	.75	.30
❑	67	James Hoey RC	.50	.20
❑	68	Dustin Moseley (RC)	.50	.20
❑	69	Peter Moylan RC	.50	.20
❑	70	Manny Delcarmen (RC)	.50	.20
❑	71	Rich Hill (RC)	.50	.20
❑	72	Boone Logan RC	.50	.20
❑	73	Cody Ross (RC)	.50	.20
❑	74	Fausto Carmona (RC)	.50	.20
❑	75	Ramon Ramirez (RC)	.50	.20
❑	76	Zach Miner (RC)	.50	.20
❑	77	Hanley Ramirez (RC)	1.25	.50
❑	78	Josh Johnson (RC)	.75	.30
❑	79	Taylor Buchholz (RC)	.50	.20
❑	80	Joe Nelson (RC)	.50	.20
❑	81	Hong-Chih Kuo (RC)	1.25	.50
❑	82	Chris Mabeus (RC)	.50	.20
❑	83	Willie Eyre (RC)	.50	.20
❑	84	John Maine (RC)	.75	.30
❑	85	Yurendell DeCaster (RC)	.50	.20
❑	86	Mike Thompson RC	.50	.20
❑	87	Brian Wilson RC	.50	.20
❑	88A	Matt Cain (RC)	.75	.30
❑	88B	Matt Cain 52 Logo	5.00	2.00
❑	89	Sean Green RC	.50	.20
❑	90	Tyler Johnson (RC)	.50	.20
❑	91	Jason Childers RC	.50	.20
❑	92	Wes Littleton (RC)	.50	.20
❑	93	Ty Taubenheim RC	.75	.30
❑	94	Saul Rivera (RC)	.50	.20
❑	95	Reggie Willits RC	2.00	.75
❑	96	Carlos Quentin (RC)	.75	.30
❑	97	Macay McBride (RC)	.50	.20
❑	98	Brandon Fahey RC	.50	.20
❑	99	Sean Marshall (RC)	.50	.20
❑	100	Sean Tracey (RC)	.50	.20
❑	101	Brian Slocum (RC)	.50	.20
❑	102	Choo Freeman (RC)	.50	.20
❑	103	Brent Clevlen (RC)	.75	.30
❑	104	Josh Willingham (RC)	.50	.20
❑	105	Chris Resop (RC)	.50	.20
❑	106	Chris Sampson RC	.50	.20
❑	107A	James Loney (RC)	.75	.30
❑	107B	James Loney 52 Logo	5.00	2.00
❑	108	Matt Kemp (RC)	.75	.30
❑	109	Jason Kubel (RC)	.50	.20
❑	110	Brian Bannister (RC)	.50	.20
❑	111	Kevin Thompson (RC)	.50	.20
❑	112	Jeremy Brown (RC)	.50	.20
❑	113	Brian Sanches (RC)	.50	.20
❑	114	Nate McLouth (RC)	.50	.20
❑	115	Ben Johnson (RC)	.50	.20
❑	116	Jonathan Sanchez (RC)	.50	.20
❑	117	Mark Lowe (RC)	.50	.20
❑	118	Skip Schumaker (RC)	.50	.20
❑	119	Jason Hammel (RC)	.50	.20
❑	120	Drew Meyer (RC)	.50	.20
❑	121	Melvin Dorta RC	.50	.20
❑	122	Jeff Mathis (RC)	.50	.20
❑	123	Davis Romero (RC)	.50	.20
❑	124	Joey Devine RC	.50	.20
❑	125	Sendy Rleal RC	.50	.20
❑	126	Freddie Bynum (RC)	.50	.20
❑	127	Brian Anderson (RC)	.50	.20
❑	128	Jeremy Sowers (RC)	.50	.20
❑	129	Ryan Shealy (RC)	.50	.20
❑	130	Reggie Abercrombie (RC)	.50	.20
❑	131	Matt Albers (RC)	.50	.20
❑	132	Lastings Milledge (RC)	.75	.30
❑	133	Robert Andino RC	.50	.20
❑	134	Chris Demaria RC	.50	.20
❑	135	Boof Bonser (RC)	.75	.30
❑	136	Alay Soler RC	.50	.20
❑	137	Wil Nieves (RC)	.50	.20
❑	138	Mike Rouse (RC)	.50	.20
❑	139	Carlos Ruiz (RC)	.50	.20
❑	140	Matt Capps (RC)	.50	.20
❑	141	Travis Ishikawa (RC)	.50	.20
❑	142	Josh Kinney RC	.50	.20
❑	143	Josh Rupe (RC)	.50	.20

❑ 144 Shaun Marcum (RC) .50 .20
❑ 145 Jason Bergmann RC .50 .20
❑ 146 Tommy Murphy (RC) .50 .20
❑ 147 Martin Prado (RC) .50 .20
❑ 148 Val Majewski (RC) .50 .20
❑ 149 Ian Kinsler (RC) .75 .30
❑ 150 Joe Winkelsas (RC) .50 .20
❑ 151 Agustin Montero (RC) .50 .20
❑ 152 Joe Inglett RC .50 .20
❑ 153 Manuel Corpas RC .50 .20
❑ 154 Yusmeiro Petit (RC) .50 .20
❑ 155 Mark Woodyard (RC) .50 .20
❑ 156 Jeff Fulchino RC .50 .20
❑ 157 Stephen Andrade (RC) .50 .20
❑ 158 Tim Hamulack (RC) .50 .20
❑ 159 Colter Bean (RC) .50 .20
❑ 160 Anderson Hernandez (RC) .50 .20
❑ 161 Kevin Reese (RC) .50 .20
❑ 162 Jason Windsor (RC) .50 .20
❑ 163A Paul Maholm (RC) .50 .20
❑ 163B Paul Maholm 52 Logo 5.00 2.00
❑ 164 Jeremy Accardo RC .50 .20
❑ 165 Joel Guzman (RC) .50 .20
❑ 166 Erick Aybar (RC) .50 .20
❑ 167 Scott Thorman (RC) .50 .20
❑ 168 Adam Loewen (RC) .50 .20
❑ 169 Carlos Marmol RC .50 .20
❑ 170 Bill Bray (RC) .50 .20
❑ 171 Edward Mujica RC .50 .20
❑ 172 Jeremy Hermida (RC) .50 .20
❑ 173 Taylor Tankersley (RC) .50 .20
❑ 174 Bobby Keppel (RC) .50 .20
❑ 175 Chris B. Young (RC) .50 .20
❑ 176 Josh Rabe RC .50 .20
❑ 177 T.J. Beam (RC) .50 .20
❑ 178A Shane Komine RC .75 .30
❑ 178B Shane Komine 52 Logo 5.00 2.00
❑ 179 Scott Mathieson (RC) .50 .20
❑ 180 Josh Barfield (RC) .50 .20
❑ 181 Justin Knoedler (RC) .50 .20
❑ 182 Emiliano Fruto RC .50 .20
❑ 183 Adam Wainwright (RC) .50 .20
❑ 184 Nick Masset (RC) .50 .20
❑ 185 Ryan Roberts RC .50 .20
❑ 186 Brandon Watson (RC) .50 .20
❑ 187 Chris Bootcheck (RC) .50 .20
❑ 188 Dan Ortmeier (RC) .50 .20
❑ 189 Kevin Barry (RC) .50 .20
❑ 190 Cory Morris RC .50 .20
❑ 191 Kason Gabbard (RC) .50 .20
❑ 192 Tom Mastny (RC) .50 .20
❑ 193 David Aardsma (RC) .50 .20
❑ 194 Anthony Reyes (RC) .75 .30
❑ 195 Mike Jacobs (RC) .50 .20
❑ 196 Conor Jackson (RC) .75 .30
❑ 197 Kenji Johjima RC 2.50 1.00
❑ 198 Jack Taschner (RC) .50 .20
❑ 199 Renyel Pinto (RC) .50 .20
❑ 200 Chad Santos (RC) .50 .20
❑ 201 Aaron Rakers (RC) .50 .20
❑ 202 Franklin Gutierrez (RC) .50 .20
❑ 203 Chris Coste RC 2.00 .75
❑ 204 Chris Iannetta RC .50 .20
❑ 205 Mike Vento (RC) .50 .20
❑ 206 Ryan O'Malley RC .50 .20
❑ 207 Jason Botts (RC) .50 .20
❑ 208 John Hattig (RC) .50 .20
❑ 209 Brandon Harper RC .50 .20
❑ 210 Ryan Theriot RC 5.00 2.00
❑ 211 Travis Hughes (RC) .50 .20
❑ 212 Paul Hoover (RC) .50 .20
❑ 213 Brayan Pena (RC) .50 .20
❑ 214 Craig Breslow RC .50 .20
❑ 215 Eude Brito (RC) .50 .20
❑ 216A Melky Cabrera (RC) .75 .30
❑ 216B Melky Cabrera 52 Logo 5.00 2.00
❑ 217A Jonathan Broxton (RC) .50 .20
❑ 217B Jonathan Broxton 52 Logo 4.00 1.50
❑ 218 Bryan Corey (RC) .50 .20
❑ 219 Ron Flores RC .50 .20
❑ 220 Andrew Brown (RC) .50 .20
❑ 221 Jaime Bubela (RC) .50 .20
❑ 222 Jason Bulger (RC) .50 .20
❑ 223 Alberto Callaspo (RC) .50 .20
❑ 224 Jose Capellan (RC) .50 .20
❑ 225A Cole Hamels (RC) 1.25 .50
❑ 225B Cole Hamels 52 Logo 8.00 3.00
❑ 226 Bernie Castro (RC) .50 .20
❑ 227 Shin-Soo Choo (RC) .75 .30
❑ 228 Doug Clark (RC) .50 .20
❑ 229 Roy Corcoran RC .50 .20
❑ 230 Tim Corcoran RC .50 .20
❑ 231 Nelson Cruz (RC) .50 .20
❑ 232 Rajai Davis (RC) .50 .20
❑ 233A Chris Duncan (RC) .75 .30
❑ 233B Chris Duncan 52 Logo 5.00 2.00
❑ 234 Scott Dunn (RC) .50 .20
❑ 235 Mike Esposito (RC) .50 .20
❑ 236 Scott Feldman RC .50 .20
❑ 237 Luis Figueroa RC .50 .20
❑ 238 Bartolome Fortunato (RC) .50 .20
❑ 239 Alejandro Freire RC .50 .20
❑ 240 J.J. Furmaniak (RC) .50 .20
❑ 241 Nick Markakis (RC) .75 .30
❑ 242 Matt Garza (RC) .50 .20
❑ 243 Justin Germano (RC) .50 .20
❑ 244 Alexis Gomez (RC) .50 .20
❑ 245 Tom Gorzelanny (RC) .50 .20
❑ 246 Dan Uggla (RC) 1.25 .50
❑ 247 Jeremy Guthrie (RC) .50 .20
❑ 248 Stephen Drew (RC) 1.25 .50
❑ 249 Brendan Harris (RC) .50 .20
❑ 250 Jeff Harris RC .50 .20
❑ 251 Corey Hart (RC) .50 .20
❑ 252 Chris Heintz RC .50 .20
❑ 253 Prince Fielder (RC) 2.00 .75
❑ 254 Francisco Liriano (RC) 2.50 1.00
❑ 255 Jason Hirsh (RC) .50 .20
❑ 256 J.R. House (RC) .50 .20
❑ 257 Zach Jackson (RC) .50 .20
❑ 258 Charlton Jimerson (RC) .50 .20
❑ 259 Greg Jones (RC) .50 .20
❑ 260 Mitch Jones (RC) .50 .20
❑ 261 Ryan Jorgensen RC .50 .20
❑ 262 Logan Kensing (RC) .50 .20
❑ 263 John Koronka (RC) .50 .20
❑ 264 Anthony Lerew (RC) .50 .20
❑ 265 Anibal Sanchez (RC) .75 .30
❑ 266 Juan Mateo RC .50 .20
❑ 267 Paul McAnulty (RC) .50 .20
❑ 268 Dustin McGowan (RC) .50 .20
❑ 269 Marty McLeary (RC) .50 .20
❑ 270 Ryan Zimmerman (RC) 3.00 1.25
❑ 271 Dustin Nippert (RC) .50 .20
❑ 272 Eric O'Flaherty RC .50 .20
❑ 273 Ronny Paulino (RC) .50 .20
❑ 274 Tony Pena (RC) .50 .20
❑ 275 Hayden Penn (RC) .50 .20
❑ 276 Miguel Perez SP (RC) 6.00 2.50
❑ 277 Paul Phillips SP (RC) 6.00 2.50
❑ 278 Omar Quintanilla SP (RC) 6.00 2.50
❑ 279 Guillermo Quiroz SP (RC) 6.00 2.50
❑ 280 Darrell Rasner SP (RC) 6.00 2.50
❑ 281 Kenny Ray SP (RC) 6.00 2.50
❑ 282 Royce Ring SP (RC) 6.00 2.50
❑ 283 Brian Rogers SP RC 8.00 3.00
❑ 284 Ed Rogers SP (RC) 6.00 2.50
❑ 285 Danny Sandoval SP RC 6.00 2.50
❑ 286 Joe Saunders SP (RC) 6.00 2.50
❑ 287 Chris Schroder SP RC 6.00 2.50
❑ 288 Mike Smith SP (RC) 8.00 3.00
❑ 289 Travis Smith SP (RC) 6.00 2.50
❑ 290 Geovany Soto SP (RC) 6.00 2.50
❑ 291 Brian Sweeney SP (RC) 6.00 2.50
❑ 292 Jon Switzer SP (RC) 6.00 2.50
❑ 293 Joe Thurston SP (RC) 6.00 2.50
❑ 294 Jermaine Van Buren SP (RC) 6.002.50
❑ 295 Ryan Garko SP (RC) 6.00 2.50
❑ 296 Cla Meredith SP (RC) 8.00 3.00
❑ 297 Luke Scott SP (RC) 6.00 2.50
❑ 298 Andy Marte SP (RC) 6.00 2.50
❑ 299 Jered Weaver SP (RC) 10.00 4.00
❑ 300 Freddy Guzman SP (RC) 6.00 2.50
❑ 301 Jonathan Papelbon SP (RC) 10.004.00
❑ 302 John-Ford Griffin SP (RC) 6.00 2.50
❑ 303 Jon Lester SP RC 10.00 4.00
❑ 304 Shawn Hill SP (RC) 6.00 2.50
❑ 305 Brian Myrow SP RC 6.00 2.50
❑ 306 Anderson Garcia SP RC 6.00 2.50
❑ 307 Andre Ethier SP (RC) 8.00 3.00
❑ 308 Ben Hendrickson SP (RC) 6.00 2.50
❑ 309 Alejandro Machado SP (RC) 6.00 2.50
❑ 310 Justin Verlander SP (RC) 10.00 4.00
❑ 311A Mickey Mantle SP Blue 50.00 20.00
❑ 311B Mickey Mantle Black 10.00 4.00
❑ 311C Mickey Mantle Green 10.00 4.00
❑ 311D Mickey Mantle Orange 10.00 4.00
❑ 311E Mickey Mantle Red 10.00 4.00
❑ 311F Mickey Mantle Yellow 10.00 4.00
❑ 312 Steve Stemle SP RC 6.00 2.50

2007 Topps 52

❑ COMP.SET w/o SPs (202) 50.00 20.00
❑ COMMON CARD (1-227) .60 .25
❑ COMMON ACTION VARIATION 5.00 2.00
❑ ACT.VAR.STATED ODDS 1:6 H, 1:6 R
❑ COMMON SP 5.00 2.00
❑ SP STATED ODDS 1:6 H, 1:6 R
❑ 1 Akinori Iwamura RC 1.50 .60
❑ 2 Angel Sanchez RC .60 .25
❑ 3 Luis Hernandez (RC) .60 .25
❑ 4 Joaquin Arias (RC) .60 .25
❑ 5a Troy Tulowitzki (RC) 1.50 .60
❑ 5b T.Tulowitzki Action SP 6.00 2.50
❑ 6 Jesus Flores RC .60 .25
❑ 7 Mickey Mantle 6.00 2.50
❑ 8 Kory Casto (RC) .60 .25
❑ 9 Tony Abreu RC 1.50 .60
❑ 10 Kevin Kouzmanoff (RC) .60 .25
❑ 11 Travis Buck (RC) .60 .25
❑ 12 Kurt Suzuki (RC) .60 .25
❑ 13 Matt DeSalvo (RC) .60 .25
❑ 14 Jerry Owens (RC) .60 .25
❑ 15 Alex Gordon RC 3.00 1.25
❑ 16 Jeff Baker (RC) .60 .25
❑ 17 Ben Francisco (RC) .60 .25
❑ 18 Nate Schierholtz (RC) .60 .25
❑ 19 Nathan Haynes (RC) .60 .25
❑ 20a Ryan Braun (RC) 4.00 1.50
❑ 20b R.Braun Action SP 8.00 3.00
❑ 21 Brian Barden RC .60 .25
❑ 22 Sean Barker RC .60 .25
❑ 23 Alejandro De Aza RC 1.00 .40
❑ 24 Jamie Burke (RC) .60 .25
❑ 25 Michael Bourn (RC) .60 .25
❑ 26 Jeff Salazar (RC) .60 .25
❑ 27 Chase Headley (RC) .60 .25
❑ 28 Chris Basak RC .60 .25
❑ 29 Mike Fontenot (RC) .60 .25
❑ 30a Hunter Pence (RC) 3.00 1.25
❑ 30b H.Pence Action SP 8.00 3.00
❑ 31 Masumi Kuwata RC 5.00 2.00
❑ 32 Ryan Rowland-Smith RC .60 .25
❑ 33 Tyler Clippard (RC) 1.00 .40
❑ 34 Matt Lindstrom (RC) .60 .25
❑ 35 Fred Lewis (RC) 1.00 .40
❑ 36 Brett Carroll RC .60 .25
❑ 37 Alexi Casilla RC 1.00 .40
❑ 38 Nick Gorneault (RC) .60 .25
❑ 39 Dennis Sarfate (RC) .60 .25
❑ 40 Felix Pie (RC) .60 .25
❑ 41 Miguel Montero (RC) .60 .25
❑ 42 Danny Putnam (RC) .60 .25
❑ 43 Shane Youman RC .60 .25
❑ 44 Andy LaRoche (RC) .60 .25
❑ 45 Jarrod Saltalamacchia (RC) 1.00 .40
❑ 46 Kei Igawa RC 1.50 .60
❑ 47 Don Kelly (RC) .60 .25
❑ 48 Fernando Cortez (RC) .60 .25
❑ 49 Travis Metcalf RC 1.00 .40

❑ 50a Daisuke Matsuzaka RC 6.00 2.50
❑ 50b D.Matsuzaka Action SP 8.00 3.00
❑ 51 Edwar Ramirez RC 1.50 .60
❑ 52 Ryan Sweeney (RC) .60 .25
❑ 53 Shawn Riggans (RC) .60 .25
❑ 54 Billy Sadler (RC) .60 .25
❑ 55 Billy Butler (RC) 1.00 .40
❑ 56 Andy Cavazos RC .60 .25
❑ 57 Sean Henn (RC) .60 .25
❑ 58 Brian Esposito (RC) .60 .25
❑ 59 Brandon Morrow RC 1.50 .60
❑ 60 Adam Lind (RC) .60 .25
❑ 61 Joe Smith RC .60 .25
❑ 62 Chris Stewart RC .60 .25
❑ 63 Eulogio De La Cruz (RC) .60 .25
❑ 64 Sean Gallagher (RC) .60 .25
❑ 65 Carlos Gomez RC 1.00 .40
❑ 66 Jailen Peguero RC .60 .25
❑ 67 Juan Perez RC .60 .25
❑ 68 Levale Speigner RC .60 .25
❑ 69 Jamie Vermilyea RC .60 .25
❑ 70a Delmon Young (RC) 1.00 .40
❑ 70b D.Young Action SP 5.00 2.00
❑ 71 Jo-Jo Reyes (RC) .60 .25
❑ 72 Zack Segovia (RC) .60 .25
❑ 73 Andy Sonnanstine RC .60 .25
❑ 74 Chase Wright RC 1.50 .60
❑ 75 Josh Fields (RC) .60 .25
❑ 76 Jon Knott (RC) .60 .25
❑ 77 Guillermo Rodriguez RC .60 .25
❑ 78 Jon Coutlangus (RC) .60 .25
❑ 79 Kevin Cameron RC .60 .25
❑ 80 Mark Reynolds RC 2.50 1.00
❑ 81 Brian Stokes (RC) .60 .25
❑ 82 Alberto Arias RC .60 .25
❑ 83 Yoel Hernandez RC .60 .25
❑ 84 David Murphy (RC) .60 .25
❑ 85 Josh Hamilton (RC) 1.50 .60
❑ 86 Justin Hampson (RC) .60 .25
❑ 87 Doug Slaten RC .60 .25
❑ 88 Joseph Bisenius RC .60 .25
❑ 89 Troy Cate RC .60 .25
❑ 90 Homer Bailey (RC) 1.00 .40
❑ 91 Jacoby Ellsbury (RC) 6.00 2.50
❑ 92 Devern Hansack RC .60 .25
❑ 93 Zach McClellan RC .60 .25
❑ 94 Vinny Rottino (RC) .60 .25
❑ 95 Elijah Dukes RC 1.00 .40
❑ 96 Ryan Z. Braun RC .60 .25
❑ 97 Lee Gardner (RC) .60 .25
❑ 98 Joakim Soria RC .60 .25
❑ 99 Jason Miller (RC) .60 .25
❑ 100a Hideki Okajima RC 3.00 1.25
❑ 100b H.Okajima Action SP 8.00 3.00
❑ 101 John Danks RC .60 .25
❑ 102 Garrett Jones (RC) .60 .25
❑ 103 Jensen Lewis RC .60 .25
❑ 104 Clay Rapada RC .60 .25
❑ 105 Kyle Kendrick RC 1.50 .60
❑ 106 Eric Stults RC .60 .25
❑ 107 Jared Burton RC .60 .25
❑ 108 Julio DePaula RC 1.00 .40
❑ 109 Jesse Litsch RC 1.00 .40
❑ 110 Micah Owings (RC) .60 .25
❑ 111 Cory Doyne (RC) .60 .25
❑ 112 Jay Marshall RC .60 .25
❑ 113 Mike Schultz RC .60 .25
❑ 114 Juan Salas (RC) .60 .25
❑ 115 Matt Chico (RC) .60 .25
❑ 116 Brad Salmon RC .60 .25
❑ 117 Jeff Bailey (RC) .60 .25
❑ 118 Gustavo Molina RC .60 .25
❑ 119 Brian Burres (RC) .60 .25
❑ 120 Yovani Gallardo (RC) 2.00 .75
❑ 121 Hector Gimenez (RC) .60 .25
❑ 122 Kelvin Jimenez RC .60 .25
❑ 123 Rick Vanden Hurk RC 1.00 .40
❑ 124 Billy Petrick (RC) .60 .25
❑ 125 Andrew Miller RC 4.00 1.50
❑ 126 Rocky Cherry RC 1.50 .60
❑ 127 Jordan De Jong RC .60 .25
❑ 128 Eric Hull RC .60 .25
❑ 129 Kevin Mahar RC .60 .25
❑ 130a Tim Lincecum RC 5.00 2.00
❑ 130b T.Lincecum Action SP 8.00 3.00
❑ 131 Garrett Olson (RC) .60 .25
❑ 132 Neal Musser RC .60 .25
❑ 133 Mike Rabelo RC .60 .25
❑ 134 Dennis Dove (RC) .60 .25
❑ 135 J.D. Durbin (RC) .60 .25
❑ 136 Jose Garcia RC .60 .25
❑ 137 Marcus McBeth (RC) .60 .25
❑ 138 Curtis Thigpen (RC) .60 .25
❑ 139 Mike Zagurski RC .60 .25
❑ 140 Kevin Slowey (RC) 1.50 .60
❑ 141 Dewon Day RC .60 .25
❑ 142 Glen Perkins (RC) .60 .25
❑ 143 Brian Wolfe (RC) .60 .25
❑ 144 Dallas Braden RC 1.00 .40
❑ 145 J.A. Happ (RC) .60 .25
❑ 146 Lee Gronkiewicz RC .60 .25
❑ 147 Cesar Jimenez RC .60 .25
❑ 148 Mark McLemore (RC) .60 .25
❑ 149 Connor Robertson RC .60 .25
❑ 150a Phil Hughes (RC) 3.00 1.25
❑ 150b P.Hughes Action SP 8.00 3.00
❑ 151 Matthew Brown RC .60 .25
❑ 152 Ryan Feierabend (RC) .60 .25
❑ 153 Brendan Ryan (RC) .60 .25
❑ 154 Terry Evans RC .60 .25
❑ 155 Eric Patterson (RC) .60 .25
❑ 156 Patrick Misch (RC) .60 .25
❑ 157 Darren Clarke RC .60 .25
❑ 158 Kevin Melillo (RC) .60 .25
❑ 159 Edwin Bellorin RC .60 .25
❑ 160 Ubaldo Jimenez (RC) .60 .25
❑ 161 Ryan Budde (RC) .60 .25
❑ 162 Brian Buscher RC 1.00 .40
❑ 163 Juan Gutierrez RC .60 .25
❑ 164 Franklin Morales (RC) .60 .25
❑ 165 Carmen Pignatiello (RC) .60 .25
❑ 166 Jair Jurrjens (RC) .60 .25
❑ 167 Manny Acosta (RC) .60 .25
❑ 168 Ian Stewart (RC) .60 .25
❑ 169 Daniel Barone (RC) .60 .25
❑ 170a Justin Upton RC 4.00 1.50
❑ 170b J.Upton Action SP 8.00 3.00
❑ 171 Tommy Watkins RC 1.00 .40
❑ 172 Ross Wolf RC .60 .25
❑ 173 Jack Cassel RC .60 .25
❑ 174 Asdrubal Cabrera RC .60 .25
❑ 175 Mauro Zarate RC .60 .25
❑ 176 Aaron Laffey RC 1.50 .60
❑ 177 Marcus Gwyn RC .60 .25
❑ 178 Danny Richar RC .60 .25
❑ 179 Joel Hanrahan (RC) .60 .25
❑ 180 Cameron Maybin RC 3.00 1.25
❑ 181 John Lannan RC .60 .25
❑ 182 Shelley Duncan (RC) 1.50 .60
❑ 183 Brandon Wood (RC) .60 .25
❑ 184 Delwyn Young (RC) .60 .25
❑ 185 Manny Parra (RC) .60 .25
❑ 186 Ehren Wassermann RC .60 .25
❑ 187 Jose A. Reyes RC .60 .25
❑ 188 Jose Ascanio RC .60 .25
❑ 190a Alvin Colina RC 1.50 .60
❑ 190b J.Chamberlain Action SP 12.00 5.00
❑ 191 Yunel Escobar (RC) .60 .25
❑ 192 Carlos Maldonado (RC) .60 .25
❑ 193 Dan Meyer (RC) .60 .25
❑ 194 Scott Moore (RC) .60 .25
❑ 195 Romulo Sanchez RC .60 .25
❑ 196 Tom Shearn (RC) .60 .25
❑ 197 Craig Stansberry (RC) .60 .25
❑ 201 Joba Chamberlain RC 6.00 2.50
❑ 202 John Nelson SP (RC) 5.00 2.00
❑ 203 Phil Dumatrait (RC) .60 .25
❑ 204 Brandon Moss (RC) .60 .25
❑ 205 Beltran Perez (RC) .60 .25
❑ 206 Drew Anderson RC .60 .25
❑ 207 Brett Campbell RC .60 .25
❑ 208 Andy Cannizaro SP RC 5.00 2.00
❑ 209 Travis Chick SP (RC) 5.00 2.00
❑ 210 Francisco Cruceta SP (RC) 5.00 2.00
❑ 211 Jose Diaz SP (RC) 5.00 2.00
❑ 212 Jeff Fiorentino SP (RC) 5.00 2.00
❑ 213 Tim Gradoville SP RC 5.00 2.00
❑ 214 Kevin Hooper SP (RC) 5.00 2.00
❑ 215 Philip Humber SP (RC) 5.00 2.00
❑ 216 Juan Lara SP RC 5.00 2.00
❑ 217 Mitch Maier SP RC 5.00 2.00
❑ 218 Juan Morillo SP (RC) 5.00 2.00
❑ 219 A.J. Murray SP RC 5.00 2.00
❑ 220 Chris Narveson SP (RC) 5.00 2.00
❑ 221 Oswaldo Navarro SP RC 5.00 2.00

2006 Topps Allen and Ginter

❑ COMPLETE SET (350) 120.00 60.00
❑ COMP.SET w/o SP's (300) 40.00 15.00
❑ COMMON SP 3.00 1.25
❑ SP STATED ODDS 1:2 HOBBY, 1:2 RETAIL
❑ SP CL: 5/15/25/35/45/50-59/65/85/105/115
❑ SP CL: 125/135/145/150-159/165/175/185
❑ SP CL: 205/215/235/245/251/255-256/265
❑ SP CL: 285/295/305/315/325/335/345
❑ FRAMED ORIGINALS ODDS 1:3227 H, 1:3227 R
❑ 1 Albert Pujols 1.50 .60
❑ 2 Aubrey Huff .20 .07
❑ 3 Mark Teixeira .60 .25
❑ 4 Vernon Wells .40 .15
❑ 5 Ken Griffey Jr. SP 5.00 2.00
❑ 6 Nick Swisher .40 .15
❑ 7 Jose Reyes 1.00 .40
❑ 8 David Wright 1.50 .60
❑ 9 Vladimir Guerrero 1.00 .40
❑ 10 Andruw Jones .60 .25
❑ 11 Ramon Hernandez .40 .15
❑ 12 Miguel Tejada .40 .15
❑ 13 Juan Pierre .40 .15
❑ 14 Jim Thome .60 .25
❑ 15 Austin Kearns SP 3.00 1.25
❑ 16 Jhonny Peralta .40 .15
❑ 17 Clint Barmes .40 .15
❑ 18 Angel Berroa .40 .15
❑ 19 Nomar Garciaparra 1.00 .40
❑ 20 Joe Nathan .40 .15
❑ 21 Brandon Webb .40 .15
❑ 22 Chad Tracy .40 .15
❑ 23 Derek Jeter 2.50 1.00
❑ 24 Conor Jackson (RC) .60 .25
❑ 25 Jason Giambi SP 3.00 1.25
❑ 26 Johnny Estrada .40 .15
❑ 27 Luis Gonzalez .40 .15
❑ 28 Javier Vazquez .40 .15
❑ 29 Orlando Hudson .40 .15
❑ 30 Shawn Green .40 .15
❑ 31 Mark Buehrle .40 .15
❑ 32 Wily Mo Pena .40 .15
❑ 33 C.C. Sabathia .40 .15
❑ 34 Ronnie Belliard .40 .15
❑ 35 Travis Hafner SP 3.00 1.25
❑ 36 Mike Jacobs (RC) .40 .15
❑ 37 Roy Oswalt .40 .15
❑ 38 Zack Greinke .40 .15
❑ 39 J.D. Drew .40 .15
❑ 40 Jeff Kent .40 .15
❑ 41 Ben Sheets .40 .15
❑ 42 Luis Castillo .40 .15
❑ 43 Carlos Delgado .40 .15
❑ 44 Cliff Floyd .40 .15
❑ 45 Danny Haren SP 3.00 1.25
❑ 46 Bobby Abreu .40 .15
❑ 47 Jeromy Burnitz .40 .15
❑ 48 Khalil Greene .60 .25
❑ 49 Moises Alou .40 .15
❑ 50 Alex Rodriguez SP 5.00 2.00
❑ 51 Ervin Santana SP 3.00 1.25
❑ 52 Bartolo Colon SP 3.00 1.25
❑ 53 John Smoltz SP 3.00 1.25

❑	54	David Ortiz SP	3.00	1.25
❑	55	Hideki Matsui SP	3.00	1.25
❑	56	Jermaine Dye SP	3.00	1.25
❑	57	Victor Martinez SP	3.00	1.25
❑	58	Willy Taveras SP	3.00	1.25
❑	59	Brady Clark SP	3.00	1.25
❑	60	Justin Morneau	.40	.15
❑	61	Xavier Nady	.40	.15
❑	62	Rich Harden	.40	.15
❑	63	Jack Wilson	.40	.15
❑	64	Brian Giles	.40	.15
❑	65	Jon Lieber SP	3.00	1.25
❑	66	Dan Johnson	.40	.15
❑	67	Billy Wagner	.40	.15
❑	68	Rickie Weeks	.40	.15
❑	69	Chris Ray (RC)	.40	.15
❑	70	Chris Shelton	.40	.15
❑	71	Dmitri Young	.40	.15
❑	72	Ivan Rodriguez	.60	.25
❑	73	Jeremy Bonderman	.40	.15
❑	74	Justin Verlander (RC)	1.50	.60
❑	75	Randy Johnson	1.00	.40
❑	76	Maggio Ordonez	.40	.15
❑	77	Brandon Inge	.40	.15
❑	78	Placido Polanco	.40	.15
❑	79	Ryan Howard	1.50	.60
❑	80	Jason Bay	.40	.15
❑	81	Sean Casey	.40	.15
❑	82	Jeremy Hermida (RC)	.40	.15
❑	83	Mike Cameron	.40	.15
❑	84	Trevor Hoffman	.40	.15
❑	85	Mike Matheny SP	3.00	1.25
❑	86	Steve Finley	.40	.15
❑	87	Adam Everett	.40	.15
❑	88	Jason Isringhausen	.40	.15
❑	89	Jonny Gomes	.40	.15
❑	90	Barry Zito	.40	.15
❑	91	Bobby Crosby	.40	.15
❑	92	Eric Chavez	.40	.15
❑	93	Frank Thomas	1.00	.40
❑	94	Huston Street	.40	.15
❑	95	Jorge Posada	.60	.25
❑	96	Casey Kotchman	.40	.15
❑	97	Darin Erstad	.40	.15
❑	98	Chipper Jones	1.00	.40
❑	99	Jeff Francoeur	1.00	.40
❑	100	Barry Bonds	2.00	.75
❑	101	Alfonso Soriano	.40	.15
❑	102	Brandon Claussen	.40	.15
❑	103	Aaron Boone	.40	.15
❑	104	Roger Clemens	1.50	.60
❑	105	Andy Pettitte SP	3.00	1.25
❑	106	Nick Johnson	.40	.15
❑	107	Tom Gordon	.40	.15
❑	108	Orlando Hernandez	.40	.15
❑	109	Francisco Rodriguez	.40	.15
❑	110	Orlando Cabrera	.40	.15
❑	111	Edgar Renteria	.40	.15
❑	112	Tim Hudson	.40	.15
❑	113	Coco Crisp	.40	.15
❑	114	Matt Clement	.40	.15
❑	115	Greg Maddux SP	5.00	2.00
❑	116	Paul Konerko	.40	.15
❑	117	Felipe Lopez	.40	.15
❑	118	Garrett Atkins	.40	.15
❑	119	Akinori Otsuka	.40	.15
❑	120	Craig Biggio	.60	.25
❑	121	Danys Baez	.40	.15
❑	122	Brad Penny	.40	.15
❑	123	Eric Gagne	.40	.15
❑	124	Lew Ford	.40	.15
❑	125	Mariano Rivera SP	3.00	1.25
❑	126	Carlos Beltran	.40	.15
❑	127	Pedro Martinez	.60	.25
❑	128	Todd Helton	.60	.25
❑	129	Aaron Rowand	.40	.15
❑	130	Mike Lieberthal	.40	.15
❑	131	Oliver Perez	.40	.15
❑	132	Ryan Klesko	.40	.15
❑	133	Randy Winn	.40	.15
❑	134	Yuniesky Betancourt	.40	.15
❑	135	David Eckstein SP	3.00	1.25
❑	136	Chad Orvella	.40	.15
❑	137	Toby Hall	.40	.15
❑	138	Hank Blalock	.40	.15
❑	139	B.J. Ryan	.40	.15
❑	140	Roy Halladay	.40	.15
❑	141	Livan Hernandez	.40	.15
❑	142	John Patterson	.40	.15
❑	143	Bengie Molina	.40	.15
❑	144	Brad Wilkerson	.40	.15
❑	145	Jorge Cantu SP	3.00	1.25
❑	146	Mark Mulder	.40	.15
❑	147	Felix Hernandez	.60	.25
❑	148	Paul Lo Duca	.40	.15
❑	149	Prince Fielder (RC)	1.50	.60
❑	150	Johnny Damon SP	3.00	1.25
❑	151	Ryan Langerhans SP	3.00	1.25
❑	152	Kris Benson SP	3.00	1.25
❑	153	Curt Schilling SP	3.00	1.25
❑	154	Manny Ramirez SP	3.00	1.25
❑	155	Robinson Cano SP	3.00	1.25
❑	156	Derrek Lee SP	3.00	1.25
❑	157	A.J. Pierzynski SP	3.00	1.25
❑	158	Adam Dunn SP	3.00	1.25
❑	159	Cliff Lee SP	3.00	1.25
❑	160	Grady Sizemore	.60	.25
❑	161	Jeff Francis	.40	.15
❑	162	Dontrelle Willis	.40	.15
❑	163	Brad Ausmus	.40	.15
❑	164	Preston Wilson	.40	.15
❑	165	Derek Lowe SP	3.00	1.25
❑	166	Chris Capuano	.40	.15
❑	167	Joe Mauer	.60	.25
❑	168	Torii Hunter	.40	.15
❑	169	Chase Utley	1.00	.40
❑	170	Zach Duke	.40	.15
❑	171	Jason Schmidt	.40	.15
❑	172	Adrian Beltre	.40	.15
❑	173	Eddie Guardado	.40	.15
❑	174	Richie Sexson	.40	.15
❑	175	Miguel Cabrera SP	3.00	1.25
❑	176	Julio Lugo	.40	.15
❑	177	Francisco Cordero	.40	.15
❑	178	Kevin Millwood	.40	.15
❑	179	A.J. Burnett	.40	.15
❑	180	Jose Guillen	.40	.15
❑	181	Larry Bigbie	.40	.15
❑	182	Raul Ibanez	.40	.15
❑	183	Jake Peavy	.40	.15
❑	184	Pat Burrell	.40	.15
❑	185	Tom Glavine SP	3.00	1.25
❑	186	J.J. Hardy	.40	.15
❑	187	Emil Brown	.40	.15
❑	188	Lance Berkman	.40	.15
❑	189	Marcus Giles	.40	.15
❑	190	Scott Podsednik	.40	.15
❑	191	Chone Figgins	.40	.15
❑	192	Melvin Mora	.40	.15
❑	193	Mark Loretta	.40	.15
❑	194	Carlos Zambrano	.40	.15
❑	195	Chien-Ming Wang	1.50	.60
❑	196	Mark Prior	.60	.25
❑	197	Bobby Jenks	.40	.15
❑	198	Brian Fuentes	.40	.15
❑	199	Garret Anderson	.40	.15
❑	200	Ichiro Suzuki	1.50	.60
❑	201	Brian Roberts	.40	.15
❑	202	Jason Kendall	.40	.15
❑	203	Milton Bradley	.40	.15
❑	204	Jimmy Rollins	.40	.15
❑	205	Brett Myers SP	3.00	1.25
❑	206	Joe Randa	.40	.15
❑	207	Mike Piazza	1.00	.40
❑	208	Matt Morris	.40	.15
❑	209	Omar Vizquel	.60	.25
❑	210	Jeremy Reed	.40	.15
❑	211	Chris Carpenter	.40	.15
❑	212	Jim Edmonds	.60	.25
❑	213	Scott Kazmir	.60	.25
❑	214	Travis Lee	.40	.15
❑	215	Michael Young SP	3.00	1.25
❑	216	Rod Barajas	.40	.15
❑	217	Gustavo Chacin	.40	.15
❑	218	Lyle Overbay	.40	.15
❑	219	Troy Glaus	.40	.15
❑	220	Chad Cordero	.40	.15
❑	221	Jose Vidro	.40	.15
❑	222	Scott Rolen	.60	.25
❑	223	Carl Crawford	.40	.15
❑	224	Rocco Baldelli	.40	.15
❑	225	Mike Mussina	.60	.25
❑	226	Kelvim Escobar	.40	.15
❑	227	Corey Patterson	.40	.15
❑	228	Javy Lopez	.40	.15
❑	229	Jonathan Papelbon (RC)	2.00	.75
❑	230	Aramis Ramirez	.40	.15
❑	231	Tadahito Iguchi	.40	.15
❑	232	Morgan Ensberg	.40	.15
❑	233	Mark Grudzielanek	.40	.15
❑	234	Mike Sweeney	.40	.15
❑	235	Shawn Chacon SP	3.00	1.25
❑	236	Nick Punto	.40	.15
❑	237	Geoff Jenkins	.40	.15
❑	238	Carlos Lee	.40	.15
❑	239	David DeJesus	.40	.15
❑	240	Brad Lidge	.40	.15
❑	241	Bob Wickman	.40	.15
❑	242	Jon Garland	.40	.15
❑	243	Kerry Wood	.40	.15
❑	244	Bronson Arroyo	.40	.15
❑	245	Matt Holliday SP	4.00	1.50
❑	246	Josh Beckett	.40	.15
❑	247	Johan Santana	.60	.25
❑	248	Rafael Furcal	.40	.15
❑	249	Shannon Stewart	.40	.15
❑	250	Gary Sheffield	.40	.15
❑	251	Josh Barfield SP (RC)	3.00	1.25
❑	252	Kenji Johjima RC	2.00	.75
❑	253	Ian Kinsler (RC)	.60	.25
❑	254	Brian Anderson (RC)	.40	.15
❑	255	Matt Cain SP (RC)	3.00	1.25
❑	256	Josh Willingham SP (RC)	3.00	1.25
❑	257	John Koronka (RC)	.40	.15
❑	258	Chris Duffy (RC)	.40	.15
❑	259	Brian McCann (RC)	.40	.15
❑	260	Hanley Ramirez (RC)	1.00	.40
❑	261	Hong-Chih Kuo (RC)	1.00	.40
❑	262	Francisco Liriano (RC)	1.00	.40
❑	263	Anderson Hernandez (RC)	.40	.15
❑	264	Ryan Zimmerman (RC)	2.50	1.00
❑	265	Brian Bannister SP (RC)	3.00	1.25
❑	266	Nolan Ryan	2.50	1.00
❑	267	Frank Robinson	.40	.15
❑	268	Roberto Clemente	3.00	1.25
❑	269	Hank Greenberg	1.00	.40
❑	270	Napolean Lajoie	.60	.25
❑	271	Lloyd Waner	.60	.25
❑	272	Paul Waner	.60	.25
❑	273	Frankie Frisch	.60	.25
❑	274	Moose Skowron	.40	.15
❑	275	Mickey Mantle	5.00	2.00
❑	276	Brooks Robinson	.60	.25
❑	277	Carl Yastrzemski	1.50	.60
❑	278	Johnny Pesky	.40	.15
❑	279	Stan Musial	1.50	.60
❑	280	Bill Mazeroski	.60	.25
❑	281	Harmon Killebrew	1.00	.40
❑	282	Monte Irvin	.40	.15
❑	283	Bob Gibson	.60	.25
❑	284	Ted Williams	2.50	1.00
❑	285	Yogi Berra SP	3.00	1.25
❑	286	Ernie Banks	1.00	.40
❑	287	Bobby Doerr	.40	.15
❑	288	Josh Gibson	1.00	.40
❑	289	Bob Feller	.40	.15
❑	290	Cal Ripken	4.00	1.50
❑	291	Bobby Cox MG	.40	.15
❑	292	Terry Francona MG	.40	.15
❑	293	Dusty Baker MG	.40	.15
❑	294	Ozzie Guillen MG	.40	.15
❑	295	Jim Leyland MG SP	3.00	1.25
❑	296	Willie Randolph MG	.40	.15
❑	297	Joe Torre MG	.60	.25
❑	298	Felipe Alou MG	.40	.15
❑	299	Tony La Russa MG	.40	.15
❑	300	Frank Robinson MG	.40	.15
❑	301	Mike Tyson	1.50	.60
❑	302	Duke Paoa Kahanamoku	.40	.15
❑	303	Jennie Finch	2.50	1.00
❑	304	Brandi Chastain	.40	.15
❑	305	Danica Patrick SP	8.00	3.00
❑	306	Wendy Guey	.40	.15
❑	307	Hulk Hogan	1.25	.50
❑	308	Carl Lewis	.30	.10
❑	309	John Wooden	.60	.25
❑	310	Randy Couture	.40	.15
❑	311	Andy Irons	.40	.15

❑ 312 Takeru Kobayashi 1.25 .50
❑ 313 Leon Spinks .20 .10
❑ 314 Jim Thorpe .60 .25
❑ 315 Jerry Bailey SP 3.00 1.25
❑ 316 Adrian C. Anson REP .60 .25
❑ 317 John M. Ward REP .40 .15
❑ 318 Mike Kelly REP
❑ 319 Capt. Jack Glasscock REP .40 .15
❑ 320 Aaron Hill .40 .15
❑ 321 Derrick Turnbow .40 .15
❑ 322 Nick Markakis (RC) .60 .25
❑ 323 Brad Hawpe .40 .15
❑ 324 Kevin Mench .40 .15
❑ 325 John Lackey SP 3.00 1.25
❑ 326 Chester A. Arthur .20 .07
❑ 327 Ulysses S. Grant .20 .10
❑ 328 Abraham Lincoln .30 .10
❑ 329 Grover Cleveland .20 .10
❑ 330 Benjamin Harrison .20 .10
❑ 331 Theodore Roosevelt .30 .10
❑ 332 Rutherford B. Hayes .20 .10
❑ 333 Chancellor Otto Von Bismarck .40 .15
❑ 334 Kaiser Wilhelm II .40 .15
❑ 335 Queen Victoria SP 3.00 1.25
❑ 336 Pope Leo XIII .40 .15
❑ 337 Thomas Edison .20 .10
❑ 338 Orville Wright .20 .10
❑ 339 Wilbur Wright .20 .10
❑ 340 Nathaniel Hawthorne .40 .15
❑ 341 Herman Melville .40 .15
❑ 342 Stonewall Jackson .20 .10
❑ 343 Robert E. Lee .20 .10
❑ 344 Andrew Carnegie .20 .10
❑ 345 John Rockefeller SP 3.00 1.25
❑ 346 Bob Fitzsimmons .20 .10
❑ 347 Billy The Kid .20 .10
❑ 348 Buffalo Bill .40 .15
❑ 349 Jesse James .20 .10
❑ 350 Statue Of Liberty .40 .15
❑ NNO Framed Originals 120.00 60.00

2007 Topps Allen and Ginter

❑ COMPLETE SET (350) 120.00 60.00
❑ COMP.SET w/o SP's (300) 50.00 20.00
❑ COMMON CARD .30 .12
❑ COMMON RC .50 .20
❑ COMMON SP 3.00 1.25
❑ SP STATED ODDS 1:2 HOBBY, 1:2 RETAIL
❑ SP CL: 5/43/48/58/63/107/110/119/130/137
❑ SP CL: 152/159/178/193/194/203/219/222
❑ SP CL: 224/243/263/301/302/303/306/307
❑ SP CL: 308/309/310/316/317/318/319/320
❑ SP CL: 321/322/325/326/327/330/331/334
❑ SP CL: 335/336/339/340/345/348/349/350
❑ FRAMED ORIGINALS ODDS 1:17,072 HOBBY
❑ FRAMED ORIGINALS ODDS 1:34,654 RETAIL
❑ 1 Ryan Howard 1.25 .50
❑ 2 Mike Gonzalez .30 .12
❑ 3 Austin Kearns .30 .12
❑ 4 Josh Hamilton (RC) 1.25 .50
❑ 5 Stephen Drew SP 3.00 1.25
❑ 6 Matt Murton .30 .12
❑ 7 Mickey Mantle 4.00 1.50
❑ 8 Howie Kendrick .30 .12
❑ 9 Alexander Graham Bell .30 .12
❑ 10 Jason Bay .30 .12
❑ 11 Hank Blalock .30 .12
❑ 12 Johan Santana .50 .20
❑ 13 Eleanor Roosevelt .30 .12
❑ 14 Kei Igawa RC 1.25 .50
❑ 15 Jeff Francoeur .75 .30
❑ 16 Carl Crawford .30 .12
❑ 17 Jhonny Peralta .30 .12
❑ 18 Mariano Rivera .75 .30
❑ 19 Mario Andretti .75 .30
❑ 20 Vladimir Guerrero .75 .30
❑ 21 Adam Wainwright .30 .12
❑ 22 Huston Street .30 .12
❑ 23 Cael Sanderson .30 .12
❑ 24 Susan B. Anthony .30 .12
❑ 25 Jay Payton .30 .12
❑ 26 P.T. Barnum .30 .12
❑ 27 Scott Podsednik .30 .12
❑ 28 Willie Randolph .30 .12
❑ 29 Sean Casey .30 .12
❑ 30 Eiffel Tower .30 .12
❑ 31 Kenji Johjima .75 .30
❑ 32 Felix Hernandez .50 .20
❑ 33 Elijah Dukes RC .75 .30
❑ 34 Mark Grudzielanek .30 .12
❑ 35 J.D. Drew .30 .12
❑ 36 Kevin Kouzmanoff .30 .12
❑ 37 Jonathan Papelbon .75 .30
❑ 38 Bobby Crosby .30 .12
❑ 39 Brooklyn Bridge .30 .12
❑ 40 Adam Dunn .30 .12
❑ 41 Lyle Overbay .30 .12
❑ 42 Brian Fuentes .30 .12
❑ 43 Scott Rolen SP 3.00 1.25
❑ 44 Matt Lindstrom (RC) .50 .20
❑ 45 Carlos Zambrano .30 .12
❑ 46 Cole Hamels .50 .20
❑ 47 Matt Kemp .30 .12
❑ 48 Gary Matthews SP 3.00 1.25
❑ 49 J.J. Putz .30 .12
❑ 50 Albert Pujols 1.50 .60
❑ 51 Dan Haren .30 .12
❑ 52 Aaron Harang .30 .12
❑ 53 Ferris Wheel .30 .12
❑ 54 Juan Rivera .30 .12
❑ 55 Ken Griffey Jr. 1.25 .50
❑ 56 Chien-Ming Wang 1.25 .50
❑ 57 Sean Henn (RC) .50 .20
❑ 58 Mike Mussina SP 3.00 1.25
❑ 59 Ian Snell .30 .12
❑ 60 Josh Barfield .30 .12
❑ 61 Justin Morneau .30 .12
❑ 62 Dwight D. Eisenhower .30 .12
❑ 63 Bengie Molina SP 3.00 1.25
❑ 64 Brett Myers .30 .12
❑ 65 Andy Marte .30 .12
❑ 66 Bill Hall .30 .12
❑ 67 Ryan Shealy .30 .12
❑ 68 Joe B. Scott .30 .12
❑ 69 Mike Rabelo RC .50 .20
❑ 70 Jermaine Dye .30 .12
❑ 71 Andre Ethier .50 .20
❑ 72 Bruce Lee 1.25 .50
❑ 73 Nick Punto .30 .12
❑ 74 Ervin Santana .30 .12
❑ 75 Troy Tulowitzki (RC) 1.25 .50
❑ 76 Garret Anderson .30 .12
❑ 77 Ryan Freel .30 .12
❑ 78 Carlos Guillen .30 .12
❑ 79 John Smoltz .50 .20
❑ 80 Chase Utley .75 .30
❑ 81 Mike Sweeney .30 .12
❑ 82 Joe Frazier .75 .30
❑ 83 Brad Lidge .30 .12
❑ 84 Casey Blake .30 .12
❑ 85 Ivan Rodriguez .50 .20
❑ 86 Roy Oswalt .30 .12
❑ 87 Akinori Iwamura RC 1.25 .50
❑ 88 Francisco Rodriguez .30 .12
❑ 89 John Lackey .30 .12
❑ 90 Miguel Cabrera .50 .20
❑ 91 Kevin Mench .30 .12
❑ 92 Victor Martinez .30 .12
❑ 93 Chad Tracy .30 .12
❑ 94 Charlie Manuel .30 .12
❑ 95 Hanley Ramirez .50 .20
❑ 96 Dontrelle Willis .30 .12
❑ 97 Doug Slaten RC .50 .20
❑ 98 Noah Lowry .30 .12
❑ 99 Shawn Green .30 .12
❑ 100 David Ortiz .75 .30
❑ 101 Mark Reynolds RC 2.00 .75
❑ 102 Preston Wilson .30 .12
❑ 103 Mohandas Gandhi .30 .12
❑ 104 Jeff Kent .30 .12
❑ 105 Lance Berkman .30 .12
❑ 106 C.C. Sabathia .30 .12
❑ 107 Jason Varitek SP 3.00 1.25
❑ 108 Mark Twain .30 .12
❑ 109 Melvin Mora .30 .12
❑ 110 Michael Young SP 3.00 1.25
❑ 111 Scott Hatteberg .30 .12
❑ 112 Erik Bedard .30 .12
❑ 113 Sitting Bull .30 .12
❑ 114 Homer Bailey (RC) .75 .30
❑ 115 Mark Teahen .30 .12
❑ 116 Ryan Braun (RC) 2.50 1.00
❑ 117 John Miles .30 .12
❑ 118 Coco Crisp .30 .12
❑ 119 Hunter Pence SP (RC) 5.00 2.00
❑ 120 Delmon Young (RC) .75 .30
❑ 121 Aramis Ramirez .30 .12
❑ 122 Magglio Ordonez .30 .12
❑ 123 Tadahito Iguchi .30 .12
❑ 124 Mark Selby .30 .12
❑ 125 Gil Meche .30 .12
❑ 126 Curt Schilling .50 .20
❑ 127 Brandon Phillips .30 .12
❑ 128 Milton Bradley .30 .12
❑ 129 Craig Monroe .30 .12
❑ 130 Jason Schmidt SP 3.00 1.25
❑ 131 Nick Markakis .50 .20
❑ 132 Paul Konerko .30 .12
❑ 133 Carlos Gomez RC .75 .30
❑ 134 Garrett Atkins .30 .12
❑ 135 Jered Weaver .50 .20
❑ 136 Edgar Renteria .30 .12
❑ 137 Jason Isringhausen SP 3.00 1.25
❑ 138 Ray Durham .30 .12
❑ 139 Bob Baffert .30 .12
❑ 140 Nick Swisher .30 .12
❑ 141 Brian McCann .30 .12
❑ 142 Orlando Hudson .30 .12
❑ 143 Brian Bannister .30 .12
❑ 144 Manny Acta .30 .12
❑ 145 Jose Vidro .30 .12
❑ 146 Carlos Quentin .30 .12
❑ 147 Billy Butler (RC) .75 .30
❑ 148 Kenny Rogers .30 .12
❑ 149 Tom Gordon .30 .12
❑ 150 Derek Jeter 2.00 .75
❑ 151 Bob Wickman .30 .12
❑ 152 Carlos Lee SP 3.00 1.25
❑ 153 Willy Taveras .30 .12
❑ 154 Paul LoDuca .30 .12
❑ 155 Ben Sheets .30 .12
❑ 156 Brian Roberts .30 .12
❑ 157 Freddy Adu .75 .30
❑ 158 Jason Kendall .30 .12
❑ 159 Michael Barrett SP 3.00 1.25
❑ 160 Frank Thomas .75 .30
❑ 161 Manny Ramirez .50 .20
❑ 162 Stanley Glenn .30 .12
❑ 163 Robinson Cano .50 .20
❑ 164 Phil Hughes (RC) 2.50 1.00
❑ 165 Joe Mauer .50 .20
❑ 166 Derrek Lee .30 .12
❑ 167 Jeff Weaver .30 .12
❑ 168 Joe Smith RC .30 .12
❑ 169 Louis Pasteur .30 .12
❑ 170 Gary Sheffield .30 .12
❑ 171 Luis Castillo .30 .12
❑ 172 Joe Torre .50 .20
❑ 173 Andy LaRoche (RC) .50 .20
❑ 174 Jamie Fischer .30 .12
❑ 175 Carlos Beltran .30 .12
❑ 176 Bronson Arroyo .30 .12
❑ 177 Rafael Furcal .30 .12
❑ 178 Juan Pierre SP 3.00 1.25
❑ 179 Matt Cain .50 .20
❑ 180 Alfonso Soriano .30 .12
❑ 181 Joe Borowski .30 .12
❑ 182 Conor Jackson .30 .12
❑ 183 Groundhog Day .30 .12

❑ 184 Pat Burrell .30 .12
❑ 185 Troy Glaus .30 .12
❑ 186 Joel Zumaya .50 .20
❑ 187 Russell Martin .30 .12
❑ 188 Josh Willingham .30 .12
❑ 189 Jarrod Saltalamacchia (RC) .75 .30
❑ 190 Scott Kazmir .50 .20
❑ 191 Jeremy Hermida .30 .12
❑ 192 Tower Bridge .30 .12
❑ 193 Rich Hill SP 3.00 1.25
❑ 194 Francisco Cordero SP 3.00 1.25
❑ 195 Mike Piazza .75 .30
❑ 196 Brad Ausmus .30 .12
❑ 197 Greg Louganis .30 .12
❑ 198 Frank Catalanotto .30 .12
❑ 199 Alejandro De Aza RC .75 .30
❑ 200 David Wright 1.25 .50
❑ 201 Freddy Sanchez .30 .12
❑ 202 Shea Hillenbrand .30 .12
❑ 203 Justin Verlander SP 3.00 1.25
❑ 204 Alex Gordon RC 2.50 1.00
❑ 205 Jimmy Rollins .30 .12
❑ 206 Mike Napoli .30 .12
❑ 207 Chris Burke .30 .12
❑ 208 Chipper Jones .75 .30
❑ 209 Randy Johnson .75 .30
❑ 210 Daisuke Matsuzaka RC 5.00 2.00
❑ 211 Orlando Cabrera .30 .12
❑ 212 B.J. Upton .30 .12
❑ 213 Lou Piniella MG .30 .12
❑ 214 Mike Cameron .30 .12
❑ 215 Luis Gonzalez .30 .12
❑ 216 Rickie Weeks .30 .12
❑ 217 Hideki Okajima RC 2.50 1.00
❑ 218 Johnny Estrada .30 .12
❑ 219 Dan Uggla SP 3.00 1.25
❑ 220 Ryan Zimmerman .75 .30
❑ 221 Tony Gwynn Jr. .30 .12
❑ 222 Rocco Baldelli SP 3.00 1.25
❑ 223 Xavier Nady .30 .12
❑ 224 Josh Bard SP 3.00 1.25
❑ 225 Raul Ibanez .30 .12
❑ 226 Chris Carpenter .30 .12
❑ 227 Matt DeSalvo (RC) .50 .20
❑ 228 Jack the Ripper .30 .12
❑ 229 Eric Chavez .30 .12
❑ 230 Jose Reyes .75 .30
❑ 231 Glen Perkins (RC) .50 .20
❑ 232 Gregg Zaun .30 .12
❑ 233 Jim Thome .50 .20
❑ 234 Joe Crede .30 .12
❑ 235 Barry Zito .30 .12
❑ 236 Yoel Hernandez RC .50 .20
❑ 237 Kelly Johnson .30 .12
❑ 238 Chris Young .30 .12
❑ 239 Fyodor Dostoevsky .30 .12
❑ 240 Miguel Tejada .30 .12
❑ 241 Doug Mientkiewicz .30 .12
❑ 242 Bobby Jenks .30 .12
❑ 243 Brad Hawpe SP 3.00 1.25
❑ 244 Jay Marshall RC .50 .20
❑ 245 Brad Penny .30 .12
❑ 246 Johnny Damon .50 .20
❑ 247 Dave Roberts .30 .12
❑ 248 Ron Washington .30 .12
❑ 249 Mike Aponte .30 .12
❑ 250 Brandon Webb .30 .12
❑ 251 Andy Pettitte .50 .20
❑ 252 Bud Black .30 .12
❑ 253 Michael Cuddyer .30 .12
❑ 254 Chris Stewart RC .50 .20
❑ 255 Mark Teixeira .50 .20
❑ 256 Hideki Matsui .75 .30
❑ 257 Curtis Granderson .30 .12
❑ 258 A.J. Pierzynski .30 .12
❑ 259 Tony La Russa .30 .12
❑ 260 Andruw Jones .50 .20
❑ 261 Torii Hunter .30 .12
❑ 262 Mark Loretta .30 .12
❑ 263 Jim Edmonds SP 3.00 1.25
❑ 264 Aaron Rowand .30 .12
❑ 265 Roy Halladay .30 .12
❑ 266 Freddy Garcia .30 .12
❑ 267 Reggie Sanders .30 .12
❑ 268 Washington Monument .30 .12
❑ 269 Franklin D. Roosevelt .30 .12
❑ 270 Alex Rodriguez 1.25 .50
❑ 271 Wes Helms .30 .12
❑ 272 Mia Hamm .75 .30
❑ 273 Jorge Posada .50 .20
❑ 274 Tim Lincecum RC 4.00 1.50
❑ 275 Bobby Abreu .30 .12
❑ 276 Zach Duke .30 .12
❑ 277 Carlos Delgado .30 .12
❑ 278 Julio Juarez .30 .12
❑ 279 Brandon Inge .30 .12
❑ 280 Todd Helton .50 .20
❑ 281 Marcus Giles .30 .12
❑ 282 Josh Johnson .30 .12
❑ 283 Chris Capuano .30 .12
❑ 284 B.J. Ryan .30 .12
❑ 285 Nick Johnson .30 .12
❑ 286 Khalil Greene .50 .20
❑ 287 Travis Hafner .30 .12
❑ 288 Ted Lilly .30 .12
❑ 289 Jim Leyland .30 .12
❑ 290 Prince Fielder .75 .30
❑ 291 Trevor Hoffman .30 .12
❑ 292 Brian Giles .30 .12
❑ 293 Omar Vizquel .50 .20
❑ 294 Julio Lugo .30 .12
❑ 295 Jake Peavy .30 .12
❑ 296 Adrian Beltre .30 .12
❑ 297 Josh Beckett .50 .20
❑ 298 Harry S. Truman .30 .12
❑ 299 Mark Buehrle .30 .12
❑ 300 Ichiro Suzuki 1.25 .50
❑ 301 Chris Duncan SP 3.00 1.25
❑ 302 Augie Garrido SP CO 3.00 1.25
❑ 303 Tyler Clippard SP (RC) 3.00 1.25
❑ 304 Ramon Hernandez .30 .12
❑ 305 Jeremy Bonderman .30 .12
❑ 306 Morgan Ensberg SP 3.00 1.25
❑ 307 J.J. Hardy SP 3.00 1.25
❑ 308 Mark Zupan SP 3.00 1.25
❑ 309 Laila Ali SP 3.00 1.25
❑ 310 Greg Maddux SP 4.00 1.50
❑ 311 David Ross .30 .12
❑ 312 Chris Duffy .30 .12
❑ 313 Moises Alou .30 .12
❑ 314 Yadier Molina .30 .12
❑ 315 Corey Patterson .30 .12
❑ 316 Dan O'Brien SP 3.00 1.25
❑ 317 Michael Bourn SP (RC) 3.00 1.25
❑ 318 Jonny Gomes SP 3.00 1.25
❑ 319 Ken Jennings SP 3.00 1.25
❑ 320 Barry Bonds SP 4.00 1.50
❑ 321 Gary Hall Jr. SP 3.00 1.25
❑ 322 Kerri Walsh SP 3.00 1.25
❑ 323 Craig Biggio .50 .20
❑ 324 Ian Kinsler .30 .12
❑ 325 Grady Sizemore SP 3.00 1.25
❑ 326 Alex Rios SP 3.00 1.25
❑ 327 Ted Toles SP 3.00 1.25
❑ 328 Jason Jennings .30 .12
❑ 329 Vernon Wells .30 .12
❑ 330 Bob Geren SP MG 3.00 1.25
❑ 331 Dennis Rodman SP 3.00 1.25
❑ 332 Tom Glavine .50 .20
❑ 333 Pedro Martinez .50 .20
❑ 334 Gustavo Molina SP RC 3.00 1.25
❑ 335 Bartolo Colon SP 3.00 1.25
❑ 336 Misty May-Treanor SP 3.00 1.25
❑ 337 Randy Winn .30 .12
❑ 338 Eric Byrnes .30 .12
❑ 339 Jason McElwain SP 3.00 1.25
❑ 340 Placido Polanco SP 3.00 1.25
❑ 341 Adrian Gonzalez .30 .12
❑ 342 Chad Cordero .30 .12
❑ 343 Jeff Francis .30 .12
❑ 344 Lastings Milledge .50 .20
❑ 345 Sammy Sosa SP 3.00 1.25
❑ 346 Jacque Jones .30 .12
❑ 347 Anibal Sanchez .30 .12
❑ 348 Roger Clemens SP 4.00 1.50
❑ 349 Jesse Litsch SP RC 3.00 1.25
❑ 350 Adam LaRoche SP 3.00 1.25
❑ NNO Framed Originals 100.00 50.00

2008 Topps Allen and Ginter

❑ COMP.SET w/o FUKU.(350) 100.00 50.00
❑ COMP.SET w/o SPs (300) 40.00 15.00
❑ COMMON CARD (1-300) .40 .15
❑ COMMON RC (1-300) 1.00 .40
❑ COMMON SP (301-350) 3.00 1.25
❑ SP STATED ODDS 1:2 HOBBY
❑ FRAMED ORIG.ODDS 1:26,500 HOBBY
❑ 1 Alex Rodriguez 1.50 .60
❑ 2 Juan Pierre .40 .15
❑ 3 Benjamin Franklin .60 .25
❑ 4 Roy Halladay .40 .15
❑ 5 C.C. Sabathia .40 .15
❑ 6 Brian Barton RC 1.50 .60
❑ 7 Mickey Mantle 4.00 1.50
❑ 8 Brian Bass (RC) 1.00 .40
❑ 9 Ian Kinsler .60 .25
❑ 10 Manny Ramirez 1.00 .40
❑ 11 Michael Cuddyer .40 .15
❑ 12 Ian Snell .40 .15
❑ 13 Mike Lowell .40 .15
❑ 14 Adrian Gonzalez .60 .25
❑ 15 B.J. Upton .60 .25
❑ 16 Hiroki Kuroda RC 1.50 .60
❑ 17 Kenji Johjima .40 .15
❑ 18 James Loney .60 .25
❑ 19 Albert Einstein .60 .25
❑ 20 Vladimir Guerrero 1.00 .40
❑ 21 Miguel Tejada .40 .15
❑ 22 Chin-Lung Hu (RC) 1.50 .60
❑ 23 A.J. Burnett .40 .15
❑ 24 Bobby Jenks .40 .15
❑ 25 Aramis Ramirez .40 .15
❑ 26 Corey Hart .40 .15
❑ 27 Brad Hawpe .40 .15
❑ 28 Adam LaRoche .40 .15
❑ 29 Empire State Building .60 .25
❑ 30 Miguel Cabrera .60 .25
❑ 31 Ryan Zimmerman .60 .25
❑ 32 Mark Ellis .40 .15
❑ 33 Nick Swisher .40 .15
❑ 34 Bill Hall .40 .15
❑ 35 Eric Byrnes .40 .15
❑ 36 Michael Young .40 .15
❑ 37 Pedro Martinez .60 .25
❑ 38 Andruw Jones .40 .15
❑ 39 J.R. Towles RC 2.50 1.00
❑ 40 Justin Upton 1.00 .40
❑ 41 Paul Konerko .40 .15
❑ 42 Luke Scott .40 .15
❑ 43 Rickie Weeks .40 .15
❑ 44 Adam Wainwright .40 .15
❑ 45 Justin Morneau .60 .25
❑ 46 Chris Young .40 .15
❑ 47 Chad Billingsley .40 .15
❑ 48 Kazuo Matsui .40 .15
❑ 49 Shane Victorino .40 .15
❑ 50 Albert Pujols 2.00 .75
❑ 51 Brian McCann .60 .25
❑ 52 Carlos Delgado .40 .15
❑ 53 Chien-Ming Wang 1.25 .50
❑ 54 Takashi Saito .40 .15
❑ 55 Josh Beckett .60 .25
❑ 56 Nick Johnson .40 .15
❑ 57 Ben Sheets .60 .25
❑ 58 Johnny Damon .60 .25

Card		
☐ 59 Nicky Hayden	.60	.25
☐ 60 Prince Fielder	1.00	.40
☐ 61 Adam Dunn	.40	.15
☐ 62 Dustin Pedroia	.60	.25
☐ 63 Jacoby Ellsbury	1.50	.60
☐ 64 Brad Penny	.40	.15
☐ 65 Victor Martinez	.40	.15
☐ 66 Joe Mauer	.60	.25
☐ 67 Kevin Kouzmanoff	.40	.15
☐ 68 Frank Thomas	1.00	.40
☐ 69 Stevie Williams	.60	.25
☐ 70 Matt Holliday	.60	.25
☐ 71 Fausto Carmona	.40	.15
☐ 72 Clayton Kershaw RC	3.00	1.25
☐ 73 Tadahito Iguchi	.40	.15
☐ 74 Khalil Greene	.60	.25
☐ 75 Travis Hafner	.40	.15
☐ 76 Jim Thome	.60	.25
☐ 77 Joba Chamberlain	1.50	.60
☐ 78 Ivan Rodriguez	.60	.25
☐ 79 Jose Guillen	.40	.15
☐ 80 Hanley Ramirez	1.00	.40
☐ 81 Vernon Wells	.40	.15
☐ 82 Jayson Nix (RC)	1.00	.40
☐ 83 Masahide Kobayashi RC	1.50	.60
☐ 84 Bonnie Blair	.60	.25
☐ 85 Curtis Granderson	.60	.25
☐ 86 Kelvim Escobar	.40	.15
☐ 87 Aaron Rowand	.40	.15
☐ 88 Troy Glaus	.60	.25
☐ 89 Billy Wagner	.40	.15
☐ 90 Jose Reyes	.60	.25
☐ 91 Scott Rolen	.60	.25
☐ 92 Dan Jansen	.60	.25
☐ 93 David Eckstein	.40	.15
☐ 94 Tom Gorzelanny	.40	.15
☐ 95 Garrett Atkins	.40	.15
☐ 96 Carlos Zambrano	.40	.15
☐ 97 Jeff Francis	.40	.15
☐ 98 Kazuo Fukumori RC	1.50	.60
☐ 99 John Bowker (RC)	1.00	.40
☐ 100 David Wright	1.25	.50
☐ 101 Adrian Beltre	.40	.15
☐ 102 Ray Durham	.40	.15
☐ 103 Kerri Strug	.60	.25
☐ 104 Orlando Hudson	.40	.15
☐ 105 Jonathan Papelbon	.60	.25
☐ 106 Brian Schneider	.40	.15
☐ 107 Matt Biondi	.60	.25
☐ 108 Alex Romero (RC)	1.00	.40
☐ 109 Joey Chestnut	.60	.25
☐ 110 Chase Utley	1.00	.40
☐ 111 Dan Uggla	.60	.25
☐ 112 Akinori Iwamura	.40	.15
☐ 113 Curt Schilling	.60	.25
☐ 114 Trevor Hoffman	.40	.15
☐ 115 Alex Rios	.40	.15
☐ 116 Mariano Rivera	1.00	.40
☐ 117 Jeff Niemann (RC)	1.00	.40
☐ 118 Geovany Soto	.40	.15
☐ 119 Billy Mitchell	.60	.25
☐ 120 Derek Jeter	2.50	1.00
☐ 121 Yovani Gallardo	.40	.15
☐ 122 The Gateway Arch	.60	.25
☐ 123 Josh Willingham	.40	.15
☐ 124 Greg Maddux	1.25	.50
☐ 125 John Lackey	.40	.15
☐ 126 Chris Young	.40	.15
☐ 127 Billy Butler	.40	.15
☐ 128 Golden Gate Bridge	.60	.25
☐ 129 Joey Votto (RC)	1.50	.60
☐ 130 Tim Wakefield	.40	.15
☐ 131 Todd Helton	.60	.25
☐ 132 Gary Matthews	.40	.15
☐ 133 Wild Bill Hickok	.60	.25
☐ 134 Jason Varitek	1.00	.40
☐ 135 Robinson Cano	.60	.25
☐ 136 Javier Vazquez	.40	.15
☐ 137 Annie Oakley	.60	.25
☐ 138 Andy Pettitte	.60	.25
☐ 139 Greg Reynolds RC	1.50	.60
☐ 140 Jimmy Rollins	.60	.25
☐ 141 Jermaine Dye	.40	.15
☐ 142 Eugenio Velez RC	1.00	.40
☐ 143 J.J. Hardy	.40	.15
☐ 144 Grand Canyon	.60	.25
☐ 145 Bobby Abreu	.40	.15
☐ 146 Scott Kazmir	.60	.25
☐ 147 James Fenimore Cooper	.60	.25
☐ 148 Mark Buehrle	.40	.15
☐ 149 Freddy Sanchez	.40	.15
☐ 150 Johan Santana	1.00	.40
☐ 151 Orlando Cabrera	.40	.15
☐ 152 Lyle Overbay	.40	.15
☐ 153 Clay Buchholz (RC)	2.50	1.00
☐ 154 Jesse Carlson RC	1.50	.60
☐ 155 Troy Tulowitzki	.60	.25
☐ 156 Delmon Young	.60	.25
☐ 157 Ross Ohlendorf RC	1.50	.60
☐ 158 Mary Shelley	.60	.25
☐ 159 James Shields	.40	.15
☐ 160 Alfonso Soriano	.60	.25
☐ 161 Randy Winn	.40	.15
☐ 162 Austin Kearns	.40	.15
☐ 163 Jeremy Hermida	.40	.15
☐ 164 Jorge Posada	.60	.25
☐ 165 Justin Verlander	.60	.25
☐ 166 Bram Stoker	.60	.25
☐ 167 Marie Curie	.60	.25
☐ 168 Melky Cabrera	.40	.15
☐ 169 Howie Kendrick	.40	.15
☐ 170 Jake Peavy	.40	.15
☐ 171 J.D. Drew	.40	.15
☐ 172 Pablo Picasso	.60	.25
☐ 173 Rick Ankiel	.40	.15
☐ 174 Jose Valverde	.40	.15
☐ 175 Chipper Jones	1.25	.50
☐ 176 Claude Monet	.60	.25
☐ 177 Evan Longoria RC	6.00	2.50
☐ 178 Jose Vidro	.40	.15
☐ 179 Hideki Matsui	1.00	.40
☐ 180 Ryan Braun	1.25	.50
☐ 181 Moises Alou	.40	.15
☐ 182 Nate McLouth	.40	.15
☐ 183 Harriet Tubman	.60	.25
☐ 184 Felix Hernandez	.60	.25
☐ 185 Carlos Pena	.40	.15
☐ 186 Jarrod Saltalamacchia	.40	.15
☐ 187 Les Miles	.60	.25
☐ 188 Kelly Johnson	.40	.15
☐ 189 Rampage Jackson	1.00	.40
☐ 190 Grady Sizemore	.60	.25
☐ 191 Francisco Cordero	.40	.15
☐ 192 Yunel Escobar	.40	.15
☐ 193 Edwin Encarnacion	.40	.15
☐ 194 Melvin Mora	.40	.15
☐ 195 Russ Martin	.40	.15
☐ 196 Edgar Renteria	.40	.15
☐ 197 Bigfoot	1.00	.40
☐ 198 Steve Holm RC	1.00	.40
☐ 199 Daric Barton (RC)	1.00	.40
☐ 200 David Ortiz	1.00	.40
☐ 201 Tim Lincecum	1.00	.40
☐ 202 Jeff King	.60	.25
☐ 203 Jhonny Peralta	.40	.15
☐ 204 Julio Lugo	.40	.15
☐ 205 J.J. Putz	.40	.15
☐ 206 Jeff Francoeur	.60	.25
☐ 207 Yuniesky Betancourt	.40	.15
☐ 208 Bruce Jenner	.60	.25
☐ 209 Clete Thomas RC	1.50	.60
☐ 210 Carlos Lee	.40	.15
☐ 211 Josh Hamilton	1.25	.50
☐ 212 Pyotr Ilyich Tchaikovsky	.60	.25
☐ 213 Brendan Harris	.40	.15
☐ 214 Dustin McGowan	.40	.15
☐ 215 Aaron Harang	.40	.15
☐ 216 Brett Myers	.40	.15
☐ 217 Friedrich Nietzsche	.60	.25
☐ 218 John Maine	.40	.15
☐ 219 Charles Dickens	.60	.25
☐ 220 Erik Bedard	.40	.15
☐ 221 Tim Hudson	.40	.15
☐ 222 Jeremy Bonderman	.40	.15
☐ 223 Nyjer Morgan (RC)	1.00	.40
☐ 224 Johnny Cueto RC	2.50	1.00
☐ 225 Roy Oswalt	.40	.15
☐ 226 Rich Hill	.40	.15
☐ 227 Frederick Douglass	.60	.25
☐ 228 Derek Lowe	.40	.15
☐ 229 Joe Blanton	.40	.15
☐ 230 Carlos Beltran	.40	.15
☐ 231 Huston Street	.40	.15
☐ 232 Davy Crockett	.60	.25
☐ 233 Pluto	.60	.25
☐ 234 Jered Weaver	.40	.15
☐ 235 Dan Haren	.40	.15
☐ 236 Alex Gordon	1.00	.40
☐ 237 Zack Greinke	.40	.15
☐ 238 Todd Clever	.60	.25
☐ 239 Brian Bannister	.40	.15
☐ 240 Magglio Ordonez	.60	.25
☐ 241 Ryan Garko	.40	.15
☐ 242 Takudzwa Ngwenya	.60	.25
☐ 243 Gil Meche	.40	.15
☐ 244 Mark Teahen	.40	.15
☐ 245 Carlos Guillen	.40	.15
☐ 246 Jeff Kent	.40	.15
☐ 247 Lisa Leslie	1.00	.40
☐ 248 Lastings Milledge	.40	.15
☐ 249 Serena Williams	1.25	.50
☐ 250 Ichiro Suzuki	1.50	.60
☐ 251 Matt Cain	.40	.15
☐ 252 Callix Crabbe (RC)	1.00	.40
☐ 253 Nick Blackburn RC	1.50	.60
☐ 254 Hunter Pence	1.00	.40
☐ 255 Cole Hamels	.60	.25
☐ 256 Garret Anderson	.40	.15
☐ 257 Luis Gonzalez	.40	.15
☐ 258 Eric Chavez	.40	.15
☐ 259 Francisco Rodriguez	.40	.15
☐ 260 Mark Teixeira	.60	.25
☐ 261 Bob Motley	.60	.25
☐ 262 Mark Spitz	.60	.25
☐ 263 Yadier Molina	.60	.25
☐ 264 Adam Jones	.40	.15
☐ 265 Brian Roberts	.60	.25
☐ 266 Matt Kemp	.40	.15
☐ 267 Andrew Miller	.60	.25
☐ 268 Dean Karnazes	.60	.25
☐ 269 Gary Sheffield	.40	.15
☐ 270 Lance Berkman	.60	.25
☐ 271 Paul Lo Duca	.40	.15
☐ 272 Matt Tolbert RC	1.50	.60
☐ 273 Jay Bruce (RC)	4.00	1.50
☐ 274 John Smoltz	1.00	.40
☐ 275 Nick Markakis	.60	.25
☐ 276 Oscar Wilde	.60	.25
☐ 277 Dontrelle Willis	.40	.15
☐ 278 Kevin Van Dam	.60	.25
☐ 279 Jim Edmonds	.60	.25
☐ 280 Brandon Webb	.40	.15
☐ 281 Joe Nathan	.40	.15
☐ 282 Jeanette Lee	.60	.25
☐ 283 Andrew Litz	.60	.25
☐ 284 Daisuke Matsuzaka	1.50	.60
☐ 285 Brandon Phillips	.40	.15
☐ 286 Pat Burrell	.40	.15
☐ 287 Chris Carpenter	.40	.15
☐ 288 Pete Weber	.60	.25
☐ 289 Derrek Lee	.60	.25
☐ 290 Ken Griffey Jr.	1.50	.60
☐ 291 Rich Thompson RC	1.00	.40
☐ 292 Elijah Dukes	.40	.15
☐ 293 Pedro Feliz	.40	.15
☐ 294 Torii Hunter	.40	.15
☐ 295 Chone Figgins	.40	.15
☐ 296 Hideki Okajima	.40	.15
☐ 297 Max Scherzer RC	2.50	1.00
☐ 298 Greg Smith RC	1.50	.60
☐ 299 Rafael Furcal	.40	.15
☐ 300 Ryan Howard	1.25	.50
☐ 301 Felix Pie SP	3.00	1.25
☐ 302 Brad Lidge SP	3.00	1.25
☐ 303 Jason Bay SP	3.00	1.25
☐ 304 Victor Hugo SP	3.00	1.25
☐ 305 Randy Johnson SP	3.00	1.25
☐ 306 Carlos Gomez SP	3.00	1.25
☐ 307 Pat Neshek SP	3.00	1.25
☐ 308 Jed Lowrie SP (RC)	3.00	1.25
☐ 309 Ryan Church SP	3.00	1.25
☐ 310 Michael Bourn SP	3.00	1.25
☐ 311 B.J. Ryan SP	3.00	1.25
☐ 312 Brandon Wood SP	3.00	1.25
☐ 313 Harriet Beecher Stowe SP	3.00	1.25
☐ 314 Mike Cameron SP	3.00	1.25
☐ 315 Tom Glavine SP	3.00	1.25
☐ 316 Ervin Santana SP	3.00	1.25

❑	317 Geoff Jenkins SP	3.00	1.25
❑	318 Andre Ethier SP	3.00	1.25
❑	319 Jason Giambi SP	3.00	1.25
❑	320 Dmitri Young SP	3.00	1.25
❑	321 Wily Mo Pena SP	3.00	1.25
❑	322 Hank Blalock SP	3.00	1.25
❑	323 James Bowie SP	3.00	1.25
❑	324 Casey Kotchman SP	3.00	1.25
❑	325 Stephen Drew SP	3.00	1.25
❑	326 Adam Kennedy SP	3.00	1.25
❑	327 A.J. Pierzynski SP	3.00	1.25
❑	328 Richie Sexson SP	3.00	1.25
❑	329 Jeff Clement SP (RC)	3.00	1.25
❑	330 Luke Hochevar SP RC	3.00	1.25
❑	331 Luis Castillo SP	3.00	1.25
❑	332 Dave Roberts SP	3.00	1.25
❑	333 Coco Crisp SP	3.00	1.25
❑	334 Jo-Jo Reyes SP	3.00	1.25
❑	335 Phil Hughes SP	3.00	1.25
❑	336 Allen Fisher SP	3.00	1.25
❑	337 Jason Schmidt SP	3.00	1.25
❑	338 Placido Polanco SP	3.00	1.25
❑	339 Jack Cust SP	3.00	1.25
❑	340 Carl Crawford SP	3.00	1.25
❑	341 Ty Wigginton SP	3.00	1.25
❑	342 Aubrey Huff SP	3.00	1.25
❑	343 Bengie Molina SP	3.00	1.25
❑	344 Matt Diaz SP	3.00	1.25
❑	345 Francisco Liriano SP	3.00	1.25
❑	346 Brandon Boggs SP (RC)	3.00	1.25
❑	347 David DeJesus SP	3.00	1.25
❑	348 Justin Masterson SP RC	4.00	1.50
❑	349 Frank Morris SP	3.00	1.25
❑	350 Kevin Youkilis SP	3.00	1.25
❑	NNO Kosuke Fukudome	25.00	10.00
❑	NNO Framed Original	100.00	50.00

1996 Topps Chrome

❑	COMPLETE SET (165)	50.00	20.00
❑	1 Tony Gwynn STP	1.25	.50
❑	2 Mike Piazza STP	2.00	.75
❑	3 Greg Maddux STP	2.00	.75
❑	4 Jeff Bagwell STP	.75	.30
❑	5 Larry Walker STP	.75	.30
❑	6 Barry Larkin STP	.75	.30
❑	7 Mickey Mantle COMM	10.00	4.00
❑	8 Tom Glavine STP	.75	.30
❑	9 Craig Biggio STP	.75	.30
❑	10 Barry Bonds STP	2.50	1.00
❑	11 Heathcliff Slocumb STP	.75	.30
❑	12 Matt Williams STP	.75	.30
❑	13 Todd Helton	4.00	1.50
❑	14 Paul Molitor	.75	.30
❑	15 Glenallen Hill	.75	.30
❑	16 Troy Percival	.75	.30
❑	17 Albert Belle	.75	.30
❑	18 Mark Wohlers	.75	.30
❑	19 Kirby Puckett	2.00	.75
❑	20 Mark Grace	1.25	.50
❑	21 J.T. Snow	.75	.30
❑	22 David Justice	.75	.30
❑	23 Mike Mussina	1.25	.50
❑	24 Bernie Williams	1.25	.50
❑	25 Ron Gant	.75	.30
❑	26 Carlos Baerga	.75	.30
❑	27 Gary Sheffield	.75	.30
❑	28 Cal Ripken 2131	6.00	2.50
❑	29 Frank Thomas	2.00	.75
❑	30 Kevin Seitzer	.75	.30
❑	31 Joe Carter	.75	.30
❑	32 Jeff King	.75	.30
❑	33 David Cone	.75	.30
❑	34 Eddie Murray	2.00	.75
❑	35 Brian Jordan	.75	.30
❑	36 Garret Anderson	.75	.30
❑	37 Hideo Nomo	2.00	.75
❑	38 Steve Finley	.75	.30
❑	39 Ivan Rodriguez	1.25	.50
❑	40 Quilvio Veras	.75	.30
❑	41 Mark McGwire	5.00	2.00
❑	42 Greg Vaughn	.75	.30
❑	43 Randy Johnson	2.00	.75
❑	44 David Segui	.75	.30
❑	45 Derek Bell	.75	.30
❑	46 John Valentin	.75	.30
❑	47 Steve Avery	.75	.30
❑	48 Tino Martinez	1.25	.50
❑	49 Shane Reynolds	.75	.30
❑	50 Jim Edmonds	.75	.30
❑	51 Raul Mondesi	.75	.30
❑	52 Chipper Jones	2.00	.75
❑	53 Gregg Jefferies	.75	.30
❑	54 Ken Caminiti	.75	.30
❑	55 Brian McRae	.75	.30
❑	56 Don Mattingly	5.00	2.00
❑	57 Marty Cordova	.75	.30
❑	58 Vinny Castilla	.75	.30
❑	59 John Smoltz	1.25	.50
❑	60 Travis Fryman	.75	.30
❑	61 Ryan Klesko	.75	.30
❑	62 Alex Fernandez	.75	.30
❑	63 Dante Bichette	.75	.30
❑	64 Eric Karros	.75	.30
❑	65 Roger Clemens	4.00	1.50
❑	66 Randy Myers	.75	.30
❑	67 Cal Ripken	6.00	2.50
❑	68 Rod Beck	.75	.30
❑	69 Jack McDowell	.75	.30
❑	70 Ken Griffey Jr.	3.00	1.25
❑	71 Ramon Martinez	.75	.30
❑	72 Jason Giambi	.75	.30
❑	73 Nomar Garciaparra	3.00	1.25
❑	74 Billy Wagner	.75	.30
❑	75 Todd Greene	.75	.30
❑	76 Paul Wilson	.75	.30
❑	77 Johnny Damon	1.25	.50
❑	78 Alan Benes	.75	.30
❑	79 Karim Garcia	.75	.30
❑	80 Derek Jeter	5.00	2.00
❑	81 Kirby Puckett STP	1.25	.50
❑	82 Cal Ripken STP	3.00	1.25
❑	83 Albert Belle STP	.75	.30
❑	84 Randy Johnson STP	1.25	.50
❑	85 Wade Boggs STP	.75	.30
❑	86 Carlos Baerga STP	.75	.30
❑	87 Ivan Rodriguez STP	.75	.30
❑	88 Mike Mussina STP	.75	.30
❑	89 Frank Thomas STP	1.25	.50
❑	90 Ken Griffey Jr. STP	2.00	.75
❑	91 Jose Mesa STP	.75	.30
❑	92 Matt Morris RC	5.00	2.00
❑	93 Mike Piazza	3.00	1.25
❑	94 Edgar Martinez	1.25	.50
❑	95 Chuck Knoblauch	.75	.30
❑	96 Andres Galarraga	.75	.30
❑	97 Tony Gwynn	2.50	1.00
❑	98 Lee Smith	.75	.30
❑	99 Sammy Sosa	2.00	.75
❑	100 Jim Thome	1.25	.50
❑	101 Bernard Gilkey	.75	.30
❑	102 Brady Anderson	.75	.30
❑	103 Rico Brogna	.75	.30
❑	104 Len Dykstra	.75	.30
❑	105 Tom Glavine	1.25	.50
❑	106 John Olerud	.75	.30
❑	107 Terry Steinbach	.75	.30
❑	108 Brian Hunter	.75	.30
❑	109 Jay Buhner	.75	.30
❑	110 Mo Vaughn	.75	.30
❑	111 Jose Mesa	.75	.30
❑	112 Brett Butler	.75	.30
❑	113 Chili Davis	.75	.30
❑	114 Paul O'Neill	1.25	.50
❑	115 Roberto Alomar	1.25	.50
❑	116 Barry Larkin	1.25	.50
❑	117 Marquis Grissom	.75	.30
❑	118 Will Clark	1.25	.50
❑	119 Barry Bonds	5.00	2.00
❑	120 Ozzie Smith	3.00	1.25
❑	121 Pedro Martinez	1.25	.50
❑	122 Craig Biggio	1.25	.50
❑	123 Moises Alou	.75	.30
❑	124 Robin Ventura	.75	.30
❑	125 Greg Maddux	3.00	1.25
❑	126 Tim Salmon	1.25	.50
❑	127 Wade Boggs	1.25	.50
❑	128 Ismael Valdes	.75	.30
❑	129 Juan Gonzalez	.75	.30
❑	130 Ray Lankford	.75	.30
❑	131 Bobby Bonilla	.75	.30
❑	132 Reggie Sanders	.75	.30
❑	133 Alex Ochoa	.75	.30
❑	134 Mark Loretta	.75	.30
❑	135 Jason Kendall	.75	.30
❑	136 Brooks Kieschnick	.75	.30
❑	137 Chris Snopek	.75	.30
❑	138 Ruben Rivera	.75	.30
❑	139 Jeff Suppan	.75	.30
❑	140 John Wasdin	.75	.30
❑	141 Jay Payton	.75	.30
❑	142 Rick Krivda	.75	.30
❑	143 Jimmy Haynes	.75	.30
❑	144 Ryne Sandberg	3.00	1.25
❑	145 Matt Williams	.75	.30
❑	146 Jose Canseco	1.25	.50
❑	147 Larry Walker	.75	.30
❑	148 Kevin Appier	.75	.30
❑	149 Javy Lopez	.75	.30
❑	150 Dennis Eckersley	.75	.30
❑	151 Jason Isringhausen	.75	.30
❑	152 Dean Palmer	.75	.30
❑	153 Jeff Bagwell	1.25	.50
❑	154 Rondell White	.75	.30
❑	155 Wally Joyner	.75	.30
❑	156 Fred McGriff	1.25	.50
❑	157 Cecil Fielder	.75	.30
❑	158 Rafael Palmeiro	1.25	.50
❑	159 Rickey Henderson	2.00	.75
❑	160 Shawon Dunston	.75	.30
❑	161 Manny Ramirez	1.25	.50
❑	162 Alex Gonzalez	.75	.30
❑	163 Shawn Green	.75	.30
❑	164 Kenny Lofton	.75	.30
❑	165 Jeff Conine	.75	.30

1997 Topps Chrome

❑	COMPLETE SET (165)	50.00	20.00
❑	1 Barry Bonds	5.00	2.00
❑	2 Jose Valentin	.75	.30
❑	3 Brady Anderson	.75	.30
❑	4 Wade Boggs	1.25	.50
❑	5 Andres Galarraga	.75	.30
❑	6 Rusty Greer	.75	.30
❑	7 Derek Jeter	5.00	2.00
❑	8 Ricky Bottalico	.75	.30
❑	9 Mike Piazza	3.00	1.25
❑	10 Garret Anderson	.75	.30
❑	11 Jeff King	.75	.30
❑	12 Kevin Appier	.75	.30
❑	13 Mark Grace	1.25	.50
❑	14 Jeff D'Amico	.75	.30
❑	15 Jay Buhner	.75	.30

❑	16 Hal Morris	.75	.30
❑	17 Harold Baines	.75	.30
❑	18 Jeff Cirillo	.75	.30
❑	19 Tom Glavine	1.25	.50
❑	20 Andy Pettitte	1.25	.50
❑	21 Mark McGwire	5.00	2.00
❑	22 Chuck Knoblauch	.75	.30
❑	23 Raul Mondesi	.75	.30
❑	24 Albert Belle	.75	.30
❑	25 Trevor Hoffman	.75	.30
❑	26 Eric Young	.75	.30
❑	27 Brian McRae	.75	.30
❑	28 Jim Edmonds	.75	.30
❑	29 Robb Nen	.75	.30
❑	30 Reggie Sanders	.75	.30
❑	31 Mike Lansing	.75	.30
❑	32 Craig Biggio	1.25	.50
❑	33 Ray Lankford	.75	.30
❑	34 Charles Nagy	.75	.30
❑	35 Paul Wilson	.75	.30
❑	36 John Wetteland	.75	.30
❑	37 Derek Bell	.75	.30
❑	38 Edgar Martinez	1.25	.50
❑	39 Rickey Henderson	2.00	.75
❑	40 Jim Thome	1.25	.50
❑	41 Frank Thomas	2.00	.75
❑	42 Jackie Robinson	2.00	.75
❑	43 Terry Steinbach	.75	.30
❑	44 Kevin Brown	.75	.30
❑	45 Joey Hamilton	.75	.30
❑	46 Travis Fryman	.75	.30
❑	47 Juan Gonzalez	.75	.30
❑	48 Ron Gant	.75	.30
❑	49 Greg Maddux	3.00	1.25
❑	50 Wally Joyner	.75	.30
❑	51 John Valentin	.75	.30
❑	52 Bret Boone	.75	.30
❑	53 Paul Molitor	.75	.30
❑	54 Rafael Palmeiro	1.25	.50
❑	55 Todd Hundley	.75	.30
❑	56 Ellis Burks	.75	.30
❑	57 Bernie Williams	1.25	.50
❑	58 Roberto Alomar	1.25	.50
❑	59 Jose Mesa	.75	.30
❑	60 Troy Percival	.75	.30
❑	61 John Smoltz	1.25	.50
❑	62 Jeff Conine	.75	.30
❑	63 Bernard Gilkey	.75	.30
❑	64 Mickey Tettleton	.75	.30
❑	65 Justin Thompson	.75	.30
❑	66 Tony Phillips	.75	.30
❑	67 Ryne Sandberg	3.00	1.25
❑	68 Geronimo Berroa	.75	.30
❑	69 Todd Hollandsworth	.75	.30
❑	70 Rey Ordonez	.75	.30
❑	71 Marquis Grissom	.75	.30
❑	72 Tino Martinez	1.25	.50
❑	73 Steve Finley	.75	.30
❑	74 Andy Benes	.75	.30
❑	75 Jason Kendall	.75	.30
❑	76 Johnny Damon	1.25	.50
❑	77 Jason Giambi	.75	.30
❑	78 Henry Rodriguez	.75	.30
❑	79 Edgar Renteria	.75	.30
❑	80 Ray Durham	.75	.30
❑	81 Gregg Jefferies	.75	.30
❑	82 Roberto Hernandez	.75	.30
❑	83 Joe Carter	.75	.30
❑	84 Jermaine Dye	.75	.30
❑	85 Julio Franco	.75	.30
❑	86 David Justice	.75	.30
❑	87 Jose Canseco	1.25	.50
❑	88 Paul O'Neill	1.25	.50
❑	89 Mariano Rivera	2.00	.75
❑	90 Bobby Higginson	.75	.30
❑	91 Mark Grudzielanek	.75	.30
❑	92 Lance Johnson	.75	.30
❑	93 Ken Caminiti	.75	.30
❑	94 Gary Sheffield	.75	.30
❑	95 Luis Castillo	.75	.30
❑	96 Scott Rolen	1.25	.50
❑	97 Chipper Jones	2.00	.75
❑	98 Darryl Strawberry	.75	.30
❑	99 Nomar Garciaparra	3.00	1.25
❑	100 Jeff Bagwell	1.25	.50
❑	101 Ken Griffey Jr.	3.00	1.25
❑	102 Sammy Sosa	2.00	.75
❑	103 Jack McDowell	.75	.30
❑	104 James Baldwin	.75	.30
❑	105 Rocky Coppinger	.75	.30
❑	106 Manny Ramirez	1.25	.50
❑	107 Tim Salmon	1.25	.50
❑	108 Eric Karros	.75	.30
❑	109 Brett Butler	.75	.30
❑	110 Randy Johnson	2.00	.75
❑	111 Pat Hentgen	.75	.30
❑	112 Rondell White	.75	.30
❑	113 Eddie Murray	2.00	.75
❑	114 Ivan Rodriguez	1.25	.50
❑	115 Jermaine Allensworth	.75	.30
❑	116 Ed Sprague	.75	.30
❑	117 Kenny Lofton	.75	.30
❑	118 Alan Benes	.75	.30
❑	119 Fred McGriff	1.25	.50
❑	120 Alex Fernandez	.75	.30
❑	121 Al Martin	.75	.30
❑	122 Devon White	.75	.30
❑	123 David Cone	.75	.30
❑	124 Karim Garcia	.75	.30
❑	125 Chili Davis	.75	.30
❑	126 Roger Clemens	4.00	1.50
❑	127 Bobby Bonilla	.75	.30
❑	128 Mike Mussina	1.25	.50
❑	129 Todd Walker	.75	.30
❑	130 Dante Bichette	.75	.30
❑	131 Carlos Baerga	.75	.30
❑	132 Matt Williams	.75	.30
❑	133 Will Clark	1.25	.50
❑	134 Dennis Eckersley	.75	.30
❑	135 Ryan Klesko	.75	.30
❑	136 Dean Palmer	.75	.30
❑	137 Javy Lopez	.75	.30
❑	138 Greg Vaughn	.75	.30
❑	139 Vinny Castilla	.75	.30
❑	140 Cal Ripken	6.00	2.50
❑	141 Ruben Rivera	.75	.30
❑	142 Mark Wohlers	.75	.30
❑	143 Tony Clark	.75	.30
❑	144 Jose Rosado	.75	.30
❑	145 Tony Gwynn	2.50	1.00
❑	146 Cecil Fielder	.75	.30
❑	147 Brian Jordan	.75	.30
❑	148 Bob Abreu	1.25	.50
❑	149 Barry Larkin	1.25	.50
❑	150 Robin Ventura	.75	.30
❑	151 John Olerud	.75	.30
❑	152 Rod Beck	.75	.30
❑	153 Vladimir Guerrero	2.00	.75
❑	154 Marty Cordova	.75	.30
❑	155 Todd Stottlemyre	.75	.30
❑	156 Hideo Nomo	2.00	.75
❑	157 Denny Neagle	.75	.30
❑	158 John Jaha	.75	.30
❑	159 Mo Vaughn	.75	.30
❑	160 Andruw Jones	1.25	.50
❑	161 Moises Alou	.75	.30
❑	162 Larry Walker	.75	.30
❑	163 Eddie Murray SH	1.25	.50
❑	164 Paul Molitor SH	.75	.30
❑	165 Checklist	.75	.30

1998 Topps Chrome

❑	COMPLETE SET (503)	150.00	60.00
❑	COMPLETE SERIES 1 (282)	80.00	30.00
❑	COMPLETE SERIES 2 (221)	80.00	30.00
❑	1 Tony Gwynn	2.50	1.00
❑	2 Larry Walker	.75	.30
❑	3 Billy Wagner	.75	.30
❑	4 Denny Neagle	.75	.30
❑	5 Vladimir Guerrero	2.00	.75
❑	6 Kevin Brown	1.25	.50
❑	8 Mariano Rivera	2.00	.75
❑	9 Tony Clark	.75	.30
❑	10 Deion Sanders	1.25	.50
❑	11 Francisco Cordova	.75	.30
❑	12 Matt Williams	.75	.30
❑	13 Carlos Baerga	.75	.30
❑	14 Mo Vaughn	.75	.30
❑	15 Bobby Witt	.75	.30
❑	16 Matt Stairs	.75	.30
❑	17 Chan Ho Park	.75	.30
❑	18 Mike Bordick	.75	.30
❑	19 Michael Tucker	.75	.30
❑	20 Frank Thomas	2.00	.75
❑	21 Roberto Clemente	5.00	2.00
❑	22 Dmitri Young	.75	.30
❑	23 Steve Trachsel	.75	.30
❑	24 Jeff Kent	.75	.30
❑	25 Scott Rolen	1.25	.50
❑	26 John Thomson	.75	.30
❑	27 Joe Vitiello	.75	.30
❑	28 Eddie Guardado	.75	.30
❑	29 Charlie Hayes	.75	.30
❑	30 Juan Gonzalez	.75	.30
❑	31 Garret Anderson	.75	.30
❑	32 John Jaha	.75	.30
❑	33 Omar Vizquel	1.25	.50
❑	34 Brian Hunter	.75	.30
❑	35 Jeff Bagwell	1.25	.50
❑	36 Mark Lemke	.75	.30
❑	37 Doug Glanville	.75	.30
❑	38 Dan Wilson	.75	.30
❑	39 Steve Cooke	.75	.30
❑	40 Chili Davis	.75	.30
❑	41 Mike Cameron	.75	.30
❑	42 F.P. Santangelo	.75	.30
❑	43 Brad Ausmus	.75	.30
❑	44 Gary DiSarcina	.75	.30
❑	45 Pat Hentgen	.75	.30
❑	46 Wilton Guerrero	.75	.30
❑	47 Devon White	.75	.30
❑	48 Danny Patterson	.75	.30
❑	49 Pat Meares	.75	.30
❑	50 Rafael Palmeiro	1.25	.50
❑	51 Mark Gardner	.75	.30
❑	52 Jeff Blauser	.75	.30
❑	53 Dave Hollins	.75	.30
❑	54 Carlos Garcia	.75	.30
❑	55 Ben McDonald	.75	.30
❑	56 John Mabry	.75	.30
❑	57 Trevor Hoffman	.75	.30
❑	58 Tony Fernandez	.75	.30
❑	59 Rich Loiselle RC	.75	.30
❑	60 Mark Leiter	.75	.30
❑	61 Pat Kelly	.75	.30
❑	62 John Flaherty	.75	.30
❑	63 Roger Bailey	.75	.30
❑	64 Tom Gordon	.75	.30
❑	65 Ryan Klesko	.75	.30
❑	66 Darryl Hamilton	.75	.30
❑	67 Jim Eisenreich	.75	.30
❑	68 Butch Huskey	.75	.30
❑	69 Mark Grudzielanek	.75	.30
❑	70 Marquis Grissom	.75	.30
❑	71 Mark McLemore	.75	.30
❑	72 Gary Gaetti	.75	.30
❑	73 Greg Gagne	.75	.30
❑	74 Lyle Mouton	.75	.30
❑	75 Jim Edmonds	.75	.30
❑	76 Shawn Green	.75	.30
❑	77 Greg Vaughn	.75	.30
❑	78 Terry Adams	.75	.30
❑	79 Kevin Polcovich	.75	.30
❑	80 Troy O'Leary	.75	.30
❑	81 Jeff Shaw	.75	.30
❑	82 Rich Becker	.75	.30
❑	83 David Wells	.75	.30
❑	84 Steve Karsay	.75	.30
❑	85 Charles Nagy	.75	.30
❑	86 B.J. Surhoff	.75	.30

❑ 87	Jamey Wright	.75	.30
❑ 88	James Baldwin	.75	.30
❑ 89	Edgardo Alfonzo	.75	.30
❑ 90	Jay Buhner	.75	.30
❑ 91	Brady Anderson	.75	.30
❑ 92	Scott Servais	.75	.30
❑ 93	Edgar Renteria	.75	.30
❑ 94	Mike Lieberthal	.75	.30
❑ 95	Rick Aguilera	.75	.30
❑ 96	Walt Weiss	.75	.30
❑ 97	Deivi Cruz	.75	.30
❑ 98	Kurt Abbott	.75	.30
❑ 99	Henry Rodriguez	.75	.30
❑ 100	Mike Piazza	3.00	1.25
❑ 101	Billy Taylor	.75	.30
❑ 102	Todd Zeile	.75	.30
❑ 103	Rey Ordonez	.75	.30
❑ 104	Willie Greene	.75	.30
❑ 105	Tony Womack	.75	.30
❑ 106	Mike Sweeney	.75	.30
❑ 107	Jeffrey Hammonds	.75	.30
❑ 108	Kevin Orie	.75	.30
❑ 109	Alex Gonzalez	.75	.30
❑ 110	Jose Canseco	1.25	.50
❑ 111	Paul Sorrento	.75	.30
❑ 112	Joey Hamilton	.75	.30
❑ 113	Brad Radke	.75	.30
❑ 114	Steve Avery	.75	.30
❑ 115	Esteban Loaiza	.75	.30
❑ 116	Stan Javier	.75	.30
❑ 117	Chris Gomez	.75	.30
❑ 118	Royce Clayton	.75	.30
❑ 119	Orlando Merced	.75	.30
❑ 120	Kevin Appier	.75	.30
❑ 121	Mel Nieves	.75	.30
❑ 122	Joe Girardi	.75	.30
❑ 123	Rico Brogna	.75	.30
❑ 124	Kent Mercker	.75	.30
❑ 125	Manny Ramirez	1.25	.50
❑ 126	Jeromy Burnitz	.75	.30
❑ 127	Kevin Foster	.75	.30
❑ 128	Matt Morris	.75	.30
❑ 129	Jason Dickson	.75	.30
❑ 130	Tom Glavine	1.25	.50
❑ 131	Wally Joyner	.75	.30
❑ 132	Rick Reed	.75	.30
❑ 133	Todd Jones	.75	.30
❑ 134	Dave Martinez	.75	.30
❑ 135	Sandy Alomar Jr.	.75	.30
❑ 136	Mike Lansing	.75	.30
❑ 137	Sean Berry	.75	.30
❑ 138	Doug Jones	.75	.30
❑ 139	Todd Stottlemyre	.75	.30
❑ 140	Jay Bell	.75	.30
❑ 141	Jaime Navarro	.75	.30
❑ 142	Chris Hoiles	.75	.30
❑ 143	Joey Cora	.75	.30
❑ 144	Scott Spiezio	.75	.30
❑ 145	Joe Carter	.75	.30
❑ 146	Jose Guillen	.75	.30
❑ 147	Damion Easley	.75	.30
❑ 148	Lee Stevens	.75	.30
❑ 149	Alex Fernandez	.75	.30
❑ 150	Randy Johnson	2.00	.75
❑ 151	J.T. Snow	.75	.30
❑ 152	Chuck Finley	.75	.30
❑ 153	Bernard Gilkey	.75	.30
❑ 154	David Segui	.75	.30
❑ 155	Dante Bichette	.75	.30
❑ 156	Kevin Stocker	.75	.30
❑ 157	Carl Everett	.75	.30
❑ 158	Jose Valentin	.75	.30
❑ 159	Pokey Reese	.75	.30
❑ 160	Derek Jeter	5.00	2.00
❑ 161	Roger Pavlik	.75	.30
❑ 162	Mark Wohlers	.75	.30
❑ 163	Ricky Bottalico	.75	.30
❑ 164	Ozzie Guillen	.75	.30
❑ 165	Mike Mussina	1.25	.50
❑ 166	Gary Sheffield	.75	.30
❑ 167	Hideo Nomo	2.00	.75
❑ 168	Mark Grace	1.25	.50
❑ 169	Aaron Sele	.75	.30
❑ 170	Darryl Kile	.75	.30
❑ 171	Shawn Estes	.75	.30
❑ 172	Vinny Castilla	.75	.30
❑ 173	Ron Coomer	.75	.30
❑ 174	Jose Rosado	.75	.30
❑ 175	Kenny Lofton	.75	.30
❑ 176	Jason Giambi	.75	.30
❑ 177	Hal Morris	.75	.30
❑ 178	Darren Bragg	.75	.30
❑ 179	Orel Hershiser	.75	.30
❑ 180	Ray Lankford	.75	.30
❑ 181	Hideki Irabu	.75	.30
❑ 182	Kevin Young	.75	.30
❑ 183	Javy Lopez	.75	.30
❑ 184	Jeff Montgomery	.75	.30
❑ 185	Mike Holtz	.75	.30
❑ 186	George Williams	.75	.30
❑ 187	Cal Eldred	.75	.30
❑ 188	Tom Candiotti	.75	.30
❑ 189	Glenallen Hill	.75	.30
❑ 190	Brian Giles	.75	.30
❑ 191	Dave Mlicki	.75	.30
❑ 192	Garrett Stephenson	.75	.30
❑ 193	Jeff Frye	.75	.30
❑ 194	Joe Oliver	.75	.30
❑ 195	Bob Hamelin	.75	.30
❑ 196	Luis Sojo	.75	.30
❑ 197	LaTroy Hawkins	.75	.30
❑ 198	Kevin Elster	.75	.30
❑ 199	Jeff Reed	.75	.30
❑ 200	Dennis Eckersley	.75	.30
❑ 201	Bill Mueller	.75	.30
❑ 202	Russ Davis	.75	.30
❑ 203	Armando Benitez	.75	.30
❑ 204	Quilvio Veras	.75	.30
❑ 205	Tim Naehring	.75	.30
❑ 206	Quinton McCracken	.75	.30
❑ 207	Raul Casanova	.75	.30
❑ 208	Matt Lawton	.75	.30
❑ 209	Luis Alicea	.75	.30
❑ 210	Luis Gonzalez	.75	.30
❑ 211	Allen Watson	.75	.30
❑ 212	Gerald Williams	.75	.30
❑ 213	David Bell	.75	.30
❑ 214	Todd Hollandsworth	.75	.30
❑ 215	Wade Boggs	1.25	.50
❑ 216	Jose Mesa	.75	.30
❑ 217	Jamie Moyer	.75	.30
❑ 218	Darren Daulton	.75	.30
❑ 219	Mickey Morandini	.75	.30
❑ 220	Rusty Greer	.75	.30
❑ 221	Jim Bullinger	.75	.30
❑ 222	Jose Offerman	.75	.30
❑ 223	Matt Karchner	.75	.30
❑ 224	Woody Williams	.75	.30
❑ 225	Mark Loretta	.75	.30
❑ 226	Mike Hampton	.75	.30
❑ 227	Willie Adams	.75	.30
❑ 228	Scott Hatteberg	.75	.30
❑ 229	Rich Amaral	.75	.30
❑ 230	Terry Steinbach	.75	.30
❑ 231	Glendon Rusch	.75	.30
❑ 232	Bret Boone	.75	.30
❑ 233	Robert Person	.75	.30
❑ 234	Jose Hernandez	.75	.30
❑ 235	Doug Drabek	.75	.30
❑ 236	Jason McDonald	.75	.30
❑ 237	Chris Widger	.75	.30
❑ 238	Tom Martin	.75	.30
❑ 239	Dave Burba	.75	.30
❑ 240	Pete Rose Jr. RC	.75	.30
❑ 241	Bobby Ayala	.75	.30
❑ 242	Tim Wakefield	.75	.30
❑ 243	Dennis Springer	.75	.30
❑ 244	Tim Belcher	.75	.30
❑ 245	J.Garland/G.Goetz	1.00	.40
❑ 246	L.Berkman/G.Davis	1.00	.40
❑ 247	V.Wells/A.Akin	1.00	.40
❑ 248	A.Kennedy/J.Romano	1.00	.40
❑ 249	J.Dellaero/T.Cameron	1.00	.40
❑ 250	J.Sandberg/A.Sanchez	1.00	.40
❑ 251	P.Ortega/J.Manias	1.00	.40
❑ 252	Mike Stoner RC	1.00	.40
❑ 253	J.Patterson/L.Rodriguez	1.00	.40
❑ 254	R.Minor RC/A.Beltre	1.00	.40
❑ 255	B.Grieve/D.Brown	1.00	.40
❑ 256	Wood/Pavano/Meche	1.00	.40
❑ 257	D.Ortiz/Sexson/Ward	5.00	2.00
❑ 258	J.Encarnacion/Winn/Vess	1.00	.40
❑ 259	Bens/T.Smith RC/C.Dunc RC	1.00	.40
❑ 260	Warren Morris RC	1.00	.40
❑ 261	B.Davis/Marrero/R.Hern.	1.00	.40
❑ 262	E.Chavez/R.Branyan	1.00	.40
❑ 263	Ryan Jackson RC	1.00	.40
❑ 264	B.Fuentes RC/Clement/Halladay	1.00	.40
❑ 265	Randy Johnson SH	1.25	.50
❑ 266	Kevin Brown SH	.75	.30
❑ 267	Ricardo Rincon SH	.75	.30
❑ 268	Nomar Garciaparra SH	2.00	.75
❑ 269	Tino Martinez SH	.75	.30
❑ 270	Chuck Knoblauch IL	.75	.30
❑ 271	Pedro Martinez IL	1.25	.50
❑ 272	Denny Neagle IL	.75	.30
❑ 273	Juan Gonzalez IL	.75	.30
❑ 274	Andres Galarraga IL	.75	.30
❑ 275	Checklist	.75	.30
❑ 276	Checklist	.75	.30
❑ 277	Moises Alou WS	.75	.30
❑ 278	Sandy Alomar Jr. WS	.75	.30
❑ 279	Gary Sheffield WS	.75	.30
❑ 280	Matt Williams WS	.75	.30
❑ 281	Livan Hernandez WS	.75	.30
❑ 282	Chad Ogea WS	.75	.30
❑ 283	Marlins Champs	.75	.30
❑ 284	Tino Martinez	1.25	.50
❑ 285	Roberto Alomar	1.25	.50
❑ 286	Jeff King	.75	.30
❑ 287	Brian Jordan	.75	.30
❑ 288	Darin Erstad	.75	.30
❑ 289	Ken Caminiti	.75	.30
❑ 290	Jim Thome	1.25	.50
❑ 291	Paul Molitor	.75	.30
❑ 292	Ivan Rodriguez	1.25	.50
❑ 293	Bernie Williams	1.25	.50
❑ 294	Todd Hundley	.75	.30
❑ 295	Andres Galarraga	.75	.30
❑ 296	Greg Maddux	3.00	1.25
❑ 297	Edgar Martinez	1.25	.50
❑ 298	Ron Gant	.75	.30
❑ 299	Derek Bell	.75	.30
❑ 300	Roger Clemens	4.00	1.50
❑ 301	Rondell White	.75	.30
❑ 302	Barry Larkin	1.25	.50
❑ 303	Robin Ventura	.75	.30
❑ 304	Jason Kendall	.75	.30
❑ 305	Chipper Jones	2.00	.75
❑ 306	John Franco	.75	.30
❑ 307	Sammy Sosa	2.00	.75
❑ 308	Troy Percival	.75	.30
❑ 309	Chuck Knoblauch	.75	.30
❑ 310	Ellis Burks	.75	.30
❑ 311	Al Martin	.75	.30
❑ 312	Tim Salmon	1.25	.50
❑ 313	Moises Alou	.75	.30
❑ 314	Lance Johnson	.75	.30
❑ 315	Justin Thompson	.75	.30
❑ 316	Will Clark	1.25	.50
❑ 317	Barry Bonds	5.00	2.00
❑ 318	Craig Biggio	1.25	.50
❑ 319	John Smoltz	1.25	.50
❑ 320	Cal Ripken	6.00	2.50
❑ 321	Ken Griffey Jr.	3.00	1.25
❑ 322	Paul O'Neill	1.25	.50
❑ 323	Todd Helton	1.25	.50
❑ 324	John Olerud	.75	.30
❑ 325	Mark McGwire	5.00	2.00
❑ 326	Jose Cruz Jr.	.75	.30
❑ 327	Jeff Cirillo	.75	.30
❑ 328	Dean Palmer	.75	.30
❑ 329	John Wetteland	.75	.30
❑ 330	Steve Finley	.75	.30
❑ 331	Albert Belle	.75	.30
❑ 332	Curt Schilling	.75	.30
❑ 333	Raul Mondesi	.75	.30
❑ 334	Andruw Jones	1.25	.50
❑ 335	Nomar Garciaparra	3.00	1.25
❑ 336	David Justice	.75	.30
❑ 337	Andy Pettitte	1.25	.50
❑ 338	Pedro Martinez	1.25	.50
❑ 339	Travis Miller	.75	.30
❑ 340	Chris Stynes	.75	.30
❑ 341	Gregg Jefferies	.75	.30
❑ 342	Jeff Fassero	.75	.30
❑ 343	Craig Counsell	.75	.30
❑ 344	Wilson Alvarez	.75	.30

❑ 345 Bip Roberts .75 .30
❑ 346 Kelvim Escobar .75 .30
❑ 347 Mark Bellhorn .75 .30
❑ 348 Cory Lidle RC 8.00 3.00
❑ 349 Fred McGriff 1.25 .50
❑ 350 Chuck Carr .75 .30
❑ 351 Bob Abreu .75 .30
❑ 352 Juan Guzman .75 .30
❑ 353 Fernando Vina .75 .30
❑ 354 Andy Benes .75 .30
❑ 355 Dave Nilsson .75 .30
❑ 356 Bobby Bonilla .75 .30
❑ 357 Ismael Valdes .75 .30
❑ 358 Carlos Perez .75 .30
❑ 359 Kirk Rueter .75 .30
❑ 360 Bartolo Colon .75 .30
❑ 361 Mel Rojas .75 .30
❑ 362 Johnny Damon 1.25 .50
❑ 363 Geronimo Berroa .75 .30
❑ 364 Reggie Sanders .75 .30
❑ 365 Jermaine Allensworth .75 .30
❑ 366 Orlando Cabrera .75 .30
❑ 367 Jorge Fabregas .75 .30
❑ 368 Scott Stahoviak .75 .30
❑ 369 Ken Cloude .75 .30
❑ 370 Donovan Osborne .75 .30
❑ 371 Roger Cedeno .75 .30
❑ 372 Neifi Perez .75 .30
❑ 373 Chris Holt .75 .30
❑ 374 Cecil Fielder .75 .30
❑ 375 Marty Cordova .75 .30
❑ 376 Tom Goodwin .75 .30
❑ 377 Jeff Suppan .75 .30
❑ 378 Jeff Brantley .75 .30
❑ 379 Mark Langston .75 .30
❑ 380 Shane Reynolds .75 .30
❑ 381 Mike Fetters .75 .30
❑ 382 Todd Greene .75 .30
❑ 383 Ray Durham .75 .30
❑ 384 Carlos Delgado .75 .30
❑ 385 Jeff D'Amico .75 .30
❑ 386 Brian McRae .75 .30
❑ 387 Alan Benes .75 .30
❑ 388 Heathcliff Slocumb .75 .30
❑ 389 Eric Young .75 .30
❑ 390 Travis Fryman .75 .30
❑ 391 David Cone .75 .30
❑ 392 Otis Nixon .75 .30
❑ 393 Jeremi Gonzalez .75 .30
❑ 394 Jeff Juden .75 .30
❑ 395 Jose Vizcaino .75 .30
❑ 396 Ugueth Urbina .75 .30
❑ 397 Ramon Martinez .75 .30
❑ 398 Robb Nen .75 .30
❑ 399 Harold Baines .75 .30
❑ 400 Delino DeShields .75 .30
❑ 401 John Burkett .75 .30
❑ 402 Sterling Hitchcock .75 .30
❑ 403 Mark Clark .75 .30
❑ 404 Terrell Wade .75 .30
❑ 405 Scott Brosius .75 .30
❑ 406 Chad Curtis .75 .30
❑ 407 Brian Johnson .75 .30
❑ 408 Roberto Kelly .75 .30
❑ 409 Dave Dellucci RC 1.25 .50
❑ 410 Michael Tucker .75 .30
❑ 411 Mark Kotsay .75 .30
❑ 412 Mark Lewis .75 .30
❑ 413 Ryan McGuire .75 .30
❑ 414 Shawon Dunston .75 .30
❑ 415 Brad Rigby .75 .30
❑ 416 Scott Erickson .75 .30
❑ 417 Bobby Jones .75 .30
❑ 418 Darren Oliver .75 .30
❑ 419 John Smiley .75 .30
❑ 420 T.J. Mathews .75 .30
❑ 421 Dustin Hermanson .75 .30
❑ 422 Mike Timlin .75 .30
❑ 423 Willie Blair .75 .30
❑ 424 Manny Alexander .75 .30
❑ 425 Bob Tewksbury .75 .30
❑ 426 Pete Schourek .75 .30
❑ 427 Reggie Jefferson .75 .30
❑ 428 Ed Sprague .75 .30
❑ 429 Jeff Conine .75 .30
❑ 430 Roberto Hernandez .75 .30
❑ 431 Tom Pagnozzi .75 .30
❑ 432 Jaret Wright .75 .30
❑ 433 Livan Hernandez .75 .30
❑ 434 Andy Ashby .75 .30
❑ 435 Todd Dunn .75 .30
❑ 436 Bobby Higginson .75 .30
❑ 437 Rod Beck .75 .30
❑ 438 Jim Leyritz .75 .30
❑ 439 Matt Williams .75 .30
❑ 440 Brett Tomko .75 .30
❑ 441 Joe Randa .75 .30
❑ 442 Chris Carpenter .75 .30
❑ 443 Dennis Reyes .75 .30
❑ 444 Al Leiter .75 .30
❑ 445 Jason Schmidt .75 .30
❑ 446 Ken Hill .75 .30
❑ 447 Shannon Stewart .75 .30
❑ 448 Enrique Wilson .75 .30
❑ 449 Fernando Tatis .75 .30
❑ 450 Jimmy Key .75 .30
❑ 451 Darrin Fletcher .75 .30
❑ 452 John Valentin .75 .30
❑ 453 Kevin Tapani .75 .30
❑ 454 Eric Karros .75 .30
❑ 455 Jay Bell .75 .30
❑ 456 Walt Weiss .75 .30
❑ 457 Devon White .75 .30
❑ 458 Carl Pavano .75 .30
❑ 459 Mike Lansing .75 .30
❑ 460 John Flaherty .75 .30
❑ 461 Richard Hidalgo .75 .30
❑ 462 Quinton McCracken .75 .30
❑ 463 Karim Garcia .75 .30
❑ 464 Miguel Cairo .75 .30
❑ 465 Edwin Diaz .75 .30
❑ 466 Bobby Smith .75 .30
❑ 467 Yamil Benitez .75 .30
❑ 468 Rich Butler RC .75 .30
❑ 469 Ben Ford RC .75 .30
❑ 470 Bubba Trammell .75 .30
❑ 471 Brent Brede .75 .30
❑ 472 Brooks Kieschnick .75 .30
❑ 473 Carlos Castillo .75 .30
❑ 474 Brad Radke SH .75 .30
❑ 475 Roger Clemens SH 2.00 .75
❑ 476 Curt Schilling SH .75 .30
❑ 477 John Olerud SH .75 .30
❑ 478 Mark McGwire SH 2.50 1.00
❑ 479 M.Piazza/K.Griffey Jr. IL 2.00 .75
❑ 480 J.Bagwell/F.Thomas IL 1.25 .50
❑ 481 C.Jones/N.Garciaparra IL 1.25 .50
❑ 482 L.Walker/J.Gonzalez IL .75 .30
❑ 483 G.Sheffield/T.Martinez IL .75 .30
❑ 484 D.Gib/M.Colem/Hutchins 1.00 .40
❑ 485 B.Rose/Looper/Politte 1.00 .40
❑ 486 E.Milton/Marquis/C.Lee 1.00 .40
❑ 487 Rob Fick RC 1.00 .40
❑ 488 A.Ramirez/A.Gonz/Casey 1.00 .40
❑ 489 D.Bridges/T.Drew RC 1.00 .40
❑ 490 D.McDonald/N.Ndungidi RC 1.00 .40
❑ 491 Ryan Anderson RC 1.00 .40
❑ 492 Troy Glaus RC 5.00 2.00
❑ 493 Dan Reichert RC 1.00 .40
❑ 494 Michael Cuddyer RC 2.50 1.00
❑ 495 Jack Cust RC 2.00 .75
❑ 496 Brian Anderson 1.00 .40
❑ 497 Tony Saunders 1.00 .40
❑ 498 J.Sandoval/V.Nunez 1.00 .40
❑ 499 B.Penny/N.Bierbrodt 1.00 .40
❑ 500 D.Carr/L.Cruz RC 1.00 .40
❑ 501 C.Bowers/M.McCain 1.00 .40
❑ 502 Checklist .75 .30
❑ 503 Checklist .75 .30
❑ 504 Alex Rodriguez 4.00 1.50

1999 Topps Chrome

❑ COMPLETE SET (462) 120.00 50.00
❑ COMPLETE SERIES 1 (241) 60.00 25.00
❑ COMPLETE SERIES 2 (221) 60.00 25.00
❑ COMMON CARD (1-6/8-463) .50 .20
❑ COMMON (205-212/425-437) 1.00 .40
❑ 1 Roger Clemens 4.00 1.50
❑ 2 Andres Galarraga .75 .30
❑ 3 Scott Brosius .75 .30
❑ 4 John Flaherty .50 .20

❑ 5 Jim Leyritz .50 .20
❑ 6 Ray Durham .75 .30
❑ 8 Jose Vizcaino .50 .20
❑ 9 Will Clark 1.25 .50
❑ 10 David Wells .75 .30
❑ 11 Jose Guillen .75 .30
❑ 12 Scott Hatteberg .50 .20
❑ 13 Edgardo Alfonzo .50 .20
❑ 14 Mike Bordick .50 .20
❑ 15 Manny Ramirez 1.25 .50
❑ 16 Greg Maddux 3.00 1.25
❑ 17 David Segui .50 .20
❑ 18 Darryl Strawberry .75 .30
❑ 19 Brad Radke .75 .30
❑ 20 Kerry Wood .75 .30
❑ 21 Matt Anderson .50 .20
❑ 22 Derrek Lee 1.25 .50
❑ 23 Mickey Morandini .50 .20
❑ 24 Paul Konerko .75 .30
❑ 25 Travis Lee .50 .20
❑ 26 Ken Hill .50 .20
❑ 27 Kenny Rogers .75 .30
❑ 28 Paul Sorrento .50 .20
❑ 29 Quilvio Veras .50 .20
❑ 30 Todd Walker .50 .20
❑ 31 Ryan Jackson .50 .20
❑ 32 John Olerud .75 .30
❑ 33 Doug Glanville .50 .20
❑ 34 Nolan Ryan 6.00 2.50
❑ 35 Ray Lankford .75 .30
❑ 36 Mark Loretta .50 .20
❑ 37 Jason Dickson .50 .20
❑ 38 Sean Bergman .50 .20
❑ 39 Quinton McCracken .50 .20
❑ 40 Bartolo Colon .75 .30
❑ 41 Brady Anderson .75 .30
❑ 42 Chris Stynes .50 .20
❑ 43 Jorge Posada 1.25 .50
❑ 44 Justin Thompson .50 .20
❑ 45 Johnny Damon 1.25 .50
❑ 46 Armando Benitez .50 .20
❑ 47 Brant Brown .50 .20
❑ 48 Charlie Hayes .50 .20
❑ 49 Darren Dreifort .50 .20
❑ 50 Juan Gonzalez .75 .30
❑ 51 Chuck Knoblauch .75 .30
❑ 52 Todd Helton 1.25 .50
❑ 53 Rick Reed .50 .20
❑ 54 Chris Gomez .50 .20
❑ 55 Gary Sheffield .75 .30
❑ 56 Rod Beck .50 .20
❑ 57 Rey Sanchez .50 .20
❑ 58 Garret Anderson .75 .30
❑ 59 Jimmy Haynes .50 .20
❑ 60 Steve Woodard .50 .20
❑ 61 Rondell White .75 .30
❑ 62 Vladimir Guerrero 2.00 .75
❑ 63 Eric Karros .75 .30
❑ 64 Russ Davis .50 .20
❑ 65 Mo Vaughn .75 .30
❑ 66 Sammy Sosa 2.00 .75
❑ 67 Troy Percival .75 .30
❑ 68 Kenny Lofton .75 .30
❑ 69 Bill Taylor .50 .20
❑ 70 Mark McGwire 5.00 2.00
❑ 71 Roger Cedeno .50 .20
❑ 72 Javy Lopez .75 .30
❑ 73 Damion Easley .50 .20

❑ 74	Andy Pettitte	1.25	.50
❑ 75	Tony Gwynn	2.50	1.00
❑ 76	Ricardo Rincon	.50	.20
❑ 77	F.P. Santangelo	.50	.20
❑ 78	Jay Bell	.75	.30
❑ 79	Scott Servais	.50	.20
❑ 80	Jose Canseco	1.25	.50
❑ 81	Roberto Hernandez	.50	.20
❑ 82	Todd Dunwoody	.50	.20
❑ 83	John Wetteland	.75	.30
❑ 84	Mike Caruso	.50	.20
❑ 85	Derek Jeter	5.00	2.00
❑ 86	Aaron Sele	.50	.20
❑ 87	Jose Lima	.50	.20
❑ 88	Ryan Christenson	.50	.20
❑ 89	Jeff Cirillo	.50	.20
❑ 90	Jose Hernandez	.50	.20
❑ 91	Mark Kotsay	.75	.30
❑ 92	Darren Bragg	.50	.20
❑ 93	Albert Belle	.75	.30
❑ 94	Matt Lawton	.50	.20
❑ 95	Pedro Martinez	1.25	.50
❑ 96	Greg Vaughn	.50	.20
❑ 97	Neifi Perez	.50	.20
❑ 98	Gerald Williams	.50	.20
❑ 99	Derek Bell	.50	.20
❑ 100	Ken Griffey Jr.	3.00	1.25
❑ 101	David Cone	.75	.30
❑ 102	Brian Johnson	.50	.20
❑ 103	Dean Palmer	.75	.30
❑ 104	Javier Valentin	.50	.20
❑ 105	Trevor Hoffman	.75	.30
❑ 106	Butch Huskey	.50	.20
❑ 107	Dave Martinez	.50	.20
❑ 108	Billy Wagner	.75	.30
❑ 109	Shawn Green	.75	.30
❑ 110	Ben Grieve	.50	.20
❑ 111	Tom Goodwin	.50	.20
❑ 112	Jaret Wright	.50	.20
❑ 113	Aramis Ramirez	.75	.30
❑ 114	Dmitri Young	.75	.30
❑ 115	Hideki Irabu	.50	.20
❑ 116	Roberto Kelly	.50	.20
❑ 117	Jeff Fassero	.50	.20
❑ 118	Mark Clark	.50	.20
❑ 119	Jason McDonald	.50	.20
❑ 120	Matt Williams	.75	.30
❑ 121	Dave Burba	.50	.20
❑ 122	Bret Saberhagen	.75	.30
❑ 123	Deivi Cruz	.50	.20
❑ 124	Chad Curtis	.50	.20
❑ 125	Scott Rolen	1.25	.50
❑ 126	Lee Stevens	.50	.20
❑ 127	J.T. Snow	.75	.30
❑ 128	Rusty Greer	.75	.30
❑ 129	Brian Meadows	.50	.20
❑ 130	Jim Edmonds	.75	.30
❑ 131	Ron Gant	.75	.30
❑ 132	A.J. Hinch	.50	.20
❑ 133	Shannon Stewart	.75	.30
❑ 134	Brad Fullmer	.50	.20
❑ 135	Cal Eldred	.50	.20
❑ 136	Matt Walbeck	.50	.20
❑ 137	Carl Everett	.75	.30
❑ 138	Walt Weiss	.50	.20
❑ 139	Fred McGriff	1.25	.50
❑ 140	Darin Erstad	.75	.30
❑ 141	Dave Nilsson	.50	.20
❑ 142	Eric Young	.50	.20
❑ 143	Dan Wilson	.50	.20
❑ 144	Jeff Reed	.50	.20
❑ 145	Brett Tomko	.50	.20
❑ 146	Terry Steinbach	.50	.20
❑ 147	Seth Greisinger	.50	.20
❑ 148	Pat Meares	.50	.20
❑ 149	Livan Hernandez	.75	.30
❑ 150	Jeff Bagwell	1.25	.50
❑ 151	Bob Wickman	.50	.20
❑ 152	Omar Vizquel	1.25	.50
❑ 153	Eric Davis	.75	.30
❑ 154	Larry Sutton	.50	.20
❑ 155	Magglio Ordonez	.75	.30
❑ 156	Eric Milton	.50	.20
❑ 157	Darren Lewis	.50	.20
❑ 158	Rick Aguilera	.50	.20
❑ 159	Mike Lieberthal	.75	.30
❑ 160	Robb Nen	.75	.30
❑ 161	Brian Giles	.75	.30
❑ 162	Jeff Brantley	.50	.20
❑ 163	Gary DiSarcina	.50	.20
❑ 164	John Valentin	.50	.20
❑ 165	Dave Dellucci	.50	.20
❑ 166	Chan Ho Park	.75	.30
❑ 167	Masato Yoshii	.50	.20
❑ 168	Jason Schmidt	.75	.30
❑ 169	LaTroy Hawkins	.50	.20
❑ 170	Bret Boone	.75	.30
❑ 171	Jerry DiPoto	.50	.20
❑ 172	Mariano Rivera	2.00	.75
❑ 173	Mike Cameron	.50	.20
❑ 174	Scott Erickson	.50	.20
❑ 175	Charles Johnson	.75	.30
❑ 176	Bobby Jones	.50	.20
❑ 177	Francisco Cordova	.50	.20
❑ 178	Todd Jones	.50	.20
❑ 179	Jeff Montgomery	.50	.20
❑ 180	Mike Mussina	1.25	.50
❑ 181	Bob Abreu	.75	.30
❑ 182	Ismael Valdes	.50	.20
❑ 183	Andy Fox	.50	.20
❑ 184	Woody Williams	.50	.20
❑ 185	Denny Neagle	.50	.20
❑ 186	Jose Valentin	.50	.20
❑ 187	Darrin Fletcher	.50	.20
❑ 188	Gabe Alvarez	.50	.20
❑ 189	Eddie Taubensee	.50	.20
❑ 190	Edgar Martinez	1.25	.50
❑ 191	Jason Kendall	.75	.30
❑ 192	Darryl Kile	.75	.30
❑ 193	Jeff King	.50	.20
❑ 194	Rey Ordonez	.50	.20
❑ 195	Andruw Jones	1.25	.50
❑ 196	Tony Fernandez	.50	.20
❑ 197	Jamey Wright	.50	.20
❑ 198	B.J. Surhoff	.75	.30
❑ 199	Vinny Castilla	.75	.30
❑ 200	David Wells HL	.50	.20
❑ 201	Mark McGwire HL	2.50	1.00
❑ 202	Sammy Sosa HL	1.25	.50
❑ 203	Roger Clemens HL	2.00	.75
❑ 204	Kerry Wood HL	.50	.20
❑ 205	L.Berkman/G.Kapler	1.00	.40
❑ 206	Alex Escobar RC	1.00	.40
❑ 207	Peter Bergeron RC	1.00	.40
❑ 208	M.Barrett/B.Davis/R.Fick	1.00	.40
❑ 209	J.Werth/Hernandez/Cline	1.00	.40
❑ 210	Ryan Anderson	1.00	.40
❑ 211	B.Penny/Dotel/Lincoln	1.00	.40
❑ 212	Chuck Abbott RC	1.00	.40
❑ 213	C.Jones/J.Urban RC	1.00	.40
❑ 214	T.Torcato/A.McDowell RC	1.00	.40
❑ 215	J.Tyner/J.McKinley RC	1.00	.40
❑ 216	M.Burch/S.Etherton RC	1.00	.40
❑ 217	R.Elder/M.Tucker RC	1.00	.40
❑ 218	J.M.Gold/R.Mills RC	1.00	.40
❑ 219	A.Brown/C.Freeman RC	1.00	.40
❑ 220A	Mark McGwire HR 1	50.00	20.00
❑ 220B	Mark McGwire HR 2	30.00	12.50
❑ 220C	Mark McGwire HR 3	30.00	12.50
❑ 220D	Mark McGwire HR 4	30.00	12.50
❑ 220E	Mark McGwire HR 5	30.00	12.50
❑ 220F	Mark McGwire HR 6	30.00	12.50
❑ 220G	Mark McGwire HR 7	30.00	12.50
❑ 220H	Mark McGwire HR 8	30.00	12.50
❑ 220I	Mark McGwire HR 9	30.00	12.50
❑ 220J	Mark McGwire HR 10	30.00	12.50
❑ 220K	Mark McGwire HR 11	30.00	12.50
❑ 220L	Mark McGwire HR 12	30.00	12.50
❑ 220M	Mark McGwire HR 13	30.00	12.50
❑ 220N	Mark McGwire HR 14	30.00	12.50
❑ 220O	Mark McGwire HR 15	30.00	12.50
❑ 220P	Mark McGwire HR 16	30.00	12.50
❑ 220Q	Mark McGwire HR 17	30.00	12.50
❑ 220R	Mark McGwire HR 18	30.00	12.50
❑ 220S	Mark McGwire HR 19	30.00	12.50
❑ 220T	Mark McGwire HR 20	30.00	12.50
❑ 220U	Mark McGwire HR 21	30.00	12.50
❑ 220V	Mark McGwire HR 22	30.00	12.50
❑ 220W	Mark McGwire HR 23	30.00	12.50
❑ 220X	Mark McGwire HR 24	30.00	12.50
❑ 220Y	Mark McGwire HR 25	30.00	12.50
❑ 220Z	Mark McGwire HR 26	30.00	12.50
❑ 220AA	Mark McGwire HR 27	30.00	12.50
❑ 220AB	Mark McGwire HR 28	30.00	12.50
❑ 220AC	Mark McGwire HR 29	30.00	12.50
❑ 220AD	Mark McGwire HR 30	30.00	12.50
❑ 220AE	Mark McGwire HR 31	30.00	12.50
❑ 220AF	Mark McGwire HR 32	30.00	12.50
❑ 220AG	Mark McGwire HR 33	30.00	12.50
❑ 220AH	Mark McGwire HR 34	30.00	12.50
❑ 220AI	Mark McGwire HR 35	30.00	12.50
❑ 220AJ	Mark McGwire HR 36	30.00	12.50
❑ 220AK	Mark McGwire HR 37	30.00	12.50
❑ 220AL	Mark McGwire HR 38	30.00	12.50
❑ 220AM	Mark McGwire HR 39	30.00	12.50
❑ 220AN	Mark McGwire HR 40	30.00	12.50
❑ 220AO	Mark McGwire HR 41	30.00	12.50
❑ 220AP	Mark McGwire HR 42	30.00	12.50
❑ 220AQ	Mark McGwire HR 43	30.00	12.50
❑ 220AR	Mark McGwire HR 44	30.00	12.50
❑ 220AS	Mark McGwire HR 45	30.00	12.50
❑ 220AT	Mark McGwire HR 46	30.00	12.50
❑ 220AU	Mark McGwire HR 47	30.00	12.50
❑ 220AV	Mark McGwire HR 48	30.00	12.50
❑ 220AW	Mark McGwire HR 49	30.00	12.50
❑ 220AX	Mark McGwire HR 50	30.00	12.50
❑ 220AY	Mark McGwire HR 51	30.00	12.50
❑ 220AZ	Mark McGwire HR 52	30.00	12.50
❑ 220BB	Mark McGwire HR 53	30.00	12.50
❑ 220CC	Mark McGwire HR 54	30.00	12.50
❑ 220DD	Mark McGwire HR 55	30.00	12.50
❑ 220EE	Mark McGwire HR 56	30.00	12.50
❑ 220FF	Mark McGwire HR 57	30.00	12.50
❑ 220GG	Mark McGwire HR 58	30.00	12.50
❑ 220HH	Mark McGwire HR 59	30.00	12.50
❑ 220II	Mark McGwire HR 60	30.00	12.50
❑ 220JJ	Mark McGwire HR 61	50.00	20.00
❑ 220KK	Mark McGwire HR 62	80.00	40.00
❑ 220LL	Mark McGwire HR 63	50.00	20.00
❑ 220MM	Mark McGwire HR 64	50.00	20.00
❑ 220NN	Mark McGwire HR 65	50.00	20.00
❑ 220OO	Mark McGwire HR 66	50.00	20.00
❑ 220PP	Mark McGwire HR 67	50.00	20.00
❑ 220QQ	Mark McGwire HR 68	50.00	20.00
❑ 220RR	Mark McGwire HR 69	50.00	20.00
❑ 220SS	Mark McGwire HR 70	120.00	60.00
❑ 221	Larry Walker LL	.50	.20
❑ 222	Bernie Williams LL	.75	.30
❑ 223	Mark McGwire LL	2.50	1.00
❑ 224	Ken Griffey Jr. LL	2.00	.75
❑ 225	Sammy Sosa LL	1.25	.50
❑ 226	Juan Gonzalez LL	.50	.20
❑ 227	Dante Bichette LL	.50	.20
❑ 228	Alex Rodriguez LL	2.00	.75
❑ 229	Sammy Sosa LL	1.25	.50
❑ 230	Derek Jeter LL	2.50	1.00
❑ 231	Greg Maddux LL	2.00	.75
❑ 232	Roger Clemens LL	2.00	.75
❑ 233	Ricky Ledee WS	.50	.20
❑ 234	Chuck Knoblauch WS	.50	.20
❑ 235	Bernie Williams WS	.75	.30
❑ 236	Tino Martinez WS	.75	.30
❑ 237	Orlando Hernandez WS	.75	.30
❑ 238	Scott Brosius WS	.50	.20
❑ 239	Andy Pettitte WS	.75	.30
❑ 240	Mariano Rivera WS	1.25	.50
❑ 241	Checklist	.50	.20
❑ 242	Checklist	.50	.20
❑ 243	Tom Glavine	1.25	.50
❑ 244	Andy Benes	.50	.20
❑ 245	Sandy Alomar Jr.	.50	.20
❑ 246	Wilton Guerrero	.50	.20
❑ 247	Alex Gonzalez	.50	.20
❑ 248	Roberto Alomar	1.25	.50
❑ 249	Ruben Rivera	.50	.20
❑ 250	Eric Chavez	.75	.30
❑ 251	Ellis Burks	.75	.30
❑ 252	Richie Sexson	.75	.30
❑ 253	Steve Finley	.75	.30
❑ 254	Dwight Gooden	.75	.30
❑ 255	Dustin Hermanson	.50	.20
❑ 256	Kirk Rueter	.50	.20
❑ 257	Steve Trachsel	.50	.20
❑ 258	Gregg Jefferies	.50	.20
❑ 259	Matt Stairs	.50	.20
❑ 260	Shane Reynolds	.50	.20
❑ 261	Gregg Olson	.50	.20
❑ 262	Kevin Tapani	.50	.20

263	Matt Morris	.75	.30
264	Carl Pavano	.75	.30
265	Nomar Garciaparra	3.00	1.25
266	Kevin Young	.75	.30
267	Rick Helling	.50	.20
268	Matt Franco	.50	.20
269	Brian McRae	.50	.20
270	Cal Ripken	6.00	2.50
271	Jeff Abbott	.50	.20
272	Tony Batista	.50	.20
273	Bill Simas	.50	.20
274	Brian Hunter	.50	.20
275	John Franco	.75	.30
276	Devon White	.75	.30
277	Rickey Henderson	2.00	.75
278	Chuck Finley	.75	.30
279	Mike Blowers	.50	.20
280	Mark Grace	1.25	.50
281	Randy Winn	.50	.20
282	Bobby Bonilla	.75	.30
283	David Justice	.75	.30
284	Shane Monahan	.50	.20
285	Kevin Brown	1.25	.50
286	Todd Zeile	.75	.30
287	Al Martin	.50	.20
288	Troy O'Leary	.50	.20
289	Darryl Hamilton	.50	.20
290	Tino Martinez	1.25	.50
291	David Ortiz	2.00	.75
292	Tony Clark	.50	.20
293	Ryan Minor	.50	.20
294	Mark Leiter	.50	.20
295	Wally Joyner	.75	.30
296	Cliff Floyd	.75	.30
297	Shawn Estes	.50	.20
298	Pat Hentgen	.50	.20
299	Scott Elarton	.50	.20
300	Alex Rodriguez	3.00	1.25
301	Ozzie Guillen	.75	.30
302	Hideo Nomo	2.00	.75
303	Ryan McGuire	.50	.20
304	Brad Ausmus	.75	.30
305	Alex Gonzalez	.50	.20
306	Brian Jordan	.75	.30
307	John Jaha	.50	.20
308	Mark Grudzielanek	.50	.20
309	Juan Guzman	.50	.20
310	Tony Womack	.50	.20
311	Dennis Reyes	.50	.20
312	Marty Cordova	.50	.20
313	Ramiro Mendoza	.50	.20
314	Robin Ventura	.75	.30
315	Rafael Palmeiro	1.25	.50
316	Ramon Martinez	.50	.20
317	Pedro Astacio	.50	.20
318	Dave Hollins	.50	.20
319	Tom Candiotti	.50	.20
320	Al Leiter	.75	.30
321	Rico Brogna	.50	.20
322	Reggie Jefferson	.50	.20
323	Bernard Gilkey	.50	.20
324	Jason Giambi	.75	.30
325	Craig Biggio	1.25	.50
326	Troy Glaus	1.25	.50
327	Delino DeShields	.50	.20
328	Fernando Vina	.50	.20
329	John Smoltz	1.25	.50
330	Jeff Kent	.75	.30
331	Roy Halladay	.75	.30
332	Andy Ashby	.50	.20
333	Tim Wakefield	.75	.30
334	Roger Clemens	4.00	1.50
335	Bernie Williams	1.25	.50
336	Desi Relaford	.50	.20
337	John Burkett	.50	.20
338	Mike Hampton	.75	.30
339	Royce Clayton	.50	.20
340	Mike Piazza	3.00	1.25
341	Jeremi Gonzalez	.50	.20
342	Mike Lansing	.50	.20
343	Jamie Moyer	.75	.30
344	Ron Coomer	.50	.20
345	Barry Larkin	1.25	.50
346	Fernando Tatis	.50	.20
347	Chili Davis	.75	.30
348	Bobby Higginson	.75	.30
349	Hal Morris	.50	.20
350	Larry Walker	.75	.30
351	Carlos Guillen	.75	.30
352	Miguel Tejada	.75	.30
353	Travis Fryman	.75	.30
354	Jarrod Washburn	.50	.20
355	Chipper Jones	2.00	.75
356	Todd Stottlemyre	.50	.20
357	Henry Rodriguez	.50	.20
358	Eli Marrero	.50	.20
359	Alan Benes	.50	.20
360	Tim Salmon	1.25	.50
361	Luis Gonzalez	.75	.30
362	Scott Spiezio	.50	.20
363	Chris Carpenter	.75	.30
364	Bobby Howry	.50	.20
365	Raul Mondesi	.75	.30
366	Ugueth Urbina	.50	.20
367	Tom Evans	.50	.20
368	Kerry Ligtenberg RC	.75	.30
369	Adrian Beltre	.75	.30
370	Ryan Klesko	.75	.30
371	Wilson Alvarez	.50	.20
372	John Thomson	.50	.20
373	Tony Saunders	.50	.20
374	Dave Mlicki	.50	.20
375	Ken Caminiti	.75	.30
376	Jay Buhner	.75	.30
377	Bill Mueller	.75	.30
378	Jeff Blauser	.50	.20
379	Edgar Renteria	.75	.30
380	Jim Thome	1.25	.50
381	Joey Hamilton	.50	.20
382	Calvin Pickering	.50	.20
383	Marquis Grissom	.75	.30
384	Omar Daal	.50	.20
385	Curt Schilling	.75	.30
386	Jose Cruz Jr.	.50	.20
387	Chris Widger	.50	.20
388	Pete Harnisch	.50	.20
389	Charles Nagy	.50	.20
390	Tom Gordon	.50	.20
391	Bobby Smith	.50	.20
392	Derrick Gibson	.50	.20
393	Jeff Conine	.75	.30
394	Carlos Perez	.50	.20
395	Barry Bonds	5.00	2.00
396	Mark McLemore	.50	.20
397	Juan Encarnacion	.50	.20
398	Wade Boggs	1.25	.50
399	Ivan Rodriguez	1.25	.50
400	Moises Alou	.75	.30
401	Jeromy Burnitz	.75	.30
402	Sean Casey	.75	.30
403	Jose Offerman	.50	.20
404	Joe Fontenot	.50	.20
405	Kevin Millwood	.75	.30
406	Lance Johnson	.50	.20
407	Richard Hidalgo	.50	.20
408	Mike Jackson	.50	.20
409	Brian Anderson	.50	.20
410	Jeff Shaw	.50	.20
411	Preston Wilson	.75	.30
412	Todd Hundley	.50	.20
413	Jim Parque	.50	.20
414	Justin Baughman	.50	.20
415	Dante Bichette	.75	.30
416	Paul O'Neill	1.25	.50
417	Miguel Cairo	.50	.20
418	Randy Johnson	2.00	.75
419	Jesus Sanchez	.50	.20
420	Carlos Delgado	.75	.30
421	Ricky Ledee	.50	.20
422	Orlando Hernandez	.75	.30
423	Frank Thomas	2.00	.75
424	Pokey Reese	.50	.20
425	C.Lee/M.Lowell	1.00	.40
426	M.Cuddyer/DeRosa/Hairston	1.00	.40
427	M.Anderson/Belliard/Cabrera	1.00	.40
428	M.Bowie/P.Norton RC/Wolf	1.00	.40
429	J.Cressend RC/Rocker	1.00	.40
430	R.Mateo/M.Zywica RC	1.00	.40
431	J.LaRue/LeCroy/Meluskey	1.00	.40
432	Gabe Kapler	1.00	.40
433	A.Kennedy/M.Lopez RC	1.00	.40
434	Jose Fernandez RC/C.Truby	1.00	.40
435	Doug Mientkiewicz RC	1.50	.60
436	R.Brown RC/V.Wells	1.00	.40
437	A.J. Burnett RC	2.00	.75
438	M.Belisle/M.Roney RC	1.00	.40
439	A.Kearns/C.George RC	4.00	1.50
440	N.Cornejo/N.Bump RC	1.00	.40
441	B.Lidge/M.Nannini RC	4.00	1.50
442	M.Holliday/J.Winchester RC	8.00	3.00
443	A.Everett/C.Ambres RC	1.50	.60
444	P.Burrell/E.Valent RC	4.00	1.50
445	Roger Clemens SK	2.00	.75
446	Kerry Wood SK	.50	.20
447	Curt Schilling SK	.50	.20
448	Randy Johnson SK	1.25	.50
449	Pedro Martinez SK	1.25	.50
450	Bagwell/Galar/McGwire AT	2.00	.75
451	Olerud/Thome/Martinez AT	.75	.30
452	ARod/Nomar/Jeter AT	2.50	1.00
453	Castilla/Jones/Rolen AT	1.25	.50
454	Sosa/Griffey/Gonzalez AT	2.00	.75
455	Bonds/Ramirez/Walker AT	2.50	1.00
456	Thomas/Salmon/Justice AT	2.00	.75
457	Lee/Helton/Grieve AT	.75	.30
458	Guerrero/Vaughn/B.Will AT	.75	.30
459	Piazza/IRod/Kendall AT	2.00	.75
460	Clemens/Wood/Maddux AT	2.00	.75
461A	Sammy Sosa HR 1	20.00	8.00
461B	Sammy Sosa HR 2	12.00	5.00
461C	Sammy Sosa HR 3	12.00	5.00
461D	Sammy Sosa HR 4	12.00	5.00
461E	Sammy Sosa HR 5	12.00	5.00
461F	Sammy Sosa HR 6	12.00	5.00
461G	Sammy Sosa HR 7	12.00	5.00
461H	Sammy Sosa HR 8	12.00	5.00
461I	Sammy Sosa HR 9	12.00	5.00
461J	Sammy Sosa HR 10	12.00	5.00
461K	Sammy Sosa HR 11	12.00	5.00
461L	Sammy Sosa HR 12	12.00	5.00
461M	Sammy Sosa HR 13	12.00	5.00
461N	Sammy Sosa HR 14	12.00	5.00
461O	Sammy Sosa HR 15	12.00	5.00
461P	Sammy Sosa HR 16	12.00	5.00
461Q	Sammy Sosa HR 17	12.00	5.00
461R	Sammy Sosa HR 18	12.00	5.00
461S	Sammy Sosa HR 19	12.00	5.00
461T	Sammy Sosa HR 20	12.00	5.00
461U	Sammy Sosa HR 21	12.00	5.00
461V	Sammy Sosa HR 22	12.00	5.00
461W	Sammy Sosa HR 23	12.00	5.00
461X	Sammy Sosa HR 24	12.00	5.00
461Y	Sammy Sosa HR 25	12.00	5.00
461Z	Sammy Sosa HR 26	12.00	5.00
461AA	Sammy Sosa HR 27	12.00	5.00
461AB	Sammy Sosa HR 28	12.00	5.00
461AC	Sammy Sosa HR 29	12.00	5.00
461AD	Sammy Sosa HR 30	12.00	5.00
461AE	Sammy Sosa HR 31	12.00	5.00
461AF	Sammy Sosa HR 32	12.00	5.00
461AG	Sammy Sosa HR 33	12.00	5.00
461AH	Sammy Sosa HR 34	12.00	5.00
461AI	Sammy Sosa HR 35	12.00	5.00
461AJ	Sammy Sosa HR 36	12.00	5.00
461AK	Sammy Sosa HR 37	12.00	5.00
461AL	Sammy Sosa HR 38	12.00	5.00
461AM	Sammy Sosa HR 39	12.00	5.00
461AN	Sammy Sosa HR 40	12.00	5.00
461AO	Sammy Sosa HR 41	12.00	5.00
461AP	Sammy Sosa HR 42	12.00	5.00
461AR	Sammy Sosa HR 43	12.00	5.00
461AS	Sammy Sosa HR 44	12.00	5.00
461AT	Sammy Sosa HR 45	12.00	5.00
461AU	Sammy Sosa HR 46	12.00	5.00
461AV	Sammy Sosa HR 47	12.00	5.00
461AW	Sammy Sosa HR 48	12.00	5.00
461AX	Sammy Sosa HR 49	12.00	5.00
461AY	Sammy Sosa HR 50	12.00	5.00
461AZ	Sammy Sosa HR 51	12.00	5.00
461BB	Sammy Sosa HR 52	12.00	5.00
461CC	Sammy Sosa HR 53	12.00	5.00
461DD	Sammy Sosa HR 54	12.00	5.00
461EE	Sammy Sosa HR 55	12.00	5.00
461FF	Sammy Sosa HR 56	12.00	5.00
461GG	Sammy Sosa HR 57	12.00	5.00
461HH	Sammy Sosa HR 58	12.00	5.00
461II	Sammy Sosa HR 59	12.00	5.00
461JJ	Sammy Sosa HR 60	12.00	5.00

Card		
❑ 461KK Sammy Sosa HR 61	20.00	8.00
❑ 461LL Sammy Sosa HR 62	30.00	12.50
❑ 461MM Sammy Sosa HR 63	20.00	8.00
❑ 461NN Sammy Sosa HR 64	20.00	8.00
❑ 461OO Sammy Sosa HR 65	20.00	8.00
❑ 461PP Sammy Sosa HR 66	60.00	30.00
❑ 462 Checklist	.50	.20
❑ 463 Checklist	.50	.20

1999 Topps Chrome Traded

Card		
❑ COMP.FACT SET (121)	100.00	50.00
❑ T1 Seth Etherton	.40	.15
❑ T2 Mark Harriger RC	.50	.20
❑ T3 Matt Wise RC	.50	.20
❑ T4 Carlos Eduardo Hernandez RC	.75	.30
❑ T5 Julio Lugo RC	1.25	.50
❑ T6 Mike Nannini	.40	.15
❑ T7 Justin Bowles RC	.50	.20
❑ T8 Mark Mulder RC	3.00	1.25
❑ T9 Roberto Vaz RC	.50	.20
❑ T10 Felipe Lopez RC	3.00	1.25
❑ T11 Matt Belisle	.40	.15
❑ T12 Micah Bowie	.40	.15
❑ T13 Ruben Quevedo RC	.50	.20
❑ T14 Jose Garcia RC	.50	.20
❑ T15 David Kelton RC	.50	.20
❑ T16 Phil Norton	.40	.15
❑ T17 Corey Patterson RC	2.00	.75
❑ T18 Ron Walker RC	.50	.20
❑ T19 Paul Hoover RC	.50	.20
❑ T20 Ryan Rupe RC	.50	.20
❑ T21 J.D. Closser RC	.75	.30
❑ T22 Rob Ryan RC	.50	.20
❑ T23 Steve Colyer RC	.50	.20
❑ T24 Bubba Crosby RC	1.25	.50
❑ T25 Luke Prokopec RC	.50	.20
❑ T26 Matt Blank RC	.50	.20
❑ T27 Josh McKinley	.40	.15
❑ T28 Nate Bump	.50	.20
❑ T29 Giuseppe Chiaramonte RC	.50	.20
❑ T30 Arturo McDowell	.40	.15
❑ T31 Tony Torcato	.40	.15
❑ T32 Dave Roberts RC	1.25	.50
❑ T33 C.C. Sabathia RC	5.00	2.00
❑ T34 Sean Spencer RC	.50	.20
❑ T35 Chip Ambres	.40	.15
❑ T36 A.J. Burnett	2.00	.75
❑ T37 Mo Bruce RC	.50	.20
❑ T38 Jason Tyner	.40	.15
❑ T39 Mamon Tucker	.40	.15
❑ T40 Sean Burroughs RC	1.25	.50
❑ T41 Kevin Eberwein RC	.50	.20
❑ T42 Junior Herndon RC	.50	.20
❑ T43 Bryan Wolff RC	.50	.20
❑ T44 Pat Burrell	3.00	1.25
❑ T45 Eric Valent	.75	.30
❑ T46 Carlos Pena RC	1.00	.40
❑ T47 Mike Zywica	.40	.15
❑ T48 Adam Everett	1.00	.40
❑ T49 Juan Pena RC	.50	.20
❑ T50 Adam Dunn RC	8.00	3.00
❑ T51 Austin Kearns	3.00	1.25
❑ T52 Jacobo Sequea RC	.50	.20
❑ T53 Choo Freeman	.60	.25
❑ T54 Jeff Winchester	.40	.15
❑ T55 Matt Burch	.50	.20
❑ T56 Chris George	.40	.15
❑ T57 Scott Mullen RC	.50	.20
❑ T58 Kit Pellow	.50	.20
❑ T59 Mark Quinn RC	.50	.20
❑ T60 Nate Cornejo	.50	.20
❑ T61 Ryan Mills	.40	.15
❑ T62 Kevin Beirne RC	.50	.20
❑ T63 Kip Wells RC	.75	.30
❑ T64 Juan Rivera RC	2.00	.75
❑ T65 Alfonso Soriano RC	10.00	4.00
❑ T66 Josh Hamilton RC	20.00	8.00
❑ T67 Josh Girdley RC	.50	.20
❑ T68 Kyle Snyder RC	.50	.20
❑ T69 Mike Paradis RC	.50	.20
❑ T70 Jason Jennings RC	1.25	.50
❑ T71 David Walling RC	.50	.20
❑ T72 Omar Ortiz RC	.50	.20
❑ T73 Jay Gehrke RC	.50	.20
❑ T74 Casey Burns RC	.50	.20
❑ T75 Carl Crawford RC	8.00	3.00
❑ T76 Reggie Sanders	.60	.25
❑ T77 Will Clark	1.00	.40
❑ T78 David Wells	.60	.25
❑ T79 Paul Konerko	.60	.25
❑ T80 Armando Benitez	.40	.15
❑ T81 Brant Brown	.40	.15
❑ T82 Mo Vaughn	.60	.25
❑ T83 Jose Canseco	1.00	.40
❑ T84 Albert Belle	.60	.25
❑ T85 Dean Palmer	.60	.25
❑ T86 Greg Vaughn	.40	.15
❑ T87 Mark Clark	.40	.15
❑ T88 Pat Meares	.40	.15
❑ T89 Eric Davis	.60	.25
❑ T90 Brian Giles	.60	.25
❑ T91 Jeff Brantley	.40	.15
❑ T92 Bret Boone	.60	.25
❑ T93 Ron Gant	.60	.25
❑ T94 Mike Cameron	.40	.15
❑ T95 Charles Johnson	.60	.25
❑ T96 Denny Neagle	.40	.15
❑ T97 Brian Hunter	.40	.15
❑ T98 Jose Hernandez	.40	.15
❑ T99 Rick Aguilera	.40	.15
❑ T100 Tony Batista	.40	.15
❑ T101 Roger Cedeno	.40	.15
❑ T102 Creighton Gubanich RC	.50	.20
❑ T103 Tim Belcher	.40	.15
❑ T104 Bruce Aven	.40	.15
❑ T105 Brian Daubach RC	.75	.30
❑ T106 Ed Sprague	.40	.15
❑ T107 Michael Tucker	.40	.15
❑ T108 Homer Bush	.40	.15
❑ T109 Armando Reynoso	.40	.15
❑ T110 Brook Fordyce	.40	.15
❑ T111 Matt Mantei	.40	.15
❑ T112 Dave Mlicki	.40	.15
❑ T113 Kenny Rogers	.60	.25
❑ T114 Livan Hernandez	.60	.25
❑ T115 Butch Huskey	.40	.15
❑ T116 David Segui	.40	.15
❑ T117 Darryl Hamilton	.40	.15
❑ T118 Terry Mulholland	.40	.15
❑ T119 Randy Velarde	.40	.15
❑ T120 Bill Taylor	.40	.15
❑ T121 Kevin Appier	.60	.25

2000 Topps Chrome

Card		
❑ COMPLETE SET (478)	160.00	60.00
❑ COMPLETE SERIES 1 (239)	80.00	30.00
❑ COMPLETE SERIES 2 (240)	80.00	30.00
❑ MCGWIRE MM SET (5)	50.00	20.00
❑ AARON MM SET (5)	40.00	15.00
❑ RIPKEN MM SET (5)	60.00	25.00
❑ BOGGS MM SET (5)	12.00	5.00
❑ GWYNN MM SET (5)	25.00	10.00
❑ GRIFFEY MM SET (5)	30.00	12.50
❑ BONDS MM SET (5)	50.00	20.00
❑ SOSA MM SET (5)	30.00	12.50
❑ JETER MM SET (5)	50.00	20.00
❑ A.ROD MM SET (5)	40.00	15.00
❑ 1 Mark McGwire	5.00	2.00
❑ 2 Tony Gwynn	2.50	1.00
❑ 3 Wade Boggs	1.25	.50
❑ 4 Cal Ripken	6.00	2.50
❑ 5 Matt Williams	.75	.30
❑ 6 Jay Buhner	.75	.30
❑ 7 Does Not Exist		
❑ 8 Jeff Conine	.75	.30
❑ 9 Todd Greene	.75	.30
❑ 10 Mike Lieberthal	.75	.30
❑ 11 Steve Avery	.75	.30
❑ 12 Bret Saberhagen	.75	.30
❑ 13 Magglio Ordonez	.75	.30
❑ 14 Brad Radke	.75	.30
❑ 15 Derek Jeter	5.00	2.00
❑ 16 Javy Lopez	.75	.30
❑ 17 Russ Davis	.75	.30
❑ 18 Armando Benitez	.75	.30
❑ 19 B.J. Surhoff	.75	.30
❑ 20 Darryl Kile	.75	.30
❑ 21 Mark Lewis	.75	.30
❑ 22 Mike Williams	.75	.30
❑ 23 Mark McLemore	.75	.30
❑ 24 Sterling Hitchcock	.75	.30
❑ 25 Darin Erstad	.75	.30
❑ 26 Ricky Gutierrez	.75	.30
❑ 27 John Jaha	.75	.30
❑ 28 Homer Bush	.75	.30
❑ 29 Darrin Fletcher	.75	.30
❑ 30 Mark Grace	1.25	.50
❑ 31 Fred McGriff	1.25	.50
❑ 32 Omar Daal	.75	.30
❑ 33 Eric Karros	.75	.30
❑ 34 Orlando Cabrera	.75	.30
❑ 35 J.T. Snow	.75	.30
❑ 36 Luis Castillo	.75	.30
❑ 37 Rey Ordonez	.75	.30
❑ 38 Bob Abreu	.75	.30
❑ 39 Warren Morris	.75	.30
❑ 40 Juan Gonzalez	.75	.30
❑ 41 Mike Lansing	.75	.30
❑ 42 Chili Davis	.75	.30
❑ 43 Dean Palmer	.75	.30
❑ 44 Hank Aaron	4.00	1.50
❑ 45 Jeff Bagwell	1.25	.50
❑ 46 Jose Valentin	.75	.30
❑ 47 Shannon Stewart	.75	.30
❑ 48 Kent Bottenfield	.75	.30
❑ 49 Jeff Shaw	.75	.30
❑ 50 Sammy Sosa	2.00	.75
❑ 51 Randy Johnson	2.00	.75
❑ 52 Benny Agbayani	.75	.30
❑ 53 Dante Bichette	.75	.30
❑ 54 Pete Harnisch	.75	.30
❑ 55 Frank Thomas	2.00	.75
❑ 56 Jorge Posada	1.25	.50
❑ 57 Todd Walker	.75	.30
❑ 58 Juan Encarnacion	.75	.30
❑ 59 Mike Sweeney	.75	.30
❑ 60 Pedro Martinez	1.25	.50
❑ 61 Lee Stevens	.75	.30
❑ 62 Brian Giles	.75	.30
❑ 63 Chad Ogea	.75	.30
❑ 64 Ivan Rodriguez	1.25	.50
❑ 65 Roger Cedeno	.75	.30
❑ 66 David Justice	.75	.30
❑ 67 Steve Trachsel	.75	.30
❑ 68 Eli Marrero	.75	.30
❑ 69 Dave Nilsson	.75	.30
❑ 70 Ken Caminiti	.75	.30
❑ 71 Tim Raines	.75	.30
❑ 72 Brian Jordan	.75	.30
❑ 73 Jeff Blauser	.75	.30

❑	74	Bernard Gilkey	.75	.30
❑	75	John Flaherty	.75	.30
❑	76	Brent Mayne	.75	.30
❑	77	Jose Vidro	.75	.30
❑	78	David Bell	.75	.30
❑	79	Bruce Aven	.75	.30
❑	80	John Olerud	.75	.30
❑	81	Pokey Reese	.75	.30
❑	82	Woody Williams	.75	.30
❑	83	Ed Sprague	.75	.30
❑	84	Joe Girardi	.75	.30
❑	85	Barry Larkin	1.25	.50
❑	86	Mike Caruso	.75	.30
❑	87	Bobby Higginson	.75	.30
❑	88	Roberto Kelly	.75	.30
❑	89	Edgar Martinez	1.25	.50
❑	90	Mark Kotsay	.75	.30
❑	91	Paul Sorrento	.75	.30
❑	92	Eric Young	.75	.30
❑	93	Carlos Delgado	.75	.30
❑	94	Troy Glaus	.75	.30
❑	95	Ben Grieve	.75	.30
❑	96	Jose Lima	.75	.30
❑	97	Garret Anderson	.75	.30
❑	98	Luis Gonzalez	.75	.30
❑	99	Carl Pavano	.75	.30
❑	100	Alex Rodriguez	3.00	1.25
❑	101	Preston Wilson	.75	.30
❑	102	Ron Gant	.75	.30
❑	103	Brady Anderson	.75	.30
❑	104	Rickey Henderson	2.00	.75
❑	105	Gary Sheffield	.75	.30
❑	106	Mickey Morandini	.75	.30
❑	107	Jim Edmonds	.75	.30
❑	108	Kris Benson	.75	.30
❑	109	Adrian Beltre	.75	.30
❑	110	Alex Fernandez	.75	.30
❑	111	Dan Wilson	.75	.30
❑	112	Mark Clark	.75	.30
❑	113	Greg Vaughn	.75	.30
❑	114	Neifi Perez	.75	.30
❑	115	Paul O'Neill	1.25	.50
❑	116	Jermaine Dye	.75	.30
❑	117	Todd Jones	.75	.30
❑	118	Terry Steinbach	.75	.30
❑	119	Greg Norton	.75	.30
❑	120	Curt Schilling	.75	.30
❑	121	Todd Zeile	.75	.30
❑	122	Edgardo Alfonzo	.75	.30
❑	123	Ryan McGuire	.75	.30
❑	124	Rich Aurilia	.75	.30
❑	125	John Smoltz	1.25	.50
❑	126	Bob Wickman	.75	.30
❑	127	Richard Hidalgo	.75	.30
❑	128	Chuck Finley	.75	.30
❑	129	Billy Wagner	.75	.30
❑	130	Todd Hundley	.75	.30
❑	131	Dwight Gooden	.75	.30
❑	132	Russ Ortiz	.75	.30
❑	133	Mike Lowell	.75	.30
❑	134	Reggie Sanders	.75	.30
❑	135	John Valentin	.75	.30
❑	136	Brad Ausmus	.75	.30
❑	137	Chad Kreuter	.75	.30
❑	138	David Cone	.75	.30
❑	139	Brook Fordyce	.75	.30
❑	140	Roberto Alomar	1.25	.50
❑	141	Charles Nagy	.75	.30
❑	142	Brian Hunter	.75	.30
❑	143	Mike Mussina	1.25	.50
❑	144	Robin Ventura	1.25	.50
❑	145	Kevin Brown	1.25	.50
❑	146	Pat Hentgen	.75	.30
❑	147	Ryan Klesko	.75	.30
❑	148	Derek Bell	.75	.30
❑	149	Andy Sheets	.75	.30
❑	150	Larry Walker	.75	.30
❑	151	Scott Williamson	.75	.30
❑	152	Jose Offerman	.75	.30
❑	153	Doug Mientkiewicz	.75	.30
❑	154	John Snyder RC	1.00	.40
❑	155	Sandy Alomar Jr.	.75	.30
❑	156	Joe Nathan	.75	.30
❑	157	Lance Johnson	.75	.30
❑	158	Odalis Perez	.75	.30
❑	159	Hideo Nomo	2.00	.75
❑	160	Steve Finley	.75	.30
❑	161	Dave Martinez	.75	.30
❑	162	Matt Walbeck	.75	.30
❑	163	Bill Spiers	.75	.30
❑	164	Fernando Tatis	.75	.30
❑	165	Kenny Lofton	.75	.30
❑	166	Paul Byrd	.75	.30
❑	167	Aaron Sele	.75	.30
❑	168	Eddie Taubensee	.75	.30
❑	169	Reggie Jefferson	.75	.30
❑	170	Roger Clemens	4.00	1.50
❑	171	Francisco Cordova	.75	.30
❑	172	Mike Bordick	.75	.30
❑	173	Wally Joyner	.75	.30
❑	174	Marvin Benard	.75	.30
❑	175	Jason Kendall	.75	.30
❑	176	Mike Stanley	.75	.30
❑	177	Chad Allen	.75	.30
❑	178	Carlos Beltran	.75	.30
❑	179	Deivi Cruz	.75	.30
❑	180	Chipper Jones	2.00	.75
❑	181	Vladimir Guerrero	2.00	.75
❑	182	Dave Burba	.75	.30
❑	183	Tom Goodwin	.75	.30
❑	184	Brian Daubach	.75	.30
❑	185	Jay Bell	.75	.30
❑	186	Roy Halladay	.75	.30
❑	187	Miguel Tejada	.75	.30
❑	188	Armando Rios	.75	.30
❑	189	Fernando Vina	.75	.30
❑	190	Eric Davis	.75	.30
❑	191	Henry Rodriguez	.75	.30
❑	192	Joe McEwing	.75	.30
❑	193	Jeff Kent	.75	.30
❑	194	Mike Jackson	.75	.30
❑	195	Mike Morgan	.75	.30
❑	196	Jeff Montgomery	.75	.30
❑	197	Jeff Zimmerman	.75	.30
❑	198	Tony Fernandez	.75	.30
❑	199	Jason Giambi	.75	.30
❑	200	Jose Canseco	1.25	.50
❑	201	Alex Gonzalez	.75	.30
❑	202	J.Cust/Colangelo/D.Brown	1.00	.40
❑	203	A.Soriano/F.Lopez	2.00	.75
❑	204	Durazo/Burrell/Johnson	1.50	.60
❑	205	John Sneed RC/K.Wells	1.00	.40
❑	206	Kalinowski/Tejera/Mears RC	1.00	.40
❑	207	L.Berkman/C.Patterson	1.50	.60
❑	208	K.Pellow/K.Barker/R.Branyan	1.00	.40
❑	209	B.Garbe/L.Bigbie RC	2.50	1.00
❑	210	B.Bradley RC/E.Munson	1.00	.40
❑	211	J.Girdley/K.Snyder	1.00	.40
❑	212	Chance Caple RC/J.Jennings	1.00	.40
❑	213	B.Myers/R.Christianson RC	4.00	1.50
❑	214	J.Stumm/R.Purvis RC	1.00	.40
❑	215	D.Walling/M.Paradis	1.00	.40
❑	216	O.Ortiz/J.Gehrke	1.00	.40
❑	217	David Cone HL	.75	.30
❑	218	Jose Jimenez HL	.75	.30
❑	219	Chris Singleton HL	.75	.30
❑	220	Fernando Tatis HL	.75	.30
❑	221	Todd Helton HL	.75	.30
❑	222	Kevin Millwood DIV	.75	.30
❑	223	Todd Pratt DIV	.75	.30
❑	224	Orlando Hernandez DIV	.75	.30
❑	225	Pedro Martinez DIV	1.25	.50
❑	226	Tom Glavine LCS	.75	.30
❑	227	Bernie Williams LCS	.75	.30
❑	228	Mariano Rivera WS	1.25	.50
❑	229	Tony Gwynn 20CB	2.50	1.00
❑	230	Wade Boggs 20CB	1.25	.50
❑	231	Lance Johnson CB	.75	.30
❑	232	Mark McGwire 20CB	5.00	2.00
❑	233	Rickey Henderson 20CB	2.00	.75
❑	234	Rickey Henderson 20CB	2.00	.75
❑	235	Roger Clemens 20CB	4.00	1.50
❑	236A	M.McGwire MM 1st HR	12.00	5.00
❑	236B	M.McGwire MM 1987 ROY	12.00	5.00
❑	236C	M.McGwire MM 62nd HR	12.00	5.00
❑	236D	M.McGwire MM 70th HR	12.00	5.00
❑	236E	M.McGwire MM 500th HR	12.00	5.00
❑	237A	H.Aaron MM 1st Career HR	10.00	4.00
❑	237B	H.Aaron MM 1957 MVP	10.00	4.00
❑	237C	H.Aaron MM 3000th Hit	10.00	4.00
❑	237D	H.Aaron MM 715th HR	10.00	4.00
❑	237E	H.Aaron MM 755th HR	10.00	4.00
❑	238A	C.Ripken MM 1982 ROY	15.00	6.00
❑	238B	C.Ripken MM 1991 MVP	15.00	6.00
❑	238C	C.Ripken MM 2131 Game	15.00	6.00
❑	238D	C.Ripken MM Streak Ends	15.00	6.00
❑	238E	C.Ripken MM 400th HR	15.00	6.00
❑	239A	W.Boggs MM 1983 Batting	3.00	1.25
❑	239B	W.Boggs MM 1988 Batting	3.00	1.25
❑	239C	W.Boggs MM 2000th Hit	3.00	1.25
❑	239D	W.Boggs MM 1996 Champs	3.00	1.25
❑	239E	W.Boggs MM 3000th Hit	3.00	1.25
❑	240A	T.Gwynn MM 1984 Batting	6.00	2.50
❑	240B	T.Gwynn MM 1984 NLCS	6.00	2.50
❑	240C	T.Gwynn MM 1995 Batting	6.00	2.50
❑	240D	T.Gwynn MM 1998 NLCS	6.00	2.50
❑	240E	T.Gwynn MM 3000th Hit	6.00	2.50
❑	241	Tom Glavine	1.25	.50
❑	242	David Wells	.75	.30
❑	243	Kevin Appier	.75	.30
❑	244	Troy Percival	.75	.30
❑	245	Ray Lankford	.75	.30
❑	246	Marquis Grissom	.75	.30
❑	247	Randy Winn	.75	.30
❑	248	Miguel Batista	.75	.30
❑	249	Darren Dreifort	.75	.30
❑	250	Barry Bonds	4.00	1.50
❑	251	Harold Baines	.75	.30
❑	252	Cliff Floyd	.75	.30
❑	253	Freddy Garcia	.75	.30
❑	254	Kenny Rogers	.75	.30
❑	255	Ben Davis	.75	.30
❑	256	Charles Johnson	.75	.30
❑	257	Bubba Trammell	.75	.30
❑	258	Desi Relaford	.75	.30
❑	259	Al Martin	.75	.30
❑	260	Andy Pettitte	1.25	.50
❑	261	Carlos Lee	.75	.30
❑	262	Matt Lawton	.75	.30
❑	263	Andy Fox	.75	.30
❑	264	Chan Ho Park	.75	.30
❑	265	Billy Koch	.75	.30
❑	266	Dave Roberts	.75	.30
❑	267	Carl Everett	.75	.30
❑	268	Orel Hershiser	.75	.30
❑	269	Trot Nixon	.75	.30
❑	270	Rusty Greer	.75	.30
❑	271	Will Clark	1.25	.50
❑	272	Quilvio Veras	.75	.30
❑	273	Rico Brogna	.75	.30
❑	274	Devon White	.75	.30
❑	275	Tim Hudson	.75	.30
❑	276	Mike Hampton	.75	.30
❑	277	Miguel Cairo	.75	.30
❑	278	Darren Oliver	.75	.30
❑	279	Jeff Cirillo	.75	.30
❑	280	Al Leiter	.75	.30
❑	281	Shane Andrews	.75	.30
❑	282	Carlos Febles	.75	.30
❑	283	Pedro Astacio	.75	.30
❑	284	Juan Guzman	.75	.30
❑	285	Orlando Hernandez	.75	.30
❑	286	Paul Konerko	.75	.30
❑	287	Tony Clark	.75	.30
❑	288	Aaron Boone	.75	.30
❑	289	Ismael Valdes	.75	.30
❑	290	Moises Alou	.75	.30
❑	291	Kevin Tapani	.75	.30
❑	292	John Franco	.75	.30
❑	293	Todd Zeile	.75	.30
❑	294	Jason Schmidt	.75	.30
❑	295	Johnny Damon	1.25	.50
❑	296	Scott Brosius	.75	.30
❑	297	Travis Fryman	.75	.30
❑	298	Jose Vizcaino	.75	.30
❑	299	Eric Chavez	.75	.30
❑	300	Mike Piazza	3.00	1.25
❑	301	Matt Clement	.75	.30
❑	302	Cristian Guzman	.75	.30
❑	303	C.J. Nitkowski	.75	.30
❑	304	Michael Tucker	.75	.30
❑	305	Brett Tomko	.75	.30
❑	306	Mike Lansing	.75	.30
❑	307	Eric Owens	.75	.30
❑	308	Livan Hernandez	.75	.30
❑	309	Rondell White	.75	.30
❑	310	Todd Stottlemyre	.75	.30
❑	311	Chris Carpenter	.75	.30

No.	Player	Nm-Mt	Ex-Mt
☐ 312	Ken Hill	.75	.30
☐ 313	Mark Loretta	.75	.30
☐ 314	John Rocker	.75	.30
☐ 315	Richie Sexson	.75	.30
☐ 316	Ruben Mateo	.75	.30
☐ 317	Joe Randa	.75	.30
☐ 318	Mike Sirotka	.75	.30
☐ 319	Jose Rosado	.75	.30
☐ 320	Matt Mantei	.75	.30
☐ 321	Kevin Millwood	.75	.30
☐ 322	Gary Disarcina	.75	.30
☐ 323	Dustin Hermanson	.75	.30
☐ 324	Mike Stanton	.75	.30
☐ 325	Kirk Rueter	.75	.30
☐ 326	Damian Miller RC	1.50	.60
☐ 327	Doug Glanville	.75	.30
☐ 328	Scott Rolen	1.25	.50
☐ 329	Ray Durham	.75	.30
☐ 330	Butch Huskey	.75	.30
☐ 331	Mariano Rivera	2.00	.75
☐ 332	Darren Lewis	.75	.30
☐ 333	Mike Timlin	.75	.30
☐ 334	Mark Grudzielanek	.75	.30
☐ 335	Mike Cameron	.75	.30
☐ 336	Kelvim Escobar	.75	.30
☐ 337	Bret Boone	.75	.30
☐ 338	Mo Vaughn	.75	.30
☐ 339	Craig Biggio	1.25	.50
☐ 340	Michael Barrett	.75	.30
☐ 341	Marlon Anderson	.75	.30
☐ 342	Bobby Jones	.75	.30
☐ 343	John Halama	.75	.30
☐ 344	Todd Ritchie	.75	.30
☐ 345	Chuck Knoblauch	.75	.30
☐ 346	Rick Reed	.75	.30
☐ 347	Kelly Stinnett	.75	.30
☐ 348	Tim Salmon	1.25	.50
☐ 349	A.J. Hinch	.75	.30
☐ 350	Jose Cruz Jr.	.75	.30
☐ 351	Roberto Hernandez	.75	.30
☐ 352	Edgar Renteria	.75	.30
☐ 353	Jose Hernandez	.75	.30
☐ 354	Brad Fullmer	.75	.30
☐ 355	Trevor Hoffman	.75	.30
☐ 356	Troy O'Leary	.75	.30
☐ 357	Justin Thompson	.75	.30
☐ 358	Kevin Young	.75	.30
☐ 359	Hideki Irabu	.75	.30
☐ 360	Jim Thome	1.25	.50
☐ 361	Steve Karsay	.75	.30
☐ 362	Octavio Dotel	.75	.30
☐ 363	Omar Vizquel	1.25	.50
☐ 364	Raul Mondesi	.75	.30
☐ 365	Shane Reynolds	.75	.30
☐ 366	Bartolo Colon	.75	.30
☐ 367	Chris Widger	.75	.30
☐ 368	Gabe Kapler	.75	.30
☐ 369	Bill Simas	.75	.30
☐ 370	Tino Martinez	1.25	.50
☐ 371	John Thomson	.75	.30
☐ 372	Delino Deshields	.75	.30
☐ 373	Carlos Perez	.75	.30
☐ 374	Eddie Perez	.75	.30
☐ 375	Jeromy Burnitz	.75	.30
☐ 376	Jimmy Haynes	.75	.30
☐ 377	Travis Lee	.75	.30
☐ 378	Darryl Hamilton	.75	.30
☐ 379	Jamie Moyer	.75	.30
☐ 380	Alex Gonzalez	.75	.30
☐ 381	John Wetteland	.75	.30
☐ 382	Vinny Castilla	.75	.30
☐ 383	Jeff Suppan	.75	.30
☐ 384	Jim Leyritz	.75	.30
☐ 385	Robb Nen	.75	.30
☐ 386	Wilson Alvarez	.75	.30
☐ 387	Andres Galarraga	.75	.30
☐ 388	Mike Remlinger	.75	.30
☐ 389	Geoff Jenkins	.75	.30
☐ 390	Matt Stairs	.75	.30
☐ 391	Bill Mueller	.75	.30
☐ 392	Mike Lowell	.75	.30
☐ 393	Andy Ashby	.75	.30
☐ 394	Ruben Rivera	.75	.30
☐ 395	Todd Helton	1.25	.50
☐ 396	Bernie Williams	1.25	.50
☐ 397	Royce Clayton	.75	.30
☐ 398	Manny Ramirez	1.25	.50
☐ 399	Kerry Wood	.75	.30
☐ 400	Ken Griffey Jr.	3.00	1.25
☐ 401	Enrique Wilson	.75	.30
☐ 402	Joey Hamilton	.75	.30
☐ 403	Shawn Estes	.75	.30
☐ 404	Ugueth Urbina	.75	.30
☐ 405	Albert Belle	.75	.30
☐ 406	Rick Helling	.75	.30
☐ 407	Steve Parris	.75	.30
☐ 408	Eric Milton	.75	.30
☐ 409	Dave Mlicki	.75	.30
☐ 410	Shawn Green	.75	.30
☐ 411	Jaret Wright	.75	.30
☐ 412	Tony Womack	.75	.30
☐ 413	Vernon Wells	.75	.30
☐ 414	Ron Belliard	.75	.30
☐ 415	Ellis Burks	.75	.30
☐ 416	Scott Erickson	.75	.30
☐ 417	Rafael Palmeiro	1.25	.50
☐ 418	Damion Easley	.75	.30
☐ 419	Jamey Wright	.75	.30
☐ 420	Corey Koskie	.75	.30
☐ 421	Bobby Howry	.75	.30
☐ 422	Ricky Ledee	.75	.30
☐ 423	Dmitri Young	.75	.30
☐ 424	Sidney Ponson	.75	.30
☐ 425	Greg Maddux	3.00	1.25
☐ 426	Jose Guillen	.75	.30
☐ 427	Jon Lieber	.75	.30
☐ 428	Andy Benes	.75	.30
☐ 429	Randy Velarde	.75	.30
☐ 430	Sean Casey	.75	.30
☐ 431	Torii Hunter	.75	.30
☐ 432	Ryan Rupe	.75	.30
☐ 433	David Segui	.75	.30
☐ 434	Todd Pratt	.75	.30
☐ 435	Nomar Garciaparra	3.00	1.25
☐ 436	Denny Neagle	.75	.30
☐ 437	Ron Coomer	.75	.30
☐ 438	Chris Singleton	.75	.30
☐ 439	Tony Batista	.75	.30
☐ 440	Andruw Jones	1.25	.50
☐ 441	Burroughs/Piatt/Huff	.75	.30
☐ 442	Rafael Furcal	1.50	.60
☐ 443	M.Lamb RC/J.Crede	4.00	1.50
☐ 444	Julio Zuleta RC	1.00	.40
☐ 445	Garry Maddox Jr. RC	1.00	.40
☐ 446	Riley/Sabathia/Mulder	1.50	.60
☐ 447	Scott Downs RC	1.00	.40
☐ 448	D.Mirabelli/B.Petrick/J.Werth	1.00	.40
☐ 449	C.Myers RC/J.Hamilton	1.50	.60
☐ 450	B.Christensen/R.Stahl RC	1.00	.40
☐ 451	B.Zito/B.Sheets RC	10.00	4.00
☐ 452	K.Ainsworth/Howington RC	1.00	.40
☐ 453	R.Asadoorian/V.Faison RC	1.50	.60
☐ 454	K.Reed/J.Heaverlo RC	1.00	.40
☐ 455	M.MacDougal/B.Baker RC	1.00	.40
☐ 456	Mark McGwire SH	2.50	1.00
☐ 457	Cal Ripken SH	3.00	1.25
☐ 458	Wade Boggs SH	.75	.30
☐ 459	Tony Gwynn SH	1.25	.50
☐ 460	Jesse Orosco SH	.75	.30
☐ 461	L.Walker/N.Garciaparra LL	1.25	.50
☐ 462	K.Griffey Jr./M.McGwire LL	2.00	.75
☐ 463	M.Ramirez/M.McGwire LL	2.00	.75
☐ 464	P.Martinez/R.Johnson LL	1.25	.50
☐ 465	P.Martinez/R.Johnson LL	1.25	.50
☐ 466	D.Jeter/L.Gonzalez LL	2.00	.75
☐ 467	L.Walker/M.Ramirez LL	1.25	.50
☐ 468	Tony Gwynn 20CB	2.50	1.00
☐ 469	Mark McGwire 20CB	5.00	2.00
☐ 470	Frank Thomas 20CB	1.25	.50
☐ 471	Harold Baines 20CB	.75	.30
☐ 472	Roger Clemens 20CB	4.00	1.50
☐ 473	John Franco 20CB	.75	.30
☐ 474	John Franco 20CB	.75	.30
☐ 475A	K.Griffey Jr. MM 350th HR	8.00	3.00
☐ 475B	K.Griffey Jr. MM 1997 MVP	8.00	3.00
☐ 475C	K.Griffey Jr. MM HR Dad	8.00	3.00
☐ 475D	K.Griffey Jr. MM 1992 AS MVP	8.00	3.00
☐ 475E	K.Griffey Jr. MM 50 HR 1997	8.00	3.00
☐ 476A	B.Bonds MM 400HR/400SB	12.00	5.00
☐ 476B	B.Bonds MM 40HR/40SB	12.00	5.00
☐ 476C	B.Bonds MM 1993 MVP	12.00	5.00
☐ 476D	B.Bonds MM 1990 MVP	12.00	5.00
☐ 476E	B.Bonds MM 1992 MVP	12.00	5.00
☐ 477A	S.Sosa MM 20 HR June	8.00	3.00
☐ 477B	S.Sosa MM 66 HR 1998	8.00	3.00
☐ 477C	S.Sosa MM 60 HR 1999	8.00	3.00
☐ 477D	S.Sosa MM 1998 MVP	8.00	3.00
☐ 477E	S.Sosa MM HR's 61/62	8.00	3.00
☐ 478A	D.Jeter MM 1996 ROY	12.00	5.00
☐ 478B	D.Jeter MM Wins 1999 WS	12.00	5.00
☐ 478C	D.Jeter MM Wins 1998 WS	12.00	5.00
☐ 478D	D.Jeter MM Wins 1996 WS	12.00	5.00
☐ 478E	D.Jeter MM 17 GM Hit Streak	12.00	5.00
☐ 479A	A.Rodriguez MM 40HR/40SB	10.00	4.00
☐ 479B	A.Rodriguez MM 100th HR	10.00	4.00
☐ 479C	A.Rodriguez MM 1996 POY	10.00	4.00
☐ 479D	A.Rodriguez MM Wins 1 Million	10.00	4.00
☐ 479E	A.Rodriguez MM 1996 Batting Leader	10.00	4.00
☐ NNO	M.McGwire 85 Reprint	8.00	3.00

2000 Topps Chrome Traded

No.	Player	Nm-Mt	Ex-Mt
☐	COMP.FACT.SET (135)	80.00	40.00
☐ T1	Mike MacDougal	.75	.30
☐ T2	Andy Tracy RC	.50	.20
☐ T3	Brandon Phillips RC	2.50	1.00
☐ T4	Brandon Inge RC	4.00	1.50
☐ T5	Robbie Morrison RC	.50	.20
☐ T6	Josh Pressley RC	.50	.20
☐ T7	Todd Moser RC	.50	.20
☐ T8	Rob Purvis	.60	.25
☐ T9	Chance Caple	.40	.15
☐ T10	Ben Sheets	2.50	1.00
☐ T11	Russ Jacobson RC	.50	.20
☐ T12	Brian Cole RC	.50	.20
☐ T13	Brad Baker	.40	.15
☐ T14	Alex Cintron RC	.75	.30
☐ T15	Lyle Overbay RC	2.00	.75
☐ T16	Mike Edwards RC	.50	.20
☐ T17	Sean McGowan RC	.50	.20
☐ T18	Jose Molina	.40	.15
☐ T19	Marcos Castillo RC	.50	.20
☐ T20	Josue Espada RC	.50	.20
☐ T21	Alex Gordon RC	.50	.20
☐ T22	Rob Pugmire RC	.50	.20
☐ T23	Jason Stumm	.50	.20
☐ T24	Ty Howington	.40	.15
☐ T25	Brett Myers	1.50	.60
☐ T26	Maicer Izturis RC	.75	.30
☐ T27	John McDonald	.40	.15
☐ T28	Wilfredo Rodriguez RC	.50	.20
☐ T29	Carlos Zambrano RC	8.00	3.00
☐ T30	Alejandro Diaz RC	.50	.20
☐ T31	Geraldo Guzman RC	.50	.20
☐ T32	J.R. House RC	.50	.20
☐ T33	Elvin Nina RC	.50	.20
☐ T34	Juan Pierre RC	2.00	.75
☐ T35	Ben Johnson RC	3.00	1.25
☐ T36	Jeff Bailey RC	.50	.20
☐ T37	Miguel Olivo RC	1.25	.50
☐ T38	Francisco Rodriguez RC	4.00	1.50
☐ T39	Tony Pena Jr. RC	.50	.20
☐ T40	Miguel Cabrera RC	40.00	15.00
☐ T41	Asdrubal Oropeza RC	.50	.20
☐ T42	Junior Zamora RC	.75	.30
☐ T43	Jovanny Cedeno RC	.50	.20
☐ T44	John Sneed	.60	.25
☐ T45	Josh Kalinowski	.60	.25
☐ T46	Mike Young RC	10.00	4.00

- ❑ T47 Rico Washington RC .50 .20
- ❑ T48 Chad Durbin RC .50 .20
- ❑ T49 Junior Brignac RC .50 .20
- ❑ T50 Carlos Hernandez RC .75 .30
- ❑ T51 Cesar Izturis RC 1.25 .50
- ❑ T52 Oscar Salazar RC .50 .20
- ❑ T53 Pat Strange RC .50 .20
- ❑ T54 Rick Asadoorian .75 .30
- ❑ T55 Keith Reed .40 .15
- ❑ T56 Leo Estrella RC .50 .20
- ❑ T57 Wascar Serrano RC .50 .20
- ❑ T58 Richard Gomez RC .50 .20
- ❑ T59 Ramon Santiago RC .50 .20
- ❑ T60 Jovanny Sosa RC .50 .20
- ❑ T61 Aaron Rowand RC 3.00 1.25
- ❑ T62 Junior Guerrero RC .50 .20
- ❑ T63 Luis Terrero RC .75 .30
- ❑ T64 Brian Sanches RC .50 .20
- ❑ T65 Scott Sobkowiak RC .50 .20
- ❑ T66 Gary Majewski RC .75 .30
- ❑ T67 Barry Zito 3.00 1.25
- ❑ T68 Ryan Christianson .50 .20
- ❑ T69 Cristian Guerrero RC .50 .20
- ❑ T70 Tomas De La Rosa RC .50 .20
- ❑ T71 Andrew Beinbrink RC .50 .20
- ❑ T72 Ryan Knox RC .50 .20
- ❑ T73 Alex Graman RC .50 .20
- ❑ T74 Juan Guzman RC .50 .20
- ❑ T75 Ruben Salazar RC .50 .20
- ❑ T76 Luis Matos RC .75 .30
- ❑ T77 Tony Mota RC .50 .20
- ❑ T78 Doug Davis .60 .25
- ❑ T79 Ben Christensen .40 .15
- ❑ T80 Mike Lamb 1.25 .50
- ❑ T81 Adrian Gonzalez RC 5.00 2.00
- ❑ T82 Mike Stodolka RC .50 .20
- ❑ T83 Adam Johnson RC .50 .20
- ❑ T84 Matt Wheatland RC .50 .20
- ❑ T85 Corey Smith RC .50 .20
- ❑ T86 Rocco Baldelli RC 4.00 1.50
- ❑ T87 Keith Bucktrot RC .50 .20
- ❑ T88 Adam Wainwright RC 2.00 .75
- ❑ T89 Scott Thorman RC 2.00 .75
- ❑ T90 Tripper Johnson RC .50 .20
- ❑ T91 Jim Edmonds Cards .60 .25
- ❑ T92 Masato Yoshii .40 .15
- ❑ T93 Adam Kennedy .40 .15
- ❑ T94 Darryl Kile .60 .25
- ❑ T95 Mark McLemore .40 .15
- ❑ T96 Ricky Gutierrez .40 .15
- ❑ T97 Juan Gonzalez .60 .25
- ❑ T98 Melvin Mora .60 .25
- ❑ T99 Dante Bichette .60 .25
- ❑ T100 Lee Stevens .40 .15
- ❑ T101 Roger Cedeno .40 .15
- ❑ T102 John Olerud .60 .25
- ❑ T103 Eric Young .40 .15
- ❑ T104 Mickey Morandini .40 .15
- ❑ T105 Travis Lee .40 .15
- ❑ T106 Greg Vaughn .40 .15
- ❑ T107 Todd Zeile .60 .25
- ❑ T108 Chuck Finley .60 .25
- ❑ T109 Ismael Valdes .40 .15
- ❑ T110 Reggie Sanders .60 .25
- ❑ T111 Pat Hentgen .40 .15
- ❑ T112 Ryan Klesko .60 .25
- ❑ T113 Derek Bell .40 .15
- ❑ T114 Hideo Nomo 1.50 .60
- ❑ T115 Aaron Sele .40 .15
- ❑ T116 Fernando Vina .40 .15
- ❑ T117 Wally Joyner .60 .25
- ❑ T118 Brian Hunter .40 .15
- ❑ T119 Joe Girardi .40 .15
- ❑ T120 Omar Daal .40 .15
- ❑ T121 Brook Fordyce .40 .15
- ❑ T122 Jose Valentin .40 .15
- ❑ T123 Curt Schilling .60 .25
- ❑ T124 B.J. Surhoff .60 .25
- ❑ T125 Henry Rodriguez .40 .15
- ❑ T126 Mike Bordick .40 .15
- ❑ T127 David Justice .60 .25
- ❑ T128 Charles Johnson .60 .25
- ❑ T129 Will Clark 1.00 .40
- ❑ T130 Dwight Gooden .60 .25
- ❑ T131 David Segui .40 .15
- ❑ T132 Denny Neagle .60 .25
- ❑ T133 Jose Canseco 1.00 .40
- ❑ T134 Bruce Chen .40 .15
- ❑ T135 Jason Bere .40 .15

2001 Topps Chrome

- ❑ COMPLETE SET (661) 300.00 150.00
- ❑ COMPLETE SERIES 1 (331) 150.00 75.00
- ❑ COMPLETE SERIES 2 (330) 150.00 75.00
- ❑ 1 Cal Ripken 6.00 2.50
- ❑ 2 Chipper Jones 2.00 .75
- ❑ 3 Roger Cedeno .50 .20
- ❑ 4 Garret Anderson .75 .30
- ❑ 5 Robin Ventura .75 .30
- ❑ 6 Daryle Ward .50 .20
- ❑ 7 Does Not Exist
- ❑ 8 Phil Nevin .75 .30
- ❑ 9 Jermaine Dye .75 .30
- ❑ 10 Chris Singleton .50 .20
- ❑ 11 Mike Redmond .50 .20
- ❑ 12 Jim Thome 1.25 .50
- ❑ 13 Brian Jordan .75 .30
- ❑ 14 Dustin Hermanson .50 .20
- ❑ 15 Shawn Green .75 .30
- ❑ 16 Todd Stottlemyre .50 .20
- ❑ 17 Dan Wilson .50 .20
- ❑ 18 Derek Lowe .75 .30
- ❑ 19 Juan Gonzalez .75 .30
- ❑ 20 Pat Meares .50 .20
- ❑ 21 Paul O'Neill 1.25 .50
- ❑ 22 Jeffrey Hammonds .50 .20
- ❑ 23 Pokey Reese .50 .20
- ❑ 24 Mike Mussina 1.25 .50
- ❑ 25 Rico Brogna .50 .20
- ❑ 26 Jay Buhner .75 .30
- ❑ 27 Steve Cox .50 .20
- ❑ 28 Quilvio Veras .50 .20
- ❑ 29 Marquis Grissom .75 .30
- ❑ 30 Shigetoshi Hasegawa .75 .30
- ❑ 31 Shane Reynolds .50 .20
- ❑ 32 Adam Piatt .50 .20
- ❑ 33 Preston Wilson .75 .30
- ❑ 34 Ellis Burks .75 .30
- ❑ 35 Armando Rios .50 .20
- ❑ 36 Chuck Finley .75 .30
- ❑ 37 Shannon Stewart .75 .30
- ❑ 38 Mark McGwire 5.00 2.00
- ❑ 39 Gerald Williams .50 .20
- ❑ 40 Eric Young .50 .20
- ❑ 41 Peter Bergeron .50 .20
- ❑ 42 Arthur Rhodes .50 .20
- ❑ 43 Bobby Jones .50 .20
- ❑ 44 Matt Clement .75 .30
- ❑ 45 Pedro Martinez 1.25 .50
- ❑ 46 Jose Canseco 1.25 .50
- ❑ 47 Matt Anderson .50 .20
- ❑ 48 Torii Hunter .75 .30
- ❑ 49 Carlos Lee .75 .30
- ❑ 50 Eric Chavez .75 .30
- ❑ 51 Rick Helling .50 .20
- ❑ 52 John Franco .75 .30
- ❑ 53 Mike Bordick .75 .30
- ❑ 54 Andres Galarraga .75 .30
- ❑ 55 Jose Cruz Jr. .50 .20
- ❑ 56 Mike Matheny .50 .20
- ❑ 57 Randy Johnson 2.00 .75
- ❑ 58 Richie Sexson .75 .30
- ❑ 59 Vladimir Nunez .50 .20
- ❑ 60 Aaron Boone .75 .30
- ❑ 61 Darin Erstad .75 .30
- ❑ 62 Alex Gonzalez .50 .20
- ❑ 63 Gil Heredia .50 .20
- ❑ 64 Shane Andrews .50 .20
- ❑ 65 Todd Hundley .50 .20
- ❑ 66 Bill Mueller .75 .30
- ❑ 67 Mark McLemore .50 .20
- ❑ 68 Scott Spiezio .50 .20
- ❑ 69 Kevin McGlinchy .50 .20
- ❑ 70 Manny Ramirez 1.25 .50
- ❑ 71 Mike Lamb .50 .20
- ❑ 72 Brian Buchanan .50 .20
- ❑ 73 Mike Sweeney .75 .30
- ❑ 74 John Wetteland .75 .30
- ❑ 75 Rob Bell .50 .20
- ❑ 76 John Burkett .50 .20
- ❑ 77 Derek Jeter 5.00 2.00
- ❑ 78 J.D. Drew .75 .30
- ❑ 79 Jose Offerman .50 .20
- ❑ 80 Rick Reed .50 .20
- ❑ 81 Will Clark 1.25 .50
- ❑ 82 Rickey Henderson 2.00 .75
- ❑ 83 Kirk Rueter .50 .20
- ❑ 84 Lee Stevens .50 .20
- ❑ 85 Jay Bell .75 .30
- ❑ 86 Fred McGriff 1.25 .50
- ❑ 87 Julio Zuleta .50 .20
- ❑ 88 Brian Anderson .50 .20
- ❑ 89 Orlando Cabrera .75 .30
- ❑ 90 Alex Fernandez .50 .20
- ❑ 91 Derek Bell .50 .20
- ❑ 92 Eric Owens .50 .20
- ❑ 93 Dennys Reyes .50 .20
- ❑ 94 Mike Stanley .50 .20
- ❑ 95 Jorge Posada 1.25 .50
- ❑ 96 Paul Konerko .75 .30
- ❑ 97 Mike Remlinger .50 .20
- ❑ 98 Travis Lee .50 .20
- ❑ 99 Ken Caminiti .75 .30
- ❑ 100 Kevin Barker .50 .20
- ❑ 101 Ozzie Guillen .75 .30
- ❑ 102 Randy Wolf .50 .20
- ❑ 103 Michael Tucker .50 .20
- ❑ 104 Darren Lewis .50 .20
- ❑ 105 Joe Randa .75 .30
- ❑ 106 Jeff Cirillo .50 .20
- ❑ 107 David Ortiz 2.00 .75
- ❑ 108 Herb Perry .50 .20
- ❑ 109 Jeff Nelson .50 .20
- ❑ 110 Chris Stynes .50 .20
- ❑ 111 Johnny Damon 1.25 .50
- ❑ 112 Jason Schmidt .75 .30
- ❑ 113 Charles Johnson .50 .20
- ❑ 114 Pat Burrell .75 .30
- ❑ 115 Gary Sheffield .75 .30
- ❑ 116 Tom Glavine 1.25 .50
- ❑ 117 Jason Isringhausen .75 .30
- ❑ 118 Chris Carpenter .75 .30
- ❑ 119 Jeff Suppan .50 .20
- ❑ 120 Ivan Rodriguez 1.25 .50
- ❑ 121 Luis Sojo .50 .20
- ❑ 122 Ron Villone .50 .20
- ❑ 123 Mike Sirotka .50 .20
- ❑ 124 Chuck Knoblauch .75 .30
- ❑ 125 Jason Kendall .75 .30
- ❑ 126 Bobby Estalella .50 .20
- ❑ 127 Jose Guillen .75 .30
- ❑ 128 Carlos Delgado .75 .30
- ❑ 129 Benji Gil .50 .20
- ❑ 130 Einar Diaz .50 .20
- ❑ 131 Andy Benes .50 .20
- ❑ 132 Adrian Beltre .75 .30
- ❑ 133 Roger Clemens 4.00 1.50
- ❑ 134 Scott Williamson .50 .20
- ❑ 135 Brad Penny .50 .20
- ❑ 136 Troy Glaus .75 .30
- ❑ 137 Kevin Appier .75 .30
- ❑ 138 Walt Weiss .50 .20
- ❑ 139 Michael Barrett .50 .20
- ❑ 140 Mike Hampton .75 .30
- ❑ 141 Francisco Cordova .50 .20
- ❑ 142 David Segui .50 .20
- ❑ 143 Carlos Febles .50 .20
- ❑ 144 Roy Halladay .75 .30
- ❑ 145 Seth Etherton .50 .20
- ❑ 146 Fernando Tatis .50 .20

	No.	Card		
❑	147	Livan Hernandez	.75	.30
❑	148	B.J. Surhoff	.75	.30
❑	149	Barry Larkin	1.25	.50
❑	150	Bobby Howry	.50	.20
❑	151	Dmitri Young	.75	.30
❑	152	Brian Hunter	.50	.20
❑	153	Alex Rodriguez	3.00	1.25
❑	154	Hideo Nomo	2.00	.75
❑	155	Warren Morris	.50	.20
❑	156	Antonio Alfonseca	.50	.20
❑	157	Edgardo Alfonzo	.50	.20
❑	158	Mark Grudzielanek	.50	.20
❑	159	Fernando Vina	.50	.20
❑	160	Homer Bush	.50	.20
❑	161	Jason Giambi	.75	.30
❑	162	Steve Karsay	.50	.20
❑	163	Matt Lawton	.50	.20
❑	164	Rusty Greer	.75	.30
❑	165	Billy Koch	.50	.20
❑	166	Todd Hollandsworth	.50	.20
❑	167	Raul Ibanez	.50	.20
❑	168	Tony Gwynn	2.50	1.00
❑	169	Carl Everett	.75	.30
❑	170	Hector Carrasco	.50	.20
❑	171	Jose Valentin	.50	.20
❑	172	Deivi Cruz	.50	.20
❑	173	Bret Boone	.75	.30
❑	174	Melvin Mora	.75	.30
❑	175	Danny Graves	.50	.20
❑	176	Jose Jimenez	.50	.20
❑	177	James Baldwin	.50	.20
❑	178	C.J. Nitkowski	.50	.20
❑	179	Jeff Zimmerman	.50	.20
❑	180	Mike Lowell	.75	.30
❑	181	Hideki Irabu	.50	.20
❑	182	Greg Vaughn	.50	.20
❑	183	Omar Daal	.50	.20
❑	184	Darren Dreifort	.50	.20
❑	185	Gil Meche	.50	.20
❑	186	Damian Jackson	.50	.20
❑	187	Frank Thomas	2.00	.75
❑	188	Luis Castillo	.50	.20
❑	189	Bartolo Colon	.75	.30
❑	190	Craig Biggio	1.25	.50
❑	191	Scott Schoeneweis	.50	.20
❑	192	Dave Veres	.50	.20
❑	193	Ramon Martinez	.50	.20
❑	194	Jose Vidro	.50	.20
❑	195	Todd Helton	1.25	.50
❑	196	Greg Norton	.50	.20
❑	197	Jacque Jones	.75	.30
❑	198	Jason Grimsley	.50	.20
❑	199	Dan Reichert	.50	.20
❑	200	Robb Nen	.75	.30
❑	201	Scott Hatteberg	.50	.20
❑	202	Terry Shumpert	.50	.20
❑	203	Kevin Millar	.75	.30
❑	204	Ismael Valdes	.50	.20
❑	205	Richard Hidalgo	.50	.20
❑	206	Randy Velarde	.50	.20
❑	207	Bengie Molina	.50	.20
❑	208	Tony Womack	.50	.20
❑	209	Enrique Wilson	.50	.20
❑	210	Jeff Brantley	.50	.20
❑	211	Rick Ankiel	.50	.20
❑	212	Terry Mulholland	.50	.20
❑	213	Ron Belliard	.50	.20
❑	214	Terrence Long	.50	.20
❑	215	Alberto Castillo	.50	.20
❑	216	Royce Clayton	.50	.20
❑	217	Joe McEwing	.50	.20
❑	218	Jason McDonald	.50	.20
❑	219	Ricky Bottalico	.50	.20
❑	220	Keith Foulke	.75	.30
❑	221	Brad Radke	.75	.30
❑	222	Gabe Kapler	.75	.30
❑	223	Pedro Astacio	.50	.20
❑	224	Armando Reynoso	.50	.20
❑	225	Darryl Kile	.75	.30
❑	226	Reggie Sanders	.75	.30
❑	227	Esteban Yan	.50	.20
❑	228	Joe Nathan	.75	.30
❑	229	Jay Payton	.50	.20
❑	230	Francisco Cordero	.50	.20
❑	231	Gregg Jefferies	.50	.20
❑	232	LaTroy Hawkins	.50	.20
❑	233	Jacob Cruz	.50	.20
❑	234	Chris Holt	.50	.20
❑	235	Vladimir Guerrero	2.00	.75
❑	236	Marvin Benard	.50	.20
❑	237	Alex Ramirez	.50	.20
❑	238	Mike Williams	.50	.20
❑	239	Sean Bergman	.50	.20
❑	240	Juan Encarnacion	.50	.20
❑	241	Russ Davis	.50	.20
❑	242	Ramon Hernandez	.50	.20
❑	243	Sandy Alomar Jr.	.50	.20
❑	244	Eddie Guardado	.50	.20
❑	245	Shane Halter	.50	.20
❑	246	Geoff Jenkins	.50	.20
❑	247	Brian Meadows	.50	.20
❑	248	Damian Miller	.50	.20
❑	249	Darrin Fletcher	.50	.20
❑	250	Rafael Furcal	.75	.30
❑	251	Mark Grace	1.25	.50
❑	252	Mark Mulder	.75	.30
❑	253	Joe Torre MG	1.25	.50
❑	254	Bobby Cox MG	.50	.20
❑	255	Mike Scioscia MG	.50	.20
❑	256	Mike Hargrove MG	.50	.20
❑	257	Jimy Williams MG	.50	.20
❑	258	Jerry Manuel MG	.50	.20
❑	259	Charlie Manuel MG	.50	.20
❑	260	Don Baylor MG	.75	.30
❑	261	Phil Garner MG	.75	.30
❑	262	Tony Muser MG	.50	.20
❑	263	Buddy Bell MG	.75	.30
❑	264	Tom Kelly MG	.50	.20
❑	265	John Boles MG	.50	.20
❑	266	Art Howe MG	.50	.20
❑	267	Larry Dierker MG	.50	.20
❑	268	Lou Piniella MG	.75	.30
❑	269	Larry Rothschild MG	.50	.20
❑	270	Davey Lopes MG	.75	.30
❑	271	Johnny Oates MG	.50	.20
❑	272	Felipe Alou MG	.50	.20
❑	273	Bobby Valentine MG	.50	.20
❑	274	Tony LaRussa MG	.50	.20
❑	275	Bruce Bochy MG	.50	.20
❑	276	Dusty Baker MG	.75	.30
❑	277	A.Gonzalez/A.Johnson	1.00	.40
❑	278	M.Wheatland/B.Digby	1.00	.40
❑	279	T.Johnson/S.Thorman	1.00	.40
❑	280	P.Dumatrait/A.Wainwright	1.00	.40
❑	281	David Parrish RC	1.00	.40
❑	282	M.Folsom RC/R.Baldelli	1.50	.60
❑	283	Dominic Rich RC	1.00	.40
❑	284	M.Stodolka/S.Burnett	1.00	.40
❑	285	D.Thompson/C.Smith	1.00	.40
❑	286	D.Borrell RC/J.Bourgeois RC	1.00	.40
❑	287	Chen/Patterson/Hamilton	2.00	.75
❑	288	B.Zito/C.Sabathia	2.00	.75
❑	289	Ben Sheets	2.00	.75
❑	290	Howington/Kalinowski/Girdley	1.00	.40
❑	291	Hee Seop Choi RC	2.00	.75
❑	292	Bradley/Ainsworth/Tsao	1.50	.60
❑	293	Glendenning/Kelly/Silvestre	1.00	.40
❑	294	J.R. House	1.00	.40
❑	295	Rafael Soriano RC	1.50	.60
❑	296	T.Hafner RC/B.Jacobsen	10.00	4.00
❑	297	Conti/Wakeland/Cole	1.00	.40
❑	298	Seabol/Huff/Crede	2.50	1.00
❑	299	Everett/Ortiz/Ginter	1.00	.40
❑	300	Hernandez/Guzman/Eaton	1.00	.40
❑	301	Kielty/Bradley/J.Rivera	1.50	.60
❑	302	Mark McGwire GM	2.50	1.00
❑	303	Don Larsen GM	.75	.30
❑	304	Bobby Thomson GM	.75	.30
❑	305	Bill Mazeroski GM	.75	.30
❑	306	Reggie Jackson GM	1.25	.50
❑	307	Kirk Gibson GM	.75	.30
❑	308	Roger Maris GM	1.25	.50
❑	309	Cal Ripken GM	3.00	1.25
❑	310	Hank Aaron GM	2.00	.75
❑	311	Joe Carter GM	.75	.30
❑	312	Cal Ripken SH	3.00	1.25
❑	313	Randy Johnson SH	1.25	.50
❑	314	Ken Griffey Jr. SH	2.00	.75
❑	315	Troy Glaus SH	.75	.30
❑	316	Kazuhiro Sasaki SH	.75	.30
❑	317	S.Sosa/T.Glaus LL	1.25	.50
❑	318	T.Helton/E.Martinez LL	.75	.30
❑	319	T.Helton/N.Garicaparra LL	2.00	.75
❑	320	B.Bonds/J.Giambi LL	2.00	.75
❑	321	T.Helton/M.Ramirez LL	.75	.30
❑	322	T.Helton/D.Erstad LL	.75	.30
❑	323	K.Brown/P.Martinez LL	1.25	.50
❑	324	R.Johnson/P.Martinez LL	1.25	.50
❑	325	Will Clark HL	1.25	.50
❑	326	New York Mets HL	2.00	.75
❑	327	New York Yankees HL	3.00	1.25
❑	328	Seattle Mariners HL	.75	.30
❑	329	Mike Hampton HL	.75	.30
❑	330	New York Yankees HL	4.00	1.50
❑	331	New York Yankees Champs	8.00	3.00
❑	332	Jeff Bagwell	1.25	.50
❑	333	Andy Pettitte	1.25	.50
❑	334	Tony Armas Jr.	.50	.20
❑	335	Jeromy Burnitz	.75	.30
❑	336	Javier Vazquez	.75	.30
❑	337	Eric Karros	.75	.30
❑	338	Brian Giles	.75	.30
❑	339	Scott Rolen	1.25	.50
❑	340	David Justice	.75	.30
❑	341	Ray Durham	.75	.30
❑	342	Todd Zeile	.75	.30
❑	343	Cliff Floyd	.75	.30
❑	344	Barry Bonds	5.00	2.00
❑	345	Matt Williams	.75	.30
❑	346	Steve Finley	.75	.30
❑	347	Scott Elarton	.50	.20
❑	348	Bernie Williams	1.25	.50
❑	349	David Wells	.75	.30
❑	350	J.T. Snow	.75	.30
❑	351	Al Leiter	.75	.30
❑	352	Magglio Ordonez	.75	.30
❑	353	Raul Mondesi	.75	.30
❑	354	Tim Salmon	1.25	.50
❑	355	Jeff Kent	.75	.30
❑	356	Mariano Rivera	2.00	.75
❑	357	John Olerud	.75	.30
❑	358	Javy Lopez	.75	.30
❑	359	Ben Grieve	.50	.20
❑	360	Ray Lankford	.75	.30
❑	361	Ken Griffey Jr.	3.00	1.25
❑	362	Rich Aurilia	.50	.20
❑	363	Andruw Jones	1.25	.50
❑	364	Ryan Klesko	.75	.30
❑	365	Roberto Alomar	1.25	.50
❑	366	Miguel Tejada	.75	.30
❑	367	Mo Vaughn	.75	.30
❑	368	Albert Belle	.75	.30
❑	369	Jose Canseco	1.25	.50
❑	370	Kevin Brown	.75	.30
❑	371	Rafael Palmeiro	1.25	.50
❑	372	Mark Redman	.50	.20
❑	373	Larry Walker	.75	.30
❑	374	Greg Maddux	3.00	1.25
❑	375	Nomar Garciaparra	3.00	1.25
❑	376	Kevin Millwood	.75	.30
❑	377	Edgar Martinez	1.25	.50
❑	378	Sammy Sosa	2.00	.75
❑	379	Tim Hudson	.75	.30
❑	380	Jim Edmonds	.75	.30
❑	381	Mike Piazza	3.00	1.25
❑	382	Brant Brown	.50	.20
❑	383	Brad Fullmer	.50	.20
❑	384	Alan Benes	.50	.20
❑	385	Mickey Morandini	.50	.20
❑	386	Troy Percival	.75	.30
❑	387	Eddie Perez	.50	.20
❑	388	Vernon Wells	.75	.30
❑	389	Ricky Gutierrez	.50	.20
❑	390	Rondell White	.75	.30
❑	391	Kelvim Escobar	.50	.20
❑	392	Tony Batista	.50	.20
❑	393	Jimmy Haynes	.50	.20
❑	394	Billy Wagner	.75	.30
❑	395	A.J. Hinch	.50	.20
❑	396	Matt Morris	.75	.30
❑	397	Lance Berkman	.75	.30
❑	398	Jeff D'Amico	.50	.20
❑	399	Octavio Dotel	.50	.20
❑	400	Olmedo Saenz	.50	.20
❑	401	Esteban Loaiza	.50	.20
❑	402	Adam Kennedy	.50	.20
❑	403	Moises Alou	.75	.30
❑	404	Orlando Palmeiro	.50	.20

❑ 405 Kevin Young .50 .20
❑ 406 Tom Goodwin .50 .20
❑ 407 Mac Suzuki .75 .30
❑ 408 Pat Hentgen .50 .20
❑ 409 Kevin Stocker .50 .20
❑ 410 Mark Sweeney .50 .20
❑ 411 Tony Eusebio .50 .20
❑ 412 Edgar Renteria .75 .30
❑ 413 John Rocker .75 .30
❑ 414 Jose Lima .50 .20
❑ 415 Kerry Wood .75 .30
❑ 416 Mike Timlin .50 .20
❑ 417 Jose Hernandez .50 .20
❑ 418 Jeremy Giambi .50 .20
❑ 419 Luis Lopez .50 .20
❑ 420 Mitch Meluskey .50 .20
❑ 421 Garrett Stephenson .50 .20
❑ 422 Jamey Wright .50 .20
❑ 423 John Jaha .50 .20
❑ 424 Placido Polanco .50 .20
❑ 425 Marty Cordova .50 .20
❑ 426 Joey Hamilton .50 .20
❑ 427 Travis Fryman .75 .30
❑ 428 Mike Cameron .50 .20
❑ 429 Matt Mantei .50 .20
❑ 430 [illegible] .75 .30
❑ 431 Shawn Estes .50 .20
❑ 432 Danny Bautista .50 .20
❑ 433 Wilson Alvarez .50 .20
❑ 434 Kenny Lofton .75 .30
❑ 435 Russ Ortiz .50 .20
❑ 436 Dave Burba .50 .20
❑ 437 Felix Martinez .50 .20
❑ 438 Jeff Shaw .50 .20
❑ 439 Mike DiFelice .50 .20
❑ 440 Roberto Hernandez .50 .20
❑ 441 Bryan Rekar .50 .20
❑ 442 Ugueth Urbina .50 .20
❑ 443 Vinny Castilla .75 .30
❑ 444 Carlos Perez .50 .20
❑ 445 Juan Guzman .50 .20
❑ 446 Ryan Rupe .50 .20
❑ 447 Mike Mordecai .50 .20
❑ 448 Ricardo Rincon .50 .20
❑ 449 Curt Schilling .75 .30
❑ 450 Alex Cora .50 .20
❑ 451 Turner Ward .50 .20
❑ 452 Omar Vizquel 1.25 .50
❑ 453 Russ Branyan .50 .20
❑ 454 Russ Johnson .50 .20
❑ 455 Greg Colbrunn .50 .20
❑ 456 Charles Nagy .50 .20
❑ 457 Wil Cordero .50 .20
❑ 458 Jason Tyner .50 .20
❑ 459 Devon White .75 .30
❑ 460 Kelly Stinnett .50 .20
❑ 461 Wilton Guerrero .50 .20
❑ 462 Jason Bere .50 .20
❑ 463 Calvin Murray .50 .20
❑ 464 Miguel Batista .50 .20
❑ 466 Luis Gonzalez .75 .30
❑ 467 Jaret Wright .50 .20
❑ 468 Chad Kreuter .50 .20
❑ 469 Armando Benitez .50 .20
❑ 470 Erubiel Durazo .50 .20
❑ 470 Sidney Ponson .50 .20
❑ 471 Adrian Brown .50 .20
❑ 472 Sterling Hitchcock .50 .20
❑ 473 Timo Perez .50 .20
❑ 474 Jamie Moyer .75 .30
❑ 475 Delino DeShields .50 .20
❑ 476 Glendon Rusch .50 .20
❑ 477 Chris Gomez .50 .20
❑ 478 Adam Eaton .50 .20
❑ 479 Pablo Ozuna .50 .20
❑ 480 Bob Abreu .75 .30
❑ 481 Kris Benson .50 .20
❑ 482 Keith Osik .50 .20
❑ 483 Darryl Hamilton .50 .20
❑ 484 Marlon Anderson .50 .20
❑ 485 Jimmy Anderson .50 .20
❑ 486 John Halama .50 .20
❑ 487 Nelson Figueroa .50 .20
❑ 488 Alex Gonzalez .50 .20
❑ 489 Benny Agbayani .50 .20
❑ 490 Ed Sprague .50 .20
❑ 491 Scott Erickson .50 .20
❑ 492 Doug Glanville .50 .20
❑ 493 Jesus Sanchez .50 .20
❑ 494 Mike Lieberthal .75 .30
❑ 495 Aaron Sele .50 .20
❑ 496 Pat Mahomes .50 .20
❑ 497 Ruben Rivera .50 .20
❑ 498 Wayne Gomes .50 .20
❑ 499 Freddy Garcia .75 .30
❑ 500 Al Martin .50 .20
❑ 501 Woody Williams .50 .20
❑ 502 Paul Byrd .50 .20
❑ 503 Rick White .50 .20
❑ 504 Trevor Hoffman .75 .30
❑ 505 Brady Anderson .75 .30
❑ 506 Robert Person .50 .20
❑ 507 Jeff Conine .75 .30
❑ 508 Chris Truby .50 .20
❑ 509 Emil Brown .50 .20
❑ 510 Ryan Dempster .50 .20
❑ 511 Ruben Mateo .50 .20
❑ 512 Alex Ochoa .50 .20
❑ 513 Jose Rosado .50 .20
❑ 514 Masato Yoshii .50 .20
❑ 515 Brian Daubach .50 .20
❑ 516 Jeff D'Amico .50 .20
❑ 517 Brent Mayne .50 .20
❑ 518 John Thomson .50 .20
❑ 519 Todd Ritchie .50 .20
❑ 520 John VanderWal .50 .20
❑ 521 Neifi Perez .50 .20
❑ 522 Chad Curtis .50 .20
❑ 523 Kenny Rogers .75 .30
❑ 524 Trot Nixon .75 .30
❑ 525 Sean Casey .75 .30
❑ 526 Wilton Veras .50 .20
❑ 527 Troy O'Leary .50 .20
❑ 528 Dante Bichette .75 .30
❑ 529 Jose Silva .50 .20
❑ 530 Darren Oliver .50 .20
❑ 531 Steve Parris .50 .20
❑ 532 David McCarty .50 .20
❑ 533 Todd Walker .50 .20
❑ 534 Brian Rose .50 .20
❑ 535 Pete Schourek .50 .20
❑ 536 Ricky Ledee .50 .20
❑ 537 Justin Thompson .50 .20
❑ 538 Benito Santiago .75 .30
❑ 539 Carlos Beltran .75 .30
❑ 540 Gabe White .50 .20
❑ 541 Bret Saberhagen .75 .30
❑ 542 Ramon Martinez .50 .20
❑ 543 John Valentin .50 .20
❑ 544 Frank Catalanotto .50 .20
❑ 545 Tim Wakefield .75 .30
❑ 546 Michael Tucker .50 .20
❑ 547 Juan Pierre .75 .30
❑ 548 Rich Garces .50 .20
❑ 549 Luis Ordaz .50 .20
❑ 550 Jerry Spradlin .50 .20
❑ 551 Corey Koskie .50 .20
❑ 552 Cal Eldred .50 .20
❑ 553 Alfonso Soriano 1.25 .50
❑ 554 Kip Wells .50 .20
❑ 555 Orlando Hernandez .75 .30
❑ 556 Bill Simas .50 .20
❑ 557 Jim Parque .50 .20
❑ 558 Joe Mays .50 .20
❑ 559 Tim Belcher .50 .20
❑ 560 Shane Spencer .50 .20
❑ 561 Glenallen Hill .50 .20
❑ 562 Matt LeCroy .50 .20
❑ 563 Tino Martinez 1.25 .50
❑ 564 Eric Milton .50 .20
❑ 565 Ron Coomer .50 .20
❑ 566 Cristian Guzman .50 .20
❑ 567 Kazuhiro Sasaki .75 .30
❑ 568 Mark Quinn .50 .20
❑ 569 Eric Gagne .75 .30
❑ 570 Kerry Ligtenberg .50 .20
❑ 571 Rolando Arrojo .50 .20
❑ 572 Jon Lieber .50 .20
❑ 573 Jose Vizcaino .50 .20
❑ 574 Jeff Abbott .50 .20
❑ 575 Carlos Hernandez .50 .20
❑ 576 Scott Sullivan .50 .20
❑ 577 Matt Stairs .50 .20
❑ 578 Tom Lampkin .50 .20
❑ 579 Donnie Sadler .50 .20
❑ 580 Desi Relaford .50 .20
❑ 581 Scott Downs .50 .20
❑ 582 Mike Mussina 1.25 .50
❑ 583 Ramon Ortiz .50 .20
❑ 584 Mike Myers .50 .20
❑ 585 Frank Castillo .50 .20
❑ 586 Manny Ramirez Sox 1.25 .50
❑ 587 Alex Rodriguez 3.00 1.25
❑ 588 Andy Ashby .50 .20
❑ 589 Felipe Crespo .50 .20
❑ 590 Bobby Bonilla .75 .30
❑ 591 Denny Neagle .50 .20
❑ 592 Dave Martinez .50 .20
❑ 593 Mike Hampton .75 .30
❑ 594 Gary DiSarcina .50 .20
❑ 595 Tsuyoshi Shinjo RC 2.00 .75
❑ 596 Albert Pujols RC 80.00 40.00
❑ 597 Oswalt/Strange/Rauch 2.50 1.00
❑ 598 Jake Peavy RC 10.00 4.00
❑ 599 S.Smyth RC/Bynum/Haynes 1.00 .40
❑ 600 Cuddyer/Lawrence/Freeman 1.00 .40
❑ 601 C.Pena/Barnes/Wise 1.00 .40
❑ 602 E.Almonte RC/F.Lopez 1.00 .40
❑ 603 [illegible]/Wilkerson 1.00 .40
❑ 604 Hall/Barajas/Goldbach 1.00 .40
❑ 605 Romano/Giles/Ozuna 1.50 .60
❑ 606 D.Brown/Cust/V.Wells 1.00 .40
❑ 607 L.Montanez RC/D.Espinosa 1.00 .40
❑ 608 J.Wayne RC/A.Pluta RC 1.00 .40
❑ 609 J.Axelson RC/C.Cali RC 1.00 .40
❑ 610 S.Boyd RC/C.Morris RC 1.00 .40
❑ 611 T.Arko RC/D.Moylan RC 1.00 .40
❑ 612 L.Cotto RC/L.Escobar 1.00 .40
❑ 613 B.Mims RC/B.Williams RC 1.00 .40
❑ 614 C.Russ RC/B.Edwards 1.00 .40
❑ 615 J.Torres/B.Diggins 1.00 .40
❑ 616 Edwin Encarnacion RC 10.00 4.00
❑ 617 B.Bass RC/O.Ayala RC 1.00 .40
❑ 618 M.Matthews RC/J.Kanooi 1.00 .40
❑ 619 S.McFarland RC/A.Sterrett RC 1.00 .40
❑ 620 D.Krynzel/G.Sizemore 5.00 2.00
❑ 621 K.Bucktrot/D.Sardinha 1.00 .40
❑ 622 Anaheim Angels TC .75 .30
❑ 623 Arizona Diamondbacks TC .75 .30
❑ 624 Atlanta Braves TC .75 .30
❑ 625 Baltimore Orioles TC .75 .30
❑ 626 Boston Red Sox TC .75 .30
❑ 627 Chicago Cubs TC .75 .30
❑ 628 Chicago White Sox TC .75 .30
❑ 629 Cincinnati Reds TC .75 .30
❑ 630 Cleveland Indians TC .75 .30
❑ 631 Colorado Rockies TC .75 .30
❑ 632 Detroit Tigers TC .75 .30
❑ 633 Florida Marlins TC .75 .30
❑ 634 Houston Astros TC .75 .30
❑ 635 Kansas City Royals TC .75 .30
❑ 636 Los Angeles Dodgers TC .75 .30
❑ 637 Milwaukee Brewers TC .75 .30
❑ 638 Minnesota Twins TC .75 .30
❑ 639 Montreal Expos TC .75 .30
❑ 640 New York Mets TC .75 .30
❑ 641 New York Yankees TC 4.00 1.50
❑ 642 Oakland Athletics TC .75 .30
❑ 643 Philadelphia Phillies TC .75 .30
❑ 644 Pittsburgh Pirates TC .75 .30
❑ 645 San Diego Padres TC .75 .30
❑ 646 San Francisco Giants TC .75 .30
❑ 647 Seattle Mariners TC .75 .30
❑ 648 St. Louis Cardinals TC .75 .30
❑ 649 Tampa Bay Devil Rays TC .75 .30
❑ 650 Texas Rangers TC .75 .30
❑ 651 Toronto Blue Jays TC .75 .30
❑ 652 Bucky Dent GM .50 .20
❑ 653 Jackie Robinson GM 2.00 .75
❑ 654 Roberto Clemente GM 2.50 1.00
❑ 655 Nolan Ryan GM 3.00 1.25
❑ 656 Kerry Wood GM .75 .30
❑ 657 Rickey Henderson GM 2.00 .75
❑ 658 Lou Brock GM 1.25 .50
❑ 659 David Wells GM .50 .20
❑ 660 Andruw Jones GM .75 .30
❑ 661 Carlton Fisk GM .75 .30

2001 Topps Chrome Traded

❑ COMPLETE SET (266)	150.00	75.00
❑ COMMON CARD (1-99/145-266)	.75	.30
❑ COMMON REPRINT (100-144)	1.25	.50
❑ T1 Sandy Alomar Jr.	.75	.30
❑ T2 Kevin Appier	1.25	.50
❑ T3 Brad Ausmus	1.25	.50
❑ T4 Derek Bell	.75	.30
❑ T5 Bret Boone	1.25	.50
❑ T6 Rico Brogna	.75	.30
❑ T7 Ellis Burks	1.25	.50
❑ T8 Ken Caminiti	1.25	.50
❑ T9 Roger Cedeno	.75	.30
❑ T10 Royce Clayton	.75	.30
❑ T11 Enrique Wilson	.75	.30
❑ T12 Rheal Cormier	.75	.30
❑ T13 Eric Davis	1.25	.50
❑ T14 Shawon Dunston	.75	.30
❑ T15 Andres Galarraga	1.25	.50
❑ T16 Tom Gordon	.75	.30
❑ T17 Mark Grace	2.00	.75
❑ T18 Jeffrey Hammonds	.75	.30
❑ T19 Dustin Hermanson	.75	.30
❑ T20 Quinton McCracken	.75	.30
❑ T21 Todd Hundley	.75	.30
❑ T22 Charles Johnson	1.25	.50
❑ T23 Marquis Grissom	1.25	.50
❑ T24 Jose Mesa	.75	.30
❑ T25 Brian Boehringer	.75	.30
❑ T26 John Rocker	1.25	.50
❑ T27 Jeff Frye	.75	.30
❑ T28 Reggie Sanders	1.25	.50
❑ T29 David Segui	.75	.30
❑ T30 Mike Sirotka	.75	.30
❑ T31 Fernando Tatis	.75	.30
❑ T32 Steve Trachsel	.75	.30
❑ T33 Ismael Valdes	.75	.30
❑ T34 Randy Velarde	.75	.30
❑ T35 Ryan Kohlmeier	.75	.30
❑ T36 Mike Bordick	1.25	.50
❑ T37 Kent Bottenfield	.75	.30
❑ T38 Pat Rapp	.75	.30
❑ T39 Jeff Nelson	.75	.30
❑ T40 Ricky Bottalico	.75	.30
❑ T41 Luke Prokopec	.75	.30
❑ T42 Hideo Nomo	3.00	1.25
❑ T43 Bill Mueller	1.25	.50
❑ T44 Roberto Kelly	.75	.30
❑ T45 Chris Holt	.75	.30
❑ T46 Mike Jackson	.75	.30
❑ T47 Devon White	1.25	.50
❑ T48 Gerald Williams	.75	.30
❑ T49 Eddie Taubensee	.75	.30
❑ T50 Brian Hunter	.75	.30
❑ T51 Nelson Cruz	.75	.30
❑ T52 Jeff Fassero	.75	.30
❑ T53 Bubba Trammell	.75	.30
❑ T54 Bo Porter	.75	.30
❑ T55 Greg Norton	.75	.30
❑ T56 Benito Santiago	1.25	.50
❑ T57 Ruben Rivera	.75	.30
❑ T58 Dee Brown	.75	.30
❑ T59 Jose Canseco	2.00	.75
❑ T60 Chris Michalak	.75	.30
❑ T61 Tim Worrell	.75	.30
❑ T62 Matt Clement	1.25	.50
❑ T63 Bill Pulsipher	.75	.30
❑ T64 Troy Brohawn RC	1.00	.40
❑ T65 Mark Kotsay	1.25	.50
❑ T66 Jimmy Rollins	1.25	.50
❑ T67 Shea Hillenbrand	1.25	.50
❑ T68 Ted Lilly	.75	.30
❑ T69 Jermaine Dye	1.25	.50
❑ T70 Jerry Hairston Jr.	.75	.30
❑ T71 John Mabry	.75	.30
❑ T72 Kurt Abbott	.75	.30
❑ T73 Eric Owens	.75	.30
❑ T74 Jeff Brantley	.75	.30
❑ T75 Roy Oswalt	3.00	1.25
❑ T76 Doug Mientkiewicz	1.25	.50
❑ T77 Rickey Henderson	3.00	1.25
❑ T78 Jason Grimsley	.75	.30
❑ T79 Christian Parker RC	1.00	.40
❑ T80 Donne Wall	.75	.30
❑ T81 Alex Arias	.75	.30
❑ T82 Willis Roberts	.75	.30
❑ T83 Ryan Minor	.75	.30
❑ T84 Jason LaRue	.75	.30
❑ T85 Ruben Sierra	1.25	.50
❑ T86 Johnny Damon	2.00	.75
❑ T87 Juan Gonzalez	1.25	.50
❑ T88 C.C. Sabathia	1.25	.50
❑ T89 Tony Batista	.75	.30
❑ T90 Jay Witasick	.75	.30
❑ T91 Brent Abernathy	.75	.30
❑ T92 Paul LoDuca	1.25	.50
❑ T93 Wes Helms	.75	.30
❑ T94 Mark Wohlers	.75	.30
❑ T95 Rob Bell	.75	.30
❑ T96 Tim Redding	.75	.30
❑ T97 Bud Smith RC	1.00	.40
❑ T98 Adam Dunn	2.00	.75
❑ T99 I.Suzuki/A.Pujols ROY	30.00	12.50
❑ T100 Carlton Fisk 81	2.00	.75
❑ T101 Tim Raines 81	1.25	.50
❑ T102 Juan Marichal 74	1.25	.50
❑ T103 Dave Winfield 81	1.25	.50
❑ T104 Reggie Jackson 82	2.00	.75
❑ T105 Cal Ripken 82	10.00	4.00
❑ T106 Ozzie Smith 82	5.00	2.00
❑ T107 Tom Seaver 83	2.00	.75
❑ T108 Lou Piniella 74	1.25	.50
❑ T109 Dwight Gooden 84	1.25	.50
❑ T110 Bret Saberhagen 84	1.25	.50
❑ T111 Gary Carter 85	1.25	.50
❑ T112 Jack Clark 85	1.25	.50
❑ T113 Rickey Henderson 85	3.00	1.25
❑ T114 Barry Bonds 86	8.00	3.00
❑ T115 Bobby Bonilla 86	1.25	.50
❑ T116 Jose Canseco 86	2.00	.75
❑ T117 Will Clark 86	2.00	.75
❑ T118 Andres Galarraga 86	1.25	.50
❑ T119 Bo Jackson 86	3.00	1.25
❑ T120 Wally Joyner 86	1.25	.50
❑ T121 Ellis Burks 87	1.25	.50
❑ T122 David Cone 87	1.25	.50
❑ T123 Greg Maddux 87	5.00	2.00
❑ T124 Willie Randolph 76	1.25	.50
❑ T125 Dennis Eckersley 87	1.25	.50
❑ T126 Matt Williams 87	1.25	.50
❑ T127 Joe Morgan 81	1.25	.50
❑ T128 Fred McGriff 87	2.00	.75
❑ T129 Roberto Alomar 88	2.00	.75
❑ T130 Lee Smith 88	1.25	.50
❑ T131 David Wells 88	1.25	.50
❑ T132 Ken Griffey Jr. 89	5.00	2.00
❑ T133 Deion Sanders 89	2.00	.75
❑ T134 Nolan Ryan 89	8.00	3.00
❑ T135 David Justice 90	1.25	.50
❑ T136 Joe Carter 91	1.25	.50
❑ T137 Jack Morris 92	1.25	.50
❑ T138 Mike Piazza 93	5.00	2.00
❑ T139 Barry Bonds 93	8.00	3.00
❑ T140 Terrence Long 94	1.25	.50
❑ T141 Ben Grieve 94	1.25	.50
❑ T142 Richie Sexson 95	1.25	.50
❑ T143 Sean Burroughs 99	1.25	.50
❑ T144 Alfonso Soriano 99	2.00	.75
❑ T145 Bob Boone MG	1.25	.50
❑ T146 Larry Bowa MG	1.25	.50
❑ T147 Bob Brenly MG	.75	.30
❑ T148 Buck Martinez MG	.75	.30
❑ T149 Lloyd McClendon MG	.75	.30
❑ T150 Jim Tracy MG	.75	.30
❑ T151 Jared Abruzzo RC	1.00	.40
❑ T152 Kurt Ainsworth	.75	.30
❑ T153 Willie Bloomquist	1.25	.50
❑ T154 Ben Broussard	.75	.30
❑ T155 Bobby Bradley	.75	.30
❑ T156 Mike Bynum	.75	.30
❑ T157 A.J. Hinch	.75	.30
❑ T158 Ryan Christianson	.75	.30
❑ T159 Carlos Silva	.75	.30
❑ T160 Joe Crede	3.00	1.25
❑ T161 Jack Cust	.75	.30
❑ T162 Ben Diggins	.75	.30
❑ T163 Phil Dumatrait	.75	.30
❑ T164 Alex Escobar	.75	.30
❑ T165 Miguel Olivo	.75	.30
❑ T166 Chris George	.75	.30
❑ T167 Marcus Giles	1.25	.50
❑ T168 Keith Ginter	.75	.30
❑ T169 Josh Girdley	.75	.30
❑ T170 Tony Alvarez	.75	.30
❑ T171 Scott Seabol	.75	.30
❑ T172 Josh Hamilton	1.50	.60
❑ T173 Jason Hart	.75	.30
❑ T174 Israel Alcantara	.75	.30
❑ T175 Jake Peavy	8.00	3.00
❑ T176 Stubby Clapp RC	1.00	.40
❑ T177 D'Angelo Jimenez	.75	.30
❑ T178 Nick Johnson	1.25	.50
❑ T179 Ben Johnson	1.25	.50
❑ T180 Larry Bigbie	.75	.30
❑ T181 Allen Levrault	.75	.30
❑ T182 Felipe Lopez	1.25	.50
❑ T183 Sean Burnett	.75	.30
❑ T184 Nick Neugebauer	.75	.30
❑ T185 Austin Kearns	1.25	.50
❑ T186 Corey Patterson	.75	.30
❑ T187 Carlos Pena	.75	.30
❑ T188 Ricardo Rodriguez RC	1.00	.40
❑ T189 Juan Rivera	.75	.30
❑ T190 Grant Roberts	.75	.30
❑ T191 Adam Pettyjohn RC	1.00	.40
❑ T192 Jared Sandberg	.75	.30
❑ T193 Xavier Nady	.75	.30
❑ T194 Dane Sardinha	.75	.30
❑ T195 Shawn Sonnier	.75	.30
❑ T196 Rafael Soriano	1.00	.40
❑ T197 Brian Specht RC	1.00	.40
❑ T198 Aaron Myette	.75	.30
❑ T199 Juan Uribe RC	1.25	.50
❑ T200 Jayson Werth	.75	.30
❑ T201 Brad Wilkerson	.75	.30
❑ T202 Horacio Estrada	.75	.30
❑ T203 Joel Pineiro	1.25	.50
❑ T204 Matt LeCroy	.75	.30
❑ T205 Michael Coleman	.75	.30
❑ T206 Ben Sheets	2.00	.75
❑ T207 Eric Byrnes	.75	.30
❑ T208 Sean Burroughs	.75	.30
❑ T209 Ken Harvey	.75	.30
❑ T210 Travis Hafner	8.00	3.00
❑ T211 Erick Almonte	1.00	.40
❑ T212 Jason Belcher RC	1.00	.40
❑ T213 Wilson Betemit RC	4.00	1.50
❑ T214 Hank Blalock RC	6.00	2.50
❑ T215 Danny Borrell	1.00	.40
❑ T216 John Buck RC	1.25	.50
❑ T217 Freddie Bynum RC	1.00	.40
❑ T218 Noel Devarez RC	1.00	.40
❑ T219 Juan Diaz RC	1.00	.40
❑ T220 Felix Diaz RC	1.00	.40
❑ T221 Josh Fogg RC	1.00	.40
❑ T222 Matt Ford RC	1.00	.40
❑ T223 Scott Heard	.75	.30
❑ T224 Ben Hendrickson RC	1.00	.40
❑ T225 Cody Ross RC	1.00	.40
❑ T226 Adrian Hernandez RC	1.00	.40
❑ T227 Alfredo Amezaga RC	1.00	.40
❑ T228 Bob Keppel RC	1.00	.40
❑ T229 Ryan Madson RC	2.00	.75
❑ T230 Octavio Martinez RC	1.00	.40
❑ T231 Hee Seop Choi	1.25	.50
❑ T232 Thomas Mitchell	.75	.30
❑ T233 Luis Montanez	1.00	.40
❑ T234 Andy Morales RC	1.00	.40

❑ T235 Justin Morneau RC	12.00	5.00
❑ T236 Toe Nash RC	1.00	.40
❑ T237 Valentino Pascucci RC	1.00	.40
❑ T238 Roy Smith RC	1.00	.40
❑ T239 Antonio Perez RC	1.25	.50
❑ T240 Chad Petty RC	1.00	.40
❑ T241 Steve Smyth	1.00	.40
❑ T242 Jose Reyes RC	30.00	12.50
❑ T243 Eric Reynolds RC	1.00	.40
❑ T244 Dominic Rich	1.00	.40
❑ T245 Jason Richardson RC	1.00	.40
❑ T246 Ed Rogers RC	1.00	.40
❑ T247 Albert Pujols	80.00	40.00
❑ T248 Esix Snead RC	1.00	.40
❑ T249 Luis Torres RC	1.00	.40
❑ T250 Matt White RC	1.00	.40
❑ T251 Blake Williams	1.00	.40
❑ T252 Chris Russ	1.00	.40
❑ T253 Joe Kennedy RC	1.25	.50
❑ T254 Jeff Randazzo RC	1.00	.40
❑ T255 Beau Hale RC	1.00	.40
❑ T256 Brad Hennessey RC	2.00	.75
❑ T257 Jake Gautreau RC	1.00	.40
❑ T258 Jeff Mathis RC	1.25	.50
❑ T259 Aaron Heilman RC	1.25	.50
❑ T260 Bronson Sardinha RC	1.00	.40
❑ T261 Irvin Guzman RC	8.00	3.00
❑ T262 Gabe Gross RC	1.25	.50
❑ T263 J.D. Martin RC	1.00	.40
❑ T264 Chris Smith RC	1.00	.40
❑ T265 Kenny Baugh RC	1.00	.40
❑ T266 Ichiro Suzuki RC	25.00	10.00

2002 Topps Chrome

❑ COMPLETE SET (660)	250.00	100.00
❑ COMPLETE SERIES 1 (330)	125.00	50.00
❑ COMPLETE SERIES 2 (330)	125.00	50.00
❑ COMMON (1-331/366-695)	.50	.20
❑ COMMON (307-326/671-690)	1.50	.60
❑ COMMON (327-331/691-695)	1.50	.60
❑ 1 Pedro Martinez	1.50	.60
❑ 2 Mike Stanton	.50	.20
❑ 3 Brad Penny	.50	.20
❑ 4 Mike Matheny	.50	.20
❑ 5 Johnny Damon	1.50	.60
❑ 6 Bret Boone	1.00	.40
❑ 7 Does Not Exist		
❑ 8 Chris Truby	.50	.20
❑ 9 B.J. Surhoff	1.00	.40
❑ 10 Mike Hampton	1.00	.40
❑ 11 Juan Pierre	1.00	.40
❑ 12 Mark Buehrle	1.00	.40
❑ 13 Bob Abreu	1.00	.40
❑ 14 David Cone	1.00	.40
❑ 15 Aaron Sele	.50	.20
❑ 16 Fernando Tatis	.50	.20
❑ 17 Bobby Jones	.50	.20
❑ 18 Rick Helling	.50	.20
❑ 19 Dmitri Young	1.00	.40
❑ 20 Mike Mussina	1.50	.60
❑ 21 Mike Sweeney	1.00	.40
❑ 22 Cristian Guzman	.50	.20
❑ 23 Ryan Kohlmeier	.50	.20
❑ 24 Adam Kennedy	.50	.20
❑ 25 Larry Walker	1.00	.40
❑ 26 Eric Davis	1.00	.40
❑ 27 Jason Tyner	.50	.20
❑ 28 Eric Young	.50	.20
❑ 29 Jason Marquis	.50	.20
❑ 30 Luis Gonzalez	1.00	.40
❑ 31 Kevin Tapani	.50	.20
❑ 32 Orlando Cabrera	1.00	.40
❑ 33 Marty Cordova	.50	.20
❑ 34 Brad Ausmus	1.00	.40
❑ 35 Livan Hernandez	1.00	.40
❑ 36 Alex Gonzalez	.50	.20
❑ 37 Edgar Renteria	1.00	.40
❑ 38 Bengie Molina	.50	.20
❑ 39 Frank Menechino	.50	.20
❑ 40 Rafael Palmeiro	1.50	.60
❑ 41 Brad Fullmer	.50	.20
❑ 42 Julio Zuleta	.50	.20
❑ 43 Darren Dreifort	.50	.20
❑ 44 Trot Nixon	1.00	.40
❑ 45 Trevor Hoffman	1.00	.40
❑ 46 Vladimir Nunez	.50	.20
❑ 47 Mark Kotsay	1.00	.40
❑ 48 Kenny Rogers	1.00	.40
❑ 49 Ben Petrick	.50	.20
❑ 50 Jeff Bagwell	1.50	.60
❑ 51 Juan Encarnacion	.50	.20
❑ 52 Ramiro Mendoza	.50	.20
❑ 53 Brian Meadows	.50	.20
❑ 54 Chad Curtis	.50	.20
❑ 55 Aramis Ramirez	1.00	.40
❑ 56 Mark McLemore	.50	.20
❑ 57 Dante Bichette	1.00	.40
❑ 58 Scott Schoeneweis	.50	.20
❑ 59 Jose Cruz Jr.	.50	.20
❑ 60 Roger Clemens	5.00	2.00
❑ 61 Jose Guillen	1.00	.40
❑ 62 Darren Oliver	.50	.20
❑ 63 Chris Reitsma	.50	.20
❑ 64 Jeff Abbott	.50	.20
❑ 65 Robin Ventura	1.00	.40
❑ 66 Denny Neagle	.50	.20
❑ 67 Al Martin	.50	.20
❑ 68 Benito Santiago	1.00	.40
❑ 69 Roy Oswalt	1.00	.40
❑ 70 Juan Gonzalez	1.00	.40
❑ 71 Garret Anderson	1.00	.40
❑ 72 Bobby Bonilla	1.00	.40
❑ 73 Danny Bautista	.50	.20
❑ 74 J.T. Snow	1.00	.40
❑ 75 Derek Jeter	6.00	2.50
❑ 76 John Olerud	1.00	.40
❑ 77 Kevin Appier	1.00	.40
❑ 78 Phil Nevin	1.00	.40
❑ 79 Sean Casey	1.00	.40
❑ 80 Troy Glaus	1.00	.40
❑ 81 Joe Randa	1.00	.40
❑ 82 Jose Valentin	.50	.20
❑ 83 Ricky Bottalico	.50	.20
❑ 84 Todd Zeile	1.00	.40
❑ 85 Barry Larkin	1.50	.60
❑ 86 Bob Wickman	.50	.20
❑ 87 Jeff Shaw	.50	.20
❑ 88 Greg Vaughn	.50	.20
❑ 89 Fernando Vina	.50	.20
❑ 90 Mark Mulder	1.00	.40
❑ 91 Paul Bako	.50	.20
❑ 92 Aaron Boone	1.00	.40
❑ 93 Esteban Loaiza	.50	.20
❑ 94 Richie Sexson	1.00	.40
❑ 95 Alfonso Soriano	1.00	.40
❑ 96 Tony Womack	.50	.20
❑ 97 Paul Shuey	.50	.20
❑ 98 Melvin Mora	1.00	.40
❑ 99 Tony Gwynn	3.00	1.25
❑ 100 Vladimir Guerrero	2.50	1.00
❑ 101 Keith Osik	.50	.20
❑ 102 Bud Smith	.50	.20
❑ 103 Scott Williamson	.50	.20
❑ 104 Daryle Ward	.50	.20
❑ 105 Doug Mientkiewicz	1.00	.40
❑ 106 Stan Javier	.50	.20
❑ 107 Russ Ortiz	.50	.20
❑ 108 Wade Miller	.50	.20
❑ 109 Luke Prokopec	.50	.20
❑ 110 Andruw Jones	1.50	.60
❑ 111 Ron Coomer	.50	.20
❑ 112 Dan Wilson	.50	.20
❑ 113 Luis Castillo	.50	.20
❑ 114 Derek Bell	.50	.20
❑ 115 Gary Sheffield	1.00	.40
❑ 116 Ruben Rivera	.50	.20
❑ 117 Paul O'Neill	1.50	.60
❑ 118 Craig Paquette	.50	.20
❑ 119 Kelvim Escobar	.50	.20
❑ 120 Brad Radke	1.00	.40
❑ 121 Jorge Fabregas	.50	.20
❑ 122 Randy Winn	.50	.20
❑ 123 Tom Goodwin	.50	.20
❑ 124 Jaret Wright	.50	.20
❑ 125 Barry Bonds HR 73	40.00	15.00
❑ 126 Al Leiter	.50	.20
❑ 127 Ben Davis	.50	.20
❑ 128 Frank Catalanotto	.50	.20
❑ 129 Jose Cabrera	.50	.20
❑ 130 Magglio Ordonez	1.00	.40
❑ 131 Jose Macias	.50	.20
❑ 132 Ted Lilly	.50	.20
❑ 133 Chris Holt	.50	.20
❑ 134 Eric Milton	.50	.20
❑ 135 Shannon Stewart	1.00	.40
❑ 136 Omar Olivares	.50	.20
❑ 137 David Segui	.50	.20
❑ 138 Jeff Nelson	.50	.20
❑ 139 Matt Williams	1.00	.40
❑ 140 Ellis Burks	1.00	.40
❑ 141 Jason Bere	.50	.20
❑ 142 Jimmy Haynes	.50	.20
❑ 143 Ramon Hernandez	.50	.20
❑ 144 Craig Counsell	.50	.20
❑ 145 John Smoltz	1.50	.60
❑ 146 Homer Bush	.50	.20
❑ 147 Quilvio Veras	.50	.20
❑ 148 Esteban Yan	.50	.20
❑ 149 Ramon Ortiz	.50	.20
❑ 150 Carlos Delgado	1.00	.40
❑ 151 Lee Stevens	.50	.20
❑ 152 Wil Cordero	.50	.20
❑ 153 Mike Bordick	1.00	.40
❑ 154 John Flaherty	.50	.20
❑ 155 Omar Daal	.50	.20
❑ 156 Todd Ritchie	.50	.20
❑ 157 Carl Everett	1.00	.40
❑ 158 Scott Sullivan	.50	.20
❑ 159 Deivi Cruz	.50	.20
❑ 160 Albert Pujols	5.00	2.00
❑ 161 Royce Clayton	.50	.20
❑ 162 Jeff Suppan	.50	.20
❑ 163 C.C. Sabathia	1.00	.40
❑ 164 Jimmy Rollins	1.00	.40
❑ 165 Rickey Henderson	2.50	1.00
❑ 166 Rey Ordonez	.50	.20
❑ 167 Shawn Estes	.50	.20
❑ 168 Reggie Sanders	1.00	.40
❑ 169 Jon Lieber	.50	.20
❑ 170 Armando Benitez	.50	.20
❑ 171 Mike Remlinger	.50	.20
❑ 172 Billy Wagner	1.00	.40
❑ 173 Troy Percival	1.00	.40
❑ 174 Devon White	1.00	.40
❑ 175 Ivan Rodriguez	1.50	.60
❑ 176 Dustin Hermanson	.50	.20
❑ 177 Brian Anderson	.50	.20
❑ 178 Graeme Lloyd	.50	.20
❑ 179 Russell Branyan	.50	.20
❑ 180 Bobby Higginson	1.00	.40
❑ 181 Alex Gonzalez	.50	.20
❑ 182 John Franco	1.00	.40
❑ 183 Sidney Ponson	.50	.20
❑ 184 Jose Mesa	.50	.20
❑ 185 Todd Hollandsworth	.50	.20
❑ 186 Kevin Young	.50	.20
❑ 187 Tim Wakefield	1.00	.40
❑ 188 Craig Biggio	1.50	.60
❑ 189 Jason Isringhausen	1.00	.40
❑ 190 Mark Quinn	.50	.20
❑ 191 Glendon Rusch	.50	.20
❑ 192 Damian Miller	.50	.20
❑ 193 Sandy Alomar Jr.	.50	.20
❑ 194 Scott Brosius	1.00	.40
❑ 195 Dave Martinez	.50	.20
❑ 196 Danny Graves	.50	.20
❑ 197 Shea Hillenbrand	1.00	.40
❑ 198 Jimmy Anderson	.50	.20
❑ 199 Travis Lee	.50	.20
❑ 200 Randy Johnson	2.50	1.00

No.	Player		
201	Carlos Beltran	1.00	.40
202	Jerry Hairston	.50	.20
203	Jesus Sanchez	.50	.20
204	Eddie Taubensee	.50	.20
205	David Wells	1.00	.40
206	Russ Davis	.50	.20
207	Michael Barrett	.50	.20
208	Marquis Grissom	1.00	.40
209	Byung-Hyun Kim	1.00	.40
210	Hideo Nomo	2.50	1.00
211	Ryan Rupe	.50	.20
212	Ricky Gutierrez	.50	.20
213	Darryl Kile	1.00	.40
214	Rico Brogna	.50	.20
215	Terrence Long	.50	.20
216	Mike Jackson	.50	.20
217	Jamey Wright	.50	.20
218	Adrian Beltre	1.00	.40
219	Benny Agbayani	.50	.20
220	Chuck Knoblauch	1.00	.40
221	Randy Wolf	.50	.20
222	Andy Ashby	.50	.20
223	Corey Koskie	.50	.20
224	Roger Cedeno	.50	.20
225	Ichiro Suzuki	5.00	2.00
226	Keith Foulke	1.00	.40
227	Ryan Minor	.50	.20
228	Shawon Dunston	.50	.20
229	Alex Cora	.50	.20
230	Jeromy Burnitz	1.00	.40
231	Mark Grace	1.50	.60
232	Aubrey Huff	1.00	.40
233	Jeffrey Hammonds	.50	.20
234	Olmedo Saenz	.50	.20
235	Brian Jordan	1.00	.40
236	Jeremy Giambi	.50	.20
237	Joe Girardi	.50	.20
238	Eric Gagne	1.00	.40
239	Masato Yoshii	.50	.20
240	Greg Maddux	4.00	1.50
241	Bryan Rekar	.50	.20
242	Ray Durham	1.00	.40
243	Torii Hunter	1.00	.40
244	Derrek Lee	1.50	.60
245	Jim Edmonds	1.00	.40
246	Einar Diaz	.50	.20
247	Brian Bohanon	.50	.20
248	Ron Belliard	.50	.20
249	Mike Lowell	1.00	.40
250	Sammy Sosa	2.50	1.00
251	Richard Hidalgo	.50	.20
252	Bartolo Colon	1.00	.40
253	Jorge Posada	1.50	.60
254	Latroy Hawkins	.50	.20
255	Paul LoDuca	1.00	.40
256	Carlos Febles	.50	.20
257	Nelson Cruz	.50	.20
258	Edgardo Alfonzo	.50	.20
259	Joey Hamilton	.50	.20
260	Cliff Floyd	1.00	.40
261	Wes Helms	.50	.20
262	Jay Bell	1.00	.40
263	Mike Cameron	.50	.20
264	Paul Konerko	1.00	.40
265	Jeff Kent	1.00	.40
266	Robert Fick	.50	.20
267	Allen Levrault	.50	.20
268	Placido Polanco	.50	.20
269	Marlon Anderson	.50	.20
270	Mariano Rivera	2.50	1.00
271	Chan Ho Park	1.00	.40
272	Jose Vizcaino	.50	.20
273	Jeff D'Amico	.50	.20
274	Mark Gardner	.50	.20
275	Travis Fryman	1.00	.40
276	Darren Lewis	.50	.20
277	Bruce Bochy MG	.50	.20
278	Jerry Manuel MG	.50	.20
279	Bob Brenly MG	.50	.20
280	Don Baylor MG	1.00	.40
281	Davey Lopes MG	1.00	.40
282	Jerry Narron MG	.50	.20
283	Tony Muser MG	.50	.20
284	Hal McRae MG	1.00	.40
285	Bobby Cox MG	.50	.20
286	Larry Dierker MG	.50	.20
287	Phil Garner MG	1.00	.40
288	Joe Kerrigan MG	.50	.20
289	Bobby Valentine MG	.50	.20
290	Dusty Baker MG	1.00	.40
291	Lloyd McClendon MG	.50	.20
292	Mike Scioscia MG	.50	.20
293	Buck Martinez MG	.50	.20
294	Larry Bowa MG	1.00	.40
295	Tony LaRussa MG	1.00	.40
296	Jeff Torborg MG	.50	.20
297	Tom Kelly MG	.50	.20
298	Mike Hargrove MG	.50	.20
299	Art Howe MG	.50	.20
300	Lou Piniella MG	1.00	.40
301	Charlie Manuel MG	.50	.20
302	Buddy Bell MG	1.00	.40
303	Tony Perez MG	1.00	.40
304	Bob Boone MG	1.00	.40
305	Joe Torre MG	1.50	.60
306	Jim Tracy MG	.50	.20
307	Jason Lane PROS	1.50	.60
308	Chris George PROS	1.50	.60
309	Hank Blalock PROS	2.50	1.00
310	Joe Borchard PROS	1.50	.60
311	Marlon Byrd PROS	1.50	.60
312	Raymond Cabrera PROS RC	1.50	.60
313	Freddy Sanchez PROS RC	6.00	2.50
314	Scott Wiggins PROS RC	1.50	.60
315	Jason Maule PROS RC	1.50	.60
316	Dionys Cesar PROS RC	1.50	.60
317	Boof Bonser PROS	1.50	.60
318	Juan Tolentino PROS RC	1.50	.60
319	Earl Snyder PROS RC	1.50	.60
320	Travis Wade PROS RC	1.50	.60
321	Napolean Calzado PROS RC	1.50	.60
322	Eric Glaser PROS RC	1.50	.60
323	Craig Kuzmic PROS RC	1.50	.60
324	Nic Jackson PROS RC	1.50	.60
325	Mike Rivera PROS	1.50	.60
326	Jason Bay PROS RC	8.00	3.00
327	Chris Smith DP	1.50	.60
328	Jake Gautreau DP	1.50	.60
329	Gabe Gross DP	1.50	.60
330	Kenny Baugh DP	1.50	.60
331	J.D. Martin DP	1.50	.60
366	Pat Meares	.50	.20
367	Mike Lieberthal	1.00	.40
368	Larry Bigbie	.50	.20
369	Ron Gant	1.00	.40
370	Moises Alou	1.00	.40
371	Chad Kreuter	.50	.20
372	Willis Roberts	.50	.20
373	Toby Hall	.50	.20
374	Miguel Batista	.50	.20
375	John Burkett	.50	.20
376	Cory Lidle	.50	.20
377	Nick Neugebauer	.50	.20
378	Jay Payton	.50	.20
379	Steve Karsay	.50	.20
380	Eric Chavez	1.00	.40
381	Kelly Stinnett	.50	.20
382	Jarrod Washburn	.50	.20
383	Rick White	.50	.20
384	Jeff Conine	1.00	.40
385	Fred McGriff	1.50	.60
386	Marvin Benard	.50	.20
387	Joe Crede	1.00	.40
388	Dennis Cook	.50	.20
389	Rick Reed	.50	.20
390	Tom Glavine	1.50	.60
391	Rondell White	1.00	.40
392	Matt Morris	1.00	.40
393	Pat Rapp	.50	.20
394	Robert Person	.50	.20
395	Omar Vizquel	1.50	.60
396	Jeff Cirillo	.50	.20
397	Dave Mlicki	.50	.20
398	Jose Ortiz	.50	.20
399	Ryan Dempster	.50	.20
400	Curt Schilling	1.00	.40
401	Peter Bergeron	.50	.20
402	Kyle Lohse	.50	.20
403	Craig Wilson	.50	.20
404	David Justice	1.00	.40
405	Darin Erstad	1.00	.40
406	Jose Mercedes	.50	.20
407	Carl Pavano	1.00	.40
408	Albie Lopez	.50	.20
409	Alex Ochoa	.50	.20
410	Chipper Jones	2.50	1.00
411	Tyler Houston	.50	.20
412	Dean Palmer	1.00	.40
413	Damian Jackson	.50	.20
414	Josh Towers	.50	.20
415	Rafael Furcal	1.00	.40
416	Mike Morgan	.50	.20
417	Herb Perry	.50	.20
418	Mike Sirotka	.50	.20
419	Mark Wohlers	.50	.20
420	Nomar Garciaparra	4.00	1.50
421	Felipe Lopez	.50	.20
422	Joe McEwing	.50	.20
423	Jacque Jones	1.00	.40
424	Julio Franco	1.00	.40
425	Frank Thomas	2.50	1.00
426	So Taguchi RC	2.50	1.00
427	Kazuhisa Ishii RC	2.50	1.00
428	D'Angelo Jimenez	.50	.20
429	Chris Stynes	.50	.20
430	Kerry Wood	1.00	.40
431	Chris Singleton	.50	.20
432	Erubiel Durazo	.50	.20
433	Matt Lawton	.50	.20
434	Bill Mueller	1.00	.40
435	Jose Canseco	1.50	.60
436	Ben Grieve	.50	.20
437	Terry Mulholland	.50	.20
438	David Bell	.50	.20
439	A.J. Pierzynski	1.00	.40
440	Adam Dunn	1.00	.40
441	Jon Garland	1.00	.40
442	Jeff Fassero	.50	.20
443	Julio Lugo	.50	.20
444	Carlos Guillen	1.00	.40
445	Orlando Hernandez	1.00	.40
446	Mark Loretta	.50	.20
447	Scott Spiezio	.50	.20
448	Kevin Millwood	1.00	.40
449	Jamie Moyer	1.00	.40
450	Todd Helton	1.50	.60
451	Todd Walker	.50	.20
452	Jose Lima	.50	.20
453	Brook Fordyce	.50	.20
454	Aaron Rowand	1.00	.40
455	Barry Zito	1.00	.40
456	Eric Owens	.50	.20
457	Charles Nagy	.50	.20
458	Raul Ibanez	.50	.20
459	Joe Mays	.50	.20
460	Jim Thome	1.50	.60
461	Adam Eaton	.50	.20
462	Felix Martinez	.50	.20
463	Vernon Wells	1.00	.40
464	Donnie Sadler	.50	.20
465	Tony Clark	.50	.20
466	Jose Hernandez	.50	.20
467	Ramon Martinez	.50	.20
468	Rusty Greer	1.00	.40
469	Rod Barajas	.50	.20
470	Lance Berkman	1.00	.40
471	Brady Anderson	1.00	.40
472	Pedro Astacio	.50	.20
473	Shane Halter	.50	.20
474	Bret Prinz	.50	.20
475	Edgar Martinez	1.50	.60
476	Steve Trachsel	.50	.20
477	Gary Matthews Jr.	.50	.20
478	Ismael Valdes	.50	.20
479	Juan Uribe	.50	.20
480	Shawn Green	1.00	.40
481	Kirk Rueter	.50	.20
482	Damion Easley	.50	.20
483	Chris Carpenter	1.00	.40
484	Kris Benson	.50	.20
485	Antonio Alfonseca	.50	.20
486	Kyle Farnsworth	.50	.20
487	Brandon Lyon	.50	.20
488	Hideki Irabu	.50	.20
489	David Ortiz	2.50	1.00
490	Mike Piazza	4.00	1.50
491	Derek Lowe	1.00	.40
492	Chris Gomez	.50	.20

❑ 493 Mark Johnson .50 .20
❑ 494 John Rocker 1.00 .40
❑ 495 Eric Karros 1.00 .40
❑ 496 Bill Haselman .50 .20
❑ 497 Dave Veres .50 .20
❑ 498 Pete Harnisch .50 .20
❑ 499 Tomokazu Ohka .50 .20
❑ 500 Barry Bonds 6.00 2.50
❑ 501 David Dellucci .50 .20
❑ 502 Wendell Magee .50 .20
❑ 503 Tom Gordon .50 .20
❑ 504 Javier Vazquez 1.00 .40
❑ 505 Ben Sheets 1.00 .40
❑ 506 Wilton Guerrero .50 .20
❑ 507 John Halama .50 .20
❑ 508 Mark Redman .50 .20
❑ 509 Jack Wilson .50 .20
❑ 510 Bernie Williams 1.50 .60
❑ 511 Miguel Cairo .50 .20
❑ 512 Denny Hocking .50 .20
❑ 513 Tony Batista .50 .20
❑ 514 Mark Grudzielanek .50 .20
❑ 515 Jose Vidro .50 .20
❑ 516 Sterling Hitchcock .50 .20
❑ 517 Billy Koch .50 .20
❑ 518 Matt Clement 1.00 .40
❑ 519 Bruce Chen .50 .20
❑ 520 Roberto Alomar 1.50 .60
❑ 521 Orlando Palmeiro .50 .20
❑ 522 Steve Finley 1.00 .40
❑ 523 Danny Patterson .50 .20
❑ 524 Terry Adams .50 .20
❑ 525 Tino Martinez 1.50 .60
❑ 526 Tony Armas Jr. .50 .20
❑ 527 Geoff Jenkins .50 .20
❑ 528 Kerry Robinson .50 .20
❑ 529 Corey Patterson .50 .20
❑ 530 Brian Giles 1.00 .40
❑ 531 Jose Jimenez .50 .20
❑ 532 Joe Kennedy .50 .20
❑ 533 Armando Rios .50 .20
❑ 534 Osvaldo Fernandez .50 .20
❑ 535 Ruben Sierra 1.00 .40
❑ 536 Octavio Dotel .50 .20
❑ 537 Luis Sojo .50 .20
❑ 538 Brent Butler .50 .20
❑ 539 Pablo Ozuna .50 .20
❑ 540 Freddy Garcia 1.00 .40
❑ 541 Chad Durbin .50 .20
❑ 542 Orlando Merced .50 .20
❑ 543 Michael Tucker .50 .20
❑ 544 Roberto Hernandez .50 .20
❑ 545 Pat Burrell 1.00 .40
❑ 546 A.J. Burnett 1.00 .40
❑ 547 Bubba Trammell .50 .20
❑ 548 Scott Elarton .50 .20
❑ 549 Mike Darr .50 .20
❑ 550 Ken Griffey Jr. 4.00 1.50
❑ 551 Ugueth Urbina .50 .20
❑ 552 Todd Jones .50 .20
❑ 553 Delino Deshields .50 .20
❑ 554 Adam Piatt .50 .20
❑ 555 Jason Kendall 1.00 .40
❑ 556 Hector Ortiz .50 .20
❑ 557 Turk Wendell .50 .20
❑ 558 Rob Bell .50 .20
❑ 559 Sun Woo Kim .50 .20
❑ 560 Raul Mondesi 1.00 .40
❑ 561 Brent Abernathy .50 .20
❑ 562 Seth Etherton .50 .20
❑ 563 Shawn Wooten .50 .20
❑ 564 Jay Buhner 1.00 .40
❑ 565 Andres Galarraga 1.00 .40
❑ 566 Shane Reynolds .50 .20
❑ 567 Rod Beck .50 .20
❑ 568 Dee Brown .50 .20
❑ 569 Pedro Feliz .50 .20
❑ 570 Ryan Klesko 1.00 .40
❑ 571 John Vander Wal .50 .20
❑ 572 Nick Bierbrodt .50 .20
❑ 573 Joe Nathan 1.00 .40
❑ 574 James Baldwin .50 .20
❑ 575 J.D. Drew 1.00 .40
❑ 576 Greg Colbrunn .50 .20
❑ 577 Doug Glanville .50 .20
❑ 578 Brandon Duckworth .50 .20
❑ 579 Shawn Chacon .50 .20
❑ 580 Rich Aurilia .50 .20
❑ 581 Chuck Finley 1.00 .40
❑ 582 Abraham Nunez .50 .20
❑ 583 Kenny Lofton 1.00 .40
❑ 584 Brian Daubach .50 .20
❑ 585 Miguel Tejada 1.00 .40
❑ 586 Nate Cornejo .50 .20
❑ 587 Kazuhiro Sasaki 1.00 .40
❑ 588 Chris Richard .50 .20
❑ 589 Armando Reynoso .50 .20
❑ 590 Tim Hudson 1.00 .40
❑ 591 Neifi Perez .50 .20
❑ 592 Steve Cox .50 .20
❑ 593 Henry Blanco .50 .20
❑ 594 Ricky Ledee .50 .20
❑ 595 Tim Salmon 1.50 .60
❑ 596 Luis Rivas .50 .20
❑ 597 Jeff Zimmerman .50 .20
❑ 598 Matt Stairs .50 .20
❑ 599 Preston Wilson 1.00 .40
❑ 600 Mark McGwire 6.00 2.50
❑ 601 Timo Perez .50 .20
❑ 602 Matt Anderson .50 .20
❑ 603 Todd Hundley .50 .20
❑ 604 Rick Ankiel .50 .20
❑ 605 Tsuyoshi Shinjo 1.00 .40
❑ 606 Woody Williams .50 .20
❑ 607 Jason LaRue .50 .20
❑ 608 Carlos Lee 1.00 .40
❑ 609 Russ Johnson .50 .20
❑ 610 Scott Rolen 1.50 .60
❑ 611 Brent Mayne .50 .20
❑ 612 Darrin Fletcher .50 .20
❑ 613 Ray Lankford 1.00 .40
❑ 614 Troy O'Leary .50 .20
❑ 615 Javier Lopez 1.00 .40
❑ 616 Randy Velarde .50 .20
❑ 617 Vinny Castilla 1.00 .40
❑ 618 Milton Bradley 1.00 .40
❑ 619 Ruben Mateo .50 .20
❑ 620 Jason Giambi Yankees 1.00 .40
❑ 621 Andy Benes .50 .20
❑ 622 Joe Mauer RC 15.00 6.00
❑ 623 Andy Pettitte 1.50 .60
❑ 624 Jose Offerman .50 .20
❑ 625 Mo Vaughn 1.00 .40
❑ 626 Steve Sparks .50 .20
❑ 627 Mike Matthews .50 .20
❑ 628 Robb Nen 1.00 .40
❑ 629 Kip Wells .50 .20
❑ 630 Kevin Brown 1.00 .40
❑ 631 Arthur Rhodes .50 .20
❑ 632 Gabe Kapler 1.00 .40
❑ 633 Jermaine Dye 1.00 .40
❑ 634 Josh Beckett 1.00 .40
❑ 635 Pokey Reese .50 .20
❑ 636 Benji Gil .50 .20
❑ 637 Marcus Giles 1.00 .40
❑ 638 Julian Tavarez .50 .20
❑ 639 Jason Schmidt 1.00 .40
❑ 640 Alex Rodriguez 4.00 1.50
❑ 641 Anaheim Angels TC 1.00 .40
❑ 642 Arizona Diamondbacks TC 1.50 .60
❑ 643 Atlanta Braves TC 1.00 .40
❑ 644 Baltimore Orioles TC 1.00 .40
❑ 645 Boston Red Sox TC 1.00 .40
❑ 646 Chicago Cubs TC 1.00 .40
❑ 647 Chicago White Sox TC 1.00 .40
❑ 648 Cincinnati Reds TC 1.00 .40
❑ 649 Cleveland Indians TC 1.00 .40
❑ 650 Colorado Rockies TC 1.00 .40
❑ 651 Detroit Tigers TC 1.00 .40
❑ 652 Florida Marlins TC 1.00 .40
❑ 653 Houston Astros TC 1.00 .40
❑ 654 Kansas City Royals TC 1.00 .40
❑ 655 Los Angeles Dodgers TC 1.00 .40
❑ 656 Milwaukee Brewers TC 1.00 .40
❑ 657 Minnesota Twins TC 1.00 .40
❑ 658 Montreal Expos TC 1.00 .40
❑ 659 New York Mets TC 1.00 .40
❑ 660 New York Yankees TC 2.50 1.00
❑ 661 Oakland Athletics TC 1.00 .40
❑ 662 Philadelphia Phillies TC 1.00 .40
❑ 663 Pittsburgh Pirates TC 1.00 .40
❑ 664 San Diego Padres TC 1.00 .40
❑ 665 San Francisco Giants TC 1.00 .40
❑ 666 Seattle Mariners TC 1.50 .60
❑ 667 St. Louis Cardinals TC 1.00 .40
❑ 668 Tampa Bay Devil Rays TC 1.00 .40
❑ 669 Texas Rangers TC 1.00 .40
❑ 670 Toronto Blue Jays TC 1.00 .40
❑ 671 Juan Cruz PROS 1.50 .60
❑ 672 Kevin Cash PROS RC 1.50 .60
❑ 673 Jimmy Gobble PROS RC 1.50 .60
❑ 674 Mike Hill PROS RC 1.50 .60
❑ 675 Taylor Buchholz PROS RC 1.50 .60
❑ 676 Bill Hall PROS 1.50 .60
❑ 677 Brett Roneberg PROS RC 1.50 .60
❑ 678 Royce Huffman PROS RC 1.50 .60
❑ 679 Chris Tritle PROS RC 1.50 .60
❑ 680 Nate Espy PROS 1.50 .60
❑ 681 Nick Alvarez PROS RC 1.50 .60
❑ 682 Jason Botts PROS RC 1.50 .60
❑ 683 Ryan Gripp PROS RC 1.50 .60
❑ 684 Dan Phillips PROS RC 1.50 .60
❑ 685 Pablo Arias PROS RC 1.50 .60
❑ 686 John Rodriguez PROS RC 2.50 1.00
❑ 687 Rich Harden PROS RC 8.00 3.00
❑ 688 Neal Frendling PROS RC 1.50 .60
❑ 689 Rich Thompson PROS RC 1.50 .60
❑ 690 Greg Montalbano PROS RC 1.50 .60
❑ 691 Len Dinardo DP RC 1.50 .60
❑ 692 Ryan Raburn DP RC 1.50 .60
❑ 693 Josh Barfield DP RC 5.00 2.00
❑ 694 David Bacani DP RC 1.50 .60
❑ 695 Dan Johnson DP RC 2.50 1.00

2002 Topps Chrome Traded

❑ COMPLETE SET (275) 120.00 60.00
❑ T1 Jeff Weaver .50 .20
❑ T2 Jay Powell .50 .20
❑ T3 Alex Gonzalez .50 .20
❑ T4 Jason Isringhausen .75 .30
❑ T5 Tyler Houston .50 .20
❑ T6 Ben Broussard .50 .20
❑ T7 Chuck Knoblauch .75 .30
❑ T8 Brian L. Hunter .50 .20
❑ T9 Dustan Mohr .50 .20
❑ T10 Eric Hinske .50 .20
❑ T11 Roger Cedeno .50 .20
❑ T12 Eddie Perez .50 .20
❑ T13 Jeromy Burnitz .75 .30
❑ T14 Bartolo Colon .75 .30
❑ T15 Rick Helling .50 .20
❑ T16 Dan Plesac .50 .20
❑ T17 Scott Strickland .50 .20
❑ T18 Antonio Alfonseca .50 .20
❑ T19 Ricky Gutierrez .50 .20
❑ T20 John Valentin .50 .20
❑ T21 Raul Mondesi .75 .30
❑ T22 Ben Davis .50 .20
❑ T23 Nelson Figueroa .50 .20
❑ T24 Earl Snyder .50 .20
❑ T25 Robin Ventura .75 .30
❑ T26 Jimmy Haynes .50 .20
❑ T27 Kenny Kelly .50 .20
❑ T28 Morgan Ensberg .75 .30
❑ T29 Reggie Sanders .75 .30
❑ T30 Shigetoshi Hasegawa .75 .30
❑ T31 Mike Timlin .50 .20
❑ T32 Russell Branyan .50 .20
❑ T33 Alan Embree .50 .20

❑ T34 D'Angelo Jimenez .50 .20
❑ T35 Kent Mercker .50 .20
❑ T36 Jesse Orosco .50 .20
❑ T37 Gregg Zaun .50 .20
❑ T38 Reggie Taylor .50 .20
❑ T39 Andres Galarraga .75 .30
❑ T40 Chris Truby .50 .20
❑ T41 Bruce Chen .50 .20
❑ T42 Darren Lewis .50 .20
❑ T43 Ryan Kohlmeier .50 .20
❑ T44 John McDonald .50 .20
❑ T45 Omar Daal .50 .20
❑ T46 Matt Clement .75 .30
❑ T47 Glendon Rusch .50 .20
❑ T48 Chan Ho Park .75 .30
❑ T49 Benny Agbayani .50 .20
❑ T50 Juan Gonzalez .75 .30
❑ T51 Carlos Baerga .50 .20
❑ T52 Tim Raines .75 .30
❑ T53 Kevin Appier .75 .30
❑ T54 Marty Cordova .50 .20
❑ T55 Jeff D'Amico .50 .20
❑ T56 Dmitri Young .75 .30
❑ T57 Roosevelt Brown .50 .20
❑ T58 Dustin Hermanson .50 .20
❑ T59 Jose Rijo .50 .20
❑ T60 Todd Ritchie .50 .20
❑ T61 Lee Stevens .50 .20
❑ T62 Placido Polanco .50 .20
❑ T63 Eric Young .50 .20
❑ T64 Chuck Finley .75 .30
❑ T65 Dicky Gonzalez .50 .20
❑ T66 Jose Macias .50 .20
❑ T67 Gabe Kapler .75 .30
❑ T68 Sandy Alomar Jr. .50 .20
❑ T69 Henry Blanco .50 .20
❑ T70 Julian Tavarez .50 .20
❑ T71 Paul Bako .50 .20
❑ T72 Scott Rolen 1.25 .50
❑ T73 Brian Jordan .75 .30
❑ T74 Rickey Henderson 2.00 .75
❑ T75 Kevin Mench .50 .20
❑ T76 Hideo Nomo 2.00 .75
❑ T77 Jeremy Giambi .50 .20
❑ T78 Brad Fullmer .50 .20
❑ T79 Carl Everett .75 .30
❑ T80 David Wells .75 .30
❑ T81 Aaron Sele .50 .20
❑ T82 Todd Hollandsworth .50 .20
❑ T83 Vicente Padilla .50 .20
❑ T84 Kenny Lofton .75 .30
❑ T85 Corky Miller .50 .20
❑ T86 Josh Fogg .50 .20
❑ T87 Cliff Floyd .75 .30
❑ T88 Craig Paquette .50 .20
❑ T89 Jay Payton .50 .20
❑ T90 Carlos Pena .50 .20
❑ T91 Juan Encarnacion .50 .20
❑ T92 Rey Sanchez .50 .20
❑ T93 Ryan Dempster .50 .20
❑ T94 Mario Encarnacion .50 .20
❑ T95 Jorge Julio .50 .20
❑ T96 John Mabry .50 .20
❑ T97 Todd Zeile .75 .30
❑ T98 Johnny Damon 1.25 .50
❑ T99 Deivi Cruz .50 .20
❑ T100 Gary Sheffield .75 .30
❑ T101 Ted Lilly .50 .20
❑ T102 Todd Van Poppel .50 .20
❑ T103 Shawn Estes .50 .20
❑ T104 Cesar Izturis .50 .20
❑ T105 Ron Coomer .50 .20
❑ T106 Grady Little MG RC .50 .20
❑ T107 Jimy Williams MGR .50 .20
❑ T108 Tony Pena MGR .50 .20
❑ T109 Frank Robinson MGR 1.25 .50
❑ T110 Ron Gardenhire MGR .50 .20
❑ T111 Dennis Tankersley .50 .20
❑ T112 Alejandro Cadena RC 1.00 .40
❑ T113 Justin Reid RC 1.00 .40
❑ T114 Nate Field RC 1.00 .40
❑ T115 Rene Reyes RC 1.00 .40
❑ T116 Nelson Castro RC 1.00 .40
❑ T117 Miguel Olivo .50 .20
❑ T118 David Espinosa .50 .20
❑ T119 Chris Bootcheck RC 1.00 .40
❑ T120 Rob Henkel RC 1.00 .40
❑ T121 Steve Bechler RC 1.00 .40
❑ T122 Mark Outlaw RC 1.00 .40
❑ T123 Henry Pichardo RC 1.00 .40
❑ T124 Michael Floyd RC 1.00 .40
❑ T125 Richard Lane RC 1.00 .40
❑ T126 Pete Zamora RC 1.00 .40
❑ T127 Javier Colina .50 .20
❑ T128 Greg Sain RC 1.00 .40
❑ T129 Ronnie Merrill .50 .20
❑ T130 Gavin Floyd RC 2.50 1.00
❑ T131 Josh Bonifay RC 1.00 .40
❑ T132 Tommy Marx RC 1.00 .40
❑ T133 Gary Cates Jr. RC 1.00 .40
❑ T134 Neal Cotts RC 2.50 1.00
❑ T135 Angel Berroa .50 .20
❑ T136 Elio Serrano RC 1.00 .40
❑ T137 J.J. Putz RC 1.25 .50
❑ T138 Ruben Gotay RC 1.25 .50
❑ T139 Eddie Rogers .50 .20
❑ T140 Wily Mo Pena .75 .30
❑ T141 Tyler Yates RC 1.00 .40
❑ T142 Colin Young RC .75 .30
❑ T143 Chance Caple .50 .20
❑ T144 Ben Howard RC 1.00 .40
❑ T145 Ryan Bukvich RC 1.00 .40
❑ T146 Cliff Bartosh RC 1.00 .40
❑ T147 Brandon Claussen .50 .20
❑ T148 Cristian Guerrero .50 .20
❑ T149 Derrick Lewis .50 .20
❑ T150 Eric Miller RC 1.00 .40
❑ T151 Justin Huber RC 2.00 .75
❑ T152 Adrian Gonzalez .50 .20
❑ T153 Brian West RC 1.00 .40
❑ T154 Chris Baker RC 1.00 .40
❑ T155 Drew Henson .50 .20
❑ T156 Scott Hairston RC 1.25 .50
❑ T157 Jason Simontacchi RC 1.00 .40
❑ T158 Jason Arnold RC 1.00 .40
❑ T159 Brandon Phillips .50 .20
❑ T160 Adam Roller RC 1.00 .40
❑ T161 Scotty Layfield RC 1.00 .40
❑ T162 Freddie Money RC 1.00 .40
❑ T163 Noochie Varner RC 1.00 .40
❑ T164 Terrance Hill RC 1.00 .40
❑ T165 Jeremy Hill RC 1.00 .40
❑ T166 Carlos Cabrera RC 1.00 .40
❑ T167 Jose Morban RC 1.00 .40
❑ T168 Kevin Frederick RC 1.00 .40
❑ T169 Mark Teixeira 4.00 1.50
❑ T170 Brian Rogers .50 .20
❑ T171 Anastacio Martinez RC 1.00 .40
❑ T172 Bobby Jenks RC 4.00 1.50
❑ T173 David Gil RC 1.00 .40
❑ T174 Andres Torres .50 .20
❑ T175 James Barrett RC 1.00 .40
❑ T176 Jimmy Journell .50 .20
❑ T177 Brett Kay RC 1.00 .40
❑ T178 Jason Young RC 1.00 .40
❑ T179 Mark Hamilton RC 1.00 .40
❑ T180 Jose Bautista RC 2.50 1.00
❑ T181 Blake McGinley RC 1.00 .40
❑ T182 Ryan Mottl RC 1.00 .40
❑ T183 Jeff Austin RC 1.00 .40
❑ T184 Xavier Nady .50 .20
❑ T185 Kyle Kane RC 1.00 .40
❑ T186 Travis Foley RC 1.00 .40
❑ T187 Nathan Kaup RC 1.00 .40
❑ T188 Eric Cyr .50 .20
❑ T189 Josh Cisneros RC 1.00 .40
❑ T190 Brad Nelson RC 1.00 .40
❑ T191 Clint Weibl RC 1.00 .40
❑ T192 Ron Calloway RC 1.00 .40
❑ T193 Jung Bong .50 .20
❑ T194 Rolando Viera RC 1.00 .40
❑ T195 Jason Bulger RC 1.00 .40
❑ T196 Chone Figgins RC 4.00 1.50
❑ T197 Jimmy Alvarez RC 1.00 .40
❑ T198 Joel Crump RC 1.00 .40
❑ T199 Ryan Doumit RC 1.50 .60
❑ T200 Demetrius Heath RC 1.00 .40
❑ T201 John Ennis RC 1.00 .40
❑ T202 Doug Sessions RC 1.00 .40
❑ T203 Clinton Hosford RC 1.00 .40
❑ T204 Chris Narveson RC 1.00 .40
❑ T205 Ross Peeples RC 1.00 .40
❑ T206 Alex Requena RC 1.00 .40
❑ T207 Matt Erickson RC 1.00 .40
❑ T208 Brian Forystek RC 1.00 .40
❑ T209 Dewon Brazelton .50 .20
❑ T210 Nathan Haynes .50 .20
❑ T211 Jack Cust .50 .20
❑ T212 Jesse Foppert RC 1.25 .50
❑ T213 Jesus Cota RC 1.00 .40
❑ T214 Juan M. Gonzalez RC 1.00 .40
❑ T215 Tim Kalita RC 1.00 .40
❑ T216 Manny Delcarmen RC 1.25 .50
❑ T217 Jim Kavourias RC 1.00 .40
❑ T218 C.J. Wilson RC 1.00 .40
❑ T219 Edwin Yan RC 1.00 .40
❑ T220 Andy Van Hekken .50 .20
❑ T221 Michael Cuddyer .50 .20
❑ T222 Jeff Verplancke RC 1.00 .40
❑ T223 Mike Wilson RC 1.00 .40
❑ T224 Corwin Malone RC 1.00 .40
❑ T225 Chris Snelling RC 1.50 .60
❑ T226 Joe Rogers RC 1.00 .40
❑ T227 Jason Bay 8.00 3.00
❑ T228 Ezequiel Astacio RC 1.00 .40
❑ T229 Joey Hammond RC 1.00 .40
❑ T230 Chris Duffy RC 1.00 .40
❑ T231 Mark Prior 1.25 .50
❑ T232 Hansel Izquierdo RC 1.00 .40
❑ T233 Franklyn German RC 1.00 .40
❑ T234 Alexis Gomez .50 .20
❑ T235 Jorge Padilla RC 1.00 .40
❑ T236 Ryan Snare RC 1.00 .40
❑ T237 Deivis Santos .50 .20
❑ T238 Taggert Bozied RC 1.25 .50
❑ T239 Mike Peeples RC 1.00 .40
❑ T240 Ronald Acuna RC 1.00 .40
❑ T241 Koyie Hill .50 .20
❑ T242 Garrett Guzman RC 1.00 .40
❑ T243 Ryan Church RC 2.50 1.00
❑ T244 Tony Fontana RC 1.00 .40
❑ T245 Keto Anderson RC 1.00 .40
❑ T246 Brad Bouras RC 1.00 .40
❑ T247 Jason Dubois RC 1.25 .50
❑ T248 Angel Guzman RC 2.00 .75
❑ T249 Joel Hanrahan RC 1.00 .40
❑ T250 Joe Jiannetti RC 1.00 .40
❑ T251 Sean Pierce RC 1.00 .40
❑ T252 Jake Mauer RC 1.00 .40
❑ T253 Marshall McDougall RC 1.00 .40
❑ T254 Edwin Almonte RC 1.00 .40
❑ T255 Shawn Riggans RC 1.00 .40
❑ T256 Steven Shell RC 1.00 .40
❑ T257 Kevin Hooper RC 1.00 .40
❑ T258 Michael Frick RC 1.00 .40
❑ T259 Travis Chapman RC 1.00 .40
❑ T260 Tim Hummel RC 1.00 .40
❑ T261 Adam Morrissey RC 1.00 .40
❑ T262 Dontrelle Willis RC 10.00 4.00
❑ T263 Justin Sherrod RC 1.00 .40
❑ T264 Gerald Smiley RC 1.00 .40
❑ T265 Tony Miller RC 1.00 .40
❑ T266 Nolan Ryan WW 5.00 2.00
❑ T267 Reggie Jackson WW 1.25 .50
❑ T268 Steve Garvey WW .75 .30
❑ T269 Wade Boggs WW 1.25 .50
❑ T270 Sammy Sosa WW 2.00 .75
❑ T271 Curt Schilling WW .75 .30
❑ T272 Mark Grace WW 1.25 .50
❑ T273 Jason Giambi WW .50 .20
❑ T274 Ken Griffey Jr. WW 3.00 1.25
❑ T275 Roberto Alomar WW 1.25 .50

2003 Topps Chrome

❑ COMPLETE SET (440) 200.00 80.00
❑ COMPLETE SERIES 1 (220) 100.00 40.00
❑ COMPLETE SERIES 2 (220) 100.00 40.00
❑ COMMON (1-200/221-420) 1.00 .40
❑ COMMON (201-220/421-440) 1.50 .60
❑ 1 Alex Rodriguez 4.00 1.50
❑ 2 Eddie Guardado 1.00 .40
❑ 3 Curt Schilling 1.00 .40
❑ 4 Andruw Jones 1.50 .60
❑ 5 Magglio Ordonez 1.00 .40
❑ 6 Todd Helton 1.50 .60
❑ 7 Odalis Perez 1.00 .40
❑ 8 Edgardo Alfonzo 1.00 .40
❑ 9 Eric Hinske 1.00 .40

❑ 10	Danny Bautista	1.00	.40
❑ 11	Sammy Sosa	2.50	1.00
❑ 12	Roberto Alomar	1.50	.60
❑ 13	Roger Clemens	5.00	2.00
❑ 14	Austin Kearns	1.00	.40
❑ 15	Luis Gonzalez	1.00	.40
❑ 16	Mo Vaughn	1.00	.40
❑ 17	Alfonso Soriano	1.00	.40
❑ 18	Orlando Cabrera	1.00	.40
❑ 19	Hideo Nomo	2.50	1.00
❑ 20	Omar Vizquel	1.50	.60
❑ 21	Greg Maddux	4.00	1.50
❑ 22	Fred McGriff	1.50	.60
❑ 23	Frank Thomas	2.50	1.00
❑ 24	Shawn Green	1.00	.40
❑ 25	Jacque Jones	1.00	.40
❑ 26	Bernie Williams	1.50	.60
❑ 27	Corey Patterson	1.00	.40
❑ 28	Cesar Izturis	1.00	.40
❑ 29	Larry Walker	1.00	.40
❑ 30	Darren Dreifort	1.00	.40
❑ 31	Al Leiter	1.00	.40
❑ 32	Jason Marquis	1.00	.40
❑ 33	Sean Casey	1.00	.40
❑ 34	Craig Counsell	1.00	.40
❑ 35	Albert Pujols	5.00	2.00
❑ 36	Kyle Lohse	1.00	.40
❑ 37	Paul Lo Duca	1.00	.40
❑ 38	Roy Oswalt	1.00	.40
❑ 39	Danny Graves	1.00	.40
❑ 40	Kevin Millwood	1.00	.40
❑ 41	Lance Berkman	1.00	.40
❑ 42	Denny Hocking	1.00	.40
❑ 43	Jose Valentin	1.00	.40
❑ 44	Josh Beckett	1.00	.40
❑ 45	Nomar Garciaparra	4.00	1.50
❑ 46	Craig Biggio	1.50	.60
❑ 47	Omar Daal	1.00	.40
❑ 48	Jimmy Rollins	1.00	.40
❑ 49	Jermaine Dye	1.00	.40
❑ 50	Edgar Renteria	1.00	.40
❑ 51	Brandon Duckworth	1.00	.40
❑ 52	Luis Castillo	1.00	.40
❑ 53	Andy Ashby	1.00	.40
❑ 54	Mike Williams	1.00	.40
❑ 55	Benito Santiago	1.00	.40
❑ 56	Bret Boone	1.00	.40
❑ 57	Randy Wolf	1.00	.40
❑ 58	Ivan Rodriguez	1.50	.60
❑ 59	Shannon Stewart	1.00	.40
❑ 60	Jose Cruz Jr.	1.00	.40
❑ 61	Billy Wagner	1.00	.40
❑ 62	Alex Gonzalez	1.00	.40
❑ 63	Ichiro Suzuki	5.00	2.00
❑ 64	Joe McEwing	1.00	.40
❑ 65	Mark Mulder	1.00	.40
❑ 66	Mike Cameron	1.00	.40
❑ 67	Corey Koskie	1.00	.40
❑ 68	Marlon Anderson	1.00	.40
❑ 69	Jason Kendall	1.00	.40
❑ 70	J.T. Snow	1.00	.40
❑ 71	Edgar Martinez	1.50	.60
❑ 72	Vernon Wells	1.00	.40
❑ 73	Vladimir Guerrero	2.50	1.00
❑ 74	Adam Dunn	1.00	.40
❑ 75	Barry Zito	1.00	.40
❑ 76	Jeff Kent	1.00	.40
❑ 77	Russ Ortiz	1.00	.40
❑ 78	Phil Nevin	1.00	.40
❑ 79	Carlos Beltran	1.00	.40
❑ 80	Mike Lowell	1.00	.40
❑ 81	Bob Wickman	1.00	.40
❑ 82	Junior Spivey	1.00	.40
❑ 83	Melvin Mora	1.00	.40
❑ 84	Derrek Lee	1.50	.60
❑ 85	Chuck Knoblauch	1.00	.40
❑ 86	Eric Gagne	1.00	.40
❑ 87	Orlando Hernandez	1.00	.40
❑ 88	Robert Person	1.00	.40
❑ 89	Elmer Dessens	1.00	.40
❑ 90	Wade Miller	1.00	.40
❑ 91	Adrian Beltre	1.00	.40
❑ 92	Kazuhiro Sasaki	1.00	.40
❑ 93	Timo Perez	1.00	.40
❑ 94	Jose Vidro	1.00	.40
❑ 95	Geronimo Gil	1.00	.40
❑ 96	Trot Nixon	1.00	.40
❑ 97	Denny Neagle	1.00	.40
❑ 98	Roberto Hernandez	1.00	.40
❑ 99	David Ortiz	2.50	1.00
❑ 100	Robb Nen	1.00	.40
❑ 101	Sidney Ponson	1.00	.40
❑ 102	Kevin Appier	1.00	.40
❑ 103	Javier Lopez	1.00	.40
❑ 104	Jeff Conine	1.00	.40
❑ 105	Mark Buehrle	1.00	.40
❑ 106	Jason Simontacchi	1.00	.40
❑ 107	Jose Jimenez	1.00	.40
❑ 108	Brian Jordan	1.00	.40
❑ 109	Brad Wilkerson	1.00	.40
❑ 110	Scott Hatteberg	1.00	.40
❑ 111	Matt Morris	1.00	.40
❑ 112	Miguel Tejada	1.00	.40
❑ 113	Rafael Furcal	1.00	.40
❑ 114	Steve Cox	1.00	.40
❑ 115	Roy Halladay	1.00	.40
❑ 116	David Eckstein	1.00	.40
❑ 117	Tomo Ohka	1.00	.40
❑ 118	Jack Wilson	1.00	.40
❑ 119	Randall Simon	1.00	.40
❑ 120	Jamie Moyer	1.00	.40
❑ 121	Andy Benes	1.00	.40
❑ 122	Tino Martinez	1.50	.60
❑ 123	Esteban Yan	1.00	.40
❑ 124	Jason Isringhausen	1.00	.40
❑ 125	Chris Carpenter	1.00	.40
❑ 126	Aaron Rowand	1.00	.40
❑ 127	Brandon Inge	1.00	.40
❑ 128	Jose Vizcaino	1.00	.40
❑ 129	Jose Mesa	1.00	.40
❑ 130	Troy Percival	1.00	.40
❑ 131	Jon Lieber	1.00	.40
❑ 132	Brian Giles	1.00	.40
❑ 133	Aaron Boone	1.00	.40
❑ 134	Bobby Higginson	1.00	.40
❑ 135	Luis Rivas	1.00	.40
❑ 136	Troy Glaus	1.00	.40
❑ 137	Jim Thome	1.50	.60
❑ 138	Ramon Martinez	1.00	.40
❑ 139	Jay Gibbons	1.00	.40
❑ 140	Mike Lieberthal	1.00	.40
❑ 141	Juan Uribe	1.00	.40
❑ 142	Gary Sheffield	1.00	.40
❑ 143	Ramon Santiago	1.00	.40
❑ 144	Ben Sheets	1.00	.40
❑ 145	Tony Armas Jr.	1.00	.40
❑ 146	Kazuhisa Ishii	1.00	.40
❑ 147	Erubiel Durazo	1.00	.40
❑ 148	Jerry Hairston Jr.	1.00	.40
❑ 149	Byung-Hyun Kim	1.00	.40
❑ 150	Marcus Giles	1.00	.40
❑ 151	Johnny Damon	1.50	.60
❑ 152	Terrence Long	1.00	.40
❑ 153	Juan Pierre	1.00	.40
❑ 154	Aramis Ramirez	1.00	.40
❑ 155	Brent Abernathy	1.00	.40
❑ 156	Ismael Valdes	1.00	.40
❑ 157	Mike Mussina	1.50	.60
❑ 158	Ramon Hernandez	1.00	.40
❑ 159	Adam Kennedy	1.00	.40
❑ 160	Tony Womack	1.00	.40
❑ 161	Tony Batista	1.00	.40
❑ 162	Kip Wells	1.00	.40
❑ 163	Jeromy Burnitz	1.00	.40
❑ 164	Todd Hundley	1.00	.40
❑ 165	Tim Wakefield	1.00	.40
❑ 166	Derek Lowe	1.00	.40
❑ 167	Jorge Posada	1.50	.60
❑ 168	Ramon Ortiz	1.00	.40
❑ 169	Brent Butler	1.00	.40
❑ 170	Shane Halter	1.00	.40
❑ 171	Matt Lawton	1.00	.40
❑ 172	Alex Sanchez	1.00	.40
❑ 173	Eric Milton	1.00	.40
❑ 174	Vicente Padilla	1.00	.40
❑ 175	Steve Karsay	1.00	.40
❑ 176	Mark Prior	1.50	.60
❑ 177	Kerry Wood	1.00	.40
❑ 178	Jason LaRue	1.00	.40
❑ 179	Danys Baez	1.00	.40
❑ 180	Nick Neugebauer	1.00	.40
❑ 181	Andres Galarraga	1.00	.40
❑ 182	Jason Giambi	1.00	.40
❑ 183	Aubrey Huff	1.00	.40
❑ 184	Juan Gonzalez	1.00	.40
❑ 185	Ugueth Urbina	1.00	.40
❑ 186	Rickey Henderson	2.50	1.00
❑ 187	Brad Fullmer	1.00	.40
❑ 188	Todd Zeile	1.00	.40
❑ 189	Jason Jennings	1.00	.40
❑ 190	Vladimir Nunez	1.00	.40
❑ 191	David Justice	1.00	.40
❑ 192	Brian Lawrence	1.00	.40
❑ 193	Pat Burrell	1.00	.40
❑ 194	Pokey Reese	1.00	.40
❑ 195	Robert Fick	1.00	.40
❑ 196	C.C. Sabathia	1.00	.40
❑ 197	Fernando Vina	1.00	.40
❑ 198	Sean Burroughs	1.00	.40
❑ 199	Ellis Burks	1.00	.40
❑ 200	Joe Randa	1.00	.40
❑ 201	Chris Duncan FY RC	6.00	2.50
❑ 202	Franklin Gutierrez FY RC	3.00	1.25
❑ 203	Adam LaRoche FY	1.50	.60
❑ 204	Manuel Ramirez FY RC	2.50	1.00
❑ 205	Il Kim FY RC	1.50	.60
❑ 206	Daryl Clark FY RC	1.50	.60
❑ 207	Sean Pierce FY	1.50	.60
❑ 208	Andy Marte FY RC	8.00	3.00
❑ 209	Bernie Castro FY RC	1.50	.60
❑ 210	Jason Perry FY RC	2.50	1.00
❑ 211	Jaime Bubela FY RC	1.50	.60
❑ 212	Alexis Rios FY	2.50	1.00
❑ 213	Brendan Harris FY RC	2.50	1.00
❑ 214	Ramon Nivar-Martinez FY RC	1.50	.60
❑ 215	Terry Tiffee FY RC	1.50	.60
❑ 216	Kevin Youkilis FY RC	4.00	1.50
❑ 217	Derell McCall FY RC	1.50	.60
❑ 218	Scott Tyler FY RC	2.50	1.00
❑ 219	Craig Brazell FY RC	1.50	.60
❑ 220	Walter Young FY	1.50	.60
❑ 221	Francisco Rodriguez	1.00	.40
❑ 222	Chipper Jones	2.50	1.00
❑ 223	Chris Singleton	1.00	.40
❑ 224	Cliff Floyd	1.00	.40
❑ 225	Bobby Hill	1.00	.40
❑ 226	Antonio Osuna	1.00	.40
❑ 227	Barry Larkin	1.50	.60
❑ 228	Dean Palmer	1.00	.40
❑ 229	Eric Owens	1.00	.40
❑ 230	Randy Johnson	2.50	1.00
❑ 231	Jeff Suppan	1.00	.40
❑ 232	Eric Karros	1.00	.40
❑ 233	Johan Santana	1.50	.60
❑ 234	Javier Vazquez	1.00	.40
❑ 235	John Thomson	1.00	.40
❑ 236	Nick Johnson	1.00	.40
❑ 237	Mark Ellis	1.00	.40
❑ 238	Doug Glanville	1.00	.40
❑ 239	Ken Griffey Jr.	4.00	1.50
❑ 240	Bubba Trammell	1.00	.40
❑ 241	Livan Hernandez	1.00	.40
❑ 242	Desi Relaford	1.00	.40
❑ 243	Eli Marrero	1.00	.40
❑ 244	Jared Sandberg	1.00	.40
❑ 245	Barry Bonds	6.00	2.50
❑ 246	Aaron Sele	1.00	.40
❑ 247	Derek Jeter	6.00	2.50
❑ 248	Eric Byrnes	1.00	.40
❑ 249	Rich Aurilia	1.00	.40

❑ 250 Joel Pineiro 1.00 .40
❑ 251 Chuck Finley 1.00 .40
❑ 252 Bengie Molina 1.00 .40
❑ 253 Steve Finley 1.00 .40
❑ 254 Marty Cordova 1.00 .40
❑ 255 Shea Hillenbrand 1.00 .40
❑ 256 Milton Bradley 1.00 .40
❑ 257 Carlos Pena 1.00 .40
❑ 258 Brad Ausmus 1.00 .40
❑ 259 Carlos Delgado 1.00 .40
❑ 260 Kevin Mench 1.00 .40
❑ 261 Joe Kennedy 1.00 .40
❑ 262 Mark McLemore 1.00 .40
❑ 263 Bill Mueller 1.00 .40
❑ 264 Ricky Ledee 1.00 .40
❑ 265 Ted Lilly 1.00 .40
❑ 266 Sterling Hitchcock 1.00 .40
❑ 267 Scott Strickland 1.00 .40
❑ 268 Damion Easley 1.00 .40
❑ 269 Torii Hunter 1.00 .40
❑ 270 Brad Radke 1.00 .40
❑ 271 Geoff Jenkins 1.00 .40
❑ 272 Paul Byrd 1.00 .40
❑ 273 Morgan Ensberg 1.00 .40
❑ 274 Mike Maroth 1.00 .40
❑ 275 Mike Hampton 1.00 .40
❑ 276 Flash Gordon 1.00 .40
❑ 277 John Burkett 1.00 .40
❑ 278 Rodrigo Lopez 1.00 .40
❑ 279 Tim Spooneybarger 1.00 .40
❑ 280 Quinton McCracken 1.00 .40
❑ 281 Tim Salmon 1.50 .60
❑ 282 Jarrod Washburn 1.00 .40
❑ 283 Pedro Martinez 1.50 .60
❑ 284 Julio Lugo 1.00 .40
❑ 285 Armando Benitez 1.00 .40
❑ 286 Raul Mondesi 1.00 .40
❑ 287 Robin Ventura 1.00 .40
❑ 288 Bobby Abreu 1.00 .40
❑ 289 Josh Fogg 1.00 .40
❑ 290 Ryan Klesko 1.00 .40
❑ 291 Tsuyoshi Shinjo 1.00 .40
❑ 292 Jim Edmonds 1.00 .40
❑ 293 Chan Ho Park 1.00 .40
❑ 294 John Mabry 1.00 .40
❑ 295 Woody Williams 1.00 .40
❑ 296 Scott Schoeneweis 1.00 .40
❑ 297 Brian Anderson 1.00 .40
❑ 298 Brett Tomko 1.00 .40
❑ 299 Scott Erickson 1.00 .40
❑ 300 Kevin Millar Sox 1.00 .40
❑ 301 Danny Wright 1.00 .40
❑ 302 Jason Schmidt 1.00 .40
❑ 303 Scott Williamson 1.00 .40
❑ 304 Einar Diaz 1.00 .40
❑ 305 Jay Payton 1.00 .40
❑ 306 Juan Acevedo 1.00 .40
❑ 307 Ben Grieve 1.00 .40
❑ 308 Raul Ibanez 1.00 .40
❑ 309 Richie Sexson 1.00 .40
❑ 310 Rick Reed 1.00 .40
❑ 311 Pedro Astacio 1.00 .40
❑ 312 Bud Smith 1.00 .40
❑ 313 Tomas Perez 1.00 .40
❑ 314 Rafael Palmeiro 1.50 .60
❑ 315 Jason Tyner 1.00 .40
❑ 316 Scott Rolen 1.50 .60
❑ 317 Randy Winn 1.00 .40
❑ 318 Ryan Jensen 1.00 .40
❑ 319 Trevor Hoffman 1.00 .40
❑ 320 Craig Wilson 1.00 .40
❑ 321 Jeremy Giambi 1.00 .40
❑ 322 Andy Pettitte 1.50 .60
❑ 323 John Franco 1.00 .40
❑ 324 Felipe Lopez 1.00 .40
❑ 325 Mike Piazza 4.00 1.50
❑ 326 Cristian Guzman 1.00 .40
❑ 327 Jose Hernandez 1.00 .40
❑ 328 Octavio Dotel 1.00 .40
❑ 329 Brad Penny 1.00 .40
❑ 330 Dave Veres 1.00 .40
❑ 331 Ryan Dempster 1.00 .40
❑ 332 Joe Crede 1.00 .40
❑ 333 Chad Hermansen 1.00 .40
❑ 334 Gary Matthews Jr. 1.00 .40
❑ 335 Frank Catalanotto 1.00 .40
❑ 336 Darin Erstad 1.00 .40
❑ 337 Matt Williams 1.00 .40
❑ 338 B.J. Surhoff 1.00 .40
❑ 339 Kerry Ligtenberg 1.00 .40
❑ 340 Mike Bordick 1.00 .40
❑ 341 Joe Girardi 1.00 .40
❑ 342 D'Angelo Jimenez 1.00 .40
❑ 343 Paul Konerko 1.00 .40
❑ 344 Joe Mays 1.00 .40
❑ 345 Marquis Grissom 1.00 .40
❑ 346 Neifi Perez 1.00 .40
❑ 347 Preston Wilson 1.00 .40
❑ 348 Jeff Weaver 1.00 .40
❑ 349 Eric Chavez 1.00 .40
❑ 350 Placido Polanco 1.00 .40
❑ 351 Matt Mantei 1.00 .40
❑ 352 James Baldwin 1.00 .40
❑ 353 Toby Hall 1.00 .40
❑ 354 Benji Gil 1.00 .40
❑ 355 Damian Moss 1.00 .40
❑ 356 Jorge Julio 1.00 .40
❑ 357 Matt Clement 1.00 .40
❑ 358 Lee Stevens 1.00 .40
❑ 359 Dave Roberts 1.00 .40
❑ 360 J.C. Romero 1.00 .40
❑ 361 Bartolo Colon 1.00 .40
❑ 362 Roger Cedeno 1.00 .40
❑ 363 Mariano Rivera 2.50 1.00
❑ 364 Billy Koch 1.00 .40
❑ 365 Manny Ramirez 1.50 .60
❑ 366 Travis Lee 1.00 .40
❑ 367 Oliver Perez 1.00 .40
❑ 368 Tim Worrell 1.00 .40
❑ 369 Damian Miller 1.00 .40
❑ 370 John Smoltz 1.50 .60
❑ 371 Willis Roberts 1.00 .40
❑ 372 Tim Hudson 1.00 .40
❑ 373 Moises Alou 1.00 .40
❑ 374 Corky Miller 1.00 .40
❑ 375 Ben Broussard 1.00 .40
❑ 376 Gabe Kapler 1.00 .40
❑ 377 Chris Woodward 1.00 .40
❑ 378 Todd Hollandsworth 1.00 .40
❑ 379 So Taguchi 1.00 .40
❑ 380 John Olerud 1.00 .40
❑ 381 Reggie Sanders 1.00 .40
❑ 382 Jake Peavy 1.00 .40
❑ 383 Kris Benson 1.00 .40
❑ 384 Ray Durham 1.00 .40
❑ 385 Boomer Wells 1.00 .40
❑ 386 Tom Glavine 1.50 .60
❑ 387 Antonio Alfonseca 1.00 .40
❑ 388 Keith Foulke 1.00 .40
❑ 389 Shawn Estes 1.00 .40
❑ 390 Mark Grace 1.50 .60
❑ 391 Dmitri Young 1.00 .40
❑ 392 A.J. Burnett 1.00 .40
❑ 393 Richard Hidalgo 1.00 .40
❑ 394 Mike Sweeney 1.00 .40
❑ 395 Doug Mientkiewicz 1.00 .40
❑ 396 Cory Lidle 1.00 .40
❑ 397 Jeff Bagwell 1.50 .60
❑ 398 Steve Sparks 1.00 .40
❑ 399 Sandy Alomar Jr. 1.00 .40
❑ 400 John Lackey 1.00 .40
❑ 401 Rick Helling 1.00 .40
❑ 402 Carlos Lee 1.00 .40
❑ 403 Garret Anderson 1.00 .40
❑ 404 Vinny Castilla 1.00 .40
❑ 405 David Bell 1.00 .40
❑ 406 Freddy Garcia 1.00 .40
❑ 407 Scott Spiezio 1.00 .40
❑ 408 Russell Branyan 1.00 .40
❑ 409 Jose Contreras RC 3.00 1.25
❑ 410 Kevin Brown 1.00 .40
❑ 411 Tyler Houston 1.00 .40
❑ 412 A.J. Pierzynski 1.00 .40
❑ 413 Peter Bergeron 1.00 .40
❑ 414 Brett Myers 1.00 .40
❑ 415 Kenny Lofton 1.00 .40
❑ 416 Ben Davis 1.00 .40
❑ 417 J.D. Drew 1.00 .40
❑ 418 Ricky Gutierrez 1.00 .40
❑ 419 Mark Redman 1.00 .40
❑ 420 Juan Encarnacion 1.00 .40
❑ 421 Bryan Bullington DP RC 1.50 .60
❑ 422 Jeremy Guthrie DP 1.50 .60
❑ 423 Joey Gomes DP RC 1.50 .60
❑ 424 Evel Bastida-Martinez DP RC 1.50 .60
❑ 425 Brian Wright DP RC 1.50 .60
❑ 426 B.J. Upton DP 2.50 1.00
❑ 427 Jeff Francis DP 1.50 .60
❑ 428 Jeremy Hermida DP 2.50 1.00
❑ 429 Khalil Greene DP 2.50 1.00
❑ 430 Darrell Rasner DP RC 1.50 .60
❑ 431 B.Phillips/V.Martinez 2.50 1.00
❑ 432 H.Choi/N.Jackson 1.50 .60
❑ 433 D.Willis/J.Stokes 2.50 1.00
❑ 434 C.Tracy/L.Overbay 1.50 .60
❑ 435 J.Borchard/C.Malone 1.50 .60
❑ 436 J.Mauer/J.Morneau 2.50 1.00
❑ 437 D.Henson/B.Claussen 1.50 .60
❑ 438 C.Utley/G.Floyd 2.50 1.00
❑ 439 T.Bozied/X.Nady 1.50 .60
❑ 440 A.Heilman/J.Reyes 1.50 .60

2003 Topps Chrome Traded

❑ COMPLETE SET (275) 120.00 60.00
❑ COMMON CARD (T1-T120) .75 .30
❑ COMMON CARD (121-165) 1.00 .40
❑ COMMON CARD (166-275) 1.00 .40
❑ 2 PER 2003 TOPPS TRADED HOBBY PACK
❑ 2 PER 2003 TOPPS TRADED HTA PACK
❑ 2 PER 2003 TOPPS TRADED RETAIL PACK
❑ T1 Juan Pierre .75 .30
❑ T2 Mark Grudzielanek .75 .30
❑ T3 Tanyon Sturtze .75 .30
❑ T4 Greg Vaughn .75 .30
❑ T5 Greg Myers .75 .30
❑ T6 Randall Simon .75 .30
❑ T7 Todd Hundley .75 .30
❑ T8 Marlon Anderson .75 .30
❑ T9 Jeff Reboulet .75 .30
❑ T10 Alex Sanchez .75 .30
❑ T11 Mike Rivera .75 .30
❑ T12 Todd Walker .75 .30
❑ T13 Ray King .75 .30
❑ T14 Shawn Estes .75 .30
❑ T15 Gary Matthews Jr. .75 .30
❑ T16 Jaret Wright .75 .30
❑ T17 Edgardo Alfonzo .75 .30
❑ T18 Omar Daal .75 .30
❑ T19 Ryan Rupe .75 .30
❑ T20 Tony Clark .75 .30
❑ T21 Jeff Suppan .75 .30
❑ T22 Mike Stanton .75 .30
❑ T23 Ramon Martinez .75 .30
❑ T24 Armando Rios .75 .30
❑ T25 Johnny Estrada .75 .30
❑ T26 Joe Girardi .75 .30
❑ T27 Ivan Rodriguez 1.25 .50
❑ T28 Robert Fick .75 .30
❑ T29 Rick White .75 .30
❑ T30 Robert Person .75 .30
❑ T31 Alan Benes .75 .30
❑ T32 Chris Carpenter .75 .30
❑ T33 Chris Widger .75 .30
❑ T34 Travis Hafner .75 .30
❑ T35 Mike Venafro .75 .30
❑ T36 Jon Lieber .75 .30
❑ T37 Orlando Hernandez .75 .30
❑ T38 Aaron Myette .75 .30
❑ T39 Paul Bako .75 .30

❑ T40 Erubiel Durazo .75 .30
❑ T41 Mark Guthrie .75 .30
❑ T42 Steve Avery .75 .30
❑ T43 Damian Jackson .75 .30
❑ T44 Rey Ordonez .75 .30
❑ T45 John Flaherty .75 .30
❑ T46 Byung-Hyun Kim .75 .30
❑ T47 Tom Goodwin .75 .30
❑ T48 Elmer Dessens .75 .30
❑ T49 Al Martin .75 .30
❑ T50 Gene Kingsale .75 .30
❑ T51 Lenny Harris .75 .30
❑ T52 David Ortiz Sox 2.00 .75
❑ T53 Jose Lima .75 .30
❑ T54 Mike Difelice .75 .30
❑ T55 Jose Hernandez .75 .30
❑ T56 Todd Zeile .75 .30
❑ T57 Roberto Hernandez .75 .30
❑ T58 Albie Lopez .75 .30
❑ T59 Roberto Alomar 1.25 .50
❑ T60 Russ Ortiz .75 .30
❑ T61 Brian Daubach .75 .30
❑ T62 Carl Everett .75 .30
❑ T63 Jeromy Burnitz .75 .30
❑ T64 Mark Bellhorn .75 .30
❑ T65 Ruben Sierra .75 .30
❑ T66 Mike Fetters .75 .30
❑ T67 Armando Benitez .75 .30
❑ T68 Deivi Cruz .75 .30
❑ T69 Jose Cruz Jr. .75 .30
❑ T70 Jeremy Fikac .75 .30
❑ T71 Jeff Kent .75 .30
❑ T72 Andres Galarraga .75 .30
❑ T73 Rickey Henderson 2.00 .75
❑ T74 Royce Clayton .75 .30
❑ T75 Troy O'Leary .75 .30
❑ T76 Ron Coomer .75 .30
❑ T77 Greg Colbrunn .75 .30
❑ T78 Wes Helms .75 .30
❑ T79 Kevin Millwood .75 .30
❑ T80 Damion Easley .75 .30
❑ T81 Bobby Kielty .75 .30
❑ T82 Keith Osik .75 .30
❑ T83 Ramiro Mendoza .75 .30
❑ T84 Shea Hillenbrand .75 .30
❑ T85 Shannon Stewart .75 .30
❑ T86 Eddie Perez .75 .30
❑ T87 Ugueth Urbina .75 .30
❑ T88 Orlando Palmeiro .75 .30
❑ T89 Graeme Lloyd .75 .30
❑ T90 John Vander Wal .75 .30
❑ T91 Gary Bennett .75 .30
❑ T92 Shane Reynolds .75 .30
❑ T93 Steve Parris .75 .30
❑ T94 Julio Lugo .75 .30
❑ T95 John Halama .75 .30
❑ T96 Carlos Baerga .75 .30
❑ T97 Jim Parque .75 .30
❑ T98 Mike Williams .75 .30
❑ T99 Fred McGriff 1.25 .50
❑ T100 Kenny Rogers .75 .30
❑ T101 Matt Herges .75 .30
❑ T102 Jay Bell .75 .30
❑ T103 Esteban Yan .75 .30
❑ T104 Eric Owens .75 .30
❑ T105 Aaron Fultz .75 .30
❑ T106 Rey Sanchez .75 .30
❑ T107 Jim Thome 1.25 .50
❑ T108 Aaron Boone .75 .30
❑ T109 Raul Mondesi .75 .30
❑ T110 Kenny Lofton .75 .30
❑ T111 Jose Guillen .75 .30
❑ T112 Aramis Ramirez .75 .30
❑ T113 Sidney Ponson .75 .30
❑ T114 Scott Williamson .75 .30
❑ T115 Robin Ventura .75 .30
❑ T116 Dusty Baker MG .75 .30
❑ T117 Felipe Alou MG .75 .30
❑ T118 Buck Showalter MG .75 .30
❑ T119 Jack McKeon MG .75 .30
❑ T120 Art Howe MG .75 .30
❑ T121 Bobby Crosby PROS 1.00 .40
❑ T122 Adrian Gonzalez PROS 1.00 .40
❑ T123 Kevin Cash PROS 1.00 .40
❑ T124 Shin-Soo Choo PROS 1.00 .40
❑ T125 Chin-Feng Chen PROS 2.50 1.00
❑ T126 Miguel Cabrera PROS 2.50 1.00
❑ T127 Jason Young PROS 1.00 .40
❑ T128 Alex Herrera PROS 1.00 .40
❑ T129 Jason Dubois PROS 1.00 .40
❑ T130 Jeff Mathis PROS 1.00 .40
❑ T131 Casey Kotchman PROS 1.00 .40
❑ T132 Ed Rogers PROS 1.00 .40
❑ T133 Wilson Betemit PROS 1.00 .40
❑ T134 Jim Kavourias PROS 1.00 .40
❑ T135 Taylor Buchholz PROS 1.00 .40
❑ T136 Adam LaRoche PROS 1.00 .40
❑ T137 Dallas McPherson PROS 1.00 .40
❑ T138 Jesus Cota PROS 1.00 .40
❑ T139 Clint Nageotte PROS 1.00 .40
❑ T140 Boof Bonser PROS 1.00 .40
❑ T141 Walter Young PROS 1.00 .40
❑ T142 Joe Crede PROS 1.00 .40
❑ T143 Denny Bautista PROS 1.00 .40
❑ T144 Victor Diaz PROS 1.00 .40
❑ T145 Chris Narveson PROS 1.00 .40
❑ T146 Gabe Gross PROS 1.00 .40
❑ T147 Jimmy Journell PROS 1.00 .40
❑ T148 Rafael Soriano PROS 1.00 .40
❑ T149 Jerome Williams PROS 1.00 .40
❑ T150 Aaron Cook PROS 1.00 .40
❑ T151 Anastacio Martinez PROS 1.00 .40
❑ T152 Scott Hairston PROS 1.00 .40
❑ T153 John Buck PROS 1.00 .40
❑ T154 Ryan Ludwick PROS 1.00 .40
❑ T155 Chris Bootcheck PROS 1.00 .40
❑ T156 John Rheinecker PROS 1.00 .40
❑ T157 Jason Lane PROS 1.00 .40
❑ T159 Adam Wainwright PROS 1.00 .40
❑ T160 Jason Arnold PROS 1.00 .40
❑ T161 Jonny Gomes PROS 1.50 .60
❑ T162 James Loney PROS 1.25 .50
❑ T163 Mike Fontenot PROS 1.00 .40
❑ T164 Khalil Greene PROS 2.50 1.00
❑ T165 Sean Burnett PROS 1.00 .40
❑ T166 David Martinez FY RC 1.00 .40
❑ T167 Felix Pie FY RC 10.00 4.00
❑ T168 Joe Valentine FY RC 1.00 .40
❑ T169 Brandon Webb FY RC 8.00 3.00
❑ T170 Matt Diaz FY RC 1.50 .60
❑ T171 Lew Ford FY RC 1.25 .50
❑ T172 Jeremy Griffiths FY RC 1.00 .40
❑ T173 Matt Hensley FY RC 1.00 .40
❑ T174 Charlie Manning FY RC 1.00 .40
❑ T175 Elizardo Ramirez FY RC 1.25 .50
❑ T176 Greg Aquino FY RC 1.00 .40
❑ T177 Felix Sanchez FY RC 1.00 .40
❑ T178 Kelly Shoppach FY RC 2.00 .75
❑ T179 Bubba Nelson FY RC 1.25 .50
❑ T180 Mike O'Keefe FY RC 1.00 .40
❑ T181 Hanley Ramirez FY RC 12.00 5.00
❑ T182 Todd Wellemeyer FY RC 1.00 .40
❑ T183 Dustin Moseley FY RC 1.00 .40
❑ T184 Eric Crozier FY RC 1.25 .50
❑ T185 Ryan Shealy FY RC 5.00 2.00
❑ T186 Jeremy Bonderman FY RC 8.00 3.00
❑ T187 T.Story-Harden FY RC 1.00 .40
❑ T188 Dusty Brown FY RC 1.00 .40
❑ T189 Rob Hammock FY RC 1.00 .40
❑ T190 Jorge Piedra FY RC 1.25 .50
❑ T191 Chris De La Cruz FY RC 1.00 .40
❑ T192 Eli Whiteside FY RC 1.00 .40
❑ T193 Jason Kubel FY RC 3.00 1.25
❑ T194 Jon Schuerholz FY RC 1.00 .40
❑ T195 Stephen Randolph FY RC 1.00 .40
❑ T196 Andy Sisco FY RC 1.00 .40
❑ T197 Sean Smith FY RC 1.25 .50
❑ T198 Jon-Mark Sprowl FY RC 1.00 .40
❑ T199 Matt Kata FY RC 1.00 .40
❑ T200 Robinson Cano FY RC 15.00 6.00
❑ T201 Nook Logan FY RC 1.25 .50
❑ T202 Ben Francisco FY RC 1.00 .40
❑ T203 Arnie Munoz FY RC 1.00 .40
❑ T204 Ozzie Chavez FY RC 1.00 .40
❑ T205 Eric Riggs FY RC 1.25 .50
❑ T206 Beau Kemp FY RC 1.00 .40
❑ T207 Travis Wong FY RC 1.25 .50
❑ T208 Dustin Yount FY RC 1.25 .50
❑ T209 Brian McCann FY RC 15.00 6.00
❑ T210 Wilton Reynolds FY RC 1.25 .50
❑ T211 Matt Bruback FY RC 1.00 .40
❑ T212 Andrew Brown FY RC 1.25 .50
❑ T213 Edgar Gonzalez FY RC 1.00 .40
❑ T214 Eider Torres FY RC 1.00 .40
❑ T215 Aquilino Lopez FY RC 1.00 .40
❑ T216 Bobby Basham FY RC 1.00 .40
❑ T217 Tim Olson FY RC 1.00 .40
❑ T218 Nathan Panther FY RC 1.00 .40
❑ T219 Bryan Grace FY RC 1.00 .40
❑ T220 Dusty Gomon FY RC 1.25 .50
❑ T221 Wil Ledezma FY RC 1.00 .40
❑ T222 Josh Willingham FY RC 2.50 1.00
❑ T223 David Cash FY RC 1.00 .40
❑ T224 Oscar Villarreal FY RC 1.00 .40
❑ T225 Jeff Duncan FY RC 1.00 .40
❑ T226 Kade Johnson FY RC 1.00 .40
❑ T227 Luke Steidlmayer FY RC 1.00 .40
❑ T228 Brandon Watson FY RC 1.00 .40
❑ T229 Jose Morales FY RC 1.00 .40
❑ T230 Mike Gallo FY RC 1.00 .40
❑ T231 Tyler Adamczyk FY RC 1.00 .40
❑ T232 Adam Stern FY RC 1.00 .40
❑ T233 Brennan King FY RC 1.00 .40
❑ T234 Dan Haren FY RC 2.00 .75
❑ T235 Michel Hernandez FY RC 1.00 .40
❑ T236 Ben Fritz FY RC 1.00 .40
❑ T237 Clay Hensley FY RC 1.00 .40
❑ T238 Tyler Johnson FY RC 1.00 .40
❑ T239 Pete LaForest FY RC 1.00 .40
❑ T240 Tyler Martin FY RC 1.00 .40
❑ T241 J.D. Durbin FY RC 1.00 .40
❑ T242 Shane Victorino FY RC 1.50 .60
❑ T243 Rajai Davis FY RC 1.00 .40
❑ T244 Ismael Castro FY RC 1.00 .40
❑ T245 Chien-Ming Wang FY RC 10.00 4.00
❑ T246 Travis Ishikawa FY RC 2.00 .75
❑ T247 Corey Shafer FY RC 1.00 .40
❑ T248 Gary Schneidmiller FY RC 1.00 .40
❑ T249 Dave Pember FY RC 1.00 .40
❑ T250 Keith Stamler FY RC 1.00 .40
❑ T251 Tyson Graham FY RC 1.00 .40
❑ T252 Ryan Cameron FY RC 1.00 .40
❑ T253 Eric Eckenstahler FY 1.00 .40
❑ T254 Matthew Peterson FY RC 1.00 .40
❑ T255 Dustin McGowan FY RC 1.25 .50
❑ T256 Prentice Redman FY RC 1.00 .40
❑ T257 Haj Turay FY RC 1.00 .40
❑ T258 Carlos Guzman FY RC 1.25 .50
❑ T259 Matt DeMarco FY RC 1.00 .40
❑ T260 Derek Michaelis FY RC 1.00 .40
❑ T261 Brian Burgamy FY RC 1.00 .40
❑ T262 Jay Sitzman FY RC 1.00 .40
❑ T263 Chris Fallon FY RC 1.00 .40
❑ T264 Mike Adams FY RC 1.00 .40
❑ T265 Clint Barmes FY RC 2.50 1.00
❑ T266 Eric Reed FY RC 1.00 .40
❑ T267 Willie Eyre FY RC 1.00 .40
❑ T268 Carlos Duran FY RC 1.00 .40
❑ T269 Nick Trzesniak FY RC 1.00 .40
❑ T270 Ferdin Tejeda FY RC 1.00 .40
❑ T271 Michael Garciaparra FY RC 1.00 .40
❑ T272 Michael Hinckley FY RC 1.25 .50
❑ T273 Branden Florence FY RC 1.00 .40
❑ T274 Trent Oeltjen FY RC 1.25 .50
❑ T275 Mike Neu FY RC 1.00 .40

2004 Topps Chrome

❑ COMP.SERIES 1 w/o SP's (220) 80.00 40.00
❑ COMP.SERIES 2 w/o SP's (220) 80.00 40.00
❑ COMMON (1-210/257-466) 1.00 .40

❑ COMMON (211-220/247-256) 2.00 .75
❑ COMMON AU (221-246) 10.00 4.00
❑ 1 Jim Thome 1.50 .60
❑ 2 Reggie Sanders 1.00 .40
❑ 3 Mark Kotsay 1.00 .40
❑ 4 Edgardo Alfonzo 1.00 .40
❑ 5 Tim Wakefield 1.00 .40
❑ 6 Moises Alou 1.00 .40
❑ 7 Jorge Julio 1.00 .40
❑ 8 Bartolo Colon 1.00 .40
❑ 9 Chan Ho Park 1.00 .40
❑ 10 Ichiro Suzuki 5.00 2.00
❑ 11 Kevin Millwood 1.00 .40
❑ 12 Preston Wilson 1.00 .40
❑ 13 Tom Glavine 1.50 .60
❑ 14 Junior Spivey 1.00 .40
❑ 15 Marcus Giles 1.00 .40
❑ 16 David Segui 1.00 .40
❑ 17 Kevin Millar 1.00 .40
❑ 18 Corey Patterson 1.00 .40
❑ 19 Aaron Rowand 1.00 .40
❑ 20 Derek Jeter 5.00 2.00
❑ 21 Luis Castillo 1.00 .40
❑ 22 Manny Ramirez 1.50 .60
❑ 23 Jay Payton 1.00 .40
❑ 24 Bobby Higginson 1.00 .40
❑ 25 Lance Berkman 1.00 .40
❑ 26 Juan Pierre 1.00 .40
❑ 27 Mike Mussina 1.50 .60
❑ 28 Fred McGriff 1.50 .60
❑ 29 Richie Sexson 1.00 .40
❑ 30 Tim Hudson 1.00 .40
❑ 31 Mike Piazza 4.00 1.50
❑ 32 Brad Radke 1.00 .40
❑ 33 Jeff Weaver 1.00 .40
❑ 34 Ramon Hernandez 1.00 .40
❑ 35 David Bell 1.00 .40
❑ 36 Randy Wolf 1.00 .40
❑ 37 Jake Peavy 1.00 .40
❑ 38 Tim Worrell 1.00 .40
❑ 39 Gil Meche 1.00 .40
❑ 40 Albert Pujols 5.00 2.00
❑ 41 Michael Young 1.00 .40
❑ 42 Josh Phelps 1.00 .40
❑ 43 Brendan Donnelly 1.00 .40
❑ 44 Steve Finley 1.00 .40
❑ 45 John Smoltz 1.50 .60
❑ 46 Jay Gibbons 1.00 .40
❑ 47 Trot Nixon 1.00 .40
❑ 48 Carl Pavano 1.00 .40
❑ 49 Frank Thomas 2.50 1.00
❑ 50 Mark Prior 1.50 .60
❑ 51 Danny Graves 1.00 .40
❑ 52 Milton Bradley 1.00 .40
❑ 53 Kris Benson 1.00 .40
❑ 54 Ryan Klesko 1.00 .40
❑ 55 Mike Lowell 1.00 .40
❑ 56 Geoff Blum 1.00 .40
❑ 57 Michael Tucker 1.00 .40
❑ 58 Paul Lo Duca 1.00 .40
❑ 59 Vicente Padilla 1.00 .40
❑ 60 Jacque Jones 1.00 .40
❑ 61 Fernando Tatis 1.00 .40
❑ 62 Ty Wigginton 1.00 .40
❑ 63 Rich Aurilia 1.00 .40
❑ 64 Andy Pettitte 1.50 .60
❑ 65 Terrence Long 1.00 .40
❑ 66 Cliff Floyd 1.00 .40
❑ 67 Mariano Rivera 2.50 1.00
❑ 68 Kelvim Escobar 1.00 .40
❑ 69 Marlon Byrd 1.00 .40
❑ 70 Mark Mulder 1.00 .40
❑ 71 Francisco Cordero 1.00 .40
❑ 72 Carlos Guillen 1.00 .40
❑ 73 Fernando Vina 1.00 .40
❑ 74 Lance Carter 1.00 .40
❑ 75 Hank Blalock 1.00 .40
❑ 76 Jimmy Rollins 1.00 .40
❑ 77 Francisco Rodriguez 1.00 .40
❑ 78 Javy Lopez 1.00 .40
❑ 79 Jerry Hairston Jr. 1.00 .40
❑ 80 Andruw Jones 1.50 .60
❑ 81 Rodrigo Lopez 1.00 .40
❑ 82 Johnny Damon 1.50 .60
❑ 83 Hee Seop Choi 1.00 .40
❑ 84 Kazuhiro Sasaki 1.00 .40
❑ 85 Danny Bautista 1.00 .40
❑ 86 Matt Lawton 1.00 .40
❑ 87 Juan Uribe 1.00 .40
❑ 88 Rafael Furcal 1.00 .40
❑ 89 Kyle Farnsworth 1.00 .40
❑ 90 Jose Vidro 1.00 .40
❑ 91 Luis Rivas 1.00 .40
❑ 92 Hideo Nomo 2.50 1.00
❑ 93 Javier Vazquez 1.00 .40
❑ 94 Al Leiter 1.00 .40
❑ 95 Jose Valentin 1.00 .40
❑ 96 Alex Cintron 1.00 .40
❑ 97 Zach Day 1.00 .40
❑ 98 Jorge Posada 1.50 .60
❑ 99 C.C. Sabathia 1.00 .40
❑ 100 Alex Rodriguez 4.00 1.50
❑ 101 Brad Penny 1.00 .40
❑ 102 Brad Ausmus 1.00 .40
❑ 103 Raul Ibanez 1.00 .40
❑ 104 Mike Hampton 1.00 .40
❑ 105 Adrian Beltre 1.00 .40
❑ 106 Ramiro Mendoza 1.00 .40
❑ 107 Rocco Baldelli 1.00 .40
❑ 108 Esteban Loaiza 1.00 .40
❑ 109 Russell Branyan 1.00 .40
❑ 110 Todd Helton 1.50 .60
❑ 111 Braden Looper 1.00 .40
❑ 112 Octavio Dotel 1.00 .40
❑ 113 Mike MacDougal 1.00 .40
❑ 114 Cesar Izturis 1.00 .40
❑ 115 Johan Santana 2.50 1.00
❑ 116 Jose Contreras 1.00 .40
❑ 117 Placido Polanco 1.00 .40
❑ 118 Jason Phillips 1.00 .40
❑ 119 Orlando Hudson 1.00 .40
❑ 120 Vernon Wells 1.00 .40
❑ 121 Ben Grieve 1.00 .40
❑ 122 Dave Roberts 1.00 .40
❑ 123 Ismael Valdes 1.00 .40
❑ 124 Eric Owens 1.00 .40
❑ 125 Curt Schilling 1.00 .40
❑ 126 Russ Ortiz 1.00 .40
❑ 127 Mark Buehrle 1.00 .40
❑ 128 Doug Mientkiewicz 1.00 .40
❑ 129 Dmitri Young 1.00 .40
❑ 130 Kazuhisa Ishii 1.00 .40
❑ 131 A.J. Pierzynski 1.00 .40
❑ 132 Brad Wilkerson 1.00 .40
❑ 133 Joe McEwing 1.00 .40
❑ 134 Alex Cora 1.00 .40
❑ 135 Jose Cruz Jr. 1.00 .40
❑ 136 Carlos Zambrano 1.00 .40
❑ 137 Jeff Kent 1.00 .40
❑ 138 Shigetoshi Hasegawa 1.00 .40
❑ 139 Jarrod Washburn 1.00 .40
❑ 140 Greg Maddux 4.00 1.50
❑ 141 Josh Beckett 1.00 .40
❑ 142 Miguel Batista 1.00 .40
❑ 143 Omar Vizquel 1.50 .60
❑ 144 Alex Gonzalez 1.00 .40
❑ 145 Billy Wagner 1.00 .40
❑ 146 Brian Jordan 1.00 .40
❑ 147 Wes Helms 1.00 .40
❑ 148 Deivi Cruz 1.00 .40
❑ 149 Alex Gonzalez 1.00 .40
❑ 150 Jason Giambi 1.00 .40
❑ 151 Erubiel Durazo 1.00 .40
❑ 152 Mike Lieberthal 1.00 .40
❑ 153 Jason Kendall 1.00 .40
❑ 154 Xavier Nady 1.00 .40
❑ 155 Kirk Rueter 1.00 .40
❑ 156 Mike Cameron 1.00 .40
❑ 157 Miguel Cairo 1.00 .40
❑ 158 Woody Williams 1.00 .40
❑ 159 Toby Hall 1.00 .40
❑ 160 Bernie Williams 1.50 .60
❑ 161 Darin Erstad 1.00 .40
❑ 162 Matt Mantei 1.00 .40
❑ 163 Shawn Chacon 1.00 .40
❑ 164 Bill Mueller 1.00 .40
❑ 165 Damian Miller 1.00 .40
❑ 166 Tony Graffanino 1.00 .40
❑ 167 Sean Casey 1.00 .40
❑ 168 Brandon Phillips 1.00 .40
❑ 169 Runelvys Hernandez 1.00 .40
❑ 170 Adam Dunn 1.00 .40
❑ 171 Carlos Lee 1.00 .40
❑ 172 Juan Encarnacion 1.00 .40
❑ 173 Angel Berroa 1.00 .40
❑ 174 Desi Relaford 1.00 .40
❑ 175 Joe Mays 1.00 .40
❑ 176 Ben Sheets 1.00 .40
❑ 177 Eddie Guardado 1.00 .40
❑ 178 Rocky Biddle 1.00 .40
❑ 179 Eric Gagne 1.00 .40
❑ 180 Eric Chavez 1.00 .40
❑ 181 Jason Michaels 1.00 .40
❑ 182 Dustan Mohr 1.00 .40
❑ 183 Kip Wells 1.00 .40
❑ 184 Brian Lawrence 1.00 .40
❑ 185 Bret Boone 1.00 .40
❑ 186 Tino Martinez 1.50 .60
❑ 187 Aubrey Huff 1.00 .40
❑ 188 Kevin Mench 1.00 .40
❑ 189 Tim Salmon 1.50 .60
❑ 190 Carlos Delgado 1.00 .40
❑ 191 John Lackey 1.00 .40
❑ 192 Eric Byrnes 1.00 .40
❑ 193 Luis Matos 1.00 .40
❑ 194 Derek Lowe 1.00 .40
❑ 195 Mark Grudzielanek 1.00 .40
❑ 196 Tom Gordon 1.00 .40
❑ 197 Matt Clement 1.00 .40
❑ 198 Byung-Hyun Kim 1.00 .40
❑ 199 Brandon Inge 1.00 .40
❑ 200 Nomar Garciaparra 4.00 1.50
❑ 201 Frank Catalanotto 1.00 .40
❑ 202 Cristian Guzman 1.00 .40
❑ 203 Bo Hart 1.00 .40
❑ 204 Jack Wilson 1.00 .40
❑ 205 Ray Durham 1.00 .40
❑ 206 Freddy Garcia 1.00 .40
❑ 207 J.D. Drew 1.00 .40
❑ 208 Orlando Cabrera 1.00 .40
❑ 209 Roy Halladay 1.00 .40
❑ 210 David Eckstein 1.00 .40
❑ 211 Omar Falcon FY RC 2.00 .75
❑ 212 Todd Self FY RC 3.00 1.25
❑ 213 David Murphy FY RC 3.00 1.25
❑ 214 Dioner Navarro FY RC 3.00 1.25
❑ 215 Marcus McBeth FY RC 2.00 .75
❑ 216 Chris O'Riordan FY RC 2.00 .75
❑ 217 Rodney Choy Foo FY RC 2.00 .75
❑ 218 Tim Frend FY RC 2.00 .75
❑ 219 Yadier Molina FY RC 6.00 2.50
❑ 220 Zach Duke FY RC 5.00 2.00
❑ 221 Anthony Lerew FY AU RC 15.00 6.00
❑ 222 B.Hawksworth FY AU RC 15.00 6.00
❑ 223 Brayan Pena FY AU RC 10.00 4.00
❑ 224 Craig Ansman FY AU RC 10.00 4.00
❑ 225 Jon Knott FY AU RC 10.00 4.00
❑ 226 Josh Labandeira FY AU RC 10.00 4.00
❑ 227 Khalid Ballouli FY AU RC 10.00 4.00
❑ 228 Kyle Davies FY AU RC 25.00 10.00
❑ 229 Matt Creighton FY AU RC 10.00 4.00
❑ 230 Mike Gosling FY AU RC 10.00 4.00
❑ 231 Nic Ungs FY AU RC 10.00 4.00
❑ 232 Zach Miner FY AU RC 25.00 10.00
❑ 233 Donald Levinski FY AU RC 10.00 4.00
❑ 234A Bradley Sullivan FY AU RC 15.00 6.00
❑ 234B B.Sullivan FY AU ERR 345 25.00 10.00
❑ 235 Carlos Quentin FY AU RC 40.00 15.00
❑ 236 Conor Jackson FY AU RC 30.00 12.50
❑ 237 Estee Harris FY AU RC 15.00 6.00
❑ 238 Jeffrey Allison FY AU RC 10.00 4.00
❑ 239 Kyle Sleeth FY AU RC 15.00 6.00
❑ 240 Matthew Moses FY AU RC 15.00 6.00
❑ 241 Tim Stauffer FY AU RC 10.00 4.00
❑ 242 Brad Snyder FY AU RC 12.00 5.00
❑ 243 Jason Hirsh FY AU RC 25.00 10.00
❑ 244 L.Milledge FY AU RC 50.00 20.00
❑ 245 Logan Kensing FY AU RC 10.00 4.00
❑ 246 Kory Casto FY AU RC 15.00 6.00
❑ 247 David Aardsma FY RC 3.00 1.25
❑ 248 Omar Quintanilla FY RC 3.00 1.25
❑ 249 Ervin Santana FY RC 5.00 2.00
❑ 250 Merkin Valdez FY RC 2.00 .75
❑ 251 Vito Chiaravalloti FY RC 2.00 .75
❑ 252 Travis Blackley FY RC 2.00 .75
❑ 253 Chris Shelton FY RC 3.00 1.25
❑ 254 Rudy Guillen FY RC 3.00 1.25
❑ 255 Bobby Brownlie FY RC 2.50 1.00

❑ 256 Paul Maholm FY RC 4.00 1.50
❑ 257 Roger Clemens 5.00 2.00
❑ 258 Laynce Nix 1.00 .40
❑ 259 Eric Hinske 1.00 .40
❑ 260 Ivan Rodriguez 1.50 .60
❑ 261 Brandon Webb 1.00 .40
❑ 262 Jhonny Peralta 1.00 .40
❑ 263 Adam Kennedy 1.00 .40
❑ 264 Tony Batista 1.00 .40
❑ 265 Jeff Suppan 1.00 .40
❑ 266 Kenny Lofton 1.00 .40
❑ 267 Scott Sullivan 1.00 .40
❑ 268 Ken Griffey Jr. 4.00 1.50
❑ 269 Juan Rivera 1.00 .40
❑ 270 Larry Walker 1.00 .40
❑ 271 Todd Hollandsworth 1.00 .40
❑ 272 Carlos Beltran 1.00 .40
❑ 273 Carl Crawford 1.00 .40
❑ 274 Karim Garcia 1.00 .40
❑ 275 Jose Reyes 1.00 .40
❑ 276 Brandon Duckworth 1.00 .40
❑ 277 Brian Giles 1.00 .40
❑ 278 J.T. Snow 1.00 .40
❑ 279 Jamie Moyer 1.00 .40
❑ 280 Julio Lugo 1.00 .40
❑ 281 Mark Teixeira 1.50 .60
❑ 282 Cory Lidle 1.00 .40
❑ 283 Lyle Overbay 1.00 .40
❑ 284 Troy Percival 1.00 .40
❑ 285 Robby Hammock 1.00 .40
❑ 286 Jason Johnson 1.00 .40
❑ 287 Damian Rolls 1.00 .40
❑ 288 Antonio Alfonseca 1.00 .40
❑ 289 Tom Goodwin 1.00 .40
❑ 290 Paul Konerko 1.00 .40
❑ 291 D'Angelo Jimenez 1.00 .40
❑ 292 Ben Broussard 1.00 .40
❑ 293 Magglio Ordonez 1.00 .40
❑ 294 Carlos Pena 1.00 .40
❑ 295 Chad Fox 1.00 .40
❑ 296 Jeriome Robertson 1.00 .40
❑ 297 Travis Hafner 1.00 .40
❑ 298 Joe Randa 1.00 .40
❑ 299 Brady Clark 1.00 .40
❑ 300 Barry Zito 1.00 .40
❑ 301 Ruben Sierra 1.00 .40
❑ 302 Brett Myers 1.00 .40
❑ 303 Oliver Perez 1.00 .40
❑ 304 Benito Santiago 1.00 .40
❑ 305 David Ross 1.00 .40
❑ 306 Joe Nathan 1.00 .40
❑ 307 Jim Edmonds 1.00 .40
❑ 308 Matt Kata 1.00 .40
❑ 309 Vinny Castilla 1.00 .40
❑ 310 Marty Cordova 1.00 .40
❑ 311 Aramis Ramirez 1.00 .40
❑ 312 Carl Everett 1.00 .40
❑ 313 Ryan Freel 1.00 .40
❑ 314 Mark Bellhorn Sox 1.00 .40
❑ 315 Joe Mauer 2.50 1.00
❑ 316 Tim Redding 1.00 .40
❑ 317 Jeromy Burnitz 1.00 .40
❑ 318 Miguel Cabrera 1.50 .60
❑ 319 Ramon Nivar 1.00 .40
❑ 320 Casey Blake 1.00 .40
❑ 321 Adam LaRoche 1.00 .40
❑ 322 Jermaine Dye 1.00 .40
❑ 323 Jerome Williams 1.00 .40
❑ 324 John Olerud 1.00 .40
❑ 325 Scott Rolen 1.50 .60
❑ 326 Bobby Kielty 1.00 .40
❑ 327 Travis Lee 1.00 .40
❑ 328 Jeff Cirillo 1.00 .40
❑ 329 Scott Spiezio 1.00 .40
❑ 330 Melvin Mora 1.00 .40
❑ 331 Mike Timlin 1.00 .40
❑ 332 Kerry Wood 1.00 .40
❑ 333 Tony Womack 1.00 .40
❑ 334 Jody Gerut 1.00 .40
❑ 335 Morgan Ensberg 1.00 .40
❑ 336 Odalis Perez 1.00 .40
❑ 337 Michael Cuddyer 1.00 .40
❑ 338 Jose Hernandez 1.00 .40
❑ 339 LaTroy Hawkins 1.00 .40
❑ 340 Marquis Grissom 1.00 .40
❑ 341 Matt Morris 1.00 .40
❑ 342 Juan Gonzalez 1.00 .40
❑ 343 Jose Valverde 1.00 .40
❑ 344 Joe Borowski 1.00 .40
❑ 345 Josh Bard 1.00 .40
❑ 346 Austin Kearns 1.00 .40
❑ 347 Chin-Hui Tsao 1.00 .40
❑ 348 Wil Ledezma 1.00 .40
❑ 349 Aaron Guiel 1.00 .40
❑ 350 Alfonso Soriano 1.00 .40
❑ 351 Ted Lilly 1.00 .40
❑ 352 Sean Burroughs 1.00 .40
❑ 353 Rafael Palmeiro 1.50 .60
❑ 354 Quinton McCracken 1.00 .40
❑ 355 David Ortiz 2.50 1.00
❑ 356 Randall Simon 1.00 .40
❑ 357 Wily Mo Pena 1.00 .40
❑ 358 Brian Anderson 1.00 .40
❑ 359 Corey Koskie 1.00 .40
❑ 360 Keith Foulke Sox 1.00 .40
❑ 361 Sidney Ponson 1.00 .40
❑ 362 Gary Matthews Jr. 1.00 .40
❑ 363 Herbert Perry 1.00 .40
❑ 364 Shea Hillenbrand 1.00 .40
❑ 365 Craig Biggio 1.50 .60
❑ 366 Barry Larkin 1.50 .60
❑ 367 Arthur Rhodes 1.00 .40
❑ 368 Sammy Sosa 2.50 1.00
❑ 369 Joe Crede 1.00 .40
❑ 370 Gary Sheffield 1.00 .40
❑ 371 Coco Crisp 1.00 .40
❑ 372 Torii Hunter 1.00 .40
❑ 373 Derrek Lee 1.50 .60
❑ 374 Adam Everett 1.00 .40
❑ 375 Miguel Tejada 1.00 .40
❑ 376 Jeremy Affeldt 1.00 .40
❑ 377 Robin Ventura 1.00 .40
❑ 378 Scott Podsednik 1.00 .40
❑ 379 Matthew LeCroy 1.00 .40
❑ 380 Vladimir Guerrero 2.50 1.00
❑ 381 Steve Karsay 1.00 .40
❑ 382 Jeff Nelson 1.00 .40
❑ 383 Chase Utley 1.50 .60
❑ 384 Bobby Abreu 1.00 .40
❑ 385 Josh Fogg 1.00 .40
❑ 386 Trevor Hoffman 1.00 .40
❑ 387 Matt Stairs 1.00 .40
❑ 388 Edgar Martinez 1.50 .60
❑ 389 Edgar Renteria 1.00 .40
❑ 390 Chipper Jones 2.50 1.00
❑ 391 Eric Munson 1.00 .40
❑ 392 Dewon Brazelton 1.00 .40
❑ 393 John Thomson 1.00 .40
❑ 394 Chris Woodward 1.00 .40
❑ 395 Joe Kennedy 1.00 .40
❑ 396 Reed Johnson 1.00 .40
❑ 397 Johnny Estrada 1.00 .40
❑ 398 Damian Moss 1.00 .40
❑ 399 Victor Zambrano 1.00 .40
❑ 400 Dontrelle Willis 1.50 .60
❑ 401 Troy Glaus 1.00 .40
❑ 402 Raul Mondesi 1.00 .40
❑ 403 Jeff Davanon 1.00 .40
❑ 404 Kurt Ainsworth 1.00 .40
❑ 405 Pedro Martinez 1.50 .60
❑ 406 Eric Karros 1.00 .40
❑ 407 Billy Koch 1.00 .40
❑ 408 Luis Gonzalez 1.00 .40
❑ 409 Jack Cust 1.00 .40
❑ 410 Mike Sweeney 1.00 .40
❑ 411 Jason Bay 1.00 .40
❑ 412 Mark Redman 1.00 .40
❑ 413 Jason Jennings 1.00 .40
❑ 414 Rondell White 1.00 .40
❑ 415 Todd Hundley 1.00 .40
❑ 416 Shannon Stewart 1.00 .40
❑ 417 Jae Weong Seo 1.00 .40
❑ 418 Livan Hernandez 1.00 .40
❑ 419 Mark Ellis 1.00 .40
❑ 420 Pat Burrell 1.00 .40
❑ 421 Mark Loretta 1.00 .40
❑ 422 Robb Nen 1.00 .40
❑ 423 Joel Pineiro 1.00 .40
❑ 424 Todd Walker 1.00 .40
❑ 425 Jeremy Bonderman 1.00 .40
❑ 426 A.J. Burnett 1.00 .40
❑ 427 Greg Myers 1.00 .40
❑ 428 Roy Oswalt 1.00 .40
❑ 429 Carlos Baerga 1.00 .40
❑ 430 Garret Anderson 1.00 .40
❑ 431 Horacio Ramirez 1.00 .40
❑ 432 Brian Roberts 1.00 .40
❑ 433 Kevin Brown 1.00 .40
❑ 434 Eric Milton 1.00 .40
❑ 435 Ramon Vazquez 1.00 .40
❑ 436 Alex Escobar 1.00 .40
❑ 437 Alex Sanchez 1.00 .40
❑ 438 Jeff Bagwell 1.50 .60
❑ 439 Claudio Vargas 1.00 .40
❑ 440 Shawn Green 1.00 .40
❑ 441 Geoff Jenkins 1.00 .40
❑ 442 David Wells 1.00 .40
❑ 443 Nick Johnson 1.00 .40
❑ 444 Jose Guillen 1.00 .40
❑ 445 Scott Hatteberg 1.00 .40
❑ 446 Phil Nevin 1.00 .40
❑ 447 Jason Schmidt 1.00 .40
❑ 448 Ricky Ledee 1.00 .40
❑ 449 So Taguchi 1.00 .40
❑ 450 Randy Johnson 2.50 1.00
❑ 451 Eric Young 1.00 .40
❑ 452 Chone Figgins 1.00 .40
❑ 453 Larry Bigbie 1.00 .40
❑ 454 Scott Williamson 1.00 .40
❑ 455 Ramon Martinez 1.00 .40
❑ 456 Roberto Alomar 1.50 .60
❑ 457 Ryan Dempster 1.00 .40
❑ 458 Ryan Ludwick 1.00 .40
❑ 459 Ramon Santiago 1.00 .40
❑ 460 Jeff Conine 1.00 .40
❑ 461 Brad Lidge 1.00 .40
❑ 462 Ken Harvey 1.00 .40
❑ 463 Guillermo Mota 1.00 .40
❑ 464 Rick Reed 1.00 .40
❑ 465 Armando Benitez 1.00 .40
❑ 466 Wade Miller 1.00 .40

2004 Topps Chrome Traded

❑ COMPLETE SET (220) 120.00 60.00
❑ COMMON CARD (1-70) .75 .30
❑ COMMON CARD (71-90) 1.00 .40
❑ COMMON CARD (91-110) 1.00 .40
❑ COMMON CARD (111-220) 1.00 .40
❑ 2 PER 2004 TOPPS TRADED HOBBY PACK
❑ 2 PER 2004 TOPPS TRADED HTA PACK
❑ 2 PER 2004 TOPPS TRADED RETAIL PACK
❑ PLATE ODDS 1:1151 H, 1:1173 R, 1:327 HTA
❑ PLATE PRINT RUN 1 SET PER COLOR
❑ BLACK-CYAN-MAGENTA-YELLOW ISSUED
❑ NO PLATE PRICING DUE TO SCARCITY
❑ T1 Pokey Reese .75 .30
❑ T2 Tony Womack .75 .30
❑ T3 Richard Hidalgo .75 .30
❑ T4 Juan Uribe .75 .30
❑ T5 J.D. Drew .75 .30
❑ T6 Alex Gonzalez .75 .30
❑ T7 Carlos Guillen .75 .30
❑ T8 Doug Mientkiewicz .75 .30
❑ T9 Fernando Vina .75 .30
❑ T10 Milton Bradley .75 .30
❑ T11 Kelvim Escobar .75 .30
❑ T12 Ben Grieve .75 .30
❑ T13 Brian Jordan .75 .30
❑ T14 A.J. Pierzynski .75 .30

❑ T15 Billy Wagner .75 .30
❑ T16 Terrence Long .75 .30
❑ T17 Carlos Beltran .75 .30
❑ T18 Carl Everett .75 .30
❑ T19 Reggie Sanders .75 .30
❑ T20 Javy Lopez .75 .30
❑ T21 Jay Payton .75 .30
❑ T22 Octavio Dotel .75 .30
❑ T23 Eddie Guardado .75 .30
❑ T24 Andy Pettitte 1.25 .50
❑ T25 Richie Sexson .75 .30
❑ T26 Ronnie Belliard .75 .30
❑ T27 Michael Tucker .75 .30
❑ T28 Brad Fullmer .75 .30
❑ T29 Freddy Garcia .75 .30
❑ T30 Bartolo Colon .75 .30
❑ T31 Larry Walker Cards 1.25 .50
❑ T32 Mark Kotsay .75 .30
❑ T33 Jason Marquis .75 .30
❑ T34 Dustan Mohr .75 .30
❑ T35 Javier Vazquez .75 .30
❑ T36 Nomar Garciaparra 3.00 1.25
❑ T37 Tino Martinez 1.25 .50
❑ T38 Hee Seop Choi .75 .30
❑ T39 Damian Miller .75 .30
❑ T40 Jose Lima .75 .30
❑ T41 Ty Wigginton .75 .30
❑ T42 Raul Ibanez .75 .30
❑ T43 Danys Baez .75 .30
❑ T44 Tony Clark .75 .30
❑ T45 Greg Maddux 3.00 1.25
❑ T46 Victor Zambrano .75 .30
❑ T47 Orlando Cabrera Sox .75 .30
❑ T48 Jose Cruz Jr. .75 .30
❑ T49 Kris Benson .75 .30
❑ T50 Alex Rodriguez 4.00 1.50
❑ T51 Steve Finley .75 .30
❑ T52 Ramon Hernandez .75 .30
❑ T53 Esteban Loaiza .75 .30
❑ T54 Ugueth Urbina .75 .30
❑ T55 Jeff Weaver .75 .30
❑ T56 Flash Gordon .75 .30
❑ T57 Jose Contreras .75 .30
❑ T58 Paul Lo Duca .75 .30
❑ T59 Junior Spivey .75 .30
❑ T60 Curt Schilling 1.25 .50
❑ T61 Brad Penny .75 .30
❑ T62 Braden Looper .75 .30
❑ T63 Miguel Cairo .75 .30
❑ T64 Juan Encarnacion .75 .30
❑ T65 Miguel Batista .75 .30
❑ T66 Terry Francona MG .75 .30
❑ T67 Lee Mazzilli MG .75 .30
❑ T68 Al Pedrique MG .75 .30
❑ T69 Ozzie Guillen MG 2.00 .75
❑ T70 Phil Garner MG .75 .30
❑ T71 Matt Bush DP RC 4.00 1.50
❑ T72 Homer Bailey DP RC 6.00 2.50
❑ T73 Greg Golson DP RC 3.00 1.25
❑ T74 Kyle Waldrop DP RC 2.50 1.00
❑ T75 Richie Robnett DP RC 3.00 1.25
❑ T76 Jay Rainville DP RC 4.00 1.50
❑ T77 Bill Bray DP RC 1.00 .40
❑ T78 Philip Hughes DP RC 15.00 6.00
❑ T79 Scott Elbert DP RC 2.50 1.00
❑ T80 Josh Fields DP RC 5.00 2.00
❑ T81 Justin Orenduff DP RC 2.00 .75
❑ T82 Dan Putnam DP RC 2.00 .75
❑ T83 Chris Nelson DP RC 5.00 2.00
❑ T84 Blake DeWitt DP RC 4.00 1.50
❑ T85 J.P. Howell DP RC 2.50 1.00
❑ T86 Huston Street DP RC 6.00 2.50
❑ T87 Kurt Suzuki DP RC 3.00 1.25
❑ T88 Erick San Pedro DP RC 1.00 .40
❑ T89 Matt Tuiasosopo DP RC 5.00 2.00
❑ T90 Matt Macri DP RC 2.50 1.00
❑ T91 Chad Tracy PROS 1.00 .40
❑ T92 Scott Hairston PROS 1.00 .40
❑ T93 Jonny Gomes PROS 1.00 .40
❑ T94 Chin-Feng Chen PROS 1.00 .40
❑ T95 Chien-Ming Wang PROS 3.00 1.25
❑ T96 Dustin McGowan PROS 1.00 .40
❑ T97 Chris Burke PROS 1.00 .40
❑ T98 Denny Bautista PROS 1.00 .40
❑ T99 Preston Larrison PROS 1.00 .40
❑ T100 Kevin Youkilis PROS 1.00 .40
❑ T101 John Maine PROS 1.00 .40
❑ T102 Guillermo Quiroz PROS 1.00 .40
❑ T103 Dave Krynzel PROS 1.00 .40
❑ T104 David Kelton PROS 1.00 .40
❑ T105 Edwin Encarnacion PROS 1.00 .40
❑ T106 Chad Gaudin PROS 1.00 .40
❑ T107 Sergio Mitre PROS 1.00 .40
❑ T108 Laynce Nix PROS 1.00 .40
❑ T109 David Parrish PROS 1.00 .40
❑ T110 Brandon Claussen PROS 1.00 .40
❑ T111 Frank Francisco FY RC 1.00 .40
❑ T112 Brian Dallimore FY RC 1.00 .40
❑ T113 Jim Crowell FY RC 1.25 .50
❑ T114 Andres Blanco FY RC 1.00 .40
❑ T115 Eduardo Villacis FY RC 1.00 .40
❑ T116 Kazuhito Tadano FY RC 1.25 .50
❑ T117 Aarom Baldiris FY RC 1.25 .50
❑ T118 Justin Germano FY RC 1.00 .40
❑ T119 Joey Gathright FY RC 3.00 1.25
❑ T120 Franklyn Gracesqui FY RC 1.00 .40
❑ T121 Chin-Lung Hu FY RC 3.00 1.25
❑ T122 Scott Olsen FY RC 4.00 1.50
❑ T123 Tyler Davidson FY RC 1.25 .50
❑ T124 Fausto Carmona FY RC 5.00 2.00
❑ T125 Tim Hutting FY RC 1.00 .40
❑ T126 Ryan Meaux FY RC 1.00 .40
❑ T127 Jon Connolly FY RC 2.50 1.00
❑ T128 Hector Made FY RC 2.00 .75
❑ T129 Jamie Brown FY RC 1.00 .40
❑ T130 Paul McAnulty FY RC 2.00 .75
❑ T131 Chris Saenz FY RC 1.00 .40
❑ T132 Marland Williams FY RC 1.25 .50
❑ T133 Mike Huggins FY RC 1.00 .40
❑ T134 Jesse Crain FY RC 2.00 .75
❑ T135 Chad Bentz FY RC 1.00 .40
❑ T136 Kazuo Matsui FY RC 2.00 .75
❑ T137 Paul Maholm FY 2.50 1.00
❑ T138 Brock Jacobsen FY RC 1.00 .40
❑ T139 Casey Daigle FY RC 1.00 .40
❑ T140 Nyjer Morgan FY RC 1.00 .40
❑ T141 Tom Mastny FY RC 1.00 .40
❑ T142 Kody Kirkland FY RC 1.25 .50
❑ T143 Jose Capellan FY RC 1.25 .50
❑ T144 Felix Hernandez FY RC 25.00 10.00
❑ T145 Shawn Hill FY RC 1.00 .40
❑ T146 Danny Gonzalez FY RC 1.00 .40
❑ T147 Scott Dohmann FY RC 1.00 .40
❑ T148 Tommy Murphy FY RC 1.00 .40
❑ T149 Akinori Otsuka FY RC 1.00 .40
❑ T150 Miguel Perez FY RC 1.00 .40
❑ T151 Mike Rouse FY RC 1.00 .40
❑ T152 Ramon Ramirez FY RC 1.00 .40
❑ T153 Luke Hughes FY RC 1.00 .40
❑ T154 Howie Kendrick FY RC 30.00 20.00
❑ T155 Ryan Budde FY RC 1.00 .40
❑ T156 Charlie Zink FY RC 1.00 .40
❑ T157 Warner Madrigal FY RC 2.00 .75
❑ T158 Jason Szuminski FY RC 1.00 .40
❑ T159 Chad Chop FY RC 1.00 .40
❑ T160 Shingo Takatsu FY RC 2.00 .75
❑ T161 Matt Lemanczyk FY RC 1.00 .40
❑ T162 Wardell Starling FY RC 1.00 .40
❑ T163 Nick Gorneault FY RC 1.25 .50
❑ T164 Scott Proctor FY RC 1.25 .50
❑ T165 Brooks Conrad FY RC 1.25 .50
❑ T166 Hector Gimenez FY RC 1.00 .40
❑ T167 Kevin Howard FY RC 1.25 .50
❑ T168 Vince Perkins FY RC 1.25 .50
❑ T169 Brock Peterson FY RC 1.00 .40
❑ T170 Chris Shelton FY 2.00 .75
❑ T171 Erick Aybar FY RC 2.00 .75
❑ T172 Paul Bacot FY RC 1.25 .50
❑ T173 Matt Capps FY RC 1.00 .40
❑ T174 Kory Casto FY 1.25 .50
❑ T175 Juan Cedeno FY RC 1.00 .40
❑ T176 Vito Chiaravalloti FY 1.00 .40
❑ T177 Alec Zumwalt FY RC 1.00 .40
❑ T178 J.J. Furmaniak FY RC 2.00 .75
❑ T179 Lee Gwaltney FY RC 1.00 .40
❑ T180 Donald Kelly FY RC 1.00 .40
❑ T181 Benji DeQuin FY RC 1.00 .40
❑ T182 Brant Colamarino FY RC 2.00 .75
❑ T183 Juan Gutierrez FY RC 1.00 .40
❑ T184 Carl Loadenthal FY RC 1.25 .50
❑ T185 Ricky Nolasco FY RC 3.00 1.25
❑ T186 Jeff Salazar FY RC 2.50 1.00
❑ T187 Rob Tejeda FY RC 2.00 .75
❑ T188 Alex Romero FY RC 1.00 .40
❑ T189 Yoann Torrealba FY RC 1.00 .40
❑ T190 Carlos Sosa FY RC 1.00 .40
❑ T191 Tim Bittner FY RC 1.00 .40
❑ T192 Chris Aguila FY RC 1.00 .40
❑ T193 Jason Frasor FY RC 1.00 .40
❑ T194 Reid Gorecki FY RC 1.00 .40
❑ T195 Dustin Nippert FY RC 1.25 .50
❑ T196 Javier Guzman FY RC 1.25 .50
❑ T197 Harvey Garcia FY RC 1.00 .40
❑ T198 Ivan Ochoa FY RC 1.00 .40
❑ T199 David Wallace FY RC 1.25 .50
❑ T200 Joel Zumaya FY RC 8.00 3.00
❑ T201 Casey Kopitzke FY RC 1.00 .40
❑ T202 Lincoln Holdzkom FY RC 1.00 .40
❑ T203 Chad Santos FY RC 1.00 .40
❑ T204 Brian Pilkington FY RC 1.00 .40
❑ T205 Terry Jones FY RC 1.25 .50
❑ T206 Jerome Gamble FY RC 1.00 .40
❑ T207 Brad Eldred FY RC 1.25 .50
❑ T208 David Pauley FY RC 3.00 1.25
❑ T209 Kevin Davidson FY RC 1.00 .40
❑ T210 Damaso Espino FY RC 1.00 .40
❑ T211 Tom Farmer FY RC 1.00 .40
❑ T212 Michael Mooney FY RC 1.00 .40
❑ T213 James Tomlin FY RC 1.00 .40
❑ T214 Greg Thissen FY RC 1.00 .40
❑ T215 Calvin Hayes FY RC 1.25 .50
❑ T216 Fernando Cortez FY RC 1.00 .40
❑ T217 Sergio Silva FY RC 1.00 .40
❑ T218 Jon de Vries FY RC 1.00 .40
❑ T219 Don Sutton FY RC 2.50 1.00
❑ T220 Leo Nunez FY RC 1.00 .40

2005 Topps Chrome

❑ COMP.SET w/o AU'S (440) 160.00 80.00
❑ COMP.SERIES 1 w/o AU's (220) 80.0040.00
❑ COMP.SERIES 2 w/o AU's (220) 80.0040.00
❑ COMMON (1-210/253-467) 1.00 .40
❑ COMMON (211-220/468-472) 2.00 .75
❑ 221-252 PRINT RUN PROVIDED BY TOPPS
❑ EXCHANGE DEADLINE 05/31/07
❑ 1-234 PLATE ODDS 1:310 SER.1 HOBBY
❑ 235-252 PLATE ODDS 1:350 SER.2 MINI BOX
❑ 253-472 PLATE ODDS 1:29 SER.2 MINI BOX
❑ PLATE PRINT RUN 1 SET PER COLOR
❑ BLACK-CYAN-MAGENTA-YELLOW ISSUED
❑ NO PLATE PRICING DUE TO SCARCITY
❑ 1 Alex Rodriguez 4.00 1.50
❑ 2 Placido Polanco 1.00 .40
❑ 3 Torii Hunter 1.00 .40
❑ 4 Lyle Overbay 1.00 .40
❑ 5 Johnny Damon 1.50 .60
❑ 6 Johnny Estrada 1.00 .40
❑ 7 Rich Harden 1.00 .40
❑ 8 Francisco Rodriguez 1.00 .40
❑ 9 Jarrod Washburn 1.00 .40
❑ 10 Sammy Sosa 2.50 1.00
❑ 11 Randy Wolf 1.00 .40
❑ 12 Jason Bay 1.00 .40
❑ 13 Tom Glavine 1.50 .60
❑ 14 Michael Tucker 1.00 .40
❑ 15 Brian Giles 1.00 .40
❑ 16 Chad Tracy 1.00 .40
❑ 17 Jim Edmonds 1.00 .40
❑ 18 John Smoltz 1.50 .60
❑ 19 Roy Halladay 1.00 .40

❑ 20 Hank Blalock 1.00 .40
❑ 21 Darin Erstad 1.00 .40
❑ 22 Todd Walker 1.00 .40
❑ 23 Mike Hampton 1.00 .40
❑ 24 Mark Bellhorn 1.00 .40
❑ 25 Jim Thome 1.50 .60
❑ 26 Shingo Takatsu 1.00 .40
❑ 27 Jody Gerut 1.00 .40
❑ 28 Vinny Castilla 1.00 .40
❑ 29 Luis Castillo 1.00 .40
❑ 30 Ivan Rodriguez 1.50 .60
❑ 31 Craig Biggio 1.50 .60
❑ 32 Joe Randa 1.00 .40
❑ 33 Adrian Beltre 1.00 .40
❑ 34 Scott Podsednik 1.00 .40
❑ 35 Cliff Floyd 1.00 .40
❑ 36 Livan Hernandez 1.00 .40
❑ 37 Eric Byrnes 1.00 .40
❑ 38 Jose Acevedo 1.00 .40
❑ 39 Jack Wilson 1.00 .40
❑ 40 Gary Sheffield 1.00 .40
❑ 41 Chan Ho Park 1.00 .40
❑ 42 Carl Crawford 1.00 .40
❑ 43 Shawn Estes 1.00 .40
❑ 44 David Bell 1.00 .40
❑ 45 Jeff DaVanon 1.00 .40
❑ 46 Brandon Webb 1.00 .40
❑ 47 Lance Berkman 1.00 .40
❑ 48 Melvin Mora 1.00 .40
❑ 49 David Ortiz 2.50 1.00
❑ 50 Andruw Jones 1.50 .60
❑ 51 Chone Figgins 1.00 .40
❑ 52 Danny Graves 1.00 .40
❑ 53 Preston Wilson 1.00 .40
❑ 54 Jeremy Bonderman 1.00 .40
❑ 55 Carlos Guillen 1.00 .40
❑ 56 Cesar Izturis 1.00 .40
❑ 57 Kazuo Matsui 1.00 .40
❑ 58 Jason Schmidt 1.00 .40
❑ 59 Jason Marquis 1.00 .40
❑ 60 Jose Vidro 1.00 .40
❑ 61 Al Leiter 1.00 .40
❑ 62 Javier Vazquez 1.00 .40
❑ 63 Erubiel Durazo 1.00 .40
❑ 64 Scott Spiezio 1.00 .40
❑ 65 Scot Shields 1.00 .40
❑ 66 Edgardo Alfonzo 1.00 .40
❑ 67 Miguel Tejada 1.00 .40
❑ 68 Francisco Cordero 1.00 .40
❑ 69 Brett Myers 1.00 .40
❑ 70 Curt Schilling 1.50 .60
❑ 71 Matt Kata 1.00 .40
❑ 72 Bartolo Colon 1.00 .40
❑ 73 Rodrigo Lopez 1.00 .40
❑ 74 Tim Wakefield 1.00 .40
❑ 75 Frank Thomas 2.50 1.00
❑ 76 Jimmy Rollins 1.00 .40
❑ 77 Barry Zito 1.00 .40
❑ 78 Hideo Nomo 2.50 1.00
❑ 79 Brad Wilkerson 1.00 .40
❑ 80 Adam Dunn 1.00 .40
❑ 81 Derrek Lee 1.50 .60
❑ 82 Joe Crede 1.00 .40
❑ 83 Nate Robertson 1.00 .40
❑ 84 John Thomson 1.00 .40
❑ 85 Mike Sweeney 1.00 .40
❑ 86 Kip Wells 1.00 .40
❑ 87 Eric Gagne 1.00 .40
❑ 88 Zach Day 1.00 .40
❑ 89 Alex Sanchez 1.00 .40
❑ 90 Bret Boone 1.00 .40
❑ 91 Mark Loretta 1.00 .40
❑ 92 Miguel Cabrera 1.50 .60
❑ 93 Randy Winn 1.00 .40
❑ 94 Adam Everett 1.00 .40
❑ 95 Aubrey Huff 1.00 .40
❑ 96 Kevin Mench 1.00 .40
❑ 97 Frank Catalanotto 1.00 .40
❑ 98 Flash Gordon 1.00 .40
❑ 99 Scott Hatteberg 1.00 .40
❑ 100 Albert Pujols 5.00 2.00
❑ 101 J.Molina/B.Molina 1.00 .40
❑ 102 Jason Johnson 1.00 .40
❑ 103 Jay Gibbons 1.00 .40
❑ 104 Byung-Hyun Kim 1.00 .40
❑ 105 Joe Borowski 1.00 .40
❑ 106 Mark Grudzielanek 1.00 .40
❑ 107 Mark Buehrle 1.00 .40
❑ 108 Paul Wilson 1.00 .40
❑ 109 Ronnie Belliard 1.00 .40
❑ 110 Reggie Sanders 1.00 .40
❑ 111 Tim Redding 1.00 .40
❑ 112 Brian Lawrence 1.00 .40
❑ 113 Travis Hafner 1.00 .40
❑ 114 Jose Hernandez 1.00 .40
❑ 115 Ben Sheets 1.00 .40
❑ 116 Johan Santana 2.50 1.00
❑ 117 Billy Wagner 1.00 .40
❑ 118 Mariano Rivera 2.50 1.00
❑ 119 Steve Trachsel 1.00 .40
❑ 120 Akinori Otsuka 1.00 .40
❑ 121 Jose Valentin 1.00 .40
❑ 122 Orlando Hernandez 1.00 .40
❑ 123 Raul Ibanez 1.00 .40
❑ 124 Mike Matheny 1.00 .40
❑ 125 Vernon Wells 1.00 .40
❑ 126 Jason Isringhausen 1.00 .40
❑ 127 Jose Guillen 1.00 .40
❑ 128 Danny Bautista 1.00 .40
❑ 129 Marcus Giles 1.00 .40
❑ 130 Javy Lopez 1.00 .40
❑ 131 Kevin Millar 1.00 .40
❑ 132 Kyle Farnsworth 1.00 .40
❑ 133 Carl Pavano 1.00 .40
❑ 134 Rafael Furcal 1.00 .40
❑ 135 Casey Blake 1.00 .40
❑ 136 Matt Holliday 1.25 .50
❑ 137 Bobby Higginson 1.00 .40
❑ 138 Adam Kennedy 1.00 .40
❑ 139 Alex Gonzalez 1.00 .40
❑ 140 Jeff Kent 1.00 .40
❑ 141 Aaron Guiel 1.00 .40
❑ 142 Shawn Green 1.00 .40
❑ 143 Bill Hall 1.00 .40
❑ 144 Shannon Stewart 1.00 .40
❑ 145 Juan Rivera 1.00 .40
❑ 146 Coco Crisp 1.00 .40
❑ 147 Mike Mussina 1.50 .60
❑ 148 Eric Chavez 1.00 .40
❑ 149 Jon Lieber 1.00 .40
❑ 150 Vladimir Guerrero 2.50 1.00
❑ 151 Alex Cintron 1.00 .40
❑ 152 Luis Matos 1.00 .40
❑ 153 Sidney Ponson 1.00 .40
❑ 154 Trot Nixon 1.00 .40
❑ 155 Greg Maddux 4.00 1.50
❑ 156 Edgar Renteria 1.00 .40
❑ 157 Ryan Freel 1.00 .40
❑ 158 Matt Lawton 1.00 .40
❑ 159 Mark Prior 1.50 .60
❑ 160 Josh Beckett 1.00 .40
❑ 161 Ken Harvey 1.00 .40
❑ 162 Angel Berroa 1.00 .40
❑ 163 Juan Encarnacion 1.00 .40
❑ 164 Wes Helms 1.00 .40
❑ 165 Brad Radke 1.00 .40
❑ 166 Phil Nevin 1.00 .40
❑ 167 Mike Cameron 1.00 .40
❑ 168 Billy Koch 1.00 .40
❑ 169 Bobby Crosby 1.00 .40
❑ 170 Mike Lieberthal 1.00 .40
❑ 171 Rob Mackowiak 1.00 .40
❑ 172 Sean Burroughs 1.00 .40
❑ 173 J.T. Snow 1.00 .40
❑ 174 Paul Konerko 1.00 .40
❑ 175 Luis Gonzalez 1.00 .40
❑ 176 John Lackey 1.00 .40
❑ 177 Oliver Perez 1.00 .40
❑ 178 Brian Roberts 1.00 .40
❑ 179 Bill Mueller 1.00 .40
❑ 180 Carlos Lee 1.00 .40
❑ 181 Corey Patterson 1.00 .40
❑ 182 Sean Casey 1.00 .40
❑ 183 Cliff Lee 1.00 .40
❑ 184 Jason Jennings 1.00 .40
❑ 185 Dmitri Young 1.00 .40
❑ 186 Juan Uribe 1.00 .40
❑ 187 Andy Pettitte 1.50 .60
❑ 188 Juan Gonzalez 1.00 .40
❑ 189 Orlando Hudson 1.00 .40
❑ 190 Jason Phillips 1.00 .40
❑ 191 Braden Looper 1.00 .40
❑ 192 Lew Ford 1.00 .40
❑ 193 Mark Mulder 1.00 .40
❑ 194 Bobby Abreu 1.00 .40
❑ 195 Jason Kendall 1.00 .40
❑ 196 Khalil Greene 1.50 .60
❑ 197 A.J. Pierzynski 1.00 .40
❑ 198 Tim Worrell 1.00 .40
❑ 199 So Taguchi 1.00 .40
❑ 200 Jason Giambi 1.00 .40
❑ 201 Tony Batista 1.00 .40
❑ 202 Carlos Zambrano 1.00 .40
❑ 203 Trevor Hoffman 1.00 .40
❑ 204 Odalis Perez 1.00 .40
❑ 205 Jose Cruz Jr. 1.00 .40
❑ 206 Michael Barrett 1.00 .40
❑ 207 Chris Carpenter 1.00 .40
❑ 208 Michael Young UER 1.00 .40
❑ 209 Toby Hall 1.00 .40
❑ 210 Woody Williams 1.00 .40
❑ 211 Chris Denorfia FY RC 3.00 1.25
❑ 212 Darren Fenster FY RC 2.00 .75
❑ 213 Elvys Quezada FY RC 2.00 .75
❑ 214 Ian Kinsler FY RC 5.00 2.00
❑ 215 Matthew Lindstrom FY RC 2.00 .75
❑ 216 Ryan Goleski FY RC 3.00 1.25
❑ 217 Ryan Sweeney FY RC 4.00 1.50
❑ 218 Sean Marshall FY RC 5.00 2.00
❑ 219 Steve Doetsch FY RC 3.00 1.25
❑ 220 Wade Robinson FY RC 2.00 .75
❑ 221 Andre Ethier FY AU RC 80.00 40.00
❑ 222 Brandon Moss FY AU RC 20.00 8.00
❑ 223 Chadd Blasko FY AU RC 15.00 6.00
❑ 224 Chris Roberson FY AU RC 10.00 4.00
❑ 225 Chris Seddon FY AU RC 10.00 4.00
❑ 226 Ian Bladergroen FY AU RC 15.00 6.00
❑ 227 Jake Dittler FY AU 10.00 4.00
❑ 228 Jose Vaquedano FY AU RC 10.004.00
❑ 229 Jeremy West FY AU RC 15.00 6.00
❑ 230 Kole Strayhorn FY AU RC 10.00 4.00
❑ 231 Kevin West FY AU RC 10.00 4.00
❑ 232 Luis Ramirez FY AU RC 10.00 4.00
❑ 233 Melky Cabrera FY AU RC 40.00 20.00
❑ 234 Nate Schierholtz FY AU 10.00 4.00
❑ 235 Billy Butler FY AU RC 50.00 20.00
❑ 236 B.Szymanski FY AU EXCH 10.00 4.00
❑ 237 Chad Orvella FY AU RC 10.00 4.00
❑ 238 Chip Cannon FY AU RC 20.00 8.00
❑ 239 Eric Nielsen FY AU RC 10.00 4.00
❑ 240 Erik Cordier FY AU RC 10.00 4.00
❑ 241 Glen Perkins FY AU RC 20.00 8.00
❑ 242 Justin Verlander FY AU RC 50.0030.00
❑ 243 Kevin Melillo FY AU RC 15.00 6.00
❑ 244 Landon Powell FY AU RC 15.00 6.00
❑ 245 Matt Campbell FY AU RC 10.00 4.00
❑ 246 Michael Rogers FY AU RC 10.00 4.00
❑ 247 Nate McLouth FY AU RC 20.00 8.00
❑ 248 Scott Mathieson FY AU RC 10.00 4.00
❑ 249 Shane Costa FY AU RC 10.00 4.00
❑ 250 Tony Giarratano FY AU RC 10.00 4.00
❑ 251 Tyler Pelland FY AU RC 15.00 6.00
❑ 252 Wes Swackhamer FY AU RC 10.004.00
❑ 253 Garret Anderson 1.00 .40
❑ 254 Randy Johnson 2.50 1.00
❑ 255 Charles Thomas 1.00 .40
❑ 256 Rafael Palmeiro 1.50 .60
❑ 257 Kevin Youkilis 1.00 .40
❑ 258 Freddy Garcia 1.00 .40
❑ 259 Magglio Ordonez 1.00 .40
❑ 260 Aaron Harang 1.00 .40
❑ 261 Grady Sizemore 1.50 .60
❑ 262 Chin-hui Tsao 1.00 .40
❑ 263 Eric Munson 1.00 .40
❑ 264 Juan Pierre 1.00 .40
❑ 265 Brad Lidge 1.00 .40
❑ 266 Brian Anderson 1.00 .40
❑ 267 Todd Helton 1.50 .60
❑ 268 Chad Cordero 1.00 .40
❑ 269 Kris Benson 1.00 .40
❑ 270 Brad Halsey 1.00 .40
❑ 271 Jermaine Dye 1.00 .40
❑ 272 Manny Ramirez 1.50 .60
❑ 273 Adam Eaton 1.00 .40
❑ 274 Brett Tomko 1.00 .40
❑ 275 Bucky Jacobsen 1.00 .40
❑ 276 Dontrelle Willis 1.00 .40
❑ 277 B.J. Upton 1.00 .40

❑ 278 Rocco Baldelli 1.00 .40
❑ 279 Ryan Drese 1.00 .40
❑ 280 Ichiro Suzuki 5.00 2.00
❑ 281 Brandon Lyon 1.00 .40
❑ 282 Nick Green 1.00 .40
❑ 283 Jerry Hairston Jr. 1.00 .40
❑ 284 Mike Lowell 1.00 .40
❑ 285 Kerry Wood 1.00 .40
❑ 286 Omar Vizquel 1.50 .60
❑ 287 Carlos Beltran 1.00 .40
❑ 288 Carlos Pena 1.00 .40
❑ 289 Jeff Weaver 1.00 .40
❑ 290 Chad Moeller 1.00 .40
❑ 291 Joe Mays 1.00 .40
❑ 292 Termel Sledge 1.00 .40
❑ 293 Richard Hidalgo 1.00 .40
❑ 294 Justin Duchscherer 1.00 .40
❑ 295 Eric Milton 1.00 .40
❑ 296 Ramon Hernandez 1.00 .40
❑ 297 Jose Reyes 1.00 .40
❑ 298 Joel Pineiro 1.00 .40
❑ 299 Matt Morris 1.00 .40
❑ 300 John Halama 1.00 .40
❑ 301 Gary Matthews Jr. 1.00 .40
❑ 302 Ryan Madson 1.00 .40
❑ 303 Mark Kotsay 1.00 .40
❑ 304 Carlos Delgado 1.00 .40
❑ 305 Casey Kotchman 1.00 .40
❑ 306 Greg Aquino 1.00 .40
❑ 307 LaTroy Hawkins 1.00 .40
❑ 308 Jose Contreras 1.00 .40
❑ 309 Ken Griffey Jr. 4.00 1.50
❑ 310 C.C. Sabathia 1.00 .40
❑ 311 Brandon Inge 1.00 .40
❑ 312 John Buck 1.00 .40
❑ 313 Hee Seop Choi 1.00 .40
❑ 314 Chris Capuano 1.00 .40
❑ 315 Jesse Crain 1.00 .40
❑ 316 Geoff Jenkins 1.00 .40
❑ 317 Mike Piazza 2.50 1.00
❑ 318 Jorge Posada 1.50 .60
❑ 319 Nick Swisher 1.00 .40
❑ 320 Kevin Millwood 1.00 .40
❑ 321 Mike Gonzalez 1.00 .40
❑ 322 Jake Peavy 1.00 .40
❑ 323 Dustin Hermanson 1.00 .40
❑ 324 Jeremy Reed 1.00 .40
❑ 325 Alfonso Soriano 1.00 .40
❑ 326 Alexis Rios 1.00 .40
❑ 327 David Eckstein 1.00 .40
❑ 328 Shea Hillenbrand 1.00 .40
❑ 329 Russ Ortiz 1.00 .40
❑ 330 Kurt Ainsworth 1.00 .40
❑ 331 Orlando Cabrera 1.00 .40
❑ 332 Carlos Silva 1.00 .40
❑ 333 Ross Gload 1.00 .40
❑ 334 Josh Phelps 1.00 .40
❑ 335 Mike Maroth 1.00 .40
❑ 336 Guillermo Mota 1.00 .40
❑ 337 Chris Burke 1.00 .40
❑ 338 David DeJesus 1.00 .40
❑ 339 Jose Lima 1.00 .40
❑ 340 Cristian Guzman 1.00 .40
❑ 341 Nick Johnson 1.00 .40
❑ 342 Victor Zambrano 1.00 .40
❑ 343 Rod Barajas 1.00 .40
❑ 344 Damian Miller 1.00 .40
❑ 345 Chase Utley 1.50 .60
❑ 346 Sean Burnett 1.00 .40
❑ 347 David Wells 1.00 .40
❑ 348 Dustan Mohr 1.00 .40
❑ 349 Bobby Madritsch 1.00 .40
❑ 350 Reed Johnson 1.00 .40
❑ 351 R.A. Dickey 1.00 .40
❑ 352 Scott Kazmir 1.00 .40
❑ 353 Tony Womack 1.00 .40
❑ 354 Tomas Perez 1.00 .40
❑ 355 Esteban Loaiza 1.00 .40
❑ 356 Tomokazu Ohka 1.00 .40
❑ 357 Ramon Ortiz 1.00 .40
❑ 358 Richie Sexson 1.00 .40
❑ 359 J.D. Drew 1.00 .40
❑ 360 Barry Bonds 6.00 2.50
❑ 361 Aramis Ramirez 1.00 .40
❑ 362 Wily Mo Pena 1.00 .40
❑ 363 Jeromy Burnitz 1.00 .40
❑ 364 Nomar Garciaparra 2.50 1.00
❑ 365 Brandon Backe 1.00 .40
❑ 366 Derek Lowe 1.00 .40
❑ 367 Doug Davis 1.00 .40
❑ 368 Joe Mauer 2.50 1.00
❑ 369 Endy Chavez 1.00 .40
❑ 370 Bernie Williams 1.50 .60
❑ 371 Jason Michaels 1.00 .40
❑ 372 Craig Wilson 1.00 .40
❑ 373 Ryan Klesko 1.00 .40
❑ 374 Ray Durham 1.00 .40
❑ 375 Jose Lopez 1.00 .40
❑ 376 Jeff Suppan 1.00 .40
❑ 377 David Bush 1.00 .40
❑ 378 Marlon Byrd 1.00 .40
❑ 379 Roy Oswalt 1.00 .40
❑ 380 Rondell White 1.00 .40
❑ 381 Troy Glaus 1.00 .40
❑ 382 Scott Hairston 1.00 .40
❑ 383 Chipper Jones 2.50 1.00
❑ 384 Daniel Cabrera 1.00 .40
❑ 385 Jon Garland 1.00 .40
❑ 386 Austin Kearns 1.00 .40
❑ 387 Jake Westbrook 1.00 .40
❑ 388 Aaron Miles 1.00 .40
❑ 389 Omar Infante 1.00 .40
❑ 390 Paul Lo Duca 1.00 .40
❑ 391 Morgan Ensberg 1.00 .40
❑ 392 Tony Graffanino 1.00 .40
❑ 393 Milton Bradley 1.00 .40
❑ 394 Keith Ginter 1.00 .40
❑ 395 Justin Morneau 1.00 .40
❑ 396 Tony Armas Jr. 1.00 .40
❑ 397 Kevin Brown 1.00 .40
❑ 398 Marco Scutaro 1.00 .40
❑ 399 Tim Hudson 1.00 .40
❑ 400 Pat Burrell 1.00 .40
❑ 401 Jeff Cirillo 1.00 .40
❑ 402 Larry Walker 1.50 .60
❑ 403 Dewon Brazelton 1.00 .40
❑ 404 Shigetoshi Hasegawa 1.00 .40
❑ 405 Octavio Dotel 1.00 .40
❑ 406 Michael Cuddyer 1.00 .40
❑ 407 Junior Spivey 1.00 .40
❑ 408 Zack Greinke 1.00 .40
❑ 409 Roger Clemens 4.00 1.50
❑ 410 Chris Shelton 1.50 .60
❑ 411 Ugueth Urbina 1.00 .40
❑ 412 Rafael Betancourt 1.00 .40
❑ 413 Willie Harris 1.00 .40
❑ 414 Keith Foulke 1.00 .40
❑ 415 Larry Bigbie 1.00 .40
❑ 416 Paul Byrd 1.00 .40
❑ 417 Troy Percival 1.00 .40
❑ 418 Pedro Martinez 1.50 .60
❑ 419 Matt Clement 1.00 .40
❑ 420 Ryan Wagner 1.00 .40
❑ 421 Jeff Francis 1.00 .40
❑ 422 Jeff Conine 1.00 .40
❑ 423 Wade Miller 1.00 .40
❑ 424 Gavin Floyd 1.00 .40
❑ 425 Kazuhisa Ishii 1.00 .40
❑ 426 Victor Santos 1.00 .40
❑ 427 Jacque Jones 1.00 .40
❑ 428 Hideki Matsui 4.00 1.50
❑ 429 Cory Lidle 1.00 .40
❑ 430 Jose Castillo 1.00 .40
❑ 431 Alex Gonzalez 1.00 .40
❑ 432 Kirk Rueter 1.00 .40
❑ 433 Jolbert Cabrera 1.00 .40
❑ 434 Erik Bedard 1.00 .40
❑ 435 Ricky Ledee 1.00 .40
❑ 436 Mark Hendrickson 1.00 .40
❑ 437 Laynce Nix 1.00 .40
❑ 438 Jason Frasor 1.00 .40
❑ 439 Kevin Gregg 1.00 .40
❑ 440 Derek Jeter 5.00 2.00
❑ 441 Jaret Wright 1.00 .40
❑ 442 Edwin Jackson 1.00 .40
❑ 443 Moises Alou 1.00 .40
❑ 444 Aaron Rowand 1.00 .40
❑ 445 Kazuhito Tadano 1.00 .40
❑ 446 Luis Gonzalez 1.00 .40
❑ 447 A.J. Burnett 1.00 .40
❑ 448 Jeff Bagwell 1.50 .60
❑ 449 Brad Penny 1.00 .40
❑ 450 Corey Koskie 1.00 .40
❑ 451 Mark Ellis 1.00 .40
❑ 452 Hector Luna 1.00 .40
❑ 453 Miguel Olivo 1.00 .40
❑ 454 Scott Rolen 1.50 .60
❑ 455 Ricardo Rodriguez 1.00 .40
❑ 456 Eric Hinske 1.00 .40
❑ 457 Tim Salmon 1.50 .60
❑ 458 Adam LaRoche 1.00 .40
❑ 459 B.J. Ryan 1.00 .40
❑ 460 Steve Finley 1.00 .40
❑ 461 Joe Nathan 1.00 .40
❑ 462 Vicente Padilla 1.00 .40
❑ 463 Yadier Molina 1.00 .40
❑ 464 Tino Martinez 1.50 .60
❑ 465 Mark Teixeira 1.50 .60
❑ 466 Kelvim Escobar 1.00 .40
❑ 467 Pedro Feliz 1.00 .40
❑ 468 Ryan Garko FY RC 5.00 2.00
❑ 469 Bobby Livingston FY RC 2.00 .75
❑ 470 Yorman Bazardo FY RC 2.00 .75
❑ 471 Mike Bourn FY RC 3.00 1.25
❑ 472 Andy LaRoche FY RC 8.00 3.00

2005 Topps Chrome Update

❑ COMPLETE SET (237) 300.00 200.00
❑ COMP.SET w/o SP's (220) 80.00 40.00
❑ COM (1-85/216-220) .75 .30
❑ COMMON (86-105) .75 .30
❑ COM (14/65/106-215) 1.00 .40
❑ 221-237 GROUP A ODDS 1:25 H, 1:49 R
❑ 221-237 GROUP B ODDS 1:29 H, 1:57 R
❑ 1-220 PLATE ODDS 1:347 H
❑ 221-237 PLATE AU ODDS 1:4857 H
❑ PLATE PRINT RUN 1 SET PER COLOR
❑ BLACK-CYAN-MAGENTA-YELLOW ISSUED
❑ NO PLATE PRICING DUE TO SCARCITY
❑ 1 Sammy Sosa 2.00 .75
❑ 2 Jeff Francoeur 2.50 1.00
❑ 3 Tony Clark .75 .30
❑ 4 Michael Tucker .75 .30
❑ 5 Mike Matheny .75 .30
❑ 6 Eric Young .75 .30
❑ 7 Jose Valentin .75 .30
❑ 8 Matt Lawton .75 .30
❑ 9 Juan Rivera .75 .30
❑ 10 Shawn Green .75 .30
❑ 11 Aaron Boone .75 .30
❑ 12 Woody Williams .75 .30
❑ 13 Brad Wilkerson .75 .30
❑ 14 Anthony Reyes RC 5.00 2.00
❑ 15 Gustavo Chacin .75 .30
❑ 16 Michael Restovich .75 .30
❑ 17 Humberto Quintero .75 .30
❑ 18 Matt Ginter .75 .30
❑ 19 Scott Podsednik .75 .30
❑ 20 Byung-Hyun Kim .75 .30
❑ 21 Orlando Hernandez .75 .30
❑ 22 Mark Grudzielanek .75 .30
❑ 23 Jody Gerut .75 .30
❑ 24 Adrian Beltre .75 .30
❑ 25 Scott Schoeneweis .75 .30
❑ 26 Marlon Anderson .75 .30
❑ 27 Jason Vargas .75 .30
❑ 28 Claudio Vargas .75 .30
❑ 29 Jason Kendall .75 .30
❑ 30 Aaron Small .75 .30

❑ 31 Juan Cruz .75 .30
❑ 32 Placido Polanco .75 .30
❑ 33 Jorge Sosa .75 .30
❑ 34 John Olerud .75 .30
❑ 35 Ryan Langerhans .75 .30
❑ 36 Randy Winn .75 .30
❑ 37 Zach Duke 2.00 .75
❑ 38 Garrett Atkins .75 .30
❑ 39 Al Leiter .75 .30
❑ 40 Shawn Chacon .75 .30
❑ 41 Mark DeRosa .75 .30
❑ 42 Miguel Ojeda .75 .30
❑ 43 A.J. Pierzynski .75 .30
❑ 44 Carlos Lee .75 .30
❑ 45 LaTroy Hawkins .75 .30
❑ 46 Nick Green .75 .30
❑ 47 Shawn Estes .75 .30
❑ 48 Eli Marrero .75 .30
❑ 49 Jeff Kent .75 .30
❑ 50 Joe Randa .75 .30
❑ 51 Jose Hernandez .75 .30
❑ 52 Joe Blanton .75 .30
❑ 53 Huston Street 2.00 .75
❑ 54 Marlon Byrd .75 .30
❑ 55 Alex Sanchez .75 .30
❑ 56 Livan Hernandez .75 .30
❑ 57 Chris Young .75 .30
❑ 58 Brad Eldred .75 .30
❑ 59 Terrence Long .75 .30
❑ 60 Phil Nevin .75 .30
❑ 61 Kyle Farnsworth .75 .30
❑ 62 Jon Lieber .75 .30
❑ 63 Antonio Alfonseca .75 .30
❑ 64 Tony Graffanino .75 .30
❑ 65 Tadahito Iguchi RC 3.00 1.25
❑ 66 Brad Thompson .75 .30
❑ 67 Jose Vidro .75 .30
❑ 68 Jason Phillips .75 .30
❑ 69 Carl Pavano .75 .30
❑ 70 Pokey Reese .75 .30
❑ 71 Jerome Williams .75 .30
❑ 72 Kazuhisa Ishii .75 .30
❑ 73 Felix Hernandez 3.00 1.25
❑ 74 Edgar Renteria .75 .30
❑ 75 Mike Myers .75 .30
❑ 76 Jeff Cirillo .75 .30
❑ 77 Endy Chavez .75 .30
❑ 78 Jose Guillen .75 .30
❑ 79 Ugueth Urbina .75 .30
❑ 80 Zach Day .75 .30
❑ 81 Javier Vazquez .75 .30
❑ 82 Willy Taveras .75 .30
❑ 83 Mark Mulder .75 .30
❑ 84 Vinny Castilla .75 .30
❑ 85 Russ Adams .75 .30
❑ 86 Homer Bailey PROS .75 .30
❑ 87 Ervin Santana PROS .75 .30
❑ 88 Bill Bray PROS .75 .30
❑ 89 Thomas Diamond PROS .75 .30
❑ 90 Trevor Plouffe PROS .75 .30
❑ 91 James Houser PROS .75 .30
❑ 92 Jake Stevens PROS .75 .30
❑ 93 Anthony Whittington PROS .75 .30
❑ 94 Philip Hughes PROS .75 .30
❑ 95 Greg Golson PROS .75 .30
❑ 96 Paul Maholm PROS .75 .30
❑ 97 Carlos Quentin PROS .75 .30
❑ 98 Dan Johnson PROS .75 .30
❑ 99 Mark Rogers PROS .75 .30
❑ 100 Neil Walker PROS .75 .30
❑ 101 Omar Quintanilla PROS .75 .30
❑ 102 Blake DeWitt PROS .75 .30
❑ 103 Taylor Tankersley PROS .75 .30
❑ 104 David Murphy PROS .75 .30
❑ 105 Chris Lambert PROS .75 .30
❑ 106 Drew Anderson FY RC 1.00 .40
❑ 107 Luis Hernandez FY RC 1.00 .40
❑ 108 Jim Burt FY RC 1.00 .40
❑ 109 Mike Morse FY RC 2.00 .75
❑ 110 Elliot Johnson FY RC 1.00 .40
❑ 111 C.J. Smith FY RC 1.00 .40
❑ 112 Casey McGehee FY RC 1.00 .40
❑ 113 Brian Miller FY RC 1.00 .40
❑ 114 Chris Vines FY RC 1.00 .40
❑ 115 D.J. Houlton FY RC 1.00 .40
❑ 116 Chuck Tiffany FY RC 3.00 1.25
❑ 117 Humberto Sanchez FY RC 4.00 1.50
❑ 118 Baltazar Lopez FY RC 1.00 .40
❑ 119 Russ Martin FY RC 3.00 1.25
❑ 120 Dana Eveland FY RC 1.00 .40
❑ 121 Johan Silva FY RC 1.00 .40
❑ 122 Adam Harben FY RC 1.25 .50
❑ 123 Brian Bannister FY RC 3.00 1.25
❑ 124 Adam Boeve FY RC 1.00 .40
❑ 125 Thomas Oldham FY RC 1.00 .40
❑ 126 Cody Haerther FY RC 1.00 .40
❑ 127 Dan Santin FY RC 1.00 .40
❑ 128 Daniel Haigwood FY RC 2.00 .75
❑ 129 Craig Tatum FY RC 1.00 .40
❑ 130 Martin Prado FY RC 1.00 .40
❑ 131 Errol Simonitsch FY RC 1.25 .50
❑ 132 Lorenzo Scott FY RC 1.00 .40
❑ 133 Hayden Penn FY RC 2.00 .75
❑ 134 Heath Totten FY RC 1.00 .40
❑ 135 Nick Masset FY RC 1.00 .40
❑ 136 Pedro Lopez FY RC 1.00 .40
❑ 137 Ben Harrison FY 1.00 .40
❑ 138 Mike Spidale FY RC 1.00 .40
❑ 139 Jeremy Harts FY RC 1.00 .40
❑ 140 Danny Zell FY RC 1.00 .40
❑ 141 Kevin Collins FY RC 1.00 .40
❑ 142 Tony Arnerich FY RC 1.00 .40
❑ 143 Matt Albers FY RC 2.50 1.00
❑ 144 Ricky Barrett FY RC 1.00 .40
❑ 145 Hernan Iribarren FY RC 1.25 .50
❑ 146 Sean Tracey FY RC 1.00 .40
❑ 147 Jerry Owens FY RC 1.25 .50
❑ 148 Steve Nelson FY RC 1.00 .40
❑ 149 Brandon McCarthy FY RC 2.50 1.00
❑ 150 David Shepard FY RC 1.00 .40
❑ 151 Steven Bondurant FY RC 1.00 .40
❑ 152 Billy Sadler FY RC 1.00 .40
❑ 153 Ryan Feierabend FY RC 1.00 .40
❑ 154 Stuart Pomeranz FY RC 1.00 .40
❑ 155 Shaun Marcum FY 1.00 .40
❑ 156 Erik Schindewolf FY RC 1.00 .40
❑ 157 Stefan Bailie FY RC 1.00 .40
❑ 158 Mike Esposito FY RC 1.00 .40
❑ 159 Buck Coats FY RC 1.00 .40
❑ 160 Andy Sides FY RC 1.00 .40
❑ 161 Micah Schnurstein FY RC 1.00 .40
❑ 162 Jesse Gutierrez FY RC 1.00 .40
❑ 163 Jake Postlewait FY RC 1.00 .40
❑ 164 Willy Mota FY RC 1.00 .40
❑ 165 Ryan Speier FY RC 1.00 .40
❑ 166 Frank Mata FY RC 1.00 .40
❑ 167 Jair Jurrjens FY RC 2.50 1.00
❑ 168 Nick Touchstone FY RC 1.00 .40
❑ 169 Matthew Kemp FY RC 8.00 3.00
❑ 170 Vinny Rottino FY RC 1.00 .40
❑ 171 J.B. Thurmond FY RC 1.00 .40
❑ 172 Kelvin Pichardo FY RC 1.00 .40
❑ 173 Scott Mitchinson FY RC 1.00 .40
❑ 174 Darwinson Salazar FY RC 1.00 .40
❑ 175 George Kottaras FY RC 2.00 .75
❑ 176 Kenny Durost FY RC 1.00 .40
❑ 177 Jonathan Sanchez FY RC 3.00 1.25
❑ 178 Brandon Moorhead FY RC 1.00 .40
❑ 179 Kennard Bibbs FY RC 1.00 .40
❑ 180 David Gassner FY RC 1.00 .40
❑ 181 Micah Furtado FY RC 1.00 .40
❑ 182 Ismael Ramirez FY RC 1.00 .40
❑ 183 Carlos Gonzalez FY RC 6.00 2.50
❑ 184 Brandon Sing FY RC 1.25 .50
❑ 185 Jason Motte FY RC 1.00 .40
❑ 186 Chuck James FY RC 5.00 2.00
❑ 187 Andy Santana FY RC 1.00 .40
❑ 188 Manny Parra FY RC 4.00 1.50
❑ 189 Chris B.Young FY RC 4.00 1.50
❑ 190 Juan Senreiso FY RC 1.00 .40
❑ 191 Franklin Morales FY RC 2.00 .75
❑ 192 Jared Gothreaux FY RC 1.00 .40
❑ 193 Jayce Tingler FY RC 1.00 .40
❑ 194 Matt Brown FY RC 1.00 .40
❑ 195 Frank Diaz FY RC 1.00 .40
❑ 196 Stephen Drew FY RC 10.00 4.00
❑ 197 Jered Weaver FY RC 10.00 4.00
❑ 198 Ryan Braun FY RC 20.00 8.00
❑ 199 John Mayberry Jr. FY RC 2.50 1.00
❑ 200 Aaron Thompson FY RC 2.00 .75
❑ 201 Ben Copeland FY RC 4.00 1.50
❑ 202 Jacoby Ellsbury FY RC 25.00 10.00
❑ 203 Garrett Olson FY RC 2.00 .75
❑ 204 Cliff Pennington FY RC 2.00 .75
❑ 205 Colby Rasmus FY RC 15.00 6.00
❑ 206 Chris Volstad FY RC 2.50 1.00
❑ 207 Ricky Romero FY RC 2.00 .75
❑ 208 Ryan Zimmerman FY RC 15.00 6.00
❑ 209 C.J. Henry FY RC 4.00 1.50
❑ 210 Nelson Cruz FY RC 3.00 1.25
❑ 211 Josh Wall FY RC 1.25 .50
❑ 212 Nick Webber FY RC 1.00 .40
❑ 213 Paul Kelly FY RC 1.25 .50
❑ 214 Kyle Winters FY RC 1.25 .50
❑ 215 Mitch Boggs FY RC 1.00 .40
❑ 216 Craig Biggio HL .75 .30
❑ 217 Greg Maddux HL 2.00 .75
❑ 218 Bobby Abreu HL .75 .30
❑ 219 Alex Rodriguez HL 2.00 .75
❑ 220 Trevor Hoffman HL .75 .30
❑ 221 Trevor Bell FY AU A RC 15.00 6.00
❑ 222 Jay Bruce FY AU A RC 120.00 60.00
❑ 223 Travis Buck FY AU B RC 15.00 6.00
❑ 224 Cesar Carrillo FY AU B RC 15.00 6.00
❑ 225 Mike Costanzo FY AU A RC 20.008.00
❑ 226 Brent Cox FY AU A RC 10.00 4.00
❑ 227 Matt Garza FY AU A RC 40.00 15.00
❑ 228 Josh Geer FY AU A RC 10.00 4.00
❑ 229 Tyler Greene FY AU A RC 15.00 6.00
❑ 230 Eli Iorg FY AU A RC 10.00 4.00
❑ 231 Craig Italiano FY AU B RC 10.00 4.00
❑ 232 Beau Jones FY AU A RC 15.00 6.00
❑ 233 M.McCormick FY AU B RC 10.00 4.00
❑ 234 A.McCutchen FY AU B RC 40.0020.00
❑ 235 Micah Owings FY AU B RC 20.00 8.00
❑ 236 Cesar Ramos FY AU B RC 10.00 4.00
❑ 237 Chaz Roe FY AU A RC 10.00 4.00

2006 Topps Chrome

❑ COMP.SET w/o AU's (330) 00.00 40.00
❑ COMMON CARD (1-252) .60 .25
❑ COMMON CARD (253-275) .40 .15
❑ COMMON ROOKIE (276-330) 1.00 .40
❑ COMMON AUTO (285b/331-354) 10.004.00
❑ AU 331-354 ODDS 1:15 HOBBY
❑ JOHJIMA AU ODDS 1:1650 HOBBY
❑ 1-330 PLATES 1:25 HOBBY BOX LDR
❑ 331-354 AU PLATES 1:324 HOBBY BOX LDR
❑ PLATE PRINT RUN 1 SET PER COLOR
❑ BLACK-CYAN-MAGENTA-YELLOW ISSUED
❑ NO PLATE PRICING DUE TO SCANCITY
❑ 1 Alex Rodriguez 2.50 1.00
❑ 2 Garrett Atkins .60 .25
❑ 3 Carl Crawford .60 .25
❑ 4 Clint Barmes .60 .25
❑ 5 Tadahito Iguchi .60 .25
❑ 6 Brian Roberts .60 .25
❑ 7 Mickey Mantle 8.00 3.00
❑ 8 David Wright 2.50 1.00
❑ 9 Jeremy Reed .60 .25
❑ 10 Bobby Abreu .60 .25
❑ 11 Lance Berkman .60 .25
❑ 12 Jonny Gomes .60 .25
❑ 13 Jason Marquis .60 .25
❑ 14 Chipper Jones 1.50 .60
❑ 15 Jon Garland .60 .25
❑ 16 Brad Wilkerson .60 .25
❑ 17 Rickie Weeks .60 .25
❑ 18 Jorge Posada 1.00 .40
❑ 19 Greg Maddux 2.50 1.00

❑ 20 Jeff Francis .60 .25
❑ 21 Felipe Lopez .60 .25
❑ 22 Dan Johnson .60 .25
❑ 23 Manny Ramirez 1.00 .40
❑ 24 Joe Mauer 1.00 .40
❑ 25 Randy Winn .60 .25
❑ 26 Pedro Feliz .60 .25
❑ 27 Kenny Rogers .60 .25
❑ 28 Rocco Baldelli .60 .25
❑ 29 Nomar Garciaparra 1.50 .60
❑ 30 Carlos Lee .60 .25
❑ 31 Tom Glavine 1.00 .40
❑ 32 Craig Biggio 1.00 .40
❑ 33 Steve Finley .60 .25
❑ 34 Eric Gagne .60 .25
❑ 35 Dallas McPherson .60 .25
❑ 36 Mark Kotsay .60 .25
❑ 37 Kerry Wood .60 .25
❑ 38 Huston Street .60 .25
❑ 39 Hank Blalock .60 .25
❑ 40 Brad Radke .60 .25
❑ 41 Chien-Ming Wang 2.50 1.00
❑ 42 Mark Buehrle .60 .25
❑ 43 Andy Pettitte 1.00 .40
❑ 44 Bernie Williams 1.00 .40
❑ 45 Victor Martinez .60 .25
❑ 46 Darin Erstad .60 .25
❑ 47 Gustavo Chacin .60 .25
❑ 48 Carlos Guillen .60 .25
❑ 49 Lyle Overbay .60 .25
❑ 50 Barry Bonds 3.00 1.25
❑ 51 Nook Logan .60 .25
❑ 52 Mark Teahen .60 .25
❑ 53 Mike Lamb .60 .25
❑ 54 Jayson Werth .60 .25
❑ 55 Mariano Rivera 1.50 .60
❑ 56 Julio Lugo .60 .25
❑ 57 Adam Dunn .60 .25
❑ 58 Troy Percival .60 .25
❑ 59 Chad Tracy .60 .25
❑ 60 Edgar Renteria .60 .25
❑ 61 Jason Giambi .60 .25
❑ 62 Justin Morneau .60 .25
❑ 63 Carlos Delgado .60 .25
❑ 64 John Buck .60 .25
❑ 65 Shannon Stewart .60 .25
❑ 66 Mike Cameron .60 .25
❑ 67 Richie Sexson .60 .25
❑ 68 Russ Adams .60 .25
❑ 69 Josh Beckett .60 .25
❑ 70 Ryan Freel .60 .25
❑ 71 Victor Zambrano .60 .25
❑ 72 Ronnie Belliard .60 .25
❑ 73 Brian Giles .60 .25
❑ 74 Randy Wolf .60 .25
❑ 75 Robinson Cano 1.00 .40
❑ 76 Joe Blanton .60 .25
❑ 77 Esteban Loaiza .60 .25
❑ 78 Troy Glaus .60 .25
❑ 79 Matt Clement .60 .25
❑ 80 Geoff Jenkins .60 .25
❑ 81 Roy Oswalt .60 .25
❑ 82 A.J. Pierzynski .60 .25
❑ 83 Pedro Martinez 1.00 .40
❑ 84 Roger Clemens 3.00 1.25
❑ 85 Jack Wilson .60 .25
❑ 86 Mike Piazza 1.50 .60
❑ 87 Paul Lo Duca .60 .25
❑ 88 Jeff Bagwell 1.00 .40
❑ 89 Carlos Zambrano .60 .25
❑ 90 Brandon Claussen .60 .25
❑ 91 Travis Hafner .60 .25
❑ 92 Chris Shelton .60 .25
❑ 93 Rafael Furcal .60 .25
❑ 94 Frank Thomas 1.50 .60
❑ 95 Noah Lowry .60 .25
❑ 96 Jhonny Peralta .60 .25
❑ 97 Vernon Wells .60 .25
❑ 98 Jorge Cantu .60 .25
❑ 99 Willy Taveras .60 .25
❑ 100 Ivan Rodriguez 1.00 .40
❑ 101 Jose Reyes 1.50 .60
❑ 102 Barry Zito .60 .25
❑ 103 Mark Teixeira 1.00 .40
❑ 104 Chone Figgins .60 .25
❑ 105 Todd Helton 1.00 .40
❑ 106 Tim Wakefield .60 .25
❑ 107 Mike Maroth .60 .25
❑ 108 Johnny Damon 1.00 .40
❑ 109 David DeJesus .60 .25
❑ 110 Ryan Klesko .60 .25
❑ 111 Nick Johnson .60 .25
❑ 112 Freddy Garcia .60 .25
❑ 113 Torii Hunter .60 .25
❑ 114 Mike Sweeney .60 .25
❑ 115 Scott Rolen 1.00 .40
❑ 116 Jim Thome 1.00 .40
❑ 117 Adam Kennedy .60 .25
❑ 118 Albert Pujols 3.00 1.25
❑ 119 Kazuo Matsui .60 .25
❑ 120 Zack Greinke .60 .25
❑ 121 Jimmy Rollins .60 .25
❑ 122 Edgardo Alfonzo .60 .25
❑ 123 Billy Wagner .60 .25
❑ 124 B.J. Ryan .60 .25
❑ 125 Orlando Hudson .60 .25
❑ 126 Preston Wilson .60 .25
❑ 127 Melvin Mora .60 .25
❑ 128 Alfonso Soriano .60 .25
❑ 129 Javy Lopez .60 .25
❑ 130 Wilson Betemit .60 .25
❑ 131 Garret Anderson .60 .25
❑ 132 Jason Bay .60 .25
❑ 133 Adam LaRoche .60 .25
❑ 134 C.C. Sabathia .60 .25
❑ 135 Bartolo Colon .60 .25
❑ 136 Ichiro Suzuki 2.50 1.00
❑ 137 Jim Edmonds 1.00 .40
❑ 138 David Eckstein .60 .25
❑ 139 Cristian Guzman .60 .25
❑ 140 Jeff Kent .60 .25
❑ 141 Chris Capuano .60 .25
❑ 142 Cliff Floyd .60 .25
❑ 143 Zach Duke .60 .25
❑ 144 Matt Morris .60 .25
❑ 145 Jose Vidro .60 .25
❑ 146 David Wells .60 .25
❑ 147 John Smoltz 1.00 .40
❑ 148 Felix Hernandez 1.50 .60
❑ 149 Orlando Cabrera .60 .25
❑ 150 Mark Prior 1.00 .40
❑ 151 Ted Lilly .60 .25
❑ 152 Michael Young .60 .25
❑ 153 Livan Hernandez .60 .25
❑ 154 Yadier Molina .60 .25
❑ 155 Eric Chavez .60 .25
❑ 156 Miguel Batista .60 .25
❑ 157 Ben Sheets .60 .25
❑ 158 Oliver Perez .60 .25
❑ 159 Doug Davis .60 .25
❑ 160 Andruw Jones 1.00 .40
❑ 161 Hideki Matsui 1.50 .60
❑ 162 Reggie Sanders .60 .25
❑ 163 Joe Nathan .60 .25
❑ 164 John Lackey .60 .25
❑ 165 Matt Murton .60 .25
❑ 166 Grady Sizemore 1.00 .40
❑ 167 Brad Thompson .60 .25
❑ 168 Kevin Millwood .60 .25
❑ 169 Orlando Hernandez .60 .25
❑ 170 Mark Mulder .60 .25
❑ 171 Chase Utley 1.50 .60
❑ 172 Moises Alou .60 .25
❑ 173 Wily Mo Pena .60 .25
❑ 174 Brian McCann .60 .25
❑ 175 Jermaine Dye .60 .25
❑ 176 Ryan Madson .60 .25
❑ 177 Aramis Ramirez .60 .25
❑ 178 Khalil Greene 1.00 .40
❑ 179 Mike Hampton .60 .25
❑ 180 Mike Mussina 1.00 .40
❑ 181 Rich Harden .60 .25
❑ 182 Woody Williams .60 .25
❑ 183 Chris Carpenter .60 .25
❑ 184 Brady Clark .60 .25
❑ 185 Luis Gonzalez .60 .25
❑ 186 Raul Ibanez .60 .25
❑ 187 Magglio Ordonez .60 .25
❑ 188 Adrian Beltre .60 .25
❑ 189 Marcus Giles .60 .25
❑ 190 Odalis Perez .60 .25
❑ 191 Derek Jeter 4.00 1.50
❑ 192 Jason Schmidt .60 .25
❑ 193 Toby Hall .60 .25
❑ 194 Danny Haren .60 .25
❑ 195 Tim Hudson .60 .25
❑ 196 Jake Peavy .60 .25
❑ 197 Casey Blake .60 .25
❑ 198 J.D. Drew .60 .25
❑ 199 Ervin Santana .60 .25
❑ 200 J.J. Hardy .60 .25
❑ 201 Austin Kearns .60 .25
❑ 202 Pat Burrell .60 .25
❑ 203 Jason Vargas .60 .25
❑ 204 Ryan Howard 2.50 1.00
❑ 205 Joe Crede .60 .25
❑ 206 Vladimir Guerrero 1.50 .60
❑ 207 Roy Halladay .60 .25
❑ 208 David Dellucci .60 .25
❑ 209 Brandon Webb .60 .25
❑ 210 Ryan Church .60 .25
❑ 211 Miguel Tejada .60 .25
❑ 212 Mark Loretta .60 .25
❑ 213 Kevin Youkilis .60 .25
❑ 214 Jon Lieber .60 .25
❑ 215 Miguel Cabrera 1.00 .40
❑ 216 A.J. Burnett .60 .25
❑ 217 David Bell .60 .25
❑ 218 Eric Byrnes .60 .25
❑ 219 Lance Niekro .60 .25
❑ 220 Shawn Green .60 .25
❑ 221 Ken Griffey Jr. 2.50 1.00
❑ 222 Johnny Estrada .60 .25
❑ 223 Omar Vizquel 1.00 .40
❑ 224 Gary Sheffield .60 .25
❑ 225 Brad Halsey .60 .25
❑ 226 Aaron Cook .60 .25
❑ 227 David Ortiz 1.50 .60
❑ 228 Scott Kazmir 1.00 .40
❑ 229 Dustin McGowan .60 .25
❑ 230 Gregg Zaun .60 .25
❑ 231 Carlos Beltran .60 .25
❑ 232 Bob Wickman .60 .25
❑ 233 Brett Myers .60 .25
❑ 234 Casey Kotchman .60 .25
❑ 235 Jeff Francoeur 1.50 .60
❑ 236 Paul Konerko .60 .25
❑ 237 Juan Rivera .60 .25
❑ 238 Bobby Crosby .60 .25
❑ 239 Derrek Lee .60 .25
❑ 240 Curt Schilling 1.00 .40
❑ 241 Jake Westbrook .60 .25
❑ 242 Dontrelle Willis .60 .25
❑ 243 Brad Lidge .60 .25
❑ 244 Randy Johnson 1.50 .60
❑ 245 Nick Swisher .60 .25
❑ 246 Johan Santana 1.00 .40
❑ 247 Jeremy Bonderman .60 .25
❑ 248 Ramon Hernandez .60 .25
❑ 249 Mike Lowell .60 .25
❑ 250 Javier Vazquez .60 .25
❑ 251 Jose Contreras .60 .25
❑ 252 Aubrey Huff .60 .25
❑ 253 Kenny Rogers AW .40 .15
❑ 254 Mark Teixeira AW .60 .25
❑ 255 Orlando Hudson AW .40 .15
❑ 256 Derek Jeter AW 2.50 1.00
❑ 257 Eric Chavez AW .40 .15
❑ 258 Torii Hunter AW .40 .15
❑ 259 Vernon Wells AW .40 .15
❑ 260 Ichiro Suzuki AW 1.50 .60
❑ 261 Greg Maddux AW 1.50 .60
❑ 262 Mike Matheny AW .40 .15
❑ 263 Derrek Lee AW .40 .15
❑ 264 Luis Castillo AW .40 .15
❑ 265 Omar Vizquel AW .60 .25
❑ 266 Mike Lowell AW .40 .15
❑ 267 Andruw Jones AW .60 .25
❑ 268 Jim Edmonds AW .60 .25
❑ 269 Bobby Abreu AW .40 .15
❑ 270 Bartolo Colon AW .40 .15
❑ 271 Chris Carpenter AW .40 .15
❑ 272 Alex Rodriguez AW 1.50 .60
❑ 273 Albert Pujols AW 2.00 .75
❑ 274 Huston Street AW .40 .15
❑ 275 Ryan Howard AW 1.50 .60
❑ 276 Chris Denorfia (RC) 1.00 .40
❑ 277 John Van Benschoten (RC) 1.00 .40

❑ 278 Russ Martin (RC) 1.50 .60
❑ 279 Fausto Carmona (RC) 1.00 .40
❑ 280 Freddie Bynum (RC) 1.00 .40
❑ 281 Kelly Shoppach (RC) 1.00 .40
❑ 282 Chris Demaria RC 1.00 .40
❑ 283 Jordan Tata RC 1.00 .40
❑ 284 Ryan Zimmerman (RC) 6.00 2.50
❑ 285a Kenji Johjima RC 5.00 2.00
❑ 285b Kenji Johjima AU 100.00 50.00
❑ 286 Ruddy Lugo (RC) 1.00 .40
❑ 287 Tommy Murphy (RC) 1.00 .40
❑ 288 Bobby Livingston (RC) 1.00 .40
❑ 289 Anderson Hernandez (RC) 1.00 .40
❑ 290 Brian Slocum (RC) 1.00 .40
❑ 291 Sendy Rleal RC 1.00 .40
❑ 292 Ryan Spilborghs (RC) 1.50 .60
❑ 293 Brandon Fahey RC 1.00 .40
❑ 294 Jason Kubel (RC) 1.00 .40
❑ 295 James Loney (RC) 1.50 .60
❑ 296 Jeremy Accardo RC 1.00 .40
❑ 297 Fabio Castro RC 1.00 .40
❑ 298 Matt Capps (RC) 1.00 .40
❑ 299 Casey Janssen RC 1.00 .40
❑ 300 Martin Prado (RC) 1.00 .40
❑ 301 Ronny Paulino (RC) 1.00 .40
❑ 302 Josh Barfield (RC) 1.00 .40
❑ 303 Joel Zumaya (RC) 2.50 1.00
❑ 304 Matt Cain (RC) 1.50 .60
❑ 305 Conor Jackson (RC) 1.50 .60
❑ 306 Brian Anderson (RC) 1.00 .40
❑ 307 Prince Fielder (RC) 4.00 1.50
❑ 308 Jeremy Hermida (RC) 1.00 .40
❑ 309 Justin Verlander (RC) 4.00 1.50
❑ 310 Brian Bannister (RC) 1.00 .40
❑ 311 Josh Willingham (RC) 1.00 .40
❑ 312 John Rheinecker (RC) 1.00 .40
❑ 313 Nick Markakis (RC) 1.50 .60
❑ 314 Jonathan Papelbon (RC) 5.00 2.00
❑ 315 Mike Jacobs (RC) 1.00 .40
❑ 316 Jose Capellan (RC) 1.00 .40
❑ 317 Mike Napoli RC 2.50 1.00
❑ 318 Ricky Nolasco (RC) 1.00 .40
❑ 319 Ben Johnson (RC) 1.00 .40
❑ 320 Paul Maholm (RC) 1.00 .40
❑ 321 Drew Meyer (RC) 1.00 .40
❑ 322 Jeff Mathis (RC) 1.00 .40
❑ 323 Fernando Nieve (RC) 1.00 .40
❑ 324 John Koronka (RC) 1.00 .40
❑ 325 Wil Nieves (RC) 1.00 .40
❑ 326 Nate McLouth (RC) 1.00 .40
❑ 327 Howie Kendrick (RC) 5.00 2.00
❑ 328 Sean Marshall (RC) 1.00 .40
❑ 329 Brandon Watson (RC) 1.00 .40
❑ 330 Skip Schumaker (RC) 1.00 .40
❑ 331 Ryan Garko AU (RC) 10.00 4.00
❑ 332 Jason Bergmann AU RC 10.00 4.00
❑ 333 Chuck James AU (RC) 15.00 6.00
❑ 334 Adam Wainwright AU (RC) 10.00 4.00
❑ 335 Dan Ortmeier AU (RC) 10.00 4.00
❑ 336 Francisco Liriano AU (RC) 30.00 12.50
❑ 337 Craig Breslow AU RC 10.00 4.00
❑ 338 Darrell Rasner AU (RC) 10.00 4.00
❑ 339 Jason Botts AU (RC) 10.00 4.00
❑ 340 Ian Kinsler AU (RC) 15.00 6.00
❑ 341 Joey Devine AU RC 10.00 4.00
❑ 342 Miguel Perez AU (RC) 10.00 4.00
❑ 343 Scott Olsen AU (RC) 15.00 6.00
❑ 344 Tyler Johnson AU (RC) 10.00 4.00
❑ 345 Anthony Lerew AU (RC) 10.00 4.00
❑ 346 Nelson Cruz AU (RC) 10.00 4.00
❑ 347 Willie Eyre AU (RC) 10.00 4.00
❑ 348 Josh Johnson AU (RC) 20.00 8.00
❑ 349 Shaun Marcum AU (RC) 10.00 4.00
❑ 350 Dustin Nippert AU (RC) 10.00 4.00
❑ 351 Josh Wilson AU (RC) 10.00 4.00
❑ 352 Hanley Ramirez AU (RC) 30.00 12.50
❑ 353 Reggie Abercrombie AU (RC) 10.00 4.00
❑ 354 Dan Uggla AU (RC) 20.00 8.00

2007 Topps Chrome

❑ COMP.SET w/o AU's (330) 80.00 40.00
❑ COMMON CARD .50 .20
❑ COMMON ROOKIE 1.00 .40
❑ JAPANESE VARIATION ODDS 1:82 H
❑ COMMON AUTO 8.00 3.00
❑ AUTO ODDS 1:16 HOBBY, 1:122 RETAIL

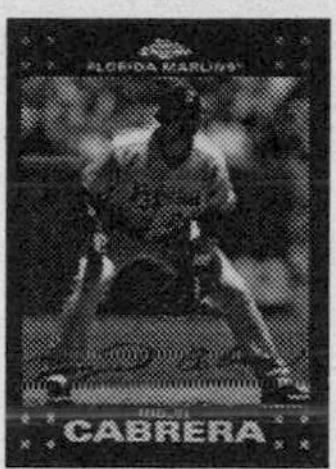

❑ PRINT.PLATE ODDS 1:36 HOBBY BOX LDR
❑ VAR.PLATES 1:1943 HOBBY BOX LDR
❑ AU PLATES 1:343 HOBBY BOX LDR
❑ PLATE PRINT RUN 1 SET PER COLOR
❑ BLACK-CYAN-MAGENTA-YELLOW ISSUED
❑ NO PLATE PRICING DUE TO SCARCITY
❑ EXCHANGE DEADLINE 07/31/09
❑ 1 Nick Swisher .50 .20
❑ 2 Bobby Abreu .50 .20
❑ 3 Edgar Renteria .50 .20
❑ 4 Mickey Mantle 4.00 1.50
❑ 5 Preston Wilson .50 .20
❑ 6 C.C. Sabathia .50 .20
❑ 7 Julio Lugo .50 .20
❑ 8 J.D. Drew .50 .20
❑ 9 Jason Varitek 1.25 .50
❑ 10 Orlando Hernandez .50 .20
❑ 11 Corey Patterson .50 .20
❑ 12 Josh Bard .50 .20
❑ 13 Gary Matthews .50 .20
❑ 14 Jason Jennings .50 .20
❑ 15 Bronson Arroyo .50 .20
❑ 16 Andy Pettitte .75 .30
❑ 17 Ervin Santana .50 .20
❑ 18 Paul Konerko .50 .20
❑ 19 Adam LaRoche .50 .20
❑ 20 Jim Edmonds .75 .30
❑ 21 Derek Jeter 3.00 1.25
❑ 22 Aubrey Huff .50 .20
❑ 23 Andre Ethier .75 .30
❑ 24 Jeremy Sowers .50 .20
❑ 25 Miguel Cabrera .75 .30
❑ 26 Carlos Lee .50 .20
❑ 27 Mike Piazza 1.25 .50
❑ 28 Cole Hamels .75 .30
❑ 29 Mark Loretta .50 .20
❑ 30 John Smoltz .75 .30
❑ 31 Dan Uggla .75 .30
❑ 32 Lyle Overbay .50 .20
❑ 33 Michael Barrett .50 .20
❑ 34 Ivan Rodriguez .75 .30
❑ 35 Jake Westbrook .50 .20
❑ 36 Moises Alou .50 .20
❑ 37 Jered Weaver .75 .30
❑ 38 Lastings Milledge .75 .30
❑ 39 Austin Kearns .50 .20
❑ 40 Adam Loewen .50 .20
❑ 41 Josh Barfield .50 .20
❑ 42 Johan Santana .75 .30
❑ 43 Ian Kinsler .50 .20
❑ 44 Mike Lowell .50 .20
❑ 45 Scott Rolen .75 .30
❑ 46 Chipper Jones 1.25 .50
❑ 47 Joe Crede .50 .20
❑ 48 Rafael Furcal .50 .20
❑ 49 Dave Bush .50 .20
❑ 50 Marcus Giles .50 .20
❑ 51 Joe Blanton .50 .20
❑ 52 Dontrelle Willis .50 .20
❑ 53 Scott Kazmir .75 .30
❑ 54 Jeff Kent .50 .20
❑ 55 Travis Hafner .50 .20
❑ 56 Ryan Garko .50 .20
❑ 57 Nick Markakis .75 .30
❑ 58 Michael Cuddyer .50 .20
❑ 59 Jason Giambi .50 .20
❑ 60 Chone Figgins .50 .20
❑ 61 Carlos Delgado .50 .20

❑ 62 Aramis Ramirez .50 .20
❑ 63 Albert Pujols 2.50 1.00
❑ 64 Gary Sheffield .50 .20
❑ 65 Adrian Gonzalez .50 .20
❑ 66 Prince Fielder 1.25 .50
❑ 67 Freddy Sanchez .50 .20
❑ 68 Jack Wilson .50 .20
❑ 69 Jake Peavy .50 .20
❑ 70 Javier Vazquez .50 .20
❑ 71 Todd Helton .75 .30
❑ 72 Bill Hall .50 .20
❑ 73 Jeremy Bonderman .50 .20
❑ 74 Rocco Baldelli .50 .20
❑ 75 Noah Lowry .50 .20
❑ 76 Justin Verlander 1.25 .50
❑ 77 Mark Buehrle .50 .20
❑ 78 Hank Blalock .50 .20
❑ 79 Mark Teahen .50 .20
❑ 80 Chien-Ming Wang 2.00 .75
❑ 81 Roy Halladay .50 .20
❑ 82 Melvin Mora .50 .20
❑ 83 Grady Sizemore .75 .30
❑ 84 Matt Cain .75 .30
❑ 85 Carl Crawford .50 .20
❑ 86 Johnny Damon .75 .30
❑ 87 Freddy Garcia .50 .20
❑ 88 Ryan Shealy .50 .20
❑ 89 Carlos Beltran .50 .20
❑ 90 Chuck James .50 .20
❑ 91 Ben Sheets .50 .20
❑ 92 Mark Mulder .50 .20
❑ 93 Carlos Quentin .50 .20
❑ 94 Richie Sexson .50 .20
❑ 95 Brian Schneider .50 .20
❑ 96a Hideki Matsui 1.25 .50
❑ 96b H.Matsui Japanese 5.00 2.00
❑ 97 Robinson Tejeda .50 .20
❑ 98 Scott Hatteberg .50 .20
❑ 99 Jeff Francis .50 .20
❑ 100 Robinson Cano .75 .30
❑ 101 Barry Zito .50 .20
❑ 102 Reed Johnson .50 .20
❑ 103 Chris Carpenter .50 .20
❑ 104 Chad Tracy .50 .20
❑ 105 Anibal Sanchez .50 .20
❑ 106 Brad Penny .50 .20
❑ 107 David Wright 2.00 .75
❑ 108 Jimmy Rollins .50 .20
❑ 109 Alfonso Soriano .50 .20
❑ 110 Greg Maddux 2.00 .75
❑ 111 Curt Schilling .75 .30
❑ 112 Stephen Drew .75 .30
❑ 113 Matt Holliday 1.25 .50
❑ 114 Jorge Posada .75 .30
❑ 115 Vladimir Guerrero 1.25 .50
❑ 116 Frank Thomas 1.25 .50
❑ 117 Jonathan Papelbon 1.25 .50
❑ 118 Manny Ramirez .75 .30
❑ 119 Magglio Ordonez .50 .20
❑ 120 Joe Mauer .75 .30
❑ 121 Ryan Howard 2.00 .75
❑ 122 Chris Young .50 .20
❑ 123 A.J. Burnett .50 .20
❑ 124 Brian McCann .50 .20
❑ 125 Juan Pierre .50 .20
❑ 126 Jonny Gomes .50 .20
❑ 127 Roger Clemens 2.00 .75
❑ 128 Chad Billingsley .50 .20
❑ 129a Kenji Johjima 1.25 .50
❑ 129b Kenji Johjima Japanese 5.00 2.00
❑ 130 Brian Giles .50 .20
❑ 131 Chase Utley 1.25 .50
❑ 132 Carl Pavano .50 .20
❑ 133 Curtis Granderson .50 .20
❑ 134 Sean Casey .50 .20
❑ 135 Jon Garland .50 .20
❑ 136 David Ortiz 1.25 .50
❑ 137 Bobby Crosby .50 .20
❑ 138 Conor Jackson .50 .20
❑ 139 Tim Hudson .50 .20
❑ 140 Rickie Weeks .50 .20
❑ 141 Mark Prior .75 .30
❑ 142 Ben Zobrist .50 .20
❑ 143 Troy Glaus .50 .20
❑ 144 Cliff Lee .50 .20
❑ 145 Adrian Beltre .50 .20

❑ 146	Endy Chavez	.50	.20
❑ 147	Ramon Hernandez	.50	.20
❑ 148	Chris Young	.50	.20
❑ 149	Jason Schmidt	.50	.20
❑ 150	Kevin Millwood	.50	.20
❑ 151	Placido Polanco	.50	.20
❑ 152	Torii Hunter	.50	.20
❑ 153	Roy Oswalt	.50	.20
❑ 154	Kelvim Escobar	.50	.20
❑ 155	Milton Bradley	.50	.20
❑ 156	Chris Capuano	.50	.20
❑ 157	Juan Encarnacion	.50	.20
❑ 158a	Ichiro Suzuki	2.00	.75
❑ 158b	Ichiro Suzuki Japanese	8.00	3.00
❑ 159	Matt Kemp	.50	.20
❑ 160	Matt Morris	.50	.20
❑ 161	Casey Blake	.50	.20
❑ 162	Josh Willingham	.50	.20
❑ 163	Nick Johnson	.50	.20
❑ 164	Khalil Greene	.75	.30
❑ 165	Tom Glavine	.75	.30
❑ 166	Jason Bay	.50	.20
❑ 167	Brandon Phillips	.50	.20
❑ 168	Jorge Cantu	.50	.20
❑ 169	Jeff Weaver	.50	.20
❑ 170	Melky Cabrera	.50	.20
❑ 171	Dan Haren	.50	.20
❑ 172	Jeff Francoeur	1.25	.50
❑ 173	Randy Wolf	.50	.20
❑ 174	Carlos Zambrano	.50	.20
❑ 175	Justin Morneau	.50	.20
❑ 176	Takashi Saito	.50	.20
❑ 177	Victor Martinez	.50	.20
❑ 178	Felix Hernandez	.75	.30
❑ 179	Paul LoDuca	.50	.20
❑ 180	Miguel Tejada	.50	.20
❑ 181	Mark Teixeira	.75	.30
❑ 182	Pat Burrell	.50	.20
❑ 183	Mike Cameron	.50	.20
❑ 184	Josh Beckett	.75	.30
❑ 185	Francisco Liriano	1.25	.50
❑ 186	Ken Griffey Jr.	2.00	.75
❑ 187	Mike Mussina	.75	.30
❑ 188	Howie Kendrick	.50	.20
❑ 189	Ted Lilly	.50	.20
❑ 190	Mike Hampton	.50	.20
❑ 191	Jeff Suppan	.50	.20
❑ 192	Jose Reyes	1.25	.50
❑ 193	Russell Martin	.50	.20
❑ 194	Jhonny Peralta	.50	.20
❑ 195	Raul Ibanez	.50	.20
❑ 196	Hanley Ramirez	.75	.30
❑ 197	Kerry Wood	.50	.20
❑ 198	Gary Sheffield	.50	.20
❑ 199	David Dellucci	.50	.20
❑ 200	Xavier Nady	.50	.20
❑ 201	Michael Young	.50	.20
❑ 202	Kevin Youkilis	.50	.20
❑ 203	Aaron Harang	.50	.20
❑ 204	Matt Garza	.50	.20
❑ 205	Jim Thome	.75	.30
❑ 206	Jose Contreras	.50	.20
❑ 207	Tadahito Iguchi	.50	.20
❑ 208	Eric Chavez	.50	.20
❑ 209	Vernon Wells	.50	.20
❑ 210	Doug Davis	.50	.20
❑ 211	Andruw Jones	.75	.30
❑ 212	David Eckstein	.50	.20
❑ 213	J.J. Hardy	.50	.20
❑ 214	Orlando Hudson	.50	.20
❑ 215	Pedro Martinez	.75	.30
❑ 216	Brian Roberts	.50	.20
❑ 217	Brett Myers	.50	.20
❑ 218	Alex Rodriguez	2.00	.75
❑ 219	Kenny Rogers	.50	.20
❑ 220	Jason Kubel	.50	.20
❑ 221	Jermaine Dye	.50	.20
❑ 222	Bartolo Colon	.50	.20
❑ 223	Craig Biggio	.75	.30
❑ 224	Alex Rios	.50	.20
❑ 225	Adam Dunn	.50	.20
❑ 226	Anthony Reyes	.50	.20
❑ 227	Derrek Lee	.50	.20
❑ 228	Jeremy Hermida	.50	.20
❑ 229	Derek Lowe	.50	.20
❑ 230	Randy Winn	.50	.20
❑ 231	Brandon Webb	.50	.20
❑ 232	Jose Vidro	.50	.20
❑ 233	Erik Bedard	.50	.20
❑ 234	Jon Lieber	.50	.20
❑ 235	Wily Mo Pena	.50	.20
❑ 236	Kelly Johnson	.50	.20
❑ 237	David DeJesus	.50	.20
❑ 238	Andy Marte	.50	.20
❑ 239	Scott Olsen	.50	.20
❑ 240	Randy Johnson	1.25	.50
❑ 241	Nelson Cruz	.50	.20
❑ 242	Carlos Guillen	.50	.20
❑ 243	Brandon McCarthy	.50	.20
❑ 244	Garret Anderson	.50	.20
❑ 245	Mike Sweeney	.50	.20
❑ 246	Brian Bannister	.50	.20
❑ 247	Jose Guillen	.50	.20
❑ 248	Brad Wilkerson	.50	.20
❑ 249	Lance Berkman	.50	.20
❑ 250	Ryan Zimmerman	1.25	.50
❑ 251	Garrett Atkins	.50	.20
❑ 252	Johan Santana	.75	.30
❑ 253	Brandon Webb	.50	.20
❑ 254	Justin Verlander	1.25	.50
❑ 255	Hanley Ramirez	.75	.30
❑ 256	Justin Morneau	.50	.20
❑ 257	Ryan Howard	2.00	.75
❑ 258	Eric Chavez	.50	.20
❑ 259	Scott Rolen	.75	.30
❑ 260	Derek Jeter	3.00	1.25
❑ 261	Omar Vizquel	.75	.30
❑ 262	Mark Grudzielanek	.50	.20
❑ 263	Orlando Hudson	.50	.20
❑ 264	Mark Teixeira	.75	.30
❑ 265	Albert Pujols	2.50	1.00
❑ 266	Ivan Rodriguez	.75	.30
❑ 267	Brad Ausmus	.50	.20
❑ 268	Torii Hunter	.50	.20
❑ 269	Mike Cameron	.50	.20
❑ 270	Ichiro Suzuki	2.00	.75
❑ 271	Carlos Beltran	.50	.20
❑ 272	Vernon Wells	.50	.20
❑ 273	Andruw Jones	.75	.30
❑ 274	Kenny Rogers	.50	.20
❑ 275	Greg Maddux	2.00	.75
❑ 276	Danny Putnam (RC)	1.00	.40
❑ 277	Chase Wright RC	2.50	1.00
❑ 278	Zach McClellan RC	1.00	.40
❑ 279	Jamie Vermilyea RC	1.00	.40
❑ 280	Felix Pie (RC)	1.00	.40
❑ 281	Phil Hughes (RC)	5.00	2.00
❑ 282	Jon Knott (RC)	1.00	.40
❑ 283	Micah Owings (RC)	1.00	.40
❑ 284	Devern Hansack RC	1.00	.40
❑ 285	Andy Cannizaro RC	1.00	.40
❑ 286	Lee Gardner (RC)	1.00	.40
❑ 287	Josh Hamilton (RC)	2.50	1.00
❑ 288a	Angel Sanchez RC		
❑ 288b	Angel Sanchez AU	8.00	3.00
❑ 289	J.D. Durbin (RC)	1.00	.40
❑ 290	Jaime Burke (RC)	1.00	.40
❑ 291	Joe Bisenius RC	1.00	.40
❑ 292	Rick Vanden Hurk RC	1.50	.60
❑ 293	Brian Barden RC	1.00	.40
❑ 294	Levale Speigner RC	1.00	.40
❑ 295	Kevin Cameron RC	1.00	.40
❑ 296	Don Kelly (RC)	1.00	.40
❑ 297a	Hideki Okajima RC	5.00	2.00
❑ 297b	Hideki Okajima Japanese	8.00	3.00
❑ 298	Andrew Miller RC	6.00	2.50
❑ 299	Delmon Young (RC)	2.50	1.00
❑ 300	Vinny Rottino (RC)	1.00	.40
❑ 301	Philip Humber (RC)	1.00	.40
❑ 302	Drew Anderson RC	1.00	.40
❑ 303	Jerry Owens (RC)	1.00	.40
❑ 304	Jose Garcia RC	1.00	.40
❑ 305	Shane Youman RC	1.00	.40
❑ 306	Ryan Feierabend (RC)	1.00	.40
❑ 307	Mike Rabelo RC	1.00	.40
❑ 308	Josh Fields (RC)	1.00	.40
❑ 309	Jon Coutlangus (RC)	1.00	.40
❑ 310	Travis Buck (RC)	1.00	.40
❑ 311	Doug Slaten RC	1.00	.40
❑ 312	Ryan Z. Braun RC	1.00	.40
❑ 313	Juan Salas (RC)	1.00	.40
❑ 314	Matt Lindstrom (RC)	1.00	.40
❑ 315	Cesar Jimenez RC	1.00	.40
❑ 316	Jay Marshall RC	1.00	.40
❑ 317	Jared Burton RC	1.00	.40
❑ 318	Juan Perez RC	1.00	.40
❑ 319	Elijah Dukes RC	1.50	.60
❑ 320	Juan Lara RC	1.00	.40
❑ 321	Justin Hampson (RC)	1.00	.40
❑ 322a	Kei Igawa RC	2.50	1.00
❑ 322b	Kei Igawa Japanese	5.00	2.00
❑ 323	Zack Segovia (RC)	1.00	.40
❑ 324	Alejandro De Aza RC	1.50	.60
❑ 325	Brandon Morrow RC	2.50	1.00
❑ 326	Gustavo Molina RC	1.00	.40
❑ 327	Joe Smith RC	1.00	.40
❑ 328	Jesus Flores RC	1.00	.40
❑ 329	Jeff Baker (RC)	1.00	.40
❑ 330a	Daisuke Matsuzaka RC	10.00	4.00
❑ 330b	Daisuke Matsuzaka Japanese	20.00	8.00
❑ 331	Troy Tulowitzki AU (RC)	30.00	12.50
❑ 332	John Danks AU RC	8.00	3.00
❑ 333	Kevin Kouzmanoff AU (RC)	8.00	3.00
❑ 334	David Murphy AU (RC)	8.00	3.00
❑ 335	Ryan Sweeney AU (RC)	8.00	3.00
❑ 336	Fred Lewis AU (RC)	10.00	4.00
❑ 337	Delwyn Young AU (RC)	8.00	3.00
❑ 338	Matt Chico AU (RC)	8.00	3.00
❑ 339	Miguel Montero AU (RC)	8.00	3.00
❑ 340	Shawn Riggans AU (RC)	8.00	3.00
❑ 341	Brian Stokes AU (RC)	8.00	3.00
❑ 342	Scott Moore AU (RC)	8.00	3.00
❑ 343	Adam Lind AU (RC)	8.00	3.00
❑ 344	Chris Narveson AU (RC)	8.00	3.00
❑ 345	Alex Gordon AU RC	40.00	15.00
❑ 346	Joaquin Arias AU (RC)	8.00	3.00
❑ 347	Brian Burres AU (RC)	8.00	3.00
❑ 348	Glen Perkins AU (RC)	8.00	3.00
❑ 349	Ubaldo Jimenez AU (RC)	25.00	10.00
❑ 350	Chris Stewart AU RC	8.00	3.00
❑ 351	Beltran Perez AU (RC)	8.00	3.00
❑ 352	Dennis Sarfate AU (RC)	8.00	3.00
❑ 353	Carlos Maldonado AU (RC)	8.00	3.00
❑ 354	Mitch Maier AU RC	8.00	3.00
❑ 355	Kory Casto AU (RC)	8.00	3.00
❑ 356	Juan Morillo AU (RC)	8.00	3.00
❑ 357	Hector Gimenez AU (RC)	8.00	3.00
❑ 358	Alexi Casilla AU RC	10.00	4.00
❑ 359	Michael Bourn AU (RC)	10.00	4.00
❑ 360	Sean Henn AU (RC)	8.00	3.00
❑ 361	Tim Gradoville AU RC	8.00	3.00
❑ 362	A.Iwamura AU RC EXCH	20.00	8.00
❑ 363	Oswaldo Navarro AU RC	8.00	3.00

2008 Topps Chrome

❑ COMP.SET w/o AU's (220)	60.00	30.00
❑ COMMON CARD	.50	.20
❑ COMMON ROOKIE	1.50	.60
❑ COMMON AUTO	10.00	4.00
❑ AUTO ODDS 1:15 HOBBY		
❑ PRINT.PLATE ODDS 1:1896 HOBBY		
❑ AU PLATES 1:10,961 HOBBY		
❑ PLATE PRINT RUN 1 SET PER COLOR		
❑ BLACK-CYAN-MAGENTA-YELLOW ISSUED		
❑ NO PLATE PRICING DUE TO SCARCITY		
❑ EXCHANGE DEADLINE 6/30/2010		
❑ 1 Alex Rodriguez	2.00	.75
❑ 2 Barry Zito	.50	.20
❑ 3 Scott Kazmir	.75	.30
❑ 4 Stephen Drew	.50	.20

	Card		
❑	5 Miguel Cabrera	.75	.30
❑	6 Daisuke Matsuzaka	2.00	.75
❑	7 Mickey Mantle	5.00	2.00
❑	8 Jimmy Rollins	.75	.30
❑	9 Joe Mauer	.75	.30
❑	10 Cole Hamels	.75	.30
❑	11 Yovani Gallardo	.50	.20
❑	12 Miguel Tejada	.50	.20
❑	13 Dontrelle Willis	.50	.20
❑	14 Orlando Cabrera	.50	.20
❑	15 Jake Peavy	.50	.20
❑	16 Erik Bedard	.50	.20
❑	17 Victor Martinez	.50	.20
❑	18 Chris Young	.50	.20
❑	19 Jose Reyes	.75	.30
❑	20 Mike Lowell	.50	.20
❑	21 Dan Uggla	.75	.30
❑	22 Garrett Atkins	.50	.20
❑	23 Felix Hernandez	.75	.30
❑	24 Ivan Rodriguez	.75	.30
❑	25 Alex Rios	.50	.20
❑	26 Jason Bay	.50	.20
❑	27 Vladimir Guerrero	1.25	.50
❑	28 John Lackey	.50	.20
❑	29 Ryan Howard	1.50	.60
❑	30 Kevin Youkilis	.75	.30
❑	31 Justin Morneau	.75	.30
❑	32 Johan Santana	1.25	.50
❑	33 Jeremy Hermida	.50	.20
❑	34 Andruw Jones	.50	.20
❑	35 Mike Cameron	.50	.20
❑	36 Jason Varitek	1.25	.50
❑	37 Tim Hudson	.50	.20
❑	38 Justin Upton	1.25	.50
❑	39 Brad Penny	.50	.20
❑	40 Robinson Cano	.75	.30
❑	41 Brandon Webb	.50	.20
❑	42 Magglio Ordonez	.75	.30
❑	43 Aaron Hill	.50	.20
❑	44 Alfonso Soriano	.75	.30
❑	45 Carlos Zambrano	.50	.20
❑	46 Ben Sheets	.75	.30
❑	47 Tim Lincecum	1.25	.50
❑	48 Phil Hughes	1.25	.50
❑	49 Scott Rolen	.75	.30
❑	50 John Maine	.50	.20
❑	51 Delmon Young	.75	.30
❑	52 Tadahito Iguchi	.50	.20
❑	53 Yunel Escobar	.50	.20
❑	54 Russell Martin	.50	.20
❑	55 Orlando Hudson	.50	.20
❑	56 Jim Edmonds	.75	.30
❑	57 Todd Helton	.75	.30
❑	58 Melky Cabrera	.50	.20
❑	59 Adrian Beltre	.50	.20
❑	60 Manny Ramirez	1.25	.50
❑	61 Gil Meche	.50	.20
❑	62 David DeJesus	.50	.20
❑	63 Roy Oswalt	.50	.20
❑	64 Mark Buehrle	.50	.20
❑	65 Hunter Pence	1.25	.50
❑	66 Dustin Pedroia	.75	.30
❑	67 Roy Halladay	.50	.20
❑	68 Rich Harden	.50	.20
❑	69 Jim Thome	.75	.30
❑	70 Akinori Iwamura	.50	.20
❑	71 Dan Haren	.50	.20
❑	72 Brandon Phillips	.50	.20
❑	73 Brett Myers	.50	.20
❑	74 James Loney	.75	.30
❑	75 C.C. Sabathia	.50	.20
❑	76 Jermaine Dye	.50	.20
❑	77 Carlos Ruiz	.50	.20
❑	78 Brian McCann	.75	.30
❑	79 Paul Konerko	.50	.20
❑	80 Jorge Posada	.75	.30
❑	81 Chien-Ming Wang	1.50	.60
❑	82 Carlos Delgado	.50	.20
❑	83 Ichiro Suzuki	2.00	.75
❑	84 Elijah Dukes	.50	.20
❑	85 David Wright	1.50	.60
❑	86 Carl Crawford	.50	.20
❑	87 Mark Teixeira	.75	.30
❑	88 Bobby Crosby	.50	.20
❑	89 Brian Roberts	.75	.30
❑	90 David Ortiz	1.25	.50
❑	91 Derrek Lee	.75	.30
❑	92 Adam Dunn	.50	.20
❑	93 Fausto Carmona	.50	.20
❑	94 Grady Sizemore	.75	.30
❑	95 Jeff Francoeur	.75	.30
❑	96 Jered Weaver	.50	.20
❑	97 Troy Tulowitzki	.75	.30
❑	98 Troy Glaus	.75	.30
❑	99 Nick Markakis	.75	.30
❑	100 Lance Berkman	.75	.30
❑	101 Randy Johnson	1.25	.50
❑	102 Kenji Johjima	.50	.20
❑	103 Jarrod Saltalamacchia	.50	.20
❑	104 Matt Holliday	.75	.30
❑	105 Travis Hafner	.50	.20
❑	106 Johnny Damon	.75	.30
❑	107 Alex Gordon	1.25	.50
❑	108 Derek Lowe	.50	.20
❑	109 Nick Swisher	.50	.20
❑	110 Aaron Harang	.50	.20
❑	111 Hanley Ramirez	1.25	.50
❑	112 Carlos Guillen	.50	.20
❑	113 Ryan Braun	1.50	.60
❑	114 Torii Hunter	.50	.20
❑	115 Joe Blanton	.50	.20
❑	116 Josh Hamilton	1.50	.60
❑	117 Pedro Martinez	.75	.30
❑	118 Hideki Matsui	1.25	.50
❑	119 Cameron Maybin	1.25	.50
❑	120 Prince Fielder	1.25	.50
❑	121 Derek Jeter	3.00	1.25
❑	122 Chone Figgins	.50	.20
❑	123 Chase Utley	1.25	.50
❑	124 Jacoby Ellsbury	2.00	.75
❑	125 Freddy Sanchez	.50	.20
❑	126 Rocco Baldelli	.50	.20
❑	127 Tom Gorzelanny	.50	.20
❑	128 Adrian Gonzalez	.75	.30
❑	129 Geovany Soto	.50	.20
❑	130 Bobby Abreu	.50	.20
❑	131 Albert Pujols	2.50	1.00
❑	132 Chipper Jones	1.50	.60
❑	133 Jeremy Bonderman	.50	.20
❑	134 B.J. Upton	.75	.30
❑	135 Justin Verlander	.75	.30
❑	136 Jeff Francis	.50	.20
❑	137 A.J. Burnett	.50	.20
❑	138 Travis Buck	.50	.20
❑	139 Vernon Wells	.50	.20
❑	140 Raul Ibanez	.50	.20
❑	141 Ryan Zimmerman	.75	.30
❑	142 John Smoltz	1.25	.50
❑	143 Carlos Lee	.50	.20
❑	144 Chris Young	.50	.20
❑	145 Francisco Liriano	.75	.30
❑	146 Curt Schilling	.75	.30
❑	147 Josh Beckett	.75	.30
❑	148 Aramis Ramirez	.50	.20
❑	149 Ronnie Belliard	.50	.20
❑	150 Homer Bailey	.75	.30
❑	151 Curtis Granderson	.75	.30
❑	152 Ken Griffey Jr.	2.00	.75
❑	153 Kazuo Matsui	.50	.20
❑	154 Brian Bannister	.50	.20
❑	155 Joba Chamberlain	2.00	.75
❑	156 Tom Glavine	.75	.30
❑	157 Carlos Beltran	.50	.20
❑	158 Kelly Johnson	.50	.20
❑	159 Rich Hill	.50	.20
❑	160 Pat Burrell	.50	.20
❑	161 Asdrubal Cabrera	.50	.20
❑	162 Gary Sheffield	.50	.20
❑	163 Greg Maddux	1.50	.60
❑	164 Eric Chavez	.50	.20
❑	165 Chris Carpenter	.50	.20
❑	166 Michael Young	.50	.20
❑	167 Carlos Pena	.50	.20
❑	168 Frank Thomas	1.25	.50
❑	169 Aaron Rowand	.50	.20
❑	170 Yadier Molina	.75	.30
❑	171 Luis Castillo	.50	.20
❑	172 Ryan Theriot	.50	.20
❑	173 Andre Ethier	.75	.30
❑	174 Casey Kotchman	.50	.20
❑	175 Rickie Weeks	.50	.20
❑	176 Milton Bradley	.50	.20
❑	177 Daniel Cabrera	.50	.20
❑	178 Jo-Jo Reyes	.50	.20
❑	179 Livan Hernandez	.50	.20
❑	180 Hideki Okajima	.50	.20
❑	181 Matt Kemp	.50	.20
❑	182 Jonny Gomes	.50	.20
❑	183 Billy Butler	.50	.20
❑	184 Adam LaRoche	.50	.20
❑	185 Brad Hawpe	.50	.20
❑	186 Paul Maholm	.50	.20
❑	187 Placido Polanco	.50	.20
❑	188 Noah Lowry	.50	.20
❑	189 Gregg Zaun	.50	.20
❑	190 Nate McLouth	.50	.20
❑	191 Edinson Volquez	.50	.20
❑	192 Jeff Niemann (RC)	1.50	.60
❑	193 Evan Longoria RC	10.00	4.00
❑	194 Adam Jones	.50	.20
❑	195 Eugenio Velez RC	1.50	.60
❑	196 Joey Votto (RC)	2.50	1.00
❑	197 Nick Blackburn RC	2.50	1.00
❑	198 Harvey Garcia (RC)	1.50	.60
❑	199 Hiroki Kuroda RC	2.50	1.00
❑	200 Elliot Johnson (RC)	1.50	.60
❑	201 Luis Mendoza (RC)	1.50	.60
❑	202 Alex Romero (RC)	1.50	.60
❑	203 Gregor Blanco (RC)	1.50	.60
❑	204 Rico Washington (RC)	1.50	.60
❑	205 Brian Bocock RC	1.50	.60
❑	206 Evan Meek RC	1.50	.60
❑	207 Stephen Holm RC	1.50	.60
❑	208 Matt Tupman RC	1.50	.60
❑	209 Fernando Hernandez RC	1.50	.60
❑	210 Randor Bierd RC	1.50	.60
❑	211 Blake DeWitt (RC)	4.00	1.50
❑	212 Randy Wells (RC)	1.50	.60
❑	213 Wesley Wright RC	1.50	.60
❑	214 Clete Thomas RC	2.50	1.00
❑	215 Kyle McClellan RC	1.50	.60
❑	216 Brian Bixler (RC)	1.50	.60
❑	217 Kazuo Fukumori RC	2.50	1.00
❑	218 Burke Badenhop RC	1.50	.60
❑	219 Denard Span (RC)	1.50	.60
❑	220 Brian Bass (RC)	1.50	.60
❑	221 J.R. Towles AU RC	10.00	4.00
❑	222 Felipe Paulino AU RC	10.00	4.00
❑	223 Sam Fuld AU (RC)	10.00	4.00
❑	224 Kevin Hart AU (RC)	10.00	4.00
❑	225 Nyjer Morgan AU (RC)	10.00	4.00
❑	226 Daric Barton AU (RC)	10.00	4.00
❑	227 Armando Galarraga AU RC	20.00	8.00
❑	228 Chin-Lung Hu AU (RC)	15.00	6.00
❑	229 Buchholz AU (RC) EXCH	25.00	10.00
❑	230 Rich Thompson AU RC	10.00	4.00
❑	231 Brian Barton AU RC	12.00	5.00
❑	232 Ross Ohlendorf AU RC	10.00	4.00
❑	233 Masahide Kobayashi AU RC	12.00	5.00
❑	234 Callix Crabbe AU (RC)	10.00	4.00
❑	235 Matt Tolbert AU RC	10.00	4.00
❑	236 Jayson Nix AU (RC)	10.00	4.00
❑	237 Johnny Cueto AU RC	25.00	10.00
❑	238 Evan Meek AU RC	10.00	4.00
❑	239 Randy Wells AU (RC)	10.00	4.00

2008 Topps Co-Signers

❑	COMP.SET w/o AU's (100)	40.00	15.00
❑	COMMON CARD (1-100)	.75	.30
❑	101-120 GROUP A ODDS 1:2025		

❑ 101-120 GROUP B ODDS 1:1625
❑ 101-120 GROUP C ODDS 1:920
❑ 101-120 GROUP D ODDS 1:81
❑ 101-120 GROUP E ODDS 1:270
❑ 101-120 GROUP F ODDS 1:68
❑ 101-120 GROUP G ODDS 1:12
❑ 101-120 GROUP A PRINT RUN 200 CARDS
❑ 101-120 GROUP B PRINT RUN 250 CARDS
❑ 101-120 GROUP C PRINT RUN 440 CARDS
❑ A-C CARDS ARE NOT SERIAL NUMBERED
❑ A-C PRINT RUNS PROVIDED BY TOPPS
❑ 1 Albert Pujols 4.00 1.50
❑ 2 Roger Clemens 4.00 1.50
❑ 3 Paul Konerko .75 .30
❑ 4 Jeff Francouer 2.00 .75
❑ 5 Miguel Tejada .75 .30
❑ 6 Curt Schilling 1.25 .50
❑ 7 Mickey Mantle 5.00 2.00
❑ 8 Miguel Cabrera 1.25 .50
❑ 9 Derrek Lee .75 .30
❑ 10 Jeff Kent .75 .30
❑ 11 Gary Sheffield .75 .30
❑ 12 Rich Harden .75 .30
❑ 13 Scott Rolen 1.25 .50
❑ 14 David Wright 3.00 1.25
❑ 15 Troy Glaus .75 .30
❑ 16 Torii Hunter .75 .30
❑ 17 Nolan Ryan 5.00 2.00
❑ 18 Alfonso Soriano .75 .30
❑ 19 Hank Blalock .75 .30
❑ 20 Chase Utley 2.00 .75
❑ 21 Ryan Howard 3.00 1.25
❑ 22 Robinson Cano 1.25 .50
❑ 23 Derek Jeter 5.00 2.00
❑ 24 Huston Street .75 .30
❑ 25 Jason Giambi .75 .30
❑ 26 Rafael Furcal .75 .30
❑ 27 Rickie Weeks .75 .30
❑ 28 Ivan Rodriguez 1.25 .50
❑ 29 Travis Hafner .75 .30
❑ 30 Greg Maddux 3.00 1.25
❑ 31 Andruw Jones 1.25 .50
❑ 32 Andy Pettitte 1.25 .50
❑ 33 Scott Podsednik .75 .30
❑ 34 Francisco Rodriguez .75 .30
❑ 35 Josh Beckett .75 .30
❑ 36 Lance Berkman .75 .30
❑ 37 Roy Oswalt .75 .30
❑ 38 Pedro Martinez 1.25 .50
❑ 39 Jimmy Rollins .75 .30
❑ 40 Johan Santana 1.25 .50
❑ 41 Randy Johnson 2.00 .75
❑ 42 Mariano Rivera 2.00 .75
❑ 43 Nick Johnson .75 .30
❑ 44 Josh Gibson 2.00 .75
❑ 45 Shawn Green .75 .30
❑ 46 Adrian Beltre .75 .30
❑ 47 Johnny Damon 1.25 .50
❑ 48 Joe Mauer 1.25 .50
❑ 49 Todd Helton 1.25 .50
❑ 50 Alex Rodriguez 3.00 1.25
❑ 51 Jake Peavy .75 .30
❑ 52 David Ortiz 2.00 .75
❑ 53 Mark Buehrle .75 .30
❑ 54 Eric Gagne .75 .30
❑ 55 Hideki Matsui 3.00 1.25
❑ 56 Bobby Abreu .75 .30
❑ 57 Victor Martinez .75 .30
❑ 58 Brian Roberts .75 .30
❑ 59 Chipper Jones 2.00 .75
❑ 60 Carlos Beltran .75 .30
❑ 61 Tim Hudson .75 .30
❑ 62 Carlos Lee .75 .30
❑ 63 Barry Zito .75 .30
❑ 64 Moises Alou .75 .30
❑ 65 Mark Teixeira 1.25 .50
❑ 66 Lyle Overbay .75 .30
❑ 67 Kerry Wood .75 .30
❑ 68 B.J. Ryan .75 .30
❑ 69 Jim Edmonds 1.25 .50
❑ 70 Carlos Delgado .75 .30
❑ 71 Magglio Ordonez .75 .30
❑ 72 Juan Pierre .75 .30
❑ 73 Manny Ramirez 1.25 .50
❑ 74 Dontrelle Willis .75 .30
❑ 75 Ichiro Suzuki 3.00 1.25
❑ 76 Nomar Garciaparra 2.00 .75
❑ 77 Zach Duke .75 .30
❑ 78 Chris Carpenter .75 .30
❑ 79 A.J. Burnett .75 .30
❑ 80 Scott Kazmir 1.25 .50
❑ 81 Carl Crawford .75 .30
❑ 82 Mark Prior 1.25 .50
❑ 83 Adam Dunn .75 .30
❑ 84 Justin Morneau .75 .30
❑ 85 Morgan Ensberg .75 .30
❑ 86 Pat Burrell .75 .30
❑ 87 Paul Lo Duca .75 .30
❑ 88 Jason Bay .75 .30
❑ 89 Aubrey Huff .75 .30
❑ 90 Kevin Millwood .75 .30
❑ 91 Vernon Wells .75 .30
❑ 92 Javy Lopez .75 .30
❑ 93 Michael Young .75 .30
❑ 94 Felix Hernandez 1.25 .50
❑ 95 Ken Griffey Jr. 3.00 1.25
❑ 96 Bartolo Colon .75 .30
❑ 97 Billy Wagner .75 .30
❑ 98 Vladimir Guerrero 2.00 .75
❑ 99 Jose Reyes 2.00 .75
❑ 100 Barry Bonds 5.00 2.00
❑ 101 Anthony LeRew AU G (RC) 10.00 4.00
❑ 102 R.Zimm AU C/440 (RC) * 50.00 20.00
❑ 103 C.Hansen AU B/250 RC * 50.00 20.00
❑ 104 F.Liriano AU G (RC) 40.00 15.00
❑ 105 Jason Botts AU G (RC) 10.00 4.00
❑ 106 Josh Johnson AU G (RC) 15.00 6.00
❑ 107 Hanley Ramirez AU G (RC) 25.00 10.00
❑ 108 A.Wainwright AU G (RC) 15.00 6.00
❑ 109 K.Johjima AU A/200 RC * 100.00 50.00
❑ 110 Dan Ortmeier AU G (RC) 10.00 4.00
❑ 111 Darrell Rasner AU G (RC) 10.00 4.00
❑ 112 Chuck James AU F (RC) 15.00 6.00
❑ 113 Nelson Cruz AU F (RC) 10.00 4.00
❑ 114 Hong-Chih Kuo AU E (RC) 40.00 15.00
❑ 115 Ryan Garko AU G (RC) 10.00 4.00
❑ 116 R.Abercrombie AU D (RC) 10.00 4.00
❑ 117 Ian Kinsler AU D (RC) 15.00 6.00
❑ 118 Joel Zumaya AU D (RC) 25.00 10.00
❑ 119 Willie Eyre AU D (RC) 10.00 4.00
❑ 120 Dan Uggla AU D (RC) 15.00 6.00

2007 Topps Co-Signers

❑ COMP.SET w/o AU's (100) 30.00 12.50
❑ COMMON CARD (1-92) .60 .25
❑ SEMISTARS 1.00 .40
❑ UNLISTED STARS 1.50 .60
❑ COMMON ROOKIE (93-100) 1.50 .60
❑ ROOKIE SEMIS 2.50 1.00
❑ ROOKIE UNLISTED 4.00 1.50
❑ COMMON ROOKIE AU (96-121) 8.00 3.00
❑ ROOKIE AUTO ODDS 1:28
❑ ROOKIE AUTO VARIATION ODDS 1:198
❑ PRINTING PLATE ODDS 1:705
❑ PRINTING PLATE AUTO ODDS 1:21,168
❑ PLATE PRINT RUN 1 SET PER COLOR
❑ BLACK-CYAN-MAGENTA-SPOT-YELLOW ISSUED
❑ NO PLATE PRICING DUE TO SCARCITY
❑ 1 Ryan Howard 2.50 1.00
❑ 2 Jered Weaver 1.00 .40
❑ 3 Brian McCann .60 .25
❑ 4 Garrett Atkins .60 .25
❑ 5 Travis Hafner .60 .25
❑ 6 Jason Schmidt .60 .25
❑ 7 Curtis Granderson .60 .25
❑ 8 Ben Sheets .60 .25
❑ 9 Chien-Ming Wang 2.50 1.00
❑ 10 Francisco Liriano 1.50 .60
❑ 11 Freddy Sanchez .60 .25
❑ 12 Roy Oswalt .60 .25
❑ 13 Jim Edmonds 1.00 .40
❑ 14 Matt Cain 1.00 .40
❑ 15 Jake Peavy .60 .25
❑ 16 Ryan Zimmerman 1.50 .60
❑ 17 Troy Glaus .60 .25
❑ 18 Kenji Johjima 1.50 .60
❑ 19 Curt Schilling 1.00 .40
❑ 20 Alfonso Soriano .60 .25
❑ 21 Adam Dunn .60 .25
❑ 22 Hanley Ramirez 1.00 .40
❑ 23 Mark Teahen .60 .25
❑ 24 Todd Helton 1.00 .40
❑ 25 Alex Rodriguez 2.50 1.00
❑ 26 Mike Mussina 1.00 .40
❑ 27 Jason Bay .60 .25
❑ 28 Carl Crawford .60 .25
❑ 29 Vernon Wells .60 .25
❑ 30 Rich Harden .60 .25
❑ 31 Justin Morneau .60 .25
❑ 32 Andre Ethier 1.00 .40
❑ 33 Ramon Hernandez .60 .25
❑ 34 Erik Bedard .60 .25
❑ 35 Vladimir Guerrero 1.50 .60
❑ 36 Stephen Drew 1.00 .40
❑ 37 Felix Hernandez 1.00 .40
❑ 38 C.C. Sabathia .60 .25
❑ 39 Adrian Gonzalez .60 .25
❑ 40 Prince Fielder 1.50 .60
❑ 41 Carlos Delgado .60 .25
❑ 42 Jimmy Rollins .60 .25
❑ 43 Raul Ibanez .60 .25
❑ 44 Jorge Cantu .60 .25
❑ 45 Michael Young .60 .25
❑ 46 Austin Kearns .60 .25
❑ 47 Ivan Rodriguez 1.00 .40
❑ 48 Mark Teixeira .60 .25
❑ 49 David Ortiz 1.50 .60
❑ 50 David Wright 2.50 1.00
❑ 51 Justin Verlander 1.50 .60
❑ 52 Nick Markakis 1.00 .40
❑ 53 Miguel Cabrera 1.00 .40
❑ 54 Lance Berkman .60 .25
❑ 55 Robinson Cano 1.00 .40
❑ 56 Jon Lieber .60 .25
❑ 57 Andruw Jones 1.00 .40
❑ 58 Dan Haren .60 .25
❑ 59 Grady Sizemore 1.00 .40
❑ 60 Gary Sheffield .60 .25
❑ 61 Paul Lo Duca .60 .25
❑ 62 Cole Hamels 1.00 .40
❑ 63 Richie Sexson .60 .25
❑ 64 David Eckstein .60 .25
❑ 65 Carlos Zambrano .60 .25
❑ 66 Scott Kazmir 1.00 .40
❑ 67 Anthony Reyes .60 .25
❑ 68 Mark Kotsay .60 .25
❑ 69 Miguel Tejada .60 .25
❑ 70 Pedro Martinez 1.00 .40
❑ 71 Jack Wilson .60 .25
❑ 72 Joe Mauer 1.00 .40
❑ 73 Brian Giles .60 .25
❑ 74 Jonathan Papelbon 1.50 .60
❑ 75 Albert Pujols 3.00 1.25
❑ 76 Nick Swisher .60 .25
❑ 77 Bill Hall .60 .25
❑ 78 Jose Contreras .60 .25
❑ 79 David DeJesus .60 .25
❑ 80 Bobby Abreu .60 .25
❑ 81 John Smoltz 1.00 .40
❑ 82 Chipper Jones 1.50 .60
❑ 83 Mark Buehrle .60 .25
❑ 84 Josh Barfield .60 .25
❑ 85 Derrek Lee .60 .25
❑ 86 Jim Thome 1.00 .40
❑ 87 Kenny Rogers .60 .25
❑ 88 Jeremy Sowers .60 .25
❑ 89 Brandon Webb .60 .25
❑ 90 Roy Halladay .60 .25
❑ 91 Tadahito Iguchi .60 .25
❑ 92 Jeff Kent .60 .25

❑ 93 Johnny Damon 1.00 .40
❑ 94 Daisuke Matsuzaka RC 8.00 3.00
❑ 95 Kei Igawa RC 2.50 1.00
❑ 96a Delmon Young (RC) 2.00 .75
❑ 96b Delmon Young AU 20.00 8.00
❑ 97a Jeff Baker (RC) 1.50 .60
❑ 97b Jeff Baker AU 8.00 3.00
❑ 98a Michael Bourn (RC) 1.50 .60
❑ 98b Michael Bourn AU 10.00 4.00
❑ 99a Ubaldo Jimenez (RC) 1.50 .60
❑ 99b Ubaldo Jimenez AU 15.00 6.00
❑ 100a Andrew Miller RC 4.00 1.50
❑ 100b Andrew Miller AU 40.00 15.00
❑ 101 Angel Sanchez AU RC 8.00 3.00
❑ 102 Troy Tulowitzki AU (RC) 30.00 12.50
❑ 103 Joaquin Arias AU (RC) 8.00 3.00
❑ 104 Beltran Perez AU (RC) 8.00 3.00
❑ 105 Josh Fields AU (RC) 10.00 4.00
❑ 106 Hector Gimenez AU (RC) 8.00 3.00
❑ 107 Kevin Kouzmanoff AU (RC) 10.00 4.00
❑ 108 Miguel Montero AU (RC) 8.00 3.00
❑ 109 Philip Humber AU (RC) 10.00 4.00
❑ 110 Jerry Owens AU (RC) 8.00 3.00
❑ 111 Shawn Riggans AU (RC) 8.00 3.00
❑ 112 Brian Stokes AU (RC) 8.00 3.00
❑ 113 Scott Moore AU (RC) 8.00 3.00
❑ 114 David Murphy AU (RC) 8.00 3.00
❑ 115 Mitch Maier AU RC 8.00 3.00
❑ 116 Adam Lind AU (RC) 10.00 4.00
❑ 117 Glen Perkins AU (RC) 10.00 4.00
❑ 118 Dennis Sarfate AU (RC) 8.00 3.00
❑ 119 Elijah Dukes AU RC 15.00 6.00
❑ 120 Josh Hamilton AU (RC) 30.00 12.50
❑ 121 Alex Gordon AU RC 40.00 15.00
❑ 122 Barry Bonds 8.00 3.00

2008 Topps Co-Signers

❑ COMP.SET w/o AU's (100) 30.00 12.50
❑ COMMON CARD (1-95) .60 .25
❑ COMMON RC (96-100) 1.50 .60
❑ AU RC VAR ODDS 1:315 HOBBY
❑ COMMON AU RC 8.00 3.00
❑ AU RC ODDS 1:22 HOBBY
❑ PRINTING PLATE VET/RC ODDS 1:446
❑ PRINTING PLATE AU RC VAR ODDS 1:29,736
❑ PRINTING PLATE AU RC ODDS 1:5216
❑ PLATE PRINT RUN 1 SET PER COLOR
❑ 5TH-BLACK-CYAN-MAGENTA-YELLOW ISSUED
❑ NO PLATE PRICING DUE TO SCARCITY
❑ 1 Jacoby Ellsbury 2.50 1.00
❑ 2 Michael Young .60 .25
❑ 3 Cameron Maybin 1.50 .60
❑ 4 Dmitri Young .60 .25
❑ 5 Grady Sizemore 1.00 .40
❑ 6 Brandon Webb .60 .25
❑ 7 Derrek Lee 1.00 .40
❑ 8 Jeff Francis .60 .25
❑ 9 Aaron Harang .60 .25
❑ 10 John Smoltz 1.50 .60
❑ 11 Nick Markakis 1.00 .40
❑ 12 Tom Gorzelanny .60 .25
❑ 13 Miguel Cabrera 1.00 .40
❑ 14 Josh Beckett 1.00 .40
❑ 15 Magglio Ordonez 1.00 .40
❑ 16 Joe Mauer 1.00 .40
❑ 17 Carl Crawford .60 .25
❑ 18 Barry Zito .60 .25
❑ 19 Brad Penny .60 .25
❑ 20 C.C. Sabathia .60 .25
❑ 21 Mark Buehrle .60 .25
❑ 22 Carlos Lee .60 .25
❑ 23 Chipper Jones 2.00 .75
❑ 24 Chase Utley 1.50 .60
❑ 25 David Ortiz 1.50 .60
❑ 26 Justin Morneau .60 .25
❑ 27 Erik Bedard .60 .25
❑ 28 Greg Maddux 2.00 .75
❑ 29 Joba Chamberlain 3.00 1.25
❑ 30 Vernon Wells .60 .25
❑ 31 Orlando Hudson .60 .25
❑ 32 Kevin Youkilis 1.00 .40
❑ 33 Curtis Granderson 1.00 .40
❑ 34 Chone Figgins .60 .25
❑ 35 Jorge Posada 1.00 .40
❑ 36 Ken Griffey Jr. 2.50 1.00
❑ 37 Tim Hudson .60 .25
❑ 38 Nick Swisher .60 .25
❑ 39 Carlos Beltran .60 .25
❑ 40 Alex Gordon 1.50 .60
❑ 41 Andre Ethier 1.00 .40
❑ 42 Todd Helton 1.00 .40
❑ 43 Miguel Tejada .60 .25
❑ 44 Yadier Molina 1.00 .40
❑ 45 Hanley Ramirez 1.50 .60
❑ 46 Justin Verlander 1.00 .40
❑ 47 Adam Dunn .60 .25
❑ 48 Raul Ibanez .60 .25
❑ 49 Scott Rolen 1.00 .40
❑ 50 Alex Rodriguez 2.50 1.00
❑ 51 Garret Anderson .60 .25
❑ 52 Andruw Jones .60 .25
❑ 53 Matt Cain .60 .25
❑ 54 Daisuke Matsuzaka 3.00 1.25
❑ 55 Ichiro Suzuki 2.50 1.00
❑ 56 Scott Kazmir 1.00 .40
❑ 57 Jeff Kent .60 .25
❑ 58 Aubrey Huff .60 .25
❑ 59 Justin Upton 1.50 .60
❑ 60 Prince Fielder 1.50 .60
❑ 61 Alex Rios .60 .25
❑ 62 Alfonso Soriano 1.00 .40
❑ 63 Paul Konerko .60 .25
❑ 64 Matt Holliday 1.00 .40
❑ 65 Felix Hernandez 1.00 .40
❑ 66 Ivan Rodriguez 1.00 .40
❑ 67 John Maine .60 .25
❑ 68 Roy Oswalt .60 .25
❑ 69 Brian McCann 1.00 .40
❑ 70 Albert Pujols 3.00 1.25
❑ 71 John Lackey .60 .25
❑ 72 Travis Hafner .60 .25
❑ 73 Gil Meche .60 .25
❑ 74 Ben Sheets 1.00 .40
❑ 75 Ryan Howard 2.00 .75
❑ 76 Hideki Matsui 1.50 .60
❑ 77 Mike Lowell .60 .25
❑ 78 Dan Haren .60 .25
❑ 79 Adrian Gonzalez 1.00 .40
❑ 80 David Wright 2.00 .75
❑ 81 Jason Bay .60 .25
❑ 82 Carlos Zambrano .60 .25
❑ 83 Johan Santana 1.50 .60
❑ 84 David DeJesus .60 .25
❑ 85 Ryan Zimmerman 1.00 .40
❑ 86 Bobby Abreu .60 .25
❑ 87 Richie Sexson .60 .25
❑ 88 Eric Chavez .60 .25
❑ 89 Derek Lowe .60 .25
❑ 90 Jake Peavy .60 .25
❑ 91 Joe Blanton .60 .25
❑ 92 Jermaine Dye .60 .25
❑ 93 Pedro Martinez 1.00 .40
❑ 94 B.J. Upton 1.00 .40
❑ 95 Vladimir Guerrero 1.50 .60
❑ 96 Ross Ohlendorf RC 2.50 1.00
❑ 97 J.R. Towles RC 4.00 1.50
❑ 98 Jonathan Meloan RC 2.50 1.00
❑ 99a Chin-Lung Hu (RC) 2.50 1.00
❑ 99b Chin-Lung Hu AU 25.00 10.00
❑ 100a Clay Buchholz (RC) 4.00 1.50
❑ 100b Clay Buchholz AU 30.00 12.50
❑ 101 Willie Collazo AU RC 8.00 3.00
❑ 102 David Davidson AU RC 8.00 3.00
❑ 103 Joe Koshansky AU (RC) 8.00 3.00
❑ 104 Sam Fuld AU (RC) 8.00 3.00
❑ 105 Nyjer Morgan AU (RC) 8.00 3.00
❑ 106 Clint Sammons AU (RC) 8.00 3.00
❑ 107 Josh Anderson AU (RC) 8.00 3.00
❑ 108 Bronson Sardinha AU (RC) 8.00 3.00
❑ 109 Wladimir Balentien AU (RC) 8.00 3.00
❑ 110 Kevin Hart AU (RC) 8.00 3.00
❑ 111 Felipe Paulino AU RC 8.00 3.00
❑ 112 Rob Johnson AU (RC) 8.00 3.00

2001 Topps Heritage

❑ COMP.MASTER SET (487) 500.00 350.00
❑ COMPLETE SET (407) 400.00 250.00
❑ COMP.BASIC SET (230) 80.00 40.00
❑ COMMON CARD (81-310) .50 .20
❑ COMMON CARD (1-80) 2.50 1.00
❑ COMMON CARD (311-407) 5.00 2.00
❑ 1 Kris Benson 2.50 1.00
❑ 1 Kris Benson Black 2.50 1.00
❑ 2 Brian Jordan 2.50 1.00
❑ 2 Brian Jordan Black 2.50 1.00
❑ 3 Fernando Vina 2.50 1.00
❑ 3 Fernando Vina Black 2.50 1.00
❑ 4 Mike Sweeney 2.50 1.00
❑ 4 Mike Sweeney Black 2.50 1.00
❑ 5 Rafael Palmeiro 2.50 1.00
❑ 5 Rafael Palmeiro Black 2.50 1.00
❑ 6 Paul O'Neill 2.50 1.00
❑ 6 Paul O'Neill Black 2.50 1.00
❑ 7 Todd Helton 2.50 1.00
❑ 7 Todd Helton Black 2.50 1.00
❑ 8 Ramiro Mendoza 2.50 1.00
❑ 8 Ramiro Mendoza Black 2.50 1.00
❑ 9 Kevin Millwood 2.50 1.00
❑ 9 Kevin Millwood Black 2.50 1.00
❑ 10 Chuck Knoblauch 2.50 1.00
❑ 10 Chuck Knoblauch Black 2.50 1.00
❑ 11 Derek Jeter 10.00 4.00
❑ 11 Derek Jeter Black 10.00 4.00
❑ 12 Alex Rodriguez Rangers 6.00 2.50
❑ 12 A.Rod Black Rangers 6.00 2.50
❑ 13 Geoff Jenkins 2.50 1.00
❑ 13 Geoff Jenkins Black 2.50 1.00
❑ 14 David Justice 2.50 1.00
❑ 14 David Justice Black 2.50 1.00
❑ 15 David Cone 2.50 1.00
❑ 15 David Cone Black 2.50 1.00
❑ 16 Andres Galarraga 2.50 1.00
❑ 16 Andres Galarraga Black 2.50 1.00
❑ 17 Garret Anderson 2.50 1.00
❑ 17 Garret Anderson Black 2.50 1.00
❑ 18 Roger Cedeno 2.50 1.00
❑ 18 Roger Cedeno Black 2.50 1.00
❑ 19 Randy Velarde 2.50 1.00
❑ 19 Randy Velarde Black 2.50 1.00
❑ 20 Carlos Delgado 2.50 1.00
❑ 20 Carlos Delgado Black 2.50 1.00
❑ 21 Quilvio Veras 2.50 1.00
❑ 21 Quilvio Veras Black 2.50 1.00
❑ 22 Jose Vidro 2.50 1.00
❑ 22 Jose Vidro Black 2.50 1.00
❑ 23 Corey Patterson 2.50 1.00
❑ 23 Corey Patterson Black 2.50 1.00
❑ 24 Jorge Posada 2.50 1.00
❑ 24 Jorge Posada Black 2.50 1.00
❑ 25 Eddie Perez 2.50 1.00
❑ 25 Eddie Perez Black 2.50 1.00
❑ 26 Jack Cust 2.50 1.00

	No.	Player		
❑	26	Jack Cust Black	2.50	1.00
❑	27	Sean Burroughs	2.50	1.00
❑	27	Sean Burroughs Black	2.50	1.00
❑	28	Randy Wolf	2.50	1.00
❑	28	Randy Wolf Black	2.50	1.00
❑	29	Mike Lamb	2.50	1.00
❑	29	Mike Lamb Black	2.50	1.00
❑	30	Rafael Furcal	2.50	1.00
❑	30	Rafael Furcal Black	2.50	1.00
❑	31	Barry Bonds	10.00	4.00
❑	31	Barry Bonds Black	10.00	4.00
❑	32	Tim Hudson	2.50	1.00
❑	32	Tim Hudson Black	2.50	1.00
❑	33	Tom Glavine	2.50	1.00
❑	33	Tom Glavine Black	2.50	1.00
❑	34	Javy Lopez	2.50	1.00
❑	34	Javy Lopez Black	2.50	1.00
❑	35	Aubrey Huff	2.50	1.00
❑	35	Aubrey Huff Black	2.50	1.00
❑	36	Wally Joyner	2.50	1.00
❑	36	Wally Joyner Black	2.50	1.00
❑	37	Magglio Ordonez	2.50	1.00
❑	37	Magglio Ordonez Black	2.50	1.00
❑	38	Matt Lawton	2.50	1.00
❑	38	Matt Lawton Black	2.50	1.00
❑	39	Mariano Rivera	4.00	1.50
❑	39	Mariano Rivera Black	4.00	1.50
❑	40	Andy Ashby	2.50	1.00
❑	40	Andy Ashby Black	2.50	1.00
❑	41	Mark Buehrle	2.50	1.00
❑	41	Mark Buehrle Black	2.50	1.00
❑	42	Esteban Loaiza	2.50	1.00
❑	42	Esteban Loaiza Black	2.50	1.00
❑	43	Mark Redman	2.50	1.00
❑	43	Mark Redman Black	2.50	1.00
❑	44	Mark Quinn	2.50	1.00
❑	44	Mark Quinn Black	2.50	1.00
❑	45	Tino Martinez	2.50	1.00
❑	45	Tino Martinez Black	2.50	1.00
❑	46	Joe Mays	2.50	1.00
❑	46	Joe Mays Black	2.50	1.00
❑	47	Walt Weiss	2.50	1.00
❑	47	Walt Weiss Black	2.50	1.00
❑	48	Roger Clemens	8.00	3.00
❑	48	Roger Clemens Black	8.00	3.00
❑	49	Greg Maddux	6.00	2.50
❑	49	Greg Maddux Black	6.00	2.50
❑	50	Richard Hidalgo	2.50	1.00
❑	50	Richard Hidalgo Black	2.50	1.00
❑	51	Orlando Hernandez	2.50	1.00
❑	51	Orlando Hernandez Black	2.50	1.00
❑	52	Chipper Jones	4.00	1.50
❑	52	Chipper Jones Black	4.00	1.50
❑	53	Ben Grieve	2.50	1.00
❑	53	Ben Grieve Black	2.50	1.00
❑	54	Jimmy Haynes	2.50	1.00
❑	54	Jimmy Haynes Black	2.50	1.00
❑	55	Ken Caminiti	2.50	1.00
❑	55	Ken Caminiti Black	2.50	1.00
❑	56	Tim Salmon	2.50	1.00
❑	56	Tim Salmon Black	2.50	1.00
❑	57	Andy Pettitte	2.50	1.00
❑	57	Andy Pettitte Black	2.50	1.00
❑	58	Darin Erstad	2.50	1.00
❑	58	Darin Erstad Black	2.50	1.00
❑	59	Marquis Grissom	2.50	1.00
❑	59	Marquis Grissom Black	2.50	1.00
❑	60	Raul Mondesi	2.50	1.00
❑	60	Raul Mondesi Black	2.50	1.00
❑	61	Bengie Molina	2.50	1.00
❑	61	Bengie Molina Black	2.50	1.00
❑	62	Miguel Tejada	2.50	1.00
❑	62	Miguel Tejada Black	2.50	1.00
❑	63	Jose Cruz Jr.	2.50	1.00
❑	63	Jose Cruz Jr. Black	2.50	1.00
❑	64	Billy Koch	2.50	1.00
❑	64	Billy Koch Black	2.50	1.00
❑	65	Troy Glaus	2.50	1.00
❑	65	Troy Glaus Black	2.50	1.00
❑	66	Cliff Floyd	2.50	1.00
❑	66	Cliff Floyd Black	2.50	1.00
❑	67	Tony Batista	2.50	1.00
❑	67	Tony Batista Black	2.50	1.00
❑	68	Jeff Bagwell	2.50	1.00
❑	68	Jeff Bagwell Black	2.50	1.00
❑	69	Billy Wagner	2.50	1.00
❑	69	Billy Wagner Black	2.50	1.00
❑	70	Eric Chavez	2.50	1.00
❑	70	Eric Chavez Black	2.50	1.00
❑	71	Troy Percival	2.50	1.00
❑	71	Troy Percival Black	2.50	1.00
❑	72	Andruw Jones	2.50	1.00
❑	72	Andruw Jones Black	2.50	1.00
❑	73	Shane Reynolds	2.50	1.00
❑	73	Shane Reynolds Black	2.50	1.00
❑	74	Barry Zito	2.50	1.00
❑	74	Barry Zito Black	2.50	1.00
❑	75	Roy Halladay	2.50	1.00
❑	75	Roy Halladay Black	2.50	1.00
❑	76	David Wells	2.50	1.00
❑	76	David Wells Black	2.50	1.00
❑	77	Jason Giambi	2.50	1.00
❑	77	Jason Giambi Black	2.50	1.00
❑	78	Scott Elarton	2.50	1.00
❑	78	Scott Elarton Black	2.50	1.00
❑	79	Moises Alou	2.50	1.00
❑	79	Moises Alou Black	2.50	1.00
❑	80	Adam Piatt	2.50	1.00
❑	80	Adam Piatt Black	2.50	1.00
❑	81	Wilton Veras	.50	.20
❑	82	Darryl Kile	.60	.25
❑	83	Johnny Damon	1.00	.40
❑	84	Tony Armas Jr.	.50	.20
❑	85	Ellis Burks	.60	.25
❑	86	Jamey Wright	.50	.20
❑	87	Jose Vizcaino	.50	.20
❑	88	Bartolo Colon	.60	.25
❑	89	Carmen Cali RC	.50	.20
❑	90	Kevin Brown	.60	.25
❑	91	Josh Hamilton	1.00	.40
❑	92	Jay Buhner	.60	.25
❑	93	Scott Pratt RC	.60	.25
❑	94	Alex Cora	.50	.20
❑	95	Luis Montanez RC	.60	.25
❑	96	Dmitri Young	.60	.25
❑	97	J.T. Snow	.60	.25
❑	98	Damion Easley	.50	.20
❑	99	Greg Norton	.50	.20
❑	100	Matt Wheatland	.50	.20
❑	101	Chin-Feng Chen	.60	.25
❑	102	Tony Womack	.50	.20
❑	103	Adam Kennedy Black	.50	.20
❑	104	J.D. Drew	.60	.25
❑	105	Carlos Febles	.50	.20
❑	106	Jim Thome	1.00	.40
❑	107	Danny Graves	.50	.20
❑	108	Dave Mlicki	.50	.20
❑	109	Ron Coomer	.50	.20
❑	110	James Baldwin	.50	.20
❑	111	Shaun Boyd RC	.50	.20
❑	112	Brian Bohanon	.50	.20
❑	113	Jacque Jones	.60	.25
❑	114	Alfonso Soriano	1.00	.40
❑	115	Tony Clark	.50	.20
❑	116	Terrence Long	.50	.20
❑	117	Todd Hundley	.50	.20
❑	118	Kazuhiro Sasaki	.60	.25
❑	119	Brian Sellier RC	.50	.20
❑	120	John Olerud	.60	.25
❑	121	Javier Vazquez	.60	.25
❑	122	Sean Burnett	.50	.20
❑	123	Matt LeCroy	.50	.20
❑	124	Erubiel Durazo	.50	.20
❑	125	Juan Encarnacion	.50	.20
❑	126	Pablo Ozuna	.50	.20
❑	127	Russ Ortiz	.50	.20
❑	128	David Segui	.50	.20
❑	129	Mark McGwire	4.00	1.50
❑	130	Mark Grace	1.00	.40
❑	131	Fred McGriff	1.00	.40
❑	132	Carl Pavano	.60	.25
❑	133	Derek Thompson	.50	.20
❑	134	Shawn Green	.60	.25
❑	135	B.J. Surhoff	.60	.25
❑	136	Michael Tucker	.50	.20
❑	137	Jason Isringhausen	.60	.25
❑	138	Eric Milton	.50	.20
❑	139	Mike Stodolka	.50	.20
❑	140	Milton Bradley	.60	.25
❑	141	Curt Schilling	.60	.25
❑	142	Sandy Alomar Jr.	.50	.20
❑	143	Brent Mayne	.50	.20
❑	144	Todd Jones	.50	.20
❑	145	Charles Johnson	.60	.25
❑	146	Dean Palmer	.60	.25
❑	147	Masato Yoshii	.50	.20
❑	148	Edgar Renteria	.60	.25
❑	149	Joe Randa	.60	.25
❑	150	Adam Johnson	.50	.20
❑	151	Greg Vaughn	.50	.20
❑	152	Adrian Beltre	.60	.25
❑	153	Glenallen Hill	.50	.20
❑	154	David Parrish RC	.50	.20
❑	155	Neifi Perez	.50	.20
❑	156	Pete Harnisch	.50	.20
❑	157	Paul Konerko	.60	.25
❑	158	Dennys Reyes	.50	.20
❑	159	Jose Lima Black	.50	.20
❑	160	Eddie Taubensee	.50	.20
❑	161	Miguel Cairo	.50	.20
❑	162	Jeff Kent	.60	.25
❑	163	Dustin Hermanson	.50	.20
❑	164	Alex Gonzalez	.50	.20
❑	165	Hideo Nomo	1.50	.60
❑	166	Sammy Sosa	1.50	.60
❑	167	C.J. Nitkowski	.50	.20
❑	168	Cal Eldred	.50	.20
❑	169	Jeff Abbott	.50	.20
❑	170	Jim Edmonds	.60	.25
❑	171	Mark Mulder Black	.60	.25
❑	172	Dominic Rich RC	.50	.20
❑	173	Ray Lankford	.60	.25
❑	174	Danny Borrell RC	.50	.20
❑	175	Rick Aguilera	.50	.20
❑	176	Shannon Stewart Black	.60	.25
❑	177	Steve Finley	.60	.25
❑	178	Jim Parque	.50	.20
❑	179	Kevin Appier Black	.60	.25
❑	180	Adrian Gonzalez	.50	.20
❑	181	Tom Goodwin	.50	.20
❑	182	Kevin Tapani	.50	.20
❑	183	Fernando Tatis	.50	.20
❑	184	Mark Grudzielanek	.50	.20
❑	185	Ryan Anderson	.50	.20
❑	186	Jeffrey Hammonds	.50	.20
❑	187	Corey Koskie	.50	.20
❑	188	Brad Fullmer Black	.50	.20
❑	189	Rey Sanchez	.50	.20
❑	190	Michael Barrett	.50	.20
❑	191	Rickey Henderson	1.50	.60
❑	192	Jermaine Dye	.60	.25
❑	193	Scott Brosius	.60	.25
❑	194	Matt Anderson	.50	.20
❑	195	Brian Buchanan	.50	.20
❑	196	Derrek Lee	1.00	.40
❑	197	Larry Walker	.60	.25
❑	198	Dan Moylan RC	.50	.20
❑	199	Vinny Castilla	.60	.25
❑	200	Ken Griffey Jr.	2.50	1.00
❑	201	Matt Stairs Black	.50	.20
❑	202	Ty Howington	.50	.20
❑	203	Andy Benes	.50	.20
❑	204	Luis Gonzalez	.60	.25
❑	205	Brian Moehler	.50	.20
❑	206	Harold Baines	.60	.25
❑	207	Pedro Astacio	.50	.20
❑	208	Cristian Guzman	.50	.20
❑	209	Kip Wells	.50	.20
❑	210	Frank Thomas	1.50	.60
❑	211	Jose Rosado	.50	.20
❑	212	Vernon Wells Black	.60	.25
❑	213	Bobby Higginson	.60	.25
❑	214	Juan Gonzalez	.60	.25
❑	215	Omar Vizquel	1.00	.40
❑	216	Bernie Williams	1.00	.40
❑	217	Aaron Sele	.50	.20
❑	218	Shawn Estes	.50	.20
❑	219	Roberto Alomar	1.00	.40
❑	220	Rick Ankiel	.50	.20
❑	221	Josh Kalinowski	.50	.20
❑	222	David Bell	.50	.20
❑	223	Keith Foulke	.60	.25
❑	224	Craig Biggio Black	1.00	.40
❑	225	Josh Axelson RC	.50	.20
❑	226	Scott Williamson	.50	.20
❑	227	Ron Belliard	.50	.20
❑	228	Chris Singleton	.50	.20
❑	229	Alex Serrano RC	.50	.20

❑ 230 Deivi Cruz .50 .20
❑ 231 Eric Munson .50 .20
❑ 232 Luis Castillo .50 .20
❑ 233 Edgar Martinez 1.00 .40
❑ 234 Jeff Shaw .50 .20
❑ 235 Jeromy Burnitz .60 .25
❑ 236 Richie Sexson .60 .25
❑ 237 Will Clark 1.00 .40
❑ 238 Ron Villone .50 .20
❑ 239 Kerry Wood .60 .25
❑ 240 Rich Aurilia .50 .20
❑ 241 Mo Vaughn Black .60 .25
❑ 242 Travis Fryman .60 .25
❑ 243 Manny Ramirez Sox 1.00 .40
❑ 244 Chris Stynes .50 .20
❑ 245 Ray Durham .60 .25
❑ 246 Juan Uribe RC 1.00 .40
❑ 247 Juan Guzman .50 .20
❑ 248 Lee Stevens .50 .20
❑ 249 Devon White .60 .25
❑ 250 Kyle Lohse RC 1.00 .40
❑ 251 Bryan Wolff .50 .20
❑ 252 Matt Galante RC .60 .25
❑ 253 Eric Young .50 .20
❑ 254 Freddy Garcia .60 .25
❑ 255 Jay Bell .60 .25
❑ 256 Steve Cox .50 .20
❑ 257 Torii Hunter .60 .25
❑ 258 Jose Canseco 1.00 .40
❑ 259 Brad Ausmus .60 .25
❑ 260 Jeff Cirillo .50 .20
❑ 261 Brad Penny .50 .20
❑ 262 Antonio Alfonseca .50 .20
❑ 263 Russ Branyan .50 .20
❑ 264 Chris Morris RC .50 .20
❑ 265 John Lackey .50 .20
❑ 266 Justin Wayne RC .60 .25
❑ 267 Brad Radke .60 .25
❑ 268 Todd Stottlemyre .50 .20
❑ 269 Mark Loretta .50 .20
❑ 270 Matt Williams .60 .25
❑ 271 Kenny Lofton .60 .25
❑ 272 Jeff D'Amico .50 .20
❑ 273 Jamie Moyer .60 .25
❑ 274 Darren Dreifort .50 .20
❑ 275 Denny Neagle .50 .20
❑ 276 Orlando Cabrera .60 .25
❑ 277 Chuck Finley .60 .25
❑ 278 Miguel Batista .60 .25
❑ 279 Carlos Beltran .60 .25
❑ 280 Eric Karros .60 .25
❑ 281 Mark Kotsay .60 .25
❑ 282 Ryan Dempster .50 .20
❑ 283 Barry Larkin 1.00 .40
❑ 284 Jeff Suppan .50 .20
❑ 285 Gary Sheffield .60 .25
❑ 286 Jose Valentin .50 .20
❑ 287 Robb Nen .60 .25
❑ 288 Chan Ho Park .60 .25
❑ 289 John Halama .50 .20
❑ 290 Steve Smyth RC .60 .25
❑ 291 Gerald Williams .50 .20
❑ 292 Preston Wilson .60 .25
❑ 293 Victor Hall RC .60 .25
❑ 294 Ben Sheets 1.00 .40
❑ 295 Eric Davis .60 .25
❑ 296 Kirk Rueter .50 .20
❑ 297 Chad Petty RC .50 .20
❑ 298 Kevin Millar .60 .25
❑ 299 Marvin Benard .50 .20
❑ 300 Vladimir Guerrero 1.50 .60
❑ 301 Livan Hernandez .60 .25
❑ 302 Travis Baptist RC .50 .20
❑ 303 Bill Mueller .60 .25
❑ 304 Mike Cameron .50 .20
❑ 305 Randy Johnson 1.50 .60
❑ 306 Alan Mahaffey RC .50 .20
❑ 307 Timo Perez UER .50 .20
❑ 308 Pokey Reese .50 .20
❑ 309 Ryan Rupe .50 .20
❑ 310 Carlos Lee .60 .25
❑ 311 Doug Glanville SP 5.00 2.00
❑ 312 Jay Payton SP 5.00 2.00
❑ 313 Troy O'Leary SP 5.00 2.00
❑ 314 Francisco Cordero SP 5.00 2.00
❑ 315 Rusty Greer SP 5.00 2.00
❑ 316 Cal Ripken SP 25.00 10.00
❑ 317 Ricky Ledee SP 5.00 2.00
❑ 318 Brian Daubach SP 5.00 2.00
❑ 319 Robin Ventura SP 5.00 2.00
❑ 320 Todd Zeile SP 5.00 2.00
❑ 321 Francisco Cordova SP 5.00 2.00
❑ 322 Henry Rodriguez SP 5.00 2.00
❑ 323 Pat Meares SP 5.00 2.00
❑ 324 Glendon Rusch SP 5.00 2.00
❑ 325 Keith Osik SP 5.00 2.00
❑ 326 Robert Keppel SP RC 5.00 2.00
❑ 327 Bobby Jones SP 5.00 2.00
❑ 328 Alex Ramirez SP 5.00 2.00
❑ 329 Robert Person SP 5.00 2.00
❑ 330 Ruben Mateo SP 5.00 2.00
❑ 331 Rob Bell SP 5.00 2.00
❑ 332 Carl Everett SP 5.00 2.00
❑ 333 Jason Schmidt SP 5.00 2.00
❑ 334 Scott Rolen SP 8.00 3.00
❑ 335 Jimmy Anderson SP 5.00 2.00
❑ 336 Bret Boone SP 5.00 2.00
❑ 337 Delino DeShields SP 5.00 2.00
❑ 338 Trevor Hoffman SP 5.00 2.00
❑ 339 Bob Abreu SP 5.00 2.00
❑ 340 Mike Williams SP 5.00 2.00
❑ 341 Mike Hampton SP 5.00 2.00
❑ 342 John Wetteland SP 5.00 2.00
❑ 343 Scott Erickson SP 5.00 2.00
❑ 344 Enrique Wilson SP 5.00 2.00
❑ 345 Tim Wakefield SP 5.00 2.00
❑ 346 Mike Lowell SP 5.00 2.00
❑ 347 Todd Pratt SP 5.00 2.00
❑ 348 Brook Fordyce SP 5.00 2.00
❑ 349 Benny Agbayani SP 5.00 2.00
❑ 350 Gabe Kapler SP 5.00 2.00
❑ 351 Sean Casey SP 5.00 2.00
❑ 352 Darren Oliver SP 5.00 2.00
❑ 353 Todd Ritchie SP 5.00 2.00
❑ 354 Kenny Rogers SP 5.00 2.00
❑ 355 Jason Kendall SP 5.00 2.00
❑ 356 John Vander Wal SP 5.00 2.00
❑ 357 Ramon Martinez SP 5.00 2.00
❑ 358 Edgardo Alfonzo SP 5.00 2.00
❑ 359 Phil Nevin SP 5.00 2.00
❑ 360 Albert Belle SP 5.00 2.00
❑ 361 Ruben Rivera SP 5.00 2.00
❑ 362 Pedro Martinez SP 8.00 3.00
❑ 363 Derek Lowe SP 5.00 2.00
❑ 364 Pat Burrell SP 5.00 2.00
❑ 365 Mike Mussina SP 8.00 3.00
❑ 366 Brady Anderson SP 5.00 2.00
❑ 367 Darren Lewis SP 5.00 2.00
❑ 368 Sidney Ponson SP 5.00 2.00
❑ 369 Adam Eaton SP 5.00 2.00
❑ 370 Eric Owens SP 5.00 2.00
❑ 371 Aaron Boone SP 5.00 2.00
❑ 372 Matt Clement SP 5.00 2.00
❑ 373 Derek Bell SP 5.00 2.00
❑ 374 Trot Nixon SP 5.00 2.00
❑ 375 Travis Lee SP 5.00 2.00
❑ 376 Mike Benjamin SP 5.00 2.00
❑ 377 Jeff Zimmerman SP 5.00 2.00
❑ 378 Mike Lieberthal SP 5.00 2.00
❑ 379 Rick Reed SP 5.00 2.00
❑ 380 Nomar Garciaparra SP 12.00 5.00
❑ 381 Omar Daal SP 5.00 2.00
❑ 382 Ryan Klesko SP 5.00 2.00
❑ 383 Rey Ordonez SP 5.00 2.00
❑ 384 Kevin Young SP 5.00 2.00
❑ 385 Rick Helling SP 5.00 2.00
❑ 386 Brian Giles SP 5.00 2.00
❑ 387 Tony Gwynn SP 10.00 4.00
❑ 388 Ed Sprague SP 5.00 2.00
❑ 389 J.R. House SP 5.00 2.00
❑ 390 Scott Hatteberg SP 5.00 2.00
❑ 391 John Valentin SP 5.00 2.00
❑ 392 Melvin Mora SP 5.00 2.00
❑ 393 Royce Clayton SP 5.00 2.00
❑ 394 Jeff Fassero SP 5.00 2.00
❑ 395 Manny Alexander SP 5.00 2.00
❑ 396 John Franco SP 5.00 2.00
❑ 397 Luis Alicea SP 5.00 2.00
❑ 398 Ivan Rodriguez SP 8.00 3.00
❑ 399 Kevin Jordan SP 5.00 2.00
❑ 400 Jose Offerman SP 5.00 2.00
❑ 401 Jeff Conine SP 5.00 2.00
❑ 402 Seth Etherton SP 5.00 2.00
❑ 403 Mike Bordick SP 5.00 2.00
❑ 404 Al Leiter SP 5.00 2.00
❑ 405 Mike Piazza SP 12.00 5.00
❑ 406 Armando Benitez SP 5.00 2.00
❑ 407 Warren Morris SP 5.00 2.00
❑ NNO 1952 Card Redemption EXCH
❑ NNO Replica Hat-Jsy EXCH

2002 Topps Heritage

❑ COMPLETE SET (440) 400.00 200.00
❑ COMP.SET w/o SP's (350) 80.00 40.00
❑ COMMON CARD (1-363) .50 .20
❑ COMMON SP (364-446) 5.00 2.00
❑ 1 Ichiro Suzuki SP 15.00 6.00
❑ 2 Darin Erstad .60 .25
❑ 3 Rod Beck .60 .25
❑ 4 Doug Mientkiewicz .60 .25
❑ 5 Mike Sweeney .60 .25
❑ 6 Roger Clemens 3.00 1.25
❑ 7 Jason Tyner .50 .20
❑ 8 Alex Gonzalez .50 .20
❑ 9 Eric Young .50 .20
❑ 10 Randy Johnson 1.50 .60
❑ 10N Randy Johnson Night SP 8.00 3.00
❑ 11 Aaron Sele .50 .20
❑ 12 Tony Clark .50 .20
❑ 13 C.C. Sabathia .60 .25
❑ 14 Melvin Mora .60 .25
❑ 15 Tim Hudson .60 .25
❑ 16 Ben Petrick .50 .20
❑ 17 Tom Glavine 1.00 .40
❑ 18 Jason Lane .60 .25
❑ 19 Larry Walker .60 .25
❑ 20 Mark Mulder .60 .25
❑ 21 Steve Finley .60 .25
❑ 22 Bengie Molina .50 .20
❑ 23 Rob Bell .50 .20
❑ 24 Nathan Haynes .50 .20
❑ 25 Rafael Furcal .60 .25
❑ 25N Rafael Furcal Night SP 5.00 2.00
❑ 26 Mike Mussina 1.00 .40
❑ 27 Paul LoDuca .60 .25
❑ 28 Torii Hunter .60 .25
❑ 29 Carlos Lee .60 .25
❑ 30 Jimmy Rollins .60 .25
❑ 31 Arthur Rhodes .50 .20
❑ 32 Ivan Rodriguez 1.00 .40
❑ 33 Wes Helms .50 .20
❑ 34 Cliff Floyd .60 .25
❑ 35 Julian Tavarez .50 .20
❑ 36 Mark McGwire 4.00 1.50
❑ 37 Chipper Jones SP 8.00 3.00
❑ 38 Denny Neagle .50 .20
❑ 39 Odalis Perez .50 .20
❑ 40 Antonio Alfonseca .50 .20
❑ 41 Edgar Renteria .60 .25
❑ 42 Troy Glaus .60 .25
❑ 43 Scott Brosius .60 .25
❑ 44 Abraham Nunez .50 .20
❑ 45 Jamey Wright .50 .20
❑ 46 Bobby Bonilla .60 .25
❑ 47 Ismael Valdes .50 .20
❑ 48 Chris Reitsma .50 .20
❑ 49 Neifi Perez .50 .20
❑ 50 Juan Cruz .50 .20
❑ 51 Kevin Brown .60 .25
❑ 52 Ben Grieve .50 .20

❑ 53 Alex Rodriguez SP 12.00 5.00
❑ 54 Charles Nagy .50 .20
❑ 55 Reggie Sanders .60 .25
❑ 56 Nelson Figueroa .50 .20
❑ 57 Felipe Lopez .50 .20
❑ 58 Bill Ortega .50 .20
❑ 59 Jeffrey Hammonds .60 .25
❑ 60 Johnny Estrada .50 .20
❑ 61 Bob Wickman .50 .20
❑ 62 Doug Glanville .50 .20
❑ 63 Jeff Cirillo .50 .20
❑ 63N Jeff Cirillo Night SP 5.00 2.00
❑ 64 Corey Patterson .50 .20
❑ 65 Aaron Myette .50 .20
❑ 66 Magglio Ordonez .60 .25
❑ 67 Ellis Burks .60 .25
❑ 68 Miguel Tejada .60 .25
❑ 69 John Olerud .60 .25
❑ 69N John Olerud Night SP 5.00 2.00
❑ 70 Greg Vaughn .50 .20
❑ 71 Andy Pettitte 1.00 .40
❑ 72 Mike Matheny .50 .20
❑ 73 Brandon Duckworth .50 .20
❑ 74 Scott Schoeneweis .50 .20
❑ 75 Mike Lowell .60 .25
❑ 76 Einar Diaz .50 .20
❑ 77 Tino Martinez 1.00 .40
❑ 78 Matt Williams .60 .25
❑ 79 Jason Young RC 1.00 .40
❑ 80 Nate Cornejo .50 .20
❑ 81 Andres Galarraga .60 .25
❑ 82 Bernie Williams SP 8.00 3.00
❑ 83 Ryan Klesko .60 .25
❑ 84 Dan Wilson .50 .20
❑ 85 Henry Pichardo RC 1.00 .40
❑ 86 Ray Durham .60 .25
❑ 87 Omar Daal .50 .20
❑ 88 Derrek Lee 1.00 .40
❑ 89 Al Leiter .60 .25
❑ 90 Darrin Fletcher .50 .20
❑ 91 Josh Beckett .60 .25
❑ 92 Johnny Damon 1.00 .40
❑ 92N Johnny Damon Night SP 8.00 3.00
❑ 93 Abraham Nunez .50 .20
❑ 94 Ricky Ledee .50 .20
❑ 95 Richie Sexson .60 .25
❑ 96 Adam Kennedy .50 .20
❑ 97 Raul Mondesi .60 .25
❑ 98 John Burkett .60 .25
❑ 99 Ben Sheets .60 .25
❑ 99N Ben Sheets Night SP 5.00 2.00
❑ 100 Preston Wilson .60 .25
❑ 100N Preston Wilson Night SP 5.00 2.00
❑ 101 Boof Bonser .50 .20
❑ 102 Shigetoshi Hasegawa .60 .25
❑ 103 Carlos Febles .50 .20
❑ 104 Jorge Posada SP 8.00 3.00
❑ 105 Michael Tucker .50 .20
❑ 106 Roberto Hernandez .60 .25
❑ 107 John Rodriguez RC 1.00 .40
❑ 108 Danny Graves .50 .20
❑ 109 Rich Aurilia .50 .20
❑ 110 Jon Lieber .50 .20
❑ 111 Tim Hummel RC 1.00 .40
❑ 112 J.T. Snow .60 .25
❑ 113 Kris Benson .50 .20
❑ 114 Derek Jeter 4.00 1.50
❑ 115 John Franco .60 .25
❑ 116 Matt Stairs .50 .20
❑ 117 Ben Davis .50 .20
❑ 118 Darryl Kile .60 .25
❑ 119 Mike Peeples RC 1.00 .40
❑ 120 Kevin Tapani .50 .20
❑ 121 Armando Benitez .50 .20
❑ 122 Damian Miller .50 .20
❑ 123 Jose Jimenez .50 .20
❑ 124 Pedro Astacio .50 .20
❑ 125 Marlyn Tisdale RC 1.00 .40
❑ 126 Deivi Cruz .50 .20
❑ 127 Paul O'Neill 1.00 .40
❑ 128 Jermaine Dye .60 .25
❑ 129 Marcus Giles .60 .25
❑ 130 Mark Loretta .50 .20
❑ 131 Garret Anderson .60 .25
❑ 132 Todd Ritchie .50 .20
❑ 133 Joe Crede .60 .25
❑ 134 Kevin Millwood .60 .25
❑ 135 Shane Reynolds .50 .20
❑ 136 Mark Grace 1.00 .40
❑ 137 Shannon Stewart .60 .25
❑ 138 Nick Neugebauer .50 .20
❑ 139 Nic Jackson RC 1.00 .40
❑ 140 Robb Nen UER .60 .25
❑ 141 Dmitri Young .60 .25
❑ 142 Kevin Appier .60 .25
❑ 143 Jack Cust .50 .20
❑ 144 Andres Torres .50 .20
❑ 145 Frank Thomas 1.50 .60
❑ 146 Jason Kendall .60 .25
❑ 147 Greg Maddux 2.50 1.00
❑ 148 David Justice .60 .25
❑ 149 Hideo Nomo 1.50 .60
❑ 150 Bret Boone .60 .25
❑ 151 Wade Miller .50 .20
❑ 152 Jeff Kent .60 .25
❑ 153 Scott Williamson .50 .20
❑ 154 Julio Lugo .50 .20
❑ 155 Bobby Higginson .60 .25
❑ 156 Geoff Jenkins .50 .20
❑ 157 Darren Dreifort .50 .20
❑ 158 Freddy Sanchez RC 3.00 1.25
❑ 159 Bud Smith .50 .20
❑ 160 Phil Nevin .60 .25
❑ 161 Cesar Izturis .50 .20
❑ 162 Sean Casey .60 .25
❑ 163 Jose Ortiz .50 .20
❑ 164 Brent Abernathy .50 .20
❑ 165 Kevin Young .50 .20
❑ 166 Daryle Ward .50 .20
❑ 167 Trevor Hoffman .60 .25
❑ 168 Rondell White .60 .25
❑ 169 Kip Wells .50 .20
❑ 170 John Vander Wal .50 .20
❑ 171 Jose Lima .50 .20
❑ 172 Wilton Guerrero .50 .20
❑ 173 Aaron Dean RC 1.00 .40
❑ 174 Rick Helling .50 .20
❑ 175 Juan Pierre .60 .25
❑ 176 Jay Bell .60 .25
❑ 177 Craig House .50 .20
❑ 178 David Bell .50 .20
❑ 179 Pat Burrell .60 .25
❑ 180 Eric Gagne .60 .25
❑ 181 Adam Pettyjohn .50 .20
❑ 182 Ugueth Urbina .50 .20
❑ 183 Peter Bergeron .50 .20
❑ 184 Adrian Gonzalez .50 .20
❑ 184N Adrian Gonzalez Night SP 5.00 2.00
❑ 185 Damion Easley .50 .20
❑ 186 Gookie Dawkins .50 .20
❑ 187 Matt Lawton .50 .20
❑ 188 Frank Catalanotto .50 .20
❑ 189 David Wells .60 .25
❑ 190 Roger Cedeno .50 .20
❑ 191 Brian Giles .60 .25
❑ 192 Julio Zuleta .50 .20
❑ 193 Timo Perez .50 .20
❑ 194 Billy Wagner .60 .25
❑ 195 Craig Counsell .50 .20
❑ 196 Bart Miadich .50 .20
❑ 197 Gary Sheffield .60 .25
❑ 198 Richard Hidalgo .50 .20
❑ 199 Juan Uribe .50 .20
❑ 200 Curt Schilling .60 .25
❑ 201 Javy Lopez .60 .25
❑ 202 Jimmy Haynes .50 .20
❑ 203 Jim Edmonds .60 .25
❑ 204 Pokey Reese .50 .20
❑ 204N Pokey Reese Night SP 5.00 2.00
❑ 205 Matt Clement .60 .25
❑ 206 Dean Palmer .60 .25
❑ 207 Nick Johnson .60 .25
❑ 208 Nate Espy RC 1.00 .40
❑ 209 Pedro Feliz .50 .20
❑ 210 Aaron Rowand .60 .25
❑ 211 Masato Yoshii .50 .20
❑ 212 Jose Cruz Jr. .50 .20
❑ 213 Paul Byrd .50 .20
❑ 214 Mark Phillips RC 1.00 .40
❑ 215 Benny Agbayani .50 .20
❑ 216 Frank Menechino .50 .20
❑ 217 John Flaherty .50 .20
❑ 218 Brian Boehringer .50 .20
❑ 219 Todd Hollandsworth .50 .20
❑ 220 Sammy Sosa SP 8.00 3.00
❑ 221 Steve Sparks .50 .20
❑ 222 Homer Bush .50 .20
❑ 223 Mike Hampton .60 .25
❑ 224 Bobby Abreu .60 .25
❑ 225 Barry Larkin 1.00 .40
❑ 226 Ryan Rupe .50 .20
❑ 227 Bubba Trammell .50 .20
❑ 228 Todd Zeile .60 .25
❑ 229 Jeff Shaw .50 .20
❑ 230 Alex Ochoa .50 .20
❑ 231 Orlando Cabrera .60 .25
❑ 232 Jeremy Giambi .50 .20
❑ 233 Tomo Ohka .50 .20
❑ 234 Luis Castillo .50 .20
❑ 235 Chris Holt .50 .20
❑ 236 Shawn Green .60 .25
❑ 237 Sidney Ponson .50 .20
❑ 238 Lee Stevens .50 .20
❑ 239 Hank Blalock 1.00 .40
❑ 240 Randy Winn .50 .20
❑ 241 Pedro Martinez 1.00 .40
❑ 242 Vinny Castilla .60 .25
❑ 243 Steve Karsay .50 .20
❑ 244 Barry Bonds SP 20.00 8.00
❑ 245 Jason Bere .50 .20
❑ 246 Scott Rolen 1.00 .40
❑ 246N Scott Rolen Night SP 8.00 3.00
❑ 247 Ryan Kohlmeier .50 .20
❑ 248 Kerry Wood .60 .25
❑ 249 Aramis Ramirez .60 .25
❑ 250 Lance Berkman .60 .25
❑ 251 Omar Vizquel 1.00 .40
❑ 252 Juan Encarnacion .50 .20
❑ 253 Does Not Exist
❑ 254 David Segui .50 .20
❑ 255 Brian Anderson .50 .20
❑ 256 Jay Payton .50 .20
❑ 257 Mark Grudzielanek .50 .20
❑ 258 Jimmy Anderson .50 .20
❑ 259 Eric Valent .50 .20
❑ 260 Chad Durbin .50 .20
❑ 261 Does Not Exist
❑ 262 Alex Gonzalez .50 .20
❑ 263 Scott Dunn .50 .20
❑ 264 Scott Elarton .50 .20
❑ 265 Tom Gordon .50 .20
❑ 266 Moises Alou .60 .25
❑ 267 Does Not Exist
❑ 268 Does Not Exist
❑ 269 Mark Buehrle .60 .25
❑ 270 Jerry Hairston .50 .20
❑ 271 Does Not Exist
❑ 272 Luke Prokopec .50 .20
❑ 273 Graeme Lloyd .50 .20
❑ 274 Bret Prinz .50 .20
❑ 275 Does Not Exist
❑ 276 Chris Carpenter .60 .25
❑ 277 Ryan Minor .50 .20
❑ 278 Jeff D'Amico .50 .20
❑ 279 Raul Ibanez .50 .20
❑ 280 Joe Mays .50 .20
❑ 281 Livan Hernandez .60 .25
❑ 282 Robin Ventura .60 .25
❑ 283 Gabe Kapler .60 .25
❑ 284 Tony Batista .50 .20
❑ 285 Ramon Hernandez .50 .20
❑ 286 Craig Paquette .50 .20
❑ 287 Mark Kotsay .60 .25
❑ 288 Mike Lieberthal .60 .25
❑ 289 Joe Borchard .50 .20
❑ 290 Cristian Guzman .50 .20
❑ 291 Craig Biggio 1.00 .40
❑ 292 Joaquin Benoit .50 .20
❑ 293 Ken Caminiti .60 .25
❑ 294 Sean Burroughs .50 .20
❑ 295 Eric Karros .60 .25
❑ 296 Eric Chavez .60 .25
❑ 297 LaTroy Hawkins .50 .20
❑ 298 Alfonso Soriano .60 .25
❑ 299 John Smoltz 1.00 .40
❑ 300 Adam Dunn .60 .25
❑ 301 Ryan Dempster .50 .20
❑ 302 Travis Hafner .60 .25

❑	303 Russell Branyan	.50	.20
❑	304 Dustin Hermanson	.50	.20
❑	305 Jim Thome	1.00	.40
❑	306 Carlos Beltran	.60	.25
❑	307 Jason Botts RC	.60	.25
❑	308 David Cone	.60	.25
❑	309 Ivanon Coffie	.50	.20
❑	310 Brian Jordan	.60	.25
❑	311 Todd Walker	.50	.20
❑	312 Jeromy Burnitz	.60	.25
❑	313 Tony Armas Jr.	.50	.20
❑	314 Jeff Conine	.60	.25
❑	315 Todd Jones	.50	.20
❑	316 Roy Oswalt	.60	.25
❑	317 Aubrey Huff	.60	.25
❑	318 Josh Fogg	.50	.20
❑	319 Jose Vidro	.50	.20
❑	320 Jace Brewer	.50	.20
❑	321 Mike Redmond	.50	.20
❑	322 Noochie Varner RC	1.00	.40
❑	323 Russ Ortiz	.50	.20
❑	324 Edgardo Alfonzo	.50	.20
❑	325 Ruben Sierra	.60	.25
❑	326 Calvin Murray	.50	.20
❑	327 Marlon Anderson	.50	.20
❑	328 Albie Lopez	.50	.20
❑	329 Chris Gomez	.50	.20
❑	330 Fernando Tatis	.50	.20
❑	331 Stubby Clapp	.50	.20
❑	332 Rickey Henderson	1.50	.60
❑	333 Brad Radke	.60	.25
❑	334 Brent Mayne	.50	.20
❑	335 Cory Lidle	.50	.20
❑	336 Edgar Martinez	1.00	.40
❑	337 Aaron Boone	.60	.25
❑	338 Jay Witasick	.50	.20
❑	339 Benito Santiago	.60	.25
❑	340 Jose Mercedes	.50	.20
❑	341 Fernando Vina	.50	.20
❑	342 A.J. Pierzynski	.60	.25
❑	343 Jeff Bagwell	1.00	.40
❑	344 Brian Bohanon	.50	.20
❑	345 Adrian Beltre	.60	.25
❑	346 Troy Percival	.60	.25
❑	347 Napoleon Calzado RC	1.00	.40
❑	348 Ruben Rivera	.50	.20
❑	349 Rafael Soriano	.50	.20
❑	350 Damian Jackson	.50	.20
❑	351 Joe Randa	.60	.25
❑	352 Chan Ho Park	.60	.25
❑	353 Dante Bichette	.60	.25
❑	354 Bartolo Colon	.60	.25
❑	355 Jason Bay RC	5.00	2.00
❑	356 Shea Hillenbrand	.60	.25
❑	357 Matt Morris	.60	.25
❑	358 Brad Penny	.50	.20
❑	359 Mark Quinn	.50	.20
❑	360 Marquis Grissom	.60	.25
❑	361 Henry Blanco	.50	.20
❑	362 Billy Koch	.50	.20
❑	363 Mike Cameron	.50	.20
❑	364 Albert Pujols SP	15.00	6.00
❑	365 Paul Konerko SP	5.00	2.00
❑	366 Eric Milton SP	5.00	2.00
❑	367 Nick Bierbrodt SP	5.00	2.00
❑	368 Rafael Palmeiro SP	8.00	3.00
❑	369 Jorge Padilla SP RC	5.00	2.00
❑	370 Jason Giambi Yankees SP	5.00	2.00
❑	371 Mike Piazza SP	12.00	5.00
❑	372 Alex Cora SP	5.00	2.00
❑	373 Todd Helton SP	8.00	3.00
❑	374 Juan Gonzalez SP	5.00	2.00
❑	375 Mariano Rivera SP	8.00	3.00
❑	376 Jason LaRue SP	5.00	2.00
❑	377 Tony Gwynn SP	10.00	4.00
❑	378 Wilson Betemit SP	5.00	2.00
❑	379 J.J. Trujillo SP RC	5.00	2.00
❑	380 Brad Ausmus SP	5.00	2.00
❑	381 Chris George SP	5.00	2.00
❑	382 Jose Canseco SP	8.00	3.00
❑	383 Ramon Ortiz SP	5.00	2.00
❑	384 John Rocker SP	5.00	2.00
❑	385 Rey Ordonez SP	5.00	2.00
❑	386 Ken Griffey Jr. SP	12.00	5.00
❑	387 Juan Pena SP	5.00	2.00
❑	388 Michael Barrett SP	5.00	2.00
❑	389 J.D. Drew SP	5.00	2.00
❑	390 Corey Koskie SP	5.00	2.00
❑	391 Vernon Wells SP	5.00	2.00
❑	392 Juan Tolentino SP RC	5.00	2.00
❑	393 Luis Gonzalez SP	5.00	2.00
❑	394 Terrence Long SP	5.00	2.00
❑	395 Travis Lee SP	5.00	2.00
❑	396 Earl Snyder SP RC	5.00	2.00
❑	397 Nomar Garciaparra SP	12.00	5.00
❑	398 Jason Schmidt SP	5.00	2.00
❑	399 David Espinosa SP	5.00	2.00
❑	400 Steve Green SP	5.00	2.00
❑	401 Jack Wilson SP	5.00	2.00
❑	402 Chris Tritle SP RC	5.00	2.00
❑	403 Angel Berroa SP	5.00	2.00
❑	404 Josh Towers SP	5.00	2.00
❑	405 Andruw Jones SP	8.00	3.00
❑	406 Brent Butler SP	5.00	2.00
❑	407 Craig Kuzmic SP	5.00	2.00
❑	408 Derek Bell SP	5.00	2.00
❑	409 Eric Glaser SP RC	5.00	2.00
❑	410 Joel Pineiro SP	5.00	2.00
❑	411 Alexis Gomez SP	5.00	2.00
❑	412 Mike Rivera SP	5.00	2.00
❑	413 Shawn Estes SP	5.00	2.00
❑	414 Milton Bradley SP	5.00	2.00
❑	415 Carl Everett SP	5.00	2.00
❑	416 Kazuhiro Sasaki SP	5.00	2.00
❑	417 Tony Fontana SP RC	5.00	2.00
❑	418 Josh Pearce SP	5.00	2.00
❑	419 Gary Matthews Jr. SP	5.00	2.00
❑	420 Raymond Cabrera SP RC	5.00	2.00
❑	421 Joe Kennedy SP	5.00	2.00
❑	422 Jason Maule SP RC	5.00	2.00
❑	423 Casey Fossum SP	5.00	2.00
❑	424 Christian Parker SP	5.00	2.00
❑	425 Laynce Nix SP RC	10.00	4.00
❑	426 Byung-Hyun Kim SP	5.00	2.00
❑	427 Freddy Garcia SP	5.00	2.00
❑	428 Herbert Perry SP	5.00	2.00
❑	429 Jason Marquis SP	5.00	2.00
❑	430 Sandy Alomar Jr. SP	5.00	2.00
❑	431 Roberto Alomar SP	8.00	3.00
❑	432 Tsuyoshi Shinjo SP	5.00	2.00
❑	433 Tim Wakefield SP	5.00	2.00
❑	434 Robert Fick SP	5.00	2.00
❑	435 Vladimir Guerrero SP	8.00	3.00
❑	436 Jose Mesa SP	5.00	2.00
❑	437 Scott Spiezio SP	5.00	2.00
❑	438 Jose Hernandez SP	5.00	2.00
❑	439 Jose Acevedo SP	5.00	2.00
❑	440 Brian West SP RC	5.00	2.00
❑	441 Barry Zito SP	5.00	2.00
❑	442 Luis Maza SP	5.00	2.00
❑	443 Marlon Byrd SP	5.00	2.00
❑	444 A.J. Burnett SP	5.00	2.00
❑	445 Dee Brown SP	5.00	2.00
❑	446 Carlos Delgado SP	5.00	2.00
❑	NNO 1953 Repurchased EXCH.		

2003 Topps Heritage

❑	COMPLETE SET (450)	300.00	175.00
❑	COMP.SET w/o SP's (350)	80.00	40.00
❑	COMMON CARD	.50	.20
❑	COMMON RC	1.00	.40
❑	COMMON SP	5.00	2.00
❑	COMMON SP RC	5.00	2.00
❑	1A Alex Rodriguez Red	2.50	1.00
❑	1B Alex Rodriguez Black SP	12.00	5.00
❑	2 Jose Cruz Jr.	.50	.20
❑	3 Ichiro Suzuki SP	15.00	6.00
❑	4 Rich Aurilia	.50	.20
❑	5 Trevor Hoffman	.60	.25
❑	6A Brian Giles New Logo	.60	.25
❑	6B Brian Giles Old Logo SP	5.00	2.00
❑	7A Albert Pujols Orange	3.00	1.25
❑	7B Albert Pujols Black SP	15.00	6.00
❑	8 Vicente Padilla	.50	.20
❑	9 Bobby Crosby	.60	.25
❑	10A Derek Jeter New Logo	4.00	1.50
❑	10B Derek Jeter Old Logo SP	15.00	6.00
❑	11A Pat Burrell New Logo	.60	.25
❑	11B Pat Burrell Old Logo SP	5.00	2.00
❑	12 Armando Benitez	.50	.20
❑	13 Javier Vazquez	.60	.25
❑	14 Justin Morneau	.60	.25
❑	15 Doug Mientkiewicz	.60	.25
❑	16 Kevin Brown	.60	.25
❑	17 Alexis Gomez	.50	.20
❑	18A Lance Berkman Blue	.60	.25
❑	18B Lance Berkman Black SP	5.00	2.00
❑	19 Adrian Gonzalez	.50	.20
❑	20A Todd Helton Green	1.00	.40
❑	20B Todd Helton Black SP	8.00	3.00
❑	21 Carlos Pena	.50	.20
❑	22 Matt Lawton	.50	.20
❑	23 Elmer Dessens	.50	.20
❑	24 Hee Seop Choi	.50	.20
❑	25 Chris Duncan SP RC	12.00	5.00
❑	26 Ugueth Urbina	.50	.20
❑	27A Rodrigo Lopez New Logo	.50	.20
❑	27B Rodrigo Lopez Old Logo SP	5.00	2.00
❑	28 Damian Moss	.50	.20
❑	29 Steve Finley	.60	.25
❑	30A Sammy Sosa New Logo	1.50	.60
❑	30B Sammy Sosa Old Logo SP	8.00	3.00
❑	31 Kevin Cash	.50	.20
❑	32 Kenny Rogers	.60	.25
❑	33 Ben Grieve	.50	.20
❑	34 Jason Simontacchi	.50	.20
❑	35 Shin-Soo Choo	.50	.20
❑	36 Freddy Garcia	.60	.25
❑	37 Jesse Foppert	.50	.20
❑	38 Tony LaRussa MG	.60	.25
❑	39 Mark Kotsay	.60	.25
❑	40 Barry Zito	.60	.25
❑	41 Josh Fogg	.50	.20
❑	42 Marlon Byrd	.50	.20
❑	43 Marcus Thames	.50	.20
❑	44 Al Leiter	.60	.25
❑	45 Michael Barrett	.50	.20
❑	46 Jake Peavy	.60	.25
❑	47 Dustan Mohr	.50	.20
❑	48 Alex Sanchez	.50	.20
❑	49 Chin-Feng Chen	.60	.25
❑	50A Kazuhisa Ishii Blue	.60	.25
❑	50B Kazuhisa Ishii Black SP	5.00	2.00
❑	51 Carlos Beltran	.60	.25
❑	52 Franklin Gutierrez RC	1.00	.40
❑	53 Miguel Cabrera	1.50	.60
❑	54 Roger Clemens	3.00	1.25
❑	55 Juan Cruz	.50	.20
❑	56 Jason Young	.50	.20
❑	57 Alex Herrera	.50	.20
❑	58 Aaron Boone	.60	.25
❑	59 Mark Buehrle	.60	.25
❑	60 Larry Walker	.60	.25
❑	61 Morgan Ensberg	.60	.25
❑	62 Barry Larkin	1.00	.40
❑	63 Joe Borchard	.50	.20
❑	64 Jason Dubois	.50	.20
❑	65 Shea Hillenbrand	.60	.25
❑	66 Jay Gibbons	.50	.20
❑	67 Vinny Castilla	.60	.25
❑	68 Jeff Mathis	.50	.20
❑	69 Curt Schilling	.60	.25
❑	70 Garret Anderson	.60	.25
❑	71 Josh Phelps	.50	.20
❑	72 Chan Ho Park	.60	.25
❑	73 Edgar Renteria	.60	.25
❑	74 Kazuhiro Sasaki	.60	.25
❑	75 Lloyd McClendon MG	.50	.20
❑	76 Jon Lieber	.50	.20
❑	77 Rolando Viera	.50	.20

❑ 78 Jeff Conine .60 .25
❑ 79 Kevin Millwood .60 .25
❑ 80A Randy Johnson Green 1.50 .60
❑ 80B Randy Johnson Black SP 12.00 5.00
❑ 81 Troy Percival .60 .25
❑ 82 Cliff Floyd .60 .25
❑ 83 Tony Graffanino .50 .20
❑ 84 Austin Kearns .50 .20
❑ 85 Manuel Ramirez SP RC 8.00 3.00
❑ 86 Jim Tracy MG .50 .20
❑ 87 Rondell White .60 .25
❑ 88 Trot Nixon .60 .25
❑ 89 Carlos Lee .60 .25
❑ 90 Mike Lowell .60 .25
❑ 91 Raul Ibanez .50 .20
❑ 92 Ricardo Rodriguez .50 .20
❑ 93 Ben Sheets .60 .25
❑ 94 Jason Perry SP RC 8.00 3.00
❑ 95 Mark Teixeira 1.00 .40
❑ 96 Brad Fullmer .50 .20
❑ 97 Casey Kotchman .60 .25
❑ 98 Craig Counsell .50 .20
❑ 99 Jason Marquis .50 .20
❑ 100A N.Garciaparra New Logo 2.50 1.00
❑ 100B N.Garciaparra Old Logo SP 12.00 5.00
❑ 101 Ed Rogers .50 .20
❑ 102 Wilson Betemit .50 .20
❑ 103 Wayne Lydon RC 1.00 .40
❑ 104 Jack Cust .50 .20
❑ 105 Derrek Lee 1.00 .40
❑ 106 Jim Kavourias .50 .20
❑ 107 Joe Randa .60 .25
❑ 108 Taylor Buchholz .50 .20
❑ 109 Gabe Kapler .60 .25
❑ 110 Preston Wilson .60 .25
❑ 111 Craig Biggio 1.00 .40
❑ 112 Paul Lo Duca .60 .25
❑ 113 Eddie Guardado .50 .20
❑ 114 Andres Galarraga 1.00 .40
❑ 115 Edgardo Alfonzo .50 .20
❑ 116 Robin Ventura .60 .25
❑ 117 Jeremy Giambi .50 .20
❑ 118 Ray Durham .60 .25
❑ 119 Mariano Rivera 1.50 .60
❑ 120 Jimmy Rollins .60 .25
❑ 121 Dennis Tankersley .50 .20
❑ 122 Jason Schmidt .60 .25
❑ 123 Bret Boone .60 .25
❑ 124 Josh Hamilton 1.00 .40
❑ 125 Scott Rolen 1.00 .40
❑ 126 Steve Cox .50 .20
❑ 127 Larry Bowa MG .60 .25
❑ 128 Adam LaRoche SP 5.00 2.00
❑ 129 Ryan Klesko .60 .25
❑ 130 Tim Hudson .60 .25
❑ 131 Brandon Claussen .50 .20
❑ 132 Craig Brazell SP RC 5.00 2.00
❑ 133 Grady Little MG .50 .20
❑ 134 Jarrod Washburn .50 .20
❑ 135 Lyle Overbay .50 .20
❑ 136 John Burkett .50 .20
❑ 137 Daryl Clark RC 1.00 .40
❑ 138 Kirk Rueter .50 .20
❑ 139A Mauer Brothers Green 1.50 .60
❑ 139B Mauer Brothers Black SP 10.00 4.00
❑ 140 Troy Glaus .60 .25
❑ 141 Trey Hodges SP 5.00 2.00
❑ 142 Dallas McPherson .60 .25
❑ 143 Art Howe MG .50 .20
❑ 144 Jesus Cota .50 .20
❑ 145 J.R. House .50 .20
❑ 146 Reggie Sanders .60 .25
❑ 147 Clint Nageotte .50 .20
❑ 148 Jim Edmonds .60 .25
❑ 149 Carl Crawford .60 .25
❑ 150A Mike Piazza Blue 2.50 1.00
❑ 150B Mike Piazza Black SP 12.00 5.00
❑ 151 Seung Song .50 .20
❑ 152 Roberto Hernandez .60 .25
❑ 153 Marquis Grissom .60 .25
❑ 154 Billy Wagner .60 .25
❑ 155 Josh Beckett .60 .25
❑ 156A Randall Simon New Logo .50 .20
❑ 156B Randall Simon Old Logo SP 5.002.00
❑ 157 Ben Broussard .50 .20
❑ 158 Russell Branyan .50 .20
❑ 159 Frank Thomas 1.50 .60
❑ 160 Alex Escobar .50 .20
❑ 161 Mark Bellhorn .60 .25
❑ 162 Melvin Mora .60 .25
❑ 163 Andruw Jones 1.00 .40
❑ 164 Danny Bautista .50 .20
❑ 165 Ramon Ortiz .50 .20
❑ 166 Wily Mo Pena .60 .25
❑ 167 Jose Jimenez .50 .20
❑ 168 Mark Redman .50 .20
❑ 169 Angel Berroa .50 .20
❑ 170 Andy Marte SP RC 12.00 5.00
❑ 171 Juan Gonzalez .60 .25
❑ 172 Fernando Vina .50 .20
❑ 173 Joel Pineiro .50 .20
❑ 174 Boof Bonser .50 .20
❑ 175 Bernie Castro SP RC 5.00 2.00
❑ 176 Bobby Cox MG .50 .20
❑ 177 Jeff Kent .60 .25
❑ 178 Oliver Perez .60 .25
❑ 179 Chase Utley 1.50 .60
❑ 180 Mark Mulder .60 .25
❑ 181 Bobby Abreu .60 .25
❑ 182 Ramiro Mendoza .50 .20
❑ 183 Aaron Heilman .50 .20
❑ 184 A.J. Pierzynski .60 .25
❑ 185 Eric Gagne .60 .25
❑ 186 Kirk Saarloos .50 .20
❑ 187 Ron Gardenhire MG .50 .20
❑ 188 Dmitri Young .60 .25
❑ 189 Todd Zeile .60 .25
❑ 190A Jim Thome New Logo 1.00 .40
❑ 190B Jim Thome Old Logo SP 8.00 3.00
❑ 191 Cliff Lee .50 .20
❑ 192 Matt Morris .60 .25
❑ 193 Robert Fick .50 .20
❑ 194 C.C. Sabathia .60 .25
❑ 195 Alexis Rios .60 .25
❑ 196 D'Angelo Jimenez .50 .20
❑ 197 Edgar Martinez 1.00 .40
❑ 198 Robb Nen .60 .25
❑ 199 Taggert Bozied .50 .20
❑ 200 Vladimir Guerrero SP 8.00 3.00
❑ 201 Walter Young SP 5.00 2.00
❑ 202 Brendan Harris RC 1.00 .40
❑ 203 Mike Hargrove MG .50 .20
❑ 204 Vernon Wells .60 .25
❑ 205 Hank Blalock .60 .25
❑ 206 Mike Cameron .50 .20
❑ 207 Tony Batista .50 .20
❑ 208 Matt Williams .60 .25
❑ 209 Tony Womack .50 .20
❑ 210 Ramon Nivar-Martinez RC 1.00 .40
❑ 211 Aaron Sele .50 .20
❑ 212 Mark Grace 1.00 .40
❑ 213 Joe Crede .60 .25
❑ 214 Ryan Dempster .50 .20
❑ 215 Omar Vizquel 1.00 .40
❑ 216 Juan Pierre .60 .25
❑ 217 Denny Bautista .50 .20
❑ 218 Chuck Knoblauch .60 .25
❑ 219 Eric Karros .60 .25
❑ 220 Victor Diaz .60 .25
❑ 221 Jacque Jones .60 .25
❑ 222 Jose Vidro .50 .20
❑ 223 Joe McEwing .50 .20
❑ 224 Nick Johnson .60 .25
❑ 225 Eric Chavez .60 .25
❑ 226 Jose Mesa .50 .20
❑ 227 Aramis Ramirez .60 .25
❑ 228 John Lackey .50 .20
❑ 229 David Bell .50 .20
❑ 230 John Olerud .60 .25
❑ 231 Tino Martinez 1.00 .40
❑ 232 Randy Winn .50 .20
❑ 233 Todd Hollandsworth .50 .20
❑ 234 Ruddy Lugo RC 1.00 .40
❑ 235 Carlos Delgado .60 .25
❑ 236 Chris Narveson .50 .20
❑ 237 Tim Salmon 1.00 .40
❑ 238 Orlando Palmeiro .50 .20
❑ 239 Jeff Clark SP RC 5.00 2.00
❑ 240 Byung-Hyun Kim .60 .25
❑ 241 Mike Remlinger .50 .20
❑ 242 Johnny Damon 1.00 .40
❑ 243 Corey Patterson .50 .20
❑ 244 Paul Konerko .60 .25
❑ 245 Danny Graves .50 .20
❑ 246 Ellis Burks .60 .25
❑ 247 Gavin Floyd .50 .20
❑ 248 Jaime Bubela RC 1.00 .40
❑ 249 Sean Burroughs .50 .20
❑ 250 Alex Rodriguez SP 12.00 5.00
❑ 251 Gabe Gross .50 .20
❑ 252 Rafael Palmeiro 1.00 .40
❑ 253 Dewon Brazelton .50 .20
❑ 254 Jimmy Journell .50 .20
❑ 255 Rafael Soriano .50 .20
❑ 256 Jerome Williams .50 .20
❑ 257 Xavier Nady .50 .20
❑ 258 Mike Williams .50 .20
❑ 259 Randy Wolf .50 .20
❑ 260A Miguel Tejada Orange .60 .25
❑ 260B Miguel Tejada Black SP 5.00 2.00
❑ 261 Juan Rivera .50 .20
❑ 262 Rey Ordonez .50 .20
❑ 263 Bartolo Colon .60 .25
❑ 264 Eric Milton .50 .20
❑ 265 Jeffrey Hammonds .50 .20
❑ 266 Odalis Perez .50 .20
❑ 267 Mike Sweeney .60 .25
❑ 268 Richard Hidalgo .50 .20
❑ 269 Alex Gonzalez .50 .20
❑ 270 Aaron Cook .50 .20
❑ 271 Earl Snyder .50 .20
❑ 272 Todd Walker .50 .20
❑ 273 Aaron Rowand .60 .25
❑ 274 Matt Clement .60 .25
❑ 275 Anastacio Martinez .50 .20
❑ 276 Mike Bordick .60 .25
❑ 277 John Smoltz 1.00 .40
❑ 278 Scott Hairston .50 .20
❑ 279 David Eckstein .60 .25
❑ 280 Shannon Stewart .60 .25
❑ 281 Carl Everett .60 .25
❑ 282 Aubrey Huff .60 .25
❑ 283 Mike Mussina 1.00 .40
❑ 284 Ruben Sierra .60 .25
❑ 285 Russ Ortiz .50 .20
❑ 286 Brian Lawrence .50 .20
❑ 287 Kip Wells .50 .20
❑ 288 Placido Polanco .50 .20
❑ 289 Ted Lilly .50 .20
❑ 290 Andy Pettitte 1.00 .40
❑ 291 John Buck .50 .20
❑ 292 Orlando Cabrera .60 .25
❑ 293 Cristian Guzman .50 .20
❑ 294 Ruben Quevedo .50 .20
❑ 295 Cesar Izturis .50 .20
❑ 296 Ryan Ludwick .50 .20
❑ 297 Roy Oswalt .60 .25
❑ 298 Jason Stokes .50 .20
❑ 299 Mike Hampton .60 .25
❑ 300 Pedro Martinez 1.00 .40
❑ 301 Nic Jackson .50 .20
❑ 302A Magglio Ordonez New Logo .60 .25
❑ 302B Magglio Ordonez Old Logo SP 5.00 2.00
❑ 303 Manny Ramirez 1.00 .40
❑ 304 Jorge Julio .50 .20
❑ 305 Javy Lopez .60 .25
❑ 306 Roy Halladay .60 .25
❑ 307 Kevin Mench .50 .20
❑ 308 Jason Isringhausen .60 .25
❑ 309 Carlos Guillen .60 .25
❑ 310 Tsuyoshi Shinjo .60 .25
❑ 311 Phil Nevin .60 .25
❑ 312 Pokey Reese .50 .20
❑ 313 Jorge Padilla .50 .20
❑ 314 Jermaine Dye .60 .25
❑ 315 David Wells .60 .25
❑ 316 Mo Vaughn .60 .25
❑ 317 Bernie Williams 1.00 .40
❑ 318 Michael Restovich .50 .20
❑ 319 Jose Hernandez .50 .20
❑ 320 Richie Sexson .60 .25
❑ 321 Daryle Ward .50 .20
❑ 322 Luis Castillo .50 .20
❑ 323 Rene Reyes .50 .20
❑ 324 Victor Martinez 1.00 .40
❑ 325A Adam Dunn New Logo .60 .25
❑ 325B Adam Dunn Old Logo SP 5.00 2.00
❑ 326 Corwin Malone .50 .20

- ❑ 327 Kerry Wood .60 .25
- ❑ 328 Rickey Henderson 1.50 .60
- ❑ 329 Marty Cordova .50 .20
- ❑ 330 Greg Maddux 2.50 1.00
- ❑ 331 Miguel Batista .50 .20
- ❑ 332 Chris Bootcheck .50 .20
- ❑ 333 Carlos Baerga .50 .20
- ❑ 334 Antonio Alfonseca .50 .20
- ❑ 335 Shane Halter .50 .20
- ❑ 336 Juan Encarnacion .50 .20
- ❑ 337 Tom Gordon .50 .20
- ❑ 338 Hideo Nomo 1.50 .60
- ❑ 339 Torii Hunter .60 .25
- ❑ 340A Alfonso Soriano Yellow .60 .25
- ❑ 340B Alfonso Soriano Black SP 5.00 2.00
- ❑ 341 Roberto Alomar 1.00 .40
- ❑ 342 David Justice .60 .25
- ❑ 343 Mike Lieberthal .60 .25
- ❑ 344 Jeff Weaver .50 .20
- ❑ 345 Timo Perez .50 .20
- ❑ 346 Travis Lee .50 .20
- ❑ 347 Sean Casey .60 .25
- ❑ 348 Willie Harris .50 .20
- ❑ 349 Derek Lowe .60 .25
- ❑ 350 Tom Glavine 1.00 .40
- ❑ 351 Eric Hinske .50 .20
- ❑ 352 Rocco Baldelli .60 .25
- ❑ 353 J.D. Drew .60 .25
- ❑ 354 Jamie Moyer .60 .25
- ❑ 355 Todd Linden .50 .20
- ❑ 356 Benito Santiago .60 .25
- ❑ 357 Brad Baker .50 .20
- ❑ 358 Alex Gonzalez .50 .20
- ❑ 359 Brandon Duckworth .50 .20
- ❑ 360 John Rheinecker .50 .20
- ❑ 361 Orlando Hernandez .60 .25
- ❑ 362 Pedro Astacio .50 .20
- ❑ 363 Brad Wilkerson .50 .20
- ❑ 364 David Ortiz SP 8.00 3.00
- ❑ 365 Geoff Jenkins SP 5.00 2.00
- ❑ 366 Brian Jordan SP 5.00 2.00
- ❑ 367 Paul Byrd SP 5.00 2.00
- ❑ 368 Jason Lane SP 5.00 2.00
- ❑ 369 Jeff Bagwell SP 8.00 3.00
- ❑ 370 Bobby Higginson SP 5.00 2.00
- ❑ 371 Juan Uribe SP 5.00 2.00
- ❑ 372 Lee Stevens SP 5.00 2.00
- ❑ 373 Jimmy Haynes SP 5.00 2.00
- ❑ 374 Jose Valentin SP 5.00 2.00
- ❑ 375 Ken Griffey Jr. SP 12.00 5.00
- ❑ 376 Barry Bonds SP 20.00 8.00
- ❑ 377 Gary Matthews Jr. SP 5.00 2.00
- ❑ 378 Gary Sheffield SP 5.00 2.00
- ❑ 379 Rick Helling SP 5.00 2.00
- ❑ 380 Junior Spivey SP 5.00 2.00
- ❑ 381 Francisco Rodriguez SP 5.00 2.00
- ❑ 382 Chipper Jones SP 8.00 3.00
- ❑ 383 Orlando Hudson SP 5.00 2.00
- ❑ 384 Ivan Rodriguez SP 8.00 3.00
- ❑ 385 Chris Snelling SP 5.00 2.00
- ❑ 386 Kenny Lofton SP 5.00 2.00
- ❑ 387 Eric Cyr SP 5.00 2.00
- ❑ 388 Jason Kendall SP 5.00 2.00
- ❑ 389 Marlon Anderson SP 5.00 2.00
- ❑ 390 Billy Koch SP 5.00 2.00
- ❑ 392 Jose Reyes SP 5.00 2.00
- ❑ 393 Fernando Tatis SP 5.00 2.00
- ❑ 394 Michael Cuddyer SP 5.00 2.00
- ❑ 395 Mark Prior SP 8.00 3.00
- ❑ 396 Dontrelle Willis SP 8.00 3.00
- ❑ 397 Jay Payton SP 5.00 2.00
- ❑ 398 Brandon Phillips SP 5.00 2.00
- ❑ 399 Dustin Moseley SP RC 5.00 2.00
- ❑ 400 Jason Giambi SP 5.00 2.00
- ❑ 401 John Mabry SP 5.00 2.00
- ❑ 402 Ron Gant SP 5.00 2.00
- ❑ 403 J.T. Snow SP 5.00 2.00
- ❑ 404 Jeff Cirillo SP 5.00 2.00
- ❑ 405 Darin Erstad SP 5.00 2.00
- ❑ 406 Luis Gonzalez SP 5.00 2.00
- ❑ 407 Marcus Giles SP 5.00 2.00
- ❑ 408 Brian Daubach SP 5.00 2.00
- ❑ 409 Moises Alou SP 5.00 2.00
- ❑ 410 Raul Mondesi SP 5.00 2.00
- ❑ 411 Adrian Beltre SP 5.00 2.00
- ❑ 412 A.J. Burnett SP 5.00 2.00
- ❑ 413 Jason Jennings SP 5.00 2.00
- ❑ 414 Edwin Almonte SP 5.00 2.00
- ❑ 415 Fred McGriff SP 8.00 3.00
- ❑ 416 Tim Raines Jr. SP 5.00 2.00
- ❑ 417 Rafael Furcal SP 5.00 2.00
- ❑ 418 Erubiel Durazo SP 5.00 2.00
- ❑ 419 Drew Henson SP 5.00 2.00
- ❑ 420 Kevin Appier SP 5.00 2.00
- ❑ 421 Chad Tracy SP 5.00 2.00
- ❑ 422 Adam Wainwright SP 5.00 2.00
- ❑ 423 Choo Freeman SP 5.00 2.00
- ❑ 424 Sandy Alomar Jr. SP 5.00 2.00
- ❑ 425 Corey Koskie SP 5.00 2.00
- ❑ 426 Jeromy Burnitz SP 5.00 2.00
- ❑ 427 Jorge Posada SP 8.00 3.00
- ❑ 428 Jason Arnold SP 5.00 2.00
- ❑ 429 Brett Myers SP 5.00 2.00
- ❑ 430 Shawn Green SP 5.00 2.00

2004 Topps Heritage

- ❑ COMPLETE SET (495) 350.00 200.00
- ❑ COMP.SET w/o SP's (385) 60.00 30.00
- ❑ 1A Jim Thome Fielding 1.00 .40
- ❑ 1B Jim Thome Hitting SP 8.00 3.00
- ❑ 2 Nomar Garciaparra SP 10.00 4.00
- ❑ 3 Aramis Ramirez .60 .25
- ❑ 4 Rafael Palmeiro SP 8.00 3.00
- ❑ 5 Danny Graves .50 .20
- ❑ 6 Casey Blake .50 .20
- ❑ 7 Juan Uribe .50 .20
- ❑ 8A Dmitri Young New Logo .60 .25
- ❑ 8B Dmitri Young Old Logo SP 5.00 2.00
- ❑ 9 Billy Wagner .60 .25
- ❑ 10A Jason Giambi Swinging .60 .25
- ❑ 10B Jason Giambi Btg Stance SP 5.00 2.00
- ❑ 11 Carlos Beltran .60 .25
- ❑ 12 Chad Hermansen .50 .20
- ❑ 13 B.J. Upton 1.00 .40
- ❑ 14 Dustan Mohr .50 .20
- ❑ 15 Endy Chavez .50 .20
- ❑ 16 Cliff Floyd .60 .25
- ❑ 17 Bernie Williams 1.00 .40
- ❑ 18 Eric Chavez .60 .25
- ❑ 19 Chase Utley 1.00 .40
- ❑ 20 Randy Johnson 1.50 .60
- ❑ 21 Vernon Wells .60 .25
- ❑ 22 Juan Gonzalez .60 .25
- ❑ 23 Joe Kennedy .50 .20
- ❑ 24 Bengie Molina .50 .20
- ❑ 25 Carlos Lee .60 .25
- ❑ 26 Horacio Ramirez .50 .20
- ❑ 27 Anthony Acevedo RC .75 .30
- ❑ 28 Sammy Sosa SP 8.00 3.00
- ❑ 29 Jon Garland .60 .25
- ❑ 30A Adam Dunn Fielding .60 .25
- ❑ 30B Adam Dunn Hitting SP 5.00 2.00
- ❑ 31 Aaron Rowand .60 .25
- ❑ 32 Jody Gerut .50 .20
- ❑ 33 Chin-Hui Tsao .60 .25
- ❑ 34 Alex Sanchez .50 .20
- ❑ 35 A.J. Burnett .60 .25
- ❑ 36 Brad Ausmus .60 .25
- ❑ 37 Blake Hawksworth RC 1.00 .40
- ❑ 38 Francisco Rodriguez .60 .25
- ❑ 39 Alex Cintron .50 .20
- ❑ 40A Chipper Jones Pointing 1.50 .60
- ❑ 40B Chipper Jones Fielding SP 8.00 3.00
- ❑ 41 Deivi Cruz .50 .20
- ❑ 42 Bill Mueller .60 .25
- ❑ 43 Joe Borowski .50 .20
- ❑ 44 Jimmy Haynes .50 .20
- ❑ 45 Mark Loretta .50 .20
- ❑ 46 Jerome Williams .50 .20
- ❑ 47 Gary Sheffield Yanks SP 8.00 3.00
- ❑ 48 Richard Hidalgo .50 .20
- ❑ 49A Jason Kendall New Logo .60 .25
- ❑ 49B Jason Kendall Old Logo SP 5.00 2.00
- ❑ 50 Ichiro Suzuki SP 12.00 5.00
- ❑ 51 Jim Edmonds .60 .25
- ❑ 52 Frank Catalanotto .50 .20
- ❑ 53 Jose Contreras .50 .20
- ❑ 54 Mo Vaughn .60 .25
- ❑ 55 Brendan Donnelly .50 .20
- ❑ 56 Luis Gonzalez .60 .25
- ❑ 57 Robert Fick .50 .20
- ❑ 58 Laynce Nix .50 .20
- ❑ 59 Johnny Damon 1.00 .40
- ❑ 60A Magglio Ordonez Running .60 .25
- ❑ 60B Magglio Ordonez Hitting SP 5.00 2.00
- ❑ 61 Matt Clement .60 .25
- ❑ 62 Ryan Ludwick .50 .20
- ❑ 63 Luis Castillo .50 .20
- ❑ 64 Dave Crouthers RC .75 .30
- ❑ 65 Dave Berg .50 .20
- ❑ 66 Kyle Davies RC 4.00 1.50
- ❑ 67 Tim Salmon 1.00 .40
- ❑ 68 Marcus Giles .60 .25
- ❑ 69 Marty Cordova .50 .20
- ❑ 70A Todd Helton White Jsy 1.00 .40
- ❑ 70B Todd Helton Purple Jsy SP 8.00 3.00
- ❑ 71 Jeff Kent .60 .25
- ❑ 72 Michael Tucker .50 .20
- ❑ 73 Cesar Izturis .50 .20
- ❑ 74 Paul Quantrill .50 .20
- ❑ 75 Conor Jackson RC 3.00 1.25
- ❑ 76 Placido Polanco .50 .20
- ❑ 77 Adam Eaton .50 .20
- ❑ 78 Ramon Hernandez .60 .25
- ❑ 79 Edgardo Alfonzo .50 .20
- ❑ 80 Dioner Navarro RC 1.00 .40
- ❑ 81 Woody Williams .50 .20
- ❑ 82 Rey Ordonez .50 .20
- ❑ 83 Randy Winn .50 .20
- ❑ 84 Casey Myers RC .75 .30
- ❑ 85A R.Choy Foo New Logo RC .75 .30
- ❑ 85B R.Choy Foo Old Logo SP 5.00 2.00
- ❑ 86 Ray Durham .60 .25
- ❑ 87 Sean Burroughs .50 .20
- ❑ 88 Tim Frend RC .75 .30
- ❑ 89 Shigetoshi Hasegawa .60 .25
- ❑ 90 Jeffrey Allison RC .75 .30
- ❑ 91 Orlando Hudson .50 .20
- ❑ 92 Matt Creighton SP RC 5.00 2.00
- ❑ 93 Tim Worrell .50 .20
- ❑ 94 Kris Benson .50 .20
- ❑ 95 Mike Lieberthal .60 .25
- ❑ 96 David Wells .60 .25
- ❑ 97 Jason Phillips .50 .20
- ❑ 98 Bobby Cox MGR .50 .20
- ❑ 99 Johan Santana 1.50 .60
- ❑ 100A Alex Rodriguez Hitting 2.50 1.00
- ❑ 100B Alex Rodriguez Throwing SP 10.00 4.00
- ❑ 101 John Vander Wal .50 .20
- ❑ 102 Orlando Cabrera .60 .25
- ❑ 103 Hideo Nomo 1.50 .60
- ❑ 104 Todd Walker .50 .20
- ❑ 105 Jason Johnson .50 .20
- ❑ 106 Matt Mantei .50 .20
- ❑ 107 Jarrod Washburn .50 .20
- ❑ 108 Preston Wilson .60 .25
- ❑ 109 Carl Pavano .60 .25
- ❑ 110 Geoff Blum .50 .20
- ❑ 111 Eric Gagne .60 .25
- ❑ 112 Geoff Jenkins .50 .20
- ❑ 113 Joe Torre MG 1.00 .40
- ❑ 114 Jon Knott RC .75 .30
- ❑ 115 Hank Blalock .60 .25
- ❑ 116 John Olerud .60 .25
- ❑ 117A Pat Burrell New Logo .60 .25
- ❑ 117B Pat Burrell Old Logo SP 5.00 2.00
- ❑ 118 Aaron Boone .60 .25
- ❑ 119 Zach Day .50 .20
- ❑ 120A Frank Thomas New Logo 1.50 .60
- ❑ 120B Frank Thomas Old Logo SP 8.00 3.00

❑ 121	Kyle Farnsworth	.50	.20
❑ 122	Derek Lowe	.60	.25
❑ 123	Zach Miner SP RC	8.00	3.00
❑ 124	Matthew Moses SP RC	8.00	3.00
❑ 125	Jesse Roman RC	.75	.30
❑ 126	Josh Phelps	.50	.20
❑ 127	Nic Ungs RC	.75	.30
❑ 128	Dan Haren	.50	.20
❑ 129	Kirk Rueter	.50	.20
❑ 130	Jack McKeon MGR	.60	.25
❑ 131	Keith Foulke	.60	.25
❑ 132	Garrett Stephenson	.50	.20
❑ 133	Wes Helms	.50	.20
❑ 134	Raul Ibanez	.50	.20
❑ 135	Morgan Ensberg	.60	.25
❑ 136	Jay Payton	.60	.25
❑ 137	Billy Koch	.50	.20
❑ 138	Mark Grudzielanek	.50	.20
❑ 139	Rodrigo Lopez	.50	.20
❑ 140	Corey Patterson	.50	.20
❑ 141	Troy Percival	.60	.25
❑ 142	Shea Hillenbrand	.60	.25
❑ 143	Brad Fullmer	.60	.25
❑ 144	Ricky Nolasco RC	1.50	.60
❑ 145	Mark Teixeira	1.00	.40
❑ 146	Tydus Meadows RC	.75	.30
❑ 147	Toby Hall	.50	.20
❑ 148	Orlando Palmeiro	.50	.20
❑ 149	Khalid Ballouli RC	.75	.30
❑ 150	Grady Little MGR	.50	.20
❑ 151	David Eckstein	.60	.25
❑ 152	Kenny Perez RC	.75	.30
❑ 153	Ben Grieve	.50	.20
❑ 154	Ismael Valdes	.50	.20
❑ 155	Bret Boone	.60	.25
❑ 156	Jesse Foppert	.50	.20
❑ 157	Vicente Padilla	.50	.20
❑ 158	Bobby Abreu	.60	.25
❑ 159	Scott Hatteberg	.50	.20
❑ 160	Carlos Quentin RC	2.50	1.00
❑ 161	Anthony Lerew RC	1.00	.40
❑ 162	Lance Carter	.50	.20
❑ 163	Robb Nen	.60	.25
❑ 164	Zach Duke SP RC	10.00	4.00
❑ 165	Xavier Nady	.50	.20
❑ 166	Kip Wells	.50	.20
❑ 167	Kevin Millwood	.60	.25
❑ 168	Jon Lieber	.50	.20
❑ 169	Jose Reyes	.60	.25
❑ 170	Eric Byrnes	.50	.20
❑ 171	Paul Konerko	.60	.25
❑ 172	Chris Lubanski	.60	.25
❑ 173	Jae Weong Seo	.50	.20
❑ 174	Corey Koskie	.50	.20
❑ 175	Tim Stauffer RC	1.00	4.00
❑ 176	John Lackey	.50	.20
❑ 177	Danny Bautista	.50	.20
❑ 178	Shane Reynolds	.50	.20
❑ 179	Jorge Julio	.50	.20
❑ 180A	Manny Ramirez New Logo	1.00	.40
❑ 180B	Manny Ramirez Old Logo SP	8.00	3.00
❑ 181	Alex Gonzalez	.50	.20
❑ 182A	Moises Alou New Logo	.60	.25
❑ 182B	Moises Alou Old Logo SP	5.00	2.00
❑ 183	Mark Buehrle	.60	.25
❑ 184	Carlos Guillen	.60	.25
❑ 185	Nate Cornejo	.50	.20
❑ 186	Billy Traber	.50	.20
❑ 187	Jason Jennings	.50	.20
❑ 188	Eric Munson	.50	.20
❑ 189	Braden Looper	.50	.20
❑ 190	Juan Encarnacion	.50	.20
❑ 191	Dusty Baker MGR	.60	.25
❑ 192	Travis Lee	.50	.20
❑ 193	Miguel Cairo	.50	.20
❑ 194	Rich Aurilia SP	5.00	2.00
❑ 195	Tom Gordon	.50	.20
❑ 196	Freddy Garcia	.60	.25
❑ 197	Brian Lawrence	.50	.20
❑ 198	Jorge Posada SP	8.00	3.00
❑ 199	Javier Vazquez	.60	.25
❑ 200A	Albert Pujols New Logo	3.00	1.25
❑ 200B	Albert Pujols Old Logo SP	12.00	5.00
❑ 201	Victor Zambrano	.50	.20
❑ 202	Eli Marrero	.50	.20
❑ 203	Joel Pineiro	.50	.20
❑ 204	Rondell White	.60	.25
❑ 205	Craig Ansman RC	.75	.30
❑ 206	Michael Young	.60	.25
❑ 207	Carlos Baerga	.50	.20
❑ 208	Andruw Jones	1.00	.40
❑ 209	Jerry Hairston Jr.	.50	.20
❑ 210	Shawn Green SP	5.00	2.00
❑ 211	Ron Gardenhire MGR	.50	.20
❑ 212	Darin Erstad	.60	.25
❑ 213A	Brandon Webb Glove Chest	.50	.20
❑ 213B	Brandon Webb Glove Out SP	5.00	2.00
❑ 214	Greg Maddux	2.50	1.00
❑ 215	Reed Johnson	.50	.20
❑ 216	John Thomson	.50	.20
❑ 217	Tino Martinez	1.00	.40
❑ 218	Mike Cameron	.50	.20
❑ 219	Edgar Martinez	1.00	.40
❑ 220	Eric Young	.50	.20
❑ 221	Reggie Sanders	.60	.25
❑ 222	Randy Wolf	.50	.20
❑ 223	Erubiel Durazo	.50	.20
❑ 224	Mike Mussina	1.00	.40
❑ 225	Tom Glavine	1.00	.40
❑ 226	Troy Glaus	.60	.25
❑ 227	Oscar Villarreal	.50	.20
❑ 228	David Segui	.50	.20
❑ 229	Jeff Suppan	.50	.20
❑ 230	Kenny Lofton	.60	.25
❑ 231	Esteban Loaiza	.50	.20
❑ 232	Felipe Lopez	.50	.20
❑ 233	Matt Lawton	.50	.20
❑ 234	Mark Bellhorn	.60	.25
❑ 235	Wil Ledezma	.50	.20
❑ 236	Todd Hollandsworth	.50	.20
❑ 237	Octavio Dotel	.50	.20
❑ 238	Darren Dreifort	.50	.20
❑ 239	Paul Lo Duca	.60	.25
❑ 240	Richie Sexson	.60	.25
❑ 241	Doug Mientkiewicz	.60	.25
❑ 242	Luis Rivas	.50	.20
❑ 243	Claudio Vargas	.50	.20
❑ 244	Mark Ellis	.50	.20
❑ 245	Brett Myers	.60	.25
❑ 246	Jake Peavy	.60	.25
❑ 247	Marquis Grissom	.60	.25
❑ 248	Armando Benitez	.50	.20
❑ 249	Ryan Franklin	.50	.20
❑ 250A	Alfonso Soriano Throwing	.60	.25
❑ 250B	Alfonso Soriano Fielding SP	5.00	2.00
❑ 251	Tim Hudson	.60	.25
❑ 252	Shannon Stewart	.60	.25
❑ 253	A.J. Pierzynski	.60	.25
❑ 254	Runelvys Hernandez	.50	.20
❑ 255	Roy Oswalt	.60	.25
❑ 256	Shawn Chacon	.50	.20
❑ 257	Tony Graffanino	.50	.20
❑ 258	Tim Wakefield	.60	.25
❑ 259	Damian Miller	.50	.20
❑ 260	Joe Crede	.60	.25
❑ 261	Jason LaRue	.50	.20
❑ 262	Jose Jimenez	.50	.20
❑ 263	Juan Pierre	.60	.25
❑ 264	Wade Miller	.50	.20
❑ 265	Odalis Perez	.50	.20
❑ 266	Eddie Guardado	.50	.20
❑ 267	Rocky Biddle	.50	.20
❑ 268	Jeff Nelson	.50	.20
❑ 269	Terrence Long	.50	.20
❑ 270	Ramon Ortiz	.50	.20
❑ 271	Raul Mondesi	.60	.25
❑ 272	Ugueth Urbina	.50	.20
❑ 273	Jeromy Burnitz	.60	.25
❑ 274	Brad Radke	.60	.25
❑ 275	Jose Vidro	.50	.20
❑ 276	Bobby Jenks	.60	.25
❑ 277	Ty Wigginton	.50	.20
❑ 278	Jose Guillen	.60	.25
❑ 279	Delmon Young	1.00	.40
❑ 280	Brian Giles	.60	.25
❑ 281	Jason Schmidt	.60	.25
❑ 282	Nick Markakis	.60	.25
❑ 283	Felipe Alou MGR	.60	.25
❑ 284	Carl Crawford	.60	.25
❑ 285	Neifi Perez	.50	.20
❑ 286	Miguel Tejada	.60	.25
❑ 287	Victor Martinez	.60	.25
❑ 288	Adam Kennedy	.50	.20
❑ 289	Kerry Ligtenberg	.50	.20
❑ 290	Scott Williamson	.50	.20
❑ 291	Tony Womack	.50	.20
❑ 292	Travis Hafner	.60	.25
❑ 293	Bobby Crosby	.60	.25
❑ 294	Chad Billingsley	.60	.25
❑ 295	Russ Ortiz	.50	.20
❑ 296	John Burkett	.50	.20
❑ 297	Carlos Zambrano	.60	.25
❑ 298	Randall Simon	.50	.20
❑ 299	Juan Castro	.50	.20
❑ 300	Mike Lowell	.60	.25
❑ 301	Fred McGriff	1.00	.40
❑ 302	Glendon Rusch	.50	.20
❑ 303	Sung Jung RC	.75	.30
❑ 304	Rocco Baldelli	.60	.25
❑ 305	Fernando Vina	.50	.20
❑ 306	Gil Meche	.50	.20
❑ 307	Jose Cruz Jr.	.50	.20
❑ 308	Bernie Castro	.50	.20
❑ 309	Scott Spiezio	.50	.20
❑ 310	Paul Byrd	.50	.20
❑ 311A	Jay Gibbons New Logo	.50	.20
❑ 311B	Jay Gibbons Old Logo SP	5.00	2.00
❑ 312	Trot Nixon	.60	.25
❑ 313	Chris O'Riordan RC	.75	.30
❑ 314	Julio Lugo	.50	.20
❑ 315	Ben Davis	.50	.20
❑ 316	Mike Williams	.50	.20
❑ 317	Trevor Hoffman	.60	.25
❑ 318	Andy Pettitte	1.00	.40
❑ 319	Orlando Hernandez	.60	.25
❑ 320	Juan Rivera	.50	.20
❑ 321	Elizardo Ramirez	.50	.20
❑ 322	Junior Spivey	.50	.20
❑ 323	Tony Batista	.50	.20
❑ 324	Mike Remlinger	.50	.20
❑ 325	Alex Gonzalez	.50	.20
❑ 326	Aaron Hill	.50	.20
❑ 327	Steve Finley	.60	.25
❑ 328	Vinny Castilla	.60	.25
❑ 329	Eric Duncan	.60	.25
❑ 330	Mike Gosling RC	.75	.30
❑ 331	Eric Hinske	.50	.20
❑ 332	Scott Rolen	1.00	.40
❑ 333	Benito Santiago	.60	.25
❑ 334	Jimmy Gobble	.50	.20
❑ 335	Bobby Higginson	.60	.25
❑ 336	Kelvim Escobar	.50	.20
❑ 337	Mike DeJean	.50	.20
❑ 338	Sidney Ponson	.50	.20
❑ 339	Todd Self RC	1.00	.40
❑ 340	Jeff Cirillo	.50	.20
❑ 341	Jimmy Rollins	.60	.25
❑ 342A	Barry Zito White Jsy	.60	.25
❑ 342B	Barry Zito Green Jsy SP	5.00	2.00
❑ 343	Felix Pie	1.00	.40
❑ 344	Matt Morris	.60	.25
❑ 345	Kazuhiro Sasaki	.60	.25
❑ 346	Jack Wilson	.50	.20
❑ 347	Nick Johnson	.60	.25
❑ 348	Wil Cordero	.50	.20
❑ 349	Ryan Madson	.50	.20
❑ 350	Torii Hunter	.60	.25
❑ 351	Andy Ashby	.50	.20
❑ 352	Aubrey Huff	.60	.25
❑ 353	Brad Lidge	.60	.25
❑ 354	Derrek Lee	1.00	.40
❑ 355	Yadier Molina RC	2.50	1.00
❑ 356	Paul Wilson	.50	.20
❑ 357	Omar Vizquel	1.00	.40
❑ 358	Rene Reyes	.50	.20
❑ 359	Marlon Anderson	.50	.20
❑ 360	Bobby Kielty	.50	.20
❑ 361A	Ryan Wagner New Logo	.50	.20
❑ 361B	Ryan Wagner Old Logo SP	5.00	2.00
❑ 362	Justin Morneau	.60	.25
❑ 363	Shane Spencer	.50	.20
❑ 364	David Bell	.50	.20
❑ 365	Matt Stairs	.50	.20
❑ 366	Joe Borchard	.50	.20
❑ 367	Mark Redman	.50	.20
❑ 368	Dave Roberts	.50	.20
❑ 369	Desi Relaford	.50	.20
❑ 370	Rich Harden	.60	.25

❑ 371	Fernando Tatis	.50	.20
❑ 372	Eric Karros	.60	.25
❑ 373	Eric Milton	.50	.20
❑ 374	Mike Sweeney	.60	.25
❑ 375	Brian Daubach	.50	.20
❑ 376	Brian Snyder	.50	.20
❑ 377	Chris Reitsma	.50	.20
❑ 378	Kyle Lohse	.50	.20
❑ 379	Livan Hernandez	.60	.25
❑ 380	Robin Ventura	.60	.25
❑ 381	Jacque Jones	.60	.25
❑ 382	Danny Kolb	.50	.20
❑ 383	Casey Kotchman	.60	.25
❑ 384	Cristian Guzman	.50	.20
❑ 385	Josh Beckett	.60	.25
❑ 386	Khalil Greene	1.00	.40
❑ 387	Greg Myers	.50	.20
❑ 388	Francisco Cordero	.50	.20
❑ 389	Donald Levinski RC	.75	.30
❑ 390	Roy Halladay	.60	.25
❑ 391	J.D. Drew	.60	.25
❑ 392	Jamie Moyer	.60	.25
❑ 393	Ken Macha MGR	.50	.20
❑ 394	Jeff Davanon	.50	.20
❑ 395	Matt Kata	.50	.20
❑ 396	Jack Cust	.50	.20
❑ 397	Mike Timlin	.50	.20
❑ 398	Zack Greinke SP	5.00	2.00
❑ 399	Byung-Hyun Kim SP	5.00	2.00
❑ 400	Kazuhisa Ishii SP	5.00	2.00
❑ 401	Brayan Pena SP RC	5.00	2.00
❑ 402	Garret Anderson SP	5.00	2.00
❑ 403	Kyle Sleeth SP RC	8.00	3.00
❑ 404	Javy Lopez SP	5.00	2.00
❑ 405	Damian Moss SP	5.00	2.00
❑ 406	David Ortiz SP	8.00	3.00
❑ 407	Pedro Martinez SP	8.00	3.00
❑ 408	Hee Seop Choi SP	5.00	2.00
❑ 409	Carl Everett SP	5.00	2.00
❑ 410	Dontrelle Willis SP	8.00	3.00
❑ 411	Ryan Harvey SP	5.00	2.00
❑ 412	Russell Branyan SP	5.00	2.00
❑ 413	Milton Bradley SP	5.00	2.00
❑ 414	Marcus McBeth SP RC	5.00	2.00
❑ 415	Carlos Pena SP	5.00	2.00
❑ 416	Ivan Rodriguez SP	8.00	3.00
❑ 417	Craig Biggio SP	8.00	3.00
❑ 418	Angel Berroa SP	5.00	2.00
❑ 419	Brian Jordan SP	5.00	2.00
❑ 420	Scott Podsednik SP	5.00	2.00
❑ 421	Omar Falcon SP RC	5.00	2.00
❑ 422	Joe Mays SP	5.00	2.00
❑ 423	Brad Wilkerson SP	5.00	2.00
❑ 424	Al Leiter SP	5.00	2.00
❑ 425	Derek Jeter SP	12.00	5.00
❑ 426	Mark Mulder SP	5.00	2.00
❑ 427	Marlon Byrd SP	5.00	2.00
❑ 428	David Murphy SP RC	8.00	3.00
❑ 429	Phil Nevin SP	5.00	2.00
❑ 430	J.T. Snow SP	5.00	2.00
❑ 431	Brad Sullivan SP RC	8.00	3.00
❑ 432	Bo Hart SP	5.00	2.00
❑ 433	Josh Labandeira SP RC	5.00	2.00
❑ 434	Chan Ho Park SP	5.00	2.00
❑ 435	Carlos Delgado SP	5.00	2.00
❑ 436	Curt Schilling Sox SP	8.00	3.00
❑ 437	John Smoltz SP	8.00	3.00
❑ 438	Luis Matos SP	5.00	2.00
❑ 439	Mark Prior SP	8.00	3.00
❑ 440	Roberto Alomar SP	8.00	3.00
❑ 441	Coco Crisp SP	5.00	2.00
❑ 442	Austin Kearns SP	5.00	2.00
❑ 443	Larry Walker SP	5.00	2.00
❑ 444	Neal Cotts SP	5.00	2.00
❑ 445	Jeff Bagwell SP	8.00	3.00
❑ 446	Adrian Beltre SP	5.00	2.00
❑ 447	Grady Sizemore SP	8.00	3.00
❑ 448	Keith Ginter SP	5.00	2.00
❑ 449	Vladimir Guerrero SP	8.00	3.00
❑ 450	Lyle Overbay SP	5.00	2.00
❑ 451	Rafael Furcal SP	5.00	2.00
❑ 452	Melvin Mora SP	5.00	2.00
❑ 453	Kerry Wood SP	5.00	2.00
❑ 454	Jose Valentin SP	5.00	2.00
❑ 455	Ken Griffey Jr. SP	10.00	4.00
❑ 456	Brandon Phillips SP	5.00	2.00
❑ 457	Miguel Cabrera SP	8.00	3.00
❑ 458	Edwin Jackson SP	5.00	2.00
❑ 459	Eric Owens SP	5.00	2.00
❑ 460	Miguel Batista SP	5.00	2.00
❑ 461	Mike Hampton SP	5.00	2.00
❑ 462	Kevin Millar SP	5.00	2.00
❑ 463	Bartolo Colon SP	5.00	2.00
❑ 464	Sean Casey SP	5.00	2.00
❑ 465	C.C. Sabathia SP	5.00	2.00
❑ 466	Rickie Weeks SP	5.00	2.00
❑ 467	Brad Penny SP	5.00	2.00
❑ 468	Mike MacDougal SP	5.00	2.00
❑ 469	Kevin Brown SP	5.00	2.00
❑ 470	Lance Berkman SP	5.00	2.00
❑ 471	Ben Sheets SP	5.00	2.00
❑ 472	Mariano Rivera SP	8.00	3.00
❑ 473	Mike Piazza SP	10.00	4.00
❑ 474	Ryan Klesko SP	5.00	2.00
❑ 475	Edgar Renteria SP	5.00	2.00

2005 Topps Heritage

❑	COMPLETE SET (495)	400.00	250.00
❑	COMP.SET w/o SP's (385)	60.00	30.00
❑	COMMON CARD	.50	.20
❑	COMMON RC	.50	.20
❑	COMMON TEAM CARD	.50	.20
❑	COMMON SP	8.00	3.00
❑	COMMON SP RC	8.00	3.00
❑	SP STATED ODDS 1:2 HOBBY/RETAIL		
❑	BASIC SP: 5/20/30/31/33/79/101/110/130		
❑	BASIC SP: 135/260/292/398-475		
❑	VARIATION SP: 3/6/7/31/50/69/78/82/118		
❑	VARIATION SP: 125/135/155/261/273/286		
❑	VARIATION SP: 296/300/312/353/389		
❑	SEE BECKETT.COM FOR VAR.DESCRIPTIONS		
❑ 1	Will Harridge	.50	.20
❑ 2	Warren Giles	.50	.20
❑ 3A	Alfonso Soriano Fldg	.50	.20
❑ 3B	Alfonso Soriano Running SP	8.00	3.00
❑ 4	Mark Mulder	.50	.20
❑ 5	Todd Helton SP	8.00	3.00
❑ 6A	Jason Bay Black Cap	.50	.20
❑ 6B	Jason Bay Yellow Cap SP	8.00	3.00
❑ 7A	Ichiro Suzuki Running	1.50	.60
❑ 7B	Ichiro Suzuki Crouch SP	10.00	4.00
❑ 8	Jim Tracy MG	.50	.20
❑ 9	Gavin Floyd	.50	.20
❑ 10	John Smoltz	.75	.30
❑ 11	Chicago Cubs TC	.75	.30
❑ 12	Darin Erstad	.50	.20
❑ 13	Chad Tracy	.50	.20
❑ 14	Charles Thomas	.50	.20
❑ 15	Miguel Tejada	.50	.20
❑ 16	Andre Ethier RC	5.00	2.00
❑ 17	Jeff Francis	.50	.20
❑ 18	Derrek Lee	.75	.30
❑ 19	Juan Uribe	.50	.20
❑ 20	Jim Edmonds SP	8.00	3.00
❑ 21	Kenny Lofton	.50	.20
❑ 22	Brad Ausmus	.50	.20
❑ 23	Jon Garland	.50	.20
❑ 24	Edwin Jackson	.50	.20
❑ 25	Joe Mauer	1.00	.40
❑ 26	Wes Helms	.50	.20
❑ 27	Brian Schneider	.50	.20
❑ 28	Kazuo Matsui	.50	.20
❑ 29	Flash Gordon	.50	.20
❑ 30	Hideo Nomo SP	8.00	3.00
❑ 31A	Albert Pujols Red Hat SP	12.00	5.00
❑ 31B	Albert Pujols Blue Hat SP	12.00	5.00
❑ 32	Carl Crawford	.50	.20
❑ 33	Vladimir Guerrero SP	8.00	3.00
❑ 34	Nick Green	.50	.20
❑ 35	Jay Gibbons	.50	.20
❑ 36	Kevin Youkilis	.50	.20
❑ 37	Billy Wagner	.50	.20
❑ 38	Terrence Long	.50	.20
❑ 39	Kevin Mench	.50	.20
❑ 40	Garret Anderson	.50	.20
❑ 41	Reed Johnson	.50	.20
❑ 42	Reggie Sanders	.50	.20
❑ 43	Kirk Rueter	.50	.20
❑ 44	Jay Payton	.50	.20
❑ 45	Tike Redman	.50	.20
❑ 46	Mike Lieberthal	.50	.20
❑ 47	Damian Miller	.50	.20
❑ 48	Zach Day	.50	.20
❑ 49	Juan Rincon	.50	.20
❑ 50A	Jim Thome At Bat	.75	.30
❑ 50B	Jim Thome Fldg SP	8.00	3.00
❑ 51	Jose Guillen	.50	.20
❑ 52	Richie Sexson	.50	.20
❑ 53	Juan Cruz	.50	.20
❑ 54	Byung-Hyun Kim	.50	.20
❑ 55	Carlos Zambrano	.50	.20
❑ 56	Carlos Lee	.50	.20
❑ 57	Adam Dunn	.50	.20
❑ 58	David Riske	.50	.20
❑ 59	Carlos Guillen	.50	.20
❑ 60	Larry Bowa MG	.50	.20
❑ 61	Barry Bonds	8.00	3.00
❑ 62	Chris Woodward	.50	.20
❑ 63	Matt DeSalvo RC	.75	.30
❑ 64	Brian Stavisky RC	.50	.20
❑ 65	Scot Shields	.50	.20
❑ 66	J.D. Drew	.50	.20
❑ 67	Erik Bedard	.50	.20
❑ 68	Scott Williamson	.50	.20
❑ 69A	M.Prior New C on Cap	.75	.30
❑ 69B	M.Prior Old C on Cap SP	8.00	3.00
❑ 70	Ken Griffey Jr.	1.50	.60
❑ 71	Kazuhito Tadano	.50	.20
❑ 72	Philadelphia Phillies TC	.50	.20
❑ 73	Jeremy Reed	.50	.20
❑ 74	Ricardo Rodriguez	.50	.20
❑ 75	Carlos Delgado	.50	.20
❑ 76	Eric Milton	.50	.20
❑ 77	Miguel Olivo	.50	.20
❑ 78A	E.Alfonzo No Socks	.50	.20
❑ 78B	E.Alfonzo Black Socks SP	8.00	3.00
❑ 79	Kazuhisa Ishii SP	8.00	3.00
❑ 80	Jason Giambi	.50	.20
❑ 81	Cliff Floyd	.50	.20
❑ 82A	Torii Hunter Twins Cap	.50	.20
❑ 82B	Torii Hunter Wash Cap SP	8.00	3.00
❑ 83	Odalis Perez	.50	.20
❑ 84	Scott Podsednik	.50	.20
❑ 85	Cleveland Indians TC	.50	.20
❑ 86	Jeff Suppan	.50	.20
❑ 87	Ray Durham	.50	.20
❑ 88	Tyler Clippard RC	20.00	8.00
❑ 89	Ryan Howard	2.50	1.00
❑ 90	Cincinnati Reds TC	.50	.20
❑ 91	Bengie Molina	.50	.20
❑ 92	Danny Bautista	.50	.20
❑ 93	Eli Marrero	.50	.20
❑ 94	Larry Bigbie	.50	.20
❑ 95	Atlanta Braves TC	.50	.20
❑ 96	Merkin Valdez	.50	.20
❑ 97	Rocco Baldelli	.50	.20
❑ 98	Woody Williams	.50	.20
❑ 99	Jason Frasor	.50	.20
❑ 100	Baltimore Orioles TC	.50	.20
❑ 101	Ivan Rodriguez SP	8.00	3.00
❑ 102	Joe Kennedy	.50	.20
❑ 103	Mike Lowell	.50	.20
❑ 104	Armando Benitez	.50	.20
❑ 105	Craig Biggio	.75	.30
❑ 106	David DeJesus	.50	.20
❑ 107	Adrian Beltre	.50	.20
❑ 108	Phil Nevin	.50	.20
❑ 109	Cristian Guzman	.50	.20
❑ 110	Jorge Posada SP	8.00	3.00
❑ 111	Boston Red Sox TC	1.00	.40

❑ 112 Jeff Mathis .50 .20
❑ 113 Bartolo Colon .50 .20
❑ 114 Alex Cintron .50 .20
❑ 115 Russ Ortiz .50 .20
❑ 116 Doug Mientkiewicz .50 .20
❑ 117 Placido Polanco .50 .20
❑ 118A M.Ordonez Black Uni .50 .20
❑ 118B M.Ordonez White Uni SP 8.00 3.00
❑ 119 Chris Seddon RC .50 .20
❑ 120 Bobby Abreu .50 .20
❑ 121 Pittsburgh Pirates TC .50 .20
❑ 122 Dallas McPherson .50 .20
❑ 123 Rodrigo Lopez .50 .20
❑ 124 Mark Bellhorn .50 .20
❑ 125A N.Garciaparra Red Cap 1.00 .40
❑ 125B N.Garciaparra Blue Cap SP 8.00 3.00
❑ 126 Sean Casey .50 .20
❑ 127 Ronnie Belliard .50 .20
❑ 128 Tom Goodwin .50 .20
❑ 129 Preston Wilson .50 .20
❑ 130 Andruw Jones SP 8.00 3.00
❑ 131 Roberto Alomar .75 .30
❑ 132 John Buck .50 .20
❑ 133 Jason LaRue .50 .20
❑ 134 St. Louis Cardinals TC .75 .30
❑ 135A Alex Rodriguez Fldg SP 10.00 4.00
❑ 135B Alex Rodriguez At Bat SP 10.00 4.00
❑ 136 Nate Robertson .50 .20
❑ 137 Juan Pierre .50 .20
❑ 138 Morgan Ensberg .50 .20
❑ 139 Vinny Castilla .50 .20
❑ 140 Jake Dittler .50 .20
❑ 141 Chan Ho Park .50 .20
❑ 142 Felix Hernandez 3.00 1.25
❑ 143 Jason Isringhausen .50 .20
❑ 144 Dustan Mohr .50 .20
❑ 145 Khalil Greene .75 .30
❑ 146 Minnesota Twins TC .50 .20
❑ 147 Vicente Padilla .50 .20
❑ 148 Oliver Perez .50 .20
❑ 149 Brian Giles .50 .20
❑ 150 Shawn Green .50 .20
❑ 151 Matt Lawton .50 .20
❑ 152 Casey Blake .50 .20
❑ 153 Frank Thomas 1.00 .40
❑ 154 Orlando Hernandez .50 .20
❑ 155A Eric Chavez Green Cap .50 .20
❑ 155B Eric Chavez Blue Cap SP 8.00 3.00
❑ 156 Chase Utley .75 .30
❑ 157 John Olerud .50 .20
❑ 158 Adam Eaton .50 .20
❑ 159 Josh Fogg .50 .20
❑ 160 Michael Tucker .50 .20
❑ 161 Kevin Brown .50 .20
❑ 162 Bobby Crosby .50 .20
❑ 163 Jason Schmidt .50 .20
❑ 164 Shannon Stewart .50 .20
❑ 165 Tony Womack .50 .20
❑ 166 Los Angeles Dodgers TC .75 .30
❑ 167 Franklin Gutierrez .50 .20
❑ 168 Ted Lilly .50 .20
❑ 169 Mark Teixeira .75 .30
❑ 170 Matt Morris .50 .20
❑ 171 Bucky Jacobsen .50 .20
❑ 172 Steve Doetsch RC .75 .30
❑ 173 Jeff Weaver .50 .20
❑ 174 Tony Graffanino .50 .20
❑ 175 Jeff Bagwell .75 .30
❑ 176 Carl Pavano .50 .20
❑ 177 Junior Spivey .50 .20
❑ 178 Carlos Silva .50 .20
❑ 179 Tim Redding .50 .20
❑ 180 Brett Myers .50 .20
❑ 181 Mike Mussina .75 .30
❑ 182 Richard Hidalgo .50 .20
❑ 183 Nick Johnson .50 .20
❑ 184 Lew Ford .50 .20
❑ 185 Barry Zito .50 .20
❑ 186 Jimmy Rollins .50 .20
❑ 187 Jack Wilson .50 .20
❑ 188 Chicago White Sox TC .50 .20
❑ 189 Guillermo Quiroz .50 .20
❑ 190 Mark Hendrickson .50 .20
❑ 191 Jeremy Bonderman .50 .20
❑ 192 Jason Jennings .50 .20
❑ 193 Paul Lo Duca .50 .20
❑ 194 A.J. Burnett .50 .20
❑ 195 Ken Harvey .50 .20
❑ 196 Geoff Jenkins .50 .20
❑ 197 Joe Mays .50 .20
❑ 198 Jose Vidro .50 .20
❑ 199 David Wright 2.00 .75
❑ 200 Randy Johnson 1.00 .40
❑ 201 Jeff DaVanon .50 .20
❑ 202 Paul Byrd .50 .20
❑ 203 David Ortiz 1.00 .40
❑ 204 Kyle Farnsworth .50 .20
❑ 205 Keith Foulke .50 .20
❑ 206 Joe Crede .50 .20
❑ 207 Austin Kearns .50 .20
❑ 208 Jody Gerut .50 .20
❑ 209 Shawn Chacon .50 .20
❑ 210 Carlos Pena .50 .20
❑ 211 Luis Castillo .50 .20
❑ 212 Chris Denorfia RC 1.00 .40
❑ 213 Detroit Tigers TC .50 .20
❑ 214 Aubrey Huff .50 .20
❑ 215 Brad Fullmer .50 .20
❑ 216 Frank Catalanotto .50 .20
❑ 217 Raul Ibanez .50 .20
❑ 218 Ryan Klesko .50 .20
❑ 219 Octavio Dotel .50 .20
❑ 220 Rob Mackowiak .50 .20
❑ 221 Scott Hatteberg .50 .20
❑ 222 Pat Burrell .50 .20
❑ 223 Bernie Williams .75 .30
❑ 224 Kris Benson .50 .20
❑ 225 Eric Gagne .50 .20
❑ 226 San Francisco Giants TC .75 .30
❑ 227 Roy Oswalt .50 .20
❑ 228 Josh Beckett .50 .20
❑ 229 Lee Mazzilli MG .50 .20
❑ 230 Rickie Weeks .50 .20
❑ 231 Troy Glaus .50 .20
❑ 232 Chone Figgins .50 .20
❑ 233 John Thomson .50 .20
❑ 234 Trot Nixon .50 .20
❑ 235 Brad Penny .50 .20
❑ 236 Oakland A's TC .50 .20
❑ 237 Miguel Batista .50 .20
❑ 238 Ryan Drese .50 .20
❑ 239 Aaron Miles .50 .20
❑ 240 Randy Wolf .50 .20
❑ 241 Brian Lawrence .50 .20
❑ 242 A.J. Pierzynski .50 .20
❑ 243 Jamie Moyer .50 .20
❑ 244 Chris Carpenter .50 .20
❑ 245 So Taguchi .50 .20
❑ 246 Rob Bell .50 .20
❑ 247 Francisco Cordero .50 .20
❑ 248 Tom Glavine .75 .30
❑ 249 Jermaine Dye .50 .20
❑ 250 Cliff Lee .50 .20
❑ 251 New York Yankees TC 1.00 .40
❑ 252 Vernon Wells .50 .20
❑ 253 R.A. Dickey .50 .20
❑ 254 Larry Walker .75 .30
❑ 255 Randy Winn .50 .20
❑ 256 Pedro Feliz .50 .20
❑ 257 Mark Loretta .50 .20
❑ 258 Tim Worrell .50 .20
❑ 259 Kip Wells .50 .20
❑ 260 Cesar Izturis SP 8.00 3.00
❑ 261A Carlos Beltran Fldg .50 .20
❑ 261B Carlos Beltran At Bat SP 8.00 3.00
❑ 262 Juan Encarnacion .50 .20
❑ 263 Luis A. Gonzalez .50 .20
❑ 264 Grady Sizemore .75 .30
❑ 265 Paul Wilson .50 .20
❑ 266 Mark Buehrle .50 .20
❑ 267 Todd Hollandsworth .50 .20
❑ 268 Orlando Cabrera .50 .20
❑ 269 Sidney Ponson .50 .20
❑ 270 Mike Hampton .50 .20
❑ 271 Luis Gonzalez .50 .20
❑ 272 Brendan Donnelly .50 .20
❑ 273A Chipper Jones Slide 1.00 .40
❑ 273B Chipper Jones Fldg SP 8.00 3.00
❑ 274 Brandon Webb .50 .20
❑ 275 Marty Cordova .50 .20
❑ 276 Greg Maddux 1.50 .60
❑ 277 Jose Contreras .50 .20
❑ 278 Aaron Harang .50 .20
❑ 279 Coco Crisp .50 .20
❑ 280 Bobby Higginson .50 .20
❑ 281 Guillermo Mota .50 .20
❑ 282 Andy Pettitte .75 .30
❑ 283 Jeremy West RC .75 .30
❑ 284 Craig Brazell .50 .20
❑ 285 Eric Hinske .50 .20
❑ 286A Hank Blalock Hitting .50 .20
❑ 286B Hank Blalock Fldg SP 8.00 3.00
❑ 287 B.J. Upton .75 .30
❑ 288 Jason Marquis .50 .20
❑ 289 Matt Herges .50 .20
❑ 290 Ramon Hernandez .50 .20
❑ 291 Marlon Byrd .50 .20
❑ 292 Ryan Sweeney SP RC 8.00 3.00
❑ 293 Esteban Loaiza .50 .20
❑ 294 Al Leiter .50 .20
❑ 295 Alex Gonzalez .50 .20
❑ 296A J.Santana Twins Cap 1.00 .40
❑ 296B J.Santana Wash Cap SP 8.00 3.00
❑ 297 Milton Bradley .50 .20
❑ 298 Mike Sweeney .50 .20
❑ 299 Wade Miller .50 .20
❑ 300A Sammy Sosa Hitting 1.00 .40
❑ 300B Sammy Sosa Standing SP 8.00 3.00
❑ 301 Wily Mo Pena .50 .20
❑ 302 Tim Wakefield .50 .20
❑ 303 Rafael Palmeiro .75 .30
❑ 304 Rafael Furcal .50 .20
❑ 305 David Eckstein .50 .20
❑ 306 David Segui .50 .20
❑ 307 Kevin Millar .50 .20
❑ 308 Matt Clement .50 .20
❑ 309 Wade Robinson RC .50 .20
❑ 310 Brad Radke .50 .20
❑ 311 Steve Finley .50 .20
❑ 312A Lance Berkman Hitting .50 .20
❑ 312B Lance Berkman Fldg SP 8.00 3.00
❑ 313 Joe Randa .50 .20
❑ 314 Miguel Cabrera .75 .30
❑ 315 Billy Koch .50 .20
❑ 316 Alex Sanchez .50 .20
❑ 317 Chin-Hui Tsao .50 .20
❑ 318 Omar Vizquel .75 .30
❑ 319 Ryan Freel .50 .20
❑ 320 LaTroy Hawkins .50 .20
❑ 321 Aaron Rowand .50 .20
❑ 322 Paul Konerko .50 .20
❑ 323 Joe Borowski .50 .20
❑ 324 Jarrod Washburn .50 .20
❑ 325 Jaret Wright .50 .20
❑ 326 Johnny Damon .75 .30
❑ 327 Corey Patterson .50 .20
❑ 328 Travis Hafner .50 .20
❑ 329 Shingo Takatsu .50 .20
❑ 330 Dmitri Young .50 .20
❑ 331 Matt Holliday .60 .25
❑ 332 Jeff Kent .50 .20
❑ 333 Desi Relaford .50 .20
❑ 334 Jose Hernandez .50 .20
❑ 335 Lyle Overbay .50 .20
❑ 336 Jacque Jones .50 .20
❑ 337 Terrmel Sledge .50 .20
❑ 338 Victor Zambrano .50 .20
❑ 339 Gary Sheffield .50 .20
❑ 340 Brad Wilkerson .50 .20
❑ 341 Ian Kinsler RC 3.00 1.25
❑ 342 Jesse Crain .50 .20
❑ 343 Orlando Hudson .50 .20
❑ 344 Laynce Nix .50 .20
❑ 345 Jose Cruz Jr. .50 .20
❑ 346 Edgar Renteria .50 .20
❑ 347 Eddie Guardado .50 .20
❑ 348 Jerome Williams .50 .20
❑ 349 Trevor Hoffman .50 .20
❑ 350 Mike Piazza 1.00 .40
❑ 351 Jason Kendall .50 .20
❑ 352 Kevin Millwood .50 .20
❑ 353A Tim Hudson Atl Cap .50 .20
❑ 353B Tim Hudson Milw Cap SP 8.00 3.00
❑ 354 Paul Quantrill .50 .20
❑ 355 Jon Lieber .50 .20
❑ 356 Braden Looper .50 .20
❑ 357 Chad Cordero .50 .20
❑ 358 Joe Nathan .50 .20

❑ 359 Doug Davis .50 .20
❑ 360 Ian Bladergroen RC .75 .30
❑ 361 Val Majewski .50 .20
❑ 362 Francisco Rodriguez .50 .20
❑ 363 Kelvim Escobar .50 .20
❑ 364 Marcus Giles .50 .20
❑ 365 Darren Fenster RC .50 .20
❑ 366 David Bell .50 .20
❑ 367 Shea Hillenbrand .50 .20
❑ 368 Manny Ramirez .75 .30
❑ 369 Ben Broussard .50 .20
❑ 370 Luis Ramirez RC .50 .20
❑ 371 Dustin Hermanson .50 .20
❑ 372 Akinori Otsuka .50 .20
❑ 373 Chadd Blasko RC .75 .30
❑ 374 Delmon Young .75 .30
❑ 375 Michael Young .50 .20
❑ 376 Bret Boone .50 .20
❑ 377 Jake Peavy .50 .20
❑ 378 Matthew Lindstrom RC .50 .20
❑ 379 Sean Burroughs .50 .20
❑ 380 Rich Harden .50 .20
❑ 381 Chris Roberson RC .50 .20
❑ 382 John Lackey .50 .20
❑ 383 Johnny Estrada .50 .20
❑ 384 Matt Rogelstad RC .50 .20
❑ 385 Toby Hall .50 .20
❑ 386 Adam LaRoche .50 .20
❑ 387 Bill Hall .50 .20
❑ 388 Tim Salmon .50 .20
❑ 389A Curt Schilling Throw .75 .30
❑ 389B Curt Schilling Glove Up SP 8.00 3.00
❑ 390 Michael Barrett .50 .20
❑ 391 Jose Acevedo .50 .20
❑ 392 Nate Schierholtz .75 .30
❑ 393 J.T. Snow Jr. .50 .20
❑ 394 Mark Redman .50 .20
❑ 395 Ryan Madson .50 .20
❑ 396 Kevin West RC .50 .20
❑ 397 Ramon Ortiz .50 .20
❑ 398 Derek Lowe SP 8.00 3.00
❑ 399 Kerry Wood SP 8.00 3.00
❑ 400 Derek Jeter SP 12.00 5.00
❑ 401 Livan Hernandez SP 8.00 3.00
❑ 402 Casey Kotchman SP 8.00 3.00
❑ 403 Chaz Lytle SP RC 8.00 3.00
❑ 404 Alexis Rios SP 8.00 3.00
❑ 405 Scott Spiezio SP 8.00 3.00
❑ 406 Craig Wilson SP 8.00 3.00
❑ 407 Felix Rodriguez SP 8.00 3.00
❑ 408 D'Angelo Jimenez SP 8.00 3.00
❑ 409 Rondell White SP 8.00 3.00
❑ 410 Shawn Estes SP 8.00 3.00
❑ 411 Troy Percival SP 8.00 3.00
❑ 412 Melvin Mora SP 8.00 3.00
❑ 413 Aramis Ramirez SP 8.00 3.00
❑ 414 Carl Everett SP 8.00 3.00
❑ 415 Elvys Quezada SP RC 8.00 3.00
❑ 416 Ben Sheets SP 8.00 3.00
❑ 417 Matt Stairs SP 8.00 3.00
❑ 418 Adam Everett SP 8.00 3.00
❑ 419 Jason Johnson SP 8.00 3.00
❑ 420 Billy Butler SP RC 10.00 4.00
❑ 421 Justin Morneau SP 8.00 3.00
❑ 422 Jose Reyes SP 8.00 3.00
❑ 423 Mariano Rivera SP 8.00 3.00
❑ 424 Jose Vaquedano SP RC 8.00 3.00
❑ 425 Gabe Gross SP 8.00 3.00
❑ 426 Scott Rolen SP 8.00 3.00
❑ 427 Ty Wigginton SP 8.00 3.00
❑ 428 James Jurries SP RC 8.00 3.00
❑ 429 Pedro Martinez SP 8.00 3.00
❑ 430 Mark Grudzielanek SP 8.00 3.00
❑ 431 Josh Phelps SP 8.00 3.00
❑ 432 Ryan Goleski SP RC 8.00 3.00
❑ 433 Mike Matheny SP 8.00 3.00
❑ 434 Bobby Kielty SP 8.00 3.00
❑ 435 Tony Batista SP 8.00 3.00
❑ 436 Corey Koskie SP 8.00 3.00
❑ 437 Brad Lidge SP 8.00 3.00
❑ 438 Dontrelle Willis SP 8.00 3.00
❑ 439 Angel Berroa SP 8.00 3.00
❑ 440 Jason Kubel SP 8.00 3.00
❑ 441 Roy Halladay SP 8.00 3.00
❑ 442 Brian Roberts SP 8.00 3.00
❑ 443 Bill Mueller SP 8.00 3.00
❑ 444 Adam Kennedy SP 8.00 3.00
❑ 445 Brandon Moss SP RC 8.00 3.00
❑ 446 Sean Burnett SP 8.00 3.00
❑ 447 Eric Byrnes SP 8.00 3.00
❑ 448 Matt Campbell SP RC 8.00 3.00
❑ 449 Ryan Webb SP 8.00 3.00
❑ 450 Jose Valentin SP 8.00 3.00
❑ 451 Jake Westbrook SP 8.00 3.00
❑ 452 Glen Perkins SP RC 8.00 3.00
❑ 453 Alex Gonzalez SP 8.00 3.00
❑ 454 Jeromy Burnitz SP 8.00 3.00
❑ 455 Zack Greinke SP 8.00 3.00
❑ 456 Sean Marshall SP RC 6.00 2.50
❑ 457 Erubiel Durazo SP 8.00 3.00
❑ 458 Michael Cuddyer SP 8.00 3.00
❑ 459 Hee Seop Choi SP 8.00 3.00
❑ 460 Melky Cabrera SP RC 10.00 4.00
❑ 461 Jerry Hairston Jr. SP 8.00 3.00
❑ 462 Moises Alou SP 8.00 3.00
❑ 463 Michael Rogers SP RC 8.00 3.00
❑ 464 Javy Lopez SP 8.00 3.00
❑ 465 Freddy Garcia SP 8.00 3.00
❑ 466 Brett Harper SP RC 8.00 3.00
❑ 467 Juan Gonzalez SP 8.00 3.00
❑ 468 Kevin Melillo SP RC 8.00 3.00
❑ 469 Todd Walker SP 8.00 3.00
❑ 470 C.C. Sabathia SP 8.00 3.00
❑ 471 Kole Strayhorn SP RC 8.00 3.00
❑ 472 Mark Kotsay SP 8.00 3.00
❑ 473 Javier Vazquez SP 8.00 3.00
❑ 474 Mike Cameron SP 8.00 3.00
❑ 475 Wes Swackhamer SP RC 8.00 3.00

2006 Topps Heritage

❑ COMPLETE SET (494) 400.00 250.00
❑ COMP.SET w/o SP's (384) 60.00 30.00
❑ COMMON CARD .50 .20
❑ COMMON RC .50 .20
❑ COMMON TEAM CARD .50 .20
❑ COMMON SP 8.00 3.00
❑ SP STATED ODDS 1:2 HOBBY/RETAIL
❑ SP CL: 1/2/10/18/20B/23B/25/35/55
❑ SP CL: 70/76/80B/91/95A/95B/99/106
❑ SP CL: 123/127/165B/200B/212B/265-269
❑ SP CL: 271-274/276-316/318-323/325A
❑ SP CL: 325B/326-328/330-349/350A/350B
❑ SP CL: 351-352/400/407/475B
❑ VARIATION CL: 20/23/80/95/165/200
❑ VARIATION CL: 212/325/350/475
❑ TWO VERSIONS OF EACH VARIATION EXIST
❑ SEE BECKETT.COM FOR VAR.DESCRIPTIONS
❑ CARD 255 NOT INTENDED FOR RELEASE
❑ COMP.SET EXCLUDES CARD 255 CUT OUT
❑ 1 David Ortiz SP 8.00 3.00
❑ 2 Mike Piazza SP 10.00 4.00
❑ 3 Daryle Ward .50 .20
❑ 4 Rafael Furcal .50 .20
❑ 5 Derek Lowe .50 .20
❑ 6 Eric Chavez .50 .20
❑ 7 Juan Uribe .50 .20
❑ 8 C.C. Sabathia .50 .20
❑ 9 Sean Casey .50 .20
❑ 10 Barry Bonds SP 12.00 5.00
❑ 11 Gary Sheffield .50 .20
❑ 12 Ted Lilly .50 .20
❑ 13 Lew Ford .50 .20
❑ 14 Tom Gordon .50 .20
❑ 15 Curt Schilling 1.00 .40
❑ 16 Jason Kendall .50 .20
❑ 17 Frank Catalanotto .50 .20
❑ 18 Pedro Martinez SP 8.00 3.00
❑ 19 David Dellucci .50 .20
❑ 20A A.Jones w/o Seats 1.00 .40
❑ 20B A.Jones w/Seats SP 8.00 3.00
❑ 21 Brad Halsey .50 .20
❑ 22 Vernon Wells .50 .20
❑ 23A D.Jeter Yellow/White Ltr 4.00 1.50
❑ 23B D.Jeter Blue Ltr SP 12.00 5.00
❑ 24 Todd Helton 1.00 .40
❑ 25 Randy Johnson SP 10.00 4.00
❑ 26 Jay Gibbons .50 .20
❑ 27 Joe Mays .50 .20
❑ 28 Paul Konerko .50 .20
❑ 29 Lyle Overbay .50 .20
❑ 30 Jorge Posada 1.00 .40
❑ 31 Brandon Webb .50 .20
❑ 32 Marcus Giles .50 .20
❑ 33 J.T. Snow .50 .20
❑ 34 Todd Walker .50 .20
❑ 35 Wily Mo Pena SP 8.00 3.00
❑ 36 Carlos Delgado .50 .20
❑ 37 David Wright 1.50 .60
❑ 38 Shea Hillenbrand .50 .20
❑ 39 Daniel Cabrera .50 .20
❑ 40 Trevor Hoffman .50 .20
❑ 41 Matt Morris .50 .20
❑ 42 Mariano Rivera 1.50 .60
❑ 43 Jeff Bagwell 1.00 .40
❑ 44 J.D. Drew .50 .20
❑ 45 Carl Pavano .50 .20
❑ 46 Placido Polanco .50 .20
❑ 47 Adrian Beltre .50 .20
❑ 48 J.D. Closser .50 .20
❑ 49 Paul Lo Duca .50 .20
❑ 50 Scott Rolen .50 .20
❑ 51 Bernie Williams 1.00 .40
❑ 52 Jose Guillen .50 .20
❑ 53 Aubrey Huff .50 .20
❑ 54 Greg Maddux 2.50 1.00
❑ 55 Derrek Lee SP 8.00 3.00
❑ 56 Hideki Matsui 1.50 .60
❑ 57 Jose Bautista .50 .20
❑ 58 Kyle Farnsworth .50 .20
❑ 59 Nate Robertson .50 .20
❑ 60 Sammy Sosa 1.50 .60
❑ 61 Javier Vazquez .50 .20
❑ 62 Jeff Mathis .50 .20
❑ 63 Mark Buehrle .50 .20
❑ 64 Orlando Hernandez .50 .20
❑ 65 Brandon Claussen .50 .20
❑ 66 Miguel Batista .50 .20
❑ 67 Eddie Guardado .50 .20
❑ 68 Alex Gonzalez .50 .20
❑ 69 Kris Benson .50 .20
❑ 70 Bobby Abreu SP 8.00 3.00
❑ 71 Vinny Castilla .50 .20
❑ 72 Ben Broussard .50 .20
❑ 73 Travis Hafner .50 .20
❑ 74 Dmitri Young .50 .20
❑ 75 Alex S. Gonzalez .50 .20
❑ 76 Jason Bay SP 8.00 3.00
❑ 77 Charlton Jimerson .50 .20
❑ 78 Ryan Garko .50 .20
❑ 79 Lance Berkman .50 .20
❑ 80A T.Hudson Red/Blue Ltr .50 .20
❑ 80B T.Hudson Blue Ltr SP 8.00 3.00
❑ 81 Guillermo Mota .50 .20
❑ 82 Chris B. Young .50 .20
❑ 83 Brad Lidge .50 .20
❑ 84 A.J. Pierzynski .50 .20
❑ 85 Maicer Izturis .50 .20
❑ 86 Vladimir Guerrero 1.50 .60
❑ 87 J.J. Hardy .50 .20
❑ 88 Cesar Izturis .50 .20
❑ 89 Mark Ellis .50 .20
❑ 90 Chipper Jones 1.50 .60
❑ 91 Chris Snelling SP 8.00 3.00
❑ 92 Jose Reyes .50 .20
❑ 93 Mike Lieberthal .50 .20
❑ 94 Octavio Dotel .50 .20
❑ 95A A.Rodriguez Fielding SP 10.00 4.00
❑ 95B A.Rodriguez w/Bat SP 10.00 4.00
❑ 96 Brett Myers .50 .20
❑ 97 New York Yankees TC 1.00 .40

❑	98	Ryan Klesko	.50	.20
❑	99	Brian Jordan SP	8.00	3.00
❑	100	W.Harridge/W.Giles	.50	.20
❑	101	Adam Eaton	.50	.20
❑	102	Aaron Boone	.50	.20
❑	103	Alex Rios	.50	.20
❑	104	Andy Pettitte	1.00	.40
❑	105	Barry Zito	.50	.20
❑	106	Bengie Molina SP	8.00	3.00
❑	107	Austin Kearns	.50	.20
❑	108	Adam Everett	.50	.20
❑	109	A.J. Burnett	.50	.20
❑	110	Mark Prior	1.00	.40
❑	111	Russ Ortiz	.50	.20
❑	112	Adam Dunn	.50	.20
❑	113	Byung-Hyun Kim	.50	.20
❑	114	Atlanta Braves TC	.50	.20
❑	115	Carlos Silva	.50	.20
❑	116	Chad Cordero	.50	.20
❑	117	Chone Figgins	.50	.20
❑	118	Chris Reitsma	.50	.20
❑	119	Coco Crisp	.50	.20
❑	120	David DeJesus	.50	.20
❑	121	Chris Snyder	.50	.20
❑	122	Brad Eldred	.50	.20
❑	123	Humberto Cota SP	8.00	3.00
❑	124	Erubiel Durazo	.50	.20
❑	125	Josh Beckett	.50	.20
❑	126	Kenny Lofton	.50	.20
❑	127	Joe Nathan SP	8.00	3.00
❑	128	Bryan Bullington	.50	.20
❑	129	Jim Thome	1.00	.40
❑	130	Shawn Green	.50	.20
❑	131	LaTroy Hawkins	.50	.20
❑	132	Mark Kotsay	.50	.20
❑	133	Matt Lawton	.50	.20
❑	134	Luis Castillo	.50	.20
❑	135	Michael Barrett	.50	.20
❑	136	Preston Wilson	.50	.20
❑	137	Orlando Cabrera	.50	.20
❑	138	Chuck James	.50	.20
❑	139	Raul Ibanez	.50	.20
❑	140	Frank Thomas	1.50	.60
❑	141	Orlando Hudson	.50	.20
❑	142	Scott Kazmir	.50	.20
❑	143	Steve Finley	.50	.20
❑	144	Danny Sandoval RC	.50	.20
❑	145	Javy Lopez	.50	.20
❑	146	Tony Giarratano	.50	.20
❑	147	Terrence Long	.50	.20
❑	148	Victor Martinez	.50	.20
❑	149	Toby Hall	.50	.20
❑	150	Fausto Carmona	.50	.20
❑	151	Tim Wakefield	.50	.20
❑	152	Troy Percival	.50	.20
❑	153	Chris Denorfia	.50	.20
❑	154	Junior Spivey	.50	.20
❑	155	Desi Relaford	.50	.20
❑	156	Francisco Liriano	3.00	1.25
❑	157	Corey Koskie	.50	.20
❑	158	Chris Carpenter	.50	.20
❑	159	Robert Andino RC	.50	.20
❑	160	Cliff Floyd	.50	.20
❑	161	Pittsburgh Pirates TC	.50	.20
❑	162	Anderson Hernandez	.50	.20
❑	163	Mike Maroth	.50	.20
❑	164	Aaron Rowand	.50	.20
❑	165A	A.Pujols Grey Shirt	3.00	1.25
❑	165B	A.Pujols Red Shirt SP	12.00	5.00
❑	166	David Bell	.50	.20
❑	167	Angel Berroa	.50	.20
❑	168	B.J. Ryan	.50	.20
❑	169	Bartolo Colon	.50	.20
❑	170	Hong-Chih Kuo	1.50	.60
❑	171	Cincinnati Reds TC	.50	.20
❑	172	Bill Mueller	.50	.20
❑	173	John Koronka	.50	.20
❑	174	Billy Wagner	.50	.20
❑	175	Zack Greinke	.50	.20
❑	176	Rick Short	.50	.20
❑	177	Yadier Molina	.50	.20
❑	178	Willy Taveras	.50	.20
❑	179	Wes Helms	.50	.20
❑	180	Wade Miller	.50	.20
❑	181	Luis Gonzalez	.50	.20
❑	182	Victor Zambrano	.50	.20
❑	183	Chicago Cubs TC	.50	.20
❑	184	Victor Santos	.50	.20
❑	185	Tyler Walker	.50	.20
❑	186	Bobby Crosby	.50	.20
❑	187	Trot Nixon	.50	.20
❑	188	Nick Johnson	.50	.20
❑	189	Nick Swisher	.50	.20
❑	190	Brian Roberts	.50	.20
❑	191	Nomar Garciaparra	1.50	.60
❑	192	Oliver Perez	.50	.20
❑	193	Ramon Hernandez	.50	.20
❑	194	Randy Winn	.50	.20
❑	195	Ryan Church	.50	.20
❑	196	Ryan Wagner	.50	.20
❑	197	Todd Hollandsworth	.50	.20
❑	198	Detroit Tigers TC	.50	.20
❑	199	Tino Martinez	1.00	.40
❑	200A	R.Clemens On Mound	3.00	1.25
❑	200B	R.Clemens Red Shirt SP	10.00	4.00
❑	201	Shawn Estes	.50	.20
❑	202	Justin Morneau	.50	.20
❑	203	Jeff Francis	.50	.20
❑	204	Oakland Athletics TC	.50	.20
❑	205	Jeff Francoeur	1.50	.60
❑	206	C.J. Wilson	.50	.20
❑	207	Francisco Rodriguez	.50	.20
❑	208	Edgardo Alfonzo	.50	.20
❑	209	David Eckstein	.50	.20
❑	210	Cory Lidle	.50	.20
❑	211	Chase Utley	1.00	.40
❑	212A	R.Baldelli Yellow/White Ltr	.50	.20
❑	212B	R.Baldelli Blue Ltr SP	8.00	3.00
❑	213	So Taguchi	.50	.20
❑	214	Philadelphia Phillies TC	.50	.20
❑	215	Brad Hawpe	.50	.20
❑	216	Walter Young	.50	.20
❑	217	Tom Gorzelanny	.50	.20
❑	218	Shaun Marcum	.50	.20
❑	219	Ryan Howard	2.50	1.00
❑	220	Damian Jackson	.50	.20
❑	221	Craig Counsell	.50	.20
❑	222	Damian Miller	.50	.20
❑	223	Derrick Turnbow	.50	.20
❑	224	Hank Blalock	.50	.20
❑	225	Brayan Pena	.50	.20
❑	226	Grady Sizemore	1.00	.40
❑	227	Ivan Rodriguez	1.00	.40
❑	228	Jason Isringhausen	.50	.20
❑	229	Brian Fuentes	.50	.20
❑	230	Jason Phillips	.50	.20
❑	231	Jason Schmidt	.50	.20
❑	232	Javier Valentin	.50	.20
❑	233	Jeff Kent	.50	.20
❑	234	John Buck	.50	.20
❑	235	Mike Matheny	.50	.20
❑	236	Jorge Cantu	.50	.20
❑	237	Jose Castillo	.50	.20
❑	238	Kenny Rogers	.50	.20
❑	239	Kerry Wood	.50	.20
❑	240	Kevin Mench	.50	.20
❑	241	Tim Stauffer	.50	.20
❑	242	Eric Milton	.50	.20
❑	243	St. Louis Cardinals TC	.50	.20
❑	244	Shawn Chacon	.50	.20
❑	245	Mike Jacobs	.50	.20
❑	246	Ryan Dempster	.50	.20
❑	247	Todd Jones	.50	.20
❑	248	Tom Glavine	1.00	.40
❑	249	Tony Graffanino	.50	.20
❑	250	Ichiro Suzuki	2.50	1.00
❑	251	Baltimore Orioles TC	.50	.20
❑	252	Brad Radke	.50	.20
❑	253	Brad Wilkerson	.50	.20
❑	254	Carlos Lee	.50	.20
❑	255	Alex Gordon Cut Out	300.00	200.00
❑	256	Gustavo Chacin	.50	.20
❑	257	Jermaine Dye	.50	.20
❑	258	Jose Mesa	.50	.20
❑	259	Julio Lugo	.50	.20
❑	260	Mark Redman	.50	.20
❑	261	Brandon Watson	.50	.20
❑	262	Pedro Feliz	.50	.20
❑	263	Esteban Loaiza	.50	.20
❑	264	Anthony Reyes	1.00	.40
❑	265	Jose Contreras SP	8.00	3.00
❑	266	Tadahito Iguchi SP	8.00	3.00
❑	267	Mark Loretta SP	8.00	3.00
❑	268	Ray Durham SP	8.00	3.00
❑	269	Neifi Perez SP	8.00	3.00
❑	270	Washington Nationals TC	.50	.20
❑	271	Troy Glaus SP	8.00	3.00
❑	272	Matt Holliday SP	10.00	4.00
❑	273	Kevin Millwood SP	8.00	3.00
❑	274	Jon Lieber SP	8.00	3.00
❑	275	Cleveland Indians TC	.50	.20
❑	276	Jeremy Reed SP	8.00	3.00
❑	277	Garrett Atkins SP	8.00	3.00
❑	278	Geoff Jenkins SP	8.00	3.00
❑	279	Joey Gathright SP	8.00	3.00
❑	280	Ben Sheets SP	8.00	3.00
❑	281	Melvin Mora SP	8.00	3.00
❑	282	Jonathan Papelbon SP	10.00	4.00
❑	283	John Smoltz SP	8.00	3.00
❑	284	Jake Peavy SP	8.00	3.00
❑	285	Felix Hernandez SP	8.00	3.00
❑	286	Alfonso Soriano SP	8.00	3.00
❑	287	Bronson Arroyo SP	8.00	3.00
❑	288	Adam LaRoche SP	8.00	3.00
❑	289	Aramis Ramirez SP	8.00	3.00
❑	290	Brad Hennessey SP	8.00	3.00
❑	291	Conor Jackson SP	8.00	3.00
❑	292	Rod Barajas SP	8.00	3.00
❑	293	Chris R. Young SP	8.00	3.00
❑	294	Jeremy Bonderman SP	8.00	3.00
❑	295	Jack Wilson SP	8.00	3.00
❑	296	Jay Payton SP	8.00	3.00
❑	297	Danys Baez SP	8.00	3.00
❑	298	Jose Lima SP	8.00	3.00
❑	299	Luis A. Gonzalez SP	8.00	3.00
❑	300	Mike Sweeney SP	8.00	3.00
❑	301	Nelson Cruz SP	8.00	3.00
❑	302	Eric Gagne SP	8.00	3.00
❑	303	Juan Castro SP	8.00	3.00
❑	304	Joe Mauer SP	8.00	3.00
❑	305	Richie Sexson SP	8.00	3.00
❑	306	Roy Oswalt SP	8.00	3.00
❑	307	Rickie Weeks SP	8.00	3.00
❑	308	Pat Borders SP	8.00	3.00
❑	309	Mike Morse SP	8.00	3.00
❑	310	Matt Stairs SP	8.00	3.00
❑	311	Chad Tracy SP	8.00	3.00
❑	312	Matt Cain SP	8.00	3.00
❑	313	Mark Mulder SP	8.00	3.00
❑	314	Mark Grudzielanek SP	8.00	3.00
❑	315	Johnny Damon Yanks SP	10.00	4.00
❑	316	Casey Kotchman SP	8.00	3.00
❑	317	San Francisco Giants TC	.50	.20
❑	318	Chris Burke SP	8.00	3.00
❑	319	Carl Crawford SP	8.00	3.00
❑	320	Edgar Renteria SP	8.00	3.00
❑	321	Chan Ho Park SP	8.00	3.00
❑	322	Boston Red Sox TC SP	8.00	3.00
❑	323	Robinson Cano SP	8.00	3.00
❑	324	Los Angeles Dodgers TC	.50	.20
❑	325A	M.Tejada w/Bat SP	8.00	3.00
❑	325B	M.Tejada Hand Up SP	8.00	3.00
❑	326	Jimmy Rollins SP	8.00	3.00
❑	327	Juan Pierre SP	8.00	3.00
❑	328	Dan Johnson SP	8.00	3.00
❑	329	Chicago White Sox TC	1.00	.40
❑	330	Pat Burrell SP	8.00	3.00
❑	331	Ramon Ortiz SP	8.00	3.00
❑	332	Rondell White SP	8.00	3.00
❑	333	David Wells SP	8.00	3.00
❑	334	Michael Young SP	8.00	3.00
❑	335	Mike Mussina SP	8.00	3.00
❑	336	Moises Alou SP	8.00	3.00
❑	337	Scott Podsednik SP	8.00	3.00
❑	338	Rich Harden SP	8.00	3.00
❑	339	Mark Teahen SP	8.00	3.00
❑	340	Jacque Jones SP	8.00	3.00
❑	341	Jason Giambi SP	8.00	3.00
❑	342	Bill Hall SP	8.00	3.00
❑	343	Jon Garland SP	8.00	3.00
❑	344	Dontrelle Willis SP	8.00	3.00
❑	345	Danny Haren SP	8.00	3.00
❑	346	Brian Giles SP	8.00	3.00
❑	347	Brad Penny SP	8.00	3.00
❑	348	Brandon McCarthy SP	8.00	3.00
❑	349	Chien-Ming Wang SP	10.00	4.00
❑	350A	T.Hunter Red/Blue Ltr SP	8.00	3.00
❑	350B	T.Hunter Blue Ltr SP	8.00	3.00

- ❑ 351 Yhency Brazoban SP 8.00 3.00
- ❑ 352 Rodrigo Lopez SP 8.00 3.00
- ❑ 353 Paul McAnulty .50 .20
- ❑ 354 Francisco Cordero .50 .20
- ❑ 355 Brandon Inge .50 .20
- ❑ 356 Jason Lane .50 .20
- ❑ 357 Brian Schneider .50 .20
- ❑ 358 Dustin Hermanson .50 .20
- ❑ 359 Eric Hinske .50 .20
- ❑ 360 Jarrod Washburn .50 .20
- ❑ 361 Jayson Werth .50 .20
- ❑ 362 Craig Breslow RC .50 .20
- ❑ 363 Jeff Weaver .50 .20
- ❑ 364 Jeromy Burnitz .50 .20
- ❑ 365 Jhonny Peralta .50 .20
- ❑ 366 Joe Crede .50 .20
- ❑ 367 Johan Santana 1.50 .60
- ❑ 368 Jose Valentin .50 .20
- ❑ 369 Keith Foulke .50 .20
- ❑ 370 Larry Bigbie .50 .20
- ❑ 371 Manny Ramirez 1.00 .40
- ❑ 372 Jim Edmonds .50 .20
- ❑ 373 Horacio Ramirez .50 .20
- ❑ 374 Garret Anderson .50 .20
- ❑ 375 Felipe Lopez .50 .20
- ❑ 376 Eric Byrnes .50 .20
- ❑ 377 Darin Erstad .50 .20
- ❑ 378 Carlos Zambrano .50 .20
- ❑ 379 Craig Biggio 1.00 .40
- ❑ 380 Darrell Rasner .50 .20
- ❑ 381 Dave Roberts .50 .20
- ❑ 382 Hanley Ramirez .50 .20
- ❑ 383 Geoff Blum .50 .20
- ❑ 384 Joel Pineiro .50 .20
- ❑ 385 Kip Wells .50 .20
- ❑ 386 Kelvim Escobar .50 .20
- ❑ 387 John Patterson .50 .20
- ❑ 388 Jody Gerut .50 .20
- ❑ 389 Marshall McDougall .50 .20
- ❑ 390 Mike MacDougal .50 .20
- ❑ 391 Orlando Palmeiro .50 .20
- ❑ 392 Rich Aurilia .50 .20
- ❑ 393 Ronnie Belliard .50 .20
- ❑ 394 Rich Hill .50 .20
- ❑ 395 Scott Hatteberg .50 .20
- ❑ 396 Ryan Langerhans .50 .20
- ❑ 397 Richard Hidalgo .50 .20
- ❑ 398 Omar Vizquel 1.00 .40
- ❑ 399 Mike Lowell .50 .20
- ❑ 400 Astros Aces SP 8.00 3.00
- ❑ 401 Mike Cameron .50 .20
- ❑ 402 Matt Clement .50 .20
- ❑ 403 Miguel Cabrera 1.00 .40
- ❑ 404 Milton Bradley .50 .20
- ❑ 405 Laynce Nix .50 .20
- ❑ 406 Rob Mackowiak .50 .20
- ❑ 407 White Sox Power Hitters SP 8.00 3.00
- ❑ 408 Mark Teixeira 1.00 .40
- ❑ 409 Brady Clark .50 .20
- ❑ 410 Johnny Estrada .50 .20
- ❑ 411 Juan Encarnacion .50 .20
- ❑ 412 Morgan Ensberg .50 .20
- ❑ 413 Nook Logan .50 .20
- ❑ 414 Phil Nevin .50 .20
- ❑ 415 Reggie Sanders .50 .20
- ❑ 416 Roy Halladay .50 .20
- ❑ 417 Livan Hernandez .50 .20
- ❑ 418 Jose Vidro .50 .20
- ❑ 419 Shannon Stewart .50 .20
- ❑ 420 Brian Bruney .50 .20
- ❑ 421 Royce Clayton .50 .20
- ❑ 422 Chris Demaria RC .50 .20
- ❑ 423 Eduardo Perez .50 .20
- ❑ 424 Jeff Suppan .50 .20
- ❑ 425 Jaret Wright .50 .20
- ❑ 426 Joe Randa .50 .20
- ❑ 427 Bobby Kielty .50 .20
- ❑ 428 Jason Ellison .50 .20
- ❑ 429 Gregg Zaun .50 .20
- ❑ 430 Runelvys Hernandez .50 .20
- ❑ 431 Joe McEwing .50 .20
- ❑ 432 Jason LaRue .50 .20
- ❑ 433 Aaron Miles .50 .20
- ❑ 434 Adam Kennedy .50 .20
- ❑ 435 Ambiorix Burgos .50 .20
- ❑ 436 Armando Benitez .50 .20
- ❑ 437 Brad Ausmus .50 .20
- ❑ 438 Brandon Backe .50 .20
- ❑ 439 Brian James Anderson .50 .20
- ❑ 440 Bruce Chen .50 .20
- ❑ 441 Carlos Guillen .50 .20
- ❑ 442 Casey Blake .50 .20
- ❑ 443 Chris Capuano .50 .20
- ❑ 444 Chris Duffy .50 .20
- ❑ 445 Chris Ray .50 .20
- ❑ 446 Clint Barmes .50 .20
- ❑ 447 Andrew Sisco .50 .20
- ❑ 448 Dallas McPherson .50 .20
- ❑ 449 Tanyon Sturtze .50 .20
- ❑ 450 Carlos Beltran .50 .20
- ❑ 451 Jason Vargas .50 .20
- ❑ 452 Ervin Santana .50 .20
- ❑ 453 Jason Marquis .50 .20
- ❑ 454 Juan Rivera .50 .20
- ❑ 455 Jake Westbrook .50 .20
- ❑ 456 Jason Johnson .50 .20
- ❑ 457 Joe Blanton .50 .20
- ❑ 458 Kevin Millar .50 .20
- ❑ 459 John Thomson .50 .20
- ❑ 460 J.P. Howell .50 .20
- ❑ 461 Justin Verlander 2.50 1.00
- ❑ 462 Kelly Johnson .50 .20
- ❑ 463 Kyle Davies .50 .20
- ❑ 464 Lance Niekro .50 .20
- ❑ 465 Magglio Ordonez .50 .20
- ❑ 466 Melky Cabrera .50 .20
- ❑ 467 Nick Punto .50 .20
- ❑ 468 Paul Byrd .50 .20
- ❑ 469 Randy Wolf .50 .20
- ❑ 470 Ruben Gotay .50 .20
- ❑ 471 Ryan Madson .50 .20
- ❑ 472 Victor Diaz .50 .20
- ❑ 473 Xavier Nady .50 .20
- ❑ 474 Zach Duke .50 .20
- ❑ 475A H.Street Yellow/White Ltr .50 .20
- ❑ 475B H.Street Blue Ltr SP 8.00 3.00
- ❑ 476 Brad Thompson .50 .20
- ❑ 477 Jonny Gomes .50 .20
- ❑ 478 B.J. Upton .50 .20
- ❑ 479 Jamey Carroll .50 .20
- ❑ 480 Mike Hampton .50 .20
- ❑ 481 Tony Clark .50 .20
- ❑ 482 Antonio Alfonseca .50 .20
- ❑ 483 Justin Duchscherer .50 .20
- ❑ 484 Mike Timlin .50 .20
- ❑ 485 Joe Saunders .50 .20

2007 Topps Heritage

- ❑ COMPLETE SET (527) 400.00 250.00
- ❑ COMP.SET w/o SP's (384) 60.00 30.00
- ❑ COMMON CARD .50 .20
- ❑ COMMON RC .50 .20
- ❑ COMMON TEAM CARD .50 .20
- ❑ COMMON SP 6.00 2.50
- ❑ SP STATED ODDS 1:2 HOBBY/RETAIL
- ❑ SEE BECKETT.COM FOR SP CHECKLIST
- ❑ COMMON YELLOW 5.00 2.00
- ❑ YELLOW STATED ODDS 1:6 HOBBY/RETAIL
- ❑ SEE BECKETT.COM FOR YELLOW CL
- ❑ CARD 145 DOES NOT EXIST
- ❑ 1 David Ortiz 1.25 .50
- ❑ 2a Roger Clemens 2.00 .75
- ❑ 2b Roger Clemens YT 8.00 3.00
- ❑ 3 David Wells .50 .20
- ❑ 4 Ronny Paulino SP 6.00 2.50
- ❑ 5 Derek Jeter SP 15.00 6.00
- ❑ 6 Felix Hernandez .75 .30
- ❑ 7 Todd Helton .75 .30
- ❑ 8a David Eckstein .50 .20
- ❑ 8b David Eckstein YN 5.00 2.00
- ❑ 9 Craig Wilson .50 .20
- ❑ 10 John Smoltz .75 .30
- ❑ 11a Rob Mackowiak .50 .20
- ❑ 11b Rob Mackowiak YT 5.00 2.00
- ❑ 12 Scott Hatteberg .50 .20
- ❑ 13a Wilfredo Ledezma SP 6.00 2.50
- ❑ 13b Wilfredo Ledezma YT 5.00 2.00
- ❑ 14 Bobby Abreu SP 6.00 2.50
- ❑ 15 Mike Stanton .50 .20
- ❑ 16 Wilson Betemit .50 .20
- ❑ 17 Darren Oliver .50 .20
- ❑ 18 Josh Beckett .75 .30
- ❑ 19 San Francisco Giants TC .50 .20
- ❑ 20a Robinson Cano .75 .30
- ❑ 20b Robinson Cano YT 6.00 2.50
- ❑ 21 Matt Cain .75 .30
- ❑ 22 Jason Kendall SP 6.00 2.50
- ❑ 23a Mark Kotsay SP 6.00 2.50
- ❑ 23b Mark Kotsay YN 5.00 2.00
- ❑ 24a Yadier Molina .50 .20
- ❑ 24b Yadier Molina YN 5.00 2.00
- ❑ 25 Brad Penny .50 .20
- ❑ 26 Adrian Gonzalez .50 .20
- ❑ 27 Danny Haren .50 .20
- ❑ 28 Brian Giles .50 .20
- ❑ 29 Jose Lopez .50 .20
- ❑ 30a Ichiro Suzuki 2.00 .75
- ❑ 30b Ichiro Suzuki YN 8.00 3.00
- ❑ 31 Beltran Perez SP (RC) 6.00 2.50
- ❑ 32 Brad Hawpe SP 6.00 2.50
- ❑ 33a Jim Thome .75 .30
- ❑ 33b Jim Thome YT 6.00 2.50
- ❑ 34 Mark DeRosa .50 .20
- ❑ 35a Woody Williams .50 .20
- ❑ 35b Woody Williams YT 5.00 2.00
- ❑ 36 Luis Gonzalez .50 .20
- ❑ 37 Billy Sadler (RC) .50 .20
- ❑ 38 Dave Roberts .50 .20
- ❑ 39 Mitch Maier RC .50 .20
- ❑ 40 Francisco Cordero SP 6.00 2.50
- ❑ 41 Anthony Reyes SP 6.00 2.50
- ❑ 42 Russell Martin .50 .20
- ❑ 43 Scott Proctor .50 .20
- ❑ 44 Washington Nationals TC .50 .20
- ❑ 45 Shane Victorino .50 .20
- ❑ 46a Joel Zumaya .75 .30
- ❑ 46b Joel Zumaya YN 6.00 2.50
- ❑ 47 Delmon Young (RC) 1.25 .50
- ❑ 48 Alex Rios .50 .20
- ❑ 49 Willy Taveras SP 6.00 2.50
- ❑ 50a Mark Buehrle SP 6.00 2.50
- ❑ 50b Mark Buehrle YT 5.00 2.00
- ❑ 51 Livan Hernandez .50 .20
- ❑ 52a Jason Bay .50 .20
- ❑ 52b Jason Bay YT 5.00 2.00
- ❑ 53a Jose Valentin .50 .20
- ❑ 53b Jose Valentin YN 5.00 2.00
- ❑ 54 Kevin Reese .50 .20
- ❑ 55 Felipe Lopez .50 .20
- ❑ 56 Ryan Sweeney (RC) .50 .20
- ❑ 57a Kelvim Escobar .50 .20
- ❑ 57b Kelvim Escobar YN 5.00 2.00
- ❑ 58a N.Swisher Sm.Print SP 6.00 2.50
- ❑ 58b N.Swisher Lg.Print YT 5.00 2.00
- ❑ 59 Kevin Millwood SP 6.00 2.50
- ❑ 60a Preston Wilson .50 .20
- ❑ 60b Preston Wilson YN 5.00 2.00
- ❑ 61a Mariano Rivera 1.25 .50
- ❑ 61b Mariano Rivera YN 6.00 2.50
- ❑ 62 Josh Barfield .50 .20
- ❑ 63 Ryan Freel .50 .20
- ❑ 64 Tim Hudson .50 .20
- ❑ 65a Chris Narveson (RC) .50 .20
- ❑ 65b Chris Narveson YN (RC) 5.00 2.00
- ❑ 66 Matt Murton .50 .20
- ❑ 67 Melvin Mora SP 6.00 2.50
- ❑ 68 Jason Jennings SP 6.00 2.50
- ❑ 69 Emil Brown .50 .20
- ❑ 70a Magglio Ordonez .50 .20
- ❑ 70b Magglio Ordonez YN 5.00 2.00

❑ 71	Los Angeles Dodgers TC	.50	.20
❑ 72	Ross Gload	.50	.20
❑ 73	David Ross	.50	.20
❑ 74	Juan Uribe	.50	.20
❑ 75	Scott Podsednik	.50	.20
❑ 76a	Cole Hamels SP	8.00	3.00
❑ 76b	Cole Hamels YT	6.00	2.50
❑ 77a	Rafael Furcal SP	6.00	2.50
❑ 77b	Rafael Furcal YT	5.00	2.00
❑ 78a	Ryan Theriot	.50	.20
❑ 78b	Ryan Theriot YN	5.00	2.00
❑ 79a	Corey Patterson	.50	.20
❑ 79b	Corey Patterson YT	5.00	2.00
❑ 80	Jered Weaver	.75	.30
❑ 81a	Stephen Drew	.75	.30
❑ 81b	Stephen Drew YT	6.00	2.50
❑ 82	Adam Kennedy	.50	.20
❑ 83	Tony Gwynn Jr.	.50	.20
❑ 84	Kazuo Matsui	.50	.20
❑ 85a	Omar Vizquel SP	8.00	3.00
❑ 85b	Omar Vizquel YT	6.00	2.50
❑ 86	Fred Lewis SP (RC)	6.00	2.50
❑ 87a	Shawn Chacon	.50	.20
❑ 87b	Shawn Chacon YN	5.00	2.00
❑ 88	Frank Catalanotto	.50	.20
❑ 89	Orlando Hudson	.50	.20
❑ 90	Pat Burrell	.50	.20
❑ 91	David DeJesus	.50	.20
❑ 92a	David Wright	2.00	.75
❑ 92b	David Wright YN	8.00	3.00
❑ 93	Conor Jackson	.50	.20
❑ 94	Xavier Nady SP	6.00	2.50
❑ 95	Bill Hall SP	6.00	2.50
❑ 96	Kip Wells	.50	.20
❑ 97a	Jeff Suppan	.50	.20
❑ 97b	Jeff Suppan YN	5.00	2.00
❑ 98a	Ryan Zimmerman	1.25	.50
❑ 98b	Ryan Zimmerman YN	6.00	2.50
❑ 99	Wes Helms	.50	.20
❑ 100a	Jose Contreras	.50	.20
❑ 100b	Jose Contreras YT	5.00	2.00
❑ 101a	Miguel Cairo	.50	.20
❑ 101b	Miguel Cairo YN	5.00	2.00
❑ 102	Brian Roberts	.50	.20
❑ 103	Carl Crawford SP	6.00	2.50
❑ 104	Mike Lamb SP	6.00	2.50
❑ 105	Mark Ellis	.50	.20
❑ 106	Scott Rolen	.75	.30
❑ 107	Garrett Atkins	.50	.20
❑ 108a	Hanley Ramirez	.75	.30
❑ 108b	Hanley Ramirez YT	6.00	2.50
❑ 109	Trot Nixon	.50	.20
❑ 110	Edgar Renteria	.50	.20
❑ 111	Jeff Francis	.50	.20
❑ 112	Marcus Thames SP	6.00	2.50
❑ 113	Brian Burres SP (RC)	6.00	2.50
❑ 114	Brian Schneider	.50	.20
❑ 115	Jeremy Bonderman	.50	.20
❑ 116	Ryan Madson	.50	.20
❑ 117	Gerald Laird	.50	.20
❑ 118	Roy Halladay	.50	.20
❑ 119	Victor Martinez	.50	.20
❑ 120	Greg Maddux	2.00	.75
❑ 121	Jay Payton SP	6.00	2.50
❑ 122	Jacque Jones SP	6.00	2.50
❑ 123	Juan Lara RC	.50	.20
❑ 124	Derrick Turnbow	.50	.20
❑ 125	Adam Everett	.50	.20
❑ 126	Michael Cuddyer	.50	.20
❑ 127	Gil Meche	.50	.20
❑ 128	Willy Aybar	.50	.20
❑ 129	Jerry Owens (RC)	.50	.20
❑ 130	Manny Ramirez SP	8.00	3.00
❑ 131	Howie Kendrick SP	6.00	2.50
❑ 132	Byung-Hyun Kim	.50	.20
❑ 133	Kevin Kouzmanoff (RC)	.50	.20
❑ 134	Philadelphia Phillies TC	.50	.20
❑ 135	Joe Blanton	.50	.20
❑ 136	Ray Durham	.50	.20
❑ 137	Luke Hudson	.50	.20
❑ 138	Eric Byrnes	.50	.20
❑ 139	Ryan Braun SP RC	6.00	2.50
❑ 140	Johnny Damon SP	8.00	3.00
❑ 141	Ambiorix Burgos	.50	.20
❑ 142	Hideki Matsui	1.25	.50
❑ 143	Josh Johnson	.50	.20
❑ 144	Miguel Cabrera	.75	.30
❑ 146	Delwyn Young (RC)	.50	.20
❑ 147	Chuck James	.50	.20
❑ 148	Morgan Ensberg	.50	.20
❑ 149	Jose Vidro SP	6.00	2.50
❑ 150	Alex Rodriguez SP	12.00	5.00
❑ 151	Carlos Maldonado (RC)	.50	.20
❑ 152	Jason Schmidt	.50	.20
❑ 153	Alex Escobar	.50	.20
❑ 154	Chris Gomez	.50	.20
❑ 155	Endy Chavez	.50	.20
❑ 156	Kris Benson	.50	.20
❑ 157	Bronson Arroyo	.50	.20
❑ 158	Cleveland Indians TC SP	6.00	2.50
❑ 159	Chris Ray SP	6.00	2.50
❑ 160	Richie Sexson	.50	.20
❑ 161	Huston Street	.50	.20
❑ 162	Kevin Youkilis	.50	.20
❑ 163	Armando Benitez	.50	.20
❑ 164	Vinny Rottino (RC)	.50	.20
❑ 165	Garret Anderson	.50	.20
❑ 166	Todd Greene	.50	.20
❑ 167	Brian Stokes SP (RC)	6.00	2.50
❑ 168	Albert Pujols SP	15.00	6.00
❑ 169	Todd Coffey	.50	.20
❑ 170	Jason Michaels	.50	.20
❑ 171	David Dellucci	.50	.20
❑ 172	Eric Milton	.50	.20
❑ 173	Austin Kearns	.50	.20
❑ 174	Oakland Athletics TC	.50	.20
❑ 175	Andy Cannizaro RC	.50	.20
❑ 176	David Weathers SP	6.00	2.50
❑ 177	Jermaine Dye SP	6.00	2.50
❑ 178	Wily Mo Pena	.50	.20
❑ 179	Chris Burke	.50	.20
❑ 180	Jeff Weaver	.50	.20
❑ 181	Edwin Encarnacion	.50	.20
❑ 182	Jeremy Hermida	.50	.20
❑ 183	Tim Wakefield	.50	.20
❑ 184	Rich Hill	.50	.20
❑ 185	Aaron Hill SP	6.00	2.50
❑ 186	Scot Shields SP	6.00	2.50
❑ 187	Randy Johnson	1.25	.50
❑ 188	Dan Johnson	.50	.20
❑ 189	Sean Marshall	.50	.20
❑ 190	Marcus Giles	.50	.20
❑ 191	Jonathan Broxton	.50	.20
❑ 192	Mike Piazza	1.25	.50
❑ 193	Carlos Quentin	.50	.20
❑ 194	Derek Lowe SP	6.00	2.50
❑ 195	Russell Branyan SP	6.00	2.50
❑ 196	Jason Marquis	.50	.20
❑ 197	Khalil Greene	.75	.30
❑ 198	Ryan Dempster	.50	.20
❑ 199	Ronnie Belliard	.50	.20
❑ 200	Josh Fogg	.50	.20
❑ 201	Carlos Lee	.50	.20
❑ 202	Chris Denorfia	.50	.20
❑ 203	Kendry Morales SP	8.00	3.00
❑ 204	Rafael Soriano SP	6.00	2.50
❑ 205	Brandon Phillips	.50	.20
❑ 206	Andrew Miller RC	3.00	1.25
❑ 207	John Koronka	.50	.20
❑ 208	Luis Castillo	.50	.20
❑ 209	Angel Guzman	.50	.20
❑ 210	Jim Edmonds	.75	.30
❑ 211	Patrick Misch (RC)	.50	.20
❑ 212	Ty Wigginton SP	6.00	2.50
❑ 213	Brandon Inge SP	6.00	2.50
❑ 214	Royce Clayton	.50	.20
❑ 215	Ben Broussard	.50	.20
❑ 216	St. Louis Cardinals TC	.50	.20
❑ 217	Mark Mulder	.50	.20
❑ 218	Kenji Johjima	1.25	.50
❑ 219	Joe Crede	.50	.20
❑ 220	Shea Hillenbrand	.50	.20
❑ 221	Josh Fields SP (RC)	6.00	2.50
❑ 222	Pat Neshek SP	8.00	3.00
❑ 223	Reed Johnson	.50	.20
❑ 224	Mike Mussina	.75	.30
❑ 225	Randy Winn	.50	.20
❑ 226	Brian Rogers	.50	.20
❑ 227	Juan Rivera	.50	.20
❑ 228	Shawn Green	.50	.20
❑ 229	Mike Napoli	.50	.20
❑ 230	Chase Utley SP	8.00	3.00
❑ 231	John Nelson SP (RC)	6.00	2.50
❑ 232	Casey Blake	.50	.20
❑ 233	Lyle Overbay	.50	.20
❑ 234	Adam LaRoche	.50	.20
❑ 235	Julio Lugo	.50	.20
❑ 236	Johnny Estrada	.50	.20
❑ 237	James Shields	.50	.20
❑ 238	Jose Castillo	.50	.20
❑ 239	Doug Davis SP	6.00	2.50
❑ 240	Jason Giambi SP	6.00	2.50
❑ 241	Mike Gonzalez	.50	.20
❑ 242	Scott Downs	.50	.20
❑ 243	Joe Inglett	.50	.20
❑ 244	Matt Kemp	.50	.20
❑ 245	Ted Lilly	.50	.20
❑ 246	New York Yankees TC	1.25	.50
❑ 247	Jamey Carroll	.50	.20
❑ 248	Adam Wainwright SP	6.00	2.50
❑ 249	Matt Thornton SP	6.00	2.50
❑ 250	Alfonso Soriano	.50	.20
❑ 251	Tom Gordon	.50	.20
❑ 252	Dennis Sarfate (RC)	.50	.20
❑ 253	Zach Duke	.50	.20
❑ 254	Hank Blalock	.50	.20
❑ 255	Johan Santana	.75	.30
❑ 256	Chicago White Sox TC	.50	.20
❑ 257	Aaron Cook SP	6.00	2.50
❑ 258	Cliff Lee SP	6.00	2.50
❑ 259	Miguel Tejada	.50	.20
❑ 260	Mike Lowell	.50	.20
❑ 261	Ian Snell	.50	.20
❑ 262	Jason Tyner	.50	.20
❑ 263	Troy Tulowitzki (RC)	1.25	.50
❑ 264	Ervin Santana	.50	.20
❑ 265	Jon Lester	.75	.30
❑ 266	Andy Pettitte SP	8.00	3.00
❑ 267	A.J. Pierzynski SP	6.00	2.50
❑ 268	Rich Aurilia	.50	.20
❑ 269	Phil Nevin	.50	.20
❑ 270	Tom Glavine	.75	.30
❑ 271	Chris Coste	.50	.20
❑ 272	Moises Alou	.50	.20
❑ 273	J.D. Drew	.50	.20
❑ 274	Abraham Nunez	.50	.20
❑ 275	Jorge Posada SP	8.00	3.00
❑ 276	Jeff Conine SP	6.00	2.50
❑ 277	Chad Cordero	.50	.20
❑ 278	Nick Johnson	.50	.20
❑ 279	Kevin Millar	.50	.20
❑ 280	Mark Grudzielanek	.50	.20
❑ 281	Chris Stewart RC	.50	.20
❑ 282	Nate Robertson	.50	.20
❑ 283	Drew Anderson RC	.50	.20
❑ 284	Doug Mientkiewicz SP	6.00	2.50
❑ 285	Ken Griffey Jr. SP	10.00	4.00
❑ 286	Cory Sullivan	.50	.20
❑ 287	Chris Carpenter	.50	.20
❑ 288	Gary Matthews	.50	.20
❑ 289	J.Verlander/Jef.Weaver	1.25	.50
❑ 290	Vicente Padilla	.50	.20
❑ 291	Chris Roberson	.50	.20
❑ 292	Chris R. Young	.50	.20
❑ 293	Ryan Garko SP	6.00	2.50
❑ 294	Miguel Batista SP	6.00	2.50
❑ 295	B.J. Upton	.50	.20
❑ 296	Justin Verlander	1.25	.50
❑ 297	Ben Zobrist	.50	.20
❑ 298	Ben Sheets	.50	.20
❑ 299	Eric Chavez	.50	.20
❑ 300	Scott Schoeneweis	.50	.20
❑ 301	Placido Polanco	.50	.20
❑ 302	Angel Sanchez SP RC	6.00	2.50
❑ 303	Freddy Sanchez SP	6.00	2.50
❑ 304	M.Ordonez/C.Monroe	.50	.20
❑ 305	A.J. Burnett	.50	.20
❑ 306	Juan Perez RC	.50	.20
❑ 307	Chris Britton	.50	.20
❑ 308	Jon Garland	.50	.20
❑ 309	Pedro Feliz	.50	.20
❑ 310	Ryan Howard	2.00	.75
❑ 311	Aaron Harang SP	6.00	2.50
❑ 312	Boston Red Sox TC SP	8.00	3.00
❑ 313	Chad Billingsley	.50	.20
❑ 314	C.Jones/B.Cox MG	1.25	.50
❑ 315	Bengie Molina	.50	.20
❑ 316	Juan Pierre	.50	.20

❑	317	Luke Scott	.50	.20
❑	318	Javier Valentin	.50	.20
❑	319	Mark Loretta	.50	.20
❑	320	Kenny Lofton SP	6.00	2.50
❑	321	V.Guerrero/I.Rodriguez SP	8.00	3.00
❑	322	Josh Willingham	.50	.20
❑	323	Lance Berkman	.50	.20
❑	324	Anibal Sanchez	.50	.20
❑	325	Maicer Izturis	.50	.20
❑	326	Brett Myers	.50	.20
❑	327	Chicago Cubs TC	.75	.30
❑	328	Francisco Liriano	2.50	1.00
❑	329	Craig Monroe SP	6.00	2.50
❑	330	Paul LoDuca SP	6.00	2.50
❑	331	Steve Trachsel	.50	.20
❑	332	Bernie Williams	.75	.30
❑	333	Carlos Guillen	.50	.20
❑	334	C.Wang/M.Mussina	2.00	.75
❑	335	Dave Bush	.50	.20
❑	336	Carlos Beltran	.50	.20
❑	337	Jason Isringhausen	.50	.20
❑	338	Todd Walker SP	6.00	2.50
❑	339	Jarrod Washburn SP	6.00	2.50
❑	340	Brandon Webb	.50	.20
❑	341	Pittsburgh Pirates TC	.50	.20
❑	342	Daryle Ward	.50	.20
❑	343	Chad Santos	.50	.20
❑	344	Brad Lidge	.50	.20
❑	345	Brad Ausmus	.50	.20
❑	346	Carlos Delgado	.50	.20
❑	347	Boone Logan SP	6.00	2.50
❑	348	Jimmy Rollins SP	6.00	2.50
❑	349	Orlando Hernandez	.50	.20
❑	350	Gary Sheffield	.50	.20
❑	351	Pujols/Duncan/Edmonds/Molina	2.50	1.00
❑	352	Jake Peavy	.50	.20
❑	353	Jason Varitek	1.25	.50
❑	354	Freddy Garcia	.50	.20
❑	355	Matt Diaz	.50	.20
❑	356	Bernie Castro SP	6.00	2.50
❑	357	Eric Stults SP RC	6.00	2.50
❑	358	John Lackey	.50	.20
❑	359	Bobby Jenks	.50	.20
❑	360	Mark Teixeira	.75	.30
❑	361	Jonathan Papelbon	1.25	.50
❑	362	Paul Konerko	.50	.20
❑	363	Erik Bedard	.50	.20
❑	364	Eliezer Alfonzo	.50	.20
❑	365	Fernando Rodney SP	6.00	2.50
❑	366	Chris Duncan SP	6.00	2.50
❑	367	Jose Diaz (RC)	.50	.20
❑	368	Travis Hafner	.50	.20
❑	369	Matt Capps	.50	.20
❑	370	Ivan Rodriguez	.75	.30
❑	371	David Murphy (RC)	.50	.20
❑	372	Carlos Zambrano	.50	.20
❑	373	Chris Iannetta	.50	.20
❑	374	Jose Mesa SP	6.00	2.50
❑	375	Michael Young SP	6.00	2.50
❑	376	Bill Bray	.50	.20
❑	377	Atlanta Braves TC	.75	.30
❑	378	Jeff Cirillo	.50	.20
❑	379	Barry Zito	.50	.20
❑	380	Clay Hensley	.50	.20
❑	381	J.J. Putz	.50	.20
❑	382	C.C. Sabathia	.50	.20
❑	383	Eduardo Perez SP	6.00	2.50
❑	384	Scott Moore SP (RC)	6.00	2.50
❑	385	Scott Olsen	.50	.20
❑	386	R.Howard/C.Utley	2.00	.75
❑	387	Aaron Rowand	.50	.20
❑	388	Mike Rouse	.50	.20
❑	389	Alexis Gomez	.50	.20
❑	390	Brian McCann	.50	.20
❑	391	Ryan Shealy	.50	.20
❑	392	Shane Youman SP RC	6.00	2.50
❑	393	Melky Cabrera SP	6.00	2.50
❑	394	Jeremy Sowers	.50	.20
❑	395	Casey Janssen	.50	.20
❑	396	Travis Chick (RC)	.50	.20
❑	397	Detroit Tigers TC	.50	.20
❑	398	Reggie Abercrombie	.50	.20
❑	399	Ricky Nolasco	.50	.20
❑	400	Tadahito Iguchi	.50	.20
❑	401	Jose Reyes SP	6.00	2.50
❑	402	Juan Encarnacion SP	6.00	2.50
❑	403	Brandon Harper	.50	.20
❑	404	Torii Hunter	.50	.20
❑	405	Dan Uggla	.75	.30
❑	406	Orlando Cabrera	.50	.20
❑	407	Jose Capellan	.50	.20
❑	408	Baltimore Orioles TC	.50	.20
❑	409	Frank Thomas	1.25	.50
❑	410	Francisco Rodriguez SP	6.00	2.50
❑	411	Ian Kinsler SP	8.00	3.00
❑	412	Billy Wagner	.50	.20
❑	413	Andy Marte	.50	.20
❑	414	Mike Jacobs	.50	.20
❑	415	Raul Ibanez	.50	.20
❑	416	Jhonny Peralta	.50	.20
❑	417	Chris B. Young	.50	.20
❑	418	A.Pujols/M.Ordonez	2.50	1.00
❑	419	Scott Kazmir SP	8.00	3.00
❑	420	Norris Hopper SP	6.00	2.50
❑	421	Chris Capuano	.50	.20
❑	422	Troy Glaus	.50	.20
❑	423	Roy Oswalt	.50	.20
❑	424	Grady Sizemore	.75	.30
❑	425	Chone Figgins	.50	.20
❑	426	Chad Tracy	.50	.20
❑	427	Brian Fuentes	.50	.20
❑	428	Cincinnati Reds TC SP	6.00	2.50
❑	429	Ramon Hernandez SP	6.00	2.50
❑	430	Mike Cameron	.50	.20
❑	431	Dontrelle Willis	.50	.20
❑	432	Josh Sharpless	.50	.20
❑	433	Adrian Beltre	.50	.20
❑	434	Curtis Granderson	.50	.20
❑	435	B.J. Ryan	.50	.20
❑	436	D.Wright/R.Howard	2.00	.75
❑	437	Vernon Wells SP	6.00	2.50
❑	438	Vladimir Guerrero SP	8.00	3.00
❑	439	Jake Westbrook	.50	.20
❑	440	Chipper Jones	1.25	.50
❑	441	James Loney	.75	.30
❑	442	Nook Logan	.50	.20
❑	443	Oswaldo Navarro RC	.50	.20
❑	444	Joe Mauer	.75	.30
❑	445	Miguel Montero (RC)	.50	.20
❑	446	Franklin Gutierrez SP	6.00	2.50
❑	447	Mark Redman SP	6.00	2.50
❑	448	Mike Rabelo RC	.50	.20
❑	449	Philip Humber (RC)	.75	.30
❑	450	Justin Morneau	.50	.20
❑	451	Hector Gimenez (RC)	.50	.20
❑	452	Matt Holliday	1.25	.50
❑	453	Akinori Otsuka	.50	.20
❑	454	Prince Fielder	1.25	.50
❑	455	Chien-Ming Wang SP	10.00	4.00
❑	456	Shawn Riggans SP	6.00	2.50
❑	457	John Maine	.50	.20
❑	458	Adam Lind (RC)	.50	.20
❑	459	Ubaldo Jimenez (RC)	.50	.20
❑	460	Jaret Wright	.50	.20
❑	461	Cla Meredith	.50	.20
❑	462	Joaquin Arias (RC)	.50	.20
❑	463	Kenny Rogers	.50	.20
❑	464	Jose Garcia SP RC	6.00	2.50
❑	465	Pedro Martinez SP	8.00	3.00
❑	466	Jeff Salazar (RC)	.50	.20
❑	467	Glen Perkins	.50	.20
❑	468	Travis Ishikawa	.50	.20
❑	469	Joe Borowski	.50	.20
❑	470	Jeremy Brown	.50	.20
❑	471	Andre Ethier	.75	.30
❑	472	Taylor Tankersley	.50	.20
❑	473	Lastings Milledge SP	8.00	3.00
❑	474	Brian Sanches SP	6.00	2.50
❑	475	O.Guillen AS MG/P.Garner AS MG	.50	.20
❑	476	Albert Pujols AS	2.50	1.00
❑	477	David Ortiz AS	1.25	.50
❑	478	Chase Utley AS	1.25	.50
❑	479	Mark Loretta AS	.50	.20
❑	480	David Wright AS	2.00	.75
❑	481	Alex Rodriguez AS	2.00	.75
❑	482	Edgar Renteria AS SP	6.00	2.50
❑	483	Derek Jeter AS SP	12.00	5.00
❑	484	Alfonso Soriano AS	.50	.20
❑	485	Vladimir Guerrero AS	1.25	.50
❑	486	Carlos Beltran AS	.50	.20
❑	487	Vernon Wells AS	.50	.20
❑	488	Jason Bay AS	.50	.20
❑	489	Ichiro Suzuki AS	2.00	.75
❑	490	Paul LoDuca AS	.50	.20
❑	491	Ivan Rodriguez AS SP	8.00	3.00
❑	492	Brad Penny AS SP	6.00	2.50
❑	493	Roy Halladay AS	.50	.20
❑	494	Brian Fuentes AS	.50	.20
❑	495	Kenny Rogers AS	.50	.20

2008 Topps Heritage

❑		COMP.SET w/o SP's (425)	80.00	40.00
❑		COMMON CARD	.40	.15
❑		COMMON RC	1.00	.40
❑		COMMON TEAM CARD	.40	.15
❑		COMMON GB SP	1.00	.40
❑		COMMON SP	6.00	2.50
❑		SP STATED ODDS 1:3 HOBBY/RETAIL		
❑	1	Vladimir Guerrero	1.00	.40
❑	2	Placido Polanco GB SP	1.00	.40
❑	3	Eric Byrnes GB SP	1.00	.40
❑	4	Mark Teixeira	.60	.25
❑	5	Javier Vazquez GB SP	1.00	.40
❑	6	Jacoby Ellsbury	1.50	.60
❑	7	Joey Gathright GB SP	1.00	.40
❑	8	Philadelphia Phillies GB SP	1.00	.40
❑	9	Andre Ethier GB SP	1.50	.60
❑	10	Alex Rodriguez	1.50	.60
❑	11	Luke Scott SP	6.00	2.50
❑	12	Curt Schilling GB SP	1.50	.60
❑	13	Billy Wagner GB SP	1.00	.40
❑	14	Gary Matthews GB SP	1.00	.40
❑	15	Sean Marshall	.40	.15
❑	16	I.Suzuki GB SP	4.00	1.50
❑	17	Wilson/Bay/Sanchez	.40	.15
❑	18	Dontrelle Willis GB SP	1.00	.40
❑	19	Josh Willingham	.40	.15
❑	20	Jeff Kent	.40	.15
❑	21	Troy Tulowitzki GB SP	1.50	.60
❑	22	Brian Fuentes GB SP	1.00	.40
❑	23	Robinson Cano GB SP	1.50	.60
❑	24	Felix Hernandez GB SP	1.50	.60
❑	25	Edwin Encarnacion	.40	.15
❑	26	Fausto Carmona	.40	.15
❑	27	Greg Maddux	1.25	.50
❑	28	Ivan Rodriguez GB SP	1.50	.60
❑	29	Joe Nathan	.40	.15
❑	30	Paul Konerko	.40	.15
❑	31	Nook Logan	.40	.15
❑	32	Derek Lowe	.40	.15
❑	33	Jose Lopez	.40	.15
❑	34	Ordonez/Granderson GB SP	1.50	.60
❑	35	Adam LaRoche GB SP	1.00	.40
❑	36	Kenny Lofton	.40	.15
❑	37	Matt Capps	.40	.15
❑	38	Mark Reynolds	.40	.15
❑	39	Joe Mauer	.60	.25
❑	40	Tim Hudson GB SP	1.00	.40
❑	41	Kelvim Escobar GB SP	1.00	.40
❑	42	Jason Jennings GB SP	1.00	.40
❑	43	Victor Martinez	.40	.15
❑	44	Jason Kendall	.40	.15
❑	45	Chris Ray GB SP	1.00	.40
❑	46	Jason Bergmann	.40	.15
❑	47	Jason Marquis	.40	.15
❑	48	Baltimore Orioles	.40	.15
❑	49	Bill Hall GB SP	1.00	.40
❑	50	Ken Griffey Jr.	1.50	.60
❑	51	Chad Cordero	.40	.15
❑	52	Omar Vizquel GB SP	1.00	.40

❑ 53 Jim Edmonds .60 .25
❑ 54 Justin Upton GB SP 2.50 1.00
❑ 55 Josh Beckett .60 .25
❑ 56 Jeff Francis .40 .15
❑ 57 Brad Lidge GB SP 1.00 .40
❑ 58 Paul Lo Duca GB SP 1.00 .40
❑ 59 John Patterson .40 .15
❑ 60 Andy Pettitte GB SP 1.50 .60
❑ 61 Brendan Harris GB SP 1.00 .40
❑ 62 Chris Young GB SP 1.00 .40
❑ 63 Eric Chavez .40 .15
❑ 64 Francisco Rodriguez .40 .15
❑ 65 Jason Giambi GB SP 1.50 .60
❑ 66 B.J. Ryan .40 .15
❑ 67 Rich Hill GB SP 1.00 .40
❑ 68 Derek Jeter 2.50 1.00
❑ 69 San Francisco Giants GB SP 1.00 .40
❑ 70 Carlos Guillen .40 .15
❑ 71 Trevor Hoffman GB SP 1.00 .40
❑ 72 Zach Duke .40 .15
❑ 73 Dustin Pedroia .60 .25
❑ 74 D.Young/R.Zimmerman .60 .25
❑ 75 Cole Hamels .60 .25
❑ 76 Carlos Delgado .40 .15
❑ 77 Jonathan Broxton .40 .15
❑ 78 Josh Hamilton GB SP 3.00 1.25
❑ 79 Mark Loretta GB SP 1.00 .40
❑ 80 Grady Sizemore .60 .25
❑ 81 Torii Hunter GB SP 1.00 .40
❑ 82 Carlos Beltran GB SP 1.00 .40
❑ 83 Jason Isringhausen GB SP 1.00 .40
❑ 84 Brad Penny GB SP 1.00 .40
❑ 85 Jayson Werth .40 .15
❑ 86 Alex Gordon 1.00 .40
❑ 87 David DeJesus .40 .15
❑ 88 Clay Buchholz 1.00 .40
❑ 89 Conor Jackson .40 .15
❑ 90 Hideki Matsui GB SP 2.50 1.00
❑ 91 Matt Garza GB SP 1.00 .40
❑ 92 P.Hughes GB SP 2.50 1.00
❑ 93 Mike Piazza 1.00 .40
❑ 94 Chicago White Sox GB SP 1.00 .40
❑ 95 Buddy Carlyle .40 .15
❑ 96 Mark DeRosa .40 .15
❑ 97 Brandon Webb .40 .15
❑ 98 Jon Garland GB SP 1.00 .40
❑ 99 Mariano Rivera 1.00 .40
❑ 100 Jack Cust .40 .15
❑ 101 Carlos Ruiz .40 .15
❑ 102 Moises Alou GB SP 1.00 .40
❑ 103 Bengie Molina .40 .15
❑ 104 Adam Jones .40 .15
❑ 105 Alfonso Soriano .60 .25
❑ 106 Troy Glaus .60 .25
❑ 107 John Maine .40 .15
❑ 108 Pat Burrell .40 .15
❑ 109 David Eckstein .40 .15
❑ 110 Homer Bailey .60 .25
❑ 111 Cincinnati Reds .40 .15
❑ 112 Corey Hart .40 .15
❑ 113 Orlando Hernandez .40 .15
❑ 114 Orlando Cabrera .40 .15
❑ 115 Ryan Garko .40 .15
❑ 116 Wladimir Balentien GB SP (RC) 1.00 .40
❑ 117 Daric Barton GB SP (RC) 1.00 .40
❑ 118 Emilio Bonifacio RC 1.50 .60
❑ 119 Lance Broadway (RC) 1.00 .40
❑ 120 Jeff Clement (RC) 1.00 .40
❑ 121 Dave Davidson RC 1.50 .60
❑ 122 Ross Detwiler GB SP RC 2.50 1.00
❑ 123 Sam Fuld (RC) 1.00 .40
❑ 124 Armando Galarraga RC 1.50 .60
❑ 125 Harvey Garcia (RC) 1.00 .40
❑ 126 Dan Giese GB SP (RC) 1.00 .40
❑ 127 Alberto Gonzalez GB SP RC 1.50 .60
❑ 128 Kevin Hart (RC) 1.00 .40
❑ 129 Luke Hochevar GB SP RC 3.00 1.25
❑ 130 Chin-Lung Hu GB SP (RC) 1.50 .60
❑ 131 Brandon Jones RC 2.50 1.00
❑ 132 Joe Koshansky (RC) 1.00 .40
❑ 133 Radhames Liz RC 1.50 .60
❑ 134 Donny Lucy (RC) 1.00 .40
❑ 135 Mitch Stetter GB SP RC 1.50 .60
❑ 136 Nyjer Morgan (RC) 1.00 .40
❑ 137 Ross Ohlendorf RC 1.50 .60
❑ 138 Steve Pearce RC 1.50 .60
❑ 139 Jeff Ridgway RC 1.50 .60
❑ 140 Bronson Sardinha (RC) 1.00 .40
❑ 141 Seth Smith (RC) 1.00 .40
❑ 142 Rich Thompson RC 1.00 .40
❑ 143 Erick Threets (RC) 1.00 .40
❑ 144 J.R. Towles RC 2.50 1.00
❑ 145 Eugenio Velez RC 1.00 .40
❑ 146 Joey Votto (RC) 1.50 .60
❑ 147 Soriano/A.Ramirez/D.Lee .60 .25
❑ 148 Hunter Pence 1.00 .40
❑ 149 Barry Zito .40 .15
❑ 150 Albert Pujols 5.00 2.00
❑ 151 Sammy Sosa .60 .25
❑ 152 Brian Bannister .40 .15
❑ 153 Reggie Willits .40 .15
❑ 154 Bobby Abreu .40 .15
❑ 155 Johnny Damon GB SP 1.50 .60
❑ 156 B.Webb/J.Peavy .40 .15
❑ 157 Aramis Ramirez .40 .15
❑ 158 Aaron Cook .40 .15
❑ 159 David Weathers .40 .15
❑ 160 Jack Wilson .40 .15
❑ 161 Josh Fogg .40 .15
❑ 162 Garrett Atkins .40 .15
❑ 163 Brad Ausmus .40 .15
❑ 164 Gil Meche .40 .15
❑ 165 Jeff Francoeur .60 .25
❑ 166 V.Mart/Hafner/Sizemore .60 .25
❑ 167 Juan Pierre .40 .15
❑ 168 Rafael Furcal .40 .15
❑ 169 J.J. Hardy .40 .15
❑ 170 Nick Markakis .60 .25
❑ 171 Delmon Young .60 .25
❑ 172 Oakland Athletics .40 .15
❑ 173 Ronny Paulino GB SP 1.00 .40
❑ 174 Mike Cameron GB SP 1.00 .40
❑ 175 Jeff Weaver GB SP 1.00 .40
❑ 176 Preston Wilson GB SP 1.00 .40
❑ 177 Robinson Tejeda GB SP 1.00 .40
❑ 178 Adam Lind GB SP 1.00 .40
❑ 179 Austin Kearns GB SP 1.00 .40
❑ 180 Jorge Posada GB SP 1.50 .60
❑ 181 Tadahito Iguchi .40 .15
❑ 182 Matt Cain .40 .15
❑ 183 Yuniesky Betancourt .40 .15
❑ 184 Bronson Arroyo .40 .15
❑ 185 Brad Hawpe GB SP 1.00 .40
❑ 186 Rickie Weeks GB SP 1.00 .40
❑ 187 Carlos Silva GB SP 1.00 .40
❑ 188 Adrian Gonzalez .60 .25
❑ 189 Kenji Johjima .40 .15
❑ 190 Chris Duncan .40 .15
❑ 191 James Shields .40 .15
❑ 192 Akinori Iwamura .40 .15
❑ 193 David Murphy .40 .15
❑ 194 Alex Rios .40 .15
❑ 195 Carlos Quentin GB SP 1.00 .40
❑ 196 Jose Valverde GB SP 1.00 .40
❑ 197 Derrek Lee GB SP 1.50 .60
❑ 198 Jerry Owens GB SP 1.00 .40
❑ 199 Russell Martin .40 .15
❑ 200 Yovani Gallardo .40 .15
❑ 201a Johan Santana Twins 1.00 .40
❑ 201b J.Santana Mets 100.00 50.00
❑ 202 Nick Swisher .40 .15
❑ 203 So Taguchi .40 .15
❑ 204 Justin Morneau .60 .25
❑ 205 Milton Bradley .40 .15
❑ 206 Jake Westbrook .40 .15
❑ 207 Dave Roberts .40 .15
❑ 208 Billy Butler .40 .15
❑ 209 Lance Berkman .60 .25
❑ 210 J.J. Putz GB SP 1.00 .40
❑ 211 Mike Sweeney GB SP 1.00 .40
❑ 212 A.Jones/C.Jones 1.25 .50
❑ 213 Ricky Nolasco .40 .15
❑ 214 Andy LaRoche .40 .15
❑ 215 Ray Durham .40 .15
❑ 216 Francisco Cordero .40 .15
❑ 217 Jered Weaver .40 .15
❑ 218 Rafael Soriano .40 .15
❑ 219 Orlando Hudson .40 .15
❑ 220 Mike Lowell .40 .15
❑ 221 Chris Snyder .40 .15
❑ 222 Cesar Izturis .40 .15
❑ 223 St. Louis Cardinals .40 .15
❑ 224 D.Wright GB SP 3.00 1.25
❑ 225 Pedro Martinez GB SP 1.50 .60
❑ 226 Rich Harden GB SP 1.00 .40
❑ 227 Shane Victorino GB SP 1.00 .40
❑ 228 Andrew Miller GB SP 1.50 .60
❑ 229 Chris Young .40 .15
❑ 230 Andruw Jones .40 .15
❑ 231 Kevin Gregg SP 6.00 2.50
❑ 232 C.C. Sabathia .40 .15
❑ 233 Hanley Ramirez 1.00 .40
❑ 234 Wandy Rodriguez .40 .15
❑ 235 Roy Oswalt .40 .15
❑ 236 Mark Grudzielanek .40 .15
❑ 237 Jeter/Wang/Cano 1.25 .50
❑ 238 Todd Helton .60 .25
❑ 239 Zack Greinke .40 .15
❑ 240 Carlos Gomez .40 .15
❑ 241 Lastings Milledge .40 .15
❑ 242 Huston Street .40 .15
❑ 243 Dan Haren .40 .15
❑ 244 Carlos Pena .40 .15
❑ 245 Brad Wilkerson .40 .15
❑ 246 Roy Halladay .40 .15
❑ 247 Dmitri Young .40 .15
❑ 248 Boston Red Sox 1.50 .60
❑ 249 Jonathan Papelbon .60 .25
❑ 250 Felix Pie .40 .15
❑ 251 Alex Gonzalez .40 .15
❑ 252 Bobby Crosby .40 .15
❑ 253 Justin Ruggiano RC 1.50 .60
❑ 254 Freddy Garcia .40 .15
❑ 255 Khalil Greene .60 .25
❑ 256 Rich Aurilia .40 .15
❑ 257 Jarrod Washburn .40 .15
❑ 258 B.J. Upton .60 .25
❑ 259 Michael Young .40 .15
❑ 260 Carlos Zambrano .40 .15
❑ 261 Livan Hernandez .40 .15
❑ 262 Billingsley/Lowe/Penny GB SP 1.00 .40
❑ 263 Melky Cabrera GB SP 1.00 .40
❑ 264 Shannon Stewart GB SP 1.00 .40
❑ 265 Aaron Rowand GB SP 1.00 .40
❑ 266 Matt Morris GB SP 1.00 .40
❑ 267 Xavier Nady GB SP 1.00 .40
❑ 268 Jim Thome .60 .25
❑ 269 Horacio Ramirez .40 .15
❑ 270 Prince Fielder 1.00 .40
❑ 271 Andy Phillips .40 .15
❑ 272 Aaron Harang .40 .15
❑ 273 Josh Barfield .40 .15
❑ 274 Ubaldo Jimenez .40 .15
❑ 275 Anibal Sanchez .40 .15
❑ 276 Carlos Lee .40 .15
❑ 277 Mark Teahen .40 .15
❑ 278 Delwyn Young .40 .15
❑ 279 Kurt Suzuki .40 .15
❑ 280 Nate Schierholtz .40 .15
❑ 281 Raul Ibanez .40 .15
❑ 282 Jose Vidro .40 .15
❑ 283 Miguel Cabrera GB SP 1.50 .60
❑ 284 Luis Gonzalez GB SP 1.00 .40
❑ 285 Chad Billingsley GB SP 1.00 .40
❑ 286 Tony Gwynn GB SP 1.00 .40
❑ 287 Matt Kemp .40 .15
❑ 288 James Loney .60 .25
❑ 289 Brett Myers .40 .15
❑ 290 Nate McLouth .40 .15
❑ 291 M.Chico/J.Bergmann GB SP 1.00 .40
❑ 292 Chad Tracy .40 .15
❑ 293 Edgar Renteria .40 .15
❑ 294 Jay Payton .40 .15
❑ 295 Josh Johnson .40 .15
❑ 296 Josh Banks (RC) 1.00 .40
❑ 297 Bill Murphy (RC) 1.00 .40
❑ 298 Ben Sheets .60 .25
❑ 299 Jose Reyes .60 .25
❑ 300 Chase Utley 1.00 .40
❑ 301 Ronnie Belliard GB SP 1.00 .40
❑ 302 Wily Mo Pena .40 .15
❑ 303 Tim Lincecum 1.00 .40
❑ 304 Chicago Cubs .60 .25
❑ 305 John Lackey .40 .15
❑ 306 Stephen Drew .40 .15
❑ 307 Kelly Johnson .40 .15
❑ 308 Daisuke Matsuzaka 1.50 .60
❑ 309 Craig Monroe .40 .15

❑	310 Jerry Owens	.40	.15
❑	311 Jeff Suppan	.40	.15
❑	312 Tom Glavine	.60	.25
❑	313 Kei Igawa	.40	.15
❑	314 Mark Kotsay	.40	.15
❑	315 Jacque Jones SP	6.00	2.50
❑	316 Melvin Mora	.40	.15
❑	317 M.Holliday/H.Ramirez	1.00	.40
❑	318 Jarrod Saltalamacchia	.40	.15
❑	319 A.J. Burnett	.40	.15
❑	320 Casey Kotchman	.40	.15
❑	321 Randy Winn GB SP	1.00	.40
❑	322 Richie Sexson GB SP	1.00	.40
❑	323 Juan Encarnacion GB SP	1.00	.40
❑	324 Rick Ankiel GB SP	1.00	.40
❑	325 Dan Wheeler GB SP	1.00	.40
❑	326 Brian Roberts	.60	.25
❑	327 David Ortiz	1.00	.40
❑	328 Garret Anderson	.40	.15
❑	329 Detroit Tigers	.40	.15
❑	330 Ty Wigginton GB SP	1.00	.40
❑	331 Travis Hafner	.40	.15
❑	332 Howie Kendrick GB SP	1.00	.40
❑	333 Kevin Kouzmanoff GB SP	1.00	.40
❑	334 Matt Holliday GB SP	1.50	.60
❑	335 Brandon Phillips GB SP	1.00	.40
❑	336 Ian Kinsler GB SP	1.50	.60
❑	337 Lyle Overbay GB SP	1.00	.40
❑	338 Justin Verlander GB SP	1.50	.60
❑	339 Ian Snell	.40	.15
❑	340 Hank Blalock	.40	.15
❑	341 Vernon Wells	.40	.15
❑	342 Matt Chico	.40	.15
❑	343 Tim Wakefield	.40	.15
❑	344 Michael Bourn	.40	.15
❑	345 Chris Carpenter	.40	.15
❑	346 Matsuzaka/Beckett	1.50	.60
❑	347 Chuck James GB SP	1.00	.40
❑	348 Joba Chamberlain	1.50	.60
❑	349 Erik Bedard	.40	.15
❑	350 Jimmy Rollins GB SP	1.50	.60
❑	351 Anthony Reyes	.40	.15
❑	352 Carl Crawford	.40	.15
❑	353 Jeremy Hermida	.40	.15
❑	354 Ervin Santana	.40	.15
❑	355 Edgar Gonzalez	.40	.15
❑	356 Yunel Escobar	.40	.15
❑	357 Yorvit Torrealba	.40	.15
❑	358 Hideki Okajima	.40	.15
❑	359 Paul Byrd	.40	.15
❑	360 Magglio Ordonez GB SP	1.50	.60
❑	361 Joe Borowski	.40	.15
❑	362 Clint Sammons (RC)	1.00	.40
❑	363 Chris Duffy	.40	.15
❑	364 Fred Lewis	.40	.15
❑	365 Adrian Beltre	.40	.15
❑	366 Alex Rodriguez BT	1.50	.60
❑	367 Troy Tulowitzki BT	.60	.25
❑	368 Prince Fielder BT	1.00	.40
❑	369 Clay Buchholz BT	1.00	.40
❑	370 Justin Verlander BT GB SP	1.50	.60
❑	371 Pedro Martinez BT GB SP	1.50	.60
❑	372 R.Howard BT GB SP	3.00	1.25
❑	373 Ichiro Suzuki BT	1.50	.60
❑	374 Kenny Lofton BT	.40	.15
❑	375 Manny Ramirez BT	1.00	.40
❑	376 Randy Johnson	1.00	.40
❑	377 Chris Capuano	.40	.15
❑	378 Johnny Estrada	.40	.15
❑	379 Franklin Morales	.40	.15
❑	380 Ryan Howard	1.25	.50
❑	381 Casey Blake SP	6.00	2.50
❑	382 Coco Crisp	.40	.15
❑	383 J.Maine/W.Randolph MG	.40	.15
❑	384 Jeremy Guthrie	.40	.15
❑	385 Geoff Jenkins	.40	.15
❑	386 Marlon Byrd	.40	.15
❑	387 Jeremy Bonderman	.40	.15
❑	388 Jason Varitek	1.00	.40
❑	389 Joe Girardi MG	.40	.15
❑	390 Ryan Braun	1.25	.50
❑	391 Ryan Zimmerman	.60	.25
❑	392 Lowell/Youkilis/Pedroia	.60	.25
❑	393 Pittsburgh Pirates	.40	.15
❑	394 Ryan Spilborghs	.40	.15
❑	395 Eric Gagne	.40	.15

❑	396 Joe Blanton	.40	.15
❑	397 Washington Nationals	4.00	.15
❑	398 Ryan Church	.40	.15
❑	399 Ted Lilly	.40	.15
❑	400 Manny Ramirez	1.00	.40
❑	401 Chad Gaudin	.40	.15
❑	402 Dustin McGowan	.40	.15
❑	403 Scott Baker	.40	.15
❑	404 Franklin Gutierrez	.40	.15
❑	405 Dave Bush	.40	.15
❑	406 Aubrey Huff	.40	.15
❑	407 Jermaine Dye	.40	.15
❑	408 C.Utley/J.Rollins	1.00	.40
❑	409 Jon Lester SP	8.00	3.00
❑	410 Mark Buehrle	.40	.15
❑	411 Sergio Mitre	.40	.15
❑	412 Jason Bartlett	.40	.15
❑	413 Edwin Jackson	.40	.15
❑	414 J.D. Drew	.40	.15
❑	415 Freddy Sanchez GB SP	1.00	.40
❑	416 Asdrubal Cabrera	.40	.15
❑	417 Nate Robertson	.40	.15
❑	418 Shaun Marcum	.40	.15
❑	419 Atlanta Braves	.60	.25
❑	420 Noah Lowry	.40	.15
❑	421 Jamie Moyer	.40	.15
❑	422 Michael Cuddyer	.40	.15
❑	423 Randy Wolf	.40	.15
❑	424 Juan Uribe	.40	.15
❑	425 Brian McCann	.60	.25
❑	426 Kyle Lohse SP	6.00	2.50
❑	427 Doug Davis SP	6.00	2.50
❑	428 Snell/Capps/Gorz/Maholm SP 6.002.50		
❑	429 Miguel Batista SP	6.00	2.50
❑	430 C.Wang SP	10.00	4.00
❑	431 Jeff Salazar SP	6.00	2.50
❑	432 Yadier Molina SP	6.00	2.50
❑	433 Adam Wainwright SP	6.00	2.50
❑	434 Scott Kazmir SP	6.00	2.50
❑	435 Adam Dunn SP	6.00	2.50
❑	436 Ryan Freel SP	6.00	2.50
❑	437 Jhonny Peralta SP	6.00	2.50
❑	438 Kazuo Matsui SP	6.00	2.50
❑	439 Daniel Cabrera	.40	.15
❑	440a John Smoltz	1.00	.40
❑	440b J.Smoltz Jon Var	150.00	75.00
❑	441 Emil Brown SP	6.00	2.50
❑	442 Gary Sheffield SP	6.00	2.50
❑	443 Jake Peavy SP	8.00	3.00
❑	444 Scott Rolen SP	8.00	3.00
❑	445 Kason Gabbard SP	6.00	2.50
❑	446 Aaron Hill SP	6.00	2.50
❑	447 Felipe Lopez SP	6.00	2.50
❑	448 Dan Uggla SP	6.00	2.50
❑	449 Willy Taveras SP	6.00	2.50
❑	450 Chipper Jones SP	8.00	3.00
❑	451 Josh Anderson SP (RC)	8.00	3.00
❑	452 Young/Upton/Byrnes SP	8.00	3.00
❑	453 Braden Looper SP	6.00	2.50
❑	454 Brandon Inge SP	6.00	2.50
❑	455 Brian Giles SP	6.00	2.50
❑	456 Corey Patterson SP	6.00	2.50
❑	457 Los Angeles Dodgers SP	8.00	3.00
❑	458 Sean Casey SP	6.00	2.50
❑	459 Pedro Feliz SP	6.00	2.50
❑	460 Tom Gorzelanny	.40	.15
❑	461 Chone Figgins SP	6.00	2.50
❑	462 Kyle Kendrick SP	6.00	2.50
❑	463 Tony Pena SP	6.00	2.50
❑	464 Marcus Giles SP	6.00	2.50
❑	465 Augie Ojeda SP	6.00	2.50
❑	466 Micah Owings SP	6.00	2.50
❑	467 Ryan Theriot SP	6.00	2.50
❑	468 Shawn Green SP	6.00	2.50
❑	469 Frank Thomas SP	8.00	3.00
❑	470 Lenny DiNardo SP	6.00	2.50
❑	471 Jose Bautista SP	6.00	2.50
❑	472 Manny Corpas SP	6.00	2.50
❑	473 Kevin Millwood SP	6.00	2.50
❑	474 Kevin Youkilis SP	6.00	2.50
❑	475 Jose Contreras SP	6.00	2.50
❑	476 Cleveland Indians	.40	.15
❑	477 Julio Lugo SP	6.00	2.50
❑	478 Jason Bay	.40	.15
❑	479 Tony LaRussa AS MG SP	6.00	2.50
❑	480 Jim Leyland AS MG SP	6.00	2.50

❑	481 Derrek Lee AS SP	6.00	2.50
❑	482 Justin Morneau AS SP	6.00	2.50
❑	483 Orlando Hudson AS SP	6.00	2.50
❑	484 Brian Roberts AS SP	6.00	2.50
❑	485 Miguel Cabrera AS SP	8.00	3.00
❑	486 Mike Lowell AS SP	6.00	2.50
❑	487 J.J. Hardy AS SP	6.00	2.50
❑	488 Carlos Guillen AS SP	6.00	2.50
❑	489 K.Griffey Jr. AS SP	10.00	4.00
❑	490 Vladimir Guerrero AS SP	8.00	3.00
❑	491 Alfonso Soriano AS SP	8.00	3.00
❑	492 I.Suzuki AS SP	10.00	4.00
❑	493 Matt Holliday AS SP	8.00	3.00
❑	494 Magglio Ordonez AS SP	8.00	3.00
❑	495 Brian McCann AS SP	6.00	2.50
❑	496 Victor Martinez AS SP	6.00	2.50
❑	497 Brad Penny AS SP	6.00	2.50
❑	498 Josh Beckett AS SP	8.00	3.00
❑	499 Cole Hamels AS SP	8.00	3.00
❑	500 Justin Verlander AS SP	8.00	3.00

2007 Topps Moments and Milestones

❑	COMMON p/r 11250-54600	.75	.30
❑	COMMON p/r 1650-10350	1.00	.40
❑	COMMON p/r 900-1500	8.00	3.00
❑	COMMON p/r 300-450	10.00	4.00
❑	COMMON ROOKIE	10.00	4.00
❑	STATED PRINT RUN 150 SER. #'d SETS		
❑	(# OF VARIATONS/TOTAL PRINT RUN)		
❑	PRICING BASED ON TOTAL PRINT RUN		
❑	OVERALL PLATE ODDS 1:473 HOBBY		
❑	PLATE PRINT RUN 1 SET PER COLOR		
❑	BLACK-CYAN-MAGENTA-YELLOW ISSUED		
❑	NO PLATE PRICING DUE TO SCARCITY		
❑	1 A.Pujols (37/5550)	2.50	1.00
❑	2 A.Pujols (130/19500)	2.00	.75
❑	3 A.Pujols (194/29100)	2.00	.75
❑	4 A.Pujols (112/16800)	2.00	.75
❑	5 A.Pujols (47/7050)	2.50	1.00
❑	6 I.Suzuki (242/36300)	1.50	.60
❑	7 I.Suzuki (34/5100)	2.00	.75
❑	8 I.Suzuki (8/1200)	10.00	4.00
❑	9 I.Suzuki (56/8400)	2.00	.75
❑	10 I.Suzuki (69/10350)	2.00	.75
❑	11 I.Suzuki (8/1200)	10.00	4.00
❑	12 G.Maddux (20/3000)	2.00	.75
❑	13 G.Maddux (199/29850)	1.50	.60
❑	14 G.Maddux (20/3000)	2.00	.75
❑	15 G.Maddux (197/29550)	1.50	.60
❑	16 R.Clemens (24/3600)	2.00	.75
❑	17 R.Clemens (10/1500)	12.00	5.00
❑	18 R.Clemens (238/35700)	1.50	.60
❑	19 R.Clemens (20/3000)	2.00	.75
❑	20 R.Clemens (256/38400)	1.50	.60
❑	21 C.Jones (45/6750)	1.50	.60
❑	22 C.Jones (110/16500)	1.25	.50
❑	23 C.Jones (181/27150)	1.25	.50
❑	24 C.Jones (116/17400)	1.25	.50
❑	25 C.Jones (41/6150)	1.50	.60
❑	26 C.Jones (25/3750)	1.50	.60
❑	27 A.Rodriguez (47/7050)	2.00	.75
❑	28 A.Rodriguez (118/17700)	1.50	.60
❑	29 A.Rodriguez (181/27150)	1.50	.60
❑	30 A.Rodriguez (124/18600)	1.50	.60
❑	31 A.Rodriguez (30/4500)	2.00	.75
❑	32 A.Rodriguez (17/2550)	2.00	.75
❑	33 A.Rodriguez (48/7200)	2.00	.75

❑ 34 A.Rodriguez (130/19500) 1.50 .60
❑ 35 A.Rodriguez (194/29100) 1.50 .60
❑ 36 A.Rodriguez (124/18600) 1.50 .60
❑ 37 A.Rodriguez (29/4350) 2.00 .75
❑ 38 A.Rodriguez (21/3150) 2.00 .75
❑ 39 V.Guerrero (39/5850) 1.50 .60
❑ 40 V.Guerrero (126/18900) 1.25 .50
❑ 41 V.Guerrero (206/30900) 1.25 .50
❑ 42 V.Guerrero (124/18600) 1.25 .50
❑ 43 V.Guerrero (39/5850) 1.50 .60
❑ 44 V.Guerrero (13/1950) 1.50 .60
❑ 45 K.Griffey Jr. (56/8400) 2.00 .75
❑ 46 K.Griffey Jr. (147/22050) 1.50 .60
❑ 47 K.Griffey Jr. (185/27750) 1.50 .60
❑ 48 Barry Zito (23/3450) 1.00 .40
❑ 49 Barry Zito (182/27300) .75 .30
❑ 50 R.Johnson (18/2700) 1.50 .60
❑ 51 R.Johnson (294/44100) 1.25 .50
❑ 52 R.Johnson (6/900) 8.00 3.00
❑ 53 R.Johnson (3/450) 60.00 30.00
❑ 54 R.Johnson (17/2550) 1.50 .60
❑ 55 R.Johnson (364/54600) 1.25 .50
❑ 56 R.Johnson (12/1800) 1.50 .60
❑ 57 R.Johnson (2/300) 60.00 30.00
❑ 58 P.Fielder (35/5250) 1.50 .60
❑ 59 P.Fielder (81/12150) 1.25 .50
❑ 60 Dan Uggla (26/3900) 1.50 .60
❑ 61 Dan Uggla (27/4050) 1.50 .60
❑ 62 Dan Uggla (172/25800) 1.25 .50
❑ 63 J.Verlander (17/2550) 1.50 .60
❑ 64 J.Verlander (124/18600) 1.25 .50
❑ 65 F.Liriano (12/1800) 1.50 .60
❑ 66 F.Liriano (144/21600) 1.25 .50
❑ 67 R.Zimmerman (176/26400) 1.25 .50
❑ 68 R.Zimmerman (110/16500) 1.25 .50
❑ 69 R.Zimmerman (84/12600) 1.25 .50
❑ 70 Hanley Ramirez (51/7650) 1.50 .60
❑ 71 Hanley Ramirez (119/17850) 1.25 .50
❑ 72 Hanley Ramirez (185/27750) 1.25 .50
❑ 73 Russ Martin (65/9750) 1.00 .40
❑ 74 Russ Martin (26/3900) 1.00 .40
❑ 75 M.Mantle (173/25950) 5.00 2.00
❑ 76 M.Mantle (121/18150) 5.00 2.00
❑ 77 M.Mantle (146/21900) 5.00 2.00
❑ 78 M.Mantle (94/14100) 5.00 2.00
❑ 79 M.Piazza (35/5250) 1.50 .60
❑ 80 M.Piazza (112/16800) 1.25 .50
❑ 81 D.Jeter (10/1500) 15.00 6.00
❑ 82 D.Jeter (78/11700) 2.50 1.00
❑ 83 D.Jeter (183/27450) 2.50 1.00
❑ 84 Dontrelle Willis (14/2100) 1.00 .40
❑ 85 Dontrelle Willis (142/21300) .75 .30
❑ 86 Dontrelle Willis (2/300) 60.00 30.00
❑ 87 Bobby Crosby (22/3300) 1.00 .40
❑ 88 Bobby Crosby (64/9600) 1.00 .40
❑ 89 R.Howard (22/3300) 2.00 .75
❑ 90 R.Howard (63/9450) 2.00 .75
❑ 91 Curt Schilling (21/3150) 1.50 .60
❑ 92 Curt Schilling (203/30450) 1.25 .50
❑ 93 Andruw Jones (52/7800) 1.50 .60
❑ 94 Andruw Jones (128/19200) 1.25 .50
❑ 95 Andruw Jones (11/1650) 1.50 .60
❑ 96 H.Matsui (23/3450) 1.50 .60
❑ 97 H.Matsui (116/17400) 1.25 .50
❑ 98 H.Matsui (192/28800) 1.25 .50
❑ 99 D.Wright (27/4050) 2.00 .75
❑ 100 D.Wright (102/15300) 1.50 .60
❑ 101 D.Wright (42/6300) 2.00 .75
❑ 102 D.Wright (17/2550) 2.00 .75
❑ 103 D.Ortiz (75/11250) 1.25 .50
❑ 104 D.Ortiz (47/7050) 1.50 .60
❑ 105 D.Ortiz (11/1650) 1.50 .60
❑ 106 F.Thomas (38/5700) 1.50 .60
❑ 107 F.Thomas (101/15150) 1.25 .50
❑ 108 Craig Biggio (40/6000) 1.50 .60
❑ 109 Miguel Cabrera (33/4950) 1.50 .60
❑ 110 Miguel Cabrera (116/17400) 1.25 .50
❑ 111 Vernon Wells (12/1800) 1.00 .40
❑ 112 Michael Young (24/3600) 1.00 .40
❑ 113 Michael Young (40/6000) 1.00 .40
❑ 114 Joe Mauer (144/21600) 1.25 .50
❑ 115 Gary Sheffield (34/5100) 1.00 .40
❑ 116 Jim Edmonds (42/6300) 1.50 .60
❑ 117 Jorge Posada (19/2850) 1.50 .60
❑ 118 Jorge Posada (23/3450) 1.50 .60
❑ 119 Pat Burrell (32/4800) 1.00 .40
❑ 120 Adam Dunn (40/6000) 1.00 .40
❑ 121 Johnny Damon (35/5250) 1.50 .60
❑ 122 Scott Rolen (34/5100) 1.50 .60
❑ 123 Paul Konerko (6/900) 8.00 3.00
❑ 124 Roy Halladay (22/3300) 1.00 .40
❑ 125 Grady Sizemore (22/3300) 1.50 .60
❑ 126 Grady Sizemore (37/5550) 1.50 .60
❑ 127 John Smoltz (24/3600) 1.50 .60
❑ 128 Jeff Kent (29/4350) 1.00 .40
❑ 129 Billy Wagner (38/5700) 1.00 .40
❑ 130 Mark Prior (18/2700) 1.50 .60
❑ 131 Eric Chavez (32/4800) 1.00 .40
❑ 132 Jimmy Rollins (41/6150) 1.00 .40
❑ 133 Manny Ramirez (7/1050) 8.00 3.00
❑ 134 Manny Ramirez (45/6750) 1.50 .60
❑ 135 Manny Ramirez (144/21600) 1.25 .50
❑ 136 Derrek Lee (46/6900) 1.00 .40
❑ 137 Derrek Lee (107/16050) .75 .30
❑ 138 Tom Glavine (14/2100) 1.50 .60
❑ 139 Tom Glavine (20/3000) 1.50 .60
❑ 140 Jose Reyes (17/2550) 1.00 .40
❑ 141 Pedro Martinez (15/2250) 1.50 .60
❑ 142 Pedro Martinez (208/31200) 1.25 .50
❑ 143 Mark Teixeira (43/6450) 1.50 .60
❑ 144 Jake Peavy (13/1950) 1.00 .40
❑ 145 Carlos Lee (32/4800) 1.00 .40
❑ 146 Josh Beckett (16/2400) 1.50 .60
❑ 147 Johan Santana (20/3000) 1.50 .60
❑ 148 Todd Helton (33/4950) 1.50 .60
❑ 149 M.Rivera (43/6450) 1.50 .60
❑ 150 Travis Hafner (33/4950) 1.00 .40
❑ 151 Jason Bay (24/3600) 1.00 .40
❑ 152 Bobby Abreu (30/4500) 1.00 .40
❑ 153 Mike Mussina (13/1950) 1.50 .60
❑ 154 Miguel Tejada (34/5100) 1.00 .40
❑ 155 Miguel Tejada (150/22500) .75 .30
❑ 156 Robinson Cano (14/2100) 1.50 .60
❑ 157 Robinson Cano (34/5100) 1.50 .60
❑ 158 R.Zimmerman (23/3450) 1.50 .60
❑ 159 Carlos Beltran (16/2400) 1.00 .40
❑ 160 Carlos Beltran (17/2550) 1.00 .40
❑ 161 R.Clemens (18/2700) 2.00 .75
❑ 162 R.Clemens (218/32700) 1.50 .60
❑ 163 M.Mantle (52/7800) 6.00 2.50
❑ 164 M.Mantle (130/19500) 5.00 2.00
❑ 165 M.Mantle (188/28200) 5.00 2.00
❑ 166 M.Mantle (132/19800) 5.00 2.00
❑ 167 M.Mantle (42/6300) 6.00 2.50
❑ 168 M.Mantle (97/14550) 5.00 2.00
❑ 169 M.Mantle (127/19050) 5.00 2.00
❑ 170 Daisuke Matsuzaka RC 60.00 30.00
❑ 171 Daisuke Matsuzaka RC 60.00 30.00
❑ 172 Daisuke Matsuzaka RC 60.00 30.00
❑ 173 Delmon Young (RC) 12.00 5.00
❑ 174 Delmon Young (RC) 12.00 5.00
❑ 175 Delmon Young (RC) 12.00 5.00
❑ 176 Andrew Miller RC 25.00 10.00
❑ 177 Andrew Miller RC 25.00 10.00
❑ 178 Andrew Miller RC 25.00 10.00
❑ 179 Troy Tulowitzki (RC) 12.00 5.00
❑ 180 Troy Tulowitzki (RC) 12.00 5.00
❑ 181 Troy Tulowitzki (RC) 12.00 5.00
❑ 182 Josh Fields (RC) 10.00 4.00
❑ 183 Josh Fields (RC) 10.00 4.00
❑ 184 Josh Fields (RC) 10.00 4.00
❑ 185 Jeff Baker (RC) 10.00 4.00
❑ 186 Jeff Baker (RC) 10.00 4.00
❑ 187 Jeff Baker (RC) 10.00 4.00
❑ 188 Philip Humber (RC) 10.00 4.00
❑ 189 Philip Humber (RC) 10.00 4.00
❑ 190 Philip Humber (RC) 10.00 4.00
❑ 191 Kevin Kouzmanoff (RC) 10.00 4.00
❑ 192 Kevin Kouzmanoff (RC) 10.00 4.00
❑ 193 Kevin Kouzmanoff (RC) 10.00 4.00

2008 Topps Moments and Milestones

❑ COMMON p/r 11250-78600 .40 .15
❑ COMMON p/r 1650-8100 .60 .25
❑ COMMON ROOKIE 5.00 2.00
❑ STATED PRINT RUN 150 SER.#'d SETS
❑ MILESTONE X 150 = TOTAL PRINT RUN
❑ PRICING BASED ON TOTAL PRINT RUN
❑ ALL VARIATIONS EQUALLY PRICED
❑ PLATES RANDOMLY INSERTED

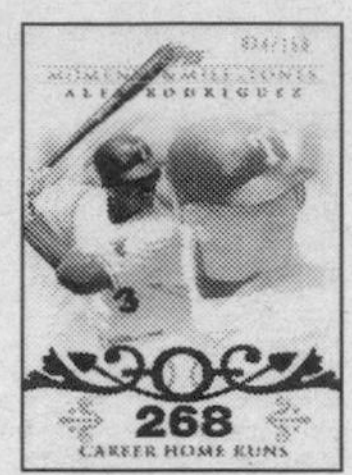

❑ PLATE PRINT RUN 1 SET PER COLOR
❑ BLACK-CYAN-MAGENTA-YELLOW ISSUED
❑ NO PLATE PRICING DUE TO SCARCITY
❑ 1-1 Alex Rodriguez 1.50 .60
❑ 145 Joey Votto (RC) 15.00 6.00
❑ 146 Joey Votto (RC) 15.00 6.00
❑ 147 Joey Votto (RC) 15.00 6.00
❑ 148 Luke Hochevar RC 15.00 6.00
❑ 149 Luke Hochevar RC 15.00 6.00
❑ 150 Luke Hochevar RC 15.00 6.00
❑ 151 Clay Buchholz (RC) 12.00 5.00
❑ 152 Clay Buchholz (RC) 12.00 5.00
❑ 153 Clay Buchholz (RC) 12.00 5.00
❑ 154 Billy Buckner (RC) 5.00 2.00
❑ 155 Billy Buckner (RC) 5.00 2.00
❑ 156 Billy Buckner (RC) 5.00 2.00
❑ 157 Jeff Clement (RC) 6.00 2.50
❑ 158 Jeff Clement (RC) 6.00 2.50
❑ 159 Jeff Clement (RC) 6.00 2.50
❑ 160 Radhames Liz RC 5.00 2.00
❑ 161 Radhames Liz RC 5.00 2.00
❑ 162 Radhames Liz RC 5.00 2.00
❑ 163 Bronson Sardinha (RC) 5.00 2.00
❑ 164 Bronson Sardinha (RC) 5.00 2.00
❑ 165 Bronson Sardinha (RC) 5.00 2.00
❑ 166 Seth Smith (RC) 5.00 2.00
❑ 167 Seth Smith (RC) 5.00 2.00
❑ 168 Seth Smith (RC) 5.00 2.00
❑ 169 Chris Seddon (RC) 5.00 2.00
❑ 170 Chris Seddon (RC) 5.00 2.00
❑ 171 Chris Seddon (RC) 5.00 2.00
❑ 172 Wladimir Balentien (RC) 6.00 2.50
❑ 173 Wladimir Balentien (RC) 6.00 2.50
❑ 174 Wladimir Balentien (RC) 6.00 2.50
❑ 175 Josh Banks (RC) 5.00 2.00
❑ 176 Josh Banks (RC) 5.00 2.00
❑ 177 Josh Banks (RC) 5.00 2.00
❑ 178 Ross Detwiler RC 5.00 2.00
❑ 179 Ross Detwiler RC 5.00 2.00
❑ 180 Ross Detwiler RC 5.00 2.00
❑ 181 Felipe Paulino RC 5.00 2.00
❑ 182 Felipe Paulino RC 5.00 2.00
❑ 183 Felipe Paulino RC 5.00 2.00
❑ 184 Troy Patton (RC) 5.00 2.00
❑ 185 Troy Patton (RC) 5.00 2.00
❑ 186 Troy Patton (RC) 5.00 2.00
❑ 187 Brandon Jones RC 5.00 2.00
❑ 188 Brandon Jones RC 5.00 2.00
❑ 189 Brandon Jones RC 5.00 2.00
❑ 2-1 Alex Rodriguez 2.50 1.00
❑ 3-1 Frank Thomas 1.00 .40
❑ 4-1 Mickey Mantle 2.00 .75
❑ 5-1 Mickey Mantle 2.00 .75
❑ 6-1 Mickey Mantle 1.50 .60
❑ 7-1 Mickey Mantle 2.00 .75
❑ 8-1 Greg Maddux 1.25 .50
❑ 9-1 Troy Tulowitzki .60 .25
❑ 10-1 Hunter Pence 1.00 .40
❑ 11-1 Hunter Pence 1.50 .60
❑ 12-1 Albert Pujols 1.50 .60
❑ 13-1 Albert Pujols 1.50 .60
❑ 14-1 Albert Pujols 2.50 1.00
❑ 15-1 Albert Pujols 1.50 .60
❑ 16-1 David Ortiz 1.50 .60
❑ 17-1 David Ortiz 1.50 .60
❑ 18-1 David Wright 2.00 .75
❑ 19-1 David Wright 2.00 .75
❑ 20-1 Aaron Hill .60 .25

- ❑ 21-1 Eric Byrnes .60 .25
- ❑ 22-1 Dmitri Young .60 .25
- ❑ 23-1 Garret Anderson .60 .25
- ❑ 24-1 Jimmy Rollins 1.00 .40
- ❑ 25-1 Jimmy Rollins 1.00 .40
- ❑ 26-1 Joba Chamberlain 6.00 2.50
- ❑ 27-1 Magglio Ordonez 1.00 .40
- ❑ 28-1 Ryan Howard 1.25 .50
- ❑ 29-1 Ryan Howard 2.00 .75
- ❑ 30-1 Ryan Howard 1.25 .50
- ❑ 31-1 Ryan Howard 2.00 .75
- ❑ 32-1 Trevor Hoffman .40 .15
- ❑ 33-1 Ken Griffey Jr. 1.50 .60
- ❑ 34-1 Travis Hafner .40 .15
- ❑ 35-1 Joe Mauer 1.00 .40
- ❑ 36-1 Daisuke Matsuzaka 100.00 50.00
- ❑ 37-1 Daisuke Matsuzaka 3.00 1.25
- ❑ 38-1 Curtis Granderson 1.00 .40
- ❑ 39-1 Curtis Granderson 1.00 .40
- ❑ 40-1 Curtis Granderson 1.00 .40
- ❑ 41-1 Curtis Granderson 1.00 .40
- ❑ 42-1 Alex Gordon 1.50 .60
- ❑ 43-1 Aramis Ramirez .40 .15
- ❑ 44-1 Jonathan Papelbon .60 .25
- ❑ 45-1 B.J. Upton 1.00 .40
- ❑ 46-1 C.C. Sabathia .60 .25
- ❑ 47-1 Carl Crawford .60 .25
- ❑ 48-1 Jason Bay .60 .25
- ❑ 49-1 Carlos Beltran .60 .25
- ❑ 50-1 Carlos Guillen .60 .25
- ❑ 51-1 C.C. Sabathia .40 .15
- ❑ 52-1 Gary Sheffield .40 .15
- ❑ 53-1 Chris Young .60 .25
- ❑ 54-1 Dontrelle Willis .60 .25
- ❑ 55-1 Dustin Pedroia 1.00 .40
- ❑ 56-1 Alfonso Soriano .60 .25
- ❑ 57-1 Derek Jeter 2.50 1.00
- ❑ 58-1 Chase Utley 1.50 .60
- ❑ 59-1 Chase Utley 1.50 .60
- ❑ 60-1 Chase Utley 1.00 .40
- ❑ 61-1 Chase Utley 1.50 .60
- ❑ 62-1 Ichiro Suzuki 80.00 40.00
- ❑ 63-1 Ichiro Suzuki 1.50 .60
- ❑ 64-1 Jorge Posada 1.00 .40
- ❑ 65-1 Jorge Posada 1.00 .40
- ❑ 66-1 Jose Reyes .60 .25
- ❑ 67-1 Miguel Tejada .60 .25
- ❑ 68-1 Miguel Tejada .60 .25
- ❑ 69-1 Nick Swisher .60 .25
- ❑ 70-1 Robinson Cano .60 .25
- ❑ 71-1 Roy Halladay .60 .25
- ❑ 72-1 Ryan Zimmerman 1.00 .40
- ❑ 73-1 Scott Rolen 1.00 .40
- ❑ 74-1 Tim Lincecum 1.00 .40
- ❑ 75-1 Vernon Wells .60 .25
- ❑ 76-1 Roger Clemens 2.00 .75
- ❑ 77-1 Roger Clemens 2.00 .75
- ❑ 78-1 Roger Clemens 2.00 .75
- ❑ 79-1 Roger Clemens 2.00 .75
- ❑ 80-1 Roger Clemens 2.00 .75
- ❑ 81-1 Roger Clemens 2.00 .75
- ❑ 82-1 Roger Clemens 2.00 .75
- ❑ 83-1 Michael Young .60 .25
- ❑ 84-1 John Smoltz 1.00 .40
- ❑ 85-1 Jim Thome .60 .25
- ❑ 86-1 Johan Santana 1.00 .40
- ❑ 87-1 Johan Santana 1.00 .40
- ❑ 88-1 Jack Cust .60 .25
- ❑ 89-1 Jack Cust .60 .25
- ❑ 90-1 Jake Peavy .60 .25
- ❑ 91-1 Hanley Ramirez 1.50 .60
- ❑ 92-1 Hanley Ramirez 1.00 .40
- ❑ 93-1 Hideki Okajima 1.00 .40
- ❑ 94-1 Grady Sizemore 1.00 .40
- ❑ 95-1 Erik Bedard .40 .15
- ❑ 96-1 Derrek Lee 1.00 .40
- ❑ 97-1 Derrek Lee 1.00 .40
- ❑ 98-1 Delmon Young 1.00 .40
- ❑ 99-1 Delmon Young 1.00 .40
- ❑ 100-1 Cole Hamels 1.00 .40
- ❑ 101-1 Brad Hawpe .40 .15
- ❑ 102-1 Mike Lowell .40 .15
- ❑ 103-1 Placido Polanco .40 .15
- ❑ 104-1 Nick Swisher .40 .15
- ❑ 105-1 Adrian Gonzalez 1.00 .40
- ❑ 106-1 Adrian Gonzalez .60 .25
- ❑ 107-1 Scott Kazmir .60 .25
- ❑ 108-1 Freddy Sanchez .40 .15
- ❑ 109-1 Jeremy Guthrie .40 .15
- ❑ 110-1 Chipper Jones 2.00 .75
- ❑ 111-1 Chris Carpenter .60 .25
- ❑ 112-1 Andy Pettitte .60 .25
- ❑ 113-1 Andruw Jones .60 .25
- ❑ 114-1 Bobby Abreu .60 .25
- ❑ 115-1 Eric Chavez .60 .25
- ❑ 116-1 Eric Chavez .60 .25
- ❑ 117-1 Josh Hamilton 2.00 .75
- ❑ 118-1 Manny Ramirez 1.00 .40
- ❑ 119-1 Manny Ramirez 1.00 .40
- ❑ 120-1 Mariano Rivera 1.50 .60
- ❑ 121-1 Kelly Johnson .60 .25
- ❑ 122-1 Jeff Kent .40 .15
- ❑ 123-1 Mark Teixeira .60 .25
- ❑ 124-1 Matt Holliday 1.00 .40
- ❑ 125-1 Matt Holliday .60 .25
- ❑ 126-1 Huston Street .60 .25
- ❑ 127-1 Carlos Lee .60 .25
- ❑ 128-1 Brian Bannister .60 .25
- ❑ 129-1 Carlos Pena .60 .25
- ❑ 130-1 Brian McCann 1.00 .40
- ❑ 131-1 Prince Fielder 1.50 .60
- ❑ 132-1 Randy Johnson 1.50 .60
- ❑ 133-1 Russell Martin .60 .25
- ❑ 134-1 Ryan Braun 2.00 .75
- ❑ 135-1 Vladimir Guerrero 1.00 .40
- ❑ 136-1 Vladimir Guerrero 1.50 .60
- ❑ 137-1 Tom Glavine .60 .25
- ❑ 138-1 Miguel Cabrera .60 .25
- ❑ 139-1 Miguel Cabrera .60 .25
- ❑ 140-1 Miguel Cabrera 1.00 .40
- ❑ 141-1 Pedro Martinez .60 .25
- ❑ 142-1 Daisuke Matsuzaka 2.00 .75
- ❑ 143-1 Garrett Atkins .60 .25
- ❑ 144-1 Brian Roberts 1.00 .40

2005 Topps Opening Day

- ❑ COMPLETE SET (165) 40.00 15.00
- ❑ COMMON CARD (1-165) .40 .15
- ❑ ISSUED IN OPENING DAY PACKS
- ❑ 1 Alex Rodriguez 1.50 .60
- ❑ 2 Placido Polanco .40 .15
- ❑ 3 Torii Hunter .40 .15
- ❑ 4 Lyle Overbay .40 .15
- ❑ 5 Johnny Damon .60 .25
- ❑ 6 Mike Cameron .40 .15
- ❑ 7 Ichiro Suzuki 2.00 .75
- ❑ 8 Francisco Rodriguez .40 .15
- ❑ 9 Bobby Crosby .40 .15
- ❑ 10 Sammy Sosa 1.00 .40
- ❑ 11 Randy Wolf .40 .15
- ❑ 12 Jason Bay .40 .15
- ❑ 13 Mike Lieberthal .40 .15
- ❑ 14 Paul Konerko .40 .15
- ❑ 15 Brian Giles .40 .15
- ❑ 16 Luis Gonzalez .40 .15
- ❑ 17 Jim Edmonds .40 .15
- ❑ 18 Carlos Lee .40 .15
- ❑ 19 Corey Patterson .40 .15
- ❑ 20 Hank Blalock .40 .15
- ❑ 21 Sean Casey .40 .15
- ❑ 22 Dmitri Young .40 .15
- ❑ 23 Mark Mulder .40 .15
- ❑ 24 Bobby Abreu .40 .15
- ❑ 25 Jim Thome .60 .25
- ❑ 26 Jason Kendall .40 .15
- ❑ 27 Jason Giambi .40 .15
- ❑ 28 Vinny Castilla .40 .15
- ❑ 29 Tony Batista .40 .15
- ❑ 30 Ivan Rodriguez .60 .25
- ❑ 31 Craig Biggio .60 .25
- ❑ 32 Chris Carpenter .40 .15
- ❑ 33 Adrian Beltre .40 .15
- ❑ 34 Scott Podsednik .40 .15
- ❑ 35 Cliff Floyd .40 .15
- ❑ 36 Chad Tracy .40 .15
- ❑ 37 John Smoltz .60 .25
- ❑ 38 Shingo Takatsu .40 .15
- ❑ 39 Jack Wilson .40 .15
- ❑ 40 Gary Sheffield .40 .15
- ❑ 41 Lance Berkman .40 .15
- ❑ 42 Carl Crawford .40 .15
- ❑ 43 Carlos Guillen .40 .15
- ❑ 44 David Bell .40 .15
- ❑ 45 Kazuo Matsui .40 .15
- ❑ 46 Jason Schmidt .40 .15
- ❑ 47 Jason Marquis .40 .15
- ❑ 48 Melvin Mora .40 .15
- ❑ 49 David Ortiz 1.00 .40
- ❑ 50 Andruw Jones .60 .25
- ❑ 51 Miguel Tejada .40 .15
- ❑ 52 Bartolo Colon .40 .15
- ❑ 53 Derrek Lee .60 .25
- ❑ 54 Eric Gagne .40 .15
- ❑ 55 Miguel Cabrera .60 .25
- ❑ 56 Travis Hafner .40 .15
- ❑ 57 Jose Valentin .40 .15
- ❑ 58 Mark Prior .60 .25
- ❑ 59 Phil Nevin .40 .15
- ❑ 60 Jose Vidro .40 .15
- ❑ 61 Khalil Greene .60 .25
- ❑ 62 Carlos Zambrano .40 .15
- ❑ 63 Erubiel Durazo .40 .15
- ❑ 64 Michael Young UER .40 .15
- ❑ 65 Woody Williams .40 .15
- ❑ 66 Edgardo Alfonzo .40 .15
- ❑ 67 Troy Glaus .40 .15
- ❑ 68 Garret Anderson .40 .15
- ❑ 69 Richie Sexson .40 .15
- ❑ 70 Curt Schilling .60 .25
- ❑ 71 Randy Johnson 1.00 .40
- ❑ 72 Chipper Jones 1.00 .40
- ❑ 73 J.D. Drew .40 .15
- ❑ 74 Russ Ortiz .40 .15
- ❑ 75 Frank Thomas 1.00 .40
- ❑ 76 Jimmy Rollins .40 .15
- ❑ 77 Barry Zito .40 .15
- ❑ 78 Rafael Palmeiro .60 .25
- ❑ 79 Brad Wilkerson .40 .15
- ❑ 80 Adam Dunn .40 .15
- ❑ 81 Doug Mientkiewicz .40 .15
- ❑ 82 Manny Ramirez .60 .25
- ❑ 83 Pedro Martinez .60 .25
- ❑ 84 Moises Alou .40 .15
- ❑ 85 Mike Sweeney .40 .15
- ❑ 86 Boston Red Sox WC 1.00 .40
- ❑ 87 Matt Clement .40 .15
- ❑ 88 Nomar Garciaparra 1.00 .40
- ❑ 89 Magglio Ordonez .40 .15
- ❑ 90 Bret Boone .40 .15
- ❑ 91 Mark Loretta .40 .15
- ❑ 92 Jose Contreras .40 .15
- ❑ 93 Randy Winn .40 .15
- ❑ 94 Austin Kearns .40 .15
- ❑ 95 Ken Griffey Jr. 1.50 .60
- ❑ 96 Jake Westbrook .40 .15
- ❑ 97 Kazuhito Tadano .40 .15
- ❑ 98 C.C. Sabathia .40 .15
- ❑ 99 Todd Helton .60 .25
- ❑ 100 Albert Pujols 2.00 .75
- ❑ 101 Jose Molina
Bengie Molina .40 .15
- ❑ 102 Aaron Miles .40 .15
- ❑ 103 Mike Lowell .40 .15
- ❑ 104 Paul Lo Duca .40 .15
- ❑ 105 Juan Pierre .40 .15
- ❑ 106 Dontrelle Willis .40 .15
- ❑ 107 Jeff Bagwell .60 .25
- ❑ 108 Carlos Beltran .40 .15
- ❑ 109 Ronnie Belliard .40 .15
- ❑ 110 Roy Oswalt .40 .15

❑ 111 Zack Greinke .40 .15
❑ 112 Steve Finley .40 .15
❑ 113 Kazuhisa Ishii .40 .15
❑ 114 Justin Morneau .40 .15
❑ 115 Ben Sheets .40 .15
❑ 116 Johan Santana 1.00 .40
❑ 117 Billy Wagner .40 .15
❑ 118 Mariano Rivera 1.00 .40
❑ 119 Corey Koskie .40 .15
❑ 120 Akinori Otsuka .40 .15
❑ 121 Joe Mauer 1.00 .40
❑ 122 Jacque Jones .40 .15
❑ 123 Joe Nathan .40 .15
❑ 124 Nick Johnson .40 .15
❑ 125 Vernon Wells .40 .15
❑ 126 Mike Piazza 1.00 .40
❑ 127 Jose Guillen .40 .15
❑ 128 Jose Reyes .40 .15
❑ 129 Marcus Giles .40 .15
❑ 130 Javy Lopez .40 .15
❑ 131 Kevin Millar .40 .15
❑ 132 Jorge Posada .60 .25
❑ 133 Carl Pavano .40 .15
❑ 134 Bernie Williams .60 .25
❑ 135 Kerry Wood .40 .15
❑ 136 Matt Holliday .50 .20
❑ 137 Kevin Brown .40 .15
❑ 138 Derek Jeter 2.00 .75
❑ 139 Barry Bonds 2.50 1.00
❑ 140 Jeff Kent .40 .15
❑ 141 Mark Kotsay .40 .15
❑ 142 Shawn Green .40 .15
❑ 143 Tim Hudson .40 .15
❑ 144 Shannon Stewart .40 .15
❑ 145 Pat Burrell .40 .15
❑ 146 Gavin Floyd .40 .15
❑ 147 Mike Mussina .60 .25
❑ 148 Eric Chavez .40 .15
❑ 149 Jon Lieber .40 .15
❑ 150 Vladimir Guerrero 1.00 .40
❑ 151 Vicente Padilla .40 .15
❑ 152 Ryan Klesko .40 .15
❑ 153 Jake Peavy .40 .15
❑ 154 Scott Rolen .60 .25
❑ 155 Greg Maddux 1.50 .60
❑ 156 Edgar Renteria .40 .15
❑ 157 Larry Walker .60 .25
❑ 158 Scott Kazmir .40 .15
❑ 159 B.J. Upton .60 .25
❑ 160 Mark Teixeira .60 .25
❑ 161 Ken Harvey .40 .15
❑ 162 Alfonso Soriano .40 .15
❑ 163 Carlos Delgado .40 .15
❑ 164 Alexis Rios .40 .15
❑ 165 Checklist .40 .15

2006 Topps Opening Day

❑ COMPLETE SET (165) 40.00 15.00
❑ COMMON CARD (1-165) .40 .15
❑ OVERALL PLATE SER.1 ODDS 1:246 HTA
❑ PLATE PRINT RUN 1 SET PER COLOR
❑ BLACK-CYAN-MAGENTA-YELLOW ISSUED
❑ NO PLATE PRICING DUE TO SCARCITY
❑ 1 Alex Rodriguez 1.50 .60
❑ 2 Jhonny Peralta .50 .20
❑ 3 Garrett Atkins .40 .15
❑ 4 Vernon Wells .40 .15
❑ 5 Carl Crawford .40 .15
❑ 6 Josh Beckett .40 .15
❑ 7 Mickey Mantle 8.00 3.00
❑ 8 Willy Taveras .40 .15
❑ 9 Ivan Rodriguez .60 .25
❑ 10 Clint Barmes .40 .15
❑ 11 Jose Reyes 1.00 .40
❑ 12 Travis Hafner .40 .15
❑ 13 Tadahito Iguchi .40 .15
❑ 14 Barry Zito .40 .15
❑ 15 Brian Roberts .40 .15
❑ 16 David Wright 1.50 .60
❑ 17 Mark Teixeira .60 .25
❑ 18 Roy Halladay .40 .15
❑ 19 Scott Rolen .60 .25
❑ 20 Bobby Abreu .40 .15
❑ 21 Lance Berkman .40 .15
❑ 22 Moises Alou .40 .15
❑ 23 Chone Figgins .40 .15
❑ 24 Aaron Rowand .40 .15
❑ 25 Chipper Jones 1.00 .40
❑ 26 Johnny Damon .60 .25
❑ 27 Matt Clement .40 .15
❑ 28 Nick Johnson .40 .15
❑ 29 Freddy Garcia .40 .15
❑ 30 Jon Garland .40 .15
❑ 31 Torii Hunter .40 .15
❑ 32 Mike Sweeney .40 .15
❑ 33 Mike Lieberthal .40 .15
❑ 34 Rafael Furcal .40 .15
❑ 35 Brad Wilkerson .40 .15
❑ 36 Brad Penny .40 .15
❑ 37 Jorge Cantu .40 .15
❑ 38 Paul Konerko .40 .15
❑ 39 Rickie Weeks .40 .15
❑ 40 Jorge Posada .60 .25
❑ 41 Albert Pujols 2.00 .75
❑ 42 Zack Greinke .40 .15
❑ 43 Jimmy Rollins .40 .15
❑ 44 Mark Prior .60 .25
❑ 45 Greg Maddux 1.50 .60
❑ 46 Jeff Francis .40 .15
❑ 47 Felipe Lopez .40 .15
❑ 48 Dan Johnson .40 .15
❑ 49 B.J. Ryan .40 .15
❑ 50 Manny Ramirez .60 .25
❑ 51 Melvin Mora .40 .15
❑ 52 Javy Lopez .40 .15
❑ 53 Garret Anderson .40 .15
❑ 54 Jason Bay .40 .15
❑ 55 Joe Mauer .60 .25
❑ 56 C.C. Sabathia .40 .15
❑ 57 Bartolo Colon .40 .15
❑ 58 Ichiro Suzuki 1.50 .60
❑ 59 Andruw Jones .60 .25
❑ 60 Rocco Baldelli .40 .15
❑ 61 Jeff Kent .40 .15
❑ 62 Cliff Floyd .40 .15
❑ 63 John Smoltz .60 .25
❑ 64 Shawn Green .40 .15
❑ 65 Nomar Garciaparra 1.00 .40
❑ 66 Miguel Cabrera .60 .25
❑ 67 Vladimir Guerrero 1.00 .40
❑ 68 Gary Sheffield .40 .15
❑ 69 Jake Peavy .40 .15
❑ 70 Carlos Lee .40 .15
❑ 71 Tom Glavine .60 .25
❑ 72 Craig Biggio .60 .25
❑ 73 Steve Finley .40 .15
❑ 74 Adrian Beltre .40 .15
❑ 75 Eric Gagne .40 .15
❑ 76 Aubrey Huff .40 .15
❑ 77 Livan Hernandez .40 .15
❑ 78 Scott Podsednik .40 .15
❑ 79 Todd Helton .60 .25
❑ 80 Kerry Wood .40 .15
❑ 81 Randy Johnson 1.00 .40
❑ 82 Huston Street .40 .15
❑ 83 Pedro Martinez .60 .25
❑ 84 Roger Clemens 2.00 .75
❑ 85 Hank Blalock .40 .15
❑ 86 Carlos Beltran .40 .15
❑ 87 Chien-Ming Wang 1.50 .60
❑ 88 Rich Harden .40 .15
❑ 89 Mike Mussina .60 .25
❑ 90 Mark Buehrle .40 .15
❑ 91 Michael Young .40 .15
❑ 92 Mark Mulder .40 .15
❑ 93 Khalil Greene .60 .25
❑ 94 Johan Santana .60 .25
❑ 95 Andy Pettitte .60 .25
❑ 96 Derek Jeter 2.50 1.00
❑ 97 Jack Wilson .40 .15
❑ 98 Ben Sheets .40 .15
❑ 99 Miguel Tejada .40 .15
❑ 100 Barry Bonds 2.50 1.00
❑ 101 Dontrelle Willis .40 .15
❑ 102 Curt Schilling .60 .25
❑ 103 Jose Contreras .40 .15
❑ 104 Jeremy Bonderman .40 .15
❑ 105 David Ortiz 1.00 .40
❑ 106 Lyle Overbay .40 .15
❑ 107 Robinson Cano .60 .25
❑ 108 Tim Hudson .40 .15
❑ 109 Paul Lo Duca .40 .15
❑ 110 Mariano Rivera .60 .25
❑ 111 Derrek Lee .40 .15
❑ 112 Morgan Ensberg .40 .15
❑ 113 Wily Mo Pena .40 .15
❑ 114 Roy Oswalt .40 .15
❑ 115 Adam Dunn .40 .15
❑ 116 Hideki Matsui 1.50 .60
❑ 117 Pat Burrell .40 .15
❑ 118 Jason Schmidt .40 .15
❑ 119 Alfonso Soriano .40 .15
❑ 120 Aramis Ramirez .40 .15
❑ 121 Jason Giambi .40 .15
❑ 122 Orlando Hernandez .40 .15
❑ 123 Magglio Ordonez .40 .15
❑ 124 Troy Glaus .40 .15
❑ 125 Carlos Delgado .40 .15
❑ 126 Kevin Millwood .40 .15
❑ 127 Shannon Stewart .40 .15
❑ 128 Luis Castillo .40 .15
❑ 129 Jim Edmonds .60 .25
❑ 130 Richie Sexson .40 .15
❑ 131 Dmitri Young .40 .15
❑ 132 Russ Adams .40 .15
❑ 133 Nick Swisher .40 .15
❑ 134 Jermaine Dye .40 .15
❑ 135 Anderson Hernandez (RC) .40 .15
❑ 136 Justin Huber (RC) .40 .15
❑ 137 Jason Botts (RC) .40 .15
❑ 138 Jeff Mathis (RC) .40 .15
❑ 139 Ryan Garko (RC) .40 .15
❑ 140 Charlton Jimerson (RC) .40 .15
❑ 141 Chris Denorfia (RC) .40 .15
❑ 142 Anthony Reyes (RC) .40 .15
❑ 143 Bryan Bullington (RC) .40 .15
❑ 144 Chuck James (RC) .60 .25
❑ 145 Danny Sandoval RC .40 .15
❑ 146 Walter Young (RC) .40 .15
❑ 147 Fausto Carmona (RC) .40 .15
❑ 148 Francisco Liriano (RC) 2.00 .75
❑ 149 Hong-Chih Kuo (RC) 1.00 .40
❑ 150 Joe Saunders (RC) .40 .15
❑ 151 John Koronka (RC) .40 .15
❑ 152 Robert Andino RC .40 .15
❑ 153 Shaun Marcum (RC) .40 .15
❑ 154 Tom Gorzelanny (RC) .40 .15
❑ 155 Craig Breslow RC .40 .15
❑ 156 Chris Demaria RC .40 .15
❑ 157 Brayan Pena (RC) .40 .15
❑ 158 Rich Hill (RC) .40 .15
❑ 159 Rick Short (RC) .40 .15
❑ 160 Darrell Rasner (RC) .40 .15
❑ 161 C.J. Wilson (RC) .40 .15
❑ 162 Brandon Watson (RC) .40 .15
❑ 163 Paul McAnulty (RC) .40 .15
❑ 164 Marshall McDougall (RC) .40 .15
❑ 165 Checklist .40 .15

2007 Topps Opening Day

❑ COMPLETE SET (220) 50.00 20.00
❑ COMMON CARD (1-220) .40 .15
❑ COMMON RC .50 .20
❑ 1 Bobby Abreu .40 .15
❑ 2 Mike Piazza 1.00 .40
❑ 3 Jake Westbrook .40 .15
❑ 4 Zach Duke .40 .15
❑ 5 David Wright 1.50 .60
❑ 6 Adrian Gonzalez .40 .15
❑ 7 Mickey Mantle 5.00 2.00

❑ 8 Bill Hall .40 .15
❑ 9 Robinson Cano .60 .25
❑ 10 Dontrelle Willis .40 .15
❑ 11 J.D. Drew .40 .15
❑ 12 Paul Konerko .40 .15
❑ 13 Austin Kearns .40 .15
❑ 14 Mike Lowell .40 .15
❑ 15 Magglio Ordonez .40 .15
❑ 16 Rafael Furcal .40 .15
❑ 17 Matt Cain .60 .25
❑ 18 Craig Monroe .40 .15
❑ 19 Matt Holliday .50 .20
❑ 20 Edgar Renteria .40 .15
❑ 21 Mark Buehrle .40 .15
❑ 22 Carlos Quentin .40 .15
❑ 23 C.C. Sabathia .40 .15
❑ 24 Nick Markakis .60 .25
❑ 25 Chipper Jones 1.00 .40
❑ 26 Jason Giambi .40 .15
❑ 27 Barry Zito .40 .15
❑ 28 Jake Peavy .40 .15
❑ 29 Hank Blalock .40 .15
❑ 30 Johnny Damon .60 .25
❑ 31 Chad Tracy .40 .15
❑ 32 Nick Swisher .40 .15
❑ 33 Willy Taveras .40 .15
❑ 34 Chuck James .40 .15
❑ 35 Carlos Delgado .40 .15
❑ 36 Livan Hernandez .40 .15
❑ 37 Freddy Garcia .40 .15
❑ 38 Bronson Arroyo .40 .15
❑ 39 Jack Wilson .40 .15
❑ 40 Dan Uggla .60 .25
❑ 41 Chris Carpenter .40 .15
❑ 42 Jorge Posada .60 .25
❑ 43 Joe Mauer .60 .25
❑ 44 Corey Patterson .40 .15
❑ 45 Chien-Ming Wang 1.50 .60
❑ 46 Derek Jeter 15.00 6.00
❑ 47 Carlos Beltran .40 .15
❑ 48 Jim Edmonds .60 .25
❑ 49 Jeremy Sowers .40 .15
❑ 50 Randy Johnson 1.00 .40
❑ 51 Jered Weaver .60 .25
❑ 52 Josh Barfield .40 .15
❑ 53 Scott Rolen .60 .25
❑ 54 Ryan Shealy .40 .15
❑ 55 Freddy Sanchez .40 .15
❑ 56 Javier Vazquez .40 .15
❑ 57 Jeremy Bonderman .40 .15
❑ 58 Miguel Cabrera .60 .25
❑ 59 Kazuo Matsui .40 .15
❑ 60 Curt Schilling .60 .25
❑ 61 Alfonso Soriano .40 .15
❑ 62 Orlando Hernandez .40 .15
❑ 63 Joe Blanton .40 .15
❑ 64 Aramis Ramirez .40 .15
❑ 65 Ben Sheets .40 .15
❑ 66 Jimmy Rollins .40 .15
❑ 67 Mark Loretta .40 .15
❑ 68 Cole Hamels .60 .25
❑ 69 Albert Pujols 2.00 .75
❑ 70 Moises Alou .40 .15
❑ 71 Mark Teahen .40 .15
❑ 72 Roy Halladay .40 .15
❑ 73 Cory Sullivan .40 .15
❑ 74 Frank Thomas 1.00 .40
❑ 75 Ryan Howard 1.50 .60
❑ 76 Rocco Baldelli .40 .15
❑ 77 Manny Ramirez .60 .25
❑ 78 Ray Durham .40 .15
❑ 79 Gary Sheffield .40 .15
❑ 80 Jay Gibbons .40 .15
❑ 81 Todd Helton .60 .25
❑ 82 Gary Matthews .40 .15
❑ 83 Brandon Inge .40 .15
❑ 84 Jonathan Papelbon 1.00 .40
❑ 85 John Smoltz .60 .25
❑ 86 Chone Figgins .40 .15
❑ 87 Hideki Matsui 1.00 .40
❑ 88 Carlos Lee .40 .15
❑ 89 Jose Reyes .40 .15
❑ 90 Lyle Overbay .40 .15
❑ 91 Johan Santana .60 .25
❑ 92 Ian Kinsler .40 .15
❑ 93 Scott Kazmir .60 .25
❑ 94 Hanley Ramirez .60 .25
❑ 95 Greg Maddux 1.50 .60
❑ 96 Johnny Estrada .40 .15
❑ 97 B.J. Upton .40 .15
❑ 98 Francisco Liriano 1.00 .40
❑ 99 Chase Utley 1.00 .40
❑ 100 Preston Wilson .40 .15
❑ 101 Marcus Giles .40 .15
❑ 102 Jeff Kent .40 .15
❑ 103 Grady Sizemore .60 .25
❑ 104 Ken Griffey 1.50 .60
❑ 105 Garret Anderson .40 .15
❑ 106 Brian McCann .40 .15
❑ 107 Jon Garland .40 .15
❑ 108 Troy Glaus .40 .15
❑ 109 Brandon Webb .40 .15
❑ 110 Jason Schmidt .40 .15
❑ 111 Ramon Hernandez .40 .15
❑ 112 Justin Morneau .40 .15
❑ 113 Mike Cameron .40 .15
❑ 114 Andruw Jones .60 .25
❑ 115 Russell Martin .40 .15
❑ 116 Vernon Wells .40 .15
❑ 117 Orlando Hudson .40 .15
❑ 118 Derek Lowe .40 .15
❑ 119 Alex Rodriguez 1.50 .60
❑ 120 Chad Billingsley .40 .15
❑ 121 Kenji Johjima 1.00 .40
❑ 122 Nick Johnson .40 .15
❑ 123 Dan Haren .40 .15
❑ 124 Mark Teixeira .60 .25
❑ 125 Jeff Francoeur 1.00 .40
❑ 126 Ted Lilly .40 .15
❑ 127 Jhonny Peralta .40 .15
❑ 128 Aaron Harang .40 .15
❑ 129 Ryan Zimmerman 1.00 .40
❑ 130 Jermaine Dye .40 .15
❑ 131 Orlando Cabrera .40 .15
❑ 132 Juan Pierre .40 .15
❑ 133 Brian Giles .40 .15
❑ 134 Jason Bay .40 .15
❑ 135 David Ortiz 1.00 .40
❑ 136 Chris Capuano .40 .15
❑ 137 Carlos Zambrano .40 .15
❑ 138 Luis Gonzalez .40 .15
❑ 139 Jeff Weaver .40 .15
❑ 140 Lance Berkman .40 .15
❑ 141 Raul Ibanez .40 .15
❑ 142 Jim Thome .60 .25
❑ 143 Jose Contreras .40 .15
❑ 144 David Eckstein .40 .15
❑ 145 Adam Dunn .40 .15
❑ 146 Alex Rios .40 .15
❑ 147 Garrett Atkins .40 .15
❑ 148 A.J. Burnett .40 .15
❑ 149 Jeremy Hermida .40 .15
❑ 150 Conor Jackson .40 .15
❑ 151 Adrian Beltre .40 .15
❑ 152 Torii Hunter .40 .15
❑ 153 Andrew Miller RC 4.00 1.50
❑ 154 Ichiro Suzuki 1.50 .60
❑ 155 Mark Redman .40 .15
❑ 156 Paul LoDuca .40 .15
❑ 157 Xavier Nady .40 .15
❑ 158 Stephen Drew .60 .25
❑ 159 Eric Chavez .40 .15
❑ 160 Pedro Martinez .60 .25
❑ 161 Derrek Lee .40 .15
❑ 162 David DeJesus .40 .15
❑ 163 Troy Tulowitzki (RC) 1.25 .50
❑ 164 Vinny Rottino (RC) .50 .20
❑ 165 Philip Humber (RC) .75 .30
❑ 166 Jerry Owens (RC) .50 .20
❑ 167 Ubaldo Jimenez (RC) .50 .20
❑ 168 Michael Young .40 .15
❑ 169 Ryan Braun RC .50 .20
❑ 170 Kevin Kouzmanoff (RC) .50 .20
❑ 171 Oswaldo Navarro RC .50 .20
❑ 172 Miguel Montero (RC) .50 .20
❑ 173 Roy Oswalt .40 .15
❑ 174 Shane Youman RC .50 .20
❑ 175 Josh Fields (RC) .50 .20
❑ 176 Adam Lind (RC) .50 .20
❑ 177 Miguel Tejada .40 .15
❑ 178 Delwyn Young (RC) .50 .20
❑ 179 Scott Moore (RC) .50 .20
❑ 180 Fred Lewis (RC) .50 .20
❑ 181 Glen Perkins (RC) .50 .20
❑ 182 Vladimir Guerrero 1.00 .40
❑ 183 Drew Anderson RC .50 .20
❑ 184 Jeff Salazar (RC) .50 .20
❑ 185 Tom Gordon .40 .15
❑ 186 The Bird .40 .15
❑ 187 Justin Verlander 1.00 .40
❑ 188 Delmon Young (RC) 1.25 .50
❑ 189 Homer .40 .15
❑ 190 Wally the Green Monster .40 .15
❑ 191 Southpaw .40 .15
❑ 192 Dinger .40 .15
❑ 193 Carl Crawford .40 .15
❑ 194 Slider .40 .15
❑ 195 Gapper .40 .15
❑ 196 Paws .40 .15
❑ 197 Billy the Marlin .40 .15
❑ 198 Ivan Rodriguez .60 .25
❑ 199 Slugger .40 .15
❑ 200 Junction Jack .40 .15
❑ 201 Bernie Brewer .40 .15
❑ 202 Travis Hafner .40 .15
❑ 203 Stomper .40 .15
❑ 204 Mr. Met .40 .15
❑ 205 The Moose .40 .15
❑ 206 Phillie Phanatic .40 .15
❑ 207 Prince Fielder 1.00 .40
❑ 208 Julio Lugo .40 .15
❑ 209 Pirate Parrot .40 .15
❑ 210 Joel Zumaya .60 .25
❑ 211 Swinging Friar .40 .15
❑ 212 Jay Payton .40 .15
❑ 213 Lou Seal .40 .15
❑ 214 Fredbird .40 .15
❑ 215 Screech .40 .15
❑ 216 TC Bear .40 .15
❑ 217 Andre Ethier .60 .25
❑ 218 Ervin Santana .40 .15
❑ 219 Melvin Mora .40 .15
❑ 220 Checklist .40 .15

2008 Topps Opening Day

❑ COMPLETE SET (220) 40.00 15.00
❑ COMMON CARD (1-194) .30 .12
❑ COMMON RC (195-220) .50 .20
❑ OVERALL PLATE ODDS 1:546 HOBBY
❑ PLATE PRINT RUN 1 SET PER COLOR
❑ BLACK-CYAN-MAGENTA-YELLOW ISSUED
❑ NO PLATE PRICING DUE TO SCARCITY

❑ 1 Alex Rodriguez	1.25	.50
❑ 2 Barry Zito	.30	.12
❑ 3 Jeff Suppan	.30	.12
❑ 4 Placido Polanco	.30	.12
❑ 5 Scott Kazmir	.50	.20
❑ 6 Ivan Rodriguez	.50	.20
❑ 7 Mickey Mantle	3.00	1.25
❑ 8 Stephen Drew	.30	.12
❑ 9 Ken Griffey Jr.	1.25	.50
❑ 10 Miguel Cabrera	.50	.20
❑ 11 Yorvit Torrealba	.30	.12
❑ 12 Daisuke Matsuzaka	1.50	.60
❑ 13 Kyle Kendrick	.30	.12
❑ 14 Jimmy Rollins	.50	.20
❑ 15 Joe Mauer	.50	.20
❑ 16 Cole Hamels	.50	.20
❑ 17 Yovani Gallardo	.30	.12
❑ 18 Miguel Tejada	.30	.12
❑ 19 Corey Hart	.30	.12
❑ 20 Nick Markakis	.50	.20
❑ 21 Zack Greinke	.30	.12
❑ 22 Orlando Cabrera	.30	.12
❑ 23 Jake Peavy	.30	.12
❑ 24 Erik Bedard	.30	.12
❑ 25 Trevor Hoffman	.30	.12
❑ 26 Derrek Lee	.50	.20
❑ 27 Hank Blalock	.30	.12
❑ 28 Victor Martinez	.30	.12
❑ 29 Chris Young	.30	.12
❑ 30 Jose Reyes	.50	.20
❑ 31 Mike Lowell	.30	.12
❑ 32 Curtis Granderson	.50	.20
❑ 33 Dan Uggla	.50	.20
❑ 34 Mike Piazza	.75	.30
❑ 35 Garrett Atkins	.30	.12
❑ 36 Felix Hernandez	.50	.20
❑ 37 Alex Rios	.30	.12
❑ 38 Mark Reynolds	.30	.12
❑ 39 Jason Bay	.30	.12
❑ 40 Josh Beckett	.50	.20
❑ 41 Jack Cust	.30	.12
❑ 42 Vladimir Guerrero	.75	.30
❑ 43 Marcus Giles	.30	.12
❑ 44 Kenny Lofton	.30	.12
❑ 45 John Lackey	.30	.12
❑ 46 Ryan Howard	1.00	.40
❑ 47 Kevin Youkilis	.50	.20
❑ 48 Gary Sheffield	.30	.12
❑ 49 Justin Morneau	.30	.12
❑ 50 Albert Pujols	1.25	.50
❑ 51 Ubaldo Jimenez	.30	.12
❑ 52 Johan Santana	.75	.30
❑ 53 Chuck James	.30	.12
❑ 54 Jeremy Hermida	.30	.12
❑ 55 Andruw Jones	.30	.12
❑ 56 Jason Varitek	.75	.30
❑ 57 Tim Hudson	.30	.12
❑ 58 Justin Upton	.75	.30
❑ 59 Brad Penny	.30	.12
❑ 60 Robinson Cano	.50	.20
❑ 61 Johnny Estrada	.30	.12
❑ 62 Brandon Webb	.30	.12
❑ 63 Chris Duncan	.30	.12
❑ 64 Aaron Hill	.30	.12
❑ 65 Alfonso Soriano	.50	.20
❑ 66 Carlos Zambrano	.30	.12
❑ 67 Ben Sheets	.50	.20
❑ 68 Andy LaRoche	.30	.12
❑ 69 Tim Lincecum	.75	.30
❑ 70 Phil Hughes	1.00	.40
❑ 71 Magglio Ordonez	.50	.20
❑ 72 Scott Rolen	.50	.20
❑ 73 John Maine	.30	.12
❑ 74 Delmon Young	.50	.20
❑ 75 Chase Utley	.75	.30
❑ 76 Jose Valverde	.30	.12
❑ 77 Tadahito Iguchi	.30	.12
❑ 78 Checklist	.30	.12
❑ 79 Russell Martin	.30	.12
❑ 80 B.J. Upton	.50	.20
❑ 81 Orlando Hudson	.30	.12
❑ 82 Jim Edmonds	.50	.20
❑ 83 J.J. Hardy	.30	.12
❑ 84 Todd Helton	.50	.20
❑ 85 Melky Cabrera	.30	.12
❑ 86 Adrian Beltre	.30	.12
❑ 87 Manny Ramirez	.75	.30
❑ 88 Rafael Furcal	.30	.12
❑ 89 Gil Meche	.30	.12
❑ 90 Grady Sizemore	.50	.20
❑ 91 Jeff Kent	.30	.12
❑ 92 David DeJesus	.30	.12
❑ 93 Lyle Overbay	.30	.12
❑ 94 Moises Alou	.30	.12
❑ 95 Frank Thomas	.75	.30
❑ 96 Ryan Garko	.30	.12
❑ 97 Kevin Kouzmanoff	.30	.12
❑ 98 Roy Oswalt	.30	.12
❑ 99 Mark Buehrle	.30	.12
❑ 100 David Ortiz	.75	.30
❑ 101 Hunter Pence	.75	.30
❑ 102 David Wright	1.00	.40
❑ 103 Dustin Pedroia	.50	.20
❑ 104 Roy Halladay	.30	.12
❑ 105 Derek Jeter	2.00	.75
❑ 106 Casey Blake	.30	.12
❑ 107 Rich Harden	.30	.12
❑ 108 Shane Victorino	.30	.12
❑ 109 Richie Sexson	.30	.12
❑ 110 Jim Thome	.50	.20
❑ 111 Akinori Iwamura	.30	.12
❑ 112 Dan Haren	.30	.12
❑ 113 Jose Contreras	.30	.12
❑ 114 Jonathan Papelbon	.50	.20
❑ 115 Prince Fielder	.75	.30
❑ 116 Dan Johnson	.30	.12
❑ 117 Dmitri Young	.30	.12
❑ 118 Brandon Phillips	.30	.12
❑ 119 Brett Myers	.30	.12
❑ 120 James Loney	.50	.20
❑ 121 C.C. Sabathia	.30	.12
❑ 122 Jermaine Dye	.30	.12
❑ 123 Aubrey Huff	.30	.12
❑ 124 Carlos Ruiz	.30	.12
❑ 125 Hanley Ramirez	.75	.30
❑ 126 Edgar Renteria	.30	.12
❑ 127 Mark Loretta	.30	.12
❑ 128 Brian McCann	.50	.20
❑ 129 Paul Konerko	.30	.12
❑ 130 Jorge Posada	.50	.20
❑ 131 Chien-Ming Wang	1.25	.50
❑ 132 Jose Vidro	.30	.12
❑ 133 Carlos Delgado	.30	.12
❑ 134 Kelvim Escobar	.30	.12
❑ 135 Pedro Martinez	.50	.20
❑ 136 Jeremy Guthrie	.30	.12
❑ 137 Ramon Hernandez	.30	.12
❑ 138 Ian Kinsler	.50	.20
❑ 139 Ichiro Suzuki	1.25	.50
❑ 140 Garret Anderson	.30	.12
❑ 141 Tom Gorzelanny	.30	.12
❑ 142 Bobby Crosby	.30	.12
❑ 143 Jeff Francoeur	.50	.20
❑ 144 Josh Hamilton	1.00	.40
❑ 145 Mark Teixeira	.50	.20
❑ 146 Fausto Carmona	.30	.12
❑ 147 Alex Gordon	.75	.30
❑ 148 Nick Swisher	.30	.12
❑ 149 Justin Verlander	.50	.20
❑ 150 Pat Burrell	.30	.12
❑ 151 Chris Carpenter	.30	.12
❑ 152 Matt Holliday	.50	.20
❑ 153 Adam Dunn	.30	.12
❑ 154 Curt Schilling	.50	.20
❑ 155 Kelly Johnson	.30	.12
❑ 156 Aaron Rowand	.30	.12
❑ 157 Brian Roberts	.50	.20
❑ 158 Bobby Abreu	.30	.12
❑ 159 Carlos Beltran	.30	.12
❑ 160 Lance Berkman	.50	.20
❑ 161 Gary Matthews	.30	.12
❑ 162 Jeff Francis	.30	.12
❑ 163 Vernon Wells	.30	.12
❑ 164 Dontrelle Willis	.30	.12
❑ 165 Travis Hafner	.30	.12
❑ 166 Brian Bannister	.30	.12
❑ 167 Carlos Pena	.30	.12
❑ 168 Raul Ibanez	.30	.12
❑ 169 Aramis Ramirez	.30	.12
❑ 170 Eric Byrnes	.30	.12
❑ 171 Greg Maddux	1.00	.40
❑ 172 John Smoltz	.75	.30
❑ 173 Jarrod Saltalamacchia	.30	.12
❑ 174 Hideki Okajima	.50	.20
❑ 175 Javier Vazquez	.30	.12
❑ 176 Aaron Harang	.30	.12
❑ 177 Jhonny Peralta	.30	.12
❑ 178 Carlos Lee	.30	.12
❑ 179 Ryan Braun	1.00	.40
❑ 180 Torii Hunter	.30	.12
❑ 181 Hideki Matsui	.75	.30
❑ 182 Eric Chavez	.30	.12
❑ 183 Freddy Sanchez	.30	.12
❑ 184 Adrian Gonzalez	.50	.20
❑ 185 Bengie Molina	.30	.12
❑ 186 Kenji Johjima	.30	.12
❑ 187 Carl Crawford	.30	.12
❑ 188 Chipper Jones	1.00	.40
❑ 189 Chris Young	.30	.12
❑ 190 Michael Young	.30	.12
❑ 191 Troy Glaus	.50	.20
❑ 192 Ryan Zimmerman	.50	.20
❑ 193 Brian Giles	.30	.12
❑ 194 Troy Tulowitzki	.50	.20
❑ 195 Chin-Lung Hu (RC)	.75	.30
❑ 196 Seth Smith (RC)	.50	.20
❑ 197 Wladimir Balentien (RC)	.50	.20
❑ 198 Rich Thompson RC	.50	.20
❑ 199 Radhames Liz RC	.75	.30
❑ 200 Ross Detwiler RC	1.25	.50
❑ 201 Sam Fuld (RC)	.50	.20
❑ 202 Clint Sammons (RC)	.50	.20
❑ 203 Ross Ohlendorf RC	.75	.30
❑ 204 Jonathan Albaladejo RC	.75	.30
❑ 205 Brandon Jones RC	1.25	.50
❑ 206 Steve Pearce RC	.75	.30
❑ 207 Kevin Hart (RC)	.50	.20
❑ 208 Luke Hochevar RC	1.50	.60
❑ 209 Troy Patton (RC)	.50	.20
❑ 210 Josh Anderson (RC)	.50	.20
❑ 211 Clay Buchholz (RC)	1.25	.50
❑ 212 Joe Koshansky (RC)	.50	.20
❑ 213 Bronson Sardinha (RC)	.50	.20
❑ 214 Emilio Bonifacio RC	.75	.30
❑ 215 Daric Barton (RC)	.50	.20
❑ 216 Lance Broadway (RC)	.50	.20
❑ 217 Jeff Clement (RC)	.50	.20
❑ 218 Joey Votto (RC)	.75	.30
❑ 219 J.R. Towles RC	1.25	.50
❑ 220 Nyjer Morgan (RC)	.50	.20

2006 Topps Sterling

Card		
❑ B.BONDS (1-19)	12.00	5.00
❑ B.BONDS ODDS 1:10		
❑ M.MANTLE (20-39)	15.00	6.00
❑ M.MANTLE ODDS 1:10		
❑ J.GIBSON (40-43)	30.00	12.50
❑ J.GIBSON ODDS 1:191		
❑ R.HENDERSON (44-53)	10.00	4.00
❑ R.HENDERSON ODDS 1:22		
❑ T.WILLIAMS (54-62)	12.00	5.00
❑ T.WILLIAMS ODDS 1:27		
❑ R.CLEMENTE (63-67)	25.00	10.00
❑ R.CLEMENTE ODDS 1:40		
❑ N.RYAN (68-77)	20.00	8.00
❑ N.RYAN ODDS 1:20		
❑ C.RIPKEN (78-96)	20.00	8.00
❑ C.RIPKEN ODDS 1:10		
❑ S.MUSIAL (97-101)	10.00	4.00
❑ S.MUSIAL ODDS 1:40		

❑ R.JACKSON (102-106)	10.00	4.00
❑ R.JACKSON ODDS 1:40		
❑ J.BENCH (107-111)	10.00	4.00
❑ J.BENCH ODDS 1:43		
❑ G.BRETT (112-121)	10.00	4.00
❑ G.BRETT ODDS 1:20		
❑ D.MATTINGLY (122-131)	12.00	5.00
❑ D.MATTINGLY ODDS 1:20		
❑ R.MARIS (132-136)	12.00	5.00
❑ R.MARIS ODDS 1:40		
❑ R.CAREW (137-146)	10.00	4.00
❑ R.CAREW ODDS 1:20		
❑ Y.BERRA (147-151)	10.00	4.00
❑ Y.BERRA ODDS 1:40		
❑ M.SCHMIDT (152-156)	10.00	4.00
❑ M.SCHMIDT ODDS 1:40		
❑ C.YASTRZEMSKI (157-175)	10.00	4.00
❑ C.YASTRZEMSKI ODDS 1:10		
❑ T.GWYNN (176-185)	10.00	4.00
❑ T.GWYNN ODDS 1:20		
❑ R.SANDBERG (186-190)	10.00	4.00
❑ R.SANDBERG ODDS 1:40		
❑ O.SMITH (191-200)	10.00	4.00
❑ O.SMITH ODDS 1:20		
❑ STATED PRINT RUN 250 SER.#'d SETS		

2007 Topps Sterling

❑ COMMON MANTLE (1-24)	12.00	5.00
❑ COMMON BONDS (25-48)	12.00	5.00
❑ COMMON ICHIRO (49-56)	10.00	4.00
❑ COMMON YAZ (57-64)	8.00	3.00
❑ COMMON WRIGHT (65-76)	8.00	3.00
❑ COMMON CLEMENTE (77-81)	15.00	6.00
❑ COMMON SANTANA (82-89)	8.00	3.00
❑ COMMON MORNEAU (90-101)	8.00	3.00
❑ COMMON R.JACKSON (102-109)	8.00	3.00
❑ COMMON CLEMENS (110-117)	10.00	4.00
❑ COMMON T.WILLIAMS (118-122)	12.00	5.00
❑ COMMON BERRA (123-130)	8.00	3.00
❑ COMMON MATSUI (131-135)	8.00	3.00
❑ COMMON HOWARD (136-143)	8.00	3.00
❑ COMMON GWYNN (144-151)	8.00	3.00
❑ COMMON ORTIZ (152-159)	6.00	2.50
❑ COMMON SEAVER (160-167)	6.00	2.50
❑ COMMON PUJOLS (168-175)	10.00	4.00
❑ COMMON MUSIAL (176-183)	8.00	3.00
❑ COMMON WANG (184-191)	12.00	5.00
❑ COMMON SANDBERG (192-199)	10.00	4.00
❑ COMMON N.RYAN (200-207)	20.00	8.00
❑ COMMON B.GIBSON (208-215)	6.00	2.50
❑ COMMON MARIS (216-220)	8.00	3.00
❑ COMMON M.RAMIREZ (221-228)	8.00	3.00
❑ COMMON SCHMIDT (229-236)	10.00	4.00
❑ COMMON A.ROD (237-244)	8.00	3.00
❑ COMMON MATSUZAKA (245-249)	15.00	6.00
❑ COMMON DIMAGGIO (250-254)	10.00	4.00
❑ THREE BASE CARDS PER BOX		
❑ STATED PRINT RUN 250 SER.#'d SETS		

2002 Topps Total

❑ COMPLETE SET (990)	150.00	75.00
❑ 1 Joe Mauer RC	10.00	4.00
❑ 2 Derek Jeter	2.00	.75
❑ 3 Shawn Green	.30	.10
❑ 4 Vladimir Guerrero	.75	.30
❑ 5 Mike Piazza	1.25	.50
❑ 6 Brandon Duckworth	.20	.07
❑ 7 Aramis Ramirez	.30	.10
❑ 8 Josh Barfield RC	2.50	1.00
❑ 9 Troy Glaus	.30	.10
❑ 10 Sammy Sosa	.75	.30
❑ 11 Rod Barajas	.20	.07
❑ 12 Tsuyoshi Shinjo	.30	.10
❑ 13 Larry Bigbie	.20	.07
❑ 14 Tino Martinez	.50	.20
❑ 15 Craig Biggio	.50	.20
❑ 16 Anastacio Martinez RC	.40	.15
❑ 17 John McDonald	.20	.07
❑ 18 Kyle Kane RC	.25	.08
❑ 19 Aubrey Huff	.30	.10
❑ 20 Juan Cruz	.20	.07
❑ 21 Doug Creek	.20	.07
❑ 22 Luther Hackman	.20	.07
❑ 23 Rafael Furcal	.30	.10
❑ 24 Andres Torres	.20	.07
❑ 25 Jason Giambi	.30	.10
❑ 26 Jose Paniagua	.20	.07
❑ 27 Jose Offerman	.20	.07
❑ 28 Alex Arias	.20	.07
❑ 29 J.M. Gold	.20	.07
❑ 30 Jeff Bagwell	.50	.20
❑ 31 Brent Cookson	.20	.07
❑ 32 Kelly Wunsch	.20	.07
❑ 33 Larry Walker	.30	.10
❑ 34 Luis Gonzalez	.30	.10
❑ 35 John Franco	.30	.10
❑ 36 Roy Oswalt	.30	.10
❑ 37 Tom Glavine	.50	.20
❑ 38 C.C. Sabathia	.30	.10
❑ 39 Jay Gibbons	.20	.07
❑ 40 Wilson Betemit	.20	.07
❑ 41 Tony Armas Jr.	.20	.07
❑ 42 Mo Vaughn	.30	.10
❑ 43 Gerard Oakes RC	.40	.15
❑ 44 Dmitri Young	.30	.10
❑ 45 Tim Salmon	.50	.20
❑ 46 Barry Zito	.30	.10
❑ 47 Adrian Gonzalez	.20	.07
❑ 48 Joe Davenport	.20	.07
❑ 49 Adrian Hernandez	.20	.07
❑ 50 Randy Johnson	.75	.30
❑ 52 Adam Pettyjohn	.20	.07
❑ 53 Alex Escobar	.20	.07
❑ 54 Stevenson Agosto RC	.25	.08
❑ 55 Omar Daal	.20	.07
❑ 56 Mike Buddie	.20	.07
❑ 57 Dave Williams	.20	.07
❑ 58 Marquis Grissom	.30	.10
❑ 59 Pat Burrell	.30	.10
❑ 60 Mark Prior	.50	.20
❑ 61 Mike Bynum	.20	.07
❑ 62 Mike Hill RC	.40	.15
❑ 63 Brandon Backe RC	.50	.20
❑ 64 Dan Wilson	.20	.07
❑ 65 Nick Johnson	.30	.10
❑ 66 Jason Grimsley	.20	.07
❑ 67 Russ Johnson	.20	.07
❑ 68 Todd Walker	.20	.07
❑ 69 Kyle Farnsworth	.20	.07
❑ 70 Ben Broussard	.20	.07
❑ 71 Garrett Guzman RC	.40	.15
❑ 72 Terry Mulholland	.20	.07
❑ 73 Tyler Houston	.20	.07
❑ 74 Jace Brewer	.20	.07
❑ 75 Chris Baker RC	.40	.15
❑ 76 Frank Catalanotto	.20	.07
❑ 77 Mike Redmond	.20	.07
❑ 78 Matt Wise	.20	.07
❑ 79 Fernando Vina	.20	.07
❑ 80 Kevin Brown	.30	.10
❑ 81 Grant Balfour	.20	.07
❑ 82 Clint Nageotte RC	.50	.20
❑ 83 Jeff Tam	.20	.07
❑ 84 Steve Trachsel	.20	.07
❑ 85 Tomo Ohka	.20	.07
❑ 86 Keith McDonald	.20	.07
❑ 87 Jose Ortiz	.20	.07
❑ 88 Rusty Greer	.30	.10
❑ 89 Jeff Suppan	.20	.07
❑ 90 Moises Alou	.30	.10
❑ 91 Juan Encarnacion	.20	.07
❑ 92 Tyler Yates RC	.40	.15
❑ 93 Scott Strickland	.20	.07
❑ 94 Brent Butler	.20	.07
❑ 95 Jon Rauch	.20	.07
❑ 96 Brian Mallette RC	.25	.08
❑ 97 Joe Randa	.30	.10
❑ 98 Cesar Crespo	.20	.07
❑ 99 Felix Rodriguez	.20	.07
❑ 100 Chipper Jones	.75	.30
❑ 101 Victor Martinez	.75	.30
❑ 102 Danny Graves	.20	.07
❑ 103 Brandon Berger	.20	.07
❑ 104 Carlos Garcia	.20	.07
❑ 105 Alfonso Soriano	.30	.10
❑ 106 Allan Simpson RC	.25	.08
❑ 107 Brad Thomas	.20	.07
❑ 108 Devon White	.30	.10
❑ 109 Scott Chiasson	.20	.07
❑ 110 Cliff Floyd	.30	.10
❑ 111 Scott Williamson	.20	.07
❑ 112 Julio Zuleta	.20	.07
❑ 113 Terry Adams	.20	.07
❑ 114 Zach Day	.20	.07
❑ 115 Ben Grieve	.20	.07
❑ 116 Mark Ellis	.20	.07
❑ 117 Bobby Jenks RC	1.50	.60
❑ 118 LaTroy Hawkins	.20	.07
❑ 119 Tim Raines Jr.	.20	.07
❑ 120 Juan Uribe	.20	.07
❑ 121 Bob Scanlan	.20	.07
❑ 122 Brad Nelson RC	.40	.15
❑ 123 Adam Johnson	.20	.07
❑ 124 Raul Casanova	.20	.07
❑ 125 Jeff D'Amico	.20	.07
❑ 126 Aaron Cook RC	.40	.15
❑ 127 Alan Benes	.20	.07
❑ 128 Mark Little	.20	.07
❑ 129 Randy Wolf	.20	.07
❑ 130 Phil Nevin	.30	.10
❑ 131 Guillermo Mota	.20	.07
❑ 132 Nick Neugebauer	.20	.07
❑ 133 Pedro Borbon Jr.	.20	.07
❑ 134 Doug Mientkiewicz	.30	.10
❑ 135 Edgardo Alfonzo	.20	.07
❑ 136 Dustan Mohr	.20	.07
❑ 137 Dan Reichert	.20	.07
❑ 138 Dewon Brazelton	.20	.07
❑ 139 Orlando Cabrera	.30	.10
❑ 140 Todd Hollandsworth	.20	.07
❑ 141 Darren Dreifort	.20	.07
❑ 142 Jose Valentin	.20	.07
❑ 143 Josh Kalinowski	.20	.07
❑ 144 Randy Keisler	.20	.07
❑ 145 Bret Boone	.30	.10
❑ 146 Roosevelt Brown	.20	.07
❑ 147 Brent Abernathy	.20	.07
❑ 148 Jorge Julio	.20	.07
❑ 149 Alex Gonzalez	.20	.07
❑ 150 Juan Pierre	.30	.10
❑ 151 Roger Cedeno	.20	.07
❑ 152 Javier Vazquez	.30	.10
❑ 153 Armando Benitez	.20	.07
❑ 154 Dave Burba	.20	.07
❑ 155 Brad Penny	.20	.07
❑ 156 Ryan Jensen	.20	.07
❑ 157 Jeromy Burnitz	.30	.10
❑ 158 Matt Childers RC	.40	.15
❑ 159 Wilmy Caceres	.20	.07
❑ 160 Roger Clemens	1.50	.60
❑ 161 Jamie Cerda RC	.40	.15
❑ 162 Jason Christiansen	.20	.07

❑ 163 Pokey Reese .20 .07
❑ 164 Ivanon Coffie .20 .07
❑ 165 Joaquin Benoit .20 .07
❑ 166 Mike Matheny .20 .07
❑ 167 Eric Cammack .20 .07
❑ 168 Alex Graman .20 .07
❑ 169 Brook Fordyce .20 .07
❑ 170 Mike Lieberthal .30 .10
❑ 171 Giovanni Carrara .20 .07
❑ 172 Antonio Perez .20 .07
❑ 173 Fernando Tatis .20 .07
❑ 174 Jason Bay RC 5.00 2.00
❑ 175 Jason Botts RC .50 .20
❑ 176 Danys Baez .20 .07
❑ 177 Shea Hillenbrand .30 .10
❑ 178 Jack Cust .20 .07
❑ 179 Clay Bellinger .20 .07
❑ 180 Roberto Alomar .50 .20
❑ 181 Graeme Lloyd .20 .07
❑ 182 Clint Weibl RC .25 .08
❑ 183 Royce Clayton .20 .07
❑ 184 Ben Davis .20 .07
❑ 185 Brian Adams RC .25 .08
❑ 186 Jack Wilson .20 .07
❑ 187 David Coggin .20 .07
❑ 188 Derrick Turnbow .20 .07
❑ 189 Vladimir Nunez .20 .07
❑ 190 Mariano Rivera .75 .30
❑ 191 Wilson Guzman .20 .07
❑ 192 Michael Barrett .20 .07
❑ 193 Corey Patterson .20 .07
❑ 194 Luis Sojo .20 .07
❑ 195 Scott Elarton .20 .07
❑ 196 Charles Thomas RC .40 .15
❑ 197 Ricky Bottalico .20 .07
❑ 198 Wilfredo Rodriguez .20 .07
❑ 199 Ricardo Rincon .20 .07
❑ 200 John Smoltz .50 .20
❑ 201 Travis Miller .20 .07
❑ 202 Ben Weber .20 .07
❑ 203 T.J. Tucker .20 .07
❑ 204 Terry Shumpert .20 .07
❑ 205 Bernie Williams .50 .20
❑ 206 Russ Ortiz .20 .07
❑ 207 Nate Rolison .20 .07
❑ 208 Jose Cruz Jr. .20 .07
❑ 209 Bill Ortega .20 .07
❑ 210 Carl Everett .30 .10
❑ 211 Luis Lopez .20 .07
❑ 212 Brian Wolfe RC .40 .15
❑ 213 Doug Davis .20 .07
❑ 214 Troy Mattes .20 .07
❑ 215 Al Leiter .30 .10
❑ 216 Joe Mays .20 .07
❑ 217 Bobby Smith .20 .07
❑ 218 J.J. Trujillo RC .40 .15
❑ 219 Hideo Nomo .75 .30
❑ 220 Jimmy Rollins .30 .10
❑ 221 Bobby Seay .20 .07
❑ 222 Mike Thurman .20 .07
❑ 223 Bartolo Colon .30 .10
❑ 224 Jesus Sanchez .20 .07
❑ 225 Ray Durham .30 .10
❑ 226 Juan Diaz .20 .07
❑ 227 Lee Stevens .20 .07
❑ 228 Ben Howard RC .40 .15
❑ 229 James Mouton .20 .07
❑ 230 Paul Quantrill .20 .07
❑ 231 Randy Knorr .20 .07
❑ 232 Abraham Nunez .20 .07
❑ 233 Mike Fetters .20 .07
❑ 234 Mario Encarnacion .20 .07
❑ 235 Jeremy Fikac .20 .07
❑ 236 Travis Lee .20 .07
❑ 237 Bob File .20 .07
❑ 238 Pete Harnisch .20 .07
❑ 239 Randy Galvez RC .40 .15
❑ 240 Geoff Goetz .20 .07
❑ 241 Gary Glover .20 .07
❑ 242 Troy Percival .30 .10
❑ 243 Len Dinardo RC .40 .15
❑ 244 Jonny Gomes RC 2.50 1.00
❑ 245 Jesus Medrano RC .40 .15
❑ 246 Rey Ordonez .20 .07
❑ 247 Juan Gonzalez .30 .10
❑ 248 Jose Guillen .30 .10
❑ 249 Franklyn German RC .40 .15
❑ 250 Mike Mussina .50 .20
❑ 251 Ugueth Urbina .20 .07
❑ 252 Melvin Mora .30 .10
❑ 253 Gerald Williams .20 .07
❑ 254 Jared Sandberg .20 .07
❑ 255 Darrin Fletcher .20 .07
❑ 256 A.J. Pierzynski .30 .10
❑ 257 Lenny Harris .20 .07
❑ 258 Blaine Neal .20 .07
❑ 259 Denny Neagle .20 .07
❑ 260 Jason Hart .20 .07
❑ 261 Henry Mateo .20 .07
❑ 262 Rheal Cormier .20 .07
❑ 263 Luis Terrero .20 .07
❑ 264 Shigetoshi Hasegawa .30 .10
❑ 265 Bill Haselman .20 .07
❑ 266 Scott Hatteberg .20 .07
❑ 267 Adam Hyzdu .20 .07
❑ 268 Mike Williams .20 .07
❑ 269 Marlon Anderson .20 .07
❑ 270 Bruce Chen .20 .07
❑ 271 Eli Marrero .20 .07
❑ 272 Jimmy Haynes .20 .07
❑ 273 Bronson Arroyo .30 .10
❑ 274 Kevin Jordan .20 .07
❑ 275 Rick Helling .20 .07
❑ 276 Mark Loretta .20 .07
❑ 277 Dustin Hermanson .20 .07
❑ 278 Pablo Ozuna .20 .07
❑ 279 Keto Anderson RC .40 .15
❑ 280 Jermaine Dye .30 .10
❑ 281 Will Smith .20 .07
❑ 282 Brian Daubach .20 .07
❑ 283 Eric Hinske .20 .07
❑ 284 Joe Jiannetti RC .40 .15
❑ 285 Chan Ho Park .30 .10
❑ 286 Curtis Legendre RC .40 .15
❑ 287 Jeff Reboulet .20 .07
❑ 288 Scott Rolen .50 .20
❑ 289 Chris Richard .20 .07
❑ 290 Eric Chavez .30 .10
❑ 291 Scot Shields .20 .07
❑ 292 Donnie Sadler .20 .07
❑ 293 Dave Veres .20 .07
❑ 294 Craig Counsell .20 .07
❑ 295 Armando Reynoso .20 .07
❑ 296 Kyle Lohse .20 .07
❑ 297 Arthur Rhodes .20 .07
❑ 298 Sidney Ponson .20 .07
❑ 299 Trevor Hoffman .30 .10
❑ 300 Kerry Wood .30 .10
❑ 301 Danny Bautista .20 .07
❑ 302 Scott Sauerbeck .20 .07
❑ 303 Johnny Estrada .20 .07
❑ 304 Mike Timlin .20 .07
❑ 305 Orlando Hernandez .30 .10
❑ 306 Tony Clark .20 .07
❑ 307 Tomas Perez .20 .07
❑ 308 Marcus Giles .30 .10
❑ 309 Mike Bordick .30 .10
❑ 310 Jorge Posada .50 .20
❑ 311 Jason Conti .20 .07
❑ 312 Kevin Millar .30 .10
❑ 313 Paul Shuey .20 .07
❑ 314 Jake Mauer RC .40 .15
❑ 315 Luke Hudson .20 .07
❑ 316 Angel Berroa .20 .07
❑ 317 Fred Bastardo RC .40 .15
❑ 318 Shawn Estes .20 .07
❑ 319 Andy Ashby .20 .07
❑ 320 Ryan Klesko .30 .10
❑ 321 Kevin Appier .30 .10
❑ 322 Juan Pena .20 .07
❑ 323 Alex Herrera .20 .07
❑ 324 Robb Nen .30 .10
❑ 325 Orlando Hudson .20 .07
❑ 326 Lyle Overbay .20 .07
❑ 327 Ben Sheets .30 .10
❑ 328 Mike DiFelice .20 .07
❑ 329 Pablo Arias RC .40 .15
❑ 330 Mike Sweeney .30 .10
❑ 331 Rick Ankiel .20 .07
❑ 332 Tomas De La Rosa .20 .07
❑ 333 Kazuhisa Ishii RC .50 .20
❑ 334 Jose Reyes .50 .20
❑ 335 Jeremy Giambi .20 .07
❑ 336 Jose Mesa .20 .07
❑ 337 Ralph Roberts RC .40 .15
❑ 338 Jose Nunez .20 .07
❑ 339 Curt Schilling .30 .10
❑ 340 Sean Casey .30 .10
❑ 341 Bob Wells .20 .07
❑ 342 Carlos Beltran .30 .10
❑ 343 Alexis Gomez .20 .07
❑ 344 Brandon Claussen .20 .07
❑ 345 Buddy Groom .20 .07
❑ 346 Mark Phillips RC .40 .15
❑ 347 Francisco Cordova .20 .07
❑ 348 Joe Oliver .20 .07
❑ 349 Danny Patterson .20 .07
❑ 350 Joel Pineiro .20 .07
❑ 351 J.R. House .20 .07
❑ 352 Benny Agbayani .20 .07
❑ 353 Jose Vidro .20 .07
❑ 354 Reed Johnson RC 1.00 .40
❑ 355 Mike Lowell .30 .10
❑ 356 Scott Schoeneweis .20 .07
❑ 357 Brian Jordan .30 .10
❑ 358 Steve Finley .30 .10
❑ 359 Randy Choate .20 .07
❑ 360 Jose Lima .20 .07
❑ 361 Miguel Olivo .20 .07
❑ 362 Kenny Rogers .30 .10
❑ 363 David Justice .30 .10
❑ 364 Brandon Knight .20 .07
❑ 365 Joe Kennedy .20 .07
❑ 366 Eric Valent .20 .07
❑ 367 Nelson Cruz .20 .07
❑ 368 Brian Giles .30 .10
❑ 369 Charles Gipson RC .25 .08
❑ 370 Juan Pena .20 .07
❑ 371 Mark Redman .20 .07
❑ 372 Billy Koch .20 .07
❑ 373 Ted Lilly .20 .07
❑ 374 Craig Paquette .20 .07
❑ 375 Kevin Jarvis .20 .07
❑ 376 Scott Erickson .20 .07
❑ 377 Josh Paul .20 .07
❑ 378 Darwin Cubillan .20 .07
❑ 379 Nelson Figueroa .20 .07
❑ 380 Darin Erstad .30 .10
❑ 381 Jeremy Hill RC .40 .15
❑ 382 Elvin Nina .20 .07
❑ 383 David Wells .30 .10
❑ 384 Jay Caligiuri RC .40 .15
❑ 385 Freddy Garcia .30 .10
❑ 386 Damian Miller .20 .07
❑ 387 Bobby Higginson .30 .10
❑ 388 Alejandro Giron RC .40 .15
❑ 389 Ivan Rodriguez .50 .20
❑ 390 Ed Rogers .20 .07
❑ 391 Andy Benes .20 .07
❑ 392 Matt Blank .20 .07
❑ 393 Ryan Vogelsong .20 .07
❑ 394 Kelly Ramos RC .25 .08
❑ 395 Eric Karros .30 .10
❑ 396 Bobby J. Jones .20 .07
❑ 397 Omar Vizquel .50 .20
❑ 398 Matt Perisho .20 .07
❑ 399 Delino DeShields .20 .07
❑ 400 Carlos Hernandez .20 .07
❑ 401 Derrek Lee .50 .20
❑ 402 Kirk Rueter .20 .07
❑ 403 David Wright RC 30.00 12.50
❑ 404 Paul LoDuca .30 .10
❑ 405 Brian Schneider .20 .07
❑ 406 Milton Bradley .30 .10
❑ 407 Daryle Ward .20 .07
❑ 408 Cody Ransom .20 .07
❑ 409 Fernando Rodney .20 .07
❑ 410 John Suomi RC .40 .15
❑ 411 Joe Girardi .20 .07
❑ 412 Demetrius Heath RC .40 .15
❑ 413 John Foster RC .40 .15
❑ 414 Doug Glanville .20 .07
❑ 415 Ryan Kohlmeier .20 .07
❑ 416 Mike Matthews .20 .07
❑ 417 Craig Wilson .20 .07
❑ 418 Jay Witasick .20 .07
❑ 419 Jay Payton .20 .07
❑ 420 Andruw Jones .50 .20

❑ 421 Benji Gil .20 .07
❑ 422 Jeff Liefer .20 .07
❑ 423 Kevin Young .20 .07
❑ 424 Richie Sexson .30 .10
❑ 425 Cory Lidle .20 .07
❑ 426 Shane Halter .20 .07
❑ 427 Jesse Foppert RC .50 .20
❑ 428 Jose Molina .20 .07
❑ 429 Nick Alvarez RC .40 .15
❑ 430 Brian L. Hunter .20 .07
❑ 431 Cliff Bartosh RC .40 .15
❑ 432 Junior Spivey .20 .07
❑ 433 Eric Good RC .40 .15
❑ 434 Chin-Feng Chen .30 .10
❑ 435 T.J. Mathews .20 .07
❑ 436 Rich Rodriguez .20 .07
❑ 437 Bobby Abreu .30 .10
❑ 438 Joe McEwing .20 .07
❑ 439 Michael Tucker .20 .07
❑ 440 Preston Wilson .30 .10
❑ 441 Mike MacDougal .20 .07
❑ 442 Shannon Stewart .30 .10
❑ 443 Bob Howry .20 .07
❑ 444 Mike Benjamin .20 .07
❑ 445 Erik Hiljus .20 .07
❑ 446 Ryan Gripp RC .40 .15
❑ 447 Jose Vizcaino .20 .07
❑ 448 Shawn Wooten .20 .07
❑ 449 Steve Kent RC .40 .15
❑ 450 Ramiro Mendoza .20 .07
❑ 451 Jake Westbrook .20 .07
❑ 452 Joe Lawrence .20 .07
❑ 453 Jae Seo .20 .07
❑ 454 Ryan Fry RC .40 .15
❑ 455 Darren Lewis .20 .07
❑ 456 Brad Wilkerson .20 .07
❑ 457 Gustavo Chacin RC 1.00 .40
❑ 458 Adrian Brown .20 .07
❑ 459 Mike Cameron .20 .07
❑ 460 Bud Smith .20 .07
❑ 461 Derrick Lewis .20 .07
❑ 462 Derek Lowe .30 .10
❑ 463 Matt Williams .30 .10
❑ 464 Jason Jennings .20 .07
❑ 465 Albie Lopez .20 .07
❑ 466 Felipe Lopez .20 .07
❑ 467 Luke Allen .20 .07
❑ 468 Brian Anderson .20 .07
❑ 469 Matt Riley .20 .07
❑ 470 Ryan Dempster .20 .07
❑ 471 Matt Ginter .20 .07
❑ 472 David Ortiz .75 .30
❑ 473 Cole Barthel RC .25 .08
❑ 474 Damian Jackson .20 .07
❑ 475 Andy Van Hekken .20 .07
❑ 476 Doug Brocail .20 .07
❑ 477 Denny Hocking .20 .07
❑ 478 Sean Douglass .20 .07
❑ 479 Eric Owens .20 .07
❑ 480 Ryan Ludwick .20 .07
❑ 481 Todd Pratt .20 .07
❑ 482 Aaron Sele .20 .07
❑ 483 Edgar Renteria .30 .10
❑ 484 Raymond Cabrera RC .40 .15
❑ 485 Brandon Lyon .20 .07
❑ 486 Chase Utley 2.50 1.00
❑ 487 Robert Fick .20 .07
❑ 488 Wilfredo Cordero .20 .07
❑ 489 Octavio Dotel .20 .07
❑ 490 Paul Abbott .20 .07
❑ 491 Jason Kendall .30 .10
❑ 492 Jarrod Washburn .20 .07
❑ 493 Dane Sardinha .20 .07
❑ 494 Jung Bong .20 .07
❑ 495 J.D. Drew .30 .10
❑ 496 Jason Schmidt .30 .10
❑ 497 Mike Magnante .20 .07
❑ 498 Jorge Padilla RC .40 .15
❑ 499 Eric Gagne .30 .10
❑ 500 Todd Helton .50 .20
❑ 501 Jeff Weaver .20 .07
❑ 502 Alex Sanchez .20 .07
❑ 503 Ken Griffey Jr. 1.25 .50
❑ 504 Abraham Nunez .20 .07
❑ 505 Reggie Sanders .30 .10
❑ 506 Casey Kotchman RC 1.00 .40
❑ 507 Jim Mann .20 .07
❑ 508 Matt LeCroy .20 .07
❑ 509 Frank Castillo .20 .07
❑ 510 Geoff Jenkins .20 .07
❑ 511 Jayson Durocher RC .25 .08
❑ 512 Ellis Burks .30 .10
❑ 513 Aaron Fultz .20 .07
❑ 514 Hiram Bocachica .20 .07
❑ 515 Nate Espy RC .40 .15
❑ 516 Placido Polanco .20 .07
❑ 517 Kerry Ligtenberg .20 .07
❑ 518 Doug Nickle .20 .07
❑ 519 Ramon Ortiz .20 .07
❑ 520 Greg Swindell .20 .07
❑ 521 J.J. Davis .20 .07
❑ 522 Sandy Alomar Jr. .20 .07
❑ 523 Chris Carpenter .30 .10
❑ 524 Vance Wilson .20 .07
❑ 525 Nomar Garciaparra 1.25 .50
❑ 526 Jim Mecir .20 .07
❑ 527 Taylor Buchholz RC .50 .20
❑ 528 Brent Mayne .20 .07
❑ 529 John Rodriguez RC .50 .20
❑ 530 David Segui .20 .07
❑ 531 Nate Cornejo .20 .07
❑ 532 Gil Heredia .20 .07
❑ 533 Esteban Loaiza .20 .07
❑ 534 Pat Mahomes .20 .07
❑ 535 Matt Morris .30 .10
❑ 536 Todd Stottlemyre .20 .07
❑ 537 Brian Lesher .20 .07
❑ 538 Arturo McDowell .20 .07
❑ 539 Felix Diaz .20 .07
❑ 540 Mark Mulder .30 .10
❑ 541 Kevin Frederick RC .40 .15
❑ 542 Andy Fox .20 .07
❑ 543 Dionys Cesar RC .25 .08
❑ 544 Justin Miller .20 .07
❑ 545 Keith Osik .20 .07
❑ 546 Shane Reynolds .20 .07
❑ 547 Mike Myers .20 .07
❑ 548 Raul Chavez RC .25 .08
❑ 549 Joe Nathan .30 .10
❑ 550 Ryan Anderson .20 .07
❑ 551 Jason Marquis .20 .07
❑ 552 Marty Cordova .20 .07
❑ 553 Kevin Tapani .20 .07
❑ 554 Jimmy Anderson .20 .07
❑ 555 Pedro Martinez .50 .20
❑ 556 Rocky Biddle .20 .07
❑ 557 Alex Ochoa .20 .07
❑ 558 D'Angelo Jimenez .20 .07
❑ 559 Wilkin Ruan .20 .07
❑ 560 Terrence Long .20 .07
❑ 561 Mark Lukasiewicz .20 .07
❑ 562 Jose Santiago .20 .07
❑ 563 Brad Fullmer .20 .07
❑ 564 Corky Miller .20 .07
❑ 565 Matt White .20 .07
❑ 566 Mark Grace .50 .20
❑ 567 Raul Ibanez .20 .07
❑ 568 Josh Towers .20 .07
❑ 569 Juan M. Gonzalez RC .40 .15
❑ 570 Brian Buchanan .20 .07
❑ 571 Ken Harvey .20 .07
❑ 572 Jeffrey Hammonds .20 .07
❑ 573 Wade Miller .20 .07
❑ 574 Elpidio Guzman .20 .07
❑ 575 Kevin Olsen .20 .07
❑ 576 Austin Kearns .20 .07
❑ 577 Tim Kalita RC .40 .15
❑ 578 David Dellucci .20 .07
❑ 579 Alex Gonzalez .20 .07
❑ 580 Joe Orloski RC .40 .15
❑ 581 Gary Matthews Jr. .20 .07
❑ 582 Ryan Mills .20 .07
❑ 583 Erick Almonte .20 .07
❑ 584 Jeremy Affeldt .20 .07
❑ 585 Chris Tritle RC .25 .08
❑ 586 Michael Cuddyer .20 .07
❑ 587 Kris Foster .20 .07
❑ 588 Russell Branyan .20 .07
❑ 589 Darren Oliver .20 .07
❑ 590 Freddie Money RC .40 .15
❑ 591 Carlos Lee .30 .10
❑ 592 Tim Wakefield .30 .10
❑ 593 Bubba Trammell .20 .07
❑ 594 John Koronka RC 1.00 .40
❑ 595 Geoff Blum .20 .07
❑ 596 Darryl Kile .30 .10
❑ 597 Neifi Perez .20 .07
❑ 598 Torii Hunter .30 .10
❑ 599 Luis Castillo .20 .07
❑ 600 Mark Buehrle .30 .10
❑ 601 Jeff Zimmerman .20 .07
❑ 602 Mike DeJean .20 .07
❑ 603 Julio Lugo .20 .07
❑ 604 Chad Hermansen .20 .07
❑ 605 Keith Foulke .30 .10
❑ 606 Lance Davis .20 .07
❑ 607 Jeff Austin RC .40 .15
❑ 608 Brandon Inge .20 .07
❑ 609 Orlando Merced .20 .07
❑ 610 Johnny Damon Sox .50 .20
❑ 611 Doug Henry .20 .07
❑ 612 Adam Kennedy .20 .07
❑ 613 Wiki Gonzalez .20 .07
❑ 614 Brian West RC .40 .15
❑ 615 Andy Pettitte .50 .20
❑ 616 Chone Figgins RC 1.50 .60
❑ 617 Matt Lawton .20 .07
❑ 618 Paul Rigdon .20 .07
❑ 619 Keith Lockhart .20 .07
❑ 620 Tim Redding .20 .07
❑ 621 John Parrish .20 .07
❑ 622 Homer Bush .20 .07
❑ 623 Todd Greene .20 .07
❑ 624 David Eckstein .30 .10
❑ 625 Greg Montalbano RC .40 .15
❑ 626 Joe Beimel .20 .07
❑ 627 Adrian Beltre .30 .10
❑ 628 Charles Nagy .20 .07
❑ 629 Cristian Guzman .20 .07
❑ 630 Toby Hall .20 .07
❑ 631 Jose Hernandez .20 .07
❑ 632 Jose Macias .30 .10
❑ 633 Jaret Wright .20 .07
❑ 634 Steve Parris .20 .07
❑ 635 Gene Kingsale .20 .07
❑ 636 Tim Worrell .20 .07
❑ 637 Billy Martin .20 .07
❑ 638 Jovanny Cedeno .20 .07
❑ 639 Curtis Leskanic .20 .07
❑ 640 Tim Hudson .30 .10
❑ 641 Juan Castro .20 .07
❑ 642 Rafael Soriano .20 .07
❑ 643 Juan Rincon .20 .07
❑ 644 Mark DeRosa .20 .07
❑ 645 Carlos Pena .20 .07
❑ 646 Robin Ventura .30 .10
❑ 647 Odalis Perez .20 .07
❑ 648 Damion Easley .20 .07
❑ 649 Benito Santiago .30 .10
❑ 650 Alex Rodriguez 1.25 .50
❑ 651 Aaron Rowand .30 .10
❑ 652 Alex Cora .20 .07
❑ 653 Bobby Kielty .20 .07
❑ 654 Jose Rodriguez RC .40 .15
❑ 655 Herbert Perry .20 .07
❑ 656 Jeff Urban .20 .07
❑ 657 Paul Bako .20 .07
❑ 658 Shane Spencer .20 .07
❑ 659 Pat Hentgen .20 .07
❑ 660 Jeff Kent .30 .10
❑ 661 Mark McLemore .20 .07
❑ 662 Chuck Knoblauch .30 .10
❑ 663 Blake Stein .20 .07
❑ 664 Brett Roneberg RC .40 .15
❑ 665 Josh Phelps .20 .07
❑ 666 Byung-Hyun Kim .30 .10
❑ 667 Dave Martinez .20 .07
❑ 668 Mike Maroth .20 .07
❑ 669 Shawn Chacon .20 .07
❑ 670 Billy Wagner .30 .10
❑ 671 Luis Alicea .20 .07
❑ 672 Sterling Hitchcock .20 .07
❑ 673 Adam Piatt .20 .07
❑ 674 Ryan Franklin .20 .07
❑ 675 Luke Prokopec .20 .07
❑ 676 Alfredo Amezaga .20 .07
❑ 677 Gookie Dawkins .20 .07
❑ 678 Eric Byrnes .20 .07

❑ 679 Barry Larkin .50 .20
❑ 680 Albert Pujols 1.50 .60
❑ 681 Edwards Guzman .20 .07
❑ 682 Jason Bere .20 .07
❑ 683 Adam Everett .20 .07
❑ 684 Greg Colbrunn .20 .07
❑ 685 Brandon Puffer RC .40 .15
❑ 686 Mark Kotsay .30 .10
❑ 687 Willie Bloomquist .30 .10
❑ 688 Hank Blalock .50 .20
❑ 689 Travis Hafner .30 .10
❑ 690 Lance Berkman .30 .10
❑ 691 Joe Crede .30 .10
❑ 692 Chuck Finley .30 .10
❑ 693 John Grabow .20 .07
❑ 694 Randy Winn .20 .07
❑ 695 Mike James .20 .07
❑ 696 Kris Benson .20 .07
❑ 697 Bret Prinz .20 .07
❑ 698 Jeff Williams .20 .07
❑ 699 Eric Munson .20 .07
❑ 700 Mike Hampton .30 .10
❑ 701 Ramon E. Martinez .20 .07
❑ 702 Hansel Izquierdo RC .40 .15
❑ 703 Nathan Haynes .20 .07
❑ 704 Eddie Taubensee .20 .07
❑ 705 Esteban German .20 .07
❑ 706 Ross Gload .20 .07
❑ 707 Matt Merricks RC .40 .15
❑ 708 Chris Piersoll RC .25 .08
❑ 709 Seth Greisinger .20 .07
❑ 710 Ichiro Suzuki 1.50 .60
❑ 711 Cesar Izturis .20 .07
❑ 712 Brad Cresse .20 .07
❑ 713 Carl Pavano .30 .10
❑ 714 Steve Sparks .20 .07
❑ 715 Dennis Tankersley .20 .07
❑ 716 Kelvim Escobar .20 .07
❑ 717 Jason LaRue .20 .07
❑ 718 Corey Koskie .20 .07
❑ 719 Vinny Castilla .30 .10
❑ 720 Tim Drew .20 .07
❑ 721 Chin-Hui Tsao .30 .10
❑ 722 Paul Byrd .20 .07
❑ 723 Alex Cintron .20 .07
❑ 724 Orlando Palmeiro .20 .07
❑ 725 Ramon Hernandez .20 .07
❑ 726 Mark Johnson .20 .07
❑ 727 B.J. Ryan .20 .07
❑ 728 Wendell Magee .20 .07
❑ 729 Michael Coleman .20 .07
❑ 730 Mario Ramos RC .40 .15
❑ 731 Mike Stanton .20 .07
❑ 732 Dee Brown .20 .07
❑ 733 Brad Ausmus .30 .10
❑ 734 Napoleon Calzado RC .40 .15
❑ 735 Woody Williams .20 .07
❑ 736 Paxton Crawford .20 .07
❑ 737 Jason Karnuth .20 .07
❑ 738 Michael Restovich .20 .07
❑ 739 Ramon Castro .20 .07
❑ 740 Magglio Ordonez .30 .10
❑ 741 Tom Gordon .20 .07
❑ 742 Mark Grudzielanek .20 .07
❑ 743 Jaime Moyer .30 .10
❑ 744 Marlyn Tisdale RC .40 .15
❑ 745 Steve Kline .20 .07
❑ 746 Adam Eaton .20 .07
❑ 747 Eric Glaser RC .40 .15
❑ 748 Sean DePaula .20 .07
❑ 749 Greg Norton .20 .07
❑ 750 Steve Reed .20 .07
❑ 751 Ricardo Aramboles .20 .07
❑ 752 Matt Mantei .20 .07
❑ 753 Gene Stechschulte .20 .07
❑ 754 Chuck McElroy .20 .07
❑ 755 Barry Bonds 2.00 .75
❑ 756 Matt Anderson .20 .07
❑ 757 Yorvit Torrealba .20 .07
❑ 758 Jason Standridge .20 .07
❑ 759 Desi Relaford .20 .07
❑ 760 Jolbert Cabrera .20 .07
❑ 761 Chris George .20 .07
❑ 762 Erubiel Durazo .20 .07
❑ 763 Paul Konerko .30 .10
❑ 764 Tike Redman .20 .07
❑ 765 Chad Ricketts RC .25 .08
❑ 766 Roberto Hernandez .20 .07
❑ 767 Mark Lewis .20 .07
❑ 768 Livan Hernandez .30 .10
❑ 769 Carlos Brackley RC .40 .15
❑ 770 Kazuhiro Sasaki .30 .10
❑ 771 Bill Hall .30 .10
❑ 772 Nelson Castro RC .40 .15
❑ 773 Eric Milton .20 .07
❑ 774 Tom Davey .20 .07
❑ 775 Todd Ritchie .20 .07
❑ 776 Seth Etherton .20 .07
❑ 777 Chris Singleton .20 .07
❑ 778 Robert Averette RC .25 .08
❑ 779 Robert Person .20 .07
❑ 780 Fred McGriff .50 .20
❑ 781 Richard Hidalgo .20 .07
❑ 782 Kris Wilson .20 .07
❑ 783 John Rocker .30 .10
❑ 784 Justin Kaye .20 .07
❑ 785 Glendon Rusch .20 .07
❑ 786 Greg Vaughn .20 .07
❑ 787 Mike Lamb .20 .07
❑ 788 Greg Myers .20 .07
❑ 789 Nate Field RC .40 .15
❑ 790 Jim Edmonds .30 .10
❑ 791 Olmedo Saenz .20 .07
❑ 792 Jason Johnson .20 .07
❑ 793 Mike Lincoln .20 .07
❑ 794 Todd Coffey RC .40 .15
❑ 795 Jesus Sanchez .20 .07
❑ 796 Aaron Myette .20 .07
❑ 797 Tony Womack .20 .07
❑ 798 Chad Kreuter .20 .07
❑ 799 Brady Clark .20 .07
❑ 800 Adam Dunn .30 .10
❑ 801 Jacque Jones .30 .10
❑ 802 Kevin Millwood .30 .10
❑ 803 Mike Rivera .20 .07
❑ 804 Jim Thome .50 .20
❑ 805 Jeff Conine .30 .10
❑ 806 Elmer Dessens .20 .07
❑ 807 Randy Velarde .20 .07
❑ 808 Carlos Delgado .30 .10
❑ 809 Steve Karsay .20 .07
❑ 810 Casey Fossum .20 .07
❑ 811 J.C. Romero .20 .07
❑ 812 Chris Truby .20 .07
❑ 813 Tony Graffanino .20 .07
❑ 814 Wascar Serrano .20 .07
❑ 815 Delvin James .20 .07
❑ 816 Pedro Feliz .20 .07
❑ 817 Damian Rolls .20 .07
❑ 818 Scott Linebrink .20 .07
❑ 819 Rafael Palmeiro .50 .20
❑ 820 Javy Lopez .30 .10
❑ 821 Larry Barnes .20 .07
❑ 822 Brian Lawrence .20 .07
❑ 823 Scotty Layfield RC .40 .15
❑ 824 Jeff Cirillo .20 .07
❑ 825 Willis Roberts .20 .07
❑ 826 Rich Harden RC 3.00 1.25
❑ 827 Chris Snelling RC .60 .25
❑ 828 Gary Sheffield .30 .10
❑ 829 Jeff Heaverlo .20 .07
❑ 830 Matt Clement .30 .10
❑ 831 Rich Garces .20 .07
❑ 832 Rondell White .30 .10
❑ 833 Henry Pichardo RC .40 .15
❑ 834 Aaron Boone .30 .10
❑ 835 Ruben Sierra .30 .10
❑ 836 Deivis Santos .20 .07
❑ 837 Tony Batista .20 .07
❑ 838 Rob Bell .20 .07
❑ 839 Frank Thomas .75 .30
❑ 840 Jose Silva .20 .07
❑ 841 Dan Johnson RC 1.00 .40
❑ 842 Steve Cox .20 .07
❑ 843 Jose Acevedo .20 .07
❑ 844 Jay Bell .30 .10
❑ 845 Mike Sirotka .20 .07
❑ 846 Garret Anderson .30 .10
❑ 847 James Shanks RC .40 .15
❑ 848 Trot Nixon .30 .10
❑ 849 Keith Ginter .20 .07
❑ 850 Tim Spooneybarger .20 .07
❑ 851 Matt Stairs .20 .07
❑ 852 Chris Stynes .20 .07
❑ 853 Marvin Benard .20 .07
❑ 854 Raul Mondesi .30 .10
❑ 855 Jeremy Owens .20 .07
❑ 856 Jon Garland .30 .10
❑ 857 Mitch Meluskey .20 .07
❑ 858 Chad Durbin .20 .07
❑ 859 John Burkett .20 .07
❑ 860 Jon Switzer RC .40 .15
❑ 861 Peter Bergeron .20 .07
❑ 862 Jesus Colome .20 .07
❑ 863 Todd Hundley .20 .07
❑ 864 Ben Petrick .20 .07
❑ 865 So Taguchi RC .50 .20
❑ 866 Ryan Drese .20 .07
❑ 867 Mike Trombley .20 .07
❑ 868 Rick Reed .20 .07
❑ 869 Mark Teixeira .75 .30
❑ 870 Corey Thurman RC .40 .15
❑ 871 Brian Roberts .30 .10
❑ 872 Mike Timlin .20 .07
❑ 873 Chris Reitsma .20 .07
❑ 874 Jeff Fassero .20 .07
❑ 875 Carlos Valderrama .20 .07
❑ 876 John Lackey .20 .07
❑ 877 Travis Fryman .30 .10
❑ 878 Ismael Valdes .20 .07
❑ 879 Rick White .20 .07
❑ 880 Edgar Martinez .50 .20
❑ 881 Dean Palmer .30 .10
❑ 882 Matt Allegra RC .40 .15
❑ 883 Greg Sain RC .40 .15
❑ 884 Carlos Silva .20 .07
❑ 885 Jose Valverde RC .40 .15
❑ 886 Dernell Stenson .20 .07
❑ 887 Todd Van Poppel .20 .07
❑ 888 Wes Anderson .20 .07
❑ 889 Bill Mueller .30 .10
❑ 890 Morgan Ensberg .30 .10
❑ 891 Marcus Thames .20 .07
❑ 892 Adam Walker RC .40 .15
❑ 893 John Halama .20 .07
❑ 894 Frank Menechino .20 .07
❑ 895 Greg Maddux 1.25 .50
❑ 896 Gary Bennett .20 .07
❑ 897 Mauricio Lara RC .40 .15
❑ 898 Mike Young .75 .30
❑ 899 Travis Phelps .20 .07
❑ 900 Rich Aurilia .20 .07
❑ 901 Henry Blanco .20 .07
❑ 902 Carlos Febles .20 .07
❑ 903 Scott MacRae .20 .07
❑ 904 Lou Merloni .20 .07
❑ 905 Dicky Gonzalez .20 .07
❑ 906 Jeff DaVanon .20 .07
❑ 907 A.J. Burnett .30 .10
❑ 908 Einar Diaz .20 .07
❑ 909 Julio Franco .30 .10
❑ 910 John Olerud .30 .10
❑ 911 Mark Hamilton RC .40 .15
❑ 912 David Riske .20 .07
❑ 913 Jason Tyner .20 .07
❑ 914 Britt Reames .20 .07
❑ 915 Vernon Wells .30 .10
❑ 916 Eddie Perez .20 .07
❑ 917 Edwin Almonte RC .40 .15
❑ 918 Enrique Wilson .20 .07
❑ 919 Chris Gomez .20 .07
❑ 920 Jayson Werth .20 .07
❑ 921 Jeff Nelson .20 .07
❑ 922 Freddy Sanchez RC 2.00 .75
❑ 923 John Vander Wal .20 .07
❑ 924 Chad Qualls RC .50 .20
❑ 925 Gabe White .20 .07
❑ 926 Chad Harville .20 .07
❑ 927 Ricky Gutierrez .20 .07
❑ 928 Carlos Guillen .30 .10
❑ 929 B.J. Surhoff .30 .10
❑ 930 Chris Woodward .20 .07
❑ 931 Ricardo Rodriguez .20 .07
❑ 932 Jimmy Gobble RC .40 .15
❑ 933 Jon Lieber .20 .07
❑ 934 Craig Kuzmic RC .40 .15
❑ 935 Eric Young .20 .07
❑ 936 Greg Zaun .20 .07

❑ 937 Miguel Batista .20 .07
❑ 938 Danny Wright .20 .07
❑ 939 Todd Zeile .30 .10
❑ 940 Chad Zerbe .20 .07
❑ 941 Jason Young RC .25 .08
❑ 942 Ronnie Belliard .20 .07
❑ 943 John Ennis RC .40 .15
❑ 944 John Flaherty .20 .07
❑ 945 Jerry Hairston Jr. .20 .07
❑ 946 Al Levine .20 .07
❑ 947 Antonio Alfonseca .20 .07
❑ 948 Brian Moehler .20 .07
❑ 949 Calvin Murray .20 .07
❑ 950 Nick Bierbrodt .20 .07
❑ 951 Sun Woo Kim .20 .07
❑ 952 Noochie Varner RC .40 .15
❑ 953 Luis Rivas .20 .07
❑ 954 Donnie Bridges .20 .07
❑ 955 Ramon Vazquez .20 .07
❑ 956 Luis Garcia .20 .07
❑ 957 Mark Quinn .20 .07
❑ 958 Armando Rios .20 .07
❑ 959 Chad Fox .20 .07
❑ 960 Hee Seop Choi .20 .07
❑ 961 Turk Wendell .20 .07
❑ 962 Adam Roller RC .40 .15
❑ 963 Grant Roberts .20 .07
❑ 964 Ben Molina .20 .07
❑ 965 Juan Rivera .20 .07
❑ 966 Matt Kinney .20 .07
❑ 967 Rod Beck .20 .07
❑ 968 Xavier Nady .20 .07
❑ 969 Masato Yoshii .20 .07
❑ 970 Miguel Tejada .30 .10
❑ 971 Danny Kolb .20 .07
❑ 972 Mike Remlinger .20 .07
❑ 973 Ray Lankford .30 .10
❑ 974 Ryan Minor .20 .07
❑ 975 J.T. Snow .30 .10
❑ 976 Brad Radke .30 .10
❑ 977 Jason Lane .30 .10
❑ 978 Jamey Wright .20 .07
❑ 979 Tom Goodwin .20 .07
❑ 980 Erik Bedard .30 .10
❑ 981 Gabe Kapler .30 .10
❑ 982 Brian Reith .20 .07
❑ 983 Nic Jackson RC .40 .15
❑ 984 Kurt Ainsworth .20 .07
❑ 985 Jason Isringhausen .30 .10
❑ 986 Willie Harris .20 .07
❑ 987 David Cone .30 .10
❑ 988 Bob Wickman .20 .07
❑ 989 Wes Helms .20 .07
❑ 990 Josh Beckett .30 .10

2003 Topps Total

❑ COMPLETE SET (990) 200.00 100.00
❑ COMMON CARD (1-990) .20 .07
❑ COMMON RC .25 .08
❑ 1 Brent Abernathy .20 .07
❑ 2 Bobby Hill .20 .07
❑ 3 Victor Martinez .50 .20
❑ 4 Chip Ambres .20 .07
❑ 5 Matt Anderson .20 .07
❑ 6 Ricardo Aramboles .20 .07
❑ 7 Carlos Pena .20 .07
❑ 8 Aaron Guiel .20 .07
❑ 9 Luke Allen .20 .07
❑ 10 Francisco Rodriguez .30 .10
❑ 11 Jason Marquis .20 .07
❑ 12 Edwin Almonte .20 .07
❑ 13 Grant Balfour .20 .07
❑ 14 Adam Piatt .20 .07
❑ 15 Andy Phillips .20 .07
❑ 16 Adrian Beltre .30 .10
❑ 17 Brandon Backe .20 .07
❑ 18 Dave Berg .20 .07
❑ 19 Brett Myers .30 .10
❑ 20 Brian Meadows .20 .07
❑ 21 Chin-Feng Chen .30 .10
❑ 22 Blake Williams .20 .07
❑ 23 Josh Bard .20 .07
❑ 24 Josh Beckett .30 .10
❑ 25 Tommy Whiteman .20 .07
❑ 26 Matt Childers .20 .07
❑ 27 Adam Everett .20 .07
❑ 28 Mike Bordick .30 .10
❑ 29 Antonio Alfonseca .20 .07
❑ 30 Doug Creek .20 .07
❑ 31 J.D. Drew .30 .10
❑ 32 Milton Bradley .30 .10
❑ 33 David Wells .30 .10
❑ 34 Vance Wilson .20 .07
❑ 35 Jeff Fassero .20 .07
❑ 36 Sandy Alomar Jr. .20 .07
❑ 37 Ryan Vogelsong .20 .07
❑ 38 Roger Clemens 1.50 .60
❑ 39 Juan Gonzalez .30 .10
❑ 40 Dustin Hermanson .20 .07
❑ 41 Andy Ashby .20 .07
❑ 42 Adam Hyzdu .20 .07
❑ 43 Ben Broussard .20 .07
❑ 44 Ryan Klesko .30 .10
❑ 45 Chris Buglovsky FY RC .40 .15
❑ 46 Bud Smith .20 .07
❑ 47 Aaron Boone .30 .10
❑ 48 Cliff Floyd .30 .10
❑ 49 Alex Cora .20 .07
❑ 50 Curt Schilling .30 .10
❑ 51 Michael Cuddyer .20 .07
❑ 52 Joe Valentine FY RC .40 .15
❑ 53 Carlos Guillen .30 .10
❑ 54 Angel Berroa .20 .07
❑ 55 Eli Marrero .20 .07
❑ 56 A.J. Burnett .30 .10
❑ 57 Oliver Perez .30 .10
❑ 58 Matt Morris .30 .10
❑ 59 Valerio De Los Santos .20 .07
❑ 60 Austin Kearns .20 .07
❑ 61 Darren Dreifort .20 .07
❑ 62 Jason Standridge .20 .07
❑ 63 Carlos Silva .20 .07
❑ 64 Moises Alou .30 .10
❑ 65 Jason Anderson .20 .07
❑ 66 Russell Branyan .20 .07
❑ 67 B.J. Ryan .20 .07
❑ 68 Cory Aldridge .20 .07
❑ 69 Ellis Burks .30 .10
❑ 70 Troy Glaus .30 .10
❑ 71 Kelly Wunsch .20 .07
❑ 72 Brad Wilkerson .20 .07
❑ 73 Jayson Durocher .20 .07
❑ 74 Tony Fiore .20 .07
❑ 75 Brian Giles .30 .10
❑ 76 Billy Wagner .30 .10
❑ 77 Neifi Perez .20 .07
❑ 78 Jose Valverde .20 .07
❑ 79 Brent Butler .20 .07
❑ 80 Mario Ramos .20 .07
❑ 81 Kerry Robinson .20 .07
❑ 82 Brent Mayne .20 .07
❑ 83 Sean Casey .30 .10
❑ 84 Danys Baez .20 .07
❑ 85 Chase Utley .75 .30
❑ 86 Jared Sandberg .20 .07
❑ 87 Terrence Long .20 .07
❑ 88 Kevin Walker .20 .07
❑ 89 Royce Clayton .20 .07
❑ 90 Shea Hillenbrand .30 .10
❑ 91 Brad Lidge .30 .10
❑ 92 Shawn Chacon .20 .07
❑ 93 Kenny Rogers .30 .10
❑ 94 Chris Snelling .20 .07
❑ 95 Omar Vizquel .50 .20
❑ 96 Joe Borchard .20 .07
❑ 97 Matt Belisle .20 .07
❑ 98 Steve Smyth .20 .07
❑ 99 Raul Mondesi .30 .10
❑ 100 Chipper Jones .75 .30
❑ 101 Victor Alvarez .20 .07
❑ 102 J.M. Gold .20 .07
❑ 103 Willis Roberts .20 .07
❑ 104 Eddie Guardado .20 .07
❑ 105 Brad Voyles .20 .07
❑ 106 Bronson Arroyo .30 .10
❑ 107 Juan Castro .20 .07
❑ 108 Dan Plesac .20 .07
❑ 109 Ramon Castro .20 .07
❑ 110 Tim Salmon .50 .20
❑ 111 Gene Kingsale .20 .07
❑ 112 J.D. Closser .20 .07
❑ 113 Mark Buehrle .30 .10
❑ 114 Steve Karsay .20 .07
❑ 115 Cristian Guerrero .20 .07
❑ 116 Brad Ausmus .30 .10
❑ 117 Cristian Guzman .20 .07
❑ 118 Dan Wilson .20 .07
❑ 119 Jake Westbrook .20 .07
❑ 120 Manny Ramirez .50 .20
❑ 121 Jason Giambi .30 .10
❑ 122 Bob Wickman .20 .07
❑ 123 Aaron Cook .20 .07
❑ 124 Alfredo Amezaga .20 .07
❑ 125 Corey Thurman .20 .07
❑ 126 Brandon Puffer .20 .07
❑ 127 Hee Seop Choi .20 .07
❑ 128 Javier Vazquez .30 .10
❑ 129 Carlos Valderrama .20 .07
❑ 130 Jerome Williams .20 .07
❑ 131 Wilson Betemit .20 .07
❑ 132 Luke Prokopec .20 .07
❑ 133 Esteban Yan .20 .07
❑ 134 Brandon Berger .20 .07
❑ 135 Bill Hall .20 .07
❑ 136 LaTroy Hawkins .20 .07
❑ 137 Nate Cornejo .20 .07
❑ 138 Jim Mecir .20 .07
❑ 139 Joe Crede .30 .10
❑ 140 Andres Galarraga .30 .10
❑ 141 Reggie Sanders .30 .10
❑ 142 Joey Eischen .20 .07
❑ 143 Mike Timlin .20 .07
❑ 144 Jose Cruz Jr. .20 .07
❑ 145 Wes Helms .20 .07
❑ 146 Brian Roberts .30 .10
❑ 147 Bret Prinz .20 .07
❑ 148 Brian Hunter .20 .07
❑ 149 Chad Hermansen .20 .07
❑ 150 Andruw Jones .50 .20
❑ 151 Kurt Ainsworth .20 .07
❑ 152 Cliff Bartosh .20 .07
❑ 153 Kyle Lohse .20 .07
❑ 154 Brian Jordan .30 .10
❑ 155 Coco Crisp .50 .20
❑ 156 Tomas Perez .20 .07
❑ 157 Keith Foulke .30 .10
❑ 158 Chris Carpenter .30 .10
❑ 159 Mike Remlinger .20 .07
❑ 160 Dewon Brazelton .20 .07
❑ 161 Brook Fordyce .20 .07
❑ 162 Rusty Greer .30 .10
❑ 163 Scott Downs .20 .07
❑ 164 Jason Dubois .20 .07
❑ 165 David Coggin .20 .07
❑ 166 Mike DeJean .20 .07
❑ 167 Carlos Hernandez .20 .07
❑ 168 Matt Williams .30 .10
❑ 169 Rheal Cormier .20 .07
❑ 170 Duaner Sanchez .20 .07
❑ 171 Craig Counsell .20 .07
❑ 172 Edgar Martinez .50 .20
❑ 173 Zack Greinke .30 .10
❑ 174 Pedro Feliz .20 .07
❑ 175 Randy Choate .20 .07
❑ 176 Jon Garland .30 .10
❑ 177 Keith Ginter .20 .07
❑ 178 Carlos Febles .20 .07
❑ 179 Kerry Wood .30 .10
❑ 180 Jack Cust .20 .07
❑ 181 Koyie Hill .20 .07

❑ 182 Ricky Gutierrez .20 .07
❑ 183 Ben Grieve .20 .07
❑ 184 Scott Eyre .20 .07
❑ 185 Jason Isringhausen .30 .10
❑ 186 Gookie Dawkins .20 .07
❑ 187 Roberto Alomar .50 .20
❑ 188 Eric Junge .20 .07
❑ 189 Carlos Beltran .30 .10
❑ 190 Denny Hocking .20 .07
❑ 191 Jason Schmidt .30 .10
❑ 192 Cory Lidle .20 .07
❑ 193 Rob Mackowiak .20 .07
❑ 194 Charlton Jimerson RC .40 .15
❑ 195 Darin Erstad .30 .10
❑ 196 Jason Davis .20 .07
❑ 197 Luis Castillo .20 .07
❑ 198 Juan Encarnacion .20 .07
❑ 199 Jeffrey Hammonds .20 .07
❑ 200 Nomar Garciaparra 1.25 .50
❑ 201 Ryan Christianson .20 .07
❑ 202 Robert Person .20 .07
❑ 203 Damian Moss .20 .07
❑ 204 Chris Richard .20 .07
❑ 205 Todd Hundley .20 .07
❑ 206 Paul Bako .20 .07
❑ 207 Adam Kennedy .20 .07
❑ 208 Scott Hatteberg .20 .07
❑ 209 Andy Pratt .20 .07
❑ 210 Ken Griffey Jr. 1.25 .50
❑ 211 Chris George .20 .07
❑ 212 Lance Niekro .20 .07
❑ 213 Greg Colbrunn .20 .07
❑ 214 Herbert Perry .20 .07
❑ 215 Cody Ransom .20 .07
❑ 216 Craig Biggio .50 .20
❑ 217 Miguel Batista .20 .07
❑ 218 Alex Escobar .20 .07
❑ 219 Willie Harris .20 .07
❑ 220 Scott Strickland .20 .07
❑ 221 Felix Rodriguez .20 .07
❑ 222 Torii Hunter .30 .10
❑ 223 Tyler Houston .20 .07
❑ 224 Darrell May .20 .07
❑ 225 Benito Santiago .30 .10
❑ 226 Ryan Dempster .20 .07
❑ 227 Andy Fox .20 .07
❑ 228 Jung Bong .20 .07
❑ 229 Jose Macias .20 .07
❑ 230 Shannon Stewart .30 .10
❑ 231 Buddy Groom .20 .07
❑ 232 Eric Valent .20 .07
❑ 233 Scott Schoenweis .20 .07
❑ 234 Corey Hart .20 .07
❑ 235 Brett Tomko .20 .07
❑ 236 Shane Bazzell RC .40 .15
❑ 237 Tim Hummel .20 .07
❑ 238 Matt Stairs .20 .07
❑ 239 Pete Munro .20 .07
❑ 240 Ismael Valdes .20 .07
❑ 241 Brian Fuentes .20 .07
❑ 242 Cesar Izturis .20 .07
❑ 243 Mark Bellhorn .30 .10
❑ 244 Geoff Jenkins .20 .07
❑ 245 Derek Jeter 2.00 .75
❑ 246 Anderson Machado .20 .07
❑ 247 Dave Roberts .20 .07
❑ 248 Jaime Cerda .20 .07
❑ 249 Woody Williams .20 .07
❑ 250 Vernon Wells .30 .10
❑ 251 Jon Lieber .20 .07
❑ 252 Franklyn German .20 .07
❑ 253 David Segui .20 .07
❑ 254 Freddy Garcia .30 .10
❑ 255 James Baldwin .20 .07
❑ 256 Tony Alvarez .20 .07
❑ 257 Walter Young .20 .07
❑ 258 Alex Herrera .20 .07
❑ 259 Robert Fick .20 .07
❑ 260 Rob Bell .20 .07
❑ 261 Ben Petrick .20 .07
❑ 262 Dee Brown .20 .07
❑ 263 Mike Bacsik .20 .07
❑ 264 Corey Patterson .20 .07
❑ 265 Marvin Benard .20 .07
❑ 266 Eddie Rogers .20 .07
❑ 267 Elio Serrano .20 .07
❑ 268 D'Angelo Jimenez .20 .07
❑ 269 Adam Johnson .20 .07
❑ 270 Gregg Zaun .20 .07
❑ 271 Nick Johnson .30 .10
❑ 272 Geoff Goetz .20 .07
❑ 273 Ryan Drese .20 .07
❑ 274 Eric Dubose .20 .07
❑ 275 Barry Zito .30 .10
❑ 276 Mike Crudale .20 .07
❑ 277 Paul Byrd .20 .07
❑ 278 Eric Gagne .30 .10
❑ 279 Aramis Ramirez .30 .10
❑ 280 Ray Durham .30 .10
❑ 281 Tony Graffanino .20 .07
❑ 282 Jeremy Guthrie .20 .07
❑ 283 Erik Bedard .20 .07
❑ 284 Vince Faison .20 .07
❑ 285 Bobby Kielty .20 .07
❑ 286 Francis Beltran .20 .07
❑ 287 Alexis Gomez .20 .07
❑ 288 Vladimir Guerrero .75 .30
❑ 289 Kevin Appier .30 .10
❑ 290 Gil Meche .20 .07
❑ 291 Marquis Grissom .30 .10
❑ 292 John Burkett .20 .07
❑ 293 Vinny Castilla .30 .10
❑ 294 Tyler Walker .20 .07
❑ 295 Shane Halter .20 .07
❑ 296 Geronimo Gil .20 .07
❑ 297 Eric Hinske .20 .07
❑ 298 Adam Dunn .30 .10
❑ 299 Mike Kinkade .20 .07
❑ 300 Mark Prior .50 .20
❑ 301 Corey Koskie .20 .07
❑ 302 David Dellucci .20 .07
❑ 303 Todd Helton .50 .20
❑ 304 Greg Miller .20 .07
❑ 305 Delvin James .20 .07
❑ 306 Humberto Cota .20 .07
❑ 307 Aaron Harang .20 .07
❑ 308 Jeremy Hill .20 .07
❑ 309 Billy Koch .20 .07
❑ 310 Brandon Claussen .20 .07
❑ 311 Matt Ginter .20 .07
❑ 312 Jason Lane .20 .07
❑ 313 Ben Weber .20 .07
❑ 314 Alan Benes .20 .07
❑ 315 Matt Walbeck .20 .07
❑ 316 Danny Graves .20 .07
❑ 317 Jason Johnson .20 .07
❑ 318 Jason Grimsley .20 .07
❑ 319 Steve Kline .20 .07
❑ 320 Johnny Damon .50 .20
❑ 321 Jay Gibbons .20 .07
❑ 322 J.J. Putz .20 .07
❑ 323 Stephen Randolph RC .40 .15
❑ 324 Bobby Higginson .30 .10
❑ 325 Kazuhisa Ishii .30 .10
❑ 326 Carlos Lee .30 .10
❑ 327 J.R. House .20 .07
❑ 328 Mark Loretta .20 .07
❑ 329 Mike Matheny .20 .07
❑ 330 Ben Diggins .20 .07
❑ 331 Seth Etherton .20 .07
❑ 332 Eli Whiteside FY RC .40 .15
❑ 333 Juan Rivera .20 .07
❑ 334 Jeff Conine .30 .10
❑ 335 John McDonald .20 .07
❑ 336 Erik Hiljus .20 .07
❑ 337 David Eckstein .30 .10
❑ 338 Jeff Bagwell .50 .20
❑ 339 Matt Holliday .25 .08
❑ 340 Jeff Liefer .20 .07
❑ 341 Greg Myers .20 .07
❑ 342 Scott Sauerbeck .20 .07
❑ 343 Omar Infante .20 .07
❑ 344 Ryan Langerhans .30 .10
❑ 345 Abraham Nunez .20 .07
❑ 346 Mike MacDougal .20 .07
❑ 347 Travis Phelps .20 .07
❑ 348 Terry Shumpert .20 .07
❑ 349 Alex Rodriguez 1.25 .50
❑ 350 Bobby Seay .20 .07
❑ 351 Ichiro Suzuki 1.50 .60
❑ 352 Brandon Inge .20 .07
❑ 353 Jack Wilson .20 .07
❑ 354 John Ennis .20 .07
❑ 355 Jamal Strong .20 .07
❑ 356 Jason Jennings .20 .07
❑ 357 Jeff Kent .30 .10
❑ 358 Scott Chiasson .20 .07
❑ 359 Jeremy Griffiths RC .40 .15
❑ 360 Paul Konerko .30 .10
❑ 361 Jeff Austin .20 .07
❑ 362 Todd Van Poppel .20 .07
❑ 363 Sun Woo Kim .20 .07
❑ 364 Jerry Hairston Jr.. .20 .07
❑ 365 Tony Torcato .20 .07
❑ 366 Arthur Rhodes .20 .07
❑ 367 Jose Jimenez .20 .07
❑ 368 Matt LeCroy .20 .07
❑ 369 Curtis Leskanic .20 .07
❑ 370 Ramon Vazquez .20 .07
❑ 371 Joe Randa .30 .10
❑ 372 John Franco .30 .10
❑ 373 Bobby Estalella .20 .07
❑ 374 Craig Wilson .20 .07
❑ 375 Michael Young .50 .20
❑ 376 Mark Ellis .20 .07
❑ 377 Joe Mauer .75 .30
❑ 378 Checklist 1 .20 .07
❑ 379 Jason Kendall .30 .10
❑ 380 Checklist 2 .20 .07
❑ 381 Alex Gonzalez .20 .07
❑ 382 Tom Gordon .20 .07
❑ 383 John Buck .20 .07
❑ 384 Shigetoshi Hasegawa .30 .10
❑ 385 Scott Stewart .20 .07
❑ 386 Luke Hudson .20 .07
❑ 387 Todd Jones .20 .07
❑ 388 Fred McGriff .50 .20
❑ 389 Mike Sweeney .30 .10
❑ 390 Marlon Anderson .20 .07
❑ 391 Terry Adams .20 .07
❑ 392 Mark DeRosa .20 .07
❑ 393 Doug Mientkiewicz .30 .10
❑ 394 Miguel Cairo .20 .07
❑ 395 Jamie Moyer .30 .10
❑ 396 Jose Leon .20 .07
❑ 397 Matt Clement .30 .10
❑ 398 Bengie Molina .20 .07
❑ 399 Marcus Thames .20 .07
❑ 400 Nick Bierbrodt .20 .07
❑ 401 Tim Kalita .20 .07
❑ 402 Corwin Malone .20 .07
❑ 403 Jesse Orosco .20 .07
❑ 404 Brandon Phillips .20 .07
❑ 405 Eric Cyr .20 .07
❑ 406 Jason Michaels .20 .07
❑ 407 Julio Lugo .20 .07
❑ 408 Gabe Kapler .30 .10
❑ 409 Mark Mulder .30 .10
❑ 410 Adam Eaton .20 .07
❑ 411 Ken Harvey .20 .07
❑ 412 Jolbert Cabrera .20 .07
❑ 413 Eric Milton .20 .07
❑ 414 Josh Hall RC .40 .15
❑ 415 Bob File .20 .07
❑ 416 Brett Evert .20 .07
❑ 417 Ron Chiavacci .20 .07
❑ 418 Jorge De La Rosa .20 .07
❑ 419 Quinton McCracken .20 .07
❑ 420 Luther Hackman .20 .07
❑ 421 Gary Knotts .20 .07
❑ 422 Kevin Brown .30 .10
❑ 423 Jeff Cirillo .20 .07
❑ 424 Damaso Marte .20 .07
❑ 425 Chan Ho Park .30 .10
❑ 426 Nathan Haynes .20 .07
❑ 427 Matt Lawton .20 .07
❑ 428 Mike Stanton .20 .07
❑ 429 Bernie Williams .50 .20
❑ 430 Kevin Jarvis .20 .07
❑ 431 Joe McEwing .20 .07
❑ 432 Mark Kotsay .30 .10
❑ 433 Juan Cruz .20 .07
❑ 434 Russ Ortiz .20 .07
❑ 435 Jeff Nelson .20 .07
❑ 436 Alan Embree .20 .07
❑ 437 Miguel Tejada .30 .10
❑ 438 Kirk Saarloos .20 .07
❑ 439 Cliff Lee .20 .07

❑ 440 Ryan Ludwick .20 .07
❑ 441 Derrek Lee .50 .20
❑ 442 Bobby Abreu .30 .10
❑ 443 Dustan Mohr .20 .07
❑ 444 Nook Logan RC .50 .20
❑ 445 Seth McClung .20 .07
❑ 446 Miguel Olivo .20 .07
❑ 447 Henry Blanco .20 .07
❑ 448 Seung Song .20 .07
❑ 449 Kris Wilson .20 .07
❑ 450 Xavier Nady .20 .07
❑ 451 Corky Miller .20 .07
❑ 452 Jim Thome .50 .20
❑ 453 George Lombard .20 .07
❑ 454 Rey Ordonez .20 .07
❑ 455 Deivis Santos .20 .07
❑ 456 Mike Myers .20 .07
❑ 457 Edgar Renteria .30 .10
❑ 458 Braden Looper .20 .07
❑ 459 Guillermo Mota .20 .07
❑ 460 Scott Rolen .50 .20
❑ 461 Lance Berkman .30 .10
❑ 462 Jeff Heaverlo .20 .07
❑ 463 Ramon Hernandez .20 .07
❑ 464 Jason Simontacchi .20 .07
❑ 465 So Taguchi .30 .10
❑ 466 Dave Veres .20 .07
❑ 467 Shane Loux .20 .07
❑ 468 Rodrigo Lopez .20 .07
❑ 469 Bubba Trammell .20 .07
❑ 470 Scott Sullivan .20 .07
❑ 471 Mike Mussina .50 .20
❑ 472 Ramon Ortiz .20 .07
❑ 473 Lyle Overbay .20 .07
❑ 474 Mike Lowell .30 .10
❑ 475 Al Martin .20 .07
❑ 476 Larry Bigbie .20 .07
❑ 477 Rey Sanchez .20 .07
❑ 478 Magglio Ordonez .30 .10
❑ 479 Rondell White .30 .10
❑ 480 Jay Witasick .20 .07
❑ 481 Jimmy Rollins .30 .10
❑ 482 Mike Maroth .20 .07
❑ 483 Alejandro Machado .20 .07
❑ 484 Nick Neugebauer .20 .07
❑ 485 Victor Zambrano .20 .07
❑ 486 Travis Lee .20 .07
❑ 487 Bobby Bradley .20 .07
❑ 488 Marcus Giles .30 .10
❑ 489 Steve Trachsel .20 .07
❑ 490 Derek Lowe .30 .10
❑ 491 Hideo Nomo .75 .30
❑ 492 Brad Hawpe .30 .10
❑ 493 Jesus Medrano .20 .07
❑ 494 Rick Ankiel .20 .07
❑ 495 Pasqual Coco .20 .07
❑ 496 Michael Barrett .20 .07
❑ 497 Joe Beimel .20 .07
❑ 498 Marty Cordova .20 .07
❑ 499 Aaron Sele .20 .07
❑ 500 Sammy Sosa .75 .30
❑ 501 Ivan Rodriguez .50 .20
❑ 502 Keith Osik .20 .07
❑ 503 Hank Blalock .30 .10
❑ 504 Hiram Bocachica .20 .07
❑ 505 Junior Spivey .20 .07
❑ 506 Edgardo Alfonzo .20 .07
❑ 507 Alex Graman .20 .07
❑ 508 J.J. Davis .20 .07
❑ 509 Roger Cedeno .20 .07
❑ 510 Joe Roa .20 .07
❑ 511 Wily Mo Pena .30 .10
❑ 512 Eric Munson .20 .07
❑ 513 Arnie Munoz RC .40 .15
❑ 514 Albie Lopez .20 .07
❑ 515 Andy Pettitte .50 .20
❑ 516 Jim Edmonds .30 .10
❑ 517 Jeff Davanon .20 .07
❑ 518 Aaron Myette .20 .07
❑ 519 C.C. Sabathia .30 .10
❑ 520 Gerardo Garcia .20 .07
❑ 521 Brian Schneider .20 .07
❑ 522 Wes Obermueller .20 .07
❑ 523 John Mabry .20 .07
❑ 524 Casey Fossum .20 .07
❑ 525 Toby Hall .20 .07
❑ 526 Denny Neagle .20 .07
❑ 527 Willie Bloomquist .30 .10
❑ 528 A.J. Pierzynski .30 .10
❑ 529 Bartolo Colon .30 .10
❑ 530 Chad Harville .20 .07
❑ 531 Blaine Neal .20 .07
❑ 532 Luis Terrero .20 .07
❑ 533 Reggie Taylor .20 .07
❑ 534 Melvin Mora .30 .10
❑ 535 Tino Martinez .50 .20
❑ 536 Peter Bergeron .20 .07
❑ 537 Jorge Padilla .20 .07
❑ 538 Oscar Villarreal RC .40 .15
❑ 539 David Weathers .20 .07
❑ 540 Mike Lamb .20 .07
❑ 541 Greg Norton .20 .07
❑ 542 Michael Tucker .20 .07
❑ 543 Ben Kozlowski .20 .07
❑ 544 Alex Sanchez .20 .07
❑ 545 Trey Lunsford .20 .07
❑ 546 Abraham Nunez .20 .07
❑ 547 Mike Lincoln .20 .07
❑ 548 Orlando Hernandez .30 .10
❑ 549 Kevin Mench .20 .07
❑ 550 Garret Anderson .30 .10
❑ 551 Kyle Farnsworth .20 .07
❑ 552 Kevin Olsen .20 .07
❑ 553 Joel Pineiro .20 .07
❑ 554 Jorge Julio .20 .07
❑ 555 Jose Mesa .20 .07
❑ 556 Jorge Posada .50 .20
❑ 557 Jose Ortiz .20 .07
❑ 558 Mike Tonis .20 .07
❑ 559 Gabe White .20 .07
❑ 560 Rafael Furcal .30 .10
❑ 561 Matt Franco .20 .07
❑ 562 Trey Hodges .20 .07
❑ 563 Esteban German .20 .07
❑ 564 Josh Fogg .20 .07
❑ 565 Fernando Tatis .20 .07
❑ 566 Alex Cintron .20 .07
❑ 567 Grant Roberts .20 .07
❑ 568 Gene Stechschulte .20 .07
❑ 569 Rafael Palmeiro .50 .20
❑ 570 Mike Hampton .30 .10
❑ 571 Ben Davis .20 .07
❑ 572 Dean Palmer .30 .10
❑ 573 Jerrod Riggan .20 .07
❑ 574 Nate Frese .20 .07
❑ 575 Josh Phelps .20 .07
❑ 576 Freddie Bynum .20 .07
❑ 577 Morgan Ensberg .30 .10
❑ 578 Juan Rincon .20 .07
❑ 579 Kazuhiro Sasaki .30 .10
❑ 580 Yorvit Torrealba .20 .07
❑ 581 Tim Wakefield .30 .10
❑ 582 Sterling Hitchcock .20 .07
❑ 583 Craig Paquette .20 .07
❑ 584 Kevin Millwood .30 .10
❑ 585 Damian Rolls .20 .07
❑ 586 Brad Baisley .20 .07
❑ 587 Kyle Snyder .20 .07
❑ 588 Paul Quantrill .20 .07
❑ 589 Trot Nixon .30 .10
❑ 590 J.T. Snow .30 .10
❑ 591 Kevin Young .20 .07
❑ 592 Tomo Ohka .20 .07
❑ 593 Brian Boehringer .20 .07
❑ 594 Danny Patterson .20 .07
❑ 595 Jeff Tam .20 .07
❑ 596 Anastacio Martinez .20 .07
❑ 597 Rod Barajas .20 .07
❑ 598 Octavio Dotel .20 .07
❑ 599 Jason Tyner .20 .07
❑ 600 Gary Sheffield .30 .10
❑ 601 Ruben Quevedo .20 .07
❑ 602 Jay Payton .20 .07
❑ 603 Mo Vaughn .30 .10
❑ 604 Pat Burrell .30 .10
❑ 605 Fernando Vina .20 .07
❑ 606 Wes Anderson .20 .07
❑ 607 Alex Gonzalez .20 .07
❑ 608 Ted Lilly .20 .07
❑ 609 Nick Punto .20 .07
❑ 610 Ryan Madson .20 .07
❑ 611 Odalis Perez .20 .07
❑ 612 Chris Woodward .20 .07
❑ 613 John Olerud .30 .10
❑ 614 Brad Cresse .20 .07
❑ 615 Chad Zerbe .20 .07
❑ 616 Brad Penny .20 .07
❑ 617 Barry Larkin .50 .20
❑ 618 Brandon Duckworth .20 .07
❑ 619 Brad Radke .30 .10
❑ 620 Troy Brohawn .20 .07
❑ 621 Juan Pierre .30 .10
❑ 622 Rick Reed .20 .07
❑ 623 Omar Daal .20 .07
❑ 624 Jose Hernandez .20 .07
❑ 625 Greg Maddux 1.25 .50
❑ 626 Henry Mateo .20 .07
❑ 627 Kip Wells .20 .07
❑ 628 Kevin Cash .20 .07
❑ 629 Wil Ledezma FY RC .40 .15
❑ 630 Luis Gonzalez .30 .10
❑ 631 Jason Conti .20 .07
❑ 632 Ricardo Rincon .20 .07
❑ 633 Mike Bynum .20 .07
❑ 634 Mike Redmond .20 .07
❑ 635 Chance Caple .20 .07
❑ 636 Chris Widger .20 .07
❑ 637 Michael Restovich .20 .07
❑ 638 Mark Grudzielanek .20 .07
❑ 639 Brandon Larson .20 .07
❑ 640 Rocco Baldelli .30 .10
❑ 641 Javy Lopez .30 .10
❑ 642 Rene Reyes .20 .07
❑ 643 Orlando Merced .20 .07
❑ 644 Jason Phillips .20 .07
❑ 645 Luis Ugueto .20 .07
❑ 646 Ron Calloway .20 .07
❑ 647 Josh Paul .20 .07
❑ 648 Todd Greene .20 .07
❑ 649 Joe Girardi .20 .07
❑ 650 Todd Ritchie .20 .07
❑ 651 Kevin Millar Sox .30 .10
❑ 652 Shawn Wooten .20 .07
❑ 653 David Riske .20 .07
❑ 654 Luis Rivas .20 .07
❑ 655 Roy Halladay .30 .10
❑ 656 Travis Driskill .20 .07
❑ 657 Ricky Ledee .20 .07
❑ 658 Timo Perez .20 .07
❑ 659 Fernando Rodney .20 .07
❑ 660 Trevor Hoffman .30 .10
❑ 661 Pat Hentgen .30 .10
❑ 662 Bret Boone .30 .10
❑ 663 Ryan Jensen .20 .07
❑ 664 Ricardo Rodriguez .20 .07
❑ 665 Jeremy Lambert .20 .07
❑ 666 Troy Percival .30 .10
❑ 667 Jon Rauch .20 .07
❑ 668 Mariano Rivera .75 .30
❑ 669 Jason LaRue .20 .07
❑ 670 J.C. Romero .20 .07
❑ 671 Cody Ross .20 .07
❑ 672 Eric Byrnes .20 .07
❑ 673 Paul Lo Duca .30 .10
❑ 674 Brad Fullmer .20 .07
❑ 675 Cliff Politte .20 .07
❑ 676 Justin Miller .20 .07
❑ 677 Nic Jackson .20 .07
❑ 678 Kris Benson .20 .07
❑ 679 Carl Sadler .20 .07
❑ 680 Joe Nathan .30 .10
❑ 681 Julio Santana .20 .07
❑ 682 Wade Miller .20 .07
❑ 683 Josh Pearce .20 .07
❑ 684 Tony Armas Jr. .20 .07
❑ 685 Al Leiter .30 .10
❑ 686 Raul Ibanez .20 .07
❑ 687 Danny Bautista .20 .07
❑ 688 Travis Hafner .30 .10
❑ 689 Carlos Zambrano .30 .10
❑ 690 Pedro Martinez .50 .20
❑ 691 Ramon Santiago .20 .07
❑ 692 Felipe Lopez .20 .07
❑ 693 David Ross .20 .07
❑ 694 Chone Figgins .20 .07
❑ 695 Antonio Osuna .20 .07
❑ 696 Jay Powell .20 .07
❑ 697 Ryan Church .30 .10

No.	Player		
698	Alexis Rios	.30	.10
699	Tanyon Sturtze	.20	.07
700	Turk Wendell	.20	.07
701	Richard Hidalgo	.20	.07
702	Joe Mays	.20	.07
703	Jorge Sosa	.20	.07
704	Eric Karros	.30	.10
705	Steve Finley	.30	.10
706	Sean Smith FY RC	.50	.20
707	Jeremy Giambi	.20	.07
708	Scott Hodges	.20	.07
709	Vicente Padilla	.20	.07
710	Erubiel Durazo	.20	.07
711	Aaron Rowand	.30	.10
712	Dennis Tankersley	.20	.07
713	Rick Bauer	.20	.07
714	Tim Olson FY RC	.40	.15
715	Jeff Urban	.20	.07
716	Steve Sparks	.20	.07
717	Glendon Rusch	.20	.07
718	Ricky Stone	.20	.07
719	Benji Gil	.20	.07
720	Pete Walker	.20	.07
721	Tim Worrell	.20	.07
722	Michael Tejera	.20	.07
723	David Kelton	.20	.07
724	Britt Reames	.20	.07
725	John Stephens	.20	.07
726	Mark McLemore	.20	.07
727	Jeff Zimmerman	.20	.07
728	Checklist 3	.20	.07
729	Andres Torres	.20	.07
730	Checklist 4	.20	.07
731	Johan Santana	.50	.20
732	Dane Sardinha	.20	.07
733	Rodrigo Rosario	.20	.07
734	Frank Thomas	.75	.30
735	Tom Glavine	.50	.20
736	Doug Mirabelli	.20	.07
737	Juan Uribe	.20	.07
738	Ryan Anderson	.20	.07
739	Sean Burroughs	.20	.07
740	Eric Chavez	.30	.10
741	Enrique Wilson	.20	.07
742	Elmer Dessens	.20	.07
743	Marlon Byrd	.20	.07
744	Brendan Donnelly	.20	.07
745	Gary Bennett	.20	.07
746	Roy Oswalt	.30	.10
747	Andy Van Hekken	.20	.07
748	Jesus Colome	.20	.07
749	Erick Almonte	.20	.07
750	Frank Catalanotto	.20	.07
751	Kenny Lofton	.30	.10
752	Carlos Delgado	.30	.10
753	Ryan Franklin	.20	.07
754	Wilkin Ruan	.20	.07
755	Kelvim Escobar	.20	.07
756	Tim Drew	.20	.07
757	Jarrod Washburn	.20	.07
758	Runelvys Hernandez	.20	.07
759	Cory Vance	.20	.07
760	Doug Glanville	.20	.07
761	Ryan Rupe	.20	.07
762	Jermaine Dye	.30	.10
763	Mike Cameron	.20	.07
764	Scott Erickson	.20	.07
765	Richie Sexson	.30	.10
766	Jose Vidro	.20	.07
767	Brian West	.20	.07
768	Shawn Estes	.20	.07
769	Brian Tallet	.20	.07
770	Larry Walker	.30	.10
771	Josh Hamilton	.40	.15
772	Orlando Hudson	.20	.07
773	Justin Morneau	.30	.10
774	Ryan Bukvich	.20	.07
775	Mike Gonzalez	.20	.07
776	Tsuyoshi Shinjo	.30	.10
777	Matt Mantei	.20	.07
778	Jimmy Journell	.20	.07
779	Brian Lawrence	.20	.07
780	Mike Lieberthal	.30	.10
781	Scott Mullen	.20	.07
782	Zach Day	.20	.07
783	John Thomson	.20	.07
784	Ben Sheets	.30	.10
785	Damon Minor	.20	.07
786	Jose Valentin	.20	.07
787	Armando Benitez	.20	.07
788	Jamie Walker RC	.25	.08
789	Preston Wilson	.30	.10
790	Josh Wilson	.20	.07
791	Phil Nevin	.30	.10
792	Roberto Hernandez	.20	.07
793	Mike Williams	.20	.07
794	Jake Peavy	.30	.10
795	Paul Shuey	.20	.07
796	Chad Bradford	.20	.07
797	Bobby Jenks	.30	.10
798	Sean Douglass	.20	.07
799	Damian Miller	.20	.07
800	Mark Wohlers	.20	.07
801	Ty Wigginton	.20	.07
802	Alfonso Soriano	.30	.10
803	Randy Johnson	.75	.30
804	Placido Polanco	.20	.07
805	Drew Henson	.20	.07
806	Tony Womack	.20	.07
807	Pokey Reese	.20	.07
808	Albert Pujols	1.50	.60
809	Henri Stanley	.20	.07
810	Mike Rivera	.20	.07
811	John Lackey	.20	.07
812	Brian Wright FY RC	.40	.15
813	Eric Good	.20	.07
814	Dernell Stenson	.20	.07
815	Kirk Rueter	.20	.07
816	Todd Zeile	.20	.07
817	Brad Thomas	.20	.07
818	Shawn Sedlacek	.20	.07
819	Garrett Stephenson	.20	.07
820	Mark Teixeira	.50	.20
821	Tim Hudson	.30	.10
822	Mike Koplove	.20	.07
823	Chris Reitsma	.20	.07
824	Rafael Soriano	.20	.07
825	Ugueth Urbina	.20	.07
826	Lance Carter	.20	.07
827	Colin Young	.20	.07
828	Pat Strange	.20	.07
829	Juan Pena	.20	.07
830	Joe Thurston	.20	.07
831	Shawn Green	.30	.10
832	Pedro Astacio	.20	.07
833	Danny Wright	.20	.07
834	Wes O'Brien FY RC	.40	.15
835	Luis Lopez	.20	.07
836	Randall Simon	.20	.07
837	Jaret Wright	.20	.07
838	Jayson Werth	.20	.07
839	Endy Chavez	.20	.07
840	Checklist 5	.20	.07
841	Chad Paronto	.20	.07
842	Randy Winn	.20	.07
843	Sidney Ponson	.20	.07
844	Robin Ventura	.30	.10
845	Rich Aurilia	.20	.07
846	Joaquin Benoit	.20	.07
847	Barry Bonds	2.00	.75
848	Carl Crawford	.30	.10
849	Jeromy Burnitz	.30	.10
850	Orlando Cabrera	.30	.10
851	Luis Vizcaino	.20	.07
852	Randy Wolf	.20	.07
853	Todd Walker	.20	.07
854	Jeremy Affeldt	.20	.07
855	Einar Diaz	.20	.07
856	Carl Everett	.30	.10
857	Wiki Gonzalez	.20	.07
858	Mike Paradis	.20	.07
859	Travis Harper	.20	.07
860	Mike Piazza	1.25	.50
861	Will Ohman	.20	.07
862	Eric Young	.20	.07
863	Jason Grabowski	.20	.07
864	Rett Johnson RC	.40	.15
865	Aubrey Huff	.30	.10
866	John Smoltz	.50	.20
867	Mickey Callaway	.20	.07
868	Joe Kennedy	.20	.07
869	Tim Redding	.20	.07
870	Colby Lewis	.20	.07
871	Salomon Torres	.20	.07
872	Marco Scutaro	.20	.07
873	Tony Batista	.20	.07
874	Dmitri Young	.30	.10
875	Scott Williamson	.20	.07
876	Scott Spiezio	.20	.07
877	John Webb	.20	.07
878	Jose Acevedo	.20	.07
879	Kevin Orie	.20	.07
880	Jacque Jones	.30	.10
881	Ben Francisco FY RC	.40	.15
882	Bobby Basham FY RC	.40	.15
883	Corey Shafer FY RC	.40	.15
884	J.D. Durbin FY RC	.40	.15
885	Chien-Ming Wang FY RC	8.00	3.00
886	Adam Stern FY RC	.25	.08
887	Wayne Lydon FY RC	.40	.15
888	Derell McCall FY RC	.40	.15
889	Jon Nelson FY RC	.50	.20
890	Willie Eyre FY RC	.40	.15
891	Ramon Nivar-Martinez FY RC	.40	.15
892	Adrian Myers FY RC	.25	.08
893	Jamie Athas FY RC	.40	.15
894	Ismael Castro FY RC	.50	.20
895	David Martinez FY RC	.40	.15
896	Terry Tiffee FY RC	.40	.15
897	Nathan Panther FY RC	.40	.15
898	Kyle Roat FY RC	.40	.15
899	Kason Gabbard FY RC	.40	.15
900	Hanley Ramirez FY RC	5.00	2.00
901	Bryan Grace FY RC	.40	.15
902	B.J. Barns FY RC	.40	.15
903	Greg Bruso FY RC	.40	.15
904	Mike Neu FY RC	.40	.15
905	Dustin Yount FY RC	.50	.20
906	Shane Victorino FY RC	.75	.30
907	Brian Burgamy FY RC	.40	.15
908	Beau Kemp FY RC	.40	.15
909	David Corrente FY RC	.40	.15
910	Dexter Cooper FY RC	.40	.15
911	Chris Colton FY RC	.40	.15
912	David Cash FY RC	.40	.15
913	Bernie Castro FY RC	.40	.15
914	Luis Hodge FY RC	.40	.15
915	Jeff Clark FY RC	.40	.15
916	Jason Kubel FY RC	1.00	.40
917	T.J. Bohn FY RC	.40	.15
918	Luke Steidlmayer FY RC	.40	.15
919	Matthew Peterson FY RC	.40	.15
920	Darrell Rasner FY RC	.40	.15
921	Scott Tyler FY RC	.50	.20
922	Gary Schneidmiller FY RC	.40	.15
923	Gregor Blanco FY RC	.40	.15
924	Ryan Cameron FY RC	.40	.15
925	Wilfredo Rodriguez FY	.20	.07
926	Rajai Davis FY RC	.40	.15
927	Evel Bastida-Martinez FY RC	.40	.15
928	Chris Duncan FY RC	4.00	1.50
929	Dave Pember FY RC	.40	.15
930	Branden Florence FY RC	.40	.15
931	Eric Eckenstahler FY	.20	.07
932	Hong-Chih Kuo FY RC	5.00	2.00
933	Il Kim FY RC	.40	.15
934	Michael Garciaparra FY RC	.40	.15
935	Kip Bouknight FY RC	.50	.20
936	Gary Harris FY RC	.40	.15
937	Derry Hammond FY RC	.40	.15
938	Joey Gomes FY RC	.40	.15
939	Donnie Hood FY RC	.50	.20
940	Clay Hensley FY RC	.40	.15
941	David Pahucki FY RC	.40	.15
942	Wilton Reynolds FY RC	.40	.15
943	Michael Hinckley FY RC	.50	.20
944	Josh Willingham FY RC	1.00	.40
945	Pete LaForest FY RC	.40	.15
946	Pete Smart FY RC	.40	.15
947	Jay Sitzman FY RC	.40	.15
948	Mark Malaska FY RC	.40	.15
949	Mike Gallo FY RC	.40	.15
950	Matt Diaz FY RC	.75	.30
951	Brennan King FY RC	.40	.15
952	Ryan Howard FY RC	15.00	6.00
953	Daryl Clark FY RC	.40	.15
954	Dayton Buller FY RC	.40	.15
955	Rylan Reed FY RC	.40	.15

❑ 956 Chris Booker FY .20 .07
❑ 957 Brandon Watson FY RC .40 .15
❑ 958 Matt DeMarco FY RC .40 .15
❑ 959 Doug Waechter FY RC .50 .20
❑ 960 Callix Crabbe FY RC .50 .20
❑ 961 Jairo Garcia FY RC .50 .20
❑ 962 Jason Perry FY RC .50 .20
❑ 963 Eric Riggs FY RC .50 .20
❑ 964 Travis Ishikawa FY RC .75 .30
❑ 965 Simon Pond FY RC .40 .15
❑ 966 Manuel Ramirez FY RC .50 .20
❑ 967 Tyler Johnson FY RC .40 .15
❑ 968 Jaime Bubela FY RC .40 .15
❑ 969 Haj Turay FY RC .25 .08
❑ 970 Tyson Graham FY RC .40 .15
❑ 971 David DeJesus FY RC .75 .30
❑ 972 Franklin Gutierrez FY RC 1.00 .40
❑ 973 Craig Brazell FY RC .40 .15
❑ 974 Keith Stamler FY RC .40 .15
❑ 975 Jemel Spearman FY RC .40 .15
❑ 976 Ozzie Chavez FY RC .40 .15
❑ 977 Nick Trzesniak FY RC .40 .15
❑ 978 Bill Simon FY RC .40 .15
❑ 979 Matthew Hagen FY RC .40 .15
❑ 980 Chris Kroski FY RC .40 .15
❑ 981 Prentice Redman FY RC .40 .15
❑ 982 Kevin Randel FY RC .40 .15
❑ 983 Thomari Story-Harden FY RC .40 .15
❑ 984 Brian Shackelford FY RC .40 .15
❑ 985 Mike Adams FY RC .40 .15
❑ 986 Brian McCann FY RC 5.00 2.00
❑ 987 Mike McNutt FY RC .40 .15
❑ 988 Aron Weston FY RC .40 .15
❑ 989 Dustin Moseley FY RC .40 .15
❑ 990 Bryan Bullington FY RC .40 .15

2004 Topps Total

❑ COMPLETE SET (880) 150.00 75.00
❑ OVERALL PRESS PLATES ODDS 1:159
❑ PLATES PRINT RUN 1 #'d SET PER COLOR
❑ PLATES: BLACK, CYAN, MAGENTA & YELLOW
❑ NO PLATES PRICING DUE TO SCARCITY
❑ 1 Kevin Brown .30 .10
❑ 2 Mike Mordecai .30 .10
❑ 3 Seung Song .30 .10
❑ 4 Mike Maroth .30 .10
❑ 5 Mike Lieberthal .30 .10
❑ 6 Billy Koch .30 .10
❑ 7 Mike Stanton .30 .10
❑ 8 Brad Penny .30 .10
❑ 9 Brooks Kieschnick .30 .10
❑ 10 Carlos Delgado .30 .10
❑ 11 Brady Clark .30 .10
❑ 12 Ramon Martinez .30 .10
❑ 13 Dan Wilson .30 .10
❑ 14 Guillermo Mota .30 .10
❑ 15 Trevor Hoffman .30 .10
❑ 16 Tony Batista .30 .10
❑ 17 Rusty Greer .30 .10
❑ 18 David Weathers .30 .10
❑ 19 Horacio Ramirez .30 .10
❑ 20 Aubrey Huff .30 .10
❑ 21 Casey Blake .30 .10
❑ 22 Ryan Bukvich .30 .10
❑ 23 Garrett Atkins .30 .10
❑ 24 Jose Contreras .30 .10
❑ 25 Chipper Jones .75 .30
❑ 26 Neifi Perez .30 .10
❑ 27 Scott Linebrink .30 .10
❑ 28 Matt Kinney .30 .10
❑ 29 Michael Restovich .30 .10
❑ 30 Scott Rolen .50 .20
❑ 31 John Franco .30 .10
❑ 32 Toby Hall .30 .10
❑ 33 Wily Mo Pena .30 .10
❑ 34 Dennis Tankersley .30 .10
❑ 35 Robb Nen .30 .10
❑ 36 Jose Valverde .30 .10
❑ 37 Chin-Feng Chen .30 .10
❑ 38 Gary Knotts .30 .10
❑ 39 Mark Sweeney .30 .10
❑ 40 Bret Boone .30 .10
❑ 41 Josh Phelps .30 .10
❑ 42 Jason LaRue .30 .10
❑ 43 Tim Redding .30 .10
❑ 44 Greg Myers .30 .10
❑ 45 Darin Erstad .30 .10
❑ 46 Kip Wells .30 .10
❑ 47 Matt Ford .30 .10
❑ 48 Jerome Williams .30 .10
❑ 49 Brian Meadows .30 .10
❑ 50 Albert Pujols 1.50 .60
❑ 51 Kirk Saarloos .30 .10
❑ 52 Scott Eyre .30 .10
❑ 53 John Flaherty .30 .10
❑ 54 Rafael Soriano .30 .10
❑ 55 Shea Hillenbrand .30 .10
❑ 56 Kyle Farnsworth .30 .10
❑ 57 Nate Cornejo .30 .10
❑ 58 Julian Tavarez .30 .10
❑ 59 Ryan Vogelsong .30 .10
❑ 60 Ryan Klesko .30 .10
❑ 61 Luke Hudson .30 .10
❑ 62 Justin Morneau .30 .10
❑ 63 Frank Catalanotto .30 .10
❑ 64 Derrick Turnbow .30 .10
❑ 65 Marcus Giles .30 .10
❑ 66 Mark Mulder .30 .10
❑ 67 Matt Anderson .30 .10
❑ 68 Mike Matheny .30 .10
❑ 69 Brian Lawrence .30 .10
❑ 70 Bobby Abreu .30 .10
❑ 71 Damian Moss .30 .10
❑ 72 Richard Hidalgo .30 .10
❑ 73 Mark Kotsay .30 .10
❑ 74 Mike Cameron .30 .10
❑ 75 Troy Glaus .30 .10
❑ 76 Matt Holliday .40 .15
❑ 77 Byung-Hyun Kim .30 .10
❑ 78 Aaron Sele .30 .10
❑ 79 Danny Graves .30 .10
❑ 80 Barry Zito .30 .10
❑ 81 Matt LeCroy .30 .10
❑ 82 Jason Isringhausen .30 .10
❑ 83 Colby Lewis .30 .10
❑ 84 Franklyn German .30 .10
❑ 85 Luis Matos .30 .10
❑ 86 Mike Timlin .30 .10
❑ 87 Miguel Batista .30 .10
❑ 88 John McDonald .30 .10
❑ 89 Joey Eischen .30 .10
❑ 90 Mike Mussina .50 .20
❑ 91 Jack Wilson .30 .10
❑ 92 Aaron Cook .30 .10
❑ 93 John Parrish .30 .10
❑ 94 Jose Valentin .30 .10
❑ 95 Johnny Damon .50 .20
❑ 96 Pat Burrell .30 .10
❑ 97 Brendan Donnelly .30 .10
❑ 98 Lance Carter .30 .10
❑ 99 Omar Daal .30 .10
❑ 100 Ichiro Suzuki 1.50 .60
❑ 101 Robin Ventura .30 .10
❑ 102 Brian Shouse .30 .10
❑ 103 Kevin Jarvis .30 .10
❑ 104 Jason Young .30 .10
❑ 105 Moises Alou .30 .10
❑ 106 Wes Obermueller .30 .10
❑ 107 David Segui .30 .10
❑ 108 Mike MacDougal .30 .10
❑ 109 John Buck .30 .10
❑ 110 Gary Sheffield .30 .10
❑ 111 Yorvit Torrealba .30 .10
❑ 112 Matt Kata .30 .10
❑ 113 David Bell .30 .10
❑ 114 Juan Gonzalez .30 .10
❑ 115 Kelvim Escobar .30 .10
❑ 116 Ruben Sierra .30 .10
❑ 117 Todd Wellemeyer .30 .10
❑ 118 Jamie Walker .30 .10
❑ 119 Will Cunnane .30 .10
❑ 120 Cliff Floyd .30 .10
❑ 121 Aramis Ramirez .30 .10
❑ 122 Damaso Marte .30 .10
❑ 123 Juan Castro .30 .10
❑ 124 Chris Woodward .30 .10
❑ 125 Andruw Jones .50 .20
❑ 126 Ben Weber .30 .10
❑ 127 Dee Brown .30 .10
❑ 128 Steve Reed .30 .10
❑ 129 Gabe Kapler .30 .10
❑ 130 Miguel Cabrera .50 .20
❑ 131 Billy McMillon .30 .10
❑ 132 Julio Mateo .30 .10
❑ 133 Preston Wilson .30 .10
❑ 134 Tony Clark .30 .10
❑ 135 Carlos Lee .30 .10
❑ 136 Carlos Baerga .30 .10
❑ 137 Mike Crudale .30 .10
❑ 138 David Ross .30 .10
❑ 139 Josh Fogg .30 .10
❑ 140 Dmitri Young .30 .10
❑ 141 Cliff Lee .30 .10
❑ 142 Mike Lowell .30 .10
❑ 143 Jason Lane .30 .10
❑ 144 Pedro Feliz .30 .10
❑ 145 Ken Griffey Jr. 1.25 .50
❑ 146 Dustin Hermanson .30 .10
❑ 147 Scott Hodges .30 .10
❑ 148 Aquilino Lopez .30 .10
❑ 149 Wes Helms .30 .10
❑ 150 Jason Giambi .30 .10
❑ 151 Erasmo Ramirez .30 .10
❑ 152 Sean Burroughs .30 .10
❑ 153 J.T. Snow .30 .10
❑ 154 Eddie Guardado .30 .10
❑ 155 C.C. Sabathia .30 .10
❑ 156 Kyle Lohse .30 .10
❑ 157 Roberto Hernandez .30 .10
❑ 158 Jason Simontacchi .30 .10
❑ 159 Tim Spooneybarger .30 .10
❑ 160 Alfonso Soriano .30 .10
❑ 161 Mike Gonzalez .30 .10
❑ 162 Alex Cora .30 .10
❑ 163 Kevin Gryboski .30 .10
❑ 164 Mike Lincoln .30 .10
❑ 165 Luis Castillo .30 .10
❑ 166 Odalis Perez .30 .10
❑ 167 Alex Sanchez .30 .10
❑ 168 Rob Mackowiak .30 .10
❑ 169 Francisco Rodriguez .30 .10
❑ 170 Roy Oswalt .30 .10
❑ 171 Omar Infante .30 .10
❑ 172 Ryan Jensen .30 .10
❑ 173 Ben Droussard .30 .10
❑ 174 Mark Hendrickson .30 .10
❑ 175 Manny Ramirez .50 .20
❑ 176 Rob Bell .30 .10
❑ 177 Adam Everett .30 .10
❑ 178 Chris George .30 .10
❑ 179 Ronnie Belliard .30 .10
❑ 180 Eric Gagne .30 .10
❑ 181 Scott Schoeneweis .30 .10
❑ 182 Kris Benson .30 .10
❑ 183 Amaury Telemaco .30 .10
❑ 184 John Riedling .30 .10
❑ 185 Juan Pierre .30 .10
❑ 186 Ramon Ortiz .30 .10
❑ 187 Luis Rivas .30 .10
❑ 188 Larry Bigbie .30 .10
❑ 189 Robby Hammock .30 .10
❑ 190 Geoff Jenkins .30 .10
❑ 191 Chad Cordero .30 .10
❑ 192 Mark Ellis .30 .10
❑ 193 Mark Loretta .30 .10
❑ 194 Ryan Drese .30 .10
❑ 195 Lance Berkman .30 .10
❑ 196 Kevin Appier .30 .10
❑ 197 Kiko Calero .30 .10
❑ 198 Mickey Callaway .30 .10

	No.	Player		
❑	199	Chase Utley	.50	.20
❑	200	Nomar Garciaparra	1.25	.50
❑	201	Kevin Cash	.30	.10
❑	202	Ramiro Mendoza	.30	.10
❑	203	Shane Reynolds	.30	.10
❑	204	Chris Spurling	.30	.10
❑	205	Aaron Guiel	.30	.10
❑	206	Mark DeRosa	.30	.10
❑	207	Adam Kennedy	.30	.10
❑	208	Andy Pettitte	.50	.20
❑	209	Rafael Palmeiro	.50	.20
❑	210	Luis Gonzalez	.30	.10
❑	211	Ryan Franklin	.30	.10
❑	212	Bob Wickman	.30	.10
❑	213	Ron Calloway	.30	.10
❑	214	Jae Weong Seo	.30	.10
❑	215	Kazuhisa Ishii	.30	.10
❑	216	Sterling Hitchcock	.30	.10
❑	217	Jimmy Gobble	.30	.10
❑	218	Chad Moeller	.30	.10
❑	219	Jake Peavy	.30	.10
❑	220	John Smoltz	.50	.20
❑	221	Donovan Osborne	.30	.10
❑	222	David Wells	.30	.10
❑	223	Brad Lidge	.30	.10
❑	224	Carlos Zambrano	.30	.10
❑	225	Kerry Wood	.30	.10
❑	226	Alex Cintron	.30	.10
❑	227	Javier A. Lopez	.30	.10
❑	228	Jeremy Griffiths	.30	.10
❑	229	Jon Garland	.30	.10
❑	230	Curt Schilling	.50	.20
❑	231	Alex Scott Gonzalez	.30	.10
❑	232	Jay Gibbons	.30	.10
❑	233	Aaron Miles	.30	.10
❑	234	Mike Gallo	.30	.10
❑	235	Johan Santana	.75	.30
❑	236	Jose Guillen	.30	.10
❑	237	Jeff Conine	.30	.10
❑	238	Matt Roney	.30	.10
❑	239	Desi Relaford	.30	.10
❑	240	Frank Thomas	.75	.30
❑	241	Danny Patterson	.30	.10
❑	242	Kevin Mench	.30	.10
❑	243	Mike Redmond	.30	.10
❑	244	Jeff Suppan	.30	.10
❑	245	Carl Everett	.30	.10
❑	246	Jack Cressend	.30	.10
❑	247	Matt Mantei	.30	.10
❑	248	Enrique Wilson	.30	.10
❑	249	Craig Counsell	.30	.10
❑	250	Mark Prior	.50	.20
❑	251	Jared Sandberg	.30	.10
❑	252	Scott Strickland	.30	.10
❑	253	Lew Ford	.30	.10
❑	254	Hee Seop Choi	.30	.10
❑	255	Jason Phillips	.30	.10
❑	256	Jason Jennings	.30	.10
❑	257	Todd Pratt	.30	.10
❑	258	Matt Herges	.30	.10
❑	259	Kerry Ligtenberg	.30	.10
❑	260	Austin Kearns	.30	.10
❑	261	Jay Witasick	.30	.10
❑	262	Tony Armas Jr.	.30	.10
❑	263	Tom Martin	.30	.10
❑	264	Oliver Perez	.30	.10
❑	265	Jorge Posada	.50	.20
❑	266	Jason Boyd	.30	.10
❑	267	Ben Hendrickson	.30	.10
❑	268	Reggie Sanders	.30	.10
❑	269	Julio Lugo	.30	.10
❑	270	Pedro Martinez	.50	.20
❑	271	Kyle Snyder	.30	.10
❑	272	Felipe Lopez	.30	.10
❑	273	Kevin Millar	.30	.10
❑	274	Travis Hafner	.30	.10
❑	275	Magglio Ordonez	.30	.10
❑	276	Marlon Byrd	.30	.10
❑	277	Scott Spiezio	.30	.10
❑	278	Mark Corey	.30	.10
❑	279	Tim Salmon	.50	.20
❑	280	Alex Gonzalez	.30	.10
❑	281	Marquis Grissom	.30	.10
❑	282	Miguel Olivo	.30	.10
❑	283	Orlando Hudson	.30	.10
❑	284	Rondell White	.30	.10
❑	285	Jermaine Dye	.30	.10
❑	286	Paul Shuey	.30	.10
❑	287	Brandon Inge	.30	.10
❑	288	B.J. Surhoff	.30	.10
❑	289	Edgar Gonzalez	.30	.10
❑	290	Angel Berroa	.30	.10
❑	291	Claudio Vargas	.30	.10
❑	292	Cesar Izturis	.30	.10
❑	293	Brandon Phillips	.30	.10
❑	294	Jeff Duncan	.30	.10
❑	295	Randy Wolf	.30	.10
❑	296	Barry Larkin	.50	.20
❑	297	Felix Rodriguez	.30	.10
❑	298	Robb Quinlan	.30	.10
❑	299	Brian Jordan	.30	.10
❑	300	Dontrelle Willis	.50	.20
❑	301	Doug Davis	.30	.10
❑	302	Ricky Stone	.30	.10
❑	303	Travis Harper	.30	.10
❑	304	Jaret Wright	.30	.10
❑	305	Edgardo Alfonzo	.30	.10
❑	306	Quinton McCracken	.30	.10
❑	307	Jason Bay	.30	.10
❑	308	Joe Randa	.30	.10
❑	309	Steve Sparks	.30	.10
❑	310	Roy Halladay	.30	.10
❑	311	Antonio Alfonseca	.30	.10
❑	312	Michael Cuddyer	.30	.10
❑	313	John Patterson	.30	.10
❑	314	Chris Widger	.30	.10
❑	315	Shigetoshi Hasegawa	.30	.10
❑	316	Tim Wakefield	.30	.10
❑	317	Scott Hatteberg	.30	.10
❑	318	Mike Remlinger	.30	.10
❑	319	Jose Vizcaino	.30	.10
❑	320	Rocco Baldelli	.30	.10
❑	321	David Riske	.30	.10
❑	322	Steve Karsay	.30	.10
❑	323	Peter Bergeron	.30	.10
❑	324	Jeff Weaver	.30	.10
❑	325	Larry Walker	.30	.10
❑	326	Jack Cust	.30	.10
❑	327	Bo Hart	.30	.10
❑	328	Rod Beck	.30	.10
❑	329	Jose Acevedo	.30	.10
❑	330	Hank Blalock	.30	.10
❑	331	Tom Gordon	.30	.10
❑	332	Brian Fuentes	.30	.10
❑	333	Tomas Perez	.30	.10
❑	334	Lenny Harris	.30	.10
❑	335	Matt Morris	.30	.10
❑	336	Jeremi Gonzalez	.30	.10
❑	337	David Eckstein	.30	.10
❑	338	Aaron Rowand	.30	.10
❑	339	Rick Bauer	.30	.10
❑	340	Jim Edmonds	.30	.10
❑	341	Joe Borowski	.30	.10
❑	342	Eric DuBose	.30	.10
❑	343	D'Angelo Jimenez	.30	.10
❑	344	Tomo Ohka	.30	.10
❑	345	Victor Zambrano	.30	.10
❑	346	Joe McEwing	.30	.10
❑	347	Jorge Sosa	.30	.10
❑	348	Keith Ginter	.30	.10
❑	349	A.J. Pierzynski	.30	.10
❑	350	Mike Sweeney	.30	.10
❑	351	Shawn Chacon	.30	.10
❑	352	Matt Clement	.30	.10
❑	353	Vance Wilson	.30	.10
❑	354	Benito Santiago	.30	.10
❑	355	Eric Hinske	.30	.10
❑	356	Vladimir Guerrero	.75	.30
❑	357	Kenny Rogers	.30	.10
❑	358	Travis Lee	.30	.10
❑	359	Jay Powell	.30	.10
❑	360	Phil Nevin	.30	.10
❑	361	Willie Harris	.30	.10
❑	362	Ty Wigginton	.30	.10
❑	363	Chad Fox	.30	.10
❑	364	Junior Spivey	.30	.10
❑	365	Brandon Webb	.30	.10
❑	366	Brett Myers	.30	.10
❑	367	Alexis Gomez	.30	.10
❑	368	Dave Roberts	.30	.10
❑	369	LaTroy Hawkins	.30	.10
❑	370	Kevin Millwood	.30	.10
❑	371	Brian Schneider	.30	.10
❑	372	Blaine Neal	.30	.10
❑	373	Jeromy Burnitz	.30	.10
❑	374	Ted Lilly	.30	.10
❑	375	Shawn Green	.30	.10
❑	376	Carlos Pena	.30	.10
❑	377	Gil Meche	.30	.10
❑	378	Jeff Bagwell	.50	.20
❑	379	Alex Escobar	.30	.10
❑	380	Erubiel Durazo	.30	.10
❑	381	Cristian Guzman	.30	.10
❑	382	Rocky Biddle	.30	.10
❑	383	Craig Wilson	.30	.10
❑	384	Rey Sanchez	.30	.10
❑	385	Russ Ortiz	.30	.10
❑	386	Freddy Garcia	.30	.10
❑	387	Luis Vizcaino	.30	.10
❑	388	David Ortiz	.75	.30
❑	389	Jose Molina	.30	.10
❑	390	Edgar Martinez	.50	.20
❑	391	Nate Bump	.30	.10
❑	392	Brent Mayne	.30	.10
❑	393	Ray King	.30	.10
❑	394	Paul Wilson	.30	.10
❑	395	Melvin Mora	.30	.10
❑	396	Morgan Ensberg	.30	.10
❑	397	Ramon Hernandez	.30	.10
❑	398	Juan Rincon	.30	.10
❑	399	Ron Mahay	.30	.10
❑	400	Jeff Kent	.30	.10
❑	401	Cal Eldred	.30	.10
❑	402	Mike Difelice	.30	.10
❑	403	Valerio De Los Santos	.30	.10
❑	404	Steve Finley	.30	.10
❑	405	Trot Nixon	.30	.10
❑	406	Akinori Otsuka RC	.40	.15
❑	407	Ryan Freel	.30	.10
❑	408	Ray Durham	.30	.10
❑	409	Aaron Heilman	.30	.10
❑	410	Edgar Renteria	.30	.10
❑	411	Mike Hampton	.30	.10
❑	412	Kirk Rueter	.30	.10
❑	413	Jim Mecir	.30	.10
❑	414	Brian Roberts	.30	.10
❑	415	Paul Konerko	.30	.10
❑	416	Reed Johnson	.30	.10
❑	417	Roger Clemens	1.50	.60
❑	418	Coco Crisp	.30	.10
❑	419	Carlos Hernandez	.30	.10
❑	420	Scott Podsednik	.30	.10
❑	421	Miguel Cairo	.30	.10
❑	422	Abraham Nunez	.30	.10
❑	423	Endy Chavez	.30	.10
❑	424	Eric Munson	.30	.10
❑	425	Torii Hunter	.30	.10
❑	426	Ben Howard	.30	.10
❑	427	Chris Gomez	.30	.10
❑	428	Francisco Cordero	.30	.10
❑	429	Jeffrey Hammonds	.30	.10
❑	430	Shannon Stewart	.30	.10
❑	431	Einar Diaz	.30	.10
❑	432	Eric Byrnes	.30	.10
❑	433	Marty Cordova	.30	.10
❑	434	Matt Ginter	.30	.10
❑	435	Victor Martinez	.30	.10
❑	436	Geronimo Gil	.30	.10
❑	437	Grant Balfour	.30	.10
❑	438	Ramon Vazquez	.30	.10
❑	439	Jose Cruz Jr.	.30	.10
❑	440	Orlando Cabrera	.30	.10
❑	441	Joe Kennedy	.30	.10
❑	442	Scott Williamson	.30	.10
❑	443	Troy Percival	.30	.10
❑	444	Derrek Lee	.50	.20
❑	445	Runelvys Hernandez	.30	.10
❑	446	Mark Grudzielanek	.30	.10
❑	447	Trey Hodges	.30	.10
❑	448	Jimmy Haynes	.30	.10
❑	449	Eric Milton	.30	.10
❑	450	Todd Helton	.50	.20
❑	451	Greg Zaun	.30	.10
❑	452	Woody Williams	.30	.10
❑	453	Todd Walker	.30	.10
❑	454	Juan Cruz	.30	.10
❑	455	Fernando Vina	.30	.10
❑	456	Omar Vizquel	.50	.20

No.	Player		
❑ 457	Roberto Alomar	.50	.20
❑ 458	Bill Hall	.30	.10
❑ 459	Juan Rivera	.30	.10
❑ 460	Tom Glavine	.50	.20
❑ 461	Ramon Castro	.30	.10
❑ 462	Cory Vance	.30	.10
❑ 463	Dan Miceli	.30	.10
❑ 464	Lyle Overbay	.30	.10
❑ 465	Craig Biggio	.50	.20
❑ 466	Ricky Ledee	.30	.10
❑ 467	Michael Barrett	.30	.10
❑ 468	Jason Anderson	.30	.10
❑ 469	Matt Stairs	.30	.10
❑ 470	Jarrod Washburn	.30	.10
❑ 471	Todd Hundley	.30	.10
❑ 472	Grant Roberts	.30	.10
❑ 473	Randy Winn	.30	.10
❑ 474	Pat Hentgen	.30	.10
❑ 475	Jose Vidro	.30	.10
❑ 476	Tony Torcato	.30	.10
❑ 477	Jeremy Affeldt	.30	.10
❑ 478	Carlos Guillen	.30	.10
❑ 479	Paul Quantrill	.30	.10
❑ 480	Rafael Furcal	.30	.10
❑ 481	Adam Melhuse	.30	.10
❑ 482	Jerry Hairston Jr.	.30	.10
❑ 483	Adam Bernero	.30	.10
❑ 484	Terrence Long	.30	.10
❑ 485	Paul Lo Duca	.30	.10
❑ 486	Corey Koskie	.30	.10
❑ 487	John Lackey	.30	.10
❑ 488	Chad Zerbe	.30	.10
❑ 489	Vinny Castilla	.30	.10
❑ 490	Corey Patterson	.30	.10
❑ 491	John Olerud	.30	.10
❑ 492	Josh Bard	.30	.10
❑ 493	Darren Dreifort	.30	.10
❑ 494	Jason Standridge	.30	.10
❑ 495	Ben Sheets	.30	.10
❑ 496	Jose Castillo	.30	.10
❑ 497	Jay Payton	.30	.10
❑ 498	Rob Bowen	.30	.10
❑ 499	Bobby Higginson	.30	.10
❑ 500	Alex Rodriguez Yanks	1.25	.50
❑ 501	Octavio Dotel	.30	.10
❑ 502	Rheal Cormier	.30	.10
❑ 503	Felix Heredia	.30	.10
❑ 504	Dan Wright	.30	.10
❑ 505	Michael Young	.30	.10
❑ 506	Wilfredo Ledezma	.30	.10
❑ 507	Sun Woo Kim	.30	.10
❑ 508	Michael Tejera	.30	.10
❑ 509	Herbert Perry	.30	.10
❑ 510	Esteban Loaiza	.30	.10
❑ 511	Alan Embree	.30	.10
❑ 512	Ben Davis	.30	.10
❑ 513	Greg Colbrunn	.30	.10
❑ 514	Josh Hall	.30	.10
❑ 515	Raul Ibanez	.30	.10
❑ 516	Jason Kershner	.30	.10
❑ 517	Corky Miller	.30	.10
❑ 518	Jason Marquis	.30	.10
❑ 519	Roger Cedeno	.30	.10
❑ 520	Adam Dunn	.30	.10
❑ 521	Paul Byrd	.30	.10
❑ 522	Sandy Alomar Jr.	.30	.10
❑ 523	Salomon Torres	.30	.10
❑ 524	John Halama	.30	.10
❑ 525	Mike Piazza	1.25	.50
❑ 526	Buddy Groom	.30	.10
❑ 527	Adrian Beltre	.30	.10
❑ 528	Chad Harville	.30	.10
❑ 529	Javier Vazquez	.30	.10
❑ 530	Jody Gerut	.30	.10
❑ 531	Elmer Dessens	.30	.10
❑ 532	B.J. Ryan	.30	.10
❑ 533	Chad Durbin	.30	.10
❑ 534	Doug Mirabelli	.30	.10
❑ 535	Bernie Williams	.50	.20
❑ 536	Jeff DaVanon	.30	.10
❑ 537	Dave Berg	.30	.10
❑ 538	Geoff Blum	.30	.10
❑ 539	John Thomson	.30	.10
❑ 540	Jeremy Bonderman	.30	.10
❑ 541	Jeff Zimmerman	.30	.10
❑ 542	Derek Lowe	.30	.10
❑ 543	Scot Shields	.30	.10
❑ 544	Michael Tucker	.30	.10
❑ 545	Tim Hudson	.30	.10
❑ 546	Ryan Ludwick	.30	.10
❑ 547	Rick Reed	.30	.10
❑ 548	Placido Polanco	.30	.10
❑ 549	Tony Graffanino	.30	.10
❑ 550	Garret Anderson	.30	.10
❑ 551	Timo Perez	.30	.10
❑ 552	Jesus Colome	.30	.10
❑ 553	R.A. Dickey	.30	.10
❑ 554	Tim Worrell	.30	.10
❑ 555	Jason Kendall	.30	.10
❑ 556	Tom Goodwin	.30	.10
❑ 557	Joaquin Benoit	.30	.10
❑ 558	Stephen Randolph	.30	.10
❑ 559	Miguel Tejada	.30	.10
❑ 560	A.J. Burnett	.30	.10
❑ 561	Ben Diggins	.30	.10
❑ 562	Kent Mercker	.30	.10
❑ 563	Zach Day	.30	.10
❑ 564	Antonio Perez	.30	.10
❑ 565	Jason Schmidt	.30	.10
❑ 566	Armando Benitez	.30	.10
❑ 567	Denny Neagle	.30	.10
❑ 568	Eric Eckenstahler	.30	.10
❑ 569	Chan Ho Park	.30	.10
❑ 570	Carlos Beltran	.30	.10
❑ 571	Brett Tomko	.30	.10
❑ 572	Henry Mateo	.30	.10
❑ 573	Ken Harvey	.30	.10
❑ 574	Matt Lawton	.30	.10
❑ 575	Mariano Rivera	.75	.30
❑ 576	Darrell May	.30	.10
❑ 577	Jamie Moyer	.30	.10
❑ 578	Paul Bako	.30	.10
❑ 579	Cory Lidle	.30	.10
❑ 580	Jacque Jones	.30	.10
❑ 581	Jolbert Cabrera	.30	.10
❑ 582	Jason Grimsley	.30	.10
❑ 583	Danny Kolb	.30	.10
❑ 584	Billy Wagner	.30	.10
❑ 585	Rich Aurilia	.30	.10
❑ 586	Vicente Padilla	.30	.10
❑ 587	Oscar Villarreal	.30	.10
❑ 588	Rene Reyes	.30	.10
❑ 589	Jon Lieber	.30	.10
❑ 590	Nick Johnson	.30	.10
❑ 591	Bobby Crosby	.30	.10
❑ 592	Steve Trachsel	.30	.10
❑ 593	Brian Boehringer	.30	.10
❑ 594	Juan Uribe	.30	.10
❑ 595	Bartolo Colon	.30	.10
❑ 596	Bobby Hill	.30	.10
❑ 597	Chris Shelton RC	1.00	.40
❑ 598	Carl Pavano	.30	.10
❑ 599	Kurt Ainsworth	.30	.10
❑ 600	Derek Jeter	1.50	.60
❑ 601	Doug Mientkiewicz	.30	.10
❑ 602	Orlando Palmeiro	.30	.10
❑ 603	J.C. Romero	.30	.10
❑ 604	Scott Sullivan	.30	.10
❑ 605	Brad Radke	.30	.10
❑ 606	Fernando Rodney	.30	.10
❑ 607	Jim Brower	.30	.10
❑ 608	Josh Towers	.30	.10
❑ 609	Brad Fullmer	.30	.10
❑ 610	Jose Reyes	.30	.10
❑ 611	Ryan Wagner	.30	.10
❑ 612	Joe Mays	.30	.10
❑ 613	Jung Bong	.30	.10
❑ 614	Curtis Leskanic	.30	.10
❑ 615	Al Leiter	.30	.10
❑ 616	Wade Miller	.30	.10
❑ 617	Keith Foulke Sox	.30	.10
❑ 618	Casey Fossum	.30	.10
❑ 619	Craig Monroe	.30	.10
❑ 620	Hideo Nomo	.75	.30
❑ 621	Bob File	.30	.10
❑ 622	Steve Kline	.30	.10
❑ 623	Bobby Kielty	.30	.10
❑ 624	Dewon Brazelton	.30	.10
❑ 625	Eric Chavez	.30	.10
❑ 626	Chris Carpenter	.30	.10
❑ 627	Alexis Rios	.30	.10
❑ 628	Jason Davis	.30	.10
❑ 629	Jose Jimenez	.30	.10
❑ 630	Vernon Wells	.30	.10
❑ 631	Kenny Lofton	.30	.10
❑ 632	Chad Bradford	.30	.10
❑ 633	Brad Wilkerson	.30	.10
❑ 634	Pokey Reese	.30	.10
❑ 635	Richie Sexson	.30	.10
❑ 636	Chin-Hui Tsao	.30	.10
❑ 637	Eli Marrero	.30	.10
❑ 638	Chris Reitsma	.30	.10
❑ 639	Daryle Ward	.30	.10
❑ 640	Mark Teixeira	.50	.20
❑ 641	Corwin Malone	.30	.10
❑ 642	Adam Eaton	.30	.10
❑ 643	Jimmy Rollins	.30	.10
❑ 644	Brian Anderson	.30	.10
❑ 645	Bill Mueller	.30	.10
❑ 646	Jake Westbrook	.30	.10
❑ 647	Bengie Molina	.30	.10
❑ 648	Jorge Julio	.30	.10
❑ 649	Billy Traber	.30	.10
❑ 650	Randy Johnson	.75	.30
❑ 651	Javy Lopez	.30	.10
❑ 652	Doug Glanville	.30	.10
❑ 653	Jeff Cirillo	.30	.10
❑ 654	Tino Martinez	.50	.20
❑ 655	Mark Buehrle	.30	.10
❑ 656	Jason Michaels	.30	.10
❑ 657	Damian Rolls	.30	.10
❑ 658	Rosman Garcia	.30	.10
❑ 659	Scott Hairston	.30	.10
❑ 660	Carl Crawford	.30	.10
❑ 661	Livan Hernandez	.30	.10
❑ 662	Danny Bautista	.30	.10
❑ 663	Brad Ausmus	.30	.10
❑ 664	Juan Acevedo	.30	.10
❑ 665	Sean Casey	.30	.10
❑ 666	Josh Beckett	.30	.10
❑ 667	Milton Bradley	.30	.10
❑ 668	Braden Looper	.30	.10
❑ 669	Paul Abbott	.30	.10
❑ 670	Joel Pineiro	.30	.10
❑ 671	Luis Terrero	.30	.10
❑ 672	Rodrigo Lopez	.30	.10
❑ 673	Joe Crede	.30	.10
❑ 674	Mike Koplove	.30	.10
❑ 675	Brian Giles	.30	.10
❑ 676	Jeff Nelson	.30	.10
❑ 677	Russell Branyan	.30	.10
❑ 678	Mike DeJean	.30	.10
❑ 679	Brian Daubach	.30	.10
❑ 680	Ellis Burks	.30	.10
❑ 681	Ryan Dempster	.30	.10
❑ 682	Cliff Politte	.30	.10
❑ 683	Brian Reith	.30	.10
❑ 684	Scott Stewart	.30	.10
❑ 685	Allan Simpson	.30	.10
❑ 686	Shawn Estes	.30	.10
❑ 687	Jason Johnson	.30	.10
❑ 688	Wil Cordero	.30	.10
❑ 689	Kelly Stinnett	.30	.10
❑ 690	Jose Lima	.30	.10
❑ 691	Gary Bennett	.30	.10
❑ 692	T.J. Tucker	.30	.10
❑ 693	Shane Spencer	.30	.10
❑ 694	Chris Hammond	.30	.10
❑ 695	Raul Mondesi	.30	.10
❑ 696	Xavier Nady	.30	.10
❑ 697	Cody Ransom	.30	.10
❑ 698	Ron Villone	.30	.10
❑ 699	Brook Fordyce	.30	.10
❑ 700	Sammy Sosa	.75	.30
❑ 701	Terry Adams	.30	.10
❑ 702	Ricardo Rincon	.30	.10
❑ 703	Tike Redman	.30	.10
❑ 704	Chris Stynes	.30	.10
❑ 705	Mark Redman	.30	.10
❑ 706	Juan Encarnacion	.30	.10
❑ 707	Jhonny Peralta	.30	.10
❑ 708	Denny Hocking	.30	.10
❑ 709	Ivan Rodriguez	.50	.20
❑ 710	Jose Hernandez	.30	.10
❑ 711	Brandon Duckworth	.30	.10
❑ 712	Dave Burba	.30	.10
❑ 713	Joe Nathan	.30	.10
❑ 714	Dan Smith	.30	.10

Card		
❑ 715 Karim Garcia	.30	.10
❑ 716 Arthur Rhodes	.30	.10
❑ 717 Shawn Wooten	.30	.10
❑ 718 Ramon Santiago	.30	.10
❑ 719 Luis Ugueto	.30	.10
❑ 720 Danys Baez	.30	.10
❑ 721 Alfredo Amezaga PROS	.30	.10
❑ 722 Sidney Ponson	.30	.10
❑ 723 Joe Mauer PROS	.75	.30
❑ 724 Jesse Foppert PROS	.30	.10
❑ 725 Todd Greene	.30	.10
❑ 726 Dan Haren PROS	.30	.10
❑ 727 Brandon Larson PROS	.30	.10
❑ 728 Bobby Jenks PROS	.30	.10
❑ 729 Grady Sizemore PROS	.75	.30
❑ 730 Ben Grieve	.30	.10
❑ 731 Khalil Greene PROS	.50	.20
❑ 732 Chad Gaudin PROS	.30	.10
❑ 733 Johnny Estrada PROS	.30	.10
❑ 734 Joe Valentine PROS	.30	.10
❑ 735 Tim Raines Jr. PROS	.30	.10
❑ 736 Brandon Claussen PROS	.30	.10
❑ 737 Sam Marsonek PROS	.30	.10
❑ 738 Delmon Young PROS	.50	.20
❑ 739 David Dellucci	.30	.10
❑ 740 Sergio Mitre PROS	.30	.10
❑ 741 Nick Neugebauer PROS	.30	.10
❑ 742 Laynce Nix PROS	.30	.10
❑ 743 Joe Thurston PROS	.30	.10
❑ 744 Ryan Langerhans PROS	.30	.10
❑ 745 Pete LaForest PROS	.30	.10
❑ 746 Arnie Munoz PROS	.30	.10
❑ 747 Rickie Weeks PROS	.30	.10
❑ 748 Neal Cotts PROS	.30	.10
❑ 749 Jonny Gomes PROS	.30	.10
❑ 750 Jim Thome	.50	.20
❑ 751 Jon Rauch PROS	.30	.10
❑ 752 Edwin Jackson PROS	.30	.10
❑ 753 Ryan Madson PROS	.30	.10
❑ 754 Andrew Good PROS	.30	.10
❑ 755 Eddie Perez	.30	.10
❑ 756 Joe Borchard PROS	.30	.10
❑ 757 Jeremy Guthrie PROS	.30	.10
❑ 758 Jose Mesa	.30	.10
❑ 759 Doug Waechter PROS	.30	.10
❑ 760 J.D. Drew	.30	.10
❑ 761 Adam LaRoche PROS	.30	.10
❑ 762 Rich Harden PROS	.30	.10
❑ 763 Justin Speier	.30	.10
❑ 764 Todd Zeile	.30	.10
❑ 765 Turk Wendell	.30	.10
❑ 766 Mark Bellhorn Sox	.30	.10
❑ 767 Mike Jackson	.30	.10
❑ 768 Chone Figgins	.30	.10
❑ 769 Mike Neu	.30	.10
❑ 770 Greg Maddux	1.25	.50
❑ 771 Frank Menechino	.30	.10
❑ 772 Alec Zumwalt RC	.30	.10
❑ 773 Eric Young	.30	.10
❑ 774 Dustan Mohr	.30	.10
❑ 775 Shane Halter	.30	.10
❑ 776 Brian Buchanan	.30	.10
❑ 777 So Taguchi	.30	.10
❑ 778 Eric Karros	.30	.10
❑ 779 Ramon Nivar	.30	.10
❑ 780 Marlon Anderson	.30	.10
❑ 781 Brayan Pena FY RC	.40	.15
❑ 782 Chris O'Riordan FY RC	.40	.15
❑ 783 Dioner Navarro FY RC	.75	.30
❑ 784 Alberto Callaspo FY RC	.75	.30
❑ 785 Hector Gimenez FY RC	.30	.10
❑ 786 Yadier Molina FY RC	2.00	.75
❑ 787 Kevin Richardson FY RC	.30	.10
❑ 788 Brian Pilkington FY RC	.30	.10
❑ 789 Adam Greenberg FY RC	.75	.30
❑ 790 Ervin Santana FY RC	2.00	.75
❑ 791 Brant Colamarino FY RC	.75	.30
❑ 792 Ben Himes FY RC	.30	.10
❑ 793 Todd Self FY RC	.50	.20
❑ 794 Brad Vericker FY RC	.40	.15
❑ 795 Donald Kelly FY RC	.40	.15
❑ 796 Brock Jacobsen FY RC	.30	.10
❑ 797 Brock Peterson FY RC	.40	.15
❑ 798 Carlos Sosa FY RC	.40	.15
❑ 799 Chad Chop FY RC	.40	.15
❑ 800 Matt Moses FY RC	1.00	.40
❑ 801 Chris Aguila FY RC	.40	.15
❑ 802 David Murphy FY RC	.75	.30
❑ 803 Don Sutton FY RC	1.00	.40
❑ 804 Jeremy Milons FY RC	.50	.20
❑ 805 Jon Coutlangus FY RC	.30	.10
❑ 806 Greg Thissen FY RC	.40	.15
❑ 807 Jose Capellan FY RC	.50	.20
❑ 808 Chad Santos FY RC	.40	.15
❑ 809 Wardell Starling FY RC	.40	.15
❑ 810 Kevin Kouzmanoff FY RC	2.00	.75
❑ 811 Kevin Davidson FY RC	.30	.10
❑ 812 Michael Mooney FY RC	.40	.15
❑ 813 Rodney Choy Foo FY RC	.30	.10
❑ 814 Reid Gorecki FY RC	.40	.15
❑ 815 Rudy Guillen FY RC	.75	.30
❑ 816 Harvey Garcia FY RC	.30	.10
❑ 817 Warner Madrigal FY RC	.75	.30
❑ 818 Kenny Perez FY RC	.40	.15
❑ 819 Joaquin Arias FY RC	.75	.30
❑ 820 Benji DeQuin FY RC	.30	.10
❑ 821 Lastings Milledge FY RC	5.00	2.00
❑ 822 Blake Hawksworth FY RC	.50	.20
❑ 823 Estee Harris FY RC	.50	.20
❑ 824 Bobby Brownlie FY RC	1.00	.40
❑ 825 Wanell Severino FY RC	.30	.10
❑ 826 Bobby Madritsch FY	.30	.10
❑ 827 Travis Hanson FY RC	.50	.20
❑ 828 Brandon Medders FY RC	.40	.15
❑ 829 Kevin Howard FY RC	.50	.20
❑ 830 Brian Steffek FY RC	.30	.10
❑ 831 Terry Jones FY RC	.50	.20
❑ 832 Anthony Acevedo FY RC	.40	.15
❑ 833 Kory Casto FY RC	.50	.20
❑ 834 Brooks Conrad FY RC	.40	.15
❑ 835 Juan Gutierrez FY RC	.40	.15
❑ 836 Charlie Zink FY RC	.30	.10
❑ 837 David Aardsma FY RC	.50	.20
❑ 838 Carl Loadenthal FY RC	.50	.20
❑ 839 Donald Levinski FY RC	.30	.10
❑ 840 Dustin Nippert FY RC	.50	.20
❑ 841 Calvin Hayes FY RC	.50	.20
❑ 842 Felix Hernandez FY RC	8.00	3.00
❑ 843 Tyler Davidson FY RC	.50	.20
❑ 844 George Sherrill FY RC	.40	.15
❑ 845 Craig Ansman FY RC	.40	.15
❑ 846 Jeff Allison FY RC	.40	.15
❑ 847 Tommy Murphy FY RC	.40	.15
❑ 848 Jerome Gamble FY RC	.30	.10
❑ 849 Jesse English FY RC	.40	.15
❑ 850 Alex Romero FY RC	.40	.15
❑ 851 Joel Zumaya FY RC	3.00	1.25
❑ 852 Carlos Quentin FY RC	2.50	1.00
❑ 853 Jose Valdez FY RC	.40	.15
❑ 854 J.J. Furmaniak FY RC	.75	.30
❑ 855 Juan Cedeno FY RC	.40	.15
❑ 856 Kyle Sleeth FY RC	.50	.20
❑ 857 Josh Labandeira FY RC	.40	.15
❑ 858 Lee Gwaltney FY RC	.30	.10
❑ 859 Lincoln Holdzkom FY RC	.40	.15
❑ 860 Ivan Ochoa FY RC	.40	.15
❑ 861 Luke Anderson FY RC	.30	.10
❑ 862 Conor Jackson FY RC	3.00	1.25
❑ 863 Matt Capps FY RC	.40	.15
❑ 864 Merkin Valdez FY RC	.50	.20
❑ 865 Paul Bacot FY RC	.50	.20
❑ 866 Erick Aybar FY RC	1.00	.40
❑ 867 Scott Proctor FY RC	.50	.20
❑ 868 Tim Stauffer FY RC	1.00	.40
❑ 869 Matt Creighton FY RC	.40	.15
❑ 870 Zach Miner FY RC	1.25	.50
❑ 871 Danny Gonzalez FY RC	.30	.10
❑ 872 Tom Farmer FY RC	.40	.15
❑ 873 John Santor FY RC	.30	.10
❑ 874 Logan Kensing FY RC	.40	.15
❑ 875 Vito Chiaravalloti FY RC	.40	.15
❑ 876 Checklist	.30	.10
❑ 877 Checklist	.30	.10
❑ 878 Checklist	.30	.10
❑ 879 Checklist	.30	.10
❑ 880 Checklist	.30	.10

2005 Topps Total

Card		
❑ COMPLETE SET (770)	150.00	75.00
❑ COMMON (1-575/666)	.30	.10
❑ COMMON CARD (576-690)	.30	.10
❑ COM (269/588/691-765)	.50	.20
❑ COMMON CL (766-770)	.30	.10
❑ OVERALL PLATE ODDS 1:85 HOBBY		
❑ PLATE PRINT RUN 1 SET PER COLOR		
❑ BLACK-CYAN-MAGENTA-YELLOW ISSUED		
❑ FRONT AND BACK PLATES PRODUCED		
❑ NO PLATE PRICING DUE TO SCARCITY		
❑ 1 Rafael Furcal	.30	.10
❑ 2 Tony Clark	.30	.10
❑ 3 Hideki Matsui	1.25	.50
❑ 4 Zach Day	.30	.10
❑ 5 Garret Anderson	.30	.10
❑ 6 B.J. Surhoff	.30	.10
❑ 7 Trevor Hoffman	.30	.10
❑ 8 Kenny Lofton	.30	.10
❑ 9 Ross Gload	.30	.10
❑ 10 Jorge Cantu	.30	.10
❑ 11 Joel Pineiro	.30	.10
❑ 12 Alex Cintron	.30	.10
❑ 13 Mike Matheny	.30	.10
❑ 14 Rod Barajas	.30	.10
❑ 15 Ray Durham	.30	.10
❑ 16 Danys Baez	.30	.10
❑ 17 Brian Schneider	.30	.10
❑ 18 Tike Redman	.30	.10
❑ 19 Ricardo Rodriguez	.30	.10
❑ 20 Mike Sweeney	.30	.10
❑ 21 Greg Myers	.30	.10
❑ 22 Chone Figgins	.30	.10
❑ 23 Brian Lawrence	.30	.10
❑ 24 Joe Nathan	.30	.10
❑ 25 Placido Polanco	.30	.10
❑ 26 Yadier Molina	.30	.10
❑ 27 Gary Bennett	.30	.10
❑ 28 Yorvit Torrealba	.30	.10
❑ 29 Javier Valentin	.30	.10
❑ 30 Jason Giambi	.30	.10
❑ 31 Brandon Claussen	.30	.10
❑ 32 Miguel Olivo	.30	.10
❑ 33 Josh Bard	.30	.10
❑ 34 Ramon Hernandez	.30	.10
❑ 35 Geoff Jenkins	.30	.10
❑ 36 Bobby Kielty	.30	.10
❑ 37 Luis A. Gonzalez	.30	.10
❑ 38 Benito Santiago	.30	.10
❑ 39 Brandon Inge	.30	.10
❑ 40 Mark Prior	.50	.20
❑ 41 Mike Lieberthal	.30	.10
❑ 42 Toby Hall	.30	.10
❑ 43 Brad Ausmus	.30	.10
❑ 44 Damian Miller	.30	.10
❑ 45 Mark Kotsay	.30	.10
❑ 46 John Buck	.30	.10
❑ 47 Oliver Perez	.30	.10
❑ 48 Matt Morris	.30	.10
❑ 49 Raul Chavez	.30	.10
❑ 50 Randy Johnson	.75	.30
❑ 51 Dave Bush	.30	.10
❑ 52 Jose Macias	.30	.10
❑ 53 Paul Wilson	.30	.10
❑ 54 Wilfredo Ledezma	.30	.10
❑ 55 J.D. Drew	.30	.10
❑ 56 Pedro Martinez	.50	.20
❑ 57 Josh Towers	.30	.10
❑ 58 Jamie Moyer	.30	.10
❑ 59 Scott Elarton	.30	.10
❑ 60 Ken Griffey Jr.	1.25	.50
❑ 61 Steve Trachsel	.30	.10
❑ 62 Bubba Crosby	.30	.10

No.	Player		
❑ 63	Michael Barrett	.30	.10
❑ 64	Odalis Perez	.30	.10
❑ 65	B.J. Upton	.30	.10
❑ 66	Eric Bruntlett	.30	.10
❑ 67	Victor Zambrano	.30	.10
❑ 68	Brandon League	.30	.10
❑ 69	Carlos Silva	.30	.10
❑ 70	Lyle Overbay	.30	.10
❑ 71	Runelvys Hernandez	.30	.10
❑ 72	Brad Penny	.30	.10
❑ 73	Ty Wigginton	.30	.10
❑ 74	Orlando Hudson	.30	.10
❑ 75	Roy Oswalt	.30	.10
❑ 76	Jason LaRue	.30	.10
❑ 77	Ismael Valdez	.30	.10
❑ 78	Calvin Pickering	.30	.10
❑ 79	Bill Hall	.30	.10
❑ 80	Carl Crawford	.30	.10
❑ 81	Tomas Perez	.30	.10
❑ 82	Joe Kennedy	.30	.10
❑ 83	Chris Woodward	.30	.10
❑ 84	Jason Lane	.30	.10
❑ 85	Steve Finley	.30	.10
❑ 86	Jeff Francis	.30	.10
❑ 87	Felipe Lopez	.30	.10
❑ 88	Chan Ho Park	.30	.10
❑ 89	Joe Crede	.30	.10
❑ 90	Jose Vidro	.30	.10
❑ 91	Casey Kotchman	.30	.10
❑ 92	Brandon Backe	.30	.10
❑ 93	Mike Hampton	.30	.10
❑ 94	Ryan Dempster	.30	.10
❑ 95	Wily Mo Pena	.30	.10
❑ 96	Matt Holliday	.40	.15
❑ 97	A.J. Pierzynski	.30	.10
❑ 98	Jason Jennings	.30	.10
❑ 99	Eli Marrero	.30	.10
❑ 100	Carlos Beltran	.30	.10
❑ 101	Scott Kazmir	.30	.10
❑ 102	Kenny Rogers	.30	.10
❑ 103	Roy Halladay	.30	.10
❑ 104	Alex Cora	.30	.10
❑ 105	Richie Sexson	.30	.10
❑ 106	Ben Sheets	.30	.10
❑ 107	Bartolo Colon	.30	.10
❑ 108	Eddie Perez	.30	.10
❑ 109	Vicente Padilla	.30	.10
❑ 110	Sammy Sosa	.75	.30
❑ 111	Mark Ellis	.30	.10
❑ 112	Woody Williams	.30	.10
❑ 113	Todd Greene	.30	.10
❑ 114	Nook Logan	.30	.10
❑ 115	Francisco Rodriguez	.30	.10
❑ 116	Miguel Batista	.30	.10
❑ 117	Livan Hernandez	.30	.10
❑ 118	Chris Aguila	.30	.10
❑ 119	Coco Crisp	.30	.10
❑ 120	Jose Reyes	.30	.10
❑ 121	Ricky Ledee	.30	.10
❑ 122	Brad Radke	.30	.10
❑ 123	Carlos Guillen	.30	.10
❑ 124	Paul Bako	.30	.10
❑ 125	Tom Glavine	.50	.20
❑ 126	Chad Moeller	.30	.10
❑ 127	Mark Buehrle	.30	.10
❑ 128	Casey Blake	.30	.10
❑ 129	Juan Rivera	.30	.10
❑ 130	Preston Wilson	.30	.10
❑ 131	Nate Robertson	.30	.10
❑ 132	Julio Franco	.30	.10
❑ 133	Derek Lowe	.30	.10
❑ 134	Rob Bell	.30	.10
❑ 135	Javy Lopez	.30	.10
❑ 136	Javier Vazquez	.30	.10
❑ 137	Desi Relaford	.30	.10
❑ 138	Danny Graves	.30	.10
❑ 139	Josh Fogg	.30	.10
❑ 140	Bobby Crosby	.30	.10
❑ 141	Ramon Castro	.30	.10
❑ 142	Jerry Hairston Jr.	.30	.10
❑ 143	Morgan Ensberg	.30	.10
❑ 144	Brandon Webb	.30	.10
❑ 145	Jack Wilson	.30	.10
❑ 146	Bill Mueller	.30	.10
❑ 147	Troy Glaus	.30	.10
❑ 148	Armando Benitez	.30	.10
❑ 149	Adam LaRoche	.30	.10
❑ 150	Hank Blalock	.30	.10
❑ 151	Ryan Franklin	.30	.10
❑ 152	Kevin Millwood	.30	.10
❑ 153	Jason Marquis	.30	.10
❑ 154	Dewon Brazelton	.30	.10
❑ 155	Al Leiter	.30	.10
❑ 156	Garrett Atkins	.30	.10
❑ 157	Todd Walker	.30	.10
❑ 158	Kris Benson	.30	.10
❑ 159	Eric Milton	.30	.10
❑ 160	Bret Boone	.30	.10
❑ 161	Matt LeCroy	.30	.10
❑ 162	Chris Widger	.30	.10
❑ 163	Ruben Gotay	.30	.10
❑ 164	Craig Monroe	.30	.10
❑ 165	Travis Hafner	.30	.10
❑ 166	Vance Wilson	.30	.10
❑ 167	Jason Grabowski	.30	.10
❑ 168	Tim Salmon	.50	.20
❑ 169	Henry Blanco	.30	.10
❑ 170	Josh Beckett	.30	.10
❑ 171	Jake Westbrook	.30	.10
❑ 172	Paul Lo Duca	.30	.10
❑ 173	Julio Lugo	.30	.10
❑ 174	Juan Cruz	.30	.10
❑ 175	Mark Mulder	.30	.10
❑ 176	Juan Castro	.30	.10
❑ 177	Damion Easley	.30	.10
❑ 178	LaTroy Hawkins	.30	.10
❑ 179	Jon Lieber	.30	.10
❑ 180	Vernon Wells	.30	.10
❑ 181	Jeff DaVanon	.30	.10
❑ 182	Dustan Mohr	.30	.10
❑ 183	Ryan Freel	.30	.10
❑ 184	Doug Davis	.30	.10
❑ 185	Sean Casey	.30	.10
❑ 186	Robb Quinlan	.30	.10
❑ 187	J.D. Closser	.30	.10
❑ 188	Tim Wakefield	.30	.10
❑ 189	Brian Jordan	.30	.10
❑ 190	Adam Dunn	.30	.10
❑ 191	Antonio Perez	.30	.10
❑ 192	Brett Tomko	.30	.10
❑ 193	John Flaherty	.30	.10
❑ 194	Michael Cuddyer	.30	.10
❑ 195	Ronnie Belliard	.30	.10
❑ 196	Tony Womack	.30	.10
❑ 197	Jason Johnson	.30	.10
❑ 198	Victor Santos	.30	.10
❑ 199	Danny Haren	.30	.10
❑ 200	Derek Jeter	1.50	.60
❑ 201	Brian Anderson	.30	.10
❑ 202	Carlos Pena	.30	.10
❑ 203	Jaret Wright	.30	.10
❑ 204	Paul Byrd	.30	.10
❑ 205	Shannon Stewart	.30	.10
❑ 206	Chris Carpenter	.30	.10
❑ 207	Matt Stairs	.30	.10
❑ 208	Brad Hawpe	.30	.10
❑ 209	Bobby Higginson	.30	.10
❑ 210	Torii Hunter	.30	.10
❑ 211	Shawn Green	.30	.10
❑ 212	Todd Hollandsworth	.30	.10
❑ 213	Scott Erickson	.30	.10
❑ 214	C.C. Sabathia	.30	.10
❑ 215	Mike Mussina	.50	.20
❑ 216	Jason Kendall	.30	.10
❑ 217	Todd Pratt	.30	.10
❑ 218	Danny Kolb	.30	.10
❑ 219	Tony Armas	.30	.10
❑ 220	Edgar Renteria	.30	.10
❑ 221	Dave Roberts	.30	.10
❑ 222	Luis Rivas	.30	.10
❑ 223	Adam Everett	.30	.10
❑ 224	Jeff Cirillo	.30	.10
❑ 225	Orlando Hernandez	.30	.10
❑ 226	Ken Harvey	.30	.10
❑ 227	Corey Patterson	.30	.10
❑ 228	Humberto Cota	.30	.10
❑ 229	A.J. Burnett	.30	.10
❑ 230	Roger Clemens	1.25	.50
❑ 231	Joe Randa	.30	.10
❑ 232	David Dellucci	.30	.10
❑ 233	Troy Percival	.30	.10
❑ 234	Dustin Hermanson	.30	.10
❑ 235	Eric Gagne	.30	.10
❑ 236	Terry Tiffee	.30	.10
❑ 237	Tony Graffanino	.30	.10
❑ 238	Jayson Werth	.30	.10
❑ 239	Mark Sweeney	.30	.10
❑ 240	Chipper Jones	.75	.30
❑ 241	Aramis Ramirez	.30	.10
❑ 242	Frank Catalanotto	.30	.10
❑ 243	Mike Maroth	.30	.10
❑ 244	Kelvim Escobar	.30	.10
❑ 245	Bobby Abreu	.30	.10
❑ 246	Kyle Lohse	.30	.10
❑ 247	Jason Isringhausen	.30	.10
❑ 248	Jose Lima	.30	.10
❑ 249	Adrian Gonzalez	.30	.10
❑ 250	Alex Rodriguez	1.25	.50
❑ 251	Ramon Ortiz	.30	.10
❑ 252	Frank Menechino	.30	.10
❑ 253	Keith Ginter	.30	.10
❑ 254	Kip Wells	.30	.10
❑ 255	Dmitri Young	.30	.10
❑ 256	Craig Biggio	.50	.20
❑ 257	Ramon E. Martinez	.30	.10
❑ 258	Jason Bartlett	.30	.10
❑ 259	Brad Lidge	.30	.10
❑ 260	Brian Giles	.30	.10
❑ 261	Luis Terrero	.30	.10
❑ 262	Miguel Ojeda	.30	.10
❑ 263	Rich Harden	.30	.10
❑ 264	Jacque Jones	.30	.10
❑ 265	Marcus Giles	.30	.10
❑ 266	Carlos Zambrano	.30	.10
❑ 267	Michael Tucker	.30	.10
❑ 268	Wes Obermueller	.30	.10
❑ 269	Pete Orr RC	.50	.20
❑ 270	Jim Thome	.50	.20
❑ 271	Omar Vizquel	.50	.20
❑ 272	Jose Valentin	.30	.10
❑ 273	Juan Uribe	.30	.10
❑ 274	Doug Mirabelli	.30	.10
❑ 275	Jeff Kent	.30	.10
❑ 276	Brad Wilkerson	.30	.10
❑ 277	Chris Burke	.30	.10
❑ 278	Endy Chavez	.30	.10
❑ 279	Richard Hidalgo	.30	.10
❑ 280	John Smoltz	.50	.20
❑ 281	Jarrod Washburn	.30	.10
❑ 282	Larry Bigbie	.30	.10
❑ 283	Edgardo Alfonzo	.30	.10
❑ 284	Cliff Lee	.30	.10
❑ 285	Carlos Lee	.30	.10
❑ 286	Olmedo Saenz	.30	.10
❑ 287	Tomo Ohka	.30	.10
❑ 288	Ruben Sierra	.30	.10
❑ 289	Nick Swisher	.30	.10
❑ 290	Frank Thomas	.75	.30
❑ 291	Aaron Cook	.30	.10
❑ 292	Cody McKay	.30	.10
❑ 293	Hee-Seop Choi	.30	.10
❑ 294	Carl Pavano	.30	.10
❑ 295	Scott Rolen	.50	.20
❑ 296	Matt Kata	.30	.10
❑ 297	Terrence Long	.30	.10
❑ 298	Jimmy Gobble	.30	.10
❑ 299	Jason Repko	.30	.10
❑ 300	Manny Ramirez	.50	.20
❑ 301	Dan Wilson	.30	.10
❑ 302	Jhonny Peralta	.30	.10
❑ 303	John Mabry	.30	.10
❑ 304	Adam Melhuse	.30	.10
❑ 305	Kerry Wood	.30	.10
❑ 306	Ryan Langerhans	.30	.10
❑ 307	Antonio Alfonseca	.30	.10
❑ 308	Marco Scutaro	.30	.10
❑ 309	Jamey Carroll	.30	.10
❑ 310	Lance Berkman	.30	.10
❑ 311	Willie Harris	.30	.10
❑ 312	Phil Nevin	.30	.10
❑ 313	Gregg Zaun	.30	.10
❑ 314	Michael Ryan	.30	.10
❑ 315	Zack Greinke	.30	.10
❑ 316	Ted Lilly	.30	.10
❑ 317	David Eckstein	.30	.10
❑ 318	Tony Torcato	.30	.10
❑ 319	Rob Mackowiak	.30	.10
❑ 320	Mark Teixeira	.50	.20

	No.	Player		
❑	321	Jason Phillips	.30	.10
❑	322	Jeremy Reed	.30	.10
❑	323	Bengie Molina	.30	.10
❑	324	Termel Sledge	.30	.10
❑	325	Justin Morneau	.30	.10
❑	326	Sandy Alomar Jr.	.30	.10
❑	327	Jon Garland	.30	.10
❑	328	Jay Payton	.30	.10
❑	329	Tino Martinez	.50	.20
❑	330	Jason Bay	.30	.10
❑	331	Jeff Conine	.30	.10
❑	332	Shawn Chacon	.30	.10
❑	333	Angel Berroa	.30	.10
❑	334	Reggie Sanders	.30	.10
❑	335	Kevin Brown	.30	.10
❑	336	Brady Clark	.30	.10
❑	337	Casey Fossum	.30	.10
❑	338	Raul Ibanez	.30	.10
❑	339	Derrek Lee	.50	.20
❑	340	Victor Martinez	.30	.10
❑	341	Kazuhisa Ishii	.30	.10
❑	342	Royce Clayton	.30	.10
❑	343	Trot Nixon	.30	.10
❑	344	Eric Young	.30	.10
❑	345	Aubrey Huff	.30	.10
❑	346	Brett Myers	.30	.10
❑	347	Joey Gathright	.30	.10
❑	348	Mark Grudzielanek	.30	.10
❑	349	Scott Spiezio	.30	.10
❑	350	Eric Chavez	.30	.10
❑	351	Einar Diaz	.30	.10
❑	352	Dallas McPherson	.30	.10
❑	353	John Thomson	.30	.10
❑	354	Neifi Perez	.30	.10
❑	355	Larry Walker	.50	.20
❑	356	Billy Wagner	.30	.10
❑	357	Mike Cameron	.30	.10
❑	358	Jimmy Rollins	.30	.10
❑	359	Kevin Mench	.30	.10
❑	360	Joe Mauer	.75	.30
❑	361	Jose Molina	.30	.10
❑	362	Joe Borchard	.30	.10
❑	363	Kevin Cash	.30	.10
❑	364	Jay Gibbons	.30	.10
❑	365	Khalil Greene	.50	.20
❑	366	Justin Leone	.30	.10
❑	367	Eddie Guardado	.30	.10
❑	368	Mike Lamb	.30	.10
❑	369	Matt Riley	.30	.10
❑	370	Luis Gonzalez	.30	.10
❑	371	Alfredo Amezaga	.30	.10
❑	372	J.J. Hardy	.30	.10
❑	373	Hector Luna	.30	.10
❑	374	Greg Aquino	.30	.10
❑	375	Jim Edmonds	.30	.10
❑	376	Joe Blanton	.30	.10
❑	377	Russell Branyan	.30	.10
❑	378	J.T. Snow	.30	.10
❑	379	Maggio Ordonez	.30	.10
❑	380	Rafael Palmeiro	.50	.20
❑	381	Andruw Jones	.50	.20
❑	382	David DeJesus	.30	.10
❑	383	Marquis Grissom	.30	.10
❑	384	Bobby Hill	.30	.10
❑	385	Kazuo Matsui	.30	.10
❑	386	Mark Loretta	.30	.10
❑	387	Chris Shelton	.40	.15
❑	388	Johnny Estrada	.30	.10
❑	389	Adam Hyzdu	.30	.10
❑	390	Nomar Garciaparra	.75	.30
❑	391	Mark Teahen	.30	.10
❑	392	Chris Capuano	.30	.10
❑	393	Ben Broussard	.30	.10
❑	394	Daniel Cabrera	.30	.10
❑	395	Jeremy Bonderman	.30	.10
❑	396	Darin Erstad	.30	.10
❑	397	Alex S. Gonzalez	.30	.10
❑	398	Kevin Millar	.30	.10
❑	399	Freddy Garcia	.30	.10
❑	400	Alfonso Soriano	.30	.10
❑	401	Koyie Hill	.30	.10
❑	402	Omar Infante	.30	.10
❑	403	Alex Gonzalez	.30	.10
❑	404	Pat Burrell	.30	.10
❑	405	Wes Helms	.30	.10
❑	406	Junior Spivey	.30	.10
❑	407	Joe Mays	.30	.10
❑	408	Jason Stanford	.30	.10
❑	409	Gil Meche	.30	.10
❑	410	Tim Hudson	.30	.10
❑	411	Chase Utley	.50	.20
❑	412	Matt Clement	.30	.10
❑	413	Nick Green	.30	.10
❑	414	Jose Vizcaino	.30	.10
❑	415	Ryan Klesko	.30	.10
❑	416	Vinny Castilla	.30	.10
❑	417	Brian Roberts	.30	.10
❑	418	Geronimo Gil	.30	.10
❑	419	Gary Matthews	.30	.10
❑	420	Jeff Weaver	.30	.10
❑	421	Jerome Williams	.30	.10
❑	422	Andy Pettitte	.50	.20
❑	423	Randy Wolf	.30	.10
❑	424	D'Angelo Jimenez	.30	.10
❑	425	Moises Alou	.30	.10
❑	426	Eric Byrnes	.30	.10
❑	427	Mark Redman	.30	.10
❑	428	Jermaine Dye	.30	.10
❑	429	Cory Lidle	.30	.10
❑	430	Jason Schmidt	.30	.10
❑	431	Jason W. Smith	.30	.10
❑	432	Jose Castillo	.30	.10
❑	433	Pokey Reese	.30	.10
❑	434	Matt Lawton	.30	.10
❑	435	Jose Guillen	.30	.10
❑	436	Craig Counsell	.30	.10
❑	437	Jose Hernandez	.30	.10
❑	438	Braden Looper	.30	.10
❑	439	Scott Hatteberg	.30	.10
❑	440	Gary Sheffield	.30	.10
❑	441	Gabe Gross	.30	.10
❑	442	Chris Gomez	.30	.10
❑	443	Dontrelle Willis	.30	.10
❑	444	Jamey Wright	.30	.10
❑	445	Rocco Baldelli	.30	.10
❑	446	Bernie Williams	.50	.20
❑	447	Sean Burroughs	.30	.10
❑	448	Willie Bloomquist	.30	.10
❑	449	Luis Castillo	.30	.10
❑	450	Mike Piazza	.75	.30
❑	451	Ryan Drese	.30	.10
❑	452	Pedro Feliz	.30	.10
❑	453	Horacio Ramirez	.30	.10
❑	454	Luis Matos	.30	.10
❑	455	Craig Wilson	.30	.10
❑	456	Russ Ortiz	.30	.10
❑	457	Xavier Nady	.30	.10
❑	458	Hideo Nomo	.75	.30
❑	459	Miguel Cairo	.30	.10
❑	460	Mike Lowell	.30	.10
❑	461	Corky Miller	.30	.10
❑	462	Bobby Madritsch	.30	.10
❑	463	Jose Contreras	.30	.10
❑	464	Johnny Damon	.50	.20
❑	465	Miguel Cabrera	.50	.20
❑	466	Eric Hinske	.30	.10
❑	467	Marlon Byrd	.30	.10
❑	468	Aaron Miles	.30	.10
❑	469	Ramon Vazquez	.30	.10
❑	470	Michael Young	.30	.10
❑	471	Alex Sanchez	.30	.10
❑	472	Shea Hillenbrand	.30	.10
❑	473	Jeff Bagwell	.50	.20
❑	474	Erik Bedard	.30	.10
❑	475	Jake Peavy	.30	.10
❑	476	Jody Gerut	.30	.10
❑	477	Randy Winn	.30	.10
❑	478	Kevin Youkilis	.30	.10
❑	479	Eric Dubose	.30	.10
❑	480	David Wright	1.25	.50
❑	481	Wilson Valdez	.30	.10
❑	482	Cliff Floyd	.30	.10
❑	483	Jose Mesa	.30	.10
❑	484	Doug Mientkiewicz	.30	.10
❑	485	Jorge Posada	.50	.20
❑	486	Sidney Ponson	.30	.10
❑	487	Dave Krynzel	.30	.10
❑	488	Octavio Dotel	.30	.10
❑	489	Matt Treanor	.30	.10
❑	490	Johan Santana	.75	.30
❑	491	John Patterson	.30	.10
❑	492	So Taguchi	.30	.10
❑	493	Carl Everett	.30	.10
❑	494	Jason Dubois	.30	.10
❑	495	Albert Pujols	1.50	.60
❑	496	Kirk Rueter	.30	.10
❑	497	Geoff Blum	.30	.10
❑	498	Juan Encarnacion	.30	.10
❑	499	Mark Hendrickson	.30	.10
❑	500	Barry Bonds	2.00	.75
❑	501	Cesar Izturis	.30	.10
❑	502	David Wells	.30	.10
❑	503	Jorge Julio	.30	.10
❑	504	Cristian Guzman	.30	.10
❑	505	Juan Pierre	.30	.10
❑	506	Adam Eaton	.30	.10
❑	507	Nick Johnson	.30	.10
❑	508	Mike Redmond	.30	.10
❑	509	Daryle Ward	.30	.10
❑	510	Adrian Beltre	.30	.10
❑	511	Laynce Nix	.30	.10
❑	512	Reed Johnson	.30	.10
❑	513	Jeremy Affeldt	.30	.10
❑	514	R.A. Dickey	.30	.10
❑	515	Alex Rios	.30	.10
❑	516	Orlando Palmeiro	.30	.10
❑	517	Mark Bellhorn	.30	.10
❑	518	Adam Kennedy	.30	.10
❑	519	Curtis Granderson	.30	.10
❑	520	Todd Helton	.50	.20
❑	521	Aaron Boone	.30	.10
❑	522	Milton Bradley	.30	.10
❑	523	Timo Perez	.30	.10
❑	524	Jeff Suppan	.30	.10
❑	525	Austin Kearns	.30	.10
❑	526	Charles Thomas	.30	.10
❑	527	Bronson Arroyo	.30	.10
❑	528	Roger Cedeno	.30	.10
❑	529	Russ Adams	.30	.10
❑	530	Barry Zito	.30	.10
❑	531	Bob Wickman	.30	.10
❑	532	Deivi Cruz	.30	.10
❑	533	Mariano Rivera	.75	.30
❑	534	J.J. Davis	.30	.10
❑	535	Greg Maddux	1.25	.50
❑	536	Ryan Vogelsong	.30	.10
❑	537	Josh Phelps	.30	.10
❑	538	Scott Hairston	.30	.10
❑	539	Vladimir Guerrero	.75	.30
❑	540	Ivan Rodriguez	.50	.20
❑	541	David Newhan	.30	.10
❑	542	David Bell	.30	.10
❑	543	Lew Ford	.30	.10
❑	544	Grady Sizemore	.50	.20
❑	545	David Ortiz	.75	.30
❑	546	Jose Cruz Jr.	.30	.10
❑	547	Aaron Rowand	.30	.10
❑	548	Marcus Thames	.30	.10
❑	549	Scott Podsednik	.30	.10
❑	550	Ichiro Suzuki	1.50	.60
❑	551	Eduardo Perez	.30	.10
❑	552	Chris Snyder	.30	.10
❑	553	Corey Koskie	.30	.10
❑	554	Miguel Tejada	.30	.10
❑	555	Orlando Cabrera	.30	.10
❑	556	Rondell White	.30	.10
❑	557	Wade Miller	.30	.10
❑	558	Rodrigo Lopez	.30	.10
❑	559	Chad Tracy	.30	.10
❑	560	Paul Konerko	.30	.10
❑	561	Wil Cordero	.30	.10
❑	562	John McDonald	.30	.10
❑	563	Jason Ellison	.30	.10
❑	564	Jason Michaels	.30	.10
❑	565	Melvin Mora	.30	.10
❑	566	Ryan Church	.30	.10
❑	567	Ryan Ludwick	.30	.10
❑	568	Erubiel Durazo	.30	.10
❑	569	Noah Lowry	.30	.10
❑	570	Curt Schilling	.50	.20
❑	571	Esteban Loaiza	.30	.10
❑	572	Freddy Sanchez	.30	.10
❑	573	Rich Aurilia	.30	.10
❑	574	Travis Lee	.30	.10
❑	575	Nick Punto	.30	.10
❑	576	J.Christiansen/K.Correia	.30	.10
❑	577	B.Baker/T.Redding	.30	.10
❑	578	T.Adams/G.Floyd	.30	.10

❑ 579 S.Etherton/D.Meyer .30 .10
❑ 580 J.Lehr/D.Turnbow .30 .10
❑ 581 M.Gosling/B.Halsey .30 .10
❑ 582 J.Mecir/L.Kensing .30 .10
❑ 583 B.Hennessey/J.Fassero .30 .10
❑ 584 J.Adkins/F.Diaz .30 .10
❑ 585 J.Crain/J.Rincon .30 .10
❑ 586 J.Cerda/N.Field .30 .10
❑ 587 B.Fortunato/J.Seo .30 .10
❑ 588 S.Schmoll RC/Y.Brazoban .50 .20
❑ 589 U.Urbina/J.Walker .30 .10
❑ 590 J.De Paula/S.Proctor .30 .10
❑ 591 J.Davis/B.Howry .30 .10
❑ 592 T.Worrell/P.Liriano .30 .10
❑ 593 J.Acevedo/K.Mercker .30 .10
❑ 594 C.Hammond/S.Linebrink .30 .10
❑ 595 F.Nieve/J.Franco .30 .10
❑ 596 R.Flores/M.Lincoln .30 .10
❑ 597 J.Borowski/S.Mitre .30 .10
❑ 598 L.Carter/J.Colome .30 .10
❑ 599 J.Halama/L.DiNardo .30 .10
❑ 600 C.Bradford/K.Calero .30 .10
❑ 601 D.Aardsma/J.Brower .30 .10
❑ 602 G.Geary/R.Madson .30 .10
❑ 603 B.Moehler/N.Bump .30 .10
❑ 604 C.Tsao/R.Speier .30 .10
❑ 605 R.Wagner/A.Harang .30 .10
❑ 606 S.Kline/H.Bauer .30 .10
❑ 607 L.Cormier/R.Choate .30 .10
❑ 608 J.Leicester/T.Wellemeyer .30 .10
❑ 609 V.Chulk/J.Frasor .30 .10
❑ 610 S.Dohmann/B.Fuentes .30 .10
❑ 611 S.Colyer/R.Hernandez .30 .10
❑ 612 I.Snell/S.Torres .30 .10
❑ 613 C.Eldred/A.Wainwright .30 .10
❑ 614 R.Bukvich/D.Brocail .30 .10
❑ 615 J.Putz/A.Sele .30 .10
❑ 616 B.Chen/T.Williams .30 .10
❑ 617 D.Weathers/B.Weber .30 .10
❑ 618 D.Reyes/R.Seanez .30 .10
❑ 619 T.Harikkala/R.Rincon .30 .10
❑ 620 S.Camp/D.Bautista .30 .10
❑ 621 J.Lopez/A.Simpson .30 .10
❑ 622 M.Remlinger/G.Rusch .30 .10
❑ 623 R.Colon/K.Gryboski .30 .10
❑ 624 T.Martin/C.Reitsma .30 .10
❑ 625 C.Qualls/D.Wheeler .30 .10
❑ 626 T.Phelps/M.Wise .30 .10
❑ 627 S.Schoeneweis/J.Speier .30 .10
❑ 628 F.Cordero/F.Francisco .30 .10
❑ 629 R.Soriano/M.Thornton .30 .10
❑ 630 M.Stanton/S.Karsay .30 .10
❑ 631 M.MacDougal/S.Sullivan .30 .10
❑ 632 B.Bruney/O.Villarreal .30 .10
❑ 633 M.Adams/R.Bottalico .30 .10
❑ 634 E.Rodriguez/D.Borkowski .30 .10
❑ 635 R.Betancourt/D.Riske .30 .10
❑ 636 J.De La Rosa/C.Glover .30 .10
❑ 637 M.Perisho/B.Howard .30 .10
❑ 638 J.Bajenaru/L.Vizcaino .30 .10
❑ 639 R.Mahay/E.Ramirez .30 .10
❑ 640 J.Grabow/M.Gonzalez .30 .10
❑ 641 J.Romero/M.Guerrier .30 .10
❑ 642 C.Hernandez/B.Duckworth .30 .10
❑ 643 T.Harper/S.McClung .30 .10
❑ 644 M.Herges/T.Walker .30 .10
❑ 645 K.Wunsch/E.Dessens .30 .10
❑ 646 M.Malaska/M.Myers .30 .10
❑ 647 K.Farnsworth/G.Knotts .30 .10
❑ 648 J.Duchscherer/J.Garcia .30 .10
❑ 649 A.Rakers/S.Reed .30 .10
❑ 650 T.Gordon/P.Quantrill .30 .10
❑ 651 B.Lyon/S.Estes .30 .10
❑ 652 P.Walker/G.Chacin .30 .10
❑ 653 J.Lackey/S.Shields .30 .10
❑ 654 D.Waechter/T.Miller .30 .10
❑ 655 L.Ayala/C.Cordero .30 .10
❑ 656 R.Villone/J.Mateo .30 .10
❑ 657 M.Mantei/B.Neal .30 .10
❑ 658 D.Marte/C.Politte .30 .10
❑ 659 J.Valentine/L.Hudson .30 .10
❑ 660 T.Jones/J.Riedling .30 .10
❑ 661 H.Bell/A.Heilman .30 .10
❑ 662 D.May/A.Otsuka .30 .10
❑ 663 J.Eischen/J.Horgan .30 .10
❑ 664 A.Sisco/M.Wood .30 .10
❑ 665 A.Embree/M.Timlin .30 .10
❑ 666 Keith Foulke .30 .10
❑ 667 R.Cormier/A.Fultz .30 .10
❑ 668 J.Woods/K.Gregg .30 .10
❑ 669 M.Ginter/F.German .30 .10
❑ 670 S.Eyre/M.Valdez .30 .10
❑ 671 B.Meadows/R.White .30 .10
❑ 672 G.Mota/T.Spooneybarger .30 .10
❑ 673 J.Grimsley/B.Ryan .30 .10
❑ 674 N.Cotts/S.Takatsu .30 .10
❑ 675 M.DeJean/F.Heredia .30 .10
❑ 676 M.Belisle/J.Hancock .30 .10
❑ 677 J.Rauch/T.Tucker .30 .10
❑ 678 N.Regilio/B.Shouse .30 .10
❑ 679 J.Tavarez/B.King .30 .10
❑ 680 C.Fox/M.Wuertz .30 .10
❑ 681 J.Sosa/A.Bernero .30 .10
❑ 682 J.Valverde/M.Koplove .30 .10
❑ 683 A.Rhodes/S.Sauerbeck .30 .10
❑ 684 F.Rodriguez/T.Sturtze .30 .10
❑ 685 G.Carrara/D.Sanchez .30 .10
❑ 686 M.Gallo/C.Harville .30 .10
❑ 687 M.Johnston/S.Burnett .30 .10
❑ 688 J.Nelson/S.Hasegawa .30 .10
❑ 689 C.Vargas/A.Osuna .30 .10
❑ 690 B.Donnelly/E.Yan .30 .10
❑ 691 J.Mathis/E.Santana .50 .20
❑ 692 C.Everts/B.Bray .50 .20
❑ 693 J.Kubel/T.Plouffe .50 .20
❑ 694 J.Stevens/A.Marte .50 .20
❑ 695 A.Hill/C.Gaudin .50 .20
❑ 696 C.Quentin/J.Cota .50 .20
❑ 697 T.Diamond/C.Young .50 .20
❑ 698 O.Quintanilla/D.Johnson .50 .20
❑ 699 J.Maine/V.Majewski .50 .20
❑ 700 J.Houser/J.Gomes .50 .20
❑ 701 D.Murphy/H.Ramirez .50 .20
❑ 702 C.Lambert/R.Ankiel .50 .20
❑ 703 F.Pie/A.Guzman .50 .20
❑ 704 F.Lewis/N.Schierholtz .50 .20
❑ 705 A.Munoz/G.Gonzalez .50 .20
❑ 706 F.Hernandez/T.Blackley 1.50 .60
❑ 707 R.Olmedo/E.Encarnacion .50 .20
❑ 708 T.Stauffer/J.Germano .50 .20
❑ 709 J.Guthrie/J.Sowers .50 .20
❑ 710 J.Cortes/T.Gorzelanny .50 .20
❑ 711 T.Tankersley/E.Reed .50 .20
❑ 712 N.Walker/P.Maholm .50 .20
❑ 713 W.Taveras/L.Scott RC 1.50 .60
❑ 714 R.Howard/G.Golson 2.00 .75
❑ 715 B.DeWitt/E.Jackson .50 .20
❑ 716 H.Street/D.Putnam .50 .20
❑ 717 R.Weeks/M.Rogers .50 .20
❑ 718 R.Cano/P.Hughes .50 .20
❑ 719 K.Waldrop/J.Rainville .50 .20
❑ 720 C.Brazell/Y.Petit .50 .20
❑ 721 B.Lopez RC/M.Brown RC .50 .20
❑ 722 D.Thomp RC/E.Chavez RC .50 .20
❑ 723 D.Uggla RC/E.Sch'wolf RC 15.00 6.00
❑ 724 I.Ramirez RC/J.Tingler RC .50 .20
❑ 725 T.G'lano RC/E.de la Cruz RC .50 .20
❑ 726 M.Campbell RC/S.Costa RC .50 .20
❑ 727 M.Prado RC/Bi.McCarthy RC .50 .20
❑ 728 I.Kinsler RC/J.Senreiso RC 2.50 1.00
❑ 729 L.Ramirez RC/Lo.Scott RC .50 .20
❑ 730 C.Seddon RC/E.Johnson RC .50 .20
❑ 731 C.Tatum RC/J.Moran RC .50 .20
❑ 732 S.Pomeranz RC/J.Motte RC .50 .20
❑ 733 J.Vaquedano RC/S.Bailie RC .50 .20
❑ 734 M.Albers RC/W.Robinson RC 1.25 .50
❑ 735 M.DeSalvo RC/Me.Cabr RC 2.00 .75
❑ 736 B.Stavisky RC/L.Powell RC .50 .20
❑ 737 S.Mathieson RC/S.Mitch RC .75 .30
❑ 738 S.Marshall RC/B.Bay RC 1.50 .60
❑ 739 B.McCarthy RC/P.Lopez RC 1.25 .50
❑ 740 A.Smit RC/R.Barrett RC .50 .20
❑ 741 M.R'stad RC/R.F'bend RC .50 .20
❑ 742 N.McLouth RC/A.Boeve RC .50 .20
❑ 743 K.Melillo RC/M.Rogers RC .75 .30
❑ 744 M.Kemp RC/H.Totten RC 4.00 1.50
❑ 745 J.Miller RC/T.Arnerich RC .50 .20
❑ 746 T.Pelland RC/J.Gutierrez RC .50 .20
❑ 747 J.West RC/W.Mota RC .50 .20
❑ 748 R.Goleski RC/R.Garko RC 1.50 .60
❑ 749 B.Triplett RC/J.Gothreaux RC .50 .20
❑ 750 K.West RC/G.Perkins RC .75 .30
❑ 751 M.Esposito RC/Z.Parker RC .50 .20
❑ 752 R.Sweeney RC/B.Miller RC 1.00 .40
❑ 753 C.McGehee RC/B.Coats RC .50 .20
❑ 754 M.Bourn RC/K.Pichardo RC .75 .30
❑ 755 M.Morse RC/B.Livingston RC .75 .30
❑ 756 W.Swack RC/B.Ryan RC .50 .20
❑ 757 M.Furtado RC/N.Masset RC .50 .20
❑ 758 P.Ramos RC/G.Kottaras RC .75 .30
❑ 759 E.Quezada RC/T.Beam RC .75 .30
❑ 760 D.Eveland RC/T.Hinton RC .50 .20
❑ 761 J.Jurries RC/C.Vines RC .50 .20
❑ 762 H.Sanch RC/J.Verlander RC 5.00 2.00
❑ 763 P.Humber RC/S.Bowman RC .75 .30
❑ 764 P.Misch RC/J.Thurmond RC .50 .20
❑ 765 C.Colonel RC/N.Wilson RC .50 .20
❑ 766 Checklist 1 .30 .10
❑ 767 Checklist 2 .30 .10
❑ 768 Checklist 3 .30 .10
❑ 769 Checklist 4 .30 .10
❑ 770 Checklist 5 .30 .10

2006 Topps Triple Threads

❑ COMMON CARD (1-100) 4.00 1.50
❑ 1-100 THREE PER PACK
❑ COMMON CARD (101-120) 15.00 6.00
❑ MINOR STARS 101-112 25.00 10.00
❑ SEMISTARS 101-112 40.00 15.00
❑ COMMON CARD (113-120) 15.00 6.00
❑ MINOR STARS 113-120 25.00 10.00
❑ SEMISTARS 113-120 40.00 15.00
❑ 101-120 ODDS 1:7 MINI
❑ 101-120 PRINT RUN 225 SERIAL #'d SETS
❑ OVERALL 1-100 PLATE ODDS 1:80 MINI
❑ PLATE PRINT RUN 1 SET PER COLOR
❑ BLACK-CYAN-MAGENTA-YELLOW ISSUED
❑ NO PLATE PRICING DUE TO SCARCITY
❑ 1 Hideki Matsui 5.00 2.00
❑ 2 Josh Gibson HOF 5.00 2.00
❑ 3 Roger Clemens 8.00 3.00
❑ 4 Paul Konerko 3.00 1.25
❑ 5 Brooks Robinson HOF 4.00 1.50
❑ 6 Stan Musial HOF 5.00 2.00
❑ 7 Dontrelle Willis 3.00 1.25
❑ 8 Yogi Berra HOF 5.00 2.00
❑ 9 John Smoltz 4.00 1.50
❑ 10 Brian Roberts 3.00 1.25
❑ 11 Gary Sheffield 3.00 1.25
❑ 12 Wade Boggs HOF 4.00 1.50
❑ 13 Alex Rodriguez 8.00 3.00
❑ 14 Ernie Banks HOF 5.00 2.00
❑ 15 Ichiro Suzuki 8.00 3.00
❑ 16 Whitey Ford HOF 4.00 1.50
❑ 17 Vladimir Guerrero 5.00 2.00
❑ 18 Tadahito Iguchi 3.00 1.25
❑ 19 Robin Yount HOF 5.00 2.00
❑ 20 Jason Schmidt 3.00 1.25
❑ 21 Roberto Clemente HOF 10.00 4.00
❑ 22 Andruw Jones 4.00 1.50
❑ 23 Don Mattingly 10.00 4.00
❑ 24 Joe Mauer 4.00 1.50
❑ 25 Barry Bonds 12.00 5.00
❑ 26 Johnny Damon 4.00 1.50
❑ 27 Chris Carpenter 3.00 1.25
❑ 28 Garret Anderson 3.00 1.25
❑ 29 Scott Rolen 4.00 1.50
❑ 30 Tim Hudson 3.00 1.25
❑ 31 Dave Winfield HOF 3.00 1.25

❑ 32 Steve Carlton HOF 3.00 1.25
❑ 33 Miguel Tejada 3.00 1.25
❑ 34 Nolan Ryan HOF 10.00 4.00
❑ 35 Mark Buehrle 3.00 1.25
❑ 36 Travis Hafner 3.00 1.25
❑ 37 Rickie Weeks 3.00 1.25
❑ 38 Sammy Sosa 5.00 2.00
❑ 39 Carlos Beltran 3.00 1.25
❑ 40 Todd Helton 4.00 1.50
❑ 41 Tom Seaver HOF 4.00 1.50
❑ 42 Ted Williams HOF 6.00 2.50
❑ 43 Alfonso Soriano 3.00 1.25
❑ 44 Reggie Jackson HOF 4.00 1.50
❑ 45 Pedro Martinez 4.00 1.50
❑ 46 Randy Johnson 5.00 2.00
❑ 47 Ted Williams HOF 6.00 2.50
❑ 48 Torii Hunter 3.00 1.25
❑ 49 Manny Ramirez 4.00 1.50
❑ 50 George Brett HOF 6.00 2.50
❑ 51 Chipper Jones 5.00 2.00
❑ 52 Nomar Garciaparra 4.00 1.50
❑ 53 Richie Sexson 3.00 1.25
❑ 54 David Ortiz 5.00 2.00
❑ 55 Derek Jeter 15.00 6.00
❑ 56 Mickey Mantle HOF 15.00 6.00
❑ 57 Michael Young 3.00 1.25
❑ 58 Aramis Ramirez 3.00 1.25
❑ 59 Bartolo Colon 3.00 1.25
❑ 60 Troy Glaus 3.00 1.25
❑ 61 Carlos Delgado 3.00 1.25
❑ 62 Mike Sweeney 3.00 1.25
❑ 63 Jorge Cantu 3.00 1.25
❑ 64 Mike Mussina 4.00 1.50
❑ 65 Hank Blalock 3.00 1.25
❑ 66 Frank Robinson HOF 3.00 1.25
❑ 67 Carl Yastrzemski HOF 5.00 2.00
❑ 68 Adam Dunn 3.00 1.25
❑ 69 Eric Chavez 3.00 1.25
❑ 70 Curt Schilling 4.00 1.50
❑ 71 Jeff Francoeur 6.00 2.50
❑ 72 C.C. Sabathia 3.00 1.25
❑ 73 Roy Oswalt 3.00 1.25
❑ 74 Carlos Lee 3.00 1.25
❑ 75 Barry Zito 3.00 1.25
❑ 76 Derrek Lee 4.00 1.50
❑ 77 Greg Maddux 6.00 2.50
❑ 78 Ivan Rodriguez 4.00 1.50
❑ 79 Jeff Kent 3.00 1.25
❑ 80 Gary Carter HOF 3.00 1.25
❑ 81 Jose Reyes 3.00 1.25
❑ 82 Johan Santana 4.00 1.50
❑ 83 Magglio Ordonez 3.00 1.25
❑ 84 Mark Prior 4.00 1.50
❑ 85 Johnny Bench HOF 5.00 2.00
❑ 86 Vernon Wells 3.00 1.25
❑ 87 Mark Mulder 3.00 1.25
❑ 88 Cal Ripken 15.00 6.00
❑ 89 Mark Teixeira 4.00 1.50
❑ 90 Miguel Cabrera 4.00 1.50
❑ 91 Duke Snider HOF 4.00 1.50
❑ 92 Jason Giambi 3.00 1.25
❑ 93 Albert Pujols 8.00 3.00
❑ 94 Carl Crawford 3.00 1.25
❑ 95 Jim Edmonds 3.00 1.25
❑ 96 Jose Contreras 3.00 1.25
❑ 97 Victor Martinez 3.00 1.25
❑ 98 Jeremy Bonderman 3.00 1.25
❑ 99 Lance Berkman 3.00 1.25
❑ 100 Rocco Baldelli 3.00 1.25
❑ 101 Zach Duke AU J-J 25.00 10.00
❑ 102 Felix Hernandez AU J-J 40.00 15.00
❑ 103 Dan Johnson AU J-J 15.00 6.00
❑ 104 Brandon McCarthy AU J-J 25.00 10.00
❑ 105 Huston Street AU J-J 25.00 10.00
❑ 106 Robinson Cano AU J-J 50.00 20.00
❑ 107 Jason Bay AU J-J 25.00 10.00
❑ 108 Ryan Howard AU B-B 120.00 60.00
❑ 109 Ervin Santana AU J-J 15.00 6.00
❑ 110 Rich Harden AU J-J 15.00 6.00
❑ 111 Aaron Hill AU J-J 15.00 6.00
❑ 112 David Wright AU J-J 60.00 30.00
❑ 114 Nelson Cruz AU J-J (RC) 15.00 6.00
❑ 115 F.Liriano AU J-J (RC) 100.00 50.00
❑ 116 Hong-Chih Kuo AU J-J (RC) 120.00 60.00
❑ 117 Ryan Garko AU J-J (RC) 25.00 10.00
❑ 118 Craig Hansen AU J-J RC 50.00 20.00
❑ 119 Shin-Soo Choo AU J-J (RC) 15.00 6.00
❑ 120 Darrell Rasner AU J-J (RC) 15.00 6.00

2007 Topps Triple Threads

❑ COMP.SET w/o AU's (125) 200.00 125.00
❑ COMMON CARD (1-125) 1.00 .40
❑ 1-125 STATED PRINT RUN 1350 SER.#'d SETS
❑ COMMON JSY AU 12.00 5.00
❑ 126-189 JSY AU ODDS 1:9 MINI
❑ 126-189 JSY AU VARIATION ODDS 1:38 MINI
❑ 126-189 JSY AU PRINT RUN 99 SER.#'d SETS
❑ TEAM INITIAL DIECUTS ARE VARIATIONS
❑ OVERALL 1-125 PLATE ODDS 1:113 MINI
❑ PLATE PRINT RUN 1 SET PER COLOR
❑ BLACK-CYAN-MAGENTA-YELLOW ISSUED
❑ NO PLATE PRICING DUE TO SCARCITY
❑ 1 Alex Rodriguez 3.00 1.25
❑ 2 Barry Zito 1.00 .40
❑ 3 Corey Patterson 1.00 .40
❑ 4 Roberto Clemente 6.00 2.50
❑ 5 David Wright 3.00 1.25
❑ 6 Dontrelle Willis 1.00 .40
❑ 7 Mickey Mantle 8.00 3.00
❑ 8 Adam Dunn 1.00 .40
❑ 9 Richie Ashburn 1.50 .60
❑ 10 Ryan Howard 3.00 1.25
❑ 11 Miguel Tejada 1.00 .40
❑ 12 Ernie Banks 2.50 1.00
❑ 13 Ken Griffey Jr. 3.00 1.25
❑ 14 Johnny Bench 2.50 1.00
❑ 15 Ichiro Suzuki 3.00 1.25
❑ 16 Gil Meche 1.00 .40
❑ 17 Kazuo Matsui 1.00 .40
❑ 18 Matt Holliday 1.25 .50
❑ 19 Juan Pierre 1.00 .40
❑ 20 Yogi Berra 2.50 1.00
❑ 21 Bill Hall 1.00 .40
❑ 22 Wade Boggs 1.50 .60
❑ 23 Jason Bay 1.00 .40
❑ 24 Troy Glaus 1.00 .40
❑ 25 Paul Konerko 1.00 .40
❑ 26 Rod Carew 1.50 .60
❑ 27 Jay Gibbons 1.00 .40
❑ 28 Frank Thomas 2.50 1.00
❑ 29 Joe Mauer 1.50 .60
❑ 30 Carlos Beltran 1.00 .40
❑ 31 Frank Robinson 1.00 .40
❑ 32 Bobby Abreu 1.00 .40
❑ 33 Roy Oswalt 1.00 .40
❑ 34 Edgar Renteria 1.00 .40
❑ 35 Magglio Ordonez 1.00 .40
❑ 36 Mike Piazza 2.50 1.00
❑ 37 Trevor Hoffman 1.00 .40
❑ 38 Eddie Mathews 2.50 1.00
❑ 39 Albert Pujols 4.00 1.50
❑ 40 Dennis Eckersley 1.00 .40
❑ 41 Andruw Jones 1.50 .60
❑ 42 Alfonso Soriano 1.00 .40
❑ 43 Bob Feller 1.00 .40
❑ 44 J.D. Drew 1.00 .40
❑ 45 Jason Schmidt 1.00 .40
❑ 46 Vladimir Guerrero 2.50 1.00
❑ 47 Reggie Jackson 1.50 .60
❑ 48 Lance Berkman 1.00 .40
❑ 49 Michael Young 1.00 .40
❑ 50 Carlton Fisk 1.50 .60
❑ 51 Brandon Webb 1.00 .40
❑ 52 Adrian Beltre 1.00 .40
❑ 53 Hideki Matsui 2.50 1.00
❑ 54 Bronson Arroyo 1.00 .40
❑ 55 Tony Gwynn 2.50 1.00
❑ 56 Ray Durham 1.00 .40
❑ 57 Garrett Atkins 1.00 .40
❑ 58 Nolan Ryan 5.00 2.00
❑ 59 Daisuke Matsuzaka RC 15.00 6.00
❑ 60 Todd Helton 1.50 .60
❑ 61 Carl Crawford 1.00 .40
❑ 62 Jake Peavy 1.00 .40
❑ 63 Rafael Furcal 1.00 .40
❑ 64 Joe Morgan 1.00 .40
❑ 65 Greg Maddux 3.00 1.25
❑ 66 Luis Aparicio 1.00 .40
❑ 67 Derrek Lee 1.00 .40
❑ 68 Johnny Damon 1.50 .60
❑ 69 Mike Lowell 1.00 .40
❑ 70 Roger Maris 2.50 1.00
❑ 71 Vernon Wells 1.00 .40
❑ 72 Monte Irvin 1.00 .40
❑ 73 Jermaine Dye 1.00 .40
❑ 74 Miguel Cabrera 1.50 .60
❑ 75 Barry Bonds 4.00 1.50
❑ 76 Stan Musial 3.00 1.25
❑ 77 Derek Lowe 1.00 .40
❑ 78 Don Mattingly 4.00 1.50
❑ 79 Lyle Overbay 1.00 .40
❑ 80 Chien-Ming Wang 3.00 1.25
❑ 81 Carlos Zambrano 1.00 .40
❑ 82 Kei Igawa RC 3.00 1.25
❑ 83 Cole Hamels 1.50 .60
❑ 84 Gary Sheffield 1.00 .40
❑ 85 Nick Johnson 1.00 .40
❑ 86 Brooks Robinson 1.50 .60
❑ 87 Curt Schilling 1.50 .60
❑ 88 Ryne Sandberg 4.00 1.50
❑ 89 Mike Cameron 1.00 .40
❑ 90 Mike Schmidt 3.00 1.25
❑ 91 Chris Carpenter 1.00 .40
❑ 92 Scott Rolen 1.50 .60
❑ 93 Rocco Baldelli 1.00 .40
❑ 94 C.C. Sabathia 1.00 .40
❑ 95 Jeff Francis 1.00 .40
❑ 96 Ozzie Smith 3.00 1.25
❑ 97 Aramis Ramirez 1.00 .40
❑ 98 Aaron Harang 1.00 .40
❑ 99 Duke Snider 1.50 .60
❑ 100 David Ortiz 2.50 1.00
❑ 101 Raul Ibanez 1.00 .40
❑ 102 Bruce Sutter 1.00 .40
❑ 103 Gary Matthews 1.00 .40
❑ 104 Chipper Jones 2.50 1.00
❑ 105 Craig Biggio 1.50 .60
❑ 106 Roy Halladay 1.00 .40
❑ 107 Hoyt Wilhelm 1.00 .40
❑ 108 Manny Ramirez 1.50 .60
❑ 109 Randy Johnson 2.50 1.00
❑ 110 Carl Yastrzemski 3.00 1.25
❑ 111 Mark Teixeira 1.50 .60
❑ 112 Derek Jeter 5.00 2.00
❑ 113 Stephen Drew 1.50 .60
❑ 114 Darryl Strawberry 1.00 .40
❑ 115 Travis Hafner 1.00 .40
❑ 116 Torii Hunter 1.00 .40
❑ 117 Jim Edmonds 1.50 .60
❑ 118 John Smoltz 1.50 .60
❑ 119 Bo Jackson 2.50 1.00
❑ 120 Roger Clemens 4.00 1.50
❑ 121 Pedro Martinez 1.50 .60
❑ 122 Rickey Henderson 2.50 1.00
❑ 123 Ivan Rodriguez 1.50 .60
❑ 124 Robin Yount 2.50 1.00
❑ 125 Johan Santana 1.50 .60
❑ 126a Robinson Cano Jsy AU 40.00 15.00
❑ 126b Robinson Cano Jsy AU 40.00 15.00
❑ 127a Jose Reyes Jsy AU 60.00 30.00
❑ 127b Jose Reyes Jsy AU 60.00 30.00
❑ 128a Justin Morneau Jsy AU 25.00 10.00
❑ 128b Justin Morneau Jsy AU 25.00 10.00
❑ 129a Curtis Granderson Jsy AU 30.00 12.50
❑ 129b Curtis Granderson Jsy AU 30.00 12.50
❑ 130a Justin Verlander Jsy AU 40.00 15.00
❑ 130b Justin Verlander Jsy AU 40.00 15.00
❑ 131 Prince Fielder Jsy AU 60.00 30.00
❑ 132a Ryan Zimmerman Jsy AU 40.00 15.00

❑ 132b Ryan Zimmerman Jsy AU 40.0015.00
❑ 133 Mike Napoli Jsy AU 12.00 5.00
❑ 134 Melky Cabrera Jsy AU 25.00 10.00
❑ 135 Jonathan Papelbon Jsy AU 40.0015.00
❑ 136a Nick Markakis Jsy AU 25.00 10.00
❑ 136b Nick Markakis Jsy AU 25.00 10.00
❑ 137 B.J. Upton Jsy AU 20.00 8.00
❑ 138a Joel Zumaya Jsy AU 25.00 10.00
❑ 138b Joel Zumaya Jsy AU 25.00 10.00
❑ 140 Nick Swisher Jsy AU 25.00 10.00
❑ 141 Andre Ethier Jsy AU 20.00 8.00
❑ 142a Jered Weaver Jsy AU 25.00 10.00
❑ 142b Jered Weaver Jsy AU 25.00 10.00
❑ 143 Matt Cain Jsy AU 30.00 12.50
❑ 144 Lastings Milledge Jsy AU 20.00 8.00
❑ 145 Brian McCann Jsy AU 40.00 15.00
❑ 146 Shin-Soo Choo Jsy AU 15.00 6.00
❑ 147a Dan Uggla Jsy AU 30.00 12.50
❑ 147b Dan Uggla Jsy AU 30.00 12.50
❑ 148 Hanley Ramirez Jsy AU 40.00 15.00
❑ 149 Russell Martin Jsy AU 40.00 15.00
❑ 150 Francisco Liriano Jsy AU 25.00 10.00
❑ 151 Anthony Reyes Jsy AU 12.00 5.00
❑ 152 Josh Barfield Jsy AU 15.00 6.00
❑ 153 Anibal Sanchez Jsy AU 12.00 5.00
❑ 154 Jeremy Hermida Jsy AU 15.00 6.00
❑ 155 Kendry Morales Jsy AU 12.00 5.00
❑ 156 Matt Kemp Jsy AU 25.00 10.00
❑ 157 Freddy Sanchez Jsy AU 15.00 6.00
❑ 158 Howie Kendrick Jsy AU 20.00 8.00
❑ 159 Scott Thorman Jsy AU 20.00 8.00
❑ 160 Franklin Gutierrez Bat AU 15.00 6.00
❑ 161 Jason Bartlett Jsy AU 15.00 6.00
❑ 162 Chris Duncan Jsy AU 50.00 20.00
❑ 163 Maicer Izturis Jsy AU 12.00 5.00
❑ 164 Jason Botts Jsy AU 12.00 5.00
❑ 165 Tony Gwynn Jr. Jsy AU 40.00 15.00
❑ 166 Jorge Cantu Jsy AU 12.00 5.00
❑ 167 Adam Jones Jsy AU 40.00 15.00
❑ 168 Edinson Volquez Jsy AU 80.00 40.00
❑ 169 Joey Gathright Jsy AU 12.00 5.00
❑ 170 Carlos Marmol Jsy AU 20.00 8.00
❑ 171 Ben Zobrist Jsy AU 15.00 6.00
❑ 172 Josh Willingham Jsy AU 12.00 5.00
❑ 173 Brad Thompson Jsy AU 25.00 10.00
❑ 174a Chris Ray Jsy AU 15.00 6.00
❑ 174b Ervin Santana Jsy AU 15.00 6.00
❑ 175 Ronny Paulino Jsy AU 12.00 5.00
❑ 176 Tyler Johnson Jsy AU 12.00 5.00
❑ 177 J.J. Hardy Jsy AU 30.00 12.50
❑ 178 Adrian Gonzalez Jsy AU 20.00 8.00
❑ 179 Scott Kazmir Jsy AU 25.00 10.00
❑ 180 Juan Morillo Jsy AU (RC) 12.00 5.00
❑ 181a Shawn Riggans JSY AU (RC) 12.00 5.00
❑ 181b Shawn Riggans JSY AU (RC) 12.00 5.00
❑ 182 Brian Stokes JSY AU (RC) 12.00 5.00
❑ 183 Delmon Young JSY AU (RC) 30.00 12.50
❑ 184a Troy Tulowitzki JSY AU (RC) 60.00 30.00
❑ 184b Troy Tulowitzki JSY AU (RC) 60.00 30.00
❑ 185 Adam Lind JSY AU (RC) 15.00 6.00
❑ 186 David Murphy JSY AU (RC) 15.00 6.00
❑ 187a Philip Humber JSY AU (RC) 15.006.00
❑ 187b Philip Humber JSY AU (RC) 15.006.00
❑ 188a Andrew Miller JSY AU RC 60.0030.00
❑ 188b Andrew Miller JSY AU RC 60.0030.00
❑ 189a Glen Perkins JSY AU (RC) 12.005.00
❑ 189b Glen Perkins JSY AU (RC) 12.005.00

2005 Topps Turkey Red

❑ COMPLETE SET (330) 300.00 200.00
❑ COMP.SET w/o SP's (275) 50.00 20.00
❑ COMMON CARD (1-270) .40 .15
❑ COMMON SP (1-270) 8.00 3.00
❑ SP CL: 160A/160B/170/175/181/184/185/193
❑ COMMON REPRINT .75 .30
❑ COMMON RC (271-300) 1.00 .40
❑ COMMON RET (301-315) 1.00 .40
❑ VAR CL: 1/5/10/16/75/83/100/102/120/125
❑ VAR CL: 130/160/225/230/270
❑ TWO VERSIONS OF EACH VARIATION EXIST
❑ 1A B.Bonds Grey Uni SP 15.00 6.00
❑ 1B B.Bonds White Uni 2.50 1.00
❑ 2 Michael Young .40 .15
❑ 3 Jim Edmonds .40 .15
❑ 4 Cliff Floyd .40 .15
❑ 5A R.Clemens Blue Sky SP 10.00 4.00
❑ 5B R.Clemens Yellow Sky SP 10.00 4.00
❑ 6 Hal Chase REP .75 .30
❑ 7 Shannon Stewart .40 .15
❑ 8 Fred Clarke REP .75 .30
❑ 9 Travis Hafner .40 .15
❑ 10A S.Sosa w/Name SP 8.00 3.00
❑ 10B S.Sosa w/o Name SP 8.00 3.00
❑ 11 Jermaine Dye .40 .15
❑ 12 Lyle Overbay .40 .15
❑ 13 Oliver Perez .40 .15
❑ 14 Red Dooin REP .75 .30
❑ 15 Kid Elberfeld REP .75 .30
❑ 16A M.Piazza Blue Uni SP 8.00 3.00
❑ 16B M.Piazza Pinstripe 1.00 .40
❑ 17 Bret Boone .40 .15
❑ 18 Hughie Jennings REP .75 .30
❑ 19 Jeff Francis .40 .15
❑ 20 Manny Ramirez SP 8.00 3.00
❑ 21 Russ Ortiz .40 .15
❑ 22 Carlos Zambrano .40 .15
❑ 23 Luis Castillo .40 .15
❑ 24 David DeJesus .40 .15
❑ 25 Carlos Beltran SP 8.00 3.00
❑ 26 Doug Davis .40 .15
❑ 27 Bobby Abreu .40 .15
❑ 28 Rich Harden SP 8.00 3.00
❑ 29 Brian Giles .40 .15
❑ 30 Richie Sexson SP 8.00 3.00
❑ 31 Nick Johnson .40 .15
❑ 32 Roy Halladay .40 .15
❑ 33 Andy Pettitte .60 .25
❑ 34 Miguel Cabrera .60 .25
❑ 35 Jeff Kent .40 .15
❑ 36 Chone Figgins .40 .15
❑ 37 Carlos Lee .40 .15
❑ 38 Greg Maddux 1.50 .60
❑ 39 Preston Wilson .40 .15
❑ 40 Chipper Jones 1.00 .40
❑ 41 Coco Crisp .40 .15
❑ 42 Adam Dunn .40 .15
❑ 43 Out At Second M.Tejada CL .40 .15
❑ 44 Sheffield At Bat CL .40 .15
❑ 45 Play At the Plate J.Lopez CL .40 .15
❑ 46 Rolen Diggin' In CL .40 .15
❑ 47 Helton With the Slap Tag CL .40 .15
❑ 48 Clemens Bringing Heat CL 1.00 .40
❑ 49 A Close Play J.Rollins CL .40 .15
❑ 50 Ichiro At Bat CL 1.00 .40
❑ 51 Can of Corn C.Floyd CL .40 .15
❑ 52 Pulling String J.Santana CL 1.00 .40
❑ 53 Mark Teixeira .60 .25
❑ 54 Chris Carpenter .40 .15
❑ 55 Roy Oswalt SP 8.00 3.00
❑ 56 Casey Kotchman .40 .15
❑ 57 Torii Hunter .40 .15
❑ 58 Jose Reyes .40 .15
❑ 59 Wily Mo Pena SP 8.00 3.00
❑ 60 Magglio Ordonez SP 8.00 3.00
❑ 61 Aaron Miles .40 .15
❑ 62 Dallas McPherson .40 .15
❑ 63 Javy Lopez .40 .15
❑ 64 Luis Gonzalez .40 .15
❑ 65 David Ortiz 1.00 .40
❑ 66 Jorge Posada .60 .25
❑ 67 Xavier Nady .40 .15
❑ 68 Larry Walker .60 .25
❑ 69 Mark Loretta .40 .15
❑ 70 Jim Thome SP 8.00 3.00
❑ 71 Livan Hernandez .40 .15
❑ 72 Garrett Atkins .40 .15
❑ 73 Milton Bradley .40 .15
❑ 74 B.J. Upton .40 .15
❑ 75A I.Suzuki w/Name SP 10.00 4.00
❑ 75B I.Suzuki w/o Name SP 10.00 4.00
❑ 76 Aramis Ramirez .40 .15
❑ 77 Eric Milton .40 .15
❑ 78 Troy Glaus SP 8.00 3.00
❑ 79 David Newhan .40 .15
❑ 80 Delmon Young .60 .25
❑ 81 Justin Morneau .40 .15
❑ 82 Ramon Ortiz .40 .15
❑ 83A E.Chavez Blue Sky .40 .15
❑ 83B E.Chavez Purple Sky SP 8.00 3.00
❑ 84 Sean Burroughs .40 .15
❑ 85 Scott Rolen SP 8.00 3.00
❑ 86 Rocco Baldelli .40 .15
❑ 87 Joe Mauer SP 10.00 4.00
❑ 88 Tony Womack .40 .15
❑ 89 Ken Griffey Jr. 1.50 .60
❑ 90 Alfonso Soriano SP 8.00 3.00
❑ 91 Paul Konerko .40 .15
❑ 92 Guillermo Mota .40 .15
❑ 93 Lance Berkman .40 .15
❑ 94 Mark Buehrle .40 .15
❑ 95 Matt Clement .40 .15
❑ 96 Melvin Mora .40 .15
❑ 97 Khalil Greene .60 .25
❑ 98 David Wright 1.50 .60
❑ 99 Jack Wilson .40 .15
❑ 100A A.Rodriguez w/Bat SP 10.00 4.00
❑ 100B A.Rodriguez w/Glove SP 10.00 4.00
❑ 101 Joe Nathan .40 .15
❑ 102A A.Beltre Grey Uni SP 8.00 3.00
❑ 102B A.Beltre White Uni .40 .15
❑ 103 Mike Sweeney .40 .15
❑ 104 Brad Lidge .40 .15
❑ 105 Shawn Green .40 .15
❑ 106 Miguel Tejada SP 8.00 3.00
❑ 107 Derrek Lee .60 .25
❑ 108 Eric Hinske .40 .15
❑ 109 Eric Byrnes .40 .15
❑ 110 Hideki Matsui SP 8.00 3.00
❑ 111 Tom Glavine .60 .25
❑ 112 Jimmy Rollins .40 .15
❑ 113 Ryan Drese .40 .15
❑ 114 Josh Beckett .40 .15
❑ 115 Curt Schilling SP 8.00 3.00
❑ 116 Jeremy Bonderman .40 .15
❑ 117 Kazuo Matsui .40 .15
❑ 118 Chase Utley .60 .25
❑ 119 Troy Percival .40 .15
❑ 120A V.Guerrero w/Bat SP 8.00 3.00
❑ 120B V.Guerrero w/Glove SP 8.00 3.00
❑ 121 Gary Sheffield .40 .15
❑ 122 Jeromy Burnitz .40 .15
❑ 123 Javier Vazquez .40 .15
❑ 124 Kevin Millar .40 .15
❑ 125A R.Johnson Blue Sky 1.00 .40
❑ 125B R.Johnson Purple Sky SP 8.00 3.00
❑ 126 Pat Burrell .40 .15
❑ 127 Jason Schmidt .40 .15
❑ 128 Jose Vidro .40 .15
❑ 129 Kip Wells .40 .15
❑ 130A I.Rodriguez w/Cap .60 .25
❑ 130B I.Rodriguez w/Helmet SP 8.00 3.00
❑ 131 C.C. Sabathia .40 .15
❑ 132 Carlos Delgado SP 8.00 3.00
❑ 133 Bartolo Colon .40 .15
❑ 134 Andruw Jones .60 .25
❑ 135 Kerry Wood .40 .15
❑ 136 Sidney Ponson .40 .15
❑ 137 Eric Gagne .40 .15
❑ 138 Rickie Weeks .40 .15
❑ 139 Mariano Rivera 1.00 .40
❑ 140 Bobby Crosby .40 .15
❑ 141 Jamie Moyer .40 .15
❑ 142 Corey Koskie .40 .15
❑ 143 John Smoltz .60 .25
❑ 144 Frank Thomas 1.00 .40
❑ 145 Cristian Guzman .40 .15
❑ 146 Paul Lo Duca .40 .15
❑ 147 Geoff Jenkins .40 .15
❑ 148 Nick Swisher .40 .15
❑ 149 Jason Bay SP 8.00 3.00

❑ 150 Albert Pujols SP 15.00 6.00
❑ 151 Edwin Jackson .40 .15
❑ 152 Carl Crawford .40 .15
❑ 153 Mark Mulder .40 .15
❑ 154 Rafael Palmeiro .60 .25
❑ 155 Pedro Martinez SP 8.00 3.00
❑ 156 Jake Westbrook .40 .15
❑ 157 Sean Casey .40 .15
❑ 158 Aaron Rowand .40 .15
❑ 159 J.D. Drew .40 .15
❑ 160A J.Sant Glove on Knee SP 8.00 3.00
❑ 160B J.Santana Throwing SP 8.00 3.00
❑ 161 Gavin Floyd .40 .15
❑ 162 Vernon Wells .40 .15
❑ 163 Aubrey Huff .40 .15
❑ 164 Jeff Bagwell .60 .25
❑ 165 Boomer Wells .40 .15
❑ 166 Brad Penny .40 .15
❑ 167 Austin Kearns .40 .15
❑ 168 Mike Mussina .60 .25
❑ 169 Randy Wolf .40 .15
❑ 170 Tim Hudson SP 8.00 3.00
❑ 171 Casey Blake .40 .15
❑ 172 Edgar Renteria .40 .15
❑ 173 Ben Sheets .40 .15
❑ 174 Kevin Brown .40 .15
❑ 175 Nomar Garciaparra SP 8.00 3.00
❑ 176 Armando Benitez .40 .15
❑ 177 Jody Gerut .40 .15
❑ 178 Craig Biggio .60 .25
❑ 179 Omar Vizquel .60 .25
❑ 180 Jake Peavy .40 .15
❑ 181 Gustavo Chacin SP 8.00 3.00
❑ 182 Johnny Damon .60 .25
❑ 183 Mike Lieberthal .40 .15
❑ 184 Felix Hernandez SP 15.00 6.00
❑ 185 Zach Day SP 8.00 3.00
❑ 186 Matt Cain 1.00 .40
❑ 187 Erubiel Durazo .40 .15
❑ 188 Zack Greinke .40 .15
❑ 189 Matt Morris .40 .15
❑ 190 Billy Wagner .40 .15
❑ 191 Al Leiter .40 .15
❑ 192 Miguel Olivo .40 .15
❑ 193 Jose Capellan SP 8.00 3.00
❑ 194 Adam Eaton .40 .15
❑ 195 Steven White SP RC 8.00 3.00
❑ 196 Joe Randa .40 .15
❑ 197 Richard Hidalgo .40 .15
❑ 198 Orlando Cabrera .40 .15
❑ 199 Joel Guzman SP 8.00 3.00
❑ 200 Garret Anderson .40 .15
❑ 201 Endy Chavez .40 .15
❑ 202 Andy Marte .40 .15
❑ 203 Jose Guillen .40 .15
❑ 204 Victor Martinez .40 .15
❑ 205 Johnny Estrada .40 .15
❑ 206 Damian Miller .40 .15
❑ 207 Ken Harvey .40 .15
❑ 208 Ronnie Belliard .40 .15
❑ 209 Chan Ho Park .40 .15
❑ 210 Laynce Nix .40 .15
❑ 211 Lew Ford .40 .15
❑ 212 Moises Alou .40 .15
❑ 213 Kris Benson .40 .15
❑ 214 Mike Gonzalez SP 8.00 3.00
❑ 215 Chris Burke .40 .15
❑ 216 Juan Pierre .40 .15
❑ 217 Phil Nevin .40 .15
❑ 218 Jerry Hairston Jr. .40 .15
❑ 219 Jeremy Reed .40 .15
❑ 220 Scott Kazmir SP 8.00 3.00
❑ 221 Mike Maroth .40 .15
❑ 222 Alex Rios .40 .15
❑ 223 Esteban Loaiza .40 .15
❑ 224 Terrmel Sledge .40 .15
❑ 225A M.Prior Blue Sky SP 8.00 3.00
❑ 225B M.Prior Yellow Sky SP 8.00 3.00
❑ 226 Hank Blalock .40 .15
❑ 227 Craig Wilson .40 .15
❑ 228 Cesar Izturis .40 .15
❑ 229 Dmitri Young .40 .15
❑ 230A D.Jeter Blue Sky SP 15.00 6.00
❑ 230B D.Jeter Purple Sky SP 15.00 6.00
❑ 231 Mark Kotsay .40 .15
❑ 232 Darin Erstad .40 .15
❑ 233 Brandon Backe SP 8.00 3.00
❑ 234 Mike Lowell .40 .15
❑ 235 Scott Podsednik .40 .15
❑ 236 Michael Barrett .40 .15
❑ 237 Chad Tracy .40 .15
❑ 238 David Dellucci .40 .15
❑ 239 Brady Clark .40 .15
❑ 240 Jorge Cantu .40 .15
❑ 241 Wil Ledezma .40 .15
❑ 242 Morgan Ensberg .40 .15
❑ 243 Omar Infante .40 .15
❑ 244 Corey Patterson .40 .15
❑ 245 Matt Holliday .50 .20
❑ 246 Vinny Castilla .40 .15
❑ 247 Jason Bartlett .40 .15
❑ 248 Noah Lowry .40 .15
❑ 249 Huston Street .60 .25
❑ 250 Russell Branyan .40 .15
❑ 251 Juan Uribe .40 .15
❑ 252 Larry Bigbie .40 .15
❑ 253 Grady Sizemore .60 .25
❑ 254 Pedro Feliz .40 .15
❑ 255 Brad Wilkerson .40 .15
❑ 256 Brandon Inge .40 .15
❑ 257 Dewon Brazelton .40 .15
❑ 258 Rodrigo Lopez .40 .15
❑ 259 Jacque Jones .40 .15
❑ 260 Jason Giambi .40 .15
❑ 261 Clint Barmes .40 .15
❑ 262 Willy Taveras .40 .15
❑ 263 Marcus Giles .40 .15
❑ 264 Joe Blanton .40 .15
❑ 265 John Thomson .40 .15
❑ 266 Steve Finley SP 8.00 3.00
❑ 267 Kevin Millwood .40 .15
❑ 268 David Eckstein .40 .15
❑ 269 Barry Zito .40 .15
❑ 270A T.Helton Purple Sky SP 8.00 3.00
❑ 270B T.Helton Yellow Sky SP 8.00 3.00
❑ 271 Landon Powell RC 1.00 .40
❑ 272 Justin Verlander RC 4.00 1.50
❑ 273 Wes Swackhamer RC 1.00 .40
❑ 274 Wladimir Balentien RC 1.00 .40
❑ 275 Philip Humber RC 1.00 .40
❑ 276 Kevin Melillo RC 1.00 .40
❑ 277 Billy Butler RC 4.00 1.50
❑ 278 Michael Rogers RC 1.00 .40
❑ 279 Bobby Livingston RC 1.00 .40
❑ 280 Glen Perkins RC 1.00 .40
❑ 281 Mike Bourn RC 1.00 .40
❑ 282 Tyler Pelland RC 1.00 .40
❑ 283 Jeremy West RC 1.00 .40
❑ 284 Brandon McCarthy RC 1.50 .60
❑ 285 Ian Kinsler RC 2.50 1.00
❑ 286 Chris Roberson RC 1.00 .40
❑ 287 Melky Cabrera RC 2.00 .75
❑ 288 Ryan Sweeney RC 1.00 .40
❑ 289 Chip Cannon RC 1.25 .50
❑ 290 Andy LaRoche RC 4.00 1.50
❑ 291 Chuck Tiffany RC 1.25 .50
❑ 292 Ian Bladergroen RC 1.00 .40
❑ 293 Bear Bay RC 1.00 .40
❑ 294 Hernan Iribarren RC 1.25 .50
❑ 295 Stuart Pomeranz RC 1.00 .40
❑ 296 Luke Scott RC 2.00 .75
❑ 297 Chuck James RC 2.00 .75
❑ 298 Kennard Bibbs RC 1.00 .40
❑ 299 Steven Bondurant RC 1.00 .40
❑ 300 Thomas Oldham RC 1.00 .40
❑ 301 Nolan Ryan RET 5.00 2.00
❑ 302 Reggie Jackson RET 1.25 .50
❑ 303 Tom Seaver RET 1.25 .50
❑ 304 Al Kaline RET 2.00 .75
❑ 305 Cal Ripken RET 6.00 2.50
❑ 306 Josh Gibson RET 2.00 .75
❑ 307 Frank Robinson RET 1.00 .40
❑ 308 Duke Snider RET 1.25 .50
❑ 309 Wade Boggs RET 1.25 .50
❑ 310 Tony Gwynn RET 2.50 1.00
❑ 311 Carl Yastrzemski RET 2.00 .75
❑ 312 Ryne Sandberg RET 3.00 1.25
❑ 313 Gary Carter RET 1.00 .40
❑ 314 Brooks Robinson RET 1.25 .50
❑ 315 Ernie Banks RET 2.00 .75

2006 Topps Turkey Red

❑ COMPLETE SET (330) 250.00 150.00
❑ COMP.SET w/o SP's (275) 40.00 15.00
❑ COMMON CARD (316-580) .40 .15
❑ COMMON SP (316-580) 8.00 3.00
❑ SP STATED ODDS 1:4 HOBBY, 1:4 RETAIL
❑ SEE BECKETT.COM FOR SP CHECKLIST
❑ COMMON CL (571-580) .20 .07
❑ CL SEMIS 571-580 .30 .12
❑ COMMON RET (581-590) .75 .30
❑ COMMON RC (591-630) 1.00 .40
❑ OVERALL PLATE ODDS 1:477 H
❑ PLATE PRINT RUN 1 SET PER COLOR
❑ BLACK-CYAN-MAGENTA-YELLOW ISSUED
❑ NO PLATE PRICING DUE TO SCARCITY
❑ 316A A.Rodriguez Yanks 1.50 .60
❑ 316B A.Rodriguez Rangers SP 10.00 4.00
❑ 316C Alex Rodriguez M's SP 10.00 4.00
❑ 317 Jeff Francoeur SP 8.00 3.00
❑ 318 Shawn Green .40 .15
❑ 319 Daniel Cabrera .40 .15
❑ 320 Craig Biggio .60 .25
❑ 321 Jeremy Bonderman .40 .15
❑ 322 Mark Kotsay .40 .15
❑ 323 Cliff Floyd .40 .15
❑ 324 Jimmy Rollins .40 .15
❑ 325A M.Ordonez Tigers .40 .15
❑ 325B M.Ordonez W.Sox SP 8.00 3.00
❑ 326 C.C. Sabathia .40 .15
❑ 327 Oliver Perez .40 .15
❑ 328 Orlando Hudson .40 .15
❑ 329 Chris Ray .40 .15
❑ 330 Manny Ramirez .60 .25
❑ 331 Paul Konerko .40 .15
❑ 332 Joe Mauer SP 8.00 3.00
❑ 333 Jorge Posada .60 .25
❑ 334 Mark Ellis .40 .15
❑ 335 A.J. Burnett .40 .15
❑ 336 Mike Sweeney .40 .15
❑ 337 Shannon Stewart .40 .15
❑ 338 Jake Peavy SP 8.00 3.00
❑ 339A C.Delgado Mets SP 8.00 3.00
❑ 339B C.Delgado B.Jays SP 8.00 3.00
❑ 340 Brian Roberts .40 .15
❑ 341 Dontrelle Willis .40 .15
❑ 342 Aaron Rowand .40 .15
❑ 343A R.Sexson M's .40 .15
❑ 343B R.Sexson Brewers SP 8.00 3.00
❑ 344 Chris Carpenter .40 .15
❑ 345 Carlos Zambrano .40 .15
❑ 346 Nomar Garciaparra 1.00 .40
❑ 347 Carlos Lee .40 .15
❑ 348A P.Wilson Astros .40 .15
❑ 348B P.Wilson Marlins SP 8.00 3.00
❑ 349 Mariano Rivera 1.00 .40
❑ 350 Ichiro Suzuki SP 10.00 4.00
❑ 351A M.Piazza Padres 1.00 .40
❑ 351B Mike Piazza Mets SP 8.00 3.00
❑ 352 Jason Schmidt .40 .15
❑ 353 Jeff Weaver .40 .15
❑ 354 Rocco Baldelli .40 .15
❑ 355 Adam Dunn .40 .15
❑ 356 Jeromy Burnitz .40 .15
❑ 357 Chris Shelton SP 8.00 3.00
❑ 358 Chone Figgins SP 8.00 3.00
❑ 359 Javier Vazquez .40 .15
❑ 360 Chipper Jones 1.00 .40

No.	Player		
❑ 361	Frank Thomas	1.00	.40
❑ 362	Mark Loretta	.40	.15
❑ 363	Hideki Matsui	1.00	.40
❑ 364	J.J. Hardy SP	8.00	3.00
❑ 365	Todd Helton	.60	.25
❑ 366	Reggie Sanders	.40	.15
❑ 367	Jay Gibbons	.40	.15
❑ 368	Johnny Estrada	.40	.15
❑ 369	Grady Sizemore	.60	.25
❑ 370	Jim Thome	.60	.25
❑ 371	Ivan Rodriguez	.60	.25
❑ 372	Jason Bay	.40	.15
❑ 373	Carl Crawford	.40	.15
❑ 374	Adrian Beltre	.40	.15
❑ 375	Derrek Lee SP	8.00	3.00
❑ 376	Miguel Olivo	.40	.15
❑ 377	Roy Oswalt	.40	.15
❑ 378	Coco Crisp	.40	.15
❑ 379	Moises Alou	.40	.15
❑ 380	Kevin Millwood	.40	.15
❑ 381	Mark Grudzielanek	.40	.15
❑ 382	Justin Morneau	.40	.15
❑ 383	Austin Kearns	.40	.15
❑ 384	Brad Penny	.40	.15
❑ 385	Troy Glaus	.40	.15
❑ 386	Cliff Lee	.40	.15
❑ 387	Armando Benitez	.40	.15
❑ 388	Clint Barmes	.40	.15
❑ 389	Orlando Cabrera	.40	.15
❑ 390	Jim Edmonds SP	8.00	3.00
❑ 391	Jermaine Dye	.40	.15
❑ 392	Morgan Ensberg SP	8.00	3.00
❑ 393	Paul LoDuca	.40	.15
❑ 394	Eric Chavez	.40	.15
❑ 395	Greg Maddux SP	10.00	4.00
❑ 396	Jack Wilson	.40	.15
❑ 397	Omar Vizquel	.60	.25
❑ 398	Joe Nathan	.40	.15
❑ 399	Bobby Abreu	.40	.15
❑ 400	Barry Bonds SP	15.00	6.00
❑ 401	Gary Sheffield	.40	.15
❑ 402	John Patterson	.40	.15
❑ 403	J.D. Drew	.40	.15
❑ 404	Bruce Chen	.40	.15
❑ 405	Johnny Damon SP	8.00	3.00
❑ 406	Aubrey Huff	.40	.15
❑ 407	Mark Mulder	.40	.15
❑ 408	Jamie Moyer	.40	.15
❑ 409	Carlos Guillen	.40	.15
❑ 410	Andruw Jones SP	8.00	3.00
❑ 411	Jhonny Peralta SP	8.00	3.00
❑ 412	Doug Davis	.40	.15
❑ 413	Aaron Miles	.40	.15
❑ 414	Jon Lieber	.40	.15
❑ 415	Aaron Hill	.40	.15
❑ 416	Josh Beckett SP	8.00	3.00
❑ 417	Bobby Crosby	.40	.15
❑ 418	Noah Lowry SP	8.00	3.00
❑ 419	Sidney Ponson	.40	.15
❑ 420	Luis Castillo	.40	.15
❑ 421	Brad Wilkerson	.40	.15
❑ 422	Felix Hernandez SP	8.00	3.00
❑ 423	Vinny Castilla	.40	.15
❑ 424	Tom Glavine	.60	.25
❑ 425	Vladimir Guerrero	1.00	.40
❑ 426	Javy Lopez	.40	.15
❑ 427	Ronnie Belliard	.40	.15
❑ 428	Dmitri Young	.40	.15
❑ 429	Johan Santana	.60	.25
❑ 430A	D.Ortiz Red Sox SP	8.00	3.00
❑ 430B	D.Ortiz Twins SP	8.00	3.00
❑ 431	Ben Sheets	.40	.15
❑ 432	Matt Holliday	1.00	.40
❑ 433	Brian McCann	.40	.15
❑ 434	Joe Blanton	.40	.15
❑ 435	Sean Casey	.40	.15
❑ 436	Brad Lidge	.40	.15
❑ 437	Chad Tracy	.40	.15
❑ 438	Brett Myers	.40	.15
❑ 439	Matt Morris	.40	.15
❑ 440	Brian Giles	.40	.15
❑ 441	Zach Duke	.40	.15
❑ 442	Jose Lopez	.40	.15
❑ 443	Kris Benson	.40	.15
❑ 444	Jose Reyes SP	8.00	3.00
❑ 445	Travis Hafner	.40	.15
❑ 446	Orlando Hernandez	.40	.15
❑ 447	Edgar Renteria	.40	.15
❑ 448	Scott Podsednik	.40	.15
❑ 449	Nick Swisher SP	8.00	3.00
❑ 450	Derek Jeter SP	15.00	6.00
❑ 451	Scott Kazmir SP	8.00	3.00
❑ 452	Hank Blalock	.40	.15
❑ 453	Jake Westbrook	.40	.15
❑ 454	Miguel Cabrera	.60	.25
❑ 455A	K.Griffey Jr. Reds	1.50	.60
❑ 455B	K.Griffey Jr. M's SP	10.00	4.00
❑ 456	Rafael Furcal	.40	.15
❑ 457	Lance Berkman	.40	.15
❑ 458	Aramis Ramirez	.40	.15
❑ 459A	X.Nady Mets	.40	.15
❑ 459B	X.Nady Padres SP	8.00	3.00
❑ 460A	R.Johnson Yanks	1.00	.40
❑ 460B	R.Johnson Astros SP	8.00	3.00
❑ 461	Khalil Greene	.60	.25
❑ 462	Bartolo Colon	.40	.15
❑ 463	Mike Lowell	.40	.15
❑ 464	David DeJesus	.40	.15
❑ 465	Ryan Howard SP	10.00	4.00
❑ 466	Tim Salmon SP	8.00	3.00
❑ 467	Mark Buehrle SP	8.00	3.00
❑ 468	Curtis Granderson	.40	.15
❑ 469	Kerry Wood	.40	.15
❑ 470	Miguel Tejada	.40	.15
❑ 471	Geoff Jenkins	.40	.15
❑ 472	Jeremy Reed	.40	.15
❑ 473	David Eckstein	.40	.15
❑ 474	Lyle Overbay	.40	.15
❑ 475	Michael Young	.40	.15
❑ 476A	N.Johnson Nats SP	8.00	3.00
❑ 476B	N.Johnson Yanks SP	8.00	3.00
❑ 477	Carlos Beltran	.40	.15
❑ 478	Huston Street	.40	.15
❑ 479	Brandon Webb	.40	.15
❑ 480	Phil Nevin	.40	.15
❑ 481	Ryan Madson SP	8.00	3.00
❑ 482	Jason Giambi	.40	.15
❑ 483	Angel Berroa	.40	.15
❑ 484	Casey Blake	.40	.15
❑ 485	Pat Burrell	.40	.15
❑ 486	B.J. Ryan	.40	.15
❑ 487	Torii Hunter	.40	.15
❑ 488	Garret Anderson	.40	.15
❑ 489	Chase Utley SP	8.00	3.00
❑ 490	Matt Murton	.40	.15
❑ 491	Rich Harden	.40	.15
❑ 492	Garrett Atkins	.40	.15
❑ 493	Tadahito Iguchi SP	8.00	3.00
❑ 494	Jarrod Washburn	.40	.15
❑ 495	Carl Everett	.40	.15
❑ 496	Kameron Loe	.40	.15
❑ 497	Jorge Cantu SP	8.00	3.00
❑ 498	Chris Young	.40	.15
❑ 499	Marcus Giles	.40	.15
❑ 500	Albert Pujols	2.00	.75
❑ 501A	A.Soriano Nats SP	8.00	3.00
❑ 501B	A.Soriano Yanks SP	8.00	3.00
❑ 502	Randy Winn	.40	.15
❑ 503	Roy Halladay	.40	.15
❑ 504	Victor Martinez	.40	.15
❑ 505	Pedro Martinez	.60	.25
❑ 506	Rickie Weeks	.40	.15
❑ 507	Dan Johnson	.40	.15
❑ 508A	T.Hudson Braves	.40	.15
❑ 508B	T.Hudson A's SP	8.00	3.00
❑ 509	Mark Prior	.60	.25
❑ 510	Melvin Mora	.40	.15
❑ 511	Matt Clement	.40	.15
❑ 512	Brandon Inge	.40	.15
❑ 513	Mike Mussina	.60	.25
❑ 514	Mike Cameron	.40	.15
❑ 515	Barry Zito	.40	.15
❑ 516	Luis Gonzalez	.40	.15
❑ 517	Jose Castillo	.40	.15
❑ 518	Andy Pettitte	.60	.25
❑ 519	Wily Mo Pena	.40	.15
❑ 520	Billy Wagner	.40	.15
❑ 521	Ervin Santana SP	8.00	3.00
❑ 522	Juan Pierre	.40	.15
❑ 523	Dan Haren	.40	.15
❑ 524	Adrian Gonzalez SP	8.00	3.00
❑ 525	Robinson Cano	.60	.25
❑ 526	Jeff Kent	.40	.15
❑ 527	Cory Sullivan	.40	.15
❑ 528	Joe Crede SP	8.00	3.00
❑ 529	John Smoltz	.60	.25
❑ 530	David Wright	1.50	.60
❑ 531	Chad Cordero	.40	.15
❑ 532	Scott Rolen SP	8.00	3.00
❑ 533	Edwin Jackson	.40	.15
❑ 534	Doug Mientkiewicz	.40	.15
❑ 535	Mark Teixeira SP	8.00	3.00
❑ 536	Kelvim Escobar	.40	.15
❑ 537	Alex Rios	.40	.15
❑ 538	Jose Vidro	.40	.15
❑ 539	Alex Gonzalez	.40	.15
❑ 540	Yadier Molina	.40	.15
❑ 541	Ronny Cedeno SP	8.00	3.00
❑ 542	Mark Hendrickson	.40	.15
❑ 543	Russ Adams	.40	.15
❑ 544	Chris Capuano	.40	.15
❑ 545	Raul Ibanez	.40	.15
❑ 546	Vicente Padilla	.40	.15
❑ 547	Chris Duffy	.40	.15
❑ 548	Bengie Molina	.40	.15
❑ 549	Chien-Ming Wang	1.50	.60
❑ 550	Curt Schilling	.60	.25
❑ 551	Craig Wilson	.40	.15
❑ 552	Mike Lieberthal	.40	.15
❑ 553	Kazuo Matsui	.40	.15
❑ 554	Jeff Francis	.40	.15
❑ 555	Brady Clark	.40	.15
❑ 556	Willy Taveras	.40	.15
❑ 557	Mike Maroth	.40	.15
❑ 558	Bernie Williams	.60	.25
❑ 559	Edwin Encarnacion	.40	.15
❑ 560	Vernon Wells	.40	.15
❑ 561A	L.Hernandez Nats	.40	.15
❑ 561B	L.Hernandez Giants SP	8.00	3.00
❑ 562	Kenny Rogers	.40	.15
❑ 563	Steve Finley	.40	.15
❑ 564	Trot Nixon	.40	.15
❑ 565	Jonny Gomes SP	8.00	3.00
❑ 566	Brandon Phillips	.40	.15
❑ 567	Shawn Chacon	.40	.15
❑ 568	Dave Bush	.40	.15
❑ 569	Jose Guillen	.40	.15
❑ 570	Gustavo Chacin	.40	.15
❑ 571	A.Rod Safe at the Plate CL	.75	.30
❑ 572	Pujols At Bat CL	1.00	.40
❑ 573	Bonds On Deck CL	1.00	.40
❑ 574	Breaking Up Two CL	.20	.07
❑ 575	Conference On The Mound CL	.50	.20
❑ 576	Touch Em All CL	.75	.30
❑ 577	Avoiding The Runner CL	.20	.07
❑ 578	Bunting The Runner Over CL	.20	.07
❑ 579	In The Hole CL	.20	.07
❑ 580	Jeter Steals Third CL	1.25	.50
❑ 581	Nolan Ryan RET	5.00	2.00
❑ 582	Cal Ripken RET	8.00	3.00
❑ 583	Carl Yastrzemski RET	3.00	1.25
❑ 584	Duke Snider RET	1.25	.50
❑ 585	Tom Seaver RET	1.25	.50
❑ 586	Mickey Mantle RET	10.00	4.00
❑ 587	Jim Palmer RET	.75	.30
❑ 588	Gary Carter RET	.75	.30
❑ 589	Stan Musial RET	3.00	1.25
❑ 590	Luis Aparicio RET	.75	.30
❑ 591	Prince Fielder (RC)	4.00	1.50
❑ 592	Conor Jackson (RC)	1.50	.60
❑ 593	Jeremy Hermida (RC)	1.00	.40
❑ 594	Jeff Mathis (RC)	1.00	.40
❑ 595	Alay Soler RC	1.00	.40
❑ 596	Ryan Spilborghs (RC)	1.50	.60
❑ 597	Chuck James (RC)	1.50	.60
❑ 598	Josh Barfield (RC)	1.00	.40
❑ 599	Ian Kinsler (RC)	1.50	.60
❑ 600	Val Majewski (RC)	1.00	.40
❑ 601	Brian Slocum (RC)	1.00	.40
❑ 602	Matt Kemp (RC)	1.50	.60
❑ 603	Nate McLouth (RC)	1.00	.40
❑ 604	Sean Marshall (RC)	1.00	.40
❑ 605	Brian Bannister (RC)	1.00	.40
❑ 606	Ryan Zimmerman (RC)	6.00	2.50
❑ 607	Kendry Morales (RC)	2.50	1.00
❑ 608	Jonathan Papelbon (RC)	5.00	2.00
❑ 609	Matt Cain (RC)	1.50	.60
❑ 610	Anderson Hernandez (RC)	1.00	.40

❑ 611 Jose Capellan (RC) 1.00 .40
❑ 612 Lastings Milledge (RC) 1.50 .60
❑ 613 Francisco Liriano (RC) 5.00 2.00
❑ 614 Hanley Ramirez (RC) 2.50 1.00
❑ 615 Brian Anderson (RC) 1.00 .40
❑ 616 Reggie Abercrombie (RC) 1.00 .40
❑ 617 Erick Aybar (RC) 1.00 .40
❑ 618 James Loney (RC) 1.50 .60
❑ 619 Joel Zumaya (RC) 2.50 1.00
❑ 620 Travis Ishikawa (RC) 1.00 .40
❑ 621 Jason Kubel (RC) 1.00 .40
❑ 622 Drew Meyer (RC) 1.00 .40
❑ 623 Kenji Johjima RC 5.00 2.00
❑ 624 Fausto Carmona (RC) 1.00 .40
❑ 625 Nick Markakis (RC) 1.50 .60
❑ 626 John Rheinecker (RC) 1.00 .40
❑ 627 Melky Cabrera (RC) 1.50 .60
❑ 628 Michael Pelfrey RC 4.00 1.50
❑ 629 Dan Uggla (RC) 2.50 1.00
❑ 630 Justin Verlander (RC) 4.00 1.50

2007 Topps Turkey Red

❑ COMPLETE SET (200) 200.00 150.00
❑ COMP.SET w/o SP's (150) 30.00 12.50
❑ COMMON CARD (1-186) .30 .12
❑ COMMON RC (1-186) .40 .15
❑ COMMON SP (1-186) 6.00 2.50
❑ SP ODDS 1:4 HOBBY, 1:4 RETAIL
❑ COMMON AD BACK (1-186) 6.00 2.50
❑ AD BACK ODDS 1:4 HOBBY,1:4 RETAIL
❑ 1 Ryan Howard 1.25 .50
❑ 1b R.Howard Ad Back SP 10.00 4.00
❑ 2 Dontrelle Willis .30 .12
❑ 3 Matt Cain .50 .20
❑ 4 John Maine .30 .12
❑ 5 Cole Hamels .50 .20
❑ 6 Corey Patterson .30 .12
❑ 7 Mickey Mantle SP 25.00 10.00
❑ 8 Servin Up Strikes Joham Santana CL .50 .20
❑ 9 Josh Beckett .30 .12
❑ 10 Jimmy Rollins .30 .12
❑ 11 Kenji Johjima .75 .30
❑ 12 Orlando Hernandez .30 .12
❑ 13 Jorge Posada Play at the Plate CL .50 .20
❑ 14 Ivan Rodriguez .50 .20
❑ 15 Ichiro Suzuki 1.25 .50
❑ 15b I.Suzuki Ad Back SP 10.00 4.00
❑ 16 Double Griffey CL 1.25 .50
❑ 17 Stephen Drew .50 .20
❑ 18 B.J. Upton .30 .12
❑ 19 Mickey Mantle 2.50 1.00
❑ 20 Alex Rodriguez 1.25 .50
❑ 20b A.Rod Ad Back SP 10.00 4.00
❑ 21 Adam Dunn .30 .12
❑ 22 Adam Lind SP (RC) 6.00 2.50
❑ 23 Adrian Gonzalez .30 .12
❑ 24 Akinori Iwamura RC 1.00 .40
❑ 25 Albert Pujols 1.50 .60
❑ 25b A.Pujols Ad Back SP 10.00 4.00
❑ 26 Frank Thomas .75 .30
❑ 27 Roy Halladay .30 .12
❑ 28 Alejandro De Aza RC .60 .25
❑ 29 Alex Gordon RC 2.00 .75
❑ 30 Barry Bonds 1.50 .60
❑ 31 Andrew Miller RC 2.50 1.00
❑ 32 Andruw Jones .50 .20
❑ 33 Kurt Suzuki SP (RC) 6.00 2.50
❑ 34 Mickey Mantle 2.50 1.00
❑ 35 Andy Pettitte .50 .20
❑ 36 Tadahito Iguchi .30 .12
❑ 37 Edgar Renteria .30 .12
❑ 38 Tim Hudson .30 .12
❑ 39 Micah Owings (RC) .40 .15
❑ 40 Chipper Jones .75 .30
❑ 40b C.Jones Ad Back SP 8.00 3.00
❑ 41 Barry Zito .30 .12
❑ 42 Dice-K CL 3.00 1.25
❑ 43 Jarrod Saltalamacchia SP (RC) 6.00 2.50
❑ 44 Bill Hall .30 .12
❑ 45 Billy Butler (RC) .60 .25
❑ 46 Billy Wagner .30 .12
❑ 47 Rich Harden SP 6.00 2.50
❑ 48 Prince Albert CL 1.50 .60
❑ 49 Brandon Inge .30 .12
❑ 50 Jason Giambi .30 .12
❑ 51 Brandon Webb .30 .12
❑ 52 Brandon Wood (RC) .40 .15
❑ 53 Swiping Second Carl Crawford CL .30 .12
❑ 54 Brian Giles .30 .12
❑ 55 Josh Hamilton (RC) 2.00 .75
❑ 56 C.Utley Ad Back SP 8.00 3.00
❑ 57 Miguel Montero (RC) .40 .15
❑ 58 Carl Crawford .30 .12
❑ 59 Carlos Beltran .30 .12
❑ 60 Mariano Rivera .75 .30
❑ 61 Carlos Delgado .30 .12
❑ 62 Carlos Lee SP 6.00 2.50
❑ 63 Carlos Zambrano SP 6.00 2.50
❑ 64 Miguel Tejada .30 .12
❑ 65 Mike Cameron .30 .12
❑ 66 Chase Utley SP 8.00 3.00
❑ 67 Chase Wright RC 1.00 .40
❑ 68 Chien-Ming Wang 1.25 .50
❑ 69 Nick Swisher .30 .12
❑ 70 David Wright 1.25 .50
❑ 71 Mike Piazza SP 8.00 3.00
❑ 72 Chris Carpenter .30 .12
❑ 73 Mark Buehrle SP 6.00 2.50
❑ 74 Torii Hunter SP 6.00 2.50
❑ 75 Tyler Clippard (RC) .60 .25
❑ 76 Nick Markakis .50 .20
❑ 77 Mickey Mantle 2.50 1.00
❑ 78 Curt Schilling .50 .20
❑ 79 Curtis Granderson .30 .12
❑ 80 Craig Biggio .50 .20
❑ 81 Juan Pierre .30 .12
❑ 82 Dallas Braden SP RC 6.00 2.50
❑ 83 Dan Haren SP 8.00 3.00
❑ 84 Dan Uggla .50 .20
❑ 85 Danny Putnam (RC) .40 .15
❑ 86 David DeJesus .30 .12
❑ 87 David Eckstein .30 .12
❑ 88 Tim Lincecum RC 3.00 1.25
❑ 89 Johnny Damon SP 6.00 2.50
❑ 90 Justin Morneau .30 .12
❑ 91 Delmon Young (RC) .60 .25
❑ 92 Homer Bailey (RC) .60 .25
❑ 93 Carlos Gomez RC .60 .25
❑ 94 Josh Fields SP (RC) 6.00 2.50
❑ 95 Derek Jeter 2.00 .75
❑ 95b D.Jeter Ad Back SP 15.00 6.00
❑ 96 Derek Lee .30 .12
❑ 97 Don Kelly (RC) .40 .15
❑ 98 Doug Slaten RC .40 .15
❑ 99 Dustin Moseley .30 .12
❑ 100 Gary Sheffield .30 .12
❑ 101 Orlando Hudson SP 6.00 2.50
❑ 102 Elijah Dukes RC .60 .25
❑ 103 Eric Byrnes SP 6.00 2.50
❑ 104 Eric Chavez .30 .12
❑ 105 Phil Hughes (RC) 2.00 .75
❑ 105b Hughes Ad Back SP (RC) 10.00 4.00
❑ 106 Felix Hernandez SP 6.00 2.50
❑ 106b Felix Hernandez Ad Back SP 6.00 2.50
❑ 107 Mickey Mantle 2.50 1.00
❑ 108 Felix Pie (RC) .40 .15
❑ 109 Captain Jeter CL 2.00 .75
❑ 110 Daisuke Matsuzaka RC 4.00 1.50
❑ 110b Dice-K Ad Back SP RC 15.00 6.00
❑ 111 Francisco Rodriguez .30 .12
❑ 112 Ramon Hernandez .30 .12
❑ 113 Randy Johnson .75 .30
❑ 114 Gary Matthews .30 .12
❑ 115 Prince Fielder .75 .30
❑ 116 Vladdy Yard CL .75 .30
❑ 117 Mickey Mantle 2.50 1.00
❑ 118 Hideki Matsui .75 .30
❑ 119 Hideki Okajima RC 2.00 .75
❑ 120 Manny Ramirez .50 .20
❑ 121 H.Pence SP (RC) 15.00 6.00
❑ 122 Roy Oswalt .30 .12
❑ 123 Josh Willingham SP 6.00 2.50
❑ 124 Tom Gordon SP 6.00 2.50
❑ 125 Michael Young .30 .12
❑ 126 J.D. Drew .30 .12
❑ 127 Ryan Zimmerman .75 .30
❑ 128 James Shields SP 8.00 3.00
❑ 129 Jack Wilson .30 .12
❑ 130 David Ortiz .75 .30
❑ 130b D.Ortiz Ad Back SP 8.00 3.00
❑ 131 Jose Reyes CL .75 .30
❑ 132 Jamie Vermilyea RC .40 .15
❑ 133 Jason Bay .30 .12
❑ 134 Scott Kazmir SP 6.00 2.50
❑ 135 Jason Isringhausen SP 8.00 3.00
❑ 136 Jason Marquis SP 6.00 2.50
❑ 137 Jason Schmidt .30 .12
❑ 138 Shawn Green .30 .12
❑ 139 Jeff Francoeur SP 8.00 3.00
❑ 140 Alfonso Soriano .30 .12
❑ 141 Kevin Kouzmanoff (RC) .40 .15
❑ 142 Jered Weaver .50 .20
❑ 143 Todd Helton SP 6.00 2.50
❑ 144 Jermaine Dye .30 .12
❑ 145 Jim Thome .50 .20
❑ 146 Tom Glavine SP 6.00 2.50
❑ 147 Joe Mauer .50 .20
❑ 148 Joe Nathan .30 .12
❑ 149 Joe Smith RC .40 .15
❑ 150 Ken Griffey Jr. 1.25 .50
❑ 150b Griffey Ad Back SP 10.00 4.00
❑ 151 Grady Sizemore .50 .20
❑ 152 Sammy Sosa SP 8.00 3.00
❑ 153 Andy LaRoche (RC) .40 .15
❑ 154 Travis Buck (RC) .40 .15
❑ 155 Alex Rios .30 .12
❑ 156 Travis Hafner .30 .12
❑ 157 Jake Peavy .30 .12
❑ 158 Jeff Kent .30 .12
❑ 159 Johan Santana .50 .20
❑ 159b Johan Santana Ad Back SP 6.00 2.50
❑ 160 Ivan Rodriguez .50 .20
❑ 161 Trevor Hoffman .30 .12
❑ 162 Troy Glaus .30 .12
❑ 163 Troy Tulowitzki (RC) 1.00 .40
❑ 164 Jorge Posada .50 .20
❑ 165 Kei Igawa SP RC 8.00 3.00
❑ 166 Jose Reyes .75 .30
❑ 167 Mickey Mantle 2.50 1.00
❑ 168 Utley Streak CL .75 .30
❑ 169 Justin Verlander .75 .30
❑ 170 Hanley Ramirez .50 .20
❑ 171 Kelly Johnson SP 6.00 2.50
❑ 172 Kelvin Jimenez RC .40 .15
❑ 173 Roger Clemens 1.50 .60
❑ 174 Khalil Greene SP 6.00 2.50
❑ 175 Lance Berkman .30 .12
❑ 176 Turning Two Hanley Ramirez CL .50 .20
❑ 177 Kyle Kendrick RC 1.00 .40
❑ 178 Magglio Ordonez .30 .12
❑ 179 Marcus Giles SP 6.00 2.50
❑ 180 Miguel Cabrera .50 .20
❑ 180b Miguel Cabrera Ad Back SP 6.00 2.50
❑ 181 Mark Teahen .30 .12
❑ 182 Mark Teixeira SP 6.00 2.50
❑ 183 Matt Chico SP (RC) 6.00 2.50
❑ 184 Matt Holliday .40 .15
❑ 185 Vladimir Guerrero .75 .30
❑ 185b V. Guerrero Ad Back SP 8.00 3.00
❑ 186 Yovani Gallardo (RC) 1.00 .40

2008 UD A Piece of History

❑ COMPLETE SET (200) 40.00 15.00
❑ COMMON CARD (1-100) .50 .20
❑ COMMON ROOKIE (101-150) 1.00 .40
❑ COMMON HM (151-200) .50 .20
❑ 1 Brandon Webb .50 .20
❑ 2 Dan Haren .50 .20

❑ 3 Justin Upton 1.25 .50
❑ 4 Chris B. Young .50 .20
❑ 5 Mark Teixeira .75 .30
❑ 6 Jeff Francoeur .75 .30
❑ 7 John Smoltz 1.25 .50
❑ 8 Tom Glavine .75 .30
❑ 9 Brian McCann .75 .30
❑ 10 Chipper Jones 1.50 .60
❑ 11 Erik Bedard .50 .20
❑ 12 Nick Markakis .75 .30
❑ 13 Josh Beckett .75 .30
❑ 14 David Ortiz 1.25 .50
❑ 15 Manny Ramirez 1.25 .50
❑ 16 Dustin Pedroia .75 .30
❑ 17 Grady Sizemore .75 .30
❑ 18 Jonathan Papelbon .75 .30
❑ 19 Daisuke Matsuzaka 2.00 .75
❑ 20 Curt Schilling .75 .30
❑ 21 Alfonso Soriano .75 .30
❑ 22 Aramis Ramirez .50 .20
❑ 23 Carlos Zambrano .50 .20
❑ 24 Nick Swisher .50 .20
❑ 25 Jim Thome .75 .30
❑ 26 Ken Griffey Jr. 2.00 .75
❑ 27 Adam Dunn .50 .20
❑ 28 Aaron Harang .50 .20
❑ 29 Matt Holliday .75 .30
❑ 30 Troy Tulowitzki .75 .30
❑ 31 Todd Helton .75 .30
❑ 32 Magglio Ordonez .75 .30
❑ 33 Justin Verlander .75 .30
❑ 34 Miguel Cabrera .75 .30
❑ 35 Gary Sheffield .50 .20
❑ 36 Ivan Rodriguez .75 .30
❑ 37 Dontrelle Willis .50 .20
❑ 38 Hanley Ramirez 1.25 .50
❑ 39 Andrew Miller .75 .30
❑ 40 Lance Berkman .75 .30
❑ 41 Roy Oswalt .50 .20
❑ 42 Carlos Lee .50 .20
❑ 43 Hunter Pence 1.25 .50
❑ 44 Alex Gordon 1.25 .50
❑ 45 Mark Teahen .50 .20
❑ 46 Torii Hunter .50 .20
❑ 47 Vladimir Guerrero 1.25 .50
❑ 48 Victor Martinez .50 .20
❑ 49 Andruw Jones .50 .20
❑ 50 James Loney .75 .30
❑ 51 Russell Martin .50 .20
❑ 52 Jeff Kent .50 .20
❑ 53 Ryan Braun 1.50 .60
❑ 54 Prince Fielder 1.25 .50
❑ 55 Joe Mauer .75 .30
❑ 56 Justin Morneau .75 .30
❑ 57 Delmon Young .75 .30
❑ 58 Jose Reyes .75 .30
❑ 59 David Wright 1.50 .60
❑ 60 Carlos Beltran .50 .20
❑ 61 Johan Santana 1.25 .50
❑ 62 Pedro Martinez .75 .30
❑ 63 Alex Rodriguez 2.00 .75
❑ 64 Derek Jeter 3.00 1.25
❑ 65 Hideki Matsui 1.25 .50
❑ 66 Robinson Cano .75 .30
❑ 67 Joba Chamberlain 2.00 .75
❑ 68 Phil Hughes 1.25 .50
❑ 69 Mariano Rivera 1.25 .50
❑ 70 Rich Harden .50 .20
❑ 71 Joe Blanton .50 .20
❑ 72 Cole Hamels .75 .30
❑ 73 Ryan Howard 1.50 .60
❑ 74 Jimmy Rollins .75 .30
❑ 75 Chase Utley 1.25 .50
❑ 76 Jason Bay .50 .20
❑ 77 Freddy Sanchez .50 .20
❑ 78 Jake Peavy .50 .20
❑ 79 Greg Maddux 1.50 .60
❑ 80 Trevor Hoffman .50 .20
❑ 81 Barry Zito .50 .20
❑ 82 Tim Lincecum 1.25 .50
❑ 83 Travis Hafner .50 .20
❑ 84 C.C. Sabathia .50 .20
❑ 85 Felix Hernandez .75 .30
❑ 86 Ichiro Suzuki 2.00 .75
❑ 87 Troy Glaus .75 .30
❑ 88 Albert Pujols 2.50 1.00
❑ 89 Chris Carpenter .50 .20
❑ 90 Scott Kazmir .75 .30
❑ 91 Carl Crawford .50 .20
❑ 92 B.J. Upton .75 .30
❑ 93 Michael Young .50 .20
❑ 94 Josh Hamilton 1.50 .60
❑ 95 Vernon Wells .50 .20
❑ 96 Alex Rios .50 .20
❑ 97 Scott Rolen .75 .30
❑ 98 Frank Thomas 1.25 .50
❑ 99 Chad Cordero .50 .20
❑ 100 Ryan Zimmerman .75 .30
❑ 101 Emilio Bonifacio RC 1.50 .60
❑ 102 Bill Murphy (RC) 1.00 .40
❑ 103 Billy Buckner (RC) 1.00 .40
❑ 104 Brandon Jones RC 2.50 1.00
❑ 105 Clint Sammons (RC) 1.00 .40
❑ 106 Clay Buchholz (RC) 2.50 1.00
❑ 107 Kevin Hart (RC) 1.00 .40
❑ 108 Lance Broadway (RC) 1.00 .40
❑ 109 Donny Lucy (RC) 1.00 .40
❑ 110 Heath Phillips RC 1.50 .60
❑ 111 Ryan Hanigan RC 1.50 .60
❑ 112 Joey Votto (RC) 1.50 .60
❑ 113 Joe Koshansky (RC) 1.00 .40
❑ 114 Josh Newman RC 1.50 .60
❑ 115 Seth Smith (RC) 1.00 .40
❑ 116 Harvey Garcia (RC) 1.00 .40
❑ 117 Chris Seddon (RC) 1.00 .40
❑ 118 Josh Anderson (RC) 1.00 .40
❑ 119 Troy Patton (RC) 1.00 .40
❑ 120 Felipe Paulino RC 1.50 .60
❑ 121 J.R. Towles RC 2.50 1.00
❑ 122 Luke Hochevar RC 3.00 1.25
❑ 123 Chin-Lung Hu (RC) 1.50 .60
❑ 124 Jonathan Meloan RC 1.50 .60
❑ 125 Sam Fuld (RC) 1.00 .40
❑ 126 Mitch Stetter RC 1.50 .60
❑ 127 Jose Morales (RC) 1.00 .40
❑ 128 Carlos Muniz RC 1.50 .60
❑ 129 Alberto Gonzalez RC 1.50 .60
❑ 130 Ian Kennedy RC 3.00 1.25
❑ 131 Ross Ohlendorf RC 1.50 .60
❑ 132 Jonathan Albaladejo RC 1.50 .60
❑ 133 Daric Barton (RC) 1.00 .40
❑ 134 Jerry Blevins RC 1.50 .60
❑ 135 Dave Davidson RC 1.50 .60
❑ 136 Nyjer Morgan (RC) 1.00 .40
❑ 137 Steve Pearce RC 1.50 .60
❑ 138 Colt Morton RC 1.50 .60
❑ 139 Eugenio Velez RC 1.00 .40
❑ 140 Erick Threets (RC) 1.00 .40
❑ 141 Bronson Sardinha (RC) 1.00 .40
❑ 142 Wladimir Balentien (RC) 1.00 .40
❑ 143 Jeff Clement (RC) 1.00 .40
❑ 144 Rob Johnson (RC) 1.00 .40
❑ 145 Jeff Ridgway RC 1.50 .60
❑ 146 Justin Ruggiano RC 1.50 .60
❑ 147 Luis Mendoza (RC) 1.00 .40
❑ 148 Bill White RC 1.00 .40
❑ 149 Ross Detwiler RC 2.50 1.00
❑ 150 Justin Maxwell RC 1.50 .60
❑ 151 Fall of the Berlin Wall .50 .20
❑ 152 Wright Brothers 1st Flight .50 .20
❑ 153 Signing of Declaration of Independence .50 .20
❑ 154 Columbus Discovers America .50 .20
❑ 155 First Space Shuttle launch .50 .20
❑ 156 Hawaii becomes 50th state .50 .20
❑ 157 Statue of Liberty given to U.S. .50 .20
❑ 158 Gettysburg Address .50 .20
❑ 159 Completion of Transcontinental Railroad .50 .20
❑ 160 Opening of Panama Canal .50 .20
❑ 161 U.S. enters World War 1 .50 .20
❑ 162 Treaty of Versailles .50 .20
❑ 163 Television invented .50 .20
❑ 164 Geneva Summit .50 .20
❑ 165 Woodstock .50 .20
❑ 166 Invention of Cotton Gin .50 .20
❑ 167 Eiffel Tower .50 .20
❑ 168 Suez Canal opens .50 .20
❑ 169 New York City Subway opens .50 .20
❑ 170 Polio Vaccine invented .50 .20
❑ 171 Bell X-1 Breaks Sound Barrier .50 .20
❑ 172 USS Enterprise Aircraft Carrier launched .50 .20
❑ 173 Hubble Telescope launches .50 .20
❑ 174 N.A.T.O. created .50 .20
❑ 175 Sputnik launched by Russia .50 .20
❑ 176 U.S.S.R. Crumbles .50 .20
❑ 177 Boston Tea Party .50 .20
❑ 178 Paul Revere's Ride .50 .20
❑ 179 Civil Rights Act Passes .50 .20
❑ 180 Hindenburg blows up .50 .20
❑ 181 Franklin discovers electricity .50 .20
❑ 182 Creation of the Internet .50 .20
❑ 183 1st World's Fair - 1851 London .50 .20
❑ 184 Pope John Paul II .50 .20
❑ 185 1st Heart Transplant .50 .20
❑ 186 California Gold Rush .50 .20
❑ 187 Creation of the personal computer .50 .20
❑ 188 Louisiana Purchase .50 .20
❑ 189 1st Dictionary published .50 .20
❑ 190 Steam Engine invented .50 .20
❑ 191 History of Nobel Prize .50 .20
❑ 192 Liberty Bell .50 .20
❑ 193 International Space Station .50 .20
❑ 194 Human Genome Project .50 .20
❑ 195 The Supreme Court .50 .20
❑ 196 Lewis and Clark .50 .20
❑ 197 Battle of the Alamo .50 .20
❑ 198 The creation of baseball .50 .20
❑ 199 Juan Ponce De Leon .50 .20
❑ 200 Jamestown - 1607 .50 .20

2007 UD Black

❑ COMMON JSY AU (1-42) 30.00 12.50
❑ 1-42 PRINT RUNS B/WN 16-75 COPIES PER
❑ NO PRICING ON QTY 25 OR LESS
❑ COMMON AU RC (43-72) 25.00 10.00
❑ 43-72 PRINT RUN 99 SER.#'d SETS
❑ EXCHANGE DEADLINE 11/26/2009
❑ AUTO PRINTING PLATES RANDOMLY INSERTED
❑ PLATE PRINT RUN 1 SET PER COLOR
❑ BLACK-CYAN-MAGENTA-YELLOW ISSUED
❑ NO PLATE PRICING DUE TO SCARCITY
❑ 1 B.Webb Jsy AU/75 50.00 20.00
❑ 2 T.Hudson Jsy AU/75 50.00 20.00
❑ 3 C.Ripken Jsy AU/75 175.00 100.00
❑ 4 N.Markakis Jsy AU/35 60.00 30.00
❑ 5 D.Ortiz Jsy AU/52 120.00 60.00
❑ 6 J.Papelbon Jsy AU/75 60.00 30.00
❑ 7 C.Crisp Jsy AU/43 40.00 15.00
❑ 8 D.Lee Jsy AU/75 50.00 20.00

❑ 9 P.Konerko Jsy AU/75	40.00	15.00
❑ 10 A.Dunn Jsy AU/75	50.00	20.00
❑ 11 K.Griffey Jr. Jsy AU/75	100.00	50.00
❑ 12 T.Hafner Jsy AU/75	60.00	30.00
❑ 13 V.Martinez Jsy AU/75	40.00	15.00
❑ 14 Garrett Atkins Jsy AU/75	30.00	12.50
❑ 15 J.Verlander Jsy AU/75	60.00	30.00
❑ 16 Jeremy Bonderman Jsy AU/75	30.00	12.50
❑ 17 C.Grand Jsy AU/75	50.00	20.00
❑ 18 H.Ramirez Jsy AU/75	50.00	20.00
❑ 19 Dan Uggla Jsy AU/75	30.00	12.50
❑ 20 L.Berkman Jsy AU/75	60.00	30.00
❑ 21 Mark Teahen Jsy AU/75	30.00	12.50
❑ 22 John Lackey Jsy AU/75	30.00	12.50
❑ 23 H.Kendrick Jsy AU/75	40.00	15.00
❑ 24 R.Martin Jsy AU/75	50.00	20.00
❑ 25 P.Fielder Jsy AU/75	80.00	40.00
❑ 26 Torii Hunter Jsy AU/75	30.00	12.50
❑ 27 J.Morneau Jsy AU/75	50.00	20.00
❑ 28 J.Maine Jsy AU/75	50.00	20.00
❑ 29 Derek Jeter Jsy AU/16		
❑ 30 Dan Haren Jsy AU/75	30.00	12.50
❑ 31 Eric Chavez Jsy AU/75	30.00	12.50
❑ 32 C.Hamels Jsy AU/75	60.00	30.00
❑ 33 J.Bay Jsy AU/75	40.00	15.00
❑ 34 Adrian Gonzalez Jsy AU/75	30.00	12.50
❑ 35 C.Young Jsy AU/75	40.00	15.00
❑ 36 M.Cain Jsy AU/75	40.00	15.00
❑ 37 F.Hernandez Jsy AU/75	50.00	20.00
❑ 38 C.Duncan Jsy AU/75	40.00	15.00
❑ 39 B.Upton Jsy AU/75	50.00	20.00
❑ 40 Ian Kinsler Jsy AU/75	50.00	20.00
❑ 41 R.Halladay Jsy AU/75	50.00	20.00
❑ 42a Chad Cordero Jsy AU/75	30.00	12.50
❑ 42b Chad Cordero Jsy AU/52	30.00	12.50
❑ 43 Adam Lind AU (RC)	25.00	10.00
❑ 44 A.Iwamura AU RC	100.00	50.00
❑ 45 Alex Gordon AU RC	120.00	60.00
❑ 46 A.LaRoche AU (RC)	40.00	15.00
❑ 47 Billy Butler AU (RC)	60.00	30.00
❑ 48 David Murphy AU (RC)	25.00	10.00
❑ 49 B.Wood AU (RC)	30.00	12.50
❑ 50 Carlos Gomez AU RC	60.00	30.00
❑ 51 Chase Headley AU (RC)	40.00	15.00
❑ 52 Curtis Thigpen AU (RC)	25.00	10.00
❑ 53 J.Chamberlain AU RC	400.00	300.00
❑ 54 Delmon Young AU (RC)	50.00	20.00
❑ 55 Felix Pie AU (RC)	30.00	12.50
❑ 56 Homer Bailey AU (RC)	50.00	20.00
❑ 57 Hunter Pence AU (RC)	80.00	40.00
❑ 58 Josh Hamilton AU (RC)	100.00	50.00
❑ 59 Kei Igawa AU RC	80.00	40.00
❑ 60 Kevin Slowey AU (RC)	50.00	20.00
❑ 61 Kurt Suzuki AU (RC)	30.00	12.50
❑ 62 Mark Reynolds AU RC	150.00	75.00
❑ 63 D.Matsuzaka AU RC	500.00	350.00
❑ 64 Justin Upton AU RC	150.00	75.00
❑ 65 Phil Hughes AU (RC)	100.00	50.00
❑ 66 Ryan Braun AU (RC)	120.00	60.00
❑ 67 Ryan Sweeney AU (RC)	25.00	10.00
❑ 68 Sean Gallagher AU (RC)	25.00	10.00
❑ 69 Tim Lincecum AU RC	250.00	150.00
❑ 70 Travis Buck AU (RC)	25.00	10.00
❑ 71 T.Tulowitzki AU (RC)	100.00	50.00
❑ 72 Y.Gallardo AU (RC)	60.00	30.00

2007 UD Masterpieces

❑ COMPLETE SET (90)	40.00	15.00
❑ COMMON CARD (1-90)	.60	.25
❑ COMMON ROOKIE (1-90)	.60	.25
❑ PRINTING PLATES RANDOMLY INSERTED		
❑ PLATE PRINT RUN 1 SET PER COLOR		
❑ BLACK-CYAN-MAGENTA-YELLOW ISSUED		
❑ NO PLATE PRICING DUE TO SCARCITY		
❑ 1 Babe Ruth	4.00	1.50
❑ 2 Babe Ruth	4.00	1.50
❑ 3 Bobby Thomson	1.00	.40
❑ 4 Bill Mazeroski	1.00	.40
❑ 5 Carlton Fisk	1.00	.40
❑ 6 Kirk Gibson	.60	.25
❑ 7 Don Larsen	.60	.25
❑ 8 Lou Gehrig	3.00	1.25
❑ 9 Roger Maris	1.50	.60
❑ 10 Cal Ripken Jr.	6.00	2.50
❑ 11 Bucky Dent	.60	.25
❑ 12 Ryan Howard	2.50	1.00
❑ 13 Brooks Robinson	1.00	.40
❑ 14 David Ortiz	1.50	.60
❑ 15 Hideki Matsui	1.50	.60
❑ 16 Roger Clemens	2.50	1.00
❑ 17 Sandy Koufax	5.00	2.00
❑ 18 Reggie Jackson	1.00	.40
❑ 19 Ozzie Smith	2.50	1.00
❑ 20 Ty Cobb	2.50	1.00
❑ 21 Walter Johnson	1.50	.60
❑ 22 Babe Ruth	4.00	1.50
❑ 23 Roy Campanella	1.50	.60
❑ 24 Jackie Robinson	1.50	.60
❑ 25 Carl Yastrzemski	2.50	1.00
❑ 26 Sandy Koufax	5.00	2.00
❑ 27 Daisuke Matsuzaka RC	6.00	2.50
❑ 28 Kei Igawa RC	1.50	.60
❑ 29 Ken Griffey Jr.	2.50	1.00
❑ 30 Derek Jeter	4.00	1.50
❑ 31 David Ortiz	1.50	.60
❑ 32 Vladimir Guerrero	1.50	.60
❑ 33 Chase Utley	1.50	.60
❑ 34 Troy Tulowitzki (RC)	1.50	.60
❑ 35 Joe Mauer	1.00	.40
❑ 36 Travis Hafner	.60	.25
❑ 37 Miguel Cabrera	1.00	.40
❑ 38 Albert Pujols	3.00	1.25
❑ 39 Frank Thomas	1.50	.60
❑ 40 Mike Piazza	1.50	.60
❑ 41 Josh Hamilton	1.50	.60
❑ 42 T.Gwynn/C.Ripken Jr.	6.00	2.50
❑ 43 Ichiro Suzuki	2.50	1.00
❑ 44 Hideki Matsui	1.50	.60
❑ 45 Ken Griffey Jr.	2.50	1.00
❑ 46 Michael Jordan	4.00	1.50
❑ 47 John F. Kennedy	2.50	1.00
❑ 48 Randy Johnson	1.50	.60
❑ 49 Albert Pujols	3.00	1.25
❑ 50 Carlos Beltran	.60	.25
❑ 51 Delmon Young (RC)	1.00	.40
❑ 52 Johan Santana	1.00	.40
❑ 53 Cal Ripken Jr.	6.00	2.50
❑ 54 Y.Berra/J.Robinson	1.50	.60
❑ 55 Cal Ripken Jr.	6.00	2.50
❑ 56 Hanley Ramirez	1.00	.40
❑ 57 Victor Martinez	.60	.25
❑ 58 Cole Hamels	1.00	.40
❑ 59 Bobby Doerr	.60	.25
❑ 60 Bruce Sutter	.60	.25
❑ 61 Jason Bay	.60	.25
❑ 62 Luis Aparicio	.60	.25
❑ 63 Stephen Drew	1.00	.40
❑ 64 Jered Weaver	1.00	.40
❑ 65 Alex Gordon RC	3.00	1.25
❑ 66 Howie Kendrick	.60	.25
❑ 67 Ryan Zimmerman	1.50	.60
❑ 68 Akinori Iwamura RC	1.50	.60
❑ 69 Chien-Ming Wang	2.50	1.00
❑ 70 David Wright	2.50	1.00
❑ 71 Ryan Howard	2.50	1.00
❑ 72 Alex Rodriguez	2.50	1.00
❑ 73 Justin Morneau	.60	.25
❑ 74 Andrew Miller RC	4.00	1.50
❑ 75 Richard Nixon	1.50	.60
❑ 76 Bill Clinton	2.50	1.00
❑ 77 Phil Hughes (RC)	3.00	1.25
❑ 78 Tom Glavine	1.00	.40
❑ 79 Chipper Jones	1.50	.60
❑ 80 Craig Biggio	1.00	.40
❑ 81 Chris Chambliss	.60	.25
❑ 82 Tim Lincecum RC	5.00	2.00
❑ 83 Billy Butler (RC)	1.00	.40
❑ 84 Andy LaRoche (RC)	.60	.25
❑ 85 1969 New York Mets	.60	.25
❑ 86 2004 Boston Red Sox	2.50	1.00
❑ 87 Roberto Clemente	5.00	2.00
❑ 88 Chase Utley	1.50	.60
❑ 89 Reggie Jackson	1.00	.40
❑ 90 Curt Schilling	1.00	.40

2001 Ultimate Collection

❑ COMMON CARD (1-90)	4.00	1.50
❑ COMMON CARD (91-100)	10.00	4.00
❑ COMMON CARD (101-110)	10.00	4.00
❑ COMMON CARD (111-120)	15.00	6.00
❑ 1 Troy Glaus	4.00	1.50
❑ 2 Darin Erstad	4.00	1.50
❑ 3 Jason Giambi	4.00	1.50
❑ 4 Barry Zito	4.00	1.50
❑ 5 Tim Hudson	4.00	1.50
❑ 6 Miguel Tejada	4.00	1.50
❑ 7 Carlos Delgado	4.00	1.50
❑ 8 Shannon Stewart	4.00	1.50
❑ 9 Greg Vaughn	4.00	1.50
❑ 10 Toby Hall	4.00	1.50
❑ 11 Roberto Alomar	4.00	1.50
❑ 12 Juan Gonzalez	4.00	1.50
❑ 13 Jim Thome	4.00	1.50
❑ 14 Edgar Martinez	4.00	1.50
❑ 15 Freddy Garcia	4.00	1.50
❑ 16 Bret Boone	4.00	1.50
❑ 17 Kazuhiro Sasaki	4.00	1.50
❑ 18 Cal Ripken	20.00	8.00
❑ 19 Tim Raines Jr.	4.00	1.50
❑ 20 Alex Rodriguez	10.00	4.00
❑ 21 Ivan Rodriguez	4.00	1.50
❑ 22 Rafael Palmeiro	4.00	1.50
❑ 23 Pedro Martinez	4.00	1.50
❑ 24 Nomar Garciaparra	10.00	4.00
❑ 25 Manny Ramirez Sox	4.00	1.50
❑ 26 Hideo Nomo	6.00	2.50
❑ 27 Mike Sweeney	4.00	1.50
❑ 28 Carlos Beltran	4.00	1.50
❑ 29 Tony Clark	4.00	1.50
❑ 30 Dean Palmer	4.00	1.50
❑ 31 Doug Mientkiewicz	4.00	1.50
❑ 32 Cristian Guzman	4.00	1.50
❑ 33 Corey Koskie	4.00	1.50
❑ 34 Frank Thomas	6.00	2.50
❑ 35 Magglio Ordonez	4.00	1.50
❑ 36 Jose Canseco	4.00	1.50
❑ 37 Roger Clemens	12.00	5.00
❑ 38 Derek Jeter	15.00	6.00
❑ 39 Bernie Williams	4.00	1.50
❑ 40 Mike Mussina	4.00	1.50
❑ 41 Tino Martinez	4.00	1.50
❑ 42 Jeff Bagwell	4.00	1.50
❑ 43 Lance Berkman	4.00	1.50
❑ 44 Roy Oswalt	6.00	2.50
❑ 45 Chipper Jones	6.00	2.50
❑ 46 Greg Maddux	10.00	4.00
❑ 47 Andruw Jones	4.00	1.50
❑ 48 Tom Glavine	4.00	1.50
❑ 49 Richie Sexson	4.00	1.50
❑ 50 Jeromy Burnitz	4.00	1.50

❑ 51 Ben Sheets 4.00 1.50
❑ 52 Mark McGwire 15.00 6.00
❑ 53 Matt Morris 4.00 1.50
❑ 54 Jim Edmonds 4.00 1.50
❑ 55 J.D. Drew 4.00 1.50
❑ 56 Sammy Sosa 6.00 2.50
❑ 57 Fred McGriff 4.00 1.50
❑ 58 Kerry Wood 4.00 1.50
❑ 59 Randy Johnson 6.00 2.50
❑ 60 Luis Gonzalez 4.00 1.50
❑ 61 Curt Schilling 4.00 1.50
❑ 62 Shawn Green 4.00 1.50
❑ 63 Kevin Brown 4.00 1.50
❑ 64 Gary Sheffield 4.00 1.50
❑ 65 Vladimir Guerrero 6.00 2.50
❑ 66 Barry Bonds 15.00 6.00
❑ 67 Jeff Kent 4.00 1.50
❑ 68 Rich Aurilia 4.00 1.50
❑ 69 Cliff Floyd 4.00 1.50
❑ 70 Charles Johnson 4.00 1.50
❑ 71 Josh Beckett 4.00 1.50
❑ 72 Mike Piazza 10.00 4.00
❑ 73 Edgardo Alfonzo 4.00 1.50
❑ 74 Robin Ventura 4.00 1.50
❑ 75 Tony Gwynn 8.00 3.00
❑ 76 Ryan Klesko 4.00 1.50
❑ 77 Phil Nevin 4.00 1.50
❑ 78 Scott Rolen 4.00 1.50
❑ 79 Bobby Abreu 4.00 1.50
❑ 80 Jimmy Rollins 4.00 1.50
❑ 81 Brian Giles 4.00 1.50
❑ 82 Jason Kendall 4.00 1.50
❑ 83 Aramis Ramirez 4.00 1.50
❑ 84 Ken Griffey Jr. 10.00 4.00
❑ 85 Adam Dunn 4.00 1.50
❑ 86 Sean Casey 4.00 1.50
❑ 87 Barry Larkin 4.00 1.50
❑ 88 Larry Walker 4.00 1.50
❑ 89 Mike Hampton 4.00 1.50
❑ 90 Todd Helton 4.00 1.50
❑ 91 Ken Harvey T1 10.00 4.00
❑ 92 Bill Ortega T1 RC 10.00 4.00
❑ 93 Juan Diaz T1 RC 10.00 4.00
❑ 94 Greg Miller T1 RC 10.00 4.00
❑ 95 Brandon Berger T1 RC 10.00 4.00
❑ 96 Brandon Lyon T1 RC 10.00 4.00
❑ 97 Jay Gibbons T1 RC 15.00 6.00
❑ 98 Rob Mackowiak T1 RC 15.00 6.00
❑ 99 Erick Almonte T1 RC 10.00 4.00
❑ 100 Jason Middlebrook T1 RC 10.00 4.00
❑ 101 Johnny Estrada T2 RC 15.00 6.00
❑ 102 Juan Uribe T2 RC 15.00 6.00
❑ 103 Travis Hafner T2 RC 30.00 12.50
❑ 104 Morgan Ensberg T2 RC 15.00 6.00
❑ 105 Mike Rivera T2 RC 10.00 4.00
❑ 106 Josh Towers T2 RC 15.00 6.00
❑ 107 Adrian Hernandez T2 RC 10.00 4.00
❑ 108 Rafael Soriano T2 RC 10.00 4.00
❑ 109 Jackson Melian T2 RC 10.00 4.00
❑ 110 Wilkin Ruan T2 RC 10.00 4.00
❑ 111 Albert Pujols T3 RC 700.00 500.00
❑ 112 Tsuyoshi Shinjo T3 RC 25.00 10.00
❑ 113 Brandon Duckworth T3 RC 15.00 6.00
❑ 114 Juan Cruz T3 RC 15.00 6.00
❑ 115 Dewon Brazelton T3 RC 15.00 6.00
❑ 116 Mark Prior T3 AU RC 200.00 125.00
❑ 117 Mark Teixeira T3 AU RC 250.00 150.00
❑ 118 Wilson Betemit T3 RC 25.00 10.00
❑ 119 Bud Smith T3 RC 15.00 6.00
❑ 120 Ichiro Suzuki T3 AU RC 2200.00 1800.00

2002 Ultimate Collection

❑ COMMON CARD (1-60) 4.00 1.50
❑ COMMON CARD (61-110) 10.00 4.00
❑ 61-110 PRINT RUN 550 SERIAL #'d SETS
❑ COMMON CARD (111-113) 15.00 6.00
❑ COMMON CARD (114-120) 15.00 6.00
❑ 1 Troy Glaus 4.00 1.50
❑ 2 Luis Gonzalez 4.00 1.50
❑ 3 Curt Schilling 4.00 1.50
❑ 4 Randy Johnson 6.00 2.50
❑ 5 Andruw Jones 4.00 1.50
❑ 6 Greg Maddux 10.00 4.00
❑ 7 Chipper Jones 6.00 2.50
❑ 8 Gary Sheffield 4.00 1.50
❑ 9 Cal Ripken 20.00 8.00

❑ 10 Manny Ramirez 4.00 1.50
❑ 11 Pedro Martinez 4.00 1.50
❑ 12 Nomar Garciaparra 10.00 4.00
❑ 13 Sammy Sosa 6.00 2.50
❑ 14 Kerry Wood 4.00 1.50
❑ 15 Mark Prior 6.00 2.50
❑ 16 Magglio Ordonez 4.00 1.50
❑ 17 Frank Thomas 6.00 2.50
❑ 18 Adam Dunn 4.00 1.50
❑ 19 Ken Griffey Jr. 10.00 4.00
❑ 20 Jim Thome 4.00 1.50
❑ 21 Larry Walker 4.00 1.50
❑ 22 Todd Helton 4.00 1.50
❑ 23 Nolan Ryan 15.00 6.00
❑ 24 Jeff Bagwell 4.00 1.50
❑ 25 Roy Oswalt 4.00 1.50
❑ 26 Lance Berkman 4.00 1.50
❑ 27 Mike Sweeney 4.00 1.50
❑ 28 Shawn Green 4.00 1.50
❑ 29 Hideo Nomo 6.00 2.50
❑ 30 Torii Hunter 4.00 1.50
❑ 31 Vladimir Guerrero 6.00 2.50
❑ 32 Tom Seaver 4.00 1.50
❑ 33 Mike Piazza 10.00 4.00
❑ 34 Roberto Alomar 4.00 1.50
❑ 35 Derek Jeter 15.00 6.00
❑ 36 Alfonso Soriano 4.00 1.50
❑ 37 Jason Giambi 4.00 1.50
❑ 38 Roger Clemens 12.00 5.00
❑ 39 Mike Mussina 4.00 1.50
❑ 40 Bernie Williams 4.00 1.50
❑ 41 Joe DiMaggio 12.00 5.00
❑ 42 Mickey Mantle 25.00 10.00
❑ 43 Miguel Tejada 4.00 1.50
❑ 44 Eric Chavez 4.00 1.50
❑ 45 Barry Zito 4.00 1.50
❑ 46 Pat Burrell 4.00 1.50
❑ 47 Jason Kendall 4.00 1.50
❑ 48 Brian Giles 4.00 1.50
❑ 49 Barry Bonds 15.00 6.00
❑ 50 Ichiro Suzuki 12.00 5.00
❑ 51 Stan Musial 10.00 4.00
❑ 52 J.D. Drew 4.00 1.50
❑ 53 Scott Rolen 4.00 1.50
❑ 54 Albert Pujols 12.00 5.00
❑ 55 Mark McGwire 15.00 6.00
❑ 56 Alex Rodriguez 10.00 4.00
❑ 57 Ivan Rodriguez 4.00 1.50
❑ 58 Juan Gonzalez 4.00 1.50
❑ 59 Rafael Palmeiro 4.00 1.50
❑ 60 Carlos Delgado 4.00 1.50
❑ 61 Jose Valverde UR RC 10.00 4.00
❑ 62 Doug Devore UR RC 10.00 4.00
❑ 63 John Ennis UR RC 10.00 4.00
❑ 64 Joey Dawley UR RC 10.00 4.00
❑ 65 Trey Hodges UR RC 10.00 4.00
❑ 66 Mike Mahoney UR 10.00 4.00
❑ 67 Aaron Cook UR RC 10.00 4.00
❑ 68 Rene Reyes UR RC 10.00 4.00
❑ 69 Mark Corey UR RC 10.00 4.00
❑ 70 Hansel Izquierdo UR RC 10.00 4.00
❑ 71 Brandon Puffer UR RC 10.00 4.00
❑ 72 Jeriome Robertson UR RC 10.00 4.00
❑ 73 Jose Diaz UR RC 10.00 4.00
❑ 74 David Ross UR RC 10.00 4.00
❑ 75 Jayson Durocher UR RC 10.00 4.00
❑ 76 Eric Good UR RC 10.00 4.00
❑ 77 Satoru Komiyama UR RC 10.00 4.00
❑ 78 Tyler Yates UR RC 10.00 4.00
❑ 79 Eric Junge UR RC 10.00 4.00
❑ 80 Anderson Machado UR RC 10.00 4.00
❑ 81 Adrian Burnside UR RC 10.00 4.00
❑ 82 Ben Howard UR RC 10.00 4.00
❑ 83 Clay Condrey UR RC 10.00 4.00
❑ 84 Nelson Castro UR RC 10.00 4.00
❑ 85 So Taguchi UR RC 15.00 6.00
❑ 86 Mike Crudale UR RC 10.00 4.00
❑ 87 Scotty Layfield UR RC 10.00 4.00
❑ 88 Steve Bechler UR RC 10.00 4.00
❑ 89 Travis Driskill UR RC 10.00 4.00
❑ 90 Howie Clark UR RC 10.00 4.00
❑ 91 Josh Hancock UR RC 12.00 5.00
❑ 92 Jorge De La Rosa UR RC 10.00 4.00
❑ 93 Anastacio Martinez UR RC 10.00 4.00
❑ 94 Brian Tallet UR RC 10.00 4.00
❑ 95 Carl Sadler UR RC 10.00 4.00
❑ 96 Cliff Lee UR RC 15.00 6.00
❑ 97 Josh Bard UR RC 10.00 4.00
❑ 98 Wes Obermueller UR RC 10.00 4.00
❑ 99 Juan Brito UR RC 10.00 4.00
❑ 100 Aaron Guiel UR RC 10.00 4.00
❑ 101 Jeremy Hill UR RC 10.00 4.00
❑ 102 Kevin Frederick UR RC 10.00 4.00
❑ 103 Nate Field UR RC 10.00 4.00
❑ 104 Julio Mateo UR RC 10.00 4.00
❑ 105 Chris Snelling UR RC 12.00 5.00
❑ 106 Felix Escalona UR RC 10.00 4.00
❑ 107 Reynaldo Garcia UR RC 10.00 4.00
❑ 108 Mike Smith UR RC 10.00 4.00
❑ 109 Ken Huckaby UR RC 10.00 4.00
❑ 110 Kevin Cash UR RC 10.00 4.00
❑ 111 Kazuhisa Ishii UR AU RC 40.00 15.00
❑ 112 Freddy Sanchez UR AU RC 40.00 15.00
❑ 113 Jas Simontacchi UR AU RC 15.00 6.00
❑ 114 Jorge Padilla UR AU RC 15.00 6.00
❑ 115 Kirk Saarloos UR AU RC 15.00 6.00
❑ 116 Rodrigo Rosario UR AU RC 15.00 6.00
❑ 117 Oliver Perez UR AU RC 40.00 15.00
❑ 118 Miguel Asencio UR AU RC 15.00 6.00
❑ 119 Franklyn German UR AU RC 15.00 6.00
❑ 120 Jaime Cerda UR AU RC 15.00 6.00
❑ MM M.McGwire Priority EXCH/100

2003 Ultimate Collection

❑ COMMON CARD (1-84) 3.00 1.25
❑ 1-84 STATED ODDS TWO PER PACK
❑ COMMON CARD (85-117) 5.00 2.00
❑ COMMON CARD (118-140) 5.00 2.00
❑ 118-140 PRINT RUN 399 SERIAL #'d SETS
❑ COMMON CARD (141-158) 6.00 2.50
❑ COMMON CARD (159-168) 12.00 5.00
❑ 159-168 PRINT RUN 100 SERIAL #'d SETS
❑ 85-168 STATED ODDS ONE PER PACK
❑ COMMON CARD (169-174) 15.00 6.00
❑ 169-174 & ULT.SIG.OVERALL ODDS 1:4
❑ COMMON CARD (175-180) 15.00 6.00
❑ 175-180 & BUYBACK OVERALL ODDS 1:8
❑ 169-180 PRINT RUN 250 SERIAL #'d SETS
❑ MATSUI PART LIVE/ PART EXCH
❑ EXCHANGE DEADLINE 12/17/06
❑ 1 Ichiro Suzuki 10.00 4.00
❑ 2 Ken Griffey Jr. 8.00 3.00
❑ 3 Sammy Sosa 5.00 2.00
❑ 4 Jason Giambi 3.00 1.25
❑ 5 Mike Piazza 8.00 3.00
❑ 6 Derek Jeter 10.00 4.00

❑ 7 Randy Johnson 5.00 2.00
❑ 8 Barry Bonds 12.00 5.00
❑ 9 Carlos Delgado 3.00 1.25
❑ 10 Mark Prior 5.00 2.00
❑ 11 Vladimir Guerrero 5.00 2.00
❑ 12 Alfonso Soriano 3.00 1.25
❑ 13 Jim Thome 5.00 2.00
❑ 14 Pedro Martinez 5.00 2.00
❑ 15 Nomar Garciaparra 8.00 3.00
❑ 16 Chipper Jones 5.00 2.00
❑ 17 Rocco Baldelli 3.00 1.25
❑ 18 Dontrelle Willis 5.00 2.00
❑ 19 Garret Anderson 3.00 1.25
❑ 20 Jeff Bagwell 5.00 2.00
❑ 21 Jim Edmonds 3.00 1.25
❑ 22 Rickey Henderson 5.00 2.00
❑ 23 Torii Hunter 3.00 1.25
❑ 24 Tom Glavine 5.00 2.00
❑ 25 Hideo Nomo 5.00 2.00
❑ 26 Luis Gonzalez 3.00 1.25
❑ 27 Alex Rodriguez 8.00 3.00
❑ 28 Albert Pujols 10.00 4.00
❑ 29 Manny Ramirez 5.00 2.00
❑ 30 Rafael Palmeiro 5.00 2.00
❑ 31 Bernie Williams 5.00 2.00
❑ 32 Curt Schilling 3.00 1.25
❑ 33 Roger Clemens 10.00 4.00
❑ 34 Andruw Jones 5.00 2.00
❑ 35 J.D. Drew 3.00 1.25
❑ 36 Kerry Wood 3.00 1.25
❑ 37 Scott Rolen 5.00 2.00
❑ 38 Darin Erstad 3.00 1.25
❑ 39 Joe DiMaggio 8.00 3.00
❑ 40 Magglio Ordonez 3.00 1.25
❑ 41 Todd Helton 5.00 2.00
❑ 42 Barry Zito 3.00 1.25
❑ 43 Mickey Mantle 15.00 6.00
❑ 44 Miguel Tejada 3.00 1.25
❑ 45 Troy Glaus 3.00 1.25
❑ 46 Kazuhisa Ishii 3.00 1.25
❑ 47 Adam Dunn 3.00 1.25
❑ 48 Ted Williams 10.00 4.00
❑ 49 Mike Mussina 5.00 2.00
❑ 50 Ivan Rodriguez 5.00 2.00
❑ 51 Jacque Jones 3.00 1.25
❑ 52 Stan Musial 8.00 3.00
❑ 53 Mariano Rivera 5.00 2.00
❑ 54 Larry Walker 3.00 1.25
❑ 55 Aaron Boone 3.00 1.25
❑ 56 Hank Blalock 3.00 1.25
❑ 57 Rich Harden 5.00 2.00
❑ 58 Lance Berkman 3.00 1.25
❑ 59 Eric Chavez 3.00 1.25
❑ 60 Carlos Beltran 3.00 1.25
❑ 61 Roy Oswalt 3.00 1.25
❑ 62 Moises Alou 3.00 1.25
❑ 63 Nolan Ryan 12.00 5.00
❑ 64 Jeff Kent 3.00 1.25
❑ 65 Roberto Alomar 5.00 2.00
❑ 66 Runelvys Hernandez 3.00 1.25
❑ 67 Roy Halladay 3.00 1.25
❑ 68 Tim Hudson 3.00 1.25
❑ 69 Tom Seaver 5.00 2.00
❑ 70 Edgardo Alfonzo 3.00 1.25
❑ 71 Andy Pettitte 5.00 2.00
❑ 72 Preston Wilson 3.00 1.25
❑ 73 Frank Thomas 5.00 2.00
❑ 74 Jerome Williams 3.00 1.25
❑ 75 Shawn Green 3.00 1.25
❑ 76 David Wells 3.00 1.25
❑ 77 John Smoltz 5.00 2.00
❑ 78 Jorge Posada 5.00 2.00
❑ 79 Marlon Byrd 3.00 1.25
❑ 80 Austin Kearns 3.00 1.25
❑ 81 Bret Boone 3.00 1.25
❑ 82 Rafael Furcal 3.00 1.25
❑ 83 Jay Gibbons 3.00 1.25
❑ 84 Shane Reynolds 3.00 1.25
❑ 85 Nate Bland UR T1 RC 5.00 2.00
❑ 86 Willie Eyre UR T1 RC 5.00 2.00
❑ 87 Jeremy Guthrie UR T1 5.00 2.00
❑ 88 Jeremy Wedel UR T1 RC 5.00 2.00
❑ 89 Jhonny Peralta UR T1 8.00 3.00
❑ 90 Luis Ayala UR T1 RC 5.00 2.00
❑ 91 Michael Hessman UR T1 RC 5.00 2.00
❑ 92 Michael Nakamura UR T1 RC 5.00 2.00
❑ 93 Nook Logan UR T1 RC 8.00 3.00
❑ 94 Rett Johnson UR T1 RC 5.00 2.00
❑ 95 Josh Hall UR T1 RC 5.00 2.00
❑ 96 Julio Manon UR T1 RC 5.00 2.00
❑ 97 Heath Bell UR T1 RC 5.00 2.00
❑ 98 Ian Ferguson UR T1 RC 5.00 2.00
❑ 99 Jason Gilfillan UR T1 RC 5.00 2.00
❑ 100 Jason Roach UR T1 RC 5.00 2.00
❑ 101 Jason Shiell UR T1 RC 5.00 2.00
❑ 102 Termel Sledge UR T1 RC 5.00 2.00
❑ 103 Phil Seibel UR T1 RC 5.00 2.00
❑ 104 Jeff Duncan UR T1 RC 5.00 2.00
❑ 105 Mike Neu UR T1 RC 5.00 2.00
❑ 106 Colin Porter UR T1 RC 5.00 2.00
❑ 107 David Matranga UR T1 RC 5.00 2.00
❑ 108 Aaron Looper UR T1 RC 5.00 2.00
❑ 109 Jeremy Bonderman UR T1 RC 15.00 6.00
❑ 110 Miguel Ojeda UR T1 RC 5.00 2.00
❑ 111 Chad Cordero UR T1 RC 10.00 4.00
❑ 112 Shane Bazzell UR T1 RC 5.00 2.00
❑ 113 Tim Olson UR T1 RC 5.00 2.00
❑ 114 Michel Hernandez UR T1 RC 5.00 2.00
❑ 115 Chien-Ming Wang UR T1 RC 50.00 20.00
❑ 116 Josh Stewart UR T1 RC 5.00 2.00
❑ 117 Clint Barmes UR T1 RC 5.00 2.00
❑ 118 Craig Brazell UR T2 RC 5.00 2.00
❑ 119 Josh Willingham UR T2 RC 10.00 4.00
❑ 120 Brent Hoard UR T2 RC 5.00 2.00
❑ 121 Francisco Rosario UR T2 RC 5.00 2.00
❑ 122 Rick Roberts UR T2 RC 5.00 2.00
❑ 123 Geoff Geary UR T2 RC 5.00 2.00
❑ 124 Edgar Gonzalez UR T2 RC 5.00 2.00
❑ 125 Kevin Correia UR T2 RC 5.00 2.00
❑ 126 Ryan Cameron UR T2 RC 5.00 2.00
❑ 127 Beau Kemp UR T2 RC 5.00 2.00
❑ 128 Tommy Phelps UR T2 5.00 2.00
❑ 129 Mark Malaska UR T2 RC 5.00 2.00
❑ 130 Kevin Ohme UR T2 RC 5.00 2.00
❑ 131 Humberto Quintero UR T2 RC 5.00 2.00
❑ 132 Aquilino Lopez UR T2 RC 5.00 2.00
❑ 133 Andrew Brown UR T2 RC 8.00 3.00
❑ 134 Wilfredo Ledezma UR T2 RC 5.00 2.00
❑ 135 Luis De Los Santos UR T2 5.00 2.00
❑ 136 Garrett Atkins UR T2 5.00 2.00
❑ 137 Fernando Cabrera UR T2 RC 5.00 2.00
❑ 138 D.J. Carrasco UR T2 RC 5.00 2.00
❑ 139 Alfredo Gonzalez UR T2 RC 5.00 2.00
❑ 140 Alex Prieto UR T2 RC 5.00 2.00
❑ 141 Matt Kata UR T3 RC 6.00 2.50
❑ 142 Chris Capuano UR T3 RC 15.00 6.00
❑ 143 Bobby Madritsch UR T3 RC 6.00 2.50
❑ 144 Greg Jones UR T3 RC 6.00 2.50
❑ 145 Pete Zoccolillo UR T3 RC 6.00 2.50
❑ 146 Chad Gaudin UR T3 RC 6.00 2.50
❑ 147 Rosman Garcia UR T3 RC 6.00 2.50
❑ 148 Gerald Laird UR T3 6.00 2.50
❑ 149 Danny Garcia UR T3 RC 6.00 2.50
❑ 150 Stephen Randolph UR T3 RC 6.00 2.50
❑ 151 Pete LaForest UR T3 RC 6.00 2.50
❑ 152 Brian Sweeney UR T3 RC 6.00 2.50
❑ 153 Aaron Miles UR T3 RC 10.00 4.00
❑ 154 Jorge DePaula UR T3 UER 6.00 2.50
❑ 155 Graham Koonce UR T3 RC 6.00 2.50
❑ 156 Tom Gregorio UR T3 RC 6.00 2.50
❑ 157 Javier A. Lopez UR T3 RC 6.00 2.50
❑ 158 Oscar Villarreal UR T3 RC 6.00 2.50
❑ 159 Prentice Redman UR T4 RC 12.00 5.00
❑ 160 Francisco Cruceta UR T4 RC 12.00 5.00
❑ 161 Guillermo Quiroz UR T4 RC 12.00 5.00
❑ 162 Jeremy Griffiths UR T4 RC 12.00 5.00
❑ 163 Lew Ford UR T4 RC 20.00 8.00
❑ 164 Rob Hammock UR T4 RC 12.00 5.00
❑ 165 Todd Wellemeyer UR T4 RC 12.00 5.00
❑ 166 Ryan Wagner UR T4 RC 12.00 5.00
❑ 167 Edwin Jackson UR T4 RC 20.00 8.00
❑ 168 Dan Haren UR T4 RC 20.00 8.00
❑ 169 Hideki Matsui AU RC 350.00 250.00
❑ 170 Jose Contreras AU RC 50.00 20.00
❑ 171 Delmon Young AU RC 325.00 225.00
❑ 172 Rickie Weeks AU RC 100.00 50.00
❑ 173 Brandon Webb AU RC 175.00 100.00
❑ 174 Bo Hart AU RC 15.00 6.00
❑ 175 Rocco Baldelli YS AU 25.00 10.00
❑ 176 Jose Reyes YS AU 25.00 10.00
❑ 177 Dontrelle Willis YS AU 50.00 20.00
❑ 178 Bobby Hill YS AU 15.00 6.00
❑ 179 Jae Weong Seo YS AU 25.00 10.00
❑ 180 Jesse Foppert YS AU 15.00 6.00

2004 Ultimate Collection

❑ COMMON CARD (1-42) 3.00 1.25
❑ COMMON CARD (43-126) 3.00 1.25
❑ 1-126 STATED ODDS TWO PER PACK
❑ 1-126 PRINT RUN 675 SERIAL #'d CARDS
❑ COMMON CARD (127-168) 5.00 2.00
❑ 127-209/222 STATED ODDS 3:4 PACKS
❑ 127-168 PRINT RUN 525 SERIAL #'d SETS
❑ COMMON CARD (169-194) 6.00 2.50
❑ 169-194 PRINT RUN 299 SERIAL #'d SETS
❑ COMMON (195-209/222) 8.00 3.00
❑ 195-209/222 PRINT RUN 199 SER.#'d SETS
❑ 210-221 STATED ODDS 1:10
❑ 210-221 PRINT RUN 75 SERIAL #'d SETS
❑ EXCHANGE DEADLINE 12/28/07
❑ 1 Al Kaline 5.00 2.00
❑ 2 Billy Williams 3.00 1.25
❑ 3 Bob Feller 3.00 1.25
❑ 4 Bob Gibson 5.00 2.00
❑ 5 Bob Lemon 3.00 1.25
❑ 6 Bobby Doerr 3.00 1.25
❑ 7 Brooks Robinson 5.00 2.00
❑ 8 Cal Ripken 15.00 6.00
❑ 9 Catfish Hunter 5.00 2.00
❑ 10 Eddie Mathews 5.00 2.00
❑ 11 Enos Slaughter 3.00 1.25
❑ 12 Ernie Banks 5.00 2.00
❑ 13 Fergie Jenkins 3.00 1.25
❑ 14 Gaylord Perry 3.00 1.25
❑ 15 Harmon Killebrew 5.00 2.00
❑ 16 Jim Bunning 3.00 1.25
❑ 17 Joe DiMaggio 8.00 3.00
❑ 18 Joe Morgan 3.00 1.25
❑ 19 Juan Marichal 3.00 1.25
❑ 20 Lou Brock 5.00 2.00
❑ 21 Luis Aparicio 3.00 1.25
❑ 22 Mickey Mantle 15.00 6.00
❑ 23 Mike Schmidt 10.00 4.00
❑ 24 Monte Irvin 3.00 1.25
❑ 25 Nolan Ryan 12.00 5.00
❑ 26 Pee Wee Reese 5.00 2.00
❑ 27 Phil Niekro 3.00 1.25
❑ 28 Phil Rizzuto 5.00 2.00
❑ 29 Ralph Kiner 5.00 2.00
❑ 30 Richie Ashburn 5.00 2.00
❑ 31 Robin Roberts 3.00 1.25
❑ 32 Robin Yount 5.00 2.00
❑ 33 Rod Carew 5.00 2.00
❑ 34 Rollie Fingers 3.00 1.25
❑ 35 Stan Musial 8.00 3.00
❑ 36 Ted Williams 10.00 4.00
❑ 37 Tom Seaver 5.00 2.00
❑ 38 Warren Spahn 5.00 2.00
❑ 39 Whitey Ford 5.00 2.00
❑ 40 Willie McCovey 5.00 2.00
❑ 41 Willie Stargell 5.00 2.00
❑ 42 Yogi Berra 5.00 2.00
❑ 43 Adrian Beltre 3.00 1.25
❑ 44 Albert Pujols 10.00 4.00
❑ 45 Alex Rodriguez 8.00 3.00
❑ 46 Alfonso Soriano 3.00 1.25
❑ 47 Andruw Jones 5.00 2.00
❑ 48 Andy Pettitte 5.00 2.00
❑ 49 Aubrey Huff 3.00 1.25
❑ 50 Barry Larkin 5.00 2.00

❑ 51 Ben Sheets 3.00 1.25
❑ 52 Bernie Williams 5.00 2.00
❑ 53 Bobby Abreu 3.00 1.25
❑ 54 Brad Penny 3.00 1.25
❑ 55 Bret Boone 3.00 1.25
❑ 56 Brian Giles 3.00 1.25
❑ 57 Carlos Beltran 3.00 1.25
❑ 58 Carlos Delgado 3.00 1.25
❑ 59 Carlos Guillen 3.00 1.25
❑ 60 Carlos Lee 3.00 1.25
❑ 61 Carlos Zambrano 3.00 1.25
❑ 62 Chipper Jones 5.00 2.00
❑ 63 Craig Biggio 5.00 2.00
❑ 64 Craig Wilson 3.00 1.25
❑ 65 Curt Schilling 5.00 2.00
❑ 66 David Ortiz 5.00 2.00
❑ 67 Derek Jeter 10.00 4.00
❑ 68 Eric Chavez 3.00 1.25
❑ 69 Eric Gagne 3.00 1.25
❑ 70 Frank Thomas 5.00 2.00
❑ 71 Garret Anderson 3.00 1.25
❑ 72 Gary Sheffield 3.00 1.25
❑ 73 Greg Maddux 8.00 3.00
❑ 74 Hank Blalock 3.00 1.25
❑ 75 Hideki Matsui 8.00 3.00
❑ 76 Ichiro Suzuki 10.00 4.00
❑ 77 Ivan Rodriguez 5.00 2.00
❑ 78 J.D. Drew 3.00 1.25
❑ 79 Jake Peavy 3.00 1.25
❑ 80 Jason Schmidt 3.00 1.25
❑ 81 Jeff Bagwell 5.00 2.00
❑ 82 Jeff Kent 3.00 1.25
❑ 83 Jim Thome 5.00 2.00
❑ 84 Joe Mauer 5.00 2.00
❑ 85 Johan Santana 5.00 2.00
❑ 86 Jose Reyes 3.00 1.25
❑ 87 Jose Vidro 3.00 1.25
❑ 88 Ken Griffey Jr. 8.00 3.00
❑ 89 Kerry Wood 3.00 1.25
❑ 90 Larry Walker Cards 5.00 2.00
❑ 91 Luis Gonzalez 3.00 1.25
❑ 92 Lyle Overbay 3.00 1.25
❑ 93 Magglio Ordonez 3.00 1.25
❑ 94 Manny Ramirez 5.00 2.00
❑ 95 Mark Mulder 3.00 1.25
❑ 96 Mark Prior 5.00 2.00
❑ 97 Mark Teixeira 5.00 2.00
❑ 98 Melvin Mora 3.00 1.25
❑ 99 Michael Young 3.00 1.25
❑ 100 Miguel Cabrera 5.00 2.00
❑ 101 Miguel Tejada 3.00 1.25
❑ 102 Mike Lowell 3.00 1.25
❑ 103 Mike Piazza 8.00 3.00
❑ 104 Mike Sweeney 3.00 1.25
❑ 105 Nomar Garciaparra 8.00 3.00
❑ 106 Oliver Perez 3.00 1.25
❑ 107 Pedro Martinez 5.00 2.00
❑ 108 Preston Wilson 3.00 1.25
❑ 109 Rafael Palmeiro 5.00 2.00
❑ 110 Randy Johnson 5.00 2.00
❑ 111 Roger Clemens 10.00 4.00
❑ 112 Roy Halladay 3.00 1.25
❑ 113 Roy Oswalt 3.00 1.25
❑ 114 Sammy Sosa 5.00 2.00
❑ 115 Scott Podsednik 3.00 1.25
❑ 116 Scott Rolen 5.00 2.00
❑ 117 Shawn Green 3.00 1.25
❑ 118 Tim Hudson 3.00 1.25
❑ 119 Todd Helton 5.00 2.00
❑ 120 Tom Glavine 5.00 2.00
❑ 121 Torii Hunter 3.00 1.25
❑ 122 Travis Hafner 3.00 1.25
❑ 123 Troy Glaus 3.00 1.25
❑ 124 Vernon Wells 3.00 1.25
❑ 125 Victor Martinez 3.00 1.25
❑ 126 Vladimir Guerrero 5.00 2.00
❑ 127 Aarom Baldiris UR T1 RC 8.00 3.00
❑ 128 Alfredo Simon UR T1 RC 5.00 2.00
❑ 129 Andres Blanco UR T1 RC 5.00 2.00
❑ 130 Jeff Bajenaru UR T1 RC 5.00 2.00
❑ 131 Bart Fortunato UR T1 RC 5.00 2.00
❑ 132 B.Medders UR T1 RC 5.00 2.00
❑ 133 Brian Dallimore UR T1 RC 5.00 2.00
❑ 134 Carlos Hines UR T1 RC 5.00 2.00
❑ 135 Carlos Vasquez UR T1 RC 8.00 3.00
❑ 136 Casey Daigle UR T1 RC 5.00 2.00
❑ 137 Chad Bentz UR T1 RC 5.00 2.00
❑ 138 Chris Aguila UR T1 RC 5.00 2.00
❑ 139 Chris Saenz UR T1 RC 5.00 2.00
❑ 140 Chris Shelton UR T1 RC 12.00 5.00
❑ 141 Colby Miller UR T1 RC 5.00 2.00
❑ 142 Dave Crouthers UR T1 RC 5.00 2.00
❑ 143 David Aardsma UR T1 RC 8.00 3.00
❑ 144 Dennis Sarfate UR T1 RC 5.00 2.00
❑ 145 Donnie Kelly UR T1 RC 5.00 2.00
❑ 146 Eddy Rodriguez UR T1 RC 8.00 3.00
❑ 147 Eduardo Villacis UR T1 RC 5.00 2.00
❑ 148 Edwardo Sierra UR T1 RC 8.00 3.00
❑ 149 Edwin Moreno UR T1 RC 8.00 3.00
❑ 150 Kyle Denney UR T1 RC 5.00 2.00
❑ 151 Evan Rust UR T1 RC 5.00 2.00
❑ 152 Fernando Nieve UR T1 RC 8.00 3.00
❑ 153 Frank Francisco UR T1 RC 5.00 2.00
❑ 154 Frank Gracesqui UR T1 RC 5.00 2.00
❑ 155 Freddy Guzman UR T1 RC 5.00 2.00
❑ 156 Greg Dobbs UR T1 RC 5.00 2.00
❑ 157 Hector Gimenez UR T1 RC 5.00 2.00
❑ 158 Jason Alfaro UR T1 RC 5.00 2.00
❑ 159 Jake Woods UR T1 RC 5.00 2.00
❑ 160 Andy Green UR T1 RC 5.00 2.00
❑ 161 Jason Bartlett UR T1 RC 8.00 3.00
❑ 162 Jason Frasor UR T1 RC 5.00 2.00
❑ 163 Jeff Bennett UR T1 RC 5.00 2.00
❑ 164 Jerome Gamble UR T1 RC 5.00 2.00
❑ 165 Jerry Gil UR T1 RC 5.00 2.00
❑ 166 Joe Hietpas UR T1 RC 5.00 2.00
❑ 167 Jorge Sequea UR T1 RC 5.00 2.00
❑ 168 Jorge Vasquez UR T1 RC 5.00 2.00
❑ 169 Josh Labandeira UR T2 RC 6.00 2.50
❑ 170 Justin Germano UR T2 RC 6.00 2.50
❑ 171 Justin Hampson UR T2 RC 6.00 2.50
❑ 172 Chris Young UR T2 RC 50.00 20.00
❑ 173 Justin Knoedler UR T2 RC 6.00 2.50
❑ 174 Justin Lehr UR T2 RC 6.00 2.50
❑ 175 Justin Leone UR T2 RC 10.00 4.00
❑ 176 Kaz Tadano UR T2 RC 10.00 4.00
❑ 177 Kevin Cave UR T2 RC 6.00 2.50
❑ 178 Linc Holdzkom UR T2 RC 6.00 2.50
❑ 179 Mike Rose UR T2 RC 6.00 2.50
❑ 180 Luis Gonzalez UR T2 RC 6.00 2.50
❑ 181 Mariano Gomez UR T2 RC 6.00 2.50
❑ 182 Rene Rivera UR T2 RC 6.00 2.50
❑ 183 Michael Wuertz UR T2 RC 10.00 4.00
❑ 184 Mike Gosling UR T2 RC 6.00 2.50
❑ 185 Mike Johnston UR T2 RC 6.00 2.50
❑ 186 Mike Rouse UR T2 RC 6.00 2.50
❑ 187 Nick Regilio UR T2 RC 6.00 2.50
❑ 188 Onil Joseph UR T2 RC 6.00 2.50
❑ 189 Orl Rodriguez UR T2 RC 6.00 2.50
❑ 190 Phil Stockman UR T2 RC 6.00 2.50
❑ 191 Renyel Pinto UR T2 RC 10.00 4.00
❑ 192 Roberto Novoa UR T2 RC 10.00 4.00
❑ 193 Roman Colon UR T2 RC 6.00 2.50
❑ 194 Ronald Belisario UR T2 RC 6.00 2.50
❑ 195 Ronny Cedeno UR T3 RC 10.00 4.00
❑ 196 Ryan Meaux UR T3 RC 8.00 3.00
❑ 197 Ryan Wing UR T3 RC 8.00 3.00
❑ 198 Scott Dohmann UR T3 RC 8.00 3.00
❑ 199 Joey Gathright UR T3 RC 12.00 5.00
❑ 200 Shawn Camp UR T3 RC 8.00 3.00
❑ 201 Shawn Hill UR T3 RC 8.00 3.00
❑ 202 Steve Andrade UR T3 RC 8.00 3.00
❑ 203 Tim Bausher UR T3 RC 8.00 3.00
❑ 204 Tim Bittner UR T3 RC 8.00 3.00
❑ 205 Brad Halsey UR T3 RC 12.00 5.00
❑ 206 William Bergolla UR T3 RC 8.00 3.00
❑ 207 Kameron Loe UR T3 RC 20.00 8.00
❑ 208 Jesse Crain UR T3 RC 12.00 5.00
❑ 209 Scott Kazmir UR T3 RC 30.00 12.50
❑ 210 Akinori Otsuka AU RC 50.00 20.00
❑ 211 Chris Oxspring AU RC 25.00 10.00
❑ 212 Ian Snell AU RC 40.00 15.00
❑ 213 John Gall AU RC 40.00 15.00
❑ 214 Jose Capellan AU RC 25.00 10.00
❑ 215 Yadier Molina AU RC 80.00 50.00
❑ 216 Merkin Valdez AU RC 25.00 10.00
❑ 217 R.Ramirez AU RC EXCH 25.00 10.00
❑ 218 Rusty Tucker AU RC 40.00 15.00
❑ 219 Scott Proctor AU RC 40.00 15.00
❑ 220 Sean Henn AU RC 25.00 10.00
❑ 221 Shingo Takatsu AU RC 40.00 15.00
❑ 222 Kazuo Matsui UR T3 RC 10.00 4.00

2005 Ultimate Collection

❑ COMMON CARD (1-100) 3.00 1.25
❑ 1-100 APPX ODDS 3:2 PACKS
❑ 1-100 PRINT RUN 475 SERIAL #'d SETS
❑ COMMON CARD (101-142) 5.00 2.00
❑ 101-142 APPX. ODDS 1:3
❑ 101-142 PRINT RUN 275 SERIAL #'d SETS
❑ COMMON CARD (143-237) 5.00 2.00
❑ COMMON RC (143-237) 5.00 2.00
❑ 143-237 STATED ODDS 3:4 PACKS
❑ 143-237 PRINT RUN 275 SERIAL #'d SETS
❑ 238-242 OVERALL AU ODDS 1:4
❑ 238-242 PRINT RUN 99 SERIAL #'d SETS
❑ 1 A.J. Burnett 3.00 1.25
❑ 2 Adam Dunn 3.00 1.25
❑ 3 Adrian Beltre 3.00 1.25
❑ 4 Albert Pujols 8.00 3.00
❑ 5 Alex Rodriguez 10.00 4.00
❑ 6 Alfonso Soriano 3.00 1.25
❑ 7 Andruw Jones 5.00 2.00
❑ 8 Andy Pettitte 5.00 2.00
❑ 9 Aramis Ramirez 3.00 1.25
❑ 10 Aubrey Huff 3.00 1.25
❑ 11 Ben Sheets 3.00 1.25
❑ 12 Bobby Abreu 3.00 1.25
❑ 13 Bobby Crosby 3.00 1.25
❑ 14 Chris Carpenter 3.00 1.25
❑ 15 Brian Giles 3.00 1.25
❑ 16 Brian Roberts 3.00 1.25
❑ 17 Carl Crawford 3.00 1.25
❑ 18 Carlos Beltran 3.00 1.25
❑ 19 Carlos Delgado 3.00 1.25
❑ 20 Carlos Zambrano 3.00 1.25
❑ 21 Chipper Jones 5.00 2.00
❑ 22 Corey Patterson 3.00 1.25
❑ 23 Craig Biggio 5.00 2.00
❑ 24 Curt Schilling 5.00 2.00
❑ 25 Dallas McPherson 3.00 1.25
❑ 26 David Ortiz 5.00 2.00
❑ 27 David Wright 8.00 3.00
❑ 28 Delmon Young 5.00 2.00
❑ 29 Derek Jeter 10.00 4.00
❑ 30 Derrek Lee 5.00 2.00
❑ 31 Dontrelle Willis 3.00 1.25
❑ 32 Eric Chavez 3.00 1.25
❑ 33 Eric Gagne 3.00 1.25
❑ 34 Francisco Rodriguez 3.00 1.25
❑ 35 Gary Sheffield 3.00 1.25
❑ 36 Greg Maddux 8.00 3.00
❑ 37 Hank Blalock 3.00 1.25
❑ 38 Hideki Matsui 6.00 2.50
❑ 39 Ichiro Suzuki 10.00 4.00
❑ 40 Ivan Rodriguez 5.00 2.00
❑ 41 J.D. Drew 3.00 1.25
❑ 42 Jake Peavy 3.00 1.25
❑ 43 Jason Bay 3.00 1.25
❑ 44 Jason Schmidt 3.00 1.25
❑ 45 Jeff Bagwell 5.00 2.00
❑ 46 Jeff Kent 3.00 1.25
❑ 47 Jeremy Bonderman 3.00 1.25
❑ 48 Jim Edmonds 3.00 1.25
❑ 49 Jim Thome 5.00 2.00
❑ 50 Joe Mauer 5.00 2.00
❑ 51 Johan Santana 5.00 2.00
❑ 52 John Smoltz 5.00 2.00
❑ 53 Johnny Damon 5.00 2.00
❑ 54 Jose Reyes 3.00 1.25

❑ 55 Jose Vidro 3.00 1.25
❑ 56 Josh Beckett 3.00 1.25
❑ 57 Justin Morneau 3.00 1.25
❑ 58 Ken Griffey Jr. 8.00 3.00
❑ 59 Kerry Wood 3.00 1.25
❑ 60 Khalil Greene 5.00 2.00
❑ 61 Lance Berkman 3.00 1.25
❑ 62 Larry Walker 5.00 2.00
❑ 63 Luis Gonzalez 3.00 1.25
❑ 64 Manny Ramirez 5.00 2.00
❑ 65 Mark Buehrle 3.00 1.25
❑ 66 Mark Mulder 3.00 1.25
❑ 67 Mark Prior 5.00 2.00
❑ 68 Mark Teixeira 5.00 2.00
❑ 69 Michael Young 3.00 1.25
❑ 70 Miguel Cabrera 5.00 2.00
❑ 71 Miguel Tejada 3.00 1.25
❑ 72 Mike Mussina 5.00 2.00
❑ 73 Mike Piazza 5.00 2.00
❑ 74 Moises Alou 3.00 1.25
❑ 75 Nomar Garciaparra 5.00 2.00
❑ 76 Oliver Perez 3.00 1.25
❑ 77 Pat Burrell 3.00 1.25
❑ 78 Paul Konerko 3.00 1.25
❑ 79 Pedro Feliz 3.00 1.25
❑ 80 Pedro Martinez 5.00 2.00
❑ 81 Randy Johnson 5.00 2.00
❑ 82 Richie Sexson 3.00 1.25
❑ 83 Rickie Weeks 3.00 1.25
❑ 84 Roger Clemens 8.00 3.00
❑ 85 Roy Halladay 3.00 1.25
❑ 86 Roy Oswalt 3.00 1.25
❑ 87 Sammy Sosa 5.00 2.00
❑ 88 Scott Kazmir 3.00 1.25
❑ 89 Scott Rolen 5.00 2.00
❑ 90 Shawn Green 3.00 1.25
❑ 91 Tim Hudson 3.00 1.25
❑ 92 Todd Helton 5.00 2.00
❑ 93 Tom Glavine 5.00 2.00
❑ 94 Torii Hunter 3.00 1.25
❑ 95 Travis Hafner 3.00 1.25
❑ 96 Troy Glaus 3.00 1.25
❑ 97 Vernon Wells 3.00 1.25
❑ 98 Victor Martinez 3.00 1.25
❑ 99 Vladimir Guerrero 5.00 2.00
❑ 100 Zack Greinke 3.00 1.25
❑ 101 Al Kaline RET 8.00 3.00
❑ 102 Babe Ruth RET 10.00 4.00
❑ 103 Bo Jackson RET 8.00 3.00
❑ 104 Bob Gibson RET 8.00 3.00
❑ 105 Brooks Robinson RET 8.00 3.00
❑ 106 Cal Ripken RET 20.00 8.00
❑ 107 Carl Yastrzemski RET 8.00 3.00
❑ 108 Carlton Fisk RET 8.00 3.00
❑ 109 Catfish Hunter RET 5.00 2.00
❑ 110 Christy Mathewson RET 8.00 3.00
❑ 111 Cy Young RET 8.00 3.00
❑ 112 Don Mattingly RET 10.00 4.00
❑ 113 Eddie Mathews RET 8.00 3.00
❑ 114 Eddie Murray RET 8.00 3.00
❑ 115 Gary Carter RET 5.00 2.00
❑ 116 Harmon Killebrew RET 8.00 3.00
❑ 117 Jim Palmer RET 5.00 2.00
❑ 118 Jimmie Foxx RET 8.00 3.00
❑ 119 Joe DiMaggio RET 8.00 3.00
❑ 120 Johnny Bench RET 8.00 3.00
❑ 121 Lefty Grove RET 8.00 3.00
❑ 122 Lou Gehrig RET 8.00 3.00
❑ 123 Mel Ott RET 8.00 3.00
❑ 124 Reggie Jackson RET 8.00 3.00
❑ 125 Mike Schmidt RET 10.00 4.00
❑ 126 Nolan Ryan RET 12.00 5.00
❑ 127 Ozzie Smith RET 8.00 3.00
❑ 128 Paul Molitor RET 5.00 2.00
❑ 129 Pee Wee Reese RET 8.00 3.00
❑ 130 Robin Yount RET 8.00 3.00
❑ 131 Ryne Sandberg RET 10.00 4.00
❑ 132 Ted Williams RET 8.00 3.00
❑ 133 Thurman Munson RET 8.00 3.00
❑ 134 Tom Seaver RET 8.00 3.00
❑ 135 Tony Gwynn RET 8.00 3.00
❑ 136 Wade Boggs RET 8.00 3.00
❑ 137 Walter Johnson RET 8.00 3.00
❑ 138 Warren Spahn RET 8.00 3.00
❑ 139 Will Clark RET 8.00 3.00
❑ 140 Willie McCovey RET 8.00 3.00
❑ 141 Willie Stargell RET 8.00 3.00
❑ 142 Yogi Berra RET 8.00 3.00
❑ 143 Ambiorix Burgos UP RC 5.00 2.00
❑ 144 Ambiorix Concepcion UP RC 5.00 2.00
❑ 145 Anibal Sanchez UP RC 15.00 6.00
❑ 146 Bill McCarthy UP RC 5.00 2.00
❑ 147 Brian Burres UP RC 5.00 2.00
❑ 148 Carlos Ruiz UP RC 5.00 2.00
❑ 149 Casey Rogowski UP RC 8.00 3.00
❑ 150 Chris Resop UP RC 5.00 2.00
❑ 151 Chris Roberson UP RC 5.00 2.00
❑ 152 Chris Seddon UP RC 5.00 2.00
❑ 153 Colter Bean UP RC 5.00 2.00
❑ 154 Dae-Sung Koo UP RC 5.00 2.00
❑ 155 Danny Rueckel UP RC 5.00 2.00
❑ 156 Dave Gassner UP RC 5.00 2.00
❑ 157 Ryan Howard UP 15.00 6.00
❑ 158 D.J. Houlton UP RC 5.00 2.00
❑ 159 Derek Wathan UP RC 5.00 2.00
❑ 160 Devon Lowery UP RC 5.00 2.00
❑ 161 Enrique Gonzalez UP RC 5.00 2.00
❑ 162 Erick Threets UP RC 5.00 2.00
❑ 163 Eude Brito UP RC 5.00 2.00
❑ 164 Francisco Butto UP RC 5.00 2.00
❑ 165 Franquelis Osoria UP RC 5.00 2.00
❑ 166 Garrett Jones UP RC 5.00 2.00
❑ 167 Geovany Soto UP RC 25.00 10.00
❑ 168 Ismael Ramirez UP RC 5.00 2.00
❑ 169 Jared Gothreaux UP RC 5.00 2.00
❑ 170 Jason Hammel UP RC 5.00 2.00
❑ 171 Jeff Housman UP RC 5.00 2.00
❑ 172 Jeff Miller UP RC 5.00 2.00
❑ 173 Jeff Francoeur UP 12.00 5.00
❑ 174 John Hattig UP RC 5.00 2.00
❑ 175 Jorge Campillo UP RC 5.00 2.00
❑ 176 Juan Morillo UP RC 5.00 2.00
❑ 177 Justin Wechsler UP RC 5.00 2.00
❑ 178 Keiichi Yabu UP RC 5.00 2.00
❑ 179 Kendry Morales UP RC 15.00 6.00
❑ 180 Luis Hernandez UP RC 5.00 2.00
❑ 181 Luis Mendoza UP RC 5.00 2.00
❑ 182 Luis Pena UP RC 5.00 2.00
❑ 183 Luis O.Rodriguez UP RC 5.00 2.00
❑ 184 Luke Scott UP RC 10.00 4.00
❑ 185 Marcos Carvajal UP RC 5.00 2.00
❑ 186 Mark Woodyard UP RC 5.00 2.00
❑ 187 Matt Smith UP RC 5.00 2.00
❑ 188 Matthew Lindstrom UP RC 5.00 2.00
❑ 189 Miguel Negron UP RC 8.00 3.00
❑ 190 Mike Morse UP RC 5.00 2.00
❑ 191 Nate McLouth UP RC 30.00 12.50
❑ 192 Nick Masset UP RC 5.00 2.00
❑ 193 Paulino Reynoso UP RC 5.00 2.00
❑ 194 Pedro Lopez UP RC 5.00 2.00
❑ 195 Pete Orr UP RC 5.00 2.00
❑ 196 Randy Messenger UP RC 5.00 2.00
❑ 197 Randy Williams UP RC 5.00 2.00
❑ 198 Raul Tablado UP RC 5.00 2.00
❑ 199 Ronny Paulino UP RC 6.00 2.50
❑ 200 Russ Rohlicek UP RC 5.00 2.00
❑ 201 Russell Martin UP RC 12.00 5.00
❑ 202 Scott Baker UP RC 8.00 3.00
❑ 203 Scott Munter UP RC 5.00 2.00
❑ 204 Sean Thompson UP RC 5.00 2.00
❑ 205 Sean Tracey UP RC 5.00 2.00
❑ 206 Steve Schmoll UP RC 5.00 2.00
❑ 207 Tony Pena UP RC 5.00 2.00
❑ 208 Travis Bowyer UP RC 5.00 2.00
❑ 209 Ubaldo Jimenez UP RC 10.00 4.00
❑ 210 Wladimir Balentien UP RC 10.00 4.00
❑ 211 Yorman Bazardo UP RC 5.00 2.00
❑ 212 Yuniesky Betancourt UP RC 10.004.00
❑ 213 Adam Shabala UP RC 5.00 2.00
❑ 214 Brandon McCarthy UP RC 10.00 4.00
❑ 215 Chad Orvella UP RC 5.00 2.00
❑ 216 Jermaine Van Buren UP 5.00 2.00
❑ 217 Anthony Reyes UP RC 25.00 10.00
❑ 218 Dana Eveland UP RC 5.00 2.00
❑ 219 Brian Anderson UP RC 8.00 3.00
❑ 220 Hayden Penn UP RC 8.00 3.00
❑ 221 Chris Denorfia UP RC 10.00 4.00
❑ 222 Joel Peralta UP RC 5.00 2.00
❑ 223 Ryan Garko UP RC 10.00 4.00
❑ 224 Felix Hernandez UP 10.00 4.00
❑ 225 Mark McLemore UP RC 5.00 2.00
❑ 226 Melky Cabrera UP RC 15.00 6.00
❑ 227 Nelson Cruz UP RC 10.00 4.00
❑ 228 Norihiro Nakamura UP RC 8.00 3.00
❑ 229 Oscar Robles UP RC 5.00 2.00
❑ 230 Rick Short UP RC 5.00 2.00
❑ 231 Ryan Zimmerman UP RC 30.00 12.50
❑ 232 Ryan Speier UP RC 5.00 2.00
❑ 233 Ryan Spilborghs UP RC 8.00 3.00
❑ 234 Shane Costa UP RC 5.00 2.00
❑ 235 Zach Duke UP 8.00 3.00
❑ 236 Tony Giarratano UP RC 5.00 2.00
❑ 237 Jeff Niemann UP RC 8.00 3.00
❑ 238 Stephen Drew AU RC 200.00 100.00
❑ 239 Justin Verlander AU RC 300.00 200.00
❑ 240 Prince Fielder AU RC 600.00 500.00
❑ 241 Philip Humber AU RC 80.00 40.00
❑ 242 Tadahito Iguchi AU RC 120.00 60.00

2006 Ultimate Collection

❑ COMMON CARD (1-274) 2.50 1.00
❑ VETERAN PRINT RUN 799 SER.#'d SETS
❑ COMMON RC (1-274) 2.50 1.00
❑ RC PRINT RUN 799 SERIAL #'d SETS
❑ COMMON AU RC (101-175) 10.00 4.00
❑ AU RC MINORS 10.00 4.00
❑ OVERALL AU ODDS 1:2
❑ AU RC PRINT RUNS B/WN 150-180
❑ EXCHANGE DEADLINE 12/20/09
❑ PLATE ODDS APPX. 7:10 BONUS PACKS
❑ PLATE PRINT RUN 1 SET PER COLOR
❑ BLACK-CYAN-MAGENTA-YELLOW ISSUED
❑ NO PLATE PRICING DUE TO SCARCITY
❑ 1 Babe Ruth 10.00 4.00
❑ 2 Chad Tracy 2.50 1.00
❑ 3 Brandon Webb 2.50 1.00
❑ 4 Andruw Jones 4.00 1.50
❑ 5 Chipper Jones 5.00 2.00
❑ 6 John Smoltz 4.00 1.50
❑ 7 Eddie Mathews 5.00 2.00
❑ 8 Miguel Tejada 2.50 1.00
❑ 9 Brian Roberts 2.50 1.00
❑ 10 Mickey Cochrane 2.50 1.00
❑ 11 Curt Schilling 4.00 1.50
❑ 12 David Ortiz 5.00 2.00
❑ 13 Manny Ramirez 4.00 1.50
❑ 14 Johnny Bench 5.00 2.00
❑ 15 Cy Young 5.00 2.00
❑ 16 Greg Maddux 6.00 2.50
❑ 17 Derrek Lee 2.50 1.00
❑ 18 Yogi Berra 5.00 2.00
❑ 19 Walter Johnson 5.00 2.00
❑ 20 Jim Thome 4.00 1.50
❑ 21 Paul Konerko 2.50 1.00
❑ 22 Lou Gehrig 8.00 3.00
❑ 23 Jose Contreras 2.50 1.00
❑ 24 Ken Griffey Jr. 6.00 2.50
❑ 25 Adam Dunn 2.50 1.00
❑ 26 Reggie Jackson 4.00 1.50
❑ 27 Travis Hafner 2.50 1.00
❑ 28 Victor Martinez 2.50 1.00
❑ 29 Grady Sizemore 4.00 1.50
❑ 30 Casey Stengel 2.50 1.00
❑ 31 Todd Helton 4.00 1.50
❑ 32 Nolan Ryan 10.00 4.00
❑ 33 Clint Barmes 2.50 1.00
❑ 34 Ivan Rodriguez 4.00 1.50
❑ 35 Chris Shelton 2.50 1.00
❑ 36 Ty Cobb 8.00 3.00
❑ 37 Miguel Cabrera 4.00 1.50

❑ 38 Dontrelle Willis 2.50 1.00
❑ 39 Lance Berkman 2.50 1.00
❑ 40 Tom Seaver 4.00 1.50
❑ 41 Roy Oswalt 2.50 1.00
❑ 42 Christy Mathewson 5.00 2.00
❑ 43 Luis Aparicio 2.50 1.00
❑ 44 Vladimir Guerrero 5.00 2.00
❑ 45 Bartolo Colon 2.50 1.00
❑ 46 Roy Campanella 5.00 2.00
❑ 47 George Sisler 2.50 1.00
❑ 48 Jeff Kent 2.50 1.00
❑ 49 J.D. Drew 2.50 1.00
❑ 50 Carlos Lee 2.50 1.00
❑ 51 Willie Stargell 4.00 1.50
❑ 52 Rickie Weeks 2.50 1.00
❑ 53 Johan Santana 4.00 1.50
❑ 54 Torii Hunter 2.50 1.00
❑ 55 Joe Mauer 4.00 1.50
❑ 56 Pedro Martinez 4.00 1.50
❑ 57 David Wright 8.00 3.00
❑ 58 Carlos Beltran 2.50 1.00
❑ 59 Jimmie Foxx 5.00 2.00
❑ 60 Jose Reyes 2.50 1.00
❑ 61 Derek Jeter 10.00 4.00
❑ 62 Alex Rodriguez 8.00 3.00
❑ 63 Randy Johnson 5.00 2.00
❑ 64 Hideki Matsui 5.00 2.00
❑ 65 Thurman Munson 5.00 2.00
❑ 66 Rich Harden 2.50 1.00
❑ 67 Eric Chavez 2.50 1.00
❑ 68 Don Drysdale 4.00 1.50
❑ 69 Bobby Crosby 2.50 1.00
❑ 70 Pee Wee Reese 4.00 1.50
❑ 71 Ryan Howard 8.00 3.00
❑ 72 Chase Utley 5.00 2.00
❑ 73 Jackie Robinson 5.00 2.00
❑ 74 Jason Bay 2.50 1.00
❑ 75 Honus Wagner 5.00 2.00
❑ 76 Lefty Grove 2.50 1.00
❑ 77 Jake Peavy 2.50 1.00
❑ 78 Brian Giles 2.50 1.00
❑ 79 Eddie Murray 5.00 2.00
❑ 80 Omar Vizquel 4.00 1.50
❑ 81 Jason Schmidt 2.50 1.00
❑ 82 Ichiro Suzuki 6.00 2.50
❑ 83 Felix Hernandez 4.00 1.50
❑ 84 Kenji Johjima RC 8.00 3.00
❑ 85 Albert Pujols 8.00 3.00
❑ 86 Chris Carpenter 2.50 1.00
❑ 87 Brooks Robinson 4.00 1.50
❑ 88 Dizzy Dean 4.00 1.50
❑ 89 Carl Crawford 2.50 1.00
❑ 90 Rogers Hornsby 4.00 1.50
❑ 91 Scott Kazmir 4.00 1.50
❑ 92 Mark Teixeira 4.00 1.50
❑ 93 Michael Young 2.50 1.00
❑ 94 Johnny Mize 2.50 1.00
❑ 95 Vernon Wells 2.50 1.00
❑ 96 Roy Halladay 2.50 1.00
❑ 97 Mel Ott 2.50 1.00
❑ 98 Alfonso Soriano 2.50 1.00
❑ 99 Joe Morgan 2.50 1.00
❑ 100 Satchel Paige 5.00 2.00
❑ 101 A.Wainwright AU/180 (RC) 25.00 10.00
❑ 102 A.Hernandez AU/180 (RC) 10.00 4.00
❑ 103 A.Ethier AU/180 (RC) 30.00 12.50
❑ 104 B.Johnson AU/180 (RC) 10.00 4.00
❑ 105 B.Bonser AU/180 (RC) 15.00 6.00
❑ 106 B.Logan AU/180 RC 10.00 4.00
❑ 107 B.Anderson AU/180 (RC) 10.00 4.00
❑ 108 B.Bannister AU/180 (RC) 50.00 20.00
❑ 109 C.Demaria AU/180 RC 10.00 4.00
❑ 110 C.Denorfia AU/180 (RC) 10.00 4.00
❑ 111 C.Ross AU/180 (RC) 10.00 4.00
❑ 112 C.Hamels AU/180 (RC) 80.00 40.00
❑ 113 C.Jackson AU/180 (RC) 15.00 6.00
❑ 114 D.Uggla AU/180 (RC) EXCH 30.00 12.50
❑ 115 D.Gassner AU/180 (RC) 10.00 4.00
❑ 116 E.Reed AU/180 (RC) 10.00 4.00
❑ 118 F.Nieve AU/180 (RC) 10.00 4.00
❑ 119 F.Liriano AU/180 (RC) 60.00 30.00
❑ 120 F.Bynum AU/180 (RC) 10.00 4.00
❑ 121 H.Ramirez AU/180 (RC) 40.00 15.00
❑ 122 H.Kuo AU/180 (RC) EXCH 80.00 40.00
❑ 123 I.Kinsler AU/180 (RC) 30.00 12.50
❑ 124 J.Hammel AU/180 (RC) 10.00 4.00
❑ 125 J.Kubel AU/180 (RC) 10.00 4.00
❑ 126 J.Harris AU/180 RC 10.00 4.00
❑ 127 J.Weaver AU/150 (RC) 50.00 20.00
❑ 128 J.Accardo AU/180 (RC) 10.00 4.00
❑ 129 J.Hermida AU/180 (RC) 15.00 6.00
❑ 130 J.Zumaya AU/180 (RC) 40.00 15.00
❑ 131 J.Devine AU/180 RC 10.00 4.00
❑ 132 J.Koronka AU/180 (RC) 10.00 4.00
❑ 133 J.Van Benschoten AU/180 (RC) 10.00 4.00
❑ 134 J.Papelbon AU/180 (RC) 50.00 20.00
❑ 135 J.Capellan AU/180 (RC) 10.00 4.00
❑ 136 J.Johnson AU/180 (RC) 15.00 6.00
❑ 137 J.Rupe AU/180 (RC) 10.00 4.00
❑ 138 J.Willingham AU/180 (RC) 10.00 4.00
❑ 139 J.Wilson AU/180 (RC) 10.00 4.00
❑ 140 J.Verlander AU/180 (RC) 50.00 20.00
❑ 141 K.Shoppach AU/180 (RC) 10.00 4.00
❑ 142 K.Morales AU/180 (RC) 15.00 6.00
❑ 143 M.McBride AU/180 (RC) 10.00 4.00
❑ 144 M.Prado AU/180 (RC) 10.00 4.00
❑ 145 M.Cain AU/180 (RC) 25.00 10.00
❑ 146 M.Jacobs AU/180 (RC) 10.00 4.00
❑ 147 M.Thompson AU/180 RC 10.00 4.00
❑ 148 N.McLouth AU/180 (RC) 20.00 8.00
❑ 149 P.Maholm AU/180 (RC) 10.00 4.00
❑ 150 P.Fielder AU/180 (RC) EXCH 120.00 60.00
❑ 151 R.Abercrombie AU/180 (RC) 10.00 4.00
❑ 152 R.Hill AU/180 (RC) 40.00 15.00
❑ 153 R.Flores AU/180 RC 10.00 4.00
❑ 154 R.Lugo AU/180 (RC) 10.00 4.00
❑ 155 R.Zimmerman AU/180 (RC) 60.00 30.00
❑ 156 S.Marshall AU/180 (RC) 25.00 10.00
❑ 157 T.Saito AU/180 RC 25.00 10.00
❑ 158 T.Buchholz AU/180 (RC) 10.00 4.00
❑ 159 T.Pena Jr. AU/180 (RC) 10.00 4.00
❑ 160 W.Nieves AU/180 (RC) 10.00 4.00
❑ 161 J.Shields AU/180 RC 10.00 4.00
❑ 162 J.Lester AU/180 RC 50.00 20.00
❑ 163 C.Hansen AU/180 RC 40.00 15.00
❑ 164 A.Rakers AU/180 (RC) 10.00 4.00
❑ 165 Y.Petit AU/180 (RC) EXCH 10.00 4.00
❑ 166 B.Livingston AU/180 (RC) 10.00 4.00
❑ 167 B.Harris AU/180 (RC) 10.00 4.00
❑ 168 C.Ruiz AU/180 (RC) 10.00 4.00
❑ 170 C.Britton AU/180 RC 10.00 4.00
❑ 171 H.Kendrick AU/180 (RC) 40.00 15.00
❑ 172 J.Van Buren AU/180 (RC) 10.00 4.00
❑ 173 K.Frandsen AU/180 (RC) 15.00 6.00
❑ 174 M.Capps AU/180 (RC) 10.00 4.00
❑ 175 P.Moylan AU/180 RC 10.00 4.00
❑ 191 Richie Ashburn 4.00 1.50
❑ 192 Lou Brock 4.00 1.50
❑ 193 Lou Boudreau 2.50 1.00
❑ 194 Orlando Cepeda 2.50 1.00
❑ 195 Bobby Doerr 2.50 1.00
❑ 196 Dennis Eckersley 2.50 1.00
❑ 197 Bob Feller 2.50 1.00
❑ 198 Rollie Fingers 2.50 1.00
❑ 199 Carlton Fisk 4.00 1.50
❑ 200 Bob Gibson 4.00 1.50
❑ 201 Catfish Hunter 2.50 1.00
❑ 202 Fergie Jenkins 2.50 1.00
❑ 203 Al Kaline 5.00 2.00
❑ 204 Harmon Killebrew 5.00 2.00
❑ 205 Ralph Kiner 4.00 1.50
❑ 206 Buck Leonard 2.50 1.00
❑ 207 Juan Marichal 2.50 1.00
❑ 208 Bill Mazeroski 4.00 1.50
❑ 209 Willie McCovey 4.00 1.50
❑ 210 Jim Palmer 2.50 1.00
❑ 211 Tony Perez 2.50 1.00
❑ 212 Gaylord Perry 2.50 1.00
❑ 213 Phil Rizzuto 4.00 1.50
❑ 214 Robin Roberts 2.50 1.00
❑ 215 Mike Schmidt 6.00 2.50
❑ 216 Enos Slaughter 2.50 1.00
❑ 217 Ozzie Smith 6.00 2.50
❑ 218 Billy Williams 2.50 1.00
❑ 219 Robin Yount 5.00 2.00
❑ 220 Carlos Quentin (RC) 4.00 1.50
❑ 221 Jeff Francoeur 5.00 2.00
❑ 222 Brian McCann 2.50 1.00
❑ 223 Nick Markakis (RC) 4.00 1.50
❑ 224 Josh Beckett 2.50 1.00
❑ 225 Jason Varitek 5.00 2.00
❑ 226 Mark Prior 4.00 1.50
❑ 227 Aramis Ramirez 2.50 1.00
❑ 228 Jermaine Dye 2.50 1.00
❑ 229 Tadahito Iguchi 2.50 1.00
❑ 230 Bobby Jenks 2.50 1.00
❑ 231 C.C. Sabathia 2.50 1.00
❑ 232 Jeff Francis 2.50 1.00
❑ 233 Matt Holliday 3.00 1.25
❑ 234 Magglio Ordonez 2.50 1.00
❑ 235 Kenny Rogers 2.50 1.00
❑ 236 Roger Clemens 8.00 3.00
❑ 237 Andy Pettitte 2.50 1.00
❑ 238 Craig Biggio 4.00 1.50
❑ 239 Chone Figgins 2.50 1.00
❑ 240 John Lackey 2.50 1.00
❑ 241 Nomar Garciaparra 5.00 2.00
❑ 242 Prince Fielder 6.00 2.50
❑ 243 Ben Sheets 2.50 1.00
❑ 244 Bill Hall 2.50 1.00
❑ 245 Justin Morneau 2.50 1.00
❑ 246 Joe Nathan 2.50 1.00
❑ 247 Carlos Delgado 2.50 1.00
❑ 248 Shawn Green 2.50 1.00
❑ 249 Billy Wagner 2.50 1.00
❑ 250 Jason Giambi 2.50 1.00
❑ 251 Mike Mussina 4.00 1.50
❑ 252 Mariano Rivera 5.00 2.00
❑ 253 Robinson Cano 4.00 1.50
❑ 254 Bobby Abreu 2.50 1.00
❑ 255 Huston Street 2.50 1.00
❑ 256 Frank Thomas 5.00 2.00
❑ 257 Danny Haren 2.50 1.00
❑ 258 Jason Kendall 2.50 1.00
❑ 259 Nick Swisher 2.50 1.00
❑ 260 Pat Burrell 2.50 1.00
❑ 261 Tom Gordon 2.50 1.00
❑ 262 Freddy Sanchez 2.50 1.00
❑ 263 Trevor Hoffman 2.50 1.00
❑ 264 Khalil Greene 4.00 1.50
❑ 265 Adrian Gonzalez 2.50 1.00
❑ 266 Moises Alou 2.50 1.00
❑ 267 Matt Morris 2.50 1.00
❑ 268 Pedro Feliz 2.50 1.00
❑ 269 Richie Sexson 2.50 1.00
❑ 270 Hoyt Wilhelm 2.50 1.00
❑ 271 Adrian Beltre 2.50 1.00
❑ 272 Jim Edmonds 4.00 1.50
❑ 273 Scott Rolen 4.00 1.50
❑ 274 Jason Isringhausen 2.50 1.00
❑ 275 Jorge Cantu 2.50 1.00
❑ 276 Hank Blalock 2.50 1.00
❑ 277 Kevin Millwood 2.50 1.00
❑ 278 Alex Rios 2.50 1.00
❑ 279 Troy Glaus 2.50 1.00
❑ 280 B.J. Ryan 2.50 1.00
❑ 281 Nick Johnson 2.50 1.00
❑ 282 Chad Cordero 2.50 1.00
❑ 283 Austin Kearns 2.50 1.00
❑ 284 Ricky Nolasco (RC) 2.50 1.00
❑ 285 Travis Ishikawa (RC) 2.50 1.00
❑ 286 Lastings Milledge (RC) 4.00 1.50
❑ 287 James Loney (RC) 4.00 1.50
❑ 288 Red Schoendienst 2.50 1.00
❑ 289 Warren Spahn 4.00 1.50
❑ 290 Early Wynn 2.50 1.00

2007 Ultimate Collection

❑ COMMON CARD (1-100) 2.00 .75
❑ 1-100 PRINT RUN 450 SER.#'d SETS

	Card	Price	Price
❑	COMMON AU RC (101-141)	10.00	4.00
❑	OVERALL AU ODDS ONE PER PACK		
❑	AU RC PRINT RUNS B/WN 289-299 COPIES PER		
❑	EXCHANGE DEADLINE 9/24/2009		
❑	1 Chipper Jones	5.00	2.00
❑	2 Andruw Jones	3.00	1.25
❑	3 Tim Hudson	2.00	.75
❑	4 Stephen Drew	3.00	1.25
❑	5 Randy Johnson	5.00	2.00
❑	6 Brandon Webb	2.00	.75
❑	7 Alfonso Soriano	2.00	.75
❑	8 Derrek Lee	2.00	.75
❑	9 Aramis Ramirez	2.00	.75
❑	10 Carlos Zambrano	2.00	.75
❑	11 Ken Griffey Jr.	8.00	3.00
❑	12 Adam Dunn	2.00	.75
❑	13 Ryan Freel	2.00	.75
❑	14 Todd Helton	3.00	1.25
❑	15 Garrett Atkins	2.00	.75
❑	16 Matt Holliday	5.00	2.00
❑	17 Hanley Ramirez	3.00	1.25
❑	18 Dontrelle Willis	2.00	.75
❑	19 Miguel Cabrera	3.00	1.25
❑	20 Lance Berkman	2.00	.75
❑	21 Roy Oswalt	2.00	.75
❑	22 Carlos Lee	2.00	.75
❑	23 Nomar Garciaparra	5.00	2.00
❑	24 Jason Schmidt	2.00	.75
❑	25 Juan Pierre	2.00	.75
❑	26 Russell Martin	2.00	.75
❑	27 Rickie Weeks	2.00	.75
❑	28 Prince Fielder	5.00	2.00
❑	29 Ben Sheets	2.00	.75
❑	30 David Wright	8.00	3.00
❑	31 Jose Reyes	5.00	2.00
❑	32 Pedro Martinez	3.00	1.25
❑	33 Carlos Beltran	2.00	.75
❑	34 Brett Myers	2.00	.75
❑	35 Jimmy Rollins	2.00	.75
❑	36 Ryan Howard	8.00	3.00
❑	37 Jason Bay	2.00	.75
❑	38 Freddy Sanchez	2.00	.75
❑	39 Ian Snell	2.00	.75
❑	40 Jake Peavy	2.00	.75
❑	41 Greg Maddux	8.00	3.00
❑	42 Brian Giles	2.00	.75
❑	43 Matt Cain	3.00	1.25
❑	44 Barry Zito	2.00	.75
❑	45 Ray Durham	2.00	.75
❑	46 Albert Pujols	10.00	4.00
❑	47 Chris Carpenter	2.00	.75
❑	48 Chris Duncan	2.00	.75
❑	49 Scott Rolen	3.00	1.25
❑	50 Ryan Zimmerman	5.00	2.00
❑	51 Chad Cordero	2.00	.75
❑	52 Ryan Church	2.00	.75
❑	53 Miguel Tejada	2.00	.75
❑	54 Erik Bedard	2.00	.75
❑	55 Brian Roberts	2.00	.75
❑	56 David Ortiz	5.00	2.00
❑	57 Josh Beckett	3.00	1.25
❑	58 Manny Ramirez	3.00	1.25
❑	59 Daisuke Matsuzaka RC	30.00	12.50
❑	60 Jim Thome	3.00	1.25
❑	61 Paul Konerko	2.00	.75
❑	62 Jermaine Dye	2.00	.75
❑	63 Grady Sizemore	3.00	1.25
❑	64 Victor Martinez	2.00	.75
❑	65 C.C. Sabathia	2.00	.75
❑	66 Ivan Rodriguez	3.00	1.25
❑	67 Justin Verlander	5.00	2.00
❑	68 Gary Sheffield	2.00	.75
❑	69 Jeremy Bonderman	2.00	.75
❑	70 Gil Meche	2.00	.75
❑	71 Mike Sweeney	2.00	.75
❑	72 Mark Teahen	2.00	.75
❑	73 Vladimir Guerrero	5.00	2.00
❑	74 Howie Kendrick	2.00	.75
❑	75 Francisco Rodriguez	2.00	.75
❑	76 Johan Santana	3.00	1.25
❑	77 Justin Morneau	2.00	.75
❑	78 Joe Mauer	3.00	1.25
❑	79 Michael Cuddyer	2.00	.75
❑	80 Alex Rodriguez	8.00	3.00
❑	81 Derek Jeter	12.00	5.00
❑	82 Johnny Damon	3.00	1.25
❑	83 Roger Clemens	8.00	3.00
❑	84 Rich Harden	2.00	.75
❑	85 Mike Piazza	5.00	2.00
❑	86 Huston Street	2.00	.75
❑	87 Ichiro Suzuki	8.00	3.00
❑	88 Felix Hernandez	3.00	1.25
❑	89 Kenji Johjima	5.00	2.00
❑	90 Adrian Beltre	2.00	.75
❑	91 Carl Crawford	2.00	.75
❑	92 Scott Kazmir	3.00	1.25
❑	93 B.J. Upton	2.00	.75
❑	94 Michael Young	2.00	.75
❑	95 Mark Teixeira	3.00	1.25
❑	96 Sammy Sosa	5.00	2.00
❑	97 Hank Blalock	2.00	.75
❑	98 Vernon Wells	2.00	.75
❑	99 Roy Halladay	2.00	.75
❑	100 Frank Thomas	5.00	2.00
❑	101 Adam Lind AU (RC)	10.00	4.00
❑	102 Akinori Iwamura AU RC	30.00	12.50
❑	103 Andrew Miller AU RC	50.00	20.00
❑	104 Michael Bourn AU (RC)	10.00	4.00
❑	105 Kory Casto AU (RC)	10.00	4.00
❑	106 Ryan Braun AU (RC)	80.00	40.00
❑	107 Sean Gallagher AU (RC)	10.00	4.00
❑	108 Billy Butler AU (RC)	40.00	15.00
❑	109 Alexi Casilla AU RC	10.00	4.00
❑	110 Chris Stewart AU RC	10.00	4.00
❑	111 Matt DeSalvo AU (RC)	15.00	6.00
❑	112 Chase Headley AU (RC)	15.00	6.00
❑	113 D.Young AU/292 (RC)	30.00	12.50
❑	114 Homer Bailey AU (RC)	15.00	6.00
❑	115 Kurt Suzuki AU (RC)	15.00	6.00
❑	116 A.Gordon AU/297 RC	60.00	30.00
❑	117 Josh Hamilton AU (RC)	50.00	20.00
❑	118 Fred Lewis AU (RC)	10.00	4.00
❑	119 Glen Perkins AU (RC)	10.00	4.00
❑	120 Hector Gimenez AU (RC)	10.00	4.00
❑	121 Phil Hughes AU (RC)	60.00	30.00
❑	122 Jeff Baker AU (RC)	10.00	4.00
❑	123 Andy LaRoche AU (RC)	10.00	4.00
❑	124 Tim Lincecum AU RC	80.00	40.00
❑	125 Joaquin Arias AU (RC)	10.00	4.00
❑	126 D.Matsuzaka AU	200.00	100.00
❑	127 Micah Owings AU (RC)	15.00	6.00
❑	128 H.Pence AU/297 (RC)	60.00	30.00
❑	129 Matt Chico AU (RC)	10.00	4.00
❑	130 Kei Igawa AU RC	30.00	12.50
❑	131 Kevin Kouzmanoff AU (RC)	10.00	4.00
❑	132 M.Montero AU/289 (RC)	10.00	4.00
❑	133 Mike Rabelo AU RC	15.00	6.00
❑	134 Felix Pie AU (RC)	10.00	4.00
❑	135 Curtis Thigpen AU (RC)	10.00	4.00
❑	136 Ryan Z. Braun AU RC	15.00	6.00
❑	137 Ryan Sweeney AU (RC)	10.00	4.00
❑	138 Brandon Wood AU (RC)	15.00	6.00
❑	139 Troy Tulowitzki AU (RC)	40.00	15.00
❑	140 Justin Upton AU RC	100.00	50.00
❑	141 J.Chamberlain AU RC EXCH	250.00	125.00

2001 Ultra

	Card	Price	Price
❑	COMPLETE SET (275)	120.00	60.00
❑	COMP.SET w/o SP's (250)	25.00	10.00
❑	COMMON CARD (1-250)	.30	.10
❑	COMMON CARD (251-275)	3.00	1.25
❑	COMMON CARD (276-280)	5.00	2.00
❑	1 Pedro Martinez	.50	.20
❑	2 Derek Jeter	2.00	.75
❑	3 Cal Ripken	2.50	1.00
❑	4 Alex Rodriguez	1.25	.50
❑	5 Vladimir Guerrero	.75	.30
❑	6 Troy Glaus	.30	.10
❑	7 Sammy Sosa	.75	.30
❑	8 Mike Piazza	1.25	.50
❑	9 Tony Gwynn	1.00	.40
❑	10 Tim Hudson	.30	.10
❑	11 John Flaherty	.30	.10
❑	12 Jeff Cirillo	.30	.10
❑	13 Ellis Burks	.30	.10
❑	14 Carlos Lee	.30	.10
❑	15 Carlos Beltran	.30	.10
❑	16 Ruben Rivera	.30	.10
❑	17 Richard Hidalgo	.30	.10
❑	18 Omar Vizquel	.50	.20
❑	19 Michael Barrett	.30	.10
❑	20 Jose Canseco	.50	.20
❑	21 Jason Giambi	.30	.10
❑	22 Greg Maddux	1.25	.50
❑	23 Charles Johnson	.30	.10
❑	24 Sandy Alomar Jr.	.30	.10
❑	25 Rick Ankiel	.30	.10
❑	26 Richie Sexson	.30	.10
❑	27 Matt Williams	.30	.10
❑	28 Joe Girardi	.30	.10
❑	29 Jason Kendall	.30	.10
❑	30 Brad Fullmer	.30	.10
❑	31 Alex Gonzalez	.30	.10
❑	32 Rick Helling	.30	.10
❑	33 Mike Mussina	.50	.20
❑	34 Joe Randa	.30	.10
❑	35 J.T. Snow	.30	.10
❑	36 Edgardo Alfonzo	.30	.10
❑	37 Dante Bichette	.30	.10
❑	38 Brad Ausmus	.30	.10
❑	39 Bobby Abreu	.30	.10
❑	40 Warren Morris	.30	.10
❑	41 Tony Womack	.30	.10
❑	42 Russell Branyan	.30	.10
❑	43 Mike Lowell	.30	.10
❑	44 Mark Grace	.50	.20
❑	45 Jeromy Burnitz	.30	.10
❑	46 J.D. Drew	.30	.10
❑	47 David Justice	.30	.10
❑	48 Alex Gonzalez	.30	.10
❑	49 Tino Martinez	.50	.20
❑	50 Raul Mondesi	.30	.10
❑	51 Rafael Furcal	.30	.10
❑	52 Marquis Grissom	.30	.10
❑	53 Kevin Young	.30	.10
❑	54 Jon Lieber	.30	.10
❑	55 Henry Rodriguez	.30	.10
❑	56 Dave Burba	.30	.10
❑	57 Shannon Stewart	.30	.10
❑	58 Preston Wilson	.30	.10
❑	59 Paul O'Neill	.50	.20
❑	60 Jimmy Haynes	.30	.10
❑	61 Darryl Kile	.30	.10
❑	62 Bret Boone	.30	.10
❑	63 Bartolo Colon	.30	.10
❑	64 Andres Galarraga	.30	.10
❑	65 Trot Nixon	.30	.10
❑	66 Steve Finley	.30	.10
❑	67 Shawn Green	.30	.10
❑	68 Robert Person	.30	.10
❑	69 Kenny Rogers	.30	.10
❑	70 Bobby Higginson	.30	.10
❑	71 Barry Larkin	.50	.20
❑	72 Al Martin	.30	.10
❑	73 Tom Glavine	.50	.20
❑	74 Rondell White	.30	.10
❑	75 Ray Lankford	.30	.10
❑	76 Moises Alou	.30	.10
❑	77 Matt Clement	.30	.10
❑	78 Geoff Jenkins	.30	.10
❑	79 David Wells	.30	.10
❑	80 Chuck Finley	.30	.10
❑	81 Andy Pettitte	.50	.20
❑	82 Travis Fryman	.30	.10
❑	83 Ron Coomer	.30	.10
❑	84 Mark McGwire	2.00	.75
❑	85 Kerry Wood	.30	.10
❑	86 Jorge Posada	.50	.20
❑	87 Jeff Bagwell	.50	.20
❑	88 Andruw Jones	.50	.20

No.	Player		
89	Ryan Klesko	.30	.10
90	Mariano Rivera	.75	.30
91	Lance Berkman	.30	.10
92	Kenny Lofton	.30	.10
93	Jacque Jones	.30	.10
94	Eric Young	.30	.10
95	Edgar Renteria	.30	.10
96	Chipper Jones	.75	.30
97	Todd Helton	.50	.20
98	Shawn Estes	.30	.10
99	Mark Mulder	.30	.10
100	Lee Stevens	.30	.10
101	Jermaine Dye	.30	.10
102	Greg Vaughn	.30	.10
103	Chris Singleton	.30	.10
104	Brady Anderson	.30	.10
105	Terrence Long	.30	.10
106	Quilvio Veras	.30	.10
107	Magglio Ordonez	.30	.10
108	Johnny Damon	.50	.20
109	Jeffrey Hammonds	.30	.10
110	Fred McGriff	.50	.20
111	Carl Pavano	.30	.10
112	Bobby Estalella	.30	.10
113	Todd Hundley	.30	.10
114	Scott Rolen	.50	.20
115	Robin Ventura	.30	.10
116	Pokey Reese	.30	.10
117	Luis Gonzalez	.30	.10
118	Jose Offerman	.30	.10
119	Edgar Martinez	.50	.20
120	Dean Palmer	.30	.10
121	David Segui	.30	.10
122	Troy O'Leary	.30	.10
123	Tony Batista	.30	.10
124	Todd Zeile	.30	.10
125	Randy Johnson	.75	.30
126	Luis Castillo	.30	.10
127	Kris Benson	.30	.10
128	John Olerud	.30	.10
129	Eric Karros	.30	.10
130	Eddie Taubensee	.30	.10
131	Neifi Perez	.30	.10
132	Matt Stairs	.30	.10
133	Luis Alicea	.30	.10
134	Jeff Kent	.30	.10
135	Javier Vazquez	.30	.10
136	Garret Anderson	.30	.10
137	Frank Thomas	.75	.30
138	Carlos Febles	.30	.10
139	Albert Belle	.30	.10
140	Tony Clark	.30	.10
141	Pat Burrell	.30	.10
142	Mike Sweeney	.30	.10
143	Jay Buhner	.30	.10
144	Gabe Kapler	.30	.10
145	Derek Bell	.30	.10
146	B.J. Surhoff	.30	.10
147	Adam Kennedy	.30	.10
148	Aaron Boone	.30	.10
149	Todd Stottlemyre	.30	.10
150	Roberto Alomar	.50	.20
151	Orlando Hernandez	.30	.10
152	Jason Varitek	.75	.30
153	Gary Sheffield	.30	.10
154	Cliff Floyd	.30	.10
155	Chad Hermansen	.30	.10
156	Carlos Delgado	.30	.10
157	Aaron Sele	.30	.10
158	Sean Casey	.30	.10
159	Ruben Mateo	.30	.10
160	Mike Bordick	.30	.10
161	Mike Cameron	.30	.10
162	Doug Glanville	.30	.10
163	Damion Easley	.30	.10
164	Carl Everett	.30	.10
165	Bengie Molina	.30	.10
166	Adrian Beltre	.30	.10
167	Tom Goodwin	.30	.10
168	Rickey Henderson	.75	.30
169	Mo Vaughn	.30	.10
170	Mike Lieberthal	.30	.10
171	Ken Griffey Jr.	1.25	.50
172	Juan Gonzalez	.30	.10
173	Ivan Rodriguez	.50	.20
174	Al Leiter	.30	.10
175	Vinny Castilla	.30	.10
176	Peter Bergeron	.30	.10
177	Pedro Astacio	.30	.10
178	Paul Konerko	.30	.10
179	Mitch Meluskey	.30	.10
180	Kevin Millwood	.30	.10
181	Ben Grieve	.30	.10
182	Barry Bonds	2.00	.75
183	Rusty Greer	.30	.10
184	Miguel Tejada	.30	.10
185	Mark Quinn	.30	.10
186	Larry Walker	.30	.10
187	Jose Valentin	.30	.10
188	Jose Vidro	.30	.10
189	Delino DeShields	.30	.10
190	Darin Erstad	.30	.10
191	Bill Mueller	.30	.10
192	Ray Durham	.30	.10
193	Ken Caminiti	.30	.10
194	Jim Thome	.50	.20
195	Javy Lopez	.30	.10
196	Fernando Vina	.30	.10
197	Eric Chavez	.30	.10
198	Eric Owens	.30	.10
199	Brad Radke	.30	.10
200	Travis Lee	.30	.10
201	Tim Salmon	.50	.20
202	Rafael Palmeiro	.50	.20
203	Nomar Garciaparra	1.25	.50
204	Mike Hampton	.30	.10
205	Kevin Brown	.30	.10
206	Juan Encarnacion	.30	.10
207	Danny Graves	.30	.10
208	Carlos Guillen	.30	.10
209	Phil Nevin	.30	.10
210	Matt Lawton	.30	.10
211	Manny Ramirez	.50	.20
212	James Baldwin	.30	.10
213	Fernando Tatis	.30	.10
214	Craig Biggio	.50	.20
215	Brian Jordan	.30	.10
216	Bernie Williams	.50	.20
217	Ryan Dempster	.30	.10
218	Roger Clemens	1.50	.60
219	Jose Cruz Jr.	.30	.10
220	John Valentin	.30	.10
221	Dmitri Young	.30	.10
222	Curt Schilling	.30	.10
223	Jim Edmonds	.30	.10
224	Chan Ho Park	.30	.10
225	Brian Giles	.30	.10
226	J.Anderson/T.Redman	.30	.10
227	A.Platt/J.Ortiz	.30	.10
228	K.Kelly/A.Huff	.30	.10
229	R.Choate/C.Dingman	.30	.10
230	E.Cammack/G.Roberts	.30	.10
231	Y.Lara/A.Tracy	.30	.10
232	W.Franklin/S.Linebrink	.30	.10
233	C.Cairncross/C.Perry	.30	.10
234	J.Romero/M.LeCroy	.30	.10
235	G.Guzman/J.Conti	.30	.10
236	M.Burkhart/P.Crawford	.30	.10
237	P.Coco/L.Estrella	.30	.10
238	J.Parrish/F.Lunar	.30	.10
239	K.McDonald/J.Brunette	.30	.10
240	C.Casimiro/I.Coffie	.30	.10
241	D.Garibay/R.Quevedo	.30	.10
242	S.Lee/T.Ohka	.30	.10
243	H.Ortiz/J.D'Amico	.30	.10
244	J.Sparks/T.Harper	.30	.10
245	J.Boyd/D.Coggin	.30	.10
246	M.Buehrle/L.Barcelo	.50	.20
247	A.Melhuse/B.Petrick	.30	.10
248	K.Davis/P.Rigdon	.30	.10
249	M.Darr/K.DeHaan	.30	.10
250	V.Padilla/M.Brownson	3.00	1.25
251	Barry Zito PROS	5.00	2.00
252	Tim Drew PROS	3.00	1.25
253	Luis Matos PROS	3.00	1.25
254	Alex Cabrera PROS	3.00	1.25
255	Jon Garland PROS	3.00	1.25
256	Milton Bradley PROS	3.00	1.25
257	Juan Pierre PROS	3.00	1.25
258	Ismael Villegas PROS	3.00	1.25
259	Eric Munson PROS	3.00	1.25
260	Tomas De la Rosa PROS	3.00	1.25
261	Chris Richard PROS	3.00	1.25
262	Jason Tyner PROS	3.00	1.25
263	B.J. Waszgis PROS	3.00	1.25
264	Jason Marquis PROS	3.00	1.25
265	Dusty Allen PROS	3.00	1.25
266	Corey Patterson PROS	3.00	1.25
267	Eric Byrnes PROS	3.00	1.25
268	Xavier Nady PROS	3.00	1.25
269	George Lombard PROS	3.00	1.25
270	Timo Perez PROS	3.00	1.25
271	Gary Matthews Jr. PROS	3.00	1.25
272	Chad Durbin PROS	3.00	1.25
273	Tony Armas Jr. PROS	3.00	1.25
274	Francisco Cordero PROS	3.00	1.25
275	Alfonso Soriano PROS	5.00	2.00
276	J.Spivey RC/J.Uribe RC	8.00	3.00
277	A.Pujols RC/B.Smith RC	80.00	40.00
278	I.Suzuki RC/T.Shinjo RC	30.00	12.50
279	D.Henson RC/J.Melian RC	8.00	3.00
280	M.White RC/A.Hernandez RC	5.00	2.00

2002 Ultra

No.	Player		
	COMPLETE SET (285)	200.00	80.00
	COMP.SET w/o SP's (200)	25.00	10.00
	COMMON CARD (1-200)	.30	.10
	COMMON CARD (201-220)	1.00	.40
	COMMON CARD (221-250)	1.00	.40
	COMMON CARD (251-285)	3.00	1.25
1	Jeff Bagwell	.50	.20
2	Derek Jeter	2.00	.75
3	Alex Rodriguez	1.25	.50
4	Eric Chavez	.30	.10
5	Tsuyoshi Shinjo	.30	.10
6	Chris Stynes	.30	.10
7	Ivan Rodriguez	.50	.20
8	Cal Ripken	2.50	1.00
9	Freddy Garcia	.30	.10
10	Chipper Jones	.75	.30
11	Hideo Nomo	.75	.30
12	Rafael Furcal	.30	.10
13	Preston Wilson	.30	.10
14	Jimmy Rollins	.30	.10
15	Cristian Guzman	.30	.10
16	Garret Anderson	.30	.10
17	Todd Helton	.50	.20
18	Moises Alou	.30	.10
19	Tony Gwynn	1.00	.40
20	Jorge Posada	.50	.20
21	Sean Casey	.30	.10
22	Kazuhiro Sasaki	.30	.10
23	Ray Lankford	.30	.10
24	Manny Ramirez	.50	.20
25	Barry Bonds	2.00	.75
26	Fred McGriff	.50	.20
27	Vladimir Guerrero	.75	.30
28	Jermaine Dye	.30	.10
29	Adrian Beltre	.30	.10
30	Ken Griffey Jr.	1.25	.50
31	Ramon Hernandez	.30	.10
32	Kerry Wood	.30	.10
33	Greg Maddux	1.25	.50
34	Rondell White	.30	.10
35	Mike Mussina	.50	.20
36	Jim Edmonds	.30	.10
37	Scott Rolen	.50	.20
38	Mike Lowell	.30	.10
39	Al Leiter	.30	.10
40	Tony Clark	.30	.10

Card		
❑ 41 Joe Mays	.30	.10
❑ 42 Mo Vaughn	.30	.10
❑ 43 Geoff Jenkins	.30	.10
❑ 44 Curt Schilling	.30	.10
❑ 45 Pedro Martinez	.50	.20
❑ 46 Andy Pettitte	.50	.20
❑ 47 Tim Salmon	.50	.20
❑ 48 Carl Everett	.30	.10
❑ 49 Lance Berkman	.30	.10
❑ 50 Troy Glaus	.30	.10
❑ 51 Ichiro Suzuki	1.50	.60
❑ 52 Alfonso Soriano	.30	.10
❑ 53 Tomo Ohka	.30	.10
❑ 54 Dean Palmer	.30	.10
❑ 55 Kevin Brown	.30	.10
❑ 56 Albert Pujols	1.50	.60
❑ 57 Homer Bush	.30	.10
❑ 58 Tim Hudson	.30	.10
❑ 59 Frank Thomas	.75	.30
❑ 60 Joe Randa	.30	.10
❑ 61 Chan Ho Park	.30	.10
❑ 62 Bobby Higginson	.30	.10
❑ 63 Bartolo Colon	.30	.10
❑ 64 Aramis Ramirez	.30	.10
❑ 65 Jeff Cirillo	.30	.10
❑ 66 Roberto Alomar	.50	.20
❑ 67 Mark Kotsay	.30	.10
❑ 68 Mike Cameron	.30	.10
❑ 69 Mike Hampton	.30	.10
❑ 70 Trot Nixon	.30	.10
❑ 71 Juan Gonzalez	.30	.10
❑ 72 Damian Rolls	.30	.10
❑ 73 Brad Fullmer	.30	.10
❑ 74 David Ortiz	.75	.30
❑ 75 Brandon Inge	.30	.10
❑ 76 Orlando Hernandez	.30	.10
❑ 77 Matt Stairs	.30	.10
❑ 78 Jay Gibbons	.30	.10
❑ 79 Greg Vaughn	.30	.10
❑ 80 Brady Anderson	.30	.10
❑ 81 Jim Thome	.50	.20
❑ 82 Ben Sheets	.30	.10
❑ 83 Rafael Palmeiro	.50	.20
❑ 84 Edgar Renteria	.30	.10
❑ 85 Doug Mientkiewicz	.30	.10
❑ 86 Raul Mondesi	.30	.10
❑ 87 Shane Reynolds	.30	.10
❑ 88 Steve Finley	.30	.10
❑ 89 Jose Cruz Jr.	.30	.10
❑ 90 Edgardo Alfonzo	.30	.10
❑ 91 Jose Valentin	.30	.10
❑ 92 Mark McGwire	2.00	.75
❑ 93 Mark Grace	.50	.20
❑ 94 Mike Lieberthal	.30	.10
❑ 95 Barry Larkin	.50	.20
❑ 96 Chuck Knoblauch	.30	.10
❑ 97 Deivi Cruz	.30	.10
❑ 98 Jeromy Burnitz	.30	.10
❑ 99 Shannon Stewart	.30	.10
❑ 100 David Wells	.30	.10
❑ 101 Brook Fordyce	.30	.10
❑ 102 Rusty Greer	.30	.10
❑ 103 Andruw Jones	.50	.20
❑ 104 Jason Kendall	.30	.10
❑ 105 Nomar Garciaparra	1.25	.50
❑ 106 Shawn Green	.30	.10
❑ 107 Craig Biggio	.50	.20
❑ 108 Masato Yoshii	.30	.10
❑ 109 Ben Petrick	.30	.10
❑ 110 Gary Sheffield	.30	.10
❑ 111 Travis Lee	.30	.10
❑ 112 Matt Williams	.30	.10
❑ 113 Billy Wagner	.30	.10
❑ 114 Robin Ventura	.30	.10
❑ 115 Jerry Hairston	.30	.10
❑ 116 Paul LoDuca	.30	.10
❑ 117 Darin Erstad	.30	.10
❑ 118 Ruben Sierra	.30	.10
❑ 119 Ricky Gutierrez	.30	.10
❑ 120 Bret Boone	.30	.10
❑ 121 John Rocker	.30	.10
❑ 122 Roger Clemens	1.50	.60
❑ 123 Eric Karros	.30	.10
❑ 124 J.D. Drew	.30	.10
❑ 125 Carlos Delgado	.30	.10
❑ 126 Jeffrey Hammonds	.30	.10
❑ 127 Jeff Kent	.30	.10
❑ 128 David Justice	.30	.10
❑ 129 Cliff Floyd	.30	.10
❑ 130 Omar Vizquel	.50	.20
❑ 131 Matt Morris	.30	.10
❑ 132 Rich Aurilia	.30	.10
❑ 133 Larry Walker	.30	.10
❑ 134 Miguel Tejada	.30	.10
❑ 135 Eric Young	.30	.10
❑ 136 Aaron Sele	.30	.10
❑ 137 Eric Milton	.30	.10
❑ 138 Travis Fryman	.30	.10
❑ 139 Magglio Ordonez	.30	.10
❑ 140 Sammy Sosa	.75	.30
❑ 141 Pokey Reese	.30	.10
❑ 142 Adam Eaton	.30	.10
❑ 143 Adam Kennedy	.30	.10
❑ 144 Mike Piazza	1.25	.50
❑ 145 Larry Barnes	.30	.10
❑ 146 Darryl Kile	.30	.10
❑ 147 Tom Glavine	.50	.20
❑ 148 Ryan Klesko	.30	.10
❑ 149 Jose Vidro	.30	.10
❑ 150 Joe Kennedy	.30	.10
❑ 151 Bernie Williams	.50	.20
❑ 152 C.C. Sabathia	.30	.10
❑ 153 Alex Ochoa	.30	.10
❑ 154 A.J. Pierzynski	.30	.10
❑ 155 Johnny Damon	.50	.20
❑ 156 Omar Daal	.30	.10
❑ 157 A.J. Burnett	.30	.10
❑ 158 Eric Munson	.30	.10
❑ 159 Fernando Vina	.30	.10
❑ 160 Chris Singleton	.30	.10
❑ 161 Juan Pierre	.30	.10
❑ 162 John Olerud	.30	.10
❑ 163 Randy Johnson	.75	.30
❑ 164 Paul Konerko	.30	.10
❑ 165 Tino Martinez	.50	.20
❑ 166 Richard Hidalgo	.30	.10
❑ 167 Luis Gonzalez	.30	.10
❑ 168 Ben Grieve	.30	.10
❑ 169 Matt Lawton	.30	.10
❑ 170 Gabe Kapler	.30	.10
❑ 171 Mariano Rivera	.75	.30
❑ 172 Kenny Lofton	.30	.10
❑ 173 Brian Jordan	.30	.10
❑ 174 Brian Giles	.30	.10
❑ 175 Mark Quinn	.30	.10
❑ 176 Neifi Perez	.30	.10
❑ 177 Ellis Burks	.30	.10
❑ 178 Bobby Abreu	.30	.10
❑ 179 Jeff Weaver	.30	.10
❑ 180 Andres Galarraga	.30	.10
❑ 181 Javy Lopez	.30	.10
❑ 182 Todd Walker	.30	.10
❑ 183 Fernando Tatis	.30	.10
❑ 184 Charles Johnson	.30	.10
❑ 185 Pat Burrell	.30	.10
❑ 186 Jay Bell	.30	.10
❑ 187 Aaron Boone	.30	.10
❑ 188 Jason Giambi	.30	.10
❑ 189 Jay Payton	.30	.10
❑ 190 Carlos Lee	.30	.10
❑ 191 Phil Nevin	.30	.10
❑ 192 Mike Sweeney	.30	.10
❑ 193 J.T. Snow	.30	.10
❑ 194 Dmitri Young	.30	.10
❑ 195 Richie Sexson	.30	.10
❑ 196 Derrek Lee	.50	.20
❑ 197 Corey Koskie	.30	.10
❑ 198 Edgar Martinez	.50	.20
❑ 199 Wade Miller	.30	.10
❑ 200 Tony Batista	.30	.10
❑ 201 John Olerud AS	1.00	.40
❑ 202 Bret Boone AS	1.00	.40
❑ 203 Cal Ripken AS	5.00	2.00
❑ 204 Alex Rodriguez AS	2.50	1.00
❑ 205 Ichiro Suzuki AS	3.00	1.25
❑ 206 Manny Ramirez AS	.50	.20
❑ 207 Juan Gonzalez AS	1.00	.40
❑ 208 Ivan Rodriguez AS	1.50	.60
❑ 209 Roger Clemens AS	3.00	1.25
❑ 210 Edgar Martinez AS	1.50	.60
❑ 211 Todd Helton AS	1.50	.60
❑ 212 Jeff Kent AS	1.00	.40
❑ 213 Chipper Jones AS	1.50	.60
❑ 214 Rich Aurilia AS	1.00	.40
❑ 215 Barry Bonds AS	4.00	1.50
❑ 216 Sammy Sosa AS	1.50	.60
❑ 217 Luis Gonzalez AS	1.00	.40
❑ 218 Mike Piazza AS	2.50	1.00
❑ 219 Randy Johnson AS	1.50	.60
❑ 220 Larry Walker AS	1.00	.40
❑ 221 T.Helton/J.Uribe	1.00	.40
❑ 222 P.Burrell/E.Valent	1.00	.40
❑ 223 E.Martinez/I.Suzuki	3.00	1.25
❑ 224 B.Grieve/J.Tyner	1.00	.40
❑ 225 M.Quinn/D.Brown	1.00	.40
❑ 226 C.Ripken/B.Roberts	5.00	2.00
❑ 227 C.Floyd/A.Nunez	1.00	.40
❑ 228 J.Bagwell/A.Everett	1.00	.40
❑ 229 M.McGwire/A.Pujols	4.00	1.50
❑ 230 D.Mientkewicz/L.Rivas	1.00	.40
❑ 231 J.Gonzalez/D.Peoples	1.00	.40
❑ 232 K.Brown/L.Prokopec	1.00	.40
❑ 233 R.Sexson/B.Sheets	1.00	.40
❑ 234 J.Giambi/J.Hart	1.00	.40
❑ 235 B.Bonds/C.Valderrama	4.00	1.50
❑ 236 T.Gwynn/C.Crespo	2.00	.75
❑ 237 K.Griffey Jr./A.Dunn	2.50	1.00
❑ 238 F.Thomas/J.Crede	1.50	.60
❑ 239 D.Jeter/D.Henson	4.00	1.50
❑ 240 C.Jones/W.Betemit	1.50	.60
❑ 241 L.Gonzalez/J.Spivey	1.00	.40
❑ 242 B.Higginson/A.Torres	1.00	.40
❑ 243 C.Delgado/V.Wells	1.00	.40
❑ 244 S.Sosa/C.Patterson	1.50	.60
❑ 245 N.Garciaparra/S.Hillenbrand	2.50	1.00
❑ 246 A.Rodriguez/J.Romano	2.50	1.00
❑ 247 T.Glaus/D.Eckstein	1.00	.40
❑ 248 M.Piazza/A.Escobar	2.50	1.00
❑ 249 B.Giles/J.Wilson	1.00	.40
❑ 250 V.Guerrero/S.Hodges	1.50	.60
❑ 251 Bud Smith PROS	3.00	1.25
❑ 252 Juan Diaz PROS	3.00	1.25
❑ 253 Wilkin Ruan PROS	3.00	1.25
❑ 254 Chris Spurling PROS RC	3.00	1.25
❑ 255 Toby Hall PROS	3.00	1.25
❑ 256 Jason Jennings PROS	3.00	1.25
❑ 257 George Perez PROS	3.00	1.25
❑ 258 D'Angelo Jimenez PROS	3.00	1.25
❑ 259 Jose Acevedo PROS	3.00	1.25
❑ 260 Josue Perez PROS	3.00	1.25
❑ 261 Brian Rogers PROS	3.00	1.25
❑ 262 Carlos Maldonado PROS RC	3.00	1.25
❑ 263 Travis Phelps PROS	3.00	1.25
❑ 264 Rob Mackowiak PROS	3.00	1.25
❑ 265 Ryan Drese PROS	3.00	1.25
❑ 266 Carlos Garcia PROS	3.00	1.25
❑ 267 Alexis Gomez PROS	3.00	1.25
❑ 268 Jeremy Affeldt PROS	3.00	1.25
❑ 269 Scott Podsednik PROS	4.00	1.50
❑ 270 Adam Johnson PROS	3.00	1.25
❑ 271 Pedro Santana PROS	3.00	1.25
❑ 272 Les Walrond PROS	3.00	1.25
❑ 273 Jackson Melian PROS	3.00	1.25
❑ 274 Carlos Hernandez PROS	3.00	1.25
❑ 275 Mark Nussbeck PROS RC	3.00	1.25
❑ 276 Cory Aldridge PROS	3.00	1.25
❑ 277 Troy Mattes PROS	3.00	1.25
❑ 278 Brent Abernathy PROS	3.00	1.25
❑ 279 J.J. Davis PROS	3.00	1.25
❑ 280 Brandon Duckworth PROS	3.00	1.25
❑ 281 Kyle Lohse PROS	3.00	1.25
❑ 282 Justin Kaye PROS	3.00	1.25
❑ 283 Cody Ransom PROS	3.00	1.25
❑ 284 Dave Williams PROS	3.00	1.25
❑ 285 Luis Lopez PROS	3.00	1.25

2003 Ultra

Card		
❑ COMP.LO SET (250)	100.00	40.00
❑ COMP.LO SET w/o SP's (200)	25.00	10.00
❑ COMMON CARD (201-220)	1.50	.60
❑ COMMON CARD (221-250)	2.00	.75
❑ COMMON CARD (251-265)	3.00	1.25
❑ 1 Barry Bonds	2.00	.75
❑ 2 Derek Jeter	2.00	.75
❑ 3 Ichiro Suzuki	1.50	.60
❑ 4 Mike Lowell	.30	.10
❑ 5 Hideo Nomo	.75	.30
❑ 6 Javier Vazquez	.30	.10

❑ 7 Jeremy Giambi .30 .10
❑ 8 Jamie Moyer .30 .10
❑ 9 Rafael Palmeiro .50 .20
❑ 10 Magglio Ordonez .30 .10
❑ 11 Trot Nixon .30 .10
❑ 12 Luis Castillo .30 .10
❑ 13 Paul Byrd .30 .10
❑ 14 Adam Kennedy .30 .10
❑ 15 Trevor Hoffman .30 .10
❑ 16 Matt Morris .30 .10
❑ 17 Nomar Garciaparra 1.25 .50
❑ 18 Matt Lawton .30 .10
❑ 19 Carlos Beltran .30 .10
❑ 20 Jason Giambi .30 .10
❑ 21 Brian Giles .30 .10
❑ 22 Jim Edmonds .30 .10
❑ 23 Garret Anderson .30 .10
❑ 24 Tony Batista .30 .10
❑ 25 Aaron Boone .30 .10
❑ 26 Mike Hampton .30 .10
❑ 27 Billy Wagner .30 .10
❑ 28 Kazuhisa Ishii .30 .10
❑ 29 Al Leiter .30 .10
❑ 30 Pat Burrell .30 .10
❑ 31 Jeff Kent .30 .10
❑ 32 Randy Johnson .75 .30
❑ 33 Ray Durham .30 .10
❑ 34 Josh Beckett .30 .10
❑ 35 Cristian Guzman .30 .10
❑ 36 Roger Clemens 1.50 .60
❑ 37 Freddy Garcia .30 .10
❑ 38 Roy Halladay .30 .10
❑ 39 David Eckstein .30 .10
❑ 40 Jerry Hairston .30 .10
❑ 41 Barry Larkin .50 .20
❑ 42 Larry Walker .30 .10
❑ 43 Craig Biggio .50 .20
❑ 44 Edgardo Alfonzo .30 .10
❑ 45 Marlon Byrd .30 .10
❑ 46 J.T. Snow .30 .10
❑ 47 Juan Gonzalez .30 .10
❑ 48 Ramon Ortiz .30 .10
❑ 49 Jay Gibbons .30 .10
❑ 50 Adam Dunn .30 .10
❑ 51 Juan Pierre .30 .10
❑ 52 Jeff Bagwell .50 .20
❑ 53 Kevin Brown .30 .10
❑ 54 Pedro Astacio .30 .10
❑ 55 Mike Lieberthal .30 .10
❑ 56 Johnny Damon .50 .20
❑ 57 Tim Salmon .50 .20
❑ 58 Mike Bordick .30 .10
❑ 59 Ken Griffey Jr. 1.25 .50
❑ 60 Jason Jennings .30 .10
❑ 61 Lance Berkman .30 .10
❑ 62 Jeromy Burnitz .30 .10
❑ 63 Jimmy Rollins .30 .10
❑ 64 Tsuyoshi Shinjo .30 .10
❑ 65 Alex Rodriguez 1.25 .50
❑ 66 Greg Maddux 1.25 .50
❑ 67 Mark Prior .50 .20
❑ 68 Mike Maroth .30 .10
❑ 69 Geoff Jenkins .30 .10
❑ 70 Tony Armas Jr. .30 .10
❑ 71 Jermaine Dye .30 .10
❑ 72 Albert Pujols 1.50 .60
❑ 73 Shannon Stewart .30 .10
❑ 74 Troy Glaus .30 .10
❑ 75 Brook Fordyce .30 .10
❑ 76 Juan Encarnacion .30 .10
❑ 77 Todd Hollandsworth .30 .10
❑ 78 Roy Oswalt .30 .10
❑ 79 Paul Lo Duca .30 .10
❑ 80 Mike Piazza 1.25 .50
❑ 81 Bobby Abreu .30 .10
❑ 82 Sean Burroughs .30 .10
❑ 83 Randy Winn .30 .10
❑ 84 Curt Schilling .30 .10
❑ 85 Chris Singleton .30 .10
❑ 86 Sean Casey .30 .10
❑ 87 Todd Zeile .30 .10
❑ 88 Richard Hidalgo .30 .10
❑ 89 Roberto Alomar .50 .20
❑ 90 Tim Hudson .30 .10
❑ 91 Ryan Klesko .30 .10
❑ 92 Greg Vaughn .30 .10
❑ 93 Tony Womack .30 .10
❑ 94 Fred McGriff .50 .20
❑ 95 Tom Glavine .50 .20
❑ 96 Todd Walker .30 .10
❑ 97 Travis Fryman .30 .10
❑ 98 Shane Reynolds .30 .10
❑ 99 Shawn Green .30 .10
❑ 100 Mo Vaughn .30 .10
❑ 101 Adam Piatt .30 .10
❑ 102 Deivi Cruz .30 .10
❑ 103 Steve Cox .30 .10
❑ 104 Luis Gonzalez .30 .10
❑ 105 Russell Branyan .30 .10
❑ 106 Daryle Ward .30 .10
❑ 107 Mariano Rivera .75 .30
❑ 108 Phil Nevin .30 .10
❑ 109 Ben Grieve .30 .10
❑ 110 Moises Alou .30 .10
❑ 111 Omar Vizquel .50 .20
❑ 112 Joe Randa .30 .10
❑ 113 Jorge Posada .50 .20
❑ 114 Mark Kotsay .30 .10
❑ 115 Ryan Rupe .30 .10
❑ 116 Javy Lopez .30 .10
❑ 117 Corey Patterson .30 .10
❑ 118 Bobby Higginson .30 .10
❑ 119 Jose Vidro .30 .10
❑ 120 Barry Zito .30 .10
❑ 121 Scott Rolen .50 .20
❑ 122 Gary Sheffield .30 .10
❑ 123 Kerry Wood .30 .10
❑ 124 Brandon Inge .30 .10
❑ 125 Jose Hernandez .30 .10
❑ 126 Michael Barrett .30 .10
❑ 127 Miguel Tejada .30 .10
❑ 128 Edgar Renteria .30 .10
❑ 129 Junior Spivey .30 .10
❑ 130 Jose Valentin .30 .10
❑ 131 Derrek Lee .50 .20
❑ 132 A.J. Pierzynski .30 .10
❑ 133 Mike Mussina .50 .20
❑ 134 Bret Boone .30 .10
❑ 135 Chan Ho Park .30 .10
❑ 136 Steve Finley .30 .10
❑ 137 Mark Buehrle .30 .10
❑ 138 A.J. Burnett .30 .10
❑ 139 Ben Sheets .30 .10
❑ 140 David Ortiz .75 .30
❑ 141 Nick Johnson .30 .10
❑ 142 Randall Simon .30 .10
❑ 143 Carlos Delgado .30 .10
❑ 144 Darin Erstad .30 .10
❑ 145 Shea Hillenbrand .30 .10
❑ 146 Todd Helton .50 .20
❑ 147 Preston Wilson .30 .10
❑ 148 Eric Gagne .30 .10
❑ 149 Vladimir Guerrero .75 .30
❑ 150 Brandon Duckworth .30 .10
❑ 151 Rich Aurilia .30 .10
❑ 152 Ivan Rodriguez .50 .20
❑ 153 Andruw Jones .50 .20
❑ 154 Carlos Lee .30 .10
❑ 155 Robert Fick .30 .10
❑ 156 Jacque Jones .30 .10
❑ 157 Bernie Williams .50 .20
❑ 158 John Olerud .30 .10
❑ 159 Eric Hinske .30 .10
❑ 160 Matt Clement .30 .10
❑ 161 Dmitri Young .30 .10
❑ 162 Torii Hunter .30 .10
❑ 163 Carlos Pena .30 .10
❑ 164 Mike Cameron .30 .10
❑ 165 Raul Mondesi .30 .10
❑ 166 Pedro Martinez .50 .20
❑ 167 Bob Wickman .30 .10
❑ 168 Mike Sweeney .30 .10
❑ 169 David Wells .30 .10
❑ 170 Jason Kendall .30 .10
❑ 171 Tino Martinez .50 .20
❑ 172 Matt Williams .30 .10
❑ 173 Frank Thomas .75 .30
❑ 174 Cliff Floyd .30 .10
❑ 175 Corey Koskie .30 .10
❑ 176 Orlando Hernandez .30 .10
❑ 177 Edgar Martinez .50 .20
❑ 178 Richie Sexson .30 .10
❑ 179 Manny Ramirez .50 .20
❑ 180 Jim Thome .50 .20
❑ 181 Andy Pettitte .50 .20
❑ 182 Aramis Ramirez .30 .10
❑ 183 J.D. Drew .30 .10
❑ 184 Brian Jordan .30 .10
❑ 185 Sammy Sosa .75 .30
❑ 186 Jeff Weaver .30 .10
❑ 187 Jeffrey Hammonds .30 .10
❑ 188 Eric Milton .30 .10
❑ 189 Eric Chavez .30 .10
❑ 190 Kazuhiro Sasaki .30 .10
❑ 191 Jose Cruz Jr. .30 .10
❑ 192 Derek Lowe .30 .10
❑ 193 C.C. Sabathia .30 .10
❑ 194 Adrian Beltre .30 .10
❑ 195 Alfonso Soriano .30 .10
❑ 196 Jack Wilson .30 .10
❑ 197 Fernando Vina .30 .10
❑ 198 Chipper Jones .75 .30
❑ 199 Paul Konerko .30 .10
❑ 200 Rusty Greer .30 .10
❑ 201 Jason Giambi AS 1.50 .60
❑ 202 Alfonso Soriano AS 1.50 .60
❑ 203 Shea Hillenbrand AS 1.50 .60
❑ 204 Alex Rodriguez AS 2.50 1.00
❑ 205 Jorge Posada AS 1.50 .60
❑ 206 Ichiro Suzuki AS 3.00 1.25
❑ 207 Manny Ramirez AS 1.50 .60
❑ 208 Torii Hunter AS 1.50 .60
❑ 209 Todd Helton AS 1.50 .60
❑ 210 Jose Vidro AS 1.50 .60
❑ 211 Scott Rolen AS 1.50 .60
❑ 212 Jimmy Rollins AS 1.50 .60
❑ 213 Mike Piazza AS 2.50 1.00
❑ 214 Barry Bonds AS 4.00 1.50
❑ 215 Sammy Sosa AS 1.50 .60
❑ 216 Vladimir Guerrero AS 1.50 .60
❑ 217 Lance Berkman AS 1.50 .60
❑ 218 Derek Jeter AS 4.00 1.50
❑ 219 Nomar Garciaparra AS 2.50 1.00
❑ 220 Luis Gonzalez AS 1.50 .60
❑ 221 Kazuhisa Ishii 02R 2.00 .75
❑ 222 Satoru Komiyama 02R 2.00 .75
❑ 223 So Taguchi 02R 2.00 .75
❑ 224 Jorge Padilla 02R 2.00 .75
❑ 225 Ben Howard 02R 2.00 .75
❑ 226 Jason Simontacchi 02R 2.00 .75
❑ 227 Barry Wesson 02R 2.00 .75
❑ 228 Howie Clark 02R 2.00 .75
❑ 229 Aaron Guiel 02R 2.00 .75
❑ 230 Oliver Perez 02R 2.00 .75
❑ 231 David Ross 02R 2.00 .75
❑ 232 Julius Matos 02R 2.00 .75
❑ 233 Chris Snelling 02R 2.00 .75
❑ 234 Rodrigo Lopez 02R 2.00 .75
❑ 235 Will Nieves 02R 2.00 .75
❑ 236 Joe Borchard 02R 2.00 .75
❑ 237 Aaron Cook 02R 2.00 .75
❑ 238 Anderson Machado 02R 2.00 .75
❑ 239 Corey Thurman 02R 2.00 .75
❑ 240 Tyler Yates 02R 2.00 .75
❑ 241 Coco Crisp 03R 3.00 1.25
❑ 242 Andy Van Hekken 03R 2.00 .75
❑ 243 Jim Rushford 03R 2.00 .75
❑ 244 Jeriome Robertson 03R 2.00 .75
❑ 245 Shane Nance 03R 2.00 .75
❑ 246 Kevin Cash 03R 2.00 .75

❑ 247 Kirk Saarloos 03R 2.00 .75
❑ 248 Josh Bard 03R 2.00 .75
❑ 249 Dave Pember 03R RC 2.00 .75
❑ 250 Freddy Sanchez 03R 2.00 .75
❑ 251 Chien-Ming Wang PROS RC 20.00 8.00
❑ 252 Rickie Weeks PROS RC 6.00 2.50
❑ 253 Brandon Webb PROS RC 8.00 3.00
❑ 254 Hideki Matsui PROS RC 10.00 4.00
❑ 255 Michael Hessman PROS RC 3.00 1.25
❑ 256 Ryan Wagner PROS RC 3.00 1.25
❑ 257 Matt Kata PROS RC 3.00 1.25
❑ 258 Edwin Jackson PROS RC 4.00 1.50
❑ 259 Jose Contreras PROS RC 4.00 1.50
❑ 260 Delmon Young PROS RC 10.00 4.00
❑ 261 Bo Hart PROS RC 3.00 1.25
❑ 262 Jeff Duncan PROS RC 3.00 1.25
❑ 263 Robby Hammock PROS RC 3.00 1.25
❑ 264 Jeremy Bonderman PROS RC 10.00 4.00
❑ 265 Clint Barmes PROS RC 2.50 1.00

2004 Ultra

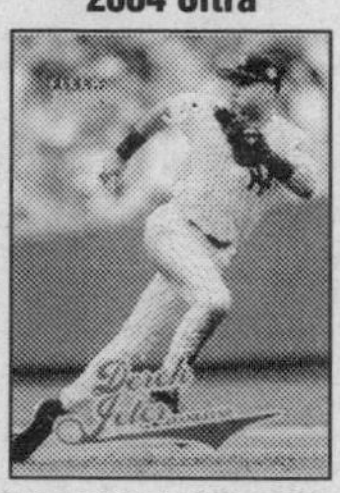

❑ COMPLETE SERIES 1 (220) 60.00 30.00
❑ COMP.SERIES 1 w/o SP's (200) 25.00 10.00
❑ COMP.SERIES 2 w/o SP's (75) 25.00 10.00
❑ COMP.SERIES 2 w/o L13 (162) 100.00 50.00
❑ COMMON CARD (1-200) .30 .10
❑ COMMON CARD (201-220) 1.25 .50
❑ 201-220 APPROXIMATE ODDS 1:2 HOBBY
❑ 201-220 RANDOM IN RETAIL PACKS
❑ COMMON CARD (296-382) 2.00 .75
❑ 296-382 ODDS TWO PER HOBBY/RETAIL
❑ COMMON CARD (383-395) 12.00 5.00
❑ 383-395 ODDS 1:28 HOBBY, 1:2000 RETAIL
❑ 383-395 PRINT RUN 500 SERIAL #'d SETS
❑ 1 Maggio Ordonez .30 .10
❑ 2 Bobby Abreu .30 .10
❑ 3 Eric Munson .30 .10
❑ 4 Eric Byrnes .30 .10
❑ 5 Bartolo Colon .30 .10
❑ 6 Juan Encarnacion .30 .10
❑ 7 Jody Gerut .30 .10
❑ 8 Eddie Guardado .30 .10
❑ 9 Shea Hillenbrand .30 .10
❑ 10 Andruw Jones .50 .20
❑ 11 Carlos Lee .30 .10
❑ 12 Pedro Martinez .50 .20
❑ 13 Barry Larkin .50 .20
❑ 14 Angel Berroa .30 .10
❑ 15 Edgar Martinez .50 .20
❑ 16 Sidney Ponson .30 .10
❑ 17 Mariano Rivera .75 .30
❑ 18 Richie Sexson .30 .10
❑ 19 Frank Thomas .75 .30
❑ 20 Jerome Williams .30 .10
❑ 21 Barry Zito .30 .10
❑ 22 Roberto Alomar .50 .20
❑ 23 Rocky Biddle .30 .10
❑ 24 Orlando Cabrera .30 .10
❑ 25 Placido Polanco .30 .10
❑ 26 Morgan Ensberg .30 .10
❑ 27 Jason Giambi .30 .10
❑ 28 Jim Thome .50 .20
❑ 29 Vladimir Guerrero .75 .30
❑ 30 Tim Hudson .30 .10
❑ 31 Jacque Jones .30 .10
❑ 32 Derrek Lee .50 .20
❑ 33 Rafael Palmeiro .50 .20
❑ 34 Mike Mussina .50 .20
❑ 35 Corey Patterson .30 .10
❑ 36 Mike Cameron .30 .10
❑ 37 Ivan Rodriguez .50 .20
❑ 38 Ben Sheets .30 .10
❑ 39 Woody Williams .30 .10
❑ 40 Ichiro Suzuki 1.50 .60
❑ 41 Moises Alou .30 .10
❑ 42 Craig Biggio .50 .20
❑ 43 Jorge Posada .50 .20
❑ 44 Craig Monroe .30 .10
❑ 45 Darin Erstad .30 .10
❑ 46 Jay Gibbons .30 .10
❑ 47 Aaron Guiel .30 .10
❑ 48 Travis Lee .30 .10
❑ 49 Jorge Julio .30 .10
❑ 50 Torii Hunter .30 .10
❑ 51 Luis Matos .30 .10
❑ 52 Brett Myers .30 .10
❑ 53 Sean Casey .30 .10
❑ 54 Mark Prior .50 .20
❑ 55 Alex Rodriguez 1.25 .50
❑ 56 Gary Sheffield .30 .10
❑ 57 Jason Varitek .75 .30
❑ 58 Dontrelle Willis .50 .20
❑ 59 Garret Anderson .30 .10
❑ 60 Casey Blake .30 .10
❑ 61 Jay Payton .30 .10
❑ 62 Carl Crawford .30 .10
❑ 63 Carl Everett .30 .10
❑ 64 Marcus Giles .30 .10
❑ 65 Jose Guillen .30 .10
❑ 66 Eric Karros .30 .10
❑ 67 Mike Lieberthal .30 .10
❑ 68 Hideki Matsui 1.25 .50
❑ 69 Xavier Nady .30 .10
❑ 70 Hank Blalock .30 .10
❑ 71 Albert Pujols 1.50 .60
❑ 72 Jose Cruz Jr. .30 .10
❑ 73 Randall Simon .30 .10
❑ 74 Javier Vazquez .30 .10
❑ 75 Preston Wilson .30 .10
❑ 76 Danys Baez .30 .10
❑ 77 Alex Cintron .30 .10
❑ 78 Jake Peavy .30 .10
❑ 79 Scott Rolen .50 .20
❑ 80 Robert Fick .30 .10
❑ 81 Brian Giles .30 .10
❑ 82 Roy Halladay .30 .10
❑ 83 Kazuhisa Ishii .30 .10
❑ 84 Austin Kearns .30 .10
❑ 85 Paul Lo Duca .30 .10
❑ 86 Darrell May .30 .10
❑ 87 Phil Nevin .30 .10
❑ 88 Carlos Pena .30 .10
❑ 89 Manny Ramirez .50 .20
❑ 90 C.C. Sabathia .30 .10
❑ 91 John Smoltz .50 .20
❑ 92 Jose Vidro .30 .10
❑ 93 Randy Wolf .30 .10
❑ 94 Jeff Bagwell .50 .20
❑ 95 Barry Bonds 2.00 .75
❑ 96 Frank Catalanotto .30 .10
❑ 97 Zach Day .30 .10
❑ 98 David Ortiz .75 .30
❑ 99 Troy Glaus .30 .10
❑ 100 Bo Hart .30 .10
❑ 101 Geoff Jenkins .30 .10
❑ 102 Jason Kendall .30 .10
❑ 103 Esteban Loaiza .30 .10
❑ 104 Doug Mientkiewicz .30 .10
❑ 105 Trot Nixon .30 .10
❑ 106 Troy Percival .30 .10
❑ 107 Aramis Ramirez .30 .10
❑ 108 Alex Sanchez .30 .10
❑ 109 Alfonso Soriano .30 .10
❑ 110 Omar Vizquel .50 .20
❑ 111 Kerry Wood .30 .10
❑ 112 Rocco Baldelli .30 .10
❑ 113 Bret Boone .30 .10
❑ 114 Shawn Chacon .30 .10
❑ 115 Carlos Delgado .30 .10
❑ 116 Shawn Green .30 .10
❑ 117 Tim Worrell .30 .10
❑ 118 Tom Glavine .50 .20
❑ 119 Shigetoshi Hasegawa .30 .10
❑ 120 Derek Jeter 1.50 .60
❑ 121 Jeff Kent .30 .10
❑ 122 Braden Looper .30 .10
❑ 123 Kevin Millwood .30 .10
❑ 124 Hideo Nomo .75 .30
❑ 125 Jason Phillips .30 .10
❑ 126 Tim Redding .30 .10
❑ 127 Reggie Sanders .30 .10
❑ 128 Sammy Sosa .75 .30
❑ 129 Billy Wagner .30 .10
❑ 130 Miguel Batista .30 .10
❑ 131 Milton Bradley .30 .10
❑ 132 Eric Chavez .30 .10
❑ 133 J.D. Drew .30 .10
❑ 134 Keith Foulke .30 .10
❑ 135 Luis Gonzalez .30 .10
❑ 136 LaTroy Hawkins .30 .10
❑ 137 Randy Johnson .75 .30
❑ 138 Byung-Hyun Kim .30 .10
❑ 139 Javy Lopez .30 .10
❑ 140 Melvin Mora .30 .10
❑ 141 Aubrey Huff .30 .10
❑ 142 Mike Piazza 1.25 .50
❑ 143 Mark Redman .30 .10
❑ 144 Kazuhiro Sasaki .30 .10
❑ 145 Shannon Stewart .30 .10
❑ 146 Larry Walker .30 .10
❑ 147 Dmitri Young .30 .10
❑ 148 Josh Beckett .30 .10
❑ 149 Jae Weong Seo .30 .10
❑ 150 Hee Seop Choi .30 .10
❑ 151 Adam Dunn .30 .10
❑ 152 Rafael Furcal .30 .10
❑ 153 Juan Gonzalez .30 .10
❑ 154 Todd Helton .50 .20
❑ 155 Carlos Zambrano .30 .10
❑ 156 Ryan Klesko .30 .10
❑ 157 Mike Lowell .30 .10
❑ 158 Jamie Moyer .30 .10
❑ 159 Russ Ortiz .30 .10
❑ 160 Juan Pierre .30 .10
❑ 161 Edgar Renteria .30 .10
❑ 162 Curt Schilling .30 .10
❑ 163 Mike Sweeney .30 .10
❑ 164 Brandon Webb .30 .10
❑ 165 Michael Young .30 .10
❑ 166 Carlos Beltran .30 .10
❑ 167 Sean Burroughs .30 .10
❑ 168 Luis Castillo .30 .10
❑ 169 David Eckstein .30 .10
❑ 170 Eric Gagne .30 .10
❑ 171 Chipper Jones .75 .30
❑ 172 Livan Hernandez .30 .10
❑ 173 Nick Johnson .30 .10
❑ 174 Corey Koskie .30 .10
❑ 175 Jason Schmidt .30 .10
❑ 176 Bill Mueller .30 .10
❑ 177 Steve Finley .30 .10
❑ 178 A.J. Pierzynski .30 .10
❑ 179 Rene Reyes .30 .10
❑ 180 Jason Johnson .30 .10
❑ 181 Mark Teixeira .50 .20
❑ 182 Kip Wells .30 .10
❑ 183 Mike MacDougal .30 .10
❑ 184 Lance Berkman .30 .10
❑ 185 Victor Zambrano .30 .10
❑ 186 Roger Clemens 1.50 .60
❑ 187 Jim Edmonds .30 .10
❑ 188 Nomar Garciaparra 1.25 .50
❑ 189 Ken Griffey Jr. 1.25 .50
❑ 190 Richard Hidalgo .30 .10
❑ 191 Cliff Floyd .30 .10
❑ 192 Greg Maddux 1.25 .50
❑ 193 Mark Mulder .30 .10
❑ 194 Roy Oswalt .30 .10
❑ 195 Marlon Byrd .30 .10
❑ 196 Jose Reyes .30 .10
❑ 197 Kevin Brown .30 .10
❑ 198 Miguel Tejada .30 .10
❑ 199 Vernon Wells .30 .10
❑ 200 Joel Pineiro .30 .10
❑ 201 Rickie Weeks AR 2.00 .75
❑ 202 Chad Gaudin AR 1.25 .50
❑ 203 Ryan Wagner AR 1.25 .50
❑ 204 Chris Bootcheck AR 1.25 .50
❑ 205 Koyie Hill AR 1.25 .50
❑ 206 Jeff Duncan AR 1.25 .50

❑	207	Rich Harden AR	2.00	.75
❑	208	Edwin Jackson AR	1.25	.50
❑	209	Robby Hammock AR	1.25	.50
❑	210	Khalil Greene AR	3.00	1.25
❑	211	Chien-Ming Wang AR	5.00	2.00
❑	212	Prentice Redman AR	1.25	.50
❑	213	Todd Wellemeyer AR	1.25	.50
❑	214	Clint Barmes AR	2.00	.75
❑	215	Matt Kata AR	1.25	.50
❑	216	Jon Leicester AR	1.25	.50
❑	217	Jeremy Guthrie AR	1.25	.50
❑	218	Chin-Hui Tsao AR	2.00	.75
❑	219	Dan Haren AR	1.25	.50
❑	220	Delmon Young AR	3.00	1.25
❑	221	Vladimir Guerrero	1.25	.50
❑	222	Andy Pettitte	.75	.30
❑	223	Gary Sheffield	.50	.20
❑	224	Javier Vazquez	.50	.20
❑	225	Alex Rodriguez	2.00	.75
❑	226	Billy Wagner	.50	.20
❑	227	Miguel Tejada	.50	.20
❑	228	Greg Maddux	2.00	.75
❑	229	Ivan Rodriguez	.75	.30
❑	230	Roger Clemens	2.50	1.00
❑	231	Alfonso Soriano	.50	.20
❑	232	Miguel Cabrera	.75	.30
❑	233	Javy Lopez	.50	.20
❑	234	David Wells	.50	.20
❑	235	Eric Milton	.50	.20
❑	236	Armando Benitez	.50	.20
❑	237	Mike Cameron	.50	.20
❑	238	J.D. Drew	.50	.20
❑	239	Carlos Beltran	.50	.20
❑	240	Bartolo Colon	.50	.20
❑	241	Jose Guillen	.50	.20
❑	242	Kevin Brown	.50	.20
❑	243	Carlos Guillen	.50	.20
❑	244	Kenny Lofton	.50	.20
❑	245	Pokey Reese	.50	.20
❑	246	Rafael Palmeiro	.75	.30
❑	247	Nomar Garciaparra	2.00	.75
❑	248	Hee Seop Choi	.50	.20
❑	249	Juan Uribe	.50	.20
❑	250	Nick Johnson	.50	.20
❑	251	Scott Podsednik	.50	.20
❑	252	Richie Sexson	.50	.20
❑	253	Keith Foulke Sox	.50	.20
❑	254	Jaret Wright	.50	.20
❑	255	Johnny Estrada	.50	.20
❑	256	Michael Barrett	.50	.20
❑	257	Bernie Williams	.75	.30
❑	258	Octavio Dotel	.50	.20
❑	259	Jeromy Burnitz	.50	.20
❑	260	Kevin Youkilis	.50	.20
❑	261	Derrek Lee	.75	.30
❑	262	Jack Wilson	.50	.20
❑	263	Craig Wilson	.50	.20
❑	264	Richard Hidalgo	.50	.20
❑	265	Royce Clayton	.50	.20
❑	266	Curt Schilling	.75	.30
❑	267	Joe Mauer	.75	.30
❑	268	Bobby Crosby	.50	.20
❑	269	Zack Greinke	.50	.20
❑	270	Victor Martinez	.50	.20
❑	271	Pedro Feliz	.50	.20
❑	272	Tony Batista	.50	.20
❑	273	Casey Kotchman	.50	.20
❑	274	Freddy Garcia	.50	.20
❑	275	Adam Everett	.50	.20
❑	276	Alexis Rios	.50	.20
❑	277	Lew Ford	.50	.20
❑	278	Adam LaRoche	.50	.20
❑	279	Lyle Overbay	.50	.20
❑	280	Juan Gonzalez	.50	.20
❑	281	A.J. Pierzynski	.50	.20
❑	282	Scott Hairston	.50	.20
❑	283	Danny Bautista	.50	.20
❑	284	Brad Penny	.50	.20
❑	285	Paul Konerko	.50	.20
❑	286	Matt Lawton	.50	.20
❑	287	Carl Pavano	.50	.20
❑	288	Pat Burrell	.50	.20
❑	289	Kenny Rogers	.50	.20
❑	290	Laynce Nix	.50	.20
❑	291	Johnny Damon	.75	.30
❑	292	Paul Wilson	.50	.20
❑	293	Vinny Castilla	.50	.20
❑	294	Aaron Miles	.50	.20
❑	295	Ken Harvey	.50	.20
❑	296	Onil Joseph RC	2.00	.75
❑	297	Kazuhito Tadano RC	3.00	1.25
❑	298	Jeff Bennett RC	2.00	.75
❑	299	Chad Bentz RC	2.00	.75
❑	300	Akinori Otsuka RC	2.00	.75
❑	301	Jon Knott RC	2.00	.75
❑	302	Ian Snell RC	3.00	1.25
❑	303	Fernando Nieve RC	3.00	1.25
❑	304	Mike Rouse RC	2.00	.75
❑	305	Dennis Sarfate RC	2.00	.75
❑	306	Josh Labandeira RC	2.00	.75
❑	307	Chris Oxspring RC	2.00	.75
❑	308	Alfredo Simon RC	2.00	.75
❑	309	Rusty Tucker RC	3.00	1.25
❑	310	Lincoln Holdzkom RC	2.00	.75
❑	311	Justin Leone RC	3.00	1.25
❑	312	Jorge Sequea RC	2.00	.75
❑	313	Brian Dallimore RC	2.00	.75
❑	314	Tim Bittner RC	2.00	.75
❑	315	Ronny Cedeno RC	3.00	1.25
❑	316	Justin Hampson RC	2.00	.75
❑	317	Ryan Wing RC	2.00	.75
❑	318	Mariano Gomez RC	2.00	.75
❑	319	Carlos Vasquez RC	3.00	1.25
❑	320	Casey Daigle RC	2.00	.75
❑	321	Renyel Pinto RC	3.00	1.25
❑	322	Chris Shelton RC	3.00	1.25
❑	323	Mike Gosling RC	2.00	.75
❑	324	Aarom Baldiris RC	3.00	1.25
❑	325	Ramon Ramirez RC	2.00	.75
❑	326	Roberto Novoa RC	3.00	1.25
❑	327	Sean Henn RC	2.00	.75
❑	328	Nick Regilio RC	2.00	.75
❑	329	Dave Crouthers RC	2.00	.75
❑	330	Greg Dobbs RC	2.00	.75
❑	331	Angel Chavez RC	2.00	.75
❑	332	Luis A. Gonzalez RC	2.00	.75
❑	333	Justin Knoedler RC	2.00	.75
❑	334	Jason Frasor RC	2.00	.75
❑	335	Jerry Gil RC	2.00	.75
❑	336	Carlos Hines RC	2.00	.75
❑	337	Ivan Ochoa RC	2.00	.75
❑	338	Jose Capellan RC	3.00	1.25
❑	339	Hector Gimenez RC	2.00	.75
❑	340	Shawn Hill RC	2.00	.75
❑	341	Freddy Guzman RC	2.00	.75
❑	342	Scott Proctor RC	3.00	1.25
❑	343	Frank Francisco RC	2.00	.75
❑	344	Brandon Medders RC	2.00	.75
❑	345	Andy Green RC	2.00	.75
❑	346	Eddy Rodriguez RC	3.00	1.25
❑	347	Tim Hamulack RC	2.00	.75
❑	348	Michael Wuertz RC	3.00	1.25
❑	349	Arnie Munoz	2.00	.75
❑	350	Enemencio Pacheco RC	2.00	.75
❑	351	Dusty Bergman RC	2.00	.75
❑	352	Charles Thomas RC	2.00	.75
❑	353	William Bergolla RC	2.00	.75
❑	354	Ramon Castro RC	2.00	.75
❑	355	Justin Lehr RC	2.00	.75
❑	356	Lino Urdaneta RC	2.00	.75
❑	357	Donnie Kelly RC	2.00	.75
❑	358	Kevin Cave RC	2.00	.75
❑	359	Franklyn Gracesqui RC	2.00	.75
❑	360	Chris Aguila RC	2.00	.75
❑	361	Jorge Vasquez RC	2.00	.75
❑	362	Andres Blanco RC	2.00	.75
❑	363	Orlando Rodriguez RC	2.00	.75
❑	364	Colby Miller RC	2.00	.75
❑	365	Shawn Camp RC	2.00	.75
❑	366	Jake Woods RC	2.00	.75
❑	367	George Sherrill RC	2.00	.75
❑	368	Justin Huisman RC	2.00	.75
❑	369	Jimmy Serrano RC	2.00	.75
❑	370	Mike Johnston RC	2.00	.75
❑	371	Ryan Meaux RC	2.00	.75
❑	372	Scott Dohmann RC	2.00	.75
❑	373	Brad Halsey RC	3.00	1.25
❑	374	Joey Gathright RC	4.00	1.50
❑	375	Yadier Molina RC	5.00	2.00
❑	376	Travis Blackley RC	2.00	.75
❑	377	Steve Andrade RC	2.00	.75
❑	378	Phil Stockman RC	2.00	.75
❑	379	Roman Colon RC	2.00	.75
❑	380	Jesse Crain RC	3.00	1.25
❑	381	Edwardo Sierra RC	3.00	1.25
❑	382	Justin Germano RC	2.00	.75
❑	383	Kaz Matsui L13 RC	10.00	4.00
❑	384	Shingo Takatsu L13 RC	10.00	4.00
❑	385	John Gall L13 RC	12.00	5.00
❑	386	Chris Saenz L13 RC	12.00	5.00
❑	387	Merkin Valdez L13 RC	10.00	4.00
❑	388	Jamie Brown L13 RC	12.00	5.00
❑	389	Jason Bartlett L13 RC	12.00	5.00
❑	390	David Aardsma L13 RC	12.00	5.00
❑	391	Scott Kazmir L13 RC	30.00	12.50
❑	392	David Wright L13	30.00	12.50
❑	393	Dioner Navarro L13 RC	10.00	4.00
❑	394	B.J. Upton L13	12.00	5.00
❑	395	Gavin Floyd L13	12.00	5.00

2005 Ultra

❑		COMPLETE SET (220)	100.00	40.00
❑		COMP.SET w/o SP's (200)	40.00	15.00
❑		COMMON CARD (1-200)	.30	.10
❑		COMMON CARD (201-220)	2.00	.75
❑		201-220 ODDS 1:4 HOBBY, 1:5 RETAIL		
❑	1	Andy Pettitte	.50	.20
❑	2	Jose Cruz Jr.	.30	.10
❑	3	Cliff Floyd	.30	.10
❑	4	Paul Konerko	.30	.10
❑	5	Joe Mauer	.75	.30
❑	6	Scott Spiezio	.30	.10
❑	7	Ben Sheets	.30	.10
❑	8	Kerry Wood	.30	.10
❑	9	Carl Pavano	.30	.10
❑	10	Matt Morris	.30	.10
❑	11	Kaz Matsui	.30	.10
❑	12	Ivan Rodriguez	.50	.20
❑	13	Victor Martinez	.30	.10
❑	14	Justin Morneau	.30	.10
❑	15	Adam Everett	.30	.10
❑	16	Carl Crawford	.30	.10
❑	17	David Ortiz	.75	.30
❑	18	Jason Giambi	.30	.10
❑	19	Derrek Lee	.50	.20
❑	20	Magglio Ordonez	.30	.10
❑	21	Bobby Abreu	.30	.10
❑	22	Milton Bradley	.30	.10
❑	23	Jeff Bagwell	.50	.20
❑	24	Jim Edmonds	.30	.10
❑	25	Garret Anderson	.30	.10
❑	26	Jacque Jones	.30	.10
❑	27	Ted Lilly	.30	.10
❑	28	Greg Maddux	1.25	.50
❑	29	Jermaine Dye	.30	.10
❑	30	Bill Mueller	.30	.10
❑	31	Roy Oswalt	.30	.10
❑	32	Tony Womack	.30	.10
❑	33	Andruw Jones	.50	.20
❑	34	Tom Glavine	.50	.20
❑	35	Mariano Rivera	.75	.30
❑	36	Sean Casey	.30	.10
❑	37	Edgardo Alfonzo	.30	.10
❑	38	Brad Penny	.30	.10
❑	39	Johan Santana	.75	.30
❑	40	Mark Teixeira	.50	.20
❑	41	Manny Ramirez	.50	.20
❑	42	Gary Sheffield	.30	.10
❑	43	Matt Lawton	.30	.10
❑	44	Troy Percival	.30	.10

❑	45	Rocco Baldelli	.30	.10
❑	46	Doug Mientkiewicz	.30	.10
❑	47	Corey Patterson	.30	.10
❑	48	Austin Kearns	.30	.10
❑	49	Edgar Martinez	.50	.20
❑	50	Brad Radke	.30	.10
❑	51	Barry Larkin	.50	.20
❑	52	Chone Figgins	.30	.10
❑	53	Alexis Rios	.30	.10
❑	54	Alex Rodriguez	1.25	.50
❑	55	Vinny Castilla	.30	.10
❑	56	Javier Vazquez	.30	.10
❑	57	Javy Lopez	.30	.10
❑	58	Mike Cameron	.30	.10
❑	59	Brian Giles	.30	.10
❑	60	Dontrelle Willis	.30	.10
❑	61	Rafael Furcal	.30	.10
❑	62	Trot Nixon	.30	.10
❑	63	Mark Mulder	.30	.10
❑	64	Josh Beckett	.30	.10
❑	65	J.D. Drew	.30	.10
❑	66	Brandon Webb	.30	.10
❑	67	Wade Miller	.30	.10
❑	68	Lyle Overbay	.30	.10
❑	69	Pedro Martinez	.50	.20
❑	70	Rich Harden	.30	.10
❑	71	Al Leiter	.30	.10
❑	72	Adam Eaton	.30	.10
❑	73	Mike Sweeney	.30	.10
❑	74	Steve Finley	.30	.10
❑	75	Kris Benson	.30	.10
❑	76	Jim Thome	.50	.20
❑	77	Juan Pierre	.30	.10
❑	78	Bartolo Colon	.30	.10
❑	79	Carlos Delgado	.30	.10
❑	80	Jack Wilson	.30	.10
❑	81	Ken Harvey	.30	.10
❑	82	Nomar Garciaparra	.75	.30
❑	83	Paul Lo Duca	.30	.10
❑	84	Cesar Izturis	.30	.10
❑	85	Adrian Beltre	.30	.10
❑	86	Brian Roberts	.30	.10
❑	87	David Eckstein	.30	.10
❑	88	Jimmy Rollins	.30	.10
❑	89	Roger Clemens	1.25	.50
❑	90	Randy Johnson	.75	.30
❑	91	Orlando Hudson	.30	.10
❑	92	Tim Hudson	.30	.10
❑	93	Dmitri Young	.30	.10
❑	94	Chipper Jones	.75	.30
❑	95	John Smoltz	.50	.20
❑	96	Billy Wagner	.30	.10
❑	97	Hideo Nomo	.75	.30
❑	98	Sammy Sosa	.75	.30
❑	99	Darin Erstad	.30	.10
❑	100	Todd Helton	.50	.20
❑	101	Aubrey Huff	.30	.10
❑	102	Alfonso Soriano	.30	.10
❑	103	Jose Vidro	.30	.10
❑	104	Carlos Lee	.30	.10
❑	105	Corey Koskie	.30	.10
❑	106	Bret Boone	.30	.10
❑	107	Torii Hunter	.30	.10
❑	108	Aramis Ramirez	.30	.10
❑	109	Chase Utley	.50	.20
❑	110	Reggie Sanders	.30	.10
❑	111	Livan Hernandez	.30	.10
❑	112	Jeromy Burnitz	.30	.10
❑	113	Carlos Zambrano	.30	.10
❑	114	Hank Blalock	.30	.10
❑	115	Sidney Ponson	.30	.10
❑	116	Zack Greinke	.30	.10
❑	117	Trevor Hoffman	.30	.10
❑	118	Jeff Kent	.30	.10
❑	119	Richie Sexson	.30	.10
❑	120	Melvin Mora	.30	.10
❑	121	Eric Chavez	.30	.10
❑	122	Miguel Cabrera	.50	.20
❑	123	Ryan Freel	.30	.10
❑	124	Russ Ortiz	.30	.10
❑	125	Craig Wilson	.30	.10
❑	126	Craig Biggio	.50	.20
❑	127	Curt Schilling	.50	.20
❑	128	Kaz Ishii	.30	.10
❑	129	Marquis Grissom	.30	.10
❑	130	Bernie Williams	.50	.20
❑	131	Travis Hafner	.30	.10
❑	132	Hee Seop Choi	.30	.10
❑	133	Scott Rolen	.50	.20
❑	134	Tony Batista	.30	.10
❑	135	Frank Thomas	.75	.30
❑	136	Jason Varitek	.75	.30
❑	137	Ichiro Suzuki	1.50	.60
❑	138	Junior Spivey	.30	.10
❑	139	Adam Dunn	.30	.10
❑	140	Jorge Posada	.50	.20
❑	141	Edgar Renteria	.30	.10
❑	142	Hideki Matsui	1.25	.50
❑	143	Carlos Guillen	.30	.10
❑	144	Jody Gerut	.30	.10
❑	145	Wily Mo Pena	.30	.10
❑	146	Derek Jeter	1.50	.60
❑	147	C.C. Sabathia	.30	.10
❑	148	Geoff Jenkins	.30	.10
❑	149	Albert Pujols	1.50	.60
❑	150	Eric Munson	.30	.10
❑	151	Moises Alou	.30	.10
❑	152	Jerry Hairston	.30	.10
❑	153	Ray Durham	.30	.10
❑	154	Mike Piazza	.75	.30
❑	155	Omar Vizquel	.30	.10
❑	156	A.J. Pierzynski	.30	.10
❑	157	Michael Young	.30	.10
❑	158	Jason Bay	.30	.10
❑	159	Mark Loretta	.30	.10
❑	160	Shawn Green	.30	.10
❑	161	Luis Gonzalez	.30	.10
❑	162	Johnny Damon	.50	.20
❑	163	Eric Milton	.30	.10
❑	164	Mike Lowell	.30	.10
❑	165	Jose Guillen	.30	.10
❑	166	Eric Hinske	.30	.10
❑	167	Jason Kendall	.30	.10
❑	168	Carlos Beltran	.30	.10
❑	169	Johnny Estrada	.30	.10
❑	170	Scott Hatteberg	.30	.10
❑	171	Laynce Nix	.30	.10
❑	172	Eric Gagne	.30	.10
❑	173	Richard Hidalgo	.30	.10
❑	174	Bobby Crosby	.30	.10
❑	175	Woody Williams	.30	.10
❑	176	Justin Leone	.30	.10
❑	177	Orlando Cabrera	.30	.10
❑	178	Mark Prior	.50	.20
❑	179	Jorge Julio	.30	.10
❑	180	Jamie Moyer	.30	.10
❑	181	Jose Reyes	.30	.10
❑	182	Ken Griffey Jr.	1.25	.50
❑	183	Mike Lieberthal	.30	.10
❑	184	Kenny Rogers	.30	.10
❑	185	Mike Mussina	.50	.20
❑	186	Preston Wilson	.30	.10
❑	187	Khalil Greene	.50	.20
❑	188	Angel Berroa	.30	.10
❑	189	Miguel Tejada	.30	.10
❑	190	Freddy Garcia	.30	.10
❑	191	Pat Burrell	.30	.10
❑	192	Luis Castillo	.30	.10
❑	193	Vladimir Guerrero	.75	.30
❑	194	Roy Halladay	.30	.10
❑	195	Barry Zito	.30	.10
❑	196	Lance Berkman	.30	.10
❑	197	Rafael Palmeiro	.50	.20
❑	198	Nate Robertson	.30	.10
❑	199	Jason Schmidt	.30	.10
❑	200	Scott Podsednik	.30	.10
❑	201	Casey Kotchman AR	3.00	1.25
❑	202	Scott Kazmir AR	5.00	2.00
❑	203	Bucky Jacobsen AR	2.00	.75
❑	204	Jeff Keppinger AR	2.00	.75
❑	205	Dave Bush AR	2.00	.75
❑	206	Gavin Floyd AR	2.00	.75
❑	207	David Wright AR	8.00	3.00
❑	208	B.J. Upton AR	5.00	2.00
❑	209	David Aardsma AR	2.00	.75
❑	210	Jason Bartlett AR	2.00	.75
❑	211	Dioner Navarro AR	3.00	1.25
❑	212	Jason Kubel AR	2.00	.75
❑	213	Ryan Howard AR	8.00	3.00
❑	214	Charles Thomas AR	2.00	.75
❑	215	Freddy Guzman AR	2.00	.75
❑	216	Brad Halsey AR	2.00	.75
❑	217	Joey Gathright AR	3.00	1.25
❑	218	Jeff Francis AR	2.00	.75
❑	219	Terry Tiffee AR	2.00	.75
❑	220	Nick Swisher AR	5.00	2.00

2006 Ultra

❑ COMP.SET w/o RL13 (200) 40.00 15.00
❑ COMMON CARD (1-180) .40 .15
❑ RL13 201-250 ODDS 1:4 HOBBY, 1:4 RETAIL
❑ 251 PRINT RUN 5000 CARDS
❑ 251 JOHJIMA IS NOT SERIAL NUMBERED
❑ 251 PRINT RUN INFO PROVIDED BY UD
❑ 251 JOHJIMA EXCH. DEADLINE 05/25/08

❑	1	Vladimir Guerrero	1.00	.40
❑	2	Bartolo Colon	.40	.15
❑	3	Francisco Rodriguez	.40	.15
❑	4	Darin Erstad	.40	.15
❑	5	Chone Figgins	.40	.15
❑	6	Bengie Molina	.40	.15
❑	7	Roger Clemens	2.00	.75
❑	8	Lance Berkman	.40	.15
❑	9	Morgan Ensberg	.40	.15
❑	10	Roy Oswalt	.40	.15
❑	11	Andy Pettitte	.60	.25
❑	12	Craig Biggio	.60	.25
❑	13	Eric Chavez	.40	.15
❑	14	Barry Zito	.40	.15
❑	15	Huston Street	.40	.15
❑	16	Bobby Crosby	.40	.15
❑	17	Nick Swisher	.40	.15
❑	18	Rich Harden	.40	.15
❑	19	Vernon Wells	.40	.15
❑	20	Roy Halladay	.40	.15
❑	21	Alex Rios	.40	.15
❑	22	Orlando Hudson	.40	.15
❑	23	Shea Hillenbrand	.40	.15
❑	24	Gustavo Chacin	.40	.15
❑	25	Chipper Jones	1.00	.40
❑	26	Andruw Jones	.60	.25
❑	27	Jeff Francoeur	1.00	.40
❑	28	John Smoltz	.60	.25
❑	29	Tim Hudson	.40	.15
❑	30	Marcus Giles	.40	.15
❑	31	Carlos Lee	.40	.15
❑	32	Ben Sheets	.40	.15
❑	33	Rickie Weeks	.40	.15
❑	34	Chris Capuano	.40	.15
❑	35	Geoff Jenkins	.40	.15
❑	36	Brady Clark	.40	.15
❑	37	Albert Pujols	2.00	.75
❑	38	Jim Edmonds	.60	.25
❑	39	Chris Carpenter	.40	.15
❑	40	Mark Mulder	.40	.15
❑	41	Yadier Molina	.40	.15
❑	42	Scott Rolen	.60	.25
❑	43	Derrek Lee	.40	.15
❑	44	Mark Prior	.60	.25
❑	45	Aramis Ramirez	.40	.15
❑	46	Carlos Zambrano	.40	.15
❑	47	Greg Maddux	1.50	.60
❑	48	Nomar Garciaparra	1.00	.40
❑	49	Jonny Gomes	.40	.15
❑	50	Carl Crawford	.40	.15
❑	51	Scott Kazmir	.60	.25
❑	52	Jorge Cantu	.40	.15
❑	53	Julio Lugo	.40	.15
❑	54	Aubrey Huff	.40	.15
❑	55	Luis Gonzalez	.40	.15

❑ 56 Brandon Webb .40 .15
❑ 57 Troy Glaus .40 .15
❑ 58 Shawn Green .40 .15
❑ 59 Craig Counsell .40 .15
❑ 60 Conor Jackson (RC) 1.50 .60
❑ 61 Jeff Kent .40 .15
❑ 62 Eric Gagne .40 .15
❑ 63 J.D. Drew .40 .15
❑ 64 Milton Bradley .40 .15
❑ 65 Jeff Weaver .40 .15
❑ 66 Cesar Izturis .40 .15
❑ 67 Jason Schmidt .40 .15
❑ 68 Moises Alou .40 .15
❑ 69 Pedro Feliz .40 .15
❑ 70 Randy Winn .40 .15
❑ 71 Omar Vizquel .60 .25
❑ 72 Noah Lowry .40 .15
❑ 73 Travis Hafner .40 .15
❑ 74 Victor Martinez .40 .15
❑ 75 C.C. Sabathia .40 .15
❑ 76 Grady Sizemore .60 .25
❑ 77 Coco Crisp .40 .15
❑ 78 Cliff Lee .40 .15
❑ 79 Raul Ibañez .40 .15
❑ 80 Ichiro Suzuki 1.50 .60
❑ 81 Richie Sexson .40 .15
❑ 82 Felix Hernandez .60 .25
❑ 83 Adrian Beltre .40 .15
❑ 84 Jamie Moyer .40 .15
❑ 85 Miguel Cabrera .60 .25
❑ 86 A.J. Burnett .40 .15
❑ 87 Juan Pierre .40 .15
❑ 88 Carlos Delgado .40 .15
❑ 89 Dontrelle Willis .40 .15
❑ 90 Juan Encarnacion .40 .15
❑ 91 Carlos Beltran .40 .15
❑ 92 Jose Reyes 1.00 .40
❑ 93 David Wright 1.50 .60
❑ 94 Tom Glavine .60 .25
❑ 95 Mike Piazza 1.00 .40
❑ 96 Pedro Martinez .60 .25
❑ 97 Ryan Zimmerman (RC) 3.00 1.25
❑ 98 Nick Johnson .40 .15
❑ 99 Jose Vidro .40 .15
❑ 100 Jose Guillen .40 .15
❑ 101 Livan Hernandez .40 .15
❑ 102 John Patterson .40 .15
❑ 103 Miguel Tejada .40 .15
❑ 104 Melvin Mora .40 .15
❑ 105 Brian Roberts .40 .15
❑ 106 Erik Bedard .40 .15
❑ 107 Javy Lopez .40 .15
❑ 108 Rodrigo Lopez .40 .15
❑ 109 Jake Peavy .40 .15
❑ 110 Mike Cameron .40 .15
❑ 111 Mark Loretta .40 .15
❑ 112 Brian Giles .40 .15
❑ 113 Trevor Hoffman .40 .15
❑ 114 Ramon Hernandez .40 .15
❑ 115 Bobby Abreu .40 .15
❑ 116 Chase Utley 1.00 .40
❑ 117 Pat Burrell .40 .15
❑ 118 Jimmy Rollins .40 .15
❑ 119 Ryan Howard 1.50 .60
❑ 120 Billy Wagner .40 .15
❑ 121 Jason Bay .40 .15
❑ 122 Oliver Perez .40 .15
❑ 123 Jack Wilson .40 .15
❑ 124 Zach Duke .40 .15
❑ 125 Rob Mackowiak .40 .15
❑ 126 Freddy Sanchez .40 .15
❑ 127 Mark Teixeira .60 .25
❑ 128 Michael Young .40 .15
❑ 129 Alfonso Soriano .40 .15
❑ 130 Hank Blalock .40 .15
❑ 131 Kenny Rogers .40 .15
❑ 132 Kevin Mench .40 .15
❑ 133 Manny Ramirez .60 .25
❑ 134 Josh Beckett .40 .15
❑ 135 David Ortiz 1.00 .40
❑ 136 Johnny Damon .60 .25
❑ 137 Edgar Renteria .40 .15
❑ 138 Curt Schilling .60 .25
❑ 139 Ken Griffey Jr. 1.50 .60
❑ 140 Adam Dunn .40 .15
❑ 141 Felipe Lopez .40 .15
❑ 142 Wily Mo Pena .40 .15
❑ 143 Aaron Harang .40 .15
❑ 144 Sean Casey .40 .15
❑ 145 Todd Helton .60 .25
❑ 146 Garrett Atkins .40 .15
❑ 147 Matt Holliday 1.00 .40
❑ 148 Jeff Francis .40 .15
❑ 149 Clint Barmes .40 .15
❑ 150 Luis Gonzalez .40 .15
❑ 151 Mike Sweeney .40 .15
❑ 152 Zack Greinke .40 .15
❑ 153 Angel Berroa .40 .15
❑ 154 Emil Brown .40 .15
❑ 155 David DeJesus .40 .15
❑ 156 Ivan Rodriguez .60 .25
❑ 157 Jeremy Bonderman .40 .15
❑ 158 Brandon Inge .40 .15
❑ 159 Craig Monroe .40 .15
❑ 160 Chris Shelton .40 .15
❑ 161 Dmitri Young .40 .15
❑ 162 Johan Santana .60 .25
❑ 163 Joe Mauer .60 .25
❑ 164 Torii Hunter .40 .15
❑ 165 Shannon Stewart .40 .15
❑ 166 Scott Baker .40 .15
❑ 167 Brad Radke .40 .15
❑ 168 Jon Garland .40 .15
❑ 169 Tadahito Iguchi .40 .15
❑ 170 Paul Konerko .40 .15
❑ 171 Scott Podsednik .40 .15
❑ 172 Mark Buehrle .40 .15
❑ 173 Joe Crede .40 .15
❑ 174 Derek Jeter 2.50 1.00
❑ 175 Alex Rodriguez 1.50 .60
❑ 176 Hideki Matsui 1.50 .60
❑ 177 Randy Johnson 1.00 .40
❑ 178 Gary Sheffield .40 .15
❑ 179 Mariano Rivera 1.00 .40
❑ 180 Jason Giambi .40 .15
❑ 181 Joey Devine RC 1.00 .40
❑ 182 Alejandro Freire RC 1.00 .40
❑ 183 Craig Hansen RC 2.00 .75
❑ 184 Robert Andino RC 1.00 .40
❑ 185 Ryan Jorgensen RC 1.00 .40
❑ 186 Chris Demaria RC 1.00 .40
❑ 187 Jonah Bayliss RC 1.00 .40
❑ 188 Ryan Theriot RC 1.00 .40
❑ 189 Steve Stemle RC 1.00 .40
❑ 190 Brian Myrow RC 1.00 .40
❑ 191 Chris Heintz RC 1.00 .40
❑ 192 Ron Flores RC 1.00 .40
❑ 193 Danny Sandoval RC 1.00 .40
❑ 194 Craig Breslow RC 1.00 .40
❑ 195 Jeremy Accardo RC 1.00 .40
❑ 196 Jeff Harris RC 1.00 .40
❑ 197 Tim Corcoran RC 1.00 .40
❑ 198 Scott Feldman RC 1.00 .40
❑ 199 Robinson Cano .60 .25
❑ 200 Jason Bergmann RC 2.00 .75
❑ 201 Ken Griffey Jr. RL13 8.00 3.00
❑ 202 Frank Thomas RL13 5.00 2.00
❑ 203 Chipper Jones RL13 5.00 2.00
❑ 204 Tony Clark RL13 2.00 .75
❑ 205 Mike Lieberthal RL13 2.00 .75
❑ 206 Manny Ramirez RL13 3.00 1.25
❑ 207 Phil Nevin RL13 2.00 .75
❑ 208 Derek Jeter RL13 10.00 4.00
❑ 209 Preston Wilson RL13 2.00 .75
❑ 210 Billy Wagner RL13 2.00 .75
❑ 211 Alex Rodriguez RL13 8.00 3.00
❑ 212 Trot Nixon RL13 2.00 .75
❑ 213 Jaret Wright RL13 2.00 .75
❑ 214 Nomar Garciaparra RL13 5.00 2.00
❑ 215 Paul Konerko RL13 2.00 .75
❑ 216 Paul Wilson RL13 2.00 .75
❑ 217 Dustin Hermanson RL13 2.00 .75
❑ 218 Todd Walker RL13 2.00 .75
❑ 219 Matt Morris RL13 2.00 .75
❑ 220 Darin Erstad RL13 2.00 .75
❑ 221 Todd Helton RL13 3.00 1.25
❑ 222 Geoff Jenkins RL13 2.00 .75
❑ 223 Eric Chavez RL13 2.00 .75
❑ 224 Kris Benson RL13 2.00 .75
❑ 225 Jon Garland RL13 2.00 .75
❑ 226 Troy Glaus RL13 2.00 .75
❑ 227 Vernon Wells RL13 2.00 .75
❑ 228 Michael Cuddyer RL13 2.00 .75
❑ 229 Justin Verlander RL13 8.00 3.00
❑ 230 Pat Burrell RL13 2.00 .75
❑ 231 Mark Mulder RL13 2.00 .75
❑ 232 Corey Patterson RL13 2.00 .75
❑ 233 J.D. Drew RL13 2.00 .75
❑ 234 Austin Kearns RL13 2.00 .75
❑ 235 Felipe Lopez RL13 2.00 .75
❑ 236 Sean Burroughs RL13 2.00 .75
❑ 237 Ben Sheets RL13 2.00 .75
❑ 238 Brett Myers RL13 2.00 .75
❑ 239 Josh Beckett RL13 2.00 .75
❑ 240 Barry Zito RL13 2.00 .75
❑ 241 Adrian Gonzalez RL13 2.00 .75
❑ 242 Rocco Baldelli RL13 2.00 .75
❑ 243 Chris Burke RL13 2.00 .75
❑ 244 Joe Mauer RL13 3.00 1.25
❑ 245 Mark Prior RL13 3.00 1.25
❑ 246 Mark Teixiera RL13 3.00 1.25
❑ 247 Khalil Greene RL13 3.00 1.25
❑ 248 Zack Greinke RL13 2.00 .75
❑ 249 Prince Fielder RL13 8.00 3.00
❑ 250 Rickie Weeks RL13 2.00 .75
❑ 251 Kenji Johjima 15.00 6.00

2007 Ultra

❑ COMP.SET w/o RC's (200) 50.00 20.00
❑ COMMON CARD .50 .20
❑ COMMON ROOKIE 2.50 1.00
❑ COMMON L13 2.50 1.00
❑ PRINTING PLATE ODDS 1:1252 HOB/RET
❑ PLATE PRINT RUN 1 SET PER COLOR
❑ BLACK-CYAN-MAGENTA-YELLOW ISSUED
❑ NO PLATE PRICING DUE TO SCARCITY
❑ 1 Brandon Webb .50 .20
❑ 2 Randy Johnson 1.25 .50
❑ 3 Conor Jackson .50 .20
❑ 4 Stephen Drew .75 .30
❑ 5 Eric Byrnes .50 .20
❑ 6 Carlos Quentin .50 .20
❑ 7 Andruw Jones .75 .30
❑ 8 Chipper Jones 1.25 .50
❑ 9 Jeff Francoeur 1.25 .50
❑ 10 Tim Hudson .50 .20
❑ 11 John Smoltz .75 .30
❑ 12 Edgar Renteria .50 .20
❑ 13 Erik Bedard .50 .20
❑ 14 Kris Benson .50 .20
❑ 15 Miguel Tejada .50 .20
❑ 16 Nick Markakis .75 .30
❑ 17 Brian Roberts .50 .20
❑ 18 Melvin Mora .50 .20
❑ 19 Aubrey Huff .50 .20
❑ 20 Curt Schilling .75 .30
❑ 21 Jonathan Papelbon 1.25 .50
❑ 22 Josh Beckett .75 .30
❑ 23 Jason Varitek 1.25 .50
❑ 24 David Ortiz 1.25 .50
❑ 25 Manny Ramirez .75 .30
❑ 26 J.D. Drew .50 .20
❑ 27 Carlos Zambrano .50 .20
❑ 28 Derrek Lee .50 .20
❑ 29 Aramis Ramirez .50 .20
❑ 30 Alfonso Soriano .50 .20
❑ 31 Rich Hill .50 .20
❑ 32 Jacque Jones .50 .20
❑ 33 A.J. Pierzynski .50 .20
❑ 34 Jermaine Dye .50 .20

❑ 35 Paul Konerko .50 .20
❑ 36 Bobby Jenks .50 .20
❑ 37 Jon Garland .50 .20
❑ 38 Mark Buehrle .50 .20
❑ 39 Tadahito Iguchi .50 .20
❑ 40 Adam Dunn .50 .20
❑ 41 Ken Griffey Jr. 2.00 .75
❑ 42 Aaron Harang .50 .20
❑ 43 Bronson Arroyo .50 .20
❑ 44 Ryan Freel .50 .20
❑ 45 Brandon Phillips .50 .20
❑ 46 Grady Sizemore .75 .30
❑ 47 Travis Hafner .50 .20
❑ 48 Victor Martinez .50 .20
❑ 49 Jhonny Peralta .50 .20
❑ 50 C.C. Sabathia .50 .20
❑ 51 Jeremy Sowers .50 .20
❑ 52 Ryan Garko .50 .20
❑ 53 Garrett Atkins .50 .20
❑ 54 Willy Taveras .50 .20
❑ 55 Todd Helton .75 .30
❑ 56 Jeff Francis .50 .20
❑ 57 Brad Hawpe .50 .20
❑ 58 Matt Holliday 1.25 .50
❑ 59 Justin Verlander 1.25 .50
❑ 60 Jeremy Bonderman .50 .20
❑ 61 Magglio Ordonez .50 .20
❑ 62 Ivan Rodriguez .75 .30
❑ 63 Gary Sheffield .50 .20
❑ 64 Kenny Rogers .50 .20
❑ 65 Brandon Inge .50 .20
❑ 66 Anibal Sanchez .50 .20
❑ 67 Scott Olsen .50 .20
❑ 68 Dontrelle Willis .50 .20
❑ 69 Dan Uggla .75 .30
❑ 70 Hanley Ramirez .75 .30
❑ 71 Miguel Cabrera .75 .30
❑ 72 Jeremy Hermida .50 .20
❑ 73 Roy Oswalt .50 .20
❑ 74 Brad Lidge .50 .20
❑ 75 Lance Berkman .50 .20
❑ 76 Carlos Lee .50 .20
❑ 77 Morgan Ensberg .50 .20
❑ 78 Craig Biggio .75 .30
❑ 79 Reggie Sanders .50 .20
❑ 80 Mike Sweeney .50 .20
❑ 81 Mark Teahen .50 .20
❑ 82 John Buck .50 .20
❑ 83 Mark Grudzielanek .50 .20
❑ 84 Gary Matthews .50 .20
❑ 85 Vladimir Guerrero 1.25 .50
❑ 86 Garret Anderson .50 .20
❑ 87 Howie Kendrick .50 .20
❑ 88 Jered Weaver .75 .30
❑ 89 Chone Figgins .50 .20
❑ 90 Bartolo Colon .50 .20
❑ 91 Francisco Rodriguez .50 .20
❑ 92 Nomar Garciaparra 1.25 .50
❑ 93 Andre Ethier .75 .30
❑ 94 Rafael Furcal .50 .20
❑ 95 Jeff Kent .50 .20
❑ 96 Derek Lowe .50 .20
❑ 97 Jason Schmidt .50 .20
❑ 98 Takashi Saito .50 .20
❑ 99 Ben Sheets .50 .20
❑ 100 Prince Fielder 1.25 .50
❑ 101 Bill Hall .50 .20
❑ 102 Rickie Weeks .50 .20
❑ 103 Francisco Cordero .50 .20
❑ 104 J.J. Hardy .50 .20
❑ 105 Johan Santana .75 .30
❑ 106 Justin Morneau .50 .20
❑ 107 Joe Mauer .75 .30
❑ 108 Joe Nathan .50 .20
❑ 109 Torii Hunter .50 .20
❑ 110 Michael Cuddyer .50 .20
❑ 111 Boof Bonser .50 .20
❑ 112 Tom Glavine .75 .30
❑ 113 Pedro Martinez .75 .30
❑ 114 Billy Wagner .50 .20
❑ 115 Jose Reyes 1.25 .50
❑ 116 David Wright 2.00 .75
❑ 117 Carlos Delgado .50 .20
❑ 118 Carlos Beltran .50 .20
❑ 119 Alex Rodriguez 2.00 .75
❑ 120 Chien-Ming Wang 2.00 .75
❑ 121 Mariano Rivera 1.25 .50
❑ 122 Bobby Abreu .50 .20
❑ 123 Hideki Matsui 1.25 .50
❑ 124 Johnny Damon .75 .30
❑ 125 Robinson Cano .75 .30
❑ 126 Derek Jeter 3.00 1.25
❑ 127 Nick Swisher .50 .20
❑ 128 Eric Chavez .50 .20
❑ 129 Jason Kendall .50 .20
❑ 130 Bobby Crosby .50 .20
❑ 131 Huston Street .50 .20
❑ 132 Dan Haren .50 .20
❑ 133 Rich Harden .50 .20
❑ 134 Mike Piazza 1.25 .50
❑ 135 Chase Utley 1.25 .50
❑ 136 Jimmy Rollins .50 .20
❑ 137 Aaron Rowand .50 .20
❑ 138 Jamie Moyer .50 .20
❑ 139 Cole Hamels .75 .30
❑ 140 Pat Burrell .50 .20
❑ 141 Ryan Howard 2.00 .75
❑ 142 Freddy Sanchez .50 .20
❑ 143 Zach Duke .50 .20
❑ 144 Ian Snell .50 .20
❑ 145 Jack Wilson .50 .20
❑ 146 Jason Bay .50 .20
❑ 147 Albert Pujols 2.50 1.00
❑ 148 Scott Rolen .75 .30
❑ 149 Jim Edmonds .75 .30
❑ 150 Chris Carpenter .50 .20
❑ 151 Yadier Molina .50 .20
❑ 152 Adam Wainwright .50 .20
❑ 153 David Eckstein .50 .20
❑ 154 Trevor Hoffman .50 .20
❑ 155 Brian Giles .50 .20
❑ 156 Adrian Gonzalez .50 .20
❑ 157 Jake Peavy .50 .20
❑ 158 Khalil Greene .75 .30
❑ 159 Chris Young .50 .20
❑ 160 Greg Maddux 2.00 .75
❑ 161 Mike Cameron .50 .20
❑ 162 Matt Cain .75 .30
❑ 163 Matt Morris .50 .20
❑ 164 Pedro Feliz .50 .20
❑ 165 Omar Vizquel .75 .30
❑ 166 Randy Winn .50 .20
❑ 167 Barry Zito .50 .20
❑ 168 Adrian Beltre .50 .20
❑ 169 Yuniesky Betancourt .50 .20
❑ 170 Richie Sexson .50 .20
❑ 171 Raul Ibanez .50 .20
❑ 172 Kenji Johjima 1.25 .50
❑ 173 Ichiro Suzuki 2.00 .75
❑ 174 Felix Hernandez .75 .30
❑ 175 Scott Kazmir .75 .30
❑ 176 Carl Crawford .50 .20
❑ 177 B.J. Upton .50 .20
❑ 178 James Shields .50 .20
❑ 179 Rocco Baldelli .50 .20
❑ 180 Jorge Cantu .50 .20
❑ 181 Ty Wigginton .50 .20
❑ 182 Mark Teixeira .75 .30
❑ 183 Hank Blalock .50 .20
❑ 184 Ian Kinsler .50 .20
❑ 185 Michael Young .50 .20
❑ 186 Vicente Padilla .50 .20
❑ 187 Akinori Otsuka .50 .20
❑ 188 Kenny Lofton .50 .20
❑ 189 A.J. Burnett .50 .20
❑ 190 Roy Halladay .50 .20
❑ 191 B.J. Ryan .50 .20
❑ 192 Vernon Wells .50 .20
❑ 193 Alex Rios .50 .20
❑ 194 Troy Glaus .50 .20
❑ 195 Frank Thomas 1.25 .50
❑ 196 Ryan Zimmerman 1.25 .50
❑ 197 Michael O'Connor .50 .20
❑ 198 Chad Cordero .50 .20
❑ 199 Nick Johnson .50 .20
❑ 200 Felipe Lopez .50 .20
❑ 201 Miguel Montero (RC) 2.50 1.00
❑ 202 Doug Slaten RC 2.50 1.00
❑ 203 Joseph Bisenius RC 2.50 1.00
❑ 204 Jared Burton RC 2.50 1.00
❑ 205 Kevin Cameron RC 2.50 1.00
❑ 206 Matt Chico (RC) 2.50 1.00
❑ 207 Chris Stewart RC 2.50 1.00
❑ 208 Joe Smith RC 2.50 1.00
❑ 209 Zack Segovia (RC) 2.50 1.00
❑ 210 John Danks RC 2.50 1.00
❑ 211 Lee Gardner (RC) 2.50 1.00
❑ 212 Jeff Baker (RC) 2.50 1.00
❑ 213 Jamie Burke (RC) 2.50 1.00
❑ 214 Phil Hughes (RC) 12.00 5.00
❑ 215 Mike Rabelo RC 2.50 1.00
❑ 216 Jose Garcia RC 2.50 1.00
❑ 217 Hector Gimenez (RC) 2.50 1.00
❑ 218 Jesus Flores RC 2.50 1.00
❑ 219 Brandon Morrow RC 6.00 2.50
❑ 220 Hideki Okajima RC 12.00 5.00
❑ 221 Jay Marshall RC 2.50 1.00
❑ 222 Matt Lindstrom (RC) 2.50 1.00
❑ 223 Juan Salas (RC) 2.50 1.00
❑ 224 Juan Perez RC 2.50 1.00
❑ 225 Sean Henn (RC) 2.50 1.00
❑ 226 Travis Buck (RC) 2.50 1.00
❑ 227 Gustavo Molina RC 2.50 1.00
❑ 228 Hunter Pence (RC) 12.00 5.00
❑ 229 Michael Bourn (RC) 2.50 1.00
❑ 230 Brian Barden RC 2.50 1.00
❑ 231 Don Kelly (RC) 2.50 1.00
❑ 232 Joakim Soria RC 2.50 1.00
❑ 233 Cesar Jimenez RC 2.50 1.00
❑ 234 Levale Speigner RC 2.50 1.00
❑ 235 Micah Owings (RC) 2.50 1.00
❑ 236 Brian Stokes (RC) 2.50 1.00
❑ 237 Joaquin Arias (RC) 2.50 1.00
❑ 238 Josh Hamilton L13 (RC) 6.00 2.50
❑ 239 Daisuke Matsuzaka L13 RC 15.00 6.00
❑ 240 Alejandro De Aza L13 RC 4.00 1.50
❑ 241 Kory Casto L13 (RC) 2.50 1.00
❑ 242 Troy Tulowitzki L13 (RC) 6.00 2.50
❑ 243 Akinori Iwamura L13 RC 6.00 2.50
❑ 244 Angel Sanchez L13 RC 2.50 1.00
❑ 245 Ryan Braun L13 (RC) 15.00 6.00
❑ 246 Alex Gordon L13 RC 12.00 5.00
❑ 247 Elijah Dukes L13 RC 4.00 1.50
❑ 248 Kei Igawa L13 RC 6.00 2.50
❑ 249 Kevin Kouzmanoff L13 (RC) 2.50 1.00
❑ 250 Delmon Young L13 (RC) 4.00 1.50

1989 Upper Deck

❑ COMPLETE SET (800) 80.00 40.00
❑ COMP.FACT.SET (800) 100.00 50.00
❑ COMP.HI FACT.SET (100) 10.00 4.00
❑ 1 Ken Griffey Jr. RC 50.00 20.00
❑ 2 Luis Medina RC .25 .08
❑ 3 Tony Chance RC .25 .08
❑ 4 Dave Otto .25 .08
❑ 5 Sandy Alomar Jr. RC 1.00 .40
❑ 6 Rolando Roomes RC .25 .08
❑ 7 Dave West RC .25 .08
❑ 8 Cris Carpenter RC .25 .08
❑ 9 Gregg Jefferies .25 .08
❑ 10 Doug Dascenzo RC .25 .08
❑ 11 Ron Jones RC .25 .08
❑ 12 Luis DeLosSantos RC .25 .08
❑ 13 Gary Sheffield RC 5.00 2.00
❑ 13A Gary Sheffield ERR 5.00 2.00
❑ 14 Mike Harkey RC .25 .08
❑ 15 Lance Blankenship RC .25 .08
❑ 16 William Brennan RC .25 .08
❑ 17 John Smoltz RC 5.00 2.00
❑ 18 Ramon Martinez RC .50 .20

❑	19 Mark Lemke RC	1.00	.40
❑	20 Juan Bell RC	.25	.08
❑	21 Rey Palacios RC	.25	.08
❑	22 Felix Jose RC	.25	.08
❑	23 Van Snider RC	.25	.08
❑	24 Dante Bichette RC	1.00	.40
❑	25 Randy Johnson RC	8.00	3.00
❑	26 Carlos Quintana RC	.25	.08
❑	27 Star Rookie CL	.25	.08
❑	28 Mike Schooler	.25	.08
❑	29 Randy St.Claire	.25	.08
❑	30 Jerald Clark RC	.25	.08
❑	31 Kevin Gross	.25	.08
❑	32 Dan Firova	.25	.08
❑	33 Jeff Calhoun	.25	.08
❑	34 Tommy Hinzo	.25	.08
❑	35 Ricky Jordan RC *	.50	.20
❑	36 Larry Parrish	.25	.08
❑	37 Bret Saberhagen UER (Hit total 931& should be 10	.40	.15
❑	38 Mike Smithson	.25	.08
❑	39 Dave Dravecky	.25	.08
❑	40 Ed Romero	.25	.08
❑	41 Jeff Musselman	.25	.08
❑	42 Ed Hearn	.25	.08
❑	43 Rance Mulliniks	.25	.08
❑	44 Jim Eisenreich	.25	.08
❑	45 Sil Campusano	.25	.08
❑	46 Mike Krukow	.25	.08
❑	47 Paul Gibson	.25	.08
❑	48 Mike LaCoss	.25	.08
❑	49 Larry Herndon	.25	.08
❑	50 Scott Garrelts	.25	.08
❑	51 Dwayne Henry	.25	.08
❑	52 Jim Acker	.25	.08
❑	53 Steve Sax	.25	.08
❑	54 Pete O'Brien	.25	.08
❑	55 Paul Runge	.25	.08
❑	56 Rick Rhoden	.25	.08
❑	57 John Dopson	.25	.08
❑	58 Casey Candaele UER (No stats for Astros for '88	.25	.08
❑	59 Dave Righetti	.40	.15
❑	60 Joe Hesketh	.25	.08
❑	61 Frank DiPino	.25	.08
❑	62 Tim Laudner	.25	.08
❑	63 Jamie Moyer	.40	.15
❑	64 Fred Toliver	.25	.08
❑	65 Mitch Webster	.25	.08
❑	66 John Tudor	.40	.15
❑	67 John Cangelosi	.25	.08
❑	68 Mike Devereaux	.25	.08
❑	69 Brian Fisher	.25	.08
❑	70 Mike Marshall	.25	.08
❑	71 Zane Smith	.25	.08
❑	72A Brian Holton ERR	1.00	.40
❑	72B Brian Holton COR	.40	.15
❑	73 Jose Guzman	.25	.08
❑	74 Rick Mahler	.25	.08
❑	75 John Shelby	.25	.08
❑	76 Jim Deshaies	.25	.08
❑	77 Bobby Meacham	.25	.08
❑	78 Bryn Smith	.25	.08
❑	79 Joaquin Andujar	.40	.15
❑	80 Richard Dotson	.25	.08
❑	81 Charlie Lea	.25	.08
❑	82 Calvin Schiraldi	.25	.08
❑	83 Les Straker	.25	.08
❑	84 Les Lancaster	.25	.08
❑	85 Allan Anderson	.25	.08
❑	86 Junior Ortiz	.25	.08
❑	87 Jesse Orosco	.25	.08
❑	88 Felix Fermin	.25	.08
❑	89 Dave Anderson	.25	.08
❑	90 Rafael Belliard UER (Born '61& not '51)	.25	.08
❑	91 Franklin Stubbs	.25	.08
❑	92 Cecil Espy	.25	.08
❑	93 Albert Hall	.25	.08
❑	94 Tim Leary	.25	.08
❑	95 Mitch Williams	.25	.08
❑	96 Tracy Jones	.25	.08
❑	97 Danny Darwin	.25	.08
❑	98 Gary Ward	.25	.08
❑	99 Neal Heaton	.25	.08
❑	100 Jim Pankovits	.25	.08
❑	101 Bill Doran	.25	.08
❑	102 Tim Wallach	.25	.08
❑	103 Joe Magrane	.25	.08
❑	104 Ozzie Virgil	.25	.08
❑	105 Alvin Davis	.25	.08
❑	106 Tom Brookens	.25	.08
❑	107 Shawon Dunston	.25	.08
❑	108 Tracy Woodson	.25	.08
❑	109 Nelson Liriano	.25	.08
❑	110 Devon White	.40	.15
❑	111 Steve Balboni	.25	.08
❑	112 Buddy Bell	.40	.15
❑	113 German Jimenez	.25	.08
❑	114 Ken Dayley	.25	.08
❑	115 Andres Galarraga	.40	.15
❑	116 Mike Scioscia	.40	.15
❑	117 Gary Pettis	.25	.08
❑	118 Ernie Whitt	.25	.08
❑	119 Bob Boone	.40	.15
❑	120 Ryne Sandberg	1.50	.60
❑	121 Bruce Benedict	.25	.08
❑	122 Hubie Brooks	.25	.08
❑	123 Mike Moore	.25	.08
❑	124 Wallace Johnson	.25	.08
❑	125 Bob Horner	.40	.15
❑	126 Chili Davis	.40	.15
❑	127 Manny Trillo	.25	.08
❑	128 Chet Lemon	.40	.15
❑	129 John Cerutti	.25	.08
❑	130 Orel Hershiser	.40	.15
❑	131 Terry Pendleton	.40	.15
❑	132 Jeff Blauser	.25	.08
❑	133 Mike Fitzgerald	.25	.08
❑	134 Henry Cotto	.25	.08
❑	135 Gerald Young	.25	.08
❑	136 Luis Salazar	.25	.08
❑	137 Alejandro Pena	.25	.08
❑	138 Jack Howell	.25	.08
❑	139 Tony Fernandez	.25	.08
❑	140 Mark Grace	1.00	.40
❑	141 Ken Caminiti	.60	.25
❑	142 Mike Jackson	.25	.08
❑	143 Larry McWilliams	.25	.08
❑	144 Andres Thomas	.25	.08
❑	145 Nolan Ryan 3X	4.00	1.50
❑	146 Mike Davis	.25	.08
❑	147 DeWayne Buice	.25	.08
❑	148 Jody Davis	.25	.08
❑	149 Jesse Barfield	.40	.15
❑	150 Matt Nokes	.25	.08
❑	151 Jerry Reuss	.25	.08
❑	152 Rick Cerone	.25	.08
❑	153 Storm Davis	.25	.08
❑	154 Marvell Wynne	.25	.08
❑	155 Will Clark	.60	.25
❑	156 Luis Aguayo	.25	.08
❑	157 Willie Upshaw	.25	.08
❑	158 Randy Bush	.25	.08
❑	159 Ron Darling	.40	.15
❑	160 Kal Daniels	.25	.08
❑	161 Spike Owen	.25	.08
❑	162 Luis Polonia	.25	.08
❑	163 Kevin Mitchell UER	.40	.15
❑	164 Dave Gallagher	.25	.08
❑	165 Benito Santiago	.40	.15
❑	166 Greg Gagne	.25	.08
❑	167 Ken Phelps	.25	.08
❑	168 Sid Fernandez	.25	.08
❑	169 Bo Diaz	.25	.08
❑	170 Cory Snyder	.25	.08
❑	171 Eric Show	.25	.08
❑	172 Robby Thompson	.25	.08
❑	173 Marty Barrett	.25	.08
❑	174 Dave Henderson	.25	.08
❑	175 Ozzie Guillen	.40	.15
❑	176 Barry Lyons	.25	.08
❑	177 Kelvin Torve	.25	.08
❑	178 Don Slaught	.25	.08
❑	179 Steve Lombardozzi	.25	.08
❑	180 Chris Sabo RC *	1.00	.40
❑	181 Jose Uribe	.25	.08
❑	182 Shane Mack	.25	.08
❑	183 Ron Karkovice	.25	.08
❑	184 Todd Benzinger	.25	.08
❑	185 Dave Stewart	.40	.15
❑	186 Julio Franco	.40	.15
❑	187 Ron Robinson	.25	.08
❑	188 Wally Backman	.25	.08
❑	189 Randy Velarde	.25	.08
❑	190 Joe Carter	.40	.15
❑	191 Bob Welch	.40	.15
❑	192 Kelly Paris	.25	.08
❑	193 Chris Brown	.25	.08
❑	194 Rick Reuschel	.40	.15
❑	195 Roger Clemens	2.00	.75
❑	196 Dave Concepcion	.40	.15
❑	197 Al Newman	.25	.08
❑	198 Brook Jacoby	.25	.08
❑	199 Mookie Wilson	.40	.15
❑	200 Don Mattingly	2.50	1.00
❑	201 Dick Schofield	.25	.08
❑	202 Mark Gubicza	.25	.08
❑	203 Gary Gaetti	.40	.15
❑	204 Dan Pasqua	.25	.08
❑	205 Andre Dawson	.40	.15
❑	206 Chris Speier	.25	.08
❑	207 Kent Tekulve	.25	.08
❑	208 Rod Scurry	.25	.08
❑	209 Scott Bailes	.25	.08
❑	210 Rickey Henderson	1.00	.40
❑	211 Harold Baines	.40	.15
❑	212 Tony Armas	.40	.15
❑	213 Kent Hrbek	.40	.15
❑	214 Darrin Jackson	.25	.08
❑	215 George Brett	2.50	1.00
❑	216 Rafael Santana	.25	.08
❑	217 Andy Allanson	.25	.08
❑	218 Brett Butler	.40	.15
❑	219 Steve Jeltz	.25	.08
❑	220 Jay Buhner	.40	.15
❑	221 Bo Jackson	1.00	.40
❑	222 Angel Salazar	.25	.08
❑	223 Kirk McCaskill	.25	.08
❑	224 Steve Lyons	.25	.08
❑	225 Bert Blyleven	.40	.15
❑	226 Scott Bradley	.25	.08
❑	227 Bob Melvin	.25	.08
❑	228 Ron Kittle	.25	.08
❑	229 Phil Bradley	.25	.08
❑	230 Tommy John	.40	.15
❑	231 Greg Walker	.25	.08
❑	232 Juan Berenguer	.25	.08
❑	233 Pat Tabler	.25	.08
❑	234 Terry Clark	.25	.08
❑	235 Rafael Palmeiro	1.00	.40
❑	236 Paul Zuvella	.25	.08
❑	237 Willie Randolph	.40	.15
❑	238 Bruce Fields	.25	.08
❑	239 Mike Aldrete	.25	.08
❑	240 Lance Parrish	.40	.15
❑	241 Greg Maddux	2.50	1.00
❑	242 John Moses	.25	.08
❑	243 Melido Perez	.25	.08
❑	244 Willie Wilson	.40	.15
❑	245 Mark McLemore	.25	.08
❑	246 Von Hayes	.25	.08
❑	247 Matt Williams	1.00	.40
❑	248 John Candelaria UER (Listed as Yankee for part o	.25	.08
❑	249 Harold Reynolds	.40	.15
❑	250 Greg Swindell	.25	.08
❑	251 Juan Agosto	.25	.08
❑	252 Mike Felder	.25	.08
❑	253 Vince Coleman	.25	.08
❑	254 Larry Sheets	.25	.08
❑	255 George Bell	.40	.15
❑	256 Terry Steinbach	.40	.15
❑	257 Jack Armstrong RC *	.50	.20
❑	258 Dickie Thon	.25	.08
❑	259 Ray Knight	.40	.15
❑	260 Darryl Strawberry	.40	.15
❑	261 Doug Sisk	.25	.08
❑	262 Alex Trevino	.25	.08
❑	263 Jeffrey Leonard	.25	.08
❑	264 Tom Henke	.25	.08
❑	265 Ozzie Smith	1.50	.60
❑	266 Dave Bergman	.25	.08
❑	267 Tony Phillips	.25	.08
❑	268 Mark Davis	.25	.08

❑	269 Kevin Elster	.25	.08
❑	270 Barry Larkin	.60	.25
❑	271 Manny Lee	.25	.08
❑	272 Tom Brunansky	.25	.08
❑	273 Craig Biggio RC	6.00	2.50
❑	274 Jim Gantner	.25	.08
❑	275 Eddie Murray	1.00	.40
❑	276 Jeff Reed	.25	.08
❑	277 Tim Teufel	.25	.08
❑	278 Rick Honeycutt	.25	.08
❑	279 Guillermo Hernandez	.25	.08
❑	280 John Kruk	.40	.15
❑	281 Luis Alicea RC *	.50	.20
❑	282 Jim Clancy	.25	.08
❑	283 Billy Ripken	.25	.08
❑	284 Craig Reynolds	.25	.08
❑	285 Robin Yount	1.50	.60
❑	286 Jimmy Jones	.25	.08
❑	287 Ron Oester	.25	.08
❑	288 Terry Leach	.25	.08
❑	289 Dennis Eckersley	.60	.25
❑	290 Alan Trammell	.40	.15
❑	291 Jimmy Key	.40	.15
❑	292 Chris Bosio	.25	.08
❑	293 Jose DeLeon	.25	.08
❑	294 Jim Traber	.25	.08
❑	295 Mike Scott	.40	.15
❑	296 Roger McDowell	.25	.08
❑	297 Garry Templeton	.40	.15
❑	298 Doyle Alexander	.25	.08
❑	299 Nick Esasky	.25	.08
❑	300 Mark McGwire	5.00	2.00
❑	301 Darryl Hamilton RC *	.50	.20
❑	302 Dave Smith	.25	.08
❑	303 Rick Sutcliffe	.40	.15
❑	304 Dave Stapleton	.25	.08
❑	305 Alan Ashby	.25	.08
❑	306 Pedro Guerrero	.40	.15
❑	307 Ron Guidry	.40	.15
❑	308 Steve Farr	.25	.08
❑	309 Curt Ford	.25	.08
❑	310 Claudell Washington	.25	.08
❑	311 Tom Prince	.25	.08
❑	312 Chad Kreuter RC	.50	.20
❑	313 Ken Oberkfell	.25	.08
❑	314 Jerry Browne	.25	.08
❑	315 R.J. Reynolds	.25	.08
❑	316 Scott Bankhead	.25	.08
❑	317 Milt Thompson	.25	.08
❑	318 Mario Diaz	.25	.08
❑	319 Bruce Ruffin	.25	.08
❑	320 Dave Valle	.25	.08
❑	321A Gary Varsho ERR	2.00	.75
❑	321B Gary Varsho COR (In road uniform)	.25	.08
❑	322 Paul Mirabella	.25	.08
❑	323 Chuck Jackson	.25	.08
❑	324 Drew Hall	.25	.08
❑	325 Don August	.25	.08
❑	326 Israel Sanchez	.25	.08
❑	327 Denny Walling	.25	.08
❑	328 Joel Skinner	.25	.08
❑	329 Danny Tartabull	.25	.08
❑	330 Tony Pena	.25	.08
❑	331 Jim Sundberg	.40	.15
❑	332 Jeff D. Robinson	.25	.08
❑	333 Oddibe McDowell	.25	.08
❑	334 Jose Lind	.25	.08
❑	335 Paul Kilgus	.25	.08
❑	336 Juan Samuel	.25	.08
❑	337 Mike Campbell	.25	.08
❑	338 Mike Maddux	.25	.08
❑	339 Darnell Coles	.25	.08
❑	340 Bob Dernier	.25	.08
❑	341 Rafael Ramirez	.25	.08
❑	342 Scott Sanderson	.25	.08
❑	343 B.J. Surhoff	.40	.15
❑	344 Billy Hatcher	.25	.08
❑	345 Pat Perry	.25	.08
❑	346 Jack Clark	.40	.15
❑	347 Gary Thurman	.25	.08
❑	348 Tim Jones	.25	.08
❑	349 Dave Winfield	.40	.15
❑	350 Frank White	.40	.15
❑	351 Dave Collins	.25	.08
❑	352 Jack Morris	.40	.15
❑	353 Eric Plunk	.25	.08
❑	354 Leon Durham	.25	.08
❑	355 Ivan DeJesus	.25	.08
❑	356 Brian Holman RC *	.25	.08
❑	357A Dale Murphy RevNeg	30.00	12.50
❑	357B Dale Murphy COR	.60	.25
❑	358 Mark Portugal	.25	.08
❑	359 Andy McGaffigan	.25	.08
❑	360 Tom Glavine	1.00	.40
❑	361 Keith Moreland	.25	.08
❑	362 Todd Stottlemyre	.25	.08
❑	363 Dave Leiper	.25	.08
❑	364 Cecil Fielder	.40	.15
❑	365 Carmelo Martinez	.25	.08
❑	366 Dwight Evans	.60	.25
❑	367 Kevin McReynolds	.25	.08
❑	368 Rich Gedman	.25	.08
❑	369 Len Dykstra	.40	.15
❑	370 Jody Reed	.25	.08
❑	371 Jose Canseco	1.00	.40
❑	372 Rob Murphy	.25	.08
❑	373 Mike Henneman	.25	.08
❑	374 Walt Weiss	.25	.08
❑	375 Rob Dibble RC	1.00	.40
❑	376 Kirby Puckett	1.00	.40
❑	377 Dennis Martinez	.40	.15
❑	378 Ron Gant	.40	.15
❑	379 Brian Harper	.25	.08
❑	380 Nelson Santovenia	.25	.08
❑	381 Lloyd Moseby	.25	.08
❑	382 Lance McCullers	.25	.08
❑	383 Dave Stieb	.40	.15
❑	384 Tony Gwynn	1.25	.50
❑	385 Mike Flanagan	.25	.08
❑	386 Bob Ojeda	.25	.08
❑	387 Bruce Hurst	.25	.08
❑	388 Dave Magadan	.25	.08
❑	389 Wade Boggs	.60	.25
❑	390 Gary Carter	.40	.15
❑	391 Frank Tanana	.40	.15
❑	392 Curt Young	.25	.08
❑	393 Jeff Treadway	.25	.08
❑	394 Darrell Evans	.40	.15
❑	395 Glenn Hubbard	.25	.08
❑	396 Chuck Cary	.25	.08
❑	397 Frank Viola	.40	.15
❑	398 Jeff Parrett	.25	.08
❑	399 Terry Blocker	.25	.08
❑	400 Dan Gladden	.25	.08
❑	401 Louie Meadows	.25	.08
❑	402 Tim Raines	.40	.15
❑	403 Joey Meyer	.25	.08
❑	404 Larry Andersen	.25	.08
❑	405 Rex Hudler	.25	.08
❑	406 Mike Schmidt	2.00	.75
❑	407 John Franco	.40	.15
❑	408 Brady Anderson RC	1.00	.40
❑	409 Don Carman	.25	.08
❑	410 Eric Davis	.40	.15
❑	411 Bob Stanley	.25	.08
❑	412 Pete Smith	.25	.08
❑	413 Jim Rice	.40	.15
❑	414 Bruce Sutter	.40	.15
❑	415 Oil Can Boyd	.25	.08
❑	416 Ruben Sierra	.40	.15
❑	417 Mike LaValliere	.25	.08
❑	418 Steve Buechele	.25	.08
❑	419 Gary Redus	.25	.08
❑	420 Scott Fletcher	.25	.08
❑	421 Dale Sveum	.25	.08
❑	422 Bob Knepper	.25	.08
❑	423 Luis Rivera	.25	.08
❑	424 Ted Higuera	.25	.08
❑	425 Kevin Bass	.25	.08
❑	426 Ken Gerhart	.25	.08
❑	427 Shane Rawley	.25	.08
❑	428 Paul O'Neill	.60	.25
❑	429 Joe Orsulak	.25	.08
❑	430 Jackie Gutierrez	.25	.08
❑	431 Gerald Perry	.25	.08
❑	432 Mike Greenwell	.25	.08
❑	433 Jerry Royster	.25	.08
❑	434 Ellis Burks	.40	.15
❑	435 Ed Olwine	.25	.08
❑	436 Dave Rucker	.25	.08
❑	437 Charlie Hough	.40	.15
❑	438 Bob Walk	.25	.08
❑	439 Bob Brower	.25	.08
❑	440 Barry Bonds	5.00	2.00
❑	441 Tom Foley	.25	.08
❑	442 Rob Deer	.25	.08
❑	443 Glenn Davis	.25	.08
❑	444 Dave Martinez	.25	.08
❑	445 Bill Wegman	.25	.08
❑	446 Lloyd McClendon	.25	.08
❑	447 Dave Schmidt	.25	.08
❑	448 Darren Daulton	.40	.15
❑	449 Frank Williams	.25	.08
❑	450 Don Aase	.25	.08
❑	451 Lou Whitaker	.40	.15
❑	452 Rich Gossage	.40	.15
❑	453 Ed Whitson	.25	.08
❑	454 Jim Walewander	.25	.08
❑	455 Damon Berryhill	.25	.08
❑	456 Tim Burke	.25	.08
❑	457 Barry Jones	.25	.08
❑	458 Joel Youngblood	.25	.08
❑	459 Floyd Youmans	.25	.08
❑	460 Mark Salas	.25	.08
❑	461 Jeff Russell	.25	.08
❑	462 Darrell Miller	.25	.08
❑	463 Jeff Kunkel	.25	.08
❑	464 Sherman Corbett	.25	.08
❑	465 Curtis Wilkerson	.25	.08
❑	466 Bud Black	.25	.08
❑	467 Cal Ripken	3.00	1.25
❑	468 John Farrell	.25	.08
❑	469 Terry Kennedy	.25	.08
❑	470 Tom Candiotti	.25	.08
❑	471 Roberto Alomar	1.00	.40
❑	472 Jeff M. Robinson	.25	.08
❑	473 Vance Law	.25	.08
❑	474 Randy Ready UER (Strikeout total 136& should be	.25	.08
❑	475 Walt Terrell	.25	.08
❑	476 Kelly Downs	.25	.08
❑	477 Johnny Paredes	.25	.08
❑	478 Shawn Hillegas	.25	.08
❑	479 Bob Brenly	.25	.08
❑	480 Otis Nixon	.25	.08
❑	481 Johnny Ray	.25	.08
❑	482 Geno Petralli	.25	.08
❑	483 Stu Cliburn	.25	.08
❑	484 Pete Incaviglia	.25	.08
❑	485 Brian Downing	.40	.15
❑	486 Jeff Stone	.25	.08
❑	487 Carmen Castillo	.25	.08
❑	488 Tom Niedenfuer	.25	.08
❑	489 Jay Bell	.40	.15
❑	490 Rick Schu	.25	.08
❑	491 Jeff Pico	.25	.08
❑	492 Mark Parent	.25	.08
❑	493 Eric King	.25	.08
❑	494 Al Nipper	.25	.08
❑	495 Andy Hawkins	.25	.08
❑	496 Daryl Boston	.25	.08
❑	497 Ernie Riles	.25	.08
❑	498 Pascual Perez	.25	.08
❑	499 Bill Long UER (Games started total 70& should be	.25	.08
❑	500 Kirt Manwaring	.25	.08
❑	501 Chuck Crim	.25	.08
❑	502 Candy Maldonado	.25	.08
❑	503 Dennis Lamp	.25	.08
❑	504 Glenn Braggs	.25	.08
❑	505 Joe Price	.25	.08
❑	506 Ken Williams	.25	.08
❑	507 Bill Pecota	.25	.08
❑	508 Rey Quinones	.25	.08
❑	509 Jeff Bittiger	.25	.08
❑	510 Kevin Seitzer	.25	.08
❑	511 Steve Bedrosian	.25	.08
❑	512 Todd Worrell	.25	.08
❑	513 Chris James	.25	.08
❑	514 Jose Oquendo	.25	.08
❑	515 David Palmer	.25	.08
❑	516 John Smiley	.25	.08
❑	517 Dave Clark	.25	.08
❑	518 Mike Dunne	.25	.08
❑	519 Ron Washington	.25	.08

520	Bob Kipper	.25	.08
521	Lee Smith	.40	.15
522	Juan Castillo	.25	.08
523	Don Robinson	.25	.08
524	Kevin Romine	.25	.08
525	Paul Molitor	.40	.15
526	Mark Langston	.25	.08
527	Donnie Hill	.25	.08
528	Larry Owen	.25	.08
529	Jerry Reed	.25	.08
530	Jack McDowell	.40	.15
531	Greg Mathews	.25	.08
532	John Russell	.25	.08
533	Dan Quisenberry	.25	.08
534	Greg Gross	.25	.08
535	Danny Cox	.25	.08
536	Terry Francona	.40	.15
537	Andy Van Slyke	.60	.25
538	Mel Hall	.25	.08
539	Jim Gott	.25	.08
540	Doug Jones	.25	.08
541	Craig Lefferts	.25	.08
542	Mike Boddicker	.25	.08
543	Greg Brock	.25	.08
544	Atlee Hammaker	.25	.08
545	Tom Bolton	.25	.08
546	Mike Macfarlane RC *	.50	.20
547	Rich Renteria	.25	.08
548	John Davis	.25	.08
549	Floyd Bannister	.25	.08
550	Mickey Brantley	.25	.08
551	Duane Ward	.25	.08
552	Dan Petry	.25	.08
553	Mickey Tettleton	.25	.08
554	Rick Leach	.25	.08
555	Mike Witt	.25	.08
556	Sid Bream	.25	.08
557	Bobby Witt	.25	.08
558	Tommy Herr	.25	.08
559	Randy Milligan	.25	.08
560	Jose Cecena	.25	.08
561	Mackey Sasser	.25	.08
562	Carney Lansford	.40	.15
563	Rick Aguilera	.25	.08
564	Ron Hassey	.25	.08
565	Dwight Gooden	.40	.15
566	Paul Assenmacher	.25	.08
567	Neil Allen	.25	.08
568	Jim Morrison	.25	.08
569	Mike Pagliarulo	.25	.08
570	Ted Simmons	.40	.15
571	Mark Thurmond	.25	.08
572	Fred McGriff	.60	.25
573	Wally Joyner	.40	.15
574	Jose Bautista RC	.25	.08
575	Kelly Gruber	.25	.08
576	Cecilio Guante	.25	.08
577	Mark Davidson	.25	.08
578	Bobby Bonilla UER	.40	.15
579	Mike Stanley	.25	.08
580	Gene Larkin	.25	.08
581	Stan Javier	.25	.08
582	Howard Johnson	.40	.15
583A	Mike Gallego Rev Neg	1.00	.40
583B	Mike Gallego COR	1.00	.40
584	David Cone	.40	.15
585	Doug Jennings	.25	.08
586	Charles Hudson	.25	.08
587	Dion James	.25	.08
588	Al Leiter	1.00	.40
589	Charlie Puleo	.25	.08
590	Roberto Kelly	.25	.08
591	Thad Bosley	.25	.08
592	Pete Stanicek	.25	.08
593	Pat Borders RC *	.50	.20
594	Bryan Harvey RC *	.50	.20
595	Jeff Ballard	.25	.08
596	Jeff Reardon	.40	.15
597	Doug Drabek	.25	.08
598	Edwin Correa	.25	.08
599	Keith Atherton	.25	.08
600	Dave LaPoint	.25	.08
601	Don Baylor	.40	.15
602	Tom Pagnozzi	.25	.08
603	Tim Flannery	.25	.08
604	Gene Walter	.25	.08
605	Dave Parker	.40	.15
606	Mike Diaz	.25	.08
607	Chris Gwynn	.25	.08
608	Odell Jones	.25	.08
609	Carlton Fisk	.60	.25
610	Jay Howell	.25	.08
611	Tim Crews	.25	.08
612	Keith Hernandez	.40	.15
613	Willie Fraser	.25	.08
614	Jim Eppard	.25	.08
615	Jeff Hamilton	.25	.08
616	Kurt Stillwell	.25	.08
617	Tom Browning	.25	.08
618	Jeff Montgomery	.25	.08
619	Jose Rijo	.40	.15
620	Jamie Quirk	.25	.08
621	Willie McGee	.40	.15
622	Mark Grant UER (Glove on wrong hand)	.25	.08
623	Bill Swift	.25	.08
624	Orlando Mercado	.25	.08
625	John Costello	.25	.08
626	Jose Gonzalez	.25	.08
627A	Bill Schroeder ERR	.60	.25
627B	Bill Schroeder COR	.60	.25
628A	Fred Manrique ERR Guillen	.60	.25
628B	Fred Manrique COR (Swinging bat on back)	.25	.08
629	Ricky Horton	.25	.08
630	Dan Plesac	.25	.08
631	Alfredo Griffin	.25	.08
632	Chuck Finley	.40	.15
633	Kirk Gibson	.40	.15
634	Randy Myers	.40	.15
635	Greg Minton	.25	.08
636A	Herm Winningham ERR (W1nningham on back)	1.00	.40
636B	Herm Winningham COR	.25	.08
637	Charlie Leibrandt	.25	.08
638	Tim Birtsas	.25	.08
639	Bill Buckner	.40	.15
640	Danny Jackson	.25	.08
641	Greg Booker	.25	.08
642	Jim Presley	.25	.08
643	Gene Nelson	.25	.08
644	Rod Booker	.25	.08
645	Dennis Rasmussen	.25	.08
646	Juan Nieves	.25	.08
647	Bobby Thigpen	.25	.08
648	Tim Belcher	.25	.08
649	Mike Young	.25	.08
650	Ivan Calderon	.25	.08
651	Oswald Peraza	.25	.08
652A	Pat Sheridan ERR NPO	15.00	6.00
652B	Pat Sheridan COR	.25	.08
653	Mike Morgan	.25	.08
654	Mike Heath	.25	.08
655	Jay Tibbs	.25	.08
656	Fernando Valenzuela	.40	.15
657	Lee Mazzilli	.40	.15
658	Frank Viola AL CY	.25	.08
659A	Jose Canseco MVP	.60	.25
659B	Jose Canseco MVP	.60	.25
660	Walt Weiss AL ROY	.25	.08
661	Orel Hershiser NL CY	.25	.08
662	Kirk Gibson NL MVP	.40	.15
663	Chris Sabo NL ROY	.40	.15
664	D.Eckersley ALCS MVP	.40	.15
665	O.Hershiser NLCS MVP	.40	.15
666	Kirk Gibson WS	1.00	.40
667	Orel Hershiser WS MVP	.25	.08
668	Wally Joyner TC California Angels	.25	.08
669	Nolan Ryan TC	1.25	.50
670	Jose Canseco TC	.60	.25
671	Fred McGriff TC	.40	.15
672	Dale Murphy TC Atlanta Braves	.40	.15
673	Paul Molitor TC	.25	.08
674	Ozzie Smith TC	1.00	.40
675	Ryne Sandberg TC	1.00	.40
676	Kirk Gibson TC	.40	.15
677	Andres Galarraga TC	.25	.08
678	Will Clark TC	.40	.15
679	Cory Snyder TC Cleveland Indians	.25	.08
680	Alvin Davis TC Seattle Mariners	.25	.08
681	Darryl Strawberry TC New York Mets	.25	.08
682	Cal Ripken TC	1.00	.40
683	Tony Gwynn TC	.60	.25
684	Mike Schmidt TC	1.00	.40
685	Andy Van Slyke TC Pittsburgh Pirates UER (96 Jun	.40	.15
686	Ruben Sierra TC	.25	.08
687	Wade Boggs TC	.40	.15
688	Eric Davis TC Cincinnati Reds	.25	.08
689	George Brett TC	1.00	.40
690	Alan Trammell TC Detroit Tigers	.25	.08
691	Frank Viola TC Minnesota Twins	.25	.08
692	Harold Baines TC Chicago White Sox	.25	.08
693	Don Mattingly TC	1.00	.40
694	Checklist 1-100	.25	.00
695	Checklist 101-200	.25	.08
696	Checklist 201-300	.25	.08
697	Checklist 301-400	.25	.08
698	Checklist UER	.25	.08
699	Checklist 501-600 UER (543 Greg Booker)	.25	.08
700	Checklist 601-700	.25	.08
701	Checklist 701-800	.25	.08
702	Jesse Barfield	.40	.15
703	Walt Terrell	.25	.08
704	Dickie Thon	.25	.08
705	Al Leiter	1.00	.40
706	Dave LaPoint	.25	.08
707	Charlie Hayes RC	.50	.20
708	Andy Hawkins	.25	.08
709	Mickey Hatcher	.25	.08
710	Lance McCullers	.25	.08
711	Ron Kittle	.25	.08
712	Bert Blyleven	.40	.15
713	Rick Dempsey	.25	.08
714	Ken Williams	.25	.08
715	Steve Rosenberg	.25	.08
716	Joe Skalski	.25	.08
717	Spike Owen	.25	.08
718	Todd Burns	.25	.08
719	Kevin Gross	.25	.08
720	Tommy Herr	.25	.08
721	Rob Ducey	.25	.08
722	Gary Green	.25	.08
723	Gregg Olson RC	.50	.20
724	Greg W.Harris RC	.25	.08
725	Craig Worthington	.25	.08
726	Thomas Howard RC	.25	.08
727	Dale Mohorcic	.25	.08
728	Rich Yett	.25	.08
729	Mel Hall	.25	.08
730	Floyd Youmans	.25	.08
731	Lonnie Smith	.25	.08
732	Wally Backman	.25	.08
733	Trevor Wilson RC	.25	.08
734	Jose Alvarez RC	.25	.08
735	Bob Milacki	.25	.00
736	Tom Gordon RC	1.50	.60
737	Wally Whitehurst RC	.25	.08
738	Mike Aldrete	.25	.08
739	Keith Miller	.25	.08
740	Randy Milligan	.25	.08
741	Jeff Parrett	.25	.08
742	Steve Finley RC	2.00	.75
743	Junior Felix RC	.25	.08
744	Pete Harnisch RC	.50	.20
745	Billy Spiers RC	.50	.20
746	Hensley Meulens RC	.25	.08
747	Juan Bell RC	.25	.08
748	Steve Sax	.25	.08
749	Phil Bradley	.25	.08
750	Rey Quinones	.25	.08
751	Tommy Gregg	.25	.08
752	Kevin Brown	1.00	.40
753	Derek Lilliquist RC	.25	.08
754	Todd Zeile RC	1.00	.40
755	Jim Abbott RC	2.00	.75

❑ 756 Ozzie Canseco	.25	.08
❑ 757 Nick Esasky	.25	.08
❑ 758 Mike Moore	.25	.08
❑ 759 Rob Murphy	.25	.08
❑ 760 Rick Mahler	.25	.08
❑ 761 Fred Lynn	.40	.15
❑ 762 Kevin Blankenship	.25	.08
❑ 763 Eddie Murray	1.00	.40
❑ 764 Steve Searcy	.25	.08
❑ 765 Jerome Walton RC	.50	.20
❑ 766 Erik Hanson RC	.50	.20
❑ 767 Bob Boone	.40	.15
❑ 768 Edgar Martinez	1.00	.40
❑ 769 Jose DeJesus	.25	.08
❑ 770 Greg Briley	.25	.08
❑ 771 Steve Peters	.25	.08
❑ 772 Rafael Palmeiro	1.00	.40
❑ 773 Jack Clark	.40	.15
❑ 774 Nolan Ryan w/FB	4.00	1.50
❑ 775 Lance Parrish	.40	.15
❑ 776 Joe Girardi RC	1.00	.40
❑ 777 Willie Randolph	.40	.15
❑ 778 Mitch Williams	.25	.08
❑ 779 Dennis Cook RC	.50	.20
❑ 780 Dwight Smith RC	.50	.20
❑ 781 Lenny Harris RC	.50	.20
❑ 782 Torey Lovullo RC	.25	.08
❑ 783 Norm Charlton RC	.50	.20
❑ 784 Chris Brown	.25	.08
❑ 785 Todd Benzinger	.25	.08
❑ 786 Shane Rawley	.25	.08
❑ 787 Omar Vizquel RC	3.00	1.25
❑ 788 LaVel Freeman	.25	.08
❑ 789 Jeffrey Leonard	.25	.08
❑ 790 Eddie Williams	.25	.08
❑ 791 Jamie Moyer	.40	.15
❑ 792 Bruce Hurst UER (Workd Series)	.25	.08
❑ 793 Julio Franco	.40	.15
❑ 794 Claudell Washington	.25	.08
❑ 795 Jody Davis	.25	.08
❑ 796 Oddibe McDowell	.25	.08
❑ 797 Paul Kilgus	.25	.08
❑ 798 Tracy Jones	.25	.08
❑ 799 Steve Wilson	.25	.08
❑ 800 Pete O'Brien	.25	.08

1990 Upper Deck

❑ COMPLETE SET (800)	25.00	10.00
❑ COMP.FACT.SET (800)	25.00	10.00
❑ COMPLETE LO SET (700)	25.00	15.00
❑ COMPLETE HI SET (100)	5.00	2.00
❑ COMP.HI FACT.SET (100)	4.00	2.00
❑ 1 Star Rookie Checklist	.10	.02
❑ 2 Randy Nosek RC	.10	.02
❑ 3 Tom Drees RC	.10	.02
❑ 4 Curt Young	.10	.02
❑ 5 Devon White TC	.10	.02
❑ 6 Luis Salazar	.10	.02
❑ 7 Von Hayes TC	.10	.02
❑ 8 Jose Bautista	.10	.02
❑ 9 Marquis Grissom RC	.50	.20
❑ 10 Orel Hershiser TC	.10	.02
❑ 11 Rick Aguilera	.20	.07
❑ 12 Benito Santiago TC	.10	.02
❑ 13 Deion Sanders	.50	.20
❑ 14 Marvell Wynne	.10	.02
❑ 15 Dave West	.10	.02
❑ 16 Bobby Bonilla TC	.10	.02
❑ 17 Sammy Sosa RC	3.00	1.25
❑ 18 Steve Sax TC	.10	.02
❑ 19 Jack Howell	.10	.02
❑ 20 Mike Schmidt SPEC	1.00	.40
❑ 21 Robin Ventura	.50	.20
❑ 22 Brian Meyer	.10	.02
❑ 23 Blaine Beatty RC	.10	.02
❑ 24 Ken Griffey Jr. TC	.60	.25
❑ 25 Greg Vaughn	.10	.02
❑ 26 Xavier Hernandez RC	.10	.02
❑ 27 Jason Grimsley RC	.10	.02
❑ 28 Eric Anthony RC	.10	.02
❑ 29 Tim Raines TC UER	.10	.02
❑ 30 David Wells	.20	.07
❑ 31 Hal Morris	.10	.02
❑ 32 Bo Jackson TC	.20	.07
❑ 33 Kelly Mann RC	.10	.02
❑ 34 Nolan Ryan SPEC	1.00	.40
❑ 35 Scott Service UER (Born Cincinnati on 7/27/67& s	.10	.02
❑ 36 Mark McGwire TC	.75	.30
❑ 37 Tino Martinez	1.00	.40
❑ 38 Chili Davis	.20	.07
❑ 39 Scott Sanderson	.10	.02
❑ 40 Kevin Mitchell TC	.10	.02
❑ 41 Lou Whitaker TC	.10	.02
❑ 42 Scott Coolbaugh RC	.10	.02
❑ 43 Jose Cano RC	.10	.02
❑ 44 Jose Vizcaino RC	.25	.08
❑ 45 Bob Hamelin RC	.25	.08
❑ 46 Jose Offerman RC	.25	.08
❑ 47 Kevin Blankenship	.10	.02
❑ 48 Kirby Puckett TC	.30	.10
❑ 49 Tommy Greene UER RC	.10	.02
❑ 50 Will Clark SPEC	.20	.07
❑ 51 Rob Nelson	.10	.02
❑ 52 Chris Hammond UER RC	.10	.02
❑ 53 Joe Carter TC	.10	.02
❑ 54A Ben McDonald ERR	2.00	.75
❑ 54B Ben McDonald COR RC	.25	.08
❑ 55 Andy Benes UER	.20	.07
❑ 56 John Olerud RC	.75	.30
❑ 57 Roger Clemens TC	.75	.30
❑ 58 Tony Armas	.10	.02
❑ 59 George Canale RC	.10	.02
❑ 60A Mickey Tettleton TC ERR	2.00	.75
❑ 60B Mickey Tettleton TC COR	.10	.02
❑ 61 Mike Stanton RC	.25	.08
❑ 62 Dwight Gooden TC	.10	.02
❑ 63 Kent Mercker RC	.25	.08
❑ 64 Francisco Cabrera	.10	.02
❑ 65 Steve Avery	.10	.02
❑ 66 Jose Canseco	.30	.10
❑ 67 Matt Merullo	.10	.02
❑ 68 Vince Coleman TC UER	.10	.02
❑ 69 Ron Karkovice	.10	.02
❑ 70 Kevin Maas RC	.25	.08
❑ 71 Dennis Cook UER (Shown with righty glove on card	.10	.02
❑ 72 Juan Gonzalez RC	1.50	.60
❑ 73 Andre Dawson TC	.10	.02
❑ 74 Dean Palmer RC	.25	.08
❑ 75 Bo Jackson SPEC	.20	.07
❑ 76 Rob Richie RC	.10	.02
❑ 77 Bobby Rose UER (Pickin& should be pick in)	.10	.02
❑ 78 Brian DuBois UER RC	.10	.02
❑ 79 Ozzie Guillen TC	.10	.02
❑ 80 Gene Nelson	.10	.02
❑ 81 Bob McClure	.10	.02
❑ 82 Julio Franco TC	.10	.02
❑ 83 Greg Minton	.10	.02
❑ 84 John Smoltz TC UER	.30	.10
❑ 85 Willie Fraser	.10	.02
❑ 86 Neal Heaton	.10	.02
❑ 87 Kevin Tapani RC	.25	.08
❑ 88 Mike Scott TC	.10	.02
❑ 89A Jim Gott ERR	2.00	.75
❑ 89B Jim Gott COR	.10	.02
❑ 90 Lance Johnson	.10	.02
❑ 91 Robin Yount TC UER	.50	.20
❑ 92 Jeff Parrett	.10	.02
❑ 93 Julio Machado RC	.10	.02
❑ 94 Ron Jones	.10	.02
❑ 95 George Bell TC	.10	.02
❑ 96 Jerry Reuss	.10	.02
❑ 97 Brian Fisher	.10	.02
❑ 98 Kevin Ritz RC	.10	.02
❑ 99 Barry Larkin TC	.20	.07
❑ 100 Checklist 1-100	.10	.02
❑ 101 Gerald Perry	.10	.02
❑ 102 Kevin Appier	.20	.07
❑ 103 Julio Franco	.20	.07
❑ 104 Craig Biggio	.50	.20
❑ 105 Bo Jackson UER	.50	.20
❑ 106 Junior Felix	.10	.02
❑ 107 Mike Harkey	.10	.02
❑ 108 Fred McGriff	.50	.20
❑ 109 Rick Sutcliffe	.20	.07
❑ 110 Pete O'Brien	.10	.02
❑ 111 Kelly Gruber	.10	.02
❑ 112 Dwight Evans	.30	.10
❑ 113 Pat Borders	.10	.02
❑ 114 Dwight Gooden	.20	.07
❑ 115 Kevin Batiste RC	.10	.02
❑ 116 Eric Davis	.20	.07
❑ 117 Kevin Mitchell UER (Career HR total 99& should b	.10	.02
❑ 118 Ron Oester	.10	.02
❑ 119 Brett Butler	.20	.07
❑ 120 Danny Jackson	.10	.02
❑ 121 Tommy Gregg	.10	.02
❑ 122 Ken Caminiti	.20	.07
❑ 123 Kevin Brown	.20	.07
❑ 124 George Brett	1.25	.50
❑ 125 Mike Scott	.10	.02
❑ 126 Cory Snyder	.10	.02
❑ 127 George Bell	.10	.02
❑ 128 Mark Grace	.30	.10
❑ 129 Devon White	.20	.07
❑ 130 Tony Fernandez	.10	.02
❑ 131 Don Aase	.10	.02
❑ 132 Rance Mulliniks	.10	.02
❑ 133 Marty Barrett	.10	.02
❑ 134 Nelson Liriano	.10	.02
❑ 135 Mark Carreon	.10	.02
❑ 136 Candy Maldonado	.10	.02
❑ 137 Tim Birtsas	.10	.02
❑ 138 Tom Brookens	.10	.02
❑ 139 John Franco	.20	.07
❑ 140 Mike LaCoss	.10	.02
❑ 141 Jeff Treadway	.10	.02
❑ 142 Pat Tabler	.10	.02
❑ 143 Darrell Evans	.20	.07
❑ 144 Rafael Ramirez	.10	.02
❑ 145 Oddibe McDowell UER (Misspelled Odibbe)	.10	.02
❑ 146 Brian Downing	.10	.02
❑ 147 Curt Wilkerson	.10	.02
❑ 148 Ernie Whitt	.10	.02
❑ 149 Bill Schroeder	.10	.02
❑ 150 Domingo Ramos UER (Says throws right& but shows	.10	.02
❑ 151 Rick Honeycutt	.10	.02
❑ 152 Don Slaught	.10	.02
❑ 153 Mitch Webster	.10	.02
❑ 154 Tony Phillips	.10	.02
❑ 155 Paul Kilgus	.10	.02
❑ 156 Ken Griffey Jr.	1.50	.60
❑ 157 Gary Sheffield	.50	.20
❑ 158 Wally Backman	.10	.02
❑ 159 B.J. Surhoff	.20	.07
❑ 160 Louie Meadows	.10	.02
❑ 161 Paul O'Neill	.30	.10
❑ 162 Jeff McKnight RC	.10	.02
❑ 163 Alvaro Espinoza	.10	.02
❑ 164 Scott Scudder	.10	.02
❑ 165 Jeff Reed	.10	.02
❑ 166 Gregg Jefferies	.20	.07
❑ 167 Barry Larkin	.30	.10
❑ 168 Gary Carter	.20	.07
❑ 169 Robby Thompson	.10	.02
❑ 170 Rolando Roomes	.10	.02
❑ 171 Mark McGwire	1.50	.60
❑ 172 Steve Sax	.10	.02
❑ 173 Mark Williamson	.10	.02

❑ 174 Mitch Williams	.10	.02
❑ 175 Brian Holton	.10	.02
❑ 176 Rob Deer	.10	.02
❑ 177 Tim Raines	.20	.07
❑ 178 Mike Felder	.10	.02
❑ 179 Harold Reynolds	.20	.07
❑ 180 Terry Francona	.20	.07
❑ 181 Chris Sabo	.10	.02
❑ 182 Darryl Strawberry	.20	.07
❑ 183 Willie Randolph	.20	.07
❑ 184 Bill Ripken	.10	.02
❑ 185 Mackey Sasser	.10	.02
❑ 186 Todd Benzinger	.10	.02
❑ 187 Kevin Elster UER (16 homers in 1989& should be 1	.10	.02
❑ 188 Jose Uribe	.10	.02
❑ 189 Tom Browning	.10	.02
❑ 190 Keith Miller	.10	.02
❑ 191 Don Mattingly	1.25	.50
❑ 192 Dave Parker	.20	.07
❑ 193 Roberto Kelly UER	.10	.02
❑ 194 Phil Bradley	.10	.02
❑ 195 Ron Hassey	.10	.02
❑ 196 Gerald Young	.10	.02
❑ 197 Hubie Brooks	.10	.02
❑ 198 Bill Doran	.10	.02
❑ 199 Al Newman	.10	.02
❑ 200 Checklist 101-200	.10	.02
❑ 201 Terry Puhl	.10	.02
❑ 202 Frank DiPino	.10	.02
❑ 203 Jim Clancy	.10	.02
❑ 204 Bob Ojeda	.10	.02
❑ 205 Alex Trevino	.10	.02
❑ 206 Dave Henderson	.10	.02
❑ 207 Henry Cotto	.10	.02
❑ 208 Rafael Belliard UER (Born 1961& not 1951)	.10	.02
❑ 209 Stan Javier	.10	.02
❑ 210 Jerry Reed	.10	.02
❑ 211 Doug Dascenzo	.10	.02
❑ 212 Andres Thomas	.10	.02
❑ 213 Greg Maddux	.75	.30
❑ 214 Mike Schooler	.10	.02
❑ 215 Lonnie Smith	.10	.02
❑ 216 Jose Rijo	.10	.02
❑ 217 Greg Gagne	.10	.02
❑ 218 Jim Gantner	.10	.02
❑ 219 Allan Anderson	.10	.02
❑ 220 Rick Mahler	.10	.02
❑ 221 Jim Deshaies	.10	.02
❑ 222 Keith Hernandez	.20	.07
❑ 223 Vince Coleman	.10	.02
❑ 224 David Cone	.20	.07
❑ 225 Ozzie Smith	.75	.30
❑ 226 Matt Nokes	.10	.02
❑ 227 Barry Bonds	1.50	.60
❑ 228 Felix Jose	.10	.02
❑ 229 Dennis Powell	.10	.02
❑ 230 Mike Gallego	.10	.02
❑ 231 Shawon Dunston UER ('89 stats are Andre Dawson's	.10	.02
❑ 232 Ron Gant	.20	.07
❑ 233 Omar Vizquel	.50	.20
❑ 234 Derek Lilliquist	.10	.02
❑ 235 Erik Hanson	.10	.02
❑ 236 Kirby Puckett	.50	.20
❑ 237 Bill Spiers	.10	.02
❑ 238 Dan Gladden	.10	.02
❑ 239 Bryan Clutterbuck	.10	.02
❑ 240 John Moses	.10	.02
❑ 241 Ron Darling	.10	.02
❑ 242 Joe Magrane	.10	.02
❑ 243 Dave Magadan	.10	.02
❑ 244 Pedro Guerrero UER (Misspelled Guererro)	.10	.02
❑ 245 Glenn Davis	.10	.02
❑ 246 Terry Steinbach	.10	.02
❑ 247 Fred Lynn	.10	.02
❑ 248 Gary Redus	.10	.02
❑ 249 Ken Williams	.10	.02
❑ 250 Sid Bream	.10	.02
❑ 251 Bob Welch UER (2587 career strike-outs& should	.10	.02
❑ 252 Bill Buckner	.10	.02
❑ 253 Carney Lansford	.20	.07
❑ 254 Paul Molitor	.20	.07
❑ 255 Jose DeJesus	.10	.02
❑ 256 Orel Hershiser	.20	.07
❑ 257 Tom Brunansky	.10	.02
❑ 258 Mike Davis	.10	.02
❑ 259 Jeff Ballard	.10	.02
❑ 260 Scott Terry	.10	.02
❑ 261 Sid Fernandez	.10	.02
❑ 262 Mike Marshall	.10	.02
❑ 263 Howard Johnson UER (192 SO& should be 592)	.10	.02
❑ 264 Kirk Gibson UER	.20	.07
❑ 265 Kevin McReynolds	.10	.02
❑ 266 Cal Ripken	1.50	.60
❑ 267 Ozzie Guillen UER	.20	.07
❑ 268 Jim Traber	.10	.02
❑ 269 Bobby Thigpen UER (31 saves in 1989& should be 3	.10	.02
❑ 270 Joe Orsulak	.10	.02
❑ 271 Bob Boone	.20	.07
❑ 272 Dave Stewart UER	.20	.07
❑ 273 Tim Wallach	.10	.02
❑ 274 Luis Aquino UER (Says throws lefty& but shows hi	.10	.02
❑ 275 Mike Moore	.10	.02
❑ 276 Tony Pena	.10	.02
❑ 277 Eddie Murray	.50	.20
❑ 278 Milt Thompson	.10	.02
❑ 279 Alejandro Pena	.10	.02
❑ 280 Ken Dayley	.10	.02
❑ 281 Carmelo Castillo	.10	.02
❑ 282 Tom Henke	.10	.02
❑ 283 Mickey Hatcher	.10	.02
❑ 284 Roy Smith	.10	.02
❑ 285 Manny Lee	.10	.02
❑ 286 Dan Pasqua	.10	.02
❑ 287 Larry Sheets	.10	.02
❑ 288 Garry Templeton	.10	.02
❑ 289 Eddie Williams	.10	.02
❑ 290 Brady Anderson	.20	.07
❑ 291 Spike Owen	.10	.02
❑ 292 Storm Davis	.10	.02
❑ 293 Chris Bosio	.10	.02
❑ 294 Jim Eisenreich	.10	.02
❑ 295 Don August	.10	.02
❑ 296 Jeff Hamilton	.10	.02
❑ 297 Mickey Tettleton	.10	.02
❑ 298 Mike Scioscia	.10	.02
❑ 299 Kevin Hickey	.10	.02
❑ 300 Checklist 201-300	.10	.02
❑ 301 Shawn Abner	.10	.02
❑ 302 Kevin Bass	.10	.02
❑ 303 Bip Roberts	.10	.02
❑ 304 Joe Girardi	.30	.10
❑ 305 Danny Darwin	.10	.02
❑ 306 Mike Heath	.10	.02
❑ 307 Mike Macfarlane	.10	.02
❑ 308 Ed Whitson	.10	.02
❑ 309 Tracy Jones	.10	.02
❑ 310 Scott Fletcher	.10	.02
❑ 311 Darnell Coles	.10	.02
❑ 312 Mike Brumley	.10	.02
❑ 313 Bill Swift	.10	.02
❑ 314 Charlie Hough	.20	.07
❑ 315 Jim Presley	.10	.02
❑ 316 Luis Polonia	.10	.02
❑ 317 Mike Morgan	.10	.02
❑ 318 Lee Guetterman	.10	.02
❑ 319 Jose Oquendo	.10	.02
❑ 320 Wayne Tolleson	.10	.02
❑ 321 Jody Reed	.10	.02
❑ 322 Damon Berryhill	.10	.02
❑ 323 Roger Clemens	1.50	.60
❑ 324 Ryne Sandberg	.75	.30
❑ 325 Benito Santiago UER	.20	.07
❑ 326 Bret Saberhagen UER (1140 hits& should be 1240;	.20	.07
❑ 327 Lou Whitaker	.20	.07
❑ 328 Dave Gallagher	.10	.02
❑ 329 Mike Pagliarulo	.10	.02
❑ 330 Doyle Alexander	.10	.02
❑ 331 Jeffrey Leonard	.10	.02
❑ 332 Torey Lovullo	.10	.02
❑ 333 Pete Incaviglia	.10	.02
❑ 334 Rickey Henderson	.50	.20
❑ 335 Rafael Palmeiro	.30	.10
❑ 336 Ken Hill	.20	.07
❑ 337 Dave Winfield UER	.20	.07
❑ 338 Alfredo Griffin	.10	.02
❑ 339 Andy Hawkins	.10	.02
❑ 340 Ted Power	.10	.02
❑ 341 Steve Wilson	.10	.02
❑ 342 Jack Clark UER (916 BB& should be 1006; 1142 SO&	.20	.07
❑ 343 Ellis Burks	.30	.10
❑ 344 Tony Gwynn	.60	.25
❑ 345 Jerome Walton UER (Total At Bats 476& should be	.10	.02
❑ 346 Roberto Alomar	.30	.10
❑ 347 Carlos Martinez UER (Born 8/11/64& should be 8/1	.10	.02
❑ 348 Chet Lemon	.10	.02
❑ 349 Willie Wilson	.10	.02
❑ 350 Greg Walker	.10	.02
❑ 351 Tom Bolton	.10	.02
❑ 352 German Gonzalez	.10	.02
❑ 353 Harold Baines	.20	.07
❑ 354 Mike Greenwell	.10	.02
❑ 355 Ruben Sierra	.20	.07
❑ 356 Andres Galarraga	.20	.07
❑ 357 Andre Dawson	.20	.07
❑ 358 Jeff Brantley	.10	.02
❑ 359 Mike Bielecki	.10	.02
❑ 360 Ken Oberkfell	.10	.02
❑ 361 Kurt Stillwell	.10	.02
❑ 362 Brian Holman	.10	.02
❑ 363 Kevin Seitzer UER (Career triples total does not	.10	.02
❑ 364 Alvin Davis	.10	.02
❑ 365 Tom Gordon	.20	.07
❑ 366 Bobby Bonilla UER (Two steals in 1987& should be	.20	.07
❑ 367 Carlton Fisk	.30	.10
❑ 368 Steve Carter UER (Charlotesville)	.10	.02
❑ 369 Joel Skinner	.10	.02
❑ 370 John Cangelosi	.10	.02
❑ 371 Cecil Espy	.10	.02
❑ 372 Gary Wayne	.10	.02
❑ 373 Jim Rice	.20	.07
❑ 374 Mike Dyer RC	.10	.02
❑ 375 Joe Carter	.20	.07
❑ 376 Dwight Smith	.10	.02
❑ 377 John Wetteland	.50	.20
❑ 378 Earnie Riles	.10	.02
❑ 379 Otis Nixon	.10	.02
❑ 380 Vance Law	.10	.02
❑ 381 Dave Bergman	.10	.02
❑ 382 Frank White	.20	.07
❑ 383 Scott Bradley	.10	.02
❑ 384 Israel Sanchez UER (Totals don't in-clude '89 s	.10	.02
❑ 385 Gary Pettis	.10	.02
❑ 386 Donn Pall	.10	.02
❑ 387 John Smiley	.10	.02
❑ 388 Tom Candiotti	.10	.02
❑ 389 Junior Ortiz	.10	.02
❑ 390 Steve Lyons	.10	.02
❑ 391 Brian Harper	.10	.02
❑ 392 Fred Manrique	.10	.02
❑ 393 Lee Smith	.20	.07
❑ 394 Jeff Kunkel	.10	.02
❑ 395 Claudell Washington	.10	.02
❑ 396 John Tudor	.10	.02
❑ 397 Terry Kennedy UER (Career totals all wrong)	.10	.02
❑ 398 Lloyd McClendon	.10	.02
❑ 399 Craig Lefferts	.10	.02
❑ 400 Checklist 301-400	.10	.02
❑ 401 Keith Moreland	.10	.02

❑	402 Rich Gedman	.10	.02
❑	403 Jeff D. Robinson	.10	.02
❑	404 Randy Ready	.10	.02
❑	405 Rick Cerone	.10	.02
❑	406 Jeff Blauser	.10	.02
❑	407 Larry Andersen	.10	.02
❑	408 Joe Boever	.10	.02
❑	409 Felix Fermin	.10	.02
❑	410 Glenn Wilson	.10	.02
❑	411 Rex Hudler	.10	.02
❑	412 Mark Grant	.10	.02
❑	413 Dennis Martinez	.20	.07
❑	414 Darrin Jackson	.10	.02
❑	415 Mike Aldrete	.10	.02
❑	416 Roger McDowell	.10	.02
❑	417 Jeff Reardon	.20	.07
❑	418 Darren Daulton	.20	.07
❑	419 Tim Laudner	.10	.02
❑	420 Don Carman	.10	.02
❑	421 Lloyd Moseby	.10	.02
❑	422 Doug Drabek	.10	.02
❑	423 Lenny Harris UER (Walks 2 in '89& should be 20)	.10	.02
❑	424 Jose Lind	.10	.02
❑	425 Dave Wayne Johnson RC	.10	.02
❑	426 Jerry Browne	.10	.02
❑	427 Eric Yelding RC	.10	.02
❑	428 Brad Komminsk	.10	.02
❑	429 Jody Davis	.10	.02
❑	430 Mariano Duncan	.10	.02
❑	431 Mark Davis	.10	.02
❑	432 Nelson Santovenia	.10	.02
❑	433 Bruce Hurst	.10	.02
❑	434 Jeff Huson RC	.10	.02
❑	435 Chris James	.10	.02
❑	436 Mark Guthrie RC	.10	.02
❑	437 Charlie Hayes	.10	.02
❑	438 Shane Rawley	.10	.02
❑	439 Dickie Thon	.10	.02
❑	440 Juan Berenguer	.10	.02
❑	441 Kevin Romine	.10	.02
❑	442 Bill Landrum	.10	.02
❑	443 Todd Frohwirth	.10	.02
❑	444 Craig Worthington	.10	.02
❑	445 Fernando Valenzuela	.20	.07
❑	446 Albert Belle	.50	.20
❑	447 Ed Whited UER RC	.10	.02
❑	448 Dave Smith	.10	.02
❑	449 Dave Clark	.10	.02
❑	450 Juan Agosto	.10	.02
❑	451 Dave Valle	.10	.02
❑	452 Kent Hrbek	.20	.07
❑	453 Von Hayes	.10	.02
❑	454 Gary Gaetti	.20	.07
❑	455 Greg Briley	.10	.02
❑	456 Glenn Braggs	.10	.02
❑	457 Kirt Manwaring	.10	.02
❑	458 Mel Hall	.10	.02
❑	459 Brook Jacoby	.10	.02
❑	460 Pat Sheridan	.10	.02
❑	461 Rob Murphy	.10	.02
❑	462 Jimmy Key	.20	.07
❑	463 Nick Esasky	.10	.02
❑	464 Rob Ducey	.10	.02
❑	465 Carlos Quintana UER (Internatinoal)	.10	.02
❑	466 Larry Walker RC	1.50	.60
❑	467 Todd Worrell	.10	.02
❑	468 Kevin Gross	.10	.02
❑	469 Terry Pendleton	.20	.07
❑	470 Dave Martinez	.10	.02
❑	471 Gene Larkin	.10	.02
❑	472 Len Dykstra UER	.20	.07
❑	473 Barry Lyons	.10	.02
❑	474 Terry Mulholland	.10	.02
❑	475 Chip Hale RC	.10	.02
❑	476 Jesse Barfield	.10	.02
❑	477 Dan Plesac	.10	.02
❑	478A Scott Garrelts ERR	2.00	.75
❑	478B Scott Garrelts COR	.10	.02
❑	479 Dave Righetti	.10	.02
❑	480 Gus Polidor UER (Wearing 14 on front& but 10 on	.10	.02
❑	481 Mookie Wilson	.20	.07
❑	482 Luis Rivera	.10	.02
❑	483 Mike Flanagan	.10	.02
❑	484 Dennis Boyd	.10	.02
❑	485 John Cerutti	.10	.02
❑	486 John Costello	.10	.02
❑	487 Pascual Perez	.10	.02
❑	488 Tommy Herr	.10	.02
❑	489 Tom Foley	.10	.02
❑	490 Curt Ford	.10	.02
❑	491 Steve Lake	.10	.02
❑	492 Tim Teufel	.10	.02
❑	493 Randy Bush	.10	.02
❑	494 Mike Jackson	.10	.02
❑	495 Steve Jeltz	.10	.02
❑	496 Paul Gibson	.10	.02
❑	497 Steve Balboni	.10	.02
❑	498 Bud Black	.10	.02
❑	499 Dale Sveum	.10	.02
❑	500 Checklist 401-500	.10	.02
❑	501 Tim Jones	.10	.02
❑	502 Mark Portugal	.10	.02
❑	503 Ivan Calderon	.10	.02
❑	504 Rick Rhoden	.10	.02
❑	505 Willie McGee	.20	.07
❑	506 Kirk McCaskill	.10	.02
❑	507 Dave LaPoint	.10	.02
❑	508 Jay Howell	.10	.02
❑	509 Johnny Ray	.10	.02
❑	510 Dave Anderson	.10	.02
❑	511 Chuck Crim	.10	.02
❑	512 Joe Hesketh	.10	.02
❑	513 Dennis Eckersley	.20	.07
❑	514 Greg Brock	.10	.02
❑	515 Tim Burke	.10	.02
❑	516 Frank Tanana	.10	.02
❑	517 Jay Bell	.20	.07
❑	518 Guillermo Hernandez	.10	.02
❑	519 Randy Kramer UER (Codiroli misspelled as Codorol	.10	.02
❑	520 Charles Hudson	.10	.02
❑	521 Jim Corsi (Word %%originally~ is misspelled on b	.10	.02
❑	522 Steve Rosenberg	.10	.02
❑	523 Cris Carpenter	.10	.02
❑	524 Matt Winters RC	.10	.02
❑	525 Melido Perez	.10	.02
❑	526 Chris Gwynn UER (Albeguergue)	.10	.02
❑	527 Bert Blyleven UER (Games career total is wrong&	.20	.07
❑	528 Chuck Cary	.10	.02
❑	529 Daryl Boston	.10	.02
❑	530 Dale Mohorcic	.10	.02
❑	531 Geronimo Berroa	.10	.02
❑	532 Edgar Martinez	.30	.10
❑	533 Dale Murphy	.30	.10
❑	534 Jay Buhner	.20	.07
❑	535 John Smoltz	.50	.20
❑	536 Andy Van Slyke	.30	.10
❑	537 Mike Henneman	.10	.02
❑	538 Miguel Garcia	.10	.02
❑	539 Frank Williams	.10	.02
❑	540 R.J. Reynolds	.10	.02
❑	541 Shawn Hillegas	.10	.02
❑	542 Walt Weiss	.10	.02
❑	543 Greg Hibbard RC	.10	.02
❑	544 Nolan Ryan	2.00	.75
❑	545 Todd Zeile	.20	.07
❑	546 Hensley Meulens	.10	.02
❑	547 Tim Belcher	.10	.02
❑	548 Mike Witt	.10	.02
❑	549 Greg Cadaret UER (Aquiring& should be Acquiring)	.10	.02
❑	550 Franklin Stubbs	.10	.02
❑	551 Tony Castillo	.10	.02
❑	552 Jeff M. Robinson	.10	.02
❑	553 Steve Olin RC	.25	.08
❑	554 Alan Trammell	.20	.07
❑	555 Wade Boggs 4X	.30	.10
❑	556 Will Clark	.30	.10
❑	557 Jeff King	.10	.02
❑	558 Mike Fitzgerald	.10	.02
❑	559 Ken Howell	.10	.02
❑	560 Bob Kipper	.10	.02
❑	561 Scott Bankhead	.10	.02
❑	562A Jeff Innis ERR	2.00	.75
❑	562B Jeff Innis COR RC	.10	.02
❑	563 Randy Johnson	1.00	.40
❑	564 Wally Whitehurst	.10	.02
❑	565 Gene Harris	.10	.02
❑	566 Norm Charlton	.10	.02
❑	567 Robin Yount UER	.75	.30
❑	568 Joe Oliver	.10	.02
❑	569 Mark Parent	.10	.02
❑	570 John Farrell UER (Loss total added wrong)	.10	.02
❑	571 Tom Glavine	.30	.10
❑	572 Rod Nichols	.10	.02
❑	573 Jack Morris	.20	.07
❑	574 Greg Swindell	.10	.02
❑	575 Steve Searcy	.10	.02
❑	576 Ricky Jordan	.10	.02
❑	577 Matt Williams	.20	.07
❑	578 Mike LaValliere	.10	.02
❑	579 Bryn Smith	.10	.02
❑	580 Bruce Ruffin	.10	.02
❑	581 Randy Myers	.20	.07
❑	582 Rick Wrona	.10	.02
❑	583 Juan Samuel	.10	.02
❑	584 Les Lancaster	.10	.02
❑	585 Jeff Musselman	.10	.02
❑	586 Rob Dibble	.20	.07
❑	587 Eric Show	.10	.02
❑	588 Jesse Orosco	.10	.02
❑	589 Herm Winningham	.10	.02
❑	590 Andy Allanson	.10	.02
❑	591 Dion James	.10	.02
❑	592 Carmelo Martinez	.10	.02
❑	593 Luis Quinones	.10	.02
❑	594 Dennis Rasmussen	.10	.02
❑	595 Rich Yett	.10	.02
❑	596 Bob Walk	.10	.02
❑	597A Andy McGaffigan ERR (Photo actually Rich Thompso	2.00	.75
❑	597B Andy McGaffigan COR	.10	.02
❑	598 Billy Hatcher	.10	.02
❑	599 Bob Knepper	.10	.02
❑	600 Checklist 501-600 UER (599 Bob Kneppers)	.10	.02
❑	601 Joey Cora	.20	.07
❑	602 Steve Finley	.20	.07
❑	603 Kal Daniels UER (12 hits in '87& should be 123;	.10	.02
❑	604 Gregg Olson	.20	.07
❑	605 Dave Stieb	.20	.07
❑	606 Kenny Rogers	.20	.07
❑	607 Zane Smith	.10	.02
❑	608 Bob Geren UER (Origionally)	.10	.02
❑	609 Chad Kreuter	.10	.02
❑	610 Mike Smithson	.10	.02
❑	611 Jeff Wetherby RC	.10	.02
❑	612 Gary Mielke RC	.10	.02
❑	613 Pete Smith	.10	.02
❑	614 Jack Daugherty RC	.10	.02
❑	615 Lance McCullers	.10	.02
❑	616 Don Robinson	.10	.02
❑	617 Jose Guzman	.10	.02
❑	618 Steve Bedrosian	.10	.02
❑	619 Jamie Moyer	.20	.07
❑	620 Atlee Hammaker	.10	.02
❑	621 Rick Luecken RC	.10	.02
❑	622 Greg W. Harris	.10	.02
❑	623 Pete Harnisch	.10	.02
❑	624 Jerald Clark	.10	.02
❑	625 Jack McDowell	.10	.02
❑	626 Frank Viola	.10	.02
❑	627 Teddy Higuera	.10	.02
❑	628 Marty Pevey RC	.10	.02
❑	629 Bill Wegman	.10	.02
❑	630 Eric Plunk	.10	.02
❑	631 Drew Hall	.10	.02
❑	632 Doug Jones	.10	.02
❑	633 Geno Petralli UER (Sacremento)	.10	.02
❑	634 Jose Alvarez	.10	.02

	No.	Player		
❑	635	Bob Milacki	.10	.02
❑	636	Bobby Witt	.10	.02
❑	637	Trevor Wilson	.10	.02
❑	638	Jeff Russell UER (Shutout stats wrong)	.10	.02
❑	639	Mike Krukow	.10	.02
❑	640	Rick Leach	.10	.02
❑	641	Dave Schmidt	.10	.02
❑	642	Terry Leach	.10	.02
❑	643	Calvin Schiraldi	.10	.02
❑	644	Bob Melvin	.10	.02
❑	645	Jim Abbott	.30	.10
❑	646	Jaime Navarro	.10	.02
❑	647	Mark Langston UER (Several errors in stats total	.10	.02
❑	648	Juan Nieves	.10	.02
❑	649	Damaso Garcia	.10	.02
❑	650	Charlie O'Brien	.10	.02
❑	651	Eric King	.10	.02
❑	652	Mike Boddicker	.10	.02
❑	653	Duane Ward	.10	.02
❑	654	Bob Stanley	.10	.02
❑	655	Sandy Alomar Jr.	.20	.07
❑	656	Danny Tartabull UER	.10	.02
❑	657	Randy McCament RC	.10	.02
❑	658	Charlie Leibrandt	.10	.02
❑	659	Dan Quisenberry	.10	.02
❑	660	Paul Assenmacher	.10	.02
❑	661	Walt Terrell	.10	.02
❑	662	Tim Leary	.10	.02
❑	663	Randy Milligan	.10	.02
❑	664	Bo Diaz	.10	.02
❑	665	Mark Lemke UER (Richmond misspelled as Richomond	.10	.02
❑	666	Jose Gonzalez	.10	.02
❑	667	Chuck Finley UER (Born 11/16/62& should be 11/26	.20	.07
❑	668	John Kruk	.20	.07
❑	669	Dick Schofield	.10	.02
❑	670	Tim Crews	.10	.02
❑	671	John Dopson	.10	.02
❑	672	John Orton RC	.10	.02
❑	673	Eric Hetzel	.10	.02
❑	674	Lance Parrish	.10	.02
❑	675	Ramon Martinez	.10	.02
❑	676	Mark Gubicza	.10	.02
❑	677	Greg Litton	.10	.02
❑	678	Greg Mathews	.10	.02
❑	679	Dave Dravecky	.20	.07
❑	680	Steve Farr	.10	.02
❑	681	Mike Devereaux	.10	.02
❑	682	Ken Griffey Sr.	.20	.07
❑	683A	Jamie Weston ERR	2.00	.75
❑	683B	Mickey Weston COR RC	.10	.02
❑	684	Jack Armstrong	.10	.02
❑	685	Steve Buechele	.10	.02
❑	686	Bryan Harvey	.10	.02
❑	687	Lance Blankenship	.10	.02
❑	688	Dante Bichette	.20	.07
❑	689	Todd Burns	.10	.02
❑	690	Dan Petry	.10	.02
❑	691	Kent Anderson	.10	.02
❑	692	Todd Stottlemyre	.20	.07
❑	693	Wally Joyner UER (Several stats errors)	.20	.07
❑	694	Mike Rochford	.10	.02
❑	695	Floyd Bannister	.10	.02
❑	696	Rick Reuschel	.10	.02
❑	697	Jose DeLeon	.10	.02
❑	698	Jeff Montgomery	.20	.07
❑	699	Kelly Downs	.10	.02
❑	700A	CL 601-700 ERR	2.00	.75
❑	700B	Checklist 601-700 (683 Mickey Weston)	.10	.02
❑	701	Jim Gott	.10	.02
❑	702	L.Walker/Grissom/DeSh	.50	.20
❑	702A	Mike Witt Black	10.00	4.00
❑	703	Alejandro Pena	.10	.02
❑	704	Willie Randolph	.20	.07
❑	705	Tim Leary	.10	.02
❑	706	Chuck McElroy RC	.10	.02
❑	707	Gerald Perry	.10	.02
❑	708	Tom Brunansky	.10	.02
❑	709	John Franco	.20	.07
❑	710	Mark Davis	.10	.02
❑	711	David Justice RC	.75	.30
❑	712	Storm Davis	.10	.02
❑	713	Scott Ruskin RC	.10	.02
❑	714	Glenn Braggs	.10	.02
❑	715	Kevin Bearse RC	.10	.02
❑	716	Jose Nunez	.10	.02
❑	717	Tim Layana RC	.10	.02
❑	718	Greg Myers	.10	.02
❑	719	Pete O'Brien	.10	.02
❑	720	John Candelaria	.10	.02
❑	721	Craig Grebeck RC	.10	.02
❑	722	Shawn Boskie RC	.10	.02
❑	723	Jim Leyritz RC	.25	.08
❑	724	Bill Sampen RC	.10	.02
❑	725	Scott Radinsky RC	.10	.02
❑	726	Todd Hundley RC	.25	.08
❑	727	Scott Hemond RC	.10	.02
❑	728	Lenny Webster RC	.10	.02
❑	729	Jeff Reardon	.20	.07
❑	730	Mitch Webster	.10	.02
❑	731	Brian Bohanon RC	.10	.02
❑	732	Rick Parker RC	.10	.02
❑	733	Terry Shumpert RC	.10	.02
❑	734A	Nolan Ryan 6th	3.00	1.25
❑	734B	Nolan Ryan 6th/300	1.00	.40
❑	735	John Burkett	.10	.02
❑	736	Derrick May RC	.10	.02
❑	737	Carlos Baerga RC	.25	.08
❑	738	Greg Smith RC	.10	.02
❑	739	Scott Sanderson	.10	.02
❑	740	Joe Kraemer RC	.10	.02
❑	741	Hector Villanueva RC	.10	.02
❑	742	Mike Fetters RC	.25	.08
❑	743	Mark Gardner RC	.10	.02
❑	744	Matt Nokes	.10	.02
❑	745	Dave Winfield	.20	.07
❑	746	Delino DeShields RC	.25	.08
❑	747	Dann Howitt RC	.10	.02
❑	748	Tony Pena	.10	.02
❑	749	Oil Can Boyd	.10	.02
❑	750	Mike Benjamin RC	.10	.02
❑	751	Alex Cole RC	.10	.02
❑	752	Eric Gunderson RC	.10	.02
❑	753	Howard Farmer RC	.10	.02
❑	754	Joe Carter	.20	.07
❑	755	Ray Lankford RC	.50	.20
❑	756	Sandy Alomar Jr.	.20	.07
❑	757	Alex Sanchez	.10	.02
❑	758	Nick Esasky	.10	.02
❑	759	Stan Belinda RC	.10	.02
❑	760	Jim Presley	.10	.02
❑	761	Gary DiSarcina RC	.25	.08
❑	762	Wayne Edwards RC	.10	.02
❑	763	Pat Combs	.10	.02
❑	764	Mickey Pina RC	.10	.02
❑	765	Wilson Alvarez RC	.25	.08
❑	766	Dave Parker	.20	.07
❑	767	Mike Blowers RC	.10	.02
❑	768	Tony Phillips	.10	.02
❑	769	Pascual Perez	.10	.02
❑	770	Gary Pettis	.10	.02
❑	771	Fred Lynn	.10	.02
❑	772	Mel Rojas RC	.10	.02
❑	773	David Segui RC	.50	.20
❑	774	Gary Carter	.20	.07
❑	775	Rafael Valdez RC	.10	.02
❑	776	Glenallen Hill	.10	.02
❑	777	Keith Hernandez	.20	.07
❑	778	Billy Hatcher	.10	.02
❑	779	Marty Clary	.10	.02
❑	780	Candy Maldonado	.10	.02
❑	781	Mike Marshall	.10	.02
❑	782	Billy Joe Robidoux	.10	.02
❑	783	Mark Langston	.10	.02
❑	784	Paul Sorrento RC	.25	.08
❑	785	Dave Hollins RC	.25	.08
❑	786	Cecil Fielder	.20	.07
❑	787	Matt Young	.10	.02
❑	788	Jeff Huson	.10	.02
❑	789	Lloyd Moseby	.10	.02
❑	790	Ron Kittle	.10	.02
❑	791	Hubie Brooks	.10	.02
❑	792	Craig Lefferts	.10	.02
❑	793	Kevin Bass	.10	.02
❑	794	Bryn Smith	.10	.02
❑	795	Juan Samuel	.10	.02
❑	796	Sam Horn	.10	.02
❑	797	Randy Myers	.20	.07
❑	798	Chris James	.10	.02
❑	799	Bill Gullickson	.10	.02
❑	800	Checklist 701-800	.10	.02

1991 Upper Deck

	No.	Player		
❑		COMPLETE SET (800)	15.00	6.00
❑		COMP.FACT.SET (800)	20.00	8.00
❑		COMPLETE LO SET (700)	15.00	6.00
❑		COMPLETE HI SET (100)	5.00	2.00
❑	1	Star Rookie Checklist	.05	.01
❑	2	Phil Plantier RC	.10	.02
❑	3	D.J. Dozier	.05	.01
❑	4	Dave Hansen	.05	.01
❑	5	Mo Vaughn	.10	.02
❑	6	Leo Gomez	.05	.01
❑	7	Scott Aldred	.05	.01
❑	8	Scott Chiamparino	.05	.01
❑	9	Lance Dickson RC	.10	.02
❑	10	Sean Berry RC	.10	.02
❑	11	Bernie Williams	.25	.08
❑	12	Brian Barnes UER RC	.10	.02
❑	13	Narciso Elvira RC	.05	.01
❑	14	Mike Gardiner RC	.05	.01
❑	15	Greg Colbrunn RC	.25	.08
❑	16	Bernard Gilkey	.05	.01
❑	17	Mark Lewis	.05	.01
❑	18	Mickey Morandini	.05	.01
❑	19	Charles Nagy	.05	.01
❑	20	Geronimo Pena	.05	.01
❑	21	Henry Rodriguez RC	.25	.08
❑	22	Scott Cooper FUDC	.05	.01
❑	23	Andujar Cedeno UER	.05	.01
❑	24	Eric Karros RC	.75	.30
❑	25	Steve Decker UER RC	.05	.01
❑	26	Kevin Belcher RC	.05	.01
❑	27	Jeff Conine RC	.50	.20
❑	28	Dave Stewart TC	.05	.01
❑	29	Carlton Fisk TC	.10	.02
❑	30	Rafael Palmeiro TC	.10	.02
❑	31	Chuck Finley TC	.05	.01
❑	32	Harold Reynolds TC	.05	.01
❑	33	Bret Saberhagen TC	.05	.01
❑	34	Gary Gaetti TC	.05	.01
❑	35	Scott Leius	.05	.01
❑	36	Neal Heaton	.05	.01
❑	37	Terry Lee RC	.05	.01
❑	38	Gary Redus	.05	.01
❑	39	Barry Jones	.05	.01
❑	40	Chuck Knoblauch	.10	.02
❑	41	Larry Andersen	.05	.01
❑	42	Darryl Hamilton	.05	.01
❑	43	Mike Greenwell TC	.05	.01
❑	44	Kelly Gruber TC	.05	.01
❑	45	Jack Morris TC	.05	.01
❑	46	Sandy Alomar Jr. TC	.05	.01
❑	47	Gregg Olson TC	.05	.01
❑	48	Dave Parker TC	.05	.01
❑	49	Roberto Kelly TC	.05	.01
❑	50	Top Prospect Checklist	.05	.01
❑	51	Kyle Abbott	.05	.01
❑	52	Jeff Juden	.05	.01
❑	53	Todd Van Poppel UER RC	.25	.08
❑	54	Steve Karsay RC	.25	.08
❑	55	Chipper Jones RC	4.00	1.50

❑ 56 Chris Johnson UER RC .10 .02
❑ 57 John Ericks .05 .01
❑ 58 Gary Scott RC .05 .01
❑ 59 Kiki Jones .05 .01
❑ 60 Wil Cordero RC .10 .02
❑ 61 Royce Clayton .05 .01
❑ 62 Tim Costo RC .10 .02
❑ 63 Roger Salkeld FUDC .05 .01
❑ 64 Brook Fordyce RC .25 .08
❑ 65 Mike Mussina RC 2.00 .75
❑ 66 Dave Staton RC .10 .02
❑ 67 Mike Lieberthal RC .50 .20
❑ 68 Kurt Miller RC .05 .01
❑ 69 Dan Peltier RC .10 .02
❑ 70 Greg Blosser FUDC .05 .01
❑ 71 Reggie Sanders RC .75 .30
❑ 72 Brent Mayne .05 .01
❑ 73 Rico Brogna .05 .01
❑ 74 Willie Banks .05 .01
❑ 75 Len Brutcher RC .05 .01
❑ 76 Pat Kelly RC .10 .02
❑ 77 Chris Sabo TC .05 .01
❑ 78 Ramon Martinez TC .05 .01
❑ 79 Matt Williams TC .05 .01
❑ 80 Roberto Alomar TC .10 .02
❑ 81 Glenn Davis TC .05 .01
❑ 82 Ron Gant TC .05 .01
❑ 83 Cecil Fielder's Feat .05 .01
❑ 84 Orlando Merced RC .10 .02
❑ 85 Domingo Ramos .05 .01
❑ 86 Tom Bolton .05 .01
❑ 87 Andres Santana .05 .01
❑ 88 John Dopson .05 .01
❑ 89 Kenny Williams .05 .01
❑ 90 Marty Barrett .05 .01
❑ 91 Tom Pagnozzi .05 .01
❑ 92 Carmelo Martinez .05 .01
❑ 93 Bobby Thigpen SAVE .05 .01
❑ 94 Barry Bonds TC .50 .20
❑ 95 Gregg Jefferies TC .05 .01
❑ 96 Tim Wallach TC .05 .01
❑ 97 Len Dykstra TC .05 .01
❑ 98 Pedro Guerrero TC .05 .01
❑ 99 Mark Grace TC .10 .02
❑ 100 Checklist 1-100 .05 .01
❑ 101 Kevin Elster .05 .01
❑ 102 Tom Brookens .05 .01
❑ 103 Mackey Sasser .05 .01
❑ 104 Felix Fermin .05 .01
❑ 105 Kevin McReynolds .05 .01
❑ 106 Dave Stieb .05 .01
❑ 107 Jeffrey Leonard .05 .01
❑ 108 Dave Henderson .05 .01
❑ 109 Sid Bream .05 .01
❑ 110 Henry Cotto .05 .01
❑ 111 Shawon Dunston .05 .01
❑ 112 Mariano Duncan .05 .01
❑ 113 Joe Girardi .05 .01
❑ 114 Billy Hatcher .05 .01
❑ 115 Greg Maddux .40 .15
❑ 116 Jerry Browne .05 .01
❑ 117 Juan Samuel .05 .01
❑ 118 Steve Olin .05 .01
❑ 119 Alfredo Griffin .05 .01
❑ 120 Mitch Webster .05 .01
❑ 121 Joel Skinner .05 .01
❑ 122 Frank Viola .10 .02
❑ 123 Cory Snyder .05 .01
❑ 124 Howard Johnson .05 .01
❑ 125 Carlos Baerga .05 .01
❑ 126 Tony Fernandez .05 .01
❑ 127 Dave Stewart .10 .02
❑ 128 Jay Buhner .10 .02
❑ 129 Mike LaValliere .05 .01
❑ 130 Scott Bradley .05 .01
❑ 131 Tony Phillips .05 .01
❑ 132 Ryne Sandberg .40 .15
❑ 133 Paul O'Neill .15 .05
❑ 134 Mark Grace .15 .05
❑ 135 Chris Sabo .05 .01
❑ 136 Ramon Martinez .05 .01
❑ 137 Brook Jacoby .05 .01
❑ 138 Candy Maldonado .05 .01
❑ 139 Mike Scioscia .05 .01
❑ 140 Chris James .05 .01
❑ 141 Craig Worthington .05 .01
❑ 142 Manny Lee .05 .01
❑ 143 Tim Raines .10 .02
❑ 144 Sandy Alomar Jr. .05 .01
❑ 145 John Olerud .10 .02
❑ 146 Ozzie Canseco w/Jose .10 .02
❑ 147 Pat Borders .05 .01
❑ 148 Harold Reynolds .10 .02
❑ 149 Tom Henke .05 .01
❑ 150 R.J. Reynolds .05 .01
❑ 151 Mike Gallego .05 .01
❑ 152 Bobby Bonilla .10 .02
❑ 153 Terry Steinbach .05 .01
❑ 154 Barry Bonds 1.00 .40
❑ 155 Jose Canseco .15 .05
❑ 156 Gregg Jefferies .05 .01
❑ 157 Matt Williams .10 .02
❑ 158 Craig Biggio .15 .05
❑ 159 Daryl Boston .05 .01
❑ 160 Ricky Jordan .05 .01
❑ 161 Stan Belinda .05 .01
❑ 162 Ozzie Smith .40 .15
❑ 163 Tom Brunansky .05 .01
❑ 164 Todd Zeile .05 .01
❑ 165 Mike Greenwell .05 .01
❑ 166 Kal Daniels .05 .01
❑ 167 Kent Hrbek .10 .02
❑ 168 Franklin Stubbs .05 .01
❑ 169 Dick Schofield .05 .01
❑ 170 Junior Ortiz .05 .01
❑ 171 Hector Villanueva .05 .01
❑ 172 Dennis Eckersley .10 .02
❑ 173 Mitch Williams .05 .01
❑ 174 Mark McGwire .75 .30
❑ 175 Fernando Valenzuela 3X .10 .02
❑ 176 Gary Carter .10 .02
❑ 177 Dave Magadan .05 .01
❑ 178 Robby Thompson .05 .01
❑ 179 Bob Ojeda .05 .01
❑ 180 Ken Caminiti .10 .02
❑ 181 Don Slaught .05 .01
❑ 182 Luis Rivera .05 .01
❑ 183 Jay Bell .10 .02
❑ 184 Jody Reed .05 .01
❑ 185 Wally Backman .05 .01
❑ 186 Dave Martinez .05 .01
❑ 187 Luis Polonia .05 .01
❑ 188 Shane Mack .05 .01
❑ 189 Spike Owen .05 .01
❑ 190 Scott Bailes .05 .01
❑ 191 John Russell .05 .01
❑ 192 Walt Weiss .05 .01
❑ 193 Jose Oquendo .05 .01
❑ 194 Carney Lansford .10 .02
❑ 195 Jeff Huson .05 .01
❑ 196 Keith Miller .05 .01
❑ 197 Eric Yelding .05 .01
❑ 198 Ron Darling .05 .01
❑ 199 John Kruk .10 .02
❑ 200 Checklist 101-200 .05 .01
❑ 201 John Shelby .05 .01
❑ 202 Bob Geren .05 .01
❑ 203 Lance McCullers .05 .01
❑ 204 Alvaro Espinoza .05 .01
❑ 205 Mark Salas .05 .01
❑ 206 Mike Pagliarulo .05 .01
❑ 207 Jose Uribe .05 .01
❑ 208 Jim Deshaies .05 .01
❑ 209 Ron Karkovice .05 .01
❑ 210 Rafael Ramirez .05 .01
❑ 211 Donnie Hill .05 .01
❑ 212 Brian Harper .05 .01
❑ 213 Jack Howell .05 .01
❑ 214 Wes Gardner .05 .01
❑ 215 Tim Burke .05 .01
❑ 216 Doug Jones .05 .01
❑ 217 Hubie Brooks .05 .01
❑ 218 Tom Candiotti .05 .01
❑ 219 Gerald Perry .05 .01
❑ 220 Jose DeLeon .05 .01
❑ 221 Wally Whitehurst .05 .01
❑ 222 Alan Mills .05 .01
❑ 223 Alan Trammell .10 .02
❑ 224 Dwight Gooden .10 .02
❑ 225 Travis Fryman .10 .02
❑ 226 Joe Carter .10 .02
❑ 227 Julio Franco .10 .02
❑ 228 Craig Lefferts .05 .01
❑ 229 Gary Pettis .05 .01
❑ 230 Dennis Rasmussen .05 .01
❑ 231A Brian Downing ERR .05 .01
❑ 231B Brian Downing COR .25 .08
❑ 232 Carlos Quintana .05 .01
❑ 233 Gary Gaetti .10 .02
❑ 234 Mark Langston .05 .01
❑ 235 Tim Wallach .05 .01
❑ 236 Greg Swindell .05 .01
❑ 237 Eddie Murray .25 .08
❑ 238 Jeff Manto .05 .01
❑ 239 Lenny Harris .05 .01
❑ 240 Jesse Orosco .05 .01
❑ 241 Scott Lusader .05 .01
❑ 242 Sid Fernandez .05 .01
❑ 243 Jim Leyritz .05 .01
❑ 244 Cecil Fielder .10 .02
❑ 245 Darryl Strawberry .10 .02
❑ 246 Frank Thomas .25 .08
❑ 247 Kevin Mitchell .05 .01
❑ 248 Lance Johnson .05 .01
❑ 249 Rick Reuschel .05 .01
❑ 250 Mark Portugal .05 .01
❑ 251 Derek Lilliquist .05 .01
❑ 252 Brian Holman .05 .01
❑ 253 Rafael Valdez UER .05 .01
❑ 254 B.J. Surhoff .10 .02
❑ 255 Tony Gwynn .30 .10
❑ 256 Andy Van Slyke .15 .05
❑ 257 Todd Stottlemyre .05 .01
❑ 258 Jose Lind .05 .01
❑ 259 Greg Myers .05 .01
❑ 260 Jeff Ballard .05 .01
❑ 261 Bobby Thigpen .05 .01
❑ 262 Jimmy Kremers .05 .01
❑ 263 Robin Ventura .10 .02
❑ 264 John Smoltz .15 .05
❑ 265 Sammy Sosa .25 .08
❑ 266 Gary Sheffield .10 .02
❑ 267 Len Dykstra .10 .02
❑ 268 Bill Spiers .05 .01
❑ 269 Charlie Hayes .05 .01
❑ 270 Brett Butler .10 .02
❑ 271 Bip Roberts .05 .01
❑ 272 Rob Deer .05 .01
❑ 273 Fred Lynn .05 .01
❑ 274 Dave Parker .10 .02
❑ 275 Andy Benes .05 .01
❑ 276 Glenallen Hill .05 .01
❑ 277 Steve Howard .05 .01
❑ 278 Doug Drabek .05 .01
❑ 279 Joe Oliver .05 .01
❑ 280 Todd Benzinger .05 .01
❑ 281 Eric King .05 .01
❑ 282 Jim Presley .05 .01
❑ 283 Ken Patterson .05 .01
❑ 284 Jack Daugherty .05 .01
❑ 285 Ivan Calderon .05 .01
❑ 286 Edgar Diaz .05 .01
❑ 287 Kevin Bass .05 .01
❑ 288 Don Carman .05 .01
❑ 289 Greg Brock .05 .01
❑ 290 John Franco .10 .02
❑ 291 Joey Cora .05 .01
❑ 292 Bill Wegman .05 .01
❑ 293 Eric Show .05 .01
❑ 294 Scott Bankhead .05 .01
❑ 295 Garry Templeton .05 .01
❑ 296 Mickey Tettleton .05 .01
❑ 297 Luis Sojo .05 .01
❑ 298 Jose Rijo .05 .01
❑ 299 Dave Johnson .05 .01
❑ 300 Checklist 201-300 .05 .01
❑ 301 Mark Grant .05 .01
❑ 302 Pete Harnisch .05 .01
❑ 303 Greg Olson .05 .01
❑ 304 Anthony Telford RC .05 .01
❑ 305 Lonnie Smith .05 .01
❑ 306 Chris Hoiles FUDC .05 .01
❑ 307 Bryn Smith .05 .01
❑ 308 Mike Devereaux .05 .01
❑ 309A Milt Thompson ERR .25 .08
❑ 309B Milt Thompson COR .05 .01
❑ 310 Bob Melvin .05 .01
❑ 311 Luis Salazar .05 .01

No.	Player		
312	Ed Whitson	.05	.01
313	Charlie Hough	.10	.02
314	Dave Clark	.05	.01
315	Eric Gunderson	.05	.01
316	Dan Petry	.05	.01
317	Dante Bichette	.10	.02
318	Mike Heath	.05	.01
319	Damon Berryhill	.05	.01
320	Walt Terrell	.05	.01
321	Scott Fletcher	.05	.01
322	Dan Plesac	.05	.01
323	Jack McDowell	.05	.01
324	Paul Molitor	.10	.02
325	Ozzie Guillen	.10	.02
326	Gregg Olson	.05	.01
327	Pedro Guerrero	.10	.02
328	Bob Milacki	.05	.01
329	John Tudor UER	.05	.01
330	Steve Finley UER	.10	.02
331	Jack Clark	.10	.02
332	Jerome Walton	.05	.01
333	Andy Hawkins	.05	.01
334	Derrick May	.05	.01
335	Roberto Alomar	.15	.05
336	Jack Morris	.10	.02
337	Dave Winfield	.10	.02
338	Steve Searcy	.05	.01
339	Chili Davis	.10	.02
340	Larry Sheets	.05	.01
341	Ted Higuera	.05	.01
342	David Segui	.05	.01
343	Greg Cadaret	.05	.01
344	Robin Yount	.40	.15
345	Nolan Ryan	1.00	.40
346	Ray Lankford	.10	.02
347	Cal Ripken	.75	.30
348	Lee Smith	.10	.02
349	Brady Anderson	.10	.02
350	Frank DiPino	.05	.01
351	Hal Morris	.05	.01
352	Deion Sanders	.15	.05
353	Barry Larkin	.15	.05
354	Don Mattingly	.60	.25
355	Eric Davis	.10	.02
356	Jose Offerman	.05	.01
357	Mel Rojas	.05	.01
358	Rudy Seanez	.05	.01
359	Oil Can Boyd	.05	.01
360	Nelson Liriano	.05	.01
361	Ron Gant	.10	.02
362	Howard Farmer	.05	.01
363	David Justice	.10	.02
364	Delino DeShields	.10	.02
365	Steve Avery	.05	.01
366	David Cone	.10	.02
367	Lou Whitaker	.10	.02
368	Von Hayes	.05	.01
369	Frank Tanana	.05	.01
370	Tim Teufel	.05	.01
371	Randy Myers	.05	.01
372	Roberto Kelly	.05	.01
373	Jack Armstrong	.05	.01
374	Kelly Gruber	.05	.01
375	Kevin Maas	.05	.01
376	Randy Johnson	.30	.10
377	David West	.05	.01
378	Brent Knackert	.05	.01
379	Rick Honeycutt	.05	.01
380	Kevin Gross	.05	.01
381	Tom Foley	.05	.01
382	Jeff Blauser	.05	.01
383	Scott Ruskin	.05	.01
384	Andres Thomas	.05	.01
385	Dennis Martinez	.10	.02
386	Mike Henneman	.05	.01
387	Felix Jose	.05	.01
388	Alejandro Pena	.05	.01
389	Chet Lemon	.05	.01
390	Craig Wilson RC	.05	.01
391	Chuck Crim	.05	.01
392	Mel Hall	.05	.01
393	Mark Knudson	.05	.01
394	Norm Charlton	.05	.01
395	Mike Felder	.05	.01
396	Tim Layana	.05	.01
397	Steve Frey	.05	.01
398	Bill Doran	.05	.01
399	Dion James	.05	.01
400	Checklist 301-400	.05	.01
401	Ron Hassey	.05	.01
402	Don Robinson	.05	.01
403	Gene Nelson	.05	.01
404	Terry Kennedy	.05	.01
405	Todd Burns	.05	.01
406	Roger McDowell	.05	.01
407	Bob Kipper	.05	.01
408	Darren Daulton	.10	.02
409	Chuck Cary	.05	.01
410	Bruce Ruffin	.05	.01
411	Juan Berenguer	.05	.01
412	Gary Ward	.05	.01
413	Al Newman	.05	.01
414	Danny Jackson	.05	.01
415	Greg Gagne	.05	.01
416	Tom Herr	.05	.01
417	Jeff Parrett	.05	.01
418	Jeff Reardon	.10	.02
419	Mark Lemke	.05	.01
420	Charlie O'Brien	.05	.01
421	Willie Randolph	.10	.02
422	Steve Bedrosian	.05	.01
423	Mike Moore	.05	.01
424	Jeff Brantley	.05	.01
425	Bob Welch	.05	.01
426	Terry Mulholland	.05	.01
427	Willie Blair	.05	.01
428	Darrin Fletcher	.05	.01
429	Mike Witt	.05	.01
430	Joe Boever	.05	.01
431	Tom Gordon	.05	.01
432	Pedro Munoz RC	.10	.02
433	Kevin Seitzer	.05	.01
434	Kevin Tapani	.05	.01
435	Bret Saberhagen	.10	.02
436	Ellis Burks	.10	.02
437	Chuck Finley	.10	.02
438	Mike Boddicker	.05	.01
439	Francisco Cabrera	.05	.01
440	Todd Hundley	.05	.01
441	Kelly Downs	.05	.01
442	Dann Howitt	.05	.01
443	Scott Garrelts	.05	.01
444	Rickey Henderson	.25	.08
445	Will Clark	.15	.05
446	Ben McDonald	.05	.01
447	Dale Murphy	.15	.05
448	Dave Righetti	.10	.02
449	Dickie Thon	.05	.01
450	Ted Power	.05	.01
451	Scott Coolbaugh	.05	.01
452	Dwight Smith	.05	.01
453	Pete Incaviglia	.05	.01
454	Andre Dawson	.10	.02
455	Ruben Sierra	.10	.02
456	Andres Galarraga	.10	.02
457	Alvin Davis	.05	.01
458	Tony Castillo	.05	.01
459	Pete O'Brien	.05	.01
460	Charlie Leibrandt	.05	.01
461	Vince Coleman	.05	.01
462	Steve Sax	.05	.01
463	Omar Olivares RC	.10	.02
464	Oscar Azocar	.05	.01
465	Joe Magrane	.05	.01
466	Karl Rhodes	.05	.01
467	Benito Santiago	.10	.02
468	Joe Klink	.05	.01
469	Sil Campusano	.05	.01
470	Mark Parent	.05	.01
471	Shawn Boskie UER	.05	.01
472	Kevin Brown	.10	.02
473	Rick Sutcliffe	.10	.02
474	Rafael Palmeiro	.15	.05
475	Mike Harkey	.05	.01
476	Jaime Navarro	.05	.01
477	Marquis Grissom	.10	.02
478	Marty Clary	.05	.01
479	Greg Briley	.05	.01
480	Tom Glavine	.15	.05
481	Lee Guetterman	.05	.01
482	Rex Hudler	.05	.01
483	Dave LaPoint	.05	.01
484	Terry Pendleton	.10	.02
485	Jesse Barfield	.05	.01
486	Jose DeJesus	.05	.01
487	Paul Abbott RC	.10	.02
488	Ken Howell	.05	.01
489	Greg W. Harris	.05	.01
490	Roy Smith	.05	.01
491	Paul Assenmacher	.05	.01
492	Geno Petralli	.05	.01
493	Steve Wilson	.05	.01
494	Kevin Reimer	.05	.01
495	Bill Long	.05	.01
496	Mike Jackson	.05	.01
497	Oddibe McDowell	.05	.01
498	Bill Swift	.05	.01
499	Jeff Treadway	.05	.01
500	Checklist 401-500	.05	.01
501	Gene Larkin	.05	.01
502	Bob Boone	.10	.02
503	Allan Anderson	.05	.01
504	Luis Aquino	.05	.01
505	Mark Guthrie	.05	.01
506	Joe Orsulak	.05	.01
507	Dana Kiecker	.05	.01
508	Dave Gallagher	.05	.01
509	Greg A. Harris	.05	.01
510	Mark Williamson	.05	.01
511	Casey Candaele	.05	.01
512	Mookie Wilson	.10	.02
513	Dave Smith	.05	.01
514	Chuck Carr FUDC	.05	.01
515	Glenn Wilson	.05	.01
516	Mike Fitzgerald	.05	.01
517	Devon White	.10	.02
518	Dave Hollins	.05	.01
519	Mark Eichhorn	.05	.01
520	Otis Nixon	.05	.01
521	Terry Shumpert	.05	.01
522	Scott Erickson	.05	.01
523	Danny Tartabull	.05	.01
524	Orel Hershiser	.10	.02
525	George Brett	.60	.25
526	Greg Vaughn	.05	.01
527	Tim Naehring FUDC	.05	.01
528	Curt Schilling	.25	.08
529	Chris Bosio	.05	.01
530	Sam Horn	.05	.01
531	Mike Scott	.05	.01
532	George Bell	.05	.01
533	Eric Anthony	.05	.01
534	Julio Valera	.05	.01
535	Glenn Davis	.05	.01
536	Larry Walker	.25	.08
537	Pat Combs	.05	.01
538	Chris Nabholz	.05	.01
539	Kirk McCaskill	.05	.01
540	Randy Ready	.05	.01
541	Mark Gubicza	.05	.01
542	Rick Aguilera	.10	.02
543	Brian McRae RC	.25	.08
544	Kirby Puckett	.25	.08
545	Bo Jackson	.25	.08
546	Wade Boggs	.15	.05
547	Tim McIntosh	.05	.01
548	Randy Milligan	.05	.01
549	Dwight Evans	.15	.05
550	Billy Ripken	.05	.01
551	Erik Hanson	.05	.01
552	Lance Parrish	.10	.02
553	Tino Martinez	.25	.08
554	Jim Abbott	.15	.05
555	Ken Griffey Jr.	.50	.20
556	Milt Cuyler	.05	.01
557	Mark Leonard RC	.05	.01
558	Jay Howell	.05	.01
559	Lloyd Moseby	.05	.01
560	Chris Gwynn	.05	.01
561	Mark Whiten FUDC	.05	.01
562	Harold Baines	.10	.02
563	Junior Felix	.05	.01
564	Darren Lewis FUDC	.05	.01
565	Fred McGriff	.15	.05
566	Kevin Appier	.10	.02
567	Luis Gonzalez RC	.75	.30
568	Frank White	.10	.02
569	Juan Agosto	.05	.01

	No.	Player		
❑	570	Mike Macfarlane	.05	.01
❑	571	Bert Blyleven	.10	.02
❑	572	Ken Griffey Sr./Jr.	.25	.08
❑	573	Lee Stevens	.05	.01
❑	574	Edgar Martinez	.15	.05
❑	575	Wally Joyner	.10	.02
❑	576	Tim Belcher	.05	.01
❑	577	John Burkett	.05	.01
❑	578	Mike Morgan	.05	.01
❑	579	Paul Gibson	.05	.01
❑	580	Jose Vizcaino	.05	.01
❑	581	Duane Ward	.05	.01
❑	582	Scott Sanderson	.05	.01
❑	583	David Wells	.10	.02
❑	584	Willie McGee	.10	.02
❑	585	John Cerutti	.05	.01
❑	586	Danny Darwin	.05	.01
❑	587	Kurt Stillwell	.05	.01
❑	588	Rich Gedman	.05	.01
❑	589	Mark Davis	.05	.01
❑	590	Bill Gullickson	.05	.01
❑	591	Matt Young	.05	.01
❑	592	Bryan Harvey	.05	.01
❑	593	Omar Vizquel	.15	.05
❑	594	Scott Lewis RC	.10	.02
❑	595	Dave Valle	.05	.01
❑	596	Tim Crews	.05	.01
❑	597	Mike Bielecki	.05	.01
❑	598	Mike Sharperson	.05	.01
❑	599	Dave Bergman	.05	.01
❑	600	Checklist 501-600	.05	.01
❑	601	Steve Lyons	.05	.01
❑	602	Bruce Hurst	.05	.01
❑	603	Donn Pall	.05	.01
❑	604	Jim Vatcher RC	.05	.01
❑	605	Dan Pasqua	.05	.01
❑	606	Kenny Rogers	.10	.02
❑	607	Jeff Schulz RC	.05	.01
❑	608	Brad Arnsberg	.05	.01
❑	609	Willie Wilson	.05	.01
❑	610	Jamie Moyer	.10	.02
❑	611	Ron Oester	.05	.01
❑	612	Dennis Cook	.05	.01
❑	613	Rick Mahler	.05	.01
❑	614	Bill Landrum	.05	.01
❑	615	Scott Scudder	.05	.01
❑	616	Tom Edens RC	.05	.01
❑	617	1917 Revisited	.10	.02
❑	618	Jim Gantner	.05	.01
❑	619	Darrel Akerfelds	.05	.01
❑	620	Ron Robinson	.05	.01
❑	621	Scott Radinsky	.05	.01
❑	622	Pete Smith	.05	.01
❑	623	Melido Perez	.05	.01
❑	624	Jerald Clark	.05	.01
❑	625	Carlos Martinez	.05	.01
❑	626	Wes Chamberlain RC	.25	.08
❑	627	Bobby Witt	.05	.01
❑	628	Ken Dayley	.05	.01
❑	629	John Barfield	.05	.01
❑	630	Bob Tewksbury	.05	.01
❑	631	Glenn Braggs	.05	.01
❑	632	Jim Neidlinger RC	.05	.01
❑	633	Tom Browning	.05	.01
❑	634	Kirk Gibson	.10	.02
❑	635	Rob Dibble	.10	.02
❑	636	R.Henderson/L.Brock	.25	.08
❑	636A	R.Henderson/L.Brock	.25	.08
❑	637	Jeff Montgomery	.05	.01
❑	638	Mike Schooler	.05	.01
❑	639	Storm Davis	.05	.01
❑	640	Rich Rodriguez RC	.05	.01
❑	641	Phil Bradley	.05	.01
❑	642	Kent Mercker	.05	.01
❑	643	Carlton Fisk	.15	.05
❑	644	Mike Bell RC	.05	.01
❑	645	Alex Fernandez	.05	.01
❑	646	Juan Gonzalez	.25	.08
❑	647	Ken Hill	.05	.01
❑	648	Jeff Russell	.05	.01
❑	649	Chuck Malone	.05	.01
❑	650	Steve Buechele	.05	.01
❑	651	Mike Benjamin	.05	.01
❑	652	Tony Pena	.05	.01
❑	653	Trevor Wilson	.05	.01
❑	654	Alex Cole	.05	.01
❑	655	Roger Clemens	.75	.30
❑	656	Mark McGwire BASH	.40	.15
❑	657	Joe Grahe RC	.10	.02
❑	658	Jim Eisenreich	.05	.01
❑	659	Dan Gladden	.05	.01
❑	660	Steve Farr	.05	.01
❑	661	Bill Sampen	.05	.01
❑	662	Dave Rohde	.05	.01
❑	663	Mark Gardner	.05	.01
❑	664	Mike Simms RC	.05	.01
❑	665	Moises Alou	.10	.02
❑	666	Mickey Hatcher	.05	.01
❑	667	Jimmy Key	.10	.02
❑	668	John Wetteland	.10	.02
❑	669	John Smiley	.05	.01
❑	670	Jim Acker	.05	.01
❑	671	Pascual Perez	.05	.01
❑	672	Reggie Harris UER	.05	.01
❑	673	Matt Nokes	.05	.01
❑	674	Rafael Novoa RC	.05	.01
❑	675	Hensley Meulens	.05	.01
❑	676	Jeff M. Robinson	.05	.01
❑	677	C.Fisk/R.Ventura	.10	.02
❑	678	Johnny Ray	.05	.01
❑	679	Greg Hibbard	.05	.01
❑	680	Paul Sorrento	.05	.01
❑	681	Mike Marshall	.05	.01
❑	682	Jim Clancy	.05	.01
❑	683	Rob Murphy	.05	.01
❑	684	Dave Schmidt	.05	.01
❑	685	Jeff Gray RC	.05	.01
❑	686	Mike Hartley	.05	.01
❑	687	Jeff King	.05	.01
❑	688	Stan Javier	.05	.01
❑	689	Bob Walk	.05	.01
❑	690	Jim Gott	.05	.01
❑	691	Mike LaCoss	.05	.01
❑	692	John Farrell	.05	.01
❑	693	Tim Leary	.05	.01
❑	694	Mike Walker	.05	.01
❑	695	Eric Plunk	.05	.01
❑	696	Mike Fetters	.05	.01
❑	697	Wayne Edwards	.05	.01
❑	698	Tim Drummond	.05	.01
❑	699	Willie Fraser	.05	.01
❑	700	Checklist 601-700	.05	.01
❑	701	Mike Heath	.05	.01
❑	702	J.Bagwell/L.Gonz/K.Rhodes	1.00	.40
❑	703	Jose Mesa	.05	.01
❑	704	Dave Smith	.05	.01
❑	705	Danny Darwin	.05	.01
❑	706	Rafael Belliard	.05	.01
❑	707	Rob Murphy	.05	.01
❑	708	Terry Pendleton	.10	.02
❑	709	Mike Pagliarulo	.05	.01
❑	710	Sid Bream	.05	.01
❑	711	Junior Felix	.05	.01
❑	712	Dante Bichette	.10	.02
❑	713	Kevin Gross	.05	.01
❑	714	Luis Sojo	.05	.01
❑	715	Bob Ojeda	.05	.01
❑	716	Julio Machado	.05	.01
❑	717	Steve Farr	.05	.01
❑	718	Franklin Stubbs	.05	.01
❑	719	Mike Boddicker	.05	.01
❑	720	Willie Randolph	.10	.02
❑	721	Willie McGee	.10	.02
❑	722	Chili Davis	.10	.02
❑	723	Danny Jackson	.05	.01
❑	724	Cory Snyder	.05	.01
❑	725	Dawson/Bell/Sandberg	.25	.08
❑	726	Rob Deer	.05	.01
❑	727	Rich DeLucia RC	.05	.01
❑	728	Mike Perez RC	.10	.02
❑	729	Mickey Tettleton	.05	.01
❑	730	Mike Blowers	.05	.01
❑	731	Gary Gaetti	.10	.02
❑	732	Brett Butler	.10	.02
❑	733	Dave Parker	.10	.02
❑	734	Eddie Zosky	.05	.01
❑	735	Jack Clark	.10	.02
❑	736	Jack Morris	.10	.02
❑	737	Kirk Gibson	.10	.02
❑	738	Steve Bedrosian	.05	.01
❑	739	Candy Maldonado	.05	.01
❑	740	Matt Young	.05	.01
❑	741	Rich Garces RC	.10	.02
❑	742	George Bell	.05	.01
❑	743	Deion Sanders	.15	.05
❑	744	Bo Jackson	.25	.08
❑	745	Luis Mercedes RC	.10	.02
❑	746	Reggie Jefferson	.05	.01
❑	747	Pete Incaviglia	.05	.01
❑	748	Chris Hammond	.05	.01
❑	749	Mike Stanton	.05	.01
❑	750	Scott Sanderson	.05	.01
❑	751	Paul Faries RC	.05	.01
❑	752	Al Osuna RC	.05	.01
❑	753	Steve Chitren RC	.05	.01
❑	754	Tony Fernandez	.05	.01
❑	755	Jeff Bagwell UER RC	1.50	.60
❑	756	Kirk Dressendorfer RC	.10	.02
❑	757	Glenn Davis	.05	.01
❑	758	Gary Carter	.10	.02
❑	759	Zane Smith	.05	.01
❑	760	Vance Law	.05	.01
❑	761	Denis Boucher RC	.10	.02
❑	762	Turner Ward RC	.10	.02
❑	763	Roberto Alomar	.15	.05
❑	764	Albert Belle	.10	.02
❑	765	Joe Carter	.10	.02
❑	766	Pete Schourek RC	.10	.02
❑	767	Heathcliff Slocumb RC	.10	.02
❑	768	Vince Coleman	.05	.01
❑	769	Mitch Williams	.05	.01
❑	770	Brian Downing	.05	.01
❑	771	Dana Allison RC	.05	.01
❑	772	Pete Harnisch	.05	.01
❑	773	Tim Raines	.10	.02
❑	774	Darryl Kile	.10	.02
❑	775	Fred McGriff	.15	.05
❑	776	Dwight Evans	.15	.05
❑	777	Joe Slusarski RC	.05	.01
❑	778	Dave Righetti	.10	.02
❑	779	Jeff Hamilton	.05	.01
❑	780	Ernest Riles	.05	.01
❑	781	Ken Dayley	.05	.01
❑	782	Eric King	.05	.01
❑	783	Devon White	.10	.02
❑	784	Beau Allred	.05	.01
❑	785	Mike Timlin RC	.25	.08
❑	786	Ivan Calderon	.05	.01
❑	787	Hubie Brooks	.05	.01
❑	788	Juan Agosto	.05	.01
❑	789	Barry Jones	.05	.01
❑	790	Wally Backman	.05	.01
❑	791	Jim Presley	.05	.01
❑	792	Charlie Hough	.10	.02
❑	793	Larry Andersen	.05	.01
❑	794	Steve Finley	.10	.02
❑	795	Shawn Abner	.05	.01
❑	796	Jeff M. Robinson	.05	.01
❑	797	Joe Bitker RC	.05	.01
❑	798	Eric Show	.05	.01
❑	799	Bud Black	.05	.01
❑	800	Checklist 701-800	.05	.01
❑	HH1	Hank Aaron Hologram	1.50	.60
❑	SP1	Michael Jordan	8.00	3.00
❑	SP2	N.Ryan/R.Henderson	2.00	.75

1991 Upper Deck Final Edition

	No.	Player		
❑		COMP.FACT.SET (100)	8.00	3.00
❑	1F	R.Klesko/R.Sanders CL	.25	.08

❏ 2F Pedro Martinez RC 8.00 3.00
❏ 3F Lance Dickson .05 .01
❏ 4F Royce Clayton .05 .01
❏ 5F Scott Bryant .05 .01
❏ 6F Dan Wilson RC .25 .08
❏ 7F Dmitri Young RC .75 .30
❏ 8F Ryan Klesko RC .50 .20
❏ 9F Tom Goodwin .05 .01
❏ 10F Rondell White RC .50 .20
❏ 11F Reggie Sanders .50 .20
❏ 12F Todd Van Poppel .05 .01
❏ 13F Arthur Rhodes RC .25 .08
❏ 14F Eddie Zosky .05 .01
❏ 15F Gerald Williams RC .25 .08
❏ 16F Robert Eenhoorn RC .10 .02
❏ 17F Jim Thome RC 4.00 1.50
❏ 18F Marc Newfield RC .10 .02
❏ 19F Kerwin Moore RC .10 .02
❏ 20F Jeff McNeely RC .10 .02
❏ 21F Frank Rodriguez RC .10 .02
❏ 22F Andy Mota RC .05 .01
❏ 23F Chris Haney RC .10 .02
❏ 24F Kenny Lofton RC .75 .30
❏ 25F Dave Nilsson RC .25 .08
❏ 26F Derek Bell .10 .02
❏ 27F Frank Castillo RC .25 .08
❏ 28F Candy Maldonado .05 .01
❏ 29F Chuck McElroy .05 .01
❏ 30F Chito Martinez RC .05 .01
❏ 31F Steve Howe .05 .01
❏ 32F Freddie Benavides RC .05 .01
❏ 33F Scott Kamieniecki RC .10 .02
❏ 34F Denny Neagle RC .25 .08
❏ 35F Mike Humphreys RC .10 .02
❏ 36F Mike Remlinger .05 .01
❏ 37F Scott Coolbaugh .05 .01
❏ 38F Darren Lewis .05 .01
❏ 39F Thomas Howard .05 .01
❏ 40F John Candelaria .05 .01
❏ 41F Todd Benzinger .05 .01
❏ 42F Wilson Alvarez .05 .01
❏ 43F Patrick Lennon RC .10 .02
❏ 44F Rusty Meacham RC .10 .02
❏ 45F Ryan Bowen RC .10 .02
❏ 46F Rick Wilkins RC .10 .02
❏ 47F Ed Sprague .05 .01
❏ 48F Bob Scanlan RC .05 .01
❏ 49F Tom Candiotti .05 .01
❏ 50F Dennis Martinez Perfect .10 .02
❏ 51F Oil Can Boyd .05 .01
❏ 52F Glenallen Hill .05 .01
❏ 53F Scott Livingstone RC .10 .02
❏ 54F Brian R.Hunter RC .25 .08
❏ 55F Ivan Rodriguez RC 2.00 .75
❏ 56F Keith Mitchell RC .10 .02
❏ 57F Roger McDowell .05 .01
❏ 58F Otis Nixon .05 .01
❏ 59F Juan Bell .05 .01
❏ 60F Bill Krueger .05 .01
❏ 61F Chris Donnels RC .05 .01
❏ 62F Tommy Greene .05 .01
❏ 63F Doug Simons RC .05 .01
❏ 64F Andy Ashby RC .25 .08
❏ 65F Anthony Young RC .10 .02
❏ 66F Kevin Morton RC .05 .01
❏ 67F Bret Barberie RC .10 .02
❏ 68F Scott Servais RC .25 .08
❏ 69F Ron Darling .05 .01
❏ 70F Tim Burke .05 .01
❏ 71F Vicente Palacios .05 .01
❏ 72F Gerald Alexander RC .05 .01
❏ 73F Reggie Jefferson .05 .01
❏ 74F Dean Palmer .10 .02
❏ 75F Mark Whiten .05 .01
❏ 76F Randy Tomlin RC .10 .02
❏ 77F Mark Wohlers RC .25 .08
❏ 78F Brook Jacoby .05 .01
❏ 79F K.Griffey Jr./R.Sandberg CL .40 .15
❏ 80F Jack Morris AS .05 .01
❏ 81F Sandy Alomar Jr. AS .05 .01
❏ 82F Cecil Fielder AS .05 .01
❏ 83F Roberto Alomar AS .10 .02
❏ 84F Wade Boggs AS .10 .02
❏ 85F Cal Ripken AS .40 .15
❏ 86F Rickey Henderson AS .15 .05
❏ 87F Ken Griffey Jr. AS .25 .08
❏ 88F Dave Henderson AS .05 .01
❏ 89F Danny Tartabull AS .05 .01
❏ 90F Tom Glavine AS .10 .02
❏ 91F Benito Santiago AS .05 .01
❏ 92F Will Clark AS .10 .02
❏ 93F Ryne Sandberg AS .25 .08
❏ 94F Chris Sabo AS .05 .01
❏ 95F Ozzie Smith AS .25 .08
❏ 96F Ivan Calderon AS .05 .01
❏ 97F Tony Gwynn AS .15 .05
❏ 98F Andre Dawson AS .05 .01
❏ 99F Bobby Bonilla AS .05 .01
❏ 100F Checklist 1-100 .05 .01

1992 Upper Deck

❏ COMPLETE SET (800) 25.00 10.00
❏ COMPLETE LO SET (700) 20.00 8.00
❏ COMPLETE HI SET (100) 5.00 2.00
❏ 1 J.Thome/R.Klesko CL .25 .08
❏ 2 Royce Clayton SR .05 .01
❏ 3 Brian Jordan RC .50 .20
❏ 4 Dave Fleming .05 .01
❏ 5 Jim Thome .25 .08
❏ 6 Jeff Juden SR .05 .01
❏ 7 Roberto Hernandez SR .05 .01
❏ 8 Kyle Abbott SR .05 .01
❏ 9 Chris George SR .05 .01
❏ 10 Rob Maurer SR .05 .01
❏ 11 Donald Harris SR .05 .01
❏ 12 Ted Wood SR .05 .01
❏ 13 Patrick Lennon SR .05 .01
❏ 14 Willie Banks SR .05 .01
❏ 15 Roger Salkeld SR UER (Bill was his grand-father .05 .01
❏ 16 Wil Cordero .05 .01
❏ 17 Arthur Rhodes SR .05 .01
❏ 18 Pedro Martinez 1.00 .40
❏ 19 Andy Ashby SR .05 .01
❏ 20 Tom Goodwin SR .05 .01
❏ 21 Braulio Castillo SR .05 .01
❏ 22 Todd Van Poppel .05 .01
❏ 23 Brian Williams RC .05 .01
❏ 24 Ryan Klesko .10 .02
❏ 25 Kenny Lofton .15 .05
❏ 26 Derek Bell .10 .02
❏ 27 Reggie Sanders .10 .02
❏ 28 Dave Winfield's 400th .05 .01
❏ 29 David Justice TC .05 .01
❏ 30 Rob Dibble TC Cincinnati Reds .05 .01
❏ 31 Craig Biggio TC .10 .02
❏ 32 Eddie Murray TC .15 .05
❏ 33 Fred McGriff TC .10 .02
❏ 34 Willie McGee TC San Francisco Giants .05 .01
❏ 35 Shawon Dunston TC Chicago Cubs .05 .01
❏ 36 Delino DeShields TC .05 .01
❏ 37 Howard Johnson TC New York Mets .05 .01
❏ 38 John Kruk TC .05 .01
❏ 39 Doug Drabek TC Pittsburgh Pirates .05 .01
❏ 40 Todd Zeile TC .05 .01
❏ 41 Steve Avery Playoff .05 .01
❏ 42 Jeremy Hernandez RC .05 .01
❏ 43 Doug Henry RC .10 .02
❏ 44 Chris Donnels .05 .01
❏ 45 Mo Sanford .05 .01
❏ 46 Scott Kamieniecki .05 .01
❏ 47 Mark Lemke .05 .01
❏ 48 Steve Farr .05 .01
❏ 49 Francisco Oliveras .05 .01
❏ 50 Ced Landrum .05 .01
❏ 51 R.White/M.Newfield CL .10 .02
❏ 52 Eduardo Perez RC .25 .08
❏ 53 Tom Nevers TP .05 .01
❏ 54 David Zancanaro TP .05 .01
❏ 55 Shawn Green RC 1.00 .40
❏ 56 Mark Wohlers TP .05 .01
❏ 57 Dave Nilsson .05 .01
❏ 58 Dmitri Young .10 .02
❏ 59 Ryan Hawblitzel RC .10 .02
❏ 60 Raul Mondesi .10 .02
❏ 61 Rondell White .10 .02
❏ 62 Steve Hosey .05 .01
❏ 63 Manny Ramirez RC 5.00 2.00
❏ 64 Marc Newfield .05 .01
❏ 65 Jeromy Burnitz .10 .02
❏ 66 Mark Smith RC .10 .02
❏ 67 Joey Hamilton RC .10 .02
❏ 68 Tyler Green RC .10 .02
❏ 69 Jon Farrell RC .10 .02
❏ 70 Kurt Miller TP .05 .01
❏ 71 Jeff Plympton TP .05 .01
❏ 72 Dan Wilson TP .05 .01
❏ 73 Joe Vitiello RC .10 .02
❏ 74 Rico Brogna TP .05 .01
❏ 75 David McCarty RC .25 .08
❏ 76 Bob Wickman .25 .08
❏ 77 Carlos Rodriguez TP .05 .01
❏ 78 Jim Abbott Stay In School .10 .02
❏ 79 P.Martinez/R.Martinez .25 .08
❏ 80 Kevin Mitchell Keith Mitchell .05 .01
❏ 81 Sandy/Roberto Alomar .10 .02
❏ 82 Ripken Brothers .50 .20
❏ 83 Tony/Chris Gwynn .15 .05
❏ 84 D.Gooden/G.Sheffield .10 .02
❏ 85 K.Griffey Jr. w/Family .25 .08
❏ 86 Jim Abbott TC California Angels .10 .02
❏ 87 Frank Thomas TC .15 .05
❏ 88 Danny Tartabull TC Kansas City Royals .05 .01
❏ 89 Scott Erickson TC Minnesota Twins .05 .01
❏ 90 Rickey Henderson TC .15 .05
❏ 91 Edgar Martinez TC .10 .02
❏ 92 Nolan Ryan TC .50 .20
❏ 93 Ben McDonald TC Baltimore Orioles .05 .01
❏ 94 Ellis Burks TC Boston Red Sox .05 .01
❏ 95 Greg Swindell TC Cleveland Indians .05 .01
❏ 96 Cecil Fielder TC .05 .01
❏ 97 Greg Vaughn TC .05 .01
❏ 98 Kevin Maas TC New York Yankees .05 .01
❏ 99 Dave Stieb TC Toronto Blue Jays .05 .01
❏ 100 Checklist 1-100 .05 .01
❏ 101 Joe Oliver .05 .01
❏ 102 Hector Villanueva .05 .01
❏ 103 Ed Whitson .05 .01
❏ 104 Danny Jackson .05 .01
❏ 105 Chris Hammond .05 .01
❏ 106 Ricky Jordan .05 .01
❏ 107 Kevin Bass .05 .01
❏ 108 Darrin Fletcher .05 .01
❏ 109 Junior Ortiz .05 .01
❏ 110 Tom Bolton .05 .01
❏ 111 Jeff King .05 .01
❏ 112 Dave Magadan .05 .01
❏ 113 Mike LaValliere .05 .01
❏ 114 Hubie Brooks .05 .01
❏ 115 Jay Bell .10 .02
❏ 116 David Wells .10 .02
❏ 117 Jim Leyritz .05 .01
❏ 118 Manuel Lee .05 .01
❏ 119 Alvaro Espinoza .05 .01

❑ 120 B.J. Surhoff .10 .02
❑ 121 Hal Morris .05 .01
❑ 122 Shawon Dawson .05 .01
❑ 123 Chris Sabo .05 .01
❑ 124 Andre Dawson .10 .02
❑ 125 Eric Davis .10 .02
❑ 126 Chili Davis .10 .02
❑ 127 Dale Murphy .15 .05
❑ 128 Kirk McCaskill .05 .01
❑ 129 Terry Mulholland .05 .01
❑ 130 Rick Aguilera .10 .02
❑ 131 Vince Coleman .05 .01
❑ 132 Andy Van Slyke .15 .05
❑ 133 Gregg Jefferies .05 .01
❑ 134 Barry Bonds 1.00 .40
❑ 135 Dwight Gooden .10 .02
❑ 136 Dave Stieb .05 .01
❑ 137 Albert Belle .10 .02
❑ 138 Teddy Higuera .05 .01
❑ 139 Jesse Barfield .05 .01
❑ 140 Pat Borders .05 .01
❑ 141 Bip Roberts .05 .01
❑ 142 Rob Dibble .10 .02
❑ 143 Mark Grace .15 .05
❑ 144 Barry Larkin .15 .05
❑ 145 Ryne Sandberg .40 .15
❑ 146 Scott Erickson .05 .01
❑ 147 Luis Polonia .05 .01
❑ 148 John Burkett .05 .01
❑ 149 Luis Sojo .05 .01
❑ 150 Dickie Thon .05 .01
❑ 151 Walt Weiss .05 .01
❑ 152 Mike Scioscia .05 .01
❑ 153 Mark McGwire .60 .25
❑ 154 Matt Williams .10 .02
❑ 155 Rickey Henderson .25 .08
❑ 156 Sandy Alomar Jr. .05 .01
❑ 157 Brian McRae .05 .01
❑ 158 Harold Baines .10 .02
❑ 159 Kevin Appier .10 .02
❑ 160 Felix Fermin .05 .01
❑ 161 Leo Gomez .05 .01
❑ 162 Craig Biggio .15 .05
❑ 163 Ben McDonald .05 .01
❑ 164 Randy Johnson .25 .08
❑ 165 Cal Ripken .75 .30
❑ 166 Frank Thomas .25 .08
❑ 167 Delino DeShields .05 .01
❑ 168 Greg Gagne .05 .01
❑ 169 Ron Karkovice .05 .01
❑ 170 Charlie Leibrandt .05 .01
❑ 171 Dave Righetti .10 .02
❑ 172 Dave Henderson .05 .01
❑ 173 Steve Decker .05 .01
❑ 174 Darryl Strawberry .10 .02
❑ 175 Will Clark .15 .05
❑ 176 Ruben Sierra .10 .02
❑ 177 Ozzie Smith .40 .15
❑ 178 Charles Nagy .05 .01
❑ 179 Gary Pettis .05 .01
❑ 180 Kirk Gibson .10 .02
❑ 181 Randy Milligan .05 .01
❑ 182 Dave Valle .05 .01
❑ 183 Chris Hoiles .05 .01
❑ 184 Tony Phillips .05 .01
❑ 185 Brady Anderson .10 .02
❑ 186 Scott Fletcher .05 .01
❑ 187 Gene Larkin .05 .01
❑ 188 Lance Johnson .05 .01
❑ 189 Greg Olson .05 .01
❑ 190 Melido Perez .05 .01
❑ 191 Lenny Harris .05 .01
❑ 192 Terry Kennedy .05 .01
❑ 193 Mike Gallego .05 .01
❑ 194 Willie McGee .10 .02
❑ 195 Juan Samuel .05 .01
❑ 196 Jeff Huson .10 .02
❑ 197 Alex Cole .05 .01
❑ 198 Ron Robinson .05 .01
❑ 199 Joel Skinner .05 .01
❑ 200 Checklist 101-200 .05 .01
❑ 201 Kevin Reimer .05 .01
❑ 202 Stan Belinda .05 .01
❑ 203 Pat Tabler .05 .01
❑ 204 Jose Guzman .05 .01
❑ 205 Jose Lind .05 .01
❑ 206 Spike Owen .05 .01
❑ 207 Joe Orsulak .05 .01
❑ 208 Charlie Hayes .05 .01
❑ 209 Mike Devereaux .05 .01
❑ 210 Mike Fitzgerald .05 .01
❑ 211 Willie Randolph .10 .02
❑ 212 Rod Nichols .05 .01
❑ 213 Mike Boddicker .05 .01
❑ 214 Bill Spiers .05 .01
❑ 215 Steve Olin .05 .01
❑ 216 David Howard .05 .01
❑ 217 Gary Varsho .05 .01
❑ 218 Mike Harkey .05 .01
❑ 219 Luis Aquino .05 .01
❑ 220 Chuck McElroy .05 .01
❑ 221 Doug Drabek .05 .01
❑ 222 Dave Winfield .10 .02
❑ 223 Rafael Palmeiro .15 .05
❑ 224 Joe Carter .10 .02
❑ 225 Bobby Bonilla .10 .02
❑ 226 Ivan Calderon .05 .01
❑ 227 Gregg Olson .05 .01
❑ 228 Tim Wallach .05 .01
❑ 229 Terry Pendleton .10 .02
❑ 230 Gilberto Reyes .05 .01
❑ 231 Carlos Baerga .05 .01
❑ 232 Greg Vaughn .05 .01
❑ 233 Bret Saberhagen .10 .02
❑ 234 Gary Sheffield .10 .02
❑ 235 Mark Lewis .05 .01
❑ 236 George Bell .05 .01
❑ 237 Danny Tartabull .05 .01
❑ 238 Willie Wilson .05 .01
❑ 239 Doug Dascenzo .05 .01
❑ 240 Bill Pecota .05 .01
❑ 241 Julio Franco .10 .02
❑ 242 Ed Sprague .05 .01
❑ 243 Juan Gonzalez .15 .05
❑ 244 Chuck Finley .10 .02
❑ 245 Ivan Rodriguez .25 .08
❑ 246 Len Dykstra .10 .02
❑ 247 Deion Sanders .15 .05
❑ 248 Dwight Evans .15 .05
❑ 249 Larry Walker .15 .05
❑ 250 Billy Ripken .05 .01
❑ 251 Mickey Tettleton .05 .01
❑ 252 Tony Pena .05 .01
❑ 253 Benito Santiago .10 .02
❑ 254 Kirby Puckett .25 .08
❑ 255 Cecil Fielder .10 .02
❑ 256 Howard Johnson .05 .01
❑ 257 Andujar Cedeno .05 .01
❑ 258 Jose Rijo .05 .01
❑ 259 Al Osuna .05 .01
❑ 260 Todd Hundley .05 .01
❑ 261 Orel Hershiser .10 .02
❑ 262 Ray Lankford .10 .02
❑ 263 Robin Ventura .10 .02
❑ 264 Felix Jose .05 .01
❑ 265 Eddie Murray .25 .08
❑ 266 Kevin Mitchell .05 .01
❑ 267 Gary Carter .10 .02
❑ 268 Mike Benjamin .05 .01
❑ 269 Dick Schofield .05 .01
❑ 270 Jose Uribe .05 .01
❑ 271 Pete Incaviglia .05 .01
❑ 272 Tony Fernandez .05 .01
❑ 273 Alan Trammell .10 .02
❑ 274 Tony Gwynn .30 .10
❑ 275 Mike Greenwell .05 .01
❑ 276 Jeff Bagwell .25 .08
❑ 277 Frank Viola .10 .02
❑ 278 Randy Myers .05 .01
❑ 279 Ken Caminiti .10 .02
❑ 280 Bill Doran .05 .01
❑ 281 Dan Pasqua .05 .01
❑ 282 Alfredo Griffin .05 .01
❑ 283 Jose Oquendo .05 .01
❑ 284 Kal Daniels .05 .01
❑ 285 Bobby Thigpen .05 .01
❑ 286 Robby Thompson .05 .01
❑ 287 Mark Eichhorn .05 .01
❑ 288 Mike Felder .05 .01
❑ 289 Dave Gallagher .05 .01
❑ 290 Dave Anderson .05 .01
❑ 291 Mel Hall .05 .01
❑ 292 Jerald Clark .05 .01
❑ 293 Al Newman .05 .01
❑ 294 Rob Deer .05 .01
❑ 295 Matt Nokes .05 .01
❑ 296 Jack Armstrong .05 .01
❑ 297 Jim Deshaies .05 .01
❑ 298 Jeff Innis .05 .01
❑ 299 Jeff Reed .05 .01
❑ 300 Checklist 201-300 .05 .01
❑ 301 Lonnie Smith .05 .01
❑ 302 Jimmy Key .10 .02
❑ 303 Junior Felix .05 .01
❑ 304 Mike Heath .05 .01
❑ 305 Mark Langston .05 .01
❑ 306 Greg W. Harris .05 .01
❑ 307 Brett Butler .10 .02
❑ 308 Luis Rivera .05 .01
❑ 309 Bruce Ruffin .05 .01
❑ 310 Paul Faries .05 .01
❑ 311 Terry Leach .05 .01
❑ 312 Scott Brosius RC .50 .20
❑ 313 Scott Leius .05 .01
❑ 314 Harold Reynolds .10 .02
❑ 315 Jack Morris .10 .02
❑ 316 David Segui .05 .01
❑ 317 Bill Gullickson .05 .01
❑ 318 Todd Frohwirth .05 .01
❑ 319 Mark Leiter .05 .01
❑ 320 Jeff M. Robinson .05 .01
❑ 321 Gary Gaetti .10 .02
❑ 322 John Smoltz .15 .05
❑ 323 Andy Benes .05 .01
❑ 324 Kelly Gruber .05 .01
❑ 325 Jim Abbott .15 .05
❑ 326 John Kruk .10 .02
❑ 327 Kevin Seitzer .05 .01
❑ 328 Darrin Jackson .05 .01
❑ 329 Kurt Stillwell .05 .01
❑ 330 Mike Maddux .05 .01
❑ 331 Dennis Eckersley .10 .02
❑ 332 Dan Gladden .05 .01
❑ 333 Jose Canseco .15 .05
❑ 334 Kent Hrbek .10 .02
❑ 335 Ken Griffey Sr. .10 .02
❑ 336 Greg Swindell .05 .01
❑ 337 Trevor Wilson .05 .01
❑ 338 Sam Horn .05 .01
❑ 339 Mike Henneman .05 .01
❑ 340 Jerry Browne .05 .01
❑ 341 Glenn Braggs .05 .01
❑ 342 Tom Glavine .15 .05
❑ 343 Wally Joyner .10 .02
❑ 344 Fred McGriff .15 .05
❑ 345 Ron Gant .10 .02
❑ 346 Ramon Martinez .05 .01
❑ 347 Wes Chamberlain .05 .01
❑ 348 Terry Shumpert .05 .01
❑ 349 Tim Teufel .05 .01
❑ 350 Wally Backman .05 .01
❑ 351 Joe Girardi .05 .01
❑ 352 Devon White .10 .02
❑ 353 Greg Maddux .40 .15
❑ 354 Ryan Bowen .05 .01
❑ 355 Roberto Alomar .15 .05
❑ 356 Don Mattingly .60 .25
❑ 357 Pedro Guerrero .10 .02
❑ 358 Steve Sax .05 .01
❑ 359 Joey Cora .05 .01
❑ 360 Jim Gantner .05 .01
❑ 361 Brian Barnes .05 .01
❑ 362 Kevin McReynolds .05 .01
❑ 363 Bret Barberie .05 .01
❑ 364 David Cone .10 .02
❑ 365 Dennis Martinez .10 .02
❑ 366 Brian Hunter .05 .01
❑ 367 Edgar Martinez .15 .05
❑ 368 Steve Finley .10 .02
❑ 369 Greg Briley .05 .01
❑ 370 Jeff Blauser .05 .01
❑ 371 Todd Stottlemyre .05 .01
❑ 372 Luis Gonzalez .10 .02
❑ 373 Rick Wilkins .05 .01
❑ 374 Darryl Kile .10 .02
❑ 375 John Olerud .10 .02
❑ 376 Lee Smith .10 .02
❑ 377 Kevin Maas .05 .01

❑ 378 Dante Bichette .10 .02
❑ 379 Tom Pagnozzi .05 .01
❑ 380 Mike Flanagan .05 .01
❑ 381 Charlie O'Brien .05 .01
❑ 382 Dave Martinez .05 .01
❑ 383 Keith Miller .05 .01
❑ 384 Scott Ruskin .05 .01
❑ 385 Kevin Elster .05 .01
❑ 386 Alvin Davis .05 .01
❑ 387 Casey Candaele .05 .01
❑ 388 Pete O'Brien .05 .01
❑ 389 Jeff Treadway .05 .01
❑ 390 Scott Bradley .05 .01
❑ 391 Mookie Wilson .10 .02
❑ 392 Jimmy Jones .05 .01
❑ 393 Candy Maldonado .05 .01
❑ 394 Eric Yelding .05 .01
❑ 395 Tom Henke .05 .01
❑ 396 Franklin Stubbs .05 .01
❑ 397 Milt Thompson .05 .01
❑ 398 Mark Carreon .05 .01
❑ 399 Randy Velarde .05 .01
❑ 400 Checklist 301-400 .05 .01
❑ 401 Omar Vizquel .15 .05
❑ 402 Joe Boever .05 .01
❑ 403 Bill Krueger .05 .01
❑ 404 Jody Reed .05 .01
❑ 405 Mike Schooler .05 .01
❑ 406 Jason Grimsley .05 .01
❑ 407 Greg Myers .05 .01
❑ 408 Randy Ready .05 .01
❑ 409 Mike Timlin .05 .01
❑ 410 Mitch Williams .05 .01
❑ 411 Garry Templeton .05 .01
❑ 412 Greg Cadaret .05 .01
❑ 413 Donnie Hill .05 .01
❑ 414 Wally Whitehurst .05 .01
❑ 415 Scott Sanderson .05 .01
❑ 416 Thomas Howard .05 .01
❑ 417 Neal Heaton .05 .01
❑ 418 Charlie Hough .10 .02
❑ 419 Jack Howell .05 .01
❑ 420 Greg Hibbard .05 .01
❑ 421 Carlos Quintana .05 .01
❑ 422 Kim Batiste .05 .01
❑ 423 Paul Molitor .10 .02
❑ 424 Ken Griffey Jr. .40 .15
❑ 425 Phil Plantier .05 .01
❑ 426 Denny Neagle .10 .02
❑ 427 Von Hayes .05 .01
❑ 428 Shane Mack .05 .01
❑ 429 Darren Daulton .10 .02
❑ 430 Dwayne Henry .05 .01
❑ 431 Lance Parrish .10 .02
❑ 432 Mike Humphreys .05 .01
❑ 433 Tim Burke .05 .01
❑ 434 Bryan Harvey .05 .01
❑ 435 Pat Kelly .05 .01
❑ 436 Ozzie Guillen .10 .02
❑ 437 Bruce Hurst .05 .01
❑ 438 Sammy Sosa .25 .08
❑ 439 Dennis Rasmussen .05 .01
❑ 440 Ken Patterson .05 .01
❑ 441 Jay Buhner .10 .02
❑ 442 Pat Combs .05 .01
❑ 443 Wade Boggs .15 .05
❑ 444 George Brett .60 .25
❑ 445 Mo Vaughn .10 .02
❑ 446 Chuck Knoblauch .10 .02
❑ 447 Tom Candiotti .05 .01
❑ 448 Mark Portugal .05 .01
❑ 449 Mickey Morandini .05 .01
❑ 450 Duane Ward .05 .01
❑ 451 Otis Nixon .05 .01
❑ 452 Bob Welch .05 .01
❑ 453 Rusty Meacham .05 .01
❑ 454 Keith Mitchell .05 .01
❑ 455 Marquis Grissom .10 .02
❑ 456 Robin Yount .40 .15
❑ 457 Harvey Pulliam .05 .01
❑ 458 Jose DeLeon .05 .01
❑ 459 Mark Gubicza .05 .01
❑ 460 Darryl Hamilton .05 .01
❑ 461 Tom Browning .05 .01
❑ 462 Monty Fariss .05 .01
❑ 463 Jerome Walton .05 .01
❑ 464 Paul O'Neill .15 .05
❑ 465 Dean Palmer .10 .02
❑ 466 Travis Fryman .10 .02
❑ 467 John Smiley .05 .01
❑ 468 Lloyd Moseby .05 .01
❑ 469 John Wehner .05 .01
❑ 470 Skeeter Barnes .05 .01
❑ 471 Steve Chitren .05 .01
❑ 472 Kent Mercker .05 .01
❑ 473 Terry Steinbach .05 .01
❑ 474 Andres Galarraga .10 .02
❑ 475 Steve Avery .05 .01
❑ 476 Tom Gordon .05 .01
❑ 477 Cal Eldred .05 .01
❑ 478 Omar Olivares .05 .01
❑ 479 Julio Machado .05 .01
❑ 480 Bob Milacki .05 .01
❑ 481 Les Lancaster .05 .01
❑ 482 John Candelaria .05 .01
❑ 483 Brian Downing .05 .01
❑ 484 Roger McDowell .05 .01
❑ 485 Scott Scudder .05 .01
❑ 486 Zane Smith .05 .01
❑ 487 John Cerutti .05 .01
❑ 488 Steve Buechele .05 .01
❑ 489 Paul Gibson .05 .01
❑ 490 Curtis Wilkerson .05 .01
❑ 491 Marvin Freeman .05 .01
❑ 492 Tom Foley .05 .01
❑ 493 Juan Berenguer .05 .01
❑ 494 Ernest Riles .05 .01
❑ 495 Sid Bream .05 .01
❑ 496 Chuck Crim .05 .01
❑ 497 Mike Macfarlane .05 .01
❑ 498 Dale Sveum .05 .01
❑ 499 Storm Davis .05 .01
❑ 500 Checklist 401-500 .05 .01
❑ 501 Jeff Reardon .10 .02
❑ 502 Shawn Abner .05 .01
❑ 503 Tony Fossas .05 .01
❑ 504 Cory Snyder .05 .01
❑ 505 Matt Young .05 .01
❑ 506 Allan Anderson .05 .01
❑ 507 Mark Lee .05 .01
❑ 508 Gene Nelson .05 .01
❑ 509 Mike Pagliarulo .05 .01
❑ 510 Rafael Belliard .05 .01
❑ 511 Jay Howell .05 .01
❑ 512 Bob Tewksbury .05 .01
❑ 513 Mike Morgan .05 .01
❑ 514 John Franco .10 .02
❑ 515 Kevin Gross .05 .01
❑ 516 Lou Whitaker .10 .02
❑ 517 Orlando Merced .05 .01
❑ 518 Todd Benzinger .05 .01
❑ 519 Gary Redus .05 .01
❑ 520 Walt Terrell .05 .01
❑ 521 Jack Clark .10 .02
❑ 522 Dave Parker .10 .02
❑ 523 Tim Naehring .05 .01
❑ 524 Mark Whiten .05 .01
❑ 525 Ellis Burks .10 .02
❑ 526 Frank Castillo .05 .01
❑ 527 Brian Harper .05 .01
❑ 528 Brook Jacoby .05 .01
❑ 529 Rick Sutcliffe .10 .02
❑ 530 Joe Klink .05 .01
❑ 531 Terry Bross .05 .01
❑ 532 Jose Offerman .05 .01
❑ 533 Todd Zeile .05 .01
❑ 534 Eric Karros .10 .02
❑ 535 Anthony Young .05 .01
❑ 536 Milt Cuyler .05 .01
❑ 537 Randy Tomlin .05 .01
❑ 538 Scott Livingstone .05 .01
❑ 539 Jim Eisenreich .05 .01
❑ 540 Don Slaught .05 .01
❑ 541 Scott Cooper .05 .01
❑ 542 Joe Grahe .05 .01
❑ 543 Tom Brunansky .05 .01
❑ 544 Eddie Zosky .05 .01
❑ 545 Roger Clemens .50 .20
❑ 546 David Justice .10 .02
❑ 547 Dave Stewart .10 .02
❑ 548 David West .05 .01
❑ 549 Dave Smith .05 .01
❑ 550 Dan Plesac .05 .01
❑ 551 Alex Fernandez .05 .01
❑ 552 Bernard Gilkey .05 .01
❑ 553 Jack McDowell .05 .01
❑ 554 Tino Martinez .15 .05
❑ 555 Bo Jackson .25 .08
❑ 556 Bernie Williams .15 .05
❑ 557 Mark Gardner .05 .01
❑ 558 Glenallen Hill .05 .01
❑ 559 Oil Can Boyd .05 .01
❑ 560 Chris James .05 .01
❑ 561 Scott Servais .05 .01
❑ 562 Rey Sanchez RC .25 .08
❑ 563 Paul McClellan .05 .01
❑ 564 Andy Mota .05 .01
❑ 565 Darren Lewis .05 .01
❑ 566 Jose Melendez .05 .01
❑ 567 Tommy Greene .05 .01
❑ 568 Rich Rodriguez .05 .01
❑ 569 Heathcliff Slocumb .05 .01
❑ 570 Joe Hesketh .05 .01
❑ 571 Carlton Fisk .15 .05
❑ 572 Erik Hanson .05 .01
❑ 573 Wilson Alvarez .05 .01
❑ 574 Rheal Cormier .05 .01
❑ 575 Tim Raines .10 .02
❑ 576 Bobby Witt .05 .01
❑ 577 Roberto Kelly .05 .01
❑ 578 Kevin Brown .10 .02
❑ 579 Chris Nabholz .05 .01
❑ 580 Jesse Orosco .05 .01
❑ 581 Jeff Brantley .05 .01
❑ 582 Rafael Ramirez .05 .01
❑ 583 Kelly Downs .05 .01
❑ 584 Mike Simms .05 .01
❑ 585 Mike Remlinger .05 .01
❑ 586 Dave Hollins .05 .01
❑ 587 Larry Andersen .05 .01
❑ 588 Mike Gardiner .05 .01
❑ 589 Craig Lefferts .05 .01
❑ 590 Paul Assenmacher .05 .01
❑ 591 Bryn Smith .05 .01
❑ 592 Donn Pall .05 .01
❑ 593 Mike Jackson .05 .01
❑ 594 Scott Radinsky .05 .01
❑ 595 Brian Holman .05 .01
❑ 596 Geronimo Pena .05 .01
❑ 597 Mike Jeffcoat .05 .01
❑ 598 Carlos Martinez .05 .01
❑ 599 Geno Petralli .05 .01
❑ 600 Checklist 501-600 .05 .01
❑ 601 Jerry Don Gleaton .05 .01
❑ 602 Adam Peterson .05 .01
❑ 603 Craig Grebeck .05 .01
❑ 604 Mark Guthrie .05 .01
❑ 605 Frank Tanana .05 .01
❑ 606 Hensley Meulens .05 .01
❑ 607 Mark Davis .05 .01
❑ 608 Eric Plunk .05 .01
❑ 609 Mark Williamson .05 .01
❑ 610 Lee Guetterman .05 .01
❑ 611 Bobby Rose .05 .01
❑ 612 Bill Wegman .05 .01
❑ 613 Mike Hartley .05 .01
❑ 614 Chris Beasley .05 .01
❑ 615 Chris Bosio .05 .01
❑ 616 Henry Cotto .05 .01
❑ 617 Chico Walker .05 .01
❑ 618 Russ Swan .05 .01
❑ 619 Bob Walk .05 .01
❑ 620 Bill Swift .05 .01
❑ 621 Warren Newson .05 .01
❑ 622 Steve Bedrosian .05 .01
❑ 623 Ricky Bones .05 .01
❑ 624 Kevin Tapani .05 .01
❑ 625 Juan Guzman .05 .01
❑ 626 Jeff Johnson .05 .01
❑ 627 Jeff Montgomery .05 .01
❑ 628 Ken Hill .05 .01
❑ 629 Gary Thurman .05 .01
❑ 630 Steve Howe .05 .01
❑ 631 Jose DeJesus .05 .01
❑ 632 Kirk Dressendorfer .05 .01
❑ 633 Jaime Navarro .05 .01
❑ 634 Lee Stevens .05 .01
❑ 635 Pete Harnisch .05 .01

	Card		
❑	636 Bill Landrum	.05	.01
❑	637 Rich DeLucia	.05	.01
❑	638 Luis Salazar	.05	.01
❑	639 Rob Murphy	.05	.01
❑	640 J.Canseco/R.Henderson CL	.15	.05
❑	641 Roger Clemens DS	.25	.08
❑	642 Jim Abbott DS	.10	.02
❑	643 Travis Fryman DS	.05	.01
❑	644 Jesse Barfield DS	.05	.01
❑	645 Cal Ripken DS	.40	.15
❑	646 Wade Boggs DS	.10	.02
❑	647 Cecil Fielder DS	.05	.01
❑	648 Rickey Henderson DS	.15	.05
❑	649 Jose Canseco DS	.10	.02
❑	650 Ken Griffey Jr. DS	.25	.08
❑	651 Kenny Rogers	.10	.02
❑	652 Luis Mercedes	.05	.01
❑	653 Mike Stanton	.05	.01
❑	654 Glenn Davis	.05	.01
❑	655 Nolan Ryan	1.00	.40
❑	656 Reggie Jefferson	.05	.01
❑	657 Javier Ortiz	.05	.01
❑	658 Greg A. Harris	.05	.01
❑	659 Mariano Duncan	.05	.01
❑	660 Jeff Shaw	.05	.01
❑	661 Mike Moore	.05	.01
❑	662 Chris Haney	.05	.01
❑	663 Joe Slusarski	.05	.01
❑	664 Wayne Housie	.05	.01
❑	665 Carlos Garcia	.05	.01
❑	666 Bob Ojeda	.05	.01
❑	667 Bryan Hickerson RC	.10	.02
❑	668 Tim Belcher	.05	.01
❑	669 Ron Darling	.05	.01
❑	670 Rex Hudler	.05	.01
❑	671 Sid Fernandez	.05	.01
❑	672 Chito Martinez	.05	.01
❑	673 Pete Schourek	.05	.01
❑	674 Armando Reynoso RC	.25	.08
❑	675 Mike Mussina	.25	.08
❑	676 Kevin Morton	.05	.01
❑	677 Norm Charlton	.05	.01
❑	678 Danny Darwin	.05	.01
❑	679 Eric King	.05	.01
❑	680 Ted Power	.05	.01
❑	681 Barry Jones	.05	.01
❑	682 Carney Lansford	.10	.02
❑	683 Mel Rojas	.05	.01
❑	684 Rick Honeycutt	.05	.01
❑	685 Jeff Fassero	.05	.01
❑	686 Cris Carpenter	.05	.01
❑	687 Tim Crews	.05	.01
❑	688 Scott Terry	.05	.01
❑	689 Chris Gwynn	.05	.01
❑	690 Gerald Perry	.05	.01
❑	691 John Barfield	.05	.01
❑	692 Bob Melvin	.05	.01
❑	693 Juan Agosto	.05	.01
❑	694 Alejandro Pena	.05	.01
❑	695 Jeff Russell	.05	.01
❑	696 Carmelo Martinez	.05	.01
❑	697 Bud Black	.05	.01
❑	698 Dave Otto	.05	.01
❑	699 Billy Hatcher	.05	.01
❑	700 Checklist 601-700	.05	.01
❑	701 Clemente Nunez RC	.05	.01
❑	702 M.Clark/Osborne/Jordan	.05	.01
❑	703 Mike Morgan	.05	.01
❑	704 Keith Miller	.05	.01
❑	705 Kurt Stillwell	.05	.01
❑	706 Damon Berryhill	.05	.01
❑	707 Von Hayes	.05	.01
❑	708 Rick Sutcliffe	.10	.02
❑	709 Hubie Brooks	.05	.01
❑	710 Ryan Turner RC	.10	.02
❑	711 B.Bonds/A.Van Slyke CL	.50	.20
❑	712 Jose Rijo DS	.05	.01
❑	713 Tom Glavine DS	.10	.02
❑	714 Shawon Dunston DS	.05	.01
❑	715 Andy Van Slyke DS	.10	.02
❑	716 Ozzie Smith DS	.25	.08
❑	717 Tony Gwynn DS	.15	.05
❑	718 Will Clark DS	.10	.02
❑	719 Marquis Grissom DS	.05	.01
❑	720 Howard Johnson DS	.05	.01
❑	721 Barry Bonds DS	.50	.20

	Card		
❑	722 Kirk McCaskill	.05	.01
❑	723 Sammy Sosa Cubs	.75	.30
❑	724 George Bell	.05	.01
❑	725 Gregg Jefferies	.05	.01
❑	726 Gary DiSarcina	.05	.01
❑	727 Mike Bordick	.05	.01
❑	728 Eddie Murray 400 HR	.15	.05
❑	729 Rene Gonzales	.05	.01
❑	730 Mike Bielecki	.05	.01
❑	731 Calvin Jones	.05	.01
❑	732 Jack Morris	.10	.02
❑	733 Frank Viola	.10	.02
❑	734 Dave Winfield	.10	.02
❑	735 Kevin Mitchell	.05	.01
❑	736 Bill Swift	.05	.01
❑	737 Dan Gladden	.05	.01
❑	738 Mike Jackson	.05	.01
❑	739 Mark Carreon	.05	.01
❑	740 Kirt Manwaring	.05	.01
❑	741 Randy Myers	.05	.01
❑	742 Kevin McReynolds	.05	.01
❑	743 Steve Sax	.05	.01
❑	744 Wally Joyner	.10	.02
❑	745 Gary Sheffield	.10	.02
❑	746 Danny Tartabull	.05	.01
❑	747 Julio Valera	.05	.01
❑	748 Denny Neagle	.10	.02
❑	749 Lance Blankenship	.05	.01
❑	750 Mike Gallego	.05	.01
❑	751 Bret Saberhagen	.10	.02
❑	752 Ruben Amaro	.05	.01
❑	753 Eddie Murray	.25	.08
❑	754 Kyle Abbott	.05	.01
❑	755 Bobby Bonilla	.10	.02
❑	756 Eric Davis	.10	.02
❑	757 Eddie Taubensee RC	.25	.08
❑	758 Andres Galarraga	.10	.02
❑	759 Pete Incaviglia	.05	.01
❑	760 Tom Candiotti	.05	.01
❑	761 Tim Belcher	.05	.01
❑	762 Ricky Bones	.05	.01
❑	763 Bip Roberts	.05	.01
❑	764 Pedro Munoz	.05	.01
❑	765 Greg Swindell	.05	.01
❑	766 Kenny Lofton	.15	.05
❑	767 Gary Carter	.10	.02
❑	768 Charlie Hayes	.05	.01
❑	769 Dickie Thon	.05	.01
❑	770 Donovan Osborne DD CL	.05	.01
❑	771 Bret Boone	.15	.05
❑	772 Archi Cianfrocco RC	.10	.02
❑	773 Mark Clark RC	.10	.02
❑	774 Chad Curtis RC	.25	.08
❑	775 Pat Listach RC	.25	.08
❑	776 Pat Mahomes RC	.25	.08
❑	777 Donovan Osborne	.05	.01
❑	778 John Patterson RC	.10	.02
❑	779 Andy Stankiewicz DD	.05	.01
❑	780 Turk Wendell RC	.25	.08
❑	781 Bill Krueger	.05	.01
❑	782 Rickey Henderson 1000	.15	.05
❑	783 Kevin Seitzer	.05	.01
❑	784 Dave Martinez	.05	.01
❑	785 John Smiley	.05	.01
❑	786 Matt Stairs RC	.25	.08
❑	787 Scott Scudder	.05	.01
❑	788 John Wetteland	.10	.02
❑	789 Jack Armstrong	.05	.01
❑	790 Ken Hill	.05	.01
❑	791 Dick Schofield	.05	.01
❑	792 Mariano Duncan	.05	.01
❑	793 Bill Pecota	.05	.01
❑	794 Mike Kelly RC	.10	.02
❑	795 Willie Randolph	.10	.02
❑	796 Butch Henry	.05	.01
❑	797 Carlos Hernandez	.05	.01
❑	798 Doug Jones	.05	.01
❑	799 Melido Perez	.05	.01
❑	800 Checklist 701-800	.05	.01
❑	HH2 Ted Williams Holo	2.00	.75
❑	SP3 Deion Sanders FB/BB	1.00	.40
❑	SP4 F.Thomas/T.Selleck	1.00	.40

1993 Upper Deck

	Card		
❑	COMPLETE SET (840)	40.00	15.00
❑	COMP.FACT.SET (840)	50.00	20.00
❑	COMPLETE SERIES 1 (420)	15.00	6.00
❑	COMPLETE SERIES 2 (420)	25.00	10.00
❑	1 Tim Salmon CL	.20	.07
❑	2 Mike Piazza	3.00	1.25
❑	3 Rene Arocha RC	.50	.20
❑	4 Willie Greene	.10	.02
❑	5 Manny Alexander	.10	.02
❑	6 Dan Wilson	.20	.07
❑	7 Dan Smith	.10	.02
❑	8 Kevin Rogers	.10	.02
❑	9 Nigel Wilson	.10	.02
❑	10 Joe Vitko	.10	.02
❑	11 Tim Costo	.10	.02
❑	12 Alan Embree	.10	.02
❑	13 Jim Tatum RC	.15	.05
❑	14 Cris Colon	.10	.02
❑	15 Steve Hosey	.10	.02
❑	16 Sterling Hitchcock RC	.50	.20
❑	17 Dave Mlicki	.10	.02
❑	18 Jessie Hollins	.10	.02
❑	19 Bobby Jones	.20	.07
❑	20 Kurt Miller	.10	.02
❑	21 Melvin Nieves	.10	.02
❑	22 Billy Ashley	.10	.02
❑	23 J.T.Snow RC	.75	.30
❑	24 Chipper Jones	.50	.20
❑	25 Tim Salmon	.30	.10
❑	26 Tim Pugh RC	.15	.05
❑	27 David Nied	.10	.02
❑	28 Mike Trombley	.10	.02
❑	29 Javier Lopez	.30	.10
❑	30 Jim Abbott CH CL	.20	.07
❑	31 Jim Abbott CH	.10	.02
❑	32 Dale Murphy CH	.30	.10
❑	33 Tony Pena CH	.10	.02
❑	34 Kirby Puckett CH	.30	.10
❑	35 Harold Reynolds CH	.10	.02
❑	36 Cal Ripken CH	.75	.30
❑	37 Nolan Ryan CH	1.00	.40
❑	38 Ryne Sandberg CH	.50	.20
❑	39 Dave Stewart CH	.10	.02
❑	40 Dave Winfield CH	.10	.02
❑	41 M.McGwire/J.Carter CL	.50	.20
❑	42 R.Alomar/J.Carter	.20	.07
❑	43 Molitor/Listach/Yount	.50	.20
❑	44 C.Ripken/B.Anderson	.50	.20
❑	45 Belle/Baerga/Thome/Lofton	.20	.07
❑	46 C.Fielder/M.Tettleton	.10	.02
❑	47 R.Kelly/D.Mattingly	.60	.25
❑	48 R.Clemens/F.Viola	.50	.20
❑	49 R.Sierra/M.McGwire	.50	.20
❑	50 K.Puckett/K.Hrbek	.30	.10
❑	51 F.Thomas/R.Ventura	.30	.10
❑	52 Cans/IRod/Gonz/Palmeiro	.30	.10
❑	53 Lethal Lefties Mark Langston Jim Abbott Chuck F	.20	.07
❑	54 Joyner/Jefferies/Brett	.50	.20
❑	55 K.Griffey/Buhner/Mitchell	.50	.20
❑	56 George Brett	1.25	.50
❑	57 Scott Cooper	.10	.02
❑	58 Mike Maddux	.10	.02
❑	59 Rusty Meacham	.10	.02

❑ 60 Wil Cordero .10 .02
❑ 61 Tim Teufel .10 .02
❑ 62 Jeff Montgomery .10 .02
❑ 63 Scott Livingstone .10 .02
❑ 64 Doug Dascenzo .10 .02
❑ 65 Bret Boone .20 .07
❑ 66 Tim Wakefield .50 .20
❑ 67 Curt Schilling .20 .07
❑ 68 Frank Tanana .10 .02
❑ 69 Len Dykstra .20 .07
❑ 70 Derek Lilliquist .10 .02
❑ 71 Anthony Young .10 .02
❑ 72 Hipolito Pichardo .10 .02
❑ 73 Rod Beck .10 .02
❑ 74 Kent Hrbek .20 .07
❑ 75 Tom Glavine .30 .10
❑ 76 Kevin Brown .20 .07
❑ 77 Chuck Finley .20 .07
❑ 78 Bob Walk .10 .02
❑ 79 Rheal Cormier UER .10 .02
❑ 80 Rick Sutcliffe .20 .07
❑ 81 Harold Baines .20 .07
❑ 82 Lee Smith .20 .07
❑ 83 Geno Petralli .10 .02
❑ 84 Jose Oquendo .10 .02
❑ 85 Mark Gubicza .10 .02
❑ 86 Mickey Tettleton .10 .02
❑ 87 Bobby Witt .10 .02
❑ 88 Mark Lewis .10 .02
❑ 89 Kevin Appier .20 .07
❑ 90 Mike Stanton .10 .02
❑ 91 Rafael Belliard .10 .02
❑ 92 Kenny Rogers .20 .07
❑ 93 Randy Velarde .10 .02
❑ 94 Luis Sojo .10 .02
❑ 95 Mark Leiter .10 .02
❑ 96 Jody Reed .10 .02
❑ 97 Pete Harnisch .10 .02
❑ 98 Tom Candiotti .10 .02
❑ 99 Mark Portugal .10 .02
❑ 100 Dave Valle .10 .02
❑ 101 Shawon Dunston .10 .02
❑ 102 B.J. Surhoff .20 .07
❑ 103 Jay Bell .20 .07
❑ 104 Sid Bream .10 .02
❑ 105 Frank Thomas CL .30 .10
❑ 106 Mike Morgan .10 .02
❑ 107 Bill Doran .10 .02
❑ 108 Lance Blankenship .10 .02
❑ 109 Mark Lemke .10 .02
❑ 110 Brian Harper .10 .02
❑ 111 Brady Anderson .20 .07
❑ 112 Bip Roberts .10 .02
❑ 113 Mitch Williams .10 .02
❑ 114 Craig Biggio .30 .10
❑ 115 Eddie Murray .50 .20
❑ 116 Matt Nokes .10 .02
❑ 117 Lance Parrish .20 .07
❑ 118 Bill Swift .10 .02
❑ 119 Jeff Innis .10 .02
❑ 120 Mike LaValliere .10 .02
❑ 121 Hal Morris .10 .02
❑ 122 Walt Weiss .10 .02
❑ 123 Ivan Rodriguez .30 .10
❑ 124 Andy Van Slyke .30 .10
❑ 125 Roberto Alomar .30 .10
❑ 126 Robby Thompson .10 .02
❑ 127 Sammy Sosa .50 .20
❑ 128 Mark Langston .10 .02
❑ 129 Jerry Browne .10 .02
❑ 130 Chuck McElroy .10 .02
❑ 131 Frank Viola .20 .07
❑ 132 Leo Gomez .10 .02
❑ 133 Ramon Martinez .10 .02
❑ 134 Don Mattingly 1.25 .50
❑ 135 Roger Clemens 1.00 .40
❑ 136 Rickey Henderson .50 .20
❑ 137 Darren Daulton .20 .07
❑ 138 Ken Hill .10 .02
❑ 139 Ozzie Guillen .20 .07
❑ 140 Jerald Clark .10 .02
❑ 141 Dave Fleming .10 .02
❑ 142 Delino DeShields .10 .02
❑ 143 Matt Williams .20 .07
❑ 144 Larry Walker .20 .07
❑ 145 Ruben Sierra .20 .07
❑ 146 Ozzie Smith .75 .30
❑ 147 Chris Sabo .10 .02
❑ 148 Carlos Hernandez .10 .02
❑ 149 Pat Borders .10 .02
❑ 150 Orlando Merced .10 .02
❑ 151 Royce Clayton .10 .02
❑ 152 Kurt Stillwell .10 .02
❑ 153 Dave Hollins .10 .02
❑ 154 Mike Greenwell .10 .02
❑ 155 Nolan Ryan 2.00 .75
❑ 156 Felix Jose .10 .02
❑ 157 Junior Felix .10 .02
❑ 158 Derek Bell .10 .02
❑ 159 Steve Buechele .10 .02
❑ 160 John Burkett .10 .02
❑ 161 Pat Howell .10 .02
❑ 162 Milt Cuyler .10 .02
❑ 163 Terry Pendleton .20 .07
❑ 164 Jack Morris .20 .07
❑ 165 Tony Gwynn .60 .25
❑ 166 Deion Sanders .30 .10
❑ 167 Mike Devereaux .10 .02
❑ 168 Ron Darling .10 .02
❑ 169 Orel Hershiser .20 .07
❑ 170 Mike Jackson .10 .02
❑ 171 Doug Jones .10 .02
❑ 172 Dan Walters .10 .02
❑ 173 Darren Lewis .10 .02
❑ 174 Carlos Baerga .10 .02
❑ 175 Ryne Sandberg .75 .30
❑ 176 Gregg Jefferies .10 .02
❑ 177 John Jaha .10 .02
❑ 178 Luis Polonia .10 .02
❑ 179 Kirt Manwaring .10 .02
❑ 180 Mike Magnante .10 .02
❑ 181 Billy Ripken .10 .02
❑ 182 Mike Moore .10 .02
❑ 183 Eric Anthony .10 .02
❑ 184 Lenny Harris .10 .02
❑ 185 Tony Pena .10 .02
❑ 186 Mike Felder .10 .02
❑ 187 Greg Olson .10 .02
❑ 188 Rene Gonzales .10 .02
❑ 189 Mike Bordick .10 .02
❑ 190 Mel Rojas .10 .02
❑ 191 Todd Frohwirth .10 .02
❑ 192 Darryl Hamilton .10 .02
❑ 193 Mike Fetters .10 .02
❑ 194 Omar Olivares .10 .02
❑ 195 Tony Phillips .10 .02
❑ 196 Paul Sorrento .10 .02
❑ 197 Trevor Wilson .10 .02
❑ 198 Kevin Gross .10 .02
❑ 199 Ron Karkovice .10 .02
❑ 200 Brook Jacoby .10 .02
❑ 201 Mariano Duncan .10 .02
❑ 202 Dennis Cook .10 .02
❑ 203 Daryl Boston .10 .02
❑ 204 Mike Perez .10 .02
❑ 205 Manuel Lee .10 .02
❑ 206 Steve Olin .10 .02
❑ 207 Charlie Hough .20 .07
❑ 208 Scott Scudder .10 .02
❑ 209 Charlie O'Brien .10 .02
❑ 210 Barry Bonds CL .75 .30
❑ 211 Jose Vizcaino .10 .02
❑ 212 Scott Leius .10 .02
❑ 213 Kevin Mitchell .10 .02
❑ 214 Brian Barnes .10 .02
❑ 215 Pat Kelly .10 .02
❑ 216 Chris Hammond .10 .02
❑ 217 Rob Deer .10 .02
❑ 218 Cory Snyder .10 .02
❑ 219 Gary Carter .20 .07
❑ 220 Danny Darwin .10 .02
❑ 221 Tom Gordon .10 .02
❑ 222 Gary Sheffield 2X .20 .07
❑ 223 Joe Carter .20 .07
❑ 224 Jay Buhner .20 .07
❑ 225 Jose Offerman .10 .02
❑ 226 Jose Rijo .10 .02
❑ 227 Mark Whiten .10 .02
❑ 228 Randy Milligan .10 .02
❑ 229 Bud Black .10 .02
❑ 230 Gary DiSarcina .10 .02
❑ 231 Steve Finley .20 .07
❑ 232 Dennis Martinez .20 .07
❑ 233 Mike Mussina .30 .10
❑ 234 Joe Oliver .10 .02
❑ 235 Chad Curtis .10 .02
❑ 236 Shane Mack .10 .02
❑ 237 Jaime Navarro .10 .02
❑ 238 Brian McRae .10 .02
❑ 239 Chili Davis .20 .07
❑ 240 Jeff King .10 .02
❑ 241 Dean Palmer .20 .07
❑ 242 Danny Tartabull .10 .02
❑ 243 Charles Nagy .10 .02
❑ 244 Ray Lankford .20 .07
❑ 245 Barry Larkin .30 .10
❑ 246 Steve Avery .10 .02
❑ 247 John Kruk .20 .07
❑ 248 Derrick May .10 .02
❑ 249 Stan Javier .10 .02
❑ 250 Roger McDowell .10 .02
❑ 251 Dan Gladden .10 .02
❑ 252 Wally Joyner .20 .07
❑ 253 Pat Listach .10 .02
❑ 254 Chuck Knoblauch .20 .07
❑ 255 Sandy Alomar Jr. .10 .02
❑ 256 Jeff Bagwell .30 .10
❑ 257 Andy Stankiewicz .10 .02
❑ 258 Darrin Jackson .10 .02
❑ 259 Brett Butler .20 .07
❑ 260 Joe Orsulak .10 .02
❑ 261 Andy Benes .10 .02
❑ 262 Kenny Lofton .20 .07
❑ 263 Robin Ventura .20 .07
❑ 264 Ron Gant .20 .07
❑ 265 Ellis Burks .20 .07
❑ 266 Juan Guzman .10 .02
❑ 267 Wes Chamberlain .10 .02
❑ 268 John Smiley .10 .02
❑ 269 Franklin Stubbs .10 .02
❑ 270 Tom Browning .10 .02
❑ 271 Dennis Eckersley .20 .07
❑ 272 Carlton Fisk .30 .10
❑ 273 Lou Whitaker .20 .07
❑ 274 Phil Plantier .10 .02
❑ 275 Bobby Bonilla .20 .07
❑ 276 Ben McDonald .10 .02
❑ 277 Bob Zupcic .10 .02
❑ 278 Terry Steinbach .10 .02
❑ 279 Terry Mulholland .10 .02
❑ 280 Lance Johnson .10 .02
❑ 281 Willie McGee .20 .07
❑ 282 Bret Saberhagen .20 .07
❑ 283 Randy Myers .10 .02
❑ 284 Randy Tomlin .10 .02
❑ 285 Mickey Morandini .10 .02
❑ 286 Brian Williams .10 .02
❑ 287 Tino Martinez .30 .10
❑ 288 Jose Melendez .10 .02
❑ 289 Jeff Huson .10 .02
❑ 290 Joe Grahe .10 .02
❑ 291 Mel Hall .10 .02
❑ 292 Otis Nixon .10 .02
❑ 293 Todd Hundley .10 .02
❑ 294 Casey Candaele .10 .02
❑ 295 Kevin Seitzer .10 .02
❑ 296 Eddie Taubensee .10 .02
❑ 297 Moises Alou .20 .07
❑ 298 Scott Radinsky .10 .02
❑ 299 Thomas Howard .10 .02
❑ 300 Kyle Abbott .10 .02
❑ 301 Omar Vizquel .30 .10
❑ 302 Keith Miller .10 .02
❑ 303 Rick Aguilera .10 .02
❑ 304 Bruce Hurst .10 .02
❑ 305 Ken Caminiti .20 .07
❑ 306 Mike Pagliarulo .10 .02
❑ 307 Frank Seminara .10 .02
❑ 308 Andre Dawson .20 .07
❑ 309 Jose Lind .10 .02
❑ 310 Joe Boever .10 .02
❑ 311 Jeff Parrett .10 .02
❑ 312 Alan Mills .10 .02
❑ 313 Kevin Tapani .10 .02
❑ 314 Darryl Kile .20 .07
❑ 315 Checklist 211-315
Will Clark .20 .07
❑ 316 Mike Sharperson .10 .02

❑ 317 John Orton .10 .02
❑ 318 Bob Tewksbury .10 .02
❑ 319 Xavier Hernandez .10 .02
❑ 320 Paul Assenmacher .10 .02
❑ 321 John Franco .20 .07
❑ 322 Mike Timlin .10 .02
❑ 323 Jose Guzman .10 .02
❑ 324 Pedro Martinez 1.00 .40
❑ 325 Bill Spiers .10 .02
❑ 326 Melido Perez .10 .02
❑ 327 Mike Macfarlane .10 .02
❑ 328 Ricky Bones .10 .02
❑ 329 Scott Bankhead .10 .02
❑ 330 Rich Rodriguez .10 .02
❑ 331 Geronimo Pena .10 .02
❑ 332 Bernie Williams .30 .10
❑ 333 Paul Molitor .20 .07
❑ 334 Carlos Garcia .10 .02
❑ 335 David Cone .20 .07
❑ 336 Randy Johnson .50 .20
❑ 337 Pat Mahomes .10 .02
❑ 338 Erik Hanson .10 .02
❑ 339 Duane Ward .10 .02
❑ 340 Al Martin .10 .02
❑ 341 Pedro Munoz .10 .02
❑ 342 Greg Colbrunn .10 .02
❑ 343 Julio Valera .10 .02
❑ 344 John Olerud .20 .07
❑ 345 George Bell .10 .02
❑ 346 Devon White .20 .07
❑ 347 Donovan Osborne .10 .02
❑ 348 Mark Gardner .10 .02
❑ 349 Zane Smith .10 .02
❑ 350 Wilson Alvarez .10 .02
❑ 351 Kevin Koslofski .10 .02
❑ 352 Roberto Hernandez .10 .02
❑ 353 Glenn Davis .10 .02
❑ 354 Reggie Sanders .20 .07
❑ 355 Ken Griffey Jr. .75 .30
❑ 356 Marquis Grissom .20 .07
❑ 357 Jack McDowell .10 .02
❑ 358 Jimmy Key .20 .07
❑ 359 Stan Belinda .10 .02
❑ 360 Gerald Williams .10 .02
❑ 361 Sid Fernandez .10 .02
❑ 362 Alex Fernandez .10 .02
❑ 363 John Smoltz .30 .10
❑ 364 Travis Fryman .20 .07
❑ 365 Jose Canseco .30 .10
❑ 366 David Justice .20 .07
❑ 367 Pedro Astacio .10 .02
❑ 368 Tim Belcher .10 .02
❑ 369 Steve Sax .10 .02
❑ 370 Gary Gaetti .20 .07
❑ 371 Jeff Frye .10 .02
❑ 372 Bob Wickman .10 .02
❑ 373 Ryan Thompson .10 .02
❑ 374 David Hulse RC .15 .05
❑ 375 Cal Eldred .10 .02
❑ 376 Ryan Klesko .20 .07
❑ 377 Damion Easley .10 .02
❑ 378 John Kiely .10 .02
❑ 379 Jim Bullinger .10 .02
❑ 380 Brian Bohanon .10 .02
❑ 381 Rod Brewer .10 .02
❑ 382 Fernando Ramsey RC .15 .05
❑ 383 Sam Militello .10 .02
❑ 384 Arthur Rhodes .10 .02
❑ 385 Eric Karros .20 .07
❑ 386 Rico Brogna .10 .02
❑ 387 John Valentin .10 .02
❑ 388 Kerry Woodson .10 .02
❑ 389 Ben Rivera .10 .02
❑ 390 Matt Whiteside RC .15 .05
❑ 391 Henry Rodriguez .10 .02
❑ 392 John Wetteland .20 .07
❑ 393 Kent Mercker .10 .02
❑ 394 Bernard Gilkey .10 .02
❑ 395 Doug Henry .10 .02
❑ 396 Mo Vaughn .20 .07
❑ 397 Scott Erickson .10 .02
❑ 398 Bill Gullickson .10 .02
❑ 399 Mark Guthrie .10 .02
❑ 400 Dave Martinez .10 .02
❑ 401 Jeff Kent .50 .20
❑ 402 Chris Hoiles .10 .02
❑ 403 Mike Henneman .10 .02
❑ 404 Chris Nabholz .10 .02
❑ 405 Tom Pagnozzi .10 .02
❑ 406 Kelly Gruber .10 .02
❑ 407 Bob Welch .10 .02
❑ 408 Frank Castillo .10 .02
❑ 409 John Dopson .10 .02
❑ 410 Steve Farr .10 .02
❑ 411 Henry Cotto .10 .02
❑ 412 Bob Patterson .10 .02
❑ 413 Todd Stottlemyre .10 .02
❑ 414 Greg A. Harris .10 .02
❑ 415 Denny Neagle .20 .07
❑ 416 Bill Wegman .10 .02
❑ 417 Willie Wilson .10 .02
❑ 418 Terry Leach .10 .02
❑ 419 Willie Randolph .20 .07
❑ 420 Checklist 316-420 McGwire .30 .10
❑ 421 Calvin Murray CL .10 .02
❑ 422 Pete Janicki RC .15 .05
❑ 423 Todd Jones TP .20 .07
❑ 424 Mike Neill .10 .02
❑ 425 Carlos Delgado .50 .20
❑ 426 Jose Oliva .10 .02
❑ 427 Tyrone Hill .10 .02
❑ 428 Dmitri Young .20 .07
❑ 429 Derek Wallace RC .15 .05
❑ 430 Michael Moore RC .15 .05
❑ 431 Cliff Floyd .20 .07
❑ 432 Calvin Murray .10 .02
❑ 433 Manny Ramirez .75 .30
❑ 434 Marc Newfield .10 .02
❑ 435 Charles Johnson .20 .07
❑ 436 Butch Huskey .10 .02
❑ 437 Brad Pennington TP .10 .02
❑ 438 Ray McDavid RC .15 .05
❑ 439 Chad McConnell .10 .02
❑ 440 Midre Cummings RC .15 .05
❑ 441 Benji Gil .10 .02
❑ 442 Frankie Rodriguez .10 .02
❑ 443 Chad Mottola RC .15 .05
❑ 444 John Burke RC .15 .05
❑ 445 Michael Tucker .10 .02
❑ 446 Rick Greene .10 .02
❑ 447 Rich Becker .10 .02
❑ 448 Mike Robertson TP .10 .02
❑ 449 Derek Jeter RC ! 10.00 4.00
❑ 450 I.Rodriguez/D.McCarty CL .30 .10
❑ 451 Jim Abbott IN .20 .07
❑ 452 Jeff Bagwell IN .20 .07
❑ 453 Jason Bere IN .10 .02
❑ 454 Delino DeShields IN .10 .02
❑ 455 Travis Fryman IN .10 .02
❑ 456 Alex Gonzalez IN .10 .02
❑ 457 Phil Hiatt IN .10 .02
❑ 458 Dave Hollins IN .10 .02
❑ 459 Chipper Jones IN .30 .10
❑ 460 David Justice IN .10 .02
❑ 461 Ray Lankford IN .10 .02
❑ 462 David McCarty IN .10 .02
❑ 463 Mike Mussina IN .20 .07
❑ 464 Jose Offerman IN .10 .02
❑ 465 Dean Palmer IN .10 .02
❑ 466 Geronimo Pena IN .10 .02
❑ 467 Eduardo Perez IN .10 .02
❑ 468 Ivan Rodriguez IN .20 .07
❑ 469 Reggie Sanders IN .10 .02
❑ 470 Bernie Williams IN .20 .07
❑ 471 Bonds/Williams/Clark CL .75 .30
❑ 472 Madd/Avery/Smolt/Glav .50 .20
❑ 473 Red October
Jose Rijo
Rob Dibble
Roberto Kelly# .20 .07
❑ 474 Sheff/Plant/Gwynn/McGrif .20 .07
❑ 475 Biggio/Drabek/Bagwell .20 .07
❑ 476 Clark/Bonds/Williams .75 .30
❑ 477 Eric Davis
Darryl Strawberry .20 .07
❑ 478 Bich/Nied/Galarraga .20 .07
❑ 479 Maga/Destr/Barbe/Conine .10 .02
❑ 480 Wakefield/Van Slyke/Bell .20 .07
❑ 481 Griss/DeSh/Mart/Walker .30 .10
❑ 482 O.Smith/Redbirds .50 .20
❑ 483 Myers/Sandberg/Grace .50 .20
❑ 484 Big Apple Power Switch .30 .10
❑ 485 Kruk/Holl/Dault/Dyks .10 .02
❑ 486 Barry Bonds AW .75 .30
❑ 487 Dennis Eckersley AW .20 .07
❑ 488 Greg Maddux AW .50 .20
❑ 489 Dennis Eckersley AW .20 .07
❑ 490 Eric Karros AW .10 .02
❑ 491 Pat Listach AW .10 .02
❑ 492 Gary Sheffield AW .10 .02
❑ 493 Mark McGwire AW .60 .25
❑ 494 Gary Sheffield AW .10 .02
❑ 495 Edgar Martinez AW .20 .07
❑ 496 Fred McGriff AW .20 .07
❑ 497 Juan Gonzalez AW .10 .02
❑ 498 Darren Daulton AW .10 .02
❑ 499 Cecil Fielder AW .10 .02
❑ 500 Brent Gates CL .10 .02
❑ 501 Tavo Alvarez .10 .02
❑ 502 Rod Bolton .10 .02
❑ 503 John Cummings RC .15 .05
❑ 504 Brent Gates .10 .02
❑ 505 Tyler Green .10 .02
❑ 506 Jose Martinez RC .15 .05
❑ 507 Troy Percival .30 .10
❑ 508 Kevin Stocker .10 .02
❑ 509 Matt Walbeck RC .15 .05
❑ 510 Rondell White .20 .07
❑ 511 Billy Ripken .10 .02
❑ 512 Mike Moore .10 .02
❑ 513 Jose Lind .10 .02
❑ 514 Chito Martinez .10 .02
❑ 515 Jose Guzman .10 .02
❑ 516 Kim Batiste .10 .02
❑ 517 Jeff Tackett .10 .02
❑ 518 Charlie Hough .20 .07
❑ 519 Marvin Freeman .10 .02
❑ 520 Carlos Martinez .10 .02
❑ 521 Eric Young .10 .02
❑ 522 Pete Incaviglia .10 .02
❑ 523 Scott Fletcher .10 .02
❑ 524 Orestes Destrade .10 .02
❑ 525 Ken Griffey Jr. CL .50 .20
❑ 526 Ellis Burks .20 .07
❑ 527 Juan Samuel .10 .02
❑ 528 Dave Magadan .10 .02
❑ 529 Jeff Parrett .10 .02
❑ 530 Bill Krueger .10 .02
❑ 531 Frank Bolick .10 .02
❑ 532 Alan Trammell .20 .07
❑ 533 Walt Weiss .10 .02
❑ 534 David Cone .20 .07
❑ 535 Greg Maddux .75 .30
❑ 536 Kevin Young .20 .07
❑ 537 Dave Hansen .10 .02
❑ 538 Alex Cole .10 .02
❑ 539 Greg Hibbard .10 .02
❑ 540 Gene Larkin .10 .02
❑ 541 Jeff Reardon .20 .07
❑ 542 Felix Jose .10 .02
❑ 543 Jimmy Key .20 .07
❑ 544 Reggie Jefferson .10 .02
❑ 545 Gregg Jefferies .10 .02
❑ 546 Dave Stewart .20 .07
❑ 547 Tim Wallach .10 .02
❑ 548 Spike Owen .10 .02
❑ 549 Tommy Greene .10 .02
❑ 550 Fernando Valenzuela .20 .07
❑ 551 Rich Amaral .10 .02
❑ 552 Bret Barberie .10 .02
❑ 553 Edgar Martinez .30 .10
❑ 554 Jim Abbott .30 .10
❑ 555 Frank Thomas .50 .20
❑ 556 Wade Boggs .30 .10
❑ 557 Tom Henke .10 .02
❑ 558 Milt Thompson .10 .02
❑ 559 Lloyd McClendon .10 .02
❑ 560 Vinny Castilla .50 .20
❑ 561 Ricky Jordan .10 .02
❑ 562 Andujar Cedeno .10 .02
❑ 563 Greg Vaughn .10 .02
❑ 564 Cecil Fielder .20 .07
❑ 565 Kirby Puckett .50 .20
❑ 566 Mark McGwire 1.25 .50
❑ 567 Barry Bonds 1.50 .60
❑ 568 Jody Reed .10 .02
❑ 569 Todd Zeile .10 .02
❑ 570 Mark Carreon .10 .02

❑ 571 Joe Girardi .10 .02
❑ 572 Luis Gonzalez .20 .07
❑ 573 Mark Grace .30 .10
❑ 574 Rafael Palmeiro .30 .10
❑ 575 Darryl Strawberry .20 .07
❑ 576 Will Clark .30 .10
❑ 577 Fred McGriff .30 .10
❑ 578 Kevin Reimer .10 .02
❑ 579 Dave Righetti .20 .07
❑ 580 Juan Bell .10 .02
❑ 581 Jeff Brantley .10 .02
❑ 582 Brian Hunter .10 .02
❑ 583 Tim Naehring .10 .02
❑ 584 Glenallen Hill .10 .02
❑ 585 Cal Ripken 1.50 .60
❑ 586 Albert Belle .20 .07
❑ 587 Robin Yount .75 .30
❑ 588 Chris Bosio .10 .02
❑ 589 Pete Smith .10 .02
❑ 590 Chuck Carr .10 .02
❑ 591 Jeff Blauser .10 .02
❑ 592 Kevin McReynolds .10 .02
❑ 593 Andres Galarraga .20 .07
❑ 594 Kevin Maas .10 .02
❑ 595 Eric Davis .20 .07
❑ 596 Brian Jordan .20 .07
❑ 597 Tim Raines .20 .07
❑ 598 Rick Wilkins .10 .02
❑ 599 Steve Cooke .10 .02
❑ 600 Mike Gallego .10 .02
❑ 601 Mike Munoz .10 .02
❑ 602 Luis Rivera .10 .02
❑ 603 Junior Ortiz .10 .02
❑ 604 Brent Mayne .10 .02
❑ 605 Luis Alicea .10 .02
❑ 606 Damon Berryhill .10 .02
❑ 607 Dave Henderson .10 .02
❑ 608 Kirk McCaskill .10 .02
❑ 609 Jeff Fassero .10 .02
❑ 610 Mike Harkey .10 .02
❑ 611 Francisco Cabrera .10 .02
❑ 612 Rey Sanchez .10 .02
❑ 613 Scott Servais .10 .02
❑ 614 Darrin Fletcher .10 .02
❑ 615 Felix Fermin .10 .02
❑ 616 Kevin Seitzer .10 .02
❑ 617 Bob Scanlan .10 .02
❑ 618 Billy Hatcher .10 .02
❑ 619 John Vander Wal .10 .02
❑ 620 Joe Hesketh .10 .02
❑ 621 Hector Villanueva .10 .02
❑ 622 Randy Milligan .10 .02
❑ 623 Tony Tarasco RC .15 .05
❑ 624 Russ Swan .10 .02
❑ 625 Willie Wilson .10 .02
❑ 626 Frank Tanana .10 .02
❑ 627 Pete O'Brien .10 .02
❑ 628 Lenny Webster .10 .02
❑ 629 Mark Clark .10 .02
❑ 630 Roger Clemens CL .50 .20
❑ 631 Alex Arias .10 .02
❑ 632 Chris Gwynn .10 .02
❑ 633 Tom Bolton .10 .02
❑ 634 Greg Briley .10 .02
❑ 635 Kent Bottenfield .10 .02
❑ 636 Kelly Downs .10 .02
❑ 637 Manuel Lee .10 .02
❑ 638 Al Leiter .20 .07
❑ 639 Jeff Gardner .10 .02
❑ 640 Mike Gardiner .10 .02
❑ 641 Mark Gardner .10 .02
❑ 642 Jeff Branson .10 .02
❑ 643 Paul Wagner .10 .02
❑ 644 Sean Berry .10 .02
❑ 645 Phil Hiatt .10 .02
❑ 646 Kevin Mitchell .10 .02
❑ 647 Charlie Hayes .10 .02
❑ 648 Jim Deshaies .10 .02
❑ 649 Dan Pasqua .10 .02
❑ 650 Mike Maddux .10 .02
❑ 651 Domingo Martinez RC .15 .05
❑ 652 Greg McMichael RC .15 .05
❑ 653 Eric Wedge RC .50 .20
❑ 654 Mark Whiten .10 .02
❑ 655 Roberto Kelly .10 .02
❑ 656 Julio Franco .20 .07
❑ 657 Gene Harris .10 .02
❑ 658 Pete Schourek .10 .02
❑ 659 Mike Bielecki .10 .02
❑ 660 Ricky Gutierrez .10 .02
❑ 661 Chris Hammond .10 .02
❑ 662 Tim Scott .10 .02
❑ 663 Norm Charlton .10 .02
❑ 664 Doug Drabek .10 .02
❑ 665 Dwight Gooden .20 .07
❑ 666 Jim Gott .10 .02
❑ 667 Randy Myers .10 .02
❑ 668 Darren Holmes .10 .02
❑ 669 Tim Spehr .10 .02
❑ 670 Bruce Ruffin .10 .02
❑ 671 Bobby Thigpen .10 .02
❑ 672 Tony Fernandez .10 .02
❑ 673 Darrin Jackson .10 .02
❑ 674 Gregg Olson .10 .02
❑ 675 Rob Dibble .20 .07
❑ 676 Howard Johnson .10 .02
❑ 677 Mike Lansing RC .50 .20
❑ 678 Charlie Leibrandt .10 .02
❑ 679 Kevin Bass .10 .02
❑ 680 Hubie Brooks .10 .02
❑ 681 Scott Brosius .20 .07
❑ 682 Randy Knorr .10 .02
❑ 683 Dante Bichette .20 .07
❑ 684 Bryan Harvey .10 .02
❑ 685 Greg Gohr .10 .02
❑ 686 Willie Banks .10 .02
❑ 687 Robb Nen .20 .07
❑ 688 Mike Scioscia .10 .02
❑ 689 John Farrell .10 .02
❑ 690 John Candelaria .10 .02
❑ 691 Damon Buford .10 .02
❑ 692 Todd Worrell .10 .02
❑ 693 Pat Hentgen .10 .02
❑ 694 John Smiley .10 .02
❑ 695 Greg Swindell .10 .02
❑ 696 Derek Bell .10 .02
❑ 697 Terry Jorgensen .10 .02
❑ 698 Jimmy Jones .10 .02
❑ 699 David Wells .20 .07
❑ 700 Dave Martinez .10 .02
❑ 701 Steve Bedrosian .10 .02
❑ 702 Jeff Russell .10 .02
❑ 703 Joe Magrane .10 .02
❑ 704 Matt Mieske .10 .02
❑ 705 Paul Molitor .20 .07
❑ 706 Dale Murphy .30 .10
❑ 707 Steve Howe .10 .02
❑ 708 Greg Gagne .10 .02
❑ 709 Dave Eiland .10 .02
❑ 710 David West .10 .02
❑ 711 Luis Aquino .10 .02
❑ 712 Joe Orsulak .10 .02
❑ 713 Eric Plunk .10 .02
❑ 714 Mike Felder .10 .02
❑ 715 Joe Klink .10 .02
❑ 716 Lonnie Smith .10 .02
❑ 717 Monty Fariss .10 .02
❑ 718 Craig Lefferts .10 .02
❑ 719 John Habyan .10 .02
❑ 720 Willie Blair .10 .02
❑ 721 Darnell Coles .10 .02
❑ 722 Mark Williamson .10 .02
❑ 723 Bryn Smith .10 .02
❑ 724 Greg W. Harris .10 .02
❑ 725 Graeme Lloyd RC .50 .20
❑ 726 Cris Carpenter .10 .02
❑ 727 Chico Walker .10 .02
❑ 728 Tracy Woodson .10 .02
❑ 729 Jose Uribe .10 .02
❑ 730 Stan Javier .10 .02
❑ 731 Jay Howell .10 .02
❑ 732 Freddie Benavides .10 .02
❑ 733 Jeff Reboulet .10 .02
❑ 734 Scott Sanderson .10 .02
❑ 735 Ryne Sandberg CL .50 .20
❑ 736 Archi Cianfrocco .10 .02
❑ 737 Daryl Boston .10 .02
❑ 738 Craig Grebeck .10 .02
❑ 739 Doug Dascenzo .10 .02
❑ 740 Gerald Young .10 .02
❑ 741 Candy Maldonado .10 .02
❑ 742 Joey Cora .10 .02
❑ 743 Don Slaught .10 .02
❑ 744 Steve Decker .10 .02
❑ 745 Blas Minor .10 .02
❑ 746 Storm Davis .10 .02
❑ 747 Carlos Quintana .10 .02
❑ 748 Vince Coleman .10 .02
❑ 749 Todd Burns .10 .02
❑ 750 Steve Frey .10 .02
❑ 751 Ivan Calderon .10 .02
❑ 752 Steve Reed RC .15 .05
❑ 753 Danny Jackson .10 .02
❑ 754 Jeff Conine .20 .07
❑ 755 Juan Gonzalez .20 .07
❑ 756 Mike Kelly .10 .02
❑ 757 John Doherty .10 .02
❑ 758 Jack Armstrong .10 .02
❑ 759 John Wehner .10 .02
❑ 760 Scott Bankhead .10 .02
❑ 761 Jim Tatum .10 .02
❑ 762 Scott Pose RC .15 .05
❑ 763 Andy Ashby .10 .02
❑ 764 Ed Sprague .10 .02
❑ 765 Harold Baines .20 .07
❑ 766 Kirk Gibson .20 .07
❑ 767 Troy Neel .10 .02
❑ 768 Dick Schofield .10 .02
❑ 769 Dickie Thon .10 .02
❑ 770 Butch Henry .10 .02
❑ 771 Junior Felix .10 .02
❑ 772 Ken Ryan RC .15 .05
❑ 773 Trevor Hoffman .50 .20
❑ 774 Phil Plantier .10 .02
❑ 775 Bo Jackson .50 .20
❑ 776 Benito Santiago .20 .07
❑ 777 Andre Dawson .20 .07
❑ 778 Bryan Hickerson .10 .02
❑ 779 Dennis Moeller .10 .02
❑ 780 Ryan Bowen .10 .02
❑ 781 Eric Fox .10 .02
❑ 782 Joe Kmak .10 .02
❑ 783 Mike Hampton .20 .07
❑ 784 Darrell Sherman RC .15 .05
❑ 785 J.T.Snow .30 .10
❑ 786 Dave Winfield .20 .07
❑ 787 Jim Austin .10 .02
❑ 788 Craig Shipley .10 .02
❑ 789 Greg Myers .10 .02
❑ 790 Todd Benzinger .10 .02
❑ 791 Cory Snyder .10 .02
❑ 792 David Segui .10 .02
❑ 793 Armando Reynoso .10 .02
❑ 794 Chili Davis .20 .07
❑ 795 Dave Nilsson .10 .02
❑ 796 Paul O'Neill .30 .10
❑ 797 Jerald Clark .10 .02
❑ 798 Jose Mesa .10 .02
❑ 799 Brain Holman .10 .02
❑ 800 Jim Eisenreich .10 .02
❑ 801 Mark McLemore .10 .02
❑ 802 Luis Sojo .10 .02
❑ 803 Harold Reynolds .20 .07
❑ 804 Dan Plesac .10 .02
❑ 805 Dave Stieb .10 .02
❑ 806 Tom Brunansky .10 .02
❑ 807 Kelly Gruber .10 .02
❑ 808 Bob Ojeda .10 .02
❑ 809 Dave Burba .10 .02
❑ 810 Joe Boever .10 .02
❑ 811 Jeremy Hernandez .10 .02
❑ 812 Tim Salmon TC .20 .07
❑ 813 Jeff Bagwell TC .20 .07
❑ 814 Dennis Eckersley TC .20 .07
❑ 815 Roberto Alomar TC .20 .07
❑ 816 Steve Avery TC .10 .02
❑ 817 Pat Listach TC .10 .02
❑ 818 Gregg Jefferies TC .10 .02
❑ 819 Sammy Sosa TC .50 .20
❑ 820 Darryl Strawberry TC .10 .02
❑ 821 Dennis Martinez TC .10 .02
❑ 822 Robby Thompson TC .10 .02
❑ 823 Albert Belle TC .20 .07
❑ 824 Randy Johnson TC .30 .10
❑ 825 Nigel Wilson TC .10 .02
❑ 826 Bobby Bonilla TC .10 .02
❑ 827 Glenn Davis TC .10 .02
❑ 828 Gary Sheffield TC .10 .02

❑ 829 Darren Daulton TC .10 .02
❑ 830 Jay Bell TC .10 .02
❑ 831 Juan Gonzalez TC .10 .02
❑ 832 Andre Dawson TC .10 .02
❑ 833 Hal Morris TC .10 .02
❑ 834 David Nied TC .10 .02
❑ 835 Felix Jose TC .10 .02
❑ 836 Travis Fryman TC .10 .02
❑ 837 Shane Mack TC .10 .02
❑ 838 Robin Ventura TC .10 .02
❑ 839 Danny Tartabull TC .10 .02
❑ 840 Roberto Alomar CL .20 .07
❑ SP5 G.Brett/R.Yount 1.00 .40
❑ SP6 Nolan Ryan 2.00 .75

1994 Upper Deck

❑ COMPLETE SET (550) 40.00 15.00
❑ COMPLETE SERIES 1 (280) 25.00 12.50
❑ COMPLETE SERIES 2 (270) 15.00 7.50
❑ 1 Brian Anderson RC .40 .15
❑ 2 Shane Andrews .15 .05
❑ 3 James Baldwin .15 .05
❑ 4 Rich Becker .15 .05
❑ 5 Greg Blosser .15 .05
❑ 6 Ricky Bottalico RC .15 .05
❑ 7 Midre Cummings .15 .05
❑ 8 Carlos Delgado .50 .20
❑ 9 Steve Dreyer RC .15 .05
❑ 10 Joey Eischen .15 .05
❑ 11 Carl Everett .30 .10
❑ 12 Cliff Floyd .30 .10
❑ 13 Alex Gonzalez .15 .05
❑ 14 Jeff Granger .15 .05
❑ 15 Shawn Green .75 .30
❑ 16 Brian L.Hunter .15 .05
❑ 17 Butch Huskey .15 .05
❑ 18 Mark Hutton .15 .05
❑ 19 Michael Jordan RC 8.00 3.00
❑ 20 Steve Karsay .15 .05
❑ 21 Jeff McNeely .15 .05
❑ 22 Marc Newfield .15 .05
❑ 23 Manny Ramirez .75 .30
❑ 24 Alex Rodriguez RC 25.00 10.00
❑ 25 Scott Ruffcorn UER .15 .05
❑ 26 Paul Spoljaric UER .15 .05
❑ 27 Salomon Torres .15 .05
❑ 28 Steve Trachsel .15 .05
❑ 29 Chris Turner .15 .05
❑ 30 Gabe White .15 .05
❑ 31 Randy Johnson FT .50 .20
❑ 32 John Wetteland FT .15 .05
❑ 33 Mike Piazza FT .75 .30
❑ 34 Rafael Palmeiro FT .30 .10
❑ 35 Roberto Alomar FT .30 .10
❑ 36 Matt Williams FT .15 .05
❑ 37 Travis Fryman FT .15 .05
❑ 38 Barry Bonds FT 1.00 .40
❑ 39 Marquis Grissom FT .15 .05
❑ 40 Albert Belle FT .30 .10
❑ 41 Steve Avery FUT .15 .05
❑ 42 Jason Bere FUT .15 .05
❑ 43 Alex Fernandez FUT .15 .05
❑ 44 Mike Mussina FUT .30 .10
❑ 45 Aaron Sele FUT .15 .05
❑ 46 Rod Beck FUT .15 .05
❑ 47 Mike Piazza FUT .75 .30
❑ 48 John Olerud FUT .15 .05
❑ 49 Carlos Baerga FUT .15 .05
❑ 50 Gary Sheffield FUT .15 .05
❑ 51 Travis Fryman FUT .15 .05
❑ 52 Juan Gonzalez FUT .15 .05
❑ 53 Ken Griffey Jr. FUT .75 .30
❑ 54 Tim Salmon FUT .30 .10
❑ 55 Frank Thomas FUT .50 .20
❑ 56 Tony Phillips .15 .05
❑ 57 Julio Franco .30 .10
❑ 58 Kevin Mitchell .15 .05
❑ 59 Raul Mondesi .30 .10
❑ 60 Rickey Henderson .75 .30
❑ 61 Jay Buhner .30 .10
❑ 62 Bill Swift .15 .05
❑ 63 Brady Anderson .30 .10
❑ 64 Ryan Klesko .30 .10
❑ 65 Darren Daulton .30 .10
❑ 66 Damion Easley .15 .05
❑ 67 Mark McGwire 2.00 .75
❑ 68 John Roper .15 .05
❑ 69 Dave Telgheder .15 .05
❑ 70 David Nied .15 .05
❑ 71 Mo Vaughn .30 .10
❑ 72 Tyler Green .15 .05
❑ 73 Dave Magadan .15 .05
❑ 74 Chili Davis .30 .10
❑ 75 Archi Cianfrocco .15 .05
❑ 76 Joe Girardi .15 .05
❑ 77 Chris Hoiles .15 .05
❑ 78 Ryan Bowen .15 .05
❑ 79 Greg Gagne .15 .05
❑ 80 Aaron Sele .15 .05
❑ 81 Dave Winfield .30 .10
❑ 82 Chad Curtis .15 .05
❑ 83 Andy Van Slyke .50 .20
❑ 84 Kevin Stocker .15 .05
❑ 85 Deion Sanders .50 .20
❑ 86 Bernie Williams .50 .20
❑ 87 John Smoltz .50 .20
❑ 88 Ruben Santana .15 .05
❑ 89 Dave Stewart .30 .10
❑ 90 Don Mattingly 2.00 .75
❑ 91 Joe Carter .30 .10
❑ 92 Ryne Sandberg 1.25 .50
❑ 93 Chris Gomez .15 .05
❑ 94 Tino Martinez .50 .20
❑ 95 Terry Pendleton .30 .10
❑ 96 Andre Dawson .30 .10
❑ 97 Wil Cordero .15 .05
❑ 98 Kent Hrbek .30 .10
❑ 99 John Olerud .30 .10
❑ 100 Kirt Manwaring .15 .05
❑ 101 Tim Bogar .15 .05
❑ 102 Mike Mussina .50 .20
❑ 103 Nigel Wilson .15 .05
❑ 104 Ricky Gutierrez .15 .05
❑ 105 Roberto Mejia .15 .05
❑ 106 Tom Pagnozzi .15 .05
❑ 107 Mike Macfarlane .15 .05
❑ 108 Jose Bautista .15 .05
❑ 109 Luis Ortiz .15 .05
❑ 110 Brent Gates .15 .05
❑ 111 Tim Salmon .50 .20
❑ 112 Wade Boggs .50 .20
❑ 113 Tripp Cromer .15 .05
❑ 114 Denny Hocking .15 .05
❑ 115 Carlos Baerga .15 .05
❑ 116 J.R. Phillips .15 .05
❑ 117 Bo Jackson .75 .30
❑ 118 Lance Johnson .15 .05
❑ 119 Bobby Jones .15 .05
❑ 120 Bobby Witt .15 .05
❑ 121 Ron Karkovice .15 .05
❑ 122 Jose Vizcaino .15 .05
❑ 123 Danny Darwin .15 .05
❑ 124 Eduardo Perez .15 .05
❑ 125 Brian Looney RC .15 .05
❑ 126 Pat Hentgen .15 .05
❑ 127 Frank Viola .30 .10
❑ 128 Darren Holmes .15 .05
❑ 129 Wally Whitehurst .15 .05
❑ 130 Matt Walbeck .15 .05
❑ 131 Albert Belle .30 .10
❑ 132 Steve Cooke .15 .05
❑ 133 Kevin Appier .30 .10
❑ 134 Joe Oliver .15 .05
❑ 135 Benji Gil .15 .05
❑ 136 Steve Buechele .15 .05
❑ 137 Devon White .30 .10
❑ 138 Sterling Hitchcock UER .15 .05
❑ 139 Phil Leftwich RC .15 .05
❑ 140 Jose Canseco .50 .20
❑ 141 Rick Aguilera .15 .05
❑ 142 Rod Beck .15 .05
❑ 143 Jose Rijo .15 .05
❑ 144 Tom Glavine .50 .20
❑ 145 Phil Plantier .15 .05
❑ 146 Jason Bere .15 .05
❑ 147 Jamie Moyer .30 .10
❑ 148 Wes Chamberlain .15 .05
❑ 149 Glenallen Hill .15 .05
❑ 150 Mark Whiten .15 .05
❑ 151 Bret Barberie .15 .05
❑ 152 Chuck Knoblauch .30 .10
❑ 153 Trevor Hoffman .50 .20
❑ 154 Rick Wilkins .15 .05
❑ 155 Juan Gonzalez .30 .10
❑ 156 Ozzie Guillen .30 .10
❑ 157 Jim Eisenreich .15 .05
❑ 158 Pedro Astacio .15 .05
❑ 159 Joe Magrane .15 .05
❑ 160 Ryan Thompson .15 .05
❑ 161 Jose Lind .15 .05
❑ 162 Jeff Conine .30 .10
❑ 163 Todd Benzinger .15 .05
❑ 164 Roger Salkeld .15 .05
❑ 165 Gary DiSarcina .15 .05
❑ 166 Kevin Gross .15 .05
❑ 167 Charlie Hayes .15 .05
❑ 168 Tim Costo .15 .05
❑ 169 Wally Joyner .30 .10
❑ 170 Johnny Ruffin .15 .05
❑ 171 Kirk Rueter .15 .05
❑ 172 Lenny Dykstra .30 .10
❑ 173 Ken Hill .15 .05
❑ 174 Mike Bordick .15 .05
❑ 175 Billy Hall .15 .05
❑ 176 Rob Butler .15 .05
❑ 177 Jay Bell .30 .10
❑ 178 Jeff Kent .50 .20
❑ 179 David Wells .30 .10
❑ 180 Dean Palmer .30 .10
❑ 181 Mariano Duncan .15 .05
❑ 182 Orlando Merced .15 .05
❑ 183 Brett Butler .30 .10
❑ 184 Milt Thompson .15 .05
❑ 185 Chipper Jones .75 .30
❑ 186 Paul O'Neill .50 .20
❑ 187 Mike Greenwell .15 .05
❑ 188 Harold Baines .30 .10
❑ 189 Todd Stottlemyre .15 .05
❑ 190 Jeromy Burnitz .30 .10
❑ 191 Rene Arocha .15 .05
❑ 192 Jeff Fassero .15 .05
❑ 193 Robby Thompson .15 .05
❑ 194 Greg W. Harris .15 .05
❑ 195 Todd Van Poppel .15 .05
❑ 196 Jose Guzman .15 .05
❑ 197 Shane Mack .15 .05
❑ 198 Carlos Garcia .15 .05
❑ 199 Kevin Roberson .15 .05
❑ 200 David McCarty .15 .05
❑ 201 Alan Trammell .30 .10
❑ 202 Chuck Carr .15 .05
❑ 203 Tommy Greene .15 .05
❑ 204 Wilson Alvarez .15 .05
❑ 205 Dwight Gooden .30 .10
❑ 206 Tony Tarasco .15 .05
❑ 207 Darren Lewis .15 .05
❑ 208 Eric Karros .30 .10
❑ 209 Chris Hammond .15 .05
❑ 210 Jeffrey Hammonds .15 .05
❑ 211 Rich Amaral .15 .05
❑ 212 Danny Tartabull .15 .05
❑ 213 Jeff Russell .15 .05
❑ 214 Dave Staton .15 .05
❑ 215 Kenny Lofton .30 .10
❑ 216 Manuel Lee .15 .05
❑ 217 Brian Koelling .15 .05
❑ 218 Scott Lydy .15 .05
❑ 219 Tony Gwynn 1.00 .40
❑ 220 Cecil Fielder .30 .10
❑ 221 Royce Clayton .15 .05

❑ 222 Reggie Sanders .30 .10
❑ 223 Brian Jordan .30 .10
❑ 224 Ken Griffey Jr. 1.25 .50
❑ 225 Fred McGriff .50 .20
❑ 226 Felix Jose .15 .05
❑ 227 Brad Pennington .15 .05
❑ 228 Chris Bosio .15 .05
❑ 229 Mike Stanley .15 .05
❑ 230 Willie Greene .15 .05
❑ 231 Alex Fernandez .15 .05
❑ 232 Brad Ausmus .50 .20
❑ 233 Darrell Whitmore .15 .05
❑ 234 Marcus Moore .15 .05
❑ 235 Allen Watson .15 .05
❑ 236 Jose Offerman .15 .05
❑ 237 Rondell White .30 .10
❑ 238 Jeff King .15 .05
❑ 239 Luis Alicea .15 .05
❑ 240 Dan Wilson .15 .05
❑ 241 Ed Sprague .15 .05
❑ 242 Todd Hundley .15 .05
❑ 243 Al Martin .15 .05
❑ 244 Mike Lansing .15 .05
❑ 245 Ivan Rodriguez .50 .20
❑ 246 Dave Fleming .15 .05
❑ 247 John Doherty .15 .05
❑ 248 Mark McLemore .15 .05
❑ 249 Bob Hamelin .15 .05
❑ 250 Curtis Pride RC .40 .15
❑ 251 Zane Smith .15 .05
❑ 252 Eric Young .15 .05
❑ 253 Brian McRae .15 .05
❑ 254 Tim Raines .30 .10
❑ 255 Javier Lopez .30 .10
❑ 256 Melvin Nieves .15 .05
❑ 257 Randy Myers .15 .05
❑ 258 Willie McGee .30 .10
❑ 259 Jimmy Key UER .30 .10
❑ 260 Tom Candiotti .15 .05
❑ 261 Eric Davis .30 .10
❑ 262 Craig Paquette .15 .05
❑ 263 Robin Ventura .30 .10
❑ 264 Pat Kelly .15 .05
❑ 265 Gregg Jefferies .15 .05
❑ 266 Cory Snyder .15 .05
❑ 267 David Justice HFA .15 .05
❑ 268 Sammy Sosa HFA .75 .30
❑ 269 Barry Larkin HFA .30 .10
❑ 270 Andres Galarraga HFA .15 .05
❑ 271 Gary Sheffield HFA .15 .05
❑ 272 Jeff Bagwell HFA .30 .10
❑ 273 Mike Piazza HFA .75 .30
❑ 274 Larry Walker HFA .15 .05
❑ 275 Bobby Bonilla HFA .15 .05
❑ 276 John Kruk HFA .15 .05
❑ 277 Jay Bell HFA .15 .05
❑ 278 Ozzie Smith HFA .75 .30
❑ 279 Tony Gwynn HFA .50 .20
❑ 280 Barry Bonds HFA 1.00 .40
❑ 281 Cal Ripken HFA 1.25 .50
❑ 282 Mo Vaughn HFA .15 .05
❑ 283 Tim Salmon HFA .30 .10
❑ 284 Frank Thomas HFA .50 .20
❑ 285 Albert Belle HFA .30 .10
❑ 286 Cecil Fielder HFA .15 .05
❑ 287 Wally Joyner HFA .15 .05
❑ 288 Greg Vaughn HFA .15 .05
❑ 289 Kirby Puckett HFA .50 .20
❑ 290 Don Mattingly HFA 1.00 .40
❑ 291 Terry Steinbach HFA .15 .05
❑ 292 Ken Griffey Jr. HFA .75 .30
❑ 293 Juan Gonzalez HFA .15 .05
❑ 294 Paul Molitor HFA .15 .05
❑ 295 Tavo Alvarez UDCA .15 .05
❑ 296 Matt Brunson UDCA .15 .05
❑ 297 Shawn Green UDCA .30 .10
❑ 298 Alex Rodriguez UDCA 6.00 2.50
❑ 299 Shannon Stewart UDCA .75 .30
❑ 300 Frank Thomas .75 .30
❑ 301 Mickey Tettleton .15 .05
❑ 302 Pedro Munoz .15 .05
❑ 303 Jose Valentin .15 .05
❑ 304 Orestes Destrade .15 .05
❑ 305 Pat Listach .15 .05
❑ 306 Scott Brosius .30 .10
❑ 307 Kurt Miller .15 .05
❑ 308 Rob Dibble .30 .10
❑ 309 Mike Blowers .15 .05
❑ 310 Jim Abbott .50 .20
❑ 311 Mike Jackson .15 .05
❑ 312 Craig Biggio .50 .20
❑ 313 Kurt Abbott RC .15 .05
❑ 314 Chuck Finley .30 .10
❑ 315 Andres Galarraga .30 .10
❑ 316 Mike Moore .15 .05
❑ 317 Doug Strange .15 .05
❑ 318 Pedro Martinez .75 .30
❑ 319 Kevin McReynolds .15 .05
❑ 320 Greg Maddux 1.25 .50
❑ 321 Mike Henneman .15 .05
❑ 322 Scott Leius .15 .05
❑ 323 John Franco .30 .10
❑ 324 Jeff Blauser .15 .05
❑ 325 Kirby Puckett .75 .30
❑ 326 Darryl Hamilton .15 .05
❑ 327 John Smiley .15 .05
❑ 328 Derrick May .15 .05
❑ 329 Jose Vizcaino .15 .05
❑ 330 Randy Johnson .75 .30
❑ 331 Jack Morris .30 .10
❑ 332 Graeme Lloyd .15 .05
❑ 333 Dave Valle .15 .05
❑ 334 Greg Myers .15 .05
❑ 335 John Wetteland .30 .10
❑ 336 Jim Gott .15 .05
❑ 337 Tim Naehring .15 .05
❑ 338 Mike Kelly .15 .05
❑ 339 Jeff Montgomery .15 .05
❑ 340 Rafael Palmeiro .50 .20
❑ 341 Eddie Murray .75 .30
❑ 342 Xavier Hernandez .15 .05
❑ 343 Bobby Munoz .15 .05
❑ 344 Bobby Bonilla .30 .10
❑ 345 Travis Fryman .30 .10
❑ 346 Steve Finley .30 .10
❑ 347 Chris Sabo .15 .05
❑ 348 Armando Reynoso .15 .05
❑ 349 Ramon Martinez .15 .05
❑ 350 Will Clark .50 .20
❑ 351 Moises Alou .30 .10
❑ 352 Jim Thome .50 .20
❑ 353 Bob Tewksbury .15 .05
❑ 354 Andujar Cedeno .15 .05
❑ 355 Orel Hershiser .30 .10
❑ 356 Mike Devereaux .15 .05
❑ 357 Mike Perez .15 .05
❑ 358 Dennis Martinez .30 .10
❑ 359 Dave Nilsson .15 .05
❑ 360 Ozzie Smith 1.25 .50
❑ 361 Eric Anthony .15 .05
❑ 362 Scott Sanders .15 .05
❑ 363 Paul Sorrento .15 .05
❑ 364 Tim Belcher .15 .05
❑ 365 Dennis Eckersley .30 .10
❑ 366 Mel Rojas .15 .05
❑ 367 Tom Henke .15 .05
❑ 368 Randy Tomlin .15 .05
❑ 369 B.J. Surhoff .30 .10
❑ 370 Larry Walker .30 .10
❑ 371 Joey Cora .15 .05
❑ 372 Mike Harkey .15 .05
❑ 373 John Valentin .15 .05
❑ 374 Doug Jones .15 .05
❑ 375 David Justice .30 .10
❑ 376 Vince Coleman .15 .05
❑ 377 David Hulse .15 .05
❑ 378 Kevin Seitzer .15 .05
❑ 379 Pete Harnisch .15 .05
❑ 380 Ruben Sierra .30 .10
❑ 381 Mark Lewis .15 .05
❑ 382 Bip Roberts .15 .05
❑ 383 Paul Wagner .15 .05
❑ 384 Stan Javier .15 .05
❑ 385 Barry Larkin .50 .20
❑ 386 Mark Portugal .15 .05
❑ 387 Roberto Kelly .15 .05
❑ 388 Andy Benes .15 .05
❑ 389 Felix Fermin .15 .05
❑ 390 Marquis Grissom .30 .10
❑ 391 Troy Neel .15 .05
❑ 392 Chad Kreuter .15 .05
❑ 393 Gregg Olson .15 .05
❑ 394 Charles Nagy .15 .05
❑ 395 Jack McDowell .15 .05
❑ 396 Luis Gonzalez .30 .10
❑ 397 Benito Santiago .30 .10
❑ 398 Chris James .15 .05
❑ 399 Terry Mulholland .15 .05
❑ 400 Barry Bonds 2.00 .75
❑ 401 Joe Grahe .15 .05
❑ 402 Duane Ward .15 .05
❑ 403 John Burkett .15 .05
❑ 404 Scott Servais .15 .05
❑ 405 Bryan Harvey .15 .05
❑ 406 Bernard Gilkey .15 .05
❑ 407 Greg McMichael .15 .05
❑ 408 Tim Wallach .15 .05
❑ 409 Ken Caminiti .30 .10
❑ 410 John Kruk .30 .10
❑ 411 Darrin Jackson .15 .05
❑ 412 Mike Gallego .15 .05
❑ 413 David Cone .30 .10
❑ 414 Lou Whitaker .30 .10
❑ 415 Sandy Alomar Jr. .15 .05
❑ 416 Bill Wegman .15 .05
❑ 417 Pat Borders .15 .05
❑ 418 Roger Pavlik .15 .05
❑ 419 Pete Smith .15 .05
❑ 420 Steve Avery .15 .05
❑ 421 David Segui .15 .05
❑ 422 Rheal Cormier .15 .05
❑ 423 Harold Reynolds .30 .10
❑ 424 Edgar Martinez .50 .20
❑ 425 Cal Ripken 2.50 1.00
❑ 426 Jaime Navarro .15 .05
❑ 427 Sean Berry .15 .05
❑ 428 Bret Saberhagen .30 .10
❑ 429 Bob Welch .15 .05
❑ 430 Juan Guzman .15 .05
❑ 431 Cal Eldred .15 .05
❑ 432 Dave Hollins .15 .05
❑ 433 Sid Fernandez .15 .05
❑ 434 Willie Banks .15 .05
❑ 435 Darryl Kile .30 .10
❑ 436 Henry Rodriguez .15 .05
❑ 437 Tony Fernandez .15 .05
❑ 438 Walt Weiss .15 .05
❑ 439 Kevin Tapani .15 .05
❑ 440 Mark Grace .50 .20
❑ 441 Brian Harper .15 .05
❑ 442 Kent Mercker .15 .05
❑ 443 Anthony Young .15 .05
❑ 444 Todd Zeile .15 .05
❑ 445 Greg Vaughn .15 .05
❑ 446 Ray Lankford .30 .10
❑ 447 Dave Weathers .15 .05
❑ 448 Bret Boone .30 .10
❑ 449 Charlie Hough .30 .10
❑ 450 Roger Clemens 1.50 .60
❑ 451 Mike Morgan .15 .05
❑ 452 Doug Drabek .15 .05
❑ 453 Danny Jackson .15 .05
❑ 454 Dante Bichette .30 .10
❑ 455 Roberto Alomar .50 .20
❑ 456 Ben McDonald .15 .05
❑ 457 Kenny Rogers .30 .10
❑ 458 Bill Gullickson .15 .05
❑ 459 Darrin Fletcher .15 .05
❑ 460 Curt Schilling .30 .10
❑ 461 Billy Hatcher .15 .05
❑ 462 Howard Johnson .15 .05
❑ 463 Mickey Morandini .15 .05
❑ 464 Frank Castillo .15 .05
❑ 465 Delino DeShields .15 .05
❑ 466 Gary Gaetti .30 .10
❑ 467 Steve Farr .15 .05
❑ 468 Roberto Hernandez .15 .05
❑ 469 Jack Armstrong .15 .05
❑ 470 Paul Molitor .30 .10
❑ 471 Melido Perez .15 .05
❑ 472 Greg Hibbard .15 .05
❑ 473 Jody Reed .15 .05
❑ 474 Tom Gordon .15 .05
❑ 475 Gary Sheffield .30 .10
❑ 476 John Jaha .15 .05
❑ 477 Shawon Dunston .15 .05
❑ 478 Reggie Jefferson .15 .05
❑ 479 Don Slaught .15 .05

❑ 480 Jeff Bagwell .50 .20
❑ 481 Tim Pugh .15 .05
❑ 482 Kevin Young .15 .05
❑ 483 Ellis Burks .30 .10
❑ 484 Greg Swindell .15 .05
❑ 485 Mark Langston .15 .05
❑ 486 Omar Vizquel .50 .20
❑ 487 Kevin Brown .30 .10
❑ 488 Terry Steinbach .15 .05
❑ 489 Mark Lemke .15 .05
❑ 490 Matt Williams .30 .10
❑ 491 Pete Incaviglia .15 .05
❑ 492 Karl Rhodes .15 .05
❑ 493 Shawn Green .75 .30
❑ 494 Hal Morris .15 .05
❑ 495 Derek Bell .15 .05
❑ 496 Luis Polonia .15 .05
❑ 497 Otis Nixon .15 .05
❑ 498 Ron Darling .15 .05
❑ 499 Mitch Williams .15 .05
❑ 500 Mike Piazza 1.50 .60
❑ 501 Pat Meares .15 .05
❑ 502 Scott Cooper .15 .05
❑ 503 Scott Erickson .15 .05
❑ 504 Jeff Juden .15 .05
❑ 505 Lee Smith .30 .10
❑ 506 Bobby Ayala .15 .05
❑ 507 Dave Henderson .15 .05
❑ 508 Erik Hanson .15 .05
❑ 509 Bob Wickman .15 .05
❑ 510 Sammy Sosa .75 .30
❑ 511 Hector Carrasco .15 .05
❑ 512 Tim Davis .15 .05
❑ 513 Joey Hamilton .15 .05
❑ 514 Robert Eenhoorn .15 .05
❑ 515 Jorge Fabregas .15 .05
❑ 516 Tim Hyers RC .15 .05
❑ 517 John Hudek RC .15 .05
❑ 518 James Mouton .15 .05
❑ 519 Herbert Perry RC .15 .05
❑ 520 Chan Ho Park RC .75 .30
❑ 521 W.VanLandingham RC .15 .05
❑ 522 Paul Shuey DD .15 .05
❑ 523 Ryan Hancock RC .15 .05
❑ 524 Billy Wagner RC 2.00 .75
❑ 525 Jason Giambi .75 .30
❑ 526 Jose Silva RC .15 .05
❑ 527 Terrell Wade RC .15 .05
❑ 528 Todd Dunn .15 .05
❑ 529 Alan Benes RC .40 .15
❑ 530 Brooks Kieschnick RC .15 .05
❑ 531 Todd Hollandsworth .15 .05
❑ 532 Brad Fullmer RC .40 .15
❑ 533 Steve Soderstrom RC .15 .05
❑ 534 Daron Kirkreit .15 .05
❑ 535 Arquimedez Pozo RC .15 .05
❑ 536 Charles Johnson .30 .10
❑ 537 Preston Wilson .30 .10
❑ 538 Alex Ochoa .15 .05
❑ 539 Derrek Lee RC 4.00 1.50
❑ 540 Wayne Gomes RC .15 .05
❑ 541 Jermaine Allensworth RC .15 .05
❑ 542 Mike Bell RC .15 .05
❑ 543 Trot Nixon RC 2.00 .75
❑ 544 Pokey Reese .15 .05
❑ 545 Neifi Perez RC .40 .15
❑ 546 Johnny Damon .75 .30
❑ 547 Matt Brunson RC .15 .05
❑ 548 LaTroy Hawkins RC .40 .15
❑ 549 Eddie Pearson RC .15 .05
❑ 550 Derek Jeter 2.50 1.00
❑ A298 Alex Rodriguez AU 700.00 350.00
❑ P224 Ken Griffey Jr. Promo 2.00 .75
❑ GM1 Griffey AU/Mantle AU/1000 900.00 700.00
❑ KG1 K.Griffey Jr. AU/1000 300.00 200.00
❑ MM1 M.Mantle AU/1000 600.00 300.00

1995 Upper Deck

❑ COMP.MASTER SET (495) 110.00 55.00
❑ COMPLETE SET (450) 50.00 20.00
❑ COMPLETE SERIES 1 (225) 25.00 10.00
❑ COMPLETE SERIES 2 (225) 25.00 10.00
❑ COMMON CARD (1-450) .15 .05
❑ COMP.TRADE SET (45) 60.00 30.00
❑ COMMON TRADE (451T-495T) 1.00 .40
❑ 1 Ruben Rivera .15 .05

❑ 2 Bill Pulsipher .15 .05
❑ 3 Ben Grieve .15 .05
❑ 4 Curtis Goodwin .15 .05
❑ 5 Damon Hollins .15 .05
❑ 6 Todd Greene .15 .05
❑ 7 Glenn Williams .15 .05
❑ 8 Bret Wagner .15 .05
❑ 9 Karim Garcia RC .15 .05
❑ 10 Nomar Garciaparra 2.00 .75
❑ 11 Raul Casanova RC .15 .05
❑ 12 Matt Smith .15 .05
❑ 13 Paul Wilson .15 .05
❑ 14 Jason Isringhausen .30 .10
❑ 15 Reid Ryan .30 .10
❑ 16 Lee Smith .30 .10
❑ 17 Chili Davis .30 .10
❑ 18 Brian Anderson .15 .05
❑ 19 Gary DiSarcina .15 .05
❑ 20 Bo Jackson .75 .30
❑ 21 Chuck Finley .30 .10
❑ 22 Darryl Kile .30 .10
❑ 23 Shane Reynolds .15 .05
❑ 24 Tony Eusebio .15 .05
❑ 25 Craig Biggio .50 .20
❑ 26 Doug Drabek .15 .05
❑ 27 Brian L.Hunter .15 .05
❑ 28 James Mouton .15 .05
❑ 29 Geronimo Berroa .15 .05
❑ 30 Rickey Henderson .75 .30
❑ 31 Steve Karsay .15 .05
❑ 32 Steve Ontiveros .15 .05
❑ 33 Ernie Young .15 .05
❑ 34 Dennis Eckersley .30 .10
❑ 35 Mark McGwire 2.00 .75
❑ 36 Dave Stewart .30 .10
❑ 37 Pat Hentgen .15 .05
❑ 38 Carlos Delgado .30 .10
❑ 39 Joe Carter .30 .10
❑ 40 Roberto Alomar .50 .20
❑ 41 John Olerud .30 .10
❑ 42 Devon White .30 .10
❑ 43 Roberto Kelly .15 .05
❑ 44 Jeff Blauser .15 .05
❑ 45 Fred McGriff .50 .20
❑ 46 Tom Glavine .50 .20
❑ 47 Mike Kelly .15 .05
❑ 48 Javier Lopez .30 .10
❑ 49 Greg Maddux 1.25 .50
❑ 50 Matt Mieske .15 .05
❑ 51 Troy O'Leary .15 .05
❑ 52 Jeff Cirillo .15 .05
❑ 53 Cal Eldred .15 .05
❑ 54 Pat Listach .15 .05
❑ 55 Jose Valentin .15 .05
❑ 56 John Mabry .15 .05
❑ 57 Bob Tewksbury .15 .05
❑ 58 Brian Jordan .30 .10
❑ 59 Gregg Jefferies .15 .05
❑ 60 Ozzie Smith 1.25 .50
❑ 61 Geronimo Pena .15 .05
❑ 62 Mark Whiten .15 .05
❑ 63 Rey Sanchez .15 .05
❑ 64 Willie Banks .15 .05
❑ 65 Mark Grace .50 .20
❑ 66 Randy Myers .15 .05
❑ 67 Steve Trachsel .15 .05
❑ 68 Derrick May .15 .05
❑ 69 Brett Butler .30 .10
❑ 70 Eric Karros .30 .10
❑ 71 Tim Wallach .15 .05
❑ 72 Delino DeShields .15 .05
❑ 73 Darren Dreifort .15 .05
❑ 74 Orel Hershiser .30 .10
❑ 75 Billy Ashley .15 .05
❑ 76 Sean Berry .15 .05
❑ 77 Ken Hill .15 .05
❑ 78 John Wetteland .30 .10
❑ 79 Moises Alou .30 .10
❑ 80 Cliff Floyd .30 .10
❑ 81 Marquis Grissom .30 .10
❑ 82 Larry Walker .30 .10
❑ 83 Rondell White .30 .10
❑ 84 William VanLandingham .15 .05
❑ 85 Matt Williams .30 .10
❑ 86 Rod Beck .15 .05
❑ 87 Darren Lewis .15 .05
❑ 88 Robby Thompson .15 .05
❑ 89 Darryl Strawberry .30 .10
❑ 90 Kenny Lofton .30 .10
❑ 91 Charles Nagy .15 .05
❑ 92 Sandy Alomar Jr. .15 .05
❑ 93 Mark Clark .15 .05
❑ 94 Dennis Martinez .30 .10
❑ 95 Dave Winfield .30 .10
❑ 96 Jim Thome .50 .20
❑ 97 Manny Ramirez .50 .20
❑ 98 Goose Gossage .30 .10
❑ 99 Tino Martinez .50 .20
❑ 100 Ken Griffey Jr. 1.25 .50
❑ 101 Greg Maddux ANA .75 .30
❑ 102 Randy Johnson ANA .50 .20
❑ 103 Barry Bonds ANA 1.00 .40
❑ 104 Juan Gonzalez ANA .15 .05
❑ 105 Frank Thomas ANA .50 .20
❑ 106 Matt Williams ANA .15 .05
❑ 107 Paul Molitor ANA .15 .05
❑ 108 Fred McGriff ANA .30 .10
❑ 109 Carlos Baerga ANA .15 .05
❑ 110 Ken Griffey Jr. ANA .75 .30
❑ 111 Reggie Jefferson .15 .05
❑ 112 Randy Johnson .75 .30
❑ 113 Marc Newfield .15 .05
❑ 114 Robb Nen .30 .10
❑ 115 Jeff Conine .30 .10
❑ 116 Kurt Abbott .15 .05
❑ 117 Charlie Hough .30 .10
❑ 118 Dave Weathers .15 .05
❑ 119 Juan Castillo .15 .05
❑ 120 Bret Saberhagen .30 .10
❑ 121 Rico Brogna .15 .05
❑ 122 John Franco .30 .10
❑ 123 Todd Hundley .15 .05
❑ 124 Jason Jacome .15 .05
❑ 125 Bobby Jones .15 .05
❑ 126 Bret Barberie .15 .05
❑ 127 Ben McDonald .15 .05
❑ 128 Harold Baines .30 .10
❑ 129 Jeffrey Hammonds .15 .05
❑ 130 Mike Mussina .50 .20
❑ 131 Chris Hoiles .15 .05
❑ 132 Brady Anderson .30 .10
❑ 133 Eddie Williams .15 .05
❑ 134 Andy Benes .15 .05
❑ 135 Tony Gwynn 1.00 .40
❑ 136 Bip Roberts .15 .05
❑ 137 Joey Hamilton .15 .05
❑ 138 Luis Lopez .15 .05
❑ 139 Ray McDavid .15 .05
❑ 140 Lenny Dykstra .30 .10
❑ 141 Mariano Duncan .15 .05
❑ 142 Fernando Valenzuela .30 .10
❑ 143 Bobby Munoz .15 .05
❑ 144 Kevin Stocker .15 .05
❑ 145 John Kruk .30 .10
❑ 146 Jon Lieber .15 .05
❑ 147 Zane Smith .15 .05
❑ 148 Steve Cooke .15 .05
❑ 149 Andy Van Slyke .50 .20
❑ 150 Jay Bell .30 .10
❑ 151 Carlos Garcia .15 .05
❑ 152 John Dettmer .15 .05
❑ 153 Darren Oliver .15 .05
❑ 154 Dean Palmer .30 .10
❑ 155 Otis Nixon .15 .05

Card	High	Low
❑ 156 Rusty Greer	.30	.10
❑ 157 Rick Helling	.15	.05
❑ 158 Jose Canseco	.50	.20
❑ 159 Roger Clemens	1.50	.60
❑ 160 Andre Dawson	.30	.10
❑ 161 Mo Vaughn	.30	.10
❑ 162 Aaron Sele	.15	.05
❑ 163 John Valentin	.15	.05
❑ 164 Brian R. Hunter	.15	.05
❑ 165 Bret Boone	.30	.10
❑ 166 Hector Carrasco	.15	.05
❑ 167 Pete Schourek	.15	.05
❑ 168 Willie Greene	.15	.05
❑ 169 Kevin Mitchell	.15	.05
❑ 170 Deion Sanders	.50	.20
❑ 171 John Roper	.15	.05
❑ 172 Charlie Hayes	.15	.05
❑ 173 David Nied	.15	.05
❑ 174 Ellis Burks	.30	.10
❑ 175 Dante Bichette	.30	.10
❑ 176 Marvin Freeman	.15	.05
❑ 177 Eric Young	.15	.05
❑ 178 David Cone	.30	.10
❑ 179 Greg Gagne	.15	.05
❑ 180 Bob Hamelin	.15	.05
❑ 181 Wally Joyner	.30	.10
❑ 182 Jeff Montgomery	.15	.05
❑ 183 Jose Lind	.15	.05
❑ 184 Chris Gomez	.15	.05
❑ 185 Travis Fryman	.30	.10
❑ 186 Kirk Gibson	.30	.10
❑ 187 Mike Moore	.15	.05
❑ 188 Lou Whitaker	.30	.10
❑ 189 Sean Bergman	.15	.05
❑ 190 Shane Mack	.15	.05
❑ 191 Rick Aguilera	.15	.05
❑ 192 Denny Hocking	.15	.05
❑ 193 Chuck Knoblauch	.30	.10
❑ 194 Kevin Tapani	.15	.05
❑ 195 Kent Hrbek	.30	.10
❑ 196 Ozzie Guillen	.30	.10
❑ 197 Wilson Alvarez	.15	.05
❑ 198 Tim Raines	.30	.10
❑ 199 Scott Ruffcorn	.15	.05
❑ 200 Michael Jordan	2.50	1.00
❑ 201 Robin Ventura	.30	.10
❑ 202 Jason Bere	.15	.05
❑ 203 Darrin Jackson	.15	.05
❑ 204 Russ Davis	.15	.05
❑ 205 Jimmy Key	.30	.10
❑ 206 Jack McDowell	.15	.05
❑ 207 Jim Abbott	.50	.20
❑ 208 Paul O'Neill	.50	.20
❑ 209 Bernie Williams	.50	.20
❑ 210 Don Mattingly	2.00	.75
❑ 211 Orlando Miller	.15	.05
❑ 212 Alex Gonzalez	.15	.05
❑ 213 Terrell Wade	.15	.05
❑ 214 Jose Oliva	.15	.05
❑ 215 Alex Rodriguez	2.00	.75
❑ 216 Garret Anderson	.30	.10
❑ 217 Alan Benes	.15	.05
❑ 218 Armando Benitez	.15	.05
❑ 219 Dustin Hermanson	.15	.05
❑ 220 Charles Johnson	.30	.10
❑ 221 Julian Tavarez	.15	.05
❑ 222 Jason Giambi	.50	.20
❑ 223 LaTroy Hawkins	.15	.05
❑ 224 Todd Hollandsworth	.15	.05
❑ 225 Derek Jeter	2.00	.75
❑ 226 Hideo Nomo RC	2.50	1.00
❑ 227 Tony Clark	.15	.05
❑ 228 Roger Cedeno	.15	.05
❑ 229 Scott Stahoviak	.15	.05
❑ 230 Michael Tucker	.15	.05
❑ 231 Joe Rosselli	.15	.05
❑ 232 Antonio Osuna	.15	.05
❑ 233 Bob Higginson RC	.75	.30
❑ 234 Mark Grudzielanek RC	.75	.30
❑ 235 Ray Durham	.30	.10
❑ 236 Frank Rodriguez	.15	.05
❑ 237 Quilvio Veras	.15	.05
❑ 238 Darren Bragg	.15	.05
❑ 239 Ugueth Urbina	.15	.05
❑ 240 Jason Bates	.15	.05
❑ 241 David Bell	.15	.05
❑ 242 Ron Villone	.15	.05
❑ 243 Joe Randa	.30	.10
❑ 244 Carlos Perez RC	.40	.15
❑ 245 Brad Clontz	.15	.05
❑ 246 Steve Rodriguez	.15	.05
❑ 247 Joe Vitiello	.15	.05
❑ 248 Ozzie Timmons	.15	.05
❑ 249 Rudy Pemberton	.15	.05
❑ 250 Marty Cordova	.15	.05
❑ 251 Tony Graffanino	.15	.05
❑ 252 Mark Johnson RC	.40	.15
❑ 253 Tomas Perez RC	.15	.05
❑ 254 Jimmy Hurst	.15	.05
❑ 255 Edgardo Alfonzo	.15	.05
❑ 256 Jose Malave	.15	.05
❑ 257 Brad Radke RC	.75	.30
❑ 258 Jon Nunnally	.15	.05
❑ 259 Dilson Torres RC	.15	.05
❑ 260 Esteban Loaiza	.15	.05
❑ 261 Freddy Adrian Garcia RC	.15	.05
❑ 262 Don Wengert	.15	.05
❑ 263 Robert Person RC	.40	.15
❑ 264 Tim Unroe RC	.15	.05
❑ 265 Juan Acevedo RC	.15	.05
❑ 266 Eduardo Perez	.15	.05
❑ 267 Tony Phillips	.15	.05
❑ 268 Jim Edmonds	.50	.20
❑ 269 Jorge Fabregas	.15	.05
❑ 270 Tim Salmon	.50	.20
❑ 271 Mark Langston	.15	.05
❑ 272 J.T. Snow	.30	.10
❑ 273 Phil Plantier	.15	.05
❑ 274 Derek Bell	.15	.05
❑ 275 Jeff Bagwell	.50	.20
❑ 276 Luis Gonzalez	.30	.10
❑ 277 John Hudek	.15	.05
❑ 278 Todd Stottlemyre	.15	.05
❑ 279 Mark Acre	.15	.05
❑ 280 Ruben Sierra	.30	.10
❑ 281 Mike Bordick	.15	.05
❑ 282 Ron Darling	.15	.05
❑ 283 Brent Gates	.15	.05
❑ 284 Todd Van Poppel	.15	.05
❑ 285 Paul Molitor	.30	.10
❑ 286 Ed Sprague	.15	.05
❑ 287 Juan Guzman	.15	.05
❑ 288 David Cone	.30	.10
❑ 289 Shawn Green	.30	.10
❑ 290 Marquis Grissom	.30	.10
❑ 291 Kent Mercker	.15	.05
❑ 292 Steve Avery	.15	.05
❑ 293 Chipper Jones	.75	.30
❑ 294 John Smoltz	.50	.20
❑ 295 David Justice	.30	.10
❑ 296 Ryan Klesko	.30	.10
❑ 297 Joe Oliver	.15	.05
❑ 298 Ricky Bones	.15	.05
❑ 299 John Jaha	.15	.05
❑ 300 Greg Vaughn	.15	.05
❑ 301 Dave Nilsson	.15	.05
❑ 302 Kevin Seitzer	.15	.05
❑ 303 Bernard Gilkey	.15	.05
❑ 304 Allen Battle	.15	.05
❑ 305 Ray Lankford	.30	.10
❑ 306 Tom Pagnozzi	.15	.05
❑ 307 Allen Watson	.15	.05
❑ 308 Danny Jackson	.15	.05
❑ 309 Ken Hill	.15	.05
❑ 310 Todd Zeile	.15	.05
❑ 311 Kevin Roberson	.15	.05
❑ 312 Steve Buechele	.15	.05
❑ 313 Rick Wilkins	.15	.05
❑ 314 Kevin Foster	.15	.05
❑ 315 Sammy Sosa	.75	.30
❑ 316 Howard Johnson	.15	.05
❑ 317 Greg Hansell	.15	.05
❑ 318 Pedro Astacio	.15	.05
❑ 319 Rafael Bournigal	.15	.05
❑ 320 Mike Piazza	1.25	.50
❑ 321 Ramon Martinez	.15	.05
❑ 322 Raul Mondesi	.30	.10
❑ 323 Ismael Valdes	.15	.05
❑ 324 Wil Cordero	.15	.05
❑ 325 Tony Tarasco	.15	.05
❑ 326 Roberto Kelly	.15	.05
❑ 327 Jeff Fassero	.15	.05
❑ 328 Mike Lansing	.15	.05
❑ 329 Pedro Martinez	.50	.20
❑ 330 Kirk Rueter	.15	.05
❑ 331 Glenallen Hill	.15	.05
❑ 332 Kirt Manwaring	.15	.05
❑ 333 Royce Clayton	.15	.05
❑ 334 J.R. Phillips	.15	.05
❑ 335 Barry Bonds	2.00	.75
❑ 336 Mark Portugal	.15	.05
❑ 337 Terry Mulholland	.15	.05
❑ 338 Omar Vizquel	.50	.20
❑ 339 Carlos Baerga	.15	.05
❑ 340 Albert Belle	.30	.10
❑ 341 Eddie Murray	.75	.30
❑ 342 Wayne Kirby	.15	.05
❑ 343 Chad Ogea	.15	.05
❑ 344 Tim Davis	.15	.05
❑ 345 Jay Buhner	.30	.10
❑ 346 Bobby Ayala	.15	.05
❑ 347 Mike Blowers	.15	.05
❑ 348 Dave Fleming	.15	.05
❑ 349 Edgar Martinez	.50	.20
❑ 350 Andre Dawson	.30	.10
❑ 351 Darrell Whitmore	.15	.05
❑ 352 Chuck Carr	.15	.05
❑ 353 John Burkett	.15	.05
❑ 354 Chris Hammond	.15	.05
❑ 355 Gary Sheffield	.30	.10
❑ 356 Pat Rapp	.15	.05
❑ 357 Greg Colbrunn	.15	.05
❑ 358 David Segui	.15	.05
❑ 359 Jeff Kent	.30	.10
❑ 360 Bobby Bonilla	.30	.10
❑ 361 Pete Harnisch	.15	.05
❑ 362 Ryan Thompson	.15	.05
❑ 363 Jose Vizcaino	.15	.05
❑ 364 Brett Butler	.30	.10
❑ 365 Cal Ripken	2.50	1.00
❑ 366 Rafael Palmeiro	.50	.20
❑ 367 Leo Gomez	.15	.05
❑ 368 Andy Van Slyke	.50	.20
❑ 369 Arthur Rhodes	.15	.05
❑ 370 Ken Caminiti	.30	.10
❑ 371 Steve Finley	.30	.10
❑ 372 Melvin Nieves	.15	.05
❑ 373 Andujar Cedeno	.15	.05
❑ 374 Trevor Hoffman	.30	.10
❑ 375 Fernando Valenzuela	.30	.10
❑ 376 Ricky Bottalico	.15	.05
❑ 377 Dave Hollins	.15	.05
❑ 378 Charlie Hayes	.15	.05
❑ 379 Tommy Greene	.15	.05
❑ 380 Darren Daulton	.30	.10
❑ 381 Curt Schilling	.30	.10
❑ 382 Midre Cummings	.15	.05
❑ 383 Al Martin	.15	.05
❑ 384 Jeff King	.15	.05
❑ 385 Orlando Merced	.15	.05
❑ 386 Denny Neagle	.30	.10
❑ 387 Don Slaught	.15	.05
❑ 388 Dave Clark	.15	.05
❑ 389 Kevin Gross	.15	.05
❑ 390 Will Clark	.50	.20
❑ 391 Ivan Rodriguez	.50	.20
❑ 392 Benji Gil	.15	.05
❑ 393 Jeff Frye	.15	.05
❑ 394 Kenny Rogers	.30	.10
❑ 395 Juan Gonzalez	.30	.10
❑ 396 Mike Macfarlane	.15	.05
❑ 397 Lee Tinsley	.15	.05
❑ 398 Tim Naehring	.15	.05
❑ 399 Tim Vanegmond	.15	.05
❑ 400 Mike Greenwell	.15	.05
❑ 401 Ken Ryan	.15	.05
❑ 402 John Smiley	.15	.05
❑ 403 Tim Pugh	.15	.05
❑ 404 Reggie Sanders	.30	.10
❑ 405 Barry Larkin	.50	.20
❑ 406 Hal Morris	.15	.05
❑ 407 Jose Rijo	.15	.05
❑ 408 Lance Painter	.15	.05
❑ 409 Joe Girardi	.15	.05
❑ 410 Andres Galarraga	.30	.10
❑ 411 Mike Kingery	.15	.05
❑ 412 Roberto Mejia	.15	.05
❑ 413 Walt Weiss	.15	.05

❑ 414	Bill Swift	.15	.05
❑ 415	Larry Walker	.30	.10
❑ 416	Billy Brewer	.15	.05
❑ 417	Pat Borders	.15	.05
❑ 418	Tom Gordon	.15	.05
❑ 419	Kevin Appier	.30	.10
❑ 420	Gary Gaetti	.30	.10
❑ 421	Greg Gohr	.15	.05
❑ 422	Felipe Lira	.15	.05
❑ 423	John Doherty	.15	.05
❑ 424	Chad Curtis	.15	.05
❑ 425	Cecil Fielder	.30	.10
❑ 426	Alan Trammell	.30	.10
❑ 427	David McCarty	.15	.05
❑ 428	Scott Erickson	.15	.05
❑ 429	Pat Mahomes	.15	.05
❑ 430	Kirby Puckett	.75	.30
❑ 431	Dave Stevens	.15	.05
❑ 432	Pedro Munoz	.15	.05
❑ 433	Chris Sabo	.15	.05
❑ 434	Alex Fernandez	.15	.05
❑ 435	Frank Thomas	.75	.30
❑ 436	Roberto Hernandez	.15	.05
❑ 437	Lance Johnson	.15	.05
❑ 438	Jim Abbott	.50	.20
❑ 439	John Wetteland	.30	.10
❑ 440	Melido Perez	.15	.05
❑ 441	Tony Fernandez	.15	.05
❑ 442	Pat Kelly	.15	.05
❑ 443	Mike Stanley	.15	.05
❑ 444	Danny Tartabull	.15	.05
❑ 445	Wade Boggs	.50	.20
❑ 446	Robin Yount TRIB	1.25	.50
❑ 447	Ryne Sandberg TRIB	1.25	.50
❑ 448	Nolan Ryan TRIB	3.00	1.25
❑ 449	George Brett TRIB	2.00	.75
❑ 450	Mike Schmidt TRIB	1.25	.50
❑ 451	Jim Abbott TRADE	2.00	.75
❑ 452	Danny Tartabull TRADE	1.00	.40
❑ 453	Ariel Prieto TRADE	1.00	.40
❑ 454	Scott Cooper TRADE	1.00	.40
❑ 455	Tom Henke TRADE	1.00	.40
❑ 456	Todd Zeile TRADE	1.00	.40
❑ 457	Brian McRae TRADE	1.00	.40
❑ 458	Luis Gonzalez TRADE	1.50	.60
❑ 459	Jaime Navarro TRADE	1.00	.40
❑ 460	Todd Worrell TRADE	1.00	.40
❑ 461	Roberto Kelly TRADE	1.00	.40
❑ 462	Chad Fonville TRADE	1.00	.40
❑ 463	Shane Andrews TRADE	1.00	.40
❑ 464	David Segui TRADE	1.00	.40
❑ 465	Deion Sanders TRADE	2.00	.75
❑ 466	Orel Hershiser TRADE	1.50	.60
❑ 467	Ken Hill TRADE	1.00	.40
❑ 468	Andy Benes TRADE	1.00	.40
❑ 469	Terry Pendleton TRADE	1.50	.60
❑ 470	Bobby Bonilla TRADE	1.50	.60
❑ 471	Scott Erickson TRADE	1.00	.40
❑ 472	Kevin Brown TRADE	1.50	.60
❑ 473	Glenn Dishman TRADE	1.00	.40
❑ 474	Phil Plantier TRADE	1.00	.40
❑ 475	Gregg Jefferies TRADE	1.00	.40
❑ 476	Tyler Green TRADE	1.00	.40
❑ 477	Heathcliff Slocumb TRADE	1.00	.40
❑ 478	Mark Whiten TRADE	1.00	.40
❑ 479	Mickey Tettleton TRADE	1.00	.40
❑ 480	Tim Wakefield TRADE	1.50	.60
❑ 481	Vaughn Eshelman TRADE	1.00	.40
❑ 482	Rick Aguilera TRADE	1.00	.40
❑ 483	Erik Hanson TRADE	1.00	.40
❑ 484	Willie McGee TRADE	1.50	.60
❑ 485	Troy O'Leary TRADE	1.00	.40
❑ 486	Benito Santiago TRADE	1.50	.60
❑ 487	Darren Lewis TRADE	1.00	.40
❑ 488	Dave Burba TRADE	1.00	.40
❑ 489	Ron Gant TRADE	1.50	.60
❑ 490	Bret Saberhagen TRADE	1.50	.60
❑ 491	Vinny Castilla TRADE	1.50	.60
❑ 492	Frank Rodriguez TRADE	1.00	.40
❑ 493	Andy Pettitte TRADE	2.00	.75
❑ 494	Ruben Sierra TRADE	1.50	.60
❑ 495	David Cone TRADE	1.50	.60
❑ J159	R.Clemens Jumbo AU	80.00	40.00
❑ J215	A.Rodriguez Jumbo AU	175.00	100.00
❑ P100	Ken Griffey Jr. Promo	2.00	.75

1996 Upper Deck

❑	COMPLETE SET (480)	50.00	20.00
❑	COMP.FACT.SET (510)	100.00	50.00
❑	COMPLETE SERIES 1 (240)	25.00	10.00
❑	COMPLETE SERIES 2 (240)	25.00	10.00
❑	COMMON CARD (1-480)	.30	.10
❑	COMP.UPDATE SET (30)	20.00	10.00
❑	COMMON UPDATE (481U-510U)	.50	.20
❑ 1	Cal Ripken 2131	4.00	1.50
❑ 2	Eddie Murray 3000 Hits	.50	.20
❑ 3	Mark Wohlers	.30	.10
❑ 4	David Justice	.30	.10
❑ 5	Chipper Jones	.75	.30
❑ 6	Javier Lopez	.30	.10
❑ 7	Mark Lemke	.30	.10
❑ 8	Marquis Grissom	.30	.10
❑ 9	Tom Glavine	.50	.20
❑ 10	Greg Maddux	1.25	.50
❑ 11	Manny Alexander	.30	.10
❑ 12	Curtis Goodwin	.30	.10
❑ 13	Scott Erickson	.30	.10
❑ 14	Chris Hoiles	.30	.10
❑ 15	Rafael Palmeiro	.50	.20
❑ 16	Rick Krivda	.30	.10
❑ 17	Jeff Manto	.30	.10
❑ 18	Mo Vaughn	.30	.10
❑ 19	Tim Wakefield	.30	.10
❑ 20	Roger Clemens	1.50	.60
❑ 21	Tim Naehring	.30	.10
❑ 22	Troy O'Leary	.30	.10
❑ 23	Mike Greenwell	.30	.10
❑ 24	Stan Belinda	.30	.10
❑ 25	John Valentin	.30	.10
❑ 26	J.T. Snow	.30	.10
❑ 27	Gary DiSarcina	.30	.10
❑ 28	Mark Langston	.30	.10
❑ 29	Brian Anderson	.30	.10
❑ 30	Jim Edmonds	.30	.10
❑ 31	Garret Anderson	.30	.10
❑ 32	Orlando Palmeiro	.30	.10
❑ 33	Brian McRae	.30	.10
❑ 34	Kevin Foster	.30	.10
❑ 35	Sammy Sosa	.75	.30
❑ 36	Todd Zeile	.30	.10
❑ 37	Jim Bullinger	.30	.10
❑ 38	Luis Gonzalez	.30	.10
❑ 39	Lyle Mouton	.30	.10
❑ 40	Ray Durham	.30	.10
❑ 41	Ozzie Guillen	.30	.10
❑ 42	Alex Fernandez	.30	.10
❑ 43	Brian Keyser	.30	.10
❑ 44	Robin Ventura	.30	.10
❑ 45	Reggie Sanders	.30	.10
❑ 46	Pete Schourek	.30	.10
❑ 47	John Smiley	.30	.10
❑ 48	Jeff Brantley	.30	.10
❑ 49	Thomas Howard	.30	.10
❑ 50	Bret Boone	.30	.10
❑ 51	Kevin Jarvis	.30	.10
❑ 52	Jeff Branson	.30	.10
❑ 53	Carlos Baerga	.30	.10
❑ 54	Jim Thome	.50	.20
❑ 55	Manny Ramirez	.50	.20
❑ 56	Omar Vizquel	.50	.20
❑ 57	Jose Mesa	.30	.10
❑ 58	Julian Tavarez UER	.30	.10
❑ 59	Orel Hershiser	.30	.10
❑ 60	Larry Walker	.30	.10
❑ 61	Bret Saberhagen	.30	.10
❑ 62	Vinny Castilla	.30	.10
❑ 63	Eric Young	.30	.10
❑ 64	Bryan Rekar	.30	.10
❑ 65	Andres Galarraga	.30	.10
❑ 66	Steve Reed	.30	.10
❑ 67	Chad Curtis	.30	.10
❑ 68	Bobby Higginson	.30	.10
❑ 69	Phil Nevin	.30	.10
❑ 70	Cecil Fielder	.30	.10
❑ 71	Felipe Lira	.30	.10
❑ 72	Chris Gomez	.30	.10
❑ 73	Charles Johnson	.30	.10
❑ 74	Quilvio Veras	.30	.10
❑ 75	Jeff Conine	.30	.10
❑ 76	John Burkett	.30	.10
❑ 77	Greg Colbrunn	.30	.10
❑ 78	Terry Pendleton	.30	.10
❑ 79	Shane Reynolds	.30	.10
❑ 80	Jeff Bagwell	.50	.20
❑ 81	Orlando Miller	.30	.10
❑ 82	Mike Hampton	.30	.10
❑ 83	James Mouton	.30	.10
❑ 84	Brian L. Hunter	.30	.10
❑ 85	Derek Bell	.30	.10
❑ 86	Kevin Appier	.30	.10
❑ 87	Joe Vitiello	.30	.10
❑ 88	Wally Joyner	.30	.10
❑ 89	Michael Tucker	.30	.10
❑ 90	Johnny Damon	.50	.20
❑ 91	Jon Nunnally	.30	.10
❑ 92	Jason Jacome	.30	.10
❑ 93	Chad Fonville	.30	.10
❑ 94	Chan Ho Park	.30	.10
❑ 95	Hideo Nomo	.75	.30
❑ 96	Ismael Valdes	.30	.10
❑ 97	Greg Gagne	.30	.10
❑ 98	Diamondbacks-Devil Rays	.75	.30
❑ 99	Raul Mondesi	.30	.10
❑ 100	Dave Winfield YH	.30	.10
❑ 101	Dennis Eckersley YH	.30	.10
❑ 102	Andre Dawson YH	.30	.10
❑ 103	Dennis Martinez YH	.30	.10
❑ 104	Lance Parrish YH	.30	.10
❑ 105	Eddie Murray YH	.50	.20
❑ 106	Alan Trammell YH	.30	.10
❑ 107	Lou Whitaker YH	.30	.10
❑ 108	Ozzie Smith YH	.75	.30
❑ 109	Paul Molitor YH	.30	.10
❑ 110	Rickey Henderson YH	.50	.20
❑ 111	Tim Raines YH	.30	.10
❑ 112	Harold Baines YH	.30	.10
❑ 113	Lee Smith YH	.30	.10
❑ 114	Fernando Valenzuela YH	.30	.10
❑ 115	Cal Ripken YH	1.25	.50
❑ 116	Tony Gwynn YH	.50	.20
❑ 117	Wade Boggs	.50	.20
❑ 118	Todd Hollandsworth	.30	.10
❑ 119	Dave Nilsson	.30	.10
❑ 120	Jose Valentin	.30	.10
❑ 121	Steve Sparks	.30	.10
❑ 122	Chuck Carr	.30	.10
❑ 123	John Jaha	.30	.10
❑ 124	Scott Karl	.30	.10
❑ 125	Chuck Knoblauch	.30	.10
❑ 126	Brad Radke	.30	.10
❑ 127	Pat Meares	.30	.10
❑ 128	Ron Coomer	.30	.10
❑ 129	Pedro Munoz	.30	.10
❑ 130	Kirby Puckett	.75	.30
❑ 131	David Segui	.30	.10
❑ 132	Mark Grudzielanek	.30	.10
❑ 133	Mike Lansing	.30	.10
❑ 134	Sean Berry	.30	.10
❑ 135	Rondell White	.30	.10
❑ 136	Pedro Martinez	.50	.20
❑ 137	Carl Everett	.30	.10
❑ 138	Dave Mlicki	.30	.10
❑ 139	Bill Pulsipher	.30	.10
❑ 140	Jason Isringhausen	.30	.10
❑ 141	Rico Brogna	.30	.10
❑ 142	Edgardo Alfonzo	.30	.10
❑ 143	Jeff Kent	.30	.10
❑ 144	Andy Pettitte	.50	.20
❑ 145	Mike Piazza BO	.75	.30

❑ 146 Cliff Floyd BO .30 .10
❑ 147 Jason Isringhausen BO .30 .10
❑ 148 Tim Wakefield BO .30 .10
❑ 149 Chipper Jones BO .50 .20
❑ 150 Hideo Nomo BO .50 .20
❑ 151 Mark McGwire BO 1.00 .40
❑ 152 Ron Gant BO .30 .10
❑ 153 Gary Gaetti BO .30 .10
❑ 154 Don Mattingly 2.00 .75
❑ 155 Paul O'Neill .50 .20
❑ 156 Derek Jeter 2.00 .75
❑ 157 Joe Girardi .30 .10
❑ 158 Ruben Sierra .30 .10
❑ 159 Jorge Posada .50 .20
❑ 160 Geronimo Berroa .30 .10
❑ 161 Steve Ontiveros .30 .10
❑ 162 George Williams .30 .10
❑ 163 Doug Johns .30 .10
❑ 164 Ariel Prieto .30 .10
❑ 165 Scott Brosius .30 .10
❑ 166 Mike Bordick .30 .10
❑ 167 Tyler Green .30 .10
❑ 168 Mickey Morandini .30 .10
❑ 169 Darren Daulton .30 .10
❑ 170 Gregg Jefferies .30 .10
❑ 171 Jim Eisenreich .30 .10
❑ 172 Heathcliff Slocumb .30 .10
❑ 173 Kevin Stocker .30 .10
❑ 174 Esteban Loaiza .30 .10
❑ 175 Jeff King .30 .10
❑ 176 Mark Johnson .30 .10
❑ 177 Denny Neagle .30 .10
❑ 178 Orlando Merced .30 .10
❑ 179 Carlos Garcia .30 .10
❑ 180 Brian Jordan .30 .10
❑ 181 Mike Morgan .30 .10
❑ 182 Mark Petkovsek .30 .10
❑ 183 Bernard Gilkey .30 .10
❑ 184 John Mabry .30 .10
❑ 185 Tom Henke .30 .10
❑ 186 Glenn Dishman .30 .10
❑ 187 Andy Ashby .30 .10
❑ 188 Bip Roberts .30 .10
❑ 189 Melvin Nieves .30 .10
❑ 190 Ken Caminiti .30 .10
❑ 191 Brad Ausmus .30 .10
❑ 192 Deion Sanders .50 .20
❑ 193 Jamie Brewington RC .30 .10
❑ 194 Glenallen Hill .30 .10
❑ 195 Barry Bonds 2.00 .75
❑ 196 Wm. Van Landingham .30 .10
❑ 197 Mark Carreon .30 .10
❑ 198 Royce Clayton .30 .10
❑ 199 Joey Cora .30 .10
❑ 200 Ken Griffey Jr. 1.25 .50
❑ 201 Jay Buhner .30 .10
❑ 202 Alex Rodriguez 1.50 .60
❑ 203 Norm Charlton .30 .10
❑ 204 Andy Benes .30 .10
❑ 205 Edgar Martinez .50 .20
❑ 206 Juan Gonzalez .30 .10
❑ 207 Will Clark .50 .20
❑ 208 Kevin Gross .30 .10
❑ 209 Roger Pavlik .30 .10
❑ 210 Ivan Rodriguez .50 .20
❑ 211 Rusty Greer .30 .10
❑ 212 Angel Martinez .30 .10
❑ 213 Tomas Perez .30 .10
❑ 214 Alex Gonzalez .30 .10
❑ 215 Joe Carter .30 .10
❑ 216 Shawn Green .30 .10
❑ 217 Edwin Hurtado .30 .10
❑ 218 E.Martinez/T.Pena CL .30 .10
❑ 219 C.Jones/B.Larkin CL .50 .20
❑ 220 Orel Hershiser CL .30 .10
❑ 221 Mike Devereaux CL .30 .10
❑ 222 Tom Glavine CL .30 .10
❑ 223 Karim Garcia .30 .10
❑ 224 Arquimedez Pozo .30 .10
❑ 225 Billy Wagner .30 .10
❑ 226 John Wasdin .30 .10
❑ 227 Jeff Suppan .30 .10
❑ 228 Steve Gibralter .30 .10
❑ 229 Jimmy Haynes .30 .10
❑ 230 Ruben Rivera .30 .10
❑ 231 Chris Snopek .30 .10
❑ 232 Alex Ochoa .30 .10
❑ 233 Shannon Stewart .30 .10
❑ 234 Quinton McCracken .30 .10
❑ 235 Trey Beamon .30 .10
❑ 236 Billy McMillon .30 .10
❑ 237 Steve Cox .30 .10
❑ 238 George Arias .30 .10
❑ 239 Yamil Benitez .30 .10
❑ 240 Todd Greene .30 .10
❑ 241 Jason Kendall .30 .10
❑ 242 Brooks Kieschnick .30 .10
❑ 243 Osvaldo Fernandez RC .30 .10
❑ 244 Livan Hernandez RC 1.00 .40
❑ 245 Rey Ordonez .30 .10
❑ 246 Mike Grace RC .30 .10
❑ 247 Jay Canizaro .30 .10
❑ 248 Bob Wolcott .30 .10
❑ 249 Jermaine Dye .30 .10
❑ 250 Jason Schmidt .50 .20
❑ 251 Mike Sweeney RC 1.00 .40
❑ 252 Marcus Jensen .30 .10
❑ 253 Mendy Lopez .30 .10
❑ 254 Wilton Guerrero RC .30 .10
❑ 255 Paul Wilson .30 .10
❑ 256 Edgar Renteria .30 .10
❑ 257 Richard Hidalgo .30 .10
❑ 258 Bob Abreu .75 .30
❑ 259 Robert Smith RC .30 .10
❑ 260 Sal Fasano .30 .10
❑ 261 Enrique Wilson .30 .10
❑ 262 Rich Hunter RC .30 .10
❑ 263 Sergio Nunez .30 .10
❑ 264 Dan Serafini .30 .10
❑ 265 David Doster .30 .10
❑ 266 Ryan McGuire .30 .10
❑ 267 Scott Spiezio .30 .10
❑ 268 Rafael Orellano .30 .10
❑ 269 Steve Avery .30 .10
❑ 270 Fred McGriff .50 .20
❑ 271 John Smoltz .50 .20
❑ 272 Ryan Klesko .30 .10
❑ 273 Jeff Blauser .30 .10
❑ 274 Brad Clontz .30 .10
❑ 275 Roberto Alomar .50 .20
❑ 276 B.J. Surhoff .30 .10
❑ 277 Jeffrey Hammonds .30 .10
❑ 278 Brady Anderson .30 .10
❑ 279 Bobby Bonilla .30 .10
❑ 280 Cal Ripken 2.50 1.00
❑ 281 Mike Mussina .50 .20
❑ 282 Wil Cordero .30 .10
❑ 283 Mike Stanley .30 .10
❑ 284 Aaron Sele .30 .10
❑ 285 Jose Canseco .50 .20
❑ 286 Tom Gordon .30 .10
❑ 287 Heathcliff Slocumb .30 .10
❑ 288 Lee Smith .30 .10
❑ 289 Troy Percival .30 .10
❑ 290 Tim Salmon .50 .20
❑ 291 Chuck Finley .30 .10
❑ 292 Jim Abbott .50 .20
❑ 293 Chili Davis .30 .10
❑ 294 Steve Trachsel .30 .10
❑ 295 Mark Grace .50 .20
❑ 296 Rey Sanchez .30 .10
❑ 297 Scott Servais .30 .10
❑ 298 Jaime Navarro .30 .10
❑ 299 Frank Castillo .30 .10
❑ 300 Frank Thomas .75 .30
❑ 301 Jason Bere .30 .10
❑ 302 Danny Tartabull .30 .10
❑ 303 Darren Lewis .30 .10
❑ 304 Roberto Hernandez .30 .10
❑ 305 Tony Phillips .30 .10
❑ 306 Wilson Alvarez .30 .10
❑ 307 Jose Rijo .30 .10
❑ 308 Hal Morris .30 .10
❑ 309 Mark Portugal .30 .10
❑ 310 Barry Larkin .50 .20
❑ 311 Dave Burba .30 .10
❑ 312 Eddie Taubensee .30 .10
❑ 313 Sandy Alomar Jr. .30 .10
❑ 314 Dennis Martinez .30 .10
❑ 315 Albert Belle .30 .10
❑ 316 Eddie Murray .75 .30
❑ 317 Charles Nagy .30 .10
❑ 318 Chad Ogea .30 .10
❑ 319 Kenny Lofton .30 .10
❑ 320 Dante Bichette .30 .10
❑ 321 Armando Reynoso .30 .10
❑ 322 Walt Weiss .30 .10
❑ 323 Ellis Burks .30 .10
❑ 324 Kevin Ritz .30 .10
❑ 325 Bill Swift .30 .10
❑ 326 Jason Bates .30 .10
❑ 327 Tony Clark .30 .10
❑ 328 Travis Fryman .30 .10
❑ 329 Mark Parent .30 .10
❑ 330 Alan Trammell .30 .10
❑ 331 C.J. Nitkowski .30 .10
❑ 332 Jose Lima .30 .10
❑ 333 Phil Plantier .30 .10
❑ 334 Kurt Abbott .30 .10
❑ 335 Andre Dawson .30 .10
❑ 336 Chris Hammond .30 .10
❑ 337 Robb Nen .30 .10
❑ 338 Pat Rapp .30 .10
❑ 339 Al Leiter .30 .10
❑ 340 Gary Sheffield .30 .10
❑ 341 Todd Jones .30 .10
❑ 342 Doug Drabek .30 .10
❑ 343 Greg Swindell .30 .10
❑ 344 Tony Eusebio .30 .10
❑ 345 Craig Biggio .50 .20
❑ 346 Darryl Kile .30 .10
❑ 347 Mike Macfarlane .30 .10
❑ 348 Jeff Montgomery .30 .10
❑ 349 Chris Haney .30 .10
❑ 350 Bip Roberts .30 .10
❑ 351 Tom Goodwin .30 .10
❑ 352 Mark Gubicza .30 .10
❑ 353 Joe Randa .30 .10
❑ 354 Ramon Martinez .30 .10
❑ 355 Eric Karros .30 .10
❑ 356 Delino DeShields .30 .10
❑ 357 Brett Butler .30 .10
❑ 358 Todd Worrell .30 .10
❑ 359 Mike Blowers .30 .10
❑ 360 Mike Piazza 1.25 .50
❑ 361 Ben McDonald .30 .10
❑ 362 Ricky Bones .30 .10
❑ 363 Greg Vaughn .30 .10
❑ 364 Matt Mieske .30 .10
❑ 365 Kevin Seitzer .30 .10
❑ 366 Jeff Cirillo .30 .10
❑ 367 LaTroy Hawkins .30 .10
❑ 368 Frank Rodriguez .30 .10
❑ 369 Rick Aguilera .30 .10
❑ 370 Roberto Alomar BG .30 .10
❑ 371 Albert Belle BG .30 .10
❑ 372 Wade Boggs BG .30 .10
❑ 373 Barry Bonds BG 1.00 .40
❑ 374 Roger Clemens BG .75 .30
❑ 375 Dennis Eckersley BG .30 .10
❑ 376 Ken Griffey Jr. BG .75 .30
❑ 377 Tony Gwynn BG .50 .20
❑ 378 Rickey Henderson BG .50 .20
❑ 379 Greg Maddux BG .75 .30
❑ 380 Fred McGriff BG .30 .10
❑ 381 Paul Molitor BG .30 .10
❑ 382 Eddie Murray BG .50 .20
❑ 383 Mike Piazza BG .75 .30
❑ 384 Kirby Puckett BG .50 .20
❑ 385 Cal Ripken BG 1.25 .50
❑ 386 Ozzie Smith BG .75 .30
❑ 387 Frank Thomas BG .50 .20
❑ 388 Matt Walbeck .30 .10
❑ 389 Dave Stevens .30 .10
❑ 390 Marty Cordova .30 .10
❑ 391 Darrin Fletcher .30 .10
❑ 392 Cliff Floyd .30 .10
❑ 393 Mel Rojas .30 .10
❑ 394 Shane Andrews .30 .10
❑ 395 Moises Alou .30 .10
❑ 396 Carlos Perez .30 .10
❑ 397 Jeff Fassero .30 .10
❑ 398 Bobby Jones .30 .10
❑ 399 Todd Hundley .30 .10
❑ 400 John Franco .30 .10
❑ 401 Jose Vizcaino .30 .10
❑ 402 Bernard Gilkey .30 .10
❑ 403 Pete Harnisch .30 .10

No.	Player	Price 1	Price 2
404	Pat Kelly	.30	.10
405	David Cone	.30	.10
406	Bernie Williams	.50	.20
407	John Wetteland	.30	.10
408	Scott Kamieniecki	.30	.10
409	Tim Raines	.30	.10
410	Wade Boggs	.50	.20
411	Terry Steinbach	.30	.10
412	Jason Giambi	.30	.10
413	Todd Van Poppel	.30	.10
414	Pedro Munoz	.30	.10
415	Eddie Murray SBT	.50	.20
416	Dennis Eckersley SBT	.30	.10
417	Bip Roberts SBT	.30	.10
418	Glenallen Hill SBT	.30	.10
419	John Hudek SBT	.30	.10
420	Derek Bell SBT	.30	.10
421	Larry Walker SBT	.30	.10
422	Greg Maddux SBT	.75	.30
423	Ken Caminiti SBT	.30	.10
424	Brent Gates	.30	.10
425	Mark McGwire	2.00	.75
426	Mark Whiten	.30	.10
427	Sid Fernandez	.30	.10
428	Ricky Bottalico	.30	.10
429	Mike Mimbs	.30	.10
430	Lenny Dykstra	.30	.10
431	Todd Zeile	.30	.10
432	Benito Santiago	.30	.10
433	Danny Miceli	.30	.10
434	Al Martin	.30	.10
435	Jay Bell	.30	.10
436	Charlie Hayes	.30	.10
437	Mike Kingery	.30	.10
438	Paul Wagner	.30	.10
439	Tom Pagnozzi	.30	.10
440	Ozzie Smith	1.25	.50
441	Ray Lankford	.30	.10
442	Dennis Eckersley	.30	.10
443	Ron Gant	.30	.10
444	Alan Benes	.30	.10
445	Rickey Henderson	.75	.30
446	Jody Reed	.30	.10
447	Trevor Hoffman	.30	.10
448	Andujar Cedeno	.30	.10
449	Steve Finley	.30	.10
450	Tony Gwynn	1.00	.40
451	Joey Hamilton	.30	.10
452	Mark Leiter	.30	.10
453	Rod Beck	.30	.10
454	Kirt Manwaring	.30	.10
455	Matt Williams	.30	.10
456	Robby Thompson	.30	.10
457	Shawon Dunston	.30	.10
458	Russ Davis	.30	.10
459	Paul Sorrento	.30	.10
460	Randy Johnson	.75	.30
461	Chris Bosio	.30	.10
462	Luis Sojo	.30	.10
463	Sterling Hitchcock	.30	.10
464	Benji Gil	.30	.10
465	Mickey Tettleton	.30	.10
466	Mark McLemore	.30	.10
467	Darryl Hamilton	.30	.10
468	Ken Hill	.30	.10
469	Dean Palmer	.30	.10
470	Carlos Delgado	.30	.10
471	Ed Sprague	.30	.10
472	Otis Nixon	.30	.10
473	Pat Hentgen	.30	.10
474	Juan Guzman	.30	.10
475	John Olerud	.30	.10
476	Buck Showalter CL	.30	.10
477	Bobby Cox CL	.30	.10
478	Tommy Lasorda CL	.30	.10
479	Buck Showalter CL	.30	.10
480	Sparky Anderson CL	.30	.10
481U	Randy Myers	.50	.20
482U	Kent Mercker	.50	.20
483U	David Wells	.75	.30
484U	Kevin Mitchell	.50	.20
485U	Randy Velarde	.50	.20
486U	Ryne Sandberg	4.00	1.50
487U	Doug Jones	.50	.20
488U	Terry Adams	.50	.20
489U	Kevin Tapani	.50	.20
490U	Harold Baines	.75	.30
491U	Eric Davis	.75	.30
492U	Julio Franco	.75	.30
493U	Jack McDowell	.50	.20
494U	Devon White	.75	.30
495U	Kevin Brown	.75	.30
496U	Rick Wilkins	.50	.20
497U	Sean Berry	.50	.20
498U	Keith Lockhart	.50	.20
499U	Mark Loretta	.50	.20
500U	Paul Molitor	.75	.30
501U	Roberto Kelly	.50	.20
502U	Lance Johnson	.50	.20
503U	Tino Martinez	1.25	.50
504U	Kenny Rogers	.75	.30
505U	Todd Stottlemyre	.50	.20
506U	Gary Gaetti	.75	.30
507U	Royce Clayton	.50	.20
508U	Andy Benes	.50	.20
509U	Wally Joyner	.75	.30
510U	Erik Hanson	.50	.20
P100	Ken Griffey Jr Promo	3.00	1.25

1997 Upper Deck

No.	Player	Price 1	Price 2
	COMP.MASTER SET (550)	200.00	80.00
	COMPLETE SET (490)	100.00	50.00
	COMPLETE SERIES 1 (240)	40.00	20.00
	COMPLETE SERIES 2 (250)	60.00	30.00
	COMP.SER.2 w/o GHL (240)	25.00	10.00
	COMMON (1-240/271-520)	.30	.10
	COMP.UPDATE SET (30)	80.00	40.00
	COMMON UPDATE (241-270)	1.00	.40
	1 UPD.SET VIA MAIL PER 10 SER.1 WRAPS		
	COMMON GHL (415-424)	1.50	.60
	COMP.TRADE SET (30)	20.00	8.00
	COMMON TRADE (521-550)	.50	.20
1	Jackie Robinson	.50	.20
2	Jackie Robinson	.50	.20
3	Jackie Robinson	.50	.20
4	Jackie Robinson	.50	.20
5	Jackie Robinson	.50	.20
6	Jackie Robinson	.50	.20
7	Jackie Robinson	.50	.20
8	Jackie Robinson	.50	.20
9	Jackie Robinson	.50	.20
10	Chipper Jones	.75	.30
11	Marquis Grissom	.30	.10
12	Jermaine Dye	.30	.10
13	Mark Lemke	.30	.10
14	Terrell Wade	.30	.10
15	Fred McGriff	.50	.20
16	Tom Glavine	.50	.20
17	Mark Wohlers	.30	.10
18	Randy Myers	.30	.10
19	Roberto Alomar	.50	.20
20	Cal Ripken	2.50	1.00
21	Rafael Palmeiro	.50	.20
22	Mike Mussina	.50	.20
23	Brady Anderson	.30	.10
24	Jose Canseco	.50	.20
25	Mo Vaughn	.30	.10
26	Roger Clemens	1.50	.60
27	Tim Naehring	.30	.10
28	Jeff Suppan	.30	.10
29	Troy Percival	.30	.10
30	Sammy Sosa	.75	.30
31	Amaury Telemaco	.30	.10
32	Rey Sanchez	.30	.10
33	Scott Servais	.30	.10
34	Steve Trachsel	.30	.10
35	Mark Grace	.50	.20
36	Wilson Alvarez	.30	.10
37	Harold Baines	.30	.10
38	Tony Phillips	.30	.10
39	James Baldwin	.30	.10
40	Frank Thomas UER	.75	.30
41	Lyle Mouton	.30	.10
42	Chris Snopek	.30	.10
43	Hal Morris	.30	.10
44	Eric Davis	.30	.10
45	Barry Larkin	.50	.20
46	Reggie Sanders	.30	.10
47	Pete Schourek	.30	.10
48	Lee Smith	.30	.10
49	Charles Nagy	.30	.10
50	Albert Belle	.30	.10
51	Julio Franco	.30	.10
52	Kenny Lofton	.30	.10
53	Orel Hershiser	.30	.10
54	Omar Vizquel	.50	.20
55	Eric Young	.30	.10
56	Curtis Leskanic	.30	.10
57	Quinton McCracken	.30	.10
58	Kevin Ritz	.30	.10
59	Walt Weiss	.30	.10
60	Dante Bichette	.30	.10
61	Mark Lewis	.30	.10
62	Tony Clark	.30	.10
63	Travis Fryman	.30	.10
64	John Smoltz SF	.30	.10
65	Greg Maddux SF	.75	.30
66	Tom Glavine SF	.30	.10
67	Mike Mussina SF	.30	.10
68	Andy Pettitte SF	.30	.10
69	Mariano Rivera SF	.50	.20
70	Hideo Nomo SF	.30	.10
71	Kevin Brown SF	.30	.10
72	Randy Johnson SF	.50	.20
73	Felipe Lira	.30	.10
74	Kimera Bartee	.30	.10
75	Alan Trammell	.30	.10
76	Kevin Brown	.30	.10
77	Edgar Renteria	.30	.10
78	Al Leiter	.30	.10
79	Charles Johnson	.30	.10
80	Andre Dawson	.30	.10
81	Billy Wagner	.30	.10
82	Donne Wall	.30	.10
83	Jeff Bagwell	.50	.20
84	Keith Lockhart	.30	.10
85	Jeff Montgomery	.30	.10
86	Tom Goodwin	.30	.10
87	Tim Belcher	.30	.10
88	Mike Macfarlane	.30	.10
89	Joe Randa	.30	.10
90	Brett Butler	.30	.10
91	Todd Worrell	.30	.10
92	Todd Hollandsworth	.30	.10
93	Ismael Valdes	.30	.10
94	Hideo Nomo	.75	.30
95	Mike Piazza	1.25	.50
96	Jeff Cirillo	.30	.10
97	Ricky Bones	.30	.10
98	Fernando Vina	.30	.10
99	Ben McDonald	.30	.10
100	John Jaha	.30	.10
101	Mark Loretta	.30	.10
102	Paul Molitor	.30	.10
103	Rick Aguilera	.30	.10
104	Marty Cordova	.30	.10
105	Kirby Puckett	.75	.30
106	Dan Naulty	.30	.10
107	Frank Rodriguez	.30	.10
108	Shane Andrews	.30	.10
109	Henry Rodriguez	.30	.10
110	Mark Grudzielanek	.30	.10
111	Pedro Martinez	.50	.20
112	Ugueth Urbina	.30	.10
113	David Segui	.30	.10
114	Rey Ordonez	.30	.10
115	Bernard Gilkey	.30	.10
116	Butch Huskey	.30	.10
117	Paul Wilson	.30	.10
118	Alex Ochoa	.30	.10

❑ 119 John Franco .30 .10
❑ 120 Dwight Gooden .30 .10
❑ 121 Ruben Rivera .30 .10
❑ 122 Andy Pettitte .50 .20
❑ 123 Tino Martinez .50 .20
❑ 124 Bernie Williams .50 .20
❑ 125 Wade Boggs .50 .20
❑ 126 Paul O'Neill .50 .20
❑ 127 Scott Brosius .30 .10
❑ 128 Ernie Young .30 .10
❑ 129 Doug Johns .30 .10
❑ 130 Geronimo Berroa .30 .10
❑ 131 Jason Giambi .30 .10
❑ 132 John Wasdin .30 .10
❑ 133 Jim Eisenreich .30 .10
❑ 134 Ricky Otero .30 .10
❑ 135 Ricky Bottalico .30 .10
❑ 136 Mark Langston DG .30 .10
❑ 137 Greg Maddux DG .75 .30
❑ 138 Ivan Rodriguez DG .30 .10
❑ 139 Charles Johnson DG .30 .10
❑ 140 J.T. Snow DG .30 .10
❑ 141 Mark Grace DG .30 .10
❑ 142 Roberto Alomar DG .30 .10
❑ 143 Craig Biggio DG .30 .10
❑ 144 Ken Caminiti DG .30 .10
❑ 145 Matt Williams DG .30 .10
❑ 146 Omar Vizquel DG .30 .10
❑ 147 Cal Ripken DG 1.25 .50
❑ 148 Ozzie Smith DG .75 .30
❑ 149 Rey Ordonez DG .30 .10
❑ 150 Ken Griffey Jr. DG .75 .30
❑ 151 Devon White DG .30 .10
❑ 152 Barry Bonds DG 1.00 .40
❑ 153 Kenny Lofton DG .30 .10
❑ 154 Mickey Morandini .30 .10
❑ 155 Gregg Jefferies .30 .10
❑ 156 Curt Schilling .30 .10
❑ 157 Jason Kendall .30 .10
❑ 158 Francisco Cordova .30 .10
❑ 159 Dennis Eckersley .30 .10
❑ 160 Ron Gant .30 .10
❑ 161 Ozzie Smith 1.25 .50
❑ 162 Brian Jordan .30 .10
❑ 163 John Mabry .30 .10
❑ 164 Andy Ashby .30 .10
❑ 165 Steve Finley .30 .10
❑ 166 Fernando Valenzuela .30 .10
❑ 167 Archi Cianfrocco .30 .10
❑ 168 Wally Joyner .30 .10
❑ 169 Greg Vaughn .30 .10
❑ 170 Barry Bonds 2.00 .75
❑ 171 William VanLandingham .30 .10
❑ 172 Marvin Benard .30 .10
❑ 173 Rich Aurilia .30 .10
❑ 174 Jay Canizaro .30 .10
❑ 175 Ken Griffey Jr. 1.25 .50
❑ 176 Bob Wells .30 .10
❑ 177 Jay Buhner .30 .10
❑ 178 Sterling Hitchcock .30 .10
❑ 179 Edgar Martinez .50 .20
❑ 180 Rusty Greer .30 .10
❑ 181 Dave Nilsson GI .30 .10
❑ 182 Larry Walker GI .30 .10
❑ 183 Edgar Renteria GI .30 .10
❑ 184 Rey Ordonez GI .30 .10
❑ 185 Rafael Palmeiro GI .30 .10
❑ 186 Osvaldo Fernandez GI .30 .10
❑ 187 Raul Mondesi GI .30 .10
❑ 188 Manny Ramirez GI .30 .10
❑ 189 Sammy Sosa GI .50 .20
❑ 190 Robert Eenhoorn GI .30 .10
❑ 191 Devon White GI .30 .10
❑ 192 Hideo Nomo GI .30 .10
❑ 193 Mac Suzuki GI .30 .10
❑ 194 Chan Ho Park GI .30 .10
❑ 195 Fernando Valenzuela GI .30 .10
❑ 196 Andruw Jones GI .30 .10
❑ 197 Vinny Castilla GI .30 .10
❑ 198 Dennis Martinez GI .30 .10
❑ 199 Ruben Rivera GI .30 .10
❑ 200 Juan Gonzalez GI .30 .10
❑ 201 Roberto Alomar GI .30 .10
❑ 202 Edgar Martinez GI .30 .10
❑ 203 Ivan Rodriguez GI .30 .10
❑ 204 Carlos Delgado GI .30 .10
❑ 205 Andres Galarraga GI .30 .10
❑ 206 Ozzie Guillen GI .30 .10
❑ 207 Midre Cummings GI .30 .10
❑ 208 Roger Pavlik .30 .10
❑ 209 Darren Oliver .30 .10
❑ 210 Dean Palmer .30 .10
❑ 211 Ivan Rodriguez .50 .20
❑ 212 Otis Nixon .30 .10
❑ 213 Pat Hentgen .30 .10
❑ 214 Ozzie/Dawson/Puckett HL/CL .50 .20
❑ 215 Bonds/Sheff/Brady HL/CL 1.00 .40
❑ 216 Ken Caminiti SH CL .30 .10
❑ 217 John Smoltz SH CL .30 .10
❑ 218 Eric Young SH CL .30 .10
❑ 219 Juan Gonzalez SH CL .30 .10
❑ 220 Eddie Murray SH CL .50 .20
❑ 221 Tommy Lasorda SH CL .30 .10
❑ 222 Paul Molitor SH CL .30 .10
❑ 223 Luis Castillo .30 .10
❑ 224 Justin Thompson .30 .10
❑ 225 Rocky Coppinger .30 .10
❑ 226 Jermaine Allensworth .30 .10
❑ 227 Jeff D'Amico .30 .10
❑ 228 Jamey Wright .30 .10
❑ 229 Scott Rolen .50 .20
❑ 230 Darin Erstad .30 .10
❑ 231 Marty Janzen .30 .10
❑ 232 Jacob Cruz .30 .10
❑ 233 Raul Ibanez .30 .10
❑ 234 Nomar Garciaparra 1.25 .50
❑ 235 Todd Walker .30 .10
❑ 236 Brian Giles RC 1.50 .60
❑ 237 Matt Beech .30 .10
❑ 238 Mike Cameron .30 .10
❑ 239 Jose Paniagua .30 .10
❑ 240 Andruw Jones .50 .20
❑ 241 Brant Brown UPD 1.00 .40
❑ 242 Robin Jennings UPD 1.00 .40
❑ 243 Willie Adams UPD 1.00 .40
❑ 244 Ken Caminiti UPD 1.50 .60
❑ 245 Brian Jordan UPD 1.50 .60
❑ 246 Chipper Jones UPD 4.00 1.50
❑ 247 Juan Gonzalez UPD 1.50 .60
❑ 248 Bernie Williams UPD 2.50 1.00
❑ 249 Roberto Alomar UPD 2.50 1.00
❑ 250 Bernie Williams UPD 2.50 1.00
❑ 251 David Wells UPD 1.50 .60
❑ 252 Cecil Fielder UPD 1.50 .60
❑ 253 Darryl Strawberry UPD 1.50 .60
❑ 254 Andy Pettitte UPD 2.50 1.00
❑ 255 Javier Lopez UPD 1.50 .60
❑ 256 Gary Gaetti UPD 1.50 .60
❑ 257 Ron Gant UPD 1.50 .60
❑ 258 Brian Jordan UPD 1.50 .60
❑ 259 John Smoltz UPD 2.50 1.00
❑ 260 Greg Maddux UPD 8.00 3.00
❑ 261 Tom Glavine UPD 2.50 1.00
❑ 262 Andruw Jones UPD 2.50 1.00
❑ 263 Greg Maddux UPD 8.00 3.00
❑ 264 David Cone UPD 1.50 .60
❑ 265 Jim Leyritz UPD 1.00 .40
❑ 266 Andy Pettitte UPD 2.50 1.00
❑ 267 John Wetteland UPD 1.50 .60
❑ 268 Dario Veras UPD 1.00 .40
❑ 269 Neifi Perez UPD 1.00 .40
❑ 270 Bill Mueller UPD 4.00 1.50
❑ 271 Vladimir Guerrero .75 .30
❑ 272 Dmitri Young .30 .10
❑ 273 Nerio Rodriguez RC .30 .10
❑ 274 Kevin Orie .30 .10
❑ 275 Felipe Crespo .30 .10
❑ 276 Danny Graves .30 .10
❑ 277 Rod Myers .30 .10
❑ 278 Felix Heredia RC .30 .10
❑ 279 Ralph Milliard .30 .10
❑ 280 Greg Norton .30 .10
❑ 281 Derek Wallace .30 .10
❑ 282 Trot Nixon .30 .10
❑ 283 Bobby Chouinard .30 .10
❑ 284 Jay Witasick .30 .10
❑ 285 Travis Miller .30 .10
❑ 286 Brian Bevil .30 .10
❑ 287 Bobby Estalella .30 .10
❑ 288 Steve Soderstrom .30 .10
❑ 289 Mark Langston .30 .10
❑ 290 Tim Salmon .50 .20
❑ 291 Jim Edmonds .30 .10
❑ 292 Garret Anderson .30 .10
❑ 293 George Arias .30 .10
❑ 294 Gary DiSarcina .30 .10
❑ 295 Chuck Finley .30 .10
❑ 296 Todd Greene .30 .10
❑ 297 Randy Velarde .30 .10
❑ 298 David Justice .30 .10
❑ 299 Ryan Klesko .30 .10
❑ 300 John Smoltz .50 .20
❑ 301 Javier Lopez .30 .10
❑ 302 Greg Maddux 1.25 .50
❑ 303 Denny Neagle .30 .10
❑ 304 B.J. Surhoff .30 .10
❑ 305 Chris Hoiles .30 .10
❑ 306 Eric Davis .30 .10
❑ 307 Scott Erickson .30 .10
❑ 308 Mike Bordick .30 .10
❑ 309 John Valentin .30 .10
❑ 310 Heathcliff Slocumb .30 .10
❑ 311 Tom Gordon .30 .10
❑ 312 Mike Stanley .30 .10
❑ 313 Reggie Jefferson .30 .10
❑ 314 Darren Bragg .30 .10
❑ 315 Troy O'Leary .30 .10
❑ 316 John Mabry SH CL .30 .10
❑ 317 Mark Whiten SH CL .30 .10
❑ 318 Edgar Martinez SH CL .30 .10
❑ 319 Alex Rodriguez SH CL .75 .30
❑ 320 Mark McGwire SH CL 1.00 .40
❑ 321 Hideo Nomo SH CL .30 .10
❑ 322 Todd Hundley SH CL .30 .10
❑ 323 Barry Bonds SH CL 1.00 .40
❑ 324 Andruw Jones SH CL .30 .10
❑ 325 Ryne Sandberg 1.25 .50
❑ 326 Brian McRae .30 .10
❑ 327 Frank Castillo .30 .10
❑ 328 Shawon Dunston .30 .10
❑ 329 Ray Durham .30 .10
❑ 330 Robin Ventura .30 .10
❑ 331 Ozzie Guillen .30 .10
❑ 332 Roberto Hernandez .30 .10
❑ 333 Albert Belle .30 .10
❑ 334 Dave Martinez .30 .10
❑ 335 Willie Greene .30 .10
❑ 336 Jeff Brantley .30 .10
❑ 337 Kevin Jarvis .30 .10
❑ 338 John Smiley .30 .10
❑ 339 Eddie Taubensee .30 .10
❑ 340 Bret Boone .30 .10
❑ 341 Kevin Seitzer .30 .10
❑ 342 Jack McDowell .30 .10
❑ 343 Sandy Alomar Jr. .30 .10
❑ 344 Chad Curtis .30 .10
❑ 345 Manny Ramirez .50 .20
❑ 346 Chad Ogea .30 .10
❑ 347 Jim Thome .50 .20
❑ 348 Mark Thompson .30 .10
❑ 349 Ellis Burks .30 .10
❑ 350 Andres Galarraga .30 .10
❑ 351 Vinny Castilla .30 .10
❑ 352 Kirt Manwaring .30 .10
❑ 353 Larry Walker .30 .10
❑ 354 Omar Olivares .30 .10
❑ 355 Bobby Higginson .30 .10
❑ 356 Melvin Nieves .30 .10
❑ 357 Brian Johnson .30 .10
❑ 358 Devon White .30 .10
❑ 359 Jeff Conine .30 .10
❑ 360 Gary Sheffield .30 .10
❑ 361 Robb Nen .30 .10
❑ 362 Mike Hampton .30 .10
❑ 363 Bob Abreu .50 .20
❑ 364 Luis Gonzalez .30 .10
❑ 365 Derek Bell .30 .10
❑ 366 Sean Berry .30 .10
❑ 367 Craig Biggio .50 .20
❑ 368 Darryl Kile .30 .10
❑ 369 Shane Reynolds .30 .10
❑ 370 Jeff Bagwell CF .30 .10
❑ 371 Ron Gant CF .30 .10
❑ 372 Andy Benes CF .30 .10
❑ 373 Gary Gaetti CF .30 .10
❑ 374 Ramon Martinez CF .30 .10
❑ 375 Raul Mondesi CF .30 .10
❑ 376 Steve Finley CF .30 .10

❑ 377 Ken Caminiti CF .30 .10
❑ 378 Tony Gwynn CF .50 .20
❑ 379 Dario Veras RC .30 .10
❑ 380 Andy Pettitte CF .30 .10
❑ 381 Ruben Rivera CF .30 .10
❑ 382 David Cone CF .30 .10
❑ 383 Roberto Alomar CF .30 .10
❑ 384 Edgar Martinez CF .30 .10
❑ 385 Ken Griffey Jr. CF .75 .30
❑ 386 Mark McGwire CF 1.00 .40
❑ 387 Rusty Greer CF .30 .10
❑ 388 Jose Rosado .30 .10
❑ 389 Kevin Appier .30 .10
❑ 390 Johnny Damon .50 .20
❑ 391 Jose Offerman .30 .10
❑ 392 Michael Tucker .30 .10
❑ 393 Craig Paquette .30 .10
❑ 394 Bip Roberts .30 .10
❑ 395 Ramon Martinez .30 .10
❑ 396 Greg Gagne .30 .10
❑ 397 Chan Ho Park .30 .10
❑ 398 Karim Garcia .30 .10
❑ 399 Wilton Guerrero .30 .10
❑ 400 Eric Karros .30 .10
❑ 401 Raul Mondesi .30 .10
❑ 402 Matt Mieske .30 .10
❑ 403 Mike Fetters .30 .10
❑ 404 Dave Nilsson .30 .10
❑ 405 Jose Valentin .30 .10
❑ 406 Scott Karl .30 .10
❑ 407 Marc Newfield .30 .10
❑ 408 Cal Eldred .30 .10
❑ 409 Rich Becker .30 .10
❑ 410 Terry Steinbach .30 .10
❑ 411 Chuck Knoblauch .30 .10
❑ 412 Pat Meares .30 .10
❑ 413 Brad Radke .30 .10
❑ 414 Kirby Puckett UER .75 .30
❑ 415 Andruw Jones GHL SP 1.50 .60
❑ 416 Chipper Jones GHL SP 2.50 1.00
❑ 417 Mo Vaughn GHL SP 1.50 .60
❑ 418 Frank Thomas GHL SP 2.50 1.00
❑ 419 Albert Belle GHL SP 1.50 .60
❑ 420 Mark McGwire GHL SP 8.00 3.00
❑ 421 Derek Jeter GHL SP 8.00 3.00
❑ 422 Alex Rodriguez GHL SP 5.00 2.00
❑ 423 Juan Gonzalez GHL SP 1.50 .60
❑ 424 Ken Griffey Jr. GHL SP 5.00 2.00
❑ 425 Rondell White .30 .10
❑ 426 Darrin Fletcher .30 .10
❑ 427 Cliff Floyd .30 .10
❑ 428 Mike Lansing .30 .10
❑ 429 F.P. Santangelo .30 .10
❑ 430 Todd Hundley .30 .10
❑ 431 Mark Clark .30 .10
❑ 432 Pete Harnisch .30 .10
❑ 433 Jason Isringhausen .30 .10
❑ 434 Bobby Jones .30 .10
❑ 435 Lance Johnson .30 .10
❑ 436 Carlos Baerga .30 .10
❑ 437 Mariano Duncan .30 .10
❑ 438 David Cone .30 .10
❑ 439 Mariano Rivera .75 .30
❑ 440 Derek Jeter 2.00 .75
❑ 441 Joe Girardi .30 .10
❑ 442 Charlie Hayes .30 .10
❑ 443 Tim Raines .30 .10
❑ 444 Darryl Strawberry .30 .10
❑ 445 Cecil Fielder .30 .10
❑ 446 Ariel Prieto .30 .10
❑ 447 Tony Batista .30 .10
❑ 448 Brent Gates .30 .10
❑ 449 Scott Spiezio .30 .10
❑ 450 Mark McGwire 2.00 .75
❑ 451 Don Wengert .30 .10
❑ 452 Mike Lieberthal .30 .10
❑ 453 Lenny Dykstra .30 .10
❑ 454 Rex Hudler .30 .10
❑ 455 Darren Daulton .30 .10
❑ 456 Kevin Stocker .30 .10
❑ 457 Trey Beamon .30 .10
❑ 458 Midre Cummings .30 .10
❑ 459 Mark Johnson .30 .10
❑ 460 Al Martin .30 .10
❑ 461 Kevin Elster .30 .10
❑ 462 Jon Lieber .30 .10
❑ 463 Jason Schmidt .30 .10
❑ 464 Paul Wagner .30 .10
❑ 465 Andy Benes .30 .10
❑ 466 Alan Benes .30 .10
❑ 467 Royce Clayton .30 .10
❑ 468 Gary Gaetti .30 .10
❑ 469 Curt Lyons RC .30 .10
❑ 470 Eugene Kingsale DD .30 .10
❑ 471 Damian Jackson DD .30 .10
❑ 472 Wendell Magee DD .30 .10
❑ 473 Kevin L. Brown DD .30 .10
❑ 474 Raul Casanova DD .30 .10
❑ 475 Ramiro Mendoza RC .30 .10
❑ 476 Todd Dunn DD .30 .10
❑ 477 Chad Mottola DD .30 .10
❑ 478 Andy Larkin DD .30 .10
❑ 479 Jaime Bluma DD .30 .10
❑ 480 Mac Suzuki DD .30 .10
❑ 481 Brian Banks DD .30 .10
❑ 482 Desi Wilson DD .30 .10
❑ 483 Einar Diaz DD .30 .10
❑ 484 Tom Pagnozzi .30 .10
❑ 485 Ray Lankford .30 .10
❑ 486 Todd Stottlemyre .30 .10
❑ 487 Donovan Osborne .30 .10
❑ 488 Trevor Hoffman .30 .10
❑ 489 Chris Gomez .30 .10
❑ 490 Ken Caminiti .30 .10
❑ 491 John Flaherty .30 .10
❑ 492 Tony Gwynn 1.00 .40
❑ 493 Joey Hamilton .30 .10
❑ 494 Rickey Henderson .75 .30
❑ 495 Glenallen Hill .30 .10
❑ 496 Rod Beck .30 .10
❑ 497 Osvaldo Fernandez .30 .10
❑ 498 Rick Wilkins .30 .10
❑ 499 Joey Cora .30 .10
❑ 500 Alex Rodriguez 1.25 .50
❑ 501 Randy Johnson .75 .30
❑ 502 Paul Sorrento .30 .10
❑ 503 Dan Wilson .30 .10
❑ 504 Jamie Moyer .30 .10
❑ 505 Will Clark .50 .20
❑ 506 Mickey Tettleton .30 .10
❑ 507 John Burkett .30 .10
❑ 508 Ken Hill .30 .10
❑ 509 Mark McLemore .30 .10
❑ 510 Juan Gonzalez .30 .10
❑ 511 Bobby Witt .30 .10
❑ 512 Carlos Delgado .30 .10
❑ 513 Alex Gonzalez .30 .10
❑ 514 Shawn Green .30 .10
❑ 515 Joe Carter .30 .10
❑ 516 Juan Guzman .30 .10
❑ 517 Charlie O'Brien .30 .10
❑ 518 Ed Sprague .30 .10
❑ 519 Mike Timlin .30 .10
❑ 520 Roger Clemens 1.50 .60
❑ 521 Eddie Murray TRADE 2.00 .75
❑ 522 Jason Dickson TRADE .50 .20
❑ 523 Jim Leyritz TRADE .50 .20
❑ 524 Michael Tucker TRADE .50 .20
❑ 525 Kenny Lofton TRADE .75 .30
❑ 526 Jimmy Key TRADE .75 .30
❑ 527 Mel Rojas TRADE .50 .20
❑ 528 Deion Sanders TRADE 1.25 .50
❑ 529 Bartolo Colon TRADE .75 .30
❑ 530 Matt Williams TRADE .75 .30
❑ 531 Marquis Grissom TRADE .75 .30
❑ 532 David Justice TRADE .75 .30
❑ 533 Bubba Trammell TRADE .75 .30
❑ 534 Moises Alou TRADE .75 .30
❑ 535 Bobby Bonilla TRADE .75 .30
❑ 536 Alex Fernandez TRADE .50 .20
❑ 537 Jay Bell TRADE .75 .30
❑ 538 Chili Davis TRADE .75 .30
❑ 539 Jeff King TRADE .50 .20
❑ 540 Todd Zeile TRADE .50 .20
❑ 541 John Olerud TRADE .75 .30
❑ 542 Jose Guillen TRADE .75 .30
❑ 543 Derrek Lee TRADE 1.25 .50
❑ 544 Dante Powell TRADE .50 .20
❑ 545 J.T. Snow TRADE .75 .30
❑ 546 Jeff Kent TRADE .75 .30
❑ 547 Jose Cruz Jr. TRADE .75 .30
❑ 548 John Wetteland TRADE .75 .30
❑ 549 Orlando Merced TRADE .50 .20
❑ 550 Hideki Irabu TRADE .75 .30

1998 Upper Deck

❑ COMPLETE SET (751) 200.00 80.00
❑ COMPLETE SERIES 1 (270) 40.00 15.00
❑ COMPLETE SERIES 2 (270) 40.00 15.00
❑ COMPLETE SERIES 3 (211) 120.00 50.00
❑ COMMON (1-600/631-750) .30 .10
❑ COMMON EP (601-630) 2.00 .75
❑ EP SER.2 ODDS APPROXIMATELY 1:4
❑ 1 Tino Martinez HIST .30 .10
❑ 2 Jimmy Key HIST .30 .10
❑ 3 Jay Buhner HIST .30 .10
❑ 4 Mark Gardner HIST .30 .10
❑ 5 Greg Maddux HIST .75 .30
❑ 6 Pedro Martinez HIST .50 .20
❑ 7 Hideo Nomo HIST .50 .20
❑ 8 Sammy Sosa HIST .50 .20
❑ 9 Mark McGwire GHL 1.00 .40
❑ 10 Ken Griffey Jr. GHL .75 .30
❑ 11 Larry Walker GHL .30 .10
❑ 12 Tino Martinez GHL .30 .10
❑ 13 Mike Piazza GHL .75 .30
❑ 14 Jose Cruz Jr. GHL .30 .10
❑ 15 Tony Gwynn GHL .50 .20
❑ 16 Greg Maddux GHL .75 .30
❑ 17 Roger Clemens GHL .75 .30
❑ 18 Alex Rodriguez GHL .75 .30
❑ 19 Shigetoshi Hasegawa .30 .10
❑ 20 Eddie Murray .75 .30
❑ 21 Jason Dickson .30 .10
❑ 22 Darin Erstad .30 .10
❑ 23 Chuck Finley .30 .10
❑ 24 Dave Hollins .30 .10
❑ 25 Garret Anderson .30 .10
❑ 26 Michael Tucker .30 .10
❑ 27 Kenny Lofton .30 .10
❑ 28 Javier Lopez .30 .10
❑ 29 Fred McGriff .50 .20
❑ 30 Greg Maddux 1.25 .50
❑ 31 Jeff Blauser .30 .10
❑ 32 John Smoltz .50 .20
❑ 33 Mark Wohlers .30 .10
❑ 34 Scott Erickson .30 .10
❑ 35 Jimmy Key .30 .10
❑ 36 Harold Baines .30 .10
❑ 37 Randy Myers .30 .10
❑ 38 B.J. Surhoff .30 .10
❑ 39 Eric Davis .30 .10
❑ 40 Rafael Palmeiro .50 .20
❑ 41 Jeffrey Hammonds .30 .10
❑ 42 Mo Vaughn .30 .10
❑ 43 Tom Gordon .30 .10
❑ 44 Tim Naehring .30 .10
❑ 45 Darren Bragg .30 .10
❑ 46 Aaron Sele .30 .10
❑ 47 Troy O'Leary .30 .10
❑ 48 John Valentin .30 .10
❑ 49 Doug Glanville .30 .10
❑ 50 Ryne Sandberg 1.25 .50
❑ 51 Steve Trachsel .30 .10
❑ 52 Mark Grace .50 .20
❑ 53 Kevin Foster .30 .10
❑ 54 Kevin Tapani .30 .10
❑ 55 Kevin Orie .30 .10
❑ 56 Lyle Mouton .30 .10
❑ 57 Ray Durham .30 .10

❑ 58 Jaime Navarro .30 .10
❑ 59 Mike Cameron .30 .10
❑ 60 Albert Belle .30 .10
❑ 61 Doug Drabek .30 .10
❑ 62 Chris Snopek .30 .10
❑ 63 Eddie Taubensee .30 .10
❑ 64 Terry Pendleton .30 .10
❑ 65 Barry Larkin .50 .20
❑ 66 Willie Greene .30 .10
❑ 67 Deion Sanders .50 .20
❑ 68 Pokey Reese .30 .10
❑ 69 Jeff Shaw .30 .10
❑ 70 Jim Thome .50 .20
❑ 71 Orel Hershiser .30 .10
❑ 72 Omar Vizquel .50 .20
❑ 73 Brian Giles .30 .10
❑ 74 David Justice .30 .10
❑ 75 Bartolo Colon .30 .10
❑ 76 Sandy Alomar Jr. .30 .10
❑ 77 Neifi Perez .30 .10
❑ 78 Dante Bichette .30 .10
❑ 79 Vinny Castilla .30 .10
❑ 80 Eric Young .30 .10
❑ 81 Quinton McCracken .30 .10
❑ 82 Jamey Wright .30 .10
❑ 83 John Thomson .30 .10
❑ 84 Damion Easley .30 .10
❑ 85 Justin Thompson .30 .10
❑ 86 Willie Blair .30 .10
❑ 87 Raul Casanova .30 .10
❑ 88 Bobby Higginson .30 .10
❑ 89 Bubba Trammell .30 .10
❑ 90 Tony Clark .30 .10
❑ 91 Livan Hernandez .30 .10
❑ 92 Charles Johnson .30 .10
❑ 93 Edgar Renteria .30 .10
❑ 94 Alex Fernandez .30 .10
❑ 95 Gary Sheffield .30 .10
❑ 96 Moises Alou .30 .10
❑ 97 Tony Saunders .30 .10
❑ 98 Robb Nen .30 .10
❑ 99 Darryl Kile .30 .10
❑ 100 Craig Biggio .50 .20
❑ 101 Chris Holt .30 .10
❑ 102 Bob Abreu .30 .10
❑ 103 Luis Gonzalez .30 .10
❑ 104 Billy Wagner .30 .10
❑ 105 Brad Ausmus .30 .10
❑ 106 Chili Davis .30 .10
❑ 107 Tim Belcher .30 .10
❑ 108 Dean Palmer .30 .10
❑ 109 Jeff King .30 .10
❑ 110 Jose Rosado .30 .10
❑ 111 Mike Macfarlane .30 .10
❑ 112 Jay Bell .30 .10
❑ 113 Todd Worrell .30 .10
❑ 114 Chan Ho Park .30 .10
❑ 115 Raul Mondesi .30 .10
❑ 116 Brett Butler .30 .10
❑ 117 Greg Gagne .30 .10
❑ 118 Hideo Nomo .75 .30
❑ 119 Todd Zeile .30 .10
❑ 120 Eric Karros .30 .10
❑ 121 Cal Eldred .30 .10
❑ 122 Jeff D'Amico .30 .10
❑ 123 Antone Williamson .30 .10
❑ 124 Doug Jones .30 .10
❑ 125 Dave Nilsson .30 .10
❑ 126 Gerald Williams .30 .10
❑ 127 Fernando Vina .30 .10
❑ 128 Ron Coomer .30 .10
❑ 129 Matt Lawton .30 .10
❑ 130 Paul Molitor .30 .10
❑ 131 Todd Walker .30 .10
❑ 132 Rick Aguilera .30 .10
❑ 133 Brad Radke .30 .10
❑ 134 Bob Tewksbury .30 .10
❑ 135 Vladimir Guerrero .75 .30
❑ 136 Tony Gwynn DG .50 .20
❑ 137 Roger Clemens DG .75 .30
❑ 138 Dennis Eckersley DG .30 .10
❑ 139 Brady Anderson DG .30 .10
❑ 140 Ken Griffey Jr. DG .75 .30
❑ 141 Derek Jeter DG 1.00 .40
❑ 142 Ken Caminiti DG .30 .10
❑ 143 Frank Thomas DG .50 .20
❑ 144 Barry Bonds DG 1.00 .40
❑ 145 Cal Ripken DG 1.25 .50
❑ 146 Alex Rodriguez DG .75 .30
❑ 147 Greg Maddux DG .75 .30
❑ 148 Kenny Lofton DG .30 .10
❑ 149 Mike Piazza DG .75 .30
❑ 150 Mark McGwire DG 1.00 .40
❑ 151 Andruw Jones DG .30 .10
❑ 152 Rusty Greer DG .30 .10
❑ 153 F.P. Santangelo DG .30 .10
❑ 154 Mike Lansing .30 .10
❑ 155 Lee Smith .30 .10
❑ 156 Carlos Perez .30 .10
❑ 157 Pedro Martinez .50 .20
❑ 158 Ryan McGuire .30 .10
❑ 159 F.P. Santangelo .30 .10
❑ 160 Rondell White .30 .10
❑ 161 Takashi Kashiwada RC .40 .15
❑ 162 Butch Huskey .30 .10
❑ 163 Edgardo Alfonzo .30 .10
❑ 164 John Franco .30 .10
❑ 165 Todd Hundley .30 .10
❑ 166 Rey Ordonez .30 .10
❑ 167 Armando Reynoso .30 .10
❑ 168 John Olerud .30 .10
❑ 169 Bernie Williams .50 .20
❑ 170 Andy Pettitte .50 .20
❑ 171 Wade Boggs .50 .20
❑ 172 Paul O'Neill .50 .20
❑ 173 Cecil Fielder .30 .10
❑ 174 Charlie Hayes .30 .10
❑ 175 David Cone .30 .10
❑ 176 Hideki Irabu .30 .10
❑ 177 Mark Bellhorn .30 .10
❑ 178 Steve Karsay .30 .10
❑ 179 Damon Mashore .30 .10
❑ 180 Jason McDonald .30 .10
❑ 181 Scott Spiezio .30 .10
❑ 182 Ariel Prieto .30 .10
❑ 183 Jason Giambi .30 .10
❑ 184 Wendell Magee .30 .10
❑ 185 Rico Brogna .30 .10
❑ 186 Garrett Stephenson .30 .10
❑ 187 Wayne Gomes .30 .10
❑ 188 Ricky Bottalico .30 .10
❑ 189 Mickey Morandini .30 .10
❑ 190 Mike Lieberthal .30 .10
❑ 191 Kevin Polcovich .30 .10
❑ 192 Francisco Cordova .30 .10
❑ 193 Kevin Young .30 .10
❑ 194 Jon Lieber .30 .10
❑ 195 Kevin Elster .30 .10
❑ 196 Tony Womack .30 .10
❑ 197 Lou Collier .30 .10
❑ 198 Mike Difelice RC .40 .15
❑ 199 Gary Gaetti .30 .10
❑ 200 Dennis Eckersley .30 .10
❑ 201 Alan Benes .30 .10
❑ 202 Willie McGee .30 .10
❑ 203 Ron Gant .30 .10
❑ 204 Fernando Valenzuela .30 .10
❑ 205 Mark McGwire 2.00 .75
❑ 206 Archi Cianfrocco .30 .10
❑ 207 Andy Ashby .30 .10
❑ 208 Steve Finley .30 .10
❑ 209 Quilvio Veras .30 .10
❑ 210 Ken Caminiti .30 .10
❑ 211 Rickey Henderson .75 .30
❑ 212 Joey Hamilton .30 .10
❑ 213 Derrek Lee .50 .20
❑ 214 Bill Mueller .30 .10
❑ 215 Shawn Estes .30 .10
❑ 216 J.T. Snow .30 .10
❑ 217 Mark Gardner .30 .10
❑ 218 Terry Mulholland .30 .10
❑ 219 Dante Powell .30 .10
❑ 220 Jeff Kent .30 .10
❑ 221 Jamie Moyer .30 .10
❑ 222 Joey Cora .30 .10
❑ 223 Jeff Fassero .30 .10
❑ 224 Dennis Martinez .30 .10
❑ 225 Ken Griffey Jr. 1.25 .50
❑ 226 Edgar Martinez .50 .20
❑ 227 Russ Davis .30 .10
❑ 228 Dan Wilson .30 .10
❑ 229 Will Clark .50 .20
❑ 230 Ivan Rodriguez .50 .20
❑ 231 Benji Gil .30 .10
❑ 232 Lee Stevens .30 .10
❑ 233 Mickey Tettleton .30 .10
❑ 234 Julio Santana .30 .10
❑ 235 Rusty Greer .30 .10
❑ 236 Bobby Witt .30 .10
❑ 237 Ed Sprague .30 .10
❑ 238 Pat Hentgen .30 .10
❑ 239 Kelvim Escobar .30 .10
❑ 240 Joe Carter .30 .10
❑ 241 Carlos Delgado .30 .10
❑ 242 Shannon Stewart .30 .10
❑ 243 Benito Santiago .30 .10
❑ 244 Tino Martinez SH .30 .10
❑ 245 Ken Griffey Jr. SH .75 .30
❑ 246 Kevin Brown SH .30 .10
❑ 247 Ryne Sandberg SH .50 .20
❑ 248 Mo Vaughn SH .30 .10
❑ 249 Darryl Hamilton SH .30 .10
❑ 250 Randy Johnson SH .50 .20
❑ 251 Steve Finley SH .30 .10
❑ 252 Bobby Higginson SH .30 .10
❑ 253 Brett Tomko .30 .10
❑ 254 Mark Kotsay .30 .10
❑ 255 Jose Guillen .30 .10
❑ 256 Eli Marrero .30 .10
❑ 257 Dennis Reyes .30 .10
❑ 258 Richie Sexson .30 .10
❑ 259 Pat Cline .30 .10
❑ 260 Todd Helton .50 .20
❑ 261 Juan Melo .30 .10
❑ 262 Matt Morris .30 .10
❑ 263 Jeremi Gonzalez .30 .10
❑ 264 Jeff Abbott .30 .10
❑ 265 Aaron Boone .30 .10
❑ 266 Todd Dunwoody .30 .10
❑ 267 Jaret Wright .30 .10
❑ 268 Derrick Gibson .30 .10
❑ 269 Mario Valdez .30 .10
❑ 270 Fernando Tatis .30 .10
❑ 271 Craig Counsell .30 .10
❑ 272 Brad Rigby .30 .10
❑ 273 Danny Clyburn .30 .10
❑ 274 Brian Rose .30 .10
❑ 275 Miguel Tejada .75 .30
❑ 276 Jason Varitek .75 .30
❑ 277 Dave Dellucci RC .60 .25
❑ 278 Michael Coleman .30 .10
❑ 279 Adam Riggs .30 .10
❑ 280 Ben Grieve .30 .10
❑ 281 Brad Fullmer .30 .10
❑ 282 Ken Cloude .30 .10
❑ 283 Tom Evans .30 .10
❑ 284 Kevin Millwood RC 1.00 .40
❑ 285 Paul Konerko .30 .10
❑ 286 Juan Encarnacion .30 .10
❑ 287 Chris Carpenter .30 .10
❑ 288 Tom Fordham .30 .10
❑ 289 Gary DiSarcina .30 .10
❑ 290 Tim Salmon .50 .20
❑ 291 Troy Percival .30 .10
❑ 292 Todd Greene .30 .10
❑ 293 Ken Hill .30 .10
❑ 294 Dennis Springer .30 .10
❑ 295 Jim Edmonds .30 .10
❑ 296 Allen Watson .30 .10
❑ 297 Brian Anderson .30 .10
❑ 298 Keith Lockhart .30 .10
❑ 299 Tom Glavine .50 .20
❑ 300 Chipper Jones .75 .30
❑ 301 Randall Simon .30 .10
❑ 302 Mark Lemke .30 .10
❑ 303 Ryan Klesko .30 .10
❑ 304 Denny Neagle .30 .10
❑ 305 Andruw Jones .50 .20
❑ 306 Mike Mussina .50 .20
❑ 307 Brady Anderson .30 .10
❑ 308 Chris Hoiles .30 .10
❑ 309 Mike Bordick .30 .10
❑ 310 Cal Ripken 2.50 1.00
❑ 311 Geronimo Berroa .30 .10
❑ 312 Armando Benitez .30 .10
❑ 313 Roberto Alomar .50 .20
❑ 314 Tim Wakefield .30 .10
❑ 315 Reggie Jefferson .30 .10

❑ 316 Jeff Frye .30 .10
❑ 317 Scott Hatteberg .30 .10
❑ 318 Steve Avery .30 .10
❑ 319 Robinson Checo .30 .10
❑ 320 Nomar Garciaparra 1.25 .50
❑ 321 Lance Johnson .30 .10
❑ 322 Tyler Houston .30 .10
❑ 323 Mark Clark .30 .10
❑ 324 Terry Adams .30 .10
❑ 325 Sammy Sosa .75 .30
❑ 326 Scott Servais .30 .10
❑ 327 Manny Alexander .30 .10
❑ 328 Norberto Martin .30 .10
❑ 329 Scott Eyre .30 .10
❑ 330 Frank Thomas .75 .30
❑ 331 Robin Ventura .30 .10
❑ 332 Matt Karchner .30 .10
❑ 333 Keith Foulke .30 .10
❑ 334 James Baldwin .30 .10
❑ 335 Chris Stynes .30 .10
❑ 336 Bret Boone .30 .10
❑ 337 Jon Nunnally .30 .10
❑ 338 Dave Burba .30 .10
❑ 339 Eduardo Perez .30 .10
❑ 340 Reggie Sanders .30 .10
❑ 341 Mike Remlinger .30 .10
❑ 342 Pat Watkins .30 .10
❑ 343 Chad Ogea .30 .10
❑ 344 John Smiley .30 .10
❑ 345 Kenny Lofton .30 .10
❑ 346 Jose Mesa .30 .10
❑ 347 Charles Nagy .30 .10
❑ 348 Enrique Wilson .30 .10
❑ 349 Bruce Aven .30 .10
❑ 350 Manny Ramirez .50 .20
❑ 351 Jerry DiPoto .30 .10
❑ 352 Ellis Burks .30 .10
❑ 353 Kirt Manwaring .30 .10
❑ 354 Vinny Castilla .30 .10
❑ 355 Larry Walker .30 .10
❑ 356 Kevin Ritz .30 .10
❑ 357 Pedro Astacio .30 .10
❑ 358 Scott Sanders .30 .10
❑ 359 Deivi Cruz .30 .10
❑ 360 Brian L. Hunter .30 .10
❑ 361 Pedro Martinez HM .50 .20
❑ 362 Tom Glavine HM .30 .10
❑ 363 Willie McGee HM .30 .10
❑ 364 J.T. Snow HM .30 .10
❑ 365 Rusty Greer HM .30 .10
❑ 366 Mike Grace HM .30 .10
❑ 367 Tony Clark HM .30 .10
❑ 368 Ben Grieve HM .30 .10
❑ 369 Gary Sheffield HM .30 .10
❑ 370 Joe Oliver .30 .10
❑ 371 Todd Jones .30 .10
❑ 372 Frank Catalanotto RC .60 .25
❑ 373 Brian Moehler .30 .10
❑ 374 Cliff Floyd .30 .10
❑ 375 Bobby Bonilla .30 .10
❑ 376 Al Leiter .30 .10
❑ 377 Josh Booty .30 .10
❑ 378 Darren Daulton .30 .10
❑ 379 Jay Powell .30 .10
❑ 380 Felix Heredia .30 .10
❑ 381 Jim Eisenreich .30 .10
❑ 382 Richard Hidalgo .30 .10
❑ 383 Mike Hampton .30 .10
❑ 384 Shane Reynolds .30 .10
❑ 385 Jeff Bagwell .50 .20
❑ 386 Derek Bell .30 .10
❑ 387 Ricky Gutierrez .30 .10
❑ 388 Bill Spiers .30 .10
❑ 389 Jose Offerman .30 .10
❑ 390 Johnny Damon .50 .20
❑ 391 Jermaine Dye .30 .10
❑ 392 Jeff Montgomery .30 .10
❑ 393 Glendon Rusch .30 .10
❑ 394 Mike Sweeney .30 .10
❑ 395 Kevin Appier .30 .10
❑ 396 Joe Vitiello .30 .10
❑ 397 Ramon Martinez .30 .10
❑ 398 Darren Dreifort .30 .10
❑ 399 Wilton Guerrero .30 .10
❑ 400 Mike Piazza 1.25 .50
❑ 401 Eddie Murray .75 .30
❑ 402 Ismael Valdes .30 .10
❑ 403 Todd Hollandsworth .30 .10
❑ 404 Mark Loretta .30 .10
❑ 405 Jeromy Burnitz .30 .10
❑ 406 Jeff Cirillo .30 .10
❑ 407 Scott Karl .30 .10
❑ 408 Mike Matheny .30 .10
❑ 409 Jose Valentin .30 .10
❑ 410 John Jaha .30 .10
❑ 411 Terry Steinbach .30 .10
❑ 412 Torii Hunter .30 .10
❑ 413 Pat Meares .30 .10
❑ 414 Marty Cordova .30 .10
❑ 415 Jaret Wright PH .30 .10
❑ 416 Mike Mussina PH .30 .10
❑ 417 John Smoltz PH .30 .10
❑ 418 Devon White PH .30 .10
❑ 419 Denny Neagle PH .30 .10
❑ 420 Livan Hernandez PH .30 .10
❑ 421 Kevin Brown PH .30 .10
❑ 422 Marquis Grissom PH .30 .10
❑ 423 Mike Mussina PH .30 .10
❑ 424 Eric Davis PH .30 .10
❑ 425 Tony Fernandez PH .30 .10
❑ 426 Moises Alou PH .30 .10
❑ 427 Sandy Alomar Jr. PH .30 .10
❑ 428 Gary Sheffield PH .30 .10
❑ 429 Jaret Wright PH .30 .10
❑ 430 Livan Hernandez PH .30 .10
❑ 431 Chad Ogea PH .30 .10
❑ 432 Edgar Renteria PH .30 .10
❑ 433 LaTroy Hawkins .30 .10
❑ 434 Rich Robertson .30 .10
❑ 435 Chuck Knoblauch .30 .10
❑ 436 Jose Vidro .30 .10
❑ 437 Dustin Hermanson .30 .10
❑ 438 Jim Bullinger .30 .10
❑ 439 Orlando Cabrera .30 .10
❑ 440 Vladimir Guerrero .75 .30
❑ 441 Ugueth Urbina .30 .10
❑ 442 Brian McRae .30 .10
❑ 443 Matt Franco .30 .10
❑ 444 Bobby Jones .30 .10
❑ 445 Bernard Gilkey .30 .10
❑ 446 Dave Mlicki .30 .10
❑ 447 Brian Bohanon .30 .10
❑ 448 Mel Rojas .30 .10
❑ 449 Tim Raines .30 .10
❑ 450 Derek Jeter 2.00 .75
❑ 451 Roger Clemens UE .75 .30
❑ 452 Nomar Garciaparra UE .75 .30
❑ 453 Mike Piazza UE .75 .30
❑ 454 Mark McGwire UE 1.00 .40
❑ 455 Ken Griffey Jr. UE .75 .30
❑ 456 Larry Walker UE .30 .10
❑ 457 Alex Rodriguez UE .75 .30
❑ 458 Tony Gwynn UE .50 .20
❑ 459 Frank Thomas UE .50 .20
❑ 460 Tino Martinez .50 .20
❑ 461 Chad Curtis .30 .10
❑ 462 Ramiro Mendoza .30 .10
❑ 463 Joe Girardi .30 .10
❑ 464 David Wells .30 .10
❑ 465 Mariano Rivera .75 .30
❑ 466 Willie Adams .30 .10
❑ 467 George Williams .30 .10
❑ 468 Dave Telgheder .30 .10
❑ 469 Dave Magadan .30 .10
❑ 470 Matt Stairs .30 .10
❑ 471 Bill Taylor .30 .10
❑ 472 Jimmy Haynes .30 .10
❑ 473 Gregg Jefferies .30 .10
❑ 474 Midre Cummings .30 .10
❑ 475 Curt Schilling .30 .10
❑ 476 Mike Grace .30 .10
❑ 477 Mark Leiter .30 .10
❑ 478 Matt Beech .30 .10
❑ 479 Scott Rolen .50 .20
❑ 480 Jason Kendall .30 .10
❑ 481 Esteban Loaiza .30 .10
❑ 482 Jermaine Allensworth .30 .10
❑ 483 Mark Smith .30 .10
❑ 484 Jason Schmidt .30 .10
❑ 485 Jose Guillen .30 .10
❑ 486 Al Martin .30 .10
❑ 487 Delino DeShields .30 .10
❑ 488 Todd Stottlemyre .30 .10
❑ 489 Brian Jordan .30 .10
❑ 490 Ray Lankford .30 .10
❑ 491 Matt Morris .30 .10
❑ 492 Royce Clayton .30 .10
❑ 493 John Mabry .30 .10
❑ 494 Wally Joyner .30 .10
❑ 495 Trevor Hoffman .30 .10
❑ 496 Chris Gomez .30 .10
❑ 497 Sterling Hitchcock .30 .10
❑ 498 Pete Smith .30 .10
❑ 499 Greg Vaughn .30 .10
❑ 500 Tony Gwynn 1.00 .40
❑ 501 Will Cunnane .30 .10
❑ 502 Darryl Hamilton .30 .10
❑ 503 Brian Johnson .30 .10
❑ 504 Kirk Rueter .30 .10
❑ 505 Barry Bonds 2.00 .75
❑ 506 Osvaldo Fernandez .30 .10
❑ 507 Stan Javier .30 .10
❑ 508 Julian Tavarez .30 .10
❑ 509 Rich Aurilia .30 .10
❑ 510 Alex Rodriguez 1.25 .50
❑ 511 David Segui .30 .10
❑ 512 Rich Amaral .30 .10
❑ 513 Raul Ibanez .30 .10
❑ 514 Jay Buhner .30 .10
❑ 515 Randy Johnson .75 .30
❑ 516 Heathcliff Slocumb .30 .10
❑ 517 Tony Saunders .30 .10
❑ 518 Kevin Elster .30 .10
❑ 519 John Burkett .30 .10
❑ 520 Juan Gonzalez .30 .10
❑ 521 John Wetteland .30 .10
❑ 522 Domingo Cedeno .30 .10
❑ 523 Darren Oliver .30 .10
❑ 524 Roger Pavlik .30 .10
❑ 525 Jose Cruz Jr. .30 .10
❑ 526 Woody Williams .30 .10
❑ 527 Alex Gonzalez .30 .10
❑ 528 Robert Person .30 .10
❑ 529 Juan Guzman .30 .10
❑ 530 Roger Clemens 1.50 .60
❑ 531 Shawn Green .30 .10
❑ 532 F.Cordova/R.Rincon/M.Smith SH .30 .10
❑ 533 Nomar Garciaparra SH .75 .30
❑ 534 Roger Clemens SH .75 .30
❑ 535 Mark McGwire SH 1.00 .40
❑ 536 Larry Walker SH .30 .10
❑ 537 Mike Piazza SH .75 .30
❑ 538 Curt Schilling SH .30 .10
❑ 539 Tony Gwynn SH .50 .20
❑ 540 Ken Griffey Jr. SH .75 .30
❑ 541 Carl Pavano .30 .10
❑ 542 Shane Monahan .30 .10
❑ 543 Gabe Kapler RC .60 .25
❑ 544 Eric Milton .30 .10
❑ 545 Gary Matthews Jr. RC .60 .25
❑ 546 Mike Kinkade RC .30 .10
❑ 547 Ryan Christenson RC .30 .10
❑ 548 Corey Koskie RC .60 .25
❑ 549 Norm Hutchins .30 .10
❑ 550 Russell Branyan .30 .10
❑ 551 Masato Yoshii RC .40 .15
❑ 552 Jesus Sanchez RC .30 .10
❑ 553 Anthony Sanders .30 .10
❑ 554 Edwin Diaz .30 .10
❑ 555 Gabe Alvarez .30 .10
❑ 556 Carlos Lee RC 2.00 .75
❑ 557 Mike Darr .30 .10
❑ 558 Kerry Wood .40 .15
❑ 559 Carlos Guillen .30 .10
❑ 560 Sean Casey .30 .10
❑ 561 Manny Aybar RC .30 .10
❑ 562 Octavio Dotel .30 .10
❑ 563 Jarrod Washburn .30 .10
❑ 564 Mark L. Johnson .30 .10
❑ 565 Ramon Hernandez .30 .10
❑ 566 Rich Butler RC .30 .10
❑ 567 Mike Caruso .30 .10
❑ 568 Cliff Politte .30 .10
❑ 569 Scott Elarton .30 .10
❑ 570 Magglio Ordonez RC 3.00 1.25
❑ 571 Adam Butler RC .30 .10
❑ 572 Marlon Anderson .30 .10
❑ 573 Julio Ramirez RC .30 .10

No.	Player		
574	Darron Ingram RC	.30	.10
575	Bruce Chen	.30	.10
576	Steve Woodard	.30	.10
577	Hiram Bocachica	.30	.10
578	Kevin Witt	.30	.10
579	Javier Vazquez	.30	.10
580	Alex Gonzalez	.30	.10
581	Brian Powell	.30	.10
582	Wes Helms	.30	.10
583	Ron Wright	.30	.10
584	Rafael Medina	.30	.10
585	Daryle Ward	.30	.10
586	Geoff Jenkins	.30	.10
587	Preston Wilson	.30	.10
588	Jim Chamblee RC	.30	.10
589	Mike Lowell RC	1.50	.60
590	A.J. Hinch	.30	.10
591	Francisco Cordero RC	.60	.25
592	Rolando Arrojo RC	.40	.15
593	Braden Looper	.30	.10
594	Sidney Ponson	.30	.10
595	Matt Clement	.30	.10
596	Carlton Loewer	.30	.10
597	Brian Meadows	.30	.10
598	Danny Klassen	.30	.10
599	Larry Sutton	.30	.10
600	Travis Lee	.30	.10
601	Randy Johnson EP	2.50	1.00
602	Greg Maddux EP	4.00	1.50
603	Roger Clemens EP	5.00	2.00
604	Jaret Wright EP	2.00	.75
605	Mike Piazza EP	4.00	1.50
606	Tino Martinez EP	2.00	.75
607	Frank Thomas EP	2.50	1.00
608	Mo Vaughn EP	2.00	.75
609	Todd Helton EP	2.00	.75
610	Mark McGwire EP	6.00	2.50
611	Jeff Bagwell EP	2.00	.75
612	Travis Lee EP	2.00	.75
613	Scott Rolen EP	2.00	.75
614	Cal Ripken EP	8.00	3.00
615	Chipper Jones EP	2.50	1.00
616	Nomar Garciaparra EP	4.00	1.50
617	Alex Rodriguez EP	4.00	1.50
618	Derek Jeter EP	6.00	2.50
619	Tony Gwynn EP	3.00	1.25
620	Ken Griffey Jr. EP	4.00	1.50
621	Kenny Lofton EP	2.00	.75
622	Juan Gonzalez EP	2.00	.75
623	Jose Cruz Jr. EP	2.00	.75
624	Larry Walker EP	2.00	.75
625	Barry Bonds EP	6.00	2.50
626	Ben Grieve EP	2.00	.75
627	Andruw Jones EP	2.00	.75
628	Vladimir Guerrero EP	2.50	1.00
629	Paul Konerko EP	2.00	.75
630	Paul Molitor EP	2.00	.75
631	Cecil Fielder	.30	.10
632	Jack McDowell	.30	.10
633	Mike James	.30	.10
634	Brian Anderson	.30	.10
635	Jay Bell	.30	.10
636	Devon White	.30	.10
637	Andy Stankiewicz	.30	.10
638	Tony Batista	.30	.10
639	Omar Daal	.30	.10
640	Matt Williams	.30	.10
641	Brent Brede	.30	.10
642	Jorge Fabregas	.30	.10
643	Karim Garcia	.30	.10
644	Felix Rodriguez	.30	.10
645	Andy Benes	.30	.10
646	Willie Blair	.30	.10
647	Jeff Suppan	.30	.10
648	Yamil Benitez	.30	.10
649	Walt Weiss	.30	.10
650	Andres Galarraga	.30	.10
651	Doug Drabek	.30	.10
652	Ozzie Guillen	.30	.10
653	Joe Carter	.30	.10
654	Dennis Eckersley	.30	.10
655	Pedro Martinez	.50	.20
656	Jim Leyritz	.30	.10
657	Henry Rodriguez	.30	.10
658	Rod Beck	.30	.10
659	Mickey Morandini	.30	.10
660	Jeff Blauser	.30	.10
661	Ruben Sierra	.30	.10
662	Mike Sirotka	.30	.10
663	Pete Harnisch	.30	.10
664	Damian Jackson	.30	.10
665	Dmitri Young	.30	.10
666	Steve Cooke	.30	.10
667	Geronimo Berroa	.30	.10
668	Shawon Dunston	.30	.10
669	Mike Jackson	.30	.10
670	Travis Fryman	.30	.10
671	Dwight Gooden	.30	.10
672	Paul Assenmacher	.30	.10
673	Eric Plunk	.30	.10
674	Mike Lansing	.30	.10
675	Darryl Kile	.30	.10
676	Luis Gonzalez	.30	.10
677	Frank Castillo	.30	.10
678	Joe Randa	.30	.10
679	Bip Roberts	.30	.10
680	Derrek Lee	.50	.20
681	M.Piazza Mets SP	3.00	1.25
681A	M.Piazza Marlins SP	3.00	1.25
682	Sean Berry	.30	.10
683	Ramon Garcia	.30	.10
684	Carl Everett	.30	.10
685	Moises Alou	.30	.10
686	Hal Morris	.30	.10
687	Jeff Conine	.30	.10
688	Gary Sheffield	.30	.10
689	Jose Vizcaino	.30	.10
690	Charles Johnson	.30	.10
691	Bobby Bonilla	.30	.10
692	Marquis Grissom	.30	.10
693	Alex Ochoa	.30	.10
694	Mike Morgan	.30	.10
695	Orlando Merced	.30	.10
696	David Ortiz	1.00	.40
697	Brent Gates	.30	.10
698	Otis Nixon	.30	.10
699	Troy Moore	.30	.10
700	Derrick May	.30	.10
701	Rich Becker	.30	.10
702	Al Leiter	.30	.10
703	Chili Davis	.30	.10
704	Scott Brosius	.30	.10
705	Chuck Knoblauch	.30	.10
706	Kenny Rogers	.30	.10
707	Mike Blowers	.30	.10
708	Mike Fetters	.30	.10
709	Tom Candiotti	.30	.10
710	Rickey Henderson	.75	.30
711	Bob Abreu	.30	.10
712	Mark Lewis	.30	.10
713	Doug Glanville	.30	.10
714	Desi Relaford	.30	.10
715	Kent Mercker	.30	.10
716	Kevin Brown	.50	.20
717	James Mouton	.30	.10
718	Mark Langston	.30	.10
719	Greg Myers	.30	.10
720	Orel Hershiser	.30	.10
721	Charlie Hayes	.30	.10
722	Robb Nen	.30	.10
723	Glenallen Hill	.30	.10
724	Tony Saunders	.30	.10
725	Wade Boggs	.50	.20
726	Kevin Stocker	.30	.10
727	Wilson Alvarez	.30	.10
728	Albie Lopez	.30	.10
729	Dave Martinez	.30	.10
730	Fred McGriff	.50	.20
731	Quinton McCracken	.30	.10
732	Bryan Rekar	.30	.10
733	Paul Sorrento	.30	.10
734	Roberto Hernandez	.30	.10
735	Bubba Trammell	.30	.10
736	Miguel Cairo	.30	.10
737	John Flaherty	.30	.10
738	Terrell Wade	.30	.10
739	Roberto Kelly	.30	.10
740	Mark McLemore	.30	.10
741	Danny Patterson	.30	.10
742	Aaron Sele	.30	.10
743	Tony Fernandez	.30	.10
744	Randy Myers	.30	.10
745	Jose Canseco	.50	.20
746	Darrin Fletcher	.30	.10
747	Mike Stanley	.30	.10
748	Marquis Grissom SH CL	.30	.10
749	Fred McGriff SH CL	.30	.10
750	Travis Lee SH CL	.30	.10

1999 Upper Deck

No.	Player		
	COMPLETE SET (525)	100.00	50.00
	COMPLETE SERIES 1 (255)	60.00	30.00
	COMPLETE SERIES 2 (270)	40.00	20.00
	COMMON (19-255/293-535)	.30	.10
	COMMON SER.1 SR (1-18)	.50	.20
	COMMON SER.2 SR (266-292)	.50	.20
1	Troy Glaus SR	1.00	.40
2	Adrian Beltre SR	.60	.25
3	Matt Anderson SR	.50	.20
4	Eric Chavez SR	.60	.25
5	Jin Ho Cho SR	.50	.20
6	Robert Smith SR	.50	.20
7	George Lombard SR	.50	.20
8	Mike Kinkade SR	.50	.20
9	Seth Greisinger SR	.50	.20
10	J.D. Drew SR	.60	.25
11	Aramis Ramirez SR	.60	.25
12	Carlos Guillen SR	.60	.25
13	Justin Baughman SR	.50	.20
14	Jim Parque SR	.50	.20
15	Ryan Jackson SR	.50	.20
16	Ramon E.Martinez SR RC	.50	.20
17	Orlando Hernandez SR	.60	.25
18	Jeremy Giambi SR	.50	.20
19	Gary DiSarcina	.30	.10
20	Darin Erstad	.30	.10
21	Troy Glaus	.50	.20
22	Chuck Finley	.30	.10
23	Dave Hollins	.30	.10
24	Troy Percival	.30	.10
25	Tim Salmon	.50	.20
26	Brian Anderson	.30	.10
27	Jay Bell	.30	.10
28	Andy Benes	.30	.10
29	Brent Brede	.30	.10
30	David Dellucci	.30	.10
31	Karim Garcia	.30	.10
32	Travis Lee	.30	.10
33	Andres Galarraga	.30	.10
34	Ryan Klesko	.30	.10
35	Keith Lockhart	.30	.10
36	Kevin Millwood	.30	.10
37	Denny Neagle	.30	.10
38	John Smoltz	.50	.20
39	Michael Tucker	.30	.10
40	Walt Weiss	.30	.10
41	Dennis Martinez	.30	.10
42	Javy Lopez	.30	.10
43	Brady Anderson	.30	.10
44	Harold Baines	.30	.10
45	Mike Bordick	.30	.10
46	Roberto Alomar	.50	.20
47	Scott Erickson	.30	.10
48	Mike Mussina	.50	.20
49	Cal Ripken	2.50	1.00
50	Darren Bragg	.30	.10
51	Dennis Eckersley	.30	.10
52	Nomar Garciaparra	1.25	.50
53	Scott Hatteberg	.30	.10
54	Troy O'Leary	.30	.10

	No.	Player		
❑	55	Bret Saberhagen	.30	.10
❑	56	John Valentin	.30	.10
❑	57	Rod Beck	.30	.10
❑	58	Jeff Blauser	.30	.10
❑	59	Brant Brown	.30	.10
❑	60	Mark Clark	.30	.10
❑	61	Mark Grace	.50	.20
❑	62	Kevin Tapani	.30	.10
❑	63	Henry Rodriguez	.30	.10
❑	64	Mike Cameron	.30	.10
❑	65	Mike Caruso	.30	.10
❑	66	Ray Durham	.30	.10
❑	67	Jaime Navarro	.30	.10
❑	68	Magglio Ordonez	.30	.10
❑	69	Mike Sirotka	.30	.10
❑	70	Sean Casey	.30	.10
❑	71	Barry Larkin	.50	.20
❑	72	Jon Nunnally	.30	.10
❑	73	Paul Konerko	.30	.10
❑	74	Chris Stynes	.30	.10
❑	75	Brett Tomko	.30	.10
❑	76	Dmitri Young	.30	.10
❑	77	Sandy Alomar Jr.	.30	.10
❑	78	Bartolo Colon	.30	.10
❑	79	Travis Fryman	.30	.10
❑	80	Brian Giles	.30	.10
❑	81	David Justice	.30	.10
❑	82	Omar Vizquel	.50	.20
❑	83	Jaret Wright	.30	.10
❑	84	Jim Thome	.50	.20
❑	85	Charles Nagy	.30	.10
❑	86	Pedro Astacio	.30	.10
❑	87	Todd Helton	.50	.20
❑	88	Darryl Kile	.30	.10
❑	89	Mike Lansing	.30	.10
❑	90	Neifi Perez	.30	.10
❑	91	John Thomson	.30	.10
❑	92	Larry Walker	.30	.10
❑	93	Tony Clark	.30	.10
❑	94	Deivi Cruz	.30	.10
❑	95	Damion Easley	.30	.10
❑	96	Brian L.Hunter	.30	.10
❑	97	Todd Jones	.30	.10
❑	98	Brian Moehler	.30	.10
❑	99	Gabe Alvarez	.30	.10
❑	100	Craig Counsell	.30	.10
❑	101	Cliff Floyd	.30	.10
❑	102	Livan Hernandez	.30	.10
❑	103	Andy Larkin	.30	.10
❑	104	Derrek Lee	.50	.20
❑	105	Brian Meadows	.30	.10
❑	106	Moises Alou	.30	.10
❑	107	Sean Berry	.30	.10
❑	108	Craig Biggio	.50	.20
❑	109	Ricky Gutierrez	.30	.10
❑	110	Mike Hampton	.30	.10
❑	111	Jose Lima	.30	.10
❑	112	Billy Wagner	.30	.10
❑	113	Hal Morris	.30	.10
❑	114	Johnny Damon	.50	.20
❑	115	Jeff King	.30	.10
❑	116	Jeff Montgomery	.30	.10
❑	117	Glendon Rusch	.30	.10
❑	118	Larry Sutton	.30	.10
❑	119	Bobby Bonilla	.30	.10
❑	120	Jim Eisenreich	.30	.10
❑	121	Eric Karros	.30	.10
❑	122	Matt Luke	.30	.10
❑	123	Ramon Martinez	.30	.10
❑	124	Gary Sheffield	.30	.10
❑	125	Eric Young	.30	.10
❑	126	Charles Johnson	.30	.10
❑	127	Jeff Cirillo	.30	.10
❑	128	Marquis Grissom	.30	.10
❑	129	Jeromy Burnitz	.30	.10
❑	130	Bob Wickman	.30	.10
❑	131	Scott Karl	.30	.10
❑	132	Mark Loretta	.30	.10
❑	133	Fernando Vina	.30	.10
❑	134	Matt Lawton	.30	.10
❑	135	Pat Meares	.30	.10
❑	136	Eric Milton	.30	.10
❑	137	Paul Molitor	.30	.10
❑	138	David Ortiz	.75	.30
❑	139	Todd Walker	.30	.10
❑	140	Shane Andrews	.30	.10
❑	141	Brad Fullmer	.30	.10
❑	142	Vladimir Guerrero	.75	.30
❑	143	Dustin Hermanson	.30	.10
❑	144	Ryan McGuire	.30	.10
❑	145	Ugueth Urbina	.30	.10
❑	146	John Franco	.30	.10
❑	147	Butch Huskey	.30	.10
❑	148	Bobby Jones	.30	.10
❑	149	John Olerud	.30	.10
❑	150	Rey Ordonez	.30	.10
❑	151	Mike Piazza	1.25	.50
❑	152	Hideo Nomo	.75	.30
❑	153	Masato Yoshii	.30	.10
❑	154	Derek Jeter	2.00	.75
❑	155	Chuck Knoblauch	.30	.10
❑	156	Paul O'Neill	.50	.20
❑	157	Andy Pettitte	.50	.20
❑	158	Mariano Rivera	.75	.30
❑	159	Darryl Strawberry	.30	.10
❑	160	David Wells	.30	.10
❑	161	Jorge Posada	.50	.20
❑	162	Ramiro Mendoza	.30	.10
❑	163	Miguel Tejada	.30	.10
❑	164	Ryan Christenson	.30	.10
❑	165	Rickey Henderson	.75	.30
❑	166	A.J. Hinch	.30	.10
❑	167	Ben Grieve	.30	.10
❑	168	Kenny Rogers	.30	.10
❑	169	Matt Stairs	.30	.10
❑	170	Bob Abreu	.30	.10
❑	171	Rico Brogna	.30	.10
❑	172	Doug Glanville	.30	.10
❑	173	Mike Grace	.30	.10
❑	174	Desi Relaford	.30	.10
❑	175	Scott Rolen	.50	.20
❑	176	Jose Guillen	.30	.10
❑	177	Francisco Cordova	.30	.10
❑	178	Al Martin	.30	.10
❑	179	Jason Schmidt	.30	.10
❑	180	Turner Ward	.30	.10
❑	181	Kevin Young	.30	.10
❑	182	Mark McGwire	2.00	.75
❑	183	Delino DeShields	.30	.10
❑	184	Eli Marrero	.30	.10
❑	185	Tom Lampkin	.30	.10
❑	186	Ray Lankford	.30	.10
❑	187	Willie McGee	.30	.10
❑	188	Matt Morris	.30	.10
❑	189	Andy Ashby	.30	.10
❑	190	Kevin Brown	.50	.20
❑	191	Ken Caminiti	.30	.10
❑	192	Trevor Hoffman	.30	.10
❑	193	Wally Joyner	.30	.10
❑	194	Greg Vaughn	.30	.10
❑	195	Danny Darwin	.30	.10
❑	196	Shawn Estes	.30	.10
❑	197	Orel Hershiser	.30	.10
❑	198	Jeff Kent	.30	.10
❑	199	Bill Mueller	.30	.10
❑	200	Robb Nen	.30	.10
❑	201	J.T. Snow	.30	.10
❑	202	Ken Cloude	.30	.10
❑	203	Russ Davis	.30	.10
❑	204	Jeff Fassero	.30	.10
❑	205	Ken Griffey Jr.	1.25	.50
❑	206	Shane Monahan	.30	.10
❑	207	David Segui	.30	.10
❑	208	Dan Wilson	.30	.10
❑	209	Wilson Alvarez	.30	.10
❑	210	Wade Boggs	.50	.20
❑	211	Miguel Cairo	.30	.10
❑	212	Bubba Trammell	.30	.10
❑	213	Quinton McCracken	.30	.10
❑	214	Paul Sorrento	.30	.10
❑	215	Kevin Stocker	.30	.10
❑	216	Will Clark	.50	.20
❑	217	Rusty Greer	.30	.10
❑	218	Rick Helling	.30	.10
❑	219	Mark McLemore	.30	.10
❑	220	Ivan Rodriguez	.50	.20
❑	221	John Wetteland	.30	.10
❑	222	Jose Canseco	.50	.20
❑	223	Roger Clemens	1.50	.60
❑	224	Carlos Delgado	.30	.10
❑	225	Darrin Fletcher	.30	.10
❑	226	Alex Gonzalez	.30	.10
❑	227	Jose Cruz Jr.	.30	.10
❑	228	Shannon Stewart	.30	.10
❑	229	Rolando Arrojo FF	.30	.10
❑	230	Livan Hernandez FF	.30	.10
❑	231	Orlando Hernandez FF	.30	.10
❑	232	Raul Mondesi FF	.30	.10
❑	233	Moises Alou FF	.30	.10
❑	234	Pedro Martinez FF	.50	.20
❑	235	Sammy Sosa FF	.50	.20
❑	236	Vladimir Guerrero FF	.75	.30
❑	237	Bartolo Colon FF	.30	.10
❑	238	Miguel Tejada FF	.30	.10
❑	239	Ismael Valdes FF	.30	.10
❑	240	Mariano Rivera FF	.50	.20
❑	241	Jose Cruz Jr. FF	.30	.10
❑	242	Juan Gonzalez FF	.30	.10
❑	243	Ivan Rodriguez FF	.50	.20
❑	244	Sandy Alomar Jr. FF	.30	.10
❑	245	Roberto Alomar FF	.50	.20
❑	246	Magglio Ordonez FF	.30	.10
❑	247	Kerry Wood SH CL	.30	.10
❑	248	Mark McGwire SH CL	2.00	.75
❑	249	David Wells SH CL	.30	.10
❑	250	Rolando Arrojo SH CL	.30	.10
❑	251	Ken Griffey Jr. SH CL	1.25	.50
❑	252	Trevor Hoffman SH CL	.30	.10
❑	253	Travis Lee SH CL	.30	.10
❑	254	Roberto Alomar SH CL	.30	.10
❑	255	Sammy Sosa SH CL	.50	.20
❑	266	Pat Burrell SR RC	3.00	1.25
❑	267	Shea Hillenbrand SR RC	1.50	.60
❑	268	Robert Fick SR	.50	.20
❑	269	Roy Halladay SR	.60	.25
❑	270	Ruben Mateo SR	.50	.20
❑	271	Bruce Chen SR	.50	.20
❑	272	Angel Pena SR	.50	.20
❑	273	Michael Barrett SR	.50	.20
❑	274	Kevin Witt SR	.50	.20
❑	275	Damon Minor SR	.50	.20
❑	276	Ryan Minor SR	.50	.20
❑	277	A.J. Pierzynski SR	.60	.25
❑	278	A.J. Burnett SR RC	1.50	.60
❑	279	Dermal Brown SR	.50	.20
❑	280	Joe Lawrence SR	.50	.20
❑	281	Derrick Gibson SR	.50	.20
❑	282	Carlos Febles SR	.50	.20
❑	283	Chris Haas SR	.50	.20
❑	284	Cesar King SR	.50	.20
❑	285	Calvin Pickering SR	.50	.20
❑	286	Mitch Meluskey SR	.50	.20
❑	287	Carlos Beltran SR	1.00	.40
❑	288	Ron Belliard SR	.50	.20
❑	289	Jerry Hairston Jr. SR	.50	.20
❑	290	Fernando Seguignol SR	.50	.20
❑	291	Kris Benson SR	.50	.20
❑	292	Chad Hutchinson SR RC	.60	.25
❑	293	Jarrod Washburn	.30	.10
❑	294	Jason Dickson	.30	.10
❑	295	Mo Vaughn	.30	.10
❑	296	Garret Anderson	.30	.10
❑	297	Jim Edmonds	.30	.10
❑	298	Ken Hill	.30	.10
❑	299	Shigetoshi Hasegawa	.30	.10
❑	300	Todd Stottlemyre	.30	.10
❑	301	Randy Johnson	.75	.30
❑	302	Omar Daal	.30	.10
❑	303	Steve Finley	.30	.10
❑	304	Matt Williams	.30	.10
❑	305	Danny Klassen	.30	.10
❑	306	Tony Batista	.30	.10
❑	307	Brian Jordan	.30	.10
❑	308	Greg Maddux	1.25	.50
❑	309	Chipper Jones	.75	.30
❑	310	Bret Boone	.30	.10
❑	311	Ozzie Guillen	.30	.10
❑	312	John Rocker	.30	.10
❑	313	Tom Glavine	.50	.20
❑	314	Andruw Jones	.50	.20
❑	315	Albert Belle	.30	.10
❑	316	Charles Johnson	.30	.10
❑	317	Will Clark	.50	.20
❑	318	B.J. Surhoff	.30	.10
❑	319	Delino DeShields	.30	.10
❑	320	Heathcliff Slocumb	.30	.10
❑	321	Sidney Ponson	.30	.10
❑	322	Juan Guzman	.30	.10

❑	323 Reggie Jefferson	.30	.10
❑	324 Mark Portugal	.30	.10
❑	325 Tim Wakefield	.30	.10
❑	326 Jason Varitek	.75	.30
❑	327 Jose Offerman	.30	.10
❑	328 Pedro Martinez	.50	.20
❑	329 Trot Nixon	.30	.10
❑	330 Kerry Wood	.30	.10
❑	331 Sammy Sosa	.75	.30
❑	332 Glenallen Hill	.30	.10
❑	333 Gary Gaetti	.30	.10
❑	334 Mickey Morandini	.30	.10
❑	335 Benito Santiago	.30	.10
❑	336 Jeff Blauser	.30	.10
❑	337 Frank Thomas	.75	.30
❑	338 Paul Konerko	.30	.10
❑	339 Jaime Navarro	.30	.10
❑	340 Carlos Lee	.30	.10
❑	341 Brian Simmons	.30	.10
❑	342 Mark Johnson	.30	.10
❑	343 Jeff Abbott	.30	.10
❑	344 Steve Avery	.30	.10
❑	345 Mike Cameron	.30	.10
❑	346 Michael Tucker	.30	.10
❑	347 Greg Vaughn	.30	.10
❑	348 Hal Morris	.30	.10
❑	349 Pete Harnisch	.30	.10
❑	350 Denny Neagle	.30	.10
❑	351 Manny Ramirez	.50	.20
❑	352 Roberto Alomar	.50	.20
❑	353 Dwight Gooden	.30	.10
❑	354 Kenny Lofton	.30	.10
❑	355 Mike Jackson	.30	.10
❑	356 Charles Nagy	.30	.10
❑	357 Enrique Wilson	.30	.10
❑	358 Russ Branyan	.30	.10
❑	359 Richie Sexson	.30	.10
❑	360 Vinny Castilla	.30	.10
❑	361 Dante Bichette	.30	.10
❑	362 Kirt Manwaring	.30	.10
❑	363 Darryl Hamilton	.30	.10
❑	364 Jamey Wright	.30	.10
❑	365 Curtis Leskanic	.30	.10
❑	366 Jeff Reed	.30	.10
❑	367 Bobby Higginson	.30	.10
❑	368 Justin Thompson	.30	.10
❑	369 Brad Ausmus	.30	.10
❑	370 Dean Palmer	.30	.10
❑	371 Gabe Kapler	.30	.10
❑	372 Juan Encarnacion	.30	.10
❑	373 Karim Garcia	.30	.10
❑	374 Alex Gonzalez	.30	.10
❑	375 Braden Looper	.30	.10
❑	376 Preston Wilson	.30	.10
❑	377 Todd Dunwoody	.30	.10
❑	378 Alex Fernandez	.30	.10
❑	379 Mark Kotsay	.30	.10
❑	380 Matt Mantei	.30	.10
❑	381 Ken Caminiti	.30	.10
❑	382 Scott Elarton	.30	.10
❑	383 Jeff Bagwell	.50	.20
❑	384 Derek Bell	.30	.10
❑	385 Ricky Gutierrez	.30	.10
❑	386 Richard Hidalgo	.30	.10
❑	387 Shane Reynolds	.30	.10
❑	388 Carl Everett	.30	.10
❑	389 Scott Service	.30	.10
❑	390 Jeff Suppan	.30	.10
❑	391 Joe Randa	.30	.10
❑	392 Kevin Appier	.30	.10
❑	393 Shane Halter	.30	.10
❑	394 Chad Kreuter	.30	.10
❑	395 Mike Sweeney	.30	.10
❑	396 Kevin Brown	.50	.20
❑	397 Devon White	.30	.10
❑	398 Todd Hollandsworth	.30	.10
❑	399 Todd Hundley	.30	.10
❑	400 Chan Ho Park	.30	.10
❑	401 Mark Grudzielanek	.30	.10
❑	402 Raul Mondesi	.30	.10
❑	403 Ismael Valdes	.30	.10
❑	404 Rafael Roque RC	.30	.10
❑	405 Sean Berry	.30	.10
❑	406 Kevin Barker	.30	.10
❑	407 Dave Nilsson	.30	.10
❑	408 Geoff Jenkins	.30	.10
❑	409 Jim Abbott	.50	.20
❑	410 Bobby Hughes	.30	.10
❑	411 Corey Koskie	.30	.10
❑	412 Rick Aguilera	.30	.10
❑	413 LaTroy Hawkins	.30	.10
❑	414 Ron Coomer	.30	.10
❑	415 Denny Hocking	.30	.10
❑	416 Marty Cordova	.30	.10
❑	417 Terry Steinbach	.30	.10
❑	418 Rondell White	.30	.10
❑	419 Wilton Guerrero	.30	.10
❑	420 Shane Andrews	.30	.10
❑	421 Orlando Cabrera	.30	.10
❑	422 Carl Pavano	.30	.10
❑	423 Javier Vazquez	.30	.10
❑	424 Chris Widger	.30	.10
❑	425 Robin Ventura	.30	.10
❑	426 Rickey Henderson	.75	.30
❑	427 Al Leiter	.30	.10
❑	428 Bobby Jones	.30	.10
❑	429 Brian McRae	.30	.10
❑	430 Roger Cedeno	.30	.10
❑	431 Bobby Bonilla	.30	.10
❑	432 Edgardo Alfonzo	.30	.10
❑	433 Bernie Williams	.50	.20
❑	434 Ricky Ledee	.30	.10
❑	435 Chili Davis	.30	.10
❑	436 Tino Martinez	.50	.20
❑	437 Scott Brosius	.30	.10
❑	438 David Cone	.30	.10
❑	439 Joe Girardi	.30	.10
❑	440 Roger Clemens	1.50	.60
❑	441 Chad Curtis	.30	.10
❑	442 Hideki Irabu	.30	.10
❑	443 Jason Giambi	.30	.10
❑	444 Scott Spiezio	.30	.10
❑	445 Tony Phillips	.30	.10
❑	446 Ramon Hernandez	.30	.10
❑	447 Mike Macfarlane	.30	.10
❑	448 Tom Candiotti	.30	.10
❑	449 Billy Taylor	.30	.10
❑	450 Bobby Estalella	.30	.10
❑	451 Curt Schilling	.30	.10
❑	452 Carlton Loewer	.30	.10
❑	453 Marlon Anderson	.30	.10
❑	454 Kevin Jordan	.30	.10
❑	455 Ron Gant	.30	.10
❑	456 Chad Ogea	.30	.10
❑	457 Abraham Nunez	.30	.10
❑	458 Jason Kendall	.30	.10
❑	459 Pat Meares	.30	.10
❑	460 Brant Brown	.30	.10
❑	461 Brian Giles	.30	.10
❑	462 Chad Hermansen	.30	.10
❑	463 Freddy Adrian Garcia	.30	.10
❑	464 Edgar Renteria	.30	.10
❑	465 Fernando Tatis	.30	.10
❑	466 Eric Davis	.30	.10
❑	467 Darren Bragg	.30	.10
❑	468 Donovan Osborne	.30	.10
❑	469 Manny Aybar	.30	.10
❑	470 Jose Jimenez	.30	.10
❑	471 Kent Mercker	.30	.10
❑	472 Reggie Sanders	.30	.10
❑	473 Ruben Rivera	.30	.10
❑	474 Tony Gwynn	1.00	.40
❑	475 Jim Leyritz	.30	.10
❑	476 Chris Gomez	.30	.10
❑	477 Matt Clement	.30	.10
❑	478 Carlos Hernandez	.30	.10
❑	479 Sterling Hitchcock	.30	.10
❑	480 Ellis Burks	.30	.10
❑	481 Barry Bonds	2.00	.75
❑	482 Marvin Benard	.30	.10
❑	483 Kirk Rueter	.30	.10
❑	484 F.P. Santangelo	.30	.10
❑	485 Stan Javier	.30	.10
❑	486 Jeff Kent	.30	.10
❑	487 Alex Rodriguez	1.25	.50
❑	488 Tom Lampkin	.30	.10
❑	489 Jose Mesa	.30	.10
❑	490 Jay Buhner	.30	.10
❑	491 Edgar Martinez	.50	.20
❑	492 Butch Huskey	.30	.10
❑	493 John Mabry	.30	.10
❑	494 Jamie Moyer	.30	.10
❑	495 Roberto Hernandez	.30	.10
❑	496 Tony Saunders	.30	.10
❑	497 Fred McGriff	.50	.20
❑	498 Dave Martinez	.30	.10
❑	499 Jose Canseco	.50	.20
❑	500 Rolando Arrojo	.30	.10
❑	501 Esteban Yan	.30	.10
❑	502 Juan Gonzalez	.30	.10
❑	503 Rafael Palmeiro	.50	.20
❑	504 Aaron Sele	.30	.10
❑	505 Royce Clayton	.30	.10
❑	506 Todd Zeile	.30	.10
❑	507 Tom Goodwin	.30	.10
❑	508 Lee Stevens	.30	.10
❑	509 Esteban Loaiza	.30	.10
❑	510 Joey Hamilton	.30	.10
❑	511 Homer Bush	.30	.10
❑	512 Willie Greene	.30	.10
❑	513 Shawn Green	.30	.10
❑	514 David Wells	.30	.10
❑	515 Kelvim Escobar	.30	.10
❑	516 Tony Fernandez	.30	.10
❑	517 Pat Hentgen	.30	.10
❑	518 Mark McGwire AR	1.00	.40
❑	519 Ken Griffey Jr. AR	.75	.30
❑	520 Sammy Sosa AR	.50	.20
❑	521 Juan Gonzalez AR	.30	.10
❑	522 J.D. Drew AR	.30	.10
❑	523 Chipper Jones AR	.50	.20
❑	524 Alex Rodriguez AR	.75	.30
❑	525 Mike Piazza AR	.75	.30
❑	526 Nomar Garciaparra AR	.75	.30
❑	527 Mark McGwire SH CL	1.00	.40
❑	528 Sammy Sosa SH CL	.50	.20
❑	529 Scott Brosius SH CL	.30	.10
❑	530 Cal Ripken SH CL	1.25	.50
❑	531 Barry Bonds SH CL	1.00	.40
❑	532 Roger Clemens SH CL	.75	.30
❑	533 Ken Griffey Jr. SH CL	.75	.30
❑	534 Alex Rodriguez SH CL	.75	.30
❑	535 Curt Schilling SH CL	.30	.10
❑	NNO K.Griffey Jr. '89 AU/100	1250.00	1000.00

2000 Upper Deck

❑	COMPLETE SET (540)	100.00	40.00
❑	COMPLETE SERIES 1 (270)	50.00	20.00
❑	COMPLETE SERIES 2 (270)	50.00	20.00
❑	COMMON CARD (1-540)	.30	.10
❑	COMMON SR (1-28/271-297)	.50	.20
❑	1 Rick Ankiel SR	.50	.20
❑	2 Vernon Wells SR	.75	.30
❑	3 Ryan Anderson SR	.50	.20
❑	4 Ed Yarnall SR	.50	.20
❑	5 Brian McNichol SR	.50	.20
❑	6 Ben Petrick SR	.50	.20
❑	7 Kip Wells SR	.50	.20
❑	8 Eric Munson SR	.50	.20
❑	9 Matt Riley SR	.50	.20
❑	10 Peter Bergeron SR	.50	.20
❑	11 Eric Gagne SR	2.00	.75
❑	12 Ramon Ortiz SR	.50	.20
❑	13 Josh Beckett SR	2.00	.75
❑	14 Alfonso Soriano SR	2.00	.75
❑	15 Jorge Toca SR	.50	.20
❑	16 Buddy Carlyle SR	.50	.20
❑	17 Chad Hermansen SR	.50	.20
❑	18 Matt Perisho SR	.50	.20
❑	19 Tomokazu Ohka SR RC	.75	.30

❑ 20 Jacque Jones SR .75 .30
❑ 21 Josh Paul SR .50 .20
❑ 22 Dermal Brown SR .50 .20
❑ 23 Adam Kennedy SR .50 .20
❑ 24 Chad Harville SR .50 .20
❑ 25 Calvin Murray SR .50 .20
❑ 26 Chad Meyers SR .50 .20
❑ 27 Brian Cooper SR .50 .20
❑ 28 Troy Glaus .30 .10
❑ 29 Ben Molina .30 .10
❑ 30 Troy Percival .30 .10
❑ 31 Ken Hill .30 .10
❑ 32 Chuck Finley .30 .10
❑ 33 Todd Greene .30 .10
❑ 34 Tim Salmon .50 .20
❑ 35 Gary DiSarcina .30 .10
❑ 36 Luis Gonzalez .30 .10
❑ 37 Tony Womack .30 .10
❑ 38 Omar Daal .30 .10
❑ 39 Randy Johnson .75 .30
❑ 40 Erubiel Durazo .30 .10
❑ 41 Jay Bell .30 .10
❑ 42 Steve Finley .30 .10
❑ 43 Travis Lee .30 .10
❑ 44 Greg Maddux 1.25 .50
❑ 45 Bret Boone .30 .10
❑ 46 Brian Jordan .30 .10
❑ 47 Kevin Millwood .30 .10
❑ 48 Odalis Perez .30 .10
❑ 49 Javy Lopez .30 .10
❑ 50 John Smoltz .50 .20
❑ 51 Bruce Chen .30 .10
❑ 52 Albert Belle .30 .10
❑ 53 Jerry Hairston Jr. .30 .10
❑ 54 Will Clark .50 .20
❑ 55 Sidney Ponson .30 .10
❑ 56 Charles Johnson .30 .10
❑ 57 Cal Ripken 2.50 1.00
❑ 58 Ryan Minor .30 .10
❑ 59 Mike Mussina .50 .20
❑ 60 Tom Gordon .30 .10
❑ 61 Jose Offerman .30 .10
❑ 62 Trot Nixon .30 .10
❑ 63 Pedro Martinez .50 .20
❑ 64 John Valentin .30 .10
❑ 65 Jason Varitek .75 .30
❑ 66 Juan Pena .30 .10
❑ 67 Troy O'Leary .30 .10
❑ 68 Sammy Sosa .75 .30
❑ 69 Henry Rodriguez .30 .10
❑ 70 Kyle Farnsworth .30 .10
❑ 71 Glenallen Hill .30 .10
❑ 72 Lance Johnson .30 .10
❑ 73 Mickey Morandini .30 .10
❑ 74 Jon Lieber .30 .10
❑ 75 Kevin Tapani .30 .10
❑ 76 Carlos Lee .30 .10
❑ 77 Ray Durham .30 .10
❑ 78 Jim Parque .30 .10
❑ 79 Bob Howry .30 .10
❑ 80 Magglio Ordonez .30 .10
❑ 81 Paul Konerko .30 .10
❑ 82 Mike Caruso .30 .10
❑ 83 Chris Singleton .30 .10
❑ 84 Sean Casey .30 .10
❑ 85 Barry Larkin .50 .20
❑ 86 Pokey Reese .30 .10
❑ 87 Eddie Taubensee .30 .10
❑ 88 Scott Williamson .30 .10
❑ 89 Jason LaRue .30 .10
❑ 90 Aaron Boone .30 .10
❑ 91 Jeffrey Hammonds .30 .10
❑ 92 Omar Vizquel .50 .20
❑ 93 Manny Ramirez .50 .20
❑ 94 Kenny Lofton .30 .10
❑ 95 Jaret Wright .30 .10
❑ 96 Einar Diaz .30 .10
❑ 97 Charles Nagy .30 .10
❑ 98 David Justice .30 .10
❑ 99 Richie Sexson .30 .10
❑ 100 Steve Karsay .30 .10
❑ 101 Todd Helton .50 .20
❑ 102 Dante Bichette .30 .10
❑ 103 Larry Walker .30 .10
❑ 104 Pedro Astacio .30 .10
❑ 105 Neifi Perez .30 .10
❑ 106 Brian Bohanon .30 .10
❑ 107 Edgard Clemente .30 .10
❑ 108 Dave Veres .30 .10
❑ 109 Gabe Kapler .30 .10
❑ 110 Juan Encarnacion .30 .10
❑ 111 Jeff Weaver .30 .10
❑ 112 Damion Easley .30 .10
❑ 113 Justin Thompson .30 .10
❑ 114 Brad Ausmus .30 .10
❑ 115 Frank Catalanotto .30 .10
❑ 116 Todd Jones .30 .10
❑ 117 Preston Wilson .30 .10
❑ 118 Cliff Floyd .30 .10
❑ 119 Mike Lowell .30 .10
❑ 120 Antonio Alfonseca .30 .10
❑ 121 Alex Gonzalez .30 .10
❑ 122 Braden Looper .30 .10
❑ 123 Bruce Aven .30 .10
❑ 124 Richard Hidalgo .30 .10
❑ 125 Mitch Meluskey .30 .10
❑ 126 Jeff Bagwell .50 .20
❑ 127 Jose Lima .30 .10
❑ 128 Derek Bell .30 .10
❑ 129 Billy Wagner .30 .10
❑ 130 Shane Reynolds .30 .10
❑ 131 Moises Alou .30 .10
❑ 132 Carlos Beltran .30 .10
❑ 133 Carlos Febles .30 .10
❑ 134 Jermaine Dye .30 .10
❑ 135 Jeremy Giambi .30 .10
❑ 136 Joe Randa .30 .10
❑ 137 Jose Rosado .30 .10
❑ 138 Chad Kreuter .30 .10
❑ 139 Jose Vizcaino .30 .10
❑ 140 Adrian Beltre .30 .10
❑ 141 Kevin Brown .50 .20
❑ 142 Ismael Valdes .30 .10
❑ 143 Angel Pena .30 .10
❑ 144 Chan Ho Park .30 .10
❑ 145 Mark Grudzielanek .30 .10
❑ 146 Jeff Shaw .30 .10
❑ 147 Geoff Jenkins .30 .10
❑ 148 Jeromy Burnitz .30 .10
❑ 149 Hideo Nomo .75 .30
❑ 150 Ron Belliard .30 .10
❑ 151 Sean Berry .30 .10
❑ 152 Mark Loretta .30 .10
❑ 153 Steve Woodard .30 .10
❑ 154 Joe Mays .30 .10
❑ 155 Eric Milton .30 .10
❑ 156 Corey Koskie .30 .10
❑ 157 Ron Coomer .30 .10
❑ 158 Brad Radke .30 .10
❑ 159 Terry Steinbach .30 .10
❑ 160 Cristian Guzman .30 .10
❑ 161 Vladimir Guerrero .75 .30
❑ 162 Wilton Guerrero .30 .10
❑ 163 Michael Barrett .30 .10
❑ 164 Chris Widger .30 .10
❑ 165 Fernando Seguignol .30 .10
❑ 166 Ugueth Urbina .30 .10
❑ 167 Dustin Hermanson .30 .10
❑ 168 Kenny Rogers .30 .10
❑ 169 Edgardo Alfonzo .30 .10
❑ 170 Orel Hershiser .30 .10
❑ 171 Robin Ventura .30 .10
❑ 172 Octavio Dotel .30 .10
❑ 173 Rickey Henderson .75 .30
❑ 174 Roger Cedeno .30 .10
❑ 175 John Olerud .30 .10
❑ 176 Derek Jeter 2.00 .75
❑ 177 Tino Martinez .50 .20
❑ 178 Orlando Hernandez .30 .10
❑ 179 Chuck Knoblauch .30 .10
❑ 180 Bernie Williams .50 .20
❑ 181 Chili Davis .30 .10
❑ 182 David Cone .30 .10
❑ 183 Ricky Ledee .30 .10
❑ 184 Paul O'Neill .50 .20
❑ 185 Jason Giambi .30 .10
❑ 186 Eric Chavez .30 .10
❑ 187 Matt Stairs .30 .10
❑ 188 Miguel Tejada .30 .10
❑ 189 Olmedo Saenz .30 .10
❑ 190 Tim Hudson .30 .10
❑ 191 John Jaha .30 .10
❑ 192 Randy Velarde .30 .10
❑ 193 Rico Brogna .30 .10
❑ 194 Mike Lieberthal .30 .10
❑ 195 Marlon Anderson .30 .10
❑ 196 Bob Abreu .30 .10
❑ 197 Ron Gant .30 .10
❑ 198 Randy Wolf .30 .10
❑ 199 Desi Relaford .30 .10
❑ 200 Doug Glanville .30 .10
❑ 201 Warren Morris .30 .10
❑ 202 Kris Benson .30 .10
❑ 203 Kevin Young .30 .10
❑ 204 Brian Giles .30 .10
❑ 205 Jason Schmidt .30 .10
❑ 206 Ed Sprague .30 .10
❑ 207 Francisco Cordova .30 .10
❑ 208 Mark McGwire 2.00 .75
❑ 209 Jose Jimenez .30 .10
❑ 210 Fernando Tatis .30 .10
❑ 211 Kent Bottenfield .30 .10
❑ 212 Eli Marrero .30 .10
❑ 213 Edgar Renteria .30 .10
❑ 214 Joe McEwing .30 .10
❑ 215 J.D. Drew .30 .10
❑ 216 Tony Gwynn 1.00 .40
❑ 217 Gary Matthews Jr. .30 .10
❑ 218 Eric Owens .30 .10
❑ 219 Damian Jackson .30 .10
❑ 220 Reggie Sanders .30 .10
❑ 221 Trevor Hoffman .30 .10
❑ 222 Ben Davis .30 .10
❑ 223 Shawn Estes .30 .10
❑ 224 F.P. Santangelo .30 .10
❑ 225 Livan Hernandez .30 .10
❑ 226 Ellis Burks .30 .10
❑ 227 J.T. Snow .30 .10
❑ 228 Jeff Kent .30 .10
❑ 229 Robb Nen .30 .10
❑ 230 Marvin Benard .30 .10
❑ 231 Ken Griffey Jr. 1.25 .50
❑ 232 John Halama .30 .10
❑ 233 Gil Meche .30 .10
❑ 234 David Bell .30 .10
❑ 235 Brian Hunter .30 .10
❑ 236 Jay Buhner .30 .10
❑ 237 Edgar Martinez .50 .20
❑ 238 Jose Mesa .30 .10
❑ 239 Wilson Alvarez .30 .10
❑ 240 Wade Boggs .50 .20
❑ 241 Fred McGriff .50 .20
❑ 242 Jose Canseco .50 .20
❑ 243 Kevin Stocker .30 .10
❑ 244 Roberto Hernandez .30 .10
❑ 245 Bubba Trammell .30 .10
❑ 246 John Flaherty .30 .10
❑ 247 Ivan Rodriguez .50 .20
❑ 248 Rusty Greer .30 .10
❑ 249 Rafael Palmeiro .50 .20
❑ 250 Jeff Zimmerman .30 .10
❑ 251 Royce Clayton .30 .10
❑ 252 Todd Zeile .30 .10
❑ 253 John Wetteland .30 .10
❑ 254 Ruben Mateo .30 .10
❑ 255 Kelvim Escobar .30 .10
❑ 256 David Wells .30 .10
❑ 257 Shawn Green .30 .10
❑ 258 Homer Bush .30 .10
❑ 259 Shannon Stewart .30 .10
❑ 260 Carlos Delgado .30 .10
❑ 261 Roy Halladay .30 .10
❑ 262 Fernando Tatis SH CL .30 .10
❑ 263 Jose Jimenez SH CL .30 .10
❑ 264 Tony Gwynn SH CL .50 .20
❑ 265 Wade Boggs SH CL .30 .10
❑ 266 Cal Ripken SH CL 1.25 .50
❑ 267 David Cone SH CL .30 .10
❑ 268 Mark McGwire SH CL 1.25 .50
❑ 269 Pedro Martinez SH CL .50 .20
❑ 270 Nomar Garciaparra SH CL .75 .30
❑ 271 Nick Johnson SR .75 .30
❑ 272 Mark Quinn SR .50 .20
❑ 273 Roosevelt Brown SR .50 .20
❑ 274 Terrence Long SR .50 .20
❑ 275 Jason Marquis SR .50 .20
❑ 276 Kazuhiro Sasaki SR RC 1.25 .50
❑ 277 Aaron Myette SR .50 .20

❑ 278 Danys Baez SR RC .75 .30
❑ 279 Travis Dawkins SR .50 .20
❑ 280 Mark Mulder SR .75 .30
❑ 281 Chris Haas SR .50 .20
❑ 282 Milton Bradley SR .75 .30
❑ 283 Brad Penny SR .50 .20
❑ 284 Rafael Furcal SR .75 .30
❑ 285 Luis Matos SR RC .75 .30
❑ 286 Victor Santos SR RC .75 .30
❑ 287 Rico Washington SR RC .50 .20
❑ 288 Rob Bell SR .50 .20
❑ 289 Joe Crede SR 2.50 1.00
❑ 290 Pablo Ozuna SR .50 .20
❑ 291 Wascar Serrano SR RC .50 .20
❑ 292 Sang-Hoon Lee SR RC .50 .20
❑ 293 Chris Wakeland SR RC .50 .20
❑ 294 Luis Rivera SR RC .50 .20
❑ 295 Mike Lamb SR RC 1.25 .50
❑ 296 Wily Mo Pena SR .75 .30
❑ 297 Mike Meyers SR RC .75 .30
❑ 298 Mo Vaughn .30 .10
❑ 299 Darin Erstad .30 .10
❑ 300 Garret Anderson .30 .10
❑ 301 Tim Belcher .30 .10
❑ 302 Scott Spiezio .30 .10
❑ 303 Kent Bottenfield .30 .10
❑ 304 Orlando Palmeiro .30 .10
❑ 305 Jason Dickson .30 .10
❑ 306 Matt Williams .30 .10
❑ 307 Brian Anderson .30 .10
❑ 308 Hanley Frias .30 .10
❑ 309 Todd Stottlemyre .30 .10
❑ 310 Matt Mantei .30 .10
❑ 311 David Dellucci .30 .10
❑ 312 Armando Reynoso .30 .10
❑ 313 Bernard Gilkey .30 .10
❑ 314 Chipper Jones .75 .30
❑ 315 Tom Glavine .50 .20
❑ 316 Quilvio Veras .30 .10
❑ 317 Andruw Jones .50 .20
❑ 318 Bobby Bonilla .30 .10
❑ 319 Reggie Sanders .30 .10
❑ 320 Andres Galarraga .30 .10
❑ 321 George Lombard .30 .10
❑ 322 John Rocker .30 .10
❑ 323 Wally Joyner .30 .10
❑ 324 B.J. Surhoff .30 .10
❑ 325 Scott Erickson .30 .10
❑ 326 Delino DeShields .30 .10
❑ 327 Jeff Conine .30 .10
❑ 328 Mike Timlin .30 .10
❑ 329 Brady Anderson .30 .10
❑ 330 Mike Bordick .30 .10
❑ 331 Harold Baines .30 .10
❑ 332 Nomar Garciaparra 1.25 .50
❑ 333 Bret Saberhagen .30 .10
❑ 334 Ramon Martinez .30 .10
❑ 335 Donnie Sadler .30 .10
❑ 336 Wilton Veras .30 .10
❑ 337 Mike Stanley .30 .10
❑ 338 Brian Rose .30 .10
❑ 339 Carl Everett .30 .10
❑ 340 Tim Wakefield .30 .10
❑ 341 Mark Grace .50 .20
❑ 342 Kerry Wood .30 .10
❑ 343 Eric Young .30 .10
❑ 344 Jose Nieves .30 .10
❑ 345 Ismael Valdes .30 .10
❑ 346 Joe Girardi .30 .10
❑ 347 Damon Buford .30 .10
❑ 348 Ricky Gutierrez .30 .10
❑ 349 Frank Thomas .75 .30
❑ 350 Brian Simmons .30 .10
❑ 351 James Baldwin .30 .10
❑ 352 Brook Fordyce .30 .10
❑ 353 Jose Valentin .30 .10
❑ 354 Mike Sirotka .30 .10
❑ 355 Greg Norton .30 .10
❑ 356 Dante Bichette .30 .10
❑ 357 Deion Sanders .50 .20
❑ 358 Ken Griffey Jr. 1.25 .50
❑ 359 Denny Neagle .30 .10
❑ 360 Dmitri Young .30 .10
❑ 361 Pete Harnisch .30 .10
❑ 362 Michael Tucker .30 .10
❑ 363 Roberto Alomar .50 .20
❑ 364 Dave Roberts .30 .10
❑ 365 Jim Thome .50 .20
❑ 366 Bartolo Colon .30 .10
❑ 367 Travis Fryman .30 .10
❑ 368 Chuck Finley .30 .10
❑ 369 Russell Branyan .30 .10
❑ 370 Alex Ramirez .30 .10
❑ 371 Jeff Cirillo .30 .10
❑ 372 Jeffrey Hammonds .30 .10
❑ 373 Scott Karl .30 .10
❑ 374 Brent Mayne .30 .10
❑ 375 Tom Goodwin .30 .10
❑ 376 Jose Jimenez .30 .10
❑ 377 Rolando Arrojo .30 .10
❑ 378 Terry Shumpert .30 .10
❑ 379 Juan Gonzalez .30 .10
❑ 380 Bobby Higginson .30 .10
❑ 381 Tony Clark .30 .10
❑ 382 Dave Mlicki .30 .10
❑ 383 Deivi Cruz .30 .10
❑ 384 Brian Moehler .30 .10
❑ 385 Dean Palmer .30 .10
❑ 386 Luis Castillo .30 .10
❑ 387 Mike Redmond .30 .10
❑ 388 Alex Fernandez .30 .10
❑ 389 Brant Brown .30 .10
❑ 390 Dave Berg .30 .10
❑ 391 A.J. Burnett .30 .10
❑ 392 Mark Kotsay .30 .10
❑ 393 Craig Biggio .50 .20
❑ 394 Daryle Ward .30 .10
❑ 395 Lance Berkman .30 .10
❑ 396 Roger Cedeno .30 .10
❑ 397 Scott Elarton .30 .10
❑ 398 Octavio Dotel .30 .10
❑ 399 Ken Caminiti .30 .10
❑ 400 Johnny Damon .50 .20
❑ 401 Mike Sweeney .30 .10
❑ 402 Jeff Suppan .30 .10
❑ 403 Rey Sanchez .30 .10
❑ 404 Blake Stein .30 .10
❑ 405 Ricky Bottalico .30 .10
❑ 406 Jay Witasick .30 .10
❑ 407 Shawn Green .30 .10
❑ 408 Orel Hershiser .30 .10
❑ 409 Gary Sheffield .30 .10
❑ 410 Todd Hollandsworth .30 .10
❑ 411 Terry Adams .30 .10
❑ 412 Todd Hundley .30 .10
❑ 413 Eric Karros .30 .10
❑ 414 F.P. Santangelo .30 .10
❑ 415 Alex Cora .30 .10
❑ 416 Marquis Grissom .30 .10
❑ 417 Henry Blanco .30 .10
❑ 418 Jose Hernandez .30 .10
❑ 419 Kyle Peterson .30 .10
❑ 420 John Snyder RC .30 .10
❑ 421 Bob Wickman .30 .10
❑ 422 Jamey Wright .30 .10
❑ 423 Chad Allen .30 .10
❑ 424 Todd Walker .30 .10
❑ 425 J.C. Romero RC .30 .10
❑ 426 Butch Huskey .30 .10
❑ 427 Jacque Jones .30 .10
❑ 428 Matt Lawton .30 .10
❑ 429 Rondell White .30 .10
❑ 430 Jose Vidro .30 .10
❑ 431 Hideki Irabu .30 .10
❑ 432 Javier Vazquez .30 .10
❑ 433 Lee Stevens .30 .10
❑ 434 Mike Thurman .30 .10
❑ 435 Geoff Blum .30 .10
❑ 436 Mike Hampton .30 .10
❑ 437 Mike Piazza 1.25 .50
❑ 438 Al Leiter .30 .10
❑ 439 Derek Bell .30 .10
❑ 440 Armando Benitez .30 .10
❑ 441 Rey Ordonez .30 .10
❑ 442 Todd Zeile .30 .10
❑ 443 Roger Clemens 1.50 .60
❑ 444 Ramiro Mendoza .30 .10
❑ 445 Andy Pettitte .50 .20
❑ 446 Scott Brosius .30 .10
❑ 447 Mariano Rivera .75 .30
❑ 448 Jim Leyritz .30 .10
❑ 449 Jorge Posada .50 .20
❑ 450 Omar Olivares .30 .10
❑ 451 Ben Grieve .30 .10
❑ 452 A.J. Hinch .30 .10
❑ 453 Gil Heredia .30 .10
❑ 454 Kevin Appier .30 .10
❑ 455 Ryan Christenson .30 .10
❑ 456 Ramon Hernandez .30 .10
❑ 457 Scott Rolen .50 .20
❑ 458 Alex Arias .30 .10
❑ 459 Andy Ashby .30 .10
❑ 460 Kevin Jordan UER 474 .30 .10
❑ 461 Robert Person .30 .10
❑ 462 Paul Byrd .30 .10
❑ 463 Curt Schilling .30 .10
❑ 464 Mike Jackson .30 .10
❑ 465 Jason Kendall .30 .10
❑ 466 Pat Meares .30 .10
❑ 467 Bruce Aven .30 .10
❑ 468 Todd Ritchie .30 .10
❑ 469 Wil Cordero .30 .10
❑ 470 Aramis Ramirez .30 .10
❑ 471 Andy Benes .30 .10
❑ 472 Ray Lankford .30 .10
❑ 473 Fernando Vina .30 .10
❑ 474 Jim Edmonds .30 .10
❑ 475 Craig Paquette .30 .10
❑ 476 Pat Hentgen .30 .10
❑ 477 Darryl Kile .30 .10
❑ 478 Sterling Hitchcock .30 .10
❑ 479 Ruben Rivera .30 .10
❑ 480 Ryan Klesko .30 .10
❑ 481 Phil Nevin .30 .10
❑ 482 Woody Williams .30 .10
❑ 483 Carlos Hernandez .30 .10
❑ 484 Brian Meadows .30 .10
❑ 485 Bret Boone .30 .10
❑ 486 Barry Bonds 2.00 .75
❑ 487 Russ Ortiz .30 .10
❑ 488 Bobby Estalella .30 .10
❑ 489 Rich Aurilia .30 .10
❑ 490 Bill Mueller .30 .10
❑ 491 Joe Nathan .30 .10
❑ 492 Russ Davis .30 .10
❑ 493 John Olerud .30 .10
❑ 494 Alex Rodriguez 1.25 .50
❑ 495 Freddy Garcia .30 .10
❑ 496 Carlos Guillen .30 .10
❑ 497 Aaron Sele .30 .10
❑ 498 Brett Tomko .30 .10
❑ 499 Jamie Moyer .30 .10
❑ 500 Mike Cameron .30 .10
❑ 501 Vinny Castilla .30 .10
❑ 502 Gerald Williams .30 .10
❑ 503 Mike DiFelice .30 .10
❑ 504 Ryan Rupe .30 .10
❑ 505 Greg Vaughn .30 .10
❑ 506 Miguel Cairo .30 .10
❑ 507 Juan Guzman .30 .10
❑ 508 Jose Guillen .30 .10
❑ 509 Gabe Kapler .30 .10
❑ 510 Rick Helling .30 .10
❑ 511 David Segui .30 .10
❑ 512 Doug Davis .30 .10
❑ 513 Justin Thompson .30 .10
❑ 514 Chad Curtis .30 .10
❑ 515 Tony Batista .30 .10
❑ 516 Billy Koch .30 .10
❑ 517 Raul Mondesi .30 .10
❑ 518 Joey Hamilton .30 .10
❑ 519 Darrin Fletcher .30 .10
❑ 520 Brad Fullmer .30 .10
❑ 521 Jose Cruz Jr. .30 .10
❑ 522 Kevin Witt .30 .10
❑ 523 Mark McGwire AUT 1.00 .40
❑ 524 Roberto Alomar AUT .30 .10
❑ 525 Chipper Jones AUT .50 .20
❑ 526 Derek Jeter AUT 1.00 .40
❑ 527 Ken Griffey Jr. AUT .75 .30
❑ 528 Sammy Sosa AUT .50 .20
❑ 529 Manny Ramirez AUT .50 .20
❑ 530 Ivan Rodriguez AUT .30 .10
❑ 531 Pedro Martinez AUT .50 .20
❑ 532 Mariano Rivera CL .50 .20
❑ 533 Sammy Sosa CL .50 .20
❑ 534 Cal Ripken CL 1.25 .50
❑ 535 Vladimir Guerrero CL .50 .20

❑ 536 Tony Gwynn CL .50 .20
❑ 537 Mark McGwire CL 1.00 .40
❑ 538 Bernie Williams CL .30 .10
❑ 539 Pedro Martinez CL .50 .20
❑ 540 Ken Griffey Jr. CL .75 .30

2001 Upper Deck

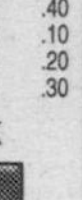

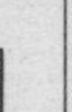
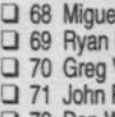

❑ COMPLETE SET (450) 150.00 90.00
❑ COMPLETE SERIES 1 (270) 40.00 20.00
❑ COMPLETE SERIES 2 (180) 100.00 60.00
❑ COMMON (46-270/300-450) .30 .10
❑ COMMON SR (1-45/271-300) .50 .20
❑ 1 Jeff DaVanon SR .50 .20
❑ 2 Aubrey Huff SR .50 .20
❑ 3 Pasqual Coco SR .50 .20
❑ 4 Barry Zito SR .60 .25
❑ 5 Augie Ojeda SR .50 .20
❑ 6 Chris Richard SR .50 .20
❑ 7 Josh Phelps SR .50 .20
❑ 8 Kevin Nicholson SR .50 .20
❑ 9 Juan Guzman SR .50 .20
❑ 10 Brandon Kolb SR .50 .20
❑ 11 Johan Santana SR 6.00 2.50
❑ 12 Josh Kalinowski SR .50 .20
❑ 13 Tike Redman SR .50 .20
❑ 14 Ivanon Coffie SR .50 .20
❑ 15 Chad Durbin SR .50 .20
❑ 16 Derrick Turnbow SR .50 .20
❑ 17 Scott Downs SR .50 .20
❑ 18 Jason Grilli SR .50 .20
❑ 19 Mark Buehrle SR .60 .25
❑ 20 Paxton Crawford SR .50 .20
❑ 21 Bronson Arroyo SR 1.00 .40
❑ 22 Tomas De la Rosa SR .50 .20
❑ 23 Paul Rigdon SR .50 .20
❑ 24 Rob Ramsay SR .50 .20
❑ 25 Damian Rolls SR .50 .20
❑ 26 Jason Conti SR .50 .20
❑ 27 John Parrish SR .50 .20
❑ 28 Geraldo Guzman SR .50 .20
❑ 29 Tony Mota SR .50 .20
❑ 30 Luis Rivas SR .50 .20
❑ 31 Brian Tollberg SR .50 .20
❑ 32 Adam Bernero SR .50 .20
❑ 33 Michael Cuddyer SR .50 .20
❑ 34 Josue Espada SR .50 .20
❑ 35 Joe Lawrence SR .50 .20
❑ 36 Chad Moeller SR .50 .20
❑ 37 Nick Bierbrodt SR .50 .20
❑ 38 DeWayne Wise SR .50 .20
❑ 39 Javier Cardona SR .50 .20
❑ 40 Hiram Bocachica SR .50 .20
❑ 41 Giuseppe Chiaramonte SR .50 .20
❑ 42 Alex Cabrera SR .50 .20
❑ 43 Jimmy Rollins SR .50 .20
❑ 44 Pat Flury SR RC .50 .20
❑ 45 Leo Estrella SR .50 .20
❑ 46 Darin Erstad .30 .10
❑ 47 Seth Etherton .30 .10
❑ 48 Troy Glaus .30 .10
❑ 49 Brian Cooper .30 .10
❑ 50 Tim Salmon .50 .20
❑ 51 Adam Kennedy .30 .10
❑ 52 Bengie Molina .30 .10
❑ 53 Jason Giambi .30 .10
❑ 54 Miguel Tejada .30 .10
❑ 55 Tim Hudson .30 .10
❑ 56 Eric Chavez .30 .10
❑ 57 Terrence Long .30 .10
❑ 58 Jason Isringhausen .30 .10
❑ 59 Ramon Hernandez .30 .10
❑ 60 Raul Mondesi .30 .10
❑ 61 David Wells .30 .10
❑ 62 Shannon Stewart .30 .10
❑ 63 Tony Batista .30 .10
❑ 64 Brad Fullmer .30 .10
❑ 65 Chris Carpenter .30 .10
❑ 66 Homer Bush .30 .10
❑ 67 Gerald Williams .30 .10
❑ 68 Miguel Cairo .30 .10
❑ 69 Ryan Rupe .30 .10
❑ 70 Greg Vaughn .30 .10
❑ 71 John Flaherty .30 .10
❑ 72 Dan Wheeler .30 .10
❑ 73 Fred McGriff .50 .20
❑ 74 Roberto Alomar .50 .20
❑ 75 Bartolo Colon .30 .10
❑ 76 Kenny Lofton .30 .10
❑ 77 David Segui .30 .10
❑ 78 Omar Vizquel .50 .20
❑ 79 Russ Branyan .30 .10
❑ 80 Chuck Finley .30 .10
❑ 81 Manny Ramirez UER .50 .20
❑ 82 Alex Rodriguez 1.25 .50
❑ 83 John Halama .30 .10
❑ 84 Mike Cameron .30 .10
❑ 85 David Bell .30 .10
❑ 86 Jay Buhner .30 .10
❑ 87 Aaron Sele .30 .10
❑ 88 Rickey Henderson .75 .30
❑ 89 Brook Fordyce .30 .10
❑ 90 Cal Ripken 2.50 1.00
❑ 91 Mike Mussina .50 .20
❑ 92 Delino DeShields .30 .10
❑ 93 Melvin Mora .30 .10
❑ 94 Sidney Ponson .30 .10
❑ 95 Brady Anderson .30 .10
❑ 96 Ivan Rodriguez .50 .20
❑ 97 Ricky Ledee .30 .10
❑ 98 Rick Helling .30 .10
❑ 99 Ruben Mateo .30 .10
❑ 100 Luis Alicea .30 .10
❑ 101 John Wetteland .30 .10
❑ 102 Mike Lamb .30 .10
❑ 103 Carl Everett .30 .10
❑ 104 Troy O'Leary .30 .10
❑ 105 Wilton Veras .30 .10
❑ 106 Pedro Martinez .50 .20
❑ 107 Rolando Arrojo .30 .10
❑ 108 Scott Hatteberg .30 .10
❑ 109 Jason Varitek .75 .30
❑ 110 Jose Offerman .30 .10
❑ 111 Carlos Beltran .30 .10
❑ 112 Johnny Damon .50 .20
❑ 113 Mark Quinn .30 .10
❑ 114 Rey Sanchez .30 .10
❑ 115 Mac Suzuki .30 .10
❑ 116 Jermaine Dye .30 .10
❑ 117 Chris Fussell .30 .10
❑ 118 Jeff Weaver .30 .10
❑ 119 Dean Palmer .30 .10
❑ 120 Robert Fick .30 .10
❑ 121 Brian Moehler .30 .10
❑ 122 Damion Easley .30 .10
❑ 123 Juan Encarnacion .30 .10
❑ 124 Tony Clark .30 .10
❑ 125 Cristian Guzman .30 .10
❑ 126 Matt LeCroy .30 .10
❑ 127 Eric Milton .30 .10
❑ 128 Jay Canizaro .30 .10
❑ 129 David Ortiz .75 .30
❑ 130 Brad Radke .30 .10
❑ 131 Jacque Jones .30 .10
❑ 132 Magglio Ordonez .30 .10
❑ 133 Carlos Lee .30 .10
❑ 134 Mike Sirotka .30 .10
❑ 135 Ray Durham .30 .10
❑ 136 Paul Konerko .30 .10
❑ 137 Charles Johnson .30 .10
❑ 138 James Baldwin .30 .10
❑ 139 Jeff Abbott .30 .10
❑ 140 Roger Clemens 1.50 .60
❑ 141 Derek Jeter 2.00 .75
❑ 142 David Justice .30 .10
❑ 143 Ramiro Mendoza .30 .10
❑ 144 Chuck Knoblauch .30 .10
❑ 145 Orlando Hernandez .30 .10
❑ 146 Alfonso Soriano .50 .20
❑ 147 Jeff Bagwell .50 .20
❑ 148 Julio Lugo .30 .10
❑ 149 Mitch Meluskey .30 .10
❑ 150 Jose Lima .30 .10
❑ 151 Richard Hidalgo .30 .10
❑ 152 Moises Alou .30 .10
❑ 153 Scott Elarton .30 .10
❑ 154 Andruw Jones .50 .20
❑ 155 Quilvio Veras .30 .10
❑ 156 Greg Maddux 1.25 .50
❑ 157 Brian Jordan .30 .10
❑ 158 Andres Galarraga .30 .10
❑ 159 Kevin Millwood .30 .10
❑ 160 Rafael Furcal .30 .10
❑ 161 Jeromy Burnitz .30 .10
❑ 162 Jimmy Haynes .30 .10
❑ 163 Mark Loretta .30 .10
❑ 164 Ron Belliard .30 .10
❑ 165 Richie Sexson .30 .10
❑ 166 Kevin Barker .30 .10
❑ 167 Jeff D'Amico .30 .10
❑ 168 Rick Ankiel .30 .10
❑ 169 Mark McGwire 2.00 .75
❑ 170 J.D. Drew .30 .10
❑ 171 Eli Marrero .30 .10
❑ 172 Darryl Kile .30 .10
❑ 173 Edgar Renteria .30 .10
❑ 174 Will Clark .50 .20
❑ 175 Eric Young .30 .10
❑ 176 Mark Grace .50 .20
❑ 177 Jon Lieber .30 .10
❑ 178 Damon Buford .30 .10
❑ 179 Kerry Wood .30 .10
❑ 180 Rondell White .30 .10
❑ 181 Joe Girardi .30 .10
❑ 182 Curt Schilling .30 .10
❑ 183 Randy Johnson .75 .30
❑ 184 Steve Finley .30 .10
❑ 185 Kelly Stinnett .30 .10
❑ 186 Jay Bell .30 .10
❑ 187 Matt Mantei .30 .10
❑ 188 Luis Gonzalez .30 .10
❑ 189 Shawn Green .30 .10
❑ 190 Todd Hundley .30 .10
❑ 191 Chan Ho Park .30 .10
❑ 192 Adrian Beltre .30 .10
❑ 193 Mark Grudzielanek .30 .10
❑ 194 Gary Sheffield .30 .10
❑ 195 Tom Goodwin .30 .10
❑ 196 Lee Stevens .30 .10
❑ 197 Javier Vazquez .30 .10
❑ 198 Milton Bradley .30 .10
❑ 199 Vladimir Guerrero .75 .30
❑ 200 Carl Pavano .30 .10
❑ 201 Orlando Cabrera .30 .10
❑ 202 Tony Armas Jr. .30 .10
❑ 203 Jeff Kent .30 .10
❑ 204 Calvin Murray .30 .10
❑ 205 Ellis Burks .30 .10
❑ 206 Barry Bonds 2.00 .75
❑ 207 Russ Ortiz .30 .10
❑ 208 Marvin Benard .30 .10
❑ 209 Joe Nathan .30 .10
❑ 210 Preston Wilson .30 .10
❑ 211 Cliff Floyd .30 .10
❑ 212 Mike Lowell .30 .10
❑ 213 Ryan Dempster .30 .10
❑ 214 Brad Penny .30 .10
❑ 215 Mike Redmond .30 .10
❑ 216 Luis Castillo .30 .10
❑ 217 Derek Bell .30 .10
❑ 218 Mike Hampton .30 .10
❑ 219 Todd Zeile .30 .10
❑ 220 Robin Ventura .30 .10
❑ 221 Mike Piazza 1.25 .50
❑ 222 Al Leiter .30 .10
❑ 223 Edgardo Alfonzo .30 .10
❑ 224 Mike Bordick .30 .10
❑ 225 Phil Nevin .30 .10
❑ 226 Ryan Klesko .30 .10
❑ 227 Adam Eaton .30 .10
❑ 228 Eric Owens .30 .10

❑ 229	Tony Gwynn	1.00	.40
❑ 230	Matt Clement	.30	.10
❑ 231	Wiki Gonzalez	.30	.10
❑ 232	Robert Person	.30	.10
❑ 233	Doug Glanville	.30	.10
❑ 234	Scott Rolen	.50	.20
❑ 235	Mike Lieberthal	.30	.10
❑ 236	Randy Wolf	.30	.10
❑ 237	Bob Abreu	.30	.10
❑ 238	Pat Burrell	.30	.10
❑ 239	Bruce Chen	.30	.10
❑ 240	Kevin Young	.30	.10
❑ 241	Todd Ritchie	.30	.10
❑ 242	Adrian Brown	.30	.10
❑ 243	Chad Hermansen	.30	.10
❑ 244	Warren Morris	.30	.10
❑ 245	Kris Benson	.30	.10
❑ 246	Jason Kendall	.30	.10
❑ 247	Pokey Reese	.30	.10
❑ 248	Rob Bell	.30	.10
❑ 249	Ken Griffey Jr.	1.25	.50
❑ 250	Sean Casey	.30	.10
❑ 251	Aaron Boone	.30	.10
❑ 252	Pete Harnisch	.30	.10
❑ 253	Barry Larkin	.50	.20
❑ 254	Dmitri Young	.30	.10
❑ 255	Todd Hollandsworth	.30	.10
❑ 256	Pedro Astacio	.30	.10
❑ 257	Todd Helton	.50	.20
❑ 258	Terry Shumpert	.30	.10
❑ 259	Neifi Perez	.30	.10
❑ 260	Jeffrey Hammonds	.30	.10
❑ 261	Ben Petrick	.30	.10
❑ 262	Mark McGwire SH	1.00	.40
❑ 263	Derek Jeter SH	1.00	.40
❑ 264	Sammy Sosa SH	.50	.20
❑ 265	Cal Ripken SH	1.25	.50
❑ 266	Pedro Martinez SH	.50	.20
❑ 267	Barry Bonds SH	1.00	.40
❑ 268	Fred McGriff SH	.30	.10
❑ 269	Randy Johnson SH	.50	.20
❑ 270	Darin Erstad SH	.30	.10
❑ 271	Ichiro Suzuki SR RC	15.00	6.00
❑ 272	Wilson Betemit SR RC	2.00	.75
❑ 273	Corey Patterson SR	.50	.20
❑ 274	Sean Douglass SR RC	.50	.20
❑ 275	Mike Penney SR RC	.50	.20
❑ 276	Nate Teut SR RC	.50	.20
❑ 277	Ricardo Rodriguez SR RC	.50	.20
❑ 278	Brandon Duckworth SR RC	.50	.20
❑ 279	Rafael Soriano SR RC	.50	.20
❑ 280	Juan Diaz SR RC	.50	.20
❑ 281	Horacio Ramirez SR RC	.60	.25
❑ 282	Tsuyoshi Shinjo SR RC	.60	.25
❑ 283	Keith Ginter SR	.50	.20
❑ 284	Esix Snead SR RC	.50	.20
❑ 285	Erick Almonte SR RC	.50	.20
❑ 286	Travis Hafner SR RC	5.00	2.00
❑ 287	Jason Smith SR RC	.50	.20
❑ 288	Jackson Melian SR RC	.50	.20
❑ 289	Tyler Walker SR RC	.50	.20
❑ 290	Jason Standridge SR	.50	.20
❑ 291	Juan Uribe SR RC	.60	.25
❑ 292	Adrian Hernandez SR RC	.50	.20
❑ 293	Jason Michaels SR RC	.50	.20
❑ 294	Jason Hart SR	.50	.20
❑ 295	Albert Pujols SR RC	50.00	20.00
❑ 296	Morgan Ensberg SR RC	2.00	.75
❑ 297	Brandon Inge SR	.50	.20
❑ 298	Jesus Colome SR	.50	.20
❑ 299	Kyle Kessel SR RC	.50	.20
❑ 300	Timo Perez SR	.50	.20
❑ 301	Mo Vaughn	.30	.10
❑ 302	Ismael Valdes	.30	.10
❑ 303	Glenallen Hill	.30	.10
❑ 304	Garret Anderson	.30	.10
❑ 305	Johnny Damon	.50	.20
❑ 306	Jose Ortiz	.30	.10
❑ 307	Mark Mulder	.30	.10
❑ 308	Adam Piatt	.30	.10
❑ 309	Gil Heredia	.30	.10
❑ 310	Mike Sirotka	.30	.10
❑ 311	Carlos Delgado	.30	.10
❑ 312	Alex Gonzalez	.30	.10
❑ 313	Jose Cruz Jr.	.30	.10
❑ 314	Darrin Fletcher	.30	.10
❑ 315	Ben Grieve	.30	.10
❑ 316	Vinny Castilla	.30	.10
❑ 317	Wilson Alvarez	.30	.10
❑ 318	Brent Abernathy	.30	.10
❑ 319	Ellis Burks	.30	.10
❑ 320	Jim Thome	.50	.20
❑ 321	Juan Gonzalez	.30	.10
❑ 322	Ed Taubensee	.30	.10
❑ 323	Travis Fryman	.30	.10
❑ 324	John Olerud	.30	.10
❑ 325	Edgar Martinez	.50	.20
❑ 326	Freddy Garcia	.30	.10
❑ 327	Bret Boone	.50	.20
❑ 328	Kazuhiro Sasaki	.30	.10
❑ 329	Albert Belle	.30	.10
❑ 330	Mike Bordick	.30	.10
❑ 331	David Segui	.30	.10
❑ 332	Pat Hentgen	.30	.10
❑ 333	Alex Rodriguez	1.25	.50
❑ 334	Andres Galarraga	.30	.10
❑ 335	Gabe Kapler	.30	.10
❑ 336	Ken Caminiti	.30	.10
❑ 337	Rafael Palmeiro	.50	.20
❑ 338	Manny Ramirez Sox	.50	.20
❑ 339	David Cone	.30	.10
❑ 340	Nomar Garciaparra	1.25	.50
❑ 341	Trot Nixon	.30	.10
❑ 342	Derek Lowe	.30	.10
❑ 343	Roberto Hernandez	.30	.10
❑ 344	Mike Sweeney	.30	.10
❑ 345	Carlos Febles	.30	.10
❑ 346	Jeff Suppan	.30	.10
❑ 347	Roger Cedeno	.30	.10
❑ 348	Bobby Higginson	.30	.10
❑ 349	Deivi Cruz	.30	.10
❑ 350	Mitch Meluskey	.30	.10
❑ 351	Matt Lawton	.30	.10
❑ 352	Mark Redman	.30	.10
❑ 353	Jay Canizaro	.30	.10
❑ 354	Corey Koskie	.30	.10
❑ 355	Matt Kinney	.30	.10
❑ 356	Frank Thomas	.75	.30
❑ 357	Sandy Alomar Jr.	.30	.10
❑ 358	David Wells	.30	.10
❑ 359	Jim Parque	.30	.10
❑ 360	Chris Singleton	.30	.10
❑ 361	Tino Martinez	.50	.20
❑ 362	Paul O'Neill	.50	.20
❑ 363	Mike Mussina	.50	.20
❑ 364	Bernie Williams	.50	.20
❑ 365	Andy Pettitte	.50	.20
❑ 366	Mariano Rivera	.75	.30
❑ 367	Brad Ausmus	.30	.10
❑ 368	Craig Biggio	.50	.20
❑ 369	Lance Berkman	.30	.10
❑ 370	Shane Reynolds	.30	.10
❑ 371	Chipper Jones	.75	.30
❑ 372	Tom Glavine	.50	.20
❑ 373	B.J. Surhoff	.30	.10
❑ 374	John Smoltz	.50	.20
❑ 375	Rico Brogna	.30	.10
❑ 376	Geoff Jenkins	.30	.10
❑ 377	Jose Hernandez	.30	.10
❑ 378	Tyler Houston	.30	.10
❑ 379	Henry Blanco	.30	.10
❑ 380	Jeffrey Hammonds	.30	.10
❑ 381	Jim Edmonds	.30	.10
❑ 382	Fernando Vina	.30	.10
❑ 383	Andy Benes	.30	.10
❑ 384	Ray Lankford	.30	.10
❑ 385	Dustin Hermanson	.30	.10
❑ 386	Todd Hundley	.30	.10
❑ 387	Sammy Sosa	.75	.30
❑ 388	Tom Gordon	.30	.10
❑ 389	Bill Mueller	.30	.10
❑ 390	Ron Coomer	.30	.10
❑ 391	Matt Stairs	.30	.10
❑ 392	Mark Grace	.50	.20
❑ 393	Matt Williams	.30	.10
❑ 394	Todd Stottlemyre	.30	.10
❑ 395	Tony Womack	.30	.10
❑ 396	Erubiel Durazo	.30	.10
❑ 397	Reggie Sanders	.30	.10
❑ 398	Andy Ashby	.30	.10
❑ 399	Eric Karros	.30	.10
❑ 400	Kevin Brown	.30	.10
❑ 401	Darren Dreifort	.30	.10
❑ 402	Fernando Tatis	.30	.10
❑ 403	Jose Vidro	.30	.10
❑ 404	Peter Bergeron	.30	.10
❑ 405	Geoff Blum	.30	.10
❑ 406	J.T. Snow	.30	.10
❑ 407	Livan Hernandez	.30	.10
❑ 408	Robb Nen	.30	.10
❑ 409	Bobby Estalella	.30	.10
❑ 410	Rich Aurilia	.30	.10
❑ 411	Eric Davis	.30	.10
❑ 412	Charles Johnson	.30	.10
❑ 413	Alex Gonzalez	.30	.10
❑ 414	A.J. Burnett	.30	.10
❑ 415	Antonio Alfonseca	.30	.10
❑ 416	Derrek Lee	.50	.20
❑ 417	Jay Payton	.30	.10
❑ 418	Kevin Appier	.30	.10
❑ 419	Steve Trachsel	.30	.10
❑ 420	Rey Ordonez	.30	.10
❑ 421	Darryl Hamilton	.30	.10
❑ 422	Ben Davis	.30	.10
❑ 423	Damian Jackson	.30	.10
❑ 424	Mark Kotsay	.30	.10
❑ 425	Trevor Hoffman	.30	.10
❑ 426	Travis Lee	.30	.10
❑ 427	Omar Daal	.30	.10
❑ 428	Paul Byrd	.30	.10
❑ 429	Reggie Taylor	.30	.10
❑ 430	Brian Giles	.30	.10
❑ 431	Derek Bell	.30	.10
❑ 432	Francisco Cordova	.30	.10
❑ 433	Pat Meares	.30	.10
❑ 434	Scott Williamson	.30	.10
❑ 435	Jason LaRue	.30	.10
❑ 436	Michael Tucker	.30	.10
❑ 437	Wilton Guerrero	.30	.10
❑ 438	Mike Hampton	.30	.10
❑ 439	Ron Gant	.30	.10
❑ 440	Jeff Cirillo	.30	.10
❑ 441	Denny Neagle	.30	.10
❑ 442	Larry Walker	.30	.10
❑ 443	Juan Pierre	.30	.10
❑ 444	Todd Walker	.30	.10
❑ 445	Jason Giambi SH CL	.30	.10
❑ 446	Jeff Kent SH CL	.30	.10
❑ 447	Mariano Rivera SH CL	.50	.20
❑ 448	Edgar Martinez SH CL	.30	.10
❑ 449	Troy Glaus SH CL	.30	.10
❑ 450	Alex Rodriguez SH CL	.75	.30

2002 Upper Deck

❑	COMPLETE SET (745)	160.00	85.00
❑	COMPLETE SERIES 1 (500)	110.00	60.00
❑	COMPLETE SERIES 2 (245)	50.00	25.00
❑	COMMON (51-500/546-745)	.30	.10
❑	COMMON SR (1-50/501-545)	1.00	.40
❑ 1	Mark Prior SR	2.00	.75
❑ 2	Mark Teixeira SR	5.00	2.00
❑ 3	Brian Roberts SR	2.00	.75
❑ 4	Jason Romano SR	1.00	.40
❑ 5	Dennis Stark SR	1.00	.40
❑ 6	Oscar Salazar SR	1.00	.40
❑ 7	John Patterson SR	1.00	.40
❑ 8	Shane Loux SR	1.00	.40
❑ 9	Marcus Giles SR	1.00	.40
❑ 10	Juan Cruz SR	1.00	.40
❑ 11	Jorge Julio SR	1.00	.40

❑ 12 Adam Dunn SR 1.00 .40
❑ 13 Delvin James SR 1.00 .40
❑ 14 Jeremy Affeldt SR 1.00 .40
❑ 15 Tim Raines Jr. SR 1.00 .40
❑ 16 Luke Hudson SR 1.00 .40
❑ 17 Todd Sears SR 1.00 .40
❑ 18 George Perez SR 1.00 .40
❑ 19 Wilmy Caceres SR 1.00 .40
❑ 20 Abraham Nunez SR 1.00 .40
❑ 21 Mike Amrhein SR RC 1.00 .40
❑ 22 Carlos Hernandez SR 1.00 .40
❑ 23 Scott Hodges SR 1.00 .40
❑ 24 Brandon Knight SR 1.00 .40
❑ 25 Geoff Goetz SR 1.00 .40
❑ 26 Carlos Garcia SR 1.00 .40
❑ 27 Luis Pineda SR 1.00 .40
❑ 28 Chris Gissell SR 1.00 .40
❑ 29 Jae Weong Seo SR 1.00 .40
❑ 30 Paul Phillips SR 1.00 .40
❑ 31 Cory Aldridge SR 1.00 .40
❑ 32 Aaron Cook SR RC 1.00 .40
❑ 33 Rendy Espina SR RC 1.00 .40
❑ 34 Jason Phillips SR 1.00 .40
❑ 35 Carlos Silva SR 1.00 .40
❑ 36 Ryan Mills SR 1.00 .40
❑ 37 Pedro Santana SR 1.00 .40
❑ 38 John Grabow SR 1.00 .40
❑ 39 Cody Ransom SR 1.00 .40
❑ 40 Orlando Woodards SR 1.00 .40
❑ 41 Bud Smith SR 1.00 .40
❑ 42 Junior Guerrero SR 1.00 .40
❑ 43 David Brous SR 1.00 .40
❑ 44 Steve Green SR 1.00 .40
❑ 45 Brian Rogers SR 1.00 .40
❑ 46 Juan Figueroa SR RC 1.00 .40
❑ 47 Nick Punto SR 1.00 .40
❑ 48 Junior Herndon SR 1.00 .40
❑ 49 Justin Kaye SR 1.00 .40
❑ 50 Jason Karnuth SR 1.00 .40
❑ 51 Troy Glaus .30 .10
❑ 52 Bengie Molina .30 .10
❑ 53 Ramon Ortiz .30 .10
❑ 54 Adam Kennedy .30 .10
❑ 55 Jarrod Washburn .30 .10
❑ 56 Troy Percival .30 .10
❑ 57 David Eckstein .30 .10
❑ 58 Ben Weber .30 .10
❑ 59 Larry Barnes .30 .10
❑ 60 Ismael Valdes .30 .10
❑ 61 Benji Gil .30 .10
❑ 62 Scott Schoeneweis .30 .10
❑ 63 Pat Rapp .30 .10
❑ 64 Jason Giambi .30 .10
❑ 65 Mark Mulder .30 .10
❑ 66 Ron Gant .30 .10
❑ 67 Johnny Damon .50 .20
❑ 68 Adam Piatt .30 .10
❑ 69 Jermaine Dye .30 .10
❑ 70 Jason Hart .30 .10
❑ 71 Eric Chavez .30 .10
❑ 72 Jim Mecir .30 .10
❑ 73 Barry Zito .30 .10
❑ 74 Jason Isringhausen .30 .10
❑ 75 Jeremy Giambi .30 .10
❑ 76 Olmedo Saenz .30 .10
❑ 77 Terrence Long .30 .10
❑ 78 Ramon Hernandez .30 .10
❑ 79 Chris Carpenter .30 .10
❑ 80 Raul Mondesi .30 .10
❑ 81 Carlos Delgado .30 .10
❑ 82 Billy Koch .30 .10
❑ 83 Vernon Wells .30 .10
❑ 84 Darrin Fletcher .30 .10
❑ 85 Homer Bush .30 .10
❑ 86 Pasqual Coco .30 .10
❑ 87 Shannon Stewart .30 .10
❑ 88 Chris Woodward .30 .10
❑ 89 Joe Lawrence .30 .10
❑ 90 Esteban Loaiza .30 .10
❑ 91 Cesar Izturis .30 .10
❑ 92 Kelvim Escobar .30 .10
❑ 93 Greg Vaughn .30 .10
❑ 94 Brent Abernathy .30 .10
❑ 95 Tanyon Sturtze .30 .10
❑ 96 Steve Cox .30 .10
❑ 97 Aubrey Huff .30 .10
❑ 98 Jesus Colome .30 .10
❑ 99 Ben Grieve .30 .10
❑ 100 Esteban Yan .30 .10
❑ 101 Joe Kennedy .30 .10
❑ 102 Felix Martinez .30 .10
❑ 103 Nick Bierbrodt .30 .10
❑ 104 Damian Rolls .30 .10
❑ 105 Russ Johnson .30 .10
❑ 106 Toby Hall .30 .10
❑ 107 Roberto Alomar .50 .20
❑ 108 Bartolo Colon .30 .10
❑ 109 John Rocker .30 .10
❑ 110 Juan Gonzalez .30 .10
❑ 111 Einar Diaz .30 .10
❑ 112 Chuck Finley .30 .10
❑ 113 Kenny Lofton .30 .10
❑ 114 Danys Baez .30 .10
❑ 115 Travis Fryman .30 .10
❑ 116 C.C. Sabathia .30 .10
❑ 117 Paul Shuey .30 .10
❑ 118 Marty Cordova .30 .10
❑ 119 Ellis Burks .30 .10
❑ 120 Bob Wickman .30 .10
❑ 121 Edgar Martinez .50 .20
❑ 122 Freddy Garcia .30 .10
❑ 123 Ichiro Suzuki 1.50 .60
❑ 124 John Olerud .30 .10
❑ 125 Gil Meche .30 .10
❑ 126 Dan Wilson .30 .10
❑ 127 Aaron Sele .30 .10
❑ 128 Kazuhiro Sasaki .30 .10
❑ 129 Mark McLemore .30 .10
❑ 130 Carlos Guillen .30 .10
❑ 131 Al Martin .30 .10
❑ 132 David Bell .30 .10
❑ 133 Jay Buhner .30 .10
❑ 134 Stan Javier .30 .10
❑ 135 Tony Batista .30 .10
❑ 136 Jason Johnson .30 .10
❑ 137 Brook Fordyce .30 .10
❑ 138 Mike Kinkade .30 .10
❑ 139 Willis Roberts .30 .10
❑ 140 David Segui .30 .10
❑ 141 Josh Towers .30 .10
❑ 142 Jeff Conine .30 .10
❑ 143 Chris Richard .30 .10
❑ 144 Pat Hentgen .30 .10
❑ 145 Melvin Mora .30 .10
❑ 146 Jerry Hairston Jr. .30 .10
❑ 147 Calvin Maduro .30 .10
❑ 148 Brady Anderson .30 .10
❑ 149 Alex Rodriguez 1.25 .50
❑ 150 Kenny Rogers .30 .10
❑ 151 Chad Curtis .30 .10
❑ 152 Ricky Ledee .30 .10
❑ 153 Rafael Palmeiro .50 .20
❑ 154 Rob Bell .30 .10
❑ 155 Rick Helling .30 .10
❑ 156 Doug Davis .30 .10
❑ 157 Mike Lamb .30 .10
❑ 158 Gabe Kapler .30 .10
❑ 159 Jeff Zimmerman .30 .10
❑ 160 Bill Haselman .30 .10
❑ 161 Tim Crabtree .30 .10
❑ 162 Carlos Pena .30 .10
❑ 163 Nomar Garciaparra 1.25 .50
❑ 164 Shea Hillenbrand .30 .10
❑ 165 Hideo Nomo .75 .30
❑ 166 Manny Ramirez .50 .20
❑ 167 Jose Offerman .30 .10
❑ 168 Scott Hatteberg .30 .10
❑ 169 Trot Nixon .30 .10
❑ 170 Darren Lewis .30 .10
❑ 171 Derek Lowe .30 .10
❑ 172 Troy O'Leary .30 .10
❑ 173 Tim Wakefield .30 .10
❑ 174 Chris Stynes .30 .10
❑ 175 John Valentin .30 .10
❑ 176 David Cone .30 .10
❑ 177 Neifi Perez .30 .10
❑ 178 Brent Mayne .30 .10
❑ 179 Dan Reichert .30 .10
❑ 180 A.J. Hinch .30 .10
❑ 181 Chris George .30 .10
❑ 182 Mike Sweeney .30 .10
❑ 183 Jeff Suppan .30 .10
❑ 184 Roberto Hernandez .30 .10
❑ 185 Joe Randa .30 .10
❑ 186 Paul Byrd .30 .10
❑ 187 Luis Ordaz .30 .10
❑ 188 Kris Wilson .30 .10
❑ 189 Dee Brown .30 .10
❑ 190 Tony Clark .30 .10
❑ 191 Matt Anderson .30 .10
❑ 192 Robert Fick .30 .10
❑ 193 Juan Encarnacion .30 .10
❑ 194 Dean Palmer .30 .10
❑ 195 Victor Santos .30 .10
❑ 196 Damion Easley .30 .10
❑ 197 Jose Lima .30 .10
❑ 198 Deivi Cruz .30 .10
❑ 199 Roger Cedeno .30 .10
❑ 200 Jose Macias .30 .10
❑ 201 Jeff Weaver .30 .10
❑ 202 Brandon Inge .30 .10
❑ 203 Brian Moehler .30 .10
❑ 204 Brad Radke .30 .10
❑ 205 Doug Mientkiewicz .30 .10
❑ 206 Cristian Guzman .30 .10
❑ 207 Corey Koskie .30 .10
❑ 208 LaTroy Hawkins .30 .10
❑ 209 J.C. Romero .30 .10
❑ 210 Chad Allen .30 .10
❑ 211 Torii Hunter .30 .10
❑ 212 Travis Miller .30 .10
❑ 213 Joe Mays .30 .10
❑ 214 Todd Jones .30 .10
❑ 215 David Ortiz .75 .30
❑ 216 Brian Buchanan .30 .10
❑ 217 A.J. Pierzynski .30 .10
❑ 218 Carlos Lee .30 .10
❑ 219 Gary Glover .30 .10
❑ 220 Jose Valentin .30 .10
❑ 221 Aaron Rowand .30 .10
❑ 222 Sandy Alomar Jr. .30 .10
❑ 223 Herbert Perry .30 .10
❑ 224 Jon Garland .30 .10
❑ 225 Mark Buehrle .30 .10
❑ 226 Chris Singleton .30 .10
❑ 227 Kip Wells .30 .10
❑ 228 Ray Durham .30 .10
❑ 229 Joe Crede .30 .10
❑ 230 Keith Foulke .30 .10
❑ 231 Royce Clayton .30 .10
❑ 232 Andy Pettitte .50 .20
❑ 233 Derek Jeter 2.00 .75
❑ 234 Jorge Posada .50 .20
❑ 235 Roger Clemens 1.50 .60
❑ 236 Paul O'Neill .50 .20
❑ 237 Nick Johnson .30 .10
❑ 238 Gerald Williams .30 .10
❑ 239 Mariano Rivera .75 .30
❑ 240 Alfonso Soriano .30 .10
❑ 241 Ramiro Mendoza .30 .10
❑ 242 Mike Mussina .50 .20
❑ 243 Luis Sojo .30 .10
❑ 244 Scott Brosius .30 .10
❑ 245 David Justice .30 .10
❑ 246 Wade Miller .30 .10
❑ 247 Brad Ausmus .30 .10
❑ 248 Jeff Bagwell .50 .20
❑ 249 Daryle Ward .30 .10
❑ 250 Shane Reynolds .30 .10
❑ 251 Chris Truby .30 .10
❑ 252 Billy Wagner .30 .10
❑ 253 Craig Biggio .50 .20
❑ 254 Moises Alou .30 .10
❑ 255 Vinny Castilla .30 .10
❑ 256 Tim Redding .30 .10
❑ 257 Roy Oswalt .30 .10
❑ 258 Julio Lugo .30 .10
❑ 259 Chipper Jones .75 .30
❑ 260 Greg Maddux 1.25 .50
❑ 261 Ken Caminiti .30 .10
❑ 262 Kevin Millwood .30 .10
❑ 263 Keith Lockhart .30 .10
❑ 264 Rey Sanchez .30 .10
❑ 265 Jason Marquis .30 .10
❑ 266 Brian Jordan .30 .10
❑ 267 Steve Karsay .30 .10
❑ 268 Wes Helms .30 .10
❑ 269 B.J. Surhoff .30 .10

❑ 270 Wilson Betemit .30 .10
❑ 271 John Smoltz .50 .20
❑ 272 Rafael Furcal .30 .10
❑ 273 Jeromy Burnitz .30 .10
❑ 274 Jimmy Haynes .30 .10
❑ 275 Mark Loretta .30 .10
❑ 276 Jose Hernandez .30 .10
❑ 277 Paul Rigdon .30 .10
❑ 278 Alex Sanchez .30 .10
❑ 279 Chad Fox .30 .10
❑ 280 Devon White .30 .10
❑ 281 Tyler Houston .30 .10
❑ 282 Ronnie Belliard .30 .10
❑ 283 Luis Lopez .30 .10
❑ 284 Ben Sheets .30 .10
❑ 285 Curtis Leskanic .30 .10
❑ 286 Henry Blanco .30 .10
❑ 287 Mark McGwire 2.00 .75
❑ 288 Edgar Renteria .30 .10
❑ 289 Matt Morris .30 .10
❑ 290 Gene Stechschulte .30 .10
❑ 291 Dustin Hermanson .30 .10
❑ 292 Eli Marrero .30 .10
❑ 293 Albert Pujols 1.50 .60
❑ 294 Luis Saturria .30 .10
❑ 295 Bobby Bonilla .30 .10
❑ 296 Garrett Stephenson .30 .10
❑ 297 Jim Edmonds .30 .10
❑ 298 Rick Ankiel .30 .10
❑ 299 Placido Polanco .30 .10
❑ 300 Dave Veres .30 .10
❑ 301 Sammy Sosa .75 .30
❑ 302 Eric Young .30 .10
❑ 303 Kerry Wood .30 .10
❑ 304 Jon Lieber .30 .10
❑ 305 Joe Girardi .30 .10
❑ 306 Fred McGriff .50 .20
❑ 307 Jeff Fassero .30 .10
❑ 308 Julio Zuleta .30 .10
❑ 309 Kevin Tapani .30 .10
❑ 310 Rondell White .30 .10
❑ 311 Julian Tavarez .30 .10
❑ 312 Tom Gordon .30 .10
❑ 313 Corey Patterson .30 .10
❑ 314 Bill Mueller .30 .10
❑ 315 Randy Johnson .75 .30
❑ 316 Chad Moeller .30 .10
❑ 317 Tony Womack .30 .10
❑ 318 Erubiel Durazo .30 .10
❑ 319 Luis Gonzalez .30 .10
❑ 320 Brian Anderson .30 .10
❑ 321 Reggie Sanders .30 .10
❑ 322 Greg Colbrunn .30 .10
❑ 323 Robert Ellis .30 .10
❑ 324 Jack Cust .30 .10
❑ 325 Bret Prinz .30 .10
❑ 326 Steve Finley .30 .10
❑ 327 Byung-Hyun Kim .30 .10
❑ 328 Albie Lopez .30 .10
❑ 329 Gary Sheffield .30 .10
❑ 330 Mark Grudzielanek .30 .10
❑ 331 Paul LoDuca .30 .10
❑ 332 Tom Goodwin .30 .10
❑ 333 Andy Ashby .30 .10
❑ 334 Hiram Bocachica .30 .10
❑ 335 Dave Hansen .30 .10
❑ 336 Kevin Brown .30 .10
❑ 337 Marquis Grissom .30 .10
❑ 338 Terry Adams .30 .10
❑ 339 Chan Ho Park .30 .10
❑ 340 Adrian Beltre .30 .10
❑ 341 Luke Prokopec .30 .10
❑ 342 Jeff Shaw .30 .10
❑ 343 Vladimir Guerrero .75 .30
❑ 344 Orlando Cabrera .30 .10
❑ 345 Tony Armas Jr. .30 .10
❑ 346 Michael Barrett .30 .10
❑ 347 Geoff Blum .30 .10
❑ 348 Ryan Minor .30 .10
❑ 349 Peter Bergeron .30 .10
❑ 350 Graeme Lloyd .30 .10
❑ 351 Jose Vidro .30 .10
❑ 352 Javier Vazquez .30 .10
❑ 353 Matt Blank .30 .10
❑ 354 Masato Yoshii .30 .10
❑ 355 Carl Pavano .30 .10
❑ 356 Barry Bonds 2.00 .75
❑ 357 Shawon Dunston .30 .10
❑ 358 Livan Hernandez .30 .10
❑ 359 Felix Rodriguez .30 .10
❑ 360 Pedro Feliz .30 .10
❑ 361 Calvin Murray .30 .10
❑ 362 Robb Nen .30 .10
❑ 363 Marvin Benard .30 .10
❑ 364 Russ Ortiz .30 .10
❑ 365 Jason Schmidt .30 .10
❑ 366 Rich Aurilia .30 .10
❑ 367 John Vander Wal .30 .10
❑ 368 Benito Santiago .30 .10
❑ 369 Ryan Dempster .30 .10
❑ 370 Charles Johnson .30 .10
❑ 371 Alex Gonzalez .30 .10
❑ 372 Luis Castillo .30 .10
❑ 373 Mike Lowell .30 .10
❑ 374 Antonio Alfonseca .30 .10
❑ 375 A.J. Burnett .30 .10
❑ 376 Brad Penny .30 .10
❑ 377 Jason Grilli .30 .10
❑ 378 Derrek Lee .50 .20
❑ 379 Matt Clement .30 .10
❑ 380 Eric Owens .30 .10
❑ 381 Vladimir Nunez .30 .10
❑ 382 Cliff Floyd .30 .10
❑ 383 Mike Piazza 1.25 .50
❑ 384 Lenny Harris .30 .10
❑ 385 Glendon Rusch .30 .10
❑ 386 Todd Zeile .30 .10
❑ 387 Al Leiter .30 .10
❑ 388 Armando Benitez .30 .10
❑ 389 Alex Escobar .30 .10
❑ 390 Kevin Appier .30 .10
❑ 391 Matt Lawton .30 .10
❑ 392 Bruce Chen .30 .10
❑ 393 John Franco .30 .10
❑ 394 Tsuyoshi Shinjo .30 .10
❑ 395 Rey Ordonez .30 .10
❑ 396 Joe McEwing .30 .10
❑ 397 Ryan Klesko .30 .10
❑ 398 Brian Lawrence .30 .10
❑ 399 Kevin Walker .30 .10
❑ 400 Phil Nevin .30 .10
❑ 401 Bubba Trammell .30 .10
❑ 402 Wiki Gonzalez .30 .10
❑ 403 D'Angelo Jimenez .30 .10
❑ 404 Rickey Henderson .75 .30
❑ 405 Mike Darr .30 .10
❑ 406 Trevor Hoffman .30 .10
❑ 407 Damian Jackson .30 .10
❑ 408 Santiago Perez .30 .10
❑ 409 Cesar Crespo .30 .10
❑ 410 Robert Person .30 .10
❑ 411 Travis Lee .30 .10
❑ 412 Scott Rolen .50 .20
❑ 413 Turk Wendell .30 .10
❑ 414 Randy Wolf .30 .10
❑ 415 Kevin Jordan .30 .10
❑ 416 Jose Mesa .30 .10
❑ 417 Mike Lieberthal .30 .10
❑ 418 Bobby Abreu .30 .10
❑ 419 Tomas Perez .30 .10
❑ 420 Doug Glanville .30 .10
❑ 421 Reggie Taylor .30 .10
❑ 422 Jimmy Rollins .30 .10
❑ 423 Brian Giles .30 .10
❑ 424 Rob Mackowiak .30 .10
❑ 425 Bronson Arroyo .30 .10
❑ 426 Kevin Young .30 .10
❑ 427 Jack Wilson .30 .10
❑ 428 Adrian Brown .30 .10
❑ 429 Chad Hermansen .30 .10
❑ 430 Jimmy Anderson .30 .10
❑ 431 Aramis Ramirez .30 .10
❑ 432 Todd Ritchie .30 .10
❑ 433 Pat Meares .30 .10
❑ 434 Warren Morris .30 .10
❑ 435 Derek Bell .30 .10
❑ 436 Ken Griffey Jr. 1.25 .50
❑ 437 Elmer Dessens .30 .10
❑ 438 Ruben Rivera .30 .10
❑ 439 Jason LaRue .30 .10
❑ 440 Sean Casey .30 .10
❑ 441 Pete Harnisch .30 .10
❑ 442 Danny Graves .30 .10
❑ 443 Aaron Boone .30 .10
❑ 444 Dmitri Young .30 .10
❑ 445 Brandon Larson .30 .10
❑ 446 Pokey Reese .30 .10
❑ 447 Todd Walker .30 .10
❑ 448 Juan Castro .30 .10
❑ 449 Todd Helton .50 .20
❑ 450 Ben Petrick .30 .10
❑ 451 Juan Pierre .30 .10
❑ 452 Jeff Cirillo .30 .10
❑ 453 Juan Uribe .30 .10
❑ 454 Brian Bohanon .30 .10
❑ 455 Terry Shumpert .30 .10
❑ 456 Mike Hampton .30 .10
❑ 457 Shawn Chacon .30 .10
❑ 458 Adam Melhuse .30 .10
❑ 459 Greg Norton .30 .10
❑ 460 Gabe White .30 .10
❑ 461 Ichiro Suzuki WS .75 .30
❑ 462 Carlos Delgado WS .30 .10
❑ 463 Manny Ramirez WS .50 .20
❑ 464 Miguel Tejada WS .30 .10
❑ 465 Tsuyoshi Shinjo WS .30 .10
❑ 466 Bernie Williams WS .30 .10
❑ 467 Juan Gonzalez WS .30 .10
❑ 468 Andruw Jones WS .30 .10
❑ 469 Ivan Rodriguez WS .30 .10
❑ 470 Larry Walker WS .30 .10
❑ 471 Hideo Nomo WS .30 .10
❑ 472 Albert Pujols WS .75 .30
❑ 473 Pedro Martinez WS .50 .20
❑ 474 Vladimir Guerrero WS .50 .20
❑ 475 Tony Batista WS .30 .10
❑ 476 Kazuhiro Sasaki WS .30 .10
❑ 477 Richard Hidalgo WS .30 .10
❑ 478 Carlos Lee WS .30 .10
❑ 479 Roberto Alomar WS .30 .10
❑ 480 Rafael Palmeiro WS .30 .10
❑ 481 Ken Griffey Jr. GG .75 .30
❑ 482 Ken Griffey Jr. GG .75 .30
❑ 483 Ken Griffey Jr. GG .75 .30
❑ 484 Ken Griffey Jr. GG .75 .30
❑ 485 Ken Griffey Jr. GG .75 .30
❑ 486 Ken Griffey Jr. GG .75 .30
❑ 487 Ken Griffey Jr. GG .75 .30
❑ 488 Ken Griffey Jr. GG .75 .30
❑ 489 Ken Griffey Jr. GG .75 .30
❑ 490 Ken Griffey Jr. GG .75 .30
❑ 491 Barry Bonds CL 1.00 .40
❑ 492 Hideo Nomo CL .30 .10
❑ 493 Ichiro Suzuki CL .75 .30
❑ 494 Cal Ripken CL 1.25 .50
❑ 495 Tony Gwynn CL .50 .20
❑ 496 Randy Johnson CL .50 .20
❑ 497 A.J. Burnett CL .30 .10
❑ 498 Rickey Henderson CL .50 .20
❑ 499 Albert Pujols CL .75 .30
❑ 500 Luis Gonzalez CL .30 .10
❑ 501 Brandon Puffer SR RC 1.00 .40
❑ 502 Rodrigo Rosario SR RC 1.00 .40
❑ 503 Tom Shearn SR RC 1.00 .40
❑ 504 Reed Johnson SR RC 1.50 .60
❑ 505 Chris Baker SR RC 1.00 .40
❑ 506 John Ennis SR RC 1.00 .40
❑ 507 Luis Martinez SR RC 1.00 .40
❑ 508 So Taguchi SR RC 1.50 .60
❑ 509 Scotty Layfield SR RC 1.00 .40
❑ 510 Francis Beltran SR RC 1.00 .40
❑ 511 Brandon Backe SR RC 1.50 .60
❑ 512 Doug Devore SR RC 1.00 .40
❑ 513 Jeremy Ward SR RC 1.00 .40
❑ 514 Jose Valverde SR RC 1.00 .40
❑ 515 P.J. Bevis SR RC 1.00 .40
❑ 516 Victor Alvarez SR RC 1.00 .40
❑ 517 Kazuhisa Ishii SR RC 1.50 .60
❑ 518 Jorge Nunez SR RC 1.00 .40
❑ 519 Eric Good SR RC 1.00 .40
❑ 520 Ron Calloway SR RC 1.00 .40
❑ 521 Val Pascucci SR 1.00 .40
❑ 522 Nelson Castro SR RC 1.00 .40
❑ 523 Deivis Santos SR 1.00 .40
❑ 524 Luis Ugueto SR RC 1.00 .40
❑ 525 Matt Thornton SR RC 1.00 .40
❑ 526 Hansel Izquierdo SR RC 1.00 .40
❑ 527 Tyler Yates SR RC 1.00 .40

❑ 528 Mark Corey SR RC 1.00 .40
❑ 529 Jaime Cerda SR RC 1.00 .40
❑ 530 Satoru Komiyama SR RC 1.00 .40
❑ 531 Steve Bechler SR RC 1.00 .40
❑ 532 Ben Howard SR RC 1.00 .40
❑ 533 Anderson Machado SR RC 1.00 .40
❑ 534 Jorge Padilla SR RC 1.00 .40
❑ 535 Eric Junge SR RC 1.00 .40
❑ 536 Adrian Burnside SR RC 1.00 .40
❑ 537 Mike Gonzalez SR RC 1.00 .40
❑ 538 Josh Hancock SR RC 1.25 .50
❑ 539 Colin Young SR RC 1.00 .40
❑ 540 Rene Reyes SR RC 1.00 .40
❑ 541 Cam Esslinger SR RC 1.00 .40
❑ 542 Tim Kalita SR RC 1.00 .40
❑ 543 Kevin Frederick SR RC 1.00 .40
❑ 544 Kyle Kane SR RC 1.00 .40
❑ 545 Edwin Almonte SR RC 1.00 .40
❑ 546 Aaron Sele .30 .10
❑ 547 Garret Anderson .30 .10
❑ 548 Darin Erstad .30 .10
❑ 549 Brad Fullmer .30 .10
❑ 550 Kevin Appier .30 .10
❑ 551 Tim Salmon .50 .20
❑ 552 David Justice .30 .10
❑ 553 Billy Koch .30 .10
❑ 554 Scott Hatteberg .30 .10
❑ 555 Tim Hudson .30 .10
❑ 556 Miguel Tejada .30 .10
❑ 557 Carlos Pena .30 .10
❑ 558 Mike Sirotka .30 .10
❑ 559 Jose Cruz Jr. .30 .10
❑ 560 Josh Phelps .30 .10
❑ 561 Brandon Lyon .30 .10
❑ 562 Luke Prokopec .30 .10
❑ 563 Felipe Lopez .30 .10
❑ 564 Jason Standridge .30 .10
❑ 565 Chris Gomez .30 .10
❑ 566 John Flaherty .30 .10
❑ 567 Jason Tyner .30 .10
❑ 568 Bobby Smith .30 .10
❑ 569 Wilson Alvarez .30 .10
❑ 570 Matt Lawton .30 .10
❑ 571 Omar Vizquel .50 .20
❑ 572 Jim Thome .50 .20
❑ 573 Brady Anderson .30 .10
❑ 574 Alex Escobar .30 .10
❑ 575 Russell Branyan .30 .10
❑ 576 Bret Boone .30 .10
❑ 577 Ben Davis .30 .10
❑ 578 Mike Cameron .30 .10
❑ 579 Jamie Moyer .30 .10
❑ 580 Ruben Sierra .30 .10
❑ 581 Jeff Cirillo .30 .10
❑ 582 Marty Cordova .30 .10
❑ 583 Mike Bordick .30 .10
❑ 584 Brian Roberts .30 .10
❑ 585 Luis Matos .30 .10
❑ 586 Geronimo Gil .30 .10
❑ 587 Jay Gibbons .30 .10
❑ 588 Carl Everett .30 .10
❑ 589 Ivan Rodriguez .50 .20
❑ 590 Chan Ho Park .30 .10
❑ 591 Juan Gonzalez .30 .10
❑ 592 Hank Blalock .50 .20
❑ 593 Todd Van Poppel .30 .10
❑ 594 Pedro Martinez .50 .20
❑ 595 Jason Varitek .75 .30
❑ 596 Tony Clark .30 .10
❑ 597 Johnny Damon Sox .50 .20
❑ 598 Dustin Hermanson .30 .10
❑ 599 John Burkett .30 .10
❑ 600 Carlos Beltran .30 .10
❑ 601 Mark Quinn .30 .10
❑ 602 Chuck Knoblauch .30 .10
❑ 603 Michael Tucker .30 .10
❑ 604 Carlos Febles .30 .10
❑ 605 Jose Rosado .30 .10
❑ 606 Dmitri Young .30 .10
❑ 607 Bobby Higginson .30 .10
❑ 608 Craig Paquette .30 .10
❑ 609 Mitch Meluskey .30 .10
❑ 610 Wendell Magee .30 .10
❑ 611 Mike Rivera .30 .10
❑ 612 Jacque Jones .30 .10
❑ 613 Luis Rivas .30 .10
❑ 614 Eric Milton .30 .10
❑ 615 Eddie Guardado .30 .10
❑ 616 Matt LeCroy .30 .10
❑ 617 Mike Jackson .30 .10
❑ 618 Magglio Ordonez .30 .10
❑ 619 Frank Thomas .75 .30
❑ 620 Rocky Biddle .30 .10
❑ 621 Paul Konerko .30 .10
❑ 622 Todd Ritchie .30 .10
❑ 623 Jon Rauch .30 .10
❑ 624 John Vander Wal .30 .10
❑ 625 Rondell White .30 .10
❑ 626 Jason Giambi .30 .10
❑ 627 Robin Ventura .30 .10
❑ 628 David Wells .30 .10
❑ 629 Bernie Williams .50 .20
❑ 630 Lance Berkman .30 .10
❑ 631 Richard Hidalgo .30 .10
❑ 632 Greg Zaun .30 .10
❑ 633 Jose Vizcaino .30 .10
❑ 634 Octavio Dotel .30 .10
❑ 635 Morgan Ensberg .30 .10
❑ 636 Andruw Jones .50 .20
❑ 637 Tom Glavine .50 .20
❑ 638 Gary Sheffield .30 .10
❑ 639 Vinny Castilla .30 .10
❑ 640 Javy Lopez .30 .10
❑ 641 Albie Lopez .30 .10
❑ 642 Geoff Jenkins .30 .10
❑ 643 Jeffrey Hammonds .30 .10
❑ 644 Alex Ochoa .30 .10
❑ 645 Richie Sexson .30 .10
❑ 646 Eric Young .30 .10
❑ 647 Glendon Rusch .30 .10
❑ 648 Tino Martinez .50 .20
❑ 649 Fernando Vina .30 .10
❑ 650 J.D. Drew .30 .10
❑ 651 Woody Williams .30 .10
❑ 652 Darryl Kile .30 .10
❑ 653 Jason Isringhausen .30 .10
❑ 654 Moises Alou .30 .10
❑ 655 Alex Gonzalez .30 .10
❑ 656 Delino DeShields .30 .10
❑ 657 Todd Hundley .30 .10
❑ 658 Chris Stynes .30 .10
❑ 659 Jason Bere .30 .10
❑ 660 Curt Schilling .30 .10
❑ 661 Craig Counsell .30 .10
❑ 662 Mark Grace .50 .20
❑ 663 Matt Williams .30 .10
❑ 664 Jay Bell .30 .10
❑ 665 Rick Helling .30 .10
❑ 666 Shawn Green .30 .10
❑ 667 Eric Karros .30 .10
❑ 668 Hideo Nomo .75 .30
❑ 669 Omar Daal .30 .10
❑ 670 Brian Jordan .30 .10
❑ 671 Cesar Izturis .30 .10
❑ 672 Fernando Tatis .30 .10
❑ 673 Lee Stevens .30 .10
❑ 674 Tomo Ohka .30 .10
❑ 675 Brian Schneider .30 .10
❑ 676 Brad Wilkerson .30 .10
❑ 677 Bruce Chen .30 .10
❑ 678 Tsuyoshi Shinjo .30 .10
❑ 679 Jeff Kent .30 .10
❑ 680 Kirk Rueter .30 .10
❑ 681 J.T. Snow .30 .10
❑ 682 David Bell .30 .10
❑ 683 Reggie Sanders .30 .10
❑ 684 Preston Wilson .30 .10
❑ 685 Vic Darensbourg .30 .10
❑ 686 Josh Beckett .30 .10
❑ 687 Pablo Ozuna .30 .10
❑ 688 Mike Redmond .30 .10
❑ 689 Scott Strickland .30 .10
❑ 690 Mo Vaughn .30 .10
❑ 691 Roberto Alomar .50 .20
❑ 692 Edgardo Alfonzo .30 .10
❑ 693 Shawn Estes .30 .10
❑ 694 Roger Cedeno .30 .10
❑ 695 Jeromy Burnitz .30 .10
❑ 696 Ray Lankford .30 .10
❑ 697 Mark Kotsay .30 .10
❑ 698 Kevin Jarvis .30 .10
❑ 699 Bobby Jones .30 .10
❑ 700 Sean Burroughs .30 .10
❑ 701 Ramon Vazquez .30 .10
❑ 702 Pat Burrell .30 .10
❑ 703 Marlon Byrd .30 .10
❑ 704 Brandon Duckworth .30 .10
❑ 705 Marlon Anderson .30 .10
❑ 706 Vicente Padilla .30 .10
❑ 707 Kip Wells .30 .10
❑ 708 Jason Kendall .30 .10
❑ 709 Pokey Reese .30 .10
❑ 710 Pat Meares .30 .10
❑ 711 Kris Benson .30 .10
❑ 712 Armando Rios .30 .10
❑ 713 Mike Williams .30 .10
❑ 714 Barry Larkin .50 .20
❑ 715 Adam Dunn .30 .10
❑ 716 Juan Encarnacion .30 .10
❑ 717 Scott Williamson .30 .10
❑ 718 Wilton Guerrero .30 .10
❑ 719 Chris Reitsma .30 .10
❑ 720 Larry Walker .30 .10
❑ 721 Denny Neagle .30 .10
❑ 722 Todd Zeile .30 .10
❑ 723 Jose Ortiz .30 .10
❑ 724 Jason Jennings .30 .10
❑ 725 Tony Eusebio .30 .10
❑ 726 Ichiro Suzuki YR .75 .30
❑ 727 Barry Bonds YR 1.00 .40
❑ 728 Randy Johnson YR .50 .20
❑ 729 Albert Pujols YR .75 .30
❑ 730 Roger Clemens YR .75 .30
❑ 731 Sammy Sosa YR .50 .20
❑ 732 Alex Rodriguez YR .75 .30
❑ 733 Chipper Jones YR .50 .20
❑ 734 Rickey Henderson YR .50 .20
❑ 735 Ichiro Suzuki YR .75 .30
❑ 736 Luis Gonzalez SH CL .30 .10
❑ 737 Derek Jeter SH CL 1.00 .40
❑ 738 Ichiro Suzuki SH CL .75 .30
❑ 739 Barry Bonds SH CL 1.00 .40
❑ 740 Curt Schilling SH CL .30 .10
❑ 741 Shawn Green SH CL .30 .10
❑ 742 Jason Giambi SH CL .30 .10
❑ 743 Roberto Alomar SH CL .30 .10
❑ 744 Larry Walker SH CL .30 .10
❑ 745 Mark McGwire SH CL 1.00 .40

2003 Upper Deck

❑ COMPLETE SERIES 1 (270) 50.00 20.00
❑ COMPLETE SERIES 2 (270) 50.00 20.00
❑ COMP.UPDATE SET (60) 20.00 10.00
❑ COMMON (31-500/531-600) .30 .10
❑ COMMON (1-30/501-530) 1.00 .40
❑ COMMON RC (541-600) .50 .20
❑ SR 1-30/501-530 ARE NOT SHORT PRINTS
❑ CARD 19 DOES NOT EXIST
❑ SCUTARO/NOMAR ARE BOTH CARD 96
❑ 541-600 ISSUED IN 04 UD1 HOBBY BOXES
❑ UPDATE SET EXCH 1:240 '04 UD1 RETAIL
❑ UPDATE SET EXCH.DEADLINE 11/10/06
❑ 1 John Lackey SR 1.00 .40
❑ 2 Alex Cintron SR 1.00 .40
❑ 3 Jose Leon SR 1.00 .40
❑ 4 Bobby Hill SR 1.00 .40
❑ 5 Brandon Larson SR 1.00 .40
❑ 6 Raul Gonzalez SR 1.00 .40
❑ 7 Ben Broussard SR 1.00 .40
❑ 8 Earl Snyder SR 1.00 .40

	No.	Player		
❑	9	Ramon Santiago SR	1.00	.40
❑	10	Jason Lane SR	1.00	.40
❑	11	Keith Ginter SR	1.00	.40
❑	12	Kirk Saarloos SR	1.00	.40
❑	13	Juan Brito SR	1.00	.40
❑	14	Runelvys Hernandez SR	1.00	.40
❑	15	Shawn Sedlacek SR	1.00	.40
❑	16	Jayson Durocher SR	1.00	.40
❑	17	Kevin Frederick SR	1.00	.40
❑	18	Zach Day SR	1.00	.40
❑	19	Marcos Scutaro SR	1.00	.40
❑	20	Marcus Thames SR	1.00	.40
❑	21	Esteban German SR	1.00	.40
❑	22	Brett Myers SR	1.00	.40
❑	23	Oliver Perez SR	1.00	.40
❑	24	Dennis Tankersley SR	1.00	.40
❑	25	Julius Matos SR	1.00	.40
❑	26	Jake Peavy SR	1.00	.40
❑	27	Eric Cyr SR	1.00	.40
❑	28	Mike Crudale SR	1.00	.40
❑	29	Josh Pearce SR	1.00	.40
❑	30	Carl Crawford SR	1.00	.40
❑	31	Tim Salmon	.50	.20
❑	32	Troy Glaus	.30	.10
❑	33	Adam Kennedy	.30	.10
❑	34	David Eckstein	.30	.10
❑	35	Ben Molina	.30	.10
❑	36	Jarrod Washburn	.30	.10
❑	37	Ramon Ortiz	.30	.10
❑	38	Eric Chavez	.30	.10
❑	39	Miguel Tejada	.30	.10
❑	40	Adam Piatt	.30	.10
❑	41	Jermaine Dye	.30	.10
❑	42	Olmedo Saenz	.30	.10
❑	43	Tim Hudson	.30	.10
❑	44	Barry Zito	.30	.10
❑	45	Billy Koch	.30	.10
❑	46	Shannon Stewart	.30	.10
❑	47	Kelvim Escobar	.30	.10
❑	48	Jose Cruz Jr.	.30	.10
❑	49	Vernon Wells	.30	.10
❑	50	Roy Halladay	.30	.10
❑	51	Esteban Loaiza	.30	.10
❑	52	Eric Hinske	.30	.10
❑	53	Steve Cox	.30	.10
❑	54	Brent Abernathy	.30	.10
❑	55	Ben Grieve	.30	.10
❑	56	Aubrey Huff	.30	.10
❑	57	Jared Sandberg	.30	.10
❑	58	Paul Wilson	.30	.10
❑	59	Tanyon Sturtze	.30	.10
❑	60	Jim Thome	.50	.20
❑	61	Omar Vizquel	.50	.20
❑	62	C.C. Sabathia	.30	.10
❑	63	Chris Magruder	.30	.10
❑	64	Ricky Gutierrez	.30	.10
❑	65	Einar Diaz	.30	.10
❑	66	Danys Baez	.30	.10
❑	67	Ichiro Suzuki	1.50	.60
❑	68	Ruben Sierra	.30	.10
❑	69	Carlos Guillen	.30	.10
❑	70	Mark McLemore	.30	.10
❑	71	Dan Wilson	.30	.10
❑	72	Jamie Moyer	.30	.10
❑	73	Joel Pineiro	.30	.10
❑	74	Edgar Martinez	.50	.20
❑	75	Tony Batista	.30	.10
❑	76	Jay Gibbons	.30	.10
❑	77	Chris Singleton	.30	.10
❑	78	Melvin Mora	.30	.10
❑	79	Geronimo Gil	.30	.10
❑	80	Rodrigo Lopez	.30	.10
❑	81	Jorge Julio	.30	.10
❑	82	Rafael Palmeiro	.50	.20
❑	83	Juan Gonzalez	.30	.10
❑	84	Mike Young	.50	.20
❑	85	Hideki Irabu	.30	.10
❑	86	Chan Ho Park	.30	.10
❑	87	Kevin Mench	.30	.10
❑	88	Doug Davis	.30	.10
❑	89	Pedro Martinez	.50	.20
❑	90	Shea Hillenbrand	.30	.10
❑	91	Derek Lowe	.30	.10
❑	92	Jason Varitek	.75	.30
❑	93	Tony Clark	.30	.10
❑	94	John Burkett	.30	.10
❑	95	Frank Castillo	.30	.10
❑	96	Nomar Garciaparra	1.25	.50
❑	97	Rickey Henderson	.75	.30
❑	98	Mike Sweeney	.30	.10
❑	99	Carlos Febles	.30	.10
❑	100	Mark Quinn	.30	.10
❑	101	Raul Ibanez	.30	.10
❑	102	A.J. Hinch	.30	.10
❑	103	Paul Byrd	.30	.10
❑	104	Chuck Knoblauch	.30	.10
❑	105	Dmitri Young	.30	.10
❑	106	Randall Simon	.30	.10
❑	107	Brandon Inge	.30	.10
❑	108	Damion Easley	.30	.10
❑	109	Carlos Pena	.30	.10
❑	110	George Lombard	.30	.10
❑	111	Juan Acevedo	.30	.10
❑	112	Torii Hunter	.30	.10
❑	113	Doug Mientkiewicz	.30	.10
❑	114	David Ortiz	.50	.20
❑	115	Eric Milton	.30	.10
❑	116	Eddie Guardado	.30	.10
❑	117	Cristian Guzman	.30	.10
❑	118	Corey Koskie	.30	.10
❑	119	Magglio Ordonez	.30	.10
❑	120	Mark Buehrle	.30	.10
❑	121	Todd Ritchie	.30	.10
❑	122	Jose Valentin	.30	.10
❑	123	Paul Konerko	.30	.10
❑	124	Carlos Lee	.30	.10
❑	125	Jon Garland	.30	.10
❑	126	Jason Giambi	.30	.10
❑	127	Derek Jeter	2.00	.75
❑	128	Roger Clemens	1.50	.60
❑	129	Raul Mondesi	.30	.10
❑	130	Jorge Posada	.50	.20
❑	131	Rondell White	.30	.10
❑	132	Robin Ventura	.30	.10
❑	133	Mike Mussina	.50	.20
❑	134	Jeff Bagwell	.50	.20
❑	135	Craig Biggio	.50	.20
❑	136	Morgan Ensberg	.30	.10
❑	137	Richard Hidalgo	.30	.10
❑	138	Brad Ausmus	.30	.10
❑	139	Roy Oswalt	.30	.10
❑	140	Carlos Hernandez	.30	.10
❑	141	Shane Reynolds	.30	.10
❑	142	Gary Sheffield	.30	.10
❑	143	Andruw Jones	.50	.20
❑	144	Tom Glavine	.50	.20
❑	145	Rafael Furcal	.30	.10
❑	146	Javy Lopez	.30	.10
❑	147	Vinny Castilla	.30	.10
❑	148	Marcus Giles	.30	.10
❑	149	Kevin Millwood	.30	.10
❑	150	Jason Marquis	.30	.10
❑	151	Ruben Quevedo	.30	.10
❑	152	Ben Sheets	.30	.10
❑	153	Geoff Jenkins	.30	.10
❑	154	Jose Hernandez	.30	.10
❑	155	Glendon Rusch	.30	.10
❑	156	Jeffrey Hammonds	.30	.10
❑	157	Alex Sanchez	.30	.10
❑	158	Jim Edmonds	.30	.10
❑	159	Tino Martinez	.50	.20
❑	160	Albert Pujols	1.50	.60
❑	161	Eli Marrero	.30	.10
❑	162	Woody Williams	.30	.10
❑	163	Fernando Vina	.30	.10
❑	164	Jason Isringhausen	.30	.10
❑	165	Jason Simontacchi	.30	.10
❑	166	Kerry Robinson	.30	.10
❑	167	Sammy Sosa	.75	.30
❑	168	Juan Cruz	.30	.10
❑	169	Fred McGriff	.50	.20
❑	170	Antonio Alfonseca	.30	.10
❑	171	Jon Lieber	.30	.10
❑	172	Mark Prior	.50	.20
❑	173	Moises Alou	.30	.10
❑	174	Matt Clement	.30	.10
❑	175	Mark Bellhorn	.30	.10
❑	176	Randy Johnson	.75	.30
❑	177	Luis Gonzalez	.30	.10
❑	178	Tony Womack	.30	.10
❑	179	Mark Grace	.50	.20
❑	180	Junior Spivey	.30	.10
❑	181	Byung Hyun Kim	.30	.10
❑	182	Danny Bautista	.30	.10
❑	183	Brian Anderson	.30	.10
❑	184	Shawn Green	.30	.10
❑	185	Brian Jordan	.30	.10
❑	186	Eric Karros	.30	.10
❑	187	Andy Ashby	.30	.10
❑	188	Cesar Izturis	.30	.10
❑	189	Dave Roberts	.30	.10
❑	190	Eric Gagne	.30	.10
❑	191	Kazuhisa Ishii	.30	.10
❑	192	Adrian Beltre	.30	.10
❑	193	Vladimir Guerrero	.75	.30
❑	194	Tony Armas Jr.	.30	.10
❑	195	Bartolo Colon	.30	.10
❑	196	Troy O'Leary	.30	.10
❑	197	Tomo Ohka	.30	.10
❑	198	Brad Wilkerson	.30	.10
❑	199	Orlando Cabrera	.30	.10
❑	200	Barry Bonds	2.00	.75
❑	201	David Bell	.30	.10
❑	202	Tsuyoshi Shinjo	.30	.10
❑	203	Benito Santiago	.30	.10
❑	204	Livan Hernandez	.30	.10
❑	205	Jason Schmidt	.30	.10
❑	206	Kirk Rueter	.30	.10
❑	207	Ramon E. Martinez	.30	.10
❑	208	Mike Lowell	.30	.10
❑	209	Luis Castillo	.30	.10
❑	210	Derrek Lee	.50	.20
❑	211	Andy Fox	.30	.10
❑	212	Eric Owens	.30	.10
❑	213	Charles Johnson	.30	.10
❑	214	Brad Penny	.30	.10
❑	215	A.J. Burnett	.30	.10
❑	216	Edgardo Alfonzo	.30	.10
❑	217	Roberto Alomar	.50	.20
❑	218	Rey Ordonez	.30	.10
❑	219	Al Leiter	.30	.10
❑	220	Roger Cedeno	.30	.10
❑	221	Timo Perez	.30	.10
❑	222	Jeromy Burnitz	.30	.10
❑	223	Pedro Astacio	.30	.10
❑	224	Joe McEwing	.30	.10
❑	225	Ryan Klesko	.30	.10
❑	226	Ramon Vazquez	.30	.10
❑	227	Mark Kotsay	.30	.10
❑	228	Bubba Trammell	.30	.10
❑	229	Wiki Gonzalez	.30	.10
❑	230	Trevor Hoffman	.30	.10
❑	231	Ron Gant	.30	.10
❑	232	Bob Abreu	.30	.10
❑	233	Marlon Anderson	.30	.10
❑	234	Jeremy Giambi	.30	.10
❑	235	Jimmy Rollins	.30	.10
❑	236	Mike Lieberthal	.30	.10
❑	237	Vicente Padilla	.30	.10
❑	238	Randy Wolf	.30	.10
❑	239	Pokey Reese	.30	.10
❑	240	Brian Giles	.30	.10
❑	241	Jack Wilson	.30	.10
❑	242	Mike Williams	.30	.10
❑	243	Kip Wells	.30	.10
❑	244	Rob Mackowiak	.30	.10
❑	245	Craig Wilson	.30	.10
❑	246	Adam Dunn	.30	.10
❑	247	Sean Casey	.30	.10
❑	248	Todd Walker	.30	.10
❑	249	Corky Miller	.30	.10
❑	250	Ryan Dempster	.30	.10
❑	251	Reggie Taylor	.30	.10
❑	252	Aaron Boone	.30	.10
❑	253	Larry Walker	.30	.10
❑	254	Jose Ortiz	.30	.10
❑	255	Todd Zeile	.30	.10
❑	256	Bobby Estalella	.30	.10
❑	257	Juan Pierre	.30	.10
❑	258	Terry Shumpert	.30	.10
❑	259	Mike Hampton	.30	.10
❑	260	Denny Stark	.30	.10
❑	261	Shawn Green SH CL	.30	.10
❑	262	Derek Lowe SH CL	.30	.10
❑	263	Barry Bonds SH CL	1.00	.40
❑	264	Mike Cameron SH CL	.30	.10
❑	265	Luis Castillo SH CL	.30	.10
❑	266	Vladimir Guerrero SH CL	.50	.20

❑ 267 Jason Giambi SH CL .30 .10
❑ 268 Eric Gagne SH CL .30 .10
❑ 269 Magglio Ordonez SH CL .30 .10
❑ 270 Jim Thome SH CL .30 .10
❑ 271 Garret Anderson .30 .10
❑ 272 Troy Percival .30 .10
❑ 273 Brad Fullmer .30 .10
❑ 274 Scott Spiezio .30 .10
❑ 275 Darin Erstad .30 .10
❑ 276 Francisco Rodriguez .30 .10
❑ 277 Kevin Appier .30 .10
❑ 278 Shawn Wooten .30 .10
❑ 279 Eric Owens .30 .10
❑ 280 Scott Hatteberg .30 .10
❑ 281 Terrence Long .30 .10
❑ 282 Mark Mulder .30 .10
❑ 283 Ramon Hernandez .30 .10
❑ 284 Ted Lilly .30 .10
❑ 285 Erubiel Durazo .30 .10
❑ 286 Mark Ellis .30 .10
❑ 287 Carlos Delgado .30 .10
❑ 288 Orlando Hudson .30 .10
❑ 289 Chris Woodward .30 .10
❑ 290 Mark Hendrickson .30 .10
❑ 291 Josh Phelps .30 .10
❑ 292 Ken Huckaby .30 .10
❑ 293 Justin Miller .30 .10
❑ 294 Travis Lee .30 .10
❑ 295 Jorge Sosa .30 .10
❑ 296 Joe Kennedy .30 .10
❑ 297 Carl Crawford .30 .10
❑ 298 Toby Hall .30 .10
❑ 299 Rey Ordonez .30 .10
❑ 300 Brandon Phillips .30 .10
❑ 301 Matt Lawton .30 .10
❑ 302 Ellis Burks .30 .10
❑ 303 Bill Selby .30 .10
❑ 304 Travis Hafner .30 .10
❑ 305 Milton Bradley .30 .10
❑ 306 Karim Garcia .30 .10
❑ 307 Cliff Lee .30 .10
❑ 308 Jeff Cirillo .30 .10
❑ 309 John Olerud .30 .10
❑ 310 Kazuhiro Sasaki .30 .10
❑ 311 Freddy Garcia .30 .10
❑ 312 Bret Boone .30 .10
❑ 313 Mike Cameron .30 .10
❑ 314 Ben Davis .30 .10
❑ 315 Randy Winn .30 .10
❑ 316 Gary Matthews Jr. .30 .10
❑ 317 Jeff Conine .30 .10
❑ 318 Sidney Ponson .30 .10
❑ 319 Jerry Hairston .30 .10
❑ 320 David Segui .30 .10
❑ 321 Scott Erickson .30 .10
❑ 322 Marty Cordova .30 .10
❑ 323 Hank Blalock .30 .10
❑ 324 Herbert Perry .30 .10
❑ 325 Alex Rodriguez 1.25 .50
❑ 326 Carl Everett .30 .10
❑ 327 Einar Diaz .30 .10
❑ 328 Ugueth Urbina .30 .10
❑ 329 Mark Teixeira .50 .20
❑ 330 Manny Ramirez .50 .20
❑ 331 Johnny Damon .50 .20
❑ 332 Trot Nixon .30 .10
❑ 333 Tim Wakefield .30 .10
❑ 334 Casey Fossum .30 .10
❑ 335 Todd Walker .30 .10
❑ 336 Jeremy Giambi .30 .10
❑ 337 Bill Mueller .30 .10
❑ 338 Ramiro Mendoza .30 .10
❑ 339 Carlos Beltran .30 .10
❑ 340 Jason Grimsley .30 .10
❑ 341 Brent Mayne .30 .10
❑ 342 Angel Berroa .30 .10
❑ 343 Albie Lopez .30 .10
❑ 344 Michael Tucker .30 .10
❑ 345 Bobby Higginson .30 .10
❑ 346 Shane Halter .30 .10
❑ 347 Jeremy Bonderman RC 4.00 1.50
❑ 348 Eric Munson .30 .10
❑ 349 Andy Van Hekken .30 .10
❑ 350 Matt Anderson .30 .10
❑ 351 Jacque Jones .30 .10
❑ 352 A.J. Pierzynski .30 .10
❑ 353 Joe Mays .30 .10
❑ 354 Brad Radke .30 .10
❑ 355 Dustan Mohr .30 .10
❑ 356 Bobby Kielty .30 .10
❑ 357 Michael Cuddyer .30 .10
❑ 358 Luis Rivas .30 .10
❑ 359 Frank Thomas .75 .30
❑ 360 Joe Borchard .30 .10
❑ 361 D'Angelo Jimenez .30 .10
❑ 362 Bartolo Colon .30 .10
❑ 363 Joe Crede .30 .10
❑ 364 Miguel Olivo .30 .10
❑ 365 Billy Koch .30 .10
❑ 366 Bernie Williams .50 .20
❑ 367 Nick Johnson .30 .10
❑ 368 Andy Pettitte .50 .20
❑ 369 Mariano Rivera .75 .30
❑ 370 Alfonso Soriano .30 .10
❑ 371 David Wells .30 .10
❑ 372 Drew Henson .30 .10
❑ 373 Juan Rivera .30 .10
❑ 374 Steve Karsay .30 .10
❑ 375 Jeff Kent .30 .10
❑ 376 Lance Berkman .30 .10
❑ 377 Octavio Dotel .30 .10
❑ 378 Julio Lugo .30 .10
❑ 379 Jason Lane .30 .10
❑ 380 Wade Miller .30 .10
❑ 381 Billy Wagner .30 .10
❑ 382 Brad Ausmus .30 .10
❑ 383 Mike Hampton .30 .10
❑ 384 Chipper Jones .75 .30
❑ 385 John Smoltz .50 .20
❑ 386 Greg Maddux 1.25 .50
❑ 387 Javy Lopez .30 .10
❑ 388 Robert Fick .30 .10
❑ 389 Mark DeRosa .30 .10
❑ 390 Russ Ortiz .30 .10
❑ 391 Julio Franco .30 .10
❑ 392 Richie Sexson .30 .10
❑ 393 Eric Young .30 .10
❑ 394 Robert Machado .30 .10
❑ 395 Mike DeJean .30 .10
❑ 396 Todd Ritchie .30 .10
❑ 397 Royce Clayton .30 .10
❑ 398 Nick Neugebauer .30 .10
❑ 399 J.D. Drew .30 .10
❑ 400 Edgar Renteria .30 .10
❑ 401 Scott Rolen .50 .20
❑ 402 Matt Morris .30 .10
❑ 403 Garrett Stephenson .30 .10
❑ 404 Eduardo Perez .30 .10
❑ 405 Mike Matheny .30 .10
❑ 406 Miguel Cairo .30 .10
❑ 407 Brett Tomko .30 .10
❑ 408 Bobby Hill .30 .10
❑ 409 Troy O'Leary .30 .10
❑ 410 Corey Patterson .30 .10
❑ 411 Kerry Wood .30 .10
❑ 412 Eric Karros .30 .10
❑ 413 Hee Seop Choi .30 .10
❑ 414 Alex Gonzalez .30 .10
❑ 415 Matt Clement .30 .10
❑ 416 Mark Grudzielanek .30 .10
❑ 417 Curt Schilling .30 .10
❑ 418 Steve Finley .30 .10
❑ 419 Craig Counsell .30 .10
❑ 420 Matt Williams .30 .10
❑ 421 Quinton McCracken .30 .10
❑ 422 Chad Moeller .30 .10
❑ 423 Lyle Overbay .30 .10
❑ 424 Miguel Batista .30 .10
❑ 425 Paul Lo Duca .30 .10
❑ 426 Kevin Brown .30 .10
❑ 427 Hideo Nomo .75 .30
❑ 428 Fred McGriff .50 .20
❑ 429 Joe Thurston .30 .10
❑ 430 Odalis Perez .30 .10
❑ 431 Darren Dreifort .30 .10
❑ 432 Todd Hundley .30 .10
❑ 433 Dave Roberts .30 .10
❑ 434 Jose Vidro .30 .10
❑ 435 Javier Vazquez .30 .10
❑ 436 Michael Barrett .30 .10
❑ 437 Fernando Tatis .30 .10
❑ 438 Peter Bergeron .30 .10
❑ 439 Endy Chavez .30 .10
❑ 440 Orlando Hernandez .30 .10
❑ 441 Marvin Benard .30 .10
❑ 442 Rich Aurilia .30 .10
❑ 443 Pedro Feliz .30 .10
❑ 444 Robb Nen .30 .10
❑ 445 Ray Durham .30 .10
❑ 446 Marquis Grissom .30 .10
❑ 447 Damian Moss .30 .10
❑ 448 Edgardo Alfonzo .30 .10
❑ 449 Juan Pierre .30 .10
❑ 450 Braden Looper .30 .10
❑ 451 Alex Gonzalez .30 .10
❑ 452 Justin Wayne .30 .10
❑ 453 Josh Beckett .30 .10
❑ 454 Juan Encarnacion .30 .10
❑ 455 Ivan Rodriguez .50 .20
❑ 456 Todd Hollandsworth .30 .10
❑ 457 Cliff Floyd .30 .10
❑ 458 Rey Sanchez .30 .10
❑ 459 Mike Piazza 1.25 .50
❑ 460 Mo Vaughn .30 .10
❑ 461 Armando Benitez .30 .10
❑ 462 Tsuyoshi Shinjo .30 .10
❑ 463 Tom Glavine .50 .20
❑ 464 David Cone .30 .10
❑ 465 Phil Nevin .30 .10
❑ 466 Sean Burroughs .30 .10
❑ 467 Jake Peavy .30 .10
❑ 468 Brian Lawrence .30 .10
❑ 469 Mark Loretta .30 .10
❑ 470 Dennis Tankersley .30 .10
❑ 471 Jesse Orosco .30 .10
❑ 472 Jim Thome .50 .20
❑ 473 Kevin Millwood .30 .10
❑ 474 David Bell .30 .10
❑ 475 Pat Burrell .30 .10
❑ 476 Brandon Duckworth .30 .10
❑ 477 Jose Mesa .30 .10
❑ 478 Marlon Byrd .30 .10
❑ 479 Reggie Sanders .30 .10
❑ 480 Jason Kendall .30 .10
❑ 481 Aramis Ramirez .30 .10
❑ 482 Kris Benson .30 .10
❑ 483 Matt Stairs .30 .10
❑ 484 Kevin Young .30 .10
❑ 485 Kenny Lofton .30 .10
❑ 486 Austin Kearns .30 .10
❑ 487 Barry Larkin .50 .20
❑ 488 Jason LaRue .30 .10
❑ 489 Ken Griffey Jr. 1.25 .50
❑ 490 Danny Graves .30 .10
❑ 491 Russell Branyan .30 .10
❑ 492 Reggie Taylor .30 .10
❑ 493 Jimmy Haynes .30 .10
❑ 494 Charles Johnson .30 .10
❑ 495 Todd Helton .50 .20
❑ 496 Juan Uribe .30 .10
❑ 497 Preston Wilson .30 .10
❑ 498 Chris Stynes .30 .10
❑ 499 Jason Jennings .30 .10
❑ 500 Jay Payton .30 .10
❑ 501 Hideki Matsui SR RC 5.00 2.00
❑ 502 Jose Contreras SR RC 1.50 .60
❑ 503 Brandon Webb SR RC 3.00 1.25
❑ 504 Robby Hammock SR RC 1.00 .40
❑ 505 Matt Kata SR RC 1.00 .40
❑ 506 Tim Olson SR RC 1.00 .40
❑ 507 Michael Hessman SR RC 1.00 .40
❑ 508 Jon Leicester SR RC 1.00 .40
❑ 509 Todd Wellemeyer SR RC 1.00 .40
❑ 510 David Sanders SR RC 1.00 .40
❑ 511 Josh Stewart SR RC 1.00 .40
❑ 512 Luis Ayala SR RC 1.00 .40
❑ 513 Clint Barmes SR RC 1.25 .50
❑ 514 Josh Willingham SR RC 2.00 .75
❑ 515 Alejandro Machado SR RC 1.00 .40
❑ 516 Felix Sanchez SR RC 1.00 .40
❑ 517 Willie Eyre SR RC 1.00 .40
❑ 518 Brent Hoard SR RC 1.00 .40
❑ 519 Lew Ford SR RC 1.50 .60
❑ 520 Termel Sledge SR RC 1.00 .40
❑ 521 Jeremy Griffiths SR RC 1.00 .40
❑ 522 Phil Seibel SR RC 1.00 .40
❑ 523 Craig Brazell SR RC 1.00 .40
❑ 524 Prentice Redman SR RC 1.00 .40

❑ 525 Jeff Duncan SR RC 1.00 .40
❑ 526 Shane Bazzell SR RC 1.00 .40
❑ 527 Bernie Castro SR RC 1.00 .40
❑ 528 Rett Johnson SR RC 1.00 .40
❑ 529 Bobby Madritsch SR RC 1.00 .40
❑ 530 Rocco Baldelli SR 1.00 .40
❑ 531 Alex Rodriguez SH CL .75 .30
❑ 532 Eric Chavez SH CL .30 .10
❑ 533 Miguel Tejada SH CL .30 .10
❑ 534 Ichiro Suzuki SH CL .75 .30
❑ 535 Sammy Sosa SH CL .50 .20
❑ 536 Barry Zito SH CL .30 .10
❑ 537 Darin Erstad SH CL .30 .10
❑ 538 Alfonso Soriano SH CL .30 .10
❑ 539 Troy Glaus SH CL .30 .10
❑ 540 Nomar Garciaparra SH CL .75 .30
❑ 541 Bo Hart RC .50 .20
❑ 542 Dan Haren RC .75 .30
❑ 543 Ryan Wagner RC .50 .20
❑ 544 Rich Harden .50 .20
❑ 545 Dontrelle Willis .75 .30
❑ 546 Jerome Williams .30 .10
❑ 547 Bobby Crosby .30 .10
❑ 548 Greg Jones RC .50 .20
❑ 549 Todd Linden .30 .10
❑ 550 Byung-Hyun Kim .30 .10
❑ 551 Rickie Weeks RC 3.00 1.25
❑ 552 Jason Roach RC .50 .20
❑ 553 Oscar Villarreal RC .50 .20
❑ 554 Justin Duchscherer .30 .10
❑ 555 Chris Capuano RC 1.50 .60
❑ 556 Josh Hall RC .50 .20
❑ 557 Luis Matos .30 .10
❑ 558 Miguel Ojeda RC .50 .20
❑ 559 Kevin Ohme RC .50 .20
❑ 560 Julio Manon RC .50 .20
❑ 561 Kevin Correia RC .50 .20
❑ 562 Delmon Young RC 5.00 2.00
❑ 563 Aaron Boone .30 .10
❑ 564 Aaron Looper RC .50 .20
❑ 565 Mike Neu RC .50 .20
❑ 566 Aquilino Lopez RC .50 .20
❑ 567 Jhonny Peralta .75 .30
❑ 568 Duaner Sanchez .30 .10
❑ 569 Stephen Randolph RC .50 .20
❑ 570 Nate Bland RC .50 .20
❑ 571 Chin-Hui Tsao .30 .10
❑ 572 Michel Hernandez RC .50 .20
❑ 573 Rocco Baldelli .30 .10
❑ 574 Robb Quinlan .30 .10
❑ 575 Aaron Heilman .30 .10
❑ 576 Jae Weong Seo .30 .10
❑ 577 Joe Borowski .30 .10
❑ 578 Chris Bootcheck .30 .10
❑ 579 Michael Ryan RC .50 .20
❑ 580 Mark Malaska RC .50 .20
❑ 581 Jose Guillen .30 .10
❑ 582 Josh Towers .30 .10
❑ 583 Tom Gregorio RC .50 .20
❑ 584 Edwin Jackson RC .50 .20
❑ 585 Jason Anderson .30 .10
❑ 586 Jose Reyes .30 .10
❑ 587 Miguel Cabrera .75 .30
❑ 588 Nate Bump .30 .10
❑ 589 Jeromy Burnitz .30 .10
❑ 590 David Ross .30 .10
❑ 591 Chase Utley .75 .30
❑ 592 Brandon Webb 1.50 .60
❑ 593 Masao Kida .30 .10
❑ 594 Jimmy Journell .30 .10
❑ 595 Eric Young .30 .10
❑ 596 Tony Womack .30 .10
❑ 597 Amaury Telemaco .30 .10
❑ 598 Rickey Henderson .75 .30
❑ 599 Esteban Loaiza .30 .10
❑ 600 Sidney Ponson .30 .10
❑ NNO Update Set Exchange Card

2004 Upper Deck

❑ COMPLETE SERIES 1 (270) 50.00 20.00
❑ COMPLETE SERIES 2 (270) 50.00 20.00
❑ COMP.UPDATE SET (50) 15.00 7.50
❑ COMMON (31-480/541-565) .30 .10
❑ COMMON (1-30/481-540) 1.00 .40
❑ COMMON CARD (566-590) .50 .20
❑ 541-590 ONE SET PER '05 UD1 HOBBY BOX

❑ UPDATE SET EXCH 1:480 '05 UD1 RETAIL
❑ UPDATE SET EXCH.DEADLINE TBD
❑ 1 Dontrelle Willis SR 1.50 .60
❑ 2 Edgar Gonzalez SR 1.00 .40
❑ 3 Jose Reyes SR 1.00 .40
❑ 4 Jae Weong Seo SR 1.00 .40
❑ 5 Miguel Cabrera SR 1.50 .60
❑ 6 Jesse Foppert SR 1.00 .40
❑ 7 Mike Neu SR 1.00 .40
❑ 8 Michael Nakamura SR 1.00 .40
❑ 9 Luis Ayala SR 1.00 .40
❑ 10 Jared Sandberg SR 1.00 .40
❑ 11 Jhonny Peralta SR 1.00 .40
❑ 12 Wil Ledezma SR 1.00 .40
❑ 13 Jason Roach SR 1.00 .40
❑ 14 Kirk Saarloos SR 1.00 .40
❑ 15 Cliff Lee SR 1.00 .40
❑ 16 Bobby Hill SR 1.00 .40
❑ 17 Lyle Overbay SR 1.00 .40
❑ 18 Josh Hall SR 1.00 .40
❑ 19 Joe Thurston SR 1.00 .40
❑ 20 Matt Kata SR 1.00 .40
❑ 21 Jeremy Bonderman SR 1.00 .40
❑ 22 Julio Manon SR 1.00 .40
❑ 23 Rodrigo Rosario SR 1.00 .40
❑ 24 Robby Hammock SR 1.00 .40
❑ 25 David Sanders SR 1.00 .40
❑ 26 Miguel Ojeda SR 1.00 .40
❑ 27 Mark Teixeira SR 1.50 .60
❑ 28 Franklyn German SR 1.00 .40
❑ 29 Ken Harvey SR 1.00 .40
❑ 30 Xavier Nady SR 1.00 .40
❑ 31 Tim Salmon .50 .20
❑ 32 Troy Glaus .30 .10
❑ 33 Adam Kennedy .30 .10
❑ 34 David Eckstein .30 .10
❑ 35 Ben Molina .30 .10
❑ 36 Jarrod Washburn .30 .10
❑ 37 Ramon Ortiz .30 .10
❑ 38 Eric Chavez .30 .10
❑ 39 Miguel Tejada .30 .10
❑ 40 Chris Singleton .30 .10
❑ 41 Jermaine Dye .30 .10
❑ 42 John Halama .30 .10
❑ 43 Tim Hudson .30 .10
❑ 44 Barry Zito .30 .10
❑ 45 Ted Lilly .30 .10
❑ 46 Bobby Kielty .30 .10
❑ 47 Kelvim Escobar .30 .10
❑ 48 Josh Phelps .30 .10
❑ 49 Vernon Wells .30 .10
❑ 50 Roy Halladay .30 .10
❑ 51 Orlando Hudson .30 .10
❑ 52 Eric Hinske .30 .10
❑ 53 Brandon Backe .30 .10
❑ 54 Dewon Brazelton .30 .10
❑ 55 Ben Grieve .30 .10
❑ 56 Aubrey Huff .30 .10
❑ 57 Toby Hall .30 .10
❑ 58 Rocco Baldelli .30 .10
❑ 59 Al Martin .30 .10
❑ 60 Brandon Phillips .30 .10
❑ 61 Omar Vizquel .50 .20
❑ 62 C.C. Sabathia .30 .10
❑ 63 Milton Bradley .30 .10
❑ 64 Ricky Gutierrez .30 .10
❑ 65 Matt Lawton .30 .10
❑ 66 Danys Baez .30 .10
❑ 67 Ichiro Suzuki 1.50 .60
❑ 68 Randy Winn .30 .10
❑ 69 Carlos Guillen .30 .10
❑ 70 Mark McLemore .30 .10
❑ 71 Dan Wilson .30 .10
❑ 72 Jamie Moyer .30 .10
❑ 73 Joel Pineiro .30 .10
❑ 74 Edgar Martinez .50 .20
❑ 75 Tony Batista .30 .10
❑ 76 Jay Gibbons .30 .10
❑ 77 Jeff Conine .30 .10
❑ 78 Melvin Mora .30 .10
❑ 79 Geronimo Gil .30 .10
❑ 80 Rodrigo Lopez .30 .10
❑ 81 Jorge Julio .30 .10
❑ 82 Rafael Palmeiro .50 .20
❑ 83 Juan Gonzalez .30 .10
❑ 84 Mike Young .30 .10
❑ 85 Alex Rodriguez 1.25 .50
❑ 86 Einar Diaz .30 .10
❑ 87 Kevin Mench .30 .10
❑ 88 Hank Blalock .30 .10
❑ 89 Pedro Martinez .50 .20
❑ 90 Byung-Hyun Kim .30 .10
❑ 91 Derek Lowe .30 .10
❑ 92 Jason Varitek .75 .30
❑ 93 Manny Ramirez .50 .20
❑ 94 John Burkett .30 .10
❑ 95 Todd Walker .30 .10
❑ 96 Nomar Garciaparra 1.25 .50
❑ 97 Trot Nixon .30 .10
❑ 98 Mike Sweeney .30 .10
❑ 99 Carlos Febles .30 .10
❑ 100 Mike MacDougal .30 .10
❑ 101 Raul Ibanez .30 .10
❑ 102 Jason Grimsley .30 .10
❑ 103 Chris George .30 .10
❑ 104 Brent Mayne .30 .10
❑ 105 Dmitri Young .30 .10
❑ 106 Eric Munson .30 .10
❑ 107 A.J. Hinch .30 .10
❑ 108 Andres Torres .30 .10
❑ 109 Bobby Higginson .30 .10
❑ 110 Shane Halter .30 .10
❑ 111 Matt Walbeck .30 .10
❑ 112 Torii Hunter .30 .10
❑ 113 Doug Mientkiewicz .30 .10
❑ 114 Lew Ford .30 .10
❑ 115 Eric Milton .30 .10
❑ 116 Eddie Guardado .30 .10
❑ 117 Cristian Guzman .30 .10
❑ 118 Corey Koskie .30 .10
❑ 119 Magglio Ordonez .30 .10
❑ 120 Mark Buehrle .30 .10
❑ 121 Billy Koch .30 .10
❑ 122 Jose Valentin .30 .10
❑ 123 Paul Konerko .30 .10
❑ 124 Carlos Lee .30 .10
❑ 125 Jon Garland .30 .10
❑ 126 Jason Giambi .30 .10
❑ 127 Derek Jeter 1.50 .60
❑ 128 Roger Clemens 1.50 .60
❑ 129 Andy Pettitte .50 .20
❑ 130 Jorge Posada .50 .20
❑ 131 David Wells .30 .10
❑ 132 Hideki Matsui 1.25 .50
❑ 133 Mike Mussina .50 .20
❑ 134 Jeff Bagwell .50 .20
❑ 135 Craig Biggio .50 .20
❑ 136 Morgan Ensberg .30 .10
❑ 137 Richard Hidalgo .30 .10
❑ 138 Brad Ausmus .30 .10
❑ 139 Roy Oswalt .30 .10
❑ 140 Billy Wagner .30 .10
❑ 141 Octavio Dotel .30 .10
❑ 142 Gary Sheffield .30 .10
❑ 143 Andruw Jones .50 .20
❑ 144 John Smoltz .50 .20
❑ 145 Rafael Furcal .30 .10
❑ 146 Javy Lopez .30 .10
❑ 147 Shane Reynolds .30 .10
❑ 148 Horacio Ramirez .30 .10
❑ 149 Mike Hampton .30 .10
❑ 150 Jung Bong .30 .10
❑ 151 Ruben Quevedo .30 .10
❑ 152 Ben Sheets .30 .10

❑ 153 Geoff Jenkins .30 .10
❑ 154 Royce Clayton .30 .10
❑ 155 Glendon Rusch .30 .10
❑ 156 John Vander Wal .30 .10
❑ 157 Scott Podsednik .30 .10
❑ 158 Jim Edmonds .30 .10
❑ 159 Tino Martinez .50 .20
❑ 160 Albert Pujols 1.50 .60
❑ 161 Matt Morris .30 .10
❑ 162 Woody Williams .30 .10
❑ 163 Edgar Renteria .30 .10
❑ 164 Jason Isringhausen .30 .10
❑ 165 Jason Simontacchi .30 .10
❑ 166 Kerry Robinson .30 .10
❑ 167 Sammy Sosa .75 .30
❑ 168 Joe Borowski .30 .10
❑ 169 Tony Womack .30 .10
❑ 170 Antonio Alfonseca .30 .10
❑ 171 Corey Patterson .30 .10
❑ 172 Mark Prior .50 .20
❑ 173 Moises Alou .30 .10
❑ 174 Matt Clement .30 .10
❑ 175 Randall Simon .30 .10
❑ 176 Randy Johnson .75 .30
❑ 177 Luis Gonzalez .30 .10
❑ 178 Craig Counsell .30 .10
❑ 179 Miguel Batista .30 .10
❑ 180 Steve Finley .30 .10
❑ 181 Brandon Webb .30 .10
❑ 182 Danny Bautista .30 .10
❑ 183 Oscar Villarreal .30 .10
❑ 184 Shawn Green .30 .10
❑ 185 Brian Jordan .30 .10
❑ 186 Fred McGriff .50 .20
❑ 187 Andy Ashby .30 .10
❑ 188 Rickey Henderson .75 .30
❑ 189 Dave Roberts .30 .10
❑ 190 Eric Gagne .30 .10
❑ 191 Kazuhisa Ishii .30 .10
❑ 192 Adrian Beltre .30 .10
❑ 193 Vladimir Guerrero .75 .30
❑ 194 Livan Hernandez .30 .10
❑ 195 Ron Calloway .30 .10
❑ 196 Sun Woo Kim .30 .10
❑ 197 Wil Cordero .30 .10
❑ 198 Brad Wilkerson .30 .10
❑ 199 Orlando Cabrera .30 .10
❑ 200 Barry Bonds 2.00 .75
❑ 201 Ray Durham .30 .10
❑ 202 Andres Galarraga .30 .10
❑ 203 Benito Santiago .30 .10
❑ 204 Jose Cruz Jr. .30 .10
❑ 205 Jason Schmidt .30 .10
❑ 206 Kirk Rueter .30 .10
❑ 207 Felix Rodriguez .30 .10
❑ 208 Mike Lowell .30 .10
❑ 209 Luis Castillo .30 .10
❑ 210 Derrek Lee .50 .20
❑ 211 Andy Fox .30 .10
❑ 212 Tommy Phelps .30 .10
❑ 213 Todd Hollandsworth .30 .10
❑ 214 Brad Penny .30 .10
❑ 215 Juan Pierre .30 .10
❑ 216 Mike Piazza 1.25 .50
❑ 217 Jae Weong Seo .30 .10
❑ 218 Ty Wigginton .30 .10
❑ 219 Al Leiter .30 .10
❑ 220 Roger Cedeno .30 .10
❑ 221 Timo Perez .30 .10
❑ 222 Aaron Heilman .30 .10
❑ 223 Pedro Astacio .30 .10
❑ 224 Joe McEwing .30 .10
❑ 225 Ryan Klesko .30 .10
❑ 226 Brian Giles .30 .10
❑ 227 Mark Kotsay .30 .10
❑ 228 Brian Lawrence .30 .10
❑ 229 Rod Beck .30 .10
❑ 230 Trevor Hoffman .30 .10
❑ 231 Sean Burroughs .30 .10
❑ 232 Bob Abreu .30 .10
❑ 233 Jim Thome .50 .20
❑ 234 David Bell .30 .10
❑ 235 Jimmy Rollins .30 .10
❑ 236 Mike Lieberthal .30 .10
❑ 237 Vicente Padilla .30 .10
❑ 238 Randy Wolf .30 .10
❑ 239 Reggie Sanders .30 .10
❑ 240 Jason Kendall .30 .10
❑ 241 Jack Wilson .30 .10
❑ 242 Jose Hernandez .30 .10
❑ 243 Kip Wells .30 .10
❑ 244 Carlos Rivera .30 .10
❑ 245 Craig Wilson .30 .10
❑ 246 Adam Dunn .30 .10
❑ 247 Sean Casey .30 .10
❑ 248 Danny Graves .30 .10
❑ 249 Ryan Dempster .30 .10
❑ 250 Barry Larkin .50 .20
❑ 251 Reggie Taylor .30 .10
❑ 252 Wily Mo Pena .30 .10
❑ 253 Larry Walker .30 .10
❑ 254 Mark Sweeney .30 .10
❑ 255 Preston Wilson .30 .10
❑ 256 Jason Jennings .30 .10
❑ 257 Charles Johnson .30 .10
❑ 258 Jay Payton .30 .10
❑ 259 Chris Stynes .30 .10
❑ 260 Juan Uribe .30 .10
❑ 261 Hideki Matsui SH CL .75 .30
❑ 262 Barry Bonds SH CL 1.00 .40
❑ 263 Dontrelle Willis SH CL .30 .10
❑ 264 Kevin Millwood SH CL .30 .10
❑ 265 Billy Wagner SH CL .30 .10
❑ 266 Rocco Baldelli SH CL .30 .10
❑ 267 Roger Clemens SH CL .75 .30
❑ 268 Rafael Palmeiro SH CL .30 .10
❑ 269 Miguel Cabrera SH CL .50 .20
❑ 270 Jose Contreras SH CL .30 .10
❑ 271 Aaron Sele .30 .10
❑ 272 Bartolo Colon .30 .10
❑ 273 Darin Erstad .30 .10
❑ 274 Francisco Rodriguez .30 .10
❑ 275 Garret Anderson .30 .10
❑ 276 Jose Guillen .30 .10
❑ 277 Troy Percival .30 .10
❑ 278 Alex Cintron .30 .10
❑ 279 Casey Fossum .30 .10
❑ 280 Elmer Dessens .30 .10
❑ 281 Jose Valverde .30 .10
❑ 282 Matt Mantei .30 .10
❑ 283 Richie Sexson .30 .10
❑ 284 Roberto Alomar .50 .20
❑ 285 Shea Hillenbrand .30 .10
❑ 286 Chipper Jones .75 .30
❑ 287 Greg Maddux 1.25 .50
❑ 288 J.D. Drew .30 .10
❑ 289 Marcus Giles .30 .10
❑ 290 Mike Hessman .30 .10
❑ 291 John Thomson .30 .10
❑ 292 Russ Ortiz .30 .10
❑ 293 Adam Loewen .30 .10
❑ 294 Jack Cust .30 .10
❑ 295 Jerry Hairston Jr. .30 .10
❑ 296 Kurt Ainsworth .30 .10
❑ 297 Luis Matos .30 .10
❑ 298 Marty Cordova .30 .10
❑ 299 Sidney Ponson .30 .10
❑ 300 Bill Mueller .30 .10
❑ 301 Curt Schilling .30 .10
❑ 302 David Ortiz .50 .20
❑ 303 Johnny Damon .50 .20
❑ 304 Keith Foulke Sox .30 .10
❑ 305 Pokey Reese .30 .10
❑ 306 Scott Williamson .30 .10
❑ 307 Tim Wakefield .30 .10
❑ 308 Alex S. Gonzalez .30 .10
❑ 309 Aramis Ramirez .30 .10
❑ 310 Carlos Zambrano .30 .10
❑ 311 Juan Cruz .30 .10
❑ 312 Kerry Wood .30 .10
❑ 313 Kyle Farnsworth .30 .10
❑ 314 Aaron Rowand .30 .10
❑ 315 Esteban Loaiza .30 .10
❑ 316 Frank Thomas .75 .30
❑ 317 Joe Borchard .30 .10
❑ 318 Joe Crede .30 .10
❑ 319 Miguel Olivo .30 .10
❑ 320 Willie Harris .30 .10
❑ 321 Aaron Harang .30 .10
❑ 322 Austin Kearns .30 .10
❑ 323 Brandon Claussen .30 .10
❑ 324 Brandon Larson .30 .10
❑ 325 Ryan Freel .30 .10
❑ 326 Ken Griffey Jr. 1.25 .50
❑ 327 Ryan Wagner .30 .10
❑ 328 Alex Escobar .30 .10
❑ 329 Coco Crisp .30 .10
❑ 330 David Riske .30 .10
❑ 331 Jody Gerut .30 .10
❑ 332 Josh Bard .30 .10
❑ 333 Travis Hafner .30 .10
❑ 334 Chin-Hui Tsao .30 .10
❑ 335 Denny Stark .30 .10
❑ 336 Jeromy Burnitz .30 .10
❑ 337 Shawn Chacon .30 .10
❑ 338 Todd Helton .50 .20
❑ 339 Vinny Castilla .30 .10
❑ 340 Alex Sanchez .30 .10
❑ 341 Carlos Pena .30 .10
❑ 342 Fernando Vina .30 .10
❑ 343 Jason Johnson .30 .10
❑ 344 Matt Anderson .30 .10
❑ 345 Mike Maroth .30 .10
❑ 346 Rondell White .30 .10
❑ 347 A.J. Burnett .30 .10
❑ 348 Alex Gonzalez .30 .10
❑ 349 Armando Benitez .30 .10
❑ 350 Carl Pavano .30 .10
❑ 351 Hee Seop Choi .30 .10
❑ 352 Ivan Rodriguez .50 .20
❑ 353 Josh Beckett .30 .10
❑ 354 Josh Willingham .30 .10
❑ 355 Adam Everett .30 .10
❑ 356 Brandon Duckworth .30 .10
❑ 357 Jason Lane .30 .10
❑ 358 Jeff Kent .30 .10
❑ 359 Jeriome Robertson .30 .10
❑ 360 Lance Berkman .30 .10
❑ 361 Wade Miller .30 .10
❑ 362 Aaron Guiel .30 .10
❑ 363 Angel Berroa .30 .10
❑ 364 Carlos Beltran .30 .10
❑ 365 David DeJesus .30 .10
❑ 366 Desi Relaford .30 .10
❑ 367 Joe Randa .30 .10
❑ 368 Runelvys Hernandez .30 .10
❑ 369 Edwin Jackson .30 .10
❑ 370 Hideo Nomo .75 .30
❑ 371 Jeff Weaver .30 .10
❑ 372 Juan Encarnacion .30 .10
❑ 373 Odalis Perez .30 .10
❑ 374 Paul Lo Duca .30 .10
❑ 375 Robin Ventura .30 .10
❑ 376 Bill Hall .30 .10
❑ 377 Chad Moeller .30 .10
❑ 378 Chris Capuano .30 .10
❑ 379 Junior Spivey .30 .10
❑ 380 Rickie Weeks .30 .10
❑ 381 Wes Helms .30 .10
❑ 382 Brad Radke .30 .10
❑ 383 Jacque Jones .30 .10
❑ 384 Joe Mays .30 .10
❑ 385 Joe Nathan .30 .10
❑ 386 Johan Santana .75 .30
❑ 387 Nick Punto .30 .10
❑ 388 Shannon Stewart .30 .10
❑ 389 Carl Everett .30 .10
❑ 390 Claudio Vargas .30 .10
❑ 391 Jose Vidro .30 .10
❑ 392 Nick Johnson .30 .10
❑ 393 Rocky Biddle .30 .10
❑ 394 Tony Armas Jr. .30 .10
❑ 395 Braden Looper .30 .10
❑ 396 Cliff Floyd .30 .10
❑ 397 Jason Phillips .30 .10
❑ 398 Mike Cameron .30 .10
❑ 399 Tom Glavine .50 .20
❑ 400 Kenny Lofton .30 .10
❑ 401 Alfonso Soriano .30 .10
❑ 402 Bernie Williams .50 .20
❑ 403 Javier Vazquez .30 .10
❑ 404 Jon Lieber .30 .10
❑ 405 Jose Contreras .30 .10
❑ 406 Kevin Brown .30 .10
❑ 407 Mariano Rivera .75 .30
❑ 408 Arthur Rhodes .30 .10
❑ 409 Eric Byrnes .30 .10
❑ 410 Erubiel Durazo .30 .10

❑ 411 Graham Koonce .30 .10
❑ 412 Marco Scutaro .30 .10
❑ 413 Mark Mulder .30 .10
❑ 414 Mark Redman .30 .10
❑ 415 Rich Harden .30 .10
❑ 416 Brett Myers .30 .10
❑ 417 Chase Utley .50 .20
❑ 418 Kevin Millwood .30 .10
❑ 419 Marlon Byrd .30 .10
❑ 420 Pat Burrell .30 .10
❑ 421 Placido Polanco .30 .10
❑ 422 Tim Worrell .30 .10
❑ 423 Jason Bay .30 .10
❑ 424 Josh Fogg .30 .10
❑ 425 Kris Benson .30 .10
❑ 426 Mike Gonzalez .30 .10
❑ 427 Oliver Perez .30 .10
❑ 428 Tike Redman .30 .10
❑ 429 Adam Eaton .30 .10
❑ 430 Ismael Valdes .30 .10
❑ 431 Jake Peavy .30 .10
❑ 432 Khalil Greene .50 .20
❑ 433 Mark Loretta .30 .10
❑ 434 Phil Nevin .30 .10
❑ 435 Ramon Hernandez .30 .10
❑ 436 A.J. Pierzynski .30 .10
❑ 437 Edgardo Alfonzo .30 .10
❑ 438 J.T. Snow .30 .10
❑ 439 Jerome Williams .30 .10
❑ 440 Marquis Grissom .30 .10
❑ 441 Robb Nen .30 .10
❑ 442 Bret Boone .30 .10
❑ 443 Freddy Garcia .30 .10
❑ 444 Gil Meche .30 .10
❑ 445 John Olerud .30 .10
❑ 446 Rich Aurilia .30 .10
❑ 447 Shigetoshi Hasegawa .30 .10
❑ 448 Bo Hart .30 .10
❑ 449 Danny Haren .30 .10
❑ 450 Jason Marquis .30 .10
❑ 451 Marlon Anderson .30 .10
❑ 452 Scott Rolen .50 .20
❑ 453 So Taguchi .30 .10
❑ 454 Carl Crawford .30 .10
❑ 455 Delmon Young .50 .20
❑ 456 Geoff Blum .30 .10
❑ 457 Jesus Colome .30 .10
❑ 458 Jonny Gomes .30 .10
❑ 459 Lance Carter .30 .10
❑ 460 Robert Fick .30 .10
❑ 461 Chan Ho Park .30 .10
❑ 462 Francisco Cordero .30 .10
❑ 463 Jeff Nelson .30 .10
❑ 464 Jeff Zimmerman .30 .10
❑ 465 Kenny Rogers .30 .10
❑ 466 Aquilino Lopez .30 .10
❑ 467 Carlos Delgado .30 .10
❑ 468 Frank Catalanotto .30 .10
❑ 469 Reed Johnson .30 .10
❑ 470 Pat Hentgen .30 .10
❑ 471 Curt Schilling SH CL .30 .10
❑ 472 Gary Sheffield SH CL .30 .10
❑ 473 Javier Vazquez SH CL .30 .10
❑ 474 Kazuo Matsui SH CL .50 .20
❑ 475 Kevin Brown SH CL .30 .10
❑ 476 Rafael Palmeiro SH CL .30 .10
❑ 477 Richie Sexson SH CL .30 .10
❑ 478 Roger Clemens SH CL .75 .30
❑ 479 Vladimir Guerrero SH CL .50 .20
❑ 480 Alex Rodriguez SH CL .75 .30
❑ 481 Jake Woods SR RC 1.00 .40
❑ 482 Tim Bittner SR RC 1.00 .40
❑ 483 Brandon Medders SR RC 1.00 .40
❑ 484 Casey Daigle SR RC 1.00 .40
❑ 485 Jerry Gil SR RC 1.00 .40
❑ 486 Mike Gosling SR RC 1.00 .40
❑ 487 Jose Capellan SR RC 1.50 .60
❑ 488 Onil Joseph SR RC 1.00 .40
❑ 489 Roman Colon SR RC 1.00 .40
❑ 490 Dave Crouthers SR RC 1.00 .40
❑ 491 Eddy Rodriguez SR RC 1.50 .60
❑ 492 Franklyn Gracesqui SR RC 1.00 .40
❑ 493 Jamie Brown SR RC 1.00 .40
❑ 494 Jerome Gamble SR RC 1.00 .40
❑ 495 Tim Hamulack SR RC 1.00 .40
❑ 496 Carlos Vasquez SR RC 1.50 .60
❑ 497 Renyel Pinto SR RC 1.50 .60
❑ 498 Ronny Cedeno SR RC 2.00 .75
❑ 499 Enemencio Pacheco SR RC 1.00 .40
❑ 500 Ryan Meaux SR RC 1.00 .40
❑ 501 Ryan Wing SR RC 1.00 .40
❑ 502 Shingo Takatsu SR RC 1.50 .60
❑ 503 William Bergolla SR RC 1.00 .40
❑ 504 Ivan Ochoa SR RC 1.00 .40
❑ 505 Mariano Gomez SR RC 1.00 .40
❑ 506 Justin Hampson SR RC 1.00 .40
❑ 507 Justin Huisman SR RC 1.00 .40
❑ 508 Scott Dohmann SR RC 1.00 .40
❑ 509 Donnie Kelly SR RC 1.00 .40
❑ 510 Chris Aguila SR RC 1.00 .40
❑ 511 Lincoln Holdzkom SR RC 1.00 .40
❑ 512 Freddy Guzman SR RC 1.00 .40
❑ 513 Hector Gimenez SR RC 1.00 .40
❑ 514 Jorge Vasquez SR RC 1.00 .40
❑ 515 Jason Frasor SR RC 1.00 .40
❑ 516 Chris Saenz SR RC 1.00 .40
❑ 517 Dennis Sarfate SR RC 1.00 .40
❑ 518 Colby Miller SR RC 1.00 .40
❑ 519 Jason Bartlett SR RC 1.50 .60
❑ 520 Chad Bentz SR RC 1.00 .40
❑ 521 Josh Labandeira SR RC 1.00 .40
❑ 522 Shawn Hill SR RC 1.00 .40
❑ 523 Kazuo Matsui SR RC 1.50 .60
❑ 524 Carlos Hines SR RC 1.00 .40
❑ 525 Mike Vento SR RC 1.50 .60
❑ 526 Scott Proctor SR RC 1.50 .60
❑ 527 Sean Henn SR RC 1.00 .40
❑ 528 David Aardsma SR RC 1.50 .60
❑ 529 Ian Snell SR RC 2.00 .75
❑ 530 Mike Johnston SR RC 1.00 .40
❑ 531 Akinori Otsuka SR RC 1.00 .40
❑ 532 Rusty Tucker SR RC 1.50 .60
❑ 533 Justin Knoedler SR RC 1.00 .40
❑ 534 Merkin Valdez SR RC 1.50 .60
❑ 535 Greg Dobbs SR RC 1.00 .40
❑ 536 Justin Leone SR RC 1.50 .60
❑ 537 Shawn Camp SR RC 1.00 .40
❑ 538 Edwin Moreno SR RC 1.00 .40
❑ 539 Angel Chavez SR RC 1.00 .40
❑ 540 Jesse Harper SR RC 1.00 .40
❑ 541 Alex Rodriguez 1.25 .50
❑ 542 Roger Clemens 1.50 .60
❑ 543 Andy Pettitte .50 .20
❑ 544 Vladimir Guerrero .75 .30
❑ 545 David Wells .30 .10
❑ 546 Derrek Lee .50 .20
❑ 547 Carlos Beltran .30 .10
❑ 548 Orlando Cabrera Sox .30 .10
❑ 549 Paul Lo Duca .30 .10
❑ 550 Dave Roberts .30 .10
❑ 551 Guillermo Mota .30 .10
❑ 552 Steve Finley .30 .10
❑ 553 Juan Encarnacion .30 .10
❑ 554 Larry Walker .30 .10
❑ 555 Ty Wigginton .30 .10
❑ 556 Doug Mientkiewicz .30 .10
❑ 557 Roberto Alomar .50 .20
❑ 558 B.J. Upton .50 .20
❑ 559 Brad Penny .30 .10
❑ 560 Hee Seop Choi .30 .10
❑ 561 David Wright 3.00 1.25
❑ 562 Nomar Garciaparra 1.25 .50
❑ 563 Felix Rodriguez .30 .10
❑ 564 Victor Zambrano .30 .10
❑ 565 Kris Benson .30 .10
❑ 566 Aarom Baldiris SR RC .50 .20
❑ 567 Joey Gathright SR RC 1.00 .40
❑ 568 Charles Thomas SR RC .50 .20
❑ 569 Brian Dallimore SR RC .50 .20
❑ 570 Chris Oxspring SR RC .50 .20
❑ 571 Chris Shelton SR RC 2.00 .75
❑ 572 Dioner Navarro SR RC 1.25 .50
❑ 573 Edwardo Sierra SR RC .50 .20
❑ 574 Fernando Nieve SR RC .75 .30
❑ 575 Frank Francisco SR RC .50 .20
❑ 576 Jeff Bennett SR RC .50 .20
❑ 577 Justin Lehr SR RC .50 .20
❑ 578 John Gall SR RC .50 .20
❑ 579 Jorge Sequea SR RC .50 .20
❑ 580 Justin Germano SR RC .50 .20
❑ 581 Kazuhito Tadano SR RC .50 .20
❑ 582 Kevin Cave SR RC .50 .20
❑ 583 Jesse Crain SR RC .75 .30
❑ 584 Luis A. Gonzalez SR RC .50 .20
❑ 585 Michael Wuertz SR RC .50 .20
❑ 586 Orlando Rodriguez SR RC .50 .20
❑ 587 Phil Stockman SR RC .50 .20
❑ 588 Ramon Ramirez SR RC .50 .20
❑ 589 Roberto Novoa SR RC .50 .20
❑ 590 Scott Kazmir SR RC 4.00 1.50
❑ NNO Update Set Exchange Card

2005 Upper Deck

❑ COMPLETE SERIES 1 (300) 50.00 30.00
❑ COMMON CARD (1-500) .30 .10
❑ COMMON (211-250/426-450) 1.00 .40
❑ OVERALL PLATES SER.1 ODDS 1:1080 H
❑ PLATES PRINT RUN 1 #'d SET PER COLOR
❑ BLACK-CYAN-MAGENTA-YELLOW ISSUED
❑ NO PLATES PRICING DUE TO SCARCITY
❑ 1 Casey Kotchman .30 .10
❑ 2 Chone Figgins .30 .10
❑ 3 David Eckstein .30 .10
❑ 4 Jarrod Washburn .30 .10
❑ 5 Robb Quinlan .30 .10
❑ 6 Troy Glaus .30 .10
❑ 7 Vladimir Guerrero .75 .30
❑ 8 Brandon Webb .30 .10
❑ 9 Danny Bautista .30 .10
❑ 10 Luis Gonzalez .30 .10
❑ 11 Matt Kata .30 .10
❑ 12 Randy Johnson .75 .30
❑ 13 Robby Hammock .30 .10
❑ 14 Shea Hillenbrand .30 .10
❑ 15 Adam LaRoche .30 .10
❑ 16 Andruw Jones .50 .20
❑ 17 Horacio Ramirez .30 .10
❑ 18 John Smoltz .50 .20
❑ 19 Johnny Estrada .30 .10
❑ 20 Mike Hampton .30 .10
❑ 21 Rafael Furcal .30 .10
❑ 22 Brian Roberts .30 .10
❑ 23 Javy Lopez .30 .10
❑ 24 Jay Gibbons .30 .10
❑ 25 Jorge Julio .30 .10
❑ 26 Melvin Mora .30 .10
❑ 27 Miguel Tejada .30 .10
❑ 28 Rafael Palmeiro .50 .20
❑ 29 Derek Lowe .30 .10
❑ 30 Jason Varitek .75 .30
❑ 31 Kevin Youkilis .30 .10
❑ 32 Manny Ramirez .50 .20
❑ 33 Curt Schilling .50 .20
❑ 34 Pedro Martinez .50 .20
❑ 35 Trot Nixon .30 .10
❑ 36 Corey Patterson .30 .10
❑ 37 Derrek Lee .50 .20
❑ 38 LaTroy Hawkins .30 .10
❑ 39 Mark Prior .50 .20
❑ 40 Matt Clement .30 .10
❑ 41 Moises Alou .30 .10
❑ 42 Sammy Sosa .75 .30
❑ 43 Aaron Rowand .30 .10
❑ 44 Carlos Lee .30 .10
❑ 45 Jose Valentin .30 .10
❑ 46 Juan Uribe .30 .10
❑ 47 Magglio Ordonez .30 .10
❑ 48 Mark Buehrle .30 .10
❑ 49 Paul Konerko .30 .10
❑ 50 Adam Dunn .30 .10

	No.	Player		
❑	51	Barry Larkin	.50	.20
❑	52	D'Angelo Jimenez	.30	.10
❑	53	Danny Graves	.30	.10
❑	54	Paul Wilson	.30	.10
❑	55	Sean Casey	.30	.10
❑	56	Wily Mo Pena	.30	.10
❑	57	Ben Broussard	.30	.10
❑	58	C.C. Sabathia	.30	.10
❑	59	Casey Blake	.30	.10
❑	60	Cliff Lee	.30	.10
❑	61	Matt Lawton	.30	.10
❑	62	Omar Vizquel	.30	.10
❑	63	Victor Martinez	.30	.10
❑	64	Charles Johnson	.30	.10
❑	65	Joe Kennedy	.30	.10
❑	66	Jeromy Burnitz	.30	.10
❑	67	Matt Holliday	.40	.15
❑	68	Preston Wilson	.30	.10
❑	69	Royce Clayton	.30	.10
❑	70	Shawn Estes	.30	.10
❑	71	Bobby Higginson	.30	.10
❑	72	Brandon Inge	.30	.10
❑	73	Carlos Guillen	.30	.10
❑	74	Dmitri Young	.30	.10
❑	75	Eric Munson	.30	.10
❑	76	Jeremy Bonderman	.30	.10
❑	77	Ugueth Urbina	.30	.10
❑	78	Josh Beckett	.30	.10
❑	79	Dontrelle Willis	.30	.10
❑	80	Jeff Conine	.30	.10
❑	81	Juan Pierre	.30	.10
❑	82	Luis Castillo	.30	.10
❑	83	Miguel Cabrera	.50	.20
❑	84	Mike Lowell	.30	.10
❑	85	Andy Pettitte	.50	.20
❑	86	Brad Lidge	.30	.10
❑	87	Carlos Beltran	.30	.10
❑	88	Craig Biggio	.50	.20
❑	89	Jeff Bagwell	.50	.20
❑	90	Roger Clemens	1.25	.50
❑	91	Roy Oswalt	.30	.10
❑	92	Benito Santiago	.30	.10
❑	93	Jeremy Affeldt	.30	.10
❑	94	Juan Gonzalez	.30	.10
❑	95	Ken Harvey	.30	.10
❑	96	Mike MacDougal	.30	.10
❑	97	Mike Sweeney	.30	.10
❑	98	Zack Greinke	.30	.10
❑	99	Adrian Beltre	.30	.10
❑	100	Alex Cora	.30	.10
❑	101	Cesar Izturis	.30	.10
❑	102	Eric Gagne	.30	.10
❑	103	Kazuhisa Ishii	.30	.10
❑	104	Milton Bradley	.30	.10
❑	105	Shawn Green	.30	.10
❑	106	Danny Kolb	.30	.10
❑	107	Ben Sheets	.30	.10
❑	108	Brooks Kieschnick	.30	.10
❑	109	Craig Counsell	.30	.10
❑	110	Geoff Jenkins	.30	.10
❑	111	Lyle Overbay	.30	.10
❑	112	Scott Podsednik	.30	.10
❑	113	Corey Koskie	.30	.10
❑	114	Johan Santana	.75	.30
❑	115	Joe Mauer	.75	.30
❑	116	Justin Morneau	.30	.10
❑	117	Lew Ford	.30	.10
❑	118	Matt LeCroy	.30	.10
❑	119	Torii Hunter	.30	.10
❑	120	Brad Wilkerson	.30	.10
❑	121	Chad Cordero	.30	.10
❑	122	Livan Hernandez	.30	.10
❑	123	Jose Vidro	.30	.10
❑	124	Termmel Sledge	.30	.10
❑	125	Tony Batista	.30	.10
❑	126	Zach Day	.30	.10
❑	127	Al Leiter	.30	.10
❑	128	Jae Weong Seo	.30	.10
❑	129	Jose Reyes	.30	.10
❑	130	Kazuo Matsui	.30	.10
❑	131	Mike Piazza	.75	.30
❑	132	Todd Zeile	.30	.10
❑	133	Cliff Floyd	.30	.10
❑	134	Alex Rodriguez	1.25	.50
❑	135	Derek Jeter	1.50	.60
❑	136	Gary Sheffield	.30	.10
❑	137	Hideki Matsui	1.25	.50
❑	138	Jason Giambi	.30	.10
❑	139	Jorge Posada	.50	.20
❑	140	Mike Mussina	.50	.20
❑	141	Barry Zito	.30	.10
❑	142	Bobby Crosby	.30	.10
❑	143	Octavio Dotel	.30	.10
❑	144	Eric Chavez	.30	.10
❑	145	Jermaine Dye	.30	.10
❑	146	Mark Kotsay	.30	.10
❑	147	Tim Hudson	.30	.10
❑	148	Billy Wagner	.30	.10
❑	149	Bobby Abreu	.30	.10
❑	150	David Bell	.30	.10
❑	151	Jim Thome	.50	.20
❑	152	Jimmy Rollins	.30	.10
❑	153	Mike Lieberthal	.30	.10
❑	154	Randy Wolf	.30	.10
❑	155	Craig Wilson	.30	.10
❑	156	Daryle Ward	.30	.10
❑	157	Jack Wilson	.30	.10
❑	158	Jason Kendall	.30	.10
❑	159	Kip Wells	.30	.10
❑	160	Oliver Perez	.30	.10
❑	161	Rob Mackowiak	.30	.10
❑	162	Brian Giles	.30	.10
❑	163	Brian Lawrence	.30	.10
❑	164	David Wells	.30	.10
❑	165	Jay Payton	.30	.10
❑	166	Ryan Klesko	.30	.10
❑	167	Sean Burroughs	.30	.10
❑	168	Trevor Hoffman	.30	.10
❑	169	Brett Tomko	.30	.10
❑	170	J.T. Snow	.30	.10
❑	171	Jason Schmidt	.30	.10
❑	172	Kirk Rueter	.30	.10
❑	173	A.J. Pierzynski	.30	.10
❑	174	Pedro Feliz	.30	.10
❑	175	Ray Durham	.30	.10
❑	176	Eddie Guardado	.30	.10
❑	177	Edgar Martinez	.50	.20
❑	178	Ichiro Suzuki	1.50	.60
❑	179	Jamie Moyer	.30	.10
❑	180	Joel Pineiro	.30	.10
❑	181	Randy Winn	.30	.10
❑	182	Raul Ibanez	.30	.10
❑	183	Albert Pujols	1.50	.60
❑	184	Edgar Renteria	.30	.10
❑	185	Jason Isringhausen	.30	.10
❑	186	Jim Edmonds	.30	.10
❑	187	Matt Morris	.30	.10
❑	188	Reggie Sanders	.30	.10
❑	189	Tony Womack	.30	.10
❑	190	Aubrey Huff	.30	.10
❑	191	Danys Baez	.30	.10
❑	192	Carl Crawford	.30	.10
❑	193	Jose Cruz Jr.	.30	.10
❑	194	Rocco Baldelli	.30	.10
❑	195	Tino Martinez	.50	.20
❑	196	Dewon Brazelton	.30	.10
❑	197	Alfonso Soriano	.30	.10
❑	198	Brad Fullmer	.30	.10
❑	199	Gerald Laird	.30	.10
❑	200	Hank Blalock	.30	.10
❑	201	Laynce Nix	.30	.10
❑	202	Mark Teixeira	.50	.20
❑	203	Michael Young	.30	.10
❑	204	Alexis Rios	.30	.10
❑	205	Eric Hinske	.30	.10
❑	206	Miguel Batista	.30	.10
❑	207	Orlando Hudson	.30	.10
❑	208	Roy Halladay	.30	.10
❑	209	Ted Lilly	.30	.10
❑	210	Vernon Wells	.30	.10
❑	211	Aarom Baldiris SR	1.00	.40
❑	212	B.J. Upton SR	1.00	.40
❑	213	Dallas McPherson SR	1.00	.40
❑	214	Brian Dallimore SR	1.00	.40
❑	215	Chris Oxspring SR	1.00	.40
❑	216	Chris Shelton SR	1.50	.60
❑	217	David Wright SR	2.00	.75
❑	218	Edwardo Sierra SR	1.00	.40
❑	219	Fernando Nieve SR	1.00	.40
❑	220	Frank Francisco SR	1.00	.40
❑	221	Jeff Bennett SR	1.00	.40
❑	222	Justin Lehr SR	1.00	.40
❑	223	John Gall SR	1.00	.40
❑	224	Jorge Sequea SR	1.00	.40
❑	225	Justin Germano SR	1.00	.40
❑	226	Kazuhito Tadano SR	1.00	.40
❑	227	Kevin Cave SR	1.00	.40
❑	228	Joe Blanton SR	1.00	.40
❑	229	Luis A. Gonzalez SR	1.00	.40
❑	230	Michael Wuertz SR	1.00	.40
❑	231	Mike Rouse SR	1.00	.40
❑	232	Nick Regilio SR	1.00	.40
❑	233	Orlando Rodriguez SR	1.00	.40
❑	234	Phil Stockman SR	1.00	.40
❑	235	Ramon Ramirez SR	1.00	.40
❑	236	Roberto Novoa SR	1.00	.40
❑	237	Dioner Navarro SR	1.00	.40
❑	238	Tim Bausher SR	1.00	.40
❑	239	Logan Kensing SR	1.00	.40
❑	240	Andy Green SR	1.00	.40
❑	241	Brad Halsey SR	1.00	.40
❑	242	Charles Thomas SR	1.00	.40
❑	243	George Sherrill SR	1.00	.40
❑	244	Jesse Crain SR	1.00	.40
❑	245	Jimmy Serrano SR	1.00	.40
❑	246	Joe Horgan SR	1.00	.40
❑	247	Chris Young SR	1.00	.40
❑	248	Joey Gathright SR	1.00	.40
❑	249	Gavin Floyd SR	1.00	.40
❑	250	Ryan Howard SR	5.00	2.00
❑	251	Lance Cormier SR	1.00	.40
❑	252	Matt Treanor SR	1.00	.40
❑	253	Jeff Francis SR	1.00	.40
❑	254	Nick Swisher SR	1.00	.40
❑	255	Scott Atchison SR	1.00	.40
❑	256	Travis Blackley SR	1.00	.40
❑	257	Travis Smith SR	1.00	.40
❑	258	Yadier Molina SR	1.00	.40
❑	259	Jeff Keppinger SR	1.00	.40
❑	260	Scott Kazmir SR	1.00	.40
❑	261	G.Anderson/V.Guerrero TL	.50	.20
❑	262	L.Gonzalez/R.Johnson TL	.50	.20
❑	263	A.Jones/C.Jones TL	.50	.20
❑	264	M.Tejada/R.Palmeiro TL	.30	.10
❑	265	C.Schilling/M.Ramirez TL	.50	.20
❑	266	M.Prior/S.Sosa TL	.50	.20
❑	267	F.Thomas/M.Ordonez TL	.50	.20
❑	268	B.Larkin/K.Griffey Jr. TL	.75	.30
❑	269	C.Sabathia/V.Martinez TL	.30	.10
❑	270	J.Burnitz/T.Helton TL	.30	.10
❑	271	D.Young/I.Rodriguez TL	.30	.10
❑	272	J.Beckett/M.Cabrera TL	.30	.10
❑	273	J.Bagwell/R.Clemens TL	.75	.30
❑	274	K.Harvey/M.Sweeney TL	.30	.10
❑	275	A.Beltre/E.Gagne TL	.30	.10
❑	276	B.Sheets/G.Jenkins TL	.30	.10
❑	277	J.Mauer/T.Hunter TL	.50	.20
❑	278	J.Vidro/L.Hernandez TL	.30	.10
❑	279	K.Matsui/M.Piazza TL	.50	.20
❑	280	A.Rodriguez/D.Jeter TL	1.50	.60
❑	281	E.Chavez/T.Hudson TL	.30	.10
❑	282	B.Abreu/J.Thome TL	.30	.10
❑	283	C.Wilson/J.Kendall TL	.30	.10
❑	284	B.Giles/P.Nevin TL	.30	.10
❑	285	A.Pierzynski/J.Schmidt TL	.30	.10
❑	286	B.Boone/I.Suzuki TL	.75	.30
❑	287	A.Pujols/S.Rolen TL	.75	.30
❑	288	A.Huff/T.Martinez TL	.30	.10
❑	289	H.Blalock/M.Teixeira TL	.30	.10
❑	290	C.Delgado/R.Halladay TL	.30	.10
❑	291	Vladimir Guerrero PR	.50	.20
❑	292	Curt Schilling PR	.30	.10
❑	293	Mark Prior PR	.50	.20
❑	294	Josh Beckett PR	.30	.10
❑	295	Roger Clemens PR	.75	.30
❑	296	Derek Jeter PR	.75	.30
❑	297	Eric Chavez PR	.30	.10
❑	298	Jim Thome PR	.30	.10
❑	299	Albert Pujols PR	.75	.30
❑	300	Hank Blalock PR	.30	.10
❑	301	Bartolo Colon	.30	.10
❑	302	Darin Erstad	.30	.10
❑	303	Garret Anderson	.30	.10
❑	304	Orlando Cabrera	.30	.10
❑	305	Steve Finley	.30	.10
❑	306	Javier Vazquez	.30	.10
❑	307	Russ Ortiz	.30	.10
❑	308	Chipper Jones	.75	.30

❑ 309 Marcus Giles .30 .10
❑ 310 Raul Mondesi .30 .10
❑ 311 B.J. Ryan .30 .10
❑ 312 Luis Matos .30 .10
❑ 313 Sidney Ponson .30 .10
❑ 314 Bill Mueller .30 .10
❑ 315 David Ortiz .75 .30
❑ 316 Johnny Damon .50 .20
❑ 317 Keith Foulke .30 .10
❑ 318 Mark Bellhorn .30 .10
❑ 319 Wade Miller .30 .10
❑ 320 Aramis Ramirez .30 .10
❑ 321 Carlos Zambrano .30 .10
❑ 322 Greg Maddux 1.25 .50
❑ 323 Kerry Wood .30 .10
❑ 324 Nomar Garciaparra .75 .30
❑ 325 Todd Walker .30 .10
❑ 326 Frank Thomas .75 .30
❑ 327 Freddy Garcia .30 .10
❑ 328 Joe Crede .30 .10
❑ 329 Jose Contreras .30 .10
❑ 330 Orlando Hernandez .30 .10
❑ 331 Shingo Takatsu .30 .10
❑ 332 Austin Kearns .30 .10
❑ 333 Eric Milton .30 .10
❑ 334 Ken Griffey Jr. 1.25 .50
❑ 335 Aaron Boone .30 .10
❑ 336 David Riske .30 .10
❑ 337 Jake Westbrook .30 .10
❑ 338 Kevin Millwood .30 .10
❑ 339 Travis Hafner .30 .10
❑ 340 Aaron Miles .30 .10
❑ 341 Jeff Baker .30 .10
❑ 342 Todd Helton .50 .20
❑ 343 Garrett Atkins .30 .10
❑ 344 Carlos Pena .30 .10
❑ 345 Ivan Rodriguez .50 .20
❑ 346 Rondell White .30 .10
❑ 347 Troy Percival .30 .10
❑ 348 A.J. Burnett .30 .10
❑ 349 Carlos Delgado .30 .10
❑ 350 Guillermo Mota .30 .10
❑ 351 Paul Lo Duca .30 .10
❑ 352 Jason Lane .30 .10
❑ 353 Lance Berkman .30 .10
❑ 354 Angel Berroa .30 .10
❑ 355 David DeJesus .30 .10
❑ 356 Ruben Gotay .30 .10
❑ 357 Jose Lima .30 .10
❑ 358 Brad Penny .30 .10
❑ 359 J.D. Drew .30 .10
❑ 360 Jayson Werth .30 .10
❑ 361 Jeff Kent .30 .10
❑ 362 Odalis Perez .30 .10
❑ 363 Brady Clark .30 .10
❑ 364 Junior Spivey .30 .10
❑ 365 Rickie Weeks .30 .10
❑ 366 Jacque Jones .30 .10
❑ 367 Joe Nathan .30 .10
❑ 368 Nick Punto .30 .10
❑ 369 Shannon Stewart .30 .10
❑ 370 Doug Mientkiewicz .30 .10
❑ 371 Kris Benson .30 .10
❑ 372 Tom Glavine .50 .20
❑ 373 Victor Zambrano .30 .10
❑ 374 Bernie Williams .50 .20
❑ 375 Carl Pavano .30 .10
❑ 376 Jaret Wright .30 .10
❑ 377 Kevin Brown .30 .10
❑ 378 Mariano Rivera .75 .30
❑ 379 Danny Haren .30 .10
❑ 380 Eric Byrnes .30 .10
❑ 381 Erubiel Durazo .30 .10
❑ 382 Rich Harden .30 .10
❑ 383 Brett Myers .30 .10
❑ 384 Chase Utley .50 .20
❑ 385 Marlon Byrd .30 .10
❑ 386 Pat Burrell .30 .10
❑ 387 Placido Polanco .30 .10
❑ 388 Freddy Sanchez .30 .10
❑ 389 Jason Bay .30 .10
❑ 390 Josh Fogg .30 .10
❑ 391 Adam Eaton .30 .10
❑ 392 Jake Peavy .30 .10
❑ 393 Khalil Greene .50 .20
❑ 394 Mark Loretta .30 .10
❑ 395 Phil Nevin .30 .10
❑ 396 Ramon Hernandez .30 .10
❑ 397 Woody Williams .30 .10
❑ 398 Armando Benitez .30 .10
❑ 399 Edgardo Alfonzo .30 .10
❑ 400 Marquis Grissom .30 .10
❑ 401 Mike Matheny .30 .10
❑ 402 Richie Sexson .30 .10
❑ 403 Bret Boone .30 .10
❑ 404 Gil Meche .30 .10
❑ 405 Chris Carpenter .30 .10
❑ 406 Jeff Suppan .30 .10
❑ 407 Larry Walker .50 .20
❑ 408 Mark Grudzielanek .30 .10
❑ 409 Mark Mulder .30 .10
❑ 410 Scott Rolen .50 .20
❑ 411 Josh Phelps .30 .10
❑ 412 Jonny Gomes .30 .10
❑ 413 Francisco Cordero .30 .10
❑ 414 Kenny Rogers .30 .10
❑ 415 Richard Hidalgo .30 .10
❑ 416 Dave Bush .30 .10
❑ 417 Frank Catalanotto .30 .10
❑ 418 Gabe Gross .30 .10
❑ 419 Guillermo Quiroz .30 .10
❑ 420 Reed Johnson .30 .10
❑ 421 Cristian Guzman .00 .10
❑ 422 Esteban Loaiza .30 .10
❑ 423 Jose Guillen .30 .10
❑ 424 Nick Johnson .30 .10
❑ 425 Vinny Castilla .30 .10
❑ 426 Pete Orr SR RC 1.00 .40
❑ 427 Tadahito Iguchi SR RC 2.50 1.00
❑ 428 Jeff Baker SR 1.00 .40
❑ 429 Marcos Carvajal SR RC 1.00 .40
❑ 430 Justin Verlander SR RC 5.00 2.00
❑ 431 Luke Scott SR RC 3.00 1.25
❑ 432 Willy Taveras SR 1.00 .40
❑ 433 Ambiorix Burgos SR RC 1.00 .40
❑ 434 Andy Sisco SR 1.00 .40
❑ 435 Denny Bautista SR 1.00 .40
❑ 436 Mark Teahen SR 1.00 .40
❑ 437 Ervin Santana SR 1.00 .40
❑ 438 Dennis Houlton SR RC 1.00 .40
❑ 439 Philip Humber SR RC 1.50 .60
❑ 440 Steve Schmoll SR RC 1.00 .40
❑ 441 J.J. Hardy SR 1.00 .40
❑ 442 Ambiorix Concepcion SR RC 1.00 .40
❑ 443 Dae-Sung Koo SR RC 1.00 .40
❑ 444 Andy Phillips SR 1.00 .40
❑ 445 Dan Meyer SR 1.00 .40
❑ 446 Huston Street SR 1.50 .60
❑ 447 Keiichi Yabu SR RC 1.00 .40
❑ 448 Jeff Niemann SR RC 1.50 .60
❑ 449 Jeremy Reed SR 1.00 .40
❑ 450 Tony Blanco SR 1.00 .40
❑ 451 Albert Pujols BG .75 .30
❑ 452 Alex Rodriguez BG .75 .30
❑ 453 Curt Schilling BG .30 .10
❑ 454 Derek Jeter BG .75 .30
❑ 455 Greg Maddux BG .75 .30
❑ 456 Ichiro Suzuki BG .75 .30
❑ 457 Ivan Rodriguez BG .30 .10
❑ 458 Jeff Bagwell BG .30 .10
❑ 459 Jim Thome BG .30 .10
❑ 460 Ken Griffey Jr. BG .75 .30
❑ 461 Manny Ramirez BG .50 .20
❑ 462 Mike Mussina BG .30 .10
❑ 463 Mike Piazza BG .50 .20
❑ 464 Pedro Martinez BG .30 .10
❑ 465 Rafael Palmeiro BG .30 .10
❑ 466 Randy Johnson BG .50 .20
❑ 467 Roger Clemens BG .75 .30
❑ 468 Sammy Sosa BG .50 .20
❑ 469 Todd Helton BG .30 .10
❑ 470 Vladimir Guerrero BG .50 .20
❑ 471 Vladimir Guerrero TC .50 .20
❑ 472 Shawn Green TC .30 .10
❑ 473 John Smoltz TC .30 .10
❑ 474 Miguel Tejada TC .30 .10
❑ 475 Curt Schilling TC .30 .10
❑ 476 Mark Prior TC .30 .10
❑ 477 Frank Thomas TC .50 .20
❑ 478 Ken Griffey Jr. TC .75 .30
❑ 479 C.C. Sabathia TC .30 .10
❑ 480 Todd Helton TC .30 .10
❑ 481 Ivan Rodriguez TC .30 .10
❑ 482 Miguel Cabrera TC .30 .10
❑ 483 Roger Clemens TC .75 .30
❑ 484 Mike Sweeney TC .30 .10
❑ 485 Eric Gagne TC .30 .10
❑ 486 Ben Sheets TC .30 .10
❑ 487 Johan Santana TC .30 .10
❑ 488 Mike Piazza TC .50 .20
❑ 489 Derek Jeter TC .75 .30
❑ 490 Eric Chavez TC .30 .10
❑ 491 Jim Thome TC .30 .10
❑ 492 Craig Wilson TC .30 .10
❑ 493 Jake Peavy TC .30 .10
❑ 494 Jason Schmidt TC .30 .10
❑ 495 Ichiro Suzuki TC .75 .30
❑ 496 Albert Pujols TC .75 .30
❑ 497 Carl Crawford TC .30 .10
❑ 498 Mark Teixeira TC .30 .10
❑ 499 Vernon Wells TC .30 .10
❑ 500 Jose Vidro TC .30 .10

2006 Upper Deck

❑ COMPLETE SET (1250) 600.00 375.00
❑ COMPLETE SERIES 1 (500) 200.00 125.00
❑ COMPLETE SERIES 2 (500) 200.00 125.00
❑ COMPLETE UPDATE (250) 200.00 125.00
❑ COMP.UPDATE w/o SP's (200) 60.00 30.00
❑ COMMON CARD (1-1250) .40 .15
❑ 1-500 ISSUED IN SERIES 1 PACKS
❑ 501-1000 ISSUED IN SERIES 2 PACKS
❑ 1001-1250 ISSUED IN UPDATE PACKS
❑ BAKER & REPKO BOTH CARD 283
❑ 1001-1250 SP STATED ODDS 1:2
❑ SP: 1005/1013/1021/1037/1045/1061/1069
❑ SP: 1077/1093/1101/1117/1125/1133/1149
❑ SP: 1157/1173/1181/1189/1205/1213
❑ SP: 1221-1250
❑ 4 MATCHED PLATES 1:2 SER.2 HOBBY CASES
❑ PLATE PRINT RUN 1 SET PER COLOR
❑ BLACK-CYAN-MAGENTA-YELLOW ISSUED
❑ NO PLATE PRICING DUE TO SCARCITY
❑ EXQUISITE EXCH 1 PER SER.2 HOBBY CASE
❑ EXQUISITE EXCH RANDOM IN UPD.CASES
❑ EXQUISITE EXCH DEADLINE 07/27/07
❑ 1 Adam Kennedy .40 .15
❑ 2 Bartolo Colon .40 .15
❑ 3 Bengie Molina .40 .15
❑ 4 Casey Kotchman .40 .15
❑ 5 Chone Figgins .40 .15
❑ 6 Dallas McPherson .40 .15
❑ 7 Darin Erstad .40 .15
❑ 8 Ervin Santana .40 .15
❑ 9 Francisco Rodriguez .40 .15
❑ 10 Garret Anderson .40 .15
❑ 11 Jarrod Washburn .40 .15
❑ 12 John Lackey .40 .15
❑ 13 Juan Rivera .40 .15
❑ 14 Orlando Cabrera .40 .15
❑ 15 Paul Byrd .40 .15
❑ 16 Steve Finley .40 .15
❑ 17 Vladimir Guerrero 1.00 .40
❑ 18 Alex Cintron .40 .15
❑ 19 Brandon Lyon .40 .15
❑ 20 Brandon Webb .40 .15
❑ 21 Chad Tracy .40 .15
❑ 22 Chris Snyder .40 .15
❑ 23 Claudio Vargas .40 .15
❑ 24 Conor Jackson .60 .25

No.	Player		
25	Craig Counsell	.40	.15
26	Javier Vazquez	.40	.15
27	Jose Valverde	.40	.15
28	Luis Gonzalez	.40	.15
29	Royce Clayton	.40	.15
30	Russ Ortiz	.40	.15
31	Shawn Green	.40	.15
32	Dustin Nippert (RC)	.75	.30
33	Tony Clark	.40	.15
34	Troy Glaus	.40	.15
35	Adam LaRoche	.40	.15
36	Andruw Jones	.60	.25
37	Craig Hansen RC	3.00	1.25
38	Chipper Jones	1.00	.40
39	Horacio Ramirez	.40	.15
40	Jeff Francoeur	1.00	.40
41	John Smoltz	.60	.25
42	Joey Devine RC	.75	.30
43	Johnny Estrada	.40	.15
44	Anthony Lerew (RC)	.75	.30
45	Julio Franco	.40	.15
46	Kyle Farnsworth	.40	.15
47	Marcus Giles	.40	.15
48	Mike Hampton	.40	.15
49	Rafael Furcal	.40	.15
50	Chuck James (RC)	1.25	.50
51	Tim Hudson	.40	.15
52	B.J. Ryan	.40	.15
53	Bernie Castro (RC)	.75	.30
54	Brian Roberts	.40	.15
55	Walter Young (RC)	.75	.30
56	Daniel Cabrera	.40	.15
57	Eric Byrnes	.40	.15
58	Alejandro Freire RC	.75	.30
59	Erik Bedard	.40	.15
60	Javy Lopez	.40	.15
61	Jay Gibbons	.40	.15
62	Jorge Julio	.40	.15
63	Luis Matos	.40	.15
64	Melvin Mora	.40	.15
65	Miguel Tejada	.40	.15
66	Rafael Palmeiro	.60	.25
67	Rodrigo Lopez	.40	.15
68	Sammy Sosa	1.00	.40
69	Alejandro Machado (RC)	.75	.30
70	Bill Mueller	.40	.15
71	Bronson Arroyo	.40	.15
72	Curt Schilling	.60	.25
73	David Ortiz	1.00	.40
74	David Wells	.40	.15
75	Edgar Renteria	.40	.15
76	Ryan Jorgensen RC	.75	.30
77	Jason Varitek	1.00	.40
78	Johnny Damon	.60	.25
79	Keith Foulke	.40	.15
80	Kevin Youkilis	.40	.15
81	Manny Ramirez	.60	.25
82	Matt Clement	.40	.15
83	Hanley Ramirez (RC)	2.00	.75
84	Tim Wakefield	.40	.15
85	Trot Nixon	.40	.15
86	Wade Miller	.40	.15
87	Aramis Ramirez	.40	.15
88	Carlos Zambrano	.40	.15
89	Corey Patterson	.40	.15
90	Derrek Lee	.40	.15
91	Geovany Soto (RC)	.75	.30
92	Greg Maddux	1.50	.60
93	Jeromy Burnitz	.40	.15
94	Jerry Hairston	.40	.15
95	Kerry Wood	.40	.15
96	Mark Prior	.60	.25
97	Matt Murton	.40	.15
98	Michael Barrett	.40	.15
99	Neifi Perez	.40	.15
100	Nomar Garciaparra	1.00	.40
101	Rich Hill	.40	.15
102	Ryan Dempster	.40	.15
103	Todd Walker	.40	.15
104	A.J. Pierzynski	.40	.15
105	Aaron Rowand	.40	.15
106	Bobby Jenks	.40	.15
107	Carl Everett	.40	.15
108	Dustin Hermanson	.40	.15
109	Frank Thomas	1.00	.40
110	Freddy Garcia	.40	.15
111	Jermaine Dye	.40	.15
112	Joe Crede	.40	.15
113	Jon Garland	.40	.15
114	Jose Contreras	.40	.15
115	Juan Uribe	.40	.15
116	Mark Buehrle	.40	.15
117	Orlando Hernandez	.40	.15
118	Paul Konerko	.40	.15
119	Scott Podsednik	.40	.15
120	Tadahito Iguchi	.40	.15
121	Aaron Harang	.40	.15
122	Adam Dunn	.40	.15
123	Austin Kearns	.40	.15
124	Brandon Claussen	.40	.15
125	Chris Denorfia (RC)	.75	.30
126	Edwin Encarnacion	.40	.15
127	Miguel Perez (RC)	.75	.30
128	Felipe Lopez	.40	.15
129	Jason LaRue	.40	.15
130	Ken Griffey Jr.	1.50	.60
131	Chris Booker (RC)	.75	.30
132	Luke Hudson	.40	.15
133	Jason Bergmann RC	.75	.30
134	Ryan Freel	.40	.15
135	Sean Casey	.40	.15
136	Wily Mo Pena	.40	.15
137	Aaron Boone	.40	.15
138	Ben Broussard	.40	.15
139	Ryan Garko (RC)	.75	.30
140	C.C. Sabathia	.40	.15
141	Casey Blake	.40	.15
142	Cliff Lee	.40	.15
143	Coco Crisp	.40	.15
144	David Riske	.40	.15
145	Grady Sizemore	.60	.25
146	Jake Westbrook	.40	.15
147	Jhonny Peralta	.40	.15
148	Josh Bard	.40	.15
149	Kevin Millwood	.40	.15
150	Ronnie Belliard	.40	.15
151	Scott Elarton	.40	.15
152	Travis Hafner	.40	.15
153	Victor Martinez	.40	.15
154	Aaron Cook	.40	.15
155	Aaron Miles	.40	.15
156	Brad Hawpe	.40	.15
157	Mike Esposito (RC)	.75	.30
158	Chin-Hui Tsao	.40	.15
159	Clint Barmes	.40	.15
160	Cory Sullivan	.40	.15
161	Garrett Atkins	.40	.15
162	J.D. Closser	.40	.15
163	Jason Jennings	.40	.15
164	Jeff Baker	.40	.15
165	Jeff Francis	.40	.15
166	Luis A. Gonzalez	.40	.15
167	Matt Holliday	1.00	.40
168	Todd Helton	.60	.25
169	Bradon Inge	.40	.15
170	Carlos Guillen	.40	.15
171	Carlos Pena	.40	.15
172	Chris Shelton	.40	.15
173	Craig Monroe	.40	.15
174	Curtis Granderson	.40	.15
175	Dmitri Young	.40	.15
176	Ivan Rodriguez	.60	.25
177	Jason Johnson	.40	.15
178	Jeremy Bonderman	.40	.15
179	Magglio Ordonez	.40	.15
180	Mark Woodyard (RC)	.75	.30
181	Nook Logan	.40	.15
182	Omar Infante	.40	.15
183	Placido Polanco	.40	.15
184	Chris Heintz RC	.75	.30
185	A.J. Burnett	.40	.15
186	Alex Gonzalez	.40	.15
187	Josh Johnson (RC)	.75	.30
188	Carlos Delgado	.40	.15
189	Dontrelle Willis	.40	.15
190	Josh Wilson (RC)	.75	.30
191	Jason Vargas	.40	.15
192	Jeff Conine	.40	.15
193	Jeremy Hermida	.40	.15
194	Josh Beckett	.40	.15
195	Juan Encarnacion	.40	.15
196	Juan Pierre	.40	.15
197	Luis Castillo	.40	.15
198	Miguel Cabrera	.60	.25
199	Mike Lowell	.40	.15
200	Paul Lo Duca	.40	.15
201	Todd Jones	.40	.15
202	Adam Everett	.40	.15
203	Andy Pettitte	.60	.25
204	Brad Ausmus	.40	.15
205	Brad Lidge	.40	.15
206	Brandon Backe	.40	.15
207	Charlton Jimerson (RC)	.75	.30
208	Chris Burke	.40	.15
209	Craig Biggio	.60	.25
210	Dan Wheeler	.40	.15
211	Jason Lane	.40	.15
212	Jeff Bagwell	.60	.25
213	Lance Berkman	.40	.15
214	Luke Scott	.40	.15
215	Morgan Ensberg	.40	.15
216	Roger Clemens	2.00	.75
217	Roy Oswalt	.40	.15
218	Willy Taveras	.40	.15
219	Andres Blanco	.40	.15
220	Angel Berroa	.40	.15
221	Ruben Gotay	.40	.15
222	David DeJesus	.40	.15
223	Emil Brown	.40	.15
224	J.P. Howell	.40	.15
225	Jeremy Affeldt	.40	.15
226	Jimmy Gobble	.40	.15
227	John Buck	.40	.15
228	Jose Lima	.40	.15
229	Mark Teahen	.40	.15
230	Matt Stairs	.40	.15
231	Mike MacDougal	.40	.15
232	Mike Sweeney	.40	.15
233	Runelvys Hernandez	.40	.15
234	Terrence Long	.40	.15
235	Zack Greinke	.40	.15
236	Ron Flores RC	.75	.30
237	Brad Penny	.40	.15
238	Cesar Izturis	.40	.15
239	D.J. Houlton	.40	.15
240	Derek Lowe	.40	.15
241	Eric Gagne	.40	.15
242	Hee Seop Choi	.40	.15
243	J.D. Drew	.40	.15
244	Jason Phillips	.40	.15
245	Jason Repko	.40	.15
246	Jayson Werth	.40	.15
247	Jeff Kent	.40	.15
248	Jeff Weaver	.40	.15
249	Milton Bradley	.40	.15
250	Odalis Perez	.40	.15
251	Hong-Chih Kuo (RC)	2.00	.75
252	Oscar Robles	.40	.15
253	Ben Sheets	.40	.15
254	Bill Hall	.40	.15
255	Brady Clark	.40	.15
256	Carlos Lee	.40	.15
257	Chris Capuano	.40	.15
258	Nelson Cruz (RC)	.75	.30
259	Derrick Turnbow	.40	.15
260	Doug Davis	.40	.15
261	Geoff Jenkins	.40	.15
262	J.J. Hardy	.40	.15
263	Lyle Overbay	.40	.15
264	Prince Fielder	1.50	.60
265	Rickie Weeks	.40	.15
266	Russell Branyan	.40	.15
267	Tomo Ohka	.40	.15
268	Jonah Bayliss (RC)	.75	.30
269	Brad Radke	.40	.15
270	Carlos Silva	.40	.15
271	Francisco Liriano (RC)	4.00	1.50
272	Jacque Jones	.40	.15
273	Joe Mauer	.60	.25
274	Travis Bowyer (RC)	.75	.30
275	Joe Nathan	.40	.15
276	Johan Santana	.60	.25
277	Justin Morneau	.40	.15
278	Kyle Lohse	.40	.15
279	Lew Ford	.40	.15
280	Matt LeCroy	.40	.15
281	Michael Cuddyer	.40	.15
282	Nick Punto	.40	.15

❑ 283a Scott Baker	.40	.15
❑ 283b Jason Repko UER	.40	.15
❑ 284 Shannon Stewart	.40	.15
❑ 285 Torii Hunter	.40	.15
❑ 286 Braden Looper	.40	.15
❑ 287 Carlos Beltran	.40	.15
❑ 288 Cliff Floyd	.40	.15
❑ 289 David Wright	1.50	.60
❑ 290 Doug Mientkiewicz	.40	.15
❑ 291 Anderson Hernandez (RC)	.75	.30
❑ 292 Jose Reyes	1.00	.40
❑ 293 Kazuo Matsui	.40	.15
❑ 294 Kris Benson	.40	.15
❑ 295 Miguel Cairo	.40	.15
❑ 296 Mike Cameron	.40	.15
❑ 297 Robert Andino RC	.75	.30
❑ 298 Mike Piazza	1.00	.40
❑ 299 Pedro Martinez	.60	.25
❑ 300 Tom Glavine	.60	.25
❑ 301 Victor Diaz	.40	.15
❑ 302 Tim Hamulack (RC)	.75	.30
❑ 303 Alex Rodriguez	1.50	.60
❑ 304 Bernie Williams	.60	.25
❑ 305 Carl Pavano	.40	.15
❑ 306 Chien-Ming Wang	1.50	.60
❑ 307 Derek Jeter	2.50	1.00
❑ 308 Gary Sheffield	.40	.15
❑ 309 Hideki Matsui	1.00	.40
❑ 310 Jason Giambi	.40	.15
❑ 311 Jorge Posada	.60	.25
❑ 312 Kevin Brown	.40	.15
❑ 313 Mariano Rivera	1.00	.40
❑ 314 Matt Lawton	.40	.15
❑ 315 Mike Mussina	.60	.25
❑ 316 Randy Johnson	1.00	.40
❑ 317 Robinson Cano	.60	.25
❑ 318 Mike Vento (RC)	.75	.30
❑ 319 Tino Martinez	.40	.15
❑ 320 Tony Womack	.40	.15
❑ 321 Barry Zito	.40	.15
❑ 322 Bobby Crosby	.40	.15
❑ 323 Bobby Kielty	.40	.15
❑ 324 Dan Johnson	.40	.15
❑ 325 Danny Haren	.40	.15
❑ 326 Eric Chavez	.40	.15
❑ 327 Erubiel Durazo	.40	.15
❑ 328 Huston Street	.40	.15
❑ 329 Jason Kendall	.40	.15
❑ 330 Jay Payton	.40	.15
❑ 331 Joe Blanton	.40	.15
❑ 332 Joe Kennedy	.40	.15
❑ 333 Kirk Saarloos	.40	.15
❑ 334 Mark Kotsay	.40	.15
❑ 335 Nick Swisher	.40	.15
❑ 336 Rich Harden	.40	.15
❑ 337 Scott Hatteberg	.40	.15
❑ 338 Billy Wagner	.40	.15
❑ 339 Bobby Abreu	.40	.15
❑ 340 Brett Myers	.40	.15
❑ 341 Chase Utley	1.00	.40
❑ 342 Danny Sandoval RC	.75	.30
❑ 343 David Bell	.40	.15
❑ 344 Gavin Floyd	.40	.15
❑ 345 Jim Thome	.60	.25
❑ 346 Jimmy Rollins	.40	.15
❑ 347 Jon Lieber	.40	.15
❑ 348 Kenny Lofton	.40	.15
❑ 349 Mike Lieberthal	.40	.15
❑ 350 Pat Burrell	.40	.15
❑ 351 Randy Wolf	.40	.15
❑ 352 Ryan Howard	1.50	.60
❑ 353 Vicente Padilla	.40	.15
❑ 354 Bryan Bullington (RC)	.75	.30
❑ 355 J.J. Furmaniak (RC)	.75	.30
❑ 356 Craig Wilson	.40	.15
❑ 357 Matt Capps (RC)	.75	.30
❑ 358 Tom Gorzelanny (RC)	.75	.30
❑ 359 Jack Wilson	.40	.15
❑ 360 Jason Bay	.40	.15
❑ 361 Jose Mesa	.40	.15
❑ 362 Josh Fogg	.40	.15
❑ 363 Kip Wells	.40	.15
❑ 364 Steve Stemle RC	.75	.30
❑ 365 Oliver Perez	.40	.15
❑ 366 Rob Mackowiak	.40	.15
❑ 367 Ronny Paulino (RC)	.75	.30
❑ 368 Tike Redman	.40	.15
❑ 369 Zach Duke	.40	.15
❑ 370 Adam Eaton	.40	.15
❑ 371 Scott Feldman RC	.75	.30
❑ 372 Brian Giles	.40	.15
❑ 373 Brian Lawrence	.40	.15
❑ 374 Damian Jackson	.40	.15
❑ 375 Dave Roberts	.40	.15
❑ 376 Jake Peavy	.40	.15
❑ 377 Joe Randa	.40	.15
❑ 378 Khalil Greene	.60	.25
❑ 379 Mark Loretta	.40	.15
❑ 380 Ramon Hernandez	.40	.15
❑ 381 Robert Fick	.40	.15
❑ 382 Ryan Klesko	.40	.15
❑ 383 Trevor Hoffman	.40	.15
❑ 384 Woody Williams	.40	.15
❑ 385 Xavier Nady	.40	.15
❑ 386 Armando Benitez	.40	.15
❑ 387 Brad Hennessey	.40	.15
❑ 388 Brian Myrow RC	.75	.30
❑ 389 Edgardo Alfonzo	.40	.15
❑ 390 J.T. Snow	.40	.15
❑ 391 Jeremy Accardo RC	.75	.30
❑ 392 Jason Schmidt	.40	.15
❑ 393 Lance Niekro	.40	.15
❑ 394 Matt Cain	.60	.25
❑ 395 Dan Ortmeier (RC)	.75	.30
❑ 396 Moises Alou	.40	.15
❑ 397 Doug Clark (RC)	.75	.30
❑ 398 Omar Vizquel	.60	.25
❑ 399 Pedro Feliz	.40	.15
❑ 400 Randy Winn	.40	.15
❑ 401 Ray Durham	.40	.15
❑ 402 Adrian Beltre	.40	.15
❑ 403 Eddie Guardado	.40	.15
❑ 404 Felix Hernandez	.60	.25
❑ 405 Gil Meche	.40	.15
❑ 406 Ichiro Suzuki	1.50	.60
❑ 407 Jamie Moyer	.40	.15
❑ 408 Jeff Nelson	.40	.15
❑ 409 Jeremy Reed	.40	.15
❑ 410 Joel Pineiro	.40	.15
❑ 411 Jaime Bubela (RC)	.75	.30
❑ 412 Raul Ibanez	.40	.15
❑ 413 Rickie Sexson	.40	.15
❑ 414 Ryan Franklin	.40	.15
❑ 415 Willie Bloomquist	.40	.15
❑ 416 Yorvit Torrealba	.40	.15
❑ 417 Yuniesky Betancourt	.40	.15
❑ 418 Jeff Harris RC	.75	.30
❑ 419 Albert Pujols	2.00	.75
❑ 420 Chris Carpenter	.40	.15
❑ 421 David Eckstein	.40	.15
❑ 422 Jason Isringhausen	.40	.15
❑ 423 Jason Marquis	.40	.15
❑ 424 Adam Wainwright (RC)	.75	.30
❑ 425 Jim Edmonds	.60	.25
❑ 426 Ryan Theriot RC	.75	.30
❑ 427 Chris Duncan (RC)	.75	.30
❑ 428 Mark Grudzielanek	.40	.15
❑ 429 Mark Mulder	.40	.15
❑ 430 Matt Morris	.40	.15
❑ 431 Reggie Sanders	.40	.15
❑ 432 Scott Rolen	.60	.25
❑ 433 Tyler Johnson (RC)	.75	.30
❑ 434 Yadier Molina	.40	.15
❑ 435 Alex S. Gonzalez	.40	.15
❑ 436 Aubrey Huff	.40	.15
❑ 437 Tim Corcoran RC	.75	.30
❑ 438 Carl Crawford	.40	.15
❑ 439 Casey Fossum	.40	.15
❑ 440 Danys Baez	.40	.15
❑ 441 Edwin Jackson	.40	.15
❑ 442 Joey Gathright	.40	.15
❑ 443 Jonny Gomes	.40	.15
❑ 444 Jorge Cantu	.40	.15
❑ 445 Julio Lugo	.40	.15
❑ 446 Nick Green	.40	.15
❑ 447 Rocco Baldelli	.40	.15
❑ 448 Scott Kazmir	.60	.25
❑ 449 Seth McClung	.40	.15
❑ 450 Toby Hall	.40	.15
❑ 451 Travis Lee	.40	.15
❑ 452 Craig Breslow RC	.75	.30
❑ 453 Alfonso Soriano	.40	.15
❑ 454 Chris R. Young	.40	.15
❑ 455 David Dellucci	.40	.15
❑ 456 Francisco Cordero	.40	.15
❑ 457 Gary Matthews	.40	.15
❑ 458 Hank Blalock	.40	.15
❑ 459 Juan Dominguez	.40	.15
❑ 460 Josh Rupe (RC)	.75	.30
❑ 461 Kenny Rogers	.40	.15
❑ 462 Kevin Mench	.40	.15
❑ 463 Laynce Nix	.40	.15
❑ 464 Mark Teixeira	.60	.25
❑ 465 Michael Young	.40	.15
❑ 466 Richard Hidalgo	.40	.15
❑ 467 Jason Botts (RC)	.75	.30
❑ 468 Aaron Hill	.40	.15
❑ 469 Alex Rios	.40	.15
❑ 470 Corey Koskie	.40	.15
❑ 471 Chris Demaria RC	.75	.30
❑ 472 Eric Hinske	.40	.15
❑ 473 Frank Catalanotto	.40	.15
❑ 474 John-Ford Griffin (RC)	.75	.30
❑ 475 Gustavo Chacin	.40	.15
❑ 476 Josh Towers	.40	.15
❑ 477 Miguel Batista	.40	.15
❑ 478 Orlando Hudson	.40	.15
❑ 479 Reed Johnson	.40	.15
❑ 480 Roy Halladay	.40	.15
❑ 481 Shaun Marcum (RC)	.75	.30
❑ 482 Shea Hillenbrand	.40	.15
❑ 483 Ted Lilly	.40	.15
❑ 484 Vernon Wells	.40	.15
❑ 485 Brad Wilkerson	.40	.15
❑ 486 Darrell Rasner (RC)	.75	.30
❑ 487 Chad Cordero	.40	.15
❑ 488 Cristian Guzman	.40	.15
❑ 489 Esteban Loaiza	.40	.15
❑ 490 John Patterson	.40	.15
❑ 491 Jose Guillen	.40	.15
❑ 492 Jose Vidro	.40	.15
❑ 493 Livan Hernandez	.40	.15
❑ 494 Marlon Byrd	.40	.15
❑ 495 Nick Johnson	.40	.15
❑ 496 Preston Wilson	.40	.15
❑ 497 Ryan Church	.40	.15
❑ 498 Ryan Zimmerman (RC)	5.00	2.00
❑ 499 Tony Armas Jr.	.40	.15
❑ 500 Vinny Castilla	.40	.15
❑ 501 Andy Green	.40	.15
❑ 502 Damion Easley	.40	.15
❑ 503 Eric Byrnes	.40	.15
❑ 504 Jason Grimsley	.40	.15
❑ 505 Jeff DaVanon	.40	.15
❑ 506 Johnny Estrada	.40	.15
❑ 507 Luis Vizcaino	.40	.15
❑ 508 Miguel Batista	.40	.15
❑ 509 Orlando Hernandez	.40	.15
❑ 510 Orlando Hudson	.40	.15
❑ 511 Terry Mulholland	.40	.15
❑ 512 Chris Reitsma	.40	.15
❑ 513 Edgar Renteria	.40	.15
❑ 514 John Thomson	.40	.15
❑ 515 Jorge Sosa	.40	.15
❑ 516 Oscar Villarreal	.40	.15
❑ 517 Pete Orr	.40	.15
❑ 518 Ryan Langerhans	.40	.15
❑ 519 Todd Pratt	.40	.15
❑ 520 Wilson Betemit	.40	.15
❑ 521 Brian Jordan	.40	.15
❑ 522 Lance Cormier	.40	.15
❑ 523 Matt Diaz	.40	.15
❑ 524 Mike Remlinger	.40	.15
❑ 525 Bruce Chen	.40	.15
❑ 526 Chris Gomez	.40	.15
❑ 527 Chris Ray	.40	.15
❑ 528 Corey Patterson	.40	.15
❑ 529 David Newhan	.40	.15
❑ 530 Ed Rogers (RC)	.75	.30
❑ 531 John Halama	.40	.15
❑ 532 Kris Benson	.40	.15
❑ 533 LaTroy Hawkins	.40	.15
❑ 534 Raul Chavez	.40	.15
❑ 535 Alex Cora	.40	.15
❑ 536 Alex Gonzalez	.40	.15
❑ 537 Coco Crisp	.40	.15
❑ 538 David Riske	.40	.15
❑ 539 Doug Mirabelli	.40	.15

☐ 540 Josh Beckett .40 .15
☐ 541 J.T. Snow .40 .15
☐ 542 Mike Timlin .40 .15
☐ 543 Julian Tavarez .40 .15
☐ 544 Rudy Seanez .40 .15
☐ 545 Wily Mo Pena .40 .15
☐ 546 Bob Howry .40 .15
☐ 547 Glendon Rusch .40 .15
☐ 548 Henry Blanco .40 .15
☐ 549 Jacque Jones .40 .15
☐ 550 Jerome Williams .40 .15
☐ 551 John Mabry .40 .15
☐ 552 Juan Pierre .40 .15
☐ 553 Scott Eyre .40 .15
☐ 554 Scott Williamson .40 .15
☐ 555 Wade Miller .40 .15
☐ 556 Will Ohman .40 .15
☐ 557 Alex Cintron .40 .15
☐ 558 Rob Mackowiak .40 .15
☐ 559 Brandon McCarthy .40 .15
☐ 560 Chris Widger .40 .15
☐ 561 Cliff Politte .40 .15
☐ 562 Javier Vazquez .40 .15
☐ 563 Jim Thome .60 .25
☐ 564 Matt Thornton .40 .15
☐ 565 Neal Cotts .40 .15
☐ 566 Pablo Ozuna .40 .15
☐ 567 Ross Gload .40 .15
☐ 568 Brandon Phillips .40 .15
☐ 569 Bronson Arroyo .40 .15
☐ 570 Dave Williams .40 .15
☐ 571 David Ross .40 .15
☐ 572 David Weathers .40 .15
☐ 573 Eric Milton .40 .15
☐ 574 Javier Valentin .40 .15
☐ 575 Kent Mercker .40 .15
☐ 576 Matt Belisle .40 .15
☐ 577 Paul Wilson .40 .15
☐ 578 Rich Aurilia .40 .15
☐ 579 Rick White .40 .15
☐ 580 Scott Hatteberg .40 .15
☐ 581 Todd Coffey .40 .15
☐ 582 Bob Wickman .40 .15
☐ 583 Danny Graves .40 .15
☐ 584 Eduardo Perez .40 .15
☐ 585 Guillermo Mota .40 .15
☐ 586 Jason Davis .40 .15
☐ 587 Jason Johnson .40 .15
☐ 588 Jason Michaels .40 .15
☐ 589 Rafael Betancourt .40 .15
☐ 590 Ramon Vazquez .40 .15
☐ 591 Scott Sauerbeck .40 .15
☐ 592 Todd Hollandsworth .40 .15
☐ 593 Brian Fuentes .40 .15
☐ 594 Danny Ardoin .40 .15
☐ 595 David Cortes .40 .15
☐ 596 Eli Marrero .40 .15
☐ 597 Jamey Carroll .40 .15
☐ 598 Jason Smith .40 .15
☐ 599 Josh Fogg .40 .15
☐ 600 Miguel Ojeda .40 .15
☐ 601 Mike DeJean .40 .15
☐ 602 Ray King .40 .15
☐ 603 Omar Quintanilla (RC) .75 .30
☐ 604 Zach Day .40 .15
☐ 605 Fernando Rodney .40 .15
☐ 606 Kenny Rogers .40 .15
☐ 607 Mike Maroth .40 .15
☐ 608 Nate Robertson .40 .15
☐ 609 Todd Jones .40 .15
☐ 610 Vance Wilson .40 .15
☐ 611 Bobby Seay .40 .15
☐ 612 Chris Spurling .40 .15
☐ 613 Roman Colon .40 .15
☐ 614 Jason Grilli .40 .15
☐ 615 Marcus Thames .40 .15
☐ 616 Ramon Santiago .40 .15
☐ 617 Alfredo Amezaga .40 .15
☐ 618 Brian Moehler .40 .15
☐ 619 Chris Aguila .40 .15
☐ 620 Franklyn German .40 .15
☐ 621 Joe Borowski .40 .15
☐ 622 Logan Kensing (RC) .75 .30
☐ 623 Matt Treanor .40 .15
☐ 624 Miguel Olivo .40 .15
☐ 625 Sergio Mitre .40 .15
☐ 626 Todd Wellemeyer .40 .15
☐ 627 Wes Helms .40 .15
☐ 628 Chad Qualls .40 .15
☐ 629 Eric Bruntlett .40 .15
☐ 630 Mike Gallo .40 .15
☐ 631 Mike Lamb .40 .15
☐ 632 Orlando Palmeiro .40 .15
☐ 633 Russ Springer .40 .15
☐ 634 Dan Wheeler .40 .15
☐ 635 Eric Munson .40 .15
☐ 636 Preston Wilson .40 .15
☐ 637 Trever Miller .40 .15
☐ 638 Ambiorix Burgos .40 .15
☐ 639 Andy Sisco .40 .15
☐ 640 Denny Bautista .40 .15
☐ 641 Doug Mientkiewicz .40 .15
☐ 642 Elmer Dessens .40 .15
☐ 643 Esteban German .40 .15
☐ 644 Joe Nelson (RC) .75 .30
☐ 645 Mark Grudzielanek .40 .15
☐ 646 Mark Redman .40 .15
☐ 647 Mike Wood .40 .15
☐ 648 Paul Bako .40 .15
☐ 649 Reggie Sanders .40 .15
☐ 650 Scott Elarton .40 .15
☐ 651 Shane Costa .40 .15
☐ 652 Tony Graffanino .40 .15
☐ 653 Jason Bulger (RC) .75 .30
☐ 654 Chris Bootcheck (RC) .75 .30
☐ 655 Esteban Yan .40 .15
☐ 656 Hector Carrasco .40 .15
☐ 657 J.C. Romero .40 .15
☐ 658 Jeff Weaver .40 .15
☐ 659 Jose Molina .40 .15
☐ 660 Kelvim Escobar .40 .15
☐ 661 Maicer Izturis .40 .15
☐ 662 Robb Quinlan .40 .15
☐ 663 Scot Shields .40 .15
☐ 664 Tim Salmon .40 .15
☐ 665 Bill Mueller .40 .15
☐ 666 Brett Tomko .40 .15
☐ 667 Dioner Navarro .40 .15
☐ 668 Jae Seo .40 .15
☐ 669 Jose Cruz Jr. .40 .15
☐ 670 Kenny Lofton .40 .15
☐ 671 Lance Carter .40 .15
☐ 672 Nomar Garciaparra 1.00 .40
☐ 673 Olmedo Saenz .40 .15
☐ 674 Rafael Furcal .40 .15
☐ 675 Ramon Martinez .40 .15
☐ 676 Ricky Ledee .40 .15
☐ 677 Sandy Alomar Jr. .40 .15
☐ 678 Yhency Brazoban .40 .15
☐ 679 Corey Koskie .40 .15
☐ 680 Dan Kolb .40 .15
☐ 681 Gabe Gross .40 .15
☐ 682 Jeff Cirillo .40 .15
☐ 683 Matt Wise .40 .15
☐ 684 Rick Helling .40 .15
☐ 685 Chad Moeller .40 .15
☐ 686 Dave Bush .40 .15
☐ 687 Jorge De La Rosa .40 .15
☐ 688 Justin Lehr .40 .15
☐ 689 Jason Bartlett .40 .15
☐ 690 Jesse Crain .40 .15
☐ 691 Juan Rincon .40 .15
☐ 692 Luis Castillo .40 .15
☐ 693 Mike Redmond .40 .15
☐ 694 Rondell White .40 .15
☐ 695 Tony Batista .40 .15
☐ 696 Juan Castro .40 .15
☐ 697 Luis Rodriguez .40 .15
☐ 698 Matt Guerrier .40 .15
☐ 699 Willie Eyre (RC) .75 .30
☐ 700 Aaron Heilman .40 .15
☐ 701 Billy Wagner .40 .15
☐ 702 Carlos Delgado .40 .15
☐ 703 Chad Bradford .40 .15
☐ 704 Chris Woodward .40 .15
☐ 705 Darren Oliver .40 .15
☐ 706 Duaner Sanchez .40 .15
☐ 707 Endy Chavez .40 .15
☐ 708 Jorge Julio .40 .15
☐ 709 Jose Valentin .40 .15
☐ 710 Julio Franco .40 .15
☐ 711 Paul Lo Duca .40 .15
☐ 712 Ramon Castro .40 .15
☐ 713 Steve Trachsel .40 .15
☐ 714 Victor Zambrano .40 .15
☐ 715 Xavier Nady .40 .15
☐ 716 Andy Phillips .40 .15
☐ 717 Bubba Crosby .40 .15
☐ 718 Jaret Wright .40 .15
☐ 719 Kelly Stinnett .40 .15
☐ 720 Kyle Farnsworth .40 .15
☐ 721 Mike Myers .40 .15
☐ 722 Octavio Dotel .40 .15
☐ 723 Ron Villone .40 .15
☐ 724 Scott Proctor .40 .15
☐ 725 Shawn Chacon .40 .15
☐ 726 Tanyon Sturtze .40 .15
☐ 727 Adam Melhuse .40 .15
☐ 728 Brad Halsey .40 .15
☐ 729 Esteban Loaiza .40 .15
☐ 730 Frank Thomas 1.00 .40
☐ 731 Jay Witasick .40 .15
☐ 732 Justin Duchscherer .40 .15
☐ 733 Kiko Calero .40 .15
☐ 734 Marco Scutaro .40 .15
☐ 735 Mark Ellis .40 .15
☐ 736 Milton Bradley .40 .15
☐ 737 Aaron Fultz .40 .15
☐ 738 Aaron Rowand .40 .15
☐ 739 Geoff Geary .40 .15
☐ 740 Arthur Rhodes .40 .15
☐ 741 Chris Coste RC .75 .30
☐ 742 Rheal Cormier .40 .15
☐ 743 Ryan Franklin .40 .15
☐ 744 Ryan Madson .40 .15
☐ 745 Sal Fasano .40 .15
☐ 746 Tom Gordon .40 .15
☐ 747 Abraham Nunez .40 .15
☐ 748 David Dellucci .40 .15
☐ 749 Julio Santana .40 .15
☐ 750 Shane Victorino .40 .15
☐ 751 Damaso Marte .40 .15
☐ 752 Freddy Sanchez .40 .15
☐ 753 Humberto Cota .40 .15
☐ 754 Jeromy Burnitz .40 .15
☐ 755 Joe Randa .40 .15
☐ 756 Jose Castillo .40 .15
☐ 757 Mike Gonzalez .40 .15
☐ 758 Ryan Doumit .40 .15
☐ 759 Sean Burnett .40 .15
☐ 760 Sean Casey .40 .15
☐ 761 Ian Snell .40 .15
☐ 762 John Grabow .40 .15
☐ 763 Jose Hernandez .40 .15
☐ 764 Roberto Hernandez .40 .15
☐ 765 Ryan Vogelsong .40 .15
☐ 766 Victor Santos .40 .15
☐ 767 Adrian Gonzalez .40 .15
☐ 768 Alan Embree .40 .15
☐ 769 Brian Sweeney (RC) .75 .30
☐ 770 Chan Ho Park .40 .15
☐ 771 Clay Hensley .40 .15
☐ 772 Dewon Brazelton .40 .15
☐ 773 Doug Brocail .40 .15
☐ 774 Eric Young .40 .15
☐ 775 Geoff Blum .40 .15
☐ 776 Josh Bard .40 .15
☐ 777 Mark Bellhorn .40 .15
☐ 778 Mike Cameron .40 .15
☐ 779 Mike Piazza 1.00 .40
☐ 780 Rob Bowen .40 .15
☐ 781 Scott Cassidy .40 .15
☐ 782 Scott Linebrink .40 .15
☐ 783 Shawn Estes .40 .15
☐ 784 Termel Sledge .40 .15
☐ 785 Vinny Castilla .40 .15
☐ 786 Jeff Fassero .40 .15
☐ 787 Jose Vizcaino .40 .15
☐ 788 Mark Sweeney .40 .15
☐ 789 Matt Morris .40 .15
☐ 790 Steve Finley .40 .15
☐ 791 Tim Worrell .40 .15
☐ 792 Jamey Wright .40 .15
☐ 793 Jason Ellison .40 .15
☐ 794 Noah Lowry .40 .15
☐ 795 Steve Kline .40 .15
☐ 796 Todd Greene .40 .15
☐ 797 Carl Everett .40 .15

❑ 798 George Sherrill .40 .15
❑ 799 J.J. Putz .40 .15
❑ 800 Jake Woods .40 .15
❑ 801 Jose Lopez .40 .15
❑ 802 Julio Mateo .40 .15
❑ 803 Mike Morse .40 .15
❑ 804 Rafael Soriano .40 .15
❑ 805 Roberto Petagine .40 .15
❑ 806 Aaron Miles .40 .15
❑ 807 Braden Looper .40 .15
❑ 808 Gary Bennett .40 .15
❑ 809 Hector Luna .40 .15
❑ 810 Jeff Suppan .40 .15
❑ 811 John Rodriguez .40 .15
❑ 812 Josh Hancock .40 .15
❑ 813 Juan Encarnacion .40 .15
❑ 814 Larry Bigbie .40 .15
❑ 815 Scott Spiezio .40 .15
❑ 816 Sidney Ponson .40 .15
❑ 817 So Taguchi .40 .15
❑ 818 Brian Meadows .40 .15
❑ 819 Damon Hollins .40 .15
❑ 820 Dan Miceli .40 .15
❑ 821 Doug Waechter .40 .15
❑ 822 Jason Childers RC .75 .30
❑ 823 Josh Paul .40 .15
❑ 824 Julio Lugo .40 .15
❑ 825 Mark Hendrickson .40 .15
❑ 826 Sean Burroughs .40 .15
❑ 827 Shawn Camp .40 .15
❑ 828 Travis Harper .40 .15
❑ 829 Ty Wigginton .40 .15
❑ 830 Adam Eaton .40 .15
❑ 831 Adrian Brown .40 .15
❑ 832 Akinori Otsuka .40 .15
❑ 833 Antonio Alfonseca .40 .15
❑ 834 Brad Wilkerson .40 .15
❑ 835 D'Angelo Jimenez .40 .15
❑ 836 Gerald Laird .40 .15
❑ 837 Joaquin Benoit .40 .15
❑ 838 Kameron Loe .40 .15
❑ 839 Kevin Millwood .40 .15
❑ 840 Mark DeRosa .40 .15
❑ 841 Phil Nevin .40 .15
❑ 842 Rod Barajas .40 .15
❑ 843 Vicente Padilla .40 .15
❑ 844 A.J. Burnett .40 .15
❑ 845 Bengie Molina .40 .15
❑ 846 Gregg Zaun .40 .15
❑ 847 John McDonald .40 .15
❑ 848 Lyle Overbay .40 .15
❑ 849 Russ Adams .40 .15
❑ 850 Troy Glaus .40 .15
❑ 851 Vinny Chulk .40 .15
❑ 852 B.J. Ryan .40 .15
❑ 853 Justin Speier .40 .15
❑ 854 Pete Walker .40 .15
❑ 855 Scott Downs .40 .15
❑ 856 Scott Schoeneweis .40 .15
❑ 857 Alfonso Soriano .40 .15
❑ 858 Brian Schneider .40 .15
❑ 859 Daryle Ward .40 .15
❑ 860 Felix Rodriguez .40 .15
❑ 861 Gary Majewski .40 .15
❑ 862 Joey Eischen .40 .15
❑ 863 Jon Rauch .40 .15
❑ 864 Marlon Anderson .40 .15
❑ 865 Matt LeCroy .40 .15
❑ 866 Mike Stanton .40 .15
❑ 867 Ramon Ortiz .40 .15
❑ 868 Robert Fick .40 .15
❑ 869 Royce Clayton .40 .15
❑ 870 Ryan Drese .40 .15
❑ 871 Vladimir Guerrero CL 1.00 .40
❑ 872 Craig Biggio CL .60 .25
❑ 873 Barry Zito CL .40 .15
❑ 874 Vernon Wells CL .40 .15
❑ 875 Chipper Jones CL 1.00 .40
❑ 876 Prince Fielder CL 1.50 .60
❑ 877 Albert Pujols CL 2.00 .75
❑ 878 Greg Maddux CL 1.50 .60
❑ 879 Carl Crawford CL .40 .15
❑ 880 Brandon Webb CL .40 .15
❑ 881 J.D. Drew CL .40 .15
❑ 882 Jason Schmidt CL .40 .15
❑ 883 Victor Martinez CL .40 .15
❑ 884 Ichiro Suzuki CL 1.50 .60
❑ 885 Miguel Cabrera CL .60 .25
❑ 886 David Wright CL 1.50 .60
❑ 887 Alfonso Soriano CL .40 .15
❑ 888 Miguel Tejada CL .40 .15
❑ 889 Khalil Greene CL .60 .25
❑ 890 Ryan Howard CL 1.50 .60
❑ 891 Jason Bay CL .40 .15
❑ 892 Mark Teixeira CL .60 .25
❑ 893 Manny Ramirez CL .60 .25
❑ 894 Ken Griffey Jr. CL 1.50 .60
❑ 895 Todd Helton CL .60 .25
❑ 896 Angel Berroa CL .40 .15
❑ 897 Ivan Rodriguez CL .60 .25
❑ 898 Johan Santana CL .60 .25
❑ 899 Paul Konerko CL .40 .15
❑ 900 Derek Jeter CL 2.50 1.00
❑ 901 Macay McBride (RC) .75 .30
❑ 902 Tony Pena (RC) .75 .30
❑ 903 Peter Moylan RC .75 .30
❑ 904 Aaron Rakers (RC) .75 .30
❑ 905 Chris Britton RC .75 .30
❑ 906 Nick Markakis (RC) 1.25 .50
❑ 907 Sendy Rleal RC .75 .30
❑ 908 Val Majewski (RC) .75 .30
❑ 909 Jermaine Van Buren (RC) .75 .30
❑ 910 Jonathan Papelbon (RC) 4.00 1.50
❑ 911 Angel Pagan (RC) .75 .30
❑ 912 David Aardsma (RC) .75 .30
❑ 913 Sean Marshall (RC) .75 .30
❑ 914 Brian Anderson (RC) .75 .30
❑ 915 Freddie Bynum (RC) .75 .30
❑ 916 Fausto Carmona (RC) .75 .30
❑ 917 Kelly Shoppach (RC) .75 .30
❑ 918 Choo Freeman (RC) .75 .30
❑ 919 Ryan Shealy (RC) .75 .30
❑ 920 Joel Zumaya (RC) 2.00 .75
❑ 921 Jordan Tata RC .75 .30
❑ 922 Justin Verlander (RC) 3.00 1.25
❑ 923 Carlos Martinez RC .75 .30
❑ 924 Chris Resop (RC) .75 .30
❑ 925 Dan Uggla (RC) 2.00 .75
❑ 926 Eric Reed (RC) .75 .30
❑ 927 Hanley Ramirez (RC) 2.00 .75
❑ 928 Yusmeiro Petit (RC) .75 .30
❑ 929 Josh Willingham (RC) .75 .30
❑ 930 Mike Jacobs (RC) .75 .30
❑ 931 Reggie Abercrombie (RC) .75 .30
❑ 932 Ricky Nolasco (RC) .75 .30
❑ 933 Scott Olsen (RC) .75 .30
❑ 934 Fernando Nieve (RC) .75 .30
❑ 935 Taylor Buchholz (RC) 1.25 .50
❑ 936 Cody Ross (RC) .75 .30
❑ 937 James Loney (RC) 1.25 .50
❑ 938 Takashi Saito RC 1.25 .50
❑ 939 Tim Hamulack (RC) .75 .30
❑ 940 Chris Demaria RC .75 .30
❑ 941 Jose Capellan (RC) .75 .30
❑ 942 David Gassner (RC) .75 .30
❑ 943 Jason Kubel (RC) .75 .30
❑ 944 Brian Bannister (RC) .75 .30
❑ 945 Mike Thompson RC .75 .30
❑ 946 Cole Hamels (RC) 2.00 .75
❑ 947 Paul Maholm (RC) .75 .30
❑ 948 John Van Benschoten (RC) .75 .30
❑ 949 Nate McLouth (RC) .75 .30
❑ 950 Ben Johnson (RC) .75 .30
❑ 951 Josh Barfield (RC) .75 .30
❑ 952 Travis Ishikawa (RC) .75 .30
❑ 953 Jack Taschner (RC) .75 .30
❑ 954 Kenji Johjima RC 4.00 1.50
❑ 955 Skip Schumaker (RC) .75 .30
❑ 956 Ruddy Lugo (RC) .75 .30
❑ 957 Jason Hammel (RC) .75 .30
❑ 958 Chris Roberson (RC) .75 .30
❑ 959 Fabio Castro RC .75 .30
❑ 960 Ian Kinsler (RC) 1.25 .50
❑ 961 John Koronka (RC) .75 .30
❑ 962 Brandon Watson (RC) .75 .30
❑ 963 Jon Lester RC 2.50 1.00
❑ 964 Ben Hendrickson (RC) .75 .30
❑ 965 Martin Prado (RC) .75 .30
❑ 966 Erick Aybar (RC) .75 .30
❑ 967 Bobby Livingston (RC) .75 .30
❑ 968 Ryan Spilborghs (RC) 1.25 .50
❑ 969 Tommy Murphy (RC) .75 .30
❑ 970 Howie Kendrick (RC) 4.00 1.50
❑ 971 Casey Janssen RC .75 .30
❑ 972 Michael O'Connor RC .75 .30
❑ 973 Conor Jackson (RC) 1.25 .50
❑ 974 Jeremy Hermida (RC) .75 .30
❑ 975 Renyel Pinto (RC) .75 .30
❑ 976 Prince Fielder (RC) 3.00 1.25
❑ 977 Kevin Frandsen (RC) 1.25 .50
❑ 978 Ty Taubenheim RC 1.25 .50
❑ 979 Rich Hill (RC) .75 .30
❑ 980 Jonathan Broxton (RC) .75 .30
❑ 981 Jamie Shields RC .75 .30
❑ 982 Carlos Villanueva RC .75 .30
❑ 983 Boone Logan RC .75 .30
❑ 984 Brian Wilson RC .75 .30
❑ 985 Andre Ethier (RC) 2.00 .75
❑ 986 Mike Napoli RC 2.00 .75
❑ 987 Agustin Montero (RC) .75 .30
❑ 988 Jack Hannahan RC .75 .30
❑ 989 Boof Bonser (RC) .75 .30
❑ 990 Carlos Ruiz (RC) .75 .30
❑ 991 Jason Botts (RC) .75 .30
❑ 992 Kendry Morales (RC) 2.00 .75
❑ 993 Alay Soler RC .75 .30
❑ 994 Santiago Ramirez (RC) .75 .30
❑ 995 Saul Rivera (RC) .75 .30
❑ 996 Anthony Reyes (RC) .75 .30
❑ 997 Matt Kemp (RC) 1.25 .50
❑ 998 Jae Kuk Ryu RC .75 .30
❑ 999 Lastings Milledge (RC) 1.25 .50
❑ NNO Exquisite Redemption
❑ 1000 Jered Weaver (RC) 4.00 1.50
❑ 1001 Stephen Drew (RC) 2.00 .75
❑ 1002 Carlos Quentin (RC) 1.25 .50
❑ 1003 Livan Hernandez .40 .15
❑ 1004 Chris B. Young (RC) .75 .30
❑ 1005 Alberto Callaspo SP (RC) 8.00 3.00
❑ 1006 Enrique Gonzalez (RC) .75 .30
❑ 1007 Tony Pena (RC) .75 .30
❑ 1008 Bob Melvin MG .40 .15
❑ 1009 Fernando Tatis .40 .15
❑ 1010 Willy Aybar (RC) .75 .30
❑ 1011 Ken Ray (RC) .75 .30
❑ 1012 Scott Thorman (RC) .75 .30
❑ 1013 Eric Hinske SP 8.00 3.00
❑ 1014 Kevin Barry (RC) .75 .30
❑ 1015 Bobby Cox MG .40 .15
❑ 1016 Phil Stockman (RC) .75 .30
❑ 1017 Brayan Pena (RC) .75 .30
❑ 1018 Adam Loewen (RC) 1.25 .50
❑ 1019 Brandon Fahey RC .75 .30
❑ 1020 Jim Hoey RC .75 .30
❑ 1021 Kurt Birkins SP RC 8.00 3.00
❑ 1022 Jim Johnson RC .75 .30
❑ 1023 Sam Perlozzo MG .40 .15
❑ 1024 Cory Morris RC .75 .30
❑ 1025 Hayden Penn (RC) .75 .30
❑ 1026 Javy Lopez .40 .15
❑ 1027 Dustin Pedroia (RC) 8.00 3.00
❑ 1028 Kason Gabbard (RC) .75 .30
❑ 1029 David Pauley (RC) .75 .30
❑ 1030 Kyle Snyder .40 .15
❑ 1031 Terry Francona MG .40 .15
❑ 1032 Craig Breslow RC .75 .30
❑ 1033 Bryan Corey (RC) .75 .30
❑ 1034 Manny Delcarmen (RC) .75 .30
❑ 1035 Carlos Marmol RC .75 .30
❑ 1036 Buck Coats (RC) .75 .30
❑ 1037 Ryan O'Malley SP RC 8.00 3.00
❑ 1038 Angel Guzman (RC) .75 .30
❑ 1039 Ronny Cedeno .40 .15
❑ 1040 Juan Mateo RC .75 .30
❑ 1041 Cesar Izturis .40 .15
❑ 1042 Les Walrond (RC) .75 .30
❑ 1043 Geovany Soto (RC) .75 .30
❑ 1044 Sean Tracey (RC) .75 .30
❑ 1045 Ozzie Guillen MG SP 8.00 3.00
❑ 1046 Royce Clayton .40 .15
❑ 1047 Norris Hopper RC .75 .30
❑ 1048 Bill Bray (RC) .75 .30
❑ 1049 Jerry Narron MG .40 .15
❑ 1050 Brendan Harris (RC) .75 .30
❑ 1051 Brian Shackelford .40 .15
❑ 1052 Jeremy Sowers (RC) .75 .30
❑ 1053 Joe Inglett RC .75 .30
❑ 1054 Brian Slocum (RC) .75 .30

❑ 1055 Andrew Brown (RC) .75 .30
❑ 1056 Rafael Perez RC .75 .30
❑ 1057 Edward Mujica RC .75 .30
❑ 1058 Andy Marte (RC) .75 .30
❑ 1059 Shin-Soo Choo (RC) .75 .30
❑ 1060 Jeremy Guthrie (RC) .75 .30
❑ 1061 Franklin Gutierrez SP (RC) 8.00 3.00
❑ 1062 Kazuo Matsui .40 .15
❑ 1063 Chris Iannetta RC .75 .30
❑ 1064 Manny Corpas RC .75 .30
❑ 1065 Clint Hurdle MG .40 .15
❑ 1066 Ramon Ramirez (RC) .75 .30
❑ 1067 Sean Casey .40 .15
❑ 1068 Zach Miner (RC) .75 .30
❑ 1069 Brent Clevlen SP (RC) 8.00 3.00
❑ 1070 Bob Wickman .40 .15
❑ 1071 Jim Leyland MG .40 .15
❑ 1072 Alexis Gomez (RC) .75 .30
❑ 1073 Anibal Sanchez (RC) 1.25 .50
❑ 1074 Taylor Tankersley (RC) .75 .30
❑ 1075 Eric Wedge MG .40 .15
❑ 1076 Jonah Bayliss RC .75 .30
❑ 1077 Paul Hoover SP (RC) 8.00 3.00
❑ 1078 Eddie Guardado .40 .15
❑ 1079 Cody Ross (RC) .75 .30
❑ 1080 Aubrey Huff .40 .15
❑ 1081 Jason Hirsh (RC) .75 .30
❑ 1082 Brandon League .40 .15
❑ 1083 Matt Albers (RC) .75 .30
❑ 1084 Chris Sampson RC .75 .30
❑ 1085 Phil Garner MG .40 .15
❑ 1086 J.R. House (RC) .75 .30
❑ 1087 Ryan Shealy (RC) .75 .30
❑ 1088 Stephen Andrade (RC) .75 .30
❑ 1089 Bob Keppel (RC) .75 .30
❑ 1090 Buddy Bell MG .40 .15
❑ 1091 Justin Huber (RC) .75 .30
❑ 1092 Paul Phillips (RC) .75 .30
❑ 1093 Greg Jones SP (RC) 8.00 3.00
❑ 1094 Jeff Mathis (RC) .75 .30
❑ 1095 Dustin Moseley (RC) .75 .30
❑ 1096 Joe Saunders (RC) .75 .30
❑ 1097 Reggie Willits RC 1.25 .50
❑ 1098 Mike Scioscia MG .40 .15
❑ 1099 Greg Maddux 1.50 .60
❑ 1100 Wilson Betemit .40 .15
❑ 1101 Chad Billingsley SP (RC) 8.00 3.00
❑ 1102 Russell Martin (RC) 1.25 .50
❑ 1103 Grady Little MG .40 .15
❑ 1104 David Bell .40 .15
❑ 1105 Kevin Mench .40 .15
❑ 1106 Laynce Nix .40 .15
❑ 1107 Chris Barnwell RC .75 .30
❑ 1108 Tony Gwynn Jr. (RC) .75 .30
❑ 1109 Corey Hart (RC) .75 .30
❑ 1110 Zach Jackson (RC) .75 .30
❑ 1111 Francisco Cordero .40 .15
❑ 1112 Joe Winkelsas (RC) .75 .30
❑ 1113 Ned Yost MG .40 .15
❑ 1114 Matt Garza (RC) .75 .30
❑ 1115 Chris Heintz .40 .15
❑ 1116 Pat Neshek RC 8.00 3.00
❑ 1117 Josh Rabe SP RC 20.00 8.00
❑ 1118 Mike Rivera .40 .15
❑ 1119 Ron Gardenhire MG .40 .15
❑ 1120 Shawn Green .40 .15
❑ 1121 Oliver Perez .40 .15
❑ 1122 Heath Bell .40 .15
❑ 1123 Bartolome Fortunato (RC) .75 .30
❑ 1124 Anderson Garcia RC .75 .30
❑ 1125 John Maine SP (RC) 8.00 3.00
❑ 1126 Henry Owens RC 1.25 .50
❑ 1127 Mike Pelfrey RC 3.00 1.25
❑ 1128 Royce Ring (RC) .75 .30
❑ 1129 Willie Randolph MG .40 .15
❑ 1130 Bobby Abreu .40 .15
❑ 1131 Craig Wilson .40 .15
❑ 1132 T.J. Beam (RC) .75 .30
❑ 1133 Colter Bean SP (RC) 8.00 3.00
❑ 1134 Melky Cabrera (RC) 1.25 .50
❑ 1135 Mitch Jones (RC) .75 .30
❑ 1136 Jeffrey Karstens RC 2.00 .75
❑ 1137 Wil Nieves (RC) .75 .30
❑ 1138 Kevin Reese (RC) 1.25 .50
❑ 1139 Kevin Thompson (RC) .75 .30
❑ 1140 Jose Veras RC .75 .30
❑ 1141 Joe Torre MG .60 .25
❑ 1142 Jeremy Brown (RC) .75 .30
❑ 1143 Santiago Casilla (RC) .75 .30
❑ 1144 Shane Komine RC 1.25 .50
❑ 1145 Mike Rouse (RC) .75 .30
❑ 1146 Jason Windsor (RC) .75 .30
❑ 1147 Ken Macha MG .40 .15
❑ 1148 Jamie Moyer .40 .15
❑ 1149 Phil Nevin SP 8.00 3.00
❑ 1150 Eude Brito (RC) .75 .30
❑ 1151 Fabio Castro .40 .15
❑ 1152 Jeff Conine .40 .15
❑ 1153 Scott Mathieson (RC) .75 .30
❑ 1154 Brian Sanches (RC) .75 .30
❑ 1155 Matt Smith RC .75 .30
❑ 1156 Joe Thurston (RC) .75 .30
❑ 1157 Marlon Anderson SP 8.00 3.00
❑ 1158 Xavier Nady .40 .15
❑ 1159 Shawn Chacon .40 .15
❑ 1160 Rajai Davis (RC) .75 .30
❑ 1161 Yurendell DeCaster (RC) .75 .30
❑ 1162 Marty McLeary (RC) .75 .30
❑ 1163 Chris Duffy .40 .15
❑ 1164 Josh Sharpless RC .75 .30
❑ 1165 Jim Tracy MG .40 .15
❑ 1166 David Wells .40 .15
❑ 1167 Russell Branyan .40 .15
❑ 1168 Todd Walker .40 .15
❑ 1169 Paul McAnulty (RC) .75 .30
❑ 1170 Bruce Bochy MG .40 .15
❑ 1171 Shea Hillenbrand .40 .15
❑ 1172 Eliezer Alfonzo RC .75 .30
❑ 1173 Justin Knoedler SP (RC) 8.00 3.00
❑ 1174 Jonathan Sanchez (RC) .75 .30
❑ 1175 Travis Smith (RC) .75 .30
❑ 1176 Cha-Seung Baek .40 .15
❑ 1177 T.J. Bohn (RC) .75 .30
❑ 1178 Emiliano Fruto RC .75 .30
❑ 1179 Sean Green RC .75 .30
❑ 1180 Jon Huber RC .75 .30
❑ 1182 Mark Lowe (RC) .75 .30
❑ 1183 Eric O'Flaherty RC .75 .30
❑ 1184 Preston Wilson .40 .15
❑ 1185 Mike Hargrove MG .40 .15
❑ 1186 Jeff Weaver .40 .15
❑ 1187 Ronnie Belliard .40 .15
❑ 1188 John Gall (RC) .75 .30
❑ 1189 Josh Kinney SP RC 8.00 3.00
❑ 1190 Tony LaRussa MG .40 .15
❑ 1191 Scott Dunn (RC) .75 .30
❑ 1192 B.J. Upton .40 .15
❑ 1193 Jon Switzer (RC) .75 .30
❑ 1194 Ben Zobrist (RC) 1.25 .50
❑ 1195 Joe Maddon .40 .15
❑ 1196 Carlos Lee .40 .15
❑ 1197 Matt Stairs .40 .15
❑ 1198 Nick Masset (RC) .75 .30
❑ 1199 Nelson Cruz (RC) .75 .30
❑ 1200 Francisco Rosario (RC) .75 .30
❑ 1201 Wes Littleton (RC) .75 .30
❑ 1202 Drew Meyer (RC) .75 .30
❑ 1203 John Rheinecker (RC) .75 .30
❑ 1204 Robinson Tejeda .40 .15
❑ 1205 Jeremy Accardo SP 8.00 3.00
❑ 1206 Luis Figueroa RC .75 .30
❑ 1207 John Hattig (RC) .75 .30
❑ 1208 Dustin McGowan (RC) .75 .30
❑ 1209 Ryan Roberts RC .75 .30
❑ 1210 Davis Romero (RC) .75 .30
❑ 1211 Ty Taubenheim 1.25 .50
❑ 1212 John Gibbons MG .40 .15
❑ 1213 Shawn Hill SP (RC) 8.00 3.00
❑ 1214 Brandon Harper RC .75 .30
❑ 1215 Travis Hughes (RC) .75 .30
❑ 1216 Chris Schroder RC .75 .30
❑ 1217 Austin Kearns .40 .15
❑ 1218 Felipe Lopez .40 .15
❑ 1219 Roy Corcoran RC .75 .30
❑ 1220 Melvin Dorta RC .75 .30
❑ 1221 Brandon Webb CL SP 5.00 2.00
❑ 1222 Andruw Jones CL SP 5.00 2.00
❑ 1223 Miguel Tejada CL SP 5.00 2.00
❑ 1224 David Ortiz CL SP 5.00 2.00
❑ 1225 Derrek Lee CL SP 5.00 2.00
❑ 1226 Jim Thome CL SP 5.00 2.00
❑ 1227 Ken Griffey Jr. CL SP 8.00 3.00
❑ 1228 Travis Hafner CL SP 5.00 2.00
❑ 1229 Todd Helton CL SP 5.00 2.00
❑ 1230 Magglio Ordonez CL SP 5.00 2.00
❑ 1231 Miguel Cabrera CL SP 5.00 2.00
❑ 1232 Lance Berkman CL SP 5.00 2.00
❑ 1233 Mike Sweeney CL SP 5.00 2.00
❑ 1234 Vladimir Guerrero CL SP 5.00 2.00
❑ 1235 Nomar Garciaparra CL SP 5.00 2.00
❑ 1236 Prince Fielder CL SP 5.00 2.00
❑ 1237 Johan Santana CL SP 5.00 2.00
❑ 1238 Pedro Martinez CL SP 5.00 2.00
❑ 1239 Derek Jeter CL SP 10.00 4.00
❑ 1240 Barry Zito CL SP 5.00 2.00
❑ 1241 Ryan Howard CL SP 8.00 3.00
❑ 1242 Jason Bay CL SP 5.00 2.00
❑ 1243 Trevor Hoffman CL SP 5.00 2.00
❑ 1244 Jason Schmidt CL SP 5.00 2.00
❑ 1245 Ichiro Suzuki CL SP 8.00 3.00
❑ 1246 Albert Pujols CL SP 8.00 3.00
❑ 1247 Carl Crawford CL SP 5.00 2.00
❑ 1248 Mark Teixeira CL SP 5.00 2.00
❑ 1249 Vernon Wells CL SP 5.00 2.00
❑ 1250 Alfonso Soriano CL SP 5.00 2.00

2007 Upper Deck

❑ COMPLETE SET (1020) 300.00 200.00
❑ COMP.SET w/o RC EXCH (1000) 200.00 120.00
❑ COMP.SER.1 w/o RC EXCH (500) 80.00 40.00
❑ COMP.SER.2 w/o RC EXCH (500) 120.00 80.00
❑ COMMON CARD (1-1020) .40 .15
❑ COMMON ROOKIE .75 .30
❑ COMMON ROOKIE (501-520) 2.50 1.00
❑ 1-500 ISSUED IN SERIES 1 PACKS
❑ 501-1020 ISSUED IN SERIES 2 PACKS
❑ MATSUZAKA JSY RANDOMLY INSERTED
❑ NO MATSUZAKA JSY PRICING AVAILABLE
❑ OVERALL PLATE SER.1 ODDS 1:192 H
❑ OVERALL PLATE SER.2 ODDS 1:96 H
❑ PLATE PRINT RUN 1 SET PER COLOR
❑ BLACK-CYAN-MAGENTA-YELLOW ISSUED
❑ NO PLATE PRICING DUE TO SCARCITY
❑ ROOKIE EXCH APPX. 1-2 PER CASE
❑ ROOKIE EXCH DEADLINE 02/27/2010
❑ 1 Doug Slaten RC .75 .30
❑ 2 Miguel Montero (RC) .75 .30
❑ 3 Brian Burres (RC) .75 .30
❑ 4 Devern Hansack RC .75 .30
❑ 5 David Murphy (RC) .75 .30
❑ 6 Jose Reyes RC .75 .30
❑ 7 Scott Moore (RC) .75 .30
❑ 8 Josh Fields (RC) .75 .30
❑ 9 Chris Stewart RC .75 .30
❑ 10 Jerry Owens (RC) .75 .30
❑ 11 Ryan Sweeney (RC) .75 .30
❑ 12 Kevin Kouzmanoff (RC) .75 .30
❑ 13 Jeff Baker (RC) .75 .30
❑ 14 Justin Hampson (RC) .75 .30
❑ 15 Jeff Salazar (RC) .75 .30
❑ 16 Alvin Colina RC 2.00 .75
❑ 17 Troy Tulowitzki (RC) 2.00 .75
❑ 18 Andrew Miller RC 5.00 2.00
❑ 19 Mike Rabelo RC .75 .30
❑ 20 Jose Diaz (RC) .75 .30
❑ 21 Angel Sanchez RC .75 .30
❑ 22 Ryan Braun RC .75 .30
❑ 23 Delwyn Young (RC) .75 .30
❑ 24 Drew Anderson RC .75 .30
❑ 25 Dennis Sarfate (RC) .75 .30

❑ 26 Vinny Rottino (RC) .75 .30
❑ 27 Glen Perkins (RC) .75 .30
❑ 28 Alexi Casilla RC 1.25 .50
❑ 29 Philip Humber (RC) .75 .30
❑ 30 Andy Cannizaro RC .75 .30
❑ 31 Jeremy Brown .40 .15
❑ 32 Sean Henn (RC) .75 .30
❑ 33 Brian Rogers .40 .15
❑ 34 Carlos Maldonado (RC) .75 .30
❑ 35 Juan Morillo (RC) .75 .30
❑ 36 Fred Lewis (RC) .75 .30
❑ 37 Patrick Misch (RC) .75 .30
❑ 38 Billy Sadler (RC) .75 .30
❑ 39 Ryan Feierabend (RC) .75 .30
❑ 40 Cesar Jimenez RC .75 .30
❑ 41 Oswaldo Navarro RC .75 .30
❑ 42 Travis Chick (RC) .75 .30
❑ 43 Delmon Young (RC) 2.00 .75
❑ 44 Shawn Riggans (RC) .75 .30
❑ 45 Brian Stokes (RC) .75 .30
❑ 46 Juan Salas (RC) .75 .30
❑ 47 Joaquin Arias (RC) .75 .30
❑ 48 Adam Lind (RC) .75 .30
❑ 49 Beltran Perez (RC) .75 .30
❑ 50 Brett Campbell RC .75 .30
❑ 51 Brian Roberts .40 .15
❑ 52 Miguel Tejada .40 .15
❑ 53 Brandon Fahey .40 .15
❑ 54 Jay Gibbons .40 .15
❑ 55 Corey Patterson .40 .15
❑ 56 Nick Markakis .60 .25
❑ 57 Ramon Hernandez .40 .15
❑ 58 Kris Benson .40 .15
❑ 59 Adam Loewen .40 .15
❑ 60 Erik Bedard .40 .15
❑ 61 Chris Ray .40 .15
❑ 62 Chris Britton .40 .15
❑ 63 Daniel Cabrera .40 .15
❑ 64 Sendy Rleal .40 .15
❑ 65 Manny Ramirez .60 .25
❑ 66 David Ortiz 1.00 .40
❑ 67 Gabe Kapler .40 .15
❑ 68 Alex Cora .40 .15
❑ 69 Dustin Pedroia .40 .15
❑ 70 Trot Nixon .40 .15
❑ 71 Doug Mirabelli .40 .15
❑ 72 Mark Loretta .40 .15
❑ 73 Curt Schilling .60 .25
❑ 74 Jonathan Papelbon 1.00 .40
❑ 75 Tim Wakefield .40 .15
❑ 76 Jon Lester .60 .25
❑ 77 Craig Hansen .40 .15
❑ 78 Keith Foulke .40 .15
❑ 79 Jermaine Dye .40 .15
❑ 80 Jim Thome .60 .25
❑ 81 Tadahito Iguchi .40 .15
❑ 82 Rob Mackowiak .40 .15
❑ 83 Brian Anderson .40 .15
❑ 84 Juan Uribe .40 .15
❑ 85 A.J. Pierzynski .40 .15
❑ 86 Alex Cintron .40 .15
❑ 87 Jon Garland .40 .15
❑ 88 Jose Contreras .40 .15
❑ 89 Neal Cotts .40 .15
❑ 90 Bobby Jenks .40 .15
❑ 91 Mike MacDougal .40 .15
❑ 92 Javier Vazquez .40 .15
❑ 93 Travis Hafner .40 .15
❑ 94 Jhonny Peralta .40 .15
❑ 95 Ryan Garko .40 .15
❑ 96 Victor Martinez .40 .15
❑ 97 Hector Luna .40 .15
❑ 98 Casey Blake .40 .15
❑ 99 Jason Michaels .40 .15
❑ 100 Shin-Soo Choo .60 .25
❑ 101 C.C. Sabathia .40 .15
❑ 102 Paul Byrd .40 .15
❑ 103 Jeremy Sowers .40 .15
❑ 104 Cliff Lee .40 .15
❑ 105 Rafael Betancourt .40 .15
❑ 106 Francisco Cruceta .40 .15
❑ 107 Sean Casey .40 .15
❑ 108 Brandon Inge .40 .15
❑ 109 Placido Polanco .40 .15
❑ 110 Omar Infante .40 .15
❑ 111 Ivan Rodriguez .60 .25
❑ 112 Magglio Ordonez .40 .15
❑ 113 Craig Monroe .40 .15
❑ 114 Marcus Thames .40 .15
❑ 115 Justin Verlander 1.00 .40
❑ 116 Todd Jones .40 .15
❑ 117 Kenny Rogers .40 .15
❑ 118 Joel Zumaya .60 .25
❑ 119 Jeremy Bonderman .40 .15
❑ 120 Nate Robertson .40 .15
❑ 121 Mark Teahen .40 .15
❑ 122 Ryan Shealy .40 .15
❑ 123 Mitch Maier RC .75 .30
❑ 124 Doug Mientkiewicz .40 .15
❑ 125 Mark Grudzielanek .40 .15
❑ 126 Shane Costa .40 .15
❑ 127 John Buck .40 .15
❑ 128 Reggie Sanders .40 .15
❑ 129 Mike Sweeney .40 .15
❑ 130 Mark Redman .40 .15
❑ 131 Todd Wellemeyer .40 .15
❑ 132 Scott Elarton .40 .15
❑ 133 Ambiorix Burgos .40 .15
❑ 134 Joe Nelson .40 .15
❑ 135 Howie Kendrick .40 .15
❑ 136 Chone Figgins .40 .15
❑ 137 Orlando Cabrera .40 .15
❑ 138 Maicer Izturis .40 .15
❑ 139 Jose Molina .40 .15
❑ 140 Vladimir Guerrero 1.00 .40
❑ 141 Darin Erstad .40 .15
❑ 142 Juan Rivera .40 .15
❑ 143 Jered Weaver .60 .25
❑ 144 John Lackey .40 .15
❑ 145 Joe Saunders .40 .15
❑ 146 Bartolo Colon .40 .15
❑ 147 Scot Shields .40 .15
❑ 148 Francisco Rodriguez .40 .15
❑ 149 Justin Morneau .40 .15
❑ 150 Jason Bartlett .40 .15
❑ 151 Luis Castillo .40 .15
❑ 152 Nick Punto .40 .15
❑ 153 Shannon Stewart .40 .15
❑ 154 Michael Cuddyer .40 .15
❑ 155 Jason Kubel .40 .15
❑ 156 Joe Mauer .60 .25
❑ 157 Francisco Liriano 1.00 .40
❑ 158 Joe Nathan .40 .15
❑ 159 Dennys Reyes .40 .15
❑ 160 Brad Radke .40 .15
❑ 161 Boof Bonser .40 .15
❑ 162 Juan Rincon .40 .15
❑ 163 Derek Jeter 2.50 1.00
❑ 164 Jason Giambi .40 .15
❑ 165 Robinson Cano .60 .25
❑ 166 Andy Phillips .40 .15
❑ 167 Bobby Abreu .40 .15
❑ 168 Gary Sheffield .40 .15
❑ 169 Bernie Williams .60 .25
❑ 170 Melky Cabrera .40 .15
❑ 171 Mike Mussina .60 .25
❑ 172 Chien Ming Wang 1.50 .60
❑ 173 Mariano Rivera 1.00 .40
❑ 174 Scott Proctor .40 .15
❑ 175 Jaret Wright .40 .15
❑ 176 Kyle Farnsworth .40 .15
❑ 177 Eric Chavez .40 .15
❑ 178 Bobby Crosby .40 .15
❑ 179 Frank Thomas 1.00 .40
❑ 180 Dan Johnson .40 .15
❑ 181 Marco Scutaro .40 .15
❑ 182 Nick Swisher .40 .15
❑ 183 Milton Bradley .40 .15
❑ 184 Jay Payton .40 .15
❑ 185 Joe Blanton .40 .15
❑ 186 Barry Zito .40 .15
❑ 187 Rich Harden .40 .15
❑ 188 Esteban Loaiza .40 .15
❑ 189 Huston Street .40 .15
❑ 190 Chad Gaudin .40 .15
❑ 191 Richie Sexson .40 .15
❑ 192 Yuniesky Betancourt .40 .15
❑ 193 Willie Bloomquist .40 .15
❑ 194 Ben Broussard .40 .15
❑ 195 Kenji Johjima 1.00 .40
❑ 196 Ichiro Suzuki 1.50 .60
❑ 197 Raul Ibanez .40 .15
❑ 198 Chris Snelling .40 .15
❑ 199 Felix Hernandez .60 .25
❑ 200 Cha-Seung Baek .40 .15
❑ 201 Joel Pineiro .40 .15
❑ 202 Julio Mateo .40 .15
❑ 203 J.J. Putz .40 .15
❑ 204 Rafael Soriano .40 .15
❑ 205 Jorge Cantu .40 .15
❑ 206 B.J. Upton .40 .15
❑ 207 Ty Wigginton .40 .15
❑ 208 Greg Norton .40 .15
❑ 209 Dioner Navarro .40 .15
❑ 210 Carl Crawford .40 .15
❑ 211 Jonny Gomes .40 .15
❑ 212 Damon Hollins .40 .15
❑ 213 Scott Kazmir .60 .25
❑ 214 Casey Fossum .40 .15
❑ 215 Ruddy Lugo .40 .15
❑ 216 James Shields .40 .15
❑ 217 Tyler Walker .40 .15
❑ 218 Shawn Camp .40 .15
❑ 219 Mark Teixeira .60 .25
❑ 220 Hank Blalock .40 .15
❑ 221 Ian Kinsler .40 .15
❑ 222 Jerry Hairston Jr. .40 .15
❑ 223 Gerald Laird .40 .15
❑ 224 Carlos Lee .40 .15
❑ 225 Gary Matthews .40 .15
❑ 226 Mark DeRosa .40 .15
❑ 227 Kip Wells .40 .15
❑ 228 Akinori Otsuka .40 .15
❑ 229 Vicente Padilla .40 .15
❑ 230 John Koronka .40 .15
❑ 231 Kevin Millwood .40 .15
❑ 232 Wes Littleton .40 .15
❑ 233 Troy Glaus .40 .15
❑ 234 Lyle Overbay .40 .15
❑ 235 Aaron Hill .40 .15
❑ 236 John McDonald .40 .15
❑ 237 Bengie Molina .40 .15
❑ 238 Vernon Wells .40 .15
❑ 239 Reed Johnson .40 .15
❑ 240 Frank Catalanotto .40 .15
❑ 241 Roy Halladay .40 .15
❑ 242 B.J. Ryan .40 .15
❑ 243 Gustavo Chacin .40 .15
❑ 244 Scott Downs .40 .15
❑ 245 Casey Janssen .40 .15
❑ 246 Justin Speier .40 .15
❑ 247 Stephen Drew .60 .25
❑ 248 Conor Jackson .40 .15
❑ 249 Orlando Hudson .40 .15
❑ 250 Chad Tracy .40 .15
❑ 251 Johnny Estrada .40 .15
❑ 252 Luis Gonzalez .40 .15
❑ 253 Eric Byrnes .40 .15
❑ 254 Carlos Quentin .40 .15
❑ 255 Brandon Webb .40 .15
❑ 256 Claudio Vargas .40 .15
❑ 257 Juan Cruz .40 .15
❑ 258 Jorge Julio .40 .15
❑ 259 Luis Vizcaino .40 .15
❑ 260 Livan Hernandez .40 .15
❑ 261 Chipper Jones 1.00 .40
❑ 262 Edgar Renteria .40 .15
❑ 263 Adam LaRoche .40 .15
❑ 264 Willy Aybar .40 .15
❑ 265 Brian McCann .40 .15
❑ 266 Ryan Langerhans .40 .15
❑ 267 Jeff Francoeur 1.00 .40
❑ 268 Matt Diaz .40 .15
❑ 269 Tim Hudson .40 .15
❑ 270 John Smoltz .60 .25
❑ 271 Oscar Villarreal .40 .15
❑ 272 Horacio Ramirez .40 .15
❑ 273 Bob Wickman .40 .15
❑ 274 Chad Paronto .40 .15
❑ 275 Derrek Lee .40 .15
❑ 276 Ryan Theriot .40 .15
❑ 277 Cesar Izturis .40 .15
❑ 278 Ronny Cedeno .40 .15
❑ 279 Michael Barrett .40 .15
❑ 280 Juan Pierre .40 .15
❑ 281 Jacque Jones .40 .15
❑ 282 Matt Murton .40 .15
❑ 283 Carlos Zambrano .40 .15

No.	Player		
284	Mark Prior	.60	.25
285	Rich Hill	.40	.15
286	Sean Marshall	.40	.15
287	Ryan Dempster	.40	.15
288	Ryan O'Malley	.40	.15
289	Scott Hatteberg	.40	.15
290	Brandon Phillips	.40	.15
291	Edwin Encarnacion	.40	.15
292	Rich Aurilia	.40	.15
293	David Ross	.40	.15
294	Ken Griffey Jr.	1.50	.60
295	Ryan Freel	.40	.15
296	Chris Denorfia	.40	.15
297	Bronson Arroyo	.40	.15
298	Aaron Harang	.40	.15
299	Brandon Claussen	.40	.15
300	Todd Coffey	.40	.15
301	David Weathers	.40	.15
302	Eric Milton	.40	.15
303	Todd Helton	.60	.25
304	Clint Barmes	.40	.15
305	Kazuo Matsui	.40	.15
306	Jamey Carroll	.40	.15
307	Yorvit Torrealba	.40	.15
308	Matt Holliday	1.00	.40
309	Choo Freeman	.40	.15
310	Brad Hawpe	.40	.15
311	Jason Jennings	.40	.15
312	Jeff Francis	.40	.15
313	Josh Fogg	.40	.15
314	Aaron Cook	.40	.15
315	Ubaldo Jimenez (RC)	.75	.30
316	Manny Corpas	.40	.15
317	Miguel Cabrera	.60	.25
318	Dan Uggla	.60	.25
319	Hanley Ramirez	.60	.25
320	Wes Helms	.40	.15
321	Miguel Olivo	.40	.15
322	Jeremy Hermida	.40	.15
323	Cody Ross	.40	.15
324	Josh Willingham	.40	.15
325	Dontrelle Willis	.40	.15
326	Anibal Sanchez	.40	.15
327	Josh Johnson	.40	.15
328	Jose Garcia RC	.75	.30
329	Joe Borowski	.40	.15
330	Taylor Tankersley	.40	.15
331	Lance Berkman	.40	.15
332	Craig Biggio	.60	.25
333	Aubrey Huff	.40	.15
334	Adam Everett	.40	.15
335	Brad Ausmus	.40	.15
336	Willy Taveras	.40	.15
337	Luke Scott	.40	.15
338	Chris Burke	.40	.15
339	Roger Clemens	1.50	.60
340	Andy Pettitte	.60	.25
341	Brandon Backe	.40	.15
342	Hector Gimenez (RC)	.75	.30
343	Brad Lidge	.40	.15
344	Dan Wheeler	.40	.15
345	Nomar Garciaparra	1.00	.40
346	Rafael Furcal	.40	.15
347	Wilson Betemit	.40	.15
348	Julio Lugo	.40	.15
349	Russell Martin	.40	.15
350	Andre Ethier	.60	.25
351	Matt Kemp	.40	.15
352	Kenny Lofton	.40	.15
353	Brad Penny	.40	.15
354	Derek Lowe	.40	.15
355	Chad Billingsley	.40	.15
356	Greg Maddux	1.50	.60
357	Takashi Saito	.40	.15
358	Jonathan Broxton	.40	.15
359	Prince Fielder	1.00	.40
360	Rickie Weeks	.40	.15
361	Bill Hall	.40	.15
362	J.J. Hardy	.40	.15
363	Jeff Cirillo	.40	.15
364	Tony Gwynn Jr.	.40	.15
365	Corey Hart	.40	.15
366	Laynce Nix	.40	.15
367	Doug Davis	.40	.15
368	Ben Sheets	.40	.15
369	Chris Capuano	.40	.15
370	Dave Bush	.40	.15
371	Derrick Turnbow	.40	.15
372	Francisco Cordero	.40	.15
373	Jose Reyes	.40	.15
374	Carlos Delgado	.40	.15
375	Julio Franco	.40	.15
376	Jose Valentin	.40	.15
377	Paul LoDuca	.40	.15
378	Carlos Beltran	.40	.15
379	Shawn Green	.40	.15
380	Lastings Milledge	.60	.25
381	Endy Chavez	.40	.15
382	Pedro Martinez	.60	.25
383	John Maine	.40	.15
384	Orlando Hernandez	.40	.15
385	Steve Trachsel	.40	.15
386	Billy Wagner	.40	.15
387	Ryan Howard	1.50	.60
388	Chase Utley	1.00	.40
389	Jimmy Rollins	.40	.15
390	Chris Coste	.40	.15
391	Jeff Conine	.40	.15
392	Aaron Rowand	.40	.15
393	Shane Victorino	.40	.15
394	David Dellucci	.40	.15
395	Cole Hamels	.60	.25
396	Jamie Moyer	.40	.15
397	Ryan Madson	.40	.15
398	Brett Myers	.40	.15
399	Tom Gordon	.40	.15
400	Geoff Geary	.40	.15
401	Freddy Sanchez	.40	.15
402	Xavier Nady	.40	.15
403	Jose Castillo	.40	.15
404	Joe Randa	.40	.15
405	Jason Bay	.40	.15
406	Chris Duffy	.40	.15
407	Jose Bautista	.40	.15
408	Ronny Paulino	.40	.15
409	Ian Snell	.40	.15
410	Zach Duke	.40	.15
411	Tom Gorzelanny	.40	.15
412	Shane Youman RC	.75	.30
413	Mike Gonzalez	.40	.15
414	Matt Capps	.40	.15
415	Adrian Gonzalez	.40	.15
416	Josh Barfield	.40	.15
417	Todd Walker	.40	.15
418	Khalil Greene	.60	.25
419	Mike Piazza	1.00	.40
420	Dave Roberts	.40	.15
421	Mike Cameron	.40	.15
422	Geoff Blum	.40	.15
423	Jake Peavy	.40	.15
424	Chris R. Young	.40	.15
425	Woody Williams	.40	.15
426	Clay Hensley	.40	.15
427	Cla Meredith	.40	.15
428	Trevor Hoffman	.40	.15
429	Shea Hillenbrand	.40	.15
430	Pedro Feliz	.40	.15
431	Ray Durham	.40	.15
432	Mark Sweeney	.40	.15
433	Eliezer Alfonzo	.40	.15
434	Moises Alou	.40	.15
435	Steve Finley	.40	.15
436	Todd Linden	.40	.15
437	Jason Schmidt	.40	.15
438	Matt Cain	.60	.25
439	Noah Lowry	.40	.15
440	Brad Hennessey	.40	.15
441	Armando Benitez	.40	.15
442	Jonathan Sanchez	.40	.15
443	Albert Pujols	2.00	.75
444	Ronnie Belliard	.40	.15
445	David Eckstein	.40	.15
446	Aaron Miles	.40	.15
447	Yadier Molina	.40	.15
448	Jim Edmonds	.60	.25
449	Chris Duncan	.40	.15
450	Juan Encarnacion	.40	.15
451	Chris Carpenter	.40	.15
452	Jeff Suppan	.40	.15
453	Jason Marquis	.40	.15
454	Jeff Weaver	.40	.15
455	Jason Isringhausen	.40	.15
456	Braden Looper	.40	.15
457	Ryan Zimmerman	1.00	.40
458	Nick Johnson	.40	.15
459	Felipe Lopez	.40	.15
460	Brian Schneider	.40	.15
461	Alfonso Soriano	.40	.15
462	Austin Kearns	.40	.15
463	Ryan Church	.40	.15
464	Alex Escobar	.40	.15
465	Ramon Ortiz	.40	.15
466	Tony Armas	.40	.15
467	Michael O'Connor	.40	.15
468	Chad Cordero	.40	.15
469	Jon Rauch	.40	.15
470	Pedro Astacio	.40	.15
471	Miguel Tejada CL	.40	.15
472	David Ortiz CL	1.00	.40
473	Jermaine Dye CL	.40	.15
474	Travis Hafner CL	.40	.15
475	Magglio Ordonez CL	.40	.15
476	Mark Teahen CL	.40	.15
477	Vladimir Guerrero CL	1.00	.40
478	Justin Morneau CL	.40	.15
479	Derek Jeter CL	2.50	1.00
480	Nick Swisher CL	.40	.15
481	Ichiro Suzuki CL	1.50	.60
482	Scott Kazmir CL	.60	.25
483	Mark Teixeira CL	.60	.25
484	Vernon Wells CL	.40	.15
485	Brandon Webb CL	.40	.15
486	Andruw Jones CL	.60	.25
487	Carlos Zambrano CL	.40	.15
488	Adam Dunn CL	.40	.15
489	Matt Holliday CL	1.00	.40
490	Miguel Cabrera CL	.60	.25
491	Lance Berkman CL	.40	.15
492	Nomar Garciaparra CL	1.00	.40
493	Prince Fielder CL	1.00	.40
494	Carlos Beltran CL	.40	.15
495	Ryan Howard CL	1.50	.60
496	Jason Bay CL	.40	.15
497	Adrian Gonzalez CL	.40	.15
498	Matt Cain CL	.60	.25
499	Albert Pujols CL	2.00	.75
500	Ryan Zimmerman CL	1.00	.40
501a	D.Matsuzaka Suit RC	50.00	20.00
501b	D.Matsuzaka Throwing RC	15.00	6.00
501c	Daisuke Matsuzaka Jsy/100		
501d	Daisuke Matsuzaka Ball/150		
502	Kei Igawa RC	4.00	1.50
503	Akinori Iwamura RC	6.00	2.50
504	Alex Gordon RC	25.00	10.00
505	Matt Chico (RC)	2.50	1.00
506	John Danks RC	2.50	1.00
507	Elijah Dukes RC	2.50	1.00
508	Gustavo Molina RC	2.50	1.00
509	Joakim Soria RC	6.00	2.50
510	Jay Marshall RC	6.00	2.50
511	Travis Buck (RC)	2.50	1.00
512	Brandon Wood (RC)	2.50	1.00
513	Kevin Cameron RC	2.50	1.00
514	Jared Burton RC	6.00	2.50
515	Kory Casto (RC)	2.50	1.00
516	Joe Smith RC	2.50	1.00
517	Jose Garcia RC	2.50	1.00
518	Hunter Pence (RC)	15.00	6.00
519	Felix Pie (RC)	2.50	1.00
520	Zach Segovia (RC)	2.50	1.00
521	Randy Johnson	1.00	.40
522	Brandon Lyon	.40	.15
523	Robby Hammock	.40	.15
524	Micah Owings (RC)	.75	.30
525	Doug Davis	.40	.15
526	Brian Barden RC	.75	.30
527	Alberto Callaspo	.40	.15
528	Stephen Drew	.60	.25
529	Chris Young	.40	.15
530	Edgar Gonzalez	.40	.15
531	Brandon Medders	.40	.15
532	Tony Pena	.40	.15
533	Jose Valverde	.40	.15
534	Chris Snyder	.40	.15
535	Tony Clark	.40	.15
536	Scott Hairston	.40	.15
537	Jeff DaVanon	.40	.15
538	Randy Johnson CL	1.00	.40

❑ 539 Mark Redman .40 .15
❑ 540 Andruw Jones .60 .25
❑ 541 Rafael Soriano .40 .15
❑ 542 Scott Thorman .40 .15
❑ 543 Chipper Jones 1.00 .40
❑ 544 Mike Gonzalez .40 .15
❑ 545 Lance Cormier .40 .15
❑ 546 Kyle Davies .40 .15
❑ 547 Mike Hampton .40 .15
❑ 548 Chuck James .40 .15
❑ 549 Macay McBride .40 .15
❑ 550 Tanyon Sturtze .40 .15
❑ 551 Tyler Yates .40 .15
❑ 552 Pete Orr .40 .15
❑ 553 Craig Wilson .40 .15
❑ 554 Chris Woodward .40 .15
❑ 555 Kelly Johnson .40 .15
❑ 556 Chipper Jones CL 1.00 .40
❑ 557 Chad Bradford .40 .15
❑ 558 John Parrish .40 .15
❑ 559 Jeremy Guthrie .40 .15
❑ 560 Steve Trachsel .40 .15
❑ 561 Scott Williamson .40 .15
❑ 562 Jaret Wright .40 .15
❑ 563 Paul Bako .40 .15
❑ 564 Chris Gomez .40 .15
❑ 565 Melvin Mora .40 .15
❑ 566 Freddie Bynum .40 .15
❑ 567 Aubrey Huff .40 .15
❑ 568 Jay Payton .40 .15
❑ 569 Miguel Tejada .40 .15
❑ 570 Kurt Birkins .40 .15
❑ 571 Danys Baez .40 .15
❑ 572 Brian Roberts CL .40 .15
❑ 573 Josh Beckett .60 .25
❑ 574 Matt Clement .40 .15
❑ 575 Hideki Okajima RC 5.00 2.00
❑ 576 Javier Lopez .40 .15
❑ 577 Joel Pineiro .40 .15
❑ 578 J.C. Romero .40 .15
❑ 579 Kyle Snyder .40 .15
❑ 580 Julian Tavarez .40 .15
❑ 581 Mike Timlin .40 .15
❑ 582 Jason Varitek 1.00 .40
❑ 583 Mike Lowell .40 .15
❑ 584 Kevin Youkilis .40 .15
❑ 585 Coco Crisp .40 .15
❑ 586 J.D. Drew .40 .15
❑ 587 Eric Hinske .40 .15
❑ 588 Wily Mo Pena .40 .15
❑ 589 Julio Lugo .40 .15
❑ 590 David Ortiz 1.00 .40
❑ 591 Manny Ramirez .60 .25
❑ 592 Daisuke Matsuzaka CL 4.00 1.50
❑ 593 Scott Eyre .40 .15
❑ 594 Angel Guzman .40 .15
❑ 595 Bob Howry .40 .15
❑ 596 Ted Lilly .40 .15
❑ 597 Juan Mateo .40 .15
❑ 598 Wade Miller .40 .15
❑ 599 Carlos Zambrano .40 .15
❑ 600 Will Ohman .40 .15
❑ 601 Michael Wuertz .40 .15
❑ 602 Henry Blanco .40 .15
❑ 603 Aramis Ramirez .40 .15
❑ 604 Cliff Floyd .40 .15
❑ 605 Kerry Wood .40 .15
❑ 606 Alfonso Soriano .40 .15
❑ 607 Daryle Ward .40 .15
❑ 608 Jason Marquis .40 .15
❑ 609 Mark DeRosa .40 .15
❑ 610 Neal Cotts .40 .15
❑ 611 Derrek Lee .40 .15
❑ 612 Aramis Ramirez CL .40 .15
❑ 613 David Aardsma .40 .15
❑ 614 Mark Buehrle .40 .15
❑ 615 Nick Masset .40 .15
❑ 616 Andrew Sisco .40 .15
❑ 617 Matt Thornton .40 .15
❑ 618 Toby Hall .40 .15
❑ 619 Joe Crede .40 .15
❑ 620 Paul Konerko .40 .15
❑ 621 Darin Erstad .40 .15
❑ 622 Pablo Ozuna .40 .15
❑ 623 Scott Podsednik .40 .15
❑ 624 Jim Thome .60 .25
❑ 625 Jermaine Dye .40 .15
❑ 626 Jim Thome CL .60 .25
❑ 627 Adam Dunn .40 .15
❑ 628 Bill Bray .40 .15
❑ 629 Alex Gonzalez .40 .15
❑ 630 Josh Hamilton (RC) 10.00 4.00
❑ 631 Matt Belisle .40 .15
❑ 632 Rheal Cormier .40 .15
❑ 633 Kyle Lohse .40 .15
❑ 634 Eric Milton .40 .15
❑ 635 Kirk Saarloos .40 .15
❑ 636 Mike Stanton .40 .15
❑ 637 Javier Valentin .40 .15
❑ 638 Juan Castro .40 .15
❑ 639 Jeff Conine .40 .15
❑ 640 Jon Coutlangus (RC) .75 .30
❑ 641 Ken Griffey Jr. 1.50 .60
❑ 642 Ken Griffey Jr. CL 1.50 .60
❑ 643 Fernando Cabrera .40 .15
❑ 644 Fausto Carmona .40 .15
❑ 645 Jason Davis .40 .15
❑ 646 Aaron Fultz .40 .15
❑ 647 Roberto Hernandez .40 .15
❑ 648 Jake Westbrook .40 .15
❑ 649 Kelly Shoppach .40 .15
❑ 650 Josh Barfield .40 .15
❑ 651 Andy Marte .40 .15
❑ 652 Joe Inglett .40 .15
❑ 653 David Dellucci .40 .15
❑ 654 Joe Borowski .40 .15
❑ 655 Franklin Gutierrez .40 .15
❑ 656 Trot Nixon .40 .15
❑ 657 Grady Sizemore .60 .25
❑ 658 Mike Rouse .40 .15
❑ 659 Travis Hafner .40 .15
❑ 660 Victor Martinez .40 .15
❑ 661 C.C. Sabathia .40 .15
❑ 662 Grady Sizemore CL .60 .25
❑ 663 Jeremy Affeldt .40 .15
❑ 664 Taylor Buchholz .40 .15
❑ 665 Brian Fuentes .40 .15
❑ 666 Latroy Hawkins .40 .15
❑ 667 Byung-Hyun Kim .40 .15
❑ 668 Brian Lawrence .40 .15
❑ 669 Rodrigo Lopez .40 .15
❑ 670 Jeff Francis .40 .15
❑ 671 Chris Ianetta .40 .15
❑ 672 Garrett Atkins .40 .15
❑ 673 Todd Helton .60 .25
❑ 674 Steve Finley .40 .15
❑ 675 John Mabry .40 .15
❑ 676 Willy Taveras .40 .15
❑ 677 Jason Hirsh .40 .15
❑ 678 Ramon Ramirez .40 .15
❑ 679 Matt Holliday 1.00 .40
❑ 680 Todd Helton CL .60 .25
❑ 681 Roman Colon .40 .15
❑ 682 Chad Durbin .40 .15
❑ 683 Jason Grilli .40 .15
❑ 684 Wilfredo Ledezma .40 .15
❑ 685 Mike Maroth .40 .15
❑ 686 Jose Mesa .40 .15
❑ 687 Justin Verlander 1.00 .40
❑ 688 Fernando Rodney .40 .15
❑ 689 Vance Wilson .40 .15
❑ 690 Carlos Guillen .40 .15
❑ 691 Neifi Perez .40 .15
❑ 692 Curtis Granderson .40 .15
❑ 693 Gary Sheffield .40 .15
❑ 694 Justin Verlander CL 1.00 .40
❑ 695 Kevin Gregg .40 .15
❑ 696 Logan Kensing .40 .15
❑ 697 Randy Messenger .40 .15
❑ 698 Sergio Mitre .40 .15
❑ 699 Ricky Nolasco .40 .15
❑ 700 Scott Olsen .40 .15
❑ 701 Renyel Pinto .40 .15
❑ 702 Matt Treanor .40 .15
❑ 703 Alfredo Amezaga .40 .15
❑ 704 Aaron Boone .40 .15
❑ 705 Mike Jacobs .40 .15
❑ 706 Miguel Cabrera .60 .25
❑ 707 Joe Borchard .40 .15
❑ 708 Jorge Julio .40 .15
❑ 709 Rick Vanden Hurk RC 1.25 .50
❑ 710 Lee Gardner (RC) .75 .30
❑ 711 Matt Lindstrom (RC) .75 .30
❑ 712 Henry Owens .40 .15
❑ 713 Hanley Ramirez .60 .25
❑ 714 Alejandro De Aza RC .75 .30
❑ 715 Hanley Ramirez CL .60 .25
❑ 716 Dave Borkowski .40 .15
❑ 717 Jason Jennings .40 .15
❑ 718 Trever Miller .40 .15
❑ 719 Roy Oswalt .40 .15
❑ 720 Wandy Rodriguez .40 .15
❑ 721 Humberto Quintero .40 .15
❑ 722 Morgan Ensberg .40 .15
❑ 723 Mike Lamb .40 .15
❑ 724 Mark Loretta .40 .15
❑ 725 Jason Lane .40 .15
❑ 726 Carlos Lee .40 .15
❑ 727 Orlando Palmeiro .40 .15
❑ 728 Woody Williams .40 .15
❑ 729 Chad Qualls .40 .15
❑ 730 Lance Berkman .40 .15
❑ 731 Rick White .40 .15
❑ 732 Chris Sampson .40 .15
❑ 733 Carlos Lee CL .40 .15
❑ 734 Jorge De La Rosa .40 .15
❑ 735 Octavio Dotel .40 .15
❑ 736 Jimmy Gobble .40 .15
❑ 737 Zack Greinke .40 .15
❑ 738 Luke Hudson .40 .15
❑ 739 Gil Meche .40 .15
❑ 740 Joel Peralta .40 .15
❑ 741 Odalis Perez .40 .15
❑ 742 David Riske .40 .15
❑ 743 Jason LaRue .40 .15
❑ 744 Tony Pena .40 .15
❑ 745 Esteban German .40 .15
❑ 746 Ross Gload .40 .15
❑ 747 Emil Brown .40 .15
❑ 748 David DeJesus .40 .15
❑ 749 Brandon Duckworth .40 .15
❑ 750 Alex Gordon CL 2.50 1.00
❑ 751 Jered Weaver .60 .25
❑ 752 Vladimir Guerrero 1.00 .40
❑ 753 Hector Carrasco .40 .15
❑ 754 Kelvim Escobar .40 .15
❑ 755 Darren Oliver .40 .15
❑ 756 Dustin Moseley .40 .15
❑ 757 Ervin Santana .40 .15
❑ 758 Mike Napoli .40 .15
❑ 759 Shea Hillenbrand .40 .15
❑ 760 Casey Kotchman .40 .15
❑ 761 Reggie Willits .40 .15
❑ 762 Robb Quinlan .40 .15
❑ 763 Garret Anderson .40 .15
❑ 764 Gary Matthews .40 .15
❑ 765 Justin Speier .40 .15
❑ 766 Jered Weaver CL .60 .25
❑ 767 Joe Beimel .40 .15
❑ 768 Yhency Brazoban .40 .15
❑ 769 Elmer Dessens .40 .15
❑ 770 Mark Hendrickson .40 .15
❑ 771 Hong-Chih Kuo .40 .15
❑ 772 Jason Schmidt .40 .15
❑ 773 Brett Tomko .40 .15
❑ 774 Randy Wolf .40 .15
❑ 775 Mike Lieberthal .40 .15
❑ 776 Marlon Anderson .40 .15
❑ 777 Jeff Kent .40 .15
❑ 778 Ramon Martinez .40 .15
❑ 779 Olmedo Saenz .40 .15
❑ 780 Luis Gonzalez .40 .15
❑ 781 Juan Pierre .40 .15
❑ 782 Jason Repko .40 .15
❑ 783 Nomar Garciaparra 1.00 .40
❑ 784 Wilson Valdez .40 .15
❑ 785 Jason Schmidt CL .40 .15
❑ 786 Greg Aquino .40 .15
❑ 787 Brian Shouse .40 .15
❑ 788 Jeff Suppan .40 .15
❑ 789 Carlos Villanueva .40 .15
❑ 790 Matt Wise .40 .15
❑ 791 Johnny Estrada .40 .15
❑ 792 Craig Counsell .40 .15
❑ 793 Tony Graffanino .40 .15
❑ 794 Corey Koskie .40 .15
❑ 795 Claudio Vargas .40 .15
❑ 796 Brady Clark .40 .15

❑ 797 Gabe Gross .40 .15
❑ 798 Geoff Jenkins .40 .15
❑ 799 Kevin Mench .40 .15
❑ 800 Bill Hall CL .40 .15
❑ 801 Sidney Ponson .40 .15
❑ 802 Jesse Crain .40 .15
❑ 803 Matt Guerrier .40 .15
❑ 804 Pat Neshek .60 .25
❑ 805 Ramon Ortiz .40 .15
❑ 806 Johan Santana .60 .25
❑ 807 Carlos Silva .40 .15
❑ 808 Mike Redmond .40 .15
❑ 809 Jeff Cirillo .40 .15
❑ 810 Luis Rodriguez .40 .15
❑ 811 Lew Ford .40 .15
❑ 812 Torii Hunter .40 .15
❑ 813 Jason Tyner .40 .15
❑ 814 Rondell White .40 .15
❑ 815 Justin Morneau .40 .15
❑ 816 Joe Mauer .60 .25
❑ 817 Johan Santana CL .60 .25
❑ 818 David Newhan .40 .15
❑ 819 Aaron Sele .40 .15
❑ 820 Ambiorix Burgos .40 .15
❑ 821 Pedro Feliciano .40 .15
❑ 822 Tom Glavine .60 .25
❑ 823 Aaron Heilman .40 .15
❑ 824 Guillermo Mota .40 .15
❑ 825 Jose Reyes .40 .15
❑ 826 Oliver Perez .40 .15
❑ 827 Duaner Sanchez .40 .15
❑ 828 Scott Schoeneweis .40 .15
❑ 829 Ramon Castro .40 .15
❑ 830 Damion Easley .40 .15
❑ 831 David Wright 1.50 .60
❑ 832 Moises Alou .40 .15
❑ 833 Carlos Beltran .40 .15
❑ 834 Dave Williams .40 .15
❑ 835 David Wright CL 1.50 .60
❑ 836 Brian Bruney .40 .15
❑ 837 Mike Myers .40 .15
❑ 838 Carl Pavano .40 .15
❑ 839 Andy Pettitte .60 .25
❑ 840 Luis Vizcaino .40 .15
❑ 841 Jorge Posada .60 .25
❑ 842 Miguel Cairo .40 .15
❑ 843 Doug Mientkiewicz .40 .15
❑ 844 Derek Jeter 2.50 1.00
❑ 845 Alex Rodriguez 1.50 .60
❑ 846 Johnny Damon .60 .25
❑ 847 Hideki Matsui 1.00 .40
❑ 848 Josh Phelps .40 .15
❑ 849 Phil Hughes (RC) 4.00 1.50
❑ 850 Roger Clemens 1.50 .60
❑ 851 Jason Giambi CL .40 .15
❑ 852 Kiko Calero .40 .15
❑ 853 Justin Duchscherer .40 .15
❑ 854 Alan Embree .40 .15
❑ 855 Todd Walker .40 .15
❑ 856 Rich Harden .40 .15
❑ 857 Dan Haren .40 .15
❑ 858 Joe Kennedy .40 .15
❑ 859 Jason Kendall .40 .15
❑ 860 Adam Melhuse .40 .15
❑ 861 Mark Ellis .40 .15
❑ 862 Bobby Kielty .40 .15
❑ 863 Mark Kotsay .40 .15
❑ 864 Shannon Stewart .40 .15
❑ 865 Mike Piazza 1.00 .40
❑ 866 Mike Piazza CL 1.00 .40
❑ 867 Antonio Alfonseca .40 .15
❑ 868 Carlos Ruiz .40 .15
❑ 869 Adam Eaton .40 .15
❑ 870 Freddy Garcia .40 .15
❑ 871 Jon Lieber .40 .15
❑ 872 Matt Smith .40 .15
❑ 873 Rod Barajas .40 .15
❑ 874 Wes Helms .40 .15
❑ 875 Abraham Nunez .40 .15
❑ 876 Pat Burrell .40 .15
❑ 877 Jayson Werth .40 .15
❑ 878 Greg Dobbs .40 .15
❑ 879 Joseph Bisenius RC .75 .30
❑ 880 Michael Bourn (RC) .75 .30
❑ 881 Chase Utley 1.00 .40
❑ 882 Ryan Howard 1.50 .60
❑ 883 Chase Utley CL 1.00 .40
❑ 884 Tony Armas .40 .15
❑ 885 Shawn Chacon .40 .15
❑ 886 John Grabow .40 .15
❑ 887 Paul Maholm .40 .15
❑ 888 Damaso Marte .40 .15
❑ 889 Salomon Torres .40 .15
❑ 890 Humberto Cota .40 .15
❑ 891 Ryan Doumit .40 .15
❑ 892 Adam LaRoche .40 .15
❑ 893 Jack Wilson .40 .15
❑ 894 Nate McLouth .40 .15
❑ 895 Brad Eldred .40 .15
❑ 896 Jonah Bayliss .40 .15
❑ 897 Juan Perez RC .75 .30
❑ 898 Jason Bay .40 .15
❑ 899 Adam LaRoche CL .40 .15
❑ 900 Doug Brocail .40 .15
❑ 901 Scott Cassidy .40 .15
❑ 902 Scott Linebrink .40 .15
❑ 903 Greg Maddux 1.50 .60
❑ 904 Jake Peavy .40 .15
❑ 905 Mike Thompson .40 .15
❑ 906 David Wells .40 .15
❑ 907 Josh Bard .40 .15
❑ 908 Rob Bowen .40 .15
❑ 909 Marcus Giles .40 .15
❑ 910 Russell Branyan .40 .15
❑ 911 Jose Cruz .40 .15
❑ 912 Termel Sledge .40 .15
❑ 913 Trevor Hoffman .40 .15
❑ 914 Brian Giles .40 .15
❑ 915 Trevor Hoffman CL .40 .15
❑ 916 Vinnie Chulk .40 .15
❑ 917 Kevin Correia .40 .15
❑ 918 Tim Lincecum RC 20.00 8.00
❑ 919 Matt Morris .40 .15
❑ 920 Russ Ortiz .40 .15
❑ 921 Barry Zito .40 .15
❑ 922 Bengie Molina .40 .15
❑ 923 Rich Aurilia .40 .15
❑ 924 Omar Vizquel .60 .25
❑ 925 Jason Ellison .40 .15
❑ 926 Ryan Klesko .40 .15
❑ 927 Dave Roberts .40 .15
❑ 928 Randy Winn .40 .15
❑ 929 Barry Zito CL .40 .15
❑ 930 Miguel Batista .40 .15
❑ 931 Horacio Ramirez .40 .15
❑ 932 Chris Reitsma .40 .15
❑ 933 George Sherrill .40 .15
❑ 934 Jarrod Washburn .40 .15
❑ 935 Jeff Weaver .40 .15
❑ 936 Jake Woods .40 .15
❑ 937 Adrian Beltre .40 .15
❑ 938 Jose Lopez .40 .15
❑ 939 Ichiro Suzuki 1.50 .60
❑ 940 Jose Vidro .40 .15
❑ 941 Jose Guillen .40 .15
❑ 942 Sean White RC .75 .30
❑ 943 Brandon Morrow RC 2.00 .75
❑ 944 Felix Hernandez .60 .25
❑ 945 Felix Hernandez CL .60 .25
❑ 946 Randy Flores .40 .15
❑ 947 Ryan Franklin .40 .15
❑ 948 Kelvin Jimenez RC .75 .30
❑ 949 Tyler Johnson .40 .15
❑ 950 Mark Mulder .40 .15
❑ 951 Anthony Reyes .40 .15
❑ 952 Russ Springer .40 .15
❑ 953 Brad Thompson .40 .15
❑ 954 Adam Wainwright .40 .15
❑ 955 Kip Wells .40 .15
❑ 956 Gary Bennett .40 .15
❑ 957 Adam Kennedy .40 .15
❑ 958 Scott Rolen .60 .25
❑ 959 Scott Spiezio .40 .15
❑ 960 So Taguchi .40 .15
❑ 961 Preston Wilson .40 .15
❑ 962 Skip Schumaker .40 .15
❑ 963 Albert Pujols 2.00 .75
❑ 964 Chris Carpenter .40 .15
❑ 965 Chris Carpenter CL .40 .15
❑ 966 Edwin Jackson .40 .15
❑ 967 Jae Kuk Ryu .40 .15
❑ 968 Jae Seo .40 .15
❑ 969 Jon Switzer .40 .15
❑ 970 Josh Paul .40 .15
❑ 971 Ben Zobrist .40 .15
❑ 972 Rocco Baldelli .40 .15
❑ 973 Scott Kazmir .60 .25
❑ 974 Carl Crawford .40 .15
❑ 975 Delmon Young CL .60 .25
❑ 976 Bruce Chen .40 .15
❑ 977 Joaquin Benoit .40 .15
❑ 978 Scott Feldman .40 .15
❑ 979 Eric Gagne .40 .15
❑ 980 Kameron Loe .40 .15
❑ 981 Brandon McCarthy .40 .15
❑ 982 Robinson Tejeda .40 .15
❑ 983 C.J. Wilson .40 .15
❑ 984 Mark Teixeira .60 .25
❑ 985 Michael Young .40 .15
❑ 986 Kenny Lofton .40 .15
❑ 987 Brad Wilkerson .40 .15
❑ 988 Nelson Cruz .40 .15
❑ 989 Sammy Sosa 1.00 .40
❑ 990 Michael Young CL .40 .15
❑ 991 Vernon Wells .40 .15
❑ 992 Matt Stairs .40 .15
❑ 993 Jeremy Accardo .40 .15
❑ 994 A.J. Burnett .40 .15
❑ 995 Jason Frasor .40 .15
❑ 996 Roy Halladay .40 .15
❑ 997 Shaun Marcum .40 .15
❑ 998 Tomo Ohka .40 .15
❑ 999 Josh Towers .40 .15
❑ 1000 Gregg Zaun .40 .15
❑ 1001 Royce Clayton .40 .15
❑ 1002 Jason Smith .40 .15
❑ 1003 Alex Rios .40 .15
❑ 1004 Frank Thomas 1.00 .40
❑ 1005 Roy Halladay CL .40 .15
❑ 1006 Jesus Flores RC .75 .30
❑ 1007 Dmitri Young .40 .15
❑ 1008 Ray King .40 .15
❑ 1009 Micah Bowie .40 .15
❑ 1010 Shawn Hill .40 .15
❑ 1011 John Patterson .40 .15
❑ 1012 Levale Speigner RC .75 .30
❑ 1013 Ryan Wagner .40 .15
❑ 1014 Jerome Williams .40 .15
❑ 1015 Ryan Zimmerman 1.00 .40
❑ 1016 Cristian Guzman .40 .15
❑ 1017 Nook Logan .40 .15
❑ 1018 Chris Snelling .40 .15
❑ 1019 Ronnie Belliard .40 .15
❑ 1020 Nick Johnson CL .40 .15
❑ NNO Rookie EXCH 60.00 30.00

2008 Upper Deck

❑ COMPLETE SET (799) 120.00 60.00
❑ COMP.SER.1 (1-400) 60.00 30.00
❑ COMP.SER.2 (401-799) 60.00 30.00
❑ COMMON CARD (1-799) .40 .15
❑ COMMON ROOKIE (1-799) 1.00 .40
❑ 1 Joe Saunders .40 .15
❑ 2 Kelvim Escobar .40 .15
❑ 3 Jered Weaver .40 .15
❑ 4 Justin Speier .40 .15
❑ 5 Scot Shields .40 .15

	No.	Player		
❑	6	Mike Napoli	.40	.15
❑	7	Orlando Cabrera	.40	.15
❑	8	Casey Kotchman	.40	.15
❑	9	Vladimir Guerrero	1.00	.40
❑	10	Garret Anderson	.40	.15
❑	11	Roy Oswalt	.40	.15
❑	12	Wandy Rodriguez	.40	.15
❑	13	Woody Williams	.40	.15
❑	14	Chad Qualls	.40	.15
❑	15	Brian Moehler	.40	.15
❑	16	Mark Loretta	.40	.15
❑	17	Brad Ausmus	.40	.15
❑	18	Ty Wigginton	.40	.15
❑	19	Carlos Lee	.40	.15
❑	20	Hunter Pence	1.00	.40
❑	21	Dan Haren	.40	.15
❑	22	Lenny DiNardo	.40	.15
❑	23	Chad Gaudin	.40	.15
❑	24	Huston Street	.40	.15
❑	25	Andrew Brown	.40	.15
❑	26	Mike Piazza	1.00	.40
❑	27	Jack Cust	.40	.15
❑	28	Mark Ellis	.40	.15
❑	29	Shannon Stewart	.40	.15
❑	30	Travis Buck	.40	.15
❑	31	Shaun Marcum	.40	.15
❑	32	A.J. Burnett	.40	.15
❑	33	Jesse Litsch	.40	.15
❑	34	Casey Janssen	.40	.15
❑	35	Jeremy Accardo	.40	.15
❑	36	Gregg Zaun	.40	.15
❑	37	Aaron Hill	.40	.15
❑	38	Frank Thomas	1.00	.40
❑	39	Matt Stairs	.40	.15
❑	40	Vernon Wells	.40	.15
❑	41	Tim Hudson	.40	.15
❑	42	Chuck James	.40	.15
❑	43	Buddy Carlyle	.40	.15
❑	44	Rafael Soriano	.40	.15
❑	45	Peter Moylan	.40	.15
❑	46	Brian McCann	.60	.25
❑	47	Edgar Renteria	.40	.15
❑	48	Mark Teixeira	.60	.25
❑	49	Willie Harris	.40	.15
❑	50	Andruw Jones	.40	.15
❑	51	Ben Sheets	.60	.25
❑	52	Dave Bush	.40	.15
❑	53	Yovani Gallardo	.40	.15
❑	54	Francisco Cordero	.40	.15
❑	55	Matt Wise	.40	.15
❑	56	Johnny Estrada	.40	.15
❑	57	Prince Fielder	1.00	.40
❑	58	J.J. Hardy	.40	.15
❑	59	Corey Hart	.40	.15
❑	60	Geoff Jenkins	.40	.15
❑	61	Adam Wainwright	.40	.15
❑	62	Joel Pineiro	.40	.15
❑	63	Brad Thompson	.40	.15
❑	64	Jason Isringhausen	.40	.15
❑	65	Troy Percival	.40	.15
❑	66	Yadier Molina	.60	.25
❑	67	Albert Pujols	2.00	.75
❑	68	David Eckstein	.40	.15
❑	69	Jim Edmonds	.60	.25
❑	70	Rick Ankiel	.40	.15
❑	71	Ted Lilly	.40	.15
❑	72	Rich Hill	.40	.15
❑	73	Jason Marquis	.40	.15
❑	74	Carlos Marmol	.40	.15
❑	75	Ryan Dempster	.40	.15
❑	76	Jason Kendall	.40	.15
❑	77	Aramis Ramirez	.40	.15
❑	78	Ryan Theriot	.40	.15
❑	79	Alfonso Soriano	.60	.25
❑	80	Jacque Jones	.40	.15
❑	81	James Shields	.40	.15
❑	82	Andy Sonnanstine	.40	.15
❑	83	Scott Dohmann	.40	.15
❑	84	Al Reyes	.40	.15
❑	85	Dioner Navarro	.40	.15
❑	86	B.J. Upton	.60	.25
❑	87	Carlos Pena	.40	.15
❑	88	Brendan Harris	.40	.15
❑	89	Josh Wilson	.40	.15
❑	90	Jonny Gomes	.40	.15
❑	91	Brandon Webb	.40	.15
❑	92	Micah Owings	.40	.15
❑	93	Livan Hernandez	.40	.15
❑	94	Doug Slaten	.40	.15
❑	95	Brandon Lyon	.40	.15
❑	96	Miguel Montero	.40	.15
❑	97	Stephen Drew	.40	.15
❑	98	Mark Reynolds	.40	.15
❑	99	Conor Jackson	.40	.15
❑	100	Chris B. Young	.40	.15
❑	101	Chad Billingsley	.40	.15
❑	102	Derek Lowe	.40	.15
❑	103	Mark Hendrickson	.40	.15
❑	104	Takashi Saito	.40	.15
❑	105	Rudy Seanez	.40	.15
❑	106	Russell Martin	.40	.15
❑	107	Jeff Kent	.40	.15
❑	108	Nomar Garciaparra	1.00	.40
❑	109	Matt Kemp	.40	.15
❑	110	Juan Pierre	.40	.15
❑	111	Matt Cain	.40	.15
❑	112	Barry Zito	.40	.15
❑	113	Kevin Correia	.40	.15
❑	114	Brad Hennessey	.40	.15
❑	115	Jack Taschner	.40	.15
❑	116	Bengie Molina	.40	.15
❑	117	Ryan Klesko	.40	.15
❑	118	Omar Vizquel	.40	.15
❑	119	Dave Roberts	.40	.15
❑	120	Rajai Davis	.40	.15
❑	121	Fausto Carmona	.40	.15
❑	122	Jake Westbrook	.40	.15
❑	123	Cliff Lee	.40	.15
❑	124	Rafael Betancourt	.40	.15
❑	125	Joe Borowski	.40	.15
❑	126	Victor Martinez	.40	.15
❑	127	Travis Hafner	.40	.15
❑	128	Ryan Garko	.40	.15
❑	129	Kenny Lofton	.40	.15
❑	130	Franklin Gutierrez	.40	.15
❑	131	Felix Hernandez	.60	.25
❑	132	Jeff Weaver	.40	.15
❑	133	J.J. Putz	.40	.15
❑	134	Brandon Morrow	.40	.15
❑	135	Sean Green	.40	.15
❑	136	Kenji Johjima	.40	.15
❑	137	Jose Vidro	.40	.15
❑	138	Richie Sexson	.40	.15
❑	139	Ichiro Suzuki	1.50	.60
❑	140	Ben Broussard	.40	.15
❑	141	Sergio Mitre	.40	.15
❑	142	Scott Olsen	.40	.15
❑	143	Rick Vanden Hurk	.40	.15
❑	144	Justin Miller	.40	.15
❑	145	Lee Gardner	.40	.15
❑	146	Miguel Olivo	.40	.15
❑	147	Hanley Ramirez	1.00	.40
❑	148	Mike Jacobs	.40	.15
❑	149	Josh Willingham	.40	.15
❑	150	Alfredo Amezaga	.40	.15
❑	151	John Maine	.40	.15
❑	152	Tom Glavine	.60	.25
❑	153	Orlando Hernandez	.40	.15
❑	154	Billy Wagner	.40	.15
❑	155	Aaron Heilman	.40	.15
❑	156	David Wright	1.25	.50
❑	157	Luis Castillo	.40	.15
❑	158	Shawn Green	.40	.15
❑	159	Damion Easley	.40	.15
❑	160	Carlos Delgado	.40	.15
❑	161	Shawn Hill	.40	.15
❑	162	Mike Bacsik	.40	.15
❑	163	John Lannan	.40	.15
❑	164	Chad Cordero	.40	.15
❑	165	Jon Rauch	.40	.15
❑	166	Jesus Flores	.40	.15
❑	167	Dmitri Young	.40	.15
❑	168	Cristian Guzman	.40	.15
❑	169	Austin Kearns	.40	.15
❑	170	Nook Logan	.40	.15
❑	171	Erik Bedard	.40	.15
❑	172	Daniel Cabrera	.40	.15
❑	173	Chris Ray	.40	.15
❑	174	Danys Baez	.40	.15
❑	175	Chad Bradford	.40	.15
❑	176	Ramon Hernandez	.40	.15
❑	177	Miguel Tejada	.40	.15
❑	178	Freddie Bynum	.40	.15
❑	179	Corey Patterson	.40	.15
❑	180	Aubrey Huff	.40	.15
❑	181	Chris Young	.40	.15
❑	182	Greg Maddux	1.25	.50
❑	183	Clay Hensley	.40	.15
❑	184	Kevin Cameron	.40	.15
❑	185	Doug Brocail	.40	.15
❑	186	Josh Bard	.40	.15
❑	187	Kevin Kouzmanoff	.40	.15
❑	188	Geoff Blum	.40	.15
❑	189	Milton Bradley	.40	.15
❑	190	Brian Giles	.40	.15
❑	191	Jamie Moyer	.40	.15
❑	192	Kyle Kendrick	.40	.15
❑	193	Kyle Lohse	.40	.15
❑	194	Antonio Alfonseca	.40	.15
❑	195	Ryan Madson	.40	.15
❑	196	Chris Coste	.40	.15
❑	197	Chase Utley	1.00	.40
❑	198	Tadahito Iguchi	.40	.15
❑	199	Aaron Rowand	.40	.15
❑	200	Shane Victorino	.40	.15
❑	201	Paul Maholm	.40	.15
❑	202	Ian Snell	.40	.15
❑	203	Shane Youman	.40	.15
❑	204	Damaso Marte	.40	.15
❑	205	Shawn Chacon	.40	.15
❑	206	Ronny Paulino	.40	.15
❑	207	Jack Wilson	.40	.15
❑	208	Adam LaRoche	.40	.15
❑	209	Ryan Doumit	.40	.15
❑	210	Xavier Nady	.40	.15
❑	211	Kevin Millwood	.40	.15
❑	212	Brandon McCarthy	.40	.15
❑	213	Joaquin Benoit	.40	.15
❑	214	Wes Littleton	.40	.15
❑	215	Mike Wood	.40	.15
❑	216	Gerald Laird	.40	.15
❑	217	Hank Blalock	.40	.15
❑	218	Ian Kinsler	.60	.25
❑	219	Marlon Byrd	.40	.15
❑	220	Brad Wilkerson	.40	.15
❑	221	Tim Wakefield	.40	.15
❑	222	Daisuke Matsuzaka	1.50	.60
❑	223	Julian Tavarez	.40	.15
❑	224	Hideki Okajima	.40	.15
❑	225	Manny Delcarmen	.40	.15
❑	226	Doug Mirabelli	.40	.15

❑ 227 Dustin Pedroia .60 .25
❑ 228 Mike Lowell .40 .15
❑ 229 Manny Ramirez 1.00 .40
❑ 230 Coco Crisp .40 .15
❑ 231 Bronson Arroyo .40 .15
❑ 232 Matt Belisle .40 .15
❑ 233 Jared Burton .40 .15
❑ 234 David Weathers .40 .15
❑ 235 Mike Gosling .40 .15
❑ 236 David Ross .40 .15
❑ 237 Jeff Keppinger .40 .15
❑ 238 Edwin Encarnacion .40 .15
❑ 239 Ken Griffey Jr. 1.50 .60
❑ 240 Adam Dunn .40 .15
❑ 241 Jeff Francis .40 .15
❑ 242 Jason Hirsh .40 .15
❑ 243 Josh Fogg .40 .15
❑ 244 Manny Corpas .40 .15
❑ 245 Jeremy Affeldt .40 .15
❑ 246 Yorvit Torrealba .40 .15
❑ 247 Todd Helton .60 .25
❑ 248 Kazuo Matsui .40 .15
❑ 249 Brad Hawpe .40 .15
❑ 250 Willy Taveras .40 .15
❑ 251 Brian Bannister .40 .15
❑ 252 Zack Greinke .40 .15
❑ 253 Kyle Davies .40 .15
❑ 254 David Riske .40 .15
❑ 255 Joel Peralta .40 .15
❑ 256 John Buck .40 .15
❑ 257 Mark Grudzielanek .40 .15
❑ 258 Ross Gload .40 .15
❑ 259 Billy Butler .40 .15
❑ 260 David DeJesus .40 .15
❑ 261 Jeremy Bonderman .40 .15
❑ 262 Chad Durbin .40 .15
❑ 263 Andrew Miller .60 .25
❑ 264 Bobby Seay .40 .15
❑ 265 Todd Jones .40 .15
❑ 266 Brandon Inge .40 .15
❑ 267 Sean Casey .40 .15
❑ 268 Placido Polanco .40 .15
❑ 269 Gary Sheffield .40 .15
❑ 270 Magglio Ordonez .60 .25
❑ 271 Matt Garza .40 .15
❑ 272 Boof Bonser .40 .15
❑ 273 Scott Baker .40 .15
❑ 274 Joe Nathan .40 .15
❑ 275 Dennys Reyes .40 .15
❑ 276 Joe Mauer .60 .25
❑ 277 Michael Cuddyer .40 .15
❑ 278 Jason Bartlett .40 .15
❑ 279 Torii Hunter .40 .15
❑ 280 Jason Tyner .40 .15
❑ 281 Mark Buehrle .40 .15
❑ 282 Jon Garland .40 .15
❑ 283 Jose Contreras .40 .15
❑ 284 Matt Thornton .40 .15
❑ 285 Ryan Bukvich .40 .15
❑ 286 Juan Uribe .40 .15
❑ 287 Jim Thome .60 .25
❑ 288 Scott Podsednik .40 .15
❑ 289 Jerry Owens .40 .15
❑ 290 Jermaine Dye .40 .15
❑ 291 Andy Pettitte .60 .25
❑ 292 Phil Hughes 1.00 .40
❑ 293 Mike Mussina .40 .15
❑ 294 Joba Chamberlain 1.50 .60
❑ 295 Brian Bruney .40 .15
❑ 296 Jorge Posada .60 .25
❑ 297 Derek Jeter 2.50 1.00
❑ 298 Jason Giambi .60 .25
❑ 299 Johnny Damon .60 .25
❑ 300 Melky Cabrera .40 .15
❑ 301 Jonathan Albaladejo RC 1.50 .60
❑ 302 Josh Anderson (RC) 1.00 .40
❑ 303 Wladimir Balentien (RC) 1.00 .40
❑ 304 Josh Banks (RC) 1.00 .40
❑ 305 Daric Barton (RC) 1.00 .40
❑ 306 Jerry Blevins RC 1.50 .60
❑ 307 Emilio Bonifacio RC 1.50 .60
❑ 308 Lance Broadway (RC) 1.00 .40
❑ 309 Clay Buchholz (RC) 2.50 1.00
❑ 310 Billy Buckner (RC) 1.00 .40
❑ 311 Jeff Clement (RC) 1.00 .40
❑ 312 Willie Collazo RC 1.50 .60
❑ 313 Ross Detwiler RC 2.50 1.00
❑ 314 Sam Fuld (RC) 1.00 .40
❑ 315 Harvey Garcia (RC) 1.00 .40
❑ 316 Alberto Gonzalez RC 1.50 .60
❑ 317 Ryan Hanigan RC 1.50 .60
❑ 318 Kevin Hart (RC) 1.00 .40
❑ 319 Luke Hochevar RC 3.00 1.25
❑ 320 Chin-Lung Hu (RC) 1.50 .60
❑ 321 Rob Johnson (RC) 1.00 .40
❑ 322 Radhames Liz RC 1.50 .60
❑ 323 Ian Kennedy RC 3.00 1.25
❑ 324 Joe Koshansky (RC) 1.00 .40
❑ 325 Donny Lucy (RC) 1.00 .40
❑ 326 Justin Maxwell RC 1.50 .60
❑ 327 Jonathan Meloan RC 1.50 .60
❑ 328 Luis Mendoza (RC) 1.00 .40
❑ 329 Jose Morales (RC) 1.00 .40
❑ 330 Nyjer Morgan (RC) 1.00 .40
❑ 331 Carlos Muniz RC 1.50 .60
❑ 332 Bill Murphy (RC) 1.00 .40
❑ 333 Josh Newman RC 1.50 .60
❑ 334 Ross Ohlendorf RC 1.50 .60
❑ 335 Troy Patton (RC) 1.00 .40
❑ 336 Felipe Paulino RC 1.50 .60
❑ 337 Steve Pearce RC 1.50 .60
❑ 338 Heath Phillips RC 1.50 .60
❑ 339 Justin Ruggiano RC 1.50 .60
❑ 340 Clint Sammons (RC) 1.00 .40
❑ 341 Bronson Sardinha (RC) 1.00 .40
❑ 342 Chris Seddon (RC) 1.00 .40
❑ 343 Seth Smith (RC) 1.00 .40
❑ 344 Mitch Stetter RC 1.50 .60
❑ 345 Dave Davidson RC 1.50 .60
❑ 346 Rich Thompson RC 1.00 .40
❑ 347 J.R. Towles RC 2.50 1.00
❑ 348 Eugenio Velez RC 1.00 .40
❑ 349 Joey Votto (RC) 1.50 .60
❑ 350 Bill White RC 1.00 .40
❑ 351 Vladimir Guerrero CL 1.00 .40
❑ 352 Lance Berkman CL .60 .25
❑ 353 Dan Haren CL .40 .15
❑ 354 Frank Thomas CL 1.00 .40
❑ 355 Chipper Jones CL 1.25 .50
❑ 356 Prince Fielder CL 1.00 .40
❑ 357 Albert Pujols CL 2.00 .75
❑ 358 Alfonso Soriano CL .60 .25
❑ 359 B.J. Upton CL .60 .25
❑ 360 Eric Byrnes CL .40 .15
❑ 361 Russell Martin CL .40 .15
❑ 362 Tim Lincecum CL 1.00 .40
❑ 363 Grady Sizemore CL .60 .25
❑ 364 Ichiro Suzuki CL 1.50 .60
❑ 365 Hanley Ramirez CL 1.00 .40
❑ 366 David Wright CL 1.25 .50
❑ 367 Ryan Zimmerman CL .60 .25
❑ 368 Nick Markakis CL .60 .25
❑ 369 Jake Peavy CL .40 .15
❑ 370 Ryan Howard CL 1.25 .50
❑ 371 Freddy Sanchez CL .40 .15
❑ 372 Michael Young CL .40 .15
❑ 373 David Ortiz CL 1.00 .40
❑ 374 Ken Griffey Jr. CL 1.50 .60
❑ 375 Matt Holliday CL .60 .25
❑ 376 Brian Bannister CL .40 .15
❑ 377 Magglio Ordonez CL .60 .25
❑ 378 Johan Santana CL 1.00 .40
❑ 379 Jim Thome CL .60 .25
❑ 380 Alex Rodriguez CL 1.50 .60
❑ 381 Alex Rodriguez HL 1.50 .60
❑ 382 Brandon Webb HL .40 .15
❑ 383 Chone Figgins HL .40 .15
❑ 384 Clay Buchholz HL 1.00 .40
❑ 385 Curtis Granderson HL .60 .25
❑ 386 Frank Thomas HL 1.00 .40
❑ 387 Fred Lewis HL .40 .15
❑ 388 Garret Anderson HL .40 .15
❑ 389 J.R. Towles HL 1.00 .40
❑ 390 Jake Peavy HL .40 .15
❑ 391 Jim Thome HL .60 .25
❑ 392 Jimmy Rollins HL .60 .25
❑ 393 Johan Santana HL 1.00 .40
❑ 394 Justin Verlander HL .60 .25
❑ 395 Mark Buehrle HL .40 .15
❑ 396 Matt Holliday HL .60 .25
❑ 397 Jarrod Saltalamacchia HL .40 .15
❑ 398 Sammy Sosa HL .60 .25
❑ 399 Tom Glavine HL .60 .25
❑ 400 Trevor Hoffman HL .40 .15
❑ 401 Dan Haren .40 .15
❑ 402 Randy Johnson 1.00 .40
❑ 403 Chris Burke .40 .15
❑ 404 Orlando Hudson .40 .15
❑ 405 Justin Upton 1.00 .40
❑ 406 Eric Byrnes .40 .15
❑ 407 Doug Davis .40 .15
❑ 408 Chad Tracy .40 .15
❑ 409 Tom Glavine .60 .25
❑ 410 Kelly Johnson .40 .15
❑ 411 Chipper Jones 1.25 .50
❑ 412 Matt Diaz .40 .15
❑ 413 Jeff Francoeur .60 .25
❑ 414 Mark Kotsay .40 .15
❑ 415 John Smoltz 1.00 .40
❑ 416 Tyler Yates .40 .15
❑ 417 Yunel Escobar .40 .15
❑ 418 Mike Hampton .40 .15
❑ 419 Luke Scott .40 .15
❑ 420 Adam Jones .40 .15
❑ 421 Jeremy Guthrie .40 .15
❑ 422 Nick Markakis .60 .25
❑ 423 Jay Payton .40 .15
❑ 424 Brian Roberts .60 .25
❑ 425 Melvin Mora .40 .15
❑ 426 Adam Loewen .40 .15
❑ 427 Luis Hernandez .40 .15
❑ 428 Steve Trachsel .40 .15
❑ 429 Josh Beckett .60 .25
❑ 430 Jon Lester .60 .25
❑ 431 Curt Schilling .60 .25
❑ 432 Jonathan Papelbon .60 .25
❑ 433 Jason Varitek 1.00 .40
❑ 434 David Ortiz 1.00 .40
❑ 435 Jacoby Ellsbury 1.50 .60
❑ 436 Julio Lugo .40 .15
❑ 437 Sean Casey .40 .15
❑ 438 Kevin Youkilis .60 .25
❑ 439 J.D. Drew .40 .15
❑ 440 Alex Cora .40 .15
❑ 441 Derrek Lee .60 .25
❑ 442 Carlos Zambrano .40 .15
❑ 443 Sean Marshall .40 .15
❑ 444 Matt Murton .40 .15
❑ 445 Kerry Wood .40 .15
❑ 446 Felix Pie .40 .15
❑ 447 Mark DeRosa .40 .15
❑ 448 Ronny Cedeno .40 .15
❑ 449 Jon Lieber .40 .15
❑ 450 Geovany Soto .40 .15
❑ 451 Gavin Floyd .40 .15
❑ 452 Bobby Jenks .40 .15
❑ 453 Scott Linebrink .40 .15
❑ 454 Javier Vazquez .40 .15
❑ 455 A.J. Pierzynski .40 .15
❑ 456 Orlando Cabrera .40 .15
❑ 457 Joe Crede .40 .15
❑ 458 Josh Fields .40 .15
❑ 459 Paul Konerko .40 .15
❑ 460 Brian Anderson .40 .15
❑ 461 Nick Swisher .40 .15
❑ 462 Carlos Quentin .40 .15
❑ 463 Homer Bailey .60 .25

	No.	Player		
❑	464	Francisco Cordero	.40	.15
❑	465	Aaron Harang	.40	.15
❑	466	Alex Gonzalez	.40	.15
❑	467	Brandon Phillips	.40	.15
❑	468	Ryan Freel	.40	.15
❑	469	Scott Hatteberg	.40	.15
❑	470	Juan Castro	.40	.15
❑	471	Norris Hopper	.40	.15
❑	472	Josh Barfield	.40	.15
❑	473	Casey Blake	.40	.15
❑	474	Paul Byrd	.40	.15
❑	475	Grady Sizemore	.60	.25
❑	476	Jason Michaels	.40	.15
❑	477	Jhonny Peralta	.40	.15
❑	478	Asdrubal Cabrera	.40	.15
❑	479	David Dellucci	.40	.15
❑	480	C.C. Sabathia	.40	.15
❑	481	Andy Marte	.40	.15
❑	482	Troy Tulowitzki	.60	.25
❑	483	Matt Holliday	.60	.25
❑	484	Garrett Atkins	.40	.15
❑	485	Aaron Cook	.40	.15
❑	486	Brian Fuentes	.40	.15
❑	487	Ryan Spilborghs	.40	.15
❑	488	Ubaldo Jimenez	.40	.15
❑	489	Jayson Nix	.40	.15
❑	490	Nate Robertson	.40	.15
❑	491	Kenny Rogers	.40	.15
❑	492	Justin Verlander	.60	.25
❑	493	Dontrelle Willis	.40	.15
❑	494	Joel Zumaya	.40	.15
❑	495	Ivan Rodriguez	.60	.25
❑	496	Miguel Cabrera	.60	.25
❑	497	Carlos Guillen	.40	.15
❑	498	Edgar Renteria	.40	.15
❑	499	Curtis Granderson	.60	.25
❑	500	Jacque Jones	.40	.15
❑	501	Marcus Thames	.40	.15
❑	502	Josh Johnson	.40	.15
❑	503	Jeremy Hermida	.40	.15
❑	504	Dan Uggla	.60	.25
❑	505	Mark Hendrickson	.40	.15
❑	506	Luis Gonzalez	.40	.15
❑	507	Dallas McPherson	.40	.15
❑	508	Cody Ross	.40	.15
❑	509	Matt Treanor	.40	.15
❑	510	Andrew Miller	.60	.25
❑	511	Jorge Cantu	.40	.15
❑	512	Kazuo Matsui	.40	.15
❑	513	Lance Berkman	.60	.25
❑	514	Darin Erstad	.40	.15
❑	515	Miguel Tejada	.40	.15
❑	516	Jose Valverde	.40	.15
❑	517	Geoff Blum	.40	.15
❑	518	Reggie Abercrombie	.40	.15
❑	519	Brandon Backe	.40	.15
❑	520	Michael Bourn	.40	.15
❑	521	Gil Meche	.40	.15
❑	522	Brett Tomko	.40	.15
❑	523	Miguel Olivo	.40	.15
❑	524	Shane Costa	.40	.15
❑	525	Joey Gathright	.40	.15
❑	526	Mark Teahen	.40	.15
❑	527	Alex Gordon	1.00	.40
❑	528	Tony Pena	.40	.15
❑	529	Jose Guillen	.40	.15
❑	530	Torii Hunter	.40	.15
❑	531	Ervin Santana	.40	.15
❑	532	Francisco Rodriguez	.40	.15
❑	533	Howie Kendrick	.40	.15
❑	534	Reggie Willits	.40	.15
❑	535	John Lackey	.40	.15
❑	536	Gary Matthews	.40	.15
❑	537	Jon Garland	.40	.15
❑	538	Kendry Morales	.40	.15
❑	539	Chone Figgins	.40	.15
❑	540	Andruw Jones	.40	.15
❑	541	Jason Schmidt	.40	.15
❑	542	James Loney	.60	.25
❑	543	Andre Ethier	.60	.25
❑	544	Rafael Furcal	.40	.15
❑	545	Brad Penny	.40	.15
❑	546	Hong-Chih Kuo	.40	.15
❑	547	Jonathan Broxton	.40	.15
❑	548	Esteban Loaiza	.40	.15
❑	549	Delwyn Young	.40	.15
❑	550	Mike Cameron	.40	.15
❑	551	Ryan Braun	1.25	.50
❑	552	Rickie Weeks	.40	.15
❑	553	Bill Hall	.40	.15
❑	554	Tony Gwynn Jr.	.40	.15
❑	555	Eric Gagne	.40	.15
❑	556	Jeff Suppan	.40	.15
❑	557	Chris Capuano	.40	.15
❑	558	Derrick Turnbow	.40	.15
❑	559	Jason Kendall	.40	.15
❑	560	Livan Hernandez	.40	.15
❑	561	Philip Humber	.40	.15
❑	562	Francisco Liriano	.60	.25
❑	563	Pat Neshek	.40	.15
❑	564	Adam Everett	.40	.15
❑	565	Brendan Harris	.40	.15
❑	566	Justin Morneau	.60	.25
❑	567	Craig Monroe	.40	.15
❑	568	Carlos Gomez	.40	.15
❑	569	Delmon Young	.60	.25
❑	570	Mike Lamb	.40	.15
❑	571	Oliver Perez	.40	.15
❑	572	Jose Reyes	.60	.25
❑	573	Moises Alou	.40	.15
❑	574	Carlos Beltran	.40	.15
❑	575	Endy Chavez	.40	.15
❑	576	Ryan Church	.40	.15
❑	577	Pedro Martinez	.60	.25
❑	578	Johan Santana	1.00	.40
❑	579	Mike Pelfrey	.40	.15
❑	580	Brian Schneider	.40	.15
❑	581	Joe Smith	.40	.15
❑	582	Matt Wise	.40	.15
❑	583	Duaner Sanchez	.40	.15
❑	584	Ramon Castro	.40	.15
❑	585	Kei Igawa	.40	.15
❑	586	Mariano Rivera	1.00	.40
❑	587	Chien-Ming Wang	1.25	.50
❑	588	Wilson Betemit	.40	.15
❑	589	Robinson Cano	.60	.25
❑	590	Alex Rodriguez	1.50	.60
❑	591	Bobby Abreu	.40	.15
❑	592	Shelley Duncan	.40	.15
❑	593	Hideki Matsui	1.00	.40
❑	594	Kyle Farnsworth	.40	.15
❑	595	Joe Blanton	.40	.15
❑	596	Bobby Crosby	.40	.15
❑	597	Eric Chavez	.40	.15
❑	598	Dan Johnson	.40	.15
❑	599	Rich Harden	.40	.15
❑	600	Justin Duchscherer	.40	.15
❑	601	Kurt Suzuki	.40	.15
❑	602	Chris Denorfia	.40	.15
❑	603	Emil Brown	.40	.15
❑	604	Ryan Howard	1.25	.50
❑	605	Jimmy Rollins	.60	.25
❑	606	Pedro Feliz	.40	.15
❑	607	Adam Eaton	.40	.15
❑	608	Brad Lidge	.40	.15
❑	609	Brett Myers	.40	.15
❑	610	Pat Burrell	.40	.15
❑	611	So Taguchi	.40	.15
❑	612	Geoff Jenkins	.40	.15
❑	613	Tom Gordon	.40	.15
❑	614	Zach Duke	.40	.15
❑	615	Matt Morris	.40	.15
❑	616	Tom Gorzelanny	.40	.15
❑	617	Jason Bay	.40	.15
❑	618	Chris Duffy	.40	.15
❑	619	Freddy Sanchez	.40	.15
❑	620	Jose Bautista	.40	.15
❑	621	Nyjer Morgan	.40	.15
❑	622	Matt Capps	.40	.15
❑	623	Paul Maholm	.40	.15
❑	624	Tadahito Iguchi	.40	.15
❑	625	Adrian Gonzalez	.60	.25
❑	626	Jim Edmonds	.60	.25
❑	627	Jake Peavy	.40	.15
❑	628	Khalil Greene	.60	.25
❑	629	Trevor Hoffman	.40	.15
❑	630	Mark Prior	.60	.25
❑	631	Randy Wolf	.40	.15
❑	632	Michael Barrett	.40	.15
❑	633	Scott Hairston	.40	.15
❑	634	Tim Lincecum	1.00	.40
❑	635	Noah Lowry	.40	.15
❑	636	Rich Aurilia	.40	.15
❑	637	Aaron Rowand	.40	.15
❑	638	Randy Winn	.40	.15
❑	639	Daniel Ortmeier	.40	.15
❑	640	Ray Durham	.40	.15
❑	641	Brian Wilson	.40	.15
❑	642	Adrian Beltre	.40	.15
❑	643	Jeremy Reed	.40	.15
❑	644	Jarrod Washburn	.40	.15
❑	645	Yuniesky Betancourt	.40	.15
❑	646	Jose Lopez	.40	.15
❑	647	Raul Ibanez	.40	.15
❑	648	Mike Morse	.40	.15
❑	649	Erik Bedard	.40	.15
❑	650	Brad Wilkerson	.40	.15
❑	651	Chris Carpenter	.40	.15
❑	652	Mark Mulder	.40	.15
❑	653	Juan Encarnacion	.40	.15
❑	654	Skip Schumaker	.40	.15
❑	655	Troy Glaus	.60	.25
❑	656	Anthony Reyes	.40	.15
❑	657	Cesar Izturis	.40	.15
❑	658	Adam Kennedy	.40	.15
❑	659	Chris Duncan	.40	.15
❑	660	Matt Clement	.40	.15
❑	661	Scott Kazmir	.60	.25
❑	662	Troy Percival	.40	.15
❑	663	Akinori Iwamura	.40	.15
❑	664	Carl Crawford	.40	.15
❑	665	Cliff Floyd	.40	.15
❑	666	Jason Bartlett	.40	.15
❑	667	Rocco Baldelli	.40	.15
❑	668	Matt Garza	.40	.15
❑	669	Edwin Jackson	.40	.15
❑	670	Vicente Padilla	.40	.15
❑	671	Josh Hamilton	1.25	.50
❑	672	Jason Botts	.40	.15
❑	673	Milton Bradley	.40	.15
❑	674	Michael Young	.40	.15
❑	675	Eddie Guardado	.40	.15
❑	676	David Murphy	.40	.15
❑	677	Ramon Vazquez	.40	.15
❑	678	Ben Broussard	.40	.15
❑	679	C.J. Wilson	.40	.15
❑	680	Jason Jennings	.40	.15
❑	681	Gustavo Chacin	.40	.15
❑	682	BJ Ryan	.40	.15
❑	683	David Eckstein	.40	.15
❑	684	Alex Rios	.40	.15
❑	685	John McDonald	.40	.15
❑	686	Rod Barajas	.40	.15
❑	687	Lyle Overbay	.40	.15
❑	688	Scott Rolen	.60	.25
❑	689	Reed Johnson	.40	.15
❑	690	Marco Scutaro	.40	.15
❑	691	Lastings Milledge	.40	.15
❑	692	Johnny Estrada	.40	.15
❑	693	Paul Lo Duca	.40	.15
❑	694	Ryan Zimmerman	.60	.25
❑	695	Odalis Perez	.40	.15
❑	696	Wily Mo Pena	.40	.15
❑	697	Elijah Dukes	.40	.15
❑	698	Aaron Boone	.40	.15
❑	699	Ronnie Belliard	.40	.15
❑	700	Nick Johnson	.40	.15

❑ 701	Randor Bierd RC	1.00	.40
❑ 702	Brian Barton RC	1.50	.60
❑ 703	Brian Bass (RC)	1.00	.40
❑ 704	Brian Bocock RC	1.00	.40
❑ 705	Gregor Blanco (RC)	1.00	.40
❑ 706	Callix Crabbe (RC)	1.00	.40
❑ 707	Johnny Cueto RC	2.50	1.00
❑ 708	Kosuke Fukudome RC	10.00	4.00
❑ 708b	K.Fukudome Japanese	80.00	40.00
❑ 709	Scott Kazmir SH	.60	.25
❑ 710	Steve Holm RC	1.00	.40
❑ 711	Fernando Hernandez RC	1.00	.40
❑ 712	Elliot Johnson (RC)	1.00	.40
❑ 713	Masahide Kobayashi RC	1.50	.60
❑ 714	Hiroki Kuroda RC	1.50	.60
❑ 715	Blake DeWitt (RC)	2.50	1.00
❑ 716	Kyle McClellan RC	1.00	.40
❑ 717	Evan Meek RC	1.00	.40
❑ 718	Denard Span (RC)	1.00	.40
❑ 719	Darren O'Day RC	1.00	.40
❑ 720	Alexei Ramirez RC	8.00	3.00
❑ 721	Alex Romero (RC)	1.00	.40
❑ 722	Clete Thomas RC	1.50	.60
❑ 723	Matt Tolbert RC	1.50	.60
❑ 724	Ramon Troncoso RC	1.00	.40
❑ 725	Matt Tupman RC	1.00	.40
❑ 726	Rico Washington (RC)	1.00	.40
❑ 727	Randy Wells (RC)	1.00	.40
❑ 728	Wesley Wright RC	1.00	.40
❑ 729	Yasuhiko Yabuta RC	1.50	.60
❑ 730	Alex Rodriguez SH	1.50	.60
❑ 731	Andruw Jones SH	.40	.15
❑ 732	C.C. Sabathia SH	.40	.15
❑ 733	Carlos Beltran SH	.40	.15
❑ 734	David Wright SH	1.25	.50
❑ 735	Derrek Lee SH	.60	.25
❑ 736	Dustin Pedroia SH	.60	.25
❑ 737	Grady Sizemore SH	.60	.25
❑ 738	Greg Maddux SH	1.25	.50
❑ 739	Ichiro Suzuki SH	1.50	.60
❑ 740	Ivan Rodriguez SH	.60	.25
❑ 741	Jake Peavy SH	.40	.15
❑ 742	Jimmy Rollins SH	.60	.25
❑ 743	Johan Santana SH	1.00	.40
❑ 744	Josh Beckett SH	.60	.25
❑ 745	Kevin Youkilis SH	.60	.25
❑ 746	Matt Holliday SH	.60	.25
❑ 747	Mike Lowell SH	.40	.15
❑ 748	Ryan Braun SH	1.25	.50
❑ 749	Torii Hunter SH	.40	.15
❑ 750	Alex Rodriguez SH	1.50	.60
❑ 751	Torii Hunter CL	.40	.15
❑ 752	Miguel Tejada CL	.40	.15
❑ 753	Huston Street CL	.40	.15
❑ 754	Scott Rolen CL	.60	.25
❑ 755	Tom Glavine CL	.60	.25
❑ 756	Ryan Braun CL	1.25	.50
❑ 757	Troy Glaus CL	.60	.25
❑ 758	Carlos Zambrano CL	.40	.15
❑ 759	Carl Crawford CL	.40	.15
❑ 760	Dan Haren CL	.40	.15
❑ 761	Andruw Jones CL	.40	.15
❑ 762	Barry Zito CL	.40	.15
❑ 763	Victor Martinez CL	.40	.15
❑ 764	Erik Bedard CL	.40	.15
❑ 765	Josh Willingham CL	.40	.15
❑ 766	Johan Santana CL	1.00	.40
❑ 767	Dmitri Young CL	.40	.15
❑ 768	Brian Roberts CL	.60	.25
❑ 769	Jim Edmonds CL	.60	.25
❑ 770	Jimmy Rollins CL	.60	.25
❑ 771	Jason Bay CL	.40	.15
❑ 772	Josh Hamilton CL	1.25	.50
❑ 773	Josh Beckett CL	.60	.25
❑ 774	Aaron Harang CL	.40	.15
❑ 775	Troy Tulowitzki CL	.60	.25
❑ 776	Jose Guillen CL	.40	.15
❑ 777	Miguel Cabrera CL	.60	.25
❑ 778	Joe Mauer CL	.60	.25
❑ 779	Nick Swisher CL	.40	.15
❑ 780	Derek Jeter CL	2.50	1.00
❑ 781	Brandon Webb SH	.40	.15
❑ 782	Brian Roberts SH	.60	.25
❑ 783	C.C. Sabathia SH	.40	.15
❑ 784	Carl Crawford SH	.40	.15
❑ 785	Curtis Granderson SH	.60	.25
❑ 786	David Ortiz SH	1.00	.40
❑ 787	Ichiro Suzuki SH	1.50	.60
❑ 788	Jake Peavy SH	.40	.15
❑ 789	Jimmy Rollins SH	.60	.25
❑ 790	Joe Borowski SH	.40	.15
❑ 791	Johan Santana SH	1.00	.40
❑ 792	John Lackey SH	.40	.15
❑ 793	Jose Reyes SH	.60	.25
❑ 794	Jose Valverde SH	.40	.15
❑ 795	Josh Beckett SH	.60	.25
❑ 796	Juan Pierre SH	.40	.15
❑ 797	Magglio Ordonez SH	.60	.25
❑ 798	Matt Holliday SH	.60	.25
❑ 799	Prince Fielder SH	1.00	.40

2007 Upper Deck Elements

❑ COMMON CARD .75 .30
❑ CARDS 1-42 FOUND IN GRIFFEY PACKS
❑ CARDS 43-84 FOUND IN RIPKEN PACKS
❑ CARDS 85-126 FOUND IN JETER PACKS
❑ ALL VETERAN VERSIONS EQUAL VALUE
❑ COMMON RC (127-168) 2.00 .75
❑ RC 127-168 FOUND IN GRIFFEY PACKS
❑ RC 169-210 FOUND IN RIPKEN PACKS
❑ COMMON RC (211-252) 2.50 1.00
❑ RC 211-252 FOUND IN JETER PACKS
❑ ROOKIE PRINT RUN 550 SER.#'d SETS
❑ PRINTING PLATES RANDOMLY INSERTED
❑ PLATE PRINT RUN 1 SET PER COLOR
❑ BLACK-CYAN-MAGENTA-YELLOW ISSUED
❑ NO PLATE PRICING DUE TO SCARCITY
❑ GIFT EXCH ODDS 1 PER CASE
❑ GIFT EXCH DEADLINE 9/30/2007

❑ 1	Stephen Drew	1.25	.50
❑ 2	Andruw Jones	1.25	.50
❑ 3	Chipper Jones	2.00	.75
❑ 4	Miguel Tejada	.75	.30
❑ 5	David Ortiz	2.00	.75
❑ 6	Manny Ramirez	1.25	.50
❑ 7	Derrek Lee	.75	.30
❑ 8	Alfonso Soriano	.75	.30
❑ 9	Jermaine Dye	.75	.30
❑ 10	Jim Thome	1.25	.50
❑ 11	Ken Griffey Jr.	3.00	1.25
❑ 12	Adam Dunn	.75	.30
❑ 13	Travis Hafner	.75	.30
❑ 14	Grady Sizemore	1.25	.50
❑ 15	Todd Helton	1.25	.50
❑ 16	Gary Sheffield	.75	.30
❑ 17	Miguel Cabrera	1.25	.50
❑ 18	Lance Berkman	.75	.30
❑ 19	Mark Teahen	.75	.30
❑ 20	Vladimir Guerrero	2.00	.75
❑ 21	Jered Weaver	1.25	.50
❑ 22	Rafael Furcal	.75	.30
❑ 23	Prince Fielder	2.00	.75
❑ 24	Justin Morneau	.75	.30
❑ 25	Johan Santana	1.25	.50
❑ 26	David Wright	3.00	1.25
❑ 27	Jose Reyes	2.00	.75
❑ 28	Derek Jeter	5.00	2.00
❑ 29	Alex Rodriguez	3.00	1.25
❑ 30	Nick Swisher	.75	.30
❑ 31	Ryan Howard	3.00	1.25
❑ 32	Jason Bay	.75	.30
❑ 33	Adrian Gonzalez	.75	.30
❑ 34	Ray Durham	.75	.30
❑ 35	Ichiro Suzuki	3.00	1.25
❑ 36	Albert Pujols	4.00	1.50
❑ 37	Scott Rolen	1.25	.50
❑ 38	Carl Crawford	.75	.30
❑ 39	Mark Teixeira	1.25	.50
❑ 40	Michael Young	.75	.30
❑ 41	Vernon Wells	.75	.30
❑ 42	Ryan Zimmerman	2.00	.75
❑ 43	Stephen Drew	1.25	.50
❑ 44	Andruw Jones	1.25	.50
❑ 45	Chipper Jones	2.00	.75
❑ 46	Miguel Tejada	.75	.30
❑ 47	David Ortiz	2.00	.75
❑ 48	Manny Ramirez	1.25	.50
❑ 49	Derrek Lee	.75	.30
❑ 50	Alfonso Soriano	.75	.30
❑ 51	Jermaine Dye	.75	.30
❑ 52	Jim Thome	1.25	.50
❑ 53	Ken Griffey Jr.	3.00	1.25
❑ 54	Adam Dunn	.75	.30
❑ 55	Travis Hafner	.75	.30
❑ 56	Grady Sizemore	1.25	.50
❑ 57	Todd Helton	1.25	.50
❑ 58	Gary Sheffield	.75	.30
❑ 59	Miguel Cabrera	1.25	.50
❑ 60	Lance Berkman	.75	.30
❑ 61	Mark Teahen	.75	.30
❑ 62	Vladimir Guerrero	2.00	.75
❑ 63	Jered Weaver	1.25	.50
❑ 64	Rafael Furcal	.75	.30
❑ 65	Prince Fielder	2.00	.75
❑ 66	Justin Morneau	.75	.30
❑ 67	Johan Santana	1.25	.50
❑ 68	David Wright	3.00	1.25
❑ 69	Jose Reyes	2.00	.75
❑ 70	Derek Jeter	5.00	2.00
❑ 71	Alex Rodriguez	3.00	1.25
❑ 72	Nick Swisher	.75	.30
❑ 73	Ryan Howard	3.00	1.25
❑ 74	Jason Bay	.75	.30
❑ 75	Adrian Gonzalez	.75	.30
❑ 76	Ray Durham	.75	.30
❑ 77	Ichiro Suzuki	3.00	1.25
❑ 78	Albert Pujols	4.00	1.50
❑ 79	Scott Rolen	1.25	.50
❑ 80	Carl Crawford	.75	.30
❑ 81	Mark Teixeira	1.25	.50
❑ 82	Michael Young	.75	.30
❑ 83	Vernon Wells	.75	.30
❑ 84	Ryan Zimmerman	2.00	.75
❑ 85	Stephen Drew	1.25	.50
❑ 86	Andruw Jones	1.25	.50
❑ 87	Chipper Jones	2.00	.75
❑ 88	Miguel Tejada	.75	.30
❑ 89	David Ortiz	2.00	.75
❑ 90	Manny Ramirez	1.25	.50
❑ 91	Derrek Lee	.75	.30
❑ 92	Alfonso Soriano	.75	.30
❑ 93	Jermaine Dye	.75	.30
❑ 94	Jim Thome	1.25	.50
❑ 95	Ken Griffey Jr.	3.00	1.25
❑ 96	Adam Dunn	.75	.30
❑ 97	Travis Hafner	.75	.30
❑ 98	Grady Sizemore	1.25	.50
❑ 99	Todd Helton	1.25	.50
❑ 100	Gary Sheffield	.75	.30
❑ 101	Miguel Cabrera	1.25	.50

❑ 102 Lance Berkman .75 .30
❑ 103 Mark Teahen .75 .30
❑ 104 Vladimir Guerrero 2.00 .75
❑ 105 Jered Weaver 1.25 .50
❑ 106 Rafael Furcal .75 .30
❑ 107 Prince Fielder 2.00 .75
❑ 108 Justin Morneau .75 .30
❑ 109 Johan Santana 1.25 .50
❑ 110 David Wright 3.00 1.25
❑ 111 Jose Reyes 2.00 .75
❑ 112 Derek Jeter 5.00 2.00
❑ 113 Alex Rodriguez 3.00 1.25
❑ 114 Nick Swisher .75 .30
❑ 115 Ryan Howard 3.00 1.25
❑ 116 Jason Bay .75 .30
❑ 117 Adrian Gonzalez .75 .30
❑ 118 Ray Durham .75 .30
❑ 119 Ichiro Suzuki 3.00 1.25
❑ 120 Albert Pujols 4.00 1.50
❑ 121 Scott Rolen 1.25 .50
❑ 122 Carl Crawford .75 .30
❑ 123 Mark Teixeira 1.25 .50
❑ 124 Michael Young .75 .30
❑ 125 Vernon Wells .75 .30
❑ 126 Ryan Zimmerman 2.00 .75
❑ 127 Miguel Montero (RC) 2.00 .75
❑ 128 Doug Slaten RC 2.00 .75
❑ 129 Hunter Pence (RC) 25.00 10.00
❑ 130 Brian Burres (RC) 2.00 .75
❑ 131 Daisuke Matsuzaka RC 15.00 6.00
❑ 132 Hideki Okajima RC 8.00 3.00
❑ 133 Devern Hansack RC 2.00 .75
❑ 134 Felix Pie (RC) 5.00 2.00
❑ 135 Ryan Sweeney (RC) 2.00 .75
❑ 136 Chris Stewart RC 3.00 1.25
❑ 137 Jarrod Saltalamacchia (RC) 3.00 1.25
❑ 138 John Danks RC 3.00 1.25
❑ 139 Travis Buck (RC) 2.00 .75
❑ 140 Troy Tulowitzki (RC) 8.00 3.00
❑ 141 Chase Wright RC 3.00 1.25
❑ 142 Matt DeSalvo (RC) 3.00 1.25
❑ 143 Micah Owings (RC) 2.00 .75
❑ 144 Jeff Baker (RC) 2.00 .75
❑ 145 Andy LaRoche (RC) 2.00 .75
❑ 146 Billy Butler (RC) 8.00 3.00
❑ 147 Jose Garcia RC 2.00 .75
❑ 148 Angel Sanchez RC 2.00 .75
❑ 149 Alex Gordon RC 15.00 6.00
❑ 150 Glen Perkins (RC) 2.00 .75
❑ 151 Alexi Casilla RC 3.00 1.25
❑ 152 Joe Smith RC 2.00 .75
❑ 153 Kei Igawa RC 8.00 3.00
❑ 154 Sean Henn (RC) 5.00 2.00
❑ 155 Phil Hughes (RC) 15.00 6.00
❑ 156 Michael Bourn (RC) 2.00 .75
❑ 157 Josh Hamilton (RC) 15.00 6.00
❑ 158 Kevin Kouzmanoff (RC) 2.00 .75
❑ 159 Tim Lincecum RC 40.00 15.00
❑ 160 Brandon Morrow RC 3.00 1.25
❑ 161 Brandon Wood (RC) 2.00 .75
❑ 162 Akinori Iwamura RC 5.00 2.00
❑ 163 Delmon Young (RC) 3.00 1.25
❑ 164 Juan Salas (RC) 2.00 .75
❑ 165 Elijah Dukes RC 3.00 1.25
❑ 166 Joaquin Arias (RC) 2.00 .75
❑ 167 Adam Lind (RC) 2.00 .75
❑ 168 Matt Chico (RC) 2.00 .75
❑ 169 Miguel Montero (RC) 2.00 .75
❑ 170 Doug Slaten RC 2.00 .75
❑ 171 Hunter Pence (RC) 25.00 10.00
❑ 172 Brian Burres (RC) 2.00 .75
❑ 173 Daisuke Matsuzaka RC 15.00 6.00
❑ 174 Hideki Okajima RC 8.00 3.00
❑ 175 Devern Hansack RC 2.00 .75
❑ 176 Felix Pie (RC) 5.00 2.00
❑ 177 Ryan Sweeney (RC) 2.00 .75
❑ 178 Chris Stewart RC 3.00 1.25
❑ 179 Jarrod Saltalamacchia (RC) 3.00 1.25
❑ 180 John Danks RC 3.00 1.25
❑ 181 Travis Buck (RC) 2.00 .75
❑ 182 Troy Tulowitzki (RC) 8.00 3.00
❑ 183 Chase Wright RC 3.00 1.25
❑ 184 Matt DeSalvo (RC) 3.00 1.25
❑ 185 Micah Owings (RC) 2.00 .75
❑ 186 Jeff Baker (RC) 2.00 .75
❑ 187 Andy LaRoche (RC) 2.00 .75
❑ 188 Billy Butler (RC) 8.00 3.00
❑ 189 Jose Garcia RC 2.00 .75
❑ 190 Angel Sanchez RC 2.00 .75
❑ 191 Alex Gordon RC 15.00 6.00
❑ 192 Glen Perkins (RC) 2.00 .75
❑ 193 Alexi Casilla RC 3.00 1.25
❑ 194 Joe Smith RC 2.00 .75
❑ 195 Kei Igawa RC 8.00 3.00
❑ 196 Sean Henn (RC) 5.00 2.00
❑ 197 Phil Hughes (RC) 15.00 6.00
❑ 198 Michael Bourn (RC) 2.00 .75
❑ 199 Josh Hamilton (RC) 15.00 6.00
❑ 200 Kevin Kouzmanoff (RC) 2.00 .75
❑ 201 Tim Lincecum RC 40.00 15.00
❑ 202 Brandon Morrow RC 3.00 1.25
❑ 203 Brandon Wood (RC) 2.00 .75
❑ 204 Akinori Iwamura RC 5.00 2.00
❑ 205 Delmon Young (RC) 3.00 1.25
❑ 206 Juan Salas (RC) 2.00 .75
❑ 207 Elijah Dukes RC 3.00 1.25
❑ 208 Joaquin Arias (RC) 2.00 .75
❑ 209 Adam Lind (RC) 2.00 .75
❑ 210 Matt Chico (RC) 2.00 .75
❑ 211 Miguel Montero (RC) 2.50 1.00
❑ 212 Doug Slaten RC 2.50 1.00
❑ 213 Hunter Pence (RC) 25.00 10.00
❑ 214 Brian Burres (RC) 2.50 1.00
❑ 215 Daisuke Matsuzaka RC 15.00 6.00
❑ 216 Hideki Okajima RC 10.00 4.00
❑ 217 Devern Hansack RC 2.50 1.00
❑ 218 Felix Pie (RC) 6.00 2.50
❑ 219 Ryan Sweeney (RC) 2.50 1.00
❑ 220 Chris Stewart RC 4.00 1.50
❑ 221 Jarrod Saltalamacchia (RC) 4.00 1.50
❑ 222 John Danks RC 4.00 1.50
❑ 223 Travis Buck (RC) 2.50 1.00
❑ 224 Troy Tulowitzki (RC) 10.00 4.00
❑ 225 Chase Wright RC 4.00 1.50
❑ 226 Matt DeSalvo (RC) 4.00 1.50
❑ 227 Micah Owings (RC) 2.50 1.00
❑ 228 Jeff Baker (RC) 2.50 1.00
❑ 229 Andy LaRoche (RC) 2.50 1.00
❑ 230 Billy Butler (RC) 10.00 4.00
❑ 231 Jose Garcia RC 2.50 1.00
❑ 232 Angel Sanchez RC 2.50 1.00
❑ 233 Alex Gordon RC 20.00 8.00
❑ 234 Glen Perkins (RC) 2.50 1.00
❑ 235 Alexi Casilla RC 4.00 1.50
❑ 236 Joe Smith RC 2.50 1.00
❑ 237 Kei Igawa RC 10.00 4.00
❑ 238 Sean Henn (RC) 6.00 2.50
❑ 239 Phil Hughes (RC) 15.00 6.00
❑ 240 Michael Bourn (RC) 2.50 1.00
❑ 241 Josh Hamilton (RC) 20.00 8.00
❑ 242 Kevin Kouzmanoff (RC) 2.50 1.00
❑ 243 Tim Lincecum RC 40.00 15.00
❑ 244 Brandon Morrow RC 4.00 1.50
❑ 245 Brandon Wood (RC) 2.50 1.00
❑ 246 Akinori Iwamura RC 6.00 2.50
❑ 247 Delmon Young (RC) 4.00 1.50
❑ 248 Juan Salas (RC) 2.50 1.00
❑ 249 Elijah Dukes RC 4.00 1.50
❑ 250 Joaquin Arias (RC) 2.50 1.00
❑ 251 Adam Lind (RC) 2.50 1.00
❑ 252 Matt Chico (RC) 2.50 1.00
❑ NNO Gift EXCH

2007 Upper Deck First Edition

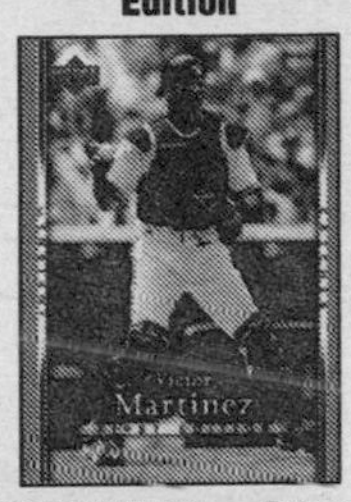

❑ COMPLETE SET (300) 50.00 20.00
❑ COMMON CARD (1-300) .30 .12
❑ COMMON ROOKIE (1-300) .40 .15
❑ PRINTING PLATE ODDS 1 PER CASE
❑ PLATE PRINT RUN 1 SET PER COLOR
❑ BLACK-CYAN-MAGENTA-YELLOW ISSUED
❑ NO PLATE PRICING DUE TO SCARCITY
❑ 1 Doug Slaten RC .40 .15
❑ 2 Miguel Montero (RC) .40 .15
❑ 3 Brian Burres (RC) .40 .15
❑ 4 Devern Hansack RC .40 .15
❑ 5 David Murphy (RC) .40 .15
❑ 6 Jose Reyes RC .40 .15
❑ 7 Scott Moore (RC) .40 .15
❑ 8 Josh Fields (RC) .40 .15
❑ 9 Chris Stewart RC .40 .15
❑ 10 Jerry Owens (RC) .40 .15
❑ 11 Ryan Sweeney (RC) .40 .15
❑ 12 Kevin Kouzmanoff (RC) .40 .15
❑ 13 Jeff Baker (RC) .40 .15
❑ 14 Justin Hampson (RC) .40 .15
❑ 15 Jeff Salazar (RC) .40 .15
❑ 16 Alvin Colina RC 1.00 .40
❑ 17 Troy Tulowitzki (RC) 1.00 .40
❑ 18 Andrew Miller RC 2.50 1.00
❑ 19 Mike Rabelo RC .40 .15
❑ 20 Jose Diaz (RC) .40 .15
❑ 21 Angel Sanchez RC .40 .15
❑ 22 Ryan Braun RC .40 .15
❑ 23 Delwyn Young (RC) .40 .15
❑ 24 Drew Anderson RC .40 .15
❑ 25 Dennis Sarfate (RC) .40 .15
❑ 26 Vinny Rottino (RC) .40 .15
❑ 27 Glen Perkins (RC) .40 .15
❑ 28 Alexi Casilla RC .60 .25
❑ 29 Philip Humber (RC) .60 .25
❑ 30 Andy Cannizaro RC .40 .15
❑ 31 Jeremy Brown .30 .12
❑ 32 Sean Henn (RC) .40 .15
❑ 33 Brian Rogers (RC) .40 .15
❑ 34 Carlos Maldonado (RC) .40 .15
❑ 35 Juan Morillo (RC) .40 .15
❑ 36 Fred Lewis (RC) .40 .15
❑ 37 Patrick Misch (RC) .40 .15
❑ 38 Billy Sadler (RC) .40 .15
❑ 39 Ryan Feierabend (RC) .40 .15
❑ 40 Cesar Jimenez RC .40 .15
❑ 41 Oswaldo Navarro RC .40 .15
❑ 42 Travis Chick (RC) .40 .15
❑ 43 Delmon Young (RC) 1.00 .40
❑ 44 Shawn Riggans (RC) .40 .15
❑ 45 Brian Stokes (RC) .40 .15
❑ 46 Juan Salas (RC) .40 .15
❑ 47 Joaquin Arias (RC) .40 .15
❑ 48 Adam Lind (RC) .40 .15
❑ 49 Beltran Perez (RC) .40 .15
❑ 50 Brett Campbell RC .40 .15
❑ 51 Miguel Tejada .30 .12
❑ 52 Brandon Fahey .30 .12
❑ 53 Jay Gibbons .30 .12

❑ 54 Nick Markakis .50 .20
❑ 55 Kris Benson .30 .12
❑ 56 Erik Bedard .30 .12
❑ 57 Chris Ray .30 .12
❑ 58 Chris Britton .30 .12
❑ 59 Manny Ramirez .50 .20
❑ 60 David Ortiz .75 .30
❑ 61 Alex Cora .30 .12
❑ 62 Trot Nixon .30 .12
❑ 63 Doug Mirabelli .30 .12
❑ 64 Curt Schilling .50 .20
❑ 65 Jonathan Papelbon .75 .30
❑ 66 Craig Hansen .30 .12
❑ 67 Jermaine Dye .30 .12
❑ 68 Jim Thome .50 .20
❑ 69 Rob Mackowiak .30 .12
❑ 70 Brian Anderson .30 .12
❑ 71 A.J. Pierzynski .30 .12
❑ 72 Alex Cintron .30 .12
❑ 73 Jose Contreras .30 .12
❑ 74 Bobby Jenks .30 .12
❑ 75 Mike MacDougal .30 .12
❑ 76 Travis Hafner .30 .12
❑ 77 Ryan Garko .30 .12
❑ 78 Victor Martinez .30 .12
❑ 79 Casey Blake .30 .12
❑ 80 Shin-Soo Choo .50 .20
❑ 81 Paul Byrd .30 .12
❑ 82 Jeremy Sowers .30 .12
❑ 83 Cliff Lee .30 .12
❑ 84 Sean Casey .30 .12
❑ 85 Brandon Inge .30 .12
❑ 86 Omar Infante .30 .12
❑ 87 Magglio Ordonez .30 .12
❑ 88 Marcus Thames .30 .12
❑ 89 Justin Verlander .75 .30
❑ 90 Todd Jones .30 .12
❑ 91 Joel Zumaya .50 .20
❑ 92 Nate Robertson .30 .12
❑ 93 Mark Teahen .30 .12
❑ 94 Ryan Shealy .30 .12
❑ 95 Mark Grudzielanek .30 .12
❑ 96 Shane Costa .30 .12
❑ 97 Reggie Sanders .30 .12
❑ 98 Mark Redman .30 .12
❑ 99 Todd Wellemeyer .30 .12
❑ 100 Ambiorix Burgos .30 .12
❑ 101 Joe Nelson .30 .12
❑ 102 Orlando Cabrera .30 .12
❑ 103 Maicer Izturis .30 .12
❑ 104 Vladimir Guerrero .75 .30
❑ 105 Juan Rivera .30 .12
❑ 106 Jered Weaver .50 .20
❑ 107 Joe Saunders .30 .12
❑ 108 Bartolo Colon .30 .12
❑ 109 Francisco Rodriguez .30 .12
❑ 110 Justin Morneau .30 .12
❑ 111 Luis Castillo .30 .12
❑ 112 Michael Cuddyer .30 .12
❑ 113 Joe Mauer .50 .20
❑ 114 Francisco Liriano .75 .30
❑ 115 Joe Nathan .30 .12
❑ 116 Brad Radke .30 .12
❑ 117 Juan Rincon .30 .12
❑ 118 Derek Jeter 2.00 .75
❑ 119 Jason Giambi .30 .12
❑ 120 Bobby Abreu .30 .12
❑ 121 Gary Sheffield .30 .12
❑ 122 Melky Cabrera .30 .12
❑ 123 Chien-Ming Wang 1.25 .50
❑ 124 Mariano Rivera .75 .30
❑ 125 Jaret Wright .30 .12
❑ 126 Kyle Farnsworth .30 .12
❑ 127 Frank Thomas .75 .30
❑ 128 Dan Johnson .30 .12
❑ 129 Marco Scutaro .30 .12
❑ 130 Jay Payton .30 .12
❑ 131 Joe Blanton .30 .12
❑ 132 Rich Harden .30 .12
❑ 133 Esteban Loaiza .30 .12
❑ 134 Chad Gaudin .30 .12
❑ 135 Yuniesky Betancourt .30 .12
❑ 136 Willie Bloomquist .30 .12
❑ 137 Ichiro Suzuki 1.25 .50
❑ 138 Raul Ibanez .30 .12
❑ 139 Chris Snelling .30 .12
❑ 140 Cha-Seung Baek .30 .12
❑ 141 Julio Mateo .30 .12
❑ 142 Rafael Soriano .30 .12
❑ 143 Jorge Cantu .30 .12
❑ 144 B.J. Upton .30 .12
❑ 145 Dioner Navarro .30 .12
❑ 146 Carl Crawford .30 .12
❑ 147 Damon Hollins .30 .12
❑ 148 Casey Fossum .30 .12
❑ 149 Ruddy Lugo .30 .12
❑ 150 Tyler Walker .30 .12
❑ 151 Shawn Camp .30 .12
❑ 152 Ian Kinsler .30 .12
❑ 153 Jerry Hairston Jr. .30 .12
❑ 154 Gerald Laird .30 .12
❑ 155 Mark DeRosa .30 .12
❑ 156 Kip Wells .30 .12
❑ 157 Vicente Padilla .30 .12
❑ 158 John Koronka .30 .12
❑ 159 Wes Littleton .30 .12
❑ 160 Lyle Overbay .30 .12
❑ 161 Aaron Hill .30 .12
❑ 162 John McDonald .30 .12
❑ 163 Vernon Wells .30 .12
❑ 164 Frank Catalanotto .30 .12
❑ 165 Roy Halladay .30 .12
❑ 166 B.J. Ryan .30 .12
❑ 167 Casey Janssen .30 .12
❑ 168 Stephen Drew .50 .20
❑ 169 Conor Jackson .30 .12
❑ 170 Chad Tracy .30 .12
❑ 171 Johnny Estrada .30 .12
❑ 172 Eric Byrnes .30 .12
❑ 173 Carlos Quentin .30 .12
❑ 174 Brandon Webb .30 .12
❑ 175 Jorge Julio .30 .12
❑ 176 Luis Vizcaino .30 .12
❑ 177 Chipper Jones .75 .30
❑ 178 Adam LaRoche .30 .12
❑ 179 Brian McCann .30 .12
❑ 180 Ryan Langerhans .30 .12
❑ 181 Matt Diaz .30 .12
❑ 182 John Smoltz .50 .20
❑ 183 Oscar Villarreal .30 .12
❑ 184 Chad Paronto .30 .12
❑ 185 Derrek Lee .30 .12
❑ 186 Ryan Theriot .30 .12
❑ 187 Ronny Cedeno .30 .12
❑ 188 Juan Pierre .30 .12
❑ 189 Matt Murton .30 .12
❑ 190 Carlos Zambrano .30 .12
❑ 191 Mark Prior .50 .20
❑ 192 Ryan Dempster .30 .12
❑ 193 Ryan O'Malley .30 .12
❑ 194 Brandon Phillips .30 .12
❑ 195 Rich Aurilia .30 .12
❑ 196 Ken Griffey Jr. 1.25 .50
❑ 197 Ryan Freel .30 .12
❑ 198 Aaron Harang .30 .12
❑ 199 Brandon Claussen .30 .12
❑ 200 David Weathers .30 .12
❑ 201 Eric Milton .30 .12
❑ 202 Kazuo Matsui .30 .12
❑ 203 Jamey Carroll .30 .12
❑ 204 Matt Holliday .75 .30
❑ 205 Brad Hawpe .30 .12
❑ 206 Jason Jennings .30 .12
❑ 207 Josh Fogg .30 .12
❑ 208 Aaron Cook .30 .12
❑ 209 Miguel Cabrera .50 .20
❑ 210 Dan Uggla .50 .20
❑ 211 Hanley Ramirez .50 .20
❑ 212 Jeremy Hermida .30 .12
❑ 213 Cody Ross .30 .12
❑ 214 Josh Willingham .30 .12
❑ 215 Anibal Sanchez .30 .12
❑ 216 Jose Garcia RC .40 .15
❑ 217 Taylor Tankersley .30 .12
❑ 218 Lance Berkman .30 .12
❑ 219 Craig Biggio .50 .20
❑ 220 Brad Ausmus .30 .12
❑ 221 Willy Taveras .30 .12
❑ 222 Chris Burke .30 .12
❑ 223 Roger Clemens 1.25 .50
❑ 224 Brandon Backe .30 .12
❑ 225 Brad Lidge .30 .12
❑ 226 Dan Wheeler .30 .12
❑ 227 Wilson Betemit .30 .12
❑ 228 Julio Lugo .30 .12
❑ 229 Russell Martin .30 .12
❑ 230 Kenny Lofton .30 .12
❑ 231 Brad Penny .30 .12
❑ 232 Chad Billingsley .30 .12
❑ 233 Greg Maddux 1.25 .50
❑ 234 Jonathan Broxton .30 .12
❑ 235 Rickie Weeks .30 .12
❑ 236 Bill Hall .30 .12
❑ 237 Tony Gwynn Jr. .30 .12
❑ 238 Corey Hart .30 .12
❑ 239 Laynce Nix .30 .12
❑ 240 Ben Sheets .30 .12
❑ 241 Dave Bush .30 .12
❑ 242 Francisco Cordero .30 .12
❑ 243 Jose Reyes .30 .12
❑ 244 Carlos Delgado .30 .12
❑ 245 Paul Lo Duca .30 .12
❑ 246 Carlos Beltran .30 .12
❑ 247 Lastings Milledge .50 .20
❑ 248 Pedro Martinez .50 .20
❑ 249 John Maine .30 .12
❑ 250 Steve Trachsel .30 .12
❑ 251 Ryan Howard 1.25 .50
❑ 252 Jimmy Rollins .30 .12
❑ 253 Chris Coste .30 .12
❑ 254 Jeff Conine .30 .12
❑ 255 David Dellucci .30 .12
❑ 256 Cole Hamels .50 .20
❑ 257 Ryan Madson .30 .12
❑ 258 Brett Myers .30 .12
❑ 259 Freddy Sanchez .30 .12
❑ 260 Xavier Nady .30 .12
❑ 261 Jose Castillo .30 .12
❑ 262 Jason Bay .30 .12
❑ 263 Jose Bautista .30 .12
❑ 264 Ronny Paulino .30 .12
❑ 265 Zach Duke .30 .12
❑ 266 Shane Youman RC .40 .15
❑ 267 Matt Capps .30 .12
❑ 268 Adrian Gonzalez .30 .12
❑ 269 Josh Barfield .30 .12
❑ 270 Mike Piazza .75 .30
❑ 271 Dave Roberts .30 .12
❑ 272 Geoff Blum .30 .12
❑ 273 Chris Young .30 .12
❑ 274 Woody Williams .30 .12
❑ 275 Cla Meredith .30 .12
❑ 276 Trevor Hoffman .30 .12
❑ 277 Ray Durham .30 .12
❑ 278 Mark Sweeney .30 .12
❑ 279 Eliezer Alfonzo .30 .12
❑ 280 Todd Linden .30 .12
❑ 281 Jason Schmidt .30 .12
❑ 282 Noah Lowry .30 .12
❑ 283 Brad Hennessey .30 .12
❑ 284 Jonathan Sanchez .30 .12
❑ 285 Albert Pujols 1.50 .60
❑ 286 David Eckstein .30 .12
❑ 287 Jim Edmonds .50 .20
❑ 288 Chris Duncan .30 .12
❑ 289 Juan Encarnacion .30 .12
❑ 290 Jeff Suppan .30 .12

❑ 291 Jeff Weaver .30 .12
❑ 292 Braden Looper .30 .12
❑ 293 Ryan Zimmerman .75 .30
❑ 294 Nick Johnson .30 .12
❑ 295 Alfonso Soriano .30 .12
❑ 296 Austin Kearns .30 .12
❑ 297 Alex Escobar .30 .12
❑ 298 Tony Armas .30 .12
❑ 299 Chad Cordero .30 .12
❑ 300 Jon Rauch .30 .12

2008 Upper Deck First Edition

❑ COMPLETE SET (300) 50.00 20.00
❑ COMMON CARD (1-250) .30 .12
❑ COMMON ROOKIE (250-300) .50 .20
❑ 1 Joe Saunders .30 .12
❑ 2 Kelvim Escobar .30 .12
❑ 3 Jered Weaver .30 .12
❑ 4 Justin Speier .30 .12
❑ 5 Scot Shields .30 .12
❑ 6 Orlando Cabrera .30 .12
❑ 7 Casey Kotchman .30 .12
❑ 8 Vladimir Guerrero .75 .30
❑ 9 Garret Anderson .30 .12
❑ 10 Roy Oswalt .30 .12
❑ 11 Wandy Rodriguez .30 .12
❑ 12 Woody Williams .30 .12
❑ 13 Chad Qualls .30 .12
❑ 14 Mark Loretta .30 .12
❑ 15 Brad Ausmus .30 .12
❑ 16 Carlos Lee .30 .12
❑ 17 Hunter Pence .75 .30
❑ 18 Dan Haren .30 .12
❑ 19 Lenny DiNardo .30 .12
❑ 20 Chad Gaudin .30 .12
❑ 21 Huston Street .30 .12
❑ 22 Andrew Brown .30 .12
❑ 23 Mike Piazza .75 .30
❑ 24 Mark Ellis .30 .12
❑ 25 Shannon Stewart .30 .12
❑ 26 Shaun Marcum .30 .12
❑ 27 A.J. Burnett .30 .12
❑ 28 Casey Janssen .30 .12
❑ 29 Jeremy Accardo .30 .12
❑ 30 Aaron Hill .30 .12
❑ 31 Frank Thomas .75 .30
❑ 32 Matt Stairs .30 .12
❑ 33 Vernon Wells .30 .12
❑ 34 Tim Hudson .30 .12
❑ 35 Buddy Carlyle .30 .12
❑ 36 Rafael Soriano .30 .12
❑ 37 Brian McCann .50 .20
❑ 38 Edgar Renteria .30 .12
❑ 39 Mark Teixeira .50 .20
❑ 40 Willie Harris .30 .12
❑ 41 Andruw Jones .30 .12
❑ 42 Ben Sheets .50 .20
❑ 43 Dave Bush .30 .12
❑ 44 Yovani Gallardo .30 .12
❑ 45 Matt Wise .30 .12
❑ 46 Johnny Estrada .30 .12
❑ 47 Prince Fielder .75 .30
❑ 48 J.J. Hardy .30 .12
❑ 49 Corey Hart .30 .12
❑ 50 Adam Wainwright .30 .12
❑ 51 Joel Pineiro .30 .12
❑ 52 Jason Isringhausen .30 .12
❑ 53 Troy Percival .30 .12
❑ 54 Albert Pujols 1.25 .50
❑ 55 David Eckstein .30 .12
❑ 56 Jim Edmonds .50 .20
❑ 57 Rick Ankiel .30 .12
❑ 58 Ted Lilly .30 .12
❑ 59 Rich Hill .30 .12
❑ 60 Jason Marquis .30 .12
❑ 61 Carlos Marmol .30 .12
❑ 62 Jason Kendall .30 .12
❑ 63 Aramis Ramirez .30 .12
❑ 64 Ryan Theriot .30 .12
❑ 65 Alfonso Soriano .50 .20
❑ 66 Jacque Jones .30 .12
❑ 67 James Shields .30 .12
❑ 68 Andy Sonnanstine .30 .12
❑ 69 Scott Dohmann .30 .12
❑ 70 Dioner Navarro .30 .12
❑ 71 B.J. Upton .50 .20
❑ 72 Carlos Pena .30 .12
❑ 73 Brendan Harris .30 .12
❑ 74 Josh Wilson .30 .12
❑ 75 Brandon Webb .30 .12
❑ 76 Micah Owings .30 .12
❑ 77 Doug Slaten .30 .12
❑ 78 Brandon Lyon .30 .12
❑ 79 Miguel Montero .30 .12
❑ 80 Stephen Drew .30 .12
❑ 81 Mark Reynolds .30 .12
❑ 82 Chris B. Young .30 .12
❑ 83 Chad Billingsley .30 .12
❑ 84 Derek Lowe .30 .12
❑ 85 Mark Hendrickson .30 .12
❑ 86 Takashi Saito .30 .12
❑ 87 Russell Martin .30 .12
❑ 88 Jeff Kent .30 .12
❑ 89 Matt Kemp .30 .12
❑ 90 Juan Pierre .30 .12
❑ 91 Matt Cain .30 .12
❑ 92 Barry Zito .30 .12
❑ 93 Kevin Correia .30 .12
❑ 94 Jack Taschner .30 .12
❑ 95 Bengie Molina .30 .12
❑ 96 Omar Vizquel .30 .12
❑ 97 Dave Roberts .30 .12
❑ 98 Rajai Davis .30 .12
❑ 99 Fausto Carmona .30 .12
❑ 100 Jake Westbrook .30 .12
❑ 101 Rafael Betancourt .30 .12
❑ 102 Joe Borowski .30 .12
❑ 103 Victor Martinez .30 .12
❑ 104 Travis Hafner .30 .12
❑ 105 Ryan Garko .30 .12
❑ 106 Kenny Lofton .30 .12
❑ 107 Franklin Gutierrez .30 .12
❑ 108 Felix Hernandez .50 .20
❑ 109 J.J. Putz .30 .12
❑ 110 Brandon Morrow .30 .12
❑ 111 Kenji Johjima .30 .12
❑ 112 Jose Vidro .30 .12
❑ 113 Richie Sexson .30 .12
❑ 114 Ichiro Suzuki 1.25 .50
❑ 115 Ben Broussard .30 .12
❑ 116 Sergio Mitre .30 .12
❑ 117 Scott Olsen .30 .12
❑ 118 Rick Vanden Hurk .30 .12
❑ 119 Lee Gardner .30 .12
❑ 120 Miguel Olivo .30 .12
❑ 121 Hanley Ramirez .75 .30
❑ 122 Mike Jacobs .30 .12
❑ 123 Josh Willingham .30 .12
❑ 124 John Maine .30 .12
❑ 125 Tom Glavine .50 .20
❑ 126 Billy Wagner .30 .12
❑ 127 Aaron Heilman .30 .12
❑ 128 David Wright 1.00 .40
❑ 129 Luis Castillo .30 .12
❑ 130 Shawn Green .30 .12
❑ 131 Damion Easley .30 .12
❑ 132 Carlos Delgado .30 .12
❑ 133 Shawn Hill .30 .12
❑ 134 John Lannan .30 .12
❑ 135 Chad Cordero .30 .12
❑ 136 Jon Rauch .30 .12
❑ 137 Jesus Flores .30 .12
❑ 138 Dmitri Young .30 .12
❑ 139 Cristian Guzman .30 .12
❑ 140 Austin Kearns .30 .12
❑ 141 Nook Logan .30 .12
❑ 142 Erik Bedard .30 .12
❑ 143 Daniel Cabrera .30 .12
❑ 144 Chris Ray .30 .12
❑ 145 Chad Bradford .30 .12
❑ 146 Ramon Hernandez .30 .12
❑ 147 Miguel Tejada .30 .12
❑ 148 Freddie Bynum .30 .12
❑ 149 Corey Patterson .30 .12
❑ 150 Chris Young .30 .12
❑ 151 Greg Maddux 1.00 .40
❑ 152 Kevin Cameron .30 .12
❑ 153 Doug Brocail .30 .12
❑ 154 Kevin Kouzmanoff .30 .12
❑ 155 Geoff Blum .30 .12
❑ 156 Milton Bradley .30 .12
❑ 157 Brian Giles .30 .12
❑ 158 Jamie Moyer .30 .12
❑ 159 Kyle Kendrick .30 .12
❑ 160 Kyle Lohse .30 .12
❑ 161 Antonio Alfonseca .30 .12
❑ 162 Chris Coste .30 .12
❑ 163 Chase Utley .75 .30
❑ 164 Tadahito Iguchi .30 .12
❑ 165 Aaron Rowand .30 .12
❑ 166 Shane Victorino .30 .12
❑ 167 Ian Snell .30 .12
❑ 168 Shane Youman .30 .12
❑ 169 Shawn Chacon .30 .12
❑ 170 Ronny Paulino .30 .12
❑ 171 Jack Wilson .30 .12
❑ 172 Adam LaRoche .30 .12
❑ 173 Ryan Doumit .30 .12
❑ 174 Xavier Nady .30 .12
❑ 175 Kevin Millwood .30 .12
❑ 176 Brandon McCarthy .30 .12
❑ 177 Wes Littleton .30 .12
❑ 178 Mike Wood .30 .12
❑ 179 Hank Blalock .30 .12
❑ 180 Ian Kinsler .50 .20
❑ 181 Marlon Byrd .30 .12
❑ 182 Brad Wilkerson .30 .12
❑ 183 Tim Wakefield .30 .12
❑ 184 Daisuke Matsuzaka 1.50 .60
❑ 185 Julian Tavarez .30 .12
❑ 186 Hideki Okajima .50 .20
❑ 187 Doug Mirabelli .30 .12
❑ 188 Dustin Pedroia .50 .20
❑ 189 Mike Lowell .30 .12
❑ 190 Manny Ramirez .75 .30
❑ 191 Coco Crisp .30 .12
❑ 192 Bronson Arroyo .30 .12
❑ 193 Matt Belisle .30 .12
❑ 194 Jared Burton .30 .12
❑ 195 Mike Gosling .30 .12
❑ 196 David Ross .30 .12
❑ 197 Edwin Encarnacion .30 .12
❑ 198 Ken Griffey Jr. 1.25 .50
❑ 199 Adam Dunn .30 .12
❑ 200 Jeff Francis .30 .12
❑ 201 Jason Hirsh .30 .12
❑ 202 Manny Corpas .30 .12
❑ 203 Jeremy Affeldt .30 .12
❑ 204 Yorvit Torrealba .30 .12
❑ 205 Todd Helton .50 .20

Card		
❑ 206 Kazuo Matsui	.30	.12
❑ 207 Brad Hawpe	.30	.12
❑ 208 Willy Taveras	.30	.12
❑ 209 Brian Bannister	.30	.12
❑ 210 Zack Greinke	.30	.12
❑ 211 Kyle Davies	.30	.12
❑ 212 David Riske	.30	.12
❑ 213 John Buck	.30	.12
❑ 214 Mark Grudzielanek	.30	.12
❑ 215 Billy Butler	.30	.12
❑ 216 David DeJesus	.30	.12
❑ 217 Jeremy Bonderman	.30	.12
❑ 218 Chad Durbin	.30	.12
❑ 219 Andrew Miller	.50	.20
❑ 220 Todd Jones	.30	.12
❑ 221 Brandon Inge	.30	.12
❑ 222 Placido Polanco	.30	.12
❑ 223 Gary Sheffield	.30	.12
❑ 224 Maggio Ordonez	.50	.20
❑ 225 Matt Garza	.30	.12
❑ 226 Boof Bonser	.30	.12
❑ 227 Joe Nathan	.30	.12
❑ 228 Dennys Reyes	.30	.12
❑ 229 Joe Mauer	.50	.20
❑ 230 Michael Cuddyer	.30	.12
❑ 231 Jason Bartlett	.30	.12
❑ 232 Torii Hunter	.30	.12
❑ 233 Jason Tyner	.30	.12
❑ 234 Mark Buehrle	.30	.12
❑ 235 Jon Garland	.30	.12
❑ 236 Jose Contreras	.30	.12
❑ 237 Matt Thornton	.30	.12
❑ 238 Juan Uribe	.30	.12
❑ 239 Jim Thome	.50	.20
❑ 240 Jerry Owens	.30	.12
❑ 241 Jermaine Dye	.30	.12
❑ 242 Andy Pettitte	.50	.20
❑ 243 Phil Hughes	1.00	.40
❑ 244 Mike Mussina	.30	.12
❑ 245 Joba Chamberlain	3.00	1.25
❑ 246 Brian Bruney	.30	.12
❑ 247 Jorge Posada	.50	.20
❑ 248 Derek Jeter	2.00	.75
❑ 249 Jason Giambi	.50	.20
❑ 250 Johnny Damon	.50	.20
❑ 251 Jonathan Albaladejo RC	.75	.30
❑ 252 Josh Anderson (RC)	.50	.20
❑ 253 Wladimir Balentien (RC)	.50	.20
❑ 254 Josh Banks (RC)	.50	.20
❑ 255 Daric Barton (RC)	.50	.20
❑ 256 Jerry Blevins RC	.75	.30
❑ 257 Emilio Bonifacio RC	.75	.30
❑ 258 Lance Broadway (RC)	.50	.20
❑ 259 Clay Buchholz (RC)	1.25	.50
❑ 260 Billy Buckner (RC)	.50	.20
❑ 261 Jeff Clement (RC)	.50	.20
❑ 262 Willie Collazo RC	.75	.30
❑ 263 Ross Detwiler RC	1.25	.50
❑ 264 Sam Fuld (RC)	.50	.20
❑ 265 Harvey Garcia (RC)	.50	.20
❑ 266 Alberto Gonzalez RC	.75	.30
❑ 267 Ryan Hanigan RC	.75	.30
❑ 268 Kevin Hart (RC)	.50	.20
❑ 269 Luke Hochevar RC	1.50	.60
❑ 270 Chin-Lung Hu (RC)	.75	.30
❑ 271 Rob Johnson (RC)	.50	.20
❑ 272 Radhames Liz RC	.75	.30
❑ 273 Ian Kennedy RC	1.50	.60
❑ 274 Joe Koshansky (RC)	.50	.20
❑ 275 Donny Lucy (RC)	.50	.20
❑ 276 Justin Maxwell RC	.75	.30
❑ 277 Jonathan Meloan RC	.75	.30
❑ 278 Luis Mendoza (RC)	.50	.20
❑ 279 Jose Morales (RC)	.50	.20
❑ 280 Nyjer Morgan (RC)	.50	.20
❑ 281 Carlos Muniz RC	.75	.30
❑ 282 Bill Murphy (RC)	.50	.20
❑ 283 Josh Newman RC	.75	.30
❑ 284 Ross Ohlendorf RC	.75	.30
❑ 285 Troy Patton (RC)	.50	.20
❑ 286 Felipe Paulino RC	.75	.30
❑ 287 Steve Pearce RC	.75	.30
❑ 288 Heath Phillips RC	.75	.30
❑ 289 Justin Ruggiano RC	.75	.30
❑ 290 Clint Sammons (RC)	.50	.20
❑ 291 Bronson Sardinha (RC)	.50	.20
❑ 292 Chris Seddon (RC)	.50	.20
❑ 293 Seth Smith (RC)	.50	.20
❑ 294 Mitch Stetter RC	.75	.30
❑ 295 Dave Davidson RC	.75	.30
❑ 296 Rich Thompson RC	.50	.20
❑ 297 J.R. Towles RC	1.25	.50
❑ 298 Eugenio Velez RC	.50	.20
❑ 299 Joey Votto (RC)	.75	.30
❑ 300 Bill White RC	.50	.20

2006 Upper Deck First Pitch

Card		
❑ COMPLETE SET (220)	50.00	20.00
❑ 1 Chad Tracy	.30	.10
❑ 2 Conor Jackson	.30	.10
❑ 3 Craig Counsell	.30	.10
❑ 4 Javier Vazquez	.30	.10
❑ 5 Luis Gonzalez	.30	.10
❑ 6 Shawn Green	.30	.10
❑ 7 Troy Glaus	.30	.10
❑ 8 Joey Devine RC	.50	.20
❑ 9 Andruw Jones	.50	.20
❑ 10 Chipper Jones	.75	.30
❑ 11 John Smoltz	.50	.20
❑ 12 Marcus Giles	.30	.10
❑ 13 Jeff Francoeur	.75	.30
❑ 14 Tim Hudson	.30	.10
❑ 15 Brian Roberts	.30	.10
❑ 16 Erik Bedard	.30	.10
❑ 17 Javy Lopez	.30	.10
❑ 18 Melvin Mora	.30	.10
❑ 19 Miguel Tejada	.30	.10
❑ 20 Alejandro Freire RC	.50	.20
❑ 21 Sammy Sosa	.75	.30
❑ 22 Craig Hansen RC	3.00	1.25
❑ 23 Curt Schilling	.50	.20
❑ 24 David Ortiz	.75	.30
❑ 25 Edgar Renteria	.30	.10
❑ 26 Johnny Damon	.50	.20
❑ 27 Manny Ramirez	.50	.20
❑ 28 Matt Clement	.30	.10
❑ 29 Trot Nixon	.30	.10
❑ 30 Aramis Ramirez	.30	.10
❑ 31 Carlos Zambrano	.30	.10
❑ 32 Derrek Lee	.50	.20
❑ 33 Greg Maddux	1.25	.50
❑ 34 Jeromy Burnitz	.30	.10
❑ 35 Kerry Wood	.30	.10
❑ 36 Mark Prior	.50	.20
❑ 37 Nomar Garciaparra	.75	.30
❑ 38 Aaron Rowand	.30	.10
❑ 39 Chris DeMaria RC	.50	.20
❑ 40 Jon Garland	.30	.10
❑ 41 Mark Buehrle	.30	.10
❑ 42 Paul Konerko	.30	.10
❑ 43 Scott Podsednik	.30	.10
❑ 44 Tadahito Iguchi	.30	.10
❑ 45 Adam Dunn	.30	.10
❑ 46 Austin Kearns	.30	.10
❑ 47 Felipe Lopez	.30	.10
❑ 48 Ken Griffey Jr.	1.25	.50
❑ 49 Ryan Freel	.30	.10
❑ 50 Sean Casey	.30	.10
❑ 51 Wily Mo Pena	.30	.10
❑ 52 C.C. Sabathia	.30	.10
❑ 53 Cliff Lee	.30	.10
❑ 54 Coco Crisp	.30	.10
❑ 55 Grady Sizemore	.50	.20
❑ 56 Jake Westbrook	.30	.10
❑ 57 Travis Hafner	.30	.10
❑ 58 Victor Martinez	.30	.10
❑ 59 Aaron Miles	.30	.10
❑ 60 Clint Barmes	.30	.10
❑ 61 Garrett Atkins	.30	.10
❑ 62 Jeff Baker	.30	.10
❑ 63 Jeff Francis	.30	.10
❑ 64 Matt Holliday	.40	.15
❑ 65 Todd Helton	.50	.20
❑ 66 Carlos Guillen	.30	.10
❑ 67 Chris Shelton	.30	.10
❑ 68 Dmitri Young	.30	.10
❑ 69 Ivan Rodriguez	.50	.20
❑ 70 Jeremy Bonderman	.30	.10
❑ 71 Magglio Ordonez	.30	.10
❑ 72 Placido Polanco	.30	.10
❑ 73 A.J. Burnett	.30	.10
❑ 74 Carlos Delgado	.30	.10
❑ 75 Dontrelle Willis	.30	.10
❑ 76 Josh Beckett	.30	.10
❑ 77 Juan Pierre	.30	.10
❑ 78 Ryan Jorgensen RC	.50	.20
❑ 79 Miguel Cabrera	.50	.20
❑ 80 Robert Andino RC	.50	.20
❑ 81 Andy Pettitte	.50	.20
❑ 82 Brad Lidge	.30	.10
❑ 83 Craig Biggio	.50	.20
❑ 84 Jeff Bagwell	.50	.20
❑ 85 Lance Berkman	.30	.10
❑ 86 Morgan Ensberg	.30	.10
❑ 87 Roger Clemens	1.50	.60
❑ 88 Roy Oswalt	.30	.10
❑ 89 Angel Berroa	.30	.10
❑ 90 David DeJesus	.30	.10
❑ 91 Steve Stemle RC	.30	.10
❑ 92 Jonah Bayliss RC	.30	.10
❑ 93 Mike Sweeney	.30	.10
❑ 94 Ryan Theriot RC	.50	.20
❑ 95 Zack Greinke	.30	.10
❑ 96 Brad Penny	.30	.10
❑ 97 Cesar Izturis	.30	.10
❑ 98 Brian Myrow RC	.30	.10
❑ 99 Eric Gagne	.30	.10
❑ 100 J.D. Drew	.30	.10
❑ 101 Jeff Kent	.30	.10
❑ 102 Milton Bradley	.30	.10
❑ 103 Odalis Perez	.30	.10
❑ 104 Ben Sheets	.30	.10
❑ 105 Brady Clark	.30	.10
❑ 106 Carlos Lee	.30	.10
❑ 107 Geoff Jenkins	.30	.10
❑ 108 Lyle Overbay	.30	.10
❑ 109 Prince Fielder	.75	.30
❑ 110 Rickie Weeks	.30	.10
❑ 111 Jacque Jones	.30	.10
❑ 112 Joe Mauer	.75	.30
❑ 113 Joe Nathan	.30	.10
❑ 114 Johan Santana	.75	.30
❑ 115 Justin Morneau	.30	.10
❑ 116 Chris Heintz RC	.30	.10
❑ 117 Torii Hunter	.30	.10
❑ 118 Carlos Beltran	.30	.10
❑ 119 Cliff Floyd	.30	.10
❑ 120 David Wright	.75	.30
❑ 121 Jose Reyes	.30	.10
❑ 122 Mike Cameron	.30	.10

❑ 123 Mike Piazza .75 .30
❑ 124 Pedro Martinez .50 .20
❑ 125 Tom Glavine .50 .20
❑ 126 Alex Rodriguez 1.25 .50
❑ 127 Derek Jeter 2.00 .75
❑ 128 Gary Sheffield .30 .10
❑ 129 Hideki Matsui .75 .30
❑ 130 Jason Giambi .30 .10
❑ 131 Jorge Posada .50 .20
❑ 132 Mariano Rivera .75 .30
❑ 133 Mike Mussina .50 .20
❑ 134 Randy Johnson .75 .30
❑ 135 Barry Zito .30 .10
❑ 136 Bobby Crosby .30 .10
❑ 137 Danny Haren .30 .10
❑ 138 Eric Chavez .30 .10
❑ 139 Huston Street .30 .10
❑ 140 Ron Flores RC .50 .20
❑ 141 Nick Swisher .30 .10
❑ 142 Rich Harden .30 .10
❑ 143 Bobby Abreu .30 .10
❑ 144 Danny Sandoval RC .50 .20
❑ 145 Chase Utley .50 .20
❑ 146 Jim Thome .50 .20
❑ 147 Jimmy Rollins .30 .10
❑ 148 Pat Burrell .30 .10
❑ 149 Ryan Howard 1.25 .50
❑ 150 Craig Wilson .30 .10
❑ 151 Jack Wilson .30 .10
❑ 152 Jason Bay .30 .10
❑ 153 Matt Lawton .30 .10
❑ 154 Oliver Perez .30 .10
❑ 155 Rob Mackowiak .30 .10
❑ 156 Zach Duke .50 .20
❑ 157 Brian Giles .30 .10
❑ 158 Jake Peavy .30 .10
❑ 159 Craig Breslow RC .50 .20
❑ 160 Khalil Greene .50 .20
❑ 161 Mark Loretta .30 .10
❑ 162 Ryan Klesko .30 .10
❑ 163 Trevor Hoffman .30 .10
❑ 164 J.T. Snow .30 .10
❑ 165 Jason Schmidt .30 .10
❑ 166 Marquis Grissom .30 .10
❑ 167 Moises Alou .30 .10
❑ 168 Omar Vizquel .50 .20
❑ 169 Pedro Feliz .30 .10
❑ 170 Jeremy Accardo RC .50 .20
❑ 171 Adrian Beltre .30 .10
❑ 172 Ichiro Suzuki 1.25 .50
❑ 173 Felix Hernandez .50 .20
❑ 174 Jeff Harris RC .30 .10
❑ 175 Randy Winn .30 .10
❑ 176 Raul Ibanez .30 .10
❑ 177 Richie Sexson .30 .10
❑ 178 Albert Pujols 1.50 .60
❑ 179 Chris Carpenter .30 .10
❑ 180 David Eckstein .30 .10
❑ 181 Jim Edmonds .30 .10
❑ 182 Larry Walker .50 .20
❑ 183 Matt Morris .30 .10
❑ 184 Reggie Sanders .30 .10
❑ 185 Scott Rolen .50 .20
❑ 186 Aubrey Huff .30 .10
❑ 187 Jonny Gomes .30 .10
❑ 188 Carl Crawford .30 .10
❑ 189 Tim Corcoran RC .50 .20
❑ 190 Julio Lugo .30 .10
❑ 191 Rocco Baldelli .30 .10
❑ 192 Scott Kazmir .30 .10
❑ 193 Alfonso Soriano .30 .10
❑ 194 Hank Blalock .30 .10
❑ 195 Kenny Rogers .30 .10
❑ 196 Scott Feldman RC .30 .10
❑ 197 Laynce Nix .30 .10
❑ 198 Mark Teixeira .50 .20
❑ 199 Michael Young .30 .10
❑ 200 Aaron Hill .30 .10
❑ 201 Alex Rios .30 .10
❑ 202 Eric Hinske .30 .10
❑ 203 Gustavo Chacin .30 .10
❑ 204 Roy Halladay .30 .10
❑ 205 Shea Hillenbrand .30 .10
❑ 206 Vernon Wells .30 .10
❑ 207 Brad Wilkerson .30 .10
❑ 208 Chad Cordero .30 .10
❑ 209 Jose Guillen .30 .10
❑ 210 Jose Vidro .30 .10
❑ 211 Livan Hernandez .30 .10
❑ 212 Preston Wilson .30 .10
❑ 213 Jason Bergmann RC .30 .10
❑ 214 Bartolo Colon .30 .10
❑ 215 Chone Figgins .30 .10
❑ 216 Darin Erstad .30 .10
❑ 217 Francisco Rodriguez .30 .10
❑ 218 Garret Anderson .30 .10
❑ 219 Steve Finley .30 .10
❑ 220 Vladimir Guerrero .75 .30

2006 Upper Deck Future Stars

❑ COMP.SET w/o AU's (75) 25.00 10.00
❑ COMMON CARD (1-75) .40 .15
❑ COMMON AU RC (76-159) 8.00 3.00
❑ FIVE AU RC PER BOX ON AVERAGE
❑ NO SP PRICING DUE TO SCARCITY
❑ PRINTING PLATE ODDS 1:2 CASES
❑ PLATE PRINT RUN 1 SET PER COLOR
❑ BLACK-CYAN-MAGENTA-YELLOW ISSUED
❑ NO PLATE PRICING DUE TO SCARCITY
❑ 1 Miguel Tejada .40 .15
❑ 2 Brian Roberts .40 .15
❑ 3 Brandon Webb .40 .15
❑ 4 Luis Gonzalez .40 .15
❑ 5 Andruw Jones .60 .25
❑ 6 Chipper Jones 1.00 .40
❑ 7 John Smoltz .60 .25
❑ 8 Curt Schilling .60 .25
❑ 9 Josh Beckett .40 .15
❑ 10 David Ortiz 1.00 .40
❑ 11 Manny Ramirez .60 .25
❑ 12 Jim Thome .60 .25
❑ 13 Paul Konerko .40 .15
❑ 14 Jermaine Dye .40 .15
❑ 15 Derrek Lee .40 .15
❑ 16 Greg Maddux 1.50 .60
❑ 17 Ken Griffey Jr. 1.50 .60
❑ 18 Adam Dunn .40 .15
❑ 19 Felipe Lopez .40 .15
❑ 20 Travis Hafner .40 .15
❑ 21 Victor Martinez .40 .15
❑ 22 Grady Sizemore .60 .25
❑ 23 Todd Helton .60 .25
❑ 24 Matt Holliday 1.00 .40
❑ 25 Jeremy Bonderman .40 .15
❑ 26 Ivan Rodriguez .60 .25
❑ 27 Miguel Cabrera .60 .25
❑ 28 Dontrelle Willis .40 .15
❑ 29 Roger Clemens 2.00 .75
❑ 30 Roy Oswalt .40 .15
❑ 31 Lance Berkman .40 .15
❑ 32 Reggie Sanders .40 .15
❑ 33 Vladimir Guerrero 1.00 .40
❑ 34 Chone Figgins .40 .15
❑ 35 Jeff Kent .40 .15
❑ 36 Eric Gagne .40 .15
❑ 37 Carlos Lee .40 .15
❑ 38 Rickie Weeks .40 .15
❑ 39 Johan Santana .60 .25
❑ 40 Torii Hunter .40 .15
❑ 41 Alex Rodriguez 1.50 .60
❑ 42 Derek Jeter 2.50 1.00
❑ 43 Randy Johnson 1.00 .40
❑ 44 Hideki Matsui 1.00 .40
❑ 45 Johnny Damon .60 .25
❑ 46 Pedro Martinez .60 .25
❑ 47 David Wright 1.50 .60
❑ 48 Carlos Beltran .40 .15
❑ 49 Rich Harden .40 .15
❑ 50 Eric Chavez .40 .15
❑ 51 Huston Street .40 .15
❑ 52 Ryan Howard 1.50 .60
❑ 53 Bobby Abreu .40 .15
❑ 54 Chase Utley 1.00 .40
❑ 55 Jason Bay .40 .15
❑ 56 Jake Peavy .40 .15
❑ 57 Brian Giles .40 .15
❑ 58 Trevor Hoffman .40 .15
❑ 59 Jason Schmidt .40 .15
❑ 60 Randy Winn .40 .15
❑ 61 Kenji Johjima RC 2.00 .75
❑ 62 Ichiro Suzuki 1.50 .60
❑ 63 Felix Hernandez .60 .25
❑ 64 Albert Pujols 2.00 .75
❑ 65 Chris Carpenter .40 .15
❑ 66 Jim Edmonds .60 .25
❑ 67 Carl Crawford .40 .15
❑ 68 Scott Kazmir .60 .25
❑ 69 Jonny Gomes .40 .15
❑ 70 Mark Teixeira .60 .25
❑ 71 Michael Young .40 .15
❑ 72 Vernon Wells .40 .15
❑ 73 Roy Halladay .40 .15
❑ 74 Nick Johnson .40 .15
❑ 75 Alfonso Soriano .40 .15
❑ 76 A.Wainwright AU (RC) 20.00 8.00
❑ 77 A.Hernandez AU (RC) 8.00 3.00
❑ 78 A.Ethier AU SP (RC) 25.00 10.00
❑ 79 Colter Bean AU SP (RC) 10.00 4.00
❑ 80 Ben Johnson AU (RC) 8.00 3.00
❑ 81 Boof Bonser AU SP (RC) 12.00 5.00
❑ 82 Boone Logan AU RC 8.00 3.00
❑ 83 Brian Anderson AU (RC) 8.00 3.00
❑ 84 B.Bannister AU (RC) 12.00 5.00
❑ 85 C.Denorfia AU SP (RC) 10.00 4.00
❑ 86 C.Billingsley AU SP (RC) 20.00 8.00
❑ 87 Cody Ross AU (RC) 8.00 3.00
❑ 88 Cole Hamels AU SP (RC) 40.00 15.00
❑ 89 Conor Jackson AU (RC) 12.00 5.00
❑ 90 Dan Uggla AU SP (RC)
❑ 91 D.Gassner AU SP (RC) 8.00 3.00
❑ 92 Jordan Tata AU RC 8.00 3.00
❑ 93 Eric Reed AU (RC) 8.00 3.00
❑ 94 Fausto Carmona AU (RC) 25.00 10.00
❑ 95 Luis Figueroa AU SP RC
❑ 96 F.Liriano AU SP (RC) 25.00 10.00
❑ 97 Freddie Bynum AU (RC) 8.00 3.00
❑ 98 H.Ramirez AU SP (RC) 20.00 8.00
❑ 99 H.Kuo AU SP (RC) 60.00 30.00
❑ 100 Ian Kinsler AU (RC) 15.00 6.00
❑ 101 N.Cruz AU SP (RC) 8.00 3.00
❑ 102 Ruddy Lugo AU (RC) 8.00 3.00
❑ 103 J.Kubel AU SP (RC) 8.00 3.00
❑ 104 Jeff Harris AU RC 8.00 3.00
❑ 105 S.Ramirez AU (RC) 8.00 3.00
❑ 106 Jer.Weaver AU SP (RC) 50.00 20.00
❑ 107 J.Accardo AU SP RC 15.00 6.00
❑ 108 J.Willingham AU SP (RC) 8.00 3.00
❑ 109 J.Zumaya AU SP (RC) 25.00 10.00
❑ 110 Joey Devine AU RC 8.00 3.00

❑ 111 John Koronka AU (RC) 8.00 3.00
❑ 112 J.Papelbon AU (RC) 40.00 15.00
❑ 113 Jose Capellan AU (RC) 8.00 3.00
❑ 114 Josh Johnson AU (RC) 12.00 5.00
❑ 115 Josh Rupe AU SP (RC) 8.00 3.00
❑ 116 J.Hermida AU SP (RC) 8.00 3.00
❑ 117 Josh Wilson AU (RC) 8.00 3.00
❑ 118 J.Verlander AU SP (RC)
❑ 119 K.Shoppach AU (RC) 8.00 3.00
❑ 120 K.Morales AU (RC) 12.00 5.00
❑ 121 Sean Tracey AU (RC) 8.00 3.00
❑ 122 Macay McBride AU (RC) 8.00 3.00
❑ 123 M.Prado AU SP (RC)
❑ 124 Matt Cain AU (RC) 12.00 5.00
❑ 125 R.Martin AU (RC) 12.00 5.00
❑ 126 T.Hamulack AU SP (RC) 8.00 3.00
❑ 127 M.Jacobs AU (RC) 12.00 5.00
❑ 128 B.Hendrickson AU (RC) 8.00 3.00
❑ 129 Jack Taschner AU (RC) 8.00 3.00
❑ 130 N.McLouth AU (RC) 15.00 6.00
❑ 131 J.Sowers AU SP (RC) 20.00 8.00
❑ 132 Paul Maholm AU (RC) 8.00 3.00
❑ 133 S.Drew AU SP (RC)
❑ 134 Jason Bergmann AU RC 8.00 3.00
❑ 135 Rich Hill AU SP (RC) 30.00 12.50
❑ 136 M.Cabrera AU SP (RC)
❑ 137 Scott Dunn AU (RC) 8.00 3.00
❑ 138 R.Zimmerman AU (RC) 50.00 20.00
❑ 139 A.Sanchez AU (RC) 12.00 5.00
❑ 140 Sean Marshall AU (RC) 12.00 5.00
❑ 141 T.Saito AU SP RC
❑ 142 T.Buchholz AU (RC) 8.00 3.00
❑ 143 C.Quentin AU SP (RC) 15.00 6.00
❑ 144 Matt Garza AU (RC) 12.00 5.00
❑ 145 Wil Nieves AU (RC) 8.00 3.00
❑ 146 Jamie Shields AU RC 8.00 3.00
❑ 147 Jon Lester AU SP RC 30.00 12.50
❑ 148 Craig Hansen AU SP RC
❑ 149 Aaron Rakers AU (RC) 8.00 3.00
❑ 150 B.Livingston AU (RC) 8.00 3.00
❑ 151 B.Harris AU (RC) 8.00 3.00
❑ 152 Alay Soler AU SP RC 8.00 3.00
❑ 153 Chris Britton AU RC 8.00 3.00
❑ 154 H.Kendrick AU SP (RC) 40.00 15.00
❑ 155 J.Van Buren AU (RC) 8.00 3.00
❑ 156 C.Freeman AU SP (RC) 8.00 3.00
❑ 157 Matt Capps AU (RC) 8.00 3.00
❑ 158 Peter Moylan AU RC 8.00 3.00
❑ 159 Ty Taubenheim AU RC 12.00 5.00

2007 Upper Deck Future Stars

❑ COMP.SET w/o AU's (100) 25.00 10.00
❑ COMMON CARD (1-100) .40 .15
❑ COMMON AU RC (101-190) 8.00 3.00
❑ 101-190 ODDS 1:6 HOB,1:24 RET,1:350 WALMART
❑ EXCHANGE DEADLINE 9/5/2009
❑ 1 Brandon Webb .40 .15
❑ 2 Conor Jackson .40 .15
❑ 3 Stephen Drew .60 .25
❑ 4 Chipper Jones 1.00 .40
❑ 5 Andruw Jones .60 .25
❑ 6 Jeff Francoeur 1.00 .40
❑ 7 John Smoltz .60 .25
❑ 8 Miguel Tejada .40 .15
❑ 9 Nick Markakis .60 .25
❑ 10 Brian Roberts .40 .15
❑ 11 David Ortiz 1.00 .40
❑ 12 Manny Ramirez .60 .25
❑ 13 Josh Beckett .40 .15
❑ 14 Curt Schilling .60 .25
❑ 15 Derrek Lee .40 .15
❑ 16 Aramis Ramirez .40 .15
❑ 17 Carlos Zambrano .40 .15
❑ 18 Alfonso Soriano .40 .15
❑ 19 Jim Thome .60 .25
❑ 20 Paul Konerko .40 .15
❑ 21 Jon Garland .40 .15
❑ 22 Ken Griffey Jr. 1.50 .60
❑ 23 Adam Dunn .40 .15
❑ 24 Aaron Harang .40 .15
❑ 25 Travis Hafner .40 .15
❑ 26 Victor Martinez .40 .15
❑ 27 Grady Sizemore .60 .25
❑ 28 C.C. Sabathia .40 .15
❑ 29 Todd Helton .60 .25
❑ 30 Matt Holliday .50 .20
❑ 31 Garrett Atkins .40 .15
❑ 32 Ivan Rodriguez .60 .25
❑ 33 Magglio Ordonez .40 .15
❑ 34 Gary Sheffield .40 .15
❑ 35 Justin Verlander 1.00 .40
❑ 36 Miguel Cabrera .60 .25
❑ 37 Hanley Ramirez .60 .25
❑ 38 Dontrelle Willis .40 .15
❑ 39 Lance Berkman .40 .15
❑ 40 Roy Oswalt .40 .15
❑ 41 Carlos Lee .40 .15
❑ 42 Gil Meche .40 .15
❑ 43 Emil Brown .40 .15
❑ 44 Mark Teahen .40 .15
❑ 45 Vladimir Guerrero 1.00 .40
❑ 46 Jered Weaver .60 .25
❑ 47 Howie Kendrick .40 .15
❑ 48 Juan Pierre .40 .15
❑ 49 Nomar Garciaparra 1.00 .40
❑ 50 Rafael Furcal .40 .15
❑ 51 Jeff Kent .40 .15
❑ 52 Prince Fielder 1.00 .40
❑ 53 Ben Sheets .40 .15
❑ 54 Rickie Weeks .40 .15
❑ 55 Justin Morneau .40 .15
❑ 56 Joe Mauer .60 .25
❑ 57 Torii Hunter .40 .15
❑ 58 Johan Santana .60 .25
❑ 59 Jose Reyes 1.00 .40
❑ 60 David Wright 1.50 .60
❑ 61 Carlos Delgado .40 .15
❑ 62 Carlos Beltran .40 .15
❑ 63 Derek Jeter 2.50 1.00
❑ 64 Alex Rodriguez 1.50 .60
❑ 65 Johnny Damon .60 .25
❑ 66 Jason Giambi .40 .15
❑ 67 Bobby Abreu .40 .15
❑ 68 Mike Piazza 1.00 .40
❑ 69 Nick Swisher .40 .15
❑ 70 Eric Chavez .40 .15
❑ 71 Ryan Howard 1.50 .60
❑ 72 Chase Utley 1.00 .40
❑ 73 Jimmy Rollins .40 .15
❑ 74 Jason Bay .40 .15
❑ 75 Freddy Sanchez .40 .15
❑ 76 Zach Duke .40 .15
❑ 77 Greg Maddux 1.50 .60
❑ 78 Adrian Gonzalez .40 .15
❑ 79 Jake Peavy .40 .15
❑ 80 Ray Durham .40 .15
❑ 81 Barry Zito .40 .15
❑ 82 Matt Cain .60 .25
❑ 83 Ichiro Suzuki 1.50 .60
❑ 84 Felix Hernandez .60 .25
❑ 85 Richie Sexson .40 .15
❑ 86 Albert Pujols 2.00 .75
❑ 87 Scott Rolen .60 .25
❑ 88 Chris Carpenter .40 .15
❑ 89 Chris Duncan .40 .15
❑ 90 Carl Crawford .40 .15
❑ 91 Rocco Baldelli .40 .15
❑ 92 Scott Kazmir .60 .25
❑ 93 Michael Young .40 .15
❑ 94 Mark Teixeira .60 .25
❑ 95 Ian Kinsler .40 .15
❑ 96 Troy Glaus .40 .15
❑ 97 Vernon Wells .40 .15
❑ 98 Roy Halladay .40 .15
❑ 99 Ryan Zimmerman 1.00 .40
❑ 100 Nick Johnson .40 .15
❑ 101 Zack Segovia AU (RC) 8.00 3.00
❑ 102 Joaquin Arias AU (RC) 8.00 3.00
❑ 103 T.Tulowitzki AU SP (RC)
❑ 104 Travis Buck AU (RC) 10.00 4.00
❑ 105 Mike Schultz AU RC 8.00 3.00
❑ 106 Sean White AU SP RC
❑ 107 Sean Henn AU (RC) 8.00 3.00
❑ 108 Ryan Z. Braun AU RC 15.00 6.00
❑ 109 Rick Vanden Hurk AU RC 8.00 3.00
❑ 110 Carlos Gomez AU SP RC
❑ 111 Mike Rabelo AU RC 10.00 4.00
❑ 112 Felix Pie AU (RC) 10.00 4.00
❑ 113 Miguel Montero AU (RC) 10.00 4.00
❑ 114 Michael Bourn AU (RC) 10.00 4.00
❑ 115 M.Owings AU SP (RC) EXCH
❑ 116 Matt Lindstrom AU (RC) 8.00 3.00
❑ 117 Matt Chico AU (RC) 8.00 3.00
❑ 118 Levale Speigner AU RC 8.00 3.00
❑ 119 Lee Gardner AU (RC) 8.00 3.00
❑ 120 Kory Casto AU (RC) 10.00 4.00
❑ 121 Kevin Kouzmanoff AU (RC) 10.00 4.00
❑ 122 Kevin Cameron AU RC 8.00 3.00
❑ 123 Kei Igawa AU SP RC
❑ 124 Tyler Clippard AU (RC) 15.00 6.00
❑ 125 Juan Perez AU RC 8.00 3.00
❑ 126 Josh Hamilton AU SP (RC) 40.00 15.00
❑ 127 Joseph Bisenius AU RC 8.00 3.00
❑ 128 Jose Luis Garcia AU RC 8.00 3.00
❑ 129 Jon Knott AU RC 8.00 3.00
❑ 130 Jon Coutlangus AU (RC) 10.00 4.00
❑ 131 John Danks AU RC 8.00 3.00
❑ 132 Joe Smith AU RC 8.00 3.00
❑ 133 Matt Brown AU RC 8.00 3.00
❑ 134 Joakim Soria AU RC 10.00 4.00
❑ 135 Jesus Flores AU RC 15.00 6.00
❑ 136 Jeff Baker AU (RC) 8.00 3.00
❑ 137 Jay Marshall AU RC 8.00 3.00
❑ 138 Jared Burton AU RC 10.00 4.00
❑ 139 Jamie Vermilyea AU RC 10.00 4.00
❑ 140 Jamie Burke AU (RC) 10.00 4.00
❑ 141 Ryan Rowland-Smith AU RC 10.00 4.00
❑ 142 Connor Robertson AU RC 8.00 3.00
❑ 143 Hector Gimenez AU (RC) 8.00 3.00
❑ 144 Gustavo Molina AU RC 10.00 4.00
❑ 145 Glen Perkins AU (RC) 8.00 3.00
❑ 146 J.Chamberlain AU SP RC EXCH 200.00 150.00
❑ 147 Doug Slaten AU RC 8.00 3.00
❑ 148 Ryan Braun AU (RC) 50.00 20.00
❑ 149 Delmon Young AU SP (RC)
❑ 150 Garrett Jones AU (RC) 8.00 3.00
❑ 151 Chris Stewart AU SP RC
❑ 152 Cesar Jimenez AU RC 10.00 4.00
❑ 153 Brian Stokes AU (RC) 8.00 3.00
❑ 154 Brian Burres AU (RC) 10.00 4.00
❑ 155 Brian Barden AU SP RC
❑ 156 Kyle Kendrick AU RC 30.00 12.50
❑ 157 Andrew Miller AU RC 20.00 8.00
❑ 158 Alexi Casilla AU RC 8.00 3.00
❑ 159 Alex Gordon AU SP RC 70.00 35.00
❑ 160 A.J. Murray AU RC 10.00 4.00
❑ 161 A.Iwamura AU SP RC

❑ 162 Adam Lind AU (RC) 10.00 4.00
❑ 163 Chase Wright AU RC 12.00 5.00
❑ 164 Dallas Braden AU RC 8.00 3.00
❑ 165 Rocky Cherry AU RC 12.00 5.00
❑ 166 Andy Gonzalez AU RC 8.00 3.00
❑ 167 Neal Musser AU RC 8.00 3.00
❑ 168 Mark Reynolds AU RC 60.00 30.00
❑ 169 Dennis Dove AU (RC) 8.00 3.00
❑ 170 Justin Hampson AU (RC) 10.00 4.00
❑ 171 Phil Hughes AU SP (RC)
❑ 172 Kelvin Jimenez AU RC 8.00 3.00
❑ 173 Hunter Pence AU SP (RC)
❑ 174 Brad Salmon AU RC 15.00 6.00
❑ 175 Ryan Sweeney AU (RC) 8.00 3.00
❑ 176 Brandon Wood AU (RC) 15.00 6.00
❑ 177 Billy Butler AU SP (RC)
❑ 178 Ben Francisco AU (RC) 8.00 3.00
❑ 179 Devern Hansack AU SP RC
❑ 180 Yoel Hernandez AU RC 8.00 3.00
❑ 181 Tim Lincecum AU SP RC 100.00 50.00
❑ 182 Danny Putnam AU (RC) 12.00 5.00
❑ 183 J.Salta AU SP (RC) 15.00 6.00
❑ 184 Andy LaRoche AU SP (RC)
❑ 185 Matt DeSalvo AU (RC) 12.00 5.00
❑ 186 Fred Lewis AU (RC) 8.00 3.00
❑ 187 Anthony Lerew AU (RC) 8.00 3.00
❑ 188 Jesse Litsch AU RC 10.00 4.00
❑ 189a Daisuke Matsuzaka RC
❑ 189b Daisuke Matsuzaka AU SP 300.00 250.00

2007 Upper Deck Goudey

❑ COMP.SET w/o SPs (200) 50.00 20.00
❑ COMMON CARD (1-200) .50 .20
❑ COMMON ROOKIE (1-200) .75 .30
❑ COMMON SP (201-240) 5.00 2.00
❑ SP ODDS 1:6 HOBBY,1:6 RETAIL
❑ 1933 ORIGINALS ODDS TWO PER CASE
❑ SEE 1933 GOUDEY PRICING FOR ORIGINALS
❑ 1 A.J. Burnett .50 .20
❑ 2 Aaron Boone .50 .20
❑ 3 Aaron Rowand .50 .20
❑ 4 Adam Dunn .50 .20
❑ 5 Adrian Beltre .50 .20
❑ 6 Albert Pujols 2.50 1.00
❑ 7 Ivan Rodriguez .75 .30
❑ 8 Alfonso Soriano .50 .20
❑ 9 Andruw Jones .75 .30
❑ 10 Andy Pettitte .75 .30
❑ 11 Aramis Ramirez .50 .20
❑ 12 B.J. Upton .50 .20
❑ 13 Barry Zito .50 .20
❑ 14 Bartolo Colon .50 .20
❑ 15 Ben Sheets .50 .20
❑ 16 Bobby Abreu .50 .20
❑ 17 Bobby Crosby .50 .20
❑ 18 Brian Giles .50 .20
❑ 19 Brian Roberts .50 .20
❑ 20 C.C. Sabathia .50 .20
❑ 21 Carlos Beltran .50 .20
❑ 22 Carlos Delgado .50 .20
❑ 23 Carlos Lee .50 [illegible]
❑ 24 Carlos Zambrano .50 .20
❑ 25 Chad Cordero .50 .20
❑ 26 Chad Tracy .50 .20
❑ 27 Chipper Jones 1.25 .50
❑ 28 Craig Biggio .75 .30
❑ 29 Curt Schilling .75 .30
❑ 30 Danny Haren .50 .20
❑ 31 Darin Erstad .50 .20
❑ 32 David Ortiz 1.25 .50
❑ 33 Billy Wagner .50 .20
❑ 34 Derek Jeter 3.00 1.25
❑ 35 Derek Lee .50 .20
❑ 36 Dontrelle Willis .50 .20
❑ 37 Edgar Renteria .50 .20
❑ 38 Eric Chavez .50 .20
❑ 39 Felix Hernandez .75 .30
❑ 40 Garret Anderson .50 .20
❑ 41 Garrett Atkins .50 .20
❑ 42 Gary Sheffield .50 .20
❑ 43 Grady Sizemore .75 .30
❑ 44 Greg Maddux 2.00 .75
❑ 45 Hank Blalock .50 .20
❑ 46 Hanley Ramirez .75 .30
❑ 47 J.D. Drew .50 .20
❑ 48 Jacque Jones .50 .20
❑ 49 Jake Peavy .50 .20
❑ 50 Jake Westbrook .50 .20
❑ 51 Jason Bay .50 .20
❑ 52 Jason Giambi .50 .20
❑ 53 Jason Schmidt .50 .20
❑ 54 Jason Varitek 1.25 .50
❑ 55 Troy Tulowitzki (RC) 2.00 .75
❑ 56 Jeff Francoeur 1.25 .50
❑ 57 Jeff Kent .50 .20
❑ 58 Jeremy Bonderman .50 .20
❑ 59 Jim Edmonds .75 .30
❑ 60 Jim Thome .75 .30
❑ 61 Jimmy Rollins .50 .20
❑ 62 Joe Mauer .75 .30
❑ 63 Johan Santana .75 .30
❑ 64 John Smoltz .75 .30
❑ 65 Johnny Damon .75 .30
❑ 66 Jose Reyes 1.25 .50
❑ 67 Josh Beckett .75 .30
❑ 68 Justin Morneau .50 .20
❑ 69 Ken Griffey Jr. 2.00 .75
❑ 70 Kerry Wood .50 .20
❑ 71 Khalil Greene .75 .30
❑ 72 Lance Berkman .50 .20
❑ 73 Livan Hernandez .50 .20
❑ 74 Manny Ramirez .75 .30
❑ 75 Mark Mulder .50 .20
❑ 76 Chase Utley 1.25 .50
❑ 77 Mark Teixeira .75 .30
❑ 78 Miguel Tejada .50 .20
❑ 79 Miguel Cabrera .75 .30
❑ 80 Mike Piazza 1.25 .50
❑ 81 Pat Burrell .50 .20
❑ 82 Paul LoDuca .50 .20
❑ 83 Pedro Martinez .75 .30
❑ 84 Prince Fielder 1.25 .50
❑ 85 Rafael Furcal .50 .20
❑ 86 Randy Johnson 1.25 .50
❑ 87 Richie Sexson .50 .20
❑ 88 Robinson Cano .75 .30
❑ 89 Roy Halladay .50 .20
❑ 90 Roy Oswalt .50 .20
❑ 91 Scott Rolen .75 .30
❑ 92 Tim Hudson .50 .20
❑ 93 Todd Helton .75 .30
❑ 94 Tom Glavine .75 .30
❑ 95 Torii Hunter .50 .20
❑ 96 Travis Hafner .50 .20
❑ 97 Trevor Hoffman .50 .20
❑ 98 [illegible] Wells .50 .20
❑ 99 Vladimir Gue[illegible] 1.25 .50
❑ 100 Zach Duke [illegible] .20
❑ 101 Alex Rodriguez 2.00 [illegible]
❑ 102 Ryan Howard 2.00 .75
❑ 103 Michael Barrett .50 .20
❑ 104 Ichiro Suzuki 2.00 .75
❑ 105 Hideki Matsui 1.25 .50
❑ 106 Jered Weaver .75 .30
❑ 107 Dan Uggla .75 .30
❑ 108 Ryan Freel .50 .20
❑ 109 Bill Hall .50 .20
❑ 110 Ray Durham .50 .20
❑ 111 Morgan Ensberg .50 .20
❑ 112 Shawn Green .50 .20
❑ 113 Brandon Webb .50 .20
❑ 114 Frank Thomas 1.25 .50
❑ 115 Corey Patterson .50 .20
❑ 116 Edwin Encarnacion .50 .20
❑ 117 Mike Cameron .50 .20
❑ 118 Matt Holliday 1.25 .50
❑ 119 Jhonny Peralta .50 .20
❑ 120 Nick Swisher .50 .20
❑ 121 Brad Penny .50 .20
❑ 122 Kenji Johjima 1.25 .50
❑ 123 Francisco Rodriguez .50 .20
❑ 124 Mark Teahen .50 .20
❑ 125 Jonathan Papelbon 1.25 .50
❑ 126 Carlos Guillen .50 .20
❑ 127 Freddy Sanchez .50 .20
❑ 128 Chien-Ming Wang 2.00 .75
❑ 129 Andre Ethier .75 .30
❑ 130 Matt Cain .75 .30
❑ 131 Austin Kearns .50 .20
❑ 132 Ramon Hernandez .50 .20
❑ 133 Chris Carpenter .50 .20
❑ 134 Michael Cuddyer .50 .20
❑ 135 Stephen Drew .75 .30
❑ 136 David Wright 2.00 .75
❑ 137 David DeJesus .50 .20
❑ 138 Gary Matthews .50 .20
❑ 139 Brandon Phillips .50 .20
❑ 140 Josh Barfield .50 .20
❑ 141 Alex Gordon RC 4.00 1.50
❑ 142 Scott Kazmir .75 .30
❑ 143 Luis Gonzalez .50 .20
❑ 144 Mike Sweeney .50 .20
❑ 145 Luis Castillo .50 .20
❑ 146 Huston Street .50 .20
❑ 147 Phil Hughes (RC) 4.00 1.50
❑ 148 Adrian Gonzalez .50 .20
❑ 149 Raul Ibanez .50 .20
❑ 150 Joe Crede .50 .20
❑ 151 Mark Loretta .50 .20
❑ 152 Adam LaRoche (RC) .75 .30
❑ 153 Troy Glaus .50 .20
❑ 154 Conor Jackson .50 .20
❑ 155 Michael Young .50 .20
❑ 156 Scott Podsednik .50 .20
❑ 157 David Eckstein .50 .20
❑ 158 Mike Jacobs .50 .20
❑ 159 Nomar Garciaparra 1.25 .50
❑ 160 Mariano Rivera 1.25 .50
❑ 161 Pedro Feliz .50 .20
❑ 162 Josh Hamilton (RC) 2.00 .75
❑ 163 Ryan Langerhans .50 .20
❑ 164 Willy Taveras .50 .20
❑ 165 Carl Crawford .50 .20
❑ 166 Melvin Mora .50 .20
❑ 167 Francisco Liriano 1.25 .50
❑ 168 Orlando Cabrera .50 .20
❑ 169 Chris Duncan .50 .20
❑ 170 Johnny Estrada .50 .20

❑ 171 Ryan Zimmerman 1.25 .50
❑ 172 Rickie Weeks .50 .20
❑ 173 Paul Konerko .50 .20
❑ 174 Jack Wilson .50 .20
❑ 175 Jorge Posada .75 .30
❑ 176 Magglio Ordonez .50 .20
❑ 177 Nick Johnson .50 .20
❑ 178 Geoff Jenkins .50 .20
❑ 179 Reggie Sanders .50 .20
❑ 180 Moises Alou .50 .20
❑ 181 Glen Perkins (RC) .75 .30
❑ 182 Brad Lidge .50 .20
❑ 183 Kevin Kouzmanoff (RC) .75 .30
❑ 184 Jorge Cantu .50 .20
❑ 185 Carlos Quentin .50 .20
❑ 186 Rich Harden .50 .20
❑ 187 Jose Vidro .50 .20
❑ 188 Aaron Harang .50 .20
❑ 189 Noah Lowry .50 .20
❑ 190 Jermaine Dye .50 .20
❑ 191 Victor Martinez .50 .20
❑ 192 Chone Figgins .50 .20
❑ 193 Aubrey Huff .50 .20
❑ 194 Jason Isringhausen .50 .20
❑ 195 Brian McCann .50 .20
❑ 196 Juan Pierre .50 .20
❑ 197 Delmon Young (RC) 1.25 .50
❑ 198 Felipe Lopez .50 .20
❑ 199 Brad Hawpe .50 .20
❑ 200 Justin Verlander 1.25 .50
❑ 201 Mike Schmidt SP 10.00 4.00
❑ 202 Nolan Ryan SP 12.00 5.00
❑ 203 Cal Ripken Jr. SP 10.00 4.00
❑ 204 Harmon Killebrew SP 6.00 2.50
❑ 205 Reggie Jackson SP 6.00 2.50
❑ 206 Johnny Bench SP 6.00 2.50
❑ 207 Carlton Fisk SP 6.00 2.50
❑ 208 Yogi Berra SP 6.00 2.50
❑ 209 Al Kaline SP 6.00 2.50
❑ 210 Alan Trammell SP 5.00 2.00
❑ 211 Bill Mazeroski SP 6.00 2.50
❑ 212 Bob Gibson SP 6.00 2.50
❑ 213 Brooks Robinson SP 6.00 2.50
❑ 214 Carl Yastrzemski SP 8.00 3.00
❑ 215 Don Mattingly SP 12.00 5.00
❑ 216 Fergie Jenkins SP 5.00 2.00
❑ 217 Jim Rice SP 5.00 2.00
❑ 218 Lou Brock SP 6.00 2.50
❑ 219 Rod Carew SP 6.00 2.50
❑ 220 Stan Musial SP 8.00 3.00
❑ 221 Tom Seaver SP 6.00 2.50
❑ 222 Tony Gwynn SP 6.00 2.50
❑ 223 Wade Boggs SP 6.00 2.50
❑ 224 Alex Rodriguez SP 8.00 3.00
❑ 225 David Wright SP 8.00 3.00
❑ 226 Ryan Howard SP 8.00 3.00
❑ 227 Ichiro Suzuki SP 8.00 3.00
❑ 228 Ken Griffey Jr. SP 8.00 3.00
❑ 229 Daisuke Matsuzaka SP RC 10.00 4.00
❑ 230 Kei Igawa SP RC 6.00 2.50
❑ 231 Akinori Iwamura SP RC 8.00 3.00
❑ 232 Derek Jeter SP 10.00 4.00
❑ 233 Albert Pujols SP 10.00 4.00
❑ 234 Greg Maddux SP 8.00 3.00
❑ 235 David Ortiz SP 6.00 2.50
❑ 236 Manny Ramirez SP 6.00 2.50
❑ 237 Johan Santana SP 6.00 2.50
❑ 238 Pedro Martinez SP 6.00 2.50
❑ 239 Roger Clemens SP 10.00 4.00
❑ 240 Vladimir Guerrero SP 6.00 2.50

2008 Upper Deck Goudey

❑ COMP.SET w/o HIGH #s (200) 50.00 20.00
❑ COMMON CARD (1-200) .50 .20

❑ COMMON ROOKIE (1-200) .75 .30
❑ COMMON SP (201-230) 5.00 2.00
❑ COMMON SP (231-250) 4.00 1.50
❑ COMMON SP (251-270) 5.00 2.00
❑ COMMON CARD (271-330) 5.00 2.00
❑ 1 Eric Byrnes .50 .20
❑ 2 Randy Johnson 1.25 .50
❑ 3 Brandon Webb .50 .20
❑ 4 Dan Haren .50 .20
❑ 5 Chris B. Young .50 .20
❑ 6 Max Scherzer RC 2.00 .75
❑ 7 Mark Teixeira .75 .30
❑ 8 John Smoltz 1.25 .50
❑ 9 Jeff Francoeur .75 .30
❑ 10 Phil Niekro .50 .20
❑ 11 Chipper Jones 1.50 .60
❑ 12 Kelly Johnson .50 .20
❑ 13 Tom Glavine .75 .30
❑ 14 Yunel Escobar .50 .20
❑ 15 Erik Bedard .50 .20
❑ 16 Melvin Mora .50 .20
❑ 17 Brian Roberts .75 .30
❑ 18 Eddie Murray 1.25 .50
❑ 19 Jim Palmer .50 .20
❑ 20 Jeremy Guthrie .50 .20
❑ 21 Nick Markakis .75 .30
❑ 22 David Ortiz 1.25 .50
❑ 23 Manny Ramirez 1.25 .50
❑ 24 Josh Beckett .75 .30
❑ 25 Dustin Pedroia .75 .30
❑ 26 Bobby Doerr .50 .20
❑ 27 Clay Buchholz (RC) 2.00 .75
❑ 28 Daisuke Matsuzaka 2.00 .75
❑ 29 Jonathan Papelbon .75 .30
❑ 30 Kevin Youkilis .75 .30
❑ 31 Pee Wee Reese .75 .30
❑ 32 Billy Williams .50 .20
❑ 33 Alfonso Soriano .75 .30
❑ 34 Derrek Lee .75 .30
❑ 35 Rich Hill .50 .20
❑ 36 Kosuke Fukudome RC 5.00 2.00
❑ 37 Aramis Ramirez .50 .20
❑ 38 Carlos Zambrano .50 .20
❑ 39 Luis Aparicio .50 .20
❑ 40 Mark Buehrle .50 .20
❑ 41 Orlando Cabrera .50 .20
❑ 42 Paul Konerko .50 .20
❑ 43 Jermaine Dye .50 .20
❑ 44 Jim Thome .75 .30
❑ 45 Nick Swisher .50 .20
❑ 46 Sparky Anderson .50 .20
❑ 47 Johnny Bench 1.25 .50
❑ 48 Joe Morgan .50 .20
❑ 49 Tony Perez .50 .20
❑ 50 Adam Dunn .50 .20
❑ 51 Aaron Harang .50 .20
❑ 52 Brandon Phillips .50 .20
❑ 53 Edwin Encarnacion .50 .20
❑ 54 Ken Griffey Jr. 2.00 .75
❑ 55 Larry Doby .50 .20
❑ 56 Bob Feller .50 .20
❑ 57 C.C. Sabathia .50 .20
❑ 58 Travis Hafner .50 .20
❑ 59 Grady Sizemore .75 .30
❑ 60 Fausto Carmona .50 .20
❑ 61 Victor Martinez .50 .20
❑ 62 Brad Hawpe .50 .20
❑ 63 Todd Helton .75 .30
❑ 64 Garrett Atkins .50 .20
❑ 65 Troy Tulowitzki .75 .30
❑ 66 Matt Holliday .75 .30
❑ 67 Jeff Francis .50 .20
❑ 68 Justin Verlander .75 .30
❑ 69 Curtis Granderson .75 .30
❑ 70 Miguel Cabrera .75 .30
❑ 71 Gary Sheffield .50 .20
❑ 72 Magglio Ordonez .75 .30
❑ 73 Jack Morris .50 .20
❑ 74 Andrew Miller .75 .30
❑ 75 Clayton Kershaw RC 2.50 1.00
❑ 76 Dan Uggla .75 .30
❑ 77 Hanley Ramirez 1.25 .50
❑ 78 Jeremy Hermida .50 .20
❑ 79 Josh Willingham .50 .20
❑ 80 Lance Berkman .75 .30
❑ 81 Roy Oswalt .50 .20
❑ 82 Miguel Tejada .50 .20
❑ 83 Hunter Pence 1.25 .50
❑ 84 Carlos Lee .50 .20
❑ 85 J.R. Towles RC 2.00 .75
❑ 86 Brian Bannister .50 .20
❑ 87 Luke Hochevar RC 2.50 1.00
❑ 88 Billy Butler .50 .20
❑ 89 Alex Gordon 1.25 .50
❑ 90 Kelvim Escobar .50 .20
❑ 91 John Lackey .50 .20
❑ 92 Chone Figgins .50 .20
❑ 93 Jered Weaver .50 .20
❑ 94 Torii Hunter .50 .20
❑ 95 Vladimir Guerrero 1.25 .50
❑ 96 Brad Penny .50 .20
❑ 97 James Loney .75 .30
❑ 98 Andruw Jones .50 .20
❑ 99 Chad Billingsley .50 .20
❑ 100 Chin-Lung Hu (RC) 1.25 .50
❑ 101 Russell Martin .50 .20
❑ 102 Eddie Mathews 1.25 .50
❑ 103 Warren Spahn .75 .30
❑ 104 Prince Fielder 1.25 .50
❑ 105 Ryan Braun 1.50 .60
❑ 106 J.J. Hardy .50 .20
❑ 107 Ben Sheets .75 .30
❑ 108 Corey Hart .50 .20
❑ 109 Yovani Gallardo .50 .20
❑ 110 Joe Mauer .75 .30
❑ 111 Delmon Young .75 .30
❑ 112 Johan Santana 1.25 .50
❑ 113 Glen Perkins .50 .20
❑ 114 Justin Morneau .75 .30
❑ 115 Carlos Beltran .50 .20
❑ 116 Jose Reyes .75 .30
❑ 117 David Wright 1.50 .60
❑ 118 Pedro Martinez .75 .30
❑ 119 Tom Seaver .75 .30
❑ 120 Billy Wagner .50 .20
❑ 121 John Maine .50 .20
❑ 122 Alex Rodriguez 2.00 .75
❑ 123 Chien-Ming Wang 1.50 .60
❑ 124 Hideki Matsui 1.25 .50
❑ 125 Jorge Posada .75 .30
❑ 126 Mariano Rivera 1.25 .50
❑ 127 Phil Rizzuto .75 .30
❑ 128 Bucky Dent .50 .20

❑ 129 Derek Jeter 3.00 1.25
❑ 130 Graig Nettles .50 .20
❑ 131 Ian Kennedy RC 2.50 1.00
❑ 132 Don Larsen .50 .20
❑ 133 Joe Blanton .50 .20
❑ 134 Mark Ellis .50 .20
❑ 135 Dennis Eckersley .50 .20
❑ 136 Rollie Fingers .50 .20
❑ 137 Catfish Hunter .50 .20
❑ 138 Daric Barton (RC) .75 .30
❑ 139 Jack Cust .50 .20
❑ 140 Ryan Howard 1.50 .60
❑ 141 Jimmy Rollins .75 .30
❑ 142 Chase Utley 1.25 .50
❑ 143 Shane Victorino .50 .20
❑ 144 Cole Hamels .75 .30
❑ 145 Richie Ashburn .75 .30
❑ 146 Jason Bay .50 .20
❑ 147 Freddy Sanchez .50 .20
❑ 148 Adam LaRoche .50 .20
❑ 149 Jack Wilson .50 .20
❑ 150 Ralph Kiner .75 .30
❑ 151 Bill Mazeroski .75 .30
❑ 152 Tom Gorzelanny .50 .20
❑ 153 Jay Bruce (RC) 3.00 1.25
❑ 154 Jake Peavy .50 .20
❑ 155 Chris Young .50 .20
❑ 156 Trevor Hoffman .50 .20
❑ 157 Khalil Greene .75 .30
❑ 158 Adrian Gonzalez .75 .30
❑ 159 Tim Lincecum 1.25 .50
❑ 160 Matt Cain .50 .20
❑ 161 Aaron Rowand .50 .20
❑ 162 Orlando Cepeda .50 .20
❑ 163 Juan Marichal .50 .20
❑ 164 Noah Lowry .50 .20
❑ 165 Ichiro Suzuki 2.00 .75
❑ 166 Felix Hernandez .75 .30
❑ 167 J.J. Putz .50 .20
❑ 168 Jose Vidro .50 .20
❑ 169 Raul Ibanez .50 .20
❑ 170 Wladimir Balentien .50 .20
❑ 171 Albert Pujols 2.50 1.00
❑ 172 Scott Rolen .75 .30
❑ 173 Lou Brock .75 .30
❑ 174 Chris Duncan .50 .20
❑ 175 Vince Coleman .50 .20
❑ 176 B.J. Upton .75 .30
❑ 177 Carl Crawford .50 .20
❑ 178 Carlos Pena .50 .20
❑ 179 Scott Kazmir .75 .30
❑ 180 Akinori Iwamura .50 .20
❑ 181 James Shields .50 .20
❑ 182 Michael Young .50 .20
❑ 183 Jarrod Saltalamacchia .50 .20
❑ 184 Hank Blalock .50 .20
❑ 185 Ian Kinsler .75 .30
❑ 186 Josh Hamilton 1.50 .60
❑ 187 Marlon Byrd .50 .20
❑ 188 David Murphy .50 .20
❑ 189 Vernon Wells .50 .20
❑ 190 Roy Halladay .50 .20
❑ 191 Frank Thomas 1.25 .50
❑ 192 Alex Rios .50 .20
❑ 193 Troy Glaus .75 .30
❑ 194 David Eckstein .50 .20
❑ 195 Ryan Zimmerman .75 .30
❑ 196 Dmitri Young .50 .20
❑ 197 Austin Kearns .50 .20
❑ 198 Chad Cordero .50 .20
❑ 199 Ryan Church .50 .20
❑ 200 Evan Longoria RC 5.00 2.00
❑ 201 Brooks Robinson SP 5.00 2.00
❑ 202 Cal Ripken Jr. SP 12.00 5.00
❑ 203 Frank Robinson SP 5.00 2.00
❑ 204 Carl Yastrzemski SP 8.00 3.00
❑ 205 Carlton Fisk SP 5.00 2.00
❑ 206 Fred Lynn SP 5.00 2.00
❑ 207 Wade Boggs SP 6.00 2.50
❑ 208 Nolan Ryan SP 12.00 5.00
❑ 209 Ernie Banks SP 6.00 2.50
❑ 210 Ryne Sandberg SP 10.00 4.00
❑ 211 Al Kaline SP 6.00 2.50
❑ 212 Bo Jackson SP 6.00 2.50
❑ 213 Paul Molitor SP 6.00 2.50
❑ 214 Robin Yount SP 6.00 2.50
❑ 215 Harmon Killebrew SP 6.00 2.50
❑ 216 Rod Carew SP 5.00 2.00
❑ 217 Bobby Thomson SP 5.00 2.00
❑ 218 Gaylord Perry SP 5.00 2.00
❑ 219 Dave Winfield SP 5.00 2.00
❑ 220 Don Mattingly SP 8.00 3.00
❑ 221 Reggie Jackson SP 5.00 2.00
❑ 222 Roger Clemens SP 8.00 3.00
❑ 223 Whitey Ford SP 5.00 2.00
❑ 224 Mike Schmidt SP 8.00 3.00
❑ 225 Steve Carlton SP 5.00 2.00
❑ 226 Tony Gwynn SP 5.00 2.00
❑ 227 Willie McCovey SP 5.00 2.00
❑ 228 Bob Gibson SP 5.00 2.00
❑ 229 Ozzie Smith SP 8.00 3.00
❑ 230 Stan Musial SP 8.00 3.00
❑ 231 George Washington SP 5.00 2.00
❑ 232 Thomas Jefferson SP 5.00 2.00
❑ 233 James Madison SP 4.00 1.50
❑ 234 James Monroe SP 4.00 1.50
❑ 235 Andrew Jackson SP 4.00 1.50
❑ 236 John Tyler SP 4.00 1.50
❑ 237 Abraham Lincoln SP 5.00 2.00
❑ 238 Ulysses S. Grant SP 4.00 1.50
❑ 239 Grover Cleveland SP 4.00 1.50
❑ 240 Theodore Roosevelt SP 4.00 1.50
❑ 241 Calvin Coolidge SP 4.00 1.50
❑ 242 John Adams SP 4.00 1.50
❑ 243 Martin Van Buren SP 4.00 1.50
❑ 244 William McKinley SP 4.00 1.50
❑ 245 Woodrow Wilson SP 4.00 1.50
❑ 246 James K. Polk SP 4.00 1.50
❑ 247 Rutherford B. Hayes SP 4.00 1.50
❑ 248 William H. Taft SP 4.00 1.50
❑ 249 Andrew Johnson SP 4.00 1.50
❑ 250 James Buchanan SP 4.00 1.50
❑ 251 A.Pujols 36 BW SP 8.00 3.00
❑ 252 A.Rodriguez 36 BW SP 8.00 3.00
❑ 253 Alfonso Soriano 36 BW SP 6.00 2.50
❑ 254 C.C. Sabathia 36 BW SP 5.00 2.00
❑ 255 Chase Utley 36 BW SP 6.00 2.50
❑ 256 David Ortiz 36 BW SP 6.00 2.50
❑ 257 D Wright 36 BW SP 6.00 2.50
❑ 258 D.Jeter 36 BW SP 10.00 4.00
❑ 259 Hanley Ramirez 36 BW SP 6.00 2.50
❑ 260 I.Suzuki 36 BW SP 8.00 3.00
❑ 261 Jake Peavy 36 BW SP 6.00 2.50
❑ 262 Johan Santana 36 BW SP 6.00 2.50
❑ 263 Jose Reyes 36 BW SP 6.00 2.50
❑ 264 K.Griffey Jr. 36 BW SP 8.00 3.00
❑ 265 Magglio Ordonez 36 BW SP 6.00 2.50
❑ 266 Matt Holliday 36 BW SP 6.00 2.50
❑ 267 Prince Fielder 36 BW SP 6.00 2.50
❑ 268 R.Braun 36 BW SP 6.00 2.50
❑ 269 R.Howard 36 BW SP 6.00 2.50
❑ 270 Vladimir Guerrero 36 BW SP 6.00 2.50
❑ 271 Carl Yastrzemski SR 5.00 2.00
❑ 272 Albert Pujols SR 8.00 3.00
❑ 273 Amy Van Dyken SR 5.00 2.00
❑ 274 Tom Seaver SR 5.00 2.00
❑ 275 Brett Favre SR 10.00 4.00
❑ 276 Bruce Jenner SR 5.00 2.00
❑ 277 Bill Russell SR 8.00 3.00
❑ 278 Barry Sanders SR 8.00 3.00
❑ 279 Cynthia Cooper SR 5.00 2.00
❑ 280 Mike Schmidt SR 6.00 2.50
❑ 281 Chipper Jones SR 6.00 2.50
❑ 282 Cal Ripken Jr. SR 10.00 4.00
❑ 283 Cael Sanderson SR 5.00 2.00
❑ 284 Dan Gable SR 5.00 2.00
❑ 285 Derek Jeter SR 10.00 4.00
❑ 286 Andre Dawson SR 5.00 2.00
❑ 287 Dan O'Brien SR 5.00 2.00
❑ 288 Julius Erving SR 6.00 2.50
❑ 289 Emmitt Smith SR 8.00 3.00
❑ 290 Janet Evans SR 5.00 2.00
❑ 291 Chase Utley SR 5.00 2.00
❑ 292 Gary Hall Jr. SR 5.00 2.00
❑ 293 Gordie Howe SR 8.00 3.00
❑ 294 Josh Beckett SR 5.00 2.00
❑ 295 John Elway SR 8.00 3.00
❑ 296 Julie Foudy SR 5.00 2.00
❑ 297 Jackie Joyner-Kersee SR 5.00 2.00
❑ 298 Jack Nicklaus SR 10.00 4.00
❑ 299 Magic Johnson SR 8.00 3.00
❑ 300 Michael Jordan SR 10.00 4.00
❑ 301 Bo Jackson SR 6.00 2.50
❑ 302 Tom Brady SR 10.00 4.00
❑ 303 Wade Boggs SR 6.00 2.50
❑ 304 Dan Marino SR 10.00 4.00
❑ 305 Dave Winfield SR 5.00 2.00
❑ 306 Jenny Thompson SR 5.00 2.00
❑ 307 Kobe Bryant SR 8.00 3.00
❑ 308 Kevin Durant SR 8.00 3.00
❑ 309 Ken Griffey Jr. SR 8.00 3.00
❑ 310 Kerri Strug SR 6.00 2.50
❑ 311 Kerri Walsh SR 6.00 2.50
❑ 312 Larry Bird SR 10.00 4.00
❑ 313 LeBron James SR 10.00 4.00
❑ 314 Matt Biondi SR 5.00 2.00
❑ 315 Mark Messier SR 6.00 2.50
❑ 316 Michael Johnson SR 5.00 2.00
❑ 317 Misty May-Treanor SR 6.00 2.50
❑ 318 Bob Gibson SR 5.00 2.00
❑ 319 Nolan Ryan SR 10.00 4.00
❑ 320 Ozzie Smith SR 8.00 3.00
❑ 321 Prince Fielder SR 6.00 2.50
❑ 322 Rulon Gardner SR 5.00 2.00
❑ 323 Reggie Jackson SR 6.00 2.50
❑ 324 Emile Danko SR 8.00 3.00
❑ 325 Sidney Crosby SR 15.00 6.00
❑ 326 Sanya Richards SR 5.00 2.00
❑ 327 Terry Bradshaw SR 6.00 2.50
❑ 328 Tony Gwynn SR 6.00 2.50
❑ 329 Stan Musial SR 10.00 4.00
❑ 330 Tiger Woods SR 60.00 30.00

2008 Upper Deck Heroes

❑ COMPLETE SET (200) 50.00 20.00
❑ COMMON CARD (1-200) .50 .20
❑ COMMON ROOKIE (1-200) 1.00 .40
❑ 1 Brandon Webb .50 .20
❑ 2 Dan Haren .50 .20
❑ 3 Chris B. Young .50 .20
❑ 4 Justin Upton 1.25 .50
❑ 5 Randy Johnson 1.25 .50
❑ 6 Chipper Jones 1.50 .60
❑ 7 John Smoltz 1.25 .50
❑ 8 Tom Glavine .75 .30
❑ 9 Mark Teixeira .75 .30
❑ 10 Brian McCann .75 .30
❑ 11 Jeff Francoeur .75 .30

- ❑ 12 Josh Hamilton 1.50 .60
- ❑ 13 Tim Hudson .50 .20
- ❑ 14 Nick Markakis .75 .30
- ❑ 15 Brian Roberts .75 .30
- ❑ 16 Cal Ripken Jr. 5.00 2.00
- ❑ 17 John Maine .50 .20
- ❑ 18 Frank Robinson .50 .20
- ❑ 19 Mike Lowell .50 .20
- ❑ 20 Jason Varitek 1.25 .50
- ❑ 21 David Ortiz 1.25 .50
- ❑ 22 Manny Ramirez 1.25 .50
- ❑ 23 Jonathan Papelbon .75 .30
- ❑ 24 Jacoby Ellsbury 2.00 .75
- ❑ 25 Kevin Youkilis .75 .30
- ❑ 26 Curt Schilling .75 .30
- ❑ 27 Josh Beckett .75 .30
- ❑ 28 Daisuke Matsuzaka 2.00 .75
- ❑ 29 Clay Buchholz (RC) 2.50 1.00
- ❑ 30 Dustin Pedroia .75 .30
- ❑ 31 Ryan Theriot .50 .20
- ❑ 32 Carlton Fisk .75 .30
- ❑ 33 Carl Yastrzemski 2.00 .75
- ❑ 34 Wade Boggs .50 .20
- ❑ 35 Nolan Ryan 3.00 1.25
- ❑ 36 Alfonso Soriano .75 .30
- ❑ 37 Kosuke Fukudome RC 6.00 2.50
- ❑ 38 Derrek Lee .75 .30
- ❑ 39 Carlos Zambrano .50 .20
- ❑ 40 Aramis Ramirez .50 .20
- ❑ 41 Ernie Banks 1.25 .50
- ❑ 42 Jim Thome .75 .30
- ❑ 43 Jermaine Dye .50 .20
- ❑ 44 Paul Konerko .50 .20
- ❑ 45 Nick Swisher .50 .20
- ❑ 46 Corey Hart .50 .20
- ❑ 47 Ken Griffey Jr. 2.00 .75
- ❑ 48 Adam Dunn .50 .20
- ❑ 49 Aaron Harang .50 .20
- ❑ 50 Johnny Bench 1.25 .50
- ❑ 51 Grady Sizemore .75 .30
- ❑ 52 Victor Martinez .50 .20
- ❑ 53 C.C. Sabathia .50 .20
- ❑ 54 Travis Hafner .50 .20
- ❑ 55 Jeff Francis .50 .20
- ❑ 56 Matt Holliday .75 .30
- ❑ 57 Troy Tulowitzki .75 .30
- ❑ 58 Garrett Atkins .50 .20
- ❑ 59 Todd Helton .75 .30
- ❑ 60 Curtis Granderson .75 .30
- ❑ 61 Dontrelle Willis .50 .20
- ❑ 62 Magglio Ordonez .75 .30
- ❑ 63 Gary Sheffield .50 .20
- ❑ 64 Miguel Cabrera .75 .30
- ❑ 65 Justin Verlander .75 .30
- ❑ 66 Ivan Rodriguez .75 .30
- ❑ 67 Al Kaline 1.25 .50
- ❑ 68 Hanley Ramirez 1.25 .50
- ❑ 69 Edinson Volquez .50 .20
- ❑ 70 Dan Uggla .75 .30
- ❑ 71 Andrew Miller .75 .30
- ❑ 72 Josh Willingham .50 .20
- ❑ 73 J.R. Towles RC 2.50 1.00
- ❑ 74 Lance Berkman .75 .30
- ❑ 75 Carlos Lee .50 .20
- ❑ 76 Roy Oswalt .50 .20
- ❑ 77 Hunter Pence 1.25 .50
- ❑ 78 Luke Hochevar RC 3.00 1.25
- ❑ 79 Alex Gordon 1.25 .50
- ❑ 80 Matt Cain .50 .20
- ❑ 81 Bo Jackson 1.25 .50
- ❑ 82 Vladimir Guerrero 1.25 .50
- ❑ 83 Torii Hunter .50 .20
- ❑ 84 Howie Kendrick .50 .20
- ❑ 85 John Lackey .50 .20
- ❑ 86 Chone Figgins .50 .20
- ❑ 87 Andruw Jones .50 .20
- ❑ 88 Brad Penny .50 .20
- ❑ 89 James Loney .75 .30
- ❑ 90 Matt Kemp .50 .20
- ❑ 91 Nomar Garciaparra 1.25 .50
- ❑ 92 Jon Lester .75 .30
- ❑ 93 Chin-Lung Hu (RC) 1.50 .60
- ❑ 94 Chad Billingsley .50 .20
- ❑ 95 Kelly Johnson .50 .20
- ❑ 96 Prince Fielder 1.25 .50
- ❑ 97 Ryan Braun 1.50 .60
- ❑ 98 Ben Sheets .75 .30
- ❑ 99 Robin Yount 1.25 .50
- ❑ 100 Justin Morneau .75 .30
- ❑ 101 Joe Mauer .75 .30
- ❑ 102 Delmon Young .75 .30
- ❑ 103 Rod Carew .75 .30
- ❑ 104 Carlos Beltran .50 .20
- ❑ 105 Jose Reyes .75 .30
- ❑ 106 Pedro Martinez .75 .30
- ❑ 107 David Wright 1.50 .60
- ❑ 108 Johan Santana 1.25 .50
- ❑ 109 Billy Wagner .50 .20
- ❑ 110 Carlos Delgado .50 .20
- ❑ 111 Mariano Rivera 1.25 .50
- ❑ 112 Chien-Ming Wang 1.50 .60
- ❑ 113 Phil Hughes 1.25 .50
- ❑ 114 Derek Jeter 3.00 1.25
- ❑ 115 Alex Rodriguez 2.00 .75
- ❑ 116 Robinson Cano .75 .30
- ❑ 117 Jorge Posada .75 .30
- ❑ 118 Hideki Matsui 1.25 .50
- ❑ 119 Joba Chamberlain 2.00 .75
- ❑ 120 Ian Kennedy RC 3.00 1.25
- ❑ 121 Yogi Berra 1.25 .50
- ❑ 122 Reggie Jackson .75 .30
- ❑ 123 Roger Clemens 1.50 .60
- ❑ 124 Ozzie Smith 2.00 .75
- ❑ 125 Don Mattingly 2.50 1.00
- ❑ 126 Dave Winfield .50 .20
- ❑ 127 Joe DiMaggio 2.50 1.00
- ❑ 128 Eric Chavez .50 .20
- ❑ 129 Bill Hall .50 .20
- ❑ 130 Rich Harden .50 .20
- ❑ 131 Andre Ethier .75 .30
- ❑ 132 Daric Barton (RC) 1.00 .40
- ❑ 133 Ryan Howard 1.50 .60
- ❑ 134 Jimmy Rollins .75 .30
- ❑ 135 Chase Utley 1.25 .50
- ❑ 136 Cole Hamels .75 .30
- ❑ 137 Pat Burrell .50 .20
- ❑ 138 Mike Schmidt 2.00 .75
- ❑ 139 Steve Carlton .50 .20
- ❑ 140 Freddy Sanchez .50 .20
- ❑ 141 Joe Blanton .50 .20
- ❑ 142 Felix Pie .50 .20
- ❑ 143 Roberto Clemente 4.00 1.50
- ❑ 144 Jake Peavy .50 .20
- ❑ 145 Greg Maddux 1.50 .60
- ❑ 146 Tom Gorzelanny .50 .20
- ❑ 147 Tony Gwynn 1.50 .60
- ❑ 148 Barry Zito .50 .20
- ❑ 149 Tim Lincecum 1.25 .50
- ❑ 150 Rich Hill .50 .20
- ❑ 151 Omar Vizquel .50 .20
- ❑ 152 Ichiro Suzuki 2.00 .75
- ❑ 153 Felix Hernandez .75 .30
- ❑ 154 Kenji Johjima .50 .20
- ❑ 155 Erik Bedard .50 .20
- ❑ 156 Albert Pujols 2.50 1.00
- ❑ 157 Troy Glaus .75 .30
- ❑ 158 Chris Carpenter .50 .20
- ❑ 159 Chris Duncan .50 .20
- ❑ 160 Mark Mulder .50 .20
- ❑ 161 Scott Rolen .75 .30
- ❑ 162 Stan Musial 2.00 .75
- ❑ 163 Bob Gibson .75 .30
- ❑ 164 B.J. Upton .75 .30
- ❑ 165 Carl Crawford .50 .20
- ❑ 166 Scott Kazmir .75 .30
- ❑ 167 Michael Young .50 .20
- ❑ 168 Luke Scott .50 .20
- ❑ 169 Roy Halladay .50 .20
- ❑ 170 Vernon Wells .50 .20
- ❑ 171 Kevin Kouzmanoff .50 .20
- ❑ 172 Frank Thomas 1.25 .50
- ❑ 173 Ryan Zimmerman .75 .30
- ❑ 174 Lastings Milledge .50 .20
- ❑ 175 Ian Kinsler .75 .30
- ❑ 176 D.Mattingly/W.Boggs 2.50 1.00
- ❑ 177 C.Fisk/C.Yastrzemski 2.00 .75
- ❑ 178 A.Pujols/S.Musial 2.50 1.00
- ❑ 179 J.Reyes/D.Jeter 3.00 1.25
- ❑ 180 C.Ripken/T.Gwynn 1.50 .60
- ❑ 181 Eddie Murray/Prince Fielder 1.25 .50
- ❑ 182 I.Suzuki/K.Fukudome 3.00 1.25
- ❑ 183 Steve Carlton/Johan Santana 1.25 .50
- ❑ 184 Bob Gibson/Jake Peavy .75 .30
- ❑ 185 Johnny Bench/Ivan Rodriguez 1.25 .50
- ❑ 186 Vlad/Ichiro/Manny 2.00 .75
- ❑ 187 Yaz/Fisk/Boggs 2.00 .75
- ❑ 188 ARod/Jeter/Cano 3.00 1.25
- ❑ 189 Chipper/Braun/Mig.Cabrera 1.50 .60
- ❑ 190 Mattingly/Winfield/Reggie 2.50 1.00
- ❑ 191 Utley/Howard/Rollins 1.50 .60
- ❑ 192 Joe Mauer/Hanley Ramirez /Troy Tulowitzki 1.25 .50
- ❑ 193 Ryan/Maddux/Unit 3.00 1.25
- ❑ 194 Brandon Webb/Justin Verlander /Felix Hernandez .75 .30
- ❑ 195 Schmidt/Banks/F.Robinson 2.00 .75
- ❑ 196 Jeter/Griffey/Ripken/Ichiro 5.00 2.00
- ❑ 197 Yogi/Reggie/Joe D/Jeter 3.00 1.25
- ❑ 198 Jonathan Papelbon/Manny Ramirez/Jason Varitek/David Ortiz 1.25 .50
- ❑ 199 Griffey/Clemente/Vlad/Joe D 4.00 1.50
- ❑ 200 Pujols/Jeter/Prince/Papi 3.00 1.25

1999 Upper Deck Ovation

- ❑ COMPLETE SET (90) 80.00 30.00
- ❑ COMP.SET w/o SP's (60) 25.00 10.00
- ❑ COMMON CARD (1-60) .40 .15
- ❑ COMMON WP (61-80) 2.00 .75
- ❑ COMMON SS (81-90) 2.50 1.00
- ❑ 1 Ken Griffey Jr. 1.50 .60
- ❑ 2 Rondell White .40 .15
- ❑ 3 Tony Clark .40 .15
- ❑ 4 Barry Bonds 2.50 1.00
- ❑ 5 Larry Walker .40 .15
- ❑ 6 Greg Vaughn .40 .15
- ❑ 7 Mark Grace .60 .25

❑ 8 John Olerud	.40	.15
❑ 9 Matt Williams	.40	.15
❑ 10 Craig Biggio	.60	.25
❑ 11 Quinton McCracken	.40	.15
❑ 12 Kerry Wood	.40	.15
❑ 13 Derek Jeter	2.50	1.00
❑ 14 Frank Thomas	1.00	.40
❑ 15 Tino Martinez	.60	.25
❑ 16 Albert Belle	.40	.15
❑ 17 Ben Grieve	.40	.15
❑ 18 Cal Ripken	3.00	1.25
❑ 19 Johnny Damon	.60	.25
❑ 20 Jose Cruz Jr.	.40	.15
❑ 21 Barry Larkin	.60	.25
❑ 22 Jason Giambi	.40	.15
❑ 23 Sean Casey	.40	.15
❑ 24 Scott Rolen	.60	.25
❑ 25 Jim Thome	.60.	.25
❑ 26 Curt Schilling	.40	.15
❑ 27 Moises Alou	.40	.15
❑ 28 Alex Rodriguez	1.50	.60
❑ 29 Mark Kotsay	.40	.15
❑ 30 Darin Erstad	.40	.15
❑ 31 Mike Mussina	.60	.25
❑ 32 Todd Walker	.40	.15
❑ 33 Nomar Garciaparra	1.50	.60
❑ 34 Vladimir Guerrero	1.00	.40
❑ 35 Jeff Bagwell	.60	.25
❑ 36 Mark McGwire	2.50	1.00
❑ 37 Travis Lee	.40	.15
❑ 38 Dean Palmer	.40	.15
❑ 39 Fred McGriff	.60	.25
❑ 40 Sammy Sosa	1.00	.40
❑ 41 Mike Piazza	1.50	.60
❑ 42 Andres Galarraga	.40	.15
❑ 43 Pedro Martinez	.60	.25
❑ 44 Juan Gonzalez	.40	.15
❑ 45 Greg Maddux	1.50	.60
❑ 46 Jeromy Burnitz	.40	.15
❑ 47 Roger Clemens	2.00	.75
❑ 48 Vinny Castilla	.40	.15
❑ 49 Kevin Brown	.60	.25
❑ 50 Mo Vaughn	.40	.15
❑ 51 Raul Mondesi	.40	.15
❑ 52 Randy Johnson	1.00	.40
❑ 53 Ray Lankford	.40	.15
❑ 54 Jaret Wright	.40	.15
❑ 55 Tony Gwynn	1.25	.50
❑ 56 Chipper Jones	1.00	.40
❑ 57 Gary Sheffield	.40	.15
❑ 58 Ivan Rodriguez	.60	.25
❑ 59 Kenny Lofton	.40	.15
❑ 60 Jason Kendall	.40	.15
❑ 61 J.D. Drew WP	2.00	.75
❑ 62 Gabe Kapler WP	2.00	.75
❑ 63 Adrian Beltre WP	2.00	.75
❑ 64 Carlos Beltran WP	2.50	1.00
❑ 65 Eric Chavez WP	2.00	.75
❑ 66 Mike Lowell WP	2.00	.75
❑ 67 Troy Glaus WP	2.50	1.00
❑ 68 George Lombard WP	2.00	.75
❑ 69 Alex Gonzalez WP	2.00	.75
❑ 70 Mike Kinkade WP	2.00	.75
❑ 71 Jeremy Giambi WP	2.00	.75
❑ 72 Bruce Chen WP	2.00	.75
❑ 73 Preston Wilson WP	2.00	.75
❑ 74 Kevin Witt WP	2.00	.75
❑ 75 Carlos Guillen WP	2.00	.75
❑ 76 Ryan Minor WP	2.00	.75
❑ 77 Corey Koskie WP	2.00	.75
❑ 78 Robert Fick WP	2.50	1.00
❑ 79 Michael Barrett WP	2.00	.75
❑ 80 Calvin Pickering WP	2.00	.75
❑ 81 Ken Griffey Jr. SS	4.00	1.50
❑ 82 Mark McGwire SS	6.00	2.50
❑ 83 Cal Ripken SS	8.00	3.00
❑ 84 Derek Jeter SS	6.00	2.50
❑ 85 Chipper Jones SS	2.50	1.00
❑ 86 Nomar Garciaparra SS	4.00	1.50
❑ 87 Sammy Sosa SS	2.50	1.00
❑ 88 Juan Gonzalez SS	2.50	1.00
❑ 89 Mike Piazza SS	4.00	1.50
❑ 90 Alex Rodriguez SS	4.00	1.50

2000 Upper Deck Ovation

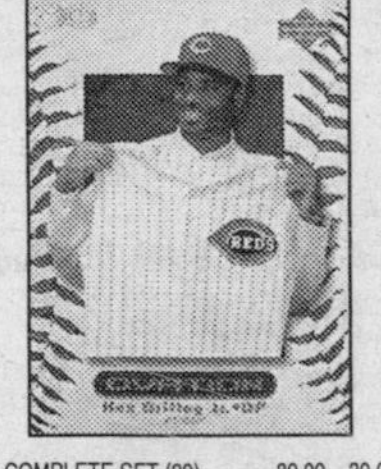

❑ COMPLETE SET (89)	80.00	30.00
❑ COMP.SET w/o SP's (60)	20.00	8.00
❑ COMMON CARD (1-60)	.40	.15
❑ COMMON WP (61-80)	2.00	.75
❑ COMMON SS (81-90)	3.00	1.25
❑ 1 Mo Vaughn	.40	.15
❑ 2 Troy Glaus	.40	.15
❑ 3 Jeff Bagwell	.60	.25
❑ 4 Craig Biggio	.60	.25
❑ 5 Mike Hampton	.40	.15
❑ 6 Jason Giambi	.40	.15
❑ 7 Tim Hudson	.40	.15
❑ 8 Chipper Jones	1.00	.40
❑ 9 Greg Maddux	1.50	.60
❑ 10 Kevin Millwood	.40	.15
❑ 11 Brian Jordan	.40	.15
❑ 12 Jeromy Burnitz	.40	.15
❑ 13 David Wells	.40	.15
❑ 14 Carlos Delgado	.40	.15
❑ 15 Sammy Sosa	1.00	.40
❑ 16 Mark McGwire	2.50	1.00
❑ 17 Matt Williams	.40	.15
❑ 18 Randy Johnson	1.00	.40
❑ 19 Erubiel Durazo	.40	.15
❑ 20 Kevin Brown	.60	.25
❑ 21 Shawn Green	.40	.15
❑ 22 Gary Sheffield	.40	.15
❑ 23 Jose Canseco	.60	.25
❑ 24 Vladimir Guerrero	1.00	.40
❑ 25 Barry Bonds	2.50	1.00
❑ 26 Manny Ramirez	.60	.25
❑ 27 Roberto Alomar	.60	.25
❑ 28 Richie Sexson	.40	.15
❑ 29 Jim Thome	.60	.25
❑ 30 Alex Rodriguez	1.50	.60
❑ 31 Ken Griffey Jr.	1.50	.60
❑ 32 Preston Wilson	.40	.15
❑ 33 Mike Piazza	1.50	.60
❑ 34 Al Leiter	.40	.15
❑ 35 Robin Ventura	.60	.25
❑ 36 Cal Ripken	3.00	1.25
❑ 37 Albert Belle	.40	.15
❑ 38 Tony Gwynn	1.25	.50
❑ 39 Brian Giles	.40	.15
❑ 40 Jason Kendall	.40	.15
❑ 41 Scott Rolen	.60	.25
❑ 42 Bob Abreu	.40	.15
❑ 43 Ken Griffey Jr. Reds	1.50	.60
❑ 44 Sean Casey	.40	.15
❑ 45 Carlos Beltran	.40	.15
❑ 46 Gabe Kapler	.40	.15
❑ 47 Ivan Rodriguez	.60	.25
❑ 48 Rafael Palmeiro	.60	.25
❑ 49 Larry Walker	.40	.15
❑ 50 Nomar Garciaparra	1.50	.60
❑ 51 Pedro Martinez	.60	.25
❑ 52 Eric Milton	.40	.15
❑ 53 Juan Gonzalez	.40	.15
❑ 54 Tony Clark	.40	.15
❑ 55 Frank Thomas	1.00	.40
❑ 56 Magglio Ordonez	.40	.15
❑ 57 Roger Clemens	2.00	.75
❑ 58 Derek Jeter	2.50	1.00
❑ 59 Bernie Williams	.60	.25
❑ 60 Orlando Hernandez	.40	.15
❑ 61 Rick Ankiel WP	2.00	.75
❑ 62 Josh Beckett WP	5.00	2.00
❑ 63 Vernon Wells WP	2.50	1.00
❑ 64 Alfonso Soriano WP	5.00	2.00
❑ 65 Pat Burrell WP	2.50	1.00
❑ 66 Eric Munson WP	2.00	.75
❑ 67 Chad Hutchinson WP	2.00	.75
❑ 68 Eric Gagne WP	5.00	2.00
❑ 69 Peter Bergeron WP	2.00	.75
❑ 70 Ryan Anderson WP SP	150.00	75.00
❑ 71 A.J. Burnett WP	2.50	1.00
❑ 72 Jorge Toca WP	2.00	.75
❑ 73 Matt Riley WP	2.00	.75
❑ 74 Chad Hermansen WP	2.00	.75
❑ 75 Doug Davis WP	2.50	1.00
❑ 76 Jim Morris WP	5.00	2.00
❑ 77 Ben Petrick WP	2.00	.75
❑ 78 Mark Quinn WP	2.00	.75
❑ 79 Ed Yarnall WP	2.00	.75
❑ 80 Ramon Ortiz WP	2.00	.75
❑ 81 Ken Griffey Jr. SS	5.00	2.00
❑ 82 Mark McGwire SS	8.00	3.00
❑ 83 Derek Jeter SS	8.00	3.00
❑ 84 Jeff Bagwell SS	3.00	1.25
❑ 85 Nomar Garciaparra SS	5.00	2.00
❑ 86 Sammy Sosa SS	3.00	1.25
❑ 87 Mike Piazza SS	5.00	2.00
❑ 88 Alex Rodriguez SS	5.00	2.00
❑ 89 Cal Ripken SS	10.00	4.00
❑ 90 Pedro Martinez SS	3.00	1.25

2001 Upper Deck Ovation

❑ COMP.SET w/o SP'S (60)	20.00	8.00
❑ COMMON CARD (1-60)	.40	.15
❑ COMMON WP (61-90)	5.00	2.00
❑ 1 Troy Glaus	.40	.15
❑ 2 Darin Erstad	.40	.15
❑ 3 Jason Giambi	.40	.15
❑ 4 Tim Hudson	.40	.15
❑ 5 Eric Chavez	.40	.15
❑ 6 Carlos Delgado	.40	.15
❑ 7 David Wells	.40	.15
❑ 8 Greg Vaughn	.40	.15
❑ 9 Omar Vizquel UER	.60	.25
❑ 10 Jim Thome	.60	.25
❑ 11 Roberto Alomar	.60	.25
❑ 12 John Olerud	.40	.15
❑ 13 Edgar Martinez	.60	.25
❑ 14 Cal Ripken	3.00	1.25
❑ 15 Alex Rodriguez	1.50	.60
❑ 16 Ivan Rodriguez	.60	.25
❑ 17 Manny Ramirez Sox	.60	.25
❑ 18 Nomar Garciaparra	1.50	.60
❑ 19 Pedro Martinez	.60	.25
❑ 20 Jermaine Dye	.40	.15
❑ 21 Juan Gonzalez	.40	.15
❑ 22 Matt Lawton	.40	.15
❑ 23 Frank Thomas	1.00	.40
❑ 24 Magglio Ordonez	.40	.15
❑ 25 Bernie Williams	.60	.25
❑ 26 Derek Jeter	2.50	1.00
❑ 27 Roger Clemens	2.00	.75
❑ 28 Jeff Bagwell	.60	.25
❑ 29 Richard Hidalgo	.40	.15
❑ 30 Chipper Jones	1.00	.40
❑ 31 Greg Maddux	1.50	.60
❑ 32 Andruw Jones	.60	.25
❑ 33 Jeromy Burnitz	.40	.15
❑ 34 Mark McGwire	2.50	1.00
❑ 35 Jim Edmonds	.40	.15
❑ 36 Sammy Sosa	1.00	.40
❑ 37 Kerry Wood	.40	.15
❑ 38 Randy Johnson	1.00	.40
❑ 39 Steve Finley	.40	.15
❑ 40 Gary Sheffield	.40	.15
❑ 41 Kevin Brown	.40	.15
❑ 42 Shawn Green	.40	.15
❑ 43 Vladimir Guerrero	1.00	.40
❑ 44 Jose Vidro	.40	.15
❑ 45 Barry Bonds	2.50	1.00
❑ 46 Jeff Kent	.40	.15
❑ 47 Preston Wilson	.40	.15
❑ 48 Luis Castillo	.40	.15
❑ 49 Mike Piazza	1.50	.60
❑ 50 Edgardo Alfonzo	.40	.15
❑ 51 Tony Gwynn	1.25	.50
❑ 52 Ryan Klesko	.40	.15
❑ 53 Scott Rolen	.60	.25
❑ 54 Bob Abreu	.40	.15
❑ 55 Jason Kendall	.40	.15
❑ 56 Brian Giles	.40	.15
❑ 57 Ken Griffey Jr.	1.50	.60
❑ 58 Barry Larkin	.60	.25
❑ 59 Todd Helton	.60	.25
❑ 60 Mike Hampton	.40	.15
❑ 61 Corey Patterson WP	5.00	2.00
❑ 62 Timo Perez WP	5.00	2.00
❑ 63 Toby Hall WP	5.00	2.00
❑ 64 Brandon Inge WP	5.00	2.00
❑ 65 Joe Crede WP	8.00	3.00
❑ 66 Xavier Nady WP	5.00	2.00
❑ 67 Adam Pettyjohn WP RC	5.00	2.00
❑ 68 Keith Ginter WP	5.00	2.00
❑ 69 Brian Cole WP	5.00	2.00
❑ 70 Tyler Walker WP RC	5.00	2.00
❑ 71 Juan Uribe WP RC	5.00	2.00
❑ 72 Alex Hernandez WP	5.00	2.00
❑ 73 Leo Estrella WP	5.00	2.00
❑ 74 Joey Nation WP	5.00	2.00
❑ 75 Aubrey Huff WP	5.00	2.00
❑ 76 Ichiro Suzuki WP RC	50.00	25.00
❑ 77 Jay Spurgeon WP	5.00	2.00
❑ 78 Sun Woo Kim WP	5.00	2.00
❑ 79 Pedro Feliz WP	5.00	2.00
❑ 80 Pablo Ozuna WP	5.00	2.00
❑ 81 Hiram Bocachica WP	5.00	2.00
❑ 82 Brad Wilkerson WP	5.00	2.00
❑ 83 Rocky Biddle WP	5.00	2.00
❑ 84 Aaron McNeal WP	5.00	2.00
❑ 85 Adam Bernero WP	5.00	2.00
❑ 86 Danys Baez WP	5.00	2.00
❑ 87 Dee Brown WP	5.00	2.00
❑ 88 Jimmy Rollins WP	5.00	2.00
❑ 89 Jason Hart WP	5.00	2.00
❑ 90 Ross Gload WP	5.00	2.00

2002 Upper Deck Ovation

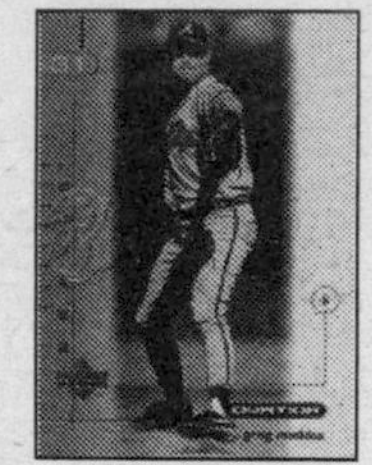

❑ COMP.LOW w/o SP's (90)	25.00	10.00
❑ COMP.UPDATE w/o SP's (30)	15.00	6.00
❑ COMMON CARD (1-60)	.40	.15
❑ COMMON (61-89/120/151-180)	4.00	1.50
❑ COMMON CARD (90-119)	.50	.20
❑ COMMON CARD (121-150)	.60	.25
❑ 1 Troy Glaus	.40	.15
❑ 2 David Justice	.40	.15
❑ 3 Tim Hudson	.40	.15
❑ 4 Jermaine Dye	.40	.15
❑ 5 Carlos Delgado	.40	.15
❑ 6 Greg Vaughn	.40	.15
❑ 7 Jim Thome	.60	.25
❑ 8 C.C. Sabathia	.40	.15
❑ 9 Ichiro Suzuki	2.00	.75
❑ 10 Edgar Martinez	.60	.25
❑ 11 Chris Richard	.40	.15
❑ 12 Rafael Palmeiro	.60	.25
❑ 13 Alex Rodriguez	1.50	.60
❑ 14 Ivan Rodriguez	.60	.25
❑ 15 Nomar Garciaparra	1.50	.60
❑ 16 Manny Ramirez	.60	.25
❑ 17 Pedro Martinez	.60	.25
❑ 18 Mike Sweeney	.40	.15
❑ 19 Dmitri Young	.40	.15
❑ 20 Doug Mientkiewicz	.40	.15
❑ 21 Brad Radke	.40	.15
❑ 22 Cristian Guzman	.40	.15
❑ 23 Frank Thomas	1.00	.40
❑ 24 Magglio Ordonez	.40	.15
❑ 25 Bernie Williams	.60	.25
❑ 26 Derek Jeter	2.50	1.00
❑ 27 Jason Giambi	.40	.15
❑ 28 Roger Clemens	2.00	.75
❑ 29 Jeff Bagwell	.60	.25
❑ 30 Lance Berkman	.40	.15
❑ 31 Chipper Jones	1.00	.40
❑ 32 Gary Sheffield	.40	.15
❑ 33 Greg Maddux	1.50	.60
❑ 34 Richie Sexson	.40	.15
❑ 35 Albert Pujols	2.00	.75
❑ 36 Tino Martinez	.60	.25
❑ 37 J.D. Drew	.40	.15
❑ 38 Sammy Sosa	1.00	.40
❑ 39 Moises Alou	.40	.15
❑ 40 Randy Johnson	1.00	.40
❑ 41 Luis Gonzalez	.40	.15
❑ 42 Shawn Green	.40	.15
❑ 43 Kevin Brown	.40	.15
❑ 44 Vladimir Guerrero	1.00	.40
❑ 45 Barry Bonds	2.50	1.00
❑ 46 Jeff Kent	.40	.15
❑ 47 Cliff Floyd	.40	.15
❑ 48 Josh Beckett	.40	.15
❑ 49 Mike Piazza	1.50	.60
❑ 50 Mo Vaughn	.40	.15
❑ 51 Jeromy Burnitz	.40	.15
❑ 52 Roberto Alomar	.60	.25
❑ 53 Phil Nevin	.40	.15
❑ 54 Scott Rolen	.60	.25
❑ 55 Jimmy Rollins	.40	.15
❑ 56 Brian Giles	.40	.15
❑ 57 Ken Griffey Jr.	1.50	.60
❑ 58 Sean Casey	.40	.15
❑ 59 Larry Walker	.40	.15
❑ 60 Todd Helton	.60	.25
❑ 61 Rodrigo Rosario WP RC	4.00	1.50
❑ 62 Reed Johnson WP RC	5.00	2.00
❑ 63 John Ennis WP RC	4.00	1.50
❑ 64 Luis Martinez WP RC	4.00	1.50
❑ 65 So Taguchi WP RC	5.00	2.00
❑ 66 Brandon Backe WP RC	5.00	2.00
❑ 67 Doug Devore WP RC	4.00	1.50
❑ 68 Victor Alvarez WP RC	4.00	1.50
❑ 69 Kazuhisa Ishii WP RC	5.00	2.00
❑ 70 Eric Good WP RC	4.00	1.50
❑ 71 Deivis Santos WP	4.00	1.50
❑ 72 Matt Thornton WP RC	4.00	1.50
❑ 73 Hansel Izquierdo WP RC	4.00	1.50
❑ 74 Tyler Yates WP RC	4.00	1.50
❑ 75 Jaime Cerda WP RC	4.00	1.50
❑ 76 Satoru Komiyama WP RC	4.00	1.50
❑ 77 Steve Bechler WP RC	4.00	1.50
❑ 78 Ben Howard WP RC	4.00	1.50
❑ 79 Jorge Padilla WP RC	4.00	1.50
❑ 80 Eric Junge WP RC	4.00	1.50
❑ 81 Anderson Machado WP RC	4.00	1.50
❑ 82 Adrian Burnside WP RC	4.00	1.50
❑ 83 Josh Hancock WP RC	5.00	2.00
❑ 84 Anastacio Martinez WP RC	4.00	1.50
❑ 85 Rene Reyes WP RC	4.00	1.50
❑ 86 Nate Field WP RC	4.00	1.50
❑ 87 Tim Kalita WP RC	4.00	1.50
❑ 88 Kevin Frederick WP RC	4.00	1.50
❑ 89 Edwin Almonte WP RC	4.00	1.50

❑ 90 Ichiro Suzuki SS 1.00 .40
❑ 91 Ichiro Suzuki SS 1.00 .40
❑ 92 Ichiro Suzuki SS 1.00 .40
❑ 93 Ichiro Suzuki SS 1.00 .40
❑ 94 Ichiro Suzuki SS 1.00 .40
❑ 95 Ken Griffey Jr. SS .75 .30
❑ 96 Ken Griffey Jr. SS .75 .30
❑ 97 Ken Griffey Jr. SS .75 .30
❑ 98 Ken Griffey Jr. SS .75 .30
❑ 99 Ken Griffey Jr. SS .75 .30
❑ 100 Jason Giambi A's SS .50 .20
❑ 101 Jason Giambi A's SS .50 .20
❑ 102 Jason Giambi A's SS .50 .20
❑ 103 Jason Giambi Yankees SS .50 .20
❑ 104 Jason Giambi Yankees SS .60 .25
❑ 105 Sammy Sosa SS .60 .25
❑ 106 Sammy Sosa SS .60 .25
❑ 107 Sammy Sosa SS .60 .25
❑ 108 Sammy Sosa SS .60 .25
❑ 109 Sammy Sosa SS .60 .25
❑ 110 Alex Rodriguez SS .75 .30
❑ 111 Alex Rodriguez SS .75 .30
❑ 112 Alex Rodriguez SS .75 .30
❑ 113 Alex Rodriguez SS .75 .30
❑ 114 Alex Rodriguez SS .75 .30
❑ 115 Mark McGwire SS 1.25 .50
❑ 116 Mark McGwire SS 1.25 .50
❑ 117 Mark McGwire SS 1.25 .50
❑ 118 Mark McGwire SS 1.25 .50
❑ 119 Mark McGwire SS 1.25 .50
❑ 120 Six Spokesmen SP/2002 15.00 6.00
❑ 121 Curt Schilling .60 .25
❑ 122 Cliff Floyd .60 .25
❑ 123 Derek Lowe .60 .25
❑ 124 Hee Seop Choi .60 .25
❑ 125 Mark Prior 1.00 .40
❑ 126 Joe Borchard .60 .25
❑ 127 Austin Kearns .60 .25
❑ 128 Adam Dunn .60 .25
❑ 129 Jay Payton .60 .25
❑ 130 Carlos Pena .60 .25
❑ 131 Andy Van Hekken .60 .25
❑ 132 Andres Torres .60 .25
❑ 133 Ben Diggins .60 .25
❑ 134 Torii Hunter .60 .25
❑ 135 Bartolo Colon .60 .25
❑ 136 Raul Mondesi .60 .25
❑ 137 Alfonso Soriano .60 .25
❑ 138 Miguel Tejada .60 .25
❑ 139 Ray Durham .60 .25
❑ 140 Eric Chavez .60 .25
❑ 141 Marlon Byrd .60 .25
❑ 142 Brett Myers .60 .25
❑ 143 Sean Burroughs .60 .25
❑ 144 Kenny Lofton .60 .25
❑ 145 Scott Rolen 1.00 .40
❑ 146 Carl Crawford .60 .25
❑ 147 Jayson Werth .60 .25
❑ 148 Josh Phelps .60 .25
❑ 149 Eric Hinske .60 .25
❑ 150 Orlando Hudson .60 .25
❑ 151 Jose Valverde WP RC 4.00 1.50
❑ 152 Trey Hodges WP RC 4.00 1.50
❑ 153 Joey Dawley WP RC 4.00 1.50
❑ 154 Travis Driskill WP RC 4.00 1.50
❑ 155 Howie Clark WP RC 4.00 1.50
❑ 156 Jorge De La Rosa WP RC 4.00 1.50
❑ 157 Freddy Sanchez WP RC 5.00 2.00
❑ 158 Earl Snyder WP RC 4.00 1.50
❑ 159 Cliff Lee WP RC 5.00 2.00
❑ 160 Josh Bard WP RC 4.00 1.50
❑ 161 Aaron Cook WP RC 4.00 1.50
❑ 162 Franklyn German WP RC 4.00 1.50
❑ 163 Brandon Puffer WP RC 4.00 1.50
❑ 164 Kirk Saarloos WP RC 4.00 1.50
❑ 165 Jeriome Robertson WP RC 4.00 1.50
❑ 166 Miguel Asencio WP RC 4.00 1.50
❑ 167 Shawn Sedlacek WP RC 4.00 1.50
❑ 168 Jayson Durocher WP RC 4.00 1.50
❑ 169 Shane Nance WP RC 4.00 1.50
❑ 170 Jamey Carroll WP RC 5.00 2.00
❑ 171 Oliver Perez WP RC 5.00 2.00
❑ 172 Wil Nieves WP RC 4.00 1.50
❑ 173 Clay Condrey WP RC 4.00 1.50
❑ 174 Chris Snelling WP RC 4.00 1.50
❑ 175 Mike Crudale WP RC 4.00 1.50
❑ 176 Jason Simontacchi WP RC 4.00 1.50
❑ 177 Felix Escalona WP RC 4.00 1.50
❑ 178 Lance Carter WP RC 4.00 1.50
❑ 179 Scott Wiggins WP RC 4.00 1.50
❑ 180 Kevin Cash WP RC 4.00 1.50

2006 Upper Deck Ovation

❑ COMP.SET w/o RC's (84) 25.00 10.00
❑ COMMON CARD (1-84) .50 .20
❑ COMMON ROOKIE (85-126) 5.00 2.00
❑ 85-126 STATED ODDS 1:18
❑ 85-126 PRINT RUN 999 SERIAL #'d SETS
❑ EXQUISITE EXCH ODDS 1:144
❑ EXQUISITE EXCH DEADLINE 07/27/07
❑ 1 Vladimir Guerrero 1.25 .50
❑ 2 Bartolo Colon .50 .20
❑ 3 Chone Figgins .50 .20
❑ 4 Lance Berkman .50 .20
❑ 5 Roy Oswalt .50 .20
❑ 6 Craig Biggio .75 .30
❑ 7 Rich Harden .50 .20
❑ 8 Eric Chavez .50 .20
❑ 9 Huston Street .50 .20
❑ 10 Vernon Wells .50 .20
❑ 11 Roy Halladay .50 .20
❑ 12 Troy Glaus .50 .20
❑ 13 Andruw Jones .75 .30
❑ 14 Chipper Jones 1.25 .50
❑ 15 John Smoltz .75 .30
❑ 16 Carlos Lee .50 .20
❑ 17 Rickie Weeks .50 .20
❑ 18 J.J. Hardy .50 .20
❑ 19 Albert Pujols 2.50 1.00
❑ 20 Chris Carpenter .50 .20
❑ 21 Scott Rolen .75 .30
❑ 22 Derrek Lee .50 .20
❑ 23 Mark Prior .75 .30
❑ 24 Aramis Ramirez .50 .20
❑ 25 Carl Crawford .50 .20
❑ 26 Scott Kazmir .75 .30
❑ 27 Luis Gonzalez .50 .20
❑ 28 Brandon Webb .50 .20
❑ 29 Chad Tracy .50 .20
❑ 30 Jeff Kent .50 .20
❑ 31 J.D. Drew .50 .20
❑ 32 Jason Schmidt .50 .20
❑ 33 Randy Winn .50 .20
❑ 34 Travis Hafner .50 .20
❑ 35 Victor Martinez .50 .20
❑ 36 Grady Sizemore .75 .30
❑ 37 Ichiro Suzuki 2.00 .75
❑ 38 Felix Hernandez .75 .30
❑ 39 Adrian Beltre .50 .20
❑ 40 Miguel Cabrera .75 .30
❑ 41 Dontrelle Willis .50 .20
❑ 42 David Wright 2.00 .75
❑ 43 Jose Reyes 1.25 .50
❑ 44 Pedro Martinez .75 .30
❑ 45 Carlos Beltran .50 .20
❑ 46 Alfonso Soriano .50 .20
❑ 47 Livan Hernandez .50 .20
❑ 48 Jose Guillen .50 .20
❑ 49 Miguel Tejada .50 .20
❑ 50 Brian Roberts .50 .20
❑ 51 Melvin Mora .50 .20
❑ 52 Jake Peavy .50 .20
❑ 53 Brian Giles .50 .20
❑ 54 Khalil Greene .75 .30
❑ 55 Bobby Abreu .50 .20
❑ 56 Ryan Howard 2.00 .75
❑ 57 Chase Utley 1.25 .50
❑ 58 Jason Bay .50 .20
❑ 59 Sean Casey .50 .20
❑ 60 Mark Teixeira .75 .30
❑ 61 Michael Young .50 .20
❑ 62 Hank Blalock .50 .20
❑ 63 Manny Ramirez .75 .30
❑ 64 David Ortiz 1.25 .50
❑ 65 Josh Beckett .50 .20
❑ 66 Jason Varitek 1.25 .50
❑ 67 Ken Griffey Jr. 2.00 .75
❑ 68 Adam Dunn .50 .20
❑ 69 Todd Helton .75 .30
❑ 70 Garrett Atkins .50 .20
❑ 71 Reggie Sanders .50 .20
❑ 72 Mike Sweeney .50 .20
❑ 73 Chris Shelton .50 .20
❑ 74 Ivan Rodriguez .75 .30
❑ 75 Johan Santana .75 .30
❑ 76 Torii Hunter .50 .20
❑ 77 Justin Morneau .50 .20
❑ 78 Jim Thome .75 .30
❑ 79 Paul Konerko .50 .20
❑ 80 Scott Podsednik .50 .20
❑ 81 Derek Jeter 3.00 1.25
❑ 82 Hideki Matsui 1.25 .50
❑ 83 Johnny Damon .75 .30
❑ 84 Alex Rodriguez 2.00 .75
❑ 85 Conor Jackson (RC) 8.00 3.00
❑ 86 Joey Devine RC 5.00 2.00
❑ 87 Jonathan Papelbon (RC) 15.00 6.00
❑ 88 Freddie Bynum (RC) 5.00 2.00
❑ 89 Chris Denorfia (RC) 5.00 2.00
❑ 90 Ryan Shealy (RC) 5.00 2.00
❑ 91 Josh Wilson (RC) 8.00 3.00
❑ 92 Brian Anderson (RC) 5.00 2.00
❑ 93 Justin Verlander (RC) 12.00 5.00
❑ 94 Jeremy Hermida (RC) 8.00 3.00
❑ 95 Mike Jacobs (RC) 5.00 2.00
❑ 96 Josh Johnson (RC) 8.00 3.00
❑ 97 Hanley Ramirez (RC) 10.00 4.00
❑ 98 Josh Willingham (RC) 5.00 2.00
❑ 99 Cole Hamels (RC) 10.00 4.00
❑ 100 Hong-Chih Kuo (RC) 15.00 6.00
❑ 101 Cody Ross (RC) 5.00 2.00
❑ 102 Jose Capellan (RC) 5.00 2.00
❑ 103 Prince Fielder (RC) 12.00 5.00
❑ 104 David Gassner (RC) 5.00 2.00
❑ 105 Jason Kubel (RC) 5.00 2.00
❑ 106 Francisco Liriano (RC) 15.00 6.00
❑ 107 Anderson Hernandez (RC) 5.00 2.00

❑ 108 Boof Bonser (RC) 5.00 2.00
❑ 109 Jered Weaver (RC) 15.00 6.00
❑ 110 Ben Johnson (RC) 5.00 2.00
❑ 111 Jeff Harris RC 5.00 2.00
❑ 112 Stephen Drew (RC) 10.00 4.00
❑ 113 Matt Cain (RC) 8.00 3.00
❑ 114 Skip Schumaker (RC) 5.00 2.00
❑ 115 Adam Wainwright (RC) 8.00 3.00
❑ 116 Jeremy Sowers (RC) 5.00 2.00
❑ 117 Jason Bergmann RC 5.00 2.00
❑ 118 Chad Billingsley (RC) 15.00 6.00
❑ 119 Ryan Zimmerman (RC) 20.00 8.00
❑ 120 Macay McBride (RC) 5.00 2.00
❑ 121 Aaron Rakers (RC) 5.00 2.00
❑ 122 Alay Soler RC 5.00 2.00
❑ 123 Melky Cabrera (RC) 15.00 6.00
❑ 124 Tim Hamulack (RC) 5.00 2.00
❑ 125 Andre Ethier (RC) 12.00 5.00
❑ 126 Kenji Johjima RC 15.00 6.00
❑ NNO Exquisite Redemption

2007 Upper Deck Premier

❑ COMMON CARD (1-200) 5.00 2.00
❑ BASE CARD ODDS ONE PER PACK
❑ 1-200 STATED PRINT RUN 99 SER.#'d SETS
❑ COMMON ROOKIE (201-244) 5.00 2.00
❑ RC ODDS ONE PER PACK
❑ 201-244 STATED PRINT RUN 199 SER.#'d SETS
❑ PRINT.PLATES RANDOM INSERTS IN PACKS
❑ PLATE PRINT RUN 1 SET PER COLOR
❑ BLACK-CYAN-MAGENTA-YELLOW ISSUED
❑ NO PLATE PRICING DUE TO SCARCITY
❑ 1 Roy Campanella 10.00 4.00
❑ 2 Ty Cobb 12.00 5.00
❑ 3 Mickey Cochrane 5.00 2.00
❑ 4 Dizzy Dean 8.00 3.00
❑ 5 Don Drysdale 8.00 3.00
❑ 6 Jimmie Foxx 10.00 4.00
❑ 7 Lou Gehrig 15.00 6.00
❑ 8 Lefty Grove 5.00 2.00
❑ 9 Rogers Hornsby 10.00 4.00
❑ 10 Walter Johnson 10.00 4.00
❑ 11 Eddie Mathews 10.00 4.00
❑ 12 Christy Mathewson 10.00 4.00
❑ 13 Johnny Mize 8.00 3.00
❑ 14 Thurman Munson 12.00 5.00
❑ 15 Mel Ott 8.00 3.00
❑ 16 Satchel Paige 10.00 4.00
❑ 17 Jackie Robinson 12.00 5.00
❑ 18 Babe Ruth 20.00 8.00
❑ 19 George Sisler 5.00 2.00
❑ 20 Honus Wagner 10.00 4.00
❑ 21 Cy Young 10.00 4.00
❑ 22 Luis Aparicio 5.00 2.00
❑ 23 Johnny Bench 10.00 4.00
❑ 24 Yogi Berra 10.00 4.00
❑ 25 Rod Carew 8.00 3.00
❑ 26 Orlando Cepeda 5.00 2.00
❑ 27 Bob Feller 8.00 3.00
❑ 28 Carlton Fisk 8.00 3.00
❑ 29 Bob Gibson 8.00 3.00
❑ 30 Catfish Hunter 5.00 2.00
❑ 31 Reggie Jackson 8.00 3.00
❑ 32 Al Kaline 10.00 4.00
❑ 33 Harmon Killebrew 10.00 4.00
❑ 34 Buck Leonard 5.00 2.00
❑ 35 Juan Marichal 5.00 2.00
❑ 36 Bill Mazeroski 8.00 3.00
❑ 37 Willie McCovey 8.00 3.00
❑ 38 Joe Morgan 8.00 3.00
❑ 39 Eddie Murray 10.00 4.00
❑ 40 Jim Palmer 8.00 3.00
❑ 41 Tony Perez 8.00 3.00
❑ 42 Pee Wee Reese 8.00 3.00
❑ 43 Brooks Robinson 10.00 4.00
❑ 44 Nolan Ryan 20.00 8.00
❑ 45 Mike Schmidt 10.00 4.00
❑ 46 Tom Seaver 8.00 3.00
❑ 47 Enos Slaughter 5.00 2.00
❑ 48 Willie Stargell 8.00 3.00
❑ 49 Early Wynn 5.00 2.00
❑ 50 Robin Yount 10.00 4.00
❑ 51 Tony Gwynn 10.00 4.00
❑ 52 Cal Ripken Jr. 25.00 10.00
❑ 53 Ernie Banks 10.00 4.00
❑ 54 Wade Boggs 8.00 3.00
❑ 55 Steve Carlton 5.00 2.00
❑ 56 Will Clark 8.00 3.00
❑ 57 Fergie Jenkins 5.00 2.00
❑ 58 Bo Jackson 10.00 4.00
❑ 59 Don Mattingly 15.00 6.00
❑ 60 Stan Musial 12.00 5.00
❑ 61 Frank Robinson 5.00 2.00
❑ 62 Ryne Sandberg 12.00 5.00
❑ 63 Ozzie Smith 15.00 6.00
❑ 64 Carl Yastrzemski 12.00 5.00
❑ 65 Dave Winfield 8.00 3.00
❑ 66 Paul Molitor 5.00 2.00
❑ 67 Jason Bay 5.00 2.00
❑ 68 Freddy Sanchez 5.00 2.00
❑ 69 Josh Beckett 5.00 2.00
❑ 70 Carlos Beltran 5.00 2.00
❑ 71 Craig Biggio 10.00 4.00
❑ 72 Matt Holliday 6.00 2.50
❑ 73 A.J. Burnett 5.00 2.00
❑ 74 Miguel Cabrera 8.00 3.00
❑ 75 Dontrelle Willis 5.00 2.00
❑ 76 Chris Carpenter 8.00 3.00
❑ 77 Roger Clemens 15.00 6.00
❑ 78 Johnny Damon 8.00 3.00
❑ 79 Jermaine Dye 5.00 2.00
❑ 80 Jim Thome 8.00 3.00
❑ 81 Vladimir Guerrero 10.00 4.00
❑ 82 Travis Hafner 5.00 2.00
❑ 83 Victor Martinez 5.00 2.00
❑ 84 Trevor Hoffman 5.00 2.00
❑ 85 Derek Jeter 20.00 8.00
❑ 86 Ken Griffey Jr. 12.00 5.00
❑ 87 Randy Johnson 10.00 4.00
❑ 88 Andruw Jones 8.00 3.00
❑ 89 Derrek Lee 5.00 2.00
❑ 90 Greg Maddux 12.00 5.00
❑ 91 Magglio Ordonez 8.00 3.00
❑ 92 David Ortiz 10.00 4.00
❑ 93 Jake Peavy 5.00 2.00
❑ 94 Roy Oswalt 5.00 2.00
❑ 95 Mike Piazza 10.00 4.00
❑ 96 Jose Reyes 10.00 4.00
❑ 97 Ivan Rodriguez 10.00 4.00
❑ 98 Johan Santana 8.00 3.00
❑ 99 Scott Rolen 8.00 3.00
❑ 100 Curt Schilling 8.00 3.00
❑ 101 John Smoltz 8.00 3.00
❑ 102 Alfonso Soriano 5.00 2.00
❑ 103 Miguel Tejada 8.00 3.00
❑ 104 Frank Thomas 12.00 5.00
❑ 105 Chase Utley 10.00 4.00
❑ 106 Joe Mauer 8.00 3.00
❑ 107 Alex Rodriguez 15.00 6.00
❑ 108 Alex Rios 8.00 3.00
❑ 109 Justin Verlander 10.00 4.00
❑ 110 Ryan Howard 12.00 5.00
❑ 111 Jered Weaver 8.00 3.00
❑ 112 Francisco Liriano 10.00 4.00
❑ 113 David Wright 12.00 5.00
❑ 114 Felix Hernandez 8.00 3.00
❑ 115 Jeremy Sowers 8.00 3.00
❑ 116 Cole Hamels 8.00 3.00
❑ 117 B.J. Upton 5.00 2.00
❑ 118 Chien-Ming Wang 50.00 20.00
❑ 119 Justin Morneau 8.00 3.00
❑ 120 Jonny Gomes 5.00 2.00
❑ 121 Adrian Gonzalez 5.00 2.00
❑ 122 Bill Hall 8.00 3.00
❑ 123 Rich Harden 8.00 3.00
❑ 124 Rich Hill 5.00 2.00
❑ 125 Tadahito Iguchi 5.00 2.00
❑ 126 Scott Kazmir 8.00 3.00
❑ 127 Howie Kendrick 5.00 2.00
❑ 128 Dan Uggla 8.00 3.00
❑ 129 Hanley Ramirez 8.00 3.00
❑ 130 Josh Willingham 5.00 2.00
❑ 131 Nick Markakis 8.00 3.00
❑ 132 Grady Sizemore 10.00 4.00
❑ 133 Ian Kinsler 8.00 3.00
❑ 134 Jonathan Papelbon 12.00 5.00
❑ 135 Ryan Zimmerman 10.00 4.00
❑ 136 Stephen Drew 8.00 3.00
❑ 137 Adam Wainwright 5.00 2.00
❑ 138 Joel Zumaya 8.00 3.00
❑ 139 Prince Fielder 10.00 4.00
❑ 140 Carl Crawford 8.00 3.00
❑ 141 Huston Street 5.00 2.00
❑ 142 Matt Cain 8.00 3.00
❑ 143 Andre Ethier 8.00 3.00
❑ 144 Brian McCann 8.00 3.00
❑ 145 Josh Barfield 5.00 2.00
❑ 146 Anibal Sanchez 5.00 2.00
❑ 147 Brian Roberts 8.00 3.00
❑ 148 Brandon Webb 5.00 2.00
❑ 149 Chipper Jones 10.00 4.00
❑ 150 Tim Hudson 8.00 3.00
❑ 151 Adam LaRoche 5.00 2.00
❑ 152 Jeff Francoeur 10.00 4.00
❑ 153 Marcus Giles 5.00 2.00
❑ 154 Jason Varitek 12.00 5.00
❑ 155 Coco Crisp 8.00 3.00
❑ 156 Manny Ramirez 8.00 3.00
❑ 157 Trot Nixon 8.00 3.00
❑ 158 Carlos Zambrano 5.00 2.00
❑ 159 Mark Prior 8.00 3.00
❑ 160 Aramis Ramirez 5.00 2.00
❑ 161 Mark Buehrle 5.00 2.00
❑ 162 Paul Konerko 5.00 2.00
❑ 163 Adam Dunn 8.00 3.00
❑ 164 C.C. Sabathia 5.00 2.00
❑ 165 Todd Helton 8.00 3.00
❑ 166 Garrett Atkins 8.00 3.00
❑ 167 Jeremy Bonderman 10.00 4.00
❑ 168 Curtis Granderson 8.00 3.00
❑ 169 Sean Casey 8.00 3.00
❑ 170 Lance Berkman 8.00 3.00
❑ 171 Brad Lidge 5.00 2.00
❑ 172 Reggie Sanders 5.00 2.00
❑ 173 Brad Penny 5.00 2.00

❑ 174	Nomar Garciaparra	12.00	5.00
❑ 175	Jeff Kent	8.00	3.00
❑ 176	Chone Figgins	5.00	2.00
❑ 177	Ben Sheets	8.00	3.00
❑ 178	Rickie Weeks	8.00	3.00
❑ 179	Joe Nathan	8.00	3.00
❑ 180	Torii Hunter	8.00	3.00
❑ 181	Carlos Delgado	8.00	3.00
❑ 182	Tom Glavine	10.00	4.00
❑ 183	Paul Lo Duca	5.00	2.00
❑ 184	Mariano Rivera	12.00	5.00
❑ 185	Robinson Cano	10.00	4.00
❑ 186	Bobby Abreu	8.00	3.00
❑ 187	Hideki Matsui	12.00	5.00
❑ 188	Barry Zito	5.00	2.00
❑ 189	Eric Chavez	8.00	3.00
❑ 190	Jimmy Rollins	8.00	3.00
❑ 191	Khalil Greene	10.00	4.00
❑ 192	Brian Giles	5.00	2.00
❑ 193	Jason Schmidt	5.00	2.00
❑ 194	Ichiro Suzuki	30.00	12.50
❑ 195	David Eckstein	10.00	4.00
❑ 196	Jim Edmonds	8.00	3.00
❑ 197	Mark Teixeira	8.00	3.00
❑ 198	Michael Young	5.00	2.00
❑ 199	Vernon Wells	8.00	3.00
❑ 200	Roy Halladay	8.00	3.00
❑ 201	Delmon Young (RC)	8.00	3.00
❑ 202	Andrew Miller RC	20.00	8.00
❑ 203	Troy Tulowitzki (RC)	8.00	3.00
❑ 204	Jeff Fiorentino (RC)	5.00	2.00
❑ 205	David Murphy (RC)	5.00	2.00
❑ 206	Jeff Baker (RC)	5.00	2.00
❑ 207	Kevin Hooper (RC)	5.00	2.00
❑ 208	Kevin Kouzmanoff (RC)	5.00	2.00
❑ 209	Adam Lind (RC)	8.00	3.00
❑ 210	Mike Rabelo RC	8.00	3.00
❑ 211	John Nelson (RC)	5.00	2.00
❑ 212	Mitch Maier RC	5.00	2.00
❑ 213	Ryan Braun RC	5.00	2.00
❑ 214	Vinny Rottino (RC)	5.00	2.00
❑ 215	Drew Anderson RC	5.00	2.00
❑ 216	Alexi Casilla RC	8.00	3.00
❑ 217	Glen Perkins (RC)	5.00	2.00
❑ 218	Cesar Jimenez RC	5.00	2.00
❑ 219	Tim Gradoville RC	5.00	2.00
❑ 220	Shane Youman RC	5.00	2.00
❑ 221	Billy Sadler (RC)	5.00	2.00
❑ 222	Patrick Misch (RC)	5.00	2.00
❑ 223	Juan Salas (RC)	5.00	2.00
❑ 224	Beltran Perez (RC)	5.00	2.00
❑ 225	Hector Gimenez (RC)	5.00	2.00
❑ 226	Philip Humber (RC)	8.00	3.00
❑ 227	Eric Stults RC	5.00	2.00
❑ 228	Dennis Sarfate (RC)	5.00	2.00
❑ 229	Andy Cannizaro RC	8.00	3.00
❑ 230	Juan Morillo (RC)	5.00	2.00
❑ 231	Fred Lewis (RC)	5.00	2.00
❑ 232	Ryan Sweeney (RC)	5.00	2.00
❑ 233	Chris Narveson (RC)	5.00	2.00
❑ 234	Michael Bourn (RC)	5.00	2.00
❑ 235	Joaquin Arias (RC)	5.00	2.00
❑ 236	Carlos Maldonado (RC)	5.00	2.00
❑ 237	Alvin Colina RC	5.00	2.00
❑ 238	Jon Knott (RC)	5.00	2.00
❑ 239	Justin Hampson (RC)	5.00	2.00
❑ 240	Jeff Salazar (RC)	5.00	2.00
❑ 241	Josh Fields (RC)	5.00	2.00
❑ 242	Delwyn Young (RC)	5.00	2.00
❑ 243	Daisuke Matsuzaka RC	30.00	12.50
❑ 244	Kei Igawa RC	20.00	8.00

2008 Upper Deck Premier

❑ COMMON CARD (1-178)	5.00	2.00
❑ COMMON RET (179-200)	3.00	1.25
❑ ONE BASE CARD PER PACK		
❑ 1-200 STATED PRINT RUN 99 SER.#'d SETS		
❑ COMMON AU RC p/r 299 (201-241)	10.00	4.00
❑ COMMON AU RC p/r 99 (201-241)	12.00	5.00
❑ OVERALL RC AUTO ONE PER PACK		
❑ 201-241 PRINT RUNS b/w 99-299 SER.#'d SETS		
❑ EXCHANGE DEADLINE 3/13/2010		

❑ 1	Chipper Jones	15.00	6.00
❑ 2	Andruw Jones	5.00	2.00
❑ 3	John Smoltz	12.00	5.00
❑ 4	Mark Teixeira	8.00	3.00
❑ 5	Edgar Renteria	5.00	2.00
❑ 6	Jeff Francoeur	8.00	3.00
❑ 7	Tim Hudson	5.00	2.00
❑ 8	Miguel Cabrera	8.00	3.00
❑ 9	Hanley Ramirez	12.00	5.00
❑ 10	Dan Uggla	8.00	3.00
❑ 11	Dontrelle Willis	5.00	2.00
❑ 12	Josh Willingham	5.00	2.00
❑ 13	Pedro Martinez	8.00	3.00
❑ 14	Carlos Delgado	5.00	2.00
❑ 15	Carlos Beltran	5.00	2.00
❑ 16	David Wright	15.00	6.00
❑ 17	Tom Glavine	8.00	3.00
❑ 18	Jose Reyes	8.00	3.00
❑ 19	Paul Lo Duca	5.00	2.00
❑ 20	John Maine	5.00	2.00
❑ 21	Chase Utley	12.00	5.00
❑ 22	Cole Hamels	8.00	3.00
❑ 23	Jimmy Rollins	8.00	3.00
❑ 24	Shane Victorino	5.00	2.00
❑ 25	Ryan Howard	15.00	6.00
❑ 26	Pat Burrell	5.00	2.00
❑ 27	Aaron Rowand	5.00	2.00
❑ 28	Ryan Zimmerman	8.00	3.00
❑ 29	Ryan Church	5.00	2.00
❑ 30	Matt Chico	5.00	2.00
❑ 31	Dmitri Young	5.00	2.00
❑ 32	Derrek Lee	8.00	3.00
❑ 33	Aramis Ramirez	5.00	2.00
❑ 34	Carlos Zambrano	5.00	2.00
❑ 35	Rich Hill	5.00	2.00
❑ 36	Alfonso Soriano	8.00	3.00
❑ 37	Kerry Wood	5.00	2.00
❑ 38	Ted Lilly	5.00	2.00
❑ 39	Ryan Theriot	5.00	2.00
❑ 40	Ken Griffey Jr.	20.00	8.00
❑ 41	Adam Dunn	5.00	2.00
❑ 42	Homer Bailey	8.00	3.00
❑ 43	Aaron Harang	5.00	2.00
❑ 44	Brandon Phillips	5.00	2.00
❑ 45	Josh Hamilton	15.00	6.00
❑ 46	Lance Berkman	8.00	3.00
❑ 47	Carlos Lee	5.00	2.00
❑ 48	Hunter Pence	12.00	5.00
❑ 49	Mark Loretta	5.00	2.00
❑ 50	Roy Oswalt	5.00	2.00
❑ 51	Prince Fielder	12.00	5.00
❑ 52	Ryan Braun	15.00	6.00
❑ 53	J.J. Hardy	5.00	2.00
❑ 54	Ben Sheets	8.00	3.00
❑ 55	Rickie Weeks	5.00	2.00
❑ 56	Corey Hart	5.00	2.00
❑ 57	Johnny Estrada	5.00	2.00
❑ 58	Jason Bay	5.00	2.00
❑ 59	Freddy Sanchez	5.00	2.00
❑ 60	Adam LaRoche	5.00	2.00
❑ 61	Ian Snell	5.00	2.00
❑ 62	Xavier Nady	5.00	2.00
❑ 63	Tom Gorzelanny	5.00	2.00
❑ 64	Scott Rolen	8.00	3.00
❑ 65	Albert Pujols	20.00	8.00
❑ 66	Jim Edmonds	8.00	3.00
❑ 67	Chris Duncan	5.00	2.00
❑ 68	Adam Wainwright	5.00	2.00
❑ 69	Brandon Webb	5.00	2.00
❑ 70	Orlando Hudson	5.00	2.00
❑ 71	Chris B. Young	5.00	2.00
❑ 72	Stephen Drew	5.00	2.00
❑ 73	Matt Holliday	8.00	3.00
❑ 74	Jeff Francis	5.00	2.00
❑ 75	Brad Hawpe	5.00	2.00
❑ 76	Todd Helton	8.00	3.00
❑ 77	Troy Tulowitzki	8.00	3.00
❑ 78	Russell Martin	5.00	2.00
❑ 79	Nomar Garciaparra	12.00	5.00
❑ 80	James Loney	8.00	3.00
❑ 81	Andre Ethier	8.00	3.00
❑ 82	Brad Penny	5.00	2.00
❑ 83	Rafael Furcal	5.00	2.00
❑ 84	Jeff Kent	5.00	2.00
❑ 85	Greg Maddux	15.00	6.00
❑ 86	Chris Young	5.00	2.00
❑ 87	Khalil Greene	8.00	3.00
❑ 88	Trevor Hoffman	5.00	2.00
❑ 89	Adrian Gonzalez	8.00	3.00
❑ 90	Jake Peavy	5.00	2.00
❑ 91	Noah Lowry	5.00	2.00
❑ 92	Omar Vizquel	5.00	2.00
❑ 93	Tim Lincecum	12.00	5.00
❑ 94	Matt Cain	5.00	2.00
❑ 95	Randy Winn	5.00	2.00
❑ 96	Miguel Tejada	5.00	2.00
❑ 97	Brian Roberts	8.00	3.00
❑ 98	Nick Markakis	8.00	3.00
❑ 99	Erik Bedard	5.00	2.00
❑ 100	Melvin Mora	5.00	2.00
❑ 101	David Ortiz	12.00	5.00
❑ 102	Manny Ramirez	12.00	5.00
❑ 103	Josh Beckett	8.00	3.00
❑ 104	Jonathan Papelbon	8.00	3.00
❑ 105	Curt Schilling	8.00	3.00
❑ 106	Daisuke Matsuzaka	25.00	10.00
❑ 107	Jason Varitek	12.00	5.00
❑ 108	Kevin Youkilis	8.00	3.00
❑ 109	Derek Jeter	30.00	12.00
❑ 110	Hideki Matsui	12.00	5.00
❑ 111	Alex Rodriguez	20.00	8.00
❑ 112	Johnny Damon	8.00	3.00
❑ 113	Robinson Cano	8.00	3.00
❑ 114	Jorge Posada	8.00	3.00
❑ 115	Mariano Rivera	12.00	5.00
❑ 116	Roger Clemens	15.00	6.00
❑ 117	Chien-Ming Wang	20.00	8.00
❑ 118	Carl Crawford	5.00	2.00
❑ 119	Delmon Young	8.00	3.00
❑ 120	B.J. Upton	8.00	3.00
❑ 121	Akinori Iwamura	5.00	2.0
❑ 122	Scott Kazmir	8.00	3.0

	No.	Player		
❑	123	Alex Rios	5.00	2.00
❑	124	Frank Thomas	12.00	5.00
❑	125	Roy Halladay	5.00	2.00
❑	126	Vernon Wells	5.00	2.00
❑	127	Troy Glaus	8.00	3.00
❑	128	Jeremy Accardo	5.00	2.00
❑	129	A.J. Burnett	5.00	2.00
❑	130	Paul Konerko	5.00	2.00
❑	131	Jim Thome	8.00	3.00
❑	132	Jermaine Dye	5.00	2.00
❑	133	Mark Buehrle	5.00	2.00
❑	134	Javier Vazquez	5.00	2.00
❑	135	Grady Sizemore	8.00	3.00
❑	136	Travis Hafner	5.00	2.00
❑	137	Victor Martinez	5.00	2.00
❑	138	C.C. Sabathia	5.00	2.00
❑	139	Ryan Garko	5.00	2.00
❑	140	Fausto Carmona	5.00	2.00
❑	141	Justin Verlander	8.00	3.00
❑	142	Jeremy Bonderman	5.00	2.00
❑	143	Magglio Ordonez	8.00	3.00
❑	144	Gary Sheffield	5.00	2.00
❑	145	Carlos Guillen	5.00	2.00
❑	146	Ivan Rodriguez	8.00	3.00
❑	147	Curtis Granderson	8.00	3.00
❑	148	Alex Gordon	12.00	5.00
❑	149	Mark Teahen	5.00	2.00
❑	150	Brian Bannister	5.00	2.00
❑	151	Billy Butler	5.00	2.00
❑	152	Johan Santana	12.00	5.00
❑	153	Torii Hunter	5.00	2.00
❑	154	Joe Mauer	8.00	3.00
❑	155	Justin Morneau	5.00	2.00
❑	156	Vladimir Guerrero	12.00	5.00
❑	157	Chone Figgins	5.00	2.00
❑	158	Jered Weaver	5.00	2.00
❑	159	Kelvim Escobar	5.00	2.00
❑	160	John Lackey	5.00	2.00
❑	161	Dan Haren	5.00	2.00
❑	162	Mike Piazza	12.00	5.00
❑	163	Nick Swisher	5.00	2.00
❑	164	Eric Chavez	5.00	2.00
❑	165	Huston Street	5.00	2.00
❑	166	Joe Blanton	5.00	2.00
❑	167	Kenji Johjima	5.00	2.00
❑	168	J.J. Putz	5.00	2.00
❑	169	Felix Hernandez	8.00	3.00
❑	170	Jose Guillen	5.00	2.00
❑	171	Adrian Beltre	5.00	2.00
❑	172	Ichiro	20.00	8.00
❑	173	Marlon Byrd	5.00	2.00
❑	174	Hank Blalock	5.00	2.00
❑	175	Michael Young	5.00	2.00
❑	176	Ian Kinsler	8.00	3.00
❑	177	Sammy Sosa	8.00	3.00
❑	178	Kevin Millwood	5.00	2.00
❑	179	Luis Aparicio	3.00	1.25
❑	180	Johnny Bench	8.00	3.00
❑	181	Yogi Berra	8.00	3.00
❑	182	Lou Brock	5.00	2.00
❑	183	Jim Bunning	3.00	1.25
❑	184	Rod Carew	5.00	2.00
❑	185	Orlando Cepeda	3.00	1.25
❑	186	Bobby Doerr	3.00	1.25
❑	187	Bob Feller	3.00	1.25
❑	188	Dennis Eckersley	3.00	1.25
❑	189	Carlton Fisk	5.00	2.00
❑	190	Monte Irvin	3.00	1.25
❑	191	Rollie Fingers	3.00	1.25
❑	192	Al Kaline	8.00	3.00
❑	193	Nolan Ryan	20.00	8.00
❑	194	Mike Schmidt	12.00	5.00
	195	Ryne Sandberg	15.00	6.00
	196	Robin Yount	8.00	3.00
❑	197	Brooks Robinson	5.00	2.00
❑	198	Bill Mazeroski	5.00	2.00
❑	199	Reggie Jackson	5.00	2.00
❑	200	Babe Ruth	20.00	8.00
❑	201	Ian Kennedy AU RC/299	30.00	12.50
❑	202	Jonathan Albaladejo AU RC/299	12.00	5.00
❑	203	Josh Anderson AU (RC)/299	10.00	4.00
❑	204	Wladimir Balentien AU (RC)/299	12.00	5.00
❑	205	Daric Barton AU (RC)/299	12.00	5.00
❑	206	Jerry Blevins AU RC/99	12.00	5.00
❑	207	Emilio Bonifacio AU RC/99	12.00	5.00
❑	208	Lance Broadway AU (RC)/299	10.00	4.00
❑	209	Clay Buchholz AU (RC)/299	40.00	15.00
❑	210	Billy Buckner AU (RC)/299	10.00	4.00
❑	212	Ross Detwiler AU RC/299	12.00	5.00
❑	213	Harvey Garcia AU (RC)/99	12.00	5.00
❑	214	Alberto Gonzalez AU RC/99	30.00	12.50
❑	215	Ryan Hanigan AU RC/99	12.00	5.00
❑	216	Kevin Hart AU (RC)/299	10.00	4.00
❑	217	Luke Hochevar AU RC/299	15.00	6.00
❑	218	Chin-Lung Hu AU (RC)/299	40.00	15.00
❑	219	Rob Johnson AU (RC)/99	12.00	5.00
❑	220	Brandon Jones AU RC/299	15.00	6.00
❑	221	Joe Koshansky AU (RC)/299	10.00	4.00
❑	222	Donny Lucy AU (RC)/299	10.00	4.00
❑	223	Justin Maxwell AU RC/299	15.00	6.00
❑	224	Jonathan Meloan AU RC/299	10.00	4.00
❑	225	Luis Mendoza AU (RC)/299	10.00	4.00
❑	226	Jose Morales AU (RC)/299	10.00	4.00
❑	227	Nyjer Morgan AU (RC)/99	12.00	5.00
❑	228	Bill Murphy AU (RC)/99	12.00	5.00
❑	229	Josh Newman AU RC/99	12.00	5.00
❑	230	Ross Ohlendorf AU RC/299	12.00	5.00
❑	231	Troy Patton AU (RC)/299	10.00	4.00
❑	232	Felipe Paulino AU RC/99 EXCH	12.00	5.00
❑	233	Steve Pearce AU RC/299	12.00	5.00
❑	234	Justin Ruggiano AU RC/99	12.00	5.00
❑	235	Clint Sammons AU (RC)/299	10.00	4.00
❑	236	Bronson Sardinha AU (RC)/299	10.00	4.00
❑	237	Chris Seddon AU (RC)/99	12.00	5.00
❑	238	Seth Smith AU (RC)/299	10.00	4.00
❑	239	J.R. Towles AU RC/299	12.00	5.00
❑	240	Eugenio Velez AU RC/99	40.00	15.00
❑	241	Joey Votto AU (RC)/299	20.00	8.00
❑	242	Bill White AU RC/99	12.00	5.00

2001 Upper Deck Prospect Premieres

	No.	Player		
❑		COMP.SET w/o SP's (90)	80.00	50.00
❑		COMMON CARD (1-90)	.40	.15
❑		COMMON AUTO (91-102)	15.00	6.00
❑	1	Jeff Mathis XRC	.50	.20
❑	2	Jake Woods XRC	.40	.15
❑	3	Dallas McPherson XRC	1.00	.40
❑	4	Steven Shell XRC	.40	.15
❑	5	Ryan Budde XRC	.40	.15
❑	6	Kirk Saarloos XRC	.40	.15
❑	7	Ryan Stegall XRC	.40	.15
❑	8	Bobby Crosby XRC	3.00	1.25
❑	9	J.T. Stotts XRC	.40	.15
❑	10	Neal Cotts XRC	1.00	.40
❑	11	Jeremy Bonderman XRC	4.00	1.50
❑	12	Brandon League XRC	.40	.15
❑	13	Tyrell Godwin XRC	.40	.15
❑	14	Gabe Gross XRC	.50	.20
❑	15	Chris Neylan XRC	.40	.15
❑	16	Macay McBride XRC	.75	.30
❑	17	Josh Burrus XRC	.40	.15
❑	18	Adam Stern XRC	.40	.15
❑	19	Richard Lewis XRC	.40	.15
❑	20	Cole Barthel XRC	.40	.15
❑	21	Mike Jones XRC	.50	.20
❑	22	J.J. Hardy XRC	6.00	2.50
❑	23	Jon Steitz XRC	.40	.15
❑	24	Brad Nelson XRC	.40	.15
❑	25	Justin Pope XRC	.40	.15
❑	26	Dan Haren XRC	2.00	.75
❑	27	Andy Sisco XRC	.40	.15
❑	28	Ryan Theriot XRC	3.00	1.25
❑	29	Ricky Nolasco XRC	2.00	.75
❑	30	Jon Switzer XRC	.40	.15
❑	31	Justin Wechsler XRC	.40	.15
❑	32	Mike Gosling XRC	.40	.15
❑	33	Scott Hairston XRC	.50	.20
❑	34	Brian Pilkington XRC	.40	.15
❑	35	Kole Strayhorn XRC	.40	.15
❑	36	David Taylor XRC	.40	.15
❑	37	Donald Levinski XRC	.40	.15
❑	38	Mike Hinckley XRC	.50	.20
❑	39	Nick Long XRC	.40	.15
❑	40	Brad Hennessey XRC	.50	.20
❑	41	Noah Lowry XRC	2.00	.75
❑	42	Josh Cram XRC	.40	.15
❑	43	Jesse Foppert XRC	.50	.20
❑	44	Julian Benavidez XRC	.40	.15
❑	45	Dan Denham XRC	.40	.15
❑	46	Travis Foley XRC	.40	.15
❑	47	Mike Conroy XRC	.40	.15
❑	48	Jake Dittler XRC	.40	.15
❑	49	Rene Rivera XRC	.40	.15
❑	50	John Cole XRC	.40	.15
❑	51	Lazaro Abreu XRC	.40	.15
❑	52	David Wright XRC	30.00	12.50
❑	53	Aaron Heilman XRC	.50	.20
❑	54	Len DiNardo XRC	.40	.15
❑	55	Alhaji Turay XRC	.40	.15
❑	56	Chris Smith XRC	.40	.15
❑	57	Rommie Lewis XRC	.40	.15
❑	58	Bryan Bass XRC	.40	.15
❑	59	David Crouthers XRC	.40	.15
❑	60	Josh Barfield XRC	3.00	1.25
❑	61	Jake Peavy XRC	6.00	2.50
❑	62	Ryan Howard XRC	25.00	10.00
❑	63	Gavin Floyd XRC	1.00	.40
❑	64	Michael Floyd XRC	.40	.15
❑	65	Stefan Bailie XRC	.40	.15
❑	66	Jon DeVries XRC	.40	.15
❑	67	Steve Kelly XRC	.40	.15
❑	68	Alan Moye XRC	.40	.15
❑	69	Justin Gillman XRC	.40	.15
❑	70	Jayson Nix XRC	.40	.15
❑	71	John Draper XRC	.40	.15
❑	72	Kenny Baugh XRC	.40	.15
❑	73	Michael Woods XRC	.40	.15
❑	74	Preston Larrison XRC	.50	.20
❑	75	Matt Coenen XRC	.40	.15
❑	76	Scott Tyler XRC	.50	.20
❑	77	Jose Morales XRC	.40	.15
❑	78	Corwin Malone XRC	.40	.15
❑	79	Dennis Ulacia XRC	.40	.15
❑	80	Andy Gonzalez XRC	.40	.15
❑	81	Kris Honel XRC	.40	.15

❑ 82 Wyatt Allen XRC	.40	.15
❑ 83 Ryan Wing XRC	.40	.15
❑ 84 Sean Henn XRC	.40	.15
❑ 85 John-Ford Griffin XRC	.40	.15
❑ 86 Bronson Sardinha XRC	.40	.15
❑ 87 Jon Skaggs XRC	.40	.15
❑ 88 Shelley Duncan XRC	4.00	1.50
❑ 89 Jason Arnold XRC	.40	.15
❑ 90 Aaron Rifkin XRC	.40	.15
❑ 91 Colt Griffin AU XRC	15.00	6.00
❑ 92 J.D. Martin AU XRC	15.00	6.00
❑ 93 Justin Wayne AU XRC	15.00	6.00
❑ 94 J.VanBenschoten AU XRC	15.00	6.00
❑ 95 Chris Burke AU XRC	25.00	10.00
❑ 96 Casey Kotchman AU XRC	50.00	20.00
❑ 97 Michael Garciaparra AU XRC	15.00	6.00
❑ 98 Jake Gautreau AU XRC	15.00	6.00
❑ 99 Jerome Williams AU XRC	15.00	6.00
❑ 100 Toe Nash AU XRC	15.00	6.00
❑ 101 Joe Borchard AU XRC	15.00	6.00
❑ 102 Mark Prior AU XRC	60.00	35.00

2002 Upper Deck Prospect Premieres

❑ COMP.SET w/o SP's (72)	40.00	25.00
❑ COMMON CARD (1-60)	.40	.15
❑ COMMON CARD (61-85)	5.00	2.00
❑ COMMON CARD (86-97)	8.00	3.00
❑ COMMON RIPKEN (98-99)	2.00	.75
❑ COMMON MCGWIRE (100-105)	2.00	.75
❑ COMMON DIMAGGIO (106-109)	1.50	.60
❑ PENDER COR AVAIL.VIA MAIL EXCHANGE		
❑ 1 Josh Rupe XRC	.40	.15
❑ 2 Blair Johnson XRC	.40	.15
❑ 3 Jason Pridie XRC	.40	.15
❑ 4 Tim Gilhooly XRC	.40	.15
❑ 5 Kennard Jones XRC	.40	.15
❑ 6 Darrell Rasner XRC	.40	.15
❑ 7 Adam Donachie XRC	.40	.15
❑ 8 Josh Murray XRC	.40	.15
❑ 9 Brian Dopirak XRC	1.00	.40
❑ 10 Jason Cooper XRC	.40	.15
❑ 11 Zach Hammes XRC	.40	.15
❑ 12 Jon Lester XRC	15.00	6.00
❑ 13 Kevin Jepsen XRC	.50	.20
❑ 14 Curtis Granderson XRC	4.00	1.50
❑ 15 David Bush XRC	1.00	.40
❑ 16 Joel Guzman	.75	.30
❑ 17A M.Pender UER Granderson	1.50	.60
❑ 17B Matt Pender COR	1.00	.40
❑ 18 Derick Grigsby XRC	.40	.15
❑ 19 Jeremy Reed XRC	1.00	.40
❑ 20 Jonathan Broxton XRC	1.00	.40
❑ 21 Jesse Crain XRC	.75	.30
❑ 22 Justin Jones XRC	.50	.20
❑ 23 Brian Slocum XRC	.40	.15
❑ 24 Brian McCann XRC	8.00	3.00
❑ 25 Francisco Liriano XRC	8.00	3.00
❑ 26 Fred Lewis XRC	.40	.15
❑ 27 Steve Stanley XRC	.40	.15
❑ 28 Chris Snyder XRC	.50	.20
❑ 29 Dan Cevette XRC	.40	.15
❑ 30 Kiel Fisher XRC	.50	.20
❑ 31 Brandon Weeden XRC	.40	.15
❑ 32 Pat Osborn XRC	.40	.15
❑ 33 Taber Lee XRC	.40	.15
❑ 34 Dan Ortmeier XRC	.50	.20
❑ 35 Josh Johnson XRC	4.00	1.50
❑ 36 Val Majewski XRC	.40	.15
❑ 37 Larry Broadway XRC	.40	.15
❑ 38 Joey Gomes XRC	.40	.15
❑ 39 Eric Thomas XRC	.40	.15
❑ 40 James Loney XRC	5.00	2.00
❑ 41 Charlie Morton XRC	.40	.15
❑ 42 Mark McLemore XRC	.40	.15
❑ 43 Matt Craig XRC	.50	.20
❑ 44 Ryan Rodriguez XRC	.40	.15
❑ 45 Rich Hill XRC	3.00	1.25
❑ 46 Bob Malek XRC	.40	.15
❑ 47 Justin Maureau XRC	.40	.15
❑ 48 Randy Braun XRC	.40	.15
❑ 49 Brian Grant XRC	.40	.15
❑ 50 Tyler Davidson XRC	.50	.20
❑ 51 Travis Hanson XRC	.50	.20
❑ 52 Kyle Boyer XRC	.40	.15
❑ 53 James Holcomb XRC	.40	.15
❑ 54 Ryan Williams XRC	.40	.15
❑ 55 Ben Crockett XRC	.40	.15
❑ 56 Adam Greenberg XRC	.75	.30
❑ 57 John Baker XRC	.40	.15
❑ 58 Matt Carson XRC	.40	.15
❑ 59 Jonathan George XRC	.40	.15
❑ 60 David Jensen XRC	.40	.15
❑ 61 Nick Swisher JSY XRC	15.00	6.00
❑ 62 Brent Clevlen JSY UER XRC	12.00	5.00
❑ 63 Royce Ring JSY XRC	5.00	2.00
❑ 64 Mike Nixon JSY XRC	5.00	2.00
❑ 65 Ricky Barrett JSY XRC	5.00	2.00
❑ 66 Russ Adams JSY XRC	5.00	2.00
❑ 67 Joe Mauer JSY XRC	25.00	10.00
❑ 68 Jeff Francoeur JSY XRC	30.00	12.50
❑ 69 Joe Blanton JSY XRC	8.00	3.00
❑ 70 Micah Schilling JSY XRC	5.00	2.00
❑ 71 John McCurdy JSY XRC	5.00	2.00
❑ 72 Sergio Santos JSY XRC	8.00	3.00
❑ 73 Josh Womack JSY XRC	5.00	2.00
❑ 74 Jared Doyle JSY XRC	5.00	2.00
❑ 75 Ben Fritz JSY XRC	5.00	2.00
❑ 76 Greg Miller JSY XRC	5.00	2.00
❑ 77 Luke Hagerty JSY XRC	5.00	2.00
❑ 78 Matt Whitney JSY XRC	5.00	2.00
❑ 79 Dan Meyer JSY XRC	8.00	3.00
❑ 80 Bill Murphy JSY XRC	5.00	2.00
❑ 81 Zach Segovia JSY XRC	5.00	2.00
❑ 82 Steve Obenchain JSY XRC	5.00	2.00
❑ 83 Matt Clanton JSY XRC	5.00	2.00
❑ 84 Mark Teahen JSY XRC	8.00	3.00
❑ 85 Kyle Pawelczyk JSY XRC	5.00	2.00
❑ 86 Khalil Greene AU XRC	30.00	12.50
❑ 87 Joe Saunders AU XRC	20.00	8.00
❑ 88 Jeremy Hermida AU XRC	50.00	30.00
❑ 89 Drew Meyer AU XRC	8.00	3.00
❑ 90 Jeff Francis AU XRC	30.00	12.50
❑ 91 Scott Moore AU XRC	8.00	3.00
❑ 92 Prince Fielder AU XRC	120.00	60.00
❑ 93 Zack Greinke AU XRC	30.00	12.50
❑ 94 Chris Gruler AU XRC	8.00	3.00
❑ 95 Scott Kazmir AU XRC	60.00	30.00
❑ 96 B.J. Upton AU XRC	50.00	20.00
❑ 97 Clint Everts AU XRC	8.00	3.00
❑ 98 Cal Ripken TRIB	2.00	.75
❑ 99 Cal Ripken TRIB	2.00	.75
❑ 100 Mark McGwire TRIB	2.00	.75
❑ 101 Mark McGwire TRIB	2.00	.75
❑ 102 Mark McGwire TRIB	2.00	.75
❑ 103 Mark McGwire TRIB	2.00	.75
❑ 104 Mark McGwire TRIB	2.00	.75
❑ 105 Joe DiMaggio TRIB	1.50	.60
❑ 106 Joe DiMaggio TRIB	1.50	.60
❑ 107 Joe DiMaggio TRIB	1.50	.60
❑ 108 Joe DiMaggio TRIB	1.50	.60
❑ 109 Joe DiMaggio TRIB	1.50	.60

2003 Upper Deck Prospect Premieres

❑ COMPLETE SET (90)	40.00	20.00
❑ 1 Bryan Opdyke XRC	.40	.15
❑ 2 Gabriel Sosa XRC	.40	.15
❑ 3 Tila Reynolds XRC	.40	.15
❑ 4 Aaron Hill XRC	1.00	.40
❑ 5 Aaron Marsden XRC	.50	.20
❑ 6 Abe Alvarez XRC	.50	.20
❑ 7 Adam Jones XRC	5.00	2.00
❑ 8 Adam Miller XRC	3.00	1.25
❑ 9 Andre Ethier XRC	8.00	3.00
❑ 10 Anthony Gwynn XRC	1.25	.50
❑ 11 Brad Snyder XRC	.75	.30
❑ 12 Brad Sullivan XRC	.50	.20
❑ 13 Brian Anderson XRC	2.00	.75
❑ 14 Brian Buscher XRC	.40	.15
❑ 15 Brian Snyder XRC	.50	.20
❑ 16 Carlos Quentin XRC	3.00	1.25
❑ 17 Chad Billingsley XRC	4.00	1.50
❑ 18 Fraser Dizard XRC	.40	.15
❑ 19 Chris Durbin XRC	.40	.15
❑ 20 Chris Ray XRC	1.00	.40
❑ 21 Conor Jackson XRC	3.00	1.25
❑ 22 Kory Casto XRC	.50	.20
❑ 23 Craig Whitaker XRC	.50	.20
❑ 24 Daniel Moore XRC	.40	.15
❑ 25 Daric Barton XRC	3.00	1.25
❑ 26 Darin Downs XRC	.50	.20
❑ 27 David Murphy XRC	.75	.30
❑ 28 Dustin Majewski XRC	.50	.20
❑ 29 Edgardo Baez XRC	.50	.20
❑ 30 Jake Fox XRC	.75	.30
❑ 31 Jake Stevens XRC	.50	.20
❑ 32 Jamie D'Antona XRC	.75	.30
❑ 33 James Houser XRC	.50	.20
❑ 34 Jarrod Saltalamacchia XRC	5.00	2.00
❑ 35 Jason Hirsh XRC	2.00	.75
❑ 36 Javi Herrera XRC	.50	.20
❑ 37 Jeff Allison XRC	.40	.15
❑ 38 John Hudgins XRC	.40	.15
❑ 39 Jo Jo Reyes XRC	1.00	.40
❑ 40 Justin James XRC	.40	.15
❑ 41 Kurt Isenberg XRC	.40	.15
❑ 42 Kyle Boyer XRC	.40	.15
❑ 43 Lastings Milledge XRC	5.00	2.00
❑ 44 Luis Atilano XRC	.40	.15

❑ 45 Matt Murton XRC 2.00 .75
❑ 46 Matt Moses XRC .75 .30
❑ 47 Matt Harrison XRC .75 .30
❑ 48 Michael Bourn XRC .75 .30
❑ 49 Miguel Vega XRC .40 .15
❑ 50 Mitch Maier XRC .50 .20
❑ 51 Omar Quintanilla XRC .50 .20
❑ 52 Ryan Sweeney XRC 2.00 .75
❑ 53 Scott Baker XRC 1.00 .40
❑ 54 Sean Rodriguez XRC 2.00 .75
❑ 55 Steve Lerud XRC .50 .20
❑ 56 Thomas Pauly XRC .40 .15
❑ 57 Tom Gorzelanny XRC 1.50 .60
❑ 58 Tim Moss XRC .40 .15
❑ 59 Robbie Wooley XRC .50 .20
❑ 60 Trey Webb XRC .40 .15
❑ 61 Wes Littleton XRC .50 .20
❑ 62 Beau Vaughan XRC .50 .20
❑ 63 Willy Jo Ronda XRC .50 .20
❑ 64 Chris Lubanski XRC 1.25 .50
❑ 65 Ian Stewart XRC 5.00 2.00
❑ 66 John Danks XRC 3.00 1.25
❑ 67 Kyle Sleeth XRC .50 .20
❑ 68 Michael Aubrey XRC .75 .30
❑ 69 Kevin Kouzmanoff XRC 5.00 2.00
❑ 70 Ryan Harvey XRC 2.00 .75
❑ 71 Tim Stauffer XRC .75 .30
❑ 72 Tony Richie XRC .40 .15
❑ 73 Brandon Wood XRC 8.00 3.00
❑ 74 David Aardsma XRC .50 .20
❑ 75 David Shinskie XRC .40 .15
❑ 76 Dennis Dove XRC .50 .20
❑ 77 Eric Sultemeier XRC .40 .15
❑ 78 Jay Sborz XRC .40 .15
❑ 79 Jimmy Barthmaier XRC .40 .15
❑ 80 Josh Whitesell XRC .40 .15
❑ 81 Josh Anderson XRC .50 .20
❑ 82 Kenny Lewis XRC .50 .20
❑ 83 Mateo Miramontes XRC .40 .15
❑ 84 Nick Markakis XRC 5.00 2.00
❑ 85 Paul Bacot XRC .50 .20
❑ 86 Peter Stonard XRC .40 .15
❑ 87 Reggie Willits XRC 2.50 1.00
❑ 88 Shane Costa XRC .40 .15
❑ 89 Billy Sadler XRC .40 .15
❑ 90 Delmon Young XRC 8.00 3.00

2007 Upper Deck SP Rookie Edition

❑ COMP.SET w/o RC's (100) 15.00 6.00
❑ COMMON CARD (1-100) .30 .12
❑ COMMON RC (101-142) .60 .25
❑ COMMON SP (143-234) 1.00 .40
❑ SP ODDS 1:2
❑ COMMON CARD (235-284) .30 .12
❑ 1 Chipper Jones .75 .30
❑ 2 Andruw Jones .50 .20
❑ 3 Jeff Francoeur .75 .30
❑ 4 Stephen Drew .50 .20
❑ 5 Randy Johnson .75 .30
❑ 6 Brandon Webb .30 .12
❑ 7 Alfonso Soriano .30 .12
❑ 8 Derrek Lee .30 .12
❑ 9 Aramis Ramirez .30 .12
❑ 10 Carlos Zambrano .30 .12
❑ 11 Ken Griffey Jr. 1.25 .50
❑ 12 Adam Dunn .30 .12
❑ 13 Bronson Arroyo .30 .12
❑ 14 Todd Helton .50 .20
❑ 15 Jeff Francis .30 .12
❑ 16 Matt Holliday .75 .30
❑ 17 Hanley Ramirez .50 .20
❑ 18 Dontrelle Willis .30 .12
❑ 19 Miguel Cabrera .50 .20
❑ 20 Lance Berkman .30 .12
❑ 21 Roy Oswalt .30 .12
❑ 22 Carlos Lee .30 .12
❑ 23 Nomar Garciaparra .75 .30
❑ 24 Jason Schmidt .30 .12
❑ 25 Juan Pierre .30 .12
❑ 26 Rafael Furcal .30 .12
❑ 27 Rickie Weeks .30 .12
❑ 28 Prince Fielder .75 .30
❑ 29 Ben Sheets .30 .12
❑ 30 David Wright 1.25 .50
❑ 31 Jose Reyes .75 .30
❑ 32 Pedro Martinez .50 .20
❑ 33 Carlos Beltran .30 .12
❑ 34 Cole Hamels .50 .20
❑ 35 Jimmy Rollins .30 .12
❑ 36 Ryan Howard 1.25 .50
❑ 37 Jason Bay .30 .12
❑ 38 Freddy Sanchez .30 .12
❑ 39 Zach Duke .30 .12
❑ 40 Jake Peavy .30 .12
❑ 41 Greg Maddux 1.25 .50
❑ 42 Trevor Hoffman .30 .12
❑ 43 Matt Cain .50 .20
❑ 44 Barry Zito .30 .12
❑ 45 Omar Vizquel .50 .20
❑ 46 Albert Pujols 1.50 .60
❑ 47 Chris Carpenter .30 .12
❑ 48 Jim Edmonds .50 .20
❑ 49 Scott Rolen .50 .20
❑ 50 Ryan Zimmerman .75 .30
❑ 51 Felipe Lopez .30 .12
❑ 52 Austin Kearns .30 .12
❑ 53 Miguel Tejada .30 .12
❑ 54 Erik Bedard .30 .12
❑ 55 Chris Ray .30 .12
❑ 56 David Ortiz .75 .30
❑ 57 Curt Schilling .50 .20
❑ 58 Manny Ramirez .50 .20
❑ 59 Jonathan Papelbon .75 .30
❑ 60 Jim Thome .50 .20
❑ 61 Paul Konerko .30 .12
❑ 62 Bobby Jenks .30 .12
❑ 63 Grady Sizemore .50 .20
❑ 64 Victor Martinez .30 .12
❑ 65 C.C. Sabathia .30 .12
❑ 66 Ivan Rodriguez .50 .20
❑ 67 Justin Verlander .75 .30
❑ 68 Joel Zumaya .50 .20
❑ 69 Jeremy Bonderman .30 .12
❑ 70 Gil Meche .30 .12
❑ 71 Mike Sweeney .30 .12
❑ 72 Mark Teahen .30 .12
❑ 73 Vladimir Guerrero .75 .30
❑ 74 Howie Kendrick .30 .12
❑ 75 Francisco Rodriguez .30 .12
❑ 76 Johan Santana .50 .20
❑ 77 Justin Morneau .30 .12
❑ 78 Joe Mauer .50 .20
❑ 79 Joe Nathan .30 .12
❑ 80 Alex Rodriguez 1.25 .50
❑ 81 Derek Jeter 2.00 .75
❑ 82 Johnny Damon .50 .20
❑ 83 Mariano Rivera .75 .30
❑ 84 Rich Harden .30 .12
❑ 85 Mike Piazza .75 .30
❑ 86 Nick Swisher .30 .12
❑ 87 Ichiro Suzuki 1.25 .50
❑ 88 Felix Hernandez .50 .20
❑ 89 Kenji Johjima .75 .30
❑ 90 Richie Sexson .30 .12
❑ 91 Carl Crawford .30 .12
❑ 92 Scott Kazmir .50 .20
❑ 93 B.J. Upton .30 .12
❑ 94 Michael Young .30 .12
❑ 95 Mark Teixeira .50 .20
❑ 96 Eric Gagne .30 .12
❑ 97 Hank Blalock .30 .12
❑ 98 Vernon Wells .30 .12
❑ 99 Roy Halladay .30 .12
❑ 100 Frank Thomas .75 .30
❑ 101 Joaquin Arias (RC) .60 .25
❑ 102 Jeff Baker (RC) .60 .25
❑ 103 Brian Barden RC .60 .25
❑ 104 Michael Bourn (RC) .60 .25
❑ 105 Kevin Slowey (RC) 1.50 .60
❑ 106 Chase Wright RC 1.50 .60
❑ 107 Kory Casto (RC) .60 .25
❑ 108 Matt Chico (RC) .60 .25
❑ 109 Matt DeSalvo (RC) .60 .25
❑ 110 Homer Bailey (RC) 1.00 .40
❑ 111 Ryan Braun (RC) 4.00 1.50
❑ 112 Felix Pie (RC) .60 .25
❑ 113 Jesus Flores RC .60 .25
❑ 114 Ryan Sweeney (RC) .60 .25
❑ 115 Ryan Z. Braun RC .60 .25
❑ 116 Alex Gordon RC 3.00 1.25
❑ 117 Josh Hamilton (RC) 1.50 .60
❑ 118 Sean Henn (RC) .60 .25
❑ 119 Kei Igawa RC 1.50 .60
❑ 120 Akinori Iwamura RC 1.50 .60
❑ 121 Andy LaRoche (RC) .60 .25
❑ 122 Kevin Kouzmanoff (RC) .60 .25
❑ 123 Matt Lindstrom (RC) .60 .25
❑ 124 Tim Lincecum RC 5.00 2.00
❑ 125 Daisuke Matsuzaka RC 6.00 2.50
❑ 126 Gustavo Molina RC .60 .25
❑ 127 Miguel Montero (RC) .60 .25
❑ 128 Brandon Morrow RC 1.50 .60
❑ 129 Hideki Okajima RC 3.00 1.25
❑ 130 Adam Lind (RC) .60 .25
❑ 131 Mike Rabelo RC .60 .25
❑ 132 Micah Owings (RC) .60 .25
❑ 133 Brandon Wood (RC) .60 .25
❑ 134 Alexi Casilla RC 1.00 .40
❑ 135 Joe Smith RC .60 .25
❑ 136 Hunter Pence (RC) 3.00 1.25
❑ 137 Glen Perkins (RC) .60 .25
❑ 138 Chris Stewart RC .60 .25
❑ 139 Troy Tulowitzki (RC) 1.50 .60
❑ 140 Billy Butler (RC) 1.00 .40
❑ 141 Delmon Young (RC) 1.00 .40
❑ 142 Phil Hughes (RC) 3.00 1.25
❑ 143 Joaquin Arias 95 1.00 .40

❑ 144 Jeff Baker 95	1.00	.40
❑ 145 Brian Barden 95	1.00	.40
❑ 146 Michael Bourn 95	1.00	.40
❑ 147 Kevin Slowey 95	2.50	1.00
❑ 148 Chase Wright 95	2.50	1.00
❑ 149 Kory Casto 95	1.00	.40
❑ 150 Matt Chico 95	1.00	.40
❑ 151 Shawn Riggans 95	1.00	.40
❑ 152 Juan Salas 95	1.00	.40
❑ 153 Ryan Braun 95	6.00	2.50
❑ 154 Felix Pie 95	1.00	.40
❑ 155 Jesus Flores 95	1.00	.40
❑ 156 Ryan Sweeney 95	1.00	.40
❑ 157 Ryan Z. Braun 95	1.00	.40
❑ 158 Alex Gordon 95	5.00	2.00
❑ 159 Josh Hamilton 95	2.50	1.00
❑ 160 Sean Henn 95	1.00	.40
❑ 161 Kei Igawa 95	2.50	1.00
❑ 162 Akinori Iwamura 95	2.50	1.00
❑ 163 Andy LaRoche 95	1.00	.40
❑ 164 Kevin Kouzmanoff 95	1.00	.40
❑ 165 Matt Lindstrom 95	1.00	.40
❑ 166 Tim Lincecum 95	8.00	3.00
❑ 167 Daisuke Matsuzaka 95	10.00	4.00
❑ 168 Gustavo Molina 95	1.00	.40
❑ 169 Miguel Montero 95	1.00	.40
❑ 170 Brandon Morrow 95	2.50	1.00
❑ 171 Hideki Okajima 95	5.00	2.00
❑ 172 Adam Lind 95	1.00	.40
❑ 173 Mike Rabelo 95	1.00	.40
❑ 174 Micah Owings 95	1.00	.40
❑ 175 Brandon Wood 95	1.00	.40
❑ 176 Alexi Casilla 95	1.50	.60
❑ 177 Joe Smith 95	1.00	.40
❑ 178 Hunter Pence 95	6.00	2.50
❑ 179 Glen Perkins 95	1.00	.40
❑ 180 Chris Stewart 95	1.00	.40
❑ 181 Troy Tulowitzki 95	2.50	1.00
❑ 182 Billy Butler 95	1.50	.60
❑ 183 Delmon Young 95	1.50	.60
❑ 184 Phil Hughes 95	5.00	2.00
❑ 185 Joaquin Arias 93	1.00	.40
❑ 186 Jeff Baker 93	1.00	.40
❑ 187 Mark Reynolds 93	4.00	1.50
❑ 188 Joseph Bisenius 93	1.00	.40
❑ 189 Michael Bourn 93	1.00	.40
❑ 190 Zack Segovia 93	1.00	.40
❑ 191 Kevin Slowey 93	2.50	1.00
❑ 192 Chase Wright 93	2.50	1.00
❑ 193 Rocky Cherry 93	2.50	1.00
❑ 194 Danny Putnam 93	1.00	.40
❑ 195 Kory Casto 93	1.00	.40
❑ 196 Matt Chico 93	1.00	.40
❑ 197 John Danks 93	1.00	.40
❑ 198 Homer Bailey 93	1.50	.60
❑ 199 Ryan Braun 93	6.00	2.50
❑ 200 Felix Pie 93	1.00	.40
❑ 201 Jesus Flores 93	1.00	.40
❑ 202 Andy Gonzalez 93	1.00	.40
❑ 203 Ryan Sweeney 93	1.00	.40
❑ 204 Jarrod Saltalamacchia 93	1.50	.60
❑ 205 Alex Gordon 93	5.00	2.00
❑ 206 Josh Hamilton 93	2.50	1.00
❑ 207 Sean Henn 93	1.00	.40
❑ 208 Kei Igawa 93	2.50	1.00
❑ 209 Akinori Iwamura 93	2.50	1.00
❑ 210 Andy LaRoche 93	1.00	.40
❑ 211 Rick Vanden Hurk 93	1.50	.60
❑ 212 Kevin Kouzmanoff 93	1.00	.40
❑ 213 Matt Lindstrom 93	1.00	.40
❑ 214 Tim Lincecum 93	8.00	3.00
❑ 215 Daisuke Matsuzaka 93	10.00	4.00
❑ 216 Gustavo Molina 93	1.00	.40
❑ 217 Miguel Montero 93	1.00	.40
❑ 218 Brandon Morrow 93	2.50	1.00
❑ 219 Hideki Okajima 93	5.00	2.00
❑ 220 Adam Lind 93	1.00	.40
❑ 221 Mike Rabelo 93	1.00	.40
❑ 222 Brian Burres 93	1.00	.40
❑ 223 Micah Owings 93	1.00	.40
❑ 224 Brandon Wood 93	1.00	.40
❑ 225 Alexi Casilla 93	1.50	.60
❑ 226 Joe Smith 93	1.00	.40
❑ 227 Hunter Pence 93	6.00	2.50
❑ 228 Glen Perkins 93	1.00	.40
❑ 229 Chris Stewart 93	1.00	.40
❑ 230 Ben Francisco 93	1.00	.40
❑ 231 Troy Tulowitzki 93	2.50	1.00
❑ 232 Billy Butler 93	1.50	.60
❑ 233 Delmon Young 93	1.50	.60
❑ 234 Phil Hughes 93	5.00	2.00
❑ 235 Joaquin Arias 96	.60	.25
❑ 236 Jeff Baker 96	.60	.25
❑ 237 Mark Reynolds 96	2.50	1.00
❑ 238 Joseph Bisenius 96	.60	.25
❑ 239 Michael Bourn 96	.60	.25
❑ 240 Zack Segovia 96	.60	.25
❑ 241 Travis Buck 96	.60	.25
❑ 242 Chase Wright 96	1.50	.60
❑ 243 Rocky Cherry 96	1.50	.60
❑ 244 Danny Putnam 96	.60	.25
❑ 245 Kory Casto 96	.60	.25
❑ 246 Matt Chico 96	.60	.25
❑ 247 John Danks 96	.60	.25
❑ 248 Juan Salas 96	.60	.25
❑ 249 Ryan Braun 96	4.00	1.50
❑ 250 Felix Pie 96	.60	.25
❑ 251 Jesus Flores 96	.60	.25
❑ 252 Andy Gonzalez 96	.60	.25
❑ 253 Ryan Sweeney 96	.60	.25
❑ 254 Jarrod Saltalamacchia 96	1.00	.40
❑ 255 Alex Gordon 96	3.00	1.25
❑ 256 Josh Hamilton 96	1.50	.60
❑ 257 Sean Henn 96	.60	.25
❑ 258 Kei Igawa 96	1.50	.60
❑ 259 Akinori Iwamura 96	1.50	.60
❑ 260 Andy LaRoche 96	.60	.25
❑ 261 Rick Vanden Hurk 96	1.00	.40
❑ 262 Kevin Kouzmanoff 96	.60	.25
❑ 263 Matt Lindstrom 96	.60	.25
❑ 264 Tim Lincecum 96	5.00	2.00
❑ 265 Daisuke Matsuzaka 96	6.00	2.50
❑ 266 Gustavo Molina 96	.60	.25
❑ 267 Miguel Montero 96	.60	.25
❑ 268 Brandon Morrow 96	1.50	.60
❑ 269 Hideki Okajima 96	3.00	1.25
❑ 270 Adam Lind 96	.60	.25
❑ 271 Mike Rabelo 96	.60	.25
❑ 272 Brian Burres 96	.60	.25
❑ 273 Micah Owings 96	.60	.25
❑ 274 Brandon Wood 96	.60	.25
❑ 275 Alexi Casilla 96	1.00	.40
❑ 276 Joe Smith 96	.60	.25
❑ 277 Hunter Pence 96	4.00	1.50
❑ 278 Glen Perkins 96	.60	.25
❑ 279 Chris Stewart 96	.60	.25
❑ 280 Ben Francisco 96	.60	.25
❑ 281 Troy Tulowitzki 96	1.50	.60
❑ 282 Billy Butler 96	1.00	.40
❑ 283 Delmon Young 96	1.00	.40
❑ 284 Phil Hughes 96	3.00	1.25

2006 Upper Deck Special F/X

❑ COMMON CARD (1-900)	.75	.30
❑ COMMON RC (901-1025)	1.25	.50
❑ 1 Adam Kennedy	.75	.30
❑ 2 Bartolo Colon	.75	.30
❑ 3 Bengie Molina	.75	.30
❑ 4 Casey Kotchman	.75	.30
❑ 5 Chone Figgins	.75	.30
❑ 6 Dallas McPherson	.75	.30
❑ 7 Darin Erstad	.75	.30
❑ 8 Ervin Santana	.75	.30
❑ 9 Francisco Rodriguez	.75	.30
❑ 10 Garret Anderson	.75	.30
❑ 11 Jarrod Washburn	.75	.30
❑ 12 John Lackey	.75	.30
❑ 13 Juan Rivera	.75	.30
❑ 14 Orlando Cabrera	.75	.30
❑ 15 Paul Byrd	.75	.30
❑ 16 Steve Finley	.75	.30
❑ 17 Vladimir Guerrero	2.00	.75
❑ 18 Alex Cintron	.75	.30
❑ 19 Brandon Lyon	.75	.30
❑ 20 Brandon Webb	.75	.30
❑ 21 Chad Tracy	.75	.30
❑ 22 Chris Snyder	.75	.30
❑ 23 Claudio Vargas	.75	.30
❑ 24 Conor Jackson	1.25	.50
❑ 25 Craig Counsell	.75	.30
❑ 26 Javier Vazquez	.75	.30
❑ 27 Jose Valverde	.75	.30
❑ 28 Luis Gonzalez	.75	.30
❑ 29 Royce Clayton	.75	.30
❑ 30 Russ Ortiz	.75	.30
❑ 31 Shawn Green	.75	.30
❑ 32 Dustin Nippert (RC)	1.25	.50
❑ 33 Tony Clark	.75	.30
❑ 34 Troy Glaus	.75	.30
❑ 35 Adam LaRoche	.75	.30
❑ 36 Andruw Jones	1.25	.50
❑ 37 Craig Hansen RC	5.00	2.00
❑ 38 Chipper Jones	2.00	.75
❑ 39 Horacio Ramirez	.75	.30
❑ 40 Jeff Francoeur	2.00	.75
❑ 41 John Smoltz	1.25	.50
❑ 42 Joey Devine RC	1.25	.50
❑ 43 Johnny Estrada	.75	.30
❑ 44 Anthony Lerew (RC)	1.25	.50
❑ 45 Julio Franco	.75	.30
❑ 46 Kyle Farnsworth	.75	.30
❑ 47 Marcus Giles	.75	.30
❑ 48 Mike Hampton	.75	.30
❑ 49 Rafael Furcal	.75	.30
❑ 50 Chuck James (RC)	2.00	.75
❑ 51 Tim Hudson	.75	.30
❑ 52 B.J. Ryan	.75	.30
❑ 53 Bernie Castro (RC)	1.25	.50
❑ 54 Brian Roberts	.75	.30

❑ 55 Walter Young (RC) 1.25 .50
❑ 56 Daniel Cabrera .75 .30
❑ 57 Eric Byrnes .75 .30
❑ 58 Alejandro Freire RC 1.25 .50
❑ 59 Erik Bedard .75 .30
❑ 60 Javy Lopez .75 .30
❑ 61 Jay Gibbons .75 .30
❑ 62 Jorge Julio .75 .30
❑ 63 Luis Matos .75 .30
❑ 64 Melvin Mora .75 .30
❑ 65 Miguel Tejada .75 .30
❑ 66 Rafael Palmeiro 1.25 .50
❑ 67 Rodrigo Lopez .75 .30
❑ 68 Sammy Sosa 2.00 .75
❑ 69 Alejandro Machado (RC) 1.25 .50
❑ 70 Bill Mueller .75 .30
❑ 71 Bronson Arroyo .75 .30
❑ 72 Curt Schilling 1.25 .50
❑ 73 David Ortiz 2.00 .75
❑ 74 David Wells .75 .30
❑ 75 Edgar Renteria .75 .30
❑ 76 Ryan Jorgensen RC 1.25 .50
❑ 77 Jason Varitek 2.00 .75
❑ 78 Johnny Damon 1.25 .50
❑ 79 Keith Foulke .75 .30
❑ 80 Kevin Youkilis .75 .30
❑ 81 Manny Ramirez 1.25 .50
❑ 82 Matt Clement .75 .30
❑ 83 Hanley Ramirez (RC) 3.00 1.25
❑ 84 Tim Wakefield .75 .30
❑ 85 Trot Nixon .75 .30
❑ 86 Wade Miller .75 .30
❑ 87 Aramis Ramirez .75 .30
❑ 88 Carlos Zambrano .75 .30
❑ 89 Corey Patterson .75 .30
❑ 90 Derrek Lee .75 .30
❑ 91 Geovany Soto (RC) 1.25 .50
❑ 92 Greg Maddux 3.00 1.25
❑ 93 Jeromy Burnitz .75 .30
❑ 94 Jerry Hairston Jr. .75 .30
❑ 95 Kerry Wood .75 .30
❑ 96 Mark Prior 1.25 .50
❑ 97 Matt Murton .75 .30
❑ 98 Michael Barrett .75 .30
❑ 99 Neifi Perez .75 .30
❑ 100 Nomar Garciaparra 2.00 .75
❑ 101 Rich Hill .75 .30
❑ 102 Ryan Dempster .75 .30
❑ 103 Todd Walker .75 .30
❑ 104 A.J. Pierzynski .75 .30
❑ 105 Aaron Rowand .75 .30
❑ 106 Bobby Jenks .75 .30
❑ 107 Carl Everett .75 .30
❑ 108 Dustin Hermanson .75 .30
❑ 109 Frank Thomas 2.00 .75
❑ 110 Freddy Garcia .75 .30
❑ 111 Jermaine Dye .75 .30
❑ 112 Joe Crede .75 .30
❑ 113 Jon Garland .75 .30
❑ 114 Jose Contreras .75 .30
❑ 115 Juan Uribe .75 .30
❑ 116 Mark Buehrle .75 .30
❑ 117 Orlando Hernandez .75 .30
❑ 118 Paul Konerko .75 .30
❑ 119 Scott Podsednik .75 .30
❑ 120 Tadahito Iguchi .75 .30
❑ 121 Aaron Harang .75 .30
❑ 122 Adam Dunn .75 .30
❑ 123 Austin Kearns .75 .30
❑ 124 Brandon Claussen .75 .30
❑ 125 Chris Denorfia (RC) 1.25 .50
❑ 126 Edwin Encarnacion .75 .30
❑ 127 Miguel Perez (RC) 1.25 .50
❑ 128 Felipe Lopez .75 .30
❑ 129 Jason LaRue .75 .30
❑ 130 Ken Griffey Jr. 3.00 1.25
❑ 131 Chris Booker (RC) 1.25 .50
❑ 132 Luke Hudson .75 .30
❑ 133 Jason Bergmann RC 1.25 .50
❑ 134 Ryan Freel .75 .30
❑ 135 Sean Casey .75 .30
❑ 136 Wily Mo Pena .75 .30
❑ 137 Aaron Boone .75 .30
❑ 138 Ben Broussard .75 .30
❑ 139 Ryan Garko (RC) 1.25 .50
❑ 140 C.C. Sabathia .75 .30
❑ 141 Casey Blake .75 .30
❑ 142 Cliff Lee .75 .30
❑ 143 Coco Crisp .75 .30
❑ 144 David Riske .75 .30
❑ 145 Grady Sizemore 1.25 .50
❑ 146 Jake Westbrook .75 .30
❑ 147 Jhonny Peralta .75 .30
❑ 148 Josh Bard .75 .30
❑ 149 Kevin Millwood .75 .30
❑ 150 Ronnie Belliard .75 .30
❑ 151 Scott Elarton .75 .30
❑ 152 Travis Hafner .75 .30
❑ 153 Victor Martinez .75 .30
❑ 154 Aaron Cook .75 .30
❑ 155 Aaron Miles .75 .30
❑ 156 Brad Hawpe .75 .30
❑ 157 Mike Esposito (RC) 1.25 .50
❑ 158 Chin-Hui Tsao .75 .30
❑ 159 Clint Barmes .75 .30
❑ 160 Cory Sullivan .75 .30
❑ 161 Garrett Atkins .75 .30
❑ 162 J.D. Closser .75 .30
❑ 163 Jason Jennings .75 .30
❑ 164 Jeff Baker .75 .30
❑ 165 Jeff Francis .75 .30
❑ 166 Luis Gonzalez .75 .30
❑ 167 Matt Holliday 1.00 .40
❑ 168 Todd Helton 1.25 .50
❑ 169 Brandon Inge .75 .30
❑ 170 Carlos Guillen .75 .30
❑ 171 Carlos Pena .75 .30
❑ 172 Chris Shelton .75 .30
❑ 173 Craig Monroe .75 .30
❑ 174 Curtis Granderson .75 .30
❑ 175 Dmitri Young .75 .30
❑ 176 Ivan Rodriguez 1.25 .50
❑ 177 Jason Johnson .75 .30
❑ 178 Jeremy Bonderman .75 .30
❑ 179 Magglio Ordonez .75 .30
❑ 180 Mark Woodyard (RC) 1.25 .50
❑ 181 Nook Logan .75 .30
❑ 182 Omar Infante .75 .30
❑ 183 Placido Polanco .75 .30
❑ 184 Chris Heintz RC 1.25 .50
❑ 185 A.J. Burnett .75 .30
❑ 186 Alex Gonzalez .75 .30
❑ 187 Josh Johnson (RC) 2.00 .75
❑ 188 Carlos Delgado .75 .30
❑ 189 Dontrelle Willis .75 .30
❑ 190 Josh Wilson (RC) 1.25 .50
❑ 191 Jason Vargas .75 .30
❑ 192 Jeff Conine .75 .30
❑ 193 Jeremy Hermida .75 .30
❑ 194 Josh Beckett .75 .30
❑ 195 Juan Encarnacion .75 .30
❑ 196 Juan Pierre .75 .30
❑ 197 Luis Castillo .75 .30
❑ 198 Miguel Cabrera 1.25 .50
❑ 199 Mike Lowell .75 .30
❑ 200 Paul Lo Duca .75 .30
❑ 201 Todd Jones .75 .30
❑ 202 Adam Everett .75 .30
❑ 203 Andy Pettitte .75 .30
❑ 204 Brad Ausmus .75 .30
❑ 205 Brad Lidge .75 .30
❑ 206 Brandon Backe .75 .30
❑ 207 Charlton Jimerson (RC) 1.25 .50
❑ 208 Chris Burke .75 .30
❑ 209 Craig Biggio 1.25 .50
❑ 210 Dan Wheeler .75 .30
❑ 211 Jason Lane .75 .30
❑ 212 Jeff Bagwell 1.25 .50
❑ 213 Lance Berkman .75 .30
❑ 214 Luke Scott .75 .30
❑ 215 Morgan Ensberg .75 .30
❑ 216 Roger Clemens 4.00 1.50
❑ 217 Roy Oswalt .75 .30
❑ 218 Willy Taveras .75 .30
❑ 219 Andres Blanco .75 .30
❑ 220 Angel Berroa .75 .30
❑ 221 Ruben Gotay .75 .30
❑ 222 David DeJesus .75 .30
❑ 223 Emil Brown .75 .30
❑ 224 J.P. Howell .75 .30
❑ 225 Jeremy Affeldt .75 .30
❑ 226 Jimmy Gobble .75 .30
❑ 227 John Buck .75 .30
❑ 228 Jose Lima .75 .30
❑ 229 Mark Teahen .75 .30
❑ 230 Matt Stairs .75 .30
❑ 231 Mike MacDougal .75 .30
❑ 232 Mike Sweeney .75 .30
❑ 233 Runelvys Hernandez .75 .30
❑ 234 Terrence Long .75 .30
❑ 235 Zack Greinke .75 .30
❑ 236 Ron Flores RC 1.25 .50
❑ 237 Brad Penny .75 .30
❑ 238 Cesar Izturis .75 .30
❑ 239 D.J. Houlton .75 .30
❑ 240 Derek Lowe .75 .30
❑ 241 Eric Gagne .75 .30
❑ 242 Hee Seop Choi .75 .30
❑ 243 J.D. Drew .75 .30
❑ 244 Jason Phillips .75 .30
❑ 245 Jason Repko .75 .30
❑ 246 Jayson Werth .75 .30
❑ 247 Jeff Kent .75 .30
❑ 248 Jeff Weaver .75 .30
❑ 249 Milton Bradley .75 .30
❑ 250 Odalis Perez .75 .30
❑ 251 Hong-Chih Kuo (RC) 3.00 1.25
❑ 252 Oscar Robles .75 .30
❑ 253 Ben Sheets .75 .30
❑ 254 Bill Hall .75 .30
❑ 255 Brady Clark .75 .30
❑ 256 Carlos Lee .75 .30
❑ 257 Chris Capuano .75 .30
❑ 258 Nelson Cruz (RC) 1.25 .50
❑ 259 Derrick Turnbow .75 .30
❑ 260 Doug Davis .75 .30
❑ 261 Geoff Jenkins .75 .30
❑ 262 J.J. Hardy .75 .30
❑ 263 Lyle Overbay .75 .30
❑ 264 Prince Fielder 3.00 1.25
❑ 265 Rickie Weeks .75 .30
❑ 266 Russell Branyan .75 .30
❑ 267 Tomo Ohka .75 .30
❑ 268 Jonah Bayliss (RC) 1.25 .50
❑ 269 Brad Radke .75 .30
❑ 270 Carlos Silva .75 .30
❑ 271 Francisco Liriano (RC) 6.00 2.50
❑ 272 Jacque Jones .75 .30
❑ 273 Joe Mauer 1.25 .50
❑ 274 Travis Bowyer (RC) 1.25 .50
❑ 275 Joe Nathan .75 .30
❑ 276 Johan Santana 1.25 .50

❑	277	Justin Morneau	.75	.30
❑	278	Kyle Lohse	.75	.30
❑	279	Lew Ford	.75	.30
❑	280	Matthew LeCroy	.75	.30
❑	281	Michael Cuddyer	.75	.30
❑	282	Nick Punto	.75	.30
❑	283	Scott Baker	.75	.30
❑	284	Shannon Stewart	.75	.30
❑	285	Torii Hunter	.75	.30
❑	286	Braden Looper	.75	.30
❑	287	Carlos Beltran	.75	.30
❑	288	Cliff Floyd	.75	.30
❑	289	David Wright	3.00	1.25
❑	290	Doug Mientkiewicz	.75	.30
❑	291	Anderson Hernandez (RC)	1.25	.50
❑	292	Jose Reyes	.75	.30
❑	293	Kazuo Matsui	.75	.30
❑	294	Kris Benson	.75	.30
❑	295	Miguel Cairo	.75	.30
❑	296	Mike Cameron	.75	.30
❑	297	Robert Andino RC	1.25	.50
❑	298	Mike Piazza	2.00	.75
❑	299	Pedro Martinez	1.25	.50
❑	300	Tom Glavine	1.25	.50
❑	301	Victor Diaz	.75	.30
❑	302	Tim Hamulack (RC)	1.25	.50
❑	303	Alex Rodriguez	3.00	1.25
❑	304	Bernie Williams	1.25	.50
❑	305	Carl Pavano	.75	.30
❑	306	Chien-Ming Wang	3.00	1.25
❑	307	Derek Jeter	5.00	2.00
❑	308	Gary Sheffield	.75	.30
❑	309	Hideki Matsui	2.00	.75
❑	310	Jason Giambi	.75	.30
❑	311	Jorge Posada	1.25	.50
❑	312	Kevin Brown	.75	.30
❑	313	Mariano Rivera	2.00	.75
❑	314	Matt Lawton	.75	.30
❑	315	Mike Mussina	1.25	.50
❑	316	Randy Johnson	2.00	.75
❑	317	Robinson Cano	1.25	.50
❑	318	Mike Vento (RC)	1.25	.50
❑	319	Tino Martinez	.75	.30
❑	320	Tony Womack	.75	.30
❑	321	Barry Zito	.75	.30
❑	322	Bobby Crosby	.75	.30
❑	323	Bobby Kielty	.75	.30
❑	324	Dan Johnson	.75	.30
❑	325	Danny Haren	.75	.30
❑	326	Eric Chavez	.75	.30
❑	327	Erubiel Durazo	.75	.30
❑	328	Huston Street	.75	.30
❑	329	Jason Kendall	.75	.30
❑	330	Jay Payton	.75	.30
❑	331	Joe Blanton	.75	.30
❑	332	Joe Kennedy	.75	.30
❑	333	Kirk Saarloos	.75	.30
❑	334	Mark Kotsay	.75	.30
❑	335	Nick Swisher	.75	.30
❑	336	Rich Harden	.75	.30
❑	337	Scott Hatteberg	.75	.30
❑	338	Billy Wagner	.75	.30
❑	339	Bobby Abreu	.75	.30
❑	340	Brett Myers	.75	.30
❑	341	Chase Utley	2.00	.75
❑	342	Danny Sandoval RC	1.25	.50
❑	343	David Bell	.75	.30
❑	344	Gavin Floyd	.75	.30
❑	345	Jim Thome	1.25	.50
❑	346	Jimmy Rollins	.75	.30
❑	347	Jon Lieber	.75	.30
❑	348	Kenny Lofton	.75	.30
❑	349	Mike Lieberthal	.75	.30
❑	350	Pat Burrell	.75	.30
❑	351	Randy Wolf	.75	.30
❑	352	Ryan Howard	3.00	1.25
❑	353	Vicente Padilla	.75	.30
❑	354	Bryan Bullington (RC)	1.25	.50
❑	355	J.J. Furmaniak (RC)	1.25	.50
❑	356	Craig Wilson	.75	.30
❑	357	Matt Capps (RC)	1.25	.50
❑	358	Tom Gorzelanny (RC)	1.25	.50
❑	359	Jack Wilson	.75	.30
❑	360	Jason Bay	.75	.30
❑	361	Jose Mesa	.75	.30
❑	362	Josh Fogg	.75	.30
❑	363	Kip Wells	.75	.30
❑	364	Steve Stemle RC	1.25	.50
❑	365	Oliver Perez	.75	.30
❑	366	Rob Mackowiak	.75	.30
❑	367	Ronny Paulino (RC)	1.25	.50
❑	368	Tike Redman	.75	.30
❑	369	Zach Duke	.75	.30
❑	370	Adam Eaton	.75	.30
❑	371	Scott Feldman (RC)	1.25	.50
❑	372	Brian Giles	.75	.30
❑	373	Brian Lawrence	.75	.30
❑	374	Damian Jackson	.75	.30
❑	375	Dave Roberts	.75	.30
❑	376	Jake Peavy	.75	.30
❑	377	Joe Randa	.75	.30
❑	378	Khalil Greene	1.25	.50
❑	379	Mark Loretta	.75	.30
❑	380	Ramon Hernandez	.75	.30
❑	381	Robert Fick	.75	.30
❑	382	Ryan Klesko	.75	.30
❑	383	Trevor Hoffman	.75	.30
❑	384	Woody Williams	.75	.30
❑	385	Xavier Nady	.75	.30
❑	386	Armando Benitez	.75	.30
❑	387	Brad Hennessey	.75	.30
❑	388	Brian Myrow RC	1.25	.50
❑	389	Edgardo Alfonzo	.75	.30
❑	390	J.T. Snow	.75	.30
❑	391	Jeremy Accardo RC	1.25	.50
❑	392	Jason Schmidt	.75	.30
❑	393	Lance Niekro	.75	.30
❑	394	Matt Cain	1.25	.50
❑	395	Daniel Ortmeier (RC)	1.25	.50
❑	396	Moises Alou	.75	.30
❑	397	Doug Clark (RC)	1.25	.50
❑	398	Omar Vizquel	1.25	.50
❑	399	Pedro Feliz	.75	.30
❑	400	Randy Winn	.75	.30
❑	401	Ray Durham	.75	.30
❑	402	Adrian Beltre	.75	.30
❑	403	Eddie Guardado	.75	.30
❑	404	Felix Hernandez	1.25	.50
❑	405	Gil Meche	.75	.30
❑	406	Ichiro Suzuki	3.00	1.25
❑	407	Jamie Moyer	.75	.30
❑	408	Jeff Nelson	.75	.30
❑	409	Jeremy Reed	.75	.30
❑	410	Joel Pineiro	.75	.30
❑	411	Jaime Bubela (RC)	1.25	.50
❑	412	Raul Ibanez	.75	.30
❑	413	Richie Sexson	.75	.30
❑	414	Ryan Franklin	.75	.30
❑	415	Willie Bloomquist	.75	.30
❑	416	Yorvit Torrealba	.75	.30
❑	417	Yuniesky Betancourt	.75	.30
❑	418	Jeff Harris RC	1.25	.50
❑	419	Albert Pujols	4.00	1.50
❑	420	Chris Carpenter	.75	.30
❑	421	David Eckstein	.75	.30
❑	422	Jason Isringhausen	.75	.30
❑	423	Jason Marquis	.75	.30
❑	424	Adam Wainwright (RC)	1.25	.50
❑	425	Jim Edmonds	1.25	.50
❑	426	Ryan Theriot RC	1.25	.50
❑	427	Chris Duncan (RC)	2.00	.75
❑	428	Mark Grudzielanek	.75	.30
❑	429	Mark Mulder	.75	.30
❑	430	Matt Morris	.75	.30
❑	431	Reggie Sanders	.75	.30
❑	432	Scott Rolen	1.25	.50
❑	433	Tyler Johnson (RC)	1.25	.50
❑	434	Yadier Molina	.75	.30
❑	435	Alex Gonzalez	.75	.30
❑	436	Aubrey Huff	.75	.30
❑	437	Tim Corcoran RC	1.25	.50
❑	438	Carl Crawford	.75	.30
❑	439	Casey Fossum	.75	.30
❑	440	Danys Baez	.75	.30
❑	441	Edwin Jackson	.75	.30
❑	442	Joey Gathright	.75	.30
❑	443	Jonny Gomes	.75	.30
❑	444	Jorge Cantu	.75	.30
❑	445	Julio Lugo	.75	.30
❑	446	Nick Green	.75	.30
❑	447	Rocco Baldelli	.75	.30
❑	448	Scott Kazmir	1.25	.50
❑	449	Seth McClung	.75	.30
❑	450	Toby Hall	.75	.30
❑	451	Travis Lee	.75	.30
❑	452	Craig Breslow RC	1.25	.50
❑	453	Alfonso Soriano	.75	.30
❑	454	Chris R. Young	.75	.30
❑	455	David Dellucci	.75	.30
❑	456	Francisco Cordero	.75	.30
❑	457	Gary Matthews	.75	.30
❑	458	Hank Blalock	.75	.30
❑	459	Juan Dominguez	.75	.30
❑	460	Josh Rupe (RC)	1.25	.50
❑	461	Kenny Rogers	.75	.30
❑	462	Kevin Mench	.75	.30
❑	463	Laynce Nix	.75	.30
❑	464	Mark Teixeira	1.25	.50
❑	465	Michael Young	.75	.30
❑	466	Richard Hidalgo	.75	.30
❑	467	Jason Botts (RC)	1.25	.50
❑	468	Aaron Hill	.75	.30
❑	469	Alex Rios	.75	.30
❑	470	Corey Koskie	.75	.30
❑	471	Chris Demaria RC	1.25	.50
❑	472	Eric Hinske	.75	.30
❑	473	Frank Catalanotto	.75	.30
❑	474	John-Ford Griffin (RC)	1.25	.50
❑	475	Gustavo Chacin	.75	.30
❑	476	Josh Towers	.75	.30
❑	477	Miguel Batista	.75	.30
❑	478	Orlando Hudson	.75	.30
❑	479	Reed Johnson	.75	.30
❑	480	Roy Halladay	.75	.30
❑	481	Shaun Marcum (RC)	1.25	.50
❑	482	Shea Hillenbrand	.75	.30
❑	483	Ted Lilly	.75	.30
❑	484	Vernon Wells	.75	.30
❑	485	Brad Wilkerson	.75	.30
❑	486	Darrell Rasner (RC)	1.25	.50
❑	487	Chad Cordero	.75	.30
❑	488	Cristian Guzman	.75	.30
❑	489	Esteban Loaiza	.75	.30
❑	490	John Patterson	.75	.30
❑	491	Jose Guillen	.75	.30
❑	492	Jose Vidro	.75	.30
❑	493	Livan Hernandez	.75	.30
❑	494	Marlon Byrd	.75	.3
❑	495	Nick Johnson	.75	
❑	496	Preston Wilson	.75	
❑	497	Ryan Church	.75	
❑	498	Ryan Zimmerman (RC)	8.00	

	No.	Player		
❑	499	Tony Armas	.75	.30
❑	500	Vinny Castilla	.75	.30
❑	501	Andy Green	.75	.30
❑	502	Damion Easley	.75	.30
❑	503	Eric Byrnes	.75	.30
❑	504	Jason Grimsley	.75	.30
❑	505	Jeff DaVanon	.75	.30
❑	506	Johnny Estrada	.75	.30
❑	507	Luis Vizcaino	.75	.30
❑	508	Miguel Batista	.75	.30
❑	509	Orlando Hernandez	.75	.30
❑	510	Orlando Hudson	.75	.30
❑	511	Terry Mulholland	.75	.30
❑	512	Chris Reitsma	.75	.30
❑	513	Edgar Renteria	.75	.30
❑	514	John Thomson	.75	.30
❑	515	Jorge Sosa	.75	.30
❑	516	Oscar Villarreal	.75	.30
❑	517	Pete Orr	.75	.30
❑	518	Ryan Langerhans	.75	.30
❑	519	Todd Pratt	.75	.30
❑	520	Wilson Betemit	.75	.30
❑	521	Brian Jordan	.75	.30
❑	522	Lance Cormier	.75	.30
❑	523	Matt Diaz	.75	.30
❑	524	Mike Remlinger	.75	.30
❑	525	Bruce Chen	.75	.30
❑	526	Chris Gomez	.75	.30
❑	527	Chris Ray	.75	.30
❑	528	Corey Patterson	.75	.30
❑	529	David Newhan	.75	.30
❑	530	Ed Rogers (RC)	1.25	.50
❑	531	John Halama	.75	.30
❑	532	Kris Benson	.75	.30
❑	533	LaTroy Hawkins	.75	.30
❑	534	Raul Chavez	.75	.30
❑	535	Alex Cora	.75	.30
❑	536	Alex Gonzalez	.75	.30
❑	537	Coco Crisp	.75	.30
❑	538	David Riske	.75	.30
❑	539	Doug Mirabelli	.75	.30
❑	540	Josh Beckett	.75	.30
❑	541	J.T. Snow	.75	.30
❑	542	Mike Timlin	.75	.30
❑	543	Julian Tavarez	.75	.30
❑	544	Rudy Seanez	.75	.30
❑	545	Wily Mo Pena	.75	.30
❑	546	Bob Howry	.75	.30
❑	547	Glendon Rusch	.75	.30
❑	548	Henry Blanco	.75	.30
❑	549	Jacque Jones	.75	.30
❑	550	Jerome Williams	.75	.30
❑	551	John Mabry	.75	.30
❑	552	Juan Pierre	.75	.30
❑	553	Scott Eyre	.75	.30
❑	554	Scott Williamson	.75	.30
❑	555	Wade Miller	.75	.30
❑	556	Will Ohman	.75	.30
❑	557	Alex Cintron	.75	.30
❑	558	Rob Mackowiak	.75	.30
❑	559	Brandon McCarthy	.75	.30
❑	560	Chris Widger	.75	.30
❑	561	Cliff Politte	.75	.30
❑	562	Javier Vazquez	.75	.30
❑	563	Jim Thome	1.25	.50
❑	564	Matt Thornton	.75	.30
❑	565	Neal Cotts	.75	.30
❑	566	Pablo Ozuna	.75	.30
	567	Ross Gload	.75	.30
	68	Brandon Phillips	.75	.30
	9	Bronson Arroyo	.75	.30
		Dave Williams	.75	.30
		)avid Ross	.75	.30
		vid Weathers	.75	.30
❑	573	Eric Milton	.75	.30
❑	574	Javier Valentin	.75	.30
❑	575	Kent Mercker	.75	.30
❑	576	Matt Belisle	.75	.30
❑	577	Paul Wilson	.75	.30
❑	578	Rich Aurilia	.75	.30
❑	579	Rick White	.75	.30
❑	580	Scott Hatteberg	.75	.30
❑	581	Todd Coffey	.75	.30
❑	582	Bob Wickman	.75	.30
❑	583	Danny Graves	.75	.30
❑	584	Eduardo Perez	.75	.30
❑	585	Guillermo Mota	.75	.30
❑	586	Jason Davis	.75	.30
❑	587	Jason Johnson	.75	.30
❑	588	Jason Michaels	.75	.30
❑	589	Rafael Betancourt	.75	.30
❑	590	Ramon Vazquez	.75	.30
❑	591	Scott Sauerbeck	.75	.30
❑	592	Todd Hollandsworth	.75	.30
❑	593	Brian Fuentes	.75	.30
❑	594	Danny Ardoin	.75	.30
❑	595	David Cortes	.75	.30
❑	596	Eli Marrero	.75	.30
❑	597	Jamey Carroll	.75	.30
❑	598	Jason Smith	.75	.30
❑	599	Josh Fogg	.75	.30
❑	600	Miguel Ojeda	.75	.30
❑	601	Mike DeJean	.75	.30
❑	602	Ray King	.75	.30
❑	603	Omar Quintanilla (RC)	1.25	.50
❑	604	Zach Day	.75	.30
❑	605	Fernando Rodney	.75	.30
❑	606	Kenny Rogers	.75	.30
❑	607	Mike Maroth	.75	.30
❑	608	Nate Robertson	.75	.30
❑	609	Todd Jones	.75	.30
❑	610	Vance Wilson	.75	.30
❑	611	Bobby Seay	.75	.30
❑	612	Chris Spurling	.75	.30
❑	613	Roman Colon	.75	.30
❑	614	Jason Grilli	.75	.30
❑	615	Marcus Thames	.75	.30
❑	616	Ramon Santiago	.75	.30
❑	617	Alfredo Amezaga	.75	.30
❑	618	Brian Moehler	.75	.30
❑	619	Chris Aguila	.75	.30
❑	620	Franklyn German	.75	.30
❑	621	Joe Borowski	.75	.30
❑	622	Logan Kensing (RC)	1.25	.50
❑	623	Matt Treanor	.75	.30
❑	624	Miguel Olivo	.75	.30
❑	625	Sergio Mitre	.75	.30
❑	626	Todd Wellemeyer	.75	.30
❑	627	Wes Helms	.75	.30
❑	628	Chad Qualls	.75	.30
❑	629	Eric Bruntlett	.75	.30
❑	630	Mike Gallo	.75	.30
❑	631	Mike Lamb	.75	.30
❑	632	Orlando Palmeiro	.75	.30
❑	633	Russ Springer	.75	.30
❑	634	Dan Wheeler	.75	.30
❑	635	Eric Munson	.75	.30
❑	636	Preston Wilson	.75	.30
❑	637	Trever Miller	.75	.30
❑	638	Ambiorix Burgos	.75	.30
❑	639	Andy Sisco	.75	.30
❑	640	Denny Bautista	.75	.30
❑	641	Doug Mientkiewicz	.75	.30
❑	642	Elmer Dessens	.75	.30
❑	643	Esteban German	.75	.30
❑	644	Joe Nelson (RC)	1.25	.50
❑	645	Mark Grudzielanek	.75	.30
❑	646	Mark Redman	.75	.30
❑	647	Mike Wood	.75	.30
❑	648	Paul Bako	.75	.30
❑	649	Reggie Sanders	.75	.30
❑	650	Scott Elarton	.75	.30
❑	651	Shane Costa	.75	.30
❑	652	Tony Graffanino	.75	.30
❑	653	Jason Bulger (RC)	1.25	.50
❑	654	Chris Bootcheck (RC)	1.25	.50
❑	655	Esteban Yan	.75	.30
❑	656	Hector Carrasco	.75	.30
❑	657	J.C. Romero	.75	.30
❑	658	Jeff Weaver	.75	.30
❑	659	Jose Molina	.75	.30
❑	660	Kelvim Escobar	.75	.30
❑	661	Maicer Izturis	.75	.30
❑	662	Robb Quinlan	.75	.30
❑	663	Scot Shields	.75	.30
❑	664	Tim Salmon	.75	.30
❑	665	Bill Mueller	.75	.30
❑	666	Brett Tomko	.75	.30
❑	667	Dioner Navarro	.75	.30
❑	668	Jae Seo	.75	.30
❑	669	Jose Cruz	.75	.30
❑	670	Kenny Lofton	.75	.30
❑	671	Lance Carter	.75	.30
❑	672	Nomar Garciaparra	2.00	.75
❑	673	Olmedo Saenz	.75	.30
❑	674	Rafael Furcal	.75	.30
❑	675	Ramon Martinez	.75	.30
❑	676	Ricky Ledee	.75	.30
❑	677	Sandy Alomar	.75	.30
❑	678	Yhency Brazoban	.75	.30
❑	679	Corey Koskie	.75	.30
❑	680	Dan Kolb	.75	.30
❑	681	Gabe Gross	.75	.30
❑	682	Jeff Cirillo	.75	.30
❑	683	Matt Wise	.75	.30
❑	684	Rick Helling	.75	.30
❑	685	Chad Moeller	.75	.30
❑	686	Dave Bush	.75	.30
❑	687	Jorge De La Rosa	.75	.30
❑	688	Justin Lehr	.75	.30
❑	689	Jason Bartlett	.75	.30
❑	690	Jesse Crain	.75	.30
❑	691	Juan Rincon	.75	.30
❑	692	Luis Castillo	.75	.30
❑	693	Mike Redmond	.75	.30
❑	694	Rondell White	.75	.30
❑	695	Tony Batista	.75	.30
❑	696	Juan Castro	.75	.30
❑	697	Luis Rodriguez	.75	.30
❑	698	Matt Guerrier	.75	.30
❑	699	Willie Eyre (RC)	1.25	.50
❑	700	Aaron Heilman	.75	.30
❑	701	Billy Wagner	.75	.30
❑	702	Carlos Delgado	.75	.30
❑	703	Chad Bradford	.75	.30
❑	704	Chris Woodward	.75	.30
❑	705	Darren Oliver	.75	.30
❑	706	Duaner Sanchez	.75	.30
❑	707	Endy Chavez	.75	.30
❑	708	Jorge Julio	.75	.30
❑	709	Jose Valentin	.75	.30
❑	710	Julio Franco	.75	.30
❑	711	Paul Lo Duca	.75	.30
❑	712	Ramon Castro	.75	.30
❑	713	Steve Trachsel	.75	.30
❑	714	Victor Zambrano	.75	.30
❑	715	Xavier Nady	.75	.30
❑	716	Andy Phillips	.75	.30
❑	717	Bubba Crosby	.75	.30
❑	718	Jaret Wright	.75	.30
❑	719	Kelly Stinnett	.75	.30
❑	720	Kyle Farnsworth	.75	.30

❑ 721 Mike Meyers .75 .30
❑ 722 Octavio Dotel .75 .30
❑ 723 Ron Villone .75 .30
❑ 724 Scott Proctor .75 .30
❑ 725 Shawn Chacon .75 .30
❑ 726 Tanyon Sturtze .75 .30
❑ 727 Adam Melhuse .75 .30
❑ 728 Brad Halsey .75 .30
❑ 729 Esteban Loaiza .75 .30
❑ 730 Frank Thomas 2.00 .75
❑ 731 Jay Witasick .75 .30
❑ 732 Justin Duchscherer .75 .30
❑ 733 Kiko Calero .75 .30
❑ 734 Marco Scutaro .75 .30
❑ 735 Mark Ellis .75 .30
❑ 736 Milton Bradley .75 .30
❑ 737 Aaron Fultz .75 .30
❑ 738 Aaron Rowand .75 .30
❑ 739 Geoff Geary .75 .30
❑ 740 Arthur Rhodes .75 .30
❑ 741 Chris Coste RC 1.25 .50
❑ 742 Rheal Cormier .75 .30
❑ 743 Ryan Franklin .75 .30
❑ 744 Ryan Madson .75 .30
❑ 745 Sal Fasano .75 .30
❑ 746 Tom Gordon .75 .30
❑ 747 Abraham Nunez .75 .30
❑ 748 David Dellucci .75 .30
❑ 749 Julio Santana .75 .30
❑ 750 Shane Victorino .75 .30
❑ 751 Damaso Marte .75 .30
❑ 752 Freddy Sanchez .75 .30
❑ 753 Humberto Cota .75 .30
❑ 754 Jeromy Burnitz .75 .30
❑ 755 Joe Randa .75 .30
❑ 756 Jose Castillo .75 .30
❑ 757 Mike Gonzalez .75 .30
❑ 758 Ryan Doumit .75 .30
❑ 759 Sean Burnett .75 .30
❑ 760 Sean Casey .75 .30
❑ 761 Ian Snell .75 .30
❑ 762 John Grabow .75 .30
❑ 763 Jose Hernandez .75 .30
❑ 764 Roberto Hernandez .75 .30
❑ 765 Ryan Vogelsong .75 .30
❑ 766 Victor Sanchez .75 .30
❑ 767 Adrian Gonzalez .75 .30
❑ 768 Alan Embree .75 .30
❑ 769 Brian Sweeney (RC) 1.25 .50
❑ 770 Chan Ho Park .75 .30
❑ 771 Clay Hensley .75 .30
❑ 772 Dewon Brazelton .75 .30
❑ 773 Doug Brocail .75 .30
❑ 774 Eric Young .75 .30
❑ 775 Geoff Blum .75 .30
❑ 776 Josh Bard .75 .30
❑ 777 Mark Bellhorn .75 .30
❑ 778 Mike Cameron .75 .30
❑ 779 Mike Piazza 2.00 .75
❑ 780 Rob Bowen .75 .30
❑ 781 Scott Cassidy .75 .30
❑ 782 Scott Linebrink .75 .30
❑ 783 Shawn Estes .75 .30
❑ 784 Terrmel Sledge .75 .30
❑ 785 Vinny Castilla .75 .30
❑ 786 Jeff Fassero .75 .30
❑ 787 Jose Vizcaino .75 .30
❑ 788 Mark Sweeney .75 .30
❑ 789 Matt Morris .75 .30
❑ 790 Steve Finley .75 .30
❑ 791 Tim Worrell .75 .30
❑ 792 Jamey Wright .75 .30
❑ 793 Jason Ellison .75 .30
❑ 794 Noah Lowry .75 .30
❑ 795 Steve Kline .75 .30
❑ 796 Todd Greene .75 .30
❑ 797 Carl Everett .75 .30
❑ 798 George Sherrill .75 .30
❑ 799 J.J. Putz .75 .30
❑ 800 Jake Woods .75 .30
❑ 801 Jose Lopez .75 .30
❑ 802 Julio Mateo .75 .30
❑ 803 Mike Morse .75 .30
❑ 804 Rafael Soriano .75 .30
❑ 805 Roberto Petagine .75 .30
❑ 806 Aaron Miles .75 .30
❑ 807 Braden Looper .75 .30
❑ 808 Gary Bennett .75 .30
❑ 809 Hector Luna .75 .30
❑ 810 Jeff Suppan .75 .30
❑ 811 John Rodriguez .75 .30
❑ 812 Josh Hancock .75 .30
❑ 813 Juan Encarnacion .75 .30
❑ 814 Larry Bigbie .75 .30
❑ 815 Scott Spiezio .75 .30
❑ 816 Sidney Ponson .75 .30
❑ 817 So Taguchi .75 .30
❑ 818 Brian Meadows .75 .30
❑ 819 Damon Hollins .75 .30
❑ 820 Dan Miceli .75 .30
❑ 821 Doug Waechter .75 .30
❑ 822 Jason Childers (RC) 1.25 .50
❑ 823 Josh Paul .75 .30
❑ 824 Julio Lugo .75 .30
❑ 825 Mark Hendrickson .75 .30
❑ 826 Sean Burroughs .75 .30
❑ 827 Shawn Camp .75 .30
❑ 828 Travis Harper .75 .30
❑ 829 Ty Wigginton .75 .30
❑ 830 Adam Eaton .75 .30
❑ 831 Adrian Brown .75 .30
❑ 832 Akinori Otsuka .75 .30
❑ 833 Antonio Alfonseca .75 .30
❑ 834 Brad Wilkerson .75 .30
❑ 835 D'Angelo Jimenez .75 .30
❑ 836 Gerald Laird .75 .30
❑ 837 Joaquin Benoit .75 .30
❑ 838 Kameron Loe .75 .30
❑ 839 Kevin Millwood .75 .30
❑ 840 Mark DeRosa .75 .30
❑ 841 Phil Nevin .75 .30
❑ 842 Rod Barajas .75 .30
❑ 843 Vicente Padilla .75 .30
❑ 844 A.J. Burnett .75 .30
❑ 845 Bengie Molina .75 .30
❑ 846 Gregg Zaun .75 .30
❑ 847 John McDonald .75 .30
❑ 848 Lyle Overbay .75 .30
❑ 849 Russ Adams .75 .30
❑ 850 Troy Glaus .75 .30
❑ 851 Vinnie Chulk .75 .30
❑ 852 B.J. Ryan .75 .30
❑ 853 Justin Speier .75 .30
❑ 854 Pete Walker .75 .30
❑ 855 Scott Downs .75 .30
❑ 856 Scott Schoeneweis .75 .30
❑ 857 Alfonso Soriano .75 .30
❑ 858 Brian Schneider .75 .30
❑ 859 Daryle Ward .75 .30
❑ 860 Felix Rodriguez .75 .30
❑ 861 Gary Majewski .75 .30
❑ 862 Joey Eischen .75 .30
❑ 863 Jon Rauch .75 .30
❑ 864 Marlon Anderson .75 .30
❑ 865 Matt LeCroy .75 .30
❑ 866 Mike Stanton .75 .30
❑ 867 Ramon Ortiz .75 .30
❑ 868 Robert Fick .75 .30
❑ 869 Royce Clayton .75 .30
❑ 870 Ryan Drese .75 .30
❑ 871 Vladimir Guerrero CL 2.00 .75
❑ 872 Craig Biggio CL 1.25 .50
❑ 873 Barry Zito CL .75 .30
❑ 874 Vernon Wells CL .75 .30
❑ 875 Chipper Jones CL 2.00 .75
❑ 876 Prince Fielder CL 3.00 1.25
❑ 877 Albert Pujols CL 4.00 1.50
❑ 878 Greg Maddux CL 3.00 1.25
❑ 879 Carl Crawford CL .75 .30
❑ 880 Brandon Webb CL .75 .30
❑ 881 J.D. Drew CL .75 .30
❑ 882 Jason Schmidt CL .75 .30
❑ 883 Victor Martinez CL .75 .30
❑ 884 Ichiro Suzuki CL 3.00 1.25
❑ 885 Miguel Cabrera CL 1.25 .50
❑ 886 David Wright CL 3.00 1.25
❑ 887 Alfonso Soriano CL .75 .30
❑ 888 Miguel Tejada CL .75 .30
❑ 889 Khalil Greene CL 1.25 .50
❑ 890 Ryan Howard CL 3.00 1.25
❑ 891 Jason Bay CL .75 .30
❑ 892 Mark Teixeira CL 1.25 .50
❑ 893 Manny Ramirez CL 1.25 .50
❑ 894 Ken Griffey Jr. CL 3.00 1.25
❑ 895 Todd Helton CL 1.25 .50
❑ 896 Angel Berroa CL .75 .30
❑ 897 Ivan Rodriguez CL 1.25 .50
❑ 898 Johan Santana CL 1.25 .50
❑ 899 Paul Konerko CL .75 .30
❑ 900 Derek Jeter CL 5.00 2.00
❑ 901 Macay McBride (RC) 1.25 .50
❑ 902 Tony Pena Jr. (RC) 1.25 .50
❑ 903 Peter Moylan RC 1.25 .50
❑ 904 Aaron Rakers (RC) 1.25 .50
❑ 905 Chris Britton RC 1.25 .50
❑ 906 Nick Markakis (RC) 2.00 .75
❑ 907 Sendy Rleal RC 1.25 .50
❑ 908 Val Majewski (RC) 1.25 .50
❑ 909 Jermaine Van Buren (RC) 1.25 .50
❑ 910 Jonathan Papelbon (RC) 6.00 2.50
❑ 911 Angel Pagan (RC) 1.25 .50
❑ 912 David Aardsma (RC) 1.25 .50
❑ 913 Sean Marshall (RC) 1.25 .50
❑ 914 Brian Anderson (RC) 1.25 .50
❑ 915 Freddie Bynum (RC) 1.25 .50
❑ 916 Fausto Carmona (RC) 1.25 .50
❑ 917 Kelly Shoppach (RC) 1.25 .50
❑ 918 Choo Freeman (RC) 1.25 .50
❑ 919 Ryan Shealy (RC) 1.25 .50
❑ 920 Joel Zumaya (RC) 3.00 1.25
❑ 921 Jordan Tata RC 1.25 .50
❑ 922 Justin Verlander (RC) 5.00 2.00
❑ 923 Carlos Martinez RC 1.25 .50
❑ 924 Chris Resop (RC) 1.25 .50
❑ 925 Dan Uggla (RC) 3.00 1.25
❑ 926 Eric Reed (RC) 1.25 .50
❑ 927 Hanley Ramirez (RC) 3.00 1.25
❑ 928 Yusmeiro Petit (RC) 1.25 .50
❑ 929 Josh Willingham (RC) 1.25 .50
❑ 930 Mike Jacobs (RC) 1.25 .50
❑ 931 Reggie Abercrombie (RC) 1.25 .50
❑ 932 Ricky Nolasco (RC) 1.25 .50
❑ 933 Scott Olsen (RC) 1.25 .50
❑ 934 Fernando Nieve (RC) 1.25 .50
❑ 935 Taylor Buchholz (RC) 1.25 .50
❑ 936 Cody Ross (RC) 1.25 .50
❑ 937 James Loney (RC) 2.00 .75
❑ 938 Takashi Saito RC 2.00 .75
❑ 939 Tim Hamulack (RC) 1.25 .5[illegible]
❑ 940 Chris Demaria RC 1.25 [illegible]
❑ 941 Jose Capellan (RC) 1.25
❑ 942 David Gassner (RC) 1.25

❑ 943	Jason Kubel (RC)	1.25	.50
❑ 944	Brian Bannister (RC)	1.25	.50
❑ 945	Mike Thompson RC	1.25	.50
❑ 946	Cole Hamels (RC)	3.00	1.25
❑ 947	Paul Maholm (RC)	1.25	.50
❑ 948	John Van Benschoten (RC)	1.25	.50
❑ 949	Nate McLouth (RC)	1.25	.50
❑ 950	Ben Johnson (RC)	1.25	.50
❑ 951	Josh Barfield (RC)	1.25	.50
❑ 952	Travis Ishikawa (RC)	1.25	.50
❑ 953	Jack Taschner (RC)	1.25	.50
❑ 954	Kenji Johjima RC	6.00	2.50
❑ 955	Skip Schumaker (RC)	1.25	.50
❑ 956	Ruddy Lugo (RC)	1.25	.50
❑ 957	Jason Hammel (RC)	1.25	.50
❑ 958	Chris Roberson (RC)	1.25	.50
❑ 959	Fabio Castro RC	1.25	.50
❑ 960	Ian Kinsler (RC)	2.00	.75
❑ 961	John Koronka (RC)	1.25	.50
❑ 962	Brandon Watson (RC)	1.25	.50
❑ 963	Jon Lester RC	4.00	1.50
❑ 964	Ben Hendrickson (RC)	1.25	.50
❑ 965	Martin Prado (RC)	1.25	.50
❑ 966	Erick Aybar (RC)	1.25	.50
❑ 967	Bobby Livingston (RC)	1.25	.50
❑ 968	Ryan Spilborghs (RC)	2.00	.75
❑ 969	Tommy Murphy (RC)	1.25	.50
❑ 970	Howie Kendrick (RC)	3.00	1.25
❑ 971	Casey Janssen RC	2.00	.75
❑ 972	Michael O'Connor RC	1.25	.50
❑ 973	Conor Jackson (RC)	2.00	.75
❑ 974	Jeremy Hermida (RC)	1.25	.50
❑ 975	Renyel Pinto (RC)	1.25	.50
❑ 976	Prince Fielder (RC)	5.00	2.00
❑ 977	Kevin Frandsen (RC)	1.25	.50
❑ 978	Ty Taubenheim RC	2.00	.75
❑ 979	Rich Hill (RC)	1.25	.50
❑ 980	Jonathan Broxton (RC)	1.25	.50
❑ 981	James Shields RC	1.25	.50
❑ 982	Carlos Villanueva RC	1.25	.50
❑ 983	Boone Logan RC	1.25	.50
❑ 984	Brian Wilson RC	1.25	.50
❑ 985	Andre Ethier (RC)	3.00	1.25
❑ 986	Mike Napoli RC	3.00	1.25
❑ 987	Agustin Montero (RC)	1.25	.50
❑ 988	Jack Hannahan RC	1.25	.50
❑ 989	Boof Bonser (RC)	2.00	.75
❑ 990	Carlos Ruiz (RC)	1.25	.50
❑ 991	Jason Botts (RC)	1.25	.50
❑ 992	Kendry Morales (RC)	2.00	.75
❑ 993	Alay Soler RC	1.25	.50
❑ 994	Santiago Ramirez (RC)	1.25	.50
❑ 995	Saul Rivera (RC)	1.25	.50
❑ 996	Anthony Reyes (RC)	2.00	.75
❑ 997	Matt Kemp (RC)	2.00	.75
❑ 998	Jae Kuk Ryu RC	1.25	.50
❑ 999	Lastings Milledge (RC)	2.00	.75
❑ 1000	Jered Weaver (RC)	4.00	1.50
❑ 1001	Jeremy Sowers (RC)	1.25	.50
❑ 1002	Chad Billingsley (RC)	2.00	.75
❑ 1003	Stephen Drew (RC)	3.00	1.25
❑ 1004	Tony Gwynn Jr. (RC)	3.00	1.25
❑ 1005	Melky Cabrera (RC)	2.00	.75
❑ 1006	Eliezer Alfonzo RC	1.25	.50
❑ 1007	Dana Eveland (RC)	1.25	.50
❑ 1008	Luis Figueroa RC	1.25	.50
❑ 1009	Emiliano Fruto RC	1.25	.50
❑ 1010	Clay Hensley (RC)	1.25	.50
❑ 1011	Zach Jackson (RC)	1.25	.50
1012	Bob Keppel (RC)	1.25	.50
013	Carlos Marmol RC	1.25	.50
14	Russell Martin (RC)	2.00	.75
5	Leo Nunez (RC)	1.25	.50
	Ken Ray (RC)	1.25	.50
❑ 1017	Mike Rouse (RC)	1.25	.50
❑ 1018	Kevin Thompson (RC)	1.25	.50
❑ 1019	C.J. Wilson (RC)	1.25	.50
❑ 1020	Stephen Andrade (RC)	1.25	.50
❑ 1021	Ed Rogers (RC)	1.25	.50
❑ 1022	Joe Nelson (RC)	1.25	.50
❑ 1023	Omar Quintanilla (RC)	1.25	.50
❑ 1024	Chris Bootcheck (RC)	1.25	.50
❑ 1025	Jason Childers RC	1.25	.50

2007 Upper Deck Spectrum

❑	COMP.SET w/o RCs (100)	25.00	10.00
❑	COMMON CARD (1-100)	.40	.15
❑	COMMON AU RC (101-149)	8.00	3.00
❑	AU RC STATED ODDS 1:18 HOBBY		
❑	COMMON ROOKIE EXCH (151-170)	25.00	10.00
❑	EXCHANGE DEADLINE 3/19/2010		
❑ 1	Miguel Tejada	.40	.15
❑ 2	Brian Roberts	.40	.15
❑ 3	Melvin Mora	.40	.15
❑ 4	David Ortiz	1.00	.40
❑ 5	Manny Ramirez	.60	.25
❑ 6	Jason Varitek	1.00	.40
❑ 7	Curt Schilling	.60	.25
❑ 8	Jim Thome	.60	.25
❑ 9	Paul Konerko	.40	.15
❑ 10	Jermaine Dye	.40	.15
❑ 11	Travis Hafner	.40	.15
❑ 12	Victor Martinez	.40	.15
❑ 13	Grady Sizemore	.60	.25
❑ 14	C.C. Sabathia	.40	.15
❑ 15	Ivan Rodriguez	.60	.25
❑ 16	Magglio Ordonez	.40	.15
❑ 17	Carlos Guillen	.40	.15
❑ 18	Justin Verlander	1.00	.40
❑ 19	Shane Costa	.40	.15
❑ 20	Emil Brown	.40	.15
❑ 21	Mark Teahen	.40	.15
❑ 22	Vladimir Guerrero	1.00	.40
❑ 23	Jered Weaver	.60	.25
❑ 24	Juan Rivera	.40	.15
❑ 25	Justin Morneau	.40	.15
❑ 26	Joe Mauer	.60	.25
❑ 27	Torii Hunter	.40	.15
❑ 28	Johan Santana	.60	.25
❑ 29	Derek Jeter	2.50	1.00
❑ 30	Alex Rodriguez	1.50	.60
❑ 31	Johnny Damon	.60	.25
❑ 32	Jason Giambi	.40	.15
❑ 33	Frank Thomas	1.00	.40
❑ 34	Nick Swisher	.40	.15
❑ 35	Eric Chavez	.40	.15
❑ 36	Ichiro Suzuki	1.50	.60
❑ 37	Raul Ibanez	.40	.15
❑ 38	Richie Sexson	.40	.15
❑ 39	Carl Crawford	.40	.15
❑ 40	Rocco Baldelli	.40	.15
❑ 41	Scott Kazmir	.60	.25
❑ 42	Michael Young	.40	.15
❑ 43	Mark Teixeira	.60	.25
❑ 44	Carlos Lee	.40	.15
❑ 45	Gary Matthews	.40	.15
❑ 46	Vernon Wells	.40	.15
❑ 47	Roy Halladay	.40	.15
❑ 48	Lyle Overbay	.40	.15
❑ 49	Brandon Webb	.40	.15
❑ 50	Conor Jackson	.40	.15
❑ 51	Stephen Drew	.60	.25
❑ 52	Chipper Jones	1.00	.40
❑ 53	Andruw Jones	.60	.25
❑ 54	Adam LaRoche	.40	.15
❑ 55	John Smoltz	.60	.25
❑ 56	Derrek Lee	.40	.15
❑ 57	Aramis Ramirez	.40	.15
❑ 58	Carlos Zambrano	.40	.15
❑ 59	Ken Griffey Jr.	1.50	.60
❑ 60	Adam Dunn	.40	.15
❑ 61	Aaron Harang	.40	.15
❑ 62	Todd Helton	.60	.25
❑ 63	Matt Holliday	1.00	.40
❑ 64	Garrett Atkins	.40	.15
❑ 65	Miguel Cabrera	.60	.25
❑ 66	Hanley Ramirez	.60	.25
❑ 67	Dontrelle Willis	.40	.15
❑ 68	Lance Berkman	.40	.15
❑ 69	Roy Oswalt	.40	.15
❑ 70	Roger Clemens	1.50	.60
❑ 71	J.D. Drew	.40	.15
❑ 72	Nomar Garciaparra	1.00	.40
❑ 73	Rafael Furcal	.40	.15
❑ 74	Jeff Kent	.40	.15
❑ 75	Prince Fielder	1.00	.40
❑ 76	Bill Hall	.40	.15
❑ 77	Rickie Weeks	.40	.15
❑ 78	Jose Reyes	.40	.15
❑ 79	David Wright	1.50	.60
❑ 80	Carlos Delgado	.40	.15
❑ 81	Carlos Beltran	.40	.15
❑ 82	Ryan Howard	1.50	.60
❑ 83	Chase Utley	1.00	.40
❑ 84	Jimmy Rollins	.40	.15
❑ 85	Jason Bay	.40	.15
❑ 86	Freddy Sanchez	.40	.15
❑ 87	Zach Duke	.40	.15
❑ 88	Trevor Hoffman	.40	.15
❑ 89	Adrian Gonzalez	.40	.15
❑ 90	Mike Piazza	1.00	.40
❑ 91	Ray Durham	.40	.15
❑ 92	Omar Vizquel	.60	.25
❑ 93	Jason Schmidt	.40	.15
❑ 94	Albert Pujols	2.00	.75
❑ 95	Scott Rolen	.60	.25
❑ 96	Jim Edmonds	.60	.25
❑ 97	Chris Carpenter	.40	.15
❑ 98	Alfonso Soriano	.40	.15
❑ 99	Ryan Zimmerman	1.00	.40
❑ 100	Nick Johnson	.40	.15
❑ 101	Adam Lind AU (RC)	10.00	4.00
❑ 102	Alexi Casilla AU RC EXCH	40.00	15.00
❑ 103	Andrew Miller AU RC	40.00	15.00
❑ 104	Andy Cannizaro AU RC	10.00	4.00
❑ 105	Angel Sanchez AU RC EXCH	15.00	6.00
❑ 106	Brian Stokes AU (RC)	8.00	3.00
❑ 107	Carlos Maldonado AU (RC) EXCH	8.00	3.00
❑ 108	Cesar Jimenez AU RC EXCH	8.00	3.00
❑ 109	Chris Stewart AU RC	8.00	3.00
❑ 111	David Murphy AU (RC)	8.00	3.00
❑ 112	Delmon Young AU (RC)	30.00	12.50
❑ 113	Delwyn Young AU (RC)	8.00	3.00
❑ 114	Dennis Sarfate AU (RC)	8.00	3.00
❑ 116	Drew Anderson AU RC	8.00	3.00

❑ 117 Fred Lewis AU (RC) 8.00 3.00
❑ 118 Glen Perkins AU (RC) 10.00 4.00
❑ 119 Hector Gimenez AU (RC) EXCH
❑ 120 Jeff Baker AU (RC) 8.00 3.00
❑ 121 Jeff Fiorentino AU (RC) 8.00 3.00
❑ 122 Jeff Salazar AU (RC) 8.00 3.00
❑ 124 Joaquin Arias AU (RC) 8.00 3.00
❑ 125 Jon Knott AU (RC) 8.00 3.00
❑ 128 Juan Morillo AU (RC) 8.00 3.00
❑ 129 Juan Perez AU RC EXCH 8.00 3.00
❑ 130 Juan Salas AU (RC) 8.00 3.00
❑ 131 Justin Hampson AU (RC) 8.00 3.00
❑ 132 Kevin Hooper AU (RC) 15.00 6.00
❑ 133 Kevin Kouzmanoff AU (RC) 10.00 4.00
❑ 134 Michael Bourn AU (RC) 8.00 3.00
❑ 135 Miguel Montero AU (RC) EXCH 8.00 3.00
❑ 136 Mike Rabelo AU RC EXCH 25.00 10.00
❑ 137 Mitch Maier AU RC 8.00 3.00
❑ 138 Oswaldo Navarro AU RC EXCH 15.00 6.00
❑ 139 Patrick Misch AU (RC) 8.00 3.00
❑ 140 Philip Humber AU (RC) 15.00 6.00
❑ 141 Ryan Braun AU RC 8.00 3.00
❑ 143 Ryan Sweeney AU (RC) 8.00 3.00
❑ 144 Scott Moore AU (RC) 8.00 3.00
❑ 145 Sean Henn AU (RC) 10.00 4.00
❑ 146 Shawn Riggans AU (RC) 8.00 3.00
❑ 148 Troy Tulowitzki AU (RC) 30.00 12.50
❑ 149 Ubaldo Jimenez AU (RC) 8.00 3.00
❑ 151 Rookie EXCH 25.00 10.00
❑ 152 Rookie EXCH 25.00 10.00
❑ 153 Rookie EXCH 25.00 10.00
❑ 154 Rookie EXCH 25.00 10.00
❑ 155 Rookie EXCH 25.00 10.00
❑ 156 Rookie EXCH 25.00 10.00
❑ 157 Elijah Dukes RC 25.00 10.00
❑ 158 Rookie EXCH 25.00 10.00
❑ 159 Rookie EXCH 25.00 10.00
❑ 160 Rookie EXCH 25.00 10.00
❑ 161 Rookie EXCH 25.00 10.00
❑ 162 Rookie EXCH 25.00 10.00
❑ 163 Rookie EXCH 25.00 10.00
❑ 164 Rookie EXCH 25.00 10.00
❑ 165 Rookie EXCH 25.00 10.00
❑ 166 Rookie EXCH 25.00 10.00
❑ 167 Rookie EXCH 25.00 10.00
❑ 168 Rookie EXCH 25.00 10.00
❑ 169 Rookie EXCH 25.00 10.00
❑ 170 Rookie EXCH 25.00 10.00

2008 Upper Deck Spectrum

❑ COMP.SET w/o AUs (100) 25.00 10.00
❑ COMMON CARD .50 .20
❑ COMMOM AU RC 8.00 3.00
❑ OVERALL AUTO ODDS 1:10
❑ PRINTING PLATES RANDOMLY INSERTED
❑ PLATE PRINT RUN 1 SET PER COLOR
❑ BLACK-CYAN-MAGENTA-YELLOW ISSUED
❑ NO PLATE PRICING DUE TO SCARCITY
❑ 1 Chris B. Young .50 .20
❑ 2 Brandon Webb .50 .20
❑ 3 Eric Byrnes .50 .20
❑ 4 John Smoltz 1.25 .50
❑ 5 Chipper Jones 1.50 .60
❑ 6 Jeff Francoeur .75 .30
❑ 7 Mark Teixeira .75 .30
❑ 8 Brian Roberts .75 .30
❑ 9 Erik Bedard .50 .20
❑ 10 Miguel Tejada .50 .20
❑ 11 Nick Markakis .75 .30
❑ 12 David Ortiz 1.25 .50
❑ 13 Daisuke Matsuzaka 2.50 1.00
❑ 14 Manny Ramirez 1.25 .50
❑ 15 Jonathan Papelbon .75 .30
❑ 16 Josh Beckett .75 .30
❑ 17 Alfonso Soriano .75 .30
❑ 18 Carlos Zambrano .50 .20
❑ 19 Derrek Lee .75 .30
❑ 20 Aramis Ramirez .50 .20
❑ 21 Paul Konerko .50 .20
❑ 22 Jermaine Dye .50 .20
❑ 23 Jim Thome .75 .30
❑ 24 Ken Griffey Jr. 2.00 .75
❑ 25 Brandon Phillips .50 .20
❑ 26 Adam Dunn .50 .20
❑ 27 Grady Sizemore .75 .30
❑ 28 Fausto Carmona .50 .20
❑ 29 Victor Martinez .50 .20
❑ 30 Travis Hafner .50 .20
❑ 31 Matt Holliday .75 .30
❑ 32 Troy Tulowitzki .75 .30
❑ 33 Todd Helton .75 .30
❑ 34 Magglio Ordonez .75 .30
❑ 35 Justin Verlander .75 .30
❑ 36 Gary Sheffield .50 .20
❑ 37 Miguel Cabrera .75 .30
❑ 38 Hanley Ramirez 1.25 .50
❑ 39 Dan Uggla .75 .30
❑ 40 Carlos Lee .50 .20
❑ 41 Roy Oswalt .50 .20
❑ 42 Lance Berkman .75 .30
❑ 43 Hunter Pence 1.25 .50
❑ 44 Alex Gordon 1.25 .50
❑ 45 David DeJesus .50 .20
❑ 46 Vladimir Guerrero 1.25 .50
❑ 47 Kelvim Escobar .50 .20
❑ 48 Chone Figgins .50 .20
❑ 49 Brad Penny .50 .20
❑ 50 Takashi Saito .50 .20
❑ 51 Russell Martin .50 .20
❑ 52 Prince Fielder 1.25 .50
❑ 53 Ryan Braun 1.50 .60
❑ 54 JJ Hardy .50 .20
❑ 55 Johan Santana 1.25 .50
❑ 56 Justin Morneau .50 .20
❑ 57 Torii Hunter .50 .20
❑ 58 Joe Mauer .75 .30
❑ 59 Carlos Beltran .50 .20
❑ 60 David Wright 1.50 .60
❑ 61 Carlos Delgado .50 .20
❑ 62 Jose Reyes .75 .30
❑ 63 Derek Jeter 3.00 1.25
❑ 64 Alex Rodriguez 2.00 .75
❑ 65 Robinson Cano .75 .30
❑ 66 Hideki Matsui 1.25 .50
❑ 67 Mariano Rivera 1.25 .50
❑ 68 Dan Haren .50 .20
❑ 69 Nick Swisher .50 .20
❑ 70 Eric Chavez .50 .20
❑ 71 Jimmy Rollins .75 .30
❑ 72 Ryan Howard 1.50 .60
❑ 73 Cole Hamels .75 .30
❑ 74 Chase Utley 1.25 .50
❑ 75 Freddy Sanchez .50 .20
❑ 76 Jason Bay .50 .20
❑ 77 Ian Snell .50 .20
❑ 78 Greg Maddux 1.50 .60
❑ 79 Jake Peavy .50 .20
❑ 80 Chris Young .50 .20
❑ 81 Barry Zito .50 .20
❑ 82 Tim Lincecum 1.25 .50
❑ 83 Omar Vizquel .50 .20
❑ 84 Felix Hernandez .75 .30
❑ 85 Ichiro Suzuki 2.00 .75
❑ 86 Richie Sexson .50 .20
❑ 87 Albert Pujols 2.50 1.00
❑ 88 Scott Rolen .75 .30
❑ 89 Chris Carpenter .50 .20
❑ 90 Delmon Young .75 .30
❑ 91 Carl Crawford .50 .20
❑ 92 B.J. Upton .75 .30
❑ 93 Michael Young .50 .20
❑ 94 Hank Blalock .50 .20
❑ 95 Sammy Sosa .75 .30
❑ 96 Roy Halladay .50 .20
❑ 97 Alex Rios .50 .20
❑ 98 Vernon Wells .50 .20
❑ 99 Ryan Zimmerman .75 .30
❑ 100 Dmitri Young .50 .20
❑ 101 Alberto Gonzalez AU RC 25.00 10.00
❑ 102 Bill Murphy AU (RC) 8.00 3.00
❑ 103 Bill White AU RC 8.00 3.00
❑ 104 Billy Buckner AU (RC) 8.00 3.00
❑ 105 Brandon Jones AU RC 8.00 3.00
❑ 106 Bronson Sardinha AU (RC) 8.00 3.00
❑ 107 Chin-Lung Hu AU (RC) 25.00 10.00
❑ 108 Chris Seddon AU (RC) 8.00 3.00
❑ 109 Clay Buchholz AU (RC) 25.00 10.00
❑ 110 Clint Sammons AU (RC) 8.00 3.00
❑ 111 Daric Barton AU (RC) 10.00 4.00
❑ 112 Dave Davidson AU RC 10.00 4.00
❑ 113 Donny Lucy AU (RC) 8.00 3.00
❑ 114 Emilio Bonifacio AU RC 8.00 3.00
❑ 115 Eugenio Velez AU RC 10.00 4.00
❑ 116 Felipe Paulino AU RC
❑ 117 Harvey Garcia AU (RC) 8.00 3.00
❑ 118 Ian Kennedy AU RC 40.00 15.00
❑ 119 J.R. Towles AU RC 15.00 6.00
❑ 120 Jeff Clement AU (RC)
❑ 121 Jerry Blevins AU RC 8.00 3.00
❑ 122 Joe Koshansky AU (RC) 8.00 3.00
❑ 123 Joey Votto AU (RC) 15.00 6.00
❑ 124 Jonathan Albaladejo AU RC 10.00 4.00
❑ 125 Jonathan Meloan AU RC 8.00 3.00
❑ 126 Jose Morales AU (RC) 8.00 3.00
❑ 127 Josh Anderson AU (RC) 8.00 3.00
❑ 128 Josh Newman AU RC 8.00 3.00
❑ 129 Justin Maxwell AU RC 10.00 4.00
❑ 130 Justin Ruggiano AU RC 8.00 3.00
❑ 131 Kevin Hart AU (RC) 8.00 3.00
❑ 132 Lance Broadway AU (RC) 8.00 3.00
❑ 133 Luis Mendoza AU (RC) 8.00 3.00
❑ 134 Luke Hochevar AU RC 15.00 6.00
❑ 135 Nyjer Morgan AU (RC) 8.00 3.00
❑ 136 Rob Johnson AU (RC) 8.00 3.00
❑ 137 Ross Detwiler AU RC 8.00 3.00
❑ 138 Ross Ohlendorf AU RC 10.00 4.00
❑ 139 Ryan Hanigan AU RC 8.00 3.00
❑ 140 Seth Smith AU (RC) 8.00 3.00
❑ 141 Steve Pearce AU RC 10.00 4.00
❑ 142 Troy Patton AU (RC) 8.00 3.00
❑ 143 Wladimir Balentien AU (RC) 10.00 4.00
❑ 144 Colt Morton AU RC 8.00 3.00
❑ 145 Carlos Muniz AU RC

Each year we refine the process of developing the most accurate and up-to-date information for this book. I believe this year's Price Guide is our best yet. Thanks again to all the contributors nationwide (listed below) as well as our staff here in Dallas.

Those who have worked closely with us on this and many other books have again proven themselves invaluable: Ed Allan, Frank and Vivian Barning, Levi Bleam and Jim Fleck (707 Sportscards), T. Scott Brandon, Peter Brennan, Ray Bright, Card Collectors Co., Dwight Chapin, Theo Chen, Barry Colla, Bill and Diane Dodge, Brett Domue, Dan Even, David Festberg, Fleer/SkyBox (Josh Perlman), Steve Freedman, Gervise Ford, Larry and Jeff Fritsch, Tony Galovich, Georgia Music and Sports (Dick DeCourcey), Dick Gilkeson, Steve Gold (AU Sports), Bill Goodwin (St. Louis Baseball Cards), Mike and Howard Gordon, George Grauer, Steve Green (STB Sports), John Greenwald, Bill Henderson, Jerry and Etta Hersh, Mike Hersh, Neil Hoppenworth, Hunt Auction, Mike Jaspersen, Jay and Mary Kasper (Jay's Emporium), Jerry Katz, Pete Kennedy, David Kohler (SportsCards Plus), Terry Knouse (Tik and Tik), Tom Leon, Lew Lipset (Four Base Hits), Mike Livingston (U-Trading Cards), Mark Macrae, Bill Madden, Bill Mastro, Dr.William McAvoy, Michael McDonald, Mid-Atlantic Sports Cards (Bill Bossert), Gary Mills, Ernie Montella, Brian Morris, Mike Mosier (Columbia City Collectibles Co.), B.A. Murry, Ralph Nozaki, Mike O'Brien, Oldies and Goodies (Nigel Spill), Oregon Trail Auctions, Pacific Trading Cards (Mike Cramer and Mike Monson), Playoff Trading Cards (Ben Ecklar, Steve Judd, and Tracy Hackler), Jack Pollard, Jeff Prillaman, Pat Quinn, Jerald Reichstein (Fabulous Cardboard), Tom Reid, Gavin Riley, Clifton Rouse, John Rumierz, Pat Blandford, Lonn Passon and Kevin Savage (Sports Gallery), Gary Sawatski and Jim Justus (The Wizards of Odd), Mike Schechter, Bill and Darlene Shafer, Barry Sloate, John E. Spalding, Phil Spector, Murvin Sterling, Ted Taylor, Lee Temanson, Topps (Marty Appel), Treat (Harold Anderson), Ed Twombly, Upper Deck (Justin Kanoya), Wayne Varner, Rob Veres, Bill Vizas, Waukesha Sportscards, Bill Wesslund (Portland Sports Card Co.), Kit Young, Rick Young, Ted Zanidakis, Robert Zanze (Z-Cards and Sports), Bill Zimpleman, and Dean Zindler. Finally we give a special acknowledgment to the late Dennis W. Eckes, "Mr. Sport Americana." The success of the Beckett Price Guides has always been the result of a team effort.

It is very difficult to be "accurate" — one can only do one's best. But this job is especially difficult since we're shooting at a moving target: Prices are fluctuating all the time. Having several full-time pricing experts has definitely proven to be better than just one, and I thank all of them for working together to provide you, our readers, with the most accurate prices possible.

Many people have provided price input, illustrative material, checklist verifications, errata, and/or background information. We should like to individually thank AbD Cards (Dale Wesolewski), Action Card Sales, Jerry Adamic, Johnny and Sandy Adams, Mehdi Ahlei, Alex's MVP Cards & Comics, Doug Allen, Will Allison, Dennis Anderson, Ed Anderson, Shane Anderson, Ellis Anmuth, Alan Applegate, Ric Apter, Clyde Archer, Randy Archer, Burl Armstrong, Neil Armstrong, Carlos Ayala, B and J Sportscards, Jeremy Bachman, Dave Bailey, Ball Four Cards (Frank and Steve Pemper), Bob Bartosz, Bubba Bennett, Carl Berg, Beulah Sports (Jeff Blatt), B.J. Sportscollectables, David Boedicker (The Wild Pitch Inc.), Louis Bollman, Tim Bond, Andrew Bosarge, Terry Boyd, Dan Brandenberry, Jeff Breitenfield, Scott Brockleman, John Broggi, Virgil Burns, Greg Bussineau, David Byer, California Card Co., Capital Cards, Danny Cariseo, Carl Carlson (C.T.S.), Jim Carr, Ira Cetron, Sandy Chan, Ric Chandgie, Ray Cherry, Bigg Wayne Christian, Josh Chidester, Michael and Abe Citron, Dr. Jeffrey Clair, Michael Cohen, Tom Cohoon (Cardboard Dreams), Gary Collett, Rick Cosmen (RC Card Co.), Lou Costanzo (Champion Sports), Mike Coyne, Tony Craig (T.C. Card Co.), Solomon Cramer, Kevin Crane, Taylor Crane, Chad Cripe, Scott Crump, Allen Custer, Dave Dame, Scott Dantio, Dee's Baseball Cards (Dee Robinson), Joe Delgrippo, Mike DeLuca, Ken Dinerman (California Cruizers), Rob DiSalvatore, Cliff Dolgins, Discount Dorothy, Richard Dolloff (Dolloff Coin Center), Joe Donato, Jerry Dong, Pat Dorsey, Double Play Baseball Cards, Joe Drelich, Richard Duglin (Baseball Cards-N-More), The Dugout, Ken Edick (Home Plate of Utah), Brad Englehardt, Doak Ewing, Terry Falkner, Mike and Chris Fanning, Linda Ferrigno and Mark Mezzardi, Jay Finglass, Bob Flitter, Fremont Fong, Paul Franzetti, Ron Frasier, Tom Freeman, Bob Frye, Bill Fusaro, Chris Gala, Richard Galasso, David Garza, David Gaumer, Georgetown Card Exchange, David Giove, Dick Goddard, Jeff Goldstein, Ron Gomez, Rich Gove, Jay and Jan Grinsby, Bob Grissett, Gerry Guenther, Neil Gubitz (What-A-Card), Hall's Nostalgia, Hershell Hanks, Gregg Hara, Todd Harrell, Robert Harrison, Steve Hart, Floyd Haynes (H and H Baseball Cards), Kevin Heffner, Joel Hellman, Hit and Run Cards (Jon, David, and Kirk Peterson), Vinny Ho, Johnny Hustle Card Co., John Inouye, Vern Isenberg, Dale Jackson, Marshall Jackson, Mike Jardina, Paul Jastrzembski, Jeff's Sports Cards, Donn Jennings Cards, George Johnson, Craig Jones, Chuck Juliana, Nick Kardoulias, Scott Kashner, Frank and Rose Katen, Kevin's Kards, Kingdom Collectibles, Inc., John Klassnik, Steve Kluback,Don Knutsen, Gregg Kohn,

Mike Kohlhas, Bob & Bryan Kornfield, Carl and Maryanne Laron, Howard Lau, Richard S. Lawrence, William Lawrence, Brent Lee, Morley Leeking, Irv Lerner, Larry and Sally Levine, Larry Loeschen (A and J Sportscards), Neil Lopez, Kendall Loyd (Orlando Sportscards South), Steve Lowe, Jim Macie, Peter Maltin, Paul Marchant, Brian Marcy, Scott Martinez, James S. Maxwell Jr., McDag Productions Inc., Bob McDonald, Steve McHenry, Tony McLaughlin, Mendal Mearkle, Carlos Medina, Ken Melanson, William Mendel, Blake Meyer (Lone Star Sportscards), Tim Meyer, Joe Michalowicz, Lee Milazzo, Cary S. Miller, George Miller, Wayne Miller, Dick Millerd, Frank Mineo, Mitchell's Baseball Cards, John Morales, William Munn, Mark Murphy, Robert Nappe, National Sportscard Exchange, Roger Neufeldt, Steve Novella, Bud Obermeyer, John O'Hara, Glenn Olson, Scott Olson, Ron Oser, Luther Owen, Earle Parrish, Clay Pasternack, Michael Perrotta, Tom Pfirrmann, Don Phlong, Loran Pulver, Bob Ragonese, Bryan Rappaport, Don and Tom Ras, Robert M. Ray, Phil Regli, Rob Resnick, Dave Reynolds, Carson Ritchey, Bill Rodman, Craig Roehrig, Mike Sablow, Terry Sack, Thomas Salem, Barry Sanders, Jon Sands, Tony Scarpa, John Schad, Dave Schau (Baseball Cards), Masa Shinohara, Eddie Silard, Mike Slepcevic, Sam Sliheet, Art Smith, Lynn and Todd Solt, Jerry Sorice, Don Spagnolo, Sports Card Fan-Attic, The Sport Hobbyist, Norm Stapleton, Bill Steinberg, Lisa Stellato (Never Enough Cards), Rob Stenzel, Jason Stern, Andy Stoltz, Rob Stenzel, Bill Stone, Ted Straka, Tim Strandberg (East Texas Sports Cards), Edward Strauss, Strike Three, Richard Strobino, Kevin Struss, Superior Sport Card, Dr. Richard Swales, George Tahinos, Brent Thorton, Ian Taylor, The The Thirdhand Shoppe, Brent Thornton, Paul Thornton, Jim and Sally Thurtell, Bud Tompkins (Minnesota Connection), Philip J. Tremont, Ralph Triplette, Umpire's Choice Inc., Eric Unglaub, Hoyt Vanderpool, Steven Wagman, T. Wall, Gary A. Walter, Joe and John Weisenburger (The Wise Guys), Brian and Mike Wentz (BMW Sportscards), Richard West, Mike Wheat, Richard Wiercinski, Don Williams (Robin's Nest of Dolls), Jeff Williams, John Williams, Kent and Louise Williams, Craig Williamson, Rich Wojtasick, John Wolf Jr., Jay Wolt (Cavalcade of Sports), Joe Yanello, Peter Yee, Tom Zocco, Mark Zubrensky, and Tim Zwick.

Every year we make active solicitations for expert input. We are particularly appreciative of help (however extensive or cursory) provided for this volume. We receive many inquiries, comments, and questions regarding material within this book. In fact, each and every one is read and digested. Time constraints, however, prevent us from personally replying. But keep sharing your knowledge. Your letters and input are part of the "big picture" of hobby information we can pass along to readers in our books and magazines. Even though we cannot respond to each letter, you are making significant contributions to the hobby through your interest and comments.

The effort to continually refine and improve this book also involves a growing number of people and types of expertise on our home team. Our company boasts a substantial Sports Data Publishing team, which strengthens our ability to provide comprehensive analysis of the marketplace. SDP capably handled numerous technical details and provided able assistance in the preparation of this edition.

Our baseball analysts played a major part in compiling this year's book, traveling thousands of miles during the past year to attend sports card shows and visit card shops around the United States and Canada. The Beckett baseball specialists are: Gabe Harro, Rich Klein, Dave Porter, and Grant Sandground (Senior Price Guide Editor). Their pricing analysis and careful proofreading were key contributions to the accuracy of this annual.

Grant Sandground's coordination and reconciling of prices as Beckett Baseball Card Monthly Price Guide Editor helped immeasurably. Rich Klein, as research analyst, contributed detailed pricing analysis and hours of proofing.

The effort was led by Dan Hitt, the Senior Manager of Sports Data Publishing. He was ably assisted by the rest of the Price Guide analysts: Clint Hall, Keith Hower, Tony Joseph, Beverly Mills, Bill Sutherland, Tim Trout, and Joe White.

The price gathering and analytical talents of this fine group of hobbyists have helped make our Beckett team stronger, while making this guide and its companion monthly Price Guide more widely recognized as the hobby's most reliable and relied upon sources of pricing information.

The Beckett Interactive Division played a critical role in technology. They spent countless hours programming, testing, and implementing it to simplify the handling of thousands of prices that must be checked and updated for each edition.

In the years since this guide debuted, Beckett Publications has grown beyond any rational expectation. A great many talented and hard working individuals have been instrumental in this growth and success. Our whole team is to be congratulated for what we together have accomplished.

The whole Beckett Publications team has my thanks for jobs well done. Thank you, everyone.